BEST'S
KEY RATING GUIDE®

Life/Health
United States & Canada

(Including Bermuda & Caribbean)

2010 Edition

Best's Financial Strength Ratings
are as of publication date
June 15, 2010

For Current Ratings and Reports access www.ambest.com

Published Continuously Since 1928

A.M. BEST COMPANY
Oldwick, New Jersey 08858 USA • (908) 439-2200 • Fax: (908) 439-3296
www.ambest.com

IMPORTANT NOTICE

The information presented herein is prepared solely for the confidential use of A.M. Best Company (A.M. Best) subscribers. For most insurance companies domiciled in the United States, the data contained within is based on each insurance company's sworn annual and quarterly (if available) financial statement as prescribed by the National Association of Insurance Commissioners (NAIC) and as filed with the Insurance Commissioners of the states in which the companies are licensed to do business. These official financial statements are presented in accordance with statutory accounting requirements.

Data related to companies operating outside the United States is presented in accordance with customs or regulatory requirements of the country of domicile, and there may be significant variations in accounting standards or methods of reporting from one country to another. These differences are imbedded in the accounting principles used, the valuation of assets and liabilities and the treatment of taxes. Financial data is usually received in the currency of the country where the company is domiciled, and our reports are generally presented in that currency and may be presented in U.S. dollars as well. Our non-U.S. reports represent a variety of reporting dates as the fiscal year utilized by companies varies according to traditional reporting periods or regulatory requirements. Within some of the Canadian company presentations, portions of the Canadian data are provided by Beyond 20/20 Inc., Ottawa, Canada.

In addition, our products may include supplemental information obtained by us, such as data supplied in response to our questionnaires; data contained in state examination reports; audit reports prepared by certified public accountants; loss reserve reports prepared by loss reserve specialists; annual reports to stockholders and policyholders; Generally Accepted Accounting Principles (GAAP) or International Accounting Standards (IAS) financial statements; and reports filed with the Securities and Exchange Commission (SEC) in the United States. Meetings between A.M. Best senior staff personnel and company management also provide additional and valuable in-depth information on the company's current performance and future objectives.

While the information obtained from these sources is believed to be reliable, its accuracy is not guaranteed. We do submit the data to a rigorous, computerized cross-checking routine to verify its arithmetic accuracy. However, we do not audit the company's financial records or statements and therefore cannot attest as to the accuracy of the information provided to us. Consequently, no representations or warranties are made or given as to the accuracy or completeness of the information presented herein, and no responsibility can be accepted for any error, omission or inaccuracy in our reports.

A Financial Strength Rating is an independent opinion of an insurer's financial strength and ability to meet its ongoing insurance policy and contract obligations. It is based on a comprehensive quantitative and qualitative evaluation of a company's balance sheet strength, operating performance and business profile.

The Financial Strength Rating opinion addresses the relative ability of an insurer to meet its ongoing insurance obligations. The ratings are not assigned to specific insurance policies or contracts and do not address any other risk, including, but not limited to, an insurer's claims-payment policies or procedures; the ability of the insurer to dispute or deny claims payment on grounds of misrepresentation or fraud; or any specific liability contractually borne by the policy or contract holder. A Financial Strength Rating is not a recommendation to purchase, hold or terminate any insurance policy, contract or any other financial obligation issued by an insurer, nor does it address the suitability of any particular policy or contract for a specific purpose or purchaser.

In arriving at a rating decision, A.M. Best relies on third-party audited financial data and/or other information provided to it. While this information is believed to be reliable, A.M. Best does not independently verify the accuracy or reliability of the information. Any and all ratings, opinions and information contained herein are provided "as is," without any express or implied warranty. A rating may be changed, suspended or withdrawn at any time for any reason at the sole discretion of A.M. Best. For additional details, see A.M. Best's *Terms of Use* at www.ambest.com/terms.html.

A.M. Best does not sell securities nor provide investment advice. It is compensated for its interactive ratings from the insurance companies it rates.

ISSN 2152-5633
ISBN 978-1-936105-07-6

PRINTED IN THE UNITED STATES OF AMERICA
And produced with Best's Publishing System

BEST'S® PUBLICATIONS & SERVICES

RATINGS & ANALYSIS PRODUCTS

Best's Insurance Reports®
- Property/Casualty — US & Canada
- Life/Health — US & Canada
- Non-US

Best's Capital Adequacy Ratio Adjustment System
- Property/Casualty — US

Best's Pocket Key Rating Guide™
- Property/Casualty — US & Canada
- Life/Health — US & Canada

Best's Key Rating Guide®
- Property/Casualty — US & Canada
- Life/Health — US & Canada

FINANCIAL DATA PRODUCTS

Best's Statement File
- Property/Casualty — US & Canada
- Life/Health — US & Canada

Best's State/Line — (P/C Lines) — US
Best's State/Line (Life Lines) — L/H — US
Best's State/Line (A&H Lines) — L/H — US
Best's Insurance Expense Exhibit — P/C — US
Best's Schedule D — P/C & L/H — US
Best's Schedule F — P/C — US
Best's Schedule P — P/C — US
Best's Schedule S — L/H — US

Best's Statement File
- Property/Casualty — Canada
- Life/Health — Canada
- UK
- Global

Best's State/Line Reports
- P/C — US (Print)
- L/H — US (Print)

Best's Aggregates & Averages
- Property/Casualty — US & Canada
- Life/Health — US & Canada

ONLINE CENTERS

Best's Property/Casualty Center
Best's Banking Center
Best's Insurance Professionals Center
Best's Health Center
Best's Underwriting & Loss Control Center
Best's Life/Health Center
Best's Consumer Insurance Center
Best's Captive Center

NEWS PRODUCTS

Best's Review®
BestWeek®
The Guide to Understanding the Insurance Industry
BestWire®
BestDay®

RISK ASSESSMENT PRODUCTS

Best's Underwriting Guide
Best's Loss Control Manual

DIRECTORIES

Best's Directory of Recommended Insurance Attorneys
Best's Directory of Recommended Insurance Adjusters
Best's Directory of Recommended Expert Service Providers
Best's Directory of Captive Managers
Best's Directory of Third Party Administrators
Best's Directory of Insurance Actuaries
Best's Directory of Insurance Auditors

REGULATORY FILING SOFTWARE

BestESP® Services — US
BestESP Services — UK

RATE FILING INFORMATION

Best's State Rate Filings® Online — P/C — US

SPECIAL SERVICES

Best's Custom Data Services
BestAlert® Service
Member Center
Best's Online Account
Best's Product Training Workshops

CORPORATE PROGRAMS & SERVICES

Article Reprints
BestMark™ Programs
Best's Preferred Publisher Program
Best's Rating Referral Program
Certificate Programs
Corporate Complimentary Subscription Program

ONLINE REPORTS

AMB Credit Reports
Best's Key Rating Guide Presentation Reports
Best's Market Share Reports
Best's Executive Summary Reports
Best's Rating Reports
Best's State Banking Reports

TABLE OF CONTENTS

PREFACE

2010 LIFE/HEALTH EDITION

AN OVERVIEW OF BEST'S CREDIT RATING METHODOLOGY

SECTION I

INTRODUCTION

The Preface provides an overview of A.M. Best's credit rating system. This overview includes a summary of our rating definitions and objectives, the interactive credit rating process, the primary sources of information that serve as the foundation for Best's quantitative and qualitative analyses, our core credit rating methodologies, and statistics regarding the distribution of our ratings. The primary purpose of the Preface is to summarize Best's rating approach and the key components of our analytical framework, including risk management and other qualitative factors, as they relate to the assignment of a Best's Credit Rating on operating insurance companies.

The Preface also covers other key elements of the broader rating assessment process — such as the impact of parents and affiliated non-insurance subsidiaries, and the analysis of holding companies, debt and other securities issued by insurance groups. However, for a comprehensive review of Best's credit rating system, please refer to *Best's Credit Rating Methodology* (BCRM). The BCRM provides in greater detail an explanation of Best's rating process, including highlights of the detailed rating criteria employed by A.M. Best Company in determining Best's Credit Ratings, which include Best's Financial Strength, Issuer Credit and Debt Ratings within the insurance industry.

A.M. Best utilizes a broad and deep portfolio of both quantitative and qualitative measures to analyze the organizations we rate. These measures and the credit rating processes are regularly reviewed and enhanced through a formalized criteria review process. Enhancements are then disseminated through criteria papers addressing specific issues or components of the rating process. The BCRM and our most current rating criteria can be accessed through A.M. Best's website at *www.ambest.com/ratings/methodology*.

SECTION II

ABOUT A.M. BEST

A.M. Best Company is a global, full-service credit rating agency dedicated to serving the financial and health care services industries. It began assigning credit ratings in 1906, making it the first of today's credit rating agencies to use symbols to differentiate the relative creditworthiness of companies. Within the insurance segment, Best's Credit Ratings cover property/casualty, life, annuity, reinsurance, captive, title and health insurance companies and health maintenance organizations (HMOs). A.M. Best provides the most comprehensive insurance ratings coverage of any credit rating agency, with reports and ratings maintained on over 10,000 insurance entities worldwide, in approximately 95 countries. A.M. Best is also a well-known and highly regarded source of information and commentary on global insurance trends and issues through a host of other products and services.

In 1900, A.M. Best first published what became known as *Best's Insurance Reports® - Property/Casualty* edition which reported on 850 property/casualty insurers operating in the United States. This was soon followed by its companion volume, *Best's Insurance Reports® - Life/Health* edition, which was published in 1906 reporting on 95 legal reserve life insurers in the United States. Over the better part of a century, these two annual publications have represented the most comprehensive source of financial information on domestic insurers.

The Property/Casualty and Life/Health editions of *Best's Insurance Reports® - United States & Canada* contain over 3,300 and 1,800 insurance companies, respectively, representing virtually all active insurers operating in the United States. In addition, these editions contain Canadian and Carribean property/casualty and life insurers and reports on United States, European, and Canadian branches.

In 1984, A.M. Best embarked on completing global coverage of the insurance industry with the publication of *Best's Insurance Reports® - Non-US* edition, which currently reports, in CD-ROM format, on over 5,400 international property/casualty and life/health companies.

In 1999, A.M. Best expanded its rating assignments to include debt and insurance-linked securities. The issuance of securities ratings for insurers and insurance holding companies is a natural extension of our expertise in providing financial strength ratings and reports on insurance organizations to investors, analysts and policyholders. This focus also serves as the foundation for which ratings are issued to other risk-bearing institutions and entities, including captive insurers and alternative risk transfer facilities.

Within the insurance segment, A.M. Best assigns ratings to various instruments including debt, hybrid debt, surplus notes, preferred stock, commercial paper, collateralized debt obligations, insurance-based liability or asset-backed securitizations and monetizations, risk-linked securities, closed block securities and institutional investment products.

In addition to our rating products and services, A.M. Best also publishes a host of other complementary products that are an extension of our knowledge of the industry. Some of these products include *Best's Aggregates and Averages* (industry-wide aggregate totals), *Best's Underwriting Guide* (an underwriter's guide to assessing over 500 commercial risks), and *Best's Loss Control Manual* (a safety engineer's guide to assessing insurance exposures and requirements). These products add to the understanding of the complexities of the insurance industry and enhance our rating evaluations as well as the value and scope of information we provide our subscribers.

A.M. Best currently provides over 50 publications and services to meet the needs of our customers who require timely, accurate and comprehensive information on this dynamic industry. A.M. Best is dedicated to providing our subscribers with the most useful and up-to-date information and ratings available in the insurance industry.

SECTION III

BEST'S CREDIT RATINGS

BEST'S CREDIT RATINGS OF LIFE/HEALTH INSURERS

Best's Credit Ratings are independent opinions regarding the creditworthiness of insurance entities, issuers, and securities. Best's Credit Ratings are based on a comprehensive quantitative and qualitative evaluation of a company's balance sheet strength, operating performance and business profile, and, where appropriate, the specific nature and details of a security. A.M. Best assigns various types of credit ratings within the insurance industry, including Financial Strength Ratings, Long-Term and Short-Term Issuer Credit Ratings, and Long-Term and Short-Term Debt Ratings on corporate securities and insurance-related securitizations.

Best's Financial Strength Ratings

The Best's Financial Strength Rating (FSR) is an independent opinion of an insurer's financial strength and ability to meet its ongoing insurance policy and contract obligations. The FSR scale is comprised of 16 individual ratings grouped into 10 categories, consisting of three Secure categories of "Superior," "Excellent" and "Good" and seven Vulnerable categories of "Fair," "Marginal," "Weak," "Poor," "Under Regulatory Supervision," "In Liquidation," and "Suspended."

Secure

A++ and A+ **(Superior)**
Assigned to companies that have, in our opinion, a superior ability to meet their ongoing insurance obligations.

A and A- **(Excellent)**
Assigned to companies that have, in our opinion, an excellent ability to meet their ongoing insurance obligations.

B++ and B+ **(Good)**
Assigned to companies that have, in our opinion, a good ability to meet their ongoing insurance obligations.

Vulnerable

B and B- **(Fair)**
Assigned to companies that have, in our opinion, a fair ability to meet their ongoing insurance obligations, but are financially vulnerable to adverse changes in underwriting and economic conditions.

C++ and C+ **(Marginal)**
Assigned to companies that have, in our opinion, a marginal ability to meet their ongoing insurance obligations, but are financially vulnerable to adverse changes in underwriting and economic conditions.

C and C- **(Weak)**
Assigned to companies that have, in our opinion, a weak ability to meet their ongoing insurance obligations, but are financially very vulnerable to adverse changes in underwriting and economic conditions.

D **(Poor)**
Assigned to companies that have, in our opinion, a poor ability to meet their ongoing insurance obligations and are financially extremely vulnerable to adverse changes in underwriting and economic conditions.

E **(Under Regulatory Supervision)**
Assigned to companies (and possibly their subsidiaries/affiliates) placed under a significant form of regulatory supervision, control or restraint - including cease and desist orders, conservatorship or rehabilitation, but not liquidation - that prevents conduct of normal, ongoing insurance operations.

F **(In Liquidation)**
Assigned to companies that have been placed under an order of liquidation by a court of law or whose owners have voluntarily agreed to liquidate the company. Note: Companies that voluntarily liquidate or dissolve their charters are generally not insolvent.

S **(Suspended)**
Assigned to rated companies that have experienced sudden and significant events affecting their balance sheet strength or operating performance whereby the rating implications cannot be evaluated due to a lack of timely or adequate information.

BEST'S ISSUER CREDIT AND DEBT RATINGS

Long-Term Issuer Credit Ratings and Long-Term Debt Ratings

Best's Long-Term Issuer Credit Rating (ICR) is an opinion of an issuer/entity's ability to meet its ongoing senior financial obligations. Best's Long-Term Debt Rating is an independent opinion of an issuer/entity's ability to meet its ongoing financial obligations to security holders when due. Best's rating scale used for Long-Term ICRs and Long-Term Debt Ratings is comprised of 22 individual ratings grouped into 8 categories, consisting of four Investment Grade categories of "Exceptional," "Very Strong," "Strong," and "Adequate" and four Non-Investment Grade categories of "Speculative," "Very Speculative," "Extremely Speculative," and "In Default."

Investment Grade

aaa **(Exceptional)**
Assigned to issues where, in our opinion, the issuer has an exceptional ability to meet the terms of the obligation.

aa+ and **aa** and **aa-** **(Very Strong)**
Assigned to issues where, in our opinion, the issuer has a very strong ability to meet the terms of the obligation.

a+ and **a** and **a-** **(Strong)**
Assigned to issues where, in our opinion, the issuer has a strong ability to meet the terms of the obligation.

bbb+ and **bbb** and **bbb-** **(Adequate)**
Assigned to issues where, in our opinion, the issuer has an adequate ability to meet the terms of the obligation; however, the issue is more susceptible to changes in economic or other conditions.

Non-Investment Grade

bb+ and **bb** and **bb-** **(Speculative)**
Assigned to issues where, in our opinion, the issuer has speculative credit characteristics, generally due to a moderate margin of principal and interest payment protection and vulnerability to economic changes.

b+ and **b** and **b-** **(Very Speculative)**
Assigned to issues where, in our opinion, the issuer has very speculative credit characteristics, generally due to a modest margin of principal and interest payment protection and extreme vulnerability to economic changes.

ccc+ and **ccc** and **ccc-**
and **cc** and **c** **(Extremely Speculative)**
Assigned to issues where, in our opinion, the issuer has extremely speculative credit characteristics, generally due to a minimal margin of principal and interest payment protection and extreme vulnerability to economic changes.

d **(In Default)**
Assigned to issues in default on payment of principal, interest or other terms and conditions, or when a bankruptcy petition or similar action has been filed.

While the above definitions apply to entities which do not issue insurance obligations, A.M. Best also assigns Issuer Credit Ratings to all rated insurance companies. In addition, it should be noted that A.M. Best assigns Issuer Credit Ratings to publicly traded holding companies, where a significant portion of cash flow is provided by insurance operations. The definitions applied to insurance companies that are assigned an Issuer Credit Rating are as follows: (aaa) - Exceptional; (aa) - Superior; (a) - Excellent; (bbb) - Good; (bb) - Fair; (b) - Marginal; (ccc, cc) - Weak; (c) - Poor; (rs) - Regulatory Supervision/ Liquidation.

Short-Term Issuer Credit Ratings and Short-Term Debt Ratings

Best's Short-Term ICR and Short-Term Debt Ratings are an opinion of an issuer/entity's ability to meet its senior financial obligations having original maturities of generally less than one year. Best's Short-Term ICR and Debt Rating scale is comprised of 6 individual ratings grouped into 6 categories, consisting of four Investment Grade categories of "Strongest," "Outstanding," "Satisfactory," and "Adequate" and two Non-Investment Grade categories of "Speculative" and "In Default."

Investment Grade

AMB-1+ **(Strongest)**
Assigned to issues where, in our opinion, the issuer has the strongest ability to repay short-term debt obligations.

AMB-1 **(Outstanding)**
Assigned to issues where, in our opinion, the issuer has an outstanding ability to repay short-term debt obligations.

AMB-2 **(Satisfactory)**
Assigned to issues where, in our opinion, the issuer has a satisfactory ability to repay short-term debt obligations.

AMB-3 **(Adequate)**
Assigned to issues where, in our opinion, the issuer has an adequate ability to repay short-term debt obligations; however, adverse economic conditions will likely reduce the issuer's capacity to meet its financial commitments.

Non-Investment Grade

AMB-4 **(Speculative)**
Assigned to issues where, in our opinion, the issuer has speculative credit characteristics and is vulnerable to adverse economic or other external changes, which could have a marked impact on the company's ability to meet its financial commitments.

d **(In Default)**
Assigned to issues in default on payment of principal, interest or other terms and conditions, or when a bankruptcy petition or similar action has been filed.

Rating Translation Table - FSRs and Long-Term ICRs

As highlighted in the summary definition above, an FSR is an opinion of an insurer's ability to meet its ongoing insurance policy and contract obligations. The analysis required for this reflects various sources of risk, including non-insurance risks, to which the legal entity issuing the policies is exposed. Since policyholders typically are among the senior-most creditors of an insurer, FSRs, in practice, have been the equivalent of the ICR for operating insurers. See the rating translation table below.

Rating Translation Table

FSR Secure	Long-Term ICR Investment Grade	FSR Vulnerable	Long-Term ICR Non-Investment Grade
A++	aaa, aa+	B	bb+, bb
A+	aa, aa-	B-	bb-
A	a+, a	C++	b+, b
A-	a-	C+	b-
B++	bbb+, bbb	C	ccc+, ccc
B+	bbb-	C-	ccc-, cc
		D	c
		E and F	rs

With the growing interest by non-policyholders in insurers' creditworthiness, A.M. Best draws a distinction between the Financial Strength and Issuer Credit Ratings. The FSR remains an opinion specific to the insurer's ability to meet ongoing insurance policy and contract obligations, while the ICR is an opinion as to the overall creditworthiness of an insurer from the perspective of its senior creditors. This distinction is important when considering ratings other than an FSR within an insurance organization, since ratings both of an organization's debt issues and of related legal entities, such as holding companies, are tied to and based on the overall creditworthiness of the operating insurer.

Best's Rating Outlooks and Under Review Modifier

A.M. Best uses various other designations to provide users of our long-term ratings additional information about a rated entity or security, including Rating Outlooks and Under Review modifiers. When assigned to a company or security, the Rating Outlook indicates the potential future direction of the rating - FSR, ICR or Debt — over an intermediate period, generally defined as the next 12 to 36 months. A Rating Outlook can be positive, negative or stable.

- A positive outlook indicates that a company is experiencing favorable financial and market trends, relative to its current rating level. If these trends continue, the company has a good possibility of having its rating upgraded.

- A negative outlook indicates that a company is experiencing unfavorable financial and market trends, relative to its current rating level. If these trends continue, the company has a good possibility of having its rating downgraded.
- A stable outlook indicates that a company is experiencing stable financial and market trends, and that there is a low likelihood the company's rating will change over an intermediate period.

Positive and negative outlooks do not necessarily lead to a change in a company's rating. Similarly, a stable rating outlook does not preclude a rating upgrade or downgrade.

Potential near-term rating changes (typically within six months) due to a recent event or abrupt change in a company's financial condition are signaled through the use of an Under Review ("u") modifier. This modifier is assigned once A.M. Best initiates a review to determine the impact on the company's rating. An Under Review status can have positive, negative or developing implications. When a rating is under review, there is no Rating Outlook until the outcome of the review is determined.

- A positive implication indicates that, based on information currently available, there is a reasonable likelihood the company's rating will be raised as a result of A.M. Best's analysis of the recent event.
- A negative implication indicates that, based on information currently available, there is a reasonable likelihood the company's rating will be lowered as a result of A.M. Best's analysis of the recent event.
- A developing implication indicates that, based on information currently available, there is uncertainty as to the final rating outcome, but there is a reasonable likelihood the company's rating will change as a result of A.M. Best's analysis of the recent event.

A company's rating remains under review until A.M. Best is able to fully determine the rating implications of the event before affirming, upgrading or downgrading the rating. Generally, a company's rating is placed under review for less than six months.

SECTION IV

BEST'S INTERACTIVE CREDIT RATING PROCESS

The foundation of Best's interactive credit rating process is an ongoing dialogue with the rated company's management, which is facilitated by Best's primary credit analysts. Each interactively rated entity is assigned to a primary analyst, who is supervised by a team leader. The primary analyst is charged with managing the ongoing relationship with company management and performing the fundamental credit analysis prescribed in our rating criteria. It is the primary analyst's responsibility to monitor the financial and non-financial results and significant developments for each rated entity in his/her portfolio. A rating action or review can be considered any time A.M. Best becomes aware of a significant development, regardless of the annual review cycle. This process typically includes the review of the following items:

- All annual and quarterly financial statement filings (statutory and GAAP, where available, or applicable standard in the specific market/jurisdiction), including footnotes and other disclosures;
- Interim management reports provided by the rated entity;
- Significant public announcements made by the rated entity;
- Information requested by A.M. Best;
- Information provided by management.

This ongoing monitoring and dialogue with management occurs through formal annual rating meetings, as well as interim discussions on key trends and emerging issues, as needed. Management meetings afford A.M. Best's analysts the opportunity to review with the company factors that may affect its rating, including strategic goals, financial objectives and management practices. It is during these interactive meetings that a company typically will share information that may be extremely sensitive or proprietary in nature.

The dialogue with management continues throughout the entire rating process, which is described in more detail below.

1. Compile Information. The rating assessment begins with the compilation of detailed public and proprietary financial information, including annual and quarterly financial statements, regulatory filings, certified actuarial and loss reserve reports, investment detail and guidelines, reinsurance transactions, annual business plans and Best's Supplemental Rating Questionnaire (if necessary). This information is used by the primary credit analyst to develop a tailored meeting agenda for the annual rating meeting. The annual meeting is a key source of quantitative and qualitative information.

2. Perform Analysis. A.M. Best's analytical process incorporates a host of quantitative and qualitative measures that evaluate various sources of risk to an organization's financial health, including underwriting, credit, interest rate, country and market risks, as well as economic and regulatory factors. The analysis includes comparisons to peers, industry standards and proprietary benchmarks, as well as assessments of operating plans, philosophy, management, risk appetite, and the implicit or explicit support of a parent or affiliate.

3. Determine Best's Credit Rating. An initial rating recommendation is developed based on the analytical process outlined above. Each rating recommendation is reviewed and modified, as appropriate, through a rigorous committee process that involves A.M. Best's analysts and senior rating officers who possess relevant expertise. This committee approach ensures rating consistency across different business segments and maintains the integrity of the rating process and methodologies. The final rating outcome is determined by one or more rating committees after a robust discussion of the pertinent rating issues and financial data.

Prior to public dissemination, the rating outcome is communicated to the company to which it is being assigned. If the company disagrees with the rating and believes that the information on which it was based was incomplete or misunderstood, the rating can be appealed. If material new information is forthcoming in a timely manner, the rating may be reconsidered by the rating committee.

4. Disseminate Best's Credit Rating. Best's Credit Ratings are disseminated as soon as practicable following the finalization of the rating review process. The ratings are made available to the public via A.M. Best's website and through a number of different data providers and news vendors.

5. Monitor Best's Credit Rating. Once an interactive credit rating is published, A.M. Best monitors and updates the rating by regularly reviewing the company's creditworthiness. A.M. Best's analysts continually monitor current developments (e.g., financial statements, public documents, news events) to evaluate the potential impact on a company's rating. Significant developments can result in a rating review, as well as modification of the rating or outlook. The primary analyst will typically initiate a formal review of the rating upon becoming aware of any information that might reasonably be expected to result in a rating action.

Conducting a Rating Meeting

As highlighted above, meeting with the management of a company is an integral part of A.M. Best's interactive rating process. Key executives of the rated entity should be present at the annual rating meeting to discuss their areas of responsibility, including strategy, capital and risk management, distribution, underwriting, reserving, investments, claims and overall financial results and projections. Companies should be prepared to provide in advance and discuss, in detail, a broad range of information that can vary depending on the company and the industry in which they operate. The primary analyst typically provides a meeting agenda, outlining discussion topics that will guide the preparation effort. Sample agendas and lists of the information typically requested can be accessed through our website at *www.ambest.com/ratings/MeetingPreparation*.

The typical meeting agenda demonstrates the breadth and depth of the annual rating meeting and the rating process itself. Topics addressed usually include organization structure; corporate governance; operating company and holding company capital structure; underwriting and product development; marketing and business production; claims management; reinsurance; investment strategy and asset allocation; asset/liability management; financial results and projections; and risk management. The ongoing interactive dialogue is intended to provide a thorough understanding of not only the rated entity's published financial statements, but the underlying strategic and operational elements that A.M. Best believes are critical to the long-term viability of an organization.

Information Requirements

The primary source of the information presented in this publication is each insurance company's official annual and quarterly (if available) financial statements as filed with the regulator of the state, province, territory or country in which the company is domiciled. In the United States, most of these financial statements are prepared in accordance with statutory accounting requirements established by the National Association of Insurance Commissioners (NAIC) and administered by the respective states. Other sources of information include, but are not limited to interim management reports on emerging issues; supplemental information requested by A.M. Best; information provided through the annual rating meeting and other discussions with management; and information available in the public domain, such as Securities and Exchange Commission (SEC) filings in the United States, Generally Accepted Accounting Principles (GAAP) or International Financial Reporting Standards (IFRS) financial statements. In addition, audit reports prepared by certified public accountants or actuaries and loss reserve reports prepared by loss reserve specialists are often considered in the rating evaluation process.

A.M. Best expects all information submitted by a company to be accurate and complete. Information provided by a company during a rating meeting, or other interim discussions, may be extremely sensitive and/or proprietary. A.M. Best analysts are held to the highest standards of ethical and professional conduct in handling such information. A.M. Best has established policies and procedures to prevent unauthorized disclosure of confidential information and ratings prior to release. A.M. Best allows the use of confidential information only for purposes related to its rating activities or in accordance with any confidentiality agreements with the rated company.

Advance notification, including background information, of significant transactions should be provided to the primary credit analyst. This gives the analyst, and Best's rating committees, an opportunity to evaluate the impact of the transaction on the company's operations, and render a rating decision in a timely manner, if appropriate. All non-public information is considered proprietary and will be held in the strictest confidence by A.M. Best.

SECTION V

BEST'S INTERACTIVE CREDIT RATING METHODOLOGY

OVERVIEW OF BEST'S CREDIT RATING EVALUATION

The primary objective of Best's Credit Ratings within the insurance industry is to provide an opinion of the rated entity's ability to meet its senior financial obligations, which for an operating insurance company are its ongoing insurance policy and contract obligations. The assignment of an interactive rating is derived from an in-depth evaluation of a company's balance sheet strength, operating performance and business profile, as compared with A.M. Best's quantitative and qualitative standards.

In determining a company's ability to meet its current and ongoing obligations, the most important area to evaluate is its balance sheet strength, since it is the foundation for financial security. Balance sheet strength measures the exposure of a company's equity or surplus to volatility based on its operating and financial practices, and can be a reflection of its capital generation capabilities resulting from earnings quality. One of the primary tools used in the evaluation of balance sheet strength for an insurer is Best's Capital Adequacy Ratio (BCAR), which provides a quantitative measure of the risks inherent in a company's investment and insurance profile, relative to its risk-adjusted capital. A.M. Best's analysis of the balance sheet also encompasses a thorough review of various financial tests and ratios over five-year and, in some cases, ten-year periods.

The assessment of balance sheet strength includes an analysis of an organization's regulatory filings, including the GAAP or IFRS balance sheet, at the operating insurance company, holding company, and consolidated levels. To assess the financial strength and financial flexibility of a rated entity, a variety of balance sheet, income statement, and cash flow metrics are reviewed, including corporate capital structure, financial leverage, interest expense coverage, cash coverage, liquidity, capital generation, and historical sources and uses of capital.

While balance sheet strength is the foundation for financial security, the balance sheet provides an assessment of capital adequacy at a point in time. A.M. Best views operating performance and business profile as leading indicators when measuring future balance sheet strength and long-term financial stability.

The term "future" is the key, since ratings are prospective and go well beyond a "static" balance sheet view. Profitability is the engine that ultimately drives capital, and looking into the future enables the analyst to gauge a company's ability to preserve and/or generate new capital over time. In many respects, what determines the relative strength or weakness of a company's operating performance is a combination of its business profile and the ability of a company to effectively execute its strategy.

A company exhibiting strong performance, over time, will generate earnings sufficient to maintain a prudent level of risk-adjusted capital and optimize stakeholder value. Strong performers are those companies whose earnings are relatively consistent and deemed to be sustainable. Companies with a stable track record and better-than-average earnings power may receive higher ratings and have lower risk-adjusted capital relative to their peers.

On the other hand, companies that have demonstrated weaknesses in their earnings — through either consistent losses or volatility — are more likely to struggle to maintain or improve capital in the future. For these reasons, these companies typically are rated lower than their counterparts that perform well and usually are held to higher capital requirements to minimize the chance of being downgraded if current trends continue.

A.M. Best believes that risk management is the common thread that links balance sheet strength, operating performance and business profile. Risk management fundamentals can be found in the strategic decision-making process used by a company to define its business profile, and in the various financial management practices and operating elements of an insurer that dictate the sustainability of its operating performance and, ultimately, its exposure to capital volatility. As such, if a company is practicing sound risk management and executing its strategy effectively, it will preserve and build its balance sheet strength and perform successfully over the long term —both key elements of Best's ratings and the evaluation of risk management.

BEST'S CREDIT RATING APPROACH: TOP-DOWN AND BOTTOM-UP

A.M. Best assigns various types of credit ratings (FSRs, ICRs, and debt ratings) to organizations of all different shapes and sizes — from single legal-entity organizations to complex multi-national organizations with diversified insurance and non-insurance operations, and/or multiple intermediate holding companies, all under a publicly traded or privately held ultimate holding company.

Best's fundamental rating approach for the assignment of any Best's Credit Rating is to examine an organization from both the top-down and the bottom-up. As a result, the analysis performed incorporates an assessment of material sources of risk to the rated entity.

The top-down analysis includes the exposure to risk generated by activities at the parent/holding company; such as the potential strain on the operating entity from debt-servicing requirements related to the parent's borrowings, as well as the benefits of earnings diversification that may come from being a member of a diversified organization. For the non-rated subsidiaries, A.M. Best performs a detailed internal analysis of their risk profile and the resulting effect on the rated entities within the group, including A.M. Best's judgment as to the exposure of that entity to debt or other borrowings at the holding company level.

The bottom-up analysis focuses on an assessment of the risks generated directly by the operations of the rated entity itself, as well as any other rated affiliates. For insurers, this analysis includes an assessment of underwriting, credit, interest rate, market and other risks at the operating company level. The primary objective of this overall approach is to gain a broad understanding of the potential impact on the current and future balance sheet of the rated operating entity — both from its own operations and those of its parent and affiliates — in support of the assignment of a credit rating.

KEY COMPONENTS OF BEST'S CREDIT RATING EVALUATION — OPERATING COMPANY ANALYSIS

As the starting point for Best's ***bottom-up*** rating approach a rated entity's strengths and weaknesses typically are first analyzed without any benefit or drag from its affiliation with a larger organization. Employing this approach allows A.M. Best to gauge the level of policyholder security with no benefit from parental support. After the stand-alone analysis is completed, the potential impact of the operations of the holding company, non-rated affiliates and other rated affiliates is incorporated into the rating evaluation.

As mentioned earlier, the assignment of an interactive Best's Credit Rating involves a comprehensive quantitative and qualitative analysis of a company's ***balance sheet strength, operating performance and business profile***. We believe this balanced method of evaluating a company on both quantitative and qualitative levels provides better insight of a company and results in a more discerning and credible rating opinion.

The interpretation of quantitative measurements involves the incorporation of more qualitative considerations into the process that may impact prospective financial strength. Our quantitative evaluation is based on an analysis of each company's reported financial performance, utilizing over 100 key financial tests and supporting data. These tests, which underlie our evaluation of balance sheet strength and operating performance, vary in importance depending upon a company's characteristics.

In assigning a Best's FSR, additional consideration is given to balance sheet strength for those companies that are exposed to shorter-duration liabilities (less than 2-3 years) or those companies maintaining an extremely strong balance sheet. Companies with short-duration liabilities are exposed to fewer potential losses, reducing long-term risk. Alternatively, those companies exposed to long-duration liabilities (over 7 years) face greater uncertainty and risk; hence, more importance is placed on operating performance, which will need to be strong to sustain or enhance balance sheet strength over the long term. Companies with an extremely strong balance sheet are given additional consideration if their weak profitability improves.

A company's quantitative results are compared with industry composites as established by A.M. Best. Composite standards are based on the performance of many insurance companies with comparable business mix and organizational structure. In addition, industry composite benchmarks are adjusted from time to time for systemic changes in underwriting, economic and regulatory market conditions to ensure the most effective and appropriate analysis.

Balance Sheet Strength

In determining a company's ability to meet its current and ongoing senior obligations, the most important area to evaluate is its balance sheet strength. An analysis of a company's underwriting, financial, operating and asset leverage is very important in assessing its overall balance sheet strength.

Balance sheet strength measures the exposure of a company's surplus to its operating and financial practices. A highly leveraged, or poorly capitalized company can show a high return on equity/surplus, but may be exposed to a high risk of instability. Conservative leverage or capitalization enables an insurer to better withstand catastrophes, unexpected losses and adverse changes in underwriting results, fluctuating investment returns or investment losses, and changes in regulatory or economic conditions.

Underwriting leverage is generated from current premium writings, loss or policy reserves and also from reinsurance recoverables for property/casualty companies and annuity deposits and reinsurance for life/health companies. A.M. Best reviews these forms of leverage to analyze changes in trends and magnitudes. To measure exposure to pricing errors in a company's book of business, we review the ratio of gross and net premiums written to capital. To measure credit exposure and dependence on reinsurance, we review the credit quality of a company's reinsurers and ratio of reinsurance premiums and reserves ceded and related reinsurance recoverables to surplus. To measure exposure to unpaid obligations, unearned premiums and exposure to reserving errors, we analyze the ratio of net liabilities to surplus.

In order to assess whether or not a company's underwriting leverage is prudent, a number of factors unique to the company are taken into consideration. These factors include type of business written, spread of risk, quality and appropriateness of its reinsurance program, quality and diversification of assets, and adequacy of loss reserves.

A.M. Best reviews a company's ***financial leverage*** in conjunction with its underwriting leverage in forming an overall opinion of a company's balance sheet strength. Financial leverage through debt or debt-like instruments (including financial reinsurance) may place a call on an insurer's earnings and strain its cash flow. Similar to underwriting leverage, excessive financial leverage at the operating or holding company can lead to financial instability. As such, the analysis is conducted both at the operating company and holding company levels, if applicable.

To supplement its assessment of financial leverage, A.M. Best also reviews a company's ***operating leverage***. A.M. Best broadly defines operating leverage as debt (or debt-like instruments) used to fund a specific pool of matched assets. Cash flows from the pool of assets are expected to be sufficient to fund the interest and principal payments associated with the obligations, substantially reducing the potential call on an insurer's earnings and cash flow. In other words, the residual risk to the insurer would be insignificant as long as the insurer possesses sound asset/liability, liquidity and investment risk management capabilities; exhibits low duration mismatches; and minimizes repayment and liquidity risk relative to these obligations. Best has established specific tolerances for operating leverage activities that are applied at each operating company, as well as at the consolidated level. Generally, debt obligations viewed by A.M. Best as eligible for operating leverage treatment would be excluded from the calculation of financial leverage, unless one of the tolerance levels is exceeded.

A.M. Best also evaluates ***asset leverage***, which measures the exposure of a company's surplus to investment, interest rate and credit risks. Investment and interest rate risks measure the credit quality and volatility associated with the company's investment portfolio and the potential impact on its balance sheet strength.

A company's underwriting, financial and asset leverage is also subjected to an evaluation by BCAR, which calculates the net required capital to support the financial risks of the company. This encompasses the exposure of its investments, assets and underwriting to adverse economic and market conditions such as a rise in interest rates, decline in the equity markets and above-normal catastrophes. This integrated stress analysis evaluation permits a more discerning view of a company's relative balance sheet strength compared to its operating risks. The BCAR is based on audited financial statements and supplemental information provided by companies. The BCAR result is an important component in determining a company's balance sheet strength. A.M. Best also views insurance groups on a consolidated basis and assigns a common BCAR result to group consolidations or multiple member companies that are linked together through intercompany pooling or reinsurance arrangements.

Capitalization Tests for Life Companies

- **Change in Net Premiums Written (NPW) and Deposits:** The annual percentage change in net premiums written and deposits. This test is a measure of growth in underwriting commitments.
- **NPW and Deposits to Total Capital:** Net premiums written and deposits related to capital and surplus funds, including asset valuation reserve (AVR). This reflects the leverage, after reinsurance assumed and ceded, of the company's current volume of net business in relation to its capital and surplus. This test measures the company's exposure to pricing errors in its current book of business.
- **Capital & Surplus to Liabilities:** The ratio of capital and surplus (including AVR) to total liabilities (excluding AVR). This test measures the relationship of capital and surplus to the company's unpaid obligations after reinsurance assumed and ceded. It reflects the extent to which the company has leveraged its capital and surplus base. On an individual company basis, this ratio will vary due to differences in product mix, balance sheet quality and spread of insurance risk.
- **Surplus Relief:** The relationship of commissions and expense allowances on reinsurance ceded to capital and surplus funds. The use of surplus relief can be the result of "surplus strain," a term used to describe any insurance transaction wherein the funds collected are not sufficient under regulatory accounting guidelines to cover the liabilities established.
- **Reinsurance Leverage:** The relationship of total reserves ceded plus commissions and expenses due on reinsurance ceded plus experience rating and other refunds due from reinsurers, plus amounts recoverable from reinsurers to total capital and surplus.
- **Change in Capital:** The annual percentage change in the sum of current year capital and surplus, plus AVR, plus voluntary investment reserves, over the prior year's sum.
- **Best's Capital Adequacy Ratio (BCAR):** The BCAR compares an insurer's adjusted surplus relative to the required capital necessary to support its operating and investment risks. Companies deemed to have "adequate" balance sheet strength normally generate a BCAR score of over 100% and will usually carry a Secure Best's Credit Rating. However, the level of capital required to support a given rating level varies by company, depending on its operating performance and business profile.

Adjusted surplus is reported surplus plus/minus adjustments made to provide a more comparable basis for evaluating balance sheet strength. Such modifications include adjustments related to equity in unearned premiums, loss reserves and assets. Certain off-balance sheet items are also deducted from reported surplus, such as encumbered capital, debt-servicing requirements, potential catastrophe losses and future operating losses.

Net Required Capital is calculated as the necessary level of capital to support four broad risk categories, including C1 (Asset Risk); C2 (Underwriting Risk); C3 (Market/Interest Rate Risk); and C4 (Business Risk). Net Required Capital represents the arithmetic sum of capital required to support each of the risk categories reduced by a covariance adjustment. The covariance adjustment reduces a company's total capital requirement by recognizing that risks associated with many of the four categories are independent and do not occur at the same time.

Generally, over two-thirds of a life insurance company's net capital requirement is generated by C1 and C3 risks. Conversely, over two-thirds of a health company's net capital requirement is generated by C1 and C2 risks. The Underwriting Risk components are influenced by a company's business profile which includes distribution of premium by line and size.

Capitalization Tests for Health Companies

- **Liabilities to Assets:** The ratio of total liabilities to total assets. This test measures the proportion of liabilities covered by a company's asset base.
- **Net Premiums Written to Capital:** The ratio of premiums to total capital and surplus. This test measures the leverage associated with the level of premiums compared to the total capital and surplus of the company. The higher the number, the more leveraged the company.
- **Debt to Capital & Surplus:** The ratio of a company's total debt to its total capital and surplus. In this ratio, debt is defined as loans and notes payable on both a current and long-term basis, as well as surplus notes.
- **Equity PMPM:** The ratio of capital and surplus to member months. This test measures the amount of capital and surplus spread over a company's membership base.
- **Capital & Surplus to Total Assets:** The ratio of total capital and surplus to total assets. This test measures the relationship of a company's asset base to its capital and surplus.
- **Months Reserves:** The ratio of a company's total capital and surplus to monthly average total expenses. This test provides a measure of the duration of a particular company's capital and surplus versus its expense commitments.
- **Best's Capital Adequacy Ratio (BCAR):** Refer to description above for Life Companies.

Quality and Appropriateness of Reinsurance and Other Risk Mitigation Programs

Reinsurance plays an essential role in the risk-spreading process and provides insurers with varying degrees of financial stability. As a result, we evaluate a company's reinsurance program to determine its appropriateness and credit quality. A company's reinsurance program should be appropriate relative to its policy limits and underwriting risks, catastrophe exposures, business, and financial capacity. In addition, a reinsurance program should involve true risk transfer and include reinsurers of good credit quality, since in the event of a reinsurer's failure to respond to its share of a loss, the reinsured or counterparty would have to absorb a potentially large loss in its entirety.

For life/health companies, a reliable reinsurance program must consider sound risk management practices to provide the company with protection against adverse fluctuations in experience. Since these risk transfer agreements on an underlying policy or policies indemnify the company for insurance risks, prudent evaluation of the economic impact on a company's life, health, and annuity operations is critical. Incorporating reinsurance to manage a company's financial risk that includes mortality, morbidity, lapse or surrender, expense, and investment performance presents a competitive risk to a counterparty's future growth prospects and long-term viability. Therefore, the range of reinsurance must be evaluated with the company's ability to manage its growth relative to demands for life and health insurance coverages under existing economic and regulatory environments.

An insurer's ability to meet its financial obligations can become overly dependent upon the performance of its reinsurers. A company can also become exposed to the state of reinsurance markets in general. A significant dependency on reinsurance can become problematic if a major reinsurer of the company becomes insolvent or disputes coverage for claims. It also can become a problem if general reinsurance rates, capacity, terms and conditions change dramatically following an industry event. The more a company is dependent upon reinsurance, the more vulnerable its underwriting capacity becomes to adverse changes in the reinsurance market. The greater this dependency, the greater our scrutiny of a company's reinsurance program to determine its appropriateness and credit quality and whether it is temporary or permanent in nature.

Over the past several years, direct life/health writers have been searching for other cost-effective capital solutions to fund reserves and/or transfer risk on a variety of products, including certain term and universal life products that are subject to reserve requirements of the Valuation of Life Insurance Policies Model Regulation, more commonly referred to as Regulation XXX. A number of life/health companies have developed capital markets solutions through a securitized transaction utilizing a captive company. These securitizations are typically intended to fund the difference between the statutory reserve and the economic reserve required to support the business according to the direct writer's own analysis.

These transactions impact a company's financial strength as measured by the BCAR calculation, and also impact a company's operating leverage. By ceding reserves to a captive company, the direct insurer's insurance risk is reduced on the BCAR. However, the captive is typically more thinly capitalized than the direct writer for these reserves (though within regulatory guidelines), and the capital structure is typically supported primarily through surplus notes, not equity contribution. Additionally, the transfer of the reserves from the direct writer's balance sheet reduces surplus strain, freeing the company to write even more business. These various factors are considered in evaluating the appropriateness of the insurer's overall reinsurance and risk mitigation program.

Adequacy of Loss/Policy Reserves

For life/health companies, an evaluation of the adequacy of an insurer's reported reserves is essential to an evaluation of its profitability, leverage, capitalization and liquidity. Net income and policyholders' surplus are directly affected by changes in reported reserves. While we do not audit a company's reserves, we rely on the reserve adequacy opinions of certified actuaries (internal and third party) to supplement our review.

A.M. Best reviews the valuation methodology, interest assumptions and degree of conservation in the establishment of life, health and annuity reserves. We also evaluate the degree of uncertainty in policy reserves, recognizing that they are only actuarial estimates of future events. If the degree of uncertainty exceeds any equity in the reserves, and is large in relation to net income and policyholders' surplus, our confidence declines in a company's reported profitability, liquidity, and leverage (capitalization).

Quality and Diversification of Assets

The quality and diversification of assets contribute to a company's financial stability. Invested assets (principally bonds, common stocks, mortgages and real estate) are evaluated to assess the risk of default and the potential impact on surplus if the sale of these assets occurred unexpectedly. The higher the liquidity, diversification and/or quality of the asset portfolio, the less uncertainty there is in the value to be realized upon an asset sale and the lesser the likelihood of default. Therefore, a company's investment guidelines are reviewed to identify a lack of diversification among industries or geographic regions, with particular attention paid to large single investments that exceed 10% of a company's total capital. Companies that hold illiquid, undiversified and/or speculative assets and have a significant underwriting exposure to volatile lines of business that are vulnerable to unfavorable changes in underwriting and/or economic conditions can jeopardize policyholders' surplus.

Liquidity

Liquidity measures a company's ability to meet its anticipated short- and long-term obligations to policyholders and other creditors. A company's liquidity depends upon the degree to which it can satisfy its financial obligations by holding cash and investments that are sound, diversified and liquid or through operating cash flow. A high degree of liquidity enables an insurer to meet unexpected needs for cash without the untimely sale of investments or fixed assets, which may result in substantial realized losses due to temporary market conditions and/or tax consequences.

To measure a company's ability to satisfy its financial obligations without having to resort to selling long-term investments or affiliated assets, we review a company's quick liquidity, which measures the amount of cash and quickly convertible investments that have a low exposure to fluctuations in market value. We also review current liquidity to measure the proportion of a company's total liabilities that are covered by cash and unaffiliated invested assets. Operational and net cash flows are reviewed since they, by themselves, can meet some liquidity needs provided cash flows are positive, large and stable relative to cash requirements. Finally, we evaluate the quality, market value and diversification of assets, particularly the exposure of large single investments relative to capital.

For life and annuity companies, in order to measure a life insurer's potential vulnerability to all surrenderable liabilities, it is necessary to review the impact of asset and liability maturations under normal and stressed cycles in the event of a crisis of confidence. A loss of confidence in the financial strength of an insurer on the part of distributors or policyholders, which can lead to a "run on the bank," can be triggered by adverse changes in the company's financial strength, the economy, the financial markets and/or a company's media profile.

The immediate liquidity analysis begins with an assessment of a life insurer's liability structure and the withdrawal characteristics of its policies and contracts. Companies that maintain a significant concentration of immediately surrenderable liabilities, which may be subject to unexpected calls on their assets, require greater levels of short-term liquidity. As a result, an evaluation is made to determine how vulnerable a company is to a potential "run" and its ability to satisfy its obligations to policyholders in the event a "run" is triggered. Included in our review is the size of the contracts issued, applicable surrender charges or market value adjustments, withdrawal restrictions, the types of distribution systems utilized, financial incentives which may exist for the replacement of policies, the level of highly liquid assets maintained, the strength and trends of cash flows and an individual company's reputation/franchise.

A.M. Best's review of liquidity for U.S. life companies utilizes A.M. Best's Liquidity Model for U.S. Life Insurers. Using statutory data, the model quantitatively measures a company's short-term (30 days) and longer-term (six to twelve months) cash needs positions under stressed scenarios. The model allows for conservative, standardized comparisons to be calculated and determines whether a company's calculated liquidity is within the range of its peers relative to its size, type of business and A.M. Best rating. A.M. Best's initial analysis has focused on companies with a preponderance of interest-sensitive liabilities. Refer to the Criteria piece "A.M. Best's Liquidity Model For U.S. Life Insurers" for more on this topic.

Key Liquidity Tests For Life Companies

- **Quick Liquidity:** The ratio of unaffiliated quick assets to liabilities. Quick assets include cash and short-term investments and a percentage of unaffiliated common stocks and unaffiliated public investment grade bonds. This test measures the proportion of liabilities (excluding AVR, conditional reserves and separate accounts) covered by cash and quickly convertible investments. It indicates a company's ability to meet its maturing obligations without requiring the sale of long-term investments or the borrowing of money.
- **Current Liquidity:** The ratio of total current assets to total liabilities. This test measures the proportion of liabilities (excluding AVR, conditional reserves and separate

account liabilities) covered by cash and unaffiliated holdings, excluding mortgages and real estate.

- **Non-Investment Grade Bonds to Capital:** The sum of NAIC Classes three, four, five, and six bonds as a percentage of capital and surplus funds (including AVR).
- **Delinquent & Foreclosed Mortgages to Capital:** The sum of long-term mortgages upon which interest is overdue more than three months, in process of foreclosure and foreclosed real estate as a percentage of capital and surplus funds (including AVR).
- **Mortgages & Credit Tenant Loans & Real Estate to Capital:** Mortgage loans and credit tenant loans and real estate (home office property, property held for income and property held for sale) as a percentage of capital and surplus funds (including AVR).
- **Affiliated Investments to Capital:** Affiliated investments (including home office property) as a percentage of capital and surplus funds (including AVR).

Key Liquidity Tests For Health Companies

- **Current Liquidity:** The ratio of total current assets to total liabilities. This test measures the proportion of liabilities (excluding AVR, conditional reserves and separate account liabilities) covered by cash, and unaffiliated holdings, excluding mortgages and real estate.
- **Overall Liquidity:** This ratio measures the proportion of total liabilities covered by a company's total assets, to reflect a company's ability to meet its maturing obligations.
- **Premium Receivable Turnover:** The ratio of premium receivables to commercial revenue. This ratio is expressed in months and measures the liquidity level of a company's total premium and fee-for-service revenue in light of its premium receivables for a specific period.
- **Cash and Assets to Claims & Payables:** The ratio of total cash, short-term investments and long-term investments to the sum of accounts payable and claims payable.
- **Claims to Net Premium Earned:** The ratio of total claims payable to net premiums earned.
- **Health Average Claims Payment Period (days):** The ratio of claims payable to total health expenses per year in days (365).
- **Total Health IBNR Pay Period (days):** The ratio of total incurred but not reported claims divided by total health expenses in days (365).

Operating Performance

Profitable insurance operations are essential for a company to operate as an ongoing concern. For an insurer to remain viable in the marketplace, it must perpetuate a financially strong balance sheet for its policyholders. When evaluating operating performance, Best's analysis centers on the stability and sustainability of the company's sources of earnings in relation to the liabilities that are retained by the company. Since long-term balance sheet strength is generally driven by operating performance, greater importance is placed on operating performance when evaluating insurers writing long-duration business. Conversely, operating performance is weighted less heavily for those insurers writing predominantly short-duration business that also possess very strong capitalization and a stable business profile.

A.M. Best reviews the components of a company's statutory earnings over the past five-year period to make an evaluation of the sources of profits and the degree and trend of various profitability measures. Areas reviewed include underwriting, investments, capital gains/losses and total operating earnings, both before and after taxes. Profitability measures are easily distorted by operational changes; therefore, we review the mix and trends of premium volume, investment income, net income and surplus. Also important to evaluating profitability is the structure of the company (stock vs. mutual), the length and nature of its insurance liability risks and how these elements relate to the company's operating mission. The degree of volatility in a company's earnings and the impact that this could have on capitalization and balance sheet strength is of particular interest to A.M. Best.

To supplement our review of profitability, A.M. Best analyzes the company's earnings on a GAAP basis, IFRS basis, and any other regulatory or accounting reporting in order to understand the company's forms and measurements of profitability. This review generally extends beyond the scope of publicly traded companies, since an increasing number of non-public insurers also prepare, monitor and/or manage to GAAP, IFRS or other forms of accounting reporting. A.M. Best recognizes that a proper assessment of an insurer's current and prospective profitability may involve a review of multiple accounting forms and results to ascertain the true economic picture.

Key Profitability Tests For Life Companies

- **Benefits Paid to NPW and Deposits:** Total benefits paid as a percentage of net premiums written and deposits. Benefits paid include death benefits, matured endowments, annuity benefits, accident and health benefits, disability and surrender benefits, group conversions, coupons and payments on supplementary contracts, interest on policy or contract funds and other miscellaneous benefits.
- **Commissions and Expenses to NPW and Deposits:** Commissions and expenses incurred as a percentage of net premiums written and deposits. Commissions and expenses include payments on both direct and assumed business, general insurance expenses, insurance taxes, licenses and fees, increase in loading and other miscellaneous expenses, and exclude commissions and expense allowances received on reinsurance ceded.
- **NOG to Total Assets:** Net operating gain (after taxes) as a percentage of the mean of current and prior year admitted

assets. This test measures insurance earnings in relation to the company's total asset base.

- **NOG to Total Revenue:** Net operating gain (after taxes) as a percentage of total revenues. This test measures insurance earnings in relation to total funds provided from operations.
- **Operating Return on Equity:** Net operating gain (after taxes) as a percentage of the mean of current and prior year capital and surplus. This test measures insurance earnings in relation to the company's policyholders' surplus base.
- **Net Yield:** Net investment income as a percentage of mean cash and invested assets plus accrued investment income minus borrowed money. This test does not reflect realized and unrealized capital gains or income taxes.
- **Total Return:** The net yield plus realized and unrealized capital gains and losses, minus transfers to IMR, plus amortization of IMR

Key Profitability Tests For Health Companies

- **Benefits Paid to Net Premiums Written & Fee for Service:** Total medical and hospital or dental expenses as a percentage of net premiums written and fee for service. Also included with net premiums written and fee for service are risk revenues and changes in unearned premium reserves.
- **Commissions and Expenses to Net Premiums Written & Fee for Service:** Total claims adjustment expense and general administrative expenses as a percentage of net premiums written and fee for service. Also included with net premiums written and fee for service are risk revenues and changes in unearned premium reserves.
- **NOG to Total Assets:** Net income excluding net realized capital gains (losses) as a percentage of the average between prior year and current year assets. This test measures post-tax insurance earnings in relation to the mean of the company's current and prior year total admitted assets.
- **NOG to Revenue:** Net income excluding net realized capital gains (losses) as a percentage of total revenue. This ratio measures post-tax earnings in relationship to total funds provided from operations.
- **Operating Return on Equity:** Net income excluding net realized capital gains (losses) as a percentage of the average between prior year and current year capital and surplus. This test measures earnings in relation to the company's total capital and contingency reserve base.
- **Net Yield:** Net investment income as a percentage of the average between prior year and current year invested assets and accrued investment income less borrowed money. It does not reflect the impact of realized and unrealized capital gains or income taxes.
- **Total Return:** The net yield plus realized and unrealized capital gains and losses.

Business Profile

Business profile is the qualitative component of Best's rating evaluation which directly impacts the quantitative measures. The factors that comprise an insurer's business profile drive current and future operating performance and, in turn, can impact long-term financial strength and the company's ability to meet its obligations to policyholders.

Business profile is influenced by the degree of risk inherent in the company's mix of business, an insurer's competitive market position and the depth and experience of its management. Lack of size or growth are not typically considered negative rating factors unless A.M. Best believes these issues have a negative influence on the company's prospective operating performance and balance sheet strength.

A.M. Best places greater emphasis on business profile issues for insurers writing long-duration business, such as life, retirement savings, casualty lines, and reinsurance where long-term financial strength is critical. Conversely, less business profile emphasis is placed on auto and property writers, as well as indemnity health insurers writing shorter-duration contracts where short- to medium-term financial strength is of greater importance.

In addition, business profile issues increase in their importance at A.M. Best's highest rating levels. At the "Superior" level, insurers are expected to have strong balance sheets and adequate operating performance, and exhibit stable operating trends. What differentiates these companies is the strength of their business profile, which typically translates into defensible competitive advantages. This rating approach is consistent with the requirements of today's marketplace, which is concerned with an insurer's financial strength and market viability.

Key Business Profile Tests

Spread of Risk: A company's book of business must be analyzed by line in terms of its geographic, product and distribution diversification. However, the size of a company, measured solely by its premium volume, cannot be used to judge its spread of risk.

Generally, large companies have a natural spread of risk. Similarly, a small company, which is conservatively managed, writes conservative lines of business and avoids a concentration of risk, can attain the same degree of stability in its book of business as that experienced by a large company, with the exception of regulatory or residual market risks.

For life/health companies, the mix of business must be evaluated with respect to the distribution and performance of the underlying assets, as well as a company's susceptibility to economic business cycles or regulatory pressures, such as minimum loss ratios, market conduct regulation or financial services and health care reform initiatives.

The geographic location and lines of business written by a company also determine its exposure or vulnerability to regulatory or residual market risks that exist within certain jurisdictions. In addition, the mix of business must also be carefully evaluated. Because the underwriting experience between lines of business varies dramatically, the underwriting risk profile of a company must be determined since high-risk lines with volatile loss experience can impact the financial stability of an insurer, particularly one that is poorly capitalized and/or has poor liquidity.

Revenue Composition: A by-line analysis of net premium volume is important to determine changes in the amount, type, geographic distribution, diversification and volatility of business written by a company, which can either have a beneficial or adverse effect on its prospective profitability. Underwriting income, investment income, capital gains, asset values and, consequently, surplus can be significantly affected by external changes in economic, regulatory, legal and financial market environments, as well as by natural and man-made catastrophes.

Competitive Market Position: Analysis of an insurer's operating strategy and competitive advantages by line is essential to assess a company's ability to respond to competitive market challenges, economic volatility and regulatory change in relation to its book of business. Defensible and sustainable competitive advantages include control over distribution, multiple distribution channels, a low-cost structure, effective utilization and leveraging of technology, superior service, strong franchise recognition, a captive market of insureds, easy and inexpensive access to capital, and underwriting expertise within the book of business.

Management: The experience and depth of management are important determinants for achieving success because the insurance business is based on an underlying foundation of trust and fiscal responsibility. Competitive pressures within virtually every insurance market segment have amplified the importance of management's ability to develop and execute defensible strategic plans. A.M. Best's understanding of the operating objectives of a company's management team plays an important role in its qualitative evaluation of the current and future operating performance of a company. This is particularly true when a company is undergoing a restructuring to address operational issues, balance sheet problems or is actively raising capital.

Insurance Market Risk: Insurance market risk reflects the potential financial volatility that is introduced by, and associated with, the segment(s) of the insurance industry and/or the financial services sphere within which an organization operates. Such risks may also be considered systemic risks and are generally common to all market participants (i.e., financial services reform, health care reform, expansion of alternative markets, and integration of health care providers). Insurance market risk can be biased either positively or negatively by a number of company-specific business factors.

Event Risk: Event risk can encompass a variety of sudden or unexpected circumstances that may arise and can potentially impact an insurer's financial strength and its Best's rating. When a sudden or unexpected event occurs, we evaluate the financial and market impact to the insurer. For example, the potential exists for major business and distribution disruption associated with significant litigation; the potential for a "run-on-the-bank" due to a loss of policyholder/distributor confidence; economic collapse or the enactment of significant legislation. In addition, constraints imposed by regulators in the form of mandated rate rollbacks, extraordinary assessments, and mandatory market lock-in arrangements in catastrophe-prone areas can adversely affect a company. Event risk may include changes in management, ownership, parental commitment, distribution, a legal ruling or regulatory development. Finally, event risk can also be influenced by potential regulatory or legislative reforms, economic conditions, interest rate levels, and financial market performance, as well as societal changes. For international companies, as well as domestic insurers operating abroad, political climates and sovereignty risks may also have a significant bearing on event risk.

KEY COMPONENTS OF BEST'S CREDIT RATING EVALUATION — HOLDING COMPANY ANALYSIS

The analysis performed in the assignment of interactive credit ratings incorporates an assessment of material sources of risk to the rated entity. This includes the exposure to risk generated by activities at the parent/holding company and non-rated affiliates (which are discussed later). Understanding the potential effect on a rated entity of the activities of the ultimate parent/holding company is key to developing a comprehensive view of the risk profile of the rated entity. As a result, all ultimate parents are reviewed and analyzed to determine, at a minimum, if the parent's activities could reasonably be expected to place a call on the capital of the rated operating company, or expose the rated entity to material risk — even in cases where no public rating of the parent is assigned.

Corporate Capital Structure

Holding companies (if present) and their associated capital structures can have a significant impact on the overall financial strength of an insurance company subsidiary. Holding companies can provide subsidiaries with a level of financial flexibility including capital infusions, access to capital markets and, in some cases, additional cash flow sources from other operations. Likewise, debt and other securities are typically obligations of a holding company, which depending on the magnitude of these obligations, can reduce the financial flexibility of the enterprise and potentially place a strain on future earnings and inhibit surplus growth at a subsidiary.

A.M. Best reviews both an insurer's capital structure and its holding company's capital structure to determine if they are sound and unencumbered. This review includes an assessment of the quality of capital with a focus on the amount, composition, and amortization schedule of intangible assets as well as the presence of surplus notes at the operating company.

A holding company can have various types of financial instruments, including debt securities, preferred stocks or hybrid securities in its capital structure. For mutual companies, surplus notes can exist as a component of overall surplus. A.M. Best reviews the relative debt and equity characteristics of a particular security in determining overall financial leverage. Our review focuses on specific terms and features of securities, including the coupon and dividend rate, repayment terms and financial and other covenants. Insurance subsidiaries generally fund debt service and other obligations of their holding company through a combination of dividends, tax-sharing payments and other expense allocation agreements with their holding company. As such, A.M. Best measures the extent to which an insurance company's earnings or the holding company's cash flow can cover interest and other fixed obligations.

Integral to an insurer's rating assignment is our assessment of a company's ability to meet the debt service and other obligations associated with its parent's capital structure and the risks that a capital structure imposes on a company.

Holding Company Methodology

For complex organizations, the core of A.M. Best's top-down analytical approach is the assessment of the holding company on a consolidated and parent-only basis, which provides an understanding of the organization as a whole. A.M. Best reviews the parent and consolidated entity to capture the entire group's performance and capital position. At these levels, financial leverage and fixed charge coverage, liquidity, asset quality and diversification, as well as other factors are reviewed to ensure that the group, as a whole, is in good financial standing. Also, if the entity issues debt or hybrid securities to the public market, A.M. Best analyzes and rates these securities.

Financial Leverage and Interest Coverage

A.M. Best takes into consideration the quality of the capital structure, the permanency of capital, as well as the diversity and sustainability of earnings sources available to the holding company. As part of its quality of capital analysis, A.M. Best reviews the terms and conditions of securities issued, the maturity schedule of the capital structure, and the level of goodwill, value in force, deferred acquisition costs and other intangible assets relative to reported equity and total capitalization. The level of intangible assets is of particular importance when such items constitute a significant portion of an organization's capital base, thereby distorting financial leverage ratios relative to its peers.

The ability to service financial obligations over time is a function of the organization's current capitalization and ability to generate earnings from operations. Unencumbered cash and equivalents and short-term investments held at the holding company may also support the parent company's debt service and other short-term obligations. In evaluating a holding company's ability to service its financial obligations, A.M. Best considers interest and fixed charge coverage, as well as cashflow coverage.

Equity Credit for Hybrid Securities

The increased use of nontraditional debt securities within the insurance industry reflects, in part, the generally more favorable treatment they receive in the analysis of an issuer's capital structure by regulators and rating agencies. The more favorable treatment of hybrid securities relative to traditional debt instruments is principally due to the existence of equity-like features or characteristics. Many of these instruments also provide a lower after-tax cost of capital to the issuer, while at the same time they are a less expensive form of accessing capital than through the equity markets.

A.M. Best's assessment of these securities, and the resulting impact on financial leverage and coverage ratios, focuses on the use of these instruments within an entity's capital structure and their impact on financial ratios and financial flexibility and highlights the importance of debt-service capabilities. Hybrid securities, typically in the form of a preferred stock, trust preferred or convertible security, share basic characteristics associated with common equity. Hybrids can include a variety of features that, over time, allow them to exhibit changing proportions of debt and equity characteristics.

A.M. Best's analysis of a hybrid's equity credit focuses on the features of a particular security and the amount of equity credit it may receive. A.M. Best's perspective on how debt-like or equity-like a given hybrid security is based on seniority (loss absorption), maturity (permanency of capital) and the cash-flow flexibility (deferability) provided by its terms and features. In ranking equity-credit-afforded securities, A.M. Best typically gives straight debt and securities with a cash put option no equity credit, while perpetual preferred securities are granted close to full equity credit. All other hybrid securities fall in between, based on loss absorption characteristics and their cash-flow flexibility. It is important to note that A.M. Best's rating committees have flexibility to adjust equity credit attribution based on individual circumstances.

In general, the longer the maturity, the longer interest/dividend payments may be deferred and the deeper the subordination, the higher will be the equity credit given to a hybrid security. Those factors are blended in an overall preliminary equity-credit score before other factors are considered. That said, these instruments can be extremely complex and require extensive further rating analysis that goes well beyond that of any simple matrix. Consider the category of hybrid instruments referred to as convertible securities, which can receive equity credit ranging from 0% to close to 100% depending on the terms and structure of the particular instrument.

Debt Rating Methodology

If an insurance organization issues public debt, A.M. Best will typically assign a rating specific to its view of the credit quality of the debt issue. The debt rating is established by reference to the underlying credit rating of the issuing entity, whether it is an operating or holding company.

For debt issued by an operating company, the rating will reflect the degree of subordination of the debt issue to the senior obligations of the insurer, typically insurance policies and contracts. For highly rated insurers, senior unsecured debt most frequently would be one rating notch below the entity's issuer credit rating (reflecting debt-holder subordination to policyholders), subordinated debt two notches, and so forth. However, for issuers in the lower rating categories, notching between policy and contract obligations and senior debt-holder obligations may be expanded as the issuer credit rating moves further down the rating scale. The increase in notching at the lower issuer credit rating levels reflects the generally increased probability of default.

Similarly, for debt issued by a holding company, debt ratings are assigned to reflect the degree of subordination of the debt obligation to senior obligations of the holding company. Since a holding company does not have policyholders, senior unsecured debt holders usually will be the senior-most creditors, and hence, ratings of senior unsecured debt issues will be at the same rating level as the corresponding issuer credit rating, with subordinated debt one notch below.

The risk of financial concerns at the operating level increasing the probability of regulatory intervention to the disadvantage of holding company creditors already is factored by the increase on notching between the operating company ICR and holding company ICR at the lower end of the rating scale.

KEY COMPONENTS OF BEST'S CREDIT RATING EVALUATION — ASSESSING NON-RATED AFFILIATES

Another important part of Best's top-down rating approach is the review and analysis of non-rated affiliates. This will typically be incorporated into the assessment of the ultimate parent's activities through the review of information — such as the organization chart and consolidated financials — with company management. However, in cases where the primary analyst or rating committee believes the non-rated affiliate represents a potential material exposure to the rated entity, additional analysis may be performed to determine the potential impact of the non-rated operations on the rated entity.

The analysis may include interaction with management, basic financial analysis of the ultimate parent's and the non-rated affiliate's financial statements and other public documents, and non-public information, if provided. When the non-rated entity is engaged in a business line where A.M. Best does not have a published rating methodology, the assessment can include ratings and reports from third-party sources, as well as other information in the public domain.

SECTION VI
RISK MANAGEMENT AND THE RATING PROCESS

Risk management is the process by which companies systematically identify, measure and manage the various types of risk inherent within their operations. The fundamental objectives of a sound risk management program are to manage the organization's exposure to potential earnings and capital volatility, and maximize value to the organization's various stakeholders.

Insurance companies are in the business of managing various types of risk. Where there is risk, there is uncertainty, and where there is uncertainty, there is exposure to volatility. It is important to note that the objective of risk management is not to eliminate risk and volatility, but to understand it and manage it. Risk management allows organizations to identify and quantify their risks; set risk tolerances based on their overall corporate objectives; and take the necessary actions to manage risk in light of those objectives. Proper risk management fosters an operating environment that supports both strong financial controls and risk mitigation, as well as prudent risk-taking to seize market opportunities.

Risk management tools and practices across the insurance industry continue to evolve. The industry has experienced a number of events and trends since the turn of the millennium that have exposed, and will continue to expose, insurers to increased levels of risk and uncertainty. Developments such as the implementation of enterprise risk management programs (ERM), including economic capital (EC) models, more sophisticated catastrophe management and dynamic hedging programs, have headlined efforts of the insurance industry to manage its growing exposure to potential volatility in earnings and capital.

A.M. Best believes that ERM — establishing a risk-aware culture, using sophisticated tools to consistently identify and manage, as well as measure risk and risk correlations — is an increasingly important component of an insurer's risk management framework. The foundation of any risk management framework is the compilation of traditional risk management practices and controls that historically have helped companies monitor and manage their exposure to the five key categories of risk: credit, market, underwriting, operational and strategic.

The analysis of ERM is an integral part of the rating analysis and discussions with all rated companies. A company's risk management capabilities are considered in the qualitative assessment of all three rating areas: balance sheet strength, operating performance, and business profile. A.M. Best believes that ERM encompasses a wide range of activities, from traditional risk management practices to the use of sophisticated tools to identify and quantify risks. One of the tools often used to quantify risks, and measure the volatility and correlation of risks is an EC model. A.M. Best believes that a strong EC model — capturing and quantifying all the material risks and risk interdependencies of an organization — can be a valuable tool to an insurer, but it is just one of many tools and processes utilized within the overall risk management framework.

ASSESSING RISK MANAGEMENT

As mentioned earlier, A.M. Best believes that risk management is the common thread that links balance sheet strength, operating performance and business profile. As such, if a company is practicing sound risk management and executing its strategy effectively, it will maintain a prudent level of risk-adjusted capital and perform successfully over the long term — common objectives of both Best's ratings and risk management.

A.M. Best believes that assessing an insurer's risk management capabilities — within the context of determining an insurer's financial strength — should be viewed in light of a company's scope of operations and the complexity of its business.

- A.M. Best believes that to remain competitive in today's dynamic environment, build sustainable earnings, accumulate capital, and ultimately, maintain high ratings, complex organizations — such as insurers participating in the global reinsurance and retirement savings markets — must develop and constantly refine an ERM framework, including the development of internal economic capital modeling.
- For organizations with a more limited operating scope focusing on more stable, traditional lines of business, the ERM process may be less comprehensive or complex at this time. However, the development of principles-based solvency approaches, such as Solvency II in Europe, and the significant efforts of sophisticated insurers to raise the bar on the risk management front, ultimately will become a competitive issue driving continued improvement and integration of ERM concepts for all insurers regardless of size.

Whether utilizing a formalized ERM framework, integrating selected elements of ERM into an insurer's operating practices or relying solely on a traditional risk management process, A.M. Best perceives risk management as paramount to an insurer's long-term success. As such, within the rating process, each company — regardless of its size or complexity — is expected to explain how it identifies, measures, monitors and manages risk. An insurer that can demonstrate strong risk management practices integrated into its core operating processes, and effectively execute its business plan, will maintain favorable ratings in an increasingly dynamic operating environment. A.M. Best believes that risk management is embedded in an insurer's "Corporate DNA" when risk metrics are integrated into corporate, business line and functional area objectives, and when risk-return measures are incorporated into financial planning and budgeting, strategic planning, performance measurement and incentive compensation.

RISK MANAGEMENT AND BEST'S CAPITAL ADEQUACY RATIO (BCAR)

BCAR is an important quantitative tool that helps A.M. Best differentiate between companies and indicate whether a company's capitalization is appropriate for a particular rating level. However, BCAR by itself never has been the sole basis for determining any Best's Credit Rating. Other considerations include the various financial management practices and operating elements of an insurer that ultimately dictate the sustainability of its operating performance, and its exposure to capital volatility. In other words, a company's relative risk management capabilities are a key factor in determining the BCAR capital requirement for each rated insurer.

In many cases, companies with similar capital positions (e.g., BCAR scores) might be assigned different ratings based on the integration of other important considerations unique to each insurance company. One of these considerations is a company's exposure to volatility, and its ability to measure, monitor and manage that volatility through its risk management practices. In assessing a company's exposure to earnings and capital volatility, A.M. Best considers both the inherent volatility in a company's business mix and the volatility in reported results.

Companies with strong risk management, and/or low relative exposure to volatility, may be allowed to maintain lower BCAR levels relative to the guideline for their ratings based on a case-by-case evaluation of an insurer's overall risk management capabilities relative to its risk profile. Conversely, companies with weak risk management need to maintain a higher level of required capital, relative to similar entities with commensurate exposure to volatility.

SECTION VII

GROUP RATING METHODOLOGY

Regulatory requirements and market dynamics often require insurers to set up subsidiaries or branch offices in foreign countries. These overseas subsidiaries carry differing levels of importance and risk to their parent companies. Some are crucial to the success of the franchise, yet they may require significant investment before they turn a profit. For other insurers, the foreign operation may simply be an ancillary investment with a relatively short time horizon.

These factors and others weigh heavily in A.M. Best's ratings of insurance companies that are members of a group. The need for international insurers to set up operations in numerous jurisdictions to maintain access to market intelligence has brought into focus the notion of fungibility of capital — that is, an organization's ability to allocate and deploy capital in the most efficient way where it is most needed. A.M. Best recognizes that to sustain a competitive advantage, these groups must allocate their capital with maximum efficiency. However, to obtain a secure credit rating, a certain minimum level of capitalization must be maintained at the insurance company level.

A.M. Best evaluates insurance groups to determine what levels of rating enhancement or drag are placed on the ratings of members of insurance groups. One of the main themes is the implicit and explicit support a parent provides its insurance subsidiaries. This support together with any legal constraints on the free flow of capital among affiliates, will be key factors in determining an insurance subsidiary's rating enhancement or drag and its ultimate rating assignment.

Rating members of complex, domestic or multinational insurance organizations is a difficult task. A.M. Best performs comprehensive quantitative and qualitative analyses of an organization's balance sheet strength, operating performance and business profile. Every legal entity that maintains an A.M. Best rating is reviewed on a stand-alone basis. The entity's strengths and weaknesses are analyzed, without any benefit or drag from its affiliation with a larger organization. Employing this approach allows A.M. Best to gauge the level of policyholder security with no benefit from parental support. Through this analysis, a stand-alone rating is determined for all entities except those that possess a pooled (p) or reinsured (r) rating modifier.

Recognizing that an insurer very often benefits greatly from its inclusion within a strong, diversified group, the published ratings of these entities often include some element of rating enhancement. This enhancement points to the insurer's greater ability to compete successfully, generate earnings and sustain a strong balance sheet over time through the support of its parent or affiliate companies. To determine this level of support, in addition to the stand-alone analysis, A.M. Best conducts a thorough, top-down evaluation of the organization's strength on a consolidated basis.

A.M. Best uses its consolidated view of the organization to conduct an enterprise-level analysis. This determines the highest possible rating for the lead insurer within the group, accounting for strengths and weaknesses that may reside not only within the insurance entities but also at the holding company or at a non-insurance affiliate. With this information, A.M. Best determines whether or not the individual insurance subsidiaries qualify for enhancement or drag to their stand-alone ratings.

SECTION VIII

COUNTRY RISK ANALYSIS

A.M. Best defines country risk as the risk that country-specific factors could adversely affect the claims-paying ability of an insurer. Country risk is evaluated and factored into all A.M. Best ratings. As part of the country risk evaluation process, A.M. Best identifies the various factors within a country that may directly or indirectly affect an insurance company. In doing so, A.M. Best separates the risks into three main categories: economic risk, political risk and financial system risk. Given A.M. Best's particular focus on and expertise in the insurance industry, financial system risk is further divided into two sections: insurance and non-insurance financial system risk.

A.M. Best's evaluation of country risk is not directly comparable to a sovereign debt rating, which evaluates the ability and willingness of a government to service its debt obligations. Though country risk analysis does take into consideration the finances and policies of a sovereign government, the final assessment is not guided by this sole purpose. Additionally, A.M. Best's country risk evaluation does not impose a ceiling on ratings in a given domicile.

A.M. Best's approach to country risk analysis employs a data-driven model that scores the level of risk present in a given country, plus a qualitative assessment of country-specific conditions that affect the operating environment for an insurer. Countries are placed into one of five Country Risk Tiers (CRTs), ranging from countries with a CRT-1 stable environment with the least amount of risk, to CRT-5 countries that exhibit the most risk and, therefore, offer the greatest challenge to an insurer's financial stability, strength and performance; i.e. higher risk exposure pressures financial stability.

Key elements of country risk can be managed or mitigated, effectively reducing the impact on the rating of an insurer. As a result, it is possible that our highest ratings can be achieved in any country. Country risk is not a ceiling or cap on insurer ratings, it is one of many rating factors.

CRT assignments are reviewed annually, though significant events and developments are tracked continuously and may cause an interim change to a country's tier assignment. CRTs are assessments of the current conditions in a country, but are designed to remain stable through the business cycle. Therefore, political and industry outlooks as well as economic forecasts are integrated into the assessment process.

SECTION IX

RATING DISTRIBUTIONS

The following table provides the distribution of Best's Financial Strength Ratings on both an individual company and rating unit basis as of the latest annual publication of the Life/Health edition of *Best's Insurance Reports® - United States & Canada*. In addition, this section provides the distribution of companies assigned to Not Rated (NR) Categories.

The term "rating unit" applies to either individual insurers or a consolidation of member companies. The rating unit forms the financial basis on which A.M. Best performs its credit rating evaluation. The financial results of rating units more accurately represent the way insurance groups operate and manage their businesses. Therefore, the rating distribution based on a rating unit basis is the more appropriate rating distribution to gauge A.M. Best's overall opinion of the financial health of the universe of insurance companies we rate.

2010 LIFE/HEALTH RATING DISTRIBUTION* BY INDIVIDUAL COMPANIES

Best's FSR	Rating Category	Number	Percent
	Secure Ratings		
A++	Superior	26	2.6%
A+	Superior	122	12.0
	Subtotal	**148**	**14.6**
A	Excellent	256	25.2
A-	Excellent	301	29.6
	Subtotal	**557**	**54.8**
B++	Good	117	11.5
B+	Good	102	10.0
	Subtotal	**219**	**21.5**
	Total Secure Ratings	**924**	**90.9%**
	Vulnerable Ratings		
B	Fair	36	3.5%
B-	Fair	18	1.8
	Subtotal	**54**	**5.3**
C++	Marginal	3	0.3
C+	Marginal	4	0.4
	Subtotal	**7**	**0.7**
C	Weak	3	0.3
C-	Weak	0	0.0
	Subtotal	**3**	**0.3**
D	Poor	3	0.3
E	Under Regulatory Supervision	17	1.7
F	In Liquidation	9	0.9
	Subtotal	**29**	**2.9**
	Total Vulnerable Ratings	**93**	**9.1%**
	Total Rating Opinions	**1,017**	**100.0%**
	No Rating Opinions		
NR-1	Insufficient Data	143	18.0%
NR-2	Insufficient Size/ Operating Experience	84	10.6
NR-3	Rating Procedure Inapplicable	83	10.4
NR-4	Company Request	19	2.4
NR-5	Not Formally Followed	466	58.6
	Total No Rating Opinions	**795**	**100.0%**
	Total Reported Companies	**1,812**	

*As of June 15, 2010

2010 LIFE/HEALTH RATING DISTRIBUTION* BY RATING UNITS

Best's FSR	Rating Category	Number	Percent
	Secure Ratings		
A++	Superior	10	1.4%
A+	Superior	45	6.5
	Subtotal	**55**	**8.0**
A	Excellent	154	22.3
A-	Excellent	216	31.3
	Subtotal	**370**	**53.5**
B++	Good	94	13.6
B+	Good	93	13.5
	Subtotal	**187**	**27.1**
	Total Secure Ratings	**612**	**88.6%**
	Vulnerable Ratings		
B	Fair	28	4.1%
B-	Fair	14	2.0
	Subtotal	**42**	**6.1**
C++	Marginal	3	0.4
C+	Marginal	4	0.6
	Subtotal	**7**	**1.0**
C	Weak	2	0.3
C-	Weak	0	0.0
	Subtotal	**2**	**0.3**
D	Poor	2	0.3
E	Under Regulatory Supervision	17	2.5
F	In Liquidation	9	1.3
	Subtotal	**28**	**4.1**
	Total Vulnerable Ratings	**79**	**11.4%**
	Total Rating Opinions	**691**	**100.0%**
	No Rating Opinions		
NR-1	Insufficient Data	143	18.0%
NR-2	Insufficient Size/ Operating Experience	84	10.6
NR-3	Rating Procedure Inapplicable	83	10.4
NR-4	Company Request	19	2.4
NR-5	Not Formally Followed	466	58.6
	Total No Rating Opinions	**795**	**100.0%**
	Total Reported Units	**1,486**	

*As of June 15, 2010

SECTION X

AFFILIATION CODES AND RATING MODIFIERS

Affiliation Codes and Rating Modifiers are added to Best's Financial Strength Ratings to identify companies whose assigned rating is based on a Group (g), Pooled (p), or Reinsured (r) affiliation with other insurers. In addition, a company's rating may be placed Under Review and be subject to a near-term change, as indicated by the "u" rating modifier. A Best's Financial Strength Rating may carry a "pd" rating modifier, indicating that the company did not subscribe to our interactive rating process. The "s" rating modifier is assigned to syndicates operating at Lloyd's that have subscribed to our interactive rating process. These affiliation codes or modifiers appear as a lowercase suffix to the rating (i.e., A g, A u, A pd, etc.).

Insurers with affiliation codes (g, p, r) indicate that their rating is based on the consolidated performance of the company and its affiliation with one or more insurers, which collectively operate, in Best's opinion, as one coordinated insurance group and meets our criteria for the same rating. Accordingly, the Financial Size Category of these member companies usually equals that of the group.

Affiliation Codes

"g" Group Rating: Assigned to members of a group and is based on the consolidation of the lead company and its insurance subsidiaries or affiliates where there is common ownership or board control. Assigned if A.M. Best views the company to be integral to the group's primary business through its financial, operational and/or strategic importance. A.M. Best expects that under almost any scenario, the parent would continue to support the company to the extent of its financial ability. The sale or closure of such a subsidiary or affiliate would imply an unexpected shift in the group's strategy. As a result, these entities are given full rating enhancement and assigned the lead company's rating and receive a group (g) affiliation code.

Group rated subsidiaries typically demonstrate a combination of the following characteristics. They are critical to the group's strategy and ongoing success; fully integrated into the group's strategic plan; carry the group name or are easily identified with the group; are material to the business profile of the group; are significant contributors to the group's earnings; currently benefit from some form of explicit parental support and have a history of receiving explicit support when needed. In certain cases, group ratings are also assigned to sister companies owned by a common holding company, or companies necessary for licensing or rate flexibility.

A stand-alone analysis is conducted on all insurance subsidiaries to assess each legal entity's stand-alone operating performance and capitalization, before consideration is given to any rating enhancement.

"p" Pooled Rating: Assigned to a group whose member companies pool assets, liabilities and operating results and maintain, in theory, the same operating performance and balance sheet strength as other companies within the pool. Pooling is viewed as explicit financial support. The assets of each pool participant are available for the protection of all pool members' policyholders. In many cases, pooled affiliates market under a common brand name and generally operate under common management and/or ownership.

The pooled (p) affiliation code is typically assigned if the pooling agreement is joint and several; pure/net; stand-alone capitalization supports the assigned rating after the pool is considered; includes coverage for any prior year loss reserve development, and the run-off of all liabilities incurred on policies incepted prior to termination; ownership or board control exceeds 50% and includes a 12-month notice of termination.

"r" Reinsured Rating: Assigned to a company that reinsures substantially all its insurance risk with an affiliated reinsurer. Reinsurance is viewed as explicit financial support. In many cases, reinsured affiliates market under a common brand name and generally operate under common management and/or ownership.

The reinsured (r) affiliation code is typically assigned if the company quota shares all gross premiums, losses and expenses (unless regulatory restrictions apply); stand-alone capitalization supports the assigned rating after the reinsurance is considered; the contract contains no loss caps or loss corridors; includes coverage for any prior year loss reserve development, and the run-off of all liabilities incurred on policies incepted prior to termination; ownership or board control exceeds 50% and includes a 12-month notice of termination.

Rating Modifiers

"u" Under Review: Assigned to companies with potential near-term rating changes (typically within six months) due to a recent event or abrupt change in their financial condition, which may have positive, developing, or negative rating implications.

"pd" Public Data Rating: Assigned to Canadian property/casualty insurers and HMOs and health insurers (United States) that do not subscribe to our interactive rating process. Best's Public Data Ratings reflect both qualitative and quantitative analyses using publicly available data and other public information. Public Data Ratings will be assigned where, in Best's view, ratings are needed due to market demand.

"s" Syndicate Rating: Assigned to syndicates operating at Lloyd's that meet our minimum size and operating experience requirements for a Best's Credit Rating and subscribe to our interactive rating process.

RATING MODIFIER/AFFILIATION CODE DISTRIBUTION

Of the 1,017 individual total ratings assigned in Best's 2010 life/health publications, 484 or 48% were also assigned a Rating Modifier or Affiliation Code. Their distribution follows.

RATING MODIFIER/ AFFILIATION CODE	NUMBER OF COMPANIES
g - Group	464
p - Pooled	0
r - Reinsured	8
pd - Public Data	0
u - Under Review	29
Subtotal	**501**
Dual Assignment	(17)
Total Modifier/ Affiliation Code Ratings	**484**

SECTION XI

"NOT RATED" (NR) CATEGORIES

The current universe of rated life/health companies account for roughly 95% of the premium volume in the United States. However, A.M. Best also reports on life/health companies that are not assigned a rating opinion. Because of their small size, Not Rated (NR) insurers constitute only 5% of the industry's premium writings.

Not Rated (NR) Categories

For Not Rated (NR) companies, a condition exists that makes it difficult for A.M. Best to develop an opinion on the company's balance sheet strength and operating performance. Generally, these companies do not qualify for a Best's Credit Rating because of their limited financial information, small level of surplus, lack of sufficient operating experience, or due to their dormant or run-off status.

NR-1 (Insufficient Data)

Assigned predominantly to small companies for which A.M. Best does not have sufficient financial information required to assign rating opinions. The information contained in these limited reports is obtained from several sources, which include the individual companies, the National Association of Insurance Commissioners (NAIC) and other data providers. Data received from the NAIC, in some cases, is prior to the completion of its cross-checking and validation process.

NR-2 (Insufficient Size and/or Operating Experience)

Assigned to companies that do not meet A.M. Best's minimum size and/or operating experience requirements. To be eligible for a letter rating, a company must generally have a minimum of $2 million in policyholders' surplus to assure reasonable financial stability and have sufficient operating experience to adequately evaluate its financial performance, usually two to five years. General exceptions to these requirements include companies that have financial or strategic affiliations with Best-rated companies; companies that have demonstrated long histories of financial performance; companies that have achieved significant market positions; and newly formed companies with experienced management that have acquired seasoned books of business and/or developed credible business plans.

NR-3 (Rating Procedure Inapplicable)

Assigned to companies that are not rated by A.M. Best, because our normal rating procedures do not apply due to a company's unique or unusual business features. This category includes companies that are in run-off with no active business writings, are effectively dormant, or underwrite financial or mortgage guaranty insurance. Exceptions to the assignment of the NR-3 designation include run-off companies that commenced run-off plans in the current year or inactive companies that have been structurally separated from active affiliates within group structures that pose potential credit, legal or market risks to the group's active companies.

NR-4 (Company Request)

Assigned to companies that are assigned a Best's Credit Rating following a review of their financial performance, but request that the assigned letter rating not be published on their company. The NR-4 is assigned following the publication of a final letter-rating opinion.

NR-5 (Not Formally Followed)

Assigned to insurers that are not formally evaluated for the purposes of assigning a rating opinion. It is also assigned retroactively to the rating history of traditional U.S. insurers when they provide prior year(s) financial information to A.M. Best and receive a Best's Credit Rating or another NR designation in more recent years. Finally, it is assigned currently to those companies that historically had been rated, but no longer provide financial information to A.M. Best because they have been liquidated, dissolved, or merged out of existence.

SECTION XII

FINANCIAL SIZE CATEGORIES

To provide a convenient indicator of the size of a company in terms of its statutory surplus and related accounts, A.M. Best assigns a Financial Size Category (FSC) to every company that is assigned an FSR. The FSC is based on reported policyholders' surplus plus conditional or technical reserve funds, such as the asset valuation reserve (AVR), other investment and operating contingency funds and miscellaneous voluntary reserves.

Many insurance buyers consider buying insurance coverage from companies that they believe have the sufficient financial capacity to provide the necessary policy limits to insure their risks. Although companies utilize reinsurance to reduce their net retention on the policy limits they underwrite, many buyers still feel more comfortable buying from companies perceived to have greater financial capacity.

2010 FINANCIAL SIZE CATEGORY (FSC) BY INDIVIDUAL COMPANIES

Financial Size Category	Adjusted Policyholders' Surplus ($ Millions)		Number of Companies	Distribution Percentage	Distribution Cumulative
Class I	Less than	1	2	0.2 %	0.2 %
Class II	1 to	2	5	0.5	0.7
Class III	2 to	5	37	3.7	4.4
Class IV	5 to	10	60	6.1	10.5
Class V	10 to	25	114	11.5	22.0
Class VI	25 to	50	107	10.8	32.8
Class VII	50 to	100	92	9.3	42.1
Class VIII	100 to	250	134	13.5	55.6
Class IX	250 to	500	112	11.3	66.9
Class X	500 to	750	52	5.2	72.1
Class XI	750 to	1,000	35	3.5	75.7
Class XII	1,000 to	1,250	9	0.9	76.6
Class XIII	1,250 to	1,500	23	2.3	78.9
Class XIV	1,500 to	2,000	29	2.9	81.8
Class XV	2,000 or greater		180	18.2	100.0 %
	Subtotal		991		
	E & F Rated Companies		26		
	Grand Total		1,017		

SECTION XIII

ORGANIZATION TYPES

Insurance transactions are conducted primarily through four types of organizations — stock companies, mutual companies, fraternal societies, and non-profit organizations.

- **Stock Companies:** Stock companies are corporations, the financial ownership of which is comprised of capital stock which is divided into shares. Ultimate control of stock insurance companies is vested in the shareholders.
- **Mutual Companies:** Mutual companies are corporations without capital stock. Ultimate control of mutual insurance companies is vested in the policyholders.
- **Fraternal Societies:** Fraternal life insurance societies are purely mutual organizations. The major fraternal societies furnish life insurance benefits to their members on a basis essentially the same as that utilized by legal reserve life insurance companies. The fraternal life insurance society is characterized by its lodge system, a representative form of government and its fraternal or benevolent activities.
- **Non-Profit Organizations:** Insurance companies that have no individuals/organizations with an ownership interest. Control of these companies rests with the board of directors. Non-profit companies reported on by Best are typically health or dental insurers.

SECTION XIV

INSURANCE LICENSES

States have the authority to regulate insurance companies and have controlled insurance mainly through the licensing power. The license is a document that indicates an insurer has met the minimum requirements established by statute and is authorized to engage in the lines of business for which it has applied.

The importance of a company being licensed in a particular domicile also determines not only the protection to the insured provided by the regulatory authorities to assist if a problem arises, but also the protection afforded the insured by guaranty fund laws, which generally apply only to licensed insurers. Each jurisdiction has its own statutes, and there are a number of different licensing requirements.

In addition to licensed insurers, there are other specialty types of companies that exist in the field of insurance such as reinsurers.

A reinsurer is a company that agrees to indemnify, for consideration, the ceding company against all or part of a loss that the latter may sustain under policies that it has issued. Reinsurers do not always have to be licensed and may operate on an approved basis in some states.

Since there are a number of different licensing requirements, we have used seven descriptions to signify the general status of a company in a particular jurisdiction.

- **State of Domicile:** The state in which the company is incorporated or chartered. The company is also licensed (admitted) under the state's insurance statutes for those lines of business for which it qualifies.
- **Licensed:** Indicates the company is incorporated (or chartered) in another state but is a licensed (admitted or chartered) insurer for this state to write specific lines of business for which it qualifies.
- **Licensed for Reinsurance Only:** Indicates the company is licensed (admitted) to write reinsurance on risks in this state. Indicates the company is incorporated (or chartered) in another state but is a licensed (admitted) reinsurer for this state.
- **Approved for Reinsurance:** Indicates the company is approved (or authorized) to write reinsurance on risks in this state. A license to write reinsurance may not be required in these states. Indicates that the company is accredited or credit is allowed for reinsurers domiciled and licensed in another state. These reinsurers meet size and regulatory filing requirements that were included as part of the NAIC Model Law on Credit for Reinsurance.
- **Credit for Reinsurance (Other):** Indicates that the company meets state requirements other than licensing or accreditation. Included are reinsurers that maintain trust funds, reinsurance arrangements that are required by law (pools, joint underwriting associations, state-owned or controlled companies) and qualified trust agreements and letters of credit arrangements. These requirements were also specified under the NAIC Model Law.
- **Approved or not Disapproved for Surplus Lines:** Indicates the company is approved (or not disapproved) to write excess or surplus lines in this state.

- **Authorized under federal Liability Risk Retention Acts (Risk Retention Groups):** Indicates companies operating under the federal Products Liability Risk Retention Act of 1981 and the Liability Risk Retention Act of 1986. Indicates states in which the company operates for members whose business or activities are similar or related with respect to the liability to which members are exposed by virtue of any related, similar, or common business, trade, product, services, premises, or operations. Companies are licensed in the state of domicile only.

Index

U.S. & Caribbean Companies

COMPANY NAME	ULTIMATE PARENT NAME	KRG	BAG
A			
AAA Life Insurance Company, Livonia, MI	ACLI Acquisition Company	2	1
AAA Life Re, Ltd., Hamilton HM 11, Bermuda	American Automobile Association Inc.	2	
Ability Insurance Company, Omaha, NE	Ability Reinsurance Holdings Limited	2	1
Ability Reinsurance (Bermuda) Ltd, Hamilton HM 12, Bermuda	Ability Reinsurance Holdings Limited	2	
Abri Health Plan, Inc., West Allis, WI	Avatar Partners, LLC	2	
Absolute Total Care, Inc., St. Louis, MO	Centene Corporation	2	
Acacia Life Insurance Company, Bethesda, MD	UNIFI Mutual Holding Company	2	1
Access Dental Plan, Sacramento, CA	Abbaszadeh Dental Group Inc	2	
ACE Life Insurance Company, Stamford, CT	ACE Limited	2	1
ACE Tempest Life Reinsurance Ltd., Philadelphia, PA	ACE Limited	4	
ACN Group of California, Inc., San Diego, CA	UnitedHealth Group Inc	4	
Admiral Life Insurance Company of America, Rome, GA	State Mutual Insurance Company	4	
Advance Insurance Company of Kansas, Topeka, KS	Blue Cross and Blue Shield of Kansas Inc	4	2
Advanta Life Insurance Company, Spring House, PA		4	
Advantage Dental Plan, Inc., Redmond, OR		4	
ADVANTAGE Health Solutions, Inc., Indianapolis, IN		4	
Advantage Healthplan, Inc., Washington, DC		4	
AECC Total Vision Health Plan of Texas, Inc., Dallas, TX	Centene Corporation	4	
Aetna Better Health Inc. (a Connecticut corporation), Blue Bell, PA	Aetna Inc	6	
Aetna Dental Inc. (a New Jersey corporation), Blue Bell, PA	Aetna Inc	6	
Aetna Dental Inc. (a Texas corporation), Sugar Land, TX	Aetna Inc	6	
Aetna Dental of California Inc., Thousand Oaks, CA	Aetna Inc	6	
Aetna Health and Life Insurance Company, Hartford, CT	Aetna Inc	6	
Aetna Health Inc. (a Colorado corporation), Blue Bell, PA	Aetna Inc	6	
Aetna Health Inc. (a Connecticut corporation), Blue Bell, PA	Aetna Inc	6	
Aetna Health Inc. (a Delaware corporation), Blue Bell, PA	Aetna Inc	6	
Aetna Health Inc. (a Florida corporation), Blue Bell, PA	Aetna Inc	6	
Aetna Health Inc. (a Georgia corporation), Blue Bell, PA	Aetna Inc	8	
Aetna Health Inc. (a Maine corporation), Blue Bell, PA	Aetna Inc	8	
Aetna Health Inc. (a Michigan corporation), Southfield, MI	Aetna Inc	8	
Aetna Health Inc. (a New Jersey corporation), Blue Bell, PA	Aetna Inc	8	
Aetna Health Inc. (a New York corporation), Blue Bell, PA	Aetna Inc	8	
Aetna Health Inc. (a Pennsylvania corporation), Blue Bell, PA	Aetna Inc	8	
Aetna Health Inc. (a Texas corporation), Dallas, TX	Aetna Inc	8	
Aetna Health Inc. (a Washington corporation), Blue Bell, PA	Aetna Inc	8	
Aetna Health Insurance Company, Blue Bell, PA	Aetna Inc	8	
Aetna Health Insurance Company of New York, Blue Bell, PA	Aetna Inc	10	
Aetna Health of California Inc., Walnut Creek, CA	Aetna Inc	10	
Aetna Health of the Carolinas Inc., Blue Bell, PA	Aetna Inc	10	
Aetna Insurance Company of Connecticut, Hartford, CT	Aetna Inc	10	
Aetna Life & Casualty (Bermuda) Ltd., Hartford, CT	Aetna Inc	10	
Aetna Life Insurance Company, Hartford, CT	Aetna Inc	10	2
AF&L Insurance Company, Warminster, PA	AF&L Holdings, LLC	10	
AGC Life Insurance Company, Houston, TX	American International Group, Inc	10	2
AGL Life Assurance Company, Hartford, CT	Phoenix Companies Inc	10	2
AIDS Healthcare Foundation, Los Angeles, CA		12	
Alabama Life Reinsurance Company Inc, Tuscaloosa, AL		12	
Alameda Alliance for Health, Alameda, CA		12	
Alaska Vision Services, Inc., Rancho Cordova, CA	Vision Service Plan	12	
Alfa Life Insurance Corporation, Montgomery, AL	Alfa Mutual Insurance Company	12	3
All Savers Insurance Company, Indianapolis, IN	UnitedHealth Group Inc	12	
All Savers Life Insurance Company of California, Indianapolis, IN	UnitedHealth Group Inc	12	
Allegiance Life Insurance Company, Springfield, IL	Horace Mann Educators Corporation	12	
Alliance for Community Health, LLC, St. Louis, MO	Molina Healthcare Inc.	12	
Alliance Health and Life Insurance Company, Detroit, MI	Henry Ford Health System	14	
Alliant Health Plans, Inc., Calhoun, GA	Health One Alliance, LLC	14	
Allianz Life and Annuity Company, Minneapolis, MN	Allianz Societas Europaea	14	
Allianz Life Insurance Company of New York, Minneapolis, MN	Allianz Societas Europaea	14	3
Allianz Life Insurance Company of North America, Minneapolis, MN	Allianz Societas Europaea	14	3
Allied Financial Insurance Company, Houston, TX		14	

COMPANY NAME	ULTIMATE PARENT NAME	KRG	BAG
Allstate Assurance Company, Northbrook, IL	Allstate Corporation	14	
Allstate Life Insurance Company, Northbrook, IL	Allstate Corporation	14	3
Allstate Life Insurance Company of New York, Hauppauge, NY	Allstate Corporation	14	4
Aloha Care, Honolulu, HI		16	
Alpha Dental Programs, Inc., Cerritos, CA	Dentegra Group Inc.	16	
Altius Health Plans, South Jordan, UT	Coventry Health Care Inc	16	
Altus Dental Insurance Company Inc., Providence, RI	Delta Dental of Rhode Island	16	
Amalgamated Life and Health Insurance Company, Chicago, IL	Amalgamated Social Benefits Association	16	
The Amalgamated Life Insurance Company, White Plains, NY	UNITE HERE National Retirement Fund	16	4
Ambassador Life Insurance Company, Houston, TX		16	
Amedex Insurance Company (Bermuda) Ltd., Hamilton HM12, Bermuda	British United Provident Association Ltd.	16	
American-Amicable Life Insurance Company of Texas, Waco, TX	Thoma Cressey Bravo Inc.	16	4
American Bankers Life Assurance Company of Florida, Miami, FL	Assurant Inc	18	4
American Benefit Life Insurance Company, Dallas, TX	Realty Advisors Inc.	18	5
American Capitol Insurance Company, Springfield, IL		18	
American Century Life Insurance Company, Tulsa, OK		18	
American Century Life Insurance Company of Texas, Austin, TX		18	
American Community Mutual Insurance Company, Livonia, MI		18	
American Continental Insurance Company, Brentwood, TN	Genworth Financial, Inc	18	
American Creditors Life Insurance Company, Costa Mesa, CA		18	
American Dental Plan of North Carolina, Inc., Roswell, GA	Humana Inc	18	
American Dental Plan of Wisconsin, Inc., Madison, WI		20	
American Dental Providers of Arkansas, Inc., Roswell, GA	Humana Inc	20	
American Equity Investment Life Insurance Company, West Des Moines, IA	American Equity Investment Life Hldg Co	20	5
American Equity Investment Life Insurance Company of New York, West Des Moines, IA	American Equity Investment Life Hldg Co	20	5
American Exchange Life Insurance Company, Lake Mary, FL		20	
American Family Life Assurance Company of Columbus (Aflac), Columbus, GA	Aflac Incorporated	20	5
American Family Life Assurance Company of New York, Columbus, GA	Aflac Incorporated	20	6
American Family Life Insurance Company, Madison, WI	American Family Mutual Insurance Company	20	6
American Farm Life Insurance Company, Fort Worth, TX	National Farm Life Insurance Company	20	
American Farmers & Ranchers Life Insurance Company, Oklahoma City, OK	American Farmers & Ranchers Mutual Ins	22	
American Federated Life Insurance Company, Flowood, MS	Galaxie Corporation	22	6
American Fidelity Assurance Company, Oklahoma City, OK	Cameron Associates Inc	22	6
American Fidelity Life Insurance Company, Pensacola, FL	AMFI Corporation	22	7
American Financial Security Life Insurance Company, Jefferson City, MO		22	
American General Assurance Company, Neptune, NJ	American International Group, Inc	22	7
American General Life and Accident Insurance Company, Nashville, TN	American International Group, Inc	22	7
American General Life Insurance Company, Houston, TX	American International Group, Inc	22	7
American General Life Insurance Company of Delaware, Houston, TX	American International Group, Inc	22	8
American Health and Life Insurance Company, Fort Worth, TX	Citigroup Inc.	24	8
American Health Network of Indiana, LLC, Indianapolis, IN	AHN Acquisition LLC	24	
American HealthGuard Corporation, Arcadia, CA		24	
American Heritage Life Insurance Company, Jacksonville, FL	Allstate Corporation	24	8
The American Home Life Insurance Company, Topeka, KS		24	8
American Home Life Insurance Company, North Little Rock, AR		24	
American Income Life Insurance Company, Waco, TX	Torchmark Corporation	24	9
American Independent Network Insurance Company of New York, Allentown, PA	Penn Treaty American Corporation	24	
American Industries Life Insurance Company, Houston, TX		24	
American International Life Assurance Company of New York, New York, NY	American International Group, Inc	26	9
American Labor Life Insurance Company, Lancaster, PA		26	
American Life and Accident Insurance Company of Kentucky, Louisville, KY		26	
American Life and Annuity Company, Hot Springs, AR		26	
American Life & Security Corp, Lincoln, NE		26	
American Life Insurance Company, Wilmington, DE	American International Group, Inc	26	9
American Life Insurance Company, Chicago, IL		26	
American Maturity Life Insurance Company, Simsbury, CT	Hartford Financial Services Group Inc	26	
American Medical and Life Insurance Company, New York, NY	TREK Holdings Inc	26	9
American Medical Security Life Insurance Company, Green Bay, WI	UnitedHealth Group Inc	28	10
American Memorial Life Insurance Company, Rapid City, SD	Assurant Inc	28	10
American Modern Life Insurance Company, Amelia, OH	Munich Reinsurance Company	28	10
American National Insurance Company, Galveston, TX	American National Insurance Company	28	10
American National Life Insurance Company of New York, Galveston, TX	American National Insurance Company	28	11
American National Life Insurance Company of Texas, Galveston, TX	American National Insurance Company	28	11
American Network Insurance Company, Allentown, PA	Penn Treaty American Corporation	28	
American Phoenix Life and Reassurance Company, Hartford, CT	Phoenix Companies Inc	28	11
American Pioneer Life Insurance Company, Lake Mary, FL	Universal American Corp.	28	11
American Progressive Life & Health Insurance Company of New York, Rye Brook, NY	Universal American Corp.	30	12
American Public Life Insurance Company, Jackson, MS	Cameron Associates Inc	30	12
American Republic Corp Insurance Company, Omaha, NE	American Enterprise Mutual Holding Co.	30	
American Republic Insurance Company, Des Moines, IA	American Enterprise Mutual Holding Co.	30	12

COMPANY NAME	ULTIMATE PARENT NAME	KRG	BAG
American Retirement Life Insurance Company, Austin, TX	American Financial Group, Inc.	30	
American Savings Life Insurance Company, Mesa, AZ		30	
American Service Life Insurance Company, Kansas City, MO	Richard F Jones	30	
American Specialty Health Plans of California, Inc., San Diego, CA		30	
American Underwriters Life Insurance Company, Goddard, KS	Norma J Hawkins	30	12
American United Life Insurance Company, Indianapolis, IN	American United Mutual Insurance Hldg Co.	32	13
America's Health Choice Medical Plans, Inc., Vero Beach, FL		32	
AmeriChoice of Connecticut, Inc., Rocky Hill, CT	UnitedHealth Group Inc	32	
AmeriChoice of Georgia, Inc., Norcross, GA	UnitedHealth Group Inc	32	
AmeriChoice of New Jersey, Inc., Newark, NJ	UnitedHealth Group Inc	32	
AmeriChoice of Pennsylvania, Inc., Philadelphia, PA	UnitedHealth Group Inc	32	
Americo Financial Life and Annuity Insurance Company, Kansas City, MO	Financial Holding Corporation	32	13
AMERIGROUP New Jersey, Inc., Virginia Beach, VA	AMERIGROUP Corporation	32	
AMERIGROUP Ohio Inc, Virginia Beach, VA	AMERIGROUP Corporation	32	
AMERIGROUP South Carolina, Inc., Virginia Beach, VA	AMERIGROUP Corporation	34	
AMERIGROUP Tennessee, Inc., Virginia Beach, VA	AMERIGROUP Corporation	34	
AMERIGROUP Texas, Inc., Virginia Beach, VA	AMERIGROUP Corporation	34	
AMERIGROUP Virginia, Inc., Virginia Beach, VA	AMERIGROUP Corporation	34	
AmeriHealth HMO, Inc., Philadelphia, PA	Independence Blue Cross	34	
AmeriHealth Insurance Company of New Jersey, Mt. Laurel, NJ	Independence Blue Cross	34	
Ameritas Life Insurance Corp., Lincoln, NE	UNIFI Mutual Holding Company	34	13
AmFirst Insurance Company, Jackson, MS	AmFirst Holdings, Inc.	34	
AMGP Georgia Managed Care Company, Inc., Virginia Beach, VA	AMERIGROUP Corporation	34	
Amica Life Insurance Company, Lincoln, RI	Amica Mutual Insurance Company	36	13
Annuity Investors Life Insurance Company, Cincinnati, OH	American Financial Group, Inc.	36	14
Anthem Blue Cross Life and Health Insurance Company, Woodland Hills, CA	WellPoint Inc.	36	
Anthem Health Plans, Inc., North Haven, CT	WellPoint Inc.	36	
Anthem Health Plans of Kentucky, Inc., Louisville, KY	WellPoint Inc.	36	
Anthem Health Plans of Maine, Inc., South Portland, ME	WellPoint Inc.	36	
Anthem Health Plans of New Hampshire, Inc., Manchester, NH	WellPoint Inc.	36	
Anthem Health Plans of Virginia, Richmond, VA	WellPoint Inc.	36	
Anthem Insurance Companies, Inc., Indianapolis, IN	WellPoint Inc.	36	
Anthem Life & Disability Insurance Company, New York, NY	WellPoint Inc.	38	14
Anthem Life Insurance Company, Worthington, OH	WellPoint Inc.	38	14
Arcadian Health Plan, Inc., Oakland, CA	Arcadian Management Services Inc	38	
Arcadian Health Plan of Georgia, Inc., Oakland, CA	Arcadian Management Services Inc	38	
Arcadian Health Plan of Louisiana, Inc., Oakland, CA	Arcadian Management Services Inc	38	
Arcadian Health Plan of North Carolina, Inc., Oakland, CA	Arcadian Management Services Inc	38	
Arizona Dental Insurance Service, Inc., Glendale, AZ		38	
Arkansas Bankers Life Insurance Company, Texarkana, AR		38	
Arkansas Community Care, Inc., Oakland, CA	Arcadian Management Services Inc	38	
Arkansas Life Insurance Company, Amelia, OH	Munich Reinsurance Company	40	
Associated Mutual, Grand Rapids, MI		40	
Assurity Life Insurance Company, Lincoln, NE	Assurity Security Group	40	14
Asuris Northwest Health, Seattle, WA	Regence Group	40	
Athens Area Health Plan Select, Inc., Athens, GA	Athens Regional Health Services Inc	40	
Atlanta Life Insurance Company, Atlanta, GA	Atlanta Life Financial Group Inc	40	15
Atlantic Coast Life Insurance Company, Charleston, SC		40	15
Atlantic Medical Insurance Limited, Nassau, New Providence, Bahamas	Edmund Gibbons Limited	40	
Atlantic Southern Dental Foundation, Philadelphia, PA		40	
Atlantic Southern Insurance Company, San Juan, PR	R D Tips Inc	42	15
ATRIO Health Plans, Inc., Roseburg, OR		42	
Aurigen Reinsurance Limited, Hamilton HM MX, Bermuda	Aurigen Capital Limited	42	
Aurora National Life Assurance Company, East Hartford, CT	New California Life Holdings Inc	42	
Auto Club Life Insurance Company, Livonia, MI	Auto Club Insurance Association	42	15
Auto-Owners Life Insurance Company, Lansing, MI	Auto-Owners Insurance Company	42	16
Automobile Club of Southern California Life Insurance Company, Livonia, MI	Automobile Club of Southern California	42	16
Avalon Insurance Company, Harrisburg, PA	Capital Blue Cross	42	
Avante Behavioral Health Plan, Fresno, CA		42	
Avera Health Plans, Inc., Sioux Falls, SD	Avera Health	44	
Aviva Life and Annuity Company, Des Moines, IA	AVIVA plc	44	16
Aviva Life and Annuity Company of New York, Woodbury, NY	AVIVA plc	44	16
AvMed, Inc., Miami, FL	SantaFe HealthCare, Inc.	44	
AXA Corporate Solutions Life Reinsurance, New York, NY	AXA S.A.	44	17
AXA Equitable Life and Annuity Company, Charlotte, NC	AXA S.A.	44	17
AXA Equitable Life Insurance Company, New York, NY	AXA S.A.	44	17

B

Balboa Life Insurance Company, Irvine, CA	Bank of America Corporation	44	17
Balboa Life Insurance Company of New York, Irvine, CA	Bank of America Corporation	44	18
The Baltimore Life Insurance Company, Owings Mills, MD	Baltimore Life Holdings Inc	46	18
Bank of Montreal Insurance (Barbados) Limited, St. Michael, Barbados	Bank of Montreal	46	
Bankers Conseco Life Insurance Company, Carmel, IN	CNO Financial Group, Inc.	46	18

COMPANY NAME	ULTIMATE PARENT NAME	KRG	BAG
Bankers Fidelity Life Insurance Company, Atlanta, GA	J. Mack Robinson & Family	46	18
Bankers Life and Casualty Company, Carmel, IN	CNO Financial Group, Inc.	46	19
Bankers Life Insurance Company, St. Petersburg, FL	Bankers International Financial Corp Ltd.	46	19
Bankers Life Insurance Company of America, Dallas, TX		46	
Bankers Life of Louisiana, Jacksonville, FL	Summit Partners LP	46	19
Bankers Reserve Life Insurance Company of Wisconsin, St. Louis, MO	Centene Corporation	46	
Banner Life Insurance Company, Rockville, MD	Legal & General Group plc	48	19
BCBSD, Inc., Wilmington, DE		48	
BCI HMO, Inc., Chicago, IL	Health Care Svc Corp Mut Legal Reserve	48	
BCS Insurance Company, Oakbrook Terrace, IL	BCS Financial Corporation	48	
BCS Life Insurance Company, Oakbrook Terrace, IL	BCS Financial Corporation	48	20
Beneficial Life Insurance Company, Salt Lake City, UT	DMC Reserve Trust	48	20
Berkley Life and Health Insurance Company, Greenwich, CT	W. R. Berkley Corporation	48	
Berkshire Hathaway Life Insurance Company of Nebraska, Omaha, NE	Berkshire Hathaway Inc	48	20
Berkshire Life Insurance Company of America, Pittsfield, MA	Guardian Life Ins Co of America	48	20
Bermuda International Insurance Services Limited, Hamilton HM 08, Bermuda	BF&M Limited	50	
Bermuda Life Insurance Company Limited, Hamilton HM EX, Bermuda	Argus Group Holdings Limited	50	
Bermuda Life Worldwide Limited, Hamilton HM EX, Bermuda	Argus Group Holdings Limited	50	
BEST Life and Health Insurance Company, Irvine, CA	Lawrenz Family Trust	50	21
Best Meridian Insurance Company, Coral Gables, FL	BMI Financial Group, Inc.	50	21
Best Meridian International Insurance Company SPC, Grand Cayman, Cayman Islands	BMI Financial Group, Inc.	50	
Better Life and Health Company, New Rochelle, NY		50	
BF&M Life Insurance Company Limited, Hamilton HM DX, Bermuda	BF&M Limited	50	
Big Sky Life Inc., Helena, MT		50	
Bird Insurance Company, Phoenix, AZ		52	
Block Vision of Texas, Inc., Dallas, TX	Block Vision Holdings LLC	52	
Blue Advantage Plus of Kansas City, Inc, Kansas City, MO	Blue Cross & Blue Shield of Kansas City	52	
Blue Care Health Plan, North Haven, CT		52	
Blue Care Network of Michigan, Southfield, MI	Blue Cross Blue Shield of Michigan	52	
Blue Care of Michigan, Inc., Southfield, MI	Blue Cross Blue Shield of Michigan	52	
Blue Cross and Blue Shield of Alabama, Birmingham, AL	Blue Cross and Blue Shield of Alabama	52	
Blue Cross and Blue Shield of Florida, Inc., Jacksonville, FL	Blue Cross and Blue Shield of FL Inc	52	
Blue Cross and Blue Shield of Georgia, Inc., Atlanta, GA	WellPoint Inc.	52	
Blue Cross & Blue Shield of Kansas City, Kansas City, MO	Blue Cross & Blue Shield of Kansas City	54	
Blue Cross and Blue Shield of Kansas, Inc., Topeka, KS	Blue Cross and Blue Shield of Kansas Inc	54	
Blue Cross and Blue Shield of Massachusetts HMO Blue, Inc., Boston, MA	Blue Cross and Blue Shield of MA.	54	
Blue Cross and Blue Shield of Massachusetts, Inc., Boston, MA	Blue Cross and Blue Shield of MA.	54	
Blue Cross and Blue Shield of Minnesota, Eagan, MN	Aware Integrated Inc.	54	
Blue Cross & Blue Shield of Mississippi, a Mutual Insurance Company, Flowood, MS	Blue Cross & BS of MS a Mutual Ins Co.	54	
Blue Cross and Blue Shield of Montana, Helena, MT	Blue Cross and Blue Shield of Montana	54	
Blue Cross and Blue Shield of Nebraska, Omaha, NE		54	
Blue Cross and Blue Shield of North Carolina, Durham, NC	Blue Cross & BS of NC	54	
Blue Cross & Blue Shield of Rhode Island, Providence, RI		56	
Blue Cross and Blue Shield of South Carolina, Columbia, SC	Blue Cross&Blue Shield of South Carolina	56	
Blue Cross and Blue Shield of Vermont, Berlin, VT	Blue Cross and Blue Shield of Vermont	56	
Blue Cross Blue Shield Healthcare Plan of Georgia, Inc., Atlanta, GA	WellPoint Inc.	56	
Blue Cross Blue Shield MT (HMO), Helena, MT		56	
Blue Cross Blue Shield of Michigan, Detroit, MI	Blue Cross Blue Shield of Michigan	56	
Blue Cross Blue Shield of Wisconsin, Milwaukee, WI	WellPoint Inc.	56	
Blue Cross Blue Shield of Wyoming, Cheyenne, WY		56	
Blue Cross of California, Woodland Hills, CA	WellPoint Inc.	56	
Blue Cross of ID Health Service, Inc., Meridian, ID		58	
Blue Shield of California Life & Health Insurance Company, San Francisco, CA	California Physicians' Service	58	21
Bluebonnet Life Insurance Company, Flowood, MS	Blue Cross & BS of MS a Mutual Ins Co.	58	21
BlueCaid of Michigan, Southfield, MI	Blue Cross Blue Shield of Michigan	58	
BlueChoice HealthPlan of South Carolina, Inc., Columbia, SC	Blue Cross&Blue Shield of South Carolina	58	
BlueCross BlueShield of Tennessee, Inc., Chattanooga, TN	BlueCross BlueShield of Tennessee Inc.	58	
Bluegrass Family Health, Inc., Lexington, KY	Baptist Healthcare System, Inc.	58	
Boston Medical Center Health Plan, Inc., Boston, MA	Boston Medical Center	58	
Boston Mutual Life Insurance Company, Canton, MA	Boston Mutual Life Insurance Company	58	22
Bravo Health Insurance Company, Inc., Baltimore, MD	Bravo Health Inc	60	
Bravo Health Mid-Atlantic, Inc., Baltimore, MD	Bravo Health Inc	60	
Bravo Health Pennsylvania, Inc., Baltimore, MD	Bravo Health Inc	60	
Bravo Health Texas, Inc., Baltimore, MD	Bravo Health Inc	60	
Brokers National Life Assurance Company, Austin, TX	BNL Financial Corporation	60	22
Brooke Life Insurance Company, Lansing, MI	Prudential plc	60	22
Buckeye Community Health Plan, Inc., St. Louis, MO	Centene Corporation	60	
Bupa Insurance Company, Miami, FL	British United Provident Association Ltd.	60	22

COMPANY NAME	ULTIMATE PARENT NAME	KRG	BAG
C			
C.M. Life Insurance Company, Springfield, MA	Massachusetts Mutual Life Insurance Co.	60	23
California Benefits Dental Plan, Santa Ana, CA	Sun Life Financial Inc.	62	
California Dental Network, Inc., Santa Ana, CA		62	
California Physicians' Service, San Francisco, CA	California Physicians' Service	62	
Cambridge Life Insurance Company, Downers Grove, IL	Coventry Health Care Inc	62	23
Canyon State Life Insurance Company, Phoenix, AZ		62	
Capital Advantage Insurance Company, Harrisburg, PA	Capital Blue Cross	62	
Capital Blue Cross, Harrisburg, PA	Capital Blue Cross	62	
Capital District Physicians' Health Plan, Inc., Albany, NY	Capital District Physicians' Health Plan	62	
Capital Health Plan, Inc., Tallahassee, FL	Blue Cross and Blue Shield of FL Inc	62	
Capital Reserve Life Insurance Company, Jefferson City, MO	Security National Financial	64	
CapitalCare, Inc., Owings Mills, MD	CareFirst Inc	64	
Capitol Life and Accident Insurance Company, Amelia, OH	Munich Reinsurance Company	64	
The Capitol Life Insurance Company, Dallas, TX	Realty Advisors Inc.	64	
Capitol Security Life Insurance Company, North Richland Hills, TX		64	
Cardif Life Insurance Company, Miami, FL	BNP Paribas SA	64	23
Care 1st Health Plan, Inc., Monterey Park, CA		64	
Care Improvement Plus of Maryland Inc, Baltimore, MD		64	
Care Plus Dental Plans, Inc., Wauwatosa, WI		64	
CareAmerica Life Insurance Company, San Francisco, CA	California Physicians' Service	66	23
CareFirst BlueChoice, Inc., Washington, DC	CareFirst Inc	66	
CareFirst of Maryland, Inc., Owings Mills, MD	CareFirst Inc	66	
Carelink Health Plans, Inc., Charleston, WV	Coventry Health Care Inc	66	
CareMore Health Plan, Cerritos, CA		66	
CarePlus Health Plans, Inc., Doral, FL	Humana Inc	66	
CareSource, Dayton, OH	CareSource Management Group Company	66	
CareSource Michigan, Okemos, MI	CareSource Management Group Company	66	
Caribbean American Life Assurance Company, San Juan, PR	Assurant Inc	66	24
Cariten Health Plan Inc., Knoxville, TN	Humana Inc	68	
Cariten Insurance Company, Knoxville, TN	Humana Inc	68	
Cass County Life Insurance Company, Atlanta, TX		68	
Caterpillar Life Insurance Company, Nashville, TN	Caterpillar Inc	68	
Catholic Knights, Milwaukee, WI		68	24
Catholic Life Insurance, San Antonio, TX		68	24
Catholic Order of Foresters, Naperville, IL		68	24
CDPHP Universal Benefits, Inc., Albany, NY	Capital District Physicians' Health Plan	68	
Celtic Insurance Company, Chicago, IL	Centene Corporation	68	25
CeltiCare Health Plan of Massachusetts, Inc., St. Louis, MO	Centene Corporation	70	
Cenpatico Behavioral Health of Texas, Inc., Austin, TX	Centene Corporation	70	
Censtat Life Assurance Company, Omaha, NE	Central States Health & Life Co of Omaha	70	25
Central Health Plan of California, Inc., Covina, CA		70	
Central Reserve Life Insurance Company, Austin, TX	American Financial Group, Inc.	70	25
Central Security Life Insurance Company, Richardson, TX	Maximum Corporation	70	
Central States Health & Life Co. of Omaha, Omaha, NE	Central States Health & Life Co of Omaha	70	25
Central United Life Insurance Company, Houston, TX	Harris Insurance Holdings Inc	70	26
Centre Life Insurance Company, New York, NY	Zurich Financial Services Ltd.	70	
Centurion Life Insurance Company, Des Moines, IA	Wells Fargo & Company	72	26
Century Credit Life Insurance Company, Tupelo, MS		72	
Century Life Assurance Company, Goddard, KS	Norma J Hawkins	72	26
CHA HMO, Inc., Louisville, KY	Humana Inc	72	
Champions Life Insurance Company, Richardson, TX	Maximum Corporation	72	
Charleston Capital Reinsurance LLC, Southborough, MA	Goldman Sachs Group Inc	72	26
Charter National Life Insurance Company, Northbrook, IL	Allstate Corporation	72	27
Cherokee National Life Insurance Company, Macon, GA	Minnesota Mutual Companies Inc	72	27
The Chesapeake Life Insurance Company, North Richland Hills, TX	Blackstone Investor Group	72	27
Children's Mercy's Family Health Partners, Kansas City, MO	Children's Mercy Hospital	74	
Chinese Community Health Plan, San Francisco, CA		74	
Christian Fidelity Life Insurance Company, Phoenix, AZ	AMERCO	74	27
Church Life Insurance Corporation, New York, NY	Church Pension Fund	74	28
CIBC Reinsurance Company Limited, Warrens, St. Michael, Barbados	Canadian Imperial Bank of Commerce	74	
CICA Life Insurance Company of America, Austin, TX	Citizens Inc	74	
CIGNA Arbor Life Insurance Company, Bloomfield, CT	CIGNA Corporation	74	
CIGNA Behavioral Health of California, Inc., Glendale, CA	CIGNA Corporation	74	
CIGNA Dental Health of California, Inc., Van Nuys, CA	CIGNA Corporation	74	
CIGNA Dental Health of Colorado, Inc., Sunrise, FL	CIGNA Corporation	76	
CIGNA Dental Health of Delaware, Inc., Sunrise, FL	CIGNA Corporation	76	
CIGNA Dental Health of Florida, Inc., Sunrise, FL	CIGNA Corporation	76	
CIGNA Dental Health of Kansas, Inc., Sunrise, FL	CIGNA Corporation	76	
CIGNA Dental Health of Kentucky, Inc., Sunrise, FL	CIGNA Corporation	76	
CIGNA Dental Health of Maryland, Inc., Sunrise, FL	CIGNA Corporation	76	

COMPANY NAME	ULTIMATE PARENT NAME	KRG	BAG
CIGNA Dental Health of Missouri, Inc, Sunrise, FL	CIGNA Corporation	76	
CIGNA Dental Health of New Jersey, Inc., Sunrise, FL	CIGNA Corporation	76	
CIGNA Dental Health of North Carolina, Inc., Sunrise, FL	CIGNA Corporation	76	
CIGNA Dental Health of Ohio, Inc., Sunrise, FL	CIGNA Corporation	78	
CIGNA Dental Health of Pennsylvania, Inc., Sunrise, FL	CIGNA Corporation	78	
CIGNA Dental Health of Texas, Inc., Sunrise, FL	CIGNA Corporation	78	
CIGNA Dental Health of Virginia, Inc., Sunrise, FL	CIGNA Corporation	78	
CIGNA Dental Health Plan of Arizona, Inc., Sunrise, FL	CIGNA Corporation	78	
CIGNA Health and Life Insurance Company, Greenwood Village, CO	CIGNA Corporation	78	
CIGNA Healthcare-Centennial State, Inc., Greenwood Village, CO	CIGNA Corporation	78	
CIGNA HealthCare Mid-Atlantic, Inc., Columbia, MD	CIGNA Corporation	78	
CIGNA HealthCare of Arizona, Inc., Hartford, CT	CIGNA Corporation	78	
CIGNA HealthCare of California, Inc., Hartford, CT	CIGNA Corporation	80	
CIGNA HealthCare of Colorado, Inc., Denver, CO	CIGNA Corporation	80	
CIGNA HealthCare of Connecticut, Inc., Bloomfield, CT	CIGNA Corporation	80	
CIGNA HealthCare of Delaware, Inc., Blue Bell, PA	CIGNA Corporation	80	
CIGNA HealthCare of Florida, Inc., Bloomfield, CT	CIGNA Corporation	80	
CIGNA HealthCare of Georgia, Inc., Bloomfield, CT	CIGNA Corporation	80	
CIGNA HealthCare of Illinois, Inc., Bloomfield, CT	CIGNA Corporation	80	
CIGNA HealthCare of Indiana, Inc., Bloomfield, CT	CIGNA Corporation	80	
CIGNA HealthCare of Maine, Inc., Bloomfield, CT	CIGNA Corporation	80	
CIGNA HealthCare of Massachusetts, Inc., Newton, MA	CIGNA Corporation	82	
CIGNA HealthCare of New Hampshire, Inc., Hooksett, NH	CIGNA Corporation	82	
CIGNA HealthCare of New Jersey, Inc., Bloomfield, CT	CIGNA Corporation	82	
CIGNA HealthCare of New York, Inc., Bloomfield, CT	CIGNA Corporation	82	
CIGNA HealthCare of North Carolina, Inc., Raleigh, NC	CIGNA Corporation	82	
CIGNA HealthCare of Ohio, Inc., Bloomfield, CT	CIGNA Corporation	82	
CIGNA HealthCare of Pennsylvania, Inc., Blue Bell, PA	CIGNA Corporation	82	
CIGNA HealthCare of St. Louis, Inc., Bloomfield, CT	CIGNA Corporation	82	
CIGNA HealthCare of South Carolina, Inc., Charleston, SC	CIGNA Corporation	82	
CIGNA HealthCare of Tennessee, Inc., Bloomfield, CT	CIGNA Corporation	84	
CIGNA HealthCare of Texas, Inc., Bloomfield, CT	CIGNA Corporation	84	
CIGNA HealthCare of Utah, Inc., Hartford, CT	CIGNA Corporation	84	
CIGNA Healthcare - Pacific, Inc., Greenwood Village, CO	CIGNA Corporation	84	
CIGNA Insurance Group, Inc., Bloomfield, CT	CIGNA Corporation	84	
CIGNA Life Insurance Company of New York, Philadelphia, PA	CIGNA Corporation	84	28
CIGNA Worldwide Insurance Company, Claymont, DE	CIGNA Corporation	84	28
Cincinnati Equitable Life Insurance Company, Cincinnati, OH	Alpha Investment Partnership	84	28
The Cincinnati Life Insurance Company, Fairfield, OH	Cincinnati Financial Corporation	84	29
Citizens Accident & Health Insurance Company, Birmingham, AL	Protective Life Corporation	86	
Citizens Fidelity Insurance Company, Little Rock, AR		86	
Citizens National Life Insurance Company, Austin, TX	Citizens Inc	86	
Citizens Security Life Insurance Company, Louisville, KY	Citizens Financial Corporation	86	29
Claria Life and Health Insurance Company, Tamarac, FL		86	
Clarian Health Plans Inc., Indianapolis, IN	Clarian Health Partners, Inc.	86	
ClearOne Health Plans, Inc., Bend, OR		86	
CLICO (Bahamas) Limited, Nassau, Bahamas	C L Financial Limited	86	
Colina Insurance Limited, Nassau, Bahamas	A F Holdings Ltd	86	
Colonial American Life Insurance Company, Souderton, PA	Coventry Resources Corp.	88	
Colonial Life & Accident Insurance Company, Columbia, SC	Unum Group	88	29
Colonial Life Assurance Company Limited, Hamilton HM 12, Bermuda	Edmund Gibbons Limited	88	
Colonial Life Insurance Company of Texas, Fort Worth, TX	CICO Holding Corp	88	
Colonial Life Insurance Company (Trinidad) Limited, Port of Spain, Trinidad And Tobago	C L Financial Limited	88	
Colonial Medical Insurance Company Limited, Hamilton HM 12, Bermuda	Edmund Gibbons Limited	88	
Colonial Penn Life Insurance Company, Carmel, IN	CNO Financial Group, Inc.	88	29
Colonial Security Life Insurance Company, Dallas, TX	Gibraltar Group, Inc.	88	
Colorado Access, Denver, CO		88	
Colorado Bankers Life Insurance Company, Greenwood Village, CO	Health Care Svc Corp Mut Legal Reserve	90	30
Colorado Choice Health Plans, Alamosa, CO		90	
Colorado Dental Service, Inc., Denver, CO		90	
Columbia Capital Life Reinsurance Company, Southborough, MA	Goldman Sachs Group Inc	90	
Columbia United Providers, Inc., Vancouver, WA	Southwest Washington Health Systems	90	
Columbian Life Insurance Company, Binghamton, NY	Columbian Mutual Life Insurance Company	90	30
Columbian Mutual Life Insurance Company, Binghamton, NY	Columbian Mutual Life Insurance Company	90	30
Columbus Life Insurance Company, Cincinnati, OH	Western & Southern Mutual Holding Co	90	30
Combined Insurance Company of America, Glenview, IL	ACE Limited	90	31
Combined Life Insurance Company of New York, Glenview, IL	ACE Limited	92	31
Commencement Bay Life Insurance Company, Seattle, WA	Regence Group	92	
Commercial Travelers Mutual Insurance Company, Utica, NY	Commercial Travelers Mutual Insurance Co	92	31
Commonwealth Annuity and Life Insurance Company, Southborough, MA	Goldman Sachs Group Inc	92	31

COMPANY NAME	ULTIMATE PARENT NAME	KRG	BAG
Commonwealth Dealers Life Insurance Company, Richmond, VA		92	32
Community Care Behavioral Health, Pittsburgh, PA	University of Pittsburgh Medical Center	92	
Community Care Health Plan, Inc., Milwaukee, WI		92	
Community Dental Associates, Inc., Vineland, NJ		92	
Community First Group Hospital Service Corp., San Antonio, TX	Bexar County Hospital District	92	
Community First Health Plans, Inc., San Antonio, TX	Bexar County Hospital District	94	
Community Health Choice, Inc., Houston, TX		94	
Community Health Group, Chula Vista, CA		94	
Community Health Plan, St. Joseph, MO	Heartland Health	94	
Community Health Plan Insurance Company, St. Joseph, MO	Heartland Health	94	
Community Health Plan of Washington, Seattle, WA	Community Health Network of Washington	94	
Community Insurance Company, Mason, OH	WellPoint Inc.	94	
CommunityCare HMO, Inc., Tulsa, OK		94	
Companion Life Insurance Company, Omaha, NE	Mutual of Omaha Insurance Company	94	32
Companion Life Insurance Company, Columbia, SC	Blue Cross&Blue Shield of South Carolina	96	32
CompBenefits Company, Roswell, GA	Humana Inc	96	
CompBenefits Dental, Inc., Roswell, GA	Humana Inc	96	
CompBenefits Insurance Company, Roswell, GA	Humana Inc	96	
Compcare Health Services Insurance Corporation, Milwaukee, WI	WellPoint Inc.	96	
CONCERN: Employee Assistance Program, Mountain View, CA		96	
Concert Health Plan Insurance Co, Oak Brook, IL		96	
Congress Life Insurance Company, Scottsdale, AZ		96	
ConnectiCare, Inc., Farmington, CT	EmblemHealth Inc	96	
ConnectiCare Insurance Company, Inc., Farmington, CT	EmblemHealth Inc	98	
ConnectiCare of Massachusetts, Farmington, CT	EmblemHealth Inc	98	
ConnectiCare of New York, Inc., Farmington, CT	EmblemHealth Inc	98	
Connecticut General Life Insurance Company, Bloomfield, CT	CIGNA Corporation	98	32
Connecticut Life Insurance and Annuity Corporation, Scottsdale, AZ		98	
Conseco Health Insurance Company, Carmel, IN	CNO Financial Group, Inc.	98	33
Conseco Insurance Company, Carmel, IN	CNO Financial Group, Inc.	98	33
Conseco Life Insurance Company, Carmel, IN	CNO Financial Group, Inc.	98	33
Conseco Life Insurance Company of Texas, Carmel, IN	CNO Financial Group, Inc.	98	
Constitution Life Insurance Company, Lake Mary, FL	Universal American Corp.	100	33
ConsumerHealth, Inc., Santa Ana, CA	Ivory Holdco Inc	100	
Consumers Life Insurance Company, Cleveland, OH	Medical Mutual of Ohio	100	
Continental American Insurance Company, Columbia, SC	Aflac Incorporated	100	34
Continental Assurance Company, Chicago, IL	Loews Corporation	100	34
Continental General Insurance Company, Austin, TX	American Financial Group, Inc.	100	34
Continental Life Insurance Company, Upper Darby, PA	Burlen Corporation	100	
Continental Life Insurance Company of Brentwood, Tennessee, Brentwood, TN	Genworth Financial, Inc	100	34
Continental Life Insurance Company of South Carolina, Columbia, SC		100	
Contra Costa Health Plan, Martinez, CA		102	
Cook Children's Health Plan, Fort Worth, TX	Cook Children's Health Care System	102	
Cooperativa de Seguros de Vida de Puerto Rico, San Juan, PR		102	35
Cooperative Life Insurance Company, Pine Bluff, AR		102	
Coordinated Care Corporation Indiana, Inc., St. Louis, MO	Centene Corporation	102	
Cornhusker Life Insurance Company, Lincoln, NE		102	
Cosmopolitan Life Insurance Company, Little Rock, AR		102	
Cotton States Life Insurance Company, Atlanta, GA	Illinois Agricultural Association	102	35
COUNTRY Investors Life Assurance Company, Bloomington, IL	Illinois Agricultural Association	102	35
COUNTRY Life Insurance Company, Bloomington, IL	Illinois Agricultural Association	104	35
County of Los Angeles, Alhambra, CA		104	
County of Ventura, Ventura, CA		104	
Coventry Health and Life Insurance Company, Bethesda, MD	Coventry Health Care Inc	104	
Coventry Health Care of Delaware, Inc., Bethesda, MD	Coventry Health Care Inc	104	
Coventry Health Care of Georgia, Inc., Bethesda, MD	Coventry Health Care Inc	104	
Coventry Health Care of Iowa, Inc., Bethesda, MD	Coventry Health Care Inc	104	
Coventry Health Care of Kansas, Inc., Wichita, KS	Coventry Health Care Inc	104	
Coventry Health Care of Louisiana, Inc., Metairie, LA	Coventry Health Care Inc	104	
Coventry Health Care of Nebraska, Inc., Bethesda, MD	Coventry Health Care Inc	106	
Coventry Health Care of Pennsylvania, Inc., Harrisburg, PA	Coventry Health Care Inc	106	
Cox Health Systems HMO, Springfield, MO	Cox Health	106	
CSI Life Insurance Company, Omaha, NE	Berkshire Hathaway Inc	106	
CUNA Mutual Insurance Society, Madison, WI	CUNA Mutual Insurance Society	106	36

D

COMPANY NAME	ULTIMATE PARENT NAME	KRG	BAG
Dallas General Life Insurance Company, Phoenix, AZ	AMERCO	106	
DaVita VillageHealth Insurance of Alabama, Inc., Birmingham, AL	DaVita Inc	106	
DaVita VillageHealth of Georgia, Inc., Atlanta, GA	DaVita Inc	106	
DaVita VillageHealth of Ohio, Inc., Tacoma, WA	DaVita Inc	106	
DaVita VillageHealth of Virginia, Inc., Glen Allen, VA	DaVita Inc	108	

COMPANY NAME	ULTIMATE PARENT NAME	KRG	BAG
DC Chartered Health Plan, Inc., Washington, DC	DC Healthcare Systems Inc	108	
Dean Health Insurance, Inc., Madison, WI	Dean Health Systems, Inc.	108	
Dean Health Plan Inc., Madison, WI	Dean Health Systems, Inc.	108	
Dedicated Dental Systems, Inc., Bakersfield, CA	InterDent Service Corporation	108	
Delaware American Life Insurance Company, Houston, TX	American International Group, Inc.	108	36
Delta Dental Insurance Company, San Francisco, CA	Dentegra Group Inc.	108	
Delta Dental of California, San Francisco, CA	Dentegra Group Inc.	108	
Delta Dental of Delaware, Mechanicsburg, PA	Dentegra Group Inc.	108	
Delta Dental of Iowa, Ankeny, IA		110	
Delta Dental of Kentucky, Inc., Louisville, KY	Renaissance Health Service Corp	110	
Delta Dental of Minnesota, Eagan, MN	DeCare International	110	
Delta Dental of Missouri, St. Louis, MO		110	
Delta Dental of Nebraska, Eagan, MN		110	
Delta Dental of New Jersey, Inc., Parsippany, NJ	Delta Dental of New Jersey Inc	110	
Delta Dental of New York, Mechanicsburg, PA	Dentegra Group Inc.	110	
Delta Dental of Pennsylvania, Mechanicsburg, PA	Dentegra Group Inc.	110	
Delta Dental of Rhode Island, Providence, RI	Delta Dental of Rhode Island	110	
Delta Dental of Tennessee, Nashville, TN	Renaissance Health Service Corp	112	
Delta Dental of Virginia, Roanoke, VA		112	
Delta Dental of West Virginia, Mechanicsburg, PA	Dentegra Group Inc.	112	
Delta Dental of Wisconsin, Inc., Stevens Point, WI	Delta Dental of Wisconsin Inc	112	
Delta Dental Plan of Arkansas, Inc., Sherwood, AR		112	
Delta Dental Plan of Idaho, Inc., Boise, ID		112	
Delta Dental Plan of Indiana, Inc., Okemos, MI	Renaissance Health Service Corp	112	
Delta Dental Plan of Kansas, Inc., Wichita, KS		112	
Delta Dental Plan of Michigan, Inc., Okemos, MI	Renaissance Health Service Corp	112	
Delta Dental Plan of New Hampshire, Concord, NH		114	
Delta Dental Plan of New Mexico, Inc., Albuquerque, NM	Renaissance Health Service Corp	114	
Delta Dental Plan of North Carolina, Inc., Raleigh, NC		114	
Delta Dental Plan of Ohio, Inc., Okemos, MI	Renaissance Health Service Corp	114	
Delta Dental Plan of Oklahoma, Oklahoma City, OK		114	
Delta Dental Plan of South Dakota, Pierre, SD		114	
Delta Life Insurance Company, Atlanta, GA	J. Mack Robinson & Family	114	
Denta-Chek of Maryland, Inc., Columbia, MD		114	
Dental Benefit Providers of California, Inc., Minnetonka, MN	UnitedHealth Group Inc	114	
Dental Benefit Providers of Illinois, Inc, Columbia, MD	UnitedHealth Group Inc	116	
Dental Care Plus, Inc., Cincinnati, OH	DCP Holding Company	116	
Dental Choice, Inc., Louisville, KY		116	
The Dental Concern, Inc., Louisville, KY	Humana Inc	116	
The Dental Concern, Ltd., Chicago, IL	Humana Inc	116	
Dental Delivery Systems, Inc., Glenside, PA		116	
Dental Group of New Jersey, Inc., Linden, NJ		116	
Dental Health Services (California), Long Beach, CA	Dental Health Services of America Inc	116	
Dental Health Services (Washington), Long Beach, CA	Dental Health Services of America Inc	116	
Dental Practice Association of New Jersey, Inc., Philadelphia, PA		118	
Dental Protection Plan, Inc., Milwaukee, WI		118	
Dental Service Corporation of North Dakota, Fargo, ND	Noridian Mutual Insurance Company	118	
Dental Service of Massachusetts, Inc., Boston, MA	Dental Service of Massachusetts Inc	118	
Dental Services Organization, Inc., Avenel, NJ		118	
Dental Source of Missouri and Kansas, Inc., Kansas City, MO	Dental Economics L P.	118	
DentaQuest Dental Plan of Wisconsin, Inc., Mequon, WI	Dental Service of Massachusetts Inc	118	
DentaQuest Mid-Atlantic, Inc., Calverton, MD	Dental Service of Massachusetts Inc	118	
DentaQuest USA Insurance Company, Inc., Austin, TX	Dental Service of Massachusetts Inc	118	
DentaQuest Virginia, Inc., Calverton, MD	Dental Service of Massachusetts Inc	120	
Dentcare Delivery Systems, Inc., Uniondale, NY		120	
Dentegra Insurance Company, San Francisco, CA	Dentegra Group Inc.	120	
Dentegra Insurance Company of New England, San Francisco, CA	Dentegra Group Inc.	120	
DentiCare, Inc., Roswell, GA	Humana Inc	120	
Denver Health Medical Plan, Inc., Denver, CO		120	
Deseret Mutual Insurance Company, Salt Lake City, UT	DMC Reserve Trust	120	
Destiny Health Insurance Company, Chicago, IL		120	
Direct Dental Service Plan, Inc., Racine, WI		120	
Direct General Life Insurance Company, Nashville, TN	Elara Holdings, Inc.	122	36
Direct Life Insurance Company, Nashville, TN	Elara Holdings, Inc.	122	
Directors Life Assurance Company, Oklahoma City, OK	Aegis Insurance Holdings Company LP.	122	
Dixie Life Insurance Company Inc., Bogalusa, LA		122	
The Doctors Life Insurance Company, Napa, CA	Doctors Company An Interinsurance Exch	122	
Dorsey Life Insurance Company, Marlin, TX		122	
Driscoll Children's Health Plan, Corpus Christi, TX		122	

COMPANY NAME	ULTIMATE PARENT NAME	KRG	BAG
E			
Eagle Life Insurance Company, West Des Moines, IA	American Equity Investment Life Hldg Co	122	
Eastern Life and Health Insurance Company, Lancaster, PA	Eastern Insurance Holdings, Inc.	122	36
Eastern Vision Service Plan, Inc., Rancho Cordova, CA	Vision Service Plan	124	
Easy Choice Health Plan, Newport Beach, CA		124	
Educators Health Plans Life Accident and Health, Murray, UT	Educators Mutual Insurance Association	124	
Educators Life Insurance Company of America, Springfield, IL	Horace Mann Educators Corporation	124	
Educators Mutual Insurance Association, Murray, UT	Educators Mutual Insurance Association	124	
El Paso First Health Plans, El Paso, TX		124	
Elderplan, Inc., Brooklyn, NY		124	
EMC National Life Company, Urbandale, IA	Employers Mutual Casualty Company	124	37
Emphesys Insurance Company, Louisville, KY	Humana Inc	124	
Empire Fidelity Investments Life Insurance Company, Boston, MA	FMR LLC	126	37
Empire HealthChoice Assurance, Inc., New York, NY	WellPoint Inc.	126	
Empire HealthChoice HMO, Inc., New York, NY	WellPoint Inc.	126	
Employees Life Company (Mutual), Lake Bluff, IL		126	37
Employees Life Insurance Company, San Antonio, TX		126	37
Employers Reassurance Corporation, Mission, KS	General Electric Company	126	38
Enterprise Life Insurance Company, Irving, TX	Enterprise Financial Group, Inc.	126	
Envision Insurance Company, Twinsburg, OH	Envision Pharmaceutical Holdings Inc.	126	
The EPIC Life Insurance Company, Madison, WI	Wisconsin Physicians Service Ins Corp	126	
Equitable Life & Casualty Insurance Company, Salt Lake City, UT	Insurance Investment Company	128	38
EquiTrust Life Insurance Company, West Des Moines, IA	Iowa Farm Bureau Federation	128	38
Erie Family Life Insurance Company, Erie, PA	Erie Indemnity Company	128	38
Escude Life Insurance Company, Mansura, LA		128	
Essence Healthcare, Inc., St. Louis, MO	Essence Group Holdings Corporation	128	
Essex Dental Benefits, Inc., St. Louis, MO		128	
Evangeline Life Insurance Company, New Iberia, LA		128	
Evercare of New Mexico, Inc., Albuquerque, NM	UnitedHealth Group Inc	128	
Evercare of Texas, LLC, Phoenix, AZ	UnitedHealth Group Inc	128	
Excellus Health Plan, Inc., Rochester, NY	Lifetime Healthcare Inc	130	
EYEXAM of California, Inc., Mission Viejo, CA		130	
F			
Fallon Community Health Plan, Inc., Worcester, MA	Fallon Community Health Plan Inc	130	
Family Benefit Life Insurance Company, Jefferson City, MO		130	
The Family Guardian Insurance Company Limited, Nassau, Bahamas	Famguard Corporation Limited	130	
Family Heritage Life Insurance Company of America, Cleveland, OH	Southwestern/Great American, Inc.	130	39
Family Liberty Life Insurance Company, Texarkana, TX		130	
Family Life Insurance Company, Houston, TX	Harris Insurance Holdings Inc	130	39
Family Security Life Insurance Company, Incorporated, Natchez, MS		130	
Family Service Life Insurance Company, New York, NY	Guardian Life Ins Co of America	132	39
FamilyCare Health Plans, Inc., Portland, OR		132	
Farm Bureau Life Insurance Company, West Des Moines, IA	Iowa Farm Bureau Federation	132	39
Farm Bureau Life Insurance Company of Michigan, Lansing, MI	Michigan Farm Bureau	132	40
Farm Bureau Life Insurance Company of Missouri, Jefferson City, MO	Missouri Farm Bureau Federation	132	40
Farm Family Life Insurance Company, Glenmont, NY	American National Insurance Company	132	40
Farmers New World Life Insurance Company, Mercer Island, WA	Zurich Financial Services Ltd	132	40
Federal Life Insurance Company (Mutual), Riverwoods, IL		132	
Federated Life Insurance Company, Owatonna, MN	Federated Mutual Insurance Company	132	41
Fidelis SecureCare of Michigan, Inc., Schaumburg, IL	Fidelis SeniorCare Inc.	134	
Fidelis SecureCare of North Carolina Inc., Schaumburg, IL	Fidelis SeniorCare Inc.	134	
Fidelis SecureCare of Texas Inc., Houston, TX	Fidelis SeniorCare Inc.	134	
Fidelity Investments Life Insurance Company, Boston, MA	FMR LLC	134	41
Fidelity Life Association, A Legal Reserve Life Insurance Company, Oak Brook, IL	Members Mutual Holding Company	134	41
Fidelity Security Life Insurance Company, Kansas City, MO	Richard F Jones	134	41
Fidelity Standard Life Insurance Company, Colorado Springs, CO		134	
Financial Assurance Life Insurance Company, Kansas City, MO	Financial Holding Corporation	134	
Financial Life Insurance Company of Georgia, Charlotte, NC	Wells Fargo & Company	134	
First Allmerica Financial Life Insurance Company, Southborough, MA	Goldman Sachs Group Inc	136	42
First Ameritas Life Insurance Corp. of New York, Suffern, NY	UNIFI Mutual Holding Company	136	42
First Assurance Life of America, Baton Rouge, LA	Louisiana Dealer Services Insurance Inc	136	42
First Berkshire Hathaway Life Insurance Company, Omaha, NE	Berkshire Hathaway Inc	136	
First Catholic Slovak Ladies Association of the United States of America, Beachwood, OH		136	42
First Catholic Slovak Union of the United States of America and Canada, Independence, OH		136	
First Central National Life Insurance Company of New York, Bridgewater, NJ	HSBC Holdings plc	136	43
First Command LIC, McKinney, TX	First Command Financial Services, Inc.	136	
First Commonwealth Insurance Company, Chicago, IL	Guardian Life Ins Co of America	136	
First Commonwealth Limited Health Service Corporation, Chicago, IL	Guardian Life Ins Co of America	138	

COMPANY NAME	ULTIMATE PARENT NAME	KRG	BAG
First Commonwealth Limited Health Services Corporation, Chicago, IL	Guardian Life Ins Co of America	138	
First Commonwealth Limited Health Services Corporation of Michigan, Chicago, IL	Guardian Life Ins Co of America	138	
First Commonwealth of Missouri, Inc., Chicago, IL	Guardian Life Ins Co of America	138	
First Continental Life & Accident Insurance Company, Sugar Land, TX	Dental Economics L P.	138	
First Dental Health, San Diego, CA		138	
First Dimension Life Insurance Company, Inc., Stillwater, OK		138	
First Dominion Mutual Life Insurance Company, Philadelphia, PA		138	
First Financial Assurance Company, Fayetteville, AR		138	
First Great-West Life & Annuity Insurance Company, Greenwood Village, CO	Power Corporation of Canada	140	43
First Guaranty Insurance Company, Ashdown, AR		140	
First Health Life & Health Insurance Company, Downers Grove, IL	Coventry Health Care Inc	140	43
First Investors Life Insurance Company, Edison, NJ	First Investors Consolidated Corporation	140	43
First Landmark Life Insurance Company, Omaha, NE		140	
First M & F Insurance Company, Kosciusko, MS		140	
First MetLife Investors Insurance Company, Irvine, CA	MetLife Inc	140	44
First National Indemnity Life Insurance Company, Richardson, TX		140	
First National Life Insurance Company of the U.S.A., Lincoln, NE	Nelnet, Inc.	140	
First Penn-Pacific Life Insurance Company, Fort Wayne, IN	Lincoln National Corporation	142	44
First Priority Life Insurance Company, Wilkes-Barre, PA	Hospital Service Assn of Northeastern PA	142	
The First Rehabilitation Life Insurance Company of America, Great Neck, NY	Rehab Services Corporation	142	44
First Reliance Standard Life Insurance Company, Philadelphia, PA	R & Co Capital Management, L.L.C.	142	44
First Security Benefit Life Insurance and Annuity Company of New York, Topeka, KS	Security Benefit Mutual Holding Company	142	45
First SunAmerica Life Insurance Company, New York, NY	American International Group, Inc.	142	45
First Symetra National Life Insurance Company of New York, New York, NY	Symetra Financial Corporation	142	45
First United American Life Insurance Company, Liverpool, NY	Torchmark Corporation	142	45
First Unum Life Insurance Company, Chattanooga, TN	Unum Group	142	46
First Virginia Life Insurance Company, Winston-Salem, NC		144	
FirstCare, Inc., Owings Mills, MD	CareFirst Inc	144	
FirstCarolinaCare Insurance Company, Inc., Pinehurst, NC	FirstHealth of the Carolinas Inc	144	
FirstCommunity Health Plan, Inc., Huntsville, AL		144	
FirstSight Vision Services, Inc., Upland, CA	National Vision Inc	144	
5 Star Life Insurance Company, Alexandria, VA	Armed Forces Benefit Assn Invstmnt Trust	144	46
Flagship Health Systems, Inc., Parsippany, NJ	Delta Dental of New Jersey Inc	144	
Florida Combined Life Insurance Company, Jacksonville, FL	LSV Partners LLC	144	46
Florida Health Care Plan, Inc., Holly Hill, FL	Blue Cross and Blue Shield of FL Inc	144	
For Eyes Vision Plan, Inc., Berkeley, CA		146	
Forethought Life Insurance Company, Indianapolis, IN	Forethought Financial Group, Inc.	146	46
Forethought National Life Insurance Company, Indianapolis, IN	Forethought Financial Group, Inc.	146	
Fort Dearborn Life Insurance Company, Downers Grove, IL	Health Care Svc Corp Mut Legal Reserve	146	47
Fort Dearborn Life Insurance Company of New York, Downers Grove, IL	Health Care Svc Corp Mut Legal Reserve	146	47
Fortis Insurance Company (Asia) Limited, Hong Kong		146	
Foundation Life Insurance Company of Arkansas, Fort Smith, AR		146	
Fox Insurance Company, CA		146	
Frandisco Life Insurance Company, Toccoa, GA		146	
Freedom Life Insurance Company of America, Fort Worth, TX	Credit Suisse Holdings (USA) Inc	148	47
Freelancers Insurance Company, Inc., Brooklyn, NY		148	
Fringe Benefit Life Insurance Company, Fort Worth, TX		148	
Funeral Directors Life Insurance Company, Abilene, TX	Directors Investment Group Inc	148	47
Futural Life Insurance Company, Phoenix, AZ		148	

G

COMPANY NAME	ULTIMATE PARENT NAME	KRG	BAG
Garden State Life Insurance Company, Galveston, TX	American National Insurance Company	148	48
Gateway Health Plan, Inc., Pittsburgh, PA	Gateway Health Plan L.P.	148	
Geisinger Health Plan, Danville, PA	Geisinger Health System Foundation	148	
GEMCare Health Plan, Inc., Bakersfield, CA		148	
General American Life Insurance Company, St. Louis, MO	MetLife Inc	150	48
General Fidelity Life Insurance Company, Irvine, CA	Bank of America Corporation	150	48
General Re Life Corporation, Stamford, CT	Berkshire Hathaway Inc	150	48
Generali USA Life Reassurance Company, Lenexa, KS	Assicurazioni Generali S.p.A.	150	49
Genworth Life and Annuity Insurance Company, Richmond, VA	Genworth Financial, Inc	150	49
Genworth Life Insurance Company, Richmond, VA	Genworth Financial, Inc	150	49
Genworth Life Insurance Company of New York, New York, NY	Genworth Financial, Inc	150	49
Gerber Life Insurance Company, White Plains, NY	Nestle S A	150	50
Germania Life Insurance Company, Brenham, TX	Germania Farm Mutual Insurance Assn	150	50
GHI HMO Select, Inc., Lake Katrine, NY	EmblemHealth Inc	152	
GHS Health Maintenance Organization, Tulsa, OK	Health Care Svc Corp Mut Legal Reserve	152	
Gleaner Life Insurance Society, Adrian, MI		152	50
GlobalHealth, Inc., Houston, TX	Universal American Corp.	152	
Globe Life and Accident Insurance Company, Oklahoma City, OK	Torchmark Corporation	152	50
Gmhp Health Insurance Limited, Tamuning, GU		152	
Golden Rule Insurance Company, Indianapolis, IN	UnitedHealth Group Inc	152	51

COMPANY NAME	ULTIMATE PARENT NAME	KRG	BAG
Golden Security Insurance Company, Chattanooga, TN.	BlueCross BlueShield of Tennessee Inc	152	
Golden State Mutual Life Insurance Company, Los Angeles, CA		152	
Golden West Health Plan, Inc., Thousand Oaks, CA	WellPoint Inc.	154	
Good Health HMO, Inc., Kansas City, MO.	Blue Cross & Blue Shield of Kansas City	154	
Government Personnel Mutual Life Insurance Company, San Antonio, TX		154	51
Grand Valley Health Plan, Inc., Grand Rapids, MI.	Grand Valley Health Corporation	154	
Grange Life Insurance Company, Columbus, OH.	Grange Mutual Casualty Pool	154	51
Graphics Arts Benefit Corporation, Greenbelt, MD		154	
Great American Life Assurance Company, Austin, TX	American Financial Group, Inc.	154	51
Great American Life Insurance Company, Cincinnati, OH	American Financial Group, Inc.	154	52
Great American Life Insurance Company of New York, New York, NY	American Financial Group, Inc.	154	52
Great Central Life Insurance Company, Oakdale, LA.		156	
Great Cornerstone Life and Health Insurance Company, Edmond, OK.	Great Cornerstone Corporation	156	
Great Fidelity Life Insurance Company, Goddard, KS	Norma J Hawkins	156	
Great Lakes Health Plan, Inc., Southfield, MI.	UnitedHealth Group Inc	156	
Great Republic Life Insurance Company, Seattle, WA.	Empire Insurance Agency, Inc.	156	
Great Southern Life Insurance Company, Kansas City, MO	Financial Holding Corporation	156	52
Great-West Healthcare of Illinois, Inc., Greenwood Village, CO.	CIGNA Corporation	156	
Great-West Life & Annuity Insurance Company, Greenwood Village, CO.	Power Corporation of Canada	156	52
Great Western Insurance Company, Ogden, UT	JAMEL Ltd.	156	53
Great Western Life Insurance Company, Ogden, UT	JAMEL Ltd.	158	
Greater Beneficial Union of Pittsburgh, Pittsburgh, PA		158	53
Greater Georgia Life Insurance Company, Atlanta, GA	WellPoint Inc.	158	53
Greek Catholic Union of the U.S.A., Beaver, PA		158	
Griffin Leggett Burial Insurance Company, Little Rock, AR		158	
Group Dental Health Administrators, Inc., Roselle Park, NJ		158	
Group Dental Service of Maryland, Inc., Rockville, MD	Coventry Health Care Inc	158	
Group Health Cooperative, Seattle, WA	Group Health Cooperative	158	
Group Health Cooperative of Eau Claire, Altoona, WI.		158	
Group Health Cooperative of South Central Wisconsin, Madison, WI.		160	
Group Health Incorporated, New York, NY	EmblemHealth Inc	160	
Group Health Options, Seattle, WA	Group Health Cooperative	160	
Group Health Plan, Inc., St. Louis, MO	Coventry Health Care Inc	160	
Group Health Plan, Inc., Minneapolis, MN.	HealthPartners Inc.	160	
Group Hospitalization and Medical Services, Inc., Owings Mills, MD	CareFirst Inc	160	
Group Insurance Trust of the California Society of Certified Public Accountants, Redwood City, CA		160	
Guarantee Security Life Insurance Company of Arizona, Scottsdale, AZ	Guarantee Trust Life Insurance Company	160	
Guarantee Trust Life Insurance Company, Glenview, IL	Guarantee Trust Life Insurance Company	160	53
Guaranty Income Life Insurance Company, Baton Rouge, LA	Guaranty Corporation	162	54
Guardian Insurance & Annuity Company, Inc., New York, NY.	Guardian Life Ins Co of America	162	54
Guardian Life Insurance Company of America, New York, NY	Guardian Life Ins Co of America	162	54
Guardian Life of the Caribbean Limited, Port of Spain, Trinidad And Tobago	Guardian Holdings Limited	162	
Guggenheim Life and Annuity Company, Schererville, IN	Guggenheim Capital LLC.	162	
Gulf Guaranty Life Insurance Company, Jackson, MS.	Gulf Guaranty Life Insurance Company.	162	54
Gulf States Life Insurance Company, Inc., Opelousas, LA.		162	
Gundersen Lutheran Health Plan, Inc., La Crosse, WI	Gundersen Lutheran, Inc.	162	

H

COMPANY NAME	ULTIMATE PARENT NAME	KRG	BAG
Hallmark Life Insurance Company, Newport Beach, CA.	Centene Corporation	162	
Hannover Life Reassurance Bermuda Limited, Hamilton HM 10, Bermuda	HDI V.a.G.	164	
Hannover Life Reassurance Company of America, Orlando, FL	HDI V.a.G.	164	55
Harleysville Life Insurance Company, Harleysville, PA	Harleysville Mutual Insurance Company	164	55
Hartford International Life Reassurance Corporation, Simsbury, CT.	Hartford Financial Services Group Inc.	164	55
Hartford Life and Accident Insurance Company, Simsbury, CT	Hartford Financial Services Group Inc.	164	55
Hartford Life and Annuity Insurance Company, Simsbury, CT	Hartford Financial Services Group Inc.	164	56
Hartford Life Insurance Company, Simsbury, CT	Hartford Financial Services Group Inc.	164	56
Harvard Pilgrim Health Care, Inc., Wellesley, MA	Harvard Pilgrim Health Care Inc	164	
Harvard Pilgrim Health Care of New England, Inc., Wellesley, MA.	Harvard Pilgrim Health Care Inc	164	
Hawaii Dental Service, Honolulu, HI		166	
Hawaii Management Alliance Association, Honolulu, HI		166	
Hawaii Medical Service Association, Honolulu, HI.	Hawaii Medical Service Association	166	
Hawkeye Life Insurance Group, Inc., West Des Moines, IA		166	
Hawthorn Life Insurance Company, Carthage, TX.		166	
HCC Life Insurance Company, Kennesaw, GA	HCC Insurance Holdings, Inc.	166	56
HCSC Insurance Services Company, Chicago, IL	Health Care Svc Corp Mut Legal Reserve	166	
Health Alliance Medical Plans, Inc., Urbana, IL.	Carle Clinic Association PC	166	
Health Alliance-Midwest, Inc., Urbana, IL.	Carle Clinic Association PC	166	
Health Alliance Plan of Michigan, Detroit, MI.	Henry Ford Health System	168	
Health and Human Resource Center, Inc., San Diego, CA.		168	
Health Care Service Corporation, a Mutual Legal Reserve Company, Chicago, IL.	Health Care Svc Corp Mut Legal Reserve	168	
Health Care Service Corporation - Illinois HMO Line of Business, Chicago, IL.		168	
Health Care Service Corporation - Texas HMO Line of Business, Richardson, TX		168	
Health First Health Plans, Rockledge, FL.	Health First, Inc.	168	

COMPANY NAME	ULTIMATE PARENT NAME	KRG	BAG
Health Insurance Plan of Greater New York, New York, NY	EmblemHealth Inc	168	
Health Net Health Plan of Oregon, Inc., Woodland Hills, CA	Health Net Inc	168	
Health Net Insurance of New York, Inc., Shelton, CT	UnitedHealth Group Inc	168	
Health Net Life Insurance Company, Woodland Hills, CA	Health Net Inc	170	56
Health Net of Arizona, Inc., Woodland Hills, CA.	Health Net Inc	170	
Health Net of California, Inc., Woodland Hills, CA	Health Net Inc	170	
Health Net of Connecticut, Inc., Woodland Hills, CA	UnitedHealth Group Inc	170	
Health Net of New Jersey, Inc., Shelton, CT.	UnitedHealth Group Inc	170	
Health Net of New York, Inc., Woodland Hills, CA.	UnitedHealth Group Inc	170	
Health New England, Inc., Springfield, MA	Baystate Health Inc.	170	
Health Options, Inc., Jacksonville, FL.	Blue Cross and Blue Shield of FL Inc	170	
Health Partners of Philadelphia, Inc., Philadelphia, PA		170	
Health Plan for Community Living, Inc., Madison, WI		172	
Health Plan of CareOregon, Inc., Portland, OR.		172	
Health Plan of Michigan, Southfield, MI.		172	
Health Plan of Nevada, Inc., Las Vegas, NV	UnitedHealth Group Inc	172	
The Health Plan of the Upper Ohio Valley, Inc., St. Clairsville, OH	Health Plan of the Upper Ohio Valley	172	
Health Plus of Louisiana, Inc., Shreveport, LA.	Willis-Knighton Medical Center.	172	
Health Resources, Inc., Evansville, IN		172	
Health Right, Inc., Washington, DC		172	
Health Tradition Health Plan, Rochester, MN.		172	
Health Ventures Network, Eagan, MN	DeCare International	174	
HealthAmerica Pennsylvania, Inc., Harrisburg, PA	Coventry Health Care Inc	174	
HealthAssurance Pennsylvania, Inc., Harrisburg, PA.	Coventry Health Care Inc	174	
HealthCare USA of Missouri, LLC, St. Louis, MO	Coventry Health Care Inc	174	
Healthfirst Health Plan of New Jersey, Inc., New York, NY	HF Management Services LLC	174	
HealthKeepers, Inc., Richmond, VA.	WellPoint Inc.	174	
HealthLink HMO, Inc., St. Louis, MO	WellPoint Inc.	174	
HealthMarkets Insurance Company, North Richland Hills, TX	Blackstone Investor Group	174	
HealthNow New York Inc., Buffalo, NY		174	
HealthPartners, Inc., Minneapolis, MN.	HealthPartners Inc.	176	
Healthplex Insurance Company, Uniondale, NY	Healthplex Inc	176	
Healthplex of NJ, Inc., Uniondale, NY	Healthplex Inc	176	
HealthPlus Insurance Company, Flint, MI	HealthPlus of Michigan Inc	176	
HealthPlus of Michigan, Inc., Flint, MI.	HealthPlus of Michigan Inc	176	
HealthPlus Partners, Inc., Flint, MI.	HealthPlus of Michigan Inc	176	
HealthSpring Life and Health Insurance Company Inc, Nashville, TN	HealthSpring, Inc.	176	
HealthSpring of Alabama, Inc., Birmingham, AL.	HealthSpring, Inc.	176	
HealthSpring of Tennessee, Inc., Nashville, TN.	HealthSpring, Inc.	176	
HealthWise, Salt Lake City, UT	Regence Group	178	
Healthy Alliance Life Insurance Company, St Louis, MO.	WellPoint Inc.	178	57
Heart of America Health Plan, Rugby, ND		178	
Heartland Fidelity Insurance Company, Washington, DC		178	
Heartland National Life Insurance Company, Blue Springs, MO.	Heartland Holding Company Inc	178	
Heritage Provider Network, Inc., Northridge, CA.		178	
Heritage Union Life Insurance Company, Richmond, VA		178	
HHS Health of Oklahoma, Inc., Houston, TX.	Universal American Corp.	178	
Higginbotham Burial Insurance Company, Walnut Ridge, AR.		178	
Highmark Inc., Pittsburgh, PA.	Highmark Inc.	180	
Highmark Senior Resources Inc., Pittsburgh, PA	Highmark Inc.	180	
Highmark West Virginia Inc., Parkersburg, WV.		180	
HIP Insurance Company of New York, New York, NY	EmblemHealth Inc	180	
HM Health Insurance Company, Pittsburgh, PA.	Highmark Inc.	180	
HM Life Insurance Company, Pittsburgh, PA.	Highmark Inc.	180	57
HM Life Insurance Company of New York, New York, NY	Highmark Inc.	180	57
HMO Colorado, Inc., Denver, CO.	WellPoint Inc.	180	
HMO Louisiana, Inc., Baton Rouge, LA.	Louisiana Health Service & Indemnity Co.	180	
HMO Maine, Indianapolis, IN		182	
HMO Minnesota, Eagan, MN	Aware Integrated Inc.	182	
HMO Missouri, Inc., St. Louis, MO	WellPoint Inc.	182	
HMO of Mississippi, Inc., Flowood, MS	Blue Cross & BS of MS a Mutual Ins Co.	182	
HMO of Northeastern Pennsylvania, Wilkes-Barre, PA.	Hospital Service Assn of Northeastern PA.	182	
HMO Partners, Inc., Little Rock, AR	USAble Mutual Insurance Company	182	
Holman Professional Counseling Centers, Northridge, CA		182	
Homesteaders Life Company, West Des Moines, IA		182	57
Hometown Health Plan, Massillon, OH	Health Plan of the Upper Ohio Valley	182	
Honored Citizens Choice Health Plan, Los Angeles, CA		184	
Horace Mann Life Insurance Company, Springfield, IL.	Horace Mann Educators Corporation	184	58
Horizon Healthcare Dental, Inc., Newark, NJ.	Horizon Healthcare Services Inc	184	
Horizon Healthcare of Delaware, Inc., Newark, NJ	Horizon Healthcare Services Inc	184	

COMPANY NAME	ULTIMATE PARENT NAME	KRG	BAG
Horizon Healthcare of New Jersey, Inc., Newark, NJ	Horizon Healthcare Services Inc	184	
Hospital Service Association of Northeastern Pennsylvania, Wilkes-Barre, PA	Hospital Service Assn of Northeastern PA	184	
Household Life Insurance Company, Bridgewater, NJ	HSBC Holdings plc	184	58
Household Life Insurance Company of Arizona, Bridgewater, NJ	HSBC Holdings plc	184	
Household Life Insurance Company of Delaware, Bridgewater, NJ	HSBC Holdings plc	184	
HPHC Insurance Company Inc, Wellesley, MA	Harvard Pilgrim Health Care Inc	186	
Human Affairs International of California, Inc., El Segundo, CA		186	
Humana AdvantageCare Plan, Miramar, FL	Humana Inc	186	
Humana Benefit Plan of Illinois, Inc., Peoria, IL	Humana Inc	186	
Humana Employers Health Plan of Georgia, Inc., Atlanta, GA	Humana Inc	186	
Humana Health Benefit Plan of Louisiana, Inc., Metairie, LA	Humana Inc	186	
Humana Health Insurance Company of Florida, Inc., Miramar, FL	Humana Inc	186	
Humana Health Plan, Inc., Louisville, KY	Humana Inc	186	
Humana Health Plan of Ohio, Inc., Cincinnati, OH	Humana Inc	186	
Humana Health Plan of Texas, Inc., Austin, TX	Humana Inc	188	
Humana Health Plans of Puerto Rico, Inc., Sn Juan, PR	Humana Inc	188	
Humana Insurance Company, DePere, WI	Humana Inc	188	58
Humana Insurance Company of Kentucky, Louisville, KY	Humana Inc	188	58
Humana Insurance Company of New York, Albany, NY	Humana Inc	188	
Humana Insurance of Puerto Rico, Inc., San Juan, PR	Humana Inc	188	59
Humana Medical Plan, Inc., Miramar, FL	Humana Inc	188	
Humana Medical Plan of Utah, Inc., Sandy, UT	Humana Inc	188	
Humana Wisconsin Health Organization Insurance Corporation, Waukesha, WI	Humana Inc	188	
HumanaDental Insurance Company, DePere, WI	Humana Inc	190	59
Hungarian Reformed Federation of America, Washington, DC		190	

I

COMPANY NAME	ULTIMATE PARENT NAME	KRG	BAG
IA American Life Insurance Company, Scottsdale, AZ	Industrial Alliance Ins & Financial Svcs	190	59
IBA Health and Life Assurance Company, Kalamazoo, MI	UnitedHealth Group Inc	190	
IBC Life Insurance Company, Laredo, TX		190	
IdeaLife Insurance Company, Stamford, CT	Berkshire Hathaway Inc	190	59
Illinois Mutual Life Insurance Company, Peoria, IL		190	60
Imerica Life and Health Insurance Company, Englewood, CO		190	
Independence American Insurance Company, New York, NY	Geneve Holdings, Inc.	190	
Independence Blue Cross, Philadelphia, PA	Independence Blue Cross	192	
Independence Insurance Inc., Philadelphia, PA	Independence Blue Cross	192	
Independence Life & Annuity Company, Wellesley Hills, MA	Sun Life Financial Inc.	192	60
Independent Care Health Plan, Milwaukee, WI	Humana Inc	192	
Independent Health Association, Buffalo, NY		192	
Independent Health Benefits Corp., Buffalo, NY		192	
Indiana Vision Services, Inc., Rancho Cordova, CA	Vision Service Plan	192	
Individual Assurance Company, Life, Health & Accident, Prairie Village, KS	IAC Group Inc.	192	60
ING Life Insurance and Annuity Company, Atlanta, GA	ING Groep N.V.	192	60
ING USA Annuity and Life Insurance Company, Atlanta, GA	ING Groep N.V.	194	61
Inland Empire Health Plan, San Bernardino, CA		194	
INRECO International Reinsurance Company, Grand Cayman, Cayman Islands	Pan-American Life Mutual Holding Company	194	
InStil Health Insurance Company, Columbia, SC	Blue Cross&Blue Shield of South Carolina	194	
Insurance Company of Scott & White, Temple, TX	Scott & White Health Plan	194	
Integrity Capital Insurance Company, Greenwood, IN	Citizens Inc	194	
Integrity Life Insurance Company, Cincinnati, OH	Western & Southern Mutual Holding Co	194	61
Inter-County Health Plan, Inc., Horsham, PA	Independence Blue Cross	194	
Inter-County Hospitalization Plan, Inc., Horsham, PA	Independence Blue Cross	194	
Inter Valley Health Plan, Inc., Pomona, CA		196	
International American Life Insurance Company, North Richland Hills, TX		196	
International HealthCare Services, Inc., Uniondale, NY	Healthplex Inc	196	
Interstate Bankers Life Insurance Company, Chicago, IL		196	
Intramerica Life Insurance Company, Hauppauge, NY	Allstate Corporation	196	61
Investors Consolidated Insurance Company, Houston, TX	Harris Insurance Holdings Inc	196	61
Investors Growth Life Insurance Company, Stillwater, MN	Student Assurance Services Inc	196	
Investors Heritage Life Insurance Company, Frankfort, KY	Investors Heritage Capital Corporation	196	62
Investors Insurance Corporation, Plano, TX	SCOR S.E.	196	62
Investors Life Insurance Company of North America, Kansas City, MO	Financial Holding Corporation	198	62
Investors Trust Assurance SPC, Grand Cayman KY1-1208, Cayman Islands		198	
Island Insurance Corp, San Juan, PR		198	

J

COMPANY NAME	ULTIMATE PARENT NAME	KRG	BAG
J.M.I.C. Life Insurance Company, Deerfield Beach, FL	JM Family Enterprises, Inc	198	
Jackson Griffin Insurance Company, Harrisburg, AR		198	
Jackson National Life Insurance Company, Lansing, MI	Prudential plc	198	62
Jackson National Life Insurance Company of New York, Lansing, MI	Prudential plc	198	63
Jaimini Health Inc., Rancho Cucamonga, CA		198	

COMPANY NAME	ULTIMATE PARENT NAME	KRG	BAG
Jamestown Life Insurance Company, Lynchburg, VA	Genworth Financial, Inc	198	
Jeff Davis Mortuary Benefit Association, Jennings, LA		200	
Jefferson Life Insurance Company, Dallas, TX	DNIC Insurance Holdings, Inc.	200	
Jefferson National Life Insurance Company, Louisville, KY	Jefferson National Financial Corp	200	63
John Alden Life Insurance Company, Milwaukee, WI	Assurant Inc	200	63
John D. Kernan, DMD, PA, Westmont, NJ		200	
John Hancock Life & Health Insurance Company, Boston, MA	Manulife Financial Corporation	200	63
John Hancock Life Insurance Company of New York, Valhalla, NY	Manulife Financial Corporation	200	64
John Hancock Life Insurance Company (USA), Boston, MA	Manulife Financial Corporation	200	64
Jordan Funeral & Insurance Company Inc., Centre, AL		200	

K

Kaiser Foundation Health Plan, Inc., Oakland, CA	Kaiser Foundation Health Plan Inc	202	
Kaiser Foundation Health Plan of Colorado, Denver, CO	Kaiser Foundation Health Plan Inc	202	
Kaiser Foundation Health Plan of Georgia, Inc., Oakland, CA	Kaiser Foundation Health Plan Inc	202	
Kaiser Foundation Health Plan of Ohio, Cleveland, OH	Kaiser Foundation Health Plan Inc	202	
Kaiser Foundation Health Plan of the Mid-Atlantic States, Inc., Oakland, CA	Kaiser Foundation Health Plan Inc	202	
Kaiser Foundation Health Plan of the Northwest, Portland, OR	Kaiser Foundation Health Plan Inc	202	
Kanawha Insurance Company, Louisville, KY	Humana Inc	202	64
Kansas City Life Insurance Company, Kansas City, MO	Kansas City Life Insurance Company	202	64
Kemper Investors Life Insurance Company, Bellevue, WA	Zurich Financial Services Ltd.	202	65
Kentucky Funeral Directors Life Insurance Company, Lexington, KY	Directors Investment Group Inc	204	65
Kentucky Home Life Insurance Company, Frankfort, KY	KHL Holdings LLC	204	
Keokuk Area Hospital Organized Delivery System, Inc., Keokuk, IA		204	
Kern Health Systems, Bakersfield, CA		204	
Kern Health Systems Group Health Plan, Bakersfield, CA		204	
Keystone Health Plan Central, Inc., Harrisburg, PA	Capital Blue Cross	204	
Keystone Health Plan East, Inc., Philadelphia, PA	Independence Blue Cross	204	
Keystone Health Plan West, Inc., Pittsburgh, PA	Highmark Inc.	204	
Kilpatrick Life Insurance Company of Louisiana, Shreveport, LA		204	
Knights of Columbus, New Haven, CT		206	65
KPS Health Plans, Bremerton, WA	Group Health Cooperative	206	
KS Plan Administrators, L.L.C., Houston, TX	St Lukes Episcopal Health System Corp	206	

L

The Lafayette Life Insurance Company	Western & Southern Mutual Holding Co	206	65
Lafourche Life Insurance Company, Raceland, LA		206	
Landcar Life Insurance Company, Sandy, UT		206	
Landmark Healthplan of California, Inc., Sacramento, CA		206	
Landmark Life Insurance Company, Brownwood, TX		206	
Laurel Life Insurance Company, Scottsdale, AZ	Sagicor Financial Corporation	206	
Leaders Life Insurance Company, Tulsa, OK		208	
Legacy Health Solutions, San Angelo, TX	Trustees of Shannon W TX Memorial Hosp	208	
Lehman Re Limited, Hamilton HM AX, Bermuda		208	
Lewer Life Insurance Company, Kansas City, MO	Lewer Financial Services L. P.	208	66
Lewis Life Insurance Company, Marshall, TX		208	
Liberty Bankers Life Insurance Company, Dallas, TX	Realty Advisors Inc.	208	66
Liberty Dental Plan of California, Irvine, CA		208	
Liberty Life Assurance Company of Boston, Dover, NH	Liberty Mutual Holding Company Inc.	208	66
Liberty Life Insurance Company, Greenville, SC	Royal Bank of Canada	208	66
Liberty National Life Insurance Company, Birmingham, AL	Torchmark Corporation	210	67
Liberty Union Life Assurance Company, Madison Heights, MI		210	67
Life Assurance Company, Inc., Oklahoma City, OK		210	
Life Assurance Company of America, Oak Brook, IL		210	
Life Insurance Company of Alabama, Gadsden, AL		210	67
Life Insurance Company of Boston & New York, Canton, MA	Boston Mutual Life Insurance Company	210	67
Life Insurance Company of Louisiana, Shreveport, LA		210	68
Life Insurance Company of North America, Philadelphia, PA	CIGNA Corporation	210	68
Life Insurance Company of the Southwest, Dallas, TX	National Life Holding Company	210	68
Life of America Insurance Company, Dallas, TX		212	
Life of the South Insurance Company, Jacksonville, FL	Summit Partners LP	212	68
Life Protection Insurance Company, Dallas, TX	Wright Titus Agency	212	
LifeCare Assurance Company, Woodland Hills, CA	21st Century Life and Health Company Inc.	212	
LifeSecure Insurance Company, Brighton, MI	Blue Cross Blue Shield of Michigan	212	
LifeShield National Insurance Co., Oklahoma City, OK	HCC Holdings LLC	212	69
LifeWise Assurance Company, Mountlake Terrace, WA	Premera	212	69
LifeWise Health Plan of Arizona, Inc., Scottsdale, AZ	Premera	212	
LifeWise Health Plan of Oregon, Inc., Mountlake Terrace, WA	Premera	212	
LifeWise Health Plan of Washington, Mountlake Terrace, WA	Premera	214	
Lincoln Benefit Life Company, Lincoln, NE	Allstate Corporation	214	69

COMPANY NAME	ULTIMATE PARENT NAME	KRG	BAG
Lincoln Heritage Life Insurance Company, Phoenix, AZ		214	69
Lincoln Life & Annuity Company of New York, Greensboro, NC	Lincoln National Corporation	214	70
Lincoln Memorial Life Insurance Company, West Lake Hills, TX		214	
Lincoln Mutual Life and Casualty Insurance Company, Fargo, ND	Noridian Mutual Insurance Company	214	
The Lincoln National Life Insurance Company, Fort Wayne, IN	Lincoln National Corporation	214	70
Local Initiative Health Authority of Los Angeles County, Los Angeles, CA		214	
Locomotive Engineers and Conductors Mutual Protection Association, Southfield, MI		214	
London Life and Casualty (Barbados) Corporation, St. Michael, Barbados	Power Corporation of Canada	216	
London Life and Casualty Reinsurance Corporation, Wildey, St. Michael, Barbados	Power Corporation of Canada	216	
London Life International Reinsurance Corporation, St. Michael, Barbados	Power Corporation of Canada	216	
London Life Reinsurance Company, Blue Bell, PA	Power Corporation of Canada	216	70
Longevity Insurance Company, New York, NY	Morgan Stanley	216	
Louisiana Health Service and Indemnity Company, Baton Rouge, LA	Louisiana Health Service & Indemnity Co.	216	
Loyal American Life Insurance Company, Cincinnati, OH	American Financial Group, Inc.	216	70

M

COMPANY NAME	ULTIMATE PARENT NAME	KRG	BAG
M Life Insurance Company, Portland, OR		216	
M-Plan, Inc., Indianapolis, IN	Clarian Health Partners, Inc.	216	
Madison National Life Insurance Company, Inc., Madison, WI	Geneve Holdings, Inc.	218	71
Magellan Behavioral Health of Iowa, Inc., West Des Moines, IA		218	
Magellan Behavioral Health of Pennsylvania, Inc., Newtown, PA		218	
Magellan Health Services of California, El Segundo, CA	Magellan Health Services Inc	218	
Magna Insurance Company, Gulfport, MS		218	
Maine Dental Service Corporation, Concord, NH		218	
Majestic Life Insurance Company, New Orleans, LA		218	
MAMSI Life and Health Insurance Company, Rockville, MD	UnitedHealth Group Inc	218	
Managed Dental Care of California, Woodland Hills, CA	Guardian Life Ins Co of America	218	
Managed DentalGuard, Inc., Woodland Hills, CA	Guardian Life Ins Co of America	220	
Managed DentalGuard, Inc., Woodland Hills, CA	Guardian Life Ins Co of America	220	
Managed Health, Inc., New York, NY	Healthfirst Inc	220	
Managed Health Network, San Rafael, CA	Health Net Inc	220	
Managed Health Services Insurance Corporation, St. Louis, MO	Centene Corporation	220	
The Manhattan Life Insurance Company, Houston, TX	Harris Insurance Holdings Inc	220	71
Manhattan National Life Insurance Company, Schaumburg, IL	American Financial Group, Inc.	220	71
MAPFRE Life Insurance Company, San Juan, PR	MAPFRE S.A.	220	
March Vision Care, Inc., Los Angeles, CA		220	
Marion Polk Community Health Plan Advantage Inc., Salem, OR		222	
Marquette Indemnity & Life Insurance Company, St. Louis, MO		222	
Marquette National Life Insurance Company, Lake Mary, FL	Universal American Corp.	222	
Maryland Care, Inc., Linthicum, MD		222	
Massachusetts Mutual Life Insurance Company, Springfield, MA	Massachusetts Mutual Life Insurance Co.	222	71
Massachusetts Vision Service Plan, Rancho Cordova, CA	Vision Service Plan	222	
Matthew Thornton Health Plan, Manchester, NH	WellPoint Inc.	222	
Max Vision Care, Inc., Whittier, CA		222	
McDonald Life Insurance Company, Austin, TX		222	
McKinley Life Insurance Company, Canton, OH	Aultman Health Foundation	224	
McLaren Health Plan, Inc., Flint, MI		224	
MCS Life Insurance Company, San Juan, PR	MCS Inc	224	
MD-Individual Practice Association, Inc., Rockville, MD	UnitedHealth Group Inc	224	
MDNY Healthcare, Inc., Melville, NY		224	
MDwise, Inc., Indianapolis, IN	Clarian Health Partners, Inc.	224	
MedAmerica Insurance Company, Rochester, NY	Lifetime Healthcare Inc	224	72
MedAmerica Insurance Company of Florida, Rochester, NY	Lifetime Healthcare Inc	224	72
MedAmerica Insurance Company of New York, Rochester, NY	Lifetime Healthcare Inc	224	72
Medco Containment Insurance Company of New York, Franklin Lakes, NJ	Medco Health Solutions Inc	226	
Medco Containment Life Insurance Company, Franklin Lakes, NJ	Medco Health Solutions Inc	226	
Medcore HP, Stockton, CA		226	
Medica Health Plans, Minnetonka, MN	Medica Holding Company	226	
Medica Health Plans of Wisconsin, Minnetonka, MN	Medica Holding Company	226	
Medica Insurance Company, Minnetonka, MN	Medica Holding Company	226	
Medical Associates Clinic Health Plan of Wisconsin, Dubuque, IA	Medical Associates Clinic P C	226	
Medical Associates Health Plan, Inc., Dubuque, IA	Medical Associates Clinic P C	226	
Medical Benefits Mutual Life Insurance Company, Newark, OH		226	72
Medical Eye Services, Inc., Costa Mesa, CA		228	
Medical Health Insuring Corporation of Ohio, Cleveland, OH	Medical Mutual of Ohio	228	
Medical Mutual of Ohio, Cleveland, OH	Medical Mutual of Ohio	228	
Medical Savings Insurance Company, Indianapolis, IN	Medical Savings Investment Inc.	228	
Medico Insurance Company, Omaha, NE	Medico Mutual Insurance Holding Company.	228	73
The MEGA Life and Health Insurance Company, North Richland Hills, TX	Blackstone Investor Group	228	73
Melancon Life Insurance Company, Carencro, LA		228	
Mellon Life Insurance Company, Pittsburgh, PA		228	

COMPANY NAME	ULTIMATE PARENT NAME	KRG	BAG
MEMBERS Life Insurance Company, Madison, WI	CUNA Mutual Insurance Society	228	73
Memorial Insurance Company of America, Salt Lake City, UT	Security National Financial	230	
Memorial Life Insurance Company, Homer, LA		230	
Memorial Service Life Insurance Company, Austin, TX		230	
Mercy Health Plans, Chesterfield, MO	Sisters of Mercy Health System Inc	230	
Mercy Health Plans of Missouri, Inc., Chesterfield, MO	Sisters of Mercy Health System Inc	230	
MercyCare Insurance Company, Janesville, WI		230	
Merit Life Insurance Co., Evansville, IN	American International Group, Inc	230	73
Merrill Lynch Life Insurance Company, Cedar Rapids, IA	AEGON N.V.	230	74
MetLife Insurance Company of Connecticut, Bloomfield, CT	MetLife Inc	230	74
MetLife Insurance Limited (Guam), Sydney, Australia		232	
MetLife Investors Insurance Company, Irvine, CA	MetLife Inc	232	74
MetLife Investors USA Insurance Company, Irvine, CA	MetLife Inc	232	74
Metropolitan Health Plan, Minneapolis, MN		232	
Metropolitan Life Insurance Company, New York, NY	MetLife Inc	232	75
Metropolitan Tower Life Insurance Company, New York, NY	MetLife Inc	232	75
MHNet Life and Health Insurance Company, Austin, TX	Coventry Health Care Inc	232	
Mid-Atlantic Vision Service Plan, Inc., Rancho Cordova, CA	Vision Service Plan	232	
Mid Rogue Health Plan, Grants Pass, OR		232	
Mid-West National Life Insurance Company of Tennessee, North Richland Hills, TX	Blackstone Investor Group	234	75
Midland National Life Insurance Company, Sioux Falls, SD	Sammons Enterprises, Inc.	234	75
Midwest Health Plan, Inc., Dearborn, MI	RJM Company LLC	234	
Midwest Security Life Insurance Company, Onalaska, WI	UnitedHealth Group Inc	234	76
Midwestern United Life Insurance Company, Atlanta, GA	ING Groep N.V.	234	76
MII Life, Incorporated, St. Paul, MN	Aware Integrated Inc.	234	76
Mililani Life Insurance Company, Honolulu, HI		234	
Minnesota Life Insurance Company, St. Paul, MN	Minnesota Mutual Companies Inc	234	76
Missouri Care Incorporated, Columbia, MO	Aetna Inc	234	
Missouri Valley Life and Health Insurance Company, Kansas City, MO	Blue Cross & Blue Shield of Kansas City	236	
ML Life Insurance Company of New York, Cedar Rapid, IA	AEGON N.V.	236	77
MMA Insurance Company, Goshen, IN		236	
MML Bay State Life Insurance Company, Springfield, MA	Massachusetts Mutual Life Insurance Co.	236	77
MNM-1997, Inc., Sugar Land, TX	Dental Economics L P.	236	
Modern Life Insurance Company of Arizona, Inc., Amelia, OH	Munich Reinsurance Company	236	
Modern Woodmen of America, Rock Island, IL	Modern Woodmen of America	236	77
Molina Healthcare Insurance Company, Long Beach, CA	Molina Healthcare Inc.	236	
Molina Healthcare of California, Inc., Long Beach, CA	Molina Healthcare Inc.	236	
Molina Healthcare of Michigan, Inc., Troy, MI	Molina Healthcare Inc.	238	
Molina Healthcare of New Mexico, Albuquerque, NM	Molina Healthcare Inc.	238	
Molina Healthcare of Ohio Inc., Columbus, OH	Molina Healthcare Inc.	238	
Molina Healthcare of Texas, Inc., Grand Prairie, TX	Molina Healthcare Inc.	238	
Molina Healthcare of Washington, Inc., Bothell, WA	Molina Healthcare Inc.	238	
Monarch Health Plan, Irvine, CA		238	
Monarch Life Insurance Company, Holyoke, MA		238	
Monitor Life Insurance Company of New York, Utica, NY	Commercial Travelers Mutual Insurance Co	238	77
Monumental Life Insurance Company, Cedar Rapids, IA	AEGON N.V.	238	78
MONY Life Insurance Company, New York, NY	AXA S.A.	240	78
MONY Life Insurance Company of America, New York, NY	AXA S.A.	240	78
Mothe Life Insurance Company, Gretna, LA		240	
Motorists Life Insurance Company, Columbus, OH	Motorists Insurance Pool	240	78
Mount Carmel Health Plan, Inc., Columbus, OH		240	
Mountain Life Insurance Company, Alcoa, TN	Mountain Services Corporation	240	79
MTL Insurance Company, Oak Brook, IL	Mutual Trust Holding Company	240	79
Mulhearn Protective Insurance Company, Monroe, LA	Mulhearn Corporation	240	
Munich American Reassurance Company, Atlanta, GA	Munich Reinsurance Company	240	79
The Mutual Beneficial Association, Inc., Berwyn, PA		242	
Mutual of America Life Insurance Company, New York, NY		242	79
Mutual of Omaha Insurance Company, Omaha, NE	Mutual of Omaha Insurance Company	242	80
Mutual Savings Life Insurance Company, St. Louis, MO	Unitrin, Inc	242	80
MVP Health Insurance Company, Schenectady, NY	MVP Health Care Inc	242	
MVP Health Insurance Company of NH, Inc., Schenectady, NY	MVP Health Care Inc	242	
MVP Health Plan, Inc., Schenectady, NY	MVP Health Care Inc	242	
MVP Health Plan of New Hampshire, Inc., Schenectady, NY	MVP Health Care Inc	242	
MVP Health Services Corp, Schenectady, NY	MVP Health Care Inc	242	

N

COMPANY NAME	ULTIMATE PARENT NAME	KRG	BAG
NAP Life Insurance Company, Austin, TX		244	
National Benefit Life Insurance Company, Long Island City, NY	Citigroup Inc.	244	80
National Family Care Life Insurance Company, Dallas, TX		244	
National Farm Life Insurance Company, Fort Worth, TX	National Farm Life Insurance Company	244	80
National Farmers Union Life Insurance Company, Kansas City, MO	Financial Holding Corporation	244	81

COMPANY NAME	ULTIMATE PARENT NAME	KRG	BAG
National Foundation Life Insurance Company, Fort Worth, TX	Credit Suisse Holdings (USA) Inc	244	81
National Guardian Life Insurance Company, Madison, WI	National Guardian Life Insurance Company	244	81
National Health Insurance Company, Grand Prairie, TX	Southwest Insurance Partners, Inc.	244	
National Income Life Insurance Company, Liverpool, NY	Torchmark Corporation	244	81
National Insurance Company of Wisconsin, Inc., Brookfield, WI	National Services Inc	246	
National Integrity Life Insurance Company, Goshen, NY	Western & Southern Mutual Holding Co	246	82
National Life Insurance Company, Montpelier, VT	National Life Holding Company	246	82
National Life Insurance Company, Hato Rey, PR	National Promoters & Services Inc.	246	82
National Masonic Provident Association, Columbus, OH		246	
National Pacific Dental, Inc., Houston, TX	UnitedHealth Group Inc	246	
National Safety Life Insurance Company, Binghamton, NY	Columbian Mutual Life Insurance Company	246	82
National Security Insurance Company, Elba, AL	National Security Group, Inc	246	83
National Security Life and Annuity Company, Cincinnati, OH	Ohio National Mutual Holdings Inc	246	83
National States Insurance Company, St. Louis, MO		248	
National Teachers Associates Life Insurance Company, Addison, TX	Ellard Enterprises, Inc.	248	83
National Western Life Insurance Company, Austin, TX		248	83
Nationwide Life and Annuity Insurance Company, Columbus, OH	Nationwide Mutual Insurance Company	248	84
Nationwide Life Insurance Company, Columbus, OH	Nationwide Mutual Insurance Company	248	84
Neighborhood Health Partnership, Inc., Miami, FL	UnitedHealth Group Inc	248	
Neighborhood Health Plan, Inc., Boston, MA		248	
Neighborhood Health Plan of Rhode Island, Inc., Providence, RI		248	
Netcare Life and Health Insurance Company, Hagatna, GU		248	
Network Health Insurance Corporation, Menasha, WI	Affinity Health System	250	
Network Health Plan, Menasha, WI	Affinity Health System	250	
Nevada Pacific Dental, Inc., Columbia, MD	UnitedHealth Group Inc	250	
New England Life Insurance Company, Boston, MA	MetLife Inc	250	84
New Era Life Insurance Company, Houston, TX	New Era Enterprises Inc	250	84
New Era Life Insurance Company of the Midwest, Houston, TX	New Era Enterprises Inc	250	85
New Foundation Life Insurance Company, Little Rock, AR		250	
New West Health Services, Helena, MT		250	
New York Life Insurance and Annuity Corporation, New York, NY	New York Life Insurance Company	250	85
New York Life Insurance Company, New York, NY	New York Life Insurance Company	252	85
NHP of Indiana LLC, Evansville, IN		252	
Niagara Life and Health Insurance Company, Columbia, SC	Blue Cross&Blue Shield of South Carolina	252	
Nippon Life Insurance Company of America, New York, NY	Nippon Life Insurance Company	252	85
Noridian Mutual Insurance Company, Fargo, ND	Noridian Mutual Insurance Company	252	
North American Company for Life and Health Insurance, Sioux Falls, SD	Sammons Enterprises, Inc.	252	86
North American Insurance Company, Phoenix, AZ	AMERCO	252	86
North American Life Insurance Company of Texas, Austin, TX	R D Tips Inc	252	
North American National Re Insurance Company, Greenwood Village, CO	Gardiner Limited Partnership	252	
North Carolina Mutual Life Insurance Company, Durham, NC		254	86
North Coast Life Insurance Company, Spokane, WA	R J Martin Mortgage Company	254	86
Northern National Life Insurance Company of Rhode Island, Warwick, RI		254	
Northwestern Long Term Care Insurance Company, Milwaukee, WI	Northwestern Mutual Life Ins Co	254	87
The Northwestern Mutual Life Insurance Company, Milwaukee, WI	Northwestern Mutual Life Ins Co	254	87
NYLIFE Insurance Company of Arizona, New York, NY	New York Life Insurance Company	254	87

O

COMPANY NAME	ULTIMATE PARENT NAME	KRG	BAG
Occidental Life Insurance Company of North Carolina, Waco, TX	Thoma Cressey Bravo Inc	254	87
ODS Health Plan, Inc., Portland, OR	Oregon Dental Association	254	
Ohio Motorists Life Insurance Company, Independence, OH	AAA East Central	254	
Ohio National Life Assurance Corporation, Cincinnati, OH	Ohio National Mutual Holdings Inc	256	88
The Ohio National Life Insurance Company, Cincinnati, OH	Ohio National Mutual Holdings Inc	256	88
The Ohio State Life Insurance Company, Kansas City, MO	Financial Holding Corporation	256	88
Old American Insurance Company, Kansas City, MO	Kansas City Life Insurance Company	256	88
Old Reliance Insurance Company, Colorado Springs, CO		256	
Old Republic Life Insurance Company, Chicago, IL	Old Republic International Corporation	256	89
Old Spartan Life Insurance Company, Inc., Spartanburg, SC		256	
Old Surety Life Insurance Company, Oklahoma City, OK		256	
Old United Life Insurance Company, Merriam, KS	Van Enterprises	256	89
OM Financial Life Insurance Company, Baltimore, MD	Old Mutual plc	258	89
OM Financial Life Insurance Company of New York, Baltimore, MD	Old Mutual plc	258	89
Omaha Insurance Company, Omaha, NE	Mutual of Omaha Insurance Company	258	
Omaha Life Insurance Company, Omaha, NE	Mutual of Omaha Insurance Company	258	
OmniCare Health Plan, Inc., Detroit, MI	Coventry Health Care Inc	258	
On Lok Senior Health Services, San Francisco, CA		258	
OneNation Insurance Company, Indianapolis, IN	WellPoint Inc.	258	
Optima Health Insurance Company, Norfolk, VA	Sentara Healthcare	258	
OPTIMA Health Plan, Virginia Beach, VA	Sentara Healthcare	258	
Optimum Choice, Inc., Rockville, MD	UnitedHealth Group Inc	260	
Optimum Re Insurance Company, Dallas, TX	Optimum Group Inc	260	90
Orange Prevention & Treatment Integrated Medical Assistance, Orange, CA		260	
Oregon Dental Service, Portland, OR	Oregon Dental Association	260	

COMPANY NAME	ULTIMATE PARENT NAME	KRG	BAG
Orkney Re, Inc., Charlotte, NC	Scottish Re Group Limited	260	
Ouachita Life Insurance Company, Amelia, OH	Munich Reinsurance Company	260	
Oxford Health Insurance, Incorporated, Trumbull, CT	UnitedHealth Group Inc	260	
Oxford Health Plans (CT), Inc., Trumbull, CT	UnitedHealth Group Inc	260	
Oxford Health Plans (NJ), Inc., Trumbull, CT	UnitedHealth Group Inc	260	
Oxford Health Plans (NY), Inc., Trumbull, CT	UnitedHealth Group Inc	262	
Oxford Life Insurance Company, Phoenix, AZ	AMERCO	262	90
Ozark National Life Insurance Company, Kansas City, MO	Charles N. Sharpe Trust	262	90

P

COMPANY NAME	ULTIMATE PARENT NAME	KRG	BAG
Pacific Beacon Life Reassurance Inc, Honolulu, HI	California State Auto Assn Inter-Ins Bur	262	90
Pacific Century Life Insurance Corp., Phoenix, AZ		262	
Pacific Guardian Life Insurance Company, Ltd., Honolulu, HI	Meiji Yasuda Life Insurance Company	262	91
Pacific Life & Annuity Company, Newport Beach, CA	Pacific Mutual Holding Company	262	91
Pacific Life Insurance Company, Newport Beach, CA	Pacific Mutual Holding Company	262	91
Pacific Visioncare Washington, Inc., Chehalis, WA		262	
PacifiCare Behavioral Health of California, Inc., Cypress, CA	UnitedHealth Group Inc	264	
PacifiCare Dental of Colorado, Inc., Santa Ana, CA	UnitedHealth Group Inc	264	
PacifiCare Life and Health Insurance Company, Cypress, CA	UnitedHealth Group Inc	264	91
PacifiCare Life Assurance Company, Cypress, CA	UnitedHealth Group Inc	264	
PacifiCare of Arizona, Inc., Phoenix, AZ	UnitedHealth Group Inc	264	
PacifiCare of California, Cypress, CA	UnitedHealth Group Inc	264	
PacifiCare of Colorado, Inc., Centennial, CO	UnitedHealth Group Inc	264	
PacifiCare of Nevada, Inc., Las Vegas, NV	UnitedHealth Group Inc	264	
PacifiCare of Oklahoma, Inc., Tulsa, OK	UnitedHealth Group Inc	264	
PacifiCare of Oregon, Inc., Lake Oswego, OR	UnitedHealth Group Inc	266	
PacifiCare of Texas, Inc., Plano, TX	UnitedHealth Group Inc	266	
PacifiCare of Washington, Inc., Mercer Island, WA	UnitedHealth Group Inc	266	
PacificSource Health Plans, Springfield, OR		266	
Pan-American Assurance Company, New Orleans, LA	Pan-American Life Mutual Holding Company	266	92
Pan-American Life Insurance Company, New Orleans, LA	Pan-American Life Mutual Holding Company	266	92
Pan-American Life Insurance Company of Puerto Rico, Guaynabo, PR	Pan-American Life Mutual Holding Company	266	
Paramount Advantage, Maumee, OH	ProMedica Health System, Inc.	266	
Paramount Care Inc., Maumee, OH	ProMedica Health System, Inc.	266	
Paramount Care of Michigan, Dundee, MI	ProMedica Health System, Inc.	268	
Paramount Insurance Company, Maumee, OH	ProMedica Health System, Inc.	268	
Park Avenue Life Insurance Company, New York, NY	Guardian Life Ins Co of America	268	92
Parker Centennial Assurance Company, Stevens Point, WI	Sentry Insurance a Mutual Company	268	92
Parkland Community Health Plan, Inc., Dallas, TX		268	
PARTNERS National Health Plans of North Carolina, Inc., Winston-Salem, NC	Blue Cross & BS of NC	268	
Patriot Life Insurance Company, Brunswick, ME	Frankenmuth Mutual Insurance Company	268	
The Paul Revere Life Insurance Company, Chattanooga, TN	Unum Group	268	93
The Paul Revere Variable Annuity Insurance Company, Chattanooga, TN	Unum Group	268	93
Peach State Health Plan, Inc., St. Louis, MO	Centene Corporation	270	
Pearle Vision Managed Care - HMO of Texas, Inc., Dallas, TX	Luxottica US Holdings Corporation	270	
Pekin Financial Life Insurance Company, Pekin, IL	Farmers Automobile Insurance Assn	270	
Pekin Life Insurance Company, Pekin, IL	Farmers Automobile Insurance Assn	270	93
Pellerin Life Insurance Company, Breaux Bridge, LA		270	
PEMCO Life Insurance Company, Seattle, WA	PEMCO Mutual Insurance Company	270	93
Peninsula Health Care, Inc., Newport News, VA	WellPoint Inc.	270	
The Penn Insurance and Annuity Company, Horsham, PA	Penn Mutual Life Insurance Company	270	94
The Penn Mutual Life Insurance Company, Horsham, PA	Penn Mutual Life Insurance Company	270	94
Penn Treaty Network America Insurance Company, Allentown, PA	Penn Treaty American Corporation	272	
Pennsylvania Life Insurance Company, Lake Mary, FL	Universal American Corp.	272	94
Peoples Savings Life Insurance Company, Alexander City, AL		272	
Performance Life of America, Baton Rouge, LA	Louisiana Dealer Services Insurance Inc	272	94
Perico Life Insurance Company, St. Louis, MO	HCC Insurance Holdings, Inc.	272	95
PersonalCare Insurance of Illinois, Inc., Champaign, IL	Coventry Health Care Inc	272	
The Pharmacists Life Insurance Company, Algona, IA	Pharmacists Mutual Insurance Company	272	95
Philadelphia American Life Insurance Company, Houston, TX	New Era Enterprises Inc	272	95
Philadelphia-United Life Insurance Company, Bala Cynwyd, PA	Philadelphia-United Life Insurance Co	272	95
PHL Variable Insurance Company, Hartford, CT	Phoenix Companies Inc	274	96
Phoenix Life and Annuity Company, Hartford, CT	Phoenix Companies Inc	274	96
Phoenix Life and Reassurance Company of New York, Hartford, CT	Phoenix Companies Inc	274	
Phoenix Life Insurance Company, Hartford, CT	Phoenix Companies Inc	274	96
PHP Insurance Company of Indiana, Inc., Fort Wayne, IN	Physicians Health Pl of Northern IN Inc	274	
PHPMM Insurance Company, Lansing, MI	Sparrow Health System	274	
Physicians' Benefits Trust Life Insurance Company, Chicago, IL	ISMIE Mutual Insurance Company	274	
Physicians Health Choice of Texas, Inc., San Antonio, TX		274	
Physicians Health Plan of Mid-Michigan, Lansing, MI	Sparrow Health System	274	

COMPANY NAME	ULTIMATE PARENT NAME	KRG	BAG
Physicians Health Plan of Mid-Michigan FamilyCare, Lansing, MI	Sparrow Health System	276	
Physicians Health Plan of Northern Indiana, Inc., Fort Wayne, IN	Physicians Health Pl of Northern IN Inc	276	
Physicians Life Insurance Company, Omaha, NE	Physicians Mutual Insurance Company	276	96
Physicians Mutual Insurance Company, Omaha, NE	Physicians Mutual Insurance Company	276	97
Physicians Plus Insurance Corporation, Madison, WI	Meriter Health Services Inc	276	
Physicians United Plan, Inc., Orlando, FL		276	
PhysiciansPlus Baptist & St. Dominic, Inc., Jackson, MS		276	
Piedmont Community Healthcare, Inc., Lynchburg, VA		276	
Pine Belt Life Insurance Company, Bay Springs, MS		276	
Pioneer American Insurance Company, Waco, TX	Thoma Cressey Bravo Inc	278	97
Pioneer Military Insurance Company, Kansas City, MO		278	
Pioneer Mutual Life Insurance Company, Fargo, ND	American United Mutual Insurance Hldg Co	278	97
Pioneer Security Life Insurance Company, Waco, TX	Thoma Cressey Bravo Inc	278	97
Plateau Insurance Company, Crossville, TN	Plateau Group Inc	278	98
Polish Roman Catholic Union of America, Chicago, IL		278	98
Popular Life Re, Guaynabo, PR	Popular Inc	278	98
Port-O-Call Life Insurance Company, Pine Bluff, AR		278	
Preferred Assurance Company, Inc., Schenectady, NY	MVP Health Care Inc	278	
Preferred Health Partnership of Tennessee, Inc., Knoxville, TN	Humana Inc	280	
Preferred Health Plan, Inc., Klamath Falls, OR		280	
Preferred Health Systems Insurance Company, Wichita, KS	Coventry Health Care Inc	280	
Preferred Plus of Kansas, Inc., Wichita, KS	Coventry Health Care Inc	280	
Preferred Security Life Insurance Company, Dallas, TX		280	
PreferredOne Community Health Plan, Golden Valley, MN	Fairview Health Services	280	
PreferredOne Insurance Company, Golden Valley, MN	Fairview Health Services	280	
Premera Blue Cross, Mountlake Terrace, WA	Premera	280	
Premier Access Insurance Company, Sacramento, CA	Abbaszadeh Dental Group Inc	280	
Premier Behavioral Systems of Tennessee, LLC, Nashville, TN	Magellan Health Services Inc	282	
Premier Choice Dental, Inc., Orange, CA	Premier Dental Services Inc	282	
Preneed Reinsurance Company of America, Madison, WI	National Guardian Life Insurance Company	282	
Presbyterian Health Plan, Inc., Albuquerque, NM	Southwest Health Foundation	282	
Presbyterian Insurance Company, Inc., Albuquerque, NM	Southwest Health Foundation	282	
Preservation Life Insurance Company, Jefferson City, MO	PFHC Medical Management LLC	282	
Presidential Life Insurance Company, Nyack, NY	Presidential Life Corporation	282	98
Presidential Life Insurance Company, Dallas, TX		282	
PrimeCare Medical Network, Inc., Ontario, CA	Aveta Inc	282	
Primerica Life Insurance Company, Duluth, GA	Citigroup Inc.	284	99
Principal Life Insurance Company, Des Moines, IA	Principal Financial Group Inc.	284	99
Principal National Life Insurance Company, Des Moines, IA	Principal Financial Group Inc.	284	
Priority Health, Grand Rapids, MI	Spectrum Health System	284	
Priority Health Care, Inc., Richmond, VA	WellPoint Inc.	284	
Priority Health Government Programs, Grand Rapids, MI	Spectrum Health System	284	
Priority Health Insurance Company, Grand Rapids, MI	Spectrum Health System	284	
ProCare Health Plan, Detroit, MI		284	
Professional Insurance Company, Wellesley Hills, MA	Sun Life Financial Inc.	284	99
Professional Life & Casualty Company, Chicago, IL		286	99
Programmed Life Insurance Company, Greenwood Village, CO	Gardiner Limited Partnership	286	
Protective Life and Annuity Insurance Company, Birmingham, AL	Protective Life Corporation	286	100
Protective Life Insurance Company, Birmingham, AL	Protective Life Corporation	286	100
Protective Life Insurance Company of New York, Melville, NY	Protective Life Corporation	286	100
Providence Health Plan, Beaverton, OR	Providence Health & Services	286	
Provident American Insurance Company, Dallas, TX		286	
Provident American Life & Health Insurance Company, Austin, TX	American Financial Group, Inc.	286	100
Provident Life and Accident Insurance Company, Chattanooga, TN	Unum Group	286	101
Provident Life and Casualty Insurance Company, Chattanooga, TN	Unum Group	288	101
Pruco Life Insurance Company, Newark, NJ	Prudential Financial Inc	288	101
Pruco Life Insurance Company of New Jersey, Newark, NJ	Prudential Financial Inc	288	101
Prudential Annuities Life Assurance Corporation, Shelton, CT	Prudential Financial Inc	288	102
The Prudential Insurance Company of America, Newark, NJ	Prudential Financial Inc	288	102
Prudential Retirement Insurance and Annuity Company, Hartford, CT	Prudential Financial Inc	288	102
Puerto Rico Health Plan, Inc., San Juan, PR	Independence Blue Cross	288	
Pupil Benefits Plan, Inc., Glenville, NY		288	
Puritan Life Insurance Company, Addison, TX		288	
The Pyramid Life Insurance Company, Lake Mary, FL	Universal American Corp.	290	102

Q

COMPANY NAME	ULTIMATE PARENT NAME	KRG	BAG
QCA Health Plan, Inc., Little Rock, AR	QualChoice of Arkansas Inc	290	
QualChoice Life and Health Insurance Company, Inc., Little Rock, AR	QualChoice of Arkansas Inc	290	

COMPANY NAME	ULTIMATE PARENT NAME	KRG	BAG
R			
Rabenhorst Life Insurance Company, Baton Rouge, LA		290	
Rayant Insurance Company of New York, Newark, NJ	Horizon Healthcare Services Inc	290	
Reassure America Life Insurance Company, Armonk, NY	Swiss Reinsurance Company Ltd	290	103
Regal Life of America Insurance Company, North Richland Hills, TX		290	
Regal Reinsurance Company, Springfield, MA		290	
Regence BlueCross BlueShield of Oregon, Portland, OR	Regence Group	290	
Regence BlueCross BlueShield of Utah, Salt Lake City, UT	Regence Group	292	
Regence BlueShield, Seattle, WA	Regence Group	292	
Regence BlueShield of Idaho, Lewiston, ID	Regence Group	292	
Regence Health Maintenance of Oregon, Inc., Portland, OR	Regence Group	292	
Regence HMO Oregon, Portland, OR	Regence Group	292	
Regence Life and Health Insurance Company, Portland, OR	Regence Group	292	103
Region 6 Rx Corporation, Philadelphia, PA	Independence Blue Cross	292	
Reinsurance Company of Missouri Inc, Chesterfield, MO	Reinsurance Group of America Inc	292	
The Reliable Life Insurance Company, St. Louis, MO	Unitrin, Inc	292	103
Reliance Standard Life Insurance Company, Philadelphia, PA	R & Co Capital Management, L.L.C.	294	103
Reliance Standard Life Insurance Company of Texas, Philadelphia, PA	R & Co Capital Management, L.L.C.	294	
ReliaStar Life Insurance Company, Atlanta, GA	ING Groep N.V.	294	104
ReliaStar Life Insurance Company of New York, Atlanta, GA	ING Groep N.V.	294	104
Renaissance Health Insurance Company of New York, Okemos, MI	Renaissance Health Service Corp	294	
Renaissance Life & Health Insurance Company of America, Okemos, MI	Renaissance Health Service Corp	294	
Requia Life Insurance Corporation, Madison, WI		294	
Reserve National Insurance Company, Oklahoma City, OK	Unitrin, Inc	294	104
Resource Life Insurance Company, Chicago, IL	Onex Corporation	294	
RGA Reinsurance Company, Chesterfield, MO	Reinsurance Group of America Inc	296	104
Rhodes Life Insurance Company of Louisiana Inc., Baton Rouge, LA		296	
RightCHOICE Insurance Company, St. Louis, MO	WellPoint Inc.	296	
RiverSource Life Insurance Co. of New York, Minneapolis, MN	Ameriprise Financial Inc.	296	105
RiverSource Life Insurance Company, Minneapolis, MN	Ameriprise Financial Inc.	296	105
Rocky Mountain Health Maintenance Organization, Inc., Grand Junction, CO	Rocky Mountain Health Maint Org Inc.	296	
Rocky Mountain HealthCare Options, Inc., Grand Junction, CO	Rocky Mountain Health Maint Org Inc.	296	
Rocky Mountain Hospital and Medical Service, Denver, CO	WellPoint Inc.	296	
Royal Bank of Canada Insurance Company Ltd, St. Michael, Barbados	Royal Bank of Canada	296	
Royal Neighbors of America, Rock Island, IL		298	105
Royal State National Insurance Company, Ltd., Honolulu, HI	Mutual Benefit Trust	298	105
S			
S.USA Life Insurance Company, Inc., Newark, NJ	SBLI USA Mutual Life Insurance Co., Inc	298	106
Sabine Life Insurance Company, Many, LA		298	
Safeguard Health Plans, Inc. A Nevada Corporation, Aliso Viejo, CA	MetLife Inc	298	
SafeGuard Health Plans, Inc. (CA), Aliso Viejo, CA	MetLife Inc	298	
SafeGuard Health Plans, Inc. (FL), Aliso Viejo, CA	MetLife Inc	298	
SafeGuard Health Plans, Inc. (TX), Dallas, TX	MetLife Inc	298	
SafeHealth Life Insurance Company, Aliso Viejo, CA	MetLife Inc	298	
Sagicor Capital Life Insurance Company Limited, St. Michael, Barbados	Sagicor Financial Corporation	300	
Sagicor Life Inc., St. Michael, Barbados	Sagicor Financial Corporation	300	
Sagicor Life Insurance Company, Scottsdale, AZ	Sagicor Financial Corporation	300	106
Sagicor Life Jamaica Limited, Kingston 5, Jamaica	Sagicor Financial Corporation	300	
Sagicor Life of the Cayman Islands Ltd., Grand Cayman, Cayman Islands	Sagicor Financial Corporation	300	
Samaritan Health Plans, Inc., Corvallis, OR		300	
San Francisco Health Plan, San Francisco, CA		300	
San Joaquin Health Commission, French Camp, CA		300	
San Mateo Health Commission, South San Francisco, CA		300	
San Miguel Health Plan, Long Beach, CA		302	
Sanford Health Plan, Sioux Falls, SD	Sanford Health	302	
Sanford Health Plan of Minnesota, Sioux Falls, SD	Sanford Health	302	
Santa Barbara Regional Health Authority, Goleta, CA		302	
Santa Clara County, San Jose, CA		302	
Santa Clara County Health Authority, Campbell, CA		302	
Santa Cruz-Monterey Managed Medical Care Commission, Scotts Valley, CA		302	
The Savings Bank Life Insurance Company of Massachusetts, Woburn, MA	Savings Bank Life Insurance Co of MA	302	106
SBLI USA Mutual Life Insurance Company, Inc., New York, NY	SBLI USA Mutual Life Insurance Co., Inc	302	106
SCAN Health Plan, Long Beach, CA	SCAN Group	304	
SCAN Health Plan Arizona, Long Beach, CA	SCAN Group	304	
SCOR Global Life Re Insurance Company of Texas, Plano, TX	SCOR S.E.	304	107
SCOR Global Life Reinsurance Company of America, Stamford, CT	SCOR S.E.	304	107
SCOR Global Life U.S. Re Insurance Company, Plano, TX	SCOR S.E.	304	107

COMPANY NAME	ULTIMATE PARENT NAME	KRG	BAG
Scotia Insurance (Barbados) Limited, St. Michael BB22026, Barbados	Bank of Nova Scotia	304	
Scott & White Health Plan, Temple, TX	Scott & White Health Plan	304	
Scottish Annuity & Life Insurance Company (Cayman) Ltd., Grand Cayman, Cayman Islands	Scottish Re Group Limited	304	
Scottish Re Life Corporation, Charlotte, NC	Scottish Re Group Limited	304	
Scottish Re (U.S.), Inc., Charlotte, NC	Scottish Re Group Limited	306	
Scripps Clinic Health Plan Services, Inc., San Diego, CA		306	
Sears Life Insurance Company, Fort Worth, TX	Citigroup Inc.	306	107
SEB Trygg Life (USA) Assurance Limited, Phoenix, AZ		306	
Securian Life Insurance Company, St. Paul, MN	Minnesota Mutual Companies Inc	306	108
Securitas Financial Life Insurance Company, Winston-Salem, NC	Unity Mutual Life Insurance Company	306	
Security Benefit Life Insurance Company, Topeka, KS	Security Benefit Mutual Holding Company	306	108
Security Health Insurance Company of America, New York Inc., Schenectady, NY	Safe Partners, LLC	306	
Security Health Plan of Wisconsin, Inc., Marshfield, WI	Marshfield Clinic	306	
Security Life Insurance Company of America, Minnetonka, MN	Safe Partners, LLC	308	108
Security Life of Denver Insurance Company, Atlanta, GA	ING Groep N.V.	308	108
Security Mutual Life Insurance Company of New York, Binghamton, NY		308	109
Security National Life Insurance Company, Salt Lake City, UT	Security National Financial	308	
Security National Life Insurance Company of Louisiana, Jackson, MS		308	
Security Plan Life Insurance Company, Donaldsonville, LA	Citizens Inc	308	
SeeChange Health Insurance Company, Westerville, OH		308	
SelectCare Health Plans, Inc., Houston, TX	Universal American Corp.	308	
SelectCare of Maine, Houston, TX	Universal American Corp.	308	
SelectCare of Oklahoma, Inc., Houston, TX	Universal American Corp.	310	
SelectCare of Texas, LLC, Houston, TX	Universal American Corp.	310	
Selected Funeral and Life Insurance Company, Hot Springs, AR		310	
Senior American Life Insurance Company, Warminster, PA	AF&L Holdings, LLC	310	109
Senior Health Insurance Company of Pennsylvania, Carmel, IN		310	
Senior Life Insurance Company, Thomasville, GA		310	
Senior Whole Health of Connecticut, Inc., Cambridge, MA		310	
Senior Whole Health of New York, Inc., Cambridge, MA	Senior Health Holdings LLC	310	
Sentinel American Life Insurance Company, New York, NY	Guardian Life Ins Co of America	310	109
Sentinel Security Life Insurance Company, Salt Lake City, UT		312	109
Sentry Life Insurance Company, Stevens Point, WI	Sentry Insurance a Mutual Company	312	110
Sentry Life Insurance Company of New York, Syracuse, NY	Sentry Insurance a Mutual Company	312	110
Servco Life Insurance Company, Houston, TX	GS Administrators Inc	312	110
Service Life & Casualty Insurance Company, Austin, TX	Gray Family	312	110
Seton Health Plan, Inc., Austin, TX	Ascension Health	312	
Settlers Life Insurance Company, Madison, WI	National Guardian Life Insurance Company	312	111
SHA, L.L.C., Austin, TX	St Joseph Health System	312	
Sharp Health Plan, San Diego, CA		312	
Shelter Life Insurance Company, Columbia, MO	Shelter Mutual Insurance Company	314	111
Shenandoah Life Insurance Company, Roanoke, VA		314	
Sheridan Life Insurance Company, Lawton, OK	Wichita National Life Insurance Company	314	
Sierra Health and Life Insurance Company, Inc., Las Vegas, NV	UnitedHealth Group Inc	314	111
Significa Insurance Group, Inc., Wilkes-Barre, PA	Hospital Service Assn of Northeastern PA	314	
SilverScript Insurance Company, Nashville, TN	CVS Caremark Corporation	314	
Sistemas Medicos Nacionales, S.A. De C.V., Chula Vista, CA		314	
Slovene National Benefit Society, Imperial, PA		314	
Smith Burial & Life Insurance Company, Stamps, AR		314	
Solano-Napa-Yolo Commission on Medical Care, Fairfield, CA		316	
Somers Isles Insurance Company Limited, Hamilton HM EX, Bermuda	Argus Group Holdings Limited	316	
The Order of the Sons of Hermann in Texas, San Antonio, TX		316	
South Dakota State Medical Holding Co., Inc., Sioux Falls, SD		316	
Southeast Family Life Insurance Company, Omaha, NE	Central States Health & Life Co of Omaha	316	111
Southern Capital Life Insurance Company, Jackson, MS	Southern Farm Bureau Life Insurance Co	316	
Southern Farm Bureau Life Insurance Company, Jackson, MS	Southern Farm Bureau Life Insurance Co	316	112
Southern Fidelity Life Insurance Company, Stamps, AR		316	
Southern Financial Life Insurance Company, Clearwater, FL		316	
Southern Financial Life Insurance Company, Jacksonville, FL	Summit Partners LP	318	112
Southern Health Services, Inc., Richmond, VA	Coventry Health Care Inc	318	
Southern Life and Health Insurance Company, Birmingham, AL	Geneve Holdings, Inc.	318	
Southern National Life Insurance Company, Inc., Baton Rouge, LA	Louisiana Health Service & Indemnity Co.	318	
Southern Pioneer Life Insurance Company, Amelia, OH	Munich Reinsurance Company	318	112
Southern Security Life Insurance Company, Incorporated, Salt Lake City, UT	Security National Financial	318	
Southland National Insurance Corporation, Tuscaloosa, AL	Collateral Holdings Ltd.	318	112
Southwest Credit Life, Inc., Gallup, NM		318	
Southwest Life & Health Insurance Company, Austin, TX	St Joseph Health System	318	
Southwest Service Life Insurance Company, North Richland Hills, TX		320	
SPJST, Temple, TX		320	113
Standard Insurance Company, Portland, OR	StanCorp Financial Group Inc	320	113

COMPANY NAME	ULTIMATE PARENT NAME	KRG	BAG
Standard Life and Accident Insurance Company, Galveston, TX	American National Insurance Company	320	113
Standard Life & Casualty Insurance Company, Salt Lake City, UT	Fidelity Ventures Inc.	320	
Standard Life Insurance Company of Indiana, Indianapolis, IN	Capital Assurance Holdings LLC	320	
The Standard Life Insurance Company of New York, Portland, OR	StanCorp Financial Group Inc	320	113
Standard Security Life Insurance Company of New York, New York, NY	Geneve Holdings, Inc..	320	114
Starmount Life Insurance Company, Baton Rouge, LA	H & J Capital LLC	320	114
State Farm Annuity and Life Insurance Company, Bloomington, IL	State Farm Mutual Automobile Ins Co.	322	
State Farm International Life Insurance Company Ltd., Hamilton HM 08, Bermuda	State Farm Mutual Automobile Ins Co.	322	
State Farm Life and Accident Assurance Company, Bloomington, IL	State Farm Mutual Automobile Ins Co.	322	114
State Farm Life Insurance Company, Bloomington, IL	State Farm Mutual Automobile Ins Co.	322	114
The State Life Insurance Company, Indianapolis, IN	American United Mutual Insurance Hldg Co.	322	115
State Life Insurance Fund (State of Wisconsin), Madison, WI		322	
State Mutual Insurance Company, Rome, GA	State Mutual Insurance Company	322	115
Sterling Investors Life Insurance Company, Rome, GA	Sterling Holdings, Inc.	322	115
Sterling Life Insurance Company, Bellingham, WA	Munich Reinsurance Company	322	
Stonebridge Life Insurance Company, Cedar Rapids, IA	AEGON N.V.	324	115
Summa Insurance Company, Akron, OH	Summa Health System	324	
SummaCare, Inc., Akron, OH	Summa Health System	324	
Summit Health Plan, Inc., Sunrise, FL	Coventry Health Care Inc	324	
Sun Life and Health Insurance Company (U.S.), Wellesley Hills, MA	Sun Life Financial Inc.	324	116
Sun Life Assurance Company of Canada (U.S.), Wellesley Hills, MA	Sun Life Financial Inc.	324	116
Sun Life Insurance and Annuity Company of New York, Wellesley Hills, MA	Sun Life Financial Inc.	324	116
SunAmerica Annuity and Life Assurance Company, Los Angeles, CA	American International Group, Inc.	324	116
SunAmerica Life Insurance Company, Los Angeles, CA	American International Group, Inc.	324	117
Sunset Life Insurance Company of America, Kansas City, MO	Kansas City Life Insurance Company	326	117
Sunshine State Health Plan, Inc., St. Louis, MO	Centene Corporation	326	
Suntrust Insurance Company, Atlanta, GA		326	
Superior Dental Care, Inc., Dayton, OH		326	
Superior HealthPlan, Inc., St. Louis, MO	Centene Corporation	326	
Supreme Council of the Royal Arcanum, Boston, MA		326	
Surency Life & Health Insurance Company, Wichita, KS		326	
Surety Life & Casualty Insurance Company, Fargo, ND		326	
Surety Life Insurance Company, Lincoln, NE	Allstate Corporation	326	
Swiss Re Life & Health America, Inc., Armonk, NY	Swiss Reinsurance Company Ltd	328	117
swisspartners Insurance Company SPC Limited, Grand Cayman, Cayman Islands	Liechtensteinische Landesbank AG	328	
Symetra Life Insurance Company, Bellevue, WA	Symetra Financial Corporation	328	117
Symetra National Life Insurance Company, Bellevue, WA	Symetra Financial Corporation	328	

T

COMPANY NAME	ULTIMATE PARENT NAME	KRG	BAG
Tandy Life Insurance Company, Fort Worth, TX		328	
TD Reinsurance (Barbados) Inc., St. Michael, Barbados	Toronto-Dominion Bank	328	
Teachers Insurance and Annuity Association of America, New York, NY	Teachers Insurance & Ann Assn of America	328	118
Teachers Protective Mutual Life Insurance Company, Lancaster, PA		328	118
Tennessee Behavioral Health, Inc., Nashville, TN	Magellan Health Services Inc	328	
Tennessee Farmers Life Insurance Company, Columbia, TN		330	118
Tennessee Life Insurance Company, Crossville, TN	Plateau Group Inc	330	
Texas Children's Health Plan, Inc., Houston, TX	Texas Children's Hospital	330	
Texas Directors Life Insurance Company, Abilene, TX	Directors Investment Group Inc	330	
Texas HealthSpring LLC, Houston, TX	HealthSpring, Inc.	330	
Texas Imperial Life Insurance Company, Richardson, TX		330	
Texas International Life Insurance Company, Austin, TX		330	
Texas Life Insurance Company, Waco, TX	Wilton Re Holdings Limited	330	118
Texas Memorial Life Insurance Company, Austin, TX		330	
Texas Security Mutual Life Insurance Company, Shiner, TX		332	
Texas Service Life Insurance Company, Austin, TX		332	
Thrivent Financial for Lutherans, Minneapolis, MN	Thrivent Financial for Lutherans	332	119
Thrivent Life Insurance Company, Minneapolis, MN	Thrivent Financial for Lutherans	332	119
TIAA-CREF Life Insurance Company, New York, NY	Teachers Insurance & Ann Assn of America	332	119
Time Insurance Company, Milwaukee, WI	Assurant Inc	332	119
TJM Life Insurance Company, McKinney, TX		332	
Total Health Care, Inc., Detroit, MI	Total Health Care Inc	332	
Total Health Care USA, Inc., Detroit, MI	Total Health Care Inc	332	
Tower Life Insurance Company, San Antonio, TX		334	120
Town & Country Life Insurance Company, Salt Lake City, UT	Moreton & Company	334	
Trans-City Life Insurance Co., Scottsdale, AZ	Trans-City Life Insurance Co	334	120
Trans-Oceanic Life Insurance Company, Guaynabo, PR	Victory Insurance Corporation	334	120
Trans-Western Life Insurance Company, Austin, TX	R D Tips Inc	334	
Trans World Assurance Company, San Mateo, CA	TWA Corporation	334	120
TransAm Assurance Company, Pensacola, FL	TWA Corporation	334	121

COMPANY NAME	ULTIMATE PARENT NAME	KRG	BAG
Transamerica Financial Life Insurance Company, Cedar Rapids, IA	AEGON N.V.	334	121
Transamerica Life Insurance Company, Cedar Rapids, IA	AEGON N.V.	334	121
The Travelers Protective Association of America, St. Louis, MO		336	
TRH Health Insurance Company, Columbia, TN	TN Rural Health Improvement Association	336	
Trillium Community Health Plan Inc, Eugene, OR		336	
Trinity Life Insurance Company, Tulsa, OK		336	
Triple-S Salud, Inc., San Juan, PR	Triple-S Management Corporation	336	
Triple-S Vida, Inc., Rio Piedras, PR	Triple-S Management Corporation	336	121
TruAssure Insurance Company, Naperville, IL		336	
Trustmark Insurance Company, Lake Forest, IL	Trustmark Mutual Holding Company	336	122
Trustmark Life Insurance Company, Lake Forest, IL	Trustmark Mutual Holding Company	336	122
Trustmark Life Insurance Company of New York, Lake Forest, IL	Trustmark Mutual Holding Company	338	122
Tufts Associated Health Maintenance Organization, Inc., Watertown, MA	Tufts Associated Health Maint Org Inc	338	
Tufts Insurance Company, Watertown, MA	Tufts Associated Health Maint Org Inc	338	

U

COMPANY NAME	ULTIMATE PARENT NAME	KRG	BAG
UAHC Health Plan of Tennessee, Inc, Memphis, TN	United American HealthCare Corp.	338	
UBS Life Insurance Company USA, Erie, PA		338	
UCare Minnesota, Minneapolis, MN	UCare Minnesota	338	
UDC Dental California, Inc., Kansas City, MO	Assurant Inc	338	
UDC Ohio, Inc., Kansas City, MO	Assurant Inc	338	
Ukrainian National Association, Inc., Parsippany, NJ		338	
ULLICO Life Insurance Company, Washington, DC	ULLICO Inc	340	
UNICARE Health Insurance Company of Texas, Chicago, IL	WellPoint Inc.	340	
UNICARE Health Insurance Company of the Midwest, Chicago, IL	WellPoint Inc.	340	
UNICARE Health Plan of Kansas, Inc., Thousand Oaks, CA	WellPoint Inc.	340	
UNICARE Health Plan of West Virginia, Inc., Thousand Oaks, CA	WellPoint Inc.	340	
UNICARE Health Plans of Texas, Chicago, IL	WellPoint Inc.	340	
UNICARE Health Plans of the Midwest, Inc., Chicago, IL	WellPoint Inc.	340	
UNICARE Life & Health Insurance Company, Indianapolis, IN	WellPoint Inc.	340	122
Unified Life Insurance Company, Overland Park, KS		340	123
Unimerica Insurance Company, Golden Valley, MN	UnitedHealth Group Inc	342	123
Unimerica Life Insurance Company of New York, New York, NY	UnitedHealth Group Inc	342	
Union Bankers Insurance Company, Lake Mary, FL	Universal American Corp.	342	123
The Union Central Life Insurance Company, Cincinnati, OH	UNIFI Mutual Holding Company	342	123
Union Fidelity Life Insurance Company, Fort Washington, PA	General Electric Company	342	124
The Union Labor Life Insurance Company, Washington, DC	ULLICO Inc	342	124
Union Life Insurance Company, Jonesboro, AR	Munich Reinsurance Company	342	
Union National Life Insurance Company, St. Louis, MO	Unitrin, Inc	342	124
Union Security DentalCare of New Jersey, Inc., Kansas City, MO	Assurant Inc	342	
Union Security Insurance Company, Kansas City, MO	Assurant Inc	344	124
Union Security Life Insurance Company of New York, Fayetteville, NY	Assurant Inc	344	125
Unison Family Health Plan of Pennsylvania, Inc., Pittsburgh, PA	UnitedHealth Group Inc	344	
Unison Health Plan of Ohio, Inc., Pittsburgh, PA	UnitedHealth Group Inc	344	
Unison Health Plan of Pennsylvania, Inc., Pittsburgh, PA	UnitedHealth Group Inc	344	
Unison Health Plan of South Carolina, Inc., Pittsburgh, PA	UnitedHealth Group Inc	344	
Unison Health Plan of Tennessee, Inc., Pittsburgh, PA	UnitedHealth Group Inc	344	
Unison Health Plan of the Capital Area, Inc., Pittsburgh, PA	UnitedHealth Group Inc	344	
United American Insurance Company, McKinney, TX	Torchmark Corporation	344	125
United Assurance Life Insurance Company, North Richland Hills, TX		346	
United Benefit Life Insurance Company, Austin, TX	American Financial Group, Inc.	346	
United Concordia Companies, Inc., Harrisburg, PA	Highmark Inc.	346	
United Concordia Dental Corporation of Alabama, Birmingham, AL	Highmark Inc.	346	
United Concordia Dental Plans, Inc., Harrisburg, PA	Highmark Inc.	346	
United Concordia Dental Plans of California, Inc., Harrisburg, PA	Highmark Inc.	346	
United Concordia Dental Plans of Florida, Inc., Harrisburg, PA	Highmark Inc.	346	
United Concordia Dental Plans of Kentucky, Inc., Harrisburg, PA	Highmark Inc.	346	
United Concordia Dental Plans of Pennsylvania, Inc., Harrisburg, PA	Highmark Inc.	346	
United Concordia Dental Plans of Texas, Inc., Dallas, TX	Highmark Inc.	348	
United Concordia Dental Plans of the Midwest (Michigan), Inc., Harrisburg, PA	Highmark Inc.	348	
United Concordia Insurance Company, Harrisburg, PA	Highmark Inc.	348	
United Concordia Insurance Company of New York, Harrisburg, PA	Highmark Inc.	348	
United Concordia Life and Health Insurance Company, Harrisburg, PA	Highmark Inc.	348	
United Dental Care of Arizona, Inc., Kansas City, MO	Assurant Inc	348	
United Dental Care of Colorado, Inc., Kansas City, MO	Assurant Inc	348	
United Dental Care of Michigan, Inc., Kansas City, MO	Assurant Inc	348	
United Dental Care of Missouri, Inc., Kansas City, MO	Assurant Inc	348	
United Dental Care of New Mexico, Inc., Kansas City, MO	Assurant Inc	350	
United Dental Care of Texas, Inc., Plano, TX	Assurant Inc	350	
United Dental Care of Utah, Inc., Kansas City, MO	Assurant Inc	350	
United Farm Family Life Insurance Company, Indianapolis, IN	Indiana Farm Bureau Inc.	350	125

COMPANY NAME	ULTIMATE PARENT NAME	KRG	BAG
United Fidelity Life Insurance Company, Kansas City, MO	Financial Holding Corporation	350	
United Funeral Benefit Life Insurance Company, Richardson, TX		350	
United Funeral Directors Benefit Life Insurance Company, Richardson, TX		350	
United Heritage Life Insurance Company, Meridian, ID	United Heritage Mutual Holding Company	350	125
United Home Life Insurance Company, Indianapolis, IN	Indiana Farm Bureau Inc.	350	126
United Insurance Company of America, St. Louis, MO	Unitrin, Inc	352	126
United International Life Insurance, Oklahoma City, OK	United International Corporation	352	
United Investors Life Insurance Company, Birmingham, AL	Torchmark Corporation	352	126
United Life Insurance Company, Cedar Rapids, IA	United Fire & Casualty Company	352	126
United National Life Insurance Company of America, Glenview, IL	Guarantee Trust Life Insurance Company	352	
United of Omaha Life Insurance Company, Omaha, NE	Mutual of Omaha Insurance Company	352	127
United Security Assurance Company of Pennsylvania, Souderton, PA	Coventry Resources Corp.	352	127
United Security Life and Health Insurance Company, Bedford Park, IL	J and P Holdings, Inc.	352	127
United States Life Insurance Company in the City of New York, New York, NY	American International Group, Inc.	352	127
United Teacher Associates Insurance Company, Austin, TX	American Financial Group, Inc.	354	128
United Transportation Union Insurance Association, Cleveland, OH		354	
United Trust Insurance Company, Birmingham, AL	Blue Cross and Blue Shield of Alabama	354	
United World Life Insurance Company, Omaha, NE	Mutual of Omaha Insurance Company	354	128
UnitedHealthcare Insurance Company, Hartford, CT	UnitedHealth Group Inc	354	128
UnitedHealthcare Insurance Company of Illinois, Chicago, IL	UnitedHealth Group Inc	354	
UnitedHealthcare Insurance Company of New York, Islandia, NY	UnitedHealth Group Inc	354	
UnitedHealthcare Insurance Company of Ohio, Westerville, OH	UnitedHealth Group Inc	354	
UnitedHealthcare Insurance Company of the River Valley, Moline, IL	UnitedHealth Group Inc	354	
UnitedHealthcare of Alabama, Inc., Birmingham, AL	UnitedHealth Group Inc	356	
UnitedHealthcare of Arizona, Inc., Phoenix, AZ	UnitedHealth Group Inc	356	
UnitedHealthcare of Arkansas, Inc., Little Rock, AR	UnitedHealth Group Inc	356	
UnitedHealthcare of Colorado, Inc., Centennial, CO	UnitedHealth Group Inc	356	
UnitedHealthcare of Florida, Inc., Maitland, FL	UnitedHealth Group Inc	356	
UnitedHealthcare of Georgia, Inc., Norcross, GA	UnitedHealth Group Inc	356	
UnitedHealthcare of Illinois, Inc., Chicago, IL	UnitedHealth Group Inc	356	
UnitedHealthcare of Kentucky, Ltd., Lexington, KY	UnitedHealth Group Inc	356	
UnitedHealthcare of Louisiana, Inc., Metairie, LA	UnitedHealth Group Inc	356	
UnitedHealthcare of Mississippi, Inc., Ridgeland, MS	UnitedHealth Group Inc	358	
UnitedHealthcare of New England, Inc., Trumbull, CT	UnitedHealth Group Inc	358	
UnitedHealthcare of New York, Inc., Trumbull, CT	UnitedHealth Group Inc	358	
UnitedHealthcare of North Carolina, Inc., Greensboro, NC	UnitedHealth Group Inc	358	
UnitedHealthcare of Ohio, Inc., Westerville, OH	UnitedHealth Group Inc	358	
UnitedHealthcare of Tennessee, Inc., Brentwood, TN	UnitedHealth Group Inc	358	
UnitedHealthcare of Texas, Inc., Plano, TX	UnitedHealth Group Inc	358	
UnitedHealthcare of the Mid-Atlantic, Inc., Rockville, MD	UnitedHealth Group Inc	358	
UnitedHealthcare of the Midlands, Inc., Omaha, NE	UnitedHealth Group Inc	358	
UnitedHealthcare of the Midwest, Inc., Maryland Heights, MO	UnitedHealth Group Inc	360	
UnitedHealthcare of Utah, Salt Lake City, UT	UnitedHealth Group Inc	360	
UnitedHealthcare of Wisconsin, Inc., Minnetonka, MN	UnitedHealth Group Inc	360	
UnitedHealthcare Plan of the River Valley, Inc., Moline, IL	UnitedHealth Group Inc	360	
Unity DPO, Inc., Parsippany, NJ		360	
Unity Financial Life Insurance Company, Cincinnati, OH	Unity Financial Insurance Group LLC	360	128
Unity Mutual Life Insurance Company, Syracuse, NY	Unity Mutual Life Insurance Company	360	129
Univantage Insurance Company, Murray, UT	Workers Compensation Fund	360	
Universal Care, Signal Hill, CA		360	
Universal Fidelity Life Insurance Company, Oklahoma City, OK	Universal Fidelity Holding Company Inc.	362	129
Universal Guaranty Life Insurance Company, Springfield, IL		362	
Universal Life Insurance Company, Birmingham, AL		362	
Universal Life Insurance Company, Caparra Heights, PR	Universal Group, Inc.	362	129
Universal Underwriters Life Insurance Company, Overland Park, KS	Zurich Financial Services Ltd.	362	129
University Health Alliance, Honolulu, HI		362	
University Health Plans, Inc., St. Louis, MO	Centene Corporation	362	
Unum Life Insurance Company of America, Chattanooga, TN	Unum Group	362	130
UPMC For You, Inc., Pittsburgh, PA	University of Pittsburgh Medical Center	362	
UPMC Health Benefits Inc., Pittsburgh, PA	University of Pittsburgh Medical Center	364	
UPMC Health Network, Inc., Pittsburgh, PA	University of Pittsburgh Medical Center	364	
UPMC Health Plan, Inc., Pittsburgh, PA	University of Pittsburgh Medical Center	364	
Upper Peninsula Health Plan, Inc., Marquette, MI		364	
U.S. Behavioral Health Plan, California, Minnetonka, MN	UnitedHealth Group Inc	364	
U.S. Financial Life Insurance Company, New York, NY	AXA S.A.	364	130
US Health and Life Insurance Company, Sterling Heights, MI		364	
USA Life One Insurance Company of Indiana, Fishers, IN		364	
USAA Direct Life Insurance Company, San Antonio, TX	United Services Automobile Association	364	
USAA Life Insurance Company, San Antonio, TX	United Services Automobile Association	366	130
USAA Life Insurance Company of New York, San Antonio, TX	United Services Automobile Association	366	130

COMPANY NAME	ULTIMATE PARENT NAME	KRG	BAG
USAble Corporation, Little Rock, AR	USAble Mutual Insurance Company	366	
USAble Life, Little Rock, AR	LSV Partners LLC	366	131
USAble Mutual Insurance Company, Little Rock, AR	USAble Mutual Insurance Company	366	
USIC Life Insurance Company, Guaynabo, PR	USIC Group, Inc.	366	131
UTMB Health Plans, Inc., Galveston, TX	UTMB Health Care Systems Inc	366	

V

COMPANY NAME	ULTIMATE PARENT NAME	KRG	BAG
Valley Baptist Insurance Company, Harlingen, TX	Valley Baptist Health System	366	
Value Behavioral Health of Pennsylvania, Norfolk, VA	FHC Health Systems Inc.	366	
ValueOptions of California, Inc., Cypress, CA		368	
ValueOptions of Texas, Inc., Norfolk, VA	FHC Health Systems Inc.	368	
Vantage Health Plan, Inc., Monroe, LA		368	
Vantis Life Insurance Company, Windsor, CT	Vantis Life Insurance Company	368	131
Vantis Life Insurance Company of New York, Windsor, CT	Vantis Life Insurance Company	368	131
The Variable Annuity Life Insurance Company, New York, NY	American International Group, Inc.	368	132
The Vermont Health Plan, LLC, Berlin, VT	Blue Cross and Blue Shield of Vermont	368	
Versant Life Insurance Company, Baton Rouge, LA	Louisiana Dealer Services Insurance Inc	368	132
Virginia Premier Health Plan, Richmond, VA	Virginia Commonwealth University H Systs	368	
Vision Benefits of America, Pittsburgh, PA		370	
Vision Care Network Insurance Corp., Racine, WI		370	
Vision First Eye Care, Inc., San Jose, CA		370	
Vision Insurance Plan of America, Inc., West Allis, WI	Block Vision Holdings LLC	370	
Vision Plan of America, Los Angeles, CA		370	
Vision Service Plan, Rancho Cordova, CA	Vision Service Plan	370	
Vision Service Plan, Inc., Rancho Cordova, CA	Vision Service Plan	370	
Vision Service Plan Insurance Company CT, Rancho Cordova, CA	Vision Service Plan	370	
Vision Service Plan Insurance Company MO, Rancho Cordova, CA	Vision Service Plan	370	
Vision Service Plan of Idaho, Inc., Rancho Cordova, CA	Vision Service Plan	372	
Vision Service Plan of Illinois, NFP, Rancho Cordova, CA	Vision Service Plan	372	
Vision Service Plan (Ohio), Rancho Cordova, CA	Vision Service Plan	372	
Vision Service Plan (Washington), Rancho Cordova, CA	Vision Service Plan	372	
Vision Services Plan, Inc., Oklahoma, Rancho Cordova, CA	Vision Service Plan	372	
VisionCare of California, San Diego, CA		372	
Vista Health Plan, Inc., Philadelphia, PA	Independence Blue Cross	372	
VISTA Health Plan, Inc., Austin, TX	Vista Service Corporation	372	
Vista Healthplan, Inc., Sunrise, FL	Coventry Health Care Inc	372	
Vista Healthplan of South Florida, Inc., Sunrise, FL	Coventry Health Care Inc	374	
Vista Life Insurance Company, Dearborn, MI	Ford Motor Company	374	
VIVA Health, Inc., Birmingham, AL	University of Alabama Board of Trustees	374	
Volunteer State Health Plan, Inc., Chattanooga, TN	BlueCross BlueShield of Tennessee Inc.	374	

W

COMPANY NAME	ULTIMATE PARENT NAME	KRG	BAG
Washington Dental Service, Seattle, WA		374	
Washington National Insurance Company, Carmel, IN	CNO Financial Group, Inc.	374	132
Wateree Life Insurance Company, Columbia, SC		374	
WEA Insurance Corporation, Madison, WI	WEA Insurance Trust	374	
WellCare of Ohio, Inc., Tampa, FL	WellCare Health Plans, Inc.	374	
WellCare of Texas, Inc., Tampa, FL	WellCare Health Plans, Inc.	376	
Wellmark Health Plan of Iowa, Inc., Des Moines, IA	Wellmark Inc.	376	
Wellmark, Inc., Des Moines, IA	Wellmark Inc.	376	
Wellmark of South Dakota, Inc., Sioux Falls, SD	Wellmark Inc.	376	
WellPath of South Carolina, Inc., Detroit, MI	Coventry Health Care Inc	376	
WellPath Select, Inc., Morrisville, NC	Coventry Health Care Inc	376	
West Coast Life Insurance Company, Birmingham, AL	Protective Life Corporation	376	132
Western American Life Insurance Company, Richardson, TX	Maximum Corporation	376	
The Western and Southern Life Insurance Company, Cincinnati, OH	Western & Southern Mutual Holding Co	376	133
Western Dental Services, Inc., Orange, CA	Premier Dental Services Inc	378	
Western Health Advantage, Sacramento, CA		378	
Western Mutual Insurance Company, Taylorsville, UT		378	
Western National Life Insurance Company, Amarillo, TX	American International Group, Inc.	378	133
Western Reserve Life Assurance Co. of Ohio, Cedar Rapids, IA	AEGON N.V.	378	133
Western-Southern Life Assurance Company, Cincinnati, OH	Western & Southern Mutual Holding Co	378	133
Western United Life Assurance Company, Spokane, WA	Global Life Acquisition LLC	378	
Westport Life Insurance Company, Prairie Village, KS	IAC Group Inc.	378	134
Westward Life Insurance Company, Irvine, CA	MF Salta Company Inc	378	134
Wichita National Life Insurance Company, Lawton, OK	Wichita National Life Insurance Company	380	134
Willamette Dental Insurance, Inc., Hillsboro, OR	Willamette Dental of Idaho Inc.	380	
Willamette Dental of Idaho, Inc., Hillsboro, OR	Willamette Dental of Idaho Inc.	380	
Willamette Dental of Washington, Inc., Hillsboro, OR	Willamette Dental of Idaho Inc.	380	
William Penn Association, Pittsburgh, PA		380	134
William Penn Life Insurance Company of New York, Rockville, MD	Legal & General Group plc.	380	135
Williams Progressive Life and Accident Insurance Company, Opelousas, LA		380	

COMPANY NAME	ULTIMATE PARENT NAME	KRG	BAG
Wilton Reassurance Company, Wilton, CT	Wilton Re Holdings Limited.	380	135
Wilton Reassurance Life Company of New York, Wilton, CT.	Wilton Re Holdings Limited.	380	135
Wilton Reinsurance Bermuda Limited, Hamilton HM 08, Bermuda	Wilton Re Holdings Limited.	382	
Windsor Life Insurance Company, Dallas, TX.	Optimum Group Inc	382	
Winnfield Life Insurance Company, Austin, TX	Realty Advisors Inc.	382	
Wisconsin Physicians Service Insurance Corporation, Madison, WI	Wisconsin Physicians Service Ins Corp	382	
Wisconsin Vision Service Plan, Inc., Rancho Cordova, CA.	Vision Service Plan	382	
Woman's Life Insurance Society, Port Huron, MI		382	135
Wonder State Life Insurance Company, Little Rock, AR		382	
Woodmen of the World Life Insurance Society and/or Omaha Woodmen Life Insurance Society, Omaha, NE		382	136
Workmen's Life Insurance Company, Los Angeles, CA	Workmen's Holding Company	382	
World Corp Insurance Company, Omaha, NE	American Enterprise Mutual Holding Co.	384	136
World Insurance Company, Omaha, NE.	American Enterprise Mutual Holding Co.	384	136
WPS Health Plan, Inc., Green Bay, WI.	Wisconsin Physicians Service Ins Corp	384	
Wyssta Insurance Company, Inc., Stevens Point, WI	Delta Dental of Wisconsin Inc	384	

X

COMPANY NAME	ULTIMATE PARENT NAME	KRG	BAG
XL Life Insurance and Annuity Company, Schaumburg, IL	XL Capital Ltd	384	136
XL Life Ltd, Hamilton HM 11, Bermuda	XL Capital Ltd	384	

Z

COMPANY NAME	ULTIMATE PARENT NAME	KRG	BAG
Zale Life Insurance Company, Irving, TX.	Zale Corporation	384	137

Index

Canadian Companies

COMPANY NAME	ULTIMATE PARENT NAME	KRG
A		
ACE INA Life Insurance, Toronto, Canada	ACE Limited	388
Aetna Life Insurance Company (Canada Branch), Newmarket, Canada		388
Allianz Life Insurance Company of North America (Canada Branch), Willowdale, Canada		388
Allstate Life Insurance Company of Canada, Markham, Canada	Allstate Corporation	388
American Bankers Life Assurance Company of Florida (Canada Branch), North York, Canada		388
American Health and Life Insurance Company (Canada Branch), London, Canada		388
American Income Life Insurance Company (Canada Branch), Toronto, Canada		388
AMEX Assurance Company (Canada Branch), Toronto, Canada		388
Assumption Mutual Life Insurance Company, Moncton, Canada		388
Assurant Life of Canada, Toronto, Canada	Assurant Inc	390
Aurigen Reinsurance Company, Toronto, Canada	Aurigen Capital Limited	390
AXA Equitable Life Insurance Company (Canada Branch), Scarborough, Canada		390
B		
Blue Cross Life Insurance Company of Canada, Moncton, Canada		390
BMO Life Assurance Company, Toronto, Canada	Bank of Montreal	390
BMO Life Insurance Company, Toronto, Canada	Bank of Montreal	390
C		
The Canada Life Assurance Company, Toronto, Canada	Power Corporation of Canada	390
The Canada Life Insurance Company of Canada, Toronto, Canada	Power Corporation of Canada	390
Canadian Premier Life Insurance Company, Markham, Canada	AEGON N.V.	390
Canassurance Hospital Service Association, Montreal, Canada	Canassurance Hospital Service Assn	392
Canassurance Insurance Company, Montreal, Canada	Canassurance Hospital Service Assn	392
CIBC Life Insurance Company Limited, Mississauga, Canada	Canadian Imperial Bank of Commerce	392
CIGNA Life Insurance Company of Canada, Scarborough, Canada	CIGNA Corporation	392
Co-operators Life Insurance Company, Regina, Canada	The Co-operators Group Limited	392
Colisee Re (Canada Branch), Montreal, Canada		392
Combined Insurance Company of America (Canada Branch), Markham, Canada		392
CompCorp Life Insurance Company, Toronto, Canada		392
Connecticut General Life Insurance Company (Canada Branch), Scarborough, Canada		392
Crown Life Insurance Company, Regina, Canada	Power Corporation of Canada	394
CUMIS Life Insurance Company, Burlington, Canada	The Co-operators Group Limited	394
CUNA Mutual Insurance Society (Canada Branch), Burlington, Canada		394
E		
The Empire Life Insurance Company, Kingston, Canada	E-L Financial Corp Ltd	394
Employers Reassurance Corporation (Canada Branch), Toronto, Canada		394
The Equitable Life Insurance Company of Canada, Waterloo, Canada		394
L'Excellence Life Insurance Company, Montreal, Canada	Industrial Alliance Ins & Financial Svcs	394
F		
First Allmerica Financial Life Insurance Company (Canada Branch), Toronto, Canada		394
G		
GAN Vie Compagnie Francaise d'Assurance sur la vie (Canada Branch), Montreal, Canada		394
General American Life Insurance Company (Canada Branch), Montreal, Canada		396
General Re Life Corporation (Canada Branch), Toronto, Canada		396
Gerber Life Insurance Company (Canada Branch), Newmarket, Canada		396
The Great-West Life Assurance Company, Winnipeg, Canada	Power Corporation of Canada	396
H		
Hartford Life Insurance Company (Canada Branch), Newmarket, Canada		396
Household Life Insurance Company (Canada Branch), Toronto, Canada		396

COMPANY NAME	ULTIMATE PARENT NAME	KRG
I		
The Independent Order of Foresters, Toronto, Canada	Independent Order of Foresters	396
Industrial Alliance Insurance and Financial Services Inc., Quebec City, Canada	Industrial Alliance Ins & Financial Svcs	396
Industrial Alliance Pacific Insurance and Financial Services Inc., Vancouver, Canada	Industrial Alliance Ins & Financial Svcs	396
K		
Knights of Columbus (Canada Branch), Belleville, Canada		398
L		
Liberty Life Assurance Company of Boston (Canada Branch), Toronto, Canada		398
Life Insurance Company of North America (Canada Branch), Scarborough, Canada		398
London Life Insurance Company, London, Canada	Power Corporation of Canada	398
M		
The Manufacturers Life Insurance Company, Toronto, Canada	Manulife Financial Corporation	398
Manulife Canada Ltd., Waterloo, Canada	Manulife Financial Corporation	398
Massachusetts Mutual Life Insurance Company (Canada Branch), Toronto, Canada		398
MD Life Insurance Company, Ottawa, Canada		398
MetLife Canada, Ottawa, Canada	MetLife Inc	398
Metropolitan Life Insurance Company (Canada Branch), Ottawa, Canada		400
Minnesota Life Insurance Company (Canada Branch), Toronto, Canada		400
Munich Reinsurance Company (Canada Branch), Toronto, Canada		400
N		
New York Life Insurance Company (Canada Branch), Toronto, Canada		400
O		
Optimum Reassurance Inc., Montreal, Canada	Optimum Group Inc	400
P		
Partner Reinsurance Company Ltd. (Canada Branch), Toronto, Canada		400
PennCorp Life Insurance Company, Mississauga, Canada	La Capitale Civil Service Mutual	400
Phoenix Life Insurance Company (Canada Branch), Toronto, Canada		400
Primerica Life Insurance Company of Canada, Mississauga, Canada	Citigroup Inc.	400
Principal Life Insurance Company (Canada Branch), Toronto, Canada		402
R		
RBC Life Insurance Company, Mississauga, Canada	Royal Bank of Canada	402
Reassure America Life Insurance Company (Canada Branch), Toronto, Canada		402
Reliable Life Insurance Company, Hamilton, Canada	Old Republic International Corporation	402
ReliaStar Life Insurance Company (Canada Branch), Toronto, Canada		402
RGA Life Reinsurance Company of Canada, Toronto, Canada	Reinsurance Group of America Inc	402
S		
SCOR Global Life (Canada Branch), Montreal, Canada		402
Scotia Life Insurance Company, Toronto, Canada	Bank of Nova Scotia	402
The Standard Life Assurance Company of Canada, Montreal, Canada		402
Standard Life Assurance Limited (Canada Branch), Montreal, Canada		404
State Farm International Life Insurance Company Ltd. (Canada Branch), Aurora, Canada		404
Sun Life Assurance Company of Canada, Toronto, Canada	Sun Life Financial Inc.	404
Sun Life Insurance (Canada) Limited, Toronto, Canada	Sun Life Financial Inc.	404
Swiss Re Life & Health Canada, Toronto, Canada	Swiss Reinsurance Company Ltd	404
Swiss Reinsurance Company (Canada Branch), Toronto, Canada		404
T		
TD Life Insurance Company, Toronto, Canada	Toronto-Dominion Bank	404
Transamerica Life Canada, Toronto, Canada	AEGON N.V	404
U		
Ukrainian National Association, Inc. (Canada Branch), Parsippany, NJ		404
United American Insurance Company (Canada Branch), Toronto, Canada		406
Unity Life of Canada, Mississauga, Canada	Independent Order of Foresters	406

COMPANY NAME	ULTIMATE PARENT NAME	KRG

W

Wawanesa Life Insurance Company, Winnipeg, Canada . . . . . Wawanesa Mutual Insurance Company 406
Western Life Assurance Company, High River, Canada . . . . . Western Financial Group Inc 406
Woman's Life Insurance Society (Canada Branch), Sarnia, Canada 406

U.S. and Caribbean Companies
Financial and Operating Exhibits
of
LICENSED INSURANCE CARRIERS
WRITING LIFE/HEALTH INSURANCE
with
KEY RATINGS

[1] Where financial information for companies was obtained by A.M. Best from the NAIC, Kansas City, Mo., a superscript "1" will appear next to the company name in the first column of the table. The company's management has not reviewed the data reflected herein.

[2] Where financial information for companies was obtained by A.M. Best from the regulatory authority representing that legal jurisdiction wherein the company is domiciled, a superscript "2" will appear next to the company name in the first column of the table. The company's management has not reviewed the data reflected herein.

2010 BEST'S KEY RATING GUIDE — LIFE/HEALTH EDITION
ANNUAL STATEMENT DATA FOR YEARS 2005 – 2009

Data in U.S. Dollars

COMPANY NAME Ultimate Parent Association Principal Officer Mailing Address Dom. : Began Bus. : Struct. : Mktg. Specialty Phone # AMB# NAIC#	Best's Financial Strength Rating FSC	Data Year	Balance Sheet: Bonds (%)	Mort. Loans & R.E. (%)	Com & Pref. Stock (%)	All Other Assets (%)	Total Assets ($000)	Life Reserves (%)	Health Reserves %)	Ann Res. & Dep. Liabilities (%)	All Other Liabilities (%)	Capital & Surplus ($000)	Operations: Direct Premiums Written ($000)	Net Premiums Written & Deposits ($000)	Operating Cash Flow ($000)	NOG Before Taxes ($000)	NOG After Taxes ($000)	Net Income ($000)
AAA LIFE INSURANCE COMPANY ACLI Acquisition Company Harold W. Huffstetler, Jr. President & CEO 17900 N. Laurel Park Drive Livonia, MI 48152 MI : 1969 : Stock : Affinity Grp Mktg Ann, Life, A&H 800-624-1662 AMB# 007424 NAIC# 71854	A- Rating Outlook: Stable	'05	87.0	...	3.3	9.7	265,482	16.6	6.3	62.2	14.9	49,172	247,633	65,421	20,452	1,255	-628	-660
		'06	81.8	...	3.2	14.9	284,692	20.9	5.8	59.1	14.1	55,825	272,404	69,743	15,692	-606	-3,082	-2,630
		'07	80.7	...	3.8	15.5	296,328	22.9	6.2	57.2	13.7	68,738	292,226	79,756	10,672	9,086	6,856	6,648
		'08	67.3	...	1.9	30.8	369,389	40.6	4.3	43.7	11.4	71,888	370,496	150,262	77,944	7,863	-2,699	-6,207
		'09	83.0	...	2.4	14.6	402,849	40.9	4.3	42.1	12.7	84,242	436,451	110,442	22,072	7,784	2,704	2,160
	FSC VII	**Rating History: A- g, 05/26/10; A- g, 05/29/09; A- g, 03/17/08; A- g, 01/16/07; A- g, 01/03/06**																
AAA LIFE RE, LTD. American Automobile Association Inc John G. Schaffer President Clarendon House, 2 Church Street Hamilton HM 11, Bermuda BM : Stock : Not Available Life 441-295-5688 AMB# 087158	A- Rating Outlook: Stable	'05	88.3	...	...	11.7	17,153	83.2	...	...	16.8	2,187	...	10,872	...	-2,559	-2,761	-3,010
		'06	90.7	...	...	9.4	31,625	54.2	...	...	45.8	3,705	...	12,646	...	-1,509	-1,931	-2,093
		'07	91.8	...	...	8.2	27,259	65.3	...	...	34.7	4,953	...	15,751	...	1,278	1,108	1,058
		'08	36.2	...	0.0	63.8	55,618	70.5	...	...	29.6	31,111	...	17,373	2,401	2,588	1,695	1,625
		'09	42.5	...	0.0	57.5	63,218	71.8	...	...	28.2	33,976	...	19,450	3,636	2,728	1,890	1,725
	FSC VII	**Rating History: A- g, 05/26/10; A- g, 05/29/09; A- g, 03/17/08; A- g, 01/16/07; A- g, 01/03/06**																
ABILITY INSURANCE COMPANY Ability Reinsurance Holdings Limited Donald M. Charsky Chief Executive Officer PO Box 3735 Omaha, NE 68103 NE : 1968 : Stock : Agency LTC, Med supp, Life 402-391-6900 AMB# 007378 NAIC# 71471	B+ Rating Outlook: Stable	'05	84.5	...	5.1	10.4	135,172	50.5	40.9	2.6	6.0	18,308	40,855	18,780	-2,190	1,321	2,115	1,926
		'06	91.6	...	1.7	6.8	135,876	48.1	44.2	2.3	5.4	18,423	36,694	18,602	-1,749	-1,596	138	197
		'07	71.2	...	...	28.8	185,155	...	95.2	...	4.8	38,679	33,998	51,372	31,962	4,032	-7,268	-6,705
		'08	80.0	...	2.5	17.5	512,339	...	30.2	...	69.8	25,917	32,091	24,301	363,233	-29,685	-21,884	-6,294
		'09	84.0	...	3.4	12.6	195,279	...	90.5	...	9.5	21,720	38,562	22,899	-317,333	-8,021	-7,718	-7,486
	FSC V	**Rating History: B+ g, 03/11/10; B+ g, 12/18/08; C++u, 11/07/07; C++g, 05/16/06; C++g, 04/18/05**																
ABILITY REINS (BERMUDA) LTD Ability Reinsurance Holdings Limited Don Charsky Chief Executive Officer 3rd Floor, Continental Building Hamilton HM 12, Bermuda BM : Stock : Not Available Life, Non-Life AMB# 071193	B+ Rating Outlook: Stable	'05	...	...	...	...	...	...	...	...	...	...	...	...	...	...	...	...
		'06	...	...	...	...	...	...	...	...	...	...	...	...	...	...	...	...
		'07	94.9	...	0.7	4.4	480,341	...	99.4	...	0.7	88,301	...	...	...	26,419	26,419	27,320
		'08	28.3	...	2.9	68.8	504,062	...	99.3	...	0.7	79,677	...	...	...	12,695	12,695	16,697
		'09	93.6	...	2.5	3.9	669,062	22.9	75.6	...	1.5	61,062	...	...	...	-26,886	-26,886	-28,625
	FSC V	**Rating History: B+ g, 03/11/10; B+ g, 12/18/08**																
ABRI HEALTH PLAN INC[2] Avatar Partners, LLC Ronald L. Scasny President 2400 S. 102nd Street West Allis, WI 53227 WI : 2004 : Stock : Not Available Health 414-847-1777 AMB# 064811 NAIC# 12007	NR-5	'05	...	...	...	100.0	3,948	...	73.2	...	26.8	1,098	10,977	10,908	2,605	178	178	178
		'06	...	...	...	100.0	7,443	...	38.3	...	61.7	1,666	27,311	27,135	3,410	1,519	1,093	1,093
		'07	...	...	...	100.0	8,208	...	51.2	...	48.8	2,741	39,979	31,155	206	1,567	946	946
		'08	...	...	...	100.0	11,376	...	43.0	...	57.0	5,845	63,101	33,972	2,950	3,632	2,419	2,419
		'09	...	...	...	100.0	14,619	...	45.4	...	54.6	6,971	94,462	57,752	2,570	2,064	1,290	1,290
		Rating History: NR-5, 05/20/10; NR-5, 05/29/09; NR-5, 05/15/08; NR-5, 06/21/07; NR-5, 07/13/06																
ABSOLUTE TOTAL CARE INC Centene Corporation Aaron W. Brace President 7711 Carondelet Avenue, Suite 800 St. Louis, MO 63105 SC : 2007 : Stock : Broker Health 314-725-4477 AMB# 064922 NAIC# 12959	B+ Rating Outlook: Stable	'05	...	...	...	...	...	...	...	...	...	...	...	...	...	...	...	...
		'06	...	...	...	...	...	...	...	...	...	...	...	...	...	...	...	...
		'07	8.3	...	...	91.7	3,727	...	1.1	...	98.9	2,339	17	17	9,642	-1,237	-1,008	-1,008
		'08	1.1	...	...	98.9	27,395	...	55.3	...	44.7	5,785	46,101	45,625	20,331	118	-439	-656
		'09	48.3	...	0.3	51.5	50,880	...	55.7	...	44.3	14,401	139,533	138,959	14,978	2,378	1,358	1,358
	FSC V	**Rating History: B+, 02/19/10; B+, 02/10/09; NR-5, 03/20/08**																
ACACIA LIFE INSURANCE COMPANY UNIFI Mutual Holding Company Barbara J. Krumsiek Chair P.O. Box 81889 Lincoln, NE 68501-1889 DC : 1869 : Stock : General Agent Univ Life, Term Life, Whole life 800-444-1889 AMB# 006002 NAIC# 60038	A Rating Outlook: Stable	'05	66.4	12.5	11.7	9.4	1,652,576	58.0	0.0	34.7	7.2	258,775	76,152	59,502	-10,763	10,692	7,886	7,655
		'06	66.4	12.6	13.0	8.0	1,651,393	59.5	0.0	33.2	7.2	298,122	69,825	70,533	-27,591	18,962	14,844	19,303
		'07	64.1	11.7	15.5	8.7	1,647,280	60.9	0.0	31.3	7.8	341,355	60,441	82,822	-40,899	18,315	14,853	21,385
		'08	63.4	11.2	14.5	10.9	1,544,345	63.4	0.0	30.4	6.2	322,405	59,864	94,110	-72,585	30,214	28,657	-759
		'09	66.1	10.6	11.4	11.9	1,517,203	66.0	0.0	30.4	3.6	321,553	61,123	119,696	-6,470	24,201	35,946	33,819
	FSC XIII	**Rating History: A g, 04/13/10; A g, 01/30/09; A g, 05/01/08; A g, 02/02/07; A g, 01/04/06**																
ACCESS DENTAL PLAN Abbaszadeh Dental Group Inc Reza Abbaszadeh, D.D.S. President & CEO 8890 Cal Center Drive Sacramento, CA 95826 CA : 1993 : Stock : Not Available Dental 916-922-5000 AMB# 064655	A- Rating Outlook: Negative	'05	...	...	...	100.0	8,404	...	...	...	100.0	5,946	34,664	34,664	-394	6,179	6,098	6,098
		'06	...	...	...	100.0	10,765	...	...	...	100.0	7,577	33,399	33,399	2,921	5,140	5,059	5,059
		'07	...	...	...	100.0	12,686	...	...	...	100.0	10,953	34,528	34,528	2,787	6,260	6,166	6,166
		'08	...	...	...	100.0	13,980	...	...	...	100.0	12,202	38,042	38,042	-2,374	6,831	6,729	6,729
		'09	...	...	...	100.0	19,751	...	...	...	100.0	13,302	40,737	40,737	6,475	7,440	7,328	7,328
	FSC V	**Rating History: A-, 07/14/09; A-, 06/06/08; A- g, 06/13/07; A- g, 06/20/06; A- g, 06/22/05**																
ACE LIFE INSURANCE COMPANY ACE Limited Ari Lindner Chairman 436 Walnut Street, P.O. Box 1000 Philadelphia, PA 19106 CT : 1965 : Stock : General Agent Life 203-352-6602 AMB# 060599 NAIC# 60348	A- Rating Outlook: Stable	'05	...	...	...	...	...	...	...	...	...	...	...	...	...	...	...	...
		'06	72.6	...	...	27.4	17,718	38.6	...	...	61.4	15,926	...	30	6,313	-1,316	-1,316	-1,316
		'07	86.5	...	...	13.5	19,663	65.2	2.0	...	32.8	13,663	28	3,199	5,827	-6,024	-6,024	-6,046
		'08	37.6	...	...	62.4	34,324	65.1	2.0	...	32.9	19,977	1,977	4,645	10,258	-6,896	-6,896	-6,731
		'09	93.5	...	...	6.5	40,242	55.3	1.4	...	43.3	19,055	...	4,555	6,680	-6,277	-6,277	-6,277
	FSC V	**Rating History: A-, 05/03/10; A, 03/20/09; A, 11/26/07; A, 10/16/06; A, 06/14/06**																

Data in U.S. Dollars

	Profitability Tests							Leverage Tests						Liquidity Tests					
Un-Realized Capital Gains ($000)	Benefits Paid to NPW & Dep (%)	Comm. & Expenses to NPW & Dep (%)	NOG to Total Assets (%)	NOG to Total Rev (%)	Operating Return on Equity (%)	Net Yield (%)	Total Return (%)	Change in NPW & Dep (%)	NPW & Dep to Capital (X)	Capital & Surplus to Liabilities (%)	Surplus Relief (%)	Reins Leverage (%)	Change in Capital (%)	Quick Liquidity (%)	Current Liquidity (%)	Non-Invest Grade Bonds to Capital (%)	Delinq. & Foreclosed Mortgages to Capital (%)	Mort. & Credit Tenant Loans & R.E. to Capital (%)	Affiliated Invest to Capital (%)
275	46.6	51.0	-0.2	-0.6	-1.5	4.78	5.08	-16.5	1.3	23.7	65.0	999.9	41.5	82.9	93.8	9.4	...	...	...
512	54.2	50.0	-1.1	-2.6	-5.9	5.17	5.66	6.6	1.2	25.6	63.4	999.9	14.2	83.8	94.3	28.4	...	...	...
18	61.1	47.8	2.4	5.1	11.0	5.40	5.43	14.4	1.1	31.5	57.5	999.9	22.1	85.8	98.1	20.7	...	...	...
-2,091	32.0	26.7	-0.8	-1.3	-3.8	4.99	3.23	88.4	2.1	24.2	55.1	999.9	1.3	105.5	115.1	24.1	...	...	...
1,102	51.6	39.8	0.7	1.6	3.5	5.53	5.72	-26.5	1.3	26.9	51.0	999.9	18.8	76.2	87.3	25.5	...	...	2.2
	Principal Lines of Business: OrdLife (29.5%), GrpLife (28.2%), IndAnn (19.6%), GrpA&H (19.5%), IndA&H (2.4%)													Principal States: CA (51.2%), MI (11.8%), FL (4.9%)					
...	63.1	66.1	-16.9	-24.6	-99.9	4.09	2.43	16.5	497.1	14.6	...	...	-25.2	106.2	101.4	...	...	...	...
...	54.7	64.5	-7.9	-14.4	-65.6	4.09	3.37	16.3	341.3	13.3	...	...	69.4	104.8	102.8	...	...	...	...
...	33.2	65.9	3.8	6.6	25.6	4.09	3.91	24.6	318.0	22.2	...	...	33.7	115.7	112.5	...	...	...	...
-511	51.5	40.3	4.1	9.2	9.4	4.66	4.38	10.3	55.8	127.0	...	...	528.1	92.4	87.7	...	...	...	...
930	55.2	37.3	3.2	9.2	5.8	4.90	4.27	12.0	57.3	116.2	...	...	9.2	95.3	92.3	...	...	...	...
23	111.8	28.3	1.6	6.8	12.2	4.21	5.30	-10.6	1.0	16.2	26.2	251.4	12.1	79.2	93.7	19.1	...	15.7	6.6
157	101.8	32.3	0.1	0.5	0.7	4.73	5.69	-0.9	1.0	16.3	18.7	277.9	0.9	75.3	89.3	13.0	...	1.2	4.7
65	50.3	11.0	-4.5	-10.4	-25.5	4.44	5.85	176.2	1.3	26.8	27.9	999.9	105.2	100.1	109.7	1.1	...	1.1	...
-2,536	81.8	35.6	-6.3	-35.5	-67.8	5.16	9.14	-52.7	0.9	5.3	78.4	999.9	-33.7	94.8	102.2	2.1	...	1.7	...
1,963	89.0	44.9	-2.2	-12.7	-32.4	5.43	6.07	-5.8	1.0	13.5	88.3	999.9	-10.2	77.3	88.3	8.1	...	1.9	...
	Principal Lines of Business: IndA&H (100.0%)													Principal States: NE (13.6%), IA (10.6%), MN (8.3%), NC (7.2%), TX (6.0%)					
...	...	...	...	...	...	...	...	...	...	...	...	...	...	...	...	...	...	...	...
...	...	...	...	...	...	...	...	...	...	...	...	...	...	...	...	...	...	...	...
10,981	...	...	...	43.3	...	...	...	...	...	22.5	...	...	...	121.1	117.1	...	...	...	...
-17,819	...	...	2.6	9.9	15.1	4.74	5.99	...	...	18.8	...	...	-9.8	37.6	38.4	...	...	...	7.2
16,385	...	...	-4.6	-22.2	-38.2	5.73	5.31	...	...	10.0	...	...	-23.4	107.2	107.2	...	...	...	14.7
...	77.0	22.8	7.0	1.6	19.1	0.79	0.79	999.9	9.9	38.5	...	...	43.7	130.5	130.5	...	...	...	...
...	79.5	18.2	19.2	4.1	79.1	3.28	3.28	148.8	16.3	28.8	...	...	51.8	123.4	123.4	...	...	...	...
...	80.4	16.8	12.1	3.0	42.9	3.13	3.13	14.8	11.4	50.1	...	85.7	64.5	134.1	134.1	...	...	...	...
...	74.8	17.3	24.7	6.9	56.3	-0.29	-0.29	9.0	5.8	105.7	...	85.1	113.2	186.2	186.2	...	...	...	...
...	86.1	11.1	9.9	2.2	20.1	0.01	0.01	70.0	8.3	91.1	...	61.6	19.3	168.2	168.2	...	...	...	...
	Principal Lines of Business: Medicaid (99.5%), OtherHlth (0.5%)													Principal States: WI (100.0%)					
...	...	...	...	...	...	...	...	...	...	...	...	...	...	...	...	...	...	...	...
...	...	...	...	...	...	...	...	...	...	...	...	...	...	...	...	...	...	...	...
353	98.1	999.9	...	-99.9	...	...	...	...	0.0	168.6	...	...	...	156.0	156.0	...	...	...	386.1
-353	83.9	17.4	-2.8	-0.9	-10.8	5.10	1.12	999.9	7.9	26.8	...	...	147.3	207.0	217.7	...	...	...	128.4
-165	84.1	14.4	3.5	1.0	13.5	0.62	0.11	204.6	9.6	39.5	...	0.4	149.0	131.4	142.0	...	...	...	44.7
	Principal Lines of Business: Medicaid (100.0%)													Principal States: SC (100.0%)					
24,524	166.7	51.9	0.5	5.5	3.2	5.45	6.97	-14.5	0.2	22.1	2.3	17.7	10.2	54.5	67.0	12.6	...	69.4	56.7
29,515	164.6	29.5	0.9	10.9	5.3	5.49	7.60	18.5	0.2	26.2	2.0	15.3	14.7	53.9	67.7	11.9	...	60.6	57.4
31,568	155.5	18.7	0.9	12.2	4.6	5.24	7.62	17.4	0.2	31.3	1.9	13.7	14.6	55.1	69.5	10.0	...	49.2	56.8
-26,207	137.5	24.0	1.8	21.2	8.6	6.24	2.73	13.6	0.3	28.7	1.8	13.7	-12.2	56.7	70.2	14.1	...	50.0	55.9
-37,353	78.4	43.0	2.3	19.7	11.2	7.73	5.11	27.2	0.4	27.4	1.9	12.9	-5.3	57.4	70.8	16.2	...	49.2	45.3
	Principal Lines of Business: OrdLife (50.8%), GrpAnn (38.4%), IndAnn (10.7%), IndA&H (0.0%)													Principal States: CA (17.5%), PA (7.3%), VA (7.2%), DC (6.1%), TX (6.0%)					
...	67.9	15.6	29.7	17.4	52.0	0.51	0.51	-55.9	5.8	241.9	...	...	-66.0	174.2	174.2	...	...	...	...
...	68.5	19.1	52.8	14.7	74.8	2.69	2.69	-3.6	4.4	237.7	...	...	27.4	172.7	172.7	...	...	...	...
...	64.3	19.8	52.6	17.5	66.6	3.56	3.56	3.4	3.2	632.3	...	...	44.6	409.2	409.2	...	...	...	...
...	61.8	21.7	50.5	17.4	58.1	2.79	2.79	10.2	3.1	686.1	...	...	11.4	303.5	303.5	...	...	...	...
...	63.3	20.9	43.4	17.6	57.5	1.75	1.75	7.1	3.1	206.2	...	...	9.0	187.0	187.0	...	...	...	...
	Principal Lines of Business: Dental (100.0%)																		
...	...	...	...	...	...	...	...	...	...	...	...	...	...	...	...	...	...	...	...
...	8.4	999.9	...	-99.9	...	...	...	...	0.0	889.9	0.1	12.4	...	999.9	999.9	...	...	...	...
...	16.4	200.7	-32.2	-92.4	-40.7	4.61	4.52	999.9	0.2	227.9	17.4	76.0	-14.2	435.6	441.7	...	...	...	...
...	36.6	266.5	-25.5	-45.0	-41.0	2.95	3.53	45.2	0.2	139.5	19.5	120.4	46.3	287.3	288.3	...	...	...	...
...	51.3	146.8	-16.8	-64.4	-32.2	1.12	1.24	-1.9	0.2	90.0	24.8	173.0	-4.7	194.1	194.7	...	...	...	...
	Principal Lines of Business: OrdLife (93.7%), CrdLife (5.0%), CrdA&H (1.4%), GrpLife (-0.1%)																		

Data in U.S. Dollars

COMPANY NAME Ultimate Parent Association Principal Officer Mailing Address Dom. : Began Bus. : Struct. : Mktg. Specialty Phone # AMB# NAIC#	Best's Financial Strength Rating FSC	Data Year	Balance Sheet Bonds (%)	Mort. Loans & R.E. (%)	Com & Pref. Stock (%)	All Other Assets (%)	Total Assets ($000)	Life Reserves (%)	Health Reserves %)	Ann Res. & Dep. Liabilities (%)	All Other Liabilities (%)	Capital & Surplus ($000)	Operations Direct Premiums Written ($000)	Net Premiums Written & Deposits ($000)	Operating Cash Flow ($000)	NOG Before Taxes ($000)	NOG After Taxes ($000)	Net Income ($000)
ACE TEMPEST LIFE REINS LTD ACE Limited Ari Lindner President & Chief Executive Officer 436 Walnut Street Philadelphia, PA 19106 BM : Stock : Not Available Life, Non-Life 441-278-6660 AMB# 077030	**A+** Rating Outlook: Stable **FSC XV**	'05	57.2	...	3.4	39.5	10,937,092	7.5	...	...	92.5	3,835,232	...	2,925,977	1,431,754	222,649	218,153	250,242
		'06	62.3	...	1.9	35.8	13,155,276	6.4	...	...	93.6	4,884,867	...	3,653,623	1,816,665	1,105,002	1,096,938	1,038,550
		'07	65.1	...	1.0	33.9	16,572,297	5.4	...	...	94.6	6,062,672	...	3,391,505	2,715,226	1,305,928	1,299,799	1,069,237
		'08	60.5	...	0.9	38.6	15,853,492	9.1	...	...	91.0	4,365,903	...	4,324,539	2,817,010	1,272,076	1,289,450	653,371
		'09	69.1	...	0.6	30.2	17,634,363	9.2	...	...	90.8	6,218,225	...	3,644,419	890,883	1,448,435	1,470,281	1,298,004
		Rating History: A+, 05/03/10; A+, 03/20/09; A+, 11/26/07; A+, 10/16/06; A+, 08/16/05																
ACN GROUP OF CALIFORNIA INC UnitedHealth Group Inc Stephen Castro President 3111 Camino Del Rio N, Suite 1000 San Diego, CA 92122 CA : 2003 : Stock : Not Available Health 800-428-6337 AMB# 064816	**NR-2**	'05	...	...	...	100.0	4,616	...	...	...	100.0	-351	...	...	1,270	-508	-343	-343
		'06	...	...	...	100.0	7,710	...	...	...	100.0	1,047	307	307	3,283	2,202	1,302	1,302
		'07	...	...	...	100.0	12,283	...	...	...	100.0	10,595	4,452	4,452	4,589	4,353	2,575	2,575
		'08	...	...	...	100.0	15,003	...	...	...	100.0	9,370	7,304	7,304	2,391	6,386	3,775	3,775
		'09	...	...	...	100.0	10,190	...	...	...	100.0	9,538	5,769	5,769	-4,647	2,767	1,667	1,667
		Rating History: NR-2, 06/15/09; NR-2, 01/29/08; NR-2, 11/21/07; NR-2, 11/16/06; NR-2, 08/17/06																
ADMIRAL LIFE INS CO OF AMERICA State Mutual Insurance Company Delos H. Yancey III Chairman, President & CEO P.O. Box 33 Rome, GA 30162-0033 AZ : 1958 : Stock : Other Direct A&H, Credit A&H, Credit Life 800-897-1593 AMB# 007358 NAIC# 71390	**NR-2**	'05	41.3	...	20.0	38.7	9,042	...	...	...	100.0	8,820	...	...	344	212	187	208
		'06	36.7	...	...	63.3	9,221	...	...	...	100.0	9,138	...	...	296	177	162	259
		'07	56.4	20.8	2.0	20.9	9,906	...	7.1	...	92.9	9,254	949	95	292	179	144	144
		'08	52.7	12.7	1.4	33.1	13,214	...	12.9	...	87.1	9,198	19,322	2,242	966	695	385	385
		'09	41.5	12.3	1.3	44.8	13,455	...	13.9	...	86.1	9,547	34,581	3,574	-621	808	565	515
		Rating History: NR-2, 02/12/10; NR-2, 03/18/09; NR-2, 02/01/08; NR-2, 12/14/06; NR-2, 06/01/06																
ADVANCE INSURANCE CO OF KANSAS Blue Cross and Blue Shield of Kansas Inc Beryl B. Lowery-Born President 1133 SW Topeka Boulevard Topeka, KS 66629-0001 KS : 2004 : Stock : Career Agent Term Life, Disability, Accident 785-273-9804 AMB# 060404 NAIC# 12143	**A** Rating Outlook: Stable **FSC X**	'05	44.3	...	51.0	4.7	44,760	49.7	14.9	...	35.4	38,760	10,650	9,482	2,434	2,860	2,481	2,801
		'06	45.5	...	45.6	8.9	49,465	43.7	16.3	...	40.0	42,345	11,435	10,601	3,056	2,783	2,393	3,862
		'07	65.4	...	22.9	11.7	39,040	46.8	13.1	...	40.1	32,413	12,157	11,194	-9,863	2,839	2,156	2,687
		'08	70.6	...	16.8	12.7	38,056	61.6	19.9	...	18.4	33,292	12,019	11,072	-956	2,447	2,173	358
		'09	75.0	...	15.7	9.3	41,221	49.2	16.0	...	34.7	35,454	11,643	10,719	2,314	2,685	1,854	1,738
		Rating History: A g, 12/14/09; A g, 02/26/09; A g, 01/30/08; A g, 12/07/06; A g, 10/25/05																
ADVANTA LIFE INS CO[1] Philip M. Browne President, CFO & Treasurer Welsh & McKean Roads Spring House, PA 19477-0429 AZ : 1972 : Stock : Not Available 215-444-5769 AMB# 008357 NAIC# 80055	**NR-1**	'05	55.2	...	...	44.8	6,585	...	...	...	100.0	5,636	8	819	...	1,139	779	779
		'06	42.5	...	...	57.5	8,556	...	...	...	100.0	7,541	5	632	...	826	396	396
		'07	41.1	...	...	58.9	9,197	...	...	...	100.0	8,807	4	578	...	1,923	594	594
		'08	86.0	...	...	14.0	4,420	...	...	...	100.0	4,133	3	465	...	183	122	122
		'09	87.2	...	...	12.8	4,354	...	...	...	100.0	4,166	1	230	...	43	32	32
		Rating History: NR-1, 06/11/10; NR-5, 05/12/10; NR-4, 09/15/08; B+, 09/15/08; B+, 12/21/07																
ADVANTAGE DENTAL PLAN INC[2] Ralph M. Shirtcliff, D.M.D. President 442 SW Umatilla Avenue, Suite 200 Redmond, OR 97756 OR : 1995 : Stock : Agency Dental 541-504-3920 AMB# 064493 NAIC# 47006	**NR-5**	'05	2.7	...	...	97.3	3,759	...	30.2	...	69.8	2,317	12,112	12,112	731	28	13	13
		'06	6.6	...	...	93.4	3,773	...	29.9	...	70.1	2,434	13,009	13,009	178	29	24	24
		'07	31.5	...	...	68.5	3,651	...	21.9	...	78.1	2,409	14,175	14,175	-113	19	19	19
		'08	19.0	...	...	81.0	3,157	...	31.9	...	68.1	2,430	13,160	13,160	-622	11	5	5
		'09	8.9	...	...	91.1	2,260	...	28.4	...	71.6	1,366	6,266	6,266	-843	13	13	13
		Rating History: NR-5, 05/20/10; NR-5, 09/16/09; NR-5, 07/14/08; NR-5, 07/02/07; NR-5, 05/11/06																
ADVANTAGE HEALTH SOLUTIONS INC[2] Vicki F. Perry President 9490 Priority Way West Drive Indianapolis, IN 46240 IN : 2000 : Stock : Not Available Group A&H 317-573-6572 AMB# 064624 NAIC# 52568	**NR-5**	'05	...	...	...	100.0	24,645	...	63.2	...	36.8	12,271	201,764	200,703	1,678	4,559	2,940	2,940
		'06	...	...	...	100.0	26,968	...	58.1	...	41.9	13,556	234,142	232,881	6,676	2,923	1,946	1,946
		'07	...	...	...	100.0	35,839	...	51.6	...	48.4	16,255	243,742	242,616	3,941	4,135	2,860	2,860
		'08	...	...	...	100.0	40,588	...	75.4	...	24.6	16,442	363,938	361,476	1,571	2,359	1,342	1,342
		'09	...	...	...	100.0	43,783	...	63.0	...	37.0	20,579	373,412	370,983	9,858	5,151	3,221	3,221
		Rating History: NR-5, 04/26/10; NR-5, 08/26/09; C++pd, 09/03/08; C++pd, 10/08/07; C++pd, 09/25/06																
ADVANTAGE HEALTHPLAN INC Elliot R. Wolff Chairman & President P.O. Box 9596 Washington, DC 20016 DC : 1994 : Non-Profit : Other Health 202-785-7835 AMB# 064689 NAIC# 95803	**NR-5**	'05	60.2	...	28.9	10.9	2,250	...	...	...	100.0	2,186	...	...	-223	1,004	1,004	1,004
		'06	66.6	...	22.4	11.0	2,031	...	...	...	100.0	1,907	...	...	-308	-86	-86	-93
		'07	72.1	...	23.4	4.6	2,078	...	...	...	100.0	2,082	...	...	11	172	172	187
		'08	73.6	...	11.5	14.9	1,774	...	...	...	100.0	1,758	...	...	-247	-278	-278	-268
		'09	63.2	...	8.2	28.6	1,837	...	...	...	100.0	1,779	...	...	38	-14	-14	-13
		Rating History: NR-5, 03/25/10; NR-5, 03/27/09; NR-5, 04/15/08; NR-5, 05/01/07; NR-5, 04/27/06																
AECC TOTAL VISION HTH PL OF TX Centene Corporation Jason M. Harrold President 4000 McEwen Road Dallas, TX 75244-5016 TX : 1996 : Stock : Not Available Group A&H 252-937-6650 AMB# 064512 NAIC# 95302	**NR-3**	'05	...	...	...	100.0	2,194	...	32.2	...	67.8	972	...	...	452	54	36	36
		'06	...	...	...	100.0	2,434	...	30.0	...	70.0	1,473	...	...	431	766	501	501
		'07	...	...	...	100.0	3,152	...	30.9	...	69.1	2,077	...	...	596	910	659	659
		'08	...	...	...	100.0	4,293	...	33.7	...	66.3	3,046	...	...	711	1,331	922	922
		'09	...	...	...	100.0	3,876	...	33.3	...	66.7	2,918	...	...	-450	826	583	583
		Rating History: NR-3, 02/19/10; NR-3, 02/10/09; NR-5, 03/19/08; NR-5, 04/03/07; NR-5, 06/05/06																

BEST'S PROFITABILITY, LEVERAGE AND LIQUIDITY TESTS 2005 – 2009

Data in U.S. Dollars

	Profitability Tests							Leverage Tests						Liquidity Tests					
Un-Realized Capital Gains ($000)	Benefits Paid to NPW & Dep (%)	Comm. & Expenses to NPW & Dep (%)	NOG to Total Assets (%)	NOG to Total Rev (%)	Operating Return on Equity (%)	Net Yield (%)	Total Return (%)	Change in NPW & Dep (%)	NPW & Dep to Capital (X)	Capital & Surplus to Liabilities (%)	Surplus Relief (%)	Reins Leverage (%)	Change in Capital (%)	Quick Liquidity (%)	Current Liquidity (%)	Non-Invest Grade Bonds to Capital (%)	Delinq. & Foreclosed Mortgages to Capital (%)	Mort. & Credit Tenant Loans & R.E. to Capital (%)	Affiliated Invest to Capital (%)
-124,176	70.8	25.8	2.3	7.1	6.1	3.72	4.16	17.0	76.3	55.1	...	...	15.3	101.8	123.5	...	...	...	...
134,562	47.6	24.2	9.1	29.9	25.2	4.04	3.44	24.9	74.8	60.4	...	...	27.4	112.0	129.7	...	...	...	...
97,799	51.3	27.7	8.7	34.7	23.8	4.36	2.47	-7.2	55.9	59.3	...	...	24.1	116.1	133.2	...	...	...	...
-1,130,984	54.8	27.1	8.0	30.8	24.7	4.41	-0.36	27.5	99.1	39.1	...	...	-28.0	100.9	113.8	...	...	...	...
1,250,259	49.2	31.7	8.8	34.8	27.8	4.51	3.25	-15.7	58.6	56.3	...	...	42.4	114.9	128.0	...	...	...	...
...	...	...	-8.6	-20.6	177.1	...	...	...	...	-7.1	...	...	-99.9	54.5	54.5	...	...	...	...
...	47.3	415.3	21.1	35.9	373.9	-2.91	-2.91	...	0.3	15.7	...	...	398.4	89.9	89.9	...	...	...	...
...	59.7	27.3	25.8	31.3	44.2	6.00	6.00	999.9	0.4	627.7	...	...	911.7	626.5	626.5	...	...	...	...
...	26.7	38.2	27.7	33.9	37.8	2.26	2.26	64.1	0.8	166.4	...	...	-11.6	233.8	233.8	...	...	...	...
...	50.4	45.2	13.2	20.1	17.6	0.15	0.15	-21.0	0.6	999.9	...	...	1.8	999.9	999.9	...	...	...	...
Principal Lines of Business: CompHosp/Med (100.0%)																			
39	...	...	...	68.9	...	...	...	...	...	999.9	...	...	...	999.9	999.9	...	...	...	...
-152	...	...	1.8	42.5	1.8	3.66	3.08	...	...	999.9	...	...	1.1	999.9	999.9	...	...	...	...
...	41.4	345.1	1.5	12.5	1.6	5.23	5.23	...	0.0	999.9	6.2	7.2	1.3	999.9	999.9	...	1.4	22.3	...
...	59.7	23.0	3.3	3.5	4.2	5.06	5.06	999.9	0.2	229.9	90.1	79.0	-0.5	199.7	209.1	...	...	18.3	...
...	82.8	7.7	4.2	3.5	6.0	4.57	4.08	59.4	0.4	245.0	126.0	86.4	3.8	191.8	205.6	2.1	2.0	17.3	...
Principal Lines of Business: IndA&H (100.0%)													Principal States: MO (28.8%), WI (17.2%), MS (17.2%), IN (8.8%), TN (6.2%)						
-219	50.0	33.3	5.7	22.3	6.6	3.75	3.99	336.4	0.2	750.7	0.1	7.3	5.3	366.7	403.5	0.5	...	...	47.2
308	54.2	35.2	5.1	19.1	5.9	4.15	8.04	11.8	0.2	773.1	0.1	8.0	10.9	511.9	560.4	...	...	...	29.3
-103	58.6	34.6	4.9	16.6	5.8	4.03	5.05	5.6	0.3	706.5	0.1	6.9	-21.9	640.2	700.7	...	...	...	2.5
-1,285	57.5	34.9	5.6	17.2	6.6	4.11	-3.86	-1.1	0.3	705.0	0.0	7.3	-2.5	608.9	676.6	0.1	...	...	2.4
1,610	51.6	38.5	4.7	15.1	5.4	3.91	7.95	-3.2	0.3	773.0	0.0	6.6	9.5	697.9	770.7	0.0	...	...	2.4
Principal Lines of Business: GrpLife (58.3%), GrpA&H (29.8%), OrdLife (12.0%)													Principal States: KS (99.8%)						
...	26.5	67.6	13.1	40.8	14.9	...	...	-21.4	0.1	594.0	0.1	...	17.7	...	...	...	...	...	...
...	19.4	70.3	5.2	28.1	6.0	...	...	-22.8	0.1	757.6	0.0	...	34.1	...	...	...	...	...	...
...	38.4	67.4	6.7	23.5	7.3	...	...	-8.5	0.1	999.9	0.0	...	16.5	...	...	...	...	...	...
...	30.5	85.8	1.8	17.3	1.9	...	...	-19.6	0.1	999.9	0.0	...	-53.1	...	...	...	...	...	...
...	17.1	97.8	0.7	10.8	0.8	...	...	-50.6	0.1	999.9	0.0	...	0.8	...	...	...	...	...	...
Principal Lines of Business: CrdA&H (64.1%), CrdLife (35.9%)																			
0	79.7	20.8	0.4	0.1	0.6	2.86	2.86	20.0	5.2	160.6	...	...	17.6	303.7	310.6	...	...	...	9.3
...	80.5	20.3	0.6	0.2	1.0	3.87	3.87	7.4	5.3	181.8	...	...	5.1	335.0	337.9	...	...	...	11.1
...	81.0	20.1	0.5	0.1	0.8	4.99	4.99	9.0	5.9	193.9	...	...	-1.0	270.4	277.5	...	...	...	10.8
...	80.3	20.7	0.1	0.0	0.2	4.56	4.56	-7.2	5.4	334.3	...	...	0.9	287.2	287.2	...	...	...	10.7
...	87.3	48.5	0.5	0.2	0.7	3.63	3.63	-52.4	4.6	152.9	...	...	-43.8	323.7	337.9	...	...	...	19.0
Principal Lines of Business: Dental (100.0%)																			
...	88.5	7.6	13.3	1.5	27.4	3.99	3.99	4.3	16.4	99.2	...	...	33.9	140.0	140.0	...	...	...	...
...	92.0	7.1	7.5	0.8	15.1	5.80	5.80	16.0	17.2	101.1	...	...	10.5	235.2	235.2	...	...	...	...
...	92.0	6.9	9.1	1.2	19.2	5.06	5.06	4.2	14.9	83.0	...	...	19.9	142.7	142.7	...	...	...	...
...	93.8	6.3	3.5	0.4	8.2	3.25	3.25	49.0	22.0	68.1	...	...	1.1	122.2	122.2	...	...	...	...
...	92.4	6.8	7.6	0.9	17.4	0.16	0.16	2.6	18.0	88.7	...	...	25.2	169.7	169.7	...	...	...	...
Principal Lines of Business: CompHosp/Med (92.8%), Medicare (7.3%), FEHBP (-0.1%)													Principal States: IN (100.0%)						
...	...	...	40.8	197.2	58.8	4.85	4.85	-99.9	...	999.9	...	...	78.4	999.9	999.9	...	...	...	...
-8	...	...	-4.0	-23.5	-4.2	4.79	4.11	...	...	999.9	...	...	-12.8	999.9	999.9	...	...	...	...
-25	...	...	8.4	38.6	8.6	4.58	4.08	...	...	-99.9	...	...	9.2	-99.9	-99.9	...	...	...	...
-107	...	...	-14.5	-99.9	-14.5	5.01	0.12	...	...	999.9	...	...	-15.6	999.9	999.9	...	...	...	...
51	...	...	-0.8	-4.5	-0.8	3.77	6.72	...	...	999.9	...	...	1.2	999.9	999.9	...	...	...	...
...	79.4	20.2	1.8	0.4	3.8	...	...	...	...	79.5	...	...	5.8	157.3	157.3	...	...	...	...
...	62.6	28.3	21.7	6.4	41.0	2.53	2.53	...	...	153.3	...	...	51.6	244.9	244.9	...	...	...	...
...	65.2	26.8	23.6	6.3	37.2	3.07	3.07	...	...	193.0	...	...	41.0	274.2	274.2	...	...	...	...
...	72.0	18.0	24.8	7.0	36.0	0.74	0.74	...	...	244.5	...	...	46.7	293.8	293.8	...	...	...	...
...	72.8	21.7	14.3	3.9	19.6	0.24	0.24	...	...	304.7	...	...	-4.2	335.2	335.2	...	...	...	...

2010 BEST'S KEY RATING GUIDE — LIFE/HEALTH EDITION
ANNUAL STATEMENT DATA FOR YEARS 2005 – 2009

Data in U.S. Dollars

COMPANY NAME Ultimate Parent Association Principal Officer Mailing Address Dom. : Began Bus. : Struct. : Mktg. Specialty Phone # AMB# NAIC#	Best's Financial Strength Rating FSC	Data Year	Balance Sheet Bonds (%)	Mort. Loans & R.E. (%)	Com & Pref. Stock (%)	All Other Assets (%)	Total Assets ($000)	Life Reserves (%)	Health Reserves %)	Ann Res. & Dep. Liabilities (%)	All Other Liabilities (%)	Capital & Surplus ($000)	Operations Direct Premiums Written ($000)	Net Premiums Written & Deposits ($000)	Operating Cash Flow ($000)	NOG Before Taxes ($000)	NOG After Taxes ($000)	Net Income ($000)
AETNA BETTER HEALTH INC (CT) Aetna Inc Thomas L. Kelly President 980 Jolly Road, U11S Blue Bell, PA 19422-1904 CT : 2008 : Stock : Other Medicaid 800-872-3862 AMB# 064964 NAIC# 13174	NR-2	'05	...	...	...	...	...	...	...	...	...	...	...	...	...	...	...	...
		'06	...	...	...	...	...	...	...	...	...	...	...	...	...	...	...	...
		'07	...	...	...	...	...	...	...	...	...	...	...	...	...	...	...	...
		'08	5.7	...	...	94.3	8,798	...	92.5	...	7.5	3,763	5,901	5,901	5,475	-380	-247	-247
		'09	59.9	...	...	40.1	69,372	...	80.7	...	19.3	35,439	213,528	213,160	44,767	12,471	7,919	7,809
		Rating History: NR-2, 06/17/09																
AETNA DENTAL INC (A NJ CORP) Aetna Inc Patricia A. Farrell President 980 Jolly Road Blue Bell, PA 19422-1904 NJ : 1991 : Stock : Not Available Dental 800-872-3862 AMB# 064709 NAIC# 11183	A-	'05	2.6	...	...	97.4	1,912	...	96.4	...	3.6	1,590	12,212	12,212	-2,025	-617	-407	-407
		'06	2.2	...	...	97.8	2,339	...	99.4	...	0.6	2,029	13,264	13,264	571	-864	-562	-562
	Rating Outlook: Stable	'07	2.1	...	...	97.9	2,386	...	98.0	...	2.0	2,071	13,436	13,436	-579	117	75	75
		'08	1.6	...	...	98.4	3,108	...	...	...	100.0	2,817	13,026	13,026	585	95	520	520
		'09	1.8	...	...	98.2	3,424	...	...	...	100.0	3,098	12,004	12,004	241	307	278	278
	FSC III	**Rating History: A-, 06/17/09; A-, 06/16/08; A-, 06/11/07; A-, 01/20/06; A-, 03/04/05**																
AETNA DENTAL INC (A TX CORP) Aetna Inc Joel D. Hodge President & CEO 1 Prudential Circle, 4th Floor Sugar Land, TX 77478 TX : 1992 : Stock : Not Available Dental 800-872-3862 AMB# 064718 NAIC# 95910	A-	'05	32.4	...	...	67.6	15,497	...	58.9	...	41.1	10,744	73,422	73,367	1,368	18,664	12,144	12,054
		'06	38.4	...	...	61.6	13,123	...	47.3	...	52.7	7,856	71,430	71,376	-3,028	16,754	11,188	11,189
	Rating Outlook: Stable	'07	21.4	...	...	78.6	23,187	...	35.2	...	64.8	16,718	72,554	72,510	9,424	19,589	13,006	12,897
		'08	22.2	...	...	77.8	14,480	...	43.6	...	56.4	6,781	68,606	68,561	-10,158	16,693	12,819	13,071
		'09	43.0	...	...	57.0	14,299	...	39.0	...	61.0	7,612	62,282	62,236	-439	18,673	12,662	12,559
	FSC IV	**Rating History: A-, 06/17/09; A-, 06/16/08; A-, 06/11/07; A-, 01/20/06; A-, 03/04/05**																
AETNA DENTAL OF CA Aetna Inc Bryan J. Geremia President & CEO 2545 W. Hillcrest Drive Thousand Oaks, CA 91320 CA : 1993 : Stock : Broker Dental 925-948-4252 AMB# 064634	A-	'05	...	...	...	100.0	17,970	...	...	...	100.0	10,175	62,226	62,226	-3,326	26,505	16,571	16,571
		'06	...	...	...	100.0	16,633	...	...	...	100.0	8,941	59,248	59,248	1,184	24,670	14,312	14,312
	Rating Outlook: Stable	'07	...	...	...	100.0	26,251	...	...	...	100.0	13,453	56,784	56,784	3,973	22,155	13,894	13,894
		'08	...	...	...	100.0	20,564	...	...	...	100.0	14,723	54,464	54,464	-666	23,955	16,236	16,236
		'09	...	...	...	100.0	22,629	...	...	...	100.0	12,055	51,226	51,226	-2,282	21,639	13,470	13,470
	FSC V	**Rating History: A-, 06/17/09; A-, 06/16/08; A-, 06/11/07; A-, 01/20/06; A-, 03/04/05**																
AETNA HEALTH AND LIFE INS CO Aetna Inc Laurie A. Brubaker President 151 Farmington Avenue Hartford, CT 06156 CT : 1971 : Stock : Agency Group A&H, Group Life, Reins 860-273-0123 AMB# 008189 NAIC# 78700	NR-3	'05	82.9	8.4	1.0	7.7	1,394,186	0.2	92.6	...	7.2	167,723	...	254,079	126,412	-9,620	-4,518	-7,033
		'06	83.0	7.5	1.8	7.7	1,533,830	0.1	90.3	...	9.6	180,904	...	259,164	139,838	-21,436	17,183	18,991
		'07	82.5	8.8	1.5	7.2	1,581,600	0.1	93.2	...	6.7	208,530	...	304,374	38,781	16,113	22,018	16,912
		'08	81.6	9.5	1.3	7.6	1,604,314	0.1	95.4	...	4.5	161,285	...	358,963	51,770	3,996	17,360	-6,706
		'09	81.6	10.4	0.0	8.0	1,772,955	0.1	95.7	...	4.3	205,779	...	396,075	177,128	10,239	18,520	23,088
		Rating History: NR-3, 06/17/09; NR-3, 06/16/08; NR-3, 06/11/07; NR-3, 01/20/06; NR-3, 03/04/05																
AETNA HEALTH INC (A CO CORP) Aetna Inc Allan I. Greenberg President 980 Jolly Road Blue Bell, PA 19422-1904 CO : 1995 : Stock : Broker Group A&H 800-872-3862 AMB# 064071 NAIC# 95256	A-	'05	44.2	...	...	55.8	25,572	...	85.0	...	15.0	15,333	110,883	110,583	332	11,282	8,235	8,202
		'06	45.9	...	...	54.1	28,513	...	75.8	...	24.2	13,707	114,816	114,524	2,287	131	-444	-466
	Rating Outlook: Stable	'07	40.8	...	...	59.2	36,426	...	78.7	...	21.3	18,899	168,236	167,851	4,424	8,139	4,903	4,843
		'08	74.2	...	...	25.8	39,147	...	70.8	...	29.2	20,092	170,724	170,724	4,021	-266	4,166	4,225
		'09	83.5	...	...	16.5	46,201	...	85.6	...	14.4	27,039	173,428	173,428	9,079	8,455	6,147	6,223
	FSC VI	**Rating History: A-, 06/17/09; A-, 06/16/08; A-, 06/11/07; A-, 01/20/06; A-, 03/04/05**																
AETNA HEALTH INC (A CT CORP) Aetna Inc Michael W. Hudson President 980 Jolly Road Blue Bell, PA 19422-1904 CT : 1987 : Stock : Broker Group A&H 800-872-3862 AMB# 068698 NAIC# 95935	A	'05	35.4	...	...	64.6	34,135	...	69.7	...	30.3	16,860	147,041	147,041	9,612	3,543	2,740	2,745
		'06	62.5	...	...	37.5	40,531	...	61.7	...	38.3	20,260	165,996	165,996	3,443	-3,307	-2,076	-2,111
	Rating Outlook: Stable	'07	49.9	...	...	50.1	46,229	...	64.2	...	35.8	25,400	162,580	162,580	1,456	6,833	3,558	3,182
		'08	45.1	...	...	54.9	42,462	...	59.6	...	40.4	21,792	178,135	178,135	-4,686	5,859	8,299	6,557
		'09	64.2	...	...	35.8	59,634	...	71.8	...	28.2	27,651	245,338	245,338	17,234	-216	558	-204
	FSC VI	**Rating History: A, 06/17/09; A, 06/16/08; A, 06/11/07; A, 01/20/06; A, 03/04/05**																
AETNA HEALTH INC (A DE CORP) Aetna Inc Patrick R. Young President 980 Jolly Road Blue Bell, PA 19422-1904 DE : 1987 : Stock : Broker Group A&H 800-872-3862 AMB# 068697 NAIC# 95245	A-	'05	52.7	...	...	47.3	10,268	...	90.8	...	9.2	4,794	31,958	31,879	451	-3,877	-3,137	-3,137
		'06	39.7	...	...	60.3	10,069	...	67.8	...	32.2	6,829	30,791	30,721	283	58	585	599
	Rating Outlook: Stable	'07	18.6	...	...	81.4	10,651	...	65.5	...	34.5	7,111	29,426	29,371	-3,303	-1,850	-1,172	-1,158
		'08	10.9	...	...	89.1	18,016	...	24.2	...	75.8	8,360	29,518	29,518	11,076	1,447	1,618	1,618
		'09	31.9	...	...	68.1	21,683	...	29.5	...	70.5	12,532	43,725	43,725	4,899	5,831	3,975	3,970
	FSC V	**Rating History: A-, 06/17/09; A-, 06/16/08; A-, 06/11/07; A-, 01/20/06; A-, 03/04/05**																
AETNA HEALTH INC (A FL CORP) Aetna Inc Clarence C. King II President 980 Jolly Road Blue Bell, PA 19422-1904 FL : 1985 : Stock : Broker Group A&H 813-775-0000 AMB# 060120 NAIC# 95088	A	'05	90.6	...	...	9.4	424,766	...	87.9	...	12.1	231,624	1,891,483	1,886,717	-28,185	229,396	149,523	148,048
		'06	89.2	...	0.0	10.8	364,504	...	84.8	...	15.2	149,495	2,025,763	2,020,873	-53,354	94,531	62,407	61,570
	Rating Outlook: Stable	'07	85.5	...	0.0	14.5	409,047	...	83.5	...	16.5	188,430	1,992,270	1,987,645	38,476	168,113	102,614	100,135
		'08	86.2	...	0.0	13.8	391,508	...	90.4	...	9.6	186,992	2,062,921	2,062,921	-23,858	161,429	152,581	135,391
		'09	87.8	...	0.0	12.2	372,446	...	89.4	...	10.6	148,073	1,988,376	1,988,376	-11,477	44,183	40,412	43,866
	FSC VIII	**Rating History: A, 06/17/09; A, 06/16/08; A, 06/11/07; A, 01/20/06; A-, 03/04/05**																

2010 BEST'S KEY RATING GUIDE — LIFE/HEALTH EDITION
BEST'S PROFITABILITY, LEVERAGE AND LIQUIDITY TESTS 2005 – 2009

Data in U.S. Dollars

—	Profitability Tests							Leverage Tests						Liquidity Tests					
Un-Realized Capital Gains ($000)	Benefits Paid to NPW & Dep (%)	Comm. & Expenses to NPW & Dep (%)	NOG to Total Assets (%)	NOG to Total Rev (%)	Operating Return on Equity (%)	Net Yield (%)	Total Return (%)	Change in NPW & Dep (%)	NPW & Dep to Capital (X)	Capital & Surplus to Liabilities (%)	Surplus Relief (%)	Reins Leverage (%)	Change in Capital (%)	Quick Liquidity (%)	Current Liquidity (%)	Non-Invest Grade Bonds to Capital (%)	Delinq. & Foreclosed Mortgages to Capital (%)	Mort. & Credit Tenant Loans & R.E. to Capital (%)	Affiliated Invest to Capital (%)
...	...	...	...	...	...	...	...	...	...	...	...	...	...	...	...	...	...	...	...
...	...	...	...	...	...	...	...	...	...	...	...	...	...	...	...	...	...	...	...
...	...	...	...	...	...	...	...	...	...	...	...	...	...	...	...	...	...	...	...
...	97.8	9.1	...	-4.2	...	...	...	...	1.6	74.8	...	...	...	165.4	176.7	...	...	...	...
...	85.4	9.0	20.3	3.7	40.4	2.09	1.69	999.9	6.0	104.4	...	0.6	841.7	134.9	144.0	...	...	...	...
Principal Lines of Business: Medicaid (96.7%), CompHosp/Med (3.3%)													Principal States: CT (100.0%)						
...	01.8	13.7	17.8	3.3	22.7	4.00	4.00	0.4	7.7	491.7	...	...	-20.3	226.5	226.5	...	...	...	...
...	86.8	20.0	-26.5	-4.2	-31.1	6.91	6.91	8.6	6.5	653.7	...	...	27.6	601.3	601.3	...	...	...	...
...	82.2	17.7	3.2	0.6	3.7	16.21	16.21	1.3	6.5	658.2	...	...	2.1	214.7	225.0	...	...	...	...
...	83.9	15.7	18.9	4.0	21.3	5.73	5.73	-3.1	4.6	968.6	...	...	36.0	615.9	646.2	...	...	...	...
...	83.6	13.9	8.5	2.3	9.4	0.76	0.76	-7.8	3.9	949.6	...	...	10.0	653.7	701.7	...	...	...	...
Principal Lines of Business: Dental (100.0%)													Principal States: NJ (100.0%)						
...	57.2	18.0	73.3	16.4	116.6	3.82	3.08	3.4	6.8	226.1	...	...	6.4	394.2	418.9	...	...	...	...
...	58.8	18.7	78.2	15.5	120.3	5.77	5.78	-2.7	9.1	149.2	...	...	-26.9	254.3	284.4	...	...	...	...
...	53.9	20.0	71.6	17.8	105.9	4.68	3.98	1.6	4.3	258.5	...	...	112.8	413.0	484.6	...	...	...	...
...	58.0	18.7	68.1	18.5	109.1	5.20	6.87	-5.4	10.1	88.1	...	...	-59.4	150.5	186.7	...	...	...	...
...	54.6	15.8	88.0	20.3	176.0	2.71	1.68	-9.2	8.2	113.8	...	...	12.3	137.7	164.1	...	...	...	...
Principal Lines of Business: Dental (100.0%)													Principal States: TX (85.5%), NC (8.4%), MD (4.7%)						
...	45.5	12.9	87.8	26.4	151.8	3.01	3.01	6.8	6.1	130.5	...	...	-12.8	149.9	149.9	...	...	...	...
...	45.9	13.6	82.7	23.9	149.7	2.74	2.74	-4.8	6.6	116.2	...	...	-12.1	166.3	166.3	...	...	...	...
...	47.8	14.4	64.8	24.2	124.1	1.59	1.59	-4.2	4.2	105.1	...	...	50.5	131.2	131.2	...	...	...	...
...	45.9	12.1	69.4	29.2	115.2	0.79	0.79	-4.1	3.7	252.1	...	...	9.4	178.3	178.3	...	...	...	...
...	48.9	9.6	62.4	26.1	100.6	0.49	0.49	-5.9	4.2	114.0	...	...	-18.1	67.5	67.5	...	...	...	...
Principal Lines of Business: Dental (100.0%)																			
5	82.4	23.0	-0.3	-1.4	-3.1	5.81	5.74	34.3	1.4	15.0	...	...	31.6	63.1	73.1	38.2	...	64.6	35.8
63	87.3	19.5	1.2	5.0	9.9	5.59	5.85	2.0	1.3	14.9	...	...	8.9	63.2	73.4	45.5	...	58.1	29.5
-115	80.5	22.0	1.4	5.7	11.3	5.41	5.18	17.4	1.4	16.1	...	...	10.6	64.5	75.0	36.9	...	63.3	8.1
143	70.1	22.4	1.1	4.0	9.4	4.88	3.35	17.9	2.2	11.5	...	...	-24.6	60.8	70.6	38.3	...	91.8	24.6
-221	69.3	18.7	1.1	3.9	10.1	5.41	5.51	10.3	1.9	13.7	...	...	29.0	62.0	70.9	56.7	3.1	86.1	20.8
Principal Lines of Business: GrpA&H (100.0%)																			
...	79.5	13.5	33.2	7.4	69.8	4.51	4.36	6.9	7.2	149.8	...	...	85.8	250.2	283.8	...	...	...	...
...	84.7	14.6	-1.6	-0.4	-3.1	4.59	4.50	3.6	8.4	92.6	...	5.0	-10.6	186.1	212.1	...	...	...	...
...	85.2	11.4	15.1	2.9	30.1	5.54	5.32	46.6	8.9	107.8	...	0.0	37.9	194.3	217.3	...	...	...	...
...	89.1	12.1	11.0	2.4	21.4	4.25	4.44	1.7	8.5	105.4	...	...	6.3	156.0	170.2	...	...	...	...
-6	83.4	12.1	14.4	3.5	26.1	4.21	4.40	1.6	6.4	141.1	...	...	34.6	191.1	207.4	3.4	...	...	...
Principal Lines of Business: CompHosp/Med (97.6%), Medicare (2.3%), FEHBP (0.1%)													Principal States: CO (100.0%)						
...	83.4	15.4	9.2	1.8	20.3	4.87	4.89	38.3	8.7	97.6	...	...	66.9	171.2	220.7	...	...	...	...
...	85.8	17.3	-5.6	-1.2	-11.2	5.66	5.55	12.9	8.2	99.9	...	...	20.2	164.0	179.9	...	...	...	...
...	83.3	13.5	8.2	2.2	15.6	7.16	6.06	-2.1	6.4	121.9	...	...	25.4	202.5	212.9	...	...	...	...
...	83.4	14.8	18.7	4.6	35.2	7.38	2.20	9.6	8.2	105.4	...	...	-14.2	133.2	164.0	...	...	...	...
-6	87.6	13.0	1.1	0.2	2.3	5.14	3.21	37.7	8.9	86.5	...	...	26.9	131.8	152.0	3.5	...	...	...
Principal Lines of Business: CompHosp/Med (89.5%), Medicare (8.8%), FEHBP (1.7%)													Principal States: CT (100.0%)						
...	95.5	12.6	-32.3	-9.7	-59.0	5.80	5.80	8.4	6.6	87.6	...	...	-18.0	148.9	163.5	...	...	...	...
...	90.8	15.3	5.8	1.9	10.1	5.47	5.65	-3.6	4.5	210.7	...	1.8	42.5	265.0	318.7	...	...	...	...
...	96.8	11.3	-11.3	-3.9	-16.8	5.43	5.66	-4.4	4.1	200.9	...	...	4.1	140.1	176.5	...	...	...	...
...	85.5	11.4	11.3	5.4	20.9	5.37	5.37	0.5	3.5	86.6	...	...	17.6	170.7	240.8	...	...	...	...
...	75.9	11.2	20.0	9.1	38.1	1.16	1.14	48.1	3.5	136.9	...	...	49.9	240.3	308.4	...	...	...	...
Principal Lines of Business: CompHosp/Med (72.7%), Medicare (24.1%), FEHBP (3.2%)													Principal States: DE (100.0%)						
-212	75.3	14.2	34.3	7.8	65.4	5.07	4.67	12.4	8.1	119.9	...	...	2.7	149.4	173.8	1.9	...	...	...
221	80.4	15.4	15.8	3.1	32.7	5.49	5.33	7.1	13.5	69.5	...	...	-35.5	125.4	142.4	...	...	...	...
22	80.7	11.5	26.5	5.1	60.7	5.16	4.49	-1.6	10.5	85.4	...	...	26.0	138.9	159.1	0.4	...	...	...
-72	81.7	11.5	38.1	7.3	81.3	5.39	0.84	3.8	11.0	91.4	...	...	-0.8	135.6	156.2	0.4	...	...	...
42	86.8	11.8	10.6	2.0	24.1	5.11	6.10	-3.6	13.4	66.0	...	...	-20.8	119.3	137.2	0.8	...	...	...
Principal Lines of Business: CompHosp/Med (98.6%), Medicare (1.4%)													Principal States: FL (100.0%)						

Data in U.S. Dollars

COMPANY NAME Ultimate Parent Association Principal Officer Mailing Address Dom. : Began Bus. : Struct. : Mktg. Specialty Phone # AMB# NAIC#	Best's Financial Strength Rating FSC	Data Year	Balance Sheet Bonds (%)	Mort. Loans & R.E. (%)	Com & Pref. Stock (%)	All Other Assets (%)	Total Assets ($000)	Life Reserves (%)	Health Reserves %)	Ann Res. & Dep. Liabilities (%)	All Other Liabilities (%)	Capital & Surplus ($000)	Operations Direct Premiums Written ($000)	Net Premiums Written & Deposits ($000)	Operating Cash Flow ($000)	NOG Before Taxes ($000)	NOG After Taxes ($000)	Net Income ($000)
AETNA HEALTH INC (A GA CORP) Aetna Inc Clarence C. King II President 980 Jolly Road Blue Bell, PA 19422-1904 GA : 1986 : Stock : Broker Group A&H 800-872-3862	**A**	'05	68.8	...	...	31.2	69,802	...	81.3	...	18.7	22,775	272,861	272,861	-6,836	3,751	1,198	1,190
		'06	50.9	...	...	49.1	86,434	...	58.0	...	42.0	31,670	298,713	298,713	17,031	12,975	9,404	9,167
	Rating Outlook: Stable	'07	62.2	...	...	37.8	82,896	...	75.8	...	24.2	47,734	304,296	304,296	-7,461	34,707	22,328	22,118
		'08	48.3	...	...	51.7	111,327	...	49.1	...	50.9	56,769	337,075	337,075	24,980	30,858	27,331	26,715
		'09	67.5	...	...	32.5	87,447	...	63.5	...	36.5	38,029	359,173	359,173	-24,628	14,348	11,306	11,270
AMB# 068701 NAIC# 95094	**FSC VI**	**Rating History: A, 06/17/09; A-, 06/16/08; A-, 06/11/07; A-, 01/20/06; A-, 03/04/05**																
AETNA HEALTH INC (A ME CORP) Aetna Inc Michael W. Hudson President 980 Jolly Road Blue Bell, PA 19422-1904 ME : 1996 : Stock : Broker Group A&H 800-872-3862	**A-**	'05	59.9	...	...	40.1	38,222	...	83.6	...	16.4	21,075	175,108	174,723	-4,702	21,298	14,541	14,518
		'06	71.6	...	...	28.4	45,818	...	73.4	...	26.6	27,218	175,646	175,273	7,588	8,420	6,289	6,283
	Rating Outlook: Stable	'07	74.5	...	...	25.5	46,142	...	76.6	...	23.4	30,505	159,359	159,046	-890	10,694	7,026	6,479
		'08	60.1	...	...	39.9	46,884	...	45.6	...	54.4	20,551	152,271	152,271	-1,336	7,061	9,251	8,341
		'09	66.7	...	...	33.3	32,394	...	81.7	...	18.3	19,376	133,169	133,169	-14,791	4,512	4,210	3,892
AMB# 064155 NAIC# 95517	**FSC V**	**Rating History: A-, 06/17/09; A-, 06/16/08; A-, 06/11/07; A-, 01/20/06; A-, 03/04/05**																
AETNA HEALTH INC (A MI CORP) Aetna Inc Allan I. Greenberg President 28588 Northwestern Highway Southfield, MI 48034 MI : 1998 : Stock : Broker Group A&H 248-208-8600	**A-**	'05	17.3	...	...	82.7	6,314	...	45.3	...	54.7	4,416	7,857	7,835	-1,510	394	320	320
		'06	14.1	...	...	85.9	7,762	...	25.4	...	74.6	4,806	6,144	6,129	1,309	603	340	340
	Rating Outlook: Stable	'07	17.1	...	...	82.9	6,416	...	21.3	...	78.7	4,974	3,529	3,521	-1,097	234	249	249
		'08	28.5	...	...	71.5	3,851	...	4.2	...	95.8	3,662	-20	-20	-2,539	268	263	263
		'09	29.5	...	...	70.5	3,714	...	32.1	...	67.9	3,708	-6	-6	-183	67	39	39
AMB# 064366 NAIC# 95756	**FSC III**	**Rating History: A-, 06/17/09; A-, 06/16/08; A-, 06/11/07; A-, 01/20/06; A-, 03/04/05**																
AETNA HEALTH INC (A NJ CORP) Aetna Inc Patrick R. Young President 980 Jolly Road Blue Bell, PA 19422-1904 NJ : 1983 : Stock : Broker Group A&H 800-872-3862	**A**	'05	86.1	...	...	13.9	539,868	...	73.9	...	26.1	243,230	2,474,220	2,406,360	65,324	116,824	75,933	76,348
		'06	86.4	...	0.5	13.1	548,215	...	68.3	...	31.7	308,264	2,385,778	2,339,300	19,845	100,007	76,047	75,912
	Rating Outlook: Stable	'07	81.8	...	0.4	17.8	535,529	...	63.8	...	36.2	300,845	2,152,571	2,102,206	-21,285	140,790	88,114	86,097
		'08	73.4	...	0.4	26.3	523,246	...	57.7	...	42.3	273,845	2,042,281	2,004,820	-30,051	97,199	111,873	111,798
		'09	80.4	...	...	19.6	509,973	...	73.2	...	26.8	258,295	1,905,755	1,876,862	4,402	-24,548	-6,275	-5,231
AMB# 068695 NAIC# 95287	**FSC IX**	**Rating History: A, 06/17/09; A, 06/16/08; A, 06/11/07; A, 01/20/06; A, 03/04/05**																
AETNA HEALTH INC (A NY CORP) Aetna Inc Michael W. Hudson President 980 Jolly Road Blue Bell, PA 19422-1904 NY : 1986 : Stock : Broker Group A&H 800-872-3862	**A**	'05	75.9	...	...	24.1	354,381	...	69.0	...	31.0	197,195	1,033,699	1,033,699	-146,044	184,909	116,842	116,814
		'06	76.5	...	0.0	23.5	351,810	...	56.5	...	43.5	188,583	935,181	935,181	-10,733	89,960	61,678	61,444
	Rating Outlook: Stable	'07	72.7	...	0.0	27.2	323,136	...	50.6	...	49.4	187,730	873,848	873,848	-3,849	106,475	65,900	64,069
		'08	71.2	...	0.0	28.8	368,445	...	50.7	...	49.3	238,417	832,625	832,625	9,798	121,727	100,585	97,919
		'09	84.2	...	0.0	15.8	338,805	...	52.4	...	47.6	183,104	801,708	801,708	6,575	61,621	47,085	47,356
AMB# 068696 NAIC# 95234	**FSC VIII**	**Rating History: A, 06/17/09; A, 06/16/08; A, 06/11/07; A, 01/20/06; A, 03/04/05**																
AETNA HEALTH INC (A PA CORP) Aetna Inc Patrick R. Young President 980 Jolly Road Blue Bell, PA 19422 PA : 1981 : Stock : Broker Group A&H 800-872-3862	**A**	'05	65.5	...	...	34.5	771,458	...	69.1	...	30.9	339,269	3,378,259	3,371,346	-23,792	227,136	152,457	152,443
		'06	64.2	...	0.4	35.4	744,159	...	64.4	...	35.6	338,449	3,456,783	3,450,075	-29,632	196,086	138,585	137,346
	Rating Outlook: Stable	'07	61.9	...	1.4	36.7	873,262	...	61.4	...	38.6	455,044	3,635,481	3,629,158	106,753	309,639	199,236	195,937
		'08	62.4	...	0.9	36.7	847,945	...	61.8	...	38.2	408,911	3,885,670	3,885,356	-63,154	286,374	270,080	258,692
		'09	68.9	...	...	31.1	901,508	...	62.5	...	37.5	425,918	3,957,328	3,957,047	58,334	191,918	157,569	160,707
AMB# 068700 NAIC# 95109	**FSC IX**	**Rating History: A, 06/17/09; A, 06/16/08; A, 06/11/07; A, 01/20/06; A, 03/04/05**																
AETNA HEALTH INC (A TX CORP) Aetna Inc Clarence C. King II President 2777 Stemmons Freeway, Suite 400 Dallas, TX 75207 TX : 1987 : Stock : Broker Group A&H 214-200-8000	**A-**	'05	70.1	...	...	29.9	169,629	...	83.2	...	16.8	74,850	970,911	968,403	16,352	65,392	39,822	39,744
		'06	69.0	...	...	31.0	188,125	...	82.1	...	17.9	91,132	979,015	976,709	20,840	52,063	21,686	21,201
	Rating Outlook: Stable	'07	74.8	...	...	25.2	242,502	...	82.4	...	17.6	159,929	897,239	895,378	49,729	105,467	65,218	65,096
		'08	78.3	...	...	21.7	192,806	...	66.2	...	33.8	87,959	843,886	843,482	-52,955	50,875	52,310	45,305
		'09	71.8	...	...	28.2	202,262	...	74.2	...	25.8	93,407	849,783	849,783	3,965	24,045	18,296	18,942
AMB# 068913 NAIC# 95490	**FSC VII**	**Rating History: A-, 06/17/09; A-, 06/16/08; A-, 06/11/07; A-, 01/20/06; A-, 03/04/05**																
AETNA HEALTH INC (A WA CORP) Aetna Inc Phillip J. Haas President 980 Jolly Road Blue Bell, PA 19422-1904 WA : 1986 : Stock : Broker Group A&H 800-872-3862	**A-**	'05	40.3	...	...	59.7	16,250	...	75.7	...	24.3	7,691	37,410	37,410	-1,257	-4,486	-1,403	-1,307
		'06	36.7	...	...	63.3	16,135	...	74.2	...	25.8	10,404	36,152	36,152	-198	1,633	2,535	2,529
	Rating Outlook: Stable	'07	53.9	...	...	46.1	13,528	...	74.4	...	25.6	8,811	28,013	28,013	-2,822	1,536	2,301	2,279
		'08	61.8	...	...	38.2	11,386	...	67.9	...	32.1	7,243	21,097	21,097	-2,630	-1,261	1,411	1,389
		'09	76.0	...	...	24.0	7,627	...	68.0	...	32.0	7,070	5,920	5,920	-2,218	1,237	2,559	2,601
AMB# 068609 NAIC# 47060	**FSC IV**	**Rating History: A-, 06/17/09; A-, 06/16/08; A-, 06/11/07; A-, 01/20/06; A-, 03/04/05**																
AETNA HEALTH INSURANCE COMPANY Aetna Inc Patrick R. Young President 980 Jolly Road Blue Bell, PA 19422 PA : 1956 : Stock : Not Available Group A&H, Stop Loss 800-872-3862	**A-**	'05	47.8	...	...	52.2	110,326	...	48.6	...	51.4	69,113	141,874	224,881	-8,593	94,622	62,587	62,586
		'06	63.2	...	...	36.8	81,035	...	42.6	...	57.4	33,899	121,137	182,249	-21,384	19,076	12,295	12,736
	Rating Outlook: Stable	'07	68.3	...	...	31.7	80,278	...	53.6	...	46.4	41,045	117,084	180,978	7,149	31,005	20,252	19,482
		'08	62.2	...	...	37.8	66,224	...	73.4	...	26.6	40,062	136,434	174,344	-3,141	51,619	37,384	37,974
		'09	80.1	...	...	19.9	40,795	...	76.1	...	23.9	17,189	80,529	109,603	-26,355	1,114	1,499	1,913
AMB# 007443 NAIC# 72052	**FSC V**	**Rating History: A-, 06/17/09; A-, 06/16/08; A-, 06/11/07; A-, 01/20/06; A-, 03/04/05**																

2010 BEST'S KEY RATING GUIDE — LIFE/HEALTH EDITION
BEST'S PROFITABILITY, LEVERAGE AND LIQUIDITY TESTS 2005 – 2009
Data in U.S. Dollars

	Profitability Tests							Leverage Tests						Liquidity Tests					
Un-Realized Capital Gains ($000)	Benefits Paid to NPW & Dep (%)	Comm. & Expenses to NPW & Dep (%)	NOG to Total Assets (%)	NOG to Total Rev (%)	Operating Return on Equity (%)	Net Yield (%)	Total Return (%)	Change in NPW & Dep (%)	NPW & Dep to Capital (X)	Capital & Surplus to Liabilities (%)	Surplus Relief (%)	Reins Leverage (%)	Change in Capital (%)	Quick Liquidity (%)	Current Liquidity (%)	Non-Invest Grade Bonds to Capital (%)	Delinq. & Foreclosed Mortgages to Capital (%)	Mort. & Credit Tenant Loans & R.E. to Capital (%)	Affiliated Invest to Capital (%)
...	84.2	14.1	1.7	0.4	4.9	2.93	2.92	4.9	12.0	48.4	...	...	-12.2	106.7	116.1	...	...	...	...
...	82.2	15.3	12.0	3.1	34.5	3.35	2.99	9.5	9.4	57.8	...	...	39.1	138.2	145.6	...	...	...	...
...	78.7	11.4	26.4	7.3	56.2	3.84	3.55	1.9	6.4	135.8	...	...	50.7	175.9	186.6	...	...	...	...
...	79.5	12.4	28.1	8.0	52.3	3.22	2.44	10.8	5.9	104.1	...	...	18.9	208.1	215.9	...	...	...	...
...	84.7	12.3	11.4	3.1	23.9	2.81	2.76	6.6	9.4	77.0	...	...	-33.0	117.9	126.2	...	...	...	...
Principal Lines of Business: CompHosp/Med (79.7%), FEHBP (15.6%), Medicare (4.0%), Dental (0.8%)													Principal States: GA (100.0%)						
...	75.1	13.5	35.8	8.2	73.3	4.27	4.21	1.2	8.3	122.9	...	...	13.2	190.2	230.9	...	...	...	...
...	80.9	15.4	15.0	3.6	26.0	4.79	4.77	0.3	6.4	146.3	...	1.0	29.1	222.4	248.2	...	...	...	...
...	83.7	11.1	15.3	4.4	24.3	5.37	4.10	-9.3	5.2	195.1	...	0.2	12.1	261.1	284.3	...	...	...	...
...	84.0	12.5	19.9	6.0	36.2	5.74	3.59	-4.3	7.4	78.0	...	...	-32.6	142.2	169.6	...	...	...	...
...	85.6	12.0	10.6	3.1	21.1	4.40	3.48	-12.5	6.9	148.8	...	...	-5.7	195.6	211.9	...	...	...	...
Principal Lines of Business: CompHosp/Med (91.1%), Medicare (8.9%)													Principal States: ME (100.0%)						
...	86.5	14.2	4.4	4.0	7.5	3.43	3.43	-16.7	1.8	232.7	...	0.9	6.3	454.0	521.1	...	...	...	...
...	77.0	16.6	4.8	5.3	7.4	5.03	5.03	-21.8	1.3	162.6	...	...	8.8	349.7	403.0	...	...	...	...
...	97.0	19.7	3.5	6.1	5.1	8.49	8.49	-42.6	0.7	345.0	...	...	3.5	559.0	669.7	...	...	...	...
...	421.0	-99.9	5.1	125.2	6.1	4.61	4.61	-99.9	0.0	999.9	...	...	-26.4	999.9	999.9	...	...	...	...
...	477.4	-99.9	1.0	77.4	1.1	1.52	1.52	70.4	0.0	999.9	...	...	1.3	999.9	999.9	...	...	...	...
Principal Lines of Business: CompHosp/Med (100.0%)																			
-1	81.5	14.3	14.8	3.1	35.3	3.93	4.02	20.2	9.9	82.0	...	4.1	29.8	126.1	141.6	2.0	...	...	...
-18	80.8	15.8	14.0	3.2	27.6	4.29	4.26	-2.8	7.6	128.5	...	3.6	26.7	165.7	183.8	1.5	...	...	...
11	81.2	13.0	16.3	4.1	28.9	4.37	3.96	-10.1	7.0	128.2	...	3.0	-2.4	168.5	186.2	1.0	...	...	...
-446	82.8	13.2	21.1	5.5	38.9	3.92	3.81	-4.6	7.3	109.8	...	1.6	-9.0	137.2	162.2	1.9	...	...	...
332	89.5	12.7	-1.2	-0.3	-2.4	3.67	3.98	-6.4	7.3	102.6	...	1.9	-5.7	134.4	154.6	5.5	...	...	...
Principal Lines of Business: CompHosp/Med (70.0%), Medicare (23.6%), FEHBP (6.3%)													Principal States: NJ (100.0%)						
...	69.8	13.7	27.7	11.1	58.9	5.34	5.34	-14.9	5.2	125.5	...	...	-1.1	160.4	176.9	0.2	...	...	...
3	80.5	11.3	17.5	6.5	32.0	4.82	4.74	-9.5	5.0	115.5	...	...	-4.4	144.8	156.9	0.3	...	...	...
9	79.8	10.3	19.5	7.4	35.0	4.41	3.76	-6.6	4.7	138.6	...	...	-0.5	188.7	206.7	0.3	...	...	...
-12	77.6	9.7	29.1	11.9	47.2	4.71	3.76	-4.7	3.5	183.4	...	...	27.0	181.3	203.2	...	...	...	...
-2,296	85.2	8.7	13.3	5.8	22.3	4.58	3.88	-3.7	4.4	117.6	...	...	-23.2	148.9	160.6	0.5	...	...	...
Principal Lines of Business: CompHosp/Med (59.5%), Medicare (25.7%), FEHBP (14.8%)													Principal States: NY (100.0%)						
7	80.9	13.4	19.9	4.5	45.3	4.69	4.69	9.0	9.9	78.5	...	1.1	1.8	128.2	146.5	2.9	...	...	...
-254	80.5	14.1	18.3	4.0	40.9	5.21	4.96	2.3	10.2	83.4	...	1.0	-0.2	132.8	148.8	3.0	...	...	...
146	81.1	11.5	24.6	5.4	50.2	5.43	4.95	5.2	8.0	108.8	...	0.8	34.4	151.2	172.0	1.9	...	...	...
-3,083	81.6	11.8	31.4	6.9	62.5	5.23	3.08	7.1	9.5	93.1	...	...	-10.1	119.3	137.8	3.1	...	...	...
3,040	83.9	12.0	18.0	4.0	37.7	4.47	5.40	1.8	9.3	89.6	...	...	4.2	113.9	132.2	5.4	...	...	...
Principal Lines of Business: CompHosp/Med (63.7%), FEHBP (19.0%), Medicare (17.0%), Dental (0.3%)													Principal States: PA (47.3%), MD (11.0%), OH (10.2%), AZ (8.2%), VA (5.9%)						
-3	77.7	16.2	23.8	4.1	56.0	4.88	4.81	-3.3	12.9	79.0	...	6.8	11.3	126.6	138.2	0.1	...	...	...
3	78.1	17.2	12.1	2.2	26.1	4.55	4.23	0.9	10.7	94.0	...	2.0	21.8	160.1	170.1	...	...	...	...
...	76.4	12.9	30.3	7.2	52.0	5.48	5.41	-8.3	5.6	193.7	...	1.4	75.5	224.2	245.7	...	...	...	...
...	81.8	13.4	24.0	6.1	42.2	5.93	2.13	-5.8	9.6	83.9	...	...	-45.0	124.1	133.1	...	...	...	...
...	85.2	12.9	9.3	2.1	20.2	5.26	5.68	0.7	9.1	85.8	...	...	6.2	117.0	131.1	2.1	...	...	...
Principal Lines of Business: CompHosp/Med (68.9%), Medicaid (17.6%), FEHBP (7.2%), Medicare (6.4%)													Principal States: TX (100.0%)						
...	96.9	15.2	-8.1	-3.7	-14.3	4.04	4.71	-18.2	4.9	89.9	...	...	-35.4	225.2	238.8	...	...	...	...
...	83.4	14.9	15.7	6.9	28.0	5.20	5.15	-3.4	3.5	181.5	...	...	35.3	296.2	334.6	...	...	...	...
...	84.9	11.8	15.5	8.0	23.9	5.24	5.06	-22.5	3.2	186.8	...	...	-15.3	270.3	284.5	...	...	...	...
...	96.0	13.0	11.3	6.5	17.6	4.97	4.73	-24.7	2.9	174.8	...	...	-17.8	193.2	202.6	...	...	...	...
...	84.9	13.8	26.9	41.0	35.8	4.76	5.35	-71.9	0.8	999.9	...	...	-2.4	943.0	991.5	...	...	...	...
Principal Lines of Business: CompHosp/Med (98.4%), FEHBP (1.6%)													Principal States: WA (100.0%)						
...	47.3	13.1	58.5	27.1	90.3	4.60	4.60	5.7	3.3	167.7	...	...	-0.6	175.1	209.1	4.1	...	...	...
-232	78.0	13.4	12.8	6.6	23.9	5.08	5.39	-19.0	5.4	71.9	...	...	-51.0	100.5	112.3	9.4	...	...	...
232	74.5	10.1	25.1	11.0	54.0	5.07	4.21	-0.7	4.4	104.6	...	3.5	21.1	140.2	161.6	2.5	...	...	...
-17	57.3	14.9	51.0	21.1	92.2	4.96	5.86	-3.7	4.4	153.1	...	0.0	-2.4	214.3	258.9	2.5	...	...	...
-3	86.0	15.0	2.8	1.3	5.2	4.42	5.25	-37.1	6.4	72.8	...	0.8	-57.1	125.1	136.3	17.0	...	...	...
Principal Lines of Business: CompHosp/Med (99.8%), OtherHlth (0.2%)													Principal States: NJ (37.9%), PA (18.4%), TX (13.1%), GA (6.0%), DC (5.6%)						

Data in U.S. Dollars

COMPANY NAME Ultimate Parent Association Principal Officer Mailing Address Dom. : Began Bus. : Struct. : Mktg. Specialty Phone # AMB# NAIC#	Best's Financial Strength Rating FSC	Data Year	Balance Sheet Bonds (%)	Mort. Loans & R.E. (%)	Com & Pref. Stock (%)	All Other Assets (%)	Total Assets ($000)	Life Reserves (%)	Health Reserves %)	Ann Res. & Dep. Liabilities (%)	All Other Liabilities (%)	Capital & Surplus ($000)	Operations Direct Premiums Written ($000)	Net Premiums Written & Deposits ($000)	Operating Cash Flow ($000)	NOG Before Taxes ($000)	NOG After Taxes ($000)	Net Income ($000)
AETNA HEALTH INS CO OF NY Aetna Inc Michael W. Hudson President 980 Jolly Road Blue Bell, PA 19422-1904 NY : 1986 : Stock : Not Available Group A&H 800-872-3862	**A** Rating Outlook: Stable	'05	49.0	...	...	51.0	13,650	...	46.7	...	53.3	7,588	19,394	19,394	-10,075	7,160	4,728	4,855
		'06	26.2	...	...	73.8	14,492	...	23.6	...	76.4	6,388	15,297	15,297	2,357	1,144	705	818
		'07	42.8	...	...	57.2	9,754	...	75.9	...	24.1	7,131	13,787	13,787	-3,801	934	616	684
		'08	32.9	...	...	67.1	11,416	...	62.9	...	37.1	8,695	12,747	12,747	903	1,226	1,828	1,796
		'09	76.3	...	...	23.7	10,271	...	75.7	...	24.3	8,370	9,823	9,823	483	-615	-329	-330
AMB# 009541 NAIC# 84450	FSC XV	**Rating History: A g, 06/17/09; A g, 06/16/08; A g, 06/11/07; A g, 01/20/06; A g, 03/04/05**																
AETNA HEALTH OF CA Aetna Inc Curtis L. Terry President 2625 Shadelands Drive Walnut Creek, CA 94598 CA : 1981 : Stock : Broker Group A&H 925-948-4244	**A** Rating Outlook: Stable	'05	...	...	...	100.0	253,588	...	...	...	100.0	66,941	919,253	919,253	22,659	107,395	68,798	68,798
		'06	...	...	...	100.0	303,597	...	...	...	100.0	76,416	1,048,221	1,048,221	21,118	61,951	36,278	36,278
		'07	...	...	...	100.0	305,940	...	...	...	100.0	129,087	1,267,900	1,267,900	16,257	127,659	80,890	80,890
		'08	...	...	...	100.0	353,577	...	...	...	100.0	178,639	1,552,544	1,552,544	29,870	111,944	99,694	99,694
		'09	...	...	...	100.0	355,671	...	...	...	100.0	137,779	1,895,408	1,895,408	-4,495	58,529	48,169	48,169
AMB# 060119	FSC VIII	**Rating History: A, 06/17/09; A, 06/16/08; A, 06/11/07; A, 01/20/06; A, 03/04/05**																
AETNA HEALTH OF THE CAROLINAS Clarence C. King II President 980 Jolly Road Blue Bell, PA 19422-1904 NC : 1995 : Stock : Broker Group A&H 800-872-3862	**NR-5**	'05	29.1	...	...	70.9	12,616	...	87.7	...	12.3	7,626	40,334	40,234	-2,692	2,538	1,679	1,736
		'06	27.5	...	...	72.5	13,297	...	85.8	...	14.2	9,176	43,105	43,001	269	1,892	1,452	1,452
		'07	43.6	...	...	56.4	12,937	...	69.7	...	30.3	8,200	42,936	42,838	-1,212	-583	-313	-458
		'08	32.4	...	...	67.6	12,439	...	88.7	...	11.3	6,726	45,454	45,351	-1,257	-4,030	-2,138	-2,159
		'09	24.2	...	...	75.8	15,522	...	80.4	...	19.6	9,152	54,263	54,147	3,958	-2,444	-645	-652
AMB# 060134 NAIC# 95343		**Rating History: NR-5, 06/15/10; A-, 06/17/09; A-, 06/16/08; A-, 06/11/07; A-, 01/20/06**																
AETNA INSURANCE COMPANY OF CT Aetna Inc Joseph M. Zubretsky President 151 Farmington Avenue, RE2T Hartford, CT 06156 CT : 1990 : Stock : Agency Stop Loss, Ind A&H 860-273-0123	**A** Rating Outlook: Stable	'05	82.0	...	...	18.0	27,856	...	...	...	100.0	25,528	21,685	7,954	-3,644	5,840	3,946	3,931
		'06	67.2	...	...	32.8	27,208	...	...	...	100.0	25,004	8,489	489	839	604	437	381
		'07	80.0	...	...	20.0	18,985	...	...	...	100.0	17,678	8,492	492	-7,823	1,221	820	753
		'08	91.5	...	...	8.5	18,195	...	...	...	100.0	17,596	8,346	346	-952	1,329	974	168
		'09	60.1	...	...	39.9	22,862	...	...	...	100.0	17,130	14,499	6,499	1,185	-199	-421	-369
AMB# 011023 NAIC# 36153	FSC XV	**Rating History: A g, 06/17/09; A g, 06/16/08; A g, 06/11/07; A g, 01/20/06; A g, 03/04/05**																
AETNA LIFE & CASUALTY (BM) LTD Aetna Inc Martha R. Temple President 151 Farmington Avenue Hartford, CT 06156 BM : Stock : Not Available Life	**A-** Rating Outlook: Stable	'05	78.3	...	...	21.7	174,365	55.1	...	...	44.9	56,832	130,243	133,544	11,652	24,705	16,063	16,087
		'06	74.5	...	...	25.5	177,875	49.5	...	...	50.5	42,391	156,041	159,582	31,054	14,882	9,447	10,007
		'07	80.7	...	...	19.3	189,142	53.2	...	...	46.8	51,082	156,692	160,932	10,648	13,474	8,947	8,242
		'08	51.7	...	...	48.3	263,639	1.2	31.2	...	67.6	45,058	194,395	251,491	21,862	1,779	1,650	-1,443
		'09	48.3	...	...	51.7	370,173	1.0	28.4	...	70.5	89,070	263,352	371,239	54,555	-5,044	-3,888	-2,750
AMB# 077031	FSC VI	**Rating History: A-, 06/17/09; A-, 06/16/08; A-, 06/11/07; A-, 01/20/06; A-, 03/04/05**																
AETNA LIFE INS CO Aetna Inc Ronald A. Williams Chairman, President & CEO 151 Farmington Avenue, RT21 Hartford, CT 06156 CT : 1850 : Stock : Agency Ann, Group A&H, Group Life 860-273-0123	**A** Rating Outlook: Stable	'05	33.7	5.3	1.3	59.7	29,120,819	4.5	5.4	27.6	62.5	2,915,227	6,802,155	7,445,412	386,645	1,303,702	845,802	825,063
		'06	28.9	5.0	1.8	64.3	32,339,162	3.9	5.8	23.2	67.1	3,037,202	8,916,884	9,426,006	-452,973	1,500,083	994,132	981,016
		'07	28.1	4.6	1.5	65.7	33,471,046	3.4	6.6	21.9	68.1	3,239,164	11,097,076	11,522,274	25,134	1,708,956	1,194,588	1,163,187
		'08	46.9	8.4	2.1	42.5	20,880,604	5.7	12.9	36.9	44.5	3,743,547	14,176,252	14,326,199	494,812	1,611,559	1,079,060	951,199
		'09	50.6	7.7	0.2	41.5	22,490,327	4.9	14.0	34.6	46.5	4,858,175	16,318,877	16,025,905	1,117,895	1,416,000	916,521	882,619
AMB# 006006 NAIC# 60054	FSC XV	**Rating History: A g, 06/17/09; A g, 06/16/08; A g, 06/11/07; A g, 01/20/06; A g, 03/04/05**																
AF&L INSURANCE COMPANY AF&L Holdings, LLC Benedict J. Iacovetti CEO 165 Veterans Way, Suite 300 Warminster, PA 18974 PA : 1988 : Stock : Agency A&H, Ind A&H, LTC 215-918-0515	**D** Rating Outlook: Stable	'05	90.8	1.0	3.8	4.4	141,321	...	25.7	...	74.3	4,408	61,457	7,856	11,611	3,169	3,169	3,169
		'06	92.8	0.9	3.3	3.0	154,594	...	24.9	...	75.1	3,456	54,014	5,620	13,351	-1,419	-1,419	-1,419
		'07	93.8	0.9	2.8	2.6	162,813	...	24.4	...	75.6	1,599	48,425	3,933	9,565	-1,301	-1,301	-1,359
		'08	91.3	0.5	2.4	5.8	168,665	...	23.6	...	76.4	428	44,553	2,838	8,220	55	55	-177
		'09	95.1	0.9	1.8	2.2	173,561	...	7.6	...	92.4	923	39,683	-3,922	8,543	-4,738	-4,738	698
AMB# 011131 NAIC# 35963	FSC V	**Rating History: D g, 05/18/10; D g, 03/24/09; D g, 03/11/08; D g, 05/14/07; D g, 05/02/06**																
AGC LIFE INSURANCE COMPANY American International Group, Inc Mary Jane B. Fortin President & CEO 2727-A Allen Parkway Houston, TX 77019 MO : 1982 : Stock : Other Direct Reins 713-522-1111	**A** Rating Outlook: Negative	'05	3.4	0.0	96.5	0.1	10,476,967	1.8	...	1.0	97.2	7,932,524	1	335	130,496	679,487	744,712	744,712
		'06	3.2	0.0	96.7	0.1	10,958,615	1.2	...	0.7	98.1	7,353,472	2	3,039	50,539	762,607	815,800	815,792
		'07	2.8	0.0	93.1	4.1	12,330,227	0.9	...	0.5	98.6	7,743,406	1	2,702	23,335	1,203,619	1,256,307	1,257,733
		'08	2.9	0.0	86.3	10.8	11,339,434	0.6	...	...	99.4	5,901,925	1	1,484	879,747	-78,874	-10,803	-7,765
		'09	2.6	0.0	96.3	1.1	11,801,538	0.6	...	...	99.4	8,154,648	0	2,878	863,119	-233,698	-162,823	-120,797
AMB# 009199 NAIC# 97780	FSC XV	**Rating History: A, 12/16/09; A, 11/10/08; A gu, 09/15/08; A+ g, 06/17/08; A++g, 05/28/08**																
AGL LIFE ASSURANCE COMPANY Phoenix Companies Inc John K. Hillman President & CEO One American Row Hartford, CT 06115 PA : 1960 : Stock : Broker Var ann, Var life 484-530-4800	**B+ u** Under Review Implication: Developing	'05	0.3	...	...	99.7	2,814,897	0.9	...	...	99.1	11,264	821,358	816,635	1,331	-462	373	373
		'06	0.2	...	...	99.8	4,101,160	0.6	...	...	99.4	11,429	1,054,542	1,049,593	6,132	7,255	918	918
		'07	0.1	...	...	99.9	5,091,051	0.7	...	...	99.3	11,382	459,813	461,453	7,640	1,984	-4,331	-4,331
		'08	0.2	...	...	99.8	4,143,050	1.4	...	...	98.6	13,762	303,501	296,450	19,202	4,242	1,901	2,054
		'09	0.2	...	...	99.8	3,776,960	3.0	...	...	97.0	21,212	161,581	153,541	18,511	290	440	441
AMB# 007142 NAIC# 60232	FSC X	**Rating History: B+ u, 01/13/10; B++g, 03/10/09; A g, 01/15/09; A g, 11/14/08; A g, 02/08/08**																

BEST'S PROFITABILITY, LEVERAGE AND LIQUIDITY TESTS 2005 – 2009

Data in U.S. Dollars

	Profitability Tests							Leverage Tests						Liquidity Tests						
Un-Realized Capital Gains ($000)	Benefits Paid to NPW & Dep (%)	Comm. & Expenses to NPW & Dep (%)	NOG to Total Assets (%)	NOG to Total Rev (%)	Operating Return on Equity (%)	Net Yield (%)	Total Return (%)	Change in NPW & Dep (%)	NPW & Dep to Capital (X)	Capital & Surplus to Liabilities (%)	Surplus Relief (%)	Reins Leverage (%)	Change in Capital (%)	Quick Liquidity (%)	Current Liquidity (%)	Non-Invest Grade Bonds to Capital (%)	Delinq. & Foreclosed Mortgages to Capital (%)	Mort. & Credit Tenant Loans & R.E. to Capital (%)	Affiliated Invest to Capital (%)
0	54.4	13.9	26.3	23.2	52.1	6.70	7.53	-33.1	2.6	125.2	...	...	-28.2	143.4	174.1	21.2	...	...	...
2	78.2	18.4	5.0	4.4	10.1	6.46	7.47	-21.1	2.4	78.8	...	...	-15.8	175.2	211.4	19.5	...	...	...
...	85.5	12.3	5.1	4.3	9.1	5.75	6.40	-9.9	1.9	271.8	...	...	11.6	389.1	436.5	...	...	...	...
...	81.0	12.9	17.3	13.9	23.1	4.50	4.15	-7.5	1.5	319.5	...	...	21.9	365.2	449.7	...	...	...	...
...	96.4	12.6	-3.0	-3.3	-3.9	2.84	2.82	-22.9	1.2	440.3	...	...	-3.7	431.0	492.9	...	...	...	...
	Principal Lines of Business: CompHosp/Med (100.0%)													Principal States: NY (100.0%)					
...	80.2	10.0	27.3	7.3	103.3	5.89	5.89	2.4	13.7	35.9	...	...	0.9	121.5	121.5	...	...	...	...
...	83.6	12.1	13.0	3.4	50.6	5.07	5.07	14.0	13.7	33.6	...	...	14.2	112.6	112.6	...	...	...	...
...	82.4	8.8	26.5	6.3	78.7	4.77	4.77	21.0	9.8	73.0	...	...	68.9	19.3	19.3	...	...	...	...
...	83.8	9.8	30.2	6.4	64.8	5.40	5.40	22.5	8.7	102.1	...	...	38.4	25.5	25.5	...	...	...	...
...	88.4	9.7	13.6	2.5	30.4	4.73	4.73	22.1	13.8	63.2	...	...	-22.9	35.3	35.3	...	...	...	...
	Principal Lines of Business: CompHosp/Med (82.8%), Medicare (17.2%)																		
-31	81.4	13.5	12.0	4.1	19.8	3.72	3.92	-12.7	5.3	152.8	...	...	-18.6	357.7	372.9	12.4	...	...	...
-15	84.3	13.3	11.2	3.3	17.3	5.17	5.05	6.9	4.7	222.7	...	2.5	20.3	347.3	410.2	10.0	...	...	...
52	87.7	14.8	-2.4	-0.7	-3.6	5.04	4.23	-0.4	5.2	173.1	...	...	-10.6	267.4	300.6	...	...	...	...
...	91.5	14.5	-16.8	-4.7	-28.6	4.28	4.07	5.9	6.7	117.7	...	...	-18.0	193.6	231.3	...	...	...	...
...	94.3	13.9	-4.6	-1.2	-8.1	1.88	1.83	19.4	5.9	143.7	...	1.1	36.1	230.6	300.0	...	...	...	...
	Principal Lines of Business: CompHosp/Med (94.3%), FEHBP (5.7%)													Principal States: NC (100.0%)					
...	47.3	6.0	10.7	38.0	14.4	5.41	5.35	-77.1	0.3	999.9	1.2	53.8	-13.2	999.9	999.9	...	...	...	...
...	101.7	87.1	1.6	23.8	1.7	5.09	4.87	-93.9	0.0	999.9	1.2	32.0	-2.1	999.9	999.9	...	...	...	...
...	135.0	-60.9	3.6	43.2	3.8	6.53	6.23	0.7	0.0	999.9	1.8	45.3	-29.3	999.9	999.9	...	...	...	...
...	-54.5	27.2	5.2	63.1	5.5	6.74	2.36	-29.7	0.0	999.9	1.8	45.5	-0.5	999.9	999.9	3.5	...	...	...
...	31.3	14.1	-2.1	-13.8	-2.4	4.06	4.35	999.9	0.4	298.9	1.8	46.7	-2.6	342.8	378.2	...	...	...	...
														Principal States: TX (14.5%), AZ (7.4%), NJ (6.7%), PA (5.6%), IL (5.3%)					
-1,801	66.1	23.0	9.2	11.2	28.1	5.04	5.05	16.4	235.0	48.4	...	...	-1.5	132.5	116.2	...	...	...	...
-486	72.5	21.8	5.4	5.7	19.0	5.44	5.79	19.5	376.5	31.3	...	...	-25.4	121.8	97.8	...	...	...	...
-218	77.7	24.7	4.9	5.0	19.1	5.53	5.11	0.9	315.1	37.0	...	...	20.5	123.7	110.5	...	...	...	...
-3,311	68.1	30.1	0.7	0.7	3.4	4.72	3.08	56.3	558.2	20.6	...	...	-11.8	94.3	62.4	...	...	...	...
6,527	70.6	28.5	-1.2	-1.1	-5.8	3.16	3.60	47.6	416.8	31.7	...	...	97.7	111.2	63.6	...	...	...	...
17,194	81.5	5.7	3.0	10.9	31.5	5.89	6.20	26.8	2.2	28.8	2.0	74.8	17.2	62.3	74.8	24.4	0.3	46.0	28.2
197	81.5	6.5	3.2	10.2	33.4	5.76	6.05	26.6	2.8	30.2	1.7	73.1	2.7	60.0	72.8	19.4	0.2	47.2	26.3
-5,355	81.7	6.7	3.6	10.1	38.1	5.44	5.48	22.2	3.2	31.5	2.1	70.0	4.5	65.2	77.7	17.3	0.2	43.4	21.1
-2,988	82.9	7.7	4.0	7.4	30.9	4.52	3.70	24.3	3.6	34.8	2.4	62.4	10.5	65.8	77.5	15.8	0.1	44.7	17.9
-13,504	85.7	8.7	4.2	5.6	21.3	5.52	5.16	11.9	3.2	43.6	2.3	50.7	27.6	70.4	81.6	19.8	0.1	34.3	15.5
	Principal Lines of Business: GrpA&H (62.3%), IndA&H (29.2%), IndAnn (3.7%), GrpLife (3.5%), GrpAnn (1.1%)													Principal States: TX (10.6%), CA (10.1%), OH (9.9%), NY (9.1%), CT (6.3%)					
1,834	124.7	8.9	2.3	2.2	172.3	4.89	6.27	-45.1	1.7	3.4	446.9	999.9	874.7	68.6	76.5	16.2	...	30.1	114.5
-232	158.9	61.1	-1.0	-5.8	-36.1	5.02	4.91	-28.5	1.5	2.5	333.3	999.9	-17.7	66.0	74.3	23.4	...	36.6	133.2
-536	229.9	66.3	-0.8	-6.3	-51.5	5.15	4.81	-30.0	1.9	1.3	543.4	999.9	-46.6	64.7	73.2	42.0	...	68.5	223.3
-997	335.1	71.2	0.0	0.3	5.5	5.51	4.81	-27.9	3.7	0.5	999.9	999.9	-62.5	63.0	72.4	24.3	113.1	113.1	535.7
-1,051	-99.9	82.3	-2.8	-74.9	-99.9	6.00	8.62	-99.9	-0.2	0.5	643.7	999.9	999.9	72.1	83.2	...	...	6.5	12.8
	Principal Lines of Business: IndA&H (100.0%)													Principal States: FL (18.9%), PA (14.3%), TX (11.8%), OH (7.5%), IL (5.9%)					
-386,706	999.9	-99.9	7.3	109.9	9.3	6.97	3.19	-99.2	0.0	311.9	0.0	0.0	-1.2	1.7	7.9	0.0	...	0.0	131.2
-651,497	126.4	14.5	7.6	106.6	10.7	7.46	1.50	807.2	0.0	204.1	...	0.0	-7.3	1.2	5.5	...	...	0.0	148.1
-1,301,918	183.1	97.9	10.8	104.1	16.6	11.28	0.38	-11.1	0.0	168.9	...	0.0	5.3	0.7	4.1	...	...	0.0	152.0
-21,171,358	235.7	414.1	-0.1	14.6	-0.2	-0.69	-99.35	-45.1	0.0	108.6	...	0.0	-23.8	0.9	1.0	...	...	0.0	170.9
559,035	41.9	29.4	-1.4	67.8	-2.3	-2.21	3.46	93.9	0.0	225.1	...	0.0	38.4	3.5	3.5	0.0	...	0.0	142.8
	Principal Lines of Business: OrdLife (100.0%), GrpLife (0.0%)													Principal States: MO (100.0%)					
...	24.2	1.3	0.0	0.0	3.2	4.56	4.64	289.6	72.4	41.5	0.2	68.4	-5.7	40.5	42.8	...	...	...	...
...	23.3	1.0	0.0	0.1	8.1	4.39	4.46	28.5	91.7	33.9	0.3	67.9	1.5	65.2	68.5	...	...	...	...
...	40.2	2.2	-0.1	-0.9	-38.0	4.41	4.42	-56.0	40.5	27.1	0.2	70.2	-0.4	48.7	51.5	...	...	...	...
...	201.3	3.7	0.0	0.6	15.1	4.75	5.01	-35.8	21.5	23.3	0.2	61.7	20.9	17.1	18.1	...	...	...	...
...	386.6	7.0	0.0	0.3	2.5	4.40	4.40	-48.2	7.2	27.6	0.2	113.1	54.0	13.2	13.9	...	...	...	...
	Principal Lines of Business: GrpAnn (72.5%), OrdLife (16.0%), IndAnn (11.5%)													Principal States: DE (23.4%), AK (14.4%), CO (8.0%), PA (7.9%), CA (7.7%)					

Data in U.S. Dollars

COMPANY NAME Ultimate Parent Association Principal Officer Mailing Address Dom. : Began Bus. : Struct. : Mktg. Specialty Phone # AMB# NAIC#	Best's Financial Strength Rating FSC	Data Year	Balance Sheet Bonds (%)	Mort. Loans & R.E. (%)	Com & Pref. Stock (%)	All Other Assets (%)	Total Assets ($000)	Life Reserves (%)	Health Reserves (%)	Ann Res. & Dep. Liabilities (%)	All Other Liabilities (%)	Capital & Surplus ($000)	Operations Direct Premiums Written ($000)	Net Premiums Written & Deposits ($000)	Operating Cash Flow ($000)	NOG Before Taxes ($000)	NOG After Taxes ($000)	Net Income ($000)
AIDS HEALTHCARE FOUNDATION Michael Weinstein President 6255 West Sunset Boulevard, 21st Floor Los Angeles, CA 90028 CA : 2006 : Non-Profit : Not Available Health 323-860-5200 AMB# 064843	NR-5	'05	...	22.4	...	77.6	39,928	...	...	...	100.0	12,400	...	...	...	2,956	2,956	2,956
		'06	...	...	...	...	...	...	...	...	...	...	...	...	...	...	...	...
		'07	...	23.9	...	76.1	48,672	...	...	...	100.0	17,616	39,635	39,635	3,405	5,505	5,505	5,505
		'08	...	16.8	...	83.2	60,524	...	...	...	100.0	32,555	52,604	52,604	11,443	15,217	15,217	15,217
		'09	...	16.3	...	83.7	66,761	...	...	...	100.0	34,893	42,022	42,022	-3,295	2,453	2,453	2,453
		Rating History: NR-5, 05/26/10; NR-5, 06/23/09; NR-5, 06/27/08; NR-5, 05/30/06																
ALABAMA LIFE REINSURANCE CO[1] Scott M. Phelps President 1550 McFarland Boulevard North Tuscaloosa, AL 35406-2211 AL : 2007 : Stock : Not Available 205-247-3404 AMB# 060674 NAIC# 13034	NR-1	'05	...	...	...	...	...	...	...	...	...	...	...	...	...	...	...	...
		'06	...	...	...	...	...	...	...	...	...	...	...	...	...	...	...	...
		'07	...	...	13.5	86.5	48,518	...	...	...	100.0	4,037	...	42,097	...	519	340	340
		'08	12.7	...	5.9	81.4	47,823	...	...	...	100.0	4,049	...	994	...	254	224	-343
		'09	22.9	...	3.7	73.3	46,109	...	...	...	100.0	4,730	...	1,422	...	33	33	-2,127
		Rating History: NR-1, 06/10/10; NR-5, 06/10/09; NR-1, 06/12/08																
ALAMEDA ALLIANCE FOR HEALTH Michael Mahoney Chairman & President 1240 South Loop Road Alameda, CA 94502 CA : 1996 : Non-Profit : Broker Health 510-747-4500 AMB# 064142	NR-5	'05	...	19.4	...	80.6	34,370	...	...	...	100.0	18,994	140,931	140,931	-10,165	-5,656	-5,656	-5,656
		'06	...	16.4	...	83.6	39,569	...	...	...	100.0	26,282	143,129	143,129	6,136	7,289	7,289	7,289
		'07	...	15.2	...	84.8	41,475	...	...	...	100.0	25,129	141,045	141,045	2,275	-1,154	-1,154	-1,154
		'08	...	...	...	...	...	...	...	...	...	...	...	...	...	...	...	...
		'09	...	13.3	...	86.7	44,952	...	...	...	100.0	17,707	187,378	187,378	-13,717	-3,841	-3,841	-3,841
		Rating History: NR-5, 03/24/10; NR-5, 03/11/08; NR-5, 04/03/07; NR-5, 04/07/06; NR-5, 04/07/05																
ALASKA VISION SERVICES INC Vision Service Plan James Robinson Lynch President & CEO 3333 Quality Drive Rancho Cordova, CA 95670 AK : 1965 : Other : Agency Group A&H 916-851-5000 AMB# 064484 NAIC# 47201	A Rating Outlook: Stable FSC IX	'05	59.0	...	...	41.0	3,383	...	50.7	...	49.3	2,962	2,684	2,684	392	467	467	467
		'06	36.8	...	...	63.2	4,076	...	42.9	...	57.1	3,676	2,718	2,718	549	712	712	712
		'07	33.2	...	...	66.8	4,962	...	37.8	...	62.2	4,508	3,101	3,101	952	832	832	832
		'08	60.8	...	...	39.2	5,931	...	11.1	...	88.9	4,680	3,379	3,379	917	994	122	122
		'09	37.9	...	...	62.1	6,901	...	5.3	...	94.7	5,308	3,532	3,532	892	1,013	654	654
		Rating History: A g, 02/09/10; A g, 11/24/08; A g, 11/30/07; A g, 10/12/06; A g, 11/10/05																
ALFA LIFE INS CORP Alfa Mutual Insurance Company Jerry A. Newby President P.O. Box 11000 Montgomery, AL 36191-0001 AL : 1955 : Stock : Direct Response ISWL, Term Life, Univ Life 334-288-3900 AMB# 006293 NAIC# 79049	A+ Rating Outlook: Negative FSC VIII	'05	80.9	...	6.9	12.2	975,448	92.4	0.2	3.8	3.6	177,189	118,916	114,655	75,737	27,424	18,553	22,696
		'06	77.5	...	7.1	15.4	1,050,768	92.6	0.2	3.5	3.7	202,198	126,128	121,079	79,883	29,559	21,412	27,564
		'07	70.2	...	7.3	22.5	1,100,150	93.6	0.2	3.4	2.8	210,814	130,180	124,647	49,077	28,600	12,232	10,332
		'08	67.7	...	0.8	31.5	1,073,397	94.9	0.2	3.4	1.5	148,059	136,498	129,885	-29,469	20,013	-1,342	-53,181
		'09	72.2	...	1.0	26.8	1,141,858	94.5	0.1	3.7	1.6	182,988	129,292	123,875	47,907	23,185	21,548	18,311
		Rating History: A+, 03/25/10; A+, 03/03/09; A+, 01/14/08; A+, 12/08/06; A+, 03/22/06																
ALL SAVERS INSURANCE CO UnitedHealth Group Inc Richard A. Collins Chairman & President 7440 Woodland Drive Indianapolis, IN 46278-1719 IN : 1986 : Stock : Other Direct Ind A&H, Ind Life 317-290-8100 AMB# 009556 NAIC# 82406	NR-3	'05	84.0	...	...	16.0	4,227	0.2	7.8	...	92.0	3,648	0	79	318	321	233	233
		'06	85.3	...	...	14.7	4,144	0.4	13.8	...	85.8	3,820	0	31	-70	168	127	127
		'07	69.4	...	...	30.6	4,180	0.4	38.0	...	61.6	3,900	0	44	38	141	69	69
		'08	67.7	...	...	32.3	4,269	0.4	38.0	...	61.6	4,009	0	45	40	186	153	153
		'09	67.7	...	...	32.3	4,249	0.5	13.3	...	86.2	4,063	0	9	48	72	54	54
		Rating History: NR-3, 06/15/09; NR-3, 01/29/08; NR-3, 11/21/07; NR-3, 11/16/06; NR-3, 08/17/06																
ALL SAVERS LIFE INS CO OF CA UnitedHealth Group Inc Richard A. Collins Chairman, President & CEO 7440 Woodland Drive Indianapolis, IN 46278-1719 CA : 1985 : Stock : Inactive Ordinary Life 317-297-4123 AMB# 060029 NAIC# 73130	NR-3	'05	82.3	...	...	17.7	10,877	...	...	...	100.0	10,491	...	...	507	569	360	360
		'06	71.2	...	...	28.8	11,429	...	...	...	100.0	10,810	...	...	624	578	311	311
		'07	14.3	...	...	85.7	11,458	...	...	...	100.0	11,269	...	...	169	530	417	417
		'08	14.0	...	...	86.0	11,589	...	...	...	100.0	11,446	...	...	142	267	180	180
		'09	13.8	...	...	86.2	11,656	...	...	...	100.0	11,526	...	...	72	102	73	73
		Rating History: NR-3, 06/15/09; NR-3, 01/29/08; NR-3, 11/21/07; NR-3, 11/16/06; NR-3, 08/17/06																
ALLEGIANCE LIFE INS CO Horace Mann Educators Corporation Louis G. Lower, II Chairman, President & CEO One Horace Mann Plaza Springfield, IL 62715 IL : 1957 : Stock : Career Agent Whole life 217-789-2500 AMB# 006324 NAIC# 62790	NR-3	'05	4.6	...	94.6	0.9	243,983	93.9	...	0.4	5.7	231,836	...	1,639	21,313	751	767	794
		'06	4.2	...	94.9	0.9	264,697	94.0	...	0.4	5.6	251,799	...	1,558	732	544	143	363
		'07	4.1	...	95.0	0.9	291,454	93.9	...	0.3	5.8	277,804	...	1,518	1,224	624	485	733
		'08	3.7	...	95.0	1.4	285,374	95.9	...	0.3	3.8	271,346	...	1,530	190	24,640	24,407	23,955
		'09	3.3	...	95.2	1.5	323,339	95.7	...	0.3	4.0	308,530	...	1,469	774	6,015	6,076	5,990
		Rating History: NR-3, 06/03/10; NR-3, 06/10/09; NR-3, 05/23/08; NR-3, 05/18/07; NR-3, 04/19/06																
ALLIANCE FOR COMMUNITY HEALTH[2] Molina Healthcare Inc Jerry Linder CEO 10123 Corporate Square Drive St. Louis, MO 63132 MO : 1996 : Stock : Broker Ind A&H 314-432-9300 AMB# 064179 NAIC# 95609	NR-5	'05	15.6	...	...	84.4	20,168	...	63.9	...	36.1	11,000	86,121	85,487	-1,351	778	468	461
		'06	4.0	...	...	96.0	41,600	...	32.1	...	67.9	25,614	124,470	124,237	10,683	13,973	9,401	9,401
		'07	4.3	...	...	95.7	38,412	...	73.0	...	27.0	22,627	173,451	173,085	-3,125	12,797	8,134	8,134
		'08	2.0	...	...	98.0	56,184	...	66.1	...	33.9	30,072	225,280	225,091	11,198	18,474	11,734	11,734
		'09	2.3	...	...	97.7	51,279	...	78.1	...	21.9	29,960	230,222	229,991	-1,232	15,186	10,523	10,523
		Rating History: NR-5, 04/15/10; NR-5, 08/26/09; B- pd, 08/11/08; B- pd, 10/11/07; C++pd, 09/05/06																

BEST'S PROFITABILITY, LEVERAGE AND LIQUIDITY TESTS 2005 – 2009

Data in U.S. Dollars

	Profitability Tests							Leverage Tests						Liquidity Tests					
Un-Realized Capital Gains ($000)	Benefits Paid to NPW & Dep (%)	Comm. & Expenses to NPW & Dep (%)	NOG to Total Assets (%)	NOG to Total Rev (%)	Operating Return on Equity (%)	Net Yield (%)	Total Return (%)	Change in NPW & Dep (%)	NPW & Dep to Capital (X)	Capital & Surplus to Liabilities (%)	Surplus Relief (%)	Reins Leverage (%)	Change in Capital (%)	Quick Liquidity (%)	Current Liquidity (%)	Non-Invest Grade Bonds to Capital (%)	Delinq. & Foreclosed Mortgages to Capital (%)	Mort. & Credit Tenant Loans & R.E. to Capital (%)	Affiliated Invest to Capital (%)
…	…	…	…	2.4	…	…	…	…	…	45.0	…	…	…	2.4	2.4	…	…	72.0	72.0
…	…	…	…	…	…	…	…	…	…	…	…	…	…	…	…	…	…	…	…
…	295.9	66.9	…	3.7	…	…	…	…	2.2	56.7	…	…	…	4.8	4.8	…	…	66.1	66.1
…	249.5	59.2	27.9	8.6	60.7	-3.14	-3.14	32.7	1.6	116.4	…	…	84.8	38.3	38.3	…	…	31.2	31.2
…	383.5	81.8	3.9	1.2	7.3	-1.77	-1.77	-20.1	1.2	109.5	…	…	7.2	13.6	13.6	…	…	31.3	31.3
Principal Lines of Business: Medicare (82.4%), Medicaid (17.3%), CompHosp/Med (0.3%)																			
…	…	…	…	…	…	…	…	…	…	…	…	…	…	…	…	…	…	…	…
…	…	…	…	…	…	…	…	…	…	…	…	…	…	…	…	…	…	…	…
-65	3.4	0.9	…	0.8	…	…	…	…	9.9	9.6	…	…	…	…	…	…	…	…	…
-1,751	655.8	126.5	0.5	3.2	5.5	…	…	-97.6	0.2	9.3	…	…	-4.7	…	…	…	…	…	…
679	304.0	65.0	0.1	0.8	0.7	…	…	43.0	0.3	11.4	…	…	16.4	…	…	…	…	…	…
Principal Lines of Business: OrdLife (100.0%)																			
…	95.5	9.6	-14.2	-4.0	-25.9	1.33	1.33	4.4	7.4	123.5	…	…	-22.9	139.5	139.5	…	…	35.1	35.1
…	86.9	9.3	19.7	5.0	32.2	2.29	2.29	1.6	5.4	197.8	…	…	38.4	206.8	206.8	…	…	24.6	24.6
…	92.1	10.4	-2.8	-0.8	-4.5	3.53	3.53	-1.5	5.6	153.7	…	…	-4.4	178.5	178.5	…	…	25.1	25.1
…	…	…	…	…	…	…	…	…	…	…	…	…	…	…	…	…	…	…	…
…	93.1	9.1	…	-2.0	…	…	…	…	10.6	65.0	…	…	…	56.9	56.9	…	…	33.8	33.8
Principal Lines of Business: Medicaid (85.7%), Medicare (7.4%), CompHosp/Med (6.8%)																			
…	83.5	2.1	14.9	16.9	17.1	3.00	3.00	32.2	0.9	704.7	…	…	18.8	941.7	941.7	…	…	…	…
…	72.7	6.8	19.1	24.7	21.4	4.44	4.44	1.3	0.7	919.6	…	…	24.1	999.9	999.9	…	…	…	…
…	73.5	6.1	18.4	25.1	20.3	5.00	5.00	14.1	0.7	992.8	…	…	22.6	999.9	999.9	…	…	…	…
…	70.2	5.1	2.2	3.4	2.7	2.99	2.99	9.0	0.7	373.9	…	…	3.8	493.0	524.0	…	…	…	…
…	70.2	4.9	10.2	17.6	13.1	1.99	1.99	4.5	0.7	333.3	…	…	13.4	564.6	585.0	…	…	…	…
Principal Lines of Business: Vision (100.0%)														Principal States: AK (100.0%)					
-2,343	43.7	25.7	2.0	11.3	10.9	5.58	5.77	4.8	0.6	23.9	0.0	4.9	9.4	90.8	101.2	9.0	…	0.2	0.6
-89	49.5	27.9	2.1	12.2	11.3	5.65	6.22	5.6	0.6	25.5	0.0	3.1	13.5	99.7	110.1	1.4	…	…	0.6
-4,888	49.6	32.4	1.1	6.7	5.9	5.63	4.96	2.9	0.6	25.0	0.0	3.9	3.2	106.1	116.3	2.7	…	…	0.5
533	51.7	34.3	-0.1	-0.7	-0.7	5.18	0.52	4.2	0.9	16.0	0.0	4.7	-32.6	110.1	118.9	3.9	…	…	0.6
1,105	53.6	37.0	1.9	12.5	13.0	4.66	4.47	-4.6	0.7	19.3	0.0	4.7	24.4	103.6	111.2	11.7	…	…	0.6
Principal Lines of Business: OrdLife (94.3%), IndAnn (4.3%), GrpAnn (0.6%), IndA&H (0.4%), GrpLife (0.4%)														Principal States: AL (88.8%), MS (5.6%), GA (5.1%)					
…	-90.3	99.7	5.7	72.2	6.6	5.27	6.14	-11.6	0.0	629.4	…	…	6.6	639.6	641.0	…	…	…	…
…	167.9	161.5	3.0	47.3	3.4	5.18	5.83	-60.9	0.0	999.9	…	…	4.7	999.9	999.9	…	…	…	…
…	38.9	121.8	1.7	25.0	1.8	5.30	5.85	42.5	0.0	999.9	…	…	2.1	999.9	999.9	…	…	…	…
…	74.3	279.4	3.6	57.4	3.9	4.84	5.38	2.3	0.0	999.9	…	0.1	2.8	999.9	999.9	…	…	…	…
…	320.2	999.9	1.3	26.7	1.3	4.19	4.68	-79.8	0.0	999.9	…	…	1.4	999.9	999.9	…	…	…	…
Principal Lines of Business: IndA&H (99.8%), OrdLife (0.2%)														Principal States: OH (97.5%)					
…	…	…	3.4	60.0	3.5	5.46	5.80	…	…	999.9	…	…	3.5	999.9	999.9	0.2	…	…	…
…	…	…	2.8	51.8	2.9	5.24	5.51	…	…	999.9	…	…	2.9	999.9	999.9	0.4	…	…	…
…	…	…	3.6	76.2	3.8	4.72	4.89	…	…	999.9	…	…	3.9	999.9	999.9	…	…	…	…
…	…	…	1.6	52.8	1.6	2.83	3.00	…	…	999.9	…	…	1.6	999.9	999.9	…	…	…	…
…	…	…	0.6	50.3	0.6	1.08	1.26	…	…	999.9	…	…	0.6	999.9	999.9	…	…	…	…
-20,388	56.4	43.7	0.3	31.8	0.3	0.30	-7.73	6.9	0.0	999.9	…	…	0.6	29.1	29.8	4.0	…	…	99.3
20,510	36.1	35.8	0.1	6.0	0.1	0.32	8.84	-4.9	0.0	999.9	…	…	8.6	34.8	35.9	3.7	…	…	99.5
25,314	44.8	26.0	0.2	20.4	0.2	0.31	9.97	-2.6	0.0	999.9	…	…	10.3	35.8	37.2	3.6	…	…	99.3
-6,142	37.7	27.2	8.5	92.8	8.9	9.01	6.74	0.8	0.0	999.9	…	…	-2.4	54.5	57.2	3.2	…	…	99.5
37,165	64.9	28.8	2.0	74.7	2.1	2.23	15.24	-4.0	0.0	999.9	…	…	13.7	59.4	62.1	2.9	…	…	99.5
Principal Lines of Business: OrdLife (100.0%)																			
…	90.6	9.4	2.2	0.5	3.8	3.45	3.39	3.3	7.8	120.0	…	1.0	-18.7	172.2	175.7	…	…	…	…
…	81.0	8.9	30.4	7.5	51.4	7.14	7.14	45.3	4.9	160.2	…	…	132.9	129.7	189.4	…	…	…	…
…	83.1	10.3	20.3	4.7	33.7	6.89	6.89	39.3	7.6	143.3	…	…	-11.7	239.5	253.7	…	…	…	…
…	80.7	11.5	24.8	5.2	44.5	3.91	3.91	30.0	7.5	115.2	…	…	32.9	246.5	261.1	…	…	…	…
…	81.8	11.7	19.6	4.6	35.1	0.62	0.62	2.2	7.7	140.5	…	…	-0.4	297.3	302.5	…	…	…	…
Principal Lines of Business: Medicaid (100.0%)														Principal States: MO (100.0%)					

Data in U.S. Dollars

COMPANY NAME Ultimate Parent Association Principal Officer Mailing Address Dom. : Began Bus. : Struct. : Mktg. Specialty Phone # AMB# NAIC#	Best's Financial Strength Rating FSC	Data Year	Balance Sheet Bonds (%)	Mort. Loans & R.E. (%)	Com & Pref. Stock (%)	All Other Assets (%)	Total Assets ($000)	Life Reserves (%)	Health Reserves %)	Ann Res. & Dep. Liabilities (%)	All Other Liabilities (%)	Capital & Surplus ($000)	Operations Direct Premiums Written ($000)	Net Premiums Written & Deposits ($000)	Operating Cash Flow ($000)	NOG Before Taxes ($000)	NOG After Taxes ($000)	Net Income ($000)
ALLIANCE HEALTH AND LIFE INS Henry Ford Health System Francine Parker President & CEO 2850 West Grand Boulevard Detroit, MI 48202 MI : 1996 : Stock : Not Available Group A&H 313-872-8100 AMB# 060220 NAIC# 60134	NR-5	'05	0.8	...	...	99.2	38,393	...	74.4	...	25.6	26,211	82,352	82,079	1,403	3,108	2,043	2,043
		'06	0.8	...	...	99.2	40,738	...	72.5	...	27.5	24,224	95,622	95,405	1,184	-2,654	-1,710	-1,710
		'07	0.8	...	...	99.2	39,985	...	70.1	...	29.9	21,819	105,335	105,164	-1,983	-2,813	-2,162	-2,162
		'08	0.9	...	...	99.1	32,142	...	71.5	...	28.5	13,975	119,142	118,980	-4,337	-2,473	-2,469	-2,870
		'09	0.8	...	4.4	94.9	39,367	...	66.7	...	33.3	20,523	121,726	121,589	5,388	1,688	1,688	1,688
		Rating History: NR-5, 03/24/10; NR-5, 04/09/09; NR-5, 04/17/08; NR-5, 04/20/07; NR-5, 04/20/06																
ALLIANT HEALTH PLANS INC[2] Health One Alliance, LLC Jeffrey D. Myers President 401 S. Wall Street, Suite 201 Calhoun, GA 30701 GA : 1998 : Stock : Not Available Health 706-629-8848 AMB# 064891 NAIC# 11256	NR-5	'05	...	...	...	...	...	...	...	...	...	...	...	...	...	...	...	...
		'06	58.3	...	...	41.7	19,356	...	62.4	...	37.6	13,134	37,222	36,789	3,523	2,697	2,518	2,518
		'07	58.6	...	...	41.4	21,204	...	52.3	...	47.7	14,619	39,320	38,874	2,186	2,028	1,557	1,557
		'08	84.6	...	...	15.4	20,821	...	42.9	...	57.1	16,111	39,578	39,274	-273	1,766	1,539	1,525
		'09	77.5	...	...	22.5	25,470	...	66.6	...	33.4	17,125	45,928	45,428	4,347	1,519	1,041	1,014
		Rating History: NR-5, 04/19/10; NR-5, 04/02/09; NR-5, 07/10/08; NR-5, 04/10/07																
ALLIANZ LIFE AND ANNUITY CO Allianz Societas Europaea Gary C. Bhojwani President & CEO 5701 Golden Hills Drive Minneapolis, MN 55416-1297 MN : 1984 : Stock : Broker Var ann 763-765-6500 AMB# 068026 NAIC# 69604	A Rating Outlook: Stable FSC V	'05	52.0	...	...	48.0	21,654	...	...	...	100.0	11,971	...	...	351	549	406	406
		'06	47.1	...	...	52.9	21,545	...	...	...	100.0	11,281	...	...	-364	1,023	699	699
		'07	47.8	...	...	52.2	20,421	...	...	1.8	98.2	11,271	...	...	1	20	-22	-22
		'08	67.7	...	...	32.3	16,301	...	...	7.5	92.5	11,422	...	...	310	276	114	114
		'09	71.1	...	...	28.9	16,918	...	...	19.3	80.7	10,765	...	...	63	-618	-677	-677
		Rating History: A, 02/12/10; A, 12/15/08; NR-2, 10/04/07; NR-5, 05/09/07; NR-5, 05/08/06																
ALLIANZ LIFE INS CO OF NY Allianz Societas Europaea Gary C. Bhojwani Chairman & CEO 5701 Golden Hills Drive Minneapolis, MN 55416-1297 NY : 1984 : Stock : Agency Group A&H, Group Life, Ind Ann 212-586-7733 AMB# 009417 NAIC# 64190	A Rating Outlook: Stable FSC XV	'05	35.1	...	0.2	64.7	703,015	0.6	1.8	29.9	67.7	53,321	191,134	191,531	88,763	4,437	2,992	3,031
		'06	33.5	...	0.0	66.5	849,132	0.6	0.5	29.8	69.2	62,528	156,329	154,585	37,343	1,911	444	3,160
		'07	33.0	...	0.0	66.9	874,371	0.8	0.5	30.7	68.0	50,337	163,156	159,567	825	765	2,485	2,172
		'08	43.8	...	0.0	56.2	881,465	0.4	0.6	47.0	52.0	29,201	237,690	235,840	127,270	-48,003	-44,838	-47,501
		'09	39.8	...	...	60.2	1,139,490	0.3	0.6	39.5	59.6	64,830	193,600	191,699	46,054	26,797	23,238	16,702
		Rating History: A g, 02/12/10; A g, 12/15/08; A g, 10/04/07; A g, 10/10/06; A g, 09/16/05																
ALLIANZ LIFE INS CO N AMERICA Allianz Societas Europaea Gary C. Bhojwani President & CEO P.O. Box 1344 Minneapolis, MN 55440-1344 MN : 1979 : Stock : Agency Ind Ann, LTC 763-765-6500 AMB# 006830 NAIC# 90611	A Rating Outlook: Stable FSC XV	'05	61.2	4.6	1.1	33.1	53,095,742	2.5	0.5	64.1	32.9	2,164,130	13,418,192	13,227,425	8,056,893	455,163	451,379	480,391
		'06	57.7	6.1	0.5	35.7	62,860,993	2.4	0.4	64.1	33.1	2,447,865	10,681,357	10,474,083	6,504,323	-200,642	-282,571	318,528
		'07	58.8	7.0	1.1	33.0	68,688,474	2.5	0.4	65.7	31.4	2,441,338	9,252,945	9,031,846	5,253,141	158,788	116,966	78,077
		'08	68.0	7.9	1.1	23.0	66,374,757	2.9	0.6	76.6	19.9	2,009,309	8,536,814	8,351,443	5,074,245	300,501	262,359	-895,825
		'09	64.7	7.8	0.8	26.6	75,453,862	2.6	0.7	73.5	23.3	3,923,209	8,764,602	8,476,157	4,736,706	293,833	317,251	-30,706
		Rating History: A g, 02/12/10; A g, 12/15/08; A g, 10/04/07; A g, 10/10/06; A g, 09/16/05																
ALLIED FINANCIAL INS CO[1] Jim C. Hodge President 6110 Pinemont, #215 Houston, TX 77092 TX : 1966 : Stock : Not Available 713-353-0400 AMB# 068226 NAIC# 82228	NR-1	'05	...	...	...	100.0	397	...	...	...	100.0	395	2	2	...	-7	5	5
		'06	...	...	...	100.0	401	...	...	...	100.0	398	2	2	...	3	3	3
		'07	...	...	...	100.0	403	...	...	...	100.0	399	2	2	...	1	1	1
		'08	...	...	...	100.0	393	...	...	...	100.0	390	2	2	...	-9	-9	-9
		'09	...	...	...	100.0	386	...	...	...	100.0	383	2	2	...	-7	-7	-7
		Rating History: NR-1, 06/10/10; NR-1, 06/12/09; NR-1, 06/12/08; NR-1, 06/08/07; NR-1, 06/07/06																
ALLSTATE ASSURANCE COMPANY Allstate Corporation James E. Hohmann President & CEO 3075 Sanders Foad, Suite H1A Northbrook, IL 60062-7127 IL : 1967 : Stock : Broker Ann, GIC's, Group pens 847-402-5000 AMB# 007289 NAIC# 70866	NR-3	'05	64.2	...	1.8	34.0	11,273	...	...	...	100.0	7,983	132	...	322	374	368	368
		'06	64.0	...	3.4	32.6	11,207	...	...	...	100.0	8,339	96	...	469	374	370	370
		'07	62.4	...	1.8	35.7	11,369	...	...	...	100.0	8,651	113	...	375	294	315	315
		'08	68.2	...	1.9	29.9	11,275	...	...	...	100.0	8,952	191	...	399	302	333	333
		'09	71.0	...	2.0	27.0	10,835	...	...	...	100.0	9,239	89	...	100	261	309	309
		Rating History: NR-3, 11/20/09; NR-3, 10/23/08; NR-3, 01/09/08; NR-3, 02/06/07; NR-3, 11/07/05																
ALLSTATE LIFE INS CO Allstate Corporation Matthew Winter President & CEO 3100 Sanders Road Northbrook, IL 60062-7154 IL : 1957 : Stock : Exclusive Agent Life, Ann 847-402-5000 AMB# 006027 NAIC# 60186	A+ Rating Outlook: Negative FSC XV	'05	59.9	8.0	1.1	30.9	76,596,470	10.9	0.1	57.4	31.6	3,664,680	4,719,476	12,145,255	2,804,418	452,908	310,004	247,036
		'06	57.8	8.1	3.1	31.0	79,028,222	11.2	0.1	56.2	32.5	3,361,031	5,043,593	8,805,481	1,569,703	432,941	180,747	237,018
		'07	56.5	9.6	4.0	29.8	77,027,929	12.1	0.1	57.7	30.0	2,622,499	2,957,273	7,808,405	-277,921	111,656	172,023	141,733
		'08	54.4	10.4	3.8	31.4	67,552,094	14.7	0.3	59.8	25.2	3,248,888	2,644,826	9,082,618	-4,265,982	-1,664,075	-1,089,156	-1,947,193
		'09	68.2	11.1	1.5	19.2	63,008,532	16.6	0.3	70.4	12.7	3,467,413	1,437,958	3,404,166	2,697,267	-411,720	-373	-895,895
		Rating History: A+ g, 11/20/09; A+ g, 10/23/08; A+ g, 01/09/08; A+ g, 02/06/07; A+ g, 11/07/05																
ALLSTATE LIFE INS CO OF NY Allstate Corporation John C. Pintozzi Vice President and CFO 100 Motor Parkway, Suite 132 Hauppauge, NY 11788-5107 NY : 1967 : Stock : Exclusive Agent Life, Ann, Struc Sett 516-451-5300 AMB# 007291 NAIC# 70874	A+ Rating Outlook: Negative FSC XV	'05	73.4	8.3	0.2	18.1	7,301,605	7.2	0.0	74.2	18.6	410,261	1,029,855	1,070,308	589,429	79,822	43,817	35,865
		'06	70.2	9.3	2.6	18.0	7,547,191	7.8	0.0	73.1	19.1	444,615	980,725	503,955	257,426	45,898	26,203	33,413
		'07	72.2	9.2	3.1	15.5	7,785,832	8.5	0.0	73.6	17.9	462,440	633,884	606,848	213,616	39,972	30,644	38,235
		'08	72.5	9.1	2.6	15.8	7,627,457	9.4	0.1	76.6	13.9	410,472	675,583	668,005	189,418	-40,230	-23,081	-18,878
		'09	73.4	6.7	1.7	18.2	7,875,950	10.1	0.1	73.9	15.9	506,286	354,671	330,161	-206,576	46	25,015	-8,618
		Rating History: A+ g, 11/20/09; A+ g, 10/23/08; A+ g, 01/09/08; A+ g, 02/06/07; A+ g, 11/07/05																

BEST'S PROFITABILITY, LEVERAGE AND LIQUIDITY TESTS 2005 – 2009

Data in U.S. Dollars

	Profitability Tests							Leverage Tests						Liquidity Tests					
Un-Realized Capital Gains ($000)	Benefits Paid to NPW & Dep (%)	Comm. & Expenses to NPW & Dep (%)	NOG to Total Assets (%)	NOG to Total Rev (%)	Operating Return on Equity (%)	Net Yield (%)	Total Return (%)	Change in NPW & Dep (%)	NPW & Dep to Capital (X)	Capital & Surplus to Liabilities (%)	Surplus Relief (%)	Reins Leverage (%)	Change in Capital (%)	Quick Liquidity (%)	Current Liquidity (%)	Non-Invest Grade Bonds to Capital (%)	Delinq. & Foreclosed Mortgages to Capital (%)	Mort. & Credit Tenant Loans & R.E. to Capital (%)	Affiliated Invest to Capital (%)
4	86.8	10.8	5.4	2.5	8.1	3.16	3.17	17.0	3.1	222.3	...	...	8.4	225.6	225.6	...	...	...	...
1	91.2	13.8	-4.3	-1.8	-6.8	5.57	5.58	16.2	3.9	154.5	...	...	-6.6	207.4	211.0	...	...	...	...
-2	92.0	12.3	-5.4	-2.0	-9.4	4.58	4.57	10.2	4.7	128.9	...	...	-9.0	194.1	199.1	...	...	...	...
-8	90.4	11.2	-6.8	-2.1	-13.8	-2.03	-3.30	13.1	8.2	82.5	...	...	-35.5	325.5	329.9	...	...	...	...
1	87.6	11.1	4.7	1.4	9.8	0.10	0.10	2.2	5.8	114.5	...	...	44.6	391.9	393.3	...	...	...	...
	Principal Lines of Business: GrpA&H (61.3%), IndA&H (38.7%)													Principal States: MI (100.0%)					
...	...	...	...	...	...	...	...	...	...	...	...	...	...	...	...	...	...	...	...
...	74.8	20.8	...	6.6	...	...	...	...	2.8	211.1	...	...	...	342.5	350.6	...	...	...	...
...	76.7	21.1	7.7	3.9	11.2	4.94	4.94	5.7	2.7	222.0	...	...	11.3	339.1	348.3	...	...	...	...
...	74.1	23.7	7.3	3.8	10.0	3.39	3.33	1.0	2.4	342.1	...	...	10.2	384.8	395.0	...	...	...	...
...	75.3	22.7	4.5	2.2	6.3	3.58	3.46	15.7	2.7	205.2	...	...	6.3	283.5	289.5	...	...	...	...
	Principal Lines of Business: CompHosp/Med (100.0%)													Principal States: GA (100.0%)					
...	...	...	1.8	71.2	3.4	4.59	4.76	...	...	999.9	...	...	3.4	999.9	999.9	...	...	...	...
...	...	...	3.2	42.6	6.0	4.96	5.13	...	...	999.9	...	...	-5.8	999.9	999.9	...	...	...	...
...	...	...	-0.1	-3.1	-0.2	5.50	5.65	...	...	999.9	...	...	-0.1	999.9	999.9	...	...	...	...
...	...	...	0.6	15.3	1.0	5.56	5.71	...	...	999.9	...	...	1.3	999.9	999.9	...	...	...	...
...	...	...	-4.1	-99.9	-6.1	5.11	5.26	...	...	667.8	...	...	-5.8	638.8	638.8	...	...	...	...
18	31.1	10.1	0.5	1.4	5.6	4.76	4.88	90.8	3.5	26.1	2.1	10.2	-0.7	95.2	105.4	1.0	...	...	...
-244	46.0	13.5	0.1	0.2	0.8	5.41	6.35	-19.3	2.4	26.8	1.6	22.6	17.3	89.8	102.3	...	...	...	...
...	89.0	14.3	0.3	1.3	4.4	5.58	5.50	3.2	3.1	20.5	1.3	12.6	-19.2	79.8	93.1	1.5	...	...	...
-68	29.7	9.2	-5.1	-16.8	-99.9	5.32	4.58	47.8	8.1	7.3	1.4	3.9	-43.1	80.4	92.6	6.3	...	...	...
68	31.1	10.4	2.3	10.2	49.4	5.60	4.20	-18.7	3.0	15.6	0.6	2.0	122.0	79.8	92.7	13.5	...	...	...
	Principal Lines of Business: IndAnn (98.0%), IndA&H (1.6%), OrdLife (0.2%), GrpLife (0.1%), GrpA&H (0.0%)													Principal States: NY (90.3%)					
-73,559	22.9	11.8	1.0	2.9	20.5	5.40	5.33	3.1	5.4	7.1	8.3	173.9	-2.4	66.7	76.7	10.0	...	99.1	47.8
-129,749	36.7	13.6	-0.5	-2.2	-12.3	5.68	6.92	-20.8	3.8	6.7	1.5	157.9	11.4	58.9	69.8	11.4	...	140.9	67.0
-170,665	56.7	16.0	0.2	1.0	4.8	5.51	5.07	-13.8	3.5	5.7	1.0	156.1	-4.0	57.8	69.0	19.2	...	183.6	73.4
-210,136	66.3	15.8	0.4	2.3	11.8	5.56	2.91	-7.5	4.0	4.0	1.5	190.4	-20.0	55.2	66.7	37.0	...	250.1	121.5
125,628	69.3	14.6	0.4	2.7	10.7	5.57	5.20	1.5	2.1	7.3	1.8	100.9	93.7	59.6	70.8	57.6	2.0	145.8	46.3
	Principal Lines of Business: IndAnn (98.5%), IndA&H (1.5%), GrpLife (0.0%), GrpAnn (0.0%), GrpA&H (0.0%)													Principal States: CA (11.0%), FL (9.8%), TX (6.8%), MI (5.3%), PA (5.0%)					
...	...	676.2	1.2	110.7	1.2	...	...	17.5	0.0	999.9	...	...	1.3	...	...	...	...	...	...
...	...	778.7	0.8	21.3	0.8	...	...	-4.5	0.0	999.9	...	...	0.8	...	...	...	...	...	...
...	...	508.1	0.2	7.7	0.2	...	...	20.9	0.0	999.9	...	...	0.2	...	...	...	...	...	...
...	...	818.9	-2.3	-99.9	-2.3	...	...	-5.1	0.0	999.9	...	...	-2.3	...	...	...	...	...	...
...	...	594.9	-1.8	-99.9	-1.9	...	...	-7.8	0.0	999.9	...	...	-1.8	...	...	...	...	...	...
	Principal Lines of Business: OrdLife (100.0%)																		
...	...	...	3.2	85.7	4.7	5.32	5.42	...	...	999.9	-0.1	999.9	4.8	999.9	999.9	...	...	...	...
...	...	...	3.3	79.4	4.5	5.41	5.53	...	...	999.9	0.1	999.9	4.6	999.9	999.9	...	...	...	...
...	...	...	2.8	65.7	3.7	5.36	5.48	...	...	999.9	0.1	999.9	3.8	999.9	999.9	...	...	...	...
...	...	...	2.9	72.8	3.8	4.51	4.84	...	...	948.2	0.1	999.9	3.5	999.9	999.9	...	...	...	...
...	...	...	2.8	-99.9	3.4	3.23	3.77	...	...	999.9	0.1	999.9	3.2	999.9	999.9	...	...	...	...
														Principal States: NJ (22.4%), OH (20.6%), IL (20.6%), TN (12.3%), NY (8.8%)					
8,221	62.6	11.0	0.4	2.8	8.5	5.65	5.31	-11.3	3.1	7.5	0.7	13.4	0.4	45.7	64.0	69.5	...	156.4	19.7
83,611	89.3	10.4	0.2	2.0	5.1	6.10	6.02	-27.5	2.3	7.0	7.7	43.6	-3.1	42.3	61.8	67.4	...	168.6	20.1
50,231	98.0	8.6	0.2	2.8	5.7	5.93	5.79	-11.3	2.4	5.8	5.8	53.1	-16.3	33.5	52.9	97.5	...	233.1	33.4
-365,894	74.7	8.3	-1.5	-18.3	-37.1	4.89	2.83	16.3	2.6	6.9	3.5	56.2	8.1	45.4	62.8	81.1	...	203.5	31.8
78,577	182.1	17.0	0.0	0.0	0.0	4.36	2.26	-62.5	1.0	6.5	1.5	69.3	0.6	42.0	58.8	101.2	...	201.5	39.3
	Principal Lines of Business: OrdLife (42.8%), IndAnn (42.6%), GrpAnn (11.4%), IndA&H (2.3%), GrpLife (0.8%)													Principal States: NE (10.4%), CA (9.9%), FL (9.7%), TX (6.8%), IL (6.2%)					
-1,014	51.4	10.1	0.6	3.2	11.4	6.29	6.17	-31.7	2.5	7.6	0.9	8.8	14.0	50.7	68.4	44.6	...	138.5	...
-614	131.7	18.1	0.4	3.3	6.1	6.13	6.24	-52.9	1.0	8.0	6.0	75.4	10.6	50.8	69.5	31.7	...	145.2	...
-3,591	96.2	13.0	0.4	3.5	6.8	6.21	6.23	20.4	1.2	8.0	3.3	67.3	4.2	44.9	63.5	36.0	...	142.2	...
-16,975	92.4	13.4	-0.3	-2.4	-5.3	6.08	5.77	10.1	1.5	6.8	2.8	84.8	-11.4	58.2	75.3	35.0	...	155.7	...
26,438	167.3	22.7	0.3	4.0	5.5	5.46	5.63	-50.6	0.6	8.4	1.0	80.4	22.8	60.8	77.2	44.4	...	96.7	1.5
	Principal Lines of Business: IndAnn (57.7%), OrdLife (38.1%), IndA&H (2.9%), GrpAnn (1.4%)													Principal States: NY (81.0%), NE (10.4%), FL (3.0%)					

Data in U.S. Dollars

COMPANY NAME Ultimate Parent Association Principal Officer Mailing Address Dom. : Began Bus. : Struct. : Mktg. Specialty Phone # AMB# NAIC#	Best's Financial Strength Rating FSC	Data Year	Balance Sheet: Bonds (%)	Mort. Loans & R.E. (%)	Com & Pref. Stock (%)	All Other Assets (%)	Total Assets ($000)	Life Reserves (%)	Health Reserves %)	Ann Res. & Dep. Liabilities (%)	All Other Liabilities (%)	Capital & Surplus ($000)	Operations: Direct Premiums Written ($000)	Net Premiums Written & Deposits ($000)	Operating Cash Flow ($000)	NOG Before Taxes ($000)	NOG After Taxes ($000)	Net Income ($000)
ALOHA CARE[2]	NR-5	'05	12.6	...	...	87.4	68,475	...	40.8	...	59.2	42,835	109,274	109,274	16,693	7,456	7,456	7,455
Dana Howeth President		'06	12.3	...	...	87.7	85,989	...	63.5	...	36.5	55,235	116,642	116,642	577	11,462	11,462	11,462
1357 Kapiolani Blvd., Suite 1250 Honolulu, HI 96814		'07	14.0	...	...	86.0	99,801	...	74.2	...	25.8	63,407	129,375	129,375	25,508	8,112	8,112	8,112
HI : 1994 : Non-Profit : Broker Ind A&H		'08	21.3	...	...	78.7	100,191	...	75.4	...	24.6	64,531	158,877	158,757	-1,002	1,117	1,117	1,109
808-973-1650		'09	21.0	...	...	79.0	103,452	...	78.2	...	21.8	66,755	183,620	183,506	-13,975	2,440	2,440	2,441
AMB# 064224 NAIC# 95853		**Rating History: NR-5, 04/21/10; NR-5, 08/26/09; B+ pd, 06/06/08; B+ pd, 06/12/07; B pd, 06/20/06**																
ALPHA DENTAL PROGRAMS INC Dentegra Group Inc	NR-2	'05	20.4	...	...	79.6	1,232	...	39.8	...	60.2	926	4,466	4,466	-164	46	46	46
Anthony S. Barth President		'06	19.7	...	...	80.3	1,272	...	47.1	...	52.9	912	5,243	5,243	-113	-14	-14	-14
12898 Towne Center Drive Cerritos, CA 90703		'07	31.0	...	...	69.0	1,708	...	53.4	...	46.6	927	6,644	6,644	402	15	15	15
TX : 1987 : Stock : Not Available Dental		'08	32.7	...	...	67.3	2,096	...	64.2	...	35.8	1,160	8,305	8,305	311	235	233	233
562-924-8311		'09	28.8	...	...	71.2	2,395	...	52.0	...	48.0	1,367	9,490	9,490	352	468	223	223
AMB# 064509 NAIC# 95163		**Rating History: NR-2, 04/08/10; NR-2, 03/18/09; NR-2, 03/24/08; NR-2, 02/13/07; NR-2, 12/21/05**																
ALTIUS HEALTH PLANS Coventry Health Care Inc	B++	'05	42.6	...	...	57.4	70,821	...	50.1	...	49.9	36,061	288,587	287,130	10,009	12,093	11,205	11,382
Todd D. Trettin President & CEO		'06	45.5	...	...	54.5	76,667	...	29.1	...	70.9	38,636	331,277	329,700	5,478	16,232	14,045	14,008
10421 S. Jordan Gateway, Suite 400 South Jordan, UT 84095	Rating Outlook: Stable	'07	65.3	...	...	34.7	91,666	...	37.3	...	62.7	45,026	372,098	370,401	17,125	21,085	15,187	15,173
UT : 1976 : Stock : Broker Group A&H, Ind A&H		'08	70.2	...	...	29.8	91,193	...	44.4	...	55.6	44,722	420,044	418,188	484	14,675	10,286	9,422
801-933-3500		'09	80.3	...	...	19.7	95,068	...	42.1	...	57.9	50,087	429,527	427,509	3,782	6,897	4,827	5,208
AMB# 068616 NAIC# 95407	FSC VII	**Rating History: B++, 02/12/10; B++, 11/19/08; B++, 10/30/07; B++, 07/11/07; B++, 10/27/06**																
ALTUS DENTAL INSURANCE COMPANY Delta Dental of Rhode Island	NR-5	'05	98.2	...	...	1.8	5,442	...	...	...	100.0	4,096	12,387	12,387	80	622	407	407
Joseph A. Nagle President		'06	83.8	...	...	16.2	6,367	...	46.3	...	53.7	4,804	16,094	16,094	759	161	108	108
10 Charles Street Providence, RI 02904		'07	79.7	...	...	20.3	6,066	...	29.1	...	70.9	3,700	17,597	17,597	-336	571	377	377
RI : 2001 : Stock : Broker Dental		'08	85.6	...	...	14.4	8,689	...	35.4	...	64.6	5,560	21,294	21,294	2,395	28	19	19
401-752-6000		'09	65.0	...	...	35.0	11,288	...	35.0	...	65.0	6,844	28,077	28,077	1,385	-521	-369	-369
AMB# 060349 NAIC# 52632		**Rating History: NR-5, 04/06/10; NR-5, 04/14/09; NR-5, 06/30/08; NR-5, 04/12/07; NR-5, 05/11/06**																
AMALGAMATED LIFE AND HEALTH Amalgamated Social Benefits Association	NR-5	'05	84.6	...	...	15.4	7,975	15.0	46.6	...	38.4	4,688	10,012	7,515	-14	1,401	1,401	1,401
Noel Beasley President		'06	85.5	...	...	14.5	7,038	17.0	69.9	...	13.1	4,176	9,138	6,733	-673	938	938	938
333 South Ashland Avenue Chicago, IL 60607		'07	83.5	...	...	16.5	7,110	14.0	56.8	...	29.2	3,983	8,761	6,354	59	771	771	771
IL : 1940 : Stock : Not Available Group A&H		'08	80.9	...	...	19.1	6,914	14.7	45.5	...	39.8	4,143	8,486	6,325	-169	950	950	950
212-539-5000		'09	84.1	...	...	15.9	6,990	12.5	38.0	...	49.6	3,868	8,116	5,877	72	660	660	660
AMB# 006030 NAIC# 60208		**Rating History: NR-5, 03/31/10; NR-5, 04/08/09; NR-5, 04/03/08; NR-5, 04/10/07; NR-5, 04/07/06**																
AMALGAMATED LIFE INS CO UNITE HERE National Retirement Fund	A	'05	82.1	...	...	17.9	51,768	41.4	2.3	...	56.3	22,932	27,211	33,154	-450	3,071	2,647	2,647
David Walsh President & CEO		'06	83.6	...	...	16.4	51,813	47.2	2.1	...	50.7	25,665	24,270	33,248	820	3,715	3,042	3,042
333 Westchester Avenue White Plains, NY 10604	Rating Outlook: Stable	'07	73.6	...	0.3	26.1	57,375	45.9	2.0	...	52.1	30,019	27,240	36,698	5,183	5,146	4,135	4,135
NY : 1944 : Stock : Direct Response Dis inc, Group Life, Trad Life		'08	68.3	...	0.7	31.0	62,441	42.0	3.7	...	54.3	30,861	29,311	38,093	3,787	3,213	2,556	2,126
914-367-5000		'09	69.0	...	0.1	30.8	65,764	43.8	7.4	...	48.7	33,536	30,015	44,462	2,272	2,819	2,516	2,482
AMB# 006031 NAIC# 60216	FSC VI	**Rating History: A, 05/20/10; A, 05/21/09; A, 04/29/08; A, 05/03/07; A, 05/09/06**																
AMBASSADOR LIFE INS CO	NR-5	'05	...	...	...	...	...	...	...	...	...	...	...	...	...	...	...	...
Jerry E. Finger President & Treasurer		'06	66.6	...	25.5	7.9	12,402	1.8	...	...	98.2	11,508	...	240	702	394	263	643
520 Post Oak Blvd., Suite 750 Houston, TX 77027-9409		'07	62.2	...	28.3	9.5	12,813	2.2	...	...	97.8	12,059	...	300	377	433	305	382
TX : 1980 : Stock : Not Available Reins		'08	67.3	...	20.8	12.0	11,573	3.9	...	...	96.1	11,132	...	300	244	493	367	106
713-621-7525		'09	69.5	...	20.7	9.9	11,960	4.0	...	...	96.0	11,419	...	300	-142	515	485	80
AMB# 009172 NAIC# 98248		**Rating History: NR-5, 04/22/10; NR-5, 04/20/09; NR-5, 04/08/08; NR-5, 05/08/07; NR-1, 06/07/06**																
AMEDEX INSURANCE CO (BERMUDA) British United Provident Association Ltd	NR-4	'05	4.6	...	...	95.4	15,980	35.5	...	59.2	5.4	2,144	...	3,432	84	133	133	133
Alfred D. Maltby President & CEO		'06	5.1	...	...	94.9	27,810	38.0	...	54.5	7.5	3,485	...	4,028	-84	-2,170	-2,170	-2,170
Armoury Building 1st Floor Hamilton HM12, Bermuda		'07	11.2	...	...	88.8	46,088	26.4	...	58.1	15.6	2,160	...	4,994	-2,362	-9,341	-9,341	-9,341
BM : Stock : Not Available Life		'08	23.2	...	...	76.8	51,071	28.5	...	60.9	10.7	2,072	...	4,704	-1,937	-15,878	-15,878	-15,878
		'09	...	...	...	...	...	...	...	...	...	...	...	...	...	...	...	...
AMB# 073172		**Rating History: NR-4, 07/23/09; B-, 07/23/09; B, 12/10/08; B++, 09/24/07; A-, 06/19/06**																
AMERICAN-AMICABLE LIFE INS TX Thoma Cressey Bravo Inc	A-	'05	74.4	1.1	12.7	11.8	300,066	53.2	...	44.2	2.6	52,558	45,595	72,838	26,511	8,765	7,899	7,797
S. Lanny Peavy President & CEO		'06	74.1	1.0	11.1	13.8	307,761	53.1	...	45.2	1.7	47,078	43,508	67,911	12,622	6,801	7,947	7,947
425 Austin Avenue Waco, TX 76701	Rating Outlook: Stable	'07	76.3	0.9	11.5	11.2	335,744	52.7	...	44.8	2.5	57,471	41,329	63,338	23,270	5,636	5,366	5,366
TX : 1981 : Stock : Agency Trad Life, Univ Life, ISWL		'08	78.4	0.9	10.9	9.8	353,383	52.4	...	43.8	3.8	57,678	39,401	59,373	19,897	5,371	4,762	4,762
254-297-2777		'09	77.2	0.8	11.4	10.6	374,417	52.2	...	43.2	4.6	57,697	43,332	62,448	13,523	26	577	338
AMB# 009122 NAIC# 68594	FSC VII	**Rating History: A- g, 03/02/10; B++g, 01/16/09; B++g, 01/17/08; B++g, 01/10/07; B++g, 02/13/06**																

BEST'S PROFITABILITY, LEVERAGE AND LIQUIDITY TESTS 2005 – 2009

Data in U.S. Dollars

	Profitability Tests							Leverage Tests						Liquidity Tests					
Un-Realized Capital Gains ($000)	Benefits Paid to NPW & Dep (%)	Comm. & Expenses to NPW & Dep (%)	NOG to Total Assets (%)	NOG to Total Rev (%)	Operating Return on Equity (%)	Net Yield (%)	Total Return (%)	Change in NPW & Dep (%)	NPW & Dep to Capital (X)	Capital & Surplus to Liabilities (%)	Surplus Relief (%)	Reins Leverage (%)	Change in Capital (%)	Quick Liquidity (%)	Current Liquidity (%)	Non-Invest Grade Bonds to Capital (%)	Delinq. & Foreclosed Mortgages to Capital (%)	Mort. & Credit Tenant Loans & R.E. to Capital (%)	Affiliated Invest to Capital (%)
...	83.7	9.2	11.7	6.8	19.4	2.57	2.56	11.8	2.6	167.1	...	8.6	25.8	294.0	296.9	...	...	...	...
...	81.9	9.9	14.8	9.7	23.4	4.77	4.77	6.7	2.1	179.6	...	10.0	28.9	253.4	255.8	...	...	...	...
...	84.6	11.7	8.7	6.1	13.7	4.83	4.83	10.9	2.0	174.2	...	13.4	14.8	297.4	299.6	...	...	...	...
...	89.6	11.5	1.1	0.7	1.7	2.87	2.86	22.7	2.5	181.0	...	16.6	1.8	275.2	277.9	...	...	...	...
...	89.4	10.1	2.4	1.3	3.7	1.16	1.16	15.6	2.7	181.9	...	20.3	3.4	186.7	189.7	...	...	...	...
Principal Lines of Business: Medicaid (92.4%), Medicare (7.6%)														Principal States: HI (100.0%)					
...	60.0	39.4	3.6	1.0	5.1	0.78	0.78	-9.2	4.8	303.3	...	...	5.2	259.0	259.0	...	...	...	...
...	62.4	38.5	-1.1	-0.3	-1.5	1.14	1.14	17.4	5.7	253.3	...	...	-1.5	122.0	156.8	...	...	...	...
...	74.4	26.7	1.0	0.2	1.7	2.70	2.70	26.7	7.2	118.8	...	...	1.7	72.0	106.0	...	...	...	...
...	72.2	25.7	12.2	2.8	22.3	2.33	2.33	25.0	7.2	124.0	...	...	25.1	146.3	146.3	...	...	...	...
...	72.5	23.0	9.9	2.3	17.7	0.79	0.79	14.3	6.9	133.0	...	...	17.9	170.8	170.8	...	...	...	...
Principal Lines of Business: Dental (100.0%)														Principal States: TX (89.4%), NJ (4.9%), MD (4.5%)					
...	82.9	13.6	16.7	3.9	31.3	3.60	3.93	16.8	8.0	103.7	...	0.3	1.4	255.1	271.7	...	...	...	...
...	83.7	12.4	19.0	4.2	37.6	4.98	4.92	14.8	8.5	101.6	...	0.7	7.1	240.7	256.5	...	...	...	...
...	81.9	13.5	18.0	4.1	36.3	5.01	4.99	12.3	8.2	96.5	...	0.9	16.5	199.6	214.7	...	...	...	...
...	85.1	12.1	11.2	2.4	22.9	4.13	3.07	12.9	9.4	96.2	...	1.1	-0.7	195.7	210.1	...	...	...	...
...	85.4	13.6	5.2	1.1	10.2	3.21	3.67	2.2	8.5	111.4	...	1.0	12.0	204.0	221.4	...	...	...	...
Principal Lines of Business: CompHosp/Med (90.2%), Medicare (9.8%), Vision (0.0%)														Principal States: UT (94.3%), WY (3.2%)					
...	77.6	19.4	7.5	3.2	9.6	4.80	4.80	41.2	3.0	304.3	...	...	-6.2	399.1	414.2	...	...	...	...
...	81.3	19.6	1.8	0.7	2.4	5.41	5.41	29.9	3.4	307.5	...	...	17.3	388.7	404.9	...	...	...	...
...	79.3	19.2	6.1	2.1	8.9	5.23	5.23	9.3	4.8	156.4	...	...	-23.0	261.6	277.8	...	...	...	...
...	82.0	19.3	0.3	0.1	0.4	4.45	4.45	21.0	3.8	177.7	...	...	50.3	254.5	277.8	...	...	...	...
...	85.4	17.4	-3.7	-1.3	-6.0	3.60	3.60	31.9	4.1	154.0	...	...	23.1	190.6	204.9	...	...	...	...
Principal Lines of Business: Dental (100.0%)														Principal States: MA (100.0%)					
...	68.3	18.1	17.7	17.2	31.4	4.30	4.63	8.2	1.6	143.7	6.0	18.4	10.5	188.6	201.3	...	...	...	...
...	73.1	18.7	12.5	12.8	21.2	4.82	5.00	-10.4	1.6	147.1	6.1	0.1	-10.9	190.8	203.5	...	...	...	...
...	75.5	18.2	10.9	11.1	18.9	5.03	5.08	-5.6	1.6	128.5	6.5	...	-4.6	173.4	187.6	...	...	...	...
...	70.8	19.3	13.6	13.9	23.4	4.49	4.38	-0.5	1.5	150.8	5.4	13.0	4.0	114.8	175.6	...	...	...	...
...	73.5	19.8	9.5	10.4	16.5	3.81	3.64	-7.1	1.5	125.0	6.0	12.7	-6.6	189.2	203.6	...	...	...	...
Principal Lines of Business: GrpA&H (99.9%), OrdLife (0.1%)														Principal States: IL (100.0%)					
...	80.2	167.0	5.2	3.0	12.2	4.41	4.64	7.7	1.3	80.1	...	24.4	16.5	153.8	163.6	...	...	...	...
...	80.5	30.2	5.9	3.4	12.5	5.01	5.10	0.3	1.1	99.0	...	23.7	11.1	154.9	168.9	...	...	...	...
...	83.9	155.2	7.6	4.4	14.8	4.91	4.89	10.4	1.1	110.7	...	20.3	13.9	164.7	181.2	...	...	...	...
...	83.8	168.5	4.3	2.6	8.4	5.01	3.99	3.8	1.1	97.7	...	22.6	2.7	120.0	154.4	0.1	...	...	...
...	85.5	158.5	3.9	2.3	7.8	4.39	4.17	16.7	1.2	104.3	...	20.1	7.9	167.8	184.0	0.7	...	...	...
Principal Lines of Business: GrpLife (77.7%), GrpA&H (19.0%), OrdLife (3.4%)														Principal States: NY (75.5%), IL (12.4%), NJ (3.8%)					
...	...	...	...	...	...	...	...	...	...	...	...	...	...	...	...	...	...	...	...
285	29.1	56.6	...	34.2	...	...	...	...	0.0	999.9	...	0.0	...	999.9	999.9	1.8	...	...	...
-374	61.1	42.3	2.4	35.5	2.6	4.52	2.23	24.9	0.0	999.9	...	0.0	3.2	999.9	999.9	1.6	...	...	...
-1,995	20.5	43.1	3.0	39.8	3.2	5.19	-12.01	...	0.0	999.9	...	0.0	-10.1	999.9	999.9	...	...	...	...
597	33.7	49.2	4.1	50.2	4.3	5.74	7.65	...	0.0	999.9	...	0.0	3.8	999.9	999.9	3.4	...	...	...
Principal Lines of Business: CrdA&H (100.0%)																			
-26	83.3	29.1	1.1	3.3	6.4	3.23	3.23	67.7	160.1	15.5	...	...	5.3	20.1	5.3	...	...	...	...
11	96.1	85.1	-9.9	-42.3	-77.1	2.87	2.87	17.4	115.6	14.3	...	...	62.6	26.1	5.8	...	...	...	...
17	91.3	244.8	-25.3	-99.9	-99.9	2.64	2.64	24.0	231.2	4.9	...	...	-38.0	36.2	11.8	...	...	...	...
-210	105.1	418.7	-32.7	-99.9	-99.9	2.38	2.38	-5.8	227.0	4.2	...	...	-4.1	53.0	24.2	...	...	...	...
...	...	...	...	...	...	...	...	...	...	...	...	...	...	...	...	...	...	...	...
4,756	30.9	32.4	2.8	13.0	17.0	5.50	7.22	-1.4	1.4	21.6	0.0	0.9	28.7	80.7	84.6	2.8	...	6.1	77.6
-4,856	33.3	28.4	2.6	12.5	16.0	6.69	5.04	-6.8	1.4	18.2	0.0	0.7	-11.3	86.6	89.4	0.0	...	6.5	78.9
4,339	39.5	28.6	1.7	9.5	10.3	4.69	6.13	-6.7	1.1	20.8	0.0	0.7	22.2	85.3	89.2	1.6	...	5.5	72.3
-268	41.1	30.8	1.4	8.5	8.3	4.59	4.55	-6.3	1.0	19.6	0.0	0.5	0.2	80.1	87.8	0.8	...	5.3	72.1
4,514	41.3	38.1	0.2	1.0	1.0	4.60	5.85	5.2	1.1	18.5	0.0	0.7	0.8	81.7	89.1	...	...	5.1	78.2
Principal Lines of Business: OrdLife (61.1%), GrpAnn (29.3%), GrpLife (6.5%), IndAnn (3.2%)														Principal States: TX (20.7%), CA (10.3%), FL (6.5%), IL (5.9%), GA (4.4%)					

Data in U.S. Dollars

Column key: COMPANY NAME; Ultimate Parent Association; Principal Officer; Mailing Address; Dom. : Began Bus. : Struct. : Mktg.; Specialty; Phone #; AMB#; NAIC#. Best's Financial Strength Rating; FSC.

AMERICAN BANKERS LIFE ASSUR CO
Assurant Inc
S. Craig Lemasters
CEO
11222 Quail Roost Drive
Miami, FL 33157
FL : 1952 : Stock : Agency
Credit A&H, Credit Life, Group A&H
305-253-2244
AMB# 006040 NAIC# 60275

Rating: **A-** — Rating Outlook: Stable — **FSC VIII**

Data Year	Bonds (%)	Mort. Loans & R.E. (%)	Com & Pref. Stock (%)	All Other Assets (%)	Total Assets ($000)	Life Reserves (%)	Health Reserves (%)	Ann Res. & Dep. Liabilities (%)	All Other Liabilities (%)	Capital & Surplus ($000)	Direct Premiums Written ($000)	Net Premiums Written & Deposits ($000)	Operating Cash Flow ($000)	NOG Before Taxes ($000)	NOG After Taxes ($000)	Net Income ($000)
'05	70.2	8.7	6.8	14.2	949,529	41.6	25.9	7.0	25.5	211,294	548,479	200,486	-27,607	39,428	46,488	47,195
'06	61.5	10.3	11.0	17.2	776,639	41.9	25.5	7.2	25.4	105,733	466,398	172,290	-155,230	33,437	26,378	28,385
'07	60.3	9.4	9.6	20.8	789,738	42.4	24.9	6.9	25.9	127,417	515,531	164,342	3,580	23,184	13,532	14,526
'08	60.2	11.8	8.7	19.3	653,077	46.6	25.7	7.9	19.7	106,707	498,102	131,969	-73,957	14,454	17,480	1,684
'09	67.7	11.1	1.6	19.6	671,086	43.1	23.5	7.4	26.0	116,618	479,116	103,069	-36,472	29,531	28,048	26,997

Rating History: A- g, 11/18/09; A- g, 11/25/08; A- g, 06/24/08; A g, 07/17/07; A g, 06/19/06

AMERICAN BENEFIT LIFE
Realty Advisors Inc
Bradford A. Phillips
President & CEO
1605 LBJ Freeway, Suite 710
Dallas, TX 75234
OK : 1909 : Stock : Agency
Ordinary Life, Reins
972-484-6063
AMB# 060382 NAIC# 66001

Rating: **B-** — Rating Outlook: Negative — **FSC III**

Data Year	Bonds (%)	Mort. Loans & R.E. (%)	Com & Pref. Stock (%)	All Other Assets (%)	Total Assets ($000)	Life Reserves (%)	Health Reserves (%)	Ann Res. & Dep. Liabilities (%)	All Other Liabilities (%)	Capital & Surplus ($000)	Direct Premiums Written ($000)	Net Premiums Written & Deposits ($000)	Operating Cash Flow ($000)	NOG Before Taxes ($000)	NOG After Taxes ($000)	Net Income ($000)
'05	70.7	20.5	...	8.8	7,469	55.9	...	...	44.1	3,570	119	1,402	1,844	-934	-912	-912
'06	63.7	18.1	...	18.3	9,255	97.7	...	...	2.3	3,475	115	6,361	1,134	-64	-74	-74
'07	59.8	13.6	2.6	24.0	11,513	98.0	...	...	2.0	3,435	93	5,435	2,020	-39	-32	-32
'08	63.6	4.6	1.4	30.3	14,288	98.6	...	...	1.4	3,225	68	6,722	2,276	418	407	-150
'09	61.6	7.2	0.7	30.4	21,565	93.8	...	...	6.2	3,966	2	10,454	4,780	-229	-227	-250

Rating History: B-, 11/24/09; B- u, 06/18/09; B, 05/23/08; B, 11/16/06; B, 07/18/05

AMERICAN CAPITOL INS CO[1]
James P. Rousey
President
5250 S 6th Street Rd
Springfield, IL 62703-5128
TX : 1954 : Stock : Agency
217-241-6590
AMB# 006043 NAIC# 60291

Rating: **NR-1**

Data Year	Bonds (%)	Mort. Loans & R.E. (%)	Com & Pref. Stock (%)	All Other Assets (%)	Total Assets ($000)	Life Reserves (%)	Health Reserves (%)	Ann Res. & Dep. Liabilities (%)	All Other Liabilities (%)	Capital & Surplus ($000)	Direct Premiums Written ($000)	Net Premiums Written & Deposits ($000)	Operating Cash Flow ($000)	NOG Before Taxes ($000)	NOG After Taxes ($000)	Net Income ($000)
'05	84.4	...	3.3	12.3	73,017	...	...	2.1	97.9	7,414	10,198	8,799	...	3,175	2,977	2,739
'06	83.7	...	3.8	12.5	71,923	...	...	2.1	97.9	8,943	8,546	7,291	...	2,052	2,096	2,154
'07	83.7	...	7.0	9.3	70,098	...	...	2.1	97.9	8,166	4,898	2,206	...	1,037	999	999
'08	63.3	...	8.8	27.9	66,830	...	...	2.2	97.8	7,346	3,542	2,191	...	1,393	1,379	1,164
'09	67.2	10.9	3.4	18.5	69,597	...	...	2.1	97.9	9,781	3,175	2,272	...	-1,177	-1,297	4,071

Rating History: NR-1, 06/10/10; NR-5, 06/24/09; NR-1, 06/12/08; NR-1, 06/08/07; NR-4, 03/23/07

AMERICAN CENTURY LIFE INS CO[1]
Kim E. Gavlik
President
9120 S. Toledo Avenue
Tulsa, OK 74137-2700
OK : 1981 : Stock : Not Available
918-712-7770
AMB# 008932 NAIC# 97810

Rating: **NR-1**

Data Year	Bonds (%)	Mort. Loans & R.E. (%)	Com & Pref. Stock (%)	All Other Assets (%)	Total Assets ($000)	Life Reserves (%)	Health Reserves (%)	Ann Res. & Dep. Liabilities (%)	All Other Liabilities (%)	Capital & Surplus ($000)	Direct Premiums Written ($000)	Net Premiums Written & Deposits ($000)	Operating Cash Flow ($000)	NOG Before Taxes ($000)	NOG After Taxes ($000)	Net Income ($000)
'05	84.6	9.4	4.2	1.9	25,382	...	...	...	100.0	1,145	4,666	4,666	...	278	206	311
'06	83.8	9.0	4.2	3.0	26,440	...	...	...	100.0	1,155	4,031	4,031	...	51	51	42
'07	85.1	8.1	4.1	2.7	28,774	...	...	...	100.0	896	5,346	5,346	...	-89	19	19
'08	83.1	7.4	3.9	5.5	30,727	...	...	...	100.0	1,008	6,084	6,084	...	351	274	252
'09	90.2	4.9	3.2	1.6	35,388	...	...	...	100.0	1,552	8,431	8,431	...	444	397	146

Rating History: NR-1, 06/10/10; NR-1, 06/12/09; NR-1, 06/12/08; NR-1, 06/08/07; NR-1, 06/07/06

AMERICAN CENTURY LIFE OF TEXAS[1]
Kim E. Gavlik
President
1509 Gaston Avenue, Suite 200
Austin, TX 78703
TX : 1981 : Stock : Not Available
918-712-7770
AMB# 068090 NAIC# 99600

Rating: **NR-1**

Data Year	Bonds (%)	Mort. Loans & R.E. (%)	Com & Pref. Stock (%)	All Other Assets (%)	Total Assets ($000)	Life Reserves (%)	Health Reserves (%)	Ann Res. & Dep. Liabilities (%)	All Other Liabilities (%)	Capital & Surplus ($000)	Direct Premiums Written ($000)	Net Premiums Written & Deposits ($000)	Operating Cash Flow ($000)	NOG Before Taxes ($000)	NOG After Taxes ($000)	Net Income ($000)
'05	78.5	...	2.8	18.7	359	...	...	...	100.0	186	174	174	...	1	-3	-13
'06	80.4	...	2.7	16.9	373	...	...	...	100.0	188	82	82	...	-1	0	0
'07	86.2	...	2.6	11.2	389	...	...	...	100.0	199	68	68	...	14	17	17
'08	83.8	...	2.5	13.7	400	...	...	...	100.0	211	63	63	...	15	13	13
'09	83.1	...	2.2	14.7	430	...	...	...	100.0	226	66	66	...	20	16	16

Rating History: NR-1, 06/10/10; NR-1, 06/12/09; NR-1, 06/12/08; NR-1, 06/08/07; NR-1, 06/07/06

AMERICAN COMMUNITY MUTUAL INS
39201 Seven Mile Road
Livonia, MI 48152-1094
MI : 1947 : Mutual : Broker
Maj med
800-991-2642
AMB# 006044 NAIC# 60305

Rating: **E**

Data Year	Bonds (%)	Mort. Loans & R.E. (%)	Com & Pref. Stock (%)	All Other Assets (%)	Total Assets ($000)	Life Reserves (%)	Health Reserves (%)	Ann Res. & Dep. Liabilities (%)	All Other Liabilities (%)	Capital & Surplus ($000)	Direct Premiums Written ($000)	Net Premiums Written & Deposits ($000)	Operating Cash Flow ($000)	NOG Before Taxes ($000)	NOG After Taxes ($000)	Net Income ($000)
'05	89.2	5.3	2.1	3.3	183,037	0.3	64.6	...	35.0	121,369	325,691	321,585	23,021	6,751	5,684	5,359
'06	85.2	5.3	2.9	6.7	178,470	0.3	67.4	...	32.3	106,879	341,627	338,689	-9,138	-21,436	-16,349	-16,428
'07	84.6	5.5	1.9	8.0	161,585	0.6	63.9	...	35.5	102,389	343,365	340,844	-13,446	857	857	-5,936
'08	86.5	5.7	2.5	5.3	141,888	0.4	73.3	...	26.3	74,506	358,887	355,886	-21,522	-23,916	-23,918	-25,340
'09	86.4	6.1	0.0	7.5	107,071	0.3	84.2	...	15.5	21,101	367,356	363,889	-23,800	-48,552	-46,053	-49,135

Rating History: E, 05/06/10; D, 03/08/10; C+, 11/05/09; B, 02/24/09; B+, 05/23/08

AMERICAN CONTINENTAL INS CO
Genworth Financial, Inc
Christopher M. Olson
President & CEO
101 Continental Place
Brentwood, TN 37027-5033
TN : 2005 : Stock : Broker
A&H
800-264-4000
AMB# 060568 NAIC# 12321

Rating: **A-** — Rating Outlook: Negative — **FSC V**

Data Year	Bonds (%)	Mort. Loans & R.E. (%)	Com & Pref. Stock (%)	All Other Assets (%)	Total Assets ($000)	Life Reserves (%)	Health Reserves (%)	Ann Res. & Dep. Liabilities (%)	All Other Liabilities (%)	Capital & Surplus ($000)	Direct Premiums Written ($000)	Net Premiums Written & Deposits ($000)	Operating Cash Flow ($000)	NOG Before Taxes ($000)	NOG After Taxes ($000)	Net Income ($000)
'05	7.7	...	...	92.3	3,231	0.4	76.5	...	23.1	3,212	11	11	3,222	17	15	15
'06	76.8	...	...	23.2	9,081	1.6	65.3	...	33.1	8,996	172	172	438	12	5	5
'07	63.9	...	...	36.1	10,697	0.6	44.0	...	55.5	8,499	2,102	2,102	1,280	-230	-226	-226
'08	25.3	...	...	74.7	21,176	0.2	58.8	...	41.0	9,971	23,033	23,033	8,932	-7,512	-5,486	-5,488
'09	18.2	...	...	81.8	36,739	0.3	56.7	...	43.0	16,357	66,488	66,488	14,293	-12,115	-11,552	-11,552

Rating History: A-, 04/21/10; A-, 02/19/09; A- u, 11/06/08; A-, 06/16/08; NR-2, 04/04/07

AMERICAN CREDITORS LIFE INS CO[1]
Joel M. Rosenblum
Chairman & President
P.O. Box 17748
Irvine, CA 92623-7748
DE : 1980 : Stock : Agency
Credit A&H, Credit Life
949-474-7600
AMB# 009097 NAIC# 94439

Rating: **NR-1**

Data Year	Bonds (%)	Mort. Loans & R.E. (%)	Com & Pref. Stock (%)	All Other Assets (%)	Total Assets ($000)	Life Reserves (%)	Health Reserves (%)	Ann Res. & Dep. Liabilities (%)	All Other Liabilities (%)	Capital & Surplus ($000)	Direct Premiums Written ($000)	Net Premiums Written & Deposits ($000)	Operating Cash Flow ($000)	NOG Before Taxes ($000)	NOG After Taxes ($000)	Net Income ($000)
'05	69.2	...	0.9	29.9	16,066	...	...	...	100.0	11,916	-16	-17	...	625	532	519
'06	75.0	...	0.9	24.1	16,460	...	...	...	100.0	12,246	-4	-4	...	336	271	277
'07	47.5	...	1.0	51.5	17,065	...	...	...	100.0	12,563	0	0	...	362	302	307
'08	13.6	...	1.4	85.0	17,201	...	...	...	100.0	12,085	...	...	...	-441	-441	-435
'09	9.3	...	1.3	89.4	17,179	...	...	...	100.0	11,755	...	...	...	-315	-315	-315

Rating History: NR-1, 06/10/10; NR-1, 06/12/09; NR-4, 05/18/09; B+, 05/18/09; B+, 06/17/08

AMERICAN DENTAL PLAN OF NC
Humana Inc
Gerald L. Ganoni
President
100 Mansell Court East, Suite 400
Roswell, GA 30076
NC : 1993 : Stock : Broker
Dental
770-998-8936
AMB# 064631 NAIC# 95107

Rating: **NR-3**

Data Year	Bonds (%)	Mort. Loans & R.E. (%)	Com & Pref. Stock (%)	All Other Assets (%)	Total Assets ($000)	Life Reserves (%)	Health Reserves (%)	Ann Res. & Dep. Liabilities (%)	All Other Liabilities (%)	Capital & Surplus ($000)	Direct Premiums Written ($000)	Net Premiums Written & Deposits ($000)	Operating Cash Flow ($000)	NOG Before Taxes ($000)	NOG After Taxes ($000)	Net Income ($000)
'05	4.6	...	...	95.4	645	...	88.1	...	11.9	567	418	418	-48	47	30	30
'06	4.4	...	...	95.6	682	...	1.6	...	98.4	615	380	380	34	74	47	47
'07	3.9	...	...	96.1	765	...	36.2	...	63.8	633	552	552	68	34	22	22
'08	2.5	...	35.9	61.6	1,205	...	12.8	...	87.2	734	589	589	429	150	98	98
'09	2.8	...	...	97.2	1,077	...	35.5	...	64.5	810	801	801	-141	123	76	76

Rating History: NR-3, 06/02/10; NR-3, 06/05/09; NR-3, 06/05/08; NR-5, 04/02/07; NR-5, 05/11/06

BEST'S PROFITABILITY, LEVERAGE AND LIQUIDITY TESTS 2005 – 2009

Data in U.S. Dollars

	Profitability Tests							Leverage Tests						Liquidity Tests					
Un-Realized Capital Gains ($000)	Benefits Paid to NPW & Dep (%)	Comm. & Expenses to NPW & Dep (%)	NOG to Total Assets (%)	NOG to Total Rev (%)	Operating Return on Equity (%)	Net Yield (%)	Total Return (%)	Change in NPW & Dep (%)	NPW & Dep to Capital (X)	Capital & Surplus to Liabilities (%)	Surplus Relief (%)	Reins Leverage (%)	Change in Capital (%)	Quick Liquidity (%)	Current Liquidity (%)	Non-Invest Grade Bonds to Capital (%)	Delinq. & Foreclosed Mortgages to Capital (%)	Mort. & Credit Tenant Loans & R.E. to Capital (%)	Affiliated Invest to Capital (%)
-963	45.9	82.9	4.6	13.2	23.5	6.29	6.43	-34.2	0.9	30.0	45.2	223.7	17.1	68.8	85.4	23.4	0.1	36.4	10.6
4	47.3	80.4	3.1	8.6	16.6	6.54	6.89	-14.1	1.5	16.9	77.7	311.4	-50.4	51.5	66.7	34.0	...	71.1	20.5
-404	51.4	79.3	1.7	4.2	11.6	6.16	6.31	-4.6	1.2	20.4	95.7	201.3	19.0	64.2	80.1	21.5	...	55.3	17.0
-40	50.6	82.6	2.4	5.8	14.9	5.21	2.89	-19.7	1.2	20.1	131.5	191.7	-18.2	59.4	75.2	22.5	...	70.6	19.9
745	72.4	79.6	4.2	9.9	25.1	6.21	6.21	-21.9	0.9	21.8	117.5	160.3	9.9	59.0	71.4	21.4	...	62.2	18.2
Principal Lines of Business: CrdLife (42.8%), CrdA&H (18.6%), OrdLife (15.3%), GrpA&H (14.8%), GrpLife (3.3%)														Principal States: TX (6.2%), FL (4.2%), PA (3.3%)					
...	22.3	167.7	-14.2	-50.0	-27.3	7.16	7.17	-14.6	0.4	93.1	...	55.3	14.7	109.0	118.0	...	5.5	42.4	...
...	6.8	50.6	-0.9	-1.1	-2.1	7.73	7.74	353.8	1.8	61.6	-1.0	13.0	-2.1	80.7	86.9	13.6	...	47.4	...
...	11.2	59.1	-0.3	-0.5	-0.9	7.41	7.46	-14.6	1.6	43.6	...	13.4	-0.9	82.2	89.8	...	...	44.9	...
-54	11.4	49.7	3.2	5.4	12.2	7.11	1.82	23.7	2.0	29.7	...	21.8	-6.0	78.8	86.0	9.4	9.1	20.1	...
0	13.1	47.0	-1.3	-2.0	-6.3	7.41	7.29	55.5	2.6	23.0	...	46.5	22.9	61.7	70.4	15.8	...	38.7	...
Principal Lines of Business: OrdLife (100.0%)														Principal States: TX (100.0%)					
-102	82.4	40.2	4.1	19.1	44.9	...	...	-11.3	1.2	11.3	40.3	...	26.8	...	...	...	...	...	...
542	80.4	55.4	2.9	15.2	25.6	...	...	-17.1	0.8	14.7	34.9	...	24.6	...	...	...	...	...	...
-295	173.8	103.6	1.4	13.7	11.7	...	...	-69.7	0.3	13.7	15.7	...	-8.7	...	...	...	...	...	...
-878	171.8	73.4	2.0	19.9	17.8	...	...	-0.7	0.3	12.3	20.0	...	-12.9	...	...	...	...	...	...
-1,723	187.2	143.4	-1.9	-31.4	-15.1	...	...	3.7	0.2	17.0	-0.9	...	37.7	...	...	...	...	74.7	...
Principal Lines of Business: OrdLife (68.1%), IndLife (28.2%), IndAnn (3.7%)																			
-2	64.3	11.9	0.8	3.4	17.7	...	...	-4.2	3.9	5.0	...	...	-0.7	...	...	...	...	197.3	...
2	92.5	13.7	0.2	0.9	4.5	...	...	-13.6	3.3	4.8	...	...	0.0	...	...	...	...	196.3	...
4	75.6	9.2	0.1	0.3	1.8	...	...	32.6	5.5	3.5	...	...	-18.8	...	...	...	...	236.9	...
75	81.1	8.5	0.9	3.5	28.7	...	...	13.8	5.4	3.8	...	...	15.7	...	...	...	...	200.8	...
336	61.1	6.2	1.2	3.9	31.0	...	...	38.6	4.9	5.1	...	...	51.6	...	...	...	...	101.5	...
Principal Lines of Business: IndAnn (97.9%), OrdLife (2.1%)																			
...	35.4	27.9	-1.0	-1.6	-1.7	...	...	31.1	0.9	107.7	...	...	-1.3	...	...	...	...	...	...
...	99.8	22.3	-0.1	-0.3	-0.2	...	...	-53.0	0.4	102.0	...	...	1.1	...	...	...	...	...	...
...	74.5	11.5	4.4	19.0	8.7	...	...	-17.1	0.3	105.5	...	...	5.9	...	...	...	...	...	...
...	94.2	25.0	3.4	16.5	6.5	...	...	-6.6	0.3	113.0	...	...	6.3	...	...	...	...	...	...
4	36.0	33.1	3.9	18.0	7.4	...	...	4.0	0.3	111.4	...	...	6.8	...	...	...	...	...	...
Principal Lines of Business: OrdLife (84.7%), IndAnn (15.3%)																			
720	73.4	28.3	3.3	1.7	5.4	3.69	3.97	-13.1	2.6	202.7	0.3	11.1	37.8	209.2	231.8	2.0	...	8.1	8.0
-491	77.8	30.0	-9.0	-4.8	-14.3	2.68	2.39	5.3	3.1	153.7	...	12.0	-11.8	164.7	182.5	1.4	...	8.8	10.5
485	75.1	26.1	0.5	0.2	0.8	2.72	-1.17	0.6	3.3	178.2	...	12.1	-4.3	182.7	203.2	2.4	...	8.6	9.1
-422	77.9	29.4	-15.8	-6.7	-27.0	2.52	1.28	4.4	4.7	112.1	...	17.0	-27.5	113.3	136.2	2.8	...	10.8	10.8
509	79.2	33.5	-37.0	-12.5	-96.3	3.49	1.34	2.2	16.9	25.2	...	58.5	-71.2	97.9	109.3	3.6	...	30.1	30.1
Principal Lines of Business: GrpA&H (58.7%), IndA&H (40.7%), GrpLife (0.7%), OrdLife (0.0%)														Principal States: MI (21.6%), OH (14.5%), AZ (13.8%), IN (13.6%), MO (12.9%)					
...	52.9	137.1	...	31.1	...	...	...	...	0.0	999.9	...	...	...	999.9	999.9	...	...	...	...
...	88.5	70.7	0.1	1.7	0.1	2.10	2.10	999.9	0.0	999.9	...	...	180.2	999.9	999.9	...	...	...	...
...	52.3	60.8	-2.3	-8.9	-2.6	4.72	4.72	999.9	0.2	386.6	...	...	-5.6	513.1	542.8	...	...	...	...
...	60.2	66.5	-34.4	-23.2	-59.4	2.98	2.97	995.8	2.3	89.1	...	...	17.4	223.7	230.0	...	...	...	...
...	75.4	41.3	-39.9	-17.2	-87.8	1.15	1.15	188.7	4.1	80.4	...	...	64.1	276.5	288.8	...	...	...	...
Principal Lines of Business: IndA&H (99.9%), OrdLife (0.1%)														Principal States: TX (14.2%), MO (14.1%), PA (14.1%), SC (13.4%), OH (7.0%)					
1	-99.9	-99.9	3.3	71.3	4.6	...	...	75.2	0.0	290.5	0.0	...	4.3	...	...	...	...	...	...
12	-99.9	-99.9	1.7	33.4	2.2	...	...	77.8	0.0	294.1	...	...	2.8	...	...	...	...	...	...
8	999.9	999.9	1.8	36.0	2.4	...	...	101.0	0.0	281.1	...	...	2.5	...	...	...	...	...	...
-52	...	...	-2.6	-99.9	-3.6	...	...	-99.9	...	236.7	...	...	-3.9	...	...	...	...	...	...
7	...	...	-1.8	-99.9	-2.6	...	...	...	...	217.9	...	...	-2.6	...	...	...	...	...	...
...	57.7	35.1	4.5	6.7	5.2	0.13	0.13	-18.0	0.7	718.5	...	...	-4.0	811.5	811.5	...	...	...	...
...	57.2	34.9	7.1	11.0	8.0	3.46	3.46	-9.0	0.6	909.9	...	...	8.5	999.8	999.8	...	...	...	...
...	61.9	40.5	3.0	3.8	3.5	3.89	3.89	45.1	0.9	479.7	...	...	2.9	999.9	999.9	...	...	...	...
...	57.8	22.6	10.0	15.9	14.4	1.35	1.35	6.6	0.8	155.9	...	...	16.0	360.9	374.7	...	...	...	...
...	75.5	15.1	6.7	9.1	9.9	0.43	0.43	36.1	1.0	304.3	...	...	10.4	640.7	640.7	...	...	...	...
Principal Lines of Business: FEHBP (58.2%), Dental (41.8%)														Principal States: NC (100.0%)					

2010 BEST'S KEY RATING GUIDE — LIFE/HEALTH EDITION
ANNUAL STATEMENT DATA FOR YEARS 2005 – 2009

Data in U.S. Dollars

COMPANY NAME Ultimate Parent Association Principal Officer Mailing Address Dom. : Began Bus. : Struct. : Mktg. Specialty Phone # AMB# NAIC#	Best's Financial Strength Rating FSC	Data Year	Balance Sheet: Bonds (%)	Mort. Loans & R.E. (%)	Com & Pref. Stock (%)	All Other Assets (%)	Total Assets ($000)	Life Reserves (%)	Health Reserves %)	Ann Res. & Dep. Liabilities (%)	All Other Liabilities (%)	Capital & Surplus ($000)	Operations: Direct Premiums Written ($000)	Net Premiums Written & Deposits ($000)	Operating Cash Flow ($000)	NOG Before Taxes ($000)	NOG After Taxes ($000)	Net Income ($000)
AMERICAN DENTAL PLAN OF WI INC[2]	NR-5	'05	...	...	...	100.0	208	...	...	...	100.0	104	3,377	3,377	...	2	2	2
Darryl Veit, D.D.S. President P.O. Box 4496 Madison, WI 53744-4966		'06	...	...	...	100.0	213	...	...	...	100.0	105	3,211	3,211	-1	1	1	1
WI : 1994 : Other : Broker		'07	...	...	...	100.0	212	...	...	...	100.0	104	3,250	3,250	22	1	1	1
Dental		'08	...	...	...	100.0	234	...	...	...	100.0	105	3,121	3,121	22	1	1	1
608-831-1047 AMB# 064796 NAIC# 52041		'09	...	...	...	100.0	237	...	...	...	100.0	105	3,025	3,025	0	0	0	0
		Rating History: NR-5, 05/19/10; NR-5, 07/13/09; NR-5, 07/29/08; NR-5, 05/03/07; NR-5, 06/06/06																
AMERICAN DENTAL PROVIDERS AR Humana Inc	NR-3	'05	39.2	...	...	60.8	268	...	74.0	...	26.0	257	138	138	61	84	54	54
Gerald L. Ganoni President 100 Mansell Court East, Suite 400 Roswell, GA 30076		'06	34.9	...	...	65.1	301	...	3.2	...	96.8	294	95	95	34	57	37	37
AR : 1997 : Stock : Not Available		'07	30.9	...	...	69.1	340	...	10.5	...	89.5	281	137	137	34	28	20	20
Dental		'08	27.9	...	39.5	32.5	376	...	14.4	...	85.6	326	136	136	31	67	40	40
770-998-8936 AMB# 064491 NAIC# 11559		'09	24.0	...	...	76.0	436	...	11.8	...	88.2	348	163	163	58	34	22	22
		Rating History: NR-3, 06/02/10; NR-3, 06/05/09; NR-3, 06/05/08; NR-5, 04/02/07; NR-5, 05/11/06																
AMERICAN EQUITY INVEST LIFE American Equity Investment Life Hldg Co	A-	'05	82.8	12.7	1.5	3.0	10,415,535	0.7	0.0	92.1	7.1	686,841	2,871,747	2,839,395	2,209,457	111,663	46,274	40,085
Ronald J. Grensteiner President		'06	79.6	14.4	1.8	4.2	11,471,358	0.8	0.0	93.8	5.3	992,478	1,866,838	1,807,940	367,705	93,142	87,242	88,511
6000 Westown Parkway West Des Moines, IA 50266	Rating Outlook: Negative	'07	79.5	15.4	2.6	2.5	12,697,227	0.9	0.0	95.2	3.9	990,801	2,143,679	2,090,262	1,167,568	39,684	20,674	15,859
IA : 1981 : Stock : Agency Ind Ann, Term Life, Trad Life		'08	77.1	17.1	2.7	3.0	13,593,940	0.9	0.0	97.7	1.4	983,325	2,297,941	2,282,137	709,454	127,065	109,958	-6,754
515-221-0002 AMB# 009024 NAIC# 92738	FSC XII	'09	76.5	14.6	1.1	7.8	16,697,568	0.8	0.0	91.2	8.0	1,193,130	3,678,796	2,872,854	2,322,023	258,031	167,549	124,636
		Rating History: A- g, 12/18/09; A- g, 10/30/08; A- g, 10/30/07; A- g, 08/02/06; B++g, 06/21/05																
AMERICAN EQUITY INVEST LIFE NY American Equity Investment Life Hldg Co	A-	'05	96.6	...	...	3.4	96,739	0.1	...	96.9	3.0	31,056	35,709	36,635	31,686	835	455	449
David J. Noble Chairman & President		'06	96.0	...	...	4.0	108,606	0.8	...	98.1	1.1	32,314	15,302	16,236	10,551	2,074	1,364	1,364
5000 Westown Parkway, Suite 440 West Des Moines, IA 50266	Rating Outlook: Negative	'07	97.1	...	...	2.9	119,243	0.8	...	97.5	1.7	33,487	12,573	12,587	9,817	1,789	1,152	1,152
NY : 2001 : Stock : Agency Ind Ann		'08	95.3	...	...	4.7	117,102	1.2	...	97.8	1.0	33,412	3,438	3,749	-3,278	2,016	1,337	-296
866-233-6660 AMB# 060367 NAIC# 11135	FSC XII	'09	93.4	...	...	6.6	124,842	0.9	...	97.8	1.2	26,568	11,204	11,873	6,077	-4,896	-5,236	-7,368
		Rating History: A- g, 12/18/09; A- g, 10/30/08; A- g, 10/30/07; A- g, 08/02/06; B++g, 06/21/05																
AMERICAN EXCHANGE LIFE INS CO	NR-5	'05	0.2	...	96.3	3.5	157,726	8.8	11.1	0.3	79.9	155,185	3,708	907	37,945	-410	4,283	4,283
Gary W. Bryant President & CEO P.O. Box 958465		'06	0.1	...	94.0	5.9	268,195	0.8	1.2	0.0	98.0	238,414	3,303	994	94,886	34,884	28,464	28,464
Lake Mary, FL 32795-8465 TX : 1965 : Stock : Broker		'07	0.0	...	94.9	5.0	436,523	1.4	2.9	0.0	95.6	420,901	3,306	1,354	122,554	74,720	58,652	61,452
Ind A&H		'08	0.2	...	91.2	8.6	477,650	1.8	3.2	0.0	95.0	464,881	2,950	1,257	28,296	66,696	42,899	42,899
407-995-8000 AMB# 006050 NAIC# 60372		'09	0.2	...	96.1	3.7	643,506	...	...	...	100.0	636,676	2,179	633	-14,398	5,310	2,479	2,479
		Rating History: NR-5, 06/03/10; NR-3, 04/16/10; NR-3, 12/03/08; NR-3, 08/21/07; NR-3, 06/21/06																
AMERICAN FAM ASSUR COLUMBUS Aflac Incorporated	A+	'05	84.4	0.6	9.7	5.3	46,859,356	9.8	82.5	1.4	6.3	3,705,480	12,167,054	12,163,514	1,726,232	1,651,730	1,255,091	1,248,003
Daniel P. Amos Chairman & CEO		'06	78.6	0.6	16.7	4.1	50,298,815	10.4	81.5	1.8	6.4	4,186,298	12,497,627	12,501,381	4,050,054	2,058,518	1,679,638	1,714,989
1932 Wynnton Road Columbus, GA 31999	Rating Outlook: Stable	'07	81.2	0.5	14.5	3.8	55,667,865	10.9	80.2	2.2	6.8	4,208,297	13,132,254	13,136,236	3,332,451	2,313,704	1,807,768	1,790,159
NE : 1956 : Stock : Agency A&H, Group Life, Ind Life		'08	82.7	0.5	13.1	3.8	71,782,958	11.5	79.3	2.5	6.7	4,601,314	15,151,125	15,173,452	4,198,017	2,384,919	1,789,318	1,208,648
706-323-3431 AMB# 006051 NAIC# 60380	FSC XV	'09	94.7	0.4	0.2	4.7	75,798,442	12.1	78.6	2.8	6.5	5,767,939	16,845,714	16,878,884	4,660,535	2,938,029	2,140,827	1,414,136
		Rating History: A+ g, 04/09/10; A+ g, 02/02/09; A+ g, 05/14/08; A+ g, 06/26/07; A+ g, 06/27/06																
AMERICAN FAMILY LIFE ASSUR NY Aflac Incorporated	A+	'05	77.3	...	...	22.7	154,418	4.4	74.7	0.6	20.3	26,770	135,275	135,259	26,271	9,291	2,686	2,695
Paul S. Amos II President		'06	80.7	...	...	19.3	190,411	3.7	79.3	0.5	16.5	37,514	156,189	156,176	32,473	13,519	8,422	8,422
1932 Wynnton Road Columbus, GA 31999	Rating Outlook: Stable	'07	85.4	...	...	14.6	227,891	3.3	78.5	0.5	17.7	51,479	174,673	174,661	36,159	23,393	11,862	11,862
NY : 1964 : Stock : Agency A&H, Group Life, Ind Life		'08	84.8	...	...	15.2	266,525	3.1	79.8	0.4	16.7	59,335	194,089	194,062	35,704	24,587	13,915	11,593
518-438-0764 AMB# 006063 NAIC# 60526	FSC XV	'09	83.2	...	...	16.8	322,556	3.1	80.4	0.3	16.2	77,042	211,954	211,985	54,145	30,022	16,141	12,868
		Rating History: A+ g, 04/09/10; A+ g, 02/02/09; A+ g, 05/14/08; A+ g, 06/26/07; A+ g, 06/27/06																
AMERICAN FAMILY LIFE INS CO American Family Mutual Insurance Company	A	'05	79.7	6.0	2.4	12.0	3,454,058	73.9	...	18.7	7.4	364,416	417,686	414,594	173,542	73,425	48,120	57,905
David R. Anderson Chairman & CEO		'06	76.1	7.6	2.6	13.7	3,685,060	73.2	...	18.0	8.8	432,227	440,949	433,476	148,269	90,579	59,289	61,132
6000 American Parkway Madison, WI 53783-0001	Rating Outlook: Negative	'07	74.3	8.0	2.3	15.5	3,893,876	73.1	...	17.1	9.8	501,515	451,382	441,033	139,100	100,351	66,268	65,399
WI : 1957 : Stock : Career Agent Var Univ life, Var ann		'08	73.5	9.2	1.6	15.7	3,860,797	75.1	...	17.4	7.5	446,822	447,251	428,514	33,270	73,903	46,879	-81,848
608-249-2111 AMB# 006052 NAIC# 60399	FSC X	'09	71.6	8.5	1.9	18.0	4,153,238	74.1	...	17.0	8.9	556,480	434,209	416,870	183,088	84,453	61,921	76,921
		Rating History: A, 04/01/10; A, 03/18/09; A, 02/25/08; A, 03/13/07; A, 01/10/06																
AMERICAN FARM LIFE INS CO National Farm Life Insurance Company	NR-2	'05	91.2	...	...	8.8	1,669	19.3	...	14.3	66.4	1,556	88	58	17	29	23	23
Jerry D. Davis, Jr. President, CEO & Chairman		'06	93.5	...	...	6.5	1,844	15.0	...	57.4	27.6	1,584	237	213	161	37	28	28
P.O. Box 1486 Fort Worth, TX 76101-1486		'07	89.5	...	5.2	5.3	1,924	25.6	...	49.1	25.3	1,593	211	193	56	13	9	9
TX : 2000 : Stock : Agency Life		'08	76.0	...	4.7	19.3	2,134	50.0	...	33.8	16.2	1,543	612	398	189	-44	-40	-40
817-451-9550 AMB# 060346 NAIC# 99619		'09	88.7	...	...	11.3	2,381	50.5	...	37.4	12.0	1,546	890	438	191	27	14	-2
		Rating History: NR-2, 05/28/10; NR-2, 05/26/09; NR-2, 05/12/08; NR-2, 05/05/07; NR-2, 05/31/06																

BEST'S PROFITABILITY, LEVERAGE AND LIQUIDITY TESTS 2005 – 2009

Data in U.S. Dollars

—	Profitability Tests							Leverage Tests						Liquidity Tests					
Un-Realized Capital Gains ($000)	Benefits Paid to NPW & Dep (%)	Comm. & Expenses to NPW & Dep (%)	NOG to Total Assets (%)	NOG to Total Rev (%)	Operating Return on Equity (%)	Net Yield (%)	Total Return (%)	Change in NPW & Dep (%)	NPW & Dep to Capital (X)	Capital & Surplus to Liabilities (%)	Surplus Relief (%)	Reins Leverage (%)	Change in Capital (%)	Quick Liquidity (%)	Current Liquidity (%)	Non-Invest Grade Bonds to Capital (%)	Delinq. & Foreclosed Mortgages to Capital (%)	Mort. & Credit Tenant Loans & R.E. to Capital (%)	Affiliated Invest to Capital (%)
...	85.9	14.3	0.9	0.1	1.9	...	...	-0.5	32.3	101.3	...	...	-4.5	171.6	171.6	...	...	...	...
...	85.8	14.6	0.4	0.0	0.7	8.41	8.41	-4.9	30.5	97.8	...	...	0.7	164.0	164.0	...	...	...	...
...	85.8	14.6	0.6	0.0	1.2	7.42	7.42	1.2	31.1	96.5	...	...	-0.7	182.9	182.9	...	...	...	...
...	85.5	14.6	0.3	0.0	0.6	1.95	1.95	-4.0	29.7	81.3	...	...	0.6	170.0	170.0	...	...	...	...
...	85.4	14.6	0.0	0.0	0.1	0.40	0.40	-3.1	28.8	79.8	...	...	0.1	166.3	166.3	...	...	...	...
Principal Lines of Business: Dental (100.0%)													Principal States: WI (100.0%)						
...	29.0	21.6	22.3	34.4	23.7	2.69	2.69	-65.3	0.5	999.9	...	...	26.9	999.9	999.9	...	...	...	...
...	26.3	30.1	13.1	33.3	13.6	3.85	3.85	-31.2	0.3	999.9	...	...	14.5	999.9	999.9	...	...	...	...
...	43.3	45.3	6.1	13.2	6.8	3.37	3.37	43.4	0.5	480.1	...	...	-4.4	773.7	773.7	...	...	...	...
...	37.4	20.4	11.3	27.7	13.3	2.39	2.39	0.0	0.4	653.7	...	...	16.0	809.3	854.0	...	...	...	...
...	57.9	24.2	5.4	13.0	6.5	0.84	0.84	19.1	0.5	395.3	...	...	6.7	501.4	501.4	...	...	...	...
Principal Lines of Business: FEHBP (67.7%), Dental (32.3%)													Principal States: AR (100.0%)						
-20,000	28.7	11.0	0.5	1.4	7.1	5.86	5.61	65.2	4.1	7.1	9.6	267.9	12.6	70.7	73.7	17.1	...	198.5	4.6
2,448	78.8	10.6	0.8	3.3	10.4	7.56	7.62	-36.3	1.8	9.7	5.7	176.2	46.9	69.7	72.4	10.9	...	169.5	3.2
-6,643	52.8	11.8	0.2	0.8	2.1	5.27	5.20	15.6	2.0	8.7	4.1	162.2	1.1	67.8	71.9	9.6	...	199.4	3.2
460	50.4	13.5	0.8	4.0	11.1	3.75	2.90	9.2	2.3	8.0	1.1	150.4	-0.8	63.6	68.9	46.1	0.3	240.8	3.9
773	42.3	11.5	1.1	4.5	15.4	5.24	4.99	25.9	2.3	8.0	10.5	174.6	22.5	59.0	68.6	35.6	1.2	206.1	2.6
Principal Lines of Business: IndAnn (99.5%), GrpLife (0.3%), OrdLife (0.1%), IndA&H (0.0%), GrpA&H (0.0%)													Principal States: FL (12.1%), TX (9.2%), CA (8.5%), IL (7.0%), OH (4.7%)						
...	11.4	10.6	0.6	1.1	1.5	5.81	5.86	38.0	1.2	47.5	...	...	0.3	102.0	115.0	...	...	...	...
...	40.2	12.6	1.3	6.3	4.3	5.82	5.85	-55.7	0.5	42.7	...	...	4.2	100.1	111.8	...	...	...	...
...	50.2	15.2	1.0	6.0	3.5	5.77	5.80	-22.5	0.4	39.4	...	...	3.8	99.4	111.0	...	...	...	...
...	229.5	31.7	1.1	12.9	4.0	5.69	4.35	-70.2	0.1	39.9	...	...	-0.9	97.1	106.5	16.3	...	...	...
...	59.9	12.8	-4.3	-29.4	-17.5	5.58	3.86	216.7	0.4	27.0	...	...	-20.5	81.0	91.5	32.4	...	...	...
Principal Lines of Business: IndAnn (100.0%)													Principal States: NY (99.6%)						
-5,679	66.2	368.5	3.0	109.6	3.1	1.89	-2.12	-14.9	0.0	999.9	0.3	1.9	23.7	208.2	208.6	...	...	...	97.8
17,917	69.4	355.5	13.4	72.2	14.5	21.58	31.17	9.6	0.0	805.3	0.1	1.2	53.7	24.9	25.6	...	...	...	105.7
45,675	102.9	411.2	16.6	71.5	17.8	27.87	43.67	36.2	0.0	999.9	0.1	0.6	76.5	188.8	192.3	...	...	...	98.4
13,239	102.7	106.5	9.4	61.7	9.7	16.44	19.44	-7.2	0.0	999.9	0.1	0.5	10.5	443.0	461.7	...	...	...	93.7
177,348	175.8	42.9	0.4	38.1	0.5	1.02	38.89	-49.6	0.0	999.9	0.0	0.0	36.9	586.0	616.1	...	...	...	97.1
Principal Lines of Business: IndA&H (132.4%), OrdLife (-32.4%)													Principal States: TX (99.4%)						
39,376	48.5	30.0	2.6	8.8	38.6	4.42	4.51	6.3	3.1	9.0	0.0	0.1	34.3	28.0	62.6	16.3	...	7.6	8.0
-22,743	45.6	29.9	3.5	11.5	42.6	4.57	4.63	2.8	2.8	9.6	0.0	0.1	13.8	25.3	61.7	20.5	...	6.5	6.9
8,106	45.6	30.4	3.4	11.7	43.1	4.47	4.47	5.1	2.9	8.7	0.0	0.1	1.1	23.5	60.1	20.2	...	6.1	7.1
-12,477	48.7	29.8	2.8	10.1	40.6	4.12	3.19	15.5	3.3	6.9	0.0	0.1	3.6	22.6	58.5	27.4	...	7.1	8.3
25,305	49.8	29.5	2.9	10.9	41.3	3.82	2.88	11.2	2.9	8.3	0.0	0.1	25.1	25.7	60.1	96.4	...	5.5	7.6
Principal Lines of Business: IndA&H (86.1%), OrdLife (11.2%), IndAnn (2.5%), GrpAnn (0.2%), GrpA&H (0.0%)																			
...	52.4	34.4	1.9	1.9	10.6	5.68	5.67	13.5	5.0	21.2	...	0.1	11.3	73.1	82.7	1.0	...	...	...
...	51.5	33.0	4.9	5.1	26.2	6.04	6.02	15.5	4.1	24.8	...	0.0	40.1	73.2	83.8	0.7	...	...	...
-234	48.0	32.3	5.7	6.4	26.7	6.25	6.11	11.8	3.4	29.5	...	0.0	37.4	73.0	84.0	3.4	...	...	...
4	48.9	32.8	5.6	6.7	25.1	6.30	5.23	11.1	3.3	28.7	...	0.0	14.3	62.1	76.8	3.7	...	...	...
230	47.1	32.1	5.5	7.1	23.7	6.41	5.29	9.2	2.8	31.4	...	0.0	29.7	72.0	89.2	4.9	...	...	...
Principal Lines of Business: IndA&H (94.0%), GrpA&H (3.9%), OrdLife (2.0%), IndAnn (0.0%)													Principal States: NY (92.9%), NJ (4.9%)						
1,084	46.9	26.2	1.4	8.2	14.2	6.02	6.37	0.4	1.1	13.3	4.3	27.4	17.5	64.6	77.5	23.6	...	52.9	...
5,925	48.5	26.7	1.7	9.6	14.9	6.01	6.27	4.6	0.9	15.3	4.2	22.8	18.4	63.9	77.0	19.1	...	60.3	...
1,550	53.7	25.7	1.7	10.5	14.2	5.82	5.86	1.7	0.8	17.1	4.0	24.1	14.8	67.6	80.6	17.2	...	58.2	...
-12,237	56.1	26.9	1.2	7.5	9.9	5.87	2.04	-2.8	0.9	14.0	5.4	33.4	-15.4	66.0	78.0	26.9	...	78.8	...
-1,707	59.5	26.7	1.5	10.0	12.3	5.82	6.18	-2.7	0.7	17.2	3.5	29.0	27.5	60.4	82.4	16.8	...	61.2	...
Principal Lines of Business: OrdLife (85.1%), IndAnn (8.9%), GrpAnn (5.1%), GrpLife (1.0%)													Principal States: WI (17.7%), MO (11.4%), MN (10.9%), IL (10.1%), CO (6.6%)						
...	1.5	151.5	1.4	18.0	1.5	4.43	4.58	-6.5	0.0	999.9	0.0	2.3	1.5	999.9	999.9	...	...	...	...
...	0.5	50.8	1.6	9.6	1.8	4.83	4.94	268.2	0.1	615.8	0.0	2.2	1.8	575.5	607.9	...	...	...	...
...	4.0	101.9	0.5	3.5	0.6	4.86	4.95	-9.3	0.1	487.1	0.0	2.2	0.6	442.5	480.9	...	...	...	...
...	18.5	52.6	-2.0	-8.5	-2.6	4.72	4.84	106.1	0.3	263.6	0.0	43.1	-3.1	296.1	318.8	...	...	...	...
...	14.6	43.2	0.6	2.5	0.9	4.12	3.52	9.9	0.3	185.2	3.9	46.5	-0.1	202.0	218.9	...	...	...	...
Principal Lines of Business: OrdLife (70.2%), IndAnn (24.7%), GrpAnn (5.1%)													Principal States: TX (53.0%), OK (27.2%), NM (14.1%), AZ (5.1%)						

2010 BEST'S KEY RATING GUIDE — LIFE/HEALTH EDITION
ANNUAL STATEMENT DATA FOR YEARS 2005 – 2009

Data in U.S. Dollars

COMPANY NAME Ultimate Parent Association Principal Officer Mailing Address Dom. : Began Bus. : Struct. : Mktg. Specialty Phone # AMB# NAIC#	Best's Financial Strength Rating FSC	Data Year	Balance Sheet Bonds (%)	Mort. Loans & R.E. (%)	Com & Pref. Stock (%)	All Other Assets (%)	Total Assets ($000)	Life Reserves (%)	Health Reserves %)	Ann Res. & Dep. Liabilities (%)	All Other Liabilities (%)	Capital & Surplus ($000)	Operations Direct Premiums Written ($000)	Net Premiums Written & Deposits ($000)	Operating Cash Flow ($000)	NOG Before Taxes ($000)	NOG After Taxes ($000)	Net Income ($000)
AMERICAN FARMERS & RANCHERS LF American Farmers & Ranchers Mutual Ins Terry L. Detrick President P.O. Box 25968 Oklahoma City, OK 73125 OK : 2000 : Stock : Inactive Ind Ann, Life 405-218-5400 AMB# 060341 NAIC# 60004	NR-5	'05	87.7	...	...	12.3	12,185	56.0	...	41.4	2.6	3,076	1,086	939	661	-114	-30	-30
		'06	88.9	...	...	11.1	12,603	52.0	...	46.0	2.0	2,628	1,887	1,710	422	-39	-65	-65
		'07	93.6	...	...	6.4	14,077	47.7	...	51.0	1.3	2,941	2,056	1,876	1,447	113	113	113
		'08	92.5	...	...	7.5	17,894	42.6	...	54.2	3.2	5,326	2,243	2,023	3,169	176	132	132
		'09	85.5	...	...	14.5	18,677	39.8	...	57.6	2.6	4,986	2,263	2,210	771	-81	-123	-123
		Rating History: NR-5, 04/28/10; NR-5, 04/22/09; NR-5, 04/09/08; NR-5, 04/24/07; NR-5, 05/08/06																
AMERICAN FEDERATED LIFE INS Galaxie Corporation James L. Martin, Jr. President P.O. Box 321422 Flowood, MS 39232 MS : 1983 : Stock : Direct Response Credit A&H, Credit Life 601-992-6886 AMB# 068071 NAIC# 98736	B+ Rating Outlook: Stable FSC IV	'05	87.0	...	...	13.0	16,079	51.3	37.1	...	11.6	7,277	8,659	8,572	-1,983	5,574	4,163	4,179
		'06	87.1	...	...	12.9	17,370	51.7	34.9	...	13.4	6,048	10,171	9,304	1,256	5,533	3,988	3,982
		'07	81.4	...	...	18.6	18,111	52.5	36.5	...	11.0	5,967	10,744	9,931	637	6,615	4,711	4,720
		'08	86.1	...	...	13.9	17,701	53.4	37.4	...	9.1	5,843	9,956	9,329	-407	6,681	4,859	4,863
		'09	82.7	...	...	17.3	18,964	52.0	36.3	...	11.7	6,057	11,179	10,401	1,056	7,032	4,976	4,983
		Rating History: B+, 05/28/10; B+, 06/05/09; B+, 05/23/08; B+, 05/22/07; B, 06/19/06																
AMERICAN FIDELITY ASSURANCE CO Cameron Associates Inc William M. Cameron Chairman & CEO 2000 N. Classen Boulevard, Suite 10E Oklahoma City, OK 73106 OK : 1960 : Stock : Exclusive Agent Ann, Dis inc, Dread dis 405-523-2000 AMB# 006054 NAIC# 60410	A+ Rating Outlook: Stable FSC IX	'05	72.1	10.4	1.3	16.1	2,932,874	6.8	9.1	29.8	54.3	184,625	688,039	457,877	184,982	39,449	19,596	19,507
		'06	69.5	10.7	0.8	18.9	2,959,825	7.2	10.5	30.9	51.4	200,447	701,784	493,486	-12,173	35,065	23,934	25,531
		'07	71.7	10.3	0.7	17.4	3,211,690	7.0	11.4	29.2	52.4	213,644	762,391	577,943	202,732	38,450	21,607	23,006
		'08	72.6	10.0	0.8	16.6	3,311,754	7.3	12.6	30.3	49.8	239,134	811,735	652,155	193,917	88,540	64,094	38,134
		'09	72.8	9.2	0.7	17.3	3,567,593	7.3	12.3	30.6	49.8	282,119	846,362	619,732	153,224	102,128	59,432	49,489
		Rating History: A+, 03/05/10; A+, 02/17/09; A+, 02/20/08; A+, 04/02/07; A+, 03/24/06																
AMERICAN FIDELITY LIFE INS CO AMFI Corporation Ruben E. Mauch President 4060 Barrancas Avenue Pensacola, FL 32507 FL : 1956 : Stock : Agency Ind Life, Term Life, Whole life 850-456-7401 AMB# 006055 NAIC# 60429	B++ Rating Outlook: Stable FSC VII	'05	83.5	7.8	3.7	5.0	464,779	25.0	...	72.8	2.2	76,265	15,448	37,076	13,383	2,624	2,394	2,494
		'06	81.8	10.0	3.8	4.5	474,967	24.5	...	72.7	2.8	77,547	15,100	36,366	11,625	3,301	3,039	2,648
		'07	80.5	11.3	3.4	4.8	477,240	24.4	...	72.9	2.7	77,055	14,515	35,167	5,470	1,721	1,568	1,910
		'08	81.3	11.1	3.0	4.6	469,805	24.6	...	73.3	2.1	73,209	13,494	33,739	-1,935	1,266	1,152	1,154
		'09	80.3	12.7	3.3	3.7	460,907	24.8	...	73.7	1.5	71,489	12,978	31,733	-9,369	2,078	2,078	-879
		Rating History: B++, 12/16/09; B++, 03/20/09; B++, 01/16/08; B++, 11/09/06; B++, 12/15/05																
AMERICAN FINANCIAL SECURITY Michael Camilleri President & CEO 10308 Metcalf, PMB #275 Overland Park, KS 66212 MO : 1957 : Stock : Not Available Life 573-636-5057 AMB# 007111 NAIC# 69337	NR-5	'05	22.9	...	...	77.1	2,615	51.3	...	...	48.7	2,527	19	19	-15	-3	-3	-3
		'06	9.8	...	...	90.2	2,635	35.6	...	...	64.4	2,560	17	17	360	-370	-370	-370
		'07	...	...	...	100.0	2,148	48.6	...	...	51.4	2,088	18	18	-485	29	29	29
		'08	...	...	...	100.0	3,086	42.5	...	...	57.5	3,016	20	20	939	-103	-103	-102
		'09	...	...	...	100.0	1,914	38.0	...	...	62.0	1,833	19	19	-1,172	-361	-361	-361
		Rating History: NR-5, 04/20/10; NR-5, 04/14/09; NR-5, 04/21/08; NR-5, 04/24/07; NR-5, 05/02/06																
AMERICAN GENERAL ASSURANCE CO American International Group, Inc Mary Jane B. Fortin President & CEO 3600 Route 66 Neptune, NJ 07754-1580 IL : 1930 : Stock : Bank Group A&H, Group Life 847-517-6000 AMB# 006989 NAIC# 68373	A Rating Outlook: Negative FSC VII	'05	80.9	...	3.1	16.0	1,507,540	32.0	53.3	...	14.7	177,235	252,095	717,931	169,071	33,042	21,866	21,949
		'06	79.6	...	5.1	15.2	1,510,699	18.4	49.2	...	32.4	280,465	223,808	491,884	18,947	-485	-4,396	-6,050
		'07	66.4	...	17.2	16.4	287,681	9.4	53.9	...	36.6	144,673	169,922	-104,405	-1,062,556	20,449	36,446	28,461
		'08	72.1	...	8.4	19.5	193,923	9.3	62.5	0.0	28.2	74,867	141,299	79,416	-77,760	3,471	1,750	-6,538
		'09	75.1	...	6.3	18.6	184,651	10.8	65.0	0.0	24.2	91,453	101,428	67,354	-9,874	17,420	12,178	10,648
		Rating History: A, 12/16/09; A, 11/10/08; A gu, 09/15/08; A+ g, 06/17/08; A++g, 05/28/08																
AMERICAN GENERAL LF & ACCIDENT American International Group, Inc James A. Mallon President & CEO American General Center Nashville, TN 37250 TN : 1900 : Stock : Career Agent Ind Ann, Trad Life, Univ Life 615-749-1000 AMB# 006788 NAIC# 66672	A Rating Outlook: Negative FSC XI	'05	79.8	10.6	0.7	8.9	8,929,012	81.7	1.7	12.0	4.5	582,948	964,817	894,723	127,004	344,535	313,857	316,574
		'06	72.6	11.9	6.1	9.3	8,936,855	81.5	1.7	12.4	4.4	500,485	960,773	889,310	-23,000	333,424	288,764	279,270
		'07	73.2	13.2	3.4	10.3	9,134,161	80.9	1.7	12.6	4.8	546,887	951,332	887,536	40,218	337,624	275,621	203,817
		'08	71.4	12.9	3.1	12.7	9,134,531	81.2	1.7	13.7	3.3	563,502	1,017,846	958,296	-964,853	297,770	206,843	-816,947
		'09	77.2	11.4	0.9	10.4	9,359,041	81.2	1.7	13.9	3.2	751,345	963,900	906,908	184,362	324,735	165,836	108,960
		Rating History: A, 12/16/09; A, 11/10/08; A gu, 09/15/08; A+ g, 06/17/08; A++g, 05/28/08																
AMERICAN GENERAL LIFE INS CO American International Group, Inc Mary Jane B. Fortin President & CEO 2727-A Allen Parkway Houston, TX 77019-2115 TX : 1960 : Stock : Agency Ind Life, Struc Sett, Ann 713-522-1111 AMB# 006058 NAIC# 60488	A Rating Outlook: Negative FSC XV	'05	68.5	4.0	10.0	17.5	31,181,403	43.6	0.7	39.8	15.9	5,088,994	3,867,665	3,310,345	2,492,330	607,343	679,993	640,822
		'06	66.3	4.6	12.1	17.0	34,234,048	43.0	0.7	41.7	14.6	5,531,547	4,129,149	3,381,737	2,744,097	542,712	538,111	509,583
		'07	64.5	6.0	10.5	19.0	36,717,239	43.0	0.7	42.7	13.6	5,780,109	3,879,976	3,012,405	2,355,719	1,059,134	1,084,913	865,022
		'08	63.6	5.9	9.3	21.2	38,668,102	42.6	0.7	44.4	12.3	5,214,869	4,566,099	4,225,466	1,270,298	69,945	58,505	-4,103,228
		'09	67.6	5.5	9.7	17.1	39,653,080	43.4	0.6	45.3	10.7	5,954,032	3,296,416	2,243,871	1,501,079	327,104	128,789	-100,502
		Rating History: A, 12/16/09; A, 11/10/08; A gu, 09/15/08; A+ g, 06/17/08; A++g, 05/28/08																
AMERICAN GENERAL LIFE INS DE American International Group, Inc Mary Jane B. Fortin President & CEO 2727-A Allen Parkway Houston, TX 77019-2115 DE : 1962 : Stock : Broker Life, Ann, A&H 713-522-1111 AMB# 006809 NAIC# 66842	A Rating Outlook: Negative FSC X	'05	66.7	4.2	0.2	28.9	12,582,970	18.6	1.2	52.7	27.5	635,980	597,434	298,742	-917,600	246,463	170,584	151,166
		'06	60.0	4.9	2.3	32.8	11,146,805	21.7	1.6	45.3	31.5	569,988	642,577	382,475	-1,411,335	151,101	93,190	108,706
		'07	58.7	5.1	2.3	33.9	10,790,222	22.7	1.8	43.4	32.1	444,806	780,746	495,721	-354,060	113,468	92,633	48,662
		'08	61.2	5.6	2.1	31.1	9,429,399	27.4	2.2	44.9	25.5	364,387	638,640	398,392	-1,284,975	66,487	46,498	-875,552
		'09	59.8	5.4	0.7	34.1	9,357,652	27.5	2.4	43.0	27.1	454,784	385,740	218,210	-188,977	65,373	32,932	-23,177
		Rating History: A, 12/16/09; A, 11/10/08; A gu, 09/15/08; A+ g, 06/17/08; A++g, 05/28/08																

2010 BEST'S KEY RATING GUIDE — LIFE/HEALTH EDITION
BEST'S PROFITABILITY, LEVERAGE AND LIQUIDITY TESTS 2005 – 2009

Data in U.S. Dollars

	Profitability Tests							Leverage Tests						Liquidity Tests					
Un-Realized Capital Gains ($000)	Benefits Paid to NPW & Dep (%)	Comm. & Expenses to NPW & Dep (%)	NOG to Total Assets (%)	NOG to Total Rev (%)	Operating Return on Equity (%)	Net Yield (%)	Total Return (%)	Change in NPW & Dep (%)	NPW & Dep to Capital (X)	Capital & Surplus to Liabilities (%)	Surplus Relief (%)	Reins Leverage (%)	Change in Capital (%)	Quick Liquidity (%)	Current Liquidity (%)	Non-Invest Grade Bonds to Capital (%)	Delinq. & Foreclosed Mortgages to Capital (%)	Mort. & Credit Tenant Loans & R.E. to Capital (%)	Affiliated Invest to Capital (%)
...	91.1	59.9	-0.3	-2.0	-1.1	4.39	5.11	143.7	0.3	33.8	0.1	5.6	25.1	112.6	113.0	...	...	...	...
...	52.8	32.6	-0.5	-2.7	-2.3	4.57	5.08	82.2	0.7	26.4	0.1	7.3	-14.5	105.4	106.5	...	...	...	...
...	36.7	29.4	0.8	4.4	4.1	5.04	5.34	9.7	0.6	26.4	0.1	7.2	12.0	102.1	104.8	...	...	...	...
...	60.2	31.0	0.8	4.4	3.2	6.11	6.28	7.8	0.4	42.4	0.0	5.8	81.0	122.6	123.5	...	...	...	...
19	40.5	33.1	-0.7	-4.3	-2.4	4.13	4.44	9.3	0.4	36.5	0.1	5.6	-6.3	123.9	126.4	...	...	...	...
	Principal Lines of Business: IndAnn (70.0%), OrdLife (30.0%)													Principal States: OK (99.8%)					
...	22.2	7.8	25.0	45.1	49.6	3.98	4.32	27.8	1.2	83.4	...	41.3	-23.4	136.5	147.4	0.0	...	...	0.3
...	24.6	7.3	23.8	39.8	59.9	4.52	4.64	8.5	1.5	53.8	...	56.5	-16.9	115.8	123.7	0.0	...	...	...
...	24.0	6.4	26.6	44.4	78.4	4.30	4.43	6.7	1.7	49.6	...	65.2	-1.3	111.4	119.8	...	...	...	...
...	30.8	6.6	27.1	48.3	82.3	4.60	4.69	-6.1	1.6	49.8	...	68.0	-2.0	107.0	117.5	...	...	...	0.4
...	26.0	6.4	27.1	44.9	83.6	4.38	4.36	11.5	1.7	47.5	...	68.7	3.7	105.1	115.4	...	...	...	...
	Principal Lines of Business: CrdLife (55.6%), CrdA&H (44.4%)													Principal States: MS (59.6%), LA (35.5%), MO (5.0%)					
1,202	57.9	50.2	0.7	3.0	10.9	6.11	6.22	3.2	2.3	8.0	13.8	474.3	4.9	68.2	76.1	6.8	...	156.8	1.1
562	61.7	49.8	0.8	3.5	12.4	5.95	6.07	7.8	2.3	8.7	13.2	444.8	7.7	67.2	75.5	4.3	...	150.9	0.4
878	60.2	49.1	0.7	2.8	10.4	5.85	5.96	17.1	2.6	8.5	8.2	434.8	6.7	65.6	75.0	3.6	...	147.3	0.5
-1,429	54.9	41.5	2.0	7.6	28.3	5.94	4.80	12.8	2.7	8.6	10.8	399.4	8.2	63.5	74.0	18.8	...	136.2	0.5
-2,297	51.4	42.9	1.7	7.3	22.8	5.78	5.30	-5.0	2.2	9.7	5.7	359.5	18.0	62.4	72.4	42.8	...	114.0	2.3
	Principal Lines of Business: GrpA&H (48.0%), IndA&H (25.2%), IndAnn (16.4%), OrdLife (9.8%), GrpAnn (0.5%)													Principal States: CA (17.2%), TX (10.8%), OK (9.3%), MS (5.5%), KY (5.3%)					
1,461	64.5	24.2	0.5	6.6	3.2	4.48	4.82	-2.0	0.5	20.6	0.0	7.2	3.3	97.2	97.4	0.3	...	45.5	24.8
569	66.0	24.0	0.6	8.3	4.0	4.41	4.45	-1.9	0.4	20.6	0.0	6.8	1.9	94.8	95.1	0.2	...	58.4	23.8
-1,487	71.6	25.8	0.3	4.3	2.0	4.35	4.11	-3.3	0.4	20.1	0.0	6.6	-1.3	93.1	93.3	0.2	...	67.1	23.8
-4,066	66.8	26.3	0.2	3.5	1.5	3.88	3.02	-4.1	0.4	19.0	0.0	6.7	-6.1	90.6	91.8	0.3	22.3	69.4	25.2
2,452	63.0	28.6	0.4	6.7	2.9	3.71	3.61	-5.9	0.4	19.2	0.0	6.6	-1.0	87.6	89.4	0.3	28.7	79.0	36.6
	Principal Lines of Business: GrpAnn (53.6%), OrdLife (36.3%), IndAnn (5.7%), GrpLife (4.5%)													Principal States: TX (13.0%), FL (11.7%), CA (9.3%), NC (7.7%), GA (3.9%)					
...	-5.3	353.1	-0.1	-4.7	-0.1	2.04	2.05	4.6	0.0	999.9	...	...	30.9	999.9	999.9	...	...	...	...
...	560.8	999.9	-14.1	-99.9	-14.6	4.66	4.66	-11.5	0.0	999.9	...	...	1.3	999.9	999.9	...	...	...	...
...	14.6	508.1	1.2	23.2	1.2	4.58	4.57	6.1	0.0	999.9	...	...	-18.4	999.9	999.9	...	...	...	...
...	...	848.8	-3.9	-99.9	-4.0	1.76	1.76	7.9	0.0	999.9	...	...	44.5	999.9	999.9	...	...	...	...
...	41.9	999.9	-14.4	-99.9	-14.9	0.15	0.11	-1.4	0.0	999.9	...	...	-39.2	999.9	999.9	...	...	...	...
	Principal Lines of Business: OrdLife (100.0%)													Principal States: MO (56.3%), OK (26.5%), KS (11.9%)					
-3,582	60.6	40.5	1.5	2.7	13.2	6.35	6.14	6.3	3.9	13.9	16.2	47.9	14.0	43.2	65.1	26.1	...	4.0	25.3
4,985	88.0	65.6	-0.3	-0.7	-1.9	6.22	6.53	-31.5	1.7	24.0	9.2	116.8	59.5	48.0	71.9	21.9	...	3.7	17.6
893	-99.9	-78.4	4.1	-99.9	17.1	3.26	2.39	-99.9	-0.7	111.9	27.7	204.1	-48.1	57.9	89.6	10.6	...	...	35.0
4,277	56.2	67.6	0.7	1.5	1.6	6.66	4.56	176.1	1.0	67.4	32.2	294.0	-48.6	69.7	96.7	7.9	...	...	27.4
3,953	41.3	61.0	6.4	13.8	14.6	6.56	7.45	-15.2	0.7	107.4	12.2	148.4	22.4	93.1	125.1	8.1	...	...	22.2
	Principal Lines of Business: GrpA&H (72.6%), GrpLife (26.9%), OrdLife (0.2%), CrdLife (0.1%), CrdA&H (0.1%)													Principal States: PA (13.3%), NC (8.7%), CA (6.9%), GA (6.6%), FL (6.2%)					
-26,664	79.1	45.4	3.5	20.1	54.4	7.73	7.50	-4.2	1.4	7.7	2.5	30.4	6.0	32.4	51.3	108.1	0.1	156.6	23.3
-19,591	82.7	43.8	3.2	18.4	53.3	7.70	7.41	-0.6	1.6	6.7	2.5	36.1	-11.7	30.1	50.1	95.0	...	198.7	24.6
-12,884	83.1	42.1	3.1	17.6	52.6	7.72	6.79	-0.2	1.4	7.3	2.2	30.2	10.0	30.9	49.5	96.9	...	203.8	21.4
-8,410	85.9	36.8	2.3	12.8	37.3	7.44	-3.54	8.0	1.6	6.9	2.1	28.5	-4.0	34.2	52.2	86.9	...	207.4	25.0
-4,335	89.8	39.0	1.8	10.7	25.2	7.33	6.61	-5.4	1.2	9.1	1.5	15.3	31.6	36.8	54.7	69.9	...	143.5	15.6
	Principal Lines of Business: OrdLife (71.4%), IndAnn (19.2%), IndA&H (8.6%), IndLife (0.7%), GrpAnn (0.1%)													Principal States: GA (11.5%), TN (9.9%), FL (9.0%), PA (8.2%), VA (6.5%)					
181,222	57.0	22.2	2.3	12.1	13.8	7.83	8.46	5.0	0.6	23.1	6.7	71.5	7.2	38.1	56.4	32.2	0.2	28.3	77.8
190,225	64.2	21.8	1.6	9.0	10.1	7.57	8.22	2.2	0.6	22.8	7.8	86.7	9.7	34.9	53.6	35.2	0.2	31.6	74.1
-373,232	78.1	16.4	3.1	18.0	19.2	8.57	6.73	-10.9	0.5	22.1	7.4	94.2	5.8	34.1	52.6	38.9	...	39.7	66.1
-4,629,138	59.2	11.4	0.2	0.9	1.1	6.15	-18.89	40.3	0.7	18.5	8.6	109.1	-6.8	36.6	54.3	35.8	...	43.4	68.1
62,400	121.2	12.6	0.3	2.8	2.3	5.85	5.14	-46.9	0.4	20.5	6.4	100.1	11.6	38.1	55.7	36.2	0.2	37.3	72.9
	Principal Lines of Business: IndAnn (72.2%), OrdLife (27.7%), IndA&H (1.3%), GrpAnn (0.0%), GrpA&H (0.0%)													Principal States: TX (16.9%), CA (14.2%), FL (7.6%), IL (4.9%), NJ (3.7%)					
-20,418	385.2	20.3	1.3	15.4	24.8	7.56	7.30	-14.4	0.4	8.0	6.5	48.3	-10.3	45.2	63.7	91.1	2.3	78.6	4.3
-8,988	563.2	16.2	0.8	8.9	15.5	6.97	7.21	28.0	0.6	9.1	8.4	48.7	-5.0	41.7	61.5	82.1	3.2	84.5	4.5
3,246	266.3	15.0	0.8	8.3	18.3	7.12	6.70	29.6	0.9	7.5	10.1	64.6	-19.4	40.7	59.6	114.0	4.0	106.8	6.2
-28,182	300.8	18.0	0.5	4.8	11.5	6.99	-5.13	-19.6	0.9	6.8	10.1	78.3	-13.6	43.0	60.3	102.2	4.4	118.5	6.6
19,458	425.9	35.7	0.4	5.0	8.0	6.61	6.04	-45.2	0.4	8.3	6.2	78.5	18.1	48.8	65.2	94.8	...	96.1	5.5
	Principal Lines of Business: GrpA&H (26.4%), GrpAnn (25.7%), GrpLife (17.6%), IndA&H (10.6%), OrdLife (10.2%)													Principal States: CA (11.7%), MI (8.5%), TX (6.0%), IL (5.9%), PA (5.6%)					

Data in U.S. Dollars

COMPANY NAME Ultimate Parent Association Principal Officer Mailing Address Dom. : Began Bus. : Struct. : Mktg. Specialty Phone # AMB# NAIC#	Best's Financial Strength Rating FSC	Data Year	Balance Sheet: Bonds (%)	Mort. Loans & R.E. (%)	Com & Pref. Stock (%)	All Other Assets (%)	Total Assets ($000)	Life Reserves (%)	Health Reserves (%)	Ann Res. & Dep. Liabilities (%)	All Other Liabilities (%)	Capital & Surplus ($000)	Operations: Direct Premiums Written ($000)	Net Premiums Written & Deposits ($000)	Operating Cash Flow ($000)	NOG Before Taxes ($000)	NOG After Taxes ($000)	Net Income ($000)
AMERICAN HEALTH AND LIFE INS Citigroup Inc. Dava S. Carson President & CEO 3001 Meacham Boulevard, Suite 100 Fort Worth, TX 76137-4697 TX : 1954 : Stock : Direct Response Credit A&H, Credit Life 800-316-5607 AMB# 006062 NAIC# 60518	**A** Rating Outlook: Stable **FSC X**	'05	84.1	0.0	6.4	9.5	1,723,021	50.9	37.6	0.0	11.5	913,559	161,389	220,283	-234,792	251,519	178,956	180,194
		'06	88.2	0.0	6.1	5.7	1,609,844	47.4	40.5	...	12.1	880,124	172,206	214,691	-63,274	192,781	138,168	139,047
		'07	88.0	0.0	5.4	6.6	1,676,168	47.6	42.4	...	9.9	886,185	262,768	292,597	47,808	146,314	102,597	101,013
		'08	85.5	0.0	5.9	8.6	1,519,632	44.0	41.1	...	14.9	656,795	255,844	282,337	-145,420	167,504	120,414	96,308
		'09	83.3	...	7.8	8.9	1,360,547	45.6	42.2	...	12.2	623,730	128,319	148,851	-209,649	147,119	107,861	100,015
		Rating History: A, 06/04/10; A, 06/03/09; A g, 05/22/08; A g, 01/12/07; A g, 07/01/05																
AMERICAN HEALTH NETWORK IN LLC[2] AHN Acquisition LLC Ben H. Park, M.D. President & CEO 10333 N. Meridian Street Indianapolis, IN 46290 IN : 2000 : Non-Profit : Broker Health 317-580-6307 AMB# 064632 NAIC# 52623	**NR-5**	'05	2.0	1.3	...	96.7	24,395	...	1.6	...	98.4	7,286	...	...	668	390	390	326
		'06	1.7	1.8	...	96.5	29,871	...	...	...	100.0	6,634	...	...	1,449	-169	-169	-174
		'07	1.5	2.0	...	96.5	34,165	...	...	...	100.0	8,340	...	...	737	1,661	1,661	1,578
		'08	1.6	1.5	...	96.9	31,307	...	...	...	100.0	9,170	...	...	-984	745	745	670
		'09	1.8	2.4	...	95.8	28,017	...	...	...	100.0	8,786	...	...	341	178	-395	-481
		Rating History: NR-5, 04/26/10; NR-5, 04/13/09; NR-5, 03/25/08; NR-5, 04/03/07; NR-5, 06/20/06																
AMERICAN HEALTHGUARD CORP David Kutner President 30 E. Santa Clara, Suite D Arcadia, CA 91006-7023 CA : 1984 : Stock : Broker Dental 626-821-5500 AMB# 064731	**NR-5**	'05	...	...	...	100.0	841	...	...	...	100.0	30	2,079	2,079	142	-7	-8	-8
		'06	...	...	...	100.0	624	...	...	...	100.0	38	2,812	2,812	-192	9	8	8
		'07	...	...	...	100.0	590	...	...	...	100.0	93	2,782	2,782	-190	67	55	55
		'08	...	...	...	100.0	827	...	...	...	100.0	232	2,900	2,900	188	123	85	85
		'09	...	...	...	100.0	795	...	...	...	100.0	200	2,619	2,619	-118	-31	-32	-32
		Rating History: NR-5, 03/22/10; NR-5, 03/13/09; NR-5, 03/11/08; NR-5, 04/03/07; NR-5, 04/12/06																
AMERICAN HERITAGE LIFE INS CO Allstate Corporation David A. Bird President 1776 American Heritage Life Drive Jacksonville, FL 32224-6688 FL : 1956 : Stock : Agency Group Life, Group univ life 904-992-1776 AMB# 006064 NAIC# 60534	**A+** Rating Outlook: Negative **FSC XV**	'05	39.7	10.0	6.1	44.2	1,549,906	77.3	11.3	3.9	7.4	223,838	453,177	414,438	-297,064	15,163	6,258	31,104
		'06	47.1	11.2	11.5	30.2	1,326,650	68.0	14.6	4.3	13.1	211,099	458,908	414,685	-224,476	34,694	22,905	23,101
		'07	44.7	11.4	10.7	33.3	1,376,587	67.3	15.6	3.8	13.3	203,963	495,452	460,723	42,372	23,172	8,672	12,485
		'08	43.5	10.0	9.6	36.9	1,326,474	68.8	16.4	3.6	11.2	192,142	521,987	414,583	-32,226	12,961	4,820	279
		'09	48.4	8.8	8.6	34.2	1,404,488	66.9	17.8	3.4	11.9	240,911	565,037	458,349	26,375	34,849	23,902	18,197
		Rating History: A+ g, 11/20/09; A+ g, 10/23/08; A+ g, 01/09/08; A+ g, 02/06/07; A+ g, 11/07/05																
AMERICAN HOME LIFE INS CO Steven S. Lobell Chairman, President & CEO P.O. Box 1497 Topeka, KS 66601-1497 KS : 1909 : Mutual : Agency Pre-need, Term Life, Whole life 785-235-6276 AMB# 006065 NAIC# 60542	**B++** Rating Outlook: Stable **FSC V**	'05	59.1	24.1	6.0	10.7	149,098	70.8	0.1	25.7	3.5	12,483	22,579	21,844	9,188	540	307	347
		'06	58.2	21.6	6.9	13.3	156,745	71.8	0.1	24.6	3.5	13,219	20,431	19,570	7,128	1,035	704	729
		'07	56.7	21.0	10.4	11.9	164,090	72.9	0.1	23.6	3.5	14,637	20,781	19,849	7,458	1,523	1,032	1,009
		'08	57.1	16.8	10.8	15.3	165,548	75.3	0.0	21.5	3.1	14,258	20,446	19,390	2,437	1,965	2,498	150
		'09	66.5	13.7	4.3	15.6	176,385	74.0	0.0	23.2	2.8	14,390	27,863	27,153	11,012	1,047	1,002	-145
		Rating History: B++, 07/06/09; B++, 06/12/08; B++, 05/25/07; A-, 06/12/06; A-, 06/14/05																
AMERICAN HOME LIFE INS CO - AR[1] Anne P. Black President P.O. Box 715 North Little Rock, AR 72115-0715 AR : 1963 : Stock : Not Available 501-758-1778 AMB# 068161 NAIC# 83860	**NR-1**	'05	43.1	27.1	17.1	12.7	13,143	...	...	...	100.0	635	2,732	2,723	...	51	50	151
		'06	44.4	24.9	16.6	14.1	13,434	...	...	...	100.0	524	2,104	2,095	...	-88	-87	-34
		'07	46.7	19.0	19.0	15.4	13,885	...	...	...	100.0	261	2,060	2,054	...	-155	-154	-129
		'08	44.4	21.7	18.2	15.6	14,891	...	...	...	100.0	845	1,972	1,965	...	13	13	-64
		'09	59.2	17.6	13.4	9.8	15,728	...	...	...	100.0	840	2,004	1,997	...	28	28	13
		Rating History: NR-1, 06/10/10; NR-1, 06/12/09; NR-1, 06/12/08; NR-1, 06/08/07; NR-1, 06/07/06																
AMERICAN INCOME LIFE INS CO Torchmark Corporation Roger Smith President & CEO P.O. Box 2608 Waco, TX 76797 IN : 1954 : Stock : Agency Ind A&H, Ind Life, Trad Life 254-761-6400 AMB# 006069 NAIC# 60577	**A+** Rating Outlook: Stable **FSC X**	'05	76.9	0.1	4.3	18.8	1,439,317	84.5	5.5	6.6	3.4	208,151	438,217	444,934	106,658	114,683	92,137	93,912
		'06	73.2	0.1	6.6	20.1	1,542,400	85.5	5.3	6.1	3.2	193,327	468,894	475,343	101,863	122,612	77,562	75,796
		'07	73.2	0.1	6.7	20.0	1,705,887	87.5	5.2	5.5	1.9	221,186	507,299	513,007	136,773	111,780	83,624	96,322
		'08	72.1	0.1	6.3	21.6	1,828,070	87.4	4.9	5.1	2.7	228,066	532,174	538,135	74,300	165,946	128,670	98,778
		'09	73.4	0.0	2.5	24.1	1,932,816	88.4	4.8	4.7	2.2	188,073	578,051	583,908	143,287	113,998	85,141	85,462
		Rating History: A+ g, 06/15/10; A+ g, 06/11/09; A+ g, 06/11/08; A+ g, 06/08/07; A+ g, 06/08/06																
AMERICAN INDEP NETWORK OF NY Penn Treaty American Corporation Jose A. Vinas SVP & Controller 3440 Lehigh Street Allentown, PA 18103-7001 NY : 1998 : Stock : Agency Ind A&H 607-732-3008 AMB# 060292 NAIC# 60243	**NR-4**	'05	95.0	...	...	5.0	16,440	...	83.6	...	16.4	7,776	4,517	4,467	2,168	1,661	1,267	1,139
		'06	93.4	...	...	6.6	18,658	...	89.6	...	10.4	8,271	4,411	4,363	2,139	258	402	392
		'07	95.3	...	...	4.7	20,185	...	93.3	...	6.7	8,871	4,364	4,295	1,581	913	731	731
		'08	93.5	...	...	6.5	21,807	...	95.5	...	4.5	8,640	4,261	4,188	1,735	-68	-111	-157
		'09	81.1	...	...	18.9	24,335	...	96.3	...	3.7	5,140	3,834	3,766	1,767	-3,891	-4,031	-4,098
		Rating History: NR-4, 04/14/09; D, 04/14/09; D, 01/08/09; D g, 10/03/08; B- g, 02/20/08																
AMERICAN INDUSTRIES LIFE[1] John L. Gorman, Jr. President P.O. Box 2952 Houston, TX 77252-2952 TX : 1971 : Stock : Agency Ind Life, Trad Life, Whole life 713-667-7566 AMB# 008529 NAIC# 81833	**NR-1**	'05	15.7	61.9	6.9	15.4	8,301	...	...	0.5	99.5	2,265	300	288	...	-289	-331	-331
		'06	15.5	66.8	8.0	9.7	8,182	...	...	0.5	99.5	2,403	278	267	...	-11	68	68
		'07	12.4	34.9	9.2	43.5	10,164	...	...	0.4	99.6	4,346	260	248	...	-113	-113	1,574
		'08	...	79.2	2.7	18.1	3,168	...	...	...	100.0	2,988	25	29	...	408	382	896
		'09	...	88.3	1.8	9.8	2,672	...	...	...	100.0	2,458	...	7	...	-192	-172	-107
		Rating History: NR-1, 06/10/10; NR-1, 06/12/09; NR-1, 06/12/08; NR-5, 05/14/07; NR-5, 05/05/06																

BEST'S PROFITABILITY, LEVERAGE AND LIQUIDITY TESTS 2005 – 2009

Data in U.S. Dollars

	Profitability Tests							Leverage Tests						Liquidity Tests					
Un-Realized Capital Gains ($000)	Benefits Paid to NPW & Dep (%)	Comm. & Expenses to NPW & Dep (%)	NOG to Total Assets (%)	NOG to Total Rev (%)	Operating Return on Equity (%)	Net Yield (%)	Total Return (%)	Change in NPW & Dep (%)	NPW & Dep to Capital (X)	Capital & Surplus to Liabilities (%)	Surplus Relief (%)	Reins Leverage (%)	Change in Capital (%)	Quick Liquidity (%)	Current Liquidity (%)	Non-Invest Grade Bonds to Capital (%)	Delinq. & Foreclosed Mortgages to Capital (%)	Mort. & Credit Tenant Loans & R.E. to Capital (%)	Affiliated Invest to Capital (%)
782	70.6	11.9	10.0	53.8	19.4	5.87	6.30	-27.4	0.2	116.1	0.8	11.6	-2.0	134.9	159.4	12.2	...	0.0	9.5
-10,212	61.8	14.8	8.3	43.2	15.4	5.81	5.64	-2.5	0.2	124.1	0.8	11.5	-3.7	156.9	176.3	10.5	...	0.0	9.0
-4,192	46.1	13.3	6.2	26.0	11.6	5.62	5.62	36.3	0.3	115.4	1.0	10.9	0.7	151.0	170.0	12.0	...	0.0	8.6
2,985	45.1	17.3	7.5	31.6	15.6	5.41	4.55	-3.5	0.4	77.9	1.4	14.4	-25.9	104.8	128.8	14.3	...	0.0	11.4
18,965	88.3	21.4	7.5	45.5	16.8	5.49	6.86	-47.3	0.2	88.8	1.1	14.7	-3.9	104.5	129.5	14.0	...	...	14.6
Principal Lines of Business: CrdLife (35.1%), CrdA&H (32.3%), GrpLife (26.6%), GrpA&H (4.1%), OrdLife (1.7%)														Principal States: TX (8.8%), NC (8.1%), PA (5.4%), OH (4.1%)					
...	78.0	23.4	1.7	0.3	5.5	...	3.69	...	...	42.6	...	...	4.7	6.8	8.2	...	...	4.2	4.2
...	102.3	29.4	-0.6	-0.1	-2.4	-13.89	-11.11	...	...	28.6	...	...	-8.9	4.8	5.9	...	...	8.0	8.0
...	106.9	29.7	5.2	1.0	22.2	3.11	-2.33	...	...	32.3	...	...	25.7	5.5	6.5	...	...	8.3	8.3
...	100.0	29.3	2.3	0.5	8.5	4.15	1.34	...	...	41.4	...	...	10.0	3.7	3.7	...	...	5.1	5.1
...	89.6	27.1	-1.3	-0.2	-4.4	2.62	-0.41	...	...	45.7	...	...	-4.2	3.3	3.3	...	...	7.7	7.7
...	58.2	42.2	-1.0	-0.4	-24.0	13.00	13.00	101.1	68.4	3.7	...	...	-21.4	64.6	64.6	...	...	...	...
...	67.1	34.2	1.1	0.3	22.9	1.53	1.53	35.2	73.5	6.5	...	...	25.9	55.4	55.4	...	...	...	...
...	60.8	36.7	9.1	2.0	83.8	-7.11	-7.11	-1.1	29.8	18.8	...	...	144.1	26.4	26.4	...	...	...	...
...	52.1	43.7	12.0	2.9	52.1	3.36	3.36	4.2	12.5	38.9	...	...	148.2	28.9	28.9	...	...	...	...
...	55.5	45.9	-4.0	-1.2	-14.9	-46.74	-46.74	-9.7	13.1	33.5	...	...	-13.9	2.1	2.1	...	...	...	...
Principal Lines of Business: Dental (100.0%)																			
-3,318	53.0	52.2	0.4	1.2	3.6	4.87	6.21	999.9	1.8	17.4	15.2	346.4	72.0	32.1	39.5	15.7	...	67.7	52.0
11,077	124.5	48.7	1.6	4.4	10.5	5.85	6.79	0.1	1.8	20.7	13.5	274.8	-0.9	42.1	51.8	11.7	...	65.5	68.3
10,883	49.9	49.7	0.6	1.6	4.2	5.16	6.42	11.1	2.0	20.1	13.1	243.7	1.2	38.2	47.0	7.4	...	67.9	68.4
-15,842	57.0	53.9	0.4	0.9	2.4	5.16	3.54	-10.0	2.1	17.9	16.7	254.5	-12.6	41.8	49.7	10.4	0.9	66.0	71.6
11,914	55.0	49.7	1.8	4.4	11.0	5.06	5.64	10.6	1.8	22.6	10.2	189.9	28.5	42.5	51.3	15.1	...	47.6	57.5
Principal Lines of Business: IndA&H (50.0%), GrpA&H (30.3%), OrdLife (14.8%), CrdA&H (1.8%), CrdLife (1.7%)														Principal States: FL (15.7%), TX (13.5%), NC (5.7%), GA (5.3%), CA (5.3%)					
-64	46.8	39.0	0.2	1.0	2.5	6.10	6.21	-10.5	1.6	9.8	2.5	27.5	2.0	48.8	56.9	9.3	...	269.0	6.9
65	59.1	41.6	0.5	2.5	5.5	6.05	6.23	-10.4	1.4	10.0	2.0	34.5	7.1	48.9	56.9	1.5	...	236.9	6.6
-208	64.3	39.9	0.6	3.6	7.4	5.92	5.86	1.4	1.3	10.4	1.1	40.2	8.0	49.0	57.0	8.1	3.6	223.1	5.7
-532	84.7	36.9	1.5	8.5	17.3	6.18	4.47	-2.3	1.3	10.0	2.8	41.5	-2.3	48.6	58.7	8.6	7.6	184.8	5.5
-761	56.6	30.8	0.6	2.8	7.0	5.69	4.60	40.0	1.8	9.2	2.4	42.1	-1.7	48.0	58.6	55.9	...	162.9	5.2
Principal Lines of Business: OrdLife (68.5%), IndAnn (31.0%), GrpAnn (0.5%), IndA&H (0.0%)														Principal States: TX (28.8%), KS (20.6%), OH (8.5%), CO (6.4%), MO (5.9%)					
21	77.4	32.0	0.4	1.5	9.0	...	...	3.6	3.5	6.4	...	...	31.9	...	...	...	...	452.8	...
-23	70.8	42.2	-0.7	-3.2	-15.0	...	...	-23.1	3.2	5.2	...	...	-16.1	...	...	...	...	506.4	...
-12	67.2	46.3	-1.1	-5.6	-39.1	...	...	-1.9	5.8	2.6	...	...	-46.3	...	...	...	...	743.9	...
418	70.7	39.0	0.1	0.5	2.4	...	...	-4.3	2.0	6.9	...	...	172.2	...	...	...	...	335.3	...
-7	57.4	37.4	0.2	1.0	3.4	...	...	1.6	2.0	6.6	...	...	1.3	...	...	...	...	283.2	...
Principal Lines of Business: OrdLife (77.5%), IndAnn (22.5%)																			
-5,757	26.9	37.6	6.7	18.1	47.2	6.00	5.74	7.3	2.1	17.7	...	0.1	14.9	55.8	66.8	38.9	...	0.6	20.8
-447	26.6	38.2	5.2	14.2	38.6	6.00	5.87	6.8	2.3	15.1	...	0.1	-6.4	55.3	66.3	44.1	...	0.9	24.8
-6,777	26.0	38.2	5.1	14.2	40.3	5.91	6.34	7.9	2.2	15.6	...	0.2	13.8	51.9	62.9	42.5	...	0.7	18.1
-5,112	26.9	40.0	7.3	20.6	57.3	6.23	3.99	4.9	2.3	14.6	...	0.1	1.1	50.0	61.0	34.6	...	0.4	19.3
953	26.9	43.0	4.5	12.7	40.9	5.77	5.86	8.5	3.1	10.8	...	0.1	-18.9	50.9	60.6	71.9	...	0.4	25.8
Principal Lines of Business: OrdLife (86.6%), IndA&H (10.9%), GrpA&H (1.2%), GrpAnn (1.0%), GrpLife (0.3%)														Principal States: CA (10.7%), OH (6.1%), TX (4.7%), IL (4.4%)					
...	32.6	33.0	8.2	25.2	17.6	3.60	2.95	4.5	0.6	89.8	...	5.1	17.6	165.1	171.9	...	...	...	...
...	32.7	30.9	2.3	7.9	5.0	4.32	4.30	-2.3	0.5	79.7	...	4.8	6.4	156.2	163.5	...	...	...	...
...	36.0	36.7	3.8	13.9	8.5	4.59	4.68	-1.6	0.5	78.6	...	4.6	7.3	155.0	162.3	...	...	...	...
...	41.5	35.7	-0.5	-2.2	-1.3	4.52	4.37	-2.5	0.5	65.6	...	4.6	-2.7	145.6	152.3	0.6	...	...	...
...	45.4	24.6	-17.5	-86.4	-58.5	3.95	3.77	-10.1	0.7	26.8	...	16.8	-40.5	123.6	127.2	0.7	...	...	...
Principal Lines of Business: IndA&H (100.0%)														Principal States: NY (100.0%)					
55	137.5	204.1	-3.9	-53.0	-13.8	...	...	-6.6	0.1	45.2	...	...	-9.7	...	...	...	...	198.8	...
80	119.5	211.1	0.8	9.2	2.9	...	...	-7.3	0.1	50.2	...	...	5.8	...	...	...	...	199.9	...
281	141.4	202.3	-1.2	-17.9	-3.3	...	...	-7.0	0.1	82.9	...	...	68.5	...	...	...	...	76.9	...
-404	263.4	999.9	5.7	45.7	10.4	...	...	-88.2	0.0	999.9	...	...	-32.7	...	...	...	...	81.0	...
-36	83.1	999.9	-5.9	-99.9	-6.3	...	...	-76.3	0.0	999.9	...	...	-17.2	...	...	...	...	92.0	...
Principal Lines of Business: OrdLife (100.0%)																			

2010 BEST'S KEY RATING GUIDE — LIFE/HEALTH EDITION
ANNUAL STATEMENT DATA FOR YEARS 2005 – 2009

Data in U.S. Dollars

COMPANY NAME Ultimate Parent Association Principal Officer Mailing Address Dom. : Began Bus. : Struct. : Mktg. Specialty Phone # AMB# NAIC#	Best's Financial Strength Rating FSC	Data Year	Balance Sheet Bonds (%)	Mort. Loans & R.E. (%)	Com & Pref. Stock (%)	All Other Assets (%)	Total Assets ($000)	Life Reserves (%)	Health Reserves (%)	Ann Res. & Dep. Liabilities (%)	All Other Liabilities (%)	Capital & Surplus ($000)	Operations Direct Premiums Written ($000)	Net Premiums Written & Deposits ($000)	Operating Cash Flow ($000)	NOG Before Taxes ($000)	NOG After Taxes ($000)	Net Income ($000)
AMERICAN INTERN LIFE ASSUR NY American International Group, Inc Mary Jane B. Fortin President & CEO 70 Pine Street, 19th Floor New York, NY 10270 NY : 1962 : Stock : Broker Ann, A&H, Struc Sett 212-770-7000 AMB# 006072 NAIC# 60607	**A** Rating Outlook: Negative **FSC XV**	'05	89.8	4.7	0.1	5.4	8,269,779	2.9	0.3	91.3	5.5	625,836	295,342	379,370	-51,816	234,308	171,420	155,182
		'06	85.0	6.3	3.0	5.6	7,820,788	3.1	0.5	90.9	5.6	606,126	340,671	488,276	-439,440	104,842	62,994	62,079
		'07	82.7	7.1	3.5	6.6	7,092,807	3.5	0.5	89.9	6.1	552,637	414,674	487,955	-685,466	106,569	89,918	78,313
		'08	78.4	7.3	3.5	10.8	6,660,685	4.2	0.6	91.2	4.1	370,537	397,886	453,813	-1,422,362	-124,329	-146,594	-1,028,914
		'09	83.2	7.0	0.7	9.2	6,543,627	4.0	0.7	90.9	4.4	523,626	172,998	196,976	202	250,095	233,000	178,235
		Rating History: A, 12/16/09; A, 11/10/08; A gu, 09/15/08; A+ g, 06/17/08; A++g, 05/28/08																
AMERICAN LABOR LIFE INS CO' David B. Anderson President 8 Marticville Road Lancaster, PA 17603-9508 AZ : 1978 : Stock : Not Available 717-872-8576 AMB# 060390 NAIC# 89427	**NR-1**	'05	...	...	12.7	87.3	3,569	...	...	...	100.0	2,221	8	2,129	...	568	515	505
		'06	...	...	15.1	84.9	4,238	...	...	...	100.0	2,765	8	2,113	...	642	556	542
		'07	...	...	7.0	93.0	4,626	...	...	...	100.0	3,254	12	2,098	...	581	502	474
		'08	...	...	5.3	94.7	5,411	...	...	...	100.0	3,762	493	2,483	...	635	546	524
		'09	8.4	...	8.3	83.4	6,107	...	...	...	100.0	4,144	968	2,955	...	406	363	406
		Rating History: NR-1, 06/10/10; NR-1, 06/12/09; NR-1, 06/12/08; NR-1, 06/08/07; NR-1, 06/07/06																
AMERICAN LIFE AND ACC OF KY Gerald W. Gerichs President & Treasurer 3 Riverfront Plaza, 471 W. Main Street Louisville, KY 40202 KY : 1906 : Stock : Not Available Life 502-585-5347 AMB# 006077 NAIC# 60666	**NR-5**	'05	29.5	4.7	62.1	3.7	268,649	21.0	0.0	...	79.0	159,279	308	305	2,944	5,650	4,700	4,610
		'06	27.9	4.8	64.3	3.0	294,063	18.6	0.0	...	81.4	172,918	269	267	3,024	6,165	5,365	5,582
		'07	30.7	5.8	59.3	4.3	261,266	39.1	0.0	...	60.9	135,128	257	13,595	5,202	-19,634	-20,482	-19,162
		'08	34.1	7.0	44.6	14.3	216,565	54.1	17.8	...	28.2	110,431	222	28,452	3,515	-8,858	-8,997	-8,997
		'09	30.1	8.3	50.4	11.3	232,044	45.9	12.6	...	41.4	118,590	195	20,474	-6,243	7,847	7,832	7,832
		Rating History: NR-5, 04/21/10; NR-5, 04/14/09; NR-5, 02/07/08; NR-1, 06/08/07; NR-5, 05/18/06																
AMERICAN LIFE & ANNUITY CO' Phil Hale President 126 Hawthorne Street Hot Springs, AR 71901-5141 AR : 1989 : Stock : Not Available 501-623-7718 AMB# 008622 NAIC# 73881	**NR-1**	'05	87.8	0.5	7.3	4.4	31,819	...	...	...	100.0	2,144	4,453	4,452	...	183	142	109
		'06	84.2	0.4	7.1	8.3	35,540	...	...	...	100.0	2,546	5,359	5,358	...	34	34	34
		'07	81.9	0.4	14.2	3.5	37,529	...	...	...	100.0	2,847	4,859	4,857	...	483	529	583
		'08	79.8	0.4	11.9	8.0	37,089	...	...	...	100.0	1,234	4,318	4,317	...	-43	-34	-717
		'09	86.1	0.8	10.3	2.8	39,667	...	...	...	100.0	1,590	4,334	4,332	...	335	335	335
		Rating History: NR-1, 06/10/10; NR-1, 06/12/09; NR-1, 06/12/08; NR-1, 06/08/07; NR-1, 06/07/06																
AMERICAN LIFE & SECURITY CORP' Mark Oliver Chief Executive Officer 8101 'O' Street, Suite S111 Lincoln, NE 68510 NE : 2009 : Stock : Not Available 877-758-9333 AMB# 060713 NAIC# 13682	**NR-1**	'05	...	...	...	...	...	...	...	...	...	...	...	...	...	...	...	...
		'06	...	...	...	...	...	...	...	...	...	...	...	...	...	...	...	...
		'07	...	...	...	...	...	...	...	...	...	...	...	...	...	...	...	...
		'08	...	...	...	...	...	...	...	...	...	...	...	...	...	...	...	...
		'09	82.4	...	...	17.6	5,859	...	...	14.8	85.2	5,198	356	354	...	-255	-255	-256
		Rating History: NR-1, 06/10/10																
AMERICAN LIFE INS CO DE American International Group, Inc Rodney Owen Martin, Jr. Chairman of the Board of Directors & CEO 600 King Street Wilmington, DE 19801 DE : 1921 : Stock : Agency A&H, Ann, Life 302-594-2000 AMB# 006081 NAIC# 60690	**A u** Under Review Implication: Positive **FSC XV**	'05	55.6	1.7	9.3	33.4	66,178,870	23.6	4.4	29.8	42.2	5,334,301	23,361,219	20,484,049	9,372,102	674,468	562,309	549,871
		'06	51.8	1.6	8.5	38.1	84,977,058	21.9	4.1	28.4	45.5	5,733,980	25,578,074	25,485,691	7,965,853	1,016,958	572,209	579,072
		'07	49.0	1.6	7.7	41.7	101,632,307	21.9	4.1	26.8	47.2	6,720,961	34,013,486	33,823,954	6,774,177	1,603,847	962,792	736,918
		'08	58.3	2.2	4.0	35.5	86,338,053	29.6	6.5	33.8	30.1	3,902,904	29,643,963	30,367,464	4,110,891	1,765,735	1,247,493	-363,704
		'09	66.3	1.9	3.7	28.1	91,042,803	31.4	7.4	35.3	26.0	4,146,527	11,360,895	13,564,255	3,127,104	839,578	737,482	668,604
		Rating History: A u, 02/09/10; A, 12/16/09; A, 11/10/08; A gu, 09/15/08; A+ g, 06/17/08																
AMERICAN LIFE INS CO IL Robert T. Napier President 200 S. Wacker Drive, Suite 725 Chicago, IL 60606 IL : 1928 : Mutual : Direct Response A&H, Ann, Life 312-756-9999 AMB# 009091 NAIC# 84158	**NR-5**	'05	...	...	...	...	...	...	...	...	...	...	...	...	...	...	...	...
		'06	58.3	...	25.2	16.4	3,779	78.6	3.7	2.2	15.5	2,482	587	587	-73	-82	-82	-55
		'07	42.6	...	25.9	31.5	3,973	78.4	3.4	2.1	16.1	2,605	535	535	-150	-240	-240	-184
		'08	46.6	...	23.9	29.6	3,379	80.8	3.8	2.2	13.2	2,095	538	538	-323	-262	-262	-272
		'09	44.3	...	20.7	35.0	3,362	83.5	3.1	2.2	11.2	2,022	390	390	-234	-366	-366	-314
		Rating History: NR-5, 04/15/10; NR-5, 04/21/09; NR-5, 04/10/08; NR-5, 05/08/07; NR-1, 06/07/06																
AMERICAN MATURITY LIFE INS CO Hartford Financial Services Group Inc John C. Walters Chairman, President & CEO 200 Hopmeadow Street Simsbury, CT 06089 CT : 1973 : Stock : Not Available Univ Life, Life, Retirement Savings 860-525-8555 AMB# 008480 NAIC# 81213	**NR-3**	'05	53.3	...	...	46.7	69,463	...	...	3.9	96.1	38,399	1,706	31	445	1,034	1,034	1,034
		'06	56.4	...	...	43.6	67,110	...	...	3.5	96.5	39,758	2,379	27	964	1,366	1,355	1,355
		'07	54.8	...	...	45.2	65,198	...	...	3.8	96.2	41,256	3,767	102	1,561	1,450	1,452	1,452
		'08	45.2	...	...	54.8	57,672	...	...	6.0	94.0	42,408	2,040	19	1,586	1,615	1,171	1,115
		'09	67.6	...	...	32.4	60,928	...	...	6.1	93.9	45,408	1,213	14	748	1,014	1,464	1,463
		Rating History: NR-3, 03/24/10; NR-3, 02/27/09; NR-3, 12/23/08; NR-3, 10/06/08; NR-3, 05/23/08																
AMERICAN MEDICAL AND LIFE INS TREK Holdings Inc John Ollis Chairman & President 8 West 38th Street, Suite 1002 New York, NY 10018 NY : 1966 : Stock : Broker Dental, Group A&H, Stop Loss 646-223-9300 AMB# 008304 NAIC# 81418	**B-** Rating Outlook: Negative **FSC IV**	'05	34.2	...	13.1	52.7	11,618	10.5	44.5	...	45.0	7,006	19,916	14,023	117	-1,575	-1,576	-1,155
		'06	49.1	...	10.1	40.8	13,649	7.1	53.7	...	39.3	7,727	19,424	16,247	1,195	-245	-245	-245
		'07	52.1	...	...	47.9	21,691	4.3	58.6	...	37.0	12,706	22,578	19,353	4,944	785	785	982
		'08	35.9	...	...	64.1	32,050	2.0	50.3	...	47.7	12,100	41,982	28,500	7,800	2,000	1,327	1,327
		'09	37.3	...	...	62.7	27,084	1.7	55.7	...	42.6	7,569	85,686	44,865	-6,062	-6,130	-6,130	-6,130
		Rating History: B-, 03/31/10; B, 12/04/09; B u, 09/01/09; B+, 08/28/08; B+, 09/24/07																

BEST'S PROFITABILITY, LEVERAGE AND LIQUIDITY TESTS 2005 – 2009

Data in U.S. Dollars

	Profitability Tests							Leverage Tests						Liquidity Tests					
Un-Realized Capital Gains ($000)	Benefits Paid to NPW & Dep (%)	Comm. & Expenses to NPW & Dep (%)	NOG to Total Assets (%)	NOG to Total Rev (%)	Operating Return on Equity (%)	Net Yield (%)	Total Return (%)	Change in NPW & Dep (%)	NPW & Dep to Capital (X)	Capital & Surplus to Liabilities (%)	Surplus Relief (%)	Reins Leverage (%)	Change in Capital (%)	Quick Liquidity (%)	Current Liquidity (%)	Non-Invest Grade Bonds to Capital (%)	Delinq. & Foreclosed Mortgages to Capital (%)	Mort. & Credit Tenant Loans & R.E. to Capital (%)	Affiliated Invest to Capital (%)
-4,914	201.9	6.1	2.1	19.8	28.8	7.44	7.28	-38.4	0.5	9.4	0.6	6.3	14.8	48.9	68.0	69.6	2.8	66.1	2.9
2,058	222.4	7.1	0.8	7.5	10.2	6.85	6.95	28.7	0.7	10.1	0.7	5.4	0.7	44.8	64.8	74.5	3.8	80.1	2.8
-7,123	299.3	6.9	1.2	10.2	15.5	7.01	6.80	-0.1	0.7	10.5	0.9	5.3	-5.5	44.9	65.5	64.6	3.7	86.7	4.2
-9,434	217.2	6.5	-2.1	-17.8	-31.8	7.07	-5.69	-7.0	1.0	7.5	1.1	11.9	-30.8	40.7	59.8	85.4	5.2	120.7	15.3
24,734	334.3	14.6	3.5	42.4	52.1	6.59	5.95	-56.6	0.3	10.4	0.6	7.2	32.7	47.3	66.4	76.7	...	85.6	8.7
Principal Lines of Business: IndAnn (33.4%), GrpAnn (28.7%), GrpLife (18.1%), GrpA&H (13.7%), OrdLife (5.3%)														Principal States: NY (80.1%), TX (13.9%)					
-39	20.0	59.0	16.0	23.0	27.8	...	...	15.9	0.9	175.7	...	...	45.2	...	...	...	...	...	...
76	23.3	59.8	14.2	22.7	22.3	...	...	-0.8	0.7	210.4	...	...	26.3	...	...	...	...	...	...
-112	22.5	56.6	11.3	22.0	16.7	...	...	-0.7	0.6	237.7	...	...	13.4	...	...	...	...	...	...
-19	22.3	58.8	10.9	18.7	15.6	...	...	18.3	0.7	228.1	...	...	15.5	...	...	...	...	...	...
85	22.4	61.9	6.3	11.8	9.2	...	...	19.0	0.7	229.6	...	...	13.1	...	...	...	...	...	...
Principal Lines of Business: IndA&H (97.5%), OrdLife (2.5%)																			
-3,995	297.0	999.9	1.7	50.6	3.0	3.38	1.91	-12.6	0.0	249.8	...	0.0	0.8	224.5	268.8	0.1	...	6.6	3.2
25,193	291.1	999.9	1.9	55.5	3.2	3.38	13.02	-12.5	0.0	251.1	...	0.0	9.6	145.2	185.1	...	...	6.7	3.6
-36,895	48.6	42.0	-7.4	-84.3	-13.3	3.93	-8.15	999.9	0.1	171.7	...	0.0	-21.5	175.8	209.8	...	...	9.1	5.1
-66,237	74.5	25.6	-3.8	-25.2	-7.3	3.16	-21.98	109.3	0.2	146.6	...	12.4	-22.0	160.6	187.6	...	...	11.8	6.4
22,700	73.9	24.7	3.5	31.8	6.8	1.97	13.49	-28.0	0.1	156.1	...	8.8	9.9	153.8	183.9	...	...	13.6	6.7
Principal Lines of Business: OrdLife (116.1%), IndLife (0.6%), IndA&H (0.0%), CrdLife (-3.2%), CrdA&H (-13.5%)														Principal States: KY (47.7%), OH (45.8%), IN (5.3%)					
148	65.6	21.5	0.5	2.3	7.1	...	...	5.2	1.8	8.3	...	...	14.7	...	...	...	...	6.0	...
381	51.6	21.1	0.1	0.5	1.4	...	...	20.4	1.8	8.9	...	...	19.5	...	...	...	...	5.2	...
-94	73.3	21.3	1.4	7.9	19.6	...	...	-9.4	1.5	9.5	...	...	11.8	...	...	...	...	4.4	...
-1,132	86.3	22.2	-0.1	-0.5	-1.7	...	...	-11.1	3.5	3.5	...	...	-61.7	...	...	...	...	10.8	...
839	86.2	19.3	0.9	5.3	23.7	...	...	0.4	1.8	6.5	...	...	95.9	...	...	...	...	13.7	...
Principal Lines of Business: IndAnn (62.9%), OrdLife (37.1%)																			
...	...	...	...	...	...	...	...	...	...	...	...	...	...	...	...	...	...	...	...
...	...	...	...	...	...	...	...	...	...	...	...	...	...	...	...	...	...	...	...
...	...	...	...	...	...	...	...	...	...	...	...	...	...	...	...	...	...	...	...
...	...	...	...	...	...	...	...	...	...	...	...	...	...	...	...	...	...	...	...
...	1.4	150.8	...	-64.6	...	...	...	...	0.1	786.8	...	...	...	...	...	...	...	...	...
Principal Lines of Business: OrdLife (100.0%)																			
365,471	52.2	10.6	0.9	2.2	11.8	2.60	3.49	0.5	3.2	15.4	10.7	98.9	26.5	67.6	77.0	3.9	0.0	17.8	98.3
567,736	40.8	9.2	0.8	2.1	10.3	4.25	5.40	24.4	3.6	14.0	5.8	90.7	10.2	66.0	76.3	5.7	0.0	19.5	93.6
-559,742	57.5	7.0	1.0	2.7	15.5	4.61	3.34	32.7	4.3	13.7	5.3	75.0	9.6	65.8	77.3	4.3	0.0	20.9	81.9
-2,244,193	103.5	9.4	1.3	3.9	23.5	4.65	-1.23	-10.2	6.8	7.1	9.9	100.3	-42.8	66.7	77.5	7.4	0.0	43.2	71.4
442,043	85.7	22.0	0.8	4.9	18.3	4.19	4.73	-55.3	2.8	7.0	7.1	41.9	8.2	68.8	78.8	17.6	0.0	36.0	80.7
Principal Lines of Business: OrdLife (36.1%), IndAnn (28.9%), IndA&H (25.4%), GrpAnn (5.1%), GrpA&H (2.0%)																			
...	...	...	...	...	...	...	...	...	...	...	...	...	...	...	...	...	...	...	...
122	25.3	117.5	...	-11.0	...	...	...	...	0.2	243.1	...	...	...	290.7	323.6	...	...	...	...
-9	27.7	135.2	-6.2	-35.2	-9.4	3.97	5.23	-9.0	0.2	243.4	...	...	5.2	280.6	306.0	...	...	...	...
-412	38.6	141.0	-7.1	-39.9	-11.2	3.40	-7.84	0.6	0.2	202.3	...	...	-19.7	236.9	260.9	...	...	...	...
219	32.3	164.6	-10.9	-75.7	-17.8	2.92	11.51	-27.5	0.2	181.1	...	...	-4.2	226.5	245.9	...	...	...	...
Principal Lines of Business: IndA&H (55.7%), OrdLife (43.2%), IndLife (1.1%)														Principal States: IL (100.0%)					
...	999.9	648.7	1.4	-22.3	2.7	3.28	3.25	-64.5	0.0	999.9	-0.1	61.0	2.8	999.9	999.9	...	...	...	...
...	999.9	244.3	2.0	-36.5	3.5	3.71	3.69	-11.2	0.0	999.9	0.1	54.3	3.5	999.9	999.9	...	...	...	...
...	856.7	260.6	2.2	-65.2	3.6	4.28	4.26	274.4	0.0	999.9	0.0	50.6	3.8	999.9	999.9	...	...	...	...
...	999.9	577.1	1.9	-99.9	2.8	3.98	3.91	-81.0	0.0	999.9	0.0	46.0	2.7	999.9	999.9	...	...	...	...
...	999.9	392.0	2.5	-99.9	3.3	2.29	2.44	-29.0	0.0	999.9	0.0	42.0	7.1	999.9	999.9	...	...	...	...
Principal Lines of Business: GrpAnn (100.0%)														Principal States: VA (15.7%), MA (14.9%), CA (14.8%), PA (13.3%), MD (8.2%)					
-279	77.4	38.1	-12.3	-10.5	-20.8	1.83	3.67	12.2	1.9	163.8	4.0	18.3	-14.9	334.1	344.0	...	...	...	...
63	60.7	49.7	-1.9	-1.3	-3.3	2.93	4.33	15.9	2.1	138.1	4.5	10.8	9.7	234.1	241.8	...	...	...	...
-142	64.0	39.1	4.4	3.6	7.7	3.63	4.37	19.1	1.5	141.7	9.7	26.3	60.6	204.3	207.9	...	...	...	...
...	61.9	33.7	4.9	3.9	10.7	3.02	3.27	47.3	2.4	60.8	39.1	70.3	-4.7	127.2	129.6	...	...	...	...
...	78.8	36.6	-20.7	-10.6	-62.3	2.14	2.63	57.4	5.9	38.9	158.3	183.1	-37.4	92.2	93.9	...	...	...	...
Principal Lines of Business: GrpA&H (97.9%), GrpLife (2.1%), IndA&H (0.0%), OrdLife (0.0%)														Principal States: NY (19.0%), FL (11.9%), TX (8.9%), PA (5.1%), NC (4.8%)					

Data in U.S. Dollars

COMPANY NAME Ultimate Parent Association Principal Officer Mailing Address Dom. : Began Bus. : Struct. : Mktg. Specialty Phone # AMB# NAIC#	Best's Financial Strength Rating FSC	Data Year	Balance Sheet: Bonds (%)	Mort. Loans & R.E. (%)	Com & Pref. Stock (%)	All Other Assets (%)	Total Assets ($000)	Life Reserves (%)	Health Reserves (%)	Ann Res. & Dep. Liabilities (%)	All Other Liabilities (%)	Capital & Surplus ($000)	Operations: Direct Premiums Written ($000)	Net Premiums Written & Deposits ($000)	Operating Cash Flow ($000)	NOG Before Taxes ($000)	NOG After Taxes ($000)	Net Income ($000)
AMERICAN MEDICAL SECURITY LIFE UnitedHealth Group Inc	**A-**	'05	79.7	5.4	...	14.9	382,595	1.1	55.5	...	43.3	179,418	686,273	871,165	27,981	2,281	-1,993	-1,993
Patrick F. Carr President		'06	65.0	4.7	...	30.3	406,875	1.4	55.3	...	43.3	258,843	587,227	631,338	36,214	96,034	81,438	81,438
P.O. Box 19032 Green Bay, WI 54307-9032	Rating Outlook: Stable	'07	75.9	7.9	...	16.2	237,916	1.7	54.4	...	43.9	153,420	283,247	282,484	-160,482	87,245	57,713	57,713
WI : 1982 : Stock : Agency A&H, Dental, Group Life		'08	37.0	...	...	63.0	129,773	0.8	53.2	...	46.0	70,517	199,076	198,468	-111,497	47,922	33,913	56,284
800-232-5432		'09	62.5	...	...	37.5	79,638	1.2	64.3	...	34.6	39,919	166,802	166,346	-48,420	24,942	18,513	18,271
AMB# 007771 NAIC# 97179	FSC VI	Rating History: A-, 06/15/09; A-, 01/29/08; A-, 11/21/07; A-, 11/16/06; A-, 08/17/06																
AMERICAN MEMORIAL LIFE INS CO Assurant Inc	**A-**	'05	71.8	10.1	5.5	12.7	1,839,653	81.6	0.0	9.9	8.5	165,907	338,580	342,951	123,937	56,579	35,662	35,652
Christopher Reznyk President & CEO		'06	68.4	9.9	8.7	13.0	1,897,497	83.4	0.0	9.2	7.4	138,268	322,224	325,256	176,526	54,160	35,260	41,539
P.O. Box 2730 Rapid City, SD 57709-2730	Rating Outlook: Stable	'07	73.3	10.1	8.2	8.3	1,935,452	83.8	0.0	8.3	7.9	86,428	290,862	293,297	57,668	49,599	36,785	28,335
SD : 1959 : Stock : Agency Pre-need, Life		'08	70.9	9.2	5.8	14.2	1,996,141	84.3	0.0	7.6	8.0	86,055	281,637	283,641	62,075	41,950	29,548	-22,978
605-719-0999		'09	80.7	8.3	0.9	10.1	2,067,829	85.7	0.0	7.3	7.0	109,717	288,541	290,512	55,173	33,004	22,804	18,240
AMB# 006942 NAIC# 67989	FSC VIII	Rating History: A-, 11/18/09; A-, 11/25/08; A, 06/24/08; A, 07/17/07; A, 06/19/06																
AMERICAN MODERN LIFE INS CO Munich Reinsurance Company	**A-**	'05	85.2	...	3.9	10.9	59,115	51.0	32.8	...	16.2	24,520	35,672	7,654	-1,489	6,253	4,323	4,323
John W. Hayden Chairman, President & CEO		'06	61.3	...	25.5	13.2	58,061	47.7	28.5	...	23.7	21,153	39,514	9,790	-5,081	2,572	1,585	1,611
7000 Midland Blvd. Amelia, OH 45102-2607	Rating Outlook: Stable	'07	59.5	...	25.3	15.1	63,526	55.0	22.7	...	22.3	22,068	44,752	12,313	4,057	-1,583	-934	-934
OH : 1957 : Stock : Agency Credit A&H, Credit Life		'08	57.3	...	25.8	16.8	64,198	62.0	20.0	...	18.0	18,348	43,672	13,197	2,141	-1,982	-2,654	-2,687
513-943-7200		'09	63.9	...	25.1	11.0	63,389	63.0	20.6	...	16.3	20,823	37,771	11,052	781	2,802	2,829	2,792
AMB# 006680 NAIC# 65811	FSC V	Rating History: A-, 03/10/10; A-, 05/15/09; A-, 04/09/08; A- u, 10/18/07; A-, 05/31/07																
AMERICAN NATIONAL INS CO American National Insurance Company	**A**	'05	59.0	11.9	10.4	18.7	12,917,074	29.8	1.4	55.5	13.3	2,037,640	1,440,032	1,547,606	628,211	192,475	125,363	128,833
G. R. Ferdinandtsen President & COO		'06	54.5	12.4	10.9	22.2	13,239,607	28.8	1.2	56.0	14.0	2,108,109	1,429,951	1,534,432	71,574	144,768	89,902	92,177
One Moody Plaza Galveston, TX 77550-7999	Rating Outlook: Stable	'07	53.3	13.0	11.6	22.1	13,839,936	27.8	1.1	55.6	15.5	2,164,812	1,663,973	1,759,349	343,327	99,536	62,602	59,119
TX : 1905 : Stock : Agency Ann, Life, Credit		'08	56.9	15.8	8.7	18.6	13,586,041	27.2	1.0	61.6	10.2	1,805,670	2,305,671	2,382,436	457,544	32,618	11,392	-123,072
409-763-4661		'09	54.7	16.8	8.9	19.6	15,359,313	24.0	0.8	63.4	11.8	1,892,467	2,660,913	2,782,754	1,233,601	146,090	111,782	53,888
AMB# 006087 NAIC# 60739	FSC XV	Rating History: A, 05/20/10; A, 06/09/09; A+, 05/13/08; A+, 04/26/07; A+, 02/08/06																
AMERICAN NATIONAL LIFE INS NY American National Insurance Company	**A**	'05	...	...	...	...	...	...	...	...	...	...	...	...	...	...	...	...
		'06	...	...	...	...	...	...	...	...	...	...	...	...	...	...	...	...
One Moody Plaza Galveston, TX 77550	Rating Outlook: Stable	'07	...	...	...	...	...	...	...	...	...	...	...	...	...	...	...	...
TX : Stock		'08	...	...	...	...	...	...	...	...	...	...	...	...	...	...	...	...
409-766-6448		'09	...	...	...	...	...	...	...	...	...	...	...	...	...	...	...	...
AMB# 060708	FSC V	Rating History: A, 05/20/10																
AMERICAN NAT'L LIFE INS TEXAS American National Insurance Company	**A**	'05	90.5	...	2.4	7.1	141,769	56.8	21.5	3.9	17.8	43,140	83,064	80,324	7,647	-556	-212	-159
G. R. Ferdinandtsen Chairman & President		'06	90.0	...	3.8	6.2	145,558	56.1	17.5	3.7	22.7	43,000	78,737	74,433	2,972	4,405	3,327	3,120
One Moody Plaza Galveston, TX 77550-7999	Rating Outlook: Stable	'07	87.7	...	6.2	6.1	140,309	59.8	19.0	3.8	17.3	44,191	78,017	75,642	-4,101	-2,139	-1,428	-1,428
TX : 1954 : Stock : Broker A&H, Life		'08	87.2	...	2.8	10.0	137,691	57.6	24.2	3.6	14.5	36,095	97,125	93,894	-3,819	-9,182	-5,845	-8,391
409-763-4661		'09	86.7	...	2.5	10.8	125,415	60.0	25.8	3.6	10.6	26,668	109,101	105,097	-10,847	-20,950	-13,378	-14,466
AMB# 007417 NAIC# 71773	FSC VI	Rating History: A, 05/20/10; A, 06/09/09; A, 05/13/08; A, 04/26/07; A, 02/08/06																
AMERICAN NETWORK INS COMPANY Penn Treaty American Corporation	**E**	'05	84.9	...	8.1	6.9	104,502	...	5.6	...	94.4	17,510	26,342	11,976	80,404	2,134	1,449	1,336
William W. Hunt, Jr. President & CEO		'06	82.7	...	7.7	9.5	114,420	...	6.7	...	93.3	19,265	24,255	8,764	6,628	2,717	1,787	1,785
3440 Lehigh Street Allentown, PA 18103-7001		'07	82.2	...	7.5	10.2	123,804	...	8.3	...	91.7	21,222	23,712	9,224	8,837	2,539	1,422	1,426
PA : 1961 : Stock : Broker Dis inc, LTC		'08	76.2	...	7.0	16.8	123,183	...	9.3	...	90.7	4,142	24,024	8,219	-1,008	2,372	2,164	1,270
610-965-2222		'09	...	...	...	...	...	...	...	...	...	...	...	...	...	...	...	...
AMB# 007362 NAIC# 81078		Rating History: E, 01/08/09; D g, 10/03/08; B- g, 02/20/08; B gu, 07/06/06; B g, 12/19/05																
AMERICAN PHOENIX LIFE&REASSUR Phoenix Companies Inc	**B+**	'05	31.9	...	13.9	54.2	88,254	2.1	53.7	...	44.2	47,211	...	9,878	17,781	17,283	11,701	11,701
David R. Pellerin President		'06	31.0	...	19.4	49.5	70,652	9.8	33.6	...	56.6	53,391	...	-224	-7,387	9,727	6,755	6,755
One American Row Hartford, CT 06115	Rating Outlook: Negative	'07	30.8	...	20.2	49.0	69,903	8.3	59.4	...	32.3	58,566	...	299	-5,608	-963	-652	-677
CT : 1994 : Stock : Other Direct Group A&H		'08	52.9	...	3.9	43.2	26,375	10.7	88.6	...	0.7	17,628	...	2,090	-19,585	-251	-153	-152
860-403-5000		'09	63.8	...	...	36.2	22,766	1.7	97.0	...	1.3	16,658	...	16	-3,550	-852	-950	-949
AMB# 068152 NAIC# 91785	FSC V	Rating History: B+, 01/13/10; B++, 03/10/09; A-, 01/15/09; A-, 11/14/08; A-, 02/08/08																
AMERICAN PIONEER LIFE INS CO Universal American Corp.	**B+**	'05	72.2	0.0	3.2	24.6	181,110	27.8	35.7	21.4	15.1	36,479	235,699	138,403	18,862	-5,082	-7,839	-7,855
Gary W. Bryant President & CEO		'06	74.3	0.0	3.3	22.3	177,522	27.1	37.0	21.8	14.1	31,463	203,333	120,897	-6,201	-1,195	-528	-528
P.O. Box 958465 Lake Mary, FL 32795-8465	Rating Outlook: Stable	'07	66.9	0.0	...	33.1	174,097	28.3	37.8	20.2	13.7	29,494	162,422	99,440	-1,131	-5,091	-3,774	-2,133
FL : 1962 : Stock : Agency Ind A&H, LTC, Med supp		'08	70.3	0.0	...	29.7	160,573	30.2	38.8	19.0	12.0	21,076	139,965	89,471	-9,298	-5,196	-3,575	-5,081
407-995-8000		'09	76.9	0.0	...	23.1	86,465	0.4	79.4	...	20.2	20,898	118,810	10,535	-64,117	-517	-1,129	-2,941
AMB# 006090 NAIC# 60763	FSC V	Rating History: B+, 04/16/10; B++g, 12/03/08; B++g, 08/21/07; B++g, 06/21/06; B++g, 06/09/05																

2010 BEST'S KEY RATING GUIDE — LIFE/HEALTH EDITION
BEST'S PROFITABILITY, LEVERAGE AND LIQUIDITY TESTS 2005 – 2009

Data in U.S. Dollars

—	Profitability Tests							Leverage Tests						Liquidity Tests					
Un-Realized Capital Gains ($000)	Benefits Paid to NPW & Dep (%)	Comm. & Expenses to NPW & Dep (%)	NOG to Total Assets (%)	NOG to Total Rev (%)	Operating Return on Equity (%)	Net Yield (%)	Total Return (%)	Change in NPW & Dep (%)	NPW & Dep to Capital (X)	Capital & Surplus to Liabilities (%)	Surplus Relief (%)	Reins Leverage (%)	Change in Capital (%)	Quick Liquidity (%)	Current Liquidity (%)	Non-Invest Grade Bonds to Capital (%)	Delinq. & Foreclosed Mortgages to Capital (%)	Mort. & Credit Tenant Loans & R.E. to Capital (%)	Affiliated Invest to Capital (%)
...	70.6	30.7	-0.5	-0.2	-1.0	4.47	4.64	23.1	4.8	90.9	0.0	0.1	-10.3	137.2	152.3	...	...	11.3	11.3
...	68.6	21.0	20.6	12.4	37.2	4.53	4.61	-27.5	2.4	179.9	0.1	0.5	43.5	300.4	312.2	...	...	7.4	7.4
...	56.8	20.5	17.9	19.0	28.0	5.91	5.90	-55.3	1.8	190.2	0.0	0.0	-40.4	255.5	269.4	...	...	12.0	12.0
...	60.3	20.4	18.4	16.3	30.3	3.63	17.37	-29.7	2.8	120.8	0.0	0.1	-54.5	322.5	342.7	...	...	...	...
...	68.3	19.1	17.7	10.9	33.5	2.01	2.30	-16.2	4.1	101.8	0.0	...	-43.4	245.4	261.4	0.1	...	...	...

Principal Lines of Business: GrpA&H (86.2%), IndA&H (12.8%), GrpLife (1.1%), OrdLife (0.0%) — Principal States: FL (14.3%), TX (9.6%), OK (9.5%), KS (8.0%), PA (7.8%)

1,205	56.2	21.0	2.1	8.1	21.9	6.02	6.11	-2.3	2.0	10.5	0.2	11.2	6.1	44.1	58.1	48.7	...	112.6	0.1
-64	62.6	22.9	1.9	8.2	23.2	5.99	6.34	-5.2	2.2	8.6	0.1	12.3	-14.4	55.1	68.9	61.7	...	132.8	0.2
25	72.2	24.7	1.9	9.1	32.7	6.12	5.67	-9.8	3.1	5.2	0.2	18.6	-36.1	48.1	61.4	102.8	...	215.6	0.0
614	78.3	25.5	1.5	7.5	34.3	5.87	3.20	-3.3	3.2	4.6	0.2	17.8	-7.7	57.2	70.0	95.5	...	219.0	...
-165	75.3	28.2	1.1	5.7	23.3	5.70	5.38	2.4	2.6	5.8	0.1	13.3	27.9	53.6	65.7	108.4	...	160.9	...

Principal Lines of Business: GrpLife (70.1%), OrdLife (27.5%), IndAnn (1.3%), GrpAnn (1.1%), IndA&H (0.0%) — Principal States: CA (22.4%), TX (19.5%), TN (5.5%), GA (3.8%), WA (3.7%)

-25	68.4	35.0	7.2	20.1	19.3	4.75	4.71	-39.7	0.3	73.3	45.5	146.0	19.9	132.6	146.4	...	...	...	...
435	59.0	45.6	2.7	6.6	6.9	4.27	5.06	27.9	0.4	61.9	56.5	161.3	-11.2	94.1	103.8	...	...	...	54.3
968	45.9	50.6	-1.5	-3.4	-4.3	3.72	5.36	25.8	0.5	57.6	60.0	157.7	4.6	97.0	106.3	...	...	...	59.0
-180	42.5	47.6	-4.2	-9.4	-13.1	3.52	3.05	7.2	0.7	43.3	70.6	187.5	-16.4	101.4	105.4	...	...	...	75.7
-1,293	50.4	48.9	4.4	12.6	14.4	1.78	-0.70	-16.3	0.5	53.1	50.6	141.8	13.3	107.4	110.7	...	...	...	64.7

Principal Lines of Business: CrdLife (73.2%), CrdA&H (26.8%) — Principal States: OH (18.4%), MI (11.0%), MO (7.3%), WA (6.3%), OR (5.9%)

29,032	66.7	31.1	1.0	5.7	6.4	5.65	5.96	-20.4	0.7	23.6	2.2	23.1	5.4	50.2	60.6	12.6	1.6	65.1	93.4
111,627	89.8	31.3	0.7	4.0	4.3	5.47	6.42	-0.9	0.6	24.5	2.2	20.4	4.9	58.9	68.6	10.9	0.3	66.4	91.8
123,610	78.5	30.7	0.5	2.6	2.9	5.29	6.26	14.7	0.7	24.8	2.0	19.7	4.9	58.7	68.5	10.5	1.5	69.0	99.7
-420,580	69.5	25.4	0.1	0.4	0.6	5.38	1.11	35.4	1.2	17.3	2.4	24.8	-25.9	53.3	62.4	18.2	2.6	111.1	115.3
212,147	52.1	20.2	0.8	3.2	6.0	5.30	6.46	16.8	1.3	17.6	2.1	19.4	13.6	54.4	63.9	25.4	1.9	117.8	108.1

Principal Lines of Business: IndAnn (47.1%), GrpAnn (35.7%), OrdLife (12.3%), GrpA&H (2.3%), GrpLife (1.0%) — Principal States: CA (11.6%), TX (11.2%), FL (8.1%), PA (5.3%), IL (4.6%)

...	...	...	...	...	...	...	...	...	...	...	...	...	...	...	...	...	...	...	...
...	...	...	...	...	...	...	...	...	...	...	...	...	...	...	...	...	...	...	...
...	...	...	...	...	...	...	...	...	...	...	...	...	...	...	...	...	...	...	...
...	...	...	...	...	...	...	...	...	...	...	...	...	...	...	...	...	...	...	...
...	...	...	...	...	...	...	...	...	...	...	...	...	...	...	...	...	...	...	...

-13	77.3	35.3	-0.1	-0.2	-0.5	6.01	6.03	-3.2	1.8	45.9	16.1	39.8	-9.3	95.7	107.9	17.9	...	...	7.7
20	73.5	34.5	2.3	3.5	7.7	5.74	5.59	-7.3	1.7	43.8	22.7	52.7	-0.6	94.1	107.3	9.7	...	...	12.5
0	77.9	38.8	-1.0	-1.5	-3.3	5.51	5.48	1.6	1.7	48.3	15.5	41.0	3.2	96.2	109.5	7.2	...	...	18.9
94	77.5	40.5	-4.2	-5.3	-14.6	5.43	3.63	24.1	2.6	36.5	18.0	57.1	-19.5	97.7	110.4	6.1	...	...	3.4
403	81.5	45.7	-10.2	-11.1	-42.6	5.11	4.57	11.9	3.8	27.8	23.2	67.5	-25.8	93.9	107.7	8.3	...	...	0.0

Principal Lines of Business: GrpA&H (85.5%), IndA&H (13.3%), OrdLife (1.1%), IndAnn (0.0%), GrpLife (0.0%) — Principal States: TX (20.6%), MO (11.2%), MI (5.1%), OH (5.1%), IL (4.9%)

771	43.2	31.0	2.5	8.9	11.2	1.67	2.81	61.1	0.7	20.3	19.1	483.8	109.1	74.3	83.4	...	...	...	48.2
323	36.2	28.8	1.6	12.7	9.7	0.65	0.95	-26.8	0.5	20.4	21.3	477.3	9.9	76.4	85.2	...	...	...	45.6
502	25.2	32.3	1.2	10.4	7.0	0.84	1.29	5.2	0.4	20.9	16.7	443.7	10.4	78.7	87.5	...	...	...	43.6
-68	29.1	22.9	1.8	16.3	17.1	0.75	-0.04	-10.9	2.0	3.5	99.6	999.9	-80.3	66.4	73.6	24.6	...	...	205.2
...	...	...	...	...	...	...	...	...	...	...	...	...	...	...	...	...	...	...	...

189	-61.8	6.7	15.8	98.9	27.0	3.19	3.51	773.3	0.2	115.4	...	51.7	20.0	183.6	196.1	...	...	...	25.9
646	999.9	112.0	8.5	305.6	13.4	3.64	4.63	-99.9	0.0	309.3	...	31.3	12.9	381.5	408.8	...	...	...	23.8
286	999.9	39.6	-0.9	-24.9	-1.2	3.93	4.40	233.3	0.0	518.4	...	28.5	9.8	497.7	524.1	...	...	...	22.4
-55	177.7	-2.0	-0.3	-4.5	-0.4	3.32	3.20	599.4	0.1	202.8	...	31.1	-69.9	328.1	343.7	...	...	...	...
...	999.9	630.9	-3.9	-99.9	-5.5	3.36	3.40	-99.2	0.0	276.1	...	3.5	-5.4	373.9	384.2	6.1	...	...	...

Principal Lines of Business: GrpA&H (100.0%)

1	78.8	23.4	-4.5	-4.5	-24.6	5.15	5.21	5.0	3.8	25.6	76.0	279.2	33.3	80.3	88.6	8.7	...	1.9	15.9
28	84.8	22.1	-0.3	-0.3	-1.6	5.50	5.55	-12.6	3.8	21.9	70.4	319.3	-13.5	79.9	88.6	4.4	...	2.0	18.5
-569	90.4	21.7	-2.1	-3.1	-12.4	5.88	6.67	-17.7	3.3	20.7	50.4	336.6	-6.3	99.8	108.3	3.4	...	1.5	...
-95	94.6	21.1	-2.1	-3.3	-14.1	5.50	4.43	-10.0	4.2	15.1	52.8	451.6	-29.5	91.7	100.7	14.2	...	2.0	...
-1,300	666.6	100.5	-0.9	-4.3	-5.4	3.42	0.62	-88.2	0.5	31.9	58.6	725.3	-0.8	96.2	106.6	0.1	...	1.8	...

Principal Lines of Business: IndA&H (556.1%), GrpA&H (147.9%), GrpLife (-0.1%), IndAnn (-99.9%), OrdLife (-99.9%) — Principal States: FL (48.8%), TX (13.5%), MS (4.8%), NC (4.1%), MO (3.0%)

Data in U.S. Dollars

COMPANY NAME Ultimate Parent Association Principal Officer Mailing Address Dom. : Began Bus. : Struct. : Mktg. Specialty Phone # AMB# NAIC#	Best's Financial Strength Rating FSC	Data Year	Balance Sheet: Bonds (%)	Mort. Loans & R.E. (%)	Com & Pref. Stock (%)	All Other Assets (%)	Total Assets ($000)	Life Reserves (%)	Health Reserves %)	Ann Res. & Dep. Liabilities (%)	All Other Liabilities (%)	Capital & Surplus ($000)	Operations: Direct Premiums Written ($000)	Net Premiums Written & Deposits ($000)	Operating Cash Flow ($000)	NOG Before Taxes ($000)	NOG After Taxes ($000)	Net Income ($000)
AMERICAN PROGRESSIVE L&H NY Universal American Corp. Richard A. Barasch President & CEO P.O. Box 958465 Lake Mary, FL 32795-8465 NY : 1946 : Stock : Agency Ann, Ind A&H, Ind Life 914-934-8300 AMB# 008411 NAIC# 80624	**B++** Rating Outlook: Stable **FSC IX**	'05	90.6	...	0.0	9.4	198,551	14.4	16.4	65.9	3.4	19,443	119,051	96,530	10,025	-3,274	-3,113	-3,113
		'06	70.4	...	0.0	29.6	259,057	13.1	24.5	49.5	12.9	34,508	252,451	191,207	34,491	-896	-1,049	-1,049
		'07	52.7	...	0.0	47.3	419,907	10.1	28.8	30.4	30.7	93,146	518,311	451,420	64,486	22,641	14,414	14,414
		'08	60.3	...	0.0	39.7	368,567	13.5	33.1	32.5	20.9	105,456	674,978	606,801	-26,065	24,479	15,108	11,235
		'09	59.5	...	0.0	40.5	244,823	1.3	73.8	...	24.9	129,461	708,476	557,303	-57,976	49,360	32,303	25,064
		Rating History: B++g, 04/16/10; B++g, 12/03/08; B++g, 08/21/07; B++g, 06/21/06; B++g, 06/09/05																
AMERICAN PUBLIC LIFE INS CO Cameron Associates Inc Jimmy V. Pate President & Chief Operating Officer 2305 Lakeland Drive Jackson, MS 39232 OK : 1946 : Stock : Agency Dental, Dread dis, Life 601-936-6600 AMB# 006094 NAIC# 60801	**A-** Rating Outlook: Stable **FSC V**	'05	88.5	2.5	1.6	7.4	74,914	20.9	34.5	0.9	43.7	14,634	40,401	44,488	3,049	5,246	2,575	2,575
		'06	88.1	2.5	1.8	7.6	72,348	22.0	34.4	0.9	42.7	15,361	41,228	43,373	-3,831	4,589	2,833	3,016
		'07	87.0	2.7	1.9	8.4	77,027	19.8	32.3	0.8	47.1	15,052	43,930	46,391	4,601	3,628	2,030	2,030
		'08	84.4	2.7	1.9	10.9	74,494	18.9	33.5	0.8	46.8	12,861	42,082	44,094	-3,210	-3,986	-2,458	-2,501
		'09	84.8	3.2	1.9	10.1	77,202	19.4	31.8	0.8	48.0	17,582	39,280	41,458	2,433	5,013	3,497	3,516
		Rating History: A-, 03/05/10; A-, 02/17/09; A-, 02/20/08; A-, 04/02/07; A-, 03/24/06																
AMERICAN REPUBLIC CORP INS CO American Enterprise Mutual Holding Co Michael E. Abbott President & CEO P.O. Box 3160 Omaha, NE 68103-0160 NE : 1962 : Stock : Agency Group A&H 402-496-8000 AMB# 006906 NAIC# 67679	**A-** Rating Outlook: Stable **FSC VIII**	'05	89.7	...	3.8	6.5	9,078	...	...	...	100.0	8,741	...	...	142	235	197	236
		'06	96.2	...	...	3.8	8,585	...	...	...	100.0	8,272	...	...	-622	317	246	217
		'07	91.4	...	...	8.6	8,598	...	28.7	...	71.3	7,996	377	377	-158	-395	-253	-253
		'08	82.7	...	...	17.3	9,651	...	64.4	...	35.6	7,121	5,901	5,901	1,046	-509	-407	-437
		'09	82.1	...	...	17.9	14,406	0.1	57.6	...	42.3	7,834	21,721	20,613	4,320	1,376	764	709
		Rating History: A- r, 04/14/10; NR-2, 01/13/09; NR-2, 01/08/08; NR-2, 01/12/07; NR-3, 02/23/06																
AMERICAN REPUBLIC INS CO American Enterprise Mutual Holding Co Michael E. Abbott Chairman, CEO & President P.O. Box 1 Des Moines, IA 50301 IA : 1929 : Stock : Agency Ind A&H, Ind Life 515-245-2000 AMB# 006096 NAIC# 60836	**A-** Rating Outlook: Stable **FSC VIII**	'05	84.0	1.5	0.1	14.4	469,661	27.1	33.2	1.9	37.7	221,193	435,276	399,179	10,864	16,108	10,330	10,134
		'06	88.2	1.4	0.2	10.2	495,479	24.2	40.3	1.6	33.9	203,728	433,447	483,247	21,721	8,254	274	239
		'07	87.9	1.4	0.0	10.7	475,303	26.5	40.4	1.9	31.2	215,831	399,129	534,081	-16,954	43,559	29,923	29,691
		'08	85.9	1.3	1.5	11.3	475,460	28.2	39.7	1.9	30.2	235,924	374,228	459,629	7,875	29,600	19,620	17,794
		'09	76.4	1.1	1.5	21.0	521,456	22.9	32.7	1.6	42.8	240,953	348,699	399,868	10,539	37,802	21,129	19,009
		Rating History: A- g, 04/14/10; A- g, 01/13/09; A- g, 01/08/08; A- g, 01/12/07; A- g, 02/23/06																
AMERICAN RETIREMENT LIFE INS American Financial Group, Inc Billy B. Hill, Jr. President & CEO P.O. Box 26580 Austin, TX 78755 OH : 1978 : Stock : Inactive Ann, Life 512-451-2224 AMB# 008831 NAIC# 88366	**NR-3**	'05	55.5	...	...	44.5	6,936	58.1	...	0.2	41.7	5,900	20	5	172	84	85	85
		'06	53.6	...	...	46.4	7,033	60.5	...	0.2	39.3	6,010	13	4	63	138	113	113
		'07	59.3	...	...	40.7	7,144	59.5	...	0.2	40.2	6,074	17	5	154	131	60	60
		'08	51.9	...	...	48.1	6,376	74.8	...	0.1	25.1	5,519	9	3	-1,062	88	69	-433
		'09	59.4	...	...	40.6	6,403	74.3	...	0.1	25.6	5,544	10	2	12	-56	-32	-49
		Rating History: NR-3, 05/10/10; NR-3, 03/27/09; NR-3, 12/17/07; NR-3, 11/28/06; NR-3, 06/17/05																
AMERICAN SAVINGS LIFE INS CO' Byron F. Allen President 935 East Main Street, Suite 100 Mesa, AZ 85203-8849 AZ : 1954 : Stock : Not Available 480-835-5000 AMB# 006100 NAIC# 91910	**NR-1**	'05	2.4	87.6	0.2	9.8	20,668	...	...	34.3	65.7	14,223	126	126	...	1,733	1,516	1,731
		'06	2.4	85.9	0.2	11.4	20,674	...	...	31.0	69.0	14,609	137	137	...	1,690	1,461	1,711
		'07	2.3	86.1	1.9	9.7	21,418	...	...	35.5	64.5	14,607	138	138	...	1,718	1,497	1,798
		'08	2.3	85.8	1.7	10.2	21,980	...	...	25.8	74.2	12,226	267	267	...	1,785	1,544	1,628
		'09	2.0	79.1	1.6	17.4	25,269	...	...	30.4	69.6	12,786	2,535	2,535	...	2,293	2,124	2,167
		Rating History: NR-1, 06/10/10; NR-1, 06/12/09; NR-1, 06/12/08; NR-1, 06/08/07; NR-1, 06/07/06																
AMERICAN SERVICE LIFE INS CO Richard F Jones Richard F. Jones President 3130 Broadway Kansas City, MO 64111-2452 AR : 1962 : Stock : Other Direct Group A&H, Group Life, Ind Life 816-756-1060 AMB# 007899 NAIC# 76201	**NR-2**	'05	48.9	...	5.0	46.1	453	47.6	...	...	52.4	414	0	283	78	91	72	72
		'06	46.5	...	5.0	48.5	475	87.1	...	...	12.9	453	0	295	23	56	36	36
		'07	43.5	...	5.0	51.5	505	84.0	...	...	16.0	483	0	266	27	41	27	27
		'08	44.3	...	5.0	50.7	495	86.0	...	...	14.0	478	0	191	-2	-5	-3	-3
		'09	41.4	...	5.0	53.6	531	68.2	...	...	31.8	508	0	232	25	42	28	28
		Rating History: NR-2, 05/22/10; NR-2, 06/09/09; NR-2, 06/18/08; NR-2, 05/25/07; NR-2, 06/21/06																
AMERICAN SPECIALTY H PLANS CA Robert P. White President 777 Front Street San Diego, CA 92101 CA : 1994 : Stock : Broker Health 619-578-2000 AMB# 064802	**NR-5**	'05	...	8.8	...	91.2	10,841	...	...	...	100.0	2,696	4,541	4,541	1,473	9,827	5,686	5,686
		'06	...	7.8	...	92.2	9,269	...	...	...	100.0	3,042	4,737	4,737	-1,672	11,862	6,974	6,974
		'07	...	...	...	100.0	9,604	...	...	...	100.0	4,402	64,070	64,070	1,511	9,019	5,561	5,561
		'08	...	...	...	100.0	7,899	...	...	...	100.0	3,223	60,850	60,850	-1,325	6,445	3,900	3,900
		'09	...	...	...	100.0	7,600	...	...	...	100.0	3,597	62,793	62,793	-1,576	7,075	4,314	4,314
		Rating History: NR-5, 05/06/10; NR-5, 05/07/09; NR-5, 05/08/08; NR-5, 05/07/07; NR-5, 06/06/06																
AMERICAN UNDERWRITERS LIFE INS Norma J Hawkins Bruce F. Welner President P.O. Box 9510 Wichita, KS 67277-0510 AZ : 1977 : Stock : Agency Credit A&H, Credit Life, Group Life 316-794-2200 AMB# 008795 NAIC# 92649	**B-** Rating Outlook: Stable **FSC V**	'05	62.4	11.9	10.7	14.9	81,069	18.7	2.1	76.3	2.9	11,606	36,753	38,188	12,560	-629	-839	-1,422
		'06	47.3	16.2	20.6	15.9	65,296	15.9	3.1	76.3	4.7	11,903	13,201	8,227	-15,382	3,680	2,670	1,906
		'07	44.2	20.2	18.7	17.0	56,072	18.9	2.9	74.3	3.9	12,456	8,778	7,510	-5,427	66	116	3,450
		'08	45.0	15.6	26.2	13.3	77,140	12.9	1.4	81.7	4.0	13,896	14,335	31,871	23,237	685	485	-1,036
		'09	47.6	11.0	17.8	23.6	78,988	11.7	0.9	83.6	3.7	12,409	15,555	14,964	753	105	186	-2,120
		Rating History: B- g, 05/14/10; B- g, 06/16/09; B- g, 06/16/08; B-, 05/31/07; B-, 05/26/06																

BEST'S PROFITABILITY, LEVERAGE AND LIQUIDITY TESTS 2005 – 2009

Data in U.S. Dollars

	Profitability Tests							Leverage Tests						Liquidity Tests					
Un-Realized Capital Gains ($000)	Benefits Paid to NPW & Dep (%)	Comm. & Expenses to NPW & Dep (%)	NOG to Total Assets (%)	NOG to Total Rev (%)	Operating Return on Equity (%)	Net Yield (%)	Total Return (%)	Change in NPW & Dep (%)	NPW & Dep to Capital (X)	Capital & Surplus to Liabilities (%)	Surplus Relief (%)	Reins Leverage (%)	Change in Capital (%)	Quick Liquidity (%)	Current Liquidity (%)	Non-Invest Grade Bonds to Capital (%)	Delinq. & Foreclosed Mortgages to Capital (%)	Mort. & Credit Tenant Loans & R.E. to Capital (%)	Affiliated Invest to Capital (%)
0	76.7	31.6	-1.6	-2.8	-18.1	5.08	5.23	15.2	4.8	11.1	28.4	99.1	30.1	82.4	91.5	15.6	...	3.3	...
...	81.5	25.1	-0.5	-0.5	-3.9	5.41	5.49	98.1	5.5	15.7	24.2	82.2	76.2	98.9	108.3	3.6	...	1.3	...
...	85.5	14.6	4.2	3.0	22.6	6.36	6.41	136.1	4.8	28.8	10.4	34.3	167.6	94.3	102.9	1.1	...	0.5	...
-95	87.5	11.8	3.8	2.4	15.2	4.96	3.53	34.4	5.8	40.1	10.6	30.9	12.4	91.8	102.0	11.9	...	0.4	...
-1,884	100.1	13.5	10.5	5.6	27.5	3.86	-0.11	-8.2	4.3	112.2	6.5	116.4	22.8	196.1	213.1	3.2	...	0.3	...
Principal Lines of Business: IndA&H (120.2%), GrpA&H (0.1%), OrdLife (-5.6%), IndAnn (-14.7%)														Principal States: NY (68.2%), PA (16.7%), MD (3.5%)					
3	57.3	38.8	3.5	5.4	18.6	6.39	6.50	0.1	3.0	24.9	0.1	0.2	11.4	77.8	86.1	...	...	12.4	8.7
62	60.6	41.6	3.8	6.1	18.9	6.71	7.35	-2.5	2.8	27.5	0.1	1.8	4.7	78.5	86.4	...	...	11.4	7.6
71	59.2	39.6	2.7	4.1	13.3	5.73	6.00	7.0	3.0	24.9	0.0	0.2	-1.7	83.5	96.1	...	...	13.7	7.5
-3	70.1	45.3	-3.2	-5.2	-17.6	6.30	6.24	-5.0	3.4	21.4	0.1	0.1	-14.5	88.0	96.6	...	...	15.5	8.5
31	47.8	45.9	4.6	7.9	23.0	6.36	6.46	-6.0	2.3	30.2	0.0	0.1	36.3	86.2	98.0	3.6	...	13.6	6.1
Principal Lines of Business: IndA&H (49.4%), GrpA&H (43.3%), OrdLife (7.3%)														Principal States: MS (23.0%), TX (21.0%), LA (19.7%), OK (6.1%), GA (6.0%)					
...	...	...	2.2	64.2	2.3	2.92	3.92	...	...	999.9	...	...	2.8	999.9	999.9	4.6	...	...	...
...	...	...	2.8	52.4	2.9	4.61	5.09	...	...	999.9	...	...	-5.7	999.9	999.9	...	...	...	...
...	10.1	262.8	-2.9	-32.1	-3.1	4.44	4.96	...	0.0	999.9	...	...	-3.3	999.9	999.9	1.2	...	...	...
...	50.5	53.0	-4.5	-6.5	-5.4	4.09	4.08	999.9	0.8	287.2	...	...	-10.7	333.7	360.5	1.0	...	...	...
...	63.6	28.0	6.4	3.6	10.2	3.90	3.64	249.3	2.6	120.8	5.5	10.1	10.1	201.7	215.4	2.3	...	...	...
Principal Lines of Business: IndA&H (99.9%), OrdLife (0.1%)														Principal States: WI (35.7%), IA (20.8%), IL (9.4%), MO (7.5%), CO (4.8%)					
39	73.1	29.1	2.2	2.4	4.8	5.71	5.72	4.9	1.8	96.1	5.8	51.1	5.3	110.7	149.1	0.7	...	3.1	3.2
44	74.6	31.3	0.1	0.1	0.1	5.62	5.66	21.1	2.3	74.3	7.6	60.8	-7.8	91.8	126.8	...	...	3.3	3.5
9	73.5	25.1	6.2	5.2	14.3	5.68	5.67	10.5	2.4	88.1	5.4	62.2	5.8	96.1	135.0	...	...	3.0	3.1
-868	74.2	26.1	4.1	3.9	8.7	5.64	5.07	-13.9	1.9	103.2	3.8	56.9	9.4	105.1	145.5	4.5	...	2.6	5.7
696	70.8	25.7	4.2	4.6	8.9	5.36	5.05	-13.0	1.6	89.7	11.0	83.6	2.2	107.7	138.5	7.3	...	2.4	5.8
Principal Lines of Business: GrpA&H (58.1%), IndA&H (40.3%), OrdLife (1.6%), GrpLife (0.0%)														Principal States: WI (11.7%), IA (11.7%), MO (8.5%), IL (8.3%), NC (8.0%)					
...	626.8	999.9	1.2	27.7	1.5	3.58	3.51	-4.3	0.0	573.8	1.2	396.9	1.4	814.2	835.0	...	...	...	...
...	222.4	999.9	1.6	33.6	1.9	4.13	4.06	-18.5	0.0	591.5	1.0	368.7	1.9	827.6	848.4	...	...	...	...
...	336.3	999.9	0.9	17.5	1.0	4.16	4.09	3.4	0.0	572.3	0.9	345.3	1.1	795.0	812.3	...	...	...	...
176	999.9	999.9	1.0	23.9	1.2	3.72	-1.09	-36.5	0.0	644.4	0.9	361.5	-9.2	876.0	881.8	0.0	...	...	...
6	999.9	999.9	-0.5	-17.0	-0.6	2.26	2.00	-19.1	0.0	645.7	0.9	341.1	0.5	804.3	809.6	0.4	...	...	...
Principal Lines of Business: OrdLife (100.0%)														Principal States: TN (30.9%), TX (25.6%), AR (19.3%), OK (11.5%), CO (5.3%)					
10	125.5	543.2	7.5	57.9	10.8	...	...	-1.8	0.0	284.3	...	...	4.6	...	...	...	...	118.4	...
10	113.4	573.5	7.1	54.1	10.1	...	...	8.5	0.0	305.3	...	...	1.8	...	...	...	...	114.1	...
10	161.0	525.1	7.1	55.0	10.2	...	...	0.9	0.0	272.2	...	...	0.6	...	...	...	...	117.7	...
-22	67.8	226.3	7.1	56.4	11.5	...	...	93.2	0.0	154.8	...	...	-14.7	...	...	...	...	141.2	...
4	8.8	24.8	9.0	47.0	17.0	...	...	848.5	0.2	124.3	...	...	4.9	...	...	...	...	142.7	...
Principal Lines of Business: IndAnn (94.5%), OrdLife (5.5%)																			
4	29.5	42.8	17.6	24.3	19.1	2.72	4.61	-49.7	0.7	999.9	...	9.8	22.5	999.9	999.9	...	...	...	5.5
1	37.1	47.8	7.7	11.6	8.2	2.51	3.14	4.3	0.7	999.9	...	7.4	9.5	999.9	999.9	...	...	...	5.2
248	39.4	49.6	5.6	9.9	5.9	2.51	77.95	-9.8	0.6	999.9	...	6.4	6.4	999.9	999.9	...	...	...	5.2
-1	53.1	56.9	-0.7	-1.7	-0.7	2.23	2.13	-28.3	0.4	999.9	...	4.3	-1.0	999.9	999.9	...	...	...	5.2
2	37.0	49.0	5.5	11.6	5.7	2.08	2.44	21.2	0.5	999.9	...	7.3	6.4	999.9	999.9	...	...	...	5.2
Principal Lines of Business: GrpA&H (97.1%), OrdLife (2.9%)														Principal States: AR (100.0%)					
...	778.7	573.7	54.2	8.0	196.3	1.13	1.13	5.0	1.7	33.1	...	...	-12.9	82.6	82.6	...	...	35.5	35.5
...	736.9	530.5	69.4	9.7	243.1	4.52	4.52	4.3	1.6	48.9	...	...	12.8	81.6	81.6	...	...	23.7	23.7
...	50.4	36.3	58.9	8.6	149.4	5.04	5.04	999.9	14.6	84.6	...	...	44.7	126.9	126.9	...	...	...	...
...	53.6	36.3	44.6	6.4	102.3	2.45	2.45	-5.0	18.9	68.9	...	...	-26.8	112.9	112.9	...	...	...	...
...	54.4	34.6	55.7	6.9	126.5	0.58	0.58	3.2	17.5	89.9	...	...	11.6	92.6	92.6	...	...	...	...
Principal Lines of Business: CompHosp/Med (92.1%), Medicare (7.8%), Medicaid (0.1%)																			
35	62.7	10.5	-1.1	-1.9	-7.0	6.36	5.46	9.5	3.0	18.8	0.9	26.0	-6.5	56.2	63.3	91.9	2.2	75.4	49.8
435	312.3	-4.5	3.6	17.0	22.7	5.14	4.39	-78.5	0.6	24.9	32.3	69.1	1.4	54.9	62.3	16.5	1.6	81.2	96.7
-3,352	217.2	39.8	0.2	1.1	1.0	4.64	4.46	-8.7	0.6	30.8	1.0	64.1	1.5	59.3	67.8	27.4	1.5	85.7	52.6
-1,188	43.0	8.4	0.7	1.3	3.7	6.45	1.89	324.4	2.3	22.0	0.7	56.0	5.3	53.2	63.2	63.9	1.4	86.4	54.2
1,150	90.8	14.8	0.2	1.0	1.4	5.50	3.80	-53.0	1.2	19.7	0.7	62.3	-6.5	59.8	69.1	50.2	1.5	67.0	61.3
Principal Lines of Business: IndAnn (90.4%), GrpA&H (4.2%), OrdLife (2.0%), GrpAnn (1.5%), GrpLife (1.0%)														Principal States: UT (43.1%), OK (14.6%), ID (13.8%), KS (12.2%), MO (6.0%)					

Data in U.S. Dollars

COMPANY NAME Ultimate Parent Association Principal Officer Mailing Address Dom. : Began Bus. : Struct. : Mktg. Specialty Phone # AMB# NAIC#	Best's Financial Strength Rating FSC	Data Year	Balance Sheet Bonds (%)	Mort. Loans & R.E. (%)	Com & Pref. Stock (%)	All Other Assets (%)	Total Assets ($000)	Life Reserves (%)	Health Reserves %)	Ann Res. & Dep. Liabilities (%)	All Other Liabilities (%)	Capital & Surplus ($000)	Operations Direct Premiums Written ($000)	Net Premiums Written & Deposits ($000)	Operating Cash Flow ($000)	NOG Before Taxes ($000)	NOG After Taxes ($000)	Net Income ($000)
AMERICAN UNITED LIFE INS CO American United Mutual Insurance Hldg Co Dayton H. Molendorp Chairman, President & CEO P.O. Box 368 Indianapolis, IN 46206-0368 IN : 1877 : Stock : General Agent Ind Life, Ann 317-285-1877 AMB# 006109 NAIC# 60895	**A** Rating Outlook: Positive **FSC XI**	**'05**	35.4	10.7	0.5	53.3	12,122,587	9.2	3.1	33.7	54.0	633,454	1,954,373	1,913,254	44,843	54,750	47,688	42,112
		'06	32.8	9.9	0.4	57.0	12,879,129	8.7	2.8	30.6	57.9	660,521	2,030,004	1,972,176	-143,732	77,409	67,373	64,011
		'07	32.9	8.8	0.3	57.9	14,032,818	8.2	2.3	31.1	58.5	677,927	2,091,499	2,048,134	438,088	79,469	59,731	57,061
		'08	42.9	9.9	1.0	46.3	12,526,176	9.4	2.5	42.2	45.8	656,212	2,392,964	2,841,254	911,308	34,805	23,338	9,406
		'09	40.5	8.7	0.5	50.3	14,839,168	8.2	2.0	39.1	50.7	758,847	2,238,301	2,413,280	596,213	80,342	61,933	61,345
		Rating History: A g, 06/10/10; A g, 06/17/09; A g, 06/09/08; A g, 06/07/07; A g, 02/08/06																
AMERICA'S HLTH CHOICE MED PLNS[2] Walter H. Janke President 1175 South U.S. Highway 1 Vero Beach, FL 32962 FL : 2000 : Stock : Broker Health 772-794-0030 AMB# 064703 NAIC# 11122	**E**	**'05**	59.5	3.2	14.7	22.6	21,717	...	74.8	...	25.2	7,854	149,501	148,762	-3,369	1,420	1,420	1,478
		'06	50.0	2.3	...	47.7	26,950	...	61.1	...	38.9	13,486	174,523	174,523	8,222	4,377	4,377	4,909
		'07	...	...	...	...	...	...	...	...	...	...	...	...	...	...	...	...
		'08	...	...	...	...	...	...	...	...	...	...	...	...	...	...	...	...
		'09	...	...	...	...	...	...	...	...	...	...	...	...	...	...	...	...
		Rating History: E, 10/15/08; C+ pd, 07/16/07; C+ pd, 08/28/06; C+ pd, 09/29/05; C+ pd, 08/13/04																
AMERICHOICE OF CONNECTICUT INC UnitedHealth Group Inc Richard M. Jelinek Chief Executive Officer 400 Capital Street Rocky Hill, CT 06067 CT : 2008 : Stock : Other Medicaid 866-315-2323 AMB# 060689 NAIC# 13178	**NR-2**	**'05**	...	...	...	...	...	...	...	...	...	...	...	...	...	...	...	...
		'06	...	...	...	...	...	...	...	...	...	...	...	...	...	...	...	...
		'07	...	...	...	...	...	...	...	...	...	...	...	...	...	...	...	...
		'08	17.2	...	...	82.8	3,001	...	14.7	...	85.3	1,333	1,530	1,530	1,993	-160	-114	-114
		'09	1.5	...	...	98.5	34,038	...	60.3	...	39.7	16,661	93,489	93,396	22,235	1,484	875	875
		Rating History: NR-2, 06/15/09																
AMERICHOICE OF GEORGIA INC UnitedHealth Group Inc Michael P. Radu President 3720 Davinci Court, Suite 300 Norcross, GA 30092 GA : 2008 : Stock : Other Medicaid 770-417-5637 AMB# 064965 NAIC# 13168	**NR-2**	**'05**	...	...	...	...	...	...	...	...	...	...	...	...	...	...	...	...
		'06	...	...	...	...	...	...	...	...	...	...	...	...	...	...	...	...
		'07	...	...	...	...	...	...	...	...	...	...	...	...	...	...	...	...
		'08	3.4	...	...	96.6	3,001	...	...	...	100.0	3,001	...	...	3,001	1	1	1
		'09	3.2	...	...	96.8	3,101	...	...	...	100.0	3,101	...	...	100	0	0	0
		Rating History: NR-2, 06/15/09																
AMERICHOICE OF NEW JERSEY UnitedHealth Group Inc John Kirchner CEO 100 Mulberry Street, 4 Gateway Center Newark, NJ 07102 NJ : 1996 : Stock : Broker Health 973-297-5500 AMB# 064214 NAIC# 95497	**A-** Rating Outlook: Stable **FSC VII**	**'05**	44.8	...	...	55.2	102,732	...	82.8	...	17.2	40,430	385,442	385,442	9,539	16,414	14,952	14,904
		'06	24.5	...	...	75.5	204,994	...	50.3	...	49.7	81,245	477,743	477,743	86,878	34,694	23,345	23,146
		'07	40.8	...	...	59.2	194,215	...	80.8	...	19.2	98,640	543,927	543,927	-9,046	24,447	16,628	16,628
		'08	54.0	...	...	46.0	182,392	...	82.4	...	17.6	92,659	647,073	647,073	-10,178	19,848	14,182	14,656
		'09	59.9	...	...	40.1	205,801	...	82.9	...	17.1	79,506	786,278	786,278	31,297	-24,667	-13,823	-13,664
		Rating History: A-, 06/15/09; A-, 01/29/08; A-, 11/21/07; A-, 11/16/06; A-, 08/17/06																
AMERICHOICE OF PENNSYLVANIA UnitedHealth Group Inc Ernest Monfiletto CEO 450 Columbus Blvd Hartford, CT 06103 PA : 1989 : Stock : Broker Health 215-832-4500 AMB# 064159 NAIC# 95033	**A-** Rating Outlook: Stable **FSC VI**	**'05**	28.3	...	...	71.7	100,556	...	39.7	...	60.3	41,251	446,725	207,500	-30,875	20,907	14,190	14,333
		'06	11.6	...	...	88.4	90,215	...	48.6	...	51.4	29,771	339,099	134,551	-22,689	-18,626	-15,536	-15,713
		'07	20.5	...	...	79.5	85,269	...	40.9	...	59.1	38,940	328,459	130,531	32,711	4,561	6,969	6,928
		'08	10.1	...	...	89.9	80,318	...	25.2	...	74.8	37,395	257,420	102,280	-28,094	5,049	2,612	2,640
		'09	0.2	...	...	99.8	82,835	...	28.7	...	71.3	34,983	280,395	111,876	-7,931	-1,972	-877	-888
		Rating History: A-, 06/15/09; A-, 01/29/08; A-, 11/21/07; A-, 11/16/06; A-, 08/17/06																
AMERICO FINANCIAL LF & ANNUITY Financial Holding Corporation Gary L. Muller CEO P.O. Box 410288 Kansas City, MO 64141-0288 TX : 1946 : Stock : Agency Ann, Term Life, Univ Life 816-391-2000 AMB# 006233 NAIC# 61999	**A-** Rating Outlook: Stable **FSC IX**	**'05**	73.9	6.5	2.2	17.4	3,519,826	12.1	0.0	51.4	36.5	190,557	347,613	350,450	182,576	52,756	34,261	40,162
		'06	69.8	6.7	6.0	17.4	3,575,248	12.7	0.0	53.2	34.0	216,584	304,170	313,742	72,316	9,793	8,195	18,715
		'07	66.6	7.5	7.8	18.2	3,735,648	13.8	0.0	51.5	34.7	225,448	337,071	358,525	126,729	9,202	9,196	8,618
		'08	66.3	9.3	8.0	16.5	3,439,012	16.3	0.0	39.8	43.8	171,039	290,566	309,326	-186,407	68,229	42,359	-20,771
		'09	69.3	8.4	5.6	16.7	3,557,790	17.8	0.0	40.0	42.2	311,287	289,889	334,965	33,467	75,003	53,107	54,072
		Rating History: A-, 11/04/09; A- g, 09/05/08; A- g, 06/14/07; A- g, 06/21/06; A- g, 06/22/05																
AMERIGROUP NEW JERSEY INC[2] AMERIGROUP Corporation Peter D. Haytaian President & CEO 4425 Corporation Lane Virginia Beach, VA 23462 NJ : 1996 : Stock : Broker Health 757-473-2721 AMB# 064209 NAIC# 95373	**NR-5**	**'05**	56.1	...	...	43.9	54,075	...	70.8	...	29.2	18,812	230,963	230,527	4,590	-3,566	-2,923	-2,923
		'06	60.6	...	...	39.4	86,525	...	34.8	...	65.2	28,765	228,127	227,428	30,587	15,197	6,979	6,979
		'07	37.1	...	...	62.9	78,584	...	53.2	...	46.8	32,147	243,484	242,844	-7,851	14,919	11,815	11,834
		'08	35.5	...	...	64.5	74,710	...	70.4	...	29.6	33,739	272,062	271,677	-2,684	15,877	10,138	10,148
		'09	44.1	...	...	55.9	95,172	...	71.3	...	28.7	49,560	316,557	316,145	15,036	-4,844	-2,902	-2,875
		Rating History: NR-5, 04/19/10; NR-5, 08/26/09; C++pd, 09/03/08; C++pd, 10/08/07; C+ pd, 09/01/06																
AMERIGROUP OHIO INC AMERIGROUP Corporation Gary H. Fletcher President & CEO 4425 Corporation Lane Virginia Beach, VA 23462 OH : 2005 : Stock : Broker Health 757-490-6900 AMB# 064873 NAIC# 10767	**NR-5**	**'05**	3.1	...	...	96.9	13,065	...	39.9	...	60.1	3,023	10,586	10,382	9,236	-1,581	-1,581	-1,581
		'06	8.9	...	...	91.1	38,227	...	48.6	...	51.4	11,517	82,870	81,835	26,388	-4,594	-4,594	-4,594
		'07	24.8	...	...	75.2	71,889	...	49.4	...	50.6	23,913	195,809	194,106	30,154	3,303	1,398	1,413
		'08	35.4	...	...	64.6	67,025	...	66.3	...	33.7	32,796	235,042	233,328	-3,384	-5,303	-2,279	-2,266
		'09	42.0	...	...	58.0	80,940	...	43.6	...	56.4	35,844	267,168	264,841	12,479	6,951	3,194	3,200
		Rating History: NR-5, 04/07/10; NR-5, 08/26/09; C++pd, 09/03/08; NR-5, 06/30/08; NR-5, 02/07/07																

BEST'S PROFITABILITY, LEVERAGE AND LIQUIDITY TESTS 2005 – 2009

Data in U.S. Dollars

	Profitability Tests							Leverage Tests						Liquidity Tests					
Un-Realized Capital Gains ($000)	Benefits Paid to NPW & Dep (%)	Comm. & Expenses to NPW & Dep (%)	NOG to Total Assets (%)	NOG to Total Rev (%)	Operating Return on Equity (%)	Net Yield (%)	Total Return (%)	Change in NPW & Dep (%)	NPW & Dep to Capital (X)	Capital & Surplus to Liabilities (%)	Surplus Relief (%)	Reins Leverage (%)	Change in Capital (%)	Quick Liquidity (%)	Current Liquidity (%)	Non-Invest Grade Bonds to Capital (%)	Delinq. & Foreclosed Mortgages to Capital (%)	Mort. & Credit Tenant Loans & R.E. to Capital (%)	Affiliated Invest to Capital (%)
-638	85.9	13.8	0.4	2.0	7.5	6.25	6.20	5.4	2.8	12.5	21.1	263.0	-2.0	42.0	60.3	12.8	0.1	191.3	15.9
-1,678	92.8	12.5	0.5	2.7	10.4	6.30	6.27	3.1	2.8	13.4	21.3	289.1	3.8	42.7	61.1	13.3	0.1	180.3	12.3
1,559	105.3	12.6	0.4	2.3	8.9	6.22	6.23	3.9	2.8	12.8	17.0	268.4	2.9	45.2	63.4	8.9	0.1	170.8	10.1
-16,271	64.4	9.4	0.2	0.8	3.5	6.21	5.79	38.7	4.0	10.5	14.8	285.3	-2.1	47.0	65.3	16.5	0.1	173.6	9.0
7,755	69.7	11.8	0.5	2.2	8.8	5.96	6.08	-15.1	3.0	11.5	11.2	246.2	14.7	46.7	65.0	22.6	0.1	157.6	8.0
	Principal Lines of Business: GrpAnn (76.9%), IndAnn (8.2%), GrpA&H (5.5%), OrdLife (5.4%), GrpLife (4.0%)													Principal States: IN (17.8%), TX (10.7%), CA (6.0%), IL (5.2%), MO (5.0%)					
261	87.3	12.4	6.5	0.9	17.5	2.89	4.57	15.9	18.9	56.7	...	2.8	-6.6	102.7	113.5	...	...	8.8	8.8
-314	85.1	13.2	18.0	2.5	41.0	4.11	5.17	17.3	12.9	100.2	...	...	71.7	172.0	179.2	...	...	4.7	...
...	...	...	...	...	...	...	...	...	...	...	...	...	...	...	...	...	...	...	...
...	...	...	...	...	...	...	...	...	...	...	...	...	...	...	...	...	...	...	...
...	...	...	...	...	...	...	...	...	...	...	...	...	...	...	...	...	...	...	...
...	...	...	...	...	...	...	...	...	...	...	...	...	...	...	...	...	...	...	...
...	...	...	...	...	...	...	...	...	...	...	...	...	...	...	...	...	...	...	...
...	...	...	...	...	...	...	...	...	...	...	...	...	...	...	...	...	...	...	...
...	100.6	11.1	...	-7.4	...	...	...	...	1.1	79.8	...	...	...	170.8	176.8	...	...	...	...
...	87.7	10.8	4.7	0.9	9.7	0.13	0.13	999.9	5.6	95.9	...	...	999.9	139.4	139.4	...	...	...	...
	Principal Lines of Business: Medicaid (100.0%)													Principal States: CT (100.0%)					
...	...	...	...	...	...	...	...	...	...	...	...	...	...	...	...	...	...	...	...
...	...	...	...	...	...	...	...	...	...	...	...	...	...	...	...	...	...	...	...
...	...	...	...	...	...	...	...	...	...	...	...	...	...	...	...	...	...	...	...
...	...	...	...	100.0	...	...	...	...	...	...	...	...	...	...	...	...	...	...	...
...	...	...	0.0	11.6	0.0	0.07	0.07	...	...	999.9	...	...	3.3	999.9	999.9	...	...	...	...
-3,355	83.5	13.2	14.6	3.8	42.8	3.68	-0.46	4.9	9.5	64.9	...	...	37.3	196.0	207.7	...	...	...	...
-2,005	83.1	11.0	15.2	4.8	38.4	4.49	2.78	23.9	5.9	65.7	...	...	101.0	230.3	241.8	...	...	...	...
-1,532	84.4	12.7	8.3	3.0	18.5	5.04	4.12	13.9	5.5	103.2	...	...	21.4	239.8	254.8	0.2	...	...	...
-1,535	85.8	12.1	7.5	2.2	14.8	4.16	3.49	19.0	7.0	103.3	...	...	-6.1	213.0	229.6	0.0	...	...	...
3	92.3	10.6	-7.1	-1.7	-16.1	2.74	2.84	21.5	9.9	63.0	...	...	-14.2	178.8	192.5	...	...	...	...
	Principal Lines of Business: Medicaid (94.9%), Medicare (5.1%)													Principal States: NJ (100.0%)					
-311	76.0	15.2	11.9	6.8	31.8	3.77	3.52	10.1	5.0	69.6	...	121.5	-13.8	129.6	138.4	...	...	...	...
-311	96.3	16.6	-16.3	-11.4	-43.7	5.66	4.43	-35.2	4.5	49.3	...	225.3	-27.8	80.2	84.5	...	...	...	...
...	81.2	19.8	7.9	5.2	20.3	5.98	5.88	-3.0	3.4	84.1	...	105.4	30.8	214.7	225.9	...	...	...	...
...	76.2	20.5	3.2	2.5	6.8	3.87	3.93	-21.6	2.7	87.1	...	82.9	-4.0	125.5	133.6	...	...	...	...
...	82.6	19.4	-1.1	-0.8	-2.4	0.97	0.93	9.4	3.2	73.1	...	115.0	-6.5	98.5	104.1	...	...	...	...
	Principal Lines of Business: Medicaid (94.9%), CompHosp/Med (4.4%), Medicare (0.7%)													Principal States: PA (100.0%)					
-14,776	59.5	36.6	1.1	3.0	18.8	5.36	5.27	18.5	1.6	6.6	14.0	789.9	10.8	50.6	64.6	45.9	...	124.2	15.5
6,510	67.5	48.8	0.2	1.6	4.0	5.55	6.25	-10.5	1.3	7.4	13.5	670.8	12.7	50.1	64.6	28.3	...	115.1	11.4
-850	70.4	49.3	0.3	1.7	4.2	5.86	5.94	14.3	1.3	7.5	11.9	623.3	9.4	49.0	64.0	16.9	...	118.8	12.5
-25,948	75.9	55.0	1.2	1.7	21.4	5.64	3.01	-13.7	1.7	5.7	21.6	999.9	-31.3	48.1	61.4	27.1	1.9	192.7	52.5
35,085	71.8	47.3	1.5	9.7	22.0	5.69	6.93	8.3	1.0	10.6	10.6	560.8	87.2	48.1	61.5	39.5	...	101.8	31.7
	Principal Lines of Business: IndAnn (44.2%), OrdLife (42.6%), GrpLife (9.3%), GrpAnn (3.1%), GrpA&H (0.4%)													Principal States: FL (13.8%), CA (12.7%), TX (10.3%), NC (6.3%), IL (4.2%)					
...	86.7	15.5	-5.7	-1.3	-15.8	3.22	3.22	6.7	12.3	53.3	...	1.8	3.5	128.4	128.4	...	...	...	...
...	75.9	18.7	9.9	3.0	29.3	5.03	5.03	-1.3	7.9	49.8	...	...	52.9	132.6	132.6	...	...	...	...
...	76.2	19.2	14.3	4.8	38.8	5.06	5.08	6.8	7.6	69.2	...	5.5	11.8	163.5	163.5	...	...	...	...
...	80.7	14.4	13.2	3.7	30.8	3.87	3.88	11.9	8.1	82.3	...	...	5.0	241.9	247.4	...	...	...	...
...	87.4	14.5	-3.4	-0.9	-7.0	1.23	1.26	16.4	6.4	108.7	...	...	46.9	264.0	274.8	...	...	...	...
	Principal Lines of Business: Medicaid (94.4%), Medicare (5.6%)													Principal States: NJ (100.0%)					
...	94.5	21.7	...	-15.1	...	...	...	...	3.4	30.1	...	...	...	92.0	92.0	...	...	...	...
...	88.3	18.4	-17.9	-5.6	-63.2	3.99	3.99	688.3	7.1	43.1	...	...	281.0	134.7	134.7	...	...	...	...
...	84.9	14.6	2.5	0.7	7.9	4.75	4.78	137.2	8.1	49.8	...	5.1	107.6	136.4	136.8	...	...	...	...
...	88.3	14.8	-3.3	-1.0	-8.0	3.05	3.07	20.2	7.1	95.8	...	3.3	37.1	276.9	288.5	...	...	...	...
...	83.8	13.9	4.3	1.2	9.3	1.53	1.54	13.5	7.4	79.5	...	2.5	9.3	227.9	238.5	...	...	...	...
	Principal Lines of Business: Medicaid (100.0%)													Principal States: OH (100.0%)					

Data in U.S. Dollars

COMPANY NAME Ultimate Parent Association Principal Officer Mailing Address Dom. : Began Bus. : Struct. : Mktg. Specialty Phone # AMB# NAIC#	Best's Financial Strength Rating FSC		Balance Sheet										Operations					
		Data Year	Bonds (%)	Mort. Loans & R.E. (%)	Com & Pref. Stock (%)	All Other Assets (%)	Total Assets ($000)	Life Reserves (%)	Health Reserves %)	Ann Res. & Dep. Liabilities (%)	All Other Liabilities (%)	Capital & Surplus ($000)	Direct Premiums Written ($000)	Net Premiums Written & Deposits ($000)	Operating Cash Flow ($000)	NOG Before Taxes ($000)	NOG After Taxes ($000)	Net Income ($000)
AMERIGROUP SOUTH CAROLINA INC[2] AMERIGROUP Corporation James G. Carlson President & CEO 4425 Corporation Lane Virginia Beach, VA 23462 SC : Stock : Broker Health 757-490-6900	**NR-5**	'05	...	...	...	...	...	...	...	...	...	...	...	...	...	...	...	...
		'06	...	...	...	100.0	1,201	...	...	...	100.0	1,201	...	...	1,201	1	1	1
		'07	6.0	...	...	94.0	5,123	...	2.1	...	97.9	4,223	20	20	3,878	-588	-588	-588
		'08	2.1	...	...	97.9	15,038	...	51.6	...	48.4	5,104	17,531	17,507	8,690	-4,704	-4,704	-4,704
		'09	...	...	...	100.0	4,991	...	102.3	...	-2.3	4,683	9,761	9,751	-9,007	8,469	7,302	7,302
AMB# 064887 NAIC# 12765		**Rating History: NR-5, 04/15/10; NR-5, 03/17/09; NR-5, 03/24/08; NR-5, 04/11/07**																
AMERIGROUP TENNESSEE INC AMERIGROUP Corporation Charles B. Shipp President and CEO 4425 Corporation Lane Virginia Beach, VA 23462 TN : 2007 : Stock : Not Available Health 757-473-2737	**NR-5**	'05	...	...	...	...	...	...	...	...	...	...	...	...	...	...	...	...
		'06	...	...	...	...	...	...	...	...	...	...	...	...	...	...	...	...
		'07	22.4	...	...	77.6	107,603	...	70.3	...	29.7	24,061	382,865	382,865	94,933	-26,661	-26,661	-26,642
		'08	34.6	...	...	65.4	133,533	...	79.5	...	20.5	54,588	607,095	607,095	26,657	2,818	2,818	2,825
		'09	33.9	...	...	66.1	163,369	...	72.3	...	27.7	80,854	626,126	626,126	1,930	22,503	22,503	22,541
AMB# 064927 NAIC# 12941		**Rating History: NR-5, 04/08/10; NR-5, 03/13/09; NR-5, 04/25/08**																
AMERIGROUP TEXAS INC[2] AMERIGROUP Corporation Aileen McCormick President & CEO 4425 Corporation Lane Virginia Beach, VA 23462 TX : 1996 : Stock : Broker Health 757-490-6900	**NR-5**	'05	29.3	...	...	70.7	227,767	...	63.4	...	36.6	64,198	853,117	850,461	44,125	32,965	20,744	20,744
		'06	74.4	...	...	25.6	266,201	...	73.3	...	26.7	87,374	947,341	945,060	27,175	66,283	41,796	41,796
		'07	48.1	...	...	51.9	318,442	...	81.9	...	18.1	113,315	1,067,926	1,065,946	54,473	74,520	48,038	48,076
		'08	51.0	...	...	49.0	331,113	...	81.6	...	18.4	138,706	1,204,064	1,202,432	21,133	95,266	62,103	62,249
		'09	65.9	...	...	34.1	316,910	...	73.3	...	26.7	156,694	1,301,685	1,299,978	-6,899	48,456	31,328	31,381
AMB# 064238 NAIC# 95314		**Rating History: NR-5, 04/06/10; NR-5, 08/26/09; C++pd, 09/03/08; C++pd, 10/08/07; C++pd, 09/01/06**																
AMERIGROUP VIRGINIA INC[2] AMERIGROUP Corporation Peter D. Haytaian President & CEO 4425 Corporation Lane Virginia Beach, VA 23462 VA : 2005 : Stock : Broker Health 757-490-6900	**NR-5**	'05	...	...	...	...	...	...	...	...	...	...	...	...	...	...	...	...
		'06	...	...	...	100.0	21,770	...	74.1	...	25.9	10,702	60,365	60,226	6,500	11,220	7,245	7,245
		'07	50.0	...	...	50.0	19,022	...	83.4	...	16.6	8,860	61,989	61,633	-3,713	4,749	3,098	3,098
		'08	26.2	...	...	73.8	21,078	...	60.9	...	39.1	12,378	62,520	62,426	2,913	5,712	3,627	3,629
		'09	28.1	...	...	71.9	21,356	...	59.9	...	40.1	12,726	75,686	75,571	-7,726	6,296	3,860	3,864
AMB# 064899 NAIC# 10153		**Rating History: NR-5, 05/18/10; NR-5, 04/24/09; NR-5, 05/05/08; NR-5, 05/11/07**																
AMERIHEALTH HMO INC[2] Independence Blue Cross Joseph A. Frick Chairman & CEO 1901 Market Street Philadelphia, PA 19103-1480 PA : 1978 : Stock : Broker Group A&H, Health, Ind A&H 215-241-2400	**NR-5**	'05	17.1	...	77.2	5.6	819,773	...	43.6	...	56.4	586,562	499,266	491,145	127,584	14,754	10,710	10,217
		'06	15.0	...	78.5	6.5	904,990	...	47.6	...	52.4	705,494	549,070	540,888	3,391	54,246	48,955	48,906
		'07	15.1	...	79.1	5.9	979,237	...	39.1	...	60.9	788,307	497,249	490,773	10,067	19,296	29,040	28,150
		'08	13.2	...	81.0	5.8	814,379	...	28.1	...	71.9	667,263	413,540	409,800	-43,319	24,095	34,345	18,427
		'09	7.6	...	83.4	9.0	887,875	...	27.9	...	72.1	725,099	336,724	334,774	16,761	-18,622	-16,486	-11,220
AMB# 064139 NAIC# 95044		**Rating History: NR-5, 04/09/10; NR-5, 08/26/09; B pd, 10/10/08; B pd, 10/11/07; B pd, 10/03/06**																
AMERIHEALTH INS CO OF NJ[2] Independence Blue Cross Joseph A. Frick Chairman 8000 Midlantic Drive, Suite 333N Mt. Laurel, NJ 08054-1560 NJ : 1995 : Stock : Broker Health 856-778-6500	**NR-5**	'05	63.7	...	...	36.3	119,555	...	62.1	...	37.9	51,074	204,623	209,953	11,917	30,319	20,029	19,705
		'06	68.5	...	...	31.5	116,341	...	51.4	...	48.6	69,481	224,745	229,822	5,630	26,767	21,226	20,837
		'07	69.3	...	...	30.7	118,138	...	57.0	...	43.0	70,916	236,010	240,887	-1,692	3,116	2,370	2,247
		'08	61.2	...	...	38.8	121,586	...	54.8	...	45.2	70,049	279,283	282,545	-4,404	16,959	11,338	759
		'09	64.0	...	...	36.0	127,447	...	52.4	...	47.6	49,829	326,035	327,619	-11,374	-38,091	-28,023	-28,002
AMB# 007887 NAIC# 60061		**Rating History: NR-5, 04/19/10; NR-5, 06/01/09; NR-5, 05/20/08; NR-5, 06/22/07; NR-5, 06/08/06**																
AMERITAS LIFE INSURANCE CORP. UNIFI Mutual Holding Company JoAnn M. Martin Chair, President & CEO P.O. Box 81889 Lincoln, NE 68501-1889 NE : 1887 : Stock : General Agent Group A&H, Retirement Savings, Univ Life 402-467-1122	**A**	'05	29.5	7.4	4.5	58.6	5,398,147	15.3	0.8	21.6	62.3	761,540	721,611	973,583	49,344	79,738	57,810	70,403
		'06	26.8	7.0	4.7	61.5	6,006,588	13.7	0.7	18.3	67.2	826,051	938,998	1,194,027	-106,928	78,159	54,353	72,461
	Rating Outlook: Stable	'07	25.3	6.8	5.1	62.7	6,398,880	12.9	0.7	17.8	68.7	878,120	1,060,887	1,160,861	65,716	76,364	54,978	77,195
		'08	31.3	8.8	4.6	55.3	5,142,388	16.3	0.8	26.6	56.3	710,625	1,281,034	1,447,730	30,624	18,346	816	-71,982
		'09	24.8	6.9	13.3	55.0	6,529,456	13.6	0.8	22.9	62.7	1,248,997	1,198,485	1,286,456	523,222	62,076	51,861	49,927
AMB# 006152 NAIC# 61301	**FSC XIII**	**Rating History: A g, 04/13/10; A g, 01/30/09; A g, 05/01/08; A g, 02/02/07; A g, 01/04/06**																
AMFIRST INSURANCE CO AmFirst Holdings, Inc. David R. White President P.O. Box 16708 Jackson, MS 39236 OK : 1999 : Stock : Agency Group A&H 601-956-2028	**B+**	'05	65.3	...	22.8	11.9	7,362	...	45.8	...	54.2	3,669	18,722	15,682	260	1,062	852	689
		'06	64.6	3.1	15.6	16.7	6,198	...	72.0	...	28.0	3,742	8,790	12,226	-971	582	388	386
	Rating Outlook: Stable	'07	53.1	3.3	9.6	34.0	7,559	...	70.0	...	30.0	5,017	11,224	14,838	1,293	952	633	620
		'08	52.1	2.6	5.2	40.1	9,310	...	68.1	...	31.9	6,100	11,202	16,810	1,533	1,112	729	728
		'09	38.1	2.2	4.1	55.5	10,805	...	64.7	...	35.3	6,750	13,961	21,705	1,153	1,133	761	758
AMB# 012998 NAIC# 60250	**FSC IV**	**Rating History: B+, 06/09/10; B+, 05/27/09; B+, 06/09/08; NR-5, 04/18/07; NR-5, 08/30/06**																
AMGP GEORGIA MANAGED CARE CO[2] AMERIGROUP Corporation Craig L. Bass President & CEO 4425 Corporation Lane Virginia Beach, VA 23462 GA : 2006 : Stock : Not Available Health 757-473-2737	**NR-5**	'05	...	...	...	...	...	...	...	...	...	...	...	...	...	...	...	...
		'06	87.4	...	...	12.6	91,282	...	83.4	...	16.6	37,653	207,644	207,245	76,684	-17,247	-17,247	-17,247
		'07	27.9	...	...	72.1	122,154	...	80.4	...	19.6	54,514	557,279	556,410	9,830	-2,244	-2,244	-2,223
		'08	29.6	...	...	70.4	114,559	...	84.9	...	15.1	63,085	491,620	490,845	12,902	8,559	8,559	8,641
		'09	...	...	...	...	...	...	...	...	...	...	...	...	...	...	...	...
AMB# 064890 NAIC# 12229		**Rating History: NR-5, 07/08/09; NR-5, 07/10/08; NR-5, 04/11/07**																

2010 BEST'S KEY RATING GUIDE — LIFE/HEALTH EDITION
BEST'S PROFITABILITY, LEVERAGE AND LIQUIDITY TESTS 2005 – 2009

Data in U.S. Dollars

	Profitability Tests							Leverage Tests						Liquidity Tests					
Un-Realized Capital Gains ($000)	Benefits Paid to NPW & Dep (%)	Comm. & Expenses to NPW & Dep (%)	NOG to Total Assets (%)	NOG to Total Rev (%)	Operating Return on Equity (%)	Net Yield (%)	Total Return (%)	Change in NPW & Dep (%)	NPW & Dep to Capital (X)	Capital & Surplus to Liabilities (%)	Surplus Relief (%)	Reins Leverage (%)	Change in Capital (%)	Quick Liquidity (%)	Current Liquidity (%)	Non-Invest Grade Bonds to Capital (%)	Delinq. & Foreclosed Mortgages to Capital (%)	Mort. & Credit Tenant Loans & R.E. to Capital (%)	Affiliated Invest to Capital (%)
...	...	...	...	...	...	...	...	...	...	...	...	...	...	...	...	...	...	...	...
...	...	...	...	100.0	...	...	...	...	...	...	...	...	...	...	...	...	...	...	...
...	129.8	999.9	-18.6	-99.9	-21.7	2.30	2.30	...	0.0	469.2	...	...	251.7	564.3	564.3	...	...	...	...
...	96.3	31.5	-46.7	-26.6	-99.9	1.62	1.62	999.9	3.4	51.4	...	...	20.9	249.8	262.1	...	...	...	...
...	57.5	15.8	72.9	46.8	149.2	0.59	0.59	-44.3	2.1	999.9	...	...	-8.2	999.9	999.9	...	...	...	...
	Principal Lines of Business: Medicaid (100.0%)													Principal States: SC (100.0%)					
...	...	...	...	...	...	...	...	...	...	...	...	...	...	...	...	...	...	...	...
...	...	...	...	...	...	...	...	...	...	...	...	...	...	...	...	...	...	...	...
...	94.2	13.5	...	-6.9	...	...	...	...	15.9	28.8	...	...	...	191.3	191.3	...	...	...	...
...	88.3	11.8	2.3	0.5	7.2	3.13	3.14	58.6	11.1	69.1	...	0.0	126.9	216.9	224.5	...	...	...	...
...	82.4	14.2	15.2	3.6	33.2	1.32	1.35	3.1	7.7	98.0	...	...	48.1	203.1	209.5	...	...	...	...
	Principal Lines of Business: Medicaid (97.9%), Medicare (2.1%)													Principal States: TN (100.0%)					
...	79.9	16.8	10.1	2.4	35.6	3.07	3.07	15.5	13.2	39.2	...	0.1	23.0	150.2	150.7	...	...	...	...
...	77.0	17.1	16.9	4.4	55.1	5.47	5.47	11.1	10.8	48.9	...	2.8	36.1	129.6	129.7	...	...	...	...
...	77.3	17.0	16.4	4.4	47.9	5.64	5.65	12.8	9.4	55.2	...	3.1	29.7	187.8	193.5	...	...	...	...
...	76.4	16.6	19.1	5.1	49.3	3.91	3.96	12.8	8.7	72.1	...	0.2	22.4	216.9	222.6	...	...	...	...
...	81.1	15.6	9.7	2.4	21.2	2.14	2.16	8.1	8.3	97.8	...	0.5	13.0	205.9	216.0	...	...	...	...
	Principal Lines of Business: Medicaid (87.0%), CompHosp/Med (6.6%), Medicare (6.4%)													Principal States: TX (100.0%)					
...	...	...	...	...	...	...	...	...	...	...	...	...	...	...	...	...	...	...	...
...	70.1	12.9	...	11.8	...	...	...	...	5.6	96.7	...	...	...	200.3	200.3	...	...	...	...
...	81.8	12.5	15.2	4.9	31.7	6.11	6.11	2.3	7.0	87.2	...	2.3	-17.2	234.5	236.2	...	...	...	...
...	78.3	13.6	18.1	5.8	34.2	3.36	3.37	1.3	5.0	142.3	...	...	39.7	385.3	399.1	...	...	...	...
...	79.5	12.5	18.2	5.1	30.7	1.26	1.28	21.1	5.9	147.5	...	...	2.8	220.3	226.1	...	...	...	...
	Principal Lines of Business: Medicaid (100.0%)													Principal States: VA (100.0%)					
43,340	84.4	14.0	1.5	2.1	1.9	3.97	10.27	-21.6	0.8	251.5	...	0.1	13.9	39.9	42.3	10.5	...	...	111.5
78,872	85.2	12.6	5.7	8.4	7.6	5.54	15.54	10.1	0.8	353.6	...	0.2	20.3	55.6	58.8	7.8	...	...	103.9
72,913	91.5	14.8	3.1	5.5	3.9	3.92	12.22	-9.3	0.6	412.9	...	0.0	11.7	54.1	57.0	8.3	...	...	102.3
-44,109	91.3	14.7	3.8	7.8	4.7	3.26	-3.58	-16.5	0.6	453.6	...	...	-15.4	40.5	43.6	6.5	...	...	115.9
12,107	88.1	16.1	-1.9	-4.8	-2.4	0.82	2.95	-18.3	0.5	445.5	...	...	8.7	64.3	68.5	7.9	...	...	110.2
	Principal Lines of Business: CompHosp/Med (86.7%), Medicare (8.0%), FEHBP (4.9%), OtherHlth (0.5%)													Principal States: NJ (83.9%), PA (12.5%), DE (3.6%)					
-441	77.9	10.5	17.7	9.3	47.4	5.28	4.52	-7.9	4.1	74.6	...	0.2	52.8	133.4	141.4	66.4	...	...	...
41	83.7	11.8	18.0	9.0	35.2	5.10	4.78	9.5	3.3	148.3	...	0.4	36.0	163.6	171.8	52.1	...	...	...
-909	88.5	12.7	2.0	1.0	3.4	5.74	4.81	4.8	3.4	150.2	...	0.1	2.1	180.1	190.9	52.9	...	...	...
-1,495	81.9	12.3	9.5	3.9	16.1	6.46	-4.46	17.3	4.0	135.9	...	...	-1.2	176.6	189.1	36.5	...	...	...
2,602	92.7	17.8	-22.5	-8.4	-46.8	5.38	8.03	16.0	6.6	64.2	...	...	-28.9	76.8	83.3	79.8	...	...	...
	Principal Lines of Business: CompHosp/Med (100.0%)													Principal States: NJ (100.0%)					
-41,973	79.6	23.0	1.1	5.9	7.7	5.87	4.72	6.5	1.2	47.9	0.9	7.3	4.6	62.9	81.2	8.1	0.3	48.0	11.6
118,716	68.2	17.1	1.0	4.6	6.8	5.46	11.03	22.6	1.3	51.1	0.8	8.0	7.5	64.9	83.6	6.5	...	46.8	10.9
-4,637	79.4	19.1	0.9	4.3	6.5	5.47	6.17	-2.8	1.2	53.9	0.4	7.6	6.4	62.5	81.8	7.2	...	45.9	12.4
-37,589	72.1	14.5	0.0	0.1	0.1	5.48	1.31	24.7	2.0	36.3	0.5	10.4	-24.7	57.3	72.8	12.4	...	62.9	16.2
63,619	72.5	17.6	0.9	3.7	5.3	4.23	6.39	-11.1	1.0	63.9	0.3	5.5	78.5	55.1	70.3	7.3	...	35.1	58.3
	Principal Lines of Business: GrpA&H (44.2%), GrpAnn (34.6%), IndAnn (12.4%), OrdLife (8.9%)													Principal States: NE (19.6%), CA (8.7%), TX (8.4%), NC (5.8%), PA (5.0%)					
-5	49.7	46.5	11.2	4.9	25.2	5.53	3.04	-17.7	4.3	99.4	...	10.2	18.4	109.3	124.6	...	...	...	19.1
-296	49.0	48.8	5.7	3.1	10.5	5.02	0.35	-22.0	3.3	152.4	...	6.3	2.0	154.5	168.5	...	...	5.2	10.7
255	49.4	46.6	9.2	4.2	14.5	5.64	9.51	21.4	3.0	197.4	...	6.2	34.1	246.0	257.6	...	...	4.9	5.1
47	47.8	47.9	8.6	4.2	13.1	4.73	5.30	13.3	2.8	190.0	...	7.3	21.6	251.2	260.9	...	...	4.0	...
-118	49.1	47.4	7.6	3.4	11.8	3.74	2.44	29.1	3.2	166.4	0.0	12.7	10.7	226.8	235.3	5.0	...	3.6	...
	Principal Lines of Business: CompHosp/Med (78.9%), Dental (21.1%)													Principal States: MS (89.8%), OK (3.4%)					
...	...	...	...	...	...	...	...	...	...	...	...	...	...	...	...	...	...	...	...
...	87.9	21.5	...	-8.2	...	...	...	...	5.5	70.2	...	...	...	149.4	149.4	...	...	...	...
...	83.6	17.6	-2.1	-0.4	-4.9	5.84	5.86	168.5	10.2	80.6	...	0.1	44.8	84.3	84.3	...	...	...	...
...	81.7	17.3	7.2	1.7	14.6	3.70	3.78	-11.8	7.8	122.6	...	0.0	15.7	316.6	330.7	...	...	...	...
...	...	...	...	...	...	...	...	...	...	...	...	...	...	...	...	...	...	...	...

Data in U.S. Dollars

COMPANY NAME Ultimate Parent Association Principal Officer Mailing Address Dom. : Began Bus. : Struct. : Mktg. Specialty Phone # AMB# NAIC#	Best's Financial Strength Rating FSC	Data Year	Balance Sheet Bonds (%)	Mort. Loans & R.E. (%)	Com & Pref. Stock (%)	All Other Assets (%)	Total Assets ($000)	Life Reserves (%)	Health Reserves (%)	Ann Res. & Dep. Liabilities (%)	All Other Liabilities (%)	Capital & Surplus ($000)	Operations Direct Premiums Written ($000)	Net Premiums Written & Deposits ($000)	Operating Cash Flow ($000)	NOG Before Taxes ($000)	NOG After Taxes ($000)	Net Income ($000)
AMICA LIFE INS CO Amica Mutual Insurance Company Robert A. DiMuccio President & CEO P.O. Box 6008 Providence, RI 02940-6008 RI : 1970 : Stock : Direct Response FPDA's, Term Life, Struc Sett 800-652-6422 AMB# 007464 NAIC# 72222	**A+** Rating Outlook: Stable **FSC VIII**	'05	88.9	...	3.8	7.3	847,460	23.1	...	69.9	7.0	143,297	71,744	82,781	43,398	21,651	13,336	13,527
		'06	88.6	...	4.1	7.3	891,439	23.8	...	68.9	7.3	147,450	73,170	76,141	36,130	16,648	10,382	11,410
		'07	88.5	...	4.3	7.2	923,146	24.6	...	67.9	7.5	158,641	74,516	75,009	25,218	16,095	9,503	10,051
		'08	89.7	...	3.1	7.1	940,142	25.6	...	67.9	6.4	156,354	83,683	79,953	27,804	14,811	8,809	8,723
		'09	87.0	...	3.8	9.2	989,219	26.5	...	66.3	7.2	167,748	110,603	103,457	35,413	16,609	9,858	8,850
		Rating History: A+, 02/08/10; A+, 05/07/09; A+, 04/15/08; A+, 05/23/07; A+, 06/12/06																
ANNUITY INVESTORS LIFE INS CO American Financial Group, Inc Charles R. Scheper President P.O. Box 5423 Cincinnati, OH 45201-5423 OH : 1981 : Stock : Agency Ann, Var ann 513-357-3300 AMB# 009088 NAIC# 93661	**A** Rating Outlook: Stable **FSC XI**	'05	50.5	...	...	49.5	1,383,662	...	...	53.0	47.0	43,125	206,574	208,267	72,378	-3,310	-3,310	-3,394
		'06	48.0	...	0.6	51.4	1,601,778	...	...	54.1	45.9	65,433	276,495	277,236	158,895	5,254	24,844	25,201
		'07	53.3	...	0.8	45.9	1,739,485	...	...	58.7	41.3	65,936	318,927	319,271	147,297	-2,134	290	-1,202
		'08	66.6	...	0.3	33.1	1,746,239	...	...	75.1	24.9	82,408	417,193	418,514	274,842	-7,535	-3,031	-21,858
		'09	65.0	...	0.3	34.7	2,167,233	...	...	73.4	26.6	129,596	421,944	422,449	265,891	12,997	11,632	-2,994
		Rating History: A g, 05/10/10; A g, 03/27/09; A g, 12/17/07; A g, 11/28/06; A g, 06/17/05																
ANTHEM BC LIFE & HEALTH INS CO WellPoint Inc. Nicholas L. Brecker III President 1 Wellpoint Way Thousand Oaks, CA 91362 CA : 1991 : Stock : Not Available Group A&H 818-703-2345 AMB# 060057 NAIC# 62825	**A** Rating Outlook: Stable **FSC XIII**	'05	73.5	...	1.9	24.6	1,248,325	1.5	49.8	...	48.6	662,773	2,321,082	2,291,119	160,678	468,258	287,838	287,618
		'06	69.1	...	0.4	30.5	1,582,082	0.7	46.3	...	53.0	762,073	2,865,000	2,835,095	272,783	501,101	330,726	329,644
		'07	77.7	...	1.1	21.3	1,667,795	0.8	58.7	...	40.5	892,351	3,429,841	3,396,586	110,391	607,409	388,579	380,882
		'08	63.6	...	4.9	31.5	1,671,072	0.7	59.3	...	40.0	760,113	3,867,772	3,828,393	-90,123	469,097	313,886	194,508
		'09	66.1	...	0.9	33.0	2,181,364	1.2	45.8	...	53.0	813,779	4,314,370	4,277,799	371,612	282,155	170,174	170,533
		Rating History: A g, 04/27/10; A g, 01/23/09; A g, 03/20/08; A g, 11/06/06; A g, 12/29/05																
ANTHEM HEALTH PLANS INC WellPoint Inc. David R. Fusco President 370 Bassett Road North Haven, CT 06473-4201 CT : 1977 : Stock : Agency Group A&H 203-239-4911 AMB# 068044 NAIC# 60217	**A** Rating Outlook: Stable **FSC IX**	'05	73.2	5.0	2.2	19.5	921,856	...	50.3	...	49.7	404,001	2,949,901	2,936,210	-8,956	296,147	192,969	194,853
		'06	67.2	5.2	2.3	25.2	918,442	...	42.6	...	57.4	423,052	2,862,277	2,855,708	19,031	379,864	256,791	253,214
		'07	75.6	...	2.4	22.0	898,381	...	32.9	...	67.1	388,504	2,918,118	2,910,521	-18,074	343,795	233,671	225,760
		'08	73.2	...	1.6	25.2	929,296	...	39.6	...	60.4	370,018	2,747,237	2,735,650	115	272,385	231,690	225,278
		'09	75.4	...	1.7	22.8	906,962	...	39.7	...	60.3	387,305	2,639,574	2,628,849	-76,234	193,451	132,813	135,506
		Rating History: A g, 04/27/10; A, 01/23/09; A, 03/20/08; A, 11/06/06; A, 12/29/05																
ANTHEM HEALTH PLANS OF KY INC WellPoint Inc. Deborah Wolfe Moessner Chairman & President 6775 West Washington Street Milwaukee, WI 53214 KY : 1993 : Non-Profit : Broker A&H, Group A&H 502-423-2011 AMB# 060150 NAIC# 95120	**A** Rating Outlook: Stable **FSC IX**	'05	81.6	4.1	1.0	13.3	803,676	...	46.6	...	53.4	415,218	1,514,137	1,514,137	74,075	165,240	100,621	103,409
		'06	66.5	4.3	14.1	15.1	739,284	...	46.0	...	54.0	358,487	1,529,535	1,529,535	-89,634	188,244	122,787	122,653
		'07	60.2	5.0	14.2	20.6	614,113	...	56.0	...	44.0	260,315	1,616,392	1,616,392	-107,309	173,645	115,809	105,944
		'08	66.2	5.1	8.2	20.5	584,654	...	42.5	...	57.5	245,779	1,698,569	1,698,569	-34,102	190,843	137,510	96,808
		'09	76.4	4.1	9.3	10.2	707,103	...	31.7	...	68.3	291,708	1,699,873	1,699,873	115,316	137,744	98,143	98,672
		Rating History: A, 04/27/10; A, 01/23/09; A, 03/20/08; A, 11/06/06; A, 12/29/05																
ANTHEM HEALTH PLANS OF ME INC WellPoint Inc. Erin P. Hoeflinger President 2 Gannett Drive South Portland, ME 04106-6911 ME : 1938 : Stock : Agency Group A&H, A&H 207-822-7000 AMB# 064391 NAIC# 52618	**A** Rating Outlook: Stable **FSC VIII**	'05	47.7	3.7	1.5	47.1	458,859	...	65.3	...	34.7	214,761	1,034,423	1,034,419	21,489	55,702	35,957	35,642
		'06	52.4	2.8	0.1	44.7	541,695	...	51.5	...	48.5	215,296	1,073,744	1,073,744	25,452	60,481	40,559	40,433
		'07	32.8	2.4	0.1	64.7	457,797	...	50.3	...	49.7	252,059	1,047,524	1,047,524	-89,687	99,652	74,470	75,718
		'08	36.6	2.3	0.1	61.0	451,133	...	50.1	...	49.9	227,973	1,020,411	1,020,411	9,936	76,788	49,803	47,727
		'09	44.2	2.4	0.1	53.3	412,837	...	60.9	...	39.1	209,506	994,288	994,288	-76,174	33,175	20,502	20,782
		Rating History: A g, 04/27/10; A, 01/23/09; A, 03/20/08; A, 11/06/06; A, 12/29/05																
ANTHEM HEALTH PLANS OF NH INC WellPoint Inc. Lisa M. Guertin President 3000 Goffs Falls Road Manchester, NH 03111 NH : 1977 : Non-Profit : Not Available Group A&H 603-695-7000 AMB# 064173 NAIC# 53759	**A** Rating Outlook: Stable **FSC VIII**	'05	23.5	...	53.0	23.5	303,184	...	42.6	...	57.4	196,791	413,031	413,031	1,105	49,333	35,476	35,716
		'06	25.7	...	54.1	20.2	379,954	...	55.8	...	44.2	268,605	443,632	442,011	23,402	36,679	26,463	26,156
		'07	30.9	...	44.4	24.7	373,195	...	30.5	...	69.5	229,350	455,057	452,828	44,254	109,787	97,845	98,035
		'08	38.6	...	31.5	29.9	306,864	0.7	33.0	...	66.3	154,880	523,460	521,978	-37,458	125,410	117,590	117,508
		'09	25.2	...	32.5	42.3	258,247	...	45.9	...	54.1	140,794	509,040	509,104	-67,345	52,658	42,174	43,557
		Rating History: A g, 04/27/10; A, 01/23/09; A, 03/20/08; A, 11/06/06; A, 12/29/05																
ANTHEM HEALTH PLANS OF VA WellPoint Inc. Thomas R. Byrd President P.O. Box 27401 Richmond, VA 23279 VA : 1935 : Stock : Agency Group A&H 804-354-7000 AMB# 068315 NAIC# 71835	**A** Rating Outlook: Stable **FSC X**	'05	61.5	1.8	3.5	33.2	2,001,503	...	35.1	...	64.9	983,643	3,263,377	3,265,473	208,477	483,616	310,209	307,085
		'06	52.8	1.8	9.4	36.1	1,907,326	...	33.2	...	66.8	934,101	3,478,642	3,482,432	-230,041	531,700	357,512	349,706
		'07	50.4	2.0	12.4	35.2	1,602,924	...	35.6	...	64.4	662,933	3,730,730	3,736,269	-188,974	531,955	337,909	330,513
		'08	40.0	1.8	8.1	50.1	1,627,261	...	35.3	...	64.7	541,420	3,844,330	3,848,436	-17,673	548,213	371,383	321,358
		'09	50.6	1.7	10.2	37.5	1,608,487	...	36.9	...	63.1	625,739	3,768,382	3,774,149	-112,723	547,834	360,175	333,983
		Rating History: A g, 04/27/10; A, 01/23/09; A, 03/20/08; A, 11/06/06; A, 12/29/05																
ANTHEM INSURANCE COMPANIES INC WellPoint Inc. Robert W. Hillman Chairperson, President and Chief Executive Officer 120 Monument Circle Indianapolis, IN 46204-4903 IN : 1944 : Mutual : Broker Group A&H 317-488-6000 AMB# 000607 NAIC# 28207	**A** Rating Outlook: Stable **FSC X**	'05	26.5	0.0	6.4	67.1	4,371,511	...	22.3	...	77.7	2,964,733	2,623,802	2,624,996	-152,837	750,463	709,679	706,492
		'06	38.6	0.0	15.9	45.5	2,229,756	...	23.6	...	76.4	726,854	3,299,883	3,335,572	-119,651	958,266	863,500	855,236
		'07	36.8	0.0	7.7	55.5	1,897,358	...	20.5	...	79.5	559,160	4,014,795	4,062,041	-362,600	419,061	316,759	359,655
		'08	32.5	0.0	5.7	61.8	2,204,027	...	18.9	...	81.1	472,175	4,897,917	4,941,490	-13,435	372,325	324,065	318,439
		'09	35.4	0.0	3.7	60.8	2,158,292	...	58.3	...	41.7	710,878	4,907,438	4,949,943	79,174	458,857	271,006	267,185
		Rating History: A, 04/27/10; A, 01/23/09; A, 03/20/08; A, 11/06/06; A, 12/29/05																

2010 BEST'S KEY RATING GUIDE — LIFE/HEALTH EDITION
BEST'S PROFITABILITY, LEVERAGE AND LIQUIDITY TESTS 2005 – 2009

Data in U.S. Dollars

—	Profitability Tests							Leverage Tests						Liquidity Tests					
Un-Realized Capital Gains ($000)	Benefits Paid to NPW & Dep (%)	Comm. & Expenses to NPW & Dep (%)	NOG to Total Assets (%)	NOG to Total Rev (%)	Operating Return on Equity (%)	Net Yield (%)	Total Return (%)	Change in NPW & Dep (%)	NPW & Dep to Capital (X)	Capital & Surplus to Liabilities (%)	Surplus Relief (%)	Reins Leverage (%)	Change in Capital (%)	Quick Liquidity (%)	Current Liquidity (%)	Non-Invest Grade Bonds to Capital (%)	Delinq. & Foreclosed Mortgages to Capital (%)	Mort. & Credit Tenant Loans & R.E. to Capital (%)	Affiliated Invest to Capital (%)
1,390	52.7	16.3	1.6	12.2	9.8	5.32	5.61	-6.4	0.6	21.5	3.9	8.4	11.5	93.5	102.5	7.5	...	...	...
2,475	68.6	18.0	1.2	9.5	7.1	5.30	5.79	-8.0	0.5	21.0	4.5	14.1	3.2	92.9	102.2	1.3	...	...	...
1,887	74.3	18.8	1.0	8.8	6.2	5.30	5.63	-1.5	0.5	22.0	4.5	19.4	7.6	92.3	101.6	...	...	...	...
-10,133	69.4	18.6	0.9	7.4	5.6	5.43	4.37	6.6	0.5	20.4	4.8	26.8	-4.5	90.5	99.5	...	...	...	...
6,438	72.2	14.8	1.0	6.8	6.1	5.33	6.01	29.4	0.6	21.6	4.8	40.4	10.5	93.5	102.1	8.0	...	...	...
Principal Lines of Business: IndAnn (54.7%), OrdLife (43.3%), GrpLife (1.9%)														Principal States: RI (24.3%), FL (9.8%), MA (9.7%), CT (9.1%), NY (6.9%)					
...	78.3	15.1	-0.2	-1.3	-7.2	5.69	5.75	-2.5	4.6	6.5	0.0	1.0	-8.5	72.0	81.8	37.8	...	...	...
131	70.9	13.5	1.7	7.4	45.8	5.60	5.68	33.1	4.0	8.4	0.0	0.7	53.9	80.9	89.9	65.1	...	...	...
-4,054	78.8	14.3	0.0	0.1	0.4	5.87	5.30	15.2	4.6	7.2	0.0	0.3	0.2	76.2	85.9	44.7	...	...	...
-1,688	53.6	11.8	-0.2	-0.6	-4.1	5.68	3.92	31.1	5.1	6.6	...	...	18.0	78.8	87.8	63.0	...	...	...
10,931	45.1	11.6	0.6	2.3	11.0	5.70	5.46	0.9	3.2	8.8	...	...	58.6	84.8	94.1	40.0	...	3.9	...
Principal Lines of Business: IndAnn (90.1%), GrpAnn (9.9%)														Principal States: CA (23.0%), TX (16.4%), OH (8.8%), MI (6.3%), FL (5.7%)					
455	70.7	10.4	25.3	12.3	47.2	4.76	4.78	26.1	3.5	113.2	...	4.8	19.3	132.0	150.4	10.8	...	...	...
-75	70.7	13.7	23.4	11.4	46.4	4.90	4.81	23.7	3.7	92.9	...	4.7	15.0	132.2	149.8	10.0	...	...	...
-247	71.3	13.1	23.9	11.1	47.0	5.74	5.17	19.8	3.8	115.1	...	4.5	17.1	123.3	142.3	20.6	...	...	...
-12,556	75.1	15.3	18.8	8.0	38.0	5.82	-3.51	12.7	5.0	83.4	...	6.6	-14.8	105.6	119.8	23.7	...	...	...
10,327	78.0	17.0	8.8	3.9	21.6	5.19	5.91	11.7	5.3	59.5	0.0	6.4	7.1	94.8	106.4	22.1	...	...	...
Principal Lines of Business: CompHosp/Med (78.1%), Medicare (8.2%), OtherHlth (7.3%), Dental (5.2%), Life (0.7%)														Principal States: CA (100.0%)					
-1,448	82.3	8.8	21.1	6.5	50.5	5.83	5.90	3.6	7.3	78.0	...	0.9	11.9	87.8	100.0	14.5	...	11.5	11.5
2,237	79.9	8.3	27.9	8.9	62.1	5.90	5.71	-2.7	6.8	85.4	...	4.7	4.7	105.9	118.6	12.5	...	11.4	11.4
758	82.3	7.3	25.7	7.9	57.6	6.13	5.08	1.9	7.5	76.2	...	8.2	-8.2	96.9	110.0	13.6	...	...	0.1
2,265	84.5	7.0	25.4	8.4	61.1	5.63	5.00	-6.0	7.4	66.2	...	7.6	-4.8	84.0	95.6	12.1	...	...	2.9
-2,969	86.8	7.7	14.5	5.0	35.1	7.54	7.49	-3.9	6.8	74.5	...	1.8	4.7	74.5	86.2	15.5	...	...	0.7
Principal Lines of Business: CompHosp/Med (83.8%), MedSup (6.0%), FEHBP (6.0%), OtherHlth (1.8%), Dental (1.2%)														Principal States: CT (100.0%)					
331	78.8	12.1	13.4	6.5	26.5	4.77	5.23	4.0	3.6	106.9	...	...	20.5	147.0	164.3	...	...	8.0	8.0
10,576	77.1	13.0	15.9	7.9	31.7	5.04	6.59	1.0	4.3	94.1	...	...	-13.7	123.0	139.9	...	...	8.9	8.9
-10,004	80.6	10.9	17.1	7.0	37.4	6.32	2.89	5.7	6.2	73.6	...	...	-27.4	106.9	121.2	...	...	11.9	11.9
568	79.1	10.9	22.9	8.0	54.3	4.33	-3.53	5.1	6.9	72.5	...	...	-5.6	101.4	114.9	0.0	...	12.2	12.2
9,014	81.4	12.2	15.2	5.7	36.5	4.76	6.55	0.1	5.8	70.2	...	...	18.7	105.4	119.7	...	...	10.0	10.0
Principal Lines of Business: CompHosp/Med (83.9%), MedSup (8.6%), Medicare (6.3%), Dental (0.8%), Vision (0.3%)														Principal States: KY (100.0%)					
-119	86.0	10.1	8.2	3.5	18.3	5.88	5.72	12.6	4.8	88.0	...	0.0	21.2	112.2	121.2	...	...	7.9	10.9
105	87.3	8.7	8.1	3.7	18.9	6.00	5.99	3.8	5.0	66.0	...	...	0.2	73.4	81.7	0.0	...	7.0	10.5
350	85.5	6.7	14.9	6.8	31.9	6.13	6.74	-2.4	4.2	122.5	...	...	17.1	110.0	120.3	...	...	4.3	7.4
29	86.6	6.9	11.0	4.9	20.7	5.39	4.47	-2.6	4.5	102.2	...	...	-9.6	93.7	102.6	0.3	...	4.6	8.0
-127	89.2	7.8	4.7	2.0	9.4	5.55	5.63	-2.6	4.7	103.0	...	...	-8.1	56.5	65.2	0.4	...	4.6	4.6
Principal Lines of Business: CompHosp/Med (77.3%), FEHBP (16.1%), MedSup (6.1%), Dental (0.3%), OtherHlth (0.2%)														Principal States: ME (100.0%)					
32,048	84.0	7.7	12.7	8.2	21.0	6.86	22.56	16.3	2.1	185.0	...	...	39.9	70.0	76.8	...	...	...	81.5
46,046	84.4	8.2	7.7	6.1	11.4	1.59	19.97	7.0	1.6	241.2	...	1.3	36.5	76.3	83.3	...	...	...	76.4
-39,667	84.6	8.2	26.0	17.9	39.3	28.01	15.98	2.4	2.0	159.4	...	1.2	-14.6	105.2	115.9	...	...	...	72.2
-69,114	87.0	8.5	34.6	18.9	61.2	49.43	25.68	15.3	3.4	101.9	...	0.6	-32.5	54.4	62.7	0.1	...	...	62.4
-12,716	85.6	8.7	14.9	8.0	28.5	16.05	9.38	-2.5	3.6	119.9	...	0.0	-9.1	26.0	31.6	0.3	...	...	59.6
Principal Lines of Business: CompHosp/Med (47.1%), FEHBP (39.6%), MedSup (12.2%), OtherHlth (0.7%), Dental (0.3%)														Principal States: NH (100.0%)					
-1,329	78.9	7.9	16.5	9.3	33.5	3.67	3.37	7.6	3.3	96.6	...	0.0	13.6	127.8	140.8	11.8	...	3.7	4.6
18,266	79.6	7.2	18.3	10.1	37.3	4.38	5.11	6.6	3.7	96.0	...	0.1	-5.0	97.8	110.0	19.2	...	3.6	5.3
-2,386	81.4	6.1	19.3	8.9	42.3	5.25	4.46	7.3	5.6	70.5	...	0.2	-29.0	68.4	78.3	33.7	...	4.9	7.4
-100,293	81.2	5.5	23.0	9.6	61.7	3.54	-9.86	3.0	7.1	49.9	...	0.1	-18.3	63.5	70.6	35.5	...	5.4	7.8
65,029	79.5	7.3	22.3	9.4	61.7	4.87	8.99	-1.9	6.0	63.7	...	0.1	15.6	51.1	59.6	38.7	...	4.3	6.5
Principal Lines of Business: CompHosp/Med (63.2%), FEHBP (29.4%), MedSup (7.0%), Medicare (0.3%), Medicaid (0.1%)														Principal States: VA (100.0%)					
331,414	83.1	7.3	16.6	22.8	24.7	14.78	24.25	12.0	0.9	210.7	...	0.0	6.5	66.6	77.7	3.7	...	0.0	78.0
347,801	81.5	8.3	26.2	22.0	46.8	28.08	42.65	27.1	4.6	48.4	...	0.3	-75.5	54.6	63.7	16.4	...	0.1	6.6
-47,792	84.6	6.2	15.4	7.8	49.3	4.69	4.41	21.8	7.3	41.8	...	0.3	-23.1	36.3	43.1	22.8	...	0.1	9.4
-80,683	86.9	5.9	15.8	6.5	62.8	7.14	-2.71	21.7	10.5	27.3	...	0.4	-15.6	21.4	26.3	33.6	...	0.1	10.0
54,964	84.3	7.3	12.4	5.5	45.8	4.10	10.21	0.2	7.0	49.1	...	0.2	50.6	32.4	37.9	26.6	...	0.1	6.6
Principal Lines of Business: CompHosp/Med (33.4%), FEHBP (29.0%), Medicare (13.5%), OtherHlth (11.9%), Medicaid (8.9%)														Principal States: IN (63.7%), OH (16.9%), KY (10.5%)					

Data in U.S. Dollars

COMPANY NAME Ultimate Parent Association Principal Officer Mailing Address Dom. : Began Bus. : Struct. : Mktg. Specialty Phone # AMB# NAIC#	Best's Financial Strength Rating FSC	Data Year	Balance Sheet: Bonds (%)	Mort. Loans & R.E. (%)	Com & Pref. Stock (%)	All Other Assets (%)	Total Assets ($000)	Life Reserves (%)	Health Reserves (%)	Ann Res. & Dep. Liabilities (%)	All Other Liabilities (%)	Capital & Surplus ($000)	Operations: Direct Premiums Written ($000)	Net Premiums Written & Deposits ($000)	Operating Cash Flow ($000)	NOG Before Taxes ($000)	NOG After Taxes ($000)	Net Income ($000)
ANTHEM LF & DISABILITY INS CO WellPoint Inc. Kenneth R. Goulet Chairperson One Liberty Plaza, 1665 Broadway New York, NY 10006 NY : 2009 : Stock : Broker Group Life 212-476-6666 AMB# 060687 NAIC# 13573	**A** Rating Outlook: Stable **FSC VII**	'05	...	...	...	...	...	...	...	...	...	...	...	...	...	...	...	...
		'06	...	...	...	...	...	...	...	...	...	...	...	...	...	...	...	...
		'07	...	...	...	...	...	...	...	...	...	...	...	...	...	...	...	...
		'08	...	...	...	...	...	...	...	...	...	...	...	...	...	...	...	...
		'09	24.8	...	...	75.2	18,582	8.3	3.5	...	88.2	18,344	107	107	2,408	271	229	229
		Rating History: A g, 04/27/10; A g, 02/03/09																
ANTHEM LIFE INSURANCE COMPANY WellPoint Inc. Kenneth R. Goulet Chairperson & President PO Box 182361 Columbus, OH 43218 IN : 1956 : Stock : Agency Group A&H, Group Life, Ind Life 614-433-8800 AMB# 006126 NAIC# 61069	**A** Rating Outlook: Stable **FSC VII**	'05	88.9	...	0.1	11.0	263,486	55.3	10.1	21.6	13.1	66,410	144,964	160,673	12,462	5,450	2,637	2,637
		'06	77.8	...	...	22.2	258,083	55.6	11.0	18.6	14.9	57,773	165,179	174,337	-6,764	25,801	15,722	15,568
		'07	84.2	...	0.9	15.0	276,394	53.3	12.6	16.5	17.6	64,145	189,994	206,041	17,102	34,294	21,929	20,404
		'08	80.5	...	0.6	18.9	288,278	51.9	11.7	19.6	16.9	65,434	201,426	225,719	7,660	42,579	27,415	23,770
		'09	85.2	...	...	14.8	285,246	51.2	12.4	23.3	13.1	60,796	191,769	199,766	682	29,483	19,994	18,295
		Rating History: A g, 04/27/10; A g, 01/23/09; A, 03/20/08; A, 11/06/06; A, 12/29/05																
ARCADIAN HEALTH PLAN INC Arcadian Management Services Inc John H. Austin CEO 825 Washington Street, Suite 300 Oakland, CA 94607 WA : 2004 : Non-Profit : Other Health 510-832-0311 AMB# 064812 NAIC# 12151	**NR-5**	'05	...	...	21.2	78.8	14,469	...	56.6	...	43.4	8,333	9,319	9,227	7,040	-7,458	-7,458	-7,458
		'06	31.4	...	4.6	64.0	36,310	...	67.5	...	32.5	7,382	80,515	80,026	19,591	-5,084	-5,084	-5,083
		'07	54.2	...	3.0	42.7	71,207	...	66.8	...	33.2	21,719	159,582	158,279	27,668	4,585	4,585	4,598
		'08	62.4	...	8.3	29.3	75,489	...	69.4	...	30.6	30,667	232,267	230,338	-6,345	5,102	3,880	3,976
		'09	47.5	...	11.1	41.5	80,959	...	58.3	...	41.7	45,183	274,954	272,763	-2,224	20,347	14,252	14,291
		Rating History: NR-5, 03/22/10; NR-5, 03/17/09; NR-5, 06/30/08; NR-5, 04/05/07; NR-5, 06/13/06																
ARCADIAN HEALTH PLAN OF GA INC[2] Arcadian Management Services Inc John H. Austin CEO 825 Washington Street, Suite 300 Oakland, CA 94607 GA : 2006 : Stock : Not Available Health 510-832-0311 AMB# 064888 NAIC# 12628	**NR-5**	'05	...	...	...	...	...	...	...	...	...	...	...	...	...	...	...	...
		'06	3.2	...	...	96.8	3,534	...	...	...	100.0	3,183	...	...	3,532	-278	-278	-277
		'07	10.6	...	...	89.4	4,713	...	41.2	...	58.8	2,812	1,783	1,774	1,004	-1,059	-1,059	-1,059
		'08	31.2	...	...	68.8	9,762	...	66.1	...	33.9	3,784	27,296	27,127	3,560	-1,048	-1,048	-1,046
		'09	...	...	...	...	...	...	...	...	...	...	...	...	...	...	...	...
		Rating History: NR-5, 04/02/09; NR-5, 07/29/08; NR-5, 04/18/07																
ARCADIAN HEALTH PLAN OF LA INC[2] Arcadian Management Services Inc John H. Austin Chief Executive Officer 825 Washington Street, Suite 300 Oakland, CA 94607 LA : 2007 : Stock : Not Available Health 510-832-0311 AMB# 064945 NAIC# 11954	**NR-5**	'05	...	...	...	...	...	...	...	...	...	...	...	...	...	...	...	...
		'06	...	...	...	...	...	...	...	...	...	...	...	...	...	...	...	...
		'07	...	...	...	...	...	...	...	...	...	...	...	...	...	...	...	...
		'08	4.3	...	...	95.7	16,485	...	60.1	...	39.9	7,187	37,593	37,247	11,187	3,893	2,498	2,499
		'09	80.2	...	...	19.8	16,593	...	51.7	...	48.3	8,818	41,546	41,269	325	3,629	2,422	2,425
		Rating History: NR-5, 04/23/10; NR-5, 04/24/09																
ARCADIAN HEALTH PLAN OF NC INC[2] Arcadian Management Services Inc John H. Austin Chief Executive Officer 825 Washington Street, #300 Oakland, CA 94607 NC : 2007 : Stock : Other Health 510-832-0311 AMB# 064946 NAIC# 12999	**NR-5**	'05	...	...	...	...	...	...	...	...	...	...	...	...	...	...	...	...
		'06	...	...	...	...	...	...	...	...	...	...	...	...	...	...	...	...
		'07	...	...	...	...	...	...	...	...	...	...	...	...	...	...	...	...
		'08	5.2	...	...	94.8	10,456	...	69.1	...	30.9	4,242	29,373	29,175	4,158	-3,006	-3,006	-3,006
		'09	50.0	...	...	50.0	8,275	...	60.8	...	39.2	3,221	24,905	24,690	-1,528	-1,334	-1,334	-1,333
		Rating History: NR-5, 04/27/10; NR-5, 04/14/09																
ARIZONA DENTAL INSURANCE SVC Mark Anderson Vice President - CFO 5656 W Talvai Boulevard Glendale, AZ 85306 AZ : 1977 : Non-Profit : Not Available Dental 602-588-3976 AMB# 064971 NAIC# 53597	**NR-4**	'05	36.9	3.1	12.2	47.8	31,947	...	39.8	...	60.2	22,050	72,249	72,249	5,312	5,287	5,287	5,287
		'06	21.9	7.9	10.4	59.8	39,639	...	43.5	...	56.5	30,292	84,840	84,840	7,643	7,816	7,816	8,437
		'07	11.5	15.6	23.7	49.2	49,307	...	42.8	...	57.2	39,555	84,370	84,370	9,448	8,935	8,935	9,728
		'08	3.8	15.0	18.1	63.1	52,933	...	33.2	...	66.8	43,103	87,507	87,507	5,927	7,771	7,771	7,685
		'09	12.0	14.2	24.1	49.7	54,863	...	41.8	...	58.2	46,723	90,715	90,715	3,014	3,399	3,399	3,130
		Rating History: NR-4, 06/02/10; A-, 06/02/10; A-, 10/02/09; NR-5, 06/10/09																
ARKANSAS BANKERS LIFE INS CO[1] James Barron President P.O. Box 1947 Texarkana, TX 75504-1947 AR : 1975 : Stock : Not Available 870-772-7324 AMB# 068164 NAIC# 86118	**NR-1**	'05	33.0	0.8	23.4	42.8	5,549	...	...	...	100.0	1,835	2,404	1,820	...	39	47	29
		'06	38.8	0.8	18.1	42.2	5,283	...	...	...	100.0	1,844	2,129	1,542	...	116	117	-32
		'07	48.1	0.8	10.8	40.4	5,167	...	...	...	100.0	1,773	2,121	1,498	...	86	73	39
		'08	54.6	...	7.8	37.6	4,889	...	...	...	100.0	1,614	2,048	1,469	...	-23	-16	-59
		'09	60.1	...	9.6	30.3	4,656	...	...	...	100.0	1,681	1,493	1,089	...	-27	-26	-57
		Rating History: NR-1, 06/10/10; NR-1, 06/12/09; NR-1, 06/12/08; NR-1, 06/08/07; NR-1, 06/07/06																
ARKANSAS COMMUNITY CARE INC Arcadian Management Services Inc John H. Austin Chief Executive Officer 825 Washington Street, Suite 300 Oakland, CA 94607 AR : 2005 : Stock : Not Available Health 510-832-0311 AMB# 064868 NAIC# 12282	**NR-5**	'05	6.9	...	...	93.1	5,070	...	...	...	100.0	5,006	...	...	5,055	61	61	61
		'06	27.8	...	...	72.2	8,790	...	59.4	...	40.6	2,755	14,665	14,584	3,367	-2,323	-2,323	-2,323
		'07	48.5	...	...	51.5	24,775	...	68.2	...	31.8	7,209	50,930	50,532	10,382	-1,631	-1,631	-1,627
		'08	64.3	...	...	35.7	22,231	...	69.1	...	30.9	10,478	68,104	67,746	-665	2,145	2,145	2,183
		'09	53.8	...	...	46.2	28,436	...	50.5	...	49.5	14,956	81,832	81,172	5,383	9,097	6,726	6,747
		Rating History: NR-5, 04/19/10; NR-5, 03/20/09; NR-5, 06/30/08; NR-5, 04/02/07; NR-5, 11/28/06																

BEST'S PROFITABILITY, LEVERAGE AND LIQUIDITY TESTS 2005 – 2009

Data in U.S. Dollars

	Profitability Tests							Leverage Tests						Liquidity Tests					
Un-Realized Capital Gains ($000)	Benefits Paid to NPW & Dep (%)	Comm. & Expenses to NPW (%)	NOG to Total Assets (%)	NOG to Total Rev (%)	Operating Return on Equity (%)	Net Yield (%)	Total Return (%)	Change in NPW & Dep (%)	NPW & Dep to Capital (X)	Capital & Surplus to Liabilities (%)	Surplus Relief (%)	Reins Leverage (%)	Change in Capital (%)	Quick Liquidity (%)	Current Liquidity (%)	Non-Invest Grade Bonds to Capital (%)	Delinq. & Foreclosed Mortgages to Capital (%)	Mort. & Credit Tenant Loans & R.E. to Capital (%)	Affiliated Invest to Capital (%)
...	...	...	...	...	...	...	...	...	...	...	...	...	...	...	...	...	...	...	...
...	...	...	...	...	...	...	...	...	...	...	...	...	...	...	...	...	...	...	...
...	...	...	...	...	...	...	...	...	...	...	...	...	...	...	...	...	...	...	...
...	...	...	...	...	...	...	...	...	...	...	...	...	...	...	...	...	...	...	...
...	38.6	14.9	...	67.4	...	...	...	...	0.0	999.9	...	0.0	...	999.9	999.9	...	...	...	...
	Principal Lines of Business: GrpLife (74.7%), GrpA&H (25.3%)													Principal States: NY (100.0%)					
...	50.6	24.7	1.0	2.0	4.1	4.56	4.57	5.4	2.4	34.2	0.2	139.1	4.4	105.6	117.2	...	...	...	...
...	43.7	24.2	6.0	10.6	25.3	5.26	5.12	8.5	3.0	29.3	0.2	168.8	-12.9	116.3	127.7	...	...	...	...
...	44.6	20.6	8.2	12.6	36.0	5.51	4.80	18.2	3.2	30.3	0.1	171.6	9.8	103.0	115.3	0.5	...	...	...
...	44.9	19.2	9.7	14.6	42.3	5.45	3.99	9.6	3.4	29.4	0.1	172.5	1.9	102.6	114.3	0.3	...	...	...
...	48.4	25.2	7.0	11.2	31.7	5.35	4.62	-11.5	3.3	27.2	0.1	190.6	-6.7	93.9	105.9	...	...	...	...
	Principal Lines of Business: GrpLife (58.6%), GrpA&H (23.0%), IndAnn (17.4%), OrdLife (1.0%), IndA&H (0.0%)													Principal States: IN (21.8%), OH (21.2%), VA (9.5%), KY (9.0%), MO (5.9%)					
...	67.8	115.5	-75.8	-78.9	-99.9	2.81	2.81	...	1.1	135.8	...	...	62.0	274.7	286.8	...	...	...	36.8
-1,412	74.1	33.4	-20.0	-6.3	-64.7	4.34	-2.01	767.3	10.8	25.5	...	3.4	-11.4	167.0	168.6	...	...	...	22.4
511	76.8	21.9	8.5	2.9	31.5	5.72	6.89	97.8	7.3	43.9	...	1.3	194.2	148.9	150.5	...	...	...	10.0
1,961	81.2	17.7	5.3	1.7	14.8	4.65	8.25	45.5	7.5	68.4	...	2.0	41.2	119.7	122.9	0.6	...	...	20.5
2,620	78.0	15.4	18.2	5.2	37.6	4.05	8.83	18.4	6.0	126.3	...	2.8	47.3	143.4	147.8	0.8	...	...	19.9
	Principal Lines of Business: Medicare (100.0%)													Principal States: TX (41.4%), SC (20.4%), ME (15.3%), WA (11.8%), AZ (11.1%)					
...	...	...	...	...	...	...	...	...	...	...	...	...	...	...	...	...	...	...	...
...	...	...	...	-99.9	...	...	...	...	...	906.7	...	...	...	973.8	990.1	...	...	...	...
...	80.1	87.8	-25.7	-55.1	-35.3	3.66	3.66	...	0.6	147.9	...	...	-11.7	443.9	443.9	...	...	...	...
...	80.9	23.5	-14.5	-3.8	-31.8	2.37	2.40	999.9	7.2	63.3	...	1.5	34.6	224.4	224.4	...	...	...	...
...	...	...	...	...	...	...	...	...	...	...	...	...	...	...	...	...	...	...	...
...	...	...	...	...	...	...	...	...	...	...	...	...	...	...	...	...	...	...	...
...	...	...	...	...	...	...	...	...	...	...	...	...	...	...	...	...	...	...	...
...	...	...	...	...	...	...	...	...	...	...	...	...	...	...	...	...	...	...	...
...	70.3	19.7	...	6.7	...	...	...	...	5.2	77.3	...	3.0	...	302.2	302.3	...	...	...	...
...	78.5	13.3	14.6	5.8	30.3	1.69	1.71	10.8	4.7	113.4	...	2.2	22.7	190.8	193.1	...	...	...	...
	Principal Lines of Business: Medicare (100.0%)													Principal States: LA (100.0%)					
...	...	...	...	...	...	...	...	...	...	...	...	...	...	...	...	...	...	...	...
...	...	...	...	...	...	...	...	...	...	...	...	...	...	...	...	...	...	...	...
...	...	...	...	...	...	...	...	...	...	...	...	...	...	...	...	...	...	...	...
...	84.8	25.8	...	-10.3	...	...	...	...	6.9	68.3	...	12.5	...	273.6	273.6	...	...	...	...
...	89.1	16.6	-14.2	-5.4	-35.7	0.97	0.98	-15.4	7.7	63.7	...	4.7	-24.1	147.9	147.9	...	...	...	...
	Principal Lines of Business: Medicare (100.0%)													Principal States: NC (100.0%)					
-318	85.2	10.7	18.3	7.1	27.0	3.75	2.28	7.7	3.3	222.8	...	...	28.9	192.2	204.1	...	...	4.5	8.4
-176	83.8	11.0	21.8	8.9	29.9	4.00	5.63	17.4	2.8	324.1	...	...	37.4	264.5	275.8	...	...	10.3	13.0
-805	81.1	10.3	20.1	10.4	25.6	3.67	3.69	-0.6	2.1	405.6	...	...	30.6	266.0	286.6	...	...	19.4	24.7
-3,733	82.7	10.2	15.2	8.7	18.8	2.12	-6.71	3.7	2.0	438.5	...	...	9.0	292.1	305.0	...	...	18.4	24.1
2,842	86.0	9.7	6.3	3.8	7.6	0.69	6.75	3.7	1.9	574.1	...	...	8.4	392.3	427.5	...	...	16.6	18.3
	Principal Lines of Business: Dental (100.0%)													Principal States: AZ (100.0%)					
...	48.1	65.7	0.8	2.0	2.7	...	...	0.5	1.0	51.4	15.0	...	13.0	...	...	...	...	2.4	...
...	51.3	72.5	2.2	5.7	6.4	...	...	-15.3	0.8	54.8	14.9	...	-0.8	...	...	...	...	2.3	...
...	44.9	71.4	1.4	3.6	4.0	...	...	-2.9	0.8	53.8	16.6	...	-3.3	...	...	...	...	2.2	...
...	39.3	75.9	-0.3	-0.8	-1.0	...	...	-1.9	0.9	50.3	16.9	...	-9.6	...	...	...	...	...	...
...	37.5	82.9	-0.6	-1.8	-1.6	...	...	-25.9	0.6	59.0	11.3	...	5.7	...	...	...	...	...	...
	Principal Lines of Business: CrdLife (79.1%), CrdA&H (20.9%)																		
...	...	...	...	89.8	...	...	...	...	...	999.9	...	...	...	999.9	999.9	...	...	...	...
...	74.1	43.8	-33.5	-15.6	-59.9	4.33	4.33	...	5.3	45.7	...	...	-45.0	233.5	234.6	...	...	...	...
...	83.7	21.1	-9.7	-3.2	-32.7	6.10	6.14	246.5	7.0	41.0	...	1.4	161.6	138.0	139.9	...	...	...	...
...	80.5	17.6	9.1	3.1	24.3	4.74	4.95	34.1	6.5	89.1	...	1.6	45.3	173.0	178.7	...	...	...	...
-21	75.6	14.0	26.6	8.2	52.9	3.26	3.26	19.8	5.4	110.9	...	3.1	42.7	191.4	197.7	0.5	...	...	...
	Principal Lines of Business: Medicare (100.0%)													Principal States: AR (80.7%), TX (10.0%), OK (9.3%)					

ANNUAL STATEMENT DATA FOR YEARS 2005 – 2009

Data in U.S. Dollars

Column key — COMPANY NAME: Ultimate Parent Association; Principal Officer; Mailing Address; Dom. : Began Bus. : Struct. : Mktg.; Specialty; Phone #; AMB#; NAIC#. Best's Financial Strength Rating; FSC.

Balance Sheet: Bonds (%), Mort. Loans & R.E. (%), Com & Pref. Stock (%), All Other Assets (%), Total Assets ($000), Life Reserves (%), Health Reserves (%), Ann Res. & Dep. Liabilities (%), All Other Liabilities (%), Capital & Surplus ($000). Operations: Direct Premiums Written ($000), Net Premiums Written & Deposits ($000), Operating Cash Flow ($000), NOG Before Taxes ($000), NOG After Taxes ($000), Net Income ($000).

ARKANSAS LIFE INS CO
Munich Reinsurance Company
John W. Hayden
Chairman & CEO
P.O. Box 5323
Cincinnati, OH 45201-5323
AZ : 1983 : Stock : Other Direct
Credit A&H, Credit Life
513-943-7200
AMB# 068314 NAIC# 97551

Rating: NR-3

Data Year	Bonds (%)	Mort. Loans & R.E. (%)	Com & Pref. Stock (%)	All Other Assets (%)	Total Assets ($000)	Life Reserves (%)	Health Reserves (%)	Ann Res. & Dep. Liabilities (%)	All Other Liabilities (%)	Capital & Surplus ($000)	Direct Premiums Written ($000)	Net Premiums Written & Deposits ($000)	Operating Cash Flow ($000)	NOG Before Taxes ($000)	NOG After Taxes ($000)	Net Income ($000)
'05	...	...	...	100.0	1,141	86.4	9.4	...	4.2	537	...	746	-494	56	48	48
'06	...	...	...	100.0	1,206	84.7	9.6	...	5.7	569	...	726	64	156	105	105
'07	...	...	...	100.0	1,109	91.6	8.3	...	0.2	588	...	617	-199	160	110	110
'08	...	...	...	100.0	1,010	87.4	12.4	...	0.2	688	...	427	23	261	183	183
'09	...	...	...	100.0	897	87.7	11.7	...	0.6	647	...	372	-104	65	47	47

Rating History: NR-3, 03/10/10; NR-3, 05/15/09; NR-3, 04/09/08; NR-3, 10/18/07; NR-3, 05/31/07

ASSOCIATED MUTUAL
John Jacobitz
President
5800 Foremost Drive S.E., Suite 207
Grand Rapids, MI 49546
MI : 1938 : Mutual : Agency
A&H, Ind A&H, Med supp
616-458-3884
AMB# 068042 NAIC# 87882

Rating: B+ — Rating Outlook: Stable — FSC IV

Data Year	Bonds (%)	Mort. Loans & R.E. (%)	Com & Pref. Stock (%)	All Other Assets (%)	Total Assets ($000)	Life Reserves (%)	Health Reserves (%)	Ann Res. & Dep. Liabilities (%)	All Other Liabilities (%)	Capital & Surplus ($000)	Direct Premiums Written ($000)	Net Premiums Written & Deposits ($000)	Operating Cash Flow ($000)	NOG Before Taxes ($000)	NOG After Taxes ($000)	Net Income ($000)
'05	59.9	...	0.0	40.1	9,192	1.1	57.6	...	41.3	5,688	15,928	15,455	791	1,172	782	780
'06	55.3	...	0.0	44.7	10,573	1.7	46.4	...	51.9	6,485	15,374	14,900	60	1,258	818	819
'07	53.0	...	1.3	45.7	11,099	1.7	51.7	...	46.6	6,596	16,143	15,525	2,253	261	171	172
'08	47.5	...	0.7	51.9	12,762	2.2	52.1	...	45.8	8,439	18,868	18,296	2,034	63	-37	-147
'09	59.8	...	0.2	40.0	13,521	1.9	60.9	...	37.2	8,291	24,108	23,533	-1,449	153	-127	-127

Rating History: B+, 10/27/09; NR-5, 04/16/09; NR-5, 04/22/08; NR-5, 04/20/07; NR-5, 04/07/06

ASSURITY LIFE INS CO
Assurity Security Group
Thomas E. Henning
Chairman, President & CEO
P.O. Box 82533
Lincoln, NE 68501-2533
NE : 1964 : Stock : Agency
Dis inc, Ind Ann, Ind Life
402-476-6500
AMB# 007374 NAIC# 71439

Rating: A- — Rating Outlook: Stable — FSC IX

Data Year	Bonds (%)	Mort. Loans & R.E. (%)	Com & Pref. Stock (%)	All Other Assets (%)	Total Assets ($000)	Life Reserves (%)	Health Reserves (%)	Ann Res. & Dep. Liabilities (%)	All Other Liabilities (%)	Capital & Surplus ($000)	Direct Premiums Written ($000)	Net Premiums Written & Deposits ($000)	Operating Cash Flow ($000)	NOG Before Taxes ($000)	NOG After Taxes ($000)	Net Income ($000)
'05	73.9	15.8	2.2	8.1	2,111,749	50.9	10.9	34.1	4.1	214,276	279,174	263,267	81,854	11,974	10,243	11,034
'06	73.1	15.7	2.8	8.4	2,158,992	52.4	10.9	32.6	4.1	227,778	268,565	245,298	47,396	13,260	9,401	12,393
'07	73.9	15.3	2.8	8.0	2,189,168	54.5	10.7	30.5	4.3	245,521	273,856	243,685	26,329	22,402	13,172	14,637
'08	72.1	15.9	2.7	9.3	2,161,105	56.4	10.5	29.5	3.6	223,151	274,153	239,790	-567	24,545	18,640	1,947
'09	73.6	14.8	2.1	9.4	2,237,619	56.4	10.2	29.7	3.7	248,678	299,060	276,204	42,605	12,910	5,412	-5,842

Rating History: A-, 10/16/09; A-, 09/16/08; A-, 08/20/07; A-, 08/17/06; A-, 06/17/06

ASURIS NORTHWEST HEALTH
Regence Group
Murphy J. Hensley
President
P.O. Box 1271
Portland, OR 97207-1271
WA : 1933 : Non-Profit : Broker
Group A&H, Ind A&H
206-464-3600
AMB# 064414 NAIC# 47350

Rating: A — Rating Outlook: Stable — FSC XI

Data Year	Bonds (%)	Mort. Loans & R.E. (%)	Com & Pref. Stock (%)	All Other Assets (%)	Total Assets ($000)	Life Reserves (%)	Health Reserves (%)	Ann Res. & Dep. Liabilities (%)	All Other Liabilities (%)	Capital & Surplus ($000)	Direct Premiums Written ($000)	Net Premiums Written & Deposits ($000)	Operating Cash Flow ($000)	NOG Before Taxes ($000)	NOG After Taxes ($000)	Net Income ($000)
'05	42.6	3.5	...	53.9	29,587	...	73.5	...	26.5	17,591	80,668	80,668	1,473	2,443	2,443	2,377
'06	38.7	...	...	61.3	48,681	...	33.5	...	66.5	14,209	154,280	132,388	1,864	-2,304	-1,749	-1,865
'07	50.4	...	...	49.6	68,134	...	53.6	...	46.4	34,190	190,206	169,246	27,679	5,476	5,630	5,787
'08	59.3	...	...	40.7	63,286	...	66.1	...	33.9	32,976	199,837	194,959	-2,958	-2,778	-2,244	-2,119
'09	49.1	...	...	50.9	85,395	...	62.6	...	37.4	43,808	225,475	218,865	16,722	-14,202	-9,341	-9,392

Rating History: A g, 06/11/10; A-, 06/17/09; A-, 11/19/08; A-, 10/16/07; A-, 08/28/06

ATHENS AREA HEALTH PLAN SELECT
Athens Regional Health Services Inc
W. Larry Webb
President
295 West Clayton Street
Athens, GA 30601-2711
GA : 1996 : Non-Profit : Agency
Group A&H, Health
706-549-0549
AMB# 064556 NAIC# 95691

Rating: NR-5

Data Year	Bonds (%)	Mort. Loans & R.E. (%)	Com & Pref. Stock (%)	All Other Assets (%)	Total Assets ($000)	Life Reserves (%)	Health Reserves (%)	Ann Res. & Dep. Liabilities (%)	All Other Liabilities (%)	Capital & Surplus ($000)	Direct Premiums Written ($000)	Net Premiums Written & Deposits ($000)	Operating Cash Flow ($000)	NOG Before Taxes ($000)	NOG After Taxes ($000)	Net Income ($000)
'05	33.3	...	...	66.7	11,041	...	67.0	...	33.0	5,845	44,616	44,071	-366	-5,755	-5,755	-5,753
'06	25.9	...	...	74.1	15,000	...	59.0	...	41.0	9,004	47,504	47,025	3,561	-840	-840	-840
'07	18.8	...	...	81.2	20,551	...	57.5	...	42.5	15,146	44,223	43,867	6,313	5,955	5,836	5,836
'08	14.8	...	...	85.2	20,505	...	57.9	...	42.1	14,921	42,757	42,438	-45	-1,047	-1,047	-1,032
'09	23.5	...	...	76.5	18,884	...	55.6	...	44.4	13,533	44,081	43,737	-1,688	-2,323	-2,323	-2,323

Rating History: NR-5, 04/07/10; NR-5, 08/26/09; C++pd, 07/01/08; C+ pd, 06/26/07; C pd, 07/25/06

ATLANTA LIFE INS CO
Atlanta Life Financial Group Inc
William A. Clement
President & CEO
100 Auburn Avenue, N.E.
Atlanta, GA 30303-2599
GA : 1916 : Stock : Agency
Group Life, Reins, Pre-need
404-659-2100
AMB# 006130 NAIC# 61093

Rating: C+ — Rating Outlook: Negative — FSC V

Data Year	Bonds (%)	Mort. Loans & R.E. (%)	Com & Pref. Stock (%)	All Other Assets (%)	Total Assets ($000)	Life Reserves (%)	Health Reserves (%)	Ann Res. & Dep. Liabilities (%)	All Other Liabilities (%)	Capital & Surplus ($000)	Direct Premiums Written ($000)	Net Premiums Written & Deposits ($000)	Operating Cash Flow ($000)	NOG Before Taxes ($000)	NOG After Taxes ($000)	Net Income ($000)
'05	28.9	5.1	2.7	63.3	90,331	76.6	...	13.7	9.7	19,681	5,699	64,542	-6,236	1,216	1,741	1,777
'06	22.1	4.4	3.0	70.5	97,008	76.9	...	11.9	11.2	18,933	5,149	53,893	-703	842	1,009	1,177
'07	26.1	5.2	4.2	64.5	75,639	73.3	...	14.8	11.9	19,375	5,011	52,830	-5,248	302	293	551
'08	21.0	4.8	2.7	71.5	75,434	77.2	...	9.6	13.2	17,341	4,654	62,508	-4,556	-321	-330	-695
'09	15.7	4.4	3.7	76.2	74,928	82.7	...	6.7	10.5	11,152	3,856	58,042	-3,243	-2,604	-2,604	-2,842

Rating History: C+, 06/04/10; B- u, 03/09/10; B, 05/07/09; B+, 06/13/08; B+, 06/19/07

ATLANTIC COAST LIFE INS CO
Yancey W. Scarborough III
President & CEO
P.O. Box 20010
Charleston, SC 29413-0010
SC : 1925 : Stock : Career Agent
Ind Life, Pre-need
843-763-8680
AMB# 006132 NAIC# 61115

Rating: B+ — Rating Outlook: Stable — FSC V

Data Year	Bonds (%)	Mort. Loans & R.E. (%)	Com & Pref. Stock (%)	All Other Assets (%)	Total Assets ($000)	Life Reserves (%)	Health Reserves (%)	Ann Res. & Dep. Liabilities (%)	All Other Liabilities (%)	Capital & Surplus ($000)	Direct Premiums Written ($000)	Net Premiums Written & Deposits ($000)	Operating Cash Flow ($000)	NOG Before Taxes ($000)	NOG After Taxes ($000)	Net Income ($000)
'05	61.9	19.3	9.7	9.0	60,544	88.9	0.6	0.0	10.4	14,361	7,195	7,180	2,378	677	543	640
'06	62.4	17.9	10.5	9.3	64,704	88.9	0.6	0.0	10.5	16,072	7,698	7,631	2,772	758	750	1,229
'07	64.3	17.0	9.1	9.5	67,521	89.3	0.5	0.0	10.2	15,712	8,487	8,431	3,559	261	162	210
'08	68.0	16.5	4.0	11.5	69,018	91.1	0.4	0.0	8.5	14,075	10,144	10,090	4,614	183	236	818
'09	72.3	15.2	1.3	11.2	75,505	89.3	0.3	2.2	8.1	13,755	14,207	14,135	5,373	-381	-159	514

Rating History: B+, 12/07/09; B+, 11/06/08; B+, 09/28/07; B+, 09/15/06; B+, 09/16/05

ATLANTIC MEDICAL INSURANCE LTD
Edmund Gibbons Limited
Alan Peacock
President and CEO
Atlantic House, 61 Collins Avenue
Nassau, New Providence, Bahamas
BS : 1995 : Stock : Not Available
Health
242-326-8191
AMB# 086819

Rating: A- — Rating Outlook: Stable — FSC VI

Data Year	Bonds (%)	Mort. Loans & R.E. (%)	Com & Pref. Stock (%)	All Other Assets (%)	Total Assets ($000)	Life Reserves (%)	Health Reserves (%)	Ann Res. & Dep. Liabilities (%)	All Other Liabilities (%)	Capital & Surplus ($000)	Direct Premiums Written ($000)	Net Premiums Written & Deposits ($000)	Operating Cash Flow ($000)	NOG Before Taxes ($000)	NOG After Taxes ($000)	Net Income ($000)
'05	...	38.5	...	61.5	26,926	49.1	...	...	50.9	12,158	...	37,278	...	2,793	2,793	2,793
'06	23.0	29.3	...	47.7	28,438	53.1	...	...	46.9	12,262	...	39,634	3,265	2,648	2,648	2,648
'07	28.1	24.9	...	47.0	33,849	60.8	...	...	39.2	15,411	...	47,256	1,790	3,182	3,182	3,182
'08	44.1	24.3	...	31.6	34,654	63.1	...	...	37.0	19,317	...	53,523	6,993	4,043	4,043	4,043
'09	42.7	21.8	...	35.5	38,741	64.4	...	...	35.6	22,998	...	62,346	-203	3,786	3,786	3,786

Rating History: A- g, 07/02/09; A- g, 01/16/09; A- g, 12/05/06; A- g, 01/26/04; A- g, 09/30/03

ATLANTIC SOUTHERN DENTAL FNDN[2]
Bertram Serota
Chairman, Management Committee
615 Chestnut Street
Philadelphia, PA 19106-4404
NJ : 1984 : Other : Broker
Dental
215-440-1013
AMB# 064783 NAIC# 11217

Rating: NR-5

Data Year	Bonds (%)	Mort. Loans & R.E. (%)	Com & Pref. Stock (%)	All Other Assets (%)	Total Assets ($000)	Life Reserves (%)	Health Reserves (%)	Ann Res. & Dep. Liabilities (%)	All Other Liabilities (%)	Capital & Surplus ($000)	Direct Premiums Written ($000)	Net Premiums Written & Deposits ($000)	Operating Cash Flow ($000)	NOG Before Taxes ($000)	NOG After Taxes ($000)	Net Income ($000)
'05	8.8	...	...	91.2	4,340	...	31.1	...	68.9	1,800	12,600	12,600	202	343	343	343
'06	18.6	...	...	81.4	4,362	...	21.5	...	78.5	1,732	13,033	13,033	257	-80	-80	-80
'07	26.4	...	...	73.6	2,707	...	20.9	...	79.1	1,810	12,971	12,971	-1,569	86	86	86
'08	57.1	...	...	42.9	2,663	...	36.7	...	63.3	1,487	12,463	12,463	-65	-32	-32	-32
'09	59.4	...	...	40.6	3,206	...	38.4	...	61.6	1,933	12,041	12,041	514	446	446	446

Rating History: NR-5, 04/19/10; NR-5, 06/01/09; NR-5, 05/21/08; NR-5, 06/22/07; NR-5, 05/11/06

—	Profitability Tests							Leverage Tests						Liquidity Tests					
Un-Realized Capital Gains ($000)	Benefits Paid to NPW & Dep (%)	Comm. & Expenses to NPW & Dep (%)	NOG to Total Assets (%)	NOG to Total Rev (%)	Operating Return on Equity (%)	Net Yield (%)	Total Return (%)	Change in NPW & Dep (%)	NPW & Dep to Capital (X)	Capital & Surplus to Liabilities (%)	Surplus Relief (%)	Reins Leverage (%)	Change in Capital (%)	Quick Liquidity (%)	Current Liquidity (%)	Non-Invest Grade Bonds to Capital (%)	Delinq. & Foreclosed Mortgages to Capital (%)	Mort. & Credit Tenant Loans & R.E. to Capital (%)	Affiliated Invest to Capital (%)
...	52.5	58.0	3.5	6.2	7.0	1.91	1.91	-7.4	1.4	89.0	...	...	-34.7	182.6	182.6	...	...	...	...
...	16.4	56.3	8.9	13.8	19.0	3.16	3.16	-2.6	1.3	89.4	...	...	5.9	183.3	183.3	...	...	...	...
...	35.5	55.3	9.5	16.7	19.0	3.78	3.78	-15.1	1.0	113.1	...	...	3.4	194.8	194.8	...	...	...	...
...	34.8	56.1	17.3	40.1	28.6	2.92	2.92	-30.7	0.6	214.0	...	0.9	17.0	392.7	392.7	...	...	...	...
...	44.9	58.8	4.9	12.2	7.0	1.24	1.24	-12.8	0.6	259.1	...	0.3	-5.9	419.4	419.4	...	...	...	...

Principal Lines of Business: CrdLife (88.3%), CrdA&H (11.7%)

0	83.9	10.3	9.3	5.0	14.8	2.06	2.03	11.4	2.7	162.4	0.4	0.1	15.8	190.4	199.2	...	...	...	...
0	79.7	12.7	8.3	5.3	13.4	3.35	3.36	-3.6	2.3	158.8	0.4	7.3	14.0	163.1	170.6	...	...	...	...
0	82.9	18.2	1.6	1.1	2.6	3.23	3.23	4.2	2.4	146.6	0.4	30.1	1.7	196.7	203.0	...	...	...	2.2
-57	83.8	16.9	-0.3	-0.2	-0.5	1.41	-0.12	17.8	2.2	195.4	0.1	19.2	27.9	250.6	257.8	...	...	...	1.0
-63	81.6	16.1	-1.0	-0.5	-1.5	2.24	1.66	28.6	2.8	158.8	...	16.4	-1.7	163.1	171.6	1.4	...	...	0.3

Principal Lines of Business: GrpA&H (97.4%), GrpLife (2.6%), OrdLife (0.0%) Principal States: MI (89.7%), OH (10.3%)

-208	65.2	37.5	0.5	2.7	4.8	6.16	6.29	5.1	1.1	12.5	4.6	20.9	2.6	42.5	61.3	26.9	...	171.2	4.5
3,504	82.7	38.8	0.4	2.5	4.3	6.06	6.46	-6.8	1.0	13.1	4.7	22.0	7.1	43.9	63.0	18.3	...	160.6	4.1
942	84.7	39.5	0.6	3.5	5.6	5.89	6.08	-0.7	0.9	14.0	4.5	21.1	7.4	39.3	61.9	16.2	0.7	155.7	0.6
-16,920	85.5	37.1	0.9	5.0	8.0	5.85	4.38	-1.6	1.0	12.1	5.3	22.8	-13.4	42.6	62.3	26.1	0.4	181.6	0.9
11,740	75.3	34.6	0.2	1.3	2.3	5.75	5.85	15.2	1.0	13.5	5.2	21.4	14.2	42.7	62.2	23.4	1.9	157.9	0.7

Principal Lines of Business: OrdLife (48.0%), IndA&H (24.1%), IndAnn (16.4%), GrpA&H (9.0%), GrpLife (1.9%) Principal States: MI (12.2%), CA (7.6%), NE (7.3%), KS (6.5%), PA (5.1%)

...	80.2	18.0	8.5	3.0	14.9	3.81	3.57	4.8	4.6	146.6	...	...	15.8	253.6	256.4	...	...	5.9	...
...	86.1	16.7	-4.5	-1.3	-11.0	4.57	4.16	64.1	9.3	41.2	...	9.6	-19.2	113.9	114.7	...	...	...	...
...	80.3	17.3	9.6	3.3	23.3	4.91	5.27	27.8	5.0	100.7	...	2.5	140.6	204.1	211.8	...	...	...	...
...	84.7	17.7	-3.4	-1.1	-6.7	3.62	3.85	15.2	5.9	108.8	...	1.9	-3.6	206.0	214.7	...	...	...	...
...	89.6	17.4	-12.6	-4.2	-24.3	2.45	2.37	12.3	5.0	105.3	...	1.5	32.8	220.1	227.5	...	...	...	...

Principal Lines of Business: CompHosp/Med (82.3%), Medicare (7.5%), OtherHlth (6.1%), Medicaid (1.8%), MedSup (1.5%) Principal States: WA (97.1%)

...	99.3	14.7	-51.9	-13.0	-95.9	3.23	3.24	10.1	7.5	112.5	...	0.5	-5.0	200.3	200.7	...	...	...	...
...	89.2	14.0	-6.4	-1.8	-11.3	4.96	4.96	6.7	5.2	150.2	...	...	54.0	227.9	227.9	...	...	...	...
...	75.0	13.1	32.8	13.1	48.3	4.39	4.39	-6.7	2.9	280.2	...	...	68.2	370.1	370.1	...	...	...	...
...	89.3	14.2	-5.1	-2.4	-7.0	2.11	2.18	-3.3	2.8	267.2	...	...	-1.5	369.1	369.1	...	...	...	...
...	92.3	13.3	-11.8	-5.3	-16.3	0.61	0.61	3.1	3.2	252.9	...	0.3	-9.3	341.5	341.5	...	...	...	...

Principal Lines of Business: CompHosp/Med (100.0%) Principal States: GA (100.0%)

135	89.4	14.9	1.9	2.5	8.5	2.23	3.03	31.1	3.2	29.3	1.7	509.8	-7.0	32.4	35.1	4.9	...	22.4	0.1
115	92.5	13.9	1.1	1.8	5.2	2.41	3.53	-16.5	2.7	25.6	2.5	514.1	-3.4	31.4	33.4	10.1	...	21.5	...
27	83.4	20.7	0.3	0.5	1.5	2.02	3.14	-2.0	2.6	36.3	3.1	486.0	1.8	35.0	38.1	...	...	19.5	...
-917	87.6	19.6	-0.4	-0.5	-1.8	1.02	-3.74	18.3	3.5	31.1	2.9	542.4	-11.0	27.2	29.5	...	...	20.2	...
855	96.6	11.5	-3.5	-4.5	-18.3	-1.60	1.65	-7.1	4.9	18.7	-2.4	807.0	-34.2	20.9	22.8	...	...	27.9	...

Principal Lines of Business: GrpLife (99.4%), OrdLife (0.6%), IndAnn (0.0%), IndLife (0.0%) Principal States: IL (30.5%), GA (23.8%), TX (7.7%), AL (7.2%), MI (4.5%)

113	49.3	61.8	0.9	5.2	3.9	5.74	6.17	11.2	0.5	35.5	...	0.5	4.5	68.5	76.8	8.8	...	73.5	0.1
567	44.0	63.3	1.2	6.7	4.9	5.93	7.75	6.3	0.4	38.0	...	0.3	12.2	73.3	81.9	5.7	...	65.0	0.1
-439	45.0	63.9	0.2	1.3	1.0	5.87	5.31	10.5	0.5	34.2	...	0.4	-3.2	74.9	83.3	4.2	...	66.8	0.1
-2,113	42.0	54.6	0.3	1.7	1.6	5.48	3.21	19.7	0.7	27.6	...	0.4	-13.4	73.1	82.1	0.5	...	76.4	0.1
-622	39.1	43.7	-0.2	-0.9	-1.1	5.20	5.30	40.1	1.0	24.3	...	0.4	-1.1	68.3	77.2	5.9	...	77.8	0.1

Principal Lines of Business: OrdLife (80.6%), GrpLife (9.9%), IndAnn (5.7%), GrpAnn (1.7%), IndA&H (1.7%) Principal States: SC (60.4%), AL (12.4%), TN (11.8%), GA (10.2%), NC (5.1%)

...	74.5	22.2	11.8	7.2	25.8	1.90	1.90	9.6	306.6	82.3	...	...	27.9	62.7	70.2	...	...	85.2	...
...	76.0	21.5	9.6	6.4	21.7	1.91	1.91	6.3	323.2	88.4	...	...	0.9	69.0	107.2	...	...	67.9	...
...	76.4	20.4	10.2	6.5	23.0	2.50	2.50	19.2	306.6	95.7	...	...	25.7	73.2	111.4	...	...	54.7	...
...	76.0	20.4	11.8	7.3	23.3	3.38	3.38	13.3	277.1	137.8	...	...	25.4	114.2	169.1	...	...	43.6	...
...	78.1	20.6	10.3	5.8	17.9	4.22	4.22	16.5	271.1	159.4	...	...	19.1	117.5	173.2	...	...	36.6	...

...	84.1	13.3	8.3	2.7	21.1	0.42	0.42	4.4	7.0	70.9	...	...	24.7	148.0	149.5	...	...	...	5.6
...	88.0	13.2	-1.8	-0.6	-4.5	1.89	1.89	3.4	7.5	65.9	...	...	-3.8	150.3	153.4	...	...	...	5.8
...	86.8	13.5	2.4	0.7	4.9	3.54	3.54	-0.5	7.2	202.0	...	...	4.5	267.5	275.5	...	...	...	5.5
...	88.1	12.6	-1.2	-0.3	-1.9	2.64	2.64	-3.9	8.4	126.4	...	...	-17.9	188.1	201.0	...	...	...	6.7
...	85.1	11.9	15.2	3.7	26.1	2.79	2.79	-3.4	6.2	151.8	...	...	30.0	209.6	224.6	...	...	...	5.2

Principal Lines of Business: Dental (100.0%) Principal States: NJ (99.1%)

COMPANY NAME Ultimate Parent Association Principal Officer Mailing Address Dom. : Began Bus. : Struct. : Mktg. Specialty Phone # AMB# NAIC#	Best's Financial Strength Rating FSC	Data Year	Balance Sheet Bonds (%)	Mort. Loans & R.E. (%)	Com & Pref. Stock (%)	All Other Assets (%)	Total Assets ($000)	Life Reserves (%)	Health Reserves %)	Ann Res. & Dep. Liabilities (%)	All Other Liabilities (%)	Capital & Surplus ($000)	Operations Direct Premiums Written ($000)	Net Premiums Written & Deposits ($000)	Operating Cash Flow ($000)	NOG Before Taxes ($000)	NOG After Taxes ($000)	Net Income ($000)
ATLANTIC SOUTHERN INS CO R D Tips Inc Alexis Gonzalez President & CEO P.O. Box 362889 San Juan, PR 00936-2889 PR : 1947 : Stock : Agency A&H, Life, Maj med 787-767-9750 AMB# 006135 NAIC# 61158	**C++** Rating Outlook: Stable **FSC IV**	'05	65.9	8.6	8.0	17.5	17,539	25.8	8.1	39.5	26.6	7,849	19,341	8,621	-74	1,123	1,123	1,123
		'06	65.9	8.4	7.0	18.7	18,004	27.7	6.6	39.3	26.4	8,283	19,945	9,323	807	226	226	226
		'07	62.1	8.2	6.0	23.7	18,133	29.0	8.1	28.6	34.3	8,207	22,202	10,951	-839	211	211	133
		'08	66.5	7.8	4.6	21.1	18,502	30.9	11.3	25.4	32.4	8,530	22,820	11,672	-810	463	463	310
		'09	65.7	7.3	0.1	26.9	19,311	32.4	14.7	12.6	40.3	8,729	22,741	12,159	1,905	523	523	401
		Rating History: C++, 06/24/08; C++, 06/20/07; C++, 06/16/06; C++, 04/05/05; C++, 04/06/04																
ATRIO HEALTH PLANS INC[2] Pamela Johnson CEO 500 SE Cass, Suite 230 Roseburg, OR 97470 OR : 2005 : Stock : Not Available Health 541-672-8620 AMB# 064904 NAIC# 10123	**NR-5**	'05	...	...	...	...	...	...	...	...	...	...	...	...	...	...	...	...
		'06	...	...	...	100.0	13,373	...	49.2	...	50.8	4,452	38,918	38,654	7,808	1,430	1,348	1,348
		'07	2.0	...	...	98.0	12,867	...	45.8	...	54.2	5,760	42,299	42,299	-405	2,434	1,385	1,385
		'08	1.6	...	...	98.4	16,782	...	33.0	...	67.0	7,046	52,304	52,304	449	1,187	807	807
		'09	1.9	...	...	98.1	13,776	...	26.6	...	73.4	5,592	44,983	44,983	-1,139	96	71	71
		Rating History: NR-5, 05/20/10; NR-5, 09/16/09; NR-5, 07/14/08; NR-5, 07/02/07																
AURIGEN REINSURANCE LTD Aurigen Capital Limited Caspar Young Managing Director The Armoury Building, 37 Reid Street Hamilton HM MX, Bermuda BM : Stock : Not Available Life Reins 441-278-3500 AMB# 088598	**A-** Rating Outlook: Stable **FSC VII**	'05	...	...	...	...	...	...	...	...	...	...	...	...	...	...	...	...
		'06	...	...	...	...	...	...	...	...	...	...	...	...	...	...	...	...
		'07	...	...	...	100.0	286	...	...	...	...	286	...	...	...	...	...	...
		'08	40.4	...	...	59.6	83,464	46.9	...	...	53.1	78,932	...	2,051	236	-1,385	-1,385	-1,385
		'09	...	...	...	...	...	...	...	...	...	...	...	...	...	...	...	...
		Rating History: A- g, 10/27/09; A- g, 08/19/08																
AURORA NATIONAL LIFE ASSUR New California Life Holdings Inc Steven W. Turner President, Treasurer & CFO 55 Hartland Street East Hartford, CT 06108 CA : 1961 : Stock : Broker Ann, Life 800-265-2652 AMB# 006139 NAIC# 61182	**NR-5**	'05	87.9	...	0.2	11.9	3,354,262	43.8	...	52.6	3.6	271,431	61,739	40,855	-197,446	27,017	51,229	48,620
		'06	85.3	...	1.1	13.6	3,292,062	43.1	...	51.4	5.5	285,548	56,542	31,536	-53,831	30,536	25,062	18,809
		'07	87.0	...	1.0	12.0	3,246,604	42.5	...	51.0	6.5	300,880	49,103	26,162	-52,290	30,842	24,308	22,027
		'08	88.1	...	1.1	10.8	3,129,411	42.7	...	51.5	5.9	320,179	42,041	17,132	-118,694	42,373	30,339	11,458
		'09	82.1	...	...	17.9	2,999,844	42.4	...	53.6	4.0	336,719	37,153	20,204	-171,193	38,637	17,228	-1,354
		Rating History: NR-5, 04/12/10; NR-5, 04/27/09; NR-5, 04/07/08; NR-5, 05/11/07; NR-5, 05/09/06																
AUTO CLUB LIFE INSURANCE CO Auto Club Insurance Association Charles H. Podowski President & CEO 17900 N. Laurel Park Drive Livonia, MI 48152 MI : 1974 : Stock : Agency SPDA's, Term Life, Univ Life 734-779-2600 AMB# 008525 NAIC# 84522	**A-** Rating Outlook: Stable **FSC VII**	'05	92.2	0.2	0.2	7.4	423,472	23.0	1.1	74.3	1.6	23,243	18,882	51,013	11,445	594	-1,472	-1,765
		'06	87.0	1.9	-0.4	11.5	423,257	25.9	1.1	71.1	1.9	33,671	16,736	51,342	7,982	-28	895	918
		'07	81.6	2.9	4.9	10.7	430,009	29.6	1.2	67.4	1.7	58,039	14,875	45,822	-4,071	5,385	4,333	4,269
		'08	82.6	...	4.9	12.6	423,260	31.9	1.2	65.6	1.3	48,803	15,088	55,282	4,702	3,936	-1,107	-3,547
		'09	83.7	...	5.1	11.1	450,264	33.1	1.2	64.2	1.5	62,962	14,374	64,329	16,651	6,891	4,862	4,610
		Rating History: A- g, 05/26/10; A- g, 05/29/09; A- g, 03/17/08; A- g, 01/16/07; A- g, 01/03/06																
AUTO-OWNERS LIFE INS CO Auto-Owners Insurance Company Ronald H. Simon Chairman & CEO P.O. Box 30660 Lansing, MI 48909-8160 MI : 1966 : Stock : Agency Ind Life, Ind Ann, Group pens 517-323-1200 AMB# 006140 NAIC# 61190	**A+** Rating Outlook: Stable **FSC IX**	'05	81.9	11.7	2.7	3.7	1,686,405	18.1	1.5	77.5	2.9	183,805	226,537	244,408	183,049	21,434	12,616	12,395
		'06	81.2	11.7	2.9	4.2	1,840,812	18.3	1.5	77.9	2.3	202,982	210,731	227,363	155,479	27,595	16,636	16,857
		'07	80.8	12.1	2.9	4.2	2,009,921	18.4	1.4	77.8	2.3	224,668	207,581	226,657	165,066	32,104	19,413	20,165
		'08	78.5	13.9	2.4	5.1	2,110,939	19.2	1.6	77.1	2.1	229,577	183,981	240,749	122,693	23,457	16,759	13,444
		'09	72.1	13.1	2.3	12.4	2,338,753	18.8	1.5	67.2	12.4	240,547	247,047	283,475	22,304	30,356	13,203	9,189
		Rating History: A+, 05/21/10; A+, 05/29/09; A+, 05/28/08; A+, 05/30/07; A+, 06/09/06																
AUTOMOBILE CLUB OF STHRN CA LF Automobile Club of Southern California Thomas V. McKernan President & CEO 17900 N. Laurel Park Drive Livonia, MI 48152 CA : 1999 : Stock : Agency Reins 714-850-5111 AMB# 060325 NAIC# 60256	**A-** Rating Outlook: Stable **FSC VII**	'05	91.8	...	0.2	7.9	272,995	10.8	0.9	84.8	3.5	17,929	...	51,409	32,582	-4,999	-5,037	-5,201
		'06	86.0	...	0.1	13.9	317,155	14.5	0.8	81.6	3.1	25,996	...	61,099	46,632	-11,929	-12,521	-12,496
		'07	85.2	...	1.0	13.7	349,410	18.0	0.8	78.9	2.3	32,200	...	69,855	31,227	-4,359	-4,466	-4,768
		'08	79.8	...	0.5	19.7	410,669	20.2	0.9	78.2	0.7	37,560	...	115,044	61,780	-6,175	-9,666	-13,516
		'09	91.1	...	0.2	8.7	501,153	19.4	0.9	78.9	0.9	48,163	...	145,573	83,256	-1,737	-2,489	-3,084
		Rating History: A- g, 05/26/10; A- g, 05/29/09; A- g, 03/17/08; A- g, 01/16/07; A- g, 01/03/06																
AVALON INSURANCE COMPANY Capital Blue Cross William Lehr, Jr. President & CEO 2500 Elmerton Avenue Harrisburg, PA 17177-9799 PA : 2006 : Stock : Agency Health 717-541-7000 AMB# 064854 NAIC# 12358	**NR-5**	'05	6.1	...	...	93.9	2,100	...	...	...	100.0	2,035	...	...	2,100	-65	-65	-65
		'06	35.6	...	...	64.4	13,031	...	12.4	...	87.6	2,344	20,961	20,961	6,268	-5,340	-3,478	-3,478
		'07	14.1	...	...	85.9	23,262	...	20.4	...	79.6	11,549	21,822	21,822	7,558	-4,164	-2,699	-2,699
		'08	20.0	...	...	80.0	30,543	...	21.5	...	78.5	6,792	27,340	27,340	6,941	-4,889	-4,406	-4,406
		'09	0.6	...	...	99.4	20,415	...	34.0	...	66.0	10,376	30,728	30,728	-4,862	3,179	3,209	3,209
		Rating History: NR-5, 04/13/10; NR-5, 07/01/09; NR-5, 05/05/08; NR-2, 01/10/07																
AVANTE BEHAVIORAL HEALTH PLAN D. Duane Oswald President 1111 E. Herndon Avenue, #308 Fresno, CA 93720 CA : 2000 : Stock : Broker Health 559-261-9060 AMB# 064803	**NR-5**	'05	...	...	...	100.0	246	...	...	...	100.0	103	930	930	93	-5	-6	-6
		'06	...	...	...	100.0	274	...	...	...	100.0	184	939	939	25	32	31	31
		'07	...	...	...	100.0	298	...	...	...	100.0	159	1,031	1,031	-13	-24	-25	-25
		'08	...	...	...	100.0	321	...	...	...	100.0	82	1,166	1,166	-6	-113	-113	-113
		'09	...	...	...	100.0	284	...	...	...	100.0	166	1,137	1,137	11	86	85	85
		Rating History: NR-5, 05/06/10; NR-5, 05/07/09; NR-5, 05/09/08; NR-5, 05/07/07; NR-5, 06/21/06																

2010 BEST'S KEY RATING GUIDE — LIFE/HEALTH EDITION
BEST'S PROFITABILITY, LEVERAGE AND LIQUIDITY TESTS 2005 – 2009

Data in U.S. Dollars

	Profitability Tests							Leverage Tests						Liquidity Tests					
Un-Realized Capital Gains ($000)	Benefits Paid to NPW & Dep (%)	Comm. & Expenses to NPW & Dep (%)	NOG to Total Assets (%)	NOG to Total Rev (%)	Operating Return on Equity (%)	Net Yield (%)	Total Return (%)	Change in NPW & Dep (%)	NPW & Dep to Capital (X)	Capital & Surplus to Liabilities (%)	Surplus Relief (%)	Reins Leverage (%)	Change in Capital (%)	Quick Liquidity (%)	Current Liquidity (%)	Non-Invest Grade Bonds to Capital (%)	Delinq. & Foreclosed Mortgages to Capital (%)	Mort. & Credit Tenant Loans & R.E. to Capital (%)	Affiliated Invest to Capital (%)
…	53.8	41.5	6.5	8.8	15.2	5.36	5.81	-12.1	1.1	83.1	42.1	241.3	13.9	126.0	140.8	…	…	19.0	19.0
…	52.9	48.3	1.3	1.7	2.8	4.35	4.61	8.1	1.1	88.0	36.1	219.9	5.9	140.1	154.0	…	…	17.9	17.9
…	62.0	47.5	1.2	1.4	2.6	4.35	4.10	17.5	1.3	85.8	38.8	220.0	-0.7	120.6	135.0	…	…	17.7	17.7
…	61.4	42.5	2.5	2.9	5.5	5.22	4.80	6.6	1.3	88.9	40.2	214.9	4.0	111.0	126.1	…	…	16.6	16.6
…	65.2	42.0	2.8	3.1	6.1	6.14	5.93	4.2	1.4	85.8	37.6	186.9	2.4	127.1	136.4	…	…	15.9	15.9
Principal Lines of Business: IndA&H (45.8%), GrpA&H (39.5%), OrdLife (11.7%), CrdLife (1.5%), IndAnn (0.8%)														Principal States: PR (35.1%), VI (6.8%)					
…	…	…	…	…	…	…	…	…	…	…	…	…	…	…	…	…	…	…	…
…	88.7	9.0	…	3.4	…	…	…	…	8.7	49.9	…	5.3	…	261.2	261.2	…	…	…	…
…	84.6	11.6	10.6	3.2	27.1	6.76	6.76	9.4	7.3	81.0	…	7.0	29.4	253.4	253.4	…	…	…	…
…	85.2	13.4	5.4	1.5	12.6	3.41	3.41	23.7	7.4	72.4	…	7.8	22.3	125.2	125.2	…	…	…	…
…	84.3	15.9	0.5	0.2	1.1	1.57	1.57	-14.0	8.0	68.3	…	0.5	-20.6	138.0	138.0	…	…	…	…
Principal Lines of Business: Medicare (100.0%)														Principal States: OR (100.0%)					
…	…	…	…	…	…	…	…	…	…	…	…	…	…	…	…	…	…	…	…
…	…	…	…	…	…	…	…	…	…	…	…	…	…	…	…	…	…	…	…
…	…	…	…	…	…	…	…	…	…	…	…	…	…	…	…	…	…	…	…
-200	103.6	68.3	-3.3	-64.7	-3.5	0.23	0.23	…	2.6	999.9	…	…	999.9	999.9	999.9	…	…	…	…
…	…	…	…	…	…	…	…	…	…	…	…	…	…	…	…	…	…	…	…
…	37.1	6.0	1.5	-84.8	19.1	6.07	6.06	20.6	0.1	9.2	2.0	9.8	3.4	68.0	77.6	49.1	…	…	…
…	47.5	0.3	0.8	-46.3	9.0	6.00	5.90	-22.8	0.1	9.8	1.6	10.6	4.1	72.9	82.7	28.5	…	…	…
…	54.4	1.9	0.7	-83.7	8.3	6.03	6.05	-17.0	0.1	10.5	1.2	9.4	5.5	71.5	82.3	19.6	…	…	…
…	76.9	2.3	1.0	-82.7	9.8	5.75	5.25	-34.5	0.1	11.4	1.0	8.1	3.6	74.9	83.2	7.8	…	…	…
-495	65.3	7.7	0.6	-74.9	5.2	5.60	5.19	17.9	0.1	12.6	0.8	15.1	5.2	85.8	93.5	4.4	…	…	…
Principal Lines of Business: GrpAnn (90.1%), OrdLife (5.2%), IndAnn (4.4%), GrpLife (0.2%)														Principal States: CA (17.6%), TX (10.1%), FL (6.3%), IL (6.2%), MA (4.6%)					
-3,641	77.1	34.2	-0.3	-2.2	-5.9	5.15	4.23	-10.3	2.1	6.0	1.8	54.7	-11.9	80.3	88.8	14.9	…	3.5	1.3
-5,025	102.1	32.1	0.2	1.5	3.1	5.22	4.00	0.6	1.4	9.1	1.2	28.4	47.6	80.4	88.7	85.3	…	22.4	-6.3
1,744	104.0	34.1	1.0	8.5	9.4	5.45	5.84	-10.8	0.8	16.4	0.6	21.1	70.8	77.4	86.5	50.5	…	20.3	30.8
-1,472	81.6	30.1	-0.3	-1.6	-2.1	5.31	4.29	20.6	1.1	13.3	0.6	21.2	-17.9	74.3	82.7	55.9	…	…	38.7
1,880	70.6	25.4	1.1	5.9	8.7	5.40	5.71	16.4	1.0	16.9	0.4	16.1	31.4	69.7	79.2	56.2	…	…	34.1
Principal Lines of Business: OrdLife (41.7%), IndAnn (38.4%), GrpLife (10.0%), GrpA&H (7.6%), IndA&H (1.8%)														Principal States: MI (60.5%), CA (29.9%)					
-770	44.4	11.2	0.8	4.0	7.1	5.78	5.72	8.1	1.2	13.4	0.4	1.5	6.1	76.3	84.6	5.8	0.0	99.0	32.9
3,061	51.8	13.2	0.9	5.4	8.6	5.70	5.89	-7.0	1.0	13.6	0.3	1.2	10.8	77.1	85.5	3.6	0.1	97.6	28.5
1,419	51.3	14.2	1.0	6.2	9.1	5.70	5.82	-0.3	0.9	13.9	0.3	1.9	10.8	75.6	84.4	3.7	0.1	98.9	25.8
-9,880	53.7	13.4	0.8	5.6	7.4	5.64	4.99	6.2	1.0	13.0	0.3	2.1	-0.5	75.0	83.7	2.5	0.8	120.7	34.2
4,590	108.6	13.0	0.6	2.4	5.6	5.49	5.53	17.7	1.1	13.9	0.4	2.6	7.9	69.0	79.7	19.5	2.2	116.5	38.0
Principal Lines of Business: IndAnn (54.5%), OrdLife (28.3%), GrpAnn (11.9%), IndA&H (4.2%), GrpA&H (0.6%)														Principal States: MI (45.4%), MN (8.3%), OH (6.3%), FL (5.6%), IL (4.6%)					
13	48.7	35.4	-1.9	-7.6	-27.9	4.66	4.88	-1.9	2.8	7.2	…	22.4	-0.6	75.8	85.7	27.8	…	…	…
12	56.8	36.2	-4.2	-15.0	-57.0	4.95	5.15	18.8	2.3	9.3	…	12.4	46.9	84.2	93.9	64.4	…	…	…
-62	73.3	35.9	-1.3	-4.6	-15.3	5.37	5.41	14.3	2.1	10.6	…	6.8	23.7	83.0	94.1	53.6	…	…	…
-259	49.3	24.9	-2.5	-7.0	-27.7	5.26	4.24	64.7	3.1	10.1	…	9.4	12.3	88.0	98.4	51.9	…	…	…
281	37.9	22.6	-0.5	-1.5	-5.8	5.53	5.52	26.5	3.0	10.8	…	11.3	29.6	71.3	82.6	51.8	…	…	…
Principal Lines of Business: IndAnn (63.1%), OrdLife (23.2%), GrpLife (8.7%), GrpA&H (4.4%), IndA&H (0.6%)																			
…	…	…	…	-99.9	…	…	…	…	…	999.9	…	…	…	999.9	999.9	…	…	…	…
…	101.9	24.6	-46.0	-16.4	-99.9	4.27	4.27	…	8.9	21.9	…	…	15.2	110.6	112.6	…	…	…	…
…	107.1	14.4	-14.9	-12.1	-38.8	4.26	4.26	4.1	1.9	98.6	…	…	392.7	221.6	233.2	…	…	…	…
…	102.7	14.8	-16.4	-15.9	-48.0	2.05	2.05	25.3	4.0	28.6	…	…	-41.2	140.2	147.2	…	…	…	…
…	75.0	14.6	12.6	10.4	37.4	0.55	0.55	12.4	3.0	103.4	…	…	52.8	327.3	343.9	…	…	…	…
Principal Lines of Business: OtherHlth (99.8%), MedSup (0.2%)														Principal States: PA (98.0%)					
…	65.7	96.3	-2.6	-0.4	-6.5	0.66	0.66	519.1	9.0	71.7	…	…	22.1	67.1	67.1	…	…	…	…
…	65.1	90.1	11.9	2.1	21.5	0.28	0.28	0.9	5.1	204.0	…	…	78.6	134.6	134.6	…	…	…	…
…	68.2	87.7	-8.7	-1.6	-14.5	0.63	0.63	9.8	6.5	114.0	…	…	-13.5	77.6	77.6	…	…	…	…
…	81.2	80.0	-36.6	-6.4	-94.3	1.47	1.47	13.1	14.3	34.1	…	…	-48.7	42.8	42.8	…	…	…	…
…	94.1	105.4	28.0	3.6	68.4	-0.02	-0.02	-2.5	6.8	141.6	…	…	103.9	96.7	96.7	…	…	…	…
Principal Lines of Business: CompHosp/Med (100.0%)																			

2010 BEST'S KEY RATING GUIDE — LIFE/HEALTH EDITION
ANNUAL STATEMENT DATA FOR YEARS 2005 – 2009
Data in U.S. Dollars

COMPANY NAME / Ultimate Parent Association / Principal Officer / Mailing Address / Dom. : Began Bus. : Struct. : Mktg. / Specialty / Phone # / AMB# / NAIC#

Best's Financial Strength Rating / FSC

Balance Sheet: Data Year; Bonds (%); Mort. Loans & R.E. (%); Com & Pref. Stock (%); All Other Assets (%); Total Assets ($000); Life Reserves (%); Health Reserves (%); Ann Res. & Dep. Liabilities (%); All Other Liabilities (%); Capital & Surplus ($000)

Operations: Direct Premiums Written ($000); Net Premiums Written & Deposits ($000); Operating Cash Flow ($000); NOG Before Taxes ($000); NOG After Taxes ($000); Net Income ($000)

AVERA HEALTH PLANS INC
Avera Health
Robin O. Bates
President
3816 S. Elmwood Avenue, Suite 100
Sioux Falls, SD 57105
SD : 1999 : Stock : Not Available
Health
605-322-4500
AMB# 064515 NAIC# 95839

NR-5

Data Year	Bonds (%)	Mort. Loans & R.E. (%)	Com & Pref. Stock (%)	All Other Assets (%)	Total Assets ($000)	Life Reserves (%)	Health Reserves (%)	Ann Res. & Dep. Liabilities (%)	All Other Liabilities (%)	Capital & Surplus ($000)	Direct Premiums Written ($000)	Net Premiums Written & Deposits ($000)	Operating Cash Flow ($000)	NOG Before Taxes ($000)	NOG After Taxes ($000)	Net Income ($000)
'05	76.0	...	...	24.0	16,540	...	86.0	...	14.0	8,542	42,625	41,895	4,064	976	960	971
'06	62.4	...	...	37.6	18,906	...	81.7	...	18.3	10,643	43,343	42,656	1,801	269	267	228
'07	56.4	...	15.9	27.7	18,407	...	82.8	...	17.2	11,231	40,059	39,370	-347	542	531	536
'08	63.7	...	8.2	28.1	16,898	...	73.8	...	26.2	9,348	41,630	40,744	-1,978	-648	-470	-589
'09	63.2	...	10.2	26.6	17,047	...	82.3	...	17.7	6,797	49,092	48,080	770	-3,088	-3,238	-3,232

Rating History: NR-5, 03/22/10; NR-5, 08/26/09; B- pd, 07/21/08; B- pd, 07/20/07; B- pd, 08/29/06

AVIVA LIFE AND ANNUITY COMPANY
AVIVA plc
Christopher J. Littlefield
President
P.O. Box 1555, Mailstop H73
Des Moines, IA 50306-1555
IA : 1896 : Stock : Agency
SPDA's, Univ Life, Term Life
800-800-9882
AMB# 006199 NAIC# 61689

A
Rating Outlook: Stable
FSC XV

Data Year	Bonds (%)	Mort. Loans & R.E. (%)	Com & Pref. Stock (%)	All Other Assets (%)	Total Assets ($000)	Life Reserves (%)	Health Reserves (%)	Ann Res. & Dep. Liabilities (%)	All Other Liabilities (%)	Capital & Surplus ($000)	Direct Premiums Written ($000)	Net Premiums Written & Deposits ($000)	Operating Cash Flow ($000)	NOG Before Taxes ($000)	NOG After Taxes ($000)	Net Income ($000)
'05	80.4	4.2	3.1	12.3	26,293,439	21.6	0.1	70.2	8.1	1,484,914	4,065,511	4,317,886	2,049,626	204,317	147,464	143,594
'06	77.0	4.3	3.5	15.2	28,640,894	21.2	0.1	68.6	10.1	1,546,004	4,107,412	4,456,258	1,540,001	32,916	27,276	61,139
'07	76.3	5.0	3.1	15.6	32,533,890	19.6	0.0	69.4	11.0	1,780,634	5,809,468	5,744,679	3,368,785	66,539	55,649	87,160
'08	71.5	5.8	2.9	19.9	39,019,896	17.0	0.0	72.2	10.8	2,196,563	8,453,984	8,955,998	5,431,410	-141,497	-130,842	-511,061
'09	75.4	6.5	2.1	16.0	41,990,392	16.4	0.0	73.4	10.1	2,282,876	6,678,472	-62,738	3,051,716	147,262	169,081	-95,868

Rating History: A g, 11/12/09; A g, 03/12/09; A+ g, 09/18/08; A+ g, 10/09/07; A g, 11/15/06

AVIVA LIFE & ANNUITY CO OF NY
AVIVA plc
Christopher J. Littlefield
Chairman, President & CEO
P.O. Box 1555, Mailstop H73
Des Moines, IA 50306-1555
NY : 1958 : Stock : Agency
Ann, Univ Life, Term Life
800-252-4467
AMB# 006467 NAIC# 63932

A
Rating Outlook: Stable
FSC XV

Data Year	Bonds (%)	Mort. Loans & R.E. (%)	Com & Pref. Stock (%)	All Other Assets (%)	Total Assets ($000)	Life Reserves (%)	Health Reserves (%)	Ann Res. & Dep. Liabilities (%)	All Other Liabilities (%)	Capital & Surplus ($000)	Direct Premiums Written ($000)	Net Premiums Written & Deposits ($000)	Operating Cash Flow ($000)	NOG Before Taxes ($000)	NOG After Taxes ($000)	Net Income ($000)
'05	91.1	1.7	-2.5	9.7	1,046,552	47.4	0.3	48.6	3.7	50,398	190,111	175,340	72,285	-1,454	-3,698	-5,459
'06	89.1	1.3	-2.4	12.0	1,171,741	49.4	0.4	46.9	3.4	50,196	238,801	228,182	110,184	-13,061	-13,236	-14,257
'07	88.2	1.1	0.8	9.9	1,335,950	48.7	0.2	47.6	3.5	90,425	243,393	200,693	130,666	-8,448	-17,472	-18,386
'08	88.7	1.0	0.7	9.5	1,394,307	49.5	0.2	48.6	1.7	80,410	191,127	169,077	64,692	-2,678	-538	-22,873
'09	83.3	3.1	0.3	13.3	1,474,773	51.6	0.3	46.0	2.1	98,156	145,332	117,317	71,663	-9,776	-10,512	-18,835

Rating History: A g, 11/12/09; A g, 03/12/09; A+ g, 09/18/08; A+ g, 10/09/07; A g, 11/15/06

AVMED INC
SantaFe HealthCare, Inc.
Michael P. Gallagher
CEO
P.O. Box 749
Gainesville, FL 32602-0749
FL : 1977 : Non-Profit : Broker
Group A&H, Health
352-372-8400
AMB# 064074 NAIC# 95263

B++
Rating Outlook: Stable
FSC VIII

Data Year	Bonds (%)	Mort. Loans & R.E. (%)	Com & Pref. Stock (%)	All Other Assets (%)	Total Assets ($000)	Life Reserves (%)	Health Reserves (%)	Ann Res. & Dep. Liabilities (%)	All Other Liabilities (%)	Capital & Surplus ($000)	Direct Premiums Written ($000)	Net Premiums Written & Deposits ($000)	Operating Cash Flow ($000)	NOG Before Taxes ($000)	NOG After Taxes ($000)	Net Income ($000)
'05	67.2	7.7	...	25.1	279,898	...	50.8	...	49.2	137,453	764,668	760,033	40,867	38,064	38,064	37,077
'06	29.2	6.7	...	64.1	305,361	...	52.5	...	47.5	147,522	884,878	880,741	18,217	34,528	34,528	33,171
'07	64.6	5.4	9.7	20.4	363,241	...	47.1	...	52.9	194,059	963,283	960,156	59,686	56,051	56,051	56,[illegible]42
'08	70.3	5.2	9.5	15.0	354,040	...	44.0	...	56.0	185,217	919,662	916,827	932	43,712	43,712	39,021
'09	69.2	4.8	10.0	16.0	371,955	...	40.6	...	59.4	190,004	1,068,017	1,064,604	-9,558	4,820	4,820	8,560

Rating History: B++, 05/25/10; B++, 07/08/09; B++, 06/12/08; B+, 05/24/07; B+, 06/13/06

AXA CORPORATE SOLUTIONS LF RE
AXA S.A.
Kevin Byrne
President and Chief Investment Officer
1290 Avenue of the Americas
New York, NY 10104
DE : 1983 : Stock : Other Direct
Reins
212-314-4168
AMB# 009083 NAIC# 68365

B++
Rating Outlook: Stable
FSC IX

Data Year	Bonds (%)	Mort. Loans & R.E. (%)	Com & Pref. Stock (%)	All Other Assets (%)	Total Assets ($000)	Life Reserves (%)	Health Reserves (%)	Ann Res. & Dep. Liabilities (%)	All Other Liabilities (%)	Capital & Surplus ($000)	Direct Premiums Written ($000)	Net Premiums Written & Deposits ($000)	Operating Cash Flow ($000)	NOG Before Taxes ($000)	NOG After Taxes ($000)	Net Income ($000)
'05	85.9	...	...	14.1	666,335	2.3	16.7	78.4	2.6	350,016	...	127,237	17,501	51,305	34,824	24,466
'06	79.1	...	...	20.9	770,303	1.4	18.1	75.4	5.1	475,515	...	112,291	69,399	106,323	85,806	62,763
'07	81.4	...	...	18.6	817,071	5.7	14.6	75.7	4.1	487,875	...	101,921	65,971	33,503	25,509	19,839
'08	51.6	...	...	48.4	1,540,933	0.9	2.6	96.0	0.5	254,539	...	98,711	845,575	-909,382	-753,530	-518,635
'09	76.3	...	...	23.7	1,433,393	1.4	2.7	92.1	3.9	401,438	...	88,251	-306,640	255,868	262,874	-8,306

Rating History: B++, 06/04/10; B++, 05/12/09; B++, 12/05/07; B++, 11/09/06; B++, 10/21/05

AXA EQUITABLE LIFE & ANNUITY
AXA S.A.
Christopher M. Condron
Chairman, President & CEO
10840 Ballantyne Commons Parkway
Charlotte, NC 28277
CO : 1984 : Stock : Agency
Whole life, ISWL
212-554-1234
AMB# 009516 NAIC# 62880

A
Rating Outlook: Stable
FSC VII

Data Year	Bonds (%)	Mort. Loans & R.E. (%)	Com & Pref. Stock (%)	All Other Assets (%)	Total Assets ($000)	Life Reserves (%)	Health Reserves (%)	Ann Res. & Dep. Liabilities (%)	All Other Liabilities (%)	Capital & Surplus ($000)	Direct Premiums Written ($000)	Net Premiums Written & Deposits ($000)	Operating Cash Flow ($000)	NOG Before Taxes ($000)	NOG After Taxes ($000)	Net Income ($000)
'05	48.3	...	...	51.7	533,681	96.2	...	0.0	3.8	91,896	58,215	10,280	-12,245	12,645	6,314	6,105
'06	45.7	...	...	54.3	541,688	97.1	...	0.0	2.9	97,619	54,206	7,741	31,438	10,074	6,291	6,116
'07	45.6	...	...	54.4	554,701	97.2	...	...	2.8	105,245	54,842	10,520	-695	9,807	7,245	7,245
'08	40.1	...	...	59.9	512,844	93.2	...	...	6.8	48,771	49,827	7,830	-50,367	12,267	9,744	8,639
'09	41.7	...	...	58.3	517,713	93.2	...	...	6.8	55,487	47,783	4,630	28,149	6,014	4,979	5,442

Rating History: A, 06/04/10; A, 06/12/09; A+ g, 05/29/08; A+ g, 01/25/07; A+ g, 08/12/05

AXA EQUITABLE LIFE INS CO
AXA S.A.
Christopher M. Condron
Chairman, President & CEO
1290 Avenue of the Americas
New York, NY 10104
NY : 1859 : Stock : Agency
Var ann, Var life, Whole life
212-554-1234
AMB# 006341 NAIC# 62944

A+
Rating Outlook: Stable
FSC XV

Data Year	Bonds (%)	Mort. Loans & R.E. (%)	Com & Pref. Stock (%)	All Other Assets (%)	Total Assets ($000)	Life Reserves (%)	Health Reserves (%)	Ann Res. & Dep. Liabilities (%)	All Other Liabilities (%)	Capital & Surplus ($000)	Direct Premiums Written ($000)	Net Premiums Written & Deposits ($000)	Operating Cash Flow ($000)	NOG Before Taxes ($000)	NOG After Taxes ($000)	Net Income ($000)
'05	24.3	3.0	3.7	69.0	115,385,611	15.5	0.5	19.0	65.0	5,111,139	14,616,756	14,826,682	59,688	963,167	861,363	774,279
'06	20.5	2.7	4.5	72.2	131,779,702	14.0	0.4	16.0	69.6	6,497,613	16,801,870	17,003,830	-1,119,852	1,005,622	807,242	526,188
'07	18.2	2.8	3.8	75.2	142,433,163	13.4	0.4	13.9	72.3	6,569,263	19,610,981	19,578,800	-853,006	807,120	641,776	598,578
'08	22.8	3.7	2.4	71.1	111,795,878	17.1	0.5	19.2	63.2	3,155,026	17,774,322	14,818,692	3,219,574	-4,291,951	-2,763,000	-1,074,785
'09	21.5	3.1	1.5	73.9	126,783,596	15.2	0.5	14.4	70.0	3,115,942	10,874,947	10,465,809	-1,544,154	3,328,743	2,420,956	1,782,902

Rating History: A+ g, 06/04/10; A+ g, 06/12/09; A+ g, 05/29/08; A+ g, 01/25/07; A+ g, 08/12/05

BALBOA LIFE INSURANCE COMPANY
Bank of America Corporation
Mark A. McElroy
Senior Vice President
3349 Michelson Drive, Suite 200
Irvine, CA 92612-1627
CA : 1969 : Stock : Agency
Term Life, Credit
949-222-8000
AMB# 006965 NAIC# 68160

A-
Rating Outlook: Stable
FSC VI

Data Year	Bonds (%)	Mort. Loans & R.E. (%)	Com & Pref. Stock (%)	All Other Assets (%)	Total Assets ($000)	Life Reserves (%)	Health Reserves (%)	Ann Res. & Dep. Liabilities (%)	All Other Liabilities (%)	Capital & Surplus ($000)	Direct Premiums Written ($000)	Net Premiums Written & Deposits ($000)	Operating Cash Flow ($000)	NOG Before Taxes ($000)	NOG After Taxes ($000)	Net Income ($000)
'05	72.1	...	20.3	7.6	71,922	41.8	17.6	12.2	28.3	47,166	20,326	19,043	-42,232	9,189	7,722	7,487
'06	46.7	...	40.2	13.1	38,917	47.8	22.2	16.6	13.4	22,390	18,978	17,576	-34,041	4,674	4,609	4,362
'07	44.9	...	39.5	15.6	41,329	43.0	21.9	19.6	15.5	27,888	17,168	15,522	3,071	5,223	5,360	5,360
'08	38.4	...	40.2	21.5	43,255	37.7	25.1	18.5	18.7	30,692	17,603	16,156	1,480	3,428	3,958	3,958
'09	52.7	...	37.2	10.1	48,100	38.8	24.4	18.0	18.8	37,077	15,964	14,778	5,777	6,143	5,727	5,565

Rating History: A- g, 11/17/09; A- g, 11/24/08; A- gu, 01/11/08; A- g, 11/21/07; A- gu, 08/16/07

BALBOA LIFE INSURANCE CO OF NY
Bank of America Corporation
Mark A. McElroy
Senior Vice President
3349 Michelson Drive, Suite 200
Irvine, CA 92612-1627
NY : 2001 : Stock : Agency
Term Life, Credit
949-222-8000
AMB# 060347 NAIC# 10097

A-
Rating Outlook: Stable
FSC VI

Data Year	Bonds (%)	Mort. Loans & R.E. (%)	Com & Pref. Stock (%)	All Other Assets (%)	Total Assets ($000)	Life Reserves (%)	Health Reserves (%)	Ann Res. & Dep. Liabilities (%)	All Other Liabilities (%)	Capital & Surplus ($000)	Direct Premiums Written ($000)	Net Premiums Written & Deposits ($000)	Operating Cash Flow ($000)	NOG Before Taxes ($000)	NOG After Taxes ($000)	Net Income ($000)
'05	89.9	...	...	10.1	15,715	8.9	61.9	...	29.2	14,573	2,305	2,255	339	1,063	707	707
'06	95.3	...	...	4.7	16,445	12.1	70.6	...	17.2	15,610	2,181	2,091	1,051	1,591	1,037	1,037
'07	76.9	...	...	23.1	17,595	10.5	57.2	...	32.3	16,291	1,846	1,711	1,277	1,024	696	696
'08	56.3	...	...	43.7	18,088	17.8	44.1	...	38.1	17,318	1,837	1,702	-817	1,612	1,069	1,069
'09	87.7	...	...	12.3	18,390	25.7	41.6	...	32.7	17,834	996	858	815	1,009	1,411	1,238

Rating History: A- g, 11/17/09; A- g, 11/24/08; A- gu, 01/11/08; A- g, 11/21/07; A- gu, 08/16/07

BEST'S PROFITABILITY, LEVERAGE AND LIQUIDITY TESTS 2005 – 2009

Data in U.S. Dollars

—	Profitability Tests							Leverage Tests						Liquidity Tests					
Un-Realized Capital Gains ($000)	Benefits Paid to NPW & Dep (%)	Comm. & Expenses to NPW & Dep (%)	NOG to Total Assets (%)	NOG to Total Rev (%)	Operating Return on Equity (%)	Net Yield (%)	Total Return (%)	Change in NPW & Dep (%)	NPW & Dep to Capital (X)	Capital & Surplus to Liabilities (%)	Surplus Relief (%)	Reins Leverage (%)	Change in Capital (%)	Quick Liquidity (%)	Current Liquidity (%)	Non-Invest Grade Bonds to Capital (%)	Delinq. & Foreclosed Mortgages to Capital (%)	Mort. & Credit Tenant Loans & R.E. to Capital (%)	Affiliated Invest to Capital (%)
...	83.2	15.7	6.1	2.3	12.4	4.01	4.10	9.3	4.9	106.8	...	2.8	22.8	213.7	228.9	...	...	...	...
...	87.0	14.4	1.5	0.6	2.8	4.16	3.92	1.8	4.0	128.8	...	5.1	24.6	254.1	268.1	...	...	...	...
...	88.9	11.8	2.8	1.3	4.9	4.15	4.18	-7.7	3.5	156.5	...	2.7	5.5	259.9	283.5	...	...	...	...
-637	92.0	12.2	-2.7	-1.1	-4.6	3.52	-1.28	3.5	4.4	123.8	...	13.6	-16.8	160.6	172.9	...	...	...	...
361	98.4	9.3	-19.1	-6.7	-40.1	2.81	5.33	18.0	7.1	66.3	...	1.5	-27.3	127.1	137.3	...	...	...	...
Principal Lines of Business: CompHosp/Med (72.6%), MedSup (27.4%)													Principal States: SD (94.5%), IA (5.5%)						
-28,539	50.7	15.5	0.6	3.0	10.4	5.69	5.62	28.7	2.6	7.1	1.6	53.8	10.1	55.4	68.6	96.1	...	76.4	5.7
38,314	64.5	15.7	0.1	0.5	1.8	6.08	6.41	3.2	2.5	7.0	1.4	52.1	6.3	52.9	66.8	97.8	...	79.8	6.3
-109,722	50.4	14.8	0.2	0.8	3.3	5.70	5.45	28.9	2.9	7.1	4.9	56.3	12.9	53.8	67.7	100.4	...	89.4	6.3
-165,515	34.0	12.8	-0.4	-1.4	-6.6	3.51	1.81	55.9	3.9	6.8	3.4	49.7	14.2	57.2	70.4	99.7	...	105.4	14.5
54,303	-99.9	-99.9	0.4	2.1	7.5	4.97	4.38	-99.9	0.0	6.3	1.4	43.9	2.2	53.4	66.7	88.8	...	123.2	18.5
Principal Lines of Business: IndAnn (999.9%), IndA&H (-1.4%), GrpLife (-4.1%), GrpAnn (-99.9%), OrdLife (-99.9%)													Principal States: CA (12.1%), FL (9.9%), TX (6.3%), MI (5.7%), OH (5.3%)						
4,951	50.4	25.0	-0.4	-1.7	-7.8	6.29	6.75	11.8	3.1	5.7	24.0	468.0	14.6	61.1	73.6	85.5	...	34.4	-53.9
12,544	43.3	19.8	-1.2	-5.0	-26.3	6.15	7.33	30.1	4.1	4.9	17.6	544.6	-1.5	61.0	73.8	91.0	...	30.2	-69.4
-573	70.7	14.8	-1.4	-6.8	-24.9	6.17	6.11	-12.0	2.0	8.0	20.2	380.7	78.7	68.3	79.6	66.3	...	16.0	...
-3,847	65.9	14.6	0.0	-0.2	-0.6	5.59	3.66	-15.8	2.1	6.2	19.0	471.4	-17.9	66.3	77.2	117.7	...	18.8	...
6,543	84.1	25.8	-0.7	-5.7	-11.8	5.69	5.55	-30.6	1.2	7.3	12.2	410.0	23.8	70.0	81.8	61.2	...	46.4	...
Principal Lines of Business: OrdLife (67.9%), GrpAnn (18.4%), IndAnn (10.2%), GrpLife (3.3%), IndA&H (0.2%)													Principal States: NY (86.4%), NJ (3.3%), FL (3.1%)						
...	83.0	11.9	14.6	5.0	28.9	2.82	2.43	7.9	5.5	96.5	...	1.2	9.4	183.5	192.4	...	...	15.7	7.2
...	86.1	12.5	11.8	3.9	24.2	3.97	3.48	15.9	6.0	93.5	...	1.7	7.3	253.2	267.8	...	...	13.8	6.4
1,001	84.0	11.9	16.8	5.8	32.8	4.16	4.63	9.0	4.9	114.7	...	0.5	31.5	180.0	195.1	...	...	10.0	4.7
-14,268	83.7	12.6	12.2	4.7	23.1	3.89	-1.62	-4.5	5.0	109.7	...	0.3	-4.6	157.0	172.4	0.1	...	10.0	4.7
10,358	87.5	13.6	1.3	0.4	2.6	3.23	7.57	16.1	5.6	104.4	...	0.3	2.6	149.6	164.7	0.1	...	9.3	4.4
Principal Lines of Business: CompHosp/Med (68.0%), Medicare (30.6%), FEHBP (1.4%)													Principal States: FL (100.0%)						
891	73.5	4.6	5.3	22.3	10.2	4.75	3.28	-8.1	0.4	111.1	0.1	9.8	5.8	153.7	171.6	...	...	...	...
-1,669	49.2	5.3	11.9	59.8	20.8	4.64	1.09	-11.7	0.2	162.8	0.0	6.1	36.1	208.0	227.9	...	...	...	...
-5,044	60.6	4.4	3.2	19.0	5.3	4.32	2.92	-9.2	0.2	149.5	0.0	6.9	2.6	214.1	234.3	...	...	...	...
-32,066	105.5	5.5	-63.9	-99.9	-99.9	3.09	24.36	-3.1	0.4	20.0	0.0	16.9	-47.5	104.7	110.2	0.9	...	...	...
7,738	161.4	7.1	17.7	230.6	80.1	1.89	-15.54	-10.6	0.2	39.3	0.0	9.4	57.1	128.0	136.9	2.8	...	...	...
Principal Lines of Business: IndAnn (97.7%), OrdLife (2.3%), GrpA&H (0.0%), CrdLife (0.0%)																			
...	268.4	-0.7	1.2	13.3	7.1	6.29	6.25	-28.4	0.1	21.2	6.6	999.9	7.4	46.2	54.5	22.9	...	...	...
...	243.2	11.1	1.2	14.0	6.6	6.21	6.18	-24.7	0.1	22.4	5.9	999.9	6.1	55.2	62.1	14.1	...	...	...
...	217.5	6.8	1.3	15.3	7.1	5.97	5.99	35.9	0.1	23.8	5.3	999.9	7.4	54.7	62.1	2.6	...	...	...
...	377.4	13.8	1.8	22.3	12.7	6.07	5.90	-25.6	0.2	10.7	11.1	999.9	-53.5	45.8	51.6	3.5	...	...	...
...	620.1	-12.3	1.0	12.9	9.6	5.88	6.02	-40.9	0.1	12.2	9.4	999.9	13.9	45.9	52.2	3.6	...	...	...
Principal Lines of Business: OrdLife (100.0%)													Principal States: NY (16.2%), NJ (12.0%), PA (11.7%), CT (8.9%), IL (5.4%)						
861,303	67.2	11.7	0.8	4.7	18.2	6.49	8.39	3.2	2.4	16.3	0.3	65.2	20.0	44.6	58.2	11.8	1.8	57.9	83.4
1,388,589	68.1	11.7	0.7	3.9	13.9	6.42	9.01	14.7	2.2	20.7	0.3	50.2	26.7	43.7	57.6	6.7	2.6	46.9	92.4
-305,365	69.0	12.7	0.5	2.7	9.8	6.60	5.83	15.1	2.5	21.0	0.4	63.2	-1.2	42.3	56.5	6.4	1.5	52.2	90.1
-2,978,338	77.6	15.3	-2.2	-14.5	-56.8	6.48	3.73	-24.3	4.1	9.0	1.1	333.3	-54.1	42.2	55.5	20.0	...	117.3	55.3
-537,841	90.9	15.9	2.0	17.4	77.2	5.25	2.39	-29.4	2.7	10.1	1.0	336.3	7.0	42.6	56.5	49.9	0.0	104.5	66.0
Principal Lines of Business: GrpAnn (46.2%), IndAnn (31.5%), OrdLife (21.8%), IndA&H (0.5%)													Principal States: NY (13.9%), NJ (8.4%), CA (7.8%), FL (6.6%), PA (5.9%)						
707	30.3	63.5	8.3	31.6	11.7	4.34	5.08	17.3	0.4	191.8	1.6	21.3	-44.2	190.7	210.1	...	...	...	30.9
678	44.8	59.1	8.3	22.8	13.3	3.60	4.54	-7.7	0.8	136.0	2.4	39.4	-52.6	107.6	115.2	...	...	...	69.7
449	28.6	61.8	13.4	30.8	21.3	3.04	4.50	-11.7	0.6	208.5	1.8	30.4	24.6	173.1	184.6	...	...	...	58.5
707	32.8	59.1	9.4	22.6	13.5	2.30	4.41	4.1	0.5	245.7	1.1	26.3	10.1	170.3	182.7	...	...	...	56.5
1,816	27.2	47.2	12.5	35.6	16.9	2.06	6.30	-8.5	0.4	336.3	0.8	20.6	20.6	224.9	241.8	1.6	...	...	48.3
Principal Lines of Business: GrpA&H (53.3%), CrdA&H (21.0%), CrdLife (9.2%), IndA&H (8.2%), OrdLife (7.1%)													Principal States: CA (12.9%), TX (11.7%), FL (4.4%), MI (4.2%), OH (3.6%)						
...	28.8	48.2	4.6	24.5	5.0	4.09	4.18	-0.6	0.2	999.9	0.2	0.1	5.0	999.9	999.9	...	...	...	...
...	24.2	37.6	6.5	36.3	6.9	4.73	4.76	-7.3	0.1	999.9	0.3	0.3	7.1	999.9	999.9	...	...	...	...
...	42.4	50.4	4.1	26.7	4.4	5.21	5.20	-18.2	0.1	999.9	0.3	0.4	4.5	999.9	999.9	...	...	...	...
...	15.6	39.0	6.0	42.9	6.4	4.19	4.26	-0.5	0.1	999.9	0.3	0.6	6.3	999.9	999.9	...	...	...	...
...	27.0	41.5	7.7	90.6	8.0	3.84	2.94	-49.6	0.0	999.9	0.2	0.7	2.8	999.9	999.9	5.1	...	...	...
Principal Lines of Business: CrdA&H (51.3%), CrdLife (26.9%), OrdLife (15.6%), GrpA&H (6.2%)													Principal States: NY (100.0%)						

Data in U.S. Dollars

COMPANY NAME / Ultimate Parent Association / Principal Officer / Mailing Address / Dom. : Began Bus. : Struct. : Mktg. / Specialty / Phone # / AMB# NAIC#	Best's Financial Strength Rating / FSC	Data Year	Balance Sheet: Bonds (%)	Mort. Loans & R.E. (%)	Com & Pref. Stock (%)	All Other Assets (%)	Total Assets ($000)	Life Reserves (%)	Health Reserves (%)	Ann Res. & Dep. Liabilities (%)	All Other Liabilities (%)	Capital & Surplus ($000)	Operations: Direct Premiums Written ($000)	Net Premiums Written & Deposits ($000)	Operating Cash Flow ($000)	NOG Before Taxes ($000)	NOG After Taxes ($000)	Net Income ($000)
BALTIMORE LIFE INS CO Baltimore Life Holdings Inc	**B++**	'05	80.1	10.8	0.2	8.9	805,524	73.6	0.7	19.8	5.8	55,342	83,060	69,651	11,977	7,857	7,857	7,570
David K. Ficca, President & CEO		'06	74.2	10.7	5.7	9.4	801,540	75.1	0.8	19.1	5.0	64,131	81,464	71,744	-5,562	5,174	5,174	5,600
10075 Red Run Boulevard, Owings Mills, MD 21117-6050	Rating Outlook: Stable	'07	74.5	10.5	5.8	9.2	810,287	75.9	0.9	17.6	5.6	72,389	82,817	81,310	5,225	5,749	5,599	8,466
MD : 1882 : Stock : Career Agent		'08	73.8	11.2	5.8	9.2	834,794	75.7	0.8	16.7	6.8	71,538	88,815	100,794	28,424	7,193	6,244	1,109
Term Life, Trad Life, Univ Life; 410-581-6600		'09	78.2	10.0	0.5	11.2	856,828	76.5	0.7	16.5	6.2	80,274	107,459	113,759	18,334	6,645	5,058	1,334
AMB# 006143 NAIC# 61212	**FSC VII**	**Rating History: B++, 03/26/10; B++, 06/15/09; B++, 05/19/08; B++, 02/06/07; B++, 03/15/06**																
BANK OF MONTREAL INS (BB) LTD Bank of Montreal	**A**	'05	35.4	...	...	64.6	703,173	10.9	...	...	89.1	446,202	3,668	234,537	139,643	98,040	98,040	98,527
Wayne Fields, Chairman		'06	34.6	...	...	65.4	800,763	8.8	...	...	91.2	479,469	3,836	178,946	130,201	131,794	131,794	132,074
Culloden Office Complex, St. Michael, Barbados	Rating Outlook: Stable	'07	47.9	...	...	52.2	605,672	58.7	...	...	41.3	535,323	1,155	426,428	98,354	168,704	168,704	169,202
BB : Stock : Not Available		'08	74.4	...	...	25.6	401,806	84.8	...	...	15.2	346,953	...	206,613	134,886	146,761	146,761	146,943
Life, Non-Life; 246-436-6972		'09	53.2	...	...	46.8	426,287	85.5	...	...	14.6	377,551	...	199,636	132,100	138,602	138,602	138,514
AMB# 056229	**FSC IX**	**Rating History: A, 06/29/09; A, 09/16/08; A, 07/02/07; A, 04/20/06; A, 03/22/05**																
BANKERS CONSECO LIFE INSURANCE CNO Financial Group, Inc.	**B**	'05	88.9	...	3.8	7.3	181,585	30.9	52.2	13.6	3.2	13,968	23,775	25,130	12,350	-2,666	-2,362	-2,362
Scott R. Perry, President		'06	68.9	...	2.3	28.8	237,057	23.5	51.9	9.4	15.2	14,644	23,617	24,772	42,427	-17,212	-16,309	-16,309
11825 N. Pennsylvania Street, Carmel, IN 46032	Rating Outlook: Stable	'07	84.0	...	1.8	14.2	241,205	24.2	64.6	9.2	2.0	21,389	24,713	25,863	-3,248	-16,895	-16,614	-17,273
NY : 1987 : Stock : Agency		'08	85.9	...	1.9	12.2	254,306	24.0	64.4	9.2	2.4	27,818	28,326	29,212	29,808	6,781	7,853	5,616
Ind Life, Health, Annuity; 317-817-6100		'09	88.2	...	...	11.8	277,107	22.2	63.2	10.2	4.5	24,984	34,030	34,834	18,625	-3,970	-3,273	-4,138
AMB# 060002 NAIC# 68560	**FSC X**	**Rating History: B g, 03/23/10; B g, 10/16/09; B gu, 03/04/09; B+ g, 11/20/08; B+ gu, 08/12/08**																
BANKERS FIDELITY LIFE INS CO J. Mack Robinson & Family	**B++**	'05	56.5	1.7	26.3	15.6	118,100	59.0	22.5	6.6	11.9	33,881	65,366	65,534	2,036	6,611	5,121	5,135
Eugene Choate, President		'06	54.1	1.2	23.3	21.4	115,187	62.4	23.4	5.7	8.5	34,467	58,065	58,286	-4,486	4,819	3,944	3,173
P.O. Box 105185, Atlanta, GA 30348	Rating Outlook: Stable	'07	61.9	0.0	8.2	29.9	119,805	59.3	22.2	5.4	13.1	33,810	56,021	55,924	14,521	4,797	4,049	11,961
GA : 1955 : Stock : Agency		'08	77.2	0.0	6.6	16.2	110,664	64.1	24.3	5.4	6.1	29,876	55,034	55,157	-5,147	3,703	2,934	1,269
A&H, Med supp, Burial Expense; 404-266-5600		'09	82.5	0.0	6.1	11.4	116,032	62.2	24.6	5.1	8.1	31,493	57,080	57,162	3,361	2,345	2,379	2,469
AMB# 006145 NAIC# 61239	**FSC VI**	**Rating History: B++, 09/09/09; B++, 08/28/08; B++, 10/02/07; B++, 07/13/06; B++, 06/21/06**																
BANKERS LIFE AND CASUALTY CO CNO Financial Group, Inc.	**B**	'05	90.3	3.0	2.9	3.9	8,929,230	6.2	32.9	57.2	3.6	587,282	2,379,015	2,353,694	1,006,718	40,867	20,551	26,805
Scott R. Perry, President		'06	89.6	4.1	2.4	3.8	9,908,157	6.6	33.3	56.6	3.5	639,712	2,470,174	2,570,054	886,221	96,120	56,153	55,816
11825 N. Pennsylvania Street, Carmel, IN 46032	Rating Outlook: Stable	'07	87.4	6.2	2.1	4.2	10,612,763	7.9	34.7	54.2	3.2	685,899	2,407,589	2,689,625	667,742	198,645	125,578	113,730
IL : 1879 : Stock : Career Agent		'08	80.9	7.9	2.0	9.1	11,442,369	7.8	34.9	54.5	2.8	607,131	2,734,465	2,986,868	730,368	135,413	80,226	-27,315
LTC, Med supp, Annuity; 312-396-6000		'09	86.3	6.7	0.9	6.1	12,318,840	6.7	34.0	54.9	4.4	730,238	2,603,001	2,710,123	821,817	314,232	189,613	86,696
AMB# 006149 NAIC# 61263	**FSC X**	**Rating History: B g, 03/23/10; B g, 10/16/09; B gu, 03/04/09; B+ g, 11/20/08; B+ gu, 08/12/08**																
BANKERS LIFE INSURANCE CO Bankers International Financial Corp Ltd	**B-**	'05	94.9	0.1	1.7	3.4	120,982	0.0	0.1	95.8	4.1	9,129	13,400	2,582	3,175	1,301	992	876
David K. Meehan, President & Chairman		'06	95.4	0.0	1.4	3.2	150,471	0.0	0.0	97.9	2.0	8,038	43,644	43,531	30,427	-841	-667	-1,123
11101 Roosevelt Blvd N, St. Petersburg, FL 33716	Rating Outlook: Negative	'07	95.1	0.5	0.7	3.7	179,893	0.3	0.0	98.4	1.3	8,616	55,662	58,649	29,673	-129	-88	169
FL : 1973 : Stock : Agency		'08	94.4	0.4	1.3	3.8	213,300	0.3	0.0	98.5	1.1	8,993	42,785	43,831	34,635	2,963	2,464	1,301
Ind Life, Annuity, Medical; 727-823-4000		'09	90.1	0.4	2.1	7.3	209,953	0.4	0.0	98.4	1.2	11,479	22,182	23,001	-5,747	3,047	2,992	-1,695
AMB# 008448 NAIC# 81043	**FSC V**	**Rating History: B-, 06/24/09; B, 06/23/08; B, 06/19/07; B, 06/20/06; B, 04/20/05**																
BANKERS LIFE INS CO OF AMERICA'	**NR-1**	'05	70.9	13.9	0.6	14.6	5,110	...	...	7.7	92.3	411	852	780	...	37	37	37
Louis P. Bickel, Jr., President		'06	71.2	13.3	0.6	14.9	5,215	...	...	6.3	93.7	423	816	738	...	10	10	10
4925 McKinney Avenue, Dallas, TX 75205-3423		'07	69.2	13.0	0.7	17.0	5,289	...	...	4.8	95.2	472	796	737	...	60	60	60
TX : 1951 : Stock : Not Available		'08	65.6	19.2	0.5	14.7	5,206	...	...	3.8	96.2	725	819	767	...	14	14	15
214-521-7100		'09	65.1	19.5	0.9	14.5	5,128	...	...	2.5	97.5	684	856	798	...	-29	-29	-21
AMB# 006153 NAIC# 61328		**Rating History: NR-1, 06/10/10; NR-1, 06/12/09; NR-1, 06/12/08; NR-1, 06/08/07; NR-1, 06/07/06**																
BANKERS LIFE OF LOUISIANA Summit Partners LP	**B++**	'05	83.2	...	3.4	13.4	24,569	30.8	23.3	...	45.9	11,247	27,919	9,185	-1,443	1,460	1,277	1,315
Richard S. Kahlbaugh, CEO		'06	82.2	...	3.1	14.6	26,491	27.1	23.0	...	49.9	12,162	30,617	9,602	2,281	870	730	824
P.O. Box 44130, Jacksonville, FL 32231-4130	Rating Outlook: Stable	'07	71.9	...	1.5	26.6	29,389	22.2	22.3	...	55.5	14,070	30,535	9,367	2,816	1,924	1,680	1,692
LA : 1959 : Stock : Agency		'08	73.6	...	2.0	24.3	13,578	51.3	40.4	...	8.3	4,902	27,308	15,268	-15,220	5,398	3,748	3,757
Ind Life; 904-350-9660		'09	72.0	...	3.4	24.6	11,541	51.0	40.7	...	8.4	3,228	26,895	12,393	-2,528	801	605	488
AMB# 006151 NAIC# 61298	**FSC V**	**Rating History: B++g, 03/23/10; B++g, 02/03/09; B++g, 12/20/07; B++g, 11/01/06; B+ g, 08/05/05**																
BANKERS RESERVE LIFE INS OF WI Centene Corporation	**B+**	'05	58.7	...	...	41.3	56,657	...	62.0	...	38.0	26,824	69,752	138,040	3,488	21,862	14,206	14,206
Michael F. Neidorff, President		'06	58.6	...	...	41.4	80,582	...	61.5	...	38.5	37,795	69,216	159,721	22,796	16,452	10,535	10,535
7711 Carondelet Avenue, Suite 800, St. Louis, MO 63105	Rating Outlook: Stable	'07	57.8	...	...	42.2	101,395	...	36.6	...	63.4	46,981	88,370	164,595	16,360	25,805	15,188	15,188
WI : 1964 : Stock : Not Available		'08	49.4	...	...	50.6	132,437	...	45.5	...	54.5	58,093	322,094	379,426	12,716	15,868	8,026	7,980
Group A&H; 314-725-4477		'09	37.2	...	...	62.8	114,793	...	77.5	...	22.5	56,439	397,789	459,358	-17,147	-777	6,311	6,588
AMB# 060401 NAIC# 71013	**FSC VII**	**Rating History: B+, 02/19/10; B+, 02/10/09; NR-1, 06/12/08; NR-5, 04/30/07; NR-1, 06/07/06**																

2010 BEST'S KEY RATING GUIDE — LIFE/HEALTH EDITION
BEST'S PROFITABILITY, LEVERAGE AND LIQUIDITY TESTS 2005 – 2009

Data in U.S. Dollars

	Profitability Tests							Leverage Tests						Liquidity Tests					
Un-Realized Capital Gains ($000)	Benefits Paid to NPW & Dep (%)	Comm. & Expenses to NPW & Dep (%)	NOG to Total Assets (%)	NOG to Total Rev (%)	Operating Return on Equity (%)	Net Yield (%)	Total Return (%)	Change in NPW & Dep (%)	NPW & Dep to Capital (X)	Capital & Surplus to Liabilities (%)	Surplus Relief (%)	Reins Leverage (%)	Change in Capital (%)	Quick Liquidity (%)	Current Liquidity (%)	Non-Invest Grade Bonds to Capital (%)	Delinq. & Foreclosed Mortgages to Capital (%)	Mort. & Credit Tenant Loans & R.E. to Capital (%)	Affiliated Invest to Capital (%)
-41	111.8	44.6	1.0	6.0	15.5	6.13	6.26	-8.2	1.1	8.3	8.4	184.7	17.6	61.1	69.4	23.2	...	141.4	19.3
78	113.2	48.3	0.6	4.1	8.7	6.13	6.35	3.0	1.0	9.5	5.8	162.7	13.4	56.7	67.2	19.5	...	123.1	16.7
-9	103.6	45.6	0.7	4.0	8.2	6.37	6.86	13.3	1.0	10.6	4.9	142.2	11.9	56.9	67.0	22.6	...	109.5	14.5
-660	74.4	37.6	0.8	4.0	8.7	6.06	5.44	24.0	1.4	9.6	4.2	124.5	-6.0	55.8	64.6	31.2	...	127.4	15.1
22	75.4	35.7	0.6	3.0	6.7	6.04	5.68	12.9	1.4	10.5	3.6	101.0	10.7	55.4	63.4	58.0	...	105.9	15.6
Principal Lines of Business: OrdLife (76.9%), IndAnn (18.4%), GrpLife (2.1%), GrpA&H (1.9%), IndA&H (0.3%)														Principal States: PA (44.7%), MD (8.8%), FL (4.6%), TX (4.5%)					
...	41.6	55.6	14.2	30.0	22.8	3.74	3.82	-7.5	52.6	173.6	...	...	7.9	225.2	216.1	...	...	...	...
...	47.6	36.3	17.5	46.7	28.5	3.97	4.02	-23.7	37.3	149.2	...	...	7.5	194.4	187.2	...	...	...	...
-1,193	133.2	-52.5	24.0	32.9	33.3	4.36	4.44	138.3	79.7	761.0	...	...	11.7	825.8	725.2	...	...	...	...
5,337	51.0	14.4	29.1	52.0	33.3	4.44	4.48	-51.6	59.6	632.5	...	...	-35.2	690.5	644.1	...	...	...	...
2,564	45.3	29.0	33.5	48.4	38.3	2.31	2.29	-3.4	52.9	774.7	...	...	8.8	823.9	643.7	...	...	...	...
...	80.7	27.7	-1.4	-6.7	-20.4	5.70	6.01	-2.4	1.7	8.6	...	0.1	51.3	71.5	85.2	...	...	...	...
...	78.5	26.7	-7.8	-46.0	-99.9	5.20	5.45	-1.4	1.6	6.8	...	0.1	5.1	85.4	98.6	...	...	...	...
...	80.1	29.9	-6.9	-43.6	-92.2	5.56	5.41	4.4	1.2	9.8	...	0.6	41.9	59.6	73.1	2.6	...	...	...
...	74.8	31.7	3.2	18.1	31.9	6.11	5.28	12.9	1.1	12.3	...	0.3	29.1	64.5	78.1	5.1	...	...	...
...	67.7	31.1	-1.2	-6.5	-12.4	5.78	5.57	19.2	1.4	9.9	...	0.2	-10.2	60.1	73.5	16.0	...	...	...
Principal Lines of Business: OrdLife (49.0%), IndA&H (28.7%), IndAnn (22.3%), GrpLife (0.0%)														Principal States: NY (98.0%)					
-214	68.7	28.0	4.4	7.2	14.8	5.36	5.24	-1.9	1.8	46.0	...	0.4	-3.6	89.0	99.6	34.9	0.1	5.3	...
-17	70.8	30.1	3.4	6.1	11.5	5.73	5.07	-11.1	1.6	47.1	...	0.6	-0.9	106.4	116.0	15.4	0.1	3.8	...
-14,032	65.5	31.7	3.4	6.5	11.9	5.72	1.26	-4.1	1.6	40.2	...	1.0	-6.8	125.9	131.1	16.3	0.1	0.1	...
-1,799	70.3	31.8	2.5	4.8	9.2	5.73	2.60	-1.4	1.8	37.3	...	0.4	-12.6	92.1	97.4	14.5	0.1	0.1	...
904	69.7	33.2	2.1	3.8	7.8	5.34	6.32	3.6	1.8	38.4	...	0.4	7.1	94.2	101.2	7.5	0.1	0.1	...
Principal Lines of Business: IndA&H (80.6%), OrdLife (18.2%), GrpA&H (0.8%), IndAnn (0.4%), GrpLife (0.0%)														Principal States: PA (15.2%), GA (14.3%), OH (11.2%), IN (8.1%), UT (6.0%)					
1,002	57.9	19.6	0.2	0.7	4.0	5.80	6.06	4.6	3.7	7.6	3.6	71.9	36.2	59.1	73.7	52.3	...	67.6	4.0
1,297	61.9	18.7	0.6	1.8	9.2	6.01	6.11	9.2	3.7	7.6	2.8	66.3	10.7	56.3	71.4	65.0	...	82.7	9.6
-2,382	73.2	18.6	1.2	3.9	18.9	5.87	5.79	4.7	3.6	7.6	2.6	65.9	7.1	51.3	67.4	76.9	...	114.8	7.8
-1,360	70.0	14.5	0.7	2.2	12.4	5.26	4.27	11.1	4.7	5.8	19.5	83.8	-16.3	47.2	62.3	127.3	1.3	174.5	11.9
-6,203	69.8	13.9	1.6	5.5	28.4	6.11	5.12	-9.3	3.7	6.4	22.6	87.4	17.9	47.1	63.4	72.0	1.9	133.4	6.4
Principal Lines of Business: IndA&H (48.0%), IndAnn (42.1%), OrdLife (8.5%), GrpA&H (1.4%), GrpLife (0.0%)														Principal States: FL (8.1%), PA (6.6%), CA (5.8%), NC (4.8%), TX (4.8%)					
1,121	258.1	23.8	0.8	7.4	12.0	6.50	7.42	-47.0	0.3	8.9	32.2	130.6	26.7	62.7	76.8	83.9	...	0.7	18.1
-530	35.7	11.5	-0.5	-1.3	-7.8	6.36	5.70	999.9	5.3	5.8	5.3	92.5	-15.8	67.4	80.2	61.8	...	0.7	22.2
-796	58.5	8.5	-0.1	-0.1	-1.1	6.57	6.31	34.7	6.8	5.1	1.3	28.4	4.6	71.4	83.4	60.0	...	10.5	...
-199	41.0	10.2	1.3	4.2	28.0	7.51	6.96	-25.3	4.9	4.4	0.5	7.0	4.2	69.3	80.3	198.2	...	10.2	...
-20	160.2	16.5	1.4	7.9	29.2	7.66	5.59	-47.5	2.0	5.8	0.1	4.5	27.6	72.7	86.2	41.5	...	7.9	...
Principal Lines of Business: IndAnn (99.5%), IndA&H (0.5%), OrdLife (0.0%)														Principal States: TX (23.3%), FL (19.8%), UT (9.8%), PA (6.0%), MO (5.9%)					
0	57.7	51.8	0.7	3.5	9.2	...	...	-5.4	1.6	10.3	3.5	...	6.8	...	...	...	...	148.5	...
0	63.1	54.2	0.2	1.0	2.4	...	...	-5.4	1.5	10.4	4.1	...	2.9	...	...	...	...	141.3	...
-1	86.2	59.0	1.1	5.9	13.4	...	...	0.0	1.4	11.5	2.6	...	10.6	...	...	...	...	126.6	...
-64	71.4	66.4	0.3	1.4	2.4	...	...	4.0	1.0	17.7	1.2	...	43.7	...	...	...	...	127.7	...
42	74.6	77.1	-0.6	-2.5	-4.1	...	...	4.0	1.0	17.8	1.8	...	-0.9	...	...	...	...	129.2	...
Principal Lines of Business: OrdLife (99.5%), IndLife (0.5%)																			
27	25.4	79.2	5.1	5.3	11.1	4.26	4.62	4.9	0.8	86.1	123.9	117.9	-4.5	141.4	154.4	1.8	...	...	...
20	21.5	83.7	2.9	2.8	6.2	4.32	4.84	4.5	0.8	86.6	125.0	128.3	8.1	149.2	162.1	1.6	...	...	...
17	18.9	78.8	6.0	6.2	12.8	4.18	4.40	-2.4	0.7	93.7	116.2	119.6	15.6	189.4	203.5	2.8	...	...	...
-234	16.0	47.0	17.4	11.9	39.5	3.37	2.45	63.0	3.1	56.5	314.4	278.3	-65.5	147.2	161.2	0.4	...	...	0.0
243	19.0	81.4	4.8	2.4	14.9	3.50	4.88	-18.8	3.8	39.9	372.3	418.5	-32.8	130.8	143.9	...	...	...	...
Principal Lines of Business: CrdLife (60.8%), IndA&H (25.8%), CrdA&H (13.3%), OrdLife (0.0%)														Principal States: LA (100.0%)					
...	72.3	14.9	25.5	10.1	60.9	4.05	4.05	54.8	5.1	89.9	...	1.0	35.4	207.5	221.3	...	...	...	...
...	77.6	14.1	15.4	6.5	32.6	4.05	4.05	15.7	4.2	88.3	...	4.5	40.9	187.8	201.8	...	...	...	...
-186	69.9	16.3	16.7	9.1	35.8	3.52	3.30	3.1	3.5	86.3	...	2.1	24.3	150.2	160.2	...	...	...	...
-29	81.5	15.3	6.9	2.1	15.3	3.24	3.17	130.5	6.5	78.1	...	4.7	23.7	164.9	178.4	0.1	...	...	...
-286	87.2	13.3	5.1	1.4	11.0	1.84	1.83	21.1	8.1	96.7	...	3.0	-2.8	185.5	198.5	6.0	...	...	...
Principal Lines of Business: CompHosp/Med (100.0%)														Principal States: TX (100.0%)					

2010 BEST'S KEY RATING GUIDE — LIFE/HEALTH EDITION
ANNUAL STATEMENT DATA FOR YEARS 2005 – 2009

Data in U.S. Dollars

COMPANY NAME Ultimate Parent Association Principal Officer Mailing Address Dom. : Began Bus. : Struct. : Mktg. Specialty Phone # AMB# NAIC#	Best's Financial Strength Rating FSC	Data Year	Balance Sheet Bonds (%)	Mort. Loans & R.E. (%)	Com & Pref. Stock (%)	All Other Assets (%)	Total Assets ($000)	Life Reserves (%)	Health Reserves %)	Ann Res. & Dep. Liabilities (%)	All Other Liabilities (%)	Capital & Surplus ($000)	Operations Direct Premiums Written ($000)	Net Premiums Written & Deposits ($000)	Operating Cash Flow ($000)	NOG Before Taxes ($000)	NOG After Taxes ($000)	Net Income ($000)
BANNER LIFE INS CO Legal & General Group plc James D. Atkins President & CEO 1701 Research Boulevard Rockville, MD 20850 MD : 1981 : Stock : Broker Ind Life, Ind Ann 301-279-4800 AMB# 006468 NAIC# 94250	A+ Rating Outlook: Stable FSC IX	'05	71.4	...	9.9	18.7	1,200,951	88.1	0.0	5.3	6.6	232,270	439,965	229,513	45,812	-67,241	-62,737	-62,737
		'06	69.6	...	10.4	20.0	1,226,386	88.7	0.0	4.1	7.2	183,196	479,978	245,718	25,593	-45,201	-43,874	-43,874
		'07	71.1	...	10.5	18.5	1,293,366	76.3	0.0	3.3	20.4	225,446	528,058	106,812	175,273	-470,839	-475,565	-476,605
		'08	72.7	...	9.2	18.2	1,335,175	75.0	0.0	2.8	22.2	211,272	571,027	194,940	44,918	1,590	173	-16,081
		'09	68.9	...	9.2	21.9	1,414,139	73.2	0.0	2.7	24.2	311,310	603,758	206,942	20,738	102,991	102,096	101,261
		Rating History: A+ g, 05/03/10; A+ g, 03/25/09; A+ g, 01/25/08; A+ g, 02/02/07; A+ g, 12/02/05																
BCBSD INC[2] Timothy J. Constantine President 800 Delaware Avenue Wilmington, DE 19801-1368 DE : 1935 : Non-Profit : Broker Health 302-421-3000 AMB# 068578 NAIC# 53287	NR-5	'05	60.3	1.0	14.8	24.0	246,289	...	35.5	...	64.5	132,715	370,057	370,057	12,325	13,761	12,711	14,650
		'06	...	...	...	...	...	...	...	...	...	...	...	...	...	...	...	...
		'07	67.4	0.1	7.7	24.8	274,858	...	38.9	...	61.1	160,002	463,849	457,670	14,595	12,062	8,955	15,525
		'08	68.1	0.1	7.4	24.5	245,310	...	0.2	...	99.8	120,807	483,789	477,183	-32,815	-9,972	-5,744	-16,749
		'09	67.3	0.1	14.0	18.6	261,989	...	0.2	...	99.8	139,689	482,122	482,122	13,688	1,913	190	827
		Rating History: NR-5, 04/19/10; NR-5, 09/21/09; NR-5, 07/02/08; NR-5, 09/19/07; B++pd, 09/25/06																
BCI HMO INC Health Care Svc Corp Mut Legal Reserve Patricia Hemingway Hall President & CEO 300 East Randolph Street Chicago, IL 60601-5099 IL : 1984 : Stock : Broker Ind A&H 312-653-6000 AMB# 068658 NAIC# 96814	NR-3	'05	73.5	...	...	26.5	8,024	...	24.5	...	75.5	7,567	294	81	-769	110	81	81
		'06	54.2	...	...	45.8	7,181	...	...	...	100.0	6,956	238	43	-679	195	141	141
		'07	33.8	...	...	66.2	6,508	...	...	...	100.0	6,443	...	...	-675	188	177	177
		'08	8.5	...	...	91.5	5,889	...	...	...	100.0	5,862	...	...	-588	68	59	59
		'09	9.5	...	...	90.5	5,276	...	...	...	100.0	5,253	...	...	-612	-36	-29	-29
		Rating History: NR-3, 01/27/10; NR-3, 12/22/08; NR-3, 11/01/07; NR-3, 08/10/06; NR-3, 11/01/05																
BCS INSURANCE COMPANY BCS Financial Corporation H. F. (Scott) Beacham III President & CEO 2 Mid America Plaza, Suite 200 Oakbrook Terrace, IL 60181 OH : 1952 : Stock : Mng Gen Agent Stop Loss, D&O Liability, E&O Liability 630-472-7700 AMB# 003251 NAIC# 38245	A- Rating Outlook: Stable FSC VIII	'05	71.6	...	1.4	27.0	225,221	...	39.7	...	60.3	130,117	210,437	77,189	4,548	11,442	7,342	7,403
		'06	70.3	...	1.4	28.2	227,984	...	35.9	...	64.1	136,668	235,765	82,567	502	13,027	8,351	8,392
		'07	73.4	...	1.5	25.1	221,833	...	42.9	...	57.1	141,290	249,649	101,510	1,846	17,923	11,614	11,348
		'08	71.5	...	1.5	27.0	221,788	...	46.3	...	53.7	140,557	210,079	111,998	-649	15,818	10,369	6,904
		'09	70.8	...	1.5	27.7	220,245	...	40.9	...	59.1	140,423	192,074	106,971	-3,026	4,933	3,393	3,069
		Rating History: A-, 03/23/10; A-, 05/14/09; A-, 05/28/08; A-, 02/05/07; A-, 06/02/06																
BCS LIFE INSURANCE CO BCS Financial Corporation H. F. Beacham III Chairman, President & CEO 2 Mid America Plaza, Suite 200 Oakbrook Terrace, IL 60181 IL : 1949 : Stock : Broker Group A&H, Group Life, Disability 630-472-7700 AMB# 007363 NAIC# 80985	A- Rating Outlook: Stable FSC VII	'05	70.2	...	...	29.8	166,681	13.0	71.6	...	15.5	72,799	201,207	196,354	11,373	6,958	4,946	5,207
		'06	71.2	...	...	28.8	170,401	13.5	71.8	...	14.6	76,385	206,026	209,440	-144	7,782	5,295	5,496
		'07	69.4	...	...	30.6	196,902	11.0	73.1	...	15.8	80,547	204,157	207,618	19,675	10,984	7,629	7,326
		'08	73.6	...	...	26.4	180,558	14.0	73.7	...	12.4	79,727	190,619	200,941	-4,427	3,812	3,668	1,114
		'09	77.1	...	...	22.9	181,394	14.5	72.7	...	12.9	80,566	179,163	188,551	-1,435	3,326	2,907	2,435
		Rating History: A-, 03/23/10; A-, 05/14/09; A-, 06/05/08; A-, 02/05/07; A-, 01/25/06																
BENEFICIAL LIFE INS CO DMC Reserve Trust Kirby Brown President & CEO 150 E. Social Hall Avenue, Suite 500 Salt Lake City, UT 84111-1578 UT : 1905 : Stock : Career Agent Ind Life, Group Life 801-933-1100 AMB# 006162 NAIC# 61395	A- Rating Outlook: Negative FSC IX	'05	90.0	0.5	2.5	7.0	3,093,072	41.7	0.2	47.9	10.2	254,789	420,245	409,159	224,136	42,547	27,655	25,387
		'06	89.3	0.3	2.6	7.8	3,678,738	36.6	0.2	53.6	9.5	279,092	515,194	855,762	565,563	32,072	22,397	29,064
		'07	88.1	0.3	3.3	8.3	3,559,646	38.9	0.1	51.8	9.2	341,146	490,340	338,777	-126,901	58,425	43,905	-174,467
		'08	88.3	0.3	0.7	10.7	3,437,234	43.0	0.1	53.1	3.8	451,321	439,796	375,629	-135,475	74,926	91,159	-239,733
		'09	91.0	...	0.7	8.3	3,446,437	43.4	0.1	52.6	3.9	478,068	358,174	311,263	49,466	45,369	33,493	10,480
		Rating History: A-, 06/17/09; A, 01/21/09; A, 11/20/07; A u, 10/23/07; A, 11/22/06																
BERKLEY LIFE AND HEALTH INS CO W. R. Berkley Corporation Christopher C. Brown President 475 Steamboat Road Greenwich, CT 06830 IA : 1963 : Stock : Agency Ind Ann, Ind Life 203-542-3800 AMB# 006579 NAIC# 64890	A+ Rating Outlook: Stable FSC VI	'05	79.3	...	...	20.7	7,660	...	20.4	...	79.6	7,446	634	245	116	140	91	91
		'06	74.6	...	...	25.4	7,825	...	15.4	...	84.6	7,632	506	223	-584	206	143	143
		'07	42.5	...	...	57.5	25,443	...	...	...	100.0	25,200	312	100	18,421	81	66	66
		'08	59.5	...	...	40.5	26,100	...	...	...	100.0	25,717	296	33	439	601	565	565
		'09	74.8	...	...	25.2	26,630	...	...	...	100.0	26,210	263	112	548	652	569	569
		Rating History: A+, 04/30/10; NR-2, 06/22/09; NR-2, 06/16/08; NR-2, 04/23/07; NR-5, 11/16/06																
BERKSHIRE HATHAWAY LIFE OF NE Berkshire Hathaway Inc Donald F. Wurster President 3024 Harney Street Omaha, NE 68131-3580 NE : 1993 : Stock : Direct Response Ann 402-916-3000 AMB# 060060 NAIC# 62345	A++ Rating Outlook: Stable FSC XV	'05	52.5	...	23.8	23.7	3,369,431	7.3	...	85.2	7.5	479,117	866	185,591	-17,356	74,970	56,470	58,429
		'06	47.5	...	22.4	30.1	3,757,507	4.6	...	85.3	10.0	861,984	1,735	140,882	350,367	115,935	64,591	353,122
		'07	55.4	...	22.4	22.2	3,658,554	2.5	...	90.4	7.1	858,078	2,297	99,218	-91,084	82,090	55,597	56,743
		'08	72.9	...	22.7	4.4	3,528,028	...	0.1	93.3	6.6	810,409	510	57,855	-38,048	99,827	70,144	70,144
		'09	43.4	...	17.1	39.5	7,624,963	36.6	0.0	38.7	24.7	1,032,640	469	2,338,938	159,094	-1,298,669	-876,628	-878,576
		Rating History: A++, 05/06/10; A++u, 11/06/09; A++, 05/22/09; A++g, 04/29/08; A++g, 05/16/07																
BERKSHIRE LIFE INS CO OF AMER Guardian Life Ins Co of America Joan E. Bancroft President 700 South Street Pittsfield, MA 01201 MA : 2001 : Stock : Not Available Dis inc 413-499-4321 AMB# 007409 NAIC# 71714	A++ Rating Outlook: Stable FSC XV	'05	78.6	13.1	0.2	8.1	1,971,977	1.2	91.0	...	7.8	296,063	151,941	357,899	205,417	43,603	35,540	41,229
		'06	78.8	13.6	0.0	7.6	2,139,102	1.4	91.3	...	7.3	345,376	190,801	379,492	151,611	79,873	52,147	59,156
		'07	80.0	13.7	0.0	6.2	2,292,683	1.6	91.6	...	6.8	386,608	239,132	402,390	152,917	98,291	62,095	62,008
		'08	78.4	13.6	0.0	8.0	2,455,455	1.7	92.2	...	6.1	423,850	276,960	419,299	167,479	63,324	36,474	28,652
		'09	82.4	12.4	0.0	5.2	2,626,861	1.8	92.9	...	5.3	452,274	312,244	445,553	181,136	59,242	37,790	33,987
		Rating History: A++g, 10/13/09; A++g, 11/26/08; A+ g, 04/23/08; A+ g, 11/10/06; A+ g, 11/18/05																

BEST'S PROFITABILITY, LEVERAGE AND LIQUIDITY TESTS 2005 – 2009

Data in U.S. Dollars

—	Profitability Tests							Leverage Tests						Liquidity Tests						
Un-Realized Capital Gains ($000)	Benefits Paid to NPW & Dep (%)	Comm. & Expenses to NPW & Dep (%)	NOG to Total Assets (%)	NOG to Total Rev (%)	Operating Return on Equity (%)	Net Yield (%)	Total Return (%)	Change in NPW & Dep (%)	NPW & Dep to Capital (X)	Capital & Surplus to Liabilities (%)	Surplus Relief (%)	Reins Leverage (%)	Change in Capital (%)	Quick Liquidity (%)	Current Liquidity (%)	Non-Invest Grade Bonds to Capital (%)	Delinq. & Foreclosed Mortgages to Capital (%)	Mort. & Credit Tenant Loans & R.E. to Capital (%)	Affiliated Invest to Capital (%)
5,875	58.4	53.3	-5.3	-18.4	-22.7	4.86	5.68	0.6	1.0	25.0	12.7	450.1	-27.8	71.4	81.1	...	...	...	50.4
-18,379	52.6	47.5	-3.6	-12.0	-21.1	4.95	3.41	7.1	1.3	18.5	23.4	768.9	-20.3	66.9	75.5	5.2	...	...	64.2
-69,087	145.4	122.2	-37.7	-99.9	-99.9	4.55	-1.53	-56.5	0.5	21.8	20.2	871.7	21.2	71.3	81.8	4.3	...	...	48.5
-14,615	67.3	65.5	0.0	0.1	0.1	4.20	1.59	82.5	0.9	19.1	34.4	999.9	-7.1	70.8	80.8	2.9	...	...	45.4
1,011	50.8	55.4	7.4	30.0	39.1	6.37	6.49	6.2	0.7	29.0	24.1	781.5	47.7	71.6	81.1	9.2	...	...	39.7
	Principal Lines of Business: OrdLife (99.2%), IndAnn (0.7%), GrpLife (0.1%), IndA&H (0.0%)													Principal States: CA (11.6%), NJ (8.6%), FL (7.8%), PA (6.2%), TX (5.1%)					
-1,612	85.5	12.8	5.4	3.4	9.7	4.14	4.32	21.8	2.8	116.9	...	...	3.4	130.2	141.0	2.2	...	1.9	2.4
...	...	...	...	...	...	...	...	...	...	...	...	...	...	...	...	...	...	...	...
-4,977	84.8	14.1	...	1.9	...	...	...	...	2.9	139.3	...	...	...	155.4	166.0	0.2	...	0.1	0.8
-4,031	89.6	14.6	-2.2	-1.2	-4.1	4.68	-2.27	4.3	3.9	97.0	...	...	-24.5	121.2	130.8	0.3	...	0.2	1.1
8,105	87.6	14.0	0.1	0.0	0.1	4.53	8.88	1.0	3.5	114.2	...	...	15.6	137.9	150.6	1.4	...	0.2	0.3
	Principal Lines of Business: CompHosp/Med (76.6%), FEHBP (17.4%), MedSup (3.8%), OtherHlth (1.5%), Dental (0.7%)													Principal States: DE (100.0%)					
...	141.1	142.7	1.0	26.0	1.0	2.96	2.96	-63.5	0.0	999.9	...	2.8	-8.7	999.9	999.9	...	...	...	...
...	154.0	117.2	1.9	37.9	1.9	4.19	4.19	-47.3	0.0	999.9	...	0.1	-8.1	999.9	999.9	...	...	...	...
...	...	...	2.6	57.0	2.6	4.67	4.67	-99.9	...	999.9	...	...	-7.4	999.9	999.9	...	...	...	...
...	...	...	1.0	38.1	1.0	2.57	2.57	...	...	999.9	...	...	-9.0	999.9	999.9	...	...	...	...
...	...	...	-0.5	-69.9	-0.5	0.75	0.75	...	...	999.9	...	...	-10.4	999.9	999.9	...	...	...	...
223	58.7	-14.8	3.3	8.8	5.8	4.64	4.80	38.4	0.6	136.8	29.0	145.6	5.1	150.2	165.6	...	...	...	2.4
126	56.5	-18.2	3.7	9.5	6.3	5.34	5.44	7.0	0.6	149.7	31.8	149.9	5.0	158.7	175.0	0.1	...	...	2.4
-38	61.0	-9.6	5.2	9.8	8.4	5.34	5.17	22.9	0.7	175.4	34.5	146.5	3.4	179.3	197.9	0.4	...	...	2.6
-127	59.3	6.7	4.7	8.3	7.4	4.90	2.89	10.3	0.8	173.0	25.2	111.6	-0.5	170.5	188.2	1.2	...	...	2.5
60	70.9	6.2	1.5	2.9	2.4	5.01	4.86	-4.5	0.8	175.9	20.7	101.0	-0.1	178.9	198.0	...	...	...	3.2
	Principal Lines of Business: GrpA&H (97.7%)													Principal States: RI (13.8%), NY (11.3%), CA (7.8%), TX (7.3%), FL (5.2%)					
-10	84.0	15.1	3.1	2.4	6.9	4.09	4.51	11.1	2.7	78.6	4.1	12.4	4.3	121.3	133.5	2.8	...	...	...
-1	83.2	15.1	3.1	2.4	7.1	4.30	4.66	6.7	2.7	82.2	4.4	14.6	4.8	120.8	133.2	1.4	...	...	...
16	71.1	16.3	4.2	3.4	9.7	4.56	4.73	-0.9	2.6	69.8	5.7	14.4	5.3	114.9	126.3	1.8	...	...	6.3
...	84.4	16.7	1.9	1.7	4.6	4.13	2.81	-3.2	2.5	79.1	5.0	14.7	-1.5	126.9	142.3	1.5	...	...	7.1
...	85.2	18.2	1.6	1.5	3.6	4.29	4.19	-6.2	2.3	81.2	4.7	12.6	2.0	124.7	138.2	3.5	...	...	1.2
	Principal Lines of Business: GrpA&H (95.7%), GrpLife (4.3%), OrdLife (0.0%)													Principal States: MI (84.8%), PA (4.3%)					
1,558	68.6	18.6	0.9	4.6	11.3	6.86	6.93	2.6	1.5	9.9	1.3	24.2	10.9	62.0	74.8	45.1	...	5.0	0.0
6,590	48.4	9.4	0.7	3.2	8.4	6.40	6.89	109.2	2.8	9.2	1.3	20.4	11.9	66.2	78.8	37.1	...	3.8	...
-1,234	127.6	17.3	1.2	6.5	14.2	6.73	0.58	-60.4	0.9	11.2	5.6	32.6	15.0	63.9	76.5	43.4	...	2.8	0.5
-26,249	122.1	11.9	2.6	13.9	23.0	6.71	-3.26	10.9	0.8	15.4	6.5	30.9	28.1	59.3	73.9	55.4	...	2.4	0.5
-4,026	144.9	17.5	1.0	6.1	7.2	6.30	5.69	-17.1	0.6	16.3	3.2	33.2	5.5	62.9	77.0	68.5	...	...	0.4
	Principal Lines of Business: IndAnn (78.3%), OrdLife (20.5%), GrpLife (1.1%), GrpAnn (0.0%), GrpA&H (0.0%)													Principal States: UT (35.9%), ID (15.2%), CA (12.8%), WA (8.0%), OR (5.1%)					
...	40.5	95.1	1.2	16.1	1.2	3.91	4.13	12.4	0.0	999.9	1.3	36.9	1.2	999.9	999.9	...	...	...	...
...	38.2	68.2	1.9	27.2	1.9	3.65	3.81	-9.0	0.0	999.9	1.1	35.3	2.5	999.9	999.9	...	...	...	...
...	...	182.6	0.4	19.3	0.4	1.52	1.59	-55.2	0.0	999.9	0.3	10.2	230.0	999.9	999.9	...	...	...	...
...	...	766.1	2.2	60.6	2.2	3.26	3.39	-66.6	0.0	999.9	0.3	9.7	2.1	999.9	999.9	...	...	...	...
1	...	176.2	2.2	61.9	2.2	3.13	3.29	237.8	0.0	999.9	0.3	9.1	2.0	999.9	999.9	...	...	...	...
	Principal Lines of Business: IndAnn (78.3%), GrpAnn (21.7%)													Principal States: WA (32.9%), PA (23.1%), VA (14.2%), MO (7.9%), NC (5.4%)					
9,670	192.0	0.5	1.6	16.0	10.8	4.77	5.41	-8.1	0.3	20.2	...	0.2	-10.6	84.6	90.5	53.1	...	...	141.0
-233,340	224.5	0.7	1.8	19.6	9.6	5.22	7.57	-24.1	0.1	35.6	...	0.1	74.0	108.7	114.5	28.9	...	...	87.7
-18,405	279.2	2.9	1.5	19.3	6.5	5.02	4.79	-29.6	0.1	35.9	...	0.0	-2.0	73.5	81.2	26.7	...	...	89.3
-18,566	411.7	1.5	2.0	28.4	8.4	5.21	4.89	-41.7	0.1	35.3	...	...	-4.7	49.0	56.9	84.0	...	...	91.1
-8,816	25.2	57.4	-15.7	-33.4	-95.1	6.79	6.71	999.9	2.0	18.2	0.1	227.6	27.7	27.6	33.0	76.1	...	...	113.2
	Principal Lines of Business: OrdLife (100.0%), IndAnn (0.0%)													Principal States: AZ (48.1%), AK (12.5%), NJ (11.6%), GA (9.6%), PA (9.3%)					
733	38.7	45.1	1.9	6.9	12.8	6.70	7.11	5.0	1.1	18.9	11.3	60.9	14.7	50.0	66.0	13.9	...	83.2	2.1
-1,610	39.5	45.1	2.5	9.6	16.3	6.54	6.87	6.0	1.0	20.3	10.3	67.4	15.2	48.9	66.2	2.2	...	80.7	1.7
31	41.1	45.7	2.8	10.6	17.0	6.46	6.49	6.0	1.0	21.2	11.8	69.4	11.0	47.4	66.1	1.7	...	80.1	1.6
305	41.8	44.9	1.5	6.0	9.0	6.33	6.03	4.2	1.0	21.5	10.6	78.5	8.2	50.6	68.1	8.6	...	78.3	1.4
-577	43.7	45.3	1.5	5.9	8.6	6.25	6.09	6.3	1.0	21.4	10.0	88.2	6.4	43.8	63.3	14.4	...	70.5	1.3
	Principal Lines of Business: IndA&H (99.6%), OrdLife (0.4%)													Principal States: NY (16.4%), NJ (8.5%), FL (5.7%), TX (4.8%), MA (4.8%)					

2010 BEST'S KEY RATING GUIDE — LIFE/HEALTH EDITION
ANNUAL STATEMENT DATA FOR YEARS 2005 – 2009
Data in U.S. Dollars

COMPANY NAME Ultimate Parent Association Principal Officer Mailing Address Dom. : Began Bus. : Struct. : Mktg. Specialty Phone # AMB# NAIC#	Best's Financial Strength Rating FSC		Balance Sheet										Operations					
		Data Year	Bonds (%)	Mort. Loans & R.E. (%)	Com & Pref. Stock (%)	All Other Assets (%)	Total Assets ($000)	Life Reserves (%)	Health Reserves %)	Ann Res. & Dep. Liabilities (%)	All Other Liabilities (%)	Capital & Surplus ($000)	Direct Premiums Written ($000)	Net Premiums Written & Deposits ($000)	Operating Cash Flow ($000)	NOG Before Taxes ($000)	NOG After Taxes ($000)	Net Income ($000)
BERMUDA INTL INS SERVICES LTD BF&M Limited P.O. Box HM 1007 Hamilton, HM DX, Bermuda BM : Stock 441-292-2447 AMB# 071194	NR-5	'05	...	...	...	100.0	4,086	...	...	...	100.0	3,705	...	...	-907	-1,270	-1,270	-1,270
		'06	86.4	...	...	13.7	17,452	23.8	...	...	76.2	16,573	...	625	-2,083	-2,386	-2,386	-2,386
		'07	65.5	...	...	34.5	20,676	-0.2	...	...	100.2	15,995	...	566	-1,020	-696	-696	-973
		'08	40.8	12.6	...	46.6	22,317	-3.2	...	...	103.2	13,216	...	37	-1,946	-2,588	-2,588	-2,778
		'09	33.9	7.9	...	58.3	23,881	-4.2	...	...	104.2	12,522	...	-31	-154	-472	-472	-694
		Rating History: NR-5, 07/02/09; NR-5, 08/26/08																
BERMUDA LIFE INS CO LTD Argus Group Holdings Limited Gerald D. E. Simons President & CEO Argus Building, 12 Wesley St Hamilton HM EX, Bermuda BM : 1957 : Stock : Not Available Life, Ann, Pension 441-295-2021 AMB# 086636	A- Rating Outlook: Negative FSC VIII	'05	34.0	2.2	44.5	19.3	305,647	97.1	...	...	2.9	105,807	...	...	...	-1,339	-1,339	-1,609
		'06	31.9	9.9	55.2	3.1	331,283	95.6	...	...	4.4	123,295	...	...	...	2,427	2,427	1,807
		'07	29.4	9.8	58.6	2.1	371,161	97.0	...	...	3.0	146,727	...	...	...	3,825	3,825	4,046
		'08	32.1	8.2	57.4	2.3	367,392	97.7	...	...	2.3	129,498	...	...	...	-4,004	-4,004	-3,803
		'09	44.0	10.1	32.2	13.7	293,947	97.9	...	...	2.2	22,218	...	...	...	6,235	6,235	5,488
		Rating History: A- g, 07/02/09; A g, 10/17/06; A g, 12/17/04; A g, 09/30/03; A gu, 09/08/03																
BERMUDA LIFE WORLDWIDE LIMITED Argus Group Holdings Limited Gerald D.E. Simons President & CEO Argus Building, 12 Wesley Street Hamilton HM EX, Bermuda BM : Stock : Not Available Life 441-295-2021 AMB# 084137	NR-5	'05	20.7	19.0	...	60.3	26,362	93.2	...	...	6.8	8,360	...	771	...	254	254	254
		'06	21.3	37.6	...	41.2	26,538	98.5	...	...	1.5	8,643	...	728	...	181	181	181
		'07	22.2	36.5	...	41.3	27,721	98.3	...	...	1.8	9,398	...	596	...	216	216	216
		'08	21.4	66.4	...	12.2	30,567	91.6	...	...	8.4	10,008	...	282	...	-68	-68	762
		'09	19.5	64.2	...	16.3	31,172	88.4	...	...	11.6	9,676	...	-86	...	532	532	-60
		Rating History: NR-5, 06/17/09; NR-5, 06/03/03; NR-5, 03/01/02; NR-5, 12/04/00																
BEST LIFE AND HEALTH INS CO Lawrenz Family Trust Donald R. Lawrenz Chairman, President & CEO P.O. Box 19721 Irvine, CA 92623-9721 TX : 1964 : Stock : Broker Dental, Group A&H, Stop Loss 949-253-4080 AMB# 007246 NAIC# 90638	B Rating Outlook: Negative FSC IV	'05	61.4	...	2.1	36.6	19,101	8.8	66.9	...	24.3	10,036	32,341	36,133	376	949	744	744
		'06	65.7	...	1.2	33.1	16,871	9.4	75.1	...	15.5	10,301	35,263	39,656	-1,654	341	261	261
		'07	62.0	6.7	1.0	30.3	16,881	10.4	70.1	...	19.5	10,703	39,641	41,833	1,667	518	404	404
		'08	56.8	6.7	1.9	34.5	16,671	10.4	76.4	...	13.2	9,814	48,285	48,405	-398	-720	-670	-670
		'09	60.4	7.6	4.0	28.0	14,731	8.0	76.3	...	15.7	8,198	44,686	46,687	-2,212	-1,727	-1,613	-1,736
		Rating History: B, 04/20/10; B+, 04/22/09; B+, 04/28/08; B+, 05/03/07; B+, 04/14/06																
BEST MERIDIAN INS CO BMI Financial Group, Inc. Anthony F. Sierra President & CEO 1320 S. Dixie Highway, 6th Floor Coral Gables, FL 33146 FL : 1987 : Stock : Agency Ind Life, Term Life, Univ Life 305-443-2898 AMB# 060007 NAIC# 63886	B++ Rating Outlook: Positive FSC VI	'05	71.6	0.4	...	27.9	125,643	65.4	13.9	0.7	20.0	15,516	53,293	42,209	11,875	362	138	138
		'06	80.0	0.9	...	19.1	139,580	65.5	13.3	0.6	20.6	20,096	51,772	41,551	14,082	5,857	4,237	4,245
		'07	77.4	1.3	1.8	19.5	153,192	65.2	14.0	0.5	20.2	22,964	57,047	46,873	15,386	3,975	3,545	3,516
		'08	79.2	1.2	0.1	19.6	164,787	82.9	12.2	0.5	4.5	27,541	61,134	73,501	10,311	11,860	7,021	3,718
		'09	71.3	6.7	...	22.0	181,776	83.4	12.8	0.4	3.5	32,864	64,979	60,667	12,513	8,893	6,309	5,808
		Rating History: B++, 01/15/10; B++, 06/18/09; B++, 06/19/08; B++, 06/01/07; B++, 05/01/06																
BEST MERIDIAN INTL INS CO SPC BMI Financial Group, Inc. Anthony F. Sierra President & CEO P.O. Box 32345 SMB Grand Cayman, Cayman Islands KY : 1994 : Stock : General Agent Life, Disability, Annuity 305-443-2898 AMB# 086911	B++ Rating Outlook: Stable FSC V	'05	...	...	3.1	96.9	34,909	11.4	...	...	88.6	7,152	...	3,136	2,484	1,494	1,494	1,494
		'06	...	...	3.9	96.1	43,520	17.4	...	...	82.6	9,808	...	3,725	2,330	2,120	2,120	2,120
		'07	...	...	6.2	93.8	50,008	19.9	...	...	80.1	12,294	...	3,966	4,723	2,686	2,686	2,686
		'08	...	...	0.9	99.2	66,550	17.2	...	...	82.8	14,008	...	5,629	1,318	1,747	1,747	1,747
		'09	...	...	...	...	...	...	...	...	...	...	...	...	...	...	...	...
		Rating History: B++, 01/15/10; B++, 06/18/09; B+, 06/19/08; B+, 06/01/07; B+, 05/01/06																
BETTER LIFE AND HEALTH COMPANY Robert J. Leaf President & Treasurer 277 North Avenue, 2nd Floor New Rochelle, NY 10801 AZ : 1994 : Stock : Not Available Dental, Reins 917-712-0600 AMB# 060102 NAIC# 60032	NR-5	'05	54.1	...	23.2	22.7	1,334	...	...	...	100.0	1,208	...	...	38	-28	-28	-28
		'06	63.1	...	22.2	14.7	1,201	...	...	...	100.0	1,068	...	...	505	678	660	660
		'07	37.9	...	9.4	52.8	2,568	...	...	...	100.0	2,475	...	...	141	-168	-176	-176
		'08	70.4	...	11.7	17.9	1,429	...	...	...	100.0	1,410	...	...	-1,008	687	656	190
		'09	63.1	...	26.0	11.0	1,101	...	...	...	100.0	1,011	...	...	-269	454	405	408
		Rating History: NR-5, 04/26/10; NR-5, 05/13/09; NR-5, 04/23/08; NR-5, 04/27/07; NR-5, 04/05/06																
BF&M LIFE INSURANCE CO LTD BF&M Limited Lynne Woolridge Senior Vice President Insurance Building, P.O. Box HM 1007 Hamilton HM DX, Bermuda BM : Stock : Not Available Life 441-295-5566 AMB# 084740	A Rating Outlook: Stable FSC VIII	'05	24.9	12.7	2.1	60.2	236,559	48.3	...	...	51.7	36,473	...	71,578	31,059	7,393	8,698	8,698
		'06	22.0	14.0	2.0	62.1	292,888	41.7	...	...	58.3	41,064	...	78,221	6,118	12,391	12,677	12,677
		'07	21.2	12.5	3.1	63.2	329,264	39.5	...	...	60.5	53,880	...	81,814	18,174	7,714	7,809	10,553
		'08	20.8	16.6	1.9	60.7	374,625	35.8	...	...	64.2	59,499	...	90,737	12,271	8,020	8,126	7,939
		'09	20.1	17.6	1.4	60.9	414,831	33.3	...	...	66.7	62,032	...	102,344	24,540	8,680	8,587	5,929
		Rating History: A g, 07/02/09; A g, 08/26/08; A g, 08/10/07; A g, 04/04/06; A g, 05/17/04																
BIG SKY LIFE INC' Richard Olson President 501 N. Sanders Street Helena, MT 59601-4552 MT : 1986 : Stock : Not Available 406-442-1233 AMB# 068171 NAIC# 73806	NR-1	'05	70.5	...	9.2	20.3	3,435	...	...	...	100.0	1,989	...	629	...	180	169	172
		'06	53.9	...	14.8	31.3	3,141	...	...	...	100.0	1,580	...	580	...	347	311	314
		'07	59.6	...	14.9	25.5	2,556	...	...	...	100.0	1,041	...	468	...	120	92	92
		'08	45.1	...	24.1	30.8	1,642	...	...	...	100.0	768	...	347	...	347	314	321
		'09	13.6	...	63.6	22.9	1,529	...	...	...	100.0	1,001	...	-35	...	369	330	330
		Rating History: NR-1, 06/10/10; NR-1, 06/12/09; NR-1, 06/12/08; NR-1, 06/08/07; NR-1, 06/07/06																

Data in U.S. Dollars

	Profitability Tests							Leverage Tests						Liquidity Tests					
Un-Realized Capital Gains ($000)	Benefits Paid to NPW & Dep (%)	Comm. & Expenses to NPW & Dep (%)	NOG to Total Assets (%)	NOG to Total Rev (%)	Operating Return on Equity (%)	Net Yield (%)	Total Return (%)	Change in NPW & Dep (%)	NPW & Dep to Capital (X)	Capital & Surplus to Liabilities (%)	Surplus Relief (%)	Reins Leverage (%)	Change in Capital (%)	Quick Liquidity (%)	Current Liquidity (%)	Non-Invest Grade Bonds to Capital (%)	Delinq. & Foreclosed Mortgages to Capital (%)	Mort. & Credit Tenant Loans & R.E. to Capital (%)	Affiliated Invest to Capital (%)
...	...	...	...	...	...	...	...	...	...	972.3	...	...	...	999.9	...	...	...	...	...
...	33.6	515.1	-22.2	-99.9	-23.5	4.03	4.03	...	3.8	999.9	...	...	347.3	999.9	999.9	...	...	...	...
...	-38.7	492.8	-3.7	-43.6	-4.3	6.37	4.63	-9.4	3.5	341.7	...	...	-3.5	324.2	289.2	...	...	...	...
...	-99.9	999.9	-12.0	-99.9	-17.7	7.63	6.28	-93.5	0.3	145.2	...	...	-17.4	110.8	130.8	...	...	21.3	...
...	571.0	-99.9	-2.0	-28.2	-3.7	8.77	7.01	-99.9	-0.3	110.2	...	...	-5.3	92.9	87.7	...	...	15.0	...
...	...	...	-0.5	-8.3	-1.5	1.40	1.30	...	...	53.0	...	...	50.0	120.3	150.4	...	...	6.3	50.8
...	...	...	0.8	11.1	2.1	2.30	2.10	...	...	59.3	...	...	16.5	140.3	154.4	...	...	26.6	0.1
...	...	...	1.1	13.7	2.8	1.68	1.75	...	...	65.4	...	...	19.0	146.6	162.1	...	...	24.8	0.4
...	...	...	-1.1	-18.5	-2.9	0.12	0.18	...	...	54.4	...	...	-11.7	138.9	151.5	...	...	23.4	1.0
...	...	...	1.9	18.1	8.2	4.81	4.58	...	...	8.2	...	...	-82.8	85.1	103.6	...	...	134.0	125.4
233	159.5	57.9	1.0	13.2	3.1	6.26	6.26	-18.7	9.2	46.4	...	...	0.6	30.4	114.2	...	...	59.8	...
90	170.4	67.8	0.7	9.4	2.1	4.77	4.77	-5.5	8.4	48.3	...	...	3.4	32.2	147.4	...	...	115.4	35.0
409	205.8	82.9	0.8	11.1	2.4	4.74	4.74	-18.1	6.4	51.3	...	...	8.7	34.9	149.6	...	...	107.7	31.8
-175	478.1	136.7	-0.2	-2.7	-0.7	4.79	7.66	-52.7	2.8	48.7	...	...	6.5	32.5	146.1	...	...	202.8	...
-125	-99.9	-99.9	1.7	43.4	5.4	6.25	4.31	-99.9	-0.9	45.0	...	...	-3.3	28.9	142.5	...	...	206.7	...
...	69.6	30.9	4.0	2.0	7.6	4.57	4.61	12.7	3.6	111.2	...	22.6	3.8	140.6	147.8	...	...	...	...
...	71.0	30.5	1.5	0.6	2.6	4.57	4.58	9.8	3.8	157.4	...	38.4	2.6	173.5	182.0	...	...	...	...
...	66.7	34.0	2.4	0.9	3.8	4.73	4.74	5.5	3.9	173.9	...	24.6	3.9	196.7	205.0	...	...	10.5	10.5
-121	72.9	29.5	-4.0	-1.4	-6.5	3.62	2.66	15.7	4.9	145.9	...	34.0	-7.7	167.9	176.7	2.5	...	11.4	11.4
110	77.2	27.7	-10.3	-3.4	-17.9	4.15	4.07	-3.5	5.6	128.8	...	28.7	-16.1	144.5	154.5	4.7	...	13.6	13.6
	Principal Lines of Business: GrpA&H (99.1%), GrpLife (0.9%), OrdLife (0.0%)													Principal States: NV (17.1%), CA (15.7%), WA (11.8%), UT (10.7%), IN (8.5%)					
22	35.4	47.2	0.1	0.3	0.9	5.11	5.19	72.8	2.7	14.3	36.6	155.0	-6.9	75.8	83.6	2.6	...	3.2	3.2
23	36.0	47.0	3.2	7.9	23.8	5.43	5.49	-1.6	2.0	17.1	29.3	140.3	29.7	76.1	85.2	0.8	...	6.2	6.2
8	46.1	44.0	2.4	5.9	16.5	5.64	5.64	12.8	2.0	18.0	23.8	101.5	14.5	75.0	84.7	2.3	...	8.6	8.6
5	36.0	26.6	4.4	8.1	27.8	5.59	3.34	56.8	2.7	20.1	12.5	15.9	18.3	79.4	88.5	6.2	...	7.1	7.1
...	42.4	37.2	3.6	8.6	20.9	5.58	5.25	-17.5	1.8	22.2	9.1	12.5	19.8	75.2	83.5	9.9	...	36.7	38.2
	Principal Lines of Business: IndA&H (63.7%), OrdLife (33.2%), GrpA&H (2.7%), GrpLife (0.3%)																		
...	20.9	26.1	4.6	50.4	23.5	6.75	6.75	16.3	43.9	25.8	...	...	28.8	18.4	3.9	...	...	...	...
...	33.7	37.6	5.4	44.4	25.0	7.04	7.04	18.8	38.0	29.1	...	...	37.1	22.0	5.1	...	...	...	...
...	29.0	80.9	5.7	38.1	24.3	18.37	18.37	6.5	32.3	32.6	...	...	25.4	28.6	8.2	...	...	...	...
...	31.9	41.3	3.0	29.8	13.3	9.69	9.69	41.9	40.2	26.7	...	...	13.9	17.4	1.1	...	...	...	...
...	...	...	...	...	...	...	...	...	...	...	...	...	...	...	...	...	...	...	...
201	...	...	-1.9	-2.6	-2.0	9.30	23.83	...	...	953.4	...	...	-22.9	680.0	999.9	...	...	...	...
-136	...	...	52.1	33.6	58.0	28.30	18.13	...	...	802.6	...	...	-11.6	967.9	999.9	...	...	...	...
-31	...	...	-9.3	-27.6	-9.9	13.16	11.51	...	...	999.9	...	...	131.7	999.9	999.9	...	...	...	...
-348	...	...	32.8	80.7	33.8	8.03	-28.88	...	...	999.9	...	...	-43.0	999.9	999.9	...	...	...	...
137	...	...	32.1	66.5	33.5	6.35	18.04	...	...	999.9	...	...	-23.3	999.9	999.9	62.9	...	...	...
...	88.9	15.6	4.0	10.6	23.2	5.31	5.31	8.2	196.3	18.2	...	...	-5.2	46.8	49.0	...	...	82.6	...
...	83.3	18.7	4.8	13.8	32.7	7.71	7.71	9.3	190.5	16.3	...	...	12.6	33.5	45.8	...	...	99.5	...
...	91.0	18.8	2.5	7.8	16.5	7.77	9.76	4.6	151.8	19.6	...	...	31.2	36.8	45.4	...	...	76.5	...
...	88.8	19.2	2.3	7.7	14.3	6.53	6.41	10.9	152.5	18.9	...	...	10.4	32.4	47.9	...	...	104.5	...
...	84.1	21.3	2.2	7.5	14.1	5.26	3.76	12.8	165.0	17.6	...	...	4.3	30.9	47.0	...	...	117.8	...
-5	26.4	58.3	4.7	21.7	7.7	...	...	-2.9	0.3	142.2	...	...	-16.4	...	...	...	...	...	...
53	19.9	60.2	9.5	41.4	17.5	...	...	-7.8	0.4	107.7	...	...	-19.2	...	...	...	...	...	...
-8	47.7	100.6	3.2	14.9	7.0	...	...	-19.3	0.4	72.8	...	...	-33.9	...	...	...	...	...	...
-221	26.9	63.9	15.0	69.1	34.8	...	...	-26.0	0.5	87.8	...	...	-28.7	...	...	...	...	...	...
21	-99.9	454.0	20.8	999.9	37.4	...	...	-99.9	0.0	206.1	...	...	34.1	...	...	...	...	...	...
	Principal Lines of Business: CrdLife (252.3%), CrdA&H (-99.9%)																		

Data in U.S. Dollars

COMPANY NAME Ultimate Parent Association Principal Officer Mailing Address Dom. : Began Bus. : Struct. : Mktg. Specialty Phone # AMB# NAIC#	Best's Financial Strength Rating FSC	Data Year	Balance Sheet: Bonds (%)	Mort. Loans & R.E. (%)	Com & Pref. Stock (%)	All Other Assets (%)	Total Assets ($000)	Life Reserves (%)	Health Reserves %)	Ann Res. & Dep. Liabilities (%)	All Other Liabilities (%)	Capital & Surplus ($000)	Operations: Direct Premiums Written ($000)	Net Premiums Written & Deposits ($000)	Operating Cash Flow ($000)	NOG Before Taxes ($000)	NOG After Taxes ($000)	Net Income ($000)
BIRD INSURANCE COMPANY[1] Kim Huempfner President One Central Avenue, Suite 1200 Phoenix, AZ 85004-4417 AZ : 2007 : Stock 602-200-6900 AMB# 060693 NAIC# 12996	NR-1	'05	...	...	...	...	...	...	...	...	...	...	...	...	...	...	...	...
		'06	...	...	...	...	...	...	...	...	...	...	...	...	...	...	...	...
		'07	...	...	...	...	...	...	...	...	...	...	...	...	...	...	...	...
		'08	...	...	...	100.0	469	...	...	...	100.0	453	...	...	...	0	0	0
		'09	64.6	...	...	35.4	473	...	...	...	100.0	435	...	...	...	-18	-18	-18
		Rating History: NR-1, 06/10/10; NR-1, 06/12/09																
BLOCK VISION OF TEXAS INC[2] Block Vision Holdings LLC Andrew Alcorn President 14228 Midway Road, Suite 213 Dallas, TX 75244 TX : 1996 : Stock : Not Available Group A&H 972-991-8816 AMB# 064510 NAIC# 95387	NR-5	'05	...	...	...	100.0	1,323	...	84.3	...	15.7	638	326	326	-27	157	97	97
		'06	...	...	...	100.0	2,501	...	64.6	...	35.4	1,366	1,262	1,262	1,159	866	525	525
		'07	...	...	...	100.0	3,335	...	61.8	...	38.2	1,987	2,557	2,557	522	722	481	481
		'08	...	...	...	100.0	3,427	...	78.1	...	21.9	2,360	4,066	4,066	53	576	374	374
		'09	...	...	...	100.0	3,021	...	54.2	...	45.8	1,401	5,421	5,421	-276	1,061	703	703
		Rating History: NR-5, 04/15/10; NR-5, 03/25/09; NR-5, 04/29/08; NR-5, 04/11/07; NR-5, 06/05/06																
BLUE ADVANTAGE PLUS OF KC INC Blue Cross & Blue Shield of Kansas City David R. Gentile President P.O. Box 413163 Kansas City, MO 64108 MO : 2005 : Non-Profit : Not Available Health 816-395-2222 AMB# 064824 NAIC# 10753	NR-5	'05	37.5	...	...	62.5	20,995	...	45.6	...	54.4	6,747	36,798	36,790	8,308	-1,810	-1,177	-1,193
		'06	35.7	...	...	64.3	23,313	...	65.9	...	34.1	8,107	72,828	72,813	439	-4,802	-3,124	-3,131
		'07	52.9	...	...	47.1	22,796	...	54.0	...	46.0	8,163	76,814	76,781	6,677	-7,018	-4,608	-4,650
		'08	44.0	...	...	56.0	24,877	...	43.4	...	56.6	11,039	84,878	84,659	1,996	4,195	2,657	2,843
		'09	59.4	...	...	40.6	24,196	...	82.3	...	17.7	11,799	87,127	86,754	-1,662	1,058	702	823
		Rating History: NR-5, 03/22/10; NR-5, 03/17/09; NR-5, 03/18/08; NR-5, 04/05/07; NR-5, 06/20/06																
BLUE CARE HEALTH PLAN WellPoint Inc. Marjorie W. Dorr President 370 Bassett Road North Haven, CT 06473-4201 CT : 1995 : Stock : Broker Group A&H, Health 203-239-4911 AMB# 064073 NAIC# 60217	A Rating Outlook: Stable FSC IX	'05	...	...	...	100.0	...	...	...	...	100.0	...	...	...	...	131,419	85,422	85,422
		'06	...	...	...	100.0	...	...	...	...	100.0	...	...	...	...	160,367	104,239	104,239
		'07	...	...	...	100.0	...	...	...	...	100.0	...	...	...	...	49,046	31,880	31,880
		'08	...	...	...	100.0	...	...	...	...	100.0	...	...	...	...	108,310	70,401	70,401
		'09	...	...	...	100.0	...	...	...	...	100.0	...	...	...	52,955	80,009	52,006	52,006
		Rating History: A g, 04/27/10; A, 01/23/09; A, 03/20/08; A, 11/06/06; A, 12/29/05																
BLUE CARE NETWORK OF MICHIGAN Blue Cross Blue Shield of Michigan Jeanne H. Carlson President & CEO 20500 Civic Center Drive Southfield, MI 48076 MI : 1981 : Non-Profit : Broker Group A&H, Health 248-799-6400 AMB# 068741 NAIC# 95610	A- Rating Outlook: Negative FSC XV	'05	19.6	...	6.8	73.5	824,005	...	39.9	...	60.1	380,158	1,904,529	1,900,639	54,812	97,398	97,346	93,370
		'06	6.6	...	0.3	93.1	675,497	...	38.3	...	61.7	194,736	2,039,530	2,031,089	-136,979	44,980	44,949	81,042
		'07	18.4	...	0.6	81.0	785,302	...	35.9	...	64.1	244,110	2,162,665	2,150,302	97,087	49,396	49,365	49,847
		'08	22.0	...	0.4	77.6	841,063	...	48.5	...	51.5	336,740	2,150,160	2,138,056	56,503	85,599	85,408	85,590
		'09	22.6	...	1.1	76.3	884,963	...	45.1	...	54.9	416,611	2,235,539	2,208,251	23,371	57,557	57,731	62,769
		Rating History: A- g, 10/16/09; A- g, 09/03/08; A- g, 08/31/07; A- g, 10/04/06; A- g, 09/01/05																
BLUE CARE OF MICHIGAN INC Blue Cross Blue Shield of Michigan Jeanne H. Carlson President 20500 Civic Center Drive Southfield, MI 48076 MI : 1984 : Non-Profit : Broker Health 245-455-3410 AMB# 064870 NAIC# 52037	NR-2	'05	...	...	0.9	99.1	5,215	...	75.7	...	24.3	5,162	4,344	4,343	141	244	244	244
		'06	...	...	...	100.0	5,817	...	85.1	...	14.9	5,737	4,834	4,833	405	389	389	389
		'07	...	...	...	100.0	6,311	...	0.6	...	99.4	6,240	4,815	4,814	395	395	395	395
		'08	31.4	...	...	68.6	6,545	...	...	...	100.0	6,488	5,063	5,062	183	171	171	171
		'09	31.1	...	...	68.9	6,895	...	...	...	100.0	6,848	4,855	4,854	221	102	102	243
		Rating History: NR-2, 10/27/09; NR-2, 09/03/08; NR-2, 08/31/07																
BLUE CROSS & BLUE SHIELD OF AL[2] Blue Cross and Blue Shield of Alabama Gary P. Pope President 450 Riverchase Parkway East Birmingham, AL 35298 AL : 1936 : Stock : Career Agent Group A&H 205-220-2100 AMB# 060080 NAIC# 55433	NR-5	'05	49.2	7.0	10.6	33.3	1,610,847	...	52.1	...	47.9	587,154	3,061,217	3,059,456	79,445	60,422	43,018	48,911
		'06	46.6	6.1	13.5	33.7	1,781,603	...	51.9	...	48.1	694,587	3,344,229	3,341,984	147,780	156,643	110,740	114,058
		'07	45.3	5.6	14.8	34.4	1,917,173	...	48.2	...	51.8	744,454	3,499,176	3,495,234	176,438	81,621	62,405	71,651
		'08	46.4	5.9	11.3	36.5	1,906,945	...	48.7	...	51.3	656,361	3,996,997	3,992,026	-22,630	39,252	29,620	28,606
		'09	44.7	5.5	11.6	38.2	1,990,489	...	50.1	...	49.9	649,035	4,325,884	4,320,066	61,813	-63,513	-27,275	-52,559
		Rating History: NR-5, 04/23/10; NR-5, 08/26/09; B++pd, 09/19/08; B++pd, 09/04/07; B++pd, 09/29/06																
BLUE CROSS & BLUE SHIELD OF FL Blue Cross and Blue Shield of FL Inc Robert I. Lufrano, M.D. Chairman, President & CEO P.O. Box 60729 Jacksonville, FL 32236 FL : 1980 : Mutual : Agency Group A&H 904-791-6111 AMB# 068174 NAIC# 98167	A Rating Outlook: Stable FSC XV	'05	41.4	4.4	31.0	23.2	3,645,043	0.3	43.5	...	56.1	1,720,113	4,044,909	4,056,355	422,057	406,431	306,906	312,266
		'06	40.8	3.9	31.5	23.8	4,152,125	0.4	50.6	...	49.0	1,993,735	4,950,027	4,959,014	295,175	249,944	234,752	248,854
		'07	40.4	4.9	31.5	23.2	4,346,458	0.3	52.2	...	47.4	2,043,998	5,970,948	5,982,447	273,224	154,260	91,097	132,591
		'08	47.3	5.8	16.6	30.4	4,278,928	0.4	62.3	...	37.3	1,790,103	6,424,314	6,438,586	60,967	151,384	83,604	64,206
		'09	42.6	5.1	20.6	31.7	4,743,540	0.3	61.4	...	38.3	2,091,886	6,244,374	6,247,975	184,652	38,451	25,856	16,833
		Rating History: A g, 05/25/10; A g, 05/26/09; A g, 04/28/08; A g, 05/04/07; A g, 04/27/06																
BLUE CROSS & BLUE SHIELD OF GA WellPoint Inc. Monye M. Connolly President 3350 Peachtree Road, NE Atlanta, GA 30326 GA : 1937 : Stock : Agency Group A&H, Ind A&H 404-842-8000 AMB# 060075 NAIC# 54801	A Rating Outlook: Stable FSC IX	'05	60.3	0.4	16.3	23.0	1,149,283	...	40.1	...	59.9	480,018	2,488,412	2,474,117	129,008	253,726	170,680	185,185
		'06	51.4	0.4	17.8	30.4	1,175,536	...	42.1	...	57.9	563,105	2,594,666	2,579,413	-27,695	343,920	241,139	250,901
		'07	57.1	0.3	16.8	25.7	1,192,061	...	40.5	...	59.5	530,535	2,652,789	2,650,550	104,123	341,270	222,424	228,680
		'08	47.8	0.4	12.8	39.1	1,050,526	...	48.4	...	51.6	425,879	2,661,576	2,661,576	-269,336	277,748	252,145	192,830
		'09	51.9	0.6	15.7	31.8	1,071,897	...	41.5	...	58.5	416,506	2,524,411	2,524,203	-9,748	213,925	131,180	132,236
		Rating History: A g, 04/27/10; A g, 01/23/09; A g, 03/20/08; A g, 11/06/06; A g, 12/29/05																

2010 BEST'S KEY RATING GUIDE — LIFE/HEALTH EDITION
BEST'S PROFITABILITY, LEVERAGE AND LIQUIDITY TESTS 2005 – 2009

Data in U.S. Dollars

	Profitability Tests							Leverage Tests						Liquidity Tests					
Un-Realized Capital Gains ($000)	Benefits Paid to NPW & Dep (%)	Comm. & Expenses to NPW (%)	NOG to Total Assets (%)	NOG to Total Rev (%)	Operating Return on Equity (%)	Net Yield (%)	Total Return (%)	Change in NPW & Dep (%)	NPW & Dep to Capital (X)	Capital & Surplus to Liabilities (%)	Surplus Relief (%)	Reins Leverage (%)	Change in Capital (%)	Quick Liquidity (%)	Current Liquidity (%)	Non-Invest Grade Bonds to Capital (%)	Delinq. & Foreclosed Mortgages to Capital (%)	Mort. & Credit Tenant Loans & R.E. to Capital (%)	Affiliated Invest to Capital (%)
...	...	...	...	...	...	...	...	...	...	...	...	...	...	...	...	...	...	...	...
...	...	...	...	...	...	...	...	...	...	...	...	...	...	...	...	...	...	...	...
...	...	...	...	...	...	...	...	...	...	...	...	...	...	...	...	...	...	...	...
...	...	...	...	-3.0	...	...	...	...	...	999.9	...	...	...	...	...	...	...	...	...
...	...	...	-3.9	-99.9	-4.2	...	...	...	...	999.9	...	...	-4.1	...	...	...	...	...	...
...	78.2	20.1	7.4	1.2	15.0	1.76	1.76	874.0	0.5	93.3	...	...	-3.1	183.3	183.3	...	...	...	...
...	72.9	20.2	27.5	4.4	52.4	3.00	3.00	286.8	0.9	120.4	...	...	114.1	212.8	212.8	...	...	...	...
...	75.5	20.6	16.5	3.0	28.7	3.36	3.36	102.6	1.3	147.4	...	...	45.4	217.8	217.8	...	...	...	...
...	77.8	19.4	11.1	1.9	17.2	1.44	1.44	59.0	1.7	221.2	...	...	18.8	280.1	280.1	...	...	...	...
...	78.4	17.1	21.8	3.1	37.4	1.36	1.36	33.3	3.9	86.5	...	...	-40.6	167.4	167.4	...	...	...	...
	Principal Lines of Business: Vision (100.0%)												Principal States: TX (100.0%)						
...	93.2	11.9	...	-3.2	...	...	...	...	5.5	47.4	...	...	...	54.7	55.0	...	...	...	...
-1	91.0	13.7	-14.1	-4.3	-42.1	3.83	3.74	97.9	9.0	53.3	...	...	20.2	54.0	54.8	...	...	...	...
1	95.4	14.1	-20.0	-6.0	-56.6	4.14	3.80	5.4	9.4	55.8	...	...	0.7	119.3	122.4	...	...	...	...
...	83.5	13.8	11.1	3.1	27.7	3.32	4.44	10.3	7.7	79.8	...	...	35.2	143.1	145.4	...	...	...	...
...	80.8	13.6	2.9	0.8	6.1	3.01	3.73	2.5	7.4	95.2	...	...	6.9	126.4	130.2	...	...	...	...
	Principal Lines of Business: Medicaid (100.0%)												Principal States: MO (100.0%)						
...	82.3	10.3	...	5.5	...	...	...	-99.9	...	...	...	...	...	...	...	...	...	...	...
...	80.9	9.6	...	6.9	...	...	...	...	...	...	...	...	...	...	...	...	...	...	...
...	87.5	9.6	...	2.2	...	...	...	...	...	...	...	...	...	...	...	...	...	...	...
...	83.9	8.1	...	5.9	...	...	...	...	...	...	...	...	...	...	...	...	...	...	...
...	86.6	7.8	...	4.7	...	...	...	...	...	...	...	...	...	...	...	...	...	...	...
6,111	82.7	13.5	12.4	5.1	29.4	3.42	3.71	3.2	5.0	85.7	...	2.8	35.3	248.4	261.4	...	...	...	18.6
754	86.1	13.5	6.0	2.2	15.6	5.49	10.78	6.9	10.4	40.5	...	4.1	-48.8	213.2	220.6	...	...	...	35.0
3,496	86.5	12.8	6.8	2.3	22.5	4.89	5.46	5.9	8.8	45.1	...	3.9	25.4	202.5	213.8	...	...	...	31.8
2,394	86.3	11.2	10.5	3.9	29.4	4.29	4.62	-0.6	6.3	66.8	...	1.5	37.9	229.8	244.3	...	...	...	23.8
9,706	87.9	10.6	6.7	2.6	15.3	3.94	5.74	3.3	5.3	89.0	...	2.0	23.7	251.9	267.7	...	...	...	21.6
	Principal Lines of Business: CompHosp/Med (78.7%), Medicare (15.9%), FEHBP (3.4%), MedSup (2.0%)												Principal States: MI (99.8%)						
38	83.8	13.1	4.8	5.5	4.9	2.19	2.94	10.1	0.8	999.9	...	...	5.8	999.9	999.9	...	...	...	24.2
186	83.3	12.5	7.1	7.7	7.1	3.54	7.02	11.3	0.8	999.9	...	...	11.1	999.9	999.9	...	...	...	24.3
109	83.2	12.8	6.5	7.9	6.6	3.43	5.26	-0.4	0.8	999.9	...	...	8.8	999.9	999.9	...	...	...	24.1
77	87.1	11.9	2.7	3.3	2.7	1.85	3.07	5.2	0.8	999.9	...	...	4.0	999.9	999.9	...	...	...	24.3
117	88.9	11.0	1.5	2.1	1.5	1.53	5.44	-4.1	0.7	999.9	...	...	5.6	999.9	999.9	...	...	...	24.8
	Principal Lines of Business: CompHosp/Med (100.0%)												Principal States: MI (100.0%)						
-1,205	92.4	7.0	2.8	1.4	7.5	3.65	4.06	9.4	5.2	57.4	0.1	0.2	5.9	94.4	102.1	...	...	19.1	21.6
13,241	90.5	6.3	6.5	3.3	17.3	4.28	5.61	9.2	4.8	63.9	0.1	0.4	18.3	100.0	108.1	...	...	15.8	23.8
-14,069	91.9	7.5	3.4	1.7	8.7	4.50	4.16	4.6	4.7	63.5	0.0	0.8	7.2	106.3	115.3	...	...	14.4	21.0
-82,338	92.5	8.1	1.5	0.7	4.2	4.49	-1.17	14.2	6.1	52.5	0.0	1.4	-11.8	80.7	91.6	0.2	...	17.0	24.2
50,396	94.7	7.9	-1.4	-0.6	-4.2	3.51	5.38	8.2	6.7	48.4	0.0	2.2	-1.1	84.6	93.5	0.9	...	16.8	24.6
	Principal Lines of Business: CompHosp/Med (61.6%), FEHBP (15.2%), Medicare (15.2%), MedSup (4.4%), Dental (2.8%)												Principal States: AL (100.0%)						
-10,391	79.7	14.3	8.9	7.1	19.5	9.77	9.57	15.3	2.4	89.4	0.3	1.5	20.8	77.8	89.9	7.8	...	9.3	34.8
10,584	82.7	15.7	6.0	4.5	12.6	8.52	9.36	22.3	2.5	92.4	0.2	1.7	15.9	75.6	89.1	11.5	...	8.1	28.4
-68,947	84.6	16.1	2.1	1.5	4.5	7.40	6.58	20.6	2.9	88.8	0.0	2.1	2.5	71.4	87.4	10.8	...	10.3	28.5
-240,545	83.1	15.7	1.9	1.3	4.4	3.18	-4.72	7.6	3.6	71.9	0.0	3.1	-12.4	63.7	72.5	10.1	...	13.9	40.4
148,936	85.6	15.2	0.6	0.4	1.3	3.44	7.92	-3.0	3.0	78.9	0.0	3.2	16.9	66.7	76.0	12.3	...	11.5	37.1
	Principal Lines of Business: CompHosp/Med (62.1%), FEHBP (27.8%), MedSup (5.7%), Medicare (2.4%), OtherHlth (1.8%)												Principal States: FL (100.0%)						
-27,907	86.6	6.4	15.7	6.7	38.5	4.60	2.97	9.5	5.2	71.7	...	0.2	17.9	94.6	108.5	...	...	1.0	5.6
540	84.8	5.0	20.7	9.1	46.2	5.17	6.43	4.3	4.6	91.9	...	0.7	17.3	99.4	114.9	0.7	...	0.8	4.8
-24,852	85.0	5.1	18.8	8.2	40.7	5.16	3.00	2.8	5.0	80.2	...	0.0	-5.8	101.1	116.5	0.3	...	0.8	4.9
-11,061	86.7	4.7	22.5	9.3	52.7	4.67	-4.66	0.4	6.2	68.2	...	...	-19.7	64.0	74.7	0.2	...	1.0	6.4
31,603	85.0	7.3	12.4	5.1	31.1	4.89	10.62	-5.2	6.1	63.6	...	0.0	-2.2	58.7	69.9	...	...	1.7	6.6
	Principal Lines of Business: CompHosp/Med (58.8%), FEHBP (32.9%), MedSup (4.0%), Medicare (2.4%), OtherHlth (1.4%)												Principal States: GA (100.0%)						

Data in U.S. Dollars

COMPANY NAME Ultimate Parent Association Principal Officer Mailing Address Dom. : Began Bus. : Struct. : Mktg. Specialty Phone # AMB# NAIC#	Best's Financial Strength Rating FSC		Balance Sheet										Operations					
		Data Year	Bonds (%)	Mort. Loans & R.E. (%)	Com & Pref. Stock (%)	All Other Assets (%)	Total Assets ($000)	Life Reserves (%)	Health Reserves %)	Ann Res. & Dep. Liabilities (%)	All Other Liabilities (%)	Capital & Surplus ($000)	Direct Premiums Written ($000)	Net Premiums Written & Deposits ($000)	Operating Cash Flow ($000)	NOG Before Taxes ($000)	NOG After Taxes ($000)	Net Income ($000)
BLUE CROSS&BLUE SHIELD OF K C Blue Cross & Blue Shield of Kansas City Tom E. Bowser President P.O. Box 419169 Kansas City, MO 64141-6169 MO : 1982 : Non-Profit : Agency Group A&H 816-395-2222 AMB# 064015 NAIC# 47171	**NR-5**	**'05**	40.7	4.3	33.5	21.5	589,885	...	38.8	...	61.2	328,106	837,389	846,098	34,658	48,364	27,943	32,776
		'06	40.5	4.0	34.6	20.9	641,311	...	39.2	...	60.8	375,138	821,000	830,942	33,176	40,702	36,327	39,507
		'07	37.7	3.5	36.5	22.3	707,244	...	42.2	...	57.8	467,776	832,702	842,101	27,590	51,470	79,864	91,430
		'08	51.8	3.2	19.5	25.5	740,622	...	34.9	...	65.1	483,154	852,726	858,103	20,319	55,367	36,048	14,943
		'09	60.6	2.7	13.9	22.8	829,284	...	43.3	...	56.7	554,459	943,835	947,442	111,851	60,917	42,623	49,695
		Rating History: NR-5, 03/22/10; NR-5, 03/13/09; NR-5, 03/11/08; NR-5, 04/02/07; NR-5, 04/20/06																
BLUE CROSS AND BLUE SHIELD KS Blue Cross and Blue Shield of Kansas Inc Andrew C. Corbin President & CEO 1133 SW Topeka Boulevard Topeka, KS 66629-0001 KS : 1942 : Mutual : Exclusive Agent A&H, Ind A&H, Med supp 785-291-7000 AMB# 060070 NAIC# 70729	**A** Rating Outlook: Stable **FSC X**	**'05**	53.1	4.0	27.1	15.7	890,670	...	41.0	0.6	58.4	458,798	1,168,809	1,166,556	14,154	81,751	51,507	61,394
		'06	50.3	4.4	33.4	11.9	968,281	...	47.4	0.6	52.0	455,484	1,325,108	1,289,870	13,445	-29,114	-33,548	-27,134
		'07	50.9	2.6	32.2	14.2	1,053,140	...	44.1	0.6	55.3	497,990	1,442,773	1,396,277	71,335	-19,587	-3,742	13,171
		'08	54.3	2.8	25.3	17.5	1,001,847	...	42.5	0.8	56.7	518,975	1,557,609	1,514,289	-55,107	70,229	80,441	24,679
		'09	61.1	2.7	17.4	18.7	1,073,112	...	40.6	0.8	58.6	589,919	1,662,466	1,620,369	27,455	57,925	38,365	19,929
		Rating History: A g, 12/14/09; A g, 02/26/09; A g, 01/30/08; A g, 12/07/06; A g, 10/25/05																
BLUE CR & BLUE SH OF MA HMO BL[2] Blue Cross and Blue Shield of MA Cleve L. Killingsworth President & CEO 401 Park Drive Boston, MA 02215 MA : 2005 : Non-Profit : Agency Health 617-246-5000 AMB# 064847 NAIC# 12219	**NR-5**	**'05**	38.7	4.3	16.9	40.1	1,253,837	...	47.4	...	52.6	763,781	3,641,564	3,641,564	348,333	96,592	96,592	137,055
		'06	36.2	8.2	14.6	41.0	1,397,810	...	45.4	...	54.6	839,662	4,223,732	4,223,732	95,679	61,190	61,190	70,272
		'07	33.9	7.7	15.3	43.1	1,445,584	...	45.0	...	55.0	880,593	4,457,631	4,457,631	64,293	27,208	27,208	63,097
		'08	36.8	8.6	16.4	38.2	1,268,808	...	48.3	...	51.7	707,041	4,447,988	4,447,988	9,299	20,315	20,308	21,685
		'09	39.0	8.6	11.5	40.9	1,258,039	...	45.2	...	54.8	705,830	4,400,791	4,400,791	-118,847	-67,943	-67,946	-127,910
		Rating History: NR-5, 05/03/10; NR-5, 04/01/09; NR-5, 05/13/08; NR-5, 06/25/07; NR-5, 05/30/06																
BLUE CROSS & BLUE SHIELD OF MA[2] Blue Cross and Blue Shield of MA Cleve L. Killingsworth President 401 Park Drive Boston, MA 02215 MA : 1937 : Non-Profit : Agency Group A&H 617-246-5000 AMB# 064562 NAIC# 53228	**NR-5**	**'05**	25.5	3.8	11.8	59.0	1,604,632	...	18.9	...	81.1	465,367	1,976,829	1,976,829	-138,589	117,096	105,941	127,723
		'06	24.1	7.1	8.5	60.4	1,841,974	...	20.1	...	79.9	628,188	2,098,317	2,098,280	98,330	95,676	146,826	157,250
		'07	22.6	6.8	10.2	60.4	1,848,962	...	20.6	...	79.4	705,748	2,266,038	2,264,944	-22,943	126,916	126,246	145,628
		'08	21.5	6.7	9.6	62.2	1,841,061	...	16.3	...	83.7	614,167	2,276,572	2,208,074	121,209	88,661	79,134	83,703
		'09	28.3	7.7	8.2	55.8	1,576,769	...	20.8	...	79.2	723,896	2,396,076	2,315,615	1,064	31,523	29,278	-21,306
		Rating History: NR-5, 04/06/10; NR-5, 04/16/09; NR-5, 05/12/08; NR-5, 09/27/07; NR-3, 09/21/06																
BLUE CROSS & BLUE SHIELD OF MN Aware Integrated Inc Patrick J. Geraghty President & CEO 3535 Blue Cross Road Eagan, MN 55122 MN : 1972 : Non-Profit : Broker Group A&H, Group Life, Stop Loss 651-662-8000 AMB# 060077 NAIC# 55026	**B++** Rating Outlook: Stable **FSC X**	**'05**	32.6	5.8	25.8	35.8	1,689,018	...	35.1	...	64.9	692,929	2,148,172	2,178,268	-7,529	27,418	45,210	59,524
		'06	38.4	5.2	27.9	28.5	1,831,259	...	32.1	...	67.9	712,646	2,471,010	2,504,101	72,991	-18,183	-2,607	893
		'07	39.4	5.2	22.9	32.5	1,785,388	...	32.4	...	67.6	645,660	2,691,648	2,689,396	-82,728	-64,131	-52,674	-3,884
		'08	37.0	5.1	15.6	42.3	1,753,683	...	34.7	...	65.3	518,128	2,810,920	2,825,881	-14,374	50,533	36,293	-2,102
		'09	38.9	4.6	21.7	34.7	1,880,046	...	35.3	...	64.7	628,802	2,798,674	2,812,069	173,364	32,808	41,158	33,457
		Rating History: B++g, 06/08/10; B++g, 05/20/09; A- g, 06/11/08; A g, 06/13/07; A g, 06/09/06																
BLUE CROSS & BLUE SHIELD OF MS Blue Cross & BS of MS a Mutual Ins Co Richard J. Hale President & CEO 3545 Lakeland Drive Flowood, MS 39232-9799 MS : 1948 : Mutual : Broker Group A&H 601-932-3704 AMB# 060217 NAIC# 60111	**A** Rating Outlook: Stable **FSC X**	**'05**	71.2	5.2	7.1	16.5	579,245	...	42.9	...	57.1	370,639	955,104	955,104	79,577	50,003	40,216	40,679
		'06	69.4	4.7	7.9	18.0	627,275	...	39.1	...	60.9	407,906	1,042,890	1,042,889	53,727	53,539	36,635	36,820
		'07	67.8	4.2	8.2	19.7	693,556	...	40.2	...	59.8	454,945	1,124,629	1,124,192	47,338	71,035	43,703	44,474
		'08	68.0	4.2	8.0	19.8	721,736	...	42.9	...	57.1	479,671	1,183,793	1,183,210	51,072	59,816	51,004	50,579
		'09	63.9	4.1	9.5	22.5	741,269	...	45.3	...	54.7	502,405	1,248,114	1,247,441	5,034	33,171	18,068	19,245
		Rating History: A g, 06/16/09; A g, 06/02/08; A g, 05/25/07; A g, 06/20/06; A g, 06/22/05																
BLUE CROSS & BLUE SHIELD OF MT Blue Cross and Blue Shield of Montana Sherry Cladouhos President & CEO P.O. Box 4309 Helena, MT 59604 MT : 1946 : Mutual : Agency Group A&H 406-444-8820 AMB# 064338 NAIC# 53686	**NR-5**	**'05**	29.5	4.5	30.5	35.5	225,310	...	33.4	...	66.6	96,272	408,578	406,238	-10,831	1,150	-391	-22
		'06	27.5	4.0	33.6	34.9	238,444	...	44.7	...	55.3	117,330	482,008	479,873	17,374	2,074	4,854	6,702
		'07	29.8	3.2	35.0	32.0	265,667	...	40.1	...	59.9	144,987	511,605	509,972	23,152	21,776	18,743	21,220
		'08	29.3	4.6	30.2	35.8	242,623	...	38.9	...	61.1	118,010	519,121	517,916	-11,518	16,987	18,314	17,687
		'09	28.3	4.5	35.6	31.6	242,936	...	37.9	...	62.1	122,556	504,821	504,821	-3,049	-11,428	-9,525	-9,783
		Rating History: NR-5, 07/01/09; NR-5, 04/29/08; NR-5, 04/20/07; NR-5, 05/03/06; NR-5, 05/09/05																
BLUE CROSS & BLUE SHIELD OF NE Steven S. Martin President P.O. Box 3248 Main P.O. Station Omaha, NE 68180 NE : 1939 : Mutual : Broker Group A&H, Ind A&H, Med supp 402-390-1800 AMB# 068172 NAIC# 77780	**A** Rating Outlook: Negative **FSC IX**	**'05**	56.6	7.6	18.5	17.3	631,628	...	56.7	...	43.3	405,847	834,520	831,508	18,591	39,290	25,097	26,923
		'06	53.3	7.2	21.0	18.5	706,977	...	56.1	...	43.9	439,353	946,161	943,331	49,547	25,265	15,568	16,596
		'07	53.2	7.0	22.3	17.5	755,023	...	58.9	...	41.1	460,414	1,095,487	1,092,473	27,416	12,200	7,987	8,112
		'08	52.3	7.4	16.7	23.6	733,292	...	59.1	...	40.9	402,308	1,193,445	1,188,076	-1,737	-5,835	-1,079	-2,575
		'09	48.1	5.4	19.8	26.7	775,627	...	55.2	...	44.8	372,378	1,295,661	1,290,030	26,691	-32,916	-32,426	-39,607
		Rating History: A, 11/12/09; A, 07/25/08; NR-5, 03/11/08; NR-5, 04/05/07; NR-5, 04/20/06																
BLUE CROSS & BLUE SHIELD OF NC[2] Blue Cross & BS of NC Robert J. Greczyn, Jr. President & CEO P.O. Box 2291 Durham, NC 27702-2291 NC : 1968 : Non-Profit : Agency Group A&H 919-489-7431 AMB# 064070 NAIC# 54631	**NR-5**	**'05**	50.6	1.9	25.4	22.1	2,138,970	...	51.0	...	49.0	980,156	3,223,326	3,217,230	263,323	196,395	118,089	119,272
		'06	49.4	2.1	27.2	21.3	2,312,620	...	58.7	...	41.3	1,110,986	3,666,950	3,658,032	205,988	179,263	116,689	125,394
		'07	53.2	1.9	25.7	19.1	2,555,859	...	60.8	...	39.2	1,285,907	4,039,244	4,027,833	195,599	278,531	186,856	198,051
		'08	57.2	2.8	20.8	19.2	2,568,597	...	62.1	...	37.9	1,258,696	4,298,258	4,496,842	162,286	265,787	177,707	157,768
		'09	53.4	3.4	25.1	18.1	2,807,638	...	60.9	...	39.1	1,423,751	4,270,693	4,716,353	121,129	134,773	80,496	58,982
		Rating History: NR-5, 04/29/10; NR-5, 08/26/09; A- pd, 09/19/08; A- pd, 08/27/07; A- pd, 09/21/06																

BEST'S PROFITABILITY, LEVERAGE AND LIQUIDITY TESTS 2005 – 2009

Data in U.S. Dollars

	Profitability Tests							Leverage Tests						Liquidity Tests					
Un-Realized Capital Gains ($000)	Benefits Paid to NPW & Dep (%)	Comm. & Expenses to NPW & Dep (%)	NOG to Total Assets (%)	NOG to Total Rev (%)	Operating Return on Equity (%)	Net Yield (%)	Total Return (%)	Change in NPW & Dep (%)	NPW & Dep to Capital (X)	Capital & Surplus to Liabilities (%)	Surplus Relief (%)	Reins Leverage (%)	Change in Capital (%)	Quick Liquidity (%)	Current Liquidity (%)	Non-Invest Grade Bonds to Capital (%)	Delinq. & Foreclosed Mortgages to Capital (%)	Mort. & Credit Tenant Loans & R.E. to Capital (%)	Affiliated Invest to Capital (%)
-1,909	82.1	14.2	4.9	3.2	8.9	3.68	4.31	4.3	2.6	125.3	...	0.7	9.7	132.6	147.4	...	...	7.7	28.0
5,285	84.0	13.6	5.9	4.3	10.3	4.20	5.86	-1.8	2.2	140.9	...	1.2	14.3	143.3	160.2	...	...	6.8	26.1
-1,420	83.7	13.1	11.8	9.2	18.9	4.97	6.83	1.3	1.8	195.3	...	1.2	24.7	163.8	184.0	...	...	5.3	21.7
-11,068	83.1	13.8	5.0	4.1	7.6	5.29	-0.18	1.9	1.8	187.7	...	1.1	3.3	153.9	167.5	0.0	...	4.9	23.1
15,779	82.0	14.3	5.4	4.4	8.2	4.30	7.86	10.4	1.7	201.7	...	1.1	14.8	192.5	208.5	0.0	...	4.1	23.1
	Principal Lines of Business: CompHosp/Med (68.9%), FEHBP (22.3%), MedSup (5.2%), OtherHlth (2.2%), Dental (1.5%)												Principal States: MO (73.8%), KS (26.2%)						
10,971	86.0	9.3	5.9	4.3	12.1	4.00	6.75	2.7	2.3	132.0	...	...	14.9	152.3	165.5	0.2	...	7.0	19.2
43,366	95.8	9.8	-3.6	-2.5	-7.3	4.52	10.58	10.6	2.5	113.9	...	...	1.7	125.5	139.8	0.0	...	8.3	27.5
19,779	95.3	9.1	-0.4	-0.3	-0.8	4.32	8.39	8.2	2.5	111.4	...	...	7.7	140.9	156.3	...	...	5.0	19.0
-25,209	88.8	9.4	7.8	5.1	15.8	4.34	-4.00	8.5	2.9	112.1	...	2.3	-4.6	140.0	157.3	0.5	...	5.4	20.3
43,767	89.1	9.7	3.7	2.3	6.9	3.92	6.97	7.0	2.6	135.7	...	2.2	16.6	176.9	194.3	0.2	...	4.8	10.5
	Principal Lines of Business: GrpA&H (75.8%), IndA&H (24.2%), GrpAnn (0.0%)												Principal States: KS (100.0%)						
-29,879	88.3	10.0	...	2.6	...	...	...	...	4.8	155.9	...	...	...	121.3	135.6	1.3	...	7.0	7.0
38,679	89.6	10.0	4.6	1.4	7.6	3.83	7.59	16.0	5.0	150.4	...	...	9.9	114.0	126.7	1.1	...	13.7	13.7
3,552	90.5	10.0	1.9	0.6	3.2	3.94	6.83	5.5	5.1	155.9	...	...	4.9	119.8	135.4	0.3	...	12.6	12.6
-185,810	90.5	10.3	1.5	0.5	2.6	4.48	-8.62	-0.2	6.3	125.9	...	...	-19.7	112.6	125.1	0.1	...	15.4	15.5
37,217	92.1	10.4	-5.4	-1.5	-9.6	3.47	1.77	-1.1	6.2	127.8	...	...	-0.2	112.7	123.1	0.1	...	15.2	15.8
	Principal Lines of Business: CompHosp/Med (89.4%), Medicare (9.9%), OtherHlth (0.7%)												Principal States: MA (99.5%)						
-11,722	85.7	10.1	5.0	5.3	13.6	2.19	2.84	-59.9	4.2	40.8	...	...	-57.3	46.3	51.7	1.6	...	13.0	13.0
17,984	85.2	12.0	8.5	6.9	26.9	3.63	6.19	6.1	3.3	51.8	...	...	35.0	49.3	54.4	1.2	...	20.7	20.7
4,602	85.1	11.4	6.8	5.5	18.9	4.10	6.15	7.9	3.2	61.7	0.0	0.0	12.3	44.4	50.9	0.3	...	17.8	17.8
-93,123	87.4	10.8	4.3	3.5	12.0	4.26	-3.07	-2.5	3.6	50.1	0.0	1.6	-13.0	44.2	48.9	0.1	...	20.0	25.1
-10,802	89.0	11.2	1.7	1.2	4.4	3.04	-2.00	4.9	3.2	84.9	0.0	1.7	17.9	81.9	88.7	0.1	...	16.8	22.9
	Principal Lines of Business: CompHosp/Med (47.1%), FEHBP (24.6%), MedSup (18.4%), OtherHlth (6.6%), Dental (3.3%)												Principal States: MA (99.8%)						
40,704	87.2	12.9	2.7	2.0	6.5	2.52	6.53	11.1	3.1	69.6	...	...	0.2	103.2	112.4	1.3	...	14.0	20.7
38,842	89.9	12.6	-0.1	-0.1	-0.4	3.44	6.42	15.0	3.5	63.7	...	...	2.8	98.2	108.4	0.7	...	13.5	18.1
-9,172	89.4	13.7	-2.9	-1.9	-7.8	3.82	6.61	7.4	4.2	56.7	...	...	-9.4	87.7	100.9	1.0	...	14.5	18.5
-92,849	85.7	13.6	2.1	1.3	6.2	3.24	-5.95	5.1	5.5	41.9	...	...	-19.8	80.4	90.4	0.9	...	17.4	22.0
76,402	85.0	14.5	2.3	1.5	7.2	2.69	7.65	-0.5	4.5	50.3	...	...	21.4	94.4	106.5	1.9	...	13.8	17.5
	Principal Lines of Business: CompHosp/Med (58.9%), FEHBP (13.4%), MedSup (12.5%), OtherHlth (10.8%), Medicare (4.3%)												Principal States: MN (100.0%)						
3,417	88.1	8.8	7.4	4.1	11.5	4.38	5.19	2.5	2.6	177.7	...	...	13.0	181.2	195.6	0.6	...	8.1	15.9
3,084	86.7	10.6	6.1	3.4	9.4	4.74	5.34	9.2	2.6	185.9	...	...	10.1	186.8	204.7	0.4	...	7.2	15.0
2,600	85.7	9.9	6.6	3.8	10.1	5.13	5.70	7.8	2.5	190.7	...	0.1	11.5	176.9	197.7	0.4	...	6.5	14.4
-8,342	89.7	8.5	7.2	4.2	10.9	4.94	3.58	5.2	2.5	198.2	...	0.2	5.4	183.1	203.5	0.9	...	6.4	14.7
1,389	91.1	8.5	2.5	1.4	3.7	4.44	4.82	5.4	2.5	210.3	...	0.1	4.7	184.4	204.1	1.1	...	6.0	14.7
	Principal Lines of Business: CompHosp/Med (71.7%), FEHBP (21.8%), MedSup (3.5%), Dental (3.0%)												Principal States: MS (100.0%)						
6,671	82.5	18.0	-0.2	-0.1	-0.4	2.88	7.29	5.7	4.2	74.6	...	0.8	1.9	74.9	81.1	0.5	...	10.4	50.0
14,135	85.6	15.7	2.1	1.0	4.5	4.15	13.62	18.1	4.1	96.9	...	3.6	21.9	112.9	120.9	...	...	8.1	42.8
5,338	81.1	17.6	7.4	3.6	14.3	6.96	10.83	6.3	3.5	120.1	...	0.4	23.6	124.9	134.0	...	...	5.9	36.3
-20,531	83.8	16.3	7.2	3.4	13.9	9.07	-0.98	1.6	4.4	94.7	...	1.5	-18.6	89.8	97.3	0.2	...	9.6	37.7
12,624	86.8	16.7	-3.9	-1.9	-7.9	3.30	10.14	-2.5	4.1	101.8	...	0.3	3.9	87.2	96.8	0.0	...	8.9	41.2
	Principal Lines of Business: CompHosp/Med (64.6%), FEHBP (24.3%), MedSup (5.9%), OtherHlth (3.7%), Medicare (0.7%)												Principal States: MT (100.0%)						
1,461	87.6	9.9	4.1	3.0	6.4	3.53	4.15	11.1	2.0	179.8	0.1	2.2	6.4	169.0	196.7	2.3	...	11.8	7.5
10,370	88.0	11.6	2.3	1.6	3.7	3.83	5.81	13.4	2.1	164.2	0.1	2.5	8.3	166.9	192.5	1.2	...	11.6	6.6
7,965	89.9	11.4	1.1	0.7	1.8	4.16	5.45	15.8	2.4	156.3	0.0	3.0	4.8	154.5	180.8	1.1	...	11.5	7.6
-32,553	89.6	13.0	-0.1	-0.1	-0.3	4.04	-1.31	8.8	3.0	121.5	0.0	4.0	-12.6	128.4	148.1	1.7	...	13.4	11.2
1,132	87.1	11.8	-4.3	-2.6	-8.4	3.06	2.07	8.6	3.5	92.3	0.0	5.0	-7.4	109.1	124.1	0.7	...	11.3	17.5
	Principal Lines of Business: CompHosp/Med (69.1%), FEHBP (14.3%), MedSup (10.8%), OtherHlth (4.6%), Medicare (1.2%)												Principal States: NE (100.0%)						
26,658	77.9	18.2	5.8	3.5	12.8	2.92	4.59	10.0	3.3	84.6	0.1	0.5	13.2	102.3	116.1	0.2	...	4.3	23.3
48,002	78.7	17.4	5.2	3.1	11.2	3.31	6.24	13.7	3.3	92.5	0.1	0.5	13.3	112.9	127.4	0.0	...	4.4	22.9
1,119	79.7	14.6	7.7	4.5	15.6	3.48	4.05	10.1	3.1	101.3	0.0	0.6	15.7	127.6	145.2	0.0	...	3.8	20.4
-99,252	81.7	13.7	6.9	3.8	14.0	3.74	-1.44	11.6	3.6	96.1	0.0	0.6	-2.1	119.0	134.8	0.0	...	5.7	23.7
87,081	84.4	14.0	3.0	1.7	6.0	3.64	6.46	4.9	3.3	102.9	0.0	0.7	13.1	131.3	148.3	...	...	6.8	22.9
	Principal Lines of Business: CompHosp/Med (65.5%), FEHBP (15.3%), Medicare (9.8%), MedSup (5.9%), OtherHlth (2.5%)												Principal States: NC (100.0%)						

2010 BEST'S KEY RATING GUIDE — LIFE/HEALTH EDITION
ANNUAL STATEMENT DATA FOR YEARS 2005 – 2009

Data in U.S. Dollars

COMPANY NAME Ultimate Parent Association Principal Officer Mailing Address Dom. : Began Bus. : Struct. : Mktg. Specialty Phone # AMB# NAIC#	Best's Financial Strength Rating FSC	Data Year	Balance Sheet: Bonds (%)	Mort. Loans & R.E. (%)	Com & Pref. Stock (%)	All Other Assets (%)	Total Assets ($000)	Life Reserves (%)	Health Reserves %)	Ann Res. & Dep. Liabilities (%)	All Other Liabilities (%)	Capital & Surplus ($000)	Operations: Direct Premiums Written ($000)	Net Premiums Written & Deposits ($000)	Operating Cash Flow ($000)	NOG Before Taxes ($000)	NOG After Taxes ($000)	Net Income ($000)
BLUE CROSS & BLUE SHIELD OF RI James E. Purcell President & CEO 444 Westminster Street Providence, RI 02903 RI : 1939 : Stock : Agency Group A&H 401-459-1000 AMB# 064570 NAIC# 53473	NR-5	'05	78.8	3.2	3.9	14.1	594,437	...	34.5	...	65.5	315,902	1,587,834	1,586,311	20,603	36,243	29,342	31,055
		'06	73.7	2.8	7.1	16.3	659,734	...	33.7	...	66.3	371,768	1,696,909	1,696,754	56,052	61,564	47,675	49,980
		'07	69.5	2.7	9.6	18.2	728,694	...	33.3	...	66.7	428,810	1,766,357	1,768,935	55,537	74,892	60,654	61,314
		'08	66.5	4.6	8.5	20.4	710,567	...	30.9	...	69.1	414,835	1,761,764	1,755,801	9,609	69,302	65,690	46,056
		'09	60.4	4.5	11.3	23.7	678,812	...	44.5	...	55.5	298,721	1,708,227	1,703,432	-26,922	-101,162	-96,051	-99,944
		Rating History: NR-5, 04/06/10; NR-5, 08/26/09; B+ pd, 09/19/08; B+ pd, 08/27/07; B+ pd, 09/21/06																
BLUE CROSS & BLUE SHIELD OF SC Blue Cross&Blue Shield of South Carolina M. Edward Sellers Chairman, President & CEO 2501 Faraway Drive Columbia, SC 29219 SC : 1947 : Mutual : Agency Group A&H 803-788-0222 AMB# 001727 NAIC# 38520	A+ Rating Outlook: Stable FSC XIV	'05	30.0	6.1	24.9	39.1	1,634,684	0.2	26.0	...	73.8	972,294	1,391,099	1,388,856	129,715	165,517	118,538	78,786
		'06	27.6	5.4	27.1	39.9	1,864,582	0.3	20.9	...	78.9	1,078,637	1,543,208	1,550,398	135,988	141,598	75,864	99,080
		'07	27.1	4.9	27.7	40.3	2,091,145	0.2	19.4	...	80.4	1,299,510	1,535,879	1,535,140	191,629	142,185	122,704	148,136
		'08	27.2	5.5	28.7	38.7	2,087,613	0.2	21.4	...	78.4	1,322,727	1,641,434	1,643,516	121,849	158,783	137,927	119,565
		'09	25.9	6.4	29.9	37.8	2,328,125	1.6	24.1	...	74.3	1,500,109	1,677,067	1,772,505	109,970	131,726	114,114	66,089
		Rating History: A+ g, 12/16/09; A+ g, 12/18/08; A+ g, 11/16/07; A+ g, 01/25/07; A+ g, 01/12/06																
BLUE CROSS & BLUE SHIELD OF VT Blue Cross and Blue Shield of Vermont Don C. George President & CEO P.O. Box 186 Montpelier, VT 05601-0186 VT : 1980 : Non-Profit : Agency Health 802-223-6131 AMB# 064541 NAIC# 53295	B++ Rating Outlook: Stable FSC VII	'05	49.8	4.2	11.8	34.3	160,969	...	60.6	...	39.4	75,525	285,291	282,663	2,592	10,101	7,697	7,774
		'06	56.9	4.2	9.8	29.2	161,151	...	61.1	...	38.9	77,714	316,655	313,824	3,316	8,012	6,253	6,079
		'07	57.0	5.2	14.0	23.8	135,195	...	35.3	...	64.7	69,875	259,250	256,120	3,927	4,032	2,676	2,747
		'08	42.6	5.1	20.4	31.9	139,951	...	34.8	...	65.2	71,489	293,450	290,623	-6,310	-1,160	1,155	-75
		'09	44.1	5.6	25.8	24.5	135,908	...	30.9	...	69.1	80,960	287,427	284,012	-11,812	3,261	3,874	3,622
		Rating History: B++g, 02/19/10; B++g, 02/03/09; B++g, 03/21/08; B++g, 02/22/07; B++g, 03/08/06																
BC BS HEALTHCARE PLAN OF GA WellPoint Inc. Monye M. Connolly President 3350 Peachtree Road, NE Atlanta, GA 30326 GA : 1986 : Stock : Broker Group A&H, Health 404-842-8000 AMB# 068527 NAIC# 96962	A Rating Outlook: Stable FSC IX	'05	68.9	...	...	31.1	329,768	...	62.3	...	37.7	161,433	1,534,762	1,534,762	-46,098	94,147	62,086	61,745
		'06	57.9	...	...	42.1	353,197	...	57.0	...	43.0	173,671	1,428,573	1,428,573	18,883	128,817	76,387	75,700
		'07	61.0	...	0.2	38.8	389,060	...	51.3	...	48.7	187,373	1,397,084	1,397,084	-5,003	136,687	88,170	87,071
		'08	60.8	...	0.2	39.0	379,680	...	52.1	...	47.9	182,551	1,393,519	1,393,519	14,985	90,021	63,303	59,943
		'09	70.1	...	...	29.9	378,399	...	55.1	...	44.9	207,860	1,345,518	1,345,518	5,163	93,499	61,848	61,380
		Rating History: A g, 04/27/10; A g, 01/23/09; A g, 03/20/08; A g, 11/06/06; A g, 12/29/05																
BLUE CROSS BLUE SHIELD MT(HMO) Blue Cross and Blue Shield of Montana Sherry Cladouhos President & CEO P.O. Box 4309 Helena, MT 59604 MT : 1987 : Non-Profit : Broker Health 406-444-8820 AMB# 064138 NAIC# 53686	NR-5	'05	...	...	...	100.0	...	...	...	...	100.0	...	73,604	71,475	...	1,438	1,150	1,150
		'06	...	...	...	100.0	...	...	...	...	100.0	...	68,989	67,141	...	103	83	83
		'07	...	...	...	100.0	...	...	...	...	100.0	...	68,053	67,722	...	3,364	2,692	2,692
		'08	...	...	...	100.0	...	...	...	...	100.0	...	45,307	45,186	...	-307	-246	-246
		'09	...	...	...	100.0	...	...	...	...	100.0	...	33,731	33,731	...	1,906	1,525	1,525
		Rating History: NR-5, 07/01/09; NR-5, 04/29/08; NR-5, 04/20/07; NR-5, 05/18/06; NR-5, 05/11/05																
BLUE CROSS BLUE SHIELD OF MI Blue Cross Blue Shield of Michigan Daniel J. Loepp President & CEO 600 E. Lafayette Detroit, MI 48226 MI : 1975 : Non-Profit : Agency Group A&H 313-225-9000 AMB# 060081 NAIC# 54291	A- Rating Outlook: Negative FSC XV	'05	52.7	3.7	23.7	19.8	4,846,089	...	55.1	...	44.9	2,461,021	5,614,913	5,614,913	410,626	279,287	209,161	193,004
		'06	52.4	3.8	28.4	15.4	5,237,887	...	52.1	...	47.9	2,501,444	5,865,134	5,865,134	58,408	204,878	169,234	158,926
		'07	50.4	3.6	30.1	16.0	5,418,152	...	52.8	...	47.2	2,406,089	6,184,770	6,184,770	343,787	-44,269	-3,413	16,184
		'08	54.9	3.6	27.7	13.7	5,127,545	...	53.9	...	46.1	2,227,407	6,837,195	6,835,648	-174,805	169,740	146,166	4,125
		'09	49.4	3.1	27.0	20.5	6,182,477	...	41.4	...	58.6	2,562,230	6,857,124	6,855,338	361,111	-58,622	-34,286	12,579
		Rating History: A- g, 10/16/09; A- g, 09/03/08; A- g, 08/31/07; A- g, 10/04/06; A- g, 09/01/05																
BLUE CROSS BLUE SHIELD OF WI WellPoint Inc. Steven J. Martenet President & CEO 6775 West Washington Street Milwaukee, WI 53214 WI : 1939 : Non-Profit : Not Available Group A&H 414-226-5000 AMB# 064315 NAIC# 54003	A Rating Outlook: Stable FSC VIII	'05	51.2	1.0	29.6	18.2	456,914	...	38.4	...	61.6	234,998	735,205	736,559	21,757	36,061	10,906	10,717
		'06	44.8	1.0	19.7	34.5	480,556	...	49.8	...	50.2	235,370	859,456	861,191	-57,802	74,607	53,947	35,112
		'07	50.1	1.1	13.3	35.5	448,553	...	52.6	...	47.4	179,084	968,581	970,621	20,529	63,557	88,616	84,116
		'08	50.7	0.9	11.2	37.2	508,419	...	48.6	...	51.4	179,179	1,012,000	1,013,678	-18,128	12,128	205	-5,798
		'09	54.0	1.0	12.7	32.3	503,499	...	41.1	...	58.9	218,364	866,813	867,997	-5,530	117,635	88,399	85,315
		Rating History: A g, 04/27/10; A- g, 01/23/09; A- g, 03/20/08; A- g, 11/06/06; A- g, 12/29/05																
BLUE CROSS BLUE SHIELD OF WY[2] Timothy J. Crilly President & Secretary 4000 House Avenue Cheyenne, WY 82001 WY : 1976 : Stock : Agency Group A&H 307-634-1393 AMB# 064567 NAIC# 53767	NR-5	'05	38.0	0.9	38.3	22.8	160,624	...	44.9	...	55.1	94,901	175,937	174,247	10,031	10,424	6,714	6,468
		'06	38.4	0.7	38.1	22.7	187,400	...	47.3	...	52.7	109,615	194,044	191,843	19,606	15,214	9,626	10,918
		'07	40.3	0.7	38.1	20.9	195,355	...	44.1	...	55.9	118,539	208,011	204,626	10,273	9,484	6,998	7,266
		'08	40.2	0.7	31.6	27.5	191,127	...	55.3	...	44.7	112,150	241,351	237,666	4,400	24,889	18,417	16,420
		'09	37.7	0.8	39.4	22.1	219,283	...	55.2	...	44.8	144,040	235,933	231,823	14,632	27,410	21,981	21,331
		Rating History: NR-5, 05/11/10; NR-5, 05/07/09; NR-5, 04/25/08; NR-5, 04/09/07; NR-5, 05/16/06																
BLUE CROSS OF CALIFORNIA WellPoint Inc. Brian A. Sassi President 21555 Oxnard Street Woodland Hills, CA 91367 CA : 1982 : Stock : Broker Group A&H, Health 805-557-6655 AMB# 068970	A Rating Outlook: Stable FSC XIII	'05	...	...	...	100.0	5,357,451	...	...	...	100.0	1,941,638	11,125,715	11,125,715	96,078	1,140,223	680,397	680,397
		'06	...	...	...	100.0	5,000,677	...	...	...	100.0	2,075,217	11,219,922	11,219,922	220,131	995,226	635,347	635,347
		'07	...	...	...	100.0	4,593,901	...	...	...	100.0	1,843,793	11,488,937	11,488,937	-284,541	1,159,256	716,865	716,865
		'08	...	...	...	100.0	3,804,226	...	...	...	100.0	1,217,752	11,429,625	11,429,625	64,824	489,213	285,885	285,885
		'09	...	...	...	100.0	3,692,956	...	...	...	100.0	1,377,338	11,079,124	11,079,124	-262,759	757,194	450,473	450,473
		Rating History: A g, 04/27/10; A g, 01/23/09; A g, 03/20/08; A g, 11/06/06; A g, 12/29/05																

	Profitability Tests							Leverage Tests						Liquidity Tests					
Un-Realized Capital Gains ($000)	Benefits Paid to NPW & Dep (%)	Comm. & Expenses to NPW & Dep (%)	NOG to Total Assets (%)	NOG to Total Rev (%)	Operating Return on Equity (%)	Net Yield (%)	Total Return (%)	Change in NPW & Dep (%)	NPW & Dep to Capital (X)	Capital & Surplus to Liabilities (%)	Surplus Relief (%)	Reins Leverage (%)	Change in Capital (%)	Quick Liquidity (%)	Current Liquidity (%)	Non-Invest Grade Bonds to Capital (%)	Delinq. & Foreclosed Mortgages to Capital (%)	Mort. & Credit Tenant Loans & R.E. to Capital (%)	Affiliated Invest to Capital (%)
-1,559	87.6	10.5	4.6	1.8	9.8	3.18	3.21	-1.4	5.0	113.4	...	0.1	11.0	159.4	169.7	...	...	6.0	6.0
2,280	85.5	10.9	7.6	2.8	13.9	4.01	4.86	7.0	4.6	129.1	...	0.1	17.7	173.9	184.8	...	...	5.0	5.0
-690	84.7	11.3	8.7	3.4	15.2	4.28	4.27	4.3	4.1	143.0	...	0.0	15.3	179.4	191.5	...	...	4.6	4.7
-12,332	84.0	13.3	9.1	3.7	15.6	4.13	-1.03	-0.7	4.2	140.3	...	0.2	-3.3	166.6	179.0	...	...	7.9	1.0
21,635	86.2	15.3	-13.8	-5.6	-26.9	3.69	6.90	-3.0	5.7	78.6	...	0.1	-28.0	111.4	121.2	0.7	...	10.3	12.0
Principal Lines of Business: CompHosp/Med (60.2%), Medicare (25.9%), FEHBP (5.8%), MedSup (2.9%), Medicaid (2.6%)														Principal States: RI (99.9%)					
73,773	79.6	13.3	7.8	8.1	12.8	2.52	5.49	14.3	1.4	146.8	0.5	0.1	10.8	82.2	92.2	0.7	...	10.2	55.1
71,266	80.7	13.8	4.3	4.7	7.4	2.07	8.80	11.6	1.4	137.2	0.5	0.1	10.9	76.2	85.9	0.5	...	9.3	57.3
36,375	80.4	16.2	6.2	7.6	10.3	3.94	7.71	-1.0	1.2	164.2	0.0	0.1	20.5	86.4	96.9	0.4	...	7.8	55.5
-90,577	80.1	15.9	6.6	7.9	10.5	4.37	-1.67	7.1	1.2	172.9	0.0	0.1	1.8	77.4	87.3	0.1	...	8.7	61.8
112,946	79.9	17.9	5.2	6.1	8.1	4.66	8.33	7.8	1.2	181.2	0.0	0.1	13.4	78.3	87.4	0.1	...	9.9	62.6
Principal Lines of Business: CompHosp/Med (59.1%), FEHBP (20.5%), MedSup (6.5%), Prop/Cas (4.7%), Medicare (3.9%)														Principal States: SC (100.0%)					
787	85.2	13.6	5.0	2.7	10.6	3.16	4.02	5.9	3.7	88.4	...	4.0	8.8	84.8	93.4	...	...	8.9	32.6
-3,255	86.5	12.9	3.9	1.9	8.2	4.57	1.26	11.0	4.0	93.1	...	3.4	2.9	86.3	95.8	...	...	8.7	27.4
3,291	87.4	14.3	1.8	0.9	3.6	4.81	8.05	-18.4	3.7	107.0	...	3.9	-10.1	123.5	134.2	2.7	...	10.0	35.6
8,796	86.5	16.6	0.8	0.4	1.6	4.49	11.75	13.5	4.1	104.4	...	3.7	2.3	120.0	130.0	2.1	...	10.0	48.0
5,276	87.3	14.3	2.8	1.3	5.1	3.60	8.44	-2.3	3.5	147.3	...	2.6	13.2	116.4	126.3	1.6	...	9.4	48.4
Principal Lines of Business: CompHosp/Med (71.3%), FEHBP (19.4%), MedSup (5.5%), OtherHlth (3.8%)														Principal States: VT (98.9%)					
...	81.7	16.3	18.2	3.9	42.2	4.35	4.22	-3.9	9.5	95.9	...	...	21.7	117.3	130.9	...	...	...	...
-45	79.1	18.0	22.4	5.0	45.6	4.84	4.55	-6.9	8.2	96.7	...	...	7.6	141.5	155.2	0.8	...	...	...
-3	78.7	18.0	23.8	5.9	48.8	5.45	5.02	-2.2	7.5	92.9	...	...	7.9	99.7	112.2	0.3	...	...	...
23	80.5	18.9	16.5	4.3	34.2	4.32	3.03	-0.3	7.6	92.6	...	...	-2.6	119.6	132.9	0.2	...	...	...
9	79.7	16.6	16.3	4.5	31.7	4.09	3.92	-3.4	6.5	121.9	...	...	13.9	124.8	140.1	...	...	...	...
Principal Lines of Business: CompHosp/Med (98.0%), Medicare (1.2%), OtherHlth (0.8%)														Principal States: GA (100.0%)					
...	80.1	18.0	...	1.6	...	...	...	-0.6	...	...	...	...	...	...	...	...	...	...	...
...	83.0	18.1	...	0.1	...	...	...	-6.1	...	...	...	...	...	...	...	...	...	...	...
...	78.0	16.0	...	4.0	...	...	...	0.9	...	...	...	...	...	...	...	...	...	...	...
...	84.2	16.3	...	-0.5	...	...	...	-33.3	...	...	...	...	...	...	...	...	...	...	...
...	79.4	15.0	...	4.5	...	...	...	-25.4	...	...	...	...	...	...	...	...	...	...	...
Principal Lines of Business: CompHosp/Med (100.0%)																			
72,085	86.3	9.9	4.6	3.7	8.9	4.04	5.41	2.1	2.3	103.2	...	...	9.7	116.6	130.0	5.6	...	7.4	44.8
72,044	89.7	10.8	3.4	2.8	6.8	4.36	5.75	4.5	2.3	91.4	...	...	1.6	80.6	92.4	6.2	...	8.0	49.0
118,294	92.2	11.2	-0.1	-0.1	-0.1	4.55	7.58	5.4	2.6	79.9	...	...	-3.8	84.1	95.3	6.5	...	8.0	61.3
-142,265	89.7	10.7	2.8	2.1	6.3	4.85	-1.62	10.5	3.1	76.8	...	...	-7.4	34.0	65.5	4.8	...	8.4	53.0
322,207	91.5	12.0	-0.6	-0.5	-1.4	4.71	13.73	0.3	2.7	70.8	...	...	15.0	51.8	72.7	5.5	...	7.4	52.3
Principal Lines of Business: CompHosp/Med (68.1%), Medicare (17.2%), FEHBP (5.1%), OtherHlth (4.1%), MedSup (4.0%)														Principal States: MI (100.0%)					
43,318	82.6	12.9	2.6	1.5	4.9	2.82	15.08	5.4	3.1	105.9	0.0	0.2	13.6	91.0	102.2	0.0	...	2.0	72.3
14,968	81.6	11.9	11.5	6.2	22.9	3.60	2.79	16.9	3.7	96.0	0.0	0.0	0.2	75.5	85.9	1.2	...	2.1	56.3
-22,692	87.4	8.7	19.1	8.8	42.8	9.19	1.61	12.7	5.4	66.5	0.0	0.3	-23.9	100.9	112.4	0.9	...	2.8	49.3
-3,954	90.1	8.2	0.0	0.0	0.1	4.53	1.47	4.4	5.7	54.4	0.0	0.4	0.1	58.4	66.9	1.8	...	2.6	47.4
7,384	81.0	9.8	17.5	10.0	44.5	4.76	6.14	-14.4	4.0	76.6	0.0	0.4	21.9	61.8	73.9	2.8	...	2.3	41.1
Principal Lines of Business: FEHBP (37.7%), Medicare (32.6%), CompHosp/Med (16.2%), MedSup (9.1%), OtherHlth (2.2%)														Principal States: WI (100.0%)					
1,444	85.5	11.0	4.4	3.8	7.4	3.90	4.85	10.0	1.8	144.4	...	0.7	9.1	154.8	177.3	...	...	1.5	1.3
3,082	84.0	10.7	5.5	5.0	9.4	4.59	7.64	10.1	1.8	140.9	...	1.0	15.5	158.0	180.7	...	...	1.3	1.1
-24	88.8	11.1	3.7	3.2	6.1	4.61	4.76	6.7	1.7	154.3	...	7.8	8.1	167.9	192.6	0.3	...	1.1	1.0
-18,685	81.8	8.4	9.5	7.8	16.0	4.18	-8.42	16.1	2.1	142.0	...	3.9	-5.4	143.2	164.5	0.4	...	1.2	1.1
10,960	83.4	9.2	10.7	9.3	17.2	3.84	10.51	-2.5	1.6	191.4	...	1.6	28.4	167.0	195.3	0.3	...	1.2	1.1
Principal Lines of Business: CompHosp/Med (63.1%), FEHBP (27.4%), MedSup (5.6%), OtherHlth (2.4%), Dental (1.1%)														Principal States: WY (100.0%)					
...	80.9	11.3	12.9	6.0	37.5	...	...	6.1	5.7	56.8	...	...	15.4	100.5	100.5	...	...	...	...
...	81.5	11.7	12.3	5.5	31.6	...	...	0.8	5.4	70.9	...	...	6.9	109.2	109.2	...	...	...	...
...	80.4	11.3	14.9	6.1	36.6	...	...	2.4	6.2	67.0	...	...	-11.2	88.5	88.5	...	...	...	...
...	83.4	10.3	6.8	2.6	18.7	...	...	-0.5	9.4	47.1	...	...	-34.0	77.6	77.6	...	...	...	...
...	83.3	10.3	12.0	4.0	34.7	...	...	-3.1	8.0	59.5	...	...	13.1	93.9	93.9	...	...	...	...
Principal Lines of Business: CompHosp/Med (78.9%), Medicaid (18.3%), Medicare (2.7%)																			

2010 BEST'S KEY RATING GUIDE — LIFE/HEALTH EDITION
ANNUAL STATEMENT DATA FOR YEARS 2005 – 2009

Data in U.S. Dollars

COMPANY NAME Ultimate Parent Association Principal Officer Mailing Address Dom. : Began Bus. : Struct. : Mktg. Specialty Phone # AMB# NAIC#	Best's Financial Strength Rating FSC	Data Year	Balance Sheet Bonds (%)	Mort. Loans & R.E. (%)	Com & Pref. Stock (%)	All Other Assets (%)	Total Assets ($000)	Life Reserves (%)	Health Reserves %)	Ann Res. & Dep. Liabilities (%)	All Other Liabilities (%)	Capital & Surplus ($000)	Operations Direct Premiums Written ($000)	Net Premiums Written & Deposits ($000)	Operating Cash Flow ($000)	NOG Before Taxes ($000)	NOG After Taxes ($000)	Net Income ($000)
BLUE CROSS OF ID HLTH SERVICE Ray Flachbart President & CEO 3000 E. Pine Avenue Meridian, ID 83642 ID : 1978 : Mutual : Broker Group A&H 208-345-4550 AMB# 008805 NAIC# 60095	NR-5	'05	60.1	2.2	22.2	15.5	334,278	...	58.9	...	41.1	196,463	800,055	800,055	40,237	60,286	47,703	49,139
		'06	56.7	5.0	24.8	13.5	386,577	...	54.5	...	45.5	224,202	889,311	889,311	44,178	38,023	28,825	31,749
		'07	52.9	5.0	26.9	15.2	424,391	...	61.0	...	39.0	260,890	974,281	966,313	24,048	35,182	27,170	33,794
		'08	47.6	4.8	22.1	25.6	443,804	...	55.7	...	44.3	263,131	1,025,882	998,285	36,768	49,701	41,195	13,928
		'09	39.5	4.0	32.3	24.3	534,276	...	51.6	...	48.4	355,577	1,083,036	1,054,119	49,800	61,252	47,590	49,685
		Rating History: NR-5, 04/07/10; NR-5, 03/13/09; NR-5, 04/03/08; NR-5, 05/03/07; NR-5, 05/17/06																
BLUE SHIELD OF CA LIFE & HLTH California Physicians' Service Duncan Ross President & CEO 50 Beale Street San Francisco, CA 94105 CA : 1954 : Stock : Broker Group A&H, Group Life, Ind A&H 888-800-2742 AMB# 006181 NAIC# 61557	A	'05	93.0	...	...	7.0	197,877	15.2	54.7	...	30.1	141,330	200,792	198,656	33,335	27,440	21,787	21,787
		'06	82.6	...	...	17.4	235,675	4.2	29.3	...	66.5	82,639	308,602	302,623	35,118	29,553	23,901	23,901
	Rating Outlook: Stable	'07	88.3	...	...	11.7	218,807	5.7	54.2	0.0	40.1	105,444	477,264	470,935	-15,964	38,257	22,597	22,597
		'08	74.7	...	...	25.3	324,328	3.4	61.7	0.0	34.9	138,487	758,444	750,525	96,605	5,059	4,690	2,967
	FSC XV	'09	78.8	...	...	21.2	521,027	2.4	69.7	0.0	27.9	247,857	1,224,308	1,214,179	180,359	-96,586	-62,892	-63,235
		Rating History: A g, 05/26/10; A-, 07/10/09; A-, 06/26/08; A-, 06/28/07; A-, 06/21/06																
BLUEBONNET LIFE INS CO Blue Cross & BS of MS a Mutual Ins Co Richard J. Hale President & CEO 3545 Lakeland Drive Flowood, MS 39232-9799 MS : 1984 : Stock : Agency Accidental Death, Dismemberment, Term Life 601-664-4218 AMB# 068175 NAIC# 68535	A	'05	79.4	...	...	20.6	28,165	31.1	0.4	...	68.5	23,688	9,130	7,581	3,348	4,480	3,009	3,009
		'06	75.8	...	...	24.2	31,215	31.3	0.4	...	68.2	26,852	9,280	7,753	3,201	4,756	3,139	3,139
	Rating Outlook: Stable	'07	77.0	...	...	23.0	34,637	29.8	0.4	...	69.7	30,282	8,753	7,685	3,552	5,100	3,444	3,444
		'08	79.1	...	...	20.9	38,395	25.5	0.3	...	74.2	33,719	8,419	7,401	3,799	5,315	3,662	3,662
	FSC X	'09	76.5	...	...	23.5	40,771	31.9	0.3	...	67.8	36,898	7,710	6,912	2,743	4,590	3,062	3,062
		Rating History: A g, 06/16/09; A g, 06/02/08; A g, 05/25/07; A g, 06/20/06; A g, 06/22/05																
BLUECAID OF MICHIGAN Blue Cross Blue Shield of Michigan Jeanne H. Carlson President & CEO 20500 Civic Center Drive Southfield, MI 48076 MI : 2003 : Non-Profit : Broker Health 248-799-6400 AMB# 064738 NAIC# 11557	NR-2	'05	32.9	...	...	67.1	3,367	...	88.5	...	11.5	2,037	34,725	34,721	-285	595	595	595
		'06	30.9	...	...	69.1	3,760	...	95.8	...	4.2	1,874	34,136	34,132	221	-100	-100	-100
		'07	...	...	...	100.0	11,773	...	18.0	...	82.0	2,980	44,655	44,299	7,930	-1,311	-1,311	-1,312
		'08	...	...	...	100.0	6,988	...	48.4	...	51.6	3,247	51,354	51,271	-4,956	-80	-80	-80
		'09	...	...	...	100.0	6,885	...	32.2	...	67.8	3,770	59,759	59,378	-170	462	462	462
		Rating History: NR-2, 10/16/09; NR-2, 09/03/08; NR-3, 03/24/08; NR-3, 01/08/07; NR-5, 05/08/06																
BLUECHOICE HEALTHPLAN OF SC Blue Cross&Blue Shield of South Carolina Mary P. Mazzola Spivey President & COO 4101 Percival Road Columbia, SC 29229 SC : 1984 : Stock : Broker Group A&H, Ind A&H 803-786-8466 AMB# 068593 NAIC# 95741	A+	'05	47.9	0.4	21.2	30.5	120,856	...	54.5	...	45.5	86,933	221,696	224,477	9,919	14,322	9,169	11,017
		'06	42.4	0.1	21.6	35.9	140,454	...	50.3	...	49.7	102,165	248,919	252,214	12,468	19,774	13,524	14,046
	Rating Outlook: Stable	'07	44.0	0.1	24.3	31.7	156,720	...	56.5	...	43.5	115,609	305,570	311,249	19,589	17,463	12,085	11,969
		'08	41.6	0.1	17.3	41.0	170,473	...	54.6	...	45.4	118,341	333,312	333,518	13,383	16,883	11,722	9,584
	FSC XIV	'09	52.1	0.1	16.4	31.5	206,752	...	36.4	...	63.6	131,284	377,289	341,968	32,047	13,370	9,568	7,867
		Rating History: A+ g, 12/16/09; A+ g, 12/18/08; A+ g, 11/16/07; A+ g, 01/25/07; A+ g, 01/12/06																
BLUECROSS BLUESHIELD OF TN[2] BlueCross BlueShield of Tennessee Inc Vicky B. Gregg President & CEO 801 Pine Street Chattanooga, TN 37402 TN : 1945 : Non-Profit : Not Available Medical, Dental, Med supp 423-755-5600 AMB# 064002 NAIC# 54518	NR-5	'05	53.0	3.3	22.6	21.1	1,452,509	...	48.9	...	51.1	907,948	2,189,900	2,186,435	180,720	202,814	114,808	147,606
		'06	52.3	2.9	20.7	24.1	1,499,826	...	54.8	...	45.2	936,119	2,483,092	2,480,054	88,324	131,710	77,553	85,372
		'07	48.4	9.1	18.4	24.0	1,776,763	...	55.4	...	44.6	1,152,585	2,710,435	2,710,435	199,950	191,447	106,741	144,323
		'08	40.6	5.5	14.9	39.0	1,604,716	...	46.0	...	54.0	903,889	2,942,268	2,942,268	101,089	190,967	138,597	112,070
		'09	44.2	6.7	12.3	36.8	1,741,371	...	46.5	...	53.5	1,137,123	3,159,668	3,159,668	19,823	128,717	104,304	80,879
		Rating History: NR-5, 04/15/10; NR-5, 08/26/09; A- pd, 11/24/08; A- pd, 09/04/07; A- pd, 09/29/06																
BLUEGRASS FAMILY HEALTH INC Baptist Healthcare System, Inc James Fritz CEO 651 Perimeter Drive, Suite 300 Lexington, KY 40517 KY : 1993 : Stock : Broker Group A&H 859-269-4475 AMB# 068747 NAIC# 95071	B++	'05	49.1	...	23.4	27.5	106,744	...	75.2	...	24.8	43,908	493,384	492,310	31,993	17,994	11,266	13,595
		'06	43.8	...	46.5	9.7	73,696	...	55.0	...	45.0	44,332	162,291	161,768	-31,993	12,897	8,376	11,018
	Rating Outlook: Stable	'07	49.4	...	40.9	9.7	76,013	...	60.8	...	39.2	47,598	162,399	161,945	2,931	2,959	1,607	3,244
		'08	42.7	...	42.3	15.0	68,845	...	54.4	...	45.6	38,198	164,380	163,501	1,541	1,475	-975	210
	FSC VI	'09	41.0	...	40.6	18.5	76,615	...	63.5	...	36.5	47,451	185,107	182,749	-271	1,561	4,598	4,928
		Rating History: B++, 06/14/10; B++, 06/05/09; B++, 06/11/08; B++, 08/23/07; B++, 06/12/07																
BOSTON MEDICAL CENTER HTH PLAN[2] Boston Medical Center Elaine Ullian President Two Copley Place, Suite 600 Boston, MA 02116 MA : 1997 : Non-Profit : Not Available Health 617-748-6000 AMB# 064973 NAIC# 13203	NR-5	'05	...	...	...	...	...	...	...	...	...	...	...	...	...	...	...	...
		'06	...	...	...	...	...	...	...	...	...	...	...	...	...	...	...	...
		'07	...	...	...	...	...	...	...	...	...	...	...	...	...	...	...	...
		'08	...	...	...	100.0	271,695	...	82.4	...	17.6	164,645	1,090,465	1,090,465	55,240	56,710	56,710	56,714
		'09	...	...	...	...	...	...	...	...	...	...	...	...	...	...	...	...
		Rating History: NR-5, 05/14/09																
BOSTON MUTUAL LIFE INS CO Boston Mutual Life Insurance Company Paul E. Petry Chairman, President & CEO 120 Royall Street Canton, MA 02021-1098 MA : 1892 : Mutual : Broker Group A&H, Group Life, Ind Life 781-828-7000 AMB# 006170 NAIC# 61476	A-	'05	62.1	16.5	2.2	19.3	788,179	89.6	2.1	3.0	5.3	79,416	236,293	189,887	37,987	13,472	7,913	7,977
		'06	61.2	15.6	2.7	20.6	841,514	89.9	1.9	2.7	5.4	89,411	230,066	185,604	49,929	14,175	7,490	7,169
	Rating Outlook: Stable	'07	60.1	15.8	2.5	21.6	893,465	90.6	1.5	2.5	5.4	102,139	222,821	170,372	45,218	20,535	10,550	10,335
		'08	60.2	15.7	2.2	21.9	929,127	88.9	1.4	2.2	7.5	77,722	221,594	171,585	35,849	17,678	11,145	9,605
	FSC VIII	'09	61.4	13.6	2.7	22.3	995,277	89.7	1.2	2.1	7.0	108,146	215,604	171,505	50,560	16,707	10,384	9,985
		Rating History: A- g, 04/06/10; A- g, 05/21/09; A- g, 06/30/08; A- g, 06/14/07; A- g, 06/01/06																

2010 BEST'S KEY RATING GUIDE — LIFE/HEALTH EDITION
BEST'S PROFITABILITY, LEVERAGE AND LIQUIDITY TESTS 2005 – 2009

Data in U.S. Dollars

—	Profitability Tests							Leverage Tests						Liquidity Tests					
Un-Realized Capital Gains ($000)	Benefits Paid to NPW & Dep (%)	Comm. & Expenses to NPW & Dep (%)	NOG to Total Assets (%)	NOG to Total Rev (%)	Operating Return on Equity (%)	Net Yield (%)	Total Return (%)	Change in NPW & Dep (%)	NPW & Dep to Capital (X)	Capital & Surplus to Liabilities (%)	Surplus Relief (%)	Reins Leverage (%)	Change in Capital (%)	Quick Liquidity (%)	Current Liquidity (%)	Non-Invest Grade Bonds to Capital (%)	Delinq. & Foreclosed Mortgages to Capital (%)	Mort. & Credit Tenant Loans & R.E. to Capital (%)	Affiliated Invest to Capital (%)
1,710	81.0	13.0	15.3	5.8	28.1	3.56	4.66	15.1	4.1	142.6	...	...	37.3	187.2	206.8	...	...	3.7	3.8
6,188	84.7	12.7	8.0	3.2	13.7	4.21	6.97	11.2	4.0	138.1	...	...	14.1	174.4	194.9	...	...	8.6	8.7
-1,175	85.9	12.3	6.7	2.8	11.2	4.22	5.72	8.7	3.7	159.6	...	0.7	16.4	176.9	197.8	...	...	8.1	8.5
-12,883	84.8	12.0	9.5	4.1	15.7	4.26	-5.89	3.3	3.8	145.6	...	0.5	0.9	191.0	210.0	0.0	...	8.0	8.1
19,545	83.9	11.9	9.7	4.4	15.4	3.66	8.78	5.6	3.0	199.0	...	0.4	35.1	213.9	242.9	0.1	...	25.4	6.0
	Principal Lines of Business: CompHosp/Med (64.8%), Medicare (20.3%), FEHBP (8.8%), Dental (2.7%), MedSup (1.9%)													Principal States: ID (100.0%)					
...	65.6	26.4	12.0	10.5	16.7	3.94	4.27	85.9	1.4	251.9	0.4	2.6	18.2	281.7	310.7	...	...	...	...
...	68.4	25.4	11.0	7.6	21.3	4.66	4.82	52.3	3.6	54.4	0.9	5.3	-41.4	124.6	136.0	...	...	...	...
...	68.3	26.2	9.9	4.7	24.0	5.53	5.62	55.6	4.4	93.9	1.0	4.2	27.6	142.5	160.8	...	...	...	...
-43	75.4	25.4	1.7	0.6	3.8	4.35	3.78	59.4	5.4	74.5	1.0	6.2	30.7	143.2	155.0	0.1	...	...	...
43	85.2	24.1	-14.9	-5.1	-32.6	3.67	3.76	61.8	4.9	91.0	0.7	3.3	79.2	145.2	161.0	0.7	...	...	...
	Principal Lines of Business: GrpA&H (64.1%), IndA&H (35.2%), GrpLife (0.6%), OrdLife (0.1%)													Principal States: CA (100.0%)					
...	35.4	22.7	11.2	34.0	13.5	4.42	4.52	-2.9	0.3	535.8	...	1.8	12.8	521.3	566.8	...	...	...	...
...	35.9	22.3	10.6	34.0	12.4	4.73	4.78	2.3	0.3	625.1	...	5.8	13.4	589.9	643.6	...	...	...	...
...	33.8	22.4	10.5	36.9	12.1	4.84	4.88	-0.9	0.3	708.1	...	6.1	12.8	663.9	723.4	...	...	...	...
-137	29.2	21.5	10.0	40.7	11.4	4.35	4.00	-3.7	0.2	732.4	...	4.4	11.3	649.4	711.4	0.5	...	...	...
90	32.2	23.0	7.7	36.1	8.7	4.07	4.33	-6.6	0.2	966.3	...	4.6	9.4	818.7	885.7	3.2	...	...	...
	Principal Lines of Business: GrpLife (97.6%), GrpA&H (1.3%), OrdLife (1.1%), IndA&H (0.0%)													Principal States: MS (99.2%)					
...	84.1	8.2	17.8	1.8	29.0	5.13	5.13	24.0	17.0	153.1	...	...	-1.1	152.7	152.7	...	...	...	...
...	82.9	11.8	-2.8	-0.3	-5.1	9.60	9.60	-1.7	18.2	99.4	...	...	-8.0	128.4	128.4	...	...	...	...
46	85.1	12.4	-16.9	-3.1	-54.0	4.29	5.10	29.8	14.9	33.9	...	2.8	59.0	210.3	216.7	...	...	...	2.0
42	88.0	6.8	-0.9	-0.2	-2.6	1.33	1.92	15.7	15.8	86.8	...	11.6	9.0	238.7	248.6	...	...	...	3.1
85	87.4	10.5	6.7	0.8	13.2	-0.09	1.76	15.8	15.8	121.0	...	14.7	16.1	269.5	280.1	...	...	...	4.9
	Principal Lines of Business: Medicaid (100.0%)													Principal States: MI (100.0%)					
3,165	81.9	12.1	8.0	4.1	11.6	2.41	8.10	16.2	2.6	256.3	...	1.3	21.0	208.1	232.1	0.5	...	0.5	10.1
1,894	81.8	11.4	10.4	5.2	14.3	3.45	5.83	12.4	2.5	266.8	...	1.5	17.5	207.1	228.6	0.5	...	0.1	10.5
1,987	85.4	10.6	8.1	3.8	11.1	4.96	6.53	23.4	2.7	281.2	...	0.5	13.2	228.6	253.7	0.4	...	0.1	10.4
-5,848	85.6	11.0	7.2	3.5	10.0	4.40	-1.49	7.2	2.8	227.0	...	4.4	2.4	188.0	207.4	...	...	0.1	11.0
3,629	85.6	12.0	5.1	2.8	7.7	3.55	4.84	2.5	2.6	174.0	...	13.5	10.9	176.2	194.1	...	...	0.1	8.8
	Principal Lines of Business: CompHosp/Med (93.2%), Medicaid (6.6%), Dental (0.2%)													Principal States: SC (100.0%)					
-14,959	83.0	8.8	8.5	5.2	13.5	4.00	5.51	16.0	2.4	166.7	0.1	0.0	15.3	207.1	227.6	...	...	5.2	12.3
20,608	84.9	10.5	5.3	3.1	8.4	4.63	6.81	13.4	2.6	166.1	0.1	...	3.1	227.6	251.2	...	...	4.7	3.3
26,405	81.6	12.7	6.5	3.9	10.2	4.83	9.24	9.3	2.4	184.7	...	...	23.1	69.6	77.8	...	...	14.0	18.4
-216,994	81.7	12.7	8.2	4.7	13.5	3.17	-12.19	8.6	3.3	129.0	...	...	-21.6	157.1	175.7	...	...	9.8	27.6
37,007	82.8	14.1	6.2	3.3	10.2	3.39	4.40	7.4	2.8	188.2	...	...	25.8	182.9	204.6	0.1	...	10.2	30.4
	Principal Lines of Business: CompHosp/Med (71.0%), FEHBP (11.8%), Medicare (10.2%), MedSup (4.3%), Dental (2.3%)													Principal States: TN (100.0%)					
-488	90.1	6.9	12.1	2.3	29.7	3.14	5.33	19.4	11.2	69.9	...	0.7	36.9	133.2	147.8	...	...	...	...
657	80.7	13.4	9.3	5.1	19.0	3.01	6.92	-67.1	3.6	151.0	...	0.3	1.0	166.7	195.2	...	...	...	...
-1,092	85.2	13.7	2.1	1.0	3.5	3.09	3.90	0.1	3.4	167.5	...	0.1	7.4	181.9	211.7	...	...	...	...
-8,397	90.1	12.0	-1.3	-0.6	-2.3	3.09	-7.03	1.0	4.3	124.6	...	0.7	-19.7	147.6	165.0	...	...	...	...
3,991	91.7	9.0	6.3	2.5	10.7	2.80	9.84	11.8	3.9	162.7	...	1.6	24.2	172.7	193.9	...	...	...	...
	Principal Lines of Business: CompHosp/Med (99.9%), FEHBP (0.1%)													Principal States: KY (89.5%), TN (9.3%)					
...	...	...	...	...	...	...	...	...	...	...	...	...	...	...	...	...	...	...	...
...	...	...	...	...	...	...	...	...	...	...	...	...	...	...	...	...	...	...	...
...	...	...	...	...	...	...	...	...	...	...	...	...	...	...	...	...	...	...	...
...	91.4	7.7	...	5.0	...	...	...	...	6.6	153.8	...	...	...	252.7	252.7	...	...	...	...
...	...	...	...	...	...	...	...	...	...	...	...	...	...	...	...	...	...	...	...
996	57.0	35.9	1.0	3.3	10.8	5.80	6.07	-0.1	2.2	12.0	16.5	94.3	17.3	45.9	55.4	...	...	153.4	9.5
2,173	57.4	34.3	0.9	3.1	8.9	5.80	6.15	-2.3	2.0	12.7	14.0	89.0	12.2	45.7	55.4	...	...	137.9	9.3
997	55.7	35.4	1.2	4.6	11.0	5.76	5.94	-8.2	1.6	13.7	13.5	74.1	13.6	45.8	55.2	...	...	130.8	8.9
-3,603	56.5	36.8	1.2	4.8	12.4	5.78	5.23	0.7	2.1	9.8	18.5	98.7	-23.1	43.0	51.6	0.7	...	176.0	13.9
4,258	56.7	38.6	1.1	4.4	11.2	5.52	6.01	0.0	1.5	13.0	13.6	65.2	37.7	50.0	57.3	10.8	...	118.9	11.6
	Principal Lines of Business: OrdLife (71.1%), GrpLife (13.4%), GrpA&H (12.4%), IndA&H (2.7%), GrpAnn (0.4%)													Principal States: MA (21.5%), NJ (8.0%), PA (5.5%), CT (5.1%), NC (3.6%)					

2010 BEST'S KEY RATING GUIDE — LIFE/HEALTH EDITION
ANNUAL STATEMENT DATA FOR YEARS 2005 – 2009

Data in U.S. Dollars

COMPANY NAME Ultimate Parent Association Principal Officer Mailing Address Dom. : Began Bus. : Struct. : Mktg. Specialty Phone # AMB# NAIC#	Best's Financial Strength Rating FSC	Data Year	Balance Sheet Bonds (%)	Mort. Loans & R.E. (%)	Com & Pref. Stock (%)	All Other Assets (%)	Total Assets ($000)	Life Reserves (%)	Health Reserves %)	Ann Res. & Dep. Liabilities (%)	All Other Liabilities (%)	Capital & Surplus ($000)	Operations Direct Premiums Written ($000)	Net Premiums Written & Deposits ($000)	Operating Cash Flow ($000)	NOG Before Taxes ($000)	NOG After Taxes ($000)	Net Income ($000)
BRAVO HEALTH INSURANCE COMPANY Bravo Health Inc Jeffrey M. Folick President 3601 O'Donnell Street Baltimore, MD 21224-5238 DE : 2007 : Stock : Broker Health 800-235-9188 AMB# 060649 NAIC# 12784	NR-5	'05	...	...	...	...	...	...	...	...	...	...	...	...	...	...	...	...
		'06	...	...	...	100.0	7,645	...	...	...	100.0	7,645	...	...	7,645	145	145	145
		'07	35.3	...	...	64.7	19,232	...	17.7	...	82.3	7,639	11,965	11,965	9,592	625	328	328
		'08	13.8	...	...	86.2	53,145	...	65.8	...	34.2	13,887	122,870	122,870	-8,352	-5,778	-3,874	-3,822
		'09	6.6	...	...	93.4	47,900	...	29.7	...	70.3	23,854	241,855	241,848	5,684	3,979	2,993	2,876
		Rating History: NR-5, 03/24/10; NR-5, 03/13/09; NR-5, 03/11/08; NR-5, 09/07/07; NR-1, 06/08/07																
BRAVO HEALTH MID-ATLANTIC INC Bravo Health Inc Ace M. Hodgin, Jr. President 3601 O'Donnell Street Baltimore, MD 21224 MD : 2001 : Non-Profit : Broker Health 800-235-9188 AMB# 064697 NAIC# 10095	NR-5	'05	...	...	...	100.0	22,221	...	60.7	...	39.3	6,696	79,288	79,136	6,652	968	968	968
		'06	...	...	...	100.0	44,291	...	37.4	...	62.6	8,765	118,951	118,787	19,089	1,623	881	881
		'07	42.3	...	...	57.7	35,542	...	64.2	...	35.8	10,717	134,084	133,929	-9,929	1,264	926	926
		'08	43.8	...	...	56.2	41,129	...	76.7	...	23.3	13,229	163,986	163,435	1,364	-4,946	-3,176	-3,249
		'09	43.7	...	...	56.3	47,858	...	50.3	...	49.7	14,918	186,432	185,939	4,351	2,200	1,629	1,481
		Rating History: NR-5, 03/24/10; NR-5, 08/26/09; C+ pd, 09/03/08; C+ pd, 09/21/07; C+ pd, 09/05/06																
BRAVO HEALTH PENNSYLVANIA INC Bravo Health Inc Jason H. Feuerman President 3601 O'Donnell Street Baltimore, MD 21224-5238 PA : 2002 : Non-Profit : Broker Health 800-235-9188 AMB# 064743 NAIC# 11524	NR-5	'05	...	...	...	100.0	35,740	...	60.0	...	40.0	8,224	107,971	107,745	18,986	648	648	648
		'06	...	...	...	100.0	62,849	...	54.4	...	45.6	15,699	184,513	184,220	22,522	9,025	5,793	5,793
		'07	31.3	...	...	68.7	124,672	...	62.2	...	37.8	36,248	315,329	314,946	54,145	-3,564	-8,270	-8,270
		'08	38.2	...	...	61.8	156,158	...	70.7	...	29.3	71,158	550,042	549,636	15,672	13,517	-2,245	-2,295
		'09	38.3	...	...	61.7	154,056	...	72.4	...	27.6	71,622	624,857	624,455	-26,542	24,577	9,796	9,576
		Rating History: NR-5, 03/24/10; NR-5, 08/26/09; C+ pd, 09/03/08; C+ pd, 09/21/07; C+ pd, 09/05/06																
BRAVO HEALTH TEXAS INC Bravo Health Inc Patrick E. Feyen President 3601 O'Donnell Street Baltimore, MD 21224-5238 TX : 2005 : Non-Profit : Broker Health 800-235-9188 AMB# 064838 NAIC# 10134	NR-5	'05	...	...	...	...	...	...	...	...	...	...	...	...	...	...	...	...
		'06	...	...	...	100.0	43,010	...	11.7	...	88.3	2,907	37,120	37,088	36,143	357	98	98
		'07	45.3	...	...	54.7	49,648	...	21.3	...	78.7	5,618	63,369	63,278	6,305	6,806	4,549	4,549
		'08	31.3	...	...	68.7	30,328	...	70.4	...	29.6	11,045	117,079	116,948	-23,589	8,730	5,753	5,793
		'09	21.1	...	...	78.9	40,705	...	72.9	...	27.1	16,467	167,311	167,144	7,247	12,695	8,442	8,395
		Rating History: NR-5, 03/24/10; NR-5, 03/17/09; NR-5, 03/18/08; NR-5, 09/04/07																
BROKERS NATIONAL LIFE ASSUR BNL Financial Corporation Wayne E. Ahart Chairman P.O. Box 92529 Austin, TX 78709-2529 AR : 1964 : Stock : Broker Dental, Hosp Ind, Term Life 512-383-0220 AMB# 006023 NAIC# 74900	B+ Rating Outlook: Stable FSC V	'05	81.7	...	1.7	16.6	23,399	10.5	32.7	27.2	29.7	12,114	44,469	44,363	-1,724	2,658	2,235	2,263
		'06	82.4	...	2.4	15.2	23,701	11.1	33.5	26.2	29.2	13,223	44,814	44,680	968	2,970	2,466	2,491
		'07	72.3	...	2.2	25.5	26,976	10.6	28.5	23.8	37.1	15,834	44,732	44,592	2,868	4,080	3,339	3,350
		'08	74.7	...	1.9	23.4	26,577	12.6	25.9	28.5	33.0	16,965	43,644	43,539	409	3,555	2,918	2,630
		'09	64.9	...	2.6	32.5	28,383	13.3	22.1	29.6	35.1	19,130	41,793	41,635	1,569	3,369	2,761	2,733
		Rating History: B+, 11/03/09; B+, 11/11/08; B+, 12/12/07; B+, 11/30/06; B+, 11/28/05																
BROOKE LIFE INSURANCE CO Prudential plc Clark P. Manning, Jr. President & CEO 1 Corporate Way Lansing, MI 48951 MI : 1987 : Stock : Not Available Ind Ann 517-381-5500 AMB# 068117 NAIC# 78620	A+ u Under Review Implication: Negative FSC XV	'05	5.4	...	94.3	0.3	3,639,733	2.7	...	11.1	86.2	2,207,993	6,817	7,248	261,530	330,745	330,745	330,745
		'06	4.6	...	95.2	0.2	3,864,214	2.2	...	8.5	89.4	2,202,585	2,705	3,104	7,550	122,103	122,103	122,103
		'07	4.0	...	95.6	0.4	4,210,876	2.0	...	8.3	89.7	2,508,309	21,137	20,879	760	160,189	160,189	160,189
		'08	8.2	...	90.8	1.0	4,128,859	1.8	...	18.4	79.8	2,244,925	218,347	218,634	194,868	216,748	216,748	216,027
		'09	8.6	...	91.0	0.4	4,365,025	1.9	...	21.1	77.0	2,674,214	20,978	21,188	577,852	181,317	181,317	180,661
		Rating History: A+ gu, 03/04/10; A+ g, 07/14/09; A+ g, 02/15/08; A+ g, 10/16/06; A+ g, 02/08/05																
BUCKEYE COMMUNITY HEALTH PLAN Centene Corporation Richard Fredrickson President 7711 Carondelet Avenue, Suite 800 St. Louis, MO 63105-3389 OH : 2004 : Stock : Broker Health 314-725-4706 AMB# 064768 NAIC# 11834	B+ Rating Outlook: Stable FSC VII	'05	20.8	...	...	79.2	43,274	...	45.2	...	54.8	15,001	102,942	99,677	21,947	-2,786	-1,469	-1,473
		'06	21.2	...	...	78.8	65,166	...	37.1	...	62.9	19,925	185,069	181,821	23,377	-3,496	-3,492	-3,488
		'07	62.2	...	...	37.8	155,802	...	46.9	...	53.1	49,751	476,521	465,547	75,764	-37,846	-28,389	-28,393
		'08	47.7	...	...	52.3	124,185	...	70.8	...	29.2	61,024	523,152	517,405	-24,125	-30,551	-16,902	-17,293
		'09	53.9	...	0.3	45.7	187,356	...	30.4	...	69.6	71,100	567,995	558,759	60,964	8,406	3,428	3,515
		Rating History: B+, 02/19/10; B+, 02/10/09; NR-5, 06/30/08; NR-5, 04/05/07; NR-5, 06/13/06																
BUPA INSURANCE COMPANY British United Provident Association Ltd Alfred D. Maltby President 7001 S.W. 97th Avenue Miami, FL 33173 FL : 1973 : Stock : Agency Group A&H, Life, Maj med 305-275-1400 AMB# 008449 NAIC# 81647	B++ Rating Outlook: Stable FSC VI	'05	56.1	...	4.7	39.3	77,367	6.7	82.2	0.7	10.3	31,599	73,811	80,188	3,341	1,636	1,337	1,437
		'06	4.1	...	1.3	94.6	82,000	5.7	83.7	0.6	10.0	21,233	84,221	94,359	8,286	-6,217	-5,285	-6,349
		'07	1.4	...	1.9	96.7	91,286	4.5	77.1	0.5	18.0	19,128	89,920	104,585	-3,331	-2,956	-1,952	-1,952
		'08	1.3	...	5.4	93.3	101,521	3.9	83.2	0.4	12.4	23,141	89,756	111,981	4,332	1,813	1,602	1,602
		'09	52.3	...	6.0	41.7	111,272	3.6	86.2	0.4	9.8	27,709	112,867	129,745	17,995	5,275	2,596	2,596
		Rating History: B++, 06/04/10; A-, 12/10/08; A-, 09/24/07; A-, 06/19/06; A, 05/13/05																
C M LIFE INSURANCE COMPANY Massachusetts Mutual Life Insurance Co Roger W. Crandall Chairman, President & CEO 1295 State Street Springfield, MA 01111 CT : 1981 : Stock : Agency Ind Life, Ann 413-788-8411 AMB# 009062 NAIC# 93432	A++ Rating Outlook: Negative FSC XV	'05	40.4	10.6	3.1	46.0	9,166,987	17.1	...	40.6	42.3	434,197	946,892	798,053	323,137	130,297	95,007	93,001
		'06	37.9	11.7	3.2	47.1	9,123,636	18.1	...	40.0	41.8	502,983	814,991	652,377	32,391	118,249	112,628	118,417
		'07	37.7	14.3	2.9	45.1	8,625,435	19.8	...	38.0	42.1	607,849	698,535	541,318	-257,782	112,477	107,165	85,716
		'08	44.2	15.6	2.8	37.4	7,539,867	24.2	...	46.1	29.6	707,773	940,873	783,359	378,215	-3,312	-14,915	-76,592
		'09	48.1	13.3	2.2	36.4	8,170,601	22.7	...	46.3	31.0	717,528	1,026,192	884,824	557,303	98,595	93,476	43,752
		Rating History: A++g, 06/04/10; A++g, 06/11/09; A++g, 03/25/08; A++g, 05/25/07; A++g, 05/02/06																

2010 BEST'S KEY RATING GUIDE — LIFE/HEALTH EDITION
BEST'S PROFITABILITY, LEVERAGE AND LIQUIDITY TESTS 2005 – 2009

Data in U.S. Dollars

	Profitability Tests							Leverage Tests						Liquidity Tests					
Un-Realized Capital Gains ($000)	Benefits Paid to NPW & Dep (%)	Comm. & Expenses to NPW & Dep (%)	NOG to Total Assets (%)	NOG to Total Rev (%)	Operating Return on Equity (%)	Net Yield (%)	Total Return (%)	Change in NPW & Dep (%)	NPW & Dep to Capital (X)	Capital & Surplus to Liabilities (%)	Surplus Relief (%)	Reins Leverage (%)	Change in Capital (%)	Quick Liquidity (%)	Current Liquidity (%)	Non-Invest Grade Bonds to Capital (%)	Delinq. & Foreclosed Mortgages to Capital (%)	Mort. & Credit Tenant Loans & R.E. to Capital (%)	Affiliated Invest to Capital (%)
...	...	...	...	...	...	...	...	...	...	...	...	...	...	...	...	...	...	...	...
...	...	...	...	100.0	...	...	...	...	...	...	...	...	...	...	...	...	...	...	...
...	81.7	16.5	2.4	2.7	4.3	3.36	3.36	...	1.6	65.9	...	...	-0.1	174.1	178.4	...	...	...	...
-118	90.2	15.2	-10.7	-3.1	-36.0	6.44	5.94	926.9	8.8	35.4	...	...	81.8	22.7	24.2	1.9	...	...	...
118	87.2	11.3	5.9	1.2	15.9	3.13	3.15	96.8	10.1	99.2	...	...	71.8	59.3	59.6	...	...	...	...

Principal Lines of Business: OtherHlth (96.4%), Medicare (3.6%) — Principal States: CA (32.6%), NY (20.4%), TX (17.1%), MI (5.7%), IL (5.5%)

...	78.8	20.5	5.3	1.2	17.0	2.59	2.59	62.4	11.8	43.1	...	...	42.9	128.7	128.7	...	...	...	...
...	83.8	16.0	2.6	0.7	11.4	4.74	4.74	50.1	13.6	24.7	...	0.3	30.9	109.7	109.7	...	...	...	...
...	85.3	15.1	2.3	0.7	9.5	5.22	5.22	12.7	12.5	43.2	...	...	22.3	148.0	155.1	...	...	...	...
-113	88.5	15.3	-8.3	-1.9	-26.5	4.48	3.85	22.0	12.4	47.4	...	...	23.4	148.7	158.5	1.9	...	...	...
113	84.8	14.6	3.7	0.9	11.6	3.21	3.10	13.8	12.5	45.3	...	...	12.8	131.8	140.0	...	...	...	...

Principal Lines of Business: Medicare (100.0%) — Principal States: MD (92.0%), DC (7.2%)

...	85.1	14.8	2.5	0.6	9.2	2.31	2.31	110.0	13.1	29.9	...	...	40.9	254.2	268.8	...	...	...	...
...	82.2	14.3	11.8	3.1	48.4	5.72	5.72	71.0	11.7	33.3	...	...	90.9	119.1	119.1	...	...	...	...
...	82.1	20.1	-8.8	-2.6	-31.8	4.27	4.27	71.0	8.7	41.0	...	...	130.9	153.2	158.2	...	...	...	...
-174	77.3	21.2	-1.6	-0.4	-4.2	4.16	3.97	74.5	7.7	83.7	...	...	96.3	219.5	232.3	0.6	...	...	...
174	77.9	18.6	6.3	1.6	13.7	2.74	2.70	13.6	8.7	86.9	...	...	0.7	152.4	161.5	...	...	...	...

Principal Lines of Business: Medicare (100.0%) — Principal States: PA (100.0%)

...	...	...	...	...	...	...	...	...	...	...	...	...	...	...	...	...	...	...	...
...	73.8	27.3	...	0.3	...	...	...	...	12.8	7.2	...	0.9	...	100.7	100.7	...	...	...	...
...	70.8	21.9	9.8	7.0	106.7	5.10	5.10	70.6	11.3	12.8	...	...	93.2	136.9	142.8	...	...	...	...
-45	74.1	19.6	14.4	4.9	69.0	4.09	4.07	84.8	10.6	57.3	...	...	96.6	184.3	195.3	0.9	...	...	...
45	73.5	19.2	23.8	5.0	61.4	2.19	2.18	42.9	10.2	67.9	...	...	49.1	199.2	210.3	...	...	...	...

Principal Lines of Business: Medicare (100.0%) — Principal States: TX (100.0%)

-31	62.7	34.0	9.4	4.9	17.5	3.87	3.97	4.5	3.6	109.3	0.1	0.4	-9.8	146.3	159.4	4.9	...	...	5.0
70	64.7	34.2	10.5	5.3	19.5	4.64	5.17	0.7	3.3	129.4	0.1	0.5	9.4	167.9	184.1	2.1	...	...	2.8
100	62.0	34.6	13.2	7.1	23.0	4.83	5.41	-0.2	2.8	145.7	0.0	0.3	19.6	187.3	203.1	1.2	...	...	1.0
-425	62.0	35.3	10.9	6.4	17.8	3.86	1.19	-2.4	2.6	176.5	0.1	0.3	6.0	232.9	250.5	0.7	...	...	0.8
237	62.5	35.5	10.0	6.3	15.3	3.58	4.57	-4.4	2.2	211.7	0.1	0.3	13.6	295.7	309.5	2.3	...	...	0.3

Principal Lines of Business: GrpA&H (95.6%), IndA&H (3.9%), OrdLife (0.3%), IndAnn (0.2%), GrpLife (0.0%) — Principal States: GA (8.6%), LA (7.5%), AR (6.7%), IN (5.8%), OH (5.7%)

32,637	209.2	15.2	9.5	96.5	16.1	16.07	17.53	-80.8	0.0	154.4	0.0	0.8	15.6	9.6	11.1	0.7	...	...	155.5
222,214	872.9	24.5	3.3	93.9	5.5	5.54	15.27	-57.2	0.0	132.7	0.0	0.8	-0.2	7.7	8.9	0.5	...	...	166.8
347,160	126.2	6.8	4.0	85.6	6.8	6.82	21.52	572.6	0.0	147.5	0.0	0.7	13.9	8.1	9.3	0.5	...	...	160.3
-278,371	11.7	4.7	5.2	47.4	9.1	9.45	-0.54	947.1	0.1	119.3	0.0	0.7	-10.5	15.7	18.3	0.6	...	...	166.7
-343,991	147.2	7.9	4.3	82.3	7.4	7.31	-4.11	-90.3	0.0	158.4	0.0	0.6	19.1	16.0	19.0	0.4	...	...	148.5

Principal Lines of Business: IndAnn (95.2%), GrpLife (3.8%), OrdLife (1.0%) — Principal States: MI (99.8%)

...	89.5	13.9	-5.1	-1.5	-14.9	2.43	2.42	115.0	6.6	53.1	...	6.4	216.0	179.3	188.6	...	...	...	...
...	84.5	18.0	-6.4	-1.9	-20.0	3.11	3.12	82.4	9.1	44.0	...	3.6	32.8	200.7	211.5	...	...	...	...
...	89.3	18.5	-25.7	-6.1	-81.5	3.80	3.80	156.0	9.4	46.9	...	3.7	149.7	135.4	147.8	...	...	...	...
...	87.7	18.3	-12.1	-3.2	-30.5	2.89	2.57	11.1	8.5	96.6	...	1.9	22.7	231.6	248.9	5.6	...	...	...
...	80.5	19.4	2.2	0.6	5.2	1.76	1.82	8.0	7.9	61.2	...	4.3	16.5	148.1	158.6	5.6	...	...	...

Principal Lines of Business: Medicaid (99.7%), Medicare (0.3%) — Principal States: OH (100.0%)

-23	50.6	46.2	1.8	1.6	4.4	4.46	4.59	14.1	2.5	69.8	0.0	13.8	7.8	107.3	117.4	0.6	...	...	5.2
-240	57.1	44.7	-6.6	-5.5	-20.0	4.11	1.72	17.7	4.4	35.1	0.1	25.9	-33.1	110.9	111.2	...	...	...	4.8
-70	60.9	41.5	-2.3	-1.8	-9.7	4.95	4.40	10.8	5.5	26.5	0.1	42.4	-10.1	86.3	86.3	...	...	...	8.9
1,494	65.4	35.8	1.7	1.3	7.6	3.27	5.11	7.1	4.7	30.7	0.0	26.8	24.7	83.2	83.2	...	...	...	22.9
-1,793	58.2	40.5	2.4	1.9	10.2	1.33	-1.19	15.9	4.7	33.2	0.1	23.1	16.4	85.2	92.0	...	...	...	24.0

Principal Lines of Business: IndA&H (97.6%), GrpA&H (2.3%), GrpLife (0.0%), OrdLife (0.0%), IndAnn (0.0%)

-25,830	113.4	18.3	1.0	7.9	22.9	6.56	5.95	-53.5	1.7	9.4	5.6	207.7	10.2	45.4	60.2	81.4	...	204.2	62.4
6,084	186.0	18.3	1.2	10.6	24.0	6.54	6.60	-18.3	1.1	11.6	4.6	186.7	22.0	46.7	62.0	56.1	0.4	183.7	70.7
-598	282.7	18.8	1.2	11.4	19.3	6.54	5.95	-17.0	0.8	14.4	3.8	162.4	16.7	35.5	50.9	49.7	...	180.3	68.8
72,628	155.6	13.2	-0.2	-1.3	-2.3	5.43	5.46	44.7	1.1	14.1	3.3	147.8	5.5	41.4	55.6	47.7	...	162.9	66.9
-102,690	103.0	11.4	1.2	7.5	13.1	5.56	2.99	13.0	1.2	13.0	3.1	146.7	0.5	46.9	62.8	47.1	...	149.6	64.3

Principal Lines of Business: IndAnn (83.9%), OrdLife (15.9%), GrpLife (0.2%) — Principal States: CA (11.4%), FL (8.5%), PA (7.3%), MA (6.7%), TX (6.1%)

Data in U.S. Dollars

COMPANY NAME Ultimate Parent Association Principal Officer Mailing Address Dom. : Began Bus. : Struct. : Mktg. Specialty Phone # AMB# NAIC#	Best's Financial Strength Rating FSC	Data Year	Balance Sheet: Bonds (%)	Mort. Loans & R.E. (%)	Com & Pref. Stock (%)	All Other Assets (%)	Total Assets ($000)	Life Reserves (%)	Health Reserves %)	Ann Res. & Dep. Liabilities (%)	All Other Liabilities (%)	Capital & Surplus ($000)	Operations: Direct Premiums Written ($000)	Net Premiums Written & Deposits ($000)	Operating Cash Flow ($000)	NOG Before Taxes ($000)	NOG After Taxes ($000)	Net Income ($000)
CALIFORNIA BENEFITS DENTAL PLN Sun Life Financial Inc Valerie A. Clark President 3611 S. Harbor Blvd., Suite 150 Santa Ana, CA 92704 CA : 1992 : Stock : Broker Dental 714-540-4255 AMB# 064722	NR-2	'05	...	...	...	100.0	1,590	...	...	...	100.0	766	2,013	2,013	-103	53	28	28
		'06	...	...	...	100.0	1,554	...	...	...	100.0	815	2,196	2,196	-13	93	50	50
		'07	...	...	...	100.0	1,322	...	...	...	100.0	749	2,265	2,265	-114	53	-66	-66
		'08	...	...	...	100.0	1,186	...	...	...	100.0	649	1,972	1,972	-139	-287	-100	-100
		'09	...	...	...	100.0	797	...	...	...	100.0	318	1,728	1,728	-347	-532	-332	-332
		Rating History: NR-2, 02/27/09; NR-5, 06/19/08; NR-5, 06/12/07; NR-5, 05/25/06; NR-5, 06/01/05																
CALIFORNIA DENTAL NETWORK INC Stephen R. Casey President 1971 East 4th Street, Suite 184 Santa Ana, CA 92705 CA : 1988 : Stock : Broker Dental 714-479-0777 AMB# 064350	NR-5	'05	...	0.2	...	99.8	986	...	...	...	100.0	84	3,658	3,658	227	112	111	111
		'06	...	0.1	...	99.9	1,022	...	...	...	100.0	62	4,767	4,767	66	-21	-22	-22
		'07	...	0.1	...	99.9	947	...	...	...	100.0	82	4,105	4,105	23	21	20	20
		'08	...	...	...	100.0	910	...	...	...	100.0	118	3,596	3,596	6	37	36	36
		'09	...	...	...	100.0	1,061	...	...	...	100.0	198	3,813	3,813	72	80	80	80
		Rating History: NR-5, 03/22/10; NR-5, 05/05/09; NR-5, 05/06/08; NR-5, 05/09/07; NR-5, 05/25/06																
CALIFORNIA PHYSICIANS' SERVICE California Physicians' Service Bruce G. Bodaken Chairman, President & CEO 50 Beale Street San Francisco, CA 94105-1808 CA : 1939 : Non-Profit : Agency Group A&H, Health 415-229-5000 AMB# 064012 NAIC# 47732	A Rating Outlook: Stable FSC XV	'05	...	1.7	...	98.3	3,244,607	...	...	...	100.0	1,764,838	7,233,259	7,233,259	228,604	370,089	307,140	307,140
		'06	...	1.5	6.0	92.5	3,757,423	...	...	...	100.0	2,214,812	7,609,536	7,609,536	399,840	440,526	357,309	357,309
		'07	...	1.9	4.4	93.6	4,480,766	...	...	...	100.0	2,918,836	7,812,649	7,812,649	598,778	493,193	704,175	704,175
		'08	...	2.5	4.4	93.1	4,772,464	...	...	...	100.0	2,818,453	8,056,956	8,056,956	410,966	275,300	165,509	165,509
		'09	...	2.5	6.6	90.8	4,977,861	...	...	...	100.0	3,189,653	8,369,551	8,369,551	96,190	286,230	206,718	206,718
		Rating History: A g, 05/26/10; A, 07/10/09; A, 06/26/08; A, 06/28/07; A, 06/21/06																
CAMBRIDGE LIFE INS CO Coventry Health Care Inc Harvey C. DeMovick, Jr. President & CEO 3200 Highland Avenue Downers Grove, IL 60515 MO : 1974 : Stock : Agency A&H, Dental, Ind A&H 630-737-5750 AMB# 008545 NAIC# 81000	B++ Rating Outlook: Negative FSC VI	'05	61.7	...	...	38.3	10,233	1.2	37.9	...	60.9	8,446	1,275	1,521	2,111	497	497	497
		'06	27.9	...	...	72.1	25,274	0.1	96.2	...	3.7	7,546	60,921	61,559	3,033	-1,800	-923	-923
		'07	14.5	...	...	85.5	45,706	0.1	56.2	...	43.7	26,164	55,501	55,625	837	-7,784	-6,057	-6,057
		'08	8.8	...	...	91.2	80,361	0.1	53.3	...	46.6	41,953	55,592	56,664	19,417	-16,259	-12,587	-12,761
		'09	22.2	...	...	77.8	74,670	0.1	57.7	...	42.2	47,988	56,651	56,553	12,516	-5,057	-562	-552
		Rating History: B++, 02/12/10; B++, 11/19/08; B++, 10/30/07; B++, 07/11/07; B++, 10/27/06																
CANYON STATE LIFE INS CO' Milford P. Christenson President 312 E. Alvarado Road Phoenix, AZ 85004 AZ : 1966 : Stock : Not Available 602-258-2422 AMB# 007537 NAIC# 72958	NR-1	'05	60.7	11.2	19.1	9.0	2,219	...	...	6.3	93.7	1,797	0	30	...	177	174	204
		'06	22.1	7.4	6.6	63.9	6,804	...	...	1.3	98.7	3,941	0	24	...	-9	-7	5,579
		'07	31.6	14.8	30.4	23.2	4,492	...	...	8.8	91.2	3,933	0	-6	...	273	252	282
		'08	37.7	21.1	30.5	10.7	2,960	...	...	13.2	86.8	2,543	0	-1	...	229	215	207
		'09	44.4	23.7	24.2	7.7	2,467	...	...	7.9	92.1	1,606	0	-3	...	138	130	131
		Rating History: NR-1, 06/10/10; NR-1, 06/12/09; NR-1, 06/12/08; NR-1, 06/08/07; NR-1, 06/07/06																
CAPITAL ADVANTAGE INSURANCE CO Capital Blue Cross William Lehr, Jr. President & CEO 2500 Elmerton Avenue Harrisburg, PA 17177-9799 PA : 1982 : Stock : Agency Group A&H 717-541-7000 AMB# 001783 NAIC# 41203	NR-5	'05	53.2	...	18.1	28.7	603,991	...	62.5	...	37.5	392,992	995,639	997,949	127,398	97,663	59,372	58,961
		'06	51.6	...	16.2	32.2	644,851	...	57.1	...	42.9	424,343	978,849	980,536	29,687	59,985	53,189	51,058
		'07	55.9	...	18.2	25.9	575,873	...	53.9	...	46.1	348,253	1,134,950	1,136,591	-59,963	-20,614	248	-942
		'08	58.9	...	21.7	19.4	493,613	...	34.4	...	65.6	304,830	1,319,414	1,320,998	-40,490	-81,889	-70,835	-80,891
		'09	54.1	...	23.3	22.6	546,747	...	34.5	...	65.5	349,443	1,356,848	1,357,473	12,640	-67,141	-692	-2,315
		Rating History: NR-5, 04/13/10; NR-5, 07/01/09; NR-5, 05/05/08; NR-5, 01/10/07; NR-5, 09/29/05																
CAPITAL BLUE CROSS Capital Blue Cross William Lehr, Jr. President & CEO 2500 Elmerton Avenue Harrisburg, PA 17177-9799 PA : 1938 : Stock : Agency Group A&H 717-541-7000 AMB# 064554 NAIC# 54720	NR-5	'05	32.6	3.8	22.7	40.9	1,019,263	...	17.8	...	82.2	658,120	348,678	348,151	41,172	27,772	46,171	48,198
		'06	29.6	3.4	26.3	40.6	1,091,104	...	14.1	...	85.9	794,006	286,911	286,412	-8,770	5,864	14,684	21,488
		'07	34.7	3.4	20.5	41.4	1,055,385	...	12.2	...	87.8	797,570	194,865	194,388	-40,122	26,419	48,906	61,783
		'08	34.1	4.2	17.8	43.9	814,201	...	11.8	...	88.2	624,798	197,938	197,478	-46,540	28,432	42,302	5,420
		'09	31.4	3.8	32.3	32.5	871,918	...	13.6	...	86.4	654,317	213,194	212,799	-2,215	15,199	-44,335	-44,169
		Rating History: NR-5, 04/13/10; NR-5, 07/01/09; NR-5, 05/05/08; NR-5, 01/10/07; NR-5, 09/29/05																
CAPITAL DISTRICT PHYS' HLTH PL Capital District Physicians' Health Plan John D. Bennet, MD President & CEO 500 Patroon Creek Blvd. Albany, NY 12206-1057 NY : 1984 : Non-Profit : Broker Group A&H, Health 518-641-3000 AMB# 068563 NAIC# 95491	B+ Rating Outlook: Negative FSC VIII	'05	54.4	...	2.3	43.3	259,709	...	36.2	...	63.8	147,193	774,180	772,747	-833	24,572	24,572	24,638
		'06	69.9	...	1.3	28.8	301,525	...	35.6	...	64.4	179,883	845,571	844,041	51,985	34,796	34,796	34,450
		'07	62.0	...	1.1	36.9	338,341	...	62.9	...	37.1	209,319	888,147	886,674	-6,240	38,477	38,477	38,349
		'08	55.3	...	2.0	42.7	345,856	...	56.5	...	43.5	206,531	962,842	960,443	4,456	15,911	15,911	14,377
		'09	49.3	...	1.7	49.0	404,456	...	45.9	...	54.1	230,310	1,027,664	1,025,074	41,175	31,099	31,099	30,698
		Rating History: B+, 06/05/09; B++u, 01/30/09; B++, 11/12/07; B++, 10/10/06; NR-5, 06/15/06																
CAPITAL HEALTH PLAN INC Blue Cross and Blue Shield of FL Inc Wallace K. Boutwell, Jr. Chairman 2140 Centerville Place Tallahassee, FL 32308 FL : 1982 : Non-Profit : Broker Group A&H, Health 850-383-3333 AMB# 064116 NAIC# 95112	A Rating Outlook: Stable FSC VIII	'05	69.0	6.9	...	24.1	180,470	...	43.9	...	56.1	117,313	388,396	385,111	44,837	39,496	39,496	37,530
		'06	60.1	10.1	...	29.8	221,000	...	47.1	...	52.9	147,970	433,552	429,949	29,631	31,966	31,966	31,289
		'07	68.5	7.8	...	23.6	278,778	...	45.8	...	54.2	184,396	468,206	464,499	57,318	35,230	35,230	36,218
		'08	66.4	7.1	...	26.6	306,601	...	45.2	...	54.8	215,471	501,687	497,773	31,242	32,037	32,037	33,857
		'09	73.1	6.6	...	20.2	319,517	...	51.4	...	48.6	220,454	537,599	533,885	27,780	9,997	9,997	14,596
		Rating History: A, 05/25/10; A, 05/26/09; A, 04/28/08; A-, 05/04/07; A-, 04/27/06																

BEST'S PROFITABILITY, LEVERAGE AND LIQUIDITY TESTS 2005 – 2009

Data in U.S. Dollars

	Profitability Tests							Leverage Tests						Liquidity Tests					
Un-Realized Capital Gains ($000)	Benefits Paid to NPW & Dep (%)	Comm. & Expenses to NPW & Dep (%)	NOG to Total Assets (%)	NOG to Total Rev (%)	Operating Return on Equity (%)	Net Yield (%)	Total Return (%)	Change in NPW & Dep (%)	NPW & Dep to Capital (X)	Capital & Surplus to Liabilities (%)	Surplus Relief (%)	Reins Leverage (%)	Change in Capital (%)	Quick Liquidity (%)	Current Liquidity (%)	Non-Invest Grade Bonds to Capital (%)	Delinq. & Foreclosed Mortgages to Capital (%)	Mort. & Credit Tenant Loans & R.E. to Capital (%)	Affiliated Invest to Capital (%)
...	36.0	66.9	1.7	1.3	3.7	3.28	3.28	-2.5	2.6	92.9	...	...	3.7	153.3	153.3	...	...	...	...
...	39.0	62.2	3.2	2.1	6.3	4.51	4.51	9.1	2.7	110.3	...	...	6.5	169.2	169.2	...	...	...	...
...	40.6	62.3	-4.6	-2.8	-8.5	5.39	5.39	3.2	3.0	130.8	...	...	-8.1	198.6	198.6	...	...	...	...
...	38.2	80.8	-8.0	-4.8	-14.3	2.64	2.64	-13.0	3.0	121.1	...	...	-13.3	186.1	186.1	...	...	...	...
...	37.5	96.1	-33.5	-18.7	-68.6	0.68	0.68	-12.4	5.4	66.2	...	...	-51.1	135.8	135.8	...	...	...	...
Principal Lines of Business: Dental (100.0%)																			
...	44.7	54.1	12.8	3.0	232.6	-99.90	-99.90	30.0	43.6	9.3	...	...	599.0	39.1	39.1	...	...	2.2	2.2
...	52.6	49.3	-2.2	-0.5	-30.1	-21.48	-21.48	30.3	77.0	6.4	...	...	-26.2	37.4	37.4	...	...	2.2	2.2
...	51.1	49.8	2.0	0.5	27.5	-16.29	-16.29	-13.9	50.3	9.4	...	...	31.9	45.6	45.6	...	...	0.7	0.7
...	45.2	55.2	3.9	1.0	36.6	-13.42	-13.42	-12.4	30.5	14.9	...	...	44.7	47.3	47.3	...	...	...	...
...	42.3	57.2	8.1	2.1	50.4	-7.91	-7.91	6.0	19.3	22.9	...	...	67.5	56.2	56.2	...	...	...	...
Principal Lines of Business: Dental (100.0%)																			
22,352	86.2	11.7	9.9	4.1	18.9	6.51	7.51	8.8	4.1	119.3	...	...	18.9	5.0	5.0	...	...	3.1	3.1
24,276	85.7	11.4	10.2	4.6	18.0	5.78	6.72	5.2	3.4	143.6	...	...	25.5	11.3	11.3	...	...	2.5	2.5
22,608	85.3	12.0	17.1	8.7	27.4	6.46	7.16	2.7	2.7	186.9	...	...	31.8	13.3	13.3	...	...	3.0	3.0
6,528	85.0	12.3	3.6	2.0	5.8	-0.86	-0.68	3.1	2.9	144.2	...	...	-3.4	17.4	17.4	...	...	4.3	4.3
-58,169	87.6	11.5	4.2	2.4	6.9	3.33	1.75	3.9	2.6	178.4	...	...	13.2	13.9	13.9	...	...	3.9	3.9
Principal Lines of Business: CompHosp/Med (93.4%), Medicare (6.0%), Medicaid (0.7%)																			
...	77.6	11.8	5.2	24.6	6.2	4.10	4.06	-29.7	0.2	476.6	2.0	1.2	9.8	485.5	508.5	...	...	...	...
...	96.8	7.1	-5.2	-1.5	-11.5	5.82	5.75	999.9	8.1	42.7	0.7	0.2	-10.6	65.2	67.4	...	...	...	...
...	101.8	7.8	-17.1	-10.8	-35.9	5.31	5.24	-9.6	2.1	134.0	0.0	0.1	246.3	66.2	68.4	...	...	...	...
...	111.8	7.7	-20.0	-22.0	-37.0	2.56	1.79	1.9	1.4	109.2	...	0.0	60.3	122.3	126.0	...	...	...	...
...	117.9	6.2	-0.7	-1.0	-1.2	1.10	1.13	-0.2	1.2	180.1	...	0.0	14.4	166.2	171.8	...	...	...	...
Principal Lines of Business: IndA&H (98.8%), GrpA&H (1.2%), GrpLife (0.0%)													Principal States: NY (99.9%)						
-24	196.2	222.0	8.1	67.2	10.1	...	...	4.3	0.0	448.3	0.3	...	9.7	...	...	...	...	13.7	...
-3,324	260.5	999.9	-0.1	-1.6	-0.2	...	...	-20.5	0.0	141.9	0.0	...	120.0	...	...	...	...	12.6	...
-214	-99.9	-99.9	4.5	66.2	6.4	...	...	-99.9	0.0	984.4	0.0	...	2.2	...	...	...	...	16.3	...
-793	-99.9	-99.9	5.8	59.7	6.6	...	...	78.5	0.0	629.7	0.0	...	-37.4	...	...	...	...	24.5	...
241	-99.9	-99.9	4.8	54.1	6.3	...	...	-99.9	0.0	191.7	0.0	...	-36.5	...	...	...	...	36.0	...
Principal Lines of Business: CrdA&H (91.8%), CrdLife (14.2%), OrdLife (-5.9%)																			
-49	77.7	15.3	11.2	5.9	19.3	3.30	3.20	3.8	2.5	186.3	...	...	78.0	190.2	202.6	...	...	...	27.7
-19,833	78.1	19.8	8.5	5.2	13.0	9.88	5.62	-1.7	2.3	192.4	...	...	8.0	188.8	205.7	...	...	...	21.8
-14,982	85.5	18.3	0.0	0.0	0.1	3.96	0.61	15.9	3.3	153.0	...	0.0	-17.9	117.5	133.8	...	...	...	25.6
-5,127	87.7	19.0	-13.2	-5.3	-21.7	1.41	-2.21	16.2	4.3	161.5	...	0.0	-12.5	110.2	126.7	0.1	...	...	32.4
16,806	88.0	17.8	-0.1	-0.1	-0.2	2.43	6.25	2.8	3.9	177.1	...	...	14.6	119.6	134.2	0.4	...	...	33.6
Principal Lines of Business: CompHosp/Med (74.6%), OtherHlth (15.5%), Medicare (7.5%), MedSup (2.1%), Dental (0.3%)													Principal States: PA (100.0%)						
-16,444	88.4	16.7	4.8	11.9	7.6	6.47	4.73	-1.5	0.5	182.2	...	0.5	16.6	126.2	141.7	2.9	...	5.9	67.9
38,206	92.4	18.7	1.4	4.4	2.0	4.32	9.18	-17.7	0.4	267.3	...	0.5	20.6	140.9	161.7	1.9	...	4.7	60.1
-31,676	93.2	24.3	4.6	19.0	6.1	5.20	3.36	-32.1	0.2	309.4	...	0.5	0.4	162.6	186.1	1.4	...	4.5	50.5
-118,338	95.5	6.9	4.5	17.7	5.9	4.26	-12.89	1.6	0.3	329.9	...	0.7	-21.7	190.9	215.8	1.5	...	5.5	55.7
41,288	98.0	8.3	-5.3	-18.9	-6.9	2.73	8.13	7.8	0.3	300.7	...	...	4.7	146.6	168.5	1.9	...	5.0	59.5
Principal Lines of Business: FEHBP (65.1%), CompHosp/Med (18.8%), MedSup (12.9%), OtherHlth (3.1%)													Principal States: PA (100.0%)						
-1,772	87.5	10.4	9.6	3.2	18.1	3.24	2.41	-11.3	5.2	130.8	...	0.6	18.9	206.0	215.8	...	...	...	9.3
-1,790	86.3	10.8	12.4	4.1	21.3	4.45	3.52	9.2	4.7	147.9	...	0.3	22.2	214.3	228.5	...	...	...	6.6
-4,954	85.9	11.0	12.0	4.3	19.8	4.66	2.63	5.1	4.2	162.2	...	0.8	16.4	176.6	190.0	...	...	...	10.5
-4,655	88.9	10.5	4.7	1.6	7.7	4.33	1.79	8.3	4.7	148.2	...	0.9	-1.3	174.1	184.7	0.3	...	...	25.9
-1,627	86.7	11.1	8.3	3.0	14.2	3.26	2.49	6.7	4.5	132.3	...	0.4	11.5	147.5	155.3	...	...	...	22.2
Principal Lines of Business: CompHosp/Med (56.9%), Medicare (22.6%), Medicaid (13.2%), OtherHlth (7.3%)													Principal States: NY (100.0%)						
...	85.6	6.3	25.0	10.0	39.4	4.98	3.68	10.0	3.3	185.7	...	0.2	40.8	254.3	268.0	...	...	10.7	10.7
...	88.9	6.5	15.9	7.2	24.1	6.24	5.89	11.6	2.9	202.6	...	0.2	26.1	200.4	214.7	...	...	15.0	15.0
...	89.6	5.9	14.1	7.3	21.2	5.67	6.08	8.0	2.5	195.4	...	0.5	24.6	218.0	234.0	0.2	...	11.9	11.9
...	90.4	5.9	10.9	6.2	16.0	4.69	5.33	7.2	2.3	236.4	...	0.1	16.9	247.8	268.8	1.6	...	10.1	10.1
...	94.7	5.7	3.2	1.8	4.6	4.00	5.51	7.3	2.4	222.5	...	0.0	2.3	229.5	245.3	6.3	...	9.6	9.6
Principal Lines of Business: CompHosp/Med (79.3%), Medicare (18.5%), FEHBP (2.3%)													Principal States: FL (100.0%)						

2010 BEST'S KEY RATING GUIDE — LIFE/HEALTH EDITION
ANNUAL STATEMENT DATA FOR YEARS 2005 – 2009

Data in U.S. Dollars

COMPANY NAME Ultimate Parent Association Principal Officer Mailing Address Dom. : Began Bus. : Struct. : Mktg. Specialty Phone # AMB# NAIC#	Best's Financial Strength Rating FSC	Data Year	Balance Sheet Bonds (%)	Mort. Loans & R.E. (%)	Com & Pref. Stock (%)	All Other Assets (%)	Total Assets ($000)	Life Reserves (%)	Health Reserves (%)	Ann Res. & Dep. Liabilities (%)	All Other Liabilities (%)	Capital & Surplus ($000)	Operations Direct Premiums Written ($000)	Net Premiums Written & Deposits ($000)	Operating Cash Flow ($000)	NOG Before Taxes ($000)	NOG After Taxes ($000)	Net Income ($000)
CAPITAL RESERVE LIFE INS CO Security National Financial Scott M. Quist President P.O. Box 896 Jefferson City, MO 65102-0896 MO : 1922 : Stock : Not Available Life 801-264-1060 AMB# 006184 NAIC# 61573	NR-5	'05	...	...	...	...	...	...	...	...	...	...	...	...	...	...	...	...
		'06	...	...	...	...	...	...	...	...	...	...	...	...	...	...	...	...
		'07	71.4	...	...	28.6	1,674	...	...	...	100.0	1,500	3,531	3,422	-22,137	1,112	1,112	1,024
		'08	18.8	...	...	81.2	6,346	99.0	...	...	1.0	1,657	1,830	122	4,421	46	9	9
		'09	38.2	...	...	61.8	1,692	...	...	...	100.0	1,681	848	176	-3,939	17	17	17
		Rating History: NR-5, 03/25/10; NR-5, 04/14/09; NR-5, 04/09/08; NR-1, 06/08/07; NR-1, 06/07/06																
CAPITALCARE INC CareFirst Inc Jon P. Shematek, M.D. President 10455 Mill Run Circle Owings Mills, MD 21117 VA : 2002 : Stock : Broker Health 410-581-3000 AMB# 064862 NAIC# 11227	NR-5	'05	87.4	...	...	12.6	3,397	...	38.4	...	61.6	2,366	3,873	4,063	-276	-52	-41	-50
		'06	88.3	...	...	11.7	3,239	...	44.8	...	55.2	2,696	3,727	3,702	-143	410	323	323
		'07	76.6	...	...	23.4	2,890	...	54.1	...	45.9	2,405	2,703	2,693	-457	-347	-278	-291
		'08	31.2	...	...	68.8	4,664	...	86.4	...	13.6	3,366	2,279	2,216	1,766	-1,260	-1,008	-1,036
		'09	...	...	...	...	...	...	...	...	...	...	...	...	...	...	...	...
		Rating History: NR-5, 03/26/09; NR-5, 03/24/08; NR-5, 05/15/07																
CAPITOL LIFE & ACCIDENT INS CO Munich Reinsurance Company John W. Hayden Chairman & CEO P.O. Box 5323 Cincinnati, OH 45201-5323 AR : 1957 : Stock : Not Available Inactive 513-943-7200 AMB# 068179 NAIC# 90840	NR-3	'05	...	...	...	...	...	...	...	...	...	...	...	...	...	...	...	...
		'06	...	...	...	100.0	356	...	...	...	100.0	319	13	13	-3,484	2	-137	-52
		'07	...	...	...	100.0	341	...	...	...	100.0	324	...	...	-15	9	6	6
		'08	...	...	...	100.0	353	...	...	...	100.0	330	...	...	12	8	6	6
		'09	...	...	...	100.0	351	...	...	...	100.0	328	...	...	0	-2	-2	-2
		Rating History: NR-3, 03/10/10; NR-3, 05/15/09; NR-3, 04/09/08; NR-3, 05/31/07; NR-1, 06/07/06																
CAPITOL LIFE INS CO Realty Advisors Inc Elton L. Bomer President 1605 LBJ Freeway, Suite 710 Dallas, TX 75234 TX : 1905 : Stock : Broker Ann, Struc Sett 469-522-4400 AMB# 006186 NAIC# 61581	NR-2	'05	91.0	0.1	0.2	8.7	254,766	35.4	...	60.1	4.5	6,847	...	3,746	-22,978	152	140	-5,275
		'06	92.3	...	0.0	7.7	236,156	36.2	...	58.9	4.9	4,956	...	2,082	-17,016	-1,353	-1,331	-1,470
		'07	88.4	...	4.6	7.0	221,989	35.5	...	58.6	6.0	7,159	...	3,339	-12,946	2,496	2,496	2,319
		'08	76.6	1.7	5.1	16.7	209,480	36.1	...	56.7	7.2	8,273	6,363	9,051	-19,667	4,768	4,624	572
		'09	81.9	3.1	3.9	11.1	226,288	31.2	...	60.6	8.3	10,793	22,532	23,940	23,617	1,231	848	-517
		Rating History: NR-2, 11/24/09; NR-2, 06/18/09; NR-2, 05/23/08; E, 03/03/04; NR-3, 05/16/03																
CAPITOL SECURITY LIFE INS CO[1] Frank M. Croy President P.O. Box 982005 Fort Worth, TX 76182-8005 TX : 1976 : Stock : Not Available 817-284-4888 AMB# 068087 NAIC# 85332	NR-1	'05	75.2	...	...	24.8	1,928	...	...	...	100.0	426	1,630	971	...	-23	-23	-23
		'06	81.1	...	...	18.9	3,634	...	...	...	100.0	592	1,641	2,533	...	12	32	32
		'07	83.1	...	...	16.9	3,860	...	...	...	100.0	640	1,564	1,381	...	54	41	41
		'08	76.8	...	...	23.2	4,133	...	...	...	100.0	831	1,424	1,271	...	151	131	131
		'09	63.7	...	...	36.3	4,325	...	...	...	100.0	994	1,311	1,176	...	182	154	154
		Rating History: NR-1, 06/10/10; NR-1, 06/12/09; NR-1, 06/12/08; NR-1, 06/08/07; NR-1, 06/07/06																
CARDIF LIFE INSURANCE COMPANY BNP Paribas SA Manuel J. Millor Chairman & CEO 12485 SW 137th Avenue, Suite 300 Miami, FL 33186 KS : 1964 : Stock : Agency Credit Life, Disability 305-234-1771 AMB# 007376 NAIC# 71455	B++ u Under Review Implication: Negative FSC V	'05	72.6	...	0.5	26.9	40,769	47.6	40.7	...	11.7	12,005	22,348	11,534	7,869	-2,157	-2,157	-2,113
		'06	69.5	...	0.3	30.2	53,112	35.6	33.6	...	30.8	10,795	29,552	11,839	7,779	-2,250	-2,280	-2,280
		'07	74.7	...	0.5	24.8	62,019	31.2	29.7	...	39.1	10,833	34,462	12,233	6,808	-3,453	-3,453	-3,460
		'08	86.7	...	0.6	12.7	61,054	34.5	32.6	...	33.0	14,219	29,450	10,193	3,322	-971	-971	-1,926
		'09	89.1	...	0.3	10.7	54,227	37.3	35.2	...	27.5	17,468	17,500	5,359	-4,737	747	747	682
		Rating History: B++u, 06/01/10; A-, 04/30/08; B++, 02/16/07; B++, 01/30/06; B++, 12/21/04																
CARE 1ST HEALTH PLAN INC Anna Tran President 601 Potrero Grande Drive, 2nd Floor Monterey Park, CA 91755 CA : 1996 : Stock : Broker Health 323-889-6638 AMB# 064143	NR-5	'05	...	11.6	...	88.4	127,898	...	...	...	100.0	50,561	272,464	272,464	23,580	11,704	5,483	5,483
		'06	...	7.5	...	92.5	194,759	...	...	...	100.0	73,668	351,995	351,995	60,177	11,915	7,107	7,107
		'07	...	8.2	...	91.8	203,942	...	...	...	100.0	84,164	453,912	453,912	6,601	16,932	10,497	10,497
		'08	...	7.3	...	92.7	223,804	...	...	...	100.0	91,103	554,744	554,744	19,623	9,701	6,936	6,936
		'09	...	6.1	...	93.9	261,279	...	...	...	100.0	102,625	663,307	663,307	47,919	19,610	11,637	11,637
		Rating History: NR-5, 05/04/10; NR-5, 08/26/09; B- pd, 07/21/08; B- pd, 07/20/07; B- pd, 08/29/06																
CARE IMPROVEMENT PLUS OF MD Patrick Henry President 351 W. Camden Street, Suite 100 Baltimore, MD 21201 MD : 2006 : Stock : Not Available Health 410-625-2200 AMB# 064894 NAIC# 12313	NR-5	'05	...	...	...	...	...	...	...	...	...	...	...	...	...	...	...	...
		'06	1.8	...	...	98.2	5,647	...	75.9	...	24.1	1,658	7,324	7,324	61	-1,553	-1,553	-1,553
		'07	5.9	...	47.5	46.7	29,212	...	78.3	...	21.7	7,981	53,102	52,697	23,584	-11,480	-11,480	-11,480
		'08	...	...	...	100.0	24,221	...	90.4	...	9.6	7,641	78,285	77,799	-3,069	-13,640	-13,640	-13,639
		'09	...	...	...	100.0	17,417	...	55.1	...	44.9	11,054	23,968	23,869	-5,799	6,639	3,556	3,556
		Rating History: NR-5, 03/24/10; NR-5, 06/17/09; NR-5, 07/29/08; NR-5, 04/25/07																
CARE PLUS DENTAL PLANS INC[2] John G. Gonis President 11711 West Burleigh Street Wauwatosa, WI 53222 WI : 1983 : Non-Profit : Not Available Dental 414-771-1711 AMB# 065736 NAIC# 55450	NR-5	'05	...	...	...	100.0	1,327	...	65.4	...	34.6	...	16,567	16,567	5	...	...	...
		'06	...	...	...	100.0	1,283	...	67.9	...	32.1	...	18,096	18,096	-5	...	...	...
		'07	...	...	...	100.0	1,354	...	63.7	...	36.3	...	18,897	18,897	-2	...	...	...
		'08	...	...	...	100.0	1,279	...	68.1	...	31.9	...	19,524	19,524	7	...	...	...
		'09	...	...	...	100.0	1,261	...	70.0	...	30.0	...	19,317	19,317	-1	...	...	...
		Rating History: NR-5, 05/20/10; NR-5, 07/13/09; NR-5, 05/16/08; NR-5, 06/20/07; NR-5, 07/12/06																

Data in U.S. Dollars

	Profitability Tests							Leverage Tests						Liquidity Tests					
Un-Realized Capital Gains ($000)	Benefits Paid to NPW & Dep (%)	Comm. & Expenses to NPW & Dep (%)	NOG to Total Assets (%)	NOG to Total Rev (%)	Operating Return on Equity (%)	Net Yield (%)	Total Return (%)	Change in NPW & Dep (%)	NPW & Dep to Capital (X)	Capital & Surplus to Liabilities (%)	Surplus Relief (%)	Reins Leverage (%)	Change in Capital (%)	Quick Liquidity (%)	Current Liquidity (%)	Non-Invest Grade Bonds to Capital (%)	Delinq. & Foreclosed Mortgages to Capital (%)	Mort. & Credit Tenant Loans & R.E. to Capital (%)	Affiliated Invest to Capital (%)
...	...	...	...	...	...	...	...	...	...	...	...	...	...	...	...	...	...	...	...
...	...	...	...	...	...	...	...	...	...	...	...	...	...	...	...	...	...	...	...
...	78.0	667.4	...	16.4	...	...	...	...	2.3	873.6	116.1	999.9	...	513.0	545.0	...	...	...	...
...	25.3	162.1	0.2	0.2	0.6	2.46	2.46	-96.4	0.1	35.4	3.7	999.9	10.5	114.5	115.7	...	...	...	...
...	83.2	999.9	0.4	2.7	1.0	8.17	8.18	44.5	0.1	999.9	2.6	999.9	1.4	999.9	999.9	...	...	...	...
Principal Lines of Business: OrdLife (100.0%)														Principal States: MO (88.1%), KS (11.7%)					
...	91.6	13.4	-1.2	-1.0	-1.7	4.46	4.21	1.3	1.7	229.5	...	...	-2.6	297.2	314.7	...	...	...	...
...	80.2	12.8	9.7	8.4	12.8	4.88	4.87	-8.9	1.4	496.4	...	...	13.9	539.3	568.3	...	...	...	...
...	105.5	12.9	-9.1	-9.8	-10.9	5.28	4.82	-27.3	1.1	495.9	...	...	-10.8	567.7	597.3	...	...	...	...
...	114.7	11.0	-26.7	-66.0	-34.9	3.49	2.69	-17.7	0.7	259.3	...	1.8	40.0	530.2	555.0	...	...	...	...
...	...	...	...	...	...	...	...	...	...	...	...	...	...	...	...	...	...	...	...
...	...	...	...	...	...	...	...	...	...	...	...	...	...	...	...	...	...	...	...
-14	387.4	368.4	...	-99.9	...	...	...	...	0.0	853.5	...	...	...	945.3	945.3	...	...	...	...
...	...	...	1.6	40.8	1.7	4.00	4.00	-99.9	...	999.9	...	...	1.7	999.9	999.9	...	...	...	...
...	...	...	1.6	69.5	1.7	2.33	2.33	...	...	999.9	...	...	1.7	999.9	999.9	...	...	...	...
...	...	...	-0.4	-99.9	-0.5	0.10	0.10	...	...	999.9	...	...	-0.5	999.9	999.9	...	...	...	...
5,053	825.8	27.3	0.1	0.8	2.0	6.44	6.41	-3.5	0.5	3.2	...	144.7	-3.2	71.5	82.1	197.3	...	4.3	6.9
-54	999.9	64.4	-0.5	-8.4	-22.6	5.79	5.68	-44.4	0.3	2.8	...	182.6	-20.0	74.8	85.1	215.5	...	...	...
60	736.5	36.6	1.1	17.8	41.2	5.69	5.59	60.4	0.4	4.2	...	114.3	40.3	68.4	80.8	160.4	...	...	...
-1,154	326.8	10.2	2.1	20.3	59.9	6.35	3.79	171.1	1.1	4.3	0.0	88.3	0.4	61.1	72.9	138.2	...	40.5	...
1,130	98.1	6.3	0.4	2.2	8.9	6.55	6.54	164.5	2.0	5.7	0.0	63.4	38.2	60.7	75.9	98.2	...	58.8	...
Principal Lines of Business: IndAnn (100.0%), OrdLife (0.0%)														Principal States: TX (94.0%)					
...	47.5	44.3	-1.2	-1.9	-5.0	...	...	27.9	2.3	28.4	49.9	...	-12.9	...	...	...	...	...	...
...	17.9	24.4	1.2	1.2	6.3	...	...	160.8	4.3	19.5	-1.7	...	38.9	...	...	...	...	...	...
...	62.6	32.5	1.1	2.6	6.7	...	...	-45.5	2.2	19.9	9.2	...	8.1	...	...	...	...	...	...
...	62.9	28.2	3.3	9.2	17.9	...	...	-7.9	1.5	25.2	5.6	...	29.9	...	...	...	...	...	...
...	63.7	24.6	3.6	11.8	16.9	...	...	-7.5	1.2	29.8	3.9	...	19.6	...	...	...	...	...	...
Principal Lines of Business: OrdLife (100.0%)																			
132	11.1	77.8	-5.6	-12.5	-21.9	2.76	3.65	-4.2	1.0	41.9	38.6	297.5	54.8	112.4	120.3	...	...	...	...
-99	19.7	90.1	-4.9	-9.3	-20.0	3.46	3.33	2.6	1.1	25.7	104.6	407.6	-9.9	90.9	98.2	...	...	...	...
-99	24.7	90.0	-6.0	-12.0	-31.9	4.02	3.85	3.3	1.1	21.3	135.3	507.0	0.6	88.6	96.9	3.0	...	...	...
-99	28.8	104.7	-1.6	-3.8	-7.8	4.72	2.88	-16.7	0.7	30.4	88.2	370.7	30.3	96.3	106.3	1.4	...	...	...
0	39.2	168.8	1.3	4.8	4.7	4.44	4.42	-47.4	0.3	47.5	45.0	246.8	22.8	111.0	122.5	5.6	...	...	...
Principal Lines of Business: CrdLife (66.3%), CrdA&H (33.7%)														Principal States: TX (31.8%), OH (18.1%), MI (16.6%), LA (5.7%), IL (4.8%)					
...	93.9	11.2	4.7	1.8	11.5	2.77	2.77	0.4	5.4	65.4	...	...	12.2	78.8	78.8	...	...	29.4	29.4
...	90.5	11.1	4.4	1.9	11.4	3.45	3.45	29.2	4.8	60.8	...	...	45.7	72.7	72.7	...	...	19.9	19.9
...	96.1	11.5	5.3	2.1	13.3	2.79	2.79	29.0	5.4	70.3	...	...	14.2	75.0	75.0	...	...	19.8	19.8
...	90.8	10.5	3.2	1.2	7.9	1.49	1.49	22.2	6.1	68.7	...	...	8.2	82.2	82.2	...	...	17.9	17.9
...	89.4	9.6	4.8	1.7	12.0	0.57	0.57	19.6	6.5	64.7	...	...	12.6	98.5	98.5	...	...	15.5	15.5
Principal Lines of Business: Medicaid (76.1%), Medicare (23.6%), CompHosp/Med (0.3%)																			
...	...	...	...	...	...	...	...	...	...	...	...	...	...	...	...	...	...	...	...
...	111.4	10.6	...	-21.0	...	...	...	...	4.4	41.6	...	1.0	...	41.8	41.8	...	...	...	...
...	106.6	15.6	-65.9	-21.7	-99.9	1.90	1.90	619.6	6.6	37.6	...	...	381.3	141.8	157.9	...	...	...	...
...	105.4	12.7	-51.1	-17.4	-99.9	2.10	2.10	47.6	10.2	46.1	...	0.5	-4.3	277.3	277.3	...	...	...	...
...	56.2	13.9	17.1	15.2	38.0	-0.04	-0.04	-69.3	2.2	173.7	...	1.8	44.7	411.6	411.6	...	...	...	...
Principal Lines of Business: Medicare (100.0%)														Principal States: MD (100.0%)					
...	99.2	0.8	...	...	...	...	...	1.1	...	...	...	...	...	0.5	0.5	...	...	...	...
...	98.6	1.4	...	...	...	...	...	9.2	...	...	...	...	...	0.1	0.1	...	...	...	...
...	98.2	1.8	...	...	...	...	...	4.4	...	...	...	...	...	0.0	0.0	...	...	...	...
...	98.5	1.5	...	...	...	...	...	3.3	...	...	...	...	...	0.5	0.5	...	...	...	...
...	98.7	1.3	...	...	...	...	...	-1.1	...	...	...	...	...	0.5	0.5	...	...	...	...
Principal Lines of Business: Dental (100.0%)														Principal States: WI (100.0%)					

2010 BEST'S KEY RATING GUIDE — LIFE/HEALTH EDITION
ANNUAL STATEMENT DATA FOR YEARS 2005 – 2009

Data in U.S. Dollars

COMPANY NAME Ultimate Parent Association Principal Officer Mailing Address Dom. : Began Bus. : Struct. : Mktg. Specialty Phone # AMB# NAIC#	Best's Financial Strength Rating FSC		Balance Sheet										Operations					
		Data Year	Bonds (%)	Mort. Loans & R.E. (%)	Com & Pref. Stock (%)	All Other Assets (%)	Total Assets ($000)	Life Reserves (%)	Health Reserves %)	Ann Res. & Dep. Liabilities (%)	All Other Liabilities (%)	Capital & Surplus ($000)	Direct Premiums Written ($000)	Net Premiums Written & Deposits ($000)	Operating Cash Flow ($000)	NOG Before Taxes ($000)	NOG After Taxes ($000)	Net Income ($000)
CAREAMERICA LIFE INS CO California Physicians' Service	**A-**	'05	92.4	...	...	7.6	29,380	13.6	44.5	...	41.9	26,295	4,947	5,352	952	1,268	1,234	1,234
Duncan Ross President & CEO		'06	91.1	...	...	8.9	30,569	2.2	4.8	...	93.0	9,460	2,736	4,765	1,319	2,094	1,685	1,685
50 Beale Street San Francisco, CA 94105	Rating Outlook: Stable	'07	90.4	...	...	9.6	25,533	15.2	45.5	...	39.2	22,201	2,317	3,560	-4,711	1,839	1,157	1,157
CA : 1968 : Stock : Broker		'08	84.8	...	...	15.2	27,900	14.5	18.8	...	66.6	24,123	2,398	3,632	2,114	2,879	1,971	1,863
Ind A&H, Term Life 888-646-0789		'09	88.5	...	...	11.5	26,949	13.7	23.6	...	62.6	23,547	2,438	3,443	-996	2,649	1,940	1,864
AMB# 007351 NAIC# 71331	**FSC XV**	**Rating History: A-, 05/26/10; A-, 07/10/09; A-, 06/26/08; A-, 06/28/07; A-, 06/21/06**																
CAREFIRST BLUECHOICE INC CareFirst Inc	**NR-5**	'05	56.2	...	15.4	28.3	452,462	...	57.1	...	42.9	252,077	1,299,078	1,299,078	23,212	32,195	25,532	33,134
Jon P. Shematek, M.D. Senior Vice President & Chief Medical Officer		'06	63.3	...	13.3	23.5	520,232	...	58.4	...	41.6	324,281	1,418,074	1,418,074	56,441	82,067	65,056	64,344
840 First Street, Northeast Washington, DC 20065		'07	63.8	...	9.3	26.8	623,745	...	57.9	...	42.1	399,421	1,591,350	1,591,325	80,032	102,625	80,907	80,599
DC : 1985 : Stock : Broker		'08	58.0	...	10.6	31.4	645,508	...	60.4	...	39.6	406,675	1,735,310	1,743,314	29,331	30,517	32,645	19,313
Group A&H, Ind A&H 410-581-3000		'09	63.2	...	6.1	30.7	709,225	...	55.7	...	44.3	470,736	1,864,662	1,874,054	36,528	48,732	40,545	48,411
AMB# 068605 NAIC# 96202		**Rating History: NR-5, 05/11/10; NR-5, 08/26/09; B++pd, 09/19/08; B+ pd, 09/04/07; B+ pd, 09/25/06**																
CAREFIRST OF MARYLAND INC CareFirst Inc	**NR-5**	'05	34.1	...	24.0	41.9	1,002,143	...	20.6	...	79.4	400,659	1,380,655	1,380,541	56,858	21,993	16,262	21,771
Chet Burrell President & CEO		'06	36.0	...	24.9	39.0	1,158,194	...	16.3	...	83.7	466,648	1,372,461	1,401,329	22,167	26,807	14,148	12,866
10455 Mill Run Circle Owings Mills, MD 21117		'07	37.3	...	27.3	35.5	1,135,067	...	29.3	...	70.7	513,480	1,348,719	1,387,307	-30,741	35,055	30,257	32,638
MD : 1985 : Stock : Agency		'08	26.4	...	25.6	48.0	1,149,945	...	34.8	...	65.2	394,251	1,476,031	1,833,811	-107,676	-12,053	-243	-10,047
Group A&H 410-581-3000		'09	22.9	...	27.7	49.4	1,155,353	...	39.3	...	60.7	407,903	1,483,292	1,871,225	-64,055	-9,552	-2,480	-1,791
AMB# 064470 NAIC# 47058		**Rating History: NR-5, 05/19/10; NR-5, 08/26/09; B+ pd, 09/19/08; B+ pd, 09/04/07; B+ pd, 09/25/06**																
CARELINK HEALTH PLANS INC Coventry Health Care Inc	**A-**	'05	75.5	...	...	24.5	41,166	...	68.1	...	31.9	21,742	126,386	124,195	7,348	7,212	5,525	5,631
Drew A. Joyce President & CEO		'06	69.0	...	...	31.0	44,891	...	62.9	...	37.1	22,654	135,021	132,863	2,458	9,586	7,521	7,509
500 Virginia Street East, Suite 400 Charleston, WV 25301	Rating Outlook: Negative	'07	74.1	...	...	25.9	43,762	...	52.5	...	47.5	26,147	134,156	132,081	-644	15,251	10,727	10,721
WV : 1995 : Stock : Broker		'08	50.2	...	...	49.8	49,497	...	47.7	...	52.3	26,607	147,109	145,031	-455	14,790	9,499	8,358
Group A&H, Health 804-747-3700		'09	51.4	...	...	48.6	58,843	...	56.6	...	43.4	33,690	170,140	167,835	12,677	10,025	7,241	7,639
AMB# 064186 NAIC# 95408	**FSC VI**	**Rating History: A-, 02/12/10; A- g, 11/19/08; A- g, 10/30/07; B++g, 07/11/07; B++g, 10/27/06**																
CAREMORE HEALTH PLAN	**NR-5**	'05	...	0.7	...	99.3	42,931	...	...	...	100.0	12,131	35,078	35,078	13,233	30,846	18,146	18,146
Leeba Lessin President		'06	...	0.5	...	99.5	56,302	...	...	...	100.0	26,000	171,348	171,348	15,006	42,842	25,369	25,369
12900 Park Plaza Drive, Suite 150 Cerritos, CA 90703		'07	...	1.7	...	98.3	65,321	...	...	...	100.0	21,023	309,303	309,303	13,190	49,875	29,523	29,523
CA : 2002 : Stock : Broker		'08	...	...	...	100.0	77,391	...	...	...	100.0	28,349	388,372	388,372	2,573	55,933	33,161	33,161
Health 562-741-4340		'09	...	...	...	100.0	123,303	...	...	...	100.0	49,098	483,057	483,057	46,040	80,469	47,649	47,649
AMB# 064751		**Rating History: NR-5, 03/25/10; NR-5, 03/20/09; NR-5, 06/30/08; NR-5, 05/07/07; NR-5, 05/30/06**																
CAREPLUS HEALTH PLANS INC Humana Inc	**A-**	'05	92.7	...	...	7.3	113,387	...	60.9	...	39.1	63,435	556,148	556,148	33,288	35,026	21,909	21,972
Michael B. McCallister President		'06	55.7	...	0.4	43.9	187,229	...	35.2	...	64.8	69,813	641,523	641,523	67,871	53,729	35,160	35,060
11430 NW 20th Street, Suite 300 Doral, FL 33172	Rating Outlook: Stable	'07	62.5	...	0.3	37.2	175,114	...	64.3	...	35.7	80,723	733,630	733,630	-16,397	83,659	56,474	56,242
FL : 1986 : Stock : Broker		'08	57.6	...	11.4	31.0	177,962	...	36.3	...	63.7	54,255	823,460	823,460	10,832	35,226	23,792	22,348
Group A&H 305-441-2245		'09	75.8	...	...	24.2	252,147	...	41.1	...	58.9	99,804	992,478	992,478	64,812	105,812	67,299	67,472
AMB# 068925 NAIC# 95092	**FSC XV**	**Rating History: A- g, 06/02/10; B++, 06/05/09; B++, 06/05/08; B++, 06/05/07; B++, 05/19/06**																
CARESOURCE CareSource Management Group Company	**NR-5**	'05	46.6	...	...	53.4	247,829	...	48.9	...	51.1	76,774	778,878	777,861	52,963	15,810	15,810	15,786
Pamela B. Morris President & CEO		'06	38.6	...	2.0	59.4	330,470	...	42.0	...	58.0	122,677	1,059,779	1,059,021	69,083	45,211	45,211	45,193
One South Main Street Dayton, OH 45402		'07	47.6	...	2.2	50.1	406,078	...	42.5	...	57.5	126,368	1,501,984	1,500,437	63,145	20,390	20,390	21,335
OH : 1988 : Non-Profit : Broker		'08	59.0	...	4.3	36.8	354,999	...	72.5	...	27.5	132,409	1,873,994	1,871,619	-75,247	-408	-408	-819
Health 937-531-3300		'09	30.3	0.3	2.8	66.6	683,477	...	35.1	...	64.9	178,530	2,446,005	2,440,659	320,722	35,603	35,603	34,913
AMB# 068574 NAIC# 95201		**Rating History: NR-5, 04/06/10; NR-5, 08/26/09; C++pd, 07/28/08; C++pd, 08/22/07; C++pd, 09/15/06**																
CARESOURCE MICHIGAN CareSource Management Group Company	**NR-5**	'05	...	...	0.1	99.9	32,654	...	...	...	100.0	16,242	102,242	101,984	5,536	6,857	6,857	6,885
Sharon R. Williams President		'06	22.0	...	...	78.0	25,141	...	62.7	...	37.3	11,877	103,906	103,596	-7,952	3,564	3,564	3,592
2369 Woodlake Drive, Suite 200 Okemos, MI 48864-6024		'07	10.9	...	...	89.1	37,365	...	49.2	...	50.8	9,487	137,641	137,337	8,521	4,447	4,447	4,447
MI : 1996 : Non-Profit : Broker		'08	41.9	...	...	58.1	46,289	...	48.5	...	51.5	19,532	154,823	154,534	12,801	14,241	14,241	14,268
Health 517-349-9922		'09	41.8	...	...	58.2	44,500	...	45.7	...	54.3	21,609	162,779	162,268	-2,874	20,284	20,284	20,285
AMB# 064042 NAIC# 95562		**Rating History: NR-5, 05/21/10; NR-5, 08/26/09; C pd, 07/28/08; C+ pd, 06/28/07; NR-5, 07/18/06**																
CARIBBEAN AMERICAN LIFE ASSUR Assurant Inc	**A-**	'05	85.9	...	2.0	12.1	119,503	45.0	47.6	...	7.5	30,009	58,424	44,147	9,840	9,236	8,212	8,195
Eduardo A. Arthur President		'06	75.0	...	3.7	21.3	78,163	39.7	52.2	...	8.1	17,589	52,132	25,700	-41,239	9,257	8,343	8,346
273 Ponce de Leon Avenue, Suite 1300 San Juan, PR 00917-1838	Rating Outlook: Stable	'07	71.4	...	5.7	22.8	69,296	43.1	50.2	...	6.7	13,848	50,445	31,649	-10,206	3,868	3,275	3,402
PR : 1988 : Stock : Agency		'08	74.8	...	5.4	19.8	64,001	43.4	46.6	...	10.0	18,725	40,149	14,919	-3,238	8,029	7,709	7,769
Credit A&H, Credit Life, Term Life 787-250-6470		'09	68.1	...	5.6	26.3	54,001	42.6	46.0	...	11.4	16,669	25,672	12,836	-9,488	6,135	5,728	5,752
AMB# 068045 NAIC# 73156	**FSC VIII**	**Rating History: A- g, 11/18/09; A- g, 11/25/08; A- g, 06/24/08; A g, 07/17/07; A g, 06/19/06**																

2010 BEST'S KEY RATING GUIDE — LIFE/HEALTH EDITION
BEST'S PROFITABILITY, LEVERAGE AND LIQUIDITY TESTS 2005 – 2009

Data in U.S. Dollars

	Profitability Tests							Leverage Tests						Liquidity Tests					
Un-Realized Capital Gains ($000)	Benefits Paid to NPW & Dep (%)	Comm. & Expenses to NPW & Dep (%)	NOG to Total Assets (%)	NOG to Total Rev (%)	Operating Return on Equity (%)	Net Yield (%)	Total Return (%)	Change in NPW & Dep (%)	NPW & Dep to Capital (X)	Capital & Surplus to Liabilities (%)	Surplus Relief (%)	Reins Leverage (%)	Change in Capital (%)	Quick Liquidity (%)	Current Liquidity (%)	Non-Invest Grade Bonds to Capital (%)	Delinq. & Foreclosed Mortgages to Capital (%)	Mort. & Credit Tenant Loans & R.E. to Capital (%)	Affiliated Invest to Capital (%)
...	56.2	46.8	4.3	18.3	4.8	4.15	4.55	5.2	0.2	868.7	...	...	4.9	767.2	846.7	...	...	...	...
...	62.8	25.1	5.6	27.3	9.4	4.67	4.95	-11.0	0.5	45.3	...	...	-63.9	115.2	127.4	...	...	...	...
...	62.2	26.0	4.1	23.2	7.3	5.09	5.31	-25.3	0.2	682.9	...	...	133.8	585.8	652.4	...	...	...	...
-2	28.8	26.0	7.4	40.4	8.5	4.51	4.40	2.0	0.2	638.6	...	...	8.3	613.8	668.3	0.0	...	...	...
2	29.3	29.1	7.1	41.6	8.1	4.21	4.34	-5.2	0.1	692.0	...	...	-2.4	613.2	682.9	0.2	...	...	...
	Principal Lines of Business: GrpLife (64.1%), GrpA&H (29.0%), OrdLife (6.7%), IndA&H (0.1%)													Principal States: CA (90.4%), AZ (9.6%)					
192	81.6	16.9	5.9	1.9	10.8	3.99	6.18	22.8	5.2	125.8	...	...	14.4	162.4	178.9	1.5	...	...	0.9
5,809	79.7	15.8	13.4	4.5	22.6	4.47	5.74	9.2	4.4	165.5	...	...	28.6	180.1	200.3	0.1	...	...	0.8
-4,491	79.3	15.7	14.1	5.0	22.4	4.87	3.86	12.2	4.0	178.1	...	...	23.2	199.6	219.1	0.0	...	...	0.7
-8,824	83.7	15.9	5.1	1.8	8.1	4.90	0.68	9.6	4.3	170.3	...	0.2	1.8	193.8	215.7	2.6	...	...	0.9
7,074	80.9	17.7	6.0	2.1	9.2	4.07	6.82	7.5	4.0	197.4	...	0.2	15.8	215.8	235.9	1.1	...	...	0.9
	Principal Lines of Business: CompHosp/Med (93.1%), FEHBP (5.9%), Dental (1.0%)													Principal States: MD (72.1%), DC (16.2%), VA (11.7%)					
8,882	86.8	12.7	1.6	1.2	4.3	3.89	6.47	4.1	3.4	66.6	...	...	13.7	63.8	71.9	1.1	...	...	37.6
51,213	86.3	13.5	1.3	1.0	3.3	3.76	11.84	1.5	3.0	67.5	...	0.7	16.5	60.4	68.1	...	...	...	41.9
42,172	87.3	12.5	2.6	2.1	6.2	3.53	10.16	-1.0	2.7	82.6	...	0.8	10.0	58.9	66.8	...	...	...	47.4
-3,006	89.1	13.1	0.0	0.0	-0.1	3.51	1.51	32.2	4.7	52.2	...	16.6	-23.2	36.5	41.8	3.2	...	...	63.5
41,383	87.2	14.4	-0.2	-0.1	-0.6	2.08	9.74	2.0	4.6	54.6	...	15.8	3.5	29.6	33.4	0.9	...	...	72.0
	Principal Lines of Business: FEHBP (49.6%), CompHosp/Med (36.0%), MedSup (7.4%), OtherHlth (4.0%), Dental (2.8%)													Principal States: MD (100.0%)					
...	83.4	12.9	14.0	4.4	28.9	3.96	4.27	-3.9	5.7	111.9	...	0.7	31.9	190.4	207.3	...	...	...	...
...	81.1	12.9	17.5	5.6	33.9	4.15	4.12	7.0	5.9	101.9	...	1.2	4.2	161.2	175.3	...	...	...	...
...	76.4	13.3	24.2	8.0	44.0	4.27	4.26	-0.6	5.1	148.4	...	0.2	15.4	198.8	217.1	...	...	...	...
...	79.6	10.9	20.4	6.5	36.0	3.57	0.71	9.8	5.5	116.2	...	3.0	1.8	175.2	185.3	...	...	...	...
...	84.5	10.1	13.4	4.3	24.0	1.67	2.55	15.7	5.0	133.9	...	0.4	26.6	209.1	220.9	...	...	...	...
	Principal Lines of Business: Medicaid (60.1%), CompHosp/Med (39.9%)													Principal States: WV (100.0%)					
...	357.4	109.1	56.1	9.3	276.7	3.31	3.31	166.9	2.9	39.4	...	...	999.9	107.9	107.9	...	...	2.3	2.3
...	100.6	20.2	51.1	10.2	133.1	5.27	5.27	388.5	6.6	85.8	...	...	114.3	155.9	155.9	...	...	1.0	1.0
...	71.6	13.2	48.5	9.5	125.6	5.62	5.62	80.5	14.7	47.5	...	...	-19.1	131.6	131.6	...	...	5.4	5.4
...	73.9	12.3	46.5	8.5	134.3	4.24	4.24	25.6	13.7	57.8	...	...	34.8	107.3	107.3	...	...	...	...
...	72.7	11.2	47.5	9.8	123.0	2.28	2.28	24.4	9.8	66.2	...	...	73.2	119.2	119.2	...	...	...	...
	Principal Lines of Business: Medicare (100.0%)																		
...	79.9	14.5	23.0	3.9	42.5	4.19	4.25	14.8	8.8	127.0	...	...	60.4	204.6	210.5	...	...	...	...
-1	82.4	10.4	23.4	5.4	52.8	5.34	5.27	15.4	9.2	59.5	...	...	10.1	185.2	194.1	...	...	...	...
-92	79.5	10.5	31.2	7.6	75.0	6.55	6.36	14.4	9.1	85.5	...	...	15.6	180.0	192.0	...	...	...	...
-231	85.9	10.8	13.5	2.9	35.3	4.81	3.79	12.2	15.2	43.9	...	...	-32.8	138.5	148.1	2.2	...	...	...
324	81.3	8.8	31.3	6.7	87.4	3.76	4.01	20.5	9.9	65.5	...	...	84.0	154.9	167.2	...	...	...	...
	Principal Lines of Business: Medicare (100.0%)													Principal States: FL (100.0%)					
...	92.8	6.1	7.2	2.1	22.8	3.51	3.50	15.8	10.1	44.9	...	...	24.1	120.3	123.1	...	...	...	...
...	86.7	10.0	15.6	4.2	45.3	4.14	4.14	36.1	8.6	59.0	...	0.6	59.8	130.2	132.7	1.2	...	...	...
-1,335	89.7	10.0	5.5	1.3	16.4	4.89	4.77	41.7	11.9	45.2	...	4.6	3.0	111.1	114.7	...	...	...	...
-8,713	90.9	10.0	-0.1	0.0	-0.3	4.98	2.07	24.7	14.1	59.5	...	3.9	4.8	99.6	106.2	2.2	...	...	...
2,534	88.3	10.7	6.9	1.5	22.9	2.67	3.10	30.4	13.7	35.4	...	6.1	34.8	102.0	107.5	...	...	1.2	1.2
	Principal Lines of Business: Medicaid (99.8%), Medicare (0.2%), OtherHlth (0.0%)													Principal States: OH (100.0%)					
-25	77.7	10.1	22.7	7.1	50.9	1.84	1.85	0.6	6.3	99.0	...	1.2	51.4	189.2	189.2	...	...	...	...
-8	80.3	11.1	12.3	3.6	25.4	3.14	3.21	1.6	8.7	89.5	...	1.1	-26.9	206.7	207.6	...	...	...	...
...	82.7	9.0	14.2	3.4	41.6	4.91	4.91	32.6	14.5	34.0	...	1.1	-20.1	112.9	113.1	...	...	...	...
...	79.7	6.3	34.0	9.7	98.1	2.56	2.63	12.5	7.9	73.0	...	0.3	105.9	159.5	164.8	...	...	...	...
...	75.8	11.0	44.7	12.6	98.6	2.53	2.53	5.0	7.5	94.4	...	1.3	10.6	100.7	100.7	...	...	...	...
	Principal Lines of Business: Medicaid (99.2%), Medicare (0.8%)													Principal States: MI (100.0%)					
244	28.6	58.9	7.2	13.7	31.2	5.03	5.13	-12.1	1.5	34.0	33.9	81.9	30.5	100.8	112.5	...	...	...	7.8
511	55.5	75.1	8.4	19.8	35.1	4.91	5.29	-41.8	1.4	29.8	67.7	165.1	-40.8	102.6	110.9	...	...	...	16.0
1,102	38.9	68.5	4.4	7.4	20.8	4.82	6.25	23.1	2.2	26.4	66.1	223.0	-19.4	99.2	106.7	...	...	...	27.5
-542	70.1	77.1	11.6	24.9	47.3	7.89	6.80	-52.9	0.8	43.2	60.5	194.1	33.3	105.8	116.8	...	...	...	17.8
-409	63.8	73.7	9.7	24.9	32.4	7.82	6.82	-14.0	0.7	46.7	36.2	191.2	-11.0	113.1	124.0	...	...	...	17.6
	Principal Lines of Business: CrdLife (51.1%), CrdA&H (41.5%), GrpA&H (4.4%), GrpLife (3.0%)													Principal States: PR (97.6%)					

COMPANY NAME Ultimate Parent Association Principal Officer Mailing Address Dom. : Began Bus. : Struct. : Mktg. Specialty Phone # AMB# NAIC#	Best's Financial Strength Rating FSC	Data Year	Balance Sheet: Bonds (%)	Mort. Loans & R.E. (%)	Com & Pref. Stock (%)	All Other Assets (%)	Total Assets ($000)	Life Reserves (%)	Health Reserves (%)	Ann Res. & Dep. Liabilities (%)	All Other Liabilities (%)	Capital & Surplus ($000)	Operations: Direct Premiums Written ($000)	Net Premiums Written & Deposits ($000)	Operating Cash Flow ($000)	NOG Before Taxes ($000)	NOG After Taxes ($000)	Net Income ($000)
CARITEN HEALTH PLAN INC Humana Inc Michael B. McCallister President & CEO P.O. Box 740036 Louisville, KY 40201-7436 TN : 1995 : Stock : Broker Group A&H, Health 865-470-7470 AMB# 064425 NAIC# 95754	A- Rating Outlook: Stable FSC XV	'05	91.3	...	...	8.7	76,637	...	54.1	...	45.9	27,698	226,035	226,035	11,849	14,639	7,952	7,930
		'06	85.9	...	...	14.1	125,610	...	42.1	...	57.9	33,086	413,735	413,735	47,986	19,915	9,536	9,610
		'07	73.7	...	...	26.3	123,654	...	44.9	...	55.1	33,589	463,653	463,653	-2,132	19,907	16,499	16,361
		'08	50.4	...	...	49.6	167,155	...	76.1	...	23.9	108,321	549,813	549,813	2,234	74,399	58,905	56,054
		'09	46.2	...	...	53.8	125,248	...	77.2	...	22.8	78,982	588,967	588,967	-14,016	34,644	21,436	22,868
		Rating History: A- g, 06/02/10; B++, 06/05/09; C+ pd, 07/21/08; C+ pd, 06/28/07; C++pd, 08/08/06																
CARITEN INSURANCE COMPANY Humana Inc Michael B. McCallister President & CEO 1420 Centerpoint Boulevard Knoxville, TN 37932 TN : 1994 : Stock : Not Available Health 865-470-7470 AMB# 007835 NAIC# 82740	A- Rating Outlook: Stable FSC XV	'05	90.2	...	...	9.8	57,765	...	56.0	...	44.0	33,176	118,726	118,726	4,544	8,525	7,254	7,326
		'06	89.9	...	...	10.1	60,182	...	51.9	...	48.1	36,484	120,727	120,727	1,899	3,218	1,371	1,416
		'07	85.9	...	...	14.1	61,890	...	45.2	...	54.8	38,184	114,513	114,513	3,898	1,957	1,581	1,485
		'08	61.1	...	...	38.9	62,218	...	40.9	...	59.1	46,810	87,408	87,408	871	12,084	10,296	8,218
		'09	81.0	...	...	19.0	25,162	...	56.0	...	44.0	17,744	68,769	68,769	-36,955	1,667	1,834	2,334
		Rating History: A- g, 06/02/10; B++, 06/05/09; NR-5, 06/03/03; NR-1, 06/06/02; NR-1, 06/13/01																
CASS COUNTY LIFE INS CO[1] John M. Hanner President P.O. Box 1070 Atlanta, TX 75551-1070 TX : 1994 : Stock : Not Available 903-796-2833 AMB# 060089 NAIC# 60019	NR-1	'05	34.4	16.5	10.1	39.0	3,964	...	...	...	100.0	297	157	158	...	61	58	62
		'06	34.3	16.9	8.6	40.2	3,972	...	...	...	100.0	359	153	153	...	37	37	37
		'07	34.6	14.9	6.9	43.7	3,873	...	...	...	100.0	333	154	154	...	42	40	40
		'08	43.2	14.2	5.6	37.0	3,554	...	...	...	100.0	133	144	144	...	56	55	-25
		'09	47.4	12.9	2.9	36.8	3,554	...	...	...	100.0	136	132	132	...	-23	-26	-26
		Rating History: NR-1, 06/10/10; NR-1, 06/12/09; NR-1, 06/12/08; NR-1, 06/08/07; NR-1, 06/07/06																
CATERPILLAR LIFE INSURANCE CO Caterpillar Inc Michael D. Reeves President P.O. Box 340001 Nashville, TN 37203 MO : 1980 : Stock : Agency Inactive 615-341-8147 AMB# 060402 NAIC# 11997	NR-5	'05	83.6	...	11.2	5.2	158,631	...	96.7	...	3.3	51,881	...	...	12,039	3,656	4,304	4,867
		'06	83.8	...	13.0	3.2	155,264	...	95.8	...	4.2	45,339	...	...	-5,525	2,281	2,633	2,954
		'07	83.3	...	13.4	3.3	161,373	...	94.2	...	5.8	50,282	...	...	5,112	5,335	4,742	5,623
		'08	86.1	...	8.8	5.1	155,564	...	98.0	...	2.0	46,858	...	...	-1,116	1,238	574	-1,759
		'09	81.6	...	10.1	8.3	160,761	...	96.7	...	3.3	48,880	...	...	2,997	1,813	649	-507
		Rating History: NR-5, 04/20/10; NR-5, 04/23/09; NR-5, 04/18/08; NR-5, 05/09/07; NR-5, 04/24/06																
CATHOLIC KNIGHTS William R. O'Toole President & CEO 1100 West Wells Street Milwaukee, WI 53233-2316 WI : 1885 : Fraternal : Career Agent Ind Ann, Ind Life 414-273-6266 AMB# 008188 NAIC# 56030	B u Under Review Implication: Negative FSC VI	'05	85.5	3.3	3.9	7.3	782,353	46.6	0.1	50.6	2.7	46,827	51,934	53,830	24,482	951	951	990
		'06	86.8	3.8	4.5	4.9	800,541	47.1	0.1	50.0	2.8	50,273	42,408	45,031	11,111	2,047	2,047	-4,007
		'07	85.2	4.1	5.3	5.4	817,567	47.8	0.1	49.2	2.8	51,873	42,378	43,162	23,736	2,073	2,073	9,281
		'08	83.2	4.3	4.6	7.9	831,150	47.6	0.1	49.8	2.5	36,284	56,768	58,344	25,261	2,606	2,606	-7,239
		'09	87.8	4.5	1.6	6.1	873,716	46.6	0.1	50.9	2.5	32,058	67,369	70,234	32,171	3,194	3,194	-12,267
		Rating History: B u, 12/22/09; B+, 05/29/09; B++, 12/17/08; NR-5, 04/22/08; NR-5, 05/08/07																
CATHOLIC LIFE INSURANCE J. Michael Belz President & CEO 1635 N.E. Loop 410 San Antonio, TX 78209-1694 TX : 1902 : Fraternal : Agency Ann, Univ Life, Whole life 210-828-9921 AMB# 008827 NAIC# 57347	A- Rating Outlook: Stable FSC VII	'05	92.9	1.6	2.2	3.3	624,673	23.7	...	74.9	1.4	43,813	50,662	51,120	36,472	4,948	4,948	4,707
		'06	93.3	1.2	2.3	3.1	650,447	23.8	...	74.9	1.3	47,444	35,664	35,917	25,967	3,555	3,555	3,515
		'07	92.5	1.1	2.1	4.4	671,496	24.2	...	74.5	1.2	51,279	34,360	34,917	21,963	3,784	3,784	4,048
		'08	93.4	0.8	2.0	3.9	704,237	23.9	...	75.3	0.7	50,909	51,608	53,056	34,060	2,900	2,900	-2,015
		'09	95.6	0.6	0.1	3.7	770,595	22.9	...	76.2	0.9	54,072	70,341	71,636	65,263	5,092	5,092	3,139
		Rating History: A-, 05/27/10; A-, 04/30/09; A-, 04/29/08; A-, 06/14/07; A-, 06/12/06																
CATHOLIC ORDER OF FORESTERS David E. Huber High Chief Ranger & President P.O. Box 3012 Naperville, IL 60566-7012 IL : 1883 : Fraternal : Agency Ind Life, Term Life, Ann 630-983-4900 AMB# 006191 NAIC# 57487	B++ Rating Outlook: Stable FSC VI	'05	91.2	1.7	2.7	4.3	562,575	52.7	0.7	40.7	5.9	36,064	55,109	62,201	20,493	278	278	830
		'06	92.2	1.9	2.1	3.8	573,666	52.8	1.0	40.6	5.6	39,337	66,116	72,364	9,283	1,250	1,250	908
		'07	91.2	2.1	2.4	4.2	618,796	51.1	1.1	42.4	5.4	39,053	49,397	55,206	11,892	228	228	721
		'08	88.2	2.1	3.5	6.2	632,921	51.1	1.4	43.3	4.3	35,673	71,562	76,970	19,335	1,908	1,908	-1,728
		'09	90.3	2.2	2.7	4.8	685,405	48.7	1.4	44.6	5.3	38,125	109,213	111,627	44,620	4,071	4,071	2,780
		Rating History: B++, 04/23/10; B++, 05/27/09; A-, 06/05/08; A-, 05/04/07; A-, 05/25/06																
CDPHP UNIVERSAL BENEFITS INC Capital District Physicians' Health Plan John D. Bennet, MD President & CEO 500 Patroon Creek Blvd. Albany, NY 12206-1057 NY : 1998 : Other : Agency Group A&H 518-641-3000 AMB# 064596 NAIC# 47027	B Rating Outlook: Negative FSC VI	'05	...	...	...	100.0	17,741	...	55.4	...	44.6	6,325	74,328	74,052	3,651	-287	-287	-287
		'06	...	...	...	100.0	15,974	...	65.0	...	35.0	2,726	129,994	129,834	3,458	-964	-964	-964
		'07	...	...	...	100.0	41,678	...	53.8	...	46.2	20,993	159,593	159,209	21,866	1,709	1,709	1,709
		'08	...	...	...	100.0	60,610	...	57.1	...	42.9	34,799	208,083	207,313	19,220	-11,459	-11,459	-11,459
		'09	41.1	...	...	58.9	56,508	...	64.6	...	35.4	28,331	246,069	245,202	-23,644	-7,981	-7,981	-7,931
		Rating History: B, 06/05/09; B+ u, 01/30/09; B+, 11/12/07; B+, 10/10/06; NR-5, 06/20/06																
CELTIC INSURANCE COMPANY Centene Corporation Mark Ponder Director, Financial Reporting & Treasury 233 South Wacker Drive, Suite 700 Chicago, IL 60606-6393 IL : 1950 : Stock : Broker A&H, Ind A&H 312-332-5401 AMB# 006999 NAIC# 80799	B++ Rating Outlook: Stable FSC V	'05	88.4	...	...	11.6	100,889	0.1	56.6	10.8	32.6	48,261	148,016	117,871	970	8,387	5,545	5,545
		'06	88.0	...	0.3	11.7	103,982	0.1	56.7	10.0	33.2	48,207	129,057	106,381	2,201	6,552	4,393	4,393
		'07	88.1	...	0.3	11.7	99,645	0.1	57.1	10.8	32.0	49,055	112,609	93,080	-4,599	7,716	5,079	5,079
		'08	87.6	...	0.4	12.0	66,800	0.2	54.2	12.1	33.5	22,378	101,107	83,210	-31,434	8,826	5,796	4,705
		'09	80.5	...	0.5	19.1	58,158	0.2	52.2	13.5	34.1	19,797	95,086	79,363	-9,206	3,846	2,332	2,332
		Rating History: B++, 02/19/10; B++, 02/10/09; A- u, 03/19/08; A-, 03/30/07; A-, 03/27/06																

2010 BEST'S KEY RATING GUIDE — LIFE/HEALTH EDITION
BEST'S PROFITABILITY, LEVERAGE AND LIQUIDITY TESTS 2005 – 2009

Data in U.S. Dollars

	Profitability Tests							Leverage Tests						Liquidity Tests					
Un-Realized Capital Gains ($000)	Benefits Paid to NPW & Dep (%)	Comm. & Expenses to NPW & Dep (%)	NOG to Total Assets (%)	NOG to Total Rev (%)	Operating Return on Equity (%)	Net Yield (%)	Total Return (%)	Change in NPW & Dep (%)	NPW & Dep to Capital (X)	Capital & Surplus to Liabilities (%)	Surplus Relief (%)	Reins Leverage (%)	Change in Capital (%)	Quick Liquidity (%)	Current Liquidity (%)	Non-Invest Grade Bonds to Capital (%)	Delinq. & Foreclosed Mortgages to Capital (%)	Mort. & Credit Tenant Loans & R.E. to Capital (%)	Affiliated Invest to Capital (%)
...	89.0	6.0	11.2	3.5	29.1	4.60	4.57	32.3	8.2	56.6	...	...	2.7	136.1	142.3	1.7	...	...	...
...	91.9	4.8	9.4	2.3	31.4	6.30	6.37	83.0	12.5	35.8	...	...	19.5	108.9	117.9	...	...	...	...
...	92.1	5.0	13.2	3.5	49.5	5.25	5.14	12.1	13.8	37.3	...	...	1.5	127.5	136.3	...	...	...	...
...	84.6	4.5	40.5	10.4	83.0	3.52	1.22	18.6	5.1	184.1	...	...	222.5	274.1	281.4	...	...	...	...
...	86.9	7.7	14.7	3.6	22.9	2.45	3.70	7.1	7.5	170.7	...	...	-27.1	334.3	351.1	...	...	...	...
	Principal Lines of Business: Medicare (88.7%), CompHosp/Med (11.3%)													Principal States: TN (100.0%)					
...	81.4	13.3	13.3	6.0	23.7	4.28	4.41	-3.0	3.6	134.9	...	...	18.7	194.1	203.6	1.9	...	...	...
...	85.9	13.8	2.3	1.1	3.9	5.10	5.18	1.7	3.3	154.0	...	...	10.0	205.3	218.9	...	...	...	...
...	87.0	13.7	2.6	1.3	4.2	4.72	4.56	-5.1	3.0	161.1	...	...	4.7	29.3	29.3	...	...	...	...
150	80.6	15.0	16.6	11.1	24.2	3.73	0.63	-23.7	1.9	303.8	...	...	22.6	467.5	488.6	...	...	...	...
...	83.6	15.7	4.2	2.6	5.7	2.78	3.96	-21.3	3.9	239.2	...	...	-62.1	323.4	356.0	...	...	...	...
	Principal Lines of Business: CompHosp/Med (98.8%), Medicare (1.2%)													Principal States: TN (100.0%)					
-46	177.7	97.5	1.4	16.6	21.6	...	...	0.8	0.5	8.3	...	...	9.7	...	...	...	...	215.0	...
35	170.7	96.8	0.9	9.7	11.3	...	...	-3.0	0.4	10.7	...	...	25.8	...	...	...	...	175.5	...
-62	179.2	98.3	1.0	10.5	11.6	...	...	0.8	0.4	10.2	...	...	-6.7	...	...	...	...	160.9	...
-209	180.8	88.0	1.5	15.1	23.6	...	...	-6.5	1.1	3.9	...	...	-62.4	...	...	...	...	376.1	...
236	201.7	101.9	-0.7	-8.9	-19.0	...	...	-8.4	0.6	6.6	...	...	64.6	...	...	...	...	207.8	...
	Principal Lines of Business: OrdLife (100.0%)																		
322	...	...	2.8	63.8	9.5	4.51	5.10	-99.9	...	53.0	...	...	31.3	79.8	114.5	...	...	...	87.3
1,548	...	...	1.7	35.9	5.4	4.80	5.99	...	...	47.0	...	...	-9.7	80.7	110.3	...	...	...	72.7
-174	...	...	3.0	64.6	9.9	4.77	5.21	...	...	51.6	...	...	10.7	80.6	112.3	...	...	...	65.7
-3,026	...	...	0.4	10.5	1.2	3.53	0.15	...	...	45.7	...	...	-11.1	80.6	111.3	...	...	...	73.9
2,873	...	...	0.4	11.3	1.4	3.76	4.83	...	...	47.9	...	...	6.6	90.0	120.5	6.3	...	...	69.3
337	80.8	35.2	0.1	1.0	2.0	6.02	6.14	-12.2	1.0	7.7	0.0	5.9	3.7	72.2	81.6	53.6	...	46.6	2.1
7,437	109.6	39.9	0.3	2.3	4.2	5.83	6.06	-16.3	0.7	8.1	...	5.5	7.6	70.2	80.0	26.1	...	50.5	1.7
-5,993	116.7	40.3	0.3	2.4	4.1	5.77	5.99	-4.2	0.7	8.2	...	6.2	3.5	68.9	79.7	12.2	...	54.4	1.3
-11,230	81.4	31.7	0.3	2.5	5.9	5.88	3.40	35.2	1.5	5.0	...	10.4	-36.4	65.7	76.4	137.3	...	89.9	1.7
11,906	64.6	28.4	0.4	2.8	9.3	5.85	5.50	20.4	2.0	4.2	...	13.8	-11.1	61.8	71.1	284.0	0.5	111.6	1.9
	Principal Lines of Business: IndAnn (60.9%), OrdLife (39.1%), IndA&H (0.0%)													Principal States: WI (85.2%), IL (3.5%), IA (3.1%)					
278	76.2	19.6	0.8	5.8	12.0	5.73	5.90	9.0	1.1	7.7	0.4	2.7	14.5	72.8	84.9	6.4	0.0	22.0	...
261	93.1	25.7	0.6	5.0	7.8	5.66	5.79	-29.7	0.7	8.2	0.1	2.4	9.3	74.0	86.3	8.9	0.1	16.5	...
-47	121.8	26.4	0.6	5.3	7.7	5.66	5.78	-2.8	0.7	8.6	0.1	2.3	8.3	74.8	86.7	15.6	0.1	13.8	...
-269	72.8	19.5	0.4	3.2	5.7	5.64	4.96	52.0	1.0	7.8	0.0	2.4	-4.1	74.1	86.3	22.6	...	10.5	...
121	46.8	15.6	0.7	4.6	9.7	5.58	5.43	35.0	1.3	7.6	0.0	2.3	6.6	74.7	86.7	12.1	...	7.9	...
	Principal Lines of Business: IndAnn (82.2%), OrdLife (17.8%)													Principal States: TX (97.8%)					
-585	64.5	21.1	0.1	0.3	0.8	5.04	5.22	-6.4	1.5	7.9	0.8	7.4	-0.3	78.2	82.8	112.9	...	23.1	10.7
1,791	90.9	17.6	0.2	1.3	3.3	5.25	5.65	16.3	1.7	8.3	0.6	8.5	6.8	77.7	82.4	103.6	...	25.5	9.5
-531	88.0	23.9	0.0	0.3	0.6	5.60	5.72	-23.7	1.2	7.7	0.6	10.4	1.2	77.5	82.8	91.1	...	32.5	8.8
-5,457	77.3	17.3	0.3	1.8	5.1	5.50	4.16	39.4	2.1	6.2	0.6	12.6	-16.1	74.5	82.8	106.5	...	43.4	9.8
2,987	67.2	13.3	0.6	2.8	11.0	5.62	6.02	45.0	2.7	6.3	-0.7	13.3	10.1	67.1	77.7	110.4	...	44.4	8.4
	Principal Lines of Business: IndAnn (71.8%), OrdLife (27.3%), IndA&H (0.9%)													Principal States: WI (16.1%), MN (13.8%), OH (12.1%), IA (11.4%), MI (8.0%)					
...	92.1	8.3	-2.7	-0.4	-6.7	2.41	2.41	760.4	11.7	55.4	...	8.5	183.3	77.4	78.8	...	...	...	...
...	91.3	9.7	-5.7	-0.8	-21.3	4.63	4.63	75.3	47.6	20.6	...	8.7	-56.9	99.9	102.0	...	...	...	...
...	87.3	12.6	5.9	1.1	14.4	7.24	7.24	22.6	7.6	101.5	...	1.8	670.2	157.7	157.7	...	...	...	...
...	93.9	12.2	-22.4	-5.6	-41.1	2.08	2.08	30.2	6.0	134.8	...	1.6	65.8	200.8	200.8	...	...	...	...
...	90.2	13.2	-13.6	-3.2	-25.3	1.43	1.56	18.3	8.7	100.5	...	0.7	-18.6	98.6	106.2	...	...	...	...
	Principal Lines of Business: CompHosp/Med (72.0%), FEHBP (18.8%), Medicare (8.9%), Dental (0.3%)													Principal States: NY (96.8%)					
...	61.2	32.2	5.5	4.5	11.5	3.88	3.98	-16.2	2.4	92.5	5.8	24.6	-0.6	178.2	191.9	...	...	...	...
...	71.2	30.5	4.3	3.9	9.1	4.87	4.95	-9.7	2.2	87.2	4.6	19.5	-0.1	161.8	175.6	...	...	...	...
...	63.2	31.7	5.0	5.1	10.4	5.31	5.38	-12.5	1.9	97.9	4.1	19.3	1.8	159.4	175.8	...	...	...	...
...	64.5	31.5	7.0	6.5	16.2	5.04	3.76	-10.6	3.7	51.1	7.9	38.9	-54.2	120.2	135.2	...	...	...	...
...	64.4	34.8	3.7	2.8	11.1	2.99	3.09	-4.6	4.0	52.4	7.5	37.6	-11.5	122.4	135.7	1.4	...	...	...
	Principal Lines of Business: IndA&H (50.8%), GrpA&H (49.2%), GrpLife (0.0%), OrdLife (0.0%)													Principal States: FL (20.2%), NC (9.7%), IL (8.7%), TX (5.3%), GA (4.5%)					

Column key: COMPANY NAME / Ultimate Parent Association / Principal Officer / Mailing Address / Dom. : Began Bus. : Struct. : Mktg. / Specialty / Phone # / AMB# / NAIC# — Best's Financial Strength Rating / FSC — Balance Sheet: Data Year, Bonds (%), Mort. Loans & R.E. (%), Com & Pref. Stock (%), All Other Assets (%), Total Assets ($000), Life Reserves (%), Health Reserves (%), Ann Res. & Dep. Liabilities (%), All Other Liabilities (%), Capital & Surplus ($000) — Operations: Direct Premiums Written ($000), Net Premiums Written & Deposits ($000), Operating Cash Flow ($000), NOG Before Taxes ($000), NOG After Taxes ($000), Net Income ($000)

CELTICARE HEALTH PLAN OF MA
Centene Corporation
Richard D. Lynch
President & CEO
7711 Carondelet Avenue, Suite 800
St. Louis, MO 63105
MA : 2009 : Stock : Broker
Health
314-725-4706
AMB# 064978 NAIC# 13632

Rating: NR-2

Data Year	Bonds (%)	Mort. Loans & R.E. (%)	Com & Pref. Stock (%)	All Other Assets (%)	Total Assets ($000)	Life Reserves (%)	Health Reserves (%)	Ann Res. & Dep. Liabilities (%)	All Other Liabilities (%)	Capital & Surplus ($000)	Direct Premiums Written ($000)	Net Premiums Written & Deposits ($000)	Operating Cash Flow ($000)	NOG Before Taxes ($000)	NOG After Taxes ($000)	Net Income ($000)
'05	...	...	...	...	...	...	...	...	...	...	...	...	...	...	...	...
'06	...	...	...	...	...	...	...	...	...	...	...	...	...	...	...	...
'07	...	...	...	...	...	...	...	...	...	...	...	...	...	...	...	...
'08	...	...	...	...	...	...	...	...	...	...	...	...	...	...	...	...
'09	34.1	...	...	65.9	14,464	...	63.5	...	36.5	5,463	11,599	11,599	12,747	-1,084	-765	-765

Rating History: NR-2, 02/19/10

CENPATICO BEHAVIORAL HLTH TX
Centene Corporation
Samuel A. Donaldson
President
504 Lavaca Street, Suite 850
Austin, TX 78701-2939
TX : 2006 : Stock : Not Available
Health
512-406-7200
AMB# 064889 NAIC# 12525

Rating: NR-3

Data Year	Bonds (%)	Mort. Loans & R.E. (%)	Com & Pref. Stock (%)	All Other Assets (%)	Total Assets ($000)	Life Reserves (%)	Health Reserves (%)	Ann Res. & Dep. Liabilities (%)	All Other Liabilities (%)	Capital & Surplus ($000)	Direct Premiums Written ($000)	Net Premiums Written & Deposits ($000)	Operating Cash Flow ($000)	NOG Before Taxes ($000)	NOG After Taxes ($000)	Net Income ($000)
'05	...	...	...	...	...	...	...	...	...	...	...	...	...	...	...	...
'06	...	...	...	100.0	1,637	...	...	...	100.0	1,328	...	...	1,637	80	50	50
'07	...	...	...	100.0	1,718	...	...	...	100.0	1,380	...	...	77	76	52	52
'08	...	...	...	100.0	1,752	...	...	...	100.0	1,402	...	...	35	35	22	22
'09	...	...	...	100.0	1,755	...	...	...	100.0	1,389	...	...	6	6	5	5

Rating History: NR-3, 02/19/10; NR-3, 02/10/09; NR-5, 03/20/08; NR-5, 04/05/07

CENSTAT LIFE ASSURANCE COMPANY
Central States Health & Life Co of Omaha
T. Edward Kizer
President
P.O. Box 34350
Omaha, NE 68134-0350
AZ : 1987 : Stock : Other Direct
Credit A&H, Credit Life
402-397-1111
AMB# 060246 NAIC# 86240

Rating: B++ — Rating Outlook: Stable — FSC VIII

Data Year	Bonds (%)	Mort. Loans & R.E. (%)	Com & Pref. Stock (%)	All Other Assets (%)	Total Assets ($000)	Life Reserves (%)	Health Reserves (%)	Ann Res. & Dep. Liabilities (%)	All Other Liabilities (%)	Capital & Surplus ($000)	Direct Premiums Written ($000)	Net Premiums Written & Deposits ($000)	Operating Cash Flow ($000)	NOG Before Taxes ($000)	NOG After Taxes ($000)	Net Income ($000)
'05	80.8	...	...	19.2	4,000	70.7	19.8	...	9.5	2,554	...	2,046	408	460	395	395
'06	77.0	...	...	23.0	4,440	64.0	18.0	...	18.0	2,584	...	2,328	355	665	286	286
'07	69.9	...	...	30.1	4,735	66.0	27.1	...	6.9	3,094	...	2,383	104	679	699	699
'08	76.2	...	...	23.8	4,819	70.2	22.9	...	6.8	3,223	...	2,364	238	706	429	429
'09	73.0	...	...	27.0	5,064	71.6	21.8	...	6.6	3,493	...	2,277	220	685	604	604

Rating History: B++g, 05/27/10; B++g, 04/28/09; B++g, 04/18/08; B++g, 03/19/07; B++g, 02/07/06

CENTRAL HEALTH PLAN OF CA
Sam Kam, M.D.
President
1051 Park View Drive, Suite 120
Covina, CA 91724
CA : 2004 : Stock : Not Available
Medicare
626-388-2390
AMB# 064929

Rating: NR-5

Data Year	Bonds (%)	Mort. Loans & R.E. (%)	Com & Pref. Stock (%)	All Other Assets (%)	Total Assets ($000)	Life Reserves (%)	Health Reserves (%)	Ann Res. & Dep. Liabilities (%)	All Other Liabilities (%)	Capital & Surplus ($000)	Direct Premiums Written ($000)	Net Premiums Written & Deposits ($000)	Operating Cash Flow ($000)	NOG Before Taxes ($000)	NOG After Taxes ($000)	Net Income ($000)
'05	...	...	...	100.0	1,713	...	...	...	100.0	1,666	...	...	-908	-1,825	-1,826	-1,826
'06	...	...	...	100.0	1,632	...	...	...	100.0	1,399	1,814	1,814	-86	-1,916	-1,916	-1,916
'07	...	...	...	100.0	5,206	...	...	...	100.0	1,569	17,734	17,734	3,299	-80	-80	-80
'08	...	...	...	100.0	6,652	...	...	...	100.0	1,778	27,067	27,067	1,152	-2,392	-2,392	-2,392
'09	...	...	...	100.0	10,371	...	...	...	100.0	1,656	41,726	41,726	2,983	-122	-122	-122

Rating History: NR-5, 05/06/10; NR-5, 05/07/09; NR-5, 05/07/08

CENTRAL RESERVE LIFE
American Financial Group, Inc
Billy B. Hill, Jr.
President
11200 Lakeline Blvd., Suite 100
Austin, TX 78717
OH : 1965 : Stock : Agency
Maj med, Med supp, Group Life
512-451-2224
AMB# 006203 NAIC# 61727

Rating: B++ — Rating Outlook: Stable — FSC V

Data Year	Bonds (%)	Mort. Loans & R.E. (%)	Com & Pref. Stock (%)	All Other Assets (%)	Total Assets ($000)	Life Reserves (%)	Health Reserves (%)	Ann Res. & Dep. Liabilities (%)	All Other Liabilities (%)	Capital & Surplus ($000)	Direct Premiums Written ($000)	Net Premiums Written & Deposits ($000)	Operating Cash Flow ($000)	NOG Before Taxes ($000)	NOG After Taxes ($000)	Net Income ($000)
'05	77.6	...	11.1	11.3	70,767	5.2	50.6	23.9	20.3	28,083	165,452	143,323	-16,315	-3,143	2,568	2,631
'06	49.6	...	24.8	25.5	38,703	7.5	22.5	33.2	36.7	24,969	154,636	64,229	-28,447	-1,653	-3,027	-2,974
'07	44.4	...	19.4	36.2	31,942	8.0	25.6	30.5	36.0	17,389	124,115	19,755	-4,302	233	112	92
'08	40.3	...	41.7	18.0	25,029	13.5	33.2	39.5	13.9	14,622	92,743	20,307	1,250	2,291	796	793
'09	40.1	...	46.6	13.4	26,121	16.1	24.9	44.3	14.8	16,716	67,852	15,494	-46	-1,001	-532	-532

Rating History: B++, 05/10/10; B++, 03/27/09; B++, 12/17/07; B++, 11/28/06; B+ u, 05/02/06

CENTRAL SECURITY LIFE INS CO
Maximum Corporation
William H. Lewis, Jr.
Chairman & President
P.O. Box 833879
Richardson, TX 75083-3879
TX : 1955 : Stock : Broker
Ind Life, Pre-need
972-699-2770
AMB# 006204 NAIC# 61735

Rating: NR-5

Data Year	Bonds (%)	Mort. Loans & R.E. (%)	Com & Pref. Stock (%)	All Other Assets (%)	Total Assets ($000)	Life Reserves (%)	Health Reserves (%)	Ann Res. & Dep. Liabilities (%)	All Other Liabilities (%)	Capital & Surplus ($000)	Direct Premiums Written ($000)	Net Premiums Written & Deposits ($000)	Operating Cash Flow ($000)	NOG Before Taxes ($000)	NOG After Taxes ($000)	Net Income ($000)
'05	81.9	2.1	3.6	12.4	86,234	75.3	1.5	12.9	10.3	6,958	5,820	3,753	10,724	2,039	1,864	1,865
'06	82.1	2.0	3.7	12.2	85,125	75.9	1.4	12.3	10.4	7,566	6,125	4,372	-2,142	1,774	1,577	1,546
'07	82.6	2.0	4.1	11.3	83,988	75.3	1.7	12.4	10.7	8,025	5,848	4,180	-1,223	1,568	1,614	1,695
'08	81.9	2.0	4.5	11.5	81,607	75.2	1.9	12.6	10.3	7,717	5,691	4,122	-1,846	1,683	1,577	1,146
'09	76.3	2.0	4.1	17.6	80,180	75.0	2.1	12.6	10.3	7,863	5,110	3,614	-1,796	559	651	416

Rating History: NR-5, 04/14/10; NR-5, 04/14/09; NR-5, 04/07/08; NR-5, 04/24/07; NR-5, 05/10/06

CENTRAL STATES H&L CO OF OMAHA
Central States Health & Life Co of Omaha
Richard T. Kizer
Chairman & Secretary
1212 North 96th Street
Omaha, NE 68114
NE : 1932 : Mutual : Broker
Credit A&H, Credit Life
402-397-1111
AMB# 006206 NAIC# 61751

Rating: B++ — Rating Outlook: Stable — FSC VIII

Data Year	Bonds (%)	Mort. Loans & R.E. (%)	Com & Pref. Stock (%)	All Other Assets (%)	Total Assets ($000)	Life Reserves (%)	Health Reserves (%)	Ann Res. & Dep. Liabilities (%)	All Other Liabilities (%)	Capital & Surplus ($000)	Direct Premiums Written ($000)	Net Premiums Written & Deposits ($000)	Operating Cash Flow ($000)	NOG Before Taxes ($000)	NOG After Taxes ($000)	Net Income ($000)
'05	61.4	3.1	7.2	28.2	310,656	39.0	26.5	0.1	34.5	94,193	165,164	-20,260	-27,764	5,815	7,279	7,652
'06	67.0	5.3	8.6	19.1	278,123	45.9	31.4	0.1	22.6	94,233	125,416	44,263	-23,654	9,286	10,141	9,978
'07	70.5	5.8	8.2	15.5	290,811	46.2	38.7	0.1	14.9	99,050	154,102	80,714	16,123	5,150	5,606	5,606
'08	71.2	6.3	8.9	13.6	320,030	41.0	38.3	0.1	20.5	85,145	156,265	85,565	31,246	1,575	1,812	-759
'09	71.8	6.0	7.0	15.2	329,652	42.5	37.5	0.1	20.0	98,105	121,678	57,767	419	6,122	5,627	4,154

Rating History: B++g, 05/27/10; B++g, 04/28/09; B++g, 04/18/08; B++g, 03/19/07; B++g, 02/07/06

CENTRAL UNITED LIFE INS CO
Harris Insurance Holdings Inc
Daniel J. George
President
2727 Allen Parkway Wortham Tower
Houston, TX 77019
AR : 1963 : Stock : Agency
A&H, Dis inc, Dread dis
713-529-0045
AMB# 006222 NAIC# 61883

Rating: B+ — Rating Outlook: Negative — FSC VI

Data Year	Bonds (%)	Mort. Loans & R.E. (%)	Com & Pref. Stock (%)	All Other Assets (%)	Total Assets ($000)	Life Reserves (%)	Health Reserves (%)	Ann Res. & Dep. Liabilities (%)	All Other Liabilities (%)	Capital & Surplus ($000)	Direct Premiums Written ($000)	Net Premiums Written & Deposits ($000)	Operating Cash Flow ($000)	NOG Before Taxes ($000)	NOG After Taxes ($000)	Net Income ($000)
'05	63.9	3.5	8.9	23.6	371,426	32.3	60.7	4.7	2.3	36,632	70,632	113,946	-13,248	5,614	5,312	5,309
'06	61.7	3.7	8.4	26.3	350,238	34.9	57.8	4.9	2.4	32,279	68,154	108,644	-18,547	1,653	1,653	1,692
'07	58.5	3.8	9.2	28.5	332,548	37.1	55.3	5.1	2.4	37,018	64,069	102,341	-19,275	5,490	5,182	5,190
'08	43.1	3.8	8.8	44.4	321,381	37.5	54.5	5.3	2.7	38,090	64,698	93,911	-8,566	3,251	2,252	2,252
'09	45.6	4.6	15.8	33.9	332,629	37.3	55.2	4.8	2.8	44,620	69,066	99,672	7,198	6,045	4,510	4,203

Rating History: B+, 03/23/10; B+, 04/16/09; B+, 03/04/08; B+, 01/31/07; B+, 05/05/06

CENTRE LIFE INSURANCE COMPANY
Zurich Financial Services Ltd
Richard W. Grilli
President
One Liberty Plaza, 165 Broadway
New York, NY 10006-1466
MA : 1927 : Stock : Agency
Dis inc
212-859-2600
AMB# 007367 NAIC# 80896

Rating: NR-5

Data Year	Bonds (%)	Mort. Loans & R.E. (%)	Com & Pref. Stock (%)	All Other Assets (%)	Total Assets ($000)	Life Reserves (%)	Health Reserves (%)	Ann Res. & Dep. Liabilities (%)	All Other Liabilities (%)	Capital & Surplus ($000)	Direct Premiums Written ($000)	Net Premiums Written & Deposits ($000)	Operating Cash Flow ($000)	NOG Before Taxes ($000)	NOG After Taxes ($000)	Net Income ($000)
'05	96.6	...	...	3.4	1,687,859	...	0.8	...	99.2	66,897	43,832	5,170	-45,646	-10,782	-394	-394
'06	96.3	...	...	3.7	1,672,562	...	1.1	...	98.9	75,125	41,371	4,511	-23,829	4,881	6,439	6,439
'07	97.8	...	...	2.2	1,658,222	...	0.7	...	99.3	93,222	38,920	3,446	-28,628	9,701	8,955	8,955
'08	97.5	...	...	2.5	2,021,720	...	0.6	...	99.4	90,764	36,527	1,192	319,901	6,099	17,258	3,403
'09	97.1	...	...	2.9	1,969,019	...	0.6	...	99.4	77,075	34,208	10,232	-53,066	11,055	1,664	-4,801

Rating History: NR-5, 04/29/10; NR-5, 04/01/09; NR-5, 04/03/08; NR-5, 08/07/06; NR-4, 05/09/06

BEST'S PROFITABILITY, LEVERAGE AND LIQUIDITY TESTS 2005 – 2009

Data in U.S. Dollars

	Profitability Tests							Leverage Tests						Liquidity Tests					
Un-Realized Capital Gains ($000)	Benefits Paid to NPW & Dep (%)	Comm. & Expenses to NPW & Dep (%)	NOG to Total Assets (%)	NOG to Total Rev (%)	Operating Return on Equity (%)	Net Yield (%)	Total Return (%)	Change in NPW & Dep (%)	NPW & Dep to Capital (X)	Capital & Surplus to Liabilities (%)	Surplus Relief (%)	Reins Leverage (%)	Change in Capital (%)	Quick Liquidity (%)	Current Liquidity (%)	Non-Invest Grade Bonds to Capital (%)	Delinq. & Foreclosed Mortgages to Capital (%)	Mort. & Credit Tenant Loans & R.E. to Capital (%)	Affiliated Invest to Capital (%)
...	...	...	...	...	...	...	...	...	...	...	...	...	...	...	...	...	...	...	...
...	...	...	...	...	...	...	...	...	...	...	...	...	...	...	...	...	...	...	...
...	...	...	...	...	...	...	...	...	...	...	...	...	...	...	...	...	...	...	...
...	...	...	...	...	...	...	...	...	...	...	...	...	...	...	...	...	...	...	...
...	92.3	17.1	...	-6.6	...	...	...	...	2.1	60.7	...	...	...	204.2	216.8	...	...	...	...
Principal Lines of Business: CompHosp/Med (100.0%)														Principal States: MA (100.0%)					
...	...	...	...	...	...	...	...	...	...	...	...	...	...	...	...	...	...	...	...
...	...	...	...	59.6	...	...	...	...	...	429.4	...	...	...	529.4	529.4	...	...	...	...
...	...	...	3.1	67.4	3.8	4.68	4.68	...	...	408.2	...	...	3.9	507.1	507.1	...	...	...	...
...	...	...	1.3	64.2	1.6	2.03	2.03	...	...	400.4	...	...	1.6	499.4	499.4	...	...	...	...
...	...	...	0.3	83.3	0.3	0.33	0.33	...	...	379.9	...	...	-0.9	479.9	479.9	...	...	...	...
...	25.1	50.9	10.5	17.8	16.1	5.20	5.22	29.8	0.8	180.2	...	12.6	8.8	197.5	217.5	9.7	...	...	...
...	22.8	49.9	6.8	11.4	11.1	5.14	5.16	13.8	0.9	141.3	...	15.6	1.1	181.0	198.1	5.8	...	...	...
...	23.8	51.8	15.2	27.2	24.6	4.98	5.00	2.4	0.8	191.4	...	15.7	19.6	233.6	252.3	4.8	...	...	...
...	30.0	51.6	9.0	16.9	13.6	4.67	4.59	-0.8	0.7	204.5	...	13.6	4.1	243.4	268.4	...	...	...	...
...	23.6	51.8	12.2	24.7	18.0	4.21	4.06	-3.7	0.6	225.5	...	11.2	8.4	269.4	296.2	...	...	...	...
Principal Lines of Business: CrdA&H (56.1%), CrdLife (43.9%)																			
...	...	...	-82.9	-99.9	-83.8	2.14	2.14	...	...	999.9	...	...	-38.1	999.9	999.9	...	...	...	...
...	54.8	153.9	-99.9	-99.9	-99.9	3.40	3.40	...	1.3	600.3	...	...	-16.0	566.0	566.0	...	...	...	...
...	75.4	21.1	-2.3	-0.5	-5.4	2.98	2.98	877.9	11.3	43.2	...	...	12.2	122.3	122.3	...	...	...	...
...	86.6	21.0	-40.3	-8.9	-99.9	2.58	2.58	52.6	15.2	36.5	...	...	13.3	110.2	110.2	...	...	...	...
...	89.7	13.0	-1.4	-0.3	-7.1	0.94	0.94	54.2	25.2	19.0	...	...	-6.9	95.8	95.8	...	...	...	...
Principal Lines of Business: Medicare (100.0%)																			
-155	72.0	32.0	3.3	1.7	7.7	4.30	4.67	2.6	5.1	66.6	15.2	12.2	-26.7	103.4	115.4	6.5	...	...	27.6
-851	79.5	39.9	-5.5	-3.8	-11.4	4.74	3.56	-55.2	2.6	183.0	54.5	114.5	-11.6	144.0	149.8	...	...	...	38.4
-4,663	74.5	28.5	0.3	0.4	0.5	3.32	-11.57	-69.2	1.1	120.0	31.7	163.4	-30.4	121.4	127.9	0.0	...	...	35.6
-1,783	70.5	21.4	2.8	2.6	5.0	2.01	-4.71	2.8	1.4	140.8	66.7	135.8	-16.0	138.8	141.8	0.0	...	...	71.2
-798	71.4	39.2	-2.1	-2.4	-3.4	1.38	-1.44	-23.7	0.9	178.0	38.3	85.5	14.3	125.4	128.7	0.0	...	...	72.7
Principal Lines of Business: IndA&H (94.5%), OrdLife (4.2%), GrpA&H (0.7%), IndAnn (0.6%)														Principal States: OH (23.3%), IN (12.4%), VA (7.0%), AZ (6.4%), PA (6.1%)					
-17	152.8	58.6	2.3	22.2	28.5	5.54	5.55	23.3	0.5	9.1	...	325.8	14.1	71.9	80.9	13.2	...	24.7	21.5
554	154.0	40.0	1.8	17.4	21.7	5.83	6.63	16.5	0.6	10.1	...	291.9	8.5	65.8	74.8	18.1	...	22.2	26.7
428	153.3	39.0	1.9	17.7	20.7	6.03	6.88	-4.4	0.5	11.0	...	261.3	6.4	67.9	76.7	21.0	...	20.3	30.0
-375	129.0	41.8	1.9	18.2	20.0	5.84	4.88	-1.4	0.5	10.5	...	264.0	-6.8	65.4	74.5	16.0	...	21.1	30.2
486	144.8	63.3	0.8	8.4	8.4	5.48	6.06	-12.3	0.5	11.0	...	251.7	2.8	81.3	90.6	18.3	...	19.8	32.5
Principal Lines of Business: OrdLife (84.4%), IndA&H (10.0%), GrpA&H (4.4%), IndAnn (1.2%), GrpAnn (0.0%)														Principal States: TX (29.1%), OK (13.9%), MS (10.9%), MO (9.7%), NC (5.7%)					
486	-93.6	-99.9	2.2	23.4	9.1	5.01	5.75	-99.9	-0.2	48.1	37.3	99.6	40.7	80.4	93.8	3.9	...	9.6	22.3
2,490	44.6	66.0	3.4	12.8	10.8	4.98	6.20	318.5	0.4	56.7	21.5	60.2	-0.3	77.5	93.1	2.0	...	14.6	22.2
-2,275	25.2	59.9	2.0	4.7	5.8	6.25	5.68	82.4	0.8	55.2	20.6	56.8	2.7	78.2	93.9	3.4	...	16.2	15.6
-7,472	25.5	62.7	0.6	1.5	2.0	4.80	1.52	6.0	1.0	38.0	25.2	68.6	-14.8	73.3	87.4	0.2	...	22.9	22.9
8,251	38.3	78.5	1.7	6.4	6.1	4.85	7.41	-32.5	0.6	45.3	15.4	60.2	16.7	72.8	86.3	11.7	0.1	19.1	19.6
Principal Lines of Business: CrdLife (49.8%), CrdA&H (45.2%), OrdLife (4.9%), GrpLife (0.1%), GrpA&H (0.0%)														Principal States: TX (13.0%), FL (7.6%), WI (6.3%), PA (5.6%), OH (5.3%)					
1,227	94.1	30.2	1.4	4.1	14.7	3.81	4.63	20.6	3.0	11.3	0.1	147.6	3.1	73.9	76.8	...	...	34.5	103.9
-2,595	97.4	27.6	0.5	1.3	4.8	3.65	3.18	-4.7	3.3	10.5	0.2	160.5	-11.8	74.9	77.4	...	...	38.5	105.6
407	99.7	26.3	1.5	4.5	15.0	3.61	4.08	-5.8	2.7	12.9	0.3	142.5	14.4	75.3	77.7	2.6	...	32.9	95.4
-1,653	99.7	26.6	0.7	2.2	6.0	3.05	2.72	-8.2	2.4	13.9	0.3	135.8	2.9	96.8	98.7	5.2	...	31.1	86.0
4,805	90.4	29.3	1.4	4.2	10.9	2.26	4.21	6.1	2.2	15.9	0.5	121.6	16.1	77.1	78.8	4.4	...	33.7	127.7
Principal Lines of Business: IndA&H (88.2%), OrdLife (5.9%), GrpA&H (4.5%), GrpAnn (1.4%), IndAnn (0.1%)														Principal States: MS (15.4%), TX (11.3%), SC (9.3%), AR (6.8%), LA (5.2%)					
...	...	999.9	0.0	-0.3	-0.6	5.91	5.92	-3.5	0.1	4.3	60.9	999.9	-3.5	75.4	84.3	...	...	...	...
...	...	999.9	0.4	4.4	9.1	5.88	5.89	-12.7	0.1	4.9	47.5	999.9	12.5	77.1	85.4	...	...	...	...
...	...	999.9	0.5	6.8	10.6	5.94	5.95	-23.6	0.0	6.2	35.6	999.9	23.8	72.6	82.7	...	...	...	...
...	...	999.9	0.9	12.2	18.8	5.67	4.91	-65.4	0.0	4.7	41.4	999.9	-6.5	72.4	83.5	1.5	...	...	...
738	...	999.9	0.1	1.2	2.0	5.75	5.46	758.1	0.1	4.1	26.1	999.9	-15.1	71.4	81.9	17.4	...	...	...
Principal Lines of Business: GrpA&H (100.0%)														Principal States: CA (14.4%), NY (12.5%), OH (6.2%), PA (5.6%), NJ (5.1%)					

COMPANY NAME Ultimate Parent Association Principal Officer Mailing Address Dom. : Began Bus. : Struct. : Mktg. Specialty Phone # AMB# NAIC#	Best's Financial Strength Rating FSC	Data Year	Balance Sheet Bonds (%)	Mort. Loans & R.E. (%)	Com & Pref. Stock (%)	All Other Assets (%)	Total Assets ($000)	Life Reserves (%)	Health Reserves (%)	Ann Res. & Dep. Liabilities (%)	All Other Liabilities (%)	Capital & Surplus ($000)	Operations Direct Premiums Written ($000)	Net Premiums Written & Deposits ($000)	Operating Cash Flow ($000)	NOG Before Taxes ($000)	NOG After Taxes ($000)	Net Income ($000)
CENTURION LIFE INS CO Wells Fargo & Company Jolene K. Edgington President 800 Walnut Street Des Moines, IA 50309 IA : 1956 : Stock : Direct Response Credit A&H, Credit Life, Ann 515-557-2131 AMB# 006276 NAIC# 62383	**A** Rating Outlook: Stable **FSC XII**	'05	83.5	0.0	6.4	10.1	1,082,595	22.6	23.7	40.8	12.9	870,851	97,634	136,975	-6,687	56,770	37,504	37,555
		'06	84.5	0.0	6.1	9.4	1,045,257	20.9	20.4	34.7	24.0	915,675	34,836	49,317	-10,767	74,712	52,577	57,369
		'07	65.2	0.0	4.3	30.5	1,521,634	3.5	5.2	15.8	75.5	949,939	57,298	94,118	82,171	64,277	42,888	45,025
		'08	71.2	0.0	1.9	26.9	1,620,996	2.0	4.3	26.5	67.1	993,314	93,521	135,319	109,698	76,931	49,957	47,781
		'09	67.9	0.0	1.7	30.4	1,887,808	1.4	3.7	36.1	58.8	1,023,395	161,410	202,573	176,604	60,563	40,871	37,462
		Rating History: A, 09/18/09; A, 09/25/08; A, 09/28/07; A, 04/10/07; A, 02/28/06																
CENTURY CREDIT LIFE INS CO' Norman W. Bowen President P.O. Box 789 Tupelo, MS 38802-0789 MS : 1978 : Stock : Not Available 662-680-2407 AMB# 008865 NAIC# 90867	**NR-1**	'05	96.8	...	...	3.2	28,991	...	...	...	100.0	28,210	-60	84	...	1,859	1,491	1,491
		'06	98.1	...	...	1.9	29,816	...	...	...	100.0	29,534	-8	-50	...	1,577	1,349	1,349
		'07	97.2	...	...	2.8	31,001	...	...	...	100.0	30,805	-1	-7	...	1,459	1,258	1,258
		'08	96.6	...	...	3.4	32,395	...	...	...	100.0	31,923	-1	-1	...	1,405	1,124	1,124
		'09	95.9	...	...	4.1	33,683	...	...	...	100.0	33,019	...	...	...	1,343	1,100	1,100
		Rating History: NR-1, 06/10/10; NR-1, 06/12/09; NR-1, 06/12/08; NR-1, 06/08/07; NR-1, 06/07/06																
CENTURY LIFE ASSUR CO Norma J Hawkins Bruce Welner President & CEO P.O. Box 9510 Wichita, KS 67277 OK : 1980 : Stock : Direct Response Credit A&H, Credit Life, Ind Life 316-794-2200 AMB# 009124 NAIC# 94447	**B-** Rating Outlook: Stable **FSC V**	'05	71.6	0.8	9.7	17.9	10,403	59.1	23.6	7.7	9.5	3,827	4,037	2,081	-3,921	598	526	687
		'06	72.8	0.3	...	26.9	9,903	61.9	25.5	7.4	5.1	4,130	4,150	2,124	-838	378	367	514
		'07	75.4	1.3	0.0	23.3	10,027	60.3	24.8	6.2	8.7	4,208	3,647	2,053	571	44	31	36
		'08	78.3	1.3	2.2	18.2	9,376	61.3	26.4	8.7	3.6	4,761	2,971	1,663	-486	951	978	521
		'09	77.8	0.9	...	21.2	9,736	60.4	20.2	12.1	7.3	5,109	1,992	1,150	227	545	436	428
		Rating History: B- g, 05/14/10; B- g, 06/16/09; B- g, 06/16/08; B-, 05/31/07; B+ u, 11/10/06																
CHA HMO INC Humana Inc Michael B. McCallister President & CEO P.O. Box 740036 Louisville, KY 40201-7436 KY : 1995 : Stock : Broker Group A&H, Health 502-580-1000 AMB# 064403 NAIC# 95158	**NR-3**	'05	43.2	...	0.6	56.2	101,041	...	71.6	...	28.4	48,854	382,487	380,156	17,915	25,260	21,236	21,236
		'06	24.3	...	0.5	75.2	53,462	...	70.7	...	29.3	20,997	183,023	181,417	-47,401	-7,872	-7,179	-7,323
		'07	82.9	...	0.6	16.5	36,082	...	50.0	...	50.0	27,473	91,088	91,088	-12,594	9,192	11,648	11,620
		'08	27.2	...	0.4	72.4	30,452	...	...	...	100.0	25,586	642	642	-4,710	-2,714	-4,692	-4,561
		'09	82.8	...	...	17.2	26,824	...	...	...	100.0	26,799	...	...	-3,852	407	544	503
		Rating History: NR-3, 06/02/10; NR-3, 06/05/09; NR-3, 06/05/08; B++, 06/05/07; B++, 05/19/06																
CHAMPIONS LIFE INS CO Maximum Corporation James G. Lewis President P.O. Box 833879 Richardson, TX 75083-3879 TX : 1952 : Stock : Broker Ann, Ind Life, Trad Life 972-699-2770 AMB# 007559 NAIC# 73121	**NR-5**	'05	66.1	7.4	19.1	7.3	39,627	65.6	1.7	24.6	8.0	5,042	799	967	1,805	557	722	721
		'06	65.0	7.4	20.3	7.3	39,276	64.3	1.3	25.7	8.7	4,892	572	794	-1,063	470	630	617
		'07	63.8	7.3	21.7	7.1	38,674	63.2	0.7	27.6	8.6	5,181	685	805	-1,006	882	1,030	1,061
		'08	65.3	6.6	19.6	8.5	41,909	66.6	0.6	20.3	12.4	4,910	608	731	3,146	714	872	706
		'09	62.5	6.6	19.9	11.0	41,116	65.6	0.7	21.1	12.7	4,696	623	672	-939	226	338	247
		Rating History: NR-5, 04/14/10; NR-5, 04/16/09; NR-5, 04/07/08; NR-5, 04/24/07; NR-5, 04/25/06																
CHARLESTON CAPITAL RE LLC Goldman Sachs Group Inc Eleanor L. Kitzman President 132 Turnpike Road, Suite 210 Southborough, MA 01772 DC : 2004 : Stock Life 843-577-1030 AMB# 076825	**A-** Rating Outlook: Stable **FSC IX**	'05	...	...	...	...	...	...	...	...	...	...	...	...	...	...	...	...
		'06	...	...	...	100.0	399	...	...	...	100.0	353	...	...	...	-7	-5	-5
		'07	88.3	...	3.9	7.7	61,803	...	...	85.0	15.0	9,157	...	787	60,170	-1,237	-950	-979
		'08	63.8	...	1.3	34.9	724,220	78.7	...	16.9	4.5	54,520	...	19,772	508,687	-759	-3,110	-12,676
		'09	80.0	...	...	20.0	690,742	78.9	...	17.1	4.0	70,748	...	16,990	-49,237	7,830	7,323	7,178
		Rating History: A- g, 08/24/09; NR-5, 01/22/09; NR-5, 04/02/07																
CHARTER NATIONAL LIFE INS CO Allstate Corporation John C. Pintozzi Vice President and CFO 3100 Sanders Road Northbrook, IL 60062-7154 IL : 1955 : Stock : Direct Response Var ann 847-402-5000 AMB# 006211 NAIC# 61808	**B++** Rating Outlook: Stable **FSC V**	'05	2.9	...	0.0	97.1	277,820	...	...	...	100.0	8,968	1,857	22	214	526	365	365
		'06	2.9	...	0.0	97.1	269,819	...	...	...	100.0	9,330	457	5	-862	522	356	358
		'07	3.1	...	0.0	96.9	254,443	...	...	...	100.0	9,693	585	4	826	535	364	364
		'08	5.2	...	0.0	94.8	150,135	...	...	...	100.0	10,024	284	11	914	492	334	334
		'09	5.6	...	0.0	94.4	158,196	...	...	...	100.0	10,317	265	7	242	429	294	294
		Rating History: B++, 11/20/09; B++, 10/23/08; B++, 01/09/08; B++, 07/27/07; A-, 02/06/07																
CHEROKEE NATIONAL LIFE INS CO Minnesota Mutual Companies Inc Christopher R. Greene President & CEO P.O. Box 6097 Macon, GA 31208-6097 GA : 1956 : Stock : Mng Gen Agent Credit A&H, Credit Life 478-477-0400 AMB# 006214 NAIC# 61824	**A-** Rating Outlook: Stable **FSC V**	'05	53.2	9.3	0.3	37.2	36,220	49.1	42.7	...	8.1	10,525	27,153	22,379	-62	1,578	1,208	1,819
		'06	67.2	6.4	...	26.5	36,189	47.2	42.3	...	10.5	10,570	23,032	20,053	526	1,483	1,230	1,243
		'07	66.9	6.6	...	26.5	34,699	45.6	43.4	...	11.0	11,860	18,599	14,419	-2,333	1,462	1,245	1,240
		'08	73.0	7.0	...	19.9	30,991	47.1	43.8	...	9.2	11,506	15,742	12,022	-2,431	1,032	791	-180
		'09	75.0	7.3	...	17.7	28,445	50.6	38.3	...	11.0	13,244	10,281	8,685	-2,562	1,572	1,252	1,441
		Rating History: A-, 04/06/10; A, 04/10/09; A, 03/25/08; A, 06/01/07; A, 06/14/06																
CHESAPEAKE LIFE INS CO Blackstone Investor Group Phillip Hildebrand President & CEO 9151 Boulevard 26 North Richland Hills, TX 76180 OK : 1956 : Stock : Agency Life, Group A&H 817-255-3100 AMB# 006215 NAIC# 61832	**B++** Rating Outlook: Negative **FSC VIII**	'05	71.6	...	...	28.4	105,533	36.3	38.2	8.6	17.0	42,210	151,019	102,284	15,317	-14,037	-10,181	-10,186
		'06	81.2	...	...	18.8	98,860	42.0	15.8	9.9	32.4	44,821	113,839	61,085	-2,825	2,243	1,377	2,318
		'07	73.7	...	...	26.3	96,029	46.6	13.6	10.9	28.9	48,300	85,278	27,382	-9,817	-2,458	-1,910	-1,270
		'08	64.6	...	...	35.4	83,771	0.3	59.1	...	40.6	42,461	181,907	117,540	-5,472	-7,098	-6,314	-8,784
		'09	47.3	...	...	52.7	73,365	0.6	25.6	...	73.8	42,256	58,125	18,079	-5,727	-2,717	-478	-1,136
		Rating History: B++g, 06/07/10; B++g, 05/28/09; B++g, 07/24/08; A- g, 05/25/07; A- g, 03/10/06																

2010 BEST'S KEY RATING GUIDE — LIFE/HEALTH EDITION
BEST'S PROFITABILITY, LEVERAGE AND LIQUIDITY TESTS 2005 – 2009

Data in U.S. Dollars

	Profitability Tests							Leverage Tests						Liquidity Tests					
Un-Realized Capital Gains ($000)	Benefits Paid to NPW & Dep (%)	Comm. & Expenses to NPW & Dep (%)	NOG to Total Assets (%)	NOG to Total Rev (%)	Operating Return on Equity (%)	Net Yield (%)	Total Return (%)	Change in NPW & Dep (%)	NPW & Dep to Capital (X)	Capital & Surplus to Liabilities (%)	Surplus Relief (%)	Reins Leverage (%)	Change in Capital (%)	Quick Liquidity (%)	Current Liquidity (%)	Non-Invest Grade Bonds to Capital (%)	Delinq. & Foreclosed Mortgages to Capital (%)	Mort. & Credit Tenant Loans & R.E. to Capital (%)	Affiliated Invest to Capital (%)
2,958	76.4	8.4	3.5	20.2	4.3	4.50	4.87	217.7	0.2	442.7	0.1	2.1	2.1	436.9	490.0	1.4	...	0.0	...
528	212.5	16.2	4.9	51.4	5.9	5.00	5.52	-64.0	0.1	785.7	0.1	0.3	5.0	734.5	816.9	6.1	...	0.0	1.5
1,523	30.8	13.2	3.3	29.1	4.6	4.48	4.80	90.8	0.1	172.3	0.0	0.1	3.8	158.8	175.3	7.8	...	0.0	...
-10,031	26.1	10.5	3.2	26.0	5.1	3.84	2.81	43.8	0.1	160.5	0.0	0.0	3.7	156.3	170.2	6.1	...	0.0	1.2
4,150	18.7	9.4	2.3	15.3	4.1	4.68	4.93	49.7	0.2	120.7	0.0	0.0	3.4	137.9	148.3	8.0	...	0.0	...

Principal Lines of Business: IndAnn (74.7%), CrdA&H (13.2%), CrdLife (10.2%), GrpA&H (1.9%) — Principal States: CA (46.6%), MO (9.5%), MN (6.3%), AZ (4.5%), IA (3.2%)

...	357.8	131.5	5.2	99.3	5.4	...	...	-54.2	0.0	999.9	...	...	5.4	...	...	...	...	...	...
...	-99.9	-99.9	4.6	97.6	4.7	...	...	-99.9	0.0	999.9	...	...	4.7	...	...	...	...	...	...
...	-45.6	-99.9	4.1	87.2	4.2	...	...	86.8	0.0	999.9	...	...	4.2	...	...	...	...	...	...
...	110.3	-99.9	3.5	77.0	3.6	...	...	87.8	0.0	999.9	...	...	3.6	...	...	...	...	...	...
...	...	...	3.3	81.2	3.4	...	...	100.0	...	999.9	...	...	3.4	...	...	...	...	...	...

-151	46.4	64.0	4.2	15.1	9.2	4.12	4.21	0.9	0.5	63.1	22.7	85.3	-49.3	143.0	145.4	...	...	2.2	...
...	42.3	65.6	3.6	10.7	9.2	3.31	4.85	2.1	0.5	71.6	22.6	85.6	2.6	150.0	150.0	...	...	0.7	...
...	49.4	72.6	0.3	1.0	0.7	3.27	3.24	-3.4	0.5	72.4	17.0	67.0	1.9	150.1	154.5	...	...	3.2	...
...	38.9	72.9	10.1	35.9	21.8	4.75	-0.11	-19.0	0.3	103.4	12.7	55.7	13.2	173.9	182.4	0.9	...	2.6	...
...	67.5	61.4	4.6	22.3	8.8	4.60	4.50	-30.9	0.2	111.0	7.3	43.5	7.4	170.9	181.4	5.3	1.8	1.8	...

Principal Lines of Business: CrdLife (39.7%), OrdLife (30.3%), IndAnn (19.7%), CrdA&H (6.8%), IndA&H (2.4%) — Principal States: OK (79.5%), KS (11.8%), TX (8.1%)

...	84.9	9.2	23.0	5.5	53.8	3.23	3.23	11.4	7.8	93.6	...	2.9	62.4	262.6	266.1	...	...	...	...
0	87.9	14.8	-9.3	-3.9	-20.6	3.49	3.29	-52.3	8.6	64.7	...	1.1	-57.0	221.3	231.5	0.3	...	...	...
-40	83.3	17.3	26.0	12.3	48.1	4.92	4.76	-49.8	3.3	319.1	...	...	30.8	330.1	368.1	1.6	...	...	...
-8	499.5	373.1	-14.1	-99.9	-17.7	4.33	4.70	-99.3	0.0	525.8	...	...	-6.9	999.9	999.9	1.1	...	...	...
42	...	...	1.9	50.1	2.1	2.57	2.57	-99.9	...	999.9	...	...	4.7	999.9	999.9	0.9	...	...	...

843	261.0	147.2	1.9	17.8	14.8	8.25	10.56	1.7	0.2	15.2	...	12.9	7.2	63.2	71.4	...	...	56.4	175.5
617	304.2	168.8	1.6	17.6	12.7	8.04	9.71	-17.9	0.2	14.8	...	14.6	-2.7	54.9	62.7	2.9	...	56.9	191.5
468	201.0	169.0	2.6	27.2	20.4	8.42	9.92	1.4	0.1	16.3	...	13.0	6.6	55.5	63.2	4.9	...	52.1	187.2
-387	608.8	193.2	2.2	25.3	17.3	7.52	6.18	-9.2	0.1	13.8	...	16.0	-6.3	55.2	62.9	1.7	...	54.8	193.2
231	276.4	214.2	0.8	11.3	7.0	6.36	6.88	-8.1	0.1	13.4	...	16.1	-3.9	63.5	71.5	1.2	...	55.6	203.0

Principal Lines of Business: OrdLife (62.6%), IndLife (19.0%), IndA&H (13.4%), IndAnn (3.8%), GrpLife (0.8%) — Principal States: TX (99.8%)

...	...	...	...	...	...	...	...	...	...	...	...	...	...	...	...	...	...	...	...
...	...	...	...	65.0	...	...	...	...	...	763.0	...	...	...	829.9	829.9	...	...	...	...
...	892.3	307.5	-3.1	-27.5	-20.0	9.04	8.97	...	0.1	17.8	...	0.5	999.9	95.0	104.0	...	...	...	...
...	417.9	47.1	-0.8	-5.2	-9.8	8.92	6.48	999.9	0.4	8.1	...	...	483.5	84.7	90.6	...	...	...	...
...	520.3	26.5	1.0	10.8	11.7	6.24	6.27	-14.1	0.2	11.4	...	...	29.8	64.8	76.5	...	...	...	35.3

Principal Lines of Business: OrdLife (94.8%), IndAnn (5.0%), GrpLife (0.2%)

...	...	...	0.1	68.8	4.2	4.98	5.37	11.6	0.0	503.1	0.1	649.4	4.2	528.0	531.9	...	...	...	...
...	...	...	0.1	67.6	3.9	5.16	5.56	-77.2	0.0	999.9	0.0	560.7	4.0	999.9	999.9	...	...	...	...
...	...	...	0.1	67.4	3.8	5.45	5.74	-26.2	0.0	999.9	0.0	530.5	3.9	999.9	999.9	...	...	...	...
...	...	...	0.2	67.5	3.4	4.60	4.81	189.3	0.0	999.9	0.0	514.6	3.4	999.9	999.9	...	...	...	...
...	...	...	0.2	66.9	2.9	3.81	3.96	-32.2	0.0	999.9	0.1	517.3	2.9	999.9	999.9	...	...	...	...

Principal Lines of Business: GrpAnn (100.0%) — Principal States: AK (18.9%), FL (13.4%), MA (7.9%), CA (7.3%), VA (6.4%)

-50	40.9	70.7	3.3	4.7	12.9	4.69	6.34	-6.8	2.1	42.5	13.8	89.8	24.9	117.9	128.3	...	...	31.1	22.1
-13	38.9	70.1	3.4	5.5	11.7	4.10	4.17	-10.4	1.9	42.6	8.4	32.9	0.1	112.6	124.5	...	...	21.3	21.3
...	48.3	70.4	3.5	7.1	11.1	4.78	4.79	-28.1	1.2	53.5	11.7	27.7	11.9	119.7	131.7	...	...	19.0	19.0
...	51.8	70.7	2.4	5.4	6.8	4.17	1.11	-16.6	1.0	61.0	10.9	26.5	-2.9	123.2	136.2	0.4	...	18.6	18.6
...	62.4	78.7	4.2	11.4	10.1	4.89	5.50	-27.8	0.6	89.9	6.9	19.5	14.7	147.2	162.1	0.4	...	15.5	...

Principal Lines of Business: CrdLife (81.2%), CrdA&H (18.4%), IndA&H (0.3%) — Principal States: GA (39.2%), AL (20.9%), TX (11.9%), LA (10.0%), MS (5.1%)

...	80.9	34.5	-10.4	-6.5	-29.9	5.53	5.48	103.7	2.4	67.2	115.1	83.1	62.6	146.0	158.4	...	...	...	...
...	64.5	33.8	1.3	1.3	3.2	5.88	6.85	-40.3	1.4	83.7	84.4	158.6	6.2	147.8	164.2	...	...	...	...
...	65.7	61.4	-2.0	-2.9	-4.1	5.50	6.19	-55.2	0.6	102.2	68.9	238.8	7.7	148.0	166.1	...	...	...	...
...	77.3	54.1	-7.0	-4.1	-13.9	5.24	2.23	329.3	2.8	102.8	75.0	388.1	-12.5	216.0	230.4	0.8	...	...	...
...	81.1	43.9	-0.6	-1.3	-1.1	2.96	2.17	-84.6	0.4	135.8	39.4	392.7	-0.5	252.1	266.8	5.5	...	...	...

Principal Lines of Business: IndA&H (57.7%), GrpA&H (39.8%), IndAnn (2.2%), OrdLife (0.3%), GrpAnn (0.0%) — Principal States: TX (16.3%), NH (13.8%), CA (8.6%), GA (7.9%), AL (6.8%)

COMPANY NAME / Ultimate Parent Association / Principal Officer / Mailing Address / Dom. : Began Bus. : Struct. : Mktg. / Specialty / Phone # / AMB# NAIC# — Best's Financial Strength Rating / FSC

Data Year	Balance Sheet: Bonds (%)	Mort. Loans & R.E. (%)	Com & Pref. Stock (%)	All Other Assets (%)	Total Assets ($000)	Life Reserves (%)	Health Reserves (%)	Ann Res. & Dep. Liabilities (%)	All Other Liabilities (%)	Capital & Surplus ($000)	Operations: Direct Premiums Written ($000)	Net Premiums Written & Deposits ($000)	Operating Cash Flow ($000)	NOG Before Taxes ($000)	NOG After Taxes ($000)	Net Income ($000)

CHILDREN'S MERCY'S FAM H PRTNR[2]
Children's Mercy Hospital
Jo Stueve
President
215 W. Pershing Road, Suite 600
Kansas City, MO 64108
MO : 1996 : Non-Profit : Broker
Health
816-559-9400
AMB# 064183 NAIC# 95636

NR-5

Data Year	Bonds	Mort. Loans & R.E.	Com & Pref. Stock	All Other Assets	Total Assets	Life Reserves	Health Reserves	Ann Res. & Dep. Liabilities	All Other Liabilities	Capital & Surplus	Direct Premiums Written	Net Premiums Written & Deposits	Operating Cash Flow	NOG Before Taxes	NOG After Taxes	Net Income
'05	23.5	...	...	76.5	20,900	...	52.9	...	47.1	8,102	109,817	109,420	3,095	3,698	3,698	3,698
'06	30.4	...	...	69.6	18,108	...	59.2	...	40.8	8,464	97,080	96,763	2,686	1,136	1,136	1,136
'07	65.7	...	...	34.3	91,014	...	65.6	...	34.4	35,314	349,839	348,559	54,782	27,038	27,038	27,038
'08	36.4	...	...	63.6	109,416	...	66.6	...	33.4	60,951	390,398	389,180	17,810	50,264	50,264	50,264
'09	19.9	...	...	80.1	114,020	...	64.7	...	35.3	62,568	402,278	401,541	4,652	27,342	27,342	23,893

Rating History: NR-5, 04/20/10; NR-5, 08/26/09; C+ pd, 07/21/08; C+ pd, 07/16/07; C+ pd, 08/28/06

CHINESE COMMUNITY HEALTH PLAN
Joe Chan
President
445 Grant Avenue, Suite 700
San Francisco, CA 94108-3208
CA : 1987 : Stock : Broker
Group A&H
415-955-8800
AMB# 064144

NR-5

Data Year	Bonds	Mort. Loans & R.E.	Com & Pref. Stock	All Other Assets	Total Assets	Life Reserves	Health Reserves	Ann Res. & Dep. Liabilities	All Other Liabilities	Capital & Surplus	Direct Premiums Written	Net Premiums Written & Deposits	Operating Cash Flow	NOG Before Taxes	NOG After Taxes	Net Income
'05	...	37.8	...	62.2	16,823	...	...	...	100.0	7,344	59,187	59,187	-700	1,891	1,172	1,172
'06	...	42.7	...	57.3	21,645	...	...	...	100.0	9,301	84,079	84,079	3,703	3,319	1,957	1,957
'07	...	41.4	...	58.6	23,762	...	...	...	100.0	11,873	88,267	88,267	939	4,131	2,572	2,572
'08	...	38.4	...	61.6	24,826	...	...	...	100.0	14,689	93,577	93,577	1,781	2,346	1,465	1,465
'09	...	26.1	...	73.9	36,007	...	...	...	100.0	16,783	99,786	99,786	-454	2,470	1,382	1,382

Rating History: NR-5, 05/06/10; NR-5, 08/26/09; C+ pd, 07/21/08; C+ pd, 07/16/07; C+ pd, 08/29/06

CHRISTIAN FIDELITY LIFE INS CO
AMERCO
Mark A. Haydukovich
President & CEO
2721 North Central Avenue
Phoenix, AZ 85004-1172
TX : 1935 : Stock : Agency
Med supp, Life
800-527-6797
AMB# 006217 NAIC# 61859

B++
Rating Outlook: Stable
FSC VIII

Data Year	Bonds	Mort. Loans & R.E.	Com & Pref. Stock	All Other Assets	Total Assets	Life Reserves	Health Reserves	Ann Res. & Dep. Liabilities	All Other Liabilities	Capital & Surplus	Direct Premiums Written	Net Premiums Written & Deposits	Operating Cash Flow	NOG Before Taxes	NOG After Taxes	Net Income
'05	80.0	7.0	0.1	12.9	77,994	7.3	62.5	22.9	7.3	22,455	60,801	60,797	-1,592	4,101	1,820	1,470
'06	70.8	7.9	7.5	13.9	77,488	7.4	63.7	20.1	8.8	21,040	60,264	60,260	4,257	3,874	2,514	2,652
'07	72.2	7.1	8.8	11.9	79,114	8.2	66.9	18.3	6.6	25,414	58,443	58,439	1,390	6,543	4,189	4,189
'08	67.9	6.9	9.1	16.2	86,902	8.3	66.9	17.3	7.5	34,357	56,087	56,122	6,892	7,723	4,342	4,342
'09	72.8	4.9	8.5	13.8	88,089	9.5	67.3	17.2	6.1	39,784	53,897	53,893	-1,680	9,024	6,588	6,439

Rating History: B++g, 03/31/10; B++g, 03/20/09; B++g, 01/31/08; B++, 11/29/06; B+, 10/19/05

CHURCH LIFE INS CORPORATION
Church Pension Fund
T. Dennis Sullivan II
President
445 Fifth Avenue
New York, NY 10016
NY : 1922 : Stock : Direct Response
Ind Life, Group Life, Ann
212-592-1800
AMB# 006221 NAIC# 61875

A-
Rating Outlook: Stable
FSC VI

Data Year	Bonds	Mort. Loans & R.E.	Com & Pref. Stock	All Other Assets	Total Assets	Life Reserves	Health Reserves	Ann Res. & Dep. Liabilities	All Other Liabilities	Capital & Surplus	Direct Premiums Written	Net Premiums Written & Deposits	Operating Cash Flow	NOG Before Taxes	NOG After Taxes	Net Income
'05	91.7	...	4.8	3.5	201,709	13.3	...	81.6	5.1	29,559	41,204	42,455	922	-47	-47	-47
'06	91.1	...	5.7	3.2	199,385	14.3	...	80.7	5.1	34,962	40,704	41,947	-3,440	4,076	4,076	4,177
'07	87.6	...	6.5	5.9	201,279	14.7	...	80.5	4.8	37,456	27,494	31,321	1,767	2,397	2,397	2,397
'08	89.4	...	3.8	6.8	205,902	13.8	...	78.0	8.2	31,476	25,704	28,508	3,978	3,086	3,086	-3,118
'09	83.8	...	6.5	9.7	219,533	13.3	...	80.7	5.9	35,308	35,385	38,593	8,749	3,809	3,809	2,281

Rating History: A-, 04/28/10; A-, 05/04/09; A-, 01/24/08; A-, 01/19/07; A-, 12/22/05

CIBC REINSURANCE CO LIMITED
Canadian Imperial Bank of Commerce
David Gray
President & CEO
FirstCaribbean International Bank Head Office
Warrens, St. Michael, Barbados
BB : Stock : Not Available
Life Reins
246-367-2400
AMB# 072561

A
Rating Outlook: Stable
FSC VIII

Data Year	Bonds	Mort. Loans & R.E.	Com & Pref. Stock	All Other Assets	Total Assets	Life Reserves	Health Reserves	Ann Res. & Dep. Liabilities	All Other Liabilities	Capital & Surplus	Direct Premiums Written	Net Premiums Written & Deposits	Operating Cash Flow	NOG Before Taxes	NOG After Taxes	Net Income
'05	...	...	...	100.0	140,867	24.3	...	...	75.7	133,017	...	145,688	...	161,892	161,892	...
'06	...	...	...	100.0	175,749	54.1	...	...	45.9	165,781	...	154,570	175,690	182,764	182,764	...
'07	...	...	...	100.0	205,777	64.8	...	...	35.2	189,375	...	126,855	202,441	193,594	193,594	...
'08	...	...	...	100.0	235,353	74.5	...	...	25.5	213,569	...	178,436	221,050	214,195	214,195	...
'09	...	...	...	100.0	259,241	66.2	...	...	33.8	223,801	...	219,422	191,127	190,232	190,232	...

Rating History: A, 06/09/09; A, 10/13/08; A, 02/11/08

CICA LIFE INS CO OF AMERICA
Citizens Inc
Rick D. Riley
President
P.O. Box 149151
Austin, TX 78714-9151
CO : 1968 : Stock : Agency
Whole life
512-837-7100
AMB# 006228 NAIC# 71463

NR-5

Data Year	Bonds	Mort. Loans & R.E.	Com & Pref. Stock	All Other Assets	Total Assets	Life Reserves	Health Reserves	Ann Res. & Dep. Liabilities	All Other Liabilities	Capital & Surplus	Direct Premiums Written	Net Premiums Written & Deposits	Operating Cash Flow	NOG Before Taxes	NOG After Taxes	Net Income
'05	63.2	1.4	21.6	13.8	302,692	79.8	0.3	13.3	6.6	38,439	85,103	86,280	-7,378	148	386	-282
'06	65.0	1.1	18.5	15.4	341,923	79.5	0.2	12.7	7.6	42,849	95,758	102,174	36,736	6,442	4,553	4,783
'07	60.6	0.9	23.7	14.7	387,498	79.2	0.2	12.5	8.1	51,552	106,030	109,995	43,778	10,322	7,124	7,362
'08	60.0	0.8	18.4	20.8	404,026	81.3	0.2	12.6	5.9	38,255	107,133	114,150	27,860	15,650	10,504	-3,319
'09	65.9	0.7	18.9	14.5	469,608	78.7	0.1	11.8	9.4	49,295	108,413	113,318	50,153	10,390	9,545	9,545

Rating History: NR-5, 04/12/10; NR-5, 04/14/09; NR-5, 04/07/08; NR-5, 04/27/07; NR-5, 05/02/06

CIGNA ARBOR LIFE INS CO[1]
CIGNA Corporation
Mark A. Parsons
President
900 Cottage Grove Road
Bloomfield, CT 06002
CT : 2009 : Stock : Not Available
860-226-600
AMB# 060710 NAIC# 13733

NR-1

Data Year	Bonds	Mort. Loans & R.E.	Com & Pref. Stock	All Other Assets	Total Assets	Life Reserves	Health Reserves	Ann Res. & Dep. Liabilities	All Other Liabilities	Capital & Surplus	Direct Premiums Written	Net Premiums Written & Deposits	Operating Cash Flow	NOG Before Taxes	NOG After Taxes	Net Income
'05	...	...	...	...	...	...	...	...	...	...	...	...	...	...	...	...
'06	...	...	...	...	...	...	...	...	...	...	...	...	...	...	...	...
'07	...	...	...	...	...	...	...	...	...	...	...	...	...	...	...	...
'08	...	...	...	...	...	...	...	...	...	...	...	...	...	...	...	...
'09	...	...	...	100.0	5,594	...	...	...	100.0	4,461	...	6,529	...	106	106	106

Rating History: NR-1, 06/10/10

CIGNA BEHAVIORAL HEALTH OF CA
CIGNA Corporation
Susan P. Urbanski
President
450 N. Brand Boulevard, Suite 500
Glendale, CA 91203
CA : 1990 : Stock : Broker
Health
818-551-2200
AMB# 064789

NR-3

Data Year	Bonds	Mort. Loans & R.E.	Com & Pref. Stock	All Other Assets	Total Assets	Life Reserves	Health Reserves	Ann Res. & Dep. Liabilities	All Other Liabilities	Capital & Surplus	Direct Premiums Written	Net Premiums Written & Deposits	Operating Cash Flow	NOG Before Taxes	NOG After Taxes	Net Income
'05	...	...	...	100.0	20,141	...	...	...	100.0	15,857	16,136	16,136	2,352	4,535	2,853	2,853
'06	...	...	...	100.0	22,789	...	...	...	100.0	18,557	15,022	15,022	2,956	4,216	2,662	2,662
'07	...	...	...	100.0	26,487	...	...	...	100.0	21,873	24,056	24,056	3,890	13,142	8,805	8,805
'08	...	...	...	100.0	11,711	...	...	...	100.0	7,177	25,315	25,315	-14,758	12,401	8,234	8,234
'09	...	...	...	100.0	12,123	...	...	...	100.0	8,773	12,219	12,219	227	9,336	5,921	5,921

Rating History: NR-3, 01/08/10; NR-3, 11/14/08; NR-3, 02/11/08; NR-3, 12/14/06; NR-3, 12/21/05

CIGNA DENTAL HEALTH OF CA INC
CIGNA Corporation
Karen S. Rohan
Chairman
P.O. Box 453099
Sunrise, FL 33323-3099
CA : 1985 : Stock : Broker
Dental
818-379-2900
AMB# 060171

A-
Rating Outlook: Negative
FSC IV

Data Year	Bonds	Mort. Loans & R.E.	Com & Pref. Stock	All Other Assets	Total Assets	Life Reserves	Health Reserves	Ann Res. & Dep. Liabilities	All Other Liabilities	Capital & Surplus	Direct Premiums Written	Net Premiums Written & Deposits	Operating Cash Flow	NOG Before Taxes	NOG After Taxes	Net Income
'05	...	...	...	100.0	11,340	...	...	...	100.0	6,562	48,781	48,781	-489	22,930	14,789	14,789
'06	...	...	...	100.0	9,269	...	...	...	100.0	5,353	39,489	39,489	-1,030	18,259	11,841	11,841
'07	...	...	...	100.0	7,477	...	...	...	100.0	3,190	39,044	39,044	-2,562	17,627	11,228	11,228
'08	...	...	...	100.0	9,176	...	...	...	100.0	4,944	38,518	38,518	2,152	21,535	13,620	13,620
'09	...	...	...	100.0	10,566	...	...	...	100.0	6,952	35,800	35,800	2,125	20,225	12,597	12,597

Rating History: A-, 01/08/10; A- g, 11/14/08; A- g, 02/11/08; A- g, 12/14/06; A- g, 12/21/05

Data in U.S. Dollars

	Profitability Tests							Leverage Tests						Liquidity Tests					
Un-Realized Capital Gains ($000)	Benefits Paid to NPW & Dep (%)	Comm. & Expenses to NPW & Dep (%)	NOG to Total Assets (%)	NOG to Total Rev (%)	Operating Return on Equity (%)	Net Yield (%)	Total Return (%)	Change in NPW & Dep (%)	NPW & Dep to Capital (X)	Capital & Surplus to Liabilities (%)	Surplus Relief (%)	Reins Leverage (%)	Change in Capital (%)	Quick Liquidity (%)	Current Liquidity (%)	Non-Invest Grade Bonds to Capital (%)	Delinq. & Foreclosed Mortgages to Capital (%)	Mort. & Credit Tenant Loans & R.E. to Capital (%)	Affiliated Invest to Capital (%)
...	87.1	9.8	21.1	3.4	60.7	3.70	3.70	10.1	13.5	63.3	...	2.9	98.4	76.6	82.1	...	...	...	...
...	84.8	14.5	5.8	1.2	13.7	5.87	5.87	-11.6	11.4	87.8	...	0.1	4.5	49.1	49.1	...	...	...	...
...	86.5	6.5	49.6	7.7	123.5	7.30	7.30	260.2	9.9	63.4	...	0.3	317.2	81.9	93.8	...	...	...	...
...	81.2	6.7	50.2	12.8	104.4	4.08	4.08	11.7	6.4	125.8	...	0.8	72.6	238.0	245.8	...	...	...	...
...	85.7	7.7	24.5	6.8	44.3	0.93	-3.04	3.2	6.4	121.6	...	0.1	2.7	269.6	286.9	...	...	...	...
Principal Lines of Business: Medicaid (100.0%)														Principal States: KS (65.8%), MO (34.2%)					
...	86.9	12.6	7.6	1.9	17.3	1.70	1.70	14.0	8.1	77.5	...	...	19.0	80.6	80.6	...	...	86.7	86.7
...	87.9	10.4	10.2	2.3	23.5	-0.08	-0.08	42.1	9.0	75.3	...	...	26.7	64.8	64.8	...	...	99.5	99.5
...	87.4	10.4	11.3	2.8	24.3	0.34	0.34	5.0	7.4	99.9	...	...	27.7	65.2	65.2	...	...	82.9	82.9
...	88.8	11.6	6.0	1.5	11.0	-0.13	-0.13	6.0	6.4	144.9	...	...	23.7	72.3	72.3	...	...	64.8	64.8
...	88.5	12.8	4.5	1.3	8.8	-0.47	-0.47	6.6	5.9	87.3	...	...	14.3	27.7	27.7	...	...	55.9	55.9
Principal Lines of Business: Medicare (77.7%), CompHosp/Med (22.3%)																			
10	80.4	21.5	2.3	2.8	8.4	5.74	5.48	0.5	2.6	42.2	...	0.0	5.5	117.0	125.5	9.2	1.5	23.7	...
368	78.7	20.9	3.2	3.9	11.6	5.36	6.12	-0.9	2.8	38.8	...	0.0	-6.5	94.5	106.0	4.4	0.4	28.3	26.8
-274	77.4	19.6	5.4	6.7	18.0	5.18	4.91	-3.0	2.2	49.1	...	0.0	20.4	93.6	106.0	3.7	5.3	21.5	24.3
-221	78.9	17.4	5.2	7.2	14.5	5.06	4.87	-4.0	1.6	67.5	...	0.0	34.4	114.2	127.2	2.7	...	17.1	19.8
252	80.1	13.9	7.5	11.4	17.8	4.51	4.75	-4.0	1.3	84.8	...	0.0	15.5	110.2	125.8	4.8	1.4	10.7	17.8
Principal Lines of Business: IndA&H (97.9%), OrdLife (2.1%), GrpAnn (0.1%), GrpA&H (0.0%), IndAnn (0.0%)														Principal States: TX (62.6%), MO (32.6%)					
389	97.1	19.1	0.0	-0.1	-0.2	4.42	4.98	77.7	1.4	18.3	...	0.3	1.1	83.8	94.0	...	...	...	...
1,339	107.8	16.8	2.0	8.1	12.6	4.70	5.64	-1.2	1.1	22.6	...	0.2	17.7	86.6	97.2	...	...	...	...
171	93.6	21.1	1.2	6.4	6.6	4.94	5.16	-25.3	0.8	24.3	...	0.3	7.0	81.0	92.0	...	...	...	...
-3,250	81.0	22.7	1.5	8.6	9.0	5.09	0.65	-9.0	0.9	19.1	...	0.2	-16.2	82.6	92.6	2.2	...	...	...
2,981	62.9	18.5	1.8	8.3	11.4	4.85	5.81	35.4	1.0	20.8	...	0.3	14.4	86.4	96.4	2.1	...	...	...
Principal Lines of Business: GrpLife (46.8%), IndAnn (28.8%), GrpAnn (22.3%), OrdLife (2.2%)														Principal States: NY (11.1%), FL (8.3%), CA (7.3%), TX (5.7%), NC (5.4%)					
...	58.1	32.1	202.6	53.9	217.1	5.16	5.16	999.9	109.5	999.9	...	...	725.0	504.8	968.2	...	...	...	...
...	47.1	38.0	115.5	58.1	122.3	4.31	4.31	6.1	93.2	999.9	...	...	24.6	503.8	912.9	...	...	...	...
...	28.7	50.1	101.5	65.9	109.0	4.55	4.55	-17.9	67.0	999.9	...	...	14.2	625.8	432.9	...	...	...	...
...	36.2	43.0	97.1	60.3	106.3	3.44	3.44	40.7	83.6	980.4	...	...	12.8	480.2	459.1	...	...	...	...
...	50.3	36.7	76.9	49.9	87.0	1.56	1.56	23.0	98.0	631.5	...	...	4.8	326.4	282.2	...	...	...	...
-2,839	36.2	41.1	0.1	0.4	0.7	3.94	2.83	13.1	2.2	14.9	1.4	21.9	-47.7	63.9	64.8	0.8	...	10.4	174.0
-2,379	34.0	36.6	1.4	4.1	11.2	5.35	4.73	18.4	2.4	14.5	1.0	17.4	10.2	66.7	67.4	0.7	...	8.9	156.0
2,263	35.6	33.3	2.0	5.7	15.1	6.12	6.87	7.7	2.1	15.9	0.8	13.2	22.6	68.1	69.9	0.5	...	6.7	130.1
-16,290	32.2	29.3	2.7	8.3	23.4	5.97	-1.75	3.8	3.0	10.5	0.8	17.4	-27.7	69.4	70.9	0.8	...	8.6	145.5
9,914	36.8	26.7	2.2	7.7	21.8	4.29	6.71	-0.7	2.1	13.3	0.6	13.5	43.6	71.8	74.1	0.1	...	5.7	144.6
Principal Lines of Business: OrdLife (88.3%), GrpAnn (6.9%), IndAnn (2.7%), GrpLife (1.0%), CrdA&H (0.5%)																			
...	...	...	...	...	...	...	...	...	...	...	...	...	...	...	...	...	...	...	...
...	...	...	...	...	...	...	...	...	...	...	...	...	...	...	...	...	...	...	...
...	...	...	...	...	...	...	...	...	...	...	...	...	...	...	...	...	...	...	...
...	...	...	...	...	...	...	...	...	...	...	...	...	...	...	...	...	...	...	...
...	98.7	0.7	...	1.6	...	...	...	...	1.5	394.4	...	...	...	...	...	...	...	...	...
Principal Lines of Business: OrdLife (100.0%)																			
...	71.5	5.5	15.0	16.8	19.7	4.09	4.09	-14.6	1.0	370.1	...	...	20.4	457.3	457.3	...	...	...	...
...	71.8	6.8	12.4	16.6	15.5	4.97	4.97	-6.9	0.8	438.5	...	...	17.0	166.9	166.9	...	...	...	...
...	48.3	2.3	35.7	34.8	43.6	5.16	5.16	60.1	1.1	474.0	...	...	17.9	567.1	567.1	...	...	...	...
...	51.0	3.1	43.1	31.5	56.7	3.41	3.41	5.2	3.5	158.3	...	...	-67.2	254.0	254.0	...	...	...	...
...	81.3	6.2	49.7	29.6	74.2	2.50	2.50	-51.7	1.4	261.9	...	...	22.2	356.5	356.5	...	...	...	...
Principal Lines of Business: CompHosp/Med (100.0%)																			
...	44.1	9.3	127.6	30.2	214.4	4.77	4.77	-8.0	7.4	137.4	...	...	-9.3	75.6	75.6	...	...	...	...
...	41.4	13.4	114.9	29.7	198.7	6.79	6.79	-19.0	7.4	136.7	...	...	-18.4	65.7	65.7	...	...	...	...
...	41.7	14.0	134.1	28.5	262.9	7.72	7.72	-1.1	12.2	74.4	...	...	-40.4	...	...	...	...	...	...
...	38.9	5.9	163.6	35.1	334.9	4.71	4.71	-1.3	7.8	116.8	...	...	55.0	128.2	128.2	...	...	...	...
...	38.1	5.8	127.6	35.1	211.8	1.94	1.94	-7.1	5.1	192.3	...	...	40.6	205.5	205.5	...	...	...	...
Principal Lines of Business: Dental (100.0%)																			

Column key: COMPANY NAME / Ultimate Parent Association / Principal Officer / Mailing Address / Dom. : Began Bus. : Struct. : Mktg. / Specialty / Phone # / AMB# / NAIC# — Best's Financial Strength Rating — FSC. Balance Sheet: Bonds (%), Mort. Loans & R.E. (%), Com & Pref. Stock (%), All Other Assets (%), Total Assets ($000), Life Reserves (%), Health Reserves (%), Ann Res. & Dep. Liabilities (%), All Other Liabilities (%), Capital & Surplus ($000). Operations: Direct Premiums Written ($000), Net Premiums Written & Deposits ($000), Operating Cash Flow ($000), NOG Before Taxes ($000), NOG After Taxes ($000), Net Income ($000).

CIGNA DENTAL HEALTH OF CO INC
CIGNA Corporation
Karen S. Rohan
President
P.O. Box 453099
Sunrise, FL 33323-3099
CO : 1986 : Stock : Broker
Dental
954-514-6600
AMB# 060196 NAIC# 11175

Best's Financial Strength Rating: **NR-2**

Data Year	Bonds (%)	Mort. Loans & R.E. (%)	Com & Pref. Stock (%)	All Other Assets (%)	Total Assets ($000)	Life Reserves (%)	Health Reserves (%)	Ann Res. & Dep. Liabilities (%)	All Other Liabilities (%)	Capital & Surplus ($000)	Direct Premiums Written ($000)	Net Premiums Written & Deposits ($000)	Operating Cash Flow ($000)	NOG Before Taxes ($000)	NOG After Taxes ($000)	Net Income ($000)
'05	6.6	...	...	93.4	2,713	...	53.2	...	46.8	2,192	9,240	9,240	1,172	1,754	1,142	1,142
'06	5.9	...	...	94.1	2,107	...	58.0	...	42.0	1,611	9,629	9,629	-790	2,013	1,306	1,306
'07	5.4	...	...	94.6	2,324	...	49.1	...	50.9	1,663	9,769	9,769	163	81	55	56
'08	6.6	...	...	93.4	1,938	...	70.5	...	29.5	1,603	9,704	9,704	-531	1,071	697	698
'09	6.3	...	...	93.7	2,065	...	68.0	...	32.0	1,674	9,466	9,466	301	1,107	719	721

Rating History: NR-2, 01/08/10; NR-2, 11/14/08; NR-2, 02/11/08; NR-2, 12/14/06; NR-2, 12/21/05

CIGNA DENTAL HEALTH OF DE INC
CIGNA Corporation
Matthew G. Manders
President
P.O. Box 453099
Sunrise, FL 33323-3099
DE : 1986 : Stock : Broker
Dental
954-514-6600
AMB# 060172 NAIC# 95380

Best's Financial Strength Rating: **NR-2**

Data Year	Bonds (%)	Mort. Loans & R.E. (%)	Com & Pref. Stock (%)	All Other Assets (%)	Total Assets ($000)	Life Reserves (%)	Health Reserves (%)	Ann Res. & Dep. Liabilities (%)	All Other Liabilities (%)	Capital & Surplus ($000)	Direct Premiums Written ($000)	Net Premiums Written & Deposits ($000)	Operating Cash Flow ($000)	NOG Before Taxes ($000)	NOG After Taxes ($000)	Net Income ($000)
'05	...	...	...	100.0	176	...	...	...	100.0	172	6	6	0	9	6	6
'06	...	...	...	100.0	171	...	83.9	...	16.1	167	4	4	-8	-9	-7	-7
'07	...	...	...	100.0	237	...	69.3	...	30.7	215	71	71	38	-73	-51	-51
'08	...	...	...	100.0	216	...	95.4	...	4.6	205	74	74	-7	-20	-10	-10
'09	...	...	...	100.0	173	...	89.7	...	10.3	154	84	84	-58	-72	-48	-48

Rating History: NR-2, 01/08/10; NR-2, 11/14/08; NR-2, 02/11/08; NR-2, 12/14/06; NR-2, 12/21/05

CIGNA DENTAL HEALTH OF FL INC
CIGNA Corporation
Matthew G. Manders
President
1571 Sawgrass Corporate Parkway
Sunrise, FL 33323
FL : 1973 : Stock : Broker
Dental
954-514-6600
AMB# 060173 NAIC# 52021

Best's Financial Strength Rating: **A-**
Rating Outlook: Negative
FSC III

Data Year	Bonds (%)	Mort. Loans & R.E. (%)	Com & Pref. Stock (%)	All Other Assets (%)	Total Assets ($000)	Life Reserves (%)	Health Reserves (%)	Ann Res. & Dep. Liabilities (%)	All Other Liabilities (%)	Capital & Surplus ($000)	Direct Premiums Written ($000)	Net Premiums Written & Deposits ($000)	Operating Cash Flow ($000)	NOG Before Taxes ($000)	NOG After Taxes ($000)	Net Income ($000)
'05	36.0	...	...	64.0	6,926	...	70.9	...	29.1	4,563	46,746	46,746	582	12,142	7,900	7,900
'06	31.8	...	...	68.2	8,033	...	67.3	...	32.7	5,460	46,308	46,308	1,033	13,889	9,026	9,026
'07	34.5	...	...	65.5	7,280	...	61.5	...	38.5	4,972	47,093	47,093	-984	15,219	9,902	9,902
'08	39.0	...	...	61.0	6,469	...	40.1	...	59.9	3,662	42,069	42,069	-1,131	9,805	6,376	6,387
'09	40.0	...	...	60.0	6,347	...	56.2	...	43.8	4,266	37,143	37,143	296	9,929	6,447	6,451

Rating History: A-, 01/08/10; A- g, 11/14/08; A- g, 02/11/08; A- g, 12/14/06; A- g, 12/21/05

CIGNA DENTAL HEALTH OF KS INC
CIGNA Corporation
Matthew G. Manders
President
P.O. Box 453099
Sunrise, FL 33323-3099
KS : 1995 : Stock : Broker
Dental
954-514-6600
AMB# 060174 NAIC# 52024

Best's Financial Strength Rating: **NR-2**

Data Year	Bonds (%)	Mort. Loans & R.E. (%)	Com & Pref. Stock (%)	All Other Assets (%)	Total Assets ($000)	Life Reserves (%)	Health Reserves (%)	Ann Res. & Dep. Liabilities (%)	All Other Liabilities (%)	Capital & Surplus ($000)	Direct Premiums Written ($000)	Net Premiums Written & Deposits ($000)	Operating Cash Flow ($000)	NOG Before Taxes ($000)	NOG After Taxes ($000)	Net Income ($000)
'05	5.3	...	...	94.7	1,032	...	37.9	...	62.1	730	2,161	2,161	158	256	169	169
'06	4.7	...	...	95.3	1,180	...	31.2	...	68.8	953	1,974	1,974	117	349	231	231
'07	5.3	...	...	94.7	1,031	...	42.9	...	57.1	845	1,981	1,981	-168	350	223	223
'08	3.9	...	...	96.1	1,388	...	23.3	...	76.7	1,063	1,927	1,927	394	350	230	230
'09	5.7	...	...	94.3	980	...	17.9	...	82.1	535	1,759	1,759	-395	334	216	216

Rating History: NR-2, 01/08/10; NR-2, 11/14/08; NR-2, 02/11/08; NR-2, 12/14/06; NR-2, 12/21/05

CIGNA DENTAL HEALTH OF KY INC
CIGNA Corporation
Matthew G. Manders
President
P.O. Box 453099
Sunrise, FL 33323-3099
KY : 1986 : Stock : Broker
Dental
954-514-6600
AMB# 060175 NAIC# 52108

Best's Financial Strength Rating: **NR-2**

Data Year	Bonds (%)	Mort. Loans & R.E. (%)	Com & Pref. Stock (%)	All Other Assets (%)	Total Assets ($000)	Life Reserves (%)	Health Reserves (%)	Ann Res. & Dep. Liabilities (%)	All Other Liabilities (%)	Capital & Surplus ($000)	Direct Premiums Written ($000)	Net Premiums Written & Deposits ($000)	Operating Cash Flow ($000)	NOG Before Taxes ($000)	NOG After Taxes ($000)	Net Income ($000)
'05	...	...	...	100.0	774	...	18.6	...	81.4	550	1,281	1,281	209	279	181	181
'06	5.2	...	...	94.8	1,064	...	14.3	...	85.7	812	1,369	1,369	270	322	209	209
'07	8.1	...	...	91.9	792	...	26.0	...	74.0	648	1,323	1,323	-269	288	187	187
'08	64.7	...	...	35.3	949	...	33.1	...	66.9	803	1,298	1,298	127	242	157	157
'09	72.5	...	...	27.5	645	...	76.9	...	23.1	580	1,292	1,292	-293	257	167	168

Rating History: NR-2, 01/08/10; NR-2, 11/14/08; NR-2, 02/11/08; NR-2, 12/14/06; NR-2, 12/21/05

CIGNA DENTAL HEALTH OF MD INC
CIGNA Corporation
Matthew G. Manders
President
1571 Sawgrass Corporate Parkway
Sunrise, FL 33323
MD : 1987 : Stock : Broker
Dental
954-514-6600
AMB# 060176 NAIC# 48119

Best's Financial Strength Rating: **A-**
Rating Outlook: Negative
FSC III

Data Year	Bonds (%)	Mort. Loans & R.E. (%)	Com & Pref. Stock (%)	All Other Assets (%)	Total Assets ($000)	Life Reserves (%)	Health Reserves (%)	Ann Res. & Dep. Liabilities (%)	All Other Liabilities (%)	Capital & Surplus ($000)	Direct Premiums Written ($000)	Net Premiums Written & Deposits ($000)	Operating Cash Flow ($000)	NOG Before Taxes ($000)	NOG After Taxes ($000)	Net Income ($000)
'05	2.4	...	...	97.6	4,195	...	50.6	...	49.4	3,547	14,334	14,334	2,000	4,838	3,145	3,145
'06	1.7	...	...	98.3	2,818	...	53.9	...	46.1	2,268	14,152	14,152	-1,398	4,820	3,135	3,135
'07	22.7	...	...	77.3	2,930	...	64.4	...	35.6	2,426	14,098	14,098	-125	4,096	2,662	2,662
'08	23.2	...	...	76.8	2,729	...	63.5	...	36.5	2,293	12,363	12,363	-152	3,654	2,375	2,380
'09	23.4	...	...	76.6	2,651	...	73.8	...	26.2	2,258	11,743	11,743	-29	3,625	2,357	2,358

Rating History: A-, 01/08/10; A- g, 11/14/08; A- g, 02/11/08; A- g, 12/14/06; A- g, 12/21/05

CIGNA DENTAL HEALTH OF MO INC
CIGNA Corporation
Karen S. Rohan
President
P.O. Box 453099
Sunrise, FL 33323-3099
MO : 2002 : Stock : Broker
Dental
954-514-6600
AMB# 064702 NAIC# 11160

Best's Financial Strength Rating: **A-**
Rating Outlook: Negative
FSC II

Data Year	Bonds (%)	Mort. Loans & R.E. (%)	Com & Pref. Stock (%)	All Other Assets (%)	Total Assets ($000)	Life Reserves (%)	Health Reserves (%)	Ann Res. & Dep. Liabilities (%)	All Other Liabilities (%)	Capital & Surplus ($000)	Direct Premiums Written ($000)	Net Premiums Written & Deposits ($000)	Operating Cash Flow ($000)	NOG Before Taxes ($000)	NOG After Taxes ($000)	Net Income ($000)
'05	3.3	...	...	96.7	1,641	...	61.4	...	38.6	1,074	7,327	7,327	-372	855	561	561
'06	3.6	...	...	96.4	1,518	...	59.7	...	40.3	981	7,141	7,141	-306	730	475	475
'07	3.5	...	...	96.5	1,561	...	68.5	...	31.5	1,179	7,104	7,104	-153	989	644	644
'08	46.1	...	...	53.9	1,625	...	78.5	...	21.5	1,277	6,954	6,954	38	942	613	614
'09	49.7	...	...	50.3	1,513	...	77.8	...	22.2	1,155	6,083	6,083	-7	731	475	476

Rating History: A-, 01/08/10; A- g, 11/14/08; A- g, 02/11/08; A- g, 12/14/06; A- g, 12/21/05

CIGNA DENTAL HEALTH OF NJ INC
CIGNA Corporation
Matthew G. Manders
President
P.O. Box 453099
Sunrise, FL 33323-3099
NJ : 1983 : Stock : Broker
Dental
954-514-6600
AMB# 060184 NAIC# 11167

Best's Financial Strength Rating: **A-**
Rating Outlook: Negative
FSC II

Data Year	Bonds (%)	Mort. Loans & R.E. (%)	Com & Pref. Stock (%)	All Other Assets (%)	Total Assets ($000)	Life Reserves (%)	Health Reserves (%)	Ann Res. & Dep. Liabilities (%)	All Other Liabilities (%)	Capital & Surplus ($000)	Direct Premiums Written ($000)	Net Premiums Written & Deposits ($000)	Operating Cash Flow ($000)	NOG Before Taxes ($000)	NOG After Taxes ($000)	Net Income ($000)
'05	38.8	...	...	61.2	5,274	...	16.3	...	83.7	3,046	12,587	12,587	-323	563	3	3
'06	36.3	...	...	63.7	5,666	...	12.4	...	87.6	3,087	12,528	12,528	83	738	-70	-70
'07	28.5	...	...	71.5	4,383	...	17.4	...	82.6	2,414	13,601	13,601	-1,731	869	257	256
'08	30.8	...	...	69.2	4,071	...	16.5	...	83.5	2,096	12,992	12,992	135	755	101	101
'09	37.0	...	...	63.0	3,412	...	16.7	...	83.3	1,296	12,111	12,111	-672	700	-85	-84

Rating History: A-, 01/08/10; A- g, 11/14/08; A- g, 02/11/08; A- g, 12/14/06; A- g, 12/21/05

CIGNA DENTAL HEALTH OF NC INC
CIGNA Corporation
Matthew G. Manders
President
1571 Sawgrass Corporate Parkway
Sunrise, FL 33323
NC : 1992 : Stock : Broker
Dental
954-514-6600
AMB# 060178 NAIC# 95179

Best's Financial Strength Rating: **NR-2**

Data Year	Bonds (%)	Mort. Loans & R.E. (%)	Com & Pref. Stock (%)	All Other Assets (%)	Total Assets ($000)	Life Reserves (%)	Health Reserves (%)	Ann Res. & Dep. Liabilities (%)	All Other Liabilities (%)	Capital & Surplus ($000)	Direct Premiums Written ($000)	Net Premiums Written & Deposits ($000)	Operating Cash Flow ($000)	NOG Before Taxes ($000)	NOG After Taxes ($000)	Net Income ($000)
'05	...	...	...	100.0	2,042	...	41.3	...	58.7	1,431	2,851	2,851	24	-68	-25	-25
'06	...	...	...	100.0	1,580	...	88.4	...	11.6	1,277	2,994	2,994	-570	-209	-152	-152
'07	7.6	...	...	92.4	4,407	...	96.7	...	3.3	1,741	4,721	4,721	2,474	-3,963	-3,324	-3,324
'08	9.1	...	...	90.9	3,727	...	79.6	...	20.4	1,936	4,799	4,799	-496	-296	219	220
'09	12.2	...	...	87.8	2,912	...	80.6	...	19.4	1,316	4,527	4,527	-781	-1,069	-642	-642

Rating History: NR-2, 01/08/10; NR-2, 11/14/08; NR-2, 02/11/08; NR-2, 12/14/06; NR-2, 12/21/05

Data in U.S. Dollars

	Profitability Tests							Leverage Tests						Liquidity Tests					
Un-Realized Capital Gains ($000)	Benefits Paid to NPW & Dep (%)	Comm. & Expenses to NPW & Dep (%)	NOG to Total Assets (%)	NOG to Total Rev (%)	Operating Return on Equity (%)	Net Yield (%)	Total Return (%)	Change in NPW & Dep (%)	NPW & Dep to Capital (X)	Capital & Surplus to Liabilities (%)	Surplus Relief (%)	Reins Leverage (%)	Change in Capital (%)	Quick Liquidity (%)	Current Liquidity (%)	Non-Invest Grade Bonds to Capital (%)	Delinq. & Foreclosed Mortgages to Capital (%)	Mort. & Credit Tenant Loans & R.E. to Capital (%)	Affiliated Invest to Capital (%)
...	66.2	15.0	53.4	12.3	68.1	1.30	1.30	2.2	4.2	420.6	...	...	88.7	371.8	388.9	...	...	...	...
...	67.3	12.9	54.2	13.4	68.7	6.15	6.16	4.2	6.0	324.9	...	...	-26.5	495.3	500.3	...	...	...	...
...	87.4	12.4	2.5	0.6	3.4	4.41	4.41	1.5	5.9	251.9	...	...	3.3	460.8	460.8	...	...	...	...
...	76.3	13.0	32.7	7.2	42.7	2.62	2.68	-0.7	6.1	478.6	...	...	-3.6	559.6	559.6	...	...	...	...
...	76.7	11.7	35.9	7.6	43.9	0.66	0.83	-2.5	5.7	428.6	...	...	4.5	628.2	628.2	...	...	...	...
Principal Lines of Business: Dental (100.0%)														Principal States: CO (100.0%)					
...	3.3	28.6	3.4	53.2	3.5	2.77	2.77	73.7	0.0	999.9	...	...	3.5	999.9	999.9	...	...	...	...
...	379.6	27.9	-3.8	-61.3	-3.8	3.70	3.70	-31.0	0.0	999.9	...	...	-3.4	999.9	999.9	...	...	...	...
...	180.7	23.3	-25.0	-65.7	-26.8	3.64	3.64	999.9	0.3	983.0	...	...	29.0	999.9	999.9	...	...	...	...
...	130.1	4.8	-4.2	-12.6	-4.6	1.11	1.11	3.5	0.4	999.9	...	...	-4.6	999.9	999.9	...	...	...	...
...	170.3	11.9	-24.9	-56.8	-27.0	0.66	0.66	14.1	0.5	786.9	...	...	-25.1	999.9	999.9	...	...	...	...
Principal Lines of Business: Dental (100.0%)														Principal States: DE (100.0%)					
...	56.2	51.6	117.0	12.6	179.5	4.45	4.45	-4.3	10.2	193.1	...	...	7.7	231.7	231.7	...	...	...	...
...	56.9	43.2	120.7	15.0	180.1	5.88	5.88	-0.9	8.5	212.2	...	...	19.7	253.3	253.3	...	...	...	...
...	56.9	40.8	129.3	16.2	189.8	6.04	6.04	1.7	9.5	215.5	...	...	-8.9	402.8	404.0	...	...	...	...
...	52.7	57.0	92.8	11.4	147.7	4.49	4.70	-10.7	11.5	130.5	...	...	-26.3	259.2	259.2	...	...	...	...
...	50.7	55.6	100.6	13.0	162.6	2.73	2.82	-11.7	8.7	205.1	...	...	16.5	363.0	363.0	...	...	...	...
Principal Lines of Business: Dental (100.0%)														Principal States: FL (100.0%)					
...	76.9	12.3	17.9	7.7	26.0	2.81	2.81	-13.6	3.0	241.3	...	...	28.3	288.5	288.5	...	...	...	...
...	72.7	11.7	20.9	11.5	27.4	4.35	4.35	-8.7	2.1	420.4	...	...	30.7	757.4	793.0	...	...	...	...
...	72.7	11.8	20.2	11.0	24.8	4.84	4.84	0.3	2.3	456.0	...	...	-11.3	515.3	523.4	...	...	...	...
...	70.8	12.0	19.0	11.8	24.1	1.95	1.95	-2.7	1.8	327.9	...	...	25.8	730.5	730.5	...	...	...	...
...	69.4	11.8	18.3	12.3	27.0	0.38	0.42	-8.7	3.3	120.4	...	...	-49.7	338.2	338.2	...	...	...	...
Principal Lines of Business: Dental (100.0%)														Principal States: KS (84.0%), NE (16.0%)					
...	64.5	14.3	27.3	14.1	37.3	1.10	1.10	-8.7	2.3	244.5	...	...	29.7	301.1	301.1	...	...	...	...
...	65.0	14.1	22.8	14.9	30.7	4.45	4.45	6.9	1.7	323.0	...	...	47.8	684.5	687.6	...	...	...	...
...	67.8	12.7	20.2	13.8	25.6	3.69	3.69	-3.4	2.0	450.7	...	...	-20.2	809.9	816.8	...	...	...	...
...	70.4	12.3	18.1	12.0	21.7	2.28	2.28	-1.9	1.6	549.0	...	...	24.0	663.7	663.7	...	...	...	...
...	69.8	11.4	21.0	12.8	24.2	2.27	2.37	-0.5	2.2	890.3	...	...	-27.8	787.6	787.6	...	...	...	...
Principal Lines of Business: Dental (100.0%)														Principal States: KY (100.0%)					
...	51.5	15.1	99.5	21.9	120.4	2.55	2.55	-3.6	4.0	547.4	...	...	111.1	586.2	586.2	...	...	...	...
...	52.3	14.3	89.4	22.0	107.8	3.28	3.28	-1.3	6.2	412.6	...	...	-36.0	677.8	703.4	...	...	...	...
...	57.8	14.2	92.6	18.7	113.4	8.64	8.60	-0.4	5.8	481.8	...	...	7.0	484.4	485.7	...	...	...	...
...	56.0	14.9	84.0	19.1	100.7	3.59	3.87	-12.3	5.4	526.1	...	...	-5.5	559.0	559.0	...	...	...	...
...	55.6	13.7	87.6	20.0	103.6	1.15	1.20	-5.0	5.2	574.9	...	...	-1.5	669.6	669.6	...	...	...	...
Principal Lines of Business: Dental (100.0%)														Principal States: MD (100.0%)					
...	74.5	13.9	30.7	7.6	43.0	0.60	0.60	-1.8	6.8	189.4	...	...	-29.9	243.3	243.3	...	...	...	...
...	77.7	12.9	30.0	6.6	46.2	5.26	5.27	-2.5	7.3	182.6	...	...	-8.7	392.0	394.0	...	...	...	...
...	75.0	11.8	41.8	9.0	59.6	5.31	5.31	-0.5	6.0	308.7	...	...	20.2	496.0	498.2	...	...	...	...
...	75.1	11.8	38.5	8.8	49.9	3.03	3.12	-2.1	5.4	367.3	...	...	8.3	332.7	332.7	...	...	...	...
...	77.5	10.8	30.3	7.8	39.0	2.03	2.11	-12.5	5.3	322.9	...	...	-9.6	320.0	320.0	...	...	...	...
Principal Lines of Business: Dental (100.0%)														Principal States: MO (100.0%)					
...	80.0	16.6	0.1	0.0	0.1	3.52	3.52	-1.0	4.1	136.7	...	...	0.0	75.8	75.8	...	...	...	...
...	80.0	15.5	-1.3	-0.6	-2.3	4.78	4.78	-0.5	4.1	119.7	...	...	1.3	207.8	215.4	...	...	...	...
...	80.0	14.7	5.1	1.9	9.3	4.77	4.74	8.6	5.6	122.6	...	...	-21.8	134.0	137.8	...	...	...	...
...	80.0	14.8	2.4	0.8	4.5	3.79	3.82	-4.5	6.2	106.1	...	...	-13.2	168.2	168.2	...	...	...	...
...	80.0	14.7	-2.3	-0.7	-5.0	3.18	3.23	-6.8	9.3	61.3	...	...	-38.2	89.7	89.7	...	...	...	...
Principal Lines of Business: Dental (100.0%)														Principal States: NJ (100.0%)					
...	89.6	13.6	-1.2	-0.9	-1.7	2.23	2.23	2.3	2.0	234.3	...	...	-1.8	289.0	289.0	...	...	...	...
...	93.6	13.8	-8.4	-5.0	-11.2	4.32	4.32	5.0	2.3	421.9	...	...	-10.8	751.7	791.4	...	...	...	...
...	126.0	14.0	-99.9	-69.4	-99.9	2.86	2.86	57.7	2.7	65.3	...	...	36.4	255.4	255.7	...	...	...	...
...	119.3	12.9	5.4	4.5	11.9	2.20	2.22	1.7	2.5	108.1	...	...	11.2	342.1	342.1	...	...	...	...
...	116.1	11.4	-19.3	-14.1	-39.5	0.67	0.69	-5.7	3.4	82.5	...	...	-32.0	280.7	280.7	...	...	...	...
Principal Lines of Business: Dental (100.0%)														Principal States: NC (100.0%)					

Data in U.S. Dollars

COMPANY NAME / Ultimate Parent Association / Principal Officer / Mailing Address / Dom. : Began Bus. : Struct. : Mktg. / Specialty / Phone # / AMB# NAIC#	Best's Financial Strength Rating / FSC	Data Year	Balance Sheet: Bonds (%)	Mort. Loans & R.E. (%)	Com & Pref. Stock (%)	All Other Assets (%)	Total Assets ($000)	Life Reserves (%)	Health Reserves (%)	Ann Res. & Dep. Liabilities (%)	All Other Liabilities (%)	Capital & Surplus ($000)	Operations: Direct Premiums Written ($000)	Net Premiums Written & Deposits ($000)	Operating Cash Flow ($000)	NOG Before Taxes ($000)	NOG After Taxes ($000)	Net Income ($000)
CIGNA DENTAL HEALTH OF OH INC CIGNA Corporation	A-	'05	...	...	...	100.0	2,932	...	46.1	...	53.9	2,050	11,228	11,228	942	2,412	1,563	1,563
Matthew G. Manders, President		'06	4.3	...	...	95.7	1,964	...	56.5	...	43.5	1,348	10,723	10,723	-1,107	2,400	1,563	1,563
P.O. Box 453099, Sunrise, FL 33323-3099	Rating Outlook: Negative	'07	4.3	...	...	95.7	1,984	...	47.5	...	52.5	1,454	9,150	9,150	-1,823	2,159	1,408	1,408
OH : 1985 : Stock : Broker		'08	4.9	...	...	95.1	2,104	...	58.3	...	41.7	1,639	9,359	9,359	1,657	2,243	1,458	1,458
Dental, 954-514-6600		'09	3.7	...	...	96.3	2,688	...	56.7	...	43.3	2,165	9,164	9,164	580	2,344	1,521	1,521
AMB# 060179 NAIC# 47805	FSC III	Rating History: A-, 01/08/10; A- g, 11/14/08; A- g, 02/11/08; A- g, 12/14/06; A- g, 12/21/05																
CIGNA DENTAL HEALTH OF PA INC CIGNA Corporation	A-	'05	...	...	...	100.0	2,859	...	46.2	...	53.8	2,553	6,560	6,560	1,219	2,303	1,497	1,497
Matthew G. Manders, President		'06	...	...	...	100.0	2,696	...	54.3	...	45.7	2,465	6,475	6,475	-238	2,191	1,428	1,428
P.O. Box 453099, Sunrise, FL 33323-3099	Rating Outlook: Negative	'07	...	...	...	100.0	2,590	...	58.2	...	41.8	2,363	6,259	6,259	-167	2,077	1,349	1,349
PA : 1982 : Stock : Broker		'08	...	...	...	100.0	2,583	...	37.5	...	62.5	2,259	6,099	6,099	-5	1,972	1,282	1,283
Dental, 954-514-6600		'09	...	...	...	100.0	2,647	...	68.1	...	31.9	2,460	6,180	6,180	20	2,199	1,428	1,428
AMB# 060180 NAIC# 47041	FSC III	Rating History: A-, 01/08/10; A- g, 11/14/08; A- g, 02/11/08; A- g, 12/14/06; A- g, 12/21/05																
CIGNA DENTAL HEALTH OF TX INC CIGNA Corporation	A-	'05	23.2	...	...	76.8	7,317	...	57.6	...	42.4	5,216	40,373	40,373	1,876	10,696	6,955	6,955
Ronald B. Bolden, President & CEO		'06	17.0	...	...	83.0	5,952	...	59.2	...	40.8	4,301	38,817	38,817	-1,765	11,782	7,657	7,657
P.O. Box 453099, Sunrise, FL 33323-3099	Rating Outlook: Negative	'07	18.2	...	...	81.8	6,258	...	63.8	...	36.2	4,713	38,976	38,976	-504	10,996	7,158	7,158
TX : 1987 : Stock : Broker		'08	17.7	...	...	82.3	6,458	...	59.0	...	41.0	5,092	37,427	37,427	322	11,675	7,589	7,590
Dental, 954-514-6600		'09	17.7	...	...	82.3	6,559	...	67.1	...	32.9	5,483	32,772	32,772	356	11,185	7,273	7,273
AMB# 060181 NAIC# 95037	FSC IV	Rating History: A-, 01/08/10; A- g, 11/14/08; A- g, 02/11/08; A- g, 12/14/06; A- g, 12/21/05																
CIGNA DENTAL HEALTH OF VA INC CIGNA Corporation	A-	'05	13.5	...	...	86.5	2,990	...	55.5	...	44.5	2,563	8,474	8,474	456	2,347	1,527	1,527
Karen S. Rohan, President		'06	20.8	...	...	79.2	2,041	...	63.6	...	36.4	1,726	7,466	7,466	-1,025	2,056	1,338	1,338
P.O. Box 453099, Sunrise, FL 33323-3099	Rating Outlook: Negative	'07	23.4	...	...	76.6	1,817	...	75.9	...	24.1	1,562	7,266	7,266	-307	1,698	1,108	1,108
VA : 2001 : Stock : Broker		'08	45.7	...	...	54.3	1,963	...	61.6	...	38.4	1,639	6,701	6,701	196	1,317	857	860
Dental, 954-514-6600		'09	39.7	...	...	60.3	2,239	...	53.4	...	46.6	1,832	6,547	6,547	370	1,339	868	869
AMB# 064706 NAIC# 52617	FSC II	Rating History: A-, 01/08/10; A- g, 11/14/08; A- g, 02/11/08; A- g, 12/14/06; A- g, 12/21/05																
CIGNA DENTAL HEALTH PLN AZ INC CIGNA Corporation	A-	'05	...	...	...	100.0	3,809	...	36.3	...	63.7	1,879	14,731	14,731	435	4,126	2,679	2,679
Matthew G. Manders, President		'06	...	...	...	100.0	2,881	...	44.3	...	55.7	1,486	14,564	14,564	-745	4,710	3,069	3,070
P.O. Box 453099, Sunrise, FL 33323-3099	Rating Outlook: Negative	'07	...	...	...	100.0	2,544	...	42.7	...	57.3	1,266	14,683	14,683	-282	4,279	2,780	2,780
AZ : 1995 : Stock : Broker		'08	...	...	...	100.0	2,249	...	38.4	...	61.6	1,041	14,401	14,401	-467	4,595	2,987	2,988
Dental, 954-514-6600		'09	...	...	...	100.0	2,694	...	40.1	...	59.9	1,532	14,023	14,023	489	4,979	3,239	3,240
AMB# 060170 NAIC# 47013	FSC II	Rating History: A-, 01/08/10; A- g, 11/14/08; A- g, 02/11/08; A- g, 12/14/06; A- g, 12/21/05																
CIGNA HEALTH & LIFE INSURANCE CIGNA Corporation	NR-2	'05	60.3	...	0.0	39.7	136,308	47.3	9.9	0.0	42.8	41,258	51,601	40,426	-68,335	30,294	20,547	20,165
Richard F. Rivers, Chairman, President & CEO		'06	58.4	...	0.0	41.6	156,550	43.4	8.4	...	48.2	59,121	46,714	45,792	18,497	27,102	16,666	16,593
8505 East Orchard Road, Greenwood Village, CO 80111		'07	72.6	...	0.0	27.4	130,839	47.5	9.3	...	43.2	58,075	41,867	41,038	-20,024	27,353	17,962	17,962
CT : 1964 : Stock : Broker		'08	35.6	...	0.0	64.3	28,301	18.4	28.9	...	52.6	19,904	39,471	-2,419	-95,359	25,235	18,781	19,433
Group A&H, Life, 303-737-3000		'09	49.4	...	...	50.6	50,006	...	37.3	...	62.7	41,977	38,061	35,228	16,694	23,851	17,828	17,920
AMB# 006871 NAIC# 67369		Rating History: NR-2, 01/08/10; NR-3, 11/17/08; NR-3, 06/22/07; NR-3, 02/01/07; NR-3, 06/19/06																
CIGNA HTHCARE-CENTENNIAL STATE CIGNA Corporation	NR-3	'05	9.5	...	...	90.5	10,016	...	0.8	...	99.2	2,777	32,331	3,233	217	629	431	429
Mark J. Carley, President		'06	7.9	...	...	92.1	11,129	...	2.2	...	97.8	2,906	24,612	2,461	2,628	734	472	473
8505 East Orchard Road, Greenwood Village, CO 80111		'07	6.9	...	...	93.1	9,940	...	1.8	...	98.2	2,853	23,063	2,306	-354	848	554	554
CO : 1996 : Stock : Broker		'08	16.3	...	...	83.7	4,086	...	3.1	...	96.9	3,060	11,629	2,382	-3,319	296	186	186
Group A&H, 303-729-7451		'09	20.5	...	...	79.5	3,184	...	2.7	...	97.3	2,422	3,026	303	-396	160	117	117
AMB# 064024 NAIC# 95412		Rating History: NR-3, 01/08/10; A-, 11/14/08; A-, 11/27/07; A, 06/22/07; A u, 02/01/07																
CIGNA HEALTHCARE MID-ATL INC CIGNA Corporation	A-	'05	56.4	...	...	43.6	36,090	...	65.2	...	34.8	18,003	146,714	146,021	5,714	9,614	6,329	6,327
Thomas J. Martel, President		'06	70.9	...	...	29.1	34,272	...	57.2	...	42.8	18,909	169,547	169,261	501	5,980	4,201	4,201
900 Cottage Grove Road, C6ACC, Hartford, CT 06152	Rating Outlook: Negative	'07	85.6	...	...	14.4	30,953	...	49.7	...	50.3	21,862	99,462	98,869	783	5,788	4,146	4,146
MD : 1986 : Stock : Broker		'08	84.2	...	...	15.8	20,425	...	47.0	...	53.0	14,467	50,586	49,944	-8,747	6,842	4,743	4,699
Group A&H, Health, 860-226-8610		'09	54.8	...	...	45.2	15,683	...	29.2	...	70.8	9,151	30,438	29,937	-3,033	4,442	2,878	2,933
AMB# 068871 NAIC# 95599	FSC IV	Rating History: A-, 01/08/10; A-, 11/14/08; A-, 02/11/08; A-, 12/14/06; A- g, 12/21/05																
CIGNA HEALTHCARE OF AZ INC CIGNA Corporation	A-	'05	51.8	14.7	...	33.6	149,025	...	59.9	...	40.1	67,594	519,435	518,259	-20,093	44,162	32,036	31,912
Jeffrey Scott Terrill, President		'06	54.2	12.0	...	33.8	172,239	...	64.8	...	35.2	57,306	631,080	630,643	5,145	28,787	16,284	16,280
900 Cottage Grove Road, C5FIN, Hartford, CT 06152-2330	Rating Outlook: Negative	'07	63.9	13.9	...	22.2	143,045	...	65.9	...	34.1	55,219	616,713	615,254	-10,672	26,650	14,248	14,207
AZ : 1977 : Stock : Broker		'08	58.0	14.7	...	27.3	125,630	...	62.1	...	37.9	55,131	538,731	536,525	-13,221	25,869	18,286	18,307
Health, 602-942-4462		'09	47.2	18.3	...	34.5	144,600	...	63.1	...	36.9	70,146	544,123	541,651	3,652	22,287	18,790	18,791
AMB# 068726 NAIC# 95125	FSC VII	Rating History: A-, 01/08/10; A-, 11/14/08; A-, 02/11/08; A-, 12/14/06; A- g, 12/21/05																

BEST'S PROFITABILITY, LEVERAGE AND LIQUIDITY TESTS 2005 – 2009

Data in U.S. Dollars

—	Profitability Tests							Leverage Tests						Liquidity Tests					
Un-Realized Capital Gains ($000)	Benefits Paid to NPW & Dep (%)	Comm. & Expenses to NPW & Dep (%)	NOG to Total Assets (%)	NOG to Total Rev (%)	Operating Return on Equity (%)	Net Yield (%)	Total Return (%)	Change in NPW & Dep (%)	NPW & Dep to Capital (X)	Capital & Surplus to Liabilities (%)	Surplus Relief (%)	Reins Leverage (%)	Change in Capital (%)	Quick Liquidity (%)	Current Liquidity (%)	Non-Invest Grade Bonds to Capital (%)	Delinq. & Foreclosed Mortgages to Capital (%)	Mort. & Credit Tenant Loans & R.E. to Capital (%)	Affiliated Invest to Capital (%)
...	64.6	14.5	64.3	13.9	94.2	2.82	2.82	-2.9	5.5	232.3	...	...	61.3	282.6	282.6	...	...	...	...
...	64.9	13.5	63.8	14.5	92.0	4.51	4.51	-4.5	8.0	218.9	...	...	-34.2	440.3	464.3	...	...	...	...
...	64.6	12.6	71.3	15.3	100.5	16.89	16.89	-14.7	6.3	274.0	...	...	7.8	106.2	127.2	...	...	...	...
...	63.5	13.0	71.3	15.5	94.3	11.50	11.51	2.3	5.7	352.4	...	...	12.7	537.4	537.4	...	...	...	...
...	62.7	11.8	63.5	16.6	80.0	0.50	0.50	-2.1	4.2	413.5	...	...	32.1	685.5	685.5	...	...	...	...

Principal Lines of Business: Dental (100.0%) Principal States: OH (100.0%)

...	47.2	18.5	68.2	22.6	82.1	2.83	2.83	0.9	2.6	835.1	...	...	133.6	792.8	792.8	...	...	...	...
...	50.7	17.0	51.4	21.7	56.9	4.51	4.51	-1.3	2.6	999.9	...	...	-3.5	999.9	999.9	...	...	...	...
...	52.5	16.4	51.1	21.1	55.9	6.30	6.30	-3.3	2.6	999.9	...	...	-4.1	999.9	999.9	...	...	...	...
...	52.0	16.6	49.6	20.8	55.5	2.84	2.90	-2.6	2.7	698.1	...	...	-4.4	999.9	999.9	...	...	...	...
...	48.9	15.8	54.6	23.0	60.5	0.87	0.88	1.3	2.5	999.9	...	...	8.9	999.9	999.9	...	...	...	...

Principal Lines of Business: Dental (100.0%) Principal States: PA (100.0%)

...	59.3	14.5	105.5	17.2	152.1	3.25	3.25	-3.5	7.7	248.3	...	...	32.7	241.6	241.6	...	...	...	...
...	56.9	13.5	115.4	19.6	160.9	6.32	6.32	-3.9	9.0	260.5	...	...	-17.5	360.0	377.2	...	...	...	...
...	58.7	13.7	117.3	18.2	158.8	8.48	8.46	0.4	8.3	305.0	...	...	9.6	312.3	315.1	...	...	...	...
...	55.5	13.7	119.4	20.2	154.8	4.93	4.95	-4.0	7.3	372.8	...	...	8.1	418.3	418.3	...	...	...	...
...	53.3	12.7	111.7	22.2	137.5	1.55	1.54	-12.4	6.0	509.6	...	...	7.7	561.7	561.7	...	...	...	...

Principal Lines of Business: Dental (100.0%) Principal States: TX (100.0%)

...	57.3	15.7	56.0	17.9	64.6	2.79	2.79	-10.4	3.3	600.5	...	...	18.6	555.0	555.0	...	...	...	...
...	59.3	14.5	53.2	17.7	62.4	5.32	5.34	-11.9	4.3	548.1	...	...	-32.6	593.7	600.7	...	...	...	...
...	63.7	14.1	57.4	15.1	67.4	7.32	7.33	-2.7	4.7	612.0	...	...	-9.5	482.9	486.3	...	...	...	...
...	66.8	14.1	45.3	12.7	53.5	3.32	3.61	-7.8	4.1	506.9	...	...	5.0	506.4	506.4	...	...	...	...
...	65.9	14.0	41.3	13.2	50.0	1.31	1.32	-2.3	3.6	449.8	...	...	11.7	574.3	574.3	...	...	...	...

Principal Lines of Business: Dental (100.0%) Principal States: VA (100.0%)

...	62.3	12.3	81.1	17.7	158.9	1.11	1.11	-4.1	7.8	97.4	...	...	26.0	121.7	121.7	...	...	...	...
...	59.6	11.0	91.8	20.5	182.4	6.50	6.51	-1.1	9.8	106.5	...	...	-20.9	234.0	236.5	...	...	...	...
...	61.8	11.5	102.5	18.5	202.0	7.30	7.29	0.8	11.6	99.1	...	...	-14.8	213.9	215.8	...	...	...	...
...	58.3	11.7	124.6	20.4	258.9	3.75	3.85	-1.9	13.8	86.2	...	...	-17.8	153.1	153.1	...	...	...	...
...	56.7	10.4	131.1	22.5	251.7	0.74	0.80	-2.6	9.2	131.9	...	...	47.2	226.6	226.6	...	...	...	...

Principal Lines of Business: Dental (100.0%) Principal States: AZ (100.0%)

464	73.3	-13.1	12.8	39.3	37.5	4.38	4.56	-3.2	1.0	43.8	...	36.3	-39.2	123.2	134.2	0.3	...	...	...
7	79.5	-12.9	11.4	30.6	33.2	4.43	4.33	13.3	0.8	61.1	...	22.4	42.9	141.9	151.5	0.0	...	...	...
-6	85.0	-13.7	12.5	36.0	30.7	4.74	4.57	-10.4	0.7	80.4	...	22.0	-1.8	137.3	148.5	...	...	...	...
-6	-99.9	437.6	23.6	475.3	48.2	4.90	5.52	-99.9	-0.1	237.5	6.2	219.4	-65.8	255.4	271.7	...	...	...	...
-8	52.9	-41.0	45.5	60.5	57.6	2.24	1.48	999.9	0.8	524.6	4.3	72.8	110.9	463.2	485.7	...	...	...	...

Principal Lines of Business: GrpA&H (76.4%), GrpAnn (23.6%) Principal States: FL (29.7%), CA (24.4%), TX (5.5%), IL (4.9%), CO (3.8%)

...	79.1	138.1	3.7	5.6	15.3	4.98	4.92	-37.7	1.2	38.4	...	282.3	-2.3	62.0	62.4	...	...	...	...
...	72.6	138.8	4.5	7.9	16.6	4.83	4.84	-23.9	0.8	35.3	...	208.7	4.7	154.4	154.8	...	...	...	...
...	67.4	139.0	5.3	9.9	19.3	4.13	4.13	-6.3	0.8	40.2	...	159.7	-1.9	168.6	174.4	...	...	...	...
...	88.2	67.7	2.7	4.7	6.3	2.10	2.10	3.3	0.8	298.3	...	30.7	7.3	568.6	569.9	...	...	...	...
...	52.0	138.9	3.2	15.8	4.3	1.24	1.24	-87.3	0.1	318.3	...	12.9	-20.8	695.4	697.1	...	...	...	...

Principal Lines of Business: CompHosp/Med (100.0%) Principal States: CO (100.0%)

...	84.7	9.4	20.4	4.3	42.8	4.80	4.79	63.3	8.1	99.5	...	0.2	55.7	117.5	127.4	...	...	...	...
...	84.7	12.7	11.9	2.5	22.8	6.01	6.01	15.9	9.0	123.1	...	...	5.0	154.8	169.1	...	...	...	...
...	81.6	14.0	12.7	4.1	20.3	5.74	5.74	-41.6	4.5	240.5	...	...	15.6	231.2	257.7	...	...	...	...
...	75.5	13.0	18.5	9.3	26.1	5.02	4.82	-49.5	3.5	242.8	...	...	-33.8	246.8	275.4	...	...	...	...
...	71.6	15.6	15.9	9.4	24.4	4.13	4.47	-40.1	3.3	140.1	...	...	-36.7	284.4	297.3	...	...	...	...

Principal Lines of Business: CompHosp/Med (100.0%) Principal States: VA (66.7%), MD (28.9%), DC (4.4%)

...	81.7	11.3	19.3	5.8	42.6	5.06	4.96	-29.3	7.7	83.0	...	0.2	-18.2	90.0	100.4	...	...	32.4	33.6
...	84.0	12.9	10.1	2.5	26.1	7.65	7.65	21.7	11.0	49.9	...	0.1	-15.2	73.9	82.7	...	...	36.0	37.9
...	87.1	9.6	9.0	2.3	25.3	6.65	6.62	-2.4	11.1	62.9	...	...	-3.6	72.7	84.0	...	...	36.1	38.1
...	88.5	7.8	13.6	3.3	33.1	7.77	7.79	-12.8	9.7	78.2	...	...	-0.2	85.2	95.5	...	...	33.5	35.5
...	90.8	6.1	13.9	3.4	30.0	4.27	4.27	1.0	7.7	94.2	...	...	27.2	95.3	104.5	...	...	37.7	37.7

Principal Lines of Business: Medicare (74.4%), CompHosp/Med (25.6%) Principal States: AZ (100.0%)

Data in U.S. Dollars

COMPANY NAME Ultimate Parent Association Principal Officer Mailing Address Dom. : Began Bus. : Struct. : Mktg. Specialty Phone # AMB# NAIC#	Best's Financial Strength Rating FSC	Data Year	Balance Sheet: Bonds (%)	Mort. Loans & R.E. (%)	Com & Pref. Stock (%)	All Other Assets (%)	Total Assets ($000)	Life Reserves (%)	Health Reserves %)	Ann Res. & Dep. Liabilities (%)	All Other Liabilities (%)	Capital & Surplus ($000)	Operations: Direct Premiums Written ($000)	Net Premiums Written & Deposits ($000)	Operating Cash Flow ($000)	NOG Before Taxes ($000)	NOG After Taxes ($000)	Net Income ($000)
CIGNA HEALTHCARE OF CA INC CIGNA Corporation Peter B. Welch President 900 Cottage Grove Road Hartford, CT 06152-2330 CA : 1978 : Stock : Broker Group A&H, Health 818-500-6284 AMB# 068912	A- Rating Outlook: Negative FSC VI	'05	...	...	...	100.0	217,292	...	...	...	100.0	67,506	229,936	229,936	-11,627	20,256	13,142	13,142
		'06	...	...	...	100.0	158,110	...	...	...	100.0	50,993	242,860	242,860	-27,088	3,399	3,102	3,102
		'07	...	...	...	100.0	160,095	...	...	...	100.0	49,772	293,394	293,394	246	-3,893	-1,723	-1,723
		'08	...	...	...	100.0	155,706	...	...	...	100.0	43,639	331,805	331,805	2,586	-12,021	-6,668	-6,668
		'09	...	...	...	100.0	155,390	...	...	...	100.0	42,065	788,558	788,558	-10,098	-20,363	-12,029	-12,029
		Rating History: A-, 01/08/10; A-, 11/14/08; A-, 02/11/08; A-, 12/14/06; A- g, 12/21/05																
CIGNA HEALTHCARE OF CO INC CIGNA Corporation Daryl W. Edmonds President 3900 East Mexico Avenue, Suite 1100 Denver, CO 80210 CO : 1986 : Stock : Broker Health 303-782-1500 AMB# 068864 NAIC# 95604	A- Rating Outlook: Negative FSC IV	'05	81.1	...	...	18.9	37,058	...	66.1	...	33.9	25,819	129,535	128,993	-11,512	7,596	5,328	5,095
		'06	69.0	...	...	31.0	29,789	...	61.1	...	38.9	20,239	121,047	120,865	-5,723	6,430	4,534	4,418
		'07	60.5	...	...	39.5	25,492	...	62.3	...	37.7	17,484	97,612	97,046	-4,674	3,142	2,260	2,260
		'08	87.5	...	...	12.5	18,697	...	51.2	...	48.8	14,522	46,499	45,908	-4,322	4,129	2,869	2,875
		'09	51.1	...	...	48.9	13,041	...	67.7	...	32.3	6,175	29,966	29,449	-5,978	-1,339	-774	-511
		Rating History: A-, 01/08/10; A-, 11/14/08; A-, 02/11/08; A-, 12/14/06; A- g, 12/21/05																
CIGNA HEALTHCARE OF CT INC CIGNA Corporation Donald M. Curry President 900 Cottage Grove Road Bloomfield, CT 06152 CT : 1986 : Stock : Broker Group A&H, Health 860-226-2300 AMB# 068865 NAIC# 95660	A- Rating Outlook: Negative FSC V	'05	56.0	...	...	44.0	21,291	...	39.2	...	60.8	10,096	72,710	72,351	-4,790	4,225	2,765	2,759
		'06	26.0	...	...	74.0	30,558	...	41.8	...	58.2	11,486	143,730	142,998	4,549	-1,941	-3,252	-3,198
		'07	56.7	...	...	43.3	28,973	...	50.3	...	49.7	14,964	144,292	143,717	3,064	5,658	3,984	3,981
		'08	78.2	...	...	21.8	25,272	...	47.4	...	52.6	14,013	91,269	89,887	-3,299	-1,893	-1,813	-1,850
		'09	85.0	...	...	15.0	21,894	...	52.4	...	47.6	10,670	69,526	67,788	-1,033	-3,290	-1,767	-1,767
		Rating History: A-, 01/08/10; A-, 11/14/08; A-, 02/11/08; A-, 12/14/06; A- g, 12/21/05																
CIGNA HEALTHCARE OF DE INC CIGNA Corporation Vincent J. Sobocinski, Jr. President 1777 Sentry Park West Blue Bell, PA 19422 DE : 1985 : Stock : Broker Group A&H, Health 215-283-3300 AMB# 068866 NAIC# 95544	NR-3	'05	61.3	...	4.0	34.7	2,496	...	51.6	...	48.4	2,093	549	547	149	248	216	216
		'06	92.5	...	...	7.5	1,776	...	16.8	...	83.2	1,307	615	614	-421	264	209	209
		'07	67.7	...	...	32.3	1,621	...	20.3	...	79.7	1,360	258	257	-147	59	28	44
		'08	59.7	...	...	40.3	1,664	...	0.6	...	99.4	1,494	102	100	54	172	142	142
		'09	58.3	...	...	41.7	1,707	...	...	...	100.0	1,556	18	18	38	70	61	61
		Rating History: NR-3, 01/08/10; NR-3, 11/14/08; A-, 02/11/08; A-, 12/14/06; A- g, 12/21/05																
CIGNA HEALTHCARE OF FL INC CIGNA Corporation Andrew D. Crooks President 900 Cottage Grove Road Bloomfield, CT 06152 FL : 1981 : Stock : Broker Group A&H, Health 860-353-4400 AMB# 068860 NAIC# 95136	A- Rating Outlook: Negative FSC V	'05	60.4	...	...	39.6	55,877	...	65.8	...	34.2	23,385	244,000	242,880	-11,684	9,736	6,701	6,645
		'06	80.4	...	...	19.6	50,240	...	69.5	...	30.5	22,853	254,145	253,723	402	-2,948	-2,527	-2,528
		'07	87.4	...	...	12.6	44,086	...	55.0	...	45.0	26,885	165,327	164,354	-1,203	4,312	4,051	4,038
		'08	94.4	...	...	5.6	29,160	...	35.6	...	64.4	17,262	58,291	57,519	-11,152	2,097	2,239	2,223
		'09	84.0	...	...	16.0	17,504	...	26.7	...	73.3	10,050	25,430	24,994	-10,875	3,566	2,814	3,028
		Rating History: A-, 01/08/10; A-, 11/14/08; A-, 02/11/08; A-, 12/14/06; A- g, 12/21/05																
CIGNA HEALTHCARE OF GA INC CIGNA Corporation Richard Seth Novack President 900 Cottage Grove Road Bloomfield, CT 06152 GA : 1985 : Stock : Broker Group A&H, Health 404-443-8800 AMB# 068753 NAIC# 96229	A- Rating Outlook: Negative FSC IV	'05	62.1	...	...	37.9	21,888	...	61.1	...	38.9	13,646	71,596	71,260	-6,042	3,865	2,764	3,052
		'06	70.1	...	...	29.9	19,339	...	49.1	...	50.9	12,845	72,468	72,344	-1,216	1,877	1,489	1,567
		'07	81.0	...	...	19.0	16,235	...	45.7	...	54.3	11,713	45,756	45,482	-698	3,143	2,362	2,362
		'08	77.5	...	...	22.5	13,327	...	35.7	...	64.3	10,582	20,083	19,845	-1,993	1,538	944	1,108
		'09	71.4	...	...	28.6	9,200	...	28.9	...	71.1	6,626	9,738	9,581	-3,844	1,163	917	1,015
		Rating History: A-, 01/08/10; A-, 11/14/08; A-, 02/11/08; A-, 12/14/06; A- g, 12/21/05																
CIGNA HEALTHCARE OF IL INC CIGNA Corporation Sue A. Podbielski President 900 Cottage Grove Road Bloomfield, CT 06152 IL : 2007 : Stock : Broker Group A&H, Health 312-648-2460 AMB# 068867 NAIC# 95602	A- Rating Outlook: Negative FSC III	'05	62.3	...	...	37.7	10,161	...	43.0	...	57.0	5,802	14,551	14,485	-350	715	344	344
		'06	57.0	...	...	43.0	10,900	...	36.0	...	64.0	6,602	14,882	14,857	1,446	1,381	1,068	1,068
		'07	62.2	...	...	37.8	9,880	...	34.3	...	65.7	7,764	11,030	10,969	-926	728	1,162	1,162
		'08	77.2	...	...	22.8	5,221	...	13.5	...	86.5	3,546	5,716	5,648	-4,146	1,020	718	726
		'09	69.4	...	...	30.6	4,249	...	12.4	...	87.6	2,909	2,741	2,697	-923	409	297	324
		Rating History: A-, 01/08/10; A-, 11/14/08; A-, 02/11/08; A-, 12/14/06; A- g, 12/21/05																
CIGNA HEALTHCARE OF IN INC CIGNA Corporation Sue A. Podbielski President 900 Cottage Grove Road Bloomfield, CT 06152 IN : 1986 : Stock : Broker Group A&H, Health 317-685-1133 AMB# 068536 NAIC# 95525	A- Rating Outlook: Negative FSC III	'05	80.9	...	...	19.1	13,817	...	69.8	...	30.2	5,781	53,927	53,716	-2,034	-2,723	-1,937	-1,926
		'06	50.0	...	...	50.0	11,696	...	74.3	...	25.7	6,320	45,239	45,183	-1,470	-2,058	-751	-766
		'07	60.5	...	...	39.5	11,579	...	59.5	...	40.5	7,712	30,323	30,194	1,327	1,700	1,492	1,492
		'08	82.6	...	...	17.4	8,406	...	40.6	...	59.4	6,377	13,425	13,271	-1,831	271	153	152
		'09	84.6	...	...	15.4	4,303	...	25.4	...	74.6	3,281	5,101	5,019	-3,888	194	187	381
		Rating History: A-, 01/08/10; A-, 11/14/08; A-, 02/11/08; A-, 12/14/06; A- g, 12/21/05																
CIGNA HEALTHCARE OF ME INC CIGNA Corporation Donald M. Curry President 900 Cottage Grove Road Bloomfield, CT 06152 ME : 1987 : Stock : Broker Health 215-761-1000 AMB# 068549 NAIC# 95447	A- Rating Outlook: Negative FSC IV	'05	80.3	...	...	19.7	20,826	...	52.7	...	47.3	11,079	64,539	64,284	-14,013	8,027	6,014	6,267
		'06	89.6	...	...	10.4	16,674	...	51.4	...	48.6	7,995	56,413	56,331	-3,589	97	-233	-233
		'07	77.0	...	...	23.0	13,438	...	50.0	...	50.0	10,297	30,417	30,255	-1,963	2,423	2,099	2,133
		'08	87.3	...	...	12.7	9,504	...	32.1	...	67.9	7,794	12,387	12,247	-3,401	2,676	1,933	1,981
		'09	65.8	...	...	34.2	10,111	...	11.1	...	88.9	8,860	3,160	3,109	503	1,451	1,071	1,071
		Rating History: A-, 01/08/10; A-, 11/14/08; A-, 02/11/08; A-, 12/14/06; A- g, 12/21/05																

2010 BEST'S KEY RATING GUIDE — LIFE/HEALTH EDITION
BEST'S PROFITABILITY, LEVERAGE AND LIQUIDITY TESTS 2005 – 2009
Data in U.S. Dollars

	Profitability Tests							Leverage Tests						Liquidity Tests					
Un-Realized Capital Gains ($000)	Benefits Paid to NPW & Dep (%)	Comm. & Expenses to NPW & Dep (%)	NOG to Total Assets (%)	NOG to Total Rev (%)	Operating Return on Equity (%)	Net Yield (%)	Total Return (%)	Change in NPW & Dep (%)	NPW & Dep to Capital (X)	Capital & Surplus to Liabilities (%)	Surplus Relief (%)	Reins Leverage (%)	Change in Capital (%)	Quick Liquidity (%)	Current Liquidity (%)	Non-Invest Grade Bonds to Capital (%)	Delinq. & Foreclosed Mortgages to Capital (%)	Mort. & Credit Tenant Loans & R.E. to Capital (%)	Affiliated Invest to Capital (%)
...	96.3	4.3	5.5	1.5	19.7	4.23	4.23	-9.1	3.4	45.1	...	...	2.4	78.1	78.1	...	...	...	...
...	96.3	6.5	1.7	0.4	5.2	3.70	3.70	5.6	4.8	47.6	...	...	-24.5	83.4	83.4	...	...	...	...
...	97.0	6.3	-1.1	-0.2	-3.4	4.17	4.17	20.8	5.9	45.1	...	...	-2.4	81.3	81.3	...	...	...	...
...	97.7	6.4	-4.2	-0.7	-14.3	3.69	3.69	13.1	7.6	38.9	...	...	-12.3	82.2	82.2	...	...	...	...
...	98.7	5.5	-7.7	-1.5	-28.1	3.03	3.03	137.7	18.7	37.1	...	...	-3.6	73.8	73.8	...	...	...	...
Principal Lines of Business: CompHosp/Med (100.0%)																			
...	86.3	9.1	12.1	4.1	20.4	4.23	3.63	-35.6	5.0	229.7	...	...	-1.9	233.8	260.1	...	...	...	...
...	84.0	12.0	13.6	3.7	19.7	5.35	4.96	-6.3	6.0	211.9	...	...	-21.6	328.7	350.8	...	...	...	...
...	86.2	11.8	8.2	2.3	12.0	5.25	5.25	-19.7	5.6	218.3	...	...	-13.6	340.9	361.8	...	...	...	...
...	79.3	13.5	13.0	6.1	17.9	4.42	4.45	-52.7	3.2	347.8	...	...	-16.9	358.8	398.0	...	...	...	...
...	91.7	14.6	-4.9	-2.6	-7.5	4.40	6.26	-35.9	4.8	89.9	...	...	-57.5	209.3	219.0	...	...	...	...
Principal Lines of Business: CompHosp/Med (100.0%)													Principal States: CO (100.0%)						
...	82.8	12.8	11.9	3.8	23.8	5.32	5.29	-10.0	7.2	90.2	...	10.8	-23.1	125.9	136.6	...	...	...	...
...	86.7	15.5	-12.5	-2.3	-30.1	6.30	6.59	97.6	12.4	60.2	...	...	13.8	182.3	195.3	...	...	...	...
...	82.3	14.1	13.4	2.7	30.1	5.70	5.69	0.5	9.6	106.8	...	3.4	30.3	212.6	226.1	...	...	...	...
...	86.9	15.5	-6.7	-2.0	-12.5	4.16	4.00	-37.5	6.4	124.5	...	1.8	-6.4	159.8	177.3	...	...	...	...
...	91.4	15.3	-7.5	-2.6	-14.3	4.02	4.02	-24.6	6.4	95.1	...	1.5	-23.9	152.0	168.5	...	...	...	...
Principal Lines of Business: CompHosp/Med (85.7%), Dental (14.3%)													Principal States: CT (100.0%)						
...	58.1	14.4	8.7	33.5	10.8	4.78	4.78	-25.2	0.3	519.5	...	...	9.3	421.6	459.6	...	...	...	...
...	70.3	7.1	9.8	28.3	12.3	6.61	6.61	12.1	0.5	278.6	...	...	-37.6	307.2	341.5	...	...	...	...
...	85.0	24.0	1.6	8.2	2.1	4.99	5.96	-58.2	0.2	520.7	...	...	4.0	549.6	592.0	...	...	...	...
...	-22.9	15.5	8.7	86.5	10.0	4.01	4.01	-60.9	0.1	879.9	...	...	9.9	999.9	999.9	...	...	...	...
...	-10.2	24.7	3.6	84.8	4.0	3.31	3.31	-82.3	0.0	999.9	...	...	4.1	999.9	999.9	...	...	...	...
Principal Lines of Business: CompHosp/Med (100.0%)													Principal States: DE (100.0%)						
...	87.0	9.9	11.1	2.7	26.7	4.76	4.64	2.1	10.4	72.0	...	0.6	-12.9	90.6	104.5	...	...	...	...
...	87.1	14.2	-4.8	-1.0	-10.9	7.32	7.31	4.5	11.1	83.4	...	0.2	-2.3	126.0	145.8	...	...	...	...
...	86.2	13.4	8.6	2.4	16.3	5.50	5.47	-35.2	6.1	156.3	...	...	17.6	178.6	206.6	...	...	...	...
...	85.7	14.4	6.1	3.8	10.1	4.66	4.61	-65.0	3.3	145.1	...	...	-35.8	185.3	208.6	...	...	...	...
...	76.2	14.6	12.1	10.9	20.6	4.04	5.00	-56.5	2.5	134.8	...	...	-41.8	216.0	235.7	...	...	...	...
Principal Lines of Business: CompHosp/Med (100.0%)													Principal States: FL (100.0%)						
...	86.5	9.6	10.8	3.8	18.5	5.72	7.19	-2.1	5.2	165.6	...	...	-16.0	157.1	173.6	...	...	...	...
...	84.9	14.0	7.2	2.0	11.2	7.00	7.49	1.5	5.6	197.8	...	0.1	-5.9	219.3	244.3	...	...	...	...
...	81.9	13.3	13.3	5.1	19.2	6.69	6.69	-37.1	3.9	259.0	...	...	-8.8	294.6	327.9	...	...	...	...
...	82.7	13.3	6.4	4.6	8.5	5.69	6.92	-56.4	1.9	385.5	...	...	-9.7	456.0	493.6	...	...	...	...
...	74.1	16.6	8.1	9.1	10.7	4.65	5.58	-51.7	1.4	257.4	...	...	-37.4	349.9	375.4	...	...	...	...
Principal Lines of Business: CompHosp/Med (100.0%)													Principal States: GA (100.0%)						
...	86.1	12.1	3.3	2.3	5.5	3.57	3.57	-1.1	2.5	133.1	...	0.6	-12.9	172.4	185.5	...	...	...	...
...	80.4	12.9	10.1	7.0	17.2	4.15	4.15	2.6	2.3	153.6	...	...	13.8	254.8	267.9	...	...	...	...
...	82.8	14.0	11.2	10.2	16.2	3.86	3.86	-26.2	1.4	366.9	...	...	17.6	554.5	580.7	...	...	...	...
...	68.2	17.7	9.5	12.2	12.7	3.14	3.25	-48.5	1.6	211.7	...	...	-54.3	336.4	356.8	...	...	...	...
...	76.4	12.9	6.3	10.5	9.2	2.68	3.27	-52.2	0.9	217.0	...	...	-18.0	352.3	369.6	...	...	...	...
Principal Lines of Business: CompHosp/Med (100.0%)													Principal States: IL (96.3%), IN (3.7%)						
...	98.8	7.5	-12.5	-3.6	-30.8	4.90	5.00	-8.6	9.3	71.9	...	...	-15.1	94.7	108.0	...	...	...	...
...	98.4	9.5	-5.9	-1.6	-12.4	4.24	4.09	-15.9	7.1	117.6	...	...	9.3	201.9	219.1	...	...	...	...
...	89.0	8.3	12.8	4.9	21.3	5.22	5.23	-33.2	3.9	199.4	...	...	22.0	306.8	325.3	...	...	...	...
...	90.1	10.3	1.5	1.1	2.2	3.64	3.63	-56.0	2.1	314.4	...	...	-17.3	394.5	426.0	...	...	...	...
...	86.4	14.2	2.9	3.6	3.9	3.74	6.91	-62.2	1.5	321.1	...	...	-48.6	417.0	447.2	...	...	...	...
Principal Lines of Business: CompHosp/Med (100.0%)													Principal States: IN (100.0%)						
...	81.3	8.4	21.2	9.2	34.6	5.88	6.89	-26.0	5.8	113.7	...	...	-53.3	148.3	165.4	...	...	...	...
...	89.6	10.5	-1.2	-0.4	-2.4	6.26	6.26	-12.4	7.0	92.1	...	...	-27.8	138.8	157.5	...	...	...	...
...	83.0	14.1	13.9	6.8	23.0	5.48	5.73	-46.3	2.9	327.9	...	...	28.8	392.2	430.5	...	...	...	...
...	66.8	15.9	16.9	15.1	21.4	5.29	5.74	-59.5	1.6	455.9	...	...	-24.3	472.1	520.6	...	...	...	...
...	53.5	13.5	10.9	30.3	12.9	4.65	4.64	-74.6	0.4	708.6	...	...	13.7	876.4	929.6	...	...	...	...
Principal Lines of Business: CompHosp/Med (100.0%)													Principal States: ME (100.0%)						

2010 BEST'S KEY RATING GUIDE — LIFE/HEALTH EDITION
ANNUAL STATEMENT DATA FOR YEARS 2005 – 2009

Data in U.S. Dollars

COMPANY NAME / Ultimate Parent Association / Principal Officer / Mailing Address / Dom. : Began Bus. : Struct. : Mktg. / Specialty / Phone # / AMB# NAIC#	Best's Financial Strength Rating / FSC	Data Year	Balance Sheet: Bonds (%)	Mort. Loans & R.E. (%)	Com & Pref. Stock (%)	All Other Assets (%)	Total Assets ($000)	Life Reserves (%)	Health Reserves %)	Ann Res. & Dep. Liabilities (%)	All Other Liabilities (%)	Capital & Surplus ($000)	Operations: Direct Premiums Written ($000)	Net Premiums Written & Deposits ($000)	Operating Cash Flow ($000)	NOG Before Taxes ($000)	NOG After Taxes ($000)	Net Income ($000)
CIGNA HEALTHCARE OF MA INC CIGNA Corporation	A-	'05	86.7	...	...	13.3	28,519	...	63.4	...	36.6	22,932	38,204	38,051	-574	8,432	6,419	6,448
Donald M. Curry President & Chairman of the Board		'06	80.9	...	...	19.1	15,072	...	51.8	...	48.2	11,283	32,283	32,236	-12,822	1,795	1,279	1,419
2223 Washington Street, Suite 200 Newton, MA 02462	Rating Outlook: Negative	'07	73.4	...	...	26.6	13,800	...	61.9	...	38.1	12,066	20,926	20,820	191	325	572	564
MA : 1996 : Stock : Broker Health		'08	55.6	...	...	44.4	7,294	...	31.6	...	68.4	4,825	13,229	13,099	-7,140	95	134	166
508-849-4311		'09	17.9	...	...	82.1	5,812	...	27.5	...	72.5	3,522	8,887	8,771	-341	578	264	265
AMB# 060201 NAIC# 95520	FSC III	Rating History: A-, 01/08/10; A-, 11/14/08; A-, 02/11/08; A-, 12/14/06; A- g, 12/21/05																
CIGNA HEALTHCARE OF NH INC CIGNA Corporation	A-	'05	88.9	...	...	11.1	54,639	...	49.3	...	50.7	31,354	157,713	157,139	-10,799	8,530	5,802	5,952
Donald M. Curry President		'06	92.0	...	...	8.0	43,132	...	50.4	...	49.6	24,075	138,784	138,596	-10,684	-4,827	-2,578	-2,498
2 College Park Drive Hooksett, NH 03106	Rating Outlook: Negative	'07	97.7	...	...	2.3	31,183	...	59.1	...	40.9	18,805	100,857	100,353	-10,340	-7,851	-4,612	-4,512
NH : 1985 : Stock : Broker Health		'08	92.9	...	...	7.1	23,449	...	48.0	...	52.0	18,421	52,958	52,083	-6,174	-1,070	13	39
603-268-7000		'09	48.1	...	...	51.9	16,609	...	45.8	...	54.2	14,142	13,898	13,853	-7,067	532	618	618
AMB# 068675 NAIC# 95493	FSC V	Rating History: A-, 01/08/10; A-, 11/14/08; A-, 02/11/08; A-, 12/14/06; A- g, 12/21/05																
CIGNA HEALTHCARE OF NJ INC CIGNA Corporation	A-	'05	77.0	...	...	23.0	80,754	...	63.0	...	37.0	52,265	181,078	180,278	-1,177	18,450	13,600	13,603
Charles R. Catalano President		'06	85.5	...	...	14.5	66,047	...	30.8	...	69.2	35,807	149,122	148,800	-10,626	2,183	6,429	6,451
900 Cottage Grove Road Bloomfield, CT 06152	Rating Outlook: Negative	'07	87.3	...	...	12.7	42,798	...	46.1	...	53.9	33,407	76,688	75,952	-18,165	-8,006	-3,281	-3,141
NJ : 1988 : Stock : Broker Group A&H, Health		'08	78.5	...	...	21.5	33,783	...	37.1	...	62.9	27,736	39,479	38,636	-6,589	-3,595	-1,946	-1,956
201-533-5001		'09	79.8	...	...	20.2	20,522	...	19.5	...	80.5	16,648	12,317	12,008	-10,869	-2,370	-1,563	-1,566
AMB# 068862 NAIC# 95500	FSC V	Rating History: A-, 01/08/10; A-, 11/14/08; A-, 02/11/08; A-, 12/14/06; A- g, 12/21/05																
CIGNA HEALTHCARE OF NY INC CIGNA Corporation	A-	'05	55.1	...	...	44.9	61,204	...	53.9	...	46.1	35,002	131,881	131,365	-23,993	11,660	13,876	14,381
Charles R. Catalano President		'06	74.3	...	...	25.7	50,530	...	48.9	...	51.1	30,351	117,375	117,232	6,966	-6,884	-7,173	-7,173
900 Cottage Grove Road Bloomfield, CT 06152	Rating Outlook: Negative	'07	75.4	...	...	24.6	30,460	...	62.4	...	37.6	15,758	79,884	79,509	-16,669	1,308	1,558	2,073
NJ : 1986 : Stock : Broker Group A&H, Health		'08	81.5	...	...	18.5	27,928	...	48.2	...	51.8	17,186	50,105	49,624	-1,888	2,088	2,033	2,033
201-533-7000		'09	81.7	...	...	18.3	27,335	...	33.9	...	66.1	22,431	2,649	2,612	3,444	-29	478	478
AMB# 068872 NAIC# 95488	FSC V	Rating History: A-, 01/08/10; A-, 11/14/08; A-, 02/11/08; A-, 12/14/06; A- g, 12/21/05																
CIGNA HEALTHCARE OF NC INC CIGNA Corporation	A-	'05	81.5	...	...	18.5	65,123	...	70.5	...	29.5	40,582	241,235	240,156	-17,813	16,756	11,689	11,938
Charles C. Pitts President		'06	81.9	...	...	18.1	51,742	...	60.1	...	39.9	33,947	230,248	229,874	-9,767	10,549	7,389	7,384
701 Corporate Center Drive Raleigh, NC 27607	Rating Outlook: Negative	'07	84.6	...	...	15.4	45,643	...	53.8	...	46.2	33,335	164,823	163,897	-1,857	11,189	7,825	7,825
NC : 1986 : Stock : Broker Group A&H, Health		'08	70.8	...	...	29.2	30,799	...	53.4	...	46.6	22,924	99,491	98,323	-13,542	9,567	6,604	6,439
919-854-7469		'09	76.7	...	...	23.3	19,112	...	33.7	...	66.3	11,508	69,220	68,135	-10,403	3,881	2,707	2,882
AMB# 068570 NAIC# 95132	FSC V	Rating History: A-, 01/08/10; A-, 11/14/08; A-, 02/11/08; A-, 12/14/06; A- g, 12/21/05																
CIGNA HEALTHCARE OF OH INC CIGNA Corporation	A-	'05	77.9	...	...	22.1	14,630	...	12.9	...	87.1	7,641	12,734	12,668	1,506	2,925	2,019	2,019
Joseph C. Gregor President		'06	74.5	...	...	25.5	8,544	...	31.6	...	68.4	3,686	16,100	16,071	-6,429	-8	85	86
900 Cottage Grove Road Bloomfield, CT 06152	Rating Outlook: Negative	'07	88.5	...	...	11.5	6,598	...	18.4	...	81.6	3,040	11,479	11,409	-1,124	854	649	656
OH : 1986 : Stock : Broker Group A&H, Health		'08	83.5	...	...	16.5	6,988	...	15.0	...	85.0	3,427	7,677	7,575	306	491	450	450
216-642-8969		'09	82.9	...	...	17.1	7,023	...	16.4	...	83.6	3,634	6,058	5,954	347	245	230	230
AMB# 068788 NAIC# 95209	FSC III	Rating History: A-, 01/08/10; A-, 11/14/08; A-, 02/11/08; A-, 12/14/06; A- g, 12/21/05																
CIGNA HEALTHCARE OF PA INC CIGNA Corporation	NR-3	'05	83.9	...	...	16.1	3,918	...	62.0	...	38.0	2,995	3,053	3,040	-654	171	151	154
Vincent J. Sobocinski, Jr. President		'06	84.1	...	...	15.9	3,836	...	35.5	...	64.5	3,276	2,721	2,717	-94	552	382	382
1777 Sentry Park West Blue Bell, PA 19422		'07	94.6	...	...	5.4	3,345	...	33.0	...	67.0	2,853	2,165	2,153	-428	152	149	149
PA : 1987 : Stock : Broker Group A&H, Health		'08	89.7	...	2.3	8.0	3,458	...	34.3	...	65.7	3,199	1,596	1,581	197	471	347	347
215-283-3300		'09	75.9	...	16.2	8.0	2,789	...	...	...	100.0	2,598	43	42	-526	73	58	84
AMB# 068876 NAIC# 95121		Rating History: NR-3, 01/08/10; A-, 11/14/08; A-, 02/11/08; A-, 12/14/06; A- g, 12/21/05																
CIGNA HEALTHCARE OF ST LOU INC CIGNA Corporation	A-	'05	64.1	...	...	35.9	7,048	...	59.8	...	40.2	4,982	16,193	16,129	-2,425	2,156	1,547	1,536
Frank Monahan President		'06	76.2	...	...	23.8	5,078	...	47.1	...	52.9	3,052	16,101	16,077	-1,701	1,438	993	993
900 Cottage Grove Road Bloomfield, CT 06002	Rating Outlook: Negative	'07	31.2	...	...	68.8	5,423	...	40.8	...	59.2	3,641	14,714	14,639	18	628	414	421
MO : 1986 : Stock : Broker Group A&H, Health		'08	34.8	...	...	65.2	4,523	...	22.7	...	77.3	3,883	1,809	1,783	520	329	287	287
314-726-5625		'09	34.8	...	...	65.2	2,084	...	17.9	...	82.1	1,502	2,009	1,973	-2,288	132	91	92
AMB# 068877 NAIC# 95635	FSC II	Rating History: A-, 01/08/10; A-, 11/14/08; A-, 02/11/08; A-, 12/14/06; A- g, 12/21/05																
CIGNA HEALTHCARE OF SC INC CIGNA Corporation	A-	'05	74.1	...	...	25.9	29,161	...	63.6	...	36.4	18,488	84,221	83,824	-1,335	2,325	2,950	2,950
Charles C. Pitts President		'06	87.4	...	...	12.6	22,340	...	57.8	...	42.2	11,929	92,856	92,690	-7,047	-1,770	-1,088	-1,088
4000 Faber Place Drive, Suite 220 Charleston, SC 29405	Rating Outlook: Negative	'07	69.5	...	...	30.5	20,814	...	48.5	...	51.5	11,406	68,073	67,659	-205	-1,576	-724	-745
SC : 1987 : Stock : Broker Group A&H, Health		'08	87.5	...	...	12.5	14,450	...	44.3	...	55.7	9,081	39,414	38,907	-5,452	221	364	351
800-962-8811		'09	86.4	...	...	13.6	11,590	...	46.6	...	53.4	7,810	26,833	26,405	-2,309	526	400	506
AMB# 068594 NAIC# 95708	FSC IV	Rating History: A-, 01/08/10; A-, 11/14/08; A-, 02/11/08; A-, 12/14/06; A- g, 12/21/05																

BEST'S PROFITABILITY, LEVERAGE AND LIQUIDITY TESTS 2005 – 2009

Data in U.S. Dollars

	Profitability Tests							Leverage Tests						Liquidity Tests					
Un-Realized Capital Gains ($000)	Benefits Paid to NPW & Dep (%)	Comm. & Expenses to NPW & Dep (%)	NOG to Total Assets (%)	NOG to Total Rev (%)	Operating Return on Equity (%)	Net Yield (%)	Total Return (%)	Change in NPW & Dep (%)	NPW & Dep to Capital (X)	Capital & Surplus to Liabilities (%)	Surplus Relief (%)	Reins Leverage (%)	Change in Capital (%)	Quick Liquidity (%)	Current Liquidity (%)	Non-Invest Grade Bonds to Capital (%)	Delinq. & Foreclosed Mortgages to Capital (%)	Mort. & Credit Tenant Loans & R.E. to Capital (%)	Affiliated Invest to Capital (%)
...	74.3	8.7	22.6	16.4	32.5	4.70	4.81	-41.4	1.7	410.5	...	...	38.1	365.3	409.6	...	...	...	...
...	84.8	13.2	5.9	3.8	7.5	6.25	6.99	-15.3	2.9	297.8	...	...	-50.8	303.7	338.4	...	...	...	...
...	88.6	12.9	4.0	2.7	4.9	5.10	5.04	-35.4	1.7	695.7	...	...	6.9	750.7	820.6	...	...	...	...
...	89.4	12.4	1.3	1.0	1.6	3.72	4.06	-37.1	2.7	195.5	...	...	-60.0	263.3	279.8	...	...	...	...
...	75.7	16.9	4.0	3.0	6.3	2.07	2.10	-33.0	2.5	153.9	...	...	-27.0	389.4	393.9	...	...	...	...
Principal Lines of Business: CompHosp/Med (100.0%)													Principal States: MA (100.0%)						
...	85.6	11.0	9.6	3.6	16.4	5.47	5.73	-16.0	5.0	134.6	...	0.0	-20.7	147.6	183.5	...	...	2.3	...
...	90.2	14.2	-5.3	-1.8	-9.3	5.62	5.80	-11.8	5.8	126.3	...	1.3	-23.2	140.9	180.4	...	...	...	...
...	94.7	14.7	-12.4	-4.5	-21.5	5.60	5.89	-27.6	5.3	151.9	...	...	-21.9	140.0	187.1	5.3	...	...	...
...	91.2	16.4	0.0	0.0	0.1	5.72	5.82	-48.1	2.8	366.4	...	0.1	-2.0	339.3	423.4	...	...	...	...
...	88.2	14.8	3.1	4.2	3.8	4.66	4.66	-73.4	1.0	573.3	...	0.3	-23.2	771.8	856.7	...	...	...	...
Principal Lines of Business: CompHosp/Med (100.0%)													Principal States: NH (100.0%)						
...	80.5	10.9	17.0	7.4	28.3	4.89	4.90	-6.2	3.4	183.5	...	0.7	18.8	188.3	210.1	...	...	...	...
...	84.7	15.9	8.8	4.2	14.6	5.27	5.30	-17.5	4.2	118.4	...	...	-31.5	158.6	178.4	...	...	...	...
...	96.9	17.4	-6.0	-4.2	-9.5	4.77	5.07	-49.0	2.3	355.7	...	...	-6.7	361.5	403.6	...	...	...	...
...	95.9	17.8	-5.1	-4.8	-6.4	5.04	5.01	-49.1	1.4	458.6	...	...	-17.0	532.8	576.6	...	...	...	...
...	92.0	36.1	-5.8	-12.0	-7.0	3.98	3.97	-68.9	0.7	429.7	...	...	-40.0	559.7	602.0	...	...	...	...
Principal Lines of Business: CompHosp/Med (100.0%)													Principal States: NJ (100.0%)						
...	85.1	9.3	21.5	10.4	50.6	5.04	6.12	-8.7	3.8	133.6	...	7.0	76.2	99.2	112.0	...	...	...	...
...	93.9	13.4	-12.8	-6.0	-22.0	5.24	5.24	-10.8	3.9	150.4	...	0.4	-13.3	181.8	202.9	...	...	...	...
...	90.0	11.4	3.8	1.9	6.8	4.75	6.30	-32.2	5.0	107.2	...	...	-48.1	154.2	171.9	...	...	...	...
...	89.3	9.0	7.0	4.0	12.3	5.31	5.31	-37.6	2.9	160.0	...	...	9.1	175.3	196.5	...	...	...	...
...	99.2	65.0	1.7	12.7	2.4	4.66	4.66	-94.7	0.1	457.4	...	...	30.5	518.7	564.2	...	...	...	...
Principal Lines of Business: CompHosp/Med (100.0%)													Principal States: NY (100.0%)						
...	83.5	11.0	15.4	4.8	25.2	5.80	6.20	-13.5	5.9	165.4	...	0.8	-22.3	160.5	188.0	...	...	1.8	...
...	82.6	14.4	12.6	3.2	19.8	6.48	6.47	-4.3	6.8	190.8	...	...	-16.3	206.3	241.2	...	...	...	...
...	80.4	14.4	16.1	4.7	23.3	6.60	6.60	-28.7	4.9	270.8	...	...	-1.8	292.0	337.0	...	...	...	...
...	77.8	14.4	17.3	6.6	23.5	5.62	5.14	-40.0	4.3	291.1	...	...	-31.2	349.7	394.2	...	...	...	...
...	81.9	13.9	10.8	3.9	15.7	4.82	5.59	-30.7	5.9	151.3	...	...	-49.8	229.5	258.3	...	...	...	...
Principal Lines of Business: CompHosp/Med (100.0%)													Principal States: NC (100.0%)						
...	67.4	13.5	14.5	15.3	26.7	4.38	4.38	-11.3	1.7	109.3	...	...	1.9	156.1	172.0	...	...	...	...
...	88.0	16.0	0.7	0.5	1.5	5.29	5.30	26.9	4.4	75.9	...	...	-51.8	148.6	164.1	...	...	...	...
...	81.7	14.4	8.6	5.5	19.3	6.07	6.17	-29.0	3.8	85.4	...	...	-17.5	152.2	169.0	...	...	...	...
...	81.9	15.6	6.6	5.7	13.9	5.28	5.28	-33.6	2.2	96.3	...	...	12.7	176.0	191.5	...	...	...	...
...	83.1	18.5	3.3	3.7	6.5	4.72	4.72	-21.4	1.6	107.3	...	...	6.0	205.7	221.9	...	...	...	...
Principal Lines of Business: CompHosp/Med (100.0%)													Principal States: MO (52.0%), KS (48.0%)						
...	89.3	9.0	3.5	4.8	5.2	3.32	3.40	-28.4	1.0	324.5	...	...	7.0	320.5	355.0	...	...	...	...
...	72.2	12.2	9.9	13.4	12.2	3.45	3.45	-10.6	0.8	584.4	...	...	9.4	623.8	687.7	...	...	...	...
...	85.2	13.7	4.2	6.5	4.9	3.78	3.78	-20.8	0.8	579.0	...	...	-12.9	550.6	612.9	...	...	...	...
...	65.5	11.4	10.2	20.6	11.5	3.27	3.27	-26.6	0.5	999.9	...	...	12.1	999.9	999.9	...	...	...	...
...	43.9	98.3	1.9	43.9	2.0	3.04	3.88	-97.3	0.0	999.9	...	...	-18.8	999.9	999.9	...	...	...	...
Principal Lines of Business: CompHosp/Med (100.0%)													Principal States: PA (100.0%)						
...	82.4	6.5	18.0	9.4	26.0	5.75	5.59	-19.9	3.2	241.2	...	...	-28.0	294.9	315.7	...	...	...	...
...	81.8	11.2	16.4	6.1	24.7	7.43	7.43	-0.3	5.3	150.6	...	...	-38.7	165.5	184.2	...	...	...	...
...	87.4	9.8	7.9	2.8	12.4	6.20	6.41	-8.9	4.0	204.4	...	...	19.3	253.7	267.0	...	...	...	...
...	71.5	17.4	5.8	15.0	7.6	3.27	3.27	-87.8	0.5	606.9	...	...	6.6	999.9	999.9	...	...	...	...
...	77.9	17.8	2.8	4.5	3.4	1.54	1.57	10.7	1.3	258.1	...	...	-61.3	536.6	536.6	...	...	...	...
Principal Lines of Business: CompHosp/Med (100.0%)													Principal States: MO (80.0%), IL (20.0%)						
...	89.0	12.8	9.5	3.5	16.7	4.14	4.14	0.1	4.5	173.2	...	0.4	10.3	200.1	220.3	...	...	...	...
...	86.5	17.4	-4.2	-1.2	-7.2	5.17	5.17	10.6	7.8	114.6	...	0.8	-35.5	148.2	168.0	...	...	...	...
...	86.7	17.2	-3.4	-1.1	-6.2	4.78	4.66	-27.0	5.9	121.2	...	...	-4.4	213.1	230.2	...	...	...	...
...	82.5	18.9	2.1	0.9	3.6	3.71	3.64	-42.5	4.3	169.1	...	...	-20.4	213.4	237.0	...	...	...	...
...	82.4	17.8	3.1	1.5	4.7	3.79	4.67	-32.1	3.4	206.6	...	...	-14.0	261.9	288.4	...	...	...	...
Principal Lines of Business: CompHosp/Med (100.0%)													Principal States: SC (100.0%)						

Data in U.S. Dollars

COMPANY NAME Ultimate Parent Association Principal Officer Mailing Address Dom. : Began Bus. : Struct. : Mktg. Specialty Phone # AMB# NAIC#	Best's Financial Strength Rating FSC	Data Year	Balance Sheet Bonds (%)	Mort. Loans & R.E. (%)	Com & Pref. Stock (%)	All Other Assets (%)	Total Assets ($000)	Life Reserves (%)	Health Reserves (%)	Ann Res. & Dep. Liabilities (%)	All Other Liabilities (%)	Capital & Surplus ($000)	Operations Direct Premiums Written ($000)	Net Premiums Written & Deposits ($000)	Operating Cash Flow ($000)	NOG Before Taxes ($000)	NOG After Taxes ($000)	Net Income ($000)
CIGNA HEALTHCARE OF TN INC CIGNA Corporation	**A-**	'05	79.1	...	...	20.9	46,905	...	61.9	...	38.1	23,954	214,682	213,684	-8,012	12,454	8,647	8,647
John W. Sorrow President		'06	78.2	...	...	21.8	44,559	...	71.2	...	28.8	19,234	257,125	256,672	-4,699	-14,650	-10,434	-10,434
900 Cottage Grove Road Bloomfield, CT 06152	Rating Outlook: Negative	'07	69.7	...	...	30.3	44,915	...	55.5	...	44.5	22,982	248,105	246,628	4,847	6,235	5,141	5,141
TN : 1985 : Stock : Broker		'08	83.3	...	...	16.7	39,041	...	57.0	...	43.0	27,961	106,879	105,389	-4,405	6,047	4,248	4,253
Group A&H, Health 860-226-8610		'09	58.6	...	...	41.4	29,971	...	44.2	...	55.8	19,539	94,975	94,975	-9,245	6,660	4,409	4,612
AMB# 068878 NAIC# 95606	**FSC V**	**Rating History: A-, 01/08/10; A-, 11/14/08; A-, 02/11/08; A-, 12/14/06; A- g, 12/21/05**																
CIGNA HEALTHCARE OF TX INC CIGNA Corporation	**A-**	'05	59.0	...	...	41.0	83,448	...	52.3	...	47.7	54,450	260,480	229,690	602	24,270	16,736	16,780
David W. Toomey President		'06	65.4	...	...	34.6	68,666	...	39.5	...	60.5	43,318	251,687	224,085	-9,852	5,958	4,428	4,428
900 Cottage Grove Road Bloomfield, CT 06002	Rating Outlook: Negative	'07	71.4	...	...	28.6	63,602	...	47.5	...	52.5	36,682	242,811	218,687	-1,000	6,468	4,798	4,535
TX : 1980 : Stock : Broker		'08	87.2	...	...	12.8	54,551	...	51.0	...	49.0	36,104	206,081	202,166	-3,077	9,065	6,653	6,777
Health 713-552-7802		'09	76.5	...	...	23.5	52,920	...	35.5	...	64.5	33,593	136,713	134,551	-4,350	3,151	2,431	2,616
AMB# 068828 NAIC# 95383	**FSC VI**	**Rating History: A-, 01/08/10; A-, 11/14/08; A-, 02/11/08; A-, 12/14/06; A- g, 12/21/05**																
CIGNA HEALTHCARE OF UT INC CIGNA Corporation	**A-**	'05	58.9	...	...	41.1	5,746	...	29.4	...	70.6	3,637	7,102	7,059	-1,030	612	402	402
Daryl W. Edmonds President		'06	56.5	...	...	43.5	4,179	...	22.6	...	77.4	2,316	5,560	5,548	-974	178	190	190
900 Cottage Grove Road, C5FIN Hartford, CT 06152	Rating Outlook: Negative	'07	54.8	...	...	45.2	4,292	...	24.6	...	75.4	2,371	4,194	4,161	-12	49	54	54
UT : 1986 : Stock : Broker		'08	54.3	...	...	45.7	4,308	...	37.8	...	62.2	2,178	3,199	3,148	89	-341	-387	-387
Health 801-265-2777		'09	14.5	...	...	85.5	4,049	...	8.7	...	91.3	2,535	2,220	2,175	76	518	549	550
AMB# 068881 NAIC# 95518	**FSC III**	**Rating History: A-, 01/08/10; A-, 11/14/08; A-, 02/11/08; A-, 12/14/06; A- g, 12/21/05**																
CIGNA HEALTHCARE - PACIFIC INC CIGNA Corporation	**A-**	'05	...	...	...	100.0	48,058	...	...	...	100.0	16,148	160,438	160,438	7,076	10,423	6,012	6,012
Susan W. Hallett President		'06	...	...	...	100.0	63,872	...	...	...	100.0	23,028	180,991	180,991	15,636	27,233	16,032	16,032
8505 East Orchard Road Greenwood Village, CO 80111	Rating Outlook: Negative	'07	...	...	...	100.0	75,443	...	...	...	100.0	43,788	171,700	171,700	243,478	34,235	20,347	20,347
CA : 1996 : Stock : Broker		'08	...	...	...	100.0	46,781	...	...	...	100.0	17,043	127,355	127,355	-34,080	29,102	17,246	17,246
Group A&H 818-500-6742		'09	...	...	...	100.0	39,576	...	...	...	100.0	19,037	84,631	84,631	-7,047	16,941	10,746	10,746
AMB# 064023 NAIC# 95379	**FSC V**	**Rating History: A-, 01/08/10; A-, 11/14/08; A-, 11/27/07; A, 06/22/07; A u, 02/01/07**																
CIGNA INSURANCE GROUP INC CIGNA Corporation	**NR-3**	'05	48.5	...	...	51.5	2,102	...	73.9	...	26.1	1,934	26	25	51	159	119	119
Donald M. Curry President		'06	46.6	...	...	53.4	2,178	...	16.5	...	83.5	2,105	10	10	82	219	161	161
900 Cottage Grove Road Bloomfield, CT 06152-1228		'07	45.3	...	...	54.7	2,230	...	16.4	...	83.6	2,199	11	11	65	117	92	92
NH : 1990 : Stock : Not Available		'08	44.3	...	...	55.7	2,272	...	...	...	100.0	2,264	0	0	47	75	64	64
Health 603-268-7000		'09	43.3	...	...	56.7	2,313	...	...	...	100.0	2,313	...	...	45	52	49	49
AMB# 068124 NAIC# 87980		**Rating History: NR-3, 01/08/10; NR-3, 11/14/08; A-, 02/11/08; A-, 12/14/06; A- g, 12/21/05**																
CIGNA LIFE INS CO OF NEW YORK CIGNA Corporation	**A**	'05	91.2	...	0.0	8.8	362,683	4.6	88.6	...	6.8	83,058	1,212,773	91,881	5,098	26,207	18,773	17,518
Karen S. Rohan President		'06	91.4	...	...	8.6	373,509	4.6	86.0	0.9	8.5	78,729	88,313	100,794	12,297	22,314	14,591	13,286
Two Liberty Place Philadelphia, PA 19192-2362	Rating Outlook: Negative	'07	90.0	...	...	10.0	381,697	5.1	89.4	1.6	3.8	85,420	109,109	115,746	4,718	22,155	15,318	16,344
NY : 1965 : Stock : Agency		'08	88.9	...	...	11.1	401,175	5.8	85.1	2.4	6.6	100,020	122,118	123,034	27,766	49,627	33,692	25,752
Dis inc, Group A&H, Group Life 215-761-1000		'09	92.6	...	...	7.4	388,041	6.3	86.4	3.5	3.9	97,194	130,007	124,143	-7,539	26,137	15,725	15,523
AMB# 006538 NAIC# 64548	**FSC XV**	**Rating History: A g, 01/08/10; A g, 11/14/08; A g, 02/11/08; A g, 12/14/06; A- g, 12/21/05**																
CIGNA WORLDWIDE INSURANCE CO CIGNA Corporation	**A-**	'05	48.8	...	1.2	50.1	516,710	39.6	4.4	0.2	55.7	50,471	155,949	155,743	27,199	33,175	15,004	15,004
David S. Scheibe President & Treasurer		'06	35.8	...	...	64.2	50,911	1.8	39.4	2.8	55.9	15,040	127,813	132,578	17,991	119,717	112,126	112,200
P.O. Box 15050 Wilmington, DE	Rating Outlook: Negative	'07	52.2	...	...	47.8	60,733	1.8	42.7	2.3	53.2	17,427	46,852	57,368	11,928	11,328	9,095	9,095
DE : 1979 : Stock : Broker		'08	49.3	...	...	50.7	53,377	3.5	37.8	2.5	56.2	16,412	29,938	37,167	-1,863	13,196	9,475	9,441
A&H, Univ Life, Var life 215-761-6244		'09	49.2	...	...	50.8	48,188	3.8	36.7	2.2	57.3	8,965	23,776	17,470	-4,205	7,347	4,157	4,157
AMB# 008944 NAIC# 90859	**FSC IV**	**Rating History: A-, 01/08/10; A-, 11/14/08; A-, 02/11/08; A-, 12/14/06; A-, 12/21/05**																
CINCINNATI EQUITABLE LIFE Alpha Investment Partnership	**B+**	'05	73.9	...	7.2	18.9	5,236	61.9	5.8	15.9	16.4	3,353	254	260	-3,287	-1,155	-833	-852
Gregory A. Baker President, Treasurer and CFO		'06	67.1	...	7.8	25.1	5,841	63.1	4.1	15.8	17.0	4,022	275	274	907	-53	-158	-142
P.O. Box 3428 Cincinnati, OH 45201-3428	Rating Outlook: Stable	'07	29.5	...	47.7	22.8	15,558	73.0	1.1	4.9	21.0	9,524	5,404	5,404	6,207	-796	-531	-528
OH : 1978 : Stock : Agency		'08	52.1	...	32.1	15.8	19,753	84.9	0.5	2.7	11.8	8,904	8,032	8,031	4,919	-224	-189	-318
Whole life, Pre-need 513-621-1826		'09	64.7	...	24.9	10.4	25,016	91.4	0.3	1.8	6.4	8,651	10,087	10,086	4,952	-458	-258	-283
AMB# 006757 NAIC# 88064	**FSC IV**	**Rating History: B+, 04/28/10; B+, 05/20/09; B+, 06/03/08; B+, 06/12/07; B+, 06/15/06**																
CINCINNATI LIFE INSURANCE CO Cincinnati Financial Corporation	**A**	'05	53.3	0.1	21.0	25.6	2,351,689	39.3	0.8	28.1	31.8	450,779	248,968	209,611	161,278	21,903	9,913	21,002
David H. Popplewell President & COO		'06	50.4	0.1	24.5	25.0	2,521,354	41.0	0.7	26.7	31.6	478,761	205,970	168,940	80,752	5,487	-487	28,459
P.O. Box 145496 Cincinnati, OH 45250-5496	Rating Outlook: Stable	'07	53.4	...	18.1	28.5	2,549,965	45.0	0.8	26.4	27.9	476,935	210,743	173,028	100,593	14,306	6,884	39,285
OH : 1988 : Stock : Agency		'08	61.0	...	7.4	31.6	2,477,627	46.5	0.7	25.9	26.9	290,089	231,230	185,321	70,069	15,964	-17,561	-70,121
Term Life, Univ Life, Whole life 513-870-2000		'09	63.3	...	3.8	32.9	2,830,559	44.4	0.6	29.1	25.9	300,245	391,243	347,314	302,972	5,187	10,879	15,090
AMB# 006568 NAIC# 76236	**FSC IX**	**Rating History: A, 02/18/10; A, 12/22/08; A+ u, 07/03/08; A+, 03/26/08; A+, 05/21/07**																

2010 BEST'S KEY RATING GUIDE — LIFE/HEALTH EDITION
BEST'S PROFITABILITY, LEVERAGE AND LIQUIDITY TESTS 2005 – 2009

Data in U.S. Dollars

	Profitability Tests							Leverage Tests						Liquidity Tests					
Un-Realized Capital Gains ($000)	Benefits Paid to NPW & Dep (%)	Comm. & Expenses to NPW & Dep (%)	NOG to Total Assets (%)	NOG to Total Rev (%)	Operating Return on Equity (%)	Net Yield (%)	Total Return (%)	Change in NPW & Dep (%)	NPW & Dep to Capital (X)	Capital & Surplus to Liabilities (%)	Surplus Relief (%)	Reins Leverage (%)	Change in Capital (%)	Quick Liquidity (%)	Current Liquidity (%)	Non-Invest Grade Bonds to Capital (%)	Delinq. & Foreclosed Mortgages to Capital (%)	Mort. & Credit Tenant Loans & R.E. to Capital (%)	Affiliated Invest to Capital (%)
...	85.3	10.0	16.0	4.0	30.0	5.20	5.20	-13.6	8.9	104.4	...	...	-28.9	120.9	146.7	...	...	3.1	...
...	91.1	14.2	-22.8	-4.0	-48.3	5.44	5.44	20.1	13.3	75.9	...	...	-19.7	115.3	140.2	...	...	...	...
...	86.9	12.8	11.5	2.1	24.4	6.33	6.33	-3.9	10.7	104.8	...	...	19.5	186.8	211.4	4.4	...	...	...
...	80.6	15.1	10.1	4.0	16.7	4.10	4.11	-57.3	3.8	252.4	...	...	21.7	263.4	302.6	...	...	...	...
...	75.4	18.4	12.8	4.6	18.6	3.64	4.32	-9.9	4.9	187.3	...	...	-30.1	291.7	313.3	...	...	...	...
	Principal Lines of Business: CompHosp/Med (100.0%)													Principal States: TN (91.4%), MS (8.6%)					
...	79.3	13.4	19.6	7.1	32.5	4.19	4.26	-6.7	4.2	187.8	...	15.7	12.2	179.6	192.4	...	...	...	...
...	85.3	15.5	5.8	1.9	9.1	5.48	5.48	-2.4	5.2	170.9	...	14.6	-20.4	213.9	230.5	...	...	...	...
...	85.4	14.6	7.3	2.1	12.0	5.35	4.84	-2.4	6.0	136.3	...	12.1	-15.3	187.3	202.4	...	...	...	...
...	84.1	12.6	11.3	3.3	18.3	4.31	4.56	-7.6	5.6	195.7	...	0.4	-1.6	220.1	243.0	...	...	...	...
...	85.4	13.5	4.5	1.8	7.0	4.11	4.53	-33.4	4.0	173.8	...	0.3	-7.0	197.3	215.5	...	...	...	...
	Principal Lines of Business: CompHosp/Med (100.0%)													Principal States: TX (100.0%)					
...	81.6	12.9	6.6	5.5	11.7	4.19	4.18	-41.1	1.9	172.4	...	...	12.2	212.2	225.5	...	...	...	...
...	85.7	15.4	3.8	3.3	6.4	5.59	5.59	-21.4	2.4	124.3	...	...	-36.3	278.1	287.7	...	...	...	...
...	86.6	16.7	1.3	1.2	2.3	4.99	4.99	-25.0	1.8	123.5	...	...	2.4	261.2	270.5	...	...	...	...
...	79.4	20.2	-9.0	-11.7	-17.0	3.79	3.79	-24.4	1.4	102.3	...	...	-8.1	249.4	257.6	...	...	...	...
...	89.1	13.9	13.1	24.3	23.3	2.17	2.19	-30.9	0.9	167.5	...	...	16.4	483.0	483.0	...	...	...	...
	Principal Lines of Business: CompHosp/Med (100.0%)													Principal States: UT (100.0%)					
...	84.7	13.3	13.4	3.6	34.7	5.68	5.68	23.8	9.9	50.6	...	...	-12.8	145.8	145.8	...	...	...	...
...	76.8	12.6	28.6	8.5	81.8	6.16	6.16	12.8	7.9	56.4	...	...	42.6	153.4	153.4	...	...	...	...
...	72.7	12.0	29.2	11.3	60.9	5.51	5.51	-5.1	3.9	138.3	...	...	90.2	235.4	235.4	...	...	...	...
...	70.9	10.9	28.2	12.9	56.7	5.33	5.33	-25.8	7.5	57.3	...	...	-61.1	141.2	141.2	...	...	...	...
...	71.7	13.9	24.9	12.0	59.6	4.31	4.31	-33.5	4.4	92.7	...	...	11.7	173.7	173.7	...	...	...	...
	Principal Lines of Business: CompHosp/Med (100.0%)																		
...	-99.9	-5.6	5.7	98.2	6.4	3.96	3.95	19.8	0.0	999.9	...	...	6.6	999.9	999.9	...	...	...	...
...	-99.9	-30.8	7.5	126.0	8.0	4.91	4.91	-60.6	0.0	999.9	...	...	8.9	999.9	999.9	...	...	...	...
...	4.6	100.8	4.2	71.6	4.3	4.72	4.72	5.9	0.0	999.9	...	...	4.5	999.9	999.9	...	...	...	...
...	999.9	999.9	2.9	91.8	2.9	3.17	3.17	-99.9	0.0	999.9	...	...	2.9	999.9	999.9	...	...	...	...
...	...	...	2.1	84.3	2.1	2.57	2.57	100.0	...	999.9	...	...	2.2	999.9	999.9	...	...	...	...
28	72.0	19.6	5.2	12.0	23.9	6.13	5.89	-8.7	1.1	30.2	52.4	300.0	13.0	52.5	82.9	7.8	...	...	...
-53	72.7	23.4	4.0	12.9	18.0	6.42	6.10	9.7	1.3	27.3	-11.8	231.9	-4.8	62.1	88.2	7.9	...	...	...
...	69.1	19.9	4.1	11.4	18.7	6.15	6.48	14.8	1.3	29.2	-2.4	197.4	7.7	64.3	89.9	5.1	...	...	...
-3	62.7	20.8	8.6	22.9	36.3	6.65	4.53	6.3	1.2	33.2	0.5	159.2	15.9	76.5	101.5	3.4	...	...	...
2	71.4	22.8	4.0	10.8	15.9	5.75	5.70	0.9	1.3	33.5	0.6	164.3	-2.7	72.7	99.2	2.9	...	...	...
	Principal Lines of Business: GrpA&H (71.9%), GrpLife (27.8%), IndA&H (0.3%)													Principal States: NY (99.7%)					
-1,429	38.5	27.2	3.1	8.5	30.4	4.37	3.87	4.1	2.9	23.3	2.2	50.2	4.9	87.7	97.7	29.0	...	...	11.4
9,056	60.2	30.2	39.5	45.5	342.3	5.84	11.84	-14.9	8.8	42.3	5.6	209.0	-71.5	117.9	125.2	...	...	...	...
2,458	67.4	17.3	16.3	15.0	56.0	5.47	11.84	-56.7	3.3	40.6	0.8	213.5	15.9	103.6	126.6	...	...	...	...
-2,748	48.9	18.1	16.6	23.4	56.0	4.54	-0.93	-35.2	2.3	44.7	1.0	204.9	-6.0	167.4	176.7	1.0	...	...	...
16,960	45.6	19.4	8.2	21.4	32.8	2.82	50.50	-53.0	1.9	23.2	0.0	365.9	-45.0	134.6	147.8	...	...	...	...
	Principal Lines of Business: GrpA&H (81.5%), GrpLife (18.5%), OrdLife (0.1%), IndA&H (0.0%)																		
-36	573.2	104.4	-11.7	-99.9	-21.8	4.11	3.81	-97.8	0.1	191.7	...	0.1	-21.8	194.5	211.2	16.1	...	...	...
22	60.7	161.3	-2.9	-29.2	-4.3	4.72	6.09	5.4	0.1	239.4	...	0.1	19.7	292.4	311.5	10.9	...	...	...
3,164	10.5	49.6	-5.0	-9.3	-7.8	2.79	39.31	999.9	0.5	207.4	...	0.0	154.8	176.5	182.6	3.3	...	...	65.4
-1,274	18.1	36.3	-1.1	-2.1	-2.1	5.47	-2.46	48.6	0.9	86.5	...	0.0	-12.7	108.2	117.5	2.1	...	...	62.3
79	26.1	35.0	-1.2	-2.2	-2.9	6.87	7.24	25.6	1.1	56.8	...	0.0	-1.1	94.2	103.8	1.9	...	...	61.8
	Principal Lines of Business: OrdLife (98.5%), IndA&H (1.5%), IndAnn (0.0%)													Principal States: IN (38.2%), KY (33.7%), OH (28.1%)					
-4,871	40.7	24.5	0.4	3.2	2.2	5.78	6.36	5.1	0.4	37.3	2.5	59.2	4.1	86.4	99.1	18.4	...	0.6	...
25,715	63.8	33.4	0.0	-0.2	-0.1	5.78	8.66	-19.4	0.3	37.8	1.7	60.0	8.7	85.0	99.5	16.4	...	0.5	...
-91,536	62.1	33.7	0.3	2.4	1.4	5.98	3.04	2.4	0.3	33.2	1.9	66.3	-8.9	85.9	98.5	24.0	...	...	...
-112,304	63.6	32.8	-0.7	-5.8	-4.6	6.52	-2.07	7.1	0.6	17.7	2.8	118.4	-42.7	74.4	86.4	24.5	...	...	...
2,934	33.7	18.9	0.4	2.3	3.7	6.58	6.62	87.4	1.1	16.3	2.5	118.3	9.0	75.1	86.0	28.8	...	...	...
	Principal Lines of Business: IndAnn (53.5%), OrdLife (43.7%), GrpAnn (1.4%), IndA&H (0.6%), GrpLife (0.5%)													Principal States: OH (15.9%), IA (11.1%), PA (8.2%), IL (7.9%), IN (7.0%)					

COMPANY NAME Ultimate Parent Association Principal Officer Mailing Address Dom. : Began Bus. : Struct. : Mktg. Specialty Phone # AMB# NAIC#	Best's Financial Strength Rating FSC	Data Year	Balance Sheet: Bonds (%)	Mort. Loans & R.E. (%)	Com & Pref. Stock (%)	All Other Assets (%)	Total Assets ($000)	Life Reserves (%)	Health Reserves (%)	Ann Res. & Dep. Liabilities (%)	All Other Liabilities (%)	Capital & Surplus ($000)	Operations: Direct Premiums Written ($000)	Net Premiums Written & Deposits ($000)	Operating Cash Flow ($000)	NOG Before Taxes ($000)	NOG After Taxes ($000)	Net Income ($000)
CITIZENS ACCIDENT AND HEALTH Protective Life Corporation Brent E. Griggs Chairman, President & CEO 2801 Highway 280 South Birmingham, AL 35223 AZ : 1975 : Stock : Other Direct Credit A&H 847-948-8988 AMB# 008642 NAIC# 85960	NR-5	'05	57.3	...	...	42.7	3,118	...	...	...	100.0	658	...	117	-3,296	71	53	53
		'06	36.0	...	...	64.0	2,927	...	...	...	100.0	750	...	-143	-56	148	93	93
		'07	28.1	...	...	71.9	2,936	...	...	...	100.0	858	...	-141	153	140	102	102
		'08	20.3	...	...	79.7	3,058	...	...	...	100.0	861	...	-142	294	20	14	14
		'09	46.4	...	...	53.6	2,533	...	...	...	100.0	550	...	-93	-387	86	57	57
		Rating History: NR-5, 10/09/09; NR-3, 02/11/09; NR-3, 06/02/08; NR-3, 04/02/07; NR-3, 02/08/06																
CITIZENS FIDELITY INS CO George W. Booker, II President P.O. Box 25440 Little Rock, AR 72211 AR : 1959 : Stock : Agency Ann, Life, Pre-need 501-228-5134 AMB# 068321 NAIC# 83968	NR-5	'05	78.6	3.3	5.4	12.7	57,673	64.8	0.0	31.8	3.5	6,775	4,822	6,210	1,898	331	279	281
		'06	77.3	3.1	4.2	15.3	59,659	64.8	0.0	32.0	3.2	7,675	4,192	5,620	1,914	651	525	649
		'07	77.6	3.5	6.3	12.6	52,316	77.3	0.0	19.4	3.4	7,485	3,982	5,142	-7,285	556	454	494
		'08	66.9	3.0	5.4	24.7	50,900	80.0	0.0	18.3	1.7	6,500	4,394	5,622	268	126	126	16
		'09	78.3	4.6	5.8	11.4	53,742	78.6	0.0	18.4	3.0	7,125	4,655	5,700	2,054	640	549	549
		Rating History: NR-5, 04/20/10; NR-5, 04/23/09; NR-5, 04/09/08; NR-5, 05/08/07; NR-5, 05/08/06																
CITIZENS NATIONAL LIFE INS CO Citizens Inc Rick D. Riley President 400 East Anderson Lane Austin, TX 78752 TX : 1966 : Stock : Broker A&H, Life 512-837-7100 AMB# 008947 NAIC# 82082	NR-5	'05	87.5	...	0.0	12.5	14,581	92.5	...	5.9	1.6	5,328	9,517	1,979	80	83	80	80
		'06	85.4	...	0.0	14.6	13,960	73.8	...	3.5	22.7	2,281	7,755	1,844	-239	-245	-245	-245
		'07	90.1	...	0.0	9.9	11,466	94.2	...	4.5	1.4	2,114	7,001	1,721	-2,462	-110	-110	-110
		'08	86.6	...	...	13.4	11,665	92.9	...	6.0	1.2	1,963	5,485	1,741	330	-94	-94	-159
		'09	92.1	...	...	7.9	11,387	92.9	...	6.0	1.1	1,549	5,617	1,561	35	-273	-273	-273
		Rating History: NR-5, 04/12/10; NR-5, 04/20/09; NR-5, 04/08/08; NR-5, 04/27/07; NR-5, 05/02/06																
CITIZENS SECURITY LIFE INS CO Citizens Financial Corporation John D. Cornett President & COO 12910 Shelbyville Road, Suite 300 Louisville, KY 40243 KY : 1965 : Stock : Agency Dental, Group Life, Ind Life 502-244-2420 AMB# 006227 NAIC# 61921	C++ Rating Outlook: Negative FSC IV	'05	78.6	4.3	7.5	9.6	139,473	88.2	1.5	6.6	3.7	11,561	26,457	25,292	1,519	589	579	1,431
		'06	74.0	4.4	8.5	13.1	135,781	89.4	1.2	6.6	2.9	11,297	23,366	21,614	-3,654	214	214	165
		'07	75.8	4.3	9.1	10.8	134,969	88.6	1.2	6.4	3.8	10,684	24,436	21,777	1,646	-1,021	-1,046	879
		'08	64.2	6.3	4.4	25.2	127,482	89.6	1.3	6.4	2.7	6,115	28,387	24,517	-14,368	-1,836	-1,451	-9,458
		'09	67.6	7.3	6.1	19.1	108,411	87.9	2.1	6.9	3.0	8,014	32,436	29,170	2,044	-2,895	-2,895	-1,084
		Rating History: C++, 12/07/09; C++, 11/06/08; B-, 10/16/07; B-, 12/11/06; B-, 12/15/05																
CLARIA LIFE & HEALTH INS CO[1] Chaim Druin President 7491 West Oakland Park Blvd. Tamarac, FL 33319 FL : 2009 : Stock : Not Available 954-749-1025 AMB# 060714 NAIC# 13192	NR-1	'05	...	...	...	...	...	...	...	...	...	...	...	...	...	...	...	...
		'06	...	...	...	...	...	...	...	...	...	...	...	...	...	...	...	...
		'07	...	...	...	...	...	...	...	...	...	...	...	...	...	...	...	...
		'08	...	...	...	...	...	...	...	...	...	...	...	...	...	...	...	...
		'09	...	...	...	100.0	4,018	...	...	...	100.0	1,059	6,272	619	...	281	183	183
		Rating History: NR-1, 06/10/10																
CLARIAN HEALTH PLANS INC[2] Clarian Health Partners, Inc. Alex P. Slabosky President 1776 N. Meridian Street, Suite 300 Indianapolis, IN 46204 IN : 2008 : Stock : Not Available Medicare 317-963-9780 AMB# 064984 NAIC# 13164	NR-5	'05	...	...	...	...	...	...	...	...	...	...	...	...	...	...	...	...
		'06	...	...	...	...	...	...	...	...	...	...	...	...	...	...	...	...
		'07	...	...	...	...	...	...	...	...	...	...	...	...	...	...	...	...
		'08	...	...	...	...	...	...	...	...	...	...	...	...	...	...	...	...
		'09	...	...	...	100.0	9,339	...	...	...	100.0	2,569	35,306	35,306	-242	-8,619	-8,619	-8,619
		Rating History: NR-5, 06/15/10																
CLEARONE HEALTH PLANS INC[2] Patricia Jean Gibford President/CEO 2650 NE Courtney Drive Bend, OR 97701 OR : 2007 : Stock : Not Available Medicare, Health 541-382-5920 AMB# 064961 NAIC# 12595	NR-5	'05	...	...	...	...	...	...	...	...	...	...	...	...	...	...	...	...
		'06	...	...	...	...	...	...	...	...	...	...	...	...	...	...	...	...
		'07	32.6	...	47.8	19.6	92,197	...	48.7	...	51.3	51,154	132,909	130,694	-8,088	-512	-1,447	1,587
		'08	31.4	...	29.4	39.2	77,485	...	59.5	...	40.5	45,651	154,978	153,543	-10,513	13,655	12,965	11,652
		'09	31.9	...	45.2	22.9	75,326	...	58.2	...	41.8	39,378	149,374	146,912	5,217	-12,212	-7,785	-7,495
		Rating History: NR-5, 05/21/10; NR-5, 09/16/09; NR-5, 09/23/08																
CLICO (BAHAMAS) LIMITED C L Financial Limited Mount Royal Avenue, P.O. Box N-3942 Nassau, Bahamas BS : Stock : Not Available Life 242-322-8937 AMB# 087843	E	'05	2.5	7.2	...	90.2	78,199	93.6	...	...	6.4	7,887	...	38,389	...	1,844	1,867	1,867
		'06	4.0	8.9	...	87.2	98,431	68.0	...	...	32.0	11,930	...	32,098	20,839	1,740	1,269	1,269
		'07	2.9	11.2	...	85.9	98,569	94.3	...	...	5.7	12,024	...	47,446	446	700	95	95
		'08	...	...	...	...	...	...	...	...	...	...	...	...	...	...	...	...
		'09	...	...	...	...	...	...	...	...	...	...	...	...	...	...	...	...
		Rating History: E, 02/26/09; B u, 02/02/09; B, 08/21/08; B+, 07/13/07; B+, 03/16/06																
COLINA INSURANCE LIMITED A F Holdings Ltd Emanuel M. Alexiou Executive Vice-Chairman 308 East Bay Street, P.O. Box N-4728 Nassau, Bahamas BS : Stock : Not Available Life, Health 242-396-2100 AMB# 089077	A- Rating Outlook: Stable FSC VII	'05	24.9	24.7	4.6	45.9	419,470	85.6	...	...	14.4	62,641	121,518	127,088	...	2,297	766	766
		'06	33.9	24.1	4.5	37.6	457,992	57.5	4.8	9.6	28.2	68,958	130,778	134,300	6,043	8,443	8,443	8,443
		'07	34.8	24.2	5.7	35.3	466,581	60.0	5.0	9.6	25.5	73,753	134,646	137,511	-10,649	4,734	4,734	4,734
		'08	34.1	24.3	5.0	36.6	474,207	62.7	4.7	9.5	23.1	81,134	137,409	137,495	-1,323	8,576	8,141	8,141
		'09	34.5	26.3	3.8	35.5	499,691	63.9	4.7	8.5	22.9	86,337	140,765	135,070	3,237	14,065	13,055	13,055
		Rating History: A-, 04/23/10; A-, 03/30/09; A-, 03/28/08; A-, 01/11/07; A-, 02/17/06																

BEST'S PROFITABILITY, LEVERAGE AND LIQUIDITY TESTS 2005 – 2009

Data in U.S. Dollars

	Profitability Tests							Leverage Tests						Liquidity Tests					
Un-Realized Capital Gains ($000)	Benefits Paid to NPW & Dep (%)	Comm. & Expenses to NPW & Dep (%)	NOG to Total Assets (%)	NOG to Total Rev (%)	Operating Return on Equity (%)	Net Yield (%)	Total Return (%)	Change in NPW & Dep (%)	NPW & Dep to Capital (X)	Capital & Surplus to Liabilities (%)	Surplus Relief (%)	Reins Leverage (%)	Change in Capital (%)	Quick Liquidity (%)	Current Liquidity (%)	Non-Invest Grade Bonds to Capital (%)	Delinq. & Foreclosed Mortgages to Capital (%)	Mort. & Credit Tenant Loans & R.E. to Capital (%)	Affiliated Invest to Capital (%)
...	...	445.2	1.1	4.1	2.1	12.48	12.53	-73.9	0.2	26.9	106.6	211.5	-85.0	83.4	88.6	...	...	...	...
...	...	49.4	3.1	9.4	13.2	9.51	9.62	-99.9	-0.2	34.6	121.4	150.5	13.8	94.8	99.6	...	...	...	...
...	...	45.0	3.5	12.6	12.7	9.31	9.43	1.2	-0.2	41.5	85.7	107.4	14.3	105.3	109.3	...	...	...	...
...	...	10.5	0.5	2.7	1.7	5.55	5.68	-1.1	-0.2	39.3	60.4	69.8	0.3	143.5	149.9	...	...	...	...
...	...	93.9	2.0	13.0	8.1	3.37	3.51	34.5	-0.2	28.0	80.1	68.1	-35.9	152.6	159.8	...	...	...	...

Principal Lines of Business: CrdA&H (100.0%)

4	59.9	29.7	0.5	3.7	3.9	5.21	5.28	-0.4	0.8	15.5	...	4.9	-7.1	79.2	89.3	46.9	...	24.3	...
71	72.4	30.7	0.9	7.3	7.3	5.43	5.81	-9.5	0.7	16.7	...	4.8	10.1	89.4	99.6	31.5	...	21.9	...
-30	69.3	33.4	0.8	6.6	6.0	5.60	5.67	-8.5	0.6	18.8	...	5.5	-3.0	86.5	97.9	20.7	...	22.1	...
-1,466	71.0	30.5	0.2	1.8	1.8	5.19	2.17	9.3	0.8	15.3	...	7.3	-18.2	98.7	109.6	18.0	...	22.6	...
708	62.5	29.3	1.0	7.7	8.1	5.19	6.59	1.4	0.7	17.5	...	7.4	18.3	86.2	97.1	19.4	...	30.8	...

Principal Lines of Business: OrdLife (74.7%), GrpAnn (20.8%), IndAnn (4.5%), IndA&H (0.0%)
Principal States: AR (100.0%)

0	52.5	94.3	0.5	1.6	1.5	4.23	4.39	-36.5	0.4	57.8	34.5	51.3	-0.2	121.6	125.0	...	...	...	...
0	69.9	80.6	-1.7	-6.5	-6.4	5.32	5.35	-6.8	0.8	19.6	55.3	124.2	-57.1	94.2	94.4	4.4	...	...	...
0	63.6	63.2	-0.9	-3.3	-5.0	4.95	4.87	-6.7	0.8	22.7	47.1	114.1	-7.3	94.2	94.2	4.7	...	...	...
0	58.3	61.2	-0.8	-3.2	-4.6	5.64	4.95	1.1	0.9	20.2	32.5	103.2	-7.5	94.9	94.9	1.8	...	...	...
...	76.6	62.3	-2.4	-10.5	-15.5	4.35	4.20	-10.3	1.0	15.8	38.4	99.7	-21.0	93.2	93.5	2.3	...	...	...

Principal Lines of Business: OrdLife (95.0%), IndAnn (4.9%), GrpAnn (0.1%)
Principal States: TX (74.7%), OK (12.0%), LA (5.6%), MS (3.5%)

-616	80.5	44.1	0.4	1.8	5.2	5.37	5.64	-8.2	1.9	10.4	3.7	25.8	2.6	64.8	74.3	31.5	...	45.9	18.5
207	87.3	50.2	0.2	0.7	1.9	5.07	5.28	-14.5	1.7	10.4	9.6	28.1	-2.6	68.2	77.0	31.4	...	47.0	19.6
-635	85.2	54.7	-0.8	-3.4	-9.5	5.04	6.13	0.8	1.7	10.5	26.9	36.9	0.5	64.2	72.7	77.9	...	45.5	19.8
-850	85.8	50.0	-1.1	-4.3	-17.3	4.67	-2.09	12.6	3.7	5.5	53.4	75.4	-47.9	72.1	77.1	116.5	...	119.4	40.0
-663	86.6	39.8	-2.5	-8.2	-41.0	3.10	4.09	19.0	3.2	9.3	29.4	303.8	37.1	69.1	71.4	88.6	...	85.6	29.3

Principal Lines of Business: GrpA&H (62.3%), OrdLife (28.0%), IndA&H (5.9%), GrpLife (2.8%), IndLife (0.7%)
Principal States: NC (20.4%), MS (10.5%), KY (9.2%), TN (6.1%), PA (5.7%)

...	...	...	...	...	...	...	...	...	...	...	...	...	...	...	...	...	...	...	...
...	...	...	...	...	...	...	...	...	...	...	...	...	...	...	...	...	...	...	...
...	...	...	...	...	...	...	...	...	...	...	...	...	...	...	...	...	...	...	...
...	...	...	...	...	...	...	...	...	...	...	...	...	...	...	...	...	...	...	...
...	24.3	51.1	...	4.6	...	...	...	...	0.6	35.8	276.2	...	...	...	...	...	...	...	...

Principal Lines of Business: IndA&H (100.0%)

...	...	...	...	...	...	...	...	...	...	...	...	...	...	...	...	...	...	...	...
...	...	...	...	...	...	...	...	...	...	...	...	...	...	...	...	...	...	...	...
...	...	...	...	...	...	...	...	...	...	...	...	...	...	...	...	...	...	...	...
...	...	...	...	...	...	...	...	...	...	...	...	...	...	...	...	...	...	...	...
...	89.5	35.1	...	-24.4	...	...	...	...	13.7	37.9	...	...	...	130.6	130.6	...	...	...	...

Principal Lines of Business: Medicare (100.0%)
Principal States: IN (100.0%)

...	...	...	...	...	...	...	...	...	...	...	...	...	...	...	...	...	...	...	...
...	...	...	...	...	...	...	...	...	...	...	...	...	...	...	...	...	...	...	...
712	90.0	11.8	...	-1.1	...	...	...	...	2.6	124.6	...	8.4	...	122.6	133.5	...	...	...	46.1
-12,442	84.8	13.9	15.3	7.9	26.8	18.46	-0.12	17.5	3.4	143.4	...	3.2	-10.8	29.4	33.9	...	...	...	43.8
11,346	91.4	17.6	-10.2	-5.3	-18.3	1.64	21.40	-4.3	3.7	109.5	...	0.9	-13.7	118.4	129.0	...	...	...	70.2

Principal Lines of Business: Medicare (78.2%), CompHosp/Med (21.8%)
Principal States: OR (98.7%)

...	81.1	27.3	2.6	4.3	26.8	8.09	8.09	-27.8	486.7	11.2	...	...	29.9	6.1	98.9	...	...	71.8	681.7
...	79.0	40.1	1.4	3.1	12.8	10.74	10.74	-16.4	269.1	13.8	...	...	51.3	7.2	106.3	...	...	73.4	579.7
...	93.0	22.3	0.1	0.2	0.8	10.82	10.82	47.8	394.6	13.9	...	...	0.8	15.3	96.0	...	...	91.6	480.1
...	...	...	...	...	...	...	...	...	...	...	...	...	...	...	...	...	...	...	...
...	...	...	...	...	...	...	...	...	...	...	...	...	...	...	...	...	...	...	...

...	83.0	39.3	0.2	0.5	1.4	10.04	10.04	72.3	202.9	17.9	...	...	31.1	50.3	86.4	...	...	165.1	3.7
380	80.3	35.3	1.9	5.1	12.8	7.54	7.54	5.7	194.8	18.0	...	...	10.1	51.7	94.3	...	...	159.8	...
3,180	85.5	34.7	1.0	2.8	6.6	8.18	8.18	2.4	186.5	19.1	...	...	7.0	53.5	98.7	...	...	153.4	4.7
2,506	79.8	34.0	1.7	4.9	10.5	5.94	5.94	-0.0	169.5	21.1	...	...	10.0	55.6	98.5	...	...	142.3	4.7
-1,563	80.9	33.1	2.7	7.8	15.6	6.68	6.68	-1.8	156.4	21.6	...	...	6.4	54.0	100.8	...	...	152.0	10.1

Data in U.S. Dollars

COMPANY NAME Ultimate Parent Association Principal Officer Mailing Address Dom. : Began Bus. : Struct. : Mktg. Specialty Phone # AMB# NAIC#	Best's Financial Strength Rating FSC	Data Year	Balance Sheet Bonds (%)	Mort. Loans & R.E. (%)	Com & Pref. Stock (%)	All Other Assets (%)	Total Assets ($000)	Life Reserves (%)	Health Reserves (%)	Ann Res. & Dep. Liabilities (%)	All Other Liabilities (%)	Capital & Surplus ($000)	Operations Direct Premiums Written ($000)	Net Premiums Written & Deposits ($000)	Operating Cash Flow ($000)	NOG Before Taxes ($000)	NOG After Taxes ($000)	Net Income ($000)
COLONIAL AMERICAN LIFE INS CO Coventry Resources Corp. William J. Neugroschel CEO & President 673 East Cherry Lane Souderton, PA 18964 PA : 1926 : Stock : Agency Life, LTC 215-723-3044 AMB# 007578 NAIC# 73326	NR-3	'05	50.2	...	...	49.8	22,258	3.2	93.1	...	3.7	8,135	3,909	5,053	1,932	1,378	1,065	1,065
		'06	52.6	...	...	47.4	24,480	3.6	94.2	...	2.2	8,946	4,138	5,181	1,583	895	620	620
		'07	56.2	...	...	43.8	26,536	3.6	94.4	...	2.1	10,236	4,508	5,495	1,867	1,548	1,204	1,203
		'08	53.8	...	...	46.2	4,546	...	...	...	100.0	4,542	4,827	5,701	-12,297	1,627	1,676	1,676
		'09	85.4	...	...	14.6	4,555	...	...	...	100.0	4,549	...	...	609	8	7	7
		Rating History: NR-3, 03/17/10; B+, 10/30/08; B+, 10/18/07; B+, 11/02/06; B+, 09/14/05																
COLONIAL LIFE & ACCIDENT INS Unum Group Randall C. Horn President & CEO 1200 Colonial Life Blvd. Columbia, SC 29210 SC : 1939 : Stock : Other Agency Ind A&H, Univ Life 803-798-7000 AMB# 006238 NAIC# 62049	A- Rating Outlook: Positive FSC XIV	'05	86.8	3.3	0.6	9.3	1,668,810	41.7	50.7	0.0	7.5	351,166	860,172	822,083	155,682	151,584	89,326	99,442
		'06	85.5	5.6	0.6	8.3	1,773,900	41.9	51.2	0.0	7.0	370,451	909,411	879,043	104,207	173,662	108,823	110,640
		'07	81.8	7.6	1.7	8.9	1,902,121	41.4	49.7	0.0	8.9	369,259	975,693	945,545	111,008	191,001	114,421	116,436
		'08	79.8	9.1	1.7	9.4	1,988,846	42.9	49.4	0.0	7.6	379,589	1,039,043	1,011,687	67,190	207,773	124,125	109,294
		'09	78.0	8.9	1.1	12.0	2,141,799	44.0	49.2	0.0	6.9	459,733	1,068,202	1,042,960	96,197	217,549	131,969	124,365
		Rating History: A- g, 03/08/10; A- g, 03/13/09; A- g, 01/29/08; A- g, 11/07/06; A- g, 06/07/06																
COLONIAL LIFE ASSURANCE CO LTD Edmund Gibbons Limited Alan Peacock President & CEO Jardine House, 33-35 Reid Street Hamilton HM 12, Bermuda BM : Stock : Not Available Life 441-296-3700 AMB# 086817	A- Rating Outlook: Stable FSC VI	'05	2.2	...	7.2	90.6	12,470	57.8	...	...	42.2	5,053	...	4,195	-1,172	-1,218	-1,218	-939
		'06	2.1	...	8.1	89.9	13,443	44.0	...	...	56.0	3,910	...	4,280	-1,082	-1,440	-1,440	-1,132
		'07	2.0	...	9.2	88.9	14,354	46.6	...	...	53.4	247	...	3,256	-1,003	-3,843	-3,843	-3,722
		'08	...	...	8.6	91.4	14,045	63.6	...	...	36.4	1,731	...	3,895	-1,825	-1,641	-1,641	-1,525
		'09	...	...	5.5	94.5	17,504	78.7	...	...	21.3	4,298	...	4,401	55	-6,261	-6,261	-6,234
		Rating History: A- g, 07/02/09; A- g, 01/16/09; A- g, 12/05/06; A- g, 01/26/04; A- g, 09/30/03																
COLONIAL LIFE INS CO OF TEXAS CICO Holding Corp Richard D. Wallace President P.O. Box 2543 Fort Worth, TX 76113-2543 TX : 1978 : Stock : Direct Response A&H, Mtge Guaranty, Term Life 817-390-2239 AMB# 008864 NAIC# 88153	NR-5	'05	89.4	...	1.6	9.0	15,812	87.5	1.1	2.2	9.2	12,254	1,543	1,201	426	470	413	365
		'06	91.6	...	1.7	6.7	16,065	89.8	0.6	2.1	7.4	12,537	1,501	1,152	470	290	265	273
		'07	89.9	...	1.7	8.4	16,730	87.9	0.4	1.9	9.8	13,022	1,495	1,151	619	547	502	505
		'08	87.9	...	3.4	8.7	16,079	85.2	0.2	2.6	12.0	13,466	1,286	1,100	-720	510	444	402
		'09	86.6	...	2.7	10.8	16,426	90.4	0.3	1.9	7.4	13,719	1,276	1,039	589	386	241	199
		Rating History: NR-5, 04/22/10; NR-5, 04/20/09; NR-5, 04/08/08; NR-5, 05/11/07; NR-5, 05/09/06																
COLONIAL LIFE INS CO TRINIDAD C L Financial Limited Nigel Chinapoo Chief Information Officer 29 St. Vincent Street Port of Spain, Trinidad And Tobago TT : Stock : Career Agent Ann, Life, Pension 868-623-1421 AMB# 084414	C u Under Review Implication: Negative FSC XII	'05	10.7	4.0	3.1	82.2	2,544,806	66.0	...	7.6	26.4	691,801	...	465,751	...	-12,325	-15,060	12,860
		'06	7.5	1.8	6.0	84.7	3,047,737	64.0	...	...	36.0	797,595	...	526,225	-93,240	14,807	10,965	8,270
		'07	9.7	1.8	5.9	82.7	3,584,031	75.0	...	...	25.0	1,024,962	...	819,754	503,153	10,101	5,397	12,322
		'08	...	...	...	...	...	...	...	...	...	...	...	...	...	...	...	...
		'09	...	...	...	...	...	...	...	...	...	...	...	...	...	...	...	...
		Rating History: C u, 08/07/09; B u, 02/02/09; B++, 08/21/08; B++, 07/13/07; A-, 03/16/06																
COLONIAL MEDICAL INS CO LTD Edmund Gibbons Limited Alan Peacock President & CEO Jardine House, 33-35 Reid Street Hamilton HM 12, Bermuda BM : 1991 : Stock : Not Available Health 441-296-3200 AMB# 086818	A- Rating Outlook: Stable FSC VI	'05	12.7	...	...	87.3	29,142	...	...	...	100.0	13,719	32,161	44,979	...	6,732	6,732	6,732
		'06	12.3	...	...	87.7	33,410	...	...	...	100.0	19,740	38,947	53,407	8,152	6,375	6,375	6,375
		'07	11.3	...	...	88.7	41,589	...	...	...	100.0	26,228	46,741	65,849	8,231	8,186	8,186	8,186
		'08	13.3	...	...	86.8	44,840	...	...	...	100.0	28,527	57,565	74,578	2,859	4,862	4,862	4,862
		'09	11.2	...	...	88.8	41,955	...	...	...	100.0	26,883	81,204	83,075	13,722	5,205	5,205	5,205
		Rating History: A- g, 07/02/09; A- g, 01/16/09; A- g, 12/05/06; A- g, 01/26/04; A- g, 09/30/03																
COLONIAL PENN LIFE INSURANCE CNO Financial Group, Inc. Gregory R. Barstead President 11825 N. Pennsylvania Street Carmel, IN 46032 PA : 1959 : Stock : Direct Response A&H, Ind Ann, Whole life 215-928-8000 AMB# 006240 NAIC# 62065	B Rating Outlook: Stable FSC X	'05	84.8	3.2	3.8	8.2	725,570	72.3	4.3	18.2	5.1	35,279	147,478	90,051	-43,710	7,465	8,897	9,513
		'06	83.1	4.7	2.9	9.3	716,714	73.8	3.9	17.4	4.8	44,468	150,897	99,816	-10,041	7,574	9,197	9,025
		'07	80.1	7.1	2.0	10.8	710,859	74.4	3.7	16.6	5.3	47,226	160,507	124,785	-7,834	-71,414	-55,332	-55,388
		'08	77.7	8.4	1.2	12.7	692,246	75.4	3.4	15.9	5.3	37,575	171,866	174,546	-21,008	-4,158	2,094	-353
		'09	80.7	7.7	0.7	10.9	683,579	76.1	3.2	15.2	5.6	32,651	175,446	182,276	-12,190	2,530	-239	-3,776
		Rating History: B g, 03/23/10; B g, 10/16/09; B gu, 03/04/09; B+ g, 11/20/08; B+ gu, 08/12/08																
COLONIAL SECURITY LIFE INS CO Gibraltar Group, Inc. Cecil A. Nettle President & CEO 4308 Avondale Avenue, Suite 100 Dallas, TX 75219-1029 TX : 1954 : Stock : Direct Response Univ Life 214-252-0313 AMB# 007604 NAIC# 73547	NR-5	'05	81.7	...	6.1	12.2	3,257	85.5	...	...	14.5	1,995	369	807	-39	222	185	185
		'06	74.0	...	3.2	22.8	3,641	66.0	...	...	34.0	2,027	369	802	100	239	196	231
		'07	84.3	...	5.1	10.6	3,158	85.5	...	...	14.5	1,948	350	763	-42	182	153	152
		'08	88.9	...	0.6	10.5	3,053	85.1	...	...	14.9	1,902	351	725	-41	156	133	126
		'09	86.8	...	0.2	13.1	2,968	87.5	...	...	12.5	1,840	343	715	-82	163	124	130
		Rating History: NR-5, 04/12/10; NR-5, 04/16/09; NR-5, 04/10/08; NR-5, 04/27/07; NR-5, 05/03/06																
COLORADO ACCESS[2] Marshall Thomas, M.D. President & CFO 10065 E. Harvard Avenue, Suite 600 Denver, CO 80231-5963 CO : 1995 : Non-Profit : Broker Health 720-744-5100 AMB# 064310 NAIC# 95733	NR-5	'05	1.6	...	...	98.4	26,863	...	60.5	...	39.5	4,719	158,595	157,869	-16,558	-10,989	-10,989	-10,989
		'06	...	...	...	100.0	21,479	...	45.2	...	54.8	5,831	167,471	167,191	-4,328	1,563	1,563	1,563
		'07	2.0	...	...	98.0	21,628	...	64.3	...	35.7	7,398	99,900	99,662	-968	2,804	2,804	2,804
		'08	1.6	...	7.4	91.0	27,137	...	63.0	...	37.0	6,834	127,660	127,332	-2,720	-955	-955	-955
		'09	1.9	...	...	98.1	23,279	...	73.7	...	26.3	4,602	147,911	147,430	-8,154	-1,601	-1,601	-1,601
		Rating History: NR-5, 04/19/10; NR-5, 08/26/09; C pd, 09/03/08; C- pd, 07/09/07; C- pd, 08/28/06																

BEST'S PROFITABILITY, LEVERAGE AND LIQUIDITY TESTS 2005 – 2009

Data in U.S. Dollars

—	Profitability Tests							Leverage Tests						Liquidity Tests					
Un-Realized Capital Gains ($000)	Benefits Paid to NPW & Dep (%)	Comm. & Expenses to NPW & Dep (%)	NOG to Total Assets (%)	NOG to Total Rev (%)	Operating Return on Equity (%)	Net Yield (%)	Total Return (%)	Change in NPW & Dep (%)	NPW & Dep to Capital (X)	Capital & Surplus to Liabilities (%)	Surplus Relief (%)	Reins Leverage (%)	Change in Capital (%)	Quick Liquidity (%)	Current Liquidity (%)	Non-Invest Grade Bonds to Capital (%)	Delinq. & Foreclosed Mortgages to Capital (%)	Mort. & Credit Tenant Loans & R.E. to Capital (%)	Affiliated Invest to Capital (%)
...	37.2	38.6	5.0	17.4	14.0	4.49	4.49	13.2	0.6	57.6	...	114.6	15.0	85.5	86.0	...	...	...	...
...	39.4	38.9	2.7	9.7	7.3	4.74	4.74	2.5	0.6	57.6	...	108.4	10.0	87.0	87.2	...	...	...	...
...	35.2	39.5	4.7	17.7	12.6	4.92	4.91	6.1	0.5	62.8	...	96.4	14.5	90.2	92.7	...	...	...	...
...	25.4	58.7	10.8	23.7	22.7	8.62	8.62	3.7	1.3	...	...	31.2	-55.6	...	...	...	...	...	...
...	...	...	0.2	5.7	0.2	3.10	3.10	-99.9	...	999.9	...	...	0.2	999.9	999.9	...	...	...	...
1,115	45.6	39.0	5.6	9.4	27.7	7.09	7.89	6.3	2.3	27.6	5.9	14.4	20.9	50.6	71.6	30.2	...	15.4	2.9
0	45.5	39.4	6.3	10.9	30.2	6.78	6.92	6.9	2.3	27.5	2.1	13.2	6.1	47.0	67.8	39.1	0.2	25.8	2.8
-307	41.2	41.0	6.2	10.7	30.9	6.68	6.79	7.6	2.4	25.7	2.5	12.4	1.6	44.9	65.0	40.6	...	38.3	3.2
-82	41.3	40.3	6.4	10.9	33.2	6.61	5.79	7.0	2.5	25.0	2.2	11.2	2.4	44.1	63.6	38.0	...	46.7	4.4
-548	42.9	39.6	6.4	11.2	31.4	6.76	6.34	3.1	2.2	28.4	1.6	7.9	19.2	42.7	63.9	31.6	...	41.3	3.5
Principal Lines of Business: IndA&H (77.9%), OrdLife (18.7%), GrpA&H (2.7%), GrpLife (0.7%)													Principal States: CA (11.5%), NC (10.9%), FL (8.5%), TX (8.1%), LA (4.7%)						
...	23.8	149.8	-9.9	-19.2	-22.1	0.22	3.77	1.0	83.0	68.1	...	...	-15.6	38.1	55.0	...	...	...	...
...	18.2	168.6	-11.1	-21.0	-32.1	0.43	5.54	2.0	109.5	41.0	...	...	-22.6	37.9	43.0	...	...	...	...
...	117.6	195.9	-27.7	-59.3	-99.9	0.32	2.08	-23.9	999.9	1.8	...	...	-93.7	29.3	34.9	...	...	...	...
...	52.0	171.5	-11.6	-22.9	-99.9	-1.17	0.57	19.6	225.0	14.1	...	...	600.7	25.9	31.8	...	...	...	...
...	90.0	175.8	-39.7	-99.9	-99.9	0.24	0.70	13.0	102.4	32.6	...	...	148.3	30.2	21.0	...	...	...	...
-1	30.6	73.9	2.7	21.8	3.4	3.90	3.94	-2.0	0.1	346.9	0.3	4.3	3.1	339.9	374.1	3.4	...	...	...
9	34.7	83.5	1.7	14.5	2.1	3.88	4.18	-4.1	0.1	358.8	0.3	3.3	2.4	347.8	385.5	2.4	...	...	...
-24	29.1	77.1	3.1	25.4	3.9	4.01	4.68	-0.1	0.1	355.1	0.2	3.5	3.9	341.7	377.5	4.4	...	...	...
19	122.3	79.5	2.7	24.9	3.4	3.80	3.54	-4.4	0.1	519.3	0.2	2.5	3.3	449.2	499.2	3.8	...	...	...
-12	45.2	73.4	1.5	13.1	1.8	4.06	4.20	-5.5	0.1	508.8	0.2	2.5	1.8	454.9	502.5	4.4	...	...	...
Principal Lines of Business: OrdLife (76.7%), GrpA&H (16.8%), IndA&H (6.3%), GrpLife (0.3%)													Principal States: TX (96.2%), OH (3.2%)						
...	116.8	12.9	-0.6	-2.4	-2.3	2.93	4.15	17.1	67.3	37.3	...	...	13.2	48.7	95.2	...	...	14.7	181.5
91,775	69.9	37.9	0.4	1.7	1.5	3.32	3.21	13.0	66.0	35.5	...	...	15.3	39.2	116.1	...	...	6.9	182.0
215,045	44.0	70.5	0.2	0.5	0.6	5.80	6.04	55.8	80.0	40.1	...	...	28.5	36.1	118.2	...	...	6.2	161.8
...	...	...	...	...	...	...	...	...	...	...	...	...	...	...	...	...	...	...	...
...	...	...	...	...	...	...	...	...	...	...	...	...	...	...	...	...	...	...	...
...	69.3	23.5	27.2	13.9	51.1	33.55	33.55	18.4	327.9	89.0	...	...	8.5	33.1	24.0	...	...	...	...
...	70.1	26.9	20.4	11.0	38.1	24.09	24.09	18.7	270.6	144.4	...	...	43.9	43.2	30.0	...	...	...	...
...	69.2	26.3	21.8	11.5	35.6	33.19	33.19	23.3	251.1	170.7	...	...	32.9	45.3	30.6	...	...	...	...
...	74.0	25.8	11.3	6.1	17.8	26.51	26.51	13.3	261.4	174.9	...	...	8.8	42.0	36.4	...	...	...	...
...	73.1	24.4	12.0	6.0	18.8	1.05	1.05	11.4	309.0	178.4	...	...	-5.8	64.2	31.3	...	...	...	...
-14	75.8	42.7	1.2	7.1	24.8	6.24	6.32	10.1	2.3	5.8	70.2	39.0	-3.3	53.5	66.4	63.2	...	79.3	10.2
-31	71.1	48.0	1.3	6.8	23.1	6.37	6.42	10.8	2.0	7.4	52.1	31.8	23.7	55.6	69.8	45.8	...	84.9	13.5
45	69.0	113.5	-7.8	-34.5	-99.9	6.21	6.35	25.0	2.4	8.0	33.1	29.3	6.4	51.6	66.5	56.0	...	120.0	14.3
-76	75.8	56.1	0.3	1.0	4.9	6.23	6.02	39.9	4.0	6.6	2.0	37.7	-17.7	42.4	57.7	84.5	...	163.1	19.2
-733	73.3	42.2	0.0	-0.1	-0.7	3.64	3.19	4.4	5.0	5.6	2.0	51.5	-15.8	44.1	59.6	58.7	...	177.9	17.2
Principal Lines of Business: OrdLife (53.2%), GrpLife (42.4%), IndA&H (3.6%), GrpA&H (0.5%), IndLife (0.2%)													Principal States: PA (8.7%), CA (8.4%), FL (6.2%), TX (5.9%), IL (5.4%)						
34	111.7	52.3	5.7	19.8	9.3	4.32	5.41	-7.4	0.4	172.7	...	5.7	1.5	195.8	211.0	5.0	...	...	...
-44	79.7	58.8	5.7	20.9	9.7	4.26	4.00	-0.6	0.4	130.6	...	7.7	0.0	177.4	185.3	...	...	...	...
-12	91.1	61.2	4.5	17.0	7.7	4.28	3.87	-4.8	0.4	168.2	...	13.1	-4.0	206.1	216.1	...	...	...	...
-14	88.0	56.4	4.3	16.0	6.9	3.61	2.93	-4.9	0.4	167.4	...	6.6	-3.5	202.4	213.0	1.0	...	...	...
2	92.3	53.3	4.1	14.7	6.6	4.73	4.99	-1.4	0.4	166.2	...	10.0	-3.0	201.0	213.8	1.1	...	...	...
Principal Lines of Business: OrdLife (59.2%), GrpLife (40.8%)													Principal States: TX (100.0%)						
...	88.9	16.9	-31.5	-7.0	-98.5	2.37	2.37	-12.8	33.5	21.3	...	4.8	-73.2	101.2	101.2	...	...	...	...
...	86.5	16.3	6.5	0.9	29.6	4.79	4.79	5.9	28.7	37.3	...	1.6	23.6	227.2	227.2	...	...	...	...
...	80.6	17.4	13.0	2.8	42.4	4.30	4.30	-40.4	13.5	52.0	...	...	26.9	120.5	120.5	...	...	...	...
...	86.3	14.4	-3.9	-0.7	-13.4	0.64	0.64	27.8	18.6	33.7	...	...	-7.6	127.1	128.6	...	...	...	...
...	90.5	12.2	-6.3	-1.1	-28.0	-1.79	-1.79	15.8	32.0	24.6	...	...	-32.7	36.3	36.3	...	...	...	...
Principal Lines of Business: Medicaid (39.9%), CompHosp/Med (31.6%), Medicare (28.5%)													Principal States: CO (100.0%)						

Data in U.S. Dollars

COMPANY NAME Ultimate Parent Association Principal Officer Mailing Address Dom. : Began Bus. : Struct. : Mktg. Specialty Phone # AMB# NAIC#	Best's Financial Strength Rating FSC	Data Year	Balance Sheet: Bonds (%)	Mort. Loans & R.E. (%)	Com & Pref. Stock (%)	All Other Assets (%)	Total Assets ($000)	Life Reserves (%)	Health Reserves %)	Ann Res. & Dep. Liabilities (%)	All Other Liabilities (%)	Capital & Surplus ($000)	Operations: Direct Premiums Written ($000)	Net Premiums Written & Deposits ($000)	Operating Cash Flow ($000)	NOG Before Taxes ($000)	NOG After Taxes ($000)	Net Income ($000)
COLORADO BANKERS LIFE INS CO Health Care Svc Corp Mut Legal Reserve Stephen Clabaugh President & CEO 5990 Greenwood Plaza Blvd., #325 Greenwood Village, CO 80111 CO : 1974 : Stock : Agency Ind A&H, Ind Ann, Ind Life 303-220-8500 AMB# 008502 NAIC# 84786	A Rating Outlook: Negative FSC V	'05	89.8	...	...	10.2	122,491	29.1	0.6	67.9	2.4	16,195	41,236	41,352	7,634	4,162	3,058	2,858
		'06	88.7	...	...	11.3	132,204	30.3	0.7	66.4	2.5	18,494	44,953	44,808	8,113	3,317	1,701	1,736
		'07	87.5	...	...	12.5	140,920	31.2	0.7	65.3	2.9	21,263	50,001	49,977	8,169	3,050	1,635	1,497
		'08	86.9	...	...	13.1	144,871	32.3	0.9	64.2	2.6	17,484	58,400	58,130	715	946	-48	-757
		'09	75.4	...	...	24.6	154,632	34.1	0.8	62.7	2.4	14,172	71,200	70,659	8,007	-2,018	-2,417	-4,192
		Rating History: A, 01/27/10; A, 12/22/08; A, 11/01/07; A, 08/10/06; A, 11/01/05																
COLORADO CHOICE HEALTH PLANS Cynthia A. Palmer CEO 700 Main Street, Suite 100 Alamosa, CO 81101 CO : 1975 : Non-Profit : Broker Health 719-589-3696 AMB# 068945 NAIC# 95774	B+ Rating Outlook: Stable FSC III	'05	28.0	...	...	72.0	7,748	...	44.1	...	55.9	5,331	14,442	14,442	-166	978	978	978
		'06	8.9	...	...	91.1	8,489	...	49.8	...	50.2	5,856	15,441	15,441	1,431	750	750	750
		'07	4.2	...	...	95.8	7,346	...	42.6	...	57.4	4,811	17,008	16,588	-1,242	-979	-979	-979
		'08	12.0	...	...	88.0	6,770	...	43.4	...	56.6	4,566	17,385	16,887	-780	-387	-387	-387
		'09	11.9	...	...	88.1	6,805	...	38.8	...	61.2	4,839	18,528	17,961	116	143	143	142
		Rating History: B+, 03/18/10; B+, 04/20/09; B+, 05/01/08; B+, 03/22/07; B+, 03/10/06																
COLORADO DENTAL SERVICE INC Kathryn A. Paul President P.O. Box 5468 Denver, CO 80217-5468 CO : 1966 : Stock : Career Agent Dental 303-741-9300 AMB# 064558 NAIC# 55875	NR-5	'05	59.3	...	17.3	23.4	37,593	...	28.6	...	71.4	27,582	97,250	96,169	5,309	1,420	1,420	2,839
		'06	56.9	...	17.2	25.8	42,068	...	37.4	...	62.6	31,886	96,981	95,090	2,787	3,332	3,332	3,595
		'07	53.6	...	16.1	30.3	54,162	...	24.4	...	75.6	39,980	91,923	89,537	14,226	2,621	2,621	3,858
		'08	56.5	...	13.8	29.7	53,824	...	28.3	...	71.7	42,080	94,273	91,674	-1,804	4,275	4,275	2,080
		'09	58.0	...	18.7	23.3	59,163	...	35.2	...	64.8	45,001	111,261	107,787	2,819	4,411	4,411	2,741
		Rating History: NR-5, 03/22/10; NR-5, 12/01/09; B+ pd, 09/24/08; B+ pd, 09/18/07; B+ pd, 10/03/06																
COLUMBIA CAPITAL LIFE REINS CO Goldman Sachs Group Inc Eleanor L. Kitzman President 132 Turnpike Road, Suite 210 Southborough, MA 01772 DC : 2005 : Stock : Agency Life 508-460-2400 AMB# 060579 NAIC# 12276	A- Rating Outlook: Stable FSC IX	'05	0.9	...	...	99.1	21,633	...	...	...	100.0	21,570	...	...	21,645	85	55	55
		'06	0.2	...	...	99.8	84,475	...	...	97.1	2.9	30,131	...	95	62,817	-1,166	-756	-756
		'07	56.9	...	4.7	38.4	36,436	...	...	44.7	55.3	31,167	...	88	-49,513	812	608	604
		'08	31.4	...	1.0	67.6	138,130	44.1	...	8.7	47.2	69,643	...	1,041	80,509	-6,101	-5,545	-6,077
		'09	28.8	...	...	71.2	145,582	46.8	...	9.3	43.9	85,543	...	894	-3,476	950	-607	-535
		Rating History: A- g, 08/24/09; NR-3, 01/19/09; NR-2, 10/16/08; NR-2, 08/23/07; NR-2, 05/31/07																
COLUMBIA UNITED PROVIDERS INC Southwest Washington Health Systems Ann K. Wheelock President & CEO 19120 SE 34th Street, Suite 201 Vancouver, WA 98683 WA : 1994 : Stock : Agency Group A&H 360-449-8861 AMB# 064106 NAIC# 47047	NR-5	'05	54.6	...	5.4	40.0	15,515	...	56.1	...	43.9	10,421	70,752	69,145	1,488	700	414	450
		'06	52.4	...	5.7	41.9	16,433	...	73.2	...	26.8	9,702	71,785	70,783	443	-1,069	-774	-772
		'07	55.5	...	2.5	42.0	16,355	...	58.9	...	41.1	7,595	74,938	74,168	193	-2,652	-2,398	-2,281
		'08	43.5	...	1.1	55.4	20,605	...	58.4	...	41.6	11,098	85,175	84,367	3,600	4,237	3,496	3,501
		'09	40.6	...	1.4	58.1	22,465	...	57.3	...	42.7	14,476	97,519	96,935	970	5,201	3,447	3,257
		Rating History: NR-5, 05/11/10; NR-5, 08/26/09; C+ pd, 06/06/08; C++pd, 06/05/07; B- pd, 06/13/06																
COLUMBIAN LIFE INSURANCE CO Columbian Mutual Life Insurance Company Thomas E. Rattmann Chairman, President & CEO P.O. Box 1381 Binghamton, NY 13902-1381 IL : 1988 : Stock : Agency Home serv, Ind Life, Pre-need 607-724-2472 AMB# 068009 NAIC# 76023	A- Rating Outlook: Stable FSC VII	'05	78.3	12.2	...	9.6	240,835	93.3	0.2	0.1	6.5	16,808	97,378	80,219	7,090	-7,260	-4,668	-4,695
		'06	69.6	18.2	...	12.1	239,026	92.7	0.2	0.1	6.9	14,866	104,937	40,971	-1,246	-779	-271	-83
		'07	74.0	18.1	...	7.9	242,456	94.2	0.3	0.1	5.3	22,260	118,342	39,866	8,090	-2,125	-2,457	-2,465
		'08	74.4	16.8	...	8.8	245,170	94.3	0.3	0.1	5.3	19,228	123,727	38,587	2,400	-5,066	-3,481	-5,668
		'09	74.2	15.1	...	10.7	248,445	93.2	0.3	0.1	6.3	19,024	138,924	42,543	1,397	-2,036	-1,661	-725
		Rating History: A- g, 06/10/10; A- g, 06/12/09; A- g, 06/11/08; A- g, 06/18/07; A- g, 06/20/06																
COLUMBIAN MUTUAL LIFE INS CO Columbian Mutual Life Insurance Company Thomas E. Rattmann Chairman, President & CEO 4704 Vestal Parkway East Binghamton, NY 13902-1381 NY : 1883 : Mutual : Agency Home serv, Ind Life, Pre-need 607-724-2472 AMB# 006243 NAIC# 62103	A- Rating Outlook: Stable FSC VII	'05	75.0	9.7	2.7	12.6	889,008	67.6	0.2	27.7	4.4	92,370	102,283	84,019	-9,416	9,378	7,922	7,544
		'06	76.9	8.5	2.1	12.5	936,062	71.0	0.2	23.9	4.8	92,313	97,870	138,222	44,546	2,253	255	362
		'07	76.4	9.6	2.7	11.4	969,050	73.8	0.2	21.2	4.9	92,033	93,066	139,477	28,289	1,966	2,472	2,386
		'08	69.2	14.0	2.4	14.4	846,269	88.1	0.2	5.2	6.5	79,424	87,128	144,786	-126,681	12,104	9,172	6,083
		'09	67.7	14.9	2.8	14.6	872,777	88.5	0.2	4.9	6.5	86,529	81,882	147,123	17,052	9,692	7,704	6,651
		Rating History: A- g, 06/10/10; A- g, 06/12/09; A- g, 06/11/08; A- g, 06/18/07; A- g, 06/20/06																
COLUMBUS LIFE INSURANCE CO Western & Southern Mutual Holding Co Jimmy Joe Miller President & CEO 400 East 4th Street Cincinnati, OH 45202-3302 OH : 1988 : Stock : Agency Ind Ann, Ind Life 513-361-6700 AMB# 006244 NAIC# 99937	A+ Rating Outlook: Stable FSC XV	'05	75.1	3.9	3.5	17.4	2,538,844	62.0	0.3	24.5	13.2	229,767	230,844	213,272	58,694	-2,281	895	2,565
		'06	79.2	3.5	4.0	13.3	2,550,330	64.8	0.3	24.1	10.8	253,239	220,070	200,555	149,450	15,680	15,958	23,884
		'07	79.5	3.1	4.0	13.4	2,507,354	67.0	0.3	23.2	9.5	229,061	195,488	171,480	-57,717	26,907	23,026	15,905
		'08	79.6	2.8	3.8	13.8	2,500,566	67.3	0.2	24.1	8.4	208,958	237,863	211,303	17,078	25,625	28,633	16,963
		'09	81.8	2.5	1.8	13.9	2,719,124	63.5	0.2	29.6	6.7	271,591	282,011	393,102	146,392	17,817	19,929	3,857
		Rating History: A+ g, 05/18/10; A+ g, 06/29/09; A++g, 07/09/08; A++g, 06/14/07; A++g, 06/21/06																
COMBINED INS CO OF AMERICA ACE Limited Douglas R. Wendt Chairman, President & CEO 1000 North Milwaukee Avenue Glenview, IL 60025 IL : 1922 : Stock : Agency Ind A&H, Ind Life 847-953-2025 AMB# 006246 NAIC# 62146	A Rating Outlook: Stable FSC X	'05	68.8	1.7	11.1	18.4	2,786,305	31.9	54.3	0.1	13.7	868,327	1,338,053	1,217,172	57,511	173,004	106,067	100,863
		'06	72.1	1.4	11.3	15.1	2,878,446	29.7	56.5	0.1	13.8	809,253	1,355,421	1,237,996	72,045	218,295	152,337	176,879
		'07	70.1	0.6	12.8	16.5	3,214,961	27.5	59.9	0.1	12.5	933,732	1,400,824	1,246,673	307,178	312,633	237,478	232,971
		'08	77.3	0.6	8.6	13.5	2,382,484	27.6	56.3	0.1	16.0	593,513	1,390,233	695,056	-671,672	235,336	167,791	383,473
		'09	82.2	0.4	5.0	12.4	2,508,210	26.8	59.7	0.1	13.4	642,729	1,236,057	870,479	71,381	255,398	200,287	178,890
		Rating History: A g, 05/03/10; A g, 03/20/09; A g, 04/11/08; A gu, 12/17/07; A gu, 08/01/07																

BEST'S PROFITABILITY, LEVERAGE AND LIQUIDITY TESTS 2005 – 2009

Data in U.S. Dollars

	Profitability Tests							Leverage Tests						Liquidity Tests					
Un-Realized Capital Gains ($000)	Benefits Paid to NPW & Dep (%)	Comm. & Expenses to NPW & Dep (%)	NOG to Total Assets (%)	NOG to Total Rev (%)	Operating Return on Equity (%)	Net Yield (%)	Total Return (%)	Change in NPW & Dep (%)	NPW & Dep to Capital (X)	Capital & Surplus to Liabilities (%)	Surplus Relief (%)	Reins Leverage (%)	Change in Capital (%)	Quick Liquidity (%)	Current Liquidity (%)	Non-Invest Grade Bonds to Capital (%)	Delinq. & Foreclosed Mortgages to Capital (%)	Mort. & Credit Tenant Loans & R.E. to Capital (%)	Affiliated Invest to Capital (%)
49	40.9	49.5	2.6	6.5	20.2	5.81	5.73	7.2	2.5	15.5	...	12.1	14.9	64.5	83.0	...	...	6.8	...
...	41.2	49.7	1.3	3.4	9.8	5.70	5.79	8.4	2.4	16.6	...	14.4	14.5	63.6	82.7	2.6	...	5.5	...
...	44.5	50.8	1.2	3.0	8.2	5.50	5.44	11.5	2.3	18.1	...	12.1	14.7	65.1	84.7	...	...	4.5	...
...	42.6	53.9	0.0	-0.1	-0.2	5.59	5.10	16.3	3.3	13.7	...	16.3	-18.9	60.7	80.0	7.2	...	5.1	...
...	36.0	59.6	-1.6	-3.2	-15.3	5.30	4.05	21.6	5.0	10.1	...	20.8	-19.0	65.4	85.1	26.8	...	6.0	...
	Principal Lines of Business: OrdLife (67.7%), IndAnn (24.7%), IndA&H (3.8%), GrpAnn (2.4%), GrpA&H (1.3%)												Principal States: CA (19.5%), MD (14.8%), IL (6.6%), FL (6.0%), OH (5.4%)						
...	75.0	19.4	13.0	6.7	19.0	2.78	2.78	-0.6	2.7	220.5	...	15.8	7.7	204.3	238.9	...	...	...	...
...	76.4	20.6	9.2	4.8	13.4	4.07	4.07	6.9	2.6	222.5	...	...	9.8	353.9	353.9	...	...	...	...
...	88.9	19.0	-12.4	-5.8	-18.4	4.55	4.55	7.4	3.4	189.8	...	1.1	-17.8	340.3	340.3	...	...	...	...
...	84.3	19.1	-5.5	-2.3	-8.3	3.55	3.55	1.8	3.7	207.1	...	6.2	-5.1	287.1	287.1	...	...	...	...
...	81.4	18.6	2.1	0.8	3.0	2.27	2.25	6.4	3.7	246.2	...	0.9	6.0	324.3	324.3	...	...	...	...
	Principal Lines of Business: CompHosp/Med (91.1%), Medicare (8.9%)												Principal States: CO (100.0%)						
-864	82.2	14.6	4.0	1.5	5.4	5.44	7.48	-11.6	3.5	275.5	0.6	...	11.1	284.5	314.5	...	...	...	0.2
1,216	80.6	16.0	8.4	3.5	11.2	5.56	10.06	-1.1	3.0	313.2	0.9	...	15.6	310.2	343.1	...	...	...	0.2
-1,209	78.3	15.4	5.4	3.0	7.3	5.85	5.99	-5.8	2.2	281.9	0.0	...	25.4	314.0	338.1	...	...	...	0.1
-2,889	79.1	15.9	7.9	4.7	10.4	4.04	-5.83	2.4	2.2	358.3	0.0	...	5.3	359.8	384.4	...	...	...	...
4,504	80.5	14.3	7.8	4.1	10.1	3.49	9.47	17.6	2.4	317.8	0.0	...	6.9	319.1	348.8	...	...	...	...
	Principal Lines of Business: Dental (100.0%)												Principal States: CO (100.0%)						
-17	...	...	...	29.4	...	...	...	...	...	999.9	...	...	...	999.9	999.9	...	...	...	1.7
-5	999.9	999.9	-1.4	-55.3	-2.9	2.43	2.42	...	0.0	55.4	...	...	39.7	154.4	154.4	...	...	...	1.2
-1,195	999.9	442.4	1.0	42.8	2.0	2.27	0.27	-7.2	0.0	593.4	0.0	151.0	3.5	379.0	410.0	...	...	...	29.4
-14,629	417.9	645.6	-6.4	-86.2	-11.0	3.29	-16.20	999.9	0.0	101.8	0.9	876.9	123.5	58.3	59.8	...	...	...	78.2
16,228	520.3	18.6	-0.4	-9.8	-0.8	2.10	17.65	-14.1	0.0	142.7	2.7	652.7	22.9	60.9	65.2	...	...	...	82.6
	Principal Lines of Business: OrdLife (94.8%), IndAnn (5.0%), GrpLife (0.2%)																		
11	86.9	13.1	2.8	0.6	4.1	3.56	3.92	9.9	6.6	204.6	...	3.8	4.1	321.7	327.4	...	...	...	...
62	89.9	12.7	-4.8	-1.1	-7.7	5.24	5.70	2.4	7.3	144.1	...	4.1	-6.9	270.9	274.2	...	...	...	...
-177	92.7	12.1	-14.6	-3.2	-27.7	5.97	5.56	4.8	9.8	86.7	...	5.2	-21.7	199.6	201.6	...	...	...	...
-183	85.4	10.4	18.9	4.1	37.4	3.62	2.51	13.8	7.6	116.7	...	7.7	46.1	278.3	281.2	...	...	...	...
274	85.1	10.0	16.0	3.5	27.0	1.39	1.87	14.9	6.7	181.2	...	1.9	30.4	328.7	333.6	...	...	...	...
	Principal Lines of Business: Medicaid (86.8%), CompHosp/Med (13.2%)												Principal States: WA (100.0%)						
...	46.6	51.4	-2.0	-5.0	-22.7	5.15	5.21	16.9	4.6	7.8	13.2	249.2	-29.5	60.4	68.3	5.9	...	168.2	...
...	83.0	52.0	-0.1	-0.4	-1.7	5.59	5.74	-48.9	2.6	7.1	137.7	471.8	-9.7	56.7	63.8	...	...	276.5	...
...	88.0	47.6	-1.0	-3.1	-13.2	5.29	5.33	-2.7	1.7	10.6	126.0	443.8	47.8	57.5	65.5	4.4	...	188.9	...
...	87.7	54.0	-1.4	-4.3	-16.8	5.38	4.47	-3.2	2.0	8.7	160.5	683.4	-15.7	59.6	67.5	4.3	...	209.4	...
...	76.6	54.1	-0.7	-1.8	-8.7	5.58	6.01	10.3	2.1	8.8	193.9	864.5	2.3	61.9	69.5	5.5	...	186.9	...
	Principal Lines of Business: OrdLife (71.8%), GrpA&H (16.6%), GrpLife (11.5%), IndA&H (0.0%), IndAnn (0.0%)												Principal States: TX (9.8%), OH (9.4%), NC (9.3%), MA (8.8%), SC (6.3%)						
-9,188	100.4	51.0	0.9	5.8	8.3	5.74	4.78	-4.1	0.9	12.2	4.0	145.2	-5.8	66.3	73.3	12.4	...	89.2	23.7
-1,905	63.3	47.5	0.0	0.1	0.3	5.45	5.35	64.5	1.4	11.5	3.6	112.7	-0.4	67.5	74.6	11.2	...	82.6	21.0
-3,714	70.0	50.2	0.3	1.3	2.7	5.55	5.19	0.9	1.4	11.1	3.6	86.9	0.7	63.0	71.7	8.7	...	95.4	28.0
-12,123	64.1	47.0	1.0	4.6	10.7	6.16	4.46	3.8	1.8	10.8	4.0	263.0	-15.0	56.4	64.2	8.0	...	149.5	27.6
1,478	57.3	48.7	0.9	3.9	9.3	5.90	5.99	1.6	1.6	11.6	4.3	224.0	10.3	57.1	64.2	6.4	...	148.5	27.9
	Principal Lines of Business: OrdLife (85.3%), GrpLife (12.6%), IndAnn (0.8%), GrpA&H (0.6%), IndLife (0.4%)												Principal States: NY (54.8%), MI (6.7%), PA (5.3%), NJ (3.9%), NC (3.0%)						
1,604	83.2	40.9	0.0	0.3	0.4	6.18	6.42	-4.8	0.8	11.2	0.0	32.4	-10.0	52.1	65.1	35.7	...	42.8	3.7
1,593	100.7	27.5	0.6	4.7	6.6	6.15	6.62	-6.0	0.7	12.4	0.0	28.1	9.3	56.1	71.9	25.1	...	35.3	21.7
687	120.3	33.5	0.9	7.3	9.5	6.34	6.11	-14.5	0.7	11.2	0.0	35.4	-10.2	55.1	71.2	17.5	...	34.1	27.9
-14,482	86.1	26.1	1.1	8.2	13.1	6.19	5.09	23.2	1.0	9.8	0.0	38.8	-12.5	57.8	71.5	30.7	...	35.3	31.2
10,035	52.8	12.3	0.8	5.1	8.3	5.75	5.51	86.0	1.4	12.0	0.0	33.8	30.3	57.4	72.0	59.7	...	25.9	30.0
	Principal Lines of Business: GrpAnn (35.4%), IndAnn (34.8%), OrdLife (29.7%), IndA&H (0.1%)												Principal States: OH (26.7%), FL (7.0%), PA (6.3%), CA (6.3%), TX (4.6%)						
47,905	40.9	49.5	3.9	7.6	12.4	4.31	6.26	-0.8	1.3	48.4	7.2	43.7	4.5	88.2	100.2	5.7	...	5.2	26.2
-26,181	41.3	49.6	5.4	10.3	18.2	6.96	7.14	1.7	1.5	41.4	6.1	40.7	-7.2	87.9	100.5	0.5	...	4.9	40.4
10,865	40.7	47.0	7.8	16.1	27.2	5.91	6.30	0.7	1.3	44.0	5.5	30.5	16.4	101.4	114.4	0.6	...	1.8	42.0
-23,220	58.7	74.6	6.0	18.3	22.0	5.86	13.53	-44.2	1.1	35.7	11.1	123.4	-36.1	81.9	93.5	1.0	...	2.3	29.5
-31,870	46.1	41.3	8.2	16.7	32.4	8.02	6.14	25.2	1.3	34.8	22.1	114.6	3.3	90.7	100.9	1.7	...	1.4	19.9
	Principal Lines of Business: IndA&H (78.9%), GrpA&H (13.1%), OrdLife (7.8%), IndAnn (0.2%), GrpLife (0.0%)												Principal States: CA (3.7%), OH (3.6%), PA (3.5%), MN (3.0%)						

Data in U.S. Dollars

COMPANY NAME Ultimate Parent Association Principal Officer Mailing Address Dom. : Began Bus. : Struct. : Mktg. Specialty Phone # AMB# NAIC#	Best's Financial Strength Rating FSC	Data Year	Balance Sheet Bonds (%)	Mort. Loans & R.E. (%)	Com & Pref. Stock (%)	All Other Assets (%)	Total Assets ($000)	Life Reserves (%)	Health Reserves %)	Ann Res. & Dep. Liabilities (%)	All Other Liabilities (%)	Capital & Surplus ($000)	Operations Direct Premiums Written ($000)	Net Premiums Written & Deposits ($000)	Operating Cash Flow ($000)	NOG Before Taxes ($000)	NOG After Taxes ($000)	Net Income ($000)
COMBINED LIFE INS CO OF NY ACE Limited Douglas R. Wendt Chairman, CEO & President 1000 North Milwaukee Avenue Glenview, IL 60025 NY : 1971 : Stock : Agency Ind A&H, Ind Life 518-220-9333 AMB# 008187 NAIC# 78697	**A** Rating Outlook: Stable **FSC X**	'05	88.1	...	0.1	11.8	326,061	30.0	50.0	...	19.9	52,109	142,759	132,911	27,803	15,544	8,101	8,101
		'06	87.9	...	0.1	12.0	337,712	30.1	50.1	...	19.8	50,954	144,421	138,669	13,597	24,026	14,835	14,824
		'07	83.1	...	2.0	15.0	359,855	29.6	64.1	...	6.3	60,071	148,543	145,033	19,278	24,047	17,177	16,856
		'08	82.7	...	1.9	15.5	375,950	28.1	63.4	...	8.6	59,122	150,497	145,429	13,952	40,461	28,580	26,369
		'09	89.7	...	0.1	10.2	391,081	27.7	62.9	...	9.3	61,635	139,003	138,014	16,692	33,275	21,851	20,531
		Rating History: A g, 05/03/10; A g, 03/20/09; A g, 04/11/08; A gu, 12/17/07; A gu, 08/01/07																
COMMENCEMENT BAY LIFE INS CO Regence Group Murphy J. Hensley President P.O. Box 1271 Portland, OR 97207-1271 WA : 1992 : Non-Profit : Other Inactive 206-464-3600 AMB# 068406 NAIC# 78879	**NR-3**	'05	32.7	...	...	67.3	22,306	...	65.2	...	34.8	21,671	...	...	499	586	405	405
		'06	56.8	...	...	43.2	22,693	...	...	...	100.0	22,323	...	...	687	1,001	734	734
		'07	53.9	...	...	46.1	23,578	...	...	...	100.0	23,073	...	...	765	1,125	713	713
		'08	67.5	...	...	32.5	7,064	...	...	...	100.0	5,957	...	...	-16,997	671	344	344
		'09	97.6	...	...	2.4	6,608	...	...	...	100.0	6,280	...	...	-511	342	330	330
		Rating History: NR-3, 06/11/10; NR-3, 06/17/09; NR-3, 11/19/08; NR-3, 10/16/07; NR-3, 08/28/06																
COMMERCIAL TRAVELERS MUTUAL Commercial Travelers Mutual Insurance Co Paul H. Trevvett President & CEO 70 Genesee Street Utica, NY 13502-3502 NY : 1883 : Mutual : Agency Student A&H, Group A&H, Dis inc 315-797-5200 AMB# 007361 NAIC# 81426	**B+** Rating Outlook: Negative **FSC IV**	'05	54.6	0.8	17.7	26.9	38,016	...	88.8	...	11.2	11,307	20,804	36,086	2,668	835	696	673
		'06	42.8	0.8	18.6	37.8	35,551	...	92.9	...	7.1	11,917	20,862	34,004	-2,206	535	505	467
		'07	44.1	0.7	16.7	38.5	37,617	...	92.6	...	7.4	12,829	20,995	36,532	1,495	1,965	1,452	1,540
		'08	34.2	0.7	15.6	49.5	35,203	...	93.0	...	7.0	12,418	19,147	33,404	-827	1,671	1,259	988
		'09	26.6	0.6	14.7	58.0	33,773	...	89.1	...	10.9	8,780	19,809	34,797	-2,250	-3,231	-2,668	-2,654
		Rating History: B+, 04/30/10; B+ g, 05/19/09; B+ g, 06/13/08; B+ g, 05/17/07; B g, 06/02/06																
COMMONWEALTH ANNUITY AND LIFE Goldman Sachs Group Inc Michael A. Reardon President & CEO 132 Turnpike Road, Suite 210 Southborough, MA 01772 MA : 1967 : Stock : Agency Ann, Var Univ life 508-460-2400 AMB# 008491 NAIC# 84824	**A-** Rating Outlook: Stable **FSC IX**	'05	11.9	...	...	88.1	10,084,391	2.0	0.0	10.8	87.2	374,091	181,568	138,006	125,179	-8,369	3,825	-2,335
		'06	9.4	...	0.5	90.2	10,556,864	1.7	...	9.2	89.1	368,937	148,640	212,957	-212,464	-13,177	-13,177	-35,525
		'07	8.8	...	0.7	90.4	9,653,746	1.6	...	8.8	89.6	461,351	113,418	617,013	-41,022	72,475	72,475	58,163
		'08	16.2	...	1.2	82.6	5,334,786	3.2	0.0	22.8	74.0	390,622	178,428	189,846	248,884	-253,872	-253,872	-247,090
		'09	31.8	...	2.3	65.9	6,929,434	21.5	0.0	15.9	62.6	455,862	177,892	1,559,433	1,271,564	-104,899	-104,899	-140,553
		Rating History: A- g, 08/24/09; A- g, 01/19/09; A-, 10/16/08; A-, 08/23/07; A-, 07/17/06																
COMMONWEALTH DEALERS LIFE INS Richard Barkhauser President & Treasurer 8001 W. Broad Street Richmond, VA 23294 VA : 1989 : Stock : Agency Credit A&H, Credit Life 800-229-0121 AMB# 068105 NAIC# 88374	**B+** Rating Outlook: Stable **FSC IV**	'05	79.7	1.6	3.3	15.4	25,014	47.2	35.8	...	17.0	6,716	1,700	3,884	-4,792	2,492	2,079	2,077
		'06	81.2	1.8	3.6	13.4	21,140	41.5	26.9	...	31.5	5,240	357	2,551	-4,367	2,599	2,238	2,237
		'07	80.6	2.2	3.3	13.9	16,452	50.9	27.6	...	21.5	5,545	70	3,042	-4,243	626	490	417
		'08	76.2	2.5	4.3	17.0	13,878	46.1	25.6	...	28.3	7,411	-76	476	-2,261	2,574	2,094	1,772
		'09	63.2	2.8	1.5	32.6	11,861	29.5	16.7	...	53.8	7,328	-104	200	-2,356	1,097	993	969
		Rating History: B+, 08/04/09; B+, 09/24/08; B+, 10/22/07; B+, 11/02/06; B+, 09/20/05																
COMMUNITY CARE BEHAVIORAL HLTH University of Pittsburgh Medical Center James Gavin CEO 112 Washington Place Pittsburgh, PA 15219 PA : 1997 : Non-Profit : Agency Health 412-454-2120 AMB# 064549 NAIC# 47024	**B++** Rating Outlook: Stable **FSC VIII**	'05	26.6	...	9.6	63.8	101,118	...	47.9	...	52.1	52,246	304,425	303,972	-8,739	9,211	9,211	9,124
		'06	32.0	...	10.2	57.7	111,470	...	63.7	...	36.3	66,169	340,739	340,307	16,914	13,736	13,736	14,150
		'07	18.3	...	6.8	74.9	160,396	...	60.3	...	39.7	82,414	541,425	541,108	6,862	18,065	18,065	18,322
		'08	12.7	...	3.9	83.4	166,563	...	61.6	...	38.4	84,283	593,445	593,002	13,270	7,029	7,029	1,958
		'09	15.9	...	4.4	79.7	186,054	...	66.2	...	33.8	101,785	641,219	640,680	27,899	15,726	15,726	15,868
		Rating History: B++, 01/29/10; B++, 02/26/09; B++, 08/24/07; B++, 01/12/07; NR-2, 02/17/06																
COMMUNITY CARE HEALTH PLAN INC[2] Kirby G. Shoaf CEO 1555 S. Layton Blvd. Milwaukee, WI 53215-1924 WI : 2005 : Stock : Not Available Health 414-385-6600 AMB# 064919 NAIC# 10756	**NR-5**	'05	...	...	...	...	...	...	...	...	...	...	...	...	...	...	...	...
		'06	32.3	...	...	67.7	10,867	...	73.0	...	27.0	6,612	58,326	58,163	784	4,485	4,485	4,485
		'07	34.5	...	1.4	64.1	19,611	...	66.5	...	33.5	12,808	69,174	68,965	9,342	5,835	5,835	5,847
		'08	39.6	...	0.8	59.5	18,822	...	63.2	...	36.8	11,223	72,832	72,562	-1,288	4,757	4,757	4,946
		'09	38.6	...	0.3	61.1	20,557	...	79.1	...	20.9	12,273	74,155	73,875	1,871	968	968	968
		Rating History: NR-5, 05/19/10; NR-5, 06/01/09; NR-5, 05/22/08; NR-5, 06/21/07																
COMMUNITY DENTAL ASSOCIATES[2] Melvyn N. Gorsen, D.D.S. President P.O. Box 1648 Paramus, NJ 07653-1648 NJ : 1981 : Stock : Broker Dental 856-692-4670 AMB# 064771 NAIC# 11214	**NR-5**	'05	...	...	...	100.0	327	...	...	...	100.0	103	939	939	13	1	1	1
		'06	...	...	...	100.0	357	...	...	...	100.0	103	1,026	1,026	47	0	0	0
		'07	...	...	...	100.0	360	...	...	...	100.0	103	998	998	3	0	0	0
		'08	...	...	...	100.0	362	...	...	...	100.0	103	1,010	1,010	1	0	0	0
		'09	...	...	...	100.0	378	...	...	...	100.0	103	1,042	1,042	-2	0	0	0
		Rating History: NR-5, 04/19/10; NR-5, 06/01/09; NR-5, 05/20/08; NR-5, 06/19/07; NR-5, 05/11/06																
COMMUNITY FIRST GRP HOSP SVC Bexar County Hospital District Charles L. Kight President 4801 NW Loop 410, Suite 1000 San Antonio, TX 78229 TX : 2001 : Stock : Broker Health 210-227-2347 AMB# 064787 NAIC# 11143	**NR-5**	'05	64.3	...	...	35.7	776	...	92.6	...	7.4	569	427	414	165	11	11	11
		'06	71.5	...	...	28.5	769	...	86.3	...	13.7	532	1,041	1,002	-28	-282	-282	-282
		'07	21.0	...	...	79.0	713	...	93.0	...	7.0	562	946	902	-54	0	0	0
		'08	2.3	...	...	97.7	2,257	...	88.5	...	11.5	996	3,608	3,427	764	-690	-690	-690
		'09	3.0	...	...	97.0	1,691	...	87.0	...	13.0	534	6,155	5,769	-514	-2,189	-2,189	-2,189
		Rating History: NR-5, 04/21/10; NR-5, 04/08/09; NR-5, 06/26/08; NR-5, 05/03/07; NR-5, 06/05/06																

BEST'S PROFITABILITY, LEVERAGE AND LIQUIDITY TESTS 2005 – 2009

Data in U.S. Dollars

	Profitability Tests							Leverage Tests						Liquidity Tests					
Un-Realized Capital Gains ($000)	Benefits Paid to NPW & Dep (%)	Comm. & Expenses to NPW & Dep (%)	NOG to Total Assets (%)	NOG to Total Rev (%)	Operating Return on Equity (%)	Net Yield (%)	Total Return (%)	Change in NPW & Dep (%)	NPW & Dep to Capital (X)	Capital & Surplus to Liabilities (%)	Surplus Relief (%)	Reins Leverage (%)	Change in Capital (%)	Quick Liquidity (%)	Current Liquidity (%)	Non-Invest Grade Bonds to Capital (%)	Delinq. & Foreclosed Mortgages to Capital (%)	Mort. & Credit Tenant Loans & R.E. to Capital (%)	Affiliated Invest to Capital (%)
...	57.6	33.2	2.6	5.4	17.1	4.41	4.77	-3.8	2.5	19.2	4.3	58.0	22.9	89.3	98.4	...	...	...	...
...	54.4	32.9	4.5	9.5	28.8	4.82	5.10	4.3	2.7	18.1	2.4	56.7	-1.8	85.5	95.9	3.7	...	...	...
...	30.5	32.3	4.9	10.5	30.9	5.30	5.41	4.6	2.4	20.4	1.0	46.6	18.0	85.6	97.9	2.9	...	...	...
...	49.9	29.1	7.8	17.5	48.0	5.24	4.74	0.3	2.4	18.8	0.4	47.9	-2.6	82.1	94.2	2.4	...	...	...
...	56.5	25.7	5.7	14.1	36.2	4.89	4.60	-5.1	2.2	18.8	0.1	44.1	4.3	81.6	92.4	5.9	...	...	...
Principal Lines of Business: IndA&H (74.4%), GrpA&H (12.8%), OrdLife (12.8%)														Principal States: NY (97.5%)					
...	...	...	1.8	67.1	1.9	2.83	2.83	-99.9	...	999.9	...	1.9	1.9	999.9	999.9	...	...	...	...
...	...	...	3.3	72.2	3.3	4.67	4.67	...	...	999.9	...	...	3.0	999.9	999.9	...	...	...	...
...	...	...	3.1	62.4	3.1	5.03	5.06	...	...	999.9	...	...	3.4	999.9	999.9	...	...	...	...
...	...	...	2.2	50.0	2.4	4.21	4.58	...	...	538.2	...	...	-74.2	791.3	792.9	...	...	...	...
...	...	...	4.8	92.0	5.4	3.94	5.34	...	...	999.9	...	...	5.5	999.9	999.9	...	...	...	...
-142	54.3	39.7	1.9	1.9	6.4	1.45	0.98	8.4	3.2	42.3	...	33.0	7.4	126.2	135.7	...	...	2.8	54.7
-29	68.3	37.6	1.4	1.4	4.3	2.16	1.97	-5.8	2.9	50.4	...	43.0	5.4	150.7	159.8	...	...	2.4	50.8
-477	59.6	38.1	4.0	3.9	11.7	2.22	1.11	7.4	2.8	51.8	...	40.6	7.7	149.8	159.6	...	...	2.1	44.3
-466	61.8	41.3	3.5	3.7	10.0	1.95	-0.19	-8.6	2.7	54.5	...	33.6	-3.2	151.3	158.2	...	...	2.0	43.5
-333	66.9	40.9	-7.7	-7.6	-25.2	0.82	-0.17	4.2	4.0	35.1	...	47.4	-29.3	121.9	125.8	...	...	2.5	57.1
Principal Lines of Business: GrpA&H (98.6%), IndA&H (1.4%)														Principal States: OH (19.7%), NJ (14.8%), ME (9.4%), NY (7.3%), AL (6.6%)					
27,668	999.9	72.9	0.0	1.5	0.8	4.82	6.45	-34.1	0.4	35.2	0.9	216.5	-32.9	91.8	105.2	2.0	...	...	...
-25,148	982.3	78.2	-0.1	-3.8	-3.5	5.69	2.39	54.3	0.6	16.6	0.8	588.1	-0.8	35.8	40.2	1.3	...	...	...
43,727	359.4	15.4	0.7	9.1	17.5	5.26	7.97	189.7	1.3	20.9	0.8	223.0	25.8	34.2	38.9	0.4	...	...	...
123,726	858.4	34.2	-3.4	-65.3	-59.6	4.53	14.48	-69.2	0.5	31.8	0.9	369.1	-15.6	80.6	87.9	0.4	...	...	...
-41,634	86.3	22.9	-1.7	-5.4	-24.8	6.84	3.45	721.4	3.4	18.3	3.9	307.3	17.0	70.3	80.5	0.5	...	...	34.0
Principal Lines of Business: OrdLife (86.0%), IndAnn (13.8%), GrpAnn (0.2%), GrpLife (0.0%), IndA&H (0.0%)														Principal States: CA (9.2%), PA (9.1%), TX (8.3%), FL (7.5%), IL (6.1%)					
47	74.5	104.7	7.6	34.4	32.7	3.70	4.32	-23.7	0.6	37.6	5.7	42.5	11.0	98.0	110.3	19.1	...	5.8	5.8
...	94.0	113.7	9.7	53.6	37.4	3.83	4.33	-34.3	0.5	34.3	5.2	45.8	-21.0	96.2	108.7	21.7	...	7.1	7.1
...	56.6	130.0	2.6	12.7	9.1	3.15	3.35	19.3	0.5	52.5	-3.1	13.8	4.9	118.4	131.0	18.0	...	6.5	6.5
-97	307.9	257.7	13.8	132.6	32.3	3.49	1.40	-84.3	0.1	116.0	1.2	2.7	31.7	181.3	198.6	10.6	...	4.7	4.7
97	624.8	337.7	7.7	142.0	13.5	2.88	4.07	-58.0	0.0	168.6	0.8	1.3	-0.1	269.0	286.9	9.5	...	4.5	4.5
Principal Lines of Business: CrdA&H (162.4%), CrdLife (-62.4%)																			
421	90.2	8.0	10.0	3.0	19.3	2.29	2.87	12.8	5.8	106.9	...	...	21.2	139.2	151.0	1.9	...	...	...
1,113	90.1	8.0	12.9	4.0	23.2	4.04	6.49	12.0	5.1	146.1	...	...	26.6	201.9	218.4	...	...	...	...
-711	90.6	8.1	13.3	3.3	24.3	3.97	3.37	59.0	6.6	105.7	...	...	24.6	147.2	158.4	...	...	...	...
-1,833	91.3	8.2	4.3	1.2	8.4	2.57	-5.52	9.6	7.0	102.4	...	...	2.3	164.3	175.3	0.1	...	...	7.1
2,665	90.7	7.9	8.9	2.4	16.9	1.29	4.03	8.0	6.3	120.8	...	...	20.8	215.1	229.9	1.7	...	...	5.9
Principal Lines of Business: Medicaid (99.4%), Life (0.6%)														Principal States: PA (100.0%)					
...	...	...	...	...	...	...	...	...	...	...	...	...	...	...	...	...	...	...	...
...	78.2	14.8	...	7.7	...	...	...	...	8.8	155.3	...	2.6	...	226.4	226.4	...	...	...	...
...	80.3	12.1	38.3	8.4	60.1	4.07	4.16	18.6	5.4	188.3	...	...	93.7	273.1	273.7	...	...	...	...
...	78.0	16.3	24.8	6.5	39.6	3.34	4.38	5.2	6.5	147.7	...	1.7	-12.4	224.8	225.1	...	...	...	...
...	85.7	13.4	4.9	1.3	8.2	1.54	1.54	1.8	6.0	148.2	...	2.0	9.4	229.4	229.5	...	...	...	...
Principal Lines of Business: Medicaid (55.2%), Medicare (44.8%)														Principal States: WI (100.0%)					
...	96.3	4.0	0.2	0.1	0.6	1.44	1.44	6.0	9.1	46.2	...	...	0.6	129.6	129.6	...	...	...	...
...	96.8	4.1	-0.1	0.0	-0.2	2.97	2.97	9.3	10.0	40.6	...	...	-0.2	132.8	132.8	...	...	...	...
...	96.5	4.4	0.0	0.0	0.0	2.66	2.66	-2.8	9.7	40.1	...	...	0.0	132.2	132.2	...	...	...	...
...	96.1	4.2	0.0	0.0	0.0	0.85	0.85	1.2	9.8	39.7	...	...	0.0	131.4	131.4	...	...	...	...
...	96.7	3.4	0.0	0.0	-0.1	0.19	0.19	3.2	10.1	37.4	...	...	-0.1	123.5	123.5	...	...	...	...
Principal Lines of Business: Dental (100.0%)														Principal States: NJ (100.0%)					
...	73.5	28.9	1.6	2.6	2.1	3.13	3.13	-1.2	0.7	274.9	...	...	13.7	478.2	491.6	...	...	...	...
...	115.2	16.4	-36.5	-27.2	-51.2	4.70	4.70	142.3	1.9	223.9	...	1.3	-6.6	394.2	403.9	...	...	...	...
...	88.9	14.3	-0.1	0.0	-0.1	4.04	4.04	-10.1	1.6	373.3	...	...	5.8	451.5	451.5	...	...	...	...
...	103.0	17.9	-46.5	-20.0	-88.5	2.56	2.56	280.2	3.4	79.0	...	1.2	77.1	114.6	114.6	...	...	...	...
...	120.1	18.0	-99.9	-37.9	-99.9	0.18	0.18	68.3	10.8	46.1	...	85.4	-46.4	80.1	80.1	...	...	...	...
Principal Lines of Business: CompHosp/Med (100.0%)														Principal States: TX (100.0%)					

Data in U.S. Dollars

COMPANY NAME Ultimate Parent Association Principal Officer Mailing Address Dom. : Began Bus. : Struct. : Mktg. Specialty Phone # AMB# NAIC#	Best's Financial Strength Rating FSC	Data Year	Balance Sheet Bonds (%)	Mort. Loans & R.E. (%)	Com & Pref. Stock (%)	All Other Assets (%)	Total Assets ($000)	Life Reserves (%)	Health Reserves %)	Ann Res. & Dep. Liabilities (%)	All Other Liabilities (%)	Capital & Surplus ($000)	Operations Direct Premiums Written ($000)	Net Premiums Written & Deposits ($000)	Operating Cash Flow ($000)	NOG Before Taxes ($000)	NOG After Taxes ($000)	Net Income ($000)
COMMUNITY FIRST HEALTH PLANS Bexar County Hospital District Charles L. Kight President 4801 NW Loop 410, Suite 1000 San Antonio, TX 78229 TX : 1995 : Non-Profit : Broker Group A&H, Health 210-227-2347 AMB# 064049 NAIC# 95248	NR-5	'05	64.5	...	...	35.5	35,236	...	88.0	...	12.0	18,476	129,932	127,083	3,159	5,636	5,636	5,634
		'06	48.5	...	...	51.5	41,865	...	91.2	...	8.8	15,378	156,991	153,579	4,163	-1,693	-1,693	-1,693
		'07	41.2	...	...	58.8	52,454	...	85.1	...	14.9	19,139	204,271	198,802	11,911	4,469	4,469	4,469
		'08	32.9	...	...	67.1	63,582	...	86.3	...	13.7	25,270	220,925	216,294	11,380	7,938	7,938	7,399
		'09	49.0	...	...	51.0	56,450	...	91.7	...	8.3	17,176	251,852	249,283	-7,785	-5,790	-5,790	-5,678
		Rating History: NR-5, 04/22/10; NR-5, 08/26/09; C+ pd, 09/03/08; C+ pd, 06/28/07; C++pd, 08/08/06																
COMMUNITY HEALTH CHOICE INC[2] Glen R. Johnson, M.D. President 2636 South Loop West, Suite 700 Houston, TX 77054 TX : 1997 : Non-Profit : Broker Health 713-295-2200 AMB# 064454 NAIC# 95615	NR-5	'05	...	...	...	100.0	44,804	...	52.3	...	47.7	20,578	115,715	113,316	6,875	7,601	7,601	7,601
		'06	...	...	...	100.0	72,432	...	60.3	...	39.7	24,284	183,062	180,548	19,656	7,204	7,204	7,204
		'07	...	...	...	100.0	115,627	...	71.4	...	28.6	31,112	323,400	320,579	46,804	8,333	8,333	8,333
		'08	17.2	...	...	82.8	165,008	...	73.4	...	26.6	60,647	387,055	384,620	44,443	25,763	25,763	25,763
		'09	40.2	...	...	59.8	148,903	...	45.4	...	54.6	76,813	427,432	424,993	-12,996	11,680	11,680	11,680
		Rating History: NR-5, 04/07/10; NR-5, 08/26/09; C+ pd, 06/06/08; C++pd, 06/12/07; C++pd, 07/10/06																
COMMUNITY HEALTH GROUP Norma Diaz President 740 Bay Boulevard Chula Vista, CA 91910 CA : 1986 : Non-Profit : Broker Group A&H, Health 619-422-0422 AMB# 064145	NR-5	'05	...	8.4	...	91.6	36,345	...	...	...	100.0	4,838	122,516	122,516	-9,250	-1,413	-1,413	-1,413
		'06	...	9.8	...	90.2	29,296	...	...	...	100.0	12,392	121,129	121,129	-130	7,554	7,554	7,554
		'07	...	7.1	...	92.9	37,685	...	...	...	100.0	16,844	123,862	123,862	12,949	4,452	4,452	4,452
		'08	...	6.9	...	93.1	39,927	...	...	...	100.0	15,664	145,838	145,838	-4,304	-1,180	-1,180	-1,180
		'09	...	5.7	...	94.3	45,106	...	...	...	100.0	19,204	165,074	165,074	11,516	3,540	3,540	3,540
		Rating History: NR-5, 05/05/10; NR-5, 08/26/09; C+ pd, 07/28/08; C+ pd, 07/20/07; C pd, 08/29/06																
COMMUNITY HEALTH PLAN Heartland Health Lowell C. Kruse President & CEO 137 North Belt Highway St. Joseph, MO 64506 MO : 1994 : Non-Profit : Broker Health 816-271-1247 AMB# 064182 NAIC# 95145	NR-4	'05	42.6	...	21.7	35.6	14,883	...	43.6	...	56.4	6,055	62,323	62,021	-665	221	221	196
		'06	53.1	...	21.4	25.5	9,595	...	53.6	...	46.4	2,875	45,729	45,515	-3,271	-2,881	-2,835	-2,746
		'07	39.4	...	28.6	31.9	8,280	...	42.6	...	57.4	3,593	32,261	32,002	-1,392	-1,147	-868	-748
		'08	39.9	...	30.0	30.1	8,026	...	43.5	...	56.5	3,299	28,951	28,674	-576	-1,789	-1,596	-1,855
		'09	...	...	...	...	...	...	...	...	...	...	...	...	...	...	...	...
		Rating History: NR-4, 06/04/09; C++g, 06/04/09; C++g, 06/18/08; C++g, 05/23/07; B gu, 04/06/07																
COMMUNITY HEALTH PLAN INS CO Heartland Health Lowell C. Kruse President 137 North Belt Highway St. Joseph, MO 64506 MO : 1981 : Stock : Broker Group A&H, Ind A&H 816-271-1247 AMB# 009101 NAIC# 92681	NR-4	'05	55.5	...	5.5	39.0	3,849	...	52.0	...	48.0	1,966	7,300	7,269	972	454	374	376
		'06	47.3	...	6.9	45.7	3,538	...	53.3	...	46.7	1,272	10,022	9,960	-314	-911	-826	-818
		'07	30.5	...	6.5	63.0	3,686	...	46.0	...	54.0	1,743	7,414	7,092	330	558	358	398
		'08	37.4	...	3.9	58.7	3,843	...	43.1	...	56.9	2,024	9,631	9,240	156	549	358	258
		'09	...	...	...	...	...	...	...	...	...	...	...	...	...	...	...	...
		Rating History: NR-4, 06/04/09; C++g, 06/04/09; C++g, 06/18/08; C++g, 05/23/07; B gu, 04/06/07																
COMMUNITY HEALTH PLAN OF WA Community Health Network of Washington Darnell Dent President & CEO 720 Olive Way, Suite 300 Seattle, WA 98101-1866 WA : 1996 : Non-Profit : Other Direct Health 206-521-8833 AMB# 064472 NAIC# 47049	NR-5	'05	22.0	...	20.8	57.1	129,903	...	25.6	...	74.4	83,025	451,193	441,813	2,329	9,652	9,652	10,755
		'06	23.1	...	20.3	56.6	141,024	...	25.9	...	74.1	79,506	472,945	464,786	11,967	-5,021	-5,021	-4,550
		'07	20.9	...	3.7	75.4	147,173	...	43.5	...	56.5	77,583	528,883	521,334	12,943	-3,481	-3,481	5,548
		'08	18.4	...	14.5	67.1	131,425	...	55.9	...	44.1	63,431	541,736	533,495	-10,023	-3,495	-3,495	-4,260
		'09	34.5	...	16.1	49.4	150,862	...	53.5	...	46.5	69,451	568,564	558,581	17,261	5,876	5,876	4,149
		Rating History: NR-5, 04/06/10; NR-5, 08/26/09; B pd, 05/23/08; B+ pd, 05/30/07; B+ pd, 05/30/06																
COMMUNITY INSURANCE COMPANY WellPoint Inc. Charles L. Slater Chairman & President 6775 W. Washington Street Milwaukee, WI 53214 OH : 1995 : Stock : Agency Group A&H 513-872-8100 AMB# 011803 NAIC# 10345	A Rating Outlook: Stable FSC X	'05	77.8	2.5	7.3	12.3	1,391,739	...	52.5	...	47.5	593,193	3,611,042	3,609,889	77,976	498,435	314,982	316,713
		'06	64.9	2.4	8.5	24.1	1,398,289	...	54.8	...	45.2	573,694	4,098,492	4,096,508	-119,826	536,891	381,698	374,588
		'07	56.7	1.8	12.2	29.4	1,772,187	...	52.6	...	47.4	642,520	4,657,259	4,656,948	407,223	565,272	396,096	385,844
		'08	61.5	1.8	9.5	27.1	1,738,041	...	34.9	...	65.1	658,817	4,470,409	4,470,332	-93,805	641,006	702,907	554,117
		'09	37.1	1.0	6.4	55.5	2,919,438	...	16.3	...	83.7	626,514	4,067,941	4,073,144	-45,214	290,690	189,134	2,516,320
		Rating History: A, 04/27/10; A, 01/23/09; A, 03/20/08; A, 11/06/06; A, 12/29/05																
COMMUNITYCARE HMO INC[2] Richard W. Todd President & CEO 218 West 6th Street Tulsa, OK 74119 OK : 1994 : Stock : Broker Group A&H, Health 918-594-5200 AMB# 064165 NAIC# 11691	NR-5	'05	7.7	...	...	92.3	109,982	...	39.6	...	60.4	43,294	490,595	486,215	26,818	11,140	5,596	5,596
		'06	12.1	...	...	87.9	130,470	...	32.1	...	67.9	51,968	516,555	513,755	16,835	19,078	13,549	13,549
		'07	19.0	...	...	81.0	114,312	...	60.4	...	39.6	57,128	543,784	540,533	-18,397	10,759	7,064	7,064
		'08	15.7	...	...	84.3	112,267	...	62.6	...	37.4	63,617	555,009	551,369	-2,102	6,648	4,799	3,840
		'09	21.0	...	...	79.0	126,209	...	48.4	...	51.6	69,954	567,585	562,166	17,835	7,241	4,310	4,310
		Rating History: NR-5, 04/26/10; NR-5, 08/26/09; C++pd, 07/14/08; C++pd, 06/19/07; C++pd, 07/17/06																
COMPANION LIFE INS COMPANY Mutual of Omaha Insurance Company Daniel P. Neary Chairman & President Mutual of Omaha Plaza Omaha, NE 68175 NY : 1949 : Stock : Agency Ind Ann, Ind Life, SPDA's 402-342-7600 AMB# 006258 NAIC# 62243	A+ Rating Outlook: Stable FSC XIII	'05	89.7	0.4	...	9.9	663,790	40.5	0.0	33.5	26.0	54,361	88,852	74,214	15,173	3,227	1,859	-742
		'06	90.1	1.3	...	8.5	673,757	45.0	0.0	31.2	23.8	57,989	92,606	77,166	10,030	8,649	4,407	4,093
		'07	87.3	1.6	...	11.0	672,853	49.9	0.0	39.6	10.5	58,047	89,894	74,308	-13,101	8,124	3,934	3,932
		'08	85.4	6.5	...	8.1	699,427	52.6	0.0	36.8	10.5	61,471	91,184	80,711	42,131	8,414	3,829	2,941
		'09	81.8	5.8	...	12.4	751,040	53.1	0.0	34.8	12.1	65,407	99,153	94,935	30,823	5,212	2,001	750
		Rating History: A+ g, 01/20/10; A+ g, 04/08/09; A+ g, 06/09/08; A+ g, 06/06/07; A g, 06/07/06																

Data in U.S. Dollars

—	Profitability Tests							Leverage Tests						Liquidity Tests					
Un-Realized Capital Gains ($000)	Benefits Paid to NPW & Dep (%)	Comm. & Expenses to NPW & Dep (%)	NOG to Total Assets (%)	NOG to Total Rev (%)	Operating Return on Equity (%)	Net Yield (%)	Total Return (%)	Change in NPW & Dep (%)	NPW & Dep to Capital (X)	Capital & Surplus to Liabilities (%)	Surplus Relief (%)	Reins Leverage (%)	Change in Capital (%)	Quick Liquidity (%)	Current Liquidity (%)	Non-Invest Grade Bonds to Capital (%)	Delinq. & Foreclosed Mortgages to Capital (%)	Mort. & Credit Tenant Loans & R.E. to Capital (%)	Affiliated Invest to Capital (%)
...	85.9	11.1	16.1	4.4	36.4	3.57	3.56	-4.1	6.9	110.2	...	3.0	47.8	230.7	240.5	...	...	...	6.0
...	91.3	10.7	-4.4	-1.1	-10.0	3.98	3.98	20.8	10.0	58.1	...	2.1	-16.8	179.2	187.3	...	...	...	8.8
...	88.7	10.0	9.5	2.2	25.9	4.88	4.88	29.4	10.4	57.4	...	11.9	24.5	211.9	222.5	...	...	...	7.2
...	86.2	10.9	13.7	3.6	35.7	3.15	2.11	8.8	8.6	66.0	...	2.7	32.0	140.7	142.2	...	...	...	9.9
...	91.9	10.6	-9.6	-2.3	-27.3	1.14	1.36	15.3	14.5	43.7	...	1.4	-32.0	113.3	113.7	...	...	...	24.6
Principal Lines of Business: Medicaid (78.1%), CompHosp/Med (21.9%)														Principal States: TX (100.0%)					
...	82.4	12.1	18.6	6.6	45.5	3.33	3.33	11.6	5.5	84.9	...	0.5	60.2	306.2	310.3	...	...	...	...
...	86.7	11.0	12.3	3.9	32.1	6.13	6.13	59.3	7.4	50.4	...	1.2	18.0	194.0	195.4	...	...	...	...
...	89.6	9.1	8.9	2.6	30.1	4.98	4.98	77.6	10.3	36.8	...	0.8	28.1	194.7	197.6	...	...	...	...
...	85.7	9.0	18.4	6.6	56.2	4.03	4.03	20.0	6.3	58.1	...	2.3	94.9	242.6	243.6	...	...	...	...
...	88.3	9.1	7.4	2.7	17.0	0.28	0.28	10.5	5.5	106.6	...	0.4	26.7	250.0	256.9	...	...	...	...
Principal Lines of Business: Medicaid (67.6%), CompHosp/Med (32.4%)														Principal States: TX (100.0%)					
...	91.7	9.7	-3.6	-1.2	-25.5	0.38	0.38	2.9	25.3	15.4	...	...	-22.6	49.5	49.5	...	...	63.4	63.4
...	85.3	9.2	23.0	6.2	87.7	0.83	0.83	-1.1	9.8	73.3	...	...	156.1	93.2	93.2	...	...	23.2	23.2
...	88.7	8.6	13.3	3.6	30.5	0.77	0.77	2.3	7.4	80.8	...	...	35.9	140.9	140.9	...	...	15.9	15.9
...	94.3	7.2	-3.0	-0.8	-7.3	0.50	0.50	17.7	9.3	64.6	...	...	-7.0	103.3	103.3	...	...	17.7	17.7
...	91.6	6.6	8.3	2.1	20.3	0.22	0.22	13.2	8.6	74.1	...	...	22.6	140.6	140.6	...	...	13.5	13.5
Principal Lines of Business: Medicaid (95.2%), Medicare (4.8%)																			
-204	88.5	11.8	1.6	0.4	4.4	3.13	1.14	-1.0	10.2	68.6	...	...	47.5	115.8	118.5	...	...	...	32.5
-686	93.4	13.7	-23.2	-6.2	-63.5	3.64	-1.98	-26.6	15.8	42.8	...	...	-52.5	110.2	113.0	...	...	...	44.3
392	91.0	13.5	-9.7	-2.7	-26.8	3.68	10.46	-29.7	8.9	76.7	...	...	25.0	130.8	133.9	...	...	...	48.5
294	94.9	13.6	-19.6	-5.4	-46.3	2.74	3.39	-10.4	8.7	69.8	...	...	-8.2	109.1	113.0	...	...	...	61.3
...	...	...	...	...	...	...	...	...	...	...	...	...	...	...	...	...	...	...	...
9	88.4	12.4	11.5	4.8	20.7	2.78	3.13	85.7	3.7	104.4	...	...	19.0	212.0	214.2	...	...	...	...
10	104.1	12.5	-22.4	-7.7	-51.0	4.15	4.69	37.0	7.8	56.2	...	7.2	-35.3	162.0	164.2	...	...	...	...
-25	75.4	18.7	9.9	5.0	23.8	3.97	4.41	-28.8	4.1	89.7	...	...	37.0	231.3	233.9	...	...	...	...
5	76.4	18.7	9.5	3.8	19.0	2.71	0.21	30.3	4.6	111.2	...	...	16.1	237.3	241.6	...	...	...	...
...	...	...	...	...	...	...	...	...	...	...	...	...	...	...	...	...	...	...	...
375	84.1	14.3	7.5	2.2	12.5	2.60	3.85	17.7	5.3	177.1	...	6.8	15.6	338.8	351.8	...	...	...	...
2,028	86.5	15.7	-3.7	-1.1	-6.2	4.37	6.35	5.2	5.8	129.2	...	6.4	-4.2	292.4	304.9	...	...	...	...
-8,482	86.2	15.6	-2.4	-0.7	-4.4	4.57	5.39	12.2	6.7	111.5	...	7.0	-2.4	323.9	331.4	...	...	...	...
-10,031	85.0	15.1	-2.5	-0.7	-5.0	2.94	-5.14	2.3	8.4	93.3	...	9.9	-18.2	272.8	279.0	0.0	...	...	...
17,804	86.1	13.4	4.2	1.0	8.8	1.32	14.67	4.7	8.0	85.3	...	7.7	9.5	231.9	239.0	0.1	...	...	...
Principal Lines of Business: Medicaid (64.2%), CompHosp/Med (29.7%), Medicare (6.0%)														Principal States: WA (100.0%)					
15,547	78.8	10.2	24.4	8.5	61.2	11.29	12.97	5.1	6.1	74.3	...	...	35.8	89.1	104.4	13.4	...	5.8	15.0
27,240	80.4	9.8	27.4	9.1	65.4	13.71	15.69	13.5	7.1	69.6	...	...	-3.3	72.9	85.7	14.3	...	5.8	17.1
-7,104	82.8	8.1	25.0	8.2	65.1	14.04	12.59	13.7	7.2	56.9	...	...	12.0	92.8	107.2	13.4	...	4.9	16.2
34,415	81.6	8.3	40.0	15.2	108.0	14.18	6.31	-4.0	6.8	61.0	...	...	2.5	78.1	89.9	17.9	...	4.7	18.0
-7,909	83.6	10.9	8.1	4.6	29.4	3.58	331.12	-8.9	6.5	27.3	0.0	0.1	-4.9	131.5	141.6	22.6	...	4.7	4.7
Principal Lines of Business: CompHosp/Med (71.5%), Medicare (23.1%), MedSup (2.6%), OtherHlth (1.7%), Dental (1.1%)														Principal States: OH (100.0%)					
...	90.0	8.4	6.0	1.1	14.0	3.39	3.39	32.3	11.2	64.9	...	0.3	18.7	258.1	267.5	...	...	...	...
...	89.8	7.6	11.3	2.6	28.4	5.26	5.26	5.7	9.9	66.2	...	4.1	20.0	251.6	261.1	...	...	...	...
...	90.3	8.9	5.8	1.3	13.0	5.61	5.61	5.2	9.5	99.9	...	1.1	9.9	274.4	278.1	8.0	...	...	...
...	90.7	8.7	4.2	0.9	7.9	3.31	2.25	2.0	8.7	130.8	...	2.9	11.4	334.0	338.1	4.8	...	...	...
...	90.4	8.6	3.6	0.8	6.5	0.96	0.96	2.0	8.0	124.4	...	0.1	10.0	242.1	242.1	3.5	...	...	...
Principal Lines of Business: CompHosp/Med (55.3%), Medicare (44.7%)														Principal States: OK (100.0%)					
226	67.1	38.8	0.3	1.7	3.3	6.00	5.65	15.9	1.3	9.8	4.1	248.5	-6.9	51.9	74.7	50.8	...	5.2	...
28	80.4	33.2	0.7	3.8	7.8	5.94	5.92	4.0	1.3	10.4	2.9	215.4	7.0	50.9	73.4	40.1	...	14.7	...
...	-8.2	33.5	0.6	3.7	6.8	5.86	5.89	-3.7	1.2	10.4	-0.8	85.1	0.6	49.3	71.7	32.7	...	17.8	...
...	71.1	25.7	0.6	3.5	6.4	5.99	5.88	8.6	1.2	10.5	2.8	76.4	4.9	47.8	68.6	45.0	...	69.6	...
-258	56.8	27.4	0.3	1.7	3.2	5.69	5.50	17.6	1.4	10.6	2.6	74.2	6.1	47.5	69.5	31.8	...	63.1	7.2
Principal Lines of Business: OrdLife (66.6%), GrpAnn (18.1%), IndAnn (14.5%), GrpLife (0.9%), IndA&H (0.0%)														Principal States: NY (97.3%)					

Data in U.S. Dollars

COMPANY NAME Ultimate Parent Association Principal Officer Mailing Address Dom. : Began Bus. : Struct. : Mktg. Specialty Phone # AMB# NAIC#	Best's Financial Strength Rating FSC	Data Year	Balance Sheet Bonds (%)	Mort. Loans & R.E. (%)	Com & Pref. Stock (%)	All Other Assets (%)	Total Assets ($000)	Life Reserves (%)	Health Reserves (%)	Ann Res. & Dep. Liabilities (%)	All Other Liabilities (%)	Capital & Surplus ($000)	Operations Direct Premiums Written ($000)	Net Premiums Written & Deposits ($000)	Operating Cash Flow ($000)	NOG Before Taxes ($000)	NOG After Taxes ($000)	Net Income ($000)
COMPANION LIFE INSURANCE CO Blue Cross&Blue Shield of South Carolina	A+	'05	55.7	...	15.2	29.1	87,616	22.1	31.9	0.5	45.5	47,352	253,188	113,129	2,918	8,582	6,013	6,557
Trescott N. Hinton, Jr. President & COO		'06	54.9	...	15.1	30.1	95,850	22.0	29.1	0.8	48.1	54,363	286,803	124,045	8,313	9,844	6,939	7,427
P.O. Box 100102 Columbia, SC 29202-3102	Rating Outlook: Stable	'07	52.6	...	14.4	33.1	122,047	15.9	24.2	0.4	59.5	63,045	304,492	135,530	21,693	13,606	9,194	9,477
SC : 1970 : Stock : Broker Dental, Group A&H, Group Life		'08	47.8	...	8.0	44.2	130,402	15.0	23.0	0.5	61.6	67,499	312,026	137,872	14,805	12,103	7,940	6,696
803-735-1251		'09	56.4	...	14.8	28.7	140,246	17.5	26.0	0.4	56.0	84,831	332,564	152,212	7,280	10,755	7,549	6,992
AMB# 008064 NAIC# 77828	FSC XIV	**Rating History: A+ g, 12/16/09; A+ g, 12/18/08; A+ g, 11/16/07; A+ g, 01/25/07; A+ g, 01/12/06**																
COMPBENEFITS COMPANY Humana Inc	A-	'05	0.5	...	...	99.5	17,406	...	89.7	...	10.3	2,117	135,698	135,698	-6,353	3,235	2,345	2,345
Gerald L. Ganoni President		'06	0.4	...	...	99.6	23,027	...	52.6	...	47.4	5,646	139,694	164,771	4,943	5,447	3,595	3,595
100 Mansell Court East, Suite 400 Roswell, GA 30076	Rating Outlook: Stable	'07	0.3	...	...	99.7	28,050	...	74.2	...	25.8	12,564	153,342	184,241	-133	4,695	4,017	4,017
FL : 1978 : Stock : Broker Dental		'08	0.3	...	3.4	96.3	30,545	...	53.1	...	46.9	15,178	141,069	170,114	9,456	-3,608	-365	-365
770-998-8936		'09	0.3	...	...	99.7	37,582	...	44.2	...	55.8	18,593	128,245	157,446	8,380	5,058	2,965	2,964
AMB# 064760 NAIC# 52015	FSC XV	**Rating History: A- g, 06/02/10; B++, 06/05/09; B++, 06/05/08; NR-5, 09/05/07; NR-5, 10/11/06**																
COMPBENEFITS DENTAL INC Humana Inc	A-	'05	14.6	...	...	85.4	3,030	...	36.0	...	64.0	877	19,108	19,108	-733	1,202	795	795
Gerald L. Ganoni President		'06	10.5	...	...	89.5	4,180	...	25.6	...	74.4	1,401	16,663	16,663	1,034	811	540	540
100 Mansell Court East, Suite 400 Roswell, GA 30076	Rating Outlook: Stable	'07	9.6	...	...	90.4	4,601	...	41.1	...	58.9	2,344	17,576	17,576	349	932	614	614
IL : 1990 : Stock : Not Available Dental		'08	7.3	...	29.8	62.9	6,039	...	37.9	...	62.1	3,705	19,239	19,239	1,391	2,083	1,609	1,609
770-998-8936		'09	6.8	...	...	93.2	6,491	...	30.7	...	69.3	3,138	15,920	15,920	399	1,491	1,007	1,007
AMB# 064759 NAIC# 11228	FSC XV	**Rating History: A- g, 06/02/10; B++, 06/05/09; B++, 06/05/08; NR-5, 04/02/07; NR-5, 06/05/06**																
COMPBENEFITS INSURANCE CO Humana Inc	A-	'05	8.6	...	...	91.4	37,576	...	77.9	...	22.1	24,301	108,490	108,096	9,747	14,825	9,691	9,691
Gerald L. Ganoni President		'06	7.5	...	...	92.5	43,056	...	75.9	...	24.1	28,764	128,163	128,065	-3,819	14,885	9,704	9,704
100 Mansell Court East, Suite 400 Roswell, GA 30076	Rating Outlook: Stable	'07	7.9	...	...	92.1	63,557	...	33.0	...	67.0	35,049	134,659	135,052	35,051	24,166	16,692	16,692
TX : 1959 : Stock : Not Available Ann, Group A&H, Ind Life		'08	8.4	...	2.3	89.3	59,863	...	76.8	...	23.2	48,129	132,994	133,408	-3,999	20,190	10,488	10,490
770-998-8936		'09	10.8	...	...	89.2	46,972	...	59.9	...	40.1	32,205	127,430	127,401	-11,038	6,070	3,261	3,262
AMB# 006118 NAIC# 60984	FSC XV	**Rating History: A- g, 06/02/10; B++, 06/05/09; B++, 06/05/08; NR-5, 04/09/07; NR-5, 05/11/06**																
COMPCARE HEALTH SERVICES INS WellPoint Inc.	A	'05	40.4	0.2	...	59.3	209,296	...	33.1	...	66.9	121,664	397,507	397,507	64,367	2,771	-10,547	43,418
Steven J. Martenet President & CEO		'06	87.3	...	0.3	12.4	155,129	...	31.3	...	68.7	92,882	426,059	426,059	-54,833	12,931	12,558	12,137
6775 West Washington Street Milwaukee, WI 53214	Rating Outlook: Stable	'07	84.1	...	...	15.9	109,917	...	61.9	...	38.1	59,051	359,100	359,100	-41,248	8,347	8,192	7,538
WI : 1976 : Stock : Broker Group A&H, Ind A&H		'08	89.3	...	...	10.7	120,570	...	37.1	...	62.9	56,307	421,920	421,920	12,374	-3,465	-2,512	-4,889
414-459-5000		'09	96.1	...	...	3.9	128,397	...	2.5	...	97.5	63,739	473,290	473,290	6,560	17,073	13,936	13,116
AMB# 068610 NAIC# 95693	FSC VIII	**Rating History: A g, 04/27/10; A- g, 01/23/09; A- g, 03/20/08; A- g, 11/06/06; A- g, 12/29/05**																
CONCERN: EMPLOYEE ASSIST PROG	NR-5	'05	...	...	...	100.0	3,539	...	...	...	100.0	2,553	3,606	3,606	-272	525	525	525
Cecile Currier President		'06	...	...	...	100.0	4,240	...	...	...	100.0	3,261	4,117	4,117	314	709	709	709
2500 Grant Road Mountain View, CA 94040		'07	...	...	...	100.0	5,576	...	...	...	100.0	4,240	4,743	4,743	613	979	979	979
CA : 2001 : Mutual : Not Available Health		'08	...	...	...	100.0	7,283	...	...	...	100.0	5,775	5,401	5,401	806	1,535	1,535	1,535
650-940-7100		'09	...	...	...	100.0	8,754	...	...	...	100.0	7,312	5,849	5,849	456	1,514	1,514	1,514
AMB# 064737		**Rating History: NR-5, 03/22/10; NR-5, 03/13/09; NR-5, 03/11/08; NR-5, 04/05/07; NR-5, 04/11/06**																
CONCERT HEALTH PLAN INS CO[1]	NR-1	'05	17.4	...	...	82.6	14,009	...	...	...	100.0	8,252	28,895	28,846	...	2,646	2,646	2,645
Kianoosh Jafari, M.D. President		'06	24.3	...	...	75.7	16,369	...	...	...	100.0	9,469	30,434	30,384	...	52	52	52
2605 West 22nd Street, Suite 25 Oak Brook, IL 60523-4625		'07	19.4	...	...	80.6	15,868	...	...	...	100.0	8,572	28,432	28,383	...	144	66	66
IL : 2000 : Stock : Not Available		'08	32.5	...	...	67.5	12,962	...	...	...	100.0	7,549	29,115	29,066	...	2	-59	-59
630-990-1090		'09	25.7	...	...	74.3	11,120	...	...	...	100.0	6,955	28,624	28,574	...	-320	-320	-320
AMB# 060374 NAIC# 87718		**Rating History: NR-1, 06/10/10; NR-1, 06/12/09; NR-1, 06/12/08; NR-1, 06/08/07; NR-1, 06/07/06**																
CONGRESS LIFE INS CO[1]	NR-1	'05	86.3	...	...	13.7	6,246	...	...	...	100.0	6,212	...	134	...	183	152	152
Peter C. Mitchell President		'06	80.9	...	...	19.1	6,315	...	...	...	100.0	6,312	...	83	...	107	101	101
6900 E Camelback Rd, Suite 935 Scottsdale, AZ 85251		'07	8.4	...	...	91.6	58,974	...	...	...	100.0	56,529	...	1,922	...	106	71	71
AZ : 1966 : Stock : Inactive Credit A&H, Credit Life, Life		'08	7.7	...	...	92.3	60,150	...	...	...	100.0	57,111	...	1,117	...	858	617	617
602-370-3625		'09	7.5	...	...	92.5	58,654	...	...	...	100.0	57,948	...	-2,188	...	1,150	887	887
AMB# 007600 NAIC# 73504		**Rating History: NR-1, 06/10/10; NR-1, 06/12/09; NR-3, 05/07/08; NR-3, 02/06/07; NR-3, 02/08/06**																
CONNECTICARE INC EmblemHealth Inc	B	'05	72.6	...	...	27.4	200,431	...	45.6	...	54.4	107,164	725,405	718,802	32,747	40,872	26,947	26,905
Michael Herbert President & CEO		'06	73.3	...	...	26.7	208,820	...	50.9	...	49.1	129,846	723,310	716,754	8,890	34,673	22,799	22,758
175 Scott Swamp Road Farmington, CT 06032	Rating Outlook: Negative	'07	76.0	...	...	24.0	216,801	...	50.0	...	50.0	118,046	780,948	774,116	11,862	21,087	14,753	14,730
CT : 1999 : Stock : Broker Group A&H, Health		'08	73.0	...	...	27.0	207,011	...	52.8	...	47.2	107,553	810,170	802,549	-24,103	8,373	7,322	4,812
860-674-5700		'09	76.6	...	...	23.4	226,407	...	55.0	...	45.0	103,153	868,911	860,504	24,513	-15,912	-6,885	-6,118
AMB# 068517 NAIC# 95675	FSC VIII	**Rating History: B g, 06/09/10; B, 05/29/09; B+, 06/06/08; B+, 05/10/07; B+ u, 11/16/06**																

2010 BEST'S KEY RATING GUIDE — LIFE/HEALTH EDITION
BEST'S PROFITABILITY, LEVERAGE AND LIQUIDITY TESTS 2005 – 2009

Data in U.S. Dollars

—	Profitability Tests							Leverage Tests						Liquidity Tests					
Un-Realized Capital Gains ($000)	Benefits Paid to NPW & Dep (%)	Comm. & Expenses to NPW & Dep (%)	NOG to Total Assets (%)	NOG to Total Rev (%)	Operating Return on Equity (%)	Net Yield (%)	Total Return (%)	Change in NPW & Dep (%)	NPW & Dep to Capital (X)	Capital & Surplus to Liabilities (%)	Surplus Relief (%)	Reins Leverage (%)	Change in Capital (%)	Quick Liquidity (%)	Current Liquidity (%)	Non-Invest Grade Bonds to Capital (%)	Delinq. & Foreclosed Mortgages to Capital (%)	Mort. & Credit Tenant Loans & R.E. to Capital (%)	Affiliated Invest to Capital (%)
361	61.4	32.8	6.8	5.2	12.2	2.34	3.25	12.1	2.3	131.2	0.1	93.3	-6.1	188.0	204.3	1.0	...	...	0.1
295	60.0	34.2	7.6	5.5	13.6	3.26	4.17	9.6	2.2	148.7	0.1	85.6	15.3	197.4	214.9	...	...	...	...
631	61.7	31.7	8.4	6.5	15.7	4.65	5.54	9.3	2.0	120.1	1.5	83.3	16.2	170.5	185.5	...	...	...	...
-4,111	60.7	33.8	6.3	5.6	12.2	3.97	-0.48	1.7	2.0	114.9	0.3	79.7	4.7	175.2	191.0	...	...	...	...
2,236	62.7	32.7	5.6	4.8	9.9	3.02	4.36	10.4	1.7	166.2	0.4	115.0	25.6	205.8	223.6	...	...	...	7.4
	Principal Lines of Business: GrpA&H (83.9%), GrpLife (16.0%), IndAnn (0.1%), IndA&H (0.0%)												Principal States: SC (10.7%), FL (6.5%), MI (4.8%), NC (4.5%), OH (4.2%)						
...	77.1	43.9	12.4	1.4	65.0	2.11	2.11	3.8	64.1	13.8	...	...	-58.5	88.5	91.7	...	...	...	...
...	66.5	34.7	17.8	2.1	92.6	6.99	6.99	21.4	29.2	32.5	...	...	166.8	89.8	90.8	...	...	...	...
...	64.3	35.3	15.7	2.2	44.1	4.93	4.93	11.8	14.7	81.1	...	...	122.5	176.9	176.9	...	...	...	...
...	67.3	37.3	-1.2	-0.2	-2.6	1.45	1.45	-7.7	11.2	98.8	...	...	20.8	298.4	301.3	...	...	...	...
...	75.6	23.8	8.7	1.8	17.6	0.11	0.11	-7.4	8.5	97.9	...	2.3	22.5	336.1	336.1	...	...	...	...
	Principal Lines of Business: Dental (56.4%), Vision (38.4%), FEHBP (5.2%)												Principal States: FL (100.0%)						
...	66.9	27.6	21.6	4.1	48.6	2.53	2.53	29.8	21.8	40.7	...	...	-63.4	111.2	111.2	...	...	...	...
...	77.2	19.1	15.0	3.2	47.4	4.23	4.23	-12.8	11.9	50.4	...	...	59.7	139.9	141.7	...	...	...	...
...	65.9	30.3	14.0	3.5	32.8	5.93	5.93	5.5	7.5	103.9	...	...	67.3	287.4	287.4	...	...	...	...
...	66.1	23.9	30.2	8.3	53.2	1.77	1.77	9.5	5.2	158.8	...	...	58.1	299.0	313.0	...	...	...	...
...	69.7	22.1	16.1	6.3	29.4	0.47	0.47	-17.3	5.1	93.6	...	...	-15.3	306.2	306.2	...	...	...	...
	Principal Lines of Business: Dental (76.2%), FEHBP (23.8%)												Principal States: IL (43.2%), MO (27.8%), KY (19.0%), MD (9.4%)						
...	72.3	14.9	28.2	8.9	43.1	3.15	3.15	24.4	4.4	183.1	0.0	33.3	17.8	237.2	244.8	...	...	...	...
...	71.3	18.2	24.1	7.5	36.6	4.54	4.54	18.5	4.5	201.3	0.0	27.4	18.4	177.6	182.8	...	...	...	...
...	66.2	16.5	31.3	12.3	52.3	2.48	2.48	5.5	3.9	122.9	...	21.9	21.8	365.3	365.3	...	...	...	...
...	70.7	15.2	17.0	7.8	25.2	1.44	1.45	-1.2	2.8	411.9	...	15.7	37.4	809.4	814.7	...	...	...	...
...	71.2	24.6	6.1	2.5	8.1	0.49	0.49	-4.5	4.0	218.1	...	22.9	-33.1	502.6	502.6	...	...	...	...
	Principal Lines of Business: GrpA&H (100.0%)												Principal States: FL (28.6%), TX (13.8%), GA (9.1%), OH (9.0%), AL (8.3%)						
-15,680	87.5	12.7	-5.7	-2.6	-9.5	4.22	33.15	18.9	3.3	138.8	...	...	21.9	315.3	335.6	0.0	...	0.4	3.1
2,709	86.3	13.3	6.9	2.9	11.7	4.79	6.18	7.2	4.6	149.2	...	...	-23.7	179.9	204.8	1.6	...	...	7.0
-2,199	87.5	14.4	6.2	2.2	10.8	13.98	11.57	-15.7	6.1	116.1	...	...	-36.4	158.9	179.1	1.7	...	...	7.4
4,480	88.0	14.1	-2.2	-0.6	-4.4	5.51	7.69	17.5	7.5	87.6	...	...	-4.6	134.9	152.9	2.8	...	...	16.3
-4,781	86.3	13.3	11.2	2.9	23.2	14.72	9.78	12.2	7.4	98.6	...	...	13.2	132.3	155.3	4.4	...	...	6.6
	Principal Lines of Business: CompHosp/Med (83.7%), Medicaid (12.2%), Dental (3.7%), MedSup (0.2%), Medicare (0.1%)												Principal States: WI (100.0%)						
...	47.8	65.6	16.4	9.9	22.9	5.27	5.27	26.8	1.4	258.9	...	...	25.9	264.4	264.4	...	...	...	...
...	59.3	46.7	18.2	12.7	24.4	4.52	4.52	14.2	1.3	333.3	...	...	27.8	340.9	340.9	...	...	...	...
...	63.2	42.1	19.9	15.1	26.1	4.89	4.89	15.2	1.1	317.3	...	...	30.0	361.0	361.0	...	...	...	...
...	60.6	38.3	23.9	19.8	30.7	5.79	5.79	13.9	0.9	382.9	...	...	36.2	438.0	438.0	...	...	...	...
...	59.5	57.8	18.9	16.3	23.1	4.53	4.53	8.3	0.8	506.9	...	...	26.6	509.9	509.9	...	...	...	...
	Principal Lines of Business: CompHosp/Med (100.0%)																		
...	75.7	16.3	20.6	9.1	35.5	...	...	9.9	3.5	143.5	...	...	23.7	...	...	...	...	...	...
...	80.5	16.3	0.3	0.2	0.6	...	...	5.3	3.2	137.4	...	...	14.8	...	...	...	...	...	...
...	79.3	19.6	0.4	0.2	0.7	...	...	-6.6	3.3	117.6	...	...	-9.5	...	...	...	...	...	...
...	79.5	21.1	-0.4	-0.2	-0.7	...	...	2.4	3.8	139.7	...	...	-11.9	...	...	...	...	...	...
...	80.2	20.4	-2.7	-1.1	-4.4	...	...	-1.7	4.1	167.2	...	...	-7.9	...	...	...	...	...	...
	Principal Lines of Business: GrpA&H (99.9%), GrpLife (0.1%)																		
...	71.8	74.7	2.5	43.5	2.5	...	...	-26.2	0.0	999.9	...	...	2.5	...	...	...	...	...	...
...	38.7	223.0	1.6	31.3	1.6	...	...	-37.9	0.0	999.9	...	...	1.6	...	...	...	...	...	...
...	15.3	69.8	0.2	1.9	0.2	...	...	999.9	0.0	999.9	...	...	795.5	...	...	...	...	...	...
...	73.4	64.1	1.0	23.6	1.1	...	...	-41.9	0.0	999.9	...	...	1.1	...	...	...	...	...	...
...	...	40.8	1.5	-46.0	1.5	...	...	-99.9	0.0	999.9	...	...	1.5	...	...	...	...	...	...
	Principal Lines of Business: OrdLife (100.0%)																		
3	80.3	14.9	14.8	3.7	28.9	4.12	4.09	-2.3	6.7	114.9	...	6.5	34.8	161.6	181.4	...	...	...	...
...	80.7	15.4	11.1	3.1	19.2	4.49	4.46	-0.3	5.5	164.4	...	6.1	21.2	204.1	227.6	...	...	...	...
...	83.5	14.9	6.9	1.9	11.9	5.04	5.03	8.0	6.6	119.5	...	8.5	-9.1	165.5	185.4	...	...	...	...
...	85.1	15.0	3.5	0.9	6.5	4.46	2.99	3.7	7.5	108.1	...	7.2	-8.9	139.9	157.2	0.1	...	...	...
...	88.9	13.8	-3.2	-0.8	-6.5	4.25	4.70	7.2	8.3	83.7	...	8.0	-4.1	121.8	136.5	0.1	...	...	...
	Principal Lines of Business: CompHosp/Med (81.6%), Medicare (17.6%), FEHBP (0.8%)												Principal States: CT (99.6%)						

COMPANY NAME Ultimate Parent Association Principal Officer Mailing Address Dom. : Began Bus. : Struct. : Mktg. Specialty Phone # AMB# NAIC#	Best's Financial Strength Rating FSC	Data Year	Balance Sheet Bonds (%)	Mort. Loans & R.E. (%)	Com & Pref. Stock (%)	All Other Assets (%)	Total Assets ($000)	Life Reserves (%)	Health Reserves (%)	Ann Res. & Dep. Liabilities (%)	All Other Liabilities (%)	Capital & Surplus ($000)	Operations Direct Premiums Written ($000)	Net Premiums Written & Deposits ($000)	Operating Cash Flow ($000)	NOG Before Taxes ($000)	NOG After Taxes ($000)	Net Income ($000)
CONNECTICARE INSURANCE CO INC EmblemHealth Inc	NR-2	'05	62.4	...	...	37.6	9,469	...	26.6	...	73.4	6,049	6,500	6,469	1,196	794	483	468
Michael Herbert President & CEO		'06	61.8	...	...	38.2	10,130	...	38.2	...	61.8	6,228	12,929	12,876	310	371	189	185
175 Scott Swamp Road Farmington, CT 06032		'07	53.3	...	...	46.7	12,148	...	39.7	...	60.3	6,753	19,567	19,192	2,036	1,135	717	705
CT : 2002 : Stock : Broker		'08	35.9	...	...	64.1	18,876	...	58.1	...	41.9	6,947	53,096	52,086	3,057	833	429	432
Dental, Health 860-674-5700		'09	46.3	...	...	53.7	31,530	...	56.9	...	43.1	9,116	147,553	144,849	6,763	-10,257	-6,551	-6,511
AMB# 064784 NAIC# 11209		Rating History: NR-2, 06/09/10; NR-2, 05/29/09; NR-2, 06/06/08; NR-2, 05/10/07; NR-2, 11/16/06																
CONNECTICARE OF MASSACHUSETTS EmblemHealth Inc	NR-2	'05	92.3	...	...	7.7	8,835	...	51.3	...	48.7	5,439	29,106	28,971	519	2,187	1,456	1,431
Michael Herbert President & CEO		'06	81.8	...	...	18.2	9,725	...	71.2	...	28.8	6,266	26,212	26,115	623	1,366	824	824
175 Scott Swamp Road Farmington, CT 06032		'07	82.4	...	...	17.6	10,527	...	54.8	...	45.2	6,716	30,429	29,901	233	1,221	761	754
MA : 2000 : Stock : Broker		'08	87.4	...	...	12.6	10,617	...	53.0	...	47.0	8,287	27,744	27,199	345	2,336	1,548	1,548
Health 860-674-5700		'09	82.7	...	...	17.3	11,804	...	60.6	...	39.4	9,596	20,643	20,228	636	1,508	1,344	1,345
AMB# 064464 NAIC# 95299		Rating History: NR-2, 06/09/10; NR-2, 05/29/09; NR-2, 06/06/08; NR-2, 05/10/07; NR-2, 11/16/06																
CONNECTICARE OF NEW YORK INC EmblemHealth Inc	NR-2	'05	86.1	...	...	13.9	5,317	...	2.9	...	97.1	4,983	27	27	222	42	27	27
Michael Herbert President & CEO		'06	91.4	...	...	8.6	5,395	...	28.6	...	71.4	5,285	136	136	112	213	302	302
175 Scott Swamp Road Farmington, CT 06032		'07	88.0	...	...	12.0	5,845	...	6.1	...	93.9	5,691	142	134	405	619	405	405
NY : 1997 : Stock : Broker		'08	82.9	...	...	17.1	6,376	...	16.1	...	83.9	6,243	144	136	501	844	551	551
Health 914-366-3840		'09	85.0	...	...	15.0	6,609	...	49.3	...	50.7	6,506	150	142	233	230	247	264
AMB# 064450 NAIC# 95768		Rating History: NR-2, 06/09/10; NR-2, 05/29/09; NR-2, 06/06/08; NR-2, 05/10/07; NR-2, 11/16/06																
CONNECTICUT GENERAL LIFE INS CIGNA Corporation	A	'05	35.5	14.2	0.3	50.1	20,748,727	24.4	5.4	22.9	47.3	2,309,080	4,566,434	6,514,160	-805,900	823,512	707,028	718,559
David M. Cordani President		'06	28.9	15.4	0.3	55.3	17,765,388	26.8	5.2	16.2	51.8	1,990,162	5,333,224	5,602,563	-1,285,413	1,052,038	866,854	1,032,778
Two Liberty Plaza Philadelphia, PA 19192-2362	Rating Outlook: Negative	'07	31.3	13.4	0.3	55.1	16,582,319	28.3	5.6	17.5	48.5	1,897,090	6,599,069	6,655,060	-274,260	856,645	636,669	668,236
CT : 1865 : Stock : Agency		'08	30.5	14.1	1.0	54.3	17,733,121	31.2	5.5	18.6	44.7	2,030,228	7,020,607	7,841,861	1,246,096	7,610	3,702	978
Ann, Group A&H, Group Life 860-226-6000		'09	32.2	12.9	0.8	54.1	19,036,994	19.6	5.4	25.2	49.8	2,919,212	6,964,752	7,739,348	117,153	937,970	669,565	647,088
AMB# 006266 NAIC# 62308	FSC XV	Rating History: A g, 01/08/10; A g, 11/14/08; A g, 02/11/08; A g, 12/14/06; A- g, 12/21/05																
CONNECTICUT LIFE INS & ANNUITY	NR-5	'05	55.4	...	40.1	4.5	311	74.3	...	...	25.7	284	...	32	18	22	22	22
Frederick S. Townsend, Jr. President		'06	28.7	...	57.4	14.0	217	53.7	...	...	46.3	175	...	35	19	48	47	47
7238 E. Montebello Avenue Scottsdale, AZ 85250		'07	17.8	...	35.5	46.7	244	71.4	...	...	28.6	209	...	38	42	21	21	24
AZ : 1989 : Stock : Other Direct		'08	16.8	...	33.6	49.6	291	48.6	...	...	51.4	223	...	42	-35	2	2	7
Ind Life 312-332-0430		'09	18.0	...	35.9	46.1	323	65.5	...	...	34.5	277	...	46	1	58	57	54
AMB# 068095 NAIC# 74454		Rating History: NR-5, 04/21/10; NR-5, 04/23/09; NR-5, 04/11/08; NR-5, 04/30/07; NR-5, 05/11/06																
CONSECO HEALTH INS CO CNO Financial Group, Inc.	B	'05	87.4	3.4	5.6	3.6	2,077,671	0.2	93.2	1.3	5.2	102,934	443,495	372,775	92,905	22,918	17,174	17,351
Steven M. Stecher President		'06	87.5	4.5	5.1	2.9	2,187,859	0.3	93.9	1.4	4.4	105,151	403,098	342,229	104,214	18,890	15,632	17,443
11825 N. Pennsylvania Street Carmel, IN 46032	Rating Outlook: Stable	'07	87.2	6.0	3.0	3.8	2,361,268	0.3	92.8	2.3	4.6	108,497	385,617	389,065	165,425	21,797	11,257	9,943
AZ : 1970 : Stock : Agency		'08	84.3	8.0	3.0	4.7	2,472,317	0.3	91.7	3.3	4.7	128,610	379,046	415,070	123,126	24,352	21,149	1,377
A&H, Dread dis, Med supp 317-817-4300		'09	86.4	7.6	1.1	4.8	2,558,880	0.3	90.1	4.4	5.2	150,574	377,226	438,503	82,701	18,812	13,607	-6,468
AMB# 008101 NAIC# 78174	FSC VIII	Rating History: B g, 03/23/10; B g, 10/16/09; B gu, 03/04/09; B+ g, 11/20/08; B+ gu, 08/12/08																
CONSECO INSURANCE COMPANY CNO Financial Group, Inc.	B	'05	86.8	3.2	5.3	4.7	4,326,687	8.1	0.3	88.9	2.6	346,131	184,220	264,057	-534,441	23,503	25,556	34,780
Steven M. Stecher President		'06	83.8	3.8	5.2	7.2	4,011,740	8.3	0.5	88.5	2.7	314,076	255,506	344,288	-310,667	8,165	5,771	8,573
11825 N. Pennsylvania Street Carmel, IN 46032	Rating Outlook: Stable	'07	66.9	8.9	11.7	12.5	1,242,277	28.6	1.9	61.3	8.3	232,968	199,303	248,510	-2,697,001	-22,817	-10,923	-10,788
IL : 1951 : Stock : Agency		'08	72.4	7.8	8.1	11.6	1,044,458	31.2	2.1	61.4	5.3	159,078	125,766	133,898	-169,760	31,061	31,189	18,664
Ann 317-817-4000		'09	72.2	8.3	9.0	10.6	759,442	10.5	3.2	76.3	10.0	137,694	119,697	120,266	-261,005	-6,631	2,941	-6,933
AMB# 006080 NAIC# 60682	FSC VIII	Rating History: B g, 03/23/10; B g, 10/16/09; B gu, 03/04/09; B+ g, 11/20/08; B+ gu, 08/12/08																
CONSECO LIFE INSURANCE COMPANY CNO Financial Group, Inc.	B-	'05	84.6	3.2	4.2	8.0	3,935,635	82.4	0.5	13.9	3.2	263,223	324,874	550,533	-29,571	50,379	42,481	46,807
Steven M. Stecher President		'06	81.2	4.5	4.3	10.0	3,983,169	83.8	0.4	12.7	3.0	160,893	307,863	519,440	56,529	-152,040	-159,276	-157,061
11825 N. Pennsylvania Street Carmel, IN 46032	Rating Outlook: Negative	'07	80.1	6.5	4.0	9.3	4,256,095	77.8	0.4	19.8	2.0	148,160	286,222	945,896	215,981	-38,958	-31,364	-54,329
IN : 1962 : Stock : Agency		'08	79.5	8.4	4.4	7.7	4,529,499	73.6	6.9	17.9	1.6	162,350	279,705	464,925	285,200	-32,230	-27,293	-68,199
Ind Ann, Univ Life 317-817-6400		'09	81.9	8.0	2.3	7.8	4,382,162	73.1	6.2	18.4	2.4	111,499	292,310	476,083	-159,272	-6,679	7,329	-21,176
AMB# 006692 NAIC# 65900	FSC VIII	Rating History: B-, 03/23/10; B g, 10/16/09; B gu, 03/04/09; B+ g, 11/20/08; B+ gu, 08/12/08																
CONSECO LIFE INS CO OF TEXAS CNO Financial Group, Inc.	NR-3	'05	0.9	...	96.1	3.0	1,669,071	18.6	...	7.9	73.4	1,602,119	445	532	81,599	-56,578	-43,845	-43,055
Steven M. Stecher President		'06	1.2	...	88.0	10.8	1,524,982	9.1	...	3.7	87.2	1,392,763	411	482	38,040	-67,083	-32,035	-32,017
11825 N. Pennsylvania Street Carmel, IN 46032		'07	1.4	...	97.7	1.0	1,291,213	9.9	...	4.1	86.0	1,174,372	395	461	144,452	-5,355	2,824	2,891
TX : 2003 : Stock : Inactive		'08	3.0	...	85.3	11.7	600,962	40.5	...	17.3	42.3	573,243	314	361	-2,188,737	55,959	91,685	-1,483,066
Life 317-817-3700		'09	2.4	...	84.2	13.3	745,355	24.0	...	10.4	65.7	700,027	290	394	18,623	-40,366	46,432	46,234
AMB# 068083 NAIC# 11804		Rating History: NR-3, 03/23/10; NR-3, 10/16/09; NR-3, 03/04/09; NR-3, 11/20/08; NR-3, 08/12/08																

BEST'S PROFITABILITY, LEVERAGE AND LIQUIDITY TESTS 2005 – 2009

Data in U.S. Dollars

	Profitability Tests							Leverage Tests						Liquidity Tests					
Un-Realized Capital Gains ($000)	Benefits Paid to NPW & Dep (%)	Comm. & Expenses to NPW & Dep (%)	NOG to Total Assets (%)	NOG to Total Rev (%)	Operating Return on Equity (%)	Net Yield (%)	Total Return (%)	Change in NPW & Dep (%)	NPW & Dep to Capital (X)	Capital & Surplus to Liabilities (%)	Surplus Relief (%)	Reins Leverage (%)	Change in Capital (%)	Quick Liquidity (%)	Current Liquidity (%)	Non-Invest Grade Bonds to Capital (%)	Delinq. & Foreclosed Mortgages to Capital (%)	Mort. & Credit Tenant Loans & R.E. to Capital (%)	Affiliated Invest to Capital (%)
...	76.9	15.1	5.3	7.2	8.3	3.39	3.21	388.9	1.1	176.9	...	0.2	8.6	281.1	300.9	...	...	...	...
...	72.7	27.3	1.9	1.4	3.1	4.28	4.23	99.0	2.1	159.6	...	...	3.0	248.2	264.7	...	...	...	...
...	76.6	19.7	6.4	3.7	11.0	4.40	4.29	49.1	2.8	125.2	...	3.4	8.4	244.2	257.9	...	...	...	...
...	88.0	11.1	2.8	0.8	6.3	3.13	3.15	171.4	7.5	58.2	...	9.2	2.9	155.9	164.5	...	...	...	...
...	96.0	11.3	-26.0	-4.5	-81.6	1.85	2.07	178.1	15.9	40.7	...	21.6	31.2	82.8	88.1	...	...	...	...
	Principal Lines of Business: CompHosp/Med (60.7%), FEHBP (37.9%), Dental (1.4%), Medicare (0.0%)													Principal States: CT (100.0%)					
...	74.6	18.9	16.3	5.0	30.8	3.98	3.68	-22.1	5.3	160.1	...	1.5	35.6	227.9	237.1	...	...	...	...
...	78.1	18.1	8.9	3.1	14.1	4.12	4.12	-9.9	4.2	181.1	...	1.8	15.2	245.2	254.5	...	...	...	...
...	79.7	17.5	7.5	2.5	11.7	4.28	4.21	14.5	4.5	176.3	...	4.9	7.2	230.3	240.4	...	...	...	...
...	74.5	18.6	14.6	5.6	20.6	4.77	4.76	-9.0	3.3	355.6	...	3.9	23.4	382.0	399.7	...	...	...	...
...	77.2	17.7	12.0	6.5	15.0	4.76	4.77	-25.6	2.1	434.6	...	3.1	15.8	421.2	437.2	...	...	...	...
	Principal Lines of Business: CompHosp/Med (100.0%)													Principal States: MA (100.0%)					
...	15.3	999.9	0.5	2.5	0.5	2.67	2.67	44.9	0.0	999.9	...	0.0	0.5	999.9	999.9	...	...	...	...
...	64.5	684.4	5.6	24.6	5.9	4.38	4.38	405.6	0.0	999.9	...	...	6.1	999.9	999.9	...	...	...	...
...	56.3	361.5	7.2	34.4	7.4	4.56	4.56	-1.1	0.0	999.9	...	0.1	7.7	999.9	999.9	...	...	...	...
...	114.9	205.7	9.0	43.0	9.2	3.89	3.89	1.7	0.0	999.9	...	0.1	9.7	999.9	999.9	...	...	...	...
...	159.2	84.7	3.8	42.9	3.9	3.52	3.78	3.9	0.0	999.9	...	0.1	4.2	999.9	999.9	...	...	...	...
	Principal Lines of Business: CompHosp/Med (100.0%)													Principal States: NY (100.0%)					
12,615	93.2	9.9	2.0	11.2	29.8	7.66	7.93	-40.0	2.6	21.4	6.0	292.8	-4.2	22.7	39.4	23.7	0.5	117.3	20.9
18,475	80.6	12.5	4.5	14.5	40.3	7.05	8.71	-14.0	2.5	24.3	6.1	387.5	-11.6	19.6	35.5	25.7	0.0	122.7	18.5
-13,036	86.9	8.5	3.7	9.3	32.8	7.50	7.67	18.8	3.1	23.9	5.8	393.1	-3.0	22.8	39.4	24.8	...	102.2	16.2
23,016	81.9	9.0	0.0	0.0	0.2	6.72	6.88	17.8	3.3	22.3	5.4	372.1	8.1	27.8	43.2	30.4	...	106.9	19.1
-34,946	81.9	9.9	3.6	9.0	27.1	6.24	5.59	-1.3	2.4	32.8	3.5	239.0	36.9	22.9	40.6	25.5	2.0	76.6	16.4
	Principal Lines of Business: GrpA&H (75.7%), GrpAnn (11.9%), IndA&H (7.1%), GrpLife (4.1%), OrdLife (1.0%)													Principal States: NY (10.2%), FL (9.2%), CA (9.0%), TX (6.8%), NJ (6.1%)					
-10	51.6	54.1	7.0	37.7	7.8	9.10	5.88	5.1	0.1	999.9	...	...	-0.1	999.9	999.9	27.3	...	...	...
33	...	46.6	17.8	70.0	20.5	13.90	28.48	9.2	0.2	559.8	...	...	-35.6	701.4	999.9	46.6	...	...	-45.7
-25	93.3	44.4	9.2	27.6	11.0	19.47	9.70	8.8	0.2	622.2	...	...	14.3	999.9	999.9	44.8	...	...	...
-103	4.0	161.0	0.6	2.2	0.8	16.06	-15.88	9.0	0.2	328.9	...	...	5.9	479.2	598.5	20.2	...	...	...
68	...	49.7	18.6	73.1	22.9	12.84	40.31	9.2	0.2	813.7	...	...	29.3	955.8	999.9	39.5	...	...	...
	Principal Lines of Business: OrdLife (100.0%)																		
-141	49.1	35.2	0.8	3.5	16.1	6.15	6.32	-6.2	3.2	5.9	38.1	...	-4.5	55.3	69.8	65.4	...	91.4	...
577	49.9	34.5	0.7	3.5	15.0	6.10	6.37	-8.2	2.8	5.9	32.7	0.3	5.6	51.7	67.2	64.2	...	110.8	11.8
-950	40.9	35.8	0.5	2.6	10.5	6.17	6.22	13.7	3.1	5.7	21.0	0.0	3.4	49.8	65.8	80.1	...	144.0	11.1
-1,279	38.6	29.9	0.9	5.0	17.8	6.10	5.34	6.7	2.9	6.0	23.3	...	11.3	45.8	62.2	101.8	...	170.5	13.6
-177	37.5	35.8	0.5	3.3	9.7	5.96	5.23	5.6	2.8	6.5	11.0	...	10.4	46.6	62.9	69.1	...	149.2	4.0
	Principal Lines of Business: IndA&H (50.0%), IndAnn (32.0%), GrpA&H (17.7%), OrdLife (0.4%)													Principal States: IL (9.0%), IA (7.8%), TX (7.2%), OH (5.4%), FL (4.9%)					
-172	239.5	29.2	0.6	5.9	7.3	5.45	5.92	64.2	0.7	9.4	0.1	5.5	0.9	60.0	75.8	36.5	0.0	70.3	5.6
311	194.2	30.3	0.1	1.1	1.7	6.20	6.53	30.4	1.0	9.4	0.2	6.1	-6.9	65.1	81.0	42.7	0.4	78.9	15.2
-2,808	54.6	30.1	-0.4	-3.7	-4.0	2.96	2.86	-27.8	1.0	24.7	20.2	999.9	-28.9	56.5	78.6	15.2	0.0	64.3	19.1
748	113.1	32.0	2.7	16.5	15.9	4.49	3.70	-46.1	0.8	19.0	17.4	999.9	-32.1	50.9	71.6	22.4	...	66.3	27.5
-1,929	122.6	48.6	0.3	1.9	2.0	5.64	3.72	-10.2	0.9	22.5	10.9	999.9	-16.5	50.5	72.8	17.9	...	64.3	16.0
	Principal Lines of Business: IndA&H (60.7%), IndAnn (30.2%), OrdLife (4.4%), GrpAnn (3.5%), GrpLife (0.8%)													Principal States: IL (15.0%), TX (9.5%), CA (8.9%), NC (6.9%), IA (5.6%)					
-1,300	92.2	23.3	1.1	6.9	17.6	6.33	6.45	-6.6	1.9	8.0	0.7	77.9	19.4	50.1	64.8	44.6	0.7	72.8	3.4
2	102.1	21.2	-4.0	-26.1	-75.1	6.28	6.37	-5.6	2.7	5.0	0.5	112.8	-34.7	51.7	66.8	74.2	...	141.0	16.0
-647	56.0	10.3	-0.8	-5.6	-20.3	6.28	5.58	82.1	5.4	4.3	1.9	174.7	-6.8	47.6	63.3	86.6	...	212.7	14.6
-2,781	122.4	28.3	-0.6	-4.9	-17.6	5.90	4.71	-50.8	2.8	3.8	0.3	160.9	-6.5	41.9	57.9	151.9	...	291.6	20.3
-2,421	141.9	22.2	0.2	1.3	5.4	6.01	5.11	2.4	4.1	2.7	1.4	226.0	-30.5	41.8	57.9	155.1	2.8	386.0	15.7
	Principal Lines of Business: OrdLife (40.9%), IndAnn (33.4%), IndA&H (20.1%), GrpA&H (5.3%), GrpLife (0.3%)													Principal States: CA (18.0%), TX (14.6%), FL (6.3%), PA (5.1%), GA (3.6%)					
27,633	181.3	490.5	-2.7	82.9	-2.8	-3.28	-1.49	1.9	0.0	999.9	0.0	0.0	6.2	106.0	112.7	0.0	...	...	100.1
-231,772	304.7	191.1	-2.0	49.0	-2.1	-4.15	-18.02	-9.3	0.0	999.9	0.0	0.0	-13.1	123.2	142.4	...	...	...	96.4
-321,105	243.4	220.9	0.2	-78.6	0.2	-0.29	-21.28	-4.5	0.0	999.9	0.0	0.0	-15.7	11.2	12.9	0.0	...	...	107.4
1,492,894	250.9	425.8	9.7	157.9	10.5	6.40	721.91	-21.7	0.0	999.9	0.0	0.0	-51.2	218.7	227.6	0.1	...	...	89.4
115,370	234.8	-99.9	6.9	-99.9	7.3	-6.45	13.04	9.3	0.0	999.9	0.0	0.0	22.1	175.9	180.5	...	...	...	89.7
	Principal Lines of Business: OrdLife (75.0%), IndAnn (25.0%), IndLife (0.0%)													Principal States: TX (89.3%)					

Data in U.S. Dollars

COMPANY NAME Ultimate Parent Association Principal Officer Mailing Address Dom. : Began Bus. : Struct. : Mktg. Specialty Phone # AMB# NAIC#	Best's Financial Strength Rating FSC	Data Year	Balance Sheet Bonds (%)	Mort. Loans & R.E. (%)	Com & Pref. Stock (%)	All Other Assets (%)	Total Assets ($000)	Life Reserves (%)	Health Reserves %)	Ann Res. & Dep. Liabilities (%)	All Other Liabilities (%)	Capital & Surplus ($000)	Operations Direct Premiums Written ($000)	Net Premiums Written & Deposits ($000)	Operating Cash Flow ($000)	NOG Before Taxes ($000)	NOG After Taxes ($000)	Net Income ($000)
CONSTITUTION LIFE INS CO Universal American Corp. Gary W. Bryant President & CEO 1001 Heathrow Park Lane, Suite 5001 Lake Mary, FL 32746 TX : 1929 : Stock : Agency Ind A&H, Life, LTC 407-995-8000 AMB# 006273 NAIC# 62359	B+ Rating Outlook: Stable FSC VI	'05	79.3	0.0	8.3	12.4	84,622	65.6	14.6	10.3	9.6	11,850	107,661	39,428	-1,820	-1,361	-2,408	-2,408
		'06	74.6	0.0	7.2	18.2	87,464	63.5	14.7	9.7	12.1	14,562	105,286	41,349	2,330	766	-1,229	-1,229
		'07	62.0	0.0	0.5	37.4	87,691	64.1	14.5	8.8	12.6	17,469	88,810	35,534	-865	3,181	1,075	235
		'08	71.1	...	0.6	28.3	87,358	64.3	14.9	7.9	13.0	19,055	75,681	31,599	601	2,727	1,601	1,325
		'09	59.7	...	...	40.3	54,702	1.6	19.4	...	79.1	27,507	64,830	-3,763	-47,288	4,079	3,928	3,735
		Rating History: B+, 04/16/10; B+, 12/03/08; B++g, 08/21/07; B++g, 06/21/06; B++g, 06/09/05																
CONSUMERHEALTH INC Ivory Holdco Inc Steven C. Bilt President 201 East Sandpointe, Suite 800 Santa Ana, CA 92707 CA : 1979 : Stock : Broker Dental 714-668-1300 AMB# 060166	NR-5	'05	...	...	...	100.0	14,097	...	...	...	100.0	11,011	8,324	8,324	540	3,354	2,017	2,017
		'06	...	...	...	100.0	15,028	...	...	...	100.0	11,826	8,375	8,375	205	4,845	2,915	2,915
		'07	...	...	...	100.0	15,594	...	...	...	100.0	11,301	8,944	8,944	1,851	3,949	2,375	2,375
		'08	...	...	...	100.0	14,655	...	...	...	100.0	10,315	9,506	9,506	-230	3,182	1,913	1,913
		'09	...	...	...	100.0	14,610	...	...	...	100.0	10,772	10,109	10,109	497	2,758	1,658	1,658
		Rating History: NR-5, 05/04/10; NR-5, 04/30/09; NR-5, 05/09/08; NR-5, 05/02/07; NR-5, 08/23/06																
CONSUMERS LIFE INS CO[1] Medical Mutual of Ohio Richard A. Chiricosta President 2060 East Ninth Street Cleveland, OH 44115-1313 OH : 1955 : Stock : Direct Response 216-687-7000 AMB# 006275 NAIC# 62375	NR-1	'05	59.5	...	...	40.5	12,785	...	...	...	100.0	8,322	13,629	13,618	...	-806	-806	-806
		'06	38.8	...	...	61.2	22,307	...	...	...	100.0	8,029	80,118	30,275	...	-263	-263	-263
		'07	25.1	...	...	74.9	34,618	...	...	...	100.0	17,065	104,465	37,252	...	-2,854	-2,867	-2,867
		'08	43.3	...	...	56.7	31,949	...	...	...	100.0	17,104	89,339	36,443	...	-4,646	-4,646	-4,646
		'09	58.0	...	...	42.0	31,048	...	...	...	100.0	14,903	91,886	42,291	...	-2,177	-2,177	-2,177
		Rating History: NR-1, 06/10/10; NR-1, 06/12/09; NR-1, 06/12/08; NR-1, 06/08/07; NR-1, 06/07/06																
CONTINENTAL AMERICAN INS CO Aflac Incorporated Eugene C. Sorrell, Sr. President P.O. Box 427 Columbia, SC 29202 SC : 1969 : Stock : Worksite Mktg Dis inc, Group A&H, Ind A&H 803-256-6265 AMB# 007411 NAIC# 71730	A+ Rating Outlook: Stable FSC XV	'05	56.2	1.8	2.0	40.0	72,747	37.9	47.3	0.3	14.6	18,874	28,432	53,487	7,839	4,279	3,349	3,359
		'06	46.6	2.6	1.6	49.2	86,234	36.8	49.4	0.3	13.5	22,693	25,989	61,718	13,498	6,036	4,772	4,772
		'07	53.8	2.2	1.1	42.9	102,769	37.3	41.0	0.2	21.5	26,959	36,389	64,928	14,173	7,568	5,163	5,129
		'08	59.9	2.1	1.7	36.3	104,027	35.5	50.1	0.2	14.2	32,646	47,783	69,127	8,683	11,115	7,626	6,918
		'09	56.2	1.6	0.2	41.9	117,984	32.7	47.8	0.2	19.3	38,471	64,979	87,345	11,873	11,300	6,498	5,803
		Rating History: A+ g, 04/09/10; A, 10/14/09; A- u, 07/30/09; A-, 06/04/09; B++, 05/28/08																
CONTINENTAL ASSURANCE CO Loews Corporation Thomas F. Motamed Chairman, President & CEO 333 S. Wabash Avenue Chicago, IL 60604 IL : 1911 : Stock : Agency A&H, Ann, Ind Life 312-822-5000 AMB# 006280 NAIC# 62413	A- Rating Outlook: Stable FSC IX	'05	46.6	1.6	0.7	51.1	5,092,011	0.4	1.6	41.6	56.4	627,002	279,423	29,845	-630,086	117,055	81,325	64,661
		'06	42.9	2.2	6.6	48.3	4,481,614	0.4	1.6	47.0	51.0	686,640	123,165	24,661	-115,005	103,718	89,489	67,373
		'07	42.4	0.0	6.7	50.9	4,120,081	0.4	1.6	46.3	51.7	471,190	84,912	19,323	-364,621	56,844	49,265	27,260
		'08	51.7	0.0	7.4	41.0	3,333,560	0.5	1.4	58.3	39.9	487,288	101,142	17,873	-51,486	9,202	-2,239	-50,740
		'09	60.8	0.0	1.2	38.1	3,208,225	0.5	1.0	60.7	37.8	447,634	85,407	17,669	23,177	-24,543	-46,982	-65,086
		Rating History: A-, 02/08/10; A-, 02/13/09; A-, 12/16/08; A-, 12/18/07; A-, 04/18/07																
CONTINENTAL GENERAL INS CO American Financial Group, Inc Billy B. Hill, Jr. President 11200 Lakeline Blvd., Suite 100 Austin, TX 78717 OH : 1961 : Stock : Broker Med supp, Maj med, Life 512-451-2224 AMB# 007360 NAIC# 71404	B++ Rating Outlook: Stable FSC VI	'05	82.3	1.7	5.9	10.1	467,229	15.3	45.2	29.5	9.9	65,901	358,974	313,537	23,865	13,436	5,357	5,402
		'06	64.7	3.2	0.9	31.2	308,446	13.1	33.2	26.1	27.7	63,578	349,439	36,904	-193,639	35,548	19,389	19,372
		'07	69.1	2.1	0.5	28.3	262,038	15.7	39.7	28.4	16.2	51,310	277,805	90,317	-18,255	13,361	9,674	11,770
		'08	76.9	2.3	0.6	20.2	227,247	18.6	48.1	28.6	4.7	44,577	224,596	78,783	-14,731	9,151	5,337	3,853
		'09	82.4	2.4	0.0	15.2	214,082	18.7	51.5	26.1	3.7	32,144	184,337	67,144	-11,162	5,682	5,538	-2,884
		Rating History: B++, 05/10/10; B++, 03/27/09; B++, 12/17/07; B++, 11/28/06; B+ u, 05/02/06																
CONTINENTAL LIFE INS CO PA Burlen Corporation Walter H. Lenhard III CEO 8049 West Chester Pike Upper Darby, PA 19082-1317 PA : 1958 : Stock : Agency A&H, Home serv, Life 610-853-2100 AMB# 007603 NAIC# 73539	NR-5	'05	79.4	3.8	2.7	14.2	19,676	79.2	0.1	...	20.8	2,309	4,151	4,259	291	47	37	37
		'06	80.7	3.6	2.4	13.3	19,826	79.8	0.1	...	20.1	2,361	4,306	4,382	197	68	58	58
		'07	76.4	6.5	4.3	12.8	20,157	81.3	0.1	...	18.7	2,387	4,289	4,374	468	44	41	41
		'08	74.5	6.2	2.5	16.8	20,502	98.5	0.1	...	1.5	2,412	4,361	4,448	373	118	150	-5
		'09	72.2	6.1	1.0	20.7	20,563	98.2	0.1	...	1.7	2,238	4,375	4,448	400	-140	-146	-146
		Rating History: NR-5, 04/12/10; NR-5, 04/16/09; NR-5, 04/18/08; NR-5, 05/09/07; NR-5, 05/11/06																
CONTINENTAL LIFE BRENTWOOD TN Genworth Financial, Inc Christopher M. Olson President & CEO P.O. Box 1188 Brentwood, TN 37024 TN : 1983 : Stock : Agency Ind A&H, Ind Life, Med supp 800-264-4000 AMB# 009502 NAIC# 68500	A- Rating Outlook: Negative FSC VII	'05	88.6	...	2.5	8.9	129,339	13.3	77.2	0.0	9.6	44,527	167,935	166,982	17,452	14,758	7,325	7,175
		'06	89.2	...	6.1	4.7	147,697	14.6	70.8	0.0	14.6	54,181	171,754	170,871	16,757	14,340	10,238	10,265
		'07	80.3	...	5.4	14.2	155,922	16.6	68.3	...	15.0	60,108	176,482	175,604	8,656	17,258	7,058	7,055
		'08	80.1	...	6.5	13.4	152,963	19.5	65.9	...	14.6	59,993	172,005	171,113	3,121	23,132	12,542	11,893
		'09	74.3	...	11.5	14.1	146,042	23.7	64.6	...	11.8	61,387	152,994	152,193	-161	17,283	11,315	11,131
		Rating History: A-, 04/21/10; A-, 02/19/09; A u, 11/06/08; A, 06/16/08; A, 04/04/07																
CONTINENTAL LIFE INS CO SC Frank K. Graham, Jr. Chairman & President P.O. Box 6138 Columbia, SC 29260-6138 SC : 1958 : Stock : Agency Ann, Hosp Ind, Life 803-782-4947 AMB# 006286 NAIC# 62480	F	'05	77.5	5.0	...	17.5	2,437	82.8	0.3	14.8	2.2	314	178	153	-11	-28	-28	-24
		'06	72.2	5.0	...	22.8	2,397	83.0	0.3	15.1	1.7	290	178	143	-31	-25	-25	-23
		'07	73.3	5.0	...	21.7	2,359	83.2	0.2	14.9	1.7	229	170	138	-31	-60	-60	-60
		'08	68.1	5.2	...	26.7	2,204	82.7	0.2	15.4	1.7	87	162	110	-150	-142	-142	-143
		'09	...	...	...	...	...	...	...	...	...	...	...	...	...	...	...	...
		Rating History: F, 04/29/09; NR-5, 04/14/09; NR-5, 04/07/08; NR-5, 05/09/07; NR-5, 05/09/06																

2010 BEST'S KEY RATING GUIDE — LIFE/HEALTH EDITION
BEST'S PROFITABILITY, LEVERAGE AND LIQUIDITY TESTS 2005 – 2009
Data in U.S. Dollars

—	Profitability Tests							Leverage Tests						Liquidity Tests					
Un-Realized Capital Gains ($000)	Benefits Paid to NPW & Dep (%)	Comm. & Expenses to NPW & Dep (%)	NOG to Total Assets (%)	NOG to Total Rev (%)	Operating Return on Equity (%)	Net Yield (%)	Total Return (%)	Change in NPW & Dep (%)	NPW & Dep to Capital (X)	Capital & Surplus to Liabilities (%)	Surplus Relief (%)	Reins Leverage (%)	Change in Capital (%)	Quick Liquidity (%)	Current Liquidity (%)	Non-Invest Grade Bonds to Capital (%)	Delinq. & Foreclosed Mortgages to Capital (%)	Mort. & Credit Tenant Loans & R.E. to Capital (%)	Affiliated Invest to Capital (%)
-616	81.3	35.1	-2.8	-3.4	-21.2	4.91	4.46	20.5	3.2	16.7	224.3	285.5	9.6	77.7	85.3	16.6	...	0.0	53.8
-711	78.8	33.9	-1.4	-1.8	-9.3	5.25	4.66	4.9	2.8	20.5	158.9	208.4	22.7	90.2	98.6	13.5	...	0.0	39.1
2,415	83.1	27.0	1.2	1.9	6.7	5.38	7.54	-14.1	2.0	25.5	100.1	159.4	19.7	131.5	140.6	16.9	...	0.0	...
-76	82.4	27.9	1.8	3.3	8.8	4.93	4.71	-11.1	1.6	28.3	69.8	141.3	8.2	126.1	136.3	8.4	...	...	...
76	-99.9	-99.9	5.5	57.3	16.9	2.93	3.10	-99.9	-0.1	101.8	31.4	231.5	43.1	135.4	144.4	...	...	...	...
	Principal Lines of Business: OrdLife (999.9%), IndAnn (111.3%), IndA&H (-99.9%)													Principal States: VA (18.6%), MS (16.1%), WI (15.2%), FL (11.3%), IL (9.5%)					
...	257.1	32.1	14.3	6.5	17.9	0.18	0.18	5.5	0.8	356.7	...	...	-4.2	16.9	16.9	...	...	...	...
...	262.7	36.0	20.0	8.6	25.5	0.11	0.11	0.6	0.7	369.3	...	...	7.4	13.0	13.0	...	...	...	...
...	265.4	38.0	15.5	6.7	20.5	0.08	0.08	6.8	0.8	263.3	...	...	-4.4	34.0	34.0	...	...	...	...
...	247.1	37.6	12.6	5.6	17.7	0.12	0.12	6.3	0.9	237.6	...	...	-8.7	14.5	14.5	...	...	...	...
...	212.0	36.6	11.3	5.4	15.7	0.10	0.10	6.3	0.9	280.7	...	...	4.4	15.5	15.5	...	...	...	...
	Principal Lines of Business: Dental (100.0%)																		
...	62.3	28.5	-7.0	-5.8	-9.2	...	...	704.2	1.6	186.5	...	...	-10.1	...	...	...	...	...	...
...	56.9	49.1	-1.5	-0.8	-3.2	...	...	122.3	3.8	56.2	...	...	-3.5	...	...	...	...	...	...
...	49.7	57.3	-10.1	-7.5	-22.9	...	...	23.0	2.2	97.2	...	...	112.5	...	...	...	...	...	...
...	51.1	63.3	-14.0	-12.4	-27.2	...	...	-2.2	2.1	115.2	...	...	0.2	...	...	...	...	...	...
...	49.6	59.5	-6.9	-5.1	-13.6	...	...	16.0	2.8	92.4	...	...	-12.8	...	...	...	...	...	...
	Principal Lines of Business: GrpA&H (70.5%), GrpLife (20.5%), IndA&H (8.8%), OrdLife (0.1%)																		
-25	31.5	59.3	5.0	5.3	19.3	4.31	4.45	26.1	2.8	35.9	1.7	114.7	18.6	76.4	81.8	...	...	6.8	4.5
173	33.9	62.8	6.0	6.3	23.0	4.53	4.90	15.4	2.7	36.6	0.8	91.7	20.1	85.0	89.4	1.4	...	9.7	8.0
-31	37.6	64.1	5.5	6.6	20.8	4.83	4.75	5.2	2.4	36.4	0.3	115.0	18.7	86.9	92.3	1.5	...	8.1	8.1
-266	33.8	60.5	7.4	9.6	25.6	3.52	2.38	6.5	2.1	46.0	0.0	69.4	19.4	99.2	106.6	5.6	...	6.7	6.7
143	31.9	58.9	5.9	6.9	18.3	2.95	2.29	26.4	2.3	48.7	0.0	53.9	18.0	116.8	125.1	...	...	4.9	4.9
	Principal Lines of Business: GrpA&H (85.9%), GrpLife (9.3%), IndA&H (4.2%), OrdLife (0.6%), IndAnn (0.0%)													Principal States: NC (11.5%), TX (11.4%), SC (10.2%), FL (7.2%), VA (6.1%)					
663	606.9	101.0	1.5	28.5	9.0	5.50	5.52	-90.8	0.0	33.1	3.9	225.4	-43.7	53.2	73.4	33.8	0.0	11.5	11.5
1,181	840.8	-16.4	1.9	34.2	13.6	6.34	6.03	-17.4	0.0	38.9	1.4	174.1	7.6	56.0	78.8	23.8	0.0	13.0	12.9
480	796.6	20.8	1.1	25.5	8.5	6.59	6.07	-21.6	0.0	28.2	2.1	242.4	-31.1	47.4	69.1	29.8	...	-0.2	-0.3
-393	995.0	39.3	-0.1	-1.8	-0.5	6.92	4.98	-7.5	0.0	26.0	1.1	206.9	-7.5	45.0	63.9	38.9	...	-0.2	-0.3
-632	972.5	259.2	-1.4	-29.7	-10.1	7.36	6.81	-1.1	0.0	24.7	0.8	214.2	-8.1	58.6	78.6	28.3	...	-0.3	-0.4
	Principal Lines of Business: GrpAnn (74.7%), IndAnn (15.2%), OrdLife (6.7%), IndA&H (2.0%), GrpLife (1.6%)													Principal States: NY (24.7%), TN (20.0%), NC (10.0%), IL (8.9%), NJ (4.7%)					
-778	69.6	27.4	1.2	1.5	7.9	5.67	5.69	-1.5	4.6	17.1	13.7	270.8	-3.5	77.5	88.9	25.6	...	11.5	2.8
1,145	377.3	121.5	5.0	19.8	29.9	6.11	6.58	-88.2	0.6	26.7	56.4	636.8	-5.0	77.5	85.4	1.6	...	15.1	1.2
409	78.6	25.6	3.4	7.3	16.8	5.77	6.91	144.7	1.7	25.8	50.8	689.2	-17.2	80.4	89.0	3.1	...	10.1	16.3
391	84.3	20.3	2.2	4.7	11.1	5.32	4.75	-12.8	1.7	25.7	54.7	748.2	-13.7	80.1	89.1	5.6	...	11.4	...
622	85.2	17.4	2.5	5.7	14.4	5.66	1.66	-14.8	2.1	17.7	61.4	999.9	-30.8	70.6	79.7	12.6	...	16.1	...
	Principal Lines of Business: IndA&H (87.8%), OrdLife (11.1%), IndAnn (0.7%), GrpA&H (0.4%)													Principal States: FL (10.9%), TX (8.2%), OH (7.2%), NE (6.2%), PA (5.1%)					
...	38.0	78.2	0.2	0.7	1.6	4.91	5.07	1.6	1.8	14.0	...	154.3	1.6	81.3	86.0	5.2	...	30.8	28.0
...	37.2	79.7	0.3	1.1	2.5	5.10	5.26	2.9	1.8	14.2	...	145.3	2.4	78.4	83.8	4.2	...	29.3	26.6
...	35.4	78.2	0.2	0.7	1.7	5.20	5.33	-0.2	1.7	14.2	...	138.3	1.6	75.7	81.2	...	...	51.9	25.4
...	41.1	70.5	0.7	1.8	6.3	5.07	4.33	1.7	1.8	13.9	...	...	-0.1	76.5	81.7	6.0	...	51.2	24.6
...	38.7	78.8	-0.7	-2.8	-6.3	4.79	4.88	0.0	1.9	13.0	...	...	-5.8	76.7	81.5	6.6	...	53.5	25.3
	Principal Lines of Business: OrdLife (88.1%), IndLife (10.0%), IndA&H (1.9%)													Principal States: PA (99.2%)					
12	68.1	23.5	6.0	4.2	18.1	5.51	5.48	9.4	3.7	52.6	0.6	10.5	21.3	117.4	120.8	6.7	...	...	7.2
1	69.6	23.5	7.4	5.7	20.7	5.60	5.67	2.3	3.1	58.1	0.4	9.6	21.8	114.5	120.8	5.1	...	...	16.6
-500	70.0	23.4	4.6	3.8	12.4	5.28	4.97	2.8	2.9	62.9	0.4	8.7	10.9	132.7	140.9	5.2	...	...	14.1
-5,525	68.9	22.1	8.1	7.0	20.9	4.98	0.89	-2.6	2.9	64.5	0.4	9.2	-0.4	122.3	138.9	5.0	...	...	16.6
-13,168	74.7	19.4	7.6	7.1	18.6	4.07	-5.13	-11.1	2.5	72.5	0.3	10.0	2.3	111.9	128.0	0.4	...	...	27.4
	Principal Lines of Business: IndA&H (88.3%), GrpA&H (7.8%), OrdLife (3.9%)													Principal States: MO (13.6%), OH (10.9%), FL (10.6%), SC (9.6%), GA (6.3%)					
...	148.4	120.5	-1.2	-10.1	-10.2	5.49	5.67	-3.4	0.5	15.6	...	12.4	26.4	71.4	73.4	23.1	...	37.1	37.1
...	79.7	120.1	-1.0	-9.3	-8.2	5.26	5.31	-6.6	0.5	14.4	...	13.4	-8.0	73.1	75.1	8.4	...	39.7	39.7
...	72.7	143.3	-2.5	-23.4	-23.1	5.43	5.43	-3.3	0.6	11.4	...	16.8	-20.1	73.4	75.4	...	...	49.0	49.0
...	120.2	220.0	-6.2	-62.8	-89.7	5.23	5.16	-20.1	1.1	4.6	...	47.0	-59.7	59.6	64.3	26.8	...	118.5	118.5
...	...	...	...	...	...	...	...	...	...	...	...	...	...	...	...	...	...	...	...

Data in U.S. Dollars

COMPANY NAME Ultimate Parent Association Principal Officer Mailing Address Dom. : Began Bus. : Struct. : Mktg. Specialty Phone # AMB# NAIC#	Best's Financial Strength Rating FSC	Data Year	Balance Sheet: Bonds (%)	Mort. Loans & R.E. (%)	Com & Pref. Stock (%)	All Other Assets (%)	Total Assets ($000)	Life Reserves (%)	Health Reserves %)	Ann Res. & Dep. Liabilities (%)	All Other Liabilities (%)	Capital & Surplus ($000)	Operations: Direct Premiums Written ($000)	Net Premiums Written & Deposits ($000)	Operating Cash Flow ($000)	NOG Before Taxes ($000)	NOG After Taxes ($000)	Net Income ($000)
CONTRA COSTA HEALTH PLAN Richard Harrison Executive Director 595 Center Avenue, Suite 100 Martinez, CA 94553 CA : 1973 : Non-Profit : Broker Group A&H, Health 925-957-5405 AMB# 064085	NR-5	'05	...	...	...	100.0	42,708	...	...	...	100.0	10,075	109,325	109,325	1,455	328	328	328
		'06	...	...	...	100.0	42,122	...	...	...	100.0	9,826	119,573	119,573	1,653	-249	-249	-249
		'07	...	...	...	100.0	39,707	...	...	...	100.0	6,239	136,911	136,911	-9,764	-3,587	-3,587	-3,587
		'08	...	...	...	100.0	36,432	...	...	...	100.0	6,485	149,834	149,834	-11,142	246	246	246
		'09	...	...	...	100.0	48,435	...	...	...	100.0	4,622	163,131	163,131	-5,073	223	223	223
		Rating History: NR-5, 03/22/10; NR-5, 03/13/09; NR-5, 06/26/08; NR-5, 04/03/07; NR-5, 04/07/06																
COOK CHILDREN'S HEALTH PLAN[2] Cook Children's Health Care System David Lamkin President P.O. Box 2488 Fort Worth, TX 76101-2488 TX : 1999 : Non-Profit : Agency Group A&H 817-334-2247 AMB# 064508 NAIC# 95822	NR-5	'05	53.2	...	23.7	23.1	15,636	...	66.0	...	34.0	12,266	28,418	28,197	-462	-647	-647	-634
		'06	44.5	...	21.5	34.0	20,284	...	85.2	...	14.8	12,457	35,220	34,488	3,589	-780	-780	-289
		'07	48.2	...	24.9	26.9	19,347	...	84.7	...	15.3	10,157	66,561	63,756	-719	-2,464	-2,464	-2,404
		'08	42.5	...	14.0	43.4	22,515	...	87.3	...	12.7	8,757	99,191	95,853	-1,727	-10,593	-10,593	-10,151
		'09	38.2	...	13.7	48.1	28,565	...	86.5	...	13.5	9,348	134,810	131,518	13,598	-6,210	-6,210	-4,067
		Rating History: NR-5, 04/19/10; NR-5, 08/26/09; C+ pd, 07/01/08; C++pd, 06/19/07; C++pd, 07/17/06																
COOPERATIVA DE SEGUROS DE VIDA Ricardo A. Rivera Cardona President 400 Americo Miranda Avenue San Juan, PR 00936-3428 PR : 1960 : Stock : Career Agent A&H, Ann, Ind Life 787-751-5656 AMB# 007607 NAIC# 79715	B- Rating Outlook: Stable FSC VI	'05	68.6	8.3	8.1	14.9	305,461	19.9	8.8	63.3	8.1	36,119	142,747	151,507	37,088	2,388	2,388	3,126
		'06	68.2	10.5	7.8	13.5	317,603	19.7	8.8	61.2	10.4	39,895	158,645	168,043	10,864	6,067	6,067	4,100
		'07	69.7	11.0	7.7	11.6	327,243	19.9	9.1	61.8	9.1	38,786	155,999	166,332	7,271	-365	-365	-504
		'08	66.1	11.5	6.5	15.9	316,367	20.4	10.5	61.4	7.7	19,175	201,996	214,678	-8,046	-16,632	-16,632	-28,698
		'09	71.7	11.6	5.0	11.7	379,819	17.8	4.0	57.1	21.1	23,721	123,372	140,975	77,197	-230	-230	1,296
		Rating History: B-, 12/10/09; B, 02/27/09; B+, 10/10/08; B+, 10/08/07; B+, 08/10/06																
COOPERATIVE LIFE INS CO[1] Adam B. Robinson, Jr. President 721 Cherry Street Pine Bluff, AR 71601 AR : 1925 : Stock : Not Available 870-534-3134 AMB# 068326 NAIC# 83933	NR-1	'05	79.5	0.3	12.6	7.6	5,934	...	...	...	100.0	1,769	587	587	...	75	70	63
		'06	75.5	0.3	13.9	10.3	6,273	...	...	...	100.0	1,891	599	599	...	39	37	36
		'07	73.8	0.3	13.7	12.2	6,357	...	...	...	100.0	1,933	484	484	...	45	43	43
		'08	79.7	0.3	13.0	7.0	6,309	...	...	...	100.0	1,887	476	476	...	44	42	42
		'09	81.3	0.3	12.2	6.2	6,376	...	...	...	100.0	1,926	431	431	...	51	47	48
		Rating History: NR-1, 06/10/10; NR-1, 06/12/09; NR-1, 06/12/08; NR-1, 06/08/07; NR-1, 06/07/06																
COORDINATED CARE CORP INDIANA Centene Corporation Patricia A. Liebman President & CEO 7711 Carondelet Avenue, Suite 800 St. Louis, MO 63105 IN : 1996 : Stock : Broker Health 314-725-4477 AMB# 064266 NAIC# 95831	B+ Rating Outlook: Stable FSC VI	'05	28.1	...	...	71.9	55,996	...	69.7	...	30.3	21,763	276,818	264,127	7,496	-3,985	-1,025	-1,026
		'06	23.1	...	...	76.9	60,285	...	80.4	...	19.6	28,697	352,161	337,708	3,693	-3,407	-3,327	-3,327
		'07	51.9	...	...	48.1	62,295	...	67.1	...	32.9	30,715	326,153	314,968	5,697	10,949	7,420	7,420
		'08	50.1	...	...	49.9	71,273	...	72.2	...	27.8	35,810	332,115	326,309	9,333	6,386	4,498	4,535
		'09	51.4	...	...	48.6	77,988	...	73.6	...	26.4	37,032	389,773	382,280	1,914	2,524	1,778	1,864
		Rating History: B+, 02/19/10; B+, 02/10/09; C+ pd, 07/09/07; C+ pd, 08/08/06; C+ pd, 09/29/05																
CORNHUSKER LIFE INSURANCE CO[1] A. Loy Todd, Jr. President P.O. Box 95023 Lincoln, NE 68509-5023 NE : 1987 : Stock : Not Available 402-475-1079 AMB# 068186 NAIC# 71030	NR-1	'05	73.0	...	21.9	5.1	2,382	...	...	...	100.0	2,017	...	361	...	194	174	178
		'06	71.8	...	24.3	3.8	2,448	...	...	...	100.0	2,046	...	346	...	176	156	164
		'07	70.3	...	26.1	3.6	2,464	...	...	...	100.0	2,082	...	297	...	191	164	193
		'08	77.7	...	19.0	3.3	2,147	...	...	...	100.0	1,961	...	255	...	129	180	184
		'09	71.0	...	24.3	4.7	2,139	...	...	...	100.0	1,931	...	229	...	161	139	139
		Rating History: NR-1, 06/10/10; NR-1, 06/12/09; NR-1, 06/12/08; NR-1, 06/08/07; NR-1, 06/07/06																
COSMOPOLITAN LIFE INS CO[1] J. Matt Lile, III President 1525 Merrill Drive Little Rock, AR 72211-1821 AR : 1931 : Stock : Not Available In Rehabilitation 501-312-4605 AMB# 008755 NAIC# 83941	E	'05	...	...	...	100.0	2,161	...	...	...	100.0	808	570	5,637	...	-30	-30	-30
		'06	...	...	...	100.0	3,966	...	...	...	100.0	2,809	437	4,510	...	519	535	535
		'07	...	...	...	100.0	3,628	...	...	...	100.0	2,278	4,018	3,931	...	-506	-506	-506
		'08	...	...	...	100.0	2,579	...	...	...	100.0	835	4,021	4,509	...	-1,106	-1,106	-1,106
		'09	...	...	...	...	...	...	...	...	...	...	...	...	...	...	...	...
		Rating History: E, 03/19/09; NR-1, 06/12/08; NR-1, 06/08/07; NR-1, 06/07/06; NR-1, 06/07/05																
COTTON STATES LIFE INS CO Illinois Agricultural Association John D. Blackburn Chairman P.O. Box 2000 Bloomington, IL 61702-2000 GA : 1955 : Stock : Exclusive Agent Term Life, Univ Life, Whole life 770-391-8789 AMB# 006292 NAIC# 62537	A- Rating Outlook: Stable FSC VI	'05	82.6	0.2	4.7	12.6	246,162	93.2	0.0	2.1	4.7	27,565	52,844	49,686	24,045	-2,072	341	403
		'06	80.8	0.1	4.5	14.6	261,085	93.7	0.0	1.9	4.3	28,092	54,436	50,630	16,560	505	661	905
		'07	80.8	0.1	5.0	14.1	273,720	95.4	0.0	1.6	3.0	31,059	52,646	48,105	9,682	1,112	2,094	2,390
		'08	81.4	0.0	4.0	14.5	281,158	96.6	0.0	1.6	1.8	31,691	50,197	45,686	14,839	3,098	2,796	1,370
		'09	82.7	0.0	2.6	14.6	291,707	96.3	0.2	1.5	2.1	34,820	47,557	41,982	5,106	3,123	2,699	-1,061
		Rating History: A-, 03/17/10; A-, 03/18/09; A-, 03/14/08; A-, 02/20/07; A-, 02/08/06																
COUNTRY INVESTORS LIFE ASSUR Illinois Agricultural Association Philip T. Nelson President 1701 N. Towanda Avenue Bloomington, IL 61701-2090 IL : 1981 : Stock : Exclusive Agent Univ Life, Ind Ann 309-821-3000 AMB# 009084 NAIC# 94218	A+ Rating Outlook: Stable FSC XI	'05	84.9	...	...	15.1	152,466	0.3	...	9.1	90.6	133,866	67,763	14,705	3,399	1,325	344	344
		'06	73.8	...	...	26.2	158,041	0.7	...	8.7	90.6	133,776	81,081	15,332	-4,173	-258	-128	-77
		'07	71.4	...	...	28.6	167,570	0.6	...	7.1	92.3	132,395	73,092	13,192	-1,098	-1,071	-1,357	-1,357
		'08	57.7	...	...	42.3	199,151	0.6	...	8.6	90.8	152,157	126,090	14,604	38,303	6,583	3,806	4,058
		'09	68.4	...	...	31.6	205,383	0.9	...	15.3	83.8	154,947	266,584	15,272	-8,390	6,631	1,768	1,798
		Rating History: A+ r, 03/17/10; A+ r, 03/18/09; A+ r, 03/14/08; A+ r, 02/20/07; A+ r, 02/08/06																

BEST'S PROFITABILITY, LEVERAGE AND LIQUIDITY TESTS 2005 – 2009

Data in U.S. Dollars

	Profitability Tests							Leverage Tests						Liquidity Tests					
Un-Realized Capital Gains ($000)	Benefits Paid to NPW & Dep (%)	Comm. & Expenses to NPW & Dep (%)	NOG to Total Assets (%)	NOG to Total Rev (%)	Operating Return on Equity (%)	Net Yield (%)	Total Return (%)	Change in NPW & Dep (%)	NPW & Dep to Capital (X)	Capital & Surplus to Liabilities (%)	Surplus Relief (%)	Reins Leverage (%)	Change in Capital (%)	Quick Liquidity (%)	Current Liquidity (%)	Non-Invest Grade Bonds to Capital (%)	Delinq. & Foreclosed Mortgages to Capital (%)	Mort. & Credit Tenant Loans & R.E. to Capital (%)	Affiliated Invest to Capital (%)
...	121.2	9.8	0.8	0.2	3.3	1.92	1.92	5.6	10.9	30.9	...	...	3.4	105.4	105.4	...	...	...	...
...	119.0	9.3	-0.6	-0.2	-2.5	4.01	4.01	9.4	12.2	30.4	...	...	-2.5	111.6	111.6	...	...	...	...
...	118.2	7.9	-8.8	-2.1	-44.7	4.27	4.27	14.5	21.9	18.6	...	...	-36.5	78.5	78.5	...	...	...	...
...	117.0	7.7	0.6	0.1	3.9	2.50	2.50	9.4	23.1	21.7	...	...	4.0	50.5	50.5	...	...	...	...
...	121.9	7.2	0.5	0.1	4.0	1.29	1.29	8.9	35.3	10.5	...	...	-28.7	23.0	23.0	...	...	...	...
Principal Lines of Business: Medicaid (58.4%), CompHosp/Med (39.3%), Medicare (2.3%)																			
-8	72.3	32.0	-3.9	-2.2	-5.1	3.53	3.55	-5.5	2.3	364.0	...	0.0	-5.0	406.9	423.4	...	...	...	...
480	78.4	24.4	-4.3	-2.2	-6.3	0.98	6.63	22.3	2.8	159.1	...	3.2	1.6	217.9	229.4	...	...	...	...
104	86.8	18.7	-12.4	-3.8	-21.8	5.42	6.27	84.9	6.3	110.5	...	...	-18.5	206.1	217.7	...	...	...	...
-201	94.8	14.0	-50.6	-11.0	-99.9	1.10	2.53	50.3	10.9	63.7	...	0.0	-13.8	95.5	102.8	...	...	...	...
509	92.0	11.1	-24.3	-4.7	-68.6	0.33	13.76	37.2	14.1	48.6	...	7.1	6.8	120.3	126.5	...	...	...	...
Principal Lines of Business: Medicaid (76.9%), CompHosp/Med (23.1%) — Principal States: TX (100.0%)																			
-1,068	65.8	22.2	0.8	1.6	8.2	4.66	4.56	18.4	3.4	15.0	...	18.4	34.9	78.7	84.9	...	...	57.4	30.9
1,358	75.2	24.3	1.9	3.5	16.0	4.81	4.62	10.9	3.5	15.6	...	5.9	7.7	74.0	79.7	...	...	69.6	30.8
-1,911	71.8	25.8	-0.1	-0.2	-0.9	4.95	4.26	-1.0	3.6	14.1	...	7.7	-4.6	72.5	78.5	...	...	79.2	39.9
-1,129	78.8	23.2	-5.2	-7.7	-57.4	5.62	1.30	29.1	8.4	7.1	...	11.6	-43.9	67.9	73.8	...	...	142.7	71.2
76	63.2	23.7	-0.1	-0.2	-1.1	5.13	5.72	-34.3	4.6	7.3	...	8.6	20.0	70.5	78.2	...	...	143.0	92.1
Principal Lines of Business: GrpA&H (35.7%), IndAnn (23.2%), GrpAnn (10.0%), IndA&H (9.0%), GrpLife (8.0%) — Principal States: PR (100.0%)																			
6	92.0	27.8	1.2	8.2	4.0	...	...	2.2	0.3	49.5	...	...	3.7	...	...	...	...	1.0	...
125	85.3	28.1	0.6	4.1	2.0	...	...	2.0	0.3	51.3	...	...	8.2	...	...	...	...	0.9	...
-1	116.2	34.1	0.7	5.3	2.2	...	...	-19.2	0.2	51.7	...	...	2.0	...	...	...	...	0.9	...
-88	118.4	34.4	0.7	5.2	2.2	...	...	-1.7	0.2	50.7	...	...	-2.1	...	...	...	...	0.9	...
-8	118.6	39.0	0.7	6.3	2.5	...	...	-9.3	0.2	51.3	...	...	1.9	...	...	...	...	0.8	...
Principal Lines of Business: IndAnn (71.1%), OrdLife (28.9%)																			
...	88.7	13.2	-2.0	-0.4	-5.4	2.56	2.56	20.3	12.1	63.6	...	14.0	32.3	173.3	184.4	...	...	...	...
...	88.6	12.9	-5.7	-1.0	-13.2	3.13	3.13	27.9	11.8	90.8	...	17.7	31.9	205.3	217.8	...	...	...	...
...	83.9	13.3	12.1	2.3	25.0	3.99	3.99	-6.7	10.3	97.3	...	12.4	7.0	185.1	200.6	...	...	...	...
...	85.0	13.5	6.7	1.4	13.5	2.60	2.67	3.6	9.1	101.0	...	4.5	16.6	209.9	227.4	...	...	...	...
...	86.4	13.2	2.4	0.5	4.9	2.10	2.25	17.2	10.3	90.4	...	5.3	3.4	163.9	177.3	9.5	...	...	...
Principal Lines of Business: Medicaid (100.0%) — Principal States: IN (100.0%)																			
-2	21.3	53.0	7.4	38.6	8.8	...	...	158.7	0.2	776.2	...	...	3.1	...	...	...	...	...	...
37	24.8	53.3	6.4	35.4	7.7	...	...	-4.2	0.2	760.0	...	...	2.5	...	...	...	...	...	...
2	17.3	56.4	6.7	42.1	8.0	...	...	-14.0	0.1	835.0	...	...	1.7	...	...	...	...	...	...
-247	29.9	57.1	7.8	55.6	8.9	...	...	-14.1	0.1	999.9	...	...	-10.9	...	...	...	...	...	...
104	20.3	59.1	6.5	50.7	7.2	...	...	-10.5	0.1	999.9	...	...	3.1	...	...	...	...	...	...
Principal Lines of Business: CrdA&H (64.0%), CrdLife (36.0%)																			
...	93.8	9.6	-1.3	-0.5	-3.6	...	...	6.9	7.0	59.7	...	...	-2.2	...	...	...	...	...	...
...	82.6	13.3	17.4	11.0	29.6	...	...	-20.0	1.6	242.7	...	...	247.7	...	...	...	...	...	...
...	104.3	14.9	-13.3	-12.1	-19.9	...	...	-12.8	1.7	168.7	...	...	-18.9	...	...	...	...	...	...
...	108.3	17.7	-35.6	-23.6	-71.1	...	...	14.7	5.4	47.9	...	...	-63.3	...	...	...	...	...	...
...	...	...	...	...	...	...	...	...	...	...	...	...	...	...	...	...	...	...	...
190	52.1	44.8	0.1	0.5	0.4	5.53	5.97	5.4	1.7	13.6	...	22.7	-81.2	76.7	84.6	7.8	0.2	1.4	2.7
252	61.6	34.3	0.3	1.0	2.4	5.53	5.98	1.9	1.7	13.1	2.2	24.2	3.1	72.3	82.5	10.8	...	4.3	2.5
-161	69.9	31.6	0.8	3.3	7.1	5.53	5.78	-5.0	1.4	14.0	2.3	26.3	11.0	65.9	77.9	8.4	...	3.5	2.1
-2,730	75.2	27.1	1.0	4.6	8.9	5.46	4.04	-5.0	1.4	12.8	2.7	28.9	-5.4	63.4	76.3	11.1	...	6.7	2.2
1,917	82.1	27.8	0.9	4.7	8.1	5.42	4.87	-8.1	1.2	14.0	2.6	39.9	12.6	60.9	74.8	39.8	...	8.6	1.9
Principal Lines of Business: OrdLife (99.4%), IndAnn (0.5%), IndA&H (0.1%), GrpLife (0.0%) — Principal States: GA (48.7%), AL (18.9%), FL (11.6%), NC (5.1%), TN (4.9%)																			
...	...	...	0.2	1.5	0.3	5.39	5.16	18.8	0.1	999.9	9.9	925.5	0.3	999.9	999.9	...	...	3.6	...
...	...	...	-0.1	-0.6	-0.1	5.23	5.08	4.3	0.1	999.9	9.8	941.0	0.0	999.9	999.9	...	...	3.2	...
...	...	...	-0.8	-5.4	-1.0	5.31	5.28	-14.0	0.1	999.9	12.1	951.8	-1.0	999.9	999.9	...	...	2.8	...
...	...	0.0	2.1	11.9	2.7	4.61	4.77	10.7	0.1	749.5	11.8	869.0	15.0	905.1	983.8	...	...	2.1	...
-51	...	0.0	0.9	4.1	1.2	4.22	4.23	4.6	0.1	999.9	15.1	977.2	1.9	999.9	999.9	0.4	...	1.7	...
Principal Lines of Business: IndAnn (100.0%) — Principal States: IL (76.0%), OR (6.1%)																			

COMPANY NAME / Ultimate Parent Association / Principal Officer / Mailing Address / Dom. : Began Bus. : Struct. : Mktg. / Specialty / Phone # / AMB# / NAIC#	Best's Financial Strength Rating / FSC	Data Year	Balance Sheet: Bonds (%)	Mort. Loans & R.E. (%)	Com & Pref. Stock (%)	All Other Assets (%)	Total Assets ($000)	Life Reserves (%)	Health Reserves (%)	Ann Res. & Dep. Liabilities (%)	All Other Liabilities (%)	Capital & Surplus ($000)	Operations: Direct Premiums Written ($000)	Net Premiums Written & Deposits ($000)	Operating Cash Flow ($000)	NOG Before Taxes ($000)	NOG After Taxes ($000)	Net Income ($000)
COUNTRY LIFE INS CO / Illinois Agricultural Association / Philip T. Nelson / President / 1701 N. Towanda Avenue / Bloomington, IL 61701-2090 / IL : 1928 : Stock : Exclusive Agent / Life, A&H / 309-821-3000 / AMB# 006294 / NAIC# 62553	A+ / Rating Outlook: Stable / FSC XI	'05	69.3	6.0	5.5	19.1	6,704,996	50.5	3.4	28.9	17.2	902,886	405,269	639,706	165,415	67,549	49,080	54,021
		'06	67.1	5.9	6.5	20.5	7,060,048	50.3	3.5	27.4	18.8	945,499	406,032	652,007	202,049	67,139	44,181	58,529
		'07	65.3	5.7	7.5	21.5	7,356,243	50.6	3.7	26.0	19.7	980,992	435,354	662,749	173,071	56,259	38,906	36,029
		'08	66.5	5.7	6.9	20.9	7,270,651	53.6	4.0	26.7	15.7	944,900	447,956	730,439	168,139	51,858	32,002	-9,745
		'09	66.4	4.7	6.4	22.5	7,895,262	51.1	3.9	26.6	18.5	918,023	460,564	920,470	296,100	47,282	35,160	-38,786
		Rating History: A+ g, 03/17/10; A+ g, 03/18/09; A+ g, 03/14/08; A+ g, 02/20/07; A+ g, 02/08/06																
COUNTY OF LOS ANGELES / 1000 South Fremont Avenue / Alhambra, CA 91803 / CA : 1983 : Non-Profit : Broker / Group A&H, Health / 626-299-5300 / AMB# 068680	NR-5	'05	...	...	...	100.0	64,588	...	...	...	100.0	29,943	200,169	200,169	-56,823	15,691	15,691	15,691
		'06	...	...	...	100.0	59,849	...	...	...	100.0	24,723	200,885	200,885	-2,583	16,011	16,011	16,011
		'07	...	...	...	100.0	71,676	...	...	...	100.0	18,623	224,537	224,537	8,106	20,644	20,644	20,644
		'08	...	...	...	100.0	80,029	...	...	...	100.0	27,214	241,520	241,520	-3,717	27,514	27,514	27,514
		'09	...	...	...	100.0	68,292	...	...	...	100.0	17,275	262,930	262,930	-11,167	23,620	23,620	23,620
		Rating History: NR-5, 03/22/10; NR-5, 03/13/09; NR-5, 03/11/08; NR-5, 04/03/07; NR-5, 04/07/06																
COUNTY OF VENTURA / Karen Davis / CFO / 2323 Knoll Drive / Ventura, CA 93003 / CA : 1996 : Stock : Not Available / Health / 806-677-5157 / AMB# 064574	NR-5	'05	...	...	...	100.0	5,469	...	...	...	100.0	1,440	17,541	17,541	-1,230	15	15	15
		'06	...	...	...	100.0	5,319	...	...	...	100.0	1,752	21,346	21,346	-380	312	312	312
		'07	...	...	...	100.0	9,017	...	...	...	100.0	2,661	26,971	26,971	3,711	909	909	909
		'08	...	...	...	100.0	13,355	...	...	...	100.0	3,971	30,497	30,497	4,694	1,309	1,309	1,309
		'09	...	...	...	100.0	14,264	...	...	...	100.0	6,100	33,884	33,884	271	2,130	2,130	2,130
		Rating History: NR-5, 03/22/10; NR-5, 03/13/09; NR-5, 03/11/08; NR-5, 04/03/07; NR-5, 04/20/06																
COVENTRY HLTH AND LIFE INS CO / Coventry Health Care Inc / Michael D. Bahr / President / 6705 Rockledge Drive, Suite 900 / Bethesda, MD 20817 / DE : 1968 : Stock : Direct Response / Group A&H / 800-843-7421 / AMB# 008812 / NAIC# 81973	A- / Rating Outlook: Negative / FSC IX	'05	29.6	...	...	70.4	186,603	...	45.5	...	54.5	76,104	452,261	538,674	52,211	55,706	36,319	36,252
		'06	15.2	...	...	84.8	400,766	...	28.8	...	71.2	118,543	895,525	952,562	186,289	67,589	45,639	45,455
		'07	38.1	...	...	61.9	407,844	...	45.2	...	54.8	128,313	1,396,177	1,371,366	-16,482	92,535	62,080	62,083
		'08	40.7	...	...	59.3	506,971	...	57.6	...	42.4	197,701	1,889,074	1,789,841	74,512	29,439	19,023	15,214
		'09	32.8	...	...	67.2	871,964	...	58.7	...	41.3	388,726	3,215,925	3,198,751	325,342	10,413	257	1,628
		Rating History: A-, 02/12/10; A- g, 11/19/08; A- g, 10/30/07; B++g, 07/11/07; B++g, 10/27/06																
COVENTRY HEALTH CARE OF DE / Coventry Health Care Inc / David L. Reynolds / President & CEO / 6705 Rockledge Drive, Suite 900 / Bethesda, MD 20817 / DE : 1986 : Stock : Broker / Group A&H, Health, Ind A&H / 302-995-6100 / AMB# 068687 / NAIC# 96460	B+ / Rating Outlook: Negative / FSC VI	'05	67.7	...	...	32.3	66,139	...	57.4	...	42.6	33,700	194,242	188,854	649	9,804	8,303	8,315
		'06	56.0	...	...	44.0	82,450	...	61.5	...	38.5	36,250	323,957	314,242	12,064	19,747	15,292	15,273
		'07	58.8	...	...	41.2	85,553	...	59.4	...	40.6	31,545	367,047	357,947	10,243	12,153	9,009	8,985
		'08	62.8	...	...	37.2	78,380	...	57.4	...	42.6	33,149	355,772	346,818	-8,171	5,977	3,135	824
		'09	63.6	...	...	36.4	72,735	...	62.5	...	37.5	32,611	329,003	320,865	-3,777	-425	575	1,626
		Rating History: B+, 02/12/10; B+, 11/19/08; B+, 10/30/07; B+, 07/11/07; B+, 10/27/06																
COVENTRY HEALTH CARE OF GA INC / Coventry Health Care Inc / Thomas A. Davis / Chairman, President & CEO / 6705 Rockledge Drive, Suite 900 / Bethesda, MD 20817 / GA : 1994 : Stock : Broker / Group A&H, Ind A&H / 678-202-2100 / AMB# 068980 / NAIC# 95282	A- / Rating Outlook: Negative / FSC VI	'05	43.0	...	...	57.0	34,889	...	55.7	...	44.3	20,122	90,899	89,553	-71	14,607	10,755	10,694
		'06	33.4	...	...	66.6	40,680	...	58.5	...	41.5	23,146	126,677	124,924	3,031	18,363	12,542	12,539
		'07	43.9	...	...	56.1	50,717	...	66.0	...	34.0	25,240	193,005	190,196	11,590	22,626	16,525	16,525
		'08	37.8	...	...	62.2	66,263	...	63.4	...	36.6	31,656	258,082	254,802	16,031	19,475	12,847	12,732
		'09	50.1	...	...	49.9	75,555	...	61.1	...	38.9	43,478	281,526	278,176	9,155	21,466	13,986	14,166
		Rating History: A-, 02/12/10; A- g, 11/19/08; A- g, 10/30/07; B++g, 07/11/07; B++g, 10/27/06																
COVENTRY HEALTH CARE OF IOWA / Coventry Health Care Inc / Charles R. Stark / President & CEO / 6705 Rockledge Drive, Suite 900 / Bethesda, MD 20817 / IA : 1986 : Stock : Broker / Group A&H, Health, Ind A&H / 515-225-1234 / AMB# 068541 / NAIC# 95241	B++ / Rating Outlook: Stable / FSC V	'05	74.5	...	...	25.5	40,010	...	65.7	...	34.3	19,159	144,851	141,819	176	7,975	5,236	5,329
		'06	69.2	...	...	30.8	44,974	...	59.9	...	40.1	26,073	155,664	152,772	5,142	18,594	13,328	13,326
		'07	63.3	...	...	36.7	39,046	...	66.7	...	33.3	18,476	144,936	142,103	-5,706	9,385	6,725	6,727
		'08	56.2	...	...	43.8	43,562	...	54.5	...	45.5	13,840	159,604	156,572	3,947	935	943	-37
		'09	57.3	...	...	42.7	46,153	...	54.6	...	45.4	19,344	170,189	167,297	-1,055	7,690	4,837	5,462
		Rating History: B++, 02/12/10; B++, 11/19/08; B++, 10/30/07; B++, 07/11/07; B++, 10/27/06																
COVENTRY HEALTH CARE OF KANSAS / Coventry Health Care Inc / Michael G. Murphy / President & CEO / 8301 East 21st Street North, Suite 300 / Wichita, KS 67206 / KS : 1981 : Stock : Broker / Group A&H, Health, Ind A&H / 816-941-3030 / AMB# 064126 / NAIC# 95489	B++ / Rating Outlook: Negative / FSC VII	'05	71.0	...	...	29.0	153,955	...	59.0	...	41.0	85,613	458,025	458,025	5,814	65,872	48,562	48,362
		'06	68.3	...	...	31.7	160,200	...	47.0	...	53.0	79,776	480,020	480,020	5,637	61,129	43,116	43,080
		'07	88.6	...	...	11.4	121,694	...	50.9	...	49.1	69,636	392,797	392,797	-34,209	51,488	36,261	36,194
		'08	69.7	...	...	30.3	98,319	...	54.9	...	45.1	55,748	320,952	315,571	-19,902	31,828	22,517	19,515
		'09	68.3	...	...	31.7	102,025	...	50.5	...	49.5	62,471	279,732	275,311	3,213	25,862	16,530	17,328
		Rating History: B++, 02/12/10; B++, 11/19/08; B++, 10/30/07; B++, 07/11/07; B++, 10/27/06																
COVENTRY HEALTH CARE OF LA / Coventry Health Care Inc / John R. Pegues / President & CEO / 3838 N. Causeway Blvd., Suite 3350 / Metairie, LA 70002 / LA : 1980 : Stock : Broker / Group A&H, Health, Ind A&H / 504-834-0840 / AMB# 068689 / NAIC# 95173	B+ / Rating Outlook: Negative / FSC V	'05	53.6	...	...	46.4	78,180	...	87.1	...	12.9	21,620	225,435	222,106	23,860	-10,316	-5,651	-5,656
		'06	63.1	...	...	36.9	68,373	...	52.5	...	47.5	47,037	152,585	150,642	-7,480	37,969	25,472	25,468
		'07	76.8	...	...	23.2	56,299	...	39.9	...	60.1	38,187	105,647	104,204	-11,842	8,276	6,397	6,339
		'08	72.9	...	...	27.1	40,635	...	44.5	...	55.5	23,867	99,596	98,123	-13,532	15,474	10,435	10,428
		'09	63.8	...	...	36.2	44,004	...	57.9	...	42.1	23,593	110,718	108,970	3,280	8,216	5,919	5,885
		Rating History: B+, 02/12/10; B+, 11/19/08; B+, 10/30/07; B+, 07/11/07; B+, 10/27/06																

2010 BEST'S KEY RATING GUIDE — LIFE/HEALTH EDITION
BEST'S PROFITABILITY, LEVERAGE AND LIQUIDITY TESTS 2005 – 2009
Data in U.S. Dollars

—	Profitability Tests							Leverage Tests						Liquidity Tests					
Un-Realized Capital Gains ($000)	Benefits Paid to NPW & Dep (%)	Comm. & Expenses to NPW & Dep (%)	NOG to Total Assets (%)	NOG to Total Rev (%)	Operating Return on Equity (%)	Net Yield (%)	Total Return (%)	Change in NPW & Dep (%)	NPW & Dep to Capital (X)	Capital & Surplus to Liabilities (%)	Surplus Relief (%)	Reins Leverage (%)	Change in Capital (%)	Quick Liquidity (%)	Current Liquidity (%)	Non-Invest Grade Bonds to Capital (%)	Delinq. & Foreclosed Mortgages to Capital (%)	Mort. & Credit Tenant Loans & R.E. to Capital (%)	Affiliated Invest to Capital (%)
-67,495	55.7	22.4	0.7	5.7	5.2	5.74	4.76	1.5	0.7	19.7	1.3	9.2	-8.2	54.2	70.9	15.9	0.1	63.9	24.2
2,993	53.0	20.8	0.6	5.1	4.8	5.95	6.31	1.9	0.6	20.2	1.3	11.6	5.8	51.6	70.0	14.2	0.1	63.7	22.7
36,733	54.4	21.4	0.5	4.4	4.0	6.02	6.61	1.6	0.6	20.3	1.4	14.8	3.1	49.2	68.3	13.7	0.1	63.1	28.1
-63,457	51.6	19.4	0.4	3.4	3.3	5.85	4.17	10.2	0.8	17.5	1.3	19.4	-10.3	48.5	67.2	18.8	0.1	73.5	33.2
26,180	40.9	16.9	0.5	3.2	3.8	5.77	5.05	26.0	1.0	16.6	1.3	21.5	0.8	46.9	64.7	34.4	0.6	68.2	33.3

Principal Lines of Business: OrdLife (37.9%), IndAnn (36.4%), GrpAnn (11.4%), IndA&H (9.1%), GrpA&H (4.6%) — Principal States: IL (66.6%), OR (3.1%)

...	81.9	10.6	16.3	7.8	31.4	1.07	1.07	0.8	6.7	86.4	...	...	-57.3	115.6	115.6	...	...	...	...
...	81.6	11.2	25.7	7.9	58.6	4.25	4.25	0.4	8.1	70.4	...	...	-17.4	106.7	106.7	...	...	...	...
...	80.2	11.6	31.4	9.1	95.3	5.24	5.24	11.8	12.1	35.1	...	...	-24.7	85.9	85.9	...	...	...	...
...	78.2	12.7	36.3	11.1	120.1	3.66	3.66	7.6	8.9	51.5	...	...	46.1	79.3	79.3	...	...	...	...
...	81.2	10.6	31.9	8.9	106.2	1.72	1.72	8.9	15.2	33.9	...	...	-36.5	60.2	60.2	...	...	...	...

Principal Lines of Business: Medicaid (64.4%), CompHosp/Med (35.6%)

...	88.2	12.6	0.2	0.1	1.0	2.41	2.41	4.5	12.2	35.7	...	...	1.0	78.2	78.2	...	...	...	...
...	88.0	11.2	5.8	1.5	19.6	2.52	2.52	21.7	12.2	49.1	...	...	21.7	77.6	77.6	...	...	...	...
...	88.1	9.7	12.7	3.3	41.2	4.76	4.76	26.3	10.1	41.9	...	...	51.9	101.9	101.9	...	...	...	...
...	84.5	12.9	11.7	4.2	39.5	4.91	4.91	13.1	7.7	42.3	...	...	49.2	119.1	119.1	...	...	...	...
...	90.2	4.7	15.4	6.2	42.3	3.09	3.09	11.1	5.6	74.7	...	...	53.6	140.2	140.2	...	...	...	...

Principal Lines of Business: CompHosp/Med (100.0%)

...	79.6	11.1	22.7	6.7	52.6	3.07	3.03	53.0	7.1	68.9	...	...	22.6	221.3	234.0	...	...	...	...
...	82.4	11.9	15.5	4.7	46.9	5.08	5.01	76.8	8.0	42.0	...	2.0	55.8	171.7	178.7	...	...	...	...
...	83.1	11.5	15.4	4.5	50.3	5.65	5.66	44.0	10.7	45.9	...	12.7	8.2	165.5	176.2	...	...	...	...
...	86.5	12.2	4.2	1.1	11.7	3.35	2.38	30.5	9.1	63.9	...	12.9	54.1	186.1	194.9	...	...	...	...
...	89.9	9.9	0.0	0.0	0.1	1.52	1.75	78.7	8.2	80.4	...	1.4	96.6	234.7	247.1	...	...	...	...

Principal Lines of Business: Medicare (50.1%), CompHosp/Med (32.0%), OtherHlth (17.4%), Medicaid (0.5%), FEHBP (0.0%) — Principal States: WV (21.4%), MO (18.0%), NC (9.9%), VA (6.1%), KS (5.8%)

...	80.7	15.4	12.9	4.3	24.9	4.50	4.52	22.7	5.6	103.9	...	1.6	2.5	200.1	217.4	1.5	...	...	...
...	81.2	13.6	20.6	4.8	43.7	5.98	5.95	66.4	8.7	78.5	...	7.2	7.6	189.8	205.3	1.4	...	...	...
...	83.8	13.4	10.7	2.5	26.6	5.92	5.89	13.9	11.3	58.4	...	8.5	-13.0	186.0	201.0	...	...	...	...
...	86.4	13.2	3.8	0.9	9.7	4.09	1.05	-3.1	10.5	73.3	...	1.7	5.1	193.7	209.1	...	...	...	...
...	86.1	14.5	0.8	0.2	1.7	2.81	4.34	-7.5	9.8	81.3	...	8.7	-1.6	214.3	230.0	...	...	...	...

Principal Lines of Business: CompHosp/Med (86.7%), Medicaid (10.8%), FEHBP (2.5%) — Principal States: MD (65.1%), DE (34.9%)

...	70.3	17.6	30.7	11.5	51.7	3.17	2.98	-9.4	4.5	136.3	...	2.2	-6.4	311.4	329.9	...	...	...	...
...	69.3	16.7	33.2	9.9	58.0	4.67	4.66	39.5	5.4	132.0	...	2.3	15.0	200.1	207.7	...	...	...	...
...	72.8	17.4	36.2	8.6	68.3	5.77	5.77	52.2	7.5	99.1	...	4.2	9.0	244.2	259.7	...	...	...	...
...	76.5	16.9	22.0	5.0	45.2	3.48	3.27	34.0	8.0	91.5	...	2.6	25.4	268.3	281.1	...	...	...	...
...	74.2	18.7	19.7	5.0	37.2	1.78	2.05	9.2	6.4	135.5	...	2.7	37.3	290.3	309.0	...	...	...	...

Principal Lines of Business: CompHosp/Med (96.1%), Medicare (3.9%) — Principal States: GA (100.0%)

-2	83.6	12.0	13.5	3.6	25.8	5.07	5.32	19.2	7.4	91.9	...	3.8	-10.8	193.3	211.6	0.0	...	...	...
1	79.0	10.5	31.4	8.6	58.9	5.49	5.49	7.7	5.9	138.0	...	2.4	36.1	246.2	268.6	...	...	...	...
...	81.9	12.8	16.0	4.7	30.2	5.08	5.08	-7.0	7.7	89.8	...	3.9	-29.1	207.6	225.5	...	...	...	...
...	88.4	12.0	2.3	0.6	5.8	4.07	1.53	10.2	11.3	46.6	...	8.5	-25.1	107.2	115.2	...	...	...	...
...	85.0	10.9	10.8	2.9	29.2	2.52	4.13	6.8	8.6	72.2	...	6.2	39.8	174.7	188.4	...	...	...	...

Principal Lines of Business: CompHosp/Med (54.3%), Medicare (34.1%), FEHBP (11.2%), Medicaid (0.4%) — Principal States: IA (100.0%)

...	74.7	12.3	31.8	10.5	59.5	3.71	3.57	-6.8	5.3	125.3	...	...	10.3	233.4	255.4	...	...	...	...
...	76.4	12.2	27.4	8.9	52.1	4.68	4.65	4.8	6.0	99.2	...	...	-6.8	202.0	220.0	...	...	...	...
...	74.3	14.3	25.7	9.1	48.5	4.90	4.85	-18.2	5.6	133.8	...	...	-12.7	184.6	206.3	...	...	...	...
...	78.9	12.2	20.5	7.0	35.9	3.94	1.00	-19.7	5.7	131.0	...	2.5	-19.9	227.6	249.5	...	...	...	...
...	78.6	13.1	16.5	5.9	28.0	3.14	4.02	-12.8	4.4	157.9	...	2.4	12.1	254.1	280.8	...	...	...	...

Principal Lines of Business: CompHosp/Med (52.3%), Medicare (30.2%), FEHBP (17.5%) — Principal States: MO (53.4%), KS (46.1%)

...	94.2	11.3	-8.6	-2.5	-24.4	3.20	3.19	8.1	10.3	38.2	...	6.8	-12.1	159.1	171.4	...	...	...	...
...	64.4	12.3	34.8	16.6	74.2	4.35	4.34	-32.2	3.2	220.5	...	1.3	117.6	345.4	374.0	...	...	...	...
...	83.1	11.4	10.3	6.0	15.0	4.41	4.31	-30.8	2.7	210.8	...	0.5	-18.8	316.2	348.3	...	...	...	...
...	74.8	11.1	21.5	10.5	33.6	3.79	3.78	-5.8	4.1	142.3	...	0.0	-37.5	328.0	353.5	...	...	...	...
...	77.9	15.6	14.0	5.4	24.9	2.88	2.80	11.1	4.6	115.6	...	0.0	-1.1	241.9	261.6	...	...	...	...

Principal Lines of Business: CompHosp/Med (87.9%), FEHBP (12.1%) — Principal States: LA (100.0%)

2010 BEST'S KEY RATING GUIDE — LIFE/HEALTH EDITION
ANNUAL STATEMENT DATA FOR YEARS 2005 – 2009

Data in U.S. Dollars

COMPANY NAME Ultimate Parent Association Principal Officer Mailing Address Dom. : Began Bus. : Struct. : Mktg. Specialty Phone # AMB# NAIC#	Best's Financial Strength Rating FSC	Data Year	Balance Sheet Bonds (%)	Mort. Loans & R.E. (%)	Com & Pref. Stock (%)	All Other Assets (%)	Total Assets ($000)	Life Reserves (%)	Health Reserves (%)	Ann Res. & Dep. Liabilities (%)	All Other Liabilities (%)	Capital & Surplus ($000)	Operations Direct Premiums Written ($000)	Net Premiums Written & Deposits ($000)	Operating Cash Flow ($000)	NOG Before Taxes ($000)	NOG After Taxes ($000)	Net Income ($000)
COVENTRY HEALTH CARE OF NE Coventry Health Care Inc Charles R. Stark President & CEO 6705 Rockledge Drive, Suite 900 Bethesda, MD 20817 NE : 1987 : Stock : Broker Group A&H, Ind A&S 402-498-9030 AMB# 068544 NAIC# 95925	**B+** Rating Outlook: Negative **FSC V**	'05	66.5	...	...	33.5	61,502	...	64.6	...	35.4	34,626	148,072	145,171	-1,331	2,737	2,162	2,156
		'06	60.4	...	...	39.6	65,177	...	61.1	...	38.9	43,258	176,179	173,280	138	12,220	9,100	9,098
		'07	46.2	...	...	53.8	68,348	...	62.7	...	37.3	42,523	161,359	159,910	-418	1,958	1,646	1,620
		'08	38.3	...	...	61.7	48,871	...	68.8	...	31.2	21,412	174,771	171,950	-4,726	5,007	3,858	2,884
		'09	58.8	...	...	41.2	46,218	...	60.2	...	39.8	20,457	158,228	155,700	-9,004	-911	563	682
		Rating History: B+, 02/12/10; B+, 11/19/08; B+, 10/30/07; B+, 07/11/07; B+, 10/27/06																
COVENTRY HEALTH CARE OF PA INC Coventry Health Care Inc Timothy E. Nolan President P.O. Box 67103 Harrisburg, PA 17106-7103 PA : 1997 : Stock : Broker Health, Group A&H, Ind A&H 800-788-6445 AMB# 064429 NAIC# 95283	**NR-3**	'05	92.9	...	...	7.1	2,101	...	...	...	100.0	2,086	...	...	54	73	44	46
		'06	94.3	...	...	5.7	2,154	...	...	...	100.0	2,138	...	...	56	74	54	52
		'07	94.3	...	...	5.7	2,200	...	...	...	100.0	2,180	...	...	65	73	38	42
		'08	84.4	...	...	15.6	2,272	...	...	...	100.0	2,238	...	...	89	70	44	66
		'09	83.3	...	...	16.7	2,295	...	...	...	100.0	2,252	...	...	28	62	6	6
		Rating History: NR-3, 02/12/10; NR-3, 11/19/08; NR-3, 10/30/07; NR-3, 07/11/07; NR-3, 10/27/06																
COX HEALTH SYSTEMS HMO[2] Cox Health Jeffrey C. Bond President P.O. Box 5750 Springfield, MO 65801-5750 MO : 1997 : Stock : Broker Group A&H 417-269-2990 AMB# 064421 NAIC# 95530	**NR-5**	'05	...	...	47.8	52.2	13,173	...	77.3	...	22.7	10,715	11,698	11,573	595	-1,993	-1,993	-1,993
		'06	...	...	45.2	54.8	14,956	...	69.5	...	30.5	11,433	20,354	20,109	744	-2,454	-2,454	-2,454
		'07	...	...	42.3	57.7	19,148	...	74.7	...	25.3	14,464	20,085	19,949	1,749	-559	-559	-559
		'08	...	...	40.6	59.4	20,970	...	78.9	...	21.1	16,215	18,188	18,057	271	882	945	945
		'09	...	...	39.4	60.6	23,265	...	77.4	...	22.6	18,936	15,719	15,609	-445	1,497	1,857	1,857
		Rating History: NR-5, 04/15/10; NR-5, 08/26/09; C++pd, 07/28/08; C++pd, 07/31/07; C++pd, 09/15/06																
CSI LIFE INSURANCE COMPANY Berkshire Hathaway Inc William M. Kizer Chairman, President & Treasurer P.O. Box 34888 Omaha, NE 68134 NE : 1974 : Stock : Bank Specialty Lines 402-997-8000 AMB# 008488 NAIC# 82880	**NR-5**	'05	30.4	...	...	69.6	21,215	38.1	13.8	...	48.2	13,401	0	10,409	-2,767	1,364	908	908
		'06	35.2	...	...	64.8	19,171	50.2	17.5	...	32.3	14,245	0	8,425	-1,783	1,293	845	845
		'07	33.7	...	...	66.3	19,975	49.6	14.8	...	35.7	14,936	0	7,866	1,004	1,061	681	681
		'08	36.6	...	...	63.4	20,169	54.9	15.7	...	29.4	15,276	0	7,231	320	529	395	395
		'09	45.0	...	...	55.0	17,602	59.6	14.1	...	26.4	12,965	254	6,133	-3,624	-3,672	-2,354	-2,354
		Rating History: NR-5, 04/22/10; NR-5, 04/20/09; NR-5, 04/08/08; NR-5, 04/24/07; NR-5, 06/02/06																
CUNA MUTUAL INS SOCIETY CUNA Mutual Insurance Society Jeff H. Post President & CEO PO Box 391 Madison, WI 53701-0391 IA : 1935 : Mutual : Direct Response Credit A&H, Credit Life, Group pens 608-238-5851 AMB# 006302 NAIC# 62626	**A** Rating Outlook: Negative **FSC XII**	'05	40.9	3.3	8.1	47.7	11,005,648	15.6	5.0	27.5	51.9	1,046,487	2,499,486	2,492,467	413,490	140,739	130,292	150,292
		'06	37.3	4.8	8.4	49.5	11,581,454	15.9	4.7	26.7	52.7	1,065,288	2,689,181	2,727,737	157,232	74,083	57,718	71,433
		'07	36.1	6.4	8.3	49.2	12,215,107	16.3	4.3	29.4	50.0	1,035,435	2,268,868	2,872,091	642,705	87,687	50,751	10,605
		'08	43.9	7.3	7.6	41.2	11,002,454	18.2	4.8	37.2	39.7	985,178	2,458,230	2,482,919	674,919	272,342	251,936	-37,828
		'09	43.8	6.5	7.2	42.5	12,441,231	16.6	4.7	37.5	41.2	1,201,075	2,605,249	2,596,531	822,914	514,620	432,270	281,644
		Rating History: A, 04/06/10; A, 03/24/09; A, 01/30/08; A g, 01/05/07; A g, 11/23/05																
DALLAS GENERAL LIFE INS CO AMERCO Mark A. Haydukovich President & CEO 2721 North Central Avenue Phoenix, AZ 85004-1172 TX : 1982 : Stock : Agency Med supp, Life, Ind A&H 602-263-6666 AMB# 009442 NAIC# 99767	**B++** Rating Outlook: Stable **FSC VIII**	'05	...	...	...	100.0	8,058	...	62.9	...	37.1	1,615	28,466	20,228	-3,142	39	-39	893
		'06	20.8	...	...	79.2	10,852	0.3	88.0	...	11.7	4,354	17,025	16,110	5,904	-1,183	-700	-700
		'07	48.3	...	1.1	50.7	10,674	0.9	88.3	...	10.8	4,414	16,033	15,024	431	337	486	486
		'08	78.4	...	1.6	20.0	10,212	1.1	90.1	...	8.8	4,528	14,488	13,662	-375	301	299	299
		'09	73.1	...	0.4	26.5	11,650	1.5	90.0	...	8.5	5,115	12,814	13,832	1,168	359	351	347
		Rating History: B++g, 03/31/10; B++g, 03/20/09; B++g, 01/31/08; NR-2, 11/29/06; NR-2, 06/02/06																
DAVITA VILLAGEHEALTH INS OF AL[2] DaVita Inc Andrew P. Hayek President 3500 Colonnade Parkway #525 Birmingham, AL 35243 AL : 2007 : Stock : Not Available Medicare 253-382-1794 AMB# 064941 NAIC# 12974	**NR-5**	'05	...	...	...	...	...	...	...	...	...	...	...	...	...	...	...	...
		'06	...	...	...	...	...	...	...	...	...	...	...	...	...	...	...	...
		'07	...	...	95.2	4.8	2,708	...	...	...	100.0	2,672	...	...	2,696	92	56	56
		'08	...	...	56.8	43.2	6,410	...	69.2	...	30.8	4,138	4,118	4,091	1,296	-6,073	-3,705	-3,705
		'09	...	...	15.2	84.8	4,549	...	87.0	...	13.0	2,631	7,059	7,000	468	-3,423	-1,924	-1,924
		Rating History: NR-5, 04/26/10; NR-5, 04/27/09; NR-5, 04/21/08																
DAVITA VILLAGEHEALTH OF GA INC[2] DaVita Inc Jess I. Parks President P.O. Box 2076 Tacoma, WA 98401-2076 GA : 2007 : Stock : Not Available Health 770-393-0751 AMB# 064938 NAIC# 12981	**NR-5**	'05	...	...	...	...	...	...	...	...	...	...	...	...	...	...	...	...
		'06	...	...	...	...	...	...	...	...	...	...	...	...	...	...	...	...
		'07	...	...	...	100.0	5,178	...	...	...	100.0	5,148	...	...	5,176	76	46	46
		'08	...	...	1.4	98.6	7,035	...	87.4	...	12.6	5,107	1,642	1,631	284	-3,790	-2,312	-2,312
		'09	...	...	...	...	...	...	...	...	...	...	...	...	...	...	...	...
		Rating History: NR-5, 04/02/09; NR-5, 07/14/08																
DAVITA VILLAGEHEALTH OF OH INC DaVita Inc Andrew P. Hayek President 1423 Pacific Avenue Tacoma, WA 98401-2076 OH : Stock : Not Available Medicare 253-382-1794 AMB# 064939 NAIC# 12975	**NR-5**	'05	...	...	...	...	...	...	...	...	...	...	...	...	...	...	...	...
		'06	...	...	...	...	...	...	...	...	...	...	...	...	...	...	...	...
		'07	...	...	...	100.0	3,481	...	...	...	100.0	3,444	...	...	3,438	94	57	57
		'08	...	...	16.2	83.8	5,762	...	92.6	...	7.4	3,855	2,279	2,264	796	-4,288	-3,163	-3,163
		'09	...	...	25.9	74.1	5,805	...	81.0	...	19.0	4,717	3,388	3,360	865	-820	-266	-266
		Rating History: NR-5, 04/07/10; NR-5, 03/19/09; NR-5, 04/29/08																

BEST'S PROFITABILITY, LEVERAGE AND LIQUIDITY TESTS 2005 – 2009

Data in U.S. Dollars

—	Profitability Tests							Leverage Tests						Liquidity Tests					
Un-Realized Capital Gains ($000)	Benefits Paid to NPW & Dep (%)	Comm. & Expenses to NPW & Dep (%)	NOG to Total Assets (%)	NOG to Total Rev (%)	Operating Return on Equity (%)	Net Yield (%)	Total Return (%)	Change in NPW & Dep (%)	NPW & Dep to Capital (X)	Capital & Surplus to Liabilities (%)	Surplus Relief (%)	Reins Leverage (%)	Change in Capital (%)	Quick Liquidity (%)	Current Liquidity (%)	Non-Invest Grade Bonds to Capital (%)	Delinq. & Foreclosed Mortgages to Capital (%)	Mort. & Credit Tenant Loans & R.E. to Capital (%)	Affiliated Invest to Capital (%)
...	87.7	12.3	3.5	1.5	6.1	3.78	3.77	-1.8	4.2	128.8	...	6.0	-4.1	255.9	271.7	...	...	...	...
...	83.1	11.3	14.4	5.2	23.4	4.43	4.43	19.4	4.0	197.4	...	4.8	24.9	300.6	322.7	...	...	...	...
...	88.3	12.3	2.5	1.0	3.8	5.12	5.08	-7.7	3.8	164.7	...	1.7	-1.7	250.1	264.7	...	...	...	...
...	87.2	10.8	6.6	2.2	12.1	2.79	1.05	7.5	8.0	78.0	...	7.8	-49.6	175.1	180.6	...	...	...	...
...	83.9	17.1	1.2	0.4	2.7	1.33	1.58	-9.5	7.6	79.4	...	3.6	-4.5	197.6	208.2	...	...	...	...
Principal Lines of Business: CompHosp/Med (90.9%), Medicare (9.0%), Dental (0.1%)														Principal States: NE (98.8%)					
...	...	...	2.1	51.7	2.1	4.16	4.25	...	...	999.9	...	...	2.2	999.9	999.9	...	...	...	...
...	...	...	2.5	61.1	2.6	4.27	4.17	...	...	999.9	...	...	2.5	999.9	999.9	...	...	...	...
...	...	...	1.7	42.5	1.7	4.14	4.37	...	...	999.9	...	...	2.0	999.9	999.9	...	...	...	...
...	...	...	2.0	54.5	2.0	3.66	4.63	...	...	999.9	...	...	2.7	999.9	999.9	...	...	...	...
...	...	...	0.3	9.4	0.3	2.91	2.91	...	...	999.9	...	...	0.6	999.9	999.9	...	...	...	...
1,899	108.5	14.4	-16.5	-16.1	-19.9	0.97	18.92	1.5	1.1	436.0	...	...	15.4	162.2	162.2	...	...	...	98.1
977	104.2	13.4	-17.4	-11.6	-22.2	1.48	8.99	73.8	1.8	324.5	...	...	6.7	135.1	135.1	...	...	...	88.5
2,633	94.1	12.3	-3.3	-2.7	-4.3	1.47	18.77	-0.8	1.4	308.8	...	0.5	26.5	139.5	139.5	...	...	...	88.1
1,728	84.8	13.0	4.7	5.1	6.2	0.56	9.72	-9.5	1.1	341.0	...	...	12.1	143.3	143.3	...	...	...	89.3
2,721	82.4	11.8	8.4	11.5	10.6	0.48	13.75	-13.6	0.8	437.4	...	...	16.8	147.2	147.2	...	...	...	90.8
Principal Lines of Business: CompHosp/Med (100.0%)														Principal States: MO (100.0%)					
...	46.1	52.4	3.9	8.3	7.0	2.87	2.96	-45.9	0.8	171.5	...	...	7.2	369.0	369.0	...	...	...	...
...	36.2	57.7	4.2	9.3	6.1	3.85	3.96	-19.1	0.6	289.2	...	...	6.3	529.8	529.8	...	...	...	...
...	37.4	61.1	3.5	7.8	4.7	4.97	5.09	-6.6	0.5	296.4	...	...	4.9	556.5	556.5	...	...	...	...
...	39.5	63.5	2.0	5.0	2.6	3.33	3.45	-8.1	0.5	315.4	...	...	2.5	569.2	569.2	4.4	...	...	...
...	48.0	119.5	-12.5	-36.3	-16.7	2.07	2.21	-15.2	0.5	283.8	...	...	-15.0	421.9	421.9	5.5	...	...	...
Principal Lines of Business: CrdLife (69.1%), CrdA&H (17.0%), OrdLife (6.1%), GrpLife (5.4%), GrpA&H (2.4%)														Principal States: TX (12.5%), CA (11.1%), FL (10.6%), GA (6.3%), NJ (6.1%)					
-151,160	74.3	20.7	1.2	4.4	12.7	5.22	3.11	-6.0	2.1	22.5	8.7	91.4	-3.7	61.2	70.9	24.4	...	31.1	75.2
60,572	80.9	23.7	0.5	1.8	5.5	5.30	6.56	9.4	2.1	23.3	4.2	87.3	7.2	52.0	64.2	39.5	...	44.0	72.5
10,109	68.8	22.7	0.4	1.6	4.8	5.35	4.84	5.3	2.3	20.7	-0.7	7.6	-1.4	46.3	59.6	41.8	...	62.0	84.8
-121,363	73.2	23.0	2.2	8.3	24.9	8.02	2.26	-13.6	2.2	16.8	0.3	15.6	-11.3	49.7	61.7	42.4	1.0	72.1	85.5
-235,290	61.9	23.2	3.7	12.7	39.5	9.62	4.61	4.6	2.1	17.1	0.7	15.1	10.2	45.4	57.8	53.2	0.9	67.3	84.9
Principal Lines of Business: GrpAnn (30.0%), IndAnn (27.5%), CrdA&H (13.3%), GrpLife (8.2%), CrdLife (7.9%)														Principal States: TX (7.4%), WI (7.3%), CA (6.0%), PA (5.8%), MI (5.0%)					
-626	71.1	35.6	-0.5	-0.2	-2.7	1.48	8.49	5.4	12.5	25.1	-62.6	171.5	10.9	58.2	58.2	...	...	...	...
...	82.4	27.1	-7.4	-4.2	-23.5	5.06	5.06	-20.4	3.7	67.5	3.3	9.6	170.7	213.0	224.7	...	...	...	...
...	79.9	24.0	4.5	3.0	11.1	5.64	5.64	-6.7	3.4	71.1	3.4	39.1	1.4	168.2	181.5	...	...	...	...
...	82.5	21.0	2.9	2.1	6.7	5.03	5.03	-9.1	3.0	80.6	2.6	36.6	2.7	126.7	143.3	...	...	...	...
...	74.7	17.7	3.2	2.4	7.3	4.78	4.75	1.2	2.7	79.4	1.6	5.0	13.2	131.7	148.5	3.0	...	...	...
Principal Lines of Business: GrpA&H (54.5%), IndA&H (44.7%), OrdLife (0.8%)														Principal States: TX (96.5%)					
...	...	...	...	...	...	...	...	...	...	...	...	...	...	...	...	...	...	...	...
...	...	...	...	...	...	...	...	...	...	...	...	...	...	...	...	...	...	...	...
...	...	...	...	61.0	...	...	...	...	...	999.9	...	...	...	999.9	999.9	...	...	...	...
...	91.0	133.0	-81.3	-89.5	-99.9	1.46	1.46	...	1.0	182.1	...	...	54.9	116.1	140.1	...	...	...	...
...	119.9	44.0	-35.1	-27.5	-56.9	-0.10	-0.10	71.1	2.7	137.2	...	1.8	-36.4	390.3	395.7	...	...	...	...
Principal Lines of Business: Medicare (100.0%)														Principal States: AL (100.0%)					
...	...	...	...	...	...	...	...	...	...	...	...	...	...	...	...	...	...	...	...
...	...	...	...	...	...	...	...	...	...	...	...	...	...	...	...	...	...	...	...
...	...	...	...	61.0	...	...	...	...	...	999.9	...	...	...	999.9	999.9	...	...	...	...
...	136.6	147.3	-37.9	-99.9	-45.1	2.75	2.75	...	0.3	264.8	...	...	-0.8	546.1	547.8	...	...	...	...
...	...	...	...	...	...	...	...	...	...	...	...	...	...	...	...	...	...	...	...
...	...	...	...	...	...	...	...	...	...	...	...	...	...	...	...	...	...	...	...
...	...	...	...	...	...	...	...	...	...	...	...	...	...	...	...	...	...	...	...
...	...	...	...	61.0	...	...	...	...	...	999.9	...	...	...	999.9	999.9	...	...	...	...
...	109.8	152.3	-68.4	-99.9	-86.7	2.16	2.16	...	0.6	202.1	...	...	11.9	375.0	382.4	...	...	...	...
...	99.8	46.6	-4.6	-7.9	-6.2	0.50	0.50	48.4	0.7	433.4	...	...	22.4	716.0	736.7	...	...	...	...
Principal Lines of Business: Medicare (100.0%)														Principal States: OH (100.0%)					

Data in U.S. Dollars

COMPANY NAME Ultimate Parent Association Principal Officer Mailing Address Dom. : Began Bus. : Struct. : Mktg. Specialty Phone # AMB# NAIC#	Best's Financial Strength Rating FSC	Data Year	Balance Sheet: Bonds (%)	Mort. Loans & R.E. (%)	Com & Pref. Stock (%)	All Other Assets (%)	Total Assets ($000)	Life Reserves (%)	Health Reserves (%)	Ann Res. & Dep. Liabilities (%)	All Other Liabilities (%)	Capital & Surplus ($000)	Operations: Direct Premiums Written ($000)	Net Premiums Written & Deposits ($000)	Operating Cash Flow ($000)	NOG Before Taxes ($000)	NOG After Taxes ($000)	Net Income ($000)
DAVITA VILLAGEHEALTH OF VA INC[2] DaVita Inc Andrew P. Hayek President 4510 Cox Road, Suite 106 Glen Allen, VA 23060 VA : 2007 : Stock : Not Available Medicare 253-382-1794 AMB# 064940 NAIC# 12972	NR-5	'05	...	...	...	...	...	...	...	...	...	...	...	...	...	...	...	...
		'06	...	...	...	...	...	...	...	...	...	...	...	...	...	...	...	...
		'07	...	...	...	100.0	6,047	...	...	...	100.0	5,982	...	...	5,995	167	102	102
		'08	...	...	...	100.0	8,048	...	51.1	...	48.9	6,960	1,985	1,960	900	-2,698	-1,646	-1,646
		'09	...	...	...	100.0	8,126	...	94.4	...	5.6	7,442	2,658	2,640	679	-745	-366	-366
		Rating History: NR-5, 05/18/10; NR-5, 04/27/09; NR-5, 04/21/08																
DC CHARTERED HEALTH PLAN INC DC Healthcare Systems Inc Jeffrey E. Thompson Chairman 1025 15th Street NW Washington, DC 20005-2601 DC : 1986 : Stock : Not Available Group A&H 202-408-4720 AMB# 064625 NAIC# 95748	NR-5	'05	26.0	...	63.6	10.4	32,926	...	65.7	...	34.3	15,365	99,191	98,681	4,870	5,595	3,634	3,634
		'06	32.2	...	51.1	16.8	43,032	...	76.1	...	23.9	20,227	131,757	131,198	3,904	8,816	6,005	6,005
		'07	20.5	...	...	79.5	44,505	...	85.4	...	14.6	21,620	165,965	165,104	726	8,345	5,464	5,464
		'08	...	...	...	100.0	44,410	...	60.1	...	39.9	19,724	182,038	180,992	385	6,556	4,193	4,193
		'09	...	...	...	100.0	41,462	...	67.6	...	32.4	13,760	230,814	229,536	-5,466	-8,752	-5,470	-5,470
		Rating History: NR-5, 03/22/10; NR-5, 08/26/09; B- pd, 07/14/08; B- pd, 06/19/07; B- pd, 07/17/06																
DEAN HEALTH INSURANCE INC Dean Health Systems, Inc. Robert L. Palmer CEO 1277 Deming Way Madison, WI 53717 WI : 1997 : Stock : Agency Group A&H, Medicare, Med supp 608-836-1400 AMB# 060218 NAIC# 60067	NR-2	'05	5.3	...	91.7	3.0	45,634	...	...	...	100.0	45,289	2,384	2,384	357	39	54	54
		'06	...	...	75.7	24.3	61,346	...	...	...	100.0	44,334	37,897	37,897	-3,729	-5,001	-3,598	-3,610
		'07	...	...	74.1	25.9	71,818	...	6.7	...	93.3	49,171	43,942	43,942	-403	-2,687	-2,107	-2,107
		'08	...	...	87.3	12.7	55,458	...	16.6	...	83.4	49,129	40,300	40,300	738	-2,485	-1,500	-1,500
		'09	...	...	92.7	7.3	76,468	...	3.5	...	96.5	72,456	26,495	26,495	2,887	1,629	1,236	1,236
		Rating History: NR-2, 07/09/09; NR-2, 06/06/08; NR-2, 05/21/07; NR-2, 03/23/06; NR-2, 06/17/05																
DEAN HEALTH PLAN INC Dean Health Systems, Inc. Robert L. Palmer CEO 1277 Deming Way Madison, WI 53717 WI : 1984 : Stock : Broker Medicare, Med supp, Medicaid 608-836-1400 AMB# 064203 NAIC# 96156	B++ Rating Outlook: Stable FSC VII	'05	33.1	13.7	16.3	36.9	75,364	...	...	...	100.0	41,634	653,752	653,752	-11,603	567	1,366	2,767
		'06	35.5	11.5	14.7	38.3	88,344	...	...	...	100.0	46,228	690,171	690,171	14,418	5,005	1,502	2,057
		'07	26.0	9.3	14.3	50.4	115,669	...	...	...	100.0	53,019	744,476	744,476	2,730	2,319	-802	-228
		'08	34.4	12.7	12.1	40.7	95,003	...	...	...	100.0	48,394	811,285	811,285	-3,033	5,069	6,826	6,357
		'09	27.8	6.6	14.9	50.7	121,477	...	...	...	100.0	70,885	938,345	938,345	25,534	16,697	9,026	8,786
		Rating History: B++, 07/09/09; B++, 06/06/08; B++, 05/21/07; B++, 03/23/06; B++, 01/19/05																
DEDICATED DENTAL SYSTEMS INC InterDent Service Corporation Scott Breman President 3990 Ming Avenue Bakersfield, CA 93309 CA : 1988 : Stock : Not Available Dental 661-397-5513 AMB# 064720	NR-5	'05	...	...	...	100.0	4,850	...	...	...	100.0	3,642	10,556	10,556	400	869	530	530
		'06	...	13.1	...	86.9	4,608	...	...	...	100.0	3,186	2,086	2,086	297	414	252	252
		'07	...	11.2	...	88.8	4,574	...	...	...	100.0	1,280	1,944	1,944	344	-1,481	-889	-889
		'08	...	...	...	100.0	4,120	...	...	...	100.0	402	1,814	1,814	-1,423	-711	-711	-711
		'09	...	...	...	100.0	3,072	...	...	...	100.0	2,141	1,528	1,528	-2,012	223	223	223
		Rating History: NR-5, 03/22/10; NR-5, 04/30/09; NR-5, 05/08/08; NR-5, 05/07/07; NR-5, 08/23/06																
DELAWARE AMERICAN LIFE INS CO American International Group, Inc Matthew E. Winter President & CEO P.O. Box 1591 Houston, TX 77251 DE : 1966 : Stock : Broker Group Life, Group A&H, Life 713-522-1111 AMB# 006305 NAIC# 62634	A Rating Outlook: Negative FSC VI	'05	77.4	...	0.4	22.2	77,955	56.9	5.2	26.5	11.4	23,374	20,699	21,938	-15,665	6,015	3,381	3,307
		'06	66.8	...	4.9	28.3	80,450	54.2	5.8	20.2	19.8	25,812	20,701	20,034	2,705	7,771	2,749	2,803
		'07	71.2	...	4.8	24.0	76,362	61.0	6.7	21.2	11.0	26,317	20,175	17,553	-5,012	2,085	1,414	883
		'08	60.5	...	4.4	35.1	83,876	61.5	7.7	18.2	12.5	27,313	29,243	26,809	3,517	3,538	3,044	2,281
		'09	78.0	...	...	22.0	65,311	5.2	24.5	...	70.3	25,880	33,074	-5,659	-18,833	4,809	2,505	2,683
		Rating History: A, 12/16/09; A, 11/10/08; A gu, 09/15/08; A+ g, 06/17/08; A++g, 05/28/08																
DELTA DENTAL INSURANCE CO Dentegra Group Inc Anthony S. Barth President 100 First Street San Francisco, CA 94105 DE : 1970 : Stock : Agency Dental 415-972-8353 AMB# 009147 NAIC# 81396	B++ Rating Outlook: Stable FSC IX	'05	35.7	...	5.8	58.4	105,063	...	14.7	...	85.3	34,347	177,938	151,640	27,269	221	137	137
		'06	35.1	...	11.3	53.6	111,377	...	21.5	...	78.5	44,753	261,623	207,620	-9,371	110	89	89
		'07	36.3	...	15.2	48.5	96,632	...	27.4	...	72.6	40,592	325,013	247,174	-3,269	-502	-1,223	89
		'08	39.0	...	9.8	51.2	101,031	...	28.0	...	72.0	46,443	414,443	293,437	-9,032	-1,222	-576	-576
		'09	50.6	...	11.6	37.8	103,855	...	24.4	...	75.6	49,120	458,349	322,405	36	-622	-690	-692
		Rating History: B++g, 04/08/10; B++g, 03/18/09; A- g, 03/24/08; A- g, 02/13/07; A- g, 12/21/05																
DELTA DENTAL OF CA Dentegra Group Inc Gary D. Radine President & CEO 100 First Street San Francisco, CA 94105 CA : 1978 : Non-Profit : Broker Dental 415-972-8300 AMB# 068800	B++ Rating Outlook: Stable FSC IX	'05	...	...	...	100.0	1,086,225	...	...	...	100.0	368,333	2,051,603	2,051,603	106,549	22,771	22,771	22,771
		'06	...	...	...	100.0	1,164,484	...	...	...	100.0	388,258	2,131,522	2,131,522	66,567	14,562	14,562	14,562
		'07	...	...	...	100.0	1,177,125	...	...	...	100.0	375,354	2,469,735	2,469,735	143,313	39,536	39,536	39,536
		'08	...	...	...	100.0	1,090,283	...	...	...	100.0	347,960	2,688,492	2,688,492	-58,282	20,467	20,467	20,467
		'09	...	...	...	100.0	1,050,424	...	...	...	100.0	376,839	2,846,970	2,846,970	-20,378	13,738	13,738	13,738
		Rating History: B++g, 04/08/10; B++g, 03/18/09; A- g, 03/24/08; A- g, 02/13/07; A- g, 12/21/05																
DELTA DENTAL OF DELAWARE Dentegra Group Inc Gary D. Radine President One Delta Drive Mechanicsburg, PA 17055 DE : 1987 : Non-Profit : Broker Dental 717-766-8500 AMB# 064642 NAIC# 11132	NR-2	'05	...	...	...	100.0	682	...	2.2	...	97.8	273	2,295	487	-333	-29	-29	-29
		'06	...	...	...	100.0	781	...	2.5	...	97.5	286	2,269	493	378	7	7	7
		'07	...	...	...	100.0	2,889	...	3.7	...	96.3	1,272	7,197	1,392	2,238	2	2	2
		'08	...	...	...	100.0	4,518	...	1.4	...	98.6	1,289	10,688	1,980	-702	2	2	2
		'09	...	...	...	100.0	2,822	...	2.3	...	97.7	1,362	12,965	2,420	448	70	70	70
		Rating History: NR-2, 04/08/10; NR-2, 03/18/09; NR-2, 03/24/08; NR-2, 02/13/07; NR-2, 12/21/05																

BEST'S PROFITABILITY, LEVERAGE AND LIQUIDITY TESTS 2005 – 2009

Data in U.S. Dollars

	Profitability Tests							Leverage Tests						Liquidity Tests					
Un-Realized Capital Gains ($000)	Benefits Paid to NPW & Dep (%)	Comm. & Expenses to NPW & Dep (%)	NOG to Total Assets (%)	NOG to Total Rev (%)	Operating Return on Equity (%)	Net Yield (%)	Total Return (%)	Change in NPW & Dep (%)	NPW & Dep to Capital (X)	Capital & Surplus to Liabilities (%)	Surplus Relief (%)	Reins Leverage (%)	Change in Capital (%)	Quick Liquidity (%)	Current Liquidity (%)	Non-Invest Grade Bonds to Capital (%)	Delinq. & Foreclosed Mortgages to Capital (%)	Mort. & Credit Tenant Loans & R.E. to Capital (%)	Affiliated Invest to Capital (%)
...	...	...	...	...	...	...	...	...	...	...	...	...	...	...	...	...	...	...	...
...	...	...	...	...	...	...	...	...	...	...	...	...	...	...	...	...	...	...	...
...	...	...	...	61.0	...	...	...	...	...	999.9	...	...	...	999.9	999.9	...	...	...	...
...	88.3	139.6	-23.4	-78.2	-25.4	2.28	2.28	...	0.3	639.5	...	...	16.3	999.9	999.9	...	...	...	...
...	97.4	45.6	-4.5	-13.7	-5.1	0.35	0.35	34.7	0.4	999.9	...	...	6.9	999.9	999.9	...	...	...	...
Principal Lines of Business: Medicare (100.0%)													Principal States: DC (72.9%), VA (27.1%)						
...	80.9	14.5	12.1	3.6	27.2	4.27	4.27	10.5	6.4	87.5	...	0.5	35.2	70.2	112.5	...	...	...	...
...	82.0	13.0	15.8	4.5	33.7	5.97	5.97	33.0	6.5	88.7	...	0.5	31.6	46.2	71.7	43.7	...	...	...
...	82.3	14.0	12.5	3.3	26.1	6.53	6.53	25.8	7.6	94.5	...	1.8	6.9	108.2	108.2	42.3	...	...	...
...	83.9	13.3	9.4	2.3	20.3	3.94	3.94	9.6	9.2	79.9	...	1.4	-8.8	138.9	138.9	...	...	...	...
...	93.5	10.9	-12.7	-2.4	-32.7	3.48	3.48	26.8	16.7	49.7	...	1.5	-30.2	104.0	104.0	...	...	...	...
Principal Lines of Business: Medicaid (79.6%), CompHosp/Med (20.4%)													Principal States: DC (100.0%)						
529	95.0	9.1	0.1	2.1	0.1	0.30	1.48	24.3	0.1	999.9	...	...	1.4	999.9	999.9	...	...	...	92.4
...	92.0	22.0	-6.7	-9.4	-8.0	0.65	0.63	999.9	0.9	260.6	...	...	-2.1	3.2	3.4	...	...	...	104.3
7,148	89.6	15.2	-3.2	-4.9	-4.5	0.32	15.70	15.9	0.9	217.1	...	...	10.9	0.6	0.7	...	...	...	107.8
-4,624	90.8	13.3	-2.4	-3.8	-3.1	0.12	-8.51	-8.3	0.8	776.2	...	...	-0.1	15.1	15.1	...	...	...	98.5
22,491	77.6	15.7	1.9	4.7	2.0	-0.04	44.24	-34.3	0.4	999.9	...	...	47.5	95.7	95.7	...	...	...	97.8
Principal Lines of Business: OtherHlth (100.0%)													Principal States: WI (100.0%)						
-514	93.0	7.3	1.7	0.2	3.3	3.76	5.12	9.1	15.7	123.4	...	...	0.9	111.2	121.5	...	...	24.9	17.6
711	93.8	6.3	1.8	0.2	3.4	7.89	9.78	5.6	14.9	109.8	...	...	11.0	122.8	133.7	...	...	22.0	15.6
679	93.3	7.5	-0.8	-0.1	-1.6	8.04	9.68	7.9	14.0	84.6	...	...	14.7	77.4	85.3	...	...	20.2	25.1
-1,972	93.7	6.3	6.5	0.8	13.5	5.75	2.50	9.0	16.8	103.8	...	...	-8.7	92.5	103.0	...	...	24.9	31.3
5,188	92.8	6.0	8.3	1.0	15.1	4.03	9.94	15.7	13.2	140.1	...	...	46.5	188.0	204.9	...	...	11.4	25.6
Principal Lines of Business: CompHosp/Med (78.6%), Medicaid (11.1%), FEHBP (4.2%), Medicare (3.9%), MedSup (2.2%)													Principal States: WI (100.0%)						
...	94.7	12.1	11.0	4.4	14.2	...	...	359.6	2.9	301.4	...	...	-5.0	112.9	112.9	...	...	...	...
...	95.1	11.6	5.3	2.3	7.4	3.79	3.79	-80.2	0.7	224.0	...	...	-12.5	107.5	107.5	...	...	18.9	18.9
...	113.3	24.9	-19.4	-8.6	-39.8	3.38	3.38	-6.8	1.5	38.9	...	...	-59.8	51.0	51.0	...	...	39.9	39.9
...	133.1	48.3	-16.4	-8.1	-84.5	1.87	1.87	-6.7	4.5	10.8	...	...	-68.6	50.1	50.1	...	...	...	...
...	113.7	8.4	6.2	2.7	17.5	...	...	-15.8	0.7	230.0	...	...	432.6	134.2	134.2	...	...	...	...
Principal Lines of Business: Dental (100.0%)																			
...	87.4	17.0	3.9	13.4	10.8	5.77	5.81	29.9	0.9	43.9	0.9	39.8	-40.4	88.9	112.1	8.7	...	...	...
...	66.4	36.4	3.5	11.4	11.2	5.79	6.01	-8.7	0.8	48.3	0.7	33.7	10.2	109.4	132.9	7.9	...	...	...
...	73.4	27.8	1.8	6.6	5.4	5.46	4.86	-12.4	0.7	53.1	0.8	25.4	1.1	103.9	126.3	6.9	...	...	...
...	66.6	24.1	3.8	10.0	11.4	5.39	4.43	52.7	1.0	49.2	0.5	16.8	4.4	116.6	134.6	3.7	...	...	...
...	-99.9	-99.9	3.4	-99.9	9.4	5.37	5.74	-99.9	-0.2	67.1	0.9	179.6	-5.2	100.6	120.4	10.1	...	...	...
Principal Lines of Business: OrdLife (305.0%), IndAnn (176.3%), GrpLife (90.5%), GrpAnn (-1.8%), IndA&H (-12.8%)													Principal States: DC (21.6%), IL (13.4%), MD (11.4%), NY (8.1%), VA (5.7%)						
390	71.1	42.7	0.2	0.1	0.4	2.69	3.18	9.7	4.4	48.6	...	32.3	-1.8	151.2	158.0	...	...	...	...
1,091	71.5	30.2	0.1	0.0	0.2	3.47	4.69	36.9	4.6	67.2	...	50.7	30.3	132.3	141.3	...	...	...	...
-2,284	73.4	29.2	-1.2	-0.5	-2.9	6.04	4.92	19.1	6.1	72.4	...	47.2	-9.3	152.5	162.1	...	...	...	0.1
-3,443	75.4	26.0	-0.6	-0.2	-1.3	3.61	-0.95	18.7	6.3	85.1	...	28.9	14.4	121.9	126.7	...	...	...	0.3
2,054	75.3	26.0	-0.7	-0.2	-1.4	3.37	6.40	9.9	6.6	89.7	...	28.7	5.8	107.1	116.4	...	...	...	0.8
Principal Lines of Business: Dental (100.0%)													Principal States: TX (33.5%), FL (18.2%), GA (14.9%), AL (5.4%), MS (4.6%)						
...	87.5	16.8	2.2	1.1	6.4	3.41	3.41	4.1	5.6	51.3	...	...	7.4	43.6	43.6	...	...	...	...
...	87.2	17.7	1.3	0.6	3.8	4.50	4.50	3.9	5.5	50.0	...	...	5.4	40.6	40.6	...	...	...	...
...	85.3	19.1	3.4	1.5	10.4	4.73	4.73	15.9	6.6	46.8	...	...	-3.3	26.5	26.5	...	...	...	...
...	87.1	17.0	1.8	0.7	5.7	3.87	3.87	8.9	7.7	46.9	...	...	-7.3	13.0	13.0	...	...	...	...
...	84.0	16.0	1.3	0.5	3.8	3.62	3.62	5.9	7.6	55.9	...	...	8.3	4.3	4.3	...	...	...	...
Principal Lines of Business: Dental (100.0%)																			
...	40.8	68.4	-4.6	-5.8	-10.1	6.57	6.57	119.0	1.8	66.8	...	68.6	-11.4	17.7	17.7	...	...	...	...
...	41.1	63.0	1.0	1.4	2.7	11.10	11.10	1.4	1.7	57.6	...	110.4	4.5	90.9	90.9	...	...	...	...
...	52.8	50.2	0.1	0.2	0.3	2.84	2.84	182.1	1.1	78.6	...	55.2	345.3	166.2	166.2	...	...	...	...
...	57.6	44.3	0.1	0.1	0.2	1.72	1.72	42.2	1.5	39.9	...	216.2	1.3	61.5	61.5	...	...	...	...
...	56.2	41.1	1.9	2.9	5.3	0.32	0.32	22.2	1.8	93.2	...	52.7	5.7	166.6	166.6	...	...	...	...
Principal Lines of Business: Dental (100.0%)													Principal States: DE (100.0%)						

Data in U.S. Dollars

COMPANY NAME Ultimate Parent Association Principal Officer Mailing Address Dom. : Began Bus. : Struct. : Mktg. Specialty Phone # AMB# NAIC#	Best's Financial Strength Rating FSC	Data Year	Balance Sheet Bonds (%)	Mort. Loans & R.E. (%)	Com & Pref. Stock (%)	All Other Assets (%)	Total Assets ($000)	Life Reserves (%)	Health Reserves (%)	Ann Res. & Dep. Liabilities (%)	All Other Liabilities (%)	Capital & Surplus ($000)	Operations Direct Premiums Written ($000)	Net Premiums Written & Deposits ($000)	Operating Cash Flow ($000)	NOG Before Taxes ($000)	NOG After Taxes ($000)	Net Income ($000)
DELTA DENTAL OF IOWA Donn Hutchins President & CEO 2401 SE Tones Drive, Suite 13 Ankeny, IA 50021 IA : 1970 : Non-Profit : Agency Dental 515-261-5500	A- Rating Outlook: Stable	'05	59.9	...	30.6	9.4	29,090	...	16.1	...	83.9	22,244	42,014	42,014	3,383	3,194	3,194	3,218
		'06	61.8	...	30.6	7.6	33,528	...	17.0	...	83.0	26,126	46,278	46,278	3,612	3,059	3,059	3,119
		'07	60.7	...	28.8	10.5	38,451	...	16.4	...	83.6	30,374	49,578	49,578	5,258	4,378	4,378	4,728
		'08	62.8	...	20.9	16.3	37,397	...	17.0	...	83.0	29,581	50,987	51,149	-196	5,102	5,102	1,668
		'09	56.3	7.6	22.9	13.1	45,751	...	15.1	...	84.9	35,544	52,374	52,615	5,903	3,261	3,261	3,116
AMB# 060205 NAIC# 55786	FSC VI	**Rating History: A-, 05/26/10; A-, 05/12/09; A-, 06/09/08; A-, 06/19/07; A-, 06/07/06**																
DELTA DENTAL OF KENTUCKY INC Renaissance Health Service Corp Clifford T. Maesaka, Jr. President & CEO P.O. Box 242810 Louisville, KY 40224-2810 KY : 1966 : Non-Profit : Agency Dental 800-423-2184	NR-5	'05	41.4	4.7	43.4	10.5	30,276	...	24.0	...	76.0	19,220	55,013	55,013	3,206	2,042	2,042	2,052
		'06	38.7	4.7	48.1	8.6	28,489	...	26.7	...	73.3	17,304	61,470	61,470	1,189	2,395	2,395	2,472
		'07	46.8	4.7	40.6	7.9	35,031	...	40.1	...	59.9	28,220	69,768	69,768	828	3,881	3,881	5,292
		'08	48.5	4.9	26.9	19.6	35,979	...	38.8	...	61.2	28,041	78,885	78,885	5,212	3,669	3,669	3,538
		'09	46.5	4.8	39.1	9.6	38,388	...	37.9	...	62.1	31,415	85,555	85,555	-12	2,692	2,692	762
AMB# 064485 NAIC# 54674		**Rating History: NR-5, 12/01/09; B+ pd, 09/24/08; B pd, 09/18/07; B pd, 10/11/06; B+ pd, 10/28/05**																
DELTA DENTAL OF MN DeCare International David B. Morse President 3560 Delta Dental Drive Eagan, MN 55122-3166 MN : 1969 : Non-Profit : Agency Dental 651-406-5900	A Rating Outlook: Stable	'05	60.0	6.1	22.7	11.2	130,037	...	11.9	...	88.1	84,529	158,209	158,209	15,962	10,775	10,775	11,118
		'06	64.7	6.0	18.3	11.0	124,977	...	13.5	...	86.5	90,408	157,444	157,444	-7,335	11,911	11,911	11,729
		'07	67.2	5.0	14.9	12.9	141,397	...	14.0	...	86.0	110,938	164,334	164,334	18,866	14,521	14,521	18,606
		'08	61.8	4.3	8.3	25.6	155,392	...	10.9	...	89.1	116,952	164,699	164,699	13,236	15,282	15,282	5,638
		'09	63.4	3.5	13.6	19.5	177,523	...	7.6	...	92.4	134,710	150,491	148,272	22,264	7,537	7,537	8,631
AMB# 064440 NAIC# 55034	FSC VIII	**Rating History: A g, 10/02/09; A g, 11/24/08; A g, 10/04/07; A g, 10/19/06; A g, 10/13/05**																
DELTA DENTAL OF MISSOURI[2] Steve P. Gaal, III President 12399 Gravois Road St. Louis, MO 63127-1702 MO : 1974 : Non-Profit : Agency Dental 314-656-3000	NR-5	'05	20.4	5.1	25.7	48.8	43,094	...	37.1	...	62.9	28,278	76,060	76,060	-126	2,247	2,247	3,372
		'06	25.9	3.9	23.5	46.8	52,210	...	37.3	...	62.7	35,328	95,937	95,937	10,476	7,810	7,810	10,150
		'07	28.6	3.1	23.1	45.2	60,909	...	31.9	...	68.1	42,656	106,332	106,332	9,632	8,959	8,959	9,802
		'08	24.5	2.4	21.5	51.6	72,427	...	30.5	...	69.5	51,769	119,480	119,480	9,184	8,892	8,892	7,440
		'09	31.8	2.9	10.8	54.4	76,447	...	31.1	...	68.9	56,577	130,395	130,395	3,012	5,746	5,746	6,760
AMB# 065732 NAIC# 55697		**Rating History: NR-5, 04/09/10; NR-5, 12/01/09; B++pd, 09/24/08; B+ pd, 09/18/07; B pd, 10/11/06**																
DELTA DENTAL OF NEBRASKA David B. Morse President 3560 Delta Dental Drive Eagan, MN 55122-3166 NE : 1986 : Non-Profit : Agency Dental 800-736-0710	A Rating Outlook: Stable	'05	89.1	...	14.1	-3.1	3,926	...	35.8	...	64.2	3,391	5,612	5,612	599	453	453	453
		'06	68.0	...	18.3	13.7	4,826	...	39.3	...	60.7	4,344	6,138	6,138	987	880	880	894
		'07	77.8	...	15.9	6.3	5,873	...	29.5	...	70.5	5,259	6,819	6,819	965	897	897	955
		'08	79.6	...	13.0	7.4	6,203	...	41.1	...	58.9	5,657	6,966	6,966	711	730	730	726
		'09	68.3	...	21.1	10.6	7,290	...	27.2	...	72.8	6,499	6,795	6,795	666	502	502	485
AMB# 064448 NAIC# 47091	FSC VIII	**Rating History: A g, 10/02/09; A g, 11/24/08; A g, 10/04/07; A g, 10/19/06; A g, 10/13/05**																
DELTA DENTAL OF NEW JERSEY INC[2] Delta Dental of New Jersey Inc Walter J. Van Brunt President 1639 Route 10 Parsippany, NJ 07054 NJ : 1970 : Stock : Agency Dental 973-285-4000	NR-5	'05	78.9	...	9.4	11.7	177,853	...	48.7	...	51.3	142,533	223,600	223,600	9,339	12,106	12,106	11,453
		'06	73.9	...	10.2	15.9	198,344	...	48.7	...	51.3	161,789	231,915	231,915	15,885	11,687	11,687	11,302
		'07	71.5	...	10.9	17.6	214,972	...	33.5	...	66.5	176,230	229,147	229,147	14,745	13,833	13,833	13,942
		'08	77.7	...	9.2	13.1	208,568	...	39.5	...	60.5	180,923	228,111	228,111	3,836	8,403	8,403	7,347
		'09	79.5	...	10.8	9.6	222,764	...	40.8	...	59.2	192,905	229,305	229,305	12,393	6,111	6,111	7,024
AMB# 060194 NAIC# 55085		**Rating History: NR-5, 04/19/10; NR-5, 12/01/09; A- pd, 09/24/08; A- pd, 09/18/07; A- pd, 10/11/06**																
DELTA DENTAL OF NEW YORK Dentegra Group Inc Gary D. Radine President One Delta Drive Mechanicsburg, PA 17055 NY : 1960 : Non-Profit : Agency Dental 717-766-8500	B+ Rating Outlook: Stable	'05	9.1	...	...	90.9	13,266	...	2.7	...	97.3	2,337	56,006	11,265	1,547	463	463	463
		'06	8.5	...	3.5	88.0	14,227	...	6.3	...	93.7	3,435	59,885	20,041	500	1,060	1,060	1,060
		'07	...	...	3.0	97.0	16,446	...	9.1	...	90.9	4,556	70,277	23,540	7	1,413	1,413	1,418
		'08	5.7	...	7.7	86.6	28,055	...	8.8	...	91.2	5,385	95,019	32,112	2,699	-195	-195	-195
		'09	96.5	...	6.9	-3.3	18,487	...	12.7	...	87.3	6,091	112,857	37,765	530	450	450	448
AMB# 064594 NAIC# 55263	FSC VI	**Rating History: B+ g, 04/08/10; B+ g, 03/18/09; B+ g, 03/24/08; B+ g, 02/13/07; B+ g, 12/21/05**																
DELTA DENTAL OF PENNSYLVANIA Dentegra Group Inc Gary D. Radine President One Delta Drive Mechanicsburg, PA 17055 PA : 1966 : Non-Profit : Career Agent Dental 717-766-8500	B+ Rating Outlook: Stable	'05	2.5	11.2	31.1	55.2	48,666	...	14.9	...	85.1	23,791	112,956	127,038	9,411	2,829	2,829	2,839
		'06	8.2	11.0	34.2	46.6	52,740	...	18.8	...	81.2	27,631	123,104	140,689	5,131	2,386	2,386	2,533
		'07	4.9	17.4	33.7	44.0	56,065	...	22.5	...	77.5	30,466	129,509	148,227	3,851	5,413	5,413	6,322
		'08	15.2	17.0	36.5	31.4	55,507	...	21.7	...	78.3	28,966	141,116	161,523	12,670	5,913	5,913	5,970
		'09	35.7	13.5	27.4	23.4	67,489	...	16.3	...	83.7	39,361	148,094	172,818	10,017	8,505	8,505	8,470
AMB# 064557 NAIC# 54798	FSC VI	**Rating History: B+ g, 04/08/10; B+ g, 03/18/09; B+ g, 03/24/08; B+ g, 02/13/07; B+ g, 12/21/05**																
DELTA DENTAL OF RHODE ISLAND Delta Dental of Rhode Island Joseph A. Nagle President 10 Charles Street Providence, RI 02904 RI : 1966 : Stock : Agency Dental 401-752-6000	NR-5	'05	62.7	...	8.9	28.5	53,483	...	36.3	...	63.7	41,142	96,630	96,630	4,451	5,031	5,022	5,003
		'06	63.2	...	11.5	25.4	59,398	...	38.8	...	61.2	46,500	112,017	112,017	1,982	4,741	4,706	4,689
		'07	59.4	...	12.0	28.5	56,724	...	39.4	...	60.6	43,810	106,144	106,144	-3	3,282	3,216	3,233
		'08	57.9	...	11.7	30.4	58,457	...	40.1	...	59.9	45,512	109,584	109,584	1,421	4,286	4,258	2,579
		'09	65.6	...	13.3	21.1	63,335	...	36.3	...	63.7	49,055	100,812	100,812	6,759	3,251	3,145	2,910
AMB# 064571 NAIC# 55301		**Rating History: NR-5, 04/06/10; NR-5, 04/08/09; NR-5, 06/26/08; NR-5, 04/12/07; NR-5, 05/11/06**																

BEST'S PROFITABILITY, LEVERAGE AND LIQUIDITY TESTS 2005 – 2009

Data in U.S. Dollars

—	Profitability Tests							Leverage Tests						Liquidity Tests					
Un-Realized Capital Gains ($000)	Benefits Paid to NPW & Dep (%)	Comm. & Expenses to NPW & Dep (%)	NOG to Total Assets (%)	NOG to Total Rev (%)	Operating Return on Equity (%)	Net Yield (%)	Total Return (%)	Change in NPW & Dep (%)	NPW & Dep to Capital (X)	Capital & Surplus to Liabilities (%)	Surplus Relief (%)	Reins Leverage (%)	Change in Capital (%)	Quick Liquidity (%)	Current Liquidity (%)	Non-Invest Grade Bonds to Capital (%)	Delinq. & Foreclosed Mortgages to Capital (%)	Mort. & Credit Tenant Loans & R.E. to Capital (%)	Affiliated Invest to Capital (%)
304	78.2	17.4	11.8	7.4	15.5	3.80	5.06	8.2	1.9	324.9	...	...	16.8	287.3	328.3	...	...	...	1.0
739	80.5	15.8	9.8	6.4	12.6	4.66	7.34	10.1	1.8	353.0	...	...	17.5	302.5	345.6	...	...	...	0.9
-502	78.9	15.5	12.2	8.5	15.5	4.92	4.49	7.1	1.6	376.1	...	...	16.3	314.8	358.4	...	...	...	...
-2,480	78.7	14.2	13.5	9.7	17.0	4.12	-11.79	3.2	1.7	378.5	...	...	-2.6	315.3	351.7	...	...	...	...
2,652	80.3	15.6	7.8	6.1	10.0	3.07	9.81	2.9	1.5	348.2	...	...	20.2	308.0	340.1	0.6	...	9.8	9.8
Principal Lines of Business: Dental (100.0%)														Principal States: IA (100.0%)					
271	83.0	16.0	6.9	3.6	11.1	7.87	9.31	25.8	2.9	173.8	...	...	10.0	186.1	207.6	...	...	7.4	24.7
842	82.6	16.8	8.2	3.8	13.1	10.76	15.46	11.7	3.6	154.7	...	...	-10.0	158.9	180.1	...	...	7.7	29.1
-1,327	80.9	16.5	12.2	5.4	17.1	8.60	9.25	13.5	2.5	414.3	...	...	63.1	253.8	287.4	...	...	5.8	18.0
-4,178	82.1	15.5	10.3	4.5	13.0	5.88	-7.24	13.1	2.8	353.3	...	...	-0.6	255.0	277.0	...	...	6.3	15.7
3,390	83.3	15.5	7.2	3.1	9.1	5.19	10.34	8.5	2.7	450.5	...	...	12.0	273.8	306.1	...	...	5.8	24.0
Principal Lines of Business: Dental (100.0%)														Principal States: KY (100.0%)					
273	80.8	17.0	8.8	6.5	14.7	5.76	6.33	8.2	1.9	185.7	...	...	36.7	161.7	186.1	0.1	...	9.4	17.8
50	78.9	17.7	9.3	7.3	13.6	5.06	4.93	-0.5	1.7	261.5	...	...	7.0	227.7	263.0	0.1	...	8.3	9.0
-4,025	78.2	17.2	10.9	8.5	14.4	5.81	6.01	4.4	1.5	364.2	...	...	22.7	302.8	344.6	0.1	...	6.4	0.0
88	77.4	17.8	10.3	8.9	13.4	5.47	-1.76	0.2	1.4	304.3	...	...	5.4	326.4	360.8	0.3	...	5.7	5.7
4,696	76.7	19.2	4.5	5.0	6.0	4.12	8.09	-10.0	1.1	314.6	...	...	15.2	335.0	371.1	0.6	...	4.6	0.0
Principal Lines of Business: Dental (100.0%)														Principal States: MN (96.5%)					
-66	81.8	19.1	5.6	2.8	8.5	2.66	5.75	6.6	2.7	190.9	...	...	14.9	188.6	200.6	...	...	7.8	23.0
-673	80.7	16.1	16.4	7.8	24.6	4.92	9.31	26.1	2.7	209.3	...	...	24.9	138.3	150.5	...	...	5.8	18.5
-64	79.9	14.0	15.8	8.2	23.0	4.81	6.48	10.8	2.5	233.7	...	...	20.7	229.0	249.9	...	...	4.4	16.8
-5,804	81.4	13.2	13.3	7.3	18.8	3.84	-8.40	12.4	2.3	250.6	...	...	21.4	231.7	246.4	0.3	...	3.4	18.4
-794	84.1	12.9	7.7	4.3	10.6	2.89	3.26	9.1	2.3	284.7	...	...	9.3	349.4	374.2	0.0	...	3.9	10.3
Principal Lines of Business: Dental (100.0%)														Principal States: MO (91.1%), SC (8.9%)					
16	75.2	19.0	12.6	8.0	14.4	3.07	3.50	8.6	1.7	634.3	...	...	16.2	583.7	664.6	...	...	...	...
59	72.3	16.3	20.1	14.0	22.7	4.36	6.10	9.4	1.4	900.9	...	...	28.1	880.6	986.6	...	...	...	...
-38	74.2	15.7	16.8	12.8	18.7	4.18	4.57	11.1	1.3	857.7	...	...	21.1	733.8	831.2	...	...	...	...
-330	76.4	16.5	12.1	10.1	13.4	4.13	-1.48	2.2	1.2	999.9	...	...	7.6	902.2	999.9	...	...	...	...
358	77.4	17.9	7.4	7.2	8.3	2.91	8.40	-2.5	1.0	821.4	...	...	14.9	712.9	804.9	...	...	...	...
Principal Lines of Business: Dental (100.0%)														Principal States: NE (99.3%)					
1,291	80.5	16.7	7.0	5.3	8.9	4.02	4.44	0.5	1.6	403.5	...	...	11.1	367.6	387.1	...	...	...	3.8
2,057	81.1	17.0	6.2	4.9	7.7	4.55	5.54	3.7	1.4	442.6	...	...	13.5	390.9	412.3	...	...	...	3.6
1,444	80.6	16.9	6.7	5.8	8.2	4.62	5.45	-1.2	1.3	454.9	...	...	8.9	397.8	420.9	...	...	...	3.8
-6,100	83.9	15.6	4.0	3.6	4.7	4.49	0.84	-0.5	1.3	654.4	...	...	2.7	544.1	573.4	0.2	...	...	4.1
3,086	84.2	15.4	2.8	2.6	3.3	4.20	6.22	0.5	1.2	646.1	...	...	6.6	540.2	570.0	0.7	...	...	4.1
Principal Lines of Business: Dental (100.0%)														Principal States: NJ (100.0%)					
...	39.9	59.1	3.4	3.8	21.2	3.58	3.58	22.6	4.8	21.4	...	273.5	15.3	161.3	162.3	...	...	...	...
...	61.7	36.0	7.7	5.0	36.7	5.64	5.64	77.9	5.8	31.8	...	156.0	47.0	161.6	162.8	...	...	...	...
...	60.8	35.9	9.2	5.6	35.4	5.84	5.89	17.5	5.2	38.3	...	143.5	32.6	156.4	157.8	...	...	...	...
-152	68.8	32.7	-0.9	-0.6	-3.9	2.98	1.54	36.4	6.0	23.8	...	322.7	18.2	83.4	86.8	...	...	...	...
94	67.3	32.4	1.9	1.2	7.9	2.82	3.58	17.6	6.2	49.1	...	102.6	13.1	73.0	88.9	...	...	...	...
Principal Lines of Business: Dental (100.0%)														Principal States: NY (100.0%)					
561	81.7	17.2	6.5	2.2	13.2	5.69	8.23	10.1	5.3	95.6	...	0.8	25.5	42.6	48.1	...	...	22.9	64.9
1,428	82.1	16.5	4.7	1.7	9.3	3.52	8.70	10.7	5.1	110.0	...	0.9	16.1	52.6	59.6	...	...	20.9	63.0
-1,309	79.7	17.9	9.9	3.6	18.6	4.01	2.96	5.4	4.9	119.0	...	1.6	10.3	44.5	51.3	...	...	32.0	74.0
-6,059	81.6	15.2	10.6	3.6	19.9	3.70	-11.01	9.0	5.6	109.1	...	2.0	-4.9	56.3	64.2	...	...	32.5	78.3
1,063	80.9	14.8	13.8	4.9	24.9	3.42	5.72	7.0	4.4	139.9	...	0.4	35.9	83.4	95.5	0.3	...	23.1	52.7
Principal Lines of Business: Dental (100.0%)														Principal States: PA (88.3%), MD (11.7%)					
-290	83.1	11.9	9.8	5.2	12.9	3.98	3.30	8.7	2.3	333.4	...	...	12.2	321.5	338.4	0.6	...	...	8.1
653	85.7	10.2	8.3	4.2	10.7	4.02	5.32	15.9	2.4	360.5	...	...	13.0	376.5	398.4	...	...	...	10.3
-1,543	84.9	13.7	5.5	3.0	7.1	3.65	0.66	-5.2	2.4	339.2	...	...	-5.8	385.4	408.8	...	...	...	6.7
-663	83.9	13.8	7.4	3.8	9.5	3.66	-0.98	3.2	2.4	351.6	...	...	3.9	363.0	392.0	0.1	...	...	7.1
1,318	83.4	15.3	5.2	2.8	6.7	3.41	5.44	-8.0	2.1	343.5	...	...	7.8	331.0	359.5	0.1	...	...	7.0
Principal Lines of Business: Dental (100.0%)														Principal States: RI (100.0%)					

Data in U.S. Dollars

COMPANY NAME / Ultimate Parent Association / Principal Officer / Mailing Address / Dom. : Began Bus. : Struct. : Mktg. / Specialty / Phone # / AMB# NAIC#	Best's Financial Strength Rating / FSC	Data Year	Balance Sheet: Bonds (%)	Mort. Loans & R.E. (%)	Com & Pref. Stock (%)	All Other Assets (%)	Total Assets ($000)	Life Reserves (%)	Health Reserves (%)	Ann Res. & Dep. Liabilities (%)	All Other Liabilities (%)	Capital & Surplus ($000)	Operations: Direct Premiums Written ($000)	Net Premiums Written & Deposits ($000)	Operating Cash Flow ($000)	NOG Before Taxes ($000)	NOG After Taxes ($000)	Net Income ($000)
DELTA DENTAL OF TENNESSEE Renaissance Health Service Corp Philip A. Wenk President & CEO	**A-**	'05	56.7	5.2	16.6	21.4	29,948	...	31.9	...	68.1	22,181	63,020	63,020	3,745	4,379	4,379	4,307
240 Venture Circle Nashville, TN 37228		'06	56.5	4.3	17.4	21.7	36,948	...	32.5	...	67.5	27,473	74,127	74,127	8,153	4,790	4,790	4,771
TN : 1969 : Non-Profit : Agency	Rating Outlook: Stable	'07	53.9	3.2	23.6	19.3	41,728	...	31.6	...	68.4	31,784	82,205	82,205	4,354	3,666	3,666	3,645
Dental		'08	63.4	4.2	17.0	15.4	41,817	...	25.9	...	74.1	31,091	85,217	85,217	1,839	1,769	1,769	2,039
615-255-3175		'09	59.1	4.3	16.9	19.7	46,030	...	29.3	...	70.7	34,196	92,320	92,320	1,583	1,811	1,811	1,946
AMB# 064670 NAIC# 54526	**FSC VI**	**Rating History: A-, 03/22/10; A-, 04/02/09; A-, 01/28/08; A-, 01/03/07; A-, 01/31/06**																
DELTA DENTAL OF VIRGINIA[2] George A. Levicki, D.D.S. President	**NR-5**	'05	46.0	4.2	25.2	24.6	64,653	...	20.0	...	80.0	42,866	89,811	89,811	18,326	9,016	9,016	8,991
4818 Starkey Road SW Roanoke, VA 24018-8542		'06	44.8	3.5	24.6	27.1	76,200	...	22.8	...	77.2	53,958	111,733	111,733	7,043	9,879	9,879	10,203
VA : 1969 : Stock : Agency		'07	43.6	11.7	30.6	14.2	83,122	...	22.9	...	77.1	57,802	123,255	123,255	4,450	11,231	11,231	8,337
Dental		'08	44.7	11.5	27.5	16.3	83,546	...	23.4	...	76.6	56,015	129,646	129,646	2,027	13,179	13,179	9,326
540-989-8000		'09	39.5	10.2	39.6	10.7	92,818	...	23.6	...	76.4	63,219	144,438	144,438	6,790	13,754	13,754	13,575
AMB# 064565 NAIC# 55611		**Rating History: NR-5, 05/18/10; NR-5, 04/24/09; NR-5, 04/23/08; NR-5, 05/09/07; NR-5, 05/24/06**																
DELTA DENTAL OF WEST VIRGINIA Dentegra Group Inc Gary D. Radine President	**NR-2**	'05	...	...	6.3	93.7	3,085	...	...	...	100.0	2,145	...	...	-65	4	4	4
One Delta Drive Mechanicsburg, PA 17055		'06	...	...	6.3	93.7	3,324	...	2.5	...	97.5	2,258	4,611	1,256	329	124	124	124
WV : 1962 : Non-Profit : Broker		'07	...	...	25.2	74.8	3,561	...	2.8	...	97.2	2,183	9,469	2,541	-50	211	211	236
Dental		'08	2.4	...	22.9	74.7	4,092	...	2.5	...	97.5	2,608	11,377	3,149	715	326	326	294
717-766-8500		'09	39.3	...	16.1	44.6	4,430	...	2.4	...	97.6	2,878	13,494	3,899	850	156	156	158
AMB# 064643 NAIC# 12329		**Rating History: NR-2, 04/08/10; NR-2, 03/18/09; NR-2, 03/24/08; NR-2, 02/13/07; NR-2, 12/21/05**																
DELTA DENTAL OF WISCONSIN INC Delta Dental of Wisconsin Inc Dennis Brown President	**A**	'05	53.5	6.1	33.5	6.9	88,648	...	25.3	...	74.7	77,518	98,080	97,346	12,989	10,083	10,083	11,458
P.O. Box 828 Stevens Point, WI 54481		'06	52.1	5.5	36.9	5.4	105,876	...	22.8	...	77.2	94,144	100,566	100,937	14,402	12,816	12,816	13,747
WI : 1967 : Non-Profit : Direct Response	Rating Outlook: Stable	'07	53.5	4.7	35.2	6.6	120,705	...	15.2	...	84.8	102,614	105,817	107,074	17,078	7,797	7,797	10,268
Dental		'08	59.0	4.6	26.2	10.2	117,750	...	14.6	...	85.4	100,518	103,922	106,025	5,998	11,489	11,489	7,531
715-344-6087		'09	49.8	3.9	37.5	8.8	135,237	...	8.8	...	91.2	104,399	107,618	110,003	13,542	-2,686	-2,686	-2,063
AMB# 064409 NAIC# 54046	**FSC VIII**	**Rating History: A, 10/02/09; A, 11/21/08; A, 11/12/07; A, 11/06/06; A, 10/13/05**																
DELTA DENTAL PLAN OF ARKANSAS Eddie A. Choate President & CEO	**A-**	'05	32.4	19.0	17.8	30.9	40,082	...	28.2	...	71.8	31,360	56,705	56,705	-1,621	3,702	3,702	4,055
1513 Country Club Road Sherwood, AR 72120		'06	30.4	14.8	20.0	34.8	44,702	...	26.2	...	73.8	36,773	59,062	59,062	8,412	6,517	6,517	6,693
AR : 1982 : Stock : Other Direct	Rating Outlook: Stable	'07	34.7	13.1	19.7	32.5	50,152	...	27.0	...	73.0	42,124	65,081	65,081	8,680	7,596	7,596	8,030
Dental		'08	31.7	17.3	15.1	35.8	57,877	...	21.4	...	78.6	46,109	70,654	70,654	659	6,737	6,737	587
501-835-3400		'09	29.6	15.7	19.7	35.1	64,551	...	20.8	...	79.2	53,351	73,690	73,312	7,226	6,270	6,270	6,270
AMB# 064699 NAIC# 47155	**FSC VII**	**Rating History: A-, 11/04/09; A- pd, 09/24/08; A- pd, 09/18/07; A- pd, 10/11/06; A- pd, 11/15/05**																
DELTA DENTAL PLAN OF IDAHO INC[2] Tamara C. Brandstetter President	**NR-5**	'05	22.4	11.8	23.2	42.6	19,991	...	23.9	...	76.1	11,141	31,193	31,193	1,264	675	675	433
P.O. Box 2870 Boise, ID 83701		'06	20.3	9.7	24.0	46.0	23,946	...	18.3	...	81.7	13,649	35,569	35,569	2,099	1,662	1,662	1,749
ID : 1971 : Stock : Agency		'07	19.4	8.6	23.8	48.2	26,676	...	19.3	...	80.7	15,195	39,408	39,408	3,599	1,272	1,272	2,169
Dental		'08	23.8	9.9	18.0	48.3	22,766	...	35.5	...	64.5	14,135	43,023	43,023	-1,223	797	797	844
208-344-4546		'09	17.3	8.1	35.2	39.4	27,574	...	29.5	...	70.5	17,549	39,474	39,474	968	1,050	1,050	891
AMB# 064525 NAIC# 47791		**Rating History: NR-5, 04/07/10; NR-5, 04/08/09; NR-5, 05/06/08; NR-5, 04/02/07; NR-5, 07/11/06**																
DELTA DENTAL PLAN OF INDIANA Renaissance Health Service Corp Thomas J. Fleszar, D.D.S. President	**A-**	'05	14.3	...	65.7	20.0	33,536	...	3.1	...	96.9	29,445	1,675	1,349	-298	1,027	1,027	1,006
4100 Okemos Road Okemos, MI 48864		'06	2.9	...	69.2	27.8	20,449	...	2.3	...	97.7	17,599	1,567	1,567	-9,778	2,228	2,224	3,524
IN : 1983 : Non-Profit : Agency	Rating Outlook: Stable	'07	2.7	...	70.7	26.5	21,861	...	2.0	...	98.0	19,016	1,264	1,264	703	1,657	1,652	1,652
Dental		'08	3.0	...	73.2	23.8	19,894	...	0.3	...	99.7	17,581	148	148	761	886	883	906
517-349-6000		'09	2.7	...	43.0	54.3	22,580	...	0.3	...	99.7	19,323	116	116	-1,792	-8	-12	-2,509
AMB# 064694 NAIC# 52634	**FSC VIII**	**Rating History: A- g, 06/03/10; A- g, 06/17/09; A- g, 12/17/07; NR-5, 02/16/06; B pd, 10/15/04**																
DELTA DENTAL PLAN OF KS Linda L. Brantner President & CEO	**NR-5**	'05	53.5	...	28.1	18.5	26,092	...	42.1	...	57.9	22,146	50,377	50,377	3,162	2,791	2,791	2,789
P.O. Box 789769 Wichita, KS 67278		'06	53.2	...	25.6	21.2	29,310	...	46.4	...	53.6	24,912	56,825	56,825	3,990	3,728	3,728	3,937
KS : 1973 : Stock : Agency		'07	44.4	...	26.5	29.1	34,807	...	41.7	...	58.3	29,936	62,372	62,372	5,082	4,010	4,010	4,132
Dental		'08	51.5	...	26.4	22.0	33,418	...	36.5	...	63.5	28,709	60,750	60,750	-1,953	2,278	2,278	1,387
316-264-1099		'09	60.8	...	27.0	12.2	35,916	...	31.1	...	68.9	30,557	60,658	60,658	3,022	704	704	1,143
AMB# 064538 NAIC# 54615		**Rating History: NR-5, 03/22/10; NR-5, 12/01/09; B++pd, 09/24/08; B+ pd, 09/18/07; B+ pd, 10/11/06**																
DELTA DENTAL PLAN OF MICHIGAN Renaissance Health Service Corp Thomas J. Fleszar, D.D.S. President & CEO	**A-**	'05	11.5	6.5	48.8	33.2	251,820	...	23.4	...	76.6	178,803	378,202	378,202	15,893	22,389	22,389	24,315
P.O. Box 30416 Lansing, MI 48909-7916		'06	8.7	5.4	52.1	33.7	284,559	...	23.9	...	76.1	216,443	395,272	395,272	24,104	25,123	25,123	29,871
MI : 1968 : Non-Profit : Agency	Rating Outlook: Stable	'07	11.5	4.8	57.4	26.3	303,476	...	20.2	...	79.8	232,610	396,573	396,573	43,645	20,951	20,951	38,029
Dental		'08	8.9	10.6	50.1	30.4	265,825	...	28.2	...	71.8	191,198	482,881	482,881	-8,960	16,121	16,121	13,028
517-349-6000		'09	8.3	24.4	39.0	28.3	291,069	...	22.4	...	77.6	203,653	474,651	474,651	22,596	-13,142	-13,142	-16,858
AMB# 068575 NAIC# 54305	**FSC VIII**	**Rating History: A- g, 06/03/10; A- g, 06/17/09; A- g, 12/17/07; B+ pd, 07/03/07; B+ pd, 10/28/05**																

BEST'S PROFITABILITY, LEVERAGE AND LIQUIDITY TESTS 2005 – 2009

Data in U.S. Dollars

—	Profitability Tests							Leverage Tests						Liquidity Tests					
Un-Realized Capital Gains ($000)	Benefits Paid to NPW & Dep (%)	Comm. & Expenses to NPW & Dep (%)	NOG to Total Assets (%)	NOG to Total Rev (%)	Operating Return on Equity (%)	Net Yield (%)	Total Return (%)	Change in NPW & Dep (%)	NPW & Dep to Capital (X)	Capital & Surplus to Liabilities (%)	Surplus Relief (%)	Reins Leverage (%)	Change in Capital (%)	Quick Liquidity (%)	Current Liquidity (%)	Non-Invest Grade Bonds to Capital (%)	Delinq. & Foreclosed Mortgages to Capital (%)	Mort. & Credit Tenant Loans & R.E. to Capital (%)	Affiliated Invest to Capital (%)
38	97.7	9.9	16.5	6.1	22.6	3.31	3.16	25.0	2.8	285.6	...	...	34.4	252.6	262.5	...	...	7.1	7.1
...	96.9	10.0	14.3	5.7	19.3	2.96	2.89	17.6	2.7	290.0	...	...	23.9	254.8	261.1	...	...	5.8	14.7
681	100.1	10.7	9.3	3.9	12.4	3.87	5.82	10.9	2.6	319.6	...	...	15.7	259.7	268.3	...	...	4.2	17.2
-2,454	100.5	10.9	4.2	1.8	5.6	2.21	-3.59	3.7	2.7	289.9	...	...	-2.2	236.0	241.1	...	...	5.7	16.9
616	101.8	11.1	4.1	1.7	5.5	2.47	4.51	8.3	2.7	289.0	...	...	10.0	231.8	237.8	...	...	5.8	14.9
Principal Lines of Business: Dental (100.0%)														Principal States: TN (100.0%)					
872	78.3	13.6	16.4	9.8	23.8	3.59	5.50	28.5	2.1	196.7	...	...	30.8	181.0	196.1	...	...	6.3	3.2
450	79.6	13.5	14.0	8.7	20.4	3.66	5.00	24.4	2.1	242.6	...	...	25.9	205.2	222.5	...	...	5.0	0.6
297	79.2	13.6	14.1	9.0	20.1	4.43	0.60	10.3	2.1	228.3	...	...	7.1	175.2	193.1	...	...	16.8	2.3
-4,180	78.6	12.6	15.8	10.0	23.2	2.59	-8.62	5.2	2.3	203.5	...	...	-3.1	156.8	171.6	...	...	17.2	2.3
4,873	79.2	12.5	15.6	9.5	23.1	2.43	8.97	11.4	2.3	213.6	...	...	12.9	167.1	187.9	...	...	14.9	2.0
Principal Lines of Business: Dental (100.0%)														Principal States: VA (100.0%)					
2	...	...	0.1	100.0	0.2	2.94	3.01	...	...	228.4	...	...	0.2	247.7	250.8	...	...	...	...
11	28.4	83.3	3.9	8.1	5.6	10.32	10.77	...	0.6	211.8	...	35.8	5.3	248.2	250.7	...	...	...	1.1
-16	25.7	75.6	6.1	7.6	9.5	9.44	9.76	102.3	1.2	158.4	...	49.9	-3.3	167.0	176.5	...	...	...	1.1
-185	25.6	71.5	8.5	9.6	13.6	8.19	1.03	23.9	1.2	175.8	...	42.0	19.5	185.0	193.7	...	...	...	5.4
111	25.0	72.8	3.7	3.9	5.7	1.24	4.32	23.8	1.4	185.4	...	20.9	10.3	222.6	235.5	...	...	...	12.9
Principal Lines of Business: Dental (100.0%)														Principal States: WV (100.0%)					
-1,989	82.0	9.3	12.1	10.2	13.8	3.07	2.35	12.3	1.3	696.5	...	0.3	13.6	545.2	598.4	...	...	7.0	13.7
3,064	82.1	7.5	13.2	12.4	14.9	2.48	6.77	3.7	1.1	802.4	...	0.3	21.4	606.7	669.9	...	...	6.2	14.4
-2,042	82.0	13.6	6.9	7.1	7.9	2.81	3.24	6.1	1.0	567.2	...	0.2	9.0	454.9	494.7	...	...	5.5	14.0
-9,842	83.6	8.7	9.6	10.5	11.3	2.86	-8.61	-1.0	1.1	583.3	...	0.2	-2.0	446.5	498.9	...	...	5.4	13.5
6,006	86.2	19.0	-2.1	-2.4	-2.6	2.39	7.86	3.8	1.1	338.5	...	0.5	3.9	277.1	311.4	...	...	5.0	18.9
Principal Lines of Business: Dental (100.0%)														Principal States: WI (100.0%)					
57	78.9	16.3	9.7	6.4	12.8	2.69	4.06	7.0	1.8	359.6	...	...	17.7	225.1	237.0	...	...	24.3	22.1
874	76.3	14.1	15.4	10.9	19.1	2.47	5.53	4.2	1.6	463.8	...	...	17.3	333.0	351.8	...	...	17.9	23.1
-1,577	73.5	16.6	16.0	11.5	19.3	2.63	-0.14	10.2	1.5	524.7	...	...	14.6	400.9	425.1	...	...	15.6	17.7
584	76.6	18.4	12.5	9.1	15.3	6.93	-4.58	8.6	1.5	391.8	...	...	9.5	273.9	286.1	...	...	21.7	23.4
2,090	76.3	18.8	10.2	8.2	12.6	5.33	9.47	3.8	1.4	476.4	0.0	0.1	15.7	322.1	350.8	...	...	19.0	23.7
Principal Lines of Business: Dental (98.5%), Vision (1.5%)														Principal States: AR (100.0%)					
454	89.0	10.0	3.5	2.1	6.3	1.99	3.17	-1.2	2.8	125.9	...	...	9.0	103.5	111.4	...	...	21.2	15.9
720	86.5	10.2	7.6	4.6	13.4	2.43	6.32	14.0	2.6	132.5	...	...	22.5	110.6	119.0	...	...	17.1	12.7
-721	88.1	10.0	5.0	3.2	8.8	2.10	2.94	10.8	2.6	132.3	...	...	11.3	116.8	125.1	...	...	15.1	11.2
-1,811	89.5	9.3	3.2	1.8	5.4	1.12	-6.06	9.2	3.0	163.8	...	...	-7.0	162.9	179.2	...	...	16.0	11.8
2,499	88.4	9.5	4.2	2.6	6.6	0.83	11.12	-8.2	2.2	175.1	...	...	24.2	147.5	170.9	...	...	12.7	9.3
Principal Lines of Business: Dental (100.0%)														Principal States: ID (100.0%)					
-863	78.9	-17.3	3.1	55.3	3.5	1.76	-1.23	-14.9	0.0	719.8	...	...	1.0	292.9	323.2	...	...	...	53.7
-410	60.0	-58.6	8.2	98.9	9.5	2.96	6.94	16.2	0.1	617.4	...	...	-40.2	362.2	402.3	...	...	...	54.3
-250	64.3	-56.6	7.8	94.2	9.0	2.68	1.34	-19.3	0.1	668.6	...	...	8.1	334.1	375.6	...	...	...	48.5
-2,243	64.5	-99.9	4.2	152.3	4.8	2.42	-9.17	-88.3	0.0	759.9	...	...	-7.6	400.0	441.6	...	...	...	48.6
4,264	53.8	345.2	-0.1	-2.6	-0.1	1.82	15.23	-22.0	0.0	593.3	...	...	9.9	524.5	561.4	...	...	...	10.9
Principal Lines of Business: Dental (100.0%)														Principal States: IN (100.0%)					
128	79.4	16.6	11.0	5.5	12.9	3.16	3.72	9.4	2.3	561.3	...	...	5.6	539.3	567.4	...	...	...	3.8
-1,309	80.5	15.2	13.5	6.4	15.8	5.11	0.85	12.8	2.3	566.5	...	...	12.5	654.0	683.5	...	...	...	1.0
897	78.8	16.9	12.5	6.3	14.6	4.53	8.09	9.8	2.1	614.6	...	...	20.2	595.1	627.6	...	...	...	0.0
-2,593	81.9	16.8	6.7	3.7	7.8	3.93	-7.40	-2.6	2.1	609.7	...	...	-4.1	614.4	647.5	...	...	...	8.1
724	81.9	19.5	2.0	1.1	2.4	4.12	8.12	-0.2	2.0	570.1	...	...	6.4	462.5	500.9	...	...	...	12.5
Principal Lines of Business: Dental (100.0%)														Principal States: KS (94.4%), MO (5.6%)					
335	85.3	11.7	9.2	5.7	13.2	4.84	6.04	9.9	2.1	244.9	...	...	11.2	238.9	270.1	...	...	9.2	15.7
7,927	84.9	11.6	9.4	6.2	12.7	5.20	11.20	4.5	1.8	317.8	...	...	21.1	305.5	340.8	...	...	7.2	17.9
-19,887	84.3	13.4	7.1	5.1	9.3	5.23	4.65	0.3	1.7	328.2	...	...	7.5	296.7	336.4	...	...	6.3	14.0
-45,858	88.0	11.0	5.7	3.3	7.6	5.20	-14.62	21.8	2.5	256.2	...	...	-17.8	188.7	215.0	...	...	14.7	21.9
25,709	92.2	12.2	-4.7	-2.7	-6.7	3.76	14.39	-1.7	2.3	233.0	...	...	6.5	144.2	164.1	...	...	34.9	41.2
Principal Lines of Business: Dental (100.0%)														Principal States: MI (100.0%)					

Data in U.S. Dollars

COMPANY NAME / Ultimate Parent Association / Principal Officer / Mailing Address / Dom. : Began Bus. : Struct. : Mktg. / Specialty / Phone # / AMB# / NAIC#	Best's Financial Strength Rating / FSC	Data Year	Balance Sheet: Bonds (%)	Mort. Loans & R.E. (%)	Com & Pref. Stock (%)	All Other Assets (%)	Total Assets ($000)	Life Reserves (%)	Health Reserves (%)	Ann Res. & Dep. Liabilities (%)	All Other Liabilities (%)	Capital & Surplus ($000)	Operations: Direct Premiums Written ($000)	Net Premiums Written & Deposits ($000)	Operating Cash Flow ($000)	NOG Before Taxes ($000)	NOG After Taxes ($000)	Net Income ($000)
DELTA DENTAL PLAN OF NH	NR-5	'05	53.1	8.8	9.2	29.0	28,077	...	18.8	...	81.2	19,716	60,848	61,525	4,648	4,266	4,266	3,970
Thomas Raffio, President		'06	53.4	10.2	9.2	27.2	33,078	...	15.2	...	84.8	24,326	63,353	63,353	3,946	5,058	5,058	5,008
One Delta Drive, Concord, NH 03302-2002		'07	50.7	10.4	13.9	25.0	37,223	...	12.2	...	87.8	27,537	65,670	65,670	3,600	3,493	3,493	3,920
NH : 1966 : Non-Profit : Agency; Dental		'08	54.9	10.9	9.0	25.2	35,002	...	11.6	...	88.4	26,234	54,462	54,552	-948	1,649	1,649	388
603-223-1000		'09	...	...	...	...	...	...	...	...	...	...	...	...	...	...	...	...
AMB# 064524 NAIC# 47079		**Rating History: NR-5, 12/01/09; B++pd, 09/24/08; B++pd, 09/18/07; B++pd, 10/03/06; B++pd, 10/27/05**																
DELTA DENTAL PLAN OF NM Renaissance Health Service Corp	NR-5	'05	35.2	...	8.5	56.3	17,332	...	39.6	...	60.4	14,476	25,847	25,847	959	1,421	1,421	1,471
Walter S. Bolic, President & CEO		'06	36.0	...	8.4	55.6	18,970	...	39.3	...	60.7	16,517	29,262	29,262	-703	1,911	1,911	1,959
2500 Louisiana Blvd. N.E., Suite 300, Albuquerque, NM 87110		'07	26.0	...	8.4	65.6	20,780	...	33.2	...	66.8	18,097	28,405	28,405	4,530	1,621	1,621	1,693
NM : 1971 : Stock : Agency; Dental		'08	27.0	...	4.8	68.2	22,159	...	32.7	...	67.3	19,221	29,131	29,131	944	1,598	1,598	1,505
505-883-4777		'09	40.8	...	11.6	47.5	22,696	...	32.3	...	67.7	19,919	30,516	30,516	1,221	703	703	664
AMB# 064537 NAIC# 47287		**Rating History: NR-5, 06/17/09; NR-5, 05/05/08; NR-5, 04/02/07; NR-5, 04/26/06; NR-5, 04/26/05**																
DELTA DENTAL PLAN OF NC INC	NR-5	'05	9.4	...	...	90.6	5,387	...	68.7	...	31.3	4,476	15,755	15,755	-1,091	-271	-271	-271
Robert Rosenthal, CEO		'06	12.0	...	...	88.0	4,225	...	23.6	...	76.4	2,943	7,474	7,474	-1,255	-1,452	-1,452	-1,452
333 Six Forks Road, Suite 180, Raleigh, NC 27609		'07	9.3	...	...	90.7	5,487	...	...	...	100.0	4,476	8,951	8,951	1,457	-1,506	-1,506	-1,506
NC : 1973 : Stock : Agency; Dental		'08	35.5	...	...	64.5	5,078	...	...	...	100.0	2,772	8,539	8,539	-95	-1,660	-1,660	-1,660
919-832-6015		'09	5.9	...	...	94.1	4,378	...	25.9	...	74.1	3,026	8,015	8,015	-650	-1,316	-1,316	-1,316
AMB# 064526 NAIC# 54658		**Rating History: NR-5, 03/25/10; NR-5, 03/26/09; NR-5, 03/26/08; NR-5, 04/13/07; NR-5, 05/11/06**																
DELTA DENTAL PLAN OF OHIO INC Renaissance Health Service Corp	A-	'05	16.2	...	25.6	58.2	43,350	...	40.8	...	59.2	28,596	121,290	121,290	8,086	8,834	8,834	8,832
Thomas J. Fleszar, D.D.S., MS, President		'06	13.7	...	35.0	51.4	50,165	...	40.7	...	59.3	35,982	133,797	133,797	9,415	11,169	11,169	11,866
P.O. Box 30416, Lansing, MI 48909-7916	Rating Outlook: Stable	'07	11.3	...	32.3	56.4	60,575	...	39.1	...	60.9	47,421	137,802	137,802	10,507	10,674	10,674	10,813
OH : 1964 : Non-Profit : Agency; Dental		'08	10.8	...	27.9	61.3	63,208	...	38.6	...	61.4	49,484	129,689	129,689	2,371	8,698	8,698	8,508
517-349-6000		'09	13.3	...	35.2	51.5	75,334	...	40.0	...	60.0	56,659	131,182	131,182	16,650	3,808	3,808	3,657
AMB# 064502 NAIC# 54402	FSC VIII	**Rating History: A- g, 06/03/10; A- g, 06/17/09; A- g, 12/17/07; B- pd, 07/03/07; B- pd, 10/28/05**																
DELTA DENTAL PLAN OF OKLAHOMA[2]	NR-5	'05	38.5	11.1	9.3	41.1	25,840	...	36.8	...	63.2	21,281	41,737	41,737	2,349	883	883	1,274
John E. Gladden, President & CEO		'06	34.2	14.4	13.5	37.9	26,689	...	45.4	...	54.6	22,976	49,217	49,217	2,941	2,166	2,166	2,855
P.O. Box 54709, Oklahoma City, OK 73154		'07	34.2	14.7	10.3	40.8	32,261	...	35.4	...	64.6	27,047	57,806	57,806	3,909	4,370	4,370	4,450
OK : 1974 : Non-Profit : Broker; Dental		'08	40.3	13.8	7.2	38.7	34,453	...	38.1	...	61.9	28,635	65,828	65,828	3,421	2,821	2,821	2,190
405-607-2100		'09	44.0	13.6	8.9	33.5	35,934	...	37.7	...	62.3	29,816	77,515	77,515	-540	783	783	594
AMB# 064563 NAIC# 53937		**Rating History: NR-5, 05/21/10; NR-5, 05/11/09; NR-5, 04/25/08; NR-5, 05/01/07; NR-5, 06/20/06**																
DELTA DENTAL PLAN OF SD	NR-5	'05	22.4	5.3	54.2	18.0	25,211	...	42.7	...	57.3	21,279	39,350	39,350	1,944	2,198	2,198	2,332
Dale Gibson, D.D.S., Chairman		'06	15.1	5.4	55.5	24.0	28,746	...	43.1	...	56.9	24,542	42,740	42,740	2,054	2,412	2,412	2,412
720 N. Euclid Avenue, Pierre, SD 57501		'07	22.5	4.9	54.4	18.2	31,360	...	35.5	...	64.5	26,968	41,413	41,413	2,100	2,891	2,891	2,893
SD : 1968 : Non-Profit : Agency; Dental		'08	28.1	6.9	56.0	9.0	27,219	...	35.2	...	64.8	22,390	38,886	38,886	2,122	1,408	1,408	1,869
605-224-7345		'09	24.1	13.8	43.6	18.5	32,175	...	31.3	...	68.7	26,655	39,918	39,918	1,111	1,756	1,756	1,422
AMB# 064488 NAIC# 54097		**Rating History: NR-5, 04/15/10; NR-5, 05/05/09; NR-5, 04/25/08; NR-5, 05/03/07; NR-5, 04/26/06**																
DELTA LIFE INS CO[1] J. Mack Robinson & Family	NR-1	'05	5.2	14.7	72.3	7.8	90,265	...	...	...	100.0	29,751	15,429	15,314	...	-2,122	-2,122	-2,990
Jesse M. Robinson, President		'06	1.8	13.3	69.9	15.0	97,224	...	...	...	100.0	33,523	15,981	15,863	...	-2,072	-2,072	133
4370 Peachtree Road, N.e., Atlanta, GA 30319-3000		'07	1.3	15.8	57.6	25.3	79,124	...	...	...	100.0	24,556	16,647	16,525	...	-1,591	-1,591	-1,561
GA : 1958 : Stock : Internet; Credit Life, Ind A&H, Ind Life		'08	0.9	28.1	33.9	37.2	56,567	...	...	...	100.0	14,081	16,313	16,188	...	-3,596	-3,596	-6,163
404-231-2111		'09	0.9	28.2	33.9	37.0	53,129	...	...	...	100.0	8,798	16,462	16,333	...	-2,144	-2,144	-2,145
AMB# 006307 NAIC# 62650		**Rating History: NR-1, 06/11/10; NR-5, 05/12/10; NR-4, 04/09/08; B-, 04/09/08; B, 11/20/07**																
DENTA-CHEK OF MARYLAND INC	NR-5	'05	2.0	...	...	98.0	186	...	0.1	...	99.9	80	435	435	-54	-61	-62	-62
Robert D. Sacks, President & Treasurer		'06	1.3	...	...	98.7	192	...	0.1	...	99.9	95	441	441	2	15	15	15
7125 Thomas Edison Drive, Suite 105, Columbia, MD 21046		'07	1.2	...	...	98.8	194	...	0.1	...	99.9	108	435	435	5	13	13	13
MD : 1981 : Stock : Not Available; Dental		'08	1.2	...	...	98.8	180	...	0.1	...	99.9	105	387	387	-11	-2	-2	-2
410-997-3300		'09	1.2	...	...	98.8	171	...	0.2	...	99.8	108	340	340	-8	2	2	2
AMB# 064536 NAIC# 47074		**Rating History: NR-5, 03/24/10; NR-5, 06/23/09; NR-5, 07/29/08; NR-5, 04/12/07; NR-5, 04/20/06**																
DENTAL BENEFIT PROVIDERS OF CA UnitedHealth Group Inc	A-	'05	...	...	...	100.0	34,077	...	...	...	100.0	13,437	120,509	120,509	7,616	11,912	7,198	7,198
Kirk E. Andrews, President		'06	...	...	...	100.0	46,386	...	...	...	100.0	20,182	121,851	121,851	16,759	12,902	7,745	7,745
9900 Bren Road East, MN008-T380, Minnetonka, MN 55343	Rating Outlook: Stable	'07	...	...	...	100.0	44,959	...	...	...	100.0	21,557	122,226	122,226	-1,479	18,097	10,760	10,760
CA : 1986 : Stock : Not Available; Dental		'08	...	...	...	100.0	48,872	...	...	...	100.0	24,020	118,107	118,107	4,379	14,709	8,693	8,693
415-778-3800		'09	...	...	...	100.0	40,123	...	...	...	100.0	26,490	114,701	114,701	-10,340	15,738	9,338	9,338
AMB# 064716	FSC VI	**Rating History: A-, 06/15/09; NR-2, 01/29/08; NR-2, 11/21/07; NR-2, 11/16/06; NR-2, 08/17/06**																

Data in U.S. Dollars

—	Profitability Tests							Leverage Tests						Liquidity Tests					
Un-Realized Capital Gains ($000)	Benefits Paid to NPW & Dep (%)	Comm. & Expenses to NPW & Dep (%)	NOG to Total Assets (%)	NOG to Total Rev (%)	Operating Return on Equity (%)	Net Yield (%)	Total Return (%)	Change in NPW & Dep (%)	NPW & Dep to Capital (X)	Capital & Surplus to Liabilities (%)	Surplus Relief (%)	Reins Leverage (%)	Change in Capital (%)	Quick Liquidity (%)	Current Liquidity (%)	Non-Invest Grade Bonds to Capital (%)	Delinq. & Foreclosed Mortgages to Capital (%)	Mort. & Credit Tenant Loans & R.E. to Capital (%)	Affiliated Invest to Capital (%)
321	77.1	17.0	16.7	6.9	24.2	3.08	3.20	2.2	3.1	235.8	...	...	26.9	207.0	227.7	...	...	12.6	10.3
161	76.3	17.2	16.5	7.9	23.0	3.60	4.00	3.0	2.6	277.9	...	...	23.4	230.3	253.7	...	...	13.9	12.3
-442	78.7	17.6	9.9	5.2	13.5	3.41	3.38	3.7	2.4	284.3	...	...	13.2	225.1	251.6	...	...	14.0	12.7
-1,270	80.3	18.5	4.6	3.0	6.1	2.95	-4.65	-16.9	2.1	299.2	...	0.0	-4.7	232.5	257.9	...	...	14.5	13.3
...	...	...	...	...	...	...	...	...	...	...	...	...	...	...	...	...	...	...	...
61	80.8	18.0	8.6	5.3	10.3	3.18	3.93	-3.3	1.8	506.7	...	...	11.2	487.8	505.0	...	...	...	0.1
97	79.3	16.7	10.5	6.4	12.3	4.84	5.82	13.2	1.8	673.3	...	...	14.1	540.3	561.0	...	...	...	0.1
-10	78.8	18.4	8.2	5.5	9.4	4.77	5.13	-2.9	1.6	674.5	...	...	9.6	806.2	825.6	...	...	...	0.1
-519	78.5	18.0	7.4	5.4	8.6	2.62	-0.49	2.6	1.5	654.3	...	...	6.2	629.3	643.0	...	...	...	...
274	78.5	17.7	3.1	2.3	3.6	1.39	2.58	4.8	1.5	717.3	...	...	3.6	628.3	645.4	...	...	...	6.7

Principal Lines of Business: Dental (100.0%) — Principal States: NM (100.0%)

...	82.4	20.5	-4.8	-1.7	-5.9	1.84	1.84	24.4	3.5	491.3	...	...	-5.4	481.8	487.3	...	...	...	...
...	81.2	41.1	-30.2	-18.9	-39.2	3.57	3.57	-52.6	2.5	229.5	...	...	-34.3	238.2	242.1	...	...	...	...
...	81.3	38.2	-31.0	-16.7	-40.6	3.28	3.28	19.8	2.0	442.6	...	...	52.1	446.1	451.1	...	...	...	...
...	80.0	40.5	-31.4	-19.2	-45.8	-0.18	-0.18	-4.6	3.1	120.2	...	...	-38.1	183.1	190.9	...	...	...	...
...	80.1	40.2	-27.8	-15.8	-45.4	7.17	7.17	-6.1	2.6	223.7	...	...	9.2	281.3	283.2	...	...	...	...

Principal Lines of Business: Dental (100.0%) — Principal States: NC (100.0%)

234	86.0	7.8	22.5	7.1	37.2	4.64	5.53	9.3	4.2	193.8	...	...	50.9	253.5	274.0	...	...	...	...
386	85.3	7.2	23.9	8.3	34.6	3.36	6.46	10.3	3.7	253.7	...	...	25.8	328.6	356.8	...	...	...	8.0
-381	84.9	8.3	19.3	7.7	25.6	2.99	2.45	3.0	2.9	360.5	...	...	31.8	489.7	521.4	...	...	...	4.7
-5,942	84.8	9.6	14.1	6.6	18.0	2.98	-8.99	-5.9	2.6	360.6	...	...	4.3	470.1	497.7	...	...	...	3.4
3,725	86.9	11.0	5.5	2.9	7.2	2.07	8.58	1.2	2.3	303.4	...	...	14.5	408.1	445.7	...	...	...	2.8

Principal Lines of Business: Dental (100.0%) — Principal States: OH (100.0%)

-978	81.9	17.4	3.6	2.1	4.4	2.50	-0.16	7.6	2.0	466.8	...	...	15.3	170.7	287.8	...	...	13.4	...
-123	81.7	16.3	8.2	4.3	9.8	5.28	7.85	17.9	2.1	618.7	...	...	8.0	234.2	371.5	...	...	16.8	17.2
-176	78.8	16.2	14.8	7.4	17.5	4.77	4.40	17.5	2.1	518.7	...	...	17.7	198.2	313.4	...	...	17.5	20.1
-553	81.8	15.7	8.5	4.2	10.1	3.69	-0.36	13.9	2.3	492.1	...	...	5.9	183.2	308.6	0.1	...	16.6	15.7
711	83.1	17.6	2.2	1.0	2.7	3.90	5.64	17.8	2.6	487.3	...	...	4.1	108.9	108.9	...	...	16.4	15.5

Principal Lines of Business: Dental (100.0%) — Principal States: OK (100.0%)

151	86.2	10.5	9.1	5.5	10.9	4.43	5.74	11.1	1.8	541.2	...	...	12.5	388.0	451.0	...	...	6.3	2.3
906	85.6	12.0	8.9	5.5	10.5	5.82	9.60	8.6	1.7	583.8	...	...	15.3	407.8	473.2	...	...	6.3	2.0
-521	83.8	14.2	9.6	6.7	11.2	7.90	5.97	-3.1	1.5	614.0	...	...	9.9	414.1	479.0	...	...	5.7	1.9
-6,442	84.5	13.9	4.8	3.5	5.7	3.22	-17.64	-6.1	1.7	463.6	...	...	-17.0	295.4	347.1	...	...	8.4	2.1
3,251	83.9	13.4	5.9	4.3	7.2	1.55	14.13	2.7	1.5	482.9	...	...	19.0	295.2	339.0	...	...	16.7	13.8

Principal Lines of Business: Dental (100.0%) — Principal States: SD (100.0%)

1,789	31.0	96.0	-2.4	-10.7	-7.0	...	...	6.5	0.4	92.9	...	...	-2.4	...	...	...	...	30.5	...
3,644	28.9	91.2	-2.2	-10.5	-6.5	...	...	3.6	0.3	96.6	...	...	9.9	...	...	...	...	27.1	...
-19,521	33.3	86.0	-1.8	-7.6	-5.5	...	...	4.2	0.5	76.9	...	...	-28.0	...	...	...	...	36.3	...
-30,127	35.5	87.1	-5.3	-18.9	-18.6	...	...	-2.0	1.1	37.1	...	...	-55.5	...	...	...	...	103.8	...
-1,401	33.7	79.4	-3.9	-11.7	-18.7	...	...	0.9	1.6	23.8	...	...	-33.3	...	...	...	...	146.6	...

Principal Lines of Business: OrdLife (88.0%), CrdA&H (6.1%), IndA&H (3.3%), CrdLife (1.7%), IndLife (0.7%)

...	47.7	67.0	-28.7	-14.2	-57.5	1.08	1.08	-14.8	5.4	75.5	...	...	-40.7	172.8	172.8	...	...	...	...
...	47.2	50.4	7.8	3.3	16.8	1.65	1.65	1.4	4.7	97.4	...	...	18.3	190.2	190.2	...	...	...	...
...	46.8	51.4	6.6	2.9	12.6	1.59	1.59	-1.5	4.0	124.2	...	...	13.4	219.7	219.7	...	...	...	...
...	45.6	55.3	-1.1	-0.5	-2.0	0.82	0.82	-11.0	3.7	141.0	...	...	-2.0	237.9	237.9	...	...	...	...
...	46.7	52.8	1.3	0.7	2.2	0.36	0.36	-12.0	3.2	169.9	...	...	2.2	269.1	269.1	...	...	...	...

Principal Lines of Business: Dental (100.0%) — Principal States: MD (100.0%)

...	58.4	24.9	20.6	6.4	45.4	1.45	1.45	11.5	9.0	65.1	...	...	-26.3	128.0	128.0	...	...	...	...
...	58.9	23.3	19.3	6.9	46.1	2.69	2.69	1.1	6.0	77.0	...	...	50.2	164.4	164.4	...	...	...	...
...	68.9	19.6	23.6	8.5	51.6	2.62	2.62	0.3	5.7	92.1	...	...	6.8	177.8	177.8	...	...	...	...
...	72.1	16.3	18.5	7.3	38.1	1.75	1.75	-3.4	4.9	96.7	...	...	11.4	189.0	189.0	...	...	...	...
...	72.0	14.6	21.0	8.1	37.0	0.13	0.13	-2.9	4.3	194.3	...	...	10.3	268.6	268.6	...	...	...	...

Principal Lines of Business: Dental (100.0%)

Data in U.S. Dollars

COMPANY NAME / Ultimate Parent Association / Principal Officer / Mailing Address / Dom. : Began Bus. : Struct. : Mktg. / Specialty / Phone # / AMB# / NAIC#	Best's Financial Strength Rating / FSC	Data Year	Balance Sheet: Bonds (%)	Mort. Loans & R.E. (%)	Com & Pref. Stock (%)	All Other Assets (%)	Total Assets ($000)	Life Reserves (%)	Health Reserves (%)	Ann Res. & Dep. Liabilities (%)	All Other Liabilities (%)	Capital & Surplus ($000)	Operations: Direct Premiums Written ($000)	Net Premiums Written & Deposits ($000)	Operating Cash Flow ($000)	NOG Before Taxes ($000)	NOG After Taxes ($000)	Net Income ($000)
DENTAL BENEFIT PROVIDERS OF IL UnitedHealth Group Inc	NR-2	'05	36.9	...	...	63.1	1,290	...	21.9	...	78.1	1,089	339	339	141	96	61	61
Diane D. Souza, President		'06	51.4	...	...	48.6	902	...	8.2	...	91.8	758	311	311	-318	53	112	112
Liberty 6, Suite 200, Columbia, MD 21045		'07	40.3	...	...	59.7	1,160	...	7.3	...	92.7	1,076	166	166	265	8	18	18
IL : 1999 : Non-Profit : Not Available; Dental		'08	30.5	...	...	69.5	1,525	...	43.5	...	56.5	945	4,274	4,274	-79	73	10	10
443-896-0418; AMB# 064690 NAIC# 52053		'09	9.2	...	...	90.8	1,791	...	26.1	...	73.9	789	3,357	3,357	635	-635	-409	-394
		Rating History: NR-2, 06/15/09; NR-2, 01/29/08; NR-2, 11/21/07; NR-2, 11/16/06; NR-2, 08/17/06																
DENTAL CARE PLUS INC DCP Holding Company	B-	'05	...	10.1	...	89.9	8,280	...	70.7	...	29.3	3,894	33,581	33,581	1,060	528	311	311
Anthony A. Cook, President & CEO		'06	19.7	9.6	...	70.7	9,608	...	72.0	...	28.0	4,171	37,401	37,388	1,107	295	175	175
100 Crowne Point Place, Cincinnati, OH 45241	Rating Outlook: Stable	'07	24.5	10.8	...	64.7	8,953	...	56.5	...	43.5	4,670	39,967	39,739	-939	856	494	494
OH : 1988 : Stock : Broker; Dental		'08	22.7	4.2	...	73.1	9,594	...	58.3	...	41.7	5,174	40,506	40,385	1,626	791	641	641
513-554-1100; AMB# 064698 NAIC# 96265	FSC III	'09	21.3	5.0	...	73.7	9,530	...	49.3	...	50.7	4,921	45,422	45,422	-393	-302	-375	-375
		Rating History: B-, 04/23/10; B-, 06/16/09; B-, 05/22/08; B-, 04/26/07; B-, 01/31/06																
DENTAL CHOICE INC	NR-5	'05	61.3	...	30.7	8.1	5,610	...	20.1	...	79.9	4,742	3,981	3,981	209	-85	-55	-28
Clifford T. Maesaka, Jr., Chairman, President & CEO		'06	60.0	...	31.2	8.8	6,035	...	17.7	...	82.3	5,039	4,679	4,679	363	225	164	180
P.O. Box 242810, Louisville, KY 40224-2810		'07	62.0	...	31.0	7.0	6,175	...	15.2	...	84.8	5,074	5,086	5,086	409	39	39	327
KY : 1987 : Stock : Not Available; Dental		'08	70.2	...	22.9	6.9	5,261	...	26.3	...	73.7	4,397	5,497	5,497	-121	80	90	44
800-423-2184; AMB# 065726 NAIC# 48127		'09	63.5	...	28.9	7.6	5,893	...	54.1	...	45.9	5,664	2,974	2,974	165	-89	-89	-215
		Rating History: NR-5, 03/25/10; NR-5, 04/08/09; NR-5, 03/18/08; NR-5, 09/27/07; NR-3, 10/11/06																
DENTAL CONCERN INC Humana Inc	A-	'05	28.1	...	...	71.9	3,803	...	78.9	...	21.1	2,630	13,530	13,530	476	552	358	358
Gerald L. Ganoni, President		'06	27.8	...	...	72.2	3,832	...	70.3	...	29.7	1,767	15,318	15,318	-153	-528	-496	-496
P.O. Box 740036, Louisville, KY 40201-7436	Rating Outlook: Stable	'07	26.0	...	...	74.0	4,480	...	63.4	...	36.6	3,225	16,266	16,266	663	2,247	1,687	1,687
KY : 1978 : Stock : Broker; Dental		'08	23.0	...	...	77.0	4,637	...	56.5	...	43.5	2,761	18,137	18,137	-616	867	830	830
502-580-1000; AMB# 068645 NAIC# 54739	FSC XV	'09	17.1	...	...	82.9	6,388	...	71.9	...	28.1	4,455	22,454	22,454	2,672	3,850	2,260	2,260
		Rating History: A- g, 06/02/10; B++, 06/05/09; B++, 06/05/08; NR-3, 06/05/07; NR-3, 05/19/06																
DENTAL CONCERN LTD Humana Inc	NR-3	'05	11.5	...	...	88.5	2,267	...	20.1	...	79.9	2,122	1,041	1,041	-75	264	172	172
Gerald L. Ganoni, President		'06	17.6	...	...	82.4	1,484	...	16.7	...	83.3	1,345	977	977	-789	344	223	223
P.O. Box 740036, Louisville, KY 40201-7436		'07	10.5	...	...	89.5	1,676	...	14.8	...	85.2	1,504	1,113	1,113	190	245	154	154
IL : 1990 : Stock : Broker; Dental		'08	14.0	...	...	86.0	896	...	11.6	...	88.4	715	1,052	1,052	-773	325	285	285
920-336-1100; AMB# 060182 NAIC# 52028		'09	12.6	...	...	87.4	982	...	5.8	...	94.2	584	704	704	82	213	130	130
		Rating History: NR-3, 06/02/10; NR-3, 06/05/09; NR-3, 06/05/08; NR-3, 06/05/07; NR-3, 05/19/06																
DENTAL DELIVERY SYSTEMS INC[2]	NR-5	'05	...	...	...	...	...	...	...	...	...	...	...	...	...	...	...	...
Mario Mele, President		'06	5.3	21.0	36.3	37.4	1,273	...	...	...	100.0	1,168	3,613	3,613	125	76	36	95
2826 Mount Carmel Avenue, Glenside, PA 19038-2245		'07	8.1	29.2	40.9	21.7	849	...	...	...	100.0	785	3,701	3,701	-223	95	48	107
NJ : 1974 : Stock : Not Available; Dental		'08	...	32.5	32.2	35.3	701	...	...	...	100.0	642	4,009	4,009	27	147	96	97
215-224-8888; AMB# 064907 NAIC# 11195		'09	...	27.9	20.0	52.1	752	...	...	...	100.0	693	4,118	4,118	48	146	101	105
		Rating History: NR-5, 04/19/10; NR-5, 06/01/09; NR-5, 05/16/08; NR-5, 06/21/07																
DENTAL GROUP OF NEW JERSEY INC[2]	NR-5	'05	...	...	...	100.0	147	...	...	...	100.0	114	145	145	2	10	10	10
Richard J. Lukenda, President		'06	...	...	...	100.0	151	...	...	...	100.0	124	147	147	2	10	10	10
924 North Wood Avenue, Linden, NJ 07036-4040		'07	...	...	...	100.0	156	...	...	...	100.0	132	137	137	9	8	8	8
NJ : 1986 : Other : Broker; Dental		'08	...	...	...	100.0	151	...	...	...	100.0	129	81	81	-4	-3	-3	-3
908-276-7480; AMB# 064775 NAIC# 11241		'09	...	...	...	100.0	194	...	...	...	100.0	152	107	107	43	9	9	9
		Rating History: NR-5, 04/19/10; NR-5, 06/01/09; NR-5, 05/16/08; NR-5, 06/22/07; NR-5, 05/24/06																
DENTAL HEALTH SERVICES (CA) Dental Health Services of America Inc	NR-5	'05	...	0.2	...	99.8	4,264	...	...	...	100.0	1,854	13,277	13,277	378	255	180	180
Godfrey Pernell, DDS, President		'06	...	0.1	...	99.9	4,848	...	...	...	100.0	2,547	12,561	12,561	517	950	410	410
3833 Atlantic Avenue, Long Beach, CA 90807-3505		'07	...	0.1	...	99.9	5,780	...	...	...	100.0	3,092	11,679	11,679	826	636	176	176
CA : 1982 : Stock : Not Available; Dental		'08	...	0.0	...	100.0	5,022	...	...	...	100.0	3,317	11,649	11,649	-901	694	206	206
562-595-6000; AMB# 064730		'09	...	...	...	100.0	4,922	...	...	...	100.0	3,391	11,987	11,987	510	720	432	432
		Rating History: NR-5, 03/22/10; NR-5, 04/09/09; NR-5, 03/11/08; NR-5, 04/05/07; NR-5, 04/20/06																
DENTAL HEALTH SERVICES (WA) Dental Health Services of America Inc	NR-5	'05	...	...	...	100.0	2,186	...	...	...	100.0	1,418	3,593	3,593	114	176	129	129
Godfrey Pernell, DDS, President		'06	...	...	...	100.0	1,850	...	...	...	100.0	905	4,864	4,864	-315	-487	-366	-366
3833 Atlantic Avenue, Long Beach, CA 90807-3505		'07	...	...	...	100.0	3,262	...	...	...	100.0	1,630	6,713	6,713	1,337	-1,990	-1,412	-1,412
WA : 1984 : Stock : Not Available; Dental		'08	...	...	...	100.0	4,232	...	33.6	...	66.4	2,872	8,074	8,074	1,043	1,189	769	769
206-633-2300; AMB# 064527 NAIC# 47490		'09	...	...	...	100.0	4,948	...	29.1	...	70.9	3,514	8,144	8,144	711	1,643	1,046	1,046
		Rating History: NR-5, 03/22/10; NR-5, 03/17/09; NR-5, 04/30/08; NR-5, 04/03/07; NR-5, 04/20/06																

BEST'S PROFITABILITY, LEVERAGE AND LIQUIDITY TESTS 2005 – 2009

Data in U.S. Dollars

	Profitability Tests							Leverage Tests						Liquidity Tests					
Un-Realized Capital Gains ($000)	Benefits Paid to NPW & Dep (%)	Comm. & Expenses to NPW & Dep (%)	NOG to Total Assets (%)	NOG to Total Rev (%)	Operating Return on Equity (%)	Net Yield (%)	Total Return (%)	Change in NPW & Dep (%)	NPW & Dep to Capital (X)	Capital & Surplus to Liabilities (%)	Surplus Relief (%)	Reins Leverage (%)	Change in Capital (%)	Quick Liquidity (%)	Current Liquidity (%)	Non-Invest Grade Bonds to Capital (%)	Delinq. & Foreclosed Mortgages to Capital (%)	Mort. & Credit Tenant Loans & R.E. to Capital (%)	Affiliated Invest to Capital (%)
...	38.7	42.5	5.0	16.5	5.8	2.84	2.84	-48.8	0.3	541.2	...	...	5.9	918.1	954.5	...	...	...	...
...	38.1	59.5	10.2	31.4	12.1	4.43	4.43	-8.3	0.4	527.0	...	...	-30.4	999.9	999.9	...	...	...	...
...	57.9	63.8	1.8	8.8	2.0	4.44	4.44	-46.4	0.2	999.9	...	...	41.9	999.9	999.9	...	...	...	...
...	74.4	24.7	0.8	0.2	1.0	3.07	3.07	999.9	4.5	163.1	...	...	-12.1	272.8	283.3	...	...	...	...
-8	92.0	26.6	-24.6	-12.2	-47.1	0.62	1.10	-21.5	4.3	78.8	...	...	-16.5	169.1	169.1	...	...	...	...
	Principal Lines of Business: Dental (100.0%)													Principal States: MD (50.7%), FL (49.3%)					
10	79.9	22.5	3.9	0.9	8.3	1.49	1.63	10.2	8.6	88.8	...	...	7.4	153.9	153.9	...	...	21.5	21.5
-3	80.8	23.1	2.0	0.4	4.3	6.17	6.13	11.3	9.0	76.7	0.0	0.2	7.1	142.7	146.2	...	...	22.2	22.2
-25	78.7	25.1	5.3	1.2	11.2	6.41	6.11	6.3	8.5	109.1	0.0	4.9	12.0	158.3	162.9	...	...	20.8	20.8
-15	78.6	25.7	6.9	1.5	13.0	3.17	2.99	1.6	7.8	117.1	0.0	0.1	10.8	190.8	195.1	...	...	7.7	7.7
-18	81.5	24.3	-3.9	-0.8	-7.4	2.08	1.88	12.5	9.2	106.7	...	...	-4.9	172.5	176.4	...	...	9.7	9.7
	Principal Lines of Business: Dental (100.0%)													Principal States: OH (86.4%), KY (13.6%)					
26	72.8	33.5	-1.0	-1.3	-1.2	3.13	4.11	-68.7	0.8	546.1	...	...	0.7	490.4	541.8	...	...	...	...
117	70.8	29.0	2.8	3.3	3.4	3.84	6.19	17.5	0.9	505.8	...	...	6.3	462.7	510.8	...	...	...	...
-292	73.9	30.0	0.6	0.7	0.8	3.98	4.16	8.7	1.0	461.0	...	...	0.7	415.6	466.0	...	...	...	...
-740	74.0	28.4	1.6	1.6	1.9	3.82	-9.37	8.1	1.3	508.7	...	...	-13.4	461.7	513.9	0.0	...	...	...
482	83.0	26.5	-1.6	-2.8	-1.8	3.56	10.46	-45.9	0.5	999.9	...	...	28.8	999.9	999.9	...	...	...	...
	Principal Lines of Business: Dental (100.0%)													Principal States: KY (52.8%), WV (47.2%)					
...	75.8	21.0	9.9	2.6	13.9	2.97	2.97	51.5	5.1	224.2	...	...	4.3	536.3	537.6	...	...	...	...
...	79.0	21.2	-13.0	-3.2	-22.5	3.59	3.59	13.2	8.7	85.6	...	...	-32.8	294.7	295.5	...	...	...	...
...	81.5	9.4	40.6	10.3	67.6	3.50	3.50	6.2	5.0	257.1	...	...	82.5	548.4	549.5	...	...	...	...
...	74.0	21.7	18.2	4.6	27.7	1.89	1.89	11.5	6.6	147.2	...	...	-14.4	259.8	260.6	...	...	...	...
...	71.6	11.7	41.0	10.0	62.6	0.75	0.75	23.8	5.0	230.6	...	...	61.4	563.0	563.8	...	...	...	...
	Principal Lines of Business: Dental (74.4%), Vision (25.6%)													Principal States: KY (99.2%)					
...	54.1	38.7	7.4	14.0	7.9	2.25	2.25	-15.5	0.5	999.9	...	...	-5.7	999.9	999.9	...	...	...	...
...	48.8	37.8	11.9	18.7	12.9	3.19	3.19	-6.2	0.7	971.9	...	...	-36.6	999.9	999.9	...	...	...	...
...	59.2	35.4	9.7	11.8	10.8	3.33	3.33	14.0	0.7	879.0	...	...	11.8	999.9	999.9	...	...	...	...
...	57.5	23.4	22.2	24.2	25.7	1.22	1.22	-5.5	1.5	395.5	...	...	-52.4	487.4	487.4	...	...	...	...
...	58.6	12.5	13.8	18.2	20.0	0.49	0.49	-33.1	1.2	146.6	...	...	-18.4	367.4	367.4	...	...	...	...
	Principal Lines of Business: Dental (100.0%)													Principal States: IL (100.0%)					
...	...	...	...	...	...	...	...	...	...	...	...	...	...	...	...	...	...	...	...
-10	82.0	17.9	...	1.0	...	...	...	...	3.1	999.9	...	...	...	996.5	999.9	...	...	22.9	...
-67	82.1	17.1	4.5	1.3	4.9	5.86	5.45	2.4	4.7	999.9	...	...	-32.7	999.9	999.9	...	...	31.6	...
-322	82.5	15.3	12.4	2.4	13.5	7.78	-27.42	8.3	6.2	999.9	...	...	-18.2	981.8	999.9	...	...	35.5	...
61	83.8	13.7	13.9	2.4	15.1	6.91	17.55	2.7	5.9	999.9	...	...	7.9	999.9	999.9	...	...	30.2	...
	Principal Lines of Business: Dental (100.0%)													Principal States: NJ (100.0%)					
...	83.2	10.4	6.8	6.8	9.1	0.49	0.49	9.2	1.3	348.7	...	...	9.5	434.8	434.8	...	...	...	...
...	80.4	13.6	6.5	6.6	8.2	0.59	0.59	1.9	1.2	446.7	...	...	8.5	520.7	520.7	...	...	...	...
...	81.0	13.6	5.4	6.0	6.5	0.59	0.59	-7.1	1.0	552.7	...	...	6.5	642.7	642.7	...	...	...	...
...	79.8	30.1	-2.0	-3.6	-2.4	3.26	3.26	-41.0	0.6	565.4	...	...	-2.3	657.1	657.1	...	...	...	...
...	80.5	11.2	5.2	8.3	6.4	0.01	0.01	32.4	0.7	355.3	...	...	17.8	452.5	452.5	...	...	...	...
	Principal Lines of Business: Dental (100.0%)													Principal States: NJ (100.0%)					
...	73.7	25.2	4.5	1.3	10.4	4.13	4.13	-4.3	7.2	76.9	...	...	15.8	90.5	90.5	...	...	0.5	0.5
...	65.8	27.8	9.0	3.2	18.6	4.11	4.11	-5.4	4.9	110.7	...	...	37.4	117.6	117.6	...	...	0.2	0.2
...	65.0	32.4	3.3	1.5	6.2	3.48	3.48	-7.0	3.8	115.0	...	...	21.4	138.2	138.2	...	...	0.1	0.1
...	65.0	33.8	3.8	1.7	6.4	4.83	4.83	-0.3	3.5	194.5	...	...	7.3	150.9	150.9	...	...	0.0	0.0
...	58.7	39.7	8.7	3.5	12.9	4.78	4.78	2.9	3.5	221.5	...	...	2.2	162.0	162.0	...	...	...	...
	Principal Lines of Business: Dental (100.0%)																		
...	43.2	52.7	6.1	3.6	9.6	1.24	1.24	4.5	2.5	184.7	...	...	11.4	281.0	281.0	...	...	...	...
20	68.4	42.5	-18.1	-7.4	-31.5	2.22	3.24	35.4	5.4	95.8	...	...	-36.2	194.9	194.9	...	...	...	...
-4	98.5	32.6	-55.3	-20.7	-99.9	3.88	3.72	38.0	4.1	100.0	...	...	80.1	194.9	194.9	...	...	...	...
-16	60.0	26.3	20.5	9.4	34.1	2.12	1.68	20.3	2.8	211.1	...	...	76.1	310.4	310.4	...	...	...	...
...	52.8	27.3	22.8	12.8	32.8	0.37	0.37	0.9	2.3	244.9	...	...	22.4	343.9	343.9	...	...	...	...
	Principal Lines of Business: Dental (100.0%)													Principal States: WA (100.0%)					

Data in U.S. Dollars

COMPANY NAME Ultimate Parent Association Principal Officer Mailing Address Dom. : Began Bus. : Struct. : Mktg. Specialty Phone # AMB# NAIC#	Best's Financial Strength Rating FSC	Data Year	Balance Sheet Bonds (%)	Mort. Loans & R.E. (%)	Com & Pref. Stock (%)	All Other Assets (%)	Total Assets ($000)	Life Reserves (%)	Health Reserves (%)	Ann Res. & Dep. Liabilities (%)	All Other Liabilities (%)	Capital & Surplus ($000)	Operations Direct Premiums Written ($000)	Net Premiums Written & Deposits ($000)	Operating Cash Flow ($000)	NOG Before Taxes ($000)	NOG After Taxes ($000)	Net Income ($000)
DENTAL PRACTICE ASSOCIATION NJ[2] Harris N. Callon, D.D.S. President 615 Chestnut Street, Suite 1001 Philadelphia, PA 19106-4411 NJ : 2004 : Stock : Not Available Dental 215-440-1018 AMB# 064950 NAIC# 12213	NR-5	'05	...	...	...	...	...	...	...	...	...	...	...	...	...	...	...	...
		'06	...	...	...	...	...	...	...	...	...	...	...	...	...	...	...	...
		'07	...	...	...	100.0	204	...	44.3	...	55.7	151	348	348	28	36	36	36
		'08	...	...	...	100.0	209	...	43.1	...	56.9	166	247	247	6	19	15	15
		'09	...	...	...	100.0	192	...	44.9	...	55.1	160	162	162	-17	-4	-5	-5
		Rating History: NR-5, 04/19/10; NR-5, 06/01/09; NR-5, 05/20/08																
DENTAL PROTECTION PLAN INC[2] Douglas Persich President & Treasurer 7130 W. Greenfield Avenue Milwaukee, WI 53214 WI : 1988 : Other : Broker Dental 414-259-9522 AMB# 064797 NAIC# 53465	NR-5	'05	...	...	...	100.0	28	...	...	...	100.0	0	62	62	6	6	6	6
		'06	...	...	...	100.0	32	...	...	...	100.0	3	61	61	4	3	3	3
		'07	...	...	...	100.0	32	...	4.8	...	95.2	3	62	62	0	0	0	0
		'08	...	...	...	100.0	36	...	3.6	...	96.4	11	63	63	5	8	8	8
		'09	...	...	...	100.0	31	...	5.1	...	94.9	3	58	58	-5	-8	-8	-8
		Rating History: NR-5, 05/20/10; NR-5, 07/13/09; NR-5, 05/16/08; NR-5, 06/20/07; NR-5, 07/11/06																
DENTAL SERVICE CORP OF ND[2] Noridian Mutual Insurance Company Timothy J. Huckle President 4510 13th Avenue South Fargo, ND 58121-0001 ND : 1970 : Non-Profit : Not Available Dental 701-282-1100 AMB# 064370 NAIC# 47054	NR-5	'05	63.4	...	20.6	16.0	10,118	...	67.3	...	32.7	8,156	20,425	20,425	1,530	2,176	1,711	1,857
		'06	58.1	...	26.6	15.3	11,894	...	69.8	...	30.2	9,874	20,706	20,706	1,566	1,849	1,456	1,597
		'07	60.4	...	24.3	15.3	13,652	...	55.6	...	44.4	11,311	19,931	19,931	2,183	1,565	1,198	1,473
		'08	51.8	...	16.8	31.4	6,614	...	69.3	...	30.7	4,595	12,726	12,726	-7,283	-7,030	-6,333	-6,303
		'09	48.1	...	20.2	31.6	7,615	...	66.8	...	33.2	5,817	21,322	21,322	94	339	984	908
		Rating History: NR-5, 04/28/10; NR-5, 03/27/09; NR-5, 04/08/08; NR-5, 04/03/07; NR-5, 06/21/06																
DENTAL SERVICE OF MA[2] Dental Service of Massachusetts Inc Fay Donohue President 465 Medford Street Boston, MA 02129 MA : 1970 : Non-Profit : Broker Dental 617-886-1000 AMB# 060193 NAIC# 52060	NR-5	'05	65.6	...	20.2	14.3	273,432	...	30.9	...	69.1	196,548	312,045	312,045	11,741	11,235	11,235	14,578
		'06	63.0	...	19.5	17.5	281,539	...	32.0	...	68.0	196,357	333,361	333,361	2,420	-7,316	-7,316	-1,567
		'07	76.7	...	21.1	2.2	242,318	...	30.5	...	69.5	153,890	357,179	357,179	33,770	-4,005	-4,005	-2,169
		'08	84.7	...	12.1	3.2	225,110	...	30.8	...	69.2	147,913	362,585	362,585	-8,584	17,092	17,092	12,514
		'09	66.8	...	18.2	15.0	263,100	...	21.4	...	78.6	187,590	301,944	301,944	-7,141	30,520	30,520	25,782
		Rating History: NR-5, 05/24/10; NR-5, 12/01/09; B++pd, 09/24/08; B++pd, 09/18/07; B++pd, 10/16/06																
DENTAL SERVICES ORGANIZATION[2] Aaron Feiler President 1030 St. George Avenue Avenel, NJ 07001 NJ : 2001 : Other : Broker Dental 732-634-4810 AMB# 064773 NAIC# 11234	NR-5	'05	...	...	...	100.0	272	...	...	...	100.0	222	3,018	3,018	-109	201	130	130
		'06	...	...	...	100.0	394	...	...	...	100.0	373	3,103	3,103	114	259	259	259
		'07	...	...	...	100.0	447	...	...	...	100.0	427	3,233	3,233	51	253	253	253
		'08	...	...	...	100.0	496	...	...	...	100.0	477	3,549	3,549	45	248	248	248
		'09	...	...	...	100.0	552	...	...	...	100.0	530	3,627	3,627	52	253	253	253
		Rating History: NR-5, 04/21/10; NR-5, 06/01/09; NR-5, 05/20/08; NR-5, 06/25/07; NR-5, 05/11/06																
DENTAL SOURCE OF MISSOURI & KS[2] Dental Economics L P James A. Taylor President & Treasurer 9091 State Line Road, Ste. 101 Kansas City, MO 64114 MO : 1990 : Non-Profit : Not Available Dental 800-369-3485 AMB# 065731 NAIC# 48160	NR-5	'05	23.9	...	...	76.1	1,174	...	14.2	...	85.8	358	5,031	5,031	37	16	11	11
		'06	19.3	...	...	80.7	1,455	...	7.5	...	92.5	480	4,699	4,699	272	182	120	120
		'07	17.5	...	...	82.5	1,605	...	9.8	...	90.2	588	4,481	4,481	115	161	110	110
		'08	21.2	...	...	78.8	1,335	...	...	...	100.0	463	4,237	4,237	-276	106	73	73
		'09	20.2	...	...	79.8	1,401	...	5.3	...	94.7	526	3,672	3,672	79	92	61	61
		Rating History: NR-5, 04/06/10; NR-5, 04/23/09; NR-5, 03/28/08; NR-5, 06/21/07; NR-5, 05/22/06																
DENTAQUEST DENTAL PLAN OF WI[2] Dental Service of Massachusetts Inc Stephen J. Pollock President 12121 N. Corporate Parkway Mequon, WI 53092 WI : 1996 : Stock : Broker Dental 262-241-7140 AMB# 064799 NAIC# 95352	NR-5	'05	...	...	...	100.0	849	...	...	...	100.0	389	921	921	...	626	373	373
		'06	...	...	...	100.0	1,878	...	...	...	100.0	430	675	675	1,072	65	41	41
		'07	...	...	...	100.0	1,970	...	...	...	100.0	500	524	524	54	109	70	70
		'08	...	...	...	100.0	720	...	...	...	100.0	511	460	460	-1,941	11	11	11
		'09	32.1	...	...	67.9	788	...	...	...	100.0	549	342	342	797	60	38	38
		Rating History: NR-5, 05/19/10; NR-5, 07/17/09; NR-5, 05/16/08; NR-5, 06/20/07; NR-5, 07/06/06																
DENTAQUEST MID-ATLANTIC INC Dental Service of Massachusetts Inc Dennis J. Leonard President 4061 Powder Mill Road, #325 Calverton, MD 20705 MD : 1997 : Non-Profit : Not Available Dental 301-937-4447 AMB# 064544 NAIC# 52040	NR-5	'05	2.8	...	...	97.2	3,765	...	...	...	100.0	1,807	14,928	14,928	180	1,432	1,000	1,000
		'06	1.8	...	...	98.2	5,980	...	6.4	...	93.6	3,471	15,854	15,854	1,469	2,113	1,369	1,369
		'07	2.6	...	...	97.4	4,232	...	6.4	...	93.6	2,268	15,790	15,790	-1,140	1,855	1,206	1,206
		'08	2.2	...	...	97.8	4,825	...	35.8	...	64.2	3,410	15,298	15,298	1,809	1,523	990	990
		'09	1.9	...	...	98.1	5,659	...	46.2	...	53.8	4,295	15,608	15,608	168	1,682	1,094	1,094
		Rating History: NR-5, 03/22/10; NR-5, 06/17/09; NR-5, 07/29/08; NR-5, 04/19/07; NR-5, 05/02/06																
DENTAQUEST USA INSURANCE CO[2] Dental Service of Massachusetts Inc Steven J. Pollock President 919 Congress Avenue Austin, TX 78701-2168 TX : 2005 : Stock : Not Available Dental 282-241-7140 AMB# 060597 NAIC# 12307	NR-5	'05	...	...	...	...	...	...	...	...	...	...	...	...	...	...	...	...
		'06	...	...	...	...	...	...	...	...	...	...	...	...	...	...	...	...
		'07	...	...	...	...	...	...	...	...	...	...	...	...	...	...	...	...
		'08	62.3	...	...	37.7	4,664	...	...	...	100.0	3,071	...	...	1,540	86	49	49
		'09	18.7	...	...	81.3	16,090	...	30.4	...	69.6	9,710	25,201	32,083	4,704	1,789	1,047	1,047
		Rating History: NR-5, 04/07/10; NR-5, 04/29/09																

2010 BEST'S KEY RATING GUIDE — LIFE/HEALTH EDITION
BEST'S PROFITABILITY, LEVERAGE AND LIQUIDITY TESTS 2005 – 2009
Data in U.S. Dollars

	Profitability Tests							Leverage Tests						Liquidity Tests					
Un-Realized Capital Gains ($000)	Benefits Paid to NPW & Dep (%)	Comm. & Expenses to NPW & Dep (%)	NOG to Total Assets (%)	NOG to Total Rev (%)	Operating Return on Equity (%)	Net Yield (%)	Total Return (%)	Change in NPW & Dep (%)	NPW & Dep to Capital (X)	Capital & Surplus to Liabilities (%)	Surplus Relief (%)	Reins Leverage (%)	Change in Capital (%)	Quick Liquidity (%)	Current Liquidity (%)	Non-Invest Grade Bonds to Capital (%)	Delinq. & Foreclosed Mortgages to Capital (%)	Mort. & Credit Tenant Loans & R.E. to Capital (%)	Affiliated Invest to Capital (%)
...	...	...	...	...	...	...	...	...	...	...	...	...	...	...	...	...	...	...	...
...	...	...	...	...	...	...	...	...	...	...	...	...	...	...	...	...	...	...	...
...	80.0	12.2	...	10.0	...	...	...	...	2.3	285.7	...	...	...	382.3	382.3	...	...	...	...
...	78.4	15.1	7.1	5.9	9.2	1.38	1.38	-29.1	1.5	387.8	...	...	9.7	487.8	487.8	...	...	...	...
...	73.3	29.3	-2.7	-3.3	-3.3	0.03	0.03	-34.3	1.0	503.8	...	...	-3.2	601.6	601.6	...	...	...	...
	Principal Lines of Business: Dental (100.0%)													Principal States: NJ (100.0%)					
...	...	90.9	22.4	9.1	-99.9	...	...	-8.5	135.7	1.7	...	...	106.2	101.7	101.7	...	...	...	...
...	...	95.7	8.8	4.3	148.5	...	...	-1.1	19.7	10.8	...	...	579.8	110.8	110.8	...	...	...	...
...	...	100.1	-0.2	-0.1	-2.1	...	...	1.2	20.4	10.6	...	...	-2.1	110.6	110.6	...	...	...	...
...	...	87.3	23.5	12.7	113.6	...	...	1.4	5.7	43.7	...	...	262.8	143.7	143.7	...	...	...	...
...	...	113.6	-23.6	-13.6	-99.9	...	...	-7.4	18.9	11.1	...	...	-72.0	111.1	111.1	...	...	...	...
	Principal Lines of Business: Dental (100.0%)													Principal States: WI (100.0%)					
-28	80.5	10.2	18.6	8.3	23.6	3.29	4.75	5.4	2.5	415.5	...	...	29.1	358.6	403.4	...	...	...	...
189	81.8	11.0	13.2	6.9	16.1	3.89	7.31	1.4	2.1	488.9	...	...	21.1	420.3	472.1	0.3	...	...	...
-53	82.7	11.6	9.4	5.9	11.3	3.74	5.67	-3.7	1.8	483.3	...	...	14.6	437.1	491.5	0.3	...	...	...
-577	139.9	17.9	-62.5	-48.5	-79.6	3.75	-2.27	-36.1	2.8	227.6	...	...	-59.4	173.0	197.9	...	...	...	...
289	87.0	12.3	13.8	4.6	18.9	3.79	8.26	67.5	3.7	323.6	...	...	26.6	230.9	263.3	0.9	...	...	...
	Principal Lines of Business: Dental (100.0%)													Principal States: ND (100.0%)					
-3,713	79.0	17.2	4.2	3.6	5.9	3.97	3.83	0.3	1.6	255.6	...	...	7.0	241.4	267.1	...	...	...	...
2,125	80.4	16.6	-2.6	-2.3	-3.7	3.94	7.23	6.8	1.7	230.5	...	...	-0.1	217.9	239.7	4.6	...	...	...
20,353	80.1	16.9	-1.5	-1.2	-2.3	4.62	14.92	7.1	2.3	174.0	...	...	-21.6	201.5	222.0	5.2	...	...	...
-2,564	79.5	14.1	7.3	4.8	11.3	4.68	1.06	1.5	2.5	191.6	...	...	-3.9	211.2	229.6	5.5	...	...	-0.6
25,958	78.0	11.2	12.5	10.2	18.2	4.20	15.68	-16.7	1.6	248.4	...	...	26.8	224.3	245.5	0.5	...	...	13.1
	Principal Lines of Business: Dental (100.0%)													Principal States: MA (100.0%)					
...	88.1	4.6	38.9	4.3	46.3	0.70	0.70	8.9	13.6	444.7	...	...	-34.6	378.9	378.9	...	...	...	...
...	87.4	4.3	77.8	8.4	87.1	1.03	1.03	2.8	8.3	999.9	...	...	68.0	999.9	999.9	...	...	...	...
...	87.8	4.5	60.1	7.8	63.2	0.78	0.78	4.2	7.6	999.9	...	...	14.3	999.9	999.9	...	...	...	...
...	88.9	4.2	52.7	7.0	55.0	0.37	0.37	9.8	7.4	999.9	...	...	11.7	999.9	999.9	...	...	...	...
...	88.9	4.1	48.3	7.0	50.3	0.20	0.20	2.2	6.8	999.9	...	...	11.3	999.9	999.9	...	...	...	...
	Principal Lines of Business: Dental (100.0%)													Principal States: NJ (100.0%)					
1	57.7	43.9	1.0	0.2	3.1	0.91	1.01	-0.8	14.1	43.9	...	...	3.8	131.2	132.1	...	...	...	14.0
...	60.0	37.2	9.1	2.5	28.7	1.66	1.66	-6.6	9.8	49.2	...	...	34.0	111.2	111.2	...	...	...	10.4
...	60.0	37.8	7.2	2.4	20.5	1.54	1.54	-4.6	7.6	57.8	...	...	22.5	144.7	145.5	...	...	...	8.5
...	59.0	40.0	5.0	1.7	14.0	1.20	1.19	-5.5	9.2	53.1	...	...	-21.3	136.9	137.7	...	...	...	10.8
...	61.4	37.7	4.4	1.6	12.2	0.88	0.88	-13.3	7.0	60.2	...	...	13.7	145.0	145.8	...	...	...	9.5
	Principal Lines of Business: Dental (100.0%)													Principal States: MO (95.1%), KS (4.9%)					
...	18.2	15.9	48.1	39.6	147.4	...	7.25	6.4	2.4	84.6	...	...	235.1	...	...	...	...	...	...
...	75.1	17.9	3.0	5.9	10.0	...	...	-26.8	1.6	29.7	...	...	10.5	129.7	129.7	...	...	...	...
...	53.4	25.7	3.6	13.3	15.0	...	...	-22.3	1.0	34.0	...	...	16.2	131.4	131.4	...	...	...	...
...	76.5	21.1	0.8	2.4	2.2	...	...	-12.3	0.9	244.0	...	...	2.2	-4.6	-4.6	...	...	...	...
...	52.7	29.8	5.0	11.0	7.1	...	...	-25.6	0.6	229.3	...	...	7.4	329.0	329.0	...	...	...	...
	Principal Lines of Business: Dental (100.0%)													Principal States: WI (100.0%)					
0	61.8	29.0	30.4	6.7	55.2	3.06	3.08	11.6	8.3	92.3	80.7	...	-0.6	105.6	105.6	...	...	...	...
0	56.9	30.6	28.1	8.6	51.9	4.58	4.57	6.2	4.6	138.4	...	0.0	92.1	141.9	141.9	...	...	...	...
7	57.3	31.9	23.6	7.6	42.0	5.38	5.61	-0.4	7.0	115.4	...	...	-34.7	124.1	124.1	...	...	...	...
-7	56.4	34.0	21.9	6.4	34.9	1.57	1.36	-3.1	4.5	241.0	...	...	50.4	290.2	290.2	...	...	...	...
...	56.5	32.8	20.9	7.0	28.4	-0.01	-0.01	2.0	3.6	314.8	...	...	25.9	313.2	313.2	...	...	...	...
	Principal Lines of Business: Dental (100.0%)													Principal States: MD (79.0%), DC (21.0%)					
...	...	...	...	...	...	...	...	...	...	...	...	...	...	...	...	...	...	...	...
...	...	...	...	...	...	...	...	...	...	...	...	...	...	...	...	...	...	...	...
...	...	...	...	...	...	...	...	...	...	...	...	...	...	...	...	...	...	...	...
...	...	...	...	56.0	...	...	...	...	...	192.8	...	...	...	290.1	290.1	...	...	...	...
...	83.7	10.9	10.1	3.3	16.4	0.99	0.99	...	3.3	152.2	...	...	216.2	146.1	146.1	...	...	...	...
	Principal Lines of Business: Dental (100.0%)													Principal States: GA (100.0%)					

Data in U.S. Dollars

COMPANY NAME: Ultimate Parent Association; Principal Officer; Mailing Address; Dom. : Began Bus. : Struct. : Mktg.; Specialty; Phone #; AMB#; NAIC#

Best's Financial Strength Rating; FSC

Balance Sheet: Data Year; Bonds (%); Mort. Loans & R.E. (%); Com & Pref. Stock (%); All Other Assets (%); Total Assets ($000); Life Reserves (%); Health Reserves (%); Ann Res. & Dep. Liabilities (%); All Other Liabilities (%); Capital & Surplus ($000)

Operations: Direct Premiums Written ($000); Net Premiums Written & Deposits ($000); Operating Cash Flow ($000); NOG Before Taxes ($000); NOG After Taxes ($000); Net Income ($000)

DENTAQUEST VIRGINIA INC[2]
Dental Service of Massachusetts Inc
Dennis J. Leonard
President
4061 Powder Mill Road, #325
Calverton, MD 20705
VA : 1997 : Stock : Not Available
Dental
301-937-4447
AMB# 064637 NAIC# 95713

Rating: **NR-5**

Data Year	Bonds (%)	Mort. Loans & R.E. (%)	Com & Pref. Stock (%)	All Other Assets (%)	Total Assets ($000)	Life Reserves (%)	Health Reserves (%)	Ann Res. & Dep. Liabilities (%)	All Other Liabilities (%)	Capital & Surplus ($000)	Direct Premiums Written ($000)	Net Premiums Written & Deposits ($000)	Operating Cash Flow ($000)	NOG Before Taxes ($000)	NOG After Taxes ($000)	Net Income ($000)
'05	...	...	...	100.0	1,790	...	...	...	100.0	1,171	1,314	1,314	188	82	59	59
'06	...	...	...	100.0	1,737	...	8.3	...	91.7	1,332	1,570	1,570	-91	210	142	142
'07	...	...	...	100.0	1,188	...	...	...	100.0	994	1,706	1,706	-582	228	148	148
'08	...	...	...	100.0	1,633	...	18.4	...	81.6	1,314	2,037	2,037	414	485	315	315
'09	...	...	...	100.0	2,026	...	42.4	...	57.6	1,762	2,679	2,679	508	662	422	422

Rating History: NR-5, 05/18/10; NR-5, 04/24/09; NR-5, 04/25/08; NR-5, 05/09/07; NR-5, 05/17/06

DENTCARE DELIVERY SYSTEMS INC
Glenn J. Sobel
President
333 Earle Ovington Boulevard
Uniondale, NY 11553
NY : 1978 : Other : Agency
Dental
516-542-2200
AMB# 064600 NAIC# 47112

Rating: **NR-5**

Data Year	Bonds (%)	Mort. Loans & R.E. (%)	Com & Pref. Stock (%)	All Other Assets (%)	Total Assets ($000)	Life Reserves (%)	Health Reserves (%)	Ann Res. & Dep. Liabilities (%)	All Other Liabilities (%)	Capital & Surplus ($000)	Direct Premiums Written ($000)	Net Premiums Written & Deposits ($000)	Operating Cash Flow ($000)	NOG Before Taxes ($000)	NOG After Taxes ($000)	Net Income ($000)
'05	9.0	...	...	91.0	11,105	...	39.7	...	60.3	6,792	54,204	54,204	1,093	961	961	961
'06	11.5	...	...	88.5	13,040	...	33.3	...	66.7	7,417	54,263	54,263	1,246	956	956	956
'07	7.3	...	...	92.7	13,692	...	42.0	...	58.0	8,431	54,727	54,727	873	1,027	1,027	1,027
'08	8.4	...	...	91.6	11,863	...	55.3	...	44.7	8,297	49,300	49,300	-1,187	555	555	555
'09	...	...	...	100.0	11,354	...	41.0	...	59.0	8,169	47,302	47,302	-240	-111	-111	-111

Rating History: NR-5, 04/19/10; NR-5, 04/09/09; NR-5, 04/15/08; NR-5, 08/28/07; NR-5, 04/20/06

DENTEGRA INSURANCE COMPANY
Dentegra Group Inc
Gary D. Radine
Chairman & President
100 First Street
San Francisco, CA 94105
DE : 1966 : Stock : Agency
Dental
415-972-8353
AMB# 060383 NAIC# 73474

Rating: **NR-2**

Data Year	Bonds (%)	Mort. Loans & R.E. (%)	Com & Pref. Stock (%)	All Other Assets (%)	Total Assets ($000)	Life Reserves (%)	Health Reserves (%)	Ann Res. & Dep. Liabilities (%)	All Other Liabilities (%)	Capital & Surplus ($000)	Direct Premiums Written ($000)	Net Premiums Written & Deposits ($000)	Operating Cash Flow ($000)	NOG Before Taxes ($000)	NOG After Taxes ($000)	Net Income ($000)
'05	24.3	...	4.8	70.9	24,145	...	0.7	...	99.3	8,857	20,771	3,220	271	152	152	152
'06	56.0	...	15.7	28.3	28,491	...	1.1	...	98.9	13,522	42,590	17,873	14,407	451	451	451
'07	19.2	...	33.5	47.3	20,460	...	1.8	...	98.2	9,531	56,924	17,252	-8,163	208	208	208
'08	2.8	...	37.5	59.7	33,068	...	0.6	...	99.4	20,049	65,386	18,566	7,216	251	74	74
'09	23.0	...	13.3	63.8	28,216	...	1.1	...	98.9	17,119	79,847	25,364	-1,579	21	201	201

Rating History: NR-2, 04/08/10; NR-2, 03/18/09; NR-2, 03/24/08; NR-2, 02/13/07; NR-2, 12/21/05

DENTEGRA INS CO OF NEW ENGLAND
Dentegra Group Inc
Gary D. Radine
Chairman & President
100 First Street
San Francisco, CA 94105
MA : 2004 : Stock : Agency
Dental
415-972-8300
AMB# 010110 NAIC# 12210

Rating: **NR-2**

Data Year	Bonds (%)	Mort. Loans & R.E. (%)	Com & Pref. Stock (%)	All Other Assets (%)	Total Assets ($000)	Life Reserves (%)	Health Reserves (%)	Ann Res. & Dep. Liabilities (%)	All Other Liabilities (%)	Capital & Surplus ($000)	Direct Premiums Written ($000)	Net Premiums Written & Deposits ($000)	Operating Cash Flow ($000)	NOG Before Taxes ($000)	NOG After Taxes ($000)	Net Income ($000)
'05	21.8	...	...	78.2	5,812	...	...	...	100.0	5,799	...	...	1,996	-1	-1	-1
'06	21.5	...	...	78.5	5,897	...	0.3	...	99.7	5,791	465	230	40	-8	-8	-8
'07	21.1	...	...	78.9	6,020	...	0.2	...	99.8	5,787	895	205	42	-4	-4	-4
'08	20.9	...	...	79.1	6,080	...	0.5	...	99.5	5,786	1,875	479	-52	-1	-1	-1
'09	21.0	...	...	79.0	6,064	...	0.9	...	99.1	5,800	2,427	715	-86	14	14	14

Rating History: NR-2, 04/08/10; NR-2, 03/18/09; NR-2, 03/24/08; NR-2, 02/13/07; NR-2, 12/21/05

DENTICARE INC
Humana Inc
Gerald L. Ganoni
President
100 Mansell Court East, Suite 400
Roswell, GA 30076
TX : 1982 : Stock : Not Available
Dental
770-998-8936
AMB# 064522 NAIC# 95161

Rating: **A-**
Rating Outlook: Stable
FSC XV

Data Year	Bonds (%)	Mort. Loans & R.E. (%)	Com & Pref. Stock (%)	All Other Assets (%)	Total Assets ($000)	Life Reserves (%)	Health Reserves (%)	Ann Res. & Dep. Liabilities (%)	All Other Liabilities (%)	Capital & Surplus ($000)	Direct Premiums Written ($000)	Net Premiums Written & Deposits ($000)	Operating Cash Flow ($000)	NOG Before Taxes ($000)	NOG After Taxes ($000)	Net Income ($000)
'05	4.4	...	...	95.6	2,964	...	80.0	...	20.0	2,084	12,006	12,006	662	1,455	947	947
'06	4.2	...	...	95.8	3,120	...	47.6	...	52.4	2,325	12,263	12,263	140	1,465	971	971
'07	2.9	...	...	97.1	4,518	...	23.3	...	76.7	3,003	12,963	12,963	1,453	-3,995	-4,255	-4,255
'08	3.5	...	4.2	92.3	5,721	...	35.4	...	64.6	4,369	12,111	12,111	1,407	2,103	1,745	1,745
'09	3.1	...	...	96.9	8,853	...	14.4	...	85.6	4,090	18,833	18,833	2,091	3,303	2,377	2,377

Rating History: A- g, 06/02/10; B++, 06/05/09; B++, 06/05/08; C++pd, 06/12/07; C++pd, 06/20/06

DENVER HEALTH MEDICAL PLAN[2]
Dawn P. Bookhardt
President
777 Bannock Street, MC 6000
Denver, CO 80204
CO : 1997 : Non-Profit : Broker
Group A&H
720-956-2333
AMB# 064420 NAIC# 95750

Rating: **NR-5**

Data Year	Bonds (%)	Mort. Loans & R.E. (%)	Com & Pref. Stock (%)	All Other Assets (%)	Total Assets ($000)	Life Reserves (%)	Health Reserves (%)	Ann Res. & Dep. Liabilities (%)	All Other Liabilities (%)	Capital & Surplus ($000)	Direct Premiums Written ($000)	Net Premiums Written & Deposits ($000)	Operating Cash Flow ($000)	NOG Before Taxes ($000)	NOG After Taxes ($000)	Net Income ($000)
'05	72.3	...	...	27.7	6,949	...	89.4	...	10.6	2,880	30,211	29,547	277	-866	-866	-851
'06	44.6	...	...	55.4	11,927	...	80.7	...	19.3	3,978	44,481	43,511	6,369	880	880	1,064
'07	64.0	...	...	36.0	15,147	...	90.4	...	9.6	6,783	55,456	54,290	2,883	2,630	2,630	2,895
'08	90.1	...	...	9.9	23,577	...	89.7	...	10.3	10,585	71,903	70,635	8,868	3,743	3,743	3,746
'09	93.0	...	...	7.0	23,745	...	86.7	...	13.3	13,253	83,633	81,900	121	5,351	5,351	5,355

Rating History: NR-5, 04/19/10; NR-5, 08/26/09; C+ pd, 09/03/08; C+ pd, 06/26/07; C+ pd, 07/25/06

DESERET MUTUAL INSURANCE CO[1]
DMC Reserve Trust
Michael J. Stapley
President
P.O. Box 45530
Salt Lake City, UT 84145-0530
UT : 1969 : Mutual : Not Available
801-578-5858
AMB# 009490 NAIC# 81019

Rating: **NR-1**

Data Year	Bonds (%)	Mort. Loans & R.E. (%)	Com & Pref. Stock (%)	All Other Assets (%)	Total Assets ($000)	Life Reserves (%)	Health Reserves (%)	Ann Res. & Dep. Liabilities (%)	All Other Liabilities (%)	Capital & Surplus ($000)	Direct Premiums Written ($000)	Net Premiums Written & Deposits ($000)	Operating Cash Flow ($000)	NOG Before Taxes ($000)	NOG After Taxes ($000)	Net Income ($000)
'05	88.4	...	...	11.6	41,121	...	...	21.0	79.0	5,416	16,644	16,624	...	110	330	328
'06	83.1	...	...	16.9	43,967	...	...	19.8	80.2	6,284	17,351	17,321	...	425	340	340
'07	86.2	...	...	13.8	46,128	...	...	18.0	82.0	7,262	18,161	18,143	...	887	1,058	1,056
'08	80.1	...	0.1	19.9	43,150	...	...	16.4	83.6	4,207	20,169	19,415	...	66	-566	-1,128
'09	86.1	...	6.8	7.1	44,499	...	...	16.8	83.2	6,780	21,066	20,293	...	1,432	1,695	1,398

Rating History: NR-1, 06/10/10; NR-1, 06/12/09; NR-1, 06/12/08; NR-1, 06/08/07; NR-1, 06/07/06

DESTINY HEALTH INSURANCE CO[1]
Arthur C. Carlos
President
200 W. Monroe Street, Suite 2100
Chicago, IL 60606-5015
IL : 2000 : Stock : Broker
312-224-7100
AMB# 060357 NAIC# 89003

Rating: **NR-1**

Data Year	Bonds (%)	Mort. Loans & R.E. (%)	Com & Pref. Stock (%)	All Other Assets (%)	Total Assets ($000)	Life Reserves (%)	Health Reserves (%)	Ann Res. & Dep. Liabilities (%)	All Other Liabilities (%)	Capital & Surplus ($000)	Direct Premiums Written ($000)	Net Premiums Written & Deposits ($000)	Operating Cash Flow ($000)	NOG Before Taxes ($000)	NOG After Taxes ($000)	Net Income ($000)
'05	...	...	...	100.0	37,478	...	...	...	100.0	15,287	62,113	61,479	...	-12,013	-12,013	-12,013
'06	...	...	...	100.0	34,234	...	...	...	100.0	13,108	50,093	60,829	...	-5,113	-5,113	-5,113
'07	...	...	...	100.0	27,649	...	...	...	100.0	10,852	34,449	37,542	...	-4,156	-4,156	-4,156
'08	...	...	...	100.0	22,687	...	...	...	100.0	1,545	10,594	37,340	...	-17,896	-17,896	-17,896
'09	...	...	...	100.0	9,394	...	...	...	100.0	2,327	214	1,275	...	-1,564	-1,564	-1,564

Rating History: NR-1, 06/10/10; NR-1, 06/12/09; NR-1, 06/12/08; NR-1, 06/08/07; NR-1, 06/07/06

DIRECT DENTAL SERVICE PLAN INC[2]
Earl L. Newton, D.D.S.
President
1320 S. Green Bay Road
Racine, WI 53406
WI : 1987 : Other : Broker
Dental
262-637-9371
AMB# 064798 NAIC# 54100

Rating: **NR-5**

Data Year	Bonds (%)	Mort. Loans & R.E. (%)	Com & Pref. Stock (%)	All Other Assets (%)	Total Assets ($000)	Life Reserves (%)	Health Reserves (%)	Ann Res. & Dep. Liabilities (%)	All Other Liabilities (%)	Capital & Surplus ($000)	Direct Premiums Written ($000)	Net Premiums Written & Deposits ($000)	Operating Cash Flow ($000)	NOG Before Taxes ($000)	NOG After Taxes ($000)	Net Income ($000)
'05	...	...	...	100.0	2	...	...	...	100.0	2	2,820	2,820	-1	...	...	...
'06	...	...	...	100.0	2	...	...	...	100.0	2	2,839	2,839	0	...	...	...
'07	...	...	...	100.0	42	...	...	...	100.0	2	2,902	2,902	1	...	...	...
'08	...	...	...	100.0	2	...	...	...	100.0	2	3,013	3,013	0	...	...	...
'09	...	...	...	100.0	2	...	...	...	100.0	2	3,182	3,182	...	...	...	...

Rating History: NR-5, 05/19/10; NR-5, 07/20/09; NR-5, 05/19/08; NR-5, 06/21/07; NR-5, 07/12/06

Data in U.S. Dollars

	Profitability Tests							Leverage Tests						Liquidity Tests					
Un-Realized Capital Gains ($000)	Benefits Paid to NPW & Dep (%)	Comm. & Expenses to NPW & Dep (%)	NOG to Total Assets (%)	NOG to Total Rev (%)	Operating Return on Equity (%)	Net Yield (%)	Total Return (%)	Change in NPW & Dep (%)	NPW & Dep to Capital (X)	Capital & Surplus to Liabilities (%)	Surplus Relief (%)	Reins Leverage (%)	Change in Capital (%)	Quick Liquidity (%)	Current Liquidity (%)	Non-Invest Grade Bonds to Capital (%)	Delinq. & Foreclosed Mortgages to Capital (%)	Mort. & Credit Tenant Loans & R.E. to Capital (%)	Affiliated Invest to Capital (%)
...	60.2	33.7	3.5	4.5	5.0	0.13	0.13	-17.2	1.1	188.9	...	...	-0.8	332.4	332.4	...	...	...	...
...	58.2	29.2	8.0	8.9	11.3	0.77	0.77	19.5	1.2	328.4	...	...	13.8	485.5	485.5	...	...	...	...
...	59.9	27.7	10.1	8.6	12.8	1.30	1.30	8.7	1.7	511.7	...	...	-25.4	713.7	713.7	...	...	...	...
...	63.7	13.0	22.3	15.4	27.3	0.71	0.71	19.4	1.6	412.7	...	...	32.2	463.0	463.0	...	...	...	...
...	60.9	14.4	23.1	15.8	27.5	0.06	0.06	31.5	1.5	669.9	...	...	34.1	753.5	753.5	...	...	...	...
	Principal Lines of Business: Dental (100.0%)													Principal States: VA (100.0%)					
...	83.5	15.0	8.8	1.8	16.4	2.09	2.09	0.4	8.0	157.5	...	...	37.3	228.6	228.6	...	...	...	...
...	83.8	15.0	7.9	1.8	13.5	3.26	3.26	0.1	7.3	131.9	...	...	9.2	197.0	197.0	...	...	...	...
...	83.7	15.0	7.7	1.9	13.0	3.12	3.12	0.9	6.5	160.3	...	...	13.7	227.7	227.7	...	...	...	...
...	84.1	15.0	4.3	1.1	6.6	1.37	1.37	-9.9	5.9	232.7	...	...	-1.6	302.6	302.6	...	...	...	...
...	85.3	15.0	-1.0	-0.2	-1.4	1.04	1.04	-4.1	5.8	256.5	...	...	-1.5	332.8	332.8	...	...	...	...
	Principal Lines of Business: Dental (100.0%)													Principal States: NY (100.0%)					
...	0.6	131.0	0.9	4.4	1.7	2.61	2.61	108.5	0.4	57.9	...	110.8	1.7	19.3	40.0	...	...	...	...
...	15.1	65.5	1.7	2.5	4.0	2.08	2.08	455.1	1.3	90.3	...	127.0	52.7	40.1	97.9	...	...	...	...
-6	4.2	85.5	0.8	1.2	1.8	2.12	2.09	-3.5	1.8	87.2	...	185.0	-29.5	97.1	128.5	...	...	...	...
-5,295	6.6	94.2	0.3	0.4	0.5	2.07	-22.21	7.6	0.9	154.0	...	77.8	110.3	126.2	137.9	...	...	...	11.4
-3,120	5.4	94.8	0.7	0.8	1.1	0.37	-13.84	36.6	1.5	154.3	...	67.7	-14.6	158.8	166.5	...	...	...	18.5
	Principal Lines of Business: Dental (100.0%)													Principal States: CA (25.4%), WA (10.2%), NJ (7.8%), VA (5.7%), AZ (4.8%)					
...	...	...	0.0	-1.6	0.0	0.79	0.79	...	...	999.9	...	...	52.6	999.9	999.9	...	...	...	...
...	7.1	145.5	-0.1	-5.3	-0.1	0.82	0.82	...	0.0	999.9	...	...	-0.1	999.9	999.9	...	...	...	...
...	2.4	122.9	-0.1	-1.7	-0.1	0.81	0.81	-10.9	0.0	999.9	...	...	-0.1	999.9	999.9	...	...	...	...
...	2.2	107.4	0.0	-0.2	0.0	0.76	0.76	134.0	0.1	999.9	...	6.6	0.0	999.9	999.9	...	...	...	...
...	2.1	104.2	0.2	1.8	0.2	1.03	1.03	49.3	0.1	999.9	...	5.8	0.2	999.9	999.9	...	...	...	...
	Principal Lines of Business: Dental (100.0%)													Principal States: MA (55.2%), NH (32.2%), VT (12.6%)					
...	55.8	33.0	31.6	7.8	44.3	2.87	2.87	1.9	5.8	236.6	...	...	-4.7	406.9	427.8	...	...	...	...
...	57.6	31.9	31.9	7.8	44.0	5.94	5.94	2.1	5.3	292.4	...	...	11.6	379.5	379.5	...	...	...	...
...	56.6	75.7	-99.9	-32.7	-99.9	3.53	3.53	5.7	4.3	198.2	...	...	29.2	446.9	446.9	...	...	...	...
...	54.1	29.5	34.1	14.3	47.3	1.32	1.32	-6.6	2.8	322.9	...	...	45.5	679.8	688.8	...	...	...	...
...	60.6	22.6	32.6	12.6	56.2	0.27	0.27	55.5	4.6	85.9	...	...	-6.4	299.6	299.6	...	...	...	...
	Principal Lines of Business: Dental (87.7%), FEHBP (12.3%)													Principal States: TX (100.0%)					
0	94.2	9.3	-13.6	-2.9	-32.3	3.14	3.41	16.3	10.3	70.8	...	...	16.1	15.5	15.5	...	...	...	...
74	88.7	9.4	9.3	2.0	25.7	3.12	6.09	47.3	10.9	50.0	...	5.3	38.1	226.6	226.6	...	...	...	...
-74	87.8	8.7	19.4	4.8	48.9	3.85	5.31	24.8	8.0	81.1	...	7.5	70.5	56.8	56.8	...	...	...	...
...	87.6	8.0	19.3	5.2	43.1	4.27	4.29	30.1	6.7	81.5	...	3.2	56.1	192.6	193.5	...	...	...	...
...	84.8	7.9	22.6	6.6	44.9	2.21	2.23	15.9	6.2	126.3	...	2.5	25.2	219.8	219.8	...	...	...	...
	Principal Lines of Business: CompHosp/Med (60.2%), Medicare (39.8%)													Principal States: CO (100.0%)					
...	89.3	29.7	0.8	1.7	6.3	...	...	-2.3	2.8	16.8	...	...	6.6	...	...	...	...	...	...
...	88.0	28.1	0.8	1.6	5.8	...	...	4.2	2.5	18.4	...	...	15.5	...	...	...	...	...	...
...	85.8	32.6	2.3	4.9	15.6	...	...	4.7	2.4	19.4	...	...	9.4	...	...	...	...	...	...
...	98.9	14.7	-1.3	-2.5	-9.9	...	...	7.0	4.6	10.8	...	...	-43.8	...	...	...	...	...	...
-4	93.0	21.2	3.9	7.1	30.9	...	...	4.5	3.0	18.2	...	...	62.7	...	...	...	...	...	...
	Principal Lines of Business: GrpA&H (94.2%), GrpLife (3.6%), GrpAnn (2.3%)																		
...	93.3	26.1	-34.0	-19.2	-76.2	...	...	18.7	4.0	68.9	7.5	...	-5.9	...	...	...	...	...	...
...	86.2	22.5	-14.3	-8.3	-36.0	...	...	-1.1	4.6	62.1	6.8	...	-14.2	...	...	...	...	...	...
...	86.1	25.4	-13.4	-10.8	-34.7	...	...	-38.3	3.5	64.7	6.1	...	-17.2	...	...	...	...	...	...
...	107.4	30.7	-71.1	-48.7	-99.9	...	...	-0.5	24.0	7.4	15.4	...	-85.7	...	...	...	...	...	...
...	324.4	28.6	-9.8	-99.9	-80.8	...	...	-96.6	0.5	32.9	...	...	49.6	...	...	...	...	...	...
	Principal Lines of Business: GrpA&H (87.3%), IndA&H (12.7%)																		
...	88.0	12.0	...	...	...	...	...	-0.3	999.9	...	...	...	...	...	...	...	...	...	...
...	88.0	12.0	...	...	...	...	...	0.7	999.9	...	...	...	...	...	...	...	...	...	...
...	88.0	12.0	...	...	...	...	...	2.2	999.9	6.0	...	...	...	6.0	6.0	...	...	...	...
...	88.0	12.0	...	...	...	...	...	3.8	999.9	...	...	...	...	...	...	...	...	...	...
...	88.0	12.0	...	...	...	...	...	5.6	999.9	...	...	...	...	...	...	...	...	...	...
	Principal Lines of Business: Dental (100.0%)													Principal States: WI (100.0%)					

Data in U.S. Dollars

Column key: COMPANY NAME / Ultimate Parent Association / Principal Officer / Mailing Address / Dom. : Began Bus. : Struct. : Mktg. / Specialty / Phone # / AMB# / NAIC# — Best's Financial Strength Rating / FSC — Balance Sheet — Operations

---

DIRECT GENERAL LIFE INSURANCE
Elara Holdings, Inc.
Dan Tarantin
CEO
1281 Murfreesboro Road
Nashville, TN 37217
SC : 1982 : Stock : Not Available
Term Life
615-399-4700
AMB# 009373 NAIC# 97705

Best's Financial Strength Rating: **B** — Rating Outlook: Stable — **FSC V**

Data Year	Bonds (%)	Mort. Loans & R.E. (%)	Com & Pref. Stock (%)	All Other Assets (%)	Total Assets ($000)	Life Reserves (%)	Health Reserves (%)	Ann Res. & Dep. Liabilities (%)	All Other Liabilities (%)	Capital & Surplus ($000)	Direct Premiums Written ($000)	Net Premiums Written & Deposits ($000)	Operating Cash Flow ($000)	NOG Before Taxes ($000)	NOG After Taxes ($000)	Net Income ($000)
'05	66.8	...	...	33.2	11,234	89.4	...	...	10.6	7,079	6,757	6,757	4,135	1,737	976	976
'06	53.6	...	...	46.4	19,948	92.7	...	...	7.3	10,022	16,887	16,887	7,444	4,727	2,700	2,700
'07	38.8	...	...	61.2	26,949	94.5	...	...	5.5	15,501	19,964	19,964	6,471	9,079	5,657	5,657
'08	62.4	...	0.1	37.5	35,468	92.3	...	...	7.7	22,009	23,345	23,345	8,294	10,059	6,404	6,404
'09	50.6	...	...	49.4	29,433	89.7	...	...	10.3	17,065	21,386	21,386	-7,255	10,269	6,566	6,555

Rating History: B, 12/15/09; B, 10/21/08; B g, 09/14/07; B g, 03/06/07; NR-5, 05/11/06

DIRECT LIFE INSURANCE COMPANY
Elara Holdings, Inc.
Dan Tarantin
CEO
1281 Murfreesboro Road
Nashville, TN 37217-2432
GA : 1969 : Stock : Direct Response
Term Life
615-399-4700
AMB# 007430 NAIC# 71919

Best's Financial Strength Rating: **NR-3**

Data Year	Bonds (%)	Mort. Loans & R.E. (%)	Com & Pref. Stock (%)	All Other Assets (%)	Total Assets ($000)	Life Reserves (%)	Health Reserves (%)	Ann Res. & Dep. Liabilities (%)	All Other Liabilities (%)	Capital & Surplus ($000)	Direct Premiums Written ($000)	Net Premiums Written & Deposits ($000)	Operating Cash Flow ($000)	NOG Before Taxes ($000)	NOG After Taxes ($000)	Net Income ($000)
'05	87.4	...	...	12.6	23,241	83.4	...	...	16.6	15,628	13,107	13,107	-1,574	9,623	6,176	6,176
'06	83.8	...	...	16.2	16,187	88.1	...	...	11.9	13,433	5,795	5,795	-5,019	6,695	4,452	4,452
'07	82.5	...	...	17.5	11,676	90.8	...	...	9.2	10,883	1,812	1,812	-4,332	2,707	2,085	2,085
'08	90.3	...	0.2	9.5	9,704	73.7	...	...	26.3	9,552	350	350	-1,637	952	808	808
'09	83.9	...	...	16.1	3,640	...	...	...	100.0	3,491	-2	-2	-6,010	159	310	137

Rating History: NR-3, 12/15/09; B, 10/21/08; B g, 09/14/07; B g, 03/06/07; NR-5, 05/17/06

DIRECTORS LIFE ASSUR CO[1]
Aegis Insurance Holdings Company LP
Linda M. Sargent
Chairman, President & Treasurer
P.O. Box 20428
Oklahoma City, OK 73156
OK : 1965 : Stock : Agency
Ann, Pre-need
405-842-1234
AMB# 007616 NAIC# 73660

Best's Financial Strength Rating: **NR-1**

Data Year	Bonds (%)	Mort. Loans & R.E. (%)	Com & Pref. Stock (%)	All Other Assets (%)	Total Assets ($000)	Life Reserves (%)	Health Reserves (%)	Ann Res. & Dep. Liabilities (%)	All Other Liabilities (%)	Capital & Surplus ($000)	Direct Premiums Written ($000)	Net Premiums Written & Deposits ($000)	Operating Cash Flow ($000)	NOG Before Taxes ($000)	NOG After Taxes ($000)	Net Income ($000)
'05	90.1	...	...	9.9	22,323	...	...	...	100.0	2,117	3,999	3,509	...	254	254	258
'06	89.7	...	...	10.3	23,035	...	...	...	100.0	2,237	3,893	3,458	...	236	236	236
'07	89.1	...	...	10.9	23,708	...	...	...	100.0	2,433	3,849	3,462	...	309	289	290
'08	90.5	...	...	9.5	22,992	...	...	...	100.0	1,690	3,770	3,429	...	190	152	152
'09	88.7	...	...	11.3	24,118	...	...	...	100.0	1,854	4,278	3,996	...	27	-6	6

Rating History: NR-1, 06/10/10; NR-5, 04/20/09; NR-5, 04/23/08; NR-5, 05/14/07; NR-5, 05/11/06

DIXIE LIFE INS CO INC[1]
Dennis M. Necaise
President & Treasurer
617 Avenue F
Bogalusa, LA 70427
LA : 1934 : Stock : Not Available
985-735-1710
AMB# 007623 NAIC# 73733

Best's Financial Strength Rating: **NR-1**

Data Year	Bonds (%)	Mort. Loans & R.E. (%)	Com & Pref. Stock (%)	All Other Assets (%)	Total Assets ($000)	Life Reserves (%)	Health Reserves (%)	Ann Res. & Dep. Liabilities (%)	All Other Liabilities (%)	Capital & Surplus ($000)	Direct Premiums Written ($000)	Net Premiums Written & Deposits ($000)	Operating Cash Flow ($000)	NOG Before Taxes ($000)	NOG After Taxes ($000)	Net Income ($000)
'05	40.8	38.4	9.6	11.1	15,270	...	...	...	100.0	856	1,657	1,579	...	-338	-338	-374
'06	47.2	37.9	10.5	4.4	15,748	...	...	...	100.0	1,150	1,646	1,566	...	89	89	91
'07	50.3	35.3	11.4	3.0	16,002	...	...	...	100.0	1,211	1,617	1,525	...	132	130	130
'08	53.0	37.5	6.3	3.1	14,370	...	...	...	100.0	-453	1,558	1,467	...	132	111	-311
'09	52.8	37.0	3.9	6.4	14,179	...	...	...	100.0	-721	1,420	1,343	...	398	359	-17

Rating History: NR-1, 06/10/10; NR-1, 06/12/09; NR-1, 06/12/08; NR-1, 06/08/07; NR-1, 06/07/06

DOCTORS LIFE INSURANCE CO
Doctors Company An Interinsurance Exch
Richard Anderson, M.D.
Chairman, President & CEO
P.O. Box 2900
Napa, CA 94558
CA : 1980 : Stock : Inactive
Ind Ann, Univ Life
707-226-0100
AMB# 009026 NAIC# 92444

Best's Financial Strength Rating: **NR-5**

Data Year	Bonds (%)	Mort. Loans & R.E. (%)	Com & Pref. Stock (%)	All Other Assets (%)	Total Assets ($000)	Life Reserves (%)	Health Reserves (%)	Ann Res. & Dep. Liabilities (%)	All Other Liabilities (%)	Capital & Surplus ($000)	Direct Premiums Written ($000)	Net Premiums Written & Deposits ($000)	Operating Cash Flow ($000)	NOG Before Taxes ($000)	NOG After Taxes ($000)	Net Income ($000)
'05	32.0	...	...	68.0	27,085	0.6	...	86.0	13.4	17,313	118	180	179	142	177	157
'06	94.5	...	...	5.5	27,971	0.5	...	82.8	16.6	17,654	103	187	347	619	362	348
'07	90.7	...	...	9.3	29,535	0.4	...	68.4	31.2	16,734	102	203	1,278	692	387	540
'08	76.4	...	...	23.6	35,315	0.3	...	42.1	57.6	15,991	82	49	-891	553	178	255
'09	95.8	...	...	4.2	26,737	0.4	...	59.1	40.5	13,534	92	53	-2,450	397	327	316

Rating History: NR-5, 05/12/10; NR-4, 01/17/08; B+, 01/17/08; B+, 01/22/07; B+, 04/20/06

DORSEY LIFE INSURANCE COMPANY[1]
Robert D. Dorsey, Sr.
President
P.O. Box 431
Marlin, TX 76661-0431
TX : 1979 : Stock : Not Available
254-803-2586
AMB# 068191 NAIC# 87661

Best's Financial Strength Rating: **NR-1**

Data Year	Bonds (%)	Mort. Loans & R.E. (%)	Com & Pref. Stock (%)	All Other Assets (%)	Total Assets ($000)	Life Reserves (%)	Health Reserves (%)	Ann Res. & Dep. Liabilities (%)	All Other Liabilities (%)	Capital & Surplus ($000)	Direct Premiums Written ($000)	Net Premiums Written & Deposits ($000)	Operating Cash Flow ($000)	NOG Before Taxes ($000)	NOG After Taxes ($000)	Net Income ($000)
'05	...	...	...	100.0	470	...	...	...	100.0	153	29	29	...	-4	-4	-4
'06	...	...	...	100.0	460	...	...	...	100.0	140	28	28	...	-13	-13	-13
'07	...	...	...	100.0	462	...	...	...	100.0	149	26	26	...	9	9	9
'08	...	...	...	100.0	452	...	...	...	100.0	136	27	27	...	-13	-13	-13
'09	...	...	...	100.0	444	...	...	...	100.0	122	26	26	...	-13	-13	-13

Rating History: NR-1, 06/10/10; NR-1, 06/12/09; NR-1, 06/12/08; NR-1, 06/08/07; NR-1, 06/07/06

DRISCOLL CHILDREN'S HEALTH PLN[2]
Mary D. Peterson, M.D.
President & CEO
615 North Upper Broadway, Suite 1621
Corpus Christi, TX 78477
TX : 1997 : Non-Profit : Not Available
Group A&H
361-694-6780
AMB# 064519 NAIC# 95809

Best's Financial Strength Rating: **NR-5**

Data Year	Bonds (%)	Mort. Loans & R.E. (%)	Com & Pref. Stock (%)	All Other Assets (%)	Total Assets ($000)	Life Reserves (%)	Health Reserves (%)	Ann Res. & Dep. Liabilities (%)	All Other Liabilities (%)	Capital & Surplus ($000)	Direct Premiums Written ($000)	Net Premiums Written & Deposits ($000)	Operating Cash Flow ($000)	NOG Before Taxes ($000)	NOG After Taxes ($000)	Net Income ($000)
'05	27.7	...	...	72.3	6,141	...	26.8	...	73.2	4,680	10,532	10,472	-330	-463	-483	-465
'06	12.6	...	...	87.4	13,530	...	76.4	...	23.6	1,057	33,652	33,357	4,357	-6,780	-6,780	-6,780
'07	5.7	...	...	94.3	29,875	...	68.7	...	31.3	10,452	96,275	95,608	16,824	-8,759	-8,759	-8,759
'08	...	...	...	100.0	31,285	...	63.1	...	36.9	13,156	115,826	115,128	1,784	14,291	14,291	14,348
'09	...	...	...	100.0	28,888	...	84.5	...	15.5	12,703	134,971	134,008	-2,170	-353	-361	-275

Rating History: NR-5, 04/07/10; NR-5, 08/26/09; C- pd, 07/01/08; C- pd, 06/19/07; C++pd, 07/17/06

EAGLE LIFE INSURANCE COMPANY
American Equity Investment Life Hldg Co
David J. Noble
President
P.O. Box 71216
Des Moines, IA 50325
IA : 2008 : Stock : Agency
Ind Ann, Term Life, Trad Life
515-221-0002
AMB# 060690 NAIC# 13183

Best's Financial Strength Rating: **NR-2**

Data Year	Bonds (%)	Mort. Loans & R.E. (%)	Com & Pref. Stock (%)	All Other Assets (%)	Total Assets ($000)	Life Reserves (%)	Health Reserves (%)	Ann Res. & Dep. Liabilities (%)	All Other Liabilities (%)	Capital & Surplus ($000)	Direct Premiums Written ($000)	Net Premiums Written & Deposits ($000)	Operating Cash Flow ($000)	NOG Before Taxes ($000)	NOG After Taxes ($000)	Net Income ($000)
'05	...	...	...	...	...	...	...	...	...	...	...	...	...	...	...	...
'06	...	...	...	...	...	...	...	...	...	...	...	...	...	...	...	...
'07	...	...	...	...	...	...	...	...	...	...	...	...	...	...	...	...
'08	82.7	...	...	17.3	6,030	...	...	...	100.0	5,976	...	...	5,933	-36	-23	-23
'09	16.3	...	...	83.7	32,759	...	...	97.5	2.5	5,895	...	27,722	26,280	11	-373	-373

Rating History: NR-2, 12/18/09; NR-2, 04/10/09

EASTERN LIFE AND HEALTH INS CO
Eastern Insurance Holdings, Inc.
Michael L. Boguski
President & COO
P.O. Box 83149
Lancaster, PA 17608-3149
PA : 1911 : Stock : Broker
Disability, Life, Dental
717-391-5767
AMB# 006325 NAIC# 62804

Best's Financial Strength Rating: **A- u** — Under Review Implication: Negative — **FSC VI**

Data Year	Bonds (%)	Mort. Loans & R.E. (%)	Com & Pref. Stock (%)	All Other Assets (%)	Total Assets ($000)	Life Reserves (%)	Health Reserves (%)	Ann Res. & Dep. Liabilities (%)	All Other Liabilities (%)	Capital & Surplus ($000)	Direct Premiums Written ($000)	Net Premiums Written & Deposits ($000)	Operating Cash Flow ($000)	NOG Before Taxes ($000)	NOG After Taxes ($000)	Net Income ($000)
'05	87.4	0.1	0.3	12.2	83,453	23.2	53.7	...	23.1	57,003	40,997	38,702	-10,637	951	882	-9,500
'06	86.5	0.0	3.6	9.9	85,698	21.0	49.2	...	29.8	60,244	35,928	33,451	2,648	3,114	2,231	2,955
'07	88.1	0.0	3.2	8.7	85,667	16.8	47.0	...	36.2	60,679	38,516	35,863	-309	5,346	4,258	4,581
'08	89.5	0.0	4.1	6.3	58,541	18.0	50.9	...	31.1	37,817	39,210	36,723	-24,401	3,892	1,699	-710
'09	55.8	0.0	3.7	40.5	48,709	18.5	51.6	...	29.9	28,676	38,736	35,937	-12,044	1,178	2,239	2,122

Rating History: A- u, 05/04/10; A-, 05/14/09; A-, 04/18/08; A-, 06/18/07; B++, 06/21/06

2010 BEST'S KEY RATING GUIDE — LIFE/HEALTH EDITION
BEST'S PROFITABILITY, LEVERAGE AND LIQUIDITY TESTS 2005 – 2009

Data in U.S. Dollars

	Profitability Tests							Leverage Tests						Liquidity Tests					
Un-Realized Capital Gains ($000)	Benefits Paid to NPW & Dep (%)	Comm. & Expenses to NPW & Dep (%)	NOG to Total Assets (%)	NOG to Total Rev (%)	Operating Return on Equity (%)	Net Yield (%)	Total Return (%)	Change in NPW & Dep (%)	NPW & Dep to Capital (X)	Capital & Surplus to Liabilities (%)	Surplus Relief (%)	Reins Leverage (%)	Change in Capital (%)	Quick Liquidity (%)	Current Liquidity (%)	Non-Invest Grade Bonds to Capital (%)	Delinq. & Foreclosed Mortgages to Capital (%)	Mort. & Credit Tenant Loans & R.E. to Capital (%)	Affiliated Invest to Capital (%)
...	4.3	26.6	11.0	13.9	15.0	2.67	2.95	999.9	1.0	170.5	...	...	19.1	232.7	238.1	...	...	...	...
...	8.0	37.4	17.3	15.5	31.6	3.48	3.54	149.9	1.7	101.0	...	...	41.6	166.6	169.2	...	...	...	...
...	11.9	40.3	24.1	27.2	44.3	3.98	4.02	18.2	1.3	135.5	...	...	54.7	201.3	203.2	...	...	...	...
-7	14.7	39.8	20.5	26.6	34.1	2.56	2.63	16.9	1.1	163.5	...	...	42.0	229.0	232.3	...	...	0.1	...
-14	15.2	45.7	20.2	29.8	33.6	1.97	2.17	-8.4	1.3	138.0	...	...	-22.5	195.2	201.1	...	...	0.1	...
Principal Lines of Business: OrdLife (100.0%)														Principal States: FL (32.7%), TN (18.4%), GA (8.9%), MS (7.5%), LA (6.8%)					
...	12.0	41.1	25.9	44.4	41.1	3.60	3.64	-26.5	0.8	206.8	...	...	8.6	216.0	239.3	...	...	...	...
...	20.5	42.6	22.6	66.8	30.6	4.93	4.86	-55.8	0.4	496.5	...	...	-14.0	467.9	506.3	...	...	...	...
...	24.9	41.2	15.0	87.5	17.1	4.67	4.42	-68.7	0.2	999.9	...	...	-19.0	999.9	999.9	...	...	...	...
-3	28.6	45.2	7.6	115.1	7.9	3.66	3.44	-80.7	0.0	999.9	...	...	-12.4	999.9	999.9	...	...	0.3	...
3	-99.9	-99.9	4.7	174.4	4.8	2.90	0.21	-99.9	0.0	999.9	...	...	-63.5	999.9	999.9	...	...	...	...
Principal Lines of Business: OrdLife (100.0%)																			
...	81.7	34.5	1.2	5.4	12.9	...	...	-2.9	1.6	11.2	5.0	...	15.9	...	...	...	...	...	...
...	74.2	35.4	1.0	5.0	10.9	...	...	-1.5	1.4	11.7	4.4	...	7.6	...	...	...	...	...	...
...	73.7	35.9	1.2	6.1	12.4	...	...	0.1	1.3	12.6	3.7	...	9.6	...	...	...	...	...	...
-1,153	82.0	37.8	0.7	3.2	7.4	...	...	-1.0	2.0	7.9	4.9	...	-36.2	...	...	...	...	...	...
262	67.8	35.0	0.0	-0.1	-0.3	...	...	16.5	2.2	8.3	4.1	...	9.7	...	...	...	...	...	...
Principal Lines of Business: OrdLife (83.8%), IndAnn (16.2%)																			
-136	58.1	96.6	-2.2	-14.3	-31.6	...	...	7.3	1.5	7.3	...	...	-33.3	...	...	...	...	562.6	...
187	59.0	71.9	0.6	3.7	8.9	...	...	-0.9	1.2	9.3	...	...	28.0	...	...	...	...	446.9	...
168	68.2	71.0	0.8	5.4	11.0	...	...	-2.6	1.1	9.9	...	...	7.8	...	...	...	...	392.1	...
-1,573	75.0	73.1	0.7	4.6	29.4	...	...	-3.8	-4.0	-2.5	...	...	-99.9	...	...	...	...	-99.9	...
-326	61.3	59.7	2.5	16.5	-61.1	...	...	-8.4	-2.1	-4.4	...	...	-77.7	...	...	...	...	-99.9	...
Principal Lines of Business: OrdLife (97.3%), IndLife (2.7%)																			
...	433.7	40.9	0.7	16.3	1.0	3.27	3.75	2.3	0.0	177.8	...	0.3	0.9	449.4	456.4	...	...	...	...
-2	364.4	35.6	1.3	24.0	2.1	4.94	5.34	4.4	0.0	171.8	...	0.3	2.0	227.0	234.7	...	...	...	...
2	306.6	38.4	1.3	24.2	2.2	5.19	6.08	8.2	0.0	131.6	...	0.3	-5.1	182.1	193.6	...	...	...	...
...	999.9	109.6	0.5	12.3	1.1	4.64	5.23	-75.8	0.0	83.2	...	0.3	-4.4	123.3	130.4	0.1	...	...	...
...	999.9	352.6	1.1	23.7	2.2	4.48	4.85	8.1	0.0	103.1	...	0.4	-15.4	170.0	179.5	...	...	...	...
Principal Lines of Business: OrdLife (86.8%), IndAnn (13.2%)														Principal States: CA (89.7%), NV (10.3%)					
...	85.4	65.6	-0.9	-11.0	-2.7	...	...	-3.9	0.2	48.1	...	...	-2.6	...	...	...	...	...	...
...	94.1	80.5	-2.7	-33.5	-8.7	...	...	-4.4	0.2	43.8	...	...	-8.4	...	...	...	...	...	...
...	76.9	94.8	1.9	19.0	6.1	...	...	-7.3	0.2	47.5	...	...	6.2	...	...	...	...	...	...
...	62.5	131.8	-2.9	-30.8	-9.3	...	...	4.1	0.2	42.9	...	...	-8.9	...	...	...	...	...	...
...	81.5	96.5	-2.9	-33.5	-10.3	...	...	-4.1	0.2	38.0	...	...	-9.8	...	...	...	...	...	...
Principal Lines of Business: OrdLife (100.0%)																			
...	70.9	35.1	-7.6	-4.7	-10.1	2.52	2.80	-14.7	2.2	320.2	...	...	-4.3	402.8	402.8	...	...	...	...
...	102.2	19.2	-68.9	-20.3	-99.9	3.59	3.59	218.5	31.6	8.5	...	...	-77.4	83.5	83.5	...	...	...	...
...	98.4	11.5	-40.4	-9.1	-99.9	3.59	3.59	186.6	9.1	53.8	...	7.9	888.6	140.2	140.2	...	...	...	...
59	77.6	10.7	46.7	12.3	121.1	2.97	3.38	20.4	8.8	72.6	...	5.8	25.9	160.2	160.2	...	...	...	...
-179	89.8	10.6	-1.2	-0.3	-2.8	0.92	0.58	16.4	10.5	78.5	...	4.4	-3.4	190.9	190.9	...	...	...	...
Principal Lines of Business: Medicaid (89.9%), OtherHlth (10.1%)														Principal States: TX (100.0%)					
...	...	...	...	...	...	...	...	...	...	...	...	...	...	...	...	...	...	...	...
...	...	...	...	...	...	...	...	...	...	...	...	...	...	...	...	...	...	...	...
...	...	...	...	...	...	...	...	...	...	...	...	...	...	...	...	...	...	...	...
...	...	...	...	-26.6	...	...	...	...	...	999.9	...	...	...	999.9	999.9	...	...	...	...
...	0.1	7.3	-1.9	-1.3	-6.3	2.81	2.81	...	4.7	22.0	...	3.0	-1.0	204.2	213.9	...	...	...	...
Principal Lines of Business: IndAnn (100.0%)																			
7,025	68.3	38.1	1.1	2.1	1.6	4.49	1.86	-0.9	0.7	224.7	...	42.9	0.1	261.0	294.8	4.2	...	0.1	-0.1
86	66.9	40.5	2.6	6.0	3.8	4.32	5.64	-13.6	0.5	258.9	...	34.3	7.0	269.5	306.4	2.5	...	0.1	...
-13	68.7	30.5	5.0	10.8	7.0	3.94	4.76	7.2	0.6	260.1	...	31.5	0.1	282.8	317.3	3.8	...	0.0	...
-629	70.8	30.6	2.4	4.3	3.5	3.67	-0.02	2.4	1.0	193.6	...	48.0	-37.6	219.2	249.2	5.6	...	0.0	...
488	71.6	32.5	4.2	5.9	6.7	3.06	4.31	-2.1	1.2	151.2	...	56.2	-24.0	265.7	285.9	10.2	...	0.0	...
Principal Lines of Business: GrpA&H (84.3%), GrpLife (15.7%)														Principal States: PA (36.6%), NC (29.4%), SC (7.3%), MD (7.3%), DE (4.9%)					

Data in U.S. Dollars

COMPANY NAME / Ultimate Parent Association / Principal Officer / Mailing Address / Dom. : Began Bus. : Struct. : Mkt. / Specialty / Phone # / AMB# NAIC#

Best's Financial Strength Rating / FSC

Balance Sheet: Data Year; Bonds (%); Mort. Loans & R.E. (%); Com & Pref. Stock (%); All Other Assets (%); Total Assets ($000); Life Reserves (%); Health Reserves %); Ann Res. & Dep. Liabilities (%); All Other Liabilities (%); Capital & Surplus ($000)

Operations: Direct Premiums Written ($000); Net Premiums Written & Deposits ($000); Operating Cash Flow ($000); NOG Before Taxes ($000); NOG After Taxes ($000); Net Income ($000)

EASTERN VISION SERVICE PLAN
Vision Service Plan
James Robinson Lynch
President & CEO
3333 Quality Drive
Rancho Cordova, CA 95670
NY : 1987 : Other : Agency
Group A&H
916-851-5000
AMB# 064483 NAIC# 47029

A — Rating Outlook: Stable — FSC IX

Data Year	Bonds (%)	Mort. Loans & R.E. (%)	Com & Pref. Stock (%)	All Other Assets (%)	Total Assets ($000)	Life Reserves (%)	Health Reserves %)	Ann Res. & Dep. Liabilities (%)	All Other Liabilities (%)	Capital & Surplus ($000)	Direct Premiums Written ($000)	Net Premiums Written & Deposits ($000)	Operating Cash Flow ($000)	NOG Before Taxes ($000)	NOG After Taxes ($000)	Net Income ($000)
'05	17.1	...	6.5	76.4	23,458	...	57.8	...	42.2	18,722	34,672	34,672	2,240	6,867	4,675	4,652
'06	18.1	...	5.1	76.8	33,745	...	78.5	...	21.5	4,130	29,740	29,740	9,848	-15,727	-17,196	-17,189
'07	14.6	...	11.3	74.1	32,418	...	81.5	...	18.5	17,350	70,092	70,092	-927	14,889	13,639	13,806
'08	28.0	...	6.4	65.6	31,588	...	91.1	...	8.9	17,631	79,643	79,643	-4,987	887	790	667
'09	26.9	...	8.1	65.0	32,361	...	80.2	...	19.8	21,053	76,322	76,322	4,141	3,520	3,842	3,510

Rating History: A g, 02/09/10; A g, 11/24/08; A g, 11/30/07; A g, 10/12/06; A g, 11/10/05

EASY CHOICE HEALTH PLAN
Eric E. Spencer
President
20411 S.W. Birch Street, Suite 200
Newport Beach, CA 92660
CA : 2006 : Stock : Not Available
Medicare
866-999-3945
AMB# 064930

NR-5

Data Year	Bonds (%)	Mort. Loans & R.E. (%)	Com & Pref. Stock (%)	All Other Assets (%)	Total Assets ($000)	Life Reserves (%)	Health Reserves %)	Ann Res. & Dep. Liabilities (%)	All Other Liabilities (%)	Capital & Surplus ($000)	Direct Premiums Written ($000)	Net Premiums Written & Deposits ($000)	Operating Cash Flow ($000)	NOG Before Taxes ($000)	NOG After Taxes ($000)	Net Income ($000)
'05	...	...	...	...	...	...	...	...	...	...	...	...	...	...	...	...
'06	...	...	...	...	...	...	...	...	...	...	...	...	...	...	...	...
'07	...	...	...	100.0	1,906	...	...	...	100.0	1,414	...	...	1,399	-848	-848	-848
'08	...	...	...	100.0	3,198	...	...	...	100.0	1,252	10,383	10,383	1,161	-1,826	-1,826	-1,826
'09	...	...	...	100.0	6,487	...	...	...	100.0	1,514	44,105	44,105	2,768	-1,782	-1,783	-1,783

Rating History: NR-5, 04/21/10; NR-5, 05/07/09; NR-5, 05/05/08

EDUCATORS HTH PLANS LF ACC HTH[1]
Educators Mutual Insurance Association
Rolando I. Galano
President
852 East Arrowhead Lane
Murray, UT 84107-5211
UT : 2006 : Stock
801-262-7476
AMB# 060648 NAIC# 12515

NR-1

Data Year	Bonds (%)	Mort. Loans & R.E. (%)	Com & Pref. Stock (%)	All Other Assets (%)	Total Assets ($000)	Life Reserves (%)	Health Reserves %)	Ann Res. & Dep. Liabilities (%)	All Other Liabilities (%)	Capital & Surplus ($000)	Direct Premiums Written ($000)	Net Premiums Written & Deposits ($000)	Operating Cash Flow ($000)	NOG Before Taxes ($000)	NOG After Taxes ($000)	Net Income ($000)
'05	...	...	...	...	...	...	...	...	...	...	...	...	...	...	...	...
'06	54.4	...	5.3	40.3	2,503	...	...	...	100.0	2,199	460	460	...	38	23	23
'07	22.2	...	1.8	76.0	4,295	...	...	...	100.0	2,078	4,035	3,868	...	-109	-109	-109
'08	28.0	...	2.7	69.2	6,444	...	...	...	100.0	2,335	5,659	5,411	...	589	355	355
'09	26.3	...	0.9	72.8	8,986	...	...	...	100.0	3,109	7,553	7,256	...	-93	-39	-39

Rating History: NR-1, 06/10/10; NR-1, 06/12/09; NR-1, 06/12/08; NR-1, 06/08/07

EDUCATORS LIFE INS CO
Horace Mann Educators Corporation
Louis G. Lower, II
Chairman, President & CEO
One Horace Mann Plaza
Springfield, IL 62715
AZ : 1964 : Stock : Inactive
Inactive
217-789-2500
AMB# 007867 NAIC# 75892

NR-3

Data Year	Bonds (%)	Mort. Loans & R.E. (%)	Com & Pref. Stock (%)	All Other Assets (%)	Total Assets ($000)	Life Reserves (%)	Health Reserves %)	Ann Res. & Dep. Liabilities (%)	All Other Liabilities (%)	Capital & Surplus ($000)	Direct Premiums Written ($000)	Net Premiums Written & Deposits ($000)	Operating Cash Flow ($000)	NOG Before Taxes ($000)	NOG After Taxes ($000)	Net Income ($000)
'05	...	...	...	100.0	155	...	...	...	100.0	155	...	...	-2	-2	1	1
'06	...	...	...	100.0	155	...	...	...	100.0	155	...	...	4	-1	-1	-1
'07	...	...	...	100.0	155	...	...	...	100.0	155	...	...	0	0	0	0
'08	...	...	...	100.0	150	...	...	...	100.0	150	...	...	-11	-7	-5	-5
'09	...	...	...	100.0	147	...	...	...	100.0	147	...	...	2	-5	-3	-3

Rating History: NR-3, 06/03/10; NR-3, 06/10/09; NR-3, 05/23/08; NR-3, 05/18/07; NR-3, 04/19/06

EDUCATORS MUTUAL INS ASSOC[1]
Educators Mutual Insurance Association
Rolando I. Galano
President
852 East Arrowhead Lane
Murray, UT 84107-5211
UT : 1935 : Mutual : Agency
801-262-7476
AMB# 009123 NAIC# 81701

NR-1

Data Year	Bonds (%)	Mort. Loans & R.E. (%)	Com & Pref. Stock (%)	All Other Assets (%)	Total Assets ($000)	Life Reserves (%)	Health Reserves %)	Ann Res. & Dep. Liabilities (%)	All Other Liabilities (%)	Capital & Surplus ($000)	Direct Premiums Written ($000)	Net Premiums Written & Deposits ($000)	Operating Cash Flow ($000)	NOG Before Taxes ($000)	NOG After Taxes ($000)	Net Income ($000)
'05	58.9	2.7	13.2	25.1	50,500	...	...	...	100.0	23,996	33,474	42,973	...	4,859	4,777	4,793
'06	60.0	2.4	12.5	25.1	53,977	...	...	...	100.0	28,543	29,348	40,445	...	4,370	4,396	4,919
'07	51.0	2.2	10.7	36.1	61,773	...	...	...	100.0	33,382	28,495	39,607	...	4,815	4,704	4,704
'08	55.2	2.6	12.3	29.9	63,512	...	...	...	100.0	33,966	36,747	47,812	...	3,447	3,399	3,399
'09	44.4	2.3	11.2	42.1	72,567	...	...	...	100.0	36,200	41,527	56,024	...	2,480	2,331	2,331

Rating History: NR-1, 06/10/10; NR-1, 06/12/09; NR-1, 06/12/08; NR-1, 06/08/07; NR-1, 06/07/06

EL PASO FIRST HEALTH PLANS[2]
Carol G. Smallwood
President & CEO
2501 North Mesa Street
El Paso, TX 79902
TX : 2000 : Non-Profit : Not Available
Health
915-298-7198
AMB# 064692 NAIC# 52635

NR-5

Data Year	Bonds (%)	Mort. Loans & R.E. (%)	Com & Pref. Stock (%)	All Other Assets (%)	Total Assets ($000)	Life Reserves (%)	Health Reserves %)	Ann Res. & Dep. Liabilities (%)	All Other Liabilities (%)	Capital & Surplus ($000)	Direct Premiums Written ($000)	Net Premiums Written & Deposits ($000)	Operating Cash Flow ($000)	NOG Before Taxes ($000)	NOG After Taxes ($000)	Net Income ($000)
'05	...	...	...	100.0	3,657	...	...	...	100.0	3,501	71,671	71,671	116	65	65	65
'06	...	...	...	100.0	17,116	...	63.3	...	36.7	3,618	80,540	80,296	7,959	-1,559	-1,559	-1,559
'07	...	...	...	100.0	25,232	...	59.1	...	40.9	9,475	83,979	83,542	12,813	5,258	5,258	5,258
'08	...	...	...	100.0	27,052	...	48.8	...	51.2	15,509	86,994	86,626	2,193	8,535	8,535	8,535
'09	...	...	...	100.0	27,133	...	77.7	...	22.3	16,289	97,489	97,106	-1,025	1,772	1,772	1,772

Rating History: NR-5, 04/07/10; NR-5, 08/26/09; C+ pd, 05/23/08; C pd, 05/30/07; NR-5, 06/05/06

ELDERPLAN INC[2]
Bravo Health Inc
Eli S. Feldman
President & CEO
6323 7th Avenue
Brooklyn, NY 11220
NY : 1985 : Non-Profit : Broker
Health
718-921-7990
AMB# 064286 NAIC# 95662

NR-5

Data Year	Bonds (%)	Mort. Loans & R.E. (%)	Com & Pref. Stock (%)	All Other Assets (%)	Total Assets ($000)	Life Reserves (%)	Health Reserves %)	Ann Res. & Dep. Liabilities (%)	All Other Liabilities (%)	Capital & Surplus ($000)	Direct Premiums Written ($000)	Net Premiums Written & Deposits ($000)	Operating Cash Flow ($000)	NOG Before Taxes ($000)	NOG After Taxes ($000)	Net Income ($000)
'05	33.2	...	11.9	55.0	83,802	...	55.8	...	44.2	39,827	236,689	236,222	21,244	17,561	17,561	17,117
'06	38.2	...	10.0	51.8	108,137	...	60.8	...	39.2	53,002	264,647	264,033	26,075	14,904	14,904	14,716
'07	46.9	...	10.1	43.0	124,174	...	64.5	...	35.5	79,887	266,383	265,759	15,125	24,108	24,108	25,254
'08	56.2	...	5.1	38.7	110,332	...	62.3	...	37.7	55,672	246,356	244,988	-4,443	-19,481	-19,481	-18,903
'09	64.6	...	9.2	26.2	103,449	...	62.3	...	37.7	45,287	234,822	233,549	-8,365	-8,614	-8,614	-7,562

Rating History: NR-5, 04/30/10; NR-5, 08/26/09; B pd, 07/21/08; B- pd, 07/20/07; C++pd, 08/29/06

EMC NATIONAL LIFE COMPANY
Employers Mutual Casualty Company
Bruce G. Kelley
President & CEO
P.O. Box 9202
Des Moines, IA 50306-9202
IA : 1963 : Stock : Agency
Ann, Trad Life, Univ Life
515-237-2000
AMB# 006339 NAIC# 62928

B++ — Rating Outlook: Stable — FSC VII

Data Year	Bonds (%)	Mort. Loans & R.E. (%)	Com & Pref. Stock (%)	All Other Assets (%)	Total Assets ($000)	Life Reserves (%)	Health Reserves %)	Ann Res. & Dep. Liabilities (%)	All Other Liabilities (%)	Capital & Surplus ($000)	Direct Premiums Written ($000)	Net Premiums Written & Deposits ($000)	Operating Cash Flow ($000)	NOG Before Taxes ($000)	NOG After Taxes ($000)	Net Income ($000)
'05	87.6	0.5	0.9	11.1	684,275	23.9	5.3	66.3	4.4	71,659	122,021	104,746	25,014	2,672	3,511	3,336
'06	82.7	2.1	1.1	14.1	679,905	24.0	5.0	66.2	4.8	51,961	165,879	150,761	-11,073	-7,287	-6,335	-4,537
'07	79.1	2.7	1.2	17.0	663,411	25.8	5.0	64.4	4.8	52,982	143,800	131,197	-17,244	-1,251	-1,210	-1,190
'08	78.5	3.7	3.2	14.5	682,705	25.3	6.3	64.3	4.1	41,271	141,570	125,187	14,789	-17,945	-17,873	-21,992
'09	80.6	2.6	3.1	13.7	958,729	38.8	0.5	57.8	3.0	55,011	159,801	134,075	293,800	-28,495	-28,289	-21,962

Rating History: B++, 05/06/10; B++, 05/19/09; B++, 03/27/08; B++, 01/12/07; B++, 10/24/05

EMPHESYS INSURANCE COMPANY
Humana Inc
Michael B. McCallister
President & CEO
P.O. Box 740036
Louisville, KY 40201-7436
TX : 1978 : Stock : Agency
Group A&H
502-580-1000
AMB# 008845 NAIC# 88595

NR-3

Data Year	Bonds (%)	Mort. Loans & R.E. (%)	Com & Pref. Stock (%)	All Other Assets (%)	Total Assets ($000)	Life Reserves (%)	Health Reserves %)	Ann Res. & Dep. Liabilities (%)	All Other Liabilities (%)	Capital & Surplus ($000)	Direct Premiums Written ($000)	Net Premiums Written & Deposits ($000)	Operating Cash Flow ($000)	NOG Before Taxes ($000)	NOG After Taxes ($000)	Net Income ($000)
'05	72.0	...	...	28.0	3,899	...	81.1	...	18.9	3,711	143	101	136	-47	-32	-32
'06	62.2	...	...	37.8	4,532	...	81.7	...	18.3	3,826	2,074	2,052	615	146	65	65
'07	72.0	...	...	28.0	3,957	...	38.4	...	61.6	3,267	3,656	3,656	-583	680	713	713
'08	58.9	...	...	41.1	4,827	...	45.7	...	54.3	3,857	2,949	2,949	886	-246	-285	-285
'09	61.5	...	...	38.5	4,614	...	34.5	...	65.5	4,102	1,745	1,745	-139	382	247	247

Rating History: NR-3, 06/02/10; NR-3, 06/05/09; NR-3, 06/05/08; NR-3, 06/05/07; NR-3, 05/19/06

2010 BEST'S KEY RATING GUIDE — LIFE/HEALTH EDITION
BEST'S PROFITABILITY, LEVERAGE AND LIQUIDITY TESTS 2005 – 2009

Data in U.S. Dollars

	Profitability Tests							Leverage Tests						Liquidity Tests					
Un-Realized Capital Gains ($000)	Benefits Paid to NPW & Dep (%)	Comm. & Expenses to NPW & Dep (%)	NOG to Total Assets (%)	NOG to Total Rev (%)	Operating Return on Equity (%)	Net Yield (%)	Total Return (%)	Change in NPW & Dep (%)	NPW & Dep to Capital (X)	Capital & Surplus to Liabilities (%)	Surplus Relief (%)	Reins Leverage (%)	Change in Capital (%)	Quick Liquidity (%)	Current Liquidity (%)	Non-Invest Grade Bonds to Capital (%)	Delinq. & Foreclosed Mortgages to Capital (%)	Mort. & Credit Tenant Loans & R.E. to Capital (%)	Affiliated Invest to Capital (%)
89	94.4	-12.1	22.6	13.0	29.4	1.76	2.41	78.0	1.9	395.3	...	...	43.1	317.3	322.2	...	...	...	...
140	83.4	4.3	-60.1	-51.6	-99.9	4.69	5.58	-14.2	7.2	13.9	...	...	-77.9	114.6	116.1	...	...	...	...
273	90.4	8.4	41.2	18.6	127.0	5.03	7.12	135.7	4.0	115.1	...	...	320.1	200.3	206.4	...	...	...	...
-603	90.8	8.4	2.5	0.9	4.5	3.14	-0.85	13.6	4.5	126.3	...	...	1.6	113.3	119.7	...	...	...	...
596	90.8	9.9	12.0	4.8	19.9	1.94	3.53	-4.2	3.6	186.2	...	...	19.4	146.9	157.4	3.6	...	...	...
	Principal Lines of Business: Vision (100.0%)													Principal States: NY (100.0%)					
...	...	...	...	...	...	...	...	...	...	...	...	...	...	...	...	...	...	...	...
...	...	...	...	...	...	...	...	...	...	...	...	...	...	...	...	...	...	...	...
...	...	...	...	-99.9	...	...	...	...	...	287.4	...	...	...	262.5	262.5	...	...	...	...
...	80.4	38.6	-71.6	-17.4	-99.9	1.29	1.29	...	8.3	64.3	...	...	-11.5	120.9	120.9	...	...	...	...
...	86.3	17.7	-36.8	-4.0	-99.9	-0.22	-0.22	324.8	29.1	30.5	...	...	21.0	99.7	99.7	...	...	...	...
	Principal Lines of Business: Medicare (100.0%)																		
...	...	...	...	...	...	...	...	...	...	...	...	...	...	...	...	...	...	...	...
...	76.2	33.5	...	4.2	...	...	...	...	0.2	759.6	...	...	...	...	...	...	...	...	...
...	92.0	14.0	-3.2	-2.7	-5.1	...	...	740.2	1.8	95.7	...	...	-5.0	...	...	...	...	...	...
-87	83.6	8.5	6.6	6.4	16.1	...	...	39.9	2.3	58.0	...	...	12.6	...	...	...	...	...	...
...	94.0	9.1	-0.5	-0.5	-1.4	...	...	34.1	2.3	54.0	...	...	33.2	...	...	...	...	...	...
	Principal Lines of Business: GrpA&H (100.0%)																		
...	...	...	0.7	35.0	0.7	1.96	1.96	...	...	...	...	...	0.7	...	...	...	...	...	...
...	...	...	-0.4	-13.2	-0.4	2.79	2.79	...	...	...	...	...	-0.4	...	...	...	...	...	...
...	...	...	0.0	-0.4	0.0	3.31	3.31	...	...	...	...	...	0.0	...	...	...	...	...	...
...	...	...	-3.1	-99.9	-3.1	2.27	2.27	...	...	...	...	...	-3.1	...	...	...	...	...	...
...	...	...	-2.1	-99.9	-2.1	0.24	0.24	...	...	...	...	...	-2.0	...	...	...	...	...	...
552	96.6	12.9	9.3	10.0	22.3	...	...	14.4	1.7	96.7	...	...	26.9	...	...	...	...	5.6	...
-412	82.1	16.3	8.4	10.0	16.7	...	...	-5.9	1.4	120.0	...	...	18.6	...	...	...	...	4.4	...
-454	84.3	21.3	8.1	10.6	15.2	...	...	-2.1	1.2	120.4	...	...	14.6	...	...	...	...	4.0	...
-2,250	83.9	18.9	5.4	6.4	10.1	...	...	20.7	1.4	122.2	...	...	3.5	...	...	...	...	4.7	...
251	93.0	12.6	3.4	3.8	6.6	...	...	17.2	1.5	105.9	...	...	6.8	...	...	...	...	4.5	...
	Principal Lines of Business: GrpA&H (99.8%), OrdLife (0.2%)																		
...	92.7	7.3	1.6	0.1	1.9	3.15	3.15	25.8	20.5	999.9	...	...	1.9	999.9	999.9	...	...	...	...
...	91.7	11.2	-15.0	-1.9	-43.8	6.08	6.08	12.0	22.2	26.8	...	...	3.3	74.8	74.8	...	...	...	...
...	81.5	13.7	24.8	6.6	80.3	4.52	4.52	4.0	8.8	60.1	...	...	161.9	145.4	145.4	...	...	...	...
...	77.1	14.3	32.6	10.0	68.3	1.75	1.75	3.7	5.6	134.4	...	...	63.7	217.4	217.4	...	...	...	...
...	86.9	12.6	6.5	1.8	11.1	1.25	1.25	12.1	6.0	150.2	...	0.1	5.0	222.0	222.0	...	...	...	...
	Principal Lines of Business: Medicaid (83.9%), CompHosp/Med (16.1%)													Principal States: TX (100.0%)					
...	80.3	19.4	23.9	6.9	55.9	3.67	2.97	17.5	5.9	90.6	...	0.6	73.0	160.7	164.9	...	...	...	...
1,054	80.5	16.5	15.5	5.5	32.1	4.77	5.76	11.8	5.0	96.1	...	...	33.1	173.7	177.5	...	...	...	...
1,259	75.4	17.8	20.8	8.9	36.3	4.69	6.88	0.7	3.3	180.4	...	...	50.7	300.6	307.2	...	...	...	...
-3,912	88.7	16.7	-16.6	-7.8	-28.7	3.08	0.22	-7.8	4.4	101.9	...	0.4	-30.3	201.3	206.2	...	...	...	...
1,840	87.5	16.5	-8.1	-3.6	-17.1	1.91	4.65	-4.7	5.2	77.9	...	...	-18.7	169.7	173.4	...	...	...	...
	Principal Lines of Business: Medicare (100.0%)													Principal States: NY (100.0%)					
157	73.1	24.6	0.5	2.4	4.8	5.78	5.82	-33.6	1.4	12.4	15.5	470.7	-2.9	90.9	94.6	20.1	...	4.4	2.4
93	91.3	21.7	-0.9	-3.4	-10.2	5.93	6.27	43.9	2.8	8.8	11.1	618.2	-26.9	90.0	93.5	19.2	...	26.6	2.7
330	113.4	24.5	-0.2	-0.7	-2.3	5.84	5.94	-13.0	2.4	9.3	10.4	575.7	1.7	92.6	96.4	18.4	...	32.7	2.5
147	85.3	23.9	-2.7	-11.2	-37.9	5.81	5.22	-4.6	3.0	6.7	10.5	700.7	-23.6	83.2	89.1	7.8	...	60.7	3.1
-510	65.6	45.6	-3.4	-16.1	-58.8	5.31	6.08	7.1	2.3	6.7	9.1	109.8	41.0	81.4	90.0	5.4	1.0	41.9	2.1
	Principal Lines of Business: IndAnn (63.3%), OrdLife (19.6%), IndA&H (12.5%), GrpLife (4.5%), GrpA&H (0.0%)													Principal States: IA (33.7%), IL (8.1%), NE (6.1%), TX (4.5%), KS (4.5%)					
...	206.4	46.2	-0.8	-15.3	-0.9	2.88	2.88	...	0.0	999.9	...	0.5	-0.8	999.9	999.9	...	...	...	...
...	77.8	22.2	1.5	2.9	1.7	3.54	3.54	999.9	0.5	542.4	...	...	3.1	851.4	854.2	...	...	...	...
...	61.2	24.3	16.8	18.7	20.1	3.62	3.62	78.2	1.1	474.4	...	...	-14.6	654.1	657.0	...	...	...	...
...	89.8	23.3	-6.5	-9.2	-8.0	3.38	3.38	-19.3	0.8	397.9	...	...	18.1	649.2	651.3	...	...	...	...
...	55.7	25.0	5.2	13.2	6.2	2.64	2.64	-40.8	0.4	802.3	...	...	6.4	999.9	999.9	...	...	...	...
	Principal Lines of Business: GrpA&H (100.0%)													Principal States: IN (54.0%), AZ (46.0%)					

Data in U.S. Dollars

COMPANY NAME Ultimate Parent Association Principal Officer Mailing Address Dom. : Began Bus. : Struct. : Mktg. Specialty Phone # AMB# NAIC#	Best's Financial Strength Rating FSC	Data Year	Balance Sheet Bonds (%)	Mort. Loans & R.E. (%)	Com & Pref. Stock (%)	All Other Assets (%)	Total Assets ($000)	Life Reserves (%)	Health Reserves (%)	Ann Res. & Dep. Liabilities (%)	All Other Liabilities (%)	Capital & Surplus ($000)	Operations Direct Premiums Written ($000)	Net Premiums Written & Deposits ($000)	Operating Cash Flow ($000)	NOG Before Taxes ($000)	NOG After Taxes ($000)	Net Income ($000)
EMPIRE FIDELITY INVESTMENTS LF FMR LLC Jon J. Skillman President 82 Devonshire Street, V5A Boston, MA 02109-3605 NY : 1992 : Stock : Direct Response Var ann 212-335-5082 AMB# 060055 NAIC# 71228	**A+** Rating Outlook: Stable **FSC X**	'05	6.6	...	...	93.4	1,178,497	0.1	...	3.4	96.5	46,063	55,866	47,153	4,073	6,683	5,555	5,546
		'06	5.2	...	...	94.8	1,353,081	0.1	...	2.1	97.9	49,301	170,915	153,869	-7,936	5,563	4,240	4,238
		'07	4.0	...	...	96.0	1,613,193	0.1	...	1.3	98.6	51,161	265,477	251,036	-9,206	4,371	2,967	2,787
		'08	3.7	...	...	96.3	1,197,658	0.1	...	1.7	98.2	52,056	212,439	204,660	4,997	690	740	265
		'09	4.3	...	...	95.7	1,451,050	0.1	...	1.5	98.4	54,461	141,501	138,853	3,973	2,944	1,766	1,857
		Rating History: A+ g, 06/11/10; A+ g, 06/15/09; A+ g, 04/01/08; A+ g, 01/24/07; A+ g, 12/21/05																
EMPIRE HEALTHCHOICE ASSURANCE WellPoint Inc. Mark L. Wagar Chairman, President & CEO 11 West 42nd Street New York, NY 10036 NY : 1974 : Non-Profit : Broker Group A&H 212-476-1000 AMB# 068564 NAIC# 55093	**A** Rating Outlook: Stable **FSC XIII**	'05	41.0	...	14.1	44.8	2,301,413	...	42.3	...	57.7	1,005,378	3,674,291	3,674,291	163,466	264,766	232,050	232,050
		'06	51.3	...	14.1	34.6	2,995,488	...	39.4	...	60.6	1,322,972	5,304,476	5,333,605	346,784	456,897	339,215	322,992
		'07	56.0	...	14.3	29.7	3,174,459	...	28.7	...	71.3	1,389,894	5,511,918	5,515,477	344,084	516,879	366,603	354,825
		'08	59.5	...	15.0	25.5	2,964,633	...	37.4	...	62.6	1,310,639	5,221,193	5,223,849	-288,725	503,253	358,419	294,509
		'09	54.0	...	17.0	29.0	2,838,622	...	40.2	...	59.8	1,363,198	5,871,074	5,868,804	-332,631	301,571	244,720	199,506
		Rating History: A g, 04/27/10; A, 01/23/09; A, 03/20/08; A, 11/06/06; A-, 12/29/05																
EMPIRE HEALTHCHOICE HMO INC WellPoint Inc. Mark L. Wagar Chairman, President & CEO 11 West 42nd Street New York, NY 10036 NY : 1996 : Stock : Broker Group A&H 212-476-1000 AMB# 064368 NAIC# 95433	**A** Rating Outlook: Stable **FSC XIII**	'05	76.5	...	...	23.5	608,977	...	68.5	...	31.5	293,133	2,153,895	2,153,820	38,386	137,860	90,283	90,283
		'06	90.8	...	1.1	8.1	1,037,277	...	38.3	...	61.7	380,498	2,548,163	2,548,106	407,983	212,586	133,992	127,773
		'07	81.8	...	0.9	17.3	933,099	...	40.4	...	59.6	433,203	2,682,034	2,682,034	-94,551	227,661	147,525	143,755
		'08	90.6	...	0.9	8.5	895,162	...	46.0	...	54.0	426,883	2,642,361	2,642,361	-113,144	171,480	109,111	78,685
		'09	87.6	...	...	12.4	813,948	...	48.4	...	51.6	482,308	2,294,564	2,294,564	-91,546	251,646	167,334	138,927
		Rating History: A g, 04/27/10; A, 01/23/09; A, 03/20/08; A, 11/06/06; A-, 12/29/05																
EMPLOYEES LIFE CO (MUTUAL) William D. Bruce Chairman & CEO 916 Sherwood Drive Lake Bluff, IL 60044-2285 IL : 1946 : Mutual : Agency Annuity, Pre-need, Trad Life 847-295-6000 AMB# 008005 NAIC# 84174	**B+** Rating Outlook: Negative **FSC V**	'05	87.3	5.5	2.6	4.5	278,638	14.3	...	84.7	1.0	18,624	18,965	46,481	-10,618	5,171	4,221	4,172
		'06	87.8	5.1	2.0	5.0	271,204	17.1	...	81.8	1.1	20,935	24,361	50,581	-7,130	3,214	2,514	2,531
		'07	88.1	4.2	2.2	5.6	266,335	21.8	...	77.1	1.2	23,123	25,421	55,271	-5,337	2,850	2,300	2,105
		'08	87.6	4.6	2.0	5.8	290,663	21.0	...	78.3	0.7	18,100	59,685	114,777	31,145	1,162	732	736
		'09	88.6	3.1	1.1	7.1	477,181	13.2	...	84.9	1.8	18,554	217,809	305,868	179,347	3,024	1,325	598
		Rating History: B+, 05/19/10; B+, 05/20/09; B+, 06/12/08; B+, 06/07/07; B+, 06/19/06																
EMPLOYEES LIFE INSURANCE CO Karen L. Ware President 9311 San Pedro, Suite 550 San Antonio, TX 78216 TX : 1980 : Stock : Other Direct Credit A&H, Credit Life 210-321-7361 AMB# 009027 NAIC# 99538	**B+** Rating Outlook: Stable **FSC V**	'05	1.9	...	7.2	90.9	11,089	49.5	21.2	...	29.4	6,122	1,224	5,645	1,448	1,404	1,211	1,206
		'06	5.2	...	7.7	87.1	12,208	48.6	24.2	...	27.1	6,540	1,563	6,311	1,016	929	799	799
		'07	3.7	...	7.3	89.0	14,066	47.1	27.0	...	25.9	7,684	1,942	7,295	1,816	1,383	1,183	1,183
		'08	1.5	...	4.2	94.3	15,631	44.1	27.2	...	28.7	8,969	1,358	7,317	1,908	1,997	1,715	1,597
		'09	3.1	...	10.3	86.6	17,331	39.7	27.3	...	33.0	10,755	1,204	7,300	1,201	2,104	1,821	1,677
		Rating History: B+, 04/01/10; B+, 04/10/09; B+, 01/22/08; B+, 01/29/07; B+, 03/13/06																
EMPLOYERS REASSURANCE CORP General Electric Company Michael Barnett CEO 5700 Broadmoor, Suite 1000 Mission, KS 66201 KS : 1907 : Stock : Other Direct Reins 913-982-3700 AMB# 006976 NAIC# 68276	**A-** Rating Outlook: Stable **FSC X**	'05	78.2	...	0.7	21.1	5,341,786	44.0	26.8	21.4	7.7	252,899	...	-125,207	-692,817	-185,883	-123,735	-107,595
		'06	58.3	...	1.7	40.0	7,644,238	34.0	46.2	13.5	6.3	421,115	...	1,174,138	656,316	-337,124	-257,713	-258,763
		'07	75.4	...	6.8	17.9	8,666,442	34.2	50.7	10.8	4.4	780,301	...	1,073,985	2,067,097	-387,795	-330,686	-331,537
		'08	75.2	...	6.5	18.3	9,697,674	32.0	51.1	8.5	8.5	681,200	...	686,908	1,108,821	-605,246	-584,150	-619,051
		'09	85.0	...	6.7	8.3	9,604,673	38.8	50.0	8.0	3.2	724,509	...	671,377	618,210	-114,744	-86,803	-129,832
		Rating History: A- g, 05/27/09; A- g, 06/09/08; A-, 06/13/07; B++, 06/12/06; B++, 03/31/05																
ENTERPRISE LIFE INS CO Enterprise Financial Group, Inc. William Bigley President 122 West Carpenter Freeway, 6th Floor Irving, TX 75039 TX : 1978 : Stock : Agency Credit A&H, Credit Life 972-445-8300 AMB# 008919 NAIC# 89087	**NR-5**	'05	73.8	...	0.3	26.0	34,962	19.8	21.0	...	59.2	12,236	22,723	3,994	-3,058	1,544	1,229	1,248
		'06	80.6	...	0.3	19.1	28,827	21.4	23.1	...	55.5	11,408	19,499	2,938	-1,147	362	253	252
		'07	83.4	...	...	16.6	26,481	27.8	25.7	...	46.6	11,692	13,738	3,046	-2,565	-912	-916	25
		'08	89.9	...	...	10.1	21,036	27.0	41.9	...	31.2	5,410	6,627	4,615	-4,455	-375	-479	-479
		'09	90.6	...	...	9.4	13,049	28.4	55.1	...	16.5	4,911	-2,704	-463	-7,559	1,788	1,237	1,237
		Rating History: NR-5, 05/12/10; NR-4, 05/30/08; B+, 05/30/08; B+, 06/04/07; B+, 06/09/06																
ENVISION INSURANCE COMPANY Envision Pharmaceutical Holdings Inc Kevin M. Nagle President 2181 East Aurora Road Twinsburg, OH 44087 OH : 2007 : Stock : Not Available Health 330-405-8089 AMB# 064969 NAIC# 12747	**NR-5**	'05	...	...	...	...	...	...	...	...	...	...	...	...	...	...	...	...
		'06	6.1	...	...	93.9	3,351	...	...	...	100.0	3,155	...	...	3,351	11	11	11
		'07	13.5	...	...	86.5	24,453	...	...	...	100.0	10,230	28,105	28,105	1,248	5,162	5,159	5,159
		'08	36.0	1.8	...	62.2	12,691	...	12.4	...	87.6	5,226	21,955	21,955	674	-8,076	-8,076	-8,076
		'09	15.9	0.6	...	83.6	37,590	...	...	...	100.0	21,588	44,043	34,038	11,404	2,358	2,358	2,358
		Rating History: NR-5, 03/22/10; NR-5, 05/01/09																
EPIC LIFE INS CO Wisconsin Physicians Service Ins Corp James R. Riordan President P.O. Box 14196 Madison, WI 53708-0196 WI : 1984 : Stock : Agency Group A&H, Group Life 608-221-6882 AMB# 009476 NAIC# 64149	**NR-5**	'05	71.8	...	16.4	11.8	37,779	7.8	5.3	...	86.8	21,380	12,351	10,936	1,253	1,326	885	943
		'06	71.9	...	17.0	11.1	40,375	8.0	6.5	...	85.5	22,310	12,702	12,162	2,536	654	439	606
		'07	72.3	...	18.2	9.6	42,784	9.7	7.3	...	83.0	23,015	14,898	14,049	2,443	980	632	812
		'08	74.6	...	10.8	14.6	42,076	12.2	7.9	...	79.9	21,758	16,950	15,776	2,587	673	185	-217
		'09	73.3	...	15.6	11.0	47,788	12.9	8.2	...	78.9	23,857	19,021	18,259	3,566	2,558	1,290	1,174
		Rating History: NR-5, 04/06/10; NR-5, 03/27/09; NR-5, 04/15/08; NR-5, 05/21/07; NR-5, 05/16/06																

BEST'S PROFITABILITY, LEVERAGE AND LIQUIDITY TESTS 2005 – 2009

Data in U.S. Dollars

—	Profitability Tests							Leverage Tests						Liquidity Tests					
Un-Realized Capital Gains ($000)	Benefits Paid to NPW & Dep (%)	Comm. & Expenses to NPW & Dep (%)	NOG to Total Assets (%)	NOG to Total Rev (%)	Operating Return on Equity (%)	Net Yield (%)	Total Return (%)	Change in NPW & Dep (%)	NPW & Dep to Capital (X)	Capital & Surplus to Liabilities (%)	Surplus Relief (%)	Reins Leverage (%)	Change in Capital (%)	Quick Liquidity (%)	Current Liquidity (%)	Non-Invest Grade Bonds to Capital (%)	Delinq. & Foreclosed Mortgages to Capital (%)	Mort. & Credit Tenant Loans & R.E. to Capital (%)	Affiliated Invest to Capital (%)
...	195.8	9.2	0.5	9.8	12.8	3.86	4.04	7.2	1.0	115.6	1.7	138.8	13.8	169.9	186.4	3.7	...	...	...
...	65.6	4.4	0.3	2.6	8.9	4.20	4.32	226.3	3.1	173.5	4.0	176.6	7.1	209.2	228.7	3.1	...	...	...
...	48.7	4.0	0.2	1.1	5.9	4.32	4.11	63.1	4.9	278.5	3.9	207.1	3.6	275.9	298.7	3.5	...	...	...
...	63.0	5.0	0.1	0.3	1.4	2.99	2.44	-18.5	3.9	240.7	2.0	218.4	1.2	390.1	408.1	...	...	...	...
...	105.7	6.4	0.1	1.2	3.3	1.73	2.31	-32.2	2.5	241.2	1.3	196.3	4.7	321.8	339.6	...	...	...	...
	Principal Lines of Business: IndAnn (99.7%), OrdLife (0.3%)													Principal States: NY (100.0%)					
90,761	87.1	8.0	10.7	6.2	22.9	3.12	9.37	7.4	3.7	77.6	...	...	-1.3	110.7	121.3	...	...	...	32.3
87,202	89.2	5.3	12.8	6.2	29.1	7.13	11.15	45.2	4.0	79.1	...	...	31.6	83.6	96.8	...	...	...	30.0
53,414	90.5	4.5	11.9	6.3	27.0	9.13	11.02	3.4	4.0	77.9	...	...	5.1	101.0	115.0	0.2	...	...	32.4
-20,975	89.9	5.1	11.7	6.6	26.5	8.89	5.20	-5.3	4.0	79.2	...	...	-5.7	77.8	90.2	3.7	...	...	32.6
70,495	90.1	8.6	8.4	4.0	18.3	10.44	11.81	12.3	4.3	92.4	...	...	4.0	67.2	80.1	2.8	...	...	35.4
	Principal Lines of Business: CompHosp/Med (87.1%), FEHBP (7.8%), MedSup (2.5%), Medicare (2.1%), Dental (0.5%)													Principal States: NY (100.0%)					
...	84.0	10.6	15.6	4.1	33.7	4.08	4.08	20.2	7.3	92.8	...	...	20.7	158.8	174.9	...	...	...	...
...	83.6	9.5	16.3	5.2	39.8	5.77	4.93	18.3	6.7	57.9	...	...	29.8	110.3	126.5	0.2	...	...	...
...	84.6	8.8	15.0	5.4	36.3	5.47	5.06	5.3	6.2	86.7	...	...	13.9	150.9	168.7	0.2	...	...	...
-3,963	87.6	7.8	11.9	4.1	25.4	6.19	1.84	-1.5	6.2	91.2	...	...	-1.5	114.9	132.4	3.7	...	...	...
3,768	82.3	8.6	19.6	7.2	36.8	7.17	3.61	-13.2	4.8	145.4	...	...	13.0	142.6	165.2	2.3	...	...	...
	Principal Lines of Business: CompHosp/Med (60.1%), Medicare (39.9%)													Principal States: NY (100.0%)					
...	55.2	11.4	1.5	11.2	25.4	5.76	5.77	2.9	2.4	7.6	...	...	27.4	58.8	69.1	63.7	...	78.3	4.9
...	53.7	12.5	0.9	5.8	12.7	5.87	5.90	8.8	2.3	8.9	0.0	...	13.2	61.1	71.3	52.8	...	62.7	4.1
...	48.3	12.9	0.9	5.3	10.4	5.77	5.72	9.3	2.3	10.1	...	...	9.5	64.2	74.5	33.9	...	45.7	3.5
...	26.9	6.2	0.3	0.9	3.6	5.51	5.54	107.7	6.2	6.8	...	...	-24.4	67.4	77.2	13.5	2.2	73.4	5.6
-5,607	12.2	3.3	0.3	0.6	7.2	4.65	3.02	166.5	15.6	4.3	...	...	6.6	63.5	73.0	50.0	...	76.0	5.0
	Principal Lines of Business: IndAnn (94.7%), OrdLife (4.0%), GrpLife (1.3%)													Principal States: AZ (26.9%), FL (16.6%), CA (11.8%), IN (10.7%), WI (5.3%)					
14	21.2	55.2	11.7	20.1	21.9	3.89	3.97	22.3	0.9	127.0	...	1.1	24.2	205.3	207.8	...	...	...	...
46	30.3	55.4	6.9	11.7	12.6	4.67	5.07	11.8	0.9	120.8	...	0.2	7.7	199.4	202.0	...	...	...	...
-4	28.6	54.2	9.0	14.8	16.6	5.56	5.54	15.6	0.9	125.7	...	0.3	17.3	205.6	208.2	...	...	...	...
-323	24.9	55.0	11.6	21.4	20.6	5.11	2.06	0.3	0.8	134.6	...	0.0	14.5	217.2	219.0	0.3	...	...	...
236	29.1	53.3	11.1	22.9	18.5	4.24	4.83	-0.2	0.7	170.9	...	0.3	21.9	240.8	246.0	0.2	...	...	...
	Principal Lines of Business: CrdA&H (56.5%), CrdLife (40.8%), OrdLife (2.4%), GrpLife (0.2%), IndA&H (0.0%)													Principal States: TX (100.0%)					
-1,152	-99.9	-99.9	-2.2	-61.4	-48.3	5.91	6.43	-99.9	-0.5	5.4	10.1	256.9	-3.0	68.8	83.0	49.9	...	...	8.7
867	-34.0	23.5	-4.0	-15.9	-76.5	5.81	5.97	999.9	2.6	6.2	14.0	539.6	62.6	58.9	68.9	27.7	...	...	5.0
-302,060	114.0	22.2	-4.1	-17.9	-55.0	9.94	5.74	-8.5	1.3	10.3	7.0	116.2	82.1	52.9	64.6	29.1	...	...	53.9
-67,641	109.0	31.0	-6.4	-47.1	-79.9	5.49	4.35	-36.0	1.0	7.7	8.1	178.6	-14.8	54.8	65.6	33.4	...	...	69.4
73,163	113.7	28.0	-0.9	-7.0	-12.4	5.56	5.99	-2.3	0.9	8.2	6.3	188.6	5.4	60.1	71.2	35.4	...	...	99.0
	Principal Lines of Business: OrdLife (54.9%), IndA&H (40.6%), GrpA&H (4.0%), IndAnn (0.4%), CrdLife (0.0%)																		
...	51.1	90.1	3.6	5.0	9.7	5.54	5.75	-31.5	0.3	54.3	155.6	470.6	-6.6	95.4	105.5	...	...	...	...
...	55.6	122.8	0.8	1.5	2.1	5.43	5.56	-26.4	0.3	66.0	106.3	436.7	-6.8	120.0	132.3	...	...	...	...
...	28.6	131.7	-3.3	-7.5	-7.9	4.71	8.80	3.7	0.3	79.6	69.3	380.3	2.3	123.9	137.1	...	...	...	...
...	18.5	72.2	-2.0	-5.4	-5.6	5.80	5.82	51.5	0.8	35.1	57.6	567.3	-53.4	96.4	107.3	3.4	...	...	...
...	-99.9	-99.9	7.3	-84.7	24.0	5.40	5.43	-99.9	-0.1	61.6	-36.4	344.3	-8.9	109.3	120.9	6.0	...	...	...
	Principal Lines of Business: CrdA&H (55.9%), CrdLife (44.1%)																		
...	...	...	...	...	...	...	...	...	...	...	...	...	...	...	...	...	...	...	...
...	...	...	...	10.2	...	...	...	...	...	999.9	...	...	...	999.9	999.9	...	...	...	...
...	137.8	5.5	37.1	11.4	77.1	4.07	4.07	...	2.7	71.9	...	...	224.2	31.2	31.2	...	...	...	...
...	112.5	23.1	-43.5	-37.2	-99.9	2.86	2.86	-21.9	4.2	70.0	...	...	-48.9	66.8	66.8	...	...	4.3	4.3
-41	81.9	10.9	9.4	6.9	17.6	1.13	0.76	55.0	1.6	134.9	...	12.6	313.1	101.1	101.1	...	...	1.0	1.0
	Principal Lines of Business: OtherHlth (100.0%)													Principal States: MA (14.7%), TX (13.5%), VA (8.9%), MD (6.9%), FL (6.4%)					
16	66.2	30.4	2.4	7.3	4.2	2.40	3.07	-1.6	0.5	141.0	0.8	5.0	5.0	198.0	219.5	...	...	...	...
286	70.5	30.0	1.1	3.3	2.0	2.10	3.47	11.2	0.5	133.4	0.7	7.1	4.4	186.6	207.2	...	...	...	...
-109	66.6	32.0	1.5	4.2	2.8	2.29	2.57	15.5	0.6	126.5	0.7	9.1	3.5	181.9	202.0	...	...	...	...
-1,691	66.7	29.3	0.4	1.1	0.8	2.63	-3.86	12.3	0.7	107.1	0.8	11.7	-8.9	176.9	194.0	0.4	...	...	...
1,263	64.3	27.2	2.9	6.5	5.7	3.18	5.92	15.7	0.7	108.7	0.8	10.5	14.4	161.5	179.4	3.5	...	...	...
	Principal Lines of Business: GrpA&H (58.9%), GrpLife (40.9%), OrdLife (0.2%)													Principal States: WI (84.3%), IN (7.5%)					

Data in U.S. Dollars

COMPANY NAME Ultimate Parent Association Principal Officer Mailing Address Dom. : Began Bus. : Struct. : Mktg. Specialty Phone # AMB# NAIC#	Best's Financial Strength Rating FSC	Data Year	Balance Sheet: Bonds (%)	Mort. Loans & R.E. (%)	Com & Pref. Stock (%)	All Other Assets (%)	Total Assets ($000)	Life Reserves (%)	Health Reserves (%)	Ann Res. & Dep. Liabilities (%)	All Other Liabilities (%)	Capital & Surplus ($000)	Operations: Direct Premiums Written ($000)	Net Premiums Written & Deposits ($000)	Operating Cash Flow ($000)	NOG Before Taxes ($000)	NOG After Taxes ($000)	Net Income ($000)
EQUITABLE LIFE & CASUALTY Insurance Investment Company E. Rod Ross Chairman & CEO P.O. Box 2460 Salt Lake City, UT 84110-2460 UT : 1935 : Stock : Agency Ind Life, Med supp 801-579-3400 AMB# 006342 NAIC# 62952	**B+** Rating Outlook: Negative **FSC VI**	'05	77.1	6.5	...	16.4	173,747	21.2	71.9	0.2	6.7	34,787	131,745	116,229	15,586	7,336	4,011	4,135
		'06	77.1	6.4	...	16.5	190,574	20.8	72.6	0.2	6.3	37,214	125,783	109,316	16,334	5,703	3,647	3,669
		'07	82.3	5.8	...	11.9	207,246	20.4	73.9	0.2	5.5	40,223	124,442	107,931	16,431	4,730	3,158	3,158
		'08	81.3	5.1	...	13.7	214,517	20.4	75.5	0.2	3.9	38,078	121,170	104,173	6,181	711	616	-919
		'09	79.4	5.1	...	15.5	233,120	18.8	76.6	0.2	4.5	30,040	127,196	109,091	10,116	-3,881	85	-1,471
		Rating History: B+, 12/18/09; B++, 08/17/09; B++, 06/18/08; B++, 06/14/07; B++, 06/20/06																
EQUITRUST LIFE INSURANCE CO Iowa Farm Bureau Federation James E. Hohmann CEO 5400 University Avenue West Des Moines, IA 50266-5997 IA : 1967 : Stock : Agency Ann, Var ann, Var Univ life 877-249-3694 AMB# 060315 NAIC# 62510	**B+** Rating Outlook: Negative **FSC IX**	'05	84.4	7.4	0.3	7.9	3,657,844	6.1	...	90.1	3.7	215,649	915,967	959,389	735,243	33,960	21,201	20,155
		'06	80.9	7.6	1.9	9.7	5,477,321	4.0	...	91.7	4.2	327,960	1,821,406	1,856,010	1,610,255	36,322	25,009	24,481
		'07	80.9	9.8	2.0	7.2	6,841,531	3.1	...	93.2	3.6	391,638	1,521,162	1,624,310	1,335,201	35,077	25,168	22,285
		'08	82.6	9.8	1.9	5.7	7,779,919	2.7	...	95.8	1.5	416,978	1,476,929	1,602,774	930,471	-56,985	-37,060	-116,931
		'09	84.9	9.4	0.3	5.5	7,163,793	0.1	...	97.4	2.4	434,967	586,680	674,959	-467,823	30,784	53,227	57,224
		Rating History: B+, 12/18/09; B+, 02/27/09; A-, 09/26/08; A, 08/23/07; A, 10/10/06																
ERIE FAMILY LIFE INS CO Erie Indemnity Company Terrence W. Cavanaugh President & CEO 100 Erie Insurance Place Erie, PA 16530 PA : 1967 : Stock : Agency Trad Life, Univ Life, Ann 814-870-2000 AMB# 007276 NAIC# 70769	**A** Rating Outlook: Stable **FSC VIII**	'05	84.6	0.4	5.1	9.8	1,592,137	21.0	0.0	70.7	8.3	147,533	168,899	158,005	126,746	26,769	17,840	15,705
		'06	84.9	0.4	6.7	7.9	1,558,306	23.5	0.0	72.3	4.2	168,067	181,603	161,488	-37,026	34,294	22,236	23,464
		'07	86.8	0.4	6.5	6.2	1,563,947	25.1	0.0	70.4	4.4	183,521	163,186	134,631	3,739	33,265	23,793	12,466
		'08	87.2	0.2	5.3	7.3	1,533,697	25.9	0.0	70.7	3.3	105,817	252,047	220,152	-29,072	35,354	18,802	-66,401
		'09	89.6	0.2	2.2	8.0	1,665,915	25.3	0.0	71.4	3.2	173,543	263,629	228,294	114,539	40,810	31,812	3,245
		Rating History: A, 06/17/09; A, 06/10/08; A, 05/31/07; A, 05/30/06; A, 05/03/05																
ESCUDE LIFE INS CO[1] H. Michael Cozart President 1904 Leglise Street Mansura, LA 71350 LA : 1982 : Stock : Not Available In Rehabilitation 501-653-2727 AMB# 009341 NAIC# 91332	**E**	'05	70.7	3.2	19.4	6.8	4,507	...	...	...	100.0	462	529	506	...	-244	-241	-242
		'06	...	...	...	...	...	...	...	...	...	...	...	...	...	...	...	...
		'07	74.9	6.1	9.5	9.5	3,041	...	...	...	100.0	-1,267	574	558	...	-268	-270	-229
		'08	67.0	3.3	13.2	16.6	2,204	...	...	...	100.0	-2,182	580	565	...	-139	-141	-140
		'09	...	...	...	...	...	...	...	...	...	...	...	...	...	...	...	...
		Rating History: E, 02/09/10; NR-1, 06/12/09; NR-1, 06/12/08; NR-5, 06/06/07; NR-1, 06/07/06																
ESSENCE HEALTHCARE INC[2] Essence Group Holdings Corporation Debra K. Gribble President 12655 Olive Boulevard, 4th Floor St. Louis, MO 63141-6362 MO : 2003 : Stock : Agency Health 314-851-3680 AMB# 064763 NAIC# 11699	**NR-5**	'05	...	...	...	100.0	4,558	...	26.1	...	73.9	3,132	13,274	12,982	1,015	-1,281	-1,281	-1,281
		'06	...	...	...	100.0	10,612	...	22.4	...	77.6	4,292	32,540	31,997	6,271	824	824	824
		'07	...	...	...	100.0	40,850	...	83.1	...	16.9	11,458	126,732	125,782	28,546	6,630	2,982	2,982
		'08	3.3	...	1.0	95.7	89,811	...	50.7	...	49.3	19,756	197,127	196,246	47,539	11,862	8,394	8,394
		'09	0.5	...	3.9	95.6	105,047	...	30.5	...	69.5	24,538	318,754	317,538	10,351	1,567	1,134	1,134
		Rating History: NR-5, 04/08/10; NR-5, 05/29/09; NR-5, 03/18/08; NR-5, 04/05/07; NR-5, 04/21/06																
ESSEX DENTAL BENEFITS INC[2] Sheldon C. Cohen, D.M.D. President 9735 Landmark Parkway Drive, Suite 14 St. Louis, MO 63127 MO : 1994 : Stock : Not Available Dental 314-543-4935 AMB# 065733 NAIC# 47035	**NR-5**	'05	1.7	...	...	98.3	3,182	...	59.5	...	40.5	1,425	18,595	18,595	1,089	248	172	172
		'06	...	...	...	100.0	3,799	...	61.3	...	38.7	1,623	21,635	21,635	577	368	204	204
		'07	1.3	...	...	98.7	4,304	...	45.5	...	54.5	2,019	23,732	23,732	543	996	439	439
		'08	1.2	...	...	98.8	4,228	...	55.8	...	44.2	2,447	26,589	26,589	-744	268	465	465
		'09	...	...	...	100.0	3,831	...	50.0	...	50.0	1,829	29,317	29,317	25	-589	-665	-665
		Rating History: NR-5, 04/09/10; NR-5, 04/03/09; NR-5, 04/16/08; NR-5, 06/25/07; NR-5, 04/20/06																
EVANGELINE LIFE INS CO INC[1] Dennis M. Necaise President & Treasurer 209 West Main Street, Suite 500 New Iberia, LA 70560 LA : 1923 : Stock : Not Available 337-364-1721 AMB# 007644 NAIC# 73946	**NR-1**	'05	26.9	65.0	0.1	7.9	13,032	...	...	...	100.0	1,120	1,136	1,078	...	-198	-198	-187
		'06	30.9	65.8	0.2	3.1	12,865	...	...	...	100.0	1,273	963	902	...	55	55	62
		'07	33.2	63.1	0.2	3.5	12,843	...	...	...	100.0	1,259	985	923	...	135	100	105
		'08	32.7	64.7	0.2	2.4	11,910	...	...	...	100.0	464	859	798	...	-210	-195	-421
		'09	30.4	65.1	...	4.6	11,381	...	...	...	100.0	277	849	786	...	9	67	-251
		Rating History: NR-1, 06/10/10; NR-1, 06/12/09; NR-1, 06/12/08; NR-1, 06/08/07; NR-1, 06/07/06																
EVERCARE OF NEW MEXICO INC UnitedHealth Group Inc John L. Larsen President & Chief Executive Officer 8820 SanPedro, N.E., Suite 300 Albuquerque, NM 87113 NM : 2008 : Stock : Other Health 505-449-4131 AMB# 060688 NAIC# 13214	**NR-2**	'05	...	...	...	...	...	...	...	...	...	...	...	...	...	...	...	...
		'06	...	...	...	...	...	...	...	...	...	...	...	...	...	...	...	...
		'07	...	...	...	...	...	...	...	...	...	...	...	...	...	...	...	...
		'08	...	...	...	100.0	3,511	...	...	...	100.0	3,507	...	...	3,511	11	7	7
		'09	0.9	...	...	99.1	121,552	...	68.1	...	31.9	22,662	354,465	354,465	116,369	-43,859	-36,895	-36,895
		Rating History: NR-2, 06/07/10																
EVERCARE OF TEXAS LLC UnitedHealth Group Inc John R. Mach, Jr., M.D. President & CEO 3141 N. 3rd Avenue Phoenix, AZ 85013 TX : 2001 : Stock : Broker Health 713-778-8664 AMB# 064745 NAIC# 11141	**NR-2**	'05	60.5	...	...	39.5	85,694	...	65.4	...	34.6	30,999	239,032	239,032	24,295	24,249	15,275	15,208
		'06	37.5	...	...	62.5	140,560	...	67.9	...	32.1	51,082	385,698	385,698	54,273	32,619	21,071	21,051
		'07	79.5	...	...	20.5	182,147	...	69.7	...	30.3	79,729	481,703	481,703	35,209	44,542	29,364	29,334
		'08	64.3	...	...	35.7	176,258	...	74.8	...	25.2	59,001	590,919	590,919	-17,769	46,068	30,094	30,383
		'09	73.6	...	...	26.4	178,204	...	60.8	...	39.2	74,806	630,283	630,283	10,056	25,063	16,824	17,051
		Rating History: NR-2, 06/15/09; NR-2, 01/29/08; NR-2, 11/21/07; NR-2, 11/16/06; NR-2, 08/17/06																

Data in U.S. Dollars

	Profitability Tests							Leverage Tests						Liquidity Tests					
Un-Realized Capital Gains ($000)	Benefits Paid to NPW & Dep (%)	Comm. & Expenses to NPW & Dep (%)	NOG to Total Assets (%)	NOG to Total Rev (%)	Operating Return on Equity (%)	Net Yield (%)	Total Return (%)	Change in NPW & Dep (%)	NPW & Dep to Capital (X)	Capital & Surplus to Liabilities (%)	Surplus Relief (%)	Reins Leverage (%)	Change in Capital (%)	Quick Liquidity (%)	Current Liquidity (%)	Non-Invest Grade Bonds to Capital (%)	Delinq. & Foreclosed Mortgages to Capital (%)	Mort. & Credit Tenant Loans & R.E. to Capital (%)	Affiliated Invest to Capital (%)
-118	59.2	30.1	2.4	3.2	11.9	4.90	4.93	2.0	3.3	25.6	5.9	14.3	5.7	84.6	94.3	1.4	5.9	31.8	0.1
...	58.1	30.9	2.0	3.0	10.1	5.15	5.18	-5.9	2.9	24.7	4.7	10.8	6.6	87.2	97.3	...	0.8	32.2	0.1
...	58.1	32.8	1.6	2.6	8.2	5.21	5.23	-1.3	2.6	24.5	4.1	11.6	8.1	84.6	95.1	...	0.7	29.6	...
...	64.0	35.0	0.3	0.5	1.6	5.21	4.43	-3.5	2.7	21.7	6.3	13.3	-6.3	81.9	92.4	2.6	0.8	28.4	...
...	63.2	37.4	0.0	0.1	0.2	4.92	4.17	4.7	3.6	15.0	15.3	28.6	-20.3	73.5	83.4	10.9	6.6	38.9	1.1

Principal Lines of Business: IndA&H (89.5%), OrdLife (10.5%)

Principal States: MO (12.2%), TX (11.5%), OR (9.4%), CO (7.5%), NV (7.3%)

-290	25.0	14.1	0.7	1.9	11.1	6.01	5.98	32.6	4.2	6.9	0.5	17.3	31.0	57.3	71.2	36.1	...	131.3	...
...	18.2	9.8	0.5	1.2	9.2	6.83	6.82	93.5	5.3	7.0	0.3	16.9	51.5	56.3	70.5	30.1	...	128.9	...
...	27.7	10.4	0.4	1.3	7.0	5.51	5.46	-12.5	3.9	6.7	0.2	8.3	20.4	55.0	69.1	33.4	...	167.4	...
-1,468	45.3	9.2	-0.5	-2.1	-9.2	4.15	3.02	-1.3	3.8	5.8	0.2	4.8	0.0	54.0	68.0	53.5	0.9	196.8	...
-5,485	198.9	10.9	0.7	5.5	12.5	4.85	4.83	-57.9	1.5	6.7	0.2	3.8	4.9	55.3	68.9	90.5	1.6	166.3	9.6

Principal Lines of Business: IndAnn (82.2%), GrpAnn (16.2%), OrdLife (1.5%)

Principal States: PA (10.3%), FL (9.8%), TX (7.0%), CA (6.7%), MI (4.5%)

304	70.5	26.2	1.2	7.4	12.6	5.85	5.97	5.9	1.0	10.6	5.9	27.0	8.4	73.2	84.9	22.6	...	4.7	...
745	102.5	22.1	1.4	8.7	14.1	5.98	6.32	2.2	0.9	12.8	7.5	29.1	15.8	74.5	87.6	14.0	...	3.9	...
2,237	117.7	29.4	1.5	10.0	13.5	6.16	5.75	-16.6	0.7	13.9	7.0	31.7	7.3	73.0	85.9	23.4	...	3.5	...
-1,225	76.9	16.8	1.2	5.8	13.0	6.21	0.83	63.5	1.8	8.6	12.1	75.8	-36.0	59.0	77.0	33.9	...	2.7	...
-1,698	79.7	14.4	2.0	9.4	22.8	6.40	4.60	3.7	1.2	12.6	7.8	54.6	53.0	64.4	81.7	41.5	...	1.7	...

Principal Lines of Business: IndAnn (57.0%), OrdLife (39.8%), GrpAnn (2.0%), GrpLife (1.2%), IndA&H (0.1%)

Principal States: PA (53.5%), MD (8.5%), VA (7.6%), OH (7.5%), NC (6.7%)

-2	96.6	72.1	-5.3	-31.2	-41.4	...	...	-3.6	0.9	14.0	...	...	-30.6	...	...	...	...	25.8	...
...	...	...	...	...	...	...	...	...	...	...	...	...	...	...	...	...	...	...	...
-35	88.7	72.3	...	-35.0	...	...	...	...	-0.5	-28.9	...	...	...	...	...	...	...	-15.1	...
-242	67.0	61.3	-5.4	-19.0	8.2	...	...	1.3	-0.3	-49.7	...	...	-76.5	...	...	...	...	-3.3	...
...	...	...	...	...	...	...	...	...	...	...	...	...	...	...	...	...	...	...	...

...	78.6	32.0	-34.0	-9.8	-47.9	2.86	2.86	999.9	4.1	219.6	...	0.6	41.0	329.0	329.0	...	...	...	...
...	77.5	21.1	10.9	2.5	22.2	5.51	5.51	146.5	7.5	67.9	...	0.1	37.1	173.6	173.6	...	...	...	...
...	80.5	15.4	11.6	2.3	37.9	6.63	6.63	293.1	11.0	39.0	...	1.3	166.9	134.5	134.5	...	...	...	...
...	79.7	14.5	12.8	4.3	53.8	0.93	0.93	56.0	9.9	28.2	...	1.4	72.4	129.9	129.9	...	...	...	4.6
-1,795	85.7	13.9	1.2	0.4	5.1	0.20	-1.77	61.8	12.9	30.5	...	2.1	24.2	112.9	112.9	...	...	...	16.5

Principal Lines of Business: Medicare (100.0%)

Principal States: MO (62.6%), WA (13.6%), IL (11.5%), KY (11.3%)

...	81.8	21.5	6.7	0.9	16.3	3.94	3.94	19.3	13.0	81.1	...	...	110.0	155.5	155.5	...	...	...	...
...	83.1	20.6	5.9	0.9	13.4	5.89	5.89	16.3	13.3	74.5	...	...	13.8	152.0	152.0	...	...	...	...
...	80.0	16.6	10.8	1.8	24.1	5.49	5.49	9.7	11.8	88.4	...	...	24.4	168.6	168.6	...	...	...	...
...	82.6	16.6	10.9	1.7	20.8	1.64	1.64	12.0	10.9	137.4	...	...	21.2	174.2	174.5	...	...	...	...
...	85.8	16.2	-16.5	-2.3	-31.1	0.03	0.03	10.3	16.0	91.4	...	...	-25.2	156.4	156.4	...	...	...	...

Principal Lines of Business: Dental (100.0%)

Principal States: MO (100.0%)

-9	117.7	102.2	-1.5	-10.7	-17.1	...	...	-20.0	0.8	11.5	...	...	-13.1	...	...	...	...	629.9	...
13	108.8	97.8	0.4	3.3	4.6	...	...	-16.3	0.6	12.7	...	...	7.6	...	...	...	...	585.0	...
21	96.3	97.6	0.8	5.5	7.9	...	...	2.4	0.6	13.6	...	...	6.0	...	...	...	...	528.1	...
-415	123.0	114.5	-1.6	-12.7	-22.6	...	...	-13.6	1.3	5.6	...	...	-58.6	...	...	...	...	999.9	...
-5	128.5	96.9	0.6	4.3	18.1	...	...	-1.5	1.9	3.8	...	...	-34.0	...	...	...	...	999.9	...

Principal Lines of Business: OrdLife (80.5%), IndLife (19.5%)

...	...	...	...	...	...	...	...	...	...	...	...	...	...	...	...	...	...	...	...
...	...	...	...	...	...	...	...	...	...	...	...	...	...	...	...	...	...	...	...
...	...	...	...	...	...	...	...	...	...	...	...	...	...	...	...	...	...	...	...
...	...	...	...	62.0	...	...	...	...	...	999.9	...	...	...	999.9	999.9	...	...	...	...
...	91.8	14.2	-59.0	-10.4	-99.9	0.02	0.02	...	15.6	22.9	...	...	546.2	121.2	121.2	...	...	...	...

Principal Lines of Business: Medicaid (100.0%)

Principal States: NM (100.0%)

125	78.8	12.0	20.9	6.3	66.3	3.37	3.45	21.6	7.7	56.7	...	...	105.2	197.0	212.6	1.2	...	...	...
-134	81.1	11.9	18.6	5.4	51.3	5.36	5.22	61.4	7.6	57.1	...	...	64.8	235.7	251.3	...	...	...	...
-1,176	78.5	13.9	18.2	6.0	44.9	5.21	4.44	24.9	6.0	77.8	...	...	56.1	173.8	190.3	...	...	...	...
...	80.6	12.7	16.8	5.1	43.4	4.68	4.85	22.7	10.0	50.3	...	...	-26.0	147.3	160.3	...	...	...	...
...	83.0	13.4	9.5	2.7	25.1	3.04	3.18	6.7	8.4	72.3	...	...	26.8	163.1	179.0	...	...	...	...

Principal Lines of Business: Medicaid (58.5%), Medicare (38.2%), CompHosp/Med (3.3%)

Principal States: TX (100.0%)

Data in U.S. Dollars

COMPANY NAME Ultimate Parent Association Principal Officer Mailing Address Dom. : Began Bus. : Struct. : Mktg. Specialty Phone # AMB# NAIC#	Best's Financial Strength Rating FSC	Data Year	Balance Sheet: Bonds (%)	Mort. Loans & R.E. (%)	Com & Pref. Stock (%)	All Other Assets (%)	Total Assets ($000)	Life Reserves (%)	Health Reserves (%)	Ann Res. & Dep. Liabilities (%)	All Other Liabilities (%)	Capital & Surplus ($000)	Operations: Direct Premiums Written ($000)	Net Premiums Written & Deposits ($000)	Operating Cash Flow ($000)	NOG Before Taxes ($000)	NOG After Taxes ($000)	Net Income ($000)
EXCELLUS HEALTH PLAN INC Lifetime Healthcare Inc David H. Klein Chief Executive Officer 165 Court Street Rochester, NY 14647 NY : 1935 : Non-Profit : Direct Response Hosp Ind 585-454-1700 AMB# 060082 NAIC# 55107	B++ Rating Outlook: Stable FSC XI	'05	40.9	2.9	20.3	35.8	1,987,294	...	47.3	...	52.7	960,842	4,425,923	4,423,498	185,245	250,367	189,470	197,876
		'06	43.8	2.5	22.5	31.2	2,150,344	...	40.6	...	59.4	1,132,312	4,814,870	4,814,870	82,677	185,285	142,973	151,722
		'07	46.5	2.3	23.3	27.9	2,248,066	...	47.8	...	52.2	1,187,206	5,135,293	5,135,293	93,468	71,146	42,251	84,256
		'08	52.9	2.4	13.9	30.8	1,947,399	...	46.5	...	53.5	857,949	4,978,984	4,978,984	-99,030	17,382	16,345	-54,093
		'09	49.3	2.1	23.3	25.3	2,200,426	...	39.1	...	60.9	965,053	4,888,135	4,888,135	50,482	37,224	15,539	46,566
		Rating History: B++g, 06/07/10; B++g, 06/09/09; B++g, 01/29/09; A- g, 12/14/07; A-, 02/16/07																
EYEXAM OF CALIFORNIA INC Eliot Grossman President 29 The Shops at Mission Viejo Mission Viejo, CA 92691 CA : 1986 : Stock : Broker Group A&H 949-364-2256 AMB# 064723	NR-5	'05	...	...	...	100.0	15,921	...	...	...	100.0	11,876	25,682	25,682	1,568	2,158	1,350	1,350
		'06	...	...	...	100.0	16,900	...	...	...	100.0	12,337	27,406	27,406	984	807	461	461
		'07	...	...	...	100.0	17,487	...	...	...	100.0	12,362	27,034	27,034	834	138	25	25
		'08	...	...	...	100.0	16,452	...	...	...	100.0	11,731	27,011	27,011	-1,715	-1,005	-630	-630
		'09	...	...	...	100.0	12,138	...	...	...	100.0	5,521	28,771	28,771	-3,529	-1,914	-1,210	-1,210
		Rating History: NR-5, 05/06/10; NR-5, 05/07/09; NR-5, 05/09/08; NR-5, 06/25/07; NR-5, 07/06/06																
FALLON COMMUNITY HEALTH PLAN Fallon Community Health Plan Inc Eric H. Schultz President 10 Chestnut Street Worcester, MA 01608-2810 MA : 1977 : Non-Profit : Broker Group A&H, Health, Ind A&H 508-799-2100 AMB# 060160 NAIC# 95541	NR-5	'05	45.6	...	36.0	18.4	227,031	...	53.3	...	46.7	134,336	767,792	766,840	5,494	25,892	25,892	24,611
		'06	44.7	...	37.2	18.1	275,608	...	51.9	...	48.1	153,649	836,024	835,346	43,204	19,660	19,660	21,976
		'07	42.8	...	36.4	20.7	300,046	...	54.8	...	45.2	171,470	890,389	889,783	20,807	18,104	18,104	17,742
		'08	44.0	...	32.8	23.2	281,443	...	47.4	...	52.6	122,510	988,207	987,351	26,412	19,392	19,392	11,628
		'09	52.1	...	27.0	20.8	272,287	...	53.2	...	46.8	100,953	1,076,962	1,075,829	-22,758	-17,459	-17,459	-19,020
		Rating History: NR-5, 04/14/10; NR-5, 08/26/09; B pd, 05/23/08; B pd, 05/30/07; B pd, 05/30/06																
FAMILY BENEFIT LIFE INS - MO[1] Ross A. Walquist President P.O. Box 665 Jefferson City, MO 65101 MO : 1964 : Stock : Agency Group Life, Ind A&H, Ind Life 573-636-3181 AMB# 007273 NAIC# 70742	NR-1	'05	92.6	1.1	0.3	6.0	57,471	...	...	8.5	91.5	7,050	2,100	2,367	...	727	610	611
		'06	90.9	1.0	0.3	7.8	58,148	...	...	9.2	90.8	7,712	2,066	2,396	...	968	886	879
		'07	87.5	2.0	0.3	10.2	56,754	...	...	8.4	91.6	7,954	1,783	2,111	...	779	607	607
		'08	83.3	1.4	0.3	15.0	57,860	...	...	8.6	91.4	9,135	2,096	2,321	...	980	875	1,575
		'09	87.8	1.6	0.5	10.1	58,693	...	...	8.2	91.8	9,655	1,580	1,837	...	1,291	1,086	1,174
		Rating History: NR-1, 06/10/10; NR-1, 06/12/09; NR-1, 06/12/08; NR-5, 05/20/08; NR-4, 09/18/07																
FAMILY GUARDIAN INSURANCE CO Famguard Corporation Limited Patricia A. Hermanns President & CEO East Bay Street Nassau, Bahamas BS : Stock : Exclusive Agent Life, A&S, Health 242-396-4000 AMB# 087111	A- Rating Outlook: Negative FSC VI	'05	17.6	55.9	6.2	20.3	120,553	92.7	...	...	7.3	32,636	...	55,150	...	5,078	5,118	5,279
		'06	24.8	49.8	5.2	20.3	134,564	50.4	4.4	32.4	12.7	36,076	...	61,265	6,843	5,747	5,747	5,978
		'07	26.1	45.3	5.8	22.8	149,155	50.9	4.8	32.3	11.9	40,563	...	65,292	7,889	7,882	7,882	8,181
		'08	27.5	43.5	4.6	24.5	160,531	52.0	5.2	30.8	12.0	42,170	...	73,423	6,137	5,248	5,248	5,249
		'09	...	...	...	...	...	...	...	...	...	...	...	...	...	...	...	...
		Rating History: A-, 04/23/10; A-, 03/31/09; A-, 04/29/08; A-, 12/15/06; A-, 07/13/05																
FAMILY HERITAGE LIFE OF AMER Southwestern/Great American, Inc. Howard L. Lewis President & CEO P.O. Box 470608 Cleveland, OH 44147 OH : 1989 : Stock : Exclusive Agent Ind Life, A&H, Dread dis 440-922-5200 AMB# 068197 NAIC# 77968	B++ Rating Outlook: Stable FSC VI	'05	96.3	...	...	3.7	183,057	0.1	94.8	...	5.1	20,724	78,087	78,087	23,574	11,636	6,061	6,061
		'06	96.9	...	...	3.1	216,364	0.1	97.0	...	2.9	24,383	89,108	89,108	22,183	13,675	7,398	7,398
		'07	97.1	...	...	2.9	262,362	0.1	94.9	...	5.0	27,090	104,667	104,638	31,738	15,571	7,149	7,149
		'08	98.3	...	...	1.7	309,399	0.1	96.9	...	2.9	34,025	120,000	119,984	29,658	20,378	12,714	12,716
		'09	95.1	...	...	4.9	365,394	0.2	97.8	...	2.1	41,694	131,971	131,950	39,137	22,189	13,334	13,334
		Rating History: B++, 02/19/10; B++, 02/17/09; B++, 03/11/08; B++, 03/09/07; B++, 03/10/06																
FAMILY LIBERTY LIFE INS CO[1] Thomas H. Fuqua, Jr. President 3720 Texas Boulevard Texarkana, TX 75503 TX : 1976 : Stock : Not Available 903-794-1300 AMB# 068198 NAIC# 85928	NR-1	'05	92.6	3.1	0.4	3.9	25,484	...	...	...	100.0	8,012	1,399	1,914	...	70	68	67
		'06	88.2	3.0	0.4	8.5	25,919	...	...	...	100.0	8,005	1,569	1,985	...	27	3	0
		'07	93.1	2.7	0.4	3.8	26,793	...	...	...	100.0	8,324	1,717	2,156	...	284	275	301
		'08	89.7	2.6	5.8	1.9	27,142	...	...	...	100.0	8,361	1,484	1,793	...	116	115	125
		'09	85.0	2.4	9.7	2.9	27,628	...	...	...	100.0	8,294	1,625	1,825	...	-44	-50	-116
		Rating History: NR-1, 06/10/10; NR-1, 06/12/09; NR-1, 06/12/08; NR-1, 06/08/07; NR-1, 06/07/06																
FAMILY LIFE INS CO Harris Insurance Holdings Inc Daniel J. George President 10700 Northwest Freeway Houston, TX 77092 TX : 1949 : Stock : Exclusive Agent Mtge Guaranty 713-529-0045 AMB# 006360 NAIC# 63053	B+ Rating Outlook: Negative FSC VI	'05	67.3	...	6.2	26.5	104,422	89.7	...	2.8	7.5	17,172	26,744	21,536	-6,459	-4,057	-3,974	-3,974
		'06	59.4	...	3.9	36.6	119,120	86.0	...	11.3	2.7	17,872	23,713	40,419	16,399	-3,337	-2,861	-4,850
		'07	64.6	...	1.4	34.0	127,816	82.3	...	11.8	5.8	22,514	21,139	20,129	9,249	8,148	6,512	6,508
		'08	63.5	...	...	36.5	126,179	84.2	...	10.8	5.0	25,371	17,122	15,997	-1,045	5,733	5,831	4,915
		'09	65.6	2.7	...	31.7	122,349	84.3	0.3	10.2	5.2	25,987	21,384	16,341	-4,819	5,109	4,370	4,370
		Rating History: B+, 03/23/10; B+, 04/16/09; B+, 03/04/08; B+, 01/31/07; B u, 12/11/06																
FAMILY SECURITY LIFE INS INC[1] Charles M. Laird President P.O. Box 1226 Natchez, MS 39121-1226 MS : 1970 : Stock : Not Available 601-442-4041 AMB# 068331 NAIC# 75337	NR-1	'05	77.5	10.0	6.2	6.3	5,254	...	...	...	100.0	1,155	805	805	...	-52	-51	-51
		'06	79.3	9.0	5.0	6.7	5,544	...	...	...	100.0	1,235	886	886	...	83	83	83
		'07	79.7	8.2	5.4	6.7	5,779	...	...	...	100.0	1,269	931	931	...	54	54	54
		'08	78.5	7.6	4.0	9.9	5,847	...	...	...	100.0	1,262	843	843	...	31	31	31
		'09	82.0	7.1	4.4	6.5	5,952	...	...	...	100.0	1,314	774	774	...	64	57	57
		Rating History: NR-1, 06/10/10; NR-1, 06/12/09; NR-1, 06/12/08; NR-1, 06/08/07; NR-1, 06/07/06																

BEST'S PROFITABILITY, LEVERAGE AND LIQUIDITY TESTS 2005 – 2009

Data in U.S. Dollars

—	Profitability Tests							Leverage Tests						Liquidity Tests					
Un-Realized Capital Gains ($000)	Benefits Paid to NPW & Dep (%)	Comm. & Expenses to NPW & Dep (%)	NOG to Total Assets (%)	NOG to Total Rev (%)	Operating Return on Equity (%)	Net Yield (%)	Total Return (%)	Change in NPW & Dep (%)	NPW & Dep to Capital (X)	Capital & Surplus to Liabilities (%)	Surplus Relief (%)	Reins Leverage (%)	Change in Capital (%)	Quick Liquidity (%)	Current Liquidity (%)	Non-Invest Grade Bonds to Capital (%)	Delinq. & Foreclosed Mortgages to Capital (%)	Mort. & Credit Tenant Loans & R.E. to Capital (%)	Affiliated Invest to Capital (%)
-5,413	85.5	9.3	10.1	4.2	21.8	2.54	2.74	10.3	4.6	93.6	...	0.0	23.5	144.6	158.3	...	...	6.1	18.2
-891	87.2	10.2	6.9	2.9	13.7	3.12	3.61	8.8	4.3	111.2	...	...	17.8	124.1	138.9	...	...	4.8	15.9
-8,101	90.1	9.8	1.9	0.8	3.6	3.63	5.67	6.7	4.3	111.9	...	...	4.8	126.6	142.0	...	...	4.3	17.5
-191,725	89.8	10.6	0.8	0.3	1.6	2.47	-13.49	-3.0	5.8	78.8	...	...	-27.7	104.9	117.3	0.1	...	5.5	9.9
57,906	88.5	11.6	0.7	0.3	1.7	2.92	8.86	-1.8	5.1	78.1	...	...	12.5	89.3	101.5	0.5	...	4.7	28.5
Principal Lines of Business: CompHosp/Med (72.7%), Medicare (15.3%), Medicaid (5.6%), FEHBP (2.0%), MedSup (1.6%)													Principal States: NY (100.0%)						
...	128.9	7.5	9.0	2.9	12.1	0.96	0.96	1.9	2.2	293.5	...	...	12.8	317.9	317.9	...	...	...	...
...	139.1	10.6	2.8	0.9	3.8	1.03	1.03	6.7	2.2	270.4	...	...	3.9	303.4	303.4	...	...	...	...
...	147.8	10.0	0.1	0.0	0.2	0.75	0.75	-1.4	2.2	241.2	...	...	0.2	286.4	286.4	...	...	...	...
...	136.8	10.4	-3.7	-1.3	-5.2	0.78	0.78	-0.1	2.3	248.5	...	...	-5.1	274.6	274.6	...	...	...	...
...	127.8	9.4	-8.5	-2.4	-14.0	0.57	0.57	6.5	5.2	83.4	...	...	-52.9	142.6	142.6	...	...	...	...
Principal Lines of Business: Vision (100.0%)																			
4,306	88.9	8.5	11.8	3.3	21.6	3.59	5.08	5.0	5.7	144.9	...	...	26.9	150.7	172.8	...	...	...	2.2
394	90.4	8.3	7.8	2.3	13.7	4.02	5.19	8.9	5.4	126.0	...	...	14.4	129.8	149.8	...	...	...	2.1
1,846	90.6	8.5	6.3	2.0	11.1	4.30	4.86	6.5	5.2	133.4	...	0.5	11.6	134.8	154.2	...	...	...	2.1
-40,122	90.8	8.6	6.7	1.9	13.2	5.23	-12.00	11.0	8.1	77.1	...	0.8	-28.6	110.2	123.4	...	...	...	2.5
11,756	94.1	8.5	-6.3	-1.6	-15.6	4.35	8.74	9.0	10.7	58.9	...	0.0	-17.6	91.1	103.2	...	...	...	3.8
Principal Lines of Business: CompHosp/Med (56.8%), Medicare (35.5%), Medicaid (5.3%), FEHBP (2.3%)													Principal States: MA (100.0%)						
...	165.2	38.7	1.1	11.0	8.9	...	...	-19.0	0.3	14.5	...	...	5.5	...	...	...	...	8.9	...
...	163.6	38.4	1.5	15.6	12.0	...	...	1.2	0.3	15.7	...	...	9.0	...	...	...	...	7.4	...
...	239.3	48.8	1.1	11.3	7.7	...	...	-11.9	0.3	16.8	...	...	3.1	...	...	...	...	13.8	...
...	159.6	34.7	1.5	16.2	10.2	...	...	9.9	0.2	19.2	...	...	14.4	...	...	...	...	8.9	...
...	147.7	41.2	1.9	20.5	11.6	...	...	-20.9	0.2	20.1	...	...	5.4	...	...	...	...	9.6	...
Principal Lines of Business: OrdLife (46.0%), IndAnn (31.8%), GrpLife (22.0%), IndA&H (0.2%)																			
...	60.5	46.2	4.5	8.0	16.1	7.32	7.47	16.3	169.0	37.1	...	...	5.7	41.0	119.6	...	...	206.5	...
-41	62.7	42.9	4.5	8.1	16.7	6.65	6.84	11.1	169.8	36.6	...	...	10.5	50.7	118.4	...	...	185.6	...
-172	61.5	44.2	5.6	10.2	20.6	6.72	6.95	6.6	161.0	37.4	...	...	12.4	55.8	114.5	...	...	166.6	...
-503	65.3	40.4	3.4	6.3	12.7	6.86	6.86	12.5	174.1	35.6	...	...	4.0	56.7	110.6	...	...	165.6	...
...	...	...	...	...	...	...	...	...	...	...	...	...	...	...	...	...	...	...	...
-5	17.8	44.5	3.6	6.8	32.0	6.83	6.83	12.8	3.7	13.1	...	...	20.7	93.9	94.1	...	...	...	...
28	17.9	45.7	3.7	7.2	32.8	7.02	7.04	14.1	3.6	12.8	...	...	15.5	93.1	93.8	...	...	...	...
55	17.9	47.7	3.0	5.9	27.8	6.94	6.96	17.4	3.8	11.6	0.1	0.0	11.2	90.5	92.1	...	...	...	...
70	18.9	43.9	4.4	9.2	41.6	6.68	6.71	14.7	3.5	12.4	0.0	0.0	25.5	91.4	92.8	...	...	...	...
73	20.0	41.6	4.0	8.8	35.2	6.25	6.27	10.0	3.1	13.0	0.0	0.1	22.4	93.8	95.2	...	...	...	...
Principal Lines of Business: IndA&H (99.6%), OrdLife (0.4%)													Principal States: TX (21.0%), OH (11.0%), IL (7.7%), IN (5.8%), NC (4.5%)						
-13	82.2	34.6	0.3	2.5	0.8	...	...	-4.6	0.2	46.1	...	...	0.8	...	...	...	...	9.9	...
-2	83.4	32.9	0.0	0.1	0.0	...	...	3.7	0.2	44.9	...	...	0.0	...	...	...	...	9.6	...
3	73.6	32.6	1.0	8.8	3.4	...	...	8.7	0.3	45.2	...	...	3.9	...	...	...	...	8.8	...
-59	107.5	27.8	0.4	4.2	1.4	...	...	-16.9	0.2	44.6	...	...	0.4	...	...	...	...	8.3	...
197	92.5	33.9	-0.2	-1.8	-0.6	...	...	1.8	0.2	44.2	...	...	1.1	...	...	...	...	7.8	...
Principal Lines of Business: IndAnn (78.6%), GrpLife (11.0%), OrdLife (10.4%)																			
329	57.8	90.8	-3.7	-14.8	-20.3	4.69	5.01	2.9	1.2	20.7	6.6	148.3	-18.9	70.0	77.3	19.8	...	...	24.7
1,376	33.7	42.8	-2.6	-6.3	-16.3	4.60	4.04	87.7	2.2	18.1	2.4	21.0	1.7	106.3	113.2	13.7	...	...	...
-396	69.6	39.8	5.3	24.9	32.2	5.23	4.93	-50.2	0.9	21.8	1.1	18.1	25.6	109.5	116.0	10.9	...	...	...
407	81.8	34.9	4.6	27.3	24.4	4.44	4.07	-20.5	0.6	25.2	1.2	14.5	10.8	119.8	125.9	4.8	...	...	...
...	68.5	47.5	3.5	19.3	17.0	3.91	3.91	2.2	0.6	27.1	7.6	18.3	2.9	109.3	114.8	11.7	...	12.5	...
Principal Lines of Business: OrdLife (92.8%), IndA&H (6.1%), IndAnn (1.0%)													Principal States: TX (28.7%), CA (15.5%), MS (7.5%), LA (3.5%), FL (3.3%)						
-2	60.9	59.7	-1.0	-4.9	-4.3	...	...	-1.4	0.7	30.2	...	...	-4.2	...	...	...	...	43.3	...
1	53.7	44.5	1.5	7.2	6.9	...	...	10.1	0.7	30.7	...	...	6.9	...	...	...	...	38.4	...
-15	62.3	45.4	1.0	4.4	4.3	...	...	5.1	0.7	29.8	...	...	2.0	...	...	...	...	35.7	...
-73	60.2	40.7	0.5	3.1	2.4	...	...	-9.4	0.6	28.6	...	...	-2.2	...	...	...	...	34.4	...
24	65.4	59.3	1.0	5.3	4.5	...	...	-8.2	0.6	30.2	...	...	6.3	...	...	...	...	30.4	...
Principal Lines of Business: OrdLife (69.6%), IndLife (30.4%)																			

Data in U.S. Dollars

COMPANY NAME / Ultimate Parent Association / Principal Officer / Mailing Address / Dom. : Began Bus. : Struct. : Mktg. / Specialty / Phone # / AMB# NAIC#	Best's Financial Strength Rating / FSC	Data Year	Balance Sheet: Bonds (%)	Mort. Loans & R.E. (%)	Com & Pref. Stock (%)	All Other Assets (%)	Total Assets ($000)	Life Reserves (%)	Health Reserves (%)	Ann Res. & Dep. Liabilities (%)	All Other Liabilities (%)	Capital & Surplus ($000)	Operations: Direct Premiums Written ($000)	Net Premiums Written & Deposits ($000)	Operating Cash Flow ($000)	NOG Before Taxes ($000)	NOG After Taxes ($000)	Net Income ($000)
FAMILY SERVICE LIFE INS CO	**A**	'05	92.4	...	3.0	4.6	600,575	39.0	...	58.6	2.4	87,088	32	32	-10,013	15,718	13,753	15,953
Guardian Life Ins Co of America / Armand M. de Palo / President & CEO		'06	92.1	...	3.0	4.9	579,531	39.0	...	58.8	2.1	90,434	28	28	-19,705	11,059	7,991	7,823
7 Hanover Square / New York, NY 10004-2616	Rating Outlook: Stable	'07	93.9	...	3.2	2.8	560,761	38.8	...	59.0	2.2	94,499	18	18	-19,067	13,364	10,149	11,139
TX : 1955 : Stock : Inactive / Ind Ann, Ind Life, Pre-need		'08	94.3	...	3.0	2.7	530,615	39.1	...	59.7	1.2	90,769	21	21	-24,782	9,726	8,881	6,604
800-538-6203		'09	90.8	...	3.0	6.2	519,558	39.1	...	59.3	1.6	96,540	15	15	-6,158	8,641	6,190	7,965
AMB# 007650 NAIC# 74004	FSC VII	Rating History: A, 10/13/09; A, 11/26/08; A, 04/23/08; A, 11/10/06; A, 11/18/05																
FAMILYCARE HEALTH PLANS INC[2]	**NR-5**	'05	40.7	...	6.8	52.5	2,710	...	55.9	...	44.1	1,276	1,045	1,045	1,200	-859	-859	-859
Jeff S. Heatherington / President		'06	12.2	...	17.1	70.6	7,330	...	56.4	...	43.6	3,052	10,506	10,367	4,112	915	915	915
2121 SW Broadway, Suite 300 / Portland, OR 97201		'07	43.1	...	2.6	54.2	10,088	...	32.2	...	67.8	4,922	14,290	14,076	1,909	1,961	1,961	1,961
OR : 1997 : Non-Profit : Agency / Group A&H		'08	62.1	...	9.6	28.2	9,290	...	44.6	...	55.4	4,318	20,706	20,409	-178	109	109	146
503-222-3205		'09	77.4	...	2.8	19.8	12,386	...	41.2	...	58.8	6,278	27,198	26,908	3,014	1,051	1,051	999
AMB# 064499 NAIC# 47084		Rating History: NR-5, 09/11/09; NR-5, 07/14/08; NR-5, 07/02/07; NR-5, 05/11/06; NR-5, 05/09/05																
FARM BUREAU LIFE INS CO	**B++**	'05	71.7	8.1	3.1	17.1	5,370,716	40.2	0.0	45.8	14.0	395,855	523,872	672,363	136,860	65,143	44,921	45,972
Iowa Farm Bureau Federation / James E. Hohmann / CEO		'06	67.7	7.9	5.4	19.0	5,477,686	40.1	0.0	44.3	15.5	335,314	470,155	612,897	12,237	56,012	38,291	49,340
5400 University Avenue / West Des Moines, IA 50266-5997	Rating Outlook: Negative	'07	68.6	7.5	3.4	20.4	5,633,103	40.3	0.0	42.9	16.8	364,915	484,637	622,986	58,668	73,609	51,706	55,153
IA : 1945 : Stock : Exclusive Agent / Ann, Trad Life, Var Univ life		'08	69.5	8.1	3.2	19.2	5,591,863	42.1	0.0	46.4	11.5	385,372	585,828	727,138	143,908	54,160	38,182	-28,712
515-225-5400		'09	71.5	7.8	0.9	19.9	5,983,345	40.0	0.0	46.9	13.1	428,458	626,103	748,437	294,718	110,561	78,747	45,518
AMB# 006362 NAIC# 63088	FSC IX	Rating History: B++, 12/18/09; B++, 02/27/09; A-, 09/26/08; A, 08/23/07; A, 10/10/06																
FARM BUREAU LIFE INS CO OF MI	**A**	'05	71.3	18.2	4.4	6.1	1,609,324	33.4	...	61.7	4.9	251,022	133,461	132,506	70,636	34,586	21,869	20,827
Michigan Farm Bureau / Wayne H. Wood / President		'06	69.6	19.3	5.1	6.0	1,655,949	34.0	...	61.9	4.0	278,142	114,613	113,277	37,624	34,943	22,779	22,145
P.O. Box 30200 / Lansing, MI 48909	Rating Outlook: Stable	'07	67.9	21.0	5.2	5.9	1,695,448	34.5	...	61.0	4.4	298,980	105,822	103,666	39,861	32,260	21,201	20,970
MI : 1951 : Stock : Agency / Univ Life, Whole life, Annuity		'08	67.1	21.8	4.3	6.8	1,740,878	34.9	...	61.8	3.3	283,724	140,676	137,733	66,218	18,719	10,368	-6,462
517-323-7000		'09	68.1	20.4	4.9	6.6	1,884,159	33.7	...	61.5	4.8	300,480	169,864	166,778	123,696	26,296	16,039	18,900
AMB# 006363 NAIC# 63096	FSC IX	Rating History: A, 04/23/10; A, 06/12/09; A, 05/27/08; A, 05/07/07; A, 04/18/06																
FARM BUREAU LIFE INS CO OF MO	**A-**	'05	84.0	...	8.1	7.9	337,850	65.6	0.0	31.3	3.1	50,234	35,202	32,342	18,045	1,765	1,948	1,569
Missouri Farm Bureau Federation / Charles E. Kruse / President		'06	81.3	...	10.6	8.1	353,256	66.8	0.0	29.9	3.2	51,613	32,745	29,114	13,613	1,909	1,331	1,331
P.O. Box 658 / Jefferson City, MO 65102-0658	Rating Outlook: Stable	'07	79.5	...	12.2	8.3	363,501	69.2	0.0	27.4	3.4	52,529	34,553	30,584	10,909	2,144	1,418	1,418
MO : 1950 : Stock : Career Agent / Ind Ann, Term Life, Whole life		'08	81.5	...	10.2	8.3	367,925	70.0	0.0	27.1	2.9	45,307	38,312	33,848	12,936	4,649	2,541	-238
573-893-1400		'09	86.2	...	4.2	9.7	391,118	69.0	0.0	28.2	2.8	45,267	48,036	43,824	22,526	2,785	2,254	1,638
AMB# 006364 NAIC# 63118	FSC VI	Rating History: A-, 05/06/10; A-, 05/18/09; A-, 06/10/08; A-, 06/08/07; A-, 06/21/06																
FARM FAMILY LIFE INS CO	**A**	'05	80.6	4.5	7.3	7.6	981,025	58.3	1.1	36.3	4.3	120,924	67,444	74,263	40,191	14,860	10,339	15,399
American National Insurance Company / Timothy A. Walsh / President & CEO		'06	78.4	4.2	7.7	9.7	1,016,437	58.5	1.2	34.8	5.6	125,749	62,935	76,253	28,910	15,332	9,592	13,444
P.O. Box 656 / Albany, NY 12201-0656	Rating Outlook: Stable	'07	77.6	5.0	8.6	8.7	1,014,955	61.0	1.3	33.4	4.2	125,127	66,030	75,132	-114	14,090	9,104	11,539
NY : 1954 : Stock : Career Agent / Whole life, Term Life, Dis inc		'08	78.5	6.7	7.1	7.7	990,963	61.9	1.4	34.0	2.7	91,290	74,373	89,675	6,609	14,649	10,228	-12,517
518-431-5000		'09	74.9	7.5	8.1	9.5	1,055,361	60.5	1.5	34.2	3.8	108,683	77,513	93,109	36,612	13,161	9,556	1,906
AMB# 006365 NAIC# 63126	FSC VIII	Rating History: A, 05/20/10; A, 06/09/09; A, 05/13/08; A, 04/26/07; A, 02/08/06																
FARMERS NEW WORLD LIFE INS CO	**A**	'05	79.6	0.9	0.6	18.9	6,744,360	43.2	0.0	43.5	13.3	634,579	848,601	790,181	-310,618	211,988	161,542	175,287
Zurich Financial Services Ltd / Thomas J. White / President & CEO		'06	77.7	0.9	0.4	21.1	6,966,390	43.7	0.0	41.2	15.0	668,552	870,171	784,630	122,129	185,968	126,434	142,199
3003 77th Avenue Southeast / Mercer Island, WA 98040-2837	Rating Outlook: Stable	'07	74.4	0.8	0.7	24.0	6,987,510	45.1	0.0	39.5	15.4	641,255	906,786	783,122	42,416	137,476	89,804	97,945
WA : 1911 : Stock : Exclusive Agent / Univ Life, Trad Life, Ind Ann		'08	79.1	0.8	0.3	19.7	6,443,866	49.9	0.0	42.2	7.9	551,476	902,815	778,409	-63,131	169,135	127,934	19,206
206-232-8400		'09	80.2	0.8	0.0	19.0	6,739,594	49.1	0.0	41.5	9.4	674,128	894,766	777,682	39,519	184,700	131,048	-13,309
AMB# 006373 NAIC# 63177	FSC X	Rating History: A, 06/16/09; A, 06/18/08; A, 06/19/07; A, 06/21/06; A, 04/14/05																
FEDERAL LIFE INS CO (MUTUAL)[1]	**NR-1**	'05	73.9	1.1	2.4	22.6	233,024	...	...	5.7	94.3	35,882	17,963	19,987	...	-3,369	-3,259	-3,143
William S. Austin / President		'06	72.2	1.0	3.7	23.0	238,479	...	...	5.3	94.7	35,199	19,774	23,471	...	-943	-766	-605
3750 W. Deerfield Road / Riverwoods, IL 60015		'07	72.2	1.1	5.2	21.5	235,623	...	...	5.3	94.7	32,973	20,213	24,891	...	-1,783	-1,582	-682
IL : 1900 : Mutual : Not Available		'08	75.6	1.1	4.7	18.6	219,093	...	...	5.6	94.4	29,824	16,305	20,397	...	-988	-531	-2,621
847-520-1900		'09	74.2	1.1	4.8	20.0	219,367	...	...	5.4	94.6	25,629	17,931	22,869	...	-1,963	-1,689	-6,079
AMB# 006378 NAIC# 63223		Rating History: NR-1, 06/10/10; NR-1, 06/12/09; NR-5, 06/30/08; NR-5, 06/28/07; NR-5, 06/16/06																
FEDERATED LIFE INS CO	**A+**	'05	88.4	...	3.9	7.7	815,406	71.8	5.6	19.9	2.6	197,194	113,460	110,383	51,289	29,149	18,221	18,180
Federated Mutual Insurance Company / Jeffrey E. Fetters / President & CEO		'06	88.0	...	4.2	7.7	868,678	72.8	5.9	18.7	2.6	205,217	119,317	114,817	50,909	26,034	16,910	17,124
121 East Park Square / Owatonna, MN 55060-3046	Rating Outlook: Stable	'07	89.1	...	3.4	7.6	919,053	74.2	5.9	17.5	2.5	216,977	122,907	118,474	48,946	32,085	21,077	21,071
MN : 1959 : Stock : Exclusive Agent / Dis inc, Term Life, Univ Life		'08	89.1	...	2.5	8.4	954,854	75.4	5.8	17.3	1.6	217,960	130,249	123,618	45,314	35,027	19,860	12,249
507-455-5200		'09	89.8	...	0.7	9.5	1,018,531	75.3	5.9	17.1	1.7	234,536	142,123	136,431	56,469	36,299	26,532	19,176
AMB# 006381 NAIC# 63258	FSC VIII	Rating History: A+, 11/25/09; A+, 01/26/09; A+, 01/10/08; A+, 12/20/06; A+, 03/24/06																

BEST'S PROFITABILITY, LEVERAGE AND LIQUIDITY TESTS 2005 – 2009

Data in U.S. Dollars

	Profitability Tests							Leverage Tests						Liquidity Tests					
Un-Realized Capital Gains ($000)	Benefits Paid to NPW & Dep (%)	Comm. & Expenses to NPW & Dep (%)	NOG to Total Assets (%)	NOG to Total Rev (%)	Operating Return on Equity (%)	Net Yield (%)	Total Return (%)	Change in NPW & Dep (%)	NPW & Dep to Capital (X)	Capital & Surplus to Liabilities (%)	Surplus Relief (%)	Reins Leverage (%)	Change in Capital (%)	Quick Liquidity (%)	Current Liquidity (%)	Non-Invest Grade Bonds to Capital (%)	Delinq. & Foreclosed Mortgages to Capital (%)	Mort. & Credit Tenant Loans & R.E. to Capital (%)	Affiliated Invest to Capital (%)
1,594	999.9	999.9	2.3	37.6	17.1	6.22	6.88	-74.8	0.0	17.9	0.1	17.5	16.3	76.8	89.9	26.0	...	...	16.5
612	999.9	999.9	1.4	22.8	9.0	6.05	6.19	-10.5	0.0	19.6	0.1	15.8	3.8	77.2	90.8	26.6	...	...	16.6
1,177	999.9	999.9	1.8	29.9	11.0	6.05	6.54	-37.8	0.0	21.4	0.0	14.3	4.2	75.3	89.0	24.3	...	...	17.1
-1,786	999.9	999.9	1.6	26.9	9.6	6.18	5.52	20.5	0.0	21.3	...	13.9	-5.6	75.0	87.8	32.0	...	...	16.2
645	999.9	999.9	1.2	20.2	6.6	5.81	6.47	-30.7	0.0	23.8	...	12.4	7.0	79.7	94.0	26.6	...	...	15.8
Principal Lines of Business: OrdLife (100.0%)														Principal States: TX (54.5%), LA (13.6%), CA (12.0%), FL (5.4%), AZ (4.5%)					
...	85.1	97.1	-44.5	-82.2	-70.7	...	...	...	0.8	89.0	...	...	10.6	173.8	175.7	...	...	...	...
18	78.1	15.3	18.2	8.6	42.3	5.05	5.42	892.2	3.4	71.3	...	7.1	139.2	239.2	253.7	...	...	...	...
6	74.9	14.2	22.5	13.5	49.2	5.69	5.77	35.8	2.9	95.3	...	50.9	61.3	217.8	227.7	...	...	...	...
-57	83.4	17.6	1.1	0.5	2.3	3.75	3.53	45.0	4.7	86.8	...	4.5	-12.3	45.2	47.9	...	...	...	...
...	84.9	12.3	9.7	3.9	19.8	3.21	2.68	31.8	4.3	102.8	...	2.6	45.4	178.8	180.1	...	...	...	...
Principal Lines of Business: Medicare (100.0%)														Principal States: OR (100.0%)					
9,478	59.2	19.7	0.9	5.4	11.6	6.55	6.85	-2.2	1.5	10.3	1.8	22.6	4.6	50.7	66.5	55.2	0.5	121.6	7.1
-14,101	72.0	21.0	0.7	4.9	10.5	6.48	6.48	-8.8	1.6	8.6	2.1	32.5	-15.2	47.9	64.0	62.0	0.2	141.1	6.3
-9,690	72.2	19.9	0.9	6.4	14.8	6.47	6.40	1.6	1.5	9.1	1.8	31.1	7.3	49.0	64.7	57.7	...	126.9	5.6
-7,801	60.1	17.9	0.7	4.2	10.2	6.19	4.70	16.7	1.8	8.4	1.8	31.2	-3.0	49.9	64.9	65.2	1.4	140.0	0.0
-3,588	55.7	16.9	1.4	8.3	19.4	6.12	5.44	2.9	1.7	9.0	1.7	25.9	11.7	50.4	65.2	64.8	1.5	127.2	1.4
Principal Lines of Business: IndAnn (50.0%), OrdLife (33.7%), GrpAnn (16.0%), GrpLife (0.1%), GrpA&H (0.1%)														Principal States: IA (28.3%), KS (18.4%), OK (11.0%), MN (5.3%), NE (4.8%)					
1,008	77.2	16.1	1.4	9.6	9.0	6.21	6.26	-12.6	0.5	20.8	0.6	1.3	6.6	46.9	63.3	24.8	...	105.4	3.7
5,233	103.5	18.1	1.4	10.8	8.6	6.00	6.34	-14.5	0.4	22.7	0.5	0.8	10.4	47.6	64.6	16.0	...	104.4	4.6
1,204	125.2	19.9	1.3	10.5	7.3	5.92	6.02	-8.5	0.3	24.0	0.6	0.7	7.3	46.1	63.9	11.3	...	108.1	4.5
-18,993	82.6	16.4	0.6	4.4	3.6	5.82	3.70	32.9	0.5	20.3	0.6	0.7	-10.5	46.9	63.8	13.9	...	129.0	4.7
9,802	68.6	14.1	0.9	6.0	5.5	5.77	6.50	21.1	0.5	21.5	0.6	0.7	13.4	48.7	65.4	17.9	3.1	115.3	4.0
Principal Lines of Business: IndAnn (60.2%), OrdLife (38.3%), GrpAnn (1.2%), GrpLife (0.3%)														Principal States: MI (98.2%)					
-115	50.4	35.5	0.6	3.8	3.9	5.99	5.90	-1.1	0.6	18.3	1.2	13.0	2.3	79.8	91.4	...	...	...	3.8
464	62.4	37.7	0.4	2.8	2.6	5.84	6.03	-10.0	0.5	18.1	1.6	14.0	3.7	77.5	90.2	...	...	...	3.7
-401	75.9	38.0	0.4	2.8	2.7	5.81	5.75	5.0	0.6	17.8	1.4	12.5	1.4	74.8	87.2	...	...	...	3.7
-6,054	59.7	35.8	0.7	4.7	5.2	5.85	3.45	10.7	0.7	14.0	2.1	17.9	-17.5	71.5	83.3	5.3	...	...	4.5
-725	52.3	28.1	0.6	3.5	5.0	5.76	5.48	29.5	1.0	13.3	2.1	17.2	1.4	69.1	79.2	28.1	...	...	6.5
Principal Lines of Business: OrdLife (58.1%), IndAnn (41.6%), GrpLife (0.2%), GrpA&H (0.1%), GrpAnn (0.1%)														Principal States: MO (94.8%)					
-1,970	72.1	22.0	1.1	8.4	8.6	6.09	6.46	11.0	0.6	15.5	0.6	9.2	2.0	67.7	80.2	27.7	0.0	33.6	3.5
2,988	82.9	22.0	1.0	7.9	7.8	5.95	6.73	2.7	0.5	16.1	0.7	10.9	6.6	72.7	85.3	24.1	...	30.2	3.5
-911	89.1	24.2	0.9	7.3	7.3	5.80	6.00	-1.5	0.5	16.2	0.7	12.5	0.8	71.7	84.0	25.0	...	35.9	3.4
-17,949	76.6	20.9	1.0	8.0	9.5	5.83	1.81	19.4	1.0	10.2	0.9	19.2	-35.2	66.3	77.7	39.2	...	72.7	5.5
15,204	69.4	19.4	0.9	7.3	9.6	5.69	6.51	3.8	0.8	13.2	0.7	19.4	33.7	68.0	79.5	37.7	...	64.5	3.8
Principal Lines of Business: OrdLife (49.4%), IndAnn (27.1%), GrpAnn (18.3%), IndA&H (4.8%), GrpLife (0.4%)														Principal States: NY (38.9%), NJ (12.0%), MA (11.2%), WV (6.4%), ME (4.8%)					
-7,562	53.3	22.7	2.4	15.5	18.7	5.86	6.11	-1.2	1.2	11.4	10.4	87.2	-41.4	63.7	77.8	7.4	0.6	9.4	2.7
-3,309	58.9	24.0	1.8	12.4	19.4	5.61	5.93	-0.7	1.1	11.9	11.6	106.0	6.0	62.2	76.0	8.9	0.5	8.7	2.6
18,462	65.9	23.0	1.3	8.8	13.7	5.55	6.08	-0.2	1.1	11.9	17.1	134.0	-0.8	61.2	75.0	8.4	0.5	8.5	6.6
-60,420	67.8	21.3	1.9	12.4	21.5	5.33	2.87	-0.6	1.4	9.9	21.9	186.0	-20.3	66.5	79.4	21.0	0.6	9.8	2.5
-3,070	61.7	20.2	2.0	13.0	21.4	5.48	3.07	-0.1	1.2	11.9	18.7	176.8	22.2	63.7	77.3	26.1	0.5	7.9	0.9
Principal Lines of Business: OrdLife (61.9%), GrpAnn (21.5%), IndAnn (12.7%), GrpLife (3.1%), IndA&H (0.9%)														Principal States: CA (30.2%), TX (18.1%), IL (5.1%), AZ (4.5%), WA (4.1%)					
-16	90.7	69.5	-1.4	-10.2	-8.7	...	...	-9.0	0.5	22.4	0.3	...	-7.5	...	...	...	...	6.8	...
428	85.3	56.0	-0.3	-2.2	-2.2	...	...	17.4	0.6	22.0	0.3	...	-0.3	...	...	...	...	6.5	...
-580	96.4	50.4	-0.7	-4.3	-4.6	...	...	6.0	0.7	21.0	0.3	...	-4.5	...	...	...	...	7.1	...
-2,338	103.3	62.6	-0.2	-1.6	-1.7	...	...	-18.1	0.7	17.5	0.3	...	-16.0	...	...	...	...	8.1	...
1,895	97.5	57.9	-0.8	-4.9	-6.1	...	...	12.1	0.9	14.9	0.2	...	-14.0	...	...	...	...	9.0	...
Principal Lines of Business: OrdLife (47.7%), GrpLife (28.1%), GrpAnn (22.4%), IndA&H (1.3%), IndAnn (0.4%)																			
-75	43.6	33.0	2.3	11.7	9.4	6.20	6.24	6.7	0.5	32.8	...	1.3	4.2	82.8	103.0	11.3	...	19.3	...
1,703	48.3	34.7	2.0	10.3	8.4	6.16	6.43	4.0	0.5	32.2	...	1.3	4.9	84.3	104.0	11.0	...	20.7	...
428	47.9	36.0	2.4	12.4	10.0	6.11	6.19	3.2	0.5	32.2	...	1.7	5.9	84.1	103.2	15.6	...	18.5	...
-5,111	45.6	37.1	2.1	11.2	9.1	6.08	4.73	4.3	0.6	29.6	...	1.7	-2.5	82.1	100.3	27.5	...	18.2	...
-1,803	48.9	34.8	2.7	13.6	11.7	6.29	5.36	10.4	0.6	29.9	...	1.7	7.5	80.7	99.0	27.8	...	23.6	...
Principal Lines of Business: OrdLife (69.1%), IndA&H (17.0%), IndAnn (9.4%), GrpLife (4.5%)														Principal States: MN (12.1%), CA (6.2%), TX (6.2%), IL (5.8%), IN (5.4%)					

Data in U.S. Dollars

COMPANY NAME Ultimate Parent Association Principal Officer Mailing Address Dom. : Began Bus. : Struct. : Mktg. Specialty Phone # AMB# NAIC#	Best's Financial Strength Rating FSC	Data Year	Balance Sheet Bonds (%)	Mort. Loans & R.E. (%)	Com & Pref. Stock (%)	All Other Assets (%)	Total Assets ($000)	Life Reserves (%)	Health Reserves %)	Ann Res. & Dep. Liabilities (%)	All Other Liabilities (%)	Capital & Surplus ($000)	Operations Direct Premiums Written ($000)	Net Premiums Written & Deposits ($000)	Operating Cash Flow ($000)	NOG Before Taxes ($000)	NOG After Taxes ($000)	Net Income ($000)
FIDELIS SECURECARE OF MICHIGAN Fidelis SeniorCare Inc Cathy Kiley President 1700 East Golf Road, Suite 1115 Schaumburg, IL 60173 MI : 2005 : Stock : Broker Health 847-605-0501 AMB# 064849 NAIC# 10769	NR-5	'05	23.4	...	50.1	26.5	2,211	...	91.8	...	8.2	1,587	829	815	1,937	-13	-13	-13
		'06	10.4	...	...	89.6	5,215	...	78.3	...	21.7	1,558	8,896	8,757	2,767	58	58	58
		'07	15.8	...	...	84.2	6,622	...	79.8	...	20.2	1,718	19,589	19,290	1,877	254	207	207
		'08	12.6	...	...	87.4	8,366	...	89.5	...	10.5	3,311	25,914	25,914	1,681	583	385	385
		'09	10.8	...	...	89.2	9,796	...	64.9	...	35.1	6,188	21,029	20,898	1,403	4,487	2,962	2,962
		Rating History: NR-5, 05/21/10; NR-5, 05/13/09; NR-5, 05/12/08; NR-5, 04/11/07; NR-5, 07/12/06																
FIDELIS SECURECARE OF NC[2] Fidelis SeniorCare Inc Joseph R. Dunlap President 1700 East Golf Road, Suite 1115 Schaumburg, IL 60173 NC : 2005 : Stock : Broker Health 847-605-0501 AMB# 064861 NAIC# 12288	NR-5	'05	...	...	...	...	...	...	...	...	...	...	...	...	...	...	...	...
		'06	12.9	...	0.5	86.6	4,073	...	60.5	...	39.5	3,261	2,249	2,215	784	-1,915	-1,915	-1,915
		'07	11.8	...	0.8	87.4	4,541	...	58.5	...	41.5	2,168	8,264	8,116	471	-1,852	-1,852	-1,852
		'08	...	...	...	100.0	6,538	...	44.5	...	55.5	1,761	12,883	12,883	1,250	-4,249	-2,804	-2,804
		'09	...	...	...	100.0	5,055	...	58.7	...	41.3	2,630	12,547	12,462	-888	1,073	708	708
		Rating History: NR-5, 04/29/10; NR-5, 03/26/09; NR-5, 04/10/08; NR-5, 05/01/07																
FIDELIS SECURECARE OF TEXAS[2] Fidelis SeniorCare Inc Eddie Parades President 17625 El Camino Real Houston, TX 77058 TX : 2006 : Stock : Not Available Health 847-605-0501 AMB# 064860 NAIC# 12597	NR-5	'05	...	...	...	...	...	...	...	...	...	...	...	...	...	...	...	...
		'06	8.1	...	0.1	91.8	1,515	...	...	...	100.0	1,510	...	...	1,510	15	10	10
		'07	3.2	...	0.0	96.7	4,015	...	75.5	...	24.5	2,295	9,669	9,547	2,015	784	555	555
		'08	10.2	...	...	89.8	4,526	...	69.1	...	30.9	2,384	7,773	7,773	1,030	118	78	78
		'09	7.5	...	...	92.5	4,372	...	49.1	...	50.9	3,629	6,967	6,932	-122	1,899	1,253	1,253
		Rating History: NR-5, 04/07/10; NR-5, 03/23/09; NR-5, 04/10/08; NR-5, 04/11/07																
FIDELITY INVESTMENTS LIFE INS FMR LLC Jeff Cimini President 82 Devonshire Street, V5A Boston, MA 02109-3605 UT : 1981 : Stock : Direct Response Var ann, Var life 801-537-2070 AMB# 009138 NAIC# 93696	A+	'05	5.0	...	0.4	94.6	12,280,312	0.1	...	1.2	98.7	566,312	720,467	827,785	28,251	52,578	45,572	48,301
		'06	4.6	...	0.4	95.1	13,590,037	0.1	...	0.8	99.1	604,497	1,531,516	1,493,251	2,764	56,406	43,322	43,269
	Rating Outlook: Stable	'07	3.8	...	0.3	95.8	16,033,979	0.1	...	0.6	99.3	645,223	2,299,476	2,166,176	4,313	64,952	48,160	47,435
		'08	3.8	...	0.4	95.8	11,892,930	0.2	...	0.8	99.0	648,121	2,242,224	2,186,590	25,448	3,319	638	-8,005
		'09	3.2	...	0.4	96.4	14,513,448	0.2	...	0.8	99.0	669,319	1,221,068	1,193,998	17,848	28,194	11,504	13,303
	FSC X	**Rating History: A+ g, 06/11/10; A+ g, 06/15/09; A+ g, 04/01/08; A+ g, 01/24/07; A+ g, 12/21/05**																
FIDELITY LIFE ASSOCIATION Members Mutual Holding Company Richard A. Hemmings Chairman, President & CEO 1211 W. 22nd Street, Suite 209 Oak Brook, IL 60523 IL : 1896 : Stock : Direct Response Term Life, Whole life, Accidental Death 630-522-0392 AMB# 006386 NAIC# 63290	A-	'05	73.4	...	16.4	10.2	579,524	14.4	...	73.2	12.3	267,843	37,794	29,274	-9,838	6,206	4,696	9,715
		'06	76.5	0.4	3.4	19.7	553,161	16.2	...	79.1	4.8	279,057	40,286	31,399	-1,091	4,402	3,117	12,994
	Rating Outlook: Stable	'07	77.4	1.1	5.8	15.7	538,268	17.5	0.0	77.8	4.7	275,248	46,028	59,190	-17,147	-484	-1,371	-76
		'08	79.0	1.8	3.9	15.2	514,697	19.7	0.0	75.9	4.4	256,820	51,210	62,083	-14,177	-2,411	-2,248	-14,104
		'09	75.3	1.8	4.9	18.0	484,842	21.8	0.2	70.4	7.5	220,503	65,374	63,098	-49,146	-5,879	-3,667	-19,680
	FSC VIII	**Rating History: A-, 06/02/10; A-, 07/09/09; A-, 05/19/08; A-, 06/07/07; A-, 05/31/06**																
FIDELITY SECURITY LIFE INS CO Richard F Jones Richard F. Jones President & Treasurer 3130 Broadway Kansas City, MO 64111-2452 MO : 1969 : Stock : Broker Group A&H, Group Life, Group pens 816-756-1060 AMB# 007426 NAIC# 71870	A-	'05	85.9	2.1	0.2	11.8	469,060	21.3	5.1	62.7	10.9	58,991	315,923	155,937	19,616	9,712	6,764	6,916
		'06	88.0	1.8	0.2	10.0	480,231	22.8	5.2	60.9	11.1	68,797	355,634	165,535	12,274	12,809	8,956	9,869
	Rating Outlook: Stable	'07	87.6	1.7	1.1	9.7	488,087	23.4	6.4	59.2	11.0	77,276	374,421	313,679	9,766	13,372	9,294	9,580
		'08	87.4	1.4	1.0	10.2	538,362	20.9	5.9	54.4	18.8	84,615	415,807	299,572	48,379	12,999	8,085	8,293
		'09	85.2	1.1	1.5	12.1	608,514	19.1	5.7	50.4	24.8	93,875	473,567	362,614	71,253	16,348	10,452	10,388
	FSC VII	**Rating History: A-, 05/21/10; A-, 06/09/09; A-, 06/17/08; A-, 05/25/07; A-, 06/21/06**																
FIDELITY STANDARD LIFE INS CO[1] Margaret Hall President 1295 Kelly Johnson Blvd., #100 Colorado Springs, CO 80920 AR : 1959 : Stock : Not Available 800-715-1458 AMB# 068332 NAIC# 84018	NR-1	'05	77.4	...	...	22.6	695	...	...	...	100.0	159	87	87	...	-8	-8	-8
		'06	75.6	...	...	24.4	700	...	...	...	100.0	150	92	92	...	-9	-9	-9
		'07	79.0	...	...	21.0	689	...	...	...	100.0	161	92	92	...	12	12	11
		'08	72.9	...	...	27.1	669	...	...	...	100.0	143	104	104	...	3	3	3
		'09	68.1	...	...	31.9	713	...	...	...	100.0	164	114	114	...	-12	-12	-27
		Rating History: NR-1, 06/10/10; NR-1, 06/12/09; NR-1, 06/12/08; NR-1, 06/08/07; NR-1, 06/07/06																
FINANCIAL ASSURANCE LIFE INS Financial Holding Corporation Gary L. Muller CEO P.O. Box 410288 Kansas City, MO 64141-0288 TX : 1912 : Stock : Agency Ann, ISWL, Term Life 816-391-2000 AMB# 008094 NAIC# 78093	NR-3	'05	68.7	...	...	31.3	8,651	68.1	...	8.9	23.0	7,456	137	137	246	272	173	173
		'06	79.1	...	...	20.9	8,879	71.3	...	8.8	19.9	7,735	126	126	348	460	299	299
		'07	85.7	...	...	14.3	9,154	69.0	...	8.8	22.2	8,113	119	119	230	562	365	365
		'08	81.1	...	...	18.9	9,725	55.0	...	6.8	38.2	8,417	119	119	577	478	284	284
		'09	65.1	...	23.7	11.2	9,810	67.5	...	8.5	24.0	8,719	110	110	-22	425	295	295
		Rating History: NR-3, 11/04/09; NR-3, 09/05/08; NR-3, 06/14/07; NR-3, 06/21/06; NR-2, 06/22/05																
FINANCIAL LIFE INS CO OF GA[1] Wells Fargo & Company David C. Florian President 401 South Tryon Street, 11 Floor Charlotte, NC 28288-1207 GA : 1982 : Stock : Not Available 404-332-1320 AMB# 068201 NAIC# 86096	NR-1	'05	76.7	0.8	...	22.5	11,957	...	...	...	100.0	7,771	...	...	...	447	159	222
		'06	29.9	0.8	...	69.3	12,053	...	...	...	100.0	8,050	...	...	...	426	297	297
		'07	26.6	0.8	...	72.6	11,816	...	...	...	100.0	8,296	...	...	...	487	363	363
		'08	13.0	0.9	...	86.2	11,597	...	...	...	100.0	8,427	...	...	...	157	131	131
		'09	9.6	...	...	90.4	11,098	...	...	...	100.0	8,430	...	...	...	174	155	35
		Rating History: NR-1, 06/10/10; NR-1, 06/12/09; NR-1, 06/12/08; NR-1, 06/08/07; NR-1, 06/07/06																

2010 BEST'S KEY RATING GUIDE — LIFE/HEALTH EDITION
BEST'S PROFITABILITY, LEVERAGE AND LIQUIDITY TESTS 2005 – 2009
Data in U.S. Dollars

—	Profitability Tests							Leverage Tests						Liquidity Tests					
Un-Realized Capital Gains ($000)	Benefits Paid to NPW & Dep (%)	Comm. & Expenses to NPW & Dep (%)	NOG to Total Assets (%)	NOG to Total Rev (%)	Operating Return on Equity (%)	Net Yield (%)	Total Return (%)	Change in NPW & Dep (%)	NPW & Dep to Capital (X)	Capital & Surplus to Liabilities (%)	Surplus Relief (%)	Reins Leverage (%)	Change in Capital (%)	Quick Liquidity (%)	Current Liquidity (%)	Non-Invest Grade Bonds to Capital (%)	Delinq. & Foreclosed Mortgages to Capital (%)	Mort. & Credit Tenant Loans & R.E. to Capital (%)	Affiliated Invest to Capital (%)
...	91.7	14.3	...	-1.5	...	...	...	...	0.5	254.6	...	9.4	...	235.7	262.3	...	...	...	...
...	97.3	3.1	1.6	0.7	3.7	2.71	2.71	974.9	5.6	42.6	...	...	-1.9	136.3	136.3	...	...	...	...
...	88.5	11.0	3.5	1.1	12.7	2.96	2.96	120.3	11.2	35.0	...	...	10.3	134.2	134.2	...	...	...	...
...	91.2	7.0	5.1	1.5	15.3	1.59	1.59	34.3	7.8	65.5	...	...	92.7	164.4	164.4	...	...	...	...
...	64.8	14.0	32.6	14.1	62.4	0.58	0.58	-19.4	3.4	171.5	...	...	86.9	239.3	239.3	...	...	...	...
	Principal Lines of Business: Medicare (100.0%)													Principal States: MI (100.0%)					
...	...	...	...	...	...	...	...	...	...	...	...	...	...	...	...	...	...	...	...
...	88.5	102.4	...	-82.7	...	...	...	...	0.7	401.9	...	...	...	493.4	493.7	...	...	...	...
...	82.5	42.0	-43.0	-22.5	-68.2	3.08	3.08	266.4	3.7	91.4	...	...	-33.5	189.7	189.9	...	...	...	...
...	101.2	32.3	-50.6	-21.6	-99.9	1.36	1.36	58.7	7.3	36.9	...	...	-18.8	120.7	120.7	...	...	...	...
...	77.7	13.8	12.2	5.7	32.3	0.16	0.16	-3.3	4.7	108.5	...	...	49.4	201.2	201.2	...	...	...	...
	Principal Lines of Business: Medicare (100.0%)													Principal States: NC (100.0%)					
...	...	...	...	...	...	...	...	...	...	...	...	...	...	...	...	...	...	...	...
...	...	...	...	66.0	...	...	...	...	...	999.9	...	...	...	999.9	999.9	...	...	...	...
...	77.0	15.4	20.1	5.8	29.2	2.47	2.47	...	4.2	133.4	...	...	52.0	204.7	204.7	...	...	...	...
...	94.0	5.0	1.8	1.0	3.3	1.15	1.15	-18.6	3.3	111.3	...	...	3.9	196.6	196.6	...	...	...	...
...	57.9	15.0	28.2	18.0	41.7	0.38	0.38	-10.8	1.9	488.5	...	...	52.2	551.4	551.4	...	...	...	...
	Principal Lines of Business: Medicare (100.0%)													Principal States: TX (100.0%)					
5,559	119.3	7.6	0.4	6.7	8.4	4.42	5.87	91.0	1.4	320.4	2.2	167.9	10.7	273.2	305.9	6.6	...	...	8.1
3,238	65.3	5.0	0.3	3.2	7.4	4.59	5.20	80.4	2.5	423.2	3.0	203.8	6.7	343.8	381.1	6.4	...	...	8.1
1,860	48.9	3.8	0.3	2.2	7.7	4.86	5.11	45.1	3.3	544.0	3.5	224.9	6.7	435.9	478.3	6.5	...	...	7.9
512	59.7	4.2	0.0	0.0	0.1	3.70	2.69	0.9	3.4	512.3	1.6	235.3	-0.2	618.8	649.0	3.8	...	...	8.0
2,788	102.5	5.5	0.1	0.9	1.7	2.41	3.46	-45.4	1.8	499.3	1.3	213.6	3.4	581.1	617.3	4.6	...	...	8.1
	Principal Lines of Business: IndAnn (99.5%), OrdLife (0.5%)													Principal States: CA (21.1%), FL (9.1%), MA (9.0%), TX (8.4%), NJ (6.9%)					
-3,281	116.5	50.5	0.8	8.8	1.8	4.89	5.32	5.9	0.1	98.5	3.8	55.0	1.8	136.2	157.1	1.1	...	...	...
-9,982	107.2	42.9	0.6	5.8	1.1	4.82	4.91	7.3	0.1	105.6	4.0	59.7	-1.2	177.6	196.9	0.0	...	0.9	...
-4,961	61.8	36.7	-0.3	-2.6	-0.5	4.71	4.01	88.5	0.2	108.3	2.4	68.8	-1.5	139.5	159.0	1.3	...	2.0	...
-5,302	52.0	51.6	-0.4	-3.6	-0.8	4.46	1.12	4.9	0.2	100.9	2.4	78.1	-7.6	124.7	146.3	1.9	...	3.6	...
17,050	49.9	57.3	-0.7	-5.1	-1.5	4.67	5.03	1.6	0.3	89.6	3.3	94.0	-11.3	117.1	136.4	4.1	0.2	3.9	...
	Principal Lines of Business: OrdLife (54.4%), GrpAnn (33.1%), GrpLife (9.6%), GrpA&H (2.7%), IndAnn (0.2%)													Principal States: CA (14.0%), FL (9.9%), TX (8.7%), IL (6.0%), NC (5.0%)					
373	75.5	29.7	1.5	3.1	11.9	5.02	5.31	0.8	2.5	15.5	71.1	86.1	8.8	84.7	91.0	...	...	15.8	5.1
39	85.2	24.7	1.9	3.8	14.0	5.32	5.67	6.2	2.3	17.9	66.4	83.9	15.8	83.2	89.7	1.0	...	12.3	4.2
-602	78.1	27.0	1.9	2.6	12.7	5.29	5.34	89.5	3.9	20.0	31.8	65.6	12.3	79.7	87.1	9.1	...	10.2	3.5
-494	76.0	27.7	1.6	2.3	10.0	5.22	5.28	-4.5	3.5	19.5	38.1	57.5	9.1	78.7	87.5	2.4	...	8.5	3.0
-73	74.2	24.3	1.8	2.5	11.7	5.50	5.63	21.0	3.8	19.1	31.2	48.4	11.3	81.3	90.6	6.9	...	7.0	2.4
	Principal Lines of Business: GrpA&H (87.0%), GrpAnn (4.2%), IndAnn (3.0%), OrdLife (2.5%), GrpLife (2.4%)													Principal States: TX (12.2%), IL (10.1%), GA (7.2%), OH (6.0%), PA (5.8%)					
...	98.3	48.7	-1.1	-6.7	-4.6	...	...	-6.4	0.5	30.1	...	...	-4.5	...	...	...	...	...	...
...	92.0	48.4	-1.2	-7.3	-5.5	...	...	4.9	0.6	27.8	...	...	-5.3	...	...	...	...	...	...
...	94.0	39.5	1.7	10.1	7.7	...	...	0.1	0.6	31.1	...	...	7.2	...	...	...	...	...	...
-23	70.3	58.5	0.4	2.3	1.9	...	...	13.0	0.7	27.1	...	...	-12.5	...	...	...	...	...	...
23	85.9	49.1	-1.8	-8.9	-8.1	...	...	10.1	0.7	29.9	...	...	14.7	...	...	...	...	...	...
	Principal Lines of Business: OrdLife (100.0%)																		
...	149.5	47.2	2.0	32.6	2.3	4.74	4.75	-5.9	0.0	638.6	...	...	2.4	853.6	920.1	...	...	...	...
...	87.9	28.6	3.4	53.6	3.9	5.07	5.07	-7.9	0.0	701.2	...	...	3.9	617.5	669.0	12.8	...	...	...
...	89.3	34.1	4.0	55.0	4.6	6.27	6.25	-5.8	0.0	799.3	...	...	4.7	804.3	860.0	...	...	...	...
...	37.7	38.9	3.0	50.0	3.4	4.90	4.89	0.0	0.0	658.4	...	...	3.8	718.5	767.1	...	...	...	...
...	61.6	39.2	3.0	55.5	3.4	4.40	4.43	-7.3	0.0	825.8	...	...	3.6	645.0	792.9	...	...	...	...
	Principal Lines of Business: OrdLife (98.9%), IndAnn (1.0%), GrpAnn (0.1%)													Principal States: MN (88.8%), CA (3.7%)					
...	...	...	1.3	22.8	2.1	...	...	...	...	186.8	...	...	4.5	...	...	...	...	1.3	...
...	...	...	2.5	38.5	3.8	...	...	...	...	202.5	...	...	3.6	...	...	...	...	1.2	...
...	...	...	3.0	50.3	4.4	...	...	...	...	237.4	...	...	3.0	...	...	...	...	1.2	...
...	...	...	1.1	29.8	1.6	...	...	...	...	267.3	...	...	1.5	...	...	...	...	1.2	...
...	...	...	1.4	59.0	1.8	...	...	...	...	316.5	...	...	-0.1	...	...	...	...	...	...

Data in U.S. Dollars

COMPANY NAME Ultimate Parent Association Principal Officer Mailing Address Dom. : Began Bus. : Struct. : Mktg. Specialty Phone # AMB# NAIC#	Best's Financial Strength Rating FSC	Data Year	Balance Sheet: Bonds (%)	Mort. Loans & R.E. (%)	Com & Pref. Stock (%)	All Other Assets (%)	Total Assets ($000)	Life Reserves (%)	Health Reserves %)	Ann Res. & Dep. Liabilities (%)	All Other Liabilities (%)	Capital & Surplus ($000)	Operations: Direct Premiums Written ($000)	Net Premiums Written & Deposits ($000)	Operating Cash Flow ($000)	NOG Before Taxes ($000)	NOG After Taxes ($000)	Net Income ($000)
FIRST ALLMERICA FINANCIAL LIFE Goldman Sachs Group Inc Michael A. Reardon President & CEO 132 Turnpike Road, Suite 210 Southborough, MA 01772 MA : 1845 : Stock : Agency In Run Off 508-460-2400 AMB# 007086 NAIC# 69140	**A-** Rating Outlook: Stable **FSC IX**	**'05**	60.1	4.9	0.3	34.8	2,845,385	24.6	4.3	31.0	40.2	158,254	53,498	72,122	-749,389	1,322	21,610	34,507
		'06	55.7	4.8	0.6	38.9	2,375,920	28.7	4.8	23.2	43.3	151,831	44,532	48,969	-380,408	-33,383	7,600	12,962
		'07	53.2	5.0	1.2	40.6	2,155,843	31.3	4.7	24.9	39.2	163,729	38,556	41,056	-94,207	-37,707	16,407	16,962
		'08	58.2	...	1.3	40.5	1,714,062	38.0	8.3	26.2	27.5	113,697	35,401	37,905	-27,203	18,352	52,414	33,124
		'09	63.0	...	0.0	37.0	1,580,619	44.1	...	33.6	22.3	156,923	32,258	155,117	-21,882	20,709	12,666	10,812
		Rating History: A- g, 08/24/09; A- g, 01/19/09; B+ u, 07/31/08; B+, 06/12/08; B+, 05/23/07																
FIRST AMERITAS LIFE OF NY UNIFI Mutual Holding Company Kenneth L. VanCleave President & CEO P.O. Box 81889 Lincoln, NE 68510-1889 NY : 1994 : Stock : Broker Life, Group A&H 800-628-8889 AMB# 068545 NAIC# 60033	**A** Rating Outlook: Stable **FSC XIII**	**'05**	86.1	0.9	...	13.1	37,434	24.6	12.0	51.9	11.5	17,536	24,953	25,662	500	1,714	904	904
		'06	83.4	0.3	...	16.3	35,520	30.5	15.8	33.8	19.9	19,912	24,877	25,853	-2,333	1,869	728	728
		'07	83.2	0.1	1.3	15.4	37,557	40.5	14.1	25.7	19.8	20,679	25,874	26,799	1,925	1,354	707	723
		'08	82.4	0.0	1.3	16.4	37,809	49.1	10.5	15.6	24.7	19,832	26,944	27,357	126	-200	-555	-555
		'09	83.1	...	...	16.9	40,493	53.5	8.2	15.3	23.0	19,261	29,981	30,193	1,097	-455	-368	-425
		Rating History: A g, 04/13/10; A g, 01/30/09; A g, 05/01/08; A g, 02/02/07; A g, 01/04/06																
FIRST ASSUR LIFE OF AMERICA Louisiana Dealer Services Insurance Inc Dick S. Taylor President PO Box 83480 Baton Rouge, LA 70884-3480 LA : 1981 : Stock : Agency Credit A&H, Credit Life 225-769-9923 AMB# 009125 NAIC# 94579	**B++** Rating Outlook: Stable **FSC V**	**'05**	72.0	...	14.6	13.3	23,066	61.4	20.6	...	18.1	17,852	16,970	5,119	2,525	1,327	1,100	1,100
		'06	71.8	...	15.3	13.0	25,233	61.6	22.5	...	15.9	19,479	22,994	4,748	1,774	1,650	1,298	1,298
		'07	71.3	...	15.3	13.4	27,103	63.3	24.9	...	11.8	21,368	22,905	4,355	1,393	1,973	1,597	1,586
		'08	67.5	...	16.3	16.2	28,967	59.9	31.6	...	8.5	22,916	15,969	4,715	1,174	1,459	1,101	1,109
		'09	73.2	...	17.2	9.5	30,698	45.9	49.0	...	5.1	24,310	9,419	4,274	948	1,134	1,054	898
		Rating History: B++g, 06/03/09; B++g, 06/16/08; B++g, 06/13/07; B++g, 06/15/06; B++g, 05/31/05																
FIRST BERKSHIRE HATHAWAY LIFE Berkshire Hathaway Inc Donald F. Wurster President 3024 Harney Street Omaha, NE 68131-3580 NY : 2003 : Stock : Inactive Inactive 402-916-3000 AMB# 060389 NAIC# 11591	**NR-3**	**'05**	98.3	...	...	1.7	9,544	...	...	86.9	13.1	8,964	494	494	603	542	349	349
		'06	98.9	...	...	1.1	10,082	...	...	72.5	27.5	9,265	110	110	541	469	305	305
		'07	96.8	...	...	3.2	10,629	...	...	74.5	25.5	9,587	213	213	537	503	326	326
		'08	88.8	...	...	11.2	12,328	...	...	77.5	22.5	10,947	330	330	1,692	560	363	363
		'09	92.9	...	...	7.1	12,533	...	...	85.8	14.2	11,312	...	...	200	564	368	368
		Rating History: NR-3, 05/06/10; NR-3, 05/22/09; NR-3, 04/29/08; NR-3, 05/16/07; NR-3, 05/09/06																
FIRST CATHOLIC SLOVAK LADIES Mary Ann Sabol Johanek President 24950 Chagrin Boulevard Beachwood, OH 44122-5634 OH : 1892 : Fraternal : Not Available Life, Ann 800-464-4642 AMB# 009869 NAIC# 56332	**A-** Rating Outlook: Stable **FSC VII**	**'05**	91.6	0.4	3.2	4.9	484,580	34.6	...	62.7	2.6	87,330	21,384	21,622	28,101	4,536	4,536	5,554
		'06	87.8	1.1	2.7	8.4	514,144	34.1	...	62.9	3.0	90,665	22,873	22,987	28,372	3,668	3,668	3,674
		'07	89.7	1.5	2.2	6.5	529,123	35.3	...	62.3	2.4	90,735	21,054	21,288	16,198	1,468	1,468	732
		'08	88.8	1.5	1.9	7.8	544,660	34.8	...	62.8	2.3	84,502	21,403	21,586	17,775	2,378	2,378	-4,575
		'09	91.2	1.1	1.8	5.9	590,102	33.6	...	63.9	2.5	86,527	43,501	43,658	45,063	2,225	2,225	1,618
		Rating History: A-, 06/03/10; A-, 06/04/09; A-, 05/14/08; A-, 06/19/07; A-, 05/17/06																
FIRST CATHOLIC SLOVAK UNION Andrew M. Rajec President 6611 Rockside Road Independence, OH 44131 OH : 1890 : Fraternal : Direct Response Ind Ann, Ind Life 216-642-9406 AMB# 009804 NAIC# 56340	**NR-5**	**'05**	85.4	2.8	5.9	5.9	195,541	36.6	...	56.3	7.1	9,867	7,614	7,862	7,866	1,342	1,342	1,169
		'06	82.1	2.7	9.9	5.3	197,311	37.0	...	56.6	6.4	11,556	4,736	4,733	1,001	1,489	1,489	1,539
		'07	85.1	2.5	6.0	6.5	203,610	36.5	...	56.9	6.6	13,112	5,706	6,244	5,802	1,915	1,915	1,721
		'08	78.8	2.4	4.9	13.9	201,037	36.8	...	57.8	5.4	9,060	8,037	8,036	5,046	1,428	1,428	265
		'09	82.1	2.0	4.2	11.7	234,795	32.2	...	62.3	5.5	13,169	17,693	30,121	29,146	4,309	4,309	4,309
		Rating History: NR-5, 04/15/10; NR-5, 04/21/09; NR-5, 04/18/08; NR-5, 05/08/07; NR-5, 05/05/06																
FIRST CENTRAL NAT LIFE OF NY HSBC Holdings plc Patrick A. Cozza President & CEO 200 Somerset Corporate Blvd. Bridgewater, NJ 08807 NY : 1971 : Stock : Other Credit A&H, Credit Life 800-443-7187 AMB# 008256 NAIC# 79340	**A** Rating Outlook: Stable **FSC IX**	**'05**	92.8	...	...	7.2	54,566	44.7	50.5	0.9	3.8	34,102	12,717	12,729	6,984	4,389	2,843	2,843
		'06	94.2	...	...	5.8	60,856	44.6	49.0	0.8	5.6	38,748	12,660	13,202	6,410	7,155	4,542	4,542
		'07	96.1	...	...	3.9	55,096	50.3	46.3	0.8	2.5	33,775	12,399	13,065	-5,457	7,765	5,135	5,135
		'08	88.3	...	...	11.7	52,533	47.4	41.2	0.6	10.9	25,257	15,020	15,004	-5,848	1,038	-168	-4,255
		'09	86.6	...	...	13.4	53,986	56.0	31.9	0.6	11.5	23,588	13,685	13,103	2,318	-672	-267	-136
		Rating History: A g, 06/05/09; A+ g, 06/12/08; A+ g, 06/06/07; A+ g, 06/21/06; A+ g, 06/22/05																
FIRST COMMAND LIC First Command Financial Services, Inc. Martin R. Durbin President 3700 S. Stonebridge Drive McKinney, TX 75070 TX : 2001 : Stock : General Agent Life 972-569-3636 AMB# 068133 NAIC# 82007	**NR-5**	**'05**	53.3	...	1.6	45.2	13,151	91.8	...	...	8.2	9,098	...	2,598	1,985	-87	-87	-87
		'06	68.5	...	12.2	19.4	15,226	95.1	...	...	4.9	9,296	...	2,702	2,103	313	265	239
		'07	79.5	...	12.3	8.1	17,509	95.2	...	...	4.8	9,492	...	2,729	2,258	515	226	233
		'08	79.7	...	11.1	9.2	19,328	99.2	...	...	0.8	9,675	...	2,710	1,774	611	323	14
		'09	84.9	...	...	15.1	21,629	98.7	...	...	1.3	9,958	...	2,660	2,212	596	275	275
		Rating History: NR-5, 04/22/10; NR-5, 04/23/09; NR-5, 04/22/08; NR-5, 04/30/07; NR-5, 06/02/06																
FIRST COMMONWEALTH INS CO Guardian Life Ins Co of America Richard A. Goren President & CEO 500 West Jackson Blvd. Chicago, IL 60661 IL : 1998 : Stock : Not Available Dental 312-993-1000 AMB# 060300 NAIC# 60239	**A** Rating Outlook: Stable **FSC V**	**'05**	34.3	...	...	65.7	26,226	...	21.6	...	78.4	14,167	68,171	68,171	600	7,813	5,070	5,070
		'06	6.3	...	...	93.7	25,679	...	68.3	...	31.7	15,500	61,948	61,948	-658	9,853	6,395	6,395
		'07	7.4	...	...	92.6	21,593	...	37.0	...	63.0	14,616	60,899	60,899	2,117	8,794	5,504	5,504
		'08	41.6	...	...	58.4	20,836	...	39.0	...	61.0	15,269	57,010	57,010	-717	7,523	6,138	6,134
		'09	66.3	...	...	33.7	18,160	...	35.3	...	64.7	13,538	51,307	51,307	-2,464	6,695	4,364	4,366
		Rating History: A, 10/13/09; A, 11/26/08; A, 04/23/08; A, 11/10/06; A, 11/18/05																

BEST'S PROFITABILITY, LEVERAGE AND LIQUIDITY TESTS 2005 – 2009

Data in U.S. Dollars

	Profitability Tests							Leverage Tests						Liquidity Tests					
Un-Realized Capital Gains ($000)	Benefits Paid to NPW & Dep (%)	Comm. & Expenses to NPW & Dep (%)	NOG to Total Assets (%)	NOG to Total Rev (%)	Operating Return on Equity (%)	Net Yield (%)	Total Return (%)	Change in NPW & Dep (%)	NPW & Dep to Capital (X)	Capital & Surplus to Liabilities (%)	Surplus Relief (%)	Reins Leverage (%)	Change in Capital (%)	Quick Liquidity (%)	Current Liquidity (%)	Non-Invest Grade Bonds to Capital (%)	Delinq. & Foreclosed Mortgages to Capital (%)	Mort. & Credit Tenant Loans & R.E. to Capital (%)	Affiliated Invest to Capital (%)
-2,633	381.9	46.7	0.6	12.2	12.6	4.42	4.83	-15.3	0.4	8.5	2.0	163.5	-10.1	57.7	69.6	37.0	...	87.8	38.0
5,067	282.3	145.1	0.3	5.3	4.9	4.61	5.16	-32.1	0.3	10.2	1.1	211.3	-5.5	58.3	69.7	20.1	...	78.1	65.7
-1,493	378.2	65.1	0.7	14.8	10.4	4.76	4.73	-16.2	0.2	12.0	0.3	180.8	5.4	59.0	71.6	12.6	...	69.8	43.5
-10,145	363.1	44.7	2.7	54.6	37.8	4.45	2.52	-7.7	0.3	8.7	0.0	199.1	-35.4	67.7	78.5	6.5	...	...	85.5
10,329	73.9	9.7	0.8	5.7	9.4	5.58	6.54	309.2	1.0	13.8	0.0	156.0	36.7	89.5	98.5	1.4	...	...	...
	Principal Lines of Business: IndAnn (56.1%), OrdLife (42.6%), GrpAnn (1.3%), IndA&H (0.0%)													Principal States: NY (21.7%), PR (4.5%), MA (3.9%), PA (3.8%), CA (3.6%)					
...	82.2	19.5	2.4	3.3	5.3	4.51	4.51	13.6	1.5	91.0	0.5	1.0	5.3	152.3	169.4	3.4	...	1.8	...
...	87.7	23.6	2.0	2.7	3.9	4.60	4.60	0.7	1.3	132.6	0.3	9.8	13.4	175.2	199.3	...	...	0.5	...
...	68.7	26.0	1.9	2.5	3.5	4.47	4.52	3.7	1.3	126.9	0.3	9.9	3.9	180.0	202.9	...	...	0.1	...
...	73.7	31.9	-1.5	-1.9	-2.7	4.64	4.62	2.1	1.4	113.4	0.3	11.6	-4.1	162.7	183.1	...	...	0.0	...
...	61.3	36.2	-0.9	-1.2	-1.9	4.77	4.57	10.4	1.6	92.9	0.4	13.2	-2.9	133.6	152.2	2.6	...	...	...
	Principal Lines of Business: GrpA&H (76.4%), OrdLife (22.0%), IndAnn (1.6%)													Principal States: NY (89.2%)					
257	7.6	66.1	5.1	4.9	6.4	3.97	5.17	69.0	0.3	347.4	91.6	95.7	8.1	321.0	340.6	...	...	...	18.9
474	14.6	60.2	5.4	7.3	7.0	4.30	6.31	-7.2	0.2	343.0	61.8	95.5	9.1	315.9	333.8	...	...	...	19.7
297	15.4	59.1	6.1	9.0	7.8	4.34	5.45	-8.3	0.2	377.7	57.5	94.5	9.7	355.5	372.3	...	...	...	19.4
586	17.1	65.9	3.9	8.2	5.0	4.04	6.20	8.3	0.2	383.9	33.5	82.5	7.2	334.3	350.6	...	...	...	20.6
558	18.1	67.1	3.5	11.2	4.5	3.67	5.05	-9.3	0.2	385.4	16.6	59.4	6.1	335.5	351.0	...	...	...	21.7
	Principal Lines of Business: CrdA&H (65.6%), CrdLife (34.4%)													Principal States: LA (100.0%)					
...	2.3	5.8	3.8	33.6	4.0	6.09	6.09	999.9	0.1	999.9	...	...	4.0	936.6	999.9	...	...	...	...
...	36.1	76.6	3.1	44.7	3.3	6.00	6.00	-77.7	0.0	999.9	...	...	3.4	696.5	821.8	...	...	...	...
...	24.6	41.0	3.2	39.5	3.5	6.11	6.11	93.5	0.0	945.1	...	...	3.5	584.5	685.7	...	...	...	...
...	19.1	17.6	3.2	37.3	3.5	5.77	5.77	54.7	0.0	812.0	...	...	14.2	625.3	715.4	...	...	...	...
...	...	...	3.0	54.5	3.3	5.59	5.59	-99.9	...	954.4	...	...	3.4	668.1	772.6	...	...	...	...
-183	72.7	29.9	1.0	9.1	5.3	6.24	6.43	-3.0	0.2	23.3	...	...	6.2	69.3	81.1	34.4	...	2.1	0.2
539	70.6	32.0	0.7	6.9	4.1	6.16	6.28	6.3	0.2	22.9	...	...	4.3	68.7	79.7	36.3	...	5.9	4.1
-617	96.3	52.4	0.3	2.8	1.6	6.09	5.84	-7.4	0.2	22.0	...	...	-0.2	69.1	80.0	36.3	...	8.3	6.6
-1,899	91.2	36.1	0.4	4.5	2.7	5.99	4.37	1.4	0.2	19.6	...	...	-6.6	71.1	81.5	36.0	...	9.3	7.5
1,401	48.8	20.9	0.4	3.0	2.6	5.77	5.92	102.2	0.5	18.6	...	...	3.7	69.8	80.4	46.7	...	7.0	7.0
	Principal Lines of Business: IndAnn (79.1%), OrdLife (20.9%)													Principal States: PA (21.8%), OH (18.0%), NE (16.3%), MN (8.6%), WI (8.0%)					
320	107.5	30.7	0.7	6.8	14.6	6.36	6.56	-33.3	0.7	6.6	...	...	14.1	56.3	64.7	209.3	4.7	45.6	12.4
552	227.1	57.4	0.8	8.9	13.9	6.17	6.62	-39.8	0.3	7.7	...	...	17.6	56.3	66.4	153.1	4.0	37.4	10.9
3	144.8	39.4	1.0	10.6	15.5	6.21	6.26	31.9	0.4	8.3	...	...	9.9	62.2	70.4	123.9	3.6	32.7	9.0
-6,773	151.2	33.8	0.7	7.0	12.9	6.14	2.42	28.7	0.9	4.8	...	...	-40.2	65.2	73.3	152.7	6.1	52.7	14.6
2,194	26.4	9.3	2.0	13.2	38.8	7.10	8.14	274.8	1.9	7.2	...	...	68.7	58.9	67.0	126.4	3.6	944.5	8.3
	Principal Lines of Business: IndAnn (95.6%), OrdLife (4.4%)													Principal States: PA (41.0%), OH (32.8%), IL (12.2%), NY (4.3%)					
...	47.9	11.0	5.6	18.9	8.7	4.46	4.75	53.6	0.4	168.0	...	1.9	9.6	195.3	236.0	...	...	...	...
...	52.0	12.5	7.9	28.7	12.5	4.55	4.73	3.7	0.3	176.9	...	1.6	13.7	224.2	254.8	...	...	...	...
...	64.8	9.8	8.9	32.2	14.2	5.07	5.18	-1.0	0.4	160.2	...	2.0	-12.7	208.6	236.9	...	...	...	...
...	51.8	48.5	-0.3	-1.0	-0.6	4.82	-2.82	14.8	0.6	92.6	0.4	5.2	-25.5	138.3	156.7	1.7	...	...	...
...	75.5	56.1	-0.5	-1.6	-1.1	4.76	5.06	-12.7	0.6	78.5	5.2	14.3	-6.0	139.6	157.2	...	...	...	...
	Principal Lines of Business: CrdLife (47.0%), OrdLife (32.9%), CrdA&H (14.9%), IndA&H (5.3%), GrpAnn (0.0%)													Principal States: NY (99.3%)					
...	9.6	51.2	-0.7	-2.7	-1.0	5.11	5.11	14.2	0.3	227.3	...	1.4	3.0	373.5	409.3	4.4	...	...	...
...	7.8	40.4	1.9	7.5	2.9	6.16	5.99	4.0	0.3	158.6	...	1.3	2.2	175.2	217.8	4.0	...	...	...
...	10.1	36.2	1.4	6.0	2.4	6.64	6.69	1.0	0.3	121.0	...	1.4	2.7	114.4	149.8	7.8	...	...	...
-37	13.7	33.7	1.8	8.4	3.4	6.52	4.64	-0.7	0.3	100.4	...	1.0	1.0	105.6	137.2	6.5	...	...	...
36	15.3	33.2	1.3	7.2	2.8	5.96	6.15	-1.8	0.3	86.6	...	1.2	3.7	119.9	141.4	24.0	...	...	...
	Principal Lines of Business: OrdLife (100.0%)																		
...	71.6	17.4	19.5	7.4	36.6	1.89	1.89	100.9	4.8	117.5	...	...	4.7	148.7	148.7	...	...	...	...
...	67.8	17.2	24.6	10.2	43.1	2.77	2.77	-9.1	4.0	152.3	...	...	9.4	173.4	173.4	...	...	...	...
...	69.2	17.0	23.3	9.0	36.6	1.52	1.52	-1.7	4.2	209.5	...	...	-5.7	283.3	283.3	...	...	...	...
...	69.8	17.7	28.9	10.7	41.1	1.75	1.72	-6.4	3.7	274.3	...	...	4.5	494.3	494.3	...	...	...	...
...	69.1	18.2	22.4	8.5	30.3	0.87	0.89	-10.0	3.8	292.9	...	...	-11.3	404.0	413.6	...	...	...	...
	Principal Lines of Business: Dental (100.0%)													Principal States: IL (100.0%)					

COMPANY NAME Ultimate Parent Association Principal Officer Mailing Address Dom. : Began Bus. : Struct. : Mktg. Specialty Phone # AMB# NAIC#	Best's Financial Strength Rating FSC	Data Year	Balance Sheet Bonds (%)	Mort. Loans & R.E. (%)	Com & Pref. Stock (%)	All Other Assets (%)	Total Assets ($000)	Life Reserves (%)	Health Reserves %)	Ann Res. & Dep. Liabilities (%)	All Other Liabilities (%)	Capital & Surplus ($000)	Operations Direct Premiums Written ($000)	Net Premiums Written & Deposits ($000)	Operating Cash Flow ($000)	NOG Before Taxes ($000)	NOG After Taxes ($000)	Net Income ($000)
FIRST COMMONWEALTH LTD HTH SVC Guardian Life Ins Co of America Richard A. Goren President & CEO 550 West Jackson Blvd. Chicago, IL 60661 WI : 1996 : Stock : Broker Dental 312-993-1000 AMB# 064819 NAIC# 52036	NR-2	'05	...	...	...	100.0	4,168	...	8.7	...	91.3	2,936	11,066	11,066	-897	964	627	627
		'06	4.0	...	...	96.0	3,596	...	79.2	...	20.8	2,413	10,586	10,586	-459	371	242	242
		'07	...	...	...	100.0	5,254	...	7.8	...	92.2	2,361	10,657	10,657	2,497	-1,043	-696	-696
		'08	...	...	...	100.0	3,615	...	14.0	...	86.0	2,623	8,381	8,381	-1,373	305	281	281
		'09	...	...	...	100.0	3,008	...	11.5	...	88.5	2,103	5,541	5,541	-671	-652	-422	-422
Rating History: NR-2, 10/13/09; NR-2, 11/26/08; NR-2, 04/23/08; NR-2, 11/10/06; NR-2, 11/18/05																		
FIRST COMMONWEALTH LTD H SVCS Guardian Life Ins Co of America Richard A. Goren President & CEO 550 West Jackson Blvd. Chicago, IL 60661 IL : 1991 : Stock : Broker Health 312-993-1000 AMB# 065719 NAIC# 11221	NR-3	'05	25.0	...	...	75.0	2,625	...	9.9	...	90.1	2,497	528	528	-438	172	112	112
		'06	8.2	...	...	91.8	2,451	...	56.3	...	43.7	2,358	460	460	-131	168	109	109
		'07	8.7	...	...	91.3	2,292	...	43.4	...	56.6	2,207	451	451	-105	138	84	84
		'08	48.4	...	...	51.6	2,114	...	21.3	...	78.7	2,073	420	420	-189	119	87	87
		'09	77.7	...	...	22.3	2,064	...	6.5	...	93.5	1,949	377	377	-28	127	82	82
Rating History: NR-3, 10/13/09; NR-3, 11/26/08; NR-3, 04/23/08; NR-3, 11/10/06; NR-3, 11/18/05																		
FIRST COMMONWLTH LTD H SVCS MI Guardian Life Ins Co of America Richard A. Goren President & CEO 500 West Jackson Blvd. Chicago, IL 60661 MI : 2004 : Stock : Broker Dental 312-993-1000 AMB# 064818 NAIC# 12146	NR-3	'05	10.1	...	...	89.9	2,474	...	27.8	...	72.2	1,349	7,157	7,157	1,244	555	358	358
		'06	8.3	...	...	91.7	2,990	...	90.7	...	9.3	1,729	9,101	9,101	234	584	380	380
		'07	8.2	...	...	91.8	3,028	...	59.2	...	40.8	2,046	9,947	9,947	739	493	319	319
		'08	9.8	...	...	90.2	3,078	...	53.9	...	46.1	2,133	10,751	10,751	146	556	362	362
		'09	41.5	...	...	58.5	3,147	...	39.7	...	60.3	2,209	9,340	9,340	-41	667	435	435
Rating History: NR-3, 10/13/09; NR-3, 11/26/08; NR-3, 04/23/08; NR-3, 11/10/06; NR-3, 11/18/05																		
FIRST COMMONWEALTH OF MISSOURI Guardian Life Ins Co of America Richard A. Goren President & CEO 550 West Jackson Blvd. Chicago, IL 60661 MO : 1989 : Stock : Not Available Health 312-993-1000 AMB# 065734 NAIC# 47716	NR-2	'05	1.3	...	...	98.7	3,956	...	22.0	...	78.0	3,257	4,159	4,159	-9	468	305	305
		'06	1.2	...	...	98.8	4,286	...	76.0	...	24.0	3,438	4,894	4,894	285	369	235	235
		'07	1.3	...	...	98.7	4,122	...	47.6	...	52.4	3,518	4,958	4,958	343	289	175	175
		'08	1.4	...	...	98.6	3,794	...	47.1	...	52.9	3,329	3,485	3,485	-371	-131	-14	-14
		'09	48.4	...	...	51.6	3,637	...	44.2	...	55.8	3,323	2,677	2,677	-81	58	39	39
Rating History: NR-2, 10/13/09; NR-2, 11/26/08; NR-2, 04/23/08; NR-2, 11/10/06; NR-2, 11/18/05																		
FIRST CONTINENTAL L & A INS CO[1] Dental Economics L P James A. Taylor President 12946 Dairy Ashford Road, Suite 360 Sugar Land, TX 77478-3149 TX : 1979 : Stock : Direct Response 281-313-7150 AMB# 006557 NAIC# 64696	NR-1	'05	43.1	...	37.6	19.3	3,927	...	...	...	100.0	3,133	528	528	...	105	100	100
		'06	30.2	...	50.0	19.7	6,593	...	...	...	100.0	5,154	3,123	3,123	...	400	287	287
		'07	21.4	...	57.9	20.7	9,321	...	...	...	100.0	7,559	4,336	4,336	...	572	445	445
		'08	17.3	...	20.0	62.7	11,859	...	...	...	100.0	4,437	6,041	6,041	...	798	587	587
		'09	18.3	...	32.4	49.3	8,413	...	...	...	100.0	2,610	7,506	7,506	...	-3,271	-2,159	-2,159
Rating History: NR-1, 06/10/10; NR-1, 06/12/09; NR-1, 06/12/08; NR-1, 06/08/07; NR-1, 06/07/06																		
FIRST DENTAL HEALTH Michael S. Grossman, DDS President 7220 Trade Street #350 San Diego, CA 92121 CA : 1995 : Stock : Not Available Dental 858-689-0904 AMB# 064931	NR-5	'05	...	...	...	...	...	...	...	...	...	...	...	...	...	...	...	...
		'06	...	...	...	...	...	...	...	...	...	...	...	...	...	...	...	...
		'07	...	...	...	100.0	2,392	...	...	...	100.0	1,865	0	0	20	-203	-157	-157
		'08	...	...	...	100.0	2,471	...	...	...	100.0	1,876	0	0	124	14	10	10
		'09	...	...	...	100.0	3,052	...	...	...	100.0	2,285	0	0	399	560	607	607
Rating History: NR-5, 05/06/10; NR-5, 05/13/09; NR-5, 05/14/08																		
FIRST DIMENSION LIFE CO INC[1] Bill F. Bernhardt, Jr. President 324 West 7th Stillwater, OK 74074 OK : 1979 : Stock : Not Available 405-372-5808 AMB# 009499 NAIC# 90492	NR-1	'05	47.0	0.6	2.8	49.6	3,654	...	...	...	100.0	1,798	332	332	...	88	85	15
		'06	64.1	0.4	3.3	32.2	3,521	...	...	...	100.0	1,791	128	128	...	45	44	-45
		'07	86.7	0.3	3.5	9.4	3,394	...	...	...	100.0	1,780	35	35	...	92	83	101
		'08	72.2	0.3	1.4	26.1	3,784	...	...	...	100.0	1,992	28	28	...	195	174	133
		'09	68.5	0.1	2.1	29.2	3,262	...	...	...	100.0	1,916	23	23	...	184	167	330
Rating History: NR-1, 06/10/10; NR-1, 06/12/09; NR-1, 06/12/08; NR-1, 06/08/07; NR-1, 06/07/06																		
FIRST DOMINION MUTUAL LIFE[1] Michael McLoone Authorized Representative 1600 John F Kennedy Blvd. Philadelphia, PA 19103 VA : 1967 : Mutual : Not Available 215-832-3413 AMB# 006383 NAIC# 63266	E	'05	87.4	...	...	12.6	16,191	...	...	0.1	99.9	6,458	...	...	...	-556	-556	-556
		'06	72.2	...	...	27.8	17,010	...	...	0.1	99.9	8,442	...	...	...	926	912	2,162
		'07	17.0	...	...	83.0	9,708	...	...	0.4	99.6	7,933	...	...	...	-439	-439	-439
		'08	...	...	...	100.0	8,389	...	...	0.0	100.0	7,399	...	...	...	-836	-836	-836
		'09	...	...	...	100.0	51,211	...	...	...	100.0	-37,557	...	...	...	-1,993	-2,007	-1,992
Rating History: E, 06/10/10; NR-1, 06/12/09; NR-1, 06/12/08; NR-1, 06/08/07; NR-1, 06/07/06																		
FIRST FINANCIAL ASSURANCE CO[1] Don L. Kelly President 1200 East Joyce Boulevard Fayetteville, AR 72703 AR : 1967 : Stock : Not Available 479-695-4300 AMB# 060236 NAIC# 83976	NR-1	'05	...	...	...	100.0	121	...	...	...	100.0	121	...	...	...	-5	-5	-5
		'06	...	...	...	100.0	117	...	...	...	100.0	116	...	...	...	-5	-5	-5
		'07	...	...	...	100.0	113	...	...	...	100.0	113	...	...	...	-8	-8	-8
		'08	...	...	...	100.0	115	...	...	...	100.0	107	...	...	...	-11	-11	-11
		'09	...	...	...	100.0	116	...	...	...	100.0	116	...	...	...	-16	-16	-16
Rating History: NR-1, 06/10/10; NR-1, 06/12/09; NR-1, 06/12/08; NR-1, 06/08/07; NR-1, 06/07/06																		

BEST'S PROFITABILITY, LEVERAGE AND LIQUIDITY TESTS 2005 – 2009

Data in U.S. Dollars

—	Profitability Tests							Leverage Tests						Liquidity Tests					
Un-Realized Capital Gains ($000)	Benefits Paid to NPW & Dep (%)	Comm. & Expenses to NPW & Dep (%)	NOG to Total Assets (%)	NOG to Total Rev (%)	Operating Return on Equity (%)	Net Yield (%)	Total Return (%)	Change in NPW & Dep (%)	NPW & Dep to Capital (X)	Capital & Surplus to Liabilities (%)	Surplus Relief (%)	Reins Leverage (%)	Change in Capital (%)	Quick Liquidity (%)	Current Liquidity (%)	Non-Invest Grade Bonds to Capital (%)	Delinq. & Foreclosed Mortgages to Capital (%)	Mort. & Credit Tenant Loans & R.E. to Capital (%)	Affiliated Invest to Capital (%)
...	76.0	15.4	13.7	5.7	19.2	0.57	0.57	2.2	3.8	238.2	...	...	-18.0	235.1	235.1	...	...	...	...
...	83.7	13.1	6.2	2.3	9.0	1.33	1.33	-4.3	4.4	204.0	...	...	-17.8	205.0	206.2	...	...	...	...
...	98.5	11.5	-15.7	-6.5	-29.1	0.53	0.53	0.7	4.5	81.6	...	...	-2.1	175.3	175.9	...	...	...	...
...	85.5	11.1	6.3	3.3	11.3	0.51	0.51	-21.4	3.2	264.5	...	...	11.1	357.6	359.2	...	...	...	...
...	100.8	11.1	-12.7	-7.6	-17.9	0.04	0.04	-33.9	2.6	232.2	...	...	-19.8	317.7	319.5	...	...	...	...

Principal Lines of Business: Dental (100.0%) Principal States: WI (100.0%)

...	56.7	25.5	4.0	18.5	4.4	2.87	2.87	14.3	0.2	999.9	...	...	-2.7	999.9	999.9	...	...	...	...
...	63.9	20.0	4.3	19.7	4.5	3.87	3.87	-12.8	0.2	999.9	...	...	-5.6	999.9	999.9	...	...	...	...
...	55.7	24.4	3.5	16.8	3.7	2.00	2.00	-2.0	0.2	999.9	...	...	-6.4	999.9	999.9	...	...	...	...
...	65.3	18.8	3.9	18.4	4.1	2.29	2.29	-7.1	0.2	999.9	...	...	-6.0	999.9	999.9	...	...	...	...
...	51.1	21.5	3.9	20.6	4.1	1.03	1.03	-10.2	0.2	999.9	...	...	-6.0	999.9	999.9	...	...	...	...

Principal Lines of Business: Dental (100.0%) Principal States: IN (94.5%), IL (5.5%)

...	73.8	18.5	25.0	5.0	41.2	0.38	0.38	...	5.3	120.0	...	...	245.0	144.3	144.3	...	...	...	...
...	75.0	18.8	13.9	4.2	24.7	0.43	0.43	27.2	5.3	137.2	...	...	28.1	147.8	147.8	...	...	...	...
...	77.0	18.3	10.6	3.2	16.9	0.40	0.40	9.3	4.9	208.5	...	...	18.3	264.5	264.5	...	...	...	...
...	76.3	18.6	11.8	3.4	17.3	-0.30	-0.30	8.1	5.0	226.0	...	...	4.3	290.3	290.3	...	...	...	...
...	75.0	18.1	14.0	4.6	20.0	0.45	0.45	-13.1	4.2	235.7	...	...	3.6	380.1	389.8	...	...	...	...

Principal Lines of Business: Dental (100.0%) Principal States: MI (100.0%)

...	71.8	18.3	7.8	7.2	9.8	1.60	1.60	32.1	1.3	465.5	...	...	10.3	485.2	485.2	...	...	...	...
...	74.9	19.6	5.7	4.7	7.0	2.75	2.75	17.7	1.4	405.1	...	...	5.6	433.9	433.9	...	...	...	...
...	76.7	18.3	4.2	3.5	5.0	0.96	0.96	1.3	1.4	582.8	...	...	2.3	666.5	666.5	...	...	...	...
...	86.1	19.1	-0.3	-0.4	-0.4	1.22	1.22	-29.7	1.0	716.3	...	...	-5.4	785.8	785.8	...	...	...	...
...	81.5	16.7	1.1	1.5	1.2	0.11	0.11	-23.2	0.8	999.9	...	...	-0.2	999.9	999.9	...	...	...	...

Principal Lines of Business: Dental (100.0%) Principal States: MO (100.0%)

70	96.1	225.0	2.6	6.6	3.2	...	...	19.4	0.2	453.5	...	...	3.8	...	...	...	...	...	...
1,823	67.7	46.7	5.5	7.4	6.9	...	...	491.3	0.6	420.9	...	...	65.6	...	...	...	...	...	...
2,098	70.2	50.3	5.6	7.6	7.0	...	...	38.8	0.6	542.4	...	...	47.7	...	...	...	...	...	...
-3,028	77.7	47.0	5.5	7.2	9.8	...	...	39.3	1.3	67.1	...	...	-39.5	...	...	...	...	...	...
354	87.1	52.7	-21.3	-29.9	-61.3	...	...	24.2	2.5	54.2	...	...	-37.9	...	...	...	...	...	...

Principal Lines of Business: GrpA&H (98.0%), GrpLife (1.9%), OrdLife (0.1%)

...	...	...	...	...	...	...	...	...	...	...	...	...	...	...	...	...	...	...	...
...	...	...	...	...	...	...	...	...	...	...	...	...	...	...	...	...	...	...	...
...	...	999.9	...	-5.2	...	...	...	...	0.0	353.8	...	...	...	214.3	214.3	...	...	...	...
...	...	999.9	0.4	0.3	0.5	4.53	4.53	300.0	0.0	315.5	...	...	0.6	203.4	203.4	...	...	...	...
...	...	999.9	22.0	14.1	29.2	3.14	3.14	...	0.0	297.7	...	...	21.8	207.3	207.3	...	...	...	...

Principal Lines of Business: CompHosp/Med (100.0%)

-94	78.9	7.9	2.4	16.8	4.9	...	...	-6.2	0.2	96.9	...	...	4.0	...	...	...	...	1.2	...
11	249.6	6.6	1.2	17.7	2.5	...	...	-61.6	0.1	103.6	...	...	-0.4	...	...	...	...	0.9	...
9	859.6	141.0	2.4	42.8	4.6	...	...	-72.5	0.0	112.9	...	...	0.5	...	...	...	...	0.6	...
312	737.9	66.1	4.8	58.0	9.2	...	...	-18.9	0.0	111.1	...	...	10.7	...	...	...	...	0.5	...
-33	635.2	160.8	4.7	54.5	8.6	...	...	-19.9	0.0	143.9	...	...	-3.4	...	...	...	...	0.3	...

Principal Lines of Business: IndAnn (89.4%), OrdLife (10.6%)

495	...	...	-3.4	-80.1	-8.5	...	...	...	...	67.0	...	...	-9.1	...	...	...	...	...	...
...	...	...	5.5	90.8	12.2	...	...	...	...	99.2	...	...	30.4	...	...	...	...	...	...
...	...	...	-3.3	-66.9	-5.4	...	...	...	...	447.3	...	...	-6.3	...	...	...	...	...	...
52	...	...	-9.2	-99.9	-10.9	...	...	...	...	749.1	...	...	-6.7	...	...	...	...	...	...
...	...	...	-6.7	-99.9	13.3	...	...	...	...	-42.3	...	...	-99.9	...	...	...	...	...	...

...	...	...	-3.9	-99.9	-3.9	...	...	...	...	...	...	...	-3.8	...	...	...	...	...	...
...	...	...	-4.0	-99.9	-4.1	...	...	...	...	999.9	...	...	-4.0	...	...	...	...	...	...
...	...	...	-7.1	-99.9	-7.1	...	...	...	...	...	...	...	-2.7	...	...	...	...	...	...
...	...	...	-9.5	-99.9	-9.8	...	...	...	...	999.9	...	...	-5.3	...	...	...	...	...	...
...	...	...	-13.4	-99.9	-13.9	...	...	...	...	...	...	...	8.8	...	...	...	...	...	...

Data in U.S. Dollars

COMPANY NAME Ultimate Parent Association Principal Officer Mailing Address Dom. : Began Bus. : Struct. : Mktg. Specialty Phone # AMB# NAIC#	Best's Financial Strength Rating FSC	Data Year	Balance Sheet Bonds (%)	Mort. Loans & R.E. (%)	Com & Pref. Stock (%)	All Other Assets (%)	Total Assets ($000)	Life Reserves (%)	Health Reserves (%)	Ann Res. & Dep. Liabilities (%)	All Other Liabilities (%)	Capital & Surplus ($000)	Operations Direct Premiums Written ($000)	Net Premiums Written & Deposits ($000)	Operating Cash Flow ($000)	NOG Before Taxes ($000)	NOG After Taxes ($000)	Net Income ($000)
FIRST GREAT-WEST LF & ANNUITY Power Corporation of Canada Mitchell T. G. Graye President & CEO 8515 East Orchard Road Greenwood Village, CO 80111 NY : 1972 : Stock : Broker Ind Life, Ann 914-682-3611 AMB# 008257 NAIC# 79359	**A+** Rating Outlook: Stable **FSC XV**	'05	64.6	14.5	0.0	20.9	583,029	52.4	0.5	28.8	18.2	37,491	57,282	46,182	-40,019	9,043	8,683	8,663
		'06	62.3	15.3	0.0	22.4	605,748	52.1	0.5	26.8	20.6	45,562	59,999	49,601	4,195	10,694	8,325	8,295
		'07	63.3	12.7	0.0	24.0	650,423	49.2	0.4	29.3	21.1	47,783	104,607	93,097	19,555	8,902	5,191	5,204
		'08	58.7	12.8	0.0	28.4	656,304	37.0	0.1	41.0	22.0	53,410	148,397	127,923	-13,078	16,225	8,621	4,942
		'09	56.7	8.8	0.0	34.4	889,492	27.2	0.1	36.9	35.9	65,871	135,839	117,216	159,696	11,312	8,940	8,940
		Rating History: A+ g, 01/22/09; A+ g, 06/22/07; A+ gu, 02/01/07; A+ g, 06/19/06; A+ g, 03/09/05																
FIRST GUARANTY INSURANCE CO' Kirk Babb President P.O. Box 848 Ashdown, AR 71822-0848 AR : 1959 : Stock : Not Available 870-898-5191 AMB# 068218 NAIC# 84034	**NR-1**	'05	70.6	17.0	0.7	11.7	43,008	...	...	...	100.0	6,801	5,429	5,417	...	402	331	320
		'06	72.2	17.8	0.5	9.5	45,348	...	...	...	100.0	5,953	5,804	5,792	...	598	497	450
		'07	67.4	16.7	0.5	15.4	47,344	...	...	...	100.0	7,405	5,541	5,527	...	1,671	1,385	1,378
		'08	61.4	15.7	6.3	16.7	47,011	...	...	...	100.0	5,005	5,375	5,361	...	344	223	383
		'09	72.1	9.4	...	18.5	49,754	...	...	...	100.0	6,302	5,245	5,229	...	-45	-47	-262
		Rating History: NR-1, 06/10/10; NR-1, 06/12/09; NR-1, 06/12/08; NR-5, 04/25/07; NR-5, 05/05/06																
FIRST HEALTH LIFE & HEALTH INS Coventry Health Care Inc Harvey C. DeMovick, Jr. President and CEO 3200 Highland Avenue Downers Grove, IL 60515-1282 TX : 1979 : Stock : Agency A&H, Group A&H, Stop Loss 630-737-7900 AMB# 008951 NAIC# 90328	**B++** Rating Outlook: Negative **FSC IX**	'05	43.1	...	...	56.9	118,313	0.3	10.1	0.0	89.5	40,118	33,711	43,772	26,595	12,638	8,307	8,307
		'06	13.6	...	...	86.4	355,961	0.1	20.6	...	79.3	48,256	515,316	470,684	223,941	10,418	7,655	7,655
		'07	52.5	...	...	47.5	488,450	0.1	49.9	...	50.0	137,061	1,566,380	1,453,518	87,484	73,169	47,620	47,620
		'08	45.2	...	...	54.8	682,069	0.0	70.6	...	29.3	214,661	2,389,420	2,034,183	123,301	-107,183	-69,658	-76,803
		'09	36.9	...	...	63.1	811,138	0.0	61.9	...	38.0	269,529	3,006,248	2,729,212	69,778	-61,291	-49,445	-49,415
		Rating History: B++, 02/12/10; B++, 11/19/08; B++, 10/30/07; B++, 07/11/07; B++, 10/27/06																
FIRST INVESTORS LIFE INS CO First Investors Consolidated Corporation Carol E. Springsteen President Raritan Plaza 1, P.O. Box 7836 Edison, NJ 08818-7836 NY : 1962 : Stock : Agency Ind Life, Var ann, Var life 212-858-8200 AMB# 006413 NAIC# 63495	**A-** Rating Outlook: Stable **FSC VIII**	'05	16.1	...	0.0	83.9	1,241,150	13.3	0.0	2.7	84.0	92,600	103,973	103,009	15,716	14,623	9,069	9,069
		'06	15.9	...	0.0	84.1	1,339,038	13.1	0.0	2.4	84.5	102,804	91,965	91,307	19,568	18,175	11,670	12,012
		'07	16.5	...	0.2	83.3	1,370,125	14.0	0.0	2.3	83.8	113,027	90,313	89,382	31,546	17,763	11,869	12,174
		'08	23.1	...	0.3	76.5	1,011,132	20.8	0.0	3.1	76.1	119,664	82,381	81,145	5,440	16,751	11,253	8,757
		'09	22.8	...	0.0	77.1	1,139,212	19.0	0.0	3.3	77.7	120,027	84,259	82,755	18,401	15,598	10,696	9,737
		Rating History: A-, 06/05/09; A-, 06/05/08; A-, 06/15/07; A-, 06/20/06; A-, 04/13/05																
FIRST LANDMARK LIFE INS CO' Martin M. Oliner Chief Executive Officer 10206 Regency Parkway Drive Omaha, NE 68114-3317 NE : 1988 : Stock : Inactive 302-429-4000 AMB# 068028 NAIC# 74888	**NR-1**	'05	80.8	...	...	19.2	2,074	...	...	...	100.0	2,045	...	...	...	45	30	30
		'06	79.0	...	...	21.0	2,123	...	...	...	100.0	2,081	...	...	...	55	36	36
		'07	...	...	...	100.0	2,163	...	...	...	100.0	2,135	...	...	...	82	54	54
		'08	...	...	...	100.0	2,152	...	...	...	100.0	2,146	...	...	...	17	11	11
		'09	...	...	...	100.0	2,131	...	...	...	100.0	2,131	...	...	...	-23	-15	-15
		Rating History: NR-1, 06/10/10; NR-1, 06/12/09; NR-1, 06/12/08; NR-1, 06/08/07; NR-1, 06/07/06																
FIRST M & F INS CO' Hugh S. Potts, Jr. President P.O. Box 520 Kosciusko, MS 39090-0520 MS : 1991 : Stock : Not Available 662-289-5121 AMB# 068336 NAIC# 63117	**NR-1**	'05	17.1	...	...	82.9	3,205	...	...	...	100.0	3,200	...	0	...	83	67	67
		'06	17.0	...	...	83.0	3,223	...	...	...	100.0	3,219	...	0	...	26	22	22
		'07	23.9	...	...	76.1	2,255	...	...	...	100.0	2,254	...	...	...	21	27	27
		'08	23.9	...	...	76.1	2,263	...	...	...	100.0	2,262	...	0	...	11	10	10
		'09	23.7	...	...	76.3	2,289	...	...	...	100.0	2,286	...	0	...	26	22	22
		Rating History: NR-1, 06/10/10; NR-1, 06/12/09; NR-1, 06/12/08; NR-1, 06/08/07; NR-1, 06/07/06																
FIRST METLIFE INVESTORS INS CO MetLife Inc Michael K. Farrell Chairman, President & CEO 18210 Crane Nest Dr., 3rd Floor Tampa, FL 33647 NY : 1993 : Stock : Broker Ann, Ind Ann, SPDA's 949-717-6536 AMB# 006119 NAIC# 60992	**A+ u** Under Review Implication: Negative **FSC XV**	'05	19.5	0.9	...	79.6	877,037	1.7	...	18.6	79.8	43,134	355,165	293,997	-21,360	-16,219	-15,911	-15,871
		'06	6.8	1.0	0.4	91.8	1,474,856	3.2	...	10.3	86.5	49,425	645,506	553,174	-23,639	-42,577	-25,795	-25,136
		'07	5.5	0.7	0.3	93.5	2,025,534	4.6	...	6.4	89.1	58,867	643,641	601,030	17,096	-49,990	-41,916	-42,253
		'08	11.7	1.0	0.3	87.1	2,067,211	7.3	...	8.6	84.1	73,978	874,975	548,814	261,211	-78,845	-56,109	-56,914
		'09	15.6	1.0	...	83.4	3,013,344	2.2	...	11.5	86.3	225,876	1,097,534	642,874	124,351	-11,269	-7,444	-8,170
		Rating History: A+ gu, 02/09/10; A+ g, 02/20/09; A+ g, 06/05/08; A+ g, 05/29/07; A+ g, 05/05/06																
FIRST NATIONAL INDEMNITY' Mary T. Lane President 1212 E Arapaho Road, Suite 150 Richardson, TX 75081 TX : 1982 : Stock : Not Available 214-365-1900 AMB# 009159 NAIC# 99481	**NR-1**	'05	...	...	...	100.0	921	...	...	...	100.0	920	...	11	...	17	14	14
		'06	...	...	...	100.0	940	...	...	...	100.0	939	...	10	...	22	18	18
		'07	...	...	...	100.0	960	...	...	...	100.0	959	...	9	...	24	20	20
		'08	...	...	...	100.0	982	...	...	...	100.0	981	...	8	...	26	22	22
		'09	...	...	...	100.0	989	...	...	...	100.0	988	...	7	...	8	7	7
		Rating History: NR-1, 06/10/10; NR-1, 06/12/09; NR-1, 06/12/08; NR-1, 06/08/07; NR-1, 06/07/06																
FIRST NATIONAL LIFE OF USA Nelnet, Inc. Kenneth D. TenHulzen President & CEO 121 South 13th Street, Suite 200 Lincoln, NE 68508-1910 NE : 1908 : Stock : Direct Response Credit Life, Credit A&H 402-483-1776 AMB# 007679 NAIC# 74233	**NR-5**	'05	64.2	3.1	20.9	11.8	6,062	62.4	30.5	...	7.1	1,593	2,117	1,559	-3	-125	-99	0
		'06	61.2	2.8	22.2	13.9	6,377	61.3	30.8	...	7.8	1,618	2,462	1,821	124	-63	-28	-28
		'07	67.4	...	21.0	11.6	6,899	60.4	30.9	...	8.7	2,067	2,256	1,675	535	-19	-16	408
		'08	67.5	...	19.8	12.7	5,350	58.4	36.3	...	5.3	1,149	2,192	1,628	-1,016	-91	-79	-65
		'09	55.2	...	24.7	20.1	5,419	59.4	34.2	...	6.4	1,259	1,941	1,423	-294	-45	-34	-25
		Rating History: NR-5, 04/14/10; NR-5, 04/09/09; NR-5, 04/09/08; NR-4, 01/19/07; NR-4, 05/19/06																

BEST'S PROFITABILITY, LEVERAGE AND LIQUIDITY TESTS 2005 – 2009

Data in U.S. Dollars

	Profitability Tests							Leverage Tests						Liquidity Tests					
Un-Realized Capital Gains ($000)	Benefits Paid to NPW & Dep (%)	Comm. & Expenses to NPW & Dep (%)	NOG to Total Assets (%)	NOG to Total Rev (%)	Operating Return on Equity (%)	Net Yield (%)	Total Return (%)	Change in NPW & Dep (%)	NPW & Dep to Capital (X)	Capital & Surplus to Liabilities (%)	Surplus Relief (%)	Reins Leverage (%)	Change in Capital (%)	Quick Liquidity (%)	Current Liquidity (%)	Non-Invest Grade Bonds to Capital (%)	Delinq. & Foreclosed Mortgages to Capital (%)	Mort. & Credit Tenant Loans & R.E. to Capital (%)	Affiliated Invest to Capital (%)
-14	107.4	20.5	1.5	10.4	18.1	6.48	6.69	21.3	1.2	8.4	2.6	185.1	-33.9	45.9	64.1	47.8	0.6	227.8	...
-95	106.3	22.0	1.4	9.8	20.0	6.36	6.50	7.4	1.0	10.3	1.6	151.8	21.6	43.6	61.9	31.5	...	206.4	...
139	61.2	12.4	0.8	4.1	11.1	5.94	6.09	87.7	1.8	10.5	1.5	152.2	6.3	45.6	63.6	35.4	...	173.7	...
-3,257	101.1	4.7	1.3	5.0	17.0	6.48	5.26	37.4	2.4	11.3	9.3	151.1	5.8	50.7	69.1	28.0	...	167.0	...
2,472	57.6	8.5	1.2	5.7	15.0	5.58	6.00	-8.4	1.7	11.3	5.0	120.0	30.2	60.5	80.1	38.8	...	120.1	...
Principal Lines of Business: GrpAnn (85.5%), OrdLife (12.4%), IndAnn (1.9%), GrpA&H (0.2%), IndA&H (0.0%)														Principal States: NY (94.1%)					
-220	65.2	37.5	0.0	4.4	4.0	...	...	0.4	0.0	19.7	...	...	-2.7	...	...	...	...	103.2	...
5	62.2	35.4	1.1	6.0	7.8	...	...	6.9	0.9	16.1	...	...	-11.3	...	...	...	...	128.4	...
3	66.8	41.5	3.0	17.1	20.7	...	...	-4.6	0.7	19.4	...	...	22.3	...	...	...	...	103.0	...
-1,116	75.2	41.3	0.5	3.0	3.6	...	...	-3.0	1.0	12.5	...	...	-31.9	...	...	...	...	140.9	...
1,090	74.8	37.4	-0.1	-0.7	-0.8	...	...	-2.5	0.8	15.0	...	...	24.3	...	...	...	...	72.2	...
Principal Lines of Business: IndAnn (64.1%), OrdLife (35.9%)																			
...	73.3	-0.4	7.7	13.5	23.2	1.22	1.21	22.0	1.1	51.6	40.8	95.5	27.8	171.4	181.1	...	...	...	...
...	89.9	9.1	3.2	1.6	17.3	3.93	3.92	975.3	9.7	15.8	22.4	77.2	20.3	123.3	126.4	...	...	...	...
...	86.9	10.3	11.3	3.2	51.4	7.56	7.56	208.8	10.6	39.2	-0.1	26.2	183.7	139.7	150.8	...	...	...	...
...	98.2	7.9	-11.9	-3.4	-39.6	3.84	2.38	39.9	9.5	45.9	0.0	37.2	56.1	133.1	139.1	...	...	...	...
...	95.8	6.9	-6.6	-1.8	-20.4	1.95	1.95	34.2	10.1	49.8	0.0	12.6	25.7	158.6	165.9	...	...	...	...
Principal Lines of Business: IndA&H (78.0%), GrpA&H (22.0%), GrpAnn (0.0%), GrpLife (0.0%)														Principal States: PA (20.2%), IN (5.7%), CA (5.1%), OH (4.6%), FL (3.9%)					
-1	94.3	21.9	0.7	7.8	10.3	5.28	5.29	-1.6	1.1	52.0	0.4	5.6	11.7	81.6	91.6	15.0	...	...	0.6
-5	134.8	22.2	0.9	11.1	11.9	5.56	5.65	-11.4	0.9	55.4	0.3	6.1	11.0	86.0	96.3	10.6	...	...	0.6
7	125.0	25.1	0.9	11.3	11.0	5.53	5.62	-2.1	0.8	54.7	0.3	6.9	10.0	85.1	95.4	11.0	...	...	0.5
-239	138.6	25.0	0.9	11.5	9.7	5.56	4.65	-9.2	0.7	57.1	0.1	7.5	4.8	88.8	100.4	10.3	...	...	0.5
178	100.5	25.1	1.0	10.2	8.9	5.22	4.87	2.0	0.7	53.7	0.2	9.9	0.7	84.8	96.1	9.0	...	...	0.5
Principal Lines of Business: OrdLife (74.7%), IndAnn (22.5%), GrpLife (2.6%), GrpAnn (0.3%), IndA&H (0.0%)														Principal States: NY (25.2%), NJ (7.7%), OR (6.1%), CT (5.7%), IN (5.0%)					
1,060	...	...	1.4	51.6	1.5	...	...	...	...	999.9	...	...	-2.6	...	...	...	...	...	...
-680	...	...	1.7	52.4	1.7	...	...	...	...	999.9	...	...	1.8	...	...	...	...	...	...
521	...	...	2.5	42.6	2.6	...	...	...	...	999.9	...	...	2.6	...	...	...	...	...	...
1,861	...	...	0.5	24.9	0.5	...	...	...	...	999.9	...	...	0.5	...	...	...	...	...	...
-362	...	...	-0.7	-99.9	-0.7	...	...	...	...	...	...	...	-0.7	...	...	...	...	...	...
...	720.2	-99.9	2.1	61.8	2.1	...	...	97.0	0.0	999.9	...	...	2.9	...	...	...	...	...	...
...	212.2	-99.9	0.7	65.7	0.7	...	...	-57.6	0.0	999.9	...	...	0.6	...	...	...	...	...	...
...	...	...	1.0	78.8	1.0	...	...	100.0	...	999.9	...	...	-30.0	...	...	...	...	...	...
...	850.0	-99.9	0.4	27.5	0.4	...	...	...	0.0	999.9	...	...	0.4	...	...	...	...	...	...
...	60.0	-99.9	1.0	67.6	1.0	...	...	-25.0	0.0	999.9	...	...	1.1	...	...	...	...	...	...
Principal Lines of Business: CrdLife (100.0%)																			
-407	16.9	7.4	-2.2	-5.0	-43.5	4.64	4.61	326.8	6.6	28.7	12.2	999.9	42.7	83.8	94.4	34.8	...	17.5	14.9
-16	15.8	8.9	-2.2	-4.4	-55.7	5.41	5.79	88.2	10.9	32.0	10.7	999.9	13.4	80.1	89.5	17.1	...	28.2	27.9
503	19.4	11.0	-2.4	-6.5	-77.4	4.52	4.81	8.7	10.0	39.1	4.6	904.9	18.1	77.8	86.9	10.2	...	25.0	16.1
-36	21.9	10.8	-2.7	-9.1	-84.5	3.11	2.81	-8.7	7.3	15.1	21.7	999.9	24.9	100.8	108.1	7.6	...	26.4	13.3
36	14.4	12.7	-0.3	-1.1	-5.0	4.04	3.87	17.1	2.8	61.3	8.4	629.2	203.9	101.4	124.6	6.8	...	13.1	4.4
Principal Lines of Business: IndAnn (106.6%), OrdLife (-6.6%)														Principal States: NY (98.8%)					
...	83.1	324.2	1.6	22.8	1.6	...	...	-8.2	0.0	999.9	...	...	1.6	...	...	...	...	...	...
...	57.5	411.4	2.0	26.9	2.0	...	...	-12.1	0.0	999.9	...	...	2.0	...	...	...	...	...	...
...	90.9	434.6	2.2	29.1	2.2	...	...	-12.0	0.0	999.9	...	...	2.2	...	...	...	...	...	...
...	108.3	367.6	2.3	34.7	2.3	...	...	-8.8	0.0	999.9	...	...	2.3	...	...	...	...	...	...
...	168.1	368.3	0.7	14.7	0.7	...	...	-6.8	0.0	999.9	...	...	0.7	...	...	...	...	...	...
Principal Lines of Business: OrdLife (100.0%)																			
-170	40.0	73.2	-1.6	-5.2	-6.3	1.70	0.88	6.2	0.9	40.2	14.3	41.0	-3.5	116.9	123.1	...	...	10.8	10.8
148	29.0	69.0	-0.5	-1.3	-1.7	2.49	4.95	16.8	1.0	38.4	16.1	45.2	1.9	116.8	123.1	...	...	10.0	10.0
-50	30.2	75.4	-0.2	-0.8	-0.9	2.39	8.28	-8.0	0.8	47.8	10.3	35.7	25.9	125.2	132.3	...	...	...	...
-396	74.0	68.2	-1.3	-4.0	-4.9	2.29	-4.12	-2.8	1.3	31.2	17.5	64.8	-43.0	111.8	116.2	...	...	...	...
211	42.8	78.7	-0.6	-1.9	-2.8	3.47	7.81	-12.6	1.0	35.1	14.7	57.1	10.8	108.2	114.6	...	...	...	...
Principal Lines of Business: CrdLife (53.9%), CrdA&H (45.4%), OrdLife (0.7%)														Principal States: NE (100.0%)					

Data in U.S. Dollars

COMPANY NAME / Ultimate Parent Association / Principal Officer / Mailing Address / Dom. : Began Bus. : Struct. : Mktg. / Specialty / Phone # / AMB# NAIC#	Best's Financial Strength Rating / FSC	Data Year	Balance Sheet: Bonds (%)	Mort. Loans & R.E. (%)	Com & Pref. Stock (%)	All Other Assets (%)	Total Assets ($000)	Life Reserves (%)	Health Reserves (%)	Ann Res. & Dep. Liabilities (%)	All Other Liabilities (%)	Capital & Surplus ($000)	Operations: Direct Premiums Written ($000)	Net Premiums Written & Deposits ($000)	Operating Cash Flow ($000)	NOG Before Taxes ($000)	NOG After Taxes ($000)	Net Income ($000)
FIRST PENN-PACIFIC LIFE INS CO Lincoln National Corporation	**A+**	'05	77.9	13.5	0.0	8.6	1,856,277	93.3	...	2.8	3.9	217,711	240,188	95,825	60,550	88,155	61,989	61,629
Dennis R. Glass, President		'06	77.8	13.6	0.0	8.6	1,898,175	93.2	...	2.6	4.2	275,209	211,115	68,464	47,269	87,965	60,591	62,852
1300 South Clinton Street, Fort Wayne, IN 46802-3518	Rating Outlook: Negative	'07	77.1	13.7	0.0	9.2	1,921,633	94.5	...	2.2	3.4	186,713	197,693	61,083	17,040	92,370	62,284	58,640
IN : 1964 : Stock : Agency		'08	72.0	14.3	2.1	11.7	1,890,903	95.5	...	1.9	2.6	192,458	187,961	56,861	-55,771	75,071	50,463	27,325
Ann, Term Life, Univ Life; 260-455-2000		'09	77.2	13.7	0.1	9.0	1,857,132	94.3	...	1.9	3.8	205,404	176,391	2,471	-26,995	69,941	45,921	31,618
AMB# 006904 NAIC# 67652	FSC XV	**Rating History: A+ g, 10/21/09; A+ g, 02/20/09; A+ g, 10/05/07; A+ g, 03/28/07; A+ g, 04/03/06**																
FIRST PRIORITY LIFE INS CO Hospital Service Assn of Northeastern PA	**NR-5**	'05	...	...	...	...	...	...	...	...	...	...	...	...	...	...	...	...
Denise S. Cesare, President & CEO		'06	...	...	...	100.0	10,562	...	...	...	100.0	10,547	...	...	325	506	329	329
19 North Main Street, Wilkes-Barre, PA 18711		'07	38.5	...	9.8	51.7	92,585	...	69.6	...	30.4	34,359	109,061	109,061	64,924	-6,133	-5,879	-5,684
PA : 1998 : Stock : Agency		'08	60.0	...	7.2	32.8	183,875	...	68.0	...	32.0	109,050	387,884	387,884	81,923	2,108	2,060	1,319
Health; 800-432-8015		'09	59.4	...	17.5	23.1	179,160	...	64.1	...	35.9	122,477	402,149	402,066	-8,291	6,845	4,848	4,702
AMB# 060298 NAIC# 60147		**Rating History: NR-5, 03/22/10; NR-5, 04/09/09; NR-5, 03/24/08; NR-5, 08/20/07; NR-5, 06/03/05**																
FIRST REHABILITATION LF OF AM Rehab Services Corporation	**A-**	'05	77.9	...	1.9	20.2	83,328	...	50.1	...	49.9	49,973	77,477	77,199	6,517	9,139	6,088	6,116
Richard A. White, Chief Executive Officer		'06	76.1	...	0.5	23.3	93,978	0.0	29.9	...	70.1	32,510	46,283	45,980	10,507	-20,221	-19,127	-19,044
600 Northern Boulevard, Great Neck, NY 11021-5202	Rating Outlook: Stable	'07	74.7	...	0.6	24.8	95,199	...	33.6	...	66.4	35,512	79,783	79,494	-1,726	4,042	4,855	4,859
NY : 1972 : Stock : Broker		'08	78.8	...	...	21.2	90,701	0.0	40.8	...	59.2	42,850	84,032	83,717	-1,598	6,131	8,145	7,738
Group A&H, Group Life; 516-829-8100		'09	82.5	...	...	17.5	93,461	0.1	65.3	...	34.5	42,011	95,633	95,330	2,760	6,376	2,508	2,359
AMB# 009877 NAIC# 81434	FSC VI	**Rating History: A-, 09/23/09; A-, 08/15/08; A-, 06/28/07; A-, 06/21/06; A-, 06/15/05**																
FIRST RELIANCE STANDARD LIFE R & Co Capital Management, L.L.C.	**A**	'05	77.6	...	1.8	20.6	111,143	13.5	69.2	1.6	15.7	32,345	56,896	52,559	8,933	7,015	5,126	5,126
Lawrence E. Daurelle, President & CEO		'06	84.0	...	...	16.0	120,026	12.2	70.6	1.5	15.7	37,324	59,623	55,149	9,617	9,527	6,882	6,882
2001 Market Street, Suite 1500, Philadelphia, PA 19103	Rating Outlook: Negative	'07	79.8	...	...	20.2	128,066	13.9	73.7	2.1	10.3	44,398	65,240	61,941	8,356	13,473	9,564	9,564
NY : 1984 : Stock : Broker		'08	93.5	...	...	6.5	133,393	13.3	75.4	2.2	9.2	48,501	64,424	61,663	7,633	13,884	9,680	9,303
Dis inc, Group Life; 212-303-8400		'09	89.0	...	...	11.0	147,708	13.5	76.2	2.1	8.2	56,760	60,916	58,467	10,376	12,356	9,116	6,057
AMB# 009418 NAIC# 71005	FSC X	**Rating History: A g, 12/22/09; A g, 12/22/08; A g, 01/08/08; A g, 12/19/06; A g, 12/21/05**																
FIRST SECURITY BENEFIT L&A NY Security Benefit Mutual Holding Company	**B u**	'05	4.6	...	...	95.4	121,420	...	...	2.0	98.0	9,261	30,989	30,976	-1,603	345	184	184
Kris A. Robbins, Chairman, President & CEO		'06	5.4	...	...	94.6	154,564	...	...	4.4	95.6	11,232	36,166	36,060	4,471	-85	-20	-22
One Security Benefit Place, Topeka, KS 66636-0001	Under Review Implication: Positive	'07	5.7	...	...	94.3	188,472	...	...	4.6	95.4	11,034	42,832	42,633	1,695	-478	-197	-197
NY : 1995 : Stock : Broker		'08	8.2	...	...	91.8	151,809	...	...	8.0	92.0	9,758	27,543	27,391	3,567	-2,296	-1,371	-1,371
Var ann; 914-697-4748		'09	5.9	...	...	94.1	180,192	...	...	6.5	93.5	10,708	15,784	15,555	-551	1,604	819	819
AMB# 060104 NAIC# 60084	FSC IX	**Rating History: B gu, 02/19/10; B g, 02/27/09; B++gu, 10/13/08; A- g, 06/24/08; A g, 07/03/07**																
FIRST SUNAMERICA LIFE INS CO American International Group, Inc	**A**	'05	78.0	7.7	0.0	14.2	4,658,439	5.5	0.0	80.8	13.8	268,572	1,025,828	1,103,598	834,098	32,164	16,471	10,979
Jay S. Wintrob, President & CEO		'06	76.6	7.2	1.7	14.6	5,617,346	4.4	...	82.7	12.9	396,981	1,153,358	1,231,937	863,086	42,982	21,206	18,488
70 Pine Street, 19th Floor, New York, NY 10270	Rating Outlook: Negative	'07	72.6	7.0	2.3	18.1	6,479,345	3.7	...	83.1	13.1	503,904	1,160,875	1,156,929	656,486	76,071	62,374	-7,137
NY : 1980 : Stock : Broker		'08	65.5	6.6	1.6	26.2	7,445,660	3.1	...	88.4	8.5	547,171	1,597,816	1,594,898	115,292	-132,726	-149,649	-1,132,799
Ind Ann, SPDA's, Var ann; 310-772-6000		'09	70.1	5.3	0.3	24.4	8,949,760	2.5	...	89.4	8.1	775,623	1,806,674	1,803,220	1,324,322	56,829	126,329	43,124
AMB# 009023 NAIC# 92495	FSC XI	**Rating History: A, 12/16/09; A, 11/10/08; A gu, 09/15/08; A+ g, 06/17/08; A++g, 05/28/08**																
FIRST SYMETRA NAT LIFE INS NY Symetra Financial Corporation	**A**	'05	93.1	...	...	6.9	170,646	0.0	...	99.0	1.0	22,216	4,766	7,728	-1,604	-3,078	-2,864	-3,016
Randall H. Talbot, President		'06	94.2	...	0.6	5.2	154,646	0.0	0.5	98.3	1.2	22,967	11,582	14,273	-15,430	1,097	420	34
P.O. Box 34690, Seattle, WA 98124-1690	Rating Outlook: Stable	'07	92.1	...	0.4	7.5	123,377	0.1	1.6	95.9	2.4	25,085	16,617	18,752	-29,197	2,879	2,431	2,371
NY : 1990 : Stock : Agency		'08	93.8	...	0.2	6.0	306,671	0.3	1.1	96.1	2.5	42,673	181,791	183,138	181,850	-2,128	-2,165	-2,169
Ind Ann, Stop Loss, Term Life; 425-256-8000		'09	92.8	5.2	...	2.0	537,957	0.7	0.7	97.5	1.1	62,010	232,296	234,083	227,587	106	-107	-597
AMB# 068147 NAIC# 78417	FSC XIV	**Rating History: A g, 09/17/09; A g, 06/13/08; A g, 06/11/07; A g, 05/05/06; A g, 05/10/05**																
FIRST UNITED AMERICAN LIFE INS Torchmark Corporation	**A+**	'05	87.5	...	...	12.5	101,880	49.4	26.8	18.9	4.9	31,624	59,447	59,332	5,962	8,670	4,713	4,713
Vern D. Herbel, President & CEO		'06	80.8	...	5.1	14.1	112,326	55.8	22.5	15.5	6.2	37,439	68,252	68,149	10,222	14,349	8,526	8,469
P.O. Box 3125, Syracuse, NY 13220	Rating Outlook: Stable	'07	82.0	...	2.9	15.1	120,976	61.6	20.9	12.7	4.8	42,460	69,350	69,264	8,681	13,264	8,623	8,623
NY : 1984 : Stock : Agency		'08	79.4	...	4.7	15.9	125,418	61.8	18.4	11.5	8.3	37,806	65,161	65,079	2,125	11,303	7,312	6,505
Ind A&H, LTC, Med supp; 315-451-2544		'09	69.9	...	...	30.1	126,774	68.4	17.8	10.5	3.2	38,374	64,526	64,453	525	11,501	7,384	4,893
AMB# 009412 NAIC# 74101	FSC X	**Rating History: A+ g, 06/15/10; A+ g, 06/11/09; A+ g, 06/11/08; A+ g, 06/08/07; A+ g, 06/08/06**																
FIRST UNUM LIFE INS CO Unum Group	**A-**	'05	94.5	1.1	...	4.5	1,497,286	5.8	88.3	3.2	2.7	160,125	418,167	432,419	104,657	29,545	18,542	18,670
Thomas R. Watjen, Chairman, President & CEO		'06	89.2	2.2	1.8	6.9	1,653,827	5.7	89.6	2.3	2.4	182,763	439,683	447,191	127,543	24,121	26,763	26,153
1 Fountain Square, Chattanooga, TN 37402-1330	Rating Outlook: Positive	'07	90.9	2.5	1.7	4.9	1,779,790	5.7	90.1	2.1	2.1	184,025	431,094	446,336	143,621	27,692	17,796	20,701
NY : 1960 : Stock : Broker		'08	89.9	3.9	1.5	4.7	1,933,234	5.3	89.0	2.1	3.6	193,793	433,210	456,580	140,589	39,904	24,828	19,473
Dis inc, Group Life; 212-953-1130		'09	92.4	4.5	...	3.1	2,012,186	5.1	91.3	2.2	1.4	218,301	423,995	446,844	62,451	41,219	26,039	7,539
AMB# 006514 NAIC# 64297	FSC XIV	**Rating History: A- g, 03/08/10; A- g, 03/13/09; A- g, 01/29/08; A- g, 11/07/06; A- g, 06/07/06**																

BEST'S PROFITABILITY, LEVERAGE AND LIQUIDITY TESTS 2005 – 2009

Data in U.S. Dollars

—	Profitability Tests							Leverage Tests						Liquidity Tests							
Un-Realized Capital Gains ($000)	Benefits Paid to NPW & Dep (%)	Comm. & Expenses to NPW & Dep (%)	NOG to Total Assets (%)	NOG to Total Rev (%)	Operating Return on Equity (%)	Net Yield (%)	Total Return (%)	Change in NPW & Dep (%)	NPW & Dep to Capital (X)	Capital & Surplus to Liabilities (%)	Surplus Relief (%)	Reins Leverage (%)	Change in Capital (%)	Quick Liquidity (%)	Current Liquidity (%)	Non-Invest Grade Bonds to Capital (%)	Delinq. & Foreclosed Mortgages to Capital (%)	Mort. & Credit Tenant Loans & R.E. to Capital (%)	Affiliated Invest to Capital (%)
-1,316	123.2	-8.1	3.4	25.4	32.7	6.64	6.56	-5.2	0.4	14.0	16.8	326.7	33.6	43.9	62.9	29.7	...	112.6	...
821	183.4	-11.7	3.2	27.6	24.6	6.57	6.77	-28.6	0.2	18.1	13.2	290.3	27.3	48.0	67.1	24.1	...	91.1	...
96	206.7	-21.7	3.3	29.2	27.0	6.60	6.44	-10.8	0.3	11.8	18.6	653.5	-30.1	47.7	64.8	34.6	...	132.1	...
-1,912	229.0	-21.4	2.6	25.0	26.6	6.32	4.97	-6.9	0.3	11.8	17.0	702.2	-2.3	45.9	61.4	51.7	...	137.9	...
-1,739	999.9	-99.9	2.5	28.6	23.1	6.34	5.44	-95.7	0.0	12.6	23.7	710.5	4.7	43.9	60.0	62.0	...	124.3	...
Principal Lines of Business: OrdLife (80.2%), GrpLife (14.5%), IndAnn (5.3%)													Principal States: CA (16.5%), IL (6.3%), TX (5.6%), FL (5.2%), PA (5.0%)						
			...	...	...	...	...	...	...	...	...	...	...	...	...	...	...	...	...
...	...	...	...	65.0	...	...	...	...	...	999.9	...	...	...	999.9	999.9	...	...	...	...
-93	94.9	12.2	-11.4	-5.3	-26.2	3.90	4.14	...	3.2	59.0	...	...	225.8	147.3	159.5	...	...	...	...
-5,037	86.7	14.2	1.5	0.5	2.9	5.20	0.21	255.7	3.6	145.7	...	...	217.4	182.6	200.7	0.0	...	...	...
6,112	84.3	15.5	2.7	1.2	4.2	3.96	7.98	3.7	3.3	216.1	...	...	12.3	238.4	265.9	0.1	...	...	...
Principal Lines of Business: CompHosp/Med (100.0%)													Principal States: PA (100.0%)						
-3	55.2	36.0	7.6	7.6	12.9	3.50	3.57	10.2	1.5	151.3	...	0.7	13.4	203.4	213.1	0.4	...	...	...
-81	98.8	52.7	-21.6	-38.4	-46.4	4.52	4.57	-40.4	1.4	53.4	...	1.2	-34.8	135.9	143.2	...	...	...	...
51	65.5	31.9	5.1	5.8	14.3	4.72	4.79	72.9	2.2	60.0	...	1.9	9.2	129.2	136.8	...	...	...	...
-62	65.9	32.1	8.8	9.3	20.8	4.27	3.71	5.3	2.0	89.5	...	0.9	20.0	153.9	164.7	0.1	...	...	...
-244	60.8	34.7	2.7	2.5	5.9	4.24	3.94	13.9	2.3	81.7	...	1.9	-2.0	133.6	147.1	4.4	...	...	...
Principal Lines of Business: GrpA&H (99.7%), GrpLife (0.3%)													Principal States: NY (94.2%), NJ (4.1%)						
...	58.8	25.4	4.8	9.0	16.5	4.21	4.34	23.8	1.6	41.8	0.2	51.8	8.3	105.5	118.1	18.6	...	...	...
...	59.8	25.1	6.0	11.5	19.8	4.36	4.46	4.9	1.5	45.9	0.1	41.5	15.3	109.0	120.7	16.1	...	...	...
...	56.4	23.8	7.7	14.4	23.4	4.24	4.32	12.3	1.4	54.0	0.1	32.7	18.9	126.1	139.5	14.4	...	...	...
-1,307	59.9	23.5	7.4	14.4	20.8	4.46	3.17	-0.4	1.3	57.1	0.1	22.1	8.0	104.8	120.6	18.6	...	...	...
1,302	56.3	25.1	6.5	14.1	17.3	4.72	3.50	-5.2	1.0	62.4	0.1	14.1	17.0	122.9	139.0	1.4	...	...	...
Principal Lines of Business: GrpA&H (61.5%), GrpLife (37.7%), IndAnn (0.6%), OrdLife (0.1%), IndA&H (0.0%)													Principal States: NY (100.0%)						
...	39.3	8.2	0.2	0.5	2.0	4.20	4.20	-16.6	3.3	-99.9	...	2.0	1.9	-99.9	-99.9	...	...	...	...
...	44.3	8.7	0.0	-0.1	-0.2	3.95	3.88	16.4	3.2	-99.9	...	2.4	21.3	-99.9	-99.9	...	...	...	...
...	40.8	8.3	-0.1	-0.4	-1.8	5.33	5.33	18.2	3.9	866.7	...	4.1	-1.7	792.1	824.9	...	...	...	...
...	62.0	8.5	-0.8	-4.3	-13.2	4.38	4.38	-35.8	2.8	158.7	...	6.1	-11.5	213.6	224.3	...	...	...	...
...	100.7	13.7	0.5	4.2	8.0	4.06	4.06	-43.2	1.5	201.7	...	22.9	9.8	217.0	234.9	...	...	...	...
Principal Lines of Business: IndAnn (100.0%)													Principal States: NY (100.0%)						
698	33.7	10.4	0.4	1.3	6.2	5.44	5.33	103.7	3.9	7.4	0.0	14.1	3.1	57.1	74.9	20.4	...	127.4	...
58	43.9	8.8	0.4	1.4	6.4	5.63	5.56	11.6	3.0	9.1	0.0	9.0	47.7	60.2	78.5	22.7	...	98.8	...
53	53.1	7.0	1.0	4.3	13.8	5.83	4.48	-6.1	2.3	9.7	0.0	6.9	22.1	61.5	79.6	27.7	...	89.3	...
20,790	48.9	6.3	-2.1	-7.8	-28.5	5.55	-9.01	37.9	2.9	8.6	0.0	6.2	8.1	77.3	94.2	34.3	...	89.6	...
-54,879	44.4	6.3	1.5	5.9	19.1	4.68	2.59	13.1	2.3	10.3	0.0	4.1	41.0	78.9	97.6	34.7	...	60.8	...
Principal Lines of Business: IndAnn (99.9%), GrpAnn (0.0%), OrdLife (0.0%)													Principal States: NY (97.4%)						
...	292.5	32.4	-1.7	-21.9	-13.7	4.98	4.91	-31.5	0.3	15.5	0.1	0.3	13.6	91.3	106.5	2.6	...	...	...
...	247.1	15.9	0.3	2.2	1.9	5.05	4.79	84.7	0.6	17.9	0.0	0.4	2.7	84.2	101.8	8.7	...	...	...
...	281.0	19.6	1.7	10.4	10.1	5.08	4.98	31.4	0.7	26.3	0.1	0.5	9.4	98.8	113.3	17.2	...	...	...
...	12.7	4.8	-1.0	-1.1	-6.4	4.15	4.11	876.6	4.2	16.6	0.1	0.4	69.7	89.4	102.6	11.1	...	...	...
...	11.8	6.5	0.0	0.0	-0.2	5.67	5.53	27.8	3.7	13.4	0.0	0.3	45.3	78.7	91.7	4.5	...	43.8	...
Principal Lines of Business: IndAnn (94.5%), GrpA&H (4.3%), OrdLife (1.1%), GrpAnn (0.0%)													Principal States: NY (100.0%)						
...	62.9	23.8	4.8	7.2	15.1	6.92	6.96	0.5	1.8	46.3	0.1	2.8	3.1	75.8	93.3	10.9	...	...	...
...	60.1	21.3	8.0	11.4	24.7	6.91	6.85	14.9	1.8	51.4	0.0	2.5	18.4	72.6	93.4	11.1	...	...	...
...	61.3	23.4	7.4	11.3	21.6	6.77	6.78	1.6	1.6	55.8	0.0	2.4	13.6	74.7	93.9	13.0	...	...	...
...	62.3	22.5	5.9	10.1	18.2	6.76	6.05	-6.0	1.7	44.3	0.0	2.9	-11.2	62.3	79.7	29.1	...	...	...
0	62.2	21.3	5.9	10.4	19.4	6.11	3.92	-1.0	1.7	43.4	0.0	2.8	-0.3	68.4	81.3	31.9	...	...	...
Principal Lines of Business: IndA&H (65.6%), OrdLife (31.8%), GrpA&H (2.3%), IndAnn (0.2%)													Principal States: NY (100.0%)						
1,785	64.2	18.6	1.3	3.8	11.4	6.50	6.68	-3.5	2.6	12.3	4.1	160.0	-1.5	54.3	71.2	38.4	...	9.8	...
...	64.5	18.7	1.7	5.2	15.6	6.33	6.32	3.4	2.4	12.9	3.2	139.8	15.0	55.6	73.0	23.7	...	21.7	...
...	59.0	19.9	1.0	3.4	9.7	6.35	6.53	-0.2	2.3	12.2	1.9	132.4	2.7	58.3	75.2	17.9	...	28.5	...
...	63.9	21.7	1.3	4.7	13.1	6.30	6.01	2.3	2.2	11.9	2.5	128.3	6.4	55.9	73.1	31.6	...	41.1	...
-154	65.2	22.3	1.3	4.9	12.6	6.39	5.43	-2.1	2.0	12.5	2.4	114.9	8.7	55.4	72.2	35.4	...	44.5	...
Principal Lines of Business: GrpA&H (51.4%), IndA&H (20.8%), GrpLife (16.8%), IndAnn (9.9%), OrdLife (0.9%)													Principal States: NY (90.8%), NJ (5.7%)						

ANNUAL STATEMENT DATA FOR YEARS 2005 – 2009

Data in U.S. Dollars

COMPANY NAME Ultimate Parent Association Principal Officer Mailing Address Dom. : Began Bus. : Struct. : Mktg. Specialty Phone # AMB# NAIC#	Best's Financial Strength Rating FSC	Data Year	Balance Sheet Bonds (%)	Mort. Loans & R.E. (%)	Com & Pref. Stock (%)	All Other Assets (%)	Total Assets ($000)	Life Reserves (%)	Health Reserves (%)	Ann Res. & Dep. Liabilities (%)	All Other Liabilities (%)	Capital & Surplus ($000)	Operations Direct Premiums Written ($000)	Net Premiums Written & Deposits ($000)	Operating Cash Flow ($000)	NOG Before Taxes ($000)	NOG After Taxes ($000)	Net Income ($000)
FIRST VIRGINIA LIFE INS CO[1] Christopher L. Henson President 150 S. Stratford Road, Suite 400 Winston-Salem, NC 27104 VA : 1967 : Stock : Direct Response 336-733-3082 AMB# 006420 NAIC# 63568	**NR-1**	'05	69.3	...	...	30.7	9,819	...	...	...	100.0	6,736	-1	-253	...	1,012	671	671
		'06	40.4	...	...	59.6	9,399	...	...	...	100.0	7,380	0	-103	...	796	651	651
		'07	18.3	...	...	81.7	7,081	...	...	...	100.0	5,631	...	-43	...	543	249	255
		'08	...	...	...	100.0	6,900	...	...	...	100.0	5,898	...	-166	...	253	270	270
		'09	...	...	...	100.0	6,700	...	...	...	100.0	5,935	...	-17	...	56	37	37
		Rating History: NR-1, 06/10/10; NR-1, 06/12/09; NR-1, 06/12/08; NR-1, 06/08/07; NR-1, 06/07/06																
FIRSTCARE INC CareFirst Inc David D. Wolf President 10455 Mill Run Circle Owings Mills, MD 21117-4208 MD : 1996 : Stock : Agency Health 410-581-3000 AMB# 060307 NAIC# 60113	**NR-5**	'05	85.8	...	...	14.2	1,908	...	...	...	100.0	1,900	...	...	3	...	...	...
		'06	8.0	...	...	92.0	17,513	...	...	...	100.0	1,991	36,615	...	9,725	237	187	178
		'07	0.9	...	...	99.1	17,821	...	...	...	100.0	2,429	47,426	...	-8,599	468	368	350
		'08	1.3	...	...	98.7	20,132	...	...	...	100.0	2,535	49,173	...	3,600	67	51	106
		'09	1.6	...	...	98.4	15,859	...	...	...	100.0	3,218	49,648	...	-2,661	22	17	17
		Rating History: NR-5, 04/19/10; NR-5, 03/27/09; NR-5, 03/24/08; NR-5, 06/06/07; NR-1, 06/07/06																
FIRSTCAROLINACARE INSURANCE CO FirstHealth of the Carolinas Inc Kenneth J. Lewis President P.O. Box 909 Pinehurst, NC 28370-0909 NC : 1996 : Non-Profit : Broker Health 910-715-8100 AMB# 064268 NAIC# 12962	**NR-5**	'05	12.6	...	...	87.4	15,455	...	73.8	...	26.2	9,636	38,836	37,838	2,286	1,507	978	978
		'06	50.6	...	9.6	39.8	15,646	...	65.9	...	34.1	10,320	40,990	39,856	-185	1,435	950	951
		'07	46.1	...	8.5	45.4	18,028	...	78.9	...	21.1	11,595	47,559	46,184	1,635	1,470	995	1,047
		'08	57.1	...	7.2	35.7	16,642	...	58.1	...	41.9	12,515	27,625	27,400	-615	1,305	1,059	752
		'09	60.0	...	14.3	25.7	16,171	...	47.3	...	52.7	12,288	28,318	28,610	-1,286	-1,216	-658	-558
		Rating History: NR-5, 04/07/10; NR-5, 08/26/09; B+ pd, 07/28/08; B+ pd, 08/22/07; B+ pd, 09/15/06																
FIRSTCOMMUNITY HEALTH PLAN INC[2] Lonnie Younger President 699 Gallatin Street SW, Suite A2 Huntsville, AL 35801 AL : 1996 : Stock : Broker Med supp 256-532-2780 AMB# 064769 NAIC# 47051	**NR-5**	'05	...	...	...	100.0	6,432	...	70.1	...	29.9	5,042	5,562	5,562	569	577	577	577
		'06	...	...	...	100.0	6,955	...	73.0	...	27.0	5,520	5,626	5,626	442	457	457	457
		'07	52.4	...	...	47.6	7,639	...	71.4	...	28.6	6,137	5,833	5,833	719	645	645	645
		'08	51.3	...	...	48.7	7,863	...	65.1	...	34.9	6,469	5,713	5,713	258	394	394	392
		'09	53.0	...	...	47.0	4,569	...	56.5	...	43.5	3,355	5,578	5,578	-3,231	-1,814	-1,814	-1,814
		Rating History: NR-5, 04/21/10; NR-5, 04/09/09; NR-5, 03/27/08; NR-5, 04/03/07; NR-5, 05/18/06																
FIRSTSIGHT VISION SERVICES INC National Vision Inc Robert K. Patton Chairman, President & CEO 1202 Monte Vista Avenue, Suite 17 Upland, CA 91786 CA : 1997 : Stock : Not Available Group A&H 800-841-2790 AMB# 064717	**NR-5**	'05	...	...	...	100.0	6,517	...	...	...	100.0	4,618	8,959	8,959	467	3	3	3
		'06	...	...	...	100.0	4,626	...	...	...	100.0	2,586	9,650	9,650	-558	-1,732	-1,732	-1,732
		'07	...	...	...	100.0	4,716	...	...	...	100.0	2,393	10,540	10,540	400	-193	-193	-193
		'08	...	...	...	100.0	4,629	...	...	...	100.0	2,412	11,419	11,419	-22	1,899	1,899	1,899
		'09	...	...	...	100.0	4,497	...	...	...	100.0	2,394	10,453	10,453	123	1,383	1,257	1,257
		Rating History: NR-5, 05/06/10; NR-5, 05/08/09; NR-5, 05/06/08; NR-5, 06/28/07; NR-5, 07/07/06																
5 STAR LIFE INSURANCE CO Armed Forces Benefit Assn Invstmnt Trust Craig S. Piers President 909 N. Washington Street Alexandria, VA 22314 LA : 1943 : Stock : Affinity Grp Mktg Group Life, Ind Life, Term Life 800-776-2322 AMB# 008069 NAIC# 77879	**A-**	'05	72.6	...	0.5	26.8	149,696	89.0	1.5	...	9.5	50,104	93,593	89,914	6,580	1,364	1,032	1,076
		'06	69.5	...	1.0	29.5	154,752	92.6	0.0	...	7.4	50,847	88,126	83,744	8,945	998	747	701
	Rating Outlook: Stable	'07	73.8	...	0.9	25.3	165,974	92.5	...	...	7.5	52,275	96,747	91,756	8,671	1,370	1,241	1,102
		'08	72.2	...	1.0	26.9	174,786	92.6	...	...	7.4	48,407	100,304	94,497	4,772	1,836	-169	-5,078
		'09	72.0	...	0.5	27.4	188,378	92.6	0.0	...	7.4	50,997	105,513	98,881	6,556	4,119	3,998	499
	FSC VII	**Rating History: A-, 03/08/10; A-, 03/17/09; A-, 01/16/08; A-, 02/06/07; A-, 05/12/06**																
FLAGSHIP HEALTH SYSTEMS INC[2] Delta Dental of New Jersey Inc Walter J. Van Brunt President 1639 Route 10 Parsippany, NJ 07054 NJ : 1986 : Stock : Broker Dental 973-285-4000 AMB# 068631 NAIC# 11179	**NR-5**	'05	...	...	...	100.0	2,389	...	...	...	100.0	1,084	9,376	9,376	168	263	263	263
		'06	...	...	...	100.0	1,840	...	...	...	100.0	1,361	9,674	9,674	-493	375	375	375
		'07	...	...	...	100.0	2,301	...	...	...	100.0	1,810	9,459	9,459	599	316	316	316
		'08	...	...	...	100.0	2,732	...	...	...	100.0	2,308	9,033	9,033	464	357	357	357
		'09	...	...	...	100.0	2,921	...	...	...	100.0	2,613	9,126	9,126	183	453	453	453
		Rating History: NR-5, 04/20/10; NR-5, 06/01/09; NR-5, 05/20/08; NR-5, 06/22/07; NR-5, 05/18/06																
FLORIDA COMBINED LIFE INS CO LSV Partners LLC Jason D. Mann President & CEO 4800 Deerwood Campus Parkway Jacksonville, FL 32256 FL : 1988 : Stock : Agency Group A&H, Group Life, Ind Life 904-828-7800 AMB# 060033 NAIC# 76031	**A**	'05	73.6	...	0.9	25.4	78,416	20.5	60.9	...	18.5	37,518	82,056	67,071	-804	-642	-371	-421
		'06	71.3	...	1.6	27.1	81,959	11.9	54.8	...	33.3	35,958	89,611	70,189	8,360	-623	292	292
	Rating Outlook: Stable	'07	65.0	...	3.6	31.4	94,213	7.9	51.2	...	40.9	30,034	95,419	57,633	4,002	-5,781	-5,531	-5,561
		'08	16.8	...	...	83.2	32,270	...	...	...	100.0	18,701	98,176	8,293	-50,068	2,234	2,259	1,851
		'09	19.4	...	...	80.6	31,985	...	...	...	100.0	20,339	97,694	...	291	669	663	663
	FSC V	**Rating History: A g, 05/22/09; A g, 04/08/08; A g, 06/18/07; A g, 03/03/06; A g, 03/18/05**																
FLORIDA HEALTH CARE PLAN INC Blue Cross and Blue Shield of FL Inc Wendy A. Myers, M.D. President & Chief Medical Officer 1340 Ridgewood Avenue Holly Hill, FL 32117 FL : 2009 : Stock : Agency Health 386-676-7100 AMB# 064968 NAIC# 13567	**NR-2**	'05	...	...	...	...	...	...	...	...	...	...	...	...	...	...	...	...
		'06	...	...	...	...	...	...	...	...	...	...	...	...	...	...	...	...
		'07	...	...	...	...	...	...	...	...	...	...	...	...	...	...	...	...
		'08	...	14.0	...	86.0	67,110	...	55.8	...	44.2	22,233	...	...	50,276	...	...	...
		'09	...	13.8	...	86.2	64,859	...	59.4	...	40.6	32,991	297,454	295,495	-6,611	13,572	10,854	10,854
		Rating History: NR-2, 06/11/09																

BEST'S PROFITABILITY, LEVERAGE AND LIQUIDITY TESTS 2005 – 2009

Data in U.S. Dollars

	Profitability Tests							Leverage Tests						Liquidity Tests					
Un-Realized Capital Gains ($000)	Benefits Paid to NPW & Dep (%)	Comm. & Expenses to NPW & Dep (%)	NOG to Total Assets (%)	NOG to Total Rev (%)	Operating Return on Equity (%)	Net Yield (%)	Total Return (%)	Change in NPW & Dep (%)	NPW & Dep to Capital (X)	Capital & Surplus to Liabilities (%)	Surplus Relief (%)	Reins Leverage (%)	Change in Capital (%)	Quick Liquidity (%)	Current Liquidity (%)	Non-Invest Grade Bonds to Capital (%)	Delinq. & Foreclosed Mortgages to Capital (%)	Mort. & Credit Tenant Loans & R.E. to Capital (%)	Affiliated Invest to Capital (%)
...	-99.9	18.9	5.8	586.7	8.5	...	...	57.1	0.0	218.4	...	...	-25.7	...	...	...	...	...	...
...	-99.9	-25.3	6.8	312.8	9.2	...	...	59.4	0.0	365.6	...	...	9.6	...	...	...	...	...	...
...	-99.9	-99.9	3.0	134.1	3.8	...	...	58.2	0.0	388.4	...	...	-23.7	...	...	...	...	...	...
...	-73.5	-32.6	3.9	999.9	4.7	...	...	-99.9	0.0	588.7	...	...	4.7	...	...	...	...	...	...
...	-99.9	-99.9	0.5	-99.9	0.6	...	...	89.7	0.0	775.3	...	...	0.6	...	...	...	...	...	...
	Principal Lines of Business: GrpLife (76.7%), CrdLife (20.4%), CrdA&H (2.9%)																		
								...	...	999.9	...	...	...	999.9	999.9	...	...	...	...
...	...	...	1.9	78.6	9.6	3.83	3.71	...	...	12.8	...	214.7	4.8	131.1	137.6	...	...	...	...
...	...	...	2.1	78.6	16.7	7.20	6.97	...	...	15.8	...	255.2	22.0	35.8	37.5	...	...	...	...
...	...	...	0.3	75.8	2.0	1.77	2.94	...	...	14.4	...	221.5	4.4	69.8	72.7	...	...	...	...
...	...	...	0.1	77.7	0.6	0.40	0.40	...	...	25.5	...	188.8	26.9	56.1	58.8	...	...	...	...
														Principal States: MD (93.1%), DE (5.5%)					
...	83.0	14.0	6.8	2.6	10.7	2.74	2.74	11.2	3.9	165.6	...	3.0	12.2	365.0	377.5	...	...	...	...
52	83.2	14.7	6.1	2.3	9.5	4.18	4.54	5.3	3.9	193.7	...	0.1	7.1	245.3	261.5	...	...	...	...
78	83.7	14.3	5.9	2.1	9.1	3.68	4.52	15.9	4.0	180.2	...	1.7	12.4	230.3	244.3	...	...	...	...
-349	76.4	20.2	6.1	3.8	8.8	2.26	-1.76	-40.7	2.2	303.3	...	...	7.9	329.5	354.4	2.5	...	...	...
306	86.1	19.5	-4.0	-2.3	-5.3	2.42	5.08	4.4	2.3	316.4	...	...	-1.8	309.3	339.6	...	...	...	...
	Principal Lines of Business: CompHosp/Med (100.0%)													Principal States: NC (100.0%)					
...	66.8	24.6	9.4	10.2	12.1	1.67	1.67	12.3	1.1	362.9	...	...	12.7	455.7	455.7	...	...	...	...
...	69.8	26.4	6.8	7.8	8.7	3.79	3.79	1.2	1.0	384.5	...	...	9.5	193.2	193.2	...	...	...	...
...	68.6	25.7	8.8	10.5	11.1	4.48	4.48	3.7	1.0	408.8	...	...	11.2	458.6	469.8	...	...	...	...
...	69.9	28.4	5.1	6.6	6.3	3.95	3.91	-2.1	0.9	464.0	...	...	5.4	546.5	563.7	...	...	...	...
...	82.8	51.8	-29.2	-31.9	-36.9	1.86	1.86	-2.4	1.7	276.2	...	...	-48.1	373.9	387.3	...	...	...	...
	Principal Lines of Business: MedSup (100.0%)													Principal States: AL (100.0%)					
...	120.1	20.6	0.1	0.0	0.1	1.15	1.15	21.7	1.9	243.2	...	...	162.1	135.6	135.6	...	...	...	...
...	133.0	36.5	-31.1	-11.8	-48.1	1.66	1.66	7.7	3.7	126.8	...	...	-44.0	95.6	95.6	...	...	...	...
...	157.6	22.5	-4.1	-1.0	-7.8	2.73	2.73	9.2	4.4	103.0	...	...	-7.5	98.5	98.5	...	...	...	...
...	175.8	21.9	40.6	7.6	79.0	2.12	2.12	8.3	4.7	108.8	...	...	0.8	92.7	92.7	...	...	...	...
...	182.2	25.4	27.5	5.3	52.3	0.42	0.42	-8.5	4.4	113.8	...	...	-0.8	103.5	103.5	...	...	...	...
	Principal Lines of Business: Vision (100.0%)																		
-10	82.7	14.1	0.7	1.1	2.1	4.96	5.29	8.4	1.8	51.8	3.6	31.0	1.9	91.9	98.6	13.7	...	...	0.3
74	79.7	17.1	0.5	0.8	1.5	5.18	5.36	-6.9	1.6	50.2	3.5	40.0	1.2	93.2	100.1	16.9	...	...	0.3
-86	79.9	16.8	0.8	1.2	2.4	5.56	5.47	9.6	1.7	47.1	3.3	50.0	2.7	91.4	98.7	16.6	...	...	0.3
-144	77.9	18.5	-0.1	-0.2	-0.3	5.80	2.48	3.0	1.9	38.4	3.9	67.8	-8.8	80.9	89.2	19.2	...	...	0.4
198	76.1	18.2	2.2	3.6	8.0	6.14	4.22	4.6	1.9	37.3	4.0	77.7	5.5	77.4	87.7	12.7	...	...	2.3
	Principal Lines of Business: GrpLife (88.0%), OrdLife (12.0%), GrpA&H (0.0%)													Principal States: TX (9.7%), VA (8.7%), FL (7.6%), CA (6.4%), GA (4.3%)					
...	82.5	14.9	11.1	2.8	27.7	1.96	1.96	2.9	8.6	83.0	...	...	33.0	144.8	144.8	...	...	...	...
...	82.1	14.3	17.7	3.9	30.7	3.22	3.22	3.2	7.1	284.6	...	...	25.6	292.1	292.1	...	...	...	...
...	82.6	14.8	15.2	3.3	19.9	3.22	3.22	-2.2	5.2	368.4	...	...	33.0	406.3	406.3	...	...	...	...
...	82.5	13.2	14.2	4.0	17.3	0.50	0.50	-4.5	3.9	544.3	...	...	27.5	580.3	580.3	...	...	...	...
...	83.1	11.5	16.0	5.0	18.4	0.06	0.06	1.0	3.5	848.7	...	...	13.2	858.5	858.5	...	...	...	...
	Principal Lines of Business: Dental (100.0%)													Principal States: NJ (100.0%)					
-3	63.9	36.8	-0.5	-0.5	-1.0	3.48	3.74	-6.5	1.8	92.2	7.2	111.0	-1.2	139.3	144.6	0.8	...	...	...
-5	61.0	38.6	0.4	0.4	0.8	4.39	4.52	4.6	1.9	78.9	12.0	88.8	-3.9	141.1	145.8	...	...	...	...
384	52.5	49.0	-6.3	-8.3	-16.8	4.24	4.80	-17.9	1.9	48.2	20.1	123.9	-15.3	113.4	119.7	...	...	...	...
-887	16.5	40.1	3.6	9.3	9.3	3.41	1.20	-85.6	0.4	145.2	72.3	295.5	-37.6	116.8	120.1	...	...	...	74.4
656	...	...	2.1	5.5	3.4	3.80	6.85	-99.9	...	196.0	53.7	269.5	10.8	153.5	155.3	...	...	...	71.9
														Principal States: FL (99.7%)					
...	...	...	...	...	...	...	...	...	...	...	...	...	...	...	...	...	...	...	...
...	...	...	...	...	...	...	...	...	...	...	...	...	...	...	...	...	...	...	...
...	...	...	...	...	...	...	...	...	...	...	...	...	...	...	...	...	...	...	...
...	...	...	...	...	...	...	...	...	...	49.5	...	0.9	...	212.7	223.9	...	...	42.2	43.4
...	83.6	12.2	16.4	3.6	39.3	0.12	0.12	...	9.0	103.5	...	0.6	48.4	216.8	225.8	...	...	27.2	28.0
	Principal Lines of Business: Medicare (51.2%), CompHosp/Med (48.7%), OtherHlth (0.1%)													Principal States: FL (98.2%)					

Data in U.S. Dollars

COMPANY NAME Ultimate Parent Association Principal Officer Mailing Address Dom. : Began Bus. : Struct. : Mktg. Specialty Phone # AMB# NAIC#	Best's Financial Strength Rating FSC	Data Year	Balance Sheet: Bonds (%)	Mort. Loans & R.E. (%)	Com & Pref. Stock (%)	All Other Assets (%)	Total Assets ($000)	Life Reserves (%)	Health Reserves (%)	Ann Res. & Dep. Liabilities (%)	All Other Liabilities (%)	Capital & Surplus ($000)	Operations: Direct Premiums Written ($000)	Net Premiums Written & Deposits ($000)	Operating Cash Flow ($000)	NOG Before Taxes ($000)	NOG After Taxes ($000)	Net Income ($000)
FOR EYES VISION PLAN INC Frederick B. Hjerpe President 2112 Shattuck Avenue Berkeley, CA 94704 CA : 1996 : Stock : Not Available Health 510-843-3200 AMB# 064727	NR-5	'05	...	...	...	100.0	242	...	...	...	100.0	-121	1,237	1,237	-379	-37	-37	-37
		'06	...	...	...	100.0	370	...	...	...	100.0	1	1,315	1,315	16	126	122	122
		'07	...	...	...	100.0	558	...	...	...	100.0	68	1,197	1,197	306	94	68	68
		'08	...	...	...	100.0	468	...	...	...	100.0	109	1,057	1,057	-92	56	41	41
		'09	...	...	...	100.0	384	...	...	...	100.0	172	1,005	1,005	-101	83	63	63
		Rating History: NR-5, 05/05/10; NR-5, 06/17/09; NR-5, 05/09/08; NR-5, 05/07/07; NR-5, 05/22/06																
FORETHOUGHT LIFE INS CO Forethought Financial Group, Inc. John A. Graf President 300 North Meridian Street, Suite 1800 Indianapolis, IN 46204 IN : 1980 : Stock : Agency Group Life, Ind Life, Pre-need 317-223-2700 AMB# 009053 NAIC# 91642	A- Rating Outlook: Stable	'05	91.5	3.6	0.9	3.9	3,420,162	94.1	...	1.3	4.6	270,000	397,399	417,717	24,020	51,083	38,131	35,736
		'06	88.5	3.4	2.0	6.0	3,498,309	94.8	...	1.2	4.0	234,516	428,854	487,865	67,851	49,421	30,494	43,747
		'07	87.6	3.2	1.6	7.6	3,689,002	92.3	...	3.4	4.3	226,718	512,035	516,847	212,991	48,303	33,564	22,581
		'08	90.4	2.8	1.4	5.3	3,870,190	85.6	...	12.4	2.0	189,717	773,599	776,361	250,238	-20,099	-15,767	-71,586
		'09	92.3	2.3	0.0	5.4	4,543,351	74.7	...	22.7	2.7	346,778	920,952	922,874	663,977	90,557	60,265	68,278
	FSC IX	**Rating History: A-, 11/30/09; A- u, 05/13/09; A-, 02/25/08; A-, 12/13/06; A, 12/15/05**																
FORETHOUGHT NATIONAL LIFE INS Forethought Financial Group, Inc. John A. Graf President 300 North Meridian Street, Suite 1800 Indianapolis, IN 46204 TX : 1985 : Stock : Agency Ordinary Life, Group Life 713-212-4600 AMB# 068262 NAIC# 77127	NR-3	'05	...	...	52.5	47.5	171,344	99.9	...	...	0.1	171,266	28	28	1	1,677	4,034	4,034
		'06	...	...	48.9	51.1	222,081	0.4	...	...	99.6	182,991	121	121	112,435	76,208	80,793	80,793
		'07	...	...	73.3	26.7	157,534	8.1	...	...	91.9	155,476	17	17	-70,309	5,698	7,612	7,612
		'08	...	...	94.3	5.7	200,163	39.5	...	...	60.5	199,665	246	246	48,991	-6,877	-4,402	-10,235
		'09	...	...	98.0	2.0	353,480	98.5	...	...	1.5	353,250	178	178	112,476	-7,071	-4,486	-4,486
		Rating History: NR-3, 11/30/09; NR-3, 05/13/09; NR-3, 02/25/08; NR-3, 12/13/06; NR-3, 12/15/05																
FORT DEARBORN LIFE INS CO Health Care Svc Corp Mut Legal Reserve Anthony F. Trani President & CEO 1020 31st Street Downers Grove, IL 60515-5591 IL : 1969 : Stock : Agency Group Life, Group A&H, Dental 800-633-3696 AMB# 007322 NAIC# 71129	A+ Rating Outlook: Negative	'05	63.5	...	0.1	36.3	1,723,890	20.2	5.0	29.7	45.2	375,990	611,657	781,444	9,817	46,115	34,421	34,637
		'06	57.5	...	0.1	42.4	2,105,495	19.2	9.1	21.1	50.7	443,361	782,521	1,027,235	124,101	30,629	17,471	17,686
		'07	54.9	...	1.2	43.9	2,238,646	18.7	8.6	19.9	52.8	468,463	874,889	974,060	50,555	53,653	41,097	42,751
		'08	50.7	...	1.0	48.2	2,616,352	14.2	6.3	28.0	51.5	290,336	1,183,527	1,258,801	226,052	-21,596	-21,683	-38,470
		'09	90.1	...	0.8	9.2	3,093,100	12.3	5.4	79.8	2.5	457,396	1,046,088	1,148,482	1,483,383	12,404	12,203	-39,808
	FSC IX	**Rating History: A+, 01/27/10; A+ g, 12/22/08; A+ g, 11/01/07; A+ g, 08/10/06; A+ g, 11/01/05**																
FORT DEARBORN LIFE INS CO NY Health Care Svc Corp Mut Legal Reserve Anthony F. Trani President & CEO 1020 31st Street Downers Grove, IL 60515-5591 NY : 1991 : Stock : Agency Group Life, Group A&H, Dental 866-406-3356 AMB# 068158 NAIC# 85090	A Rating Outlook: Negative	'05	89.0	...	...	11.0	38,515	55.2	27.3	...	17.4	21,768	6,222	5,906	-1,948	2,014	1,430	1,426
		'06	82.2	...	...	17.8	38,594	55.7	21.4	...	22.9	23,742	5,281	4,933	-15	2,861	1,840	1,784
		'07	90.4	...	...	9.6	25,966	...	...	...	100.0	25,004	2,611	1,347	-11,730	2,068	1,723	1,723
		'08	74.0	...	...	26.0	44,252	25.1	38.0	20.3	16.7	24,748	9,240	20,538	14,889	-1,290	-1,305	-1,417
		'09	94.4	...	...	5.6	69,920	11.4	13.6	73.2	1.9	22,523	36,831	36,146	28,464	-2,086	-2,075	-2,317
	FSC V	**Rating History: A, 01/27/10; A, 12/22/08; A, 11/01/07; A, 07/12/07; A+ g, 06/01/07**																
FORTIS INSURANCE CO (ASIA) LTD Charles S. Fraser Executive Director 28th Floor Wing On Centre Hong Kong BM : Stock : Not Available Life 852-2866-8898 AMB# 087137	A- Rating Outlook: Stable	'05	28.4	0.2	14.2	57.2	1,319,166	65.3	...	7.1	27.7	320,681	...	211,727	13,085	2,632	862	6,199
		'06	31.3	0.2	5.1	63.5	1,504,250	63.7	...	8.9	27.4	332,991	...	233,887	154,561	5,377	3,644	39,174
		'07	39.6	11.1	0.4	48.9	1,990,011	55.7	...	15.0	29.3	363,421	...	262,597	-112,093	-9,593	-17,832	37,890
		'08	45.0	7.3	...	47.8	2,196,170	58.0	...	1.1	40.9	511,756	...	252,184	7,165	-20,909	-21,984	-54,837
		'09	45.6	7.8	...	46.7	2,414,979	54.8	...	0.2	45.0	451,328	...	267,648	-110,524	41,964	33,733	38,655
	FSC X	**Rating History: A-, 07/22/09; A-, 11/19/07; A-, 10/09/06; A-, 11/16/05; A-, 10/12/04**																
FOUNDATION LIFE INS CO OF AR' Bennie B. Westphal President 109 North Sixth Street Fort Smith, AR 72901-2103 AR : 1959 : Stock : Not Available 479-785-1714 AMB# 068338 NAIC# 83992	NR-1	'05	3.8	18.9	6.2	71.1	6,825	...	...	...	100.0	1,421	2,464	2,448	...	103	103	103
		'06	4.0	20.1	6.7	69.2	6,752	...	...	...	100.0	1,169	2,275	2,261	...	-67	-67	-59
		'07	3.8	19.4	7.9	68.9	7,170	...	...	...	100.0	1,579	2,189	2,170	...	377	377	421
		'08	10.6	18.0	6.9	64.6	7,560	...	...	...	100.0	2,000	1,968	1,949	...	162	162	519
		'09	43.9	...	10.1	46.1	6,789	...	...	...	100.0	1,467	1,889	1,874	...	-229	-229	-157
		Rating History: NR-1, 06/10/10; NR-1, 06/12/09; NR-1, 06/12/08; NR-1, 06/08/07; NR-1, 06/07/06																
FOX INSURANCE COMPANY CA CA : Stock : Not Available AMB# 064976	NR-5	'05	...	...	...	...	...	...	...	...	...	...	...	...	...	...	...	...
		'06	...	...	...	...	...	...	...	...	...	...	...	...	...	...	...	...
		'07	...	...	...	...	...	...	...	...	...	...	...	...	...	...	...	...
		'08	...	...	...	...	...	...	...	...	...	...	...	...	...	...	...	...
		'09	...	...	...	100.0	42,814	...	...	...	100.0	10,396	76,482	76,482	-1,797	952	622	622
		Rating History: NR-5, 05/26/10																
FRANDISCO LIFE INSURANCE CO' Alvin R. Guimond, Jr. President 135 East Tugalo Street Toccoa, GA 30577-2127 GA : 1977 : Stock : Not Available 706-886-7571 AMB# 008800 NAIC# 89079	NR-1	'05	80.3	...	...	19.7	36,244	...	...	...	100.0	34,737	...	8,430	...	4,796	3,690	3,690
		'06	73.6	...	...	26.4	40,653	...	...	...	100.0	38,964	...	9,413	...	5,693	4,232	4,232
		'07	73.7	...	...	26.3	45,587	...	...	...	100.0	43,583	...	10,548	...	6,227	4,628	4,628
		'08	89.1	...	...	10.9	35,873	...	...	...	100.0	33,720	...	11,011	...	6,149	4,762	4,762
		'09	69.4	...	...	30.6	40,309	...	...	...	100.0	38,074	...	10,803	...	5,418	4,362	4,362
		Rating History: NR-1, 06/10/10; NR-1, 06/12/09; NR-1, 06/12/08; NR-1, 06/08/07; NR-1, 06/07/06																

2010 BEST'S KEY RATING GUIDE — LIFE/HEALTH EDITION
BEST'S PROFITABILITY, LEVERAGE AND LIQUIDITY TESTS 2005 – 2009

Data in U.S. Dollars

—	Profitability Tests							Leverage Tests						Liquidity Tests					
Un-Realized Capital Gains ($000)	Benefits Paid to NPW & Dep (%)	Comm. & Expenses to NPW & Dep (%)	NOG to Total Assets (%)	NOG to Total Rev (%)	Operating Return on Equity (%)	Net Yield (%)	Total Return (%)	Change in NPW & Dep (%)	NPW & Dep to Capital (X)	Capital & Surplus to Liabilities (%)	Surplus Relief (%)	Reins Leverage (%)	Change in Capital (%)	Quick Liquidity (%)	Current Liquidity (%)	Non-Invest Grade Bonds to Capital (%)	Delinq. & Foreclosed Mortgages to Capital (%)	Mort. & Credit Tenant Loans & R.E. to Capital (%)	Affiliated Invest to Capital (%)
...	107.8	18.8	-8.5	-2.1	36.0	0.49	0.49	-7.3	-10.2	-33.3	...	...	-43.9	39.6	39.6	...	...	...	...
...	100.3	19.2	39.7	6.5	-99.9	102.56	102.56	6.3	999.9	0.2	...	...	100.5	43.2	43.2	...	...	...	...
...	104.8	17.5	14.6	3.8	196.3	-8.79	-8.79	-8.9	17.5	14.0	...	...	999.9	95.0	95.0	...	...	...	...
...	104.5	19.0	8.0	2.6	46.1	-5.35	-5.35	-11.8	9.7	30.5	...	...	59.9	104.2	104.2	...	...	...	...
...	104.8	13.4	14.8	4.2	44.7	-2.42	-2.42	-4.9	5.8	81.2	...	...	57.5	128.4	128.4	...	...	...	...
	Principal Lines of Business: Vision (100.0%)																		
1,160	83.3	26.1	1.1	6.1	14.0	5.62	6.88	86.0	1.4	8.3	5.1	985.1	-0.7	63.9	75.9	38.3	...	42.8	4.0
115	79.2	26.4	0.9	3.2	12.1	5.82	6.52	16.8	1.9	7.8	5.7	999.9	-12.7	63.8	75.8	41.2	...	47.4	4.5
-8,124	74.5	24.0	0.9	4.6	14.6	5.64	5.35	5.9	2.2	6.9	5.7	999.9	-6.0	67.6	79.2	57.3	...	49.0	4.5
5,812	53.7	19.7	-0.4	-1.7	-7.6	5.03	3.89	50.2	3.8	5.5	2.1	1.4	-15.3	66.8	78.1	46.8	...	54.1	5.2
-626	46.2	18.5	1.4	5.2	22.5	5.82	6.20	18.9	2.5	8.7	0.0	0.7	79.9	63.4	77.6	37.1	...	29.1	1.1
	Principal Lines of Business: IndAnn (57.4%), GrpLife (34.0%), GrpAnn (4.4%), OrdLife (4.2%)													Principal States: CA (14.0%), TX (10.1%), FL (7.7%), WA (6.3%), OH (5.8%)					
26,290	17.7	-15.3	2.6	238.6	2.6	1.07	19.51	215.0	0.0	999.9	...	...	20.2	318.3	318.3	...	...	...	98.5
-60,592	8.3	3.3	41.1	105.9	45.6	50.01	22.56	336.4	0.0	469.1	...	...	6.9	437.0	459.9	...	...	...	71.5
6,636	52.6	136.5	4.0	132.7	4.5	3.15	6.81	-85.9	0.0	999.9	...	...	-15.1	999.9	999.9	...	...	...	93.9
-19,084	25.1	212.5	-2.5	70.1	-2.5	-3.66	-17.28	999.9	0.0	999.9	...	...	28.4	220.0	231.6	...	...	...	96.3
47,325	19.9	98.2	-1.6	65.7	-1.6	-2.54	16.46	-27.7	0.0	999.9	...	...	76.9	999.9	999.9	...	...	...	98.1
	Principal Lines of Business: OrdLife (86.4%), GrpLife (13.6%)													Principal States: TX (100.0%)					
-116	72.6	19.5	2.0	4.1	9.4	5.18	5.28	2.9	2.0	46.4	0.1	27.7	2.7	105.0	120.9	16.4	...	...	0.9
-704	59.0	16.1	0.9	1.6	4.3	5.05	5.07	31.5	2.3	50.3	0.1	38.6	18.1	108.1	124.9	6.1	...	...	0.6
-1,711	78.9	16.0	1.9	4.0	9.0	4.80	5.02	-5.2	2.1	52.2	0.0	35.7	4.0	105.7	124.3	8.6	...	...	6.2
-4,561	57.3	13.9	-0.9	-1.6	-5.7	4.83	3.45	29.2	4.3	22.4	0.4	58.8	-38.2	96.6	110.0	20.4	...	...	9.6
-2,808	61.0	-74.5	0.4	1.0	3.3	4.83	2.53	-8.8	2.5	17.4	0.1	35.3	57.5	80.9	95.7	55.6	...	...	5.0
	Principal Lines of Business: GrpLife (44.2%), IndAnn (42.2%), GrpA&H (10.8%), GrpAnn (1.4%), OrdLife (1.4%)													Principal States: TX (19.0%), IL (10.1%), PA (7.4%), OH (5.9%), CT (4.3%)					
...	97.7	45.6	3.6	17.5	6.8	5.72	5.71	4.8	0.3	131.0	0.4	0.0	6.5	195.0	216.6	...	...	...	...
...	72.0	48.9	4.8	25.6	8.1	5.87	5.70	-16.5	0.2	161.3	0.4	0.0	9.1	236.6	262.9	...	...	...	...
...	80.5	78.0	5.3	34.6	7.1	6.10	6.00	-72.7	0.1	999.9	7.2	5.8	5.3	999.9	999.9	...	...	...	...
...	21.9	20.7	-3.7	-5.9	-5.2	5.66	5.16	999.9	0.8	127.2	0.0	27.8	-1.2	210.1	225.5	...	...	...	...
...	18.1	13.4	-3.6	-5.3	-8.8	6.32	5.84	76.0	1.6	47.5	0.0	25.2	-9.1	121.1	134.8	2.2	...	...	...
	Principal Lines of Business: IndAnn (84.9%), GrpLife (9.1%), GrpA&H (6.0%), OrdLife (0.0%)													Principal States: NY (100.0%)					
24,068	77.0	39.2	0.1	0.3	0.3	3.08	3.63	9.5	66.0	32.1	...	...	9.3	73.0	82.8	...	...	0.6	...
-13,261	85.2	43.5	0.3	1.1	1.1	3.00	6.21	10.5	70.2	28.4	...	...	3.8	73.8	77.0	...	...	0.7	...
-6,541	112.9	39.6	-1.0	-3.9	-5.1	3.44	7.30	12.3	72.3	22.3	...	...	9.1	58.5	93.1	...	...	60.8	...
100,355	82.9	-5.9	-1.1	-14.7	-5.0	4.07	1.98	-4.0	49.3	30.4	...	...	40.8	72.3	73.8	...	...	31.1	...
-98,885	81.8	101.8	1.5	6.2	7.0	4.55	4.88	6.1	59.3	23.0	...	...	-11.8	63.0	70.2	...	...	41.6	...
13	31.2	67.7	1.6	3.5	7.6	...	...	0.6	1.6	29.2	...	...	10.0	...	...	...	...	83.6	...
15	45.2	71.9	-1.0	-2.5	-5.2	...	...	-7.7	1.7	24.0	...	...	-15.3	...	...	...	...	103.9	...
-43	36.4	74.4	5.4	13.8	27.4	...	...	-4.0	1.3	31.8	...	...	32.5	...	...	...	...	80.4	...
-257	45.9	82.4	2.2	6.4	9.0	...	...	-10.2	0.9	39.4	...	...	23.5	...	...	...	...	63.5	...
182	43.8	82.0	-3.2	-11.2	-13.2	...	...	-3.8	1.2	31.3	...	...	-24.3	...	...	...	...	...	...
	Principal Lines of Business: CrdLife (68.0%), OrdLife (14.6%), CrdA&H (11.3%), GrpLife (5.9%), GrpA&H (0.2%)																		
...	...	...	...	...	...	...	...	...	...	...	...	...	...	...	...	...	...	...	...
...	...	...	...	...	...	...	...	...	...	...	...	...	...	...	...	...	...	...	...
...	...	...	...	...	...	...	...	...	...	...	...	...	...	...	...	...	...	...	...
...	...	...	...	...	...	...	...	...	...	...	...	...	...	...	...	...	...	...	...
...	80.2	18.9	...	0.8	...	...	...	...	7.4	32.1	...	...	...	4.3	4.3	...	...	...	...
	Principal Lines of Business: Medicare (100.0%)																		
...	30.2	28.4	10.7	37.8	11.2	...	...	1.3	0.2	999.9	...	...	11.9	...	...	...	...	...	...
...	28.0	27.4	11.0	38.3	11.5	...	...	11.7	0.2	999.9	...	...	12.2	...	...	...	...	...	...
...	28.7	27.5	10.7	37.2	11.2	...	...	12.1	0.2	999.9	...	...	11.9	...	...	...	...	...	...
...	28.9	28.7	11.7	37.7	12.3	...	...	4.4	0.3	999.9	...	...	-22.6	...	...	...	...	...	...
...	32.2	27.6	11.5	36.6	12.2	...	...	-1.9	0.3	999.9	...	...	12.9	...	...	...	...	...	...
	Principal Lines of Business: CrdA&H (69.9%), CrdLife (30.1%)																		

Data in U.S. Dollars

COMPANY NAME Ultimate Parent Association Principal Officer Mailing Address Dom. : Began Bus. : Struct. : Mktg. Specialty Phone # AMB# NAIC#	Best's Financial Strength Rating FSC	Data Year	Balance Sheet Bonds (%)	Mort. Loans & R.E. (%)	Com & Pref. Stock (%)	All Other Assets (%)	Total Assets ($000)	Life Reserves (%)	Health Reserves (%)	Ann Res. & Dep. Liabilities (%)	All Other Liabilities (%)	Capital & Surplus ($000)	Operations Direct Premiums Written ($000)	Net Premiums Written & Deposits ($000)	Operating Cash Flow ($000)	NOG Before Taxes ($000)	NOG After Taxes ($000)	Net Income ($000)
FREEDOM LIFE INS CO OF AMER Credit Suisse Holdings (USA) Inc	**B**	'05	95.0	...	...	5.0	35,812	0.4	92.7	...	6.9	10,018	39,278	19,358	1,125	839	843	665
Benjamin M. Cutler Chairman, President & CEO		'06	98.7	...	...	1.3	35,222	0.4	92.8	...	6.9	10,056	37,861	17,881	-352	175	175	175
3100 Burnett Plaza, 801 Cherry Street Fort Worth, TX 76102	Rating Outlook: Negative	'07	96.4	...	...	3.6	33,054	0.5	92.8	...	6.7	8,890	45,370	23,466	-1,936	-1,122	-1,122	-1,122
TX : 1956 : Stock : Agency		'08	79.7	...	21.3	-1.0	38,305	1.1	91.3	...	7.6	15,001	55,586	29,238	-2,995	-1,711	-1,711	-1,821
A&H, Hosp Ind, Ind A&H 817-878-3300		'09	73.5	...	24.8	1.7	31,844	3.6	54.8	...	41.6	17,825	62,248	19,651	-5,220	-6,798	-6,820	-6,843
AMB# 006269 NAIC# 62324	**FSC V**	**Rating History: B g, 02/08/10; B g, 02/04/09; B g, 04/01/08; B g, 05/31/07; B g, 05/22/06**																
FREELANCERS INSURANCE COMPANY[2]	**NR-5**	'05	...	...	...	...	...	...	...	...	...	...	...	...	...	...	...	...
Sara Horowitz President & CEO		'06	...	...	...	...	...	...	...	...	...	...	...	...	...	...	...	...
20 Jay Street, Suite 700 Brooklyn, NY 11201		'07	...	...	...	...	...	...	...	...	...	...	...	...	...	...	...	...
NY : 2009 : Non-Profit : Not Available		'08	53.9	...	43.3	2.8	16,253	...	...	...	100.0	14,760	...	...	16,184	-1,467	-1,467	-1,467
Health 718-532-1515		'09	63.1	...	...	36.9	28,913	...	35.1	...	64.9	9,472	69,618	67,361	9,909	-4,992	-4,992	-4,992
AMB# 064970 NAIC# 13564		**Rating History: NR-5, 04/30/10; NR-5, 05/07/09**																
FRINGE BENEFIT LIFE INS CO[1]	**NR-1**	'05	53.5	13.2	14.6	18.7	40,523	...	...	...	100.0	13,970	165	918	...	1,793	1,713	1,946
Kelly B. Keller President		'06	54.2	12.0	16.3	17.5	41,004	...	...	...	100.0	15,962	174	564	...	1,600	1,387	1,713
2901 Morton Street Fort Worth, TX 76107-2925		'07	54.2	14.8	16.7	14.2	41,546	...	...	...	100.0	17,996	162	293	...	2,190	1,896	2,079
TX : 1982 : Stock : Not Available		'08	53.2	20.2	9.1	17.6	38,488	...	...	...	100.0	17,913	177	50	...	1,894	1,669	1,212
817-885-8223		'09	44.3	17.5	12.8	25.4	39,819	...	...	...	100.0	19,609	142	-183	...	1,793	1,650	1,287
AMB# 068213 NAIC# 99457		**Rating History: NR-1, 06/10/10; NR-1, 06/12/09; NR-1, 06/12/08; NR-1, 06/08/07; NR-1, 06/07/06**																
FUNERAL DIRECTORS LIFE INS CO Directors Investment Group Inc	**A-**	'05	89.2	1.8	5.2	3.7	416,297	45.1	...	52.9	2.0	41,454	83,592	83,698	38,795	4,796	3,872	3,749
B. Kris Seale President		'06	81.7	2.3	5.9	10.2	453,383	44.5	...	54.0	1.6	45,429	84,718	84,857	38,493	4,325	3,332	3,315
P.O. Box 5649 Abilene, TX 79606	Rating Outlook: Negative	'07	79.7	7.4	7.9	4.9	500,389	43.6	...	54.5	1.9	48,511	99,384	99,559	46,688	5,293	3,092	3,831
TX : 1981 : Stock : Agency		'08	79.6	8.0	7.0	5.5	556,606	42.4	...	55.9	1.7	48,561	124,097	124,285	56,437	6,230	4,101	1,027
Group Life, Ind Ann, Ind Life 325-695-3412		'09	83.3	8.2	3.8	4.8	632,477	41.9	...	55.8	2.3	57,766	143,533	143,626	68,919	10,926	7,160	6,007
AMB# 009492 NAIC# 99775	**FSC VII**	**Rating History: A-, 07/01/09; A-, 06/05/08; A-, 05/16/07; A-, 06/19/06; B++, 06/21/05**																
FUTURAL LIFE INS CO[1]	**NR-1**	'05	49.3	...	19.5	31.2	10,976	...	...	...	100.0	5,428	...	2,513	...	561	495	564
Philip R. Terrell President		'06	45.5	...	21.6	32.8	10,217	...	...	...	100.0	5,739	...	1,427	...	1,040	916	965
2700 North Third Street, Suite 3050 Phoenix, AZ 85004-4620		'07	37.9	...	19.0	43.1	10,027	...	...	...	100.0	6,321	...	1,461	...	693	612	645
AZ : 1970 : Stock : Not Available		'08	29.5	...	12.0	58.5	8,666	...	...	...	100.0	5,778	...	936	...	386	345	470
602-200-6900		'09	9.9	...	14.5	75.5	8,621	...	...	...	100.0	6,134	...	669	...	456	392	380
AMB# 008138 NAIC# 78549		**Rating History: NR-1, 06/10/10; NR-1, 06/12/09; NR-1, 06/12/08; NR-1, 06/08/07; NR-1, 06/07/06**																
GARDEN STATE LIFE INS CO American National Insurance Company	**A**	'05	70.2	...	7.6	22.2	92,529	89.1	0.2	2.6	8.1	25,247	42,602	39,810	-6,998	-3,758	-2,579	-668
Ronald J. Welch President & CEO		'06	70.5	...	8.7	20.8	90,661	90.8	0.2	2.2	6.8	18,500	43,761	40,862	-1,041	-5,992	-4,467	-4,633
One Moody Plaza Galveston, TX 77550-7999	Rating Outlook: Stable	'07	64.3	...	14.1	21.6	92,179	89.8	0.1	2.1	7.9	17,269	44,596	41,232	145	-490	-795	-721
TX : 1956 : Stock : Direct Response		'08	70.9	...	4.3	24.7	91,014	93.8	0.1	2.4	3.7	17,678	43,180	39,597	149	86	-71	-1,572
Term Life, Whole life 281-538-1037		'09	64.6	...	4.8	30.6	93,243	93.2	0.1	2.2	4.5	18,690	40,313	36,445	1,306	-299	-649	-724
AMB# 006436 NAIC# 63657	**FSC V**	**Rating History: A, 05/20/10; A, 06/09/09; A, 05/13/08; A, 04/26/07; A, 02/08/06**																
GATEWAY HEALTH PLAN INC Gateway Health Plan L.P.	**NR-4**	'05	42.5	...	17.8	39.7	180,839	...	58.5	...	41.5	65,769	929,648	929,321	22,733	-13,378	-8,865	-8,115
Charles M. Blackwood President		'06	27.2	...	16.9	55.8	286,698	...	69.0	...	31.0	85,931	1,178,161	1,177,506	83,196	8,992	8,634	8,353
600 Grant Street Pittsburgh, PA 15219		'07	24.6	...	17.6	57.8	330,928	...	61.7	...	38.3	129,597	1,239,028	1,238,440	54,613	59,084	37,853	41,023
PA : 1986 : Stock : Broker		'08	30.2	...	13.6	56.2	284,792	...	74.9	...	25.1	122,314	1,263,678	1,262,879	-86,449	-2,188	-4,582	-8,692
Health 412-255-4640		'09	...	...	...	...	...	...	...	...	...	...	...	...	...	...	...	...
AMB# 060129 NAIC# 96938		**Rating History: NR-4, 08/27/09; B-, 08/27/09; B-, 10/29/08; B-, 07/03/07; B-, 06/21/06**																
GEISINGER HEALTH PLAN[2] Geisinger Health System Foundation	**NR-5**	'05	53.1	...	21.2	25.7	176,547	...	43.8	...	56.2	88,908	745,011	738,633	-9,731	22,067	22,067	21,712
Richard J. Gilfillan, M.D. President & CEO		'06	57.4	...	22.0	20.6	255,765	...	34.5	...	65.5	156,297	741,253	735,186	80,666	92,155	92,051	92,120
100 North Academy Avenue Danville, PA 17822		'07	57.1	...	22.7	20.2	254,207	...	39.8	...	60.2	152,463	755,577	751,930	-28,524	78,187	78,054	78,695
PA : 1985 : Non-Profit : Broker		'08	54.1	...	15.5	30.4	211,624	...	38.1	...	61.9	109,820	788,462	787,853	-5,448	49,607	49,671	43,212
Group A&H, Health 570-271-8777		'09	57.7	...	22.1	20.2	200,917	...	32.3	...	67.7	104,118	792,155	784,661	-14,730	43,602	43,533	39,838
AMB# 068588 NAIC# 95923		**Rating History: NR-5, 03/24/10; NR-5, 08/26/09; B+ pd, 09/03/08; B+ pd, 10/08/07; B- pd, 07/25/06**																
GEMCARE HEALTH PLAN INC	**NR-5**	'05	...	...	...	...	...	...	...	...	...	...	...	...	...	...	...	...
Michael Myers President		'06	...	...	...	100.0	1,059	...	...	...	100.0	928	...	...	-189	-1,342	-1,342	-1,342
4550 California Avenue, Suite 100 Bakersfield, CA 93309		'07	...	...	...	100.0	8,926	...	...	...	100.0	3,193	50,762	50,762	5,499	359	615	615
CA : 2005 : Stock : Not Available		'08	...	...	...	100.0	9,500	...	...	...	100.0	3,578	62,089	62,089	-766	-152	-115	-115
Health 661-716-8800		'09	...	0.3	...	99.7	9,647	...	...	...	100.0	3,441	69,328	69,328	121	-491	-704	-704
AMB# 064876		**Rating History: NR-5, 05/06/10; NR-5, 05/08/09; NR-5, 05/09/08; NR-5, 05/04/07**																

2010 BEST'S KEY RATING GUIDE — LIFE/HEALTH EDITION
BEST'S PROFITABILITY, LEVERAGE AND LIQUIDITY TESTS 2005 – 2009
Data in U.S. Dollars

—	Profitability Tests							Leverage Tests						Liquidity Tests					
Un-Realized Capital Gains ($000)	Benefits Paid to NPW & Dep (%)	Comm. & Expenses to NPW & Dep (%)	NOG to Total Assets (%)	NOG to Total Rev (%)	Operating Return on Equity (%)	Net Yield (%)	Total Return (%)	Change in NPW & Dep (%)	NPW & Dep to Capital (X)	Capital & Surplus to Liabilities (%)	Surplus Relief (%)	Reins Leverage (%)	Change in Capital (%)	Quick Liquidity (%)	Current Liquidity (%)	Non-Invest Grade Bonds to Capital (%)	Delinq. & Foreclosed Mortgages to Capital (%)	Mort. & Credit Tenant Loans & R.E. to Capital (%)	Affiliated Invest to Capital (%)
...	56.1	48.6	2.4	2.9	8.7	5.45	5.15	-17.5	1.9	38.8	73.3	59.3	5.9	108.1	119.8	4.3	...	...	...
...	55.7	53.1	0.5	0.6	1.7	5.57	5.78	-7.6	1.8	40.2	80.8	57.2	0.9	108.1	120.6	2.7	...	...	...
...	61.5	57.4	-3.3	-3.2	-11.8	5.63	5.82	31.2	2.6	37.3	109.2	56.2	-11.1	111.9	124.1	5.8	...	...	...
-768	60.7	58.2	-4.8	-4.0	-14.3	5.08	2.71	24.6	1.9	64.6	78.9	34.8	67.4	98.4	110.5	2.8	...	...	54.3
-265	101.0	94.5	-19.4	-20.1	-41.6	4.75	4.07	-32.8	1.1	128.4	70.7	93.4	19.0	145.5	160.1	7.7	...	...	44.1
	Principal Lines of Business: GrpA&H (124.2%), OrdLife (8.0%), IndA&H (-32.2%)													Principal States: FL (26.3%), TX (12.2%), MS (8.4%), CO (7.6%), PA (6.5%)					
...	...	...	...	...	...	...	...	...	...	...	...	...	...	...	...	...	...	...	...
...	...	...	...	...	...	...	...	...	...	...	...	...	...	...	...	...	...	...	...
...	...	...	...	...	...	...	...	...	...	...	...	...	...	...	...	...	...	...	...
...	...	...	...	-99.9	...	...	...	...	...	988.2	...	...	...	852.0	960.5	...	...	...	...
...	87.8	20.2	-22.1	-7.4	-41.2	1.99	1.99	...	7.1	48.7	...	0.3	-35.8	135.7	142.7	...	...	...	...
	Principal Lines of Business: CompHosp/Med (100.0%)													Principal States: NY (100.0%)					
-151	306.2	41.4	4.3	48.0	13.2	...	...	-52.8	0.1	62.5	0.0	...	18.0	...	...	...	...	34.3	...
381	527.0	58.1	3.4	42.5	9.3	...	...	-38.5	0.0	75.5	0.0	...	13.2	...	...	...	...	27.8	...
-29	740.4	94.2	4.6	57.9	11.2	...	...	-48.0	0.0	90.1	0.0	...	11.6	...	...	...	...	31.3	...
-2,646	999.9	522.4	4.2	61.2	9.3	...	...	-83.0	0.0	90.3	0.0	...	-7.3	...	...	...	...	42.5	...
1,292	-99.9	-99.9	4.2	70.0	8.8	...	...	-99.9	0.0	109.8	0.0	...	14.1	...	...	...	...	33.4	...
	Principal Lines of Business: OrdLife (100.6%), GrpLife (-0.6%)																		
435	56.0	23.3	1.0	3.6	9.9	6.13	6.27	10.3	2.0	11.4	0.0	0.0	11.5	70.2	81.0	...	...	18.0	22.2
248	57.8	23.3	0.8	3.0	7.7	6.01	6.10	1.4	1.8	11.3	0.0	0.0	8.6	80.3	91.6	...	...	22.7	21.4
581	53.9	24.4	0.6	2.4	6.6	6.15	6.47	17.3	2.0	11.3	0.0	0.0	9.9	62.9	74.0	...	...	73.3	42.4
-1,032	51.2	23.1	0.8	2.6	8.4	6.47	5.73	24.8	2.5	9.9	0.0	0.0	-1.3	57.9	70.0	21.9	...	88.5	43.4
779	50.3	22.0	1.2	4.0	13.5	6.36	6.38	15.6	2.4	10.5	0.0	0.0	19.9	60.6	70.7	27.8	...	86.3	36.9
	Principal Lines of Business: IndAnn (59.5%), OrdLife (21.5%), GrpLife (19.0%), IndLife (0.0%)													Principal States: TX (34.5%), MN (18.8%), PA (10.3%), OH (8.5%), MS (3.7%)					
60	59.8	37.4	4.5	16.8	9.0	...	...	-7.0	0.4	114.2	...	...	-1.8	...	...	...	...	...	...
-27	65.9	58.6	8.6	48.2	16.4	...	...	-43.2	0.2	149.5	...	...	4.6	...	...	...	...	...	...
19	59.8	57.3	6.0	31.7	10.2	...	...	2.4	0.2	192.4	...	...	7.8	...	...	...	...	...	...
-619	96.8	63.6	3.7	24.3	5.7	...	...	-36.0	0.2	200.0	3.0	...	-12.4	...	...	...	...	...	...
517	65.8	68.9	4.5	40.7	6.6	...	...	-28.5	0.1	283.2	2.0	...	10.3	...	...	...	...	...	...
	Principal Lines of Business: CrdLife (54.9%), CrdA&H (45.1%)																		
-1,866	48.3	67.5	-2.7	-5.7	-8.8	5.70	5.95	1.6	1.5	41.6	2.6	28.3	-22.5	71.9	82.7	27.7	...	...	5.3
471	59.5	57.5	-4.9	-9.8	-20.4	5.64	6.20	2.6	2.0	29.2	3.0	46.1	-24.6	68.4	78.7	26.4	...	...	9.8
82	47.4	56.9	-0.9	-1.7	-4.4	5.45	5.78	0.9	2.1	27.1	3.2	56.7	-4.2	61.5	71.2	22.4	...	...	35.5
-988	54.3	52.1	-0.1	-0.2	-0.4	5.42	2.19	-4.0	2.2	25.0	2.9	51.5	-7.2	75.2	85.8	8.5	...	...	0.4
611	61.0	44.3	-0.7	-1.6	-3.6	4.72	5.47	-8.0	1.8	27.0	2.4	45.4	8.8	84.5	94.8	14.4	...	...	0.0
	Principal Lines of Business: OrdLife (99.4%), IndAnn (0.2%), GrpA&H (0.2%), IndA&H (0.2%), GrpLife (0.0%)													Principal States: TX (9.1%), FL (8.4%), NY (7.4%), CA (7.0%), NJ (5.5%)					
-12	88.3	12.3	-5.1	-0.9	-13.1	3.55	4.15	13.0	14.1	57.2	...	0.3	-6.0	132.3	146.3	...	...	...	...
2,637	86.9	13.8	3.7	0.7	11.4	5.26	6.60	26.7	13.7	42.8	...	0.3	30.7	147.5	160.6	...	...	...	...
-935	81.8	14.5	12.3	3.0	35.1	3.71	4.62	5.2	9.6	64.4	...	0.3	50.8	182.7	198.8	...	...	...	...
-16,503	86.5	13.6	-1.5	-0.4	-3.6	4.21	-4.69	2.0	10.3	75.3	...	0.9	-5.6	122.7	135.7	0.2	...	...	...
...	...	...	...	...	...	...	...	...	...	...	...	...	...	...	...	...	...	...	...
1,239	81.1	16.8	12.8	3.0	27.3	2.80	3.42	3.6	8.3	101.4	...	...	22.0	134.8	151.2	0.7	...	...	...
5,806	79.3	9.3	42.6	12.4	75.1	3.91	7.16	-0.5	4.7	157.1	...	...	75.8	199.7	223.1	0.4	...	...	...
-7,233	81.9	10.2	30.6	10.1	50.6	9.37	6.34	2.3	4.9	149.9	...	...	-2.5	144.7	164.7	0.4	...	...	...
-19,224	83.4	11.4	21.3	6.2	37.9	4.70	-8.38	4.8	7.2	107.9	...	0.6	-28.0	161.5	177.5	...	...	...	...
10,809	84.7	10.7	21.1	5.5	40.7	3.48	7.77	-0.4	7.5	107.6	...	0.1	-5.2	146.3	164.6	...	...	...	...
	Principal Lines of Business: Medicare (55.0%), CompHosp/Med (44.1%), FEHBP (1.0%)													Principal States: PA (100.0%)					
...	...	...	...	...	...	...	...	...	...	...	...	...	...	...	...	...	...	...	...
...	...	...	...	-99.9	...	...	...	...	...	708.1	...	...	...	700.6	700.6	...	...	...	...
...	90.7	9.7	12.3	1.2	29.9	11.89	11.89	...	15.9	55.7	...	...	244.2	110.9	110.9	...	...	...	...
...	89.6	11.7	-1.2	-0.2	-3.4	4.93	4.93	22.3	17.4	60.4	...	...	12.1	92.0	92.0	...	...	...	...
...	92.2	9.2	-7.4	-1.0	-20.1	2.19	2.19	11.7	20.1	55.4	...	...	-3.8	89.2	89.2	...	...	0.9	0.9
	Principal Lines of Business: Medicare (100.0%)																		

Data in U.S. Dollars

COMPANY NAME Ultimate Parent Association Principal Officer Mailing Address Dom. : Began Bus. : Struct. : Mktg. Specialty Phone # AMB# NAIC#	Best's Financial Strength Rating FSC	Data Year	Balance Sheet: Bonds (%)	Mort. Loans & R.E. (%)	Com & Pref. Stock (%)	All Other Assets (%)	Total Assets ($000)	Life Reserves (%)	Health Reserves (%)	Ann Res. & Dep. Liabilities (%)	All Other Liabilities (%)	Capital & Surplus ($000)	Operations: Direct Premiums Written ($000)	Net Premiums Written & Deposits ($000)	Operating Cash Flow ($000)	NOG Before Taxes ($000)	NOG After Taxes ($000)	Net Income ($000)
GENERAL AMERICAN LIFE INS CO MetLife Inc Lisa M. Weber Chairman, President & CEO 18210 Crane Nest Dr., 3rd Floor Tampa, FL 33647 MO : 1933 : Stock : Agency A&H, Ann, Life 314-843-8700 AMB# 006439 NAIC# 63665	A+ u Under Review Implication: Negative FSC XV	'05	54.8	2.3	8.9	33.9	14,094,377	52.0	0.5	10.1	37.4	1,677,306	1,092,403	303,896	-54,556	20,767	-57,193	-33,555
		'06	50.8	2.1	11.4	35.7	14,482,980	52.7	0.5	9.1	37.7	2,141,675	884,257	688,515	218,376	188,080	221,560	316,500
		'07	52.5	2.2	11.1	34.2	14,122,917	54.6	0.5	8.7	36.2	2,279,712	796,765	648,503	-209,281	244,426	211,551	106,023
		'08	55.9	2.4	2.7	39.0	11,734,937	60.9	0.5	9.3	29.3	1,079,457	776,816	611,871	706,812	145,033	48,320	1,177,066
		'09	56.9	3.9	1.5	37.6	11,049,153	63.9	0.5	9.7	25.8	995,160	670,162	523,842	-617,202	184,330	149,235	65,499
		Rating History: A+ gu, 02/09/10; A+ g, 02/20/09; A+ g, 06/05/08; A+ g, 05/29/07; A+ g, 05/05/06																
GENERAL FIDELITY LIFE INS CO Bank of America Corporation J. Keith Pellerin President 3349 Michelson Drive, Suite 200 Irvine, CA 92612 NC : 1981 : Stock : Direct Response Credit A&H, Credit Life, Group Life 980-386-3640 AMB# 006441 NAIC# 93521	A- Rating Outlook: Stable FSC VIII	'05	84.5	...	12.0	3.5	573,758	57.6	2.6	6.7	33.1	441,736	-2,792	-4,076	-16,650	45,022	29,833	30,084
		'06	64.1	...	32.0	4.0	251,964	48.8	1.5	7.7	42.0	145,696	-608	2,050	-323,129	32,113	22,170	22,911
		'07	60.8	...	34.0	5.2	250,147	38.9	3.0	7.9	50.2	161,953	59	40,609	-8,249	20,475	13,045	13,647
		'08	67.4	...	25.7	6.8	210,242	48.0	4.4	13.2	34.4	164,414	1,997	48,659	-5,650	20,188	12,692	7,940
		'09	62.5	...	32.0	5.5	214,902	30.6	6.0	11.9	51.5	170,548	862	55,737	-13,586	13,386	7,574	2,810
		Rating History: A-, 11/17/09; A-, 04/29/09; A-, 01/17/08; A-, 12/20/06; A-, 10/20/05																
GENERAL RE LIFE CORPORATION Berkshire Hathaway Inc Steven J. Mannik Chairman, President & CEO 120 Long Ridge Road Stamford, CT 06902 CT : 1967 : Stock : Other Direct Reins 203-352-3000 AMB# 006234 NAIC# 86258	A++ Rating Outlook: Stable FSC XV	'05	16.8	...	2.6	80.6	2,219,281	38.3	52.4	0.2	9.0	368,427	...	1,010,660	180,345	26,653	18,184	18,764
		'06	13.0	...	2.1	84.9	2,382,835	39.6	53.7	0.2	6.5	392,391	...	1,039,883	149,498	45,308	24,941	28,594
		'07	9.6	...	1.6	88.8	2,637,601	39.5	53.8	0.2	6.6	440,229	...	1,055,794	215,528	-23,745	-19,762	-15,523
		'08	23.6	...	3.0	73.3	2,615,078	42.5	52.8	0.2	4.5	466,576	...	1,086,070	17,213	41,377	29,641	31,949
		'09	56.9	...	0.7	42.4	2,780,942	42.5	51.4	0.2	5.9	560,763	...	1,072,826	140,200	157,770	101,102	99,128
		Rating History: A++g, 05/06/10; A++gu, 11/06/09; A++g, 10/02/09; A++g, 08/26/08; A++g, 08/07/07																
GENERALI USA LIFE REASSURANCE Assicurazioni Generali S.p.A. Christopher J. Carnicelli Chairman & CEO P.O. Box 419076 Kansas City, MO 64141-6076 KS : 1982 : Stock : Other Direct Life, A&H, Reins 913-901-4600 AMB# 009189 NAIC# 97071	A Rating Outlook: Stable FSC IX	'05	79.0	0.0	2.0	19.0	671,260	86.9	6.5	...	6.6	244,918	...	196,031	31,236	-12,030	-12,433	-11,995
		'06	78.9	...	1.4	19.6	731,871	86.3	6.2	...	7.5	240,176	...	235,404	62,270	-10,457	-10,500	-9,230
		'07	77.7	...	2.8	19.5	801,290	87.1	5.8	...	7.2	256,201	...	245,344	79,872	4,197	3,523	3,527
		'08	84.4	...	2.0	13.6	831,112	88.8	5.7	...	5.6	259,547	...	278,055	5,476	17,053	4,734	695
		'09	83.2	...	1.7	15.1	913,098	87.4	5.6	...	7.1	311,423	...	293,010	74,533	31,188	19,900	12,371
		Rating History: A, 06/09/10; A, 06/04/09; A, 06/12/08; A, 06/06/07; A, 05/31/06																
GENWORTH LIFE AND ANNUITY INS Genworth Financial, Inc Pamela S. Schutz Chairperson of the Board, President & CEO 6610 West Broad Street Richmond, VA 23230 VA : 1871 : Stock : Agency Ann, GIC's, Ind Life 804-662-2400 AMB# 006648 NAIC# 65536	A Rating Outlook: Negative FSC XV	'05	43.2	10.6	0.9	45.3	24,512,178	22.5	0.3	32.5	44.7	1,564,385	2,905,441	3,313,114	-977,146	-68,803	166,468	144,006
		'06	37.8	9.6	2.6	50.0	28,980,487	18.9	0.2	31.7	49.2	1,323,736	3,693,326	5,563,881	1,222,647	428,092	505,883	512,224
		'07	37.3	10.2	2.7	49.8	29,146,511	21.7	0.2	32.3	45.8	1,414,244	4,481,373	4,515,502	323,424	384,296	440,923	420,707
		'08	36.0	10.4	4.2	49.3	25,963,876	24.5	0.2	37.1	38.2	1,930,920	3,823,824	3,456,859	229,288	-215,030	-116,996	-242,048
		'09	34.0	9.5	4.1	52.4	25,113,007	24.2	0.2	29.6	46.1	1,935,719	2,216,763	182,067	-2,284,516	759,307	613,637	250,877
		Rating History: A g, 04/21/10; A g, 02/19/09; A+ gu, 11/06/08; A+ g, 06/16/08; A+ g, 04/04/07																
GENWORTH LIFE INSURANCE CO Genworth Financial, Inc Michael Fraizer Chairman, President & CEO 6604 West Broad Street Richmond, VA 23230 DE : 1956 : Stock : Broker LTC, SPDA's, Struc Sett 888-322-4629 AMB# 007183 NAIC# 70025	A Rating Outlook: Negative FSC XV	'05	76.6	11.7	5.5	6.2	34,936,107	7.0	13.9	64.6	14.4	3,098,351	6,622,480	5,918,254	3,239,844	708,696	671,072	636,651
		'06	71.7	13.3	7.5	7.4	34,770,582	7.3	16.1	60.3	16.3	2,996,930	3,686,643	3,503,729	274,112	621,264	626,940	633,978
		'07	68.7	14.1	8.4	8.8	34,571,591	8.3	18.1	56.6	17.0	3,142,794	3,288,840	1,818,406	-512,289	308,974	299,722	182,207
		'08	62.1	13.3	9.5	15.1	34,733,533	8.9	16.6	48.7	25.7	3,326,835	3,783,919	2,310,425	-223,397	82,671	298,712	-349,164
		'09	69.1	12.9	7.3	10.7	32,974,558	6.0	19.6	43.9	30.5	3,164,850	2,655,581	1,407,737	-1,451,647	59,934	207,903	-199,352
		Rating History: A g, 04/21/10; A g, 02/19/09; A+ gu, 11/06/08; A+ g, 06/16/08; A+ g, 04/04/07																
GENWORTH LIFE INSURANCE CO NY Genworth Financial, Inc David J. Sloane Chairperson of the Board, President & CEO 666 Third Avenue, 9th Floor New York, NY 10017 NY : 1988 : Stock : Broker FPDA's, Struc Sett 212-895-4137 AMB# 060026 NAIC# 72990	A Rating Outlook: Negative FSC XV	'05	77.1	13.5	0.7	8.7	5,638,478	7.0	10.5	72.3	10.1	452,325	617,799	630,361	278,667	111,731	100,114	94,665
		'06	67.3	16.7	2.8	13.2	5,768,645	7.0	14.9	64.8	13.4	307,318	669,455	684,596	6,261	-117,339	-133,020	-133,655
		'07	57.7	15.2	2.9	24.1	6,465,058	6.6	13.7	56.0	23.7	408,841	881,990	878,967	8,940	131,654	112,885	110,714
		'08	55.6	12.8	2.2	29.4	6,999,427	6.5	14.8	57.6	21.2	434,358	1,263,247	1,211,101	359,937	-102,300	-111,384	-258,847
		'09	64.6	11.1	0.5	23.7	7,218,410	6.3	16.3	52.1	25.4	429,513	405,141	365,298	203,633	96,746	104,870	40,871
		Rating History: A g, 04/21/10; A g, 02/19/09; A+ gu, 11/06/08; A+ g, 06/16/08; A+ g, 04/04/07																
GERBER LIFE INS CO Nestle S A Wesley D. Protheroe President & CEO 1311 Mamaroneck Ave White Plains, NY 10605 NY : 1968 : Stock : Direct Response Group A&H, Ind Life, Stop Loss 914-272-4000 AMB# 007299 NAIC# 70939	A Rating Outlook: Negative FSC VIII	'05	84.9	...	3.2	12.0	1,101,023	84.7	5.2	...	10.0	172,753	473,063	278,792	142,719	42,214	26,047	26,040
		'06	85.3	...	3.5	11.2	1,242,847	86.6	4.8	...	8.5	190,768	472,428	310,561	137,075	32,298	19,127	22,625
		'07	84.5	...	3.5	11.9	1,422,128	85.9	5.2	...	8.9	201,154	456,429	346,276	158,649	22,550	12,269	14,064
		'08	83.9	...	1.9	14.1	1,567,859	85.0	4.1	...	10.9	160,419	453,375	368,128	103,499	17,332	9,841	-42,089
		'09	85.9	...	2.3	11.9	1,712,613	88.8	4.0	...	7.2	194,251	455,041	379,022	162,785	27,457	16,171	17,586
		Rating History: A, 06/01/10; A, 05/04/09; A, 04/30/08; A, 03/05/07; A, 04/10/06																
GERMANIA LIFE INS CO Germania Farm Mutual Insurance Assn David C. Sommer Chairman & President P.O. Box 645 Brenham, TX 77834-0645 TX : 1983 : Stock : Broker Group Life, Ind Ann, Ind Life 979-836-5224 AMB# 009530 NAIC# 67920	B++ Rating Outlook: Stable FSC V	'05	85.5	...	1.9	12.7	34,022	42.3	...	55.6	2.0	6,977	6,347	5,004	2,655	-9	-36	-96
		'06	84.0	...	1.9	14.0	35,589	46.6	...	51.6	1.9	6,722	5,718	4,177	1,017	-321	-314	-314
		'07	88.1	...	0.9	11.0	41,244	53.3	...	44.9	1.8	11,374	5,999	4,372	6,004	-282	-261	-195
		'08	88.9	...	0.7	10.4	43,306	57.2	...	41.7	1.2	10,850	6,938	5,177	1,995	-314	-316	-481
		'09	88.0	...	0.7	11.3	47,455	59.1	...	39.5	1.4	10,759	7,765	5,888	3,552	10	-16	-48
		Rating History: B++, 11/13/09; B++, 12/16/08; B++, 11/27/07; B++, 01/05/07; B++, 01/09/06																

2010 BEST'S KEY RATING GUIDE — LIFE/HEALTH EDITION
BEST'S PROFITABILITY, LEVERAGE AND LIQUIDITY TESTS 2005 – 2009

Data in U.S. Dollars

—	Profitability Tests							Leverage Tests						Liquidity Tests					
Un-Realized Capital Gains ($000)	Benefits Paid to NPW & Dep (%)	Comm. & Expenses to NPW & Dep (%)	NOG to Total Assets (%)	NOG to Total Rev (%)	Operating Return on Equity (%)	Net Yield (%)	Total Return (%)	Change in NPW & Dep (%)	NPW & Dep to Capital (X)	Capital & Surplus to Liabilities (%)	Surplus Relief (%)	Reins Leverage (%)	Change in Capital (%)	Quick Liquidity (%)	Current Liquidity (%)	Non-Invest Grade Bonds to Capital (%)	Delinq. & Foreclosed Mortgages to Capital (%)	Mort. & Credit Tenant Loans & R.E. to Capital (%)	Affiliated Invest to Capital (%)
-28,960	225.5	-46.6	-0.4	-12.2	-3.8	5.14	4.96	-68.8	0.2	17.2	24.6	166.7	26.2	53.1	62.3	13.1	0.0	18.8	73.7
205,249	94.6	5.3	1.6	18.9	11.6	4.70	7.21	126.6	0.3	21.7	6.5	145.4	26.9	52.7	62.4	9.3	...	14.0	76.0
-81,571	143.5	5.1	1.5	17.7	9.6	4.63	2.93	-5.8	0.3	23.6	4.9	147.9	4.4	51.0	61.2	9.0	...	13.5	68.7
-913,263	127.8	5.5	0.4	4.3	2.9	5.17	8.02	-5.6	0.5	12.6	8.6	329.3	-50.0	45.8	57.3	23.6	...	24.6	50.2
-63,372	140.7	4.1	1.3	15.4	14.4	5.21	3.57	-14.4	0.5	12.0	8.8	365.4	-9.8	47.6	58.0	38.5	...	41.5	31.5
Principal Lines of Business: OrdLife (71.2%), IndAnn (25.0%), GrpAnn (3.9%), IndA&H (0.0%), GrpLife (0.0%)														Principal States: CA (7.9%), PA (5.8%), TX (5.5%), MO (4.9%), FL (4.8%)					
128	-99.9	-99.9	5.1	150.1	6.9	3.78	4.23	61.2	0.0	383.7	...	0.0	5.8	347.3	384.8	0.3	...	...	0.2
5,622	643.8	249.5	5.4	93.3	7.5	4.86	6.77	150.3	0.0	180.6	...	0.0	-64.4	213.5	238.7	0.8	...	...	0.9
629	31.4	86.1	5.2	25.9	8.5	3.61	4.48	999.9	0.2	252.8	...	1.4	10.5	260.9	295.1	...	...	...	0.6
-19,835	21.7	87.4	5.5	22.1	7.8	3.76	-6.49	19.8	0.3	358.8	...	1.9	-8.3	350.5	391.5	1.1	...	...	0.2
10,307	23.5	85.4	3.6	11.8	4.5	3.76	6.85	14.5	0.3	500.2	0.0	2.5	8.9	418.3	479.1	2.2	...	...	0.7
Principal Lines of Business: CrdA&H (77.5%), CrdLife (23.0%), GrpLife (-0.6%)														Principal States: NM (33.7%), GA (29.2%), MD (25.7%), AZ (14.7%), WA (11.9%)					
383	71.6	21.3	0.9	1.6	5.0	4.13	4.24	17.5	2.7	20.1	5.3	98.7	2.8	169.7	172.5	4.9	...	...	42.1
3,481	70.5	18.1	1.1	2.1	6.6	5.21	5.61	2.9	2.6	19.8	1.4	75.4	6.2	177.3	178.8	3.8	...	...	49.1
1,351	79.3	20.1	-0.8	-1.7	-4.7	5.28	5.58	1.5	2.4	20.1	0.9	28.4	12.0	197.5	198.7	1.1	...	...	9.3
906	75.0	17.5	1.1	2.5	6.5	3.24	3.44	2.9	2.3	22.1	0.8	20.5	7.2	173.1	177.0	25.8	...	...	16.8
-755	75.3	17.6	3.7	8.1	19.7	6.41	6.35	-1.2	1.9	26.0	0.7	15.6	21.3	123.9	134.6	42.0	...	...	3.4
Principal Lines of Business: IndA&H (48.6%), OrdLife (47.1%), GrpA&H (2.9%), GrpLife (1.5%), CrdLife (0.0%)																			
215	66.2	36.2	-1.9	-4.4	-5.1	3.98	4.09	-16.0	0.8	57.9	25.8	314.4	2.5	130.4	136.1	...	...	0.0	...
341	67.1	30.7	-1.5	-3.2	-4.3	4.52	4.76	20.1	1.0	49.6	27.4	419.4	-1.5	127.7	132.9	...	...	...	...
1,650	68.5	28.7	0.5	1.0	1.4	4.69	4.89	4.2	0.9	48.1	28.7	511.2	7.4	126.7	130.8	...	...	...	...
-7,939	76.4	24.3	0.6	1.2	1.8	4.62	2.98	13.3	1.1	45.7	35.1	626.3	0.0	110.0	115.0	...	...	...	...
9,121	69.4	23.6	2.3	4.7	7.0	4.39	4.62	5.4	0.9	52.5	32.0	576.9	20.6	121.0	127.1	...	...	...	...
Principal Lines of Business: OrdLife (90.6%), GrpA&H (4.8%), GrpLife (3.3%), IndA&H (1.3%)																			
17,728	83.3	15.6	0.7	4.7	9.3	6.21	6.45	8.3	1.9	12.6	12.3	739.9	-21.4	37.8	56.0	49.0	0.0	151.7	42.5
-254,985	43.8	4.9	1.9	11.3	35.0	6.15	4.72	67.9	3.8	8.8	43.4	999.9	-14.2	26.7	44.9	57.5	0.1	189.4	49.8
-50,292	50.9	-9.1	1.5	8.4	32.2	7.08	6.78	-18.8	2.9	10.4	58.5	903.6	7.5	27.3	47.7	51.8	...	188.5	40.7
90,515	66.8	4.3	-0.4	-2.7	-7.0	5.29	5.18	-23.4	1.7	13.6	31.3	734.2	30.3	35.8	54.0	43.1	...	131.5	45.2
-193,860	980.0	-99.9	2.4	27.0	31.7	4.63	0.93	-94.7	0.1	15.3	49.7	763.3	-5.0	29.9	46.9	59.3	...	121.6	63.8
Principal Lines of Business: IndAnn (427.1%), IndA&H (37.9%), GrpAnn (3.9%), GrpA&H (2.4%), GrpLife (2.3%)														Principal States: CA (11.5%), FL (8.7%), TX (5.5%), NJ (5.1%), PA (4.9%)					
-342,347	72.7	11.2	2.0	7.6	21.4	7.24	6.18	17.3	1.8	10.5	9.6	307.1	-2.2	40.8	59.3	38.0	...	123.6	96.8
-389,171	140.6	18.9	1.8	10.8	20.6	7.32	6.28	-40.8	1.1	10.3	10.6	347.0	-2.6	39.7	57.8	36.9	...	143.1	87.1
375,370	268.4	33.3	0.9	6.2	9.8	5.91	6.73	-48.1	0.5	10.8	11.5	354.3	3.7	38.0	55.2	37.7	...	145.5	89.2
55,058	209.1	35.8	0.9	7.7	9.2	5.29	3.61	27.1	0.7	11.3	11.0	401.1	4.6	42.2	57.3	34.7	...	131.8	97.8
-286,277	326.0	54.4	0.6	6.4	6.4	4.59	2.56	-39.1	0.4	10.7	8.5	460.0	-9.1	38.0	52.8	56.2	...	133.0	104.3
Principal Lines of Business: IndA&H (58.9%), IndAnn (31.2%), OrdLife (5.0%), GrpA&H (4.2%), GrpLife (0.7%)														Principal States: CA (11.2%), FL (6.6%), TX (5.2%), IL (4.9%), NJ (4.8%)					
-100	71.5	15.5	1.8	10.9	24.5	5.80	5.83	-30.1	1.3	10.1	6.1	347.7	22.5	48.2	66.4	45.9	...	155.6	0.0
605	113.4	13.2	-2.3	-13.6	-35.0	5.85	5.91	8.6	2.0	7.0	12.3	536.1	-28.7	47.7	62.9	75.6	...	277.4	...
1,859	86.6	14.0	1.8	9.5	31.5	5.82	5.81	28.4	1.9	9.4	7.6	424.5	30.4	46.0	62.8	73.8	...	216.7	...
42,209	59.1	12.0	-1.7	-7.1	-26.4	5.76	3.79	37.8	2.7	8.1	6.6	447.6	-2.9	51.8	66.0	97.7	...	203.0	...
-48,788	152.1	19.8	1.5	15.0	24.3	5.58	3.54	-69.8	0.8	7.9	6.5	506.9	-1.6	46.1	62.0	109.8	...	185.2	...
Principal Lines of Business: IndAnn (48.2%), IndA&H (41.6%), OrdLife (9.1%), GrpA&H (1.0%), GrpAnn (0.1%)														Principal States: NY (93.2%)					
2,507	30.4	37.6	2.6	6.7	16.2	5.41	6.04	10.6	1.5	19.8	26.7	70.8	17.0	71.4	83.9	10.1	...	...	...
-5,231	31.3	40.8	1.6	4.6	10.5	5.32	5.44	11.4	1.5	19.3	20.1	59.1	10.3	70.7	83.6	6.2	...	...	...
-924	35.7	40.3	0.9	2.7	6.3	5.42	5.66	11.5	1.6	17.6	14.6	50.6	6.2	69.8	81.7	4.6	...	...	...
245	35.2	42.8	0.7	2.1	5.4	5.38	1.89	6.3	2.1	12.3	16.3	46.5	-19.6	67.1	77.9	8.1	...	...	...
6,449	37.4	38.7	1.0	3.3	9.1	5.41	6.09	3.0	1.9	13.3	12.4	37.5	17.1	68.4	78.7	11.4	...	...	...
Principal Lines of Business: OrdLife (66.2%), GrpA&H (30.2%), IndA&H (2.6%), GrpLife (1.1%)														Principal States: NY (10.8%), CA (8.1%), PA (7.6%), MD (5.8%), TX (5.4%)					
17	46.3	28.4	-0.1	-0.5	-0.5	4.66	4.59	19.7	0.7	26.2	3.9	41.1	-1.1	101.9	112.1	...	...	...	...
72	69.3	32.8	-0.9	-5.2	-4.6	4.85	5.12	-16.5	0.6	23.8	4.4	59.0	-3.1	96.5	106.8	4.0	...	...	...
-112	90.1	37.5	-0.7	-4.1	-2.9	5.00	4.91	4.7	0.4	38.6	2.2	41.5	67.9	108.6	120.4	2.4	...	...	...
-151	57.2	33.5	-0.7	-4.2	-2.8	5.12	4.38	18.4	0.5	33.4	2.6	49.3	-5.6	102.7	114.0	2.6	...	...	...
44	30.8	35.7	0.0	-0.2	-0.1	5.32	5.40	13.7	0.5	29.5	2.4	55.9	-0.3	98.6	109.2	0.4	...	...	...
Principal Lines of Business: OrdLife (78.5%), IndAnn (17.7%), GrpLife (3.8%), GrpA&H (0.0%)														Principal States: TX (100.0%)					

Data in U.S. Dollars

COMPANY NAME / Ultimate Parent Association / Principal Officer / Mailing Address / Dom. : Began Bus. : Struct. : Mktg. / Specialty / Phone # / AMB# / NAIC#	Best's Financial Strength Rating / FSC	Data Year	Balance Sheet: Bonds (%)	Mort. Loans & R.E. (%)	Com & Pref. Stock (%)	All Other Assets (%)	Total Assets ($000)	Life Reserves (%)	Health Reserves (%)	Ann Res. & Dep. Liabilities (%)	All Other Liabilities (%)	Capital & Surplus ($000)	Operations: Direct Premiums Written ($000)	Net Premiums Written & Deposits ($000)	Operating Cash Flow ($000)	NOG Before Taxes ($000)	NOG After Taxes ($000)	Net Income ($000)
GHI HMO SELECT INC / EmblemHealth Inc	C	'05	29.4	...	...	70.6	43,967	...	69.6	...	30.4	9,855	175,656	174,979	1,533	-10,780	-8,630	-8,697
Frank J. Branchini / President & COO / 789 Grant Avenue		'06	19.9	...	...	80.1	52,553	...	73.7	...	26.3	14,684	196,814	196,076	6,217	-4,855	-4,057	-4,156
Lake Katrine, NY 12449 / NY : 1999 : Stock : Agency	Rating Outlook: Negative	'07	42.7	...	0.5	56.7	52,930	...	73.0	...	27.0	17,509	174,735	174,525	4,253	1,261	815	1,428
Group A&H, Ind A&H		'08	43.4	...	2.6	54.0	51,598	...	73.5	...	26.5	12,866	182,240	181,978	-2,090	-12,873	-11,259	-10,568
845-340-2200		'09	45.8	...	...	54.2	53,854	...	69.2	...	30.8	29,762	173,549	173,378	13,178	-1,795	-1,562	-749
AMB# 064564 NAIC# 95835	FSC VIII	**Rating History: C g, 06/09/10; C++g, 05/29/09; B- g, 06/06/08; B- g, 05/10/07; C- pd, 09/01/06**																
GHS HEALTH MAINTENANCE ORG / Health Care Svc Corp Mut Legal Reserve	A+	'05	46.0	...	...	54.0	24,687	...	61.8	...	38.2	17,852	30,252	29,963	166	643	657	657
Bert E. Marshall / President & CEO / 1400 South Boston		'06	41.9	...	...	58.1	26,388	...	74.4	...	25.6	18,841	26,872	26,872	1,214	1,480	1,073	1,073
Tulsa, OK 74119 / OK : 1984 : Stock : Broker	Rating Outlook: Stable	'07	45.4	...	...	54.6	26,582	...	38.0	...	62.0	22,590	23,336	23,336	811	5,661	4,540	4,540
Group A&H, Health		'08	4.3	...	...	95.7	24,270	...	91.9	...	8.1	20,110	22,717	22,717	-1,044	-3,095	-2,485	-2,485
312-653-7844		'09	12.7	...	...	87.3	25,371	...	1.1	...	98.9	23,241	41,038	-8	-7,271	4,216	3,225	3,225
AMB# 068932 NAIC# 11814	FSC V	**Rating History: A+ g, 01/27/10; A, 12/22/08; A, 11/01/07; A, 08/10/06; A, 11/01/05**																
GLEANER LIFE INS SOCIETY	A-	'05	89.3	1.9	...	8.8	1,269,605	13.5	0.0	84.6	1.8	92,673	156,720	157,981	74,842	2,097	2,097	2,097
Ellsworth L. Stout / President & CEO / 5200 West U.S. Hwy. 223		'06	88.9	2.8	...	8.3	1,223,927	14.6	0.0	84.3	1.0	90,171	118,666	118,059	-44,206	-2,179	-2,179	-3,259
Adrian, MI 49221-7894 / MI : 1894 : Fraternal : Agency	Rating Outlook: Stable	'07	90.2	3.8	0.5	5.5	1,148,018	16.0	0.0	83.0	1.0	92,938	64,768	63,629	-72,584	2,512	2,512	2,002
Ind Ann, Term Life, Univ Life		'08	87.9	4.2	0.5	7.5	1,103,005	16.7	0.0	82.4	0.8	80,600	66,199	64,821	-40,091	2,799	2,799	-12,910
517-263-2244		'09	90.1	3.6	...	6.3	1,143,428	16.6	0.0	82.5	0.8	81,142	97,608	95,857	40,770	5,282	5,282	381
AMB# 006459 NAIC# 56154	FSC VII	**Rating History: A-, 12/03/09; A-, 11/13/08; A, 01/07/08; A, 12/19/06; A, 11/15/05**																
GLOBALHEALTH INC / Universal American Corp.	B	'05	...	...	...	100.0	2,960	...	...	...	100.0	2,963	43,849	43,849	-574	1,989	1,989	1,989
Theodore M. Carpenter, Jr. / President		'06	...	...	...	100.0	5,285	...	...	...	100.0	3,516	55,713	55,713	190	1,906	1,156	1,156
4888 Loop Central Drive, Suite 700 / Houston, TX 77081	Rating Outlook: Stable	'07	...	...	...	100.0	18,004	...	16.5	...	83.5	5,366	70,855	70,810	12,905	1,829	1,050	1,050
OK : 2003 : Stock : Broker / Health		'08	19.9	...	...	80.1	19,693	...	30.9	...	69.1	6,868	100,554	100,479	248	1,201	852	852
713-965-9444		'09	34.0	...	...	66.0	23,971	...	54.9	...	45.1	9,114	127,256	127,136	1,000	203	1	1
AMB# 064790 NAIC# 11709	FSC IV	**Rating History: B, 04/16/10; B, 12/03/08; NR-2, 08/21/07; NR-5, 05/31/06; NR-5, 05/09/05**																
GLOBE LIFE AND ACCIDENT INS CO / Torchmark Corporation	A+	'05	74.7	0.4	9.8	15.2	2,293,728	93.7	2.4	0.2	3.7	363,433	477,200	460,716	102,143	167,090	145,769	142,089
Charles F. Hudson / President & CEO / 204 North Robinson Avenue		'06	69.7	0.3	13.3	16.6	2,423,421	94.4	2.2	0.2	3.2	338,108	506,044	487,621	112,964	136,622	127,048	123,569
Oklahoma City, OK 73102 / NE : 1951 : Stock : Direct Response	Rating Outlook: Stable	'07	69.4	0.4	15.4	14.8	2,554,739	95.0	2.3	0.2	2.5	324,521	542,973	524,864	113,579	145,225	130,434	130,088
Group Life, Ind Life, Med supp		'08	68.3	0.0	15.4	16.3	2,736,764	95.3	2.4	0.2	2.2	392,687	561,891	511,680	145,301	169,681	154,217	133,709
405-270-1400		'09	75.7	...	6.5	17.9	2,899,403	96.2	1.4	0.2	2.3	479,548	587,076	498,132	195,213	279,022	247,089	225,108
AMB# 006462 NAIC# 91472	FSC X	**Rating History: A+ g, 06/15/10; A+ g, 06/11/09; A+ g, 06/11/08; A+ g, 06/08/07; A+ g, 06/08/06**																
GMHP HEALTH INSURANCE LIMITED'	NR-1	'05	...	74.5	...	25.5	2,386	...	...	...	100.0	2,014	...	...	...	-280	-280	-280
Frank B. Rosario / President		'06	...	75.0	...	25.0	2,179	...	...	...	100.0	1,844	...	...	...	-184	-184	-2,972
177 Chalan Pasaheru, Suite A / Tamuning, GU 96913-4161		'07	...	87.6	...	12.4	1,703	...	...	...	100.0	1,398	...	...	...	-125	-125	-765
GU : 1988 : Stock : Not Available		'08	...	85.6	...	14.4	1,575	...	...	...	100.0	1,324	...	...	...	-87	-87	-87
671-646-4647		'09	...	80.0	...	20.0	1,507	...	...	...	100.0	1,283	...	...	...	-73	-73	-52
AMB# 068424 NAIC# 88560		**Rating History: NR-1, 06/10/10; NR-1, 06/12/09; NR-1, 06/12/08; NR-1, 06/08/07; NR-1, 06/07/06**																
GOLDEN RULE INS CO / UnitedHealth Group Inc	A	'05	46.8	1.8	1.7	49.8	825,989	0.1	40.2	...	59.8	375,818	1,103,112	1,041,052	-1,562,586	292,276	196,254	194,462
Richard A. Collins / CEO / 7440 Woodland Drive		'06	61.2	2.5	2.5	33.9	596,607	0.1	64.7	...	35.2	291,735	1,196,068	997,978	-248,967	259,246	191,470	191,538
Indianapolis, IN 46278-1719 / IN : 1961 : Stock : Broker	Rating Outlook: Stable	'07	65.4	2.4	...	32.2	590,141	0.1	65.5	...	34.4	263,874	1,294,858	1,128,252	-2,752	235,948	162,543	162,560
Group A&H, Ind A&H		'08	63.1	0.4	...	36.6	613,699	0.1	63.0	...	36.9	267,811	1,379,102	1,260,822	29,082	219,925	139,860	144,741
618-943-8000		'09	80.7	0.9	...	18.4	524,422	0.1	63.5	...	36.3	175,793	1,378,347	1,324,415	-93,896	233,134	155,798	156,253
AMB# 006263 NAIC# 62286	FSC VIII	**Rating History: A, 06/15/09; A, 01/29/08; A, 11/21/07; A, 11/16/06; A, 08/17/06**																
GOLDEN SECURITY INS CO' / BlueCross BlueShield of Tennessee Inc	NR-1	'05	89.3	...	...	10.7	2,962	...	...	...	100.0	2,950	...	...	...	66	49	49
Vicky Brown Gregg / President & CEO / 1 Cameron Hill Circle		'06	62.5	...	...	37.5	3,040	...	...	...	100.0	3,031	...	...	...	129	84	82
Chattanooga, TN 37402 / TN : 1984 : Stock : Not Available		'07	51.7	...	...	48.3	3,146	...	...	...	100.0	3,126	...	...	...	155	103	103
		'08	30.5	...	...	69.5	3,218	...	...	...	100.0	3,203	...	...	...	116	74	74
423-535-5600		'09	52.7	...	...	47.3	3,249	...	...	...	100.0	3,239	...	...	...	55	36	36
AMB# 009420 NAIC# 65463		**Rating History: NR-1, 06/10/10; NR-1, 06/12/09; NR-1, 06/12/08; NR-1, 06/08/07; NR-1, 06/07/06**																
GOLDEN STATE MUTUAL LIFE INS'	E	'05	54.5	22.6	4.9	18.0	113,985	...	...	0.7	99.3	10,016	14,312	25,469	...	-2,037	-2,037	4,277
Larkin Teasley / President & CEO / 1999 W. Adams Boulevard		'06	49.3	23.8	4.7	22.1	103,535	...	...	0.8	99.2	10,113	12,731	25,948	...	-550	-550	524
Los Angeles, CA 90018-3514 / CA : 1925 : Mutual : Agency		'07	43.8	26.6	4.3	25.3	102,398	...	...	0.7	99.3	8,706	12,478	22,803	...	-877	-877	-710
Ind A&H, Ind Ann, Ind Life		'08	36.1	29.9	5.3	28.7	89,963	...	...	0.9	99.1	6,088	11,699	28,122	...	-406	-406	-406
323-731-1131		'09	37.0	36.5	5.9	20.6	73,477	...	...	1.0	99.0	-2,486	10,506	10,170	...	-7,845	-7,845	-8,125
AMB# 006466 NAIC# 63924		**Rating History: E, 10/01/09; NR-4, 04/24/09; C++, 04/24/09; C++, 06/04/08; C++, 06/08/07**																

BEST'S PROFITABILITY, LEVERAGE AND LIQUIDITY TESTS 2005 – 2009

Data in U.S. Dollars

	Profitability Tests							Leverage Tests						Liquidity Tests					
Un-Realized Capital Gains ($000)	Benefits Paid to NPW & Dep (%)	Comm. & Expenses to NPW & Dep (%)	NOG to Total Assets (%)	NOG to Total Rev (%)	Operating Return on Equity (%)	Net Yield (%)	Total Return (%)	Change in NPW & Dep (%)	NPW & Dep to Capital (X)	Capital & Surplus to Liabilities (%)	Surplus Relief (%)	Reins Leverage (%)	Change in Capital (%)	Quick Liquidity (%)	Current Liquidity (%)	Non-Invest Grade Bonds to Capital (%)	Delinq. & Foreclosed Mortgages to Capital (%)	Mort. & Credit Tenant Loans & R.E. to Capital (%)	Affiliated Invest to Capital (%)
...	93.8	12.6	-23.3	-4.9	-79.4	2.66	2.30	43.0	17.8	28.9	...	8.9	-17.1	54.4	54.5	...	...	...	...
...	90.0	12.8	-8.4	-2.1	-33.1	2.76	2.33	12.1	13.4	38.8	...	6.3	49.0	82.7	83.0	...	...	...	...
...	85.6	14.4	1.5	0.5	5.1	4.99	7.21	-11.0	10.0	49.4	...	3.7	19.2	89.9	90.2	...	...	...	...
...	90.8	15.1	-21.5	-6.2	-74.1	3.16	5.61	4.3	14.1	33.2	...	1.4	-26.5	63.9	64.5	...	...	...	...
...	85.6	17.1	-3.0	-0.9	-7.3	1.27	3.71	-4.7	5.8	123.5	...	13.8	131.3	200.7	205.4	...	...	...	...
Principal Lines of Business: Medicaid (64.1%), CompHosp/Med (33.4%), FEHBP (2.5%)														Principal States: NY (100.0%)					
...	74.4	25.5	2.6	2.2	3.9	2.95	2.95	-30.4	1.7	261.1	...	...	11.7	359.5	359.5	...	...	...	...
...	78.9	19.3	4.2	3.7	5.8	4.49	4.49	-10.3	1.4	249.7	...	...	5.5	288.6	288.6	...	...	...	...
...	67.7	15.3	17.1	16.6	21.9	5.69	5.69	-13.2	1.0	565.9	...	...	19.9	675.3	675.3	...	...	...	...
...	100.2	16.7	-9.8	-10.6	-11.6	2.54	2.54	-2.7	1.1	483.4	...	...	-11.0	812.7	812.7	...	...	...	...
...	...	...	13.0	38.3	14.9	1.20	1.20	-99.9	0.0	999.9	...	34.8	15.6	992.2	999.9	...	...	...	...
Principal Lines of Business: CompHosp/Med (100.0%)														Principal States: OK (100.0%)					
...	30.0	13.1	0.2	0.9	2.3	5.67	5.78	-16.3	1.6	8.2	0.4	3.5	1.4	87.5	95.2	13.5	0.1	24.9	2.1
...	169.4	18.1	-0.2	-1.2	-2.4	5.66	5.68	-25.3	1.3	8.2	0.4	4.4	-3.3	86.3	93.7	6.5	0.1	37.4	2.0
...	289.0	27.0	0.2	2.0	2.7	5.61	5.65	-46.1	0.7	9.1	0.4	4.9	2.9	83.3	91.0	4.3	0.2	45.5	1.9
...	214.3	23.2	0.2	2.2	3.2	5.67	4.34	1.9	0.8	8.1	0.5	7.7	-13.5	76.1	87.7	26.6	0.7	55.6	2.3
-192	98.2	16.9	0.5	3.4	6.5	5.50	5.09	47.9	1.1	7.9	0.6	8.7	1.3	71.9	84.1	36.6	1.1	49.4	2.2
Principal Lines of Business: IndAnn (92.4%), OrdLife (7.6%), IndA&H (0.0%)														Principal States: MI (55.3%), IL (17.3%), OH (14.3%), IN (4.4%), FL (3.4%)					
...	88.0	7.5	68.2	4.5	98.7	1.93	1.93	290.2	14.8	-99.9	...	...	178.0	-99.9	-99.9	...	...	...	...
...	87.3	9.3	28.0	2.1	35.7	5.76	5.76	27.1	15.8	198.9	...	...	18.7	51.4	51.4	...	...	...	...
...	85.1	12.8	9.0	1.5	23.6	5.43	5.43	27.1	13.2	42.5	...	...	52.6	109.3	109.3	...	...	...	...
...	83.2	16.0	4.5	0.8	13.9	2.90	2.90	41.9	14.6	53.6	...	...	28.0	172.2	180.9	...	...	...	...
...	86.1	13.9	0.0	0.0	0.0	1.75	1.75	26.5	13.9	61.3	...	...	32.7	106.8	109.8	...	...	...	...
Principal Lines of Business: Medicare (59.9%), CompHosp/Med (38.5%), FEHBP (1.7%)														Principal States: OK (100.0%)					
5,402	41.1	36.9	6.6	21.1	42.3	10.78	11.00	1.8	1.2	19.6	3.1	30.7	11.9	52.8	64.4	43.7	...	2.2	56.9
1,344	43.4	38.4	5.4	18.1	36.2	9.55	9.56	5.8	1.4	17.0	2.9	34.3	-6.5	49.7	62.6	38.2	...	2.2	56.7
24,233	43.0	40.7	5.2	17.6	39.4	9.18	10.35	7.6	1.5	15.4	2.8	30.9	-2.8	45.0	57.4	45.3	...	2.6	65.4
-419	43.9	39.3	5.8	20.9	43.0	9.24	8.45	-2.5	1.3	17.2	3.0	30.7	17.6	45.5	57.7	34.9	...	0.1	57.3
-61,247	40.3	34.2	8.8	30.8	56.7	12.33	9.16	-2.6	1.0	19.9	2.3	23.0	19.9	49.9	61.8	32.7	...	...	39.5
Principal Lines of Business: GrpLife (56.6%), OrdLife (37.1%), IndA&H (6.2%), GrpA&H (0.1%), GrpAnn (0.0%)														Principal States: TX (9.3%), CA (6.5%), FL (6.4%), IL (5.4%), OH (4.6%)					
...	...	...	-9.7	863.1	-11.3	...	...	...	...	898.8	...	...	-31.8	...	...	...	...	82.8	...
...	...	...	-8.1	999.9	-9.5	...	...	...	...	923.3	...	...	-8.4	...	...	...	...	83.2	...
...	...	...	-6.5	-99.9	-7.7	...	...	...	...	785.8	...	...	-23.2	...	...	...	...	98.8	...
...	...	...	-5.3	-99.9	-6.4	...	...	...	...	947.2	...	...	-5.7	...	...	...	...	94.6	...
...	...	...	-4.8	-96.3	-5.6	...	...	...	...	999.9	...	...	-3.6	...	...	...	...	87.8	...
452	61.9	15.7	12.3	16.5	60.3	7.11	7.12	2.5	2.7	85.0	11.2	470.0	28.5	231.1	244.0	...	...	3.8	7.5
565	59.5	17.6	26.9	18.0	57.4	5.03	5.29	-4.1	3.4	97.3	10.7	661.0	-22.5	184.5	200.6	...	...	5.0	9.9
539	60.8	21.0	27.4	13.8	58.5	5.65	5.91	13.1	4.2	82.3	4.9	750.3	-9.4	171.9	187.2	...	...	5.3	5.3
...	63.0	21.8	23.2	10.8	52.6	4.07	5.12	11.7	4.7	77.5	2.6	743.8	0.6	188.8	205.3	...	...	0.8	0.8
...	63.3	21.3	27.4	11.5	70.2	3.23	3.54	5.0	7.5	50.9	2.4	999.9	-34.0	120.9	133.9	0.0	...	2.6	2.6
Principal Lines of Business: GrpA&H (84.2%), IndA&H (15.6%), GrpLife (0.1%), OrdLife (0.0%)														Principal States: FL (22.2%), TX (8.2%), OH (5.4%), AZ (4.6%), MO (4.6%)					
...	...	...	1.7	48.0	1.7	...	...	...	...	999.9	...	...	1.5	...	...	...	...	...	...
...	...	...	2.8	61.4	2.8	...	...	...	...	999.9	...	...	2.8	...	...	...	...	...	...
...	...	...	3.3	63.3	3.3	...	...	...	...	999.9	...	...	3.3	...	...	...	...	...	...
...	...	...	2.3	59.8	2.3	...	...	...	...	999.9	...	...	2.4	...	...	...	...	...	...
...	...	...	1.1	56.7	1.1	...	...	...	...	999.9	...	...	1.1	...	...	...	...	...	...
-38	75.9	46.5	-1.8	-6.4	-22.2	...	...	-10.8	2.4	10.2	...	...	17.3	...	...	...	...	244.1	...
-86	87.4	46.5	-0.5	-2.4	-5.5	...	...	1.9	2.5	11.4	...	...	0.1	...	...	...	...	233.6	...
-108	84.2	47.0	-0.9	-3.0	-9.3	...	...	-12.1	2.5	10.0	...	...	-12.3	...	...	...	...	293.8	...
-1,117	91.2	33.9	-0.4	-1.7	-5.5	...	...	23.3	4.5	7.5	...	...	-32.4	...	...	...	...	429.4	...
701	76.4	132.5	-9.6	-57.7	-99.9	...	...	-63.8	-4.6	-2.9	...	...	-99.9	...	...	...	...	-99.9	...
Principal Lines of Business: OrdLife (83.5%), IndAnn (10.5%), IndA&H (3.7%), GrpLife (1.4%), IndLife (0.7%)																			

Data in U.S. Dollars

COMPANY NAME / Ultimate Parent Association / Principal Officer / Mailing Address / Dom. : Began Bus. : Struct. : Mktg. / Specialty / Phone # / AMB# NAIC#	Best's Financial Strength Rating / FSC	Data Year	Balance Sheet: Bonds (%)	Mort. Loans & R.E. (%)	Com & Pref. Stock (%)	All Other Assets (%)	Total Assets ($000)	Life Reserves (%)	Health Reserves (%)	Ann Res. & Dep. Liabilities (%)	All Other Liabilities (%)	Capital & Surplus ($000)	Operations: Direct Premiums Written ($000)	Net Premiums Written & Deposits ($000)	Operating Cash Flow ($000)	NOG Before Taxes ($000)	NOG After Taxes ($000)	Net Income ($000)
GOLDEN WEST HEALTH PLAN INC WellPoint Inc.	NR-2	'05	...	...	...	100.0	7,622	...	...	...	100.0	2,980	20,067	20,067	3,707	2,859	1,681	1,681
Joan E. Herman, President & CEO		'06	...	...	...	100.0	8,641	...	...	...	100.0	4,665	20,164	20,164	701	2,895	1,681	1,681
4553 La Tienda Drive, Mail Stop 1B3, Thousand Oaks, CA 91362		'07	...	...	...	100.0	11,401	...	...	...	100.0	5,699	19,016	19,016	2,772	1,686	1,048	1,048
CA : Stock : Broker; Group A&H		'08	...	...	...	100.0	12,906	...	...	...	100.0	6,894	16,547	16,547	1,955	2,285	1,259	1,259
800-995-4124		'09	...	...	...	100.0	14,582	...	...	...	100.0	7,241	14,961	14,961	233	538	332	332
AMB# 064721		**Rating History: NR-2, 04/27/10; NR-2, 01/23/09; NR-2, 03/24/08; NR-2, 11/06/06; NR-2, 12/29/05**																
GOOD HEALTH HMO INC Blue Cross & Blue Shield of Kansas City	NR-5	'05	80.6	...	...	19.4	64,183	...	64.0	...	36.0	37,381	224,658	224,569	-1,353	1,509	1,064	986
David R. Gentile, Chairman, President & CEO		'06	77.7	...	...	22.3	74,251	...	68.7	...	31.3	40,835	270,095	269,996	7,770	555	440	341
P.O. Box 413163, Kansas City, MO 64108		'07	73.2	...	...	26.8	88,600	...	63.1	...	36.9	47,277	369,614	369,503	10,007	9,907	6,476	6,471
MO : 1989 : Non-Profit : Broker; Group A&H, Health		'08	70.7	...	...	29.3	101,246	...	71.9	...	28.1	55,946	397,670	396,908	11,641	12,492	8,408	8,347
816-395-2222		'09	78.8	...	...	21.2	113,767	...	66.2	...	33.8	71,000	433,735	432,826	13,743	22,612	14,188	15,557
AMB# 068956 NAIC# 95315		**Rating History: NR-5, 03/22/10; NR-5, 08/26/09; B pd, 07/21/08; B pd, 07/09/07; B pd, 08/29/06**																
GOVERNMENT PERSONNEL MUTUAL	A-	'05	69.4	14.3	0.7	15.6	763,987	72.3	0.2	22.1	5.3	79,330	69,373	105,549	57,042	3,529	1,688	1,743
Peter J. Hennessey III, Chairman, President & CEO		'06	69.9	14.3	0.9	14.9	775,380	73.6	0.2	21.0	5.3	84,523	68,492	61,064	13,673	7,618	5,395	5,816
P.O. Box 659567, San Antonio, TX 78265-9567	Rating Outlook: Stable	'07	67.8	14.8	1.3	16.1	786,599	74.3	0.2	20.1	5.4	87,957	71,847	57,965	11,500	9,416	6,397	5,134
TX : 1934 : Mutual : General Agent; Ind Ann, Trad Life, Univ Life		'08	62.9	16.9	1.4	18.8	787,153	75.2	0.2	19.3	5.3	83,559	68,855	57,438	3,149	6,977	4,308	-3,138
210-357-2222		'09	66.3	17.6	0.7	15.4	801,887	75.0	0.2	19.5	5.3	87,788	71,427	62,099	11,394	7,778	5,861	630
AMB# 006470 NAIC# 63967	FSC VII	**Rating History: A-, 06/09/10; A-, 05/29/09; A-, 06/10/08; A-, 06/06/07; A-, 05/25/06**																
GRAND VALLEY HEALTH PLAN INC Grand Valley Health Corporation	NR-5	'05	...	8.8	...	91.2	12,865	...	30.4	...	69.6	4,907	45,603	45,117	2,030	-384	-254	-254
Roland Palmer, President		'06	...	8.9	...	91.1	11,665	...	46.6	...	53.4	5,238	39,445	38,961	-138	651	407	407
829 Forest Hill Avenue, Southeast, Grand Rapids, MI 49546		'07	...	9.6	...	90.4	10,483	...	18.2	...	81.8	5,647	33,349	32,921	-1,896	431	284	284
MI : 1982 : Stock : Broker; Group A&H		'08	...	10.5	...	89.5	9,278	...	30.8	...	69.2	3,714	30,549	30,034	-1,168	-3,002	-1,946	-1,946
616-949-2410		'09	...	14.1	...	85.9	6,720	...	35.8	...	64.2	2,602	28,501	27,955	-1,596	-1,107	-1,173	-1,173
AMB# 068632 NAIC# 95453		**Rating History: NR-5, 05/21/10; NR-5, 08/26/09; C++pd, 07/21/08; C++pd, 07/20/07; C++pd, 08/29/06**																
GRANGE LIFE INS CO Grange Mutual Casualty Pool	A-	'05	83.8	...	0.1	16.1	214,747	67.2	0.2	27.7	4.8	28,199	52,899	37,560	20,241	2,327	1,455	1,426
Michelle Benz, President		'06	80.9	...	1.3	17.8	227,572	69.1	0.2	26.5	4.3	31,112	57,919	39,903	10,399	3,885	3,016	3,017
P.O. Box 1218, Columbus, OH 43216-1218	Rating Outlook: Stable	'07	80.4	...	0.4	19.1	245,496	69.7	0.2	25.2	4.9	34,163	61,501	40,149	11,393	4,556	3,314	3,314
OH : 1968 : Stock : Agency; Term Life, Trad Life, Univ Life		'08	77.5	...	0.4	22.1	254,933	71.0	0.3	23.9	4.8	33,571	64,899	41,783	8,837	2,243	1,763	-1,212
614-445-2900		'09	79.0	...	0.0	21.0	271,857	71.5	0.2	23.3	4.9	37,911	69,184	44,781	8,897	4,787	3,566	2,896
AMB# 007332 NAIC# 71218	FSC VI	**Rating History: A-, 04/13/10; A-, 02/25/09; A-, 02/01/08; A-, 02/21/07; A-, 12/29/05**																
GRAPHICS ARTS BENEFIT CORP	NR-5	'05	70.9	...	28.2	0.9	4,613	...	72.2	...	27.8	1,844	15,031	14,336	-1,010	-1,092	-1,099	-1,103
Gerard J. McGeehan, Jr., President		'06	66.0	...	38.1	-4.1	4,053	...	74.5	...	25.5	1,637	18,166	17,238	-828	-356	-360	-360
6411 Ivy Lane, Suite 700, Greenbelt, MD 20770		'07	44.2	...	29.4	26.4	4,027	...	78.7	...	21.3	1,740	16,748	15,858	-463	-285	-333	5
MD : 1993 : Non-Profit : Agency; Group A&H		'08	42.9	...	18.3	38.8	4,276	...	77.3	...	22.7	2,465	11,491	11,072	1,500	1,262	1,246	1,246
301-474-7950		'09	52.2	...	26.3	21.5	3,796	...	89.9	...	10.1	2,739	8,806	8,191	-1,006	400	391	393
AMB# 064539 NAIC# 47000		**Rating History: NR-5, 04/19/10; NR-5, 06/17/09; NR-5, 07/29/08; NR-5, 04/12/07; NR-5, 04/27/06**																
GREAT AMERICAN LIFE ASSUR CO American Financial Group, Inc	B++	'05	72.7	...	...	27.3	22,049	38.5	...	56.8	4.7	7,737	11	11	-208	256	177	177
Billy B. Hill, Jr., President & CEO		'06	55.2	...	...	44.8	22,189	39.9	...	56.8	3.3	8,325	19	19	341	317	212	462
P.O. Box 26580, Austin, TX 78755	Rating Outlook: Stable	'07	73.5	...	...	26.5	21,374	44.8	...	51.8	3.3	8,646	6	624	-769	524	332	332
OH : 1967 : Stock : Agency; FPDA's, Ind A&H, Ind Life		'08	65.8	...	...	34.2	20,204	47.2	...	51.8	1.0	8,288	...	8	-1,178	432	268	268
512-451-2224		'09	61.3	...	...	38.7	19,762	47.3	...	52.0	0.7	7,798	4	22	-430	-379	-422	-588
AMB# 006253 NAIC# 62200	FSC IV	**Rating History: B++, 05/10/10; A-, 03/27/09; A-, 12/17/07; A-, 11/28/06; A-, 06/17/05**																
GREAT AMERICAN LIFE INS CO American Financial Group, Inc	A	'05	87.2	2.1	4.9	5.8	8,243,030	1.7	0.5	95.6	2.1	669,149	689,131	662,671	309,888	155,192	126,992	150,857
Charles R. Scheper, President		'06	83.3	2.7	5.1	9.0	8,805,808	1.6	0.8	95.5	2.1	643,816	1,129,631	1,132,649	398,751	86,975	56,232	124,178
P.O. Box 5420, Cincinnati, OH 45201-5420	Rating Outlook: Stable	'07	83.5	3.2	5.0	8.3	9,295,574	1.7	1.0	96.0	1.3	732,328	1,230,492	1,268,778	418,139	86,667	80,416	43,978
OH : 1963 : Stock : Agency; FPDA's, SPDA's, Ind Life		'08	86.7	2.6	2.4	8.3	9,648,623	1.5	1.2	96.5	0.8	794,257	1,236,751	1,214,433	373,195	168,999	160,431	-3,980
513-357-3300		'09	86.1	2.4	1.9	9.6	9,962,026	1.5	0.0	97.7	0.7	874,636	1,085,578	925,302	183,880	118,807	81,802	-54,440
AMB# 006474 NAIC# 63312	FSC XI	**Rating History: A g, 05/10/10; A g, 03/27/09; A g, 12/17/07; A g, 11/28/06; A g, 06/17/05**																
GREAT AMERICAN LIFE INS OF NY American Financial Group, Inc	A-	'05	91.9	...	...	8.1	55,680	0.0	0.0	98.3	1.7	9,588	4	4	-7,930	1,131	802	381
Charles R. Scheper, Chairman		'06	81.1	...	...	18.9	54,108	0.0	0.0	98.6	1.4	10,372	4	4	-1,026	1,021	750	760
P.O. Box 21029, New York, NY 10129	Rating Outlook: Stable	'07	89.2	...	...	10.8	52,573	0.0	0.0	99.0	1.0	10,980	4	4	-1,588	925	673	673
NY : 1964 : Stock : Inactive; FPDA's		'08	94.1	...	...	5.9	46,882	0.0	0.0	98.7	1.3	7,093	5	5	-5,578	546	123	51
212-885-1544		'09	82.8	...	...	17.2	45,035	0.0	0.0	98.8	1.1	8,011	26	26	-1,950	1,259	1,003	782
AMB# 006864 NAIC# 67288	FSC IV	**Rating History: A-, 05/10/10; A-, 03/27/09; A-, 12/17/07; A-, 11/28/06; A-, 06/17/05**																

2010 BEST'S KEY RATING GUIDE — LIFE/HEALTH EDITION
BEST'S PROFITABILITY, LEVERAGE AND LIQUIDITY TESTS 2005 – 2009

Data in U.S. Dollars

	Profitability Tests							Leverage Tests						Liquidity Tests					
Un-Realized Capital Gains ($000)	Benefits Paid to NPW & Dep (%)	Comm. & Expenses to NPW & Dep (%)	NOG to Total Assets (%)	NOG to Total Rev (%)	Operating Return on Equity (%)	Net Yield (%)	Total Return (%)	Change in NPW & Dep (%)	NPW & Dep to Capital (X)	Capital & Surplus to Liabilities (%)	Surplus Relief (%)	Reins Leverage (%)	Change in Capital (%)	Quick Liquidity (%)	Current Liquidity (%)	Non-Invest Grade Bonds to Capital (%)	Delinq. & Foreclosed Mortgages to Capital (%)	Mort. & Credit Tenant Loans & R.E. to Capital (%)	Affiliated Invest to Capital (%)
...	60.1	38.8	26.4	7.4	78.5	...	...	-1.2	6.7	64.2	...	...	129.2	129.6	129.6	...	...	...	...
...	59.7	36.3	20.7	7.6	44.0	...	...	0.5	4.3	117.4	...	...	56.6	157.7	157.7	...	...	...	...
...	59.6	44.1	10.5	4.9	20.2	...	...	-5.7	3.3	99.9	...	...	22.2	158.9	158.9	...	...	...	...
...	58.1	40.5	10.4	6.8	20.0	...	...	-13.0	2.4	114.7	...	...	21.0	183.6	183.6	...	...	...	...
...	55.5	51.6	2.4	2.0	4.7	...	...	-9.6	2.1	98.6	...	...	5.0	163.4	163.4	...	...	...	...
Principal Lines of Business: Dental (100.0%)																			
16	88.4	11.8	1.7	0.5	2.9	3.59	3.48	15.4	6.0	139.5	...	...	2.7	182.8	195.7	...	...	...	0.2
12	89.8	10.9	0.6	0.2	1.1	4.04	3.89	20.2	6.6	122.2	...	...	9.2	166.7	178.3	...	...	...	0.2
-10	87.6	10.5	8.0	1.7	14.7	4.59	4.56	36.9	7.8	114.4	...	...	15.8	160.1	169.8	...	...	...	0.1
13	86.9	10.7	8.9	2.1	16.3	4.20	4.14	7.4	7.1	123.5	...	1.3	18.3	178.5	189.7	0.0	...	...	0.1
20	85.4	10.2	13.2	3.2	22.4	3.75	5.30	9.0	6.1	166.0	...	...	26.9	205.7	217.7	0.0	...	...	0.1
Principal Lines of Business: CompHosp/Med (100.0%)														Principal States: MO (77.3%), KS (22.7%)					
-100	48.9	24.0	0.2	1.2	2.1	5.81	5.88	78.4	1.2	13.1	6.3	22.0	3.6	61.7	69.0	...	...	123.6	9.0
280	97.2	29.5	0.7	5.3	6.6	5.67	5.82	-42.1	0.6	13.9	5.6	22.7	7.2	61.7	68.9	...	...	116.9	8.2
-489	96.3	31.3	0.8	6.2	7.4	5.75	5.58	-5.1	0.6	14.4	5.4	22.7	4.9	61.7	68.9	8.9	3.3	117.4	7.7
-872	102.3	36.3	0.5	4.2	5.0	5.93	4.92	-0.9	0.6	13.5	5.2	24.3	-5.2	60.3	67.8	24.9	4.1	141.6	7.8
251	84.9	32.5	0.7	5.7	6.8	5.67	5.12	8.1	0.6	14.0	5.2	23.8	5.1	54.7	63.5	19.7	6.5	142.4	7.2
Principal Lines of Business: OrdLife (70.9%), IndAnn (12.6%), GrpLife (7.4%), GrpAnn (6.8%), GrpA&H (2.3%)														Principal States: TX (12.6%), CA (8.5%), FL (8.3%), VA (6.0%), GA (5.2%)					
...	92.2	9.7	-2.1	-0.6	-5.2	5.37	5.37	-0.4	9.2	61.7	...	6.5	1.8	103.8	103.8	...	...	23.1	38.4
...	87.8	11.6	3.3	1.0	8.0	6.44	6.44	-13.6	7.4	81.5	...	1.9	6.7	126.4	126.4	...	...	19.8	13.2
...	90.4	10.5	2.6	0.8	5.2	8.50	8.50	-15.5	5.8	116.8	...	10.4	7.8	128.8	128.8	...	...	17.8	30.7
...	101.1	10.9	-19.7	-6.2	-41.6	8.74	8.74	-8.8	8.1	66.7	...	13.3	-34.2	90.9	90.9	...	...	26.3	46.3
...	95.5	10.0	-14.7	-4.1	-37.2	7.71	7.71	-6.9	10.7	63.2	...	...	-29.9	84.1	84.1	...	...	36.5	36.5
Principal Lines of Business: CompHosp/Med (76.6%), FEHBP (23.4%)														Principal States: MI (100.0%)					
45	54.0	28.8	0.7	2.7	6.0	5.39	5.54	0.0	1.3	15.5	23.8	153.8	39.7	79.3	87.9	...	...	...	0.0
4	66.3	24.3	1.4	5.2	10.2	5.40	5.50	6.2	1.3	16.2	24.0	203.9	10.0	78.7	87.9	...	...	...	0.0
...	61.5	24.1	1.4	5.5	10.2	5.53	5.59	0.6	1.2	16.5	24.4	264.3	9.9	77.3	85.3	4.0	...	...	0.0
...	72.1	28.0	0.7	2.9	5.2	5.45	4.14	4.1	1.2	15.6	22.7	323.1	-1.3	79.7	87.8	13.3	...	...	0.0
...	62.0	28.0	1.4	5.6	10.0	5.41	5.14	7.2	1.1	16.7	17.7	337.0	13.4	75.1	83.1	15.1	...	...	0.0
Principal Lines of Business: OrdLife (87.9%), IndAnn (9.1%), GrpLife (2.6%), IndA&H (0.3%)														Principal States: OH (46.9%), KY (12.8%), TN (11.8%), GA (9.0%), IN (7.2%)					
4	98.6	10.6	-21.4	-7.5	-45.5	4.54	4.53	34.6	7.8	66.6	...	2.2	-38.3	32.9	95.4	...	...	...	...
153	91.7	11.5	-8.3	-2.1	-20.7	5.00	8.73	20.2	10.5	67.7	...	8.7	-11.2	30.4	91.2	...	...	...	...
-317	90.9	12.2	-8.3	-2.1	-19.8	6.11	7.67	-8.0	9.1	76.1	...	48.9	6.3	42.7	85.0	...	...	...	...
-454	74.4	15.5	30.0	11.1	59.3	4.10	-7.80	-30.2	4.5	136.0	...	...	41.6	120.5	172.1	...	...	...	...
191	73.8	22.3	9.7	4.7	15.0	2.19	7.48	-26.0	3.0	259.4	...	11.6	11.2	108.9	207.4	...	...	...	...
Principal Lines of Business: CompHosp/Med (100.0%)														Principal States: MD (90.0%), VA (7.0%)					
...	999.9	999.9	0.8	14.8	2.3	5.44	5.50	149.9	0.0	55.9	...	...	2.2	120.7	131.5	9.5	...	...	...
...	999.9	560.4	1.0	19.2	2.6	4.97	6.15	71.1	0.0	60.5	...	...	5.8	169.7	178.8	...	...	...	...
...	358.5	25.6	1.5	27.8	3.9	5.59	5.61	999.9	0.1	68.6	...	...	3.9	143.9	155.7	...	...	...	...
...	999.9	999.9	1.3	25.9	3.2	5.12	5.12	-98.8	0.0	70.6	...	...	-3.8	158.1	167.3	8.9	...	...	...
16	999.9	622.8	-2.1	-49.7	-5.2	4.24	3.41	190.1	0.0	65.2	...	...	-6.7	160.0	168.7	0.6	...	...	...
Principal Lines of Business: IndAnn (100.0%)														Principal States: CA (75.0%), WA (25.0%)					
-77,632	118.4	13.9	1.6	10.8	20.0	6.53	5.97	17.2	0.9	10.1	1.2	41.5	12.0	66.9	76.8	62.0	1.2	22.7	28.6
33,915	86.8	11.7	0.7	3.5	8.6	5.83	7.11	70.9	1.5	9.1	1.4	46.3	-2.9	70.9	80.2	59.0	0.7	37.8	31.5
-51,162	87.1	12.5	0.9	4.5	11.7	6.03	5.07	12.0	1.6	9.3	1.1	43.1	8.1	67.3	77.0	64.8	...	41.3	30.2
-79,764	93.0	11.4	1.7	9.0	21.0	6.21	3.57	-4.3	1.5	9.2	1.5	43.3	2.4	67.2	76.5	76.0	...	33.8	24.1
94,197	105.5	12.7	0.8	5.5	9.8	5.96	5.50	-23.8	1.0	9.8	2.3	60.4	9.4	71.0	80.3	57.7	0.1	32.4	21.7
Principal Lines of Business: IndAnn (104.6%), GrpAnn (3.5%), OrdLife (2.2%), GrpLife (0.0%), GrpA&H (-0.7%)														Principal States: OH (12.2%), MI (8.7%), CA (8.3%), FL (7.8%), WA (6.7%)					
...	999.9	999.9	1.3	23.0	6.8	5.78	5.27	-30.8	0.0	21.3	...	...	-32.1	89.6	100.7	34.4	...	...	...
...	999.9	999.9	1.4	24.3	7.5	5.52	5.72	...	0.0	24.2	...	...	7.7	112.5	124.3	14.4	...	...	...
...	999.9	999.9	1.3	21.3	6.3	5.90	6.01	13.8	0.0	27.1	...	...	6.4	104.2	116.4	9.0	...	...	...
...	999.9	999.9	0.2	4.4	1.4	5.75	5.64	24.0	0.0	18.5	...	...	-34.8	89.6	100.3	24.2	...	...	...
...	999.9	474.4	2.2	41.1	13.3	5.33	4.88	400.6	0.0	22.0	...	...	11.3	114.4	124.2	6.8	...	...	...
Principal Lines of Business: IndAnn (99.2%), OrdLife (0.8%)														Principal States: NY (99.6%)					

Data in U.S. Dollars

Column key: COMPANY NAME / Ultimate Parent Association / Principal Officer / Mailing Address / Dom. : Began Bus. : Struct. : Mktg. / Specialty / Phone # / AMB# / NAIC# — Best's Financial Strength Rating / FSC — Balance Sheet — Operations

GREAT CENTRAL LIFE INS CO' — **NR-1**

Kelly J. Rush
President
137 East 6th Avenue
Oakdale, LA 71463-2615
LA : 1966 : Stock : Not Available
318-335-0500
AMB# 007705 NAIC# 74470

Data Year	Bonds (%)	Mort. Loans & R.E. (%)	Com & Pref. Stock (%)	All Other Assets (%)	Total Assets ($000)	Life Reserves (%)	Health Reserves (%)	Ann Res. & Dep. Liabilities (%)	All Other Liabilities (%)	Capital & Surplus ($000)	Direct Premiums Written ($000)	Net Premiums Written & Deposits ($000)	Operating Cash Flow ($000)	NOG Before Taxes ($000)	NOG After Taxes ($000)	Net Income ($000)
'05	46.1	24.7	11.0	18.2	16,149	...	...	...	100.0	5,550	2,552	2,552	...	279	243	265
'06	44.9	26.2	10.9	17.9	16,576	...	...	...	100.0	5,648	2,479	2,479	...	237	197	255
'07	43.7	25.7	12.1	18.4	17,259	...	...	...	100.0	6,259	2,573	2,573	...	562	487	543
'08	25.5	29.1	14.4	31.0	17,420	...	...	...	100.0	6,422	2,016	2,016	...	231	225	138
'09	22.4	30.2	26.9	20.4	18,234	...	...	...	100.0	6,226	2,202	2,202	...	-57	-52	-89

Rating History: NR-1, 06/10/10; NR-1, 06/12/09; NR-1, 06/12/08; NR-1, 06/08/07; NR-1, 06/07/06

GREAT CORNERSTONE L&H INS CO — **NR-5**

Great Cornerstone Corporation
Brent A. Gibson
President
P.O. Box 30685
Edmond, OK 73003
OK : 2002 : Stock : General Agent
Ind A&H
405-285-0838
AMB# 060385 NAIC# 11254

Data Year	Bonds (%)	Mort. Loans & R.E. (%)	Com & Pref. Stock (%)	All Other Assets (%)	Total Assets ($000)	Life Reserves (%)	Health Reserves (%)	Ann Res. & Dep. Liabilities (%)	All Other Liabilities (%)	Capital & Surplus ($000)	Direct Premiums Written ($000)	Net Premiums Written & Deposits ($000)	Operating Cash Flow ($000)	NOG Before Taxes ($000)	NOG After Taxes ($000)	Net Income ($000)
'05	94.2	1.7	...	4.1	2,219	...	68.7	...	31.3	2,011	1,144	1,142	-1	-18	-18	-19
'06	90.3	1.5	...	8.1	2,228	...	74.6	...	25.4	2,042	1,422	1,417	3	8	8	19
'07	81.5	1.4	1.4	15.8	2,272	...	72.8	...	27.2	2,049	1,687	1,679	52	46	46	62
'08	71.5	1.2	1.1	26.2	2,324	...	66.3	...	33.7	2,108	1,794	1,780	-30	20	15	12
'09	56.8	1.0	1.4	40.7	2,419	...	71.7	...	28.3	2,176	2,099	2,079	110	26	19	37

Rating History: NR-5, 03/22/10; NR-5, 04/08/09; NR-5, 03/11/08; NR-5, 04/03/07; NR-5, 03/01/06

GREAT FIDELITY LIFE INS CO — **NR-2**

Norma J Hawkins
Bruce F. Welner
President
P.O. Box 9510
Wichita, KS 67277-0510
IN : 1952 : Stock : Broker
Ordinary Life, Group A&H, Ind A&H
316-794-2200
AMB# 006481 NAIC# 64076

Data Year	Bonds (%)	Mort. Loans & R.E. (%)	Com & Pref. Stock (%)	All Other Assets (%)	Total Assets ($000)	Life Reserves (%)	Health Reserves (%)	Ann Res. & Dep. Liabilities (%)	All Other Liabilities (%)	Capital & Surplus ($000)	Direct Premiums Written ($000)	Net Premiums Written & Deposits ($000)	Operating Cash Flow ($000)	NOG Before Taxes ($000)	NOG After Taxes ($000)	Net Income ($000)
'05	55.9	12.3	2.0	29.8	3,504	7.2	17.0	6.8	69.0	2,581	3,010	353	-75	67	76	75
'06	54.3	11.6	2.2	31.9	3,363	7.5	16.7	11.4	64.4	2,671	2,421	261	-345	175	98	98
'07	25.8	18.9	4.3	51.0	3,284	7.4	13.5	15.1	64.1	2,735	2,028	196	-841	87	82	82
'08	16.7	21.2	7.3	54.7	3,163	4.0	11.8	23.1	61.2	2,764	1,659	160	963	45	43	-7
'09	48.8	17.0	2.4	31.8	3,184	3.1	7.3	27.9	61.8	2,847	1,193	117	95	-43	-34	-34

Rating History: NR-2, 05/14/10; NR-2, 06/16/09; NR-2, 06/16/08; NR-2, 05/31/07; NR-2, 05/26/06

GREAT LAKES HEALTH PLAN INC — **A-** — Rating Outlook: Stable — **FSC VI**

UnitedHealth Group Inc
Chris A. Scherer
President
17117 West Nine Mile Road, Suite 1600
Southfield, MI 48075
MI : 1994 : Stock : Broker
Health
248-559-5656
AMB# 064439 NAIC# 95467

Data Year	Bonds (%)	Mort. Loans & R.E. (%)	Com & Pref. Stock (%)	All Other Assets (%)	Total Assets ($000)	Life Reserves (%)	Health Reserves (%)	Ann Res. & Dep. Liabilities (%)	All Other Liabilities (%)	Capital & Surplus ($000)	Direct Premiums Written ($000)	Net Premiums Written & Deposits ($000)	Operating Cash Flow ($000)	NOG Before Taxes ($000)	NOG After Taxes ($000)	Net Income ($000)
'05	...	...	...	100.0	52,420	...	81.5	...	18.5	32,198	251,900	250,794	-17,771	8,266	5,777	5,777
'06	1.4	...	...	98.6	71,334	...	57.6	...	42.4	35,376	279,689	278,749	21,392	2,405	1,391	1,391
'07	52.0	...	...	48.0	84,701	...	65.2	...	34.8	41,978	441,634	440,432	12,240	8,986	6,950	6,950
'08	34.4	...	...	65.6	97,862	...	57.2	...	42.8	49,939	541,550	540,233	12,822	9,389	5,815	5,741
'09	22.8	...	...	77.2	111,301	...	78.9	...	21.1	40,077	681,038	679,559	422	-1,529	-762	-664

Rating History: A-, 06/15/09; A-, 01/29/08; A-, 11/21/07; A-, 11/16/06; A-, 08/17/06

GREAT REPUBLIC LIFE INS CO' — **NR-4**

Empire Insurance Agency, Inc.
Patricia D. Pritchett
President
3933 Stone Way North
Seattle, WA 98103-8017
WA : 1966 : Stock : Agency
LTC, Ind A&H, Trad Life
206-285-1422
AMB# 006888 NAIC# 67482

Data Year	Bonds (%)	Mort. Loans & R.E. (%)	Com & Pref. Stock (%)	All Other Assets (%)	Total Assets ($000)	Life Reserves (%)	Health Reserves (%)	Ann Res. & Dep. Liabilities (%)	All Other Liabilities (%)	Capital & Surplus ($000)	Direct Premiums Written ($000)	Net Premiums Written & Deposits ($000)	Operating Cash Flow ($000)	NOG Before Taxes ($000)	NOG After Taxes ($000)	Net Income ($000)
'05	87.2	...	3.3	9.5	18,742	...	...	...	100.0	2,681	3,359	2,048	...	99	99	107
'06	90.2	...	3.4	6.4	18,807	...	...	...	100.0	985	3,030	1,841	...	-1,722	-1,722	-1,722
'07	84.5	...	2.9	12.6	19,089	...	...	...	100.0	1,038	2,833	1,715	...	49	49	50
'08	79.5	...	4.1	16.3	18,218	...	...	...	100.0	2,747	2,504	1,512	...	2,181	2,181	1,704
'09	89.9	...	4.9	5.1	17,790	...	...	...	100.0	1,931	2,178	1,317	...	-539	-571	-697

Rating History: NR-4, 02/24/09; C-, 02/24/09; C-, 04/02/08; C-, 03/06/07; C+, 03/17/06

GREAT SOUTHERN LIFE INS CO — **B+** — Rating Outlook: Stable — **FSC VI**

Financial Holding Corporation
Gary L. Muller
CEO
P.O. Box 410288
Kansas City, MO 64141-0288
TX : 1909 : Stock : Agency
Ann, Term Life, Univ Life
816-391-2000
AMB# 006491 NAIC# 90212

Data Year	Bonds (%)	Mort. Loans & R.E. (%)	Com & Pref. Stock (%)	All Other Assets (%)	Total Assets ($000)	Life Reserves (%)	Health Reserves (%)	Ann Res. & Dep. Liabilities (%)	All Other Liabilities (%)	Capital & Surplus ($000)	Direct Premiums Written ($000)	Net Premiums Written & Deposits ($000)	Operating Cash Flow ($000)	NOG Before Taxes ($000)	NOG After Taxes ($000)	Net Income ($000)
'05	90.5	...	0.0	9.5	331,769	3.4	...	0.0	96.6	29,126	99,294	5,237	31,270	4,437	-693	-640
'06	92.7	...	1.8	5.5	303,636	3.2	...	0.0	96.7	29,997	93,061	4,726	-27,209	2,427	-1,054	-1,177
'07	88.7	...	6.1	5.2	289,242	3.3	...	0.0	96.7	31,058	92,246	4,616	-13,383	2,061	-307	-334
'08	87.9	0.5	5.4	6.2	274,057	3.3	...	0.0	96.6	34,181	84,638	2,871	-10,004	6,814	1,513	-1,117
'09	86.5	0.5	6.5	6.5	254,776	3.4	...	0.0	96.6	34,292	79,465	2,029	-12,666	3,006	2,117	-21

Rating History: B+, 11/04/09; A- g, 09/05/08; A- g, 06/14/07; A- g, 06/21/06; A- g, 06/22/05

GREAT-WEST HEALTHCARE OF IL — **NR-3**

CIGNA Corporation
Sherry B. Husa
President
8505 East Orchard Road
Greenwood Village, CO 80111
IL : 1996 : Stock : Broker
Group A&H
800-663-9094
AMB# 064026 NAIC# 95388

Data Year	Bonds (%)	Mort. Loans & R.E. (%)	Com & Pref. Stock (%)	All Other Assets (%)	Total Assets ($000)	Life Reserves (%)	Health Reserves (%)	Ann Res. & Dep. Liabilities (%)	All Other Liabilities (%)	Capital & Surplus ($000)	Direct Premiums Written ($000)	Net Premiums Written & Deposits ($000)	Operating Cash Flow ($000)	NOG Before Taxes ($000)	NOG After Taxes ($000)	Net Income ($000)
'05	3.6	...	...	96.4	8,452	...	3.4	...	96.6	2,088	25,150	2,515	3,388	-260	-173	-173
'06	4.0	...	...	96.0	8,110	...	2.9	...	97.1	2,392	20,140	2,014	1,582	470	320	321
'07	5.8	...	...	94.2	5,420	...	1.8	...	98.2	1,991	13,808	1,381	-1,776	380	247	247
'08	15.2	...	...	84.8	2,024	...	40.5	...	59.5	1,852	888	374	-1,758	-201	-160	-160
'09	...	...	...	...	...	...	...	...	...	...	...	...	...	...	...	...

Rating History: NR-3, 01/08/10; NR-3, 11/14/08; A-, 11/27/07; A, 06/22/07; A u, 02/01/07

GREAT-WEST LIFE & ANN — **A+** — Rating Outlook: Stable — **FSC XV**

Power Corporation of Canada
Mitchell T. G. Graye
President & CEO
8515 East Orchard Road
Greenwood Village, CO 80111
CO : 1907 : Stock : Broker
Health, Life, Disability
303-737-3000
AMB# 006981 NAIC# 68322

Data Year	Bonds (%)	Mort. Loans & R.E. (%)	Com & Pref. Stock (%)	All Other Assets (%)	Total Assets ($000)	Life Reserves (%)	Health Reserves (%)	Ann Res. & Dep. Liabilities (%)	All Other Liabilities (%)	Capital & Surplus ($000)	Direct Premiums Written ($000)	Net Premiums Written & Deposits ($000)	Operating Cash Flow ($000)	NOG Before Taxes ($000)	NOG After Taxes ($000)	Net Income ($000)
'05	36.4	3.8	0.6	59.2	35,869,592	29.0	0.7	19.4	50.9	1,496,278	4,117,242	4,292,714	1,159,877	459,404	384,903	418,516
'06	36.8	3.2	1.4	58.6	39,292,240	27.6	0.7	21.5	50.1	1,831,941	4,366,614	6,750,252	1,468,397	374,965	305,677	316,245
'07	33.1	3.0	1.5	62.4	38,409,183	23.9	0.7	20.8	54.6	1,846,171	4,902,543	2,991,456	-2,422,210	598,405	547,477	550,470
'08	35.8	3.8	1.2	59.2	34,960,361	26.7	0.6	23.5	49.2	901,429	4,794,106	4,262,413	-102,845	700,540	296,152	259,348
'09	33.5	3.7	0.4	62.4	40,039,587	25.0	0.5	21.3	53.2	1,375,267	6,655,309	6,076,222	1,012,279	378,048	337,553	282,033

Rating History: A+ g, 01/22/09; A+ g, 06/22/07; A+ gu, 02/01/07; A+ g, 06/19/06; A+ g, 03/09/05

GREAT WESTERN INS CO — **B+** — Rating Outlook: Negative — **FSC VI**

JAMEL Ltd.
John E. Lindquist
President
3434 Washington Boulevard, Suite 300
Ogden, UT 84401-4108
UT : 1983 : Stock : Broker
Pre-need
801-689-1415
AMB# 009362 NAIC# 71480

Data Year	Bonds (%)	Mort. Loans & R.E. (%)	Com & Pref. Stock (%)	All Other Assets (%)	Total Assets ($000)	Life Reserves (%)	Health Reserves (%)	Ann Res. & Dep. Liabilities (%)	All Other Liabilities (%)	Capital & Surplus ($000)	Direct Premiums Written ($000)	Net Premiums Written & Deposits ($000)	Operating Cash Flow ($000)	NOG Before Taxes ($000)	NOG After Taxes ($000)	Net Income ($000)
'05	88.0	3.3	5.6	3.1	386,565	90.5	...	0.3	9.2	30,753	114,902	116,888	47,841	8,914	5,819	5,550
'06	83.3	2.9	5.1	8.8	433,847	96.4	...	0.5	3.1	37,913	128,219	130,739	46,386	10,012	6,481	6,551
'07	81.2	2.9	5.5	10.4	499,842	97.1	...	0.5	2.4	33,824	145,815	148,315	66,504	9,068	5,737	-3,426
'08	84.7	3.7	6.1	5.5	403,032	97.4	...	0.6	1.9	32,426	149,148	-13,990	-88,865	28,226	27,182	6,352
'09	84.0	3.4	4.1	8.5	462,148	97.5	...	0.6	1.9	34,308	135,460	120,951	40,729	6,672	-1,119	-4,067

Rating History: B+, 04/16/10; B+, 03/10/09; B+ u, 12/22/08; B+, 03/24/08; B++, 05/25/07

BEST'S PROFITABILITY, LEVERAGE AND LIQUIDITY TESTS 2005 – 2009

Data in U.S. Dollars

	Profitability Tests							Leverage Tests						Liquidity Tests					
Un-Realized Capital Gains ($000)	Benefits Paid to NPW & Dep (%)	Comm. & Expenses to NPW & Dep (%)	NOG to Total Assets (%)	NOG to Total Rev (%)	Operating Return on Equity (%)	Net Yield (%)	Total Return (%)	Change in NPW & Dep (%)	NPW & Dep to Capital (X)	Capital & Surplus to Liabilities (%)	Surplus Relief (%)	Reins Leverage (%)	Change in Capital (%)	Quick Liquidity (%)	Current Liquidity (%)	Non-Invest Grade Bonds to Capital (%)	Delinq. & Foreclosed Mortgages to Capital (%)	Mort. & Credit Tenant Loans & R.E. to Capital (%)	Affiliated Invest to Capital (%)
56	31.6	80.3	1.5	7.4	4.5	...	...	-12.8	0.4	57.3	...	...	5.4	...	...	...	...	67.8	...
23	29.6	86.3	1.2	5.8	3.5	...	...	-2.9	0.4	56.9	...	...	2.2	...	...	...	...	72.4	...
-13	33.8	86.2	2.9	13.6	8.2	...	...	3.8	0.4	62.5	...	...	10.4	...	...	...	...	66.9	...
-212	40.5	80.6	1.3	7.8	3.6	...	...	-21.6	0.3	61.5	...	...	0.0	...	...	...	...	76.3	...
388	32.9	81.4	-0.3	-1.7	-0.8	...	...	9.2	0.3	61.2	...	...	4.3	...	...	...	...	79.7	...
	Principal Lines of Business: CrdLife (48.8%), IndAnn (37.0%), CrdA&H (13.2%), OrdLife (1.1%), IndLife (-0.1%)																		
	55.7	58.4	-0.8	-1.4	-0.9	6.27	6.26	88.3	0.6	965.2			-0.5	725.3	735.3	14.8		1.9	
...	58.9	50.9	0.3	0.5	0.4	5.84	6.35	24.1	0.7	999.9	...	...	1.5	884.6	890.4	9.6	...	1.7	...
-55	48.4	56.6	2.0	2.6	2.3	5.73	3.96	18.5	0.8	918.7	...	...	0.4	775.2	777.3	6.9	...	1.5	...
43	49.7	56.0	0.7	0.8	0.7	5.37	7.23	6.1	0.8	979.3	...	0.2	2.9	886.5	888.3	...	...	1.3	...
8	51.8	49.5	0.8	0.9	0.9	3.08	4.23	16.8	1.0	895.3	...	...	3.2	867.2	869.3	...	...	1.1	...
	Principal Lines of Business: Dental (53.4%), OtherHlth (40.6%), Vision (6.0%)													Principal States: OK (93.6%), TX (6.4%)					
0	30.1	79.8	2.1	5.4	3.0	2.69	2.90	-12.3	0.1	289.6	35.5	54.7	2.1	247.7	257.0	4.0	...	16.5	...
0	39.0	60.9	2.9	7.1	3.7	4.13	4.45	-26.1	0.1	404.3	37.2	69.0	3.5	319.6	325.0	5.7	...	14.5	...
29	38.9	113.2	2.5	7.1	3.0	5.10	6.35	-25.0	0.1	537.3	29.6	50.2	2.7	232.7	244.3	9.1	...	22.5	...
-20	40.7	129.8	1.3	4.4	1.6	4.67	2.56	-18.1	0.1	709.4	24.2	53.3	0.1	829.8	849.6	3.8	...	24.2	...
19	15.5	231.3	-1.1	-4.8	-1.2	3.46	4.26	-26.8	0.0	902.3	16.7	44.0	3.4	794.3	808.7	3.5	...	18.9	...
	Principal Lines of Business: GrpA&H (94.9%), OrdLife (3.0%), IndA&H (2.1%)													Principal States: TX (99.8%)					
...	79.1	12.3	9.0	2.4	16.0	2.90	2.90	19.2	7.8	159.2	...	...	-19.6	460.0	485.4	...	...	...	...
...	82.3	11.9	2.2	0.5	4.1	5.30	5.30	11.1	7.9	98.4	...	...	9.9	369.2	389.2	...	...	...	...
...	83.4	9.4	8.9	1.7	18.0	5.00	5.00	58.0	10.5	98.3	...	...	18.7	253.4	272.3	...	...	...	...
...	83.1	10.2	6.4	1.1	12.7	3.50	3.42	22.7	10.8	104.2	...	3.2	19.0	298.8	318.3	...	...	...	...
...	85.1	14.2	-0.7	-0.1	-1.7	1.74	1.85	25.8	17.0	56.3	...	...	-19.7	221.6	235.9	...	...	...	...
	Principal Lines of Business: Medicaid (99.1%), Medicare (0.9%)													Principal States: MI (100.0%)					
5	87.8	43.1	0.5	3.2	3.8	...	...	-1.0	0.7	17.4	7.5	...	5.0	...	...	...	...	...	...
26	110.5	37.6	-9.2	-58.2	-94.0	...	...	-10.1	1.7	6.1	18.4	...	-60.9	...	...	...	...	...	...
4	86.0	42.9	0.3	1.7	4.8	...	...	-6.8	1.5	6.4	15.3	...	5.0	...	...	...	...	...	...
-96	122.9	56.2	11.7	86.6	115.2	...	...	-11.8	0.6	17.8	4.9	...	140.2	...	...	...	...	...	...
39	118.9	52.3	-3.2	-25.6	-24.4	...	...	-12.9	0.7	12.4	6.1	...	-28.4	...	...	...	...	...	...
	Principal Lines of Business: IndA&H (89.4%), OrdLife (7.4%), GrpA&H (3.1%)																		
-47	35.3	999.9	-0.3	-0.2	-2.5	3.42	3.89	12.3	0.2	10.0	46.4	999.9	10.5	71.3	88.0	49.5	...	...	...
48	71.2	16.4	-0.3	-3.4	-3.6	5.55	5.79	-9.8	0.2	11.5	36.8	999.9	4.2	63.1	78.8	53.7	...	...	...
1	31.0	341.5	-0.1	-1.0	-1.0	6.11	6.36	-2.3	0.1	12.7	36.0	999.9	4.6	63.5	80.7	21.3	...	...	...
-1	61.5	315.4	0.5	5.7	4.6	5.68	5.00	-37.8	0.1	14.3	27.9	999.9	4.5	64.7	81.3	16.8	...	4.2	...
1	66.9	616.7	0.8	8.7	6.2	5.93	5.41	-29.3	0.1	15.6	22.1	999.9	1.6	65.9	84.7	10.7	...	3.8	...
	Principal Lines of Business: IndAnn (61.3%), GrpAnn (19.7%), OrdLife (19.0%)													Principal States: TX (16.3%), NJ (12.9%), CA (9.1%), FL (7.4%), NC (6.2%)					
...	82.2	166.3	-2.2	-2.9	-12.1	6.31	6.31	-19.6	1.2	32.8	...	361.1	168.8	61.2	61.4	...	...	...	...
...	76.0	148.2	3.9	6.5	14.3	4.75	4.75	-19.9	0.8	41.8	...	180.0	14.6	177.1	177.2	...	...	...	...
...	71.0	149.6	3.6	7.2	11.3	4.38	4.38	-31.4	0.7	58.0	...	125.8	-16.8	179.6	185.3	...	...	...	...
...	152.6	41.6	-4.3	-30.5	-8.3	1.75	1.76	-72.9	0.2	999.9	...	0.0	-7.0	999.9	999.9	...	...	...	...
...	...	...	...	...	...	...	...	...	...	...	...	...	...	...	...	...	...	...	...
-117,349	94.0	8.4	1.1	6.7	26.3	6.19	5.86	19.4	2.6	8.4	0.3	95.7	1.3	36.6	53.0	32.0	0.3	91.3	17.0
71,642	74.1	5.3	0.8	3.8	18.4	5.29	5.73	57.2	3.4	9.7	0.1	33.5	22.9	38.7	55.6	20.5	0.6	68.3	21.6
57,335	160.8	5.9	1.4	12.3	29.8	5.53	5.83	-55.7	1.5	11.2	0.0	12.6	0.5	37.4	54.6	13.7	...	61.9	23.5
-70,391	77.1	-3.1	0.8	4.9	21.6	5.69	5.14	42.5	3.9	5.8	60.0	35.6	-46.2	34.8	50.4	45.7	...	131.5	27.1
84,743	62.5	2.1	0.9	4.5	29.7	5.65	5.83	42.6	4.0	7.9	14.5	18.8	41.0	36.2	52.4	49.1	...	105.4	17.0
	Principal Lines of Business: GrpAnn (81.6%), OrdLife (15.5%), GrpLife (1.1%), IndAnn (1.0%), GrpA&H (0.7%)													Principal States: CA (26.3%), NC (11.0%), CO (4.3%), TX (4.3%), MD (4.0%)					
664	35.1	23.2	1.6	4.2	21.2	6.45	6.54	13.4	3.5	9.5	...	...	27.7	53.4	72.8	2.6	...	44.3	15.9
439	36.4	24.4	1.6	4.2	18.9	6.43	6.57	11.9	3.2	10.3	...	...	20.4	46.6	71.6	...	...	31.6	13.0
-2,044	37.8	23.4	1.2	3.3	16.0	5.87	3.45	13.4	4.2	7.6	...	...	-13.0	54.0	73.4	9.5	...	42.7	14.7
-3,411	-99.9	-75.3	6.0	76.5	82.1	6.64	1.28	-99.9	-0.4	8.8	64.8	496.0	-7.1	44.3	66.8	61.8	...	46.4	15.5
1,204	39.2	29.1	-0.3	-0.8	-3.4	6.07	5.65	964.6	3.4	8.2	-0.4	469.3	7.3	46.9	66.8	89.5	2.9	45.8	14.2
	Principal Lines of Business: GrpLife (70.6%), OrdLife (27.8%), IndAnn (1.6%), CrdLife (0.0%)													Principal States: CA (18.6%), UT (8.4%), AZ (7.4%), WI (5.4%), MN (5.2%)					

Data in U.S. Dollars

COMPANY NAME Ultimate Parent Association Principal Officer Mailing Address Dom. : Began Bus. : Struct. : Mktg. Specialty Phone # AMB# NAIC#	Best's Financial Strength Rating FSC	Data Year	Balance Sheet: Bonds (%)	Mort. Loans & R.E. (%)	Com & Pref. Stock (%)	All Other Assets (%)	Total Assets ($000)	Life Reserves (%)	Health Reserves (%)	Ann Res. & Dep. Liabilities (%)	All Other Liabilities (%)	Capital & Surplus ($000)	Operations: Direct Premiums Written ($000)	Net Premiums Written & Deposits ($000)	Operating Cash Flow ($000)	NOG Before Taxes ($000)	NOG After Taxes ($000)	Net Income ($000)
GREAT WESTERN LIFE INS CO JAMEL Ltd. John E. Lindquist President 3434 Washington Boulevard, Suite 300 Ogden, UT 84401-4108 MT : 1980 : Stock : Inactive Inactive 801-689-1415 AMB# 006458 NAIC# 92428	NR-3	'05	94.8	...	...	5.2	2,000	60.5	...	35.8	3.7	1,409	9	15	41	45	41	41
		'06	93.7	...	...	6.3	2,009	59.4	...	35.8	4.8	1,421	9	14	22	54	32	32
		'07	92.8	...	...	7.2	2,013	59.0	...	36.3	4.8	1,421	8	14	18	33	19	19
		'08	91.9	...	...	8.1	2,018	58.9	...	38.1	3.0	1,441	9	13	19	42	38	38
		'09	92.9	...	...	7.1	2,060	54.4	...	37.4	8.3	1,451	8	13	32	50	20	28
		Rating History: NR-3, 04/16/10; NR-3, 03/10/09; NR-3, 12/22/08; NR-3, 03/24/08; NR-3, 05/25/07																
GREATER BENEFICIAL UNION James R. Stoker CEO, National Secretary & Treasurer 4254 Clairton Boulevard Pittsburgh, PA 15227-3394 PA : 1892 : Fraternal : Agency Ind Ann, Trad Life, Univ Life 800-765-4428 AMB# 008161 NAIC# 56685	B++ Rating Outlook: Negative FSC VI	'05	95.5	0.6	1.0	2.9	424,482	8.8	...	88.4	2.8	25,134	50,032	50,416	40,678	3,748	3,748	3,754
		'06	94.3	0.5	1.0	4.2	442,354	8.6	...	88.8	2.6	30,057	51,000	51,653	15,702	4,797	4,797	4,569
		'07	94.9	0.4	1.0	3.7	464,485	8.6	...	88.8	2.6	31,868	55,601	55,769	21,371	3,576	3,576	3,623
		'08	94.3	0.3	0.9	4.5	498,869	8.3	...	89.8	2.0	27,675	62,379	63,376	37,543	4,676	4,676	-1,754
		'09	95.6	0.2	0.7	3.4	602,550	6.8	...	91.2	1.9	31,005	119,524	120,286	98,887	4,489	4,489	2,104
		Rating History: B++, 06/15/10; B++, 05/01/09; B++, 06/09/08; B++, 06/19/07; B+, 06/12/06																
GREATER GEORGIA LIFE INS CO WellPoint Inc. Monye M. Connolly President 2 Gannett Drive South Portland, ME 04106 GA : 1982 : Stock : Broker Dis inc, Group Life 678-443-5200 AMB# 009177 NAIC# 97217	A Rating Outlook: Stable FSC IX	'05	82.7	...	...	17.3	42,151	37.2	9.0	24.8	29.0	22,238	32,593	38,673	913	1,392	972	972
		'06	85.1	...	...	14.9	41,869	37.0	4.8	28.3	29.8	22,214	30,425	38,278	-1,128	2,201	2,565	2,537
		'07	86.9	...	...	13.1	43,176	36.7	6.9	27.8	28.6	22,166	31,767	38,202	970	3,119	2,011	1,956
		'08	85.7	...	...	14.3	44,758	39.9	10.3	27.6	22.2	22,687	33,562	39,882	374	3,537	2,392	2,230
		'09	87.2	...	...	12.8	45,601	39.7	9.4	32.2	18.7	20,645	31,332	38,968	1,677	1,862	1,339	863
		Rating History: A g, 04/27/10; A g, 01/23/09; A g, 03/20/08; A g, 11/06/06; A g, 12/29/05																
GREEK CATHOLIC UNION OF USA George N. Juba President 5400 Tuscarawas Road Beaver, PA 15009-9513 PA : 1892 : Fraternal : Agency Ann, Life 724-495-3400 AMB# 009807 NAIC# 56693	NR-4	'05	92.4	0.7	2.0	4.8	575,478	8.5	...	88.8	2.7	25,188	43,622	44,084	9,869	1,091	1,091	1,101
		'06	88.2	0.8	5.1	6.0	574,567	8.7	...	88.5	2.8	29,058	90,437	90,755	-142	3,900	3,900	3,453
		'07	81.8	1.0	10.5	6.7	591,295	8.6	...	88.5	2.9	26,556	62,865	62,930	21,877	-1,901	-1,901	1,277
		'08	78.3	0.9	14.1	6.6	618,183	8.1	...	90.4	1.4	6,410	83,084	83,129	46,397	60	60	-5,342
		'09	...	...	...	...	...	...	...	...	...	...	...	...	...	...	...	...
		Rating History: NR-4, 07/09/09; C-, 07/09/09; C-, 03/11/09; B, 06/17/08; B, 06/07/07																
GRIFFIN LEGGETT BURIAL INS CO[1] Michael H. Kelly President 5802 W. 12th Street Little Rock, AR 72204-1607 AR : 1956 : Stock : Not Available 501-663-8775 AMB# 068426 NAIC# 84107	NR-1	'05	67.4	...	...	32.6	148	...	...	...	100.0	137	18	18	...	1	1	1
		'06	65.5	...	...	34.5	153	...	...	...	100.0	143	19	19	...	6	6	6
		'07	64.9	...	...	35.1	154	...	...	...	100.0	144	15	15	...	1	1	1
		'08	...	...	...	100.0	148	...	...	...	100.0	144	12	12	...	0	0	0
		'09	...	...	...	100.0	143	...	...	...	100.0	142	12	12	...	-2	-2	-2
		Rating History: NR-1, 06/10/10; NR-1, 06/12/09; NR-1, 06/12/08; NR-1, 06/08/07; NR-1, 06/07/06																
GROUP DENTAL H ADMINISTRATORS[2] Craig S. Abramowitz, M.D. President 236 East Westfield Avenue Roselle Park, NJ 07204 NJ : 1982 : Stock : Broker Dental 908-241-9700 AMB# 064774 NAIC# 11246	NR-5	'05	...	...	...	100.0	148	...	...	...	100.0	132	1,259	1,259	-79	34	29	29
		'06	...	...	35.0	65.0	150	...	...	...	100.0	140	1,243	1,243	52	20	16	16
		'07	...	...	1.5	98.5	176	...	...	...	100.0	160	1,184	1,184	-57	15	12	12
		'08	...	...	0.7	99.3	285	...	...	...	100.0	160	1,150	1,150	1	13	11	11
		'09	...	...	1.3	98.7	280	...	...	...	100.0	165	999	999	0	6	5	5
		Rating History: NR-5, 04/15/10; NR-5, 06/01/09; NR-5, 05/19/08; NR-5, 06/22/07; NR-5, 05/11/06																
GROUP DENTAL SERVICE OF MD INC Coventry Health Care Inc Ralph Foxman CEO 111 Rockville Pike #950 Rockville, MD 20850 MD : 2001 : Stock : Broker Dental 240-283-3500 AMB# 064791 NAIC# 95846	NR-5	'05	26.8	...	0.4	72.8	5,226	...	83.2	...	16.8	3,585	19,117	19,117	1,283	-1,360	-1,360	-1,360
		'06	23.6	...	19.8	56.6	5,862	...	81.8	...	18.2	3,471	23,700	23,700	482	-2,656	-2,656	-2,656
		'07	19.6	...	0.7	79.7	6,896	...	72.7	...	27.3	4,228	26,383	26,383	-25	-990	-990	-990
		'08	7.1	...	...	92.9	6,693	...	75.5	...	24.5	4,107	26,802	26,802	300	-1,804	-1,804	-1,804
		'09	1.3	...	...	98.7	7,484	...	71.9	...	28.1	4,436	25,700	28,847	-243	-82	-82	-82
		Rating History: NR-5, 04/06/10; NR-5, 07/08/09; NR-5, 07/02/08; NR-5, 07/03/07; NR-5, 08/15/06																
GROUP HEALTH COOPERATIVE Group Health Cooperative Scott E. Armstrong President & CEO 320 Westlake Avenue North, Suite 100 Seattle, WA 98109-5233 WA : 1945 : Non-Profit : Broker Group A&H, Health, Ind A&H 206-448-5528 AMB# 064044 NAIC# 95672	NR-5	'05	19.3	22.0	2.8	55.9	1,001,047	...	3.2	...	96.8	438,570	1,647,140	1,647,140	80,939	101,001	101,001	100,873
		'06	22.2	14.3	10.2	53.2	1,382,832	...	14.5	...	85.5	635,141	1,790,412	1,790,412	282,283	222,460	222,369	222,332
		'07	39.3	18.6	13.0	29.1	1,444,273	...	17.5	...	82.5	737,754	1,835,593	1,835,593	137,993	63,884	63,865	64,175
		'08	39.6	21.0	12.3	27.0	1,380,675	...	16.6	...	83.4	550,235	1,942,950	1,942,950	-22,564	65,368	65,368	-24,350
		'09	37.6	21.6	17.8	22.9	1,357,968	...	19.2	...	80.8	593,198	1,999,205	1,999,205	-56,751	-23,878	-23,878	16,214
		Rating History: NR-5, 03/29/10; NR-5, 08/26/09; B++pd, 06/06/08; B++pd, 06/05/07; B+ pd, 06/13/06																
GROUP HLTH COOP OF EAU CLAIRE Catherine Anderson President P.O. Box 3217 Eau Claire, WI 54702 WI : 1976 : Non-Profit : Broker Group A&H, Health 715-552-4300 AMB# 068654 NAIC# 95192	NR-5	'05	37.5	1.8	...	60.7	28,127	...	84.9	...	15.1	13,912	60,278	60,026	4,684	5,223	5,223	5,152
		'06	9.1	1.3	...	89.6	36,049	...	86.3	...	13.7	18,158	92,864	92,435	6,728	4,242	4,214	4,214
		'07	0.1	1.0	...	98.9	43,369	...	85.1	...	14.9	17,710	114,700	114,246	7,641	-399	-405	-405
		'08	16.5	0.8	...	82.7	51,735	...	83.5	...	16.5	19,766	145,639	144,601	9,046	2,038	2,031	2,031
		'09	50.6	0.7	...	48.7	58,525	...	76.7	...	23.3	22,863	201,694	200,624	6,012	3,288	3,146	3,146
		Rating History: NR-5, 04/19/10; NR-5, 08/26/09; B- pd, 06/06/08; B- pd, 06/05/07; B- pd, 06/20/06																

2010 BEST'S KEY RATING GUIDE — LIFE/HEALTH EDITION
BEST'S PROFITABILITY, LEVERAGE AND LIQUIDITY TESTS 2005 – 2009

Data in U.S. Dollars

—	Profitability Tests							Leverage Tests						Liquidity Tests					
Un-Realized Capital Gains ($000)	Benefits Paid to NPW & Dep (%)	Comm. & Expenses to NPW & Dep (%)	NOG to Total Assets (%)	NOG to Total Rev (%)	Operating Return on Equity (%)	Net Yield (%)	Total Return (%)	Change in NPW & Dep (%)	NPW & Dep to Capital (X)	Capital & Surplus to Liabilities (%)	Surplus Relief (%)	Reins Leverage (%)	Change in Capital (%)	Quick Liquidity (%)	Current Liquidity (%)	Non-Invest Grade Bonds to Capital (%)	Delinq. & Foreclosed Mortgages to Capital (%)	Mort. & Credit Tenant Loans & R.E. to Capital (%)	Affiliated Invest to Capital (%)
...	262.5	65.7	2.1	44.4	2.9	3.28	3.70	-12.9	0.0	240.4	...	0.0	1.3	291.7	291.7	...	...	...	...
...	257.0	56.5	1.6	33.1	2.3	3.52	3.83	-4.4	0.0	244.4	...	0.0	0.9	301.1	301.1	...	...	...	...
...	271.3	71.8	0.9	20.7	1.3	3.63	3.71	-1.9	0.0	242.8	...	0.0	0.0	322.0	322.0	...	...	...	...
...	240.0	102.5	1.9	45.7	2.7	3.49	3.49	-8.3	0.0	253.2	...	0.0	1.5	303.7	336.2	...	...	...	...
...	120.6	205.8	1.0	22.3	1.4	3.83	4.33	-0.9	0.0	241.9	...	0.0	0.7	269.2	300.9	...	...	...	...
Principal Lines of Business: OrdLife (100.0%)														Principal States: MT (53.3%), OH (22.2%), WY (4.1%), CO (3.8%), WA (3.0%)					
85	54.6	10.8	0.9	5.0	16.1	6.34	6.43	0.0	1.8	6.9	...	1.4	16.3	61.5	71.8	46.3		9.2	2.7
1,062	106.5	8.9	1.1	6.2	17.4	6.37	6.63	2.5	1.6	8.1	...	1.2	20.5	75.8	80.7	22.5	0.0	7.0	2.1
-17	96.5	9.3	0.8	4.3	11.5	6.28	6.35	8.0	1.6	8.2	...	1.3	6.4	76.0	80.8	27.2	...	5.4	1.5
-4,439	66.5	8.5	1.0	5.1	15.7	6.38	4.20	13.6	2.2	6.2	...	1.6	-17.6	73.3	80.4	18.9	1.2	5.8	1.7
1,807	36.1	6.0	0.8	2.9	15.3	6.35	6.30	89.8	3.7	5.8	...	1.3	13.5	66.1	75.8	55.2	0.0	4.5	1.4
Principal Lines of Business: IndAnn (98.7%), OrdLife (1.3%)														Principal States: PA (54.3%), OH (12.3%), WI (9.8%), MI (8.2%), NY (4.1%)					
...	51.1	29.5	2.3	3.1	4.1	4.30	4.51	21.4	1.7	112.9	...	25.4	-11.1	174.0	192.4	...	...	...	...
...	49.5	24.1	6.1	8.5	11.5	4.47	4.54	-1.0	1.7	114.3	...	28.2	-0.1	156.4	174.8	1.0	...	...	...
...	47.4	22.1	4.7	6.5	9.1	4.82	4.77	-0.2	1.7	106.3	2.5	29.0	-0.4	141.6	160.1	0.7	...	...	...
...	47.5	21.4	5.4	7.3	10.7	5.21	4.83	4.4	1.8	102.9	2.2	33.0	2.0	139.0	157.6	0.1	...	...	...
...	46.0	22.0	3.0	4.3	6.2	5.20	3.99	-2.3	1.9	82.7	2.1	46.0	-9.1	129.2	145.2	...	...	...	...
Principal Lines of Business: GrpLife (54.3%), IndAnn (27.2%), GrpA&H (16.9%), OrdLife (1.6%)														Principal States: GA (98.8%)					
334	125.0	12.2	0.2	1.5	4.4	4.88	5.12	-13.1	1.5	5.5	...	...	1.6	68.2	78.0	90.6	...	14.2	22.3
1,065	126.5	6.7	0.7	3.3	14.4	5.09	5.35	105.9	2.7	6.3	...	...	13.5	67.6	77.5	50.6	...	13.8	19.5
-1,048	109.9	10.5	-0.3	-2.1	-6.8	5.08	5.58	-30.7	1.9	5.9	...	...	-2.8	66.8	77.4	62.2	...	17.3	19.8
-17,950	66.7	8.0	0.0	0.1	0.4	5.21	1.49	32.1	12.7	1.1	...	...	-80.1	56.8	68.1	381.0	...	89.2	96.5
...	...	...	...	...	...	...	...	...	...	...	...	...	...	...	...	...	...	...	...
...	67.6	45.5	0.6	4.0	0.6	...	...	-28.6	0.1	999.9	...	...	0.6	...	...	...	...	...	...
...	51.1	37.3	3.8	25.8	4.1	...	...	1.8	0.1	999.9	...	...	4.2	...	...	...	...	...	...
...	70.1	44.1	0.8	6.6	0.9	...	...	-18.4	0.1	999.9	...	...	0.9	...	...	...	...	...	...
...	59.7	56.7	0.0	0.2	0.0	...	...	-19.0	0.1	999.9	...	...	0.0	...	...	...	...	...	...
...	54.1	58.0	-1.2	-14.4	-1.2	...	...	0.1	0.1	999.9	...	...	-1.2	...	...	...	...	...	...
Principal Lines of Business: OrdLife (100.0%)																			
...	85.0	12.5	15.8	2.3	17.0	1.20	1.20	0.6	9.6	799.5	...	...	-35.8	377.6	377.6	...	...	...	...
...	85.0	13.5	10.7	1.3	11.8	2.49	2.49	-1.3	8.9	999.9	...	...	6.5	928.9	999.9	...	...	...	...
...	85.0	13.8	7.6	1.1	8.3	0.18	0.18	-4.8	7.4	999.9	...	...	14.4	347.6	350.1	...	...	...	...
...	85.0	14.0	4.6	0.9	6.6	3.14	3.14	-2.8	7.2	128.2	...	...	-0.2	45.3	45.6	...	...	...	...
...	85.0	14.6	1.9	0.5	3.3	3.15	3.15	-13.2	6.0	143.2	...	...	3.2	48.8	49.3	...	...	...	...
Principal Lines of Business: Dental (100.0%)														Principal States: NJ (100.0%)					
...	75.2	32.0	-29.7	-7.1	-42.9	0.53	0.53	29.3	5.3	218.5	...	...	30.5	260.7	261.7	...	...	...	...
...	75.8	37.1	-47.9	-11.0	-75.3	3.79	3.79	24.0	6.8	145.2	...	...	-3.2	184.4	192.4	...	...	...	...
...	72.2	35.6	-15.5	-3.6	-25.7	3.95	3.95	11.3	6.2	158.5	...	...	21.8	188.0	190.1	...	...	...	...
...	79.3	30.0	-26.6	-6.5	-43.3	2.21	2.21	1.6	6.5	158.8	...	...	-2.9	201.6	201.6	...	...	...	...
5	75.2	28.8	-1.2	-0.3	-1.9	0.49	0.59	7.6	6.5	145.5	...	...	8.0	163.9	163.9	...	...	...	...
Principal Lines of Business: Dental (100.0%)														Principal States: MD (67.3%), DC (17.5%), PA (9.0%), VA (6.0%)					
118	88.1	10.3	10.6	4.7	24.7	2.97	2.97	8.5	3.8	78.0	...	...	16.0	169.2	176.8	...	...	50.1	63.8
23,152	85.4	8.8	18.7	9.5	41.4	4.74	7.31	8.7	2.8	84.9	...	...	44.8	171.4	181.1	...	...	31.2	43.2
-28,428	92.1	9.5	4.5	2.8	9.3	5.04	2.49	2.5	2.5	104.4	...	...	16.2	145.2	157.5	...	...	36.3	45.6
1,331	88.5	8.9	4.6	3.3	10.2	3.31	-4.47	5.8	3.5	66.3	...	...	-25.4	114.1	123.4	0.0	...	52.8	59.5
...	93.3	9.2	-1.7	-1.2	-4.2	2.88	6.83	2.9	3.4	77.6	...	...	7.8	99.1	109.1	0.1	...	49.5	62.6
Principal Lines of Business: CompHosp/Med (54.0%), Medicare (32.5%), FEHBP (11.6%), Medicaid (1.9%), OtherHlth (0.0%)														Principal States: WA (96.4%)					
...	83.5	12.2	19.5	4.6	46.0	3.64	3.34	9.3	4.3	97.9	...	0.1	57.8	103.2	157.0	...	...	3.6	3.6
...	86.2	11.6	13.1	2.9	26.3	5.75	5.75	54.0	5.1	101.5	...	2.4	30.5	165.9	210.4	...	...	2.6	2.6
...	89.5	10.8	-1.0	-0.2	-2.3	6.02	6.02	23.6	6.5	69.0	...	1.8	-2.5	175.7	181.1	...	...	2.6	2.6
...	90.0	10.6	4.3	1.0	10.8	4.53	4.53	26.6	7.3	61.8	...	1.7	11.6	143.0	162.6	...	...	2.2	2.2
...	90.0	9.5	5.7	1.3	14.8	2.34	2.34	38.7	8.8	64.1	...	0.5	15.7	137.3	161.0	...	...	1.8	1.8
Principal Lines of Business: CompHosp/Med (62.1%), Medicaid (37.4%), Dental (0.4%), MedSup (0.1%)														Principal States: WI (99.7%)					

Data in U.S. Dollars

COMPANY NAME / Ultimate Parent Association / Principal Officer / Mailing Address / Dom. : Began Bus. : Struct. : Mktg. / Specialty / Phone # / AMB# / NAIC#	Best's Financial Strength Rating / FSC	Data Year	Bonds (%)	Mort. Loans & R.E. (%)	Com & Pref. Stock (%)	All Other Assets (%)	Total Assets ($000)	Life Reserves (%)	Health Reserves %)	Ann Res. & Dep. Liabilities (%)	All Other Liabilities (%)	Capital & Surplus ($000)	Direct Premiums Written ($000)	Net Premiums Written & Deposits ($000)	Operating Cash Flow ($000)	NOG Before Taxes ($000)	NOG After Taxes ($000)	Net Income ($000)
			Balance Sheet										Operations					
GROUP HEALTH COOP OF S CENT WI	**NR-5**	'05	46.3	15.6	10.4	27.7	75,748	...	31.6	...	68.4	52,593	159,685	159,123	3,101	3,413	3,413	3,413
Kenneth N. Machtan, President		'06	42.8	15.9	12.8	28.5	81,008	...	40.5	...	59.5	55,316	178,135	177,467	9,425	1,962	1,962	1,962
P.O. Box 44971, Madison, WI 53744-4971		'07	46.2	15.6	25.6	12.6	88,738	...	47.4	...	52.6	61,289	201,541	200,798	8,457	4,026	4,026	4,026
WI : 1976 : Non-Profit : Broker; Group A&H, Health		'08	51.3	15.1	20.4	13.2	96,466	...	43.0	...	57.0	66,130	219,599	219,007	9,372	10,690	10,690	8,864
608-251-4156		'09	43.1	15.4	34.9	6.6	101,639	...	46.8	...	53.2	68,813	239,394	238,537	3,624	2,894	2,894	2,080
AMB# 068807 NAIC# 95311		**Rating History: NR-5, 04/07/10; NR-5, 08/26/09; B+ pd, 07/01/08; B+ pd, 06/26/07; B+ pd, 07/25/06**																
GROUP HEALTH INCORPORATED	**C**	'05	43.6	9.3	5.4	41.8	734,617	...	67.6	...	32.4	204,310	2,318,126	2,314,177	61,031	4,059	1,583	3,143
EmblemHealth Inc		'06	40.0	10.3	4.6	45.2	793,959	...	63.4	...	36.6	245,189	2,397,114	2,394,277	15,331	31,940	22,564	38,306
Frank J. Branchini, President & COO; 441 Ninth Avenue, New York, NY 10001	Rating Outlook: Negative	'07	36.4	13.7	5.0	44.8	871,142	...	63.1	...	36.9	313,581	2,522,417	2,521,391	50,000	37,308	26,180	25,635
NY : 1940 : Other : Agency; Group A&H		'08	33.3	13.9	3.1	49.7	861,558	...	61.2	...	38.8	239,456	2,774,627	2,773,870	-3,683	15,834	16,577	-21,653
212-615-0000		'09	40.3	11.2	3.7	44.8	824,484	...	59.3	...	40.7	146,386	3,160,757	3,160,112	7,549	-24,349	-23,094	-8,949
AMB# 064601 NAIC# 55239	**FSC VIII**	**Rating History: C g, 06/09/10; C++g, 05/29/09; B- g, 06/06/08; B- g, 05/10/07; NR-5, 06/26/06**																
GROUP HEALTH OPTIONS	**NR-5**	'05	...	...	...	100.0	68,979	...	13.1	...	86.9	27,647	407,098	407,098	-5,037	-958	-513	-513
Group Health Cooperative		'06	1.5	...	...	98.5	69,085	...	10.7	...	89.3	31,383	403,207	403,207	1,110	5,744	3,784	3,784
April D. Golenor, President; 320 Westlake Avenue North, Suite 100, Seattle, WA 98109-5233		'07	...	...	...	100.0	70,761	...	17.4	...	82.6	31,707	387,020	387,020	4,222	418	143	143
WA : 1990 : Stock : Agency; Group A&H		'08	1.1	...	...	98.9	88,463	...	25.4	...	74.6	29,968	483,108	483,108	-1,660	-1,161	-1,236	-1,236
206-448-2965		'09	52.0	...	...	48.0	123,767	...	55.8	...	44.2	69,648	652,876	652,876	91,263	-4,435	-4,726	-4,623
AMB# 064531 NAIC# 47055		**Rating History: NR-5, 03/30/10; NR-5, 03/18/09; NR-5, 04/09/08; NR-5, 04/02/07; NR-5, 04/20/06**																
GROUP HEALTH PLAN INC	**A-**	'05	73.6	...	...	26.4	160,591	...	54.6	...	45.4	91,731	532,385	524,739	-5,707	59,580	43,362	43,316
Coventry Health Care Inc		'06	72.2	...	...	27.8	173,210	...	41.5	...	58.5	88,025	524,674	517,275	11,340	55,746	38,548	38,497
Roman T. Kulich, President & CEO; 550 Maryville Centre Drive, Suite 300, St. Louis, MO 63141-5818	Rating Outlook: Negative	'07	84.9	...	...	15.1	181,179	...	48.4	...	51.6	108,306	532,838	526,070	5,729	82,306	55,601	55,598
MO : 1985 : Stock : Broker; Group A&H, Health, Ind A&H		'08	63.8	...	...	36.2	211,579	...	41.5	...	58.5	112,270	522,103	516,443	37,339	67,442	45,625	44,258
314-506-1700		'09	73.6	...	...	26.4	208,841	...	40.2	...	59.8	101,800	488,939	484,589	-10,379	37,882	23,239	23,926
AMB# 068534 NAIC# 96377	**FSC VIII**	**Rating History: A-, 02/12/10; A- g, 11/19/08; A- g, 10/30/07; B++g, 07/11/07; B++g, 10/27/06**																
GROUP HEALTH PLAN INC[2]	**NR-5**	'05	40.2	16.9	5.6	37.3	416,942	...	3.9	...	96.1	44,431	220,825	220,775	-4,509	-4,316	-4,316	-5,012
HealthPartners Inc		'06	33.5	13.8	6.4	46.3	480,880	...	3.5	...	96.5	60,241	158,349	158,280	57,862	2,778	2,778	1,174
Mary K. Brainerd, President & CFO; 8100-34th Avenue South, Minneapolis, MN 55440-1309		'07	35.3	14.0	4.8	45.9	476,286	...	3.5	...	96.5	61,244	135,604	135,574	8,819	5,052	5,052	5,488
MN : 1957 : Non-Profit : Broker; Group A&H		'08	38.8	16.1	4.7	40.4	424,410	...	5.4	...	94.6	75,787	210,514	210,481	-22,025	18,926	18,926	7,118
952-883-6000		'09	38.2	14.1	5.7	42.0	492,845	...	5.2	...	94.8	79,444	366,254	366,240	22,509	17,800	17,800	18,903
AMB# 068667 NAIC# 52628		**Rating History: NR-5, 06/02/10; NR-5, 08/26/09; C++pd, 09/03/08; C++pd, 09/21/07; C++pd, 09/05/06**																
GROUP HOSPITAL & MEDICAL SVCS	**NR-5**	'05	32.8	...	15.5	51.7	1,528,768	...	26.1	...	73.9	560,967	2,258,372	2,258,297	68,879	63,888	49,767	54,397
CareFirst Inc		'06	37.7	...	16.3	46.0	1,690,628	...	26.3	...	73.7	663,006	2,456,519	2,461,318	95,865	84,608	65,827	64,623
Chet Burrell, Interim CEO; 10455 Mill Run Circle, Owings Mills, MD 21117		'07	40.0	...	16.3	43.7	1,699,544	...	71.9	...	28.1	753,559	2,706,982	2,713,086	25,259	82,428	67,246	68,424
DC : 1934 : Non-Profit : Broker; Group A&H		'08	34.5	...	16.3	49.2	1,772,935	...	66.0	...	34.0	686,780	3,126,829	2,815,214	-14,411	51,851	44,280	26,260
410-581-3000		'09	37.6	...	14.4	48.1	1,887,554	...	66.4	...	33.6	761,458	3,265,597	2,927,358	22,648	32,775	33,760	44,801
AMB# 064471 NAIC# 53007		**Rating History: NR-5, 05/11/10; NR-5, 08/26/09; B++pd, 09/19/08; B++pd, 09/04/07; B++pd, 09/25/06**																
GROUP INS TRUST OF CA SOC CPAS	**B++**	'05	...	...	...	...	26,422	...	...	...	...	22,095	...	30,121	...	...	...	3,196
Susan Young, Executive Director		'06	...	...	...	...	29,530	...	...	...	...	24,088	...	31,165	...	...	...	1,993
1235 Radio Road, Redwood City, CA 94065	Rating Outlook: Stable	'07	...	...	...	...	32,670	...	...	...	...	25,375	...	33,408	...	...	...	1,287
CA : 1959 : Stock : Not Available; Health		'08	...	...	...	...	27,847	...	...	...	...	21,393	...	36,168	...	...	...	-3,982
800-556-5771		'09	...	...	...	...	28,922	...	...	...	...	22,171	...	39,454	...	...	...	777
AMB# 064924 NAIC# 73562	**FSC V**	**Rating History: B++, 06/10/10; B++, 06/02/09; B++, 05/16/08**																
GUARANTEE SECURITY LIFE OF AZ	**NR-3**	'05	26.1	...	...	73.9	771	62.7	32.0	...	5.3	684	...	89	-2	21	17	17
Guarantee Trust Life Insurance Company		'06	26.3	...	...	73.7	762	59.7	27.0	...	13.3	689	...	69	-7	5	4	4
Reed Gass, President; 7238 E. Montebello Avenue, Scottsdale, AZ 85250		'07	26.0	...	...	74.0	770	63.7	24.3	...	12.0	716	...	65	6	34	27	27
AZ : 1973 : Stock : Other Direct; Credit A&H, Credit Life, Reins		'08	16.2	...	...	83.8	772	72.2	26.0	...	1.8	721	...	54	9	5	5	5
480-607-1602		'09	16.4	...	...	83.6	760	70.9	28.5	...	0.6	724	...	54	-15	1	1	1
AMB# 008401 NAIC# 83232		**Rating History: NR-3, 05/25/10; NR-3, 05/29/09; NR-3, 06/26/08; NR-3, 06/13/07; NR-3, 02/23/06**																
GUARANTEE TRUST LIFE INS CO	**B+**	'05	69.5	6.8	1.1	22.6	199,221	53.5	35.3	1.7	9.4	34,008	278,569	170,931	-9,105	3,903	3,903	3,998
Guarantee Trust Life Insurance Company		'06	70.0	8.1	3.7	18.3	193,584	51.5	37.2	1.7	9.5	35,501	251,621	152,639	1,455	2,558	2,180	2,243
R. S. Holson III, President, Chairman & CEO; 1275 Milwaukee Avenue, Glenview, IL 60025	Rating Outlook: Negative	'07	64.8	8.2	2.9	24.1	207,663	52.2	36.5	1.7	9.6	43,517	279,849	130,741	6,129	4,752	1,012	1,012
IL : 1936 : Mutual : Agency; A&H, Life, Credit Life		'08	60.6	12.7	2.8	23.8	218,660	49.4	38.5	1.5	10.6	42,048	292,751	160,432	7,733	1,596	547	-1,261
847-699-0600		'09	68.0	11.3	1.1	19.6	232,502	47.3	41.9	1.4	9.5	40,358	276,750	164,588	14,146	3,953	3,026	1,583
AMB# 006503 NAIC# 64211	**FSC VI**	**Rating History: B+, 05/25/10; B+, 05/29/09; B+, 06/26/08; B+, 06/13/07; B+, 02/23/06**																

BEST'S PROFITABILITY, LEVERAGE AND LIQUIDITY TESTS 2005 – 2009

Data in U.S. Dollars

—	Profitability Tests							Leverage Tests						Liquidity Tests					
Un-Realized Capital Gains ($000)	Benefits Paid to NPW & Dep (%)	Comm. & Expenses to NPW & Dep (%)	NOG to Total Assets (%)	NOG to Total Rev (%)	Operating Return on Equity (%)	Net Yield (%)	Total Return (%)	Change in NPW & Dep (%)	NPW & Dep to Capital (X)	Capital & Surplus to Liabilities (%)	Surplus Relief (%)	Reins Leverage (%)	Change in Capital (%)	Quick Liquidity (%)	Current Liquidity (%)	Non-Invest Grade Bonds to Capital (%)	Delinq. & Foreclosed Mortgages to Capital (%)	Mort. & Credit Tenant Loans & R.E. to Capital (%)	Affiliated Invest to Capital (%)
-17	87.8	10.9	4.7	2.1	6.6	1.53	1.50	10.8	3.0	227.1	...	...	3.1	194.3	212.8	...	...	22.5	22.5
973	91.2	9.3	2.5	1.1	3.6	6.88	8.29	11.5	3.2	215.3	...	0.3	5.2	204.3	222.4	...	...	23.3	23.3
-278	89.1	10.8	4.7	1.9	6.9	8.04	7.69	13.1	3.3	223.3	...	...	10.8	202.2	229.1	...	...	22.6	22.6
-2,994	85.9	10.7	11.5	4.8	16.8	6.86	1.35	9.1	3.3	218.0	...	0.2	7.9	206.7	233.2	...	...	22.0	22.0
1,838	91.3	9.8	2.9	1.2	4.3	6.15	7.28	8.9	3.5	209.6	...	0.7	4.1	178.2	206.9	...	...	22.8	22.8
Principal Lines of Business: CompHosp/Med (90.0%), FEHBP (6.3%), Medicaid (3.2%), MedSup (0.5%)														Principal States: WI (100.0%)					
-10,067	90.1	10.3	0.2	0.1	0.8	4.34	1.85	0.5	11.3	38.5	365.8	0.4	5.8	49.9	56.1	0.5	...	33.3	35.5
4,577	88.5	11.0	3.0	0.9	10.0	5.31	10.78	3.5	9.8	44.7	0.2	0.1	20.0	46.5	51.6	...	...	33.2	37.1
41,620	87.4	12.0	3.1	1.0	9.4	5.14	15.19	5.3	8.0	56.2	...	0.1	27.9	58.2	65.3	0.3	...	38.2	43.8
-74,127	88.8	11.3	1.9	0.6	6.0	4.59	-18.51	10.0	11.6	38.5	...	0.1	-23.6	54.6	60.5	0.6	...	49.9	43.9
-37,955	89.8	11.4	-2.7	-0.7	-12.0	3.75	-1.56	13.9	21.6	21.6	...	0.2	-38.9	48.9	54.2	0.8	...	63.1	40.9
Principal Lines of Business: CompHosp/Med (75.4%), Medicare (8.1%), FEHBP (6.4%), OtherHlth (6.3%), Dental (3.6%)														Principal States: NY (100.0%)					
...	86.9	13.5	-0.8	-0.1	-1.8	2.34	2.34	15.8	14.7	66.9	...	...	-1.7	77.5	81.9	...	...	...	...
...	86.1	12.6	5.5	0.9	12.8	4.51	4.51	-1.0	12.8	83.2	...	...	13.5	94.5	94.5	...	...	...	...
...	86.4	13.7	0.2	0.0	0.5	4.80	4.80	-4.0	12.2	81.2	...	...	1.0	68.7	68.7	...	...	...	...
...	86.6	13.7	-1.6	-0.3	-4.0	2.33	2.33	24.8	16.1	51.2	...	...	-5.5	63.2	63.2	...	...	...	...
...	86.2	14.2	-4.5	-0.7	-9.5	1.06	1.22	35.1	9.4	128.7	...	...	132.4	275.0	289.7	...	...	...	...
Principal Lines of Business: CompHosp/Med (100.0%)														Principal States: WA (98.1%)					
-35	81.6	9.0	25.5	8.1	46.9	6.94	6.88	-17.0	5.7	133.2	...	2.2	-1.5	240.4	261.4	1.0	...	...	...
35	83.7	7.9	23.1	7.3	42.9	8.85	8.84	-1.4	5.9	103.3	...	3.0	-4.0	217.1	236.2	1.1	...	...	...
...	78.0	8.9	31.4	10.3	56.6	9.09	9.09	1.7	4.9	148.6	...	1.7	23.0	207.2	229.3	...	...	...	...
128	81.6	7.4	23.2	8.7	41.4	5.94	5.27	-1.8	4.6	113.1	...	1.8	3.7	223.7	240.3	...	...	...	58.1
2,112	85.8	7.5	11.1	4.7	21.7	3.02	4.46	-6.2	4.8	95.1	...	0.9	-9.3	171.4	187.0	...	...	...	...
Principal Lines of Business: Medicare (67.5%), CompHosp/Med (27.6%), FEHBP (4.9%)														Principal States: MO (76.3%), IL (23.5%)					
...	100.9	4.8	-1.0	-0.8	-8.4	3.44	3.10	0.1	5.0	11.9	...	...	-23.6	41.2	46.2	...	...	158.9	194.6
-3,503	106.2	4.0	0.6	0.5	5.3	8.01	5.73	-28.3	2.6	14.3	...	...	35.6	50.8	55.1	...	...	110.4	138.1
-12	102.8	5.0	1.1	0.9	8.3	5.06	5.23	-14.3	2.2	14.8	...	...	1.7	69.7	74.3	...	...	108.8	139.3
-870	98.3	6.2	4.2	2.7	27.6	4.77	-0.35	55.3	2.8	21.7	...	...	23.7	56.0	61.5	1.0	...	90.3	90.3
868	98.0	5.6	3.9	2.1	22.9	2.79	3.61	74.0	4.6	19.2	...	...	4.8	61.1	67.6	3.9	...	87.6	87.6
Principal Lines of Business: Medicare (74.6%), FEHBP (24.0%), Dental (1.2%), CompHosp/Med (0.3%)														Principal States: MN (100.0%)					
7,357	89.3	9.2	3.4	2.2	9.4	3.61	5.22	11.1	4.0	58.0	...	...	12.0	61.3	68.1	1.8	...	...	20.4
36,453	88.6	9.4	4.1	2.6	10.8	4.25	8.48	9.0	3.7	64.5	...	0.1	18.2	59.6	67.2	0.1	...	...	21.3
26,204	89.1	10.0	4.0	2.3	9.5	4.44	7.38	10.2	3.6	79.7	...	0.1	13.7	71.3	79.5	0.0	...	...	23.1
-10,492	90.3	9.8	2.6	1.6	6.1	4.56	1.58	3.8	4.1	63.2	...	8.6	-8.9	57.4	65.2	3.4	...	...	26.1
36,073	89.6	11.0	1.8	1.2	4.7	3.54	8.53	4.0	3.8	67.6	...	7.1	10.9	58.6	64.9	1.3	...	...	27.0
Principal Lines of Business: FEHBP (53.6%), CompHosp/Med (43.4%), Dental (1.2%), MedSup (1.1%), OtherHlth (0.8%)														Principal States: DC (62.0%), MD (23.3%), VA (14.7%)					
...	76.2	9.1	12.8	10.2	15.6	...	...	...	1.4	...	...	...	...	...	...	...	...	...	...
...	81.0	8.4	7.1	5.8	8.6	...	...	...	1.3	...	...	...	...	...	...	...	...	...	...
...	83.3	7.9	4.1	3.6	5.2	...	...	...	1.3	...	...	...	...	...	...	...	...	...	...
...	93.0	10.2	-13.2	-13.2	-17.0	...	...	...	1.7	...	...	...	...	...	...	...	...	...	...
...	81.4	7.7	2.7	1.7	3.6	...	...	...	1.8	...	...	...	...	...	...	...	...	...	...
...	38.8	76.2	2.3	16.6	2.6	2.26	2.26	1.1	0.1	784.5	...	0.6	2.9	999.9	999.9	...	...	...	...
...	78.1	68.5	0.6	4.8	0.7	3.19	3.19	-22.0	0.1	944.6	...	0.3	0.7	999.9	999.9	...	...	...	...
...	41.2	67.5	3.5	29.5	3.9	3.59	3.59	-5.5	0.1	999.9	...	0.7	4.0	999.9	999.9	...	...	...	...
...	64.5	72.6	0.6	6.1	0.6	2.74	2.74	-17.9	0.1	999.9	...	0.2	0.6	999.9	999.9	...	...	...	...
...	55.5	72.8	0.1	1.1	0.1	1.62	1.62	1.6	0.1	999.9	...	0.6	0.4	999.9	999.9	...	...	...	...
Principal Lines of Business: CrdLife (59.2%), CrdA&H (40.8%)																			
-106	60.6	39.4	1.9	1.8	11.9	4.48	4.63	-17.5	4.8	21.9	121.3	361.9	7.7	70.7	81.0	10.0	0.2	37.8	6.2
53	58.1	41.0	1.1	1.0	6.3	4.75	4.91	-10.7	4.0	24.3	133.1	360.0	5.5	69.2	81.7	2.3	0.7	41.4	6.1
-17	54.3	42.2	0.5	0.5	2.6	4.80	4.91	-14.3	2.8	28.5	115.9	304.9	22.0	70.2	81.5	3.3	3.1	37.1	4.6
-227	54.8	44.0	0.3	0.3	1.3	4.83	3.84	22.7	3.7	24.9	100.4	318.1	-5.5	73.0	83.3	9.2	1.9	63.9	4.2
439	49.9	43.3	1.3	1.5	7.3	5.05	4.63	2.6	3.9	22.0	80.7	309.5	-3.6	67.8	77.1	32.6	3.0	62.3	3.8
Principal Lines of Business: IndA&H (47.6%), GrpA&H (38.8%), OrdLife (10.0%), CrdA&H (1.4%), CrdLife (1.4%)														Principal States: IL (9.0%), MN (7.6%), CA (7.2%), TX (6.2%), IA (5.2%)					

Data in U.S. Dollars

COMPANY NAME Ultimate Parent Association Principal Officer Mailing Address Dom. : Began Bus. : Struct. : Mktg. Specialty Phone # AMB# NAIC#	Best's Financial Strength Rating FSC	Data Year	Balance Sheet Bonds (%)	Mort. Loans & R.E. (%)	Com & Pref. Stock (%)	All Other Assets (%)	Total Assets ($000)	Life Reserves (%)	Health Reserves (%)	Ann Res. & Dep. Liabilities (%)	All Other Liabilities (%)	Capital & Surplus ($000)	Operations Direct Premiums Written ($000)	Net Premiums Written & Deposits ($000)	Operating Cash Flow ($000)	NOG Before Taxes ($000)	NOG After Taxes ($000)	Net Income ($000)
GUARANTY INCOME LIFE INS CO Guaranty Corporation John H. Lancaster President P.O. Box 2231 Baton Rouge, LA 70821-2231 LA : 1926 : Stock : Agency Ind Ann, Ind Life, LTC 800-535-8110 AMB# 006504 NAIC# 64238	**B** Rating Outlook: Stable **FSC V**	'05	91.0	1.9	1.6	5.5	348,212	13.1	0.2	77.7	9.0	17,394	50,200	52,391	-22,381	665	614	588
		'06	92.0	1.6	1.8	4.6	354,021	12.6	0.3	82.5	4.7	22,639	53,248	53,081	6,773	1,261	1,280	1,715
		'07	89.2	1.3	1.9	7.5	373,694	11.4	0.3	85.0	3.3	23,597	61,276	59,143	18,867	772	822	914
		'08	83.1	1.7	2.2	12.9	407,337	10.2	0.4	87.0	2.5	22,716	70,922	70,531	36,506	1,478	942	-897
		'09	86.2	1.5	1.6	10.7	457,793	8.7	0.4	89.0	1.8	21,573	84,222	83,095	47,947	1,538	1,071	-1,630
		Rating History: B, 08/19/09; B+, 08/08/08; B+, 07/26/07; B, 11/30/06; B, 06/15/06																
GUARDIAN INS & ANNUITY CO INC Guardian Life Ins Co of America Scott Dolfi President 7 Hanover Square New York, NY 10004-4025 DE : 1971 : Stock : Agency Var ann, Group pens, Var life 212-598-8000 AMB# 008197 NAIC# 78778	**A++** Rating Outlook: Stable **FSC XV**	'05	19.2	0.0	0.6	80.1	9,855,131	1.1	...	20.6	78.3	244,429	1,160,326	1,091,375	180,318	8,776	20,394	21,585
		'06	17.1	...	0.4	82.4	10,291,227	1.1	...	19.2	79.7	228,579	1,279,014	1,214,022	-40,436	8,203	14,302	20,486
		'07	16.5	...	0.3	83.2	10,402,935	1.1	...	17.2	81.7	244,674	1,254,812	1,190,117	-169,231	7,674	17,723	19,993
		'08	22.9	...	0.3	76.8	7,502,709	1.7	...	23.6	74.7	212,558	1,008,112	941,133	33,505	-47,481	-33,411	-35,097
		'09	19.7	...	0.3	80.0	9,022,922	1.6	...	19.5	78.9	236,201	1,354,771	1,310,577	-48,873	35,732	36,008	9,899
		Rating History: A++g, 10/13/09; A++g, 11/26/08; A+ g, 04/23/08; A+ g, 11/10/06; A+ g, 11/18/05																
GUARDIAN LIFE INS CO OF AMER Guardian Life Ins Co of America Dennis J. Manning President & CEO 7 Hanover Square New York, NY 10004-4025 NY : 1860 : Mutual : Agency Group A&H, Group Life, Ind Life 212-598-8000 AMB# 006508 NAIC# 64246	**A++** Rating Outlook: Stable **FSC XV**	'05	62.8	10.3	11.1	15.8	24,806,542	79.6	6.5	3.2	10.7	3,158,570	5,760,574	6,024,755	1,362,882	325,474	277,576	375,227
		'06	61.7	10.7	11.8	15.8	26,706,999	80.0	6.2	2.8	11.0	3,490,207	5,944,667	6,126,078	1,651,001	302,961	260,601	375,759
		'07	61.0	11.5	10.5	17.0	28,328,340	80.8	5.6	2.6	11.0	3,750,545	6,176,668	6,066,338	1,579,030	348,997	218,614	292,026
		'08	60.4	12.6	5.4	21.6	28,973,450	83.7	5.3	2.7	8.3	3,658,868	6,319,447	6,054,735	1,370,369	269,571	311,513	437,309
		'09	64.8	11.4	5.7	18.0	30,895,175	84.3	4.8	2.5	8.3	4,187,965	6,295,235	6,059,565	1,928,497	190,811	124,193	27,732
		Rating History: A++g, 10/13/09; A++g, 11/26/08; A+ g, 04/23/08; A+ g, 11/10/06; A+ g, 11/18/05																
GUARDIAN LIFE OF THE CARIBBEAN Guardian Holdings Limited Ravi Tewari President 1 Guardian Drive, Westmoorings Port of Spain, Trinidad And Tobago TT : Stock : Not Available Life 868-632-5433 AMB# 084191	**A-** Rating Outlook: Negative **FSC VIII**	'05	15.7	9.4	37.6	37.4	749,297	89.9	...	...	10.1	175,675	...	122,200	31,882	7,746	4,968	7,071
		'06	15.1	16.9	38.3	29.7	758,571	91.5	...	...	8.5	178,807	...	118,781	-40,636	-2,860	-4,116	-4,759
		'07	14.6	15.9	35.9	33.6	812,237	92.1	...	...	7.9	174,695	...	131,880	36,187	-2,246	-4,732	-3,719
		'08	27.3	8.1	19.2	45.5	840,500	92.8	...	...	7.2	163,885	...	158,574	12,174	-22,252	-23,675	-4,792
		'09	32.9	6.7	16.1	44.3	909,159	93.9	...	...	6.2	165,545	...	173,564	42,654	7,689	10,033	10,088
		Rating History: A-, 06/17/09; A, 05/28/08; A, 04/02/07; A, 02/07/06; A, 12/15/04																
GUGGENHEIM LIFE AND ANNUITY CO Guggenheim Capital LLC Jeffrey S. Lange President 222 Indianapolis Boulevard, #100 Schererville, IN 46357 IA : 1985 : Stock : Inactive A&H, Group A&H, Med supp 219-864-6040 AMB# 009504 NAIC# 83607	**NR-5**	'05	44.0	...	48.9	7.2	19,984	0.0	...	...	100.0	15,567	...	0	482	658	504	491
		'06	47.1	...	51.0	1.8	21,168	0.0	...	...	100.0	16,843	...	0	101	663	503	696
		'07	47.5	...	48.2	4.3	22,231	0.0	...	...	100.0	17,538	...	0	547	720	538	609
		'08	58.7	...	37.4	3.9	18,307	0.0	...	...	100.0	16,055	...	0	-1,067	774	570	-762
		'09	76.7	...	1.2	22.1	1,302,828	0.0	...	99.4	0.6	115,721	...	-27	1,267,102	-29,246	-28,688	-27,938
		Rating History: NR-5, 05/03/10; NR-3, 05/19/09; NR-3, 06/16/08; NR-3, 06/01/07; NR-3, 06/20/06																
GULF GUARANTY LIFE INS CO Gulf Guaranty Life Insurance Company Jim Robertson President 4785 I-55 North, Suite 200 Jackson, MS 39206 MS : 1970 : Stock : Direct Response Credit Life 601-981-4920 AMB# 008081 NAIC# 77976	**B-** Rating Outlook: Stable **FSC IV**	'05	21.4	16.4	40.6	21.7	15,997	46.1	25.0	1.0	27.9	9,399	6,423	5,464	379	-434	-156	943
		'06	23.9	15.7	41.7	18.7	15,940	45.1	22.8	2.3	29.8	8,026	7,581	6,350	546	-969	-828	-236
		'07	23.8	14.8	41.6	19.8	16,245	46.5	23.4	2.7	27.4	7,524	7,713	6,400	43	-565	-487	-175
		'08	22.1	12.8	40.0	25.0	17,799	46.7	24.8	3.7	24.8	8,438	8,423	6,919	1,596	-517	-517	557
		'09	22.7	12.2	40.4	24.8	17,827	48.0	23.5	5.2	23.3	8,466	7,428	6,119	-288	75	45	-47
		Rating History: B-, 05/04/10; B-, 05/06/09; B-, 05/14/08; B-, 03/28/07; B-, 04/06/06																
GULF STATES LIFE INS CO INC David E. Link President P.O. Box 1969 Opelousas, LA 70571 LA : 1994 : Stock : Not Available Credit Life, Credit A&H 337-948-5058 AMB# 007838 NAIC# 75612	**NR-5**	'05	...	...	...	...	...	...	...	...	...	...	...	...	...	...	...	...
		'06	...	...	...	...	...	...	...	...	...	...	...	...	...	...	...	...
		'07	...	...	...	...	...	...	...	...	...	...	...	...	...	...	...	...
		'08	44.0	4.4	28.4	23.2	2,995	31.8	60.7	...	7.5	2,324	555	555	-87	208	147	123
		'09	37.5	4.2	32.5	25.8	3,136	26.7	43.5	...	29.8	2,425	970	970	68	230	158	151
		Rating History: NR-5, 06/14/10; NR-5, 06/08/09; NR-1, 06/12/08; NR-1, 06/08/07; NR-1, 06/07/06																
GUNDERSEN LUTHERAN HEALTH PLAN[2] Gundersen Lutheran, Inc. Marilu Bintz, M.D. President 1836 South Avenue La Crosse, WI 54601 WI : 1995 : Non-Profit : Broker Group A&H, Health 608-782-7300 AMB# 064204 NAIC# 95101	**NR-5**	'05	44.9	...	...	55.1	13,317	...	...	...	100.0	8,891	136,107	136,014	116	109	109	109
		'06	16.0	...	...	84.0	18,690	...	20.9	...	79.1	10,326	158,257	158,158	5,802	1,571	1,571	1,571
		'07	...	...	...	100.0	19,613	...	3.2	...	96.8	11,505	170,402	170,289	1,300	1,259	1,259	1,259
		'08	42.8	...	...	57.2	20,552	...	2.8	...	97.2	13,631	186,480	186,353	707	2,130	2,130	2,130
		'09	26.3	...	...	73.7	22,943	...	3.1	...	96.9	14,739	211,503	211,252	2,437	1,034	1,034	1,034
		Rating History: NR-5, 05/24/10; NR-5, 08/26/09; C+ pd, 07/21/08; C+ pd, 07/16/07; C+ pd, 08/28/06																
HALLMARK LIFE INSURANCE CO Centene Corporation Michele F. Salta Chairman & President 680 Newport Center Drive, Suite 270 Newport Beach, CA 92660 AZ : 1997 : Stock : Other Direct Ind Life, Credit A&H, Credit Life 949-720-1568 AMB# 060297 NAIC# 60078	**NR-2**	'05	81.7	...	...	18.3	743	81.2	7.6	...	11.2	613	...	69	25	132	118	118
		'06	38.6	...	...	61.4	715	11.6	4.5	...	83.9	287	...	46	-22	24	23	23
		'07	75.4	...	...	24.6	366	31.7	42.6	...	25.7	315	...	28	-351	27	27	27
		'08	...	...	...	100.0	2,233	...	100.0	...	...	630	...	825	782	-824	-549	-549
		'09	3.8	...	...	96.2	3,311	...	100.0	...	...	592	...	2,323	1,193	-827	-541	-541
		Rating History: NR-2, 02/19/10; NR-2, 02/10/09; NR-3, 10/15/07; NR-3, 03/19/07; NR-3, 01/20/06																

BEST'S PROFITABILITY, LEVERAGE AND LIQUIDITY TESTS 2005 – 2009

Data in U.S. Dollars

	Profitability Tests							Leverage Tests						Liquidity Tests					
Un-Realized Capital Gains ($000)	Benefits Paid to NPW & Dep (%)	Comm. & Expenses to NPW & Dep (%)	NOG to Total Assets (%)	NOG to Total Rev (%)	Operating Return on Equity (%)	Net Yield (%)	Total Return (%)	Change in NPW & Dep (%)	NPW & Dep to Capital (X)	Capital & Surplus to Liabilities (%)	Surplus Relief (%)	Reins Leverage (%)	Change in Capital (%)	Quick Liquidity (%)	Current Liquidity (%)	Non-Invest Grade Bonds to Capital (%)	Delinq. & Foreclosed Mortgages to Capital (%)	Mort. & Credit Tenant Loans & R.E. to Capital (%)	Affiliated Invest to Capital (%)
225	103.2	14.2	0.2	0.9	3.7	4.74	5.16	-15.9	2.8	5.6	-0.1	502.1	10.5	85.7	90.5	25.7	...	35.2	8.2
690	109.5	13.2	0.4	1.8	6.4	5.20	5.83	1.3	2.2	7.2	0.6	297.6	28.5	84.4	89.2	22.9	...	23.8	3.5
60	83.4	10.5	0.2	1.1	3.6	5.36	5.66	11.4	2.4	7.1	0.5	255.9	4.1	83.2	88.4	25.5	...	20.1	5.1
-1,214	62.5	9.0	0.2	1.1	4.1	5.52	4.93	19.3	3.1	6.0	0.8	246.6	-7.4	75.6	84.0	55.1	...	30.2	14.5
407	46.9	7.9	0.2	1.1	4.8	4.87	4.51	17.8	3.8	5.0	1.1	266.4	-4.5	78.3	86.9	70.3	...	31.3	14.7
Principal Lines of Business: IndAnn (94.1%), IndA&H (3.5%), OrdLife (2.3%)														Principal States: TX (26.4%), WA (20.4%), LA (8.7%), FL (6.1%), OR (5.7%)					
2,848	147.7	13.3	0.2	1.5	8.6	5.06	4.97	-3.6	4.1	12.9	5.2	13.8	7.4	86.4	99.4	45.0	...	0.4	13.2
-8,551	139.4	12.4	0.1	1.0	6.0	5.19	5.08	11.2	4.8	12.6	5.7	23.4	-4.3	89.7	103.5	49.7	...	...	6.2
-3,411	160.3	13.4	0.2	1.2	7.5	5.35	5.29	-2.0	4.5	14.8	5.3	12.8	5.3	82.7	97.9	36.3	...	...	7.2
-17,486	155.8	14.4	-0.4	-2.8	-14.6	5.10	4.03	-20.9	4.1	12.3	7.6	55.4	-13.4	77.5	91.0	33.2	...	...	11.8
14,439	79.8	12.5	0.4	2.4	16.0	4.97	4.30	39.3	5.1	14.5	8.4	46.3	11.7	75.3	90.0	27.8	...	...	15.7
Principal Lines of Business: IndAnn (71.8%), GrpAnn (27.5%), OrdLife (0.7%), GrpLife (0.0%)														Principal States: NY (17.0%), NJ (8.2%), FL (8.0%), CA (7.6%), PA (5.8%)					
41,101	62.6	21.9	1.2	3.8	9.2	5.82	6.75	5.1	1.7	16.9	4.4	61.2	7.5	44.1	59.1	29.7	0.1	70.8	22.9
78,541	59.5	23.0	1.0	3.5	7.8	5.75	6.83	1.7	1.5	17.6	3.3	60.5	11.4	41.9	56.9	34.4	0.0	71.6	30.6
13,887	61.6	24.2	0.8	2.9	6.0	5.72	6.36	-1.0	1.4	17.9	3.0	60.2	7.5	40.4	55.9	29.1	1.2	75.4	29.6
-607,618	61.6	22.9	1.1	4.2	8.4	5.60	4.06	-0.2	1.6	15.5	4.8	65.1	-9.4	40.2	54.9	39.4	0.0	93.3	33.2
261,748	62.2	25.1	0.4	1.6	3.2	5.65	6.35	0.1	1.3	17.3	2.6	59.9	17.1	37.0	53.1	35.9	0.0	77.2	33.3
Principal Lines of Business: OrdLife (49.0%), GrpA&H (43.5%), GrpLife (4.9%), IndAnn (2.6%), GrpAnn (0.0%)														Principal States: NY (16.2%), CA (8.4%), NJ (6.6%), FL (5.1%), TX (4.9%)					
-173	90.7	36.1	0.7	3.0	2.8	4.88	5.24	20.4	69.6	30.6	...	...	-0.1	92.0	82.5	...	...	40.0	...
949	86.9	41.9	-0.6	-2.8	-2.3	4.56	4.45	-2.8	66.4	30.8	...	...	1.8	84.1	92.6	...	...	71.8	...
-1,395	84.5	40.2	-0.6	-2.9	-2.7	4.07	4.23	11.0	75.5	27.4	...	...	-2.3	83.6	85.2	...	...	73.9	...
3,682	79.1	39.9	-2.9	-12.7	-14.0	5.29	8.13	20.2	96.8	24.2	...	...	-6.2	82.8	73.3	...	...	41.4	21.1
76	84.2	35.8	1.2	4.6	6.1	5.30	5.31	9.5	104.8	22.3	...	...	1.0	85.0	73.0	...	...	36.8	20.5
202	...	999.9	2.6	68.2	3.3	3.30	4.80	-90.1	0.0	721.7	...	...	4.0	610.3	706.2	0.7	...	...	...
681	...	999.9	2.4	68.4	3.1	3.22	7.93	9.5	0.0	843.2	...	...	7.8	646.0	751.2	0.4	...	...	...
192	...	999.9	2.5	65.9	3.1	3.55	5.04	9.5	0.0	781.9	...	...	4.2	617.1	716.8	...	...	...	...
-1,883	...	999.9	2.8	69.2	3.4	3.89	-11.14	10.0	0.0	999.9	...	...	-11.4	999.9	999.9	0.0	...	...	...
-599	-99.9	999.9	-4.3	-99.9	-43.5	2.47	2.57	-99.9	0.0	10.2	...	...	588.5	71.9	84.5	63.2	...	...	...
Principal Lines of Business: IndAnn (100.0%)																			
-872	24.3	91.3	-1.0	-2.5	-1.6	1.68	3.71	5.9	0.6	162.6	1.7	11.6	-6.3	153.7	175.0	...	...	26.5	42.6
1,655	25.7	88.3	-5.2	-11.1	-9.5	2.00	17.46	16.2	0.7	136.7	4.4	15.8	-7.1	162.1	184.9	...	...	27.3	47.3
-1,846	22.6	86.5	-3.0	-6.5	-6.3	2.07	-7.07	0.8	0.7	119.9	4.8	20.7	-3.8	134.9	151.6	...	...	27.1	48.6
-2,826	23.9	85.2	-3.0	-6.3	-6.5	2.39	-6.62	8.1	0.7	123.3	5.6	20.7	11.0	140.4	152.6	...	...	23.3	42.6
96	24.3	89.2	0.3	0.6	0.5	2.08	2.17	-11.6	0.6	123.2	5.3	24.4	0.1	131.3	142.9	1.0	...	22.1	42.4
Principal Lines of Business: CrdLife (59.6%), CrdA&H (26.2%), IndLife (8.6%), IndAnn (3.1%), GrpA&H (1.4%)														Principal States: MS (67.5%), LA (24.9%), TN (7.2%)					
...	...	...	...	...	...	...	...	...	...	...	...	...	...	...	...	...	...	...	...
...	...	...	...	...	...	...	...	...	...	...	...	...	...	...	...	...	...	...	...
...	...	...	...	...	...	...	...	...	...	...	...	...	...	...	...	...	...	...	...
-275	52.2	78.6	...	21.6	...	...	...	...	0.2	346.3	...	...	...	355.0	397.5	...	...	5.6	...
147	17.3	80.8	5.2	14.9	6.7	2.54	7.18	74.9	0.4	458.5	...	...	10.8	480.3	535.8	...	...	5.1	...
Principal Lines of Business: CrdLife (72.2%), CrdA&H (27.8%)														Principal States: LA (100.0%)					
...	93.1	7.1	0.8	0.1	1.2	3.18	3.18	15.8	15.3	200.8	...	...	0.7	336.0	345.0	...	...	...	...
...	93.1	6.5	9.8	1.0	16.4	5.82	5.82	16.3	15.3	123.5	...	0.8	16.1	341.3	356.6	...	...	...	...
...	93.0	6.9	6.6	0.7	11.5	6.08	6.08	7.7	14.8	141.9	...	...	11.4	401.6	421.3	...	...	...	...
...	92.7	6.4	10.6	1.1	16.9	2.93	2.93	9.4	13.7	197.0	...	0.3	18.5	400.1	409.9	...	...	...	...
...	93.7	5.9	4.8	0.5	7.3	0.76	0.76	13.4	14.3	179.7	...	...	8.1	422.9	437.5	...	...	...	...
Principal Lines of Business: Medicare (49.9%), CompHosp/Med (41.2%), Medicaid (8.8%)														Principal States: WI (99.6%)					
...	-1.4	78.9	15.9	122.2	21.1	3.86	3.83	-58.2	0.1	474.5	...	...	20.1	585.6	593.8	...	...	...	...
...	107.5	83.7	3.2	31.6	5.1	3.89	3.81	-33.6	0.2	66.8	...	...	-53.3	260.0	260.0	...	...	...	...
...	68.2	103.9	5.0	57.1	9.1	3.84	3.67	-37.9	0.1	615.0	...	...	9.8	836.1	836.1	...	...	...	...
...	194.8	1.7	-42.3	-65.6	-99.9	1.92	1.63	999.9	1.3	39.3	...	...	100.2	121.5	127.1	...	...	...	...
...	135.9	0.3	-19.5	-23.2	-88.7	0.52	0.75	181.4	3.9	21.8	...	124.8	-6.0	157.3	165.2	...	...	...	...
Principal Lines of Business: GrpA&H (100.0%)																			

Data in U.S. Dollars

COMPANY NAME Ultimate Parent Association Principal Officer Mailing Address Dom. : Began Bus. : Struct. : Mktg. Specialty Phone # AMB# NAIC#	Best's Financial Strength Rating FSC	Data Year	Balance Sheet										Operations					
			Bonds (%)	Mort. Loans & R.E. (%)	Com & Pref. Stock (%)	All Other Assets (%)	Total Assets ($000)	Life Reserves (%)	Health Reserves (%)	Ann Res. & Dep. Liabilities (%)	All Other Liabilities (%)	Capital & Surplus ($000)	Direct Premiums Written ($000)	Net Premiums Written & Deposits ($000)	Operating Cash Flow ($000)	NOG Before Taxes ($000)	NOG After Taxes ($000)	Net Income ($000)
HANNOVER LIFE REASR BM LTD HDI V.a.G.	**A**	'05	...	...	...	...	...	...	...	...	...	...	...	...	...	...	...	...
Colin Rainer CEO		'06	...	...	...	...	...	...	...	...	...	...	...	...	...	...	...	...
Victoria Place - 2nd Floor	Rating Outlook: Stable	'07	96.6	...	...	3.4	178,978	80.0	...	...	20.0	176,841	...	...	...	1,287	1,287	1,290
Hamilton HM 10, Bermuda BM : Stock		'08	57.1	...	...	42.9	213,978	17.0	...	...	83.0	184,874	...	...	...	10,907	10,907	12,989
Life 1-441-294-3110		'09	51.7	...	...	48.3	282,920	31.1	...	...	68.9	213,968	...	...	...	23,501	23,501	22,787
AMB# 088859	FSC XV	**Rating History: A g, 02/17/10; A g, 07/20/09; A g, 08/19/08**																
HANNOVER LIFE REASSURANCE AMER HDI V.a.G.	**A**	'05	59.3	1.5	1.4	37.9	1,305,931	17.8	10.1	6.9	65.3	113,145	...	283,775	37,794	1,278	1,278	3,406
Peter R. Schaefer President & CEO		'06	57.6	1.8	1.0	39.7	1,542,039	16.8	8.5	5.0	69.6	111,396	...	279,309	185,344	2,604	2,604	2,381
800 N. Magnolia Avenue, Suite 1400	Rating Outlook: Stable	'07	52.4	2.0	0.6	44.9	1,710,630	15.8	7.7	4.4	72.1	136,570	...	295,472	7,706	28,379	28,379	30,319
Orlando, FL 32803-3268 FL : 1988 : Stock : Other		'08	24.6	1.1	0.3	74.0	3,572,590	21.5	4.2	1.2	73.1	128,073	...	788,343	7,596	-4,680	-4,805	-11,357
Reins 407-649-8411		'09	41.2	1.1	0.0	57.7	3,499,867	14.4	4.7	9.3	71.6	140,766	...	403,006	713,958	4,195	-4,142	-6,057
AMB# 068031 NAIC# 88340	FSC XV	**Rating History: A g, 07/20/09; A g, 07/16/08; A g, 03/13/08; A g, 09/11/07; A g, 08/29/06**																
HARLEYSVILLE LIFE INS CO Harleysville Mutual Insurance Company	**A-**	'05	75.0	...	...	25.0	375,733	31.6	1.5	47.1	19.8	24,090	76,061	54,361	23,329	1,231	920	1,518
Theodore A. Majewski President & COO		'06	80.6	...	...	19.4	372,677	34.5	1.6	48.5	15.4	23,655	71,446	47,438	-4,200	-3,768	-2,765	-2,757
355 Maple Avenue	Rating Outlook: Stable	'07	85.8	...	...	14.2	374,093	37.6	1.7	47.9	12.7	21,197	78,301	52,702	1,997	-2,230	-2,015	-2,015
Harleysville, PA 19438-2297 PA : 1961 : Stock : Agency		'08	87.7	...	...	12.3	341,303	42.1	1.8	53.5	2.5	20,319	79,267	51,711	-38,622	-1,713	-1,304	-4,946
Group Life, Ind Ann, Ind Life 215-513-6400		'09	90.1	...	...	9.9	356,484	42.2	1.9	53.3	2.6	18,967	78,986	53,291	17,957	-3,040	-3,003	-2,773
AMB# 006517 NAIC# 64327	FSC V	**Rating History: A-, 04/27/10; B++, 02/04/09; B++, 01/17/08; B++, 12/14/06; B++, 05/09/06**																
HARTFORD INTERNAT LIFE REASSUR Hartford Financial Services Group Inc	**A-**	'05	32.0	...	...	68.0	1,197,755	93.9	0.1	...	6.1	82,348	...	20,261	-547,061	26,999	19,248	20,174
John C. Walters Chairman, President & CEO		'06	29.1	...	3.4	67.5	1,144,149	92.8	...	...	7.2	83,314	...	18,435	-39,720	25,802	16,979	19,114
200 Hopmeadow Street	Rating Outlook: Stable	'07	30.9	...	2.7	66.3	1,135,919	95.6	...	...	4.4	106,354	...	12,623	-2,131	13,949	4,086	3,718
Simsbury, CT 06089 CT : 1987 : Stock : Not Available		'08	29.3	...	2.1	68.7	1,115,772	96.0	...	...	4.0	102,380	...	9,780	-13,453	10,884	4,721	4,355
Reins 860-525-8555		'09	31.9	...	...	68.1	1,129,423	95.5	...	...	4.5	91,849	...	11,993	19,166	7,550	4,182	-3,299
AMB# 009117 NAIC# 93505	FSC VII	**Rating History: A-, 03/24/10; A-, 02/27/09; A, 12/23/08; A u, 10/06/08; A, 05/23/08**																
HARTFORD LIFE & ACCIDENT INS Hartford Financial Services Group Inc	**A**	'05	54.7	1.3	32.8	11.1	12,173,735	20.0	60.3	7.9	11.8	4,291,340	3,000,602	4,074,785	559,282	806,338	802,960	924,448
John C. Walters Chairman, President & CEO		'06	50.9	2.1	34.5	12.5	12,966,230	19.0	58.9	7.5	14.5	4,732,992	3,450,715	4,549,101	589,279	655,251	620,211	644,450
200 Hopmeadow Street	Rating Outlook: Stable	'07	43.3	4.0	41.3	11.4	14,187,519	18.9	59.4	7.3	14.5	5,786,073	3,604,099	4,678,071	497,623	809,864	784,440	776,753
Simsbury, CT 06089 CT : 1967 : Stock : Not Available		'08	41.7	5.2	38.5	14.6	14,413,998	19.0	60.0	8.2	12.7	6,045,731	3,743,408	4,793,349	2,586,624	685,579	613,783	263,377
Ann, Life, Retirement Savings 860-525-8555		'09	45.1	4.5	40.0	10.4	14,254,524	19.4	62.5	8.2	9.9	6,005,261	3,767,255	3,956,461	1,012,217	238,804	234,976	70,450
AMB# 007285 NAIC# 70815	FSC XV	**Rating History: A g, 03/24/10; A g, 02/27/09; A+ g, 12/23/08; A+ gu, 10/06/08; A+ g, 05/23/08**																
HARTFORD LIFE AND ANNUITY INS Hartford Financial Services Group Inc	**A**	'05	7.3	0.2	0.0	92.5	75,100,486	3.1	0.0	5.4	91.5	1,490,266	9,133,177	9,332,637	104,188	261,501	219,038	219,092
John C. Walters Chairman, President & CEO		'06	6.1	0.2	0.3	93.4	83,086,138	3.4	0.0	4.7	92.0	1,667,679	9,936,139	9,977,433	-13,185	411,329	379,367	338,711
200 Hopmeadow Street	Rating Outlook: Stable	'07	6.3	0.4	0.4	92.9	89,347,777	2.7	0.0	4.3	93.0	2,556,588	11,045,000	10,459,324	1,044,856	454,724	366,275	284,516
Simsbury, CT 06089 CT : 1965 : Stock : Not Available		'08	12.8	1.0	0.4	85.8	65,460,546	3.6	0.0	13.6	82.8	2,177,858	7,861,654	9,453,938	5,905,741	-3,190,012	-2,944,267	-1,983,105
Ann, Life, Retirement Savings 860-525-8555		'09	11.7	0.7	1.6	86.0	73,406,512	3.3	0.0	8.6	88.1	4,085,601	3,748,791	-55,059,834	577,041	3,125,390	2,678,682	2,408,611
AMB# 007325 NAIC# 71153	FSC XV	**Rating History: A g, 03/24/10; A g, 02/27/09; A+ g, 12/23/08; A+ gu, 10/06/08; A+ g, 05/23/08**																
HARTFORD LIFE INS CO Hartford Financial Services Group Inc	**A**	'05	20.2	0.7	1.4	77.6	120,590,126	2.1	0.1	19.7	78.1	3,021,666	9,872,807	13,567,281	2,795,316	211,864	172,365	171,508
John C. Walters Chairman, President & CEO		'06	17.1	1.2	2.2	79.5	146,277,717	1.7	0.1	18.1	80.1	3,275,572	11,889,753	14,470,073	3,594,993	622,902	549,944	552,982
200 Hopmeadow Street	Rating Outlook: Stable	'07	16.4	1.7	2.6	79.3	165,997,882	1.6	0.1	17.0	81.3	4,448,474	16,772,615	19,056,008	4,084,259	350,877	282,972	191,483
Simsbury, CT 06089 CT : 1979 : Stock : Not Available		'08	19.3	2.3	2.9	75.6	133,562,466	2.0	0.1	21.8	76.1	4,071,384	9,386,136	11,327,579	961,783	-2,661,209	-2,179,124	-2,533,318
Ann, Retirement Savings, Life 860-525-8555		'09	16.3	1.9	3.2	78.5	140,231,960	1.9	0.1	19.2	78.8	5,365,015	6,309,204	8,115,763	-4,105,205	1,045,982	1,194,155	-538,834
AMB# 006518 NAIC# 88072	FSC XV	**Rating History: A g, 03/24/10; A g, 02/27/09; A+ g, 12/23/08; A+ gu, 10/06/08; A+ g, 05/23/08**																
HARVARD PILGRIM HEALTH CARE Harvard Pilgrim Health Care Inc	**B++**	'05	72.3	3.5	2.7	21.5	636,191	...	17.4	...	82.6	289,920	2,034,039	2,034,039	39,318	65,570	65,570	64,984
Eric H. Schultz President & CEO		'06	69.9	1.3	4.1	24.6	731,691	...	15.9	...	84.1	321,947	2,196,295	2,196,295	67,212	69,597	69,597	68,354
93 Worcester Street	Rating Outlook: Stable	'07	69.8	1.1	6.1	22.9	754,154	...	26.1	...	73.9	373,473	2,066,256	2,066,256	55,163	36,738	36,738	38,075
Wellesley, MA 02481-9181 MA : 1969 : Non-Profit : Broker		'08	72.4	0.7	8.1	18.8	748,226	...	26.5	...	73.5	386,733	2,049,438	2,049,438	-3,667	54,831	54,831	52,292
Health 617-263-6000		'09	67.5	4.2	14.7	13.7	801,144	...	15.3	...	84.7	381,956	2,078,608	2,077,767	26,993	26,813	26,813	23,964
AMB# 068973 NAIC# 96911	FSC IX	**Rating History: B++g, 05/06/10; B++g, 02/18/09; B++g, 02/25/08; B++g, 02/13/07; B pd, 07/18/05**																
HARVARD PILGRIM HLTH CARE OFNE Harvard Pilgrim Health Care Inc	**B++**	'05	80.1	...	...	19.9	49,164	...	45.0	...	55.0	22,643	176,173	176,173	5,616	6,632	6,632	6,540
Eric H. Schultz President & CEO		'06	87.5	...	...	12.5	57,561	...	43.6	...	56.4	23,564	242,297	242,297	11,419	1,145	1,145	1,002
93 Worcester Street	Rating Outlook: Stable	'07	76.2	...	...	23.8	70,189	...	46.9	...	53.1	28,621	336,066	336,066	2,930	5,229	5,229	5,228
Wellesley, MA 02481-9181 MA : 1980 : Non-Profit : Broker		'08	91.0	...	...	9.0	81,025	...	38.2	...	61.8	33,712	344,748	344,748	20,456	-4,123	-4,123	-4,480
Group A&H, Health 781-263-6000		'09	92.8	...	...	7.2	78,689	...	36.9	...	63.1	36,554	360,040	359,877	-879	-13,624	-13,624	-12,421
AMB# 064342 NAIC# 96717	FSC IX	**Rating History: B++g, 05/06/10; B++g, 02/18/09; B++g, 02/25/08; B++g, 02/13/07; NR-5, 06/15/06**																

2010 BEST'S KEY RATING GUIDE — LIFE/HEALTH EDITION
BEST'S PROFITABILITY, LEVERAGE AND LIQUIDITY TESTS 2005 – 2009

Data in U.S. Dollars

	Profitability Tests							Leverage Tests						Liquidity Tests					
Un-Realized Capital Gains ($000)	Benefits Paid to NPW & Dep (%)	Comm. & Expenses to NPW & Dep (%)	NOG to Total Assets (%)	NOG to Total Rev (%)	Operating Return on Equity (%)	Net Yield (%)	Total Return (%)	Change in NPW & Dep (%)	NPW & Dep to Capital (X)	Capital & Surplus to Liabilities (%)	Surplus Relief (%)	Reins Leverage (%)	Change in Capital (%)	Quick Liquidity (%)	Current Liquidity (%)	Non-Invest Grade Bonds to Capital (%)	Delinq. & Foreclosed Mortgages to Capital (%)	Mort. & Credit Tenant Loans & R.E. to Capital (%)	Affiliated Invest to Capital (%)
...	...	...	...	...	...	...	...	...	...	...	...	...	...	...	...	...	...	...	...
...	...	...	...	...	...	...	...	...	...	...	...	...	...	...	...	...	...	...	...
-1,197	...	...	...	30.7	...	...	...	...	...	999.9	...	...	...	999.9	999.9	...	...	...	...
2,632	...	...	5.6	20.1	6.0	4.46	5.83	...	...	635.2	...	...	4.5	444.6	420.0	...	...	...	...
3,222	...	...	9.5	14.1	11.8	3.92	3.43	...	...	310.3	...	...	15.7	235.3	212.1	...	...	...	...
-584	80.9	31.3	0.1	0.3	1.3	4.77	5.12	-5.4	2.5	9.7	72.8	986.0	32.0	54.3	61.0	6.9	...	16.7	7.8
122	88.8	33.9	0.2	0.4	2.3	5.10	5.22	-1.6	2.4	8.0	206.3	999.9	-1.2	60.2	67.1	4.5	...	23.8	...
174	91.8	37.4	1.7	5.1	22.9	5.06	5.41	5.8	2.1	9.0	117.6	999.9	23.1	54.4	60.7	2.7	...	24.4	...
-670	39.7	13.4	-0.2	-0.1	-3.6	4.72	4.07	166.8	6.1	3.8	641.1	999.9	-7.5	25.7	28.2	3.6	...	30.3	...
576	84.6	39.4	-0.1	-0.2	-3.1	4.34	4.14	-48.9	2.8	4.3	381.6	999.9	11.6	41.6	46.5	8.3	0.6	26.0	...
Principal Lines of Business: OrdLife (41.7%), IndA&H (34.8%), GrpA&H (12.6%), IndAnn (8.6%), CrdLife (0.8%)																			
-329	61.5	29.9	0.3	1.2	3.8	4.69	4.79	5.1	2.2	7.2	18.1	240.1	-1.4	86.0	93.1	34.6	...	...	...
11	81.0	35.9	-0.7	-4.0	-11.6	4.79	4.80	-12.7	1.9	7.0	19.4	303.0	-2.6	84.4	92.1	...	...	...	...
-108	84.0	34.2	-0.5	-2.7	-9.0	4.85	4.81	11.1	2.4	6.3	26.6	431.8	-9.6	89.8	98.6	10.9	...	...	...
108	81.1	38.3	-0.4	-1.8	-6.3	5.14	4.11	-1.9	2.5	6.5	24.8	505.0	-6.4	84.4	93.6	4.5	...	...	...
...	74.7	35.4	-0.9	-4.0	-15.3	5.27	5.34	3.1	2.7	5.8	25.7	613.9	-5.6	81.8	91.1	...	...	...	...
Principal Lines of Business: IndAnn (31.6%), OrdLife (30.0%), GrpLife (21.4%), GrpA&H (17.0%), IndA&H (0.1%)														Principal States: PA (42.1%), NJ (13.3%), MA (6.4%), VA (6.2%), MD (4.9%)					
...	999.9	-23.6	1.3	22.7	23.7	5.09	5.25	-5.7	0.2	7.6	-4.0	22.5	2.6	31.9	38.6	19.4	...	4.4	...
-80	646.3	-34.0	1.5	21.2	20.5	6.00	6.24	-9.0	0.2	8.0	-2.5	20.0	0.1	33.1	40.3	...	...	...	...
80	421.8	18.9	0.4	5.2	4.3	5.98	5.98	-31.5	0.1	10.5	0.1	15.5	27.6	31.0	38.3	11.7	...	...	...
...	568.3	39.3	0.4	6.1	4.5	6.25	6.21	-22.5	0.1	10.2	...	12.8	-4.3	25.4	31.3	12.3	...	...	...
...	489.6	29.1	0.4	5.3	4.3	6.20	5.52	22.6	0.1	8.9	...	12.1	-11.4	24.4	31.0	24.1	...	...	...
Principal Lines of Business: OrdLife (79.2%), GrpLife (20.8%)																			
-324,344	60.7	27.6	6.4	17.5	17.2	8.72	7.20	0.5	0.9	54.7	0.0	5.8	-18.2	52.4	70.1	5.2	...	4.1	87.4
162,531	58.7	27.8	4.9	13.0	13.7	6.80	8.47	11.6	0.9	60.2	0.0	5.1	13.2	51.4	71.1	6.2	...	5.9	82.8
797,552	59.2	26.6	5.8	15.7	14.9	7.55	13.87	2.8	0.8	70.9	0.0	4.5	20.8	48.3	67.2	3.7	...	9.9	88.2
-2,591,237	58.4	25.3	4.3	12.8	10.4	5.57	-14.21	2.5	0.8	72.4	0.0	4.2	2.8	50.0	67.2	3.5	...	12.4	84.2
-1,111,331	58.0	30.6	1.6	6.2	3.9	3.16	-5.76	-17.5	0.7	72.9	0.0	3.4	-0.7	51.3	67.8	5.7	...	10.7	90.3
Principal Lines of Business: GrpA&H (68.5%), GrpLife (15.4%), GrpAnn (15.3%), OrdLife (0.8%), IndA&H (0.0%)														Principal States: CA (7.9%), TX (6.4%), FL (6.3%), PA (5.3%), NC (4.0%)					
-7,075	77.8	12.7	0.3	2.3	15.7	5.24	5.26	-20.8	6.1	29.0	5.7	72.4	14.0	67.3	88.3	12.5	...	9.2	6.1
-35,674	93.8	13.4	0.5	3.7	24.0	5.33	4.21	6.9	5.8	33.8	5.7	73.4	12.1	70.8	92.2	12.0	...	11.5	3.4
262,434	94.6	11.5	0.4	3.3	17.3	4.93	7.49	4.8	4.0	45.9	13.1	84.6	52.3	66.7	91.1	7.2	...	14.9	1.3
731,680	112.5	11.5	-3.8	-25.4	-99.9	3.48	19.51	-9.6	4.3	17.2	10.5	156.9	-16.1	73.9	85.7	7.5	...	29.7	1.5
-1,127,255	-11.0	-1.4	3.9	76.0	85.5	3.80	-6.14	-99.9	-13.4	40.2	5.2	108.6	88.3	64.3	87.1	5.8	...	12.8	70.5
Principal Lines of Business: IndAnn (101.5%), GrpLife (0.0%), IndA&H (0.0%), GrpAnn (-0.1%), OrdLife (-1.4%)														Principal States: CA (13.1%), TX (7.2%), FL (6.8%), IL (5.4%), PA (4.2%)					
205,136	76.2	5.9	0.1	1.3	5.5	5.37	6.19	-0.4	4.1	12.5	1.7	78.9	-3.4	50.4	68.5	24.1	...	32.6	47.8
142,943	78.4	6.4	0.4	3.8	17.5	5.77	6.29	6.7	3.9	12.3	1.7	70.5	11.2	45.7	66.2	26.7	...	49.1	47.6
978,370	67.8	5.6	0.2	1.4	7.3	6.09	8.69	31.7	3.9	14.6	2.3	53.8	32.5	41.2	62.3	21.3	...	60.2	55.2
-341,617	104.9	7.7	-1.5	-17.3	-51.2	5.00	3.15	-40.6	2.8	11.3	2.2	64.1	-15.8	48.5	65.7	28.7	...	76.7	57.9
-85,604	123.8	8.1	0.9	14.2	25.3	3.92	-1.03	-28.4	1.5	17.4	0.9	41.9	30.6	49.7	67.1	31.8	...	52.5	79.8
Principal Lines of Business: GrpAnn (72.4%), IndAnn (23.3%), OrdLife (2.1%), GrpLife (1.2%), GrpA&H (1.0%)														Principal States: CT (22.7%), NY (10.3%), CA (7.7%), TX (5.6%), FL (4.9%)					
1,639	84.3	13.4	10.6	3.2	24.6	3.89	4.09	-3.2	7.0	83.7	...	...	19.1	136.7	153.7	0.2	...	7.6	13.5
621	85.3	12.9	10.2	3.1	22.7	4.74	4.64	8.0	6.8	78.6	...	...	11.0	130.9	145.9	...	...	3.1	12.3
1,964	87.5	11.8	4.9	1.8	10.6	3.49	4.00	-5.9	5.5	98.1	...	...	16.0	162.5	178.8	0.1	...	2.2	11.3
-13,493	88.4	10.1	7.3	2.6	14.4	3.39	1.01	-0.8	5.3	107.0	...	...	3.6	157.4	175.5	2.4	...	1.4	9.1
23,500	89.6	9.8	3.5	1.3	7.0	2.99	6.04	1.4	5.4	91.1	...	0.1	-1.2	135.9	152.3	0.8	...	8.7	19.5
Principal Lines of Business: CompHosp/Med (85.7%), Medicare (14.3%)														Principal States: MA (95.0%), ME (4.4%)					
...	82.2	14.8	15.3	3.7	34.2	3.18	2.95	26.8	7.8	85.4	...	...	40.8	137.9	151.9	0.4	...	...	...
...	83.4	17.0	2.1	0.5	5.0	4.52	4.22	37.5	10.3	69.3	...	...	4.1	136.7	151.5	...	...	...	...
...	85.2	14.1	8.2	1.5	20.0	4.99	4.99	38.7	11.7	68.9	...	4.9	21.5	118.4	130.8	...	...	...	...
-355	88.9	13.1	-5.5	-1.2	-13.2	4.33	3.25	2.6	10.2	71.3	...	2.5	17.8	141.9	154.4	2.0	...	...	...
117	91.9	12.5	-17.1	-3.8	-38.8	2.71	4.48	4.4	9.8	86.8	...	1.6	8.4	136.1	158.3	0.1	...	...	...
Principal Lines of Business: CompHosp/Med (93.4%), Medicare (6.6%)														Principal States: NH (100.0%)					

Data in U.S. Dollars

COMPANY NAME / Ultimate Parent Association / Principal Officer / Mailing Address / Dom. : Began Bus. : Struct. : Mktg. / Specialty / Phone # / AMB# / NAIC# — Best's Financial Strength Rating — FSC

Balance Sheet: Bonds (%), Mort. Loans & R.E. (%), Com & Pref. Stock (%), All Other Assets (%), Total Assets ($000), Life Reserves (%), Health Reserves (%), Ann Res. & Dep. Liabilities (%), All Other Liabilities (%), Capital & Surplus ($000). Operations: Direct Premiums Written ($000), Net Premiums Written & Deposits ($000), Operating Cash Flow ($000), NOG Before Taxes ($000), NOG After Taxes ($000), Net Income ($000).

HAWAII DENTAL SERVICE
Faye W. Kurren
President & CEO
700 Bishop Street, Suite 700
Honolulu, HI 96813-4196
HI : Non-Profit : Not Available
Dental
808-521-1431
AMB# 058183

A- — Rating Outlook: Stable — FSC VIII

Data Year	Bonds (%)	Mort. Loans & R.E. (%)	Com & Pref. Stock (%)	All Other Assets (%)	Total Assets ($000)	Life Reserves (%)	Health Reserves (%)	Ann Res. & Dep. Liabilities (%)	All Other Liabilities (%)	Capital & Surplus ($000)	Direct Premiums Written ($000)	Net Premiums Written & Deposits ($000)	Operating Cash Flow ($000)	NOG Before Taxes ($000)	NOG After Taxes ($000)	Net Income ($000)
'05	...	...	...	...	82,420	...	...	...	...	69,968	...	152,865	...	...	...	13,348
'06	...	...	...	...	98,487	...	...	...	...	85,851	...	162,975	...	...	...	14,394
'07	...	...	...	...	121,042	...	...	...	...	104,848	...	168,916	...	...	...	16,847
'08	...	...	...	...	116,246	...	...	...	...	97,361	...	173,883	...	...	...	1,661
'09	...	...	...	...	128,402	...	...	...	...	110,392	...	176,777	...	...	...	12,466

Rating History: A-, 04/01/10; A-, 02/04/09; A-, 10/12/07; A-, 12/28/06; A-, 11/17/05

HAWAII MANAGEMENT ALLIANCE ASN[2]
J. Terrence Mullen
President & COO
737 Bishop Street, Suite 2390
Honolulu, HI 96813
HI : 1990 : Non-Profit : Agency
Group A&H
808-591-0088
AMB# 064547 NAIC# 48330

NR-5

Data Year	Bonds (%)	Mort. Loans & R.E. (%)	Com & Pref. Stock (%)	All Other Assets (%)	Total Assets ($000)	Life Reserves (%)	Health Reserves (%)	Ann Res. & Dep. Liabilities (%)	All Other Liabilities (%)	Capital & Surplus ($000)	Direct Premiums Written ($000)	Net Premiums Written & Deposits ($000)	Operating Cash Flow ($000)	NOG Before Taxes ($000)	NOG After Taxes ($000)	Net Income ($000)
'05	...	...	...	100.0	27,346	...	23.7	...	76.3	13,980	86,055	82,417	9,316	10,726	7,079	7,079
'06	...	...	...	100.0	25,349	...	6.5	...	93.5	15,421	88,831	24,213	-3,123	2,308	1,441	1,441
'07	12.8	...	24.7	62.5	27,181	...	5.7	...	94.3	17,663	94,228	13,449	2,158	3,283	2,189	2,189
'08	21.6	...	...	78.4	28,548	...	6.8	...	93.2	19,111	95,972	14,047	1,268	3,396	2,240	1,771
'09	21.8	...	...	78.2	28,925	...	18.7	...	81.3	19,489	92,786	37,101	417	226	218	267

Rating History: NR-5, 04/21/10; NR-5, 04/15/09; NR-5, 04/16/08; NR-5, 04/09/07; NR-5, 04/27/06

HAWAII MEDICAL SERVICE ASSN[2]
Hawaii Medical Service Association
Robert P. Hiam
President & CEO
P.O. Box 860
Honolulu, HI 96808
HI : 1938 : Non-Profit : Not Available
Group A&H
808-948-5145
AMB# 064035 NAIC# 49948

NR-5

Data Year	Bonds (%)	Mort. Loans & R.E. (%)	Com & Pref. Stock (%)	All Other Assets (%)	Total Assets ($000)	Life Reserves (%)	Health Reserves (%)	Ann Res. & Dep. Liabilities (%)	All Other Liabilities (%)	Capital & Surplus ($000)	Direct Premiums Written ($000)	Net Premiums Written & Deposits ($000)	Operating Cash Flow ($000)	NOG Before Taxes ($000)	NOG After Taxes ($000)	Net Income ($000)
'05	30.1	4.9	44.9	20.1	884,253	...	44.8	...	55.2	555,985	1,716,312	1,716,312	50,933	35,319	25,043	25,456
'06	27.2	4.6	50.8	17.4	905,912	...	51.7	...	48.3	567,649	1,805,729	1,805,729	-53,209	-4,662	16,624	17,796
'07	25.4	4.7	56.1	13.8	875,268	...	50.0	...	50.0	569,097	1,646,869	1,646,869	23,310	-30,849	-28,801	-22,588
'08	20.2	5.8	41.9	32.0	696,777	...	58.5	...	41.5	420,648	1,547,319	1,514,792	-92,742	-60,906	-59,511	-35,794
'09	21.9	5.9	45.1	27.2	664,778	...	55.1	...	44.9	356,116	1,674,996	1,643,173	-62,973	-76,937	-64,506	-64,391

Rating History: NR-5, 04/21/10; NR-5, 08/26/09; B+ pd, 09/19/08; B++pd, 08/27/07; B++pd, 09/21/06

HAWKEYE LIFE INS GROUP INS[1]
Patrick H. Clemons
President
1111 Office Park Road
West Des Moines, IA 50265-2507
IA : 1979 : Stock : Not Available
515-226-1900
AMB# 009046 NAIC# 90255

NR-1

Data Year	Bonds (%)	Mort. Loans & R.E. (%)	Com & Pref. Stock (%)	All Other Assets (%)	Total Assets ($000)	Life Reserves (%)	Health Reserves (%)	Ann Res. & Dep. Liabilities (%)	All Other Liabilities (%)	Capital & Surplus ($000)	Direct Premiums Written ($000)	Net Premiums Written & Deposits ($000)	Operating Cash Flow ($000)	NOG Before Taxes ($000)	NOG After Taxes ($000)	Net Income ($000)
'05	85.7	...	0.1	14.2	23,490	...	...	...	100.0	16,375	...	4,111	...	1,601	1,337	1,337
'06	88.1	...	0.1	11.9	19,499	...	...	...	100.0	12,675	...	3,149	...	1,145	938	938
'07	93.0	...	0.1	6.9	17,589	...	...	...	100.0	11,782	...	2,654	...	433	354	354
'08	92.3	...	...	7.7	15,272	...	...	...	100.0	10,585	...	2,631	...	1,115	907	907
'09	92.5	...	...	7.5	14,642	...	...	...	100.0	10,879	...	2,272	...	1,230	1,030	1,030

Rating History: NR-1, 06/10/10; NR-1, 06/12/09; NR-1, 06/12/08; NR-1, 06/08/07; NR-1, 06/07/06

HAWTHORN LIFE INSURANCE CO[1]
Charlie Allison
President
P.O. Box 234
Carthage, TX 75633-0234
TX : 1974 : Stock : Not Available
903-693-8441
AMB# 068222 NAIC# 82686

NR-1

Data Year	Bonds (%)	Mort. Loans & R.E. (%)	Com & Pref. Stock (%)	All Other Assets (%)	Total Assets ($000)	Life Reserves (%)	Health Reserves (%)	Ann Res. & Dep. Liabilities (%)	All Other Liabilities (%)	Capital & Surplus ($000)	Direct Premiums Written ($000)	Net Premiums Written & Deposits ($000)	Operating Cash Flow ($000)	NOG Before Taxes ($000)	NOG After Taxes ($000)	Net Income ($000)
'05	43.2	...	50.3	6.4	6,772	...	...	...	100.0	1,622	104	886	...	14	28	28
'06	65.3	...	28.8	5.9	7,717	...	...	...	100.0	617	103	600	...	155	180	180
'07	62.8	...	30.2	6.9	7,742	...	...	...	100.0	694	94	826	...	-73	-47	-47
'08	63.1	...	32.8	4.1	8,942	...	...	...	100.0	1,068	94	928	...	-278	-219	-219
'09	59.0	...	34.7	6.3	11,489	...	...	...	100.0	702	320	1,258	...	587	597	597

Rating History: NR-1, 06/10/10; NR-1, 06/12/09; NR-1, 06/12/08; NR-1, 06/08/07; NR-1, 06/07/06

HCC LIFE INSURANCE COMPANY
HCC Insurance Holdings, Inc
Craig J. Kelbel
President
225 TownPark Drive, Suite 145
Kennesaw, GA 30144
IN : 1981 : Stock : General Agent
Group Life, Medical, Stop Loss
770-973-9851
AMB# 009081 NAIC# 92711

A+ — Rating Outlook: Stable — FSC IX

Data Year	Bonds (%)	Mort. Loans & R.E. (%)	Com & Pref. Stock (%)	All Other Assets (%)	Total Assets ($000)	Life Reserves (%)	Health Reserves (%)	Ann Res. & Dep. Liabilities (%)	All Other Liabilities (%)	Capital & Surplus ($000)	Direct Premiums Written ($000)	Net Premiums Written & Deposits ($000)	Operating Cash Flow ($000)	NOG Before Taxes ($000)	NOG After Taxes ($000)	Net Income ($000)
'05	64.7	...	1.1	34.2	325,311	0.5	83.3	...	16.2	190,580	446,636	421,079	106,444	44,526	30,419	30,419
'06	76.7	...	5.6	17.7	549,104	0.6	88.7	...	10.7	268,777	421,207	494,157	237,420	70,200	47,996	47,996
'07	78.0	...	5.1	16.9	623,203	0.3	88.5	...	11.3	336,165	568,175	649,529	87,516	79,390	60,307	64,234
'08	77.8	...	6.8	15.5	584,804	0.6	89.3	...	10.1	345,370	609,319	663,429	-59,114	89,873	65,677	60,296
'09	79.1	...	8.3	12.6	598,019	0.6	90.1	...	9.3	367,721	597,332	651,838	1,586	91,102	65,955	65,955

Rating History: A+, 08/27/09; A+, 07/30/08; A+, 04/15/08; A+, 01/04/07; A+ u, 11/22/06

HCSC INSURANCE SERVICES CO
Health Care Svc Corp Mut Legal Reserve
Martha P. Mahaffey
President & CEO
300 East Randolph Street
Chicago, IL 60601-5099
IL : 1958 : Stock : Inactive
Group A&H
312-653-3117
AMB# 007048 NAIC# 78611

A+ — Rating Outlook: Stable — FSC XV

Data Year	Bonds (%)	Mort. Loans & R.E. (%)	Com & Pref. Stock (%)	All Other Assets (%)	Total Assets ($000)	Life Reserves (%)	Health Reserves (%)	Ann Res. & Dep. Liabilities (%)	All Other Liabilities (%)	Capital & Surplus ($000)	Direct Premiums Written ($000)	Net Premiums Written & Deposits ($000)	Operating Cash Flow ($000)	NOG Before Taxes ($000)	NOG After Taxes ($000)	Net Income ($000)
'05	29.6	...	...	70.4	49,594	0.4	4.8	...	94.8	30,743	514	1,265	-4,149	-21,580	-17,548	-17,548
'06	9.4	...	...	90.6	122,795	1.9	17.9	...	80.2	77,412	348,428	347,486	11,584	7,278	6,576	6,576
'07	4.2	...	...	95.8	180,235	1.0	6.0	...	93.0	82,165	404,629	400,277	-11,449	8,954	5,629	5,629
'08	3.5	...	...	96.5	112,317	2.5	24.6	...	72.9	79,952	414,152	407,557	18,594	4,892	3,693	3,693
'09	2.3	...	...	97.7	166,255	0.1	37.4	...	62.4	71,301	437,928	428,804	97,837	14,354	5,418	5,418

Rating History: A+ g, 01/27/10; A+ g, 12/22/08; A+ g, 11/01/07; NR-2, 08/10/06; NR-3, 11/01/05

HEALTH ALLIANCE MEDICAL PLANS
Carle Clinic Association PC
Jeffrey C. Ingrum
President & CEO
301 S. Vine
Urbana, IL 61801
IL : 1989 : Stock : Other
Health
800-851-3379
AMB# 068039 NAIC# 77950

B++ — Rating Outlook: Negative — FSC VIII

Data Year	Bonds (%)	Mort. Loans & R.E. (%)	Com & Pref. Stock (%)	All Other Assets (%)	Total Assets ($000)	Life Reserves (%)	Health Reserves (%)	Ann Res. & Dep. Liabilities (%)	All Other Liabilities (%)	Capital & Surplus ($000)	Direct Premiums Written ($000)	Net Premiums Written & Deposits ($000)	Operating Cash Flow ($000)	NOG Before Taxes ($000)	NOG After Taxes ($000)	Net Income ($000)
'05	38.6	...	19.1	42.3	173,914	...	37.2	...	62.8	101,057	688,283	685,950	43,013	47,005	32,687	33,430
'06	36.0	...	21.3	42.7	206,212	...	34.7	...	65.3	112,634	764,470	762,639	27,416	30,715	18,140	19,023
'07	40.5	...	23.3	36.2	207,831	...	41.0	...	59.0	114,963	806,311	804,267	-36,242	19,839	12,328	13,039
'08	32.7	8.5	19.6	39.2	210,817	...	43.2	...	56.8	112,534	875,533	873,193	15,031	22,080	9,706	5,506
'09	21.5	5.7	15.4	57.4	312,456	...	43.8	...	56.2	127,301	948,507	947,077	-9,524	14,627	10,042	11,870

Rating History: B++, 02/08/10; B++, 05/04/09; B++, 02/19/08; B++, 01/31/07; B++, 01/20/06

HEALTH ALLIANCE-MIDWEST INC
Carle Clinic Association PC
Jeffrey C. Ingrum
CEO
301 S. Vine
Urbana, IL 61801
IL : 1997 : Stock : Other
Health
800-851-3379
AMB# 064392 NAIC# 95513

B+ — Rating Outlook: Negative — FSC III

Data Year	Bonds (%)	Mort. Loans & R.E. (%)	Com & Pref. Stock (%)	All Other Assets (%)	Total Assets ($000)	Life Reserves (%)	Health Reserves (%)	Ann Res. & Dep. Liabilities (%)	All Other Liabilities (%)	Capital & Surplus ($000)	Direct Premiums Written ($000)	Net Premiums Written & Deposits ($000)	Operating Cash Flow ($000)	NOG Before Taxes ($000)	NOG After Taxes ($000)	Net Income ($000)
'05	75.2	...	...	24.8	4,827	...	28.9	...	71.1	3,228	6,133	6,053	395	0	-44	-44
'06	71.1	...	...	28.9	4,426	...	32.4	...	67.6	2,936	5,788	5,742	-490	-637	-431	-444
'07	76.7	...	...	23.3	4,415	...	46.7	...	53.3	2,698	5,909	5,886	166	-261	-242	-242
'08	69.1	...	...	30.9	4,744	...	41.6	...	58.4	2,371	8,522	8,476	70	-473	-285	-323
'09	63.9	...	...	36.1	5,343	...	43.0	...	57.0	2,387	10,587	10,557	114	-99	21	21

Rating History: B+, 02/08/10; B+, 05/04/09; B+, 02/19/08; B+, 01/31/07; B+, 01/20/06

BEST'S PROFITABILITY, LEVERAGE AND LIQUIDITY TESTS 2005 – 2009

Data in U.S. Dollars

	Profitability Tests							Leverage Tests						Liquidity Tests					
Un-Realized Capital Gains ($000)	Benefits Paid to NPW & Dep (%)	Comm. & Expenses to NPW & Dep (%)	NOG to Total Assets (%)	NOG to Total Rev (%)	Operating Return on Equity (%)	Net Yield (%)	Total Return (%)	Change in NPW & Dep (%)	NPW & Dep to Capital (X)	Capital & Surplus to Liabilities (%)	Surplus Relief (%)	Reins Leverage (%)	Change in Capital (%)	Quick Liquidity (%)	Current Liquidity (%)	Non-Invest Grade Bonds to Capital (%)	Delinq. & Foreclosed Mortgages to Capital (%)	Mort. & Credit Tenant Loans & R.E. to Capital (%)	Affiliated Invest to Capital (%)
...	84.4	7.0	17.4	8.6	21.0	...	...	...	2.2	...	...	...	...	...	...	...	...	...	...
...	84.7	6.6	15.9	8.6	18.5	...	...	...	1.9	...	...	...	...	...	...	...	...	...	...
...	84.1	6.2	15.4	9.6	17.7	...	...	...	1.6	...	...	...	...	...	...	...	...	...	...
...	91.7	7.1	1.4	1.0	1.6	...	...	...	1.8	...	...	...	...	...	...	...	...	...	...
...	85.6	7.4	10.2	6.8	12.0	...	...	...	1.6	...	...	...	...	...	...	...	...	...	...
...	60.2	27.5	30.4	8.5	64.1	2.86	2.86	12.2	5.9	104.6	...	3.8	72.6	192.0	192.0	...	...	...	...
...	63.2	31.9	5.5	5.7	9.8	4.78	4.78	-70.6	1.6	155.3	...	41.8	10.3	227.1	227.1	...	...	...	...
80	64.8	30.2	8.3	13.6	13.2	5.12	5.46	-44.5	0.8	185.6	...	34.1	14.5	223.7	238.0	...	...	...	...
-80	70.0	44.1	8.0	11.5	12.2	2.66	0.52	4.4	0.7	202.5	...	39.3	8.2	262.5	269.1	...	...	...	...
...	70.6	33.2	0.8	0.6	1.1	1.57	1.76	164.1	1.9	206.5	...	22.2	2.0	266.3	273.0	...	...	...	...
	Principal Lines of Business: CompHosp/Med (94.8%), Dental (5.2%)													Principal States: HI (100.0%)					
12,816	91.2	8.2	2.9	1.4	4.6	4.11	5.93	7.0	3.1	169.4	...	...	2.8	158.4	185.5	1.1	...	7.8	13.5
831	92.9	8.8	1.9	0.9	3.0	4.47	4.73	5.2	3.2	167.8	...	...	2.1	135.5	159.8	0.5	...	7.4	15.1
12,583	93.4	9.6	-3.2	-1.7	-5.1	4.40	6.85	-8.8	2.9	185.9	...	...	0.3	169.8	197.7	0.1	...	7.2	16.4
-83,868	96.2	10.5	-7.6	-3.9	-12.0	3.61	-4.46	-8.0	3.6	152.3	...	1.7	-26.1	154.6	172.5	0.6	...	9.7	19.5
26,480	96.3	10.0	-9.5	-3.9	-16.6	4.63	9.69	8.5	4.6	115.4	...	0.0	-15.3	117.0	134.3	0.5	...	11.0	24.7
	Principal Lines of Business: CompHosp/Med (64.9%), Medicaid (15.4%), FEHBP (14.9%), Medicare (4.5%), OtherHlth (0.3%)													Principal States: HI (99.4%)					
...	42.3	60.2	5.4	26.2	7.7	...	...	-15.0	0.2	244.0	...	...	-9.8	...	...	...	...	...	...
...	54.6	67.6	4.4	23.1	6.5	...	...	-23.4	0.2	196.4	...	...	-22.5	...	...	...	...	...	...
...	44.9	76.9	1.9	10.2	2.9	...	...	-15.7	0.2	214.8	...	...	-7.1	...	...	...	...	...	...
...	40.3	76.4	5.5	27.4	8.1	...	...	-0.9	0.2	234.2	...	...	-10.8	...	...	...	...	...	...
...	41.5	79.6	6.9	35.0	9.6	...	...	-13.7	0.2	300.2	...	...	2.6	...	...	...	...	...	...
	Principal Lines of Business: CrdA&H (60.8%), CrdLife (39.2%)																		
335	81.6	70.6	0.4	1.9	1.9	...	...	50.0	0.5	31.5	...	...	28.9	...	...	...	...	...	...
-1,188	95.1	75.2	2.5	6.0	16.1	...	...	-32.3	1.0	8.7	0.8	...	-62.0	...	...	...	...	...	...
122	86.3	49.7	-0.6	-4.3	-7.2	...	...	37.7	1.2	9.8	0.5	...	12.4	...	...	...	...	...	...
593	79.3	104.6	-2.6	-9.7	-24.9	...	...	12.4	0.9	13.6	...	...	54.0	...	...	...	...	...	...
...	72.6	31.5	5.8	28.3	67.4	...	...	35.6	1.8	6.5	...	...	-34.3	...	...	...	...	...	...
	Principal Lines of Business: OrdLife (82.3%), IndAnn (17.7%)																		
...	73.9	17.7	10.7	6.9	19.0	3.70	3.78	82.8	2.2	142.2	7.3	59.5	46.1	196.1	213.7	...	...	...	...
-12,775	103.7	15.4	11.0	7.2	20.9	3.80	0.76	17.4	1.8	96.8	3.3	40.2	41.4	156.9	174.6	...	...	...	10.2
3,992	77.0	14.0	10.3	8.8	19.9	4.25	5.69	31.4	1.9	118.4	3.9	35.9	25.1	179.0	196.6	...	...	...	9.4
7,943	76.3	13.6	10.9	9.5	19.3	3.95	4.41	2.1	1.9	144.5	2.1	29.5	2.3	189.7	208.6	...	...	...	11.4
10,300	76.1	13.2	11.2	9.7	18.5	3.63	5.56	-1.7	1.8	160.1	2.0	24.7	6.5	193.7	213.7	0.2	...	...	13.5
	Principal Lines of Business: GrpA&H (99.4%), GrpLife (0.4%), IndA&H (0.2%)													Principal States: CA (7.7%), TX (6.8%), OH (6.1%), WI (4.7%), IN (4.5%)					
...	89.8	999.9	-51.0	-99.9	-71.7	3.33	3.33	-42.2	0.0	163.1	...	4.2	68.8	76.1	76.2	...	...	...	...
...	82.8	15.6	7.6	1.9	12.2	8.05	8.05	999.9	4.5	170.6	...	1.1	151.8	60.3	60.6	...	...	...	...
...	81.9	16.2	3.7	1.4	7.1	6.77	6.77	15.2	4.9	83.8	...	1.5	6.1	19.4	19.8	...	...	...	...
...	81.9	17.1	2.5	0.9	4.6	3.59	3.59	1.8	5.1	247.0	...	1.6	-2.7	185.3	185.3	...	...	...	...
...	75.7	18.8	3.9	1.3	7.2	0.17	0.17	5.2	6.0	75.1	...	1.5	-10.8	243.1	244.5	...	...	...	...
	Principal Lines of Business: OtherHlth (82.0%), Medicaid (9.6%), Medicare (8.5%), Life (-0.1%)													Principal States: IL (46.1%), TX (22.2%), NM (16.2%), OK (14.7%)					
246	85.1	8.8	20.3	4.7	38.2	3.48	4.23	13.7	6.8	138.7	...	0.8	44.3	189.1	203.8	0.2	...	...	3.2
3,968	89.8	7.0	9.5	2.4	17.0	3.69	6.58	11.2	6.8	120.4	...	1.7	11.5	172.9	185.7	...	...	...	2.6
2,558	91.3	7.2	6.0	1.5	10.8	4.13	6.08	5.5	7.0	123.8	...	0.7	2.1	134.7	149.8	...	...	...	2.3
-7,987	90.6	7.5	4.6	1.1	8.5	3.66	-4.20	8.6	7.8	114.5	...	0.1	-2.1	110.6	121.3	0.6	...	15.9	25.5
2,589	89.7	9.5	3.8	1.1	8.4	5.13	8.88	8.5	7.4	68.8	...	0.5	13.1	54.4	59.9	0.9	...	13.9	21.2
	Principal Lines of Business: CompHosp/Med (85.4%), Medicare (11.4%), FEHBP (2.6%), MedSup (0.6%)													Principal States: IL (100.0%)					
...	88.6	14.1	-0.9	-0.7	-1.3	4.55	4.55	11.8	1.9	201.9	...	...	-1.6	226.1	245.5	...	...	...	...
...	95.8	18.2	-9.3	-7.3	-14.0	4.38	4.07	-5.1	2.0	196.9	...	...	-9.1	231.1	250.4	...	...	...	...
...	90.1	16.9	-5.5	-4.0	-8.6	4.19	4.19	2.5	2.2	157.1	...	...	-8.1	204.2	221.7	...	...	...	...
...	95.3	12.0	-6.2	-3.3	-11.2	3.85	2.85	44.0	3.6	100.0	...	...	-12.1	157.3	170.4	0.2	...	...	...
...	91.8	10.5	0.4	0.2	0.9	3.73	3.74	24.5	4.4	80.8	...	...	0.7	127.7	137.2	2.7	...	...	...
	Principal Lines of Business: CompHosp/Med (94.6%), FEHBP (5.4%)													Principal States: IA (76.4%), IL (23.6%)					

Data in U.S. Dollars

COMPANY NAME Ultimate Parent Association Principal Officer Mailing Address Dom. : Began Bus. : Struct. : Mktg. Specialty Phone # AMB# NAIC#	Best's Financial Strength Rating FSC	Data Year	Balance Sheet Bonds (%)	Mort. Loans & R.E. (%)	Com & Pref. Stock (%)	All Other Assets (%)	Total Assets ($000)	Life Reserves (%)	Health Reserves (%)	Ann Res. & Dep. Liabilities (%)	All Other Liabilities (%)	Capital & Surplus ($000)	Operations Direct Premiums Written ($000)	Net Premiums Written & Deposits ($000)	Operating Cash Flow ($000)	NOG Before Taxes ($000)	NOG After Taxes ($000)	Net Income ($000)
HEALTH ALLIANCE PLAN OF MI Henry Ford Health System Francine Parker President & CEO 2850 West Grand Boulevard Detroit, MI 48202 MI : 1979 : Non-Profit : Broker Group A&H, Health, Ind A&H 313-872-8100 AMB# 068810 NAIC# 95844	NR-5	'05	...	0.3	36.0	63.7	347,710	...	39.0	...	61.0	220,773	1,507,240	1,507,240	-12,149	30,417	30,417	34,213
		'06	...	0.2	32.7	67.1	393,976	...	41.6	...	58.4	242,352	1,587,240	1,587,240	58,495	48,894	48,894	48,892
		'07	...	0.2	33.4	66.4	402,539	...	45.0	...	55.0	238,901	1,611,525	1,611,525	11,606	35,863	35,863	35,888
		'08	...	0.3	23.9	75.8	323,229	...	49.3	...	50.7	176,224	1,655,116	1,655,116	-59,068	24,006	24,006	19,476
		'09	...	0.2	26.0	73.8	405,318	...	41.8	...	58.2	256,293	1,718,076	1,718,076	19,324	23,329	23,329	22,789
		Rating History: NR-5, 04/07/10; NR-5, 08/26/09; B++pd, 06/06/08; B++pd, 06/05/07; B++pd, 06/13/06																
HEALTH AND HUMAN RESOURCE CTR Peggy Wagner President & Secretary 9370 Sky Park Court, Suite 140 San Diego, CA 92123-5302 CA : 1979 : Stock : Broker Health 858-571-1698 AMB# 064749	NR-5	'05	...	0.6	...	99.4	5,766	...	...	...	100.0	5,392	4,564	4,564	-94	967	568	568
		'06	...	0.4	...	99.6	6,806	...	...	...	100.0	6,248	4,750	4,750	161	1,316	855	855
		'07	...	0.3	...	99.7	7,114	...	...	...	100.0	6,510	3,345	3,345	871	437	262	262
		'08	...	...	...	100.0	3,978	...	...	...	100.0	3,376	6,413	6,413	302	1,562	937	937
		'09	...	...	...	100.0	2,765	...	...	...	100.0	1,730	6,942	6,942	-665	1,655	963	963
		Rating History: NR-5, 05/05/10; NR-5, 04/30/09; NR-5, 03/11/08; NR-5, 05/03/07; NR-5, 06/13/06																
HEALTH CARE SERVICE CORP Health Care Svc Corp Mut Legal Reserve Patricia Hemingway Hall President & CEO 300 East Randolph Street Chicago, IL 60601-5099 IL : 1937 : Mutual : Broker Dental, Group A&H, Ind A&H 312-653-6000 AMB# 009193 NAIC# 70670	A+ Rating Outlook: Stable FSC XV	'05	28.5	2.9	10.1	58.4	7,783,445	...	42.3	...	57.7	4,268,276	11,940,593	11,873,718	1,246,165	1,340,592	1,147,559	1,147,838
		'06	24.4	2.8	11.2	61.6	9,173,484	...	40.4	...	59.6	5,262,751	13,114,260	13,080,209	785,499	1,407,597	1,122,994	1,119,941
		'07	21.8	3.2	11.9	63.1	10,007,660	...	39.1	...	60.9	6,095,693	14,241,552	14,206,862	558,989	1,002,740	826,343	865,686
		'08	30.8	4.6	8.8	55.9	10,528,728	...	39.7	...	60.3	6,104,793	16,220,351	16,179,722	813,689	1,114,113	919,228	742,597
		'09	28.7	6.0	9.8	55.5	11,377,915	...	48.0	...	52.0	6,692,380	17,621,207	17,619,725	366,742	562,514	517,609	514,461
		Rating History: A+ g, 01/27/10; A+ g, 12/22/08; A+ g, 11/01/07; A+ g, 08/10/06; A+ g, 11/01/05																
HEALTH CARE SERVICE-IL LOB Health Care Svc Corp Mut Legal Reserve 300 East Randolph Street Chicago, IL 60601-5099 IL : 1975 : Mutual : Broker Group A&H, Ind A&H 312-653-6000 AMB# 068771 NAIC# 70670	A+ Rating Outlook: Stable FSC XV	'05	...	...	...	100.0	...	...	...	...	100.0	...	2,030,986	2,030,986	-793	193,171	166,341	165,547
		'06	...	...	...	100.0	...	...	...	...	100.0	...	2,162,341	2,162,341	-508	263,498	210,287	209,779
		'07	...	...	...	100.0	...	...	...	...	100.0	...	2,260,896	2,260,896	6,253	237,475	196,218	202,471
		'08	...	...	...	100.0	...	...	...	...	100.0	...	2,335,396	2,335,396	-25,388	193,326	158,415	133,027
		'09	...	...	...	100.0	...	...	...	...	100.0	...	2,343,518	2,343,518	-419	141,014	129,727	129,309
		Rating History: A+ g, 01/27/10; A+ g, 12/22/08; A+ g, 11/01/07; A+ g, 08/10/06; A+ g, 11/01/05																
HEALTH CARE SERVICE-TEXAS LOB Health Care Svc Corp Mut Legal Reserve 901 South Central Expressway Richardson, TX 75080 TX : 1984 : Mutual : Broker Group A&H, Health 972-766-6900 AMB# 068718 NAIC# 70670	A+ Rating Outlook: Stable FSC XV	'05	...	...	...	100.0	...	...	...	...	100.0	...	832,166	832,166	-325	22,807	19,672	19,347
		'06	...	...	...	100.0	...	...	...	...	100.0	...	800,360	800,360	-188	46,192	36,884	36,696
		'07	...	...	...	100.0	...	...	...	...	100.0	...	714,515	714,515	1,976	39,117	32,161	34,137
		'08	...	...	...	100.0	...	...	...	...	100.0	...	630,516	630,516	-6,854	69,974	56,853	49,999
		'09	...	...	...	100.0	...	...	...	...	100.0	...	542,509	542,509	-97	51,521	47,393	47,296
		Rating History: A+ g, 01/27/10; A+ g, 12/22/08; A+ g, 11/01/07; A+ g, 08/10/06; A+ g, 11/01/05																
HEALTH FIRST HEALTH PLANS Health First, Inc. Peter Weiss, M.D. CEO & Secretary 6450 US Highway 1 Rockledge, FL 32955 FL : 1996 : Stock : Broker Group A&H, Health 321-434-5600 AMB# 064115 NAIC# 95019	NR-4	'05	53.3	11.7	...	35.1	41,780	...	65.6	...	34.4	14,374	261,741	260,992	-14,937	739	133	-145
		'06	58.2	9.6	...	32.2	50,831	...	62.7	...	37.3	18,935	314,748	313,669	8,209	7,008	5,788	5,763
		'07	70.5	6.9	...	22.6	71,490	...	68.8	...	31.2	26,524	345,576	343,479	20,426	7,028	4,546	4,513
		'08	36.7	6.0	...	57.3	82,697	...	49.6	...	50.4	41,531	373,731	370,353	11,691	23,223	16,043	16,033
		'09	42.5	6.8	...	50.7	74,098	...	49.4	...	50.6	39,008	377,922	374,671	-8,102	11,154	7,252	7,224
		Rating History: NR-4, 06/11/09; B, 06/11/09; B, 06/18/08; B, 06/27/07; B+, 06/15/06																
HEALTH INS PLAN OF GREATER NY EmblemHealth Inc Daniel T. McGowan President & COO 55 Water Street New York, NY 10041 NY : 1947 : Non-Profit : Agency Group A&H, Health, Ind A&H 646-447-5000 AMB# 068985 NAIC# 55247	B Rating Outlook: Negative FSC XI	'05	44.4	6.0	14.3	35.3	1,348,876	...	48.0	...	52.0	667,902	3,768,446	3,767,789	-318,157	135,098	139,302	142,711
		'06	41.8	4.9	17.8	35.5	1,656,966	...	53.8	...	46.2	924,532	4,070,233	4,069,829	303,836	217,872	212,883	206,575
		'07	39.8	4.6	23.4	32.2	1,701,366	...	51.8	...	48.2	993,705	4,257,396	4,257,396	-91,534	66,222	64,551	54,881
		'08	38.2	4.9	21.0	35.8	1,641,408	...	50.3	...	49.7	844,613	4,533,587	4,533,587	16,383	13,632	13,632	-84,012
		'09	46.8	5.1	17.1	31.0	1,652,272	...	56.6	...	43.4	923,059	4,766,046	4,761,800	28,771	63,234	63,163	91,779
		Rating History: B g, 06/09/10; B g, 05/29/09; B+ g, 06/06/08; B+ g, 05/10/07; B+ gu, 11/16/06																
HEALTH NET HEALTH PLAN OF OR Health Net Inc Stephen D. Lynch Chairman & President 21650 Oxnard Street, 25th Floor Woodland Hills, CA 91367-7824 OR : 1989 : Stock : Broker Group A&H, Health 503-213-5057 AMB# 068947 NAIC# 95800	B+ Rating Outlook: Negative FSC VII	'05	53.3	...	...	46.7	92,311	...	56.8	...	43.2	49,628	359,915	358,784	8,632	16,641	10,697	10,708
		'06	44.1	...	...	55.9	105,546	...	19.9	...	80.1	59,803	369,685	368,727	10,222	17,920	11,757	11,756
		'07	37.8	...	...	62.2	113,673	...	22.1	...	77.9	67,436	387,865	386,790	9,110	18,570	12,095	12,098
		'08	21.9	...	...	78.1	105,400	...	65.4	...	34.6	57,423	422,389	421,105	-11,669	9,296	6,001	3,838
		'09	50.6	...	...	49.4	120,647	...	67.3	...	32.7	73,677	434,362	434,362	19,767	-5,107	-3,293	-3,231
		Rating History: B+, 07/21/09; B+, 11/14/08; B++, 05/14/08; B++, 05/04/07; B++, 05/03/06																
HEALTH NET INS OF NEW YORK INC UnitedHealth Group Inc Steven J. Sell President 21650 Oxnard Street, 25th Floor Woodland Hills, CA 91367 NY : 1991 : Stock : Inactive Inactive 203-402-4200 AMB# 011859 NAIC# 43893	B++ Rating Outlook: Stable FSC VIII	'05	48.6	...	0.0	51.3	94,108	...	52.3	...	47.7	66,761	171,308	169,093	1,256	11,542	7,692	7,651
		'06	40.5	...	...	59.5	114,669	...	59.7	...	40.3	74,713	288,695	271,215	-28,270	19,563	12,388	12,341
		'07	25.8	...	...	74.2	187,265	...	41.0	...	59.0	128,452	467,223	345,847	61,943	7,194	658	808
		'08	37.2	...	2.1	60.7	167,772	...	45.0	...	55.0	98,938	636,951	387,180	-35,159	-10,403	-6,810	-7,607
		'09	6.1	...	0.5	93.4	220,033	...	35.9	...	64.1	124,882	759,086	448,373	108,196	-23,105	-15,074	-12,415
		Rating History: B++, 01/14/10; B+ gu, 10/29/09; B+ g, 07/21/09; B+ g, 11/14/08; B+ g, 05/14/08																

BEST'S PROFITABILITY, LEVERAGE AND LIQUIDITY TESTS 2005 – 2009

Data in U.S. Dollars

	Profitability Tests							Leverage Tests						Liquidity Tests					
Un-Realized Capital Gains ($000)	Benefits Paid to NPW & Dep (%)	Comm. & Expenses to NPW & Dep (%)	NOG to Total Assets (%)	NOG to Total Rev (%)	Operating Return on Equity (%)	Net Yield (%)	Total Return (%)	Change in NPW & Dep (%)	NPW & Dep to Capital (X)	Capital & Surplus to Liabilities (%)	Surplus Relief (%)	Reins Leverage (%)	Change in Capital (%)	Quick Liquidity (%)	Current Liquidity (%)	Non-Invest Grade Bonds to Capital (%)	Delinq. & Foreclosed Mortgages to Capital (%)	Mort. & Credit Tenant Loans & R.E. to Capital (%)	Affiliated Invest to Capital (%)
-3,685	91.1	7.5	8.6	2.0	13.9	2.98	3.03	4.5	6.8	173.9	...	...	2.0	149.8	161.5	...	...	0.4	12.5
-2,085	91.0	6.9	13.2	3.1	21.1	4.64	4.02	5.3	6.5	159.8	...	...	9.8	179.7	191.9	...	...	0.4	11.0
1,411	91.7	7.1	9.0	2.2	14.9	4.14	4.53	1.5	6.7	146.0	...	...	-1.4	219.4	236.4	...	...	0.4	10.6
-10,929	91.6	7.0	6.6	1.4	11.6	0.41	-4.06	2.7	9.4	119.9	...	...	-26.2	319.5	329.8	...	...	0.5	9.0
14,278	92.4	6.5	6.4	1.4	10.8	1.68	5.82	3.8	6.7	172.0	...	...	45.4	353.1	361.4	...	...	0.3	9.2
	Principal Lines of Business: CompHosp/Med (71.9%), Medicare (22.6%), FEHBP (5.5%)													Principal States: MI (99.7%)					
...	62.0	17.1	10.3	12.2	11.1	0.46	0.46	3.0	0.8	999.9	...	...	11.8	122.9	122.9	...	...	0.7	0.7
...	58.5	14.3	13.6	17.7	14.7	0.47	0.47	4.1	0.8	999.9	...	...	15.9	110.7	110.7	...	...	0.4	0.4
...	58.7	28.6	3.8	7.7	4.1	0.47	0.47	-29.6	0.5	999.9	...	...	4.2	246.5	246.5	...	...	0.3	0.3
...	56.4	21.1	16.9	14.0	19.0	3.34	3.34	91.7	1.9	560.6	...	...	-48.1	433.4	433.4	...	...	...	...
...	48.7	28.4	28.6	13.4	37.7	0.45	0.45	8.3	4.0	167.1	...	...	-48.8	188.2	188.2	...	...	...	...
	Principal Lines of Business: CompHosp/Med (100.0%)																		
-12,321	81.4	8.6	16.2	9.6	31.1	3.74	3.47	10.0	2.8	121.4	0.1	0.1	37.6	148.7	157.7	...	...	5.4	17.1
47,163	81.4	9.9	13.2	8.4	23.6	4.96	5.78	10.2	2.5	134.6	0.0	0.3	23.3	147.1	156.1	0.0	...	4.8	16.7
36,859	83.2	11.8	8.6	5.6	14.6	4.85	6.12	8.6	2.3	155.8	0.0	0.5	15.8	217.6	226.6	0.3	...	5.3	16.3
-180,168	83.4	11.2	9.0	5.7	15.1	3.56	-1.83	13.9	2.7	138.0	0.0	0.3	0.1	186.7	195.2	0.1	...	7.9	21.3
-219,012	86.1	11.6	4.7	3.0	8.1	2.66	-0.51	8.9	2.6	142.8	0.0	0.3	9.6	170.6	182.1	0.1	...	10.3	20.4
	Principal Lines of Business: CompHosp/Med (71.6%), FEHBP (19.9%), MedSup (6.0%), OtherHlth (1.6%), Dental (0.8%)													Principal States: IL (49.1%), TX (37.9%), OK (8.7%), NM (3.2%)					
...	87.5	4.3	...	8.1	...	...	...	5.3	...	...	...	...	...	...	...	...	...	...	...
...	84.8	5.0	...	9.5	...	...	...	6.5	...	...	...	...	...	...	...	...	...	...	...
...	86.5	5.0	...	8.5	...	...	...	4.6	...	...	...	...	...	...	...	...	...	...	...
...	88.9	4.3	...	6.7	...	...	...	3.3	...	...	...	...	...	...	...	...	...	...	...
...	90.9	4.0	...	5.5	...	...	...	0.3	...	...	...	...	...	...	...	...	...	...	...
	Principal Lines of Business: CompHosp/Med (100.0%)													Principal States: IL (100.0%)					
...	86.0	11.0	...	2.3	...	...	...	9.7	...	...	...	...	...	...	...	...	...	...	...
...	86.9	11.0	...	4.5	...	...	...	-3.8	...	...	...	...	...	...	...	...	...	...	...
...	84.9	11.6	...	4.4	...	...	...	-10.7	...	...	...	...	...	...	...	...	...	...	...
...	81.7	8.7	...	8.9	...	...	...	-11.8	...	...	...	...	...	...	...	...	...	...	...
...	84.0	7.4	...	8.7	...	...	...	-14.0	...	...	...	...	...	...	...	...	...	...	...
	Principal Lines of Business: CompHosp/Med (99.0%), FEHBP (1.0%)													Principal States: TX (100.0%)					
...	91.8	8.6	0.3	0.1	0.7	4.19	3.59	12.9	18.2	52.5	...	0.7	-32.8	104.5	111.9	...	...	33.9	33.9
...	89.7	8.8	12.5	1.8	34.8	5.23	5.17	20.2	16.6	59.4	...	1.3	31.7	133.4	141.0	...	...	25.9	25.9
...	89.5	9.4	7.4	1.3	20.0	6.39	6.33	9.5	12.9	59.0	...	0.4	40.1	110.0	119.8	...	...	18.7	18.7
...	83.3	11.2	20.8	4.3	47.1	4.00	3.98	7.8	8.9	100.9	...	0.5	56.6	223.0	235.9	...	...	12.0	12.0
...	87.7	9.8	9.3	1.9	18.0	2.46	2.42	1.2	9.6	111.2	...	1.1	-6.1	202.3	213.9	...	...	12.8	12.8
	Principal Lines of Business: Medicare (69.3%), CompHosp/Med (30.7%)													Principal States: FL (100.0%)					
-14,201	81.8	13.3	9.7	3.7	19.4	1.70	0.82	4.4	5.6	98.1	...	0.1	-13.2	132.4	143.9	...	...	12.2	61.8
28,222	84.0	12.1	14.2	5.2	26.7	2.80	4.57	8.0	4.4	126.2	...	0.0	38.4	169.7	185.2	...	...	8.8	47.5
12,772	87.3	12.2	3.8	1.5	6.7	2.99	3.22	4.6	4.3	140.4	...	...	7.5	137.7	154.9	0.1	...	7.9	44.6
-51,233	87.7	12.4	0.8	0.3	1.5	2.23	-8.69	6.5	5.4	106.0	...	...	-15.0	135.5	148.9	0.2	...	9.6	51.5
-35,663	87.4	11.8	3.8	1.3	7.1	1.21	0.73	5.0	5.2	126.6	...	0.9	9.3	138.6	150.9	0.1	...	9.2	13.9
	Principal Lines of Business: CompHosp/Med (45.6%), Medicare (40.3%), Medicaid (13.9%), OtherHlth (0.1%), MedSup (0.1%)													Principal States: NY (100.0%)					
...	82.0	14.2	12.1	3.0	24.0	3.79	3.80	15.5	7.2	116.3	...	...	25.6	263.4	280.1	...	...	...	...
...	82.2	14.0	11.9	3.2	21.5	4.92	4.92	2.8	6.2	130.7	...	1.1	20.5	293.0	309.8	...	...	...	...
...	82.2	14.1	11.0	3.1	19.0	5.13	5.14	4.9	5.7	145.8	...	1.2	12.8	341.5	351.4	...	...	...	...
...	86.9	11.5	5.5	1.4	9.6	3.18	1.04	8.9	7.3	119.7	...	3.5	-14.8	326.5	331.8	...	...	...	...
...	89.4	12.0	-2.9	-0.8	-5.0	1.39	1.44	3.1	5.9	156.9	...	...	28.3	331.6	345.9	...	...	...	...
	Principal Lines of Business: CompHosp/Med (98.8%), Vision (0.6%), Dental (0.6%), MedSup (0.1%)													Principal States: OR (94.4%), WA (5.1%)					
...	78.0	16.8	8.4	4.5	12.2	3.41	3.36	-22.8	2.5	244.1	...	0.5	12.2	374.2	397.5	...	...	...	...
...	76.4	17.6	11.9	4.5	17.5	4.82	4.75	60.4	3.6	187.0	...	5.3	11.9	137.7	148.8	...	...	...	...
...	78.9	18.1	0.4	0.2	0.6	5.20	5.34	27.5	2.7	218.4	0.0	15.0	71.9	299.1	307.2	...	...	...	...
...	88.9	14.4	-3.8	-1.7	-6.0	1.83	1.16	12.0	3.9	143.7	0.0	25.5	-23.0	123.3	132.9	...	...	...	...
...	87.7	17.9	-7.8	-3.4	-13.5	1.69	3.65	15.8	3.6	131.2	0.0	30.7	26.2	363.5	375.9	...	...	...	...
	Principal Lines of Business: CompHosp/Med (95.4%), Medicare (2.7%), OtherHlth (1.9%)													Principal States: NY (100.0%)					

Data in U.S. Dollars

COMPANY NAME Ultimate Parent Association Principal Officer Mailing Address Dom. : Began Bus. : Struct. : Mktg. Specialty Phone # AMB# NAIC#	Best's Financial Strength Rating FSC	Data Year	Balance Sheet Bonds (%)	Mort. Loans & R.E. (%)	Com & Pref. Stock (%)	All Other Assets (%)	Total Assets ($000)	Life Reserves (%)	Health Reserves (%)	Ann Res. & Dep. Liabilities (%)	All Other Liabilities (%)	Capital & Surplus ($000)	Operations Direct Premiums Written ($000)	Net Premiums Written & Deposits ($000)	Operating Cash Flow ($000)	NOG Before Taxes ($000)	NOG After Taxes ($000)	Net Income ($000)
HEALTH NET LIFE INSURANCE CO Health Net Inc James E. Woys President 21281 Burbank Blvd., B3 Woodland Hills, CA 91367-6607 CA : 1987 : Stock : Broker Group A&H, Group Life, Ind A&H 818-676-8256 AMB# 006722 NAIC# 66141	B+ Rating Outlook: Negative FSC XIII	'05	72.4	...	...	27.6	359,826	0.6	57.2	...	42.3	191,552	875,146	640,654	14,732	59,183	42,452	42,452
		'06	63.8	...	...	36.2	400,411	0.5	59.0	...	40.5	203,500	1,296,002	816,480	-44,738	95,170	61,713	61,713
		'07	41.6	...	...	58.4	656,005	0.2	39.9	...	59.8	233,580	1,700,569	1,064,976	239,038	472	-19,954	-19,954
		'08	59.2	...	0.5	40.3	650,111	0.4	52.9	...	46.7	368,802	2,031,774	1,241,223	-122,979	9,837	15,568	14,086
		'09	69.6	...	0.2	30.2	643,099	0.3	45.1	...	54.5	383,551	1,894,416	1,161,565	59,965	70,609	58,165	58,165
		Rating History: B+ g, 07/21/09; B+ g, 11/14/08; B++g, 05/14/08; B++g, 05/04/07; B++g, 05/03/06																
HEALTH NET OF ARIZONA INC Health Net Inc Charles M. Sowers President & CEO 21650 Oxnard Street, 25th Floor Woodland Hills, CA 91367-7824 AZ : 1981 : Stock : Broker Group A&H, Health, Ind A&H 602-794-1400 AMB# 068713 NAIC# 95206	B+ Rating Outlook: Negative FSC VIII	'05	72.0	6.1	...	21.9	114,713	...	64.9	...	35.1	56,986	418,313	417,731	-18,402	5,909	5,092	5,132
		'06	69.1	5.4	...	25.5	125,103	...	61.4	...	38.6	58,761	470,911	470,039	2,056	40,909	26,156	26,095
		'07	61.8	...	1.4	36.8	136,156	...	68.1	...	31.9	66,196	595,431	594,789	-12,987	19,725	13,379	17,312
		'08	43.9	...	0.3	55.8	162,732	...	57.5	...	42.5	63,741	758,452	757,705	18,279	-24,168	-15,853	-18,366
		'09	32.0	...	...	68.0	196,855	...	55.6	...	44.4	108,773	805,175	805,175	35,967	27,098	18,437	19,279
		Rating History: B+, 07/21/09; B+, 11/14/08; B++, 05/14/08; B++, 05/04/07; B++, 05/03/06																
HEALTH NET OF CALIFORNIA INC Health Net Inc Stephen D. Lynch Vice Chairman & President 21650 Oxnard Street, 24th Floor Woodland Hills, CA 91367-7824 CA : 1979 : Stock : Broker Group A&H, Health 818-676-6775 AMB# 068507 NAIC# 95567	B+ Rating Outlook: Negative FSC XIII	'05	...	5.3	...	94.7	1,448,770	...	...	...	100.0	710,377	6,352,237	6,352,237	200,389	287,445	174,631	174,631
		'06	...	0.9	...	99.1	1,826,703	...	...	...	100.0	941,845	7,133,422	7,133,422	89,603	352,400	216,851	216,851
		'07	...	0.7	...	99.3	2,120,911	...	...	...	100.0	928,923	7,766,165	7,766,165	250,034	295,217	177,341	177,341
		'08	...	0.6	...	99.4	2,314,435	...	...	...	100.0	1,130,459	8,542,157	8,542,157	-192,017	182,759	112,085	112,085
		'09	...	0.6	...	99.4	2,354,566	...	...	...	100.0	1,283,591	8,721,298	8,721,298	96,873	277,107	172,172	172,172
		Rating History: B+ g, 07/21/09; B+ g, 11/14/08; B++g, 05/14/08; B++g, 05/04/07; B++g, 05/03/06																
HEALTH NET OF CONNECTICUT INC UnitedHealth Group Inc Allen J. Sorbo President & CEO 21650 Oxnard Street, 25th Floor Woodland Hills, CA 91367-7824 CT : 1977 : Stock : Broker Group A&H, Health 203-402-4200 AMB# 068520 NAIC# 95968	B++ Rating Outlook: Stable FSC VIII	'05	53.5	...	0.0	46.5	333,560	...	55.1	...	44.9	140,176	1,251,863	1,181,043	35,278	77,654	52,733	52,654
		'06	59.8	...	...	40.2	306,145	...	49.4	...	50.6	118,760	1,249,604	1,185,535	-7,715	28,592	441	293
		'07	59.1	...	...	40.9	322,462	...	56.3	...	43.7	151,904	1,272,861	1,247,298	29,744	16,902	9,618	10,232
		'08	70.8	...	...	29.2	297,108	...	44.1	...	55.9	145,872	1,127,377	1,127,377	-24,653	8,551	7,479	5,857
		'09	12.0	...	...	88.0	258,259	...	53.3	...	46.7	122,130	1,036,604	1,036,604	-18,934	5,251	1,892	10,469
		Rating History: B++, 01/14/10; B+ gu, 10/29/09; B+ g, 07/21/09; B+ g, 11/14/08; B+ g, 05/14/08																
HEALTH NET OF NEW JERSEY INC UnitedHealth Group Inc Paul S. Lambdin President 21650 Oxnard Street, 25th Floor Woodland Hills, CA 91367-7824 NJ : 1993 : Stock : Broker Group A&H, Health 203-402-4200 AMB# 064005 NAIC# 95351	B++ Rating Outlook: Stable FSC VI	'05	64.1	...	0.0	35.9	162,105	...	46.0	...	54.0	68,687	654,770	454,924	-11,925	-484	2,098	1,846
		'06	58.7	...	...	41.3	144,296	...	44.4	...	55.6	74,920	538,918	385,504	-8,651	8,910	4,260	4,216
		'07	37.2	...	...	62.8	150,411	...	57.0	...	43.0	47,799	495,120	416,060	-7,803	-33,126	-25,344	-25,218
		'08	31.7	...	...	68.3	121,624	...	52.6	...	47.4	51,355	452,480	431,706	-12,835	20,448	11,725	11,936
		'09	8.6	...	...	91.4	109,816	...	54.8	...	45.2	41,323	473,513	447,191	-15,579	-47,821	-37,297	-35,953
		Rating History: B++, 01/14/10; B+ gu, 10/29/09; B+ g, 07/21/09; B+ g, 11/14/08; B+ g, 05/14/08																
HEALTH NET OF NEW YORK INC UnitedHealth Group Inc Paul S. Lambdin Chief Commercial Officer 21650 Oxnard Street, 25th Floor Woodland Hills, CA 91367-7824 NY : 1987 : Stock : Broker Group A&H, Health 203-381-6400 AMB# 068568 NAIC# 95305	B++ Rating Outlook: Stable FSC VII	'05	60.5	...	0.0	39.5	157,305	...	38.4	...	61.6	52,649	719,414	525,664	12,949	24,377	15,617	15,595
		'06	65.0	...	...	35.0	152,168	...	39.2	...	60.8	58,517	701,109	519,109	-10,212	14,682	9,747	9,608
		'07	51.2	...	...	48.8	161,311	...	44.8	...	55.2	61,146	618,683	549,787	15,867	-17,066	-21,882	-21,759
		'08	61.1	...	2.3	36.5	141,613	...	50.9	...	49.1	70,497	463,059	463,059	-20,151	5,338	4,991	5,123
		'09	23.9	...	0.9	75.2	116,364	...	38.5	...	61.5	61,994	387,792	387,792	-30,053	-9,322	-4,497	-2,169
		Rating History: B++, 01/14/10; B+ gu, 10/29/09; B+ g, 07/21/09; B+ g, 11/14/08; B+ g, 05/14/08																
HEALTH NEW ENGLAND INC Baystate Health Inc. Peter F. Straley President One Monarch Place, Suite 1500 Springfield, MA 01144 MA : 1986 : Stock : Broker Group A&H, Ind A&H 413-787-4000 AMB# 068553 NAIC# 95673	NR-4	'05	83.7	...	-0.3	16.6	67,473	...	42.7	...	57.3	24,695	229,119	228,150	9,853	12,456	12,370	12,237
		'06	79.1	...	5.1	15.8	70,882	...	44.8	...	55.2	30,752	248,687	247,690	2,093	8,275	5,151	5,197
		'07	68.8	...	6.5	24.7	85,279	...	45.1	...	54.9	35,969	274,993	274,049	8,893	7,114	4,190	4,077
		'08	69.6	...	2.6	27.8	86,165	...	43.6	...	56.4	38,374	289,346	288,252	3,705	8,900	6,020	3,436
		'09	70.7	...	3.5	25.8	82,417	...	48.1	...	51.9	41,660	308,684	307,576	-2,258	5,182	3,848	3,162
		Rating History: NR-4, 05/27/10; B++, 05/27/10; B++, 06/12/09; B++, 06/16/08; B+, 06/14/07																
HEALTH OPTIONS INC Blue Cross and Blue Shield of FL Inc R. Chris Doerr CEO P.O. Box 60729 Jacksonville, FL 32236 FL : 1984 : Stock : Broker Group A&H, Health 904-791-6111 AMB# 068672 NAIC# 95089	A Rating Outlook: Stable FSC XV	'05	70.3	...	19.9	9.8	578,899	...	58.4	...	41.6	355,424	1,684,667	1,684,667	-135,050	172,900	118,675	130,878
		'06	89.1	...	0.1	10.8	474,764	...	44.5	...	55.5	279,672	1,241,164	1,241,164	-64,865	80,903	55,148	92,525
		'07	87.1	...	0.1	12.8	412,041	...	36.8	...	63.2	224,987	992,133	992,133	-68,922	72,799	49,009	49,501
		'08	85.7	...	0.1	14.2	438,825	...	26.9	...	73.1	231,333	877,339	877,339	26,257	28,002	7,374	7,945
		'09	83.5	...	...	16.5	383,813	...	36.5	...	63.5	274,762	674,376	674,376	-54,709	65,280	44,270	46,584
		Rating History: A g, 05/25/10; A g, 05/26/09; A g, 04/28/08; A g, 05/04/07; A g, 04/27/06																
HEALTH PARTNERS OF PHILA[2] William S. George President & CFO 901 Market Street, Suite 500 Philadelphia, PA 19107 PA : 1988 : Non-Profit : Other Health 215-849-9606 AMB# 064160 NAIC# 95066	NR-5	'05	57.5	...	...	42.5	182,331	...	63.7	...	36.3	56,402	809,014	807,362	638	3,745	3,745	3,401
		'06	22.0	...	...	78.0	217,447	...	62.4	...	37.6	63,708	875,655	873,588	40,710	6,842	6,842	6,842
		'07	52.3	...	...	47.7	225,323	...	41.8	...	58.2	76,000	843,214	839,766	7,415	126,209	126,209	125,548
		'08	42.9	...	...	57.1	201,733	...	42.1	...	57.9	75,068	703,753	702,629	-78,966	-847	-847	-409
		'09	41.4	...	...	58.6	191,648	...	52.7	...	47.3	70,844	806,008	805,548	-30,411	865	865	2,944
		Rating History: NR-5, 03/24/10; NR-5, 08/26/09; C+ pd, 09/03/08; C+ pd, 06/05/07; C+ pd, 05/30/06																

BEST'S PROFITABILITY, LEVERAGE AND LIQUIDITY TESTS 2005 – 2009

Data in U.S. Dollars

	Profitability Tests							Leverage Tests						Liquidity Tests					
Un-Realized Capital Gains ($000)	Benefits Paid to NPW & Dep (%)	Comm. & Expenses to NPW & Dep (%)	NOG to Total Assets (%)	NOG to Total Rev (%)	Operating Return on Equity (%)	Net Yield (%)	Total Return (%)	Change in NPW & Dep (%)	NPW & Dep to Capital (X)	Capital & Surplus to Liabilities (%)	Surplus Relief (%)	Reins Leverage (%)	Change in Capital (%)	Quick Liquidity (%)	Current Liquidity (%)	Non-Invest Grade Bonds to Capital (%)	Delinq. & Foreclosed Mortgages to Capital (%)	Mort. & Credit Tenant Loans & R.E. to Capital (%)	Affiliated Invest to Capital (%)
...	76.7	16.4	11.9	6.2	23.4	3.66	3.81	-1.8	3.3	114.3	16.1	22.3	12.0	167.1	182.2	...	...	...	...
...	74.4	16.5	16.2	6.8	31.2	5.94	5.89	27.4	4.0	103.9	33.3	39.3	6.3	99.8	111.6	...	...	...	...
...	78.7	17.8	-3.8	-1.7	-9.1	5.11	5.09	30.4	4.5	55.5	42.5	40.8	14.8	153.5	160.2	...	...	...	...
...	84.8	17.4	2.4	1.1	5.2	5.48	5.17	16.5	3.2	131.2	31.8	29.7	68.2	108.9	123.9	...	...	...	...
...	80.4	16.1	9.0	4.5	15.5	4.15	4.42	-6.4	3.0	148.3	28.2	17.2	-1.8	130.6	146.6	...	...	...	...

Principal Lines of Business: IndA&H (49.9%), GrpA&H (49.7%), GrpLife (0.3%), OrdLife (0.0%) — Principal States: CA (56.6%), AZ (12.2%), OR (11.1%), CT (5.6%)

...	85.8	13.7	4.1	1.2	9.4	3.55	3.59	1.1	7.3	98.7	...	...	11.8	168.3	180.3	...	...	12.3	...
...	78.0	14.4	21.8	5.5	45.2	4.95	4.89	12.5	8.0	88.6	...	...	3.1	139.9	151.7	...	...	11.6	...
55	85.0	12.6	10.2	2.2	21.4	5.76	9.97	26.5	9.0	94.6	...	0.1	12.7	119.4	131.9	...	...	...	...
36	93.2	10.6	-10.6	-2.1	-24.4	4.47	2.02	27.4	11.9	64.4	...	1.0	-3.7	132.1	139.7	...	...	0.9	...
-181	87.7	9.3	10.3	2.3	21.4	2.84	3.37	6.3	7.4	123.5	...	0.0	70.6	231.6	240.9	0.5	...	...	...

Principal Lines of Business: Medicare (76.9%), CompHosp/Med (16.1%), FEHBP (6.9%), Vision (0.1%), Dental (0.0%) — Principal States: AZ (99.8%)

...	86.4	9.8	12.8	2.7	31.6	3.63	3.63	3.0	8.9	96.2	...	...	79.8	147.2	147.2	...	...	10.8	10.8
...	85.7	10.3	13.2	3.0	26.2	4.77	4.77	12.3	7.6	106.4	...	...	32.6	131.8	131.8	...	...	1.7	1.7
...	85.9	11.3	9.0	2.3	19.0	4.93	4.93	8.9	8.4	77.9	...	...	-1.4	119.2	119.2	...	...	1.6	1.6
...	88.7	9.9	5.1	1.3	10.9	3.37	3.37	10.0	7.6	95.5	...	...	21.7	102.6	102.6	...	...	1.3	1.3
...	87.9	10.0	7.4	2.0	14.3	4.96	4.96	2.1	6.8	119.9	...	...	13.5	123.3	123.3	...	...	1.1	1.1

Principal Lines of Business: CompHosp/Med (59.7%), Medicare (28.0%), Medicaid (12.3%)

...	80.8	13.3	17.6	4.4	46.1	3.65	3.62	-0.4	8.4	72.5	10.7	5.0	58.0	154.9	166.6	...	...	...	...
...	82.6	16.0	0.1	0.0	0.3	4.97	4.91	0.4	10.0	63.4	10.9	5.1	-15.3	150.8	162.6	...	...	...	...
...	84.8	14.6	3.1	0.8	7.1	5.12	5.35	5.2	8.2	89.1	0.0	0.5	27.9	189.4	201.8	...	...	...	...
...	85.6	14.5	2.4	0.7	5.0	4.20	3.59	-9.6	7.7	96.5	...	0.9	-4.0	170.0	184.9	...	...	...	...
...	85.1	14.4	0.7	0.2	1.4	3.22	6.84	-8.1	8.5	89.7	...	...	-16.3	295.3	301.7	...	...	...	...

Principal Lines of Business: Medicare (58.5%), CompHosp/Med (41.5%), Medicaid (0.0%) — Principal States: CT (100.0%)

...	86.4	14.8	1.2	0.5	3.2	3.91	3.73	-27.7	6.6	73.5	58.0	41.2	11.3	174.5	179.6	...	...	...	...
...	79.9	19.1	2.8	1.1	5.9	4.23	4.19	-15.3	5.1	108.0	41.3	22.4	9.1	225.2	230.6	...	...	...	...
...	85.8	22.8	-17.2	-6.1	-41.3	4.49	4.59	7.9	8.7	46.6	0.0	32.9	-36.2	165.3	168.7	...	...	...	...
...	77.5	14.7	8.6	2.8	23.7	3.33	3.52	3.8	8.4	73.1	...	17.3	7.4	237.6	242.3	...	...	...	...
...	86.9	19.7	-32.2	-8.7	-80.5	1.33	2.74	3.6	10.8	60.3	...	26.1	-19.5	241.4	243.5	...	...	...	...

Principal Lines of Business: CompHosp/Med (67.8%), Medicaid (32.2%) — Principal States: NJ (100.0%)

...	81.3	15.0	10.1	2.9	35.1	4.01	3.99	1.1	10.0	50.3	...	31.8	44.5	140.7	150.1	...	...	...	...
...	81.3	17.2	6.3	1.9	17.5	4.98	4.87	-1.2	8.9	62.5	...	24.2	11.1	148.0	157.7	...	...	...	...
...	82.8	16.2	-14.0	-4.2	-36.6	5.11	5.21	5.9	9.0	61.0	...	2.7	4.5	183.5	191.6	...	...	...	...
...	85.6	14.7	3.3	1.1	7.6	3.85	3.95	-15.8	6.6	99.1	...	...	15.3	193.2	205.8	...	...	...	...
...	85.8	17.5	-3.5	-1.1	-6.8	2.59	4.79	-16.3	6.3	114.0	...	0.5	-12.1	286.5	291.0	...	...	...	...

Principal Lines of Business: CompHosp/Med (100.0%) — Principal States: NY (100.0%)

...	83.5	11.8	19.3	5.4	59.2	3.05	2.81	1.9	9.2	57.7	...	0.0	44.6	148.2	158.8	...	...	...	2.4
158	85.2	11.7	7.4	2.1	18.6	1.02	1.34	8.6	8.1	76.6	...	...	24.5	152.1	165.6	...	...	...	2.7
34	87.3	11.1	5.4	1.5	12.6	4.17	4.06	10.6	7.6	72.9	...	1.1	17.0	128.2	141.8	0.9	...	...	2.8
-226	87.1	11.2	7.0	2.1	16.2	5.41	1.79	5.2	7.5	80.3	...	...	6.7	139.7	153.1	...	...	...	0.3
471	87.4	11.7	4.6	1.2	9.6	3.30	3.02	6.7	7.4	102.2	...	...	8.6	168.3	185.1	2.4	...	...	0.6

Principal Lines of Business: CompHosp/Med (98.5%), Medicare (1.5%), OtherHlth (0.0%) — Principal States: MA (99.2%)

-15,333	74.5	16.2	18.2	6.9	31.2	4.21	3.74	-14.9	4.7	159.0	...	...	-12.2	180.1	196.7	0.3	...	...	...
-22,728	82.0	14.3	10.5	4.3	17.4	4.63	8.13	-26.3	4.4	143.4	...	...	-21.3	183.1	193.5	...	...	...	...
-6,539	82.2	13.5	11.1	4.8	19.4	6.57	5.05	-20.1	4.4	120.3	...	...	-19.6	160.1	170.6	0.0	...	...	...
-7,035	86.7	12.1	1.7	0.8	3.2	4.04	2.32	-11.6	3.8	111.5	...	...	2.8	157.9	164.5	...	...	...	...
-1,569	82.1	11.0	10.8	6.4	17.5	4.32	4.54	-23.1	2.5	252.0	...	...	18.8	256.0	266.6	...	...	...	...

Principal Lines of Business: CompHosp/Med (59.2%), Medicare (40.8%) — Principal States: FL (100.0%)

...	87.4	12.5	2.1	0.5	6.8	2.00	1.76	17.7	14.3	44.8	...	1.1	4.4	117.1	117.4	...	...	...	...
...	88.3	11.8	3.4	0.8	11.4	4.21	4.21	8.2	13.7	41.4	...	...	13.0	122.9	123.0	...	...	...	...
...	88.6	12.0	57.0	13.0	180.7	6.47	6.14	-3.9	11.0	50.9	...	...	19.3	121.2	124.6	...	...	...	...
...	87.6	13.5	-0.4	-0.1	-1.1	4.09	4.37	-16.3	9.4	59.3	...	0.6	-1.2	85.0	88.3	...	...	...	...
...	86.4	13.9	0.4	0.1	1.2	3.48	5.51	14.6	11.4	58.6	...	...	-5.6	61.8	65.9	...	...	...	...

Principal Lines of Business: Medicaid (100.0%), OtherHlth (0.0%) — Principal States: PA (100.0%)

ANNUAL STATEMENT DATA FOR YEARS 2005 – 2009

Data in U.S. Dollars

COMPANY NAME Ultimate Parent Association Principal Officer Mailing Address Dom. : Began Bus. : Struct. : Mktg. Specialty Phone # AMB# NAIC#	Best's Financial Strength Rating FSC	Data Year	Balance Sheet: Bonds (%)	Mort. Loans & R.E. (%)	Com & Pref. Stock (%)	All Other Assets (%)	Total Assets ($000)	Life Reserves (%)	Health Reserves %	Ann Res. & Dep. Liabilities (%)	All Other Liabilities (%)	Capital & Surplus ($000)	Operations: Direct Premiums Written ($000)	Net Premiums Written & Deposits ($000)	Operating Cash Flow ($000)	NOG Before Taxes ($000)	NOG After Taxes ($000)	Net Income ($000)
HEALTH PL FOR COMMUNITY LIVING[2] Robert Brewer President P.O. Box 8028 Madison, WI 53708-8029 WI : 2006 : Stock : Not Available Health 608-242-8335 AMB# 064920 NAIC# 12493	**F**	'05	…	…	…	…	…	…	…	…	…	…	…	…	…	…	…	…
		'06	…	…	25.5	74.5	7,903	…	54.3	…	45.7	2,963	25,599	25,422	6,994	625	625	625
		'07	…	…	0.2	99.8	5,189	…	63.1	…	36.9	-2,682	27,049	26,888	-2,592	-3,158	-3,158	-3,158
		'08	…	…	…	…	…	…	…	…	…	…	…	…	…	…	…	…
		'09	…	…	…	…	…	…	…	…	…	…	…	…	…	…	…	…
		Rating History: F, 07/08/08; NR-5, 07/03/08; NR-5, 06/20/07																
HEALTH PLAN OF CAREOREGON INC[2] David E. Ford President 315 SW Fifth Avenue, Suite 900 Portland, OR 97204-1753 OR : 2005 : Stock : Not Available Health 503-416-4100 AMB# 064902 NAIC# 12277	**NR-5**	'05	…	…	…	…	…	…	…	…	…	…	…	…	…	…	…	…
		'06	31.8	…	…	68.2	32,922	…	63.7	…	36.3	8,872	67,124	67,124	21,258	3,800	2,507	2,506
		'07	40.6	…	…	59.4	37,019	…	58.4	…	41.6	20,348	66,526	65,678	-4,799	4,544	1,521	1,505
		'08	71.5	…	…	28.5	41,582	…	47.0	…	53.0	29,105	68,483	67,730	13,566	13,148	10,253	10,250
		'09	76.2	…	…	23.8	40,665	…	46.6	…	53.4	27,019	71,591	71,021	-853	5,280	3,717	3,739
		Rating History: NR-5, 05/21/10; NR-5, 07/14/08; NR-5, 07/02/07																
HEALTH PLAN OF MICHIGAN David B. Cotton, M.D. President & CEO 17515 West Nine Mile Road, Suite 500 Southfield, MI 48075 MI : 1995 : Stock : Not Available Group A&H 248-557-3700 AMB# 064615 NAIC# 52563	**NR-5**	'05	17.5	1.1	0.9	80.5	51,739	…	80.4	…	19.6	30,080	192,876	192,293	13,311	20,038	12,953	12,953
		'06	22.8	…	1.2	76.1	53,429	…	75.9	…	24.1	30,444	218,147	217,478	2,603	18,337	12,037	11,998
		'07	18.7	…	0.7	80.5	73,680	…	80.0	…	20.0	35,302	330,773	330,156	18,050	13,454	7,716	10,637
		'08	18.5	…	1.1	80.4	95,274	…	74.5	…	25.5	50,278	448,661	448,167	23,784	24,671	16,322	16,511
		'09	27.3	…	0.9	71.8	117,106	…	67.0	…	33.0	60,013	660,893	660,311	12,811	21,641	14,580	14,342
		Rating History: NR-5, 05/06/10; NR-5, 08/26/09; B- pd, 07/14/08; B- pd, 06/26/07; B- pd, 07/25/06																
HEALTH PLAN OF NEVADA INC UnitedHealth Group Inc Jonathon W. Bunker President & CEO P.O. Box 46377 Las Vegas, NV 89114-6377 NV : 1982 : Stock : Broker Group A&H, Health, Ind A&H 702-242-7700 AMB# 068619 NAIC# 96342	**A-** Rating Outlook: Stable **FSC VIII**	'05	43.4	4.3	1.3	50.9	269,388	…	51.7	…	48.3	106,231	1,198,284	1,197,177	32,615	34,133	20,903	21,321
		'06	48.4	13.3	…	38.3	324,439	…	57.0	…	43.0	117,079	1,314,574	1,313,263	47,306	32,239	21,371	21,736
		'07	46.2	4.0	0.1	49.7	325,598	…	47.1	…	52.9	139,136	1,408,691	1,407,539	-10,004	52,037	42,014	42,986
		'08	40.3	3.9	3.6	52.1	328,688	…	41.2	…	58.8	139,368	1,465,831	1,464,781	9,197	20,131	11,110	8,460
		'09	18.8	7.4	3.1	70.7	335,269	…	47.5	…	52.5	121,865	1,534,505	1,533,450	18,472	-4,849	-396	-3,214
		Rating History: A- g, 06/15/09; A- g, 03/05/08; B++gu, 03/13/07; B++g, 06/08/06; B++g, 12/19/05																
HEALTH PLAN OF UPPER OH VALLEY[2] Health Plan of the Upper Ohio Valley Philip D. Wright President 52160 National Road St. Clairsville, OH 43950 WV : 1979 : Non-Profit : Broker Group A&H, Health, Ind A&H 740-695-3585 AMB# 064201 NAIC# 95677	**NR-5**	'05	12.8	5.3	63.7	18.2	130,741	…	17.4	…	82.6	90,263	268,040	266,783	16,437	12,195	12,195	14,308
		'06	13.8	3.7	65.2	17.3	185,340	…	27.9	…	72.1	117,749	367,026	365,515	47,088	21,532	21,532	25,338
		'07	32.1	3.6	53.1	11.3	191,030	…	39.5	…	60.5	130,496	390,279	389,402	7,780	14,847	14,847	22,782
		'08	27.9	3.7	48.3	20.1	178,869	…	45.0	…	55.0	123,908	394,961	394,298	669	23,957	23,957	14,684
		'09	30.9	3.2	44.5	21.3	197,722	…	44.3	…	55.7	147,770	401,876	401,236	15,346	15,714	15,714	14,796
		Rating History: NR-5, 03/22/10; NR-5, 08/26/09; B pd, 07/14/08; B pd, 06/12/07; B- pd, 06/20/06																
HEALTH PLUS OF LOUISIANA INC[2] Willis-Knighton Medical Center Patrick F. Bicknell President P.O. Box 32625 Shreveport, LA 71103-2625 LA : 1995 : Stock : Broker Group A&H 318-212-8800 AMB# 064279 NAIC# 95009	**NR-5**	'05	18.6	…	0.0	81.4	25,928	…	52.6	…	47.4	15,107	54,082	52,345	1,559	2,196	2,151	2,145
		'06	29.9	…	0.0	70.1	27,555	…	36.9	…	63.1	17,664	54,778	52,835	2,297	2,638	2,581	2,581
		'07	38.1	…	0.0	61.8	28,511	…	47.5	…	52.5	19,254	57,227	55,118	-740	1,662	1,614	1,614
		'08	33.7	…	0.0	66.3	28,652	…	43.2	…	56.8	20,273	57,592	55,407	-171	856	844	870
		'09	17.0	…	0.1	82.9	17,108	…	54.4	…	45.6	9,167	61,002	58,562	-11,007	-11,349	-11,349	-11,011
		Rating History: NR-5, 04/23/10; NR-5, 08/26/09; B pd, 07/21/08; B pd, 06/28/07; B pd, 08/08/06																
HEALTH RESOURCES INC Allan L. Reid, D.M.D. President & CEO P.O. Box 15660 Evansville, IN 47716-0660 IN : 1987 : Stock : Broker Dental 812-424-1444 AMB# 068538 NAIC# 96687	**NR-4**	'05	…	10.3	2.9	86.9	6,667	…	44.0	…	56.0	4,814	31,137	31,137	1,276	1,252	751	751
		'06	…	12.0	3.2	84.8	7,033	…	48.4	…	51.6	5,131	35,156	35,156	312	1,201	714	712
		'07	…	20.5	2.5	77.0	8,054	…	43.6	…	56.4	5,783	38,698	38,698	1,106	1,094	667	669
		'08	11.3	16.4	1.4	70.9	9,731	…	31.5	…	68.5	6,239	43,521	43,521	1,862	988	703	672
		'09	…	…	…	…	…	…	…	…	…	…	…	…	…	…	…	…
		Rating History: NR-4, 04/21/10; B, 04/21/10; B, 06/12/09; B, 05/06/08; B, 05/18/07																
HEALTH RIGHT INC Vincent A. Keane Chairman 1101 14th Street, NW, Suite 900 Washington, DC 20005 DC : 1998 : Stock : Broker Health 202-218-0373 AMB# 064611 NAIC# 95787	**NR-5**	'05	31.9	…	…	68.1	8,697	…	83.1	…	16.9	5,081	32,552	31,850	1,616	1,196	695	695
		'06	2.9	…	…	97.1	27,941	…	89.1	…	10.9	8,247	63,436	62,459	13,956	5,305	3,142	3,167
		'07	…	…	…	100.0	39,587	…	88.4	…	11.6	15,164	105,566	104,924	11,662	9,294	6,507	6,508
		'08	…	…	…	100.0	34,055	…	94.6	…	5.4	6,388	99,963	99,963	-4,917	-4,833	-4,833	-4,833
		'09	…	…	…	100.0	33,964	…	91.0	…	9.0	7,084	106,684	106,684	-730	-3,700	-2,307	-2,307
		Rating History: NR-5, 03/22/10; NR-5, 08/26/09; C++pd, 07/01/08; C++pd, 06/26/07; B- pd, 07/25/06																
HEALTH TRADITION HEALTH PLAN[2] Karen L. Ytterberg, M.D. President P.O. Box 188 La Crosse, WI 54620-0188 WI : 1986 : Stock : Broker Group A&H, Health, Ind A&H 507-538-5212 AMB# 068620 NAIC# 96628	**NR-5**	'05	44.1	…	…	55.9	14,093	…	11.6	…	88.4	5,813	88,312	86,866	2,748	273	158	158
		'06	22.3	…	…	77.7	16,446	…	10.5	…	89.5	7,429	101,808	101,096	2,432	808	551	535
		'07	10.9	…	…	89.1	17,100	…	9.2	…	90.8	8,052	110,128	108,935	-73	1,236	755	755
		'08	7.0	…	…	93.0	17,577	…	11.6	…	88.4	8,238	112,784	111,394	966	187	30	30
		'09	12.2	…	…	87.8	16,459	…	33.1	…	66.9	8,316	133,303	131,639	-1,885	190	287	287
		Rating History: NR-5, 05/20/10; NR-5, 08/26/09; C++pd, 07/21/08; C++pd, 07/16/07; C++pd, 08/28/06																

BEST'S PROFITABILITY, LEVERAGE AND LIQUIDITY TESTS 2005 – 2009

Data in U.S. Dollars

	Profitability Tests							Leverage Tests						Liquidity Tests					
Un-Realized Capital Gains ($000)	Benefits Paid to NPW & Dep (%)	Comm. & Expenses to NPW & Dep (%)	NOG to Total Assets (%)	NOG to Total Rev (%)	Operating Return on Equity (%)	Net Yield (%)	Total Return (%)	Change in NPW & Dep (%)	NPW & Dep to Capital (X)	Capital & Surplus to Liabilities (%)	Surplus Relief (%)	Reins Leverage (%)	Change in Capital (%)	Quick Liquidity (%)	Current Liquidity (%)	Non-Invest Grade Bonds to Capital (%)	Delinq. & Foreclosed Mortgages to Capital (%)	Mort. & Credit Tenant Loans & R.E. to Capital (%)	Affiliated Invest to Capital (%)
...	...	...	...	...	...	...	...	...	...	...	...	...	...	...	...	...	...	...	...
...	84.2	15.0	...	2.4	...	...	...	...	8.6	60.0	...	...	...	125.3	131.4	...	...	...	...
...	92.5	19.1	-48.2	-11.6	-99.9	4.86	4.86	5.8	-10.0	-34.1	...	-0.6	-99.9	55.9	55.9	...	...	...	...
...	...	...	...	...	...	...	...	...	...	...	...	...	...	...	...	...	...	...	...
...	...	...	...	...	...	...	...	...	...	...	...	...	...	...	...	...	...	...	...
...	...	...	...	...	...	...	...	...	...	...	...	...	...	...	...	...	...	...	...
...	85.4	11.0	...	3.7	...	...	...	...	7.6	36.9	...	4.5	...	177.4	180.2	...	...	...	...
...	74.2	15.0	4.3	2.3	10.4	5.62	5.56	-2.2	3.2	122.1	...	12.4	129.3	138.3	143.7	...	...	...	...
...	69.7	18.1	26.1	15.0	41.5	2.95	2.94	3.1	2.3	233.3	...	0.6	43.0	70.1	70.1	...	...	...	...
...	76.9	15.7	9.0	5.2	13.2	2.72	2.78	4.9	2.6	198.0	...	1.2	-7.2	248.1	286.3	...	...	...	...
Principal Lines of Business: Medicare (100.0%)														Principal States: OR (100.0%)					
345	76.5	7.4	28.5	7.1	51.3	2.83	3.63	27.1	6.4	138.9	...	...	47.1	228.7	237.0	...	...	1.9	0.2
884	78.3	8.4	22.9	5.8	39.8	4.22	5.87	13.1	7.1	132.4	...	...	1.2	223.2	231.8	...	...	...	...
269	82.9	7.8	12.1	2.5	23.5	3.52	8.77	51.8	9.4	92.0	...	...	16.0	177.9	183.8	0.4	...	...	...
-2,035	79.0	10.4	19.3	3.8	38.1	1.74	-0.50	35.7	8.9	111.7	...	0.3	42.4	180.1	183.4	...	...	...	...
171	80.4	15.4	13.7	2.2	26.4	1.79	1.72	47.3	11.0	105.1	...	0.0	19.4	124.9	124.9	...	...	...	...
Principal Lines of Business: Medicaid (100.0%)														Principal States: MI (100.0%)					
...	77.2	20.6	8.2	1.7	21.8	3.40	3.58	15.0	11.3	65.1	...	0.2	24.6	190.2	200.7	...	...	11.0	4.5
...	77.7	20.8	7.2	1.6	19.1	5.07	5.21	9.7	11.2	56.5	...	0.2	10.2	134.3	143.8	...	0.6	36.8	3.9
...	77.2	20.1	12.9	3.0	32.8	5.30	5.64	7.2	10.1	74.6	...	0.2	18.8	163.1	171.4	1.1	...	9.3	7.5
25	80.0	19.4	3.4	0.8	8.0	3.79	2.87	4.1	10.5	73.6	...	0.2	0.2	180.2	191.5	0.7	...	9.3	12.0
-25	82.8	17.8	-0.1	0.0	-0.3	1.66	0.69	4.7	12.6	57.1	...	0.0	-12.6	203.4	212.6	1.0	...	20.5	3.4
Principal Lines of Business: CompHosp/Med (51.1%), Medicare (38.3%), Medicaid (9.1%), FEHBP (0.9%), Dental (0.5%)														Principal States: NV (99.6%)					
12,493	91.0	5.4	10.3	4.5	15.6	1.91	15.58	6.7	3.0	223.0	...	0.3	37.3	138.7	155.7	...	...	7.6	52.7
1,815	88.7	6.3	13.6	5.8	20.7	2.10	5.82	37.0	3.1	174.2	...	0.4	30.5	122.8	140.6	...	...	5.8	48.1
-6,319	91.1	6.6	7.9	3.8	12.0	2.83	3.87	6.5	3.0	215.6	...	0.2	10.8	182.0	209.9	...	...	5.2	19.8
-25,593	88.6	6.7	13.0	6.0	18.8	3.24	-15.30	1.3	3.2	225.4	...	0.3	-5.0	193.8	220.2	...	...	5.4	19.0
11,890	91.7	5.7	8.3	3.9	11.6	2.86	9.14	1.8	2.7	295.8	...	0.0	19.3	241.1	272.9	6.1	...	4.3	12.6
Principal Lines of Business: Medicare (46.7%), CompHosp/Med (37.1%), Medicaid (14.1%), FEHBP (2.1%)														Principal States: OH (50.4%), WV (49.6%)					
...	85.5	11.1	8.6	4.1	15.3	1.95	1.92	1.0	3.5	139.6	...	8.6	16.0	229.4	229.4	...	...	...	0.1
...	85.5	11.2	9.7	4.8	15.8	3.85	3.85	0.9	3.0	178.6	...	3.7	16.9	241.9	241.9	...	...	...	0.1
...	87.1	12.0	5.8	2.9	8.7	4.82	4.82	4.3	2.9	208.0	...	9.0	9.0	252.9	253.6	...	...	...	0.1
...	87.0	12.9	3.0	1.5	4.3	3.63	3.74	0.5	2.7	241.9	...	11.1	5.3	273.4	273.6	...	...	...	0.0
...	103.4	13.2	-49.6	-19.2	-77.1	2.76	4.67	5.7	6.4	115.4	...	13.8	-54.8	149.4	149.4	...	...	...	0.1
Principal Lines of Business: CompHosp/Med (100.0%)														Principal States: LA (100.0%)					
...	80.0	16.2	12.0	2.4	16.9	1.65	1.65	11.1	6.5	259.7	...	...	18.5	286.8	287.9	...	...	14.2	15.4
30	80.7	16.6	10.4	2.0	14.4	4.22	4.66	12.9	6.9	269.8	...	...	6.6	286.1	287.3	...	...	16.4	18.0
-37	80.1	18.0	8.8	1.7	12.2	5.43	4.94	10.1	6.7	254.7	...	...	12.7	251.2	252.3	...	...	28.5	29.1
-33	80.7	17.4	7.9	1.6	11.7	2.18	1.43	12.5	7.0	178.7	...	...	7.9	211.5	215.1	...	...	25.6	26.3
...	...	...	...	...	...	...	...	...	...	...	...	...	...	...	...	...	...	...	...
...	84.5	12.4	8.4	2.2	14.7	2.91	2.91	17.4	6.3	140.5	...	...	16.0	232.3	232.3	...	...	...	...
-1	85.6	7.0	17.2	5.0	47.2	4.24	4.39	96.1	7.6	41.9	...	-2.6	62.3	116.5	116.5	...	...	...	...
...	86.3	6.0	19.3	6.1	55.6	4.37	4.37	68.0	6.9	62.1	...	...	83.9	138.6	138.6	...	...	...	...
...	99.1	6.7	-13.1	-4.8	-44.8	3.13	3.13	-4.7	15.6	23.1	...	1.9	-57.9	104.6	104.6	...	...	...	...
...	95.1	8.5	-6.8	-2.2	-34.2	0.27	0.27	6.7	15.1	26.4	...	4.3	10.9	104.9	104.9	...	...	...	...
Principal Lines of Business: Medicaid (53.0%), CompHosp/Med (40.4%), OtherHlth (6.7%)														Principal States: DC (100.0%)					
...	90.5	9.7	1.2	0.2	2.8	2.28	2.28	7.1	14.9	70.2	...	3.7	3.0	172.6	172.6	...	...	...	...
...	90.9	8.8	3.6	0.5	8.3	2.50	2.39	16.4	13.6	82.4	...	0.2	27.8	192.8	192.8	...	...	...	...
...	91.1	8.3	4.5	0.7	9.7	2.90	2.90	7.8	13.5	89.0	...	10.4	8.4	231.0	231.0	...	...	...	...
...	91.5	8.7	0.2	0.0	0.4	1.56	1.56	2.3	13.5	88.2	...	1.5	2.3	180.3	180.3	...	...	...	...
...	91.2	8.8	1.7	0.2	3.5	0.31	0.31	18.2	15.8	102.1	...	0.7	0.9	183.5	183.5	...	...	...	...
Principal Lines of Business: CompHosp/Med (85.3%), Medicaid (12.2%), MedSup (2.5%)														Principal States: WI (100.0%)					

Data in U.S. Dollars

COMPANY NAME Ultimate Parent Association Principal Officer Mailing Address Dom. : Began Bus. : Struct. : Mktg. Specialty Phone # AMB# NAIC#	Best's Financial Strength Rating FSC		Balance Sheet										Operations					
		Data Year	Bonds (%)	Mort. Loans & R.E. (%)	Com & Pref. Stock (%)	All Other Assets (%)	Total Assets ($000)	Life Reserves (%)	Health Reserves (%)	Ann Res. & Dep. Liabilities (%)	All Other Liabilities (%)	Capital & Surplus ($000)	Direct Premiums Written ($000)	Net Premiums Written & Deposits ($000)	Operating Cash Flow ($000)	NOG Before Taxes ($000)	NOG After Taxes ($000)	Net Income ($000)
HEALTH VENTURES NETWORK DeCare International David B. Morse President 3560 Delta Dental Drive Eagan, MN 55122-3166 MN : 1985 : Non-Profit : Agency Group A&H 651-406-5900 AMB# 064540 NAIC# 48011	NR-2	'05	71.1	...	...	28.9	693	...	52.0	...	48.0	404	...	150	-110	17	17	17
		'06	59.3	...	...	40.7	827	...	...	...	100.0	677	...	107	61	273	273	273
		'07	88.6	...	...	11.4	777	...	...	...	100.0	755	...	77	172	100	78	78
		'08	87.3	...	...	12.7	780	...	...	...	100.0	775	...	17	8	33	27	21
		'09	85.5	...	...	14.5	793	...	...	...	100.0	782	...	...	19	7	7	7
		Rating History: NR-2, 10/02/09; NR-2, 11/24/08; NR-2, 10/04/07; NR-2, 10/19/06; NR-2, 10/13/05																
HEALTHAMERICA PENNSYLVANIA Coventry Health Care Inc Timothy E. Nolan President & CEO P.O. Box 67103 Harrisburg, PA 17106-7103 PA : 1975 : Stock : Broker Group A&H, Health, Ind A&H 800-788-6445 AMB# 068590 NAIC# 95060	A- Rating Outlook: Negative FSC VII	'05	76.7	...	...	23.3	231,634	...	63.7	...	36.3	117,209	798,023	785,811	30,516	87,929	62,225	62,179
		'06	65.0	...	...	35.0	253,929	...	50.0	...	50.0	124,895	764,421	754,350	27,945	97,074	67,207	67,157
		'07	87.9	...	...	12.1	211,140	...	59.4	...	40.6	114,103	683,807	675,391	-49,457	78,415	55,246	55,623
		'08	70.2	...	...	29.8	184,085	...	69.0	...	31.0	90,215	643,237	636,491	-24,571	48,503	33,786	32,642
		'09	77.6	...	...	22.4	206,914	...	52.3	...	47.7	97,840	613,612	608,309	19,022	41,018	21,601	23,508
		Rating History: A- g, 02/12/10; A- g, 11/19/08; A- g, 10/30/07; B++g, 07/11/07; B++g, 10/27/06																
HEALTHASSURANCE PENNSYLVANIA Coventry Health Care Inc Timothy E. Nolan President & CEO 3721 TecPort Drive Harrisburg, PA 17106-7103 PA : 2001 : Stock : Broker Group A&H, Health, Ind A&H 800-788-6445 AMB# 064719 NAIC# 11102	A- Rating Outlook: Negative FSC VII	'05	54.8	...	...	45.2	256,137	...	50.0	...	50.0	109,143	971,314	955,760	55,584	89,522	60,780	60,736
		'06	40.6	...	...	59.4	270,791	...	62.7	...	37.3	122,453	993,520	979,439	15,332	76,507	55,608	55,547
		'07	61.8	...	...	38.2	255,779	...	61.1	...	38.9	115,740	975,945	961,898	-12,016	62,410	44,991	45,163
		'08	78.8	...	...	21.2	201,017	...	69.7	...	30.3	104,440	885,796	873,054	-54,546	38,590	27,993	24,079
		'09	82.8	...	...	17.2	213,542	...	68.8	...	31.2	114,251	840,539	827,946	7,198	32,491	25,463	26,333
		Rating History: A- g, 02/12/10; A- g, 11/19/08; A- g, 10/30/07; B++g, 07/11/07; B++g, 10/27/06																
HEALTHCARE USA OF MISSOURI LLC Coventry Health Care Inc Dan Paquin President & CEO 10 South Broadway, Suite 1200 St. Louis, MO 63102 MO : 1995 : Stock : Other Health 314-241-5300 AMB# 064077 NAIC# 95318	B+ Rating Outlook: Negative FSC VII	'05	33.5	...	...	66.5	89,628	...	45.9	...	54.1	40,983	352,518	344,285	4,387	27,039	18,651	18,639
		'06	32.2	...	...	67.8	91,653	...	72.2	...	27.8	52,262	332,578	324,587	10,861	14,929	12,324	12,329
		'07	48.4	...	...	51.6	111,612	...	71.5	...	28.5	54,850	447,739	437,692	8,043	20,451	15,498	15,498
		'08	44.5	...	...	55.5	130,311	...	69.7	...	30.3	68,571	514,685	504,202	5,835	35,521	23,785	23,854
		'09	48.5	...	...	51.5	126,486	...	76.9	...	23.1	70,171	569,032	557,386	8,212	14,892	10,155	10,172
		Rating History: B+, 02/12/10; B+, 11/19/08; B+, 10/30/07; B+, 07/11/07; B+, 10/27/06																
HEALTHFIRST HEALTH PLAN OF NJ[2] HF Management Services LLC Michael Honig Chief Executive Officer 25 Broadway New York, NY 10004 NJ : 2008 : Non-Profit : Not Available Medicare, Medicaid 212-801-6000 AMB# 064974 NAIC# 13035	NR-5	'05	...	...	...	...	...	...	...	...	...	...	...	...	...	...	...	...
		'06	...	...	...	...	...	...	...	...	...	...	...	...	...	...	...	...
		'07	...	...	...	...	...	...	...	...	...	...	...	...	...	...	...	...
		'08	...	...	...	100.0	9,202	20.8	64.8	...	14.4	5,289	16,179	16,106	4,181	133	133	133
		'09	...	...	...	100.0	14,392	4.0	92.4	...	3.6	5,917	39,537	39,179	3,006	-199	-199	-199
		Rating History: NR-5, 04/26/10; NR-5, 06/01/09																
HEALTHKEEPERS INC WellPoint Inc. Thomas R. Byrd Chairman & President 2015 Staples Mill Road Richmond, VA 23230 VA : 1986 : Stock : Broker Group A&H, Health, Ind A&H 804-354-7000 AMB# 068669 NAIC# 95169	A Rating Outlook: Stable FSC X	'05	76.5	...	...	23.5	309,410	...	46.0	...	54.0	200,836	706,220	704,817	51,820	90,675	59,131	58,572
		'06	79.7	...	...	20.3	327,791	...	42.0	...	58.0	211,193	768,017	766,183	9,026	90,421	61,909	61,597
		'07	74.1	...	...	25.9	311,038	...	41.1	...	58.9	180,468	833,109	830,307	-20,091	84,942	54,631	54,383
		'08	72.5	...	...	27.5	318,293	...	34.2	...	65.8	179,341	860,099	857,711	-15,910	82,952	55,398	53,842
		'09	60.7	...	...	39.3	321,611	...	44.2	...	55.8	173,295	921,303	917,193	-34,547	72,436	44,971	42,190
		Rating History: A g, 04/27/10; A, 01/23/09; A, 03/20/08; A, 11/06/06; A, 12/29/05																
HEALTHLINK HMO INC WellPoint Inc. David W. Fields President 6775 W. Washington Street Milwaukee, WI 53214 MO : 1993 : Stock : Broker Group A&H 314-923-4444 AMB# 060152 NAIC# 96475	NR-3	'05	7.7	...	...	92.3	15,395	...	...	...	100.0	14,751	2,350	2,350	-11,726	13,676	9,205	8,943
		'06	20.3	...	...	79.7	27,964	...	...	...	100.0	24,587	1,684	1,684	13,407	15,637	10,004	10,004
		'07	77.6	...	...	22.4	25,663	...	...	...	100.0	24,964	376	346	-999	18,041	11,929	11,929
		'08	83.1	...	...	16.9	26,701	...	...	...	100.0	24,360	186	106	1,228	18,440	11,982	11,982
		'09	100.1	...	...	-0.1	23,621	...	...	...	100.0	22,968	145	75	-3,112	17,598	11,451	11,451
		Rating History: NR-3, 04/27/10; NR-3, 01/23/09; NR-3, 03/20/08; A-, 11/06/06; A-, 12/29/05																
HEALTHMARKETS INSURANCE CO Blackstone Investor Group Phillip Hildebrand President & CEO 9151 Boulevard 26 North Richland Hills, TX 76180 OK : 1981 : Stock : Not Available Inactive 817-255-3100 AMB# 009066 NAIC# 92908	NR-3	'05	75.5	...	...	24.5	9,078	...	...	...	100.0	8,988	...	...	302	257	167	167
		'06	95.9	...	...	4.1	9,291	...	...	...	100.0	9,185	...	...	250	303	197	197
		'07	73.6	...	...	26.4	9,686	...	...	...	100.0	9,568	...	...	274	266	174	174
		'08	70.6	...	...	29.4	9,406	...	...	...	100.0	9,291	...	...	-397	-482	-200	-200
		'09	87.5	...	...	12.5	8,996	...	...	...	100.0	8,793	...	...	4	-780	-380	-366
		Rating History: NR-3, 06/07/10; NR-3, 05/28/09; NR-3, 07/24/08; NR-3, 06/11/08; NR-1, 06/08/07																
HEALTHNOW NEW YORK INC Alphonso O'Neil-White President & CEO 257 West Genesee Street Buffalo, NY 14202 NY : 1940 : Non-Profit : Agency Group A&H 716-887-6900 AMB# 064602 NAIC# 55204	NR-5	'05	52.2	...	16.5	31.3	698,681	...	58.6	...	41.4	363,736	2,155,452	2,155,452	94,854	109,462	85,929	91,216
		'06	50.4	...	15.3	34.3	763,891	...	53.9	...	46.1	462,020	2,115,838	2,115,838	55,304	110,756	85,778	79,992
		'07	52.2	...	17.8	30.0	809,468	...	52.8	...	47.2	496,428	2,139,609	2,139,609	43,700	77,939	57,020	75,746
		'08	57.5	...	15.8	26.7	782,695	...	51.4	...	48.6	445,557	2,272,241	2,272,241	-3,088	74,122	67,254	25,407
		'09	50.7	...	15.6	33.8	896,604	...	50.4	...	49.6	546,244	2,444,886	2,444,886	34,907	67,926	56,354	62,034
		Rating History: NR-5, 04/07/10; NR-5, 08/26/09; B+ pd, 09/19/08; B+ pd, 09/04/07; B+ pd, 09/29/06																

BEST'S PROFITABILITY, LEVERAGE AND LIQUIDITY TESTS 2005 – 2009

Data in U.S. Dollars

—	Profitability Tests							Leverage Tests						Liquidity Tests					
Un-Realized Capital Gains ($000)	Benefits Paid to NPW & Dep (%)	Comm. & Expenses to NPW & Dep (%)	NOG to Total Assets (%)	NOG to Total Rev (%)	Operating Return on Equity (%)	Net Yield (%)	Total Return (%)	Change in NPW & Dep (%)	NPW & Dep to Capital (X)	Capital & Surplus to Liabilities (%)	Surplus Relief (%)	Reins Leverage (%)	Change in Capital (%)	Quick Liquidity (%)	Current Liquidity (%)	Non-Invest Grade Bonds to Capital (%)	Delinq. & Foreclosed Mortgages to Capital (%)	Mort. & Credit Tenant Loans & R.E. to Capital (%)	Affiliated Invest to Capital (%)
...	100.1	8.7	2.5	9.3	4.2	3.72	3.72	...	0.4	140.1	...	37.1	4.3	144.2	161.3	...	...	...	...
...	-99.9	9.0	35.9	205.8	50.5	3.43	3.43	-28.5	0.2	452.0	...	32.9	67.5	397.8	430.5	...	...	...	...
...	...	12.7	9.7	70.8	10.8	4.11	4.11	-28.2	0.1	999.9	...	0.8	11.4	999.9	999.9	...	...	...	...
...	...	58.3	3.5	62.3	3.5	2.94	2.13	-77.6	0.0	999.9	...	...	2.7	999.9	999.9	...	...	...	...
...	...	...	0.9	27.7	0.9	2.89	2.89	-99.9	...	999.9	...	...	0.9	999.9	999.9	...	...	...	...
138	81.1	8.6	28.6	7.8	60.2	3.82	3.73	5.5	6.7	102.4	...	2.5	31.0	179.5	196.8	0.7	...	...	...
116	80.7	7.7	27.7	8.8	55.5	4.38	4.41	-4.0	6.0	96.8	...	3.2	6.6	207.1	224.7	0.8	...	...	...
-92	82.1	7.7	23.8	8.1	46.2	4.53	4.67	-10.5	5.9	117.6	...	2.4	-8.6	158.4	177.4	0.8	...	...	...
114	86.5	7.0	17.1	5.3	33.1	4.14	3.55	-5.8	7.1	96.1	...	2.2	-20.9	180.4	194.5	...	...	...	...
...	86.5	7.6	11.0	3.5	23.0	3.31	4.45	-4.4	6.2	89.7	...	0.9	8.5	154.7	170.5	...	...	...	...
Principal Lines of Business: Medicare (70.5%), FEHBP (16.0%), CompHosp/Med (13.5%)														Principal States: PA (99.8%)					
...	77.9	13.2	26.8	6.3	66.9	3.07	3.05	15.8	8.8	74.2	...	3.9	50.6	185.1	198.4	...	...	...	...
...	80.9	12.5	21.1	5.6	48.0	3.84	3.82	2.5	8.0	82.6	...	3.4	12.2	218.6	231.5	...	...	...	...
...	81.8	12.8	17.1	4.6	37.8	4.26	4.33	-1.8	8.3	82.6	...	3.4	-5.5	180.7	192.7	...	...	...	...
...	84.2	12.2	12.3	3.2	25.4	3.40	1.64	-9.2	8.4	108.1	...	4.0	-9.8	206.1	224.1	...	...	...	...
...	84.0	12.7	12.3	3.1	23.3	2.81	3.26	-5.2	7.2	115.1	...	4.6	9.4	196.4	216.1	...	...	...	...
Principal Lines of Business: CompHosp/Med (79.6%), Medicare (20.4%)														Principal States: PA (100.0%)					
...	82.5	9.5	22.2	5.4	50.1	4.67	4.65	0.1	8.4	84.2	...	5.6	22.3	126.9	136.5	...	...	...	...
...	88.4	8.8	13.6	3.8	26.4	5.41	5.42	-5.7	6.2	132.7	...	8.9	27.5	202.5	217.5	...	...	...	...
...	87.8	8.2	15.2	3.5	28.9	5.05	5.05	34.8	8.0	96.6	...	8.7	5.0	118.1	129.6	...	...	...	...
...	85.8	7.7	19.7	4.7	38.5	4.40	4.50	15.2	7.4	111.1	...	5.5	25.0	122.2	132.1	...	...	...	...
...	85.0	12.7	7.9	1.8	14.6	3.02	3.04	10.5	7.9	124.6	...	5.8	2.3	158.1	172.7	...	...	...	...
Principal Lines of Business: Medicaid (100.0%)														Principal States: MO (100.0%)					
...	...	...	...	...	...	...	...	...	...	...	...	...	...	...	...	...	...	...	...
...	...	...	...	...	...	...	...	...	...	...	...	...	...	...	...	...	...	...	...
...	...	...	...	...	...	...	...	...	...	...	...	...	...	...	...	...	...	...	...
...	86.6	13.4	...	0.8	...	...	...	...	3.0	135.1	...	0.8	...	201.2	202.5	...	...	...	...
...	87.4	13.4	-1.7	-0.5	-3.5	1.34	1.34	143.3	6.6	69.8	...	11.2	11.9	163.2	167.7	...	...	...	...
Principal Lines of Business: Medicare (96.2%), Medicaid (3.8%)														Principal States: NJ (100.0%)					
...	77.1	11.4	21.0	8.3	33.2	3.97	3.75	11.6	3.5	185.0	...	...	29.3	253.0	271.8	...	...	...	...
-10	79.7	10.0	19.4	8.0	30.1	4.34	4.23	8.7	3.6	181.1	...	0.0	5.2	219.1	241.5	0.2	...	...	...
-43	82.0	8.7	17.1	6.5	27.9	4.87	4.76	8.4	4.6	138.2	...	0.7	-14.5	187.3	207.4	0.2	...	...	...
53	84.3	7.6	17.6	6.4	30.8	4.69	4.11	3.3	4.8	129.1	...	0.8	-0.6	157.7	175.4	0.1	...	...	...
-42	84.6	8.0	14.1	4.9	25.5	4.59	3.39	6.9	5.3	116.8	...	0.8	-3.4	127.4	140.7	0.6	...	...	...
Principal Lines of Business: CompHosp/Med (61.8%), Medicaid (38.2%)														Principal States: VA (100.0%)					
...	116.4	91.5	43.8	49.6	45.2	4.63	3.19	-47.7	0.2	999.9	...	...	-43.2	999.9	999.9	...	...	...	...
...	164.1	105.2	46.1	49.6	50.9	4.75	4.75	-28.4	0.1	728.0	...	...	66.7	999.9	999.9	...	...	...	...
...	331.1	311.5	44.5	58.9	48.2	5.98	5.98	-79.5	0.0	999.9	...	0.0	1.5	999.9	999.9	...	...	...	...
...	4.9	-99.9	45.8	999.9	48.6	4.07	4.07	-69.3	0.0	999.9	...	0.0	-2.4	999.9	999.9	...	...	...	...
...	...	-99.9	45.5	999.9	48.4	3.13	3.13	-29.2	0.0	999.9	...	0.0	-5.7	999.9	999.9	...	...	...	...
Principal Lines of Business: CompHosp/Med (100.0%)														Principal States: MO (100.0%)					
...	...	...	1.9	65.0	1.9	2.90	2.90	...	...	999.9	...	...	1.9	999.9	999.9	...	...	...	...
...	...	...	2.1	65.0	2.2	3.35	3.35	...	...	999.9	...	...	2.2	999.9	999.9	...	...	...	...
-1	...	...	1.8	41.5	1.9	4.56	4.55	...	...	999.9	...	...	4.2	999.9	999.9	...	...	...	...
1	...	...	-2.1	-51.4	-2.1	4.27	4.28	...	...	999.9	...	...	-2.9	999.9	999.9	...	...	...	...
...	...	...	-4.1	-99.9	-4.2	1.78	1.78	...	...	999.9	...	...	-5.4	999.9	999.9	...	...	...	...
1,418	86.3	9.9	13.2	3.9	26.9	3.55	4.92	4.5	5.9	108.6	...	...	32.1	138.5	153.4	0.2	...	...	0.0
5,582	86.7	9.9	11.7	4.0	20.8	4.57	4.54	-1.8	4.6	153.1	...	...	27.0	175.5	192.5	0.1	...	...	6.4
-13,751	87.8	10.0	7.2	2.6	11.9	4.43	5.30	1.1	4.3	158.6	...	...	7.4	174.2	192.7	...	...	...	5.1
-22,023	88.0	9.9	8.4	2.9	14.3	3.64	-6.20	6.2	5.1	132.2	...	...	-10.2	141.1	158.5	...	...	...	4.4
14,043	88.3	10.2	6.7	2.3	11.4	3.37	6.42	7.6	4.5	155.9	...	...	22.6	162.6	177.5	...	...	...	3.1
Principal Lines of Business: CompHosp/Med (65.4%), Medicare (26.8%), Medicaid (3.9%), OtherHlth (1.8%), FEHBP (1.2%)														Principal States: NY (100.0%)					

Data in U.S. Dollars

COMPANY NAME Ultimate Parent Association Principal Officer Mailing Address Dom. : Began Bus. : Struct. : Mktg. Specialty Phone # AMB# NAIC#	Best's Financial Strength Rating FSC	Data Year	Balance Sheet Bonds (%)	Mort. Loans & R.E. (%)	Com & Pref. Stock (%)	All Other Assets (%)	Total Assets ($000)	Life Reserves (%)	Health Reserves (%)	Ann Res. & Dep. Liabilities (%)	All Other Liabilities (%)	Capital & Surplus ($000)	Operations Direct Premiums Written ($000)	Net Premiums Written & Deposits ($000)	Operating Cash Flow ($000)	NOG Before Taxes ($000)	NOG After Taxes ($000)	Net Income ($000)
HEALTHPARTNERS INC[2] HealthPartners Inc Mary K. Brainerd President & CEO P.O. Box 1309 Minneapolis, MN 55440-1309 MN : 1984 : Non-Profit : Broker Group A&H, Health, Ind A&H 952-883-6584 AMB# 068731 NAIC# 95766	NR-5	'05	26.1	...	...	73.9	377,822	...	85.8	...	14.2	275,121	1,282,268	1,282,005	-30,411	17,077	17,077	16,677
		'06	19.3	...	...	80.7	427,705	...	83.1	...	16.9	296,981	1,454,456	1,453,702	8,064	22,541	22,541	21,177
		'07	18.4	...	...	81.6	498,205	...	75.9	...	24.1	344,744	1,577,923	1,577,538	77,831	34,539	34,539	34,589
		'08	18.8	...	...	81.2	491,058	...	69.9	...	30.1	335,414	1,633,698	1,633,222	-5,421	37,825	37,825	35,337
		'09	21.1	...	...	78.9	544,932	...	71.5	...	28.5	386,554	1,584,537	1,584,279	18,038	35,520	35,520	35,990
		Rating History: NR-5, 06/02/10; NR-5, 08/26/09; B+ pd, 09/03/08; B+ pd, 08/08/07; B+ pd, 09/05/06																
HEALTHPLEX INSURANCE CO[2] Healthplex Inc Martin Kane President 333 Earle Ovington Boulevard Uniondale, NY 11553 NY : 2003 : Stock : Not Available Dental 516-542-2200 AMB# 013569 NAIC# 11172	NR-5	'05	...	...	...	...	...	...	...	...	...	...	...	...	...	...	...	...
		'06	...	...	...	...	...	...	...	...	...	...	...	...	...	...	...	...
		'07	...	...	...	...	...	...	...	...	...	...	...	...	...	...	...	...
		'08	22.5	...	...	77.5	962	...	38.8	...	61.2	882	954	954	132	120	120	120
		'09	...	...	...	100.0	1,027	...	31.4	...	68.6	947	892	892	70	65	65	65
		Rating History: NR-5, 04/30/10; NR-5, 05/05/09																
HEALTHPLEX OF NJ INC[2] Healthplex Inc Martin Kane President 333 Earle Ovington Boulevard Uniondale, NY 11553 NJ : 2007 : Non-Profit : Not Available Dental 516-542-2200 AMB# 064959 NAIC# 12830	NR-5	'05	...	...	...	...	...	...	...	...	...	...	...	...	...	...	...	...
		'06	...	...	...	...	...	...	...	...	...	...	...	...	...	...	...	...
		'07	...	...	...	...	...	...	...	...	...	...	...	...	...	...	...	...
		'08	...	...	...	100.0	1,265	...	72.0	...	28.0	381	8,954	8,954	261	-3,020	-3,020	-3,020
		'09	...	...	...	100.0	1,864	...	43.5	...	56.5	1,052	9,552	9,552	606	-2,869	-2,869	-2,869
		Rating History: NR-5, 04/19/10; NR-5, 06/01/09																
HEALTHPLUS INSURANCE COMPANY[1] HealthPlus of Michigan Inc Bruce R. Hill President 2050 South Linden Road Flint, MI 48532 MI : 2007 : Stock 800-332-9161 AMB# 060672 NAIC# 12826	NR-1	'05	...	...	...	...	...	...	...	...	...	...	...	...	...	...	...	...
		'06	...	...	...	...	...	...	...	...	...	...	...	...	...	...	...	...
		'07	3.3	...	...	96.7	9,885	...	...	...	100.0	8,329	3,063	2,925	...	-289	-296	-296
		'08	5.7	...	...	94.3	18,233	...	...	...	100.0	10,898	19,164	18,270	...	-3,931	-3,931	-3,931
		'09	1.3	...	...	98.7	25,509	...	...	...	100.0	13,052	44,801	43,983	...	-3,739	-3,739	-3,739
		Rating History: NR-1, 06/10/10; NR-1, 06/12/09; NR-1, 06/12/08																
HEALTHPLUS OF MICHIGAN INC HealthPlus of Michigan Inc David P. Crosby President P.O. Box 1700 Flint, MI 48501-1700 MI : 1979 : Non-Profit : Broker Group A&H, Health 800-332-9161 AMB# 068555 NAIC# 95580	NR-5	'05	3.1	4.2	7.7	85.0	114,253	...	41.0	...	59.0	44,907	389,340	389,253	22,404	10,857	10,857	10,857
		'06	2.5	3.9	13.6	80.0	140,233	...	28.8	...	71.2	58,155	402,528	402,272	24,605	10,031	10,031	10,018
		'07	2.0	3.5	12.0	82.4	160,571	...	30.3	...	69.7	76,008	413,167	412,622	20,823	19,724	19,724	19,817
		'08	1.9	3.4	13.3	81.4	157,640	...	35.0	...	65.0	82,118	417,709	417,176	8,048	15,715	15,715	15,693
		'09	14.3	3.3	15.0	67.4	164,672	...	34.7	...	65.3	86,377	436,068	435,591	1,697	731	731	652
		Rating History: NR-5, 05/21/10; NR-5, 08/26/09; B- pd, 07/14/08; B- pd, 06/19/07; B- pd, 07/17/06																
HEALTHPLUS PARTNERS INC HealthPlus of Michigan Inc David P. Crosby Interim President P.O. Box 1700 Flint, MI 48501-1700 MI : 2003 : Non-Profit : Broker Health 800-332-9161 AMB# 064762 NAIC# 11549	NR-5	'05	...	...	36.6	63.4	15,046	...	41.2	...	58.8	8,491	135,537	135,473	1,002	156	156	156
		'06	...	...	17.2	82.8	34,955	...	35.5	...	64.5	11,482	136,334	136,224	14,942	1,797	1,797	1,809
		'07	...	...	19.6	80.4	32,543	...	43.1	...	56.9	8,604	177,613	177,421	-4,659	-2,959	-2,959	-2,959
		'08	...	...	17.3	82.7	31,701	...	41.3	...	58.7	10,142	196,586	196,414	3,137	-627	-627	-646
		'09	...	...	13.3	86.7	48,014	...	55.6	...	44.4	23,427	222,653	222,541	14,099	5,491	5,491	5,491
		Rating History: NR-5, 05/21/10; NR-5, 08/26/09; C pd, 07/14/08; C pd, 06/19/07; C pd, 06/13/06																
HEALTHSPRING LIFE AND HEALTH[2] HealthSpring, Inc. Michael G. Mirt Chairman, President & CEO 601 Mainstream Drive Nashville, TN 37228 TX : 2007 : Stock : Not Available Ind A&H 615-565-8100 AMB# 060673 NAIC# 12902	NR-5	'05	...	...	...	...	...	...	...	...	...	...	...	...	...	...	...	...
		'06	...	...	...	...	...	...	...	...	...	...	...	...	...	...	...	...
		'07	...	...	...	...	...	...	...	...	...	...	...	...	...	...	...	...
		'08	...	...	...	100.0	7,694	...	...	...	100.0	7,694	...	...	-514	186	145	145
		'09	0.8	...	...	99.2	90,686	...	64.9	...	35.1	34,576	138,201	138,201	42,824	28,703	17,454	17,454
		Rating History: NR-5, 05/06/10; NR-5, 05/11/09; NR-1, 06/12/08																
HEALTHSPRING OF ALABAMA INC[2] HealthSpring, Inc. Rene P. Moret Chairman, President & CEO 2 Chase Corporate Drive, Suite 300 Birmingham, AL 35244 AL : 1986 : Stock : Broker Group A&H, Health 205-423-1000 AMB# 068784 NAIC# 95781	NR-5	'05	19.8	...	...	80.2	39,412	...	93.6	...	6.4	10,245	195,708	195,708	15,296	3,352	2,189	2,189
		'06	9.9	...	...	90.1	88,987	...	46.2	...	53.8	30,071	285,922	286,085	44,255	28,535	18,976	18,977
		'07	12.6	...	...	87.4	79,229	...	66.5	...	33.5	36,691	305,431	305,401	-13,184	12,556	8,495	8,485
		'08	37.4	...	...	62.6	78,770	...	73.8	...	26.2	44,350	338,196	338,146	-2,699	24,603	17,612	17,594
		'09	35.3	...	...	64.7	78,667	...	71.7	...	28.3	41,923	376,531	376,482	-6,383	19,309	11,977	11,968
		Rating History: NR-5, 04/26/10; NR-5, 08/26/09; C++pd, 10/10/08; B- pd, 08/22/07; C++pd, 09/05/06																
HEALTHSPRING OF TENNESSEE HealthSpring, Inc. Shawn Morris President 44 Vantage Way, Suite 300 Nashville, TN 37228-1513 TN : 1995 : Stock : Broker Group A&H, Health 615-291-7000 AMB# 064300 NAIC# 11522	NR-5	'05	23.1	...	...	76.9	56,029	...	90.6	...	9.4	16,204	391,412	391,412	16,178	6,459	4,291	4,291
		'06	8.3	...	...	91.7	148,551	...	42.5	...	57.5	35,700	622,281	622,281	85,665	6,658	4,289	4,289
		'07	22.4	...	...	77.6	239,134	...	37.8	...	62.2	59,151	734,591	734,591	83,258	40,762	28,345	28,345
		'08	23.3	...	...	76.7	203,061	...	76.7	...	23.3	93,812	919,107	919,107	-86,764	53,253	37,793	37,793
		'09	29.6	...	...	70.4	172,280	...	58.0	...	42.0	90,314	984,343	984,343	15,651	3,229	-6,364	-6,364
		Rating History: NR-5, 04/20/10; NR-5, 08/26/09; C+ pd, 10/10/08; C+ pd, 08/22/07; C+ pd, 09/15/06																

2010 BEST'S KEY RATING GUIDE — LIFE/HEALTH EDITION
BEST'S PROFITABILITY, LEVERAGE AND LIQUIDITY TESTS 2005 – 2009

Data in U.S. Dollars

	Profitability Tests							Leverage Tests						Liquidity Tests					
Un-Realized Capital Gains ($000)	Benefits Paid to NPW & Dep (%)	Comm. & Expenses to NPW & Dep (%)	NOG to Total Assets (%)	NOG to Total Rev (%)	Operating Return on Equity (%)	Net Yield (%)	Total Return (%)	Change in NPW & Dep (%)	NPW & Dep to Capital (X)	Capital & Surplus to Liabilities (%)	Surplus Relief (%)	Reins Leverage (%)	Change in Capital (%)	Quick Liquidity (%)	Current Liquidity (%)	Non-Invest Grade Bonds to Capital (%)	Delinq. & Foreclosed Mortgages to Capital (%)	Mort. & Credit Tenant Loans & R.E. to Capital (%)	Affiliated Invest to Capital (%)
…	89.4	9.8	4.5	1.3	6.3	2.80	2.56	12.8	4.7	267.9	…	…	3.9	132.0	139.1	…	…	…	99.3
…	91.1	8.3	5.6	1.5	7.9	4.32	3.45	13.4	4.9	227.2	…	…	7.9	98.2	103.7	…	…	…	85.0
…	90.0	8.8	7.5	2.2	10.8	4.55	4.57	8.5	4.6	224.6	…	0.1	16.1	177.8	184.5	…	…	…	78.7
…	90.0	8.6	7.6	2.3	11.1	3.24	2.19	3.5	4.9	215.5	…	…	-2.7	142.1	148.1	0.1	…	…	…
-794	89.8	8.6	6.9	2.2	9.8	1.46	1.32	-3.0	4.1	244.1	…	0.1	15.2	219.7	234.8	0.5	…	…	…
	Principal Lines of Business: CompHosp/Med (70.2%), Medicaid (24.3%), Dental (4.3%), Medicare (1.2%), MedSup (0.1%)													Principal States: MN (100.0%)					
…	…	…	…	…	…	…	…	…	…	…	…	…	…	…	…	…	…	…	…
…	…	…	…	…	…	…	…	…	…	…	…	…	…	…	…	…	…	…	…
…	…	…	…	…	…	…	…	…	…	…	…	…	…	…	…	…	…	…	…
…	51.9	36.6	…	12.4	…	…	…	…	1.1	999.9	…	…	…	999.9	999.9	…	…	…	…
…	54.0	38.5	6.5	7.3	7.1	-0.21	-0.21	-6.5	0.9	999.9	…	…	7.4	999.9	999.9	…	…	…	…
	Principal Lines of Business: Dental (100.0%)													Principal States: NY (100.0%)					
…	…	…	…	…	…	…	…	…	…	…	…	…	…	…	…	…	…	…	…
…	…	…	…	…	…	…	…	…	…	…	…	…	…	…	…	…	…	…	…
…	…	…	…	…	…	…	…	…	…	…	…	…	…	…	…	…	…	…	…
…	133.8	0.1	…	-33.7	…	…	…	…	23.5	43.1	…	…	…	142.3	142.3	…	…	…	…
…	129.7	0.6	-99.9	-30.0	-99.9	1.23	1.23	6.7	9.1	129.7	…	…	176.1	229.7	229.7	…	…	…	…
	Principal Lines of Business: Dental (100.0%)													Principal States: NJ (100.0%)					
…	…	…	…	…	…	…	…	…	…	…	…	…	…	…	…	…	…	…	…
…	…	…	…	…	…	…	…	…	…	…	…	…	…	…	…	…	…	…	…
…	98.4	26.0	…	-8.8	…	…	…	…	0.4	535.4	…	…	…	…	…	…	…	…	…
…	112.1	10.9	-28.0	-21.2	-40.9	…	…	524.7	1.7	148.6	…	…	30.8	…	…	…	…	…	…
…	101.8	7.0	-17.1	-8.5	-31.2	…	…	140.7	3.4	104.8	…	…	19.8	…	…	…	…	…	…
	Principal Lines of Business: GrpA&H (100.0%)																		
1,239	90.0	7.9	10.6	2.8	27.7	2.96	4.28	6.5	8.7	64.8	…	…	34.3	225.4	238.5	0.6	…	10.8	30.9
4,000	89.2	9.3	7.9	2.5	19.5	3.28	6.66	3.3	6.9	70.9	…	0.5	29.5	226.4	239.6	…	…	9.4	45.4
-2,252	86.7	9.7	13.1	4.7	29.4	3.71	2.21	2.6	5.4	89.9	…	…	30.7	264.5	279.7	…	…	7.5	31.7
-9,847	86.7	10.4	9.9	3.7	19.9	2.32	-4.02	1.1	5.1	108.7	…	0.5	8.0	292.7	310.0	…	…	6.5	33.0
3,754	89.9	9.6	0.5	0.2	0.9	0.68	3.13	4.4	5.0	110.3	…	0.0	5.2	97.5	97.5	…	…	6.2	34.0
	Principal Lines of Business: CompHosp/Med (68.4%), Medicare (29.5%), FEHBP (2.1%)													Principal States: MI (100.0%)					
1,023	91.2	9.4	1.1	0.1	2.0	4.56	12.91	29.0	16.0	129.5	…	…	16.1	314.6	340.7	…	…	…	-1.8
1,182	84.4	9.2	7.2	1.4	18.0	5.96	11.57	0.6	11.9	48.9	…	…	35.2	208.9	222.8	…	…	…	6.5
81	88.0	8.2	-8.8	-1.8	-29.5	4.80	5.09	30.2	20.6	35.9	…	…	-25.1	172.3	184.5	…	…	…	0.1
-1,109	87.2	8.4	-2.0	-0.3	-6.7	3.35	-0.85	10.7	19.4	47.0	…	…	17.9	211.8	225.8	…	…	…	0.1
640	84.3	12.1	13.8	2.5	32.7	1.14	3.00	13.3	9.5	95.3	…	…	131.0	144.9	144.9	…	…	…	0.1
	Principal Lines of Business: Medicaid (100.0%)													Principal States: MI (100.0%)					
…	…	…	…	…	…	…	…	…	…	…	…	…	…	…	…	…	…	…	…
…	…	…	…	…	…	…	…	…	…	…	…	…	…	…	…	…	…	…	…
…	…	…	…	…	…	…	…	…	…	…	…	…	…	…	…	…	…	…	…
…	…	…	…	78.1	…	…	…	…	…	…	…	…	…	…	…	…	…	…	…
…	42.2	10.8	35.5	12.6	82.6	0.29	0.29	…	4.0	61.6	…	…	349.4	94.9	94.9	…	…	…	…
	Principal Lines of Business: IndA&H (100.0%)													Principal States: TX (22.0%), IL (8.2%), TN (8.0%), LA (4.3%), AL (4.1%)					
…	81.5	17.0	6.7	1.1	24.4	2.49	2.49	45.0	19.1	35.1	…	…	33.4	105.8	119.2	…	…	…	…
…	75.8	15.1	29.6	6.6	94.1	3.54	3.55	46.2	9.5	51.0	…	…	193.5	138.9	140.2	…	…	…	…
…	82.5	15.0	10.1	2.7	25.4	6.36	6.35	6.8	8.3	86.3	…	…	22.0	162.6	164.0	…	…	…	…
…	79.1	14.0	22.3	5.2	43.5	3.33	3.30	10.7	7.6	128.8	…	…	20.9	203.4	255.4	…	…	…	…
…	81.0	14.3	15.2	3.2	27.8	1.89	1.87	11.3	9.0	114.1	…	…	-5.5	157.0	206.9	…	…	…	…
	Principal Lines of Business: Medicare (99.2%), CompHosp/Med (0.8%)													Principal States: AL (100.0%)					
…	80.0	18.8	9.3	1.1	34.3	3.97	3.97	36.4	24.2	40.7	…	…	84.4	93.9	93.9	…	…	…	…
…	83.5	15.8	4.2	0.7	16.5	5.95	5.95	59.0	17.4	31.6	…	…	120.3	109.4	109.4	…	…	…	…
…	81.7	14.5	14.6	3.8	59.8	6.25	6.25	18.0	12.4	32.9	…	…	65.7	113.3	115.9	…	…	…	…
…	81.4	13.6	17.1	4.1	49.4	4.66	4.66	25.1	9.8	85.9	…	…	58.6	111.1	114.8	…	…	…	…
…	85.6	14.2	-3.4	-0.6	-6.9	1.57	1.57	7.1	10.9	110.2	…	…	-3.7	278.1	295.7	…	…	…	…
	Principal Lines of Business: Medicare (78.9%), OtherHlth (20.9%), CompHosp/Med (0.2%)													Principal States: TN (64.6%), IL (14.4%), MS (5.0%)					

2010 BEST'S KEY RATING GUIDE — LIFE/HEALTH EDITION
ANNUAL STATEMENT DATA FOR YEARS 2005 – 2009

Data in U.S. Dollars

COMPANY NAME Ultimate Parent Association Principal Officer Mailing Address Dom. : Began Bus. : Struct. : Mktg. Specialty Phone # AMB# NAIC#	Best's Financial Strength Rating FSC	Data Year	Balance Sheet Bonds (%)	Mort. Loans & R.E. (%)	Com & Pref. Stock (%)	All Other Assets (%)	Total Assets ($000)	Life Reserves (%)	Health Reserves %)	Ann Res. & Dep. Liabilities (%)	All Other Liabilities (%)	Capital & Surplus ($000)	Operations Direct Premiums Written ($000)	Net Premiums Written & Deposits ($000)	Operating Cash Flow ($000)	NOG Before Taxes ($000)	NOG After Taxes ($000)	Net Income ($000)
HEALTHWISE Regence Group D. Scott Ideson President P.O. Box 1271 Portland, OR 97207-1271 UT : 1982 : Non-Profit : Broker Group A&H 801-333-2000	**A-**	'05	63.6	...	14.6	21.8	56,401	...	67.3	...	32.7	47,893	67,447	62,245	2,928	10,182	6,655	6,568
		'06	59.3	...	24.5	16.2	66,281	...	63.3	...	36.7	53,722	84,146	77,852	11,332	7,252	4,190	4,182
	Rating Outlook: Negative	'07	64.5	...	21.0	14.5	80,716	...	51.0	...	49.0	63,467	98,361	91,033	13,870	14,206	9,554	9,621
		'08	69.8	...	12.2	18.0	85,408	...	46.2	...	53.8	68,119	96,484	88,627	8,575	16,424	10,107	7,625
		'09	70.8	...	19.3	9.9	91,534	...	27.4	...	72.6	77,337	65,632	60,754	4,800	9,286	6,017	5,580
AMB# 068604 NAIC# 95303	**FSC VIII**	**Rating History: A- g, 06/11/10; A- g, 06/17/09; A- g, 11/19/08; A- g, 10/16/07; A- g, 08/28/06**																
HEALTHY ALLIANCE LIFE INS CO WellPoint Inc. Dennis A. Matheis President 6775 W Washington Street Milwaukee, WI 53214 MO : 1971 : Stock : Not Available Group A&H 314-923-4444	**A**	'05	75.9	...	...	24.1	456,515	0.5	57.9	0.6	41.0	199,463	1,409,679	1,411,039	-2,225	100,771	63,742	63,227
		'06	68.1	...	0.8	31.1	529,918	0.4	63.3	0.7	35.6	222,798	1,499,164	1,501,358	55,171	110,189	67,360	67,201
	Rating Outlook: Stable	'07	69.7	...	0.5	29.8	541,529	0.1	61.0	0.5	38.5	213,983	1,478,129	1,480,923	12,618	130,122	84,918	83,029
		'08	69.3	...	0.4	30.4	598,258	0.0	69.5	0.3	30.2	268,945	1,562,695	1,553,489	28,989	179,051	116,334	107,535
		'09	73.1	...	...	26.9	624,295	0.0	61.3	0.2	38.4	252,111	1,600,073	1,591,164	14,972	169,611	114,719	106,665
AMB# 008217 NAIC# 78972	**FSC IX**	**Rating History: A g, 04/27/10; A g, 01/23/09; A g, 03/20/08; A g, 11/06/06; A g, 12/29/05**																
HEART OF AMERICA HEALTH PLAN[2] Gary Dosch President 810 South Main Rugby, ND 58368 ND : 1982 : Non-Profit : Broker Health 701-776-5848	**NR-5**	'05	55.1	...	10.0	34.9	1,320	...	63.0	...	37.0	803	5,075	4,715	-31	23	23	23
		'06	58.5	...	10.0	31.5	1,453	...	59.3	...	40.7	868	5,196	4,794	88	74	74	74
		'07	51.1	...	8.8	40.1	1,703	...	56.7	...	43.3	1,083	5,003	4,599	254	281	281	281
		'08	64.2	...	9.1	26.7	2,114	...	67.8	...	32.2	1,623	4,867	4,515	305	565	565	565
		'09	62.8	...	8.4	28.9	2,074	...	49.4	...	50.6	1,501	4,706	4,419	-100	-45	-45	-45
AMB# 064184 NAIC# 52554		**Rating History: NR-5, 04/28/10; NR-5, 03/31/09; NR-5, 03/31/08; NR-5, 05/21/07; NR-5, 05/22/06**																
HEARTLAND FIDELITY INS CO David S. Karlin President 1200 G Street, N. W. Washington, DC 20005 DC : 2003 : Stock : Exclusive Agent Group A&H 202-434-8354	**B++**	'05	...	...	...	100.0	10,084	...	...	...	100.0	9,206	17,043	16,435	...	6,764	4,438	4,438
		'06	...	...	...	100.0	13,322	...	...	...	100.0	12,229	14,432	13,894	...	4,577	3,023	3,023
	Rating Outlook: Stable	'07	...	...	...	100.0	17,078	...	...	...	100.0	13,911	16,328	16,535	...	2,533	1,682	1,682
		'08	...	...	...	100.0	16,614	...	...	...	100.0	14,361	18,223	21,783	...	696	450	450
		'09	...	...	...	100.0	17,221	...	...	...	100.0	14,885	19,991	26,090	...	781	525	525
AMB# 076359 NAIC# 11686	**FSC V**	**Rating History: B++, 06/01/10; B++, 06/03/09; B++, 06/12/08; B+, 05/18/07; B+, 06/20/06**																
HEARTLAND NATIONAL LIFE INS CO Heartland Holding Company Inc Christopher M. McDaniel Chrm, President & CEO P.O. Box 2878 Salt Lake City, UT 84110-2878 IN : 1965 : Stock : Agency Ind Life, Pre-need 816-476-0120	**NR-5**	'05	82.2	...	...	17.8	4,482	22.6	...	41.5	35.9	1,874	1,688	-28,122	-28,020	851	851	524
		'06	61.5	...	...	38.5	5,122	23.5	...	50.4	26.1	3,012	2,555	48	459	-3	-3	-3
		'07	73.8	...	...	26.2	4,879	24.3	...	52.7	22.9	3,007	1,728	16	-82	-3	-3	-3
		'08	44.1	...	...	55.9	5,641	24.8	...	52.9	22.4	4,007	1,139	7	765	-5	-5	-5
		'09	49.7	...	...	50.3	6,929	13.0	1.0	20.0	66.0	3,626	1,476	171	887	-114	-114	-114
AMB# 006730 NAIC# 66214		**Rating History: NR-5, 03/30/10; NR-5, 04/22/09; NR-5, 10/10/08; NR-3, 07/03/08; NR-3, 05/18/07**																
HERITAGE PROVIDER NETWORK INC Richard Merkin, M.D. President & Corporate Secretary 8510 Balboa Boulevard, Suite 285 Northridge, CA 91325 CA : 1996 : Stock : Agency Group A&H 818-654-3461	**NR-5**	'05	...	0.0	...	100.0	140,152	...	...	...	100.0	26,454	...	...	2,590	3,014	2,726	2,726
		'06	...	0.0	...	100.0	146,883	...	...	...	100.0	29,849	...	...	-7,548	2,904	2,611	2,611
		'07	...	0.0	...	100.0	161,851	...	...	...	100.0	31,322	...	...	-15,288	2,858	2,624	2,624
		'08	...	0.0	...	100.0	165,577	...	...	...	100.0	39,953	...	...	16,464	3,686	2,588	2,588
		'09	...	0.0	...	100.0	241,952	...	...	...	100.0	70,842	...	...	40,214	98	245	245
AMB# 064580		**Rating History: NR-5, 06/02/10; NR-5, 05/08/09; NR-5, 05/05/08; NR-5, 04/27/07; NR-5, 09/06/06**																
HERITAGE UNION LIFE INS CO[1] Julia B. Roper President 1805 Monument Avenue, Suite 201 Richmond, VA 23220-7001 AZ : 1964 : Stock : Inactive ISWL, Univ Life 804-212-2815	**NR-1**	'05	94.1	...	1.2	4.7	49,807	...	...	...	100.0	11,547	5,539	-12,411	...	-142	-142	760
		'06	86.8	...	...	13.2	12,327	...	...	...	100.0	11,662	5,216	-50	...	339	339	42
		'07	61.9	...	...	38.1	11,886	...	...	...	100.0	11,722	4,603	...	...	36	36	63
		'08	65.5	...	...	34.5	12,094	...	...	...	100.0	11,691	4,270	0	...	-3,446	-3,446	-3,446
		'09	77.3	...	...	22.7	9,344	...	...	...	100.0	9,160	3,819	3	...	-2,463	-2,463	-2,463
AMB# 006281 NAIC# 62421		**Rating History: NR-1, 06/10/10; NR-1, 06/12/09; NR-1, 06/12/08; NR-5, 05/09/07; NR-5, 05/02/06**																
HHS HEALTH OF OKLAHOMA INC Universal American Corp. Theodore M. Carpenter, Jr. President 4888 Loop Central Drive, Suite 700 Houston, TX 77081 OK : 2009 : Stock : Broker Inactive 713-770-1111	**NR-2**	'05	...	...	...	...	...	...	...	...	...	...	...	...	...	...	...	...
		'06	...	...	...	...	...	...	...	...	...	...	...	...	...	...	...	...
		'07	...	...	...	...	...	...	...	...	...	...	...	...	...	...	...	...
		'08	...	...	...	...	...	...	...	...	...	...	...	...	...	...	...	...
		'09	35.6	...	...	64.4	1,560	...	...	...	100.0	1,555	...	...	1,559	7	5	5
AMB# 064977 NAIC# 13667		**Rating History: NR-2, 04/16/10**																
HIGGINBOTHAM BURIAL INS CO[1] Mary Jo Higginbotham President P.O. Box 686 Walnut Ridge, AR 72476-0686 AR : 1959 : Stock : Not Available 870-886-7766	**NR-1**	'05	37.6	...	3.5	58.9	1,333	...	...	...	100.0	95	90	90	...	-17	-14	-14
		'06	44.4	...	3.9	51.7	1,355	...	...	...	100.0	31	104	104	...	-52	-52	-52
		'07	37.6	...	3.2	59.2	1,412	...	...	...	100.0	15	77	77	...	-84	-83	-83
		'08	26.9	...	7.1	65.9	1,443	...	...	...	100.0	34	91	91	...	-47	-47	-47
		'09	24.9	...	8.8	66.3	1,448	...	...	...	100.0	175	70	70	...	91	91	91
AMB# 068345 NAIC# 84042		**Rating History: NR-1, 06/10/10; NR-1, 06/12/09; NR-1, 06/12/08; NR-1, 06/08/07; NR-1, 06/07/06**																

BEST'S PROFITABILITY, LEVERAGE AND LIQUIDITY TESTS 2005 – 2009

Data in U.S. Dollars

—	Profitability Tests							Leverage Tests						Liquidity Tests					
Un-Realized Capital Gains ($000)	Benefits Paid to NPW & Dep (%)	Comm. & Expenses to NPW & Dep (%)	NOG to Total Assets (%)	NOG to Total Rev (%)	Operating Return on Equity (%)	Net Yield (%)	Total Return (%)	Change in NPW & Dep (%)	NPW & Dep to Capital (X)	Capital & Surplus to Liabilities (%)	Surplus Relief (%)	Reins Leverage (%)	Change in Capital (%)	Quick Liquidity (%)	Current Liquidity (%)	Non-Invest Grade Bonds to Capital (%)	Delinq. & Foreclosed Mortgages to Capital (%)	Mort. & Credit Tenant Loans & R.E. to Capital (%)	Affiliated Invest to Capital (%)
168	67.5	19.6	12.3	10.1	15.0	5.42	5.60	15.4	1.3	562.9	…	…	16.5	437.9	485.9	0.8	…	…	…
1,817	72.5	20.9	6.8	5.2	8.2	5.22	8.63	25.1	1.4	427.8	…	1.4	12.2	365.5	414.9	1.0	…	…	…
142	67.8	19.4	13.0	10.2	16.3	4.89	5.20	16.9	1.4	367.9	…	3.9	18.1	313.3	362.2	0.2	…	…	…
-2,255	67.8	16.5	12.2	11.1	15.4	4.13	-1.91	-2.6	1.3	394.0	…	1.1	7.3	391.8	435.2	0.0	…	…	…
2,346	72.6	16.9	6.8	9.5	8.3	4.04	6.40	-31.5	0.8	544.8	…	4.4	13.5	493.9	551.6	0.2	…	…	…

Principal Lines of Business: CompHosp/Med (96.5%), MedSup (2.5%), OtherHlth (1.0%) Principal States: UT (100.0%)

…	78.7	14.8	14.1	4.5	32.0	4.73	4.70	12.5	7.1	78.1	0.5	4.5	0.2	100.2	124.8	…	…	…	…
…	80.7	13.2	13.7	4.4	31.9	4.88	4.82	6.4	6.7	73.0	0.4	4.1	11.8	99.5	113.9	1.1	…	…	…
…	80.3	12.1	15.9	5.7	38.9	5.28	4.75	-1.4	6.9	65.4	0.4	4.1	-4.2	99.3	112.9	1.7	…	…	…
0	79.2	10.5	20.4	7.4	48.2	5.34	3.25	4.9	5.8	81.7	0.3	3.8	25.6	102.9	117.0	1.9	…	…	…
0	79.4	11.5	18.8	7.1	44.0	5.78	4.04	2.4	6.3	67.8	0.3	3.7	-6.2	89.8	104.3	3.6	…	…	…

Principal Lines of Business: GrpA&H (79.6%), IndA&H (20.4%) Principal States: MO (100.0%)

-22	90.1	10.1	1.8	0.5	2.9	3.00	1.25	-2.1	5.9	155.4	…	12.6	2.2	196.1	212.6	4.5	…	…	…
21	88.9	10.4	5.3	1.5	8.8	3.27	4.96	1.7	5.5	148.2	…	4.2	8.0	193.7	210.9	4.7	…	…	…
-28	84.5	10.5	17.8	6.0	28.8	3.43	1.55	-4.1	4.2	174.8	…	2.0	24.8	226.7	243.1	3.2	…	…	…
29	78.6	10.2	29.6	12.3	41.7	3.32	4.94	-1.8	2.8	330.7	…	1.7	49.9	346.9	379.7	2.0	…	…	…
-23	92.0	10.4	-2.2	-1.0	-2.9	3.19	2.01	-2.1	2.9	262.0	…	5.0	-7.5	285.0	311.6	2.6	…	…	…

Principal Lines of Business: CompHosp/Med (63.5%), OtherHlth (30.3%), FEHBP (6.1%) Principal States: ND (100.0%)

…	21.7	31.6	54.4	28.6	63.5	…	…	26.8	1.8	999.9	…	6.6	93.1	988.6	988.6	…	…	…	…
…	29.6	36.4	25.8	22.0	28.2	…	…	-15.5	1.1	999.9	…	4.4	32.8	999.9	999.9	…	…	…	…
…	53.9	32.2	11.1	10.0	12.9	…	…	19.0	1.2	439.2	…	1.6	13.8	432.8	432.8	…	…	…	…
…	68.2	29.4	2.7	2.1	3.2	…	…	31.7	1.5	637.2	…	1.6	3.2	659.6	659.6	…	…	…	…
…	68.7	27.8	3.1	2.0	3.6	…	…	19.8	1.8	637.2	…	1.5	3.7	640.5	640.5	…	…	…	…

Principal Lines of Business: GrpA&H (100.0%) Principal States: DC (100.0%)

263	-6.2	-0.3	4.3	-3.4	33.0	5.57	5.27	-99.9	-14.9	72.4	71.9	999.9	-44.1	157.7	168.3	…	…	…	…
…	363.9	383.8	-0.1	-0.9	-0.1	4.42	4.44	100.2	0.0	143.7	1.8	939.0	60.4	254.5	267.5	…	…	…	…
…	999.9	999.9	-0.1	-0.8	-0.1	5.01	5.15	-66.8	0.0	162.0	2.3	632.8	-0.1	295.1	315.8	…	…	…	…
…	999.9	999.9	-0.1	-2.6	-0.1	2.83	2.97	-58.2	0.0	246.2	0.6	462.5	33.0	330.4	340.2	…	…	…	…
…	299.0	72.6	-1.8	-15.0	-3.0	1.34	1.38	999.9	0.0	110.1	13.2	187.6	-9.5	179.4	184.1	…	…	…	…

Principal Lines of Business: IndAnn (62.5%), IndA&H (37.2%), GrpAnn (0.4%) Principal States: MO (54.6%), TX (17.4%), AR (9.2%), GA (6.0%), MS (5.8%)

…	999.9	539.9	2.0	0.4	10.5	3.69	3.69	…	…	23.3	…	…	4.1	104.0	104.0	…	…	0.1	0.1
…	999.9	567.0	1.8	0.3	9.3	3.00	3.00	…	…	25.5	…	…	12.8	101.2	101.2	…	…	0.1	0.1
…	999.9	702.6	1.7	0.3	8.6	3.39	3.39	…	…	24.0	…	…	4.9	81.8	81.8	…	…	0.1	0.1
…	999.9	745.5	1.6	0.3	7.3	3.41	3.41	…	…	31.8	…	…	27.6	70.3	70.3	…	…	0.1	0.1
…	999.9	644.5	0.1	0.0	0.4	0.84	0.84	…	…	41.4	…	…	77.3	92.1	92.1	…	…	0.1	0.1

…	-11.1	-23.2	-0.3	0.5	-1.3	…	…	-99.9	-1.1	30.6	2.9	…	7.0	…	…	…	…	…	…
…	213.7	-99.9	1.1	70.6	2.9	…	…	99.6	0.0	999.9	…	…	0.1	…	…	…	…	…	…
…	…	…	0.3	7.0	0.3	…	…	100.0	…	999.9	…	…	0.5	…	…	…	…	…	…
…	62.2	999.9	-28.7	-99.9	-29.4	…	…	…	0.0	999.9	0.0	…	-0.3	…	…	…	…	…	…
…	30.6	999.9	-23.0	-99.9	-23.6	…	…	999.9	0.0	999.9	1.7	…	-21.6	…	…	…	…	…	…

Principal Lines of Business: OrdLife (95.5%), IndA&H (4.5%)

…	…	…	…	…	…	…	…	…	…	…	…	…	…	…	…	…	…	…	…
…	…	…	…	…	…	…	…	…	…	…	…	…	…	…	…	…	…	…	…
…	…	…	…	…	…	…	…	…	…	…	…	…	…	…	…	…	…	…	…
…	…	…	…	…	…	…	…	…	…	…	…	…	…	…	…	…	…	…	…
…	…	…	…	45.8	…	…	…	…	…	999.9	…	…	…	999.9	999.9	…	…	…	…

-3	95.6	63.8	-1.0	-9.5	-13.3	…	…	-6.6	0.9	8.5	…	…	-10.0	…	…	…	…	…	…
6	82.7	51.8	-3.9	-31.9	-82.5	…	…	16.6	2.2	3.6	…	…	-54.5	…	…	…	…	…	…
-7	106.5	94.6	-6.0	-60.5	-99.9	…	…	-26.6	2.0	2.7	…	…	-20.7	…	…	…	…	…	…
-135	123.4	87.2	-3.3	-27.5	-99.9	…	…	18.7	2.5	2.6	…	…	-2.6	…	…	…	…	…	…
51	149.5	87.4	6.3	69.5	86.7	…	…	-22.8	0.4	14.0	…	…	385.9	…	…	…	…	…	…

Principal Lines of Business: OrdLife (100.0%)

ANNUAL STATEMENT DATA FOR YEARS 2005 – 2009

Data in U.S. Dollars

COMPANY NAME Ultimate Parent Association Principal Officer Mailing Address Dom. : Began Bus. : Struct. : Mktg. Specialty Phone # AMB# NAIC#	Best's Financial Strength Rating FSC	Data Year	Balance Sheet Bonds (%)	Mort. Loans & R.E. (%)	Com & Pref. Stock (%)	All Other Assets (%)	Total Assets ($000)	Life Reserves (%)	Health Reserves %)	Ann Res. & Dep. Liabilities (%)	All Other Liabilities (%)	Capital & Surplus ($000)	Operations Direct Premiums Written ($000)	Net Premiums Written & Deposits ($000)	Operating Cash Flow ($000)	NOG Before Taxes ($000)	NOG After Taxes ($000)	Net Income ($000)
HIGHMARK INC. Highmark Inc.	A	'05	29.5	1.5	41.0	28.0	4,718,513	...	26.4	...	73.6	2,844,615	4,178,403	4,209,973	130,683	220,307	105,987	157,092
Kenneth R. Melani, M.D. President & CEO		'06	29.7	1.4	51.4	17.5	5,049,556	...	27.2	...	72.8	3,206,817	4,658,925	4,690,053	-468,938	171,118	62,900	132,370
120 Fifth Avenue, Suite 924 Pittsburgh, PA 15222-3024	Rating Outlook: Negative	'07	27.5	1.4	52.0	19.0	5,267,189	...	29.9	...	70.1	3,483,388	5,175,463	5,205,550	-18,278	126,356	100,174	260,447
PA : 1996 : Non-Profit : Direct Response A&H, Hosp Ind, Maj med		'08	25.9	1.4	46.4	26.2	5,008,958	...	36.0	...	64.0	3,063,138	5,748,623	5,770,415	-267,711	-83,183	137,249	51,752
412-544-7000		'09	25.5	1.4	48.2	24.9	5,361,491	...	38.2	...	61.8	3,394,765	6,087,793	6,107,969	147,387	66,744	58,351	74,206
AMB# 064010 NAIC# 54771	FSC XV	**Rating History: A g, 03/25/10; A g, 06/15/09; A g, 06/12/08; A g, 03/05/07; A g, 02/07/06**																
HIGHMARK SENIOR RESOURCES INC Highmark Inc.	NR-2	'05	1.0	...	...	99.0	10,681	...	...	...	100.0	2,226	...	...	9,447	-20,973	-21,006	-21,006
Cynthia M. Dellecker President & CEO		'06	0.2	...	...	99.8	43,152	...	39.6	...	60.4	15,602	123,910	123,910	9,588	-10,934	-7,143	-7,143
120 Fifth Avenue Pittsburgh, PA 15222-3099		'07	0.2	...	...	99.8	62,275	...	25.5	...	74.5	13,406	156,730	156,730	-14,161	-18,302	-11,381	-11,381
PA : 2005 : Non-Profit : Broker Med supp, Health		'08	...	...	...	100.0	48,819	...	9.7	...	90.3	12,285	127,695	127,695	2,993	-16,533	-10,217	-10,217
412-544-7000		'09	0.3	...	...	99.7	40,248	...	40.0	...	60.0	24,333	109,609	109,609	15,226	4,718	5,794	5,794
AMB# 060570 NAIC# 10131		**Rating History: NR-2, 03/25/10; NR-2, 06/15/09; NR-2, 06/13/08; NR-2, 03/05/07; NR-2, 02/07/06**																
HIGHMARK WEST VIRGINIA INC Highmark Inc.	A	'05	49.3	0.4	4.4	45.8	227,750	...	67.9	...	32.1	99,149	552,566	550,026	-5,834	30,188	24,726	24,385
J. Fred Earley II President		'06	57.0	0.4	4.6	38.0	247,604	...	72.3	...	27.7	122,011	654,481	651,893	27,104	23,244	20,647	21,181
P.O. Box 1948 Parkersburg, WV 26101	Rating Outlook: Negative	'07	58.1	0.9	5.3	35.7	276,686	...	62.4	...	37.6	164,082	656,646	653,735	43,252	51,031	41,606	41,802
WV : 1983 : Non-Profit : Not Available Group A&H		'08	53.1	4.3	2.8	39.7	345,277	...	61.9	...	38.1	205,315	719,500	716,859	57,419	59,754	49,480	49,623
304-424-9813		'09	55.8	4.2	3.1	36.9	365,766	...	63.4	...	36.6	212,779	766,794	762,996	10,755	7,301	4,012	5,344
AMB# 064415 NAIC# 54828	FSC XV	**Rating History: A g, 03/25/10; A g, 06/15/09; A g, 06/12/08; A g, 03/05/07; A g, 02/07/06**																
HIP INSURANCE CO OF NEW YORK EmblemHealth Inc	B	'05	79.5	...	...	20.5	27,301	...	67.8	...	32.2	19,545	26,191	26,019	-611	-3,484	-4,005	-4,013
Anthony L. Watson Chairman & CEO		'06	65.8	...	...	34.2	30,693	...	87.8	...	12.2	21,284	50,885	50,768	1,562	2,414	2,108	2,063
55 Water Street New York, NY 10041-8190	Rating Outlook: Negative	'07	22.0	...	0.0	78.0	96,679	...	22.9	...	77.1	22,681	172,884	174,281	2,261	2,214	1,358	1,220
NY : 1995 : Stock : Not Available Group A&H		'08	30.3	...	...	69.7	68,131	...	63.9	...	36.1	35,905	146,944	149,484	23,891	-3,455	-2,537	-3,140
646-447-5000		'09	37.1	...	...	62.9	62,930	...	76.5	...	23.5	27,481	182,523	187,875	-14,145	-13,876	-10,998	-11,153
AMB# 008034 NAIC# 60094	FSC XI	**Rating History: B g, 06/09/10; B g, 05/29/09; B+ g, 06/06/08; B+ g, 05/10/07; B+ gu, 11/16/06**																
HM HEALTH INSURANCE COMPANY Highmark Inc.	NR-2	'05	90.2	...	...	9.8	13,684	...	...	...	100.0	13,019	...	...	504	459	326	326
Cynthia M. Dellecker President & CEO		'06	92.0	...	...	8.0	12,617	...	...	...	100.0	10,460	...	...	-823	-2,483	-2,517	-2,517
120 Fifth Avenue, Suite 924 Pittsburgh, PA 15222		'07	56.5	...	...	43.5	20,208	...	63.1	...	36.9	12,666	52,754	52,754	5,947	3,260	2,359	2,348
PA : 1955 : Stock : Agency Ind A&H		'08	40.5	...	...	59.5	23,304	...	82.8	...	17.2	12,652	69,912	69,912	509	-81	34	56
412-544-7000		'09	55.3	...	...	44.7	28,510	...	83.2	...	16.8	11,392	91,686	91,686	4,018	-3,075	-1,297	-1,244
AMB# 006128 NAIC# 71768		**Rating History: NR-2, 03/25/10; NR-3, 06/15/09; NR-3, 06/13/08; NR-3, 03/05/07; NR-3, 11/06/06**																
HM LIFE INSURANCE COMPANY Highmark Inc.	A-	'05	85.1	...	...	14.9	400,029	13.6	69.3	0.3	16.8	125,012	327,787	286,933	26,937	10,950	8,747	8,744
Daniel J. Lebish Chairman & CEO		'06	75.4	...	3.5	21.1	284,767	1.9	68.5	...	29.6	138,674	329,419	284,933	-113,820	13,704	10,466	10,468
P.O. Box 535061 Pittsburgh, PA 15253-5061	Rating Outlook: Stable	'07	70.4	...	2.9	26.6	317,951	2.0	71.0	...	27.0	141,816	314,797	315,886	28,829	7,495	4,620	4,447
PA : 1981 : Stock : Broker Stop Loss		'08	57.8	...	2.5	39.7	350,111	1.2	72.2	...	26.5	148,492	387,105	383,947	8,791	5,211	2,119	-34
800-328-5433		'09	63.4	...	2.1	34.4	346,167	1.4	70.9	...	27.7	157,802	375,976	394,099	17,742	17,330	12,718	12,718
AMB# 009063 NAIC# 93440	FSC VIII	**Rating History: A- g, 03/25/10; A- g, 06/15/09; A- g, 06/12/08; A- g, 03/05/07; A- g, 02/07/06**																
HM LIFE INSURANCE COMPANY NY Highmark Inc.	A-	'05	79.1	...	...	20.9	40,596	17.7	62.3	...	20.0	16,922	60,396	50,769	5,013	3,203	2,038	2,038
Daniel J. Lebish CEO		'06	51.1	...	...	48.9	47,723	13.3	55.2	...	31.5	19,614	65,245	49,761	6,667	4,065	2,744	2,744
P.O. Box 535061 Pittsburgh, PA 15253-5061	Rating Outlook: Stable	'07	41.3	...	...	58.7	50,989	11.5	65.2	...	23.3	19,574	63,849	53,666	3,446	45	72	51
NY : 1997 : Stock : Broker Stop Loss		'08	66.1	...	...	33.9	41,849	4.2	68.5	...	27.3	21,550	58,999	53,289	-8,740	2,854	2,032	2,032
800-235-6753		'09	70.4	...	...	29.6	41,082	0.5	69.3	...	30.2	20,592	65,594	61,236	-55	-1,819	-1,121	-1,121
AMB# 060209 NAIC# 60213	FSC VIII	**Rating History: A- g, 03/25/10; A- g, 06/15/09; A- g, 06/12/08; A- g, 03/05/07; A- g, 02/07/06**																
HMO COLORADO INC WellPoint Inc.	A	'05	77.4	...	...	22.6	92,313	...	51.7	...	48.3	53,510	206,082	206,183	-11,080	18,196	14,141	14,329
David S. Helwig President		'06	66.3	...	0.5	33.2	105,160	...	58.4	...	41.6	56,042	222,940	222,940	-2,128	22,049	16,509	16,475
700 Broadway Denver, CO 80273	Rating Outlook: Stable	'07	46.0	...	...	54.0	115,721	...	78.2	...	21.8	50,764	325,181	325,181	-10,701	-18,220	-13,079	-13,132
CO : 1980 : Stock : Broker Group A&H, Health		'08	53.1	...	...	46.9	104,968	...	71.1	...	28.9	50,341	383,738	383,738	10,519	9,009	10,153	9,700
303-831-2131		'09	59.9	...	...	40.1	82,473	...	57.2	...	42.8	55,932	281,040	281,040	-40,730	11,381	9,999	10,152
AMB# 068927 NAIC# 95473	FSC IX	**Rating History: A g, 04/27/10; A, 01/23/09; A, 03/20/08; A, 11/06/06; A, 12/29/05**																
HMO LOUISIANA INC[2] Louisiana Health Service & Indemnity Co	NR-5	'05	58.2	...	12.2	29.6	194,505	...	33.6	...	66.4	124,120	281,642	281,642	28,100	27,311	20,847	21,871
Gery J. Barry President & CEO		'06	62.3	...	15.7	22.0	219,976	...	41.3	...	58.7	142,757	289,817	289,817	21,986	19,623	16,954	17,025
5525 Reitz Avenue Baton Rouge, LA 70809		'07	62.0	...	15.8	22.2	238,108	...	37.8	...	62.2	162,437	323,262	323,262	15,837	23,616	19,207	20,336
LA : 1986 : Non-Profit : Broker Group A&H, Health, Ind A&H		'08	60.9	...	11.1	28.0	251,517	...	36.0	...	64.0	171,837	362,997	362,997	22,002	39,785	25,199	23,591
225-295-3307		'09	51.6	...	22.4	26.0	301,201	...	34.2	...	65.8	208,228	423,918	423,918	23,805	30,880	19,705	17,236
AMB# 068990 NAIC# 95643		**Rating History: NR-5, 04/26/10; NR-5, 08/26/09; B++pd, 09/08/08; B+ pd, 08/27/07; B+ pd, 09/25/06**																

Data in U.S. Dollars

—	Profitability Tests							Leverage Tests						Liquidity Tests					
Un-Realized Capital Gains ($000)	Benefits Paid to NPW & Dep (%)	Comm. & Expenses to NPW & Dep (%)	NOG to Total Assets (%)	NOG to Total Rev (%)	Operating Return on Equity (%)	Net Yield (%)	Total Return (%)	Change in NPW & Dep (%)	NPW & Dep to Capital (X)	Capital & Surplus to Liabilities (%)	Surplus Relief (%)	Reins Leverage (%)	Change in Capital (%)	Quick Liquidity (%)	Current Liquidity (%)	Non-Invest Grade Bonds to Capital (%)	Delinq. & Foreclosed Mortgages to Capital (%)	Mort. & Credit Tenant Loans & R.E. to Capital (%)	Affiliated Invest to Capital (%)
115,298	83.5	8.9	2.4	2.6	3.9	2.40	7.49	6.0	1.5	151.8	0.0	0.2	11.8	115.1	127.3	3.7	...	2.6	43.0
289,240	84.1	10.1	1.3	1.4	2.1	2.87	12.88	11.4	1.5	174.0	20.4	0.2	12.7	93.4	107.7	5.8	...	2.2	52.6
45,483	90.3	9.4	1.9	1.9	3.0	6.07	11.25	11.0	1.5	195.3	0.0	0.0	8.6	108.8	126.0	2.8	...	2.1	52.8
-218,329	90.4	9.3	2.7	2.4	4.2	3.72	-3.90	10.9	1.9	157.4	0.0	0.4	-12.1	81.2	90.2	2.4	...	2.3	65.4
382,202	90.1	8.7	1.1	1.0	1.8	4.43	15.20	5.8	1.8	172.6	0.0	0.5	10.8	95.2	106.8	3.1	...	2.2	64.7

Principal Lines of Business: CompHosp/Med (65.5%), Medicare (17.9%), FEHBP (9.8%), MedSup (5.9%), OtherHlth (0.4%) — Principal States: PA (100.0%)

...	...	...	...	-99.9	...	...	...	...	...	20.3	...	...	...	211.0	222.1	...	...	...	...
...	85.5	23.6	-26.5	-5.8	-80.1	4.57	4.57	...	7.9	56.6	...	...	600.8	130.6	137.5	...	...	...	...
...	93.0	18.9	-21.6	-7.2	-78.5	-10.78	-10.78	26.5	11.7	27.4	...	...	-14.1	18.7	19.7	...	...	...	...
...	95.3	16.8	-18.4	-8.1	-79.5	5.83	5.83	-18.5	10.4	33.6	...	...	-8.4	40.4	42.5	...	...	...	...
...	79.6	15.8	13.0	5.3	31.6	-5.44	-5.44	-14.2	4.5	152.9	...	...	98.1	239.3	263.8	...	...	...	...

Principal Lines of Business: OtherHlth (100.0%) — Principal States: PA (90.7%), WV (9.3%)

22	86.0	9.4	11.4	4.5	26.5	5.43	5.21	9.2	5.5	77.1	...	0.8	13.5	111.0	118.6	1.0	...	1.0	2.2
-360	88.1	10.0	8.7	3.1	18.7	7.12	7.23	18.5	5.3	97.1	...	0.7	23.1	126.6	136.2	...	...	0.7	1.5
-43	84.9	9.3	15.9	6.2	29.1	6.88	6.96	0.3	4.0	145.7	...	0.3	34.5	171.1	184.2	0.5	...	1.5	1.9
-5,281	84.6	8.6	15.9	6.8	26.8	4.93	2.77	9.7	3.5	146.7	...	0.3	25.1	180.3	190.2	0.2	...	7.3	7.3
-555	89.8	8.8	1.1	0.5	1.9	4.07	4.36	6.4	3.6	139.1	...	0.2	3.6	156.7	169.6	...	...	7.2	7.1

Principal Lines of Business: CompHosp/Med (61.4%), FEHBP (33.1%), MedSup (3.2%), OtherHlth (2.2%), Vision (0.1%) — Principal States: WV (100.0%)

...	98.2	18.5	-14.6	-14.9	-18.6	3.68	3.65	79.7	1.3	252.0	...	10.2	-17.1	261.8	283.4	...	...	...	...
207	83.9	12.7	7.3	4.1	10.3	2.93	3.59	95.1	2.4	226.2	...	...	8.9	234.5	252.3	...	...	...	...
5	89.4	9.9	2.1	0.8	6.2	4.07	3.57	243.3	7.7	30.7	...	...	6.6	30.6	33.3	...	...	...	...
-15	93.3	9.8	-3.1	-1.7	-8.7	3.11	1.54	-14.2	4.2	111.4	...	0.4	58.3	148.7	154.9	0.1	...	...	...
9	96.4	9.1	-16.8	-5.8	-34.7	2.49	2.16	25.7	6.8	77.5	...	1.0	-23.5	93.2	98.7	0.0	...	...	...

Principal Lines of Business: CompHosp/Med (82.9%), OtherHlth (17.1%) — Principal States: NY (100.0%)

...	...	...	2.4	47.4	2.6	4.38	4.38	...	...	999.9	...	...	4.4	999.9	999.9	...	...	...	...
...	...	...	-19.1	-99.9	-21.4	4.79	4.79	...	...	484.9	...	...	-19.7	505.9	543.8	...	...	...	...
...	76.6	19.9	14.4	4.4	20.4	6.48	6.40	...	4.2	167.9	...	...	21.1	299.8	317.3	...	...	...	...
...	89.4	11.8	0.2	0.0	0.3	4.12	4.23	32.5	5.5	118.8	...	...	-0.1	244.8	255.0	...	...	...	...
...	95.6	8.3	-5.0	-1.4	-10.8	2.43	2.68	31.1	8.0	66.6	...	...	-10.0	150.6	161.0	...	...	...	...

Principal Lines of Business: Medicare (100.0%) — Principal States: WV (100.0%)

...	72.4	28.4	2.3	2.7	7.2	4.36	4.47	13.8	2.2	46.8	19.2	130.3	7.0	112.2	117.9	25.0	...	...	...
...	76.8	29.0	3.1	3.0	7.9	4.95	4.97	-0.7	2.0	98.5	22.4	108.3	10.7	134.8	141.5	22.3	...	...	6.6
-88	74.4	27.4	1.5	1.3	3.3	4.98	4.91	10.9	2.2	83.8	12.3	83.6	2.6	121.9	129.5	24.3	...	...	5.7
-1,645	77.9	25.5	0.6	0.5	1.5	4.31	3.00	21.5	2.6	74.2	14.8	79.7	2.9	120.8	127.1	21.9	...	...	5.2
-330	71.6	26.8	3.7	3.0	8.3	3.71	3.61	2.6	2.4	87.0	12.4	62.9	8.0	137.7	145.9	21.9	...	...	4.6

Principal Lines of Business: GrpA&H (99.9%), OrdLife (0.1%), GrpLife (0.0%) — Principal States: PA (21.8%), TX (5.8%), TN (5.0%), MA (5.0%), NC (4.6%)

...	64.2	29.9	5.3	3.7	12.8	4.37	4.33	16.2	3.0	72.0	13.5	90.5	13.5	141.3	148.8	1.2	...	...	...
...	67.2	26.3	6.2	5.0	15.0	4.47	4.44	-2.0	2.5	70.4	18.3	103.1	16.0	178.2	198.3	1.0	...	...	...
...	81.0	24.4	0.1	0.1	0.4	4.38	4.32	7.8	2.7	62.9	12.8	101.0	-0.2	210.5	221.1	...	...	...	...
...	73.9	23.4	4.4	3.5	9.9	3.59	3.63	-0.7	2.5	107.0	5.6	51.8	9.9	204.4	213.2	...	...	...	...
...	81.7	25.3	-2.7	-1.8	-5.3	3.47	3.62	14.9	3.0	101.7	7.0	37.6	-4.3	184.5	196.1	1.1	...	...	...

Principal Lines of Business: GrpA&H (100.0%) — Principal States: NY (100.0%)

-91	79.8	13.3	14.7	6.7	25.6	4.78	4.90	-6.9	3.9	137.9	...	...	-6.3	189.4	207.7	...	...	...	...
461	80.0	11.5	16.7	7.3	30.1	4.42	4.97	8.1	4.0	114.1	...	...	4.7	127.2	142.6	...	...	...	...
...	93.1	10.5	-11.8	-4.0	-24.5	3.84	3.76	45.9	6.4	78.2	...	...	-9.4	109.4	121.6	...	...	...	...
6	90.6	9.6	9.2	2.6	20.1	5.13	4.46	18.0	7.6	92.2	...	...	-0.8	140.2	155.5	0.2	...	...	2.0
0	88.5	8.6	10.7	3.5	18.8	5.21	5.52	-26.8	5.0	210.7	...	...	11.1	90.2	108.3	0.1	...	...	1.8

Principal Lines of Business: CompHosp/Med (98.6%), Medicare (1.0%), OtherHlth (0.3%), Medicaid (0.1%) — Principal States: CO (92.9%), NV (7.1%)

244	78.9	13.1	12.2	7.3	18.6	3.35	4.24	1.8	2.3	176.3	...	...	23.7	166.7	184.7	0.5	...	...	...
2,611	82.2	13.2	8.2	5.7	12.7	3.76	5.36	2.9	2.0	184.9	...	...	15.0	174.1	196.0	0.4	...	...	...
-280	83.3	11.8	8.4	5.8	12.6	4.15	4.60	11.5	2.0	214.7	...	...	13.8	211.6	238.5	0.3	...	...	...
-12,839	79.5	11.8	10.3	6.8	15.1	4.10	-2.93	12.3	2.1	215.7	...	...	5.8	217.9	241.9	0.3	...	...	...
17,043	83.1	11.4	7.1	4.6	10.4	3.43	10.22	16.8	2.0	224.0	...	...	21.2	204.2	228.5	0.1	...	...	...

Principal Lines of Business: CompHosp/Med (100.0%) — Principal States: LA (100.0%)

COMPANY NAME / Ultimate Parent Association / Principal Officer / Mailing Address / Dom. : Began Bus. : Struct. : Mktg. / Specialty / Phone # / AMB# / NAIC# — Best's Financial Strength Rating / FSC

Balance Sheet: Bonds (%), Mort. Loans & R.E. (%), Com & Pref. Stock (%), All Other Assets (%), Total Assets ($000), Life Reserves (%), Health Reserves (%), Ann Res. & Dep. Liabilities (%), All Other Liabilities (%), Capital & Surplus ($000). Operations: Direct Premiums Written ($000), Net Premiums Written & Deposits ($000), Operating Cash Flow ($000), NOG Before Taxes ($000), NOG After Taxes ($000), Net Income ($000)

HMO MAINE
WellPoint Inc.
Marjorie W. Dorr
President
120 Monument Circle
Indianapolis, IN 46204
ME : 1938 : Stock : Broker
Group A&H, Health
207-822-7000
AMB# 064175 NAIC# 55638

A — Rating Outlook: Stable — FSC VIII

Data Year	Bonds (%)	Mort. Loans & R.E. (%)	Com & Pref. Stock (%)	All Other Assets (%)	Total Assets ($000)	Life Reserves (%)	Health Reserves (%)	Ann Res. & Dep. Liabilities (%)	All Other Liabilities (%)	Capital & Surplus ($000)	Direct Premiums Written ($000)	Net Premiums Written & Deposits ($000)	Operating Cash Flow ($000)	NOG Before Taxes ($000)	NOG After Taxes ($000)	Net Income ($000)
'05	...	...	...	100.0	...	...	...	...	100.0	...	402,418	402,418	-126	27,082	17,648	17,521
'06	...	...	...	100.0	...	...	...	...	100.0	...	428,171	428,171	-50	39,671	25,804	25,753
'07	...	...	...	100.0	...	...	...	...	100.0	...	422,104	422,104	490	47,226	30,526	31,015
'08	...	...	...	100.0	...	...	...	...	100.0	...	400,288	400,288	-786	24,038	15,900	15,114
'09	...	...	...	100.0	...	...	...	...	100.0	...	364,361	364,361	98	500	291	388

Rating History: A g, 04/27/10; A, 01/23/09; A, 03/20/08; A, 11/06/06; A, 12/29/05

HMO MINNESOTA
Aware Integrated Inc
Mark J. Hudson
President & CEO
3535 Blue Cross Road
Eagan, MN 55122
MN : 1974 : Non-Profit : Broker
Group A&H, Health
651-662-8000
AMB# 068646 NAIC# 95649

B++ — Rating Outlook: Stable — FSC X

Data Year	Bonds (%)	Mort. Loans & R.E. (%)	Com & Pref. Stock (%)	All Other Assets (%)	Total Assets ($000)	Life Reserves (%)	Health Reserves (%)	Ann Res. & Dep. Liabilities (%)	All Other Liabilities (%)	Capital & Surplus ($000)	Direct Premiums Written ($000)	Net Premiums Written & Deposits ($000)	Operating Cash Flow ($000)	NOG Before Taxes ($000)	NOG After Taxes ($000)	Net Income ($000)
'05	65.5	1.8	9.8	23.0	306,618	...	49.1	...	50.9	162,482	623,823	608,132	12,836	32,367	32,367	31,883
'06	61.7	1.3	18.4	18.6	409,526	...	57.7	...	42.3	210,242	791,712	772,693	104,902	16,897	16,897	17,320
'07	59.8	1.2	20.2	18.8	433,559	...	50.6	...	49.4	234,819	817,201	814,180	41,750	25,458	25,458	27,751
'08	65.6	1.3	14.7	18.3	368,294	...	63.7	...	36.3	200,827	875,844	875,842	-46,608	1,943	1,900	-16,250
'09	65.4	1.1	16.5	17.0	423,862	...	62.8	...	37.2	250,900	965,340	965,340	11,421	34,849	34,885	28,738

Rating History: B++g, 06/08/10; B++g, 05/20/09; A- g, 06/11/08; A g, 06/13/07; A g, 06/09/06

HMO MISSOURI INC
WellPoint Inc.
Dennis A. Matheis
President
1831 Chestnut Street
St. Louis, MO 63103-2275
MO : 1987 : Stock : Broker
Group A&H, Health, Ind A&H
414-459-6833
AMB# 068790 NAIC# 95358

A — Rating Outlook: Stable — FSC IX

Data Year	Bonds (%)	Mort. Loans & R.E. (%)	Com & Pref. Stock (%)	All Other Assets (%)	Total Assets ($000)	Life Reserves (%)	Health Reserves (%)	Ann Res. & Dep. Liabilities (%)	All Other Liabilities (%)	Capital & Surplus ($000)	Direct Premiums Written ($000)	Net Premiums Written & Deposits ($000)	Operating Cash Flow ($000)	NOG Before Taxes ($000)	NOG After Taxes ($000)	Net Income ($000)
'05	64.5	...	...	35.5	94,845	...	48.3	...	51.7	34,149	342,765	332,923	14,525	24,255	17,967	18,009
'06	49.1	...	...	50.9	123,397	...	73.7	...	26.3	53,065	398,096	387,951	-3,612	28,622	18,888	18,888
'07	42.6	...	...	57.4	115,553	...	83.7	...	16.3	32,285	377,783	365,089	-19,020	24,296	15,984	15,951
'08	35.7	...	...	64.3	131,930	...	53.0	...	47.0	59,711	334,885	334,885	33,164	25,099	15,594	15,594
'09	42.2	...	...	57.8	135,236	...	51.3	...	48.7	75,745	321,793	321,793	11,649	30,204	20,032	20,030

Rating History: A g, 04/27/10; A g, 01/23/09; A g, 03/20/08; A g, 11/06/06; A g, 12/29/05

HMO OF MISSISSIPPI INC
Blue Cross & BS of MS a Mutual Ins Co
Richard J. Hale
President & CEO
3545 Lakeland Drive
Flowood, MS 39239-9799
MS : 1995 : Stock : Broker
Health
601-932-3704
AMB# 064129 NAIC# 95289

NR-3

Data Year	Bonds (%)	Mort. Loans & R.E. (%)	Com & Pref. Stock (%)	All Other Assets (%)	Total Assets ($000)	Life Reserves (%)	Health Reserves (%)	Ann Res. & Dep. Liabilities (%)	All Other Liabilities (%)	Capital & Surplus ($000)	Direct Premiums Written ($000)	Net Premiums Written & Deposits ($000)	Operating Cash Flow ($000)	NOG Before Taxes ($000)	NOG After Taxes ($000)	Net Income ($000)
'05	82.4	...	...	17.6	2,406	...	...	...	100.0	2,322	...	...	-81	-139	-71	-71
'06	84.6	...	0.0	15.4	2,344	...	...	...	100.0	2,328	...	...	-4	-1	6	6
'07	81.5	...	0.0	18.5	2,349	...	...	...	100.0	2,337	...	...	-1	7	12	12
'08	79.2	...	0.0	20.8	2,415	...	...	...	100.0	2,389	...	...	68	66	49	49
'09	80.5	...	0.0	19.4	2,456	...	...	...	100.0	2,429	...	...	41	58	40	40

Rating History: NR-3, 06/16/09; NR-3, 06/02/08; NR-3, 05/25/07; NR-3, 06/20/06; NR-3, 06/22/05

HMO OF NORTHEASTERN PA
Hospital Service Assn of Northeastern PA
Denise S. Cesare
President & CEO
19 North Main Street
Wilkes-Barre, PA 18711
PA : 1987 : Non-Profit : Not Available
Group A&H, Health
800-432-8015
AMB# 068780 NAIC# 96601

NR-5

Data Year	Bonds (%)	Mort. Loans & R.E. (%)	Com & Pref. Stock (%)	All Other Assets (%)	Total Assets ($000)	Life Reserves (%)	Health Reserves (%)	Ann Res. & Dep. Liabilities (%)	All Other Liabilities (%)	Capital & Surplus ($000)	Direct Premiums Written ($000)	Net Premiums Written & Deposits ($000)	Operating Cash Flow ($000)	NOG Before Taxes ($000)	NOG After Taxes ($000)	Net Income ($000)
'05	56.1	...	20.0	24.0	123,420	...	73.3	...	26.7	78,499	321,004	321,004	-2,096	19,980	9,595	17,740
'06	46.1	...	17.7	36.2	173,617	...	42.1	...	57.9	100,924	329,861	329,861	49,235	28,318	19,168	18,313
'07	62.9	...	23.5	13.7	156,931	...	67.7	...	32.3	116,846	309,269	309,269	-19,446	21,187	13,276	17,303
'08	69.4	...	14.6	16.0	152,812	...	63.5	...	36.5	107,193	284,805	284,805	12,297	7,735	5,073	3,776
'09	63.0	...	23.2	13.8	140,018	...	77.7	...	22.3	111,158	228,740	228,740	-21,089	3,828	2,414	2,691

Rating History: NR-5, 03/22/10; NR-5, 08/26/09; B pd, 06/06/08; B pd, 06/05/07; B pd, 06/20/06

HMO PARTNERS INC
USAble Mutual Insurance Company
David F. Bridges
CEO
320 West Capitol
Little Rock, AR 72203-8069
AR : 1994 : Stock : Agency
Group A&H, Health
501-221-1800
AMB# 068964 NAIC# 95442

A — Rating Outlook: Stable — FSC IX

Data Year	Bonds (%)	Mort. Loans & R.E. (%)	Com & Pref. Stock (%)	All Other Assets (%)	Total Assets ($000)	Life Reserves (%)	Health Reserves (%)	Ann Res. & Dep. Liabilities (%)	All Other Liabilities (%)	Capital & Surplus ($000)	Direct Premiums Written ($000)	Net Premiums Written & Deposits ($000)	Operating Cash Flow ($000)	NOG Before Taxes ($000)	NOG After Taxes ($000)	Net Income ($000)
'05	45.5	...	14.1	40.4	95,140	...	12.5	...	87.5	56,582	165,682	113,372	3,744	13,597	8,882	9,128
'06	40.1	...	13.6	46.3	106,786	...	10.6	...	89.4	66,185	147,673	89,579	6,341	13,018	8,581	9,747
'07	30.8	...	15.0	54.2	116,104	...	6.9	...	93.1	74,845	163,942	100,895	7,838	9,718	6,322	8,347
'08	22.5	...	11.7	65.9	116,007	...	20.0	...	80.0	74,902	187,418	116,487	11,530	9,724	5,602	5,449
'09	31.5	...	16.4	52.0	128,358	...	20.9	...	79.1	84,096	198,720	122,799	5,916	8,746	5,532	5,394

Rating History: A, 06/19/09; A, 04/17/08; A, 06/15/07; A, 05/16/06; A- g, 09/21/04

HOLMAN PROFESSIONAL COUNSELING
Ron Holman, Ph.D.
President
9451 Corbin Avenue, Suite 100
Northridge, CA 91324
CA : 1984 : Non-Profit : Broker
Health
818-704-1444
AMB# 064804

NR-5

Data Year	Bonds (%)	Mort. Loans & R.E. (%)	Com & Pref. Stock (%)	All Other Assets (%)	Total Assets ($000)	Life Reserves (%)	Health Reserves (%)	Ann Res. & Dep. Liabilities (%)	All Other Liabilities (%)	Capital & Surplus ($000)	Direct Premiums Written ($000)	Net Premiums Written & Deposits ($000)	Operating Cash Flow ($000)	NOG Before Taxes ($000)	NOG After Taxes ($000)	Net Income ($000)
'05	...	1.2	...	98.8	1,860	...	...	...	100.0	678	6,919	6,919	46	-117	-117	-117
'06	...	...	...	100.0	1,672	...	...	...	100.0	721	3,712	3,712	-387	44	44	44
'07	...	...	...	100.0	1,893	...	...	...	100.0	726	3,574	3,574	-57	4	4	4
'08	...	...	...	100.0	2,474	...	...	...	100.0	948	6,185	6,185	822	222	222	222
'09	...	...	...	100.0	2,459	...	...	...	100.0	1,353	5,866	5,866	202	406	406	406

Rating History: NR-5, 05/07/10; NR-5, 05/08/09; NR-5, 06/27/08; NR-5, 05/04/07; NR-5, 06/05/06

HOMESTEADERS LIFE CO
Graham J. Cook
Chairman, President & CEO
P.O. Box 1756
Des Moines, IA 50306-1756
IA : 1906 : Mutual : Agency
Pre-need
515-440-7777
AMB# 006534 NAIC# 64505

B++ — Rating Outlook: Stable — FSC VIII

Data Year	Bonds (%)	Mort. Loans & R.E. (%)	Com & Pref. Stock (%)	All Other Assets (%)	Total Assets ($000)	Life Reserves (%)	Health Reserves (%)	Ann Res. & Dep. Liabilities (%)	All Other Liabilities (%)	Capital & Surplus ($000)	Direct Premiums Written ($000)	Net Premiums Written & Deposits ($000)	Operating Cash Flow ($000)	NOG Before Taxes ($000)	NOG After Taxes ($000)	Net Income ($000)
'05	86.5	9.9	...	3.6	1,197,652	95.7	...	1.7	2.6	63,152	318,171	304,421	125,783	9,020	5,128	3,361
'06	86.3	9.9	0.3	3.5	1,337,914	95.9	...	1.6	2.4	67,778	339,939	332,853	137,122	10,590	5,663	4,152
'07	86.5	9.9	0.3	3.3	1,473,812	96.1	...	1.5	2.3	74,720	335,314	332,558	133,956	14,546	8,581	7,766
'08	85.4	9.8	0.2	4.5	1,602,425	96.3	...	1.5	2.2	79,208	343,857	343,843	125,230	14,287	8,322	160
'09	87.8	8.3	0.2	3.8	1,762,231	96.1	...	1.4	2.5	94,432	361,300	362,261	146,369	18,099	10,412	10,326

Rating History: B++, 03/23/09; B++, 01/13/09; B++, 04/25/08; B++, 05/02/07; B++, 04/19/06

HOMETOWN HEALTH PLAN
Health Plan of the Upper Ohio Valley
Philip D. Wright
President
100 Lillian Gish Boulevard, Suite 301
Massillon, OH 44647
OH : 1987 : Non-Profit : Broker
Group A&H, Health
877-236-2289
AMB# 068576 NAIC# 95195

NR-5

Data Year	Bonds (%)	Mort. Loans & R.E. (%)	Com & Pref. Stock (%)	All Other Assets (%)	Total Assets ($000)	Life Reserves (%)	Health Reserves (%)	Ann Res. & Dep. Liabilities (%)	All Other Liabilities (%)	Capital & Surplus ($000)	Direct Premiums Written ($000)	Net Premiums Written & Deposits ($000)	Operating Cash Flow ($000)	NOG Before Taxes ($000)	NOG After Taxes ($000)	Net Income ($000)
'05	30.8	...	45.0	24.2	47,130	...	48.7	...	51.3	34,692	94,087	93,647	7,651	10,814	10,814	11,046
'06	34.1	...	54.4	11.5	43,892	...	4.7	...	95.3	42,700	26,852	26,744	-8,556	5,207	5,207	6,742
'07	24.5	...	2.4	73.2	2,509	...	1.7	...	98.3	2,394	71	71	-38,211	504	504	3,995
'08	29.0	...	3.5	67.5	2,592	...	...	...	100.0	2,586	...	...	-53	55	55	55
'09	24.9	...	4.9	70.2	2,477	...	...	...	100.0	2,468	...	...	18	15	15	15

Rating History: NR-5, 03/22/10; NR-5, 03/19/09; NR-5, 04/24/08; NR-5, 06/12/07; B pd, 07/10/06

2010 BEST'S KEY RATING GUIDE — LIFE/HEALTH EDITION
BEST'S PROFITABILITY, LEVERAGE AND LIQUIDITY TESTS 2005 – 2009
Data in U.S. Dollars

	Profitability Tests							Leverage Tests						Liquidity Tests					
Un-Realized Capital Gains ($000)	Benefits Paid to NPW & Dep (%)	Comm. & Expenses to NPW & Dep (%)	NOG to Total Assets (%)	NOG to Total Rev (%)	Operating Return on Equity (%)	Net Yield (%)	Total Return (%)	Change in NPW & Dep (%)	NPW & Dep to Capital (X)	Capital & Surplus to Liabilities (%)	Surplus Relief (%)	Reins Leverage (%)	Change in Capital (%)	Quick Liquidity (%)	Current Liquidity (%)	Non-Invest Grade Bonds to Capital (%)	Delinq. & Foreclosed Mortgages to Capital (%)	Mort. & Credit Tenant Loans & R.E. to Capital (%)	Affiliated Invest to Capital (%)
...	84.9	10.0	...	4.3	...	...	...	51.3	...	...	...	...	...	...	...	...	...	...	...
...	85.3	7.1	...	5.9	...	...	...	6.4	...	...	...	...	...	...	...	...	...	...	...
...	85.0	5.3	...	7.1	...	...	...	-1.4	...	...	...	...	...	...	...	...	...	...	...
...	92.5	2.3	...	4.2	...	...	...	-5.2	...	...	...	...	...	...	...	...	...	...	...
...	96.5	4.4	...	0.1	...	...	...	-9.0	...	...	...	...	...	...	...	...	...	...	...

Principal Lines of Business: CompHosp/Med (99.7%), OtherHlth (0.3%)

794	87.3	9.9	10.8	5.2	22.1	4.28	4.41	3.8	3.7	112.7	...	3.4	24.7	135.0	146.4	1.0	...	3.4	1.6
6,103	91.1	8.2	4.7	2.2	9.1	4.58	6.79	27.1	3.7	105.5	...	1.6	29.4	149.2	164.0	0.6	...	2.5	1.3
-3,309	92.4	8.2	6.0	3.1	11.4	4.94	4.67	5.4	3.5	118.2	...	...	11.7	161.5	184.5	0.1	...	2.1	1.1
-16,681	93.6	8.5	0.5	0.2	0.9	4.22	-5.11	7.6	4.4	119.9	...	...	-14.5	160.0	181.8	0.4	...	2.4	2.5
21,048	90.4	8.0	8.8	3.6	15.4	4.18	8.67	10.2	3.8	145.1	...	...	24.9	154.1	177.0	0.1	...	1.8	2.2

Principal Lines of Business: Medicaid (35.9%), CompHosp/Med (32.1%), Medicare (31.7%), MedSup (0.2%) Principal States: MN (100.0%)

...	82.7	10.7	20.5	5.4	47.0	4.36	4.43	22.0	9.7	56.3	...	7.3	-19.4	146.0	146.2	...	...	...	...
...	82.9	10.6	17.3	4.8	43.3	4.92	4.92	16.5	7.3	75.5	...	4.1	55.4	116.7	118.9	...	...	...	...
...	84.9	9.3	13.4	4.3	37.5	5.36	5.31	-5.9	11.3	38.8	0.0	10.2	-39.2	66.1	66.7	...	...	...	...
...	84.4	9.0	12.6	4.5	33.9	3.43	3.43	-8.3	5.6	82.7	...	...	84.9	158.5	163.4	...	...	...	...
...	82.1	9.3	15.0	6.0	29.6	2.06	2.06	-3.9	4.2	127.3	...	...	26.9	170.5	171.7	...	...	...	...

Principal Lines of Business: CompHosp/Med (72.7%), FEHBP (27.2%), Medicare (0.1%) Principal States: MO (100.0%)

...	...	...	-2.9	-90.9	-3.0	3.29	3.29	...	...	999.9	...	...	-3.0	999.9	999.9	...	...	...	...
...	...	...	0.3	7.5	0.3	3.59	3.59	...	...	999.9	...	...	0.3	999.9	999.9	...	...	...	...
0	...	...	0.5	13.2	0.5	3.84	3.84	...	...	999.9	...	...	0.4	999.9	999.9	...	...	...	...
0	...	...	2.1	52.8	2.1	4.00	4.00	...	...	999.9	...	...	2.2	999.9	999.9	...	...	...	...
0	...	...	1.6	43.6	1.7	3.82	3.82	...	...	999.9	...	...	1.7	999.9	999.9	...	...	...	...

-4,207	84.1	10.3	7.5	3.0	12.6	3.38	6.99	5.2	4.1	174.7	...	...	5.7	249.7	273.8	...	...	...	...
1,347	83.8	9.4	12.9	5.7	21.4	3.31	3.67	2.8	3.3	138.8	...	...	28.6	249.9	272.0	...	...	...	...
-439	84.5	10.7	8.0	4.2	12.2	3.74	6.06	-6.2	2.6	291.5	...	...	15.8	278.7	316.0	...	...	...	...
-10,381	87.8	10.7	3.3	1.8	4.5	2.76	-5.01	-7.9	2.7	235.0	...	...	-8.3	253.8	283.0	0.3	...	...	...
5,524	88.1	10.7	1.6	1.0	2.2	2.14	6.43	-19.7	2.1	385.2	...	...	3.7	383.8	431.7	...	...	...	...

Principal Lines of Business: CompHosp/Med (100.0%) Principal States: PA (100.0%)

1,233	80.3	10.1	9.7	7.7	17.2	3.16	5.01	-4.1	2.0	146.7	...	8.3	20.7	227.3	238.0	2.4	...	...	...
555	76.7	12.6	8.5	9.2	14.0	3.68	5.67	-21.0	1.4	163.0	...	7.1	17.0	253.1	263.7	0.6	...	...	...
1,269	82.3	12.0	5.7	6.0	9.0	3.92	7.40	12.6	1.3	181.4	...	10.1	13.1	303.1	314.4	...	...	...	...
-4,656	82.3	12.1	4.8	4.7	7.5	2.82	-1.75	15.5	1.6	182.2	...	10.9	0.1	357.8	367.6	...	...	...	...
4,284	82.2	12.4	4.5	4.4	7.0	1.64	5.45	5.4	1.5	190.0	...	7.8	12.3	343.8	357.0	0.4	...	...	...

Principal Lines of Business: CompHosp/Med (100.0%) Principal States: AR (99.5%)

...	68.6	33.5	-5.5	-1.7	-15.6	1.88	1.88	-9.0	10.2	57.3	...	...	-16.9	109.4	109.4	...	...	3.3	3.3
...	72.8	27.0	2.5	1.2	6.3	2.29	2.29	-46.4	5.1	75.9	...	...	6.5	95.4	95.4	...	...	...	...
...	74.6	26.5	0.2	0.1	0.6	5.18	5.18	-3.7	4.9	62.2	...	...	0.6	74.2	74.2	...	...	...	...
...	67.8	29.1	10.2	3.6	26.5	1.98	1.98	73.0	6.5	62.1	...	...	30.6	108.7	108.7	...	...	...	...
...	70.4	28.1	16.5	6.5	35.3	3.07	3.07	-5.2	4.3	122.4	...	...	42.8	151.1	151.1	...	...	...	...

Principal Lines of Business: CompHosp/Med (100.0%)

-319	54.4	22.3	0.5	1.4	8.3	5.83	5.67	10.9	4.4	6.1	5.4	82.9	4.4	63.3	72.8	36.2	0.7	173.0	20.6
351	53.6	22.7	0.4	1.4	8.7	5.80	5.73	9.3	4.5	5.9	0.8	84.7	8.2	62.9	72.7	28.4	...	179.1	18.5
-412	57.2	22.0	0.6	2.1	12.0	5.82	5.75	-0.1	4.1	5.9	0.8	80.0	10.6	62.9	72.9	23.8	...	177.0	15.4
-1,506	62.2	20.9	0.5	2.0	10.8	5.74	5.13	3.4	4.2	5.4	0.7	75.6	0.0	64.9	74.8	22.2	0.8	191.9	15.1
813	60.2	21.0	0.6	2.3	12.0	5.69	5.75	5.4	3.6	6.1	0.5	63.1	23.8	64.7	75.1	22.5	2.4	144.0	11.9

Principal Lines of Business: GrpLife (93.7%), OrdLife (3.7%), IndAnn (1.4%), GrpAnn (1.1%) Principal States: OH (14.6%), IN (8.9%), PA (6.4%), CA (6.1%), IA (6.1%)

657	81.0	8.6	25.2	11.4	37.6	2.53	4.67	1.3	2.7	278.9	...	0.1	51.5	286.9	317.3	...	...	...	...
819	76.7	9.2	11.4	18.5	13.5	3.26	8.56	-71.4	0.6	999.9	...	...	23.1	999.9	999.9	...	...	...	...
-2,867	85.2	108.0	2.2	78.6	2.2	2.50	7.15	-99.7	0.0	999.9	...	...	-94.4	999.9	999.9	...	...	...	...
137	...	...	2.2	94.3	2.2	2.31	7.84	-99.9	...	999.9	...	...	8.0	999.9	999.9	...	...	...	...
-133	...	...	0.6	46.3	0.6	1.30	-3.83	...	...	999.9	...	...	-4.6	999.9	999.9	...	...	...	...

Data in U.S. Dollars

COMPANY NAME Ultimate Parent Association Principal Officer Mailing Address Dom. : Began Bus. : Struct. : Mktg. Specialty Phone # AMB# NAIC#	Best's Financial Strength Rating FSC	Data Year	Balance Sheet Bonds (%)	Mort. Loans & R.E. (%)	Com & Pref. Stock (%)	All Other Assets (%)	Total Assets ($000)	Life Reserves (%)	Health Reserves %)	Ann Res. & Dep. Liabilities (%)	All Other Liabilities (%)	Capital & Surplus ($000)	Operations Direct Premiums Written ($000)	Net Premiums Written & Deposits ($000)	Operating Cash Flow ($000)	NOG Before Taxes ($000)	NOG After Taxes ($000)	Net Income ($000)
HONORED CITIZENS CHOICE HTH PL Paul Kahen President & Secretary 5400 East Olympic Boulevard, Suite 130 Los Angeles, CA 90022 CA : 2005 : Stock : Not Available Health 323-728-7232 AMB# 064815	**NR-5**	**'05**	...	...	...	100.0	1,770	...	...	...	100.0	-718	245	245	489	-993	-993	-993
		'06	...	...	...	100.0	5,391	...	...	...	100.0	-1,454	16,422	16,422	3,748	-711	-711	-711
		'07	...	...	...	100.0	7,014	...	...	...	100.0	1,278	33,014	33,014	1,229	-241	-241	-241
		'08	...	10.3	...	89.7	9,746	...	...	...	100.0	2,678	54,585	54,585	914	399	399	399
		'09	...	8.9	...	91.1	15,922	...	...	...	100.0	3,260	87,811	87,811	2,002	431	431	431
		Rating History: NR-5, 05/05/10; NR-5, 05/08/09; NR-5, 05/06/08; NR-5, 05/07/07; NR-5, 06/20/06																
HORACE MANN LIFE INS CO Horace Mann Educators Corporation Louis G. Lower, II Chairman, President & CEO One Horace Mann Plaza Springfield, IL 62715 IL : 1949 : Stock : Direct Response Ind Ann, Life, Var ann 217-789-2500 AMB# 006535 NAIC# 64513	**A-** Rating Outlook: Stable **FSC IX**	**'05**	62.6	0.4	...	37.0	4,648,971	23.0	0.2	41.3	35.5	230,720	430,597	919,977	396,365	7,436	22,994	24,501
		'06	58.8	0.3	0.7	40.1	5,102,515	21.7	0.2	40.1	38.1	251,231	434,999	456,341	291,279	29,138	24,650	28,415
		'07	60.5	0.3	1.9	37.3	5,069,884	22.6	0.1	41.9	35.3	276,611	444,733	465,924	-76,866	41,436	30,860	26,070
		'08	67.5	0.4	2.6	29.5	4,540,834	26.1	0.2	50.4	23.4	270,433	419,303	435,162	53,338	32,879	31,178	-10,743
		'09	63.8	0.3	2.1	33.9	5,087,047	23.9	0.1	48.9	27.0	307,550	455,627	468,179	258,450	50,572	37,827	39,492
		Rating History: A-, 06/03/10; A-, 06/10/09; A-, 05/23/08; A-, 05/18/07; A-, 04/19/06																
HORIZON HEALTHCARE DENTAL[2] Horizon Healthcare Services Inc George H. McMurray, DDS President & CEO 3 Penn Plaza East, Suite PP-15D Newark, NJ 07105-2248 NJ : 1994 : Stock : Broker Dental 973-466-5954 AMB# 064696 NAIC# 11146	**NR-5**	**'05**	0.9	...	...	99.1	5,782	...	0.1	...	99.9	2,730	18,517	18,517	157	693	442	442
		'06	0.9	...	...	99.1	5,905	...	0.1	...	99.9	3,315	18,587	18,587	-158	897	597	597
		'07	1.0	...	...	99.0	5,027	...	0.1	...	99.9	2,913	18,381	18,381	-970	904	613	613
		'08	1.0	...	...	99.0	5,090	...	0.1	...	99.9	3,193	18,453	18,453	248	829	569	569
		'09	1.0	...	...	99.0	5,082	...	0.2	...	99.8	3,582	18,173	18,173	-47	226	156	156
		Rating History: NR-5, 04/19/10; NR-5, 08/26/09; B+ pd, 09/08/08; B+ pd, 08/27/07; B+ pd, 09/21/06																
HORIZON HEALTHCARE OF DELAWARE[2] Horizon Healthcare Services Inc Robert E. Meehan Vice President 3 Penn Plaza East, Suite PP-15D Newark, NJ 07105-2248 DE : 1998 : Stock : Not Available Health 973-466-5954 AMB# 064397 NAIC# 95790	**NR-5**	**'05**	...	...	...	100.0	1,402	...	76.3	...	23.7	1,271	...	...	-37	-5	-4	-4
		'06	...	...	...	100.0	1,428	...	...	...	100.0	1,354	...	...	26	128	83	83
		'07	...	...	...	100.0	1,407	...	...	...	100.0	1,369	...	...	-20	24	16	16
		'08	...	...	...	100.0	1,392	...	...	...	100.0	1,362	...	...	-14	-9	-7	-7
		'09	...	...	...	100.0	1,352	...	...	...	100.0	1,322	...	...	-46	-50	-40	-40
		Rating History: NR-5, 04/19/10; NR-5, 09/21/09; NR-5, 04/29/08; NR-5, 05/16/07; NR-5, 07/11/06																
HORIZON HEALTHCARE OF NJ[2] Horizon Healthcare Services Inc Christy W. Bell President & COO 3 Penn Plaza East, Suite PP-15D Newark, NJ 07105-2248 NJ : 1986 : Stock : Broker Group A&H, Health 973-466-5954 AMB# 068960 NAIC# 95529	**NR-5**	**'05**	90.2	...	0.0	9.8	645,029	...	63.4	...	36.6	319,403	1,666,979	1,666,979	73,625	102,705	65,544	65,680
		'06	88.8	...	0.0	11.2	866,574	...	52.7	...	47.3	395,772	1,933,062	1,933,062	225,598	107,023	63,544	63,285
		'07	84.8	...	0.4	14.8	841,508	...	54.3	...	45.7	347,989	2,193,686	2,193,686	-47,498	123,929	84,366	83,125
		'08	82.7	...	0.0	17.3	853,329	...	49.1	...	50.9	313,558	2,483,819	2,483,819	15,608	71,977	57,447	47,975
		'09	89.2	...	0.0	10.8	954,194	...	49.8	...	50.2	406,095	2,766,785	2,766,785	81,506	135,524	90,095	90,810
		Rating History: NR-5, 04/19/10; NR-5, 08/26/09; B++pd, 09/08/08; B++pd, 08/27/07; B++pd, 09/21/06																
HOSPITAL SERVICE ASSN OF NE PA Hospital Service Assn of Northeastern PA Denise S. Cesare President & CEO 19 North Main Street Wilkes-Barre, PA 18711 PA : 1938 : Non-Profit : Not Available Group A&H 800-432-8015 AMB# 064307 NAIC# 54747	**NR-5**	**'05**	34.5	3.0	46.8	15.7	636,895	...	36.3	...	63.7	409,958	362,480	362,248	-2,052	-22,612	-16,358	-12,060
		'06	26.3	2.7	56.5	14.5	676,493	...	29.4	...	70.6	461,675	375,027	374,803	-704	32,394	26,559	24,752
		'07	26.6	3.1	57.0	13.4	622,153	...	23.9	...	76.1	462,315	293,844	293,623	10,700	1,514	-9,964	44,043
		'08	30.2	3.2	48.5	18.0	555,110	...	13.3	...	86.7	338,687	119,944	119,733	37,819	-18,872	-12,406	-4,427
		'09	33.4	3.4	51.9	11.4	542,161	...	10.9	...	89.1	250,745	122,770	122,565	27,773	-69,434	-70,147	-59,535
		Rating History: NR-5, 03/22/10; NR-5, 04/09/09; NR-5, 03/24/08; NR-5, 04/02/07; NR-5, 04/20/06																
HOUSEHOLD LIFE INS CO HSBC Holdings plc Patrick A. Cozza President & CEO 200 Somerset Corporate Blvd. Bridgewater, NJ 08807 MI : 1981 : Stock : Other Credit A&H, Credit Life 800-443-7187 AMB# 009129 NAIC# 93777	**A** Rating Outlook: Stable **FSC IX**	**'05**	80.6	...	3.2	16.1	1,050,447	45.6	24.9	...	29.5	490,910	221,193	223,874	4,986	131,927	103,445	103,381
		'06	79.6	...	3.7	16.7	1,043,802	49.6	25.2	...	25.2	509,081	244,748	265,061	-14,784	97,408	60,311	58,481
		'07	83.3	...	3.6	13.1	943,406	50.7	24.0	...	25.3	424,004	245,467	265,606	-58,997	95,466	59,583	59,589
		'08	80.1	...	3.0	16.8	829,108	53.8	22.0	0.0	24.2	329,513	228,617	246,982	-114,879	40,429	28,614	12,707
		'09	79.5	...	3.0	17.6	797,433	58.9	31.4	0.0	9.7	351,666	179,519	207,116	-18,770	26,258	17,278	18,673
		Rating History: A g, 06/05/09; A+ g, 06/12/08; A+ g, 06/06/07; A+ g, 06/21/06; A+ g, 06/22/05																
HOUSEHOLD LIFE INS CO OF AZ HSBC Holdings plc Patrick A. Cozza President & CEO 200 Somerset Corporate Blvd. Bridgewater, NJ 08807 AZ : 1984 : Stock : Inactive Inactive 800-443-7187 AMB# 009573 NAIC# 64360	**NR-3**	**'05**	97.6	...	...	2.4	953,823	0.1	...	91.6	8.3	24,692	...	...	-32,686	-34,861	-31,926	-33,621
		'06	97.0	...	...	3.0	915,890	0.1	...	94.1	5.8	49,560	...	...	-41,391	1,610	17,909	17,909
		'07	96.7	...	...	3.3	876,071	0.1	...	93.8	6.1	49,984	...	...	-33,432	5,566	5,059	-296
		'08	95.8	...	...	4.2	843,310	0.1	...	94.3	5.6	47,460	...	...	-39,127	1,554	2,387	-3,710
		'09	96.7	...	...	3.3	825,042	0.1	...	94.3	5.7	56,883	...	...	-9,223	10,789	8,926	8,926
		Rating History: NR-3, 06/05/09; NR-3, 06/12/08; NR-3, 06/06/07; NR-3, 06/21/06; NR-3, 06/22/05																
HOUSEHOLD LIFE INS CO OF DE HSBC Holdings plc Patrick A. Cozza President & CEO 200 Somerset Corporate Blvd. Bridgewater, NJ 08807 DE : 2000 : Stock : Inactive Credit 800-443-7187 AMB# 060344 NAIC# 89007	**NR-3**	**'05**	23.6	...	63.4	13.0	812,690	10.8	...	...	89.2	808,794	487	487	112,916	88,016	85,707	85,707
		'06	26.5	...	71.9	1.6	777,406	11.4	...	...	88.6	775,886	453	453	-84,098	48,624	52,096	52,096
		'07	22.7	...	69.3	7.9	683,584	15.4	...	...	84.6	682,217	559	559	-2,916	118,209	115,035	115,035
		'08	19.2	...	65.6	15.2	574,550	40.3	...	...	59.7	573,784	493	493	-11,784	123,817	121,032	120,114
		'09	21.6	...	72.5	6.0	563,816	11.6	...	...	88.4	562,950	346	346	-43,622	16,000	13,949	13,999
		Rating History: NR-3, 06/05/09; NR-3, 06/12/08; NR-3, 06/06/07; NR-3, 06/21/06; NR-3, 06/22/05																

BEST'S PROFITABILITY, LEVERAGE AND LIQUIDITY TESTS 2005 – 2009

Data in U.S. Dollars

	Profitability Tests							Leverage Tests						Liquidity Tests					
Un-Realized Capital Gains ($000)	Benefits Paid to NPW & Dep (%)	Comm. & Expenses to NPW & Dep (%)	NOG to Total Assets (%)	NOG to Total Rev (%)	Operating Return on Equity (%)	Net Yield (%)	Total Return (%)	Change in NPW & Dep (%)	NPW & Dep to Capital (X)	Capital & Surplus to Liabilities (%)	Surplus Relief (%)	Reins Leverage (%)	Change in Capital (%)	Quick Liquidity (%)	Current Liquidity (%)	Non-Invest Grade Bonds to Capital (%)	Delinq. & Foreclosed Mortgages to Capital (%)	Mort. & Credit Tenant Loans & R.E. to Capital (%)	Affiliated Invest to Capital (%)
...	114.6	373.3	-70.6	-99.9	448.6	-9.38	-9.38	...	-0.3	-28.9	...	...	-99.9	38.1	38.1	...	...	...	...
...	79.9	24.3	-19.9	-4.3	65.5	-4.44	-4.44	999.9	-11.3	-21.2	...	...	-99.9	65.1	65.1	...	...	...	...
...	77.3	25.3	-3.9	-0.7	274.3	10.47	10.47	101.0	25.8	22.3	...	...	187.9	95.4	95.4	...	...	...	...
...	82.5	17.2	4.8	0.7	20.2	4.19	4.19	65.3	20.4	37.9	...	...	109.4	87.1	87.1	...	...	37.3	37.3
...	86.0	13.6	3.4	0.5	14.5	1.68	1.68	60.9	26.9	25.7	...	...	21.7	62.7	62.7	...	...	43.7	43.7

Principal Lines of Business: Medicare (100.0%)

...	83.7	10.9	0.5	3.0	10.0	5.45	5.59	117.1	3.0	7.9	-2.2	0.4	1.7	77.4	87.5	52.0	...	7.3	5.8
...	78.7	20.5	0.5	3.9	10.2	5.22	5.40	-50.4	1.7	8.1	0.1	8.2	11.1	81.3	91.9	45.9	...	6.4	5.1
-634	92.5	19.1	0.6	4.7	11.7	5.44	5.34	2.1	1.6	9.2	0.1	7.6	9.3	73.1	84.2	40.9	...	5.6	4.6
355	79.7	19.7	0.6	4.9	11.4	5.76	4.62	-6.6	1.6	8.2	0.1	7.8	-8.6	73.5	84.0	39.2	...	6.0	4.9
-595	67.1	18.9	0.8	5.5	13.1	6.01	6.11	7.6	1.5	8.8	0.1	7.4	15.4	75.0	84.8	52.9	...	7.3	4.2

Principal Lines of Business: IndAnn (66.9%), OrdLife (19.8%), GrpAnn (12.0%), GrpLife (0.6%), GrpA&H (0.4%)
Principal States: IL (11.6%), VA (6.4%), NC (6.1%), CA (6.0%), SC (5.3%)

...	80.0	16.9	8.5	2.4	20.1	3.24	3.24	4.1	6.8	89.4	...	...	63.1	226.8	238.1	...	...	...	...
...	80.0	16.2	10.2	3.2	19.8	5.26	5.26	0.4	5.6	128.0	...	...	21.4	266.9	280.8	...	...	...	...
...	80.0	15.9	11.2	3.3	19.7	4.71	4.71	-1.1	6.3	137.8	...	...	-12.1	228.8	240.0	...	...	...	...
...	82.8	13.2	11.2	3.1	18.6	2.94	2.94	0.4	5.8	168.3	...	...	9.6	292.1	307.2	...	...	...	...
...	83.8	15.1	3.1	0.9	4.6	0.74	0.74	-1.5	5.1	238.9	...	...	12.2	362.4	381.1	...	...	...	...

Principal Lines of Business: Dental (100.0%)
Principal States: NJ (100.0%)

...	...	...	-0.3	-9.8	-0.3	2.78	2.78	...	...	970.0	...	...	-0.3	999.9	999.9	...	...	...	...
...	...	...	5.9	128.6	6.3	4.68	4.68	...	...	999.9	...	...	6.5	999.9	999.9	...	...	...	...
...	...	...	1.1	22.4	1.1	5.04	5.04	...	...	999.9	...	...	1.2	999.9	999.9	...	...	...	...
...	...	...	-0.5	-18.6	-0.5	2.75	2.75	...	...	999.9	...	...	-0.5	999.9	999.9	...	...	...	...
...	...	...	-2.9	-99.9	-3.0	0.55	0.55	...	...	999.9	...	...	-3.0	999.9	999.9	...	...	...	...

-416	84.4	11.7	10.4	3.8	20.7	5.06	5.01	11.3	5.2	98.1	...	...	2.3	163.3	166.9	1.4	...	...	...
368	82.9	13.7	8.4	3.2	17.8	5.36	5.37	16.0	4.9	84.1	...	...	23.9	163.3	167.0	1.2	...	...	...
106	84.3	12.2	9.9	3.8	22.7	5.37	5.22	13.5	6.3	70.5	...	...	-12.1	149.0	152.8	0.4	...	...	...
-97	85.1	13.5	6.8	2.3	17.4	4.75	3.53	13.2	7.9	58.1	...	...	-9.9	143.1	146.7	...	...	...	...
46	83.0	13.2	10.0	3.2	25.0	3.70	3.79	11.4	6.8	74.1	...	...	29.5	144.8	147.5	0.1	...	...	...

Principal Lines of Business: Medicaid (40.6%), CompHosp/Med (33.7%), Medicare (25.8%)
Principal States: NJ (100.0%)

-34,111	99.0	14.2	-2.6	-4.3	-4.1	3.06	-2.40	8.1	0.9	180.6	...	0.1	4.2	164.3	190.0	...	...	4.6	18.5
34,551	82.2	11.9	4.0	6.8	6.1	2.75	8.86	3.5	0.8	214.9	...	0.1	12.6	166.2	194.4	0.0	...	4.0	27.1
-35,826	91.0	16.9	-1.5	-3.2	-2.2	2.68	6.59	-21.7	0.6	289.2	...	0.2	0.1	181.8	211.2	0.0	...	4.1	38.7
-93,498	103.0	29.7	-2.1	-8.8	-3.1	2.79	-13.61	-59.2	0.4	156.5	...	0.3	-26.7	102.1	116.6	...	...	5.3	59.1
-17,650	99.2	64.4	-12.8	-50.9	-23.8	3.14	1.48	2.4	0.5	86.0	...	0.5	-26.0	82.7	95.4	...	...	7.3	77.6

Principal Lines of Business: FEHBP (38.3%), CompHosp/Med (33.1%), MedSup (28.6%)
Principal States: PA (100.0%)

2,984	80.6	31.4	9.8	38.0	21.9	4.33	4.94	14.7	0.5	88.6	0.6	20.6	8.4	133.9	153.0	0.6	...	...	6.9
4,645	52.1	27.1	5.8	18.7	12.1	4.45	4.90	18.4	0.5	96.2	2.7	16.7	3.7	140.2	158.8	0.0	...	...	7.6
-4,965	52.9	39.3	6.0	17.9	12.8	5.88	5.51	0.2	0.6	82.5	2.6	18.3	-16.7	134.8	151.4	0.0	...	...	7.9
-8,534	53.5	51.0	3.2	9.5	7.6	5.30	2.56	-7.0	0.7	66.0	3.1	21.6	-22.7	121.4	136.2	1.0	...	...	7.7
-1,668	49.2	49.7	2.1	6.7	5.1	4.68	4.76	-16.1	0.6	79.8	4.1	6.1	7.4	138.5	153.9	0.4	...	...	6.7

Principal Lines of Business: CrdLife (31.6%), OrdLife (28.2%), CrdA&H (23.6%), GrpLife (12.5%), GrpA&H (3.0%)
Principal States: CA (6.7%), NC (6.6%), TX (5.5%), FL (4.4%)

...	...	...	-3.3	-54.8	-75.1	5.86	6.00	...	...	2.7	...	...	-59.2	57.5	72.8	11.4	...	...	...
...	...	...	1.9	32.1	48.2	5.74	6.08	...	...	5.8	...	...	104.4	58.2	74.0	5.1	...	...	...
...	...	...	0.6	9.5	10.2	5.79	5.54	...	...	6.1	...	...	-0.9	61.5	77.0	6.3	...	...	...
...	...	...	0.3	4.6	4.9	5.84	5.49	...	...	6.0	...	...	-5.0	62.9	77.8	6.1	...	...	...
...	...	...	1.1	18.3	17.1	5.68	6.04	...	...	7.5	...	...	21.7	65.7	80.7	4.4	...	...	...

2,424	22.5	102.5	11.3	97.0	11.5	12.33	12.67	53.1	0.0	999.9	...	...	19.2	999.9	999.9	...	...	...	63.7
43,039	98.4	32.2	6.6	106.4	6.6	6.30	11.90	-6.9	0.0	999.9	...	...	-4.1	999.9	999.9	...	...	...	71.9
-84,654	54.2	10.6	15.7	97.1	15.8	17.64	6.65	23.2	0.0	999.9	...	...	-12.1	999.9	999.9	...	...	...	69.4
-97,015	85.4	138.3	19.2	96.9	19.3	21.96	7.49	-11.8	0.0	999.9	...	...	-16.0	999.9	999.9	0.2	...	...	65.7
31,576	118.6	63.3	2.5	84.0	2.5	2.89	8.64	-29.7	0.0	999.9	...	...	-1.8	999.9	999.9	0.2	...	...	72.5

Principal Lines of Business: GrpLife (96.4%), CrdLife (3.6%)
Principal States: DE (100.0%)

Data in U.S. Dollars

COMPANY NAME Ultimate Parent Association Principal Officer Mailing Address Dom. : Began Bus. : Struct. : Mktg. Specialty Phone # AMB# NAIC#	Best's Financial Strength Rating FSC	Data Year	Balance Sheet Bonds (%)	Mort. Loans & R.E. (%)	Com & Pref. Stock (%)	All Other Assets (%)	Total Assets ($000)	Life Reserves (%)	Health Reserves %)	Ann Res. & Dep. Liabilities (%)	All Other Liabilities (%)	Capital & Surplus ($000)	Operations Direct Premiums Written ($000)	Net Premiums Written & Deposits ($000)	Operating Cash Flow ($000)	NOG Before Taxes ($000)	NOG After Taxes ($000)	Net Income ($000)
HPHC INSURANCE COMPANY INC Harvard Pilgrim Health Care Inc	B++	'05	72.5	...	...	27.5	16,247	...	44.5	...	55.5	11,981	24,024	24,024	2,850	2,803	2,680	2,585
Eric H. Schultz President & CEO		'06	71.9	...	...	28.1	31,373	...	45.2	...	54.8	23,213	47,608	47,608	13,560	1,967	1,257	1,210
93 Worcester Street Wellesley, MA 02481-9181	Rating Outlook: Stable	'07	70.0	...	0.6	29.4	44,003	...	42.8	...	57.2	23,350	91,686	95,264	4,867	345	48	40
MA : 1992 : Stock : Agency Group A&H		'08	49.9	...	0.4	49.6	60,076	...	48.0	...	52.0	20,841	196,555	199,311	976	-2,671	-2,247	-2,308
781-263-6000		'09	58.0	...	...	42.0	81,799	...	42.0	...	58.0	28,954	256,620	264,577	21,370	12,401	7,936	7,906
AMB# 011367 NAIC# 18975	FSC IX	**Rating History: B++g, 05/06/10; B++g, 02/18/09; B++g, 02/25/08; B++g, 02/13/07; NR-5, 06/15/06**																
HUMAN AFFAIRS INTERNATL OF CA	NR-5	'05	...	...	...	100.0	9,079	...	...	...	100.0	3,450	23,156	23,156	1,176	2,696	1,597	1,597
Pamela Masters President		'06	...	...	...	100.0	3,454	...	...	...	100.0	1,783	13,479	13,479	-3,492	2,696	1,598	1,598
300 Continental Blvd., Suite 240 El Segundo, CA 90245		'07	...	...	...	100.0	4,497	...	...	...	100.0	2,319	11,298	11,298	1,104	3,941	2,335	2,335
CA : 1989 : Stock : Broker Health		'08	...	...	...	100.0	2,929	...	...	...	100.0	1,278	9,890	9,890	-1,493	3,288	1,948	1,948
310-726-7005		'09	...	...	...	100.0	2,673	...	...	...	100.0	913	8,054	8,054	-256	1,683	997	997
AMB# 064805		**Rating History: NR-5, 03/22/10; NR-5, 04/08/09; NR-5, 03/11/08; NR-5, 05/03/07; NR-5, 06/05/06**																
HUMANA ADVANTAGECARE PLAN Humana Inc	A-	'05	...	...	...	100.0	6,393	...	42.7	...	57.3	4,801	2,825	2,798	3,443	-6,599	-6,599	-6,599
Michael B. McCallister President & CEO		'06	...	...	...	100.0	7,040	...	44.8	...	55.2	-1,659	28,238	27,978	307	-5,188	-5,188	-5,188
501 SW 160th Avenue Miramar, FL 33027	Rating Outlook: Stable	'07	...	...	...	100.0	13,886	...	57.6	...	42.4	2,723	55,065	54,488	5,622	-1,404	-1,404	-1,404
FL : 2005 : Stock : Not Available Medicare		'08	...	...	...	100.0	19,003	...	84.1	...	15.9	9,013	83,376	80,602	3,627	-5,678	-5,537	-5,536
305-626-5616		'09	...	...	...	100.0	10,815	...	42.9	...	57.1	1,496	89,676	88,236	-6,226	-7,719	-5,612	-5,612
AMB# 064915 NAIC# 10126	FSC XV	**Rating History: A- g, 06/02/10; B++, 06/05/09; NR-5, 06/20/07**																
HUMANA BENEFIT PLAN OF IL Humana Inc	A-	'05	47.9	9.0	...	43.1	57,267	...	...	...	100.0	26,348	273,522	273,517	178	5,918	5,918	5,918
Michael B. McCallister President & CEO		'06	41.1	7.4	...	51.5	72,078	...	...	...	100.0	39,140	284,027	284,023	4,025	12,793	12,793	12,793
7915 North Hale Avenue, Suite D Peoria, IL 61615	Rating Outlook: Stable	'07	64.1	...	...	35.9	78,355	...	...	...	100.0	42,365	296,572	296,571	16,315	9,358	9,358	9,204
IL : 1995 : Stock : Not Available Health, FEHBP, Medicare		'08	33.3	...	18.6	48.1	83,386	...	0.0	...	100.0	43,310	309,917	309,916	-5,298	4,358	4,570	4,420
309-677-8274		'09	53.3	...	...	46.7	82,114	...	43.5	...	56.5	39,736	269,572	269,572	-4,150	3,346	1,008	1,126
AMB# 060099 NAIC# 60052	FSC XV	**Rating History: A- g, 06/02/10; B++, 06/05/09; B++, 06/05/08; NR-5, 03/13/08; NR-5, 04/10/07**																
HUMANA EMPLOYERS HTH PLN OF GA Humana Inc	A-	'05	75.1	...	...	24.9	28,698	...	82.9	...	17.1	7,981	49,820	49,773	-4,410	-12,660	-9,887	-9,879
Michael B. McCallister President & CEO		'06	37.3	...	0.7	62.1	36,644	...	68.2	...	31.8	20,676	70,082	70,007	11,132	3,925	4,671	4,686
P.O. Box 740036 Louisville, KY 40201-7436	Rating Outlook: Stable	'07	52.3	...	0.5	47.2	40,579	...	63.3	...	36.7	16,288	92,487	75,861	3,328	-6,833	-4,974	-4,988
GA : 1997 : Stock : Broker Group A&H, FEHBP		'08	24.1	...	3.5	72.4	52,792	...	23.1	...	76.9	27,799	167,283	81,086	14,632	17,955	17,286	17,126
770-393-9226		'09	32.9	...	...	67.1	67,746	...	9.3	...	90.7	30,584	223,169	75,798	13,951	9,132	5,807	6,022
AMB# 064068 NAIC# 95519	FSC XV	**Rating History: A- g, 06/02/10; A-, 06/05/09; A-, 06/05/08; A-, 06/05/07; A-, 05/19/06**																
HUMANA HEALTH BENEFIT PL OF LA Humana Inc	A-	'05	56.7	...	0.0	43.3	276,795	...	52.7	...	47.3	122,784	906,741	906,741	52,627	48,728	24,694	24,840
Michael B. McCallister President & CEO		'06	47.1	...	...	52.9	323,883	...	48.9	...	51.1	186,379	910,125	910,125	86,835	96,870	76,129	76,130
One Galleria Boulevard, Suite 850 Metairie, LA 70001-7542	Rating Outlook: Stable	'07	68.9	...	...	31.1	270,489	...	51.5	...	48.5	150,027	835,790	835,790	-49,534	107,149	77,378	77,378
LA : 1985 : Stock : Broker Group A&H, FEHBP, Med supp		'08	57.6	...	4.2	38.2	254,401	...	60.6	...	39.4	128,447	996,190	996,190	-18,803	73,167	43,815	43,684
504-219-6600		'09	57.2	...	...	42.8	340,466	...	50.0	...	50.0	176,756	1,189,993	1,189,993	78,516	80,852	50,697	49,903
AMB# 068835 NAIC# 95642	FSC XV	**Rating History: A- g, 06/02/10; A-, 06/05/09; B++, 06/05/08; B++, 06/05/07; B++, 05/19/06**																
HUMANA HEALTH INS CO FL INC Humana Inc	A-	'05	63.1	...	...	36.9	152,235	1.6	39.9	...	58.6	66,946	410,483	406,868	9,711	20,389	1,070	1,357
Michael B. McCallister President & CEO		'06	67.7	...	0.5	31.8	145,006	2.9	55.3	...	41.9	60,050	514,399	511,448	-18,376	18,448	15,525	15,232
P.O. Box 740036 Louisville, KY 40201-7436	Rating Outlook: Stable	'07	75.3	...	0.4	24.2	137,186	3.6	55.3	...	41.1	45,306	417,812	453,354	6,820	5,385	-1,977	-2,058
FL : 1984 : Stock : Broker Group A&H, FEHBP, Life		'08	48.4	...	1.3	50.3	156,960	4.5	55.6	...	39.9	61,814	400,040	499,645	11,910	8,244	975	-454
305-626-5616		'09	57.1	...	...	42.9	169,753	2.7	54.0	...	43.3	80,369	300,149	516,912	9,143	24,584	14,236	13,744
AMB# 009494 NAIC# 69671	FSC XV	**Rating History: A- g, 06/02/10; A-, 06/05/09; A-, 06/05/08; A-, 06/05/07; A-, 05/19/06**																
HUMANA HEALTH PLAN INC Humana Inc	A-	'05	78.8	11.4	0.8	9.0	393,711	...	56.5	...	43.5	174,883	1,676,180	1,656,186	-37,984	-4,599	-8,519	-6,825
Michael B. McCallister President & CEO		'06	71.0	8.1	9.6	11.3	410,078	...	52.4	...	47.6	207,669	1,490,982	1,490,674	57,740	74,637	62,999	62,357
P.O. Box 740036 Louisville, KY 40201-7436	Rating Outlook: Stable	'07	67.5	8.3	8.3	15.9	336,192	...	62.6	...	37.4	146,286	1,435,216	1,413,167	-86,607	6,389	-7,422	-16,118
KY : 1983 : Stock : Broker Group A&H, FEHBP, Medicare		'08	60.3	7.3	10.2	22.2	382,870	...	48.7	...	51.3	177,269	1,754,223	1,663,594	38,434	-15,219	-13,414	-14,076
502-580-1000		'09	38.7	6.8	6.6	47.9	405,428	...	43.7	...	56.3	175,615	1,903,414	1,767,234	28,454	-7,660	-8,096	-8,902
AMB# 068898 NAIC# 95885	FSC XV	**Rating History: A- g, 06/02/10; A-, 06/05/09; A-, 06/05/08; A-, 06/05/07; A-, 05/19/06**																
HUMANA HEALTH PLAN OF OHIO Humana Inc	A-	'05	57.4	...	...	42.6	98,965	...	68.3	...	31.7	41,959	313,976	309,503	9,873	-32,020	-26,908	-26,873
Michael B. McCallister President & CEO		'06	76.1	...	0.8	23.1	86,941	...	65.9	...	34.1	55,845	232,913	186,172	-4,195	12,177	14,184	14,031
P.O. Box 740036 Louisville, KY 40201-7436	Rating Outlook: Stable	'07	81.7	...	0.9	17.3	62,088	...	28.4	...	71.6	41,892	142,554	66,212	-26,616	12,184	13,634	13,520
OH : 1979 : Stock : Broker Group A&H		'08	42.2	...	3.6	54.2	50,359	...	28.1	...	71.9	24,614	279,244	65,872	-15,032	3,843	5,351	4,230
513-784-5320		'09	39.2	...	...	60.8	43,491	...	55.3	...	44.7	16,178	287,564	44,748	-13,717	-6,869	-4,933	-4,679
AMB# 068573 NAIC# 95348	FSC XV	**Rating History: A- g, 06/02/10; A-, 06/05/09; A-, 06/05/08; A-, 06/05/07; A-, 05/19/06**																

BEST'S PROFITABILITY, LEVERAGE AND LIQUIDITY TESTS 2005 – 2009

Data in U.S. Dollars

—	Profitability Tests							Leverage Tests						Liquidity Tests					
Un-Realized Capital Gains ($000)	Benefits Paid to NPW & Dep (%)	Comm. & Expenses to NPW & Dep (%)	NOG to Total Assets (%)	NOG to Total Rev (%)	Operating Return on Equity (%)	Net Yield (%)	Total Return (%)	Change in NPW & Dep (%)	NPW & Dep to Capital (X)	Capital & Surplus to Liabilities (%)	Surplus Relief (%)	Reins Leverage (%)	Change in Capital (%)	Quick Liquidity (%)	Current Liquidity (%)	Non-Invest Grade Bonds to Capital (%)	Delinq. & Foreclosed Mortgages to Capital (%)	Mort. & Credit Tenant Loans & R.E. to Capital (%)	Affiliated Invest to Capital (%)
...	77.4	12.9	19.2	10.9	24.8	4.20	3.37	78.6	2.0	280.9	...	...	24.9	259.8	286.8	...	...	...	...
...	80.6	16.8	5.3	2.6	7.1	3.71	3.47	98.2	2.1	284.5	...	...	93.7	289.8	322.2	...	...	...	...
...	83.5	17.6	0.1	0.1	0.2	5.04	5.01	100.1	4.1	113.1	...	19.4	0.6	120.2	133.0	...	...	...	...
-8	88.0	14.2	-4.3	-1.1	-10.2	5.00	4.79	109.2	9.6	53.1	...	27.9	-10.7	70.4	78.3	0.1	...	...	...
-117	83.5	12.5	11.2	3.0	31.9	4.34	3.99	32.7	9.1	54.8	...	43.5	38.9	89.6	100.5	0.4	...	...	...
Principal Lines of Business: CompHosp/Med (93.2%), MedSup (5.5%), OtherHlth (1.2%)														Principal States: MA (42.4%), ME (34.1%), NH (23.5%)					
...	65.8	22.7	20.9	6.9	49.5	0.46	0.46	6.8	0.7	61.3	...	...	14.0	117.4	117.4	...	...	...	...
...	49.6	32.1	25.5	11.7	61.1	4.78	4.78	-41.8	7.6	106.7	...	...	-48.3	186.4	186.4	...	...	...	...
...	37.3	29.4	58.7	20.4	113.9	4.89	4.89	-16.2	4.9	106.5	...	...	30.0	193.7	193.7	...	...	...	...
...	33.4	34.6	52.5	19.5	108.3	3.44	3.44	-12.5	7.7	77.4	...	...	-44.9	165.1	165.1	...	...	...	...
...	39.6	39.8	35.6	12.3	91.0	1.02	1.02	-18.6	8.8	51.9	...	...	-28.5	140.3	140.3	...	...	...	...
Principal Lines of Business: CompHosp/Med (100.0%)																			
...	86.2	252.3	...	-99.9	...	...	...	...	0.6	301.5	...	...	...	387.1	387.1	...	...	...	...
...	88.0	32.1	-77.2	-18.3	-99.9	6.95	6.95	899.8	-16.9	-19.1	...	-3.9	-99.9	74.4	74.4	...	...	...	...
...	83.7	20.1	-13.4	-2.5	-99.9	7.27	7.27	94.8	20.0	24.4	...	5.1	264.1	108.4	108.4	...	...	...	...
...	84.4	23.0	-33.7	-6.8	-94.3	2.13	2.14	47.9	8.9	90.2	...	0.3	231.0	344.1	344.9	...	...	...	...
...	94.7	14.1	-37.6	-6.4	-99.9	0.33	0.33	9.5	59.0	16.0	...	1.2	-83.4	203.6	204.1	...	...	...	...
Principal Lines of Business: Medicare (100.0%)														Principal States: FL (100.0%)					
...	0.4	10.0	10.8	17.2	25.0	3.58	3.58	19.9	10.4	85.2	...	...	25.2	136.9	139.2	...	...	19.6	19.6
...	0.3	9.7	19.8	31.1	39.1	3.86	3.86	3.8	7.3	118.8	...	...	48.6	150.4	155.2	...	...	13.6	13.6
...	0.2	9.2	12.4	25.2	23.0	4.70	4.43	4.4	7.0	117.7	...	...	8.2	192.7	199.5	...	...	...	...
...	0.1	8.5	5.7	14.7	10.7	4.19	3.95	4.5	7.2	108.1	...	...	2.2	164.7	175.0	...	...	...	...
...	90.3	9.9	1.2	0.4	2.4	3.49	3.70	-13.0	6.8	93.8	...	...	-8.3	143.0	151.0	...	...	...	...
Principal Lines of Business: Medicare (56.1%), CompHosp/Med (43.1%), FEHBP (0.7%)														Principal States: IL (100.0%)					
-12	95.2	23.0	-34.6	-19.5	-86.1	3.63	3.62	14.9	6.2	38.5	...	...	-46.7	88.9	94.7	11.5	...	...	...
6	83.9	22.6	14.3	6.6	32.6	3.91	3.99	40.7	3.4	129.5	...	...	159.1	302.2	318.7	3.6	...	...	...
-39	76.1	26.8	-12.9	-6.4	-26.9	4.38	4.23	8.4	4.7	67.1	...	9.5	-21.2	184.7	193.9	3.7	...	...	...
-39	66.9	23.3	37.0	21.0	78.4	2.79	2.33	6.9	2.9	111.2	...	22.3	70.7	313.6	319.7	1.5	...	...	...
74	70.6	18.2	9.6	7.7	19.9	1.63	2.14	-6.5	2.5	82.3	...	65.2	10.0	271.0	277.7	1.4	...	...	...
Principal Lines of Business: CompHosp/Med (95.5%), FEHBP (4.5%)														Principal States: GA (100.0%)					
...	83.8	11.6	10.4	2.7	23.0	4.18	4.25	20.5	7.4	79.7	...	...	34.1	153.5	162.9	...	...	...	0.0
...	79.8	10.3	25.3	8.2	49.2	5.11	5.11	0.4	4.9	135.5	...	...	51.8	274.5	283.8	...	...	...	0.0
...	77.1	12.3	26.0	9.1	46.0	5.73	5.73	-8.2	5.6	124.5	...	...	-19.5	210.3	223.9	...	...	...	...
...	82.6	11.0	16.7	4.4	31.5	3.93	3.88	19.2	7.8	102.0	...	...	-14.4	198.9	210.4	...	...	...	...
...	84.2	9.8	17.0	4.2	33.2	2.12	1.83	19.5	6.7	108.0	...	...	37.6	226.5	235.3	...	...	...	...
Principal Lines of Business: Medicare (77.2%), CompHosp/Med (22.5%), OtherHlth (0.1%), FEHBP (0.1%), MedSup (0.1%)														Principal States: LA (100.0%)					
-77	76.3	20.7	0.8	0.3	1.6	4.01	4.18	26.4	6.1	78.5	...	2.3	3.5	149.3	158.3	6.0	...	...	...
23	77.8	19.1	10.4	3.0	24.4	5.07	4.84	25.7	8.5	70.7	...	2.3	-10.3	97.4	109.6	6.7	...	...	...
-128	78.9	26.6	-1.4	-0.4	-3.8	4.85	4.66	-11.4	10.0	49.3	...	3.2	-24.6	90.6	101.5	7.7	...	...	...
-338	83.4	23.5	0.7	0.2	1.8	4.21	2.70	10.2	8.1	65.0	...	2.6	36.4	139.2	147.0	4.6	...	...	...
445	80.8	24.0	8.7	2.5	20.0	3.54	3.51	3.5	6.4	89.9	...	0.0	30.0	147.7	157.7	3.3	...	...	...
Principal Lines of Business: CompHosp/Med (96.3%), Medicare (1.5%), FEHBP (1.3%), OtherHlth (0.8%), Life (0.1%)														Principal States: FL (100.0%)					
-243	84.6	15.3	-2.0	-0.5	-4.6	3.62	4.00	-16.5	9.5	79.9	...	2.1	-10.7	100.7	112.7	7.9	...	25.7	...
-22,630	82.7	14.2	15.7	4.2	32.9	4.86	-1.27	-10.0	7.2	102.6	...	0.0	18.7	113.6	127.5	4.9	...	16.0	18.5
5,129	81.7	17.4	-2.0	-0.5	-4.2	4.64	3.61	-5.2	9.7	77.0	...	2.0	-29.6	86.6	97.8	4.7	...	19.1	18.8
-2,065	86.7	15.4	-3.7	-0.8	-8.3	4.77	3.88	17.7	9.4	86.2	...	4.8	21.2	98.0	107.5	2.9	...	15.7	14.4
1,717	85.7	14.5	-2.1	-0.5	-4.6	3.17	3.45	6.2	10.1	76.4	...	5.4	-0.9	167.0	172.6	2.4	...	15.8	15.3
Principal Lines of Business: Medicare (54.0%), CompHosp/Med (40.1%), FEHBP (5.9%)														Principal States: IL (27.4%), KY (26.8%), NV (16.6%), AZ (9.7%), MO (9.1%)					
44	90.8	15.6	-29.3	-8.6	-61.6	3.55	3.65	-20.5	7.4	73.6	...	0.8	-7.7	195.6	203.6	...	...	...	...
-1	84.8	15.8	15.3	7.5	29.0	4.56	4.38	-39.8	3.3	179.6	...	6.3	33.1	270.2	291.7	...	...	...	...
-92	65.1	23.4	18.3	19.7	27.9	4.12	3.83	-64.4	1.6	207.4	...	21.9	-25.0	211.7	237.9	...	...	...	...
37	77.4	21.6	9.5	7.9	16.1	4.35	2.14	-0.5	2.7	95.6	...	55.8	-41.2	189.2	198.6	0.4	...	...	...
38	83.1	18.9	-10.5	-10.7	-24.2	3.96	4.83	-32.1	2.8	59.2	...	114.2	-34.3	110.3	116.2	1.0	...	...	...
Principal Lines of Business: CompHosp/Med (100.0%)														Principal States: OH (100.0%)					

Data in U.S. Dollars

COMPANY NAME Ultimate Parent Association Principal Officer Mailing Address Dom. : Began Bus. : Struct. : Mktg. Specialty Phone # AMB# NAIC#	Best's Financial Strength Rating FSC		Balance Sheet										Operations					
		Data Year	Bonds (%)	Mort. Loans & R.E. (%)	Com & Pref. Stock (%)	All Other Assets (%)	Total Assets ($000)	Life Reserves (%)	Health Reserves %)	Ann Res. & Dep. Liabilities (%)	All Other Liabilities (%)	Capital & Surplus ($000)	Direct Premiums Written ($000)	Net Premiums Written & Deposits ($000)	Operating Cash Flow ($000)	NOG Before Taxes ($000)	NOG After Taxes ($000)	Net Income ($000)
HUMANA HEALTH PLAN OF TX Humana Inc Michael B. McCallister President & CEO P.O. Box 740036 Louisville, KY 40201-7436 TX : 1982 : Stock : Broker Group A&H, FEHBP, Medicare 512-338-6100 AMB# 068903 NAIC# 95024	**A-** Rating Outlook: Stable **FSC XV**	'05	73.8	3.6	...	22.6	139,762	...	56.6	...	43.4	77,839	496,376	496,376	-24,226	28,624	20,606	20,837
		'06	63.8	3.2	...	33.0	146,821	...	49.7	...	50.3	82,922	495,770	490,000	10,503	66,202	47,793	47,720
		'07	65.9	3.1	...	31.0	136,532	...	44.3	...	55.7	74,916	597,344	493,790	-9,836	55,768	40,661	40,685
		'08	41.9	2.6	3.2	52.3	144,518	...	41.2	...	58.8	43,511	730,430	521,761	10,359	15,281	7,321	6,311
		'09	51.4	2.0	...	46.6	182,295	...	31.2	...	68.8	35,562	837,334	482,343	46,220	-7,577	-4,734	-4,273
		Rating History: A- g, 06/02/10; B++, 06/05/09; B++, 06/05/08; B++, 06/05/07; B++, 05/19/06																
HUMANA HEALTH PLANS OF PR INC Humana Inc David M. Krebs President & COO 383 FD Roosevelt Avenue Sn Juan, PR 00918-2131 PR : 1986 : Stock : Broker Group A&H, Medicare, Medicaid 787-282-7900 AMB# 060162 NAIC# 95721	**B+** Rating Outlook: Stable **FSC VII**	'05	36.6	...	...	63.4	136,226	...	71.6	...	28.4	64,574	440,409	440,409	22,617	12,268	8,691	8,844
		'06	30.3	...	...	69.7	141,666	...	73.6	...	26.4	24,272	542,336	542,336	-9,757	-11,338	-11,286	-11,355
		'07	30.8	...	...	69.2	167,693	...	80.1	...	19.9	19,065	624,673	624,673	13,143	-6,909	-7,574	-7,629
		'08	27.9	...	0.0	72.1	207,351	...	71.6	...	28.4	49,829	588,522	588,522	17,520	51,739	38,085	38,551
		'09	35.7	...	...	64.3	192,651	...	71.7	...	28.3	61,006	592,121	592,121	-33,731	9,456	5,765	6,354
		Rating History: B+, 06/02/10; B+, 06/05/09; B+, 06/05/08; B+, 06/05/07; B+, 05/19/06																
HUMANA INSURANCE COMPANY Humana Inc Michael B. McCallister President & CEO P.O. Box 740036 Louisville, KY 40201-7436 WI : 1968 : Stock : Broker Group A&H, Ind A&H, Group Life 920-336-1100 AMB# 007574 NAIC# 73288	**A-** Rating Outlook: Stable **FSC XV**	'05	62.5	2.7	16.9	17.8	1,146,906	0.9	60.2	0.6	38.3	410,695	3,242,929	3,224,058	174,066	-99,945	-90,541	-89,350
		'06	49.0	1.0	9.4	40.6	3,250,207	0.5	44.9	0.2	54.5	1,174,581	9,115,619	9,164,075	1,286,965	38,279	71,106	73,187
		'07	53.2	0.5	6.7	39.6	3,836,602	0.5	58.0	0.2	41.3	1,879,192	11,966,081	12,199,565	648,427	701,758	488,848	492,157
		'08	62.9	0.5	7.5	29.1	4,063,225	0.7	64.3	0.2	34.9	2,189,471	13,410,306	14,067,938	268,068	432,524	344,146	320,883
		'09	82.2	0.5	6.4	11.0	4,373,948	0.6	53.6	0.1	45.6	2,182,713	13,227,049	14,244,161	562,895	506,271	324,914	308,063
		Rating History: A- g, 06/02/10; A- g, 06/05/09; A- g, 06/05/08; A- g, 06/05/07; A- g, 05/19/06																
HUMANA INSURANCE COMPANY OF KY Humana Inc Michael B. McCallister President & CEO 500 West Main Street Louisville, KY 40202 KY : 2001 : Stock : Inactive Group A&H, Group Life, Ind A&H 502-580-1000 AMB# 060248 NAIC# 60219	**A-** Rating Outlook: Stable **FSC XV**	'05	11.6	...	...	88.4	14,257	25.8	58.9	...	15.3	11,402	14,471	14,313	3,336	6,499	4,464	4,464
		'06	8.9	...	...	91.1	18,422	26.2	61.1	...	12.7	12,430	17,914	17,726	4,097	1,223	136	136
		'07	7.4	...	...	92.6	22,608	28.3	58.7	...	13.0	13,271	20,890	20,647	4,649	1,417	686	686
		'08	8.6	...	45.7	45.7	29,640	32.0	45.5	...	22.5	18,978	26,518	26,229	7,878	9,296	7,039	7,040
		'09	7.4	...	...	92.6	34,240	35.8	47.5	...	16.7	19,574	34,026	33,691	4,088	380	148	148
		Rating History: A- g, 06/02/10; A- g, 06/05/09; A- g, 06/05/08; A- g, 06/05/07; A- g, 05/19/06																
HUMANA INSURANCE COMPANY OF NY Humana Inc Michael B. McCallister President & CEO P.O. Box 740036 Louisville, KY 40201-7436 NY : 2006 : Stock : Broker Medicare, Health, Med supp 518-435-0459 AMB# 060595 NAIC# 12634	**A-** Rating Outlook: Stable **FSC XV**	'05	...	...	...	...	...	...	...	...	...	...	...	...	...	...	...	...
		'06	0.2	...	...	99.8	111,014	...	1.0	...	99.0	15,039	130,930	130,930	-1,161	-1,027	-750	-750
		'07	0.9	...	...	99.1	136,997	...	6.6	...	93.4	74,084	198,245	198,245	960	22,173	14,901	14,895
		'08	1.5	...	...	98.5	83,698	...	39.7	...	60.3	66,770	131,606	131,606	34,004	-11,584	-7,610	-7,613
		'09	0.2	...	...	99.8	110,023	...	28.4	...	71.6	75,419	120,713	120,713	65,827	13,260	8,488	8,499
		Rating History: A- g, 06/02/10; A- g, 06/05/09; A- g, 06/05/08; A- g, 06/05/07; NR-2, 11/30/06																
HUMANA INS OF PUERTO RICO INC Humana Inc David M. Krebs President & COO 383 F.D. Roosevelt Avenue, 3rd Floor San Juan, PR 00918-2131 PR : 1970 : Stock : Direct Response Group A&H 787-282-7900 AMB# 008265 NAIC# 84603	**B+** Rating Outlook: Stable **FSC VI**	'05	33.6	...	...	66.4	18,342	0.5	67.9	...	31.6	-7,200	106,280	106,280	-10,625	-15,430	-15,430	-15,399
		'06	19.0	...	...	81.0	30,616	0.8	71.7	...	27.5	17,369	90,723	90,723	17,759	3,118	3,118	3,115
		'07	17.7	...	...	82.3	36,236	0.8	61.8	...	37.5	23,608	65,567	65,567	4,191	6,526	6,014	6,012
		'08	8.0	...	0.3	91.7	44,129	0.8	63.2	...	36.0	31,098	77,208	77,208	7,755	7,595	7,186	7,195
		'09	10.4	...	...	89.6	49,793	0.6	60.8	...	38.6	32,751	80,582	80,582	-583	2,784	1,283	1,282
		Rating History: B+, 06/02/10; B+, 06/05/09; B+, 06/05/08; B+, 06/05/07; B+, 05/19/06																
HUMANA MEDICAL PLAN INC Humana Inc Michael B. McCallister President & CEO P.O. Box 740036 Louisville, KY 40201-7436 FL : 1987 : Stock : Broker Medicare, Group A&H, Medicaid 305-626-5616 AMB# 068907 NAIC# 95270	**A-** Rating Outlook: Stable **FSC XV**	'05	75.8	1.0	...	23.2	611,300	...	38.9	...	61.1	199,403	2,994,450	2,993,590	42,735	167,620	101,424	102,211
		'06	66.7	0.7	0.1	32.5	883,946	...	22.0	...	78.0	261,601	3,355,748	3,352,329	274,690	255,088	189,482	188,318
		'07	65.9	0.3	0.1	33.8	951,275	...	32.8	...	67.2	292,313	3,722,218	3,686,520	90,849	207,982	136,806	136,713
		'08	64.6	0.2	9.7	25.5	1,084,776	...	22.3	...	77.7	344,725	4,101,498	4,001,748	144,416	330,255	217,495	211,149
		'09	88.9	0.2	0.1	10.8	1,387,567	...	18.7	...	81.3	467,699	4,569,476	4,352,585	316,436	446,154	282,062	291,945
		Rating History: A- g, 06/02/10; A-, 06/05/09; A-, 06/05/08; A-, 06/05/07; A-, 05/19/06																
HUMANA MEDICAL PLAN OF UTAH Humana Inc Michael B. McCallister President & CEO P.O. Box 740036 Louisville, KY 40201-7436 UT : 2007 : Stock : Not Available Medicare 801-256-6200 AMB# 064893 NAIC# 12908	**NR-2**	'05	...	...	...	...	...	...	...	...	...	...	...	...	...	...	...	...
		'06	...	...	...	...	...	...	...	...	...	...	...	...	...	...	...	...
		'07	26.8	...	...	73.2	2,053	...	...	...	100.0	2,041	...	...	2,046	62	40	40
		'08	...	...	...	100.0	4,926	...	28.4	...	71.6	4,494	3,119	3,119	2,701	698	507	507
		'09	...	...	...	100.0	4,906	...	73.9	...	26.1	4,292	3,194	3,194	37	-296	-192	-192
		Rating History: NR-2, 06/02/10; NR-2, 06/05/09; NR-2, 06/05/08; NR-2, 06/05/07																
HUMANA WISCONSIN HEALTH Humana Inc Michael B. McCallister President & CEO P.O. Box 740036 Louisville, KY 40201-7436 WI : 1985 : Stock : Broker Group A&H 262-951-2300 AMB# 068626 NAIC# 95342	**A-** Rating Outlook: Stable **FSC XV**	'05	77.4	...	1.7	20.9	67,745	...	54.2	...	45.8	39,915	242,216	240,695	-5,153	15,589	9,836	9,980
		'06	93.0	...	0.9	6.2	43,304	...	66.0	...	34.0	25,321	173,949	173,760	-22,697	9,048	6,883	6,611
		'07	93.7	...	0.7	5.6	42,867	...	68.1	...	31.9	11,620	260,467	242,098	-2,498	-9,943	-7,713	-7,751
		'08	55.8	...	7.6	36.6	56,451	...	66.1	...	33.9	31,775	204,579	145,349	14,195	1,869	914	755
		'09	65.2	...	...	34.8	57,936	...	41.2	...	58.8	31,604	250,919	151,625	438	2,890	6	223
		Rating History: A- g, 06/02/10; A-, 06/05/09; A-, 06/05/08; A-, 06/05/07; A-, 05/19/06																

BEST'S PROFITABILITY, LEVERAGE AND LIQUIDITY TESTS 2005 – 2009

Data in U.S. Dollars

	Profitability Tests							Leverage Tests						Liquidity Tests					
Un-Realized Capital Gains ($000)	Benefits Paid to NPW & Dep (%)	Comm. & Expenses to NPW & Dep (%)	NOG to Total Assets (%)	NOG to Total Rev (%)	Operating Return on Equity (%)	Net Yield (%)	Total Return (%)	Change in NPW & Dep (%)	NPW & Dep to Capital (X)	Capital & Surplus to Liabilities (%)	Surplus Relief (%)	Reins Leverage (%)	Change in Capital (%)	Quick Liquidity (%)	Current Liquidity (%)	Non-Invest Grade Bonds to Capital (%)	Delinq. & Foreclosed Mortgages to Capital (%)	Mort. & Credit Tenant Loans & R.E. to Capital (%)	Affiliated Invest to Capital (%)
-48	82.2	14.0	13.4	4.1	25.2	1.69	1.84	-25.3	6.4	125.7	...	...	-8.9	156.4	164.5	4.1	...	6.5	6.5
23	79.1	10.2	33.4	9.6	59.5	5.32	5.28	-1.3	5.9	129.8	...	1.0	6.5	198.8	209.9	3.0	...	5.7	5.7
-6	77.2	12.7	28.7	8.1	51.5	6.13	6.14	0.8	6.6	121.6	...	13.4	-9.7	186.0	192.6	2.0	...	5.6	4.2
-247	82.1	13.6	5.2	1.4	12.4	4.33	3.25	5.7	12.0	43.1	...	34.8	-41.9	150.6	153.4	2.4	...	8.7	6.6
251	84.1	17.5	-2.9	-1.0	-12.0	2.75	3.25	-7.6	13.6	24.2	...	106.4	-18.3	148.3	152.0	2.9	...	10.1	7.9
	Principal Lines of Business: Medicare (80.9%), FEHBP (13.1%), CompHosp/Med (6.0%)													Principal States: TX (100.0%)					
-30	89.4	8.7	7.0	2.0	14.5	3.24	3.34	13.4	6.8	90.1	...	...	16.5	268.4	271.8	1.7	...	...	...
15	93.4	9.8	-8.1	-2.1	-25.4	4.75	4.71	23.1	22.3	20.7	...	...	-62.4	166.5	168.7	4.5	...	...	...
-14	93.9	8.2	-4.9	-1.2	-35.0	5.08	5.02	15.2	32.8	12.8	...	...	-21.5	139.7	141.9	5.1	...	...	...
-192	84.2	7.7	20.3	6.4	110.6	3.01	3.20	-5.8	11.8	31.6	...	...	161.4	132.9	138.1	1.3	...	...	...
199	90.3	8.5	2.9	1.0	10.4	2.05	2.64	0.6	9.7	46.3	...	...	22.4	110.0	116.7	1.1	...	...	...
	Principal Lines of Business: Medicaid (80.1%), Medicare (14.5%), CompHosp/Med (5.4%)													Principal States: PR (100.0%)					
16,355	81.2	22.8	-8.7	-2.8	-23.0	4.38	6.67	9.1	7.4	62.1	...	6.8	12.4	91.9	101.3	10.2	...	7.2	43.2
75,461	83.9	16.9	3.2	0.8	9.0	5.74	10.50	184.2	7.5	60.8	...	2.2	180.6	104.8	112.9	3.9	...	2.5	25.9
-32,957	81.6	14.7	13.8	3.9	32.0	10.36	9.34	33.1	6.4	98.8	...	1.2	55.2	142.4	153.9	2.2	...	1.1	14.0
-10,044	84.5	14.2	8.7	2.4	16.9	7.13	6.18	15.3	6.4	119.0	...	1.0	15.8	133.5	146.7	4.0	...	0.9	11.3
26,391	81.6	15.7	7.7	2.3	14.9	3.87	4.33	1.3	6.4	103.7	...	0.9	0.9	120.6	136.3	2.0	...	0.9	13.0
	Principal Lines of Business: IndA&H (72.2%), GrpA&H (27.6%), GrpLife (0.2%), OrdLife (0.0%), IndAnn (0.0%)													Principal States: TX (12.0%), IL (6.0%), WI (5.5%), NC (5.4%), OH (5.2%)					
...	50.8	3.6	37.6	30.5	48.1	2.92	2.91	21.6	1.3	399.4	...	1.2	58.8	825.4	825.4	...	...	...	...
...	83.7	8.9	0.8	0.7	1.1	4.48	4.48	23.8	1.4	207.5	...	1.6	9.0	530.3	530.5	...	...	...	...
...	82.3	9.3	3.3	3.2	5.3	4.36	4.36	16.5	1.6	142.1	...	2.9	6.8	439.0	439.0	...	...	...	...
...	50.4	11.9	26.9	26.5	43.7	1.49	1.50	27.0	1.4	187.5	...	1.4	45.7	357.0	376.7	...	...	...	...
...	87.5	12.9	0.5	0.4	0.8	0.50	0.50	28.5	1.7	133.5	...	3.3	1.3	436.4	436.4	...	...	...	...
	Principal Lines of Business: GrpA&H (50.8%), GrpLife (41.0%), IndA&H (7.9%), OrdLife (0.3%)													Principal States: KY (100.0%)					
...	...	...	...	...	...	...	...	...	...	...	...	...	...	...	...	...	...	...	...
...	92.3	8.9	...	-0.6	...	...	...	...	8.7	15.7	...	...	...	0.4	0.4	...	...	...	...
...	79.7	9.6	12.0	7.5	33.4	294.77	294.06	51.4	2.7	117.8	...	...	392.6	2.0	2.0	...	...	...	...
...	98.3	10.7	-6.9	-5.8	-10.8	1.52	1.50	-33.6	2.0	394.5	...	...	-9.9	411.5	411.5	...	...	...	...
...	78.1	11.0	8.8	7.0	11.9	0.10	0.12	-8.3	1.6	217.9	...	...	13.0	587.1	587.1	...	...	...	...
	Principal Lines of Business: OtherHlth (57.5%), Medicare (42.4%), MedSup (0.1%)													Principal States: NY (100.0%)					
...	94.8	15.3	-68.0	-14.5	-99.9	4.45	5.23	1.4	-14.8	-28.1	...	...	-99.9	13.1	14.9	-4.7	...	...	...
...	91.1	13.1	12.7	3.4	61.3	6.25	6.55	-14.6	5.2	131.8	...	...	342.7	292.8	295.8	4.2	...	...	...
...	80.1	11.8	18.0	9.0	29.4	4.72	4.87	-27.7	2.8	187.4	...	...	35.7	346.9	350.6	0.9	...	...	...
...	78.4	12.6	17.9	9.2	26.3	1.93	2.09	17.8	2.5	239.0	...	...	31.7	470.9	484.0	0.6	...	...	...
...	85.9	11.0	2.7	1.6	4.0	0.78	0.90	4.4	2.5	192.5	...	...	5.3	339.5	357.5	0.4	...	...	...
	Principal Lines of Business: GrpA&H (99.3%), GrpLife (0.7%), OrdLife (0.0%)													Principal States: PR (100.0%)					
-22	82.0	12.7	17.6	3.4	44.3	4.17	4.32	13.9	15.0	48.4	...	0.2	-22.9	122.8	132.3	...	...	3.2	...
-1	83.7	10.0	25.3	5.6	82.2	5.45	5.28	12.0	12.8	42.0	...	0.2	31.2	153.9	165.5	...	...	2.4	...
-92	84.8	10.9	14.9	3.7	49.4	5.85	5.82	10.0	12.6	44.4	...	1.7	11.7	147.7	157.4	...	...	0.8	...
-5,656	82.5	10.4	21.4	5.4	68.3	4.68	3.43	8.6	11.6	46.6	...	2.2	17.9	131.2	141.8	0.4	...	0.7	2.6
-4,456	80.4	10.2	22.8	6.4	69.4	3.36	3.82	8.8	9.3	50.8	...	5.7	35.7	115.9	128.0	0.2	...	0.5	0.3
	Principal Lines of Business: Medicare (85.5%), CompHosp/Med (9.9%), Medicaid (4.0%), FEHBP (0.7%)													Principal States: FL (100.0%)					
...	...	...	...	...	...	...	...	...	...	...	...	...	...	...	...	...	...	...	...
...	...	...	...	...	...	...	...	...	...	...	...	...	...	...	...	...	...	...	...
...	...	...	...	63.7	...	...	...	...	...	999.9	...	...	...	999.9	999.9	...	...	...	...
...	68.7	10.3	14.5	16.0	15.5	1.23	1.23	...	0.7	999.9	...	...	120.2	999.9	999.9	...	...	...	...
...	96.3	13.4	-3.9	-6.0	-4.4	0.26	0.26	2.4	0.7	697.9	...	...	-4.5	999.9	999.9	...	...	...	...
	Principal Lines of Business: Medicare (100.0%)													Principal States: UT (100.0%)					
-66	86.0	8.5	13.7	4.0	27.1	3.84	3.95	-16.4	6.0	143.4	...	...	22.1	229.3	244.2	9.1	...	...	...
60	88.8	7.4	12.4	3.9	21.1	4.72	4.33	-27.8	6.9	140.8	...	0.2	-36.6	187.2	209.9	12.3	...	...	...
-55	97.7	7.5	-17.9	-3.2	-41.8	5.50	5.27	39.3	20.8	37.2	...	18.0	-54.1	89.2	100.6	17.0	...	...	...
-138	78.8	16.9	1.8	0.6	4.2	4.49	3.85	-40.0	4.6	128.8	...	15.1	173.4	213.1	227.0	4.0	...	...	...
202	90.0	13.4	0.0	0.0	0.0	3.17	3.96	4.3	4.8	120.0	...	32.0	-0.5	228.7	242.3	3.8	...	...	...
	Principal Lines of Business: CompHosp/Med (100.0%)													Principal States: WI (100.0%)					

Data in U.S. Dollars

COMPANY NAME Ultimate Parent Association Principal Officer Mailing Address Dom. : Began Bus. : Struct. : Mktg. Specialty Phone # AMB# NAIC#	Best's Financial Strength Rating FSC	Data Year	Balance Sheet: Bonds (%)	Mort. Loans & R.E. (%)	Com & Pref. Stock (%)	All Other Assets (%)	Total Assets ($000)	Life Reserves (%)	Health Reserves %)	Ann Res. & Dep. Liabilities (%)	All Other Liabilities (%)	Capital & Surplus ($000)	Operations: Direct Premiums Written ($000)	Net Premiums Written & Deposits ($000)	Operating Cash Flow ($000)	NOG Before Taxes ($000)	NOG After Taxes ($000)	Net Income ($000)
HUMANADENTAL INSURANCE COMPANY Humana Inc Gerald L. Ganoni President P.O. Box 740036 Louisville, KY 40201-7436 WI : 1908 : Stock : Agency Dental 920-336-1100 AMB# 007254 NAIC# 70580	A- Rating Outlook: Stable FSC XV	'05	69.2	...	...	30.8	92,228	...	64.3	...	35.7	62,392	261,435	249,957	14,341	31,058	20,337	20,338
		'06	88.9	...	0.8	10.3	90,382	...	57.0	...	43.0	63,900	287,964	277,634	-4,805	32,439	21,256	21,256
		'07	79.9	...	0.8	19.4	96,611	...	43.1	...	56.9	65,630	311,801	302,447	9,443	33,261	22,502	22,489
		'08	78.2	...	3.2	18.6	93,909	...	52.7	...	47.3	63,790	305,941	296,952	-3,731	38,207	23,738	22,666
		'09	69.0	...	...	31.0	92,293	...	52.7	...	47.3	58,408	304,061	295,591	-3,373	25,264	15,421	15,582
		Rating History: A- g, 06/02/10; A- g, 06/05/09; A- g, 06/05/08; A- g, 06/05/07; A- g, 05/19/06																
HUNGARIAN REFORMED FED OF AMER Jules G. Balogh President 2001 Massachusetts Avenue N.W. Washington, DC 20036-1011 DC : 1896 : Fraternal : Career Agent Ordinary Life, Ind Ann 202-328-2630 AMB# 009872 NAIC# 56553	NR-5	'05	60.7	10.9	23.4	4.9	22,067	79.9	...	8.3	11.8	5,549	631	620	-573	-580	-580	-575
		'06	60.4	11.9	23.2	4.5	22,142	80.6	...	7.0	12.4	5,633	423	409	-473	-646	-646	-479
		'07	50.1	11.2	29.9	8.9	20,978	81.9	...	7.0	11.1	4,702	371	358	-708	-804	-804	-779
		'08	45.9	11.5	27.8	14.8	17,879	84.9	...	7.4	7.7	2,326	333	327	-1,418	-533	-533	-1,127
		'09	57.7	6.8	17.2	18.3	17,475	82.2	...	7.1	10.6	1,705	360	363	-2,704	-883	-883	-421
		Rating History: NR-5, 04/15/10; NR-5, 04/22/09; NR-5, 04/22/08; NR-5, 05/08/07; NR-5, 05/17/06																
IA AMERICAN LIFE INSURANCE CO Industrial Alliance Ins & Financial Svcs Michael L. Stickney President P.O. Box 26900 Scottsdale, AZ 85255 GA : 1980 : Stock : Mng Gen Agent Ind A&H, Ordinary Life 480-473-5540 AMB# 060682 NAIC# 91693	A- Rating Outlook: Stable FSC V	'05	42.0	...	...	58.0	9,133	71.1	...	19.3	9.6	2,024	7	596	387	205	154	169
		'06	48.4	...	...	51.6	8,891	73.0	...	19.9	7.1	2,240	7	16	-239	218	202	202
		'07	45.0	...	...	55.0	9,180	67.1	...	28.2	4.6	2,228	7	744	291	187	183	183
		'08	27.4	...	0.9	71.7	39,999	50.3	...	20.1	29.6	30,827	11,308	-38,357	-42,864	1,074	4,424	4,406
		'09	72.3	...	...	27.7	37,856	21.6	59.1	8.4	10.9	16,866	7,555	12,933	-2,999	-8,820	-8,815	-8,722
		Rating History: A-, 03/12/10; A-, 02/12/09																
IBA HEALTH AND LIFE ASSUR CO UnitedHealth Group Inc Jelka Saicic Petrovic President & CEO 106 Farmers Alley, Suite 300 Kalamazoo, MI 49005-1100 MI : 1980 : Stock : Not Available Group A&H 800-851-0404 AMB# 068102 NAIC# 81450	NR-3	'05	...	...	...	...	...	...	...	...	...	...	...	...	...	...	...	...
		'06	48.7	...	...	51.3	38,723	0.3	48.3	...	51.4	15,695	95,135	92,300	7,818	-3,212	-2,442	-2,490
		'07	51.3	...	...	48.7	29,367	7.2	72.3	...	20.5	22,585	67,523	67,508	-9,426	7,782	5,361	5,361
		'08	54.4	...	...	45.6	19,335	29.6	12.5	...	58.0	18,373	7,091	7,091	-7,821	977	931	931
		'09	56.4	...	...	43.6	9,575	27.5	33.3	...	39.2	9,284	...	...	-9,036	529	594	594
		Rating History: NR-3, 06/15/09; NR-3, 01/29/08; NR-3, 11/21/07; NR-3, 06/08/07; NR-1, 06/07/06																
IBC LIFE INSURANCE COMPANY[1] Dennis E. Nixon President P.O. Box 1359 Laredo, TX 78040 TX : 1981 : Stock : Not Available Credit Life, Credit A&H 956-722-7611 AMB# 068225 NAIC# 97888	NR-1	'05	0.1	...	...	99.9	3,017	...	...	...	100.0	2,444	...	535	...	331	309	309
		'06	0.0	...	...	100.0	3,161	...	...	...	100.0	2,714	...	583	...	346	225	225
		'07	...	...	...	100.0	3,289	...	...	...	100.0	2,909	...	472	...	332	228	228
		'08	...	...	...	100.0	3,279	...	...	...	100.0	2,995	...	344	...	204	79	79
		'09	...	...	...	100.0	3,359	...	...	...	100.0	3,062	...	395	...	116	68	68
		Rating History: NR-1, 06/10/10; NR-1, 06/12/09; NR-1, 06/12/08; NR-1, 06/08/07; NR-1, 06/07/06																
IDEALIFE INS CO Berkshire Hathaway Inc Steven J. Mannik Chairman, President & CEO 120 Long Ridge Road Stamford, CT 06902 CT : 1983 : Stock : Other Direct Life, Health 203-352-3000 AMB# 009326 NAIC# 97764	A- Rating Outlook: Stable FSC V	'05	26.5	...	...	73.5	20,566	84.5	2.0	2.7	10.8	12,433	7,735	1,587	2	975	558	558
		'06	43.3	...	...	56.7	20,106	86.3	1.9	1.4	10.4	12,745	6,491	1,634	-691	473	319	319
		'07	24.1	...	...	75.9	21,185	81.7	1.5	4.6	12.1	13,795	5,656	1,730	1,391	1,632	1,045	1,049
		'08	18.2	...	...	81.8	21,067	77.7	1.4	2.5	18.4	14,618	5,108	1,931	-224	1,159	811	811
		'09	18.8	...	...	81.2	19,853	86.9	1.4	1.2	10.4	14,347	12,991	1,886	-1,084	-206	-287	-287
		Rating History: A-, 05/06/10; A- u, 11/06/09; A-, 10/02/09; A-, 08/26/08; A-, 08/07/07																
ILLINOIS MUTUAL LIFE INS CO Michel A. McCord Chairman & President 300 S.W. Adams Street Peoria, IL 61634 IL : 1912 : Mutual : Broker Dis inc, Life, Ann 309-674-8255 AMB# 006542 NAIC# 64580	B++ Rating Outlook: Stable FSC VIII	'05	59.5	10.3	18.2	12.0	1,158,390	24.4	24.8	44.5	6.2	130,652	138,340	135,352	15,537	23,540	12,862	299
		'06	66.5	8.9	8.0	16.6	1,234,962	24.3	25.0	43.8	6.9	147,238	166,918	168,412	65,744	31,218	19,319	25,155
		'07	70.0	8.0	7.4	14.5	1,253,563	25.5	25.7	41.8	7.0	145,648	167,061	157,795	17,164	12,954	11,331	17,267
		'08	66.2	7.5	5.2	21.1	1,268,230	26.4	26.3	40.4	6.9	132,399	160,897	149,578	11,225	19,716	6,620	-9,140
		'09	70.3	7.0	4.3	18.4	1,248,028	28.4	26.6	37.3	7.7	136,360	154,367	141,633	-26,081	25,925	17,933	1,037
		Rating History: B++, 11/02/09; A-, 10/16/08; A-, 11/29/07; A-, 10/26/06; A-, 10/13/05																
IMERICA LIFE AND HEALTH INS CO John C. Herbers President & Treasurer 304 Inverness Way South, Suite 465 Englewood, CO 80112 AR : 1925 : Stock : Inactive Group A&H 303-706-1200 AMB# 006418 NAIC# 63533	F	'05	55.0	...	...	45.0	5,382	...	17.9	...	82.1	4,648	547	36	1,030	-4,254	-4,254	-4,254
		'06	63.0	...	...	37.0	4,008	5.1	55.0	...	39.8	3,619	1,878	1,689	-1,416	-2,457	-2,457	-2,457
		'07	71.0	...	...	29.0	3,689	...	77.4	...	22.6	3,121	1,582	1,389	-899	-704	-704	-704
		'08	33.7	...	...	66.3	7,636	...	73.4	...	26.6	3,079	10,231	9,015	2,565	-1,689	-1,689	-1,689
		'09	...	...	...	...	...	...	...	...	...	...	...	...	...	...	...	...
		Rating History: F, 05/26/10; E, 12/14/09; NR-5, 03/20/09; NR-5, 04/14/08; NR-5, 08/07/07																
INDEPENDENCE AMERICAN INS CO Geneve Holdings, Inc. David T. Kettig President 485 Madison Avenue, 14th Floor New York, NY 10022-5872 DE : 1973 : Stock : Mng Gen Agent Stop Loss, Maj med, Ind A&H 212-355-4141 AMB# 003552 NAIC# 26581	A- Rating Outlook: Negative FSC VIII	'05	68.9	...	3.1	28.0	60,056	...	81.1	...	18.9	39,335	1,727	66,118	6,905	3,260	2,670	2,667
		'06	69.8	...	3.5	26.8	62,840	...	81.9	...	18.1	40,778	2,295	67,908	2,363	2,592	2,118	1,897
		'07	63.7	...	4.6	31.7	73,564	...	88.6	...	11.4	41,353	27,039	106,206	6,542	1,720	1,328	1,325
		'08	70.2	...	4.3	25.5	70,840	...	94.6	...	5.4	40,365	32,342	96,947	-289	3,432	2,728	2,323
		'09	69.6	...	7.6	22.9	72,463	...	82.5	...	17.5	44,215	37,396	85,464	1,043	3,629	2,485	2,760
		Rating History: A- g, 12/18/09; A- g, 01/29/09; A- g, 11/19/07; B++, 09/05/07; B++, 06/09/06																

2010 BEST'S KEY RATING GUIDE — LIFE/HEALTH EDITION
BEST'S PROFITABILITY, LEVERAGE AND LIQUIDITY TESTS 2005 – 2009
Data in U.S. Dollars

	Profitability Tests							Leverage Tests						Liquidity Tests					
Un-Realized Capital Gains ($000)	Benefits Paid to NPW & Dep (%)	Comm. & Expenses to NPW & Dep (%)	NOG to Total Assets (%)	NOG to Total Rev (%)	Operating Return on Equity (%)	Net Yield (%)	Total Return (%)	Change in NPW & Dep (%)	NPW & Dep to Capital (X)	Capital & Surplus to Liabilities (%)	Surplus Relief (%)	Reins Leverage (%)	Change in Capital (%)	Quick Liquidity (%)	Current Liquidity (%)	Non-Invest Grade Bonds to Capital (%)	Delinq. & Foreclosed Mortgages to Capital (%)	Mort. & Credit Tenant Loans & R.E. to Capital (%)	Affiliated Invest to Capital (%)
...	69.0	19.5	24.0	8.1	34.0	3.16	3.19	21.6	4.0	210.0	...	360.5	8.8	367.0	378.4	3.1	...	...	...
...	68.8	20.7	23.3	7.6	33.7	4.26	4.31	11.1	4.3	243.3	...	342.1	2.5	265.1	291.6	3.5	...	...	...
...	68.1	22.0	24.1	7.4	34.7	4.48	4.50	8.9	4.6	214.0	...	321.2	2.8	293.1	315.7	3.2	...	...	...
...	67.0	21.4	24.9	7.9	36.7	4.36	3.31	-1.8	4.7	212.5	...	321.1	-3.0	279.8	297.0	3.2	...	...	...
...	67.6	25.1	16.6	5.2	25.2	3.21	3.60	-0.5	5.1	172.4	...	344.1	-8.5	301.8	313.2	2.9	...	...	...
	Principal Lines of Business: GrpA&H (94.0%), IndA&H (5.9%), IndAnn (0.1%), OrdLife (0.0%)													Principal States: TX (15.9%), CA (11.8%), IL (9.8%), FL (7.1%), WI (6.6%)					
-134	157.4	231.2	-2.0	-32.5	-10.1	5.03	4.00	-3.0	0.1	30.5	...	0.1	-1.7	89.4	101.0	...	...	39.2	13.4
543	210.2	352.4	-2.9	-40.0	-11.6	5.37	8.79	-34.1	0.1	38.9	...	0.1	1.1	86.9	99.4	...	...	42.5	12.8
-369	196.4	426.8	-3.7	-56.0	-15.6	4.97	3.52	-12.3	0.1	31.7	...	0.1	-18.5	79.4	92.0	...	...	46.4	15.2
-1,592	228.0	371.1	-2.7	-40.5	-15.2	5.40	-5.61	-8.7	0.1	15.0	...	0.2	-53.8	66.7	76.6	8.5	4.9	88.1	31.9
507	203.1	308.5	-5.0	-78.0	-43.8	4.98	10.20	10.8	0.2	13.8	...	0.3	-9.1	78.5	85.8	18.0	...	249.5	...
	Principal Lines of Business: OrdLife (87.6%), IndAnn (12.4%)													Principal States: PA (25.9%), NJ (25.2%), OH (18.6%), NY (10.3%), DC (6.7%)					
-8	73.8	24.6	1.7	14.8	8.1	2.60	5.22	33.3	0.3	28.5	0.1	47.4	13.6	182.5	184.2	1.8	...	...	...
...	999.9	999.9	2.2	37.3	9.5	3.77	6.02	-97.3	0.0	33.7	0.1	40.8	10.7	183.4	184.6	...	...	...	...
...	43.2	27.5	2.0	14.5	8.2	4.26	5.94	999.9	0.3	32.1	0.1	...	-0.5	181.8	186.3	...	...	...	...
-37	-1.9	-1.1	18.0	-12.0	26.8	7.54	7.82	-99.9	-1.2	374.7	-0.3	999.9	999.9	481.3	485.6	...	...	...	...
...	2.8	84.0	-22.6	-56.7	-37.0	2.53	2.94	133.7	0.7	88.5	...	999.9	-43.7	160.2	168.6	0.5	...	...	...
	Principal Lines of Business: IndA&H (95.9%), OrdLife (4.1%), IndAnn (0.0%)													Principal States: NC (36.8%), TN (30.7%), GA (18.6%)					
...	...	...	...	...	...	...	...	...	...	...	...	...	...	...	...	...	...	...	...
...	91.2	14.8	...	-2.6	...	...	...	...	5.9	68.2	...	12.1	...	220.4	228.3	...	...	...	...
...	74.8	15.6	15.7	7.7	28.0	4.41	4.56	-26.9	3.0	333.0	...	0.1	43.9	528.4	545.8	...	...	...	...
...	83.3	18.5	3.8	11.9	4.5	3.21	3.36	-89.5	0.4	999.9	...	...	-18.7	999.9	999.9	...	...	...	...
...	...	...	4.1	165.1	4.3	2.24	2.58	-99.9	...	999.9	...	4.0	-49.5	999.9	999.9	...	...	...	...
...	5.5	41.4	10.7	54.6	13.2	...	...	-8.6	0.2	425.8	...	...	9.5	...	...	...	...	...	...
...	18.1	42.0	7.3	32.1	8.7	...	...	9.0	0.2	607.4	...	...	11.1	...	...	...	...	...	...
...	28.9	46.0	7.1	36.8	8.1	...	...	-19.1	0.2	767.0	...	...	7.2	...	...	...	...	...	...
...	42.1	42.3	2.4	19.2	2.7	...	...	-27.0	0.1	999.9	...	...	2.9	...	...	...	...	...	...
...	30.9	42.1	2.0	16.1	2.2	...	...	14.7	0.1	999.9	...	...	2.2	...	...	...	...	...	...
	Principal Lines of Business: CrdLife (86.3%), CrdA&H (13.7%)																		
...	93.7	24.7	2.7	16.7	4.6	3.96	3.96	-26.1	0.1	153.1	9.4	441.1	4.8	194.4	197.8	...	...	...	...
...	146.2	24.2	1.6	8.7	2.5	4.95	4.96	3.0	0.1	173.6	7.7	414.3	2.6	185.9	188.2	...	...	...	...
...	116.1	16.7	5.1	20.3	7.9	4.88	4.90	5.9	0.1	187.1	14.7	363.9	8.2	326.5	328.8	...	...	...	...
...	95.3	13.0	3.8	20.9	5.7	3.17	3.18	11.6	0.1	226.7	8.8	332.7	5.9	414.2	416.2	...	...	...	...
...	152.3	12.8	-1.4	-3.8	-2.0	1.29	1.29	-2.3	0.1	260.5	34.4	334.4	-1.9	454.6	457.2	...	...	...	...
	Principal Lines of Business: OrdLife (85.7%), IndA&H (12.4%), IndAnn (1.2%), GrpAnn (0.7%)													Principal States: ME (65.6%), FL (12.6%)					
1,719	71.2	33.4	1.1	6.6	10.2	6.95	6.02	18.1	1.0	14.5	3.4	17.9	3.8	47.9	65.3	40.3	...	83.7	13.1
1,122	67.1	29.2	1.6	8.1	13.9	7.50	8.17	24.4	1.0	15.6	3.1	19.8	13.4	59.3	70.8	32.9	0.0	68.2	12.7
-17,427	83.3	33.1	0.9	5.1	7.7	6.14	5.23	-6.3	1.0	15.5	3.5	24.9	0.8	58.8	70.8	13.8	...	61.9	11.5
-6,017	77.3	32.5	0.5	3.0	4.8	6.19	4.43	-5.2	1.1	12.6	3.7	33.0	-15.1	59.5	71.6	60.3	...	69.1	14.7
-483	98.3	34.9	1.4	8.9	13.3	5.72	4.35	-5.3	1.0	13.5	3.5	34.5	2.8	59.5	72.1	67.0	5.8	61.4	5.0
	Principal Lines of Business: IndA&H (41.8%), IndAnn (29.4%), OrdLife (26.9%), GrpA&H (1.3%), GrpAnn (0.6%)													Principal States: IL (12.7%), FL (8.2%), WI (7.2%), IA (6.3%), OH (5.1%)					
...	569.6	999.9	-86.7	-99.9	-95.9	3.09	3.09	226.0	0.0	633.0	...	...	10.1	718.3	718.3	...	...	...	...
...	46.0	239.1	-52.3	-99.9	-59.4	2.93	2.93	999.9	0.5	931.9	...	2.4	-22.1	999.9	999.9	...	...	...	...
...	94.8	66.1	-18.3	-45.9	-20.9	3.54	3.54	-17.8	0.4	550.1	...	19.9	-13.8	563.3	563.3	...	...	...	...
...	55.8	67.9	-29.8	-17.8	-54.5	3.11	3.11	549.1	2.9	67.6	...	13.7	-1.4	119.2	119.2	...	...	...	...
...	...	...	...	...	...	...	...	...	...	...	...	...	...	...	...	...	...	...	...
-339	67.6	31.0	4.6	3.9	7.1	5.60	4.86	9.8	1.7	189.8	0.4	2.5	11.1	154.7	172.6	3.4	...	...	4.7
1,087	70.3	29.5	3.4	3.0	5.3	5.55	7.28	2.7	1.7	184.8	0.5	2.6	3.7	167.4	187.9	0.4	...	...	...
-381	73.9	27.2	1.9	1.2	3.2	5.70	5.01	56.4	2.6	128.4	0.2	17.7	1.4	140.0	155.7	0.3	...	...	...
-392	72.1	27.4	3.8	2.7	6.7	5.74	4.37	-8.7	2.4	132.5	1.9	6.3	-2.4	132.5	149.6	0.4	...	...	...
287	69.4	26.5	3.5	2.8	5.9	5.00	5.97	-11.8	1.9	156.5	5.4	19.5	9.5	135.6	161.0	...	...	...	...
	Principal Lines of Business: GrpA&H (100.0%)													Principal States: TX (42.9%), NC (20.0%), FL (5.5%), AZ (4.1%), GA (4.1%)					

Data in U.S. Dollars

COMPANY NAME: Ultimate Parent Association; Principal Officer; Mailing Address; Dom. : Began Bus. : Struct. : Mktg.; Specialty; Phone #; AMB#; NAIC#

Best's Financial Strength Rating; FSC

Column headings: Balance Sheet — Data Year; Bonds (%); Mort. Loans & R.E. (%); Com & Pref. Stock (%); All Other Assets (%); Total Assets ($000); Life Reserves (%); Health Reserves %); Ann Res. & Dep. Liabilities (%); All Other Liabilities (%); Capital & Surplus ($000). Operations — Direct Premiums Written ($000); Net Premiums Written & Deposits ($000); Operating Cash Flow ($000); NOG Before Taxes ($000); NOG After Taxes ($000); Net Income ($000).

INDEPENDENCE BLUE CROSS[2]
Independence Blue Cross
Joseph A. Frick
President & CEO
1901 Market Street
Philadelphia, PA 19103-1480
PA : 1938 : Non-Profit : Agency
Group A&H
215-241-2400
AMB# 064553 NAIC# 54704

NR-5

Data Year	Bonds (%)	Mort. Loans & R.E. (%)	Com & Pref. Stock (%)	All Other Assets (%)	Total Assets ($000)	Life Reserves (%)	Health Reserves %)	Ann Res. & Dep. Liabilities (%)	All Other Liabilities (%)	Capital & Surplus ($000)	Direct Premiums Written ($000)	Net Premiums Written & Deposits ($000)	Operating Cash Flow ($000)	NOG Before Taxes ($000)	NOG After Taxes ($000)	Net Income ($000)
'05	3.0	...	74.1	23.0	1,669,993	...	28.0	...	72.0	1,186,958	303,745	368,930	79,247	9,594	22,578	23,355
'06	2.8	...	84.5	12.7	1,773,215	...	36.0	...	64.0	1,411,621	300,103	358,792	-110,680	27,418	29,229	29,015
'07	2.6	...	86.9	10.5	1,890,581	...	30.3	...	69.7	1,490,401	296,668	350,918	35,933	-4,715	14,483	16,056
'08	3.8	...	80.7	15.5	1,568,245	...	24.0	...	76.0	1,106,768	289,437	342,984	62,486	15,571	30,279	34,117
'09	1.9	...	78.5	19.6	1,703,908	...	34.4	...	65.6	1,285,628	306,954	392,312	-42,253	-10,631	-38,478	-43,065

Rating History: NR-5, 04/07/10; NR-5, 08/26/09; B pd, 10/10/08; B pd, 10/11/07; B pd, 10/03/06

INDEPENDENCE INSURANCE INC[1]
Independence Blue Cross
Christopher D. Butler
President & CEO
1901 Market Street
Philadelphia, PA 19103-1400
DE : 1999 : Stock : Agency
215-241-2400
AMB# 060332 NAIC# 60254

NR-1

Data Year	Bonds (%)	Mort. Loans & R.E. (%)	Com & Pref. Stock (%)	All Other Assets (%)	Total Assets ($000)	Life Reserves (%)	Health Reserves %)	Ann Res. & Dep. Liabilities (%)	All Other Liabilities (%)	Capital & Surplus ($000)	Direct Premiums Written ($000)	Net Premiums Written & Deposits ($000)	Operating Cash Flow ($000)	NOG Before Taxes ($000)	NOG After Taxes ($000)	Net Income ($000)
'05	...	...	...	100.0	1,650	...	...	...	100.0	1,623	...	...	...	12	8	8
'06	...	...	...	100.0	1,675	...	...	...	100.0	1,672	...	...	...	76	49	49
'07	...	...	...	100.0	1,721	...	...	...	100.0	1,718	...	...	...	70	46	46
'08	...	...	...	100.0	1,743	...	...	...	100.0	1,742	...	...	...	37	24	24
'09	...	...	...	100.0	1,739	...	...	...	100.0	1,739	...	...	...	-6	-4	-4

Rating History: NR-1, 06/10/10; NR-1, 06/12/09; NR-1, 06/12/08; NR-1, 06/08/07; NR-1, 06/07/06

INDEPENDENCE LIFE & ANNUITY CO
Sun Life Financial Inc
Janet V. Whitehouse
President
One Sun Life Executive Park
Wellesley Hills, MA 02481-5699
RI : 1945 : Stock : Broker
Ann, Var life
781-237-6030
AMB# 006547 NAIC# 64602

A
Rating Outlook: Stable
FSC VII

Data Year	Bonds (%)	Mort. Loans & R.E. (%)	Com & Pref. Stock (%)	All Other Assets (%)	Total Assets ($000)	Life Reserves (%)	Health Reserves %)	Ann Res. & Dep. Liabilities (%)	All Other Liabilities (%)	Capital & Surplus ($000)	Direct Premiums Written ($000)	Net Premiums Written & Deposits ($000)	Operating Cash Flow ($000)	NOG Before Taxes ($000)	NOG After Taxes ($000)	Net Income ($000)
'05	31.5	...	...	68.5	171,890	38.2	...	0.3	61.4	48,740	...	-871	1,636	4,048	2,941	2,908
'06	30.9	...	0.3	68.8	171,920	39.1	...	0.3	60.6	51,258	...	-864	2,823	3,484	2,625	2,634
'07	35.1	...	0.9	63.9	162,387	33.7	...	0.2	66.1	53,251	...	-758	-8,463	2,959	2,300	1,767
'08	42.1	...	0.8	57.1	131,607	43.5	...	0.3	56.2	52,709	...	-780	-4,025	3,620	2,808	-609
'09	40.2	...	0.4	59.4	125,888	38.7	...	0.4	60.9	55,431	...	-515	-3,724	3,631	2,749	2,566

Rating History: A, 02/27/09; A+, 06/19/08; A+, 06/12/07; A+, 07/10/06; A+, 06/30/05

INDEPENDENT CARE HEALTH PLAN
Humana Inc
Thomas H. Lutzow
President
1555 N. RiverCenter Drive, Suite 206
Milwaukee, WI 53212
WI : 2003 : Stock : Other Direct
Medicaid, Medicare
414-223-4847
AMB# 064794 NAIC# 11695

NR-3

Data Year	Bonds (%)	Mort. Loans & R.E. (%)	Com & Pref. Stock (%)	All Other Assets (%)	Total Assets ($000)	Life Reserves (%)	Health Reserves %)	Ann Res. & Dep. Liabilities (%)	All Other Liabilities (%)	Capital & Surplus ($000)	Direct Premiums Written ($000)	Net Premiums Written & Deposits ($000)	Operating Cash Flow ($000)	NOG Before Taxes ($000)	NOG After Taxes ($000)	Net Income ($000)
'05	38.1	...	...	61.9	22,156	...	65.9	...	34.1	7,466	65,708	65,623	8,256	2,594	1,662	1,590
'06	32.6	...	...	67.4	26,568	...	82.8	...	17.2	8,342	75,943	75,884	3,088	1,357	873	806
'07	28.0	...	...	72.0	32,177	...	86.6	...	13.4	8,808	91,635	91,535	6,340	581	443	434
'08	26.3	...	...	73.7	35,455	...	65.6	...	34.4	13,382	86,849	86,728	3,350	8,652	5,458	5,534
'09	21.3	...	...	78.7	45,971	...	85.5	...	14.5	15,478	139,825	139,630	7,370	6,295	4,243	4,344

Rating History: NR-3, 06/02/10; NR-3, 06/05/09; NR-3, 06/05/08; NR-3, 06/05/07; NR-3, 05/19/06

INDEPENDENT HEALTH ASSOCIATION
Michael Cropp, M.D.
President
511 Farber Lakes Drive
Buffalo, NY 14221
NY : 1980 : Non-Profit : Broker
Group A&H, Health, Ind A&H
716-635-3939
AMB# 064343 NAIC# 95308

NR-5

Data Year	Bonds (%)	Mort. Loans & R.E. (%)	Com & Pref. Stock (%)	All Other Assets (%)	Total Assets ($000)	Life Reserves (%)	Health Reserves %)	Ann Res. & Dep. Liabilities (%)	All Other Liabilities (%)	Capital & Surplus ($000)	Direct Premiums Written ($000)	Net Premiums Written & Deposits ($000)	Operating Cash Flow ($000)	NOG Before Taxes ($000)	NOG After Taxes ($000)	Net Income ($000)
'05	46.8	2.4	5.7	45.0	337,753	...	8.4	...	91.6	238,163	854,554	854,554	19,544	62,978	62,483	61,996
'06	45.1	2.0	7.5	45.4	400,898	...	3.6	...	96.4	278,753	996,048	996,048	97,111	58,038	57,353	55,872
'07	43.9	1.7	7.2	47.1	442,287	...	1.9	...	98.1	304,462	1,060,899	1,060,899	11,594	30,015	30,015	28,979
'08	46.1	1.6	6.5	45.8	476,625	...	0.0	...	100.0	336,917	1,034,804	1,034,804	-19,346	54,625	54,574	42,640
'09	46.4	1.8	7.4	44.5	521,635	...	0.0	...	100.0	374,277	1,060,409	1,060,409	15,827	35,544	34,003	29,944

Rating History: NR-5, 05/07/10; NR-5, 08/26/09; B++pd, 11/24/08; B++pd, 10/08/07; B++pd, 08/28/06

INDEPENDENT HEALTH BENEFITS
Michael Cropp
President
511 Farber Lakes Drive
Buffalo, NY 14221
NY : 1995 : Other : Agency
Group A&H
716-631-3001
AMB# 064597 NAIC# 47034

NR-5

Data Year	Bonds (%)	Mort. Loans & R.E. (%)	Com & Pref. Stock (%)	All Other Assets (%)	Total Assets ($000)	Life Reserves (%)	Health Reserves %)	Ann Res. & Dep. Liabilities (%)	All Other Liabilities (%)	Capital & Surplus ($000)	Direct Premiums Written ($000)	Net Premiums Written & Deposits ($000)	Operating Cash Flow ($000)	NOG Before Taxes ($000)	NOG After Taxes ($000)	Net Income ($000)
'05	...	...	...	100.0	21,536	...	71.0	...	29.0	11,824	85,239	84,588	12,612	3,519	2,869	2,869
'06	...	...	...	100.0	34,956	...	69.1	...	30.9	18,458	135,708	134,746	12,741	4,144	2,564	2,564
'07	16.5	...	...	83.5	64,443	...	78.6	...	21.4	30,555	220,527	219,241	23,985	-6,674	-4,983	-4,983
'08	11.7	...	...	88.3	148,431	...	69.7	...	30.3	94,409	416,481	411,260	79,460	-7,399	-7,528	-8,112
'09	29.8	...	...	70.2	153,802	...	57.2	...	42.8	92,887	476,396	470,048	16,564	6,578	8,523	8,335

Rating History: NR-5, 05/07/10; NR-5, 04/09/09; NR-5, 03/19/08; NR-5, 04/02/07; NR-5, 05/11/06

INDIANA VISION SERVICES INC
Vision Service Plan
James Robinson Lynch
President & CEO
3333 Quality Drive
Rancho Cordova, CA 95670
IN : 1975 : Other : Agency
Group A&H
916-851-5000
AMB# 065725 NAIC# 52050

A
Rating Outlook: Stable
FSC IX

Data Year	Bonds (%)	Mort. Loans & R.E. (%)	Com & Pref. Stock (%)	All Other Assets (%)	Total Assets ($000)	Life Reserves (%)	Health Reserves %)	Ann Res. & Dep. Liabilities (%)	All Other Liabilities (%)	Capital & Surplus ($000)	Direct Premiums Written ($000)	Net Premiums Written & Deposits ($000)	Operating Cash Flow ($000)	NOG Before Taxes ($000)	NOG After Taxes ($000)	Net Income ($000)
'05	55.9	...	...	44.1	30,670	...	52.8	...	47.2	28,257	17,135	17,135	2,157	3,124	3,124	3,124
'06	64.8	...	...	35.2	34,246	...	45.3	...	54.7	31,786	18,078	18,078	4,092	3,535	3,535	3,535
'07	82.5	...	...	17.5	38,221	...	45.9	...	54.1	35,641	20,130	20,130	3,767	3,828	3,828	3,828
'08	68.1	...	...	31.9	21,660	...	21.5	...	78.5	14,468	21,386	21,386	-16,410	1,901	-1,654	-1,466
'09	52.9	...	...	47.1	23,318	...	17.5	...	82.5	15,199	21,243	21,243	1,626	1,950	1,048	533

Rating History: A g, 02/09/10; A g, 11/24/08; A g, 11/30/07; A g, 10/12/06; A g, 11/10/05

INDIVIDUAL ASSUR LF HLTH & ACC
IAC Group Inc
Michael M. Strickland
President
2400 West 75th Street
Prairie Village, KS 66208-3509
MO : 1974 : Stock : Agency
Credit A&H, Credit Life, Group Life
913-432-1451
AMB# 008437 NAIC# 81779

B+
Rating Outlook: Stable
FSC V

Data Year	Bonds (%)	Mort. Loans & R.E. (%)	Com & Pref. Stock (%)	All Other Assets (%)	Total Assets ($000)	Life Reserves (%)	Health Reserves %)	Ann Res. & Dep. Liabilities (%)	All Other Liabilities (%)	Capital & Surplus ($000)	Direct Premiums Written ($000)	Net Premiums Written & Deposits ($000)	Operating Cash Flow ($000)	NOG Before Taxes ($000)	NOG After Taxes ($000)	Net Income ($000)
'05	60.3	9.1	5.6	25.0	44,053	67.7	12.9	9.4	10.0	9,881	43,247	27,170	-997	-1,722	-1,440	-1,440
'06	60.1	8.7	5.5	25.8	44,983	70.2	12.0	9.4	8.4	11,310	43,953	27,999	1,086	319	289	289
'07	59.9	8.4	6.0	25.7	45,308	70.9	11.5	8.6	9.0	11,137	43,656	28,222	612	188	157	157
'08	62.5	8.0	7.3	22.2	45,695	69.2	10.0	9.0	11.8	11,329	38,445	24,749	1,003	-202	-121	-121
'09	63.7	8.0	6.8	21.6	44,823	71.1	8.7	9.9	10.3	12,131	33,656	21,037	197	132	46	46

Rating History: B+ g, 04/30/10; B+ g, 05/01/09; B+ g, 06/02/08; B+, 04/20/07; B+, 03/27/06

ING LIFE INSURANCE AND ANNUITY
ING Groep N.V.
Brian D. Comer
President
5780 Powers Ferry Road, NW
Atlanta, GA 30327-4390
CT : 1976 : Stock : Agency
Group pens, Var ann
860-580-4646
AMB# 006895 NAIC# 86509

A
Rating Outlook: Stable
FSC XIV

Data Year	Bonds (%)	Mort. Loans & R.E. (%)	Com & Pref. Stock (%)	All Other Assets (%)	Total Assets ($000)	Life Reserves (%)	Health Reserves %)	Ann Res. & Dep. Liabilities (%)	All Other Liabilities (%)	Capital & Surplus ($000)	Direct Premiums Written ($000)	Net Premiums Written & Deposits ($000)	Operating Cash Flow ($000)	NOG Before Taxes ($000)	NOG After Taxes ($000)	Net Income ($000)
'05	30.4	2.5	0.3	66.8	56,859,409	0.1	...	30.8	69.1	1,539,095	7,572,141	7,440,012	732,886	197,120	231,560	228,515
'06	24.3	3.0	0.8	71.9	63,590,647	0.1	...	26.2	73.7	1,434,857	10,446,350	10,329,963	-791,235	166,280	145,408	125,712
'07	20.2	3.3	0.7	75.9	67,000,403	0.1	...	23.1	76.8	1,388,018	10,355,997	10,239,944	-1,121,837	276,213	250,334	245,505
'08	27.3	3.8	0.4	68.4	57,306,158	0.1	...	31.6	68.3	1,524,556	10,669,724	10,591,290	1,906,250	-258,867	-188,012	-428,353
'09	24.0	3.1	0.2	72.7	62,474,626	0.1	...	29.7	70.3	1,762,126	8,478,468	8,390,204	536,146	553,855	458,315	271,647

Rating History: A g, 06/11/10; A g, 04/24/09; A+ g, 06/18/08; A+ g, 05/11/07; A+ g, 02/24/06

BEST'S PROFITABILITY, LEVERAGE AND LIQUIDITY TESTS 2005 – 2009

Data in U.S. Dollars

—	Profitability Tests							Leverage Tests						Liquidity Tests					
Un-Realized Capital Gains ($000)	Benefits Paid to NPW & Dep (%)	Comm. & Expenses to NPW & Dep (%)	NOG to Total Assets (%)	NOG to Total Rev (%)	Operating Return on Equity (%)	Net Yield (%)	Total Return (%)	Change in NPW & Dep (%)	NPW & Dep to Capital (X)	Capital & Surplus to Liabilities (%)	Surplus Relief (%)	Reins Leverage (%)	Change in Capital (%)	Quick Liquidity (%)	Current Liquidity (%)	Non-Invest Grade Bonds to Capital (%)	Delinq. & Foreclosed Mortgages to Capital (%)	Mort. & Credit Tenant Loans & R.E. to Capital (%)	Affiliated Invest to Capital (%)
143,752	92.9	9.9	1.5	5.8	2.0	1.49	13.84	-6.8	0.3	245.7	0.0	2.7	14.3	39.6	44.2	0.5	...	...	98.4
223,353	88.8	14.0	1.7	7.3	2.2	2.76	19.64	-2.7	0.3	390.4	0.0	2.5	18.9	4.4	8.8	0.5	...	...	100.5
127,784	90.5	16.9	0.8	3.9	1.0	1.55	9.99	-2.2	0.2	372.4	0.0	3.0	5.6	14.9	19.7	0.5	...	...	104.8
-354,691	95.1	14.8	1.8	7.5	2.3	3.05	-17.51	-2.3	0.3	239.8	0.0	3.6	-25.7	26.2	29.8	0.4	...	...	111.5
89,297	91.1	12.6	-2.4	-9.1	-3.2	2.98	9.26	14.4	0.3	307.4	0.0	1.2	16.2	17.1	19.1	0.3	...	...	103.8

Principal Lines of Business: CompHosp/Med (41.0%), FEHBP (34.4%), MedSup (16.2%), OtherHlth (8.4%)

Principal States: PA (100.0%)

...	...	...	0.5	18.1	0.5	...	...	...	...	999.9	...	...	0.5	...	...	...	...	...	...
...	...	...	3.0	63.8	3.0	...	...	...	...	999.9	...	...	3.0	...	...	...	...	...	...
...	...	...	2.7	60.7	2.7	...	...	...	...	999.9	...	...	2.7	...	...	...	...	...	...
...	...	...	1.4	57.9	1.4	...	...	...	...	999.9	...	...	1.4	...	...	...	...	...	...
...	...	...	-0.2	-72.6	-0.2	...	...	...	...	999.9	...	...	-0.2	...	...	...	...	...	...

...	-99.9	-29.8	1.7	51.8	6.2	4.60	4.75	2.0	0.0	102.5	...	0.7	6.6	90.9	100.7	2.4	...	...	...
-2	-99.9	-33.6	1.5	42.5	5.2	5.04	5.13	0.8	0.0	108.4	...	0.3	5.4	92.2	101.5	6.1	...	...	...
2	-99.9	-36.7	1.4	38.8	4.4	5.01	4.49	12.3	0.0	143.5	...	0.2	3.4	121.7	135.6	5.5	...	...	...
-20	-99.9	-37.3	1.9	47.1	5.3	5.37	1.59	-2.9	0.0	153.8	...	0.7	-1.2	136.8	150.5	5.5	...	...	...
-25	-99.9	-60.6	2.1	51.7	5.1	5.24	5.03	33.9	0.0	201.6	...	0.3	5.3	189.5	207.6	8.0	...	...	...

Principal Lines of Business: OrdLife (106.7%), IndAnn (-6.7%)

...	88.0	9.0	9.2	2.5	24.2	2.98	2.52	18.1	8.8	50.8	...	...	19.2	204.9	213.1	...	...	...	...
...	88.3	11.6	3.6	1.1	11.0	4.60	4.29	15.6	9.1	45.8	...	...	11.7	191.5	199.2	...	...	...	...
...	88.1	12.8	1.5	0.5	5.2	5.26	5.22	20.6	10.4	37.7	...	0.8	5.6	203.7	212.8	...	...	...	...
...	74.3	17.0	16.1	6.2	49.2	3.40	3.65	-5.3	6.5	60.6	...	0.9	51.9	239.8	250.4	...	...	...	...
...	83.4	12.6	10.4	3.0	29.4	1.07	1.36	61.0	9.0	50.8	...	0.1	15.7	217.0	227.0	...	...	...	...

Principal Lines of Business: Medicaid (70.6%), Medicare (29.4%)

Principal States: WI (100.0%)

-543	85.2	10.1	19.6	7.1	30.2	3.54	3.17	1.5	3.6	239.1	...	...	35.3	263.2	271.8	...	...	3.5	6.7
2,337	87.4	8.7	15.5	5.7	22.2	4.63	4.90	16.6	3.6	228.2	...	...	17.0	249.6	259.0	...	...	2.8	4.6
1,113	90.5	8.8	7.1	2.8	10.3	4.54	4.56	6.5	3.5	220.9	...	...	9.2	233.8	243.5	...	...	2.5	4.4
-3,719	84.7	11.7	11.9	5.2	17.0	4.17	0.34	-2.5	3.1	241.2	...	0.2	10.7	205.6	214.6	...	...	2.3	33.5
9,196	88.6	9.3	6.8	3.2	9.6	2.61	3.77	2.5	2.8	254.0	...	1.1	11.1	206.6	217.8	...	...	2.5	30.4

Principal Lines of Business: Medicare (53.8%), CompHosp/Med (29.2%), Medicaid (8.7%), FEHBP (8.3%), Dental (0.0%)

Principal States: NY (100.0%)

...	88.6	7.6	18.9	3.4	36.3	2.61	2.61	168.4	7.2	121.7	...	0.5	198.4	203.5	203.5	...	...	...	...
...	88.8	9.2	9.1	1.9	16.9	5.71	5.71	59.3	7.3	111.9	...	...	56.1	197.0	197.0	...	...	...	...
...	94.6	9.6	-10.0	-2.2	-20.3	6.01	6.01	62.7	7.2	90.2	...	...	65.5	158.3	161.4	...	...	...	...
...	89.4	11.8	-7.1	-1.8	-12.0	-2.22	-2.82	87.6	4.4	174.8	...	...	209.0	241.7	244.9	...	...	...	...
...	88.1	10.8	5.6	1.8	9.1	0.98	0.85	14.3	5.1	152.5	...	...	-1.6	235.5	244.8	...	...	...	...

Principal Lines of Business: CompHosp/Med (89.3%), Medicare (10.5%), FEHBP (0.2%)

Principal States: NY (100.0%)

...	88.9	-1.8	10.7	16.8	11.8	2.84	2.84	3.1	0.6	999.9	...	...	14.0	999.9	999.9	...	...	...	...
...	78.4	10.4	10.9	17.6	11.8	4.32	4.32	5.5	0.6	999.9	...	...	12.5	999.9	999.9	...	...	...	...
...	77.3	12.5	10.6	16.5	11.4	4.84	4.84	11.4	0.6	999.9	...	...	12.1	999.9	999.9	...	...	...	...
-110	80.4	15.2	-5.5	-6.9	-6.6	4.00	4.28	6.2	1.5	201.2	...	...	-59.4	282.3	290.4	2.7	...	...	...
110	78.8	14.4	4.7	4.5	7.1	1.86	-0.09	-0.7	1.4	187.2	...	...	5.1	239.2	251.3	3.3	...	...	...

Principal Lines of Business: Vision (100.0%)

Principal States: IN (100.0%)

-647	56.3	53.9	-3.1	-4.5	-13.2	4.50	2.87	7.2	2.6	30.4	33.7	672.9	-16.9	79.2	83.6	...	...	39.0	41.5
378	56.0	50.3	0.6	0.9	2.7	4.81	5.83	3.1	2.4	35.3	26.0	559.5	14.2	77.1	82.4	4.2	...	33.2	38.8
230	56.5	50.3	0.3	0.5	1.4	4.83	5.44	0.8	2.4	34.3	25.8	500.2	-1.3	79.1	84.1	4.3	...	32.8	40.7
62	57.7	54.8	-0.3	-0.4	-1.1	4.70	4.88	-12.3	2.1	34.8	22.5	456.8	2.0	73.6	80.0	4.2	...	31.0	39.9
-11	56.5	59.0	0.1	0.2	0.4	4.62	4.62	-15.0	1.7	39.2	22.4	392.1	7.0	77.9	84.0	2.4	...	28.3	36.6

Principal Lines of Business: GrpLife (34.7%), OrdLife (26.9%), CrdLife (20.9%), CrdA&H (13.6%), IndAnn (3.9%)

Principal States: GU (30.8%), MO (11.0%), PA (8.7%), MP (6.1%), AR (4.9%)

28,427	96.9	7.2	0.4	2.6	16.0	5.50	5.74	4.0	4.4	9.2	2.9	180.0	13.8	59.0	74.5	36.0	...	82.8	23.7
63,298	85.7	5.9	0.2	1.2	9.8	5.44	5.73	38.8	6.1	9.3	2.9	187.9	-0.1	54.3	68.9	43.2	...	111.5	27.4
654	102.3	6.1	0.4	2.1	17.7	6.02	6.01	-0.9	6.2	9.9	2.8	185.6	-2.7	48.4	62.3	68.0	...	132.8	37.8
-51,506	81.5	6.1	-0.3	-1.6	-12.9	5.94	4.34	3.4	6.6	8.3	2.4	164.1	-2.8	46.9	60.9	62.2	0.5	138.0	40.2
6,736	100.0	6.7	0.8	4.7	27.9	5.26	4.31	-20.8	4.6	9.9	2.0	137.5	15.1	49.4	64.1	62.6	...	107.1	53.2

Principal Lines of Business: GrpAnn (97.9%), IndAnn (2.1%)

Principal States: NY (10.4%), CA (10.0%), CT (9.0%), TX (8.0%), OH (5.5%)

COMPANY NAME / Ultimate Parent Association / Principal Officer / Mailing Address / Dom. : Began Bus. : Struct. : Mktg. / Specialty / Phone # / AMB# / NAIC#	Best's Financial Strength Rating / FSC	Data Year	Bonds (%)	Mort. Loans & R.E. (%)	Com & Pref. Stock (%)	All Other Assets (%)	Total Assets ($000)	Life Reserves (%)	Health Reserves (%)	Ann Res. & Dep. Liabilities (%)	All Other Liabilities (%)	Capital & Surplus ($000)	Direct Premiums Written ($000)	Net Premiums Written & Deposits ($000)	Operating Cash Flow ($000)	NOG Before Taxes ($000)	NOG After Taxes ($000)	Net Income ($000)
ING USA ANNUITY & LIFE INS CO ING Groep N.V.	A	'05	24.5	5.6	0.1	69.9	52,423,132	2.6	...	27.7	69.6	1,846,584	8,994,402	8,709,007	-1,142,291	-59,619	58,105	6,869
Robert G. Leary CEO ING Ins U.S.		'06	22.7	4.7	0.2	72.3	61,524,348	2.2	...	26.5	71.3	1,660,747	9,764,867	12,341,104	1,268,544	122,668	127,679	-1,568
5780 Powers Ferry Road, NW Atlanta, GA 30327-4390	Rating Outlook: Stable	'07	25.5	4.0	0.4	70.1	74,257,086	1.8	...	30.0	68.2	2,552,616	11,534,623	18,579,655	5,422,505	99,389	38,028	-40,140
IA : 1973 : Stock : Broker Ann, Var ann, Var life		'08	28.1	5.1	0.5	66.2	64,089,977	2.5	...	35.3	62.2	1,872,666	12,347,121	16,604,434	189,822	-1,407,096	-652,671	-831,431
515-698-7000 AMB# 008388 NAIC# 80942	FSC XIV	'09	21.9	4.0	0.3	73.8	71,917,082	2.5	...	27.2	70.2	1,485,056	6,182,970	8,197,230	-1,242,721	1,231,713	828,935	-638,279
		Rating History: A g, 06/11/10; A g, 04/24/09; A+ g, 06/18/08; A+ g, 05/11/07; A+ g, 02/24/06																
INLAND EMPIRE HEALTH PLAN	NR-5	'05	...	14.3	...	85.7	63,180	...	...	...	100.0	37,490	335,053	335,053	3,989	6,344	6,344	6,344
Richard Bruno CEO		'06	...	14.5	...	85.5	62,391	...	...	...	100.0	33,466	309,272	309,272	22,022	-4,024	-4,024	-4,024
P.O. Box 19026 San Bernardino, CA 92408-9026		'07	...	15.7	...	84.3	56,833	...	...	...	100.0	29,085	370,328	370,328	-5,260	-4,941	-4,941	-4,941
CA : 1996 : Non-Profit : Agency Health, Medicaid, Medicare		'08	...	11.5	...	88.5	73,475	...	...	...	100.0	29,631	441,515	441,515	18,519	545	545	545
909-890-2000 AMB# 064578		'09	...	9.0	...	91.0	88,930	...	...	...	100.0	34,301	514,457	514,457	15,583	4,671	4,671	4,671
		Rating History: NR-5, 03/22/10; NR-5, 08/26/09; C pd, 07/01/08; C+ pd, 06/28/07; C++pd, 08/08/06																
INRECO INTERNATIONAL REINS CO Pan-American Life Mutual Holding Company	A	'05	17.0	...	...	83.0	42,557	8.1	...	...	91.9	31,423	...	1,938	-681	5,581	5,581	5,577
Carlos Mickan President		'06	25.4	...	...	74.6	57,545	7.7	...	...	92.3	36,536	...	2,167	-2,760	5,590	5,590	5,584
P.O. Box 105 Grand Cayman, Cayman Islands KY1-1102	Rating Outlook: Stable	'07	58.6	...	...	41.4	205,597	12.0	...	...	88.0	31,686	20,827	17,049	-10,497	-5,118	-5,118	-5,152
KY : Stock : Other Life Reins		'08	56.4	...	...	43.6	217,417	11.5	...	...	88.5	32,546	28,805	29,484	9,163	6,810	6,810	6,570
345-949-7988 AMB# 075491	FSC IX	'09	62.4	...	...	37.6	257,126	15.4	...	...	84.6	54,022	28,985	31,427	19,625	12,057	12,057	13,460
		Rating History: A g, 05/18/10; A- g, 01/30/09; A- g, 10/23/07; A- g, 08/07/06; A- g, 08/08/05																
INSTIL HEALTH INSURANCE CO Blue Cross&Blue Shield of South Carolina	A-	'05	29.7	...	...	70.3	10,510	...	13.5	...	86.5	7,522	756	756	3,437	-11,305	-7,528	-7,528
Bruce W. Hughes President		'06	11.9	...	...	88.1	26,081	...	47.9	...	52.1	8,886	42,467	42,467	2,527	-12,935	-9,235	-9,235
P.O. Box 100294 Columbia, SC 29202-3298	Rating Outlook: Stable	'07	11.5	...	2.8	85.8	91,472	...	62.4	...	37.6	12,018	235,756	235,756	39,929	-17,066	-14,740	-14,740
SC : 2004 : Mutual : Agency Med supp		'08	11.8	...	1.5	86.7	114,228	...	69.9	...	30.1	38,885	279,061	279,061	24,105	-13,346	-9,394	-9,705
877-446-7845 AMB# 013586 NAIC# 12168	FSC VI	'09	56.6	...	2.1	41.2	104,017	...	75.1	...	24.9	44,060	295,671	295,671	-10,625	1,983	4,175	3,664
		Rating History: A-, 12/16/09; A-, 12/18/08; NR-2, 11/16/07; NR-2, 01/25/07																
INSURANCE CO OF SCOTT & WHITE Scott & White Health Plan	NR-2	'05	...	...	...	100.0	2,480	...	67.5	...	32.5	2,308	224	214	93	66	66	66
Allan Einboden CEO		'06	...	...	...	100.0	2,689	...	75.1	...	24.9	2,488	469	452	178	187	180	180
2401 South 31st Street Temple, TX 76508		'07	...	...	...	100.0	2,850	...	72.2	...	27.8	2,641	438	419	176	229	151	151
TX : 2003 : Stock : Not Available Health		'08	...	...	...	100.0	2,911	...	64.8	...	35.2	2,683	531	510	26	66	41	41
254-298-3000 AMB# 060393 NAIC# 11670		'09	...	...	...	100.0	2,928	...	72.3	...	27.7	2,694	708	686	20	12	10	10
		Rating History: NR-2, 07/10/09; NR-2, 01/18/08; NR-2, 11/30/06; NR-2, 11/18/05; NR-2, 01/20/05																
INTEGRITY CAPITAL INSURANCE CO Citizens Inc	NR-5	'05	...	...	...	...	...	...	...	...	...	...	...	...	...	...	...	...
Rick D. Riley President		'06	...	...	...	...	...	...	...	...	...	...	...	...	...	...	...	...
65 Airport Parkway, Suite 118 Greenwood, IN 46143-1439		'07	...	...	...	...	...	...	...	...	...	...	...	...	...	...	...	...
IN : 2003 : Stock : Not Available Ordinary Life		'08	...	...	...	100.0	6,664	61.8	...	27.0	11.1	2,510	2,480	2,774	1,539	280	255	255
317-889-9798 AMB# 060398 NAIC# 11829		'09	86.1	...	...	13.9	7,695	70.8	...	28.1	1.1	3,054	2,096	2,177	879	189	169	169
		Rating History: NR-5, 06/14/10; NR-5, 06/17/09; NR-1, 06/12/08; NR-1, 06/08/07; NR-1, 06/07/06																
INTEGRITY LIFE INS CO Western & Southern Mutual Holding Co	A+	'05	32.5	0.5	6.7	60.3	4,228,561	7.3	...	31.9	60.8	236,621	381,601	379,107	49,764	-4,605	-4,691	10,559
Jill T. McGruder President & CEO		'06	28.5	0.9	8.1	62.5	4,648,997	6.9	...	28.8	64.4	338,373	560,067	566,252	193,849	13,330	39,452	75,706
400 Broadway Cincinnati, OH 45202	Rating Outlook: Stable	'07	31.1	1.3	6.3	61.2	4,692,412	6.9	...	32.1	61.1	355,341	552,498	560,975	137,788	5,888	9,514	30,506
OH : 1966 : Stock : Broker Ann, Var ann		'08	35.9	1.3	6.1	56.7	4,850,848	6.5	...	37.7	55.7	375,422	753,519	822,620	376,848	-24,339	-11,658	-27,410
513-629-1800 AMB# 007739 NAIC# 74780	FSC XV	'09	39.2	1.1	6.6	53.1	5,414,032	5.8	...	40.6	53.7	501,528	553,872	640,543	248,042	-4,996	-3,298	-12,397
		Rating History: A+ g, 05/18/10; A+ g, 06/29/09; A++g, 07/09/08; A++g, 06/14/07; A++g, 06/21/06																
INTER-COUNTY HEALTH PLAN INC[2] Independence Blue Cross	NR-5	'05	64.9	...	...	35.1	18,330	...	...	...	100.0	4,584	36,284	...	3,130	105	95	95
Daniel J. Pedriani, Jr. President		'06	43.4	...	...	56.6	18,198	...	...	...	100.0	4,848	32,856	...	-62	392	258	258
720 Blair Mill Road Horsham, PA 19044-2244		'07	72.2	...	...	27.8	15,170	...	...	...	100.0	5,087	29,709	...	-3,040	304	240	240
PA : 1978 : Non-Profit : Not Available Health, Med supp		'08	67.1	...	...	32.9	13,693	...	...	...	100.0	5,273	25,527	...	-2,711	277	159	159
215-657-8900 AMB# 064466 NAIC# 53252		'09	43.2	...	...	56.8	12,837	...	...	...	100.0	2,053	24,970	...	-2,890	-6,114	-5,723	-5,721
		Rating History: NR-5, 04/07/10; NR-5, 04/08/09; NR-5, 04/07/08; NR-5, 06/06/06; NR-5, 06/08/05																
INTER-COUNTY HOSPITALIZATION[2] Independence Blue Cross	NR-5	'05	56.2	12.7	3.8	27.3	34,663	...	...	...	100.0	11,126	70,501	...	-3,223	132	324	324
Daniel J. Pedriani, Jr. President		'06	48.2	12.0	4.0	35.8	34,183	...	...	...	100.0	11,908	63,531	...	-1,635	486	326	737
720 Blair Mill Road Horsham, PA 19044-2244		'07	51.1	12.4	4.6	31.9	31,290	...	...	...	100.0	12,428	57,843	...	-2,917	494	454	455
PA : 1937 : Non-Profit : Agency Group A&H		'08	39.2	11.3	4.5	45.0	33,110	...	...	...	100.0	12,843	59,186	...	3,009	572	325	325
215-657-8900 AMB# 064467 NAIC# 54763		'09	23.9	12.2	5.2	58.7	29,142	...	...	...	100.0	4,198	56,419	...	-7,983	-12,557	-11,586	-11,569
		Rating History: NR-5, 04/09/10; NR-5, 04/08/09; NR-5, 04/07/08; NR-5, 06/06/06; NR-5, 06/08/05																

2010 BEST'S KEY RATING GUIDE — LIFE/HEALTH EDITION
BEST'S PROFITABILITY, LEVERAGE AND LIQUIDITY TESTS 2005 – 2009

Data in U.S. Dollars

—	Profitability Tests							Leverage Tests						Liquidity Tests					
Un-Realized Capital Gains ($000)	Benefits Paid to NPW & Dep (%)	Comm. & Expenses to NPW & Dep (%)	NOG to Total Assets (%)	NOG to Total Rev (%)	Operating Return on Equity (%)	Net Yield (%)	Total Return (%)	Change in NPW & Dep (%)	NPW & Dep to Capital (X)	Capital & Surplus to Liabilities (%)	Surplus Relief (%)	Reins Leverage (%)	Change in Capital (%)	Quick Liquidity (%)	Current Liquidity (%)	Non-Invest Grade Bonds to Capital (%)	Delinq. & Foreclosed Mortgages to Capital (%)	Mort. & Credit Tenant Loans & R.E. to Capital (%)	Affiliated Invest to Capital (%)
18,107	53.8	11.9	0.1	0.7	3.3	4.75	4.55	-24.6	4.5	13.0	-13.1	164.8	11.8	49.7	66.3	25.6	...	151.3	5.0
55,266	42.2	7.3	0.2	1.1	7.3	5.47	4.97	41.7	6.9	10.8	0.2	174.2	-8.1	52.5	67.6	26.7	...	162.2	10.6
-131,574	38.1	5.3	0.1	0.3	1.8	5.97	4.90	50.6	6.8	12.2	0.1	97.1	51.8	53.3	66.8	45.5	...	109.0	16.8
-132,708	46.6	7.9	-0.9	-4.7	-29.5	3.97	2.58	-10.6	8.5	8.4	0.7	271.5	-27.8	45.9	60.2	74.2	0.7	166.2	18.2
27,996	72.9	9.5	1.2	9.7	49.4	3.45	-2.61	-50.6	5.3	6.6	1.3	465.0	-21.3	54.1	65.5	99.9	...	185.4	51.8
Principal Lines of Business: IndAnn (56.1%), GrpAnn (35.2%), GrpLife (6.3%), OrdLife (2.4%)														Principal States: IA (14.3%), CA (8.7%), PA (7.9%), TX (6.3%), FL (5.2%)					
...	90.4	7.8	10.7	1.9	18.5	2.42	2.42	934.8	8.9	145.9	...	...	20.4	49.2	49.2	...	...	24.1	24.1
...	93.8	7.8	-6.4	-1.3	-11.3	2.34	2.34	-7.7	9.2	115.7	...	...	-10.7	105.7	105.7	...	...	27.1	27.1
...	93.3	8.3	-8.3	-1.3	-15.8	2.36	2.36	19.7	12.7	104.8	...	...	-13.1	101.3	101.3	...	...	30.7	30.7
...	92.6	7.6	0.8	0.1	1.9	1.34	1.34	19.2	14.9	67.6	...	...	1.9	102.2	102.2	...	...	28.4	28.4
...	92.4	6.8	5.8	0.9	14.6	0.68	0.68	16.5	15.0	62.8	...	...	15.8	108.4	108.4	...	...	23.2	23.2
Principal Lines of Business: Medicaid (94.0%), Medicare (6.0%)																			
-1,035	19.7	92.1	14.6	189.3	19.1	1.98	1.96	7.0	6.2	282.2	...	...	16.9	84.8	65.0	...	...	...	...
-471	23.8	74.1	11.2	138.0	16.5	5.52	5.47	11.8	5.9	173.9	...	...	16.3	82.2	70.7	...	...	...	...
221	32.6	188.4	-3.9	-15.7	-15.0	9.42	9.37	686.8	53.8	18.2	...	...	-13.3	71.3	71.4	...	...	...	...
-5,710	26.5	79.1	3.2	18.1	21.2	6.22	6.03	72.9	90.6	17.6	...	...	2.7	68.9	69.4	...	...	...	...
8,016	35.0	58.8	5.1	28.0	27.9	6.50	7.40	6.6	58.2	26.6	...	...	66.0	84.5	82.6	...	...	...	...
...	87.3	999.9	-96.9	-99.9	-99.9	2.46	2.46	...	0.1	251.8	...	...	49.8	277.8	277.8	...	...	...	...
...	79.2	52.3	-50.5	-21.5	-99.9	4.74	4.74	999.9	4.8	51.7	...	...	18.1	63.0	63.0	...	...	...	...
-18	94.0	10.1	-25.1	-6.2	-99.9	6.13	6.07	455.1	19.6	15.1	...	...	35.2	60.5	67.0	...	...	...	...
-637	93.7	12.3	-9.1	-3.3	-36.9	2.84	1.34	18.4	7.2	51.6	...	...	223.6	96.7	100.6	...	...	...	...
673	95.4	7.3	3.8	1.4	10.1	3.45	3.69	6.0	6.7	73.5	...	...	13.3	88.0	98.0	...	...	...	...
Principal Lines of Business: FEHBP (63.5%), Medicare (34.0%), OtherHlth (2.5%)														Principal States: SC (86.2%), GA (13.8%)					
...	43.8	55.7	2.7	22.8	2.9	2.73	2.73	90.6	0.1	999.9	0.4	...	2.8	999.9	999.9	...	...	...	...
...	64.0	16.5	7.0	31.7	7.5	3.96	3.96	111.2	0.2	999.9	0.7	...	7.8	999.9	999.9	...	...	...	...
...	51.5	19.2	5.5	27.7	5.9	3.97	3.97	-7.2	0.2	999.9	0.7	...	6.1	999.9	999.9	...	...	...	...
...	71.7	22.2	1.4	7.5	1.5	1.25	1.25	21.7	0.2	999.9	...	...	1.6	999.9	999.9	...	...	...	...
...	78.5	20.0	0.3	1.5	0.4	0.05	0.05	34.4	0.3	999.9	...	...	0.4	999.9	999.9	...	...	...	...
Principal Lines of Business: GrpA&H (100.0%)														Principal States: TX (100.0%)					
...	...	...	...	...	...	...	...	...	...	...	...	...	...	...	...	...	...	...	...
...	...	...	...	...	...	...	...	...	...	...	...	...	...	...	...	...	...	...	...
...	...	...	...	...	...	...	...	...	...	...	...	...	...	...	...	...	...	...	...
...	4.0	35.1	...	9.9	...	...	...	...	1.1	60.4	...	3.0	...	157.6	157.6	...	...	...	...
...	9.3	40.1	2.4	7.6	6.1	3.24	3.25	-21.5	0.7	65.8	...	3.4	21.7	138.1	138.7	...	...	...	...
Principal Lines of Business: OrdLife (100.0%)														Principal States: IN (99.5%)					
-8,847	82.2	10.9	-0.1	-1.3	-1.9	5.62	5.96	12.9	1.4	16.2	1.1	8.8	-3.8	53.4	69.0	23.5	0.1	8.3	36.5
42,992	76.8	8.3	0.9	7.5	13.7	5.53	9.71	49.4	1.5	22.6	0.7	4.5	42.7	54.8	72.0	17.2	...	12.1	33.6
-1,438	77.3	9.3	0.2	2.0	2.7	5.20	6.06	-0.9	1.4	22.7	0.6	4.9	5.5	55.9	72.9	11.8	...	16.2	49.3
-81,802	47.8	7.1	-0.2	-1.5	-3.2	5.63	1.28	46.6	2.1	17.9	0.5	0.7	-5.6	58.7	72.9	21.8	...	17.0	61.6
21,647	59.7	7.5	-0.1	-0.6	-0.8	5.24	5.65	-22.1	1.2	21.3	0.4	7.1	34.2	61.6	76.1	39.9	...	12.4	43.9
Principal Lines of Business: IndAnn (99.3%), GrpAnn (0.6%), OrdLife (0.1%)														Principal States: FL (10.0%), PA (10.0%), CA (8.0%), NJ (7.9%), OH (6.7%)					
...	...	...	0.5	1.4	2.1	1.51	1.51	...	...	33.4	-99.9	208.2	1.6	163.2	167.3	...	...	...	...
...	...	...	1.4	4.1	5.5	1.89	1.89	...	...	36.3	-99.9	77.4	5.8	196.7	200.5	...	...	...	...
...	...	...	1.4	4.5	4.8	3.03	3.03	...	...	50.5	-0.6	1.3	4.9	164.8	167.8	...	...	...	...
...	...	...	1.1	3.3	3.1	3.20	3.20	...	...	62.6	-0.5	18.3	3.7	154.7	161.8	...	...	...	...
...	...	...	-43.1	-99.9	-99.9	2.22	2.23	...	...	19.0	-1.3	34.9	-61.1	87.7	101.9	...	...	...	...
														Principal States: PA (100.0%)					
29	...	...	0.9	4.3	3.0	1.48	1.56	...	...	47.3	-99.9	165.3	3.1	125.6	127.6	...	...	39.5	51.4
56	...	...	0.9	4.5	2.8	2.43	3.96	...	...	53.5	-99.9	62.4	7.0	140.8	143.5	...	...	34.4	46.0
49	...	...	1.4	7.6	3.7	3.00	3.18	...	...	65.9	-0.5	0.8	4.4	128.1	130.2	...	...	31.2	42.6
52	...	...	1.0	6.0	2.6	2.49	2.67	...	...	63.4	-0.5	10.7	3.3	145.5	151.4	...	...	29.1	40.6
39	...	...	-37.2	-99.9	-99.9	0.65	0.87	...	...	16.8	-1.5	23.6	-67.3	78.1	87.3	...	...	84.4	120.6
														Principal States: PA (100.0%)					

Column key: COMPANY NAME / Ultimate Parent Association / Principal Officer / Mailing Address / Dom. : Began Bus. : Struct. : Mktg. / Specialty / Phone # / AMB# / NAIC# — Best's Financial Strength Rating / FSC — Balance Sheet: Data Year; Bonds (%); Mort. Loans & R.E. (%); Com & Pref. Stock (%); All Other Assets (%); Total Assets ($000); Life Reserves (%); Health Reserves (%); Ann Res. & Dep. Liabilities (%); All Other Liabilities (%); Capital & Surplus ($000) — Operations: Direct Premiums Written ($000); Net Premiums Written & Deposits ($000); Operating Cash Flow ($000); NOG Before Taxes ($000); NOG After Taxes ($000); Net Income ($000)

INTER VALLEY HEALTH PLAN INC
Ronald Bolding, President
P.O. Box 6002
Pomona, CA 91769-6002
CA : 1979 : Non-Profit : Broker
Group A&H, Health
909-623-6333
AMB# 064148

Best's Financial Strength Rating: **NR-5**

Data Year	Bonds (%)	Mort. Loans & R.E. (%)	Com & Pref. Stock (%)	All Other Assets (%)	Total Assets ($000)	Life Reserves (%)	Health Reserves (%)	Ann Res. & Dep. Liabilities (%)	All Other Liabilities (%)	Capital & Surplus ($000)	Direct Premiums Written ($000)	Net Premiums Written & Deposits ($000)	Operating Cash Flow ($000)	NOG Before Taxes ($000)	NOG After Taxes ($000)	Net Income ($000)
'05	...	0.3	...	99.7	8,794	...	...	...	100.0	-1,348	116,407	116,407	-23	4,432	4,432	4,432
'06	...	...	...	100.0	22,035	...	...	...	100.0	1,802	123,299	123,299	13,738	3,150	3,150	3,150
'07	...	0.9	...	99.1	29,689	...	...	...	100.0	7,545	130,744	130,744	8,158	5,743	5,743	5,743
'08	...	1.9	...	98.1	18,587	...	...	...	100.0	11,339	134,696	134,696	-11,126	3,794	3,794	3,794
'09	...	...	...	100.0	21,528	...	...	...	100.0	15,956	130,158	130,158	3,246	4,617	4,617	4,617

Rating History: NR-5, 03/22/10; NR-5, 08/26/09; C pd, 05/23/08; C- pd, 05/30/07; D pd, 05/30/06

INTERNATIONAL AMERICAN LIFE[1]
Frank M. Croy, President
P.O. Box 982005
Fort Worth, TX 76182-8005
TX : 1953 : Stock : Not Available
817-284-4888
AMB# 068089 NAIC# 82244

Best's Financial Strength Rating: **NR-1**

Data Year	Bonds (%)	Mort. Loans & R.E. (%)	Com & Pref. Stock (%)	All Other Assets (%)	Total Assets ($000)	Life Reserves (%)	Health Reserves (%)	Ann Res. & Dep. Liabilities (%)	All Other Liabilities (%)	Capital & Surplus ($000)	Direct Premiums Written ($000)	Net Premiums Written & Deposits ($000)	Operating Cash Flow ($000)	NOG Before Taxes ($000)	NOG After Taxes ($000)	Net Income ($000)
'05	67.9	...	...	32.1	1,589	...	...	...	100.0	405	624	405	...	-264	-207	-207
'06	83.2	...	...	16.8	1,720	...	...	...	100.0	530	545	431	...	136	119	119
'07	85.4	...	...	14.6	1,775	...	...	...	100.0	568	483	378	...	36	31	31
'08	84.0	...	...	16.0	1,856	...	...	...	100.0	647	422	329	...	73	64	64
'09	77.7	...	...	22.3	1,910	...	...	...	100.0	716	376	293	...	82	68	68

Rating History: NR-1, 06/10/10; NR-1, 06/12/09; NR-1, 06/12/08; NR-1, 06/08/07; NR-1, 06/07/06

INTERNATIONAL HEALTHCARE SVCS[2]
Healthplex Inc
Bruce H. Safran, President
333 Earle Ovington Boulevard
Uniondale, NY 11553
NJ : 1981 : Stock : Broker
Dental
516-542-2200
AMB# 064782 NAIC# 11173

Best's Financial Strength Rating: **NR-5**

Data Year	Bonds (%)	Mort. Loans & R.E. (%)	Com & Pref. Stock (%)	All Other Assets (%)	Total Assets ($000)	Life Reserves (%)	Health Reserves (%)	Ann Res. & Dep. Liabilities (%)	All Other Liabilities (%)	Capital & Surplus ($000)	Direct Premiums Written ($000)	Net Premiums Written & Deposits ($000)	Operating Cash Flow ($000)	NOG Before Taxes ($000)	NOG After Taxes ($000)	Net Income ($000)
'05	...	...	...	100.0	614	...	32.5	...	67.5	463	7,580	7,580	-405	124	124	124
'06	...	...	...	100.0	823	...	32.5	...	67.5	582	7,762	7,762	217	119	119	119
'07	...	...	...	100.0	958	...	74.7	...	25.3	694	7,861	7,861	177	113	113	113
'08	...	...	...	100.0	1,055	...	73.8	...	26.2	818	7,728	7,728	184	124	124	124
'09	...	...	...	100.0	1,221	...	66.7	...	33.3	959	7,361	7,361	125	141	141	141

Rating History: NR-5, 04/15/10; NR-5, 05/29/09; NR-5, 05/20/08; NR-5, 06/22/07; NR-5, 05/11/06

INTERSTATE BANKERS LIFE INS CO
William C. Chiaro, President & Treasurer
8501 W. Higgins Road
Chicago, IL 60631
IL : 1959 : Mutual : Agency
A&H, Credit Life
773-693-3930
AMB# 009095 NAIC# 84220

Best's Financial Strength Rating: **NR-5**

Data Year	Bonds (%)	Mort. Loans & R.E. (%)	Com & Pref. Stock (%)	All Other Assets (%)	Total Assets ($000)	Life Reserves (%)	Health Reserves (%)	Ann Res. & Dep. Liabilities (%)	All Other Liabilities (%)	Capital & Surplus ($000)	Direct Premiums Written ($000)	Net Premiums Written & Deposits ($000)	Operating Cash Flow ($000)	NOG Before Taxes ($000)	NOG After Taxes ($000)	Net Income ($000)
'05	65.5	...	...	34.5	725	24.8	21.7	...	53.4	714	0	0	-1	5	8	8
'06	67.2	...	...	32.8	707	11.0	64.0	...	24.9	684	...	...	-18	-20	-20	-20
'07	70.1	...	...	29.9	677	14.0	49.0	...	36.9	659	...	...	-29	-17	-17	-17
'08	77.9	...	...	22.1	610	64.7	...	...	35.3	606	...	0	-68	-45	-45	-45
'09	...	...	...	100.0	0	...	...	...	100.0	0	...	...	-606	-187	-187	-187

Rating History: NR-5, 04/21/10; NR-5, 04/21/09; NR-5, 04/08/08; NR-5, 04/25/07; NR-5, 05/09/06

INTRAMERICA LIFE INS CO
Allstate Corporation
Matthew E. Winter, President
100 Motor Parkway, Suite 132
Hauppauge, NY 11788-5107
NY : 1966 : Stock : Direct Response
Pre-need, Var ann
847-402-5000
AMB# 006572 NAIC# 64831

Best's Financial Strength Rating: **B++**; Rating Outlook: Stable; **FSC IV**

Data Year	Bonds (%)	Mort. Loans & R.E. (%)	Com & Pref. Stock (%)	All Other Assets (%)	Total Assets ($000)	Life Reserves (%)	Health Reserves (%)	Ann Res. & Dep. Liabilities (%)	All Other Liabilities (%)	Capital & Surplus ($000)	Direct Premiums Written ($000)	Net Premiums Written & Deposits ($000)	Operating Cash Flow ($000)	NOG Before Taxes ($000)	NOG After Taxes ($000)	Net Income ($000)
'05	29.0	...	0.0	71.0	45,097	...	...	8.8	91.2	11,501	2,193	175	-6,064	562	493	493
'06	27.0	...	0.0	73.0	45,990	...	...	3.9	96.1	12,005	1,864	121	-794	605	500	500
'07	17.4	...	0.0	82.6	42,651	...	...	5.0	95.0	8,496	1,591	56	-3,103	576	486	486
'08	30.8	...	0.0	69.2	28,640	...	...	11.2	88.8	8,810	1,359	13	827	325	334	334
'09	19.9	...	0.0	80.1	31,509	...	...	10.3	89.7	8,992	1,199	25	299	178	203	203

Rating History: B++, 11/20/09; B++, 10/23/08; B++, 01/09/08; B++, 07/27/07; A-, 02/06/07

INVESTORS CONSOLIDATED INS CO
Harris Insurance Holdings Inc
Daniel J. George, President & Treasurer
2727 Allen Parkway Wortham Tower
Houston, TX 77019-2115
NH : 1975 : Stock : Broker
A&H, Dis inc, Hosp Ind
713-529-0045
AMB# 008588 NAIC# 85189

Best's Financial Strength Rating: **B+**; Rating Outlook: Negative; **FSC IV**

Data Year	Bonds (%)	Mort. Loans & R.E. (%)	Com & Pref. Stock (%)	All Other Assets (%)	Total Assets ($000)	Life Reserves (%)	Health Reserves (%)	Ann Res. & Dep. Liabilities (%)	All Other Liabilities (%)	Capital & Surplus ($000)	Direct Premiums Written ($000)	Net Premiums Written & Deposits ($000)	Operating Cash Flow ($000)	NOG Before Taxes ($000)	NOG After Taxes ($000)	Net Income ($000)
'05	85.0	...	...	15.0	14,967	70.2	20.9	2.3	6.6	5,835	1,934	1,934	639	247	244	244
'06	82.8	...	...	17.2	15,367	70.1	20.8	2.3	6.8	6,107	1,828	1,828	361	241	237	237
'07	68.7	...	...	31.3	15,606	71.6	20.6	1.2	6.6	6,645	1,849	1,849	245	485	482	482
'08	45.8	...	...	54.2	15,746	72.6	21.3	1.2	4.9	6,900	1,669	1,669	124	203	211	211
'09	72.9	...	...	27.1	16,173	80.7	8.0	1.4	9.9	8,170	1,321	1,321	113	936	929	929

Rating History: B+, 03/23/10; B+, 04/16/09; B+, 03/04/08; B+, 01/31/07; B+, 05/05/06

INVESTORS GROWTH LIFE INS CO
Student Assurance Services Inc
Mark L. Desch, President
P.O. Box 196
Stillwater, MN 55082-0196
AZ : 1975 : Stock : Other Direct
Student A&H
651-439-7098
AMB# 008650 NAIC# 85944

Best's Financial Strength Rating: **NR-5**

Data Year	Bonds (%)	Mort. Loans & R.E. (%)	Com & Pref. Stock (%)	All Other Assets (%)	Total Assets ($000)	Life Reserves (%)	Health Reserves (%)	Ann Res. & Dep. Liabilities (%)	All Other Liabilities (%)	Capital & Surplus ($000)	Direct Premiums Written ($000)	Net Premiums Written & Deposits ($000)	Operating Cash Flow ($000)	NOG Before Taxes ($000)	NOG After Taxes ($000)	Net Income ($000)
'05	33.1	...	9.0	57.9	12,576	...	98.8	...	1.2	5,356	...	17,221	-2,524	2,339	1,632	1,632
'06	23.9	...	5.9	70.2	15,291	...	96.0	...	4.0	5,742	...	16,618	3,030	1,121	659	647
'07	24.0	...	7.1	68.9	17,683	...	98.4	...	1.6	6,175	...	20,229	2,380	837	666	657
'08	24.9	...	10.2	64.9	19,301	...	95.4	...	4.6	7,155	...	20,029	1,469	2,479	1,689	1,286
'09	25.2	...	12.0	62.8	21,246	...	95.9	...	4.1	8,531	...	22,343	418	2,252	1,492	1,326

Rating History: NR-5, 05/06/10; NR-5, 05/04/09; NR-5, 04/23/08; NR-5, 04/26/07; NR-5, 04/20/06

INVESTORS HERITAGE LIFE INS CO
Investors Heritage Capital Corporation
Harry Lee Waterfield II, Chairman & President
P.O. Box 717
Frankfort, KY 40602-0717
KY : 1961 : Stock : Broker
Credit A&H, Credit Life, Pre-need
502-223-2361
AMB# 006580 NAIC# 64904

Best's Financial Strength Rating: **B+**; Rating Outlook: Stable; **FSC V**

Data Year	Bonds (%)	Mort. Loans & R.E. (%)	Com & Pref. Stock (%)	All Other Assets (%)	Total Assets ($000)	Life Reserves (%)	Health Reserves (%)	Ann Res. & Dep. Liabilities (%)	All Other Liabilities (%)	Capital & Surplus ($000)	Direct Premiums Written ($000)	Net Premiums Written & Deposits ($000)	Operating Cash Flow ($000)	NOG Before Taxes ($000)	NOG After Taxes ($000)	Net Income ($000)
'05	79.7	6.6	1.0	12.7	347,017	80.2	0.0	12.9	6.9	16,626	53,505	43,243	5,726	1,262	1,172	4,236
'06	83.7	7.3	1.1	7.8	336,727	84.3	0.0	14.3	1.4	18,479	52,674	44,026	7,419	1,233	1,082	1,301
'07	83.1	7.3	1.3	8.3	341,832	83.2	0.0	14.7	2.0	19,083	49,246	39,747	5,081	1,062	1,028	1,135
'08	83.6	6.7	1.2	8.5	338,042	84.0	0.0	15.0	1.0	16,588	47,140	38,250	-4,411	1,323	1,170	-3,522
'09	82.9	6.1	1.3	9.7	340,960	83.9	0.0	14.9	1.2	17,911	44,666	38,512	470	1,426	1,329	587

Rating History: B+, 03/18/10; B+, 06/19/09; B+, 06/17/08; B+, 05/29/07; B+, 05/12/06

INVESTORS INSURANCE CORP
SCOR S.E.
Michael W. Pado, President & CEO
P.O. Box 56050
Jacksonville, FL 32241-6050
DE : 1987 : Stock : Broker
Ann
904-260-6990
AMB# 006583 NAIC# 64939

Best's Financial Strength Rating: **A-**; Rating Outlook: Positive; **FSC VI**

Data Year	Bonds (%)	Mort. Loans & R.E. (%)	Com & Pref. Stock (%)	All Other Assets (%)	Total Assets ($000)	Life Reserves (%)	Health Reserves (%)	Ann Res. & Dep. Liabilities (%)	All Other Liabilities (%)	Capital & Surplus ($000)	Direct Premiums Written ($000)	Net Premiums Written & Deposits ($000)	Operating Cash Flow ($000)	NOG Before Taxes ($000)	NOG After Taxes ($000)	Net Income ($000)
'05	90.6	3.7	0.5	5.2	255,610	1.3	0.0	47.7	51.0	24,721	188,024	34,650	24,126	-870	-533	-642
'06	82.3	3.3	2.0	12.4	248,016	1.5	0.0	94.9	3.6	22,322	49,626	152,703	-21,005	-2,968	-2,383	-2,383
'07	76.7	3.2	3.1	17.0	245,173	1.7	0.0	95.4	2.9	31,699	31,431	39,137	4,860	3,214	3,762	3,762
'08	79.9	2.9	3.3	13.8	246,924	1.7	...	93.9	4.4	28,351	152,705	42,846	14,595	3,509	4,318	627
'09	86.7	1.9	0.2	11.2	353,125	1.1	...	90.2	8.7	33,010	531,692	116,145	87,115	-11,096	-9,853	-12,374

Rating History: A-, 09/04/09; A-, 11/14/08; A-, 08/20/07; B++, 09/08/06; B++, 11/08/05

Data in U.S. Dollars

—	Profitability Tests							Leverage Tests						Liquidity Tests					
Un-Realized Capital Gains ($000)	Benefits Paid to NPW & Dep (%)	Comm. & Expenses to NPW & Dep (%)	NOG to Total Assets (%)	NOG to Total Rev (%)	Operating Return on Equity (%)	Net Yield (%)	Total Return (%)	Change in NPW & Dep (%)	NPW & Dep to Capital (X)	Capital & Surplus to Liabilities (%)	Surplus Relief (%)	Reins Leverage (%)	Change in Capital (%)	Quick Liquidity (%)	Current Liquidity (%)	Non-Invest Grade Bonds to Capital (%)	Delinq. & Foreclosed Mortgages to Capital (%)	Mort. & Credit Tenant Loans & R.E. to Capital (%)	Affiliated Invest to Capital (%)
...	87.4	8.7	47.6	3.8	-99.9	-14.90	-14.90	0.4	-86.4	-13.3	...	...	76.7	68.9	68.9	...	...	-1.7	-1.7
...	89.1	8.4	20.4	2.6	999.9	0.01	0.01	5.9	68.4	8.9	...	...	233.7	98.1	98.1	...	...	...	...
...	87.5	8.7	22.2	4.4	122.9	3.25	3.25	6.0	17.3	34.1	...	...	318.6	126.0	126.0	...	...	3.5	3.5
...	88.6	9.4	15.7	2.8	40.2	4.82	4.82	3.0	11.9	156.5	...	...	50.3	226.3	226.3	...	...	3.2	3.2
...	85.7	11.2	23.0	3.5	33.8	2.73	2.73	-3.4	8.2	286.4	...	...	40.7	347.1	347.1	...	...	...	...
Principal Lines of Business: Medicare (100.0%)																			
...	62.8	-49.4	-16.7	-22.7	-55.5	...	...	22.5	1.0	34.2	119.0	...	19.5	...	...	...	...	...	...
...	50.8	28.0	7.2	22.7	25.4	...	...	6.4	0.8	44.5	7.4	...	30.7	...	...	...	...	...	...
...	76.5	26.2	1.8	6.5	5.6	...	...	-12.4	0.7	47.1	6.0	...	7.2	...	...	...	...	...	...
...	68.4	25.0	3.5	15.3	10.5	...	...	-12.8	0.5	53.5	4.6	...	13.9	...	...	...	...	...	...
...	68.9	23.6	3.6	18.7	10.0	...	...	-10.9	0.4	59.9	3.4	...	10.5	...	...	...	...	...	...
Principal Lines of Business: OrdLife (100.0%)																			
...	80.3	19.7	17.2	1.6	21.6	1.08	1.08	-3.9	16.4	306.7	...	...	-32.8	206.1	206.1	...	...	...	...
...	80.1	20.0	16.5	1.5	22.7	1.11	1.11	2.4	13.3	240.3	...	...	25.6	218.0	218.0	...	...	...	...
...	80.5	19.7	12.7	1.4	17.7	0.70	0.70	1.3	11.3	263.4	...	...	19.4	267.2	267.2	...	...	...	...
...	80.5	19.6	12.3	1.6	16.3	0.20	0.20	-1.7	9.4	345.6	...	...	17.8	375.4	375.4	...	...	...	...
...	80.0	19.8	12.4	1.9	15.9	0.00	0.00	-4.7	7.7	366.6	...	...	17.3	387.2	387.2	...	...	...	...
Principal Lines of Business: Dental (100.0%)													Principal States: NJ (100.0%)						
...	42.2	-99.9	1.0	26.5	1.1	4.04	4.04	-99.9	0.0	999.9	...	...	-0.1	999.9	999.9	...	...	...	...
...	...	...	-2.7	-74.2	-2.8	3.77	3.77	100.0	...	999.9	...	...	-4.2	999.9	999.9	...	...	...	...
...	...	...	-2.4	-57.3	-2.5	4.27	4.27	...	...	999.9	...	...	-3.6	999.9	999.9	...	...	...	...
...	-99.9	-99.9	-7.0	-99.9	-7.1	4.04	4.04	...	0.0	999.9	...	...	-8.1	999.9	999.9	...	...	...	...
...	...	...	-61.3	-99.9	-61.7	1.22	1.22	100.0	...	...	...	...	-99.9	...	...	...	...	...	...
...	999.9	149.6	1.0	43.9	4.4	4.04	4.31	-22.5	0.0	359.9	...	218.1	4.5	418.2	430.4	...	...	...	...
...	999.9	194.6	1.1	47.1	4.3	4.96	5.27	-31.0	0.0	687.1	...	190.0	4.3	717.9	737.3	...	...	...	...
...	999.9	382.7	1.1	54.2	4.7	4.94	5.22	-53.9	0.0	442.4	...	251.6	-29.2	597.9	608.5	...	...	...	...
...	999.9	999.9	0.9	51.7	3.9	4.19	4.32	-77.0	0.0	375.9	...	218.6	3.7	493.2	504.2	...	...	...	...
...	999.9	732.5	0.7	41.0	2.3	2.99	3.10	91.4	0.0	376.3	...	197.4	2.1	618.5	627.9	...	...	...	...
Principal Lines of Business: IndAnn (100.0%)													Principal States: NY (58.3%), NJ (14.4%), FL (9.5%)						
...	53.5	67.5	1.6	9.5	4.3	4.16	4.71	-6.0	0.3	63.9	...	...	4.6	152.0	152.0	...	...	...	...
...	55.9	61.2	1.6	9.4	4.0	4.43	4.88	-5.5	0.3	66.0	...	...	4.7	162.9	162.9	...	...	...	...
...	54.9	69.0	3.1	18.9	7.6	4.50	4.89	1.1	0.3	74.2	...	...	8.8	194.4	194.4	...	...	...	...
...	50.9	67.7	1.3	9.4	3.1	3.59	3.93	-9.7	0.2	78.0	...	...	3.8	244.3	244.3	...	...	...	...
...	51.9	97.3	5.8	54.8	12.3	2.13	2.51	-20.8	0.2	102.1	...	...	18.4	216.1	217.4	...	...	...	...
Principal Lines of Business: IndA&H (56.5%), GrpLife (33.4%), GrpA&H (9.1%), OrdLife (0.9%), IndAnn (0.1%)													Principal States: NC (76.1%), VA (12.7%), SC (4.4%)						
-11	68.0	34.1	12.4	9.2	38.9	3.49	3.41	-18.8	3.2	76.1	...	...	75.1	200.5	211.7	5.7	...	...	...
13	60.4	25.5	4.7	3.8	11.9	4.50	4.50	-3.5	2.9	61.1	...	16.9	6.7	213.6	220.8	3.0	...	...	...
-4	62.1	29.5	4.0	3.2	11.2	4.10	4.01	21.7	3.2	54.4	...	16.1	7.4	206.6	214.1	3.9	...	...	...
-510	60.1	29.6	9.1	8.2	25.3	3.72	-1.63	-1.0	2.8	60.0	...	14.4	16.1	195.9	204.3	2.8	...	...	...
328	60.0	28.8	7.4	6.5	19.0	2.74	3.74	11.6	2.6	68.7	...	18.2	19.5	181.6	195.5	3.7	...	...	...
Principal Lines of Business: GrpA&H (100.0%)																			
-814	96.2	27.4	0.3	1.7	6.9	5.89	6.66	-2.7	2.4	5.6	33.2	335.8	-3.7	63.6	70.8	5.5	...	125.6	...
129	95.7	27.9	0.3	1.6	6.2	5.72	5.87	1.8	2.2	6.3	27.5	293.2	9.3	66.7	74.4	...	...	123.4	...
-108	106.7	29.8	0.3	1.6	5.5	5.66	5.67	-9.7	1.9	6.4	28.0	274.4	3.1	68.2	75.8	...	...	120.9	...
-206	105.9	32.1	0.3	1.9	6.6	5.59	4.10	-3.8	2.3	5.2	29.1	308.5	-19.6	67.3	75.7	3.5	...	136.5	...
-1,235	106.9	33.7	0.4	2.2	7.7	5.49	4.98	0.7	2.1	5.6	19.0	272.9	9.1	64.3	73.3	15.3	...	115.1	21.6
Principal Lines of Business: OrdLife (72.8%), IndAnn (15.8%), GrpLife (11.3%), GrpAnn (0.1%), IndA&H (0.0%)													Principal States: KY (35.5%), NC (30.4%), TN (10.1%), GA (4.9%), VA (4.2%)						
634	36.2	11.4	-0.2	-1.2	-2.2	2.86	3.11	-16.8	1.4	11.0	75.6	999.9	1.2	70.5	81.6	3.0	...	36.9	...
1,933	20.6	2.4	-0.9	-1.8	-10.1	4.18	5.01	340.7	6.6	10.3	24.2	999.9	-9.0	65.6	76.7	...	...	35.4	...
-3,446	76.1	6.6	1.5	15.0	13.9	4.97	3.56	-74.4	1.2	15.4	11.5	999.9	41.7	73.0	84.7	7.6	...	23.8	...
-5,018	61.4	12.8	1.8	8.3	14.4	4.92	1.37	9.5	1.5	13.0	49.9	999.9	-12.9	80.3	93.5	8.0	...	25.5	...
8,075	25.8	10.4	-3.3	-6.2	-32.1	4.43	6.40	171.1	3.5	10.3	128.1	999.9	16.2	72.6	84.7	28.2	...	19.8	...
Principal Lines of Business: IndAnn (100.0%), OrdLife (0.0%)													Principal States: CA (19.9%), TX (13.4%), FL (12.7%), PA (8.6%), AR (4.3%)						

2010 BEST'S KEY RATING GUIDE — LIFE/HEALTH EDITION
ANNUAL STATEMENT DATA FOR YEARS 2005 – 2009

Data in U.S. Dollars

COMPANY NAME Ultimate Parent Association Principal Officer Mailing Address Dom. : Began Bus. : Struct. : Mktg. Specialty Phone # AMB# NAIC#	Best's Financial Strength Rating FSC	Data Year	Balance Sheet Bonds (%)	Mort. Loans & R.E. (%)	Com & Pref. Stock (%)	All Other Assets (%)	Total Assets ($000)	Life Reserves (%)	Health Reserves %)	Ann Res. & Dep. Liabilities (%)	All Other Liabilities (%)	Capital & Surplus ($000)	Operations Direct Premiums Written ($000)	Net Premiums Written & Deposits ($000)	Operating Cash Flow ($000)	NOG Before Taxes ($000)	NOG After Taxes ($000)	Net Income ($000)
INVESTORS LIFE OF NORTH AMER Financial Holding Corporation Gary L. Muller CEO P.O. Box 410288 Kansas City, MO 64141-0288 TX : 1963 : Stock : Agency SPDA's, Term Life, Univ Life 816-391-2000 AMB# 006412 NAIC# 63487	**B+** Rating Outlook: Stable **FSC VI**	'05	52.7	0.1	0.7	46.6	1,016,389	48.6	0.0	14.1	37.4	39,709	39,045	35,750	-25,867	2,827	4,434	10,008
		'06	54.2	...	0.0	45.7	988,928	47.2	0.0	12.3	40.5	43,414	35,758	13,725	-27,217	5,748	5,965	6,036
		'07	54.2	...	0.0	45.7	936,375	48.2	0.0	11.9	39.9	47,755	34,342	31,605	-40,575	3,524	3,851	3,872
		'08	62.7	...	0.2	37.1	754,802	57.0	0.0	13.0	30.0	34,193	31,176	22,225	-30,113	-419	-510	-510
		'09	63.5	...	1.2	35.3	746,067	55.8	0.0	12.4	31.8	39,481	28,327	890	-29,051	209	2,478	1,869
		Rating History: B+, 11/04/09; B+, 09/05/08; B u, 01/16/08; B, 06/15/07; B-, 06/09/06																
INVESTORS TRUST ASSUR SPC Marteena Rodriguez Chief Financial Officer 23 Lime Tree Bay Ave. Grand Cayman KY1-1208, Cayman Islands KY : Stock : Agency Investment Linked, Long-term Savings, Var ann AMB# 075811	**B++** Rating Outlook: Stable **FSC VI**	'05	...	...	...	100.0	80,792	...	...	51.8	48.2	702	...	...	14,442	414	414	414
		'06	...	...	...	100.0	155,391	...	...	54.9	45.1	7,827	...	...	23,813	3,125	3,125	3,125
		'07	...	...	...	100.0	371,151	...	...	45.9	54.1	24,177	...	...	63,504	6,351	6,351	6,351
		'08	...	...	...	100.0	439,935	...	...	34.2	65.8	42,006	...	...	52,565	17,827	17,827	17,827
		'09	...	...	...	100.0	532,198	...	...	43.6	56.4	50,158	...	...	49,069	14,152	14,152	14,152
		Rating History: B++, 09/30/09																
ISLAND INSURANCE CORP Hector Calvo President P.O. Box 362589 San Juan, PR 00936-2589 PR : 2005 : Stock Inactive 787-274-7101 AMB# 060581 NAIC# 12498	**NR-5**	'05	...	...	...	...	...	...	...	...	...	...	...	...	...	...	...	...
		'06	...	...	...	...	...	...	...	...	...	...	...	...	...	...	...	...
		'07	35.3	...	...	64.7	6,000	...	...	...	100.0	5,946	...	...	230	169	169	169
		'08	13.2	...	...	86.8	6,024	...	...	...	100.0	5,984	...	...	110	98	98	98
		'09	19.6	...	...	80.4	4,024	...	...	...	100.0	3,990	...	...	-1,970	-10	-10	-10
		Rating History: NR-5, 04/15/10; NR-5, 04/23/09; NR-5, 04/09/08; NR-1, 06/08/07; NR-1, 06/07/06																
JMIC LIFE INSURANCE COMPANY[1] JM Family Enterprises, Inc Forrest W. Heathcott III President 500 Jim Moran Boulevard Deerfield Beach, FL 33442 FL : 1979 : Stock : Not Available 954-429-2333 AMB# 008994 NAIC# 89958	**NR-1**	'05	74.7	...	12.8	12.5	245,819	...	...	...	100.0	79,111	58,617	38,051	...	3,424	1,189	1,240
		'06	76.3	...	12.3	11.5	239,019	...	...	...	100.0	80,505	52,247	34,421	...	5,369	919	1,347
		'07	79.2	...	0.6	20.2	183,778	...	...	...	100.0	87,212	-4,873	-8,989	...	-9,143	849	5,621
		'08	78.5	...	1.0	20.5	95,859	...	...	...	100.0	47,216	-4,216	-6,648	...	20,673	14,874	13,851
		'09	76.5	...	0.0	23.5	54,939	...	...	...	100.0	32,338	-29,511	-23,466	...	20,544	13,531	12,279
		Rating History: NR-1, 06/10/10; NR-1, 06/12/09; NR-1, 06/12/08; NR-5, 05/22/08; NR-4, 05/24/07																
JACKSON GRIFFIN INSURANCE CO[1] Laura J. Maris President 103 Jackson Street Harrisburg, AR 72432 AR : 1957 : Stock : Not Available 870-523-5822 AMB# 068351 NAIC# 84115	**NR-1**	'05	73.8	...	20.8	5.4	9,336	...	...	...	100.0	1,793	1,059	1,059	...	66	66	183
		'06	76.2	...	17.7	6.2	9,778	...	...	...	100.0	1,792	945	945	...	-58	-58	38
		'07	81.0	...	14.7	4.4	10,072	...	...	...	100.0	1,646	899	899	...	-34	-34	-29
		'08	72.4	...	16.0	11.6	10,019	...	...	...	100.0	1,314	973	973	...	-201	-201	-150
		'09	80.0	...	15.8	4.2	10,092	...	...	...	100.0	1,042	963	963	...	-251	-251	-272
		Rating History: NR-1, 06/10/10; NR-1, 06/12/09; NR-1, 06/12/08; NR-1, 06/08/07; NR-1, 06/07/06																
JACKSON NATIONAL LIFE INS CO Prudential plc Clark P. Manning, Jr. President & CEO 1 Corporate Way Lansing, MI 48951 MI : 1961 : Stock : Broker Ind Ann, Ind Life, ISWL 517-381-5500 AMB# 006596 NAIC# 65056	**A+ u** Under Review Implication: Negative **FSC XV**	'05	61.7	8.4	1.0	28.9	60,742,602	11.9	...	61.6	26.5	3,434,049	7,609,695	9,976,034	706,728	681,220	597,227	565,099
		'06	53.9	8.1	0.9	37.1	66,835,657	10.7	...	54.9	34.3	3,676,896	9,502,991	11,876,932	-947,987	677,360	508,741	412,252
		'07	48.1	7.6	1.2	43.2	73,963,867	9.6	...	49.1	41.3	4,024,057	11,171,981	13,799,164	-203,393	670,319	537,885	490,011
		'08	53.8	9.5	1.1	35.5	68,327,271	10.4	...	58.2	31.4	3,745,686	10,509,188	13,779,251	3,507,456	-535,983	-285,486	-623,395
		'09	44.9	7.8	0.6	46.7	77,789,118	9.0	...	48.8	42.2	3,972,694	13,597,039	13,502,817	-2,441,603	1,712,180	1,397,394	373,594
		Rating History: A+ gu, 03/04/10; A+ g, 07/14/09; A+ g, 02/15/08; A+ g, 10/16/06; A+ g, 02/08/05																
JACKSON NATIONAL LF INS OF NY Prudential plc Clark P. Manning, Jr. President & CEO 1 Corporate Way Lansing, MI 48951 NY : 1996 : Stock : General Agent Ann, Life 517-381-5500 AMB# 060216 NAIC# 60140	**A+ u** Under Review Implication: Negative **FSC XV**	'05	63.7	...	0.0	36.3	2,281,679	0.1	...	63.7	36.1	132,449	344,997	347,654	-2,264	17,970	11,845	11,892
		'06	53.5	...	0.0	46.5	2,680,896	0.1	...	53.1	46.7	134,618	451,211	451,203	-21,781	8,475	3,277	3,374
		'07	41.6	...	0.0	58.4	3,039,695	0.1	...	44.6	55.2	132,086	557,291	557,548	-87,593	1,382	-2,364	-4,139
		'08	46.8	...	0.1	53.1	2,681,811	0.2	...	52.1	47.7	94,662	458,295	216,518	67,986	-284,887	-284,887	-309,370
		'09	40.7	...	0.1	59.3	3,398,281	0.2	...	42.4	57.4	212,409	792,307	784,617	92,813	72,597	53,801	44,737
		Rating History: A+ gu, 03/04/10; A+ g, 07/14/09; A+ g, 02/15/08; A+ g, 10/16/06; A+ g, 02/08/05																
JAIMINI HEALTH INC Mohender Narula, DMD President & CEO 9500 Haven Street, Suite 125 Rancho Cucamonga, CA 92730 CA : 1983 : Stock : Broker Dental 909-483-8310 AMB# 064732	**NR-5**	'05	...	...	...	100.0	749	...	...	...	100.0	-183	555	555	-107	-242	-243	-243
		'06	...	...	...	100.0	660	...	...	...	100.0	-160	477	477	-67	-164	-165	-165
		'07	...	...	...	100.0	724	...	...	...	100.0	-143	419	419	31	-149	-150	-150
		'08	...	...	...	100.0	692	...	...	...	100.0	-137	375	375	-14	-146	-146	-146
		'09	...	...	...	100.0	760	...	...	...	100.0	-81	322	322	56	-84	-84	-84
		Rating History: NR-5, 05/05/10; NR-5, 05/08/09; NR-5, 05/09/08; NR-5, 05/07/07; NR-5, 05/25/06																
JAMESTOWN LIFE INS CO Genworth Financial, Inc Leon E. Roday Chairman of the Board, President & CEO 6604 West Broad Street Richmond, VA 23230 VA : 1982 : Stock : Other Direct Reins 888-322-4629 AMB# 009188 NAIC# 97144	**NR-3**	'05	95.5	...	...	4.5	268,367	83.2	...	...	16.8	108,406	...	16,380	-72,353	3,257	4,933	4,880
		'06	87.8	...	7.3	4.9	244,459	75.6	...	...	24.4	141,947	...	-33,182	-20,459	46,868	33,075	33,301
		'07	84.3	...	3.8	11.9	149,997	82.1	...	...	17.9	47,014	...	8,110	-90,679	6,957	4,396	4,371
		'08	75.7	...	3.0	21.3	148,099	83.8	...	...	16.2	40,065	...	7,834	-1,492	4,082	3,486	-3,638
		'09	83.5	...	...	16.5	154,172	86.5	...	...	13.5	47,312	...	7,098	7,105	6,591	7,439	9,579
		Rating History: NR-3, 04/21/10; NR-3, 02/19/09; NR-3, 11/06/08; NR-3, 06/16/08; NR-3, 04/04/07																

BEST'S PROFITABILITY, LEVERAGE AND LIQUIDITY TESTS 2005 – 2009

Data in U.S. Dollars

—	Profitability Tests							Leverage Tests						Liquidity Tests					
Un-Realized Capital Gains ($000)	Benefits Paid to NPW & Dep (%)	Comm. & Expenses to NPW & Dep (%)	NOG to Total Assets (%)	NOG to Total Rev (%)	Operating Return on Equity (%)	Net Yield (%)	Total Return (%)	Change in NPW & Dep (%)	NPW & Dep to Capital (X)	Capital & Surplus to Liabilities (%)	Surplus Relief (%)	Reins Leverage (%)	Change in Capital (%)	Quick Liquidity (%)	Current Liquidity (%)	Non-Invest Grade Bonds to Capital (%)	Delinq. & Foreclosed Mortgages to Capital (%)	Mort. & Credit Tenant Loans & R.E. to Capital (%)	Affiliated Invest to Capital (%)
-879	236.9	48.0	0.4	6.9	12.0	4.23	4.99	-17.8	0.8	7.2	1.4	21.4	10.0	83.2	89.7	22.8	...	1.2	48.8
-5,516	577.0	138.0	0.6	12.7	14.4	4.79	3.99	-61.6	0.3	7.7	0.8	14.0	0.6	83.9	91.5	36.7	...	...	0.6
...	310.9	54.8	0.4	6.0	8.4	4.93	4.98	130.3	0.6	9.2	1.1	12.8	11.1	79.8	88.3	54.0	...	...	0.6
-619	606.1	79.7	-0.1	-0.1	-1.2	4.79	4.74	-29.7	0.6	7.0	1.1	13.9	-27.1	76.5	87.4	66.3	...	...	0.8
568	999.9	377.1	0.3	-13.9	6.7	5.78	5.79	-96.0	0.0	8.9	2.3	11.1	18.2	63.6	78.8	27.9	...	...	3.0
Principal Lines of Business: IndAnn (58.9%), GrpAnn (43.7%), GrpLife (-0.2%), IndA&H (-0.3%), OrdLife (-2.0%)														Principal States: PA (12.0%), CA (7.9%), OH (7.2%), TX (6.2%), NJ (5.9%)					
...	...	...	...	7.4	...	...	...	...	...	0.9	...	...	...	8.5	43.5	...	...	...	...
...	...	...	2.7	18.0	73.3	0.13	0.13	...	...	5.3	...	...	999.9	6.6	48.8	...	...	...	...
...	...	...	2.4	17.2	39.7	0.40	0.40	...	...	7.0	...	...	208.9	6.2	45.2	...	...	...	...
...	...	...	4.4	-54.5	53.9	0.51	0.51	...	...	10.6	...	...	73.7	2.5	39.7	...	...	...	...
...	...	...	2.9	21.4	30.7	0.25	0.25	...	...	10.4	...	...	19.4	5.1	43.7	...	...	...	...
...	...	...	...	...	...	...	...	...	...	...	...	...	...	...	...	...	...	...	...
...	...	...	...	...	...	...	...	...	...	...	...	...	...	...	...	...	...	...	...
...	...	...	...	61.8	...	...	...	...	...	999.9	...	...	...	999.9	999.9	...	...	...	...
...	...	...	1.6	51.0	1.6	3.30	3.26	...	...	999.9	...	...	0.6	999.9	999.9	...	...	...	...
...	...	...	-0.2	-14.9	-0.2	1.44	1.34	...	...	999.9	...	...	-33.3	999.9	999.9	...	...	...	...
1,579	55.4	74.0	0.5	2.1	1.5	...	...	0.7	0.5	51.1	13.7	...	4.3	...	...	...	...	...	...
837	55.6	80.0	0.4	1.7	1.2	...	...	-9.5	0.4	55.7	11.6	...	2.9	...	...	...	...	...	...
-3,072	-99.9	-99.9	0.4	34.6	1.0	...	...	-99.9	-0.1	91.3	2.4	...	2.5	...	...	...	...	...	...
-13	-99.9	-3.9	10.6	999.9	22.1	...	...	26.0	-0.1	97.1	3.0	...	-46.1	...	...	...	...	...	...
-122	-34.5	113.7	17.9	-57.1	34.0	...	...	-99.9	-0.7	143.3	-9.6	...	-31.5	...	...	...	...	...	...
Principal Lines of Business: CrdA&H (56.9%), CrdLife (43.1%)																			
-84	60.0	42.3	0.7	4.4	3.8	...	...	28.1	0.6	24.0	...	...	4.3	...	...	...	...	...	...
83	66.6	47.0	-0.6	-4.2	-3.2	...	...	-10.8	0.5	22.9	...	...	1.0	...	...	...	...	...	...
...	75.5	52.5	-0.3	-2.4	-2.0	...	...	-4.8	0.5	20.3	...	...	-7.0	...	...	...	...	...	...
-181	73.8	50.6	-2.0	-14.6	-13.6	...	...	8.2	0.7	16.0	...	...	-18.5	...	...	...	...	...	...
31	70.1	56.9	-2.5	-18.3	-21.3	...	...	-1.0	0.9	12.6	...	...	-18.2	...	...	...	...	...	...
Principal Lines of Business: IndAnn (67.1%), OrdLife (32.9%)																			
156,759	52.8	8.4	1.0	5.7	17.9	5.91	6.23	12.6	2.6	9.0	0.7	29.0	8.6	46.7	63.4	70.3	0.0	169.4	5.6
521	57.1	8.2	0.8	4.1	14.3	6.11	5.97	19.1	2.9	9.7	0.6	25.0	5.2	48.7	64.9	59.1	0.0	162.5	5.2
181,764	54.7	8.4	0.8	3.7	14.0	6.39	6.78	16.2	3.1	10.8	0.5	24.5	9.8	49.1	65.4	48.1	0.0	150.3	22.9
-882,709	50.1	10.8	-0.4	-2.0	-7.3	5.90	3.37	-0.1	3.5	8.9	0.5	32.3	-11.3	46.4	61.5	76.4	0.0	191.9	24.8
171,248	47.4	7.5	1.9	8.4	36.2	5.47	3.74	-2.0	3.4	9.5	0.5	21.0	1.3	46.8	61.7	71.8	0.4	178.1	25.3
Principal Lines of Business: IndAnn (85.7%), GrpAnn (11.1%), OrdLife (3.2%), GrpLife (0.0%), IndLife (0.0%)														Principal States: CA (10.3%), MI (7.2%), FL (7.1%), TX (6.0%), PA (5.6%)					
-9	46.8	8.7	0.6	2.7	9.3	6.03	6.05	6.0	2.4	10.7	0.1	1.6	8.9	61.1	80.6	71.3	...	2.7	...
71	51.9	8.5	0.1	0.6	2.5	6.12	6.13	29.8	3.1	11.2	0.1	1.4	2.5	62.8	81.8	66.6	...	2.6	...
46	51.3	8.4	-0.1	-0.4	-1.8	6.11	5.96	23.6	3.9	11.7	0.1	1.6	-3.2	72.3	92.0	45.1	...	2.6	...
-307	164.3	18.0	-10.0	-87.5	-99.9	5.80	3.97	-61.2	2.3	6.6	0.1	258.0	-33.4	71.4	87.9	68.0	...	9.1	...
-12,492	48.9	8.2	1.8	6.0	35.0	5.64	4.14	262.4	3.7	16.5	0.0	16.3	124.4	73.8	93.4	50.0	...	6.6	...
Principal Lines of Business: IndAnn (99.6%), GrpAnn (0.3%), OrdLife (0.1%)														Principal States: NY (95.1%)					
...	44.8	92.1	-29.0	-46.8	229.8	...	...	-10.2	-3.0	-19.6	...	...	-99.9	30.1	30.1	...	...	...	...
...	40.5	94.1	-23.4	-34.6	96.2	-0.13	-0.13	-14.2	-3.0	-19.5	...	...	12.7	25.8	25.8	...	...	...	...
...	41.1	95.2	-21.6	-35.4	98.7	-0.87	-0.87	-12.1	-2.9	-16.5	...	...	10.2	27.7	27.7	...	...	...	...
...	48.6	90.8	-20.7	-38.8	104.3	-0.64	-0.64	-10.5	-2.7	-16.6	...	...	4.3	27.4	27.4	...	...	...	...
...	51.1	76.2	-11.6	-25.8	77.1	-1.11	-1.11	-14.2	-4.0	-9.6	...	...	41.1	33.6	33.6	...	...	...	...
Principal Lines of Business: CompHosp/Med (100.0%)																			
...	21.4	31.2	1.6	15.2	4.4	4.90	5.40	-4.5	0.1	69.6	...	1.0	-4.6	78.7	115.9	8.8	...	...	...
...	-16.6	40.9	12.9	-99.9	26.4	5.99	6.77	-99.9	-0.2	142.1	...	2.1	30.3	124.4	177.7	4.8	...	...	...
...	61.1	35.4	2.2	20.1	4.7	6.34	7.21	124.4	0.2	46.8	...	3.7	-66.7	82.1	119.7	1.1	...	...	...
...	64.8	37.7	2.3	20.1	8.0	5.43	1.90	-3.4	0.2	37.1	...	4.2	-16.3	90.6	122.9	6.2	...	...	...
-778	61.7	35.3	4.9	46.3	17.0	4.92	7.09	-9.4	0.1	44.7	...	3.4	19.0	85.8	117.3	12.1	...	...	...
Principal Lines of Business: OrdLife (100.0%)																			

Data in U.S. Dollars

COMPANY NAME / Ultimate Parent Association / Principal Officer / Mailing Address / Dom. : Began Bus. : Struct. : Mktg. / Specialty / Phone # / AMB# / NAIC#	Best's Financial Strength Rating / FSC	Data Year	Balance Sheet: Bonds (%)	Mort. Loans & R.E. (%)	Com & Pref. Stock (%)	All Other Assets (%)	Total Assets ($000)	Life Reserves (%)	Health Reserves (%)	Ann Res. & Dep. Liabilities (%)	All Other Liabilities (%)	Capital & Surplus ($000)	Operations: Direct Premiums Written ($000)	Net Premiums Written & Deposits ($000)	Operating Cash Flow ($000)	NOG Before Taxes ($000)	NOG After Taxes ($000)	Net Income ($000)
JEFF DAVIS MORTUARY BEN ASSOC[1] Dorothy M. Bryan President 114 Shankland Avenue Jennings, LA 70546 LA : 1936 : Stock : Not Available 337-824-1862 AMB# 007750 NAIC# 69055	NR-1	'05	77.6	...	...	22.4	3,218	...	...	...	100.0	1,823	114	114	...	-14	-14	-14
		'06	76.3	...	...	23.7	3,273	...	...	...	100.0	1,846	98	98	...	25	23	23
		'07	31.3	...	...	68.7	3,350	...	...	...	100.0	1,873	115	115	...	29	26	26
		'08	58.6	...	...	41.4	3,410	...	...	...	100.0	1,887	138	138	...	15	15	15
		'09	28.7	...	...	71.3	3,460	...	...	...	100.0	1,891	179	179	...	4	4	4
		Rating History: NR-1, 06/10/10; NR-1, 06/12/09; NR-1, 06/12/08; NR-1, 06/08/07; NR-1, 06/07/06																
JEFFERSON LIFE INSURANCE CO DNIC Insurance Holdings, Inc. John W. Hagan President P.O. Box 800409 Dallas, TX 75380-0409 TX : 1985 : Stock : Not Available Group A&H 214-880-0808 AMB# 009521 NAIC# 94790	NR-5	'05	9.6	...	...	90.4	8,522	20.6	74.2	0.1	5.1	4,077	4,971	11,862	2,431	-852	-853	-211
		'06	11.9	...	...	88.1	6,430	16.6	77.3	0.1	6.0	1,254	11,890	13,892	-1,522	-3,101	-3,114	-3,114
		'07	10.3	...	...	89.7	8,514	16.7	74.4	0.1	8.8	3,364	8,716	12,554	1,995	143	130	130
		'08	14.9	...	...	85.1	4,810	36.9	59.1	0.1	3.9	2,488	6,008	5,899	-2,389	-756	-746	-746
		'09	21.0	...	...	79.0	4,754	45.8	47.7	0.2	6.3	2,943	4,213	4,245	54	318	318	318
		Rating History: NR-5, 04/06/10; NR-5, 04/09/09; NR-5, 04/18/08; NR-5, 04/24/07; NR-5, 06/07/06																
JEFFERSON NATIONAL LIFE INS CO Jefferson National Financial Corp Laurence P. Greenberg President & CEO 9920 Corporate Campus Drive Louisville, KY 40223 TX : 1937 : Stock : Agency Ann, Group A&H, Life 212-741-9311 AMB# 006475 NAIC# 64017	B- Rating Outlook: Negative FSC VI	'05	31.1	...	1.6	67.3	1,623,921	1.4	...	32.6	66.0	40,486	156,212	108,493	-72,812	-2,006	-1,302	-948
		'06	26.9	0.1	1.8	71.2	1,675,872	1.3	...	28.7	70.0	41,065	196,314	150,877	-43,635	-2,301	-2,186	-3,065
		'07	23.4	0.5	1.7	74.5	1,727,626	1.2	...	25.3	73.5	41,081	283,392	242,802	-36,749	-112	-112	-220
		'08	29.4	1.4	2.1	67.1	1,325,645	1.5	...	33.1	65.5	23,340	216,175	183,289	-7,186	-8,452	-8,452	-14,843
		'09	25.7	1.1	1.9	71.3	1,572,584	1.1	...	26.2	72.7	25,905	179,385	150,745	35,348	4,370	4,370	1,379
		Rating History: B-, 05/15/09; B, 07/24/08; B, 12/07/07; B, 10/04/06; B g, 01/19/06																
JOHN ALDEN LIFE INS CO Assurant Inc Donald G. Hamm, Jr. President & CEO P.O. Box 3050 Milwaukee, WI 53201-3050 WI : 1974 : Stock : Broker Ann, Group A&H, Maj med 414-271-3011 AMB# 006600 NAIC# 65080	A- Rating Outlook: Stable FSC VIII	'05	79.1	3.8	3.4	13.7	587,378	49.0	26.7	6.6	17.6	106,791	646,956	616,950	-88,328	77,818	48,158	48,952
		'06	72.5	2.9	8.6	16.0	540,573	53.1	25.9	6.3	14.7	102,601	594,114	565,058	-33,897	91,180	62,202	61,679
		'07	70.2	4.1	10.5	15.3	526,043	52.1	25.2	5.7	17.1	93,111	570,472	544,190	-16,955	56,688	39,239	37,585
		'08	71.3	4.9	9.2	14.5	490,584	55.3	23.8	5.7	15.2	94,328	535,367	510,909	-30,889	58,576	37,154	28,049
		'09	76.8	5.0	2.0	16.2	462,740	56.1	26.4	5.3	12.3	85,197	510,969	486,993	-28,194	9,298	3,994	1,824
		Rating History: A- g, 11/18/09; A- g, 11/25/08; A- g, 06/24/08; A- g, 07/17/07; A- g, 06/19/06																
JOHN D KERNAN DMD PA[2] John D. Kernan President 658 W. Cuthbert Blvd. Westmont, NJ 08108 NJ : 1977 : Stock : Not Available Dental 856-869-8660 AMB# 064916 NAIC# 11182	NR-5	'05	...	...	...	...	...	...	...	...	...	...	...	...	...	...	...	...
		'06	...	...	...	100.0	277	...	...	...	100.0	244	1,117	1,117	0	25	25	25
		'07	...	...	...	100.0	296	...	...	...	100.0	260	1,161	1,161	4	11	11	11
		'08	...	...	...	100.0	335	...	...	...	100.0	288	1,178	1,178	-4	21	21	21
		'09	...	...	...	100.0	348	...	...	...	100.0	301	1,130	1,130	2	6	6	6
		Rating History: NR-5, 04/19/10; NR-5, 05/29/09; NR-5, 05/20/08; NR-5, 06/19/07																
JOHN HANCOCK LIFE & HEALTH INS Manulife Financial Corporation James R. Boyle Senior Exec VP, US Div & President, JHFS P.O. Box 717 Boston, MA 02117-0717 MA : 1981 : Stock : Broker ISWL 617-572-6000 AMB# 009074 NAIC# 93610	A+ Rating Outlook: Stable FSC XV	'05	55.8	18.7	0.5	25.0	546,444	97.2	0.0	...	2.8	115,419	2,461	451	-22,807	526	-2,102	-2,401
		'06	52.9	17.2	0.4	29.5	545,708	94.9	0.1	1.0	4.0	118,642	2,528	14,369	-26,923	7,451	6,247	5,317
		'07	51.1	14.2	0.3	34.4	538,935	94.6	0.2	1.1	4.0	126,270	2,238	11,216	16,593	14,373	10,150	13,217
		'08	20.4	4.3	0.0	75.2	2,573,744	26.8	0.1	0.5	72.7	193,247	2,113	14,432	315,405	8,569	7,910	6,358
		'09	18.3	5.7	2.8	73.3	6,443,031	10.9	14.6	0.2	74.3	350,912	1,044,497	1,158,795	1,561,907	-3,808	-1,952	-1,423
		Rating History: A+ g, 01/19/10; A+ g, 07/17/09; A++g, 02/04/09; A++g, 06/06/08; A++g, 06/07/07																
JOHN HANCOCK LIFE INS CO NY Manulife Financial Corporation James D. Gallagher Executive Vice President 100 Summit Lake Drive, 2nd Floor Valhalla, NY 10595 NY : 1992 : Stock : Agency Ind Life, Ann, Group pens 914-773-0708 AMB# 060056 NAIC# 86375	A+ Rating Outlook: Stable FSC XV	'05	5.6	...	...	94.4	4,594,898	2.0	...	7.5	90.5	100,870	1,253,834	1,186,663	14,030	18,237	13,253	13,230
		'06	5.9	...	...	94.1	6,042,157	1.9	...	5.3	92.8	166,325	1,404,730	1,294,691	92,209	98,127	62,957	63,057
		'07	7.0	...	...	93.0	7,320,515	2.6	...	4.6	92.8	223,048	1,580,111	1,499,729	206,070	96,760	66,351	66,351
		'08	10.8	...	...	89.2	6,221,292	5.9	...	11.1	83.0	218,287	1,470,858	1,397,202	470,389	-323,053	-328,077	-328,055
		'09	13.9	...	...	86.1	8,770,571	7.1	...	4.5	88.3	1,016,982	1,264,641	1,176,344	670,857	386,885	309,504	309,504
		Rating History: A+ g, 01/19/10; A+ g, 07/17/09; A++g, 02/04/09; A++g, 06/06/08; A++g, 06/07/07																
JOHN HANCOCK LIFE INS CO USA Manulife Financial Corporation James R. Boyle Sr. Exec. VP (US Div) & President 601 Congress Street Boston, MA 02210 MI : 1956 : Stock : Agency Ind Life, Ann, Group pens 617-854-4300 AMB# 006681 NAIC# 65838	A+ Rating Outlook: Stable FSC XV	'05	32.0	8.6	1.3	58.2	174,145,917	17.2	2.2	22.3	58.4	4,912,521	24,200,969	15,721,243	532,700	544,006	343,881	655,622
		'06	28.4	7.5	1.7	62.3	194,486,032	16.0	2.3	18.2	63.5	5,018,739	27,933,212	17,881,273	931,072	606,569	542,805	730,328
		'07	25.9	7.0	1.5	65.6	210,291,317	15.7	2.5	16.0	65.8	5,840,788	30,549,146	19,916,553	2,124,101	881,757	919,376	1,131,662
		'08	29.4	8.6	1.5	60.5	178,632,131	19.5	3.4	18.4	58.8	4,474,155	30,910,754	13,469,998	687,530	-2,492,139	-1,869,686	-2,439,444
		'09	26.3	7.7	1.3	64.8	203,396,347	18.1	3.2	15.6	63.2	5,018,613	26,517,680	14,116,918	867,167	605,607	605,509	-71,601
		Rating History: A+ g, 01/19/10; A+ g, 07/17/09; A++g, 02/04/09; A++g, 06/06/08; A++g, 06/07/07																
JORDAN FUNERAL & INSURANCE CO[1] Mary Walden President P.O. Box 610 Centre, AL 35960-0610 AL : 1937 : Stock : Not Available 256-927-5870 AMB# 060353 NAIC# 88218	E	'05	...	62.1	14.8	23.1	1,712	...	...	...	100.0	291	74	74	...	-75	-75	-75
		'06	...	56.5	17.4	26.2	1,677	...	...	...	100.0	206	76	76	...	-109	-109	-161
		'07	...	51.6	6.9	41.5	1,666	...	...	...	100.0	250	68	68	...	17	17	40
		'08	...	...	...	...	...	...	...	...	...	...	...	...	...	...	...	...
		'09	27.7	38.8	...	33.5	1,553	...	...	...	100.0	396	56	56	...	-82	-82	-71
		Rating History: E, 06/10/10; NR-5, 06/08/09; NR-1, 06/12/08; NR-1, 06/08/07; NR-1, 06/07/06																

BEST'S PROFITABILITY, LEVERAGE AND LIQUIDITY TESTS 2005 – 2009

Data in U.S. Dollars

—	Profitability Tests							Leverage Tests						Liquidity Tests					
Un-Realized Capital Gains ($000)	Benefits Paid to NPW & Dep (%)	Comm. & Expenses to NPW & Dep (%)	NOG to Total Assets (%)	NOG to Total Rev (%)	Operating Return on Equity (%)	Net Yield (%)	Total Return (%)	Change in NPW & Dep (%)	NPW & Dep to Capital (X)	Capital & Surplus to Liabilities (%)	Surplus Relief (%)	Reins Leverage (%)	Change in Capital (%)	Quick Liquidity (%)	Current Liquidity (%)	Non-Invest Grade Bonds to Capital (%)	Delinq. & Foreclosed Mortgages to Capital (%)	Mort. & Credit Tenant Loans & R.E. to Capital (%)	Affiliated Invest to Capital (%)
...	69.9	73.6	-0.4	-6.0	-0.8	...	...	25.7	0.1	130.6	...	...	-0.7	...	...	...	...	...	...
...	77.4	88.7	0.7	10.6	1.3	...	...	-14.1	0.1	129.4	...	...	1.3	...	...	...	...	...	...
...	85.2	60.3	0.8	10.9	1.4	...	...	17.4	0.1	126.8	...	...	1.4	...	...	...	...	...	...
...	72.6	55.2	0.4	6.1	0.8	...	...	19.9	0.1	123.9	...	...	0.8	...	...	...	...	...	...
...	74.4	43.5	0.1	1.6	0.2	...	...	29.8	0.1	120.6	...	...	0.2	...	...	...	...	...	...
Principal Lines of Business: OrdLife (69.9%), IndLife (30.1%)																			
-276	117.4	-3.3	-11.7	-6.2	-21.3	1.78	9.18	10.7	2.9	91.9	...	2.4	-5.3	141.6	142.7	...	...	...	...
...	100.3	25.3	-41.7	-21.8	-99.9	3.51	3.51	17.1	11.0	24.3	1.5	65.7	-69.2	92.1	93.1	...	...	...	...
...	77.4	23.9	1.7	1.0	5.6	2.94	2.94	-9.6	3.7	65.5	2.6	5.3	167.8	131.4	132.0	...	...	...	...
...	59.2	50.5	-11.2	-12.5	-25.5	1.02	1.02	-53.0	2.4	107.4	...	5.9	-26.1	189.4	190.7	...	...	...	...
...	85.1	16.0	6.7	7.5	11.7	0.26	0.29	-28.0	1.4	162.6	...	1.0	18.2	245.2	245.2	...	...	...	...
Principal Lines of Business: IndA&H (66.7%), GrpA&H (31.4%), OrdLife (1.8%), GrpLife (0.0%)														Principal States: TX (88.2%), LA (11.8%)					
-15	173.8	16.9	-0.1	-0.8	-2.8	5.01	5.37	15.2	2.4	8.6	31.8	999.9	-18.7	68.4	81.7	72.8	...	...	...
59	156.5	13.2	-0.1	-1.1	-5.4	5.11	5.18	39.1	3.3	9.4	26.5	999.9	1.6	65.5	78.9	76.3	...	4.4	...
25	106.6	8.0	0.0	0.0	-0.3	5.44	5.50	60.9	5.5	9.9	5.7	999.9	-4.8	77.1	89.0	9.3	...	19.3	...
-70	112.6	10.4	-0.6	-4.1	-26.2	5.35	4.01	-24.5	7.7	5.2	9.9	999.9	-46.1	63.7	77.6	55.0	...	78.1	...
-688	110.8	8.5	0.3	2.5	17.7	5.66	4.84	-17.8	5.8	5.3	7.2	999.9	10.2	69.8	84.0	49.0	5.3	67.7	3.6
Principal Lines of Business: IndAnn (96.3%), GrpAnn (3.5%), OrdLife (0.2%)														Principal States: TX (13.3%), CA (8.5%), PA (6.6%), CO (5.3%), IL (5.3%)					
...	66.0	26.2	7.7	7.6	37.5	6.27	6.44	-16.3	5.5	23.4	1.4	287.3	-27.8	68.4	84.2	25.8	1.9	19.9	...
...	62.2	26.2	11.0	10.7	59.4	6.40	6.29	-8.4	5.2	25.0	1.3	317.2	-2.9	75.3	92.3	29.3	...	14.6	0.0
0	68.7	27.2	7.4	7.0	40.1	6.49	6.11	-3.7	5.5	22.9	1.3	362.9	-9.2	70.7	87.8	26.6	...	21.9	...
-55	65.7	27.3	7.3	7.1	39.6	6.24	4.31	-6.1	5.3	24.4	1.0	362.5	-2.0	73.3	87.6	24.6	...	25.0	...
56	76.7	27.8	0.8	0.8	4.4	5.93	5.37	-4.7	5.6	23.2	1.0	422.0	-9.5	76.0	90.1	30.8	...	26.5	...
Principal Lines of Business: GrpA&H (88.6%), IndA&H (10.5%), GrpLife (0.9%), IndAnn (0.0%), OrdLife (0.0%)														Principal States: TX (13.7%), MI (6.3%), IL (5.5%), NV (4.7%), WY (4.7%)					
...	...	...	...	...	...	...	...	...	...	...	...	...	...	...	...	...	...	...	...
...	86.0	12.0	...	2.2	...	...	...	...	4.6	740.1	...	...	...	163.2	163.2	...	...	...	...
...	87.7	11.6	3.7	0.9	4.2	6.03	6.03	3.9	4.5	721.7	...	...	6.4	159.9	159.9	...	...	...	...
...	87.5	11.0	6.6	1.8	7.6	5.97	5.97	1.4	4.1	608.0	...	...	10.7	112.6	112.6	...	...	...	...
...	89.4	10.4	1.6	0.5	1.9	4.50	4.50	-4.0	3.8	649.7	...	...	4.7	119.1	119.1	...	...	...	...
Principal Lines of Business: Dental (100.0%)														Principal States: NJ (100.0%)					
-5,825	999.9	410.0	-0.4	-6.0	-1.8	6.58	5.36	140.9	0.0	27.0	0.5	15.8	-4.7	27.0	45.0	22.2	...	88.0	0.3
-2,105	240.1	26.3	1.1	18.7	5.3	6.34	5.80	999.9	0.1	28.0	0.4	15.2	2.8	29.3	46.4	13.0	...	78.5	0.4
-1,161	283.9	6.0	1.9	30.7	8.3	6.23	6.82	-21.9	0.1	31.0	0.4	14.2	6.9	50.2	67.4	8.9	...	59.8	0.4
-6,244	288.3	5.8	0.5	2.6	5.0	4.37	3.41	28.7	0.1	29.3	0.3	9.9	52.1	63.2	80.5	12.3	...	57.6	...
8,568	8.7	3.4	0.0	-0.2	-0.7	2.83	3.55	999.9	3.1	16.7	1.1	221.7	93.7	69.4	85.8	12.7	...	106.1	3.8
Principal Lines of Business: GrpA&H (95.8%), IndA&H (2.5%), GrpAnn (1.6%), OrdLife (0.1%)														Principal States: NY (3.6%)					
...	31.8	8.4	0.3	1.0	17.5	19.88	19.97	22.7	11.7	26.1	16.7	130.8	95.8	142.6	148.2	...	...	...	...
...	36.8	7.7	1.2	4.0	47.1	30.82	30.89	9.1	7.8	39.4	30.3	152.2	64.4	146.4	151.0	...	...	...	...
...	43.6	11.0	1.0	3.7	34.1	29.43	29.47	15.8	6.7	38.4	8.1	147.7	34.0	143.8	148.3	...	...	...	0.4
...	46.3	13.7	-4.8	-19.5	-99.9	18.50	18.55	-6.8	6.4	19.3	1.9	158.0	-2.1	141.3	143.7	...	...	...	...
...	53.5	13.4	4.1	21.3	50.1	11.42	11.46	-15.8	1.2	92.2	0.3	38.1	364.8	206.1	209.1	...	...	...	0.1
Principal Lines of Business: GrpAnn (53.4%), IndAnn (25.2%), OrdLife (21.4%)														Principal States: NY (97.3%)					
-3,528	93.2	16.2	0.2	1.3	6.8	6.69	7.14	0.6	2.4	7.9	13.7	231.2	-3.2	32.5	49.9	62.6	0.3	227.4	22.6
71,780	91.5	14.7	0.3	1.8	10.9	6.44	6.85	13.7	2.7	8.1	14.6	273.2	2.6	36.5	54.8	43.3	0.1	218.1	23.5
316,936	93.8	14.5	0.5	2.8	16.9	6.49	7.22	11.4	2.7	8.7	14.5	247.6	9.7	41.0	59.1	35.9	0.1	199.7	23.4
-242,100	118.0	22.2	-1.0	-6.3	-36.3	5.71	4.88	-32.4	2.5	6.3	20.0	367.4	-26.5	39.2	55.2	64.0	0.4	282.9	40.9
-71,568	58.6	17.4	0.3	3.0	12.8	5.10	4.37	4.8	2.4	6.8	22.0	337.7	6.2	39.0	55.9	71.9	0.3	322.6	54.6
Principal Lines of Business: GrpAnn (53.8%), IndAnn (23.1%), OrdLife (15.8%), IndA&H (5.5%), GrpA&H (1.3%)														Principal States: CA (12.2%), FL (6.3%), TX (6.1%), PA (5.0%), CT (4.5%)					
-7	84.8	160.5	-4.4	-47.0	-23.8	...	...	-7.8	0.2	21.1	...	...	-12.7	...	...	...	...	356.6	...
64	104.0	192.0	-6.4	-77.9	-44.0	...	...	2.9	0.3	16.5	...	...	-20.4	...	...	...	...	398.9	...
-17	66.7	160.4	1.0	14.2	7.6	...	...	-11.2	0.2	19.7	...	...	15.5	...	...	...	...	313.2	...
...	...	...	...	...	...	...	...	...	...	...	...	...	...	...	...	...	...	...	...
9	108.2	167.3	...	-98.8	...	...	...	...	0.1	35.9	...	...	...	...	...	...	...	147.1	...
Principal Lines of Business: IndLife (100.0%)																			

2010 BEST'S KEY RATING GUIDE — LIFE/HEALTH EDITION
ANNUAL STATEMENT DATA FOR YEARS 2005 – 2009
Data in U.S. Dollars

Column key — COMPANY NAME · Ultimate Parent Association / Principal Officer / Mailing Address / Dom. : Began Bus. : Struct. : Mktg. / Specialty / Phone # / AMB# NAIC# — Best's Financial Strength Rating / FSC

Company	Best's Financial Strength Rating / FSC	Data Year	Bonds (%)	Mort. Loans & R.E. (%)	Com & Pref. Stock (%)	All Other Assets (%)	Total Assets ($000)	Life Reserves (%)	Health Reserves (%)	Ann Res. & Dep. Liabilities (%)	All Other Liabilities (%)	Capital & Surplus ($000)	Direct Premiums Written ($000)	Net Premiums Written & Deposits ($000)	Operating Cash Flow ($000)	NOG Before Taxes ($000)	NOG After Taxes ($000)	Net Income ($000)
KAISER FOUNDATION HEALTH PLAN Kaiser Foundation Health Plan Inc George C. Halvorson Chairman, President & CEO One Kaiser Plaza, 15th Floor Oakland, CA 94612 CA : Non-Profit : Agency Group A&H, Medicare, Medicaid 510-625-3176 AMB# 064585	NR-5	'05	...	26.4	...	73.6	23,986,196	...	...	...	100.0	10,812,426	29,154,744	29,154,744	2,909,195	1,009,019	1,009,019	1,009,019
		'06	...	23.0	...	77.0	29,747,513	...	...	...	100.0	10,331,986	32,187,678	32,187,678	6,508,631	1,351,829	1,351,829	1,351,829
		'07	...	24.6	...	75.4	33,660,518	...	...	...	100.0	13,633,065	35,309,231	35,309,231	4,713,437	2,244,036	2,244,036	2,244,036
		'08	...	32.8	...	67.2	32,917,232	...	...	...	100.0	11,430,511	37,625,355	37,625,355	3,452,558	-794,010	-794,010	-794,010
		'09	...	32.0	...	68.0	37,797,981	...	...	...	100.0	11,837,629	39,407,845	39,407,845	4,841,833	2,108,611	2,108,611	2,108,611
		Rating History: NR-5, 05/07/10; NR-5, 08/26/09; A- pd, 09/08/08; A- pd, 09/21/07; A- pd, 09/15/06																
KAISER FDN HEALTH PLAN OF CO[2] Kaiser Foundation Health Plan Inc George C. Halvorson Chairman, President & CEO 10350 East Dakota Avenue Denver, CO 80231-1314 CO : 1969 : Non-Profit : Broker Group A&H, Medicare, FEHBP 303-338-3454 AMB# 068516 NAIC# 95669	NR-5	'05	34.9	51.9	...	13.3	489,142	...	32.3	...	67.7	259,645	1,587,585	1,587,585	54,080	6,040	6,040	5,808
		'06	34.9	51.0	...	14.1	504,219	...	25.0	...	75.0	233,013	1,796,969	1,796,969	23,269	75,783	75,783	74,929
		'07	37.3	51.4	...	11.3	491,969	...	27.5	...	72.5	162,208	2,020,801	2,020,801	24,534	116,065	116,065	120,986
		'08	48.5	29.6	...	21.8	872,336	...	11.5	...	88.5	547,047	2,121,315	2,121,315	383,108	110,628	110,628	100,524
		'09	55.8	26.3	...	17.9	987,827	...	8.5	...	91.5	626,219	2,183,129	2,183,129	142,019	45,652	45,652	44,396
		Rating History: NR-5, 04/15/10; NR-5, 08/26/09; B+ pd, 09/08/08; B++pd, 09/21/07; B++pd, 09/15/06																
KAISER FOUNDATION HLTH P OF GA Kaiser Foundation Health Plan Inc Carolyn M. Kenny Regional President One Kaiser Plaza, 21B Oakland, CA 94612 GA : 1985 : Non-Profit : Broker Group A&H, Medicare, FEHBP 404-364-7000 AMB# 068528 NAIC# 96237	NR-5	'05	...	43.0	...	57.0	180,409	...	49.4	...	50.6	57,945	709,128	709,128	-30,892	-8,427	-8,427	-8,427
		'06	...	39.6	...	60.4	199,529	...	50.1	...	49.9	55,594	767,180	767,180	21,894	3,990	3,990	3,990
		'07	39.7	36.9	...	23.4	249,196	...	45.9	...	54.1	97,353	962,699	962,699	26,920	41,392	41,392	41,372
		'08	37.6	34.1	...	28.4	269,374	...	44.5	...	55.5	102,190	994,755	994,755	27,421	4,430	4,430	1,376
		'09	...	...	...	...	...	...	...	...	...	...	...	...	...	...	...	...
		Rating History: NR-5, 08/26/09; B+ pd, 09/08/08; B+ pd, 09/21/07; B+ pd, 09/15/06; B++pd, 09/02/05																
KAISER FOUNDATION HTH PL OF OH Kaiser Foundation Health Plan Inc Patricia Kennedy-Scott Regional President 1001 Lakeside Avenue, Suite 1200 Cleveland, OH 44114-1153 OH : 1976 : Non-Profit : Broker Group A&H, Medicare, FEHBP 216-621-5600 AMB# 068577 NAIC# 95204	NR-5	'05	0.2	27.8	...	71.9	182,108	...	14.3	...	85.7	59,035	495,326	495,326	6,929	-31,046	-31,046	-31,046
		'06	0.2	34.1	...	65.7	171,543	...	15.5	...	84.5	49,670	540,172	540,172	1,369	-18,489	-18,489	-18,489
		'07	50.7	33.6	...	15.7	170,612	...	13.0	...	87.0	40,876	559,572	559,572	96,550	-4,495	-4,495	-4,495
		'08	49.3	30.4	...	20.2	179,512	...	10.4	...	89.6	37,810	555,538	555,538	16,307	7,026	7,026	4,439
		'09	17.6	26.3	...	56.1	205,387	...	9.8	...	90.2	40,644	562,158	562,158	30,855	-12,600	-12,600	-6,367
		Rating History: NR-5, 03/22/10; NR-5, 08/26/09; B pd, 09/08/08; B pd, 09/21/07; B+ pd, 09/15/06																
KAISER FDN H PL OF THE MID-ATL Kaiser Foundation Health Plan Inc Marilyn Kawamura Regional President One Kaiser Plaza, 21B Oakland, CA 94612 MD : 1972 : Non-Profit : Broker Group A&H, FEHBP, Medicare 301-816-2424 AMB# 068551 NAIC# 95639	NR-5	'05	36.0	36.1	...	27.8	441,226	...	21.8	...	78.2	149,679	1,584,763	1,584,763	-21,946	24,123	24,123	22,544
		'06	36.5	34.1	...	29.4	487,075	...	21.5	...	78.5	190,886	1,721,645	1,721,645	29,050	30,648	30,648	29,737
		'07	45.8	29.8	...	24.4	553,031	...	17.1	...	82.9	188,954	1,820,611	1,820,611	93,989	53,980	53,980	53,384
		'08	55.4	24.4	...	20.2	626,073	...	16.0	...	84.0	211,000	1,888,790	1,888,790	120,014	32,738	32,738	19,970
		'09	48.6	32.3	...	19.1	695,259	...	13.3	...	86.7	218,517	1,957,089	1,957,089	62,019	-12,841	-12,841	-7,142
		Rating History: NR-5, 03/25/10; NR-5, 08/26/09; B++pd, 09/08/08; B++pd, 09/21/07; B++pd, 09/15/06																
KAISER FDN HEALTH PL OF THE NW[2] Kaiser Foundation Health Plan Inc Cynthia A. Finter Regional President 500 N.E. Multnomah Street, Suite 100 Portland, OR 97232-2099 OR : 1942 : Non-Profit : Broker Group A&H, Medicare, FEHBP 503-813-2800 AMB# 068585 NAIC# 95540	NR-5	'05	5.1	31.7	...	63.3	610,077	...	9.1	...	90.9	362,534	1,807,006	1,807,005	15,845	37,075	37,045	36,918
		'06	3.5	27.0	...	69.6	715,951	...	9.1	...	90.9	433,639	2,007,354	2,007,280	30,961	45,335	45,342	45,342
		'07	64.4	21.5	...	14.1	838,938	...	7.1	...	92.9	494,196	2,182,587	2,182,512	510,382	59,482	59,459	59,041
		'08	61.8	19.8	...	18.4	878,815	...	6.1	...	93.9	480,100	2,277,277	2,277,277	-3,033	48,430	48,550	32,592
		'09	57.9	18.5	...	23.7	941,702	...	4.4	...	95.6	494,918	2,379,593	2,379,593	114,113	28,321	28,321	36,292
		Rating History: NR-5, 05/21/10; NR-5, 08/26/09; B++pd, 09/08/08; B++pd, 09/21/07; B++pd, 09/15/06																
KANAWHA INSURANCE COMPANY Humana Inc Richard D. Vaughan President P.O. Box 740036 Louisville, KY 40201-7436 SC : 1958 : Stock : Agency Ind A&H, Group A&H, Life 803-283-5300 AMB# 006604 NAIC# 65110	B++ Rating Outlook: Stable FSC VII	'05	81.6	3.9	1.8	12.8	575,243	47.8	40.1	2.7	9.4	85,063	120,620	108,746	23,959	-10,414	-8,887	-8,887
		'06	80.7	3.1	4.7	11.5	608,840	42.9	45.0	2.4	9.7	72,284	147,376	129,968	29,475	-22,956	-14,857	-14,718
		'07	84.4	2.4	1.0	12.2	664,720	37.7	50.8	2.1	9.4	65,916	183,990	162,803	51,055	-46,657	-30,332	-30,067
		'08	64.9	1.3	0.5	33.3	823,103	28.9	63.1	1.7	6.3	59,571	166,471	148,397	189,903	-53,807	-53,807	-73,698
		'09	90.0	1.0	0.7	8.3	926,380	26.1	66.5	1.5	5.9	92,684	176,796	157,228	112,557	-70,195	-70,195	-77,113
		Rating History: B++, 06/02/10; B++, 06/05/09; A-, 06/05/08; A-, 09/11/07; A-, 03/29/07																
KANSAS CITY LIFE INS CO Kansas City Life Insurance Company R. Philip Bixby Chairman, CEO & President 3520 Broadway Kansas City, MO 64111-2565 MO : 1895 : Stock : Career Agent Ind Life, Ind Ann, Group A&H 816-753-7000 AMB# 006605 NAIC# 65129	A Rating Outlook: Stable FSC IX	'05	66.2	12.8	2.8	18.2	3,333,590	44.2	0.2	38.7	16.9	339,961	283,398	293,269	6,630	48,077	49,500	48,668
		'06	63.8	13.0	3.2	20.0	3,314,089	44.3	0.2	37.7	17.8	371,766	259,424	260,697	-50,939	48,170	46,801	49,353
		'07	63.9	12.8	2.9	20.3	3,258,283	44.7	0.3	36.1	18.9	357,332	267,841	265,786	-74,922	54,424	50,141	47,718
		'08	66.6	14.5	2.9	15.9	2,998,063	47.7	0.3	38.3	13.7	306,247	275,793	267,725	-69,707	29,566	27,301	-20,114
		'09	61.7	14.6	2.5	21.2	3,152,631	45.0	0.3	38.3	16.4	336,615	318,706	311,624	69,029	30,280	24,979	19,455
		Rating History: A g, 06/04/10; A g, 06/02/09; A g, 12/07/07; A g, 11/14/06; A g, 12/21/05																
KEMPER INVESTORS LIFE INS CO Zurich Financial Services Ltd Nicolas A. Burnet President & CEO 15375 SE 30th Place, Suite 310 Bellevue, WA 98007 IL : 1947 : Stock : Exclusive Agent Group Life, Var ann 425-577-5100 AMB# 006225 NAIC# 90557	A- Rating Outlook: Stable FSC VIII	'05	3.9	...	0.0	96.1	17,324,156	0.1	...	2.7	97.1	410,778	390,584	259,439	96,072	18,574	34,512	39,917
		'06	1.6	...	...	98.4	16,589,796	0.3	...	1.0	98.8	222,457	255,336	-872,105	-449,180	-709,797	-427,392	-422,997
		'07	2.0	...	0.0	98.0	16,700,205	0.7	...	0.9	98.4	186,926	189,673	26,037	110,770	-60,166	-19,649	-19,861
		'08	2.7	...	0.0	97.3	13,886,167	1.2	...	1.2	97.6	166,863	146,440	-79,038	67,427	-33,768	-11,692	-15,695
		'09	3.2	...	...	96.8	13,324,913	1.6	...	1.2	97.3	187,496	121,514	-101,598	48,889	13,261	19,945	17,405
		Rating History: A-, 06/16/09; A-, 06/18/08; A-, 06/17/07; A-, 06/21/06; A-, 04/15/05																

BEST'S PROFITABILITY, LEVERAGE AND LIQUIDITY TESTS 2005 – 2009

Data in U.S. Dollars

—	Profitability Tests							Leverage Tests						Liquidity Tests					
Un-Realized Capital Gains ($000)	Benefits Paid to NPW & Dep (%)	Comm. & Expenses to NPW & Dep (%)	NOG to Total Assets (%)	NOG to Total Rev (%)	Operating Return on Equity (%)	Net Yield (%)	Total Return (%)	Change in NPW & Dep (%)	NPW & Dep to Capital (X)	Capital & Surplus to Liabilities (%)	Surplus Relief (%)	Reins Leverage (%)	Change in Capital (%)	Quick Liquidity (%)	Current Liquidity (%)	Non-Invest Grade Bonds to Capital (%)	Delinq. & Foreclosed Mortgages to Capital (%)	Mort. & Credit Tenant Loans & R.E. to Capital (%)	Affiliated Invest to Capital (%)
...	100.1	3.8	4.4	3.2	9.8	2.04	2.04	10.9	2.7	82.1	...	...	9.8	35.3	35.3	...	...	58.6	58.6
...	99.6	3.8	5.0	3.9	12.8	2.53	2.53	10.4	3.1	53.2	...	...	-4.4	24.5	24.5	...	...	66.1	66.1
...	97.8	3.6	7.1	5.9	18.7	2.77	2.77	9.7	2.6	68.1	...	...	32.0	24.8	24.8	...	...	60.8	60.8
...	98.5	4.2	-2.4	-2.1	-6.3	-10.62	-10.62	6.6	3.3	53.2	...	...	-16.2	23.8	23.8	...	...	94.3	94.3
...	98.0	4.3	6.0	4.9	18.1	2.21	2.21	4.7	3.3	45.6	...	...	3.6	22.9	22.9	...	...	102.0	102.0
	Principal Lines of Business: CompHosp/Med (73.1%), Medicare (26.6%), Medicaid (0.4%)																		
...	92.7	9.2	1.3	0.4	2.7	1.69	1.63	12.7	6.1	113.1	...	...	43.6	61.2	66.3	...	...	97.7	97.7
...	88.8	9.2	15.3	4.1	30.8	3.59	3.39	13.2	7.7	85.9	...	...	-10.3	50.8	55.3	...	...	110.3	108.8
...	87.5	7.0	23.3	5.7	58.7	3.76	4.94	12.5	12.5	49.2	...	...	-30.4	45.8	49.0	...	...	156.0	156.0
...	87.6	7.6	16.2	5.2	31.2	3.29	1.63	5.0	3.9	168.2	...	...	237.2	171.5	181.9	...	...	47.3	47.3
-4	90.3	7.8	4.9	2.1	7.8	3.78	3.63	2.9	3.5	173.2	...	...	14.5	174.4	186.3	0.0	...	41.6	41.6
	Principal Lines of Business: CompHosp/Med (61.0%), Medicare (32.5%), FEHBP (6.5%)													Principal States: CO (98.5%)					
...	96.6	5.7	-4.3	-1.0	-13.3	3.46	3.46	8.2	12.2	47.3	...	...	-15.8	60.5	60.5	...	...	134.0	134.0
...	93.6	7.9	2.1	0.4	7.0	13.27	13.27	8.2	13.8	38.6	...	...	-4.1	63.2	63.2	...	...	142.0	142.0
...	90.3	8.0	18.4	4.2	54.1	8.24	8.23	25.5	9.9	64.1	...	...	75.1	60.0	65.3	...	...	94.4	94.4
...	92.9	7.9	1.7	0.4	4.4	5.93	4.45	3.3	9.7	61.1	...	...	5.0	81.8	87.8	0.3	...	89.8	89.8
...	...	...	...	...	...	...	...	...	...	...	...	...	...	...	...	...	...	...	...
...	97.6	9.8	-14.9	-6.2	-42.4	3.80	3.80	7.2	8.4	48.0	...	...	-32.4	1.5	1.5	...	...	85.9	85.9
...	96.2	9.1	-10.5	-3.3	-34.0	10.17	10.17	9.1	10.9	40.8	...	...	-15.9	-6.6	-6.6	...	...	117.8	117.8
...	93.6	9.1	-2.6	-0.8	-9.9	7.36	7.36	3.6	13.7	31.5	...	...	-17.7	59.2	64.6	...	...	140.1	140.1
...	91.0	9.7	4.0	1.2	17.9	3.69	1.99	-0.7	14.7	26.7	...	...	-7.5	75.6	81.5	0.7	...	144.5	144.5
...	93.1	10.0	-6.5	-2.2	-32.1	2.65	6.41	1.2	13.8	24.7	...	...	7.5	115.8	122.1	...	...	132.8	132.8
	Principal Lines of Business: CompHosp/Med (75.5%), Medicare (17.8%), FEHBP (6.7%)													Principal States: OH (100.0%)					
-70	91.7	8.6	5.5	1.5	18.3	-3.50	-4.02	8.9	10.6	51.3	...	...	32.2	45.7	47.9	9.5	...	106.5	106.5
54	90.9	8.2	6.6	1.7	18.0	3.16	2.88	8.6	9.0	64.4	...	...	27.5	42.4	45.3	6.8	...	87.1	87.1
111	90.1	8.0	10.4	2.9	28.4	3.50	3.36	5.7	9.6	51.9	...	...	-1.0	62.5	67.5	...	...	87.2	87.2
39	91.0	8.3	5.6	1.7	16.4	2.86	0.08	3.7	9.0	50.8	...	...	11.7	78.6	84.4	0.1	...	72.4	72.4
-342	91.4	10.5	-1.9	-0.6	-6.0	2.73	3.76	3.6	9.0	45.8	...	...	3.6	64.3	69.9	...	...	102.8	102.8
	Principal Lines of Business: CompHosp/Med (61.8%), FEHBP (28.1%), Medicare (10.1%)													Principal States: DC (45.3%), MD (27.6%), VA (24.3%)					
...	93.7	5.1	6.3	2.0	11.0	6.11	6.04	12.3	5.0	146.5	...	...	16.3	6.4	7.7	...	...	53.3	52.3
...	94.3	4.9	6.8	2.2	11.4	11.90	11.90	11.1	4.6	153.6	...	0.0	19.6	15.4	16.6	...	...	44.5	43.7
...	94.1	4.9	7.6	2.7	12.8	6.46	6.37	8.7	4.4	143.4	...	...	14.0	143.6	156.2	...	...	36.5	35.8
...	94.0	5.3	5.7	2.1	10.0	4.06	1.87	4.3	4.7	120.4	...	...	-2.9	121.7	132.0	0.3	...	36.3	35.6
...	94.2	5.4	3.1	1.2	5.8	2.31	3.36	4.5	4.8	110.8	...	...	3.1	150.2	161.7	...	...	35.1	34.4
	Principal Lines of Business: CompHosp/Med (66.4%), Medicare (23.5%), FEHBP (6.1%), Dental (3.4%), Vision (0.5%)													Principal States: OR (77.1%), WA (19.1%)					
3,405	66.4	38.7	-1.6	-6.3	-10.5	5.25	6.08	4.9	1.2	18.2	5.1	93.1	4.8	66.8	77.2	12.4	0.4	25.2	15.5
6,076	67.3	44.9	-2.5	-8.9	-18.9	5.55	6.82	19.5	1.7	14.5	6.1	133.3	-13.3	63.5	75.3	14.9	0.2	24.5	15.9
5	78.2	39.3	-4.8	-15.1	-43.9	5.66	5.87	25.3	2.3	11.9	6.0	178.0	-8.1	68.9	78.8	17.3	...	22.4	17.0
-872	82.7	46.2	-7.2	-28.8	-85.8	4.91	2.15	-8.8	2.5	7.8	5.7	254.1	-15.3	96.5	103.7	7.3	...	18.1	4.9
-1,777	76.8	48.8	-8.0	-34.5	-92.2	5.12	4.14	6.0	1.7	11.2	3.7	185.9	55.5	74.7	84.6	6.7	...	9.5	6.3
	Principal Lines of Business: IndA&H (52.3%), GrpA&H (29.2%), GrpLife (9.4%), OrdLife (9.2%), GrpAnn (0.0%)													Principal States: NC (12.5%), SC (12.0%), FL (10.8%), TX (9.5%), LA (4.7%)					
3,047	109.2	32.2	1.5	10.5	15.7	6.59	6.67	-9.6	0.8	14.2	1.7	39.6	14.2	60.9	70.5	30.7	...	116.1	20.5
1,903	138.1	38.2	1.4	10.4	13.2	6.66	6.82	-11.1	0.6	16.0	1.5	36.8	9.2	59.5	69.3	29.3	...	107.4	19.1
-1,248	139.5	36.3	1.5	11.0	13.8	6.73	6.61	2.0	0.7	15.7	1.6	44.6	-4.3	58.3	68.0	35.7	...	108.3	17.0
-9,235	128.7	36.6	0.9	6.0	8.2	6.46	4.44	0.7	0.8	13.2	1.8	57.2	-17.0	50.1	63.7	34.6	...	136.5	18.3
-993	99.1	34.0	0.8	5.2	7.8	6.35	6.15	16.4	0.9	14.3	1.5	55.4	11.1	55.8	68.1	39.3	...	131.4	16.5
	Principal Lines of Business: IndAnn (48.5%), OrdLife (35.5%), GrpA&H (12.2%), GrpLife (3.2%), GrpAnn (0.5%)													Principal States: TX (11.0%), MO (9.8%), KS (6.2%), CO (6.0%), CA (5.4%)					
-421	274.4	9.6	0.2	6.3	8.7	4.19	5.23	-21.1	0.6	81.4	6.3	865.4	6.6	114.7	135.0	0.3	...	...	...
-471	-99.9	-3.2	-2.5	76.1	-99.9	6.30	7.15	-99.9	-3.9	131.7	10.1	999.9	-45.8	122.6	142.5	...	...	...	...
...	999.9	73.5	-0.1	-5.5	-9.6	4.88	4.93	103.0	0.1	58.5	15.2	999.9	-15.8	88.7	102.8	...	...	...	...
-78	-99.9	-99.9	-0.1	-5.1	-6.6	5.74	4.85	-99.9	-0.5	44.3	14.9	999.9	-11.0	77.4	90.9	1.3	...	...	...
78	-99.9	-99.9	0.1	8.4	11.3	5.31	4.80	-28.5	-0.5	43.2	12.8	999.9	12.4	76.7	89.2	3.5	...	...	...
	Principal Lines of Business: GrpLife (182.7%), OrdLife (0.0%), GrpAnn (-37.7%), IndAnn (-45.0%)													Principal States: TX (12.9%), IL (11.7%), MI (9.7%), CA (7.4%), WA (6.8%)					

Data in U.S. Dollars

COMPANY NAME Ultimate Parent Association Principal Officer Mailing Address Dom. : Began Bus. : Struct. : Mktg. Specialty Phone # AMB# NAIC#	Best's Financial Strength Rating FSC	Data Year	Balance Sheet: Bonds (%)	Mort. Loans & R.E. (%)	Com & Pref. Stock (%)	All Other Assets (%)	Total Assets ($000)	Life Reserves (%)	Health Reserves (%)	Ann Res. & Dep. Liabilities (%)	All Other Liabilities (%)	Capital & Surplus ($000)	Operations: Direct Premiums Written ($000)	Net Premiums Written & Deposits ($000)	Operating Cash Flow ($000)	NOG Before Taxes ($000)	NOG After Taxes ($000)	Net Income ($000)
KENTUCKY FUNERAL DIRECTORS LF Directors Investment Group Inc B. Kris Seale President P.O. Box 5649 Abilene, TX 79606 KY : 2001 : Stock : Agency Ind Ann, Ordinary Life 800-692-5976	**B+** Rating Outlook: Stable	'05	92.6	...	2.0	5.4	9,881	43.0	...	55.8	1.2	3,545	1,841	1,841	1,186	45	52	53
		'06	94.8	...	1.8	3.4	11,069	40.0	...	58.9	1.1	3,596	2,002	2,002	1,197	70	60	59
		'07	84.4	...	8.2	7.4	11,574	40.8	...	57.9	1.3	3,744	1,021	1,021	546	222	169	167
		'08	83.4	...	8.3	8.3	12,073	42.8	...	56.3	0.9	3,842	1,228	1,228	535	216	165	120
		'09	89.5	...	8.0	2.6	12,559	45.2	...	54.2	0.6	4,033	1,148	1,148	491	288	230	196
AMB# 060365 NAIC# 11133	**FSC III**	**Rating History: B+, 07/01/09; B+, 06/05/08; B+, 05/16/07; B+, 06/19/06; B+, 06/21/05**																
KENTUCKY HOME LIFE INS CO KHL Holdings LLC James M. Bennett President P.O. Box 309 Frankfort, KY 40602-0309 KY : 1998 : Stock : Broker Credit Life, A&H 502-227-1677	**NR-5**	'05	47.9	...	...	52.1	3,953	80.1	3.3	...	16.6	3,511	9,675	577	901	3	2	2
		'06	62.3	...	...	37.7	4,326	87.4	7.0	...	5.6	3,553	7,901	808	413	42	39	39
		'07	45.0	...	...	55.0	4,770	87.2	8.4	...	4.4	3,673	6,685	1,119	457	131	122	122
		'08	79.2	...	...	20.8	5,073	88.0	9.1	...	2.9	3,871	6,015	1,058	329	211	194	194
		'09	93.1	...	...	6.9	5,107	76.5	15.2	...	8.3	3,853	4,721	865	-103	103	74	74
AMB# 060296 NAIC# 60244		**Rating History: NR-5, 04/26/10; NR-5, 04/22/09; NR-5, 04/09/08; NR-5, 06/01/07; NR-2, 05/13/06**																
KEOKUK AREA HOSP ORG DELIV SYS Alan W. Zastrow CEO 1600 Morgan Street Keokuk, IA 52632 IA : 1998 : Non-Profit : Not Available Group A&H, Dental, Vision 319-524-7160	**NR-5**	'05	...	...	...	100.0	1,846	...	93.5	...	6.5	1,003	3,714	3,714	...	-1,077	-1,077	-1,077
		'06	...	...	...	100.0	1,516	...	96.0	...	4.0	1,071	2,374	2,374	156	69	69	69
		'07	...	...	...	100.0	1,468	...	94.1	...	5.9	1,045	2,505	2,505	...	-26	-26	-26
		'08	...	...	...	100.0	1,482	...	97.5	...	2.5	1,066	2,580	2,580	...	21	21	21
		'09	...	...	...	100.0	2,002	...	93.8	...	6.2	1,454	2,975	2,975	...	384	384	384
AMB# 064676		**Rating History: NR-5, 03/25/10; NR-5, 03/17/09; NR-5, 09/07/07; NR-5, 10/11/06; NR-5, 06/29/05**																
KERN HEALTH SYSTEMS Carol L. Sorrell President & CEO 9700 Stockdale Highway Bakersfield, CA 93311-3617 CA : 1996 : Non-Profit : Broker Group A&H 661-664-5030	**NR-5**	'05	...	9.9	...	90.1	78,565	...	...	...	100.0	49,910	111,393	111,393	-10,695	-141	-141	-141
		'06	...	9.9	...	90.1	82,387	...	...	...	100.0	49,470	117,370	117,370	2,717	-440	-440	-440
		'07	...	8.4	...	91.6	95,294	...	...	...	100.0	59,996	123,468	123,468	11,452	10,526	10,526	10,526
		'08	...	7.4	...	92.6	105,144	...	...	...	100.0	69,179	130,497	130,497	12,398	257	257	257
		'09	...	7.1	...	92.9	106,929	...	...	...	100.0	71,186	141,790	141,790	-125	5,473	2,007	2,007
AMB# 064084		**Rating History: NR-5, 05/07/10; NR-5, 08/26/09; B pd, 07/21/08; B pd, 07/20/07; B pd, 08/29/06**																
KERN HEALTH SYSTS GR HLTH PLAN Carol L. Sorrell Chief Executive Officer 9700 Stockdale Highway Bakersfield, CA 93311-3617 CA : 2005 : Non-Profit : Broker Health 661-664-5000	**NR-5**	'05	...	...	...	100.0	13,784	...	...	...	100.0	12,357	3,288	3,288	12,647	357	357	357
		'06	...	...	...	100.0	16,399	...	...	...	100.0	13,914	6,821	6,821	3,072	1,557	1,557	1,557
		'07	...	...	...	100.0	17,848	...	...	...	100.0	15,980	7,766	7,766	1,317	2,066	2,066	2,066
		'08	...	...	...	100.0	9,147	...	...	...	100.0	7,040	8,554	8,554	-9,597	-15	-15	-15
		'09	...	...	...	100.0	6,861	...	...	...	100.0	5,014	8,715	8,715	-1,261	-2,026	-2,026	-2,026
AMB# 064851		**Rating History: NR-5, 05/05/10; NR-5, 08/26/09; B pd, 07/21/08; NR-5, 06/30/08; NR-5, 05/03/07**																
KEYSTONE HEALTH PLAN CENTRAL Capital Blue Cross William Lehr, Jr. Chairman, President & CEO 2500 Elmerton Avenue Harrisburg, PA 17177-9799 PA : 1988 : Stock : Broker Medicare, Group A&H, FEHBP 717-541-7241	**NR-5**	'05	57.8	...	2.6	39.7	184,296	...	75.0	...	25.0	101,361	496,611	494,502	7,102	63,927	45,075	44,980
		'06	67.5	...	3.5	29.0	157,690	...	61.4	...	38.6	85,018	449,004	447,316	-34,917	45,056	28,309	28,033
		'07	68.8	...	0.9	30.3	151,274	...	43.6	...	56.4	73,618	411,848	410,207	-3,426	6,481	4,046	5,446
		'08	71.6	...	0.4	28.0	129,735	...	41.2	...	58.8	77,600	424,791	423,207	-19,108	6,425	6,656	4,524
		'09	63.0	...	0.1	36.9	140,975	...	47.4	...	52.6	92,126	420,907	420,282	10,329	8,077	16,616	15,175
AMB# 064051 NAIC# 95199		**Rating History: NR-5, 04/13/10; NR-5, 07/01/09; NR-5, 05/05/08; NR-5, 01/10/07; NR-5, 09/29/05**																
KEYSTONE HEALTH PLAN EAST INC[2] Independence Blue Cross Joseph A. Frick President 1901 Market Street Philadelphia, PA 19103-1480 PA : 1987 : Stock : Broker Group A&H, Medicare, FEHBP 215-241-2193	**NR-5**	'05	43.4	...	30.4	26.2	1,179,609	...	70.3	...	29.7	507,206	3,318,243	3,318,243	-160,099	99,297	62,315	64,618
		'06	43.0	...	30.3	26.7	1,219,860	...	61.7	...	38.3	572,176	3,855,905	3,855,905	99,243	137,637	110,263	115,886
		'07	44.6	...	31.4	24.1	1,238,893	...	58.6	...	41.4	628,823	3,966,896	3,966,896	-12,007	127,626	97,629	102,884
		'08	41.9	...	23.1	35.0	1,106,157	...	42.1	...	57.9	506,147	3,983,663	3,983,663	-138,780	83,124	51,912	-8,495
		'09	40.0	...	19.2	40.8	1,072,839	...	49.6	...	50.4	557,859	4,106,077	4,106,077	-91,402	-34,646	-14,056	-18,223
AMB# 068924 NAIC# 95056		**Rating History: NR-5, 04/12/10; NR-5, 08/26/09; B pd, 10/10/08; B pd, 10/11/07; B pd, 10/03/06**																
KEYSTONE HEALTH PLAN WEST INC Highmark Inc. Cynthia M. Dellecker President & CEO 120 Fifth Avenue, Suite 924 Pittsburgh, PA 15222-3023 PA : 1986 : Stock : Direct Response Medicare, Group A&H 412-544-7000	**A** Rating Outlook: Negative	'05	62.8	...	...	37.2	586,521	...	67.4	...	32.6	323,333	2,244,216	2,244,216	-69,832	109,691	80,541	79,786
		'06	62.1	...	...	37.9	722,611	...	54.2	...	45.8	417,951	2,409,786	2,409,786	127,141	161,874	111,852	108,509
		'07	59.1	...	0.4	40.5	682,451	...	67.2	...	32.8	388,533	2,453,805	2,453,805	-48,105	115,353	73,745	73,990
		'08	56.3	...	0.5	43.2	684,719	...	68.3	...	31.7	411,445	2,456,589	2,456,589	-24,383	128,425	78,911	79,795
		'09	49.7	...	...	50.3	758,357	...	73.8	...	26.2	479,912	2,445,962	2,445,962	15,348	95,051	142,766	143,231
AMB# 068833 NAIC# 95048	**FSC XV**	**Rating History: A g, 03/25/10; A g, 06/15/09; A, 06/12/08; A, 03/05/07; A, 02/07/06**																
KILPATRICK LIFE INS CO OF LA[1] Joseph B. Morrison President 1818 Marshall Street Shreveport, LA 71101-4109 LA : 1936 : Stock : Not Available 318-222-0555	**NR-1**	'05	53.0	16.3	5.8	24.9	136,714	...	...	...	100.0	5,810	18,791	17,745	...	-180	-135	754
		'06	58.7	19.5	6.7	15.1	141,268	...	...	...	100.0	4,481	19,304	17,867	...	-230	-230	-262
		'07	55.1	23.1	7.2	14.6	148,681	...	...	...	100.0	5,247	19,553	18,408	...	-158	-182	-930
		'08	59.3	19.8	6.5	14.4	143,136	...	...	...	100.0	-4,563	20,185	18,567	...	-1,548	-1,538	-2,103
		'09	56.7	18.4	5.9	18.9	160,081	...	...	...	100.0	5,680	19,060	17,355	...	2,079	2,064	2,173
AMB# 007756 NAIC# 74918		**Rating History: NR-1, 06/10/10; NR-1, 06/12/09; NR-1, 06/12/08; NR-1, 06/08/07; NR-1, 06/07/06**																

2010 BEST'S KEY RATING GUIDE — LIFE/HEALTH EDITION
BEST'S PROFITABILITY, LEVERAGE AND LIQUIDITY TESTS 2005 – 2009

Data in U.S. Dollars

—	Profitability Tests							Leverage Tests						Liquidity Tests					
Un-Realized Capital Gains ($000)	Benefits Paid to NPW & Dep (%)	Comm. & Expenses to NPW & Dep (%)	NOG to Total Assets (%)	NOG to Total Rev (%)	Operating Return on Equity (%)	Net Yield (%)	Total Return (%)	Change in NPW & Dep (%)	NPW & Dep to Capital (X)	Capital & Surplus to Liabilities (%)	Surplus Relief (%)	Reins Leverage (%)	Change in Capital (%)	Quick Liquidity (%)	Current Liquidity (%)	Non-Invest Grade Bonds to Capital (%)	Delinq. & Foreclosed Mortgages to Capital (%)	Mort. & Credit Tenant Loans & R.E. to Capital (%)	Affiliated Invest to Capital (%)
...	41.2	20.5	0.6	2.2	1.5	5.25	5.26	-27.1	0.5	56.3	...	...	1.7	112.8	123.9	...	...	...	...
...	43.4	24.1	0.6	2.4	1.7	5.39	5.38	8.7	0.6	48.5	...	...	1.6	111.6	121.1	...	...	...	...
...	81.6	20.7	1.5	10.5	4.6	5.42	5.40	-49.0	0.3	48.2	...	...	4.2	109.6	122.6	...	...	...	...
...	67.2	33.6	1.4	8.8	4.4	5.71	5.31	20.3	0.3	46.8	...	...	2.2	103.4	119.2	1.9	...	...	...
-45	79.3	27.4	1.9	12.5	5.8	5.74	5.11	-6.5	0.3	47.3	...	...	4.8	93.1	108.8	8.2	...	...	...
Principal Lines of Business: OrdLife (58.0%), IndAnn (42.0%)													Principal States: KY (100.0%)						
...	8.2	75.6	0.1	0.0	0.1	3.36	3.37	...	0.2	794.1	190.0	424.1	11.4	999.9	999.9	...	...	...	...
...	10.8	79.8	0.9	0.6	1.1	4.80	4.82	40.0	0.2	459.9	158.2	404.8	1.2	705.0	705.0	...	...	...	...
...	14.4	75.3	2.7	2.0	3.4	5.11	5.13	38.5	0.3	335.0	124.4	348.5	3.4	639.1	639.1	...	...	...	...
...	17.8	78.2	3.9	3.5	5.1	4.09	4.10	-5.4	0.3	322.2	109.0	295.0	5.4	463.8	465.6	...	...	...	...
...	31.5	94.4	1.5	1.7	1.9	3.75	3.82	-18.2	0.2	307.3	86.2	262.1	-0.5	345.1	347.3	...	...	...	...
Principal Lines of Business: CrdLife (52.6%), CrdA&H (47.4%)													Principal States: KY (100.0%)						
...	107.6	13.6	-64.2	-28.8	-99.9	1.68	1.68	-4.3	3.7	119.0	...	1.0	0.0	132.3	132.3	...	...	...	...
...	95.4	18.8	4.1	2.9	6.6	3.69	3.69	-36.1	2.2	240.8	...	6.1	6.8	285.9	285.9	...	...	...	...
...	85.0	19.5	-1.7	-1.0	-2.5	4.85	4.85	5.5	2.4	247.1	...	1.5	-2.4	285.1	285.1	...	...	...	...
...	81.1	19.2	1.4	0.8	2.0	2.35	2.35	3.0	2.4	255.9	...	5.1	2.0	330.7	330.7	...	...	...	...
...	69.8	17.6	22.0	12.9	30.5	0.59	0.59	15.3	2.0	265.7	...	0.0	36.5	353.4	353.4	...	...	...	...
Principal Lines of Business: CompHosp/Med (92.4%), Dental (7.2%), Vision (0.4%)													Principal States: IA (100.0%)						
...	99.1	8.7	-0.2	-0.1	-0.3	2.83	2.83	11.0	2.2	174.2	...	...	-19.6	195.8	195.8	...	...	15.5	15.5
...	100.1	8.0	-0.5	-0.3	-0.9	4.26	4.26	5.4	2.4	150.3	...	...	-0.9	175.9	175.9	...	...	16.5	16.5
...	90.4	8.4	11.8	7.9	19.2	4.38	4.38	5.2	2.1	170.0	...	...	21.3	194.2	194.2	...	...	13.3	13.3
...	89.0	13.7	0.3	0.2	0.4	2.49	2.49	5.7	1.9	192.4	...	...	15.3	217.6	217.6	...	...	11.3	11.3
...	93.0	9.3	1.9	1.3	2.9	1.20	1.20	8.7	2.0	199.2	...	...	2.9	209.4	209.4	...	...	10.7	10.7
Principal Lines of Business: Medicaid (100.0%)																			
...	78.9	16.4	...	10.2	...	...	...	...	0.3	866.0	...	...	...	886.3	886.3	...	...	...	...
...	76.5	15.8	10.3	19.8	11.9	3.62	3.62	107.4	0.5	559.9	...	...	12.6	632.5	632.5	...	...	...	...
...	73.5	14.9	12.1	23.1	13.8	3.90	3.90	13.9	0.5	855.6	...	...	14.9	912.1	912.1	...	...	...	...
...	84.1	15.1	-0.1	-0.2	-0.1	3.28	3.28	10.1	1.2	334.1	...	...	-55.9	353.1	353.1	...	...	...	...
...	112.1	15.5	-25.3	-22.3	-33.6	1.34	1.34	1.9	1.7	271.5	...	...	-28.8	334.4	334.4	...	...	...	...
Principal Lines of Business: Medicaid (100.0%)																			
-57	80.2	7.2	23.7	9.0	49.9	4.00	3.90	0.8	4.9	122.2	...	...	27.7	218.4	234.7	0.1	...	...	-2.0
529	80.4	11.1	16.6	6.3	30.4	5.00	5.17	-9.5	5.3	117.0	...	0.5	-16.1	146.6	164.3	...	...	...	...
-1,233	85.1	13.9	2.6	1.0	5.1	4.98	5.12	-8.3	5.6	94.8	...	0.3	-13.4	128.7	145.0	...	...	...	...
-103	87.5	12.8	4.7	1.5	8.8	4.89	2.88	3.2	5.5	148.8	...	0.2	5.4	147.8	169.5	0.1	...	...	...
121	87.1	12.4	12.3	3.9	19.6	4.65	3.41	-0.7	4.6	188.6	...	...	18.7	207.9	232.6	1.3	...	...	...
Principal Lines of Business: Medicare (50.6%), CompHosp/Med (46.9%), FEHBP (2.5%)													Principal States: PA (100.0%)						
-1,880	85.3	11.1	5.2	1.9	12.9	3.45	3.49	-11.0	6.5	75.4	...	...	10.7	77.9	97.4	14.7	...	...	5.2
8,750	87.2	10.7	9.2	2.8	20.4	4.33	5.81	16.2	6.7	88.3	...	...	12.8	103.1	123.9	14.4	...	...	4.4
98	88.2	10.3	7.9	2.4	16.3	4.39	4.91	2.9	6.3	103.1	...	...	9.9	98.9	122.3	13.1	...	...	4.5
-49,447	88.3	10.0	4.4	1.3	9.1	4.87	-6.97	0.4	7.9	84.4	...	...	-19.5	83.1	100.5	14.1	...	...	5.1
43,120	90.3	11.6	-1.3	-0.3	-2.6	3.90	9.12	3.1	7.4	108.3	...	...	10.2	96.1	115.9	17.5	...	...	5.8
Principal Lines of Business: CompHosp/Med (55.9%), Medicare (40.2%), FEHBP (3.9%)													Principal States: PA (100.0%)						
-148	89.6	6.5	12.9	3.6	27.7	4.10	3.94	8.2	6.9	122.9	...	...	24.9	176.6	188.1	2.0	...	...	...
822	87.5	7.4	17.1	4.6	30.2	6.10	5.66	7.4	5.8	137.2	...	...	29.3	230.2	245.1	...	...	...	2.0
669	89.8	6.9	10.5	3.0	18.3	5.98	6.13	1.8	6.3	132.2	...	...	-7.0	224.0	236.9	...	...	...	2.4
-4,818	88.8	6.7	11.5	3.2	19.7	4.69	4.01	0.1	6.0	150.6	...	...	5.9	225.9	242.7	0.0	...	...	1.1
-4,326	91.2	5.7	19.8	5.8	32.0	3.33	2.65	-0.4	5.1	172.4	...	...	16.6	225.1	243.3	0.2	...	...	...
Principal Lines of Business: Medicare (86.6%), CompHosp/Med (13.4%)													Principal States: PA (100.0%)						
-724	54.3	65.5	-0.1	-0.5	-1.9	...	...	-0.3	2.0	6.8	...	...	-18.6	...	...	...	...	257.5	...
-590	56.2	65.0	-0.2	-0.9	-4.5	...	...	0.7	2.4	5.5	...	...	-14.7	...	...	...	...	373.0	...
-128	54.0	63.8	-0.1	-0.7	-3.7	...	...	3.0	2.2	6.0	...	...	14.4	...	...	...	...	405.9	...
-4,971	57.4	60.5	-1.1	-5.8	-99.9	...	...	0.9	-6.9	-1.8	...	...	-99.9	...	...	...	...	-99.9	...
187	58.4	51.5	1.4	7.8	369.4	...	...	-6.5	2.0	5.9	...	...	431.2	...	...	...	...	331.5	...
Principal Lines of Business: OrdLife (84.6%), IndAnn (11.9%), IndLife (2.1%), IndA&H (1.5%)																			

Data in U.S. Dollars

COMPANY NAME Ultimate Parent Association Principal Officer Mailing Address Dom. : Began Bus. : Struct. : Mktg. Specialty Phone # AMB# NAIC#	Best's Financial Strength Rating FSC	Data Year	Balance Sheet Bonds (%)	Mort. Loans & R.E. (%)	Com & Pref. Stock (%)	All Other Assets (%)	Total Assets ($000)	Life Reserves (%)	Health Reserves (%)	Ann Res. & Dep. Liabilities (%)	All Other Liabilities (%)	Capital & Surplus ($000)	Operations Direct Premiums Written ($000)	Net Premiums Written & Deposits ($000)	Operating Cash Flow ($000)	NOG Before Taxes ($000)	NOG After Taxes ($000)	Net Income ($000)
KNIGHTS OF COLUMBUS Carl A. Anderson President P.O. Box 1670 New Haven, CT 06507-0901 CT : 1882 : Fraternal : Career Agent Whole life, Term Life, FPDA's 203-752-4000 AMB# 006616 NAIC# 58033	**A++** Rating Outlook: Stable	'05	86.3	1.5	4.4	7.8	12,277,595	64.4	0.4	29.3	5.9	1,593,524	844,564	1,104,274	675,152	58,300	58,300	71,796
		'06	86.8	1.4	4.5	7.3	12,986,337	65.6	0.6	28.3	5.5	1,682,818	896,431	1,128,068	671,363	64,917	64,917	97,178
		'07	86.4	1.2	4.2	8.3	14,013,813	66.1	0.7	27.1	6.1	1,751,216	934,788	1,149,034	779,244	54,585	54,585	88,371
		'08	86.0	0.9	4.1	9.0	14,051,335	68.0	0.9	27.6	3.5	1,618,816	980,502	1,328,979	594,717	113,511	113,511	11,195
		'09	86.8	0.8	2.5	9.8	15,548,928	65.6	1.0	28.1	5.4	1,647,504	958,413	1,479,116	1,200,134	85,622	85,622	22,517
	FSC XIV	**Rating History: A++, 06/17/09; A++, 06/20/08; A++, 06/12/07; A++, 06/13/06; A++, 06/14/05**																
KPS HEALTH PLANS Group Health Cooperative Richard T. Marks President P.O. Box 339 Bremerton, WA 98337 WA : 1948 : Stock : Broker Group A&H, FEHBP, Med supp 360-377-5576 AMB# 064627 NAIC# 53872	**NR-5**	'05	3.0	8.2	19.2	69.6	43,219	...	51.1	...	48.9	23,306	143,482	143,272	22,302	7,118	7,012	6,625
		'06	23.0	6.9	8.2	62.0	49,132	...	50.4	...	49.6	27,126	138,240	138,008	3,673	5,793	4,131	4,707
		'07	44.4	6.5	17.1	32.1	48,032	...	55.6	...	44.4	21,667	151,172	150,899	979	-3,566	-2,572	-2,557
		'08	41.3	7.8	11.5	39.4	42,558	...	58.9	...	41.1	17,327	154,315	154,014	-3,018	-1,274	-716	-3,488
		'09	15.5	6.5	12.7	65.2	48,519	...	58.7	...	41.3	13,719	146,313	146,063	-4,640	-1,728	-1,558	-1,930
		Rating History: NR-5, 04/19/10; NR-5, 04/09/09; NR-5, 04/30/08; NR-5, 05/07/07; NR-5, 06/20/06																
KS PLAN ADMINISTRATORS L L C[2] St Lukes Episcopal Health System Corp Spencer R. Berthelsen Director 2727 West Holcombe Road Houston, TX 77025 TX : 2006 : Stock : Not Available Medicare 713-442-0757 AMB# 064972 NAIC# 12827	**NR-5**	'05	...	...	...	...	...	...	...	...	...	...	...	...	...	...	...	...
		'06	...	...	...	...	...	...	...	...	...	...	...	...	...	...	...	...
		'07	...	...	...	...	...	...	...	...	...	...	...	...	...	...	...	...
		'08	...	...	...	100.0	6,622	...	12.1	...	87.9	-297	29,210	29,062	3,858	-2,593	-2,593	-2,593
		'09	...	...	...	100.0	17,032	...	41.3	...	58.7	5,899	105,181	104,902	10,236	4,178	2,561	2,561
		Rating History: NR-5, 04/19/10; NR-5, 05/08/09																
LAFAYETTE LIFE INS CO Western & Southern Mutual Holding Co Jerry B. Stillwell President & CEO P.O. Box 7007 Lafayette, IN 47903-7007 : 1905 : Stock : Agency Ann, Ordinary Life 765-477-7411 AMB# 006617 NAIC# 65242	**A+** Rating Outlook: Stable	'05	75.5	12.2	0.3	12.0	1,762,635	47.6	0.1	43.8	8.6	114,390	344,146	317,098	85,668	7,995	4,435	3,426
		'06	72.4	11.7	0.5	15.3	1,806,950	50.2	0.1	40.5	9.2	117,423	316,850	300,408	20,236	8,057	4,556	4,680
		'07	75.1	11.1	0.8	13.1	1,937,269	51.6	0.1	40.9	7.4	118,208	364,455	411,495	133,952	8,720	3,460	-640
		'08	73.1	11.6	1.0	14.3	2,017,159	52.8	0.1	41.1	6.0	102,895	400,420	426,854	100,351	8,294	2,404	-9,627
		'09	72.5	10.4	0.4	16.7	2,268,230	51.1	0.1	41.1	7.8	115,750	443,303	445,984	167,394	17,447	8,158	221
	FSC XV	**Rating History: A+ g, 05/18/10; A+ g, 06/29/09; A++g, 07/09/08; A++g, 06/14/07; A++g, 06/21/06**																
LAFOURCHE LIFE INS CO[1] Dennis M. Necaise President & Treasurer 4634 Highway 1 Raceland, LA 70394-2623 LA : 1938 : Stock : Not Available 985-537-7537 AMB# 007759 NAIC# 74942	**NR-1**	'05	32.7	56.9	...	10.4	22,343	...	...	...	100.0	3,564	1,861	1,803	...	-21	-21	-11
		'06	38.4	56.3	...	5.4	23,089	...	...	...	100.0	4,004	2,003	1,944	...	31	31	98
		'07	41.4	53.6	...	5.0	24,317	...	...	...	100.0	4,558	2,069	2,005	...	647	641	721
		'08	46.4	48.8	...	4.8	22,504	...	...	...	100.0	2,440	2,173	2,089	...	26	-48	-1,209
		'09	53.3	38.5	...	8.1	22,218	...	...	...	100.0	1,473	3,174	3,109	...	3	-4	-1,452
		Rating History: NR-1, 06/10/10; NR-1, 06/12/09; NR-1, 06/12/08; NR-1, 06/08/07; NR-1, 06/07/06																
LANDCAR LIFE INS CO[1] 9350 South 150 East, Suite 1000 Sandy, UT 84070-2721 UT : 1981 : Stock : Not Available 801-563-4150 AMB# 009255 NAIC# 92274	**NR-1**	'05	24.6	41.7	31.5	2.2	31,016	...	...	...	100.0	18,755	4,538	4,537	...	2,015	1,755	1,817
		'06	23.4	42.5	32.0	2.2	34,195	...	...	...	100.0	19,900	4,992	4,992	...	2,289	1,974	1,978
		'07	12.4	42.0	43.4	2.2	37,390	...	...	...	100.0	21,640	6,537	6,537	...	2,489	2,174	2,191
		'08	7.3	46.3	35.2	11.2	33,686	...	...	...	100.0	19,218	4,044	4,044	...	3,617	2,752	2,750
		'09	14.6	35.7	44.0	5.8	39,429	...	...	...	100.0	25,963	1,900	1,900	...	3,607	2,986	2,666
		Rating History: NR-1, 06/10/10; NR-1, 06/12/09; NR-1, 06/12/08; NR-1, 06/08/07; NR-1, 06/07/06																
LANDMARK HEALTHPLAN OF CA George W. Vieth, Jr. President & Secretary 1750 Howe Avenue, Suite 300 Sacramento, CA 95825-3369 CA : 1997 : Non-Profit : Broker Health 916-929-7806 AMB# 064766	**NR-5**	'05	...	...	...	100.0	1,258	...	...	...	100.0	760	2,222	2,222	56	167	66	66
		'06	...	...	...	100.0	1,730	...	...	...	100.0	1,207	1,930	1,930	772	559	457	457
		'07	...	...	...	100.0	2,007	...	...	...	100.0	1,033	1,694	1,694	936	458	187	187
		'08	...	...	...	100.0	1,694	...	...	...	100.0	861	1,675	1,675	455	132	8	8
		'09	...	...	...	100.0	1,346	...	...	...	100.0	503	1,402	1,402	457	35	62	62
		Rating History: NR-5, 05/07/10; NR-5, 05/13/09; NR-5, 05/14/08; NR-5, 05/03/07; NR-5, 06/21/06																
LANDMARK LIFE INSURANCE CO[1] Thomas A. Munson President & CEO P.O. Box 40 Brownwood, TX 76804 TX : 1965 : Stock : Not Available 325-646-6579 AMB# 068055 NAIC# 82252	**NR-1**	'05	77.8	10.2	2.0	10.0	60,643	...	...	...	100.0	2,451	8,783	8,662	...	-508	-513	-957
		'06	77.7	11.7	1.7	8.9	59,854	...	...	...	100.0	3,059	9,516	7,770	...	246	226	178
		'07	76.4	13.4	1.6	8.6	60,465	...	...	...	100.0	3,074	10,238	7,163	...	519	521	511
		'08	74.1	13.1	3.1	9.7	60,567	...	...	...	100.0	2,888	11,605	7,091	...	422	422	212
		'09	74.1	14.5	1.5	10.0	61,860	...	...	...	100.0	3,256	14,196	8,248	...	915	915	561
		Rating History: NR-1, 06/10/10; NR-1, 06/12/09; NR-1, 06/12/08; NR-1, 06/08/07; NR-4, 03/30/06																
LAUREL LIFE INS CO Sagicor Financial Corporation Kendrick A. Marshall President & CEO 4343 N. Scottsdale Road, Suite 300 Scottsdale, AZ 85251-3347 TX : 1984 : Stock : Agency Trad Life 480-425-5100 AMB# 068076 NAIC# 67296	**NR-3**	'05	1.6	...	96.8	1.7	43,695	14.0	...	...	86.0	42,151	...	0	16,078	-1,970	-927	4,418
		'06	2.0	...	96.4	1.6	35,177	9.7	...	...	90.3	33,084	...	0	-237	601	936	936
		'07	1.9	...	97.3	0.8	36,120	13.1	...	...	86.9	34,575	...	0	8,265	-624	-386	-386
		'08	1.5	...	96.8	1.7	30,158	7.3	...	...	92.7	27,545	...	0	18,064	-1,063	-1,074	-1,074
		'09	1.2	...	98.1	0.8	39,397	5.1	...	...	94.9	36,031	...	0	33,236	-770	-770	-770
		Rating History: NR-3, 05/04/09; NR-3, 02/19/08; NR-3, 06/18/07; NR-3, 05/08/06; NR-3, 10/21/05																

BEST'S PROFITABILITY, LEVERAGE AND LIQUIDITY TESTS 2005 – 2009

Data in U.S. Dollars

—	Profitability Tests							Leverage Tests						Liquidity Tests					
Un-Realized Capital Gains ($000)	Benefits Paid to NPW & Dep (%)	Comm. & Expenses to NPW & Dep (%)	NOG to Total Assets (%)	NOG to Total Rev (%)	Operating Return on Equity (%)	Net Yield (%)	Total Return (%)	Change in NPW & Dep (%)	NPW & Dep to Capital (X)	Capital & Surplus to Liabilities (%)	Surplus Relief (%)	Reins Leverage (%)	Change in Capital (%)	Quick Liquidity (%)	Current Liquidity (%)	Non-Invest Grade Bonds to Capital (%)	Delinq. & Foreclosed Mortgages to Capital (%)	Mort. & Credit Tenant Loans & R.E. to Capital (%)	Affiliated Invest to Capital (%)
9,988	38.0	20.0	0.5	3.8	3.7	5.68	6.08	-2.0	0.6	16.5	0.0	0.2	4.5	74.5	88.4	20.0	...	10.5	0.8
25,898	39.8	19.8	0.5	4.0	4.0	5.68	6.29	2.2	0.6	16.3	0.0	0.2	5.1	74.3	88.3	16.7	...	10.3	0.7
-31,647	43.2	21.3	0.4	3.2	3.2	5.71	5.83	1.9	0.6	15.6	0.0	0.2	3.9	76.0	89.5	17.9	...	8.8	0.7
-241,210	39.2	20.0	0.8	6.3	6.7	5.73	3.39	15.7	0.8	13.1	0.0	0.2	-14.4	74.3	87.3	19.9	...	8.0	2.6
76,460	37.7	19.9	0.6	4.8	5.2	5.56	5.75	11.3	0.9	12.4	0.0	0.0	5.9	74.4	85.9	53.8	...	7.3	3.4
Principal Lines of Business: OrdLife (62.2%), IndAnn (35.2%), IndA&H (2.4%)														Principal States: TX (6.2%), CA (5.2%), NY (4.3%), NJ (3.7%)					
705	81.7	13.3	22.3	4.9	61.3	3.48	4.83	-5.7	6.1	117.0	...	...	999.9	144.4	152.1	...	...	16.2	17.0
74	82.6	14.5	8.9	3.0	16.4	5.72	7.46	-3.7	5.1	123.3	...	...	16.4	154.5	158.2	...	...	12.5	14.3
162	87.7	15.6	-5.3	-1.7	-10.5	5.74	6.20	9.3	7.0	82.2	...	...	-20.1	108.6	115.5	...	...	14.4	17.1
-349	86.2	15.1	-1.6	-0.5	-3.7	3.43	-5.44	2.1	8.9	68.7	...	...	-20.0	99.2	103.6	...	...	19.2	23.1
1,070	92.1	11.0	-3.4	-1.0	-10.0	1.17	3.56	-5.2	10.6	39.4	...	...	-20.8	63.6	66.8	...	...	22.9	22.9
Principal Lines of Business: CompHosp/Med (52.9%), FEHBP (43.8%), MedSup (3.3%)														Principal States: WA (99.1%)					
...	...	...	...	...	...	...	...	...	...	...	...	...	...	...	...	...	...	...	...
...	...	...	...	...	...	...	...	...	...	...	...	...	...	...	...	...	...	...	...
...	...	...	...	...	...	...	...	...	...	...	...	...	...	...	...	...	...	...	...
...	82.9	22.2	...	-9.3	...	...	...	...	-97.7	-4.3	...	...	...	82.9	82.9	...	...	...	...
...	85.2	10.8	21.7	2.4	91.4	0.05	0.05	261.0	17.8	53.0	...	1.0	999.9	143.5	143.5	...	...	...	...
Principal Lines of Business: Medicare (100.0%)														Principal States: TX (100.0%)					
83	57.1	25.3	0.3	1.1	3.9	5.72	5.68	11.7	2.5	7.6	1.9	125.0	4.2	55.2	66.2	36.8	1.1	175.7	1.0
29	75.0	26.1	0.3	1.2	3.9	6.08	6.10	-5.3	2.3	7.8	1.8	135.1	4.8	51.6	62.9	44.8	...	162.7	1.0
40	51.5	20.9	0.2	0.8	2.9	5.84	5.60	37.0	3.1	7.4	1.8	124.9	1.7	48.3	61.4	36.5	...	162.9	0.9
-1,630	59.0	21.2	0.1	0.5	2.2	5.44	4.71	3.7	3.8	5.9	2.2	144.6	-15.7	49.6	62.2	64.5	...	210.1	1.1
1,604	46.9	18.3	0.4	1.5	7.5	6.22	5.90	4.5	3.6	5.8	1.1	115.7	10.1	46.8	59.2	64.6	...	192.3	1.2
Principal Lines of Business: OrdLife (53.7%), IndAnn (35.9%), GrpAnn (10.1%), GrpLife (0.2%), GrpA&H (0.0%)														Principal States: CA (10.1%), TX (7.5%), IN (6.6%), FL (5.9%), VA (5.0%)					
...	78.1	74.1	-0.1	-0.7	-0.6	...	...	2.2	0.4	22.9	...	...	-5.2	...	...	...	...	305.2	...
...	73.1	50.2	0.1	1.1	0.8	...	...	7.9	0.4	24.4	...	...	8.8	...	...	...	...	286.7	...
...	69.9	49.5	2.7	17.9	15.0	...	...	3.1	0.4	27.3	...	...	15.1	...	...	...	...	249.9	...
-891	71.9	64.0	-0.2	-1.5	-1.4	...	...	4.2	0.7	15.0	...	...	-43.7	...	...	...	...	374.5	...
-219	53.2	40.2	0.0	-0.1	-0.2	...	...	48.8	2.1	7.1	...	...	-49.8	...	...	...	...	581.4	...
Principal Lines of Business: OrdLife (97.4%), IndLife (2.6%)																			
-249	16.4	60.1	5.9	28.5	9.7	...	...	20.4	0.2	185.7	...	...	8.4	...	...	...	...	64.2	...
668	15.9	60.3	6.1	28.5	10.2	...	...	10.0	0.2	189.4	...	...	11.0	...	...	...	...	64.9	...
-1,030	7.2	57.3	6.1	25.1	10.5	...	...	31.0	0.3	170.5	...	...	5.3	...	...	...	...	66.7	...
-6,294	18.1	68.1	7.7	42.6	13.5	...	...	-38.1	0.2	150.8	...	...	-14.1	...	...	...	...	77.0	...
5,372	33.6	96.8	8.2	73.0	13.2	...	...	-53.0	0.1	256.0	...	...	40.0	...	...	...	...	49.6	...
Principal Lines of Business: CrdLife (63.1%), CrdA&H (36.9%)																			
...	57.3	99.0	3.6	1.8	4.7	3.07	3.07	-3.5	2.9	152.8	...	...	-62.5	67.5	67.5	...	...	...	...
...	58.2	89.8	30.6	13.4	46.5	1.80	1.80	-13.1	1.6	230.6	...	...	58.7	78.9	78.9	...	...	...	...
...	68.6	121.0	10.0	5.1	16.7	2.23	2.23	-12.2	1.6	106.1	...	...	-14.4	50.0	50.0	...	...	...	...
...	57.3	132.4	0.4	0.2	0.9	0.89	0.89	-1.1	1.9	103.3	...	...	-16.7	22.2	22.2	...	...	...	...
...	60.3	151.7	4.1	2.1	9.1	0.12	0.12	-16.3	2.8	59.6	...	...	-41.6	12.5	12.5	...	...	...	...
Principal Lines of Business: CompHosp/Med (100.0%)																			
-89	56.4	69.2	-0.9	-3.7	-16.1	...	...	6.6	3.0	5.0	0.0	...	-32.2	...	...	...	...	214.3	...
74	67.5	83.7	0.4	1.8	8.2	...	...	-10.3	2.2	6.3	52.6	...	22.9	...	...	...	...	196.6	...
101	78.0	47.7	0.9	4.1	17.0	...	...	-7.8	1.9	6.5	86.3	...	4.1	...	...	...	...	219.7	...
84	83.9	46.4	0.7	3.2	14.2	...	...	-1.0	2.0	6.1	113.1	...	-5.8	...	...	...	...	228.3	...
-130	69.7	41.3	1.5	5.9	29.8	...	...	16.3	2.3	6.2	119.0	...	3.5	...	...	...	...	247.6	...
Principal Lines of Business: OrdLife (79.4%), IndAnn (20.6%)																			
950	999.9	999.9	-2.4	47.4	-2.7	-5.07	12.77	-39.9	0.0	999.9	...	...	60.4	62.3	62.6	...	...	...	100.3
-8,373	999.9	999.9	2.4	148.5	2.5	1.62	-17.68	112.7	0.0	999.9	...	...	-21.5	38.4	38.8	...	...	...	102.5
-7,074	999.9	999.9	-1.1	65.8	-1.1	-1.65	-19.87	-86.3	0.0	999.9	...	...	4.5	46.1	46.2	...	...	...	101.6
-24,012	999.9	999.9	-3.2	104.9	-3.5	-3.18	-58.11	-31.3	0.0	999.9	...	...	-20.3	36.5	37.6	...	...	...	106.0
-23,776	999.9	999.9	-2.2	104.1	-2.4	-2.30	-56.62	-90.9	0.0	999.9	...	...	30.8	28.5	29.3	...	...	...	107.2
Principal Lines of Business: IndLife (100.0%)																			

Data in U.S. Dollars

COMPANY NAME Ultimate Parent Association Principal Officer Mailing Address Dom. : Began Bus. : Struct. : Mktg. Specialty Phone # AMB# NAIC#	Best's Financial Strength Rating FSC	Data Year	Balance Sheet Bonds (%)	Mort. Loans & R.E. (%)	Com & Pref. Stock (%)	All Other Assets (%)	Total Assets ($000)	Life Reserves (%)	Health Reserves (%)	Ann Res. & Dep. Liabilities (%)	All Other Liabilities (%)	Capital & Surplus ($000)	Operations Direct Premiums Written ($000)	Net Premiums Written & Deposits ($000)	Operating Cash Flow ($000)	NOG Before Taxes ($000)	NOG After Taxes ($000)	Net Income ($000)
LEADERS LIFE INS CO[1] Russell E. Angell President P.O. Box 35768 Tulsa, OK 74153 OK : 1989 : Stock : Not Available 918-254-0200 AMB# 068017 NAIC# 74799	NR-1	'05	40.9	...	...	59.1	3,767	...	...	...	100.0	2,063	6,859	2,635	...	254	240	240
		'06	45.4	...	...	54.6	4,181	...	...	...	100.0	2,257	7,134	2,701	...	213	202	202
		'07	39.1	...	2.0	58.9	5,133	...	...	...	100.0	2,936	7,481	2,815	...	358	341	341
		'08	43.2	...	1.6	55.2	5,366	...	...	...	100.0	2,907	7,803	2,945	...	65	50	50
		'09	36.6	...	1.6	61.8	5,744	...	...	...	100.0	3,085	8,073	3,081	...	233	257	257
		Rating History: NR-1, 06/10/10; NR-1, 06/12/09; NR-1, 06/12/08; NR-1, 06/08/07; NR-5, 05/05/06																
LEGACY HEALTH SOLUTIONS[2] Trustees of Shannon W TX Memorial Hosp Marinan Williams President 2018 Pulliam Street San Angelo, TX 76905 TX : 2004 : Stock : Not Available Health 325-859-7589 AMB# 064892 NAIC# 12174	NR-5	'05	...	...	...	...	...	...	...	...	...	...	...	...	...	...	...	...
		'06	...	...	...	100.0	2,372	...	38.9	...	61.1	2,061	1,951	1,906	-94	12	8	8
		'07	...	...	...	100.0	2,387	...	59.4	...	40.6	1,983	2,169	2,120	18	-70	-46	-46
		'08	...	...	...	100.0	2,037	...	33.8	...	66.2	1,513	2,260	2,191	-603	-452	-452	-452
		'09	...	...	...	100.0	1,907	...	3.1	...	96.9	1,596	1,026	1,026	278	-301	-237	-237
		Rating History: NR-5, 04/07/10; NR-5, 03/23/09; NR-5, 03/25/08; NR-5, 04/04/07																
LEHMAN RE LIMITED Michael Gelband President HM 68 Hamilton HM AX, Bermuda BM : 1998 : Stock : Broker Property, Casualty, Life 441-296-8451 AMB# 086949	F	'05	84.4	...	...	15.6	777,531	67.6	...	...	32.4	334,794	...	1,899	...	13,698	6,979	12,427
		'06	16.8	...	...	83.2	794,334	67.5	...	...	32.5	358,479	...	3,343	-276	31,417	18,688	23,686
		'07	6.8	...	...	93.2	1,158,435	36.7	...	...	63.3	372,093	...	1,015	96,919	20,563	13,232	13,613
		'08	...	...	...	...	...	...	...	...	...	...	...	...	...	...	...	...
		'09	...	...	...	...	...	...	...	...	...	...	...	...	...	...	...	...
		Rating History: F, 09/30/08; B, 09/16/08; A-, 09/11/08; A, 05/07/08; A+, 09/18/06																
LEWER LIFE INS CO Lewer Financial Services L. P. Michael D. Lewer President & CEO P.O. Box 32395 Kansas City, MO 64171-5395 MO : 1987 : Stock : Other Direct Ind Ann, Student A&H, Univ Life 816-753-4390 AMB# 007393 NAIC# 71595	B Rating Outlook: Positive FSC IV	'05	89.3	...	1.1	9.5	26,642	40.7	4.0	48.1	7.2	7,019	49	3,049	-198	-346	-341	-232
		'06	83.4	...	...	16.6	26,887	39.8	5.4	46.3	8.6	7,101	49	4,084	187	46	47	47
		'07	88.4	...	...	11.6	27,493	41.1	6.7	44.6	7.6	7,896	33	5,085	537	724	724	724
		'08	86.3	...	...	13.7	27,564	41.1	7.7	43.0	8.2	7,973	34	5,872	87	577	561	444
		'09	89.8	...	...	10.2	27,498	41.9	6.7	43.5	7.9	8,556	32	5,332	-187	784	787	752
		Rating History: B, 05/25/10; B, 04/30/09; B, 05/30/08; B, 04/26/07; B, 05/15/06																
LEWIS LIFE INSURANCE COMPANY[1] J. W. Reeves President 512 East Bowie Street Marshall, TX 75670-4202 TX : 1982 : Stock : Not Available 903-935-5556 AMB# 068233 NAIC# 99805	NR-1	'05	...	...	...	100.0	932	...	...	...	100.0	53	148	148	...	-3	-3	-3
		'06	...	...	...	100.0	980	...	...	...	100.0	114	146	146	...	60	60	60
		'07	...	...	...	100.0	1,019	...	...	...	100.0	165	141	141	...	51	51	51
		'08	...	...	...	100.0	1,051	...	...	...	100.0	190	141	141	...	25	25	25
		'09	...	...	...	100.0	1,041	...	...	...	100.0	163	131	131	...	-27	-27	-27
		Rating History: NR-1, 06/10/10; NR-1, 06/12/09; NR-1, 06/12/08; NR-1, 06/08/07; NR-1, 06/07/06																
LIBERTY BANKERS LIFE INS CO Realty Advisors Inc Bradford A. Phillips CEO 1605 LBJ Freeway, Suite 710 Dallas, TX 75234 OK : 1958 : Stock : Agency Ind Ann, Ind Life, Term Life 972-484-6063 AMB# 007011 NAIC# 68543	B- Rating Outlook: Negative FSC VIII	'05	46.6	26.6	3.7	23.2	393,227	9.6	...	69.3	21.1	31,166	72,118	74,132	72,861	3,125	3,221	2,324
		'06	49.3	25.6	4.3	20.7	490,029	9.8	...	75.9	14.2	39,667	133,668	142,388	93,499	7,981	5,527	9,347
		'07	54.9	18.3	13.4	13.5	666,011	7.3	...	76.7	16.0	60,937	166,671	184,732	161,028	11,153	5,097	9,526
		'08	49.9	22.0	11.5	16.7	807,084	6.2	...	79.9	13.8	63,206	185,488	201,704	142,782	18,652	14,380	1,987
		'09	54.4	21.8	9.3	14.5	1,040,432	5.0	...	85.1	9.9	96,011	290,694	304,783	231,265	16,124	11,034	4,235
		Rating History: B-, 11/24/09; B- u, 06/18/09; B, 05/23/08; B, 11/16/06; B, 07/18/05																
LIBERTY DENTAL PLAN OF CA Amir Neshat, D.D.S. Chairman & President 3200 El Camino Real, Suite 290 Irvine, CA 92602 CA : 1976 : Stock : Not Available Dental 949-223-0007 AMB# 064663	NR-5	'05	...	...	...	100.0	764	...	...	...	100.0	372	1,935	1,935	76	-216	-216	-216
		'06	...	...	...	100.0	1,411	...	...	...	100.0	476	5,625	5,625	271	85	169	169
		'07	...	...	...	100.0	2,126	...	...	...	100.0	629	8,356	8,356	-99	76	148	148
		'08	...	...	...	100.0	3,719	...	...	...	100.0	815	14,828	14,828	1,165	266	179	179
		'09	...	...	...	100.0	7,488	...	...	...	100.0	1,952	26,609	26,609	3,204	1,280	745	745
		Rating History: NR-5, 03/23/10; NR-5, 04/08/09; NR-5, 03/11/08; NR-5, 04/03/07; NR-5, 04/12/06																
LIBERTY LIFE ASSUR OF BOSTON Liberty Mutual Holding Company Inc. Edmund F. Kelly Chairman, President & CEO 100 Liberty Way Dover, NH 03820-1525 MA : 1964 : Stock : Other Agency A&H, Ind Life, Struc Sett 617-357-9500 AMB# 006627 NAIC# 65315	A Rating Outlook: Negative FSC X	'05	62.3	...	0.0	37.7	9,026,133	24.3	9.0	33.1	33.5	431,685	857,916	883,197	534,097	57,479	32,538	38,489
		'06	62.2	0.6	0.0	37.1	10,457,191	22.8	8.4	34.6	34.2	449,323	1,281,827	1,325,790	887,911	30,449	20,046	12,915
		'07	61.1	1.2	0.4	37.4	11,185,421	22.8	8.5	34.1	34.5	482,667	986,479	1,038,783	376,184	26,876	21,471	35,530
		'08	61.7	1.6	0.3	36.3	11,605,062	24.0	9.3	34.8	31.9	460,448	1,153,423	1,180,637	637,893	-2,346	7,005	-27,565
		'09	61.0	1.4	0.8	36.8	12,983,175	23.7	9.4	32.7	34.2	597,543	1,274,152	1,291,648	860,631	15,982	-5,715	-23,476
		Rating History: A, 06/11/10; A, 04/09/09; A, 03/05/08; A, 02/28/07; A, 01/25/06																
LIBERTY LIFE INSURANCE COMPANY Royal Bank of Canada R. David Black President P.O. Box 1389 Greenville, SC 29602-1389 SC : 1909 : Stock : Broker Annuity 800-551-8354 AMB# 006175 NAIC# 61492	A Rating Outlook: Stable FSC IX	'05	72.6	15.8	1.9	9.7	3,745,064	48.6	1.1	44.8	5.5	274,937	611,072	570,776	191,786	31,723	32,821	32,426
		'06	72.7	14.6	2.4	10.3	3,770,946	48.3	1.2	45.7	4.9	268,504	523,886	463,856	25,634	19,794	19,767	19,988
		'07	73.4	15.4	3.4	7.9	3,722,392	48.9	1.2	45.2	4.6	261,542	388,388	320,200	-39,605	20,262	24,991	39,259
		'08	72.8	15.6	2.0	9.6	3,597,209	50.1	1.2	45.0	3.6	234,251	361,818	296,421	-73,787	16,365	16,368	-19,111
		'09	77.5	11.6	1.5	9.3	4,326,571	41.7	1.0	53.4	3.9	274,963	1,068,614	995,623	669,387	-9,875	-9,875	-31,856
		Rating History: A, 12/08/09; A, 07/02/09; A, 07/09/08; A, 06/20/07; A, 04/27/06																

BEST'S PROFITABILITY, LEVERAGE AND LIQUIDITY TESTS 2005 – 2009

Data in U.S. Dollars

—	Profitability Tests							Leverage Tests						Liquidity Tests					
Un-Realized Capital Gains ($000)	Benefits Paid to NPW & Dep (%)	Comm. & Expenses to NPW & Dep (%)	NOG to Total Assets (%)	NOG to Total Rev (%)	Operating Return on Equity (%)	Net Yield (%)	Total Return (%)	Change in NPW & Dep (%)	NPW & Dep to Capital (X)	Capital & Surplus to Liabilities (%)	Surplus Relief (%)	Reins Leverage (%)	Change in Capital (%)	Quick Liquidity (%)	Current Liquidity (%)	Non-Invest Grade Bonds to Capital (%)	Delinq. & Foreclosed Mortgages to Capital (%)	Mort. & Credit Tenant Loans & R.E. to Capital (%)	Affiliated Invest to Capital (%)
...	27.6	56.1	6.9	4.8	12.4	...	...	12.0	1.3	121.8	108.4	...	13.6	...	...	...	...	...	...
...	31.6	57.0	5.1	3.9	9.3	...	...	2.5	1.2	119.2	104.1	...	9.9	...	...	...	...	...	...
1	25.4	58.0	7.3	6.3	13.1	...	...	4.2	1.0	136.5	82.6	...	30.3	...	...	...	...	...	...
-17	29.7	63.4	1.0	0.9	1.7	...	...	4.6	1.0	121.7	86.7	...	-0.6	...	...	...	...	...	...
-120	33.8	54.1	4.6	4.4	8.6	...	...	4.6	1.0	118.5	85.2	...	5.8	...	...	...	...	...	...
Principal Lines of Business: OrdLife (98.3%), IndA&H (1.7%)																			
...	...	...	...	...	...	...	...	...	...	...	...	...	...	...	...	...	...	...	...
...	89.5	16.0	...	0.4	...	...	...	...	0.9	664.8	...	...	...	999.9	999.9	...	...	...	...
...	94.2	15.3	-1.9	-2.1	-2.3	6.33	6.33	11.2	1.1	490.8	...	...	-3.8	884.1	884.1	...	...	...	...
...	108.4	16.8	-20.4	-20.0	-25.9	3.83	3.83	3.4	1.4	288.8	...	...	-23.7	580.8	612.2	...	...	...	...
...	103.3	27.3	-12.0	-22.8	-15.2	0.72	0.72	-53.2	0.6	513.6	...	...	5.5	999.9	999.9	...	...	...	...
Principal Lines of Business: CompHosp/Med (100.0%)													Principal States: TX (100.0%)						
...	444.9	1.2	0.9	25.3	2.0	2.78	3.52	-99.9	0.6	75.6	...	...	-11.3	153.1	167.2	...	...	...	8.8
...	125.7	-30.7	2.4	41.0	5.4	4.96	5.62	76.0	0.9	82.3	...	...	7.1	35.4	170.4	...	...	...	7.4
...	784.3	999.9	1.4	25.2	3.6	4.71	4.75	-69.6	0.3	47.3	...	...	3.8	25.3	122.8	...	...	...	4.9
...	...	...	...	...	...	...	...	...	...	...	...	...	...	...	...	...	...	...	...
...	...	...	...	...	...	...	...	...	...	...	...	...	...	...	...	...	...	...	...
...	109.6	66.6	-1.3	-7.3	-4.8	5.74	6.55	10.4	0.4	36.8	0.4	0.7	-3.0	105.4	117.7	9.5	...	...	...
...	93.9	53.5	0.2	0.8	0.7	5.61	5.98	34.0	0.6	36.7	0.5	1.4	0.8	119.0	131.0	4.3	...	...	...
...	73.5	48.8	2.7	10.9	9.6	5.46	5.78	24.5	0.6	41.2	0.3	0.6	11.0	115.1	127.5	3.8	...	...	...
-271	73.8	46.3	2.0	7.6	7.1	5.31	4.22	15.5	0.7	41.1	0.3	0.6	0.1	113.9	125.8	10.6	...	...	...
...	70.5	49.2	2.9	11.3	9.5	5.49	5.84	-9.2	0.6	45.6	0.3	0.6	7.3	112.6	125.2	5.6	...	...	...
Principal Lines of Business: GrpA&H (88.8%), OrdLife (7.0%), IndAnn (4.3%)													Principal States: TX (46.8%), MO (25.3%), AZ (12.8%), OR (8.5%), OK (4.5%)						
...	43.5	50.0	-0.3	-1.6	-5.0	...	...	-2.2	2.8	6.1	...	...	-4.9	...	...	...	...	...	...
...	42.1	45.8	6.3	34.4	72.3	...	...	-1.3	1.3	13.1	...	...	113.1	...	...	...	...	...	...
...	50.7	47.9	5.1	28.9	36.7	...	...	-3.4	0.9	19.3	...	...	45.1	...	...	...	...	...	...
...	39.9	61.3	2.5	14.5	14.3	...	...	0.1	0.7	22.1	...	...	15.4	...	...	...	...	...	...
...	60.8	67.9	-2.6	-17.1	-15.4	...	...	-6.7	0.8	18.6	...	...	-14.2	...	...	...	...	...	...
Principal Lines of Business: OrdLife (100.0%)																			
2,192	56.5	14.4	0.9	3.4	12.8	7.97	8.61	54.5	2.1	9.7	0.0	181.8	70.8	45.8	50.4	26.6	9.1	299.7	46.3
2,275	39.2	9.4	1.3	3.1	15.6	9.53	11.30	92.1	3.1	10.2	0.0	115.0	30.2	48.9	54.0	51.3	10.7	276.7	41.0
10,140	36.6	9.6	0.9	2.4	10.1	8.62	11.64	29.7	2.6	12.0	0.0	49.8	56.7	48.6	58.8	11.3	7.4	171.3	34.3
-1,200	40.3	8.9	2.0	5.9	23.2	9.24	7.22	9.2	2.8	9.9	0.1	1.0	2.0	47.4	55.9	36.9	53.2	244.2	38.4
-122	35.3	8.0	1.2	3.1	13.9	7.59	6.81	51.1	2.8	11.7	0.2	0.6	50.5	43.2	54.5	61.3	24.7	207.5	32.6
Principal Lines of Business: IndAnn (96.9%), OrdLife (3.0%), IndLife (0.2%)													Principal States: TX (27.8%), FL (11.7%), CA (5.8%), AZ (4.7%), NC (3.9%)						
354	30.4	80.3	-31.7	-11.2	-63.5	2.39	-99.90	72.2	5.2	94.8	...	...	20.2	19.3	19.3	...	...	...	...
...	52.6	45.7	15.5	3.0	39.9	-1.45	-1.45	190.6	11.8	50.9	...	...	28.0	25.6	25.6	...	...	...	...
...	55.2	43.5	8.4	1.8	26.8	-7.71	-7.71	48.6	13.3	42.0	...	...	32.2	9.4	9.4	...	...	...	...
...	58.6	40.0	6.1	1.2	24.9	-0.22	-0.22	77.5	18.2	28.0	...	...	29.5	44.9	44.9	...	...	...	...
...	62.5	39.7	13.3	2.6	53.9	-0.45	-0.45	79.5	13.6	35.3	...	...	139.6	76.8	76.8	...	...	...	...
Principal Lines of Business: Dental (100.0%)																			
3,387	62.4	16.3	0.4	2.7	8.9	6.35	6.56	71.3	1.8	8.1	2.0	32.3	40.8	63.6	74.0	78.7	...	...	0.1
8,788	46.4	12.9	0.2	1.2	4.6	6.29	6.37	50.1	2.6	7.3	2.4	35.6	4.4	66.1	76.3	68.0	...	13.0	0.1
7,574	77.0	16.2	0.2	1.5	4.6	6.09	6.43	-21.6	1.9	7.5	1.6	35.0	9.0	63.4	73.9	77.4	0.0	24.4	0.1
-13,878	70.7	15.0	0.1	0.4	1.5	5.98	5.42	13.7	2.3	6.5	3.0	38.8	-6.0	66.3	76.5	71.2	...	36.5	0.0
-20,804	71.0	15.8	0.0	-0.3	-1.1	5.75	5.34	9.4	2.0	7.5	0.4	41.5	27.3	65.4	74.7	77.2	0.1	27.7	15.6
Principal Lines of Business: GrpA&H (34.7%), OrdLife (27.0%), IndAnn (24.1%), GrpLife (12.6%), GrpAnn (1.5%)													Principal States: NY (14.0%), CA (12.0%), DE (11.2%), WI (4.9%), TX (4.8%)						
-11,728	70.5	29.9	0.9	4.2	12.0	5.85	5.52	0.9	1.8	9.1	3.0	169.2	0.6	62.5	70.9	2.8	...	191.4	0.0
6,744	99.8	32.3	0.5	2.9	7.3	5.66	5.86	-18.7	1.5	8.7	6.9	182.6	-3.1	65.3	73.9	0.2	...	183.5	0.8
-9,495	132.9	44.2	0.7	4.6	9.4	5.73	5.85	-31.0	1.1	8.6	6.5	199.7	-2.9	61.2	70.6	0.2	0.0	196.4	0.3
-18,266	135.3	46.1	0.4	3.2	6.6	5.79	4.27	-7.4	1.2	7.2	5.3	220.9	-17.5	63.3	72.4	2.5	0.5	234.1	0.0
16,840	38.5	19.3	-0.2	-0.8	-3.9	5.60	5.44	235.9	3.3	7.5	5.9	206.0	25.1	67.8	77.8	10.0	3.8	167.7	0.0
Principal Lines of Business: IndAnn (82.3%), OrdLife (12.6%), GrpA&H (2.7%), GrpLife (1.1%), IndA&H (1.1%)													Principal States: CA (7.7%), FL (7.4%), SC (7.2%), MI (7.0%), TX (5.9%)						

Data in U.S. Dollars

COMPANY NAME / Ultimate Parent Association / Principal Officer / Mailing Address / Dom. : Began Bus. : Struct. : Mktg. / Specialty / Phone # / AMB# / NAIC#	Best's Financial Strength Rating / FSC	Data Year	Balance Sheet: Bonds (%)	Mort. Loans & R.E. (%)	Com & Pref. Stock (%)	All Other Assets (%)	Total Assets ($000)	Life Reserves (%)	Health Reserves (%)	Ann Res. & Dep. Liabilities (%)	All Other Liabilities (%)	Capital & Surplus ($000)	Operations: Direct Premiums Written ($000)	Net Premiums Written & Deposits ($000)	Operating Cash Flow ($000)	NOG Before Taxes ($000)	NOG After Taxes ($000)	Net Income ($000)
LIBERTY NATIONAL LIFE INS CO Torchmark Corporation	A+	'05	80.5	1.0	8.3	10.3	4,565,747	86.2	7.4	3.4	3.0	516,124	617,299	540,378	162,642	235,916	186,056	183,573
Anthony L. McWhorter, CEO		'06	75.5	0.6	14.0	10.0	4,926,695	86.7	6.4	3.2	3.7	677,787	614,723	542,103	244,665	276,255	225,060	225,045
P.O. Box 2612, Birmingham, AL 35202	Rating Outlook: Stable	'07	75.5	0.5	13.8	10.3	4,981,019	88.4	6.1	3.0	2.5	607,030	603,164	540,039	50,050	273,952	221,132	217,447
NE : 1929 : Stock : Agency		'08	71.6	0.4	16.3	11.7	5,149,123	89.6	5.8	2.8	1.8	674,133	591,269	477,814	43,745	257,889	217,586	155,252
A&H, Ind A&H, Ind Life; 205-325-2722		'09	75.4	0.3	10.8	13.5	5,514,587	87.0	5.3	5.5	2.2	721,609	723,640	598,326	331,378	202,502	168,656	62,668
AMB# 006629 NAIC# 65331	FSC X	Rating History: A+ g, 06/15/10; A+ g, 06/11/09; A+ g, 06/11/08; A+ g, 06/08/07; A+ g, 06/08/06																
LIBERTY UNION LIFE ASSURANCE	B	'05	62.2	...	3.7	34.1	11,345	1.5	74.0	0.4	24.1	4,440	24,359	26,292	1,298	654	378	378
Christopher T. Mazur, President & Treasurer		'06	67.2	...	3.8	29.0	11,068	1.4	74.1	0.4	24.1	4,301	29,212	30,685	140	-67	-82	73
30775 Barrington Street, Madison Heights, MI 48071	Rating Outlook: Negative	'07	69.8	...	0.9	29.3	11,495	1.4	74.9	0.2	23.5	4,462	28,876	30,271	859	400	202	106
MI : 1964 : Stock : Not Available		'08	74.7	0.3	2.5	22.6	10,021	1.6	80.8	0.2	17.4	4,124	24,209	25,191	-1,497	-313	-219	-915
Group A&H, Group Life; 248-583-7123		'09	72.0	3.2	2.7	22.2	10,591	1.6	79.9	0.2	18.3	4,289	20,492	21,162	817	395	261	260
AMB# 006799 NAIC# 66753	FSC III	Rating History: B, 02/02/10; B, 05/21/09; B, 04/02/08; B, 03/22/07; B, 03/13/06																
LIFE ASSURANCE COMPANY	NR-5	'05	19.1	...	...	80.9	7,900	50.9	34.7	11.9	2.5	2,235	5,056	3,309	-177	812	710	710
Danny S. Baze, Chairman & President		'06	15.4	...	...	84.6	7,822	50.7	36.0	11.1	2.3	2,373	4,924	3,175	-23	890	766	766
P.O. Box 20667, Oklahoma City, OK 73156		'07	12.1	...	...	87.9	8,166	48.3	39.2	9.9	2.5	2,552	5,760	3,458	267	812	701	701
OK : 1975 : Stock : Agency		'08	11.7	...	...	88.3	7,743	47.4	40.7	10.2	1.6	2,524	4,976	2,829	-366	690	601	601
Credit Life, Credit A&H, Ordinary Life; 405-810-1111		'09	8.1	...	...	91.9	6,886	49.7	37.9	10.6	1.9	2,316	3,282	1,881	-904	384	357	357
AMB# 008635 NAIC# 85677		Rating History: NR-5, 04/20/10; NR-5, 04/20/09; NR-5, 04/21/08; NR-5, 05/08/07; NR-5, 05/03/06																
LIFE ASSURANCE CO OF AMERICA'	NR-1	'05	66.5	...	0.0	33.4	6,758	...	...	0.8	99.2	2,324	344	167	...	131	131	131
Anthony C. Borcich, President		'06	68.5	...	...	31.5	7,166	...	...	0.7	99.3	2,442	458	309	...	146	138	138
1100 Jorie Boulevard, Suite 143, Oak Brook, IL 60523		'07	72.7	...	...	27.3	7,099	...	...	0.4	99.6	2,555	295	147	...	121	120	120
IL : 1970 : Stock : Not Available		'08	82.5	...	...	17.5	6,087	...	...	0.3	99.7	2,451	380	269	...	-40	-40	-40
630-571-2100		'09	85.7	...	...	14.3	6,401	...	...	0.2	99.8	2,533	283	184	...	93	93	93
AMB# 007768 NAIC# 75027		Rating History: NR-1, 06/10/10; NR-1, 06/12/09; NR-1, 06/12/08; NR-1, 06/08/07; NR-1, 06/07/06																
LIFE INSURANCE CO OF ALABAMA	B+	'05	82.8	0.8	5.5	11.0	68,903	49.6	37.8	7.3	5.3	12,281	35,943	34,976	3,965	2,307	1,775	1,835
Clarence W. Daugette III, Chairman of the Board & President		'06	82.4	0.8	5.7	11.1	73,822	48.7	39.3	6.9	5.0	14,443	37,406	36,455	4,504	2,425	2,058	2,058
P.O. Box 349, Gadsden, AL 35901	Rating Outlook: Stable	'07	82.7	0.7	4.8	11.9	79,199	48.0	40.1	6.5	5.4	16,632	38,230	37,272	5,613	2,895	2,425	2,425
AL : 1952 : Stock : Agency		'08	83.0	0.6	1.6	14.8	81,803	47.4	41.8	5.9	4.8	16,138	39,706	39,248	3,671	2,790	2,178	1,367
Ind A&H, Term Life, Whole life; 256-543-2022		'09	83.3	0.6	3.0	13.1	88,751	46.8	42.9	5.4	4.8	18,922	41,237	40,739	7,634	4,587	3,514	3,312
AMB# 006637 NAIC# 65412	FSC V	Rating History: B+, 02/22/10; B+, 03/10/09; B+, 03/18/08; B+, 01/29/07; B+, 02/01/06																
LIFE INS CO OF BOSTON & NY Boston Mutual Life Insurance Company	A-	'05	74.1	...	...	25.9	51,086	91.9	4.2	...	4.0	7,901	20,219	10,777	3,758	1,458	794	794
Paul E. Petry, Chairman & President		'06	73.6	...	0.2	26.2	56,849	92.7	3.4	...	3.9	8,786	20,290	10,846	5,670	1,564	976	943
120 Royall Street, Canton, MA 02021-1098	Rating Outlook: Stable	'07	71.3	...	0.2	28.5	62,967	92.9	3.4	...	3.7	9,591	20,360	11,233	6,424	1,187	791	763
NY : 1990 : Stock : Agency		'08	69.8	...	0.2	30.0	68,395	93.7	3.1	...	3.2	11,544	21,858	13,192	4,688	3,021	2,559	2,242
Group A&H, Group Life, Ind Life; 914-712-0610		'09	69.2	...	...	30.8	77,271	92.4	3.2	...	4.4	13,225	22,870	14,663	6,669	1,531	1,068	1,025
AMB# 068126 NAIC# 78140	FSC VIII	Rating History: A- g, 04/06/10; A- g, 05/21/09; A- g, 06/30/08; A- g, 06/14/07; A- g, 06/01/06																
LIFE INSURANCE CO OF LOUISIANA	B	'05	48.4	...	33.7	17.9	8,062	52.9	4.6	1.0	41.5	2,600	791	262	-225	138	138	252
George D. Nelson, Jr., President		'06	47.1	...	33.7	19.2	8,062	53.1	4.6	1.2	41.1	3,021	454	205	38	72	72	280
P.O. Box 1803, Shreveport, LA 71166	Rating Outlook: Stable	'07	46.9	...	35.0	18.2	7,894	51.1	4.1	1.6	43.2	3,582	501	220	-223	171	146	282
LA : 1964 : Stock : Agency		'08	52.2	...	30.0	17.8	6,987	63.2	3.7	2.1	31.0	3,515	418	151	218	148	140	245
Credit Life, Credit A&H; 318-221-0646		'09	53.7	...	34.1	12.2	7,246	60.8	3.1	2.3	33.8	3,716	337	90	33	92	86	116
AMB# 007775 NAIC# 75094	FSC III	Rating History: B, 03/16/10; B, 03/18/09; B-, 02/29/08; B-, 03/21/07; B-, 04/19/06																
LIFE INSURANCE OF NORTH AMER CIGNA Corporation	A	'05	28.6	17.5	25.3	28.7	5,537,877	11.5	54.5	1.4	32.6	682,399	1,626,018	1,750,866	-83,070	162,635	125,256	123,424
Karen S. Rohan, President		'06	25.0	18.5	25.0	31.5	5,776,607	12.0	52.7	1.4	33.9	615,482	1,696,269	1,795,096	-22,459	138,029	103,356	94,891
1601 Chestnut Street, 2 Liberty Place, Philadelphia, PA 19192-2362	Rating Outlook: Negative	'07	26.2	15.4	25.8	32.5	5,880,600	11.7	53.5	1.5	33.3	641,254	1,939,172	2,051,563	-20,263	243,157	179,759	172,956
PA : 1957 : Stock : Agency		'08	26.9	17.3	29.3	26.6	5,464,298	14.3	58.4	1.7	25.7	628,615	2,085,446	2,255,845	-1,384	260,822	154,345	125,023
Dis inc, A&H, Term Life; 215-761-1000		'09	27.3	15.7	28.9	28.2	5,732,662	13.6	55.9	1.5	29.0	769,441	2,201,444	2,304,661	1,638	286,871	221,975	215,628
AMB# 006645 NAIC# 65498	FSC XV	Rating History: A g, 01/08/10; A g, 11/14/08; A g, 02/11/08; A g, 12/14/06; A- g, 12/21/05																
LIFE INSURANCE CO OF SOUTHWEST National Life Holding Company	A	'05	77.8	13.0	0.9	8.4	4,658,104	5.2	0.0	92.4	2.5	240,642	806,196	802,038	621,988	45,945	34,570	35,098
Wade H. Mayo, President & CEO		'06	75.4	13.9	0.6	10.2	5,352,826	5.1	0.0	91.8	3.1	292,904	829,732	848,470	589,914	63,583	44,527	46,233
1300 West Mockingbird Lane, Dallas, TX 75247-4921	Rating Outlook: Stable	'07	78.3	13.8	0.5	7.4	5,849,880	5.4	0.0	92.4	2.1	364,627	878,338	941,529	577,335	76,863	51,363	43,494
TX : 1956 : Stock : Agency		'08	79.4	13.3	0.6	6.7	6,525,364	6.1	0.0	91.8	2.1	420,121	1,237,668	1,258,577	620,696	11,138	3,206	-37,005
FPDA's, Life, SPDA's; 214-638-7100		'09	76.0	10.2	0.1	13.7	8,209,832	5.7	0.0	87.1	7.1	492,310	1,583,304	1,619,383	1,080,856	145,823	92,359	51,775
AMB# 006647 NAIC# 65528	FSC XII	Rating History: A g, 09/21/09; A g, 11/12/08; A g, 06/15/07; A g, 06/21/06; A g, 05/06/05																

BEST'S PROFITABILITY, LEVERAGE AND LIQUIDITY TESTS 2005 – 2009

Data in U.S. Dollars

—	Profitability Tests							Leverage Tests						Liquidity Tests					
Un-Realized Capital Gains ($000)	Benefits Paid to NPW & Dep (%)	Comm. & Expenses to NPW & Dep (%)	NOG to Total Assets (%)	NOG to Total Rev (%)	Operating Return on Equity (%)	Net Yield (%)	Total Return (%)	Change in NPW & Dep (%)	NPW & Dep to Capital (X)	Capital & Surplus to Liabilities (%)	Surplus Relief (%)	Reins Leverage (%)	Change in Capital (%)	Quick Liquidity (%)	Current Liquidity (%)	Non-Invest Grade Bonds to Capital (%)	Delinq. & Foreclosed Mortgages to Capital (%)	Mort. & Credit Tenant Loans & R.E. to Capital (%)	Affiliated Invest to Capital (%)
50,419	60.8	35.8	4.2	19.9	38.8	7.97	9.19	-0.1	1.0	13.4	4.9	22.4	14.6	53.1	66.6	47.4	1.9	8.1	62.7
113,019	54.5	30.3	4.7	24.0	37.7	7.60	10.14	0.3	0.8	17.1	3.4	16.8	33.7	49.4	64.7	31.1	...	4.0	66.0
-5,307	56.6	27.6	4.5	23.9	34.4	7.54	7.44	-0.4	0.8	15.0	3.5	18.6	-10.1	46.5	60.8	40.8	...	3.9	73.5
31,667	61.8	29.0	4.3	24.0	34.0	7.59	7.05	-11.5	0.7	15.4	7.6	21.5	6.0	43.3	57.5	31.6	...	2.9	80.1
45,591	50.3	27.4	3.2	16.6	24.2	6.87	5.79	25.2	0.8	15.3	7.5	20.3	6.6	45.2	56.9	49.4	...	2.5	81.4
	Principal Lines of Business: OrdLife (53.3%), IndAnn (24.5%), IndA&H (21.8%), GrpLife (0.2%), GrpA&H (0.1%)													Principal States: AL (27.2%), GA (14.0%), FL (10.2%), NC (7.7%), SC (6.8%)					
-201	67.9	29.6	3.4	1.4	8.7	0.97	-1.12	-1.3	5.8	66.3	...	16.2	0.5	137.0	140.7	2.7	...	...	2.7
-102	72.0	28.6	-0.7	-0.3	-1.9	1.75	2.29	16.7	6.9	66.7	...	5.8	-2.1	133.0	143.7	2.3	...	...	...
-236	72.5	27.3	1.8	0.7	4.6	3.04	-0.19	-1.3	6.7	64.3	0.4	8.9	1.5	131.6	141.0	...	...	...	...
399	75.1	27.7	-2.0	-0.9	-5.1	3.65	0.99	-16.8	6.1	69.9	0.5	3.6	-8.3	151.3	164.4	0.8	...	0.6	...
25	70.3	29.3	2.5	1.2	6.2	3.12	3.37	-16.0	4.9	68.6	0.5	2.9	4.5	148.1	160.7	1.9	...	7.8	4.4
	Principal Lines of Business: GrpA&H (97.3%), GrpLife (2.2%), IndA&H (0.5%), OrdLife (0.0%)													Principal States: MI (100.0%)					
...	27.8	54.9	8.9	15.8	31.8	2.78	2.79	-2.7	1.5	39.5	47.8	143.3	0.3	131.4	132.4	...	...	...	...
...	26.7	56.4	9.7	17.4	33.2	4.02	4.03	-4.1	1.3	43.6	42.3	130.4	6.2	137.0	137.7	...	...	...	...
...	20.6	56.3	8.8	14.0	28.5	4.72	4.73	8.9	1.4	45.5	50.8	129.7	7.5	138.1	138.6	...	...	...	...
...	33.0	58.2	7.6	14.2	23.7	3.64	3.64	-18.2	1.1	48.4	49.3	130.2	-1.1	141.8	142.5	...	...	...	...
...	49.2	66.5	4.9	12.9	14.8	2.41	2.42	-33.5	0.8	50.7	31.7	142.5	-8.2	143.0	143.4	...	...	...	...
	Principal Lines of Business: CrdLife (65.3%), CrdA&H (18.1%), OrdLife (12.4%), GrpAnn (4.2%)													Principal States: OK (100.0%)					
...	63.8	69.6	2.0	23.9	5.9	...	...	-52.9	0.1	52.6	1.9	...	7.7	...	...	...	...	...	...
...	86.6	48.2	2.0	19.0	5.8	...	...	84.7	0.1	52.1	1.2	...	5.3	...	...	...	...	...	...
...	196.4	116.4	1.7	21.1	4.8	...	...	-52.4	0.1	56.9	1.2	...	4.9	...	...	...	...	...	...
-83	525.3	58.6	-0.6	-5.7	-1.6	...	...	83.3	0.1	67.4	1.3	...	-4.8	...	...	...	...	...	...
51	35.5	97.8	1.5	17.4	3.7	...	...	-31.7	0.1	67.7	1.0	...	5.4	...	...	...	...	...	...
	Principal Lines of Business: OrdLife (59.7%), IndAnn (40.3%)																		
-402	55.6	42.4	2.7	4.6	15.3	5.68	5.16	5.0	2.6	23.9	...	15.6	11.4	79.2	85.1	23.8	...	4.2	2.9
334	55.3	42.9	2.9	5.1	15.4	5.75	6.23	4.2	2.3	26.6	...	13.7	16.8	81.1	87.0	15.7	...	3.7	2.6
-391	53.7	43.0	3.2	5.9	15.6	5.73	5.20	2.2	2.1	28.2	...	12.6	12.1	82.9	88.6	16.9	...	3.2	2.3
-2,732	52.4	44.6	2.7	4.9	13.3	5.72	1.17	5.3	2.4	24.7	...	9.6	-7.0	84.3	87.6	11.1	...	3.3	2.4
453	50.3	42.1	4.1	7.8	20.0	5.30	5.65	3.8	2.1	28.1	...	3.6	20.4	92.5	95.6	9.8	...	2.7	2.0
	Principal Lines of Business: IndA&H (80.8%), OrdLife (12.6%), GrpA&H (6.6%), IndAnn (0.1%), GrpAnn (0.0%)													Principal States: AL (30.5%), TN (16.7%), GA (15.0%), MS (12.5%), KY (8.2%)					
...	34.8	30.4	1.6	5.0	10.5	5.57	5.62	1.6	1.3	18.6	31.7	211.5	9.5	61.9	73.0	...	...	...	...
...	38.1	30.3	1.8	6.0	11.7	5.68	5.65	0.6	1.2	18.5	30.2	173.5	11.1	59.4	70.8	...	...	...	...
...	40.5	33.1	1.3	4.7	8.6	5.77	5.76	3.6	1.2	18.2	25.1	179.3	9.2	59.6	70.6	...	...	...	...
...	37.0	39.9	3.9	13.4	24.2	5.73	5.26	17.4	1.1	20.5	19.8	140.6	20.2	58.4	68.9	0.6	...	...	...
...	36.1	37.4	1.5	5.2	8.6	5.56	5.53	11.1	1.1	20.9	16.6	138.0	14.4	62.9	71.0	4.8	...	...	...
	Principal Lines of Business: OrdLife (87.4%), IndA&H (6.3%), GrpA&H (5.6%), GrpLife (0.7%)													Principal States: NY (96.7%)					
81	96.4	184.8	1.7	14.0	5.8	4.45	7.30	-13.1	0.1	63.0	13.2	71.0	11.1	100.9	114.7	6.5	...	...	...
71	93.3	162.1	0.9	10.3	2.6	4.25	8.38	-21.8	0.1	78.8	5.2	49.0	14.0	114.8	130.6	5.7	...	...	-4.9
-46	63.6	156.4	1.8	19.1	4.4	4.14	5.51	7.4	0.1	108.6	5.1	32.2	15.6	130.1	148.9	4.9	...	...	...
-871	83.2	169.6	1.9	22.4	3.9	4.48	-6.27	-31.2	0.0	108.9	4.2	23.9	-11.4	124.4	140.1	1.2	...	...	22.0
388	90.0	299.8	1.2	17.6	2.4	4.05	10.80	-40.7	0.0	136.6	3.0	15.3	14.9	138.8	158.8	1.3	...	...	22.2
	Principal Lines of Business: CrdLife (69.6%), CrdA&H (16.9%), OrdLife (12.1%), IndAnn (1.4%)													Principal States: LA (100.0%)					
46,391	78.3	21.1	2.3	6.5	18.7	4.44	5.68	3.9	2.5	19.1	0.5	251.2	2.9	15.8	28.5	20.5	0.0	137.2	181.7
55,921	76.1	22.3	1.8	5.3	15.9	4.22	5.40	2.5	2.8	16.8	0.5	277.2	-8.9	15.4	27.0	23.0	0.0	165.3	207.5
57,111	71.3	20.9	3.1	8.1	28.6	4.38	5.59	14.3	3.0	17.4	0.6	260.7	4.3	15.8	28.9	21.4	...	134.1	207.3
104,220	73.7	19.1	2.7	6.3	24.3	4.51	6.21	10.0	3.4	16.7	0.5	258.4	-2.0	13.8	25.3	30.5	...	142.1	231.3
103,596	72.4	20.8	4.0	9.0	31.8	3.97	6.15	2.2	2.8	20.9	0.8	205.6	23.2	12.8	24.6	30.5	3.2	109.8	203.7
	Principal Lines of Business: GrpA&H (51.8%), GrpLife (47.8%), OrdLife (0.3%), IndA&H (0.2%), GrpAnn (0.0%)													Principal States: CA (13.5%), TX (11.3%), PA (6.4%), NJ (5.2%), MI (4.9%)					
-469	35.6	16.6	0.8	3.3	15.0	5.78	5.80	17.0	2.8	6.4	0.1	7.7	13.4	53.7	67.4	54.0	1.3	215.1	...
-46	45.6	17.1	0.9	3.8	16.7	7.46	7.51	5.8	2.6	6.5	0.1	6.9	16.3	52.2	65.0	58.0	0.8	226.8	...
-10	52.4	16.1	0.9	4.3	15.6	5.87	5.72	11.0	2.4	7.3	0.1	6.8	22.0	50.4	64.4	60.5	...	202.1	...
1	45.5	15.6	0.1	0.2	0.8	2.66	2.00	33.7	2.9	7.1	0.1	6.6	8.3	51.3	65.3	66.8	...	200.2	...
-2,459	33.7	14.1	1.3	4.4	20.2	7.50	6.92	28.7	3.2	6.5	0.1	5.8	15.3	49.4	62.3	94.6	...	168.2	...
	Principal Lines of Business: IndAnn (81.3%), OrdLife (11.4%), GrpAnn (7.3%), IndA&H (0.0%), GrpLife (0.0%)													Principal States: CA (29.0%), TX (12.7%), FL (12.0%), NC (3.3%)					

2010 BEST'S KEY RATING GUIDE — LIFE/HEALTH EDITION
ANNUAL STATEMENT DATA FOR YEARS 2005 – 2009

Data in U.S. Dollars

COMPANY NAME Ultimate Parent Association Principal Officer Mailing Address Dom. : Began Bus. : Struct. : Mktg. Specialty Phone # AMB# NAIC#	Best's Financial Strength Rating FSC	Data Year	Balance Sheet: Bonds (%)	Mort. Loans & R.E. (%)	Com & Pref. Stock (%)	All Other Assets (%)	Total Assets ($000)	Life Reserves (%)	Health Reserves %)	Ann Res. & Dep. Liabilities (%)	All Other Liabilities (%)	Capital & Surplus ($000)	Operations: Direct Premiums Written ($000)	Net Premiums Written & Deposits ($000)	Operating Cash Flow ($000)	NOG Before Taxes ($000)	NOG After Taxes ($000)	Net Income ($000)
LIFE OF AMERICA INSURANCE CO	NR-4	'05	58.3	9.9	6.2	25.6	6,486	12.2	31.1	39.3	17.4	3,162	4,769	4,296	-701	-1,717	-1,717	-1,697
Marshall W. Mordecai President & Treasurer		'06	63.9	12.8	3.8	19.5	4,945	17.0	29.3	46.3	7.5	2,486	2,741	2,349	-1,542	-683	-683	-676
8200 Brookriver Drive, Suite 600 N Dallas, TX 75247-4069		'07	58.0	14.9	1.0	26.1	4,183	12.1	48.8	30.8	8.3	717	3,893	3,362	-727	-1,630	-1,630	-1,700
TX : 1965 : Stock : Agency		'08	58.2	15.6	0.0	26.2	3,898	15.1	39.9	38.3	6.7	1,032	5,397	5,168	71	390	390	313
A&H, Life 214-631-6310		'09	19.6	5.4	0.1	74.9	10,844	77.8	5.3	11.8	5.2	1,178	1,357	1,222	-605	101	101	88
AMB# 006574 NAIC# 81132		**Rating History: NR-4, 03/12/10; D, 03/12/10; D, 07/15/09; C u, 06/02/09; C, 03/28/08**																
LIFE OF THE SOUTH INSURANCE CO Summit Partners LP	B++	'05	49.2	18.2	17.5	15.0	60,391	51.8	31.2	2.8	14.1	24,336	76,993	36,286	4,807	3,847	3,376	3,428
Richard S. Kahlbaugh CEO		'06	47.1	17.4	15.8	19.7	57,749	53.3	30.3	2.7	13.6	20,827	89,342	39,190	-4,402	1,814	1,414	2,251
P.O. Box 44130 Jacksonville, FL 32231-4130	Rating Outlook: Stable	'07	46.3	...	13.9	39.8	68,105	53.0	34.7	2.3	10.0	23,802	108,969	55,761	8,639	2,170	1,449	1,362
GA : 1982 : Stock : Agency		'08	65.4	...	12.1	22.5	70,462	59.5	29.6	2.0	8.9	19,216	92,936	68,538	-939	7,742	5,679	5,679
Credit A&H, Credit Life, Ind A&H 904-350-9660		'09	60.2	...	12.5	27.3	62,970	58.1	34.6	...	7.3	17,865	60,744	49,473	-2,931	9,662	8,261	7,886
AMB# 008921 NAIC# 97691	FSC V	**Rating History: B++g, 03/23/10; B++g, 02/03/09; B++g, 12/20/07; B++g, 11/01/06; B+ g, 08/05/05**																
LIFE PROTECTION INS CO Wright Titus Agency	NR-5	'05	64.1	0.7	25.6	9.6	15,367	36.1	...	...	63.9	13,273	1,134	490	326	207	197	342
Gary A. Dobbie President		'06	62.5	...	28.0	9.6	18,177	31.1	...	...	68.9	15,521	1,883	496	2,042	138	120	2,330
4245 N. Central Expressway, Suite 500 Dallas, TX 75205		'07	57.4	...	27.5	15.1	18,114	41.4	...	...	58.6	15,843	2,018	522	-896	311	227	633
TX : 1955 : Stock : Not Available		'08	53.3	...	22.2	24.5	14,254	55.4	...	...	44.6	12,556	1,910	457	-2,712	243	231	257
Credit Life 972-559-2200		'09	46.3	...	33.3	20.4	12,570	39.4	...	...	60.6	10,976	1,781	446	-2,203	37	35	229
AMB# 006653 NAIC# 65560		**Rating History: NR-5, 04/21/10; NR-5, 04/24/09; NR-5, 04/07/08; NR-5, 04/30/07; NR-5, 04/27/06**																
LIFECARE ASSURANCE CO 21st Century Life and Health Company Inc	NR-5	'05	89.2	...	...	10.8	352,142	0.0	96.7	...	3.3	35,964	...	146,796	135,151	19,121	5,833	5,833
James M. Glickman President & CEO		'06	81.5	...	2.5	16.0	484,599	0.0	98.0	...	2.0	42,818	...	172,978	128,168	19,864	8,465	8,465
P.O. Box 4243 Woodland Hills, CA 91365-4243		'07	85.9	...	4.6	9.5	637,032	0.0	97.9	...	2.1	48,236	...	189,865	147,894	23,236	10,873	10,872
AZ : 1980 : Stock : Other Direct		'08	86.6	...	4.8	8.6	800,030	0.0	97.9	...	2.1	58,047	...	209,325	158,315	41,189	21,304	8,725
Ind A&H 818-867-2499		'09	91.7	...	...	8.3	997,020	0.0	98.4	...	1.6	55,244	...	221,170	191,316	38,437	19,876	16,163
AMB# 009200 NAIC# 91898		**Rating History: NR-5, 03/31/10; NR-5, 04/09/09; NR-5, 04/15/08; NR-5, 04/12/07; NR-5, 04/05/06**																
LIFESECURE INSURANCE COMPANY Blue Cross Blue Shield of Michigan	NR-2	'05	22.2	...	...	77.8	24,011	...	77.5	...	22.5	12,581	39,793	39,402	7,675	-6,038	-6,038	-5,599
E. Lisa Wendt President & CEO		'06	20.1	...	...	79.9	42,152	...	59.4	...	40.6	28,500	62,012	33,876	18,183	-7,704	-7,779	-8,003
10559 Citation Drive, Suite 300 Brighton, MI 48116		'07	65.1	...	...	34.9	31,714	...	60.5	...	39.5	26,590	37,843	25,510	-10,052	-7,165	-6,700	-6,512
MI : 1954 : Stock : Agency		'08	81.6	...	...	18.4	57,386	...	94.3	...	5.7	21,282	12,214	36,912	24,047	-6,570	-6,266	-6,266
LTC 810-220-7700		'09	59.0	...	...	41.0	96,145	...	95.3	...	4.7	9,749	11,853	13,771	2,619	-11,953	-11,953	-11,953
AMB# 060645 NAIC# 77720		**Rating History: NR-2, 10/16/09; NR-2, 09/03/08; NR-2, 08/03/07; NR-3, 06/12/07**																
LIFESHIELD NATIONAL INS CO HCC Holdings LLC	B++	'05	75.7	...	5.0	19.2	58,768	39.4	1.0	55.3	4.4	21,866	140	3,769	20,106	1,521	1,186	1,177
Gary R. Peterson President		'06	77.7	...	8.5	13.8	60,881	46.6	0.8	48.9	3.7	22,210	104	9,048	1,453	760	411	417
P.O. Box 18223 Oklahoma City, OK 73154-0223	Rating Outlook: Negative	'07	71.0	...	12.0	17.0	63,324	45.5	0.7	43.8	10.0	25,345	101	4,740	2,441	3,967	3,161	3,161
OK : 1982 : Stock : Direct Response		'08	72.9	...	8.2	18.9	67,109	38.1	17.4	33.2	11.3	22,038	79	9,931	3,512	-2,088	-2,123	-2,140
A&H, Life, Ann 405-236-2640		'09	62.5	...	7.6	29.9	60,537	37.3	18.6	32.9	11.2	14,978	182	14,568	-3,505	-502	-710	-4,779
AMB# 009458 NAIC# 99724	FSC V	**Rating History: B++, 04/30/10; B++, 03/13/09; B++, 12/20/07; B++, 12/11/06; B++, 11/07/05**																
LIFEWISE ASSURANCE COMPANY Premera	A-	'05	87.1	...	...	12.9	57,248	21.4	35.5	...	43.1	30,575	35,190	31,756	685	3,894	2,489	2,489
Richard L. Grover President		'06	86.6	...	...	13.4	62,831	20.8	33.3	...	46.0	34,382	38,597	34,442	5,475	5,672	3,625	3,622
7001 220th Street S.W. Mountlake Terrace, WA 98043-2124	Rating Outlook: Stable	'07	87.8	...	...	12.2	67,073	24.0	36.1	...	39.9	39,395	43,597	39,196	6,150	8,799	5,657	5,551
WA : 1981 : Stock : Broker		'08	88.5	...	...	11.5	70,387	25.5	43.4	...	31.1	41,225	51,356	47,061	3,900	6,209	3,372	1,509
Dis inc, Group A&H, Group Life 425-918-4575		'09	86.2	...	...	13.8	76,427	26.8	44.4	...	28.8	45,418	56,118	51,574	4,469	7,054	4,672	4,412
AMB# 009086 NAIC# 94188	FSC XI	**Rating History: A- g, 06/15/09; A- g, 06/06/08; A- g, 05/23/07; B++g, 06/21/06; B++g, 06/20/05**																
LIFEWISE HEALTH PLAN OF AZ Premera	B+	'05	77.1	...	...	22.9	31,342	...	63.9	...	36.1	21,021	16,230	16,108	21,650	-9,325	-6,739	-6,628
Majd F. El-Azma President		'06	87.6	...	...	12.4	27,519	...	60.2	...	39.8	10,843	44,122	43,772	-5,986	-15,580	-10,819	-11,005
P.O. Box 327 Seattle, WA 98111-0327	Rating Outlook: Stable	'07	91.2	...	...	8.8	37,649	...	72.7	...	27.3	18,759	66,401	65,761	9,558	-22,456	-14,483	-14,426
WA : 1992 : Stock : Broker		'08	79.5	...	...	20.5	22,227	...	57.7	...	42.3	9,434	52,037	51,682	-17,073	-13,573	-8,301	-8,558
Health 480-425-2300		'09	6.0	...	...	94.0	9,123	...	55.1	...	44.9	5,651	19,769	19,724	-10,156	-6,548	-3,000	-2,858
AMB# 068458 NAIC# 65105	FSC IV	**Rating History: B+, 06/15/09; B+, 06/06/08; B+, 05/23/07; B+, 06/21/06; NR-3, 06/20/05**																
LIFEWISE HEALTH PLAN OF OREGON Premera	A-	'05	90.2	...	0.1	9.7	131,878	...	55.6	...	44.4	62,789	371,603	369,925	-22,708	19,268	13,473	11,870
Majd F. El-Azma President		'06	94.6	...	...	5.4	133,947	...	48.9	...	51.1	74,923	327,273	325,286	2,859	19,015	12,397	12,018
7001 220th Street S.W. Mountlake Terrace, WA 98043-2124	Rating Outlook: Stable	'07	91.2	...	...	8.8	126,816	...	48.0	...	52.0	69,922	322,135	320,820	-5,125	-7,319	-4,956	-5,274
OR : 1987 : Stock : Broker		'08	89.2	...	...	10.8	101,451	...	45.9	...	54.1	58,819	264,985	264,121	-30,024	-11,105	-6,664	-9,953
Group A&H, Ind A&H, Med supp 503-295-6707		'09	88.9	...	...	11.1	97,417	...	36.3	...	63.7	58,464	217,667	217,339	5,050	-188	596	767
AMB# 068259 NAIC# 84930	FSC VII	**Rating History: A- g, 06/15/09; A- g, 06/06/08; A- g, 05/23/07; B++g, 06/21/06; B++g, 06/20/05**																

BEST'S PROFITABILITY, LEVERAGE AND LIQUIDITY TESTS 2005 – 2009

Data in U.S. Dollars

	Profitability Tests							Leverage Tests						Liquidity Tests					
Un-Realized Capital Gains ($000)	Benefits Paid to NPW & Dep (%)	Comm. & Expenses to NPW & Dep (%)	NOG to Total Assets (%)	NOG to Total Rev (%)	Operating Return on Equity (%)	Net Yield (%)	Total Return (%)	Change in NPW & Dep (%)	NPW & Dep to Capital (X)	Capital & Surplus to Liabilities (%)	Surplus Relief (%)	Reins Leverage (%)	Change in Capital (%)	Quick Liquidity (%)	Current Liquidity (%)	Non-Invest Grade Bonds to Capital (%)	Delinq. & Foreclosed Mortgages to Capital (%)	Mort. & Credit Tenant Loans & R.E. to Capital (%)	Affiliated Invest to Capital (%)
-67	73.5	80.5	-25.5	-35.1	-50.5	5.55	5.00	149.3	1.3	96.9	...	4.0	-13.1	114.6	122.8	27.4	...	20.1	...
62	86.2	67.9	-12.0	-24.4	-24.2	5.81	7.24	-45.3	0.9	107.5	...	6.1	-19.8	110.2	117.6	30.1	...	24.7	...
-31	112.9	50.0	-35.7	-43.5	-99.9	6.11	3.95	43.1	4.4	22.3	0.1	61.1	-70.2	75.6	78.9	39.6	...	81.5	...
...	58.7	33.8	9.7	7.7	44.6	5.52	3.75	53.7	4.9	37.6	...	26.0	39.4	97.6	101.3	17.5	...	57.2	...
7	44.4	64.6	1.4	7.2	9.1	4.48	4.47	-76.4	1.0	12.6	...	616.0	13.7	23.2	24.1	24.3	...	48.7	...
	Principal Lines of Business: GrpA&H (64.3%), IndA&H (33.3%), OrdLife (2.0%), GrpLife (0.4%)													Principal States: MS (46.6%), TX (36.8%), GA (4.5%), IN (3.7%)					
-940	23.8	75.4	5.7	5.3	14.2	7.13	5.50	13.0	1.4	70.0	95.2	230.0	5.4	103.5	100.1	...	...	43.9	22.0
1,061	23.4	75.1	2.4	2.0	6.3	3.87	7.36	8.0	1.8	58.8	133.5	319.0	-14.6	96.2	97.6	...	1.4	47.0	31.7
1,243	18.6	67.7	2.3	1.6	6.5	3.73	5.73	42.3	2.3	55.0	127.0	321.7	13.0	148.8	158.3	...	...	...	34.0
-874	22.5	60.6	8.2	6.2	26.4	4.39	3.02	22.9	3.5	37.8	106.3	381.2	-20.0	92.8	102.3	0.0	...	...	40.5
-1,547	30.9	72.4	12.4	12.6	44.6	11.28	8.16	-27.8	2.7	40.1	53.9	324.5	-6.8	114.9	124.5	...	...	...	34.8
	Principal Lines of Business: CrdLife (40.2%), IndA&H (38.7%), CrdA&H (21.1%), OrdLife (0.0%)													Principal States: GA (68.1%), NC (14.9%), TN (10.1%), SC (6.0%), AL (4.1%)					
53	38.4	104.9	1.3	17.0	1.5	3.52	4.86	20.5	0.0	877.7	1.2	32.4	-0.2	778.4	873.8	...	...	0.8	0.8
468	42.5	136.3	0.7	9.9	0.8	3.71	20.97	1.1	0.0	801.5	0.8	18.7	17.1	737.9	824.9	...	...	...	...
131	28.2	114.5	1.3	17.5	1.4	3.76	6.79	5.3	0.0	999.9	0.7	14.6	2.0	973.9	999.9	...	...	...	...
-1,241	48.6	117.0	1.4	20.8	1.6	3.49	-3.89	-12.4	0.0	999.9	0.9	15.9	-21.2	999.9	999.9	...	...	...	...
659	64.9	185.3	0.3	3.8	0.3	2.86	9.52	-2.5	0.0	999.9	0.9	16.3	-11.4	967.4	999.9	...	...	...	...
	Principal Lines of Business: CrdLife (100.0%)													Principal States: TX (100.0%)					
...	9.6	49.6	2.0	2.9	17.7	5.81	5.84	19.7	4.0	11.7	...	...	19.8	59.0	71.0	5.7	...	...	...
...	12.5	42.0	2.0	3.5	21.5	5.67	5.68	17.8	3.9	10.0	...	...	19.5	68.2	78.8	6.5	...	...	...
...	12.6	39.8	1.9	4.1	23.9	5.86	5.88	9.8	3.8	8.5	...	...	13.4	62.1	74.2	10.0	...	...	...
...	15.5	37.7	3.0	7.1	40.1	5.99	4.20	10.2	3.6	7.8	...	36.1	16.3	58.2	72.8	10.9	...	...	...
-404	17.5	34.5	2.2	6.1	35.1	6.10	5.64	5.7	4.0	5.9	...	13.1	-4.8	61.2	74.6	51.2	...	...	...
	Principal Lines of Business: IndA&H (100.0%), OrdLife (0.0%)																		
...	108.4	7.3	-31.0	-15.3	-54.4	0.94	3.43	506.3	3.1	110.1	...	...	30.7	314.5	329.1	...	...	...	...
-6,126	134.2	29.1	-23.5	-21.5	-37.9	6.85	-11.64	-14.0	1.2	208.8	3.4	999.9	126.6	479.2	493.1	...	...	...	...
...	97.6	37.7	-18.1	-24.4	-24.3	5.21	5.72	-24.7	1.0	520.0	3.0	999.9	-6.7	669.0	681.4	...	...	...	...
...	7.5	25.4	-14.1	-16.4	-26.2	3.51	3.52	44.7	1.7	59.1	3.0	999.9	-19.9	131.9	142.8	...	...	...	...
...	46.9	119.6	-15.6	-21.7	-77.0	6.62	6.78	-62.7	1.4	11.4	5.0	999.9	-53.9	10.2	39.3	...	...	...	...
	Principal Lines of Business: IndA&H (88.4%), IndAnn (7.6%), GrpA&H (3.5%), OrdLife (0.5%), GrpAnn (0.0%)													Principal States: TX (38.2%), CA (8.2%), FL (6.6%), LA (3.8%), AL (3.7%)					
13	108.0	110.6	2.4	4.1	5.6	4.64	4.65	-6.7	0.2	60.3	0.1	5.2	6.1	128.4	136.0	0.1	...	...	4.6
51	58.1	83.8	0.7	2.6	1.9	6.86	6.96	140.0	0.4	58.9	0.0	5.7	2.1	108.4	118.6	...	...	...	4.7
235	124.8	80.8	5.1	29.2	13.3	6.17	6.57	-47.6	0.2	69.5	0.0	6.7	15.1	121.9	133.0	...	...	...	4.5
-1,046	89.2	46.5	-3.3	-14.9	-9.0	3.86	2.11	109.5	0.4	49.7	0.0	7.9	-14.2	103.9	113.1	6.2	...	...	4.0
-921	61.1	54.8	-1.1	-4.1	-3.8	0.32	-8.08	46.7	0.9	34.6	0.0	10.9	-30.1	101.6	105.7	69.7	...	...	7.2
	Principal Lines of Business: IndA&H (68.7%), OrdLife (14.1%), GrpA&H (11.9%), GrpLife (4.1%), IndAnn (1.2%)													Principal States: TX (85.6%), OK (12.6%)					
...	56.0	33.9	4.2	7.3	8.1	4.41	4.49	-0.6	1.0	116.0	...	35.3	-1.5	171.7	192.5	1.6	...	...	...
...	54.7	34.9	6.0	9.8	11.2	4.39	4.44	8.5	1.0	122.4	...	28.9	12.5	179.6	200.2	1.9	...	...	...
...	52.0	32.4	8.7	13.4	15.3	5.18	5.03	13.8	1.0	143.5	...	22.9	14.3	206.0	228.0	1.4	...	...	...
...	60.7	31.2	4.9	6.7	8.4	5.34	2.60	20.1	1.1	141.4	...	23.4	4.3	203.1	219.9	5.0	...	...	...
...	61.8	30.4	6.4	8.4	10.8	5.05	4.78	9.6	1.1	149.7	...	22.7	11.1	202.7	220.3	10.7	...	...	...
	Principal Lines of Business: GrpA&H (62.1%), GrpLife (37.8%), OrdLife (0.1%)													Principal States: WA (75.9%), AK (16.5%), OR (4.1%)					
...	91.9	63.1	-30.1	-41.6	-53.3	3.59	4.17	610.7	0.8	203.7	...	...	391.5	300.2	310.2	...	...	...	...
-3	94.8	39.4	-36.8	-24.0	-67.9	4.71	4.02	171.7	4.0	65.0	...	1.1	-48.4	122.2	132.8	...	...	...	...
9	103.8	33.2	-44.4	-21.7	-97.8	4.72	4.95	50.2	3.5	99.3	...	0.8	73.0	127.4	146.8	...	...	...	...
-6	92.6	38.3	-27.7	-15.6	-58.9	5.32	4.28	-21.4	5.5	73.7	...	6.5	-49.7	98.3	110.7	...	...	...	...
...	107.0	46.0	-19.1	-13.9	-39.8	2.32	3.59	-61.8	3.5	162.8	...	6.0	-40.1	257.4	257.4	...	...	...	...
	Principal Lines of Business: CompHosp/Med (100.0%)													Principal States: AZ (100.0%)					
66	81.0	15.3	9.0	3.6	21.8	4.47	3.35	-4.5	5.9	90.9	...	1.2	3.6	145.1	162.5	...	...	...	0.2
-33	78.2	18.0	9.3	3.7	18.0	5.40	5.07	-12.1	4.3	126.9	...	1.2	19.3	170.1	194.0	1.5	...	...	0.1
-1	88.1	16.1	-3.8	-1.5	-6.8	5.71	5.45	-1.4	4.6	122.9	...	0.6	-6.7	173.5	192.5	2.2	...	...	0.2
-556	88.0	18.7	-5.8	-2.4	-10.4	5.61	2.07	-17.7	4.5	138.0	...	1.6	-15.9	166.8	186.5	4.0	...	...	0.2
-816	82.5	20.0	0.6	0.3	1.0	5.49	4.81	-17.7	3.7	150.1	...	0.1	-0.6	197.8	218.9	5.0	...	...	...
	Principal Lines of Business: CompHosp/Med (97.2%), MedSup (2.8%)													Principal States: OR (100.0%)					

Data in U.S. Dollars

COMPANY NAME Ultimate Parent Association Principal Officer Mailing Address Dom. : Began Bus. : Struct. : Mktg. Specialty Phone # AMB# NAIC#	Best's Financial Strength Rating FSC	Data Year	Balance Sheet: Bonds (%)	Mort. Loans & R.E. (%)	Com & Pref. Stock (%)	All Other Assets (%)	Total Assets ($000)	Life Reserves (%)	Health Reserves %)	Ann Res. & Dep. Liabilities (%)	All Other Liabilities (%)	Capital & Surplus ($000)	Operations: Direct Premiums Written ($000)	Net Premiums Written & Deposits ($000)	Operating Cash Flow ($000)	NOG Before Taxes ($000)	NOG After Taxes ($000)	Net Income ($000)
LIFEWISE HEALTH PLAN OF WA Premera Jeffrey E. Roe President P.O. Box 327 Seattle, WA 98111-0327 WA : 2001 : Non-Profit : Broker Health 425-918-4000 AMB# 064608 NAIC# 52633	**B++** Rating Outlook: Stable **FSC VI**	'05	93.1	...	...	6.9	55,850	...	61.8	...	38.2	14,836	156,686	156,686	2,502	2,514	1,911	1,122
		'06	93.0	...	...	7.0	76,608	...	52.1	...	47.9	31,120	180,253	180,253	20,549	10,000	6,565	6,186
		'07	94.3	...	...	5.7	70,423	...	60.0	...	40.0	31,403	179,356	179,356	-6,771	2,150	1,270	1,149
		'08	89.8	...	...	10.2	82,651	...	47.6	...	52.4	37,283	206,893	206,893	14,491	13,632	9,208	5,692
		'09	88.7	...	...	11.3	97,258	...	47.2	...	52.8	46,867	210,235	210,235	11,861	14,862	6,557	7,079
		Rating History: B++, 06/15/09; B++, 06/06/08; B++, 05/23/07; B+, 06/21/06; B+, 06/20/05																
LINCOLN BENEFIT LIFE CO Allstate Corporation John C. Pintozzi Senior V.P. and CFO 2940 South 84th Street Lincoln, NE 68506-4142 NE : 1938 : Stock : Agency Life, Ann 800-525-9287 AMB# 006657 NAIC# 65595	**A+** Rating Outlook: Negative **FSC XV**	'05	8.7	...	0.0	91.3	3,075,173	...	...	...	100.0	267,501	3,663,097	109,523	24,039	13,629	8,800	8,800
		'06	7.8	...	0.0	92.2	3,448,631	...	...	...	100.0	274,412	3,530,360	81,043	-4,243	13,910	9,065	9,065
		'07	7.7	...	0.1	92.3	3,442,530	...	...	...	100.0	282,931	2,650,301	50,401	30,160	13,905	9,087	9,087
		'08	10.4	...	0.1	89.5	2,184,805	...	...	...	100.0	278,816	2,856,367	37,234	16,189	14,090	9,000	7,800
		'09	12.4	...	0.0	87.6	2,418,532	...	...	...	100.0	305,997	2,445,247	31,246	4,120	12,473	8,525	8,525
		Rating History: A+ r, 11/20/09; A+ r, 10/23/08; A+ r, 01/09/08; A+ r, 02/06/07; A+ r, 11/07/05																
LINCOLN HERITAGE LIFE INS CO Thomas A. Londen President 4343 East Camelback Road Phoenix, AZ 85018 IL : 1963 : Stock : Agency Ind Life, Pre-need, Trad Life 602-957-1650 AMB# 006694 NAIC# 65927	**A-** Rating Outlook: Stable **FSC VIII**	'05	77.0	6.1	0.9	16.0	514,320	89.3	0.6	7.0	3.1	79,419	172,793	142,398	24,847	12,516	8,172	9,739
		'06	76.1	6.0	1.4	16.4	549,256	89.8	0.6	6.6	3.0	89,338	191,527	155,941	36,873	13,613	8,673	10,386
		'07	76.0	5.8	2.2	16.0	587,072	90.6	0.6	6.3	2.5	88,947	217,184	182,319	37,495	6,746	4,016	4,188
		'08	75.6	5.6	1.2	17.6	621,699	91.2	0.6	6.3	1.9	86,064	239,354	201,604	36,045	8,983	6,589	2,325
		'09	69.9	5.2	1.0	23.8	697,715	91.8	0.5	6.0	1.7	109,752	271,708	219,990	43,161	17,195	10,870	166
		Rating History: A-, 04/19/10; A-, 05/13/09; A-, 04/02/08; A-, 03/15/07; A-, 04/14/06																
LINCOLN LIFE & ANNUITY CO NY Lincoln National Corporation Dennis R. Glass President & CEO 100 North Greene Street Greensboro, NC 27401 NY : 1897 : Stock : Broker Ind Life 603-226-5000 AMB# 006239 NAIC# 62057	**A+** Rating Outlook: Negative **FSC XV**	'05	64.3	5.3	0.2	30.1	5,011,283	30.8	0.4	41.5	27.3	354,498	678,208	782,857	-10,696	2,060	-12,530	-13,457
		'06	58.2	4.5	0.1	37.2	5,599,345	30.9	0.5	35.4	33.3	298,739	829,803	909,419	49,116	-55,007	-46,985	-47,969
		'07	63.9	2.9	0.1	33.1	9,000,554	46.5	0.4	24.7	28.4	832,793	922,025	1,197,494	117,730	-146,796	-162,040	-187,823
		'08	67.1	3.5	1.2	28.2	8,440,912	50.9	0.5	26.7	21.9	795,171	841,304	1,271,552	6,119	28,903	12,780	-95,022
		'09	65.8	2.4	0.1	31.7	9,375,138	46.9	0.6	26.0	26.5	818,994	801,930	1,171,296	358,405	101,115	107,387	13,175
		Rating History: A+ g, 10/21/09; A+ g, 02/20/09; A+ g, 10/05/07; A+ g, 03/28/07; A+ g, 04/03/06																
LINCOLN MEMORIAL LIFE INS CO Randall J. Singer President P.O. Box 160050 Austin, TX 78716-0050 TX : 1938 : Stock : Not Available In Liquidation 512-328-0075 AMB# 007162 NAIC# 69833	**F**	'05	...	...	...	...	...	...	...	...	...	...	...	...	...	...	...	...
		'06	...	...	...	...	...	...	...	...	...	...	...	...	...	...	...	...
		'07	...	...	...	...	...	...	...	...	...	...	...	...	...	...	...	...
		'08	...	...	...	...	...	...	...	...	...	...	...	...	...	...	...	...
		'09	...	...	...	...	...	...	...	...	...	...	...	...	...	...	...	...
		Rating History: F, 09/26/08; E, 04/25/08; NR-1, 06/08/07; NR-1, 06/07/06; NR-1, 06/07/05																
LINCOLN MUTUAL LIFE & CASUALTY' Noridian Mutual Insurance Company Lawrence J. Zich President P.O. Box 1918 Fargo, ND 58107-1918 ND : 1935 : Mutual : Agency 701-282-1807 AMB# 006662 NAIC# 65641	**NR-1**	'05	82.8	...	9.2	8.0	32,270	...	...	7.8	92.2	9,647	9,777	5,604	...	455	354	496
		'06	76.6	...	10.7	12.7	32,225	...	...	7.8	92.2	10,026	10,757	6,056	...	203	215	404
		'07	81.0	...	12.0	7.0	31,825	...	...	8.0	92.0	10,589	11,741	6,312	...	547	493	681
		'08	77.3	...	9.3	13.4	31,978	...	...	7.8	92.2	10,757	12,438	6,606	...	803	659	533
		'09	80.1	...	13.1	6.8	32,712	...	...	7.9	92.1	11,273	11,648	6,633	...	498	396	268
		Rating History: NR-1, 06/10/10; NR-1, 06/12/09; NR-1, 06/12/08; NR-1, 06/08/07; NR-1, 06/07/06																
LINCOLN NATIONAL LIFE INS CO Lincoln National Corporation Dennis R. Glass President 1300 South Clinton Street Fort Wayne, IN 46802-3518 IN : 1905 : Stock : Agency Ann, Life 260-455-2000 AMB# 006664 NAIC# 65676	**A+** Rating Outlook: Negative **FSC XV**	'05	40.2	5.9	1.0	52.8	124,659,530	21.3	1.1	25.4	52.2	5,202,010	15,924,080	16,896,004	1,369,285	1,131,236	872,936	876,428
		'06	36.6	5.1	1.0	57.3	137,232,525	20.5	1.0	21.8	56.8	4,879,762	18,608,714	19,187,528	-322,166	631,426	367,324	403,518
		'07	32.8	4.8	1.1	61.2	144,609,572	18.4	1.0	20.2	60.4	4,957,875	21,438,629	21,130,899	-120,620	1,250,662	895,906	1,204,808
		'08	37.8	6.0	2.4	53.8	119,849,817	23.0	1.2	25.4	50.4	4,585,435	20,088,116	20,735,695	1,113,845	305,051	505,212	-144,793
		'09	36.2	4.7	1.2	58.0	143,345,609	19.5	1.0	22.7	56.8	6,245,064	18,552,140	19,058,533	4,183,926	992,554	684,902	-116,195
		Rating History: A+ g, 10/21/09; A+ g, 02/20/09; A+ g, 10/05/07; A+ g, 03/28/07; A+ g, 04/03/06																
LOCAL INITIATIVE HLTH AUTH LA Howard A. Kahn President & CEO 555 West Fifth Street, 18th Floor Los Angeles, CA 90013 CA : 1997 : Non-Profit : Not Available Medicaid 213-694-1250 AMB# 064652	**NR-5**	'05	...	...	...	100.0	221,359	...	...	...	100.0	120,282	920,998	920,998	13,291	14,102	14,102	14,102
		'06	...	...	...	100.0	314,838	...	...	...	100.0	133,940	983,046	983,046	42,005	13,658	13,658	13,658
		'07	...	...	...	100.0	241,729	...	...	...	100.0	120,702	998,793	998,793	-238	-13,238	-13,238	-13,238
		'08	...	...	...	100.0	307,089	...	...	...	100.0	117,327	1,030,304	1,030,304	-104,798	-3,375	-3,375	-3,375
		'09	...	...	...	100.0	378,277	...	...	...	100.0	125,211	1,112,702	1,112,702	218,481	27,845	7,884	7,884
		Rating History: NR-5, 03/23/10; NR-5, 04/08/09; NR-5, 03/11/08; NR-5, 04/03/07; NR-5, 04/20/06																
LOCOMOTIVE ENGINEERS&CONDUCTOR' Susan Tukel President 4000 Town Center, Suite 1250 Southfield, MI 48075-1407 MI : 1910 : Mutual : Not Available 800-514-0010 AMB# 068235 NAIC# 87920	**NR-1**	'05	54.2	...	26.9	18.9	17,397	...	...	...	100.0	8,893	15,347	15,347	...	-744	-744	-767
		'06	61.9	...	25.2	12.9	18,188	...	...	...	100.0	8,142	17,170	17,170	...	-988	-988	-988
		'07	69.0	...	20.9	10.2	17,170	...	...	...	100.0	5,763	19,106	19,106	...	-2,287	-2,287	-2,287
		'08	59.0	...	11.2	29.8	21,321	...	...	...	100.0	10,571	21,783	21,783	...	5,957	5,957	5,957
		'09	50.9	...	9.0	40.0	28,402	...	...	...	100.0	20,844	19,332	19,332	...	10,160	10,160	10,046
		Rating History: NR-1, 06/10/10; NR-1, 06/12/09; NR-1, 06/12/08; NR-1, 06/08/07; NR-1, 06/07/06																

BEST'S PROFITABILITY, LEVERAGE AND LIQUIDITY TESTS 2005 – 2009

Data in U.S. Dollars

—	Profitability Tests							Leverage Tests						Liquidity Tests					
Un-Realized Capital Gains ($000)	Benefits Paid to NPW & Dep (%)	Comm. & Expenses to NPW & Dep (%)	NOG to Total Assets (%)	NOG to Total Rev (%)	Operating Return on Equity (%)	Net Yield (%)	Total Return (%)	Change in NPW & Dep (%)	NPW & Dep to Capital (X)	Capital & Surplus to Liabilities (%)	Surplus Relief (%)	Reins Leverage (%)	Change in Capital (%)	Quick Liquidity (%)	Current Liquidity (%)	Non-Invest Grade Bonds to Capital (%)	Delinq. & Foreclosed Mortgages to Capital (%)	Mort. & Credit Tenant Loans & R.E. to Capital (%)	Affiliated Invest to Capital (%)
...	76.7	22.3	3.3	1.2	12.8	4.06	2.57	32.3	10.6	36.2	...	...	-0.8	114.3	124.6	1.7	...	...	...
-10	73.5	21.4	9.9	3.6	28.6	4.72	4.11	15.0	5.8	68.4	...	...	109.8	137.7	151.7	1.6	...	...	...
-2	81.3	19.5	1.7	0.7	4.1	5.65	5.48	-0.5	5.7	80.5	...	...	0.9	136.7	150.8	1.5	...	...	...
-537	76.2	19.0	12.0	4.4	26.8	6.27	0.96	15.4	5.5	82.2	...	...	18.7	162.8	174.4	5.1	...	...	...
-193	76.6	18.9	7.3	3.1	15.6	5.06	5.44	1.6	4.5	93.0	...	...	25.7	156.2	170.4	4.7	...	...	...
Principal Lines of Business: CompHosp/Med (100.0%)													Principal States: WA (100.0%)						
...	...	...	0.3	2.1	3.4	0.70	0.70	1.2	0.4	302.7	149.0	999.9	4.7	200.5	219.2	...	...	...	...
...	...	...	0.3	2.2	3.3	6.57	6.56	-26.0	0.3	361.7	147.9	999.9	2.6	230.1	249.9	...	...	...	...
...	...	...	0.3	2.6	3.3	6.25	6.22	-37.8	0.2	309.2	118.8	999.9	3.1	225.3	247.6	...	...	...	...
...	...	0.0	0.3	2.4	3.2	5.49	5.17	-26.1	0.1	340.9	130.4	999.9	-1.4	363.5	390.4	...	...	...	0.8
...	...	...	0.4	3.1	2.9	4.37	4.72	-16.1	0.1	426.4	84.7	999.9	9.8	304.9	344.1	...	...	...	0.7
Principal Lines of Business: IndAnn (100.0%), OrdLife (0.0%)													Principal States: CA (14.1%), FL (8.3%), TX (7.1%), PA (5.3%), IL (4.6%)						
-247	51.7	39.7	1.6	4.4	10.8	5.06	5.37	26.6	1.7	19.2	19.9	87.8	9.4	66.8	76.8	11.0	...	38.1	4.3
177	49.2	46.0	1.6	4.4	10.3	5.61	5.99	9.5	1.7	20.5	14.8	75.4	12.7	67.1	77.6	9.3	...	35.5	3.8
432	44.4	47.5	0.7	1.8	4.5	5.45	5.57	16.9	1.9	18.9	15.6	73.3	0.1	65.7	76.3	16.8	...	36.3	...
-725	43.7	44.8	1.1	2.6	7.5	5.30	4.40	10.6	2.3	16.4	21.3	73.6	-6.1	63.2	73.7	25.1	...	39.7	...
-149	43.6	40.7	1.6	3.8	11.1	5.31	3.48	9.1	2.0	18.9	29.3	59.4	26.4	63.5	72.9	28.4	...	32.9	...
Principal Lines of Business: OrdLife (81.5%), GrpLife (10.0%), IndA&H (5.7%), GrpAnn (1.3%), IndAnn (1.2%)													Principal States: CA (14.5%), MI (7.4%), TX (6.9%), IL (5.5%), FL (5.5%)						
-57	62.8	14.1	-0.3	-1.3	-3.4	5.93	5.94	14.6	2.1	10.8	1.0	56.4	-3.9	56.8	73.6	29.7	...	72.8	...
479	59.1	15.4	-0.9	-4.3	-14.4	5.86	5.86	16.2	2.8	9.1	0.6	83.5	-13.3	56.5	73.0	31.5	...	79.3	1.9
-538	61.0	28.6	-2.2	-11.3	-28.6	7.17	6.66	31.7	1.4	14.6	0.4	87.0	166.2	58.6	76.5	25.1	...	33.8	...
-10,304	59.1	13.0	0.1	0.9	1.6	6.12	4.34	6.2	1.6	13.5	0.2	95.7	-6.0	55.6	72.5	27.7	...	40.2	...
-16,668	58.1	12.9	1.2	7.9	13.3	6.17	4.51	-7.9	1.4	13.1	0.2	94.4	2.4	54.8	71.3	63.5	...	31.0	...
Principal Lines of Business: GrpAnn (36.2%), IndAnn (31.1%), OrdLife (28.9%), GrpA&H (2.6%), GrpLife (1.2%)													Principal States: NY (86.2%)						
...	...	...	...	...	...	...	...	...	...	...	...	...	...	...	...	...	...	...	...
...	...	...	...	...	...	...	...	...	...	...	...	...	...	...	...	...	...	...	...
...	...	...	...	...	...	...	...	...	...	...	...	...	...	...	...	...	...	...	...
...	...	...	...	...	...	...	...	...	...	...	...	...	...	...	...	...	...	...	...
...	...	...	...	...	...	...	...	...	...	...	...	...	...	...	...	...	...	...	...
-139	63.8	59.2	1.1	4.7	3.7	...	...	0.5	0.5	46.5	2.7	...	3.4	...	...	...	...	...	...
95	71.8	62.4	0.7	2.7	2.2	...	...	8.1	0.6	50.2	3.1	...	5.1	...	...	...	...	...	...
-95	68.4	54.4	1.5	6.1	4.8	...	...	4.2	0.6	55.5	3.1	...	5.5	...	...	...	...	...	...
-853	49.8	59.3	2.1	7.5	6.2	...	...	4.7	0.6	51.2	3.9	...	-4.6	...	...	...	...	...	...
752	58.9	56.3	1.2	4.5	3.6	...	...	0.4	0.6	58.2	4.7	...	11.0	...	...	...	...	...	...
Principal Lines of Business: GrpLife (73.7%), GrpA&H (20.3%), OrdLife (5.6%), IndA&H (0.3%), IndAnn (0.1%)																			
-28,215	72.6	14.1	0.7	4.2	17.3	6.01	5.98	4.4	2.9	9.6	6.2	203.6	7.3	47.6	64.0	63.5	...	130.7	21.9
89,497	77.7	13.2	0.3	1.6	7.3	5.83	6.02	13.6	3.4	9.2	6.4	230.4	-3.2	46.3	62.9	61.4	0.0	128.1	23.0
-306,865	78.6	13.6	0.6	3.5	18.2	5.89	5.90	10.1	3.7	9.9	8.3	239.0	2.2	44.2	61.1	52.8	...	124.1	27.4
-309,310	72.9	13.3	0.4	2.1	10.6	5.75	4.19	-1.9	4.3	8.2	8.7	298.7	-14.8	46.7	62.5	60.2	...	149.3	28.1
100,875	68.0	13.1	0.5	3.2	12.6	5.41	4.32	-8.1	2.9	10.1	7.9	243.9	32.8	47.8	63.4	61.9	...	105.0	33.8
Principal Lines of Business: IndAnn (53.9%), GrpAnn (27.4%), OrdLife (10.6%), GrpA&H (5.4%), GrpLife (2.7%)													Principal States: CA (10.5%), FL (7.4%), TX (6.9%), PA (5.3%), OH (4.8%)						
...	97.4	4.2	6.8	1.5	12.5	2.13	2.13	-0.3	7.7	119.0	...	...	13.3	179.1	179.1	...	...	...	...
...	97.6	3.9	5.1	1.4	10.7	4.89	4.89	6.7	7.3	74.0	...	...	11.4	122.8	122.8	...	...	...	...
...	100.8	4.3	-4.8	-1.3	-10.4	5.40	5.40	1.6	8.3	99.7	...	...	-9.9	183.2	183.2	...	...	...	...
...	98.0	4.6	-1.2	-0.3	-2.8	3.13	3.13	3.2	8.8	61.8	...	...	-2.8	52.2	52.2	...	...	...	...
...	98.5	4.3	2.3	0.7	6.5	3.02	3.02	8.0	8.9	49.5	...	...	6.7	137.6	137.6	...	...	...	...
Principal Lines of Business: Medicaid (100.0%), CompHosp/Med (0.0%)																			
-123	73.6	36.7	-4.3	-4.6	-7.9	...	...	19.0	1.7	109.9	...	...	-10.2	...	...	...	...	...	...
248	78.9	32.1	-5.6	-5.5	-11.6	...	...	11.9	2.0	85.6	...	...	-7.9	...	...	...	...	...	...
-333	91.8	24.7	-12.9	-11.4	-32.9	...	...	11.3	3.3	51.1	...	...	-30.8	...	...	...	...	...	...
-828	51.0	25.1	31.0	26.4	72.9	...	...	14.0	2.1	98.3	...	...	81.9	...	...	...	...	...	...
475	32.5	19.0	40.9	50.5	64.7	...	...	-11.3	0.9	285.1	...	...	98.9	...	...	...	...	...	...
Principal Lines of Business: OrdLife (100.0%)																			

Data in U.S. Dollars

COMPANY NAME Ultimate Parent Association Principal Officer Mailing Address Dom. : Began Bus. : Struct. : Mktg. Specialty Phone # AMB# NAIC#	Best's Financial Strength Rating FSC	Data Year	Balance Sheet Bonds (%)	Mort. Loans & R.E. (%)	Com & Pref. Stock (%)	All Other Assets (%)	Total Assets ($000)	Life Reserves (%)	Health Reserves (%)	Ann Res. & Dep. Liabilities (%)	All Other Liabilities (%)	Capital & Surplus ($000)	Operations Direct Premiums Written ($000)	Net Premiums Written & Deposits ($000)	Operating Cash Flow ($000)	NOG Before Taxes ($000)	NOG After Taxes ($000)	Net Income ($000)
LONDON LIFE & CAS (BB) CORP Power Corporation of Canada Gabriel R. Kelly President & CEO Fourth Floor, Cedar Court St. Michael, Barbados BB : Stock : Broker Reins Finite, Reins 246-436-1200 AMB# 077342	**A** Rating Outlook: Stable **FSC IX**	'05	37.5	...	...	62.5	658,876	20.4	...	...	79.6	263,256	...	453,923	248,128	30,005	29,702	29,607
		'06	31.1	...	...	68.9	779,319	31.5	...	...	68.5	322,828	...	1,061,518	152,138	67,308	66,239	65,875
		'07	60.1	...	...	39.9	489,471	54.3	...	...	45.7	420,305	...	257,023	-387,380	108,378	107,178	106,270
		'08	43.9	...	...	56.1	672,643	87.3	...	...	12.7	478,706	...	546,624	218,486	82,648	81,830	82,648
		'09	54.2	...	...	45.8	662,293	80.9	...	...	19.1	492,670	...	210,600	-36,212	27,635	27,635	22,871
		Rating History: A, 01/22/09; A, 06/22/07; A u, 02/01/07; A, 06/19/06; A, 03/09/05																
LONDON LIFE & CAS REINS CORP Power Corporation of Canada Philip S. Young President Fourth Floor, Cedar Court Wildey, St. Michael, Barbados BB : 1989 : Stock : Direct Response Reins Property, Reins Casualty, Life 246-436-5347 AMB# 086037	**A** Rating Outlook: Stable **FSC X**	'05	26.1	...	...	73.9	2,025,097	75.4	...	...	24.6	326,027	...	546,109	-52,606	72,400	71,522	72,121
		'06	27.2	...	...	72.8	1,629,793	67.3	...	...	32.7	370,309	...	1,100,291	-337,144	80,465	79,397	79,120
		'07	36.8	...	...	63.2	1,269,643	87.5	...	...	12.5	431,488	...	308,813	-371,212	133,916	128,464	128,051
		'08	37.0	...	...	63.0	1,234,815	87.2	...	...	12.9	477,069	...	571,173	103,924	95,741	84,285	85,922
		'09	48.7	...	...	51.4	1,093,022	77.9	...	...	22.1	613,693	...	325,905	-210,600	218,223	185,823	181,059
		Rating History: A, 01/22/09; A, 06/22/07; A u, 02/01/07; A, 04/26/06; A, 01/07/05																
LONDON LIFE INTERNAT REINS CP Power Corporation of Canada David W. Allan Director Life of Barbados Building, Wildey St. Michael, Barbados BB : Stock : Not Available Life, Non-Life 246-435-3106 AMB# 086458	**NR-3**	'05	10.1	...	...	90.0	1,123,918	...	...	...	100.0	7,908	...	2,612,970	494,298	-3,215	-2,024	-2,212
		'06	9.9	...	...	90.1	1,125,823	...	...	...	100.0	6,365	...	1,794,351	5,247	-2,174	-1,344	-1,541
		'07	10.5	...	...	89.5	1,092,589	95.3	...	...	4.7	6,643	...	4,260,768	-35,836	-797	-141	-1,219
		'08	20.0	...	...	80.1	564,038	89.0	...	...	11.0	12,159	...	2,857,280	-524,884	10,100	7,347	1,551
		'09	24.5	...	...	75.5	572,949	88.7	...	...	11.3	14,346	...	3,020,083	8,123	-1,456	-2,640	2,159
		Rating History: NR-3, 01/22/09; NR-3, 06/22/07; NR-3, 02/01/07; NR-3, 06/19/06; NR-3, 03/09/05																
LONDON LIFE REINSURANCE CO Power Corporation of Canada Monica M. Hainer President & CEO P.O. Box 1120 Blue Bell, PA 19422-0319 PA : 1969 : Stock : Other Direct Reins 215-542-7200 AMB# 060237 NAIC# 76694	**A** Rating Outlook: Stable **FSC VII**	'05	28.2	...	...	71.8	1,496,120	2.9	5.9	14.2	77.1	69,618	16,156	42,328	-22,954	4,565	2,782	2,869
		'06	23.0	...	...	77.0	1,558,651	5.1	5.4	11.8	77.8	71,380	11,690	30,893	-21,984	2,121	1,650	1,676
		'07	22.0	...	...	78.0	1,502,478	5.6	4.7	10.4	79.3	75,030	14,766	20,206	-20,263	4,625	3,497	3,507
		'08	41.0	...	...	59.0	713,239	11.7	8.6	20.1	59.6	70,409	17,283	37,752	-37,060	8,411	3,715	3,385
		'09	39.2	...	...	60.8	704,488	12.1	9.2	19.4	59.4	73,996	16,062	51,054	-32,783	4,759	6,939	6,768
		Rating History: A, 01/22/09; A, 06/22/07; A u, 02/01/07; A, 06/19/06; A, 03/09/05																
LONGEVITY INSURANCE COMPANY[1] Morgan Stanley Caitlin F. Long President & Managing Director 1585 Broadway New York, NY 10036 TX : 1965 : Stock : Not Available 800-223-2440 AMB# 060701 NAIC# 68446	**NR-1**	'05	...	...	...	...	...	...	...	...	...	...	...	...	...	...	...	...
		'06	...	...	...	...	...	...	...	...	...	...	...	...	...	...	...	...
		'07	...	...	...	...	...	...	...	...	...	...	...	...	...	...	...	...
		'08	40.1	...	...	59.9	7,594	...	...	...	100.0	7,594	726	-32	...	42	86	86
		'09	36.2	...	...	63.8	8,253	...	...	...	100.0	8,222	679	...	...	-901	-586	-586
		Rating History: NR-1, 06/10/10; NR-5, 05/22/09																
LOUISIANA HLTH SVC & INDEMNITY[2] Louisiana Health Service & Indemnity Co Gery J. Barry President & CEO 5525 Reitz Avenue Baton Rouge, LA 70809 LA : 1975 : Mutual : Not Available Group A&H, FEHBP, Med supp 504-295-3307 AMB# 068440 NAIC# 81200	**NR-5**	'05	48.9	3.6	28.9	18.6	753,350	...	42.8	...	57.2	434,921	1,339,198	1,334,469	77,623	111,666	87,994	92,868
		'06	48.2	3.2	31.8	16.7	869,282	...	48.7	...	51.3	523,994	1,471,540	1,466,599	73,857	64,571	54,040	55,009
		'07	43.1	5.7	30.4	20.8	945,280	...	49.4	...	50.6	597,609	1,625,378	1,619,879	41,385	54,664	44,942	53,014
		'08	45.0	7.3	31.1	16.7	983,719	...	46.5	...	53.5	592,383	1,749,140	1,741,424	81,291	71,896	67,728	43,297
		'09	37.3	6.3	36.2	20.2	1,115,285	...	42.9	...	57.1	697,528	1,804,722	1,798,164	38,958	55,885	57,110	52,742
		Rating History: NR-5, 04/23/10; NR-5, 08/26/09; B++pd, 09/08/08; B++pd, 08/27/07; B+ pd, 09/25/06																
LOYAL AMERICAN LIFE INS CO American Financial Group, Inc Billy B. Hill, Jr. President P.O. Box 26580 Austin, TX 78755 OH : 1955 : Stock : Agency Dread dis, Ind Life, Univ Life 800-633-6752 AMB# 006671 NAIC# 65722	**A-** Rating Outlook: Stable **FSC VII**	'05	85.8	...	3.1	11.0	447,833	6.5	8.8	54.0	30.8	43,362	50,457	38,714	-49,487	8,830	4,148	4,291
		'06	80.4	...	4.4	15.2	434,856	6.7	9.4	51.8	32.2	45,354	42,943	32,938	-12,853	6,208	4,908	4,898
		'07	82.6	...	4.3	13.1	438,980	6.4	9.9	51.2	32.5	41,795	106,891	59,924	3,906	5,493	4,962	4,904
		'08	81.1	...	3.0	15.9	483,899	5.5	7.9	58.4	28.1	37,698	131,379	110,485	46,422	2,379	2,044	-4,721
		'09	82.0	...	3.5	14.6	465,849	5.6	6.0	57.5	30.9	33,330	88,386	53,515	-27,801	3,889	3,188	961
		Rating History: A-, 05/10/10; A g, 03/27/09; A g, 12/17/07; A g, 11/28/06; A g, 06/17/05																
M LIFE INSURANCE COMPANY[2] Fred H. Jonske President & CEO 1125 NW Couch Street, Suite 900 Portland, OR 97209 CO : 1981 : Stock : Not Available Ordinary Life, Ind A&H 503-232-6960 AMB# 009096 NAIC# 93580	**NR-5**	'05	49.8	...	8.8	41.5	193,249	38.7	0.0	...	61.3	98,339	...	369,481	22,169	-22,112	-22,112	-21,810
		'06	47.0	...	10.1	42.9	196,751	49.2	0.0	...	50.8	115,925	...	348,302	2,633	38,839	22,595	22,595
		'07	32.2	...	10.0	57.8	222,542	38.2	0.0	...	61.7	98,072	...	426,806	-27,977	20,034	11,705	11,326
		'08	34.5	...	5.6	59.8	229,022	32.6	0.0	...	67.4	87,164	...	387,766	31,276	204,498	125,986	122,744
		'09	60.0	...	...	40.0	121,683	112.5	0.1	...	-12.6	77,232	...	340,569	-6,252	36,088	20,812	19,161
		Rating History: NR-5, 05/04/10; NR-5, 05/11/09; NR-5, 06/30/08; NR-5, 06/28/07; NR-5, 06/16/06																
M-PLAN INC[2] Clarian Health Partners, Inc. Alex P. Slabosky President 8802 N. Meridian St., Ste. 100 Indianapolis, IN 46260 IN : 1989 : Stock : Broker Group A&H, Health 317-571-5300 AMB# 060142 NAIC# 95444	**NR-5**	'05	2.5	...	0.3	97.2	59,513	...	10.1	...	89.9	38,160	610,193	610,193	13,134	13,198	7,556	7,556
		'06	8.9	...	0.3	90.8	65,377	...	11.5	...	88.5	47,527	605,429	605,429	14,262	12,855	7,982	7,982
		'07	6.8	...	0.3	92.9	86,426	...	8.6	...	91.4	63,149	603,673	603,673	17,272	25,543	20,140	20,140
		'08	21.0	...	1.0	78.0	16,401	...	...	...	100.0	11,272	25,787	25,787	-50,696	-20,151	-17,053	-17,053
		'09	27.1	...	...	72.9	6,249	...	...	...	100.0	5,682	...	...	-5,732	-1,950	-127	-127
		Rating History: NR-5, 04/26/10; NR-5, 08/26/09; B pd, 05/23/08; B- pd, 05/30/07; C++pd, 06/13/06																

BEST'S PROFITABILITY, LEVERAGE AND LIQUIDITY TESTS 2005 – 2009

Data in U.S. Dollars

—	Profitability Tests							Leverage Tests						Liquidity Tests					
Un-Realized Capital Gains ($000)	Benefits Paid to NPW & Dep (%)	Comm. & Expenses to NPW & Dep (%)	NOG to Total Assets (%)	NOG to Total Rev (%)	Operating Return on Equity (%)	Net Yield (%)	Total Return (%)	Change in NPW & Dep (%)	NPW & Dep to Capital (X)	Capital & Surplus to Liabilities (%)	Surplus Relief (%)	Reins Leverage (%)	Change in Capital (%)	Quick Liquidity (%)	Current Liquidity (%)	Non-Invest Grade Bonds to Capital (%)	Delinq. & Foreclosed Mortgages to Capital (%)	Mort. & Credit Tenant Loans & R.E. to Capital (%)	Affiliated Invest to Capital (%)
...	73.1	22.1	6.2	6.4	12.6	2.61	2.58	999.9	172.4	66.5	...	...	26.9	95.4	62.4	...	...	...	...
...	38.1	56.9	9.2	6.2	22.6	3.16	3.08	133.9	328.8	70.7	...	...	22.6	121.6	53.2	...	...	...	...
-452	60.9	52.7	16.9	26.8	28.8	5.55	5.36	-75.8	61.2	607.7	...	...	30.2	586.5	425.3	...	...	...	...
-15,548	38.9	49.9	14.1	14.4	18.2	5.20	5.40	112.7	114.2	246.8	...	...	13.9	212.7	152.3	1.9	...	...	...
9,529	87.3	6.8	4.1	12.5	5.7	3.63	2.49	-61.5	42.8	290.5	...	...	2.9	252.3	211.8	2.7	...	...	...
...	103.0	9.2	3.6	10.4	23.1	17.19	17.27	183.1	167.5	19.2	...	...	10.8	43.0	31.1	...	...	...	...
...	49.4	52.2	4.3	6.6	22.8	12.89	12.86	101.5	297.1	29.4	...	...	13.6	62.7	35.2	...	...	...	...
-680	85.4	45.3	8.9	23.9	32.0	10.25	10.19	-71.9	71.6	51.5	...	...	16.5	76.4	55.7	...	...	...	...
-17,184	37.5	55.4	6.7	13.4	18.6	8.96	9.22	85.0	119.7	63.0	...	...	10.6	81.9	60.4	2.6	...	...	...
17,153	36.3	7.3	16.0	52.3	34.1	5.18	4.42	-42.9	53.1	128.0	...	...	28.6	131.4	110.9	2.8	...	...	...
...	51.1	49.7	-0.2	-0.1	-22.5	15.39	15.23	39.3	999.9	0.7	...	...	-21.9	10.8	10.2	...	...	...	...
...	87.3	15.6	-0.1	-0.1	-18.8	39.78	39.62	-31.3	999.9	0.6	...	...	-19.5	11.6	10.0	...	...	...	...
21	51.6	49.6	-0.0	...	-2.2	37.68	36.87	137.5	999.9	0.6	...	...	4.4	12.7	10.6	...	...	...	...
-34	73.2	27.8	0.9	0.3	78.2	27.37	23.29	-32.9	999.9	2.2	...	...	83.0	26.6	20.4	...	...	...	...
39	87.7	13.2	-0.5	-0.1	-19.9	15.50	18.60	5.7	999.9	2.6	...	...	18.0	29.1	25.2	10.3	...	...	...
...	144.1	31.9	0.2	0.8	4.0	4.78	4.89	-23.3	0.6	5.0	353.6	999.9	2.6	20.8	26.0	14.2	...	...	...
...	193.4	219.4	0.1	0.3	2.3	5.07	5.12	-27.0	0.4	4.9	698.8	999.9	2.0	22.3	27.0	3.9	...	...	...
...	219.2	281.8	0.2	1.2	4.8	4.57	4.70	-34.6	0.3	5.4	258.7	999.9	5.0	23.7	28.1	5.6	...	...	...
...	119.3	127.0	0.3	0.8	5.1	4.60	4.69	86.8	0.5	11.2	559.9	999.9	-6.2	47.6	57.1	4.3	...	...	...
-280	109.5	66.0	1.0	-2.0	9.6	4.01	4.05	35.2	0.7	12.1	-99.9	999.9	5.8	38.8	48.2	14.7	...	6.2	...
	Principal Lines of Business: GrpA&H (89.4%), OrdLife (9.8%), IndAnn (0.4%), CrdA&H (0.2%), CrdLife (0.1%)													Principal States: TN (42.6%), MS (26.9%), WI (7.7%), GA (5.1%), CO (4.3%)					
...	...	...	...	...	...	...	...	...	...	...	...	...	...	...	...	...	...	...	...
...	...	...	...	...	...	...	...	...	...	...	...	...	...	...	...	...	...	...	...
...	...	...	...	...	...	...	...	...	...	...	...	...	...	...	...	...	...	...	...
...	-99.9	-99.9	...	40.7	...	...	...	...	0.0	...	0.1	...	...	...	...	...	...	...	...
...	...	...	-7.4	-99.9	-7.4	...	...	100.0	...	999.9	0.1	...	8.3	...	...	...	...	...	...
26,690	80.5	14.8	12.8	6.4	23.1	3.64	9.10	10.2	3.1	136.6	...	0.7	33.7	116.2	129.0	0.4	...	6.3	36.6
33,141	84.7	14.5	6.7	3.6	11.3	3.97	8.96	9.9	2.8	151.8	...	0.8	20.5	125.6	141.1	0.4	...	5.4	34.2
15,230	86.1	14.1	5.0	2.7	8.0	3.96	6.97	10.5	2.7	171.9	...	1.1	14.0	150.0	167.2	0.4	...	9.1	37.9
-22,189	85.2	14.0	7.0	3.8	11.4	3.60	-1.89	7.5	2.9	151.4	...	0.9	-0.9	123.6	138.9	1.1	...	12.1	42.8
73,018	85.8	15.1	5.4	3.1	8.9	3.57	11.32	3.3	2.6	167.0	...	0.9	17.7	134.3	148.7	0.7	...	10.1	41.7
	Principal Lines of Business: CompHosp/Med (76.0%), FEHBP (17.7%), MedSup (5.3%), OtherHlth (1.0%)													Principal States: LA (100.0%)					
222	110.3	46.6	0.9	6.0	6.0	5.74	5.78	-20.4	0.8	11.5	10.0	347.0	-52.2	69.7	78.8	50.9	...	...	29.6
826	145.1	66.5	1.1	8.1	11.1	5.56	5.77	-14.9	0.7	12.6	4.0	327.1	5.5	76.0	84.8	52.8	...	...	29.4
-529	85.7	42.9	1.1	5.4	11.4	5.76	5.64	81.9	1.3	11.3	12.3	433.4	-8.2	75.1	84.1	43.4	...	...	32.9
1,381	49.2	19.7	0.4	1.5	5.1	6.04	4.86	84.4	2.8	8.8	18.1	521.8	-12.8	82.6	90.9	39.4	...	...	35.4
665	103.4	54.1	0.7	3.7	9.0	5.40	5.11	-51.6	1.6	7.9	22.6	665.7	-12.3	78.4	86.9	36.4	...	...	39.0
	Principal Lines of Business: IndA&H (90.9%), OrdLife (4.8%), IndAnn (3.6%), GrpLife (0.3%), GrpA&H (0.3%)													Principal States: TX (17.7%), AL (5.8%), IN (5.3%), NC (5.1%), SC (4.4%)					
242	32.4	30.8	-11.7	-3.2	-24.3	3.83	4.18	-3.4	3.7	109.9	22.1	-28.0	17.5	103.1	109.0	...	...	...	16.7
1,370	45.7	24.6	11.6	2.9	21.1	5.12	5.99	-5.7	2.9	153.8	17.3	-8.7	17.8	123.7	129.5	...	...	...	16.6
-26	48.0	25.7	5.6	1.4	10.9	6.22	5.68	22.5	4.2	83.6	26.0	-4.0	-15.0	52.6	56.8	0.8	...	...	21.9
-10,370	39.0	-19.5	55.8	36.5	136.0	5.32	-6.98	-9.1	4.4	61.4	251.7	36.8	-14.0	80.0	84.1	1.8	...	...	14.8
4,466	43.8	23.6	11.9	2.8	25.3	2.62	5.01	-12.2	4.4	173.7	47.7	-55.7	-11.4	297.5	308.8	4.7	...	...	...
	Principal Lines of Business: OrdLife (99.1%), IndA&H (0.9%)																		
...	90.7	8.5	13.8	1.2	23.5	3.66	3.66	-4.7	16.0	178.7	...	...	45.3	144.0	144.0	...	...	...	0.4
...	91.2	7.8	12.8	1.3	18.6	5.01	5.01	-0.8	12.7	266.3	...	...	24.5	234.0	236.5	...	...	...	0.3
...	91.9	7.8	26.5	3.2	36.4	5.07	5.07	-0.3	9.6	271.3	...	...	32.9	254.5	256.4	...	...	...	0.3
...	105.4	82.8	-33.2	-60.1	-45.8	4.04	4.04	-95.7	2.3	219.8	...	...	-82.1	172.2	176.9	...	...	...	1.5
...	...	...	-1.1	-99.9	-1.5	0.20	0.20	-99.9	...	999.9	...	...	-49.6	589.4	619.2	...	...	29.8	...

COMPANY NAME / Ultimate Parent Association / Principal Officer / Mailing Address / Dom. : Began Bus. : Struct. : Mktg. / Specialty / Phone # / AMB# / NAIC#

Best's Financial Strength Rating / FSC

Balance Sheet: Data Year; Bonds (%); Mort. Loans & R.E. (%); Com & Pref. Stock (%); All Other Assets (%); Total Assets ($000); Life Reserves (%); Health Reserves (%); Ann Res. & Dep. Liabilities (%); All Other Liabilities (%); Capital & Surplus ($000)

Operations: Direct Premiums Written ($000); Net Premiums Written & Deposits ($000); Operating Cash Flow ($000); NOG Before Taxes ($000); NOG After Taxes ($000); Net Income ($000)

MADISON NATL LIFE INS CO INC
Geneve Holdings, Inc.
Larry R. Graber
President
P.O. Box 5008
Madison, WI 53705-0008
WI : 1962 : Stock : Mng Gen Agent
Group A&H, Group Life, Life
608-830-2000
AMB# 006678 NAIC# 65781

A-
Rating Outlook: Negative
FSC VIII

Data Year	Bonds (%)	Mort. Loans & R.E. (%)	Com & Pref. Stock (%)	All Other Assets (%)	Total Assets ($000)	Life Reserves (%)	Health Reserves (%)	Ann Res. & Dep. Liabilities (%)	All Other Liabilities (%)	Capital & Surplus ($000)	Direct Premiums Written ($000)	Net Premiums Written & Deposits ($000)	Operating Cash Flow ($000)	NOG Before Taxes ($000)	NOG After Taxes ($000)	Net Income ($000)
'05	63.0	...	22.4	14.5	759,365	58.6	8.4	28.9	4.2	129,324	119,837	98,089	145,489	-5,413	-4,403	-4,179
'06	62.3	...	24.1	13.6	755,051	59.1	8.3	28.1	4.5	126,414	149,786	115,580	24,816	7,469	6,622	7,806
'07	55.0	...	29.0	16.0	757,894	57.5	8.5	27.0	7.1	136,569	225,829	135,036	6,492	9,944	6,823	7,357
'08	61.6	...	24.7	13.7	799,124	58.0	7.9	30.1	4.0	138,243	205,844	130,513	21,991	13,899	13,808	-4,824
'09	60.3	...	23.5	16.1	784,366	45.6	9.1	31.0	14.3	169,301	191,456	121,303	-33,370	20,453	19,081	21,423

Rating History: A- g, 12/18/09; A- g, 01/29/09; A- g, 11/19/07; A-, 09/05/07; A-, 06/09/06

MAGELLAN BEHAVIORAL HLTH OF IA
Russell Petrella
President
2600 Westown Parkway, Suite 200
West Des Moines, IA 50266
IA : 1995 : Stock : Not Available
Medicaid
515-223-0306
AMB# 064675

NR-5

Data Year	Bonds (%)	Mort. Loans & R.E. (%)	Com & Pref. Stock (%)	All Other Assets (%)	Total Assets ($000)	Life Reserves (%)	Health Reserves (%)	Ann Res. & Dep. Liabilities (%)	All Other Liabilities (%)	Capital & Surplus ($000)	Direct Premiums Written ($000)	Net Premiums Written & Deposits ($000)	Operating Cash Flow ($000)	NOG Before Taxes ($000)	NOG After Taxes ($000)	Net Income ($000)
'05	13.5	...	...	86.5	78,835	...	18.9	...	81.1	20,768	119,011	119,011	20,473	2,929	1,904	1,904
'06	...	...	...	...	...	...	...	...	...	...	...	...	...	...	...	...
'07	...	...	...	100.0	59,287	...	26.3	...	73.7	17,221	123,784	123,784	1,509	3,403	2,212	2,212
'08	...	...	...	100.0	56,505	...	51.7	...	48.3	15,058	139,460	139,460	-2,536	2,517	1,636	1,636
'09	35.1	...	...	64.9	52,759	...	55.8	...	44.2	12,418	146,609	146,609	-4,268	2,093	1,361	1,361

Rating History: NR-5, 04/06/10; NR-5, 03/19/09; NR-5, 05/05/08; NR-5, 07/14/06; NR-5, 07/01/05

MAGELLAN BEHAVIORAL HLTH OF PA[2]
Russell C. Petrella
President
105 Terry Drive, Suite 103
Newtown, PA 18940
PA : 1997 : Stock : Broker
Medicaid
215-504-3907
AMB# 064552 NAIC# 47019

NR-5

Data Year	Bonds (%)	Mort. Loans & R.E. (%)	Com & Pref. Stock (%)	All Other Assets (%)	Total Assets ($000)	Life Reserves (%)	Health Reserves (%)	Ann Res. & Dep. Liabilities (%)	All Other Liabilities (%)	Capital & Surplus ($000)	Direct Premiums Written ($000)	Net Premiums Written & Deposits ($000)	Operating Cash Flow ($000)	NOG Before Taxes ($000)	NOG After Taxes ($000)	Net Income ($000)
'05	...	...	...	100.0	59,488	...	69.1	...	30.9	24,224	214,106	214,106	15,163	11,877	7,720	7,720
'06	...	...	...	100.0	61,505	...	78.1	...	21.9	25,985	247,070	247,070	-1,722	8,863	5,761	5,761
'07	...	...	...	100.0	63,659	...	74.5	...	25.5	26,725	262,674	262,674	4,133	5,754	3,740	3,740
'08	...	...	...	100.0	70,983	...	75.7	...	24.3	33,898	287,805	287,805	10,142	11,035	7,173	7,173
'09	...	...	...	100.0	70,383	...	79.9	...	20.1	34,897	315,037	315,037	-1,346	6,152	3,999	3,999

Rating History: NR-5, 04/06/10; NR-5, 04/02/09; NR-5, 04/22/08; NR-5, 06/13/06; NR-5, 06/09/05

MAGELLAN HEALTH SERVICES OF CA
Magellan Health Services Inc
Pamela Masters
President
300 Continental Blvd., Suite 240
El Segundo, CA 90245
CA : 1977 : Stock : Not Available
Group A&H
310-726-7005
AMB# 064650

NR-5

Data Year	Bonds (%)	Mort. Loans & R.E. (%)	Com & Pref. Stock (%)	All Other Assets (%)	Total Assets ($000)	Life Reserves (%)	Health Reserves (%)	Ann Res. & Dep. Liabilities (%)	All Other Liabilities (%)	Capital & Surplus ($000)	Direct Premiums Written ($000)	Net Premiums Written & Deposits ($000)	Operating Cash Flow ($000)	NOG Before Taxes ($000)	NOG After Taxes ($000)	Net Income ($000)
'05	...	...	...	100.0	3,636	...	...	...	100.0	2,437	6,395	6,395	-1,450	934	553	553
'06	...	...	...	100.0	2,337	...	...	...	100.0	1,490	6,476	6,476	-895	2,784	1,648	1,648
'07	...	...	...	100.0	2,079	...	...	...	100.0	846	6,740	6,740	-224	3,132	1,856	1,856
'08	...	...	...	100.0	1,727	...	...	...	100.0	754	5,923	5,923	-349	2,392	1,417	1,417
'09	...	...	...	100.0	1,899	...	...	...	100.0	915	5,590	5,590	161	2,190	1,297	1,297

Rating History: NR-5, 03/23/10; NR-5, 04/08/09; NR-5, 03/11/08; NR-5, 05/03/07; NR-5, 05/25/06

MAGNA INSURANCE COMPANY[1]
Clifton J. Saik
President
One Hancock Plaza, 2510 14th Street
Gulfport, MS 39501-1947
MS : 1962 : Stock : Not Available
Credit A&H, Credit Life, Group A&H
602-200-6900
AMB# 068127 NAIC# 61018

NR-1

Data Year	Bonds (%)	Mort. Loans & R.E. (%)	Com & Pref. Stock (%)	All Other Assets (%)	Total Assets ($000)	Life Reserves (%)	Health Reserves (%)	Ann Res. & Dep. Liabilities (%)	All Other Liabilities (%)	Capital & Surplus ($000)	Direct Premiums Written ($000)	Net Premiums Written & Deposits ($000)	Operating Cash Flow ($000)	NOG Before Taxes ($000)	NOG After Taxes ($000)	Net Income ($000)
'05	82.4	...	10.1	7.5	72,778	...	...	...	100.0	15,529	9,082	9,045	...	2,200	1,410	1,410
'06	88.0	...	1.1	10.9	71,400	...	...	...	100.0	15,448	7,861	7,653	...	535	379	466
'07	86.5	...	1.1	12.4	59,533	...	...	...	100.0	14,895	5,734	5,496	...	-916	-449	-429
'08	85.6	...	1.0	13.5	44,715	...	...	...	100.0	12,668	2,999	2,823	...	-73	-48	32
'09	89.5	...	0.4	10.1	27,266	...	...	...	100.0	12,427	2,149	2,238	...	500	306	465

Rating History: NR-1, 06/10/10; NR-1, 06/12/09; NR-1, 06/12/08; NR-5, 05/22/08; NR-4, 12/07/07

MAINE DENTAL SERVICE CORP[2]
Thomas Raffio
President & CEO
One Delta Drive
Concord, NH 03302-2002
ME : 1966 : Non-Profit : Broker
Dental
603-223-1000
AMB# 064639

NR-5

Data Year	Bonds (%)	Mort. Loans & R.E. (%)	Com & Pref. Stock (%)	All Other Assets (%)	Total Assets ($000)	Life Reserves (%)	Health Reserves (%)	Ann Res. & Dep. Liabilities (%)	All Other Liabilities (%)	Capital & Surplus ($000)	Direct Premiums Written ($000)	Net Premiums Written & Deposits ($000)	Operating Cash Flow ($000)	NOG Before Taxes ($000)	NOG After Taxes ($000)	Net Income ($000)
'05	51.3	...	21.2	27.4	22,696	...	36.6	...	63.4	18,164	50,640	49,963	3,930	3,800	3,800	3,693
'06	56.3	...	18.5	25.2	27,773	...	29.5	...	70.5	22,576	52,713	52,713	4,589	3,942	3,942	4,012
'07	52.2	...	23.4	24.5	32,073	...	25.2	...	74.8	26,787	50,913	50,913	3,483	3,870	3,870	3,885
'08	55.6	...	14.6	29.7	31,316	...	19.0	...	81.0	24,602	53,137	53,227	426	234	234	-788
'09	51.3	...	23.0	25.7	34,572	...	18.5	...	81.5	27,554	52,956	53,219	809	978	978	1,210

Rating History: NR-5, 06/15/10; NR-5, 12/01/09; B++pd, 09/24/08; B++pd, 09/18/07; B++pd, 10/03/06

MAJESTIC LIFE INS CO[1]
Cecilia H. Robert
President
1125 N. Claiborne Ave.
New Orleans, LA 70116
LA : 1947 : Stock : Not Available
504-827-0705
AMB# 007786 NAIC# 75159

NR-1

Data Year	Bonds (%)	Mort. Loans & R.E. (%)	Com & Pref. Stock (%)	All Other Assets (%)	Total Assets ($000)	Life Reserves (%)	Health Reserves (%)	Ann Res. & Dep. Liabilities (%)	All Other Liabilities (%)	Capital & Surplus ($000)	Direct Premiums Written ($000)	Net Premiums Written & Deposits ($000)	Operating Cash Flow ($000)	NOG Before Taxes ($000)	NOG After Taxes ($000)	Net Income ($000)
'05	...	...	...	...	...	...	...	...	...	...	...	...	...	...	...	...
'06	...	...	...	...	...	...	...	...	...	...	...	...	...	...	...	...
'07	...	...	...	...	...	...	...	...	...	...	...	...	...	...	...	...
'08	...	...	...	...	...	...	...	...	...	...	...	...	...	...	...	...
'09	14.4	2.2	65.7	17.6	4,863	...	...	...	100.0	1,226	679	679	...	-85	-85	-415

Rating History: NR-1, 06/10/10; NR-5, 06/02/05; NR-1, 06/02/04; NR-5, 06/03/03; NR-1, 06/06/02

MAMSI LIFE AND HEALTH INS
UnitedHealth Group Inc
James P. Cronin, Jr.
President & CEO
4 Taft Court
Rockville, MD 20850
MD : 1955 : Stock : Agency
Group Life, Group A&H
301-762-8208
AMB# 006046 NAIC# 60321

A
Rating Outlook: Stable
FSC VI

Data Year	Bonds (%)	Mort. Loans & R.E. (%)	Com & Pref. Stock (%)	All Other Assets (%)	Total Assets ($000)	Life Reserves (%)	Health Reserves (%)	Ann Res. & Dep. Liabilities (%)	All Other Liabilities (%)	Capital & Surplus ($000)	Direct Premiums Written ($000)	Net Premiums Written & Deposits ($000)	Operating Cash Flow ($000)	NOG Before Taxes ($000)	NOG After Taxes ($000)	Net Income ($000)
'05	39.9	...	...	60.1	170,899	1.3	50.8	...	48.0	87,919	605,970	605,970	-79,951	128,620	88,775	88,306
'06	40.9	...	...	59.1	174,186	0.8	60.7	...	38.5	97,097	516,092	516,092	51,887	80,405	54,455	54,359
'07	51.0	...	...	49.0	200,746	0.7	52.1	...	47.2	143,516	375,828	375,828	3,154	72,182	47,565	47,654
'08	54.2	...	...	45.8	194,919	1.0	55.8	...	43.1	168,191	236,009	236,009	27,587	54,461	36,592	35,580
'09	35.7	...	...	64.3	51,195	2.5	60.7	...	36.8	38,018	127,657	127,657	-138,709	31,807	21,034	21,311

Rating History: A, 06/15/09; A, 01/29/08; A, 11/21/07; A, 11/16/06; A, 08/17/06

MANAGED DENTAL CARE OF CA
Guardian Life Ins Co of America
Candee Bolyog
President
6200 Canoga Avenue, Suite 100
Woodland Hills, CA 91367
CA : 1991 : Stock : Broker
Dental
800-273-3330
AMB# 064657

NR-2

Data Year	Bonds (%)	Mort. Loans & R.E. (%)	Com & Pref. Stock (%)	All Other Assets (%)	Total Assets ($000)	Life Reserves (%)	Health Reserves (%)	Ann Res. & Dep. Liabilities (%)	All Other Liabilities (%)	Capital & Surplus ($000)	Direct Premiums Written ($000)	Net Premiums Written & Deposits ($000)	Operating Cash Flow ($000)	NOG Before Taxes ($000)	NOG After Taxes ($000)	Net Income ($000)
'05	...	...	...	100.0	4,269	...	...	...	100.0	1,248	14,825	14,825	197	445	281	281
'06	...	...	...	100.0	5,232	...	...	...	100.0	2,096	16,298	16,298	917	1,430	848	848
'07	...	...	...	100.0	5,391	...	...	...	100.0	3,125	18,092	18,092	-112	1,736	1,029	1,029
'08	...	...	...	100.0	5,882	...	...	...	100.0	3,614	19,458	19,458	1,948	1,755	1,043	1,043
'09	...	...	...	100.0	6,159	...	...	...	100.0	3,847	17,458	17,458	107	1,643	973	973

Rating History: NR-2, 10/13/09; NR-2, 11/26/08; NR-2, 04/23/08; NR-2, 11/10/06; NR-2, 11/18/05

BEST'S PROFITABILITY, LEVERAGE AND LIQUIDITY TESTS 2005 – 2009

Data in U.S. Dollars

—	Profitability Tests							Leverage Tests						Liquidity Tests					
Un-Realized Capital Gains ($000)	Benefits Paid to NPW & Dep (%)	Comm. & Expenses to NPW & Dep (%)	NOG to Total Assets (%)	NOG to Total Rev (%)	Operating Return on Equity (%)	Net Yield (%)	Total Return (%)	Change in NPW & Dep (%)	NPW & Dep to Capital (X)	Capital & Surplus to Liabilities (%)	Surplus Relief (%)	Reins Leverage (%)	Change in Capital (%)	Quick Liquidity (%)	Current Liquidity (%)	Non-Invest Grade Bonds to Capital (%)	Delinq. & Foreclosed Mortgages to Capital (%)	Mort. & Credit Tenant Loans & R.E. to Capital (%)	Affiliated Invest to Capital (%)
4,239	89.7	57.4	-0.6	-3.1	-3.3	4.57	5.27	26.2	0.7	21.7	10.3	57.6	-2.9	56.0	64.8	20.5	...	...	95.3
-14,063	87.8	36.9	0.9	4.1	5.2	4.13	2.42	17.8	0.9	21.5	12.1	59.5	-1.2	60.2	68.8	3.4	...	...	107.5
-6,604	89.5	33.7	0.9	3.6	5.2	4.64	3.88	16.8	0.9	23.1	16.5	78.3	6.3	65.5	75.0	3.8	...	...	109.0
-2,135	88.0	35.1	1.8	7.4	10.0	4.76	2.06	-3.3	0.9	20.9	16.6	75.9	-2.7	52.1	60.9	2.9	...	...	115.7
-5,781	94.1	29.2	2.4	10.0	12.4	4.45	4.03	-7.1	0.7	27.6	19.0	122.6	22.5	48.7	59.9	11.4	...	...	94.6
Principal Lines of Business: GrpA&H (66.7%), OrdLife (16.7%), GrpLife (8.3%), IndAnn (7.8%), IndA&H (0.4%)														Principal States: MI (14.1%), WI (13.9%), MN (7.6%), IN (6.8%), TX (6.7%)					
...	84.7	15.2	2.8	1.6	11.4	2.75	2.75	3.7	5.7	35.8	...	...	63.2	141.1	141.1	...	...	...	...
...	...	...	...	...	...	...	...	...	...	...	...	...	...	...	...	...	...	...	...
...	85.6	14.3	...	1.7	...	...	...	...	7.2	40.9	...	...	...	204.9	208.5	...	...	...	...
...	85.5	14.3	2.8	1.2	10.1	2.25	2.25	12.7	9.3	36.3	...	...	-12.6	226.5	235.2	...	...	...	...
...	85.5	14.2	2.5	0.9	9.9	1.19	1.19	5.1	11.8	30.8	...	...	-17.5	169.3	180.1	...	...	...	...
Principal Lines of Business: Medicaid (81.5%), OtherHlth (18.5%)														Principal States: IA (100.0%)					
...	85.3	9.4	14.4	3.6	33.8	1.61	1.61	14.4	8.8	68.7	...	...	12.6	105.9	105.9	...	...	...	...
...	87.1	10.0	9.5	2.3	22.9	4.39	4.39	15.4	9.5	73.2	...	...	7.3	100.3	100.3	...	...	...	...
...	89.6	8.9	6.0	1.4	14.2	4.69	4.69	6.3	9.8	72.4	...	...	2.8	188.2	190.9	...	...	...	...
...	88.0	8.5	10.7	2.5	23.7	2.68	2.68	9.6	8.5	91.4	...	...	26.8	195.9	202.7	...	...	...	...
...	89.8	8.3	5.7	1.3	11.6	0.64	0.64	9.5	9.0	98.3	...	...	2.9	223.5	233.1	...	...	...	...
Principal Lines of Business: Medicaid (100.0%)														Principal States: PA (100.0%)					
...	47.8	37.9	12.6	8.6	19.2	0.43	0.43	-38.7	2.6	203.2	...	...	-26.5	242.8	242.8	...	...	...	...
...	26.7	31.5	55.2	25.1	83.9	3.08	3.08	1.3	4.3	176.1	...	...	-38.8	238.2	238.2	...	...	...	...
...	27.6	26.1	84.0	27.5	158.8	0.53	0.53	4.1	8.0	68.6	...	...	-43.2	145.3	145.3	...	...	...	...
...	31.4	28.4	74.5	23.9	177.2	0.44	0.44	-12.1	7.9	77.4	...	...	-10.9	148.2	148.2	...	...	...	...
...	29.5	31.5	71.6	23.2	155.5	0.81	0.81	-5.6	6.1	93.0	...	...	21.4	163.0	163.0	...	...	...	...
Principal Lines of Business: CompHosp/Med (100.0%)																			
73	81.3	44.4	1.9	11.2	9.5	...	...	-83.7	0.6	27.4	-0.7	...	10.5	...	...	...	...	...	...
20	90.1	58.6	0.5	3.4	2.4	...	...	-15.4	0.5	28.1	0.6	...	0.1	...	...	...	...	...	...
-32	658.1	88.5	-0.7	-5.0	-3.0	...	...	-28.2	0.4	34.3	0.9	...	-3.0	...	...	...	...	...	...
-80	176.5	102.6	-0.1	-1.1	-0.3	...	...	-48.6	0.2	40.5	0.8	...	-15.2	...	...	...	...	...	...
-275	265.0	86.5	0.9	9.4	2.4	...	...	-20.7	0.2	85.1	-0.4	...	-2.8	...	...	...	...	...	...
Principal Lines of Business: CrdLife (38.1%), CrdA&H (36.0%), GrpLife (18.1%), IndAnn (3.7%), GrpA&H (2.2%)																			
20	78.6	15.0	18.4	7.5	23.3	3.60	3.15	6.9	2.8	400.7	...	...	25.3	392.0	417.4	...	...	...	...
397	79.1	14.9	15.6	7.4	19.4	3.69	5.68	5.5	2.3	434.5	...	...	24.3	422.7	447.5	0.4	...	...	...
370	79.0	15.3	12.9	7.5	15.7	3.64	5.02	-3.4	1.9	506.7	...	...	18.6	467.0	501.8	0.4	...	...	...
-1,456	82.8	18.7	0.7	0.4	0.9	3.47	-4.69	4.5	2.2	366.4	...	0.0	-8.2	366.4	395.6	0.6	...	...	...
1,720	84.1	15.4	3.0	1.8	3.8	2.41	8.97	0.0	1.9	392.6	...	...	12.0	367.6	406.8	...	...	...	5.0
Principal Lines of Business: Dental (100.0%)														Principal States: ME (100.0%)					
...	...	...	...	...	...	...	...	...	...	...	...	...	...	...	...	...	...	...	...
...	...	...	...	...	...	...	...	...	...	...	...	...	...	...	...	...	...	...	...
...	...	...	...	...	...	...	...	...	...	...	...	...	...	...	...	...	...	...	...
...	...	...	...	...	...	...	...	...	...	...	...	...	...	...	...	...	...	...	...
1,039	40.5	66.8	...	-9.9	...	...	...	...	0.4	59.6	...	...	...	...	...	...	...	5.9	...
Principal Lines of Business: OrdLife (66.0%), IndLife (34.0%)																			
...	71.6	9.1	43.8	13.9	86.2	4.54	4.24	-21.8	6.9	106.0	...	...	-25.5	163.9	176.3	...	...	...	...
...	76.8	9.7	31.6	9.8	58.9	4.97	4.89	-14.8	5.3	126.0	...	...	10.4	282.7	301.8	...	...	...	...
...	74.3	9.4	25.4	11.5	39.5	5.50	5.56	-27.2	2.6	250.8	...	...	47.8	336.8	364.7	...	...	...	...
-1	72.2	8.7	18.5	15.1	23.5	4.16	3.56	-37.2	1.4	629.3	...	...	17.2	884.3	945.8	0.5	...	...	...
1	68.8	8.4	17.1	16.1	20.4	2.53	2.77	-45.9	3.4	288.5	...	...	-77.4	493.7	524.0	...	...	...	...
Principal Lines of Business: CompHosp/Med (94.1%), Dental (5.0%), Life (0.7%), OtherHlth (0.2%)														Principal States: MD (54.2%), DC (21.0%), VA (19.1%), WV (4.5%)					
...	78.5	18.9	6.8	1.9	25.3	2.50	2.50	13.4	11.9	41.3	...	...	29.0	84.5	84.5	...	...	...	...
...	72.7	19.3	17.8	5.2	50.7	4.19	4.19	9.9	7.8	66.8	...	...	67.9	110.7	110.7	...	...	...	...
...	73.6	17.8	19.4	5.6	39.4	5.24	5.24	11.0	5.8	138.0	...	...	49.1	148.3	148.3	...	...	...	...
...	71.2	20.2	18.5	5.3	31.0	1.95	1.95	7.6	5.4	159.3	...	...	15.6	233.9	233.9	...	...	...	...
...	70.6	20.1	16.2	5.6	26.1	0.11	0.11	-10.3	4.5	166.4	...	...	6.5	234.1	234.1	...	...	...	...
Principal Lines of Business: Dental (100.0%)																			

Data in U.S. Dollars

COMPANY NAME / Ultimate Parent Association / Principal Officer / Mailing Address / Dom. : Began Bus. : Struct. : Mktg. / Specialty / Phone # / AMB# / NAIC#	Best's Financial Strength Rating / FSC	Data Year	Balance Sheet: Bonds (%)	Mort. Loans & R.E. (%)	Com & Pref. Stock (%)	All Other Assets (%)	Total Assets ($000)	Life Reserves (%)	Health Reserves (%)	Ann Res. & Dep. Liabilities (%)	All Other Liabilities (%)	Capital & Surplus ($000)	Operations: Direct Premiums Written ($000)	Net Premiums Written & Deposits ($000)	Operating Cash Flow ($000)	NOG Before Taxes ($000)	NOG After Taxes ($000)	Net Income ($000)
MANAGED DENTALGUARD INC Guardian Life Ins Co of America	NR-2	'05	16.1	...	...	83.9	342	...	1.4	...	98.6	269	1,430	1,430	14	36	22	22
John P. Foley, President		'06	14.6	...	...	85.4	377	...	2.4	...	97.6	299	1,638	1,638	43	46	31	31
21255 Burbank Boulevard, Suite 120, Woodland Hills, CA 91367		'07	13.1	...	...	86.9	418	...	3.9	...	96.1	308	1,646	1,646	88	13	9	9
NJ : 2001 : Stock : Broker, Dental		'08	12.5	...	...	87.5	440	...	1.9	...	98.1	338	1,793	1,793	-26	46	30	30
818-596-5815		'09	11.3	...	...	88.7	488	...	2.9	...	97.1	367	1,843	1,843	10	44	29	29
AMB# 064822 NAIC# 11199		**Rating History: NR-2, 10/13/09; NR-2, 11/26/08; NR-2, 04/23/08; NR-2, 11/10/06; NR-2, 11/18/05**																
MANAGED DENTALGUARD INC Guardian Life Ins Co of America	NR-2	'05	42.7	...	...	57.3	2,530	...	29.9	...	70.1	2,225	4,992	4,992	108	570	384	384
John P. Foley, President & CEO		'06	1.9	...	...	98.1	2,865	...	18.9	...	81.1	2,578	5,942	5,942	320	833	558	574
21255 Burbank Boulevard, Suite 120, Woodland Hills, CA 91367		'07	1.6	...	...	98.4	3,368	...	35.6	...	64.4	3,159	6,655	6,655	462	895	581	581
TX : 2000 : Stock : Broker, Dental		'08	1.6	...	...	98.4	3,466	...	24.9	...	75.1	3,061	7,229	7,229	80	748	486	486
818-596-5815		'09	1.7	...	...	98.3	3,326	...	40.2	...	59.8	2,909	7,280	7,280	-189	501	324	324
AMB# 064646 NAIC# 52556		**Rating History: NR-2, 10/13/09; NR-2, 11/26/08; NR-2, 04/23/08; NR-2, 11/10/06; NR-2, 11/18/05**																
MANAGED HEALTH INC[2] Healthfirst Inc	NR-5	'05	...	...	...	100.0	123,436	...	75.9	...	24.1	43,087	306,410	306,410	24,090	6,673	6,673	6,673
Paul Dickstein, CEO		'06	21.4	...	...	78.6	229,539	...	68.0	...	32.0	82,018	550,964	550,964	80,779	24,850	24,850	24,850
25 Broadway, New York, NY 10004		'07	26.6	...	...	73.4	227,366	...	74.0	...	26.0	109,687	742,165	741,080	-26,468	20,499	20,499	20,513
NY : 1990 : Non-Profit : Broker, Medicare, Group A&H		'08	16.6	...	...	83.4	286,579	...	71.6	...	28.4	116,806	1,038,756	1,037,428	36,369	-4,134	-4,134	-5,680
212-801-6000		'09	15.8	...	...	84.2	373,727	-12.3	90.3	...	22.0	132,722	1,217,146	1,215,595	104,594	7,164	7,164	7,281
AMB# 064346 NAIC# 95284		**Rating History: NR-5, 04/29/10; NR-5, 08/26/09; C++pd, 06/06/08; C++pd, 06/12/07; C++pd, 07/10/06**																
MANAGED HEALTH NETWORK Health Net Inc	NR-2	'05	...	...	...	100.0	41,445	...	...	...	100.0	19,506	125,093	125,093	4,939	26,122	15,557	15,557
Gerald V. Coil, President & CEO		'06	...	...	...	100.0	40,643	...	...	...	100.0	11,427	131,149	131,149	-1,064	16,486	9,857	9,857
1600 Los Gamos Drive, Suite 300, San Rafael, CA 94903		'07	...	...	...	100.0	36,372	...	...	...	100.0	17,051	134,676	134,676	-4,306	18,979	11,317	11,317
CA : 1983 : Stock : Not Available, Health		'08	...	...	...	100.0	34,328	...	...	...	100.0	15,287	113,842	113,842	2,881	-8,109	-4,809	-4,809
415-491-7200		'09	...	...	...	100.0	11,578	...	...	...	100.0	6,937	37,155	37,155	-15,682	1,085	642	642
AMB# 064673		**Rating History: NR-2, 07/21/09; NR-2, 11/14/08; NR-2, 05/14/08; NR-2, 05/04/07; NR-2, 05/03/06**																
MANAGED HEALTH SERVICES INS CP Centene Corporation	B+	'05	40.2	...	...	59.8	67,815	...	64.1	...	35.9	38,196	242,713	230,618	7,984	15,509	15,048	15,007
Linda A. McKnew, President & CEO		'06	32.0	...	...	68.0	69,314	...	66.5	...	33.5	38,152	251,638	242,088	1,394	5,513	2,198	2,178
7711 Carondelet Avenue, Suite 800, St. Louis, MO 63105	Rating Outlook: Stable	'07	64.4	...	...	35.6	74,314	...	63.4	...	36.6	46,167	206,368	200,041	4,054	19,268	12,937	12,886
WI : 1990 : Stock : Broker, Medicaid		'08	57.1	...	...	42.9	77,263	...	46.0	...	54.0	46,815	161,499	155,009	511	26,495	17,213	16,751
314-725-4477		'09	43.5	...	0.3	56.2	77,993	...	60.6	...	39.4	51,893	243,992	236,910	-2,362	14,849	9,752	9,696
AMB# 064205 NAIC# 96822	FSC VII	**Rating History: B+, 02/19/10; B+, 02/10/09; C++pd, 07/09/07; C++pd, 08/08/06; C++pd, 09/29/05**																
MANHATTAN LIFE INS CO Harris Insurance Holdings Inc	B+	'05	59.2	12.0	...	28.8	400,457	74.1	0.0	23.4	2.5	43,647	20,496	32,916	50,686	3,695	3,548	5,533
Daniel J. George, President & Treasurer		'06	66.5	11.6	4.9	16.9	362,539	73.4	0.0	23.5	3.1	34,766	18,719	35,617	-37,003	-339	-321	15
2727 Allen Parkway Wortham Tower, Houston, TX 77019-2115	Rating Outlook: Negative	'07	61.2	11.0	6.2	21.5	363,058	71.8	...	25.4	2.8	35,742	18,137	36,295	-5,701	-1,391	404	478
NY : 1850 : Stock : Broker, Term Life, Trad Life, Univ Life		'08	50.2	10.3	7.2	32.3	354,152	70.4	...	26.7	2.9	32,017	18,256	29,355	-9,343	258	599	-1,029
888-222-0843		'09	58.2	7.9	8.1	25.8	345,166	69.0	...	28.1	2.9	34,226	18,238	22,443	-10,859	1,293	2,484	2,484
AMB# 006686 NAIC# 65870	FSC VI	**Rating History: B+, 03/23/10; B+, 04/16/09; B+, 03/04/08; B+, 01/31/07; B+, 05/05/06**																
MANHATTAN NATIONAL LIFE INS CO American Financial Group, Inc	A-	'05	85.3	...	1.8	12.9	264,969	9.1	0.0	4.1	86.8	34,246	40,968	2,988	-2,280	3,924	4,385	4,722
Charles R. Scheper, President & CEO		'06	81.8	...	1.9	16.3	254,980	9.6	0.0	4.1	86.3	32,196	38,865	3,657	-3,186	4,083	3,385	4,755
P.O. Box 5420, Cincinnati, OH 45201-5420	Rating Outlook: Stable	'07	84.6	...	1.8	13.6	265,320	9.5	0.0	3.7	86.8	48,503	34,098	1,711	502	7,560	5,376	5,522
IL : 1957 : Stock : Agency, Term Life, Univ Life		'08	80.3	...	0.4	19.3	213,681	9.2	0.0	3.8	86.9	7,878	31,152	1,704	-48,922	2,429	1,692	-81
513-357-3300		'09	81.8	...	0.1	18.1	210,736	9.3	0.0	3.8	86.9	9,523	30,036	2,481	-2,626	1,226	1,181	1,118
AMB# 006842 NAIC# 67083	FSC V	**Rating History: A-, 05/10/10; A-, 03/27/09; A-, 12/17/07; A-, 11/28/06; A-, 06/17/05**																
MAPFRE LIFE INSURANCE COMPANY[1] MAPFRE S.A.	NR-1	'05	82.6	...	1.4	16.0	53,281	...	...	...	100.0	15,221	56,227	54,957	...	179	179	-293
Raul Costilla, President & CEO		'06	83.2	...	0.9	15.9	57,072	...	...	...	100.0	17,166	81,994	80,598	...	4,159	4,159	4,127
P.O. Box 70297, San Juan, PR 00936-8297		'07	80.7	...	0.7	18.6	62,420	...	...	...	100.0	13,999	110,310	109,005	...	-1,979	-1,979	-1,979
PR : 1984 : Stock : Not Available		'08	63.9	...	0.6	35.4	75,987	...	...	4.0	96.0	7,902	179,995	178,604	...	-10,366	-10,366	-10,066
787-250-6500		'09	75.2	...	1.2	23.6	81,994	...	...	4.5	95.5	24,533	157,614	151,761	...	15,985	15,985	15,985
AMB# 007981 NAIC# 77054		**Rating History: NR-1, 06/11/10; NR-5, 05/12/10; NR-4, 10/10/08; B++, 10/10/08; B++, 07/11/08**																
MARCH VISION CARE INC	NR-5	'05	...	...	...	...	...	...	...	...	...	...	...	...	...	...	...	...
Glen March, M.D., President		'06	...	...	...	100.0	862	...	...	...	100.0	344	...	...	347	-504	-504	-504
6701 Center Drive West #790, Los Angeles, CA 90045		'07	...	...	...	100.0	1,459	...	...	...	100.0	677	8	8	971	-713	-714	-714
CA : 2005 : Stock : Not Available, Vision		'08	...	...	...	100.0	1,628	...	...	...	100.0	869	40	40	-383	142	141	141
310-216-2300		'09	...	...	...	100.0	2,678	...	...	...	100.0	1,770	50	50	1,224	999	901	901
AMB# 064933		**Rating History: NR-5, 05/07/10; NR-5, 05/13/09; NR-5, 05/05/08**																

BEST'S PROFITABILITY, LEVERAGE AND LIQUIDITY TESTS 2005 – 2009

Data in U.S. Dollars

	Profitability Tests							Leverage Tests						Liquidity Tests					
Un-Realized Capital Gains ($000)	Benefits Paid to NPW & Dep (%)	Comm. & Expenses to NPW & Dep (%)	NOG to Total Assets (%)	NOG to Total Rev (%)	Operating Return on Equity (%)	Net Yield (%)	Total Return (%)	Change in NPW & Dep (%)	NPW & Dep to Capital (X)	Capital & Surplus to Liabilities (%)	Surplus Relief (%)	Reins Leverage (%)	Change in Capital (%)	Quick Liquidity (%)	Current Liquidity (%)	Non-Invest Grade Bonds to Capital (%)	Delinq. & Foreclosed Mortgages to Capital (%)	Mort. & Credit Tenant Loans & R.E. to Capital (%)	Affiliated Invest to Capital (%)
...	80.4	17.3	6.8	1.5	8.6	1.12	1.12	57.4	5.3	368.6	...	...	8.8	342.1	342.1	...	...	...	...
...	80.3	17.0	8.6	1.9	10.9	1.01	1.01	14.5	5.5	385.2	...	...	11.3	384.0	384.0	...	...	...	...
...	82.1	17.2	2.2	0.5	2.8	0.77	0.77	0.5	5.3	281.7	...	...	3.0	353.0	353.0	...	...	...	...
...	80.3	17.3	7.0	1.7	9.3	0.74	0.74	8.9	5.3	333.1	...	...	9.7	355.0	355.0	...	...	...	...
...	80.9	16.9	6.2	1.6	8.1	0.75	0.75	2.8	5.0	302.9	...	...	8.5	305.8	305.8	...	...	...	...
Principal Lines of Business: Dental (100.0%)														Principal States: NJ (100.0%)					
...	70.0	20.0	15.6	7.6	18.9	3.18	3.18	21.9	2.2	728.2	...	...	20.8	672.4	705.9	...	...	...	...
...	67.7	20.2	20.7	9.2	23.2	4.66	5.30	19.0	2.3	897.4	...	...	15.9	920.7	920.7	...	...	...	...
...	69.1	19.7	18.7	8.5	20.3	5.29	5.29	12.0	2.1	999.9	...	...	22.6	999.9	999.9	...	...	...	...
...	70.0	20.5	14.2	6.7	15.6	2.07	2.07	8.6	2.4	755.3	...	...	-3.1	786.5	786.5	...	...	...	...
...	73.4	19.9	9.6	4.5	10.9	0.19	0.19	0.7	2.5	698.3	...	...	-4.9	719.8	719.8	...	...	...	...
Principal Lines of Business: Dental (100.0%)														Principal States: TX (100.0%)					
...	85.1	13.8	6.1	2.2	17.8	3.23	3.23	32.6	7.1	53.6	...	0.0	35.7	147.2	147.2	...	...	...	...
...	83.7	13.7	14.1	4.4	39.7	6.80	6.80	79.8	6.7	55.6	...	1.0	90.4	139.5	140.9	...	...	...	...
...	84.6	14.2	9.0	2.7	21.4	6.65	6.65	34.5	6.8	93.2	...	1.8	33.7	145.8	147.8	...	...	...	...
...	86.7	14.4	-1.6	-0.4	-3.7	3.60	2.80	40.0	8.9	68.8	...	1.5	6.5	136.1	138.8	...	...	...	...
...	86.2	13.7	2.2	0.6	5.7	2.00	2.04	17.2	9.2	55.1	...	1.1	13.6	138.4	141.0	...	...	...	...
Principal Lines of Business: Medicare (99.8%), CompHosp/Med (0.2%)														Principal States: NY (100.0%)					
...	67.7	18.2	43.0	11.6	92.8	3.12	3.12	7.9	6.4	88.9	...	...	39.2	114.9	114.9	...	...	...	...
...	70.3	18.3	24.0	7.4	63.7	6.41	6.41	4.8	11.5	39.1	...	...	-41.4	82.0	82.0	...	...	...	...
...	69.3	17.5	29.4	8.3	79.5	4.80	4.80	2.7	7.9	88.3	...	...	49.2	101.8	101.8	...	...	...	...
...	76.3	31.2	-13.6	-4.2	-29.7	2.04	2.04	-15.5	7.4	80.3	...	...	-10.3	110.7	110.7	...	...	...	...
...	62.0	35.4	2.8	1.7	5.8	0.45	0.45	-67.4	5.4	149.5	...	...	-54.6	139.6	139.6	...	...	...	...
Principal Lines of Business: CompHosp/Med (100.0%)																			
...	82.6	13.2	23.4	4.6	47.6	3.16	3.09	12.8	6.0	129.0	...	3.9	52.9	193.5	203.4	...	...	...	...
...	86.1	13.1	3.2	0.6	5.8	4.09	4.05	5.0	6.3	122.4	...	8.3	-0.1	235.5	247.9	...	...	...	...
...	81.0	13.3	18.0	4.3	30.7	3.19	3.11	-17.4	4.3	164.0	...	4.1	21.0	153.8	170.4	...	...	...	...
...	75.8	13.9	22.7	7.1	37.0	2.73	2.01	-22.5	3.3	153.8	...	3.6	1.4	164.7	181.4	2.8	...	...	...
...	87.8	8.5	12.6	2.6	19.8	1.67	1.57	52.8	4.6	198.8	...	2.4	10.8	226.3	242.6	...	...	...	...
Principal Lines of Business: Medicaid (100.0%), Medicare (0.0%)														Principal States: WI (100.0%)					
...	116.8	19.7	0.9	9.6	8.5	4.98	5.81	-14.1	0.7	12.6	0.5	12.3	8.5	84.0	86.9	0.0	1.0	107.4	...
...	137.5	16.1	-0.1	-0.9	-0.8	5.33	5.60	8.2	1.0	11.1	0.9	30.7	-18.9	63.1	66.1	0.0	1.2	116.3	49.2
3,595	131.1	15.0	0.1	1.1	1.1	5.38	6.56	1.9	1.0	11.1	2.0	33.6	0.2	69.8	72.3	...	...	109.8	61.8
1,810	145.5	22.1	0.2	1.7	1.8	5.47	5.67	-19.1	0.9	10.1	1.8	30.8	-11.1	85.4	87.7	3.1	...	113.2	78.4
-431	175.8	25.2	0.7	8.0	7.5	4.56	4.66	-23.5	0.6	11.2	2.8	27.6	7.0	80.6	82.8	11.6	...	79.0	80.3
Principal Lines of Business: OrdLife (62.6%), GrpAnn (36.5%), IndAnn (0.4%), GrpLife (0.3%), GrpA&H (0.1%)														Principal States: NY (17.5%), CA (12.1%), FL (6.4%), PA (4.8%), NJ (4.0%)					
209	151.8	-56.4	1.6	37.2	11.4	1.59	1.80	-12.5	0.1	16.1	14.6	636.4	-19.4	67.7	76.4	104.1	...	...	44.8
-702	125.2	-47.1	1.3	31.0	10.2	1.50	1.78	22.4	0.1	15.7	12.5	657.0	-6.3	73.9	83.0	103.6	...	...	67.5
149	289.3	-99.9	2.1	47.6	13.3	1.68	1.81	-53.2	0.0	23.4	6.2	440.0	46.0	80.3	90.4	21.0	...	...	20.0
-1,113	143.2	8.9	0.7	21.6	6.0	1.43	0.09	-0.4	0.2	4.3	34.2	999.9	-82.6	76.2	83.6	93.9	...	...	...
8	117.1	15.7	0.6	16.2	13.6	0.74	0.54	45.6	0.2	5.3	26.1	999.9	20.7	75.6	83.2	77.5	...	...	...
Principal Lines of Business: OrdLife (86.0%), IndAnn (13.7%), IndA&H (0.3%)														Principal States: CA (15.7%), TX (7.4%), FL (6.4%), WI (5.6%), OH (4.0%)					
491	70.4	33.0	0.3	0.3	1.1	...	...	16.9	3.5	41.6	0.0	...	-6.9	...	...	...	...	...	...
6	73.6	30.6	7.5	5.0	25.7	...	...	46.7	4.6	44.5	...	...	12.2	...	...	...	...	...	...
-51	82.5	23.9	-3.3	-1.8	-12.7	...	...	35.2	7.6	29.9	...	...	-18.2	...	...	...	...	...	...
-154	93.2	14.6	-15.0	-5.7	-94.7	...	...	63.8	21.7	12.2	0.2	...	-42.6	...	...	...	...	...	...
128	74.8	17.5	20.2	10.3	98.6	...	...	-15.0	6.1	43.6	4.5	...	201.8	...	...	...	...	...	...
Principal Lines of Business: IndA&H (55.8%), GrpA&H (40.6%), CrdLife (2.6%), GrpLife (0.7%), OrdLife (0.1%)																			
...	...	...	...	...	...	...	...	...	...	...	...	...	...	...	...	...	...	...	...
...	...	...	...	-24.2	...	...	...	...	...	66.3	...	...	...	35.0	35.0	...	...	...	...
1,049	999.9	999.9	-61.5	-11.6	-99.9	0.41	999.90	...	0.0	86.6	...	...	97.1	108.5	108.5	...	...	...	...
...	780.7	960.1	9.2	1.7	18.3	0.56	0.56	390.5	0.0	114.4	...	...	28.3	32.2	32.2	...	...	...	...
...	376.6	373.9	41.9	7.8	68.3	0.46	0.46	25.3	0.0	194.9	...	...	103.8	121.2	121.2	...	...	...	...
Principal Lines of Business: Vision (100.0%)																			

Data in U.S. Dollars

COMPANY NAME Ultimate Parent Association Principal Officer Mailing Address Dom. : Began Bus. : Struct. : Mktg. Specialty Phone # AMB# NAIC#	Best's Financial Strength Rating FSC	Data Year	Balance Sheet Bonds (%)	Mort. Loans & R.E. (%)	Com & Pref. Stock (%)	All Other Assets (%)	Total Assets ($000)	Life Reserves (%)	Health Reserves %)	Ann Res. & Dep. Liabilities (%)	All Other Liabilities (%)	Capital & Surplus ($000)	Operations Direct Premiums Written ($000)	Net Premiums Written & Deposits ($000)	Operating Cash Flow ($000)	NOG Before Taxes ($000)	NOG After Taxes ($000)	Net Income ($000)
MARION POLK COMMUNITY H PL ADV[2] Charles E. Wilson, M.D. President 245 Commercial Street SE, Suite 200 Salem, OR 97301 OR : 2005 : Stock : Not Available Health 503-371-7701 AMB# 064905 NAIC# 12310	**NR-5**	'05	...	...	...	...	...	...	...	...	...	...	...	...	...	...	...	...
		'06	...	...	...	100.0	14,269	...	40.6	...	59.4	6,664	49,893	49,893	8,894	2,099	2,099	2,099
		'07	...	...	...	100.0	15,119	...	17.1	...	82.9	7,673	43,170	43,170	-267	2,952	2,106	2,161
		'08	...	...	...	100.0	12,880	...	61.5	...	38.5	7,831	44,022	44,022	-2,979	334	209	209
		'09	...	...	...	100.0	13,542	...	51.3	...	48.7	7,431	49,313	49,313	-1,508	-612	-412	-412
		Rating History: NR-5, 05/21/10; NR-5, 09/11/09; NR-5, 07/14/08; NR-5, 07/02/07																
MARQUETTE INDEMNITY & LIFE INS Thomas J. Conley President & Treasurer 1000 Des Peres Road, Suite 350 St. Louis, MO 63131-2041 AZ : 1977 : Stock : Other Direct Dread dis, Life 314-909-9100 AMB# 008804 NAIC# 87394	**NR-5**	'05	73.6	...	21.2	5.3	10,767	31.7	32.7	...	35.6	5,723	1,281	2,082	-62	361	338	492
		'06	73.0	...	17.9	9.2	11,102	30.3	32.7	...	37.0	6,070	1,306	2,081	180	259	225	357
		'07	76.3	...	14.3	9.4	11,008	27.1	31.7	...	41.2	6,326	1,473	1,715	-188	533	388	1,034
		'08	75.5	...	13.9	10.6	10,032	25.1	31.9	...	43.0	5,706	1,546	1,397	-699	184	237	-16
		'09	72.6	...	12.7	14.7	8,948	23.1	28.0	...	48.9	5,046	1,527	810	-1,290	195	142	95
		Rating History: NR-5, 04/22/10; NR-5, 04/20/09; NR-5, 04/08/08; NR-5, 05/11/07; NR-5, 05/09/06																
MARQUETTE NATIONAL LIFE INS CO Universal American Corp. Gary W. Bryant President & CEO P.O. Box 958465 Lake Mary, FL 32795-8465 TX : 1967 : Stock : Agency A&H, Ann, Life 407-995-8000 AMB# 007311 NAIC# 71072	**B+** Rating Outlook: Stable **FSC IV**	'05	67.8	...	...	32.2	7,082	...	...	74.7	25.3	6,535	...	...	-97	67	49	49
		'06	23.1	...	...	76.9	17,658	0.0	5.9	3.6	90.4	5,824	23,969	12,533	6,341	-497	-497	-497
		'07	16.2	...	...	83.8	22,022	0.1	6.2	3.5	90.2	9,446	3,380	3,579	4,802	-1,510	-1,518	-1,518
		'08	21.9	...	...	78.1	33,113	0.1	52.0	1.7	46.2	6,122	82,892	82,530	3,284	-10,202	-10,202	-10,202
		'09	63.4	...	...	36.6	10,592	2.2	57.7	...	40.0	6,003	11,716	11,035	-13,222	768	768	768
		Rating History: B+, 04/16/10; B++g, 12/03/08; B++g, 08/21/07; NR-3, 06/21/06; NR-3, 06/09/05																
MARYLAND CARE INC Ray Grahe Chairman 509 Progress Drive Linthicum, MD 21090 MD : 1997 : Stock : Not Available Medicaid 410-401-9400 AMB# 064897	**NR-5**	'05	...	...	...	...	...	...	...	...	...	...	...	...	...	...	...	...
		'06	27.7	...	...	72.3	75,457	...	64.6	...	35.4	21,281	351,135	348,817	14,151	13,016	8,066	7,943
		'07	21.9	...	...	78.1	105,582	...	54.7	...	45.3	32,865	347,213	345,340	32,616	18,072	11,682	11,654
		'08	30.8	...	...	69.2	112,180	...	54.5	...	45.5	35,087	383,020	381,531	6,119	1,581	1,575	1,411
		'09	31.6	...	...	68.4	130,469	...	...	...	100.0	42,477	458,519	456,799	17,278	12,881	8,942	8,820
		Rating History: NR-5, 04/15/10; NR-5, 06/17/09; NR-5, 08/20/08; NR-5, 04/25/07																
MASSACHUSETTS MUTUAL LIFE INS Massachusetts Mutual Life Insurance Co Roger W. Crandall President & CEO 1295 State Street Springfield, MA 01111 MA : 1851 : Mutual : Agency Ind Life, Group pens, Annuity 413-788-8411 AMB# 006695 NAIC# 65935	**A++** Rating Outlook: Negative **FSC XV**	'05	37.0	9.8	4.1	49.2	100,693,988	40.9	2.4	17.8	38.9	6,688,466	12,109,356	12,531,291	1,348,984	521,460	448,172	663,047
		'06	36.9	10.3	4.2	48.6	109,220,587	39.3	2.2	15.8	42.7	7,026,842	12,806,012	13,611,798	2,695,957	404,757	454,444	702,798
		'07	33.8	10.6	3.6	52.1	119,085,813	38.1	2.1	15.0	44.8	8,008,148	13,247,573	15,158,403	3,797,387	689,314	570,703	140,007
		'08	39.5	11.3	2.3	46.9	114,294,059	42.0	2.3	16.9	38.8	8,462,931	13,705,469	14,469,364	6,057,670	-27,790	240,419	-993,468
		'09	38.5	10.0	3.3	48.2	121,329,281	40.5	2.2	15.3	42.0	9,258,844	12,906,670	13,251,589	-632,804	514,735	571,982	-289,365
		Rating History: A++g, 06/04/10; A++g, 06/11/09; A++g, 03/25/08; A++g, 05/25/07; A++g, 05/02/06																
MASSACHUSETTS VISION SVC PLAN Vision Service Plan James Robinson Lynch President& CEO 3333 Quality Drive Rancho Cordova, CA 95670 MA : 1981 : Other : Agency Group A&H 916-851-5000 AMB# 064479 NAIC# 47093	**A** Rating Outlook: Stable **FSC IX**	'05	19.9	...	5.8	74.2	10,006	...	31.9	...	68.1	8,188	9,416	9,416	924	2,253	1,413	1,414
		'06	22.0	...	6.1	71.9	11,355	...	45.2	...	54.8	9,797	11,615	11,615	1,809	2,373	1,650	1,665
		'07	58.2	...	13.1	28.7	13,508	...	36.8	...	63.2	11,249	13,882	13,882	1,772	2,259	1,410	1,436
		'08	65.2	...	7.3	27.5	14,525	...	50.1	...	49.9	12,607	16,416	16,416	1,171	2,701	1,838	1,690
		'09	58.0	...	7.8	34.2	17,955	...	31.3	...	68.7	15,027	17,704	17,704	3,199	3,300	2,249	2,069
		Rating History: A g, 02/09/10; A g, 11/24/08; A g, 11/30/07; A g, 10/12/06; A g, 11/10/05																
MATTHEW THORNTON HEALTH PLAN WellPoint Inc. Lisa M. Guertin President 3000 Goffs Falls Road Manchester, NH 03111-0001 NH : 1971 : Non-Profit : Broker Group A&H, Health, Ind A&H 603-695-7000 AMB# 068999 NAIC# 95527	**A** Rating Outlook: Stable **FSC VIII**	'05	80.4	...	0.2	19.4	227,821	...	36.7	...	63.3	146,610	512,483	512,483	33,874	60,653	41,115	41,509
		'06	84.6	...	0.2	15.2	253,847	...	40.0	...	60.0	191,964	490,394	484,810	12,879	72,264	48,202	47,954
		'07	68.1	...	0.2	31.7	226,521	...	40.1	...	59.9	157,968	427,851	421,738	-58,046	51,750	36,883	35,801
		'08	74.3	...	0.1	25.6	191,832	...	25.4	...	74.6	91,417	437,885	434,817	7,954	36,045	24,874	23,120
		'09	77.7	...	...	22.3	158,333	...	28.4	...	71.6	82,201	399,898	400,032	-32,501	11,310	8,996	10,531
		Rating History: A g, 04/27/10; A, 01/23/09; A, 03/20/08; A, 11/06/06; A, 12/29/05																
MAX VISION CARE INC Mark A. Galvan, O.D. President 6711 Comstock Avenue Whittier, CA 90601 CA : 1996 : Stock : Not Available Health 562-698-3607 AMB# 064934	**NR-5**	'05	...	...	...	...	...	...	...	...	...	...	...	...	...	...	...	...
		'06	...	...	...	...	...	...	...	...	...	...	...	...	...	...	...	...
		'07	...	...	...	100.0	209	...	...	...	100.0	205	...	...	-67	-69	-70	-70
		'08	...	...	...	100.0	96	...	...	...	100.0	81	...	...	-114	-122	-123	-123
		'09	...	...	...	100.0	105	...	...	...	100.0	45	...	...	-10	-111	-112	-112
		Rating History: NR-5, 03/23/10; NR-5, 04/08/09; NR-5, 03/20/08																
MCDONALD LIFE INSURANCE CO[1] Frederick E. McDonald III President 9500 Arboretum Boulevard, Suite 200 Austin, TX 78759 TX : 1983 : Stock : Not Available 512-344-6190 AMB# 009570 NAIC# 68020	**NR-1**	'05	10.8	2.8	24.9	61.4	1,846	...	...	...	100.0	1,585	121	125	...	1	1	46
		'06	10.3	2.5	29.7	57.6	1,948	...	...	...	100.0	1,710	118	116	...	36	36	66
		'07	10.8	2.4	24.9	61.9	1,844	...	...	...	100.0	1,669	110	110	...	50	50	79
		'08	1.3	5.2	44.0	49.6	757	...	...	...	100.0	701	-10	-16	...	125	138	-154
		'09	2.5	4.7	40.2	52.6	795	...	...	...	100.0	735	-1	-1	...	-35	-36	-170
		Rating History: NR-1, 06/10/10; NR-1, 06/12/09; NR-1, 06/12/08; NR-1, 06/08/07; NR-1, 06/07/06																

2010 BEST'S KEY RATING GUIDE — LIFE/HEALTH EDITION
BEST'S PROFITABILITY, LEVERAGE AND LIQUIDITY TESTS 2005 – 2009

Data in U.S. Dollars

	Profitability Tests							Leverage Tests						Liquidity Tests					
Un-Realized Capital Gains ($000)	Benefits Paid to NPW & Dep (%)	Comm. & Expenses to NPW & Dep (%)	NOG to Total Assets (%)	NOG to Total Rev (%)	Operating Return on Equity (%)	Net Yield (%)	Total Return (%)	Change in NPW & Dep (%)	NPW & Dep to Capital (X)	Capital & Surplus to Liabilities (%)	Surplus Relief (%)	Reins Leverage (%)	Change in Capital (%)	Quick Liquidity (%)	Current Liquidity (%)	Non-Invest Grade Bonds to Capital (%)	Delinq. & Foreclosed Mortgages to Capital (%)	Mort. & Credit Tenant Loans & R.E. to Capital (%)	Affiliated Invest to Capital (%)
...	...	...	...	...	...	...	...	...	...	...	...	...	...	...	...	...	...	...	...
...	89.0	7.5	...	4.2	...	...	...	...	7.5	87.6	...	...	...	176.8	176.8	...	...	...	...
...	81.5	13.4	14.3	4.8	29.4	5.78	6.20	-13.5	5.6	103.0	...	0.6	15.1	176.2	176.2	...	...	...	...
...	85.3	14.9	1.5	0.5	2.7	3.58	3.58	2.0	5.6	155.1	...	10.1	2.1	200.9	200.9	...	...	...	...
...	84.6	16.8	-3.1	-0.8	-5.4	0.82	0.82	12.0	6.6	121.6	...	5.5	-5.1	141.3	141.3	...	...	...	...
	Principal Lines of Business: Medicare (100.0%)													Principal States: OR (100.0%)					
63	36.5	81.1	3.1	10.0	5.9	4.15	6.33	2.9	0.3	136.5	15.2	18.5	1.1	153.4	178.5	2.7	...	...	...
4	32.7	81.3	2.1	6.6	3.8	4.26	5.64	0.0	0.3	142.2	14.6	16.5	4.9	166.1	191.0	1.9	...	...	...
-63	32.3	85.6	3.5	12.4	6.3	4.04	9.79	-17.6	0.3	154.2	15.7	15.5	2.4	169.9	192.9	0.5	...	...	...
-289	26.8	89.5	2.3	8.6	3.9	3.18	-2.12	-18.6	0.2	147.2	18.4	16.2	-10.5	168.3	189.4	0.6	...	...	...
141	69.6	110.5	1.5	6.5	2.6	3.41	4.53	-42.0	0.2	144.5	21.0	18.2	-11.5	174.5	195.9	0.7	...	...	...
	Principal Lines of Business: CrdA&H (50.3%), CrdLife (49.7%)													Principal States: PR (100.0%)					
...	...	...	0.7	15.2	0.7	4.39	4.61	...	...	999.9	...	...	-3.1	999.9	999.9	...	...	...	...
...	78.6	27.2	-4.0	-3.3	-8.0	3.74	3.78	...	2.1	49.3	32.6	4.3	-10.9	121.6	124.8	...	...	...	...
...	74.7	76.9	-7.7	-36.6	-19.9	2.91	2.94	-71.4	0.4	75.3	1.1	3.5	62.2	194.7	201.8	...	...	...	...
...	103.6	9.6	-37.0	-12.2	-99.9	3.86	3.88	999.9	13.4	22.8	1.9	1.2	-35.1	107.4	112.0	...	...	...	...
...	65.7	32.8	3.5	6.6	12.7	2.15	2.17	-86.6	1.8	131.5	4.6	13.0	-2.0	204.9	215.1	...	...	...	...
	Principal Lines of Business: IndA&H (101.0%), OrdLife (3.3%), IndAnn (-4.2%)													Principal States: OH (36.6%), IN (21.0%), OK (15.2%), SC (12.7%), NE (10.2%)					
...	...	...	...	...	...	...	...	...	...	...	...	...	...	...	...	...	...	...	...
...	83.6	13.3	...	2.3	...	...	...	...	16.4	39.3	...	3.9	...	93.4	97.3	...	...	...	...
...	82.4	13.1	12.9	3.4	43.2	4.83	4.78	-1.0	10.5	45.2	...	0.6	54.4	115.0	118.9	...	...	...	...
...	88.0	12.2	1.4	0.4	4.6	2.77	2.58	10.5	10.9	45.5	...	4.4	6.8	182.5	195.3	...	...	...	...
...	85.1	12.5	7.4	2.0	23.1	1.68	1.55	19.7	10.8	48.3	...	2.3	21.1	189.9	203.2	...	...	...	...
	Principal Lines of Business: Medicaid (100.0%)													Principal States: MD (100.0%)					
208,528	75.9	11.4	0.5	2.8	6.9	6.28	6.89	-12.7	1.5	13.4	1.5	17.0	9.7	44.8	57.2	43.4	0.3	123.7	62.0
84,268	74.6	12.0	0.4	2.7	6.6	6.31	6.72	8.6	1.6	13.9	1.5	20.1	6.9	36.1	48.8	40.3	0.4	131.6	79.7
455,300	69.6	10.6	0.5	3.2	7.6	6.61	6.62	11.4	1.6	14.2	1.4	20.5	9.2	36.2	49.2	38.5	0.1	134.1	81.8
-8,996	76.5	10.6	0.2	1.3	2.9	6.47	4.84	-4.5	1.6	11.9	1.3	22.4	-7.0	37.7	49.2	41.3	...	148.2	89.0
737,033	85.5	14.0	0.5	3.4	6.5	5.09	4.98	-8.4	1.3	14.2	1.2	23.0	17.4	37.6	49.9	37.8	...	118.2	88.8
	Principal Lines of Business: GrpAnn (45.6%), OrdLife (29.0%), IndAnn (21.2%), IndA&H (3.5%), GrpLife (0.8%)													Principal States: NY (11.6%), MA (7.3%), CA (6.8%), FL (6.6%), IL (5.2%)					
63	85.7	-6.1	15.4	14.7	19.8	2.77	3.60	19.0	1.2	450.2	...	...	34.9	674.7	679.5	...	...	...	...
67	76.3	7.1	15.4	13.3	18.4	4.58	5.48	23.4	1.2	628.6	...	...	19.7	999.9	999.9	...	...	...	...
73	77.7	9.8	11.3	9.6	13.4	4.43	5.33	19.5	1.2	498.0	...	...	14.8	544.0	578.9	...	...	...	...
-393	77.8	8.6	13.1	10.5	15.4	3.30	-1.06	18.3	1.3	657.1	...	...	12.1	609.0	651.0	...	...	...	...
339	75.9	7.7	13.8	12.0	16.3	2.03	3.18	7.8	1.2	513.3	...	...	19.2	590.8	635.0	...	...	...	...
	Principal Lines of Business: Vision (100.0%)													Principal States: MA (100.0%)					
...	79.3	10.3	19.7	7.9	31.5	4.29	4.51	-3.4	3.5	180.5	...	...	28.2	227.6	249.9	...	...	...	...
-1,606	77.6	9.6	20.0	9.7	28.5	4.96	4.05	-5.4	2.5	310.2	...	5.9	30.9	281.2	314.8	...	...	...	...
-18	80.9	9.1	15.4	8.6	21.1	5.43	4.82	-13.0	2.7	230.4	...	2.9	-17.7	174.3	200.5	...	...	...	0.0
30	83.6	10.0	11.9	5.6	19.9	5.27	4.16	3.1	4.8	91.0	...	2.1	-42.1	132.2	149.0	0.4	...	...	...
-14	86.9	11.9	5.1	2.2	10.4	4.69	5.78	-8.0	4.9	108.0	...	...	-10.1	141.9	157.5	2.1	...	...	...
	Principal Lines of Business: CompHosp/Med (97.3%), Medicaid (2.0%), OtherHlth (0.8%)													Principal States: NH (100.0%)					
...	...	...	...	...	...	...	...	...	...	...	...	...	...	...	...	...	...	...	...
...	...	...	...	...	...	...	...	...	...	...	...	...	...	...	...	...	...	...	...
...	...	...	...	-99.9	...	...	...	...	...	999.9	...	...	...	999.9	999.9	...	...	...	...
...	...	...	-80.8	-99.9	-86.1	1.44	1.44	...	...	563.7	...	...	-60.2	315.2	315.2	...	...	...	...
...	...	...	-99.9	-99.9	-99.9	0.15	0.15	...	...	75.3	...	...	-44.8	65.0	65.0	...	...	...	...
-21	14.4	137.2	0.1	0.5	0.1	...	...	-21.2	0.1	818.5	...	...	0.3	...	...	...	...	3.2	...
75	16.4	146.5	1.9	18.3	2.2	...	...	-7.6	0.1	999.9	...	...	8.6	...	...	...	...	2.7	...
-163	19.2	133.2	2.6	25.0	2.9	...	...	-5.4	0.1	999.9	...	...	-4.7	...	...	...	...	2.6	...
-506	-41.3	-99.9	10.6	111.0	11.6	...	...	-99.9	0.0	999.9	...	...	-58.4	...	...	...	...	5.6	...
105	-99.9	-99.9	-4.7	-71.2	-5.1	...	...	93.3	0.0	999.9	...	...	8.1	...	...	...	...	4.9	...
	Principal Lines of Business: CrdA&H (78.6%), CrdLife (21.4%)																		

COMPANY NAME Ultimate Parent Association Principal Officer Mailing Address Dom. : Began Bus. : Struct. : Mktg. Specialty Phone # AMB# NAIC#	Best's Financial Strength Rating FSC	Data Year	Balance Sheet: Bonds (%)	Mort. Loans & R.E. (%)	Com & Pref. Stock (%)	All Other Assets (%)	Total Assets ($000)	Life Reserves (%)	Health Reserves (%)	Ann Res. & Dep. Liabilities (%)	All Other Liabilities (%)	Capital & Surplus ($000)	Operations: Direct Premiums Written ($000)	Net Premiums Written & Deposits ($000)	Operating Cash Flow ($000)	NOG Before Taxes ($000)	NOG After Taxes ($000)	Net Income ($000)
MCKINLEY LIFE INS CO Aultman Health Foundation Rick L. Haines President 2600 Sixth Street Southwest Canton, OH 44710 OH : 1989 : Stock : Not Available Medicare, Group A&H, FEHBP 330-363-4057	**B++** Rating Outlook: Negative	'05	62.3	...	...	37.7	67,101	...	69.9	...	30.1	29,712	352,007	348,530	9,182	5,234	4,353	4,434
		'06	62.9	...	...	37.1	80,873	...	76.3	...	23.7	32,957	374,003	361,722	9,402	3,698	3,104	3,000
		'07	62.6	...	...	37.4	84,594	...	76.8	...	23.2	36,396	427,518	411,918	-5,471	-17,254	-14,960	-14,960
		'08	60.5	...	5.7	33.8	97,266	...	75.3	...	24.7	42,555	466,049	452,804	13,883	8,946	8,240	8,243
		'09	57.8	...	6.9	35.3	103,487	...	73.3	...	26.7	49,239	443,166	429,473	12,568	5,199	3,972	3,976
AMB# 068111 NAIC# 77216	FSC VI	**Rating History: B++, 06/08/10; B++, 06/05/09; B++, 06/16/08; B++, 06/12/07; B++, 06/21/06**																
MCLAREN HEALTH PLAN INC Kathy Kendall President G-3245 Beecher Road Flint, MI 48532 MI : 1998 : Non-Profit : Not Available Group A&H 810-733-9723	**NR-5**	'05	...	7.2	2.7	90.1	39,863	...	25.5	...	74.5	20,508	108,955	108,326	10,397	5,157	5,157	5,157
		'06	...	5.4	2.2	92.4	50,744	...	35.4	...	64.6	28,295	123,463	122,778	11,430	7,695	7,695	7,695
		'07	...	3.9	13.2	82.9	66,563	...	46.3	...	53.7	40,752	167,083	166,379	15,667	10,966	10,966	10,966
		'08	...	3.0	8.2	88.8	88,061	...	49.9	...	50.1	56,954	205,853	205,250	22,656	16,250	16,250	16,251
		'09	...	2.9	7.5	89.6	110,285	...	57.3	...	42.7	69,823	271,924	270,944	19,543	11,728	11,728	11,570
AMB# 064616 NAIC# 95848		**Rating History: NR-5, 05/21/10; NR-5, 08/26/09; B pd, 07/14/08; B pd, 06/28/07; B- pd, 07/25/06**																
MCS LIFE INSURANCE COMPANY[1] MCS Inc Julio Julia President 255 Ponce de Leon Avenue, Suite 900 San Juan, PR 00917 PR : 1996 : Stock : Not Available 787-758-2500	**NR-1**	'05	23.3	...	1.5	75.2	77,367	...	...	...	100.0	18,027	223,445	222,434	...	7,836	7,098	7,374
		'06	11.6	...	1.2	87.2	159,945	...	...	...	100.0	17,294	574,948	572,534	...	690	-433	-417
		'07	37.8	...	1.6	60.6	61,641	...	...	...	100.0	19,988	230,003	228,771	...	7,702	7,666	8,039
		'08	36.9	...	1.7	61.4	45,514	...	...	...	100.0	9,708	176,729	175,860	...	478	489	210
		'09	31.8	...	1.4	66.8	53,222	...	...	...	100.0	16,547	199,825	199,064	...	5,852	5,265	5,285
AMB# 060379 NAIC# 60030		**Rating History: NR-1, 06/10/10; NR-1, 06/12/09; NR-1, 06/12/08; NR-1, 06/08/07; NR-1, 06/07/06**																
MD-INDIVIDUAL PRACTICE ASSOC UnitedHealth Group Inc Kevin J. Ruth President & CEO 4 Taft Court Rockville, MD 20850 MD : 1980 : Stock : Broker Group A&H, FEHBP 301-762-8205	**A** Rating Outlook: Stable	'05	22.1	...	...	77.9	145,948	...	17.6	...	82.4	43,576	590,457	589,832	11,588	43,936	30,003	30,093
		'06	28.9	...	...	71.1	130,768	...	49.2	...	50.8	42,197	621,689	621,060	-22,750	70,675	44,410	44,382
		'07	18.2	...	...	81.8	192,897	...	63.5	...	36.5	107,365	651,181	650,536	62,496	99,833	67,672	67,672
		'08	27.9	...	...	72.1	251,163	...	56.5	...	43.5	156,200	639,147	638,513	48,959	75,833	51,177	51,356
		'09	10.4	...	...	89.6	123,483	...	53.4	...	46.6	42,211	590,922	590,335	-113,536	58,222	38,503	38,443
AMB# 068606 NAIC# 96310	FSC VI	**Rating History: A, 06/15/09; A, 01/29/08; A, 11/21/07; A, 11/16/06; A, 08/17/06**																
MDNY HEALTHCARE INC[2] Paul T. Accardi CEO One Huntington Quadrangle Melville, NY 11747 NY : 1996 : Stock : Broker In Liquidation 516-454-1900	**F**	'05	...	...	...	100.0	31,730	...	25.6	...	74.4	2,615	116,556	116,237	902	-2,401	-2,410	-2,410
		'06	24.6	...	...	75.4	10,130	...	44.6	...	55.4	-21,896	94,111	93,830	-3,916	-8,118	-8,119	-8,119
		'07	...	...	...	...	...	...	...	...	...	...	...	...	...	...	...	...
		'08	...	...	...	...	...	...	...	...	...	...	...	...	...	...	...	...
		'09	...	...	...	...	...	...	...	...	...	...	...	...	...	...	...	...
AMB# 064291 NAIC# 95476		**Rating History: F, 09/17/08; NR-5, 07/24/08; D pd, 10/08/07; C- pd, 09/25/06; C pd, 11/15/05**																
MDWISE INC[2] Clarian Health Partners, Inc. Charlotte MacBeth President 1099 N. Meridian Street, Suite 320 Indianapolis, IN 46204 IN : 1989 : Stock : Broker Medicaid 317-370-2824	**NR-5**	'05	80.8	...	...	19.2	13,961	...	...	...	100.0	12,206	212,301	208,543	557	406	187	187
		'06	...	...	...	100.0	16,047	...	...	...	100.0	12,432	231,549	227,946	3,435	543	352	226
		'07	9.9	...	26.8	63.3	56,450	...	48.5	...	51.5	32,144	551,302	542,632	23,416	12,081	12,081	12,078
		'08	30.9	...	2.7	66.4	49,656	...	28.4	...	71.6	37,691	601,890	593,335	5,705	9,051	9,051	9,051
		'09	31.5	...	3.1	65.4	51,153	...	15.7	...	84.3	40,520	630,654	622,715	3,776	6,582	6,582	6,965
AMB# 064386 NAIC# 95807		**Rating History: NR-5, 04/26/10; NR-5, 08/26/09; C+ pd, 09/08/08; C+ pd, 05/30/07; C+ pd, 05/30/06**																
MEDAMERICA INSURANCE CO Lifetime Healthcare Inc William E. Jones President 165 Court Street Rochester, NY 14647 PA : 1966 : Stock : Agency LTC 800-544-0327	**B++** Rating Outlook: Stable	'05	86.6	...	...	13.4	315,135	...	91.2	...	8.8	31,539	40,032	34,690	35,293	-12,531	-7,717	-5,501
		'06	90.8	...	...	9.2	367,740	...	92.2	...	7.8	33,191	48,837	49,887	52,846	-5,878	-3,595	-2,567
		'07	83.6	...	0.7	15.6	365,275	...	93.3	...	6.7	27,066	55,491	7,079	-1,020	-9,336	-4,439	-3,881
		'08	45.9	...	0.4	53.7	451,588	...	94.2	...	5.8	17,830	60,120	93,961	35,139	-5,660	-7,226	-7,753
		'09	89.9	...	0.9	9.2	497,148	...	94.7	...	5.3	33,132	61,923	42,785	98,977	1,703	6,497	4,484
AMB# 007131 NAIC# 69515	FSC VI	**Rating History: B++g, 06/07/10; B++g, 06/09/09; B++g, 01/29/09; A- g, 12/14/07; A-, 02/16/07**																
MEDAMERICA INS CO OF FLORIDA Lifetime Healthcare Inc William E. Jones President & COO 165 Court Street Rochester, NY 14647 FL : 2007 : Stock : Agency LTC 800-544-0327	**B++** Rating Outlook: Stable	'05	...	...	...	...	...	...	...	...	...	...	...	...	...	...	...	...
		'06	...	...	...	...	...	...	...	...	...	...	...	...	...	...	...	...
		'07	...	...	...	100.0	5,862	...	95.7	...	4.3	2,725	2,309	2,309	5,767	-301	-257	-257
		'08	...	...	...	100.0	8,628	...	98.1	...	1.9	1,791	2,160	4,193	1,179	-1,132	-823	-823
		'09	78.0	...	...	22.0	11,906	...	96.3	...	3.7	3,755	2,425	2,658	4,667	528	310	309
AMB# 060658 NAIC# 12967	FSC XI	**Rating History: B++g, 06/07/10; B++g, 06/09/09; B++g, 01/29/09; A- g, 12/14/07**																
MEDAMERICA INS CO OF NEW YORK Lifetime Healthcare Inc William E. Jones President & COO 165 Court Street Rochester, NY 14647 NY : 1987 : Stock : Agency LTC 800-544-0327	**B++** Rating Outlook: Stable	'05	88.7	...	...	11.3	171,239	...	91.8	...	8.2	17,811	35,098	34,985	36,052	-9,454	-6,055	-5,191
		'06	89.2	...	...	10.8	211,738	...	91.6	...	8.4	15,169	37,471	36,373	41,020	-4,826	-3,004	-2,498
		'07	82.2	...	...	17.8	250,363	...	94.8	...	5.2	17,986	40,207	38,165	38,473	-12,358	-7,028	-6,671
		'08	49.4	...	...	50.6	280,520	...	96.7	...	3.3	14,673	41,642	40,858	34,474	-8,417	-6,343	-6,784
		'09	86.1	...	...	13.9	328,970	...	96.2	...	3.8	18,739	41,531	39,536	45,892	-17,411	-8,580	-9,164
AMB# 060021 NAIC# 83437	FSC XI	**Rating History: B++g, 06/07/10; B++g, 06/09/09; B++g, 01/29/09; A- g, 12/14/07; A-, 02/16/07**																

BEST'S PROFITABILITY, LEVERAGE AND LIQUIDITY TESTS 2005 – 2009

Data in U.S. Dollars

—	Profitability Tests							Leverage Tests						Liquidity Tests					
Un-Realized Capital Gains ($000)	Benefits Paid to NPW & Dep (%)	Comm. & Expenses to NPW & Dep (%)	NOG to Total Assets (%)	NOG to Total Rev (%)	Operating Return on Equity (%)	Net Yield (%)	Total Return (%)	Change in NPW & Dep (%)	NPW & Dep to Capital (X)	Capital & Surplus to Liabilities (%)	Surplus Relief (%)	Reins Leverage (%)	Change in Capital (%)	Quick Liquidity (%)	Current Liquidity (%)	Non-Invest Grade Bonds to Capital (%)	Delinq. & Foreclosed Mortgages to Capital (%)	Mort. & Credit Tenant Loans & R.E. to Capital (%)	Affiliated Invest to Capital (%)
...	90.8	8.2	7.1	1.2	16.4	3.25	3.39	13.6	11.7	79.5	...	4.2	26.7	147.9	147.9	...	...	...	25.1
...	91.2	8.5	4.2	0.9	9.9	3.85	3.70	3.8	11.0	68.8	...	7.5	10.9	127.3	127.3	...	...	...	22.3
...	96.6	8.3	-18.1	-3.6	-43.1	4.20	4.20	13.9	11.3	75.5	...	17.7	10.4	114.2	114.2	...	...	...	19.9
-1,482	89.4	9.2	9.1	1.8	20.9	3.64	1.67	9.9	10.6	77.8	...	13.6	16.9	117.4	118.9	...	...	...	19.7
1,469	90.1	9.2	4.0	0.9	8.7	2.79	4.50	-5.2	8.7	90.8	...	6.3	15.7	123.8	126.2	...	...	...	35.1
Principal Lines of Business: Medicare (49.6%), CompHosp/Med (45.7%), FEHBP (3.0%), OtherHlth (1.6%)														Principal States: OH (100.0%)					
-139	83.6	6.5	15.0	5.0	29.1	2.28	1.84	42.8	5.3	100.0	...	0.1	36.7	173.9	174.8	...	...	14.1	14.1
-35	83.4	5.4	17.0	6.6	31.5	3.85	3.77	13.3	4.3	126.0	...	...	38.0	200.7	201.5	...	...	9.7	9.7
-20	84.5	4.2	18.7	6.9	31.8	4.98	4.95	35.5	4.1	157.9	...	0.2	44.0	223.0	228.0	...	...	6.4	6.7
-514	82.7	4.2	21.0	8.4	33.3	2.10	1.41	23.4	3.6	183.1	...	0.3	39.8	252.9	256.3	...	...	4.6	5.5
957	86.0	8.2	11.8	4.4	18.5	-0.01	0.84	32.0	3.9	172.6	...	0.4	22.6	230.7	230.7	...	...	4.5	4.5
Principal Lines of Business: Medicaid (88.6%), CompHosp/Med (11.4%)																			
-173	77.8	19.1	11.9	3.2	47.5	...	...	66.7	12.2	31.0	...	...	48.3	...	...	...	...	...	...
110	86.8	13.7	-0.4	-0.1	-2.4	...	...	157.4	32.4	12.4	...	...	-3.5	...	...	...	...	...	...
-310	84.0	13.3	6.9	3.3	41.1	...	...	-60.0	11.4	48.4	...	...	13.8	...	...	...	...	...	...
15	82.7	17.8	0.9	0.3	3.3	...	...	-23.1	17.8	27.7	...	...	-50.8	...	...	...	...	...	...
-53	78.9	18.6	10.7	2.6	40.1	...	...	13.2	11.9	45.8	...	...	69.3	...	...	...	...	...	...
Principal Lines of Business: GrpA&H (85.0%), IndA&H (13.8%), GrpLife (1.2%)																			
...	86.8	6.4	22.9	5.1	60.8	4.90	5.01	3.8	13.5	42.6	...	...	-20.9	122.5	129.5	...	...	...	...
...	84.3	5.0	32.1	7.1	103.6	6.07	6.03	5.3	14.7	47.6	...	...	-3.2	85.9	91.8	...	...	...	...
...	80.9	4.4	41.8	10.3	90.5	5.32	5.32	4.7	6.1	125.5	...	...	154.4	241.6	252.5	...	...	...	...
0	85.1	3.9	23.0	8.0	38.8	3.46	3.58	-1.8	4.1	164.5	...	...	45.5	269.6	282.7	0.1	...	...	...
0	85.8	4.6	20.6	6.5	38.8	1.77	1.71	-7.5	14.0	51.9	...	...	-73.0	119.7	125.4	...	...	...	...
Principal Lines of Business: FEHBP (92.2%), CompHosp/Med (7.8%)														Principal States: DC (94.1%), MD (4.3%)					
...	87.3	14.9	-7.2	-2.1	-60.6	...	...	-13.8	44.4	9.0	...	12.1	-51.1	27.7	27.7	...	...	...	...
-4	92.9	16.2	-38.8	-8.6	84.2	2.39	2.33	-19.3	-4.3	-68.4	...	-1.0	-99.9	12.5	12.5	...	...	...	...
...	...	...	...	...	...	...	...	...	...	...	...	...	...	...	...	...	...	...	...
...	...	...	...	...	...	...	...	...	...	...	...	...	...	...	...	...	...	...	...
...	...	...	...	...	...	...	...	...	...	...	...	...	...	...	...	...	...	...	...
...	89.6	10.4	1.4	0.1	1.5	3.36	3.36	-5.1	17.1	695.5	...	...	1.6	689.5	689.5	...	...	...	...
...	92.0	8.0	2.3	0.2	2.9	3.93	3.05	9.3	18.3	343.9	...	...	1.8	442.2	442.2	...	...	...	...
-7	91.4	6.6	33.3	2.2	54.2	5.22	5.18	138.1	16.9	132.3	...	...	158.6	166.0	175.3	...	...	...	...
-252	88.5	10.1	17.1	1.5	25.9	1.31	0.74	9.3	15.7	315.0	...	0.7	17.3	528.6	530.3	...	...	...	...
196	86.9	12.1	13.1	1.1	16.8	1.14	2.34	5.0	15.4	381.1	...	...	7.5	671.2	673.4	...	...	...	...
Principal Lines of Business: Medicaid (100.0%)														Principal States: IN (100.0%)					
...	54.9	22.6	-2.6	-12.7	-29.3	1.51	4.16	-2.4	1.1	11.1	52.6	595.6	48.6	86.3	93.8	45.2	...	...	...
...	40.8	11.8	-1.1	-3.9	-11.1	3.89	5.73	43.8	1.5	9.9	73.0	767.4	5.2	80.5	88.8	35.5	...	...	...
-275	327.9	48.1	-1.2	-9.3	-14.7	3.50	4.88	-85.8	0.3	8.0	88.9	999.9	-18.5	92.5	100.6	31.7	...	...	10.1
-934	26.9	0.1	-1.8	-5.3	-32.2	3.00	3.50	999.9	4.9	4.4	160.3	999.9	-29.2	108.8	116.5	24.5	...	...	9.3
454	66.8	2.5	1.4	7.4	25.5	4.44	4.14	-54.5	1.2	7.6	78.5	999.9	83.6	72.5	82.3	...	...	...	10.7
Principal Lines of Business: IndA&H (77.3%), GrpA&H (22.7%)														Principal States: DC (10.5%), NC (6.9%), TN (6.8%), CT (5.9%), ND (4.8%)					
...	...	...	...	...	...	...	...	...	...	...	...	...	...	...	...	...	...	...	...
...	...	...	...	...	...	...	...	...	...	...	...	...	...	...	...	...	...	...	...
...	1.6	11.0	...	-10.6	...	...	...	...	0.8	86.9	...	...	...	183.9	183.9	...	...	...	...
...	2.7	27.6	-11.4	-19.0	-36.4	2.37	2.37	81.6	2.3	26.2	...	78.3	-34.3	101.6	101.6	...	...	...	...
...	15.5	30.7	3.0	10.7	11.2	2.70	2.70	-36.6	0.7	46.3	...	...	110.4	120.0	134.1	...	...	...	...
Principal Lines of Business: IndA&H (97.2%), GrpA&H (2.8%)														Principal States: FL (100.0%)					
...	31.3	30.0	-4.0	-14.9	-37.2	1.87	4.09	9.8	2.0	11.6	2.4	1.9	20.9	88.8	96.2	37.9	...	...	...
...	35.7	20.1	-1.6	-6.4	-18.2	3.64	5.16	4.0	2.4	7.7	8.7	4.3	-14.8	84.5	93.1	40.9	...	...	...
...	38.9	20.6	-3.0	-14.0	-42.4	3.78	4.97	4.9	2.1	7.7	7.2	10.2	18.6	98.7	106.8	26.1	...	...	...
...	38.1	20.0	-2.4	-12.3	-38.8	3.31	3.78	7.1	2.6	5.9	4.7	41.3	-13.4	134.2	143.8	16.0	...	...	...
...	45.1	22.7	-2.8	-16.6	-51.4	4.00	3.86	-3.2	2.0	6.4	2.7	32.5	26.6	79.9	90.0	...	...	...	...
Principal Lines of Business: IndA&H (76.2%), GrpA&H (23.8%)														Principal States: NY (98.3%)					

Data in U.S. Dollars

COMPANY NAME Ultimate Parent Association Principal Officer Mailing Address Dom. : Began Bus. : Struct. : Mktg. Specialty Phone # AMB# NAIC#	Best's Financial Strength Rating FSC	Data Year	Balance Sheet Bonds (%)	Mort. Loans & R.E. (%)	Com & Pref. Stock (%)	All Other Assets (%)	Total Assets ($000)	Life Reserves (%)	Health Reserves (%)	Ann Res. & Dep. Liabilities (%)	All Other Liabilities (%)	Capital & Surplus ($000)	Operations Direct Premiums Written ($000)	Net Premiums Written & Deposits ($000)	Operating Cash Flow ($000)	NOG Before Taxes ($000)	NOG After Taxes ($000)	Net Income ($000)
MEDCO CONTAINMENT INS CO OF NY Medco Health Solutions Inc	**A-**	'05	7.0	...	...	93.0	10,685	...	...	...	100.0	10,117	185	185	255	748	486	486
Richard J. Rubino President		'06	6.2	...	...	93.8	12,003	...	1.5	...	98.5	10,142	2,285	2,285	959	276	173	173
100 Parsons Pond Drive Franklin Lakes, NJ 07417-2603	Rating Outlook: Stable	'07	6.2	...	...	93.8	12,062	...	2.7	...	97.3	10,362	1,961	1,961	179	412	261	261
NY : 1989 : Stock : Direct Response Stop Loss		'08	1.5	...	...	98.5	16,603	...	16.1	...	83.9	11,729	21,030	21,030	-1,188	1,862	1,166	1,166
800-426-0152 AMB# 010747 NAIC# 34720	FSC VIII	'09	23.3	...	...	76.7	23,308	...	23.6	...	76.4	12,666	48,776	48,776	-3,173	1,420	923	924
		Rating History: A- g, 06/10/10; A- g, 06/03/09; A- g, 06/18/08; A- g, 06/13/07; A- g, 06/19/06																
MEDCO CONTAINMENT LIFE INS CO Medco Health Solutions Inc	**A-**	'05	16.6	...	...	83.4	56,734	...	...	...	100.0	51,589	7	...	-1,071	-3,428	-2,228	-2,228
Richard J. Rubino President		'06	4.2	...	...	95.8	207,522	0.5	2.4	...	97.1	59,506	462,617	462,611	119,075	23,923	15,022	15,022
100 Parsons Pond Drive, Bldg F1 Franklin Lakes, NJ 07417-2603	Rating Outlook: Stable	'07	1.0	...	...	99.0	215,553	...	7.4	...	92.6	82,121	250,545	250,549	10,772	43,768	28,410	28,410
PA : 1955 : Stock : Direct Response Stop Loss		'08	2.9	...	...	97.1	143,754	...	12.6	...	87.4	95,800	295,843	296,898	-119,504	4,754	3,272	3,272
201-269-3400 AMB# 006449 NAIC# 63762	FSC VIII	'09	17.4	...	...	82.6	208,743	...	12.0	...	88.0	107,420	494,599	494,608	107,346	14,321	9,196	9,196
		Rating History: A- g, 06/10/10; A- g, 06/03/09; A- g, 06/18/08; A- g, 06/13/07; A- g, 06/19/06																
MEDCORE HP	**NR-5**	'05	...	...	...	100.0	1,543	...	...	...	100.0	-2,485	...	...	-34	-1,026	-1,027	-1,027
Kirit B. Patel, M.D. President		'06	...	...	...	100.0	1,899	...	...	...	100.0	929	4,811	4,811	743	-905	-905	-905
509 West Weber Avenue, Suite 200 Stockton, CA 95203		'07	...	...	...	100.0	4,260	...	...	...	100.0	940	17,647	17,647	1,761	10	10	10
CA : 1996 : Other : Broker Health		'08	...	...	...	100.0	5,621	...	...	...	100.0	474	27,117	27,117	1,660	-466	-466	-466
209-320-2600 AMB# 064788		'09	...	...	...	100.0	1,621	...	...	...	100.0	447	24,427	24,427	-3,912	-35	-35	-35
		Rating History: NR-5, 05/07/10; NR-5, 05/11/09; NR-5, 05/22/08; NR-5, 05/03/07; NR-5, 06/21/06																
MEDICA HEALTH PLANS[2] Medica Holding Company	**NR-5**	'05	64.7	1.7	9.4	24.1	555,915	...	37.5	...	62.5	320,997	1,220,019	1,220,019	-71,311	-14,177	-14,323	2,825
David M. Tilford President & CEO		'06	54.4	1.8	7.4	36.4	520,512	...	46.3	...	53.7	281,754	1,026,507	1,026,507	-12,425	-28,901	-30,756	-27,024
P.O. Box 9310, Rt. No. CP 475 Minneapolis, MN 55440-9310		'07	51.3	1.5	7.0	40.3	578,584	...	38.2	...	61.8	319,500	1,042,213	1,042,213	24,009	27,101	28,336	29,966
MN : 1974 : Non-Profit : Broker Group A&H, Health, Ind A&H		'08	50.1	1.5	0.5	47.8	506,233	...	50.0	...	50.0	317,704	1,053,127	1,053,127	-40,851	39,083	39,191	11,528
952-992-2900 AMB# 068559 NAIC# 52626		'09	38.4	1.3	0.4	60.0	586,326	...	59.0	...	41.0	361,273	1,201,084	1,367,530	2,079	48,405	48,465	49,657
		Rating History: NR-5, 06/02/10; NR-5, 08/26/09; B pd, 07/21/08; B- pd, 07/09/07; B pd, 08/28/06																
MEDICA HEALTH PLANS OF WI[2] Medica Holding Company	**NR-5**	'05	...	...	...	100.0	3,049	...	24.0	...	76.0	2,281	5,006	5,006	-753	-208	-208	-208
David M. Tilford President & CEO		'06	...	...	...	100.0	2,489	...	92.7	...	7.3	2,412	408	408	-543	129	129	129
P.O. Box 9310, Rt. No. CP 475 Minneapolis, MN 55440-9310		'07	...	...	...	100.0	3,227	...	80.9	...	19.1	2,777	1,788	1,788	715	365	365	365
WI : 1998 : Non-Profit : Broker Group A&H		'08	...	...	...	100.0	3,028	...	54.9	...	45.1	2,927	1,577	1,577	-175	160	160	160
952-992-2900 AMB# 064445 NAIC# 95232		'09	...	...	...	100.0	2,972	...	99.8	...	0.2	2,922	2	2	-54	-13	-13	-13
		Rating History: NR-5, 05/24/10; NR-5, 04/08/09; NR-5, 04/09/08; NR-5, 05/02/07; NR-5, 06/13/06																
MEDICA INSURANCE COMPANY[2] Medica Holding Company	**NR-5**	'05	48.2	...	...	51.8	272,258	...	52.7	...	47.3	118,925	935,505	936,066	100,865	-4,377	-1,773	-1,786
David M. Tilford President		'06	59.6	...	...	40.4	313,828	...	51.0	...	49.0	142,330	1,288,980	1,252,721	13,699	34,807	24,430	24,353
P.O. Box 9310, Rt. No. CP475 Minneapolis, MN 55440-9310		'07	52.3	...	...	47.7	367,563	...	33.9	...	66.1	159,871	1,354,793	931,670	92,420	20,348	15,108	14,867
MN : 1984 : Stock : Agency Maj med		'08	73.5	...	...	26.5	369,083	...	37.6	...	62.4	174,330	1,475,705	1,022,110	10,856	23,217	20,146	15,275
952-992-2900 AMB# 011072 NAIC# 12459		'09	63.4	...	...	36.6	449,420	...	19.5	...	80.5	198,482	1,458,410	1,064,834	78,816	22,848	13,733	17,431
		Rating History: NR-5, 06/01/10; NR-5, 04/08/09; NR-5, 04/09/08; NR-5, 04/03/07; NR-5, 04/20/06																
MEDICAL ASSOCIATES CLINIC WI[2] Medical Associates Clinic P C	**NR-5**	'05	39.7	...	5.0	55.3	2,544	...	17.4	...	82.6	1,884	22,521	22,406	106	55	55	54
Andrea Ries, M.D. President		'06	27.0	...	6.7	66.3	3,250	...	20.8	...	79.2	2,106	23,147	22,993	230	233	233	220
1605 Associates Drive, Suite 101 Dubuque, IA 52002-2270		'07	32.9	...	15.1	52.0	2,821	...	40.7	...	59.3	2,091	24,228	24,103	58	44	44	45
WI : 1985 : Non-Profit : Broker Health		'08	27.3	...	19.6	53.1	3,087	...	24.3	...	75.7	1,851	25,475	25,325	-36	-221	-221	-205
563-556-8070 AMB# 068612 NAIC# 95782		'09	35.1	...	12.8	52.0	3,299	...	10.6	...	89.4	2,282	27,117	26,958	120	254	254	294
		Rating History: NR-5, 05/21/10; NR-5, 05/29/09; NR-5, 05/16/08; NR-5, 06/21/07; NR-5, 07/12/06																
MEDICAL ASSOCIATES HEALTH PLAN Medical Associates Clinic P C	**NR-5**	'05	40.9	...	8.6	50.5	18,221	...	49.4	...	50.6	10,199	64,601	64,202	575	3,577	2,172	2,172
Andrea Ries, M.D. Chairman		'06	29.1	...	8.4	62.4	20,942	...	44.9	...	55.1	11,229	72,260	71,724	2,273	2,470	1,330	1,185
1605 Associates Drive, Suite 101 Dubuque, IA 52002-2270		'07	43.2	...	5.8	51.0	21,434	...	51.6	...	48.4	12,679	83,702	83,242	2,313	1,921	1,895	1,921
IA : 1987 : Stock : Broker Group A&H, Medicare, Med supp		'08	32.6	...	21.3	46.1	24,080	...	46.8	...	53.2	13,542	93,263	92,682	3,102	2,371	1,405	1,431
563-556-8070 AMB# 068542 NAIC# 52559		'09	47.0	...	21.3	31.7	23,994	...	53.5	...	46.5	14,228	98,202	97,571	-1,358	1,111	692	944
		Rating History: NR-5, 04/20/10; NR-5, 08/26/09; B- pd, 09/03/08; B- pd, 09/21/07; B- pd, 07/17/06																
MEDICAL BENEFITS MUTUAL LIFE	**B+**	'05	22.3	9.5	37.5	30.7	17,303	2.4	8.8	...	88.7	11,144	33,382	7,597	962	1,476	1,021	1,018
Douglas J. Freeman President		'06	26.2	9.2	10.9	53.7	18,904	2.9	9.0	...	88.1	12,676	33,670	7,090	6,129	870	549	566
P.O. Box 1009 Newark, OH 43058-1009	Rating Outlook: Stable	'07	24.2	9.1	14.6	52.0	20,642	2.8	9.2	...	87.9	13,496	34,609	6,877	1,698	429	321	336
OH : 1938 : Mutual : Broker Dental, Group A&H, Group Life		'08	22.0	10.3	12.8	55.0	19,986	2.0	9.4	...	88.6	13,380	33,022	6,488	-81	667	431	403
740-522-7324 AMB# 068036 NAIC# 74322	FSC V	'09	25.5	8.5	12.7	53.4	23,249	1.4	29.4	...	69.2	13,997	28,058	13,974	1,707	1,163	799	738
		Rating History: B+, 08/28/09; B+, 06/17/08; B+, 06/14/07; B+, 06/15/06; B+, 06/17/05																

BEST'S PROFITABILITY, LEVERAGE AND LIQUIDITY TESTS 2005 – 2009

Data in U.S. Dollars

	Profitability Tests							Leverage Tests						Liquidity Tests					
Un-Realized Capital Gains ($000)	Benefits Paid to NPW & Dep (%)	Comm. & Expenses to NPW & Dep (%)	NOG to Total Assets (%)	NOG to Total Rev (%)	Operating Return on Equity (%)	Net Yield (%)	Total Return (%)	Change in NPW & Dep (%)	NPW & Dep to Capital (X)	Capital & Surplus to Liabilities (%)	Surplus Relief (%)	Reins Leverage (%)	Change in Capital (%)	Quick Liquidity (%)	Current Liquidity (%)	Non-Invest Grade Bonds to Capital (%)	Delinq. & Foreclosed Mortgages to Capital (%)	Mort. & Credit Tenant Loans & R.E. to Capital (%)	Affiliated Invest to Capital (%)
...	-99.9	81.1	4.6	106.5	4.9	2.61	2.61	-77.0	0.0	999.9	...	...	5.1	999.9	999.9	...	...	...	...
...	87.4	19.9	1.5	6.3	1.7	4.06	4.06	999.9	0.2	544.9	...	...	0.3	999.9	999.9	...	...	...	...
...	86.0	19.8	2.2	10.5	2.5	4.60	4.60	-14.2	0.2	609.5	...	...	2.2	999.9	999.9	...	...	...	...
...	87.8	4.0	8.1	5.5	10.6	2.90	2.90	972.4	1.8	240.6	...	...	13.2	408.4	408.4	...	...	...	...
...	86.7	9.9	4.6	1.9	7.6	0.36	0.37	131.9	3.9	119.0	...	...	8.0	80.2	80.2	...	...	...	...
	Principal Lines of Business: OtherHlth (100.0%)													Principal States: NY (100.0%)					
...	...	...	-3.9	-99.9	4.2	2.51	2.51	...	...	999.9	...	1.7	-4.1	999.9	999.9	...	...	...	...
...	89.0	6.9	11.4	3.2	27.0	4.56	4.56	...	7.8	40.2	...	...	15.3	151.2	151.2	...	...	...	...
...	77.5	8.3	13.4	11.0	40.1	4.64	4.64	-45.8	3.1	61.5	...	0.8	38.0	181.7	181.7	...	...	...	...
...	88.5	6.0	1.8	1.1	3.7	2.65	2.65	18.5	3.1	199.8	...	0.7	16.7	239.2	239.5	...	...	...	...
...	87.3	8.6	5.2	1.9	9.1	0.41	0.41	66.6	4.6	106.0	...	0.6	12.1	185.2	185.3	...	...	...	...
	Principal Lines of Business: OtherHlth (100.0%)													Principal States: VA (15.5%), GA (6.5%), PA (5.4%), NC (4.5%), IL (4.3%)					
...	...	...	-64.9	-57.4	52.1	-0.88	-0.88	...	...	-61.7	...	...	-70.4	18.8	18.8	...	...	...	...
...	77.6	71.9	-52.6	-14.4	116.4	17.09	17.09	...	5.2	95.9	...	...	137.4	145.2	145.2	...	...	...	...
...	95.3	20.9	0.3	0.1	1.1	7.30	7.30	266.8	18.8	28.3	...	...	1.1	92.4	92.4	...	...	...	...
...	96.9	14.4	-9.4	-1.6	-65.9	2.90	2.90	53.7	57.2	9.2	...	...	-49.6	91.5	91.5	...	...	...	...
...	110.8	15.4	-1.0	-0.1	-7.7	-0.20	-0.20	-9.9	54.6	38.1	...	...	-5.6	81.5	81.5	...	...	...	...
	Principal Lines of Business: Medicare (64.1%), CompHosp/Med (35.9%)																		
-14,939	92.5	10.4	-2.4	-1.2	-4.4	4.04	4.53	-11.3	3.8	136.6	...	...	-2.8	124.2	152.9	5.8	...	3.0	19.6
99	97.0	8.0	-5.7	-2.9	-10.2	4.73	5.51	-15.9	3.6	118.0	...	...	-12.2	165.3	192.1	4.6	...	3.3	22.2
683	92.1	7.8	5.2	2.7	9.4	5.47	5.94	1.5	3.3	123.3	...	...	13.4	164.1	188.1	3.5	...	2.7	19.3
-9,397	90.4	7.6	7.2	3.7	12.3	3.74	-3.79	1.0	3.3	168.5	...	...	-0.6	234.5	259.0	4.8	...	2.5	19.2
-342	90.5	7.4	8.9	3.5	14.3	4.36	4.54	29.9	3.8	160.5	...	8.5	13.7	225.0	241.0	3.3	...	2.1	16.8
	Principal Lines of Business: Medicaid (55.5%), Medicare (22.6%), CompHosp/Med (21.1%), FEHBP (0.4%), MedSup (0.2%)													Principal States: MN (98.3%)					
...	93.9	12.1	-6.1	-4.1	-8.7	2.61	2.61	-34.0	2.2	296.9	...	...	-8.3	394.2	394.2	...	...	...	...
...	83.2	13.6	4.7	24.6	5.5	4.28	4.28	-91.9	0.2	999.9	...	...	5.7	999.9	999.9	...	...	...	...
...	77.9	7.9	12.8	19.2	14.1	4.02	4.02	338.3	0.6	617.1	...	...	15.1	999.9	999.9	...	...	...	...
...	86.8	8.0	5.1	9.7	5.6	2.56	2.56	-11.8	0.5	999.9	...	...	5.4	999.9	999.9	...	...	...	...
...	151.9	997.6	-0.4	-99.9	-0.4	0.26	0.26	-99.9	0.0	999.9	...	...	-0.2	999.9	999.9	...	...	...	...
	Principal Lines of Business: Medicare (100.0%)													Principal States: WI (100.0%)					
...	87.3	13.7	-0.8	-0.2	-1.9	2.91	2.91	41.7	7.9	77.6	...	...	68.4	135.3	144.1	...	...	...	...
...	85.5	12.3	8.3	1.9	18.7	2.70	2.67	33.8	8.8	83.0	2.4	15.6	19.7	165.1	181.2	...	...	...	...
...	82.3	16.4	4.4	1.6	10.0	2.79	2.71	-25.6	5.8	77.0	0.0	21.7	12.3	209.0	225.9	...	...	...	...
...	83.0	16.0	5.5	1.9	12.1	3.75	2.35	9.7	5.9	89.5	0.0	21.2	9.0	189.6	208.3	...	...	...	...
...	82.0	16.0	3.4	1.3	7.4	0.35	1.30	4.2	5.4	79.1	0.0	15.4	13.9	200.3	218.0	...	...	...	...
	Principal Lines of Business: CompHosp/Med (60.6%), Medicare (36.9%), OtherHlth (2.4%), FEHBP (0.0%)													Principal States: MN (92.7%), WI (5.6%)					
...	90.9	9.3	2.1	0.2	2.9	3.77	3.73	5.8	11.9	285.6	...	...	2.9	322.3	328.2	...	...	...	...
...	89.8	9.8	8.0	1.0	11.7	4.84	4.31	2.6	10.9	184.1	...	...	11.8	206.6	213.2	...	...	...	...
...	90.6	9.9	1.4	0.2	2.1	4.85	4.88	4.8	11.5	286.3	...	...	-0.7	305.7	319.8	...	...	...	...
-12	91.7	9.6	-7.5	-0.9	-11.2	3.64	3.80	5.1	13.7	149.8	...	...	-11.5	82.4	82.4	...	...	...	...
52	90.5	8.9	8.0	0.9	12.3	2.87	6.52	6.4	11.8	224.6	...	...	23.3	230.7	242.2	...	...	...	...
	Principal Lines of Business: CompHosp/Med (60.7%), Medicare (27.2%), MedSup (12.2%)													Principal States: WI (100.0%)					
-27	84.7	10.5	12.2	3.4	23.7	3.74	3.56	-19.8	6.3	127.1	...	2.2	25.4	162.4	165.6	...	...	...	...
65	87.3	10.3	6.8	1.8	12.4	4.64	4.13	11.7	6.4	115.6	...	...	10.1	101.7	104.5	...	...	...	...
-25	88.7	10.0	8.9	2.3	15.9	4.51	4.52	16.1	6.6	144.8	...	2.0	12.9	104.8	107.0	...	...	...	...
-74	88.9	9.4	6.2	1.5	10.7	4.07	3.83	11.3	6.8	128.5	...	1.8	6.8	85.0	85.0	...	...	...	...
351	89.8	9.8	2.9	0.7	5.0	3.34	6.14	5.3	6.9	145.7	...	2.5	5.1	49.6	49.6	...	...	...	...
	Principal Lines of Business: CompHosp/Med (64.7%), Medicare (25.7%), MedSup (9.7%)													Principal States: IA (88.2%), IL (11.8%)					
18	64.8	63.6	6.1	6.5	9.4	0.51	0.63	-13.9	0.6	240.4	40.1	35.2	6.0	163.4	178.2	...	...	13.4	56.2
289	68.0	77.9	3.0	3.5	4.6	1.38	3.48	-6.7	0.5	232.6	35.2	33.5	8.2	250.6	265.4	...	...	13.1	17.0
644	71.0	89.8	1.6	2.0	2.5	2.45	6.56	-3.0	0.5	221.1	32.0	35.6	7.5	253.2	270.2	...	...	13.2	16.1
-457	70.6	101.1	2.1	2.8	3.2	1.17	-1.69	-5.7	0.5	228.9	26.5	38.5	-2.1	247.2	262.4	...	...	14.7	20.9
-87	82.5	56.9	3.7	3.6	5.8	0.44	-0.41	115.4	1.0	168.1	10.8	11.3	4.8	160.9	170.3	...	...	13.5	16.7
	Principal Lines of Business: GrpA&H (96.0%), GrpLife (4.0%)													Principal States: IN (54.2%), OH (30.6%), WV (15.1%)					

Data in U.S. Dollars

COMPANY NAME Ultimate Parent Association Principal Officer Mailing Address Dom. : Began Bus. : Struct. : Mktg. Specialty Phone # AMB# NAIC#	Best's Financial Strength Rating FSC	Data Year	Balance Sheet: Bonds (%)	Mort. Loans & R.E. (%)	Com & Pref. Stock (%)	All Other Assets (%)	Total Assets ($000)	Life Reserves (%)	Health Reserves %)	Ann Res. & Dep. Liabilities (%)	All Other Liabilities (%)	Capital & Surplus ($000)	Operations: Direct Premiums Written ($000)	Net Premiums Written & Deposits ($000)	Operating Cash Flow ($000)	NOG Before Taxes ($000)	NOG After Taxes ($000)	Net Income ($000)
MEDICAL EYE SERVICES INC Aspasia Shappet President 345 Baker Street Costa Mesa, CA 92626 CA : 1997 : Stock : Broker Health 714-619-4660 AMB# 064712	NR-5	'05	...	44.2	...	55.8	10,279	...	...	...	100.0	4,414	4,692	4,692	1,167	610	363	363
		'06	...	44.2	...	55.8	10,083	...	...	...	100.0	4,464	3,574	3,574	202	417	268	268
		'07	...	44.0	...	56.0	9,928	...	...	...	100.0	4,461	3,446	3,446	476	409	157	157
		'08	...	45.2	...	54.8	9,495	...	...	...	100.0	4,477	3,543	3,543	-389	78	35	35
		'09	...	44.6	...	55.4	9,437	...	...	...	100.0	4,625	3,501	3,501	446	-34	-21	-21
		Rating History: NR-5, 05/07/10; NR-5, 05/07/09; NR-5, 05/12/08; NR-5, 05/14/07; NR-5, 06/13/06																
MEDICAL HEALTH INSURING OHIO Medical Mutual of Ohio Kent W. Clapp President 2060 East Ninth Street Cleveland, OH 44115-1355 OH : 1985 : Stock : Broker Group A&H, FEHBP 216-687-7000 AMB# 064217 NAIC# 95828	NR-5	'05	83.0	...	...	17.0	65,010	...	69.5	...	30.5	48,341	91,987	91,938	8,090	6,291	6,114	6,114
		'06	86.5	...	...	13.5	76,380	...	53.6	...	46.4	57,320	92,873	92,810	11,536	10,544	8,836	8,851
		'07	85.5	...	...	14.5	86,306	...	68.7	...	31.3	67,026	99,015	98,971	8,648	10,840	9,244	9,258
		'08	85.0	...	...	15.0	87,056	...	68.0	...	32.0	70,092	96,742	96,701	3,302	3,394	3,160	3,377
		'09	86.1	...	...	13.9	83,266	...	43.9	...	56.1	74,886	40,964	40,951	-2,976	6,501	4,834	4,952
		Rating History: NR-5, 03/31/10; NR-5, 08/26/09; B++pd, 07/21/08; B+ pd, 06/28/07; B+ pd, 07/25/06																
MEDICAL MUTUAL OF OHIO Medical Mutual of Ohio Richard A. Chiricosta President 2060 East Ninth Street Cleveland, OH 44115-1355 OH : 1937 : Mutual : Direct Response Group A&H 216-687-7000 AMB# 004693 NAIC# 29076	NR-5	'05	50.9	...	11.9	37.2	1,032,352	...	58.4	...	41.6	622,586	1,756,021	1,754,803	91,506	83,718	55,829	58,072
		'06	52.0	...	12.6	35.4	1,209,862	...	54.3	...	45.7	752,939	1,867,651	1,916,061	119,565	131,885	91,396	91,077
		'07	50.0	...	15.7	34.3	1,330,973	...	52.5	...	47.5	879,850	1,928,841	1,995,235	107,905	135,904	100,399	100,204
		'08	49.9	...	9.2	40.9	1,396,167	...	48.0	...	52.0	910,979	1,979,015	2,030,649	67,337	112,088	97,766	76,367
		'09	52.7	...	8.3	38.9	1,454,852	...	45.2	...	54.8	975,032	1,932,069	1,979,337	17,292	57,816	43,762	43,510
		Rating History: NR-5, 03/23/10; NR-5, 03/20/09; NR-5, 05/05/08; NR-5, 04/02/07; NR-5, 05/23/06																
MEDICAL SAVINGS INSURANCE CO Medical Savings Investment Inc J. Patrick Rooney Chairman & President 5835 West 74th Street Indianapolis, IN 46278-1757 IN : 1965 : Stock : Agency In Liquidation 317-329-8222 AMB# 007677 NAIC# 74217	F	'05	96.1	...	...	3.9	52,960	0.1	17.6	...	82.2	8,854	52,060	52,060	-3,676	257	217	279
		'06	88.9	...	...	11.1	51,757	0.1	17.7	...	82.1	5,802	45,681	45,681	-5,205	-5,008	-3,273	-3,228
		'07	85.2	...	...	14.8	43,511	0.1	15.9	...	83.9	4,295	38,968	38,968	-7,811	-4,232	-3,144	-3,123
		'08	...	...	...	...	...	...	...	...	...	...	...	...	...	...	...	...
		'09	...	...	...	...	...	...	...	...	...	...	...	...	...	...	...	...
		Rating History: F, 04/16/09; E, 12/03/08; C++, 10/15/08; B-, 03/11/08; B, 12/07/07																
MEDICO INSURANCE COMPANY Medico Mutual Insurance Holding Company Timothy J. Hall President & CEO P.O. Box 3477 Omaha, NE 68103 NE : 1930 : Stock : Agency Ind A&H, Med supp 402-391-6900 AMB# 003150 NAIC# 31119	B- Rating Outlook: Stable FSC VI	'05	77.3	...	11.6	11.1	283,679	...	93.9	...	6.1	30,295	154,436	61,403	8,788	9,752	8,148	8,794
		'06	83.3	0.3	7.9	8.4	308,119	...	94.8	...	5.2	31,241	140,190	58,720	20,272	-1,732	846	374
		'07	82.6	0.8	5.0	11.6	127,945	68.3	14.1	3.0	14.5	49,306	134,412	-131,133	-174,863	6,316	19,973	32,698
		'08	83.0	...	6.7	10.3	117,816	69.7	14.5	3.0	12.8	45,528	122,683	15,539	-6,272	-1,717	-3,514	-4,972
		'09	80.8	...	3.4	15.9	113,109	68.9	16.3	2.9	11.9	44,669	111,936	18,583	-8,806	-3,870	-3,755	-3,972
		Rating History: B-, 04/26/10; B-, 03/18/09; B-, 11/21/07; C++g, 05/16/06; C++g, 04/18/05																
MEGA LIFE AND HEALTH INS CO Blackstone Investor Group Phillip J. Hildebrand President & CEO 9151 Boulevard 26 North Richland Hills, TX 76180 OK : 1982 : Stock : Agency Group A&H, Life, Student A&H 817-255-3100 AMB# 009190 NAIC# 97055	B++ Rating Outlook: Negative FSC VIII	'05	75.5	2.2	3.9	18.4	1,254,391	18.0	58.2	8.0	15.8	366,806	1,307,995	1,346,612	27,872	194,122	132,766	130,818
		'06	79.3	2.3	4.7	13.7	1,112,325	22.5	48.3	9.0	20.2	362,192	1,278,111	1,232,164	113,724	127,524	78,600	279,838
		'07	76.9	2.2	5.2	15.6	1,061,133	25.6	45.5	8.0	20.9	274,935	1,052,507	959,797	-49,115	44,721	30,133	31,320
		'08	77.0	3.2	7.4	12.4	708,328	1.0	68.3	3.7	26.9	190,990	930,397	849,808	-310,509	9,444	-5,957	-12,813
		'09	76.4	3.3	7.6	12.7	651,185	1.2	68.6	4.3	25.9	239,119	720,419	688,554	-16,287	98,489	68,897	67,579
		Rating History: B++g, 06/07/10; B++g, 05/28/09; B++g, 07/24/08; A- g, 05/25/07; A- g, 03/10/06																
MELANCON LIFE INS CO[1] Gerald W. Melancon President 4117 N. University Avenue Carencro, LA 70520 LA : 1948 : Stock : Not Available 337-235-3315 AMB# 007794 NAIC# 75221	NR-1	'05	74.7	8.8	9.8	6.7	5,671	...	...	...	100.0	694	739	734	...	-3	-3	-1
		'06	77.0	7.9	9.8	5.2	6,079	...	...	...	100.0	800	886	881	...	87	87	94
		'07	71.4	5.5	13.7	9.4	6,369	...	...	...	100.0	820	890	885	...	-63	-63	22
		'08	75.8	2.7	10.0	11.5	6,553	...	...	...	100.0	784	947	941	...	247	234	149
		'09	83.1	2.1	10.9	3.9	6,906	...	...	...	100.0	803	987	981	...	-18	-18	-53
		Rating History: NR-1, 06/10/10; NR-1, 06/12/09; NR-1, 06/12/08; NR-1, 06/08/07; NR-1, 06/07/06																
MELLON LIFE INS CO[1] Philip K. Kocher President BNY Center, Suite 2835 Pittsburgh, PA 15258-2502 DE : 1980 : Stock : Other Direct 412-234-6398 AMB# 009048 NAIC# 92452	NR-1	'05	87.8	...	...	12.2	26,637	...	...	...	100.0	19,648	...	326	...	2,773	1,911	1,911
		'06	82.9	...	...	17.1	26,765	...	...	...	100.0	22,379	...	345	...	2,003	1,422	1,422
		'07	72.3	...	...	27.7	26,445	...	...	...	100.0	23,392	...	350	...	1,402	927	927
		'08	83.3	...	...	16.7	26,127	...	...	...	100.0	24,304	...	306	...	1,378	915	915
		'09	51.3	...	...	48.7	25,719	...	...	...	100.0	24,469	-24	283	...	965	637	637
		Rating History: NR-1, 06/10/10; NR-1, 06/12/09; NR-1, 06/12/08; NR-1, 06/08/07; NR-1, 06/07/06																
MEMBERS LIFE INS CO CUNA Mutual Insurance Society Jeffrey H. Post President & CEO P.O. Box 391 Madison, WI 53701-0391 IA : 1976 : Stock : Other Direct Ind Ann 608-238-5851 AMB# 008719 NAIC# 86126	B++ Rating Outlook: Stable FSC V	'05	93.8	1.4	...	4.8	794,891	16.2	0.0	81.5	2.3	30,926	6,561	67,233	-8,882	-4,526	-2,340	-3,207
		'06	87.8	3.6	0.5	8.0	780,097	16.9	0.0	80.4	2.7	29,511	5,954	58,504	-14,594	4,431	3,552	1,035
		'07	27.7	...	1.0	71.3	66,612	97.6	0.4	0.1	1.9	30,887	5,498	-571,316	-674,681	25,368	22,742	-8,637
		'08	81.7	...	...	18.3	45,950	98.3	0.3	0.1	1.3	12,231	4,970	4,971	-7,895	-1,686	-7,059	-5,500
		'09	64.0	...	...	36.0	54,337	97.0	0.3	0.2	2.6	21,565	4,551	4,557	10,381	-1,969	-2,822	4,531
		Rating History: B++, 04/06/10; B++, 03/24/09; A-, 01/30/08; A g, 01/05/07; A g, 11/23/05																

BEST'S PROFITABILITY, LEVERAGE AND LIQUIDITY TESTS 2005 – 2009

Data in U.S. Dollars

	Profitability Tests							Leverage Tests						Liquidity Tests					
Un-Realized Capital Gains ($000)	Benefits Paid to NPW & Dep (%)	Comm. & Expenses to NPW & Dep (%)	NOG to Total Assets (%)	NOG to Total Rev (%)	Operating Return on Equity (%)	Net Yield (%)	Total Return (%)	Change in NPW & Dep (%)	NPW & Dep to Capital (X)	Capital & Surplus to Liabilities (%)	Surplus Relief (%)	Reins Leverage (%)	Change in Capital (%)	Quick Liquidity (%)	Current Liquidity (%)	Non-Invest Grade Bonds to Capital (%)	Delinq. & Foreclosed Mortgages to Capital (%)	Mort. & Credit Tenant Loans & R.E. to Capital (%)	Affiliated Invest to Capital (%)
...	55.2	30.9	3.6	7.8	8.5	0.03	0.03	-2.6	1.1	75.3	...	...	6.4	52.9	52.9	...	...	102.9	102.9
-6	56.2	38.0	2.6	7.1	6.0	-0.41	-0.55	-23.8	0.8	79.5	...	...	1.1	50.0	50.0	...	...	99.8	99.8
...	54.0	39.9	1.6	4.3	3.5	-0.37	-0.37	-3.6	0.8	81.6	...	...	-0.1	50.6	50.6	...	...	98.0	98.0
...	57.4	37.2	0.4	1.0	0.8	-0.37	-0.37	2.8	0.8	89.2	...	...	0.4	44.5	44.5	...	...	95.9	95.9
...	59.2	36.6	-0.2	-0.6	-0.5	-0.37	-0.37	-1.2	0.8	96.1	...	...	3.3	45.9	45.9	...	...	90.9	90.9
Principal Lines of Business: Vision (100.0%)																			
...	87.8	7.6	10.0	6.5	13.5	3.70	3.70	-9.8	1.9	290.0	...	...	13.9	40.2	40.2	...	...	...	...
...	80.6	9.0	12.5	9.4	16.7	4.32	4.34	0.9	1.6	300.7	...	...	18.6	392.3	402.7	...	...	...	...
...	85.2	9.2	11.4	8.9	14.9	4.60	4.61	6.6	1.5	347.6	...	...	16.9	426.2	438.1	...	...	...	...
...	90.7	9.5	3.6	3.2	4.6	4.40	4.65	-2.3	1.4	413.2	...	...	4.6	502.4	522.2	...	...	...	...
...	82.3	9.9	5.7	10.9	6.7	4.02	4.16	-57.7	0.5	893.6	...	...	6.8	971.0	999.9	...	...	...	...
Principal Lines of Business: CompHosp/Med (65.2%), FEHBP (34.6%), MedSup (0.2%)														Principal States: OH (100.0%)					
58,354	82.6	14.0	5.8	3.1	9.7	2.77	9.59	6.7	2.8	151.9	...	...	16.7	179.3	189.4	1.1	...	...	49.7
55,659	80.8	14.3	8.2	4.7	13.3	3.38	8.71	9.2	2.5	164.8	...	0.0	20.9	175.6	184.3	1.0	...	...	50.0
29,230	81.1	14.1	7.9	4.9	12.3	3.24	5.67	4.1	2.3	195.0	...	0.0	16.9	179.7	189.2	1.0	...	...	54.1
13,936	82.0	14.8	7.2	4.7	10.9	2.89	2.34	1.8	2.2	187.8	...	0.0	3.5	191.1	198.0	1.1	...	...	59.2
22,943	83.5	15.7	3.1	2.2	4.6	2.63	4.30	-2.5	2.0	203.2	...	0.2	7.0	186.8	191.6	0.4	...	...	56.9
Principal Lines of Business: CompHosp/Med (92.1%), OtherHlth (3.7%), Medicare (2.5%), MedSup (1.6%), Dental (0.1%)														Principal States: OH (99.9%)					
...	64.6	36.2	0.4	0.4	2.5	3.98	4.10	-3.0	5.9	20.1	...	...	5.2	99.7	106.9	...	...	...	...
...	78.6	33.4	-6.3	-7.1	-44.7	4.11	4.20	-12.3	7.9	12.6	...	...	-34.5	84.5	90.5	...	...	...	...
...	72.9	39.2	-6.6	-7.9	-62.3	4.42	4.47	-14.7	9.1	11.0	...	...	-26.0	82.1	88.2	...	...	...	...
...	...	...	...	...	...	...	...	...	...	...	...	...	...	...	...	...	...	...	...
...	...	...	...	...	...	...	...	...	...	...	...	...	...	...	...	...	...	...	...
2,624	93.9	17.8	2.9	8.7	31.5	4.22	5.79	-10.3	1.9	12.7	66.7	616.8	40.6	69.2	82.7	11.6	...	6.3	62.9
-196	69.0	19.5	0.3	0.9	2.7	4.55	4.83	-4.4	1.8	11.9	52.6	666.4	2.1	65.6	78.6	9.9	...	7.6	65.2
-12,479	-33.8	-11.9	9.2	-18.5	49.6	5.44	6.70	-99.9	-2.6	65.4	20.9	999.9	54.8	83.5	109.2	13.3	...	4.0	7.5
1,118	110.7	45.7	-2.9	-9.4	-7.4	3.40	4.06	111.9	0.3	63.9	36.5	999.9	-9.2	83.6	106.7	12.4	...	2.1	12.4
-517	100.0	60.3	-3.3	-9.6	-8.3	3.98	4.48	19.6	0.4	66.3	33.6	483.5	-1.9	87.8	108.2	25.4	...	1.9	12.5
Principal Lines of Business: IndA&H (61.5%), OrdLife (20.1%), GrpA&H (18.4%), IndAnn (0.1%)														Principal States: FL (22.8%), IA (9.6%), MO (9.0%), NE (6.7%), WA (5.7%)					
-9,895	53.4	37.3	10.5	9.4	39.4	4.94	3.98	-2.5	3.6	42.2	0.8	15.5	18.9	95.2	106.8	2.9	0.0	7.3	20.3
8,654	45.5	49.2	6.6	6.1	21.6	4.94	26.61	-8.5	3.3	50.1	1.6	58.4	-0.5	89.4	106.6	1.2	0.0	6.8	20.8
-4,950	54.6	44.8	2.8	2.9	9.5	6.65	6.34	-22.1	3.4	36.6	5.8	47.7	-23.5	81.4	97.8	2.4	...	8.4	28.0
-5,360	62.6	69.2	-0.7	-0.6	-2.6	5.31	3.90	-11.5	4.4	37.6	38.5	191.9	-31.9	70.0	88.3	5.3	...	11.8	41.1
-2,121	55.3	37.0	10.1	9.4	32.0	4.71	4.24	-19.0	2.8	60.0	6.1	83.7	25.9	93.5	116.4	4.0	...	8.9	32.3
Principal Lines of Business: GrpA&H (84.4%), IndA&H (15.4%), OrdLife (0.1%), GrpLife (0.1%), IndAnn (0.0%)														Principal States: CA (10.5%), TX (8.5%), IL (6.5%), FL (5.6%), ME (4.5%)					
3	57.5	46.2	0.0	-0.2	-0.4	...	...	-4.4	0.9	17.6	...	...	-2.3	...	...	...	...	58.8	...
34	56.7	34.9	1.5	7.2	11.7	...	...	19.9	0.9	19.2	...	...	15.1	...	...	...	...	49.2	...
17	68.3	43.4	-1.0	-5.1	-7.8	...	...	0.4	0.9	18.6	...	...	1.8	...	...	...	...	35.1	...
-185	55.4	34.2	3.6	17.1	29.2	...	...	6.4	1.0	17.0	...	...	-4.3	...	...	...	...	18.8	...
73	61.3	36.1	-0.3	-1.3	-2.3	...	...	4.2	1.0	16.4	...	...	1.8	...	...	...	...	14.9	...
Principal Lines of Business: OrdLife (96.9%), IndLife (3.1%)																			
...	401.8	88.4	6.8	128.4	10.5	...	...	128.8	0.0	283.3	...	...	17.1	...	...	...	...	...	...
...	370.6	95.7	5.3	90.8	6.8	...	...	5.7	0.0	516.3	...	...	13.9	...	...	...	...	...	...
...	322.7	119.6	3.5	59.9	4.0	...	...	1.6	0.0	778.9	...	...	4.5	...	...	...	...	...	...
...	180.5	108.1	3.5	73.7	3.8	...	...	-12.5	0.0	999.9	...	...	3.9	...	...	...	...	...	...
...	84.3	117.7	2.5	61.4	2.6	...	...	-7.5	0.0	999.9	...	...	0.6	...	...	...	...	...	...
Principal Lines of Business: CrdLife (100.3%), CrdA&H (-0.3%)																			
8	143.6	28.8	-0.3	-2.1	-6.0	5.24	5.12	-33.1	1.9	4.7	0.0	11.6	-30.5	70.8	81.5	106.1	...	31.0	...
-8	178.0	22.5	0.5	3.4	11.8	5.92	5.47	-13.0	1.7	4.6	-0.2	0.7	-3.5	62.9	75.5	157.0	...	81.9	9.3
26	-25.9	1.4	5.4	-4.3	75.3	11.71	3.68	-99.9	-18.5	86.5	0.0	...	-10.1	202.7	204.7	0.0	...	...	...
...	88.3	21.9	-12.5	-99.9	-32.7	4.60	-2.29	100.9	0.4	36.4	...	...	-60.3	97.2	101.9	...	...	...	...
...	88.0	23.2	-5.6	-99.9	-16.7	4.55	13.20	-8.3	0.2	66.0	...	...	76.4	124.8	132.6	...	...	...	...
Principal Lines of Business: GrpLife (54.4%), OrdLife (45.1%), GrpA&H (0.4%), IndAnn (0.1%)														Principal States: MI (65.7%), TX (19.8%), CA (5.4%)					

Data in U.S. Dollars

COMPANY NAME Ultimate Parent Association Principal Officer Mailing Address Dom. : Began Bus. : Struct. : Mktg. Specialty Phone # AMB# NAIC#	Best's Financial Strength Rating FSC	Data Year	Balance Sheet Bonds (%)	Mort. Loans & R.E. (%)	Com & Pref. Stock (%)	All Other Assets (%)	Total Assets ($000)	Life Reserves (%)	Health Reserves %)	Ann Res. & Dep. Liabilities (%)	All Other Liabilities (%)	Capital & Surplus ($000)	Operations Direct Premiums Written ($000)	Net Premiums Written & Deposits ($000)	Operating Cash Flow ($000)	NOG Before Taxes ($000)	NOG After Taxes ($000)	Net Income ($000)
MEMORIAL INSURANCE CO OF AMER Security National Financial Scott M. Quist President P.O. Box 505 Blytheville, AR 72316 AR : 1956 : Stock : Not Available Ind A&H 801-264-1060 AMB# 068356 NAIC# 83798	**NR-5**	**'05**	59.9	0.4	25.6	14.0	34,198	0.0	0.3	...	99.7	2,138	2,063	2,063	-11,359	1,002	602	801
		'06	27.6	5.6	0.0	66.7	2,631	1.5	13.4	...	85.1	1,969	1,862	151	-28,756	-5	-5	3,109
		'07	19.3	11.0	...	69.7	1,298	3.9	33.5	...	62.6	1,046	1,672	144	-1,231	52	-16	-16
		'08	24.4	11.3	...	64.3	1,220	5.3	48.1	...	46.6	1,060	1,891	121	-83	12	12	11
		'09	25.4	11.3	...	63.3	1,174	6.7	68.1	...	25.2	1,063	1,061	124	12	1	1	1
		Rating History: NR-5, 04/19/10; NR-5, 04/27/09; NR-5, 04/11/08; NR-5, 04/27/07; NR-5, 05/03/06																
MEMORIAL LIFE INS CO[1] Lafaye C. Jackson President 4043 Highway 79 Homer, LA 71040-4700 LA : 1953 : Stock : Not Available AMB# 060053 NAIC# 91499	**NR-1**	**'05**	...	...	...	...	...	...	...	...	...	...	...	...	...	...	...	...
		'06	46.7	10.1	...	43.2	2,108	...	...	...	100.0	599	344	344	...	32	32	32
		'07	26.5	19.2	18.9	35.4	2,463	...	...	...	100.0	827	343	343	...	177	171	297
		'08	34.8	18.2	15.6	31.4	2,501	...	...	...	100.0	976	395	395	...	190	184	184
		'09	41.7	16.4	17.1	24.8	2,625	...	...	...	100.0	757	354	354	...	38	38	38
		Rating History: NR-1, 06/10/10; NR-1, 06/12/09; NR-1, 06/12/08; NR-1, 06/08/07; NR-5, 06/14/00																
MEMORIAL SERVICE LIFE INS CO Randall K. Sutton President P.O. Box 160090 Austin, TX 78716-0090 TX : 1986 : Stock : Not Available In Liquidation 512-328-0075 AMB# 068059 NAIC# 74926	**F**	**'05**	...	...	...	...	...	...	...	...	...	...	...	...	...	...	...	...
		'06	...	...	...	...	...	...	...	...	...	...	...	...	...	...	...	...
		'07	...	...	...	...	...	...	...	...	...	...	...	...	...	...	...	...
		'08	...	...	...	...	...	...	...	...	...	...	...	...	...	...	...	...
		'09	...	...	...	...	...	...	...	...	...	...	...	...	...	...	...	...
		Rating History: F, 09/26/08; E, 04/25/08; NR-1, 06/08/07; NR-1, 06/07/06; NR-1, 06/07/05																
MERCY HEALTH PLANS Sisters of Mercy Health System Inc Robert R. Vogel President & CEO 14528 South Outer Forty, Suite 300 Chesterfield, MO 63017-5705 MO : 2002 : Stock : Broker Group A&H, Medicare 314-214-8100 AMB# 060384 NAIC# 11529	**B+** Rating Outlook: Negative **FSC VI**	**'05**	2.5	...	...	97.5	24,735	...	80.8	...	19.2	12,112	77,188	77,092	7,986	-5,722	-3,325	-3,325
		'06	13.3	...	...	86.7	39,311	...	85.2	...	14.8	20,550	150,483	150,173	3,721	-10,345	-8,020	-8,020
		'07	7.1	...	...	92.9	46,067	...	65.2	...	34.8	19,874	207,930	207,422	17,370	-7,158	-6,580	-6,580
		'08	33.4	...	...	66.6	47,457	...	69.2	...	30.8	25,547	249,764	249,238	-10,491	1,900	1,482	1,482
		'09	24.7	...	...	75.3	45,907	...	70.1	...	29.9	18,458	263,129	262,382	9,113	-14,777	-12,967	-12,967
		Rating History: B+ g, 02/02/10; B++g, 06/12/09; B++g, 06/04/08; B++g, 05/07/07; B++g, 05/08/06																
MERCY HEALTH PLANS OF MO INC Sisters of Mercy Health System Inc Christopher Knackstedt Interim President & CEO 14528 South Outer Forty, Suite 300 Chesterfield, MO 63017-5705 MO : 1995 : Stock : Broker Group A&H, Medicare 314-214-8100 AMB# 064419 NAIC# 95309	**B+** Rating Outlook: Negative **FSC VI**	**'05**	68.2	...	0.6	31.2	101,825	...	57.2	...	42.8	46,852	424,928	476,310	-41,301	25,096	22,048	22,048
		'06	76.4	...	0.8	22.8	84,540	...	48.9	...	51.1	46,123	365,787	417,118	-3,461	4,483	564	564
		'07	60.2	...	1.0	38.8	68,066	...	57.4	...	42.6	30,297	340,566	340,210	-14,883	3,190	2,118	2,118
		'08	17.9	...	...	82.1	59,401	...	45.2	...	54.8	30,126	322,521	322,294	-8,562	13,365	7,162	7,162
		'09	14.3	...	...	85.7	63,898	...	36.7	...	63.3	29,801	294,396	294,150	897	12,336	8,887	8,887
		Rating History: B+ g, 02/02/10; B++g, 06/12/09; B++g, 06/04/08; B++g, 05/07/07; B++g, 05/08/06																
MERCYCARE INSURANCE COMPANY[2] Javon R. Bea President P.O. Box 2770 Janesville, WI 53547-2770 WI : 1994 : Stock : Not Available Group A&H 608-752-3431 AMB# 060254 NAIC# 60215	**NR-5**	**'05**	23.7	...	52.8	23.5	9,210	...	83.6	...	16.4	8,067	5,789	5,715	-8,148	166	170	110
		'06	28.6	...	45.4	26.0	7,373	...	85.5	...	14.5	6,246	6,477	6,394	1,810	195	150	153
		'07	28.7	...	67.4	3.9	11,439	...	93.4	...	6.6	9,591	6,641	6,563	4,109	-11	-11	-8
		'08	29.9	...	92.8	-22.7	11,674	...	86.2	...	13.8	11,301	1,353	1,333	-482	62	67	10
		'09	16.0	...	84.0	0.1	13,380	...	...	...	100.0	13,131	974	962	-1,353	-173	-176	-1,381
		Rating History: NR-5, 05/21/10; NR-5, 06/01/09; NR-5, 05/19/08; NR-5, 06/20/07; NR-5, 07/06/06																
MERIT LIFE INSURANCE CO American International Group, Inc Frederick W. Geissinger Chairman & President 601 N.W. Second Street Evansville, IN 47708-1013 IN : 1957 : Stock : Exclusive Agent Credit A&H, Credit Life, Term Life 812-424-8031 AMB# 006703 NAIC# 65951	**A-** Rating Outlook: Negative **FSC IX**	**'05**	87.6	6.9	0.0	5.5	996,920	36.8	32.7	25.0	5.4	614,548	94,848	95,420	-20,234	84,263	58,477	54,836
		'06	84.4	9.0	1.8	4.9	1,042,443	35.7	34.0	24.3	6.0	662,307	100,186	101,798	44,570	74,016	48,382	48,394
		'07	80.7	12.5	1.6	5.2	1,096,282	34.2	36.3	23.3	6.2	707,006	103,734	106,552	61,581	66,744	42,399	45,960
		'08	65.3	18.5	2.0	14.2	776,733	33.8	39.1	23.9	3.2	408,194	85,089	89,284	-343,800	63,766	43,132	-16,709
		'09	69.9	21.1	0.5	8.6	659,563	30.2	38.2	24.1	7.6	316,091	54,715	56,858	-118,365	51,113	34,792	28,016
		Rating History: A-, 12/16/09; A, 11/10/08; A u, 09/15/08; A, 05/28/08; A u, 02/14/08																
MERRILL LYNCH LIFE INS CO AEGON N.V. Lonny J. Olejniczak President 4333 Edgewood Road NE Cedar Rapids, IA 52499 AR : 1986 : Stock : Broker Ind Ann, Var ann 319-355-8511 AMB# 009537 NAIC# 79022	**A** Rating Outlook: Stable **FSC XV**	**'05**	10.9	...	0.3	88.8	14,062,480	13.1	...	4.8	82.1	400,951	710,962	686,252	-41,790	147,161	115,980	117,262
		'06	8.9	...	0.3	90.8	14,297,372	12.3	...	4.0	83.7	418,100	786,368	761,194	-122,067	232,595	193,203	193,731
		'07	8.5	...	0.2	91.3	13,911,027	12.2	...	3.9	83.9	366,011	771,535	745,442	-203,865	144,594	107,494	108,791
		'08	12.6	0.6	0.5	86.3	10,341,871	15.6	...	9.4	75.1	356,135	448,300	455,182	336,750	-294,086	-294,611	-259,862
		'09	10.8	0.5	0.1	88.6	11,102,780	15.0	...	5.3	79.7	599,014	292,039	296,802	-166,438	289,954	282,663	225,287
		Rating History: A g, 04/23/09; A+, 06/18/08; A+, 01/11/08; A gu, 08/15/07; A g, 12/26/06																
METLIFE INSURANCE CO OF CT MetLife Inc Michael K. Farrell President 18210 Crane Nest Drive, 3rd Floor Tampa, FL 33647 CT : 1864 : Stock : Agency Ind Life, Ann 860-308-1000 AMB# 007330 NAIC# 87726	**A+ u** Under Review Implication: Negative **FSC XV**	**'05**	49.9	2.2	0.7	47.2	86,992,349	6.6	0.4	38.0	54.9	4,081,299	7,140,702	9,407,729	5,438,425	1,066,087	821,598	1,000,393
		'06	45.1	3.4	2.6	48.9	85,090,231	7.1	0.5	36.9	55.5	4,089,690	4,049,720	3,721,655	-3,517,306	1,091,823	936,623	856,383
		'07	44.3	4.6	3.9	47.2	83,221,523	7.9	0.5	35.4	56.1	4,208,400	3,081,215	3,682,980	1,633,963	1,086,532	1,026,252	1,100,626
		'08	42.1	5.7	5.1	47.1	69,829,133	10.1	0.2	43.0	46.7	5,471,465	3,641,020	6,114,029	-2,349,883	864,438	714,726	242,343
		'09	42.0	6.0	3.1	48.9	67,232,743	10.5	0.2	39.1	50.2	4,928,675	3,346,756	17,439,949	-5,163,589	734,224	659,680	80,524
		Rating History: A+ gu, 02/09/10; A+ g, 02/20/09; A+ g, 06/05/08; A+ g, 05/29/07; A+ g, 05/05/06																

BEST'S PROFITABILITY, LEVERAGE AND LIQUIDITY TESTS 2005 – 2009

Data in U.S. Dollars

	Profitability Tests							Leverage Tests						Liquidity Tests					
Un-Realized Capital Gains ($000)	Benefits Paid to NPW & Dep (%)	Comm. & Expenses to NPW & Dep (%)	NOG to Total Assets (%)	NOG to Total Rev (%)	Operating Return on Equity (%)	Net Yield (%)	Total Return (%)	Change in NPW & Dep (%)	NPW & Dep to Capital (X)	Capital & Surplus to Liabilities (%)	Surplus Relief (%)	Reins Leverage (%)	Change in Capital (%)	Quick Liquidity (%)	Current Liquidity (%)	Non-Invest Grade Bonds to Capital (%)	Delinq. & Foreclosed Mortgages to Capital (%)	Mort. & Credit Tenant Loans & R.E. to Capital (%)	Affiliated Invest to Capital (%)
100	105.8	999.9	...	12.5	...	...	...	...	0.6	10.6	...	999.9	...	73.8	84.3	19.1	...	4.7	4.7
-2,487	17.7	70.0	0.0	-1.7	-0.2	-0.17	5.89	-92.7	0.1	301.2	9.2	999.9	-39.9	276.2	283.5	...	...	7.5	7.5
0	44.5	70.4	-0.8	-4.0	-1.1	4.61	4.62	-4.6	0.1	424.4	18.4	999.9	-46.8	284.3	284.3	...	...	13.6	13.6
...	37.1	85.8	1.0	3.2	1.2	3.19	3.07	-16.1	0.1	687.8	22.7	999.9	1.4	409.2	409.2	...	...	12.9	12.9
...	18.0	99.4	0.1	0.4	0.1	2.44	2.44	2.8	0.1	999.9	16.1	999.9	0.4	616.3	616.3	...	...	12.4	...
	Principal Lines of Business: IndA&H (100.0%)													Principal States: AR (100.0%)					
...	...	...	...	...	...	...	...	...	...	...	...	...	...	...	...	...	...	...	...
...	27.4	63.5	...	6.9	...	...	...	...	0.6	40.8	...	...	...	...	...	...	...	34.8	...
-12	21.7	58.5	7.5	35.8	24.0	...	...	-0.3	0.4	57.1	...	...	46.3	...	...	...	...	52.9	...
-93	24.4	60.2	7.4	37.3	20.4	...	...	15.2	0.4	65.1	...	...	10.3	...	...	...	...	46.2	...
45	28.9	84.0	1.5	7.9	4.4	...	...	-10.4	0.4	45.1	...	...	-17.3	...	...	...	...	52.8	...
	Principal Lines of Business: IndLife (80.5%), OrdLife (19.5%)																		
...	...	...	...	...	...	...	...	...	...	...	...	...	...	...	...	...	...	...	...
...	...	...	...	...	...	...	...	...	...	...	...	...	...	...	...	...	...	...	...
...	...	...	...	...	...	...	...	...	...	...	...	...	...	...	...	...	...	...	...
...	...	...	...	...	...	...	...	...	...	...	...	...	...	...	...	...	...	...	...
...	...	...	...	...	...	...	...	...	...	...	...	...	...	...	...	...	...	...	...
...	92.4	15.4	-18.1	-4.3	-39.6	2.28	2.28	226.6	6.4	95.9	...	1.4	159.2	152.1	152.1	...	...	...	...
...	91.2	15.1	-25.0	-5.3	-49.1	4.40	4.40	94.8	7.3	109.5	...	0.6	69.7	119.8	121.7	...	...	...	...
...	93.0	12.2	-15.4	-3.1	-32.6	5.97	5.97	38.1	10.4	75.9	...	0.6	-3.3	152.7	153.4	...	...	...	...
...	86.3	13.5	3.2	0.6	6.5	3.86	3.86	20.2	9.8	116.6	...	2.4	28.5	121.2	124.4	7.8	...	...	...
...	90.3	15.0	-27.8	-4.9	-58.9	2.13	2.13	5.3	14.2	67.2	...	3.2	-27.7	131.3	133.2	10.8	...	...	...
	Principal Lines of Business: CompHosp/Med (86.0%), Medicare (14.0%)													Principal States: MO (88.6%), AR (11.4%)					
...	86.7	9.6	17.7	4.6	42.4	3.48	3.48	-15.0	10.2	85.2	...	28.1	-17.9	122.7	130.7	...	...	...	1.4
...	90.8	9.5	0.6	0.1	1.2	4.72	4.72	-12.4	9.0	120.1	...	1.2	-1.6	168.6	179.1	...	...	...	1.5
...	90.2	10.0	2.8	0.6	5.5	5.75	5.75	-18.4	11.2	80.2	...	1.6	-34.3	137.8	144.9	...	...	...	2.3
...	85.8	10.6	11.2	2.2	23.7	3.48	3.48	-5.3	10.7	102.9	...	1.2	-0.6	158.0	161.1	...	...	...	...
...	87.0	10.1	14.4	3.0	29.7	1.15	1.15	-8.7	9.9	87.4	...	...	-1.1	137.8	140.1	...	...	...	...
	Principal Lines of Business: Medicare (61.5%), CompHosp/Med (38.5%)													Principal States: MO (91.8%), TX (5.9%)					
1,615	88.7	11.0	1.4	2.9	2.1	1.44	17.26	-91.1	0.7	706.2	...	0.6	-1.8	116.5	122.9	...	...	...	60.6
-4,211	92.8	5.8	1.8	2.3	2.1	1.57	-46.69	11.9	1.0	553.7	...	0.5	-22.6	277.1	283.5	...	...	...	53.5
-28	95.2	7.3	-0.1	-0.2	-0.1	1.76	1.47	2.6	0.7	519.1	...	...	53.6	178.9	189.1	...	...	...	71.3
1,205	93.7	17.0	0.6	4.3	0.6	1.84	12.72	-79.7	0.1	999.9	...	0.0	17.8	377.4	472.5	...	...	...	79.7
3,213	107.5	17.6	-1.4	-17.0	-1.4	0.55	20.92	-27.8	0.1	999.9	...	0.0	16.2	774.0	783.4	...	...	...	85.5
	Principal Lines of Business: CompHosp/Med (100.0%)													Principal States: WI (91.3%), IL (8.7%)					
-1,855	59.7	44.6	5.8	35.6	9.5	7.10	6.64	-13.6	0.2	164.2	0.0	0.0	-0.3	105.4	161.0	7.7	...	12.6	...
626	49.1	44.4	4.7	29.0	7.6	6.61	6.72	6.7	0.2	179.6	0.0	0.1	8.1	103.5	164.1	6.7	...	16.3	...
1,292	47.9	44.0	4.0	24.6	6.2	6.44	6.91	4.7	0.1	188.6	0.0	0.1	7.0	106.7	168.4	6.9	...	20.5	0.2
-2,057	60.9	46.6	4.6	28.6	7.7	7.01	0.39	-16.2	0.2	112.3	0.0	0.1	-42.6	73.9	122.6	13.2	...	37.2	0.3
2,876	89.3	52.2	4.8	37.1	9.6	5.77	4.83	-36.3	0.2	95.4	0.0	0.0	-21.6	42.8	90.3	19.0	...	46.9	...
	Principal Lines of Business: CrdA&H (35.1%), CrdLife (31.9%), OrdLife (16.7%), IndA&H (10.1%), GrpLife (6.2%)													Principal States: IL (11.8%), IN (9.6%), NC (8.3%), GA (5.9%), VA (5.5%)					
-178	249.4	12.7	0.8	11.1	33.8	4.80	4.93	-8.7	1.7	18.2	...	2.3	38.5	49.5	59.8	8.4	...	...	7.0
178	233.9	11.8	1.4	17.0	47.2	4.85	4.96	10.9	1.8	20.0	...	1.0	3.3	59.4	69.6	3.5	...	...	...
-107	264.2	12.2	0.8	9.5	27.4	5.07	5.19	-2.1	2.0	18.8	...	1.5	-12.3	54.9	63.7	2.8	...	...	...
-2,301	317.9	20.7	-2.4	-40.1	-81.6	5.15	6.51	-38.9	1.3	15.4	...	2.4	-5.0	55.3	65.2	21.0	...	21.5	...
-1,103	377.5	31.5	2.6	47.0	59.2	4.62	2.41	-34.8	0.5	30.2	...	0.7	69.8	69.8	78.1	9.2	...	11.7	6.6
	Principal Lines of Business: IndAnn (97.9%), OrdLife (2.1%)													Principal States: TX (10.9%), IL (10.6%), CA (8.7%), FL (7.6%), MI (5.7%)					
-247,894	82.0	10.0	0.9	7.9	13.7	6.13	6.05	-38.1	2.0	10.2	1.6	118.3	-44.9	62.8	75.2	57.0	0.2	40.2	17.3
-14,671	233.7	14.4	1.1	13.7	22.9	5.42	5.26	-60.4	0.8	10.7	1.3	132.7	0.6	53.3	66.2	56.2	0.1	59.8	18.0
-290,520	229.3	10.7	1.2	17.5	24.7	5.44	5.00	-1.0	0.7	11.4	1.3	139.2	6.4	52.0	65.6	69.9	0.0	75.6	26.9
-355,766	116.5	5.4	0.9	12.2	14.8	4.77	3.04	66.0	1.0	14.3	1.0	124.5	18.4	57.6	72.3	54.8	...	65.6	33.1
-456,622	28.8	1.9	1.0	13.0	12.7	4.15	1.82	185.2	3.3	14.2	1.1	140.6	-12.8	48.7	62.1	69.3	...	77.3	50.3
	Principal Lines of Business: GrpAnn (83.6%), IndAnn (14.8%), OrdLife (1.6%), IndA&H (0.0%), GrpA&H (0.0%)													Principal States: DE (81.3%)					

2010 BEST'S KEY RATING GUIDE — LIFE/HEALTH EDITION
ANNUAL STATEMENT DATA FOR YEARS 2005 – 2009

Data in U.S. Dollars

COMPANY NAME Ultimate Parent Association Principal Officer Mailing Address Dom. : Began Bus. : Struct. : Mktg. Specialty Phone # AMB# NAIC#	Best's Financial Strength Rating FSC	Data Year	Balance Sheet: Bonds (%)	Mort. Loans & R.E. (%)	Com & Pref. Stock (%)	All Other Assets (%)	Total Assets ($000)	Life Reserves (%)	Health Reserves (%)	Ann Res. & Dep. Liabilities (%)	All Other Liabilities (%)	Capital & Surplus ($000)	Operations: Direct Premiums Written ($000)	Net Premiums Written & Deposits ($000)	Operating Cash Flow ($000)	NOG Before Taxes ($000)	NOG After Taxes ($000)	Net Income ($000)
METLIFE INSURANCE LIMITED (GU)[1] Robert G. Glading President 2 Park Street, Level 9 Sydney, Australia NSW 2000 GU : 1949 : Stock : Not Available 671-475-841 AMB# 060715 NAIC# 13649	NR-1	'05	...	...	...	...	...	...	...	...	...	...	...	...	...	...	...	...
		'06	...	...	...	...	...	...	...	...	...	...	...	...	...	...	...	...
		'07	...	...	...	...	...	...	...	...	...	...	...	...	...	...	...	...
		'08	...	...	...	...	...	...	...	...	...	...	...	...	...	...	...	...
		'09	...	...	...	100.0	2,378	...	...	...	100.0	749	970	951	...	280	79	79
		Rating History: NR-1, 06/10/10																
METLIFE INVESTORS INSURANCE CO MetLife Inc Michael K. Farrell Chairman, President & CEO 18210 Crane Nest Dr., 3rd Floor Tampa, FL 33647 MO : 1981 : Stock : Broker Ann, SPDA's, Var ann 949-717-6536 AMB# 009075 NAIC# 93513	A+ u Under Review Implication: Negative FSC XV	'05	23.1	0.6	0.0	76.2	10,190,580	1.7	...	19.5	78.9	175,412	1,406,816	1,362,476	-40,927	5,591	1,386	4,166
		'06	17.8	0.8	0.6	80.7	11,341,829	1.5	...	15.8	82.7	283,962	1,413,740	1,226,663	-97,105	40,474	97,790	115,908
		'07	16.9	0.6	0.5	82.0	11,882,623	1.4	...	13.7	84.9	328,563	1,522,137	1,449,864	-85,517	30,482	39,372	39,686
		'08	19.3	0.8	0.5	79.4	9,523,373	1.8	...	18.8	79.4	397,632	2,029,221	1,504,016	375,567	-58,648	-30,154	-34,949
		'09	16.0	0.9	0.0	83.1	11,670,931	1.4	...	14.7	83.9	410,754	1,965,370	1,391,667	-456,619	71,796	64,663	49,043
		Rating History: A+ gu, 02/09/10; A+ g, 02/20/09; A+ g, 06/05/08; A+ g, 05/29/07; A+ g, 05/05/06																
METLIFE INVESTORS USA INS CO MetLife Inc Michael K. Farrell Chairman, President & CEO 18210 Crane Nest Dr., 3rd Floor Tampa, FL 33647 DE : 1961 : Stock : Broker FPDA's, SPDA's, Var ann 949-717-6536 AMB# 006125 NAIC# 61050	A+ u Under Review Implication: Negative FSC XV	'05	23.3	2.4	...	74.3	18,807,765	5.3	...	18.2	76.5	538,368	3,535,691	4,462,675	1,173,045	-300,666	-248,880	-243,673
		'06	16.4	2.0	0.5	81.1	24,029,259	5.7	...	13.1	81.2	575,049	5,716,862	5,433,348	-153,414	-197,472	-119,344	-115,784
		'07	14.2	1.4	0.4	84.1	29,684,128	5.9	...	10.3	83.7	584,168	7,580,873	7,346,706	546,833	-1,071,067	-1,092,279	-1,106,497
		'08	17.0	1.4	0.4	81.2	26,939,324	8.0	...	14.6	77.4	760,534	8,471,258	6,919,699	2,051,312	-576,081	-444,582	-482,265
		'09	19.2	1.5	0.0	79.2	40,666,152	6.1	...	12.8	81.1	1,406,057	10,687,574	9,031,817	2,392,809	25,549	11,497	-24,221
		Rating History: A+ gu, 02/09/10; A+ g, 02/20/09; A+ g, 06/05/08; A+ g, 05/29/07; A+ g, 05/05/06																
METROPOLITAN HEALTH PLAN[2] David R. Johnson Executive Director 400 South 4th Street, Suite 201 Minneapolis, MN 55415 MN : 1984 : Non-Profit : Broker Medicaid, Medicare 612-543-3397 AMB# 068558 NAIC# 52627	NR-5	'05	...	...	...	100.0	32,207	...	44.1	...	55.9	12,619	103,715	102,794	-7,490	-2,880	-2,880	-2,880
		'06	...	...	...	100.0	33,575	...	40.3	...	59.7	10,352	112,272	111,474	-135	-1,987	-1,987	-1,987
		'07	...	5.3	...	94.7	37,893	...	43.2	...	56.8	12,191	121,660	120,949	3,245	-6,467	-6,467	-6,467
		'08	...	5.3	...	94.7	26,925	...	78.0	...	22.0	4,771	152,835	152,291	-9,363	-8,432	-8,432	-8,432
		'09	...	3.5	...	96.5	27,377	...	67.3	...	32.7	8,053	140,658	140,025	728	2,473	2,473	2,473
		Rating History: NR-5, 05/12/10; NR-4, 07/15/08; B, 07/15/08; B, 06/14/07; B, 06/26/06																
METROPOLITAN LIFE INS CO MetLife Inc C. Robert Henrikson Chairman, President & CEO 18210 Crane Nest Drive, 3rd Floor Tampa, FL 33647 NY : 1868 : Stock : Career Agent Ann, Group Life, Ind Life 212-579-2211 AMB# 006704 NAIC# 65978	A+ u Under Review Implication: Negative FSC XV	'05	49.6	13.9	1.7	34.9	251,626,153	23.0	2.6	34.0	40.4	8,750,417	29,055,331	36,968,170	691,213	2,001,915	1,375,605	2,188,409
		'06	48.1	13.5	3.5	34.9	280,557,488	20.6	2.7	32.8	43.8	9,197,539	29,656,561	40,099,369	18,428,926	1,817,548	1,296,474	1,027,211
		'07	45.5	14.2	3.8	36.6	297,465,527	14.0	3.4	33.7	48.8	13,003,979	29,588,845	46,867,774	7,443,503	2,934,330	2,069,704	2,123,095
		'08	41.7	15.2	3.1	40.0	289,578,009	14.7	4.0	40.4	40.8	11,592,263	34,973,784	76,747,602	5,912,392	686,541	552,499	-337,644
		'09	45.4	14.5	3.8	36.3	289,575,344	14.9	4.8	39.3	41.0	12,633,855	31,808,006	63,434,916	-641,044	2,103,484	1,872,172	1,221,422
		Rating History: A+ gu, 02/09/10; A+ g, 02/20/09; A+ g, 06/05/08; A+ g, 05/29/07; A+ g, 05/05/06																
METROPOLITAN TOWER LIFE INS CO MetLife Inc Eric T. Steigerwalt President & Treasurer 18210 Crane Nest Dr., 3rd Floor Tampa, FL 33647 DE : 1983 : Stock : Inactive Var life 212-578-2211 AMB# 009165 NAIC# 97136	A+ u Under Review Implication: Negative FSC XV	'05	75.3	11.7	0.1	12.9	5,806,117	72.4	...	...	27.6	690,349	190,847	217,766	-792,145	132,063	85,327	352,849
		'06	53.1	5.5	2.9	38.5	7,261,999	57.7	...	...	42.3	1,042,833	179,199	203,997	155,662	121,098	73,732	2,786,763
		'07	62.2	20.3	3.2	14.3	6,179,138	69.4	...	...	30.6	1,137,780	170,906	191,422	-809,055	181,818	104,271	103,215
		'08	58.9	24.0	3.5	13.6	5,511,567	74.0	...	...	26.0	884,826	161,637	199,847	-291,926	128,416	80,030	212,196
		'09	57.6	26.6	0.3	15.5	5,000,315	80.3	...	...	19.7	866,623	157,664	223,033	-283,316	139,528	93,924	57,181
		Rating History: A+ gu, 02/09/10; A+ g, 02/20/09; A+ g, 06/05/08; A+ g, 05/29/07; A+ g, 05/05/06																
MHNET LIFE AND HEALTH INS CO Coventry Health Care Inc Susan Norris President P.O. Box 209010 Austin, TX 78720 TX : 2006 : Stock : Broker 513-340-4208 AMB# 060707 NAIC# 12509	NR-2	'05	...	...	...	...	...	...	...	...	...	...	...	...	...	...	...	...
		'06	...	...	...	...	...	...	...	...	...	...	...	...	...	...	...	...
		'07	...	...	...	...	...	...	...	...	...	...	...	...	...	...	...	...
		'08	...	...	...	...	...	...	...	...	...	...	...	...	...	...	...	...
		'09	...	...	...	100.0	3,889	...	78.9	...	21.1	3,525	...	...	-732	516	229	229
		Rating History: NR-2, 06/07/10																
MID-ATLANTIC VISION SERVICE PL Vision Service Plan James Robinson Lynch President & CEO 3333 Quality Drive Rancho Cordova, CA 95670 VA : 1960 : Other : Not Available Group A&H 916-851-5000 AMB# 064478 NAIC# 53031	A Rating Outlook: Stable FSC IX	'05	38.5	...	11.9	49.6	38,900	...	59.7	...	40.3	35,804	25,187	25,187	3,831	5,879	5,879	6,521
		'06	43.1	...	10.6	46.3	47,669	...	52.9	...	47.1	44,774	29,852	29,852	12,404	8,596	8,596	8,948
		'07	64.9	...	12.7	22.4	56,927	...	47.7	...	52.3	53,393	33,646	33,646	9,733	8,278	8,278	8,872
		'08	68.7	...	7.0	24.3	64,379	...	13.4	...	86.6	50,471	42,894	42,894	6,840	7,746	-1,419	-3,182
		'09	50.0	...	8.1	42.0	73,142	...	18.5	...	81.5	56,381	51,019	51,019	8,125	8,180	5,563	4,172
		Rating History: A g, 02/09/10; A g, 11/24/08; A g, 11/30/07; A g, 10/12/06; A g, 11/10/05																
MID ROGUE HEALTH PLAN[2] Robert M. Gentry, M.D. President 820 N.E. 7th Street Grants Pass, OR 97526-1635 OR : 2005 : Stock : Not Available Medicaid 541-471-4106 AMB# 064903 NAIC# 12253	NR-5	'05	...	...	...	...	...	...	...	...	...	...	...	...	...	...	...	...
		'06	26.2	...	11.0	62.8	10,552	...	30.5	...	69.5	5,051	31,647	31,221	4,354	1,668	1,240	1,240
		'07	16.4	...	18.9	64.7	8,528	...	43.4	...	56.6	3,519	34,965	34,558	-2,957	942	426	425
		'08	12.3	...	5.5	82.2	17,233	...	33.6	...	66.4	3,234	66,379	65,565	3,207	2,569	2,016	2,016
		'09	...	...	...	100.0	13,209	...	28.8	...	71.2	4,809	56,352	55,646	-4,555	-846	-548	-516
		Rating History: NR-5, 05/21/10; NR-5, 09/11/09; NR-5, 07/14/08; NR-5, 06/29/07																

BEST'S PROFITABILITY, LEVERAGE AND LIQUIDITY TESTS 2005 – 2009

Data in U.S. Dollars

—	Profitability Tests							Leverage Tests						Liquidity Tests					
Un-Realized Capital Gains ($000)	Benefits Paid to NPW & Dep (%)	Comm. & Expenses to NPW & Dep (%)	NOG to Total Assets (%)	NOG to Total Rev (%)	Operating Return on Equity (%)	Net Yield (%)	Total Return (%)	Change in NPW & Dep (%)	NPW & Dep to Capital (X)	Capital & Surplus to Liabilities (%)	Surplus Relief (%)	Reins Leverage (%)	Change in Capital (%)	Quick Liquidity (%)	Current Liquidity (%)	Non-Invest Grade Bonds to Capital (%)	Delinq. & Foreclosed Mortgages to Capital (%)	Mort. & Credit Tenant Loans & R.E. to Capital (%)	Affiliated Invest to Capital (%)
...	...	...	...	...	...	...	...	...	...	...	...	...	...	...	...	...	...	...	...
...	...	...	...	...	...	...	...	...	...	...	...	...	...	...	...	...	...	...	...
...	...	...	...	...	...	...	...	...	...	...	...	...	...	...	...	...	...	...	...
...	...	...	...	...	...	...	...	...	...	...	...	...	...	...	...	...	...	...	...
...	29.2	65.6	...	8.2	...	...	...	...	1.3	45.9	...	...	...	...	...	...	...	...	...

Principal Lines of Business: CrdLife (100.0%)

4,637	65.6	10.7	0.0	0.1	0.8	4.23	4.68	211.3	7.1	7.8	2.4	555.8	2.7	67.3	78.0	74.8	...	33.5	39.4
-4,699	94.1	12.0	0.9	6.6	42.6	4.22	4.81	-10.0	4.1	13.2	2.6	369.2	56.5	71.3	82.1	35.4	...	29.8	25.5
3,316	91.7	11.5	0.3	2.3	12.9	4.39	4.53	18.2	4.2	16.4	1.1	268.3	14.6	69.0	81.7	25.5	...	21.3	20.3
51,991	65.4	9.9	-0.3	-1.7	-8.3	4.26	6.00	3.7	3.6	16.6	3.7	382.2	19.4	97.6	110.8	18.6	...	18.5	0.5
-45,637	48.1	9.9	0.6	3.8	16.0	4.29	1.71	-7.5	3.4	21.5	4.6	423.2	-0.2	75.4	90.4	34.3	...	25.0	11.1

Principal Lines of Business: IndAnn (99.8%), OrdLife (0.2%), IndA&H (0.0%), GrpLife (0.0%)
Principal States: TX (7.9%), CA (6.5%), IL (6.2%), NC (5.6%), FL (5.1%)

-5,630	23.9	23.6	-1.5	-5.0	-54.1	4.17	4.15	402.6	7.8	11.5	7.3	446.0	43.1	64.7	75.8	37.1	...	78.9	23.5
-3,065	34.6	12.0	-0.6	-2.0	-21.4	4.13	4.12	21.8	9.0	12.6	2.9	563.1	6.4	54.3	66.2	33.0	...	79.1	57.9
9,700	35.6	25.1	-4.1	-13.5	-99.9	4.12	3.99	35.2	11.9	11.9	1.5	787.6	2.5	53.3	64.4	29.7	...	65.4	77.5
24,982	32.1	14.8	-1.6	-5.7	-66.1	4.03	3.77	-5.8	8.5	10.4	8.7	999.9	31.8	47.9	57.3	28.4	...	46.0	203.4
-33,356	20.0	13.2	0.0	0.1	1.1	4.15	3.33	30.5	6.4	15.2	5.3	690.0	72.7	66.6	79.9	31.7	...	44.1	28.5

Principal Lines of Business: IndAnn (92.4%), OrdLife (6.5%), GrpAnn (1.0%)
Principal States: CA (10.6%), FL (9.3%), NJ (6.8%), TX (6.1%), PA (6.1%)

...	83.8	19.5	-8.5	-2.8	-20.0	1.79	1.79	8.7	8.1	64.4	...	5.8	-22.2	120.9	120.9	...	...	...	...
...	81.3	21.2	-6.0	-1.8	-17.3	3.88	3.88	8.4	10.8	44.6	...	0.3	-18.0	101.4	101.4	...	...	...	...
...	82.1	23.1	-18.1	-5.3	-57.4	3.76	3.76	8.5	9.9	47.4	...	...	17.8	97.8	97.8	...	...	16.4	16.4
...	85.4	21.4	-26.0	-5.5	-99.4	4.50	4.50	25.9	31.9	21.5	...	...	-60.9	71.2	71.2	...	...	29.7	29.7
...	80.7	17.8	9.1	1.8	38.6	2.06	2.06	-8.1	17.4	41.7	...	...	68.8	85.5	85.5	...	...	12.0	12.0

Principal Lines of Business: Medicaid (71.6%), Medicare (21.2%), OtherHlth (7.3%)
Principal States: MN (100.0%)

501,605	66.2	8.8	0.6	3.9	14.9	5.68	6.42	-1.5	2.9	6.6	4.9	50.7	-8.3	41.6	50.8	74.3	0.2	273.8	109.6
393,246	68.4	8.8	0.5	3.7	14.4	5.71	5.77	8.5	2.9	6.3	4.5	71.1	6.2	39.8	50.0	82.0	0.3	278.7	109.9
185,511	59.5	5.5	0.7	10.7	18.6	5.72	5.82	16.9	2.7	8.1	7.2	187.8	28.5	37.3	47.7	65.8	0.1	241.2	93.5
577,126	35.8	6.4	0.2	1.2	4.5	5.77	5.61	63.8	4.8	7.2	3.8	218.7	-8.1	41.0	51.5	72.3	0.0	274.0	80.5
-2,102,160	42.8	7.6	0.6	4.8	15.5	4.74	3.44	-17.3	4.2	6.9	3.7	197.4	-5.2	36.5	47.5	98.2	...	276.6	102.3

Principal Lines of Business: GrpAnn (62.2%), IndAnn (21.9%), GrpLife (8.4%), OrdLife (4.2%), GrpA&H (3.2%)
Principal States: NY (40.3%), DE (15.4%), CA (3.5%)

-6,085	147.0	4.3	1.4	23.5	9.1	4.83	9.24	4.0	0.3	16.8	...	87.9	-41.9	59.7	71.9	18.7	...	82.8	15.7
511	156.9	19.3	1.1	20.4	8.5	4.87	60.58	-6.3	0.2	17.9	...	57.7	32.4	86.8	98.7	9.2	...	37.1	7.2
-12,762	155.2	-3.1	1.6	28.1	9.6	4.96	4.74	-6.2	0.2	24.7	0.0	48.8	10.4	51.4	64.3	8.6	...	104.9	23.6
-186,335	152.4	3.5	1.4	22.9	7.9	5.14	4.25	4.4	0.2	21.4	0.0	59.2	-20.1	45.1	58.9	12.4	...	138.2	8.6
-233,321	121.9	6.1	1.8	29.0	10.7	5.35	0.12	11.6	0.2	23.1	0.0	57.0	-3.8	43.0	55.0	27.1	...	144.7	17.5

Principal Lines of Business: IndAnn (77.8%), OrdLife (22.2%)
Principal States: NY (17.0%), IL (7.9%), PA (7.8%), FL (7.5%), NJ (6.0%)

...	...	...	...	...	...	...	...	...	...	...	...	...	...	...	...	...	...	...	...
...	...	...	...	...	...	...	...	...	...	...	...	...	...	...	...	...	...	...	...
...	...	...	...	...	...	...	...	...	...	...	...	...	...	...	...	...	...	...	...
...	...	...	...	...	...	...	...	...	...	...	...	...	...	...	...	...	...	...	...
...	35.1	37.6	...	12.2	...	...	...	...	...	968.9	...	...	...	886.7	886.7	...	...	...	...

-217	87.5	-7.8	16.9	22.3	18.6	2.72	4.16	14.7	0.7	999.9	...	...	29.8	999.9	999.9	...	...	...	...
21	73.3	6.2	19.9	26.1	21.3	4.13	5.12	18.5	0.7	999.9	...	...	25.1	999.9	999.9	...	...	...	...
-227	72.8	9.0	15.8	22.3	16.9	4.72	5.48	12.7	0.6	999.9	...	...	19.3	999.9	999.9	...	...	...	...
-1,254	76.4	10.7	-2.3	-3.0	-2.7	3.47	-1.83	27.5	0.8	362.9	...	...	-5.5	429.4	455.3	...	...	...	...
1,365	78.0	7.3	8.1	10.3	10.4	2.25	2.26	18.9	0.9	336.4	...	...	11.7	340.8	370.1	1.3	...	...	23.1

Principal Lines of Business: Vision (100.0%)
Principal States: VA (54.0%), MD (46.0%)

...	...	...	...	...	...	...	...	...	...	...	...	...	...	...	...	...	...	...	...
-64	80.4	15.4	...	3.9	...	...	...	...	6.2	91.8	...	...	...	174.4	177.5	...	...	...	...
...	75.9	22.9	4.5	1.2	9.9	4.38	4.37	10.7	9.8	70.3	...	3.7	-30.3	176.4	186.9	...	...	...	...
...	81.8	14.7	15.7	3.1	59.7	3.17	3.17	89.7	20.3	23.1	...	4.0	-8.1	52.7	52.7	...	...	...	...
...	91.8	10.3	-3.6	-1.0	-13.6	2.44	2.83	-15.1	11.6	57.2	...	10.0	48.7	86.1	87.8	...	...	...	...

Principal Lines of Business: Medicare (99.6%), Medicaid (0.4%)
Principal States: OR (100.0%)

2010 BEST'S KEY RATING GUIDE — LIFE/HEALTH EDITION
ANNUAL STATEMENT DATA FOR YEARS 2005 – 2009

Data in U.S. Dollars

COMPANY NAME Ultimate Parent Association Principal Officer Mailing Address Dom. : Began Bus. : Struct. : Mktg. Specialty Phone # AMB# NAIC#	Best's Financial Strength Rating FSC	Data Year	Balance Sheet: Bonds (%)	Mort. Loans & R.E. (%)	Com & Pref. Stock (%)	All Other Assets (%)	Total Assets ($000)	Life Reserves (%)	Health Reserves (%)	Ann Res. & Dep. Liabilities (%)	All Other Liabilities (%)	Capital & Surplus ($000)	Operations: Direct Premiums Written ($000)	Net Premiums Written & Deposits ($000)	Operating Cash Flow ($000)	NOG Before Taxes ($000)	NOG After Taxes ($000)	Net Income ($000)
MID-WEST NATIONAL LIFE OF TN Blackstone Investor Group Phillip Hildebrand President and CEO 9151 Boulevard 26 North Richland Hills, TX 76180 TX : 1965 : Stock : Agency Group A&H, Life 817-255-3100 AMB# 006715 NAIC# 66087	**B++** Rating Outlook: Negative **FSC VIII**	'05	91.9	...	...	8.1	426,143	23.2	54.6	9.8	12.5	154,418	426,296	427,842	-10,577	119,763	80,548	79,369
		'06	85.1	...	0.6	14.4	409,610	23.1	54.4	9.7	12.9	142,311	431,188	431,871	-9,276	106,035	71,239	71,047
		'07	91.3	...	0.6	8.0	374,848	26.5	47.9	10.7	15.0	145,267	365,085	364,101	-34,377	110,675	71,305	72,173
		'08	88.8	...	1.0	10.2	218,508	2.5	71.6	...	25.9	98,335	280,177	272,994	-150,398	76,623	49,823	38,467
		'09	80.2	...	0.1	19.6	197,285	2.6	75.4	...	22.1	77,820	255,657	247,608	-12,659	41,820	28,157	31,869
		Rating History: B++g, 06/07/10; B++g, 05/28/09; B++g, 07/24/08; A- g, 05/25/07; A- g, 03/10/06																
MIDLAND NATIONAL LIFE INS CO Sammons Enterprises, Inc. Michael M. Masterson Chairman One Sammons Plaza Sioux Falls, SD 57193 IA : 1906 : Stock : Agency Univ Life, Var Univ life, Term Life 605-335-5700 AMB# 006711 NAIC# 66044	**A+** Rating Outlook: Negative **FSC XIV**	'05	85.2	1.9	1.8	11.1	18,824,108	23.5	0.0	47.7	28.8	964,575	3,105,465	2,256,038	2,468,845	264,653	190,070	186,840
		'06	83.2	1.4	2.6	12.8	21,661,560	21.6	0.0	47.1	31.3	1,020,003	3,199,707	2,456,273	2,460,271	224,517	149,789	155,139
		'07	84.4	1.1	2.4	12.1	23,518,176	20.8	0.0	46.5	32.7	1,109,422	2,763,151	2,087,281	1,587,109	167,160	108,697	112,166
		'08	86.3	1.0	1.9	10.8	25,408,812	19.6	0.0	46.3	34.1	1,240,344	2,858,164	2,264,315	2,215,598	254,114	168,510	110,608
		'09	81.3	0.9	1.8	16.0	26,496,854	18.7	0.0	46.2	35.1	1,391,869	2,757,655	2,328,823	275,105	201,065	83,327	-31,253
		Rating History: A+ g, 04/16/09; A+ g, 01/04/08; A+ g, 08/31/06; A+, 06/16/05; A+, 06/07/04																
MIDWEST HEALTH PLAN INC RJM Company LLC Mark Saffer President 5050 Schaefer Road Dearborn, MI 48126 MI : 1993 : Stock : Agency Medicaid, Medicare 313-581-3700 AMB# 064518 NAIC# 95814	**NR-5**	'05	2.4	...	...	97.6	41,531	...	74.2	...	25.8	23,580	125,440	124,927	5,762	8,641	5,704	5,704
		'06	2.2	...	...	97.8	46,259	...	72.0	...	28.0	29,369	129,243	128,668	5,216	9,066	6,009	6,009
		'07	1.9	...	...	98.1	54,546	...	84.7	...	15.3	33,857	176,690	176,195	8,258	6,802	4,373	4,373
		'08	1.6	...	...	98.4	62,789	...	57.7	...	42.3	38,803	201,115	200,504	8,347	8,087	5,224	5,224
		'09	1.4	...	...	98.6	71,885	...	50.4	...	49.6	45,989	227,576	227,020	7,379	10,960	7,060	7,060
		Rating History: NR-5, 05/21/10; NR-5, 08/26/09; B pd, 07/14/08; B pd, 06/19/07; B pd, 07/17/06																
MIDWEST SECURITY LIFE INS CO UnitedHealth Group Inc Richard G. Dunlop President & CEO 2700 Midwest Drive Onalaska, WI 54650-8764 WI : 1973 : Stock : Agency Group A&H, Ann, Group Life 608-783-7130 AMB# 008297 NAIC# 79480	**A-** Rating Outlook: Stable **FSC V**	'05	67.0	5.7	...	27.3	92,093	0.6	65.5	...	33.9	44,488	219,947	221,145	-20,243	19,578	16,685	16,685
		'06	67.7	7.0	...	25.3	72,486	1.0	67.0	...	32.0	40,893	162,545	162,543	-19,055	18,131	11,740	11,740
		'07	73.0	7.7	...	19.3	64,083	1.2	68.7	...	30.1	34,843	127,690	127,690	-8,268	6,862	4,593	4,593
		'08	69.8	1.1	...	29.0	50,291	0.7	74.2	...	25.2	24,359	118,723	118,723	-13,214	2,137	1,146	2,991
		'09	81.6	1.4	...	17.0	39,759	0.9	73.5	...	25.5	20,906	90,061	90,061	-10,586	8,248	5,930	5,819
		Rating History: A-, 06/15/09; A-, 01/29/08; A-, 11/21/07; A-, 11/16/06; A-, 08/17/06																
MIDWESTERN UNITED LIFE INS CO ING Groep N.V. Donald W. Britton President 5780 Powers Ferry Road, NW Atlanta, GA 30327-4390 IN : 1948 : Stock : Agency Ann, Trad Life, Univ Life 770-980-5100 AMB# 006718 NAIC# 66109	**A-** Rating Outlook: Stable **FSC VIII**	'05	85.4	6.9	0.0	7.7	254,857	78.6	...	17.9	3.5	89,642	5,080	9,657	-3,655	8,334	5,751	5,889
		'06	80.9	4.5	1.1	13.6	251,989	79.6	...	17.9	2.4	94,704	4,874	9,613	-3,146	7,719	5,326	5,016
		'07	71.3	3.8	1.6	23.3	250,388	77.8	...	17.5	4.6	96,143	4,694	9,257	-922	6,784	817	1,456
		'08	82.0	3.1	0.5	14.4	244,724	77.7	...	17.8	4.5	96,123	4,578	9,266	-2,771	4,156	2,721	731
		'09	76.4	1.8	0.0	21.9	243,674	75.7	...	18.4	5.9	102,865	4,327	9,732	-1,090	9,541	8,031	7,473
		Rating History: A-, 06/11/10; A-, 04/24/09; A, 06/18/08; A, 05/11/07; A, 02/24/06																
MII LIFE INC Aware Integrated Inc David Spalding President & CEO 3535 Blue Cross Road St. Paul, MN 55122 MN : 1959 : Stock : Broker Dis inc, Group Life 651-662-8000 AMB# 009495 NAIC# 61522	**B++** Rating Outlook: Stable **FSC IV**	'05	34.1	...	20.0	46.0	101,558	16.8	44.7	33.2	5.3	43,422	39,628	55,351	17,484	-1,836	-1,431	-1,432
		'06	41.0	...	29.4	29.6	84,059	18.8	2.4	68.6	10.1	32,456	40,755	74,500	-22,270	-13,893	-12,670	-11,681
		'07	71.9	...	11.1	17.0	111,169	...	4.9	87.9	7.2	13,011	38,939	129,038	32,524	-7,877	-8,023	-8,082
		'08	63.8	...	6.3	29.9	139,420	...	...	93.5	6.5	10,437	26,404	119,127	30,028	-6,454	-757	-5,305
		'09	72.8	...	8.1	19.1	164,376	...	...	96.6	3.4	6,497	19,216	137,395	24,679	-1,714	2,493	-934
		Rating History: B++, 06/08/10; B++, 05/20/09; B++, 06/11/08; A-, 06/13/07; A g, 06/09/06																
MILILANI LIFE INSURANCE CO' Rex S. Kuwasaki President 38 South Kukui Street Honolulu, HI 96813-2319 HI : 1987 : Stock : Not Available 808-523-3002 AMB# 068358 NAIC# 73989	**NR-1**	'05	...	...	...	100.0	1,883	...	...	...	100.0	1,694	135	135	...	31	31	31
		'06	...	...	...	100.0	1,926	...	...	...	100.0	1,740	140	140	...	49	46	46
		'07	...	...	...	100.0	2,130	...	...	...	100.0	1,816	142	142	...	81	76	76
		'08	...	...	...	100.0	2,183	...	...	...	100.0	1,875	119	119	...	63	59	59
		'09	...	...	...	100.0	2,117	...	...	...	100.0	1,887	...	125	...	15	13	13
		Rating History: NR-1, 06/10/10; NR-1, 06/12/09; NR-1, 06/12/08; NR-1, 06/08/07; NR-1, 06/07/06																
MINNESOTA LIFE INS COMPANY Minnesota Mutual Companies Inc Robert L. Senkler Chairman & CEO 400 Robert Street North St. Paul, MN 55101-2098 MN : 1880 : Stock : Direct Response Ind Life, Ann, Group Life 651-665-3500 AMB# 006724 NAIC# 66168	**A+** Rating Outlook: Stable **FSC XIV**	'05	30.9	4.8	4.2	60.1	21,543,634	15.4	0.6	20.6	63.4	1,585,280	3,287,832	3,480,984	475,256	149,724	109,622	158,494
		'06	29.1	5.2	4.3	61.4	22,151,124	15.6	0.6	20.3	63.4	1,710,884	3,564,892	3,808,048	-1,171,407	148,178	109,970	167,976
		'07	27.1	5.3	3.3	64.3	23,829,005	15.0	0.6	18.8	65.6	1,818,067	3,940,921	4,204,455	210,244	178,472	141,531	181,760
		'08	32.8	6.4	2.5	58.3	19,697,080	18.9	0.7	25.0	55.4	1,431,990	4,442,171	4,696,543	191,234	-20,793	-20,501	-236,099
		'09	32.1	5.6	1.8	60.5	22,800,080	17.0	0.6	23.1	59.3	1,741,622	4,396,579	4,482,922	462,093	125,793	69,781	60,714
		Rating History: A+ g, 04/06/10; A+ g, 04/10/09; A+ g, 03/25/08; A+ g, 06/01/07; A+ g, 06/14/06																
MISSOURI CARE INCORPORATED Aetna Inc Tom Kelly President 2404 Forum Blvd. Columbia, MO 65203 MO : 2006 : Stock : Broker Medicaid 573-441-2100 AMB# 064921 NAIC# 12913	**NR-2**	'05	...	...	...	...	...	...	...	...	...	...	...	...	...	...	...	...
		'06	...	...	...	...	...	...	...	...	...	...	...	...	...	...	...	...
		'07	6.4	...	...	93.6	16,053	...	53.2	...	46.8	8,805	68,656	68,237	8,734	2,067	1,282	1,282
		'08	14.8	...	...	85.2	27,538	...	50.0	...	50.0	10,081	112,422	112,165	4,764	1,133	-78	-80
		'09	18.6	...	...	81.4	26,966	...	70.1	...	29.9	11,088	124,043	123,877	-502	-4,480	-4,160	-4,150
		Rating History: NR-2, 06/17/09; NR-2, 07/07/08																

BEST'S PROFITABILITY, LEVERAGE AND LIQUIDITY TESTS 2005 – 2009

Data in U.S. Dollars

—	Profitability Tests							Leverage Tests						Liquidity Tests					
Un-Realized Capital Gains ($000)	Benefits Paid to NPW & Dep (%)	Comm. & Expenses to NPW & Dep (%)	NOG to Total Assets (%)	NOG to Total Rev (%)	Operating Return on Equity (%)	Net Yield (%)	Total Return (%)	Change in NPW & Dep (%)	NPW & Dep to Capital (X)	Capital & Surplus to Liabilities (%)	Surplus Relief (%)	Reins Leverage (%)	Change in Capital (%)	Quick Liquidity (%)	Current Liquidity (%)	Non-Invest Grade Bonds to Capital (%)	Delinq. & Foreclosed Mortgages to Capital (%)	Mort. & Credit Tenant Loans & R.E. to Capital (%)	Affiliated Invest to Capital (%)
...	46.6	31.7	18.7	17.8	54.5	5.45	5.26	-0.4	2.8	57.3	0.4	6.3	9.1	117.1	131.7	7.5	...	...	...
21	51.1	30.2	17.0	15.6	48.0	5.58	5.61	0.9	3.0	54.0	0.4	8.1	-7.5	119.4	133.7	9.1	...	...	...
17	47.9	34.6	18.2	17.6	49.6	5.73	6.00	-15.7	2.5	65.1	0.4	7.1	2.9	113.4	131.5	9.5	...	...	...
-628	52.1	64.5	16.8	15.7	40.9	5.64	1.52	-25.0	2.8	81.8	4.7	92.2	-33.5	123.1	142.2	11.0	...	...	1.8
-2,142	55.0	39.4	13.5	10.2	32.0	4.59	5.55	-9.3	3.1	67.2	2.2	103.7	-19.4	140.9	156.2	15.7	...	...	0.3
Principal Lines of Business: GrpA&H (89.5%), IndA&H (10.3%), GrpLife (0.1%), OrdLife (0.1%), IndAnn (0.0%)														Principal States: CA (22.2%), MA (14.2%), FL (11.0%), WA (5.0%), TX (4.9%)					
14,962	45.4	14.2	1.1	6.1	21.4	5.34	5.50	0.6	2.1	6.3	13.0	356.1	19.1	49.2	68.3	69.8	...	48.3	0.8
2,879	53.7	14.6	0.7	4.2	15.1	6.07	6.17	8.9	2.1	5.9	10.6	403.0	7.9	53.9	70.3	79.3	...	37.6	0.7
24,388	74.4	15.3	0.5	3.5	10.2	5.27	5.46	-15.0	1.6	6.1	9.0	417.1	11.1	52.0	69.0	88.2	...	30.0	0.7
-48,371	68.4	14.6	0.7	5.3	14.3	4.31	3.75	8.5	1.6	6.2	6.7	397.2	11.5	50.6	67.5	78.7	...	24.9	2.0
88,056	67.9	15.5	0.3	2.4	6.3	5.20	4.93	2.8	1.5	6.6	3.5	406.1	8.3	49.2	66.1	84.5	0.5	24.9	1.7
Principal Lines of Business: IndAnn (56.6%), OrdLife (27.5%), GrpAnn (15.7%), GrpLife (0.2%), GrpA&H (0.0%)														Principal States: CA (14.1%), FL (7.1%), PA (6.8%), TX (5.8%), OH (5.6%)					
...	81.2	8.4	14.9	4.7	27.5	3.40	3.40	12.0	5.3	131.4	...	3.3	31.4	394.4	413.5	...	...	...	...
...	80.3	8.7	13.7	4.9	22.7	5.30	5.30	3.0	4.4	173.9	...	0.8	24.5	374.4	386.4	...	...	...	...
...	84.5	7.2	8.7	2.6	13.8	5.42	5.42	36.9	5.2	163.6	...	1.4	15.3	389.8	404.5	...	...	...	...
...	83.4	7.9	8.9	2.7	14.4	2.38	2.38	13.8	5.2	161.8	...	0.2	14.6	398.6	414.3	...	...	...	...
...	82.1	11.5	10.5	3.2	16.7	0.18	0.18	13.2	4.9	177.6	...	0.5	18.5	262.7	262.7	...	...	...	...
Principal Lines of Business: Medicaid (98.0%), Medicare (2.0%)														Principal States: MI (100.0%)					
...	84.5	12.8	16.2	7.3	33.1	4.43	4.60	-7.6	4.9	95.8	...	0.1	-20.8	179.6	194.1	...	...	11.7	11.7
...	79.3	13.4	14.3	7.0	27.5	5.14	5.24	-26.5	3.9	133.5	...	0.1	-8.0	218.7	237.2	...	...	12.3	12.3
...	85.0	14.1	6.7	3.5	12.1	5.84	5.94	-21.4	3.6	123.0	...	0.1	-14.7	189.8	205.7	...	...	14.0	14.0
...	85.7	14.3	2.0	0.9	3.9	4.85	8.50	-7.0	4.9	94.6	...	...	-30.8	205.1	222.8	...	...	2.4	2.4
...	81.3	12.9	13.2	6.4	26.2	3.31	3.33	-24.1	4.3	111.4	...	...	-14.3	191.5	210.3	...	...	2.8	2.8
Principal Lines of Business: GrpA&H (98.5%), GrpLife (1.5%), OrdLife (0.0%)														Principal States: MI (58.6%), WI (22.6%), NE (10.6%), IL (6.9%)					
-4	138.1	30.4	2.2	29.7	6.6	5.53	5.80	-15.2	0.1	55.4	0.0	5.8	6.9	89.0	106.3	4.9	...	19.3	0.5
8	141.0	31.1	2.1	27.7	5.8	5.73	5.70	-0.5	0.1	61.5	0.0	5.1	5.6	110.7	125.9	5.9	...	11.7	0.8
194	148.9	25.9	0.3	4.5	0.9	5.56	5.87	-3.7	0.1	64.2	0.0	5.0	2.0	126.6	142.7	6.1	...	9.7	1.3
-255	165.7	31.9	1.1	15.4	2.8	5.53	4.59	0.1	0.1	64.9	0.0	3.8	-1.5	115.5	132.2	5.0	...	8.0	1.4
-19	146.7	22.2	3.3	52.1	8.1	4.70	4.49	5.0	0.1	74.1	0.0	3.5	7.6	115.5	134.8	9.6	...	4.2	7.4
Principal Lines of Business: IndAnn (55.2%), OrdLife (44.8%)														Principal States: IN (24.2%), OH (18.7%), MI (9.9%), TX (7.7%), CA (6.3%)					
83	21.2	22.9	-1.6	-4.6	-3.2	4.46	4.55	56.6	1.2	77.6	...	1.1	-4.3	148.5	155.6	...	...	...	27.0
-62	17.7	25.6	-13.7	-45.8	-33.4	3.82	4.88	34.6	2.1	71.7	...	0.9	-20.9	109.7	119.9	...	...	...	34.2
-392	18.4	12.2	-8.2	-24.1	-35.3	4.25	3.72	73.2	8.2	16.4	27.7	94.7	-55.4	72.8	89.5	...	...	...	...
-2,283	1.9	12.7	-0.6	-5.6	-6.5	4.59	-1.17	-7.7	9.5	9.8	24.5	61.8	-20.3	98.3	112.5	7.0	...	...	...
1,075	1.4	8.2	1.6	17.7	29.4	3.50	1.82	15.3	14.3	6.2	39.0	63.6	-23.2	87.1	99.9	20.7	...	...	...
Principal Lines of Business: GrpAnn (99.7%), GrpA&H (0.3%)														Principal States: MN (87.8%), WI (9.5%)					
...	34.9	60.5	1.7	19.5	1.9	...	...	7.3	0.1	897.1	...	...	1.8	...	...	...	...	...	...
...	37.4	60.2	2.4	24.8	2.7	...	...	3.5	0.1	937.1	...	...	2.7	...	...	...	...	...	...
...	32.8	59.0	3.8	36.0	4.3	...	...	1.7	0.1	579.3	...	...	4.4	...	...	...	...	...	...
...	17.0	74.6	2.7	34.4	3.2	...	...	-16.5	0.1	609.3	...	...	3.2	...	...	...	...	...	...
...	27.0	83.7	0.6	8.3	0.7	...	...	5.6	0.1	821.6	...	...	0.7	...	...	...	...	...	...
Principal Lines of Business: CrdLife (100.0%)																			
14,056	79.5	14.3	0.5	2.6	7.3	4.76	5.40	7.4	1.9	19.9	2.6	47.2	10.5	60.1	82.9	9.5	0.1	59.1	18.4
40,270	84.9	13.9	0.5	2.4	6.7	4.97	5.95	9.4	2.0	24.6	2.3	47.6	7.2	54.4	73.0	8.5	...	60.0	18.5
-14,905	84.2	13.1	0.6	2.9	8.0	5.46	5.71	10.4	2.1	25.5	2.7	47.1	5.2	55.6	73.4	8.9	...	62.5	18.1
-53,305	79.9	12.7	-0.1	-0.4	-1.3	5.42	2.65	11.7	2.9	19.2	2.6	62.9	-19.2	57.4	72.9	13.3	...	77.3	22.8
4,824	79.9	13.6	0.3	1.3	4.4	5.23	5.14	-4.5	2.4	20.9	2.2	54.9	13.1	57.5	72.6	18.3	...	68.9	20.7
Principal Lines of Business: GrpLife (32.3%), GrpAnn (28.7%), IndAnn (19.2%), OrdLife (16.1%), GrpA&H (1.5%)														Principal States: MN (15.0%), CA (8.6%), IL (7.7%), VA (6.1%), FL (5.2%)					
...	...	...	...	...	...	...	...	...	...	...	...	...	...	...	...	...	...	...	...
...	...	...	...	...	...	...	...	...	...	...	...	...	...	...	...	...	...	...	...
0	85.2	12.2	...	1.9	...	...	...	...	7.7	121.5	...	1.3	...	130.6	161.6	...	...	...	...
0	85.2	11.8	-0.4	-0.1	-0.8	3.83	3.81	64.4	11.1	57.7	...	0.1	14.5	120.4	130.0	...	...	...	...
...	86.0	14.2	-15.3	-3.5	-39.3	1.54	1.62	10.4	11.2	69.8	...	...	10.0	90.2	106.8	...	...	...	...
Principal Lines of Business: Medicaid (100.0%)														Principal States: MO (100.0%)					

Data in U.S. Dollars

COMPANY NAME Ultimate Parent Association Principal Officer Mailing Address Dom. : Began Bus. : Struct. : Mktg. Specialty Phone # AMB# NAIC#	Best's Financial Strength Rating FSC	Data Year	Balance Sheet: Bonds (%)	Mort. Loans & R.E. (%)	Com & Pref. Stock (%)	All Other Assets (%)	Total Assets ($000)	Life Reserves (%)	Health Reserves %)	Ann Res. & Dep. Liabilities (%)	All Other Liabilities (%)	Capital & Surplus ($000)	Operations: Direct Premiums Written ($000)	Net Premiums Written & Deposits ($000)	Operating Cash Flow ($000)	NOG Before Taxes ($000)	NOG After Taxes ($000)	Net Income ($000)
MISSOURI VALLEY LIFE & HEALTH Blue Cross & Blue Shield of Kansas City Roger L. Foreman President P.O. Box 419169 Kansas City, MO 64141-6169 MO : 1990 : Stock : Not Available Group A&H, Group Life, Ind Life 816-395-2750 AMB# 068244 NAIC# 76040	NR-5	'05	87.9	...	...	12.1	10,308	8.9	46.9	...	44.2	9,177	2,622	2,622	372	922	645	645
		'06	95.4	...	...	4.6	10,660	7.3	75.9	...	16.9	9,219	1,878	1,878	57	4	45	45
		'07	91.6	...	...	8.4	10,389	23.8	1.6	...	74.5	9,956	1,552	1,552	5	1,126	735	735
		'08	74.4	...	...	25.6	11,117	27.1	...	...	72.9	10,767	901	901	724	1,200	840	814
		'09	86.5	...	...	13.5	11,716	31.3	...	...	68.7	11,422	844	844	610	1,061	640	640
		Rating History: NR-5, 04/06/10; NR-5, 03/27/09; NR-5, 04/15/08; NR-5, 04/09/07; NR-5, 04/20/06																
ML LIFE INS CO OF NY AEGON N.V. Lonny J. Olejniczak President 4333 Edgewood Road NE Cedar Rapid, IA 52499 NY : 1974 : Stock : Broker Ind Ann, Var ann 319-355-8511 AMB# 008487 NAIC# 82848	A	'05	7.2	...	0.0	92.8	1,206,508	7.9	...	4.5	87.6	43,307	43,061	41,216	5,942	13,250	10,662	10,662
		'06	6.1	...	0.0	93.8	1,219,426	7.9	...	3.8	88.3	56,734	61,273	59,358	-2,529	21,080	17,427	17,427
	Rating Outlook: Stable	'07	5.2	...	0.0	94.8	1,169,230	7.7	...	3.3	89.0	76,871	36,721	34,849	-5,604	23,739	19,969	19,969
		'08	9.2	...	0.2	90.6	835,362	11.0	...	6.7	82.3	51,928	9,852	11,664	7,715	-13,932	-13,744	-13,112
		'09	8.0	...	...	92.0	882,568	11.3	...	3.0	85.7	81,728	3,713	2,985	-1,167	24,795	23,940	22,257
	FSC XV	**Rating History: A g, 04/23/09; A+, 06/18/08; A+, 01/11/08; A gu, 08/15/07; A g, 12/26/06**																
MMA INSURANCE COMPANY[1] Larry D. Miller President 1110 North Main Street Goshen, IN 46528 IN : 1988 : Stock : Not Available 574-533-9511 AMB# 009580 NAIC# 74209	NR-1	'05	80.2	2.2	2.3	15.2	18,570	...	...	...	100.0	11,944	22,188	21,001	...	457	351	351
		'06	87.9	1.7	2.1	8.2	20,580	...	...	...	100.0	12,742	21,497	19,988	...	-123	-90	-92
		'07	79.5	3.3	4.7	12.5	21,923	...	...	...	100.0	12,116	20,624	18,748	...	-974	-913	-912
		'08	83.1	3.0	0.3	13.6	24,956	...	...	...	100.0	12,815	21,112	19,492	...	737	464	220
		'09	78.3	2.6	0.3	18.8	27,329	...	...	...	100.0	13,519	17,723	16,558	...	67	315	109
		Rating History: NR-1, 06/10/10; NR-1, 06/12/09; NR-1, 06/12/08; NR-1, 06/08/07; NR-1, 06/07/06																
MML BAY STATE LIFE INS CO Massachusetts Mutual Life Insurance Co Roger W. Crandall Chairman, President & CEO 1295 State Street Springfield, MA 01111 CT : 1894 : Stock : Agency Ind Life 413-788-8411 AMB# 007233 NAIC# 70416	A++	'05	4.1	0.1	...	95.9	4,377,380	2.2	...	0.2	97.6	217,758	94,109	76,568	1,449	37,894	43,582	43,519
		'06	4.1	0.2	...	95.7	4,549,928	2.3	...	0.1	97.6	211,580	84,992	66,333	2,835	39,773	37,465	37,442
	Rating Outlook: Negative	'07	3.8	0.2	0.0	96.0	4,636,984	2.4	...	0.1	97.5	183,358	67,921	51,260	-9,843	33,004	13,668	10,812
		'08	3.5	0.2	0.0	96.3	4,176,228	2.7	...	0.1	97.2	191,776	69,861	48,603	18,173	10,943	13,383	9,669
		'09	3.8	0.2	0.0	96.0	4,345,097	2.7	...	0.2	97.1	158,093	62,496	38,984	-17,487	14,074	9,705	7,725
	FSC XV	**Rating History: A++g, 06/04/10; A++g, 06/11/09; A++g, 03/25/08; A++g, 05/25/07; A++g, 05/02/06**																
MNM-1997 INC[2] Dental Economics L P James A. Taylor President & CEO 12946 Dairy Ashford Road, Suite 360 Sugar Land, TX 77478 TX : 1995 : Stock : Not Available Dental 218-313-7170 AMB# 064513 NAIC# 95247	NR-5	'05	7.5	...	...	92.5	757	...	10.7	...	89.3	553	1,545	1,545	54	32	21	21
		'06	6.8	...	...	93.2	855	...	21.5	...	78.5	602	1,759	1,759	88	67	49	49
		'07	3.3	...	...	96.7	1,828	...	12.1	...	87.9	1,049	3,230	3,230	883	669	448	448
		'08	3.1	...	...	96.9	2,022	...	...	...	100.0	964	3,740	3,740	-78	544	362	362
		'09	3.1	...	...	96.9	2,057	...	...	...	100.0	1,027	3,797	3,797	-160	91	64	64
		Rating History: NR-5, 03/24/10; NR-5, 03/31/09; NR-5, 03/28/08; NR-5, 04/17/07; NR-5, 06/06/06																
MODERN LIFE INS CO OF ARIZONA Munich Reinsurance Company John W. Hayden Chairman & CEO P.O. Box 5323 Cincinnati, OH 45201-5323 AZ : 1978 : Stock : Other Direct Credit A&H, Credit Life 513-943-7200 AMB# 008859 NAIC# 88226	NR-3	'05	48.6	...	...	51.4	1,929	...	85.6	...	14.4	1,243	...	449	72	-22	-18	-18
		'06	42.5	...	...	57.5	2,131	...	93.3	...	6.7	1,187	...	731	-82	-68	-45	-45
		'07	46.6	...	...	53.4	2,391	...	91.2	...	8.8	1,154	...	963	-7	-50	-36	-36
		'08	35.9	...	...	64.1	2,597	...	95.4	...	4.6	1,138	...	858	-68	-14	-5	-13
		'09	14.3	...	...	85.7	2,801	...	95.3	...	4.7	1,107	...	807	-47	-54	-36	-36
		Rating History: NR-3, 03/10/10; NR-3, 05/15/09; NR-5, 04/09/08; NR-3, 10/18/07; NR-3, 05/31/07																
MODERN WOODMEN OF AMERICA Modern Woodmen of America W. Kenny Massey President & CEO 1701 First Avenue Rock Island, IL 61201-8779 IL : 1883 : Fraternal : Career Agent Ind Ann, Univ Life, Whole life 309-786-6481 AMB# 006737 NAIC# 57541	A+	'05	79.9	8.2	6.4	5.6	7,456,431	33.9	0.1	61.3	4.7	960,166	668,344	714,081	490,374	43,717	43,717	69,518
		'06	79.2	7.9	7.0	5.8	7,928,882	33.2	0.1	61.3	5.4	1,063,345	641,528	681,541	424,242	53,770	53,770	99,189
	Rating Outlook: Stable	'07	78.6	7.5	7.3	6.7	8,318,153	32.9	0.1	61.2	5.9	1,170,475	628,670	663,050	317,838	66,472	66,472	96,563
		'08	81.9	7.4	4.8	5.9	8,479,198	32.7	0.1	64.5	2.8	1,104,955	793,581	843,997	422,393	62,263	62,263	-7,424
		'09	81.5	6.9	5.1	6.5	9,266,005	30.3	0.0	65.6	4.1	1,136,447	962,153	1,028,385	640,707	66,562	66,562	29,831
	FSC XII	**Rating History: A+, 01/18/10; A+, 04/08/09; A+, 02/29/08; A+, 01/23/07; A+, 02/24/06**																
MOLINA HEALTHCARE INSURANCE CO Molina Healthcare Inc Joseph M. Molina President 200 Oceangate, Suite 100 Long Beach, CA 90802 OH : 1978 : Stock : Inactive Ann, Group Life, Univ Life 562-435-3666 AMB# 007144 NAIC# 69647	NR-5	'05	67.8	...	...	32.2	8,138	...	...	...	100.0	7,718	1,566	263	-5,932	809	612	611
		'06	64.3	...	...	35.7	8,570	...	...	...	100.0	8,022	1,663	...	671	353	443	443
		'07	62.6	...	...	37.4	8,778	...	...	...	100.0	8,190	1,347	...	308	321	171	171
		'08	58.0	...	...	42.0	9,048	...	...	...	100.0	8,414	1,292	...	187	134	101	101
		'09	69.5	...	...	30.5	8,954	...	...	...	100.0	8,578	1,171	...	54	40	288	288
		Rating History: NR-5, 05/11/10; NR-5, 04/01/09; NR-5, 04/17/08; NR-5, 04/27/07; NR-5, 02/22/06																
MOLINA HEALTHCARE OF CA INC Molina Healthcare Inc Steve O'Dell President One Golden Shore Drive Long Beach, CA 90802 CA : 1989 : Stock : Broker Medicaid 562-499-6191 AMB# 064150	NR-5	'05	...	4.8	...	95.2	97,210	...	...	...	100.0	45,763	313,363	313,363	11,550	2,098	1,127	1,127
		'06	...	4.7	...	95.3	97,467	...	...	...	100.0	46,252	201,799	201,799	-6,259	-22,090	-15,511	-15,511
		'07	...	4.6	...	95.4	98,811	...	...	...	100.0	52,865	204,886	204,886	13,417	1,282	643	643
		'08	...	4.6	...	95.4	96,742	...	...	...	100.0	47,318	282,154	282,154	3,204	-16,875	-10,547	-10,547
		'09	...	4.1	...	95.9	107,321	...	...	...	100.0	49,944	323,006	323,006	1,305	-30,402	-19,374	-19,374
		Rating History: NR-5, 05/18/10; NR-5, 08/26/09; C++pd, 08/11/08; C+ pd, 08/09/07; C++pd, 09/05/06																

BEST'S PROFITABILITY, LEVERAGE AND LIQUIDITY TESTS 2005 – 2009

Data in U.S. Dollars

—	Profitability Tests							Leverage Tests						Liquidity Tests					
Un-Realized Capital Gains ($000)	Benefits Paid to NPW & Dep (%)	Comm. & Expenses to NPW & Dep (%)	NOG to Total Assets (%)	NOG to Total Rev (%)	Operating Return on Equity (%)	Net Yield (%)	Total Return (%)	Change in NPW & Dep (%)	NPW & Dep to Capital (X)	Capital & Surplus to Liabilities (%)	Surplus Relief (%)	Reins Leverage (%)	Change in Capital (%)	Quick Liquidity (%)	Current Liquidity (%)	Non-Invest Grade Bonds to Capital (%)	Delinq. & Foreclosed Mortgages to Capital (%)	Mort. & Credit Tenant Loans & R.E. to Capital (%)	Affiliated Invest to Capital (%)
...	74.5	11.4	6.4	21.0	7.3	3.76	4.58	-34.1	0.3	831.0	...	...	7.6	870.2	925.2	...	...	...	...
0	130.5	7.1	0.4	1.9	0.5	4.27	4.92	-28.4	0.2	653.9	...	...	0.5	608.7	650.5	...	...	...	...
0	53.4	7.0	7.0	35.8	7.7	4.50	4.96	-17.4	0.2	999.9	...	...	8.0	999.9	999.9	...	...	...	...
...	17.7	2.2	7.8	60.9	8.1	4.13	4.31	-41.9	0.1	999.9	...	...	7.9	999.9	999.9	0.0	...	...	...
...	21.0	5.6	5.6	49.8	5.8	3.56	3.95	-6.4	0.1	999.9	...	...	6.1	999.9	999.9	0.0	...	...	...
Principal Lines of Business: GrpLife (99.9%), OrdLife (0.1%)														Principal States: MO (100.0%)					
...	368.8	16.0	0.9	15.8	28.1	4.49	4.53	-44.7	0.9	32.4	...	0.1	31.8	56.1	65.4	4.5	...	...	...
...	263.6	12.0	1.4	20.0	34.8	4.67	4.71	44.0	1.0	47.3	...	1.6	29.9	86.5	97.3	0.9	...	...	...
...	463.2	16.3	1.7	31.2	29.9	4.87	4.88	-41.3	0.5	76.0	...	1.2	34.9	121.5	131.6	0.6	...	...	...
...	903.3	51.2	-1.4	-44.9	-21.3	4.79	5.13	-66.5	0.2	39.9	...	1.0	-32.1	77.2	91.1	3.5	...	...	...
...	999.9	202.6	2.8	99.2	35.8	4.35	3.40	-74.4	0.0	75.8	...	0.3	56.3	113.5	126.9	1.2	...	...	...
Principal Lines of Business: IndAnn (152.6%), OrdLife (-52.6%)														Principal States: NY (90.2%), FL (8.6%)					
-119	71.7	29.8	2.0	1.6	3.1	...	...	1.4	1.7	184.7	...	...	11.4	...	...	...	...	3.4	...
897	72.1	31.1	-0.5	-0.4	-0.7	...	...	-4.8	1.5	173.5	...	...	8.4	...	...	...	...	2.7	...
-126	73.8	32.2	-4.3	-4.6	-7.3	...	...	-6.2	1.5	129.6	...	...	-5.2	...	...	...	...	5.8	...
-70	56.7	24.3	2.0	2.2	3.7	...	...	4.0	1.5	107.5	...	...	4.5	...	...	...	...	5.8	...
101	75.2	28.7	1.2	1.7	2.4	...	...	-15.0	1.2	98.3	...	...	4.8	...	...	...	...	5.2	...
Principal Lines of Business: GrpA&H (86.6%), GrpAnn (12.8%), GrpLife (0.6%)																			
-31	171.9	24.4	1.0	26.1	19.8	5.32	5.30	-9.8	0.3	300.9	0.8	20.9	-1.9	215.5	262.7	1.2	...	1.2	0.5
28	196.8	27.1	0.8	24.2	17.5	5.90	5.91	-13.4	0.3	255.5	1.0	25.0	-2.7	145.2	186.2	2.4	...	3.6	0.5
8	243.5	34.0	0.3	9.5	6.9	6.09	5.07	-22.7	0.3	164.1	1.2	24.7	-14.0	90.1	121.5	3.5	...	5.2	...
-14	215.2	30.3	0.3	10.0	7.1	5.41	4.09	-5.2	0.3	158.4	1.3	24.2	3.6	122.7	149.8	3.4	...	4.5	...
2	232.3	37.7	0.2	8.1	5.5	5.11	4.42	-19.8	0.2	119.6	1.7	28.3	-17.6	54.7	85.6	4.4	...	4.8	...
Principal Lines of Business: OrdLife (99.2%), IndAnn (2.8%), GrpLife (-1.9%)														Principal States: CA (12.2%), TX (8.0%), FL (5.3%), PA (5.2%), VA (4.5%)					
...	44.2	55.5	2.9	1.3	3.9	1.51	1.51	10.7	2.8	270.5	...	...	3.9	529.0	529.0	...	...	...	...
...	42.1	56.0	6.1	2.7	8.5	2.27	2.27	13.9	2.9	238.2	...	...	8.9	467.1	467.1	...	...	...	...
...	38.5	43.6	33.4	13.5	54.2	2.62	2.62	83.6	3.1	134.8	...	...	74.4	267.8	267.8	...	...	...	...
...	39.9	53.6	18.8	9.0	36.0	2.41	2.41	15.8	3.9	91.1	...	...	-8.2	186.4	190.7	...	...	...	...
...	42.1	69.0	3.1	1.5	6.4	0.85	0.85	1.5	3.7	99.8	...	...	6.6	171.8	175.8	...	...	...	...
Principal Lines of Business: Dental (100.0%)														Principal States: TX (100.0%)					
...	42.6	38.0	-1.0	-3.6	-1.4	3.62	3.62	105.4	0.4	182.1	...	47.2	-0.3	191.8	202.6	...	...	...	...
...	31.1	47.9	-2.2	-5.8	-3.7	4.10	4.10	63.0	0.6	126.4	...	74.2	-4.5	138.2	146.6	...	...	...	...
...	25.6	59.6	-1.6	-3.5	-3.1	4.51	4.51	31.6	0.8	93.7	...	97.8	-2.8	85.5	93.5	...	...	...	...
...	33.5	43.4	-0.2	-0.6	-0.5	3.98	3.33	-10.8	0.8	78.1	...	127.5	-1.5	83.0	85.8	...	...	...	...
...	46.6	37.0	-1.3	-4.4	-3.2	0.68	1.13	-6.0	0.7	65.3	...	152.3	-2.9	103.9	103.9	...	...	...	...
Principal Lines of Business: CrdA&H (100.0%)																			
8,804	61.4	19.9	0.6	4.1	4.7	5.81	6.34	-4.3	0.6	17.7	0.5	1.6	7.4	51.6	72.9	27.5	0.1	56.7	3.6
8,624	72.6	21.6	0.7	5.0	5.3	5.68	6.45	-4.6	0.6	18.7	0.5	1.4	11.0	52.4	74.2	24.9	0.1	52.7	3.9
21,448	84.9	20.1	0.8	6.2	6.0	5.59	6.28	-2.7	0.5	19.8	0.5	2.2	9.3	53.6	76.2	18.4	0.0	47.5	3.8
-211,093	67.4	17.8	0.7	5.0	5.5	5.70	2.38	27.3	0.8	15.4	0.3	4.5	-17.1	53.7	74.2	32.1	0.0	57.5	4.6
105,778	56.2	15.7	0.8	4.6	5.9	5.72	6.53	21.8	0.8	15.8	0.2	3.5	11.4	54.1	75.0	34.7	0.0	52.9	4.1
Principal Lines of Business: IndAnn (77.8%), OrdLife (22.2%), IndA&H (0.0%)														Principal States: WI (7.8%), TX (6.7%), IL (6.3%), TN (6.1%), AR (5.3%)					
...	...	-29.3	5.5	70.4	5.8	6.88	6.93	297.9	0.0	999.9	1.8	470.5	-42.8	999.9	999.9	...	...	...	...
...	...	...	5.3	98.7	5.6	5.51	5.62	-99.9	...	999.9	...	402.5	4.0	999.9	999.9	...	...	...	...
...	...	...	2.0	36.2	2.1	5.50	5.61	...	...	999.9	...	351.7	2.1	999.9	999.9	...	...	...	...
...	...	...	1.1	36.6	1.2	2.97	3.15	...	...	999.9	...	321.3	2.7	999.9	999.9	...	...	...	...
...	...	...	3.2	139.1	3.4	2.12	2.34	...	...	999.9	...	294.5	2.0	999.9	999.9	...	...	...	...
														Principal States: OH (39.1%), CA (18.0%), KY (5.9%), FL (4.9%), TX (3.2%)					
...	96.0	11.9	1.5	0.3	3.0	2.00	2.00	22.1	6.8	89.0	...	...	49.4	63.2	63.2	...	...	10.1	10.1
...	167.4	28.1	-15.9	-4.1	-33.7	4.24	4.24	-35.6	4.4	90.3	...	...	1.1	46.9	46.9	...	...	9.9	9.9
...	155.8	28.6	0.7	0.2	1.3	5.23	5.23	1.5	3.9	115.1	...	...	14.3	80.3	80.3	...	...	8.5	8.5
...	132.5	16.5	-10.8	-2.6	-21.1	1.93	1.93	37.7	6.0	95.7	...	...	-10.5	79.8	79.8	...	...	9.4	9.4
...	136.5	13.5	-19.0	-4.2	-39.8	0.78	0.78	14.5	6.5	87.0	...	...	5.5	69.0	69.0	...	...	8.8	8.8
Principal Lines of Business: Medicaid (93.6%), Medicare (6.4%)																			

Data in U.S. Dollars

COMPANY NAME / Ultimate Parent Association / Principal Officer / Mailing Address / Dom. : Began Bus. : Struct. : Mkt. / Specialty / Phone # / AMB# NAIC#

Best's Financial Strength Rating / FSC

Balance Sheet: Bonds (%), Mort. Loans & R.E. (%), Com & Pref. Stock (%), All Other Assets (%), Total Assets ($000), Life Reserves (%), Health Reserves (%), Ann Res. & Dep. Liabilities (%), All Other Liabilities (%), Capital & Surplus ($000)

Operations: Direct Premiums Written ($000), Net Premiums Written & Deposits ($000), Operating Cash Flow ($000), NOG Before Taxes ($000), NOG After Taxes ($000), Net Income ($000)

Company	Best's FSR	Data Year	Bonds (%)	Mort. Loans & R.E. (%)	Com & Pref. Stock (%)	All Other Assets (%)	Total Assets ($000)	Life Reserves (%)	Health Reserves (%)	Ann Res. & Dep. Liabilities (%)	All Other Liabilities (%)	Capital & Surplus ($000)	Direct Premiums Written ($000)	Net Premiums Written & Deposits ($000)	Operating Cash Flow ($000)	NOG Before Taxes ($000)	NOG After Taxes ($000)	Net Income ($000)
MOLINA HEALTHCARE OF MI INC Molina Healthcare Inc	NR-5	'05	0.7	0.0	...	99.3	141,245	...	57.3	...	42.7	55,166	504,943	503,592	31,362	16,245	10,769	10,769
Roman T. Kulich, President		'06	0.8	...	...	99.2	132,720	...	59.4	...	40.6	59,828	499,317	498,632	-10,702	35,548	23,187	23,187
100 West Big Beaver, Suite 600, Troy, MI 48084-5209		'07	18.3	...	...	81.7	147,656	...	66.5	...	33.5	69,499	595,503	595,257	10,247	5,670	3,879	3,879
MI : 1998 : Stock : Broker; Medicaid		'08	31.0	...	...	69.0	149,684	...	48.0	...	52.0	78,212	649,110	648,852	1,329	25,428	16,530	16,531
248-925-1700; AMB# 064685 NAIC# 52630		'09	38.3	...	...	61.7	145,624	...	51.9	...	48.1	69,269	728,870	728,242	-9,364	16,013	9,958	9,978

Rating History: NR-5, 05/21/10; NR-5, 08/26/09; C++pd, 08/11/08; C++pd, 08/09/07; C++pd, 09/05/06

Company	Best's FSR	Data Year	Bonds (%)	Mort. Loans & R.E. (%)	Com & Pref. Stock (%)	All Other Assets (%)	Total Assets ($000)	Life Reserves (%)	Health Reserves (%)	Ann Res. & Dep. Liabilities (%)	All Other Liabilities (%)	Capital & Surplus ($000)	Direct Premiums Written ($000)	Net Premiums Written & Deposits ($000)	Operating Cash Flow ($000)	NOG Before Taxes ($000)	NOG After Taxes ($000)	Net Income ($000)
MOLINA HEALTHCARE NEW MEXICO Molina Healthcare Inc	NR-5	'05	0.9	...	...	99.1	54,946	...	85.3	...	14.7	21,665	240,219	239,415	-10,897	-4,285	-2,786	-2,786
Ann Ouellette Wehr, M.D., President & CEO		'06	0.6	...	...	99.4	75,583	...	62.5	...	37.5	26,606	220,909	220,083	20,851	6,338	4,791	4,791
8801 Horizon Blvd NE, Albuquerque, NM 87113		'07	0.3	...	...	99.7	94,540	...	55.6	...	44.4	41,059	267,954	267,809	18,660	22,223	13,936	13,936
NM : 1993 : Stock : Broker; Medicaid		'08	15.0	...	...	85.0	82,825	...	78.7	...	21.3	42,931	348,568	348,361	-12,947	26,270	16,887	16,913
505-348-0412; AMB# 064260 NAIC# 95739		'09	42.1	...	...	57.9	83,753	...	66.8	...	33.2	44,020	400,824	400,513	-5,074	7,620	5,284	5,364

Rating History: NR-5, 04/07/10; NR-5, 08/26/09; B- pd, 08/11/08; C++pd, 08/09/07; C+ pd, 09/05/06

Company	Best's FSR	Data Year	Bonds (%)	Mort. Loans & R.E. (%)	Com & Pref. Stock (%)	All Other Assets (%)	Total Assets ($000)	Life Reserves (%)	Health Reserves (%)	Ann Res. & Dep. Liabilities (%)	All Other Liabilities (%)	Capital & Surplus ($000)	Direct Premiums Written ($000)	Net Premiums Written & Deposits ($000)	Operating Cash Flow ($000)	NOG Before Taxes ($000)	NOG After Taxes ($000)	Net Income ($000)
MOLINA HEALTHCARE OF OHIO INC Molina Healthcare Inc	NR-5	'05	...	...	...	100.0	3,946	...	3.2	...	96.8	3,142	38	38	3,399	-1,511	-995	-995
Jesse Thomas, President		'06	...	...	...	100.0	60,065	...	27.1	...	72.9	21,208	94,751	94,148	44,989	-5,904	-3,845	-3,845
8101 North High Street, Suite 180, Columbus, OH 43235		'07	10.4	...	...	89.6	156,901	...	33.9	...	66.1	51,802	436,238	434,148	79,601	-6,735	-4,486	-4,486
OH : 2005 : Stock : Broker; Medicaid		'08	22.1	...	...	77.9	132,334	...	48.4	...	51.6	59,436	602,826	601,519	-30,034	-15,909	-10,347	-10,351
614-781-4300; AMB# 064865 NAIC# 12334		'09	14.7	...	...	85.3	225,812	...	21.0	...	79.0	73,596	803,521	801,858	83,565	5,544	-1,984	-2,001

Rating History: NR-5, 03/23/10; NR-5, 05/14/09; NR-5, 05/01/08; NR-5, 05/04/07; NR-5, 11/14/06

Company	Best's FSR	Data Year	Bonds (%)	Mort. Loans & R.E. (%)	Com & Pref. Stock (%)	All Other Assets (%)	Total Assets ($000)	Life Reserves (%)	Health Reserves (%)	Ann Res. & Dep. Liabilities (%)	All Other Liabilities (%)	Capital & Surplus ($000)	Direct Premiums Written ($000)	Net Premiums Written & Deposits ($000)	Operating Cash Flow ($000)	NOG Before Taxes ($000)	NOG After Taxes ($000)	Net Income ($000)
MOLINA HEALTHCARE OF TEXAS INC[2] Molina Healthcare Inc	NR-5	'05	...	...	...	...	...	...	...	...	...	...	...	...	...	...	...	...
Lillis A. Koontz, President		'06	...	...	...	100.0	9,312	...	62.4	...	37.6	5,313	4,913	4,839	4,484	-3,116	-2,027	-2,027
2505 N. Highway 360, Suite 300, Grand Prairie, TX 75050		'07	...	...	...	100.0	35,438	...	60.7	...	39.3	13,507	88,048	87,910	26,319	10,117	6,365	6,365
TX : 2005 : Stock : Broker; Medicaid, Medicare		'08	4.0	...	...	96.0	37,687	...	64.5	...	35.5	15,308	117,706	117,570	2,120	6,973	4,523	4,523
877-665-4622; AMB# 064864 NAIC# 10757		'09	...	...	...	100.0	38,842	...	71.6	...	28.4	17,253	141,671	141,255	-1,608	4,926	3,046	3,046

Rating History: NR-5, 03/29/10; NR-5, 03/31/09; NR-5, 04/17/08; NR-5, 04/23/07

Company	Best's FSR	Data Year	Bonds (%)	Mort. Loans & R.E. (%)	Com & Pref. Stock (%)	All Other Assets (%)	Total Assets ($000)	Life Reserves (%)	Health Reserves (%)	Ann Res. & Dep. Liabilities (%)	All Other Liabilities (%)	Capital & Surplus ($000)	Direct Premiums Written ($000)	Net Premiums Written & Deposits ($000)	Operating Cash Flow ($000)	NOG Before Taxes ($000)	NOG After Taxes ($000)	Net Income ($000)
MOLINA HEALTHCARE OF WA INC Molina Healthcare Inc	NR-5	'05	49.6	...	...	50.4	152,389	...	42.7	...	57.3	71,049	593,583	591,431	37,304	41,989	27,320	27,229
Dale C. Ahlskog, Chairman of the Board & President		'06	38.6	...	...	61.4	161,051	...	53.8	...	46.2	95,245	613,750	612,313	9,206	70,931	46,534	46,491
P.O. Box 1469, Bothell, WA 98041-1469		'07	45.6	...	...	54.4	175,308	...	54.5	...	45.5	113,622	652,970	652,790	11,447	69,761	45,478	45,477
WA : 1986 : Stock : Broker; Group A&H, Medicaid, Medicare		'08	55.5	...	...	44.5	152,923	...	51.7	...	48.3	94,621	709,118	708,485	-33,534	61,267	40,111	40,397
425-424-1100; AMB# 068949 NAIC# 96270		'09	63.7	...	...	36.3	124,070	...	50.2	...	49.8	80,991	725,766	724,671	-20,539	33,197	22,264	22,416

Rating History: NR-5, 04/07/10; NR-5, 08/26/09; B pd, 08/11/08; B pd, 08/09/07; B- pd, 09/05/06

Company	Best's FSR	Data Year	Bonds (%)	Mort. Loans & R.E. (%)	Com & Pref. Stock (%)	All Other Assets (%)	Total Assets ($000)	Life Reserves (%)	Health Reserves (%)	Ann Res. & Dep. Liabilities (%)	All Other Liabilities (%)	Capital & Surplus ($000)	Direct Premiums Written ($000)	Net Premiums Written & Deposits ($000)	Operating Cash Flow ($000)	NOG Before Taxes ($000)	NOG After Taxes ($000)	Net Income ($000)
MONARCH HEALTH PLAN	NR-5	'05	...	...	...	...	...	...	...	...	...	...	...	...	...	...	...	...
Jay Cohen, President		'06	...	...	...	...	...	...	...	...	...	...	...	...	...	...	...	...
7 Technology Drive, Irvine, CA 92618		'07	...	...	...	100.0	2,846	...	...	...	100.0	2,113	...	...	2,546	-687	-687	-687
CA : 2008 : Stock : Not Available; Medicare		'08	...	...	...	100.0	8,745	...	...	...	100.0	1,679	...	...	5,484	-722	-433	-433
949-923-3200; AMB# 064936		'09	...	...	...	100.0	11,417	...	...	...	100.0	2,039	...	...	2,264	600	360	360

Rating History: NR-5, 05/05/10; NR-5, 04/30/09; NR-5, 05/14/08

Company	Best's FSR	Data Year	Bonds (%)	Mort. Loans & R.E. (%)	Com & Pref. Stock (%)	All Other Assets (%)	Total Assets ($000)	Life Reserves (%)	Health Reserves (%)	Ann Res. & Dep. Liabilities (%)	All Other Liabilities (%)	Capital & Surplus ($000)	Direct Premiums Written ($000)	Net Premiums Written & Deposits ($000)	Operating Cash Flow ($000)	NOG Before Taxes ($000)	NOG After Taxes ($000)	Net Income ($000)
MONARCH LIFE INS CO	E	'05	54.4	0.0	0.0	45.6	985,104	13.2	29.1	23.7	34.0	11,630	39,961	12,846	-9,225	857	857	-234
Kevin J. McAdoo, Special Deputy Receiver		'06	54.7	0.0	0.0	45.3	968,404	12.8	29.4	24.1	33.7	11,272	37,117	11,481	-11,047	-1,233	-1,233	-479
330 Whitney Avenue, Suite 500, Holyoke, MA 01040-2857		'07	55.4	0.0	0.0	44.6	953,182	12.3	29.7	24.2	33.8	11,024	34,516	10,935	-11,282	-2,125	-2,125	-2,039
MA : 1901 : Stock : Inactive; In Rehabilitation		'08	62.5	0.0	0.0	37.5	827,647	13.6	33.5	28.0	24.9	9,496	31,676	10,194	-14,258	-2,135	-2,135	-1,628
413-784-2000; AMB# 006739 NAIC# 66265		'09	60.4	0.0	0.0	39.6	813,222	12.7	33.2	27.0	27.1	3,824	29,183	8,590	-31,537	-5,346	-5,346	-6,581

Rating History: E, 07/12/05; E, 04/14/00; E, 04/26/99; E, 04/27/98; E, 04/28/97

Company	Best's FSR	Data Year	Bonds (%)	Mort. Loans & R.E. (%)	Com & Pref. Stock (%)	All Other Assets (%)	Total Assets ($000)	Life Reserves (%)	Health Reserves (%)	Ann Res. & Dep. Liabilities (%)	All Other Liabilities (%)	Capital & Surplus ($000)	Direct Premiums Written ($000)	Net Premiums Written & Deposits ($000)	Operating Cash Flow ($000)	NOG Before Taxes ($000)	NOG After Taxes ($000)	Net Income ($000)
MONITOR LIFE INSURANCE CO Commercial Travelers Mutual Insurance Co	B+	'05	80.1	...	...	19.9	9,623	67.2	0.8	20.4	11.6	5,773	3,607	1,313	134	167	237	237
Paul H. Trevvett, Chairman, President & CEO		'06	76.8	...	...	23.2	9,468	72.8	0.5	21.3	5.4	5,686	2,916	1,258	104	67	75	75
70 Genesee Street, Utica, NY 13502-3502	Rating Outlook: Negative	'07	88.7	...	...	11.3	9,128	76.0	0.5	21.3	2.2	5,321	2,653	1,254	-313	-152	-4	-4
NY : 1972 : Stock : Broker; Group Life		'08	84.7	...	...	15.3	8,724	77.9	0.5	18.7	3.0	5,056	2,445	1,281	-414	-332	-112	-112
315-797-5200; AMB# 008664 NAIC# 81442	FSC III	'09	86.9	...	...	13.1	8,487	75.1	0.4	17.9	6.6	4,723	2,273	1,265	-371	-324	-139	-139

Rating History: B+, 04/30/10; B+ g, 05/19/09; B+ g, 06/13/08; B+ g, 05/17/07; B g, 06/02/06

Company	Best's FSR	Data Year	Bonds (%)	Mort. Loans & R.E. (%)	Com & Pref. Stock (%)	All Other Assets (%)	Total Assets ($000)	Life Reserves (%)	Health Reserves (%)	Ann Res. & Dep. Liabilities (%)	All Other Liabilities (%)	Capital & Surplus ($000)	Direct Premiums Written ($000)	Net Premiums Written & Deposits ($000)	Operating Cash Flow ($000)	NOG Before Taxes ($000)	NOG After Taxes ($000)	Net Income ($000)
MONUMENTAL LIFE INS CO AEGON N.V.	A	'05	56.5	7.7	0.5	35.4	34,389,253	18.8	1.2	30.8	49.2	1,204,144	2,849,629	5,035,451	949,573	363,169	361,850	355,289
Henry G. Hagan, Chairman, President & CEO		'06	50.5	7.4	3.6	38.5	34,891,879	19.6	1.7	25.3	53.5	1,206,359	3,063,618	6,115,000	-1,056,492	183,296	200,457	283,119
4333 Edgewood Road N.E., Cedar Rapids, IA 52499	Rating Outlook: Stable	'07	51.4	8.5	2.9	37.3	37,935,163	18.2	1.8	19.1	60.9	731,779	2,663,687	8,486,316	2,508,347	368,141	285,028	361,381
IA : 1860 : Stock : Agency; Group A&H, Home serv, Ind Life		'08	50.6	8.7	2.9	37.9	35,531,178	6.6	1.8	20.3	71.3	1,236,153	2,433,632	1,500,054	547,940	576,726	528,792	343,664
319-355-8511; AMB# 006742 NAIC# 66281	FSC XV	'09	44.6	7.6	0.2	47.6	34,727,978	18.1	1.9	16.3	63.8	1,436,586	1,786,289	-1,808,482	-2,221,992	1,020,600	435,836	191,678

Rating History: A g, 04/23/09; A+ g, 06/18/08; A+ g, 05/30/07; A+ g, 06/21/06; A+ g, 05/13/05

BEST'S PROFITABILITY, LEVERAGE AND LIQUIDITY TESTS 2005 – 2009

Data in U.S. Dollars

—	Profitability Tests							Leverage Tests						Liquidity Tests					
Un-Realized Capital Gains ($000)	Benefits Paid to NPW & Dep (%)	Comm. & Expenses to NPW & Dep (%)	NOG to Total Assets (%)	NOG to Total Rev (%)	Operating Return on Equity (%)	Net Yield (%)	Total Return (%)	Change in NPW & Dep (%)	NPW & Dep to Capital (X)	Capital & Surplus to Liabilities (%)	Surplus Relief (%)	Reins Leverage (%)	Change in Capital (%)	Quick Liquidity (%)	Current Liquidity (%)	Non-Invest Grade Bonds to Capital (%)	Delinq. & Foreclosed Mortgages to Capital (%)	Mort. & Credit Tenant Loans & R.E. to Capital (%)	Affiliated Invest to Capital (%)
...	82.5	8.8	8.6	2.3	23.1	2.92	2.92	38.5	9.1	64.1	...	...	45.4	225.2	233.0	...	...	0.0	0.0
...	77.4	10.6	16.9	4.9	40.3	4.57	4.57	-1.0	8.3	82.1	...	...	8.5	238.8	246.7	...	...	...	...
...	84.2	10.1	2.8	0.7	6.0	5.08	5.08	19.4	8.6	88.9	...	...	16.2	156.1	159.5	...	...	...	...
...	81.0	10.4	11.1	2.7	22.4	3.03	3.03	9.0	8.3	109.4	...	0.0	12.5	267.2	282.3	...	...	...	...
...	82.9	13.8	6.7	1.4	13.5	1.35	1.36	12.2	10.5	90.7	...	...	-11.4	88.7	88.7	...	...	...	...
Principal Lines of Business: Medicaid (95.1%), Medicare (4.9%), CompHosp/Med (0.0%)														Principal States: MI (100.0%)					
...	90.3	12.5	-4.6	-1.2	-10.3	1.40	1.40	-23.7	11.1	65.1	...	...	-33.5	150.3	150.3	...	...	...	...
...	83.3	15.0	7.3	2.2	19.9	4.82	4.82	-8.1	8.3	54.3	...	0.8	22.8	144.7	144.7	...	...	...	...
...	81.5	11.5	16.4	5.1	41.2	5.19	5.19	21.7	6.5	76.8	...	...	54.3	167.4	167.4	...	...	...	...
...	81.1	11.9	19.0	4.8	40.2	2.61	2.64	30.1	8.1	107.6	...	0.0	4.6	213.8	214.2	...	...	...	...
...	85.6	13.4	6.3	1.3	12.2	0.95	1.05	15.0	9.1	110.8	...	2.5	2.5	182.1	182.6	...	...	...	...
Principal Lines of Business: Medicaid (99.0%), Medicare (1.0%)														Principal States: NM (100.0%)					
...	94.0	999.9	...	-99.9	...	...	...	...	0.0	391.1	...	...	...	791.8	827.3	...	...	...	...
...	89.2	17.5	-12.0	-4.1	-31.6	1.76	1.76	999.9	4.4	54.6	...	0.5	574.9	190.3	197.5	...	...	...	...
...	89.1	13.1	-4.1	-1.0	-12.3	3.51	3.51	361.1	8.4	49.3	...	1.6	144.3	154.7	159.5	...	...	...	...
...	89.6	13.5	-7.2	-1.7	-18.6	2.60	2.59	38.6	10.1	81.5	...	0.3	14.7	184.2	193.6	...	...	...	...
...	84.3	15.1	-1.1	-0.2	-3.0	0.81	0.80	33.3	10.9	48.3	...	0.8	23.8	188.9	205.3	...	...	...	...
Principal Lines of Business: Medicaid (100.0%), Medicare (0.0%)														Principal States: OH (100.0%)					
...	...	...	...	...	...	...	...	...	...	...	...	...	...	...	...	...	...	...	...
...	86.3	80.9	...	-40.7	...	...	...	...	0.9	132.8	...	...	...	271.8	279.2	...	...	...	...
...	71.9	17.7	28.4	7.2	67.6	4.53	4.53	999.9	6.5	61.6	...	...	154.3	294.3	308.7	...	...	...	...
...	71.4	17.2	12.4	4.1	31.4	3.02	3.02	33.7	7.7	68.4	...	0.7	13.3	301.8	317.1	...	...	...	...
...	75.4	16.4	8.0	2.3	18.7	0.62	0.62	20.1	8.2	79.9	...	1.8	12.7	326.2	348.0	...	...	...	...
Principal Lines of Business: Medicaid (90.9%), OtherHlth (4.7%), Medicare (4.4%)														Principal States: TX (100.0%)					
...	82.4	11.2	20.5	4.6	41.9	3.47	3.40	28.1	8.3	87.3	...	2.9	19.7	173.0	173.0	...	...	...	...
...	77.4	12.2	29.7	7.5	56.0	5.20	5.17	3.5	6.4	144.7	...	1.0	34.1	233.2	233.2	...	...	...	...
...	78.1	12.6	27.0	6.9	43.5	5.94	5.94	6.6	5.7	184.2	...	0.9	19.3	277.4	283.3	...	...	...	...
...	79.7	12.6	24.4	5.6	38.5	3.97	4.16	8.5	7.5	162.3	0.0	1.4	-16.7	235.3	243.2	...	...	...	...
...	82.9	12.8	16.1	3.1	25.4	1.75	1.87	2.3	8.9	188.0	...	...	-14.4	255.2	299.3	...	...	...	...
Principal Lines of Business: Medicaid (87.1%), CompHosp/Med (11.0%), Medicare (2.0%)														Principal States: WA (100.0%)					
...	...	...	...	...	...	...	...	...	...	...	...	...	...	...	...	...	...	...	...
...	...	...	...	...	...	...	...	...	...	...	...	...	...	...	...	...	...	...	...
...	...	...	...	-99.9	...	...	...	...	...	288.2	...	...	...	347.2	347.2	...	...	...	...
...	...	...	-7.5	-0.9	-22.9	3.30	3.30	...	...	23.8	...	...	-20.5	113.6	113.6	...	...	...	...
...	...	...	3.6	0.5	19.4	0.23	0.23	...	...	21.7	...	...	21.4	109.7	109.7	...	...	...	...
-149	670.0	82.9	0.1	1.4	7.3	6.56	6.61	-6.1	0.8	2.2	38.0	999.9	-4.2	53.3	61.8	46.1	...	1.7	0.4
2	789.7	85.2	-0.1	-2.1	-10.8	6.48	6.84	-10.6	0.8	2.1	39.4	999.9	-2.6	54.1	62.5	80.0	...	1.6	0.5
2	771.7	89.5	-0.2	-3.7	-19.1	6.43	6.70	-4.8	0.8	2.1	37.7	999.9	-2.3	54.3	62.6	53.6	...	1.1	0.5
1	766.2	93.3	-0.2	-3.8	-20.8	6.36	6.72	-6.8	0.8	1.9	40.4	999.9	-11.1	55.4	63.8	39.3	...	1.2	0.6
0	940.6	105.5	-0.7	-10.0	-80.3	6.33	6.41	-15.7	1.4	1.0	86.1	999.9	-51.4	55.0	63.5	142.3	...	1.6	1.2
Principal Lines of Business: IndA&H (99.6%), IndAnn (1.9%), GrpLife (0.1%), OrdLife (-1.6%)														Principal States: NY (15.5%), CA (9.7%), NJ (9.0%), FL (6.8%), MI (4.5%)					
...	51.5	57.1	2.4	10.8	4.0	2.91	3.01	-22.1	0.2	150.4	7.2	190.4	-2.6	236.3	249.0	...	...	...	...
...	42.3	71.9	0.8	3.8	1.3	3.18	3.40	-4.2	0.2	150.9	4.8	87.7	-1.5	261.4	269.2	...	...	...	...
...	74.3	65.3	0.0	-0.2	-0.1	3.73	3.97	-0.3	0.2	140.5	5.6	73.1	-6.4	220.7	233.3	...	...	...	...
...	76.8	82.1	-1.3	-6.3	-2.2	3.16	3.60	2.2	0.3	138.7	4.8	68.3	-4.9	222.7	235.0	...	...	...	...
...	64.8	79.7	-1.6	-8.1	-2.8	2.65	3.18	-1.3	0.3	126.3	4.2	74.7	-6.6	200.9	212.9	...	...	...	...
Principal Lines of Business: GrpLife (99.1%), OrdLife (0.5%), IndA&H (0.4%), IndAnn (0.0%)														Principal States: NY (76.1%), PA (7.4%), OH (3.0%)					
-57,603	51.1	6.7	1.1	9.4	29.5	5.46	5.20	10.4	3.3	6.5	18.7	246.6	-0.1	45.1	61.1	93.8	0.8	175.5	11.2
32,168	41.8	8.6	0.6	4.8	16.6	5.93	6.44	21.4	4.0	6.8	16.1	260.2	-0.2	42.1	58.3	86.4	0.6	171.0	15.5
-12,236	30.2	13.4	0.8	7.4	29.4	6.23	6.52	38.8	7.3	4.7	11.6	226.7	-23.7	40.8	57.7	110.6	0.9	279.0	42.5
-26,319	168.6	68.6	1.4	-99.9	53.7	5.27	4.45	-82.3	1.0	5.8	3.9	509.0	26.0	49.3	63.5	119.2	0.7	213.7	74.9
-100,340	-99.9	-5.9	1.2	6.2	32.6	4.53	3.08	-99.9	-1.2	6.6	32.7	397.7	2.8	62.5	74.9	120.0	0.5	177.7	61.9
Principal Lines of Business: IndAnn (171.5%), IndLife (0.7%), CrdA&H (-0.3%), CrdLife (-0.7%), GrpLife (-4.3%)														Principal States: NJ (10.4%), CA (7.0%), FL (6.5%), KY (6.4%), PA (5.1%)					

2010 BEST'S KEY RATING GUIDE — LIFE/HEALTH EDITION
ANNUAL STATEMENT DATA FOR YEARS 2005 – 2009
Data in U.S. Dollars

COMPANY NAME / Ultimate Parent Association / Principal Officer / Mailing Address / Dom. : Began Bus. : Struct. : Mktg. / Specialty / Phone # / AMB# / NAIC#	Best's Financial Strength Rating / FSC	Data Year	Balance Sheet: Bonds (%)	Mort. Loans & R.E. (%)	Com & Pref. Stock (%)	All Other Assets (%)	Total Assets ($000)	Life Reserves (%)	Health Reserves (%)	Ann Res. & Dep. Liabilities (%)	All Other Liabilities (%)	Capital & Surplus ($000)	Operations: Direct Premiums Written ($000)	Net Premiums Written & Deposits ($000)	Operating Cash Flow ($000)	NOG Before Taxes ($000)	NOG After Taxes ($000)	Net Income ($000)
MONY LIFE INS CO AXA S.A.	A+	'05	54.7	12.0	7.1	26.2	11,022,768	70.8	0.1	10.8	18.2	968,559	639,091	705,082	85,339	208,125	170,705	142,328
Christopher M. Condron, Chairman, President & CEO		'06	56.8	11.9	9.7	21.6	10,270,270	76.5	0.1	10.9	12.5	1,069,547	551,909	629,060	-300,608	272,490	244,615	293,480
1290 Avenue of the Americas, New York, NY 10104	Rating Outlook: Stable	'07	54.6	12.9	9.6	22.9	9,917,633	77.5	0.1	10.2	12.1	961,274	508,258	573,788	-278,122	210,282	142,570	130,419
NY : 1843 : Stock : Agency; Ann, Trad Life, Var Univ life		'08	55.9	14.4	8.0	21.6	9,161,876	79.3	0.2	10.1	10.5	520,732	491,604	567,150	-206,399	115,669	80,760	2,878
212-554-1234		'09	58.0	13.4	7.0	21.6	9,181,461	79.8	0.1	9.5	10.5	728,706	454,947	537,736	-198,709	129,590	115,590	44,565
AMB# 006751 NAIC# 66370	FSC XV	**Rating History: A+ g, 06/04/10; A+ g, 06/12/09; A+ g, 05/29/08; A+ g, 01/25/07; A+ g, 08/12/05**																
MONY LIFE INSURANCE CO OF AMER AXA S.A.	A+	'05	24.6	4.7	1.9	68.8	6,200,371	17.5	...	16.6	65.9	239,252	423,344	453,889	-137	-26,936	-3,578	-5,615
Christopher M. Condron, Chairman, President & CEO		'06	27.0	3.7	3.3	66.1	6,004,780	19.1	...	15.6	65.3	281,252	328,441	320,211	19,314	39,811	27,962	27,656
1290 Avenue of the Americas, New York, NY 10104	Rating Outlook: Stable	'07	28.5	3.6	3.4	64.5	5,594,467	21.0	...	14.9	64.1	291,315	317,956	305,055	-52,158	26,667	24,474	7,273
AZ : 1969 : Stock : Agency; A&H, Univ Life, Var Univ life		'08	35.1	4.2	3.8	56.9	4,198,940	28.5	...	18.6	52.9	191,705	309,561	306,835	-34,166	-51,962	-40,343	-68,212
212-554-1234		'09	38.5	3.5	1.9	56.1	4,276,906	28.5	...	17.8	53.7	273,755	277,479	271,078	-18,414	52,977	37,877	11,662
AMB# 008091 NAIC# 78077	FSC XV	**Rating History: A+ g, 06/04/10; A+ g, 06/12/09; A+ g, 05/29/08; A+ g, 01/25/07; A+ g, 08/12/05**																
MOTHE LIFE INS CO[1]	NR-1	'05	23.7	54.3	11.8	10.2	45,848	...	...	...	100.0	1,337	3,411	3,360	...	-169	-169	182
Dennis M. Necaise, President & Treasurer		'06	29.2	55.3	12.6	2.9	46,340	...	...	...	100.0	2,749	3,060	2,975	...	687	687	703
1601 Belle Chasse Highway, Gretna, LA 70056-7011		'07	30.8	53.6	13.4	2.2	47,626	...	...	...	100.0	3,190	3,592	3,515	...	347	295	296
LA : 1932 : Stock : Not Available		'08	33.0	56.0	6.3	4.7	41,030	...	...	...	100.0	-3,394	3,539	3,452	...	23	-20	-1,103
504-398-0777		'09	40.1	52.8	5.3	1.8	38,964	...	...	...	100.0	-5,009	2,381	2,301	...	-145	-124	-1,593
AMB# 006743 NAIC# 66303		**Rating History: NR-1, 06/10/10; NR-1, 06/12/09; NR-1, 06/12/08; NR-1, 06/08/07; NR-1, 06/07/06**																
MOTORISTS LIFE INS CO Motorists Insurance Pool	A-	'05	88.8	...	2.9	8.3	308,583	45.4	...	51.8	2.8	49,714	46,084	38,962	15,249	-39	-185	13
John J. Bishop, Chairman, President & CEO		'06	87.3	...	3.0	9.7	322,527	47.7	...	49.5	2.8	49,944	49,064	41,070	13,215	-279	-171	732
471 East Broad Street, Columbus, OH 43215-3861	Rating Outlook: Stable	'07	87.7	...	3.2	9.2	333,633	50.7	...	46.5	2.9	50,806	51,932	43,063	10,831	1,013	600	663
OH : 1967 : Stock : Agency; Ind Ann, Ind Life		'08	87.3	...	2.0	10.7	334,026	53.3	...	44.8	1.9	43,109	55,033	46,029	1,553	-817	-748	-8,328
614-225-8358		'09	87.1	...	2.4	10.5	359,305	53.2	...	44.2	2.5	44,497	68,078	58,088	18,572	-1,381	-1,180	-1,056
AMB# 006744 NAIC# 66311	FSC VI	**Rating History: A-, 06/01/09; A-, 05/15/08; A-, 05/25/07; A-, 05/25/06; A-, 05/04/05**																
MOUNT CARMEL HEALTH PLAN INC	NR-5	'05	2.8	...	...	97.2	65,619	...	77.4	...	22.6	43,710	165,793	165,793	17,821	12,317	11,376	11,376
Mark Richardson, President & CEO		'06	1.7	...	...	98.3	106,405	...	60.3	...	39.7	73,329	223,150	223,150	36,787	44,271	28,400	28,400
6150 East Broad Street, EE320, Columbus, OH 43213		'07	30.9	...	17.2	52.0	150,582	...	59.6	...	40.4	121,892	237,187	237,187	-24,564	40,798	40,798	38,597
OH : 1997 : Stock : Broker; Medicare		'08	37.0	...	19.2	43.7	152,877	...	79.4	...	20.6	128,045	270,518	270,518	-17,354	19,313	19,366	4,375
614-546-3100		'09	36.8	...	19.8	43.4	189,242	...	83.1	...	16.9	165,939	312,635	312,635	38,252	30,736	30,736	30,618
AMB# 064112 NAIC# 95655		**Rating History: NR-5, 03/23/10; NR-5, 08/26/09; B++pd, 07/14/08; B+ pd, 06/26/07; B pd, 07/25/06**																
MOUNTAIN LIFE INS CO Mountain Services Corporation	B+	'05	24.6	4.9	...	70.5	11,415	51.6	0.0	...	48.4	3,330	10,913	2,720	-299	63	59	59
David E. Line, President & CEO		'06	15.9	4.4	...	79.7	12,145	41.9	0.2	...	57.9	3,472	9,297	2,181	-628	212	182	182
P.O. Box 240, Alcoa, TN 37701-0240	Rating Outlook: Negative	'07	20.3	4.8	...	74.9	10,502	48.6	0.1	...	51.3	3,495	9,031	2,296	-156	368	303	303
TN : 1972 : Stock : Agency; Credit Life, Credit A&H, Term Life		'08	17.8	5.2	...	77.0	9,390	50.2	...	...	49.8	3,362	7,143	1,886	-903	153	134	139
865-970-2800		'09	20.5	5.3	...	74.2	8,635	51.6	...	...	48.4	3,337	5,052	1,734	-646	35	33	33
AMB# 008354 NAIC# 80020	FSC III	**Rating History: B+, 05/10/10; B+, 05/14/09; B+, 06/09/08; B+, 05/24/07; B+, 06/06/06**																
MTL INSURANCE COMPANY Mutual Trust Holding Company	A-	'05	68.3	17.9	1.2	12.6	1,227,165	63.4	...	29.7	6.9	105,645	121,736	115,066	50,088	9,611	10,244	9,885
Stephen Batza, President & CEO		'06	64.4	18.7	1.4	15.5	1,256,788	66.6	...	26.9	6.5	106,730	131,551	127,965	20,653	3,483	765	5,803
1200 Jorie Boulevard, Oak Brook, IL 60523-2218	Rating Outlook: Stable	'07	63.5	19.0	1.5	16.0	1,273,967	71.4	...	23.3	5.3	105,276	144,984	137,489	9,635	-1,032	-913	-812
IL : 1905 : Mutual : Agency; Trad Life, Univ Life, Ann		'08	61.4	20.0	0.9	17.7	1,319,361	74.7	...	20.5	4.8	89,225	165,918	157,706	57,612	-4,818	-4,974	-11,268
630-990-1000		'09	60.8	19.2	1.1	18.8	1,398,474	76.3	...	18.8	4.9	92,138	172,106	163,122	67,466	1,294	723	-2,224
AMB# 006756 NAIC# 66427	FSC VIII	**Rating History: A-, 05/21/10; A-, 06/15/09; A-, 06/18/08; A-, 06/20/07; A-, 06/20/06**																
MULHEARN PROTECTIVE INSURANCE Mulhearn Corporation	NR-5	'05	28.1	1.4	30.0	40.4	8,982	95.2	...	...	4.8	814	1,195	1,195	336	34	28	102
Timothy M. Mulhearn, Sr., President		'06	31.7	4.3	29.7	34.3	9,728	95.4	...	...	4.6	1,220	1,299	1,299	518	154	140	199
P.O. Box 1411, Monroe, LA 71210		'07	27.7	3.9	32.5	35.9	10,023	95.1	...	...	4.9	1,169	1,250	1,247	372	187	168	244
LA : 1934 : Stock : Not Available; Ordinary Life, Ind Life		'08	30.5	4.5	33.0	32.1	9,025	99.4	...	...	0.6	402	1,135	1,134	7	120	114	-87
318-329-0141		'09	29.0	3.7	39.4	27.8	10,090	99.5	...	...	0.5	1,160	1,263	1,261	222	62	90	-71
AMB# 007823 NAIC# 75485		**Rating History: NR-5, 04/20/10; NR-5, 04/16/09; NR-5, 04/11/08; NR-5, 04/25/07; NR-5, 04/24/06**																
MUNICH AMERICAN REASSURANCE CO Munich Reinsurance Company	A+	'05	83.0	0.4	0.2	16.3	3,923,119	37.8	14.6	4.2	43.3	532,246	...	822,181	421,724	-51,478	-51,478	-51,235
Michael G. DeKoning, President & CEO		'06	82.6	0.3	3.1	14.1	4,527,185	37.9	15.1	8.1	39.0	544,274	...	960,161	587,218	-59,778	-61,562	-60,083
P.O. Box 3210, Atlanta, GA 30302-3210	Rating Outlook: Stable	'07	85.7	0.2	1.0	13.1	5,029,518	38.9	16.5	7.7	36.9	673,037	...	1,164,498	434,453	55,117	52,801	62,590
GA : 1959 : Stock : Other Direct; Reins		'08	89.0	0.2	0.8	9.9	5,506,150	38.4	18.0	7.0	36.7	649,235	...	1,278,046	551,491	-45,766	-43,937	-58,594
770-350-3200		'09	90.0	0.1	0.2	9.7	5,984,409	36.5	18.9	7.2	37.4	609,661	...	1,073,248	559,599	48,847	49,045	46,109
AMB# 006746 NAIC# 66346	FSC XV	**Rating History: A+ g, 07/20/09; A+ g, 09/25/08; A+ g, 09/07/07; A+ g, 11/07/06; A+ g, 11/03/05**																

BEST'S PROFITABILITY, LEVERAGE AND LIQUIDITY TESTS 2005 – 2009

Data in U.S. Dollars

—	Profitability Tests							Leverage Tests						Liquidity Tests					
Un-Realized Capital Gains ($000)	Benefits Paid to NPW & Dep (%)	Comm. & Expenses to NPW & Dep (%)	NOG to Total Assets (%)	NOG to Total Rev (%)	Operating Return on Equity (%)	Net Yield (%)	Total Return (%)	Change in NPW & Dep (%)	NPW & Dep to Capital (X)	Capital & Surplus to Liabilities (%)	Surplus Relief (%)	Reins Leverage (%)	Change in Capital (%)	Quick Liquidity (%)	Current Liquidity (%)	Non-Invest Grade Bonds to Capital (%)	Delinq. & Foreclosed Mortgages to Capital (%)	Mort. & Credit Tenant Loans & R.E. to Capital (%)	Affiliated Invest to Capital (%)
15,663	125.6	18.4	1.5	14.4	19.0	6.30	6.28	-20.1	0.7	12.0	0.8	57.6	18.3	40.3	53.8	23.3	1.4	123.1	55.2
-26,435	207.8	17.4	2.3	21.7	24.0	6.56	6.92	-10.8	0.5	14.4	0.5	52.1	14.1	38.5	53.7	11.2	1.1	99.5	55.6
-36,030	142.5	14.1	1.4	13.8	14.0	6.16	5.71	-8.8	0.5	13.1	0.5	56.9	-10.9	36.4	52.0	15.8	0.0	116.4	64.1
-233,112	139.4	15.0	0.8	8.2	10.9	6.06	2.61	-1.2	1.0	6.9	0.8	102.1	-47.3	33.6	48.2	36.8	...	228.7	77.9
123,699	132.6	12.4	1.3	13.2	18.5	5.53	6.19	-5.2	0.7	9.6	0.6	70.7	34.5	33.8	48.3	51.0	...	158.7	77.3
	Principal Lines of Business: OrdLife (71.6%), IndAnn (24.7%), IndA&H (3.0%), GrpA&H (0.3%), GrpLife (0.2%)													Principal States: NY (17.2%), TX (4.9%), IL (4.9%), CA (4.9%), PA (4.1%)					
12,762	174.2	30.0	-0.1	-0.6	-1.5	6.18	6.84	-48.0	1.7	13.6	4.3	92.0	7.9	51.0	69.4	19.3	1.0	108.4	19.5
14,710	285.0	28.7	0.5	5.5	10.7	6.14	6.88	-29.5	1.0	16.3	1.1	90.5	18.6	48.8	68.9	12.4	0.9	68.5	23.4
-2,939	305.3	31.2	0.4	5.1	8.5	5.96	5.08	-4.7	1.0	17.0	1.3	91.5	0.3	46.9	67.7	14.8	...	63.6	21.8
-35,120	257.6	34.5	-0.8	-9.0	-16.7	5.67	2.69	0.6	1.6	10.2	1.4	165.2	-38.7	49.5	67.7	32.6	...	89.8	20.8
7,523	203.7	28.3	0.9	9.6	16.3	5.49	4.59	-11.7	1.0	15.5	0.9	113.0	44.0	47.2	65.3	58.3	...	52.8	19.5
	Principal Lines of Business: OrdLife (65.2%), IndAnn (32.0%), GrpLife (2.8%), IndA&H (0.0%)													Principal States: CA (13.1%), PA (7.6%), TX (7.4%), IL (7.4%), FL (7.1%)					
-1,366	89.2	109.2	-0.4	-2.5	-10.5	...	...	36.6	1.6	4.9	...	...	-15.0	...	...	...	...	999.9	...
721	107.5	67.8	1.5	11.8	33.6	...	...	-11.5	0.9	8.1	...	...	60.8	...	...	...	...	739.2	...
578	85.9	70.9	0.6	4.8	9.9	...	...	18.1	0.8	9.9	...	...	24.1	...	...	...	...	593.4	...
-5,941	95.2	64.9	0.0	-0.3	19.8	...	...	-1.8	-1.2	-6.6	...	...	-99.9	...	...	...	...	-99.9	...
-475	142.8	75.1	-0.3	-2.7	2.9	...	...	-33.3	-0.5	-10.8	...	...	-60.9	...	...	...	...	-99.9	...
	Principal Lines of Business: OrdLife (93.4%), IndLife (6.6%)																		
266	59.7	33.5	-0.1	-0.3	-0.4	4.72	4.95	1.8	0.8	20.1	5.9	33.8	1.0	83.2	93.9	...	...	...	0.1
181	66.0	36.9	-0.1	-0.3	-0.3	4.84	5.28	5.4	0.8	19.5	5.8	45.2	1.8	86.2	96.1	2.1	...	...	0.2
-162	74.2	34.7	0.2	1.0	1.2	4.96	4.99	4.9	0.8	19.1	5.6	58.1	1.8	84.0	95.1	...	...	...	0.1
-1,674	74.7	35.0	-0.2	-1.2	-1.6	4.95	2.13	6.9	1.1	14.8	7.0	82.6	-19.5	80.8	91.7	5.2	...	...	0.0
400	59.0	31.6	-0.3	-1.5	-2.7	4.81	5.05	26.2	1.3	14.8	7.4	97.4	7.3	77.8	87.7	5.4	...	...	0.1
	Principal Lines of Business: OrdLife (67.1%), IndAnn (31.6%), GrpLife (0.7%), GrpAnn (0.6%)													Principal States: OH (48.2%), PA (15.9%), KY (8.1%), IN (7.0%), MI (5.7%)					
...	84.9	8.3	20.1	6.8	30.0	2.07	2.07	22.8	3.8	199.5	...	...	36.0	293.6	293.6	...	...	...	...
...	74.5	7.2	33.0	12.5	48.5	4.18	4.18	34.6	3.0	221.7	...	...	67.8	305.7	305.7	...	...	...	...
...	77.8	7.7	31.8	16.7	41.8	5.43	3.69	6.3	1.9	424.9	...	...	66.2	466.6	487.4	...	...	...	...
...	86.1	8.7	12.8	7.0	15.5	3.57	-5.97	14.1	2.1	515.7	...	...	5.0	762.6	816.6	...	...	...	...
...	84.0	7.6	18.0	9.7	20.9	2.50	2.43	15.6	1.9	712.1	...	...	29.6	999.9	999.9	...	...	...	...
	Principal Lines of Business: Medicare (100.0%)													Principal States: OH (100.0%)					
...	46.8	73.5	0.5	0.8	1.8	2.11	2.11	1.1	0.8	41.2	134.8	477.0	-1.4	101.5	107.2	...	...	16.7	16.7
...	51.2	77.6	1.5	2.9	5.4	3.40	3.40	-19.8	0.6	40.0	108.7	440.8	4.3	94.7	96.6	...	...	15.3	15.3
...	34.2	78.2	2.7	4.8	8.7	4.07	4.07	5.3	0.7	49.9	102.7	364.3	0.7	119.0	119.0	...	...	14.5	14.5
...	42.1	85.6	1.4	2.7	3.9	3.28	3.34	-17.9	0.6	55.8	83.2	327.5	-3.8	108.9	116.5	...	...	14.4	14.4
...	48.9	81.8	0.4	0.8	1.0	2.49	2.49	-8.1	0.5	63.0	58.5	281.2	-0.7	109.6	119.1	...	...	13.8	13.8
	Principal Lines of Business: CrdLife (66.5%), OrdLife (29.0%), GrpA&H (4.6%)													Principal States: TN (61.6%), AL (18.8%), GA (8.8%), AR (5.9%), MO (4.9%)					
672	67.2	31.5	0.9	5.8	10.1	5.75	5.96	-12.6	1.0	10.4	1.7	30.8	8.6	38.5	55.9	44.4	...	194.2	6.4
-1,691	75.6	32.1	0.1	0.4	0.7	5.93	6.35	11.2	1.1	10.6	1.7	35.9	3.7	35.7	53.0	50.2	...	198.5	6.1
1,022	78.3	33.4	-0.1	-0.4	-0.9	5.95	6.10	7.4	1.2	10.2	1.8	41.2	-1.4	33.2	50.0	48.0	...	208.0	...
-7,422	58.5	30.4	-0.4	-2.3	-5.1	5.92	4.88	14.7	1.6	7.8	2.0	55.6	-19.0	35.0	49.9	43.6	...	278.4	...
3,556	54.1	30.8	0.1	0.3	0.8	5.85	5.97	3.4	1.6	7.7	1.8	53.4	4.7	34.6	48.2	44.9	0.6	270.1	...
	Principal Lines of Business: OrdLife (89.3%), IndAnn (6.7%), GrpAnn (3.9%)													Principal States: IL (12.4%), TX (6.4%), CA (6.3%), PA (6.2%), MI (6.1%)					
-58	56.5	44.9	0.3	1.9	3.2	3.65	3.83	-20.0	1.0	14.8	...	...	-9.0	94.9	101.1	4.3	...	11.1	...
179	54.7	39.2	1.5	8.2	13.8	4.60	7.18	8.6	0.8	19.2	...	...	34.9	105.9	112.5	...	...	26.8	...
-125	57.4	37.6	1.7	10.1	14.0	4.41	3.92	-4.0	0.8	18.4	...	0.0	-0.5	104.7	111.9	...	...	25.3	...
-1,083	68.2	40.5	1.2	7.7	14.5	3.63	-9.39	-9.0	2.8	4.8	...	0.0	-73.7	85.2	94.2	...	...	98.3	...
884	59.3	32.7	0.9	5.7	11.5	3.35	11.52	11.2	1.1	13.1	...	0.0	185.4	80.2	91.1	...	...	32.3	...
	Principal Lines of Business: OrdLife (96.4%), IndLife (3.6%)													Principal States: LA (100.0%)					
430	82.7	16.1	-1.4	-3.9	-10.0	4.58	4.93	12.1	1.5	16.2	40.4	389.4	8.3	87.2	94.8	13.3	...	3.1	1.2
2,285	89.8	16.2	-1.5	-3.9	-11.4	5.14	5.41	16.8	1.7	14.2	32.1	428.0	2.8	79.6	87.1	10.0	...	2.3	...
-2,617	79.4	13.4	1.1	3.4	8.7	5.25	5.48	21.3	1.7	15.9	25.8	404.3	22.9	79.6	86.1	9.3	...	1.6	1.1
-1,173	85.7	15.1	-0.8	-2.7	-6.6	5.12	4.80	9.8	2.0	13.5	27.6	498.8	-5.1	77.8	86.5	6.4	...	1.5	1.2
1,667	102.1	14.7	0.9	3.3	7.8	4.32	4.13	-16.0	1.7	11.5	33.2	587.2	-6.1	83.0	87.7	0.2	...	1.3	1.2
	Principal Lines of Business: OrdLife (61.8%), IndA&H (24.0%), IndAnn (5.0%), GrpA&H (4.6%), GrpLife (4.4%)																		

Data in U.S. Dollars

COMPANY NAME Ultimate Parent Association Principal Officer Mailing Address Dom. : Began Bus. : Struct. : Mktg. Specialty Phone # AMB# NAIC#	Best's Financial Strength Rating FSC	Data Year	Balance Sheet Bonds (%)	Mort. Loans & R.E. (%)	Com & Pref. Stock (%)	All Other Assets (%)	Total Assets ($000)	Life Reserves (%)	Health Reserves %)	Ann Res. & Dep. Liabilities (%)	All Other Liabilities (%)	Capital & Surplus ($000)	Operations Direct Premiums Written ($000)	Net Premiums Written & Deposits ($000)	Operating Cash Flow ($000)	NOG Before Taxes ($000)	NOG After Taxes ($000)	Net Income ($000)
MUTUAL BENEFICIAL ASSOC INC Stephen M. Santarlasci President 1301 Lancaster Avenue, Suite 102 Berwyn, PA 19312-1290 DE : 1914 : Fraternal : Not Available Ind Ann, Ordinary Life 610-722-0253 AMB# 009812 NAIC# 56251	NR-5	'05	96.8	...	...	3.2	37,361	16.8	...	81.6	1.6	773	5,089	5,023	3,917	30	30	30
		'06	97.1	...	...	2.9	40,057	16.2	...	83.1	0.8	798	4,918	4,841	2,642	22	22	22
		'07	96.4	...	...	3.6	41,707	15.9	...	83.3	0.9	825	3,952	3,873	1,611	20	20	20
		'08	95.4	...	...	4.6	42,733	15.9	...	83.6	0.5	831	4,246	4,163	1,213	71	71	84
		'09	97.0	...	...	3.0	45,369	15.4	...	83.9	0.7	752	4,640	4,556	2,556	5	5	5
		Rating History: NR-5, 04/15/10; NR-5, 04/24/09; NR-5, 04/11/08; NR-5, 05/08/07; NR-5, 04/25/06																
MUTUAL OF AMERICA LIFE INS CO Thomas J. Moran Chairman, President & CEO 320 Park Avenue New York, NY 10022 NY : 1945 : Mutual : Direct Response Ann 212-224-1600 AMB# 008851 NAIC# 88668	A+ Rating Outlook: Stable FSC XI	'05	46.6	2.4	3.1	47.8	11,838,778	0.4	0.4	47.4	51.7	801,828	1,170,990	1,206,921	-193,564	133,210	133,210	124,567
		'06	43.1	2.3	3.3	51.2	12,437,899	0.4	0.4	44.6	54.5	811,938	1,283,566	1,289,337	-91,593	13,626	13,626	16,821
		'07	42.4	2.1	2.6	52.9	13,016,898	0.4	0.4	43.0	56.2	831,510	1,406,086	1,406,782	-25,261	-14,780	-14,780	7,286
		'08	54.8	2.5	0.6	42.2	10,971,697	0.4	0.4	55.2	43.9	783,832	1,372,254	1,372,582	201,537	1,244	1,244	-54,045
		'09	50.2	2.1	0.6	47.1	12,427,574	0.4	0.3	49.8	49.5	796,924	1,442,518	1,453,241	104,930	3,310	3,310	-2,730
		Rating History: A+, 01/15/10; A+, 12/05/08; A+, 10/24/07; A+, 06/21/06; A+, 06/21/05																
MUTUAL OF OMAHA INS CO Mutual of Omaha Insurance Company Daniel P. Neary Chairman & CEO Mutual of Omaha Plaza Omaha, NE 68175 NE : 1910 : Mutual : Agency Med supp 402-342-7600 AMB# 007369 NAIC# 71412	A+ Rating Outlook: Stable FSC XIII	'05	56.5	1.7	30.7	11.1	4,150,151	...	74.8	1.0	24.3	1,749,375	1,525,195	1,868,801	158,777	80,923	79,599	73,612
		'06	56.7	3.3	27.3	12.7	4,752,902	...	75.7	1.0	23.3	2,140,907	1,611,636	2,183,544	627,398	74,669	85,854	93,422
		'07	50.3	4.5	35.8	9.3	4,541,725	...	73.8	0.0	26.2	2,217,383	1,243,280	1,824,822	-4,623	102,004	60,083	89,625
		'08	43.2	5.9	39.0	11.9	4,700,084	...	71.2	0.0	28.8	2,098,578	1,000,300	1,554,254	131,731	199,299	182,560	152,034
		'09	41.9	5.7	39.1	13.3	4,730,154	...	75.8	...	24.2	2,237,934	938,263	1,620,392	-85,753	105,988	82,217	26,034
		Rating History: A+ g, 01/20/10; A+ g, 04/08/09; A+ g, 06/09/08; A+ g, 06/06/07; A g, 06/07/06																
MUTUAL SAVINGS LIFE INS CO Unitrin, Inc Don M. Royster, Sr. President 12115 Lackland Road St. Louis, MO 63146-4003 AL : 1927 : Stock : Career Agent Home serv, Ind Life, Ind A&H 256-552-7011 AMB# 006753 NAIC# 66397	A- Rating Outlook: Stable FSC IX	'05	88.5	1.1	0.8	9.6	414,032	88.7	3.8	5.5	2.0	19,318	47,435	50,793	2,074	7,638	5,996	6,040
		'06	84.1	1.1	3.6	11.3	417,778	88.8	3.8	5.3	2.1	20,969	47,068	49,633	4,816	8,962	6,741	6,745
		'07	85.2	0.2	3.4	11.2	425,913	88.7	3.7	5.1	2.5	23,596	46,579	49,023	7,297	8,903	6,946	8,680
		'08	85.9	0.2	1.4	12.5	424,531	89.7	3.6	4.9	1.7	22,624	45,038	46,799	4,134	7,455	6,557	1,280
		'09	82.0	0.2	1.2	16.6	439,467	88.9	3.5	4.9	2.6	33,824	42,614	43,720	10,000	11,747	7,494	7,183
		Rating History: A- g, 05/25/10; A-, 04/10/09; B++, 05/05/08; B- u, 11/13/07; B-, 04/09/07																
MVP HEALTH INSURANCE COMPANY MVP Health Care Inc David W. Oliker President 625 State Street Schenectady, NY 12305 NY : 2001 : Non-Profit : Not Available Group A&H, Health 518-370-4793 AMB# 060369 NAIC# 11125	B Rating Outlook: Negative FSC VII	'05	38.7	...	...	61.3	27,253	...	32.0	...	68.0	17,040	73,662	73,187	4,299	5,002	4,967	4,967
		'06	35.9	...	...	64.1	26,317	...	31.7	...	68.3	19,400	49,558	49,034	-10	2,392	2,309	2,309
		'07	42.1	...	...	57.9	29,108	...	34.5	...	65.5	22,632	47,902	47,632	1,747	3,259	3,299	3,299
		'08	59.8	...	...	40.2	46,923	...	43.7	...	56.3	19,238	139,465	138,242	14,594	-3,774	-3,774	-3,528
		'09	26.1	...	9.6	64.3	143,792	...	38.6	...	61.4	56,161	430,449	428,987	87,215	-68,778	-66,653	-65,649
		Rating History: B, 06/11/10; B u, 11/19/09; B+ g, 06/11/09; B+ g, 03/05/08; B+ g, 02/15/07																
MVP HEALTH INS CO OF NH INC MVP Health Care Inc David Oliker President 625 State Street Schenectady, NY 12305 NH : Other : Broker Group A&H, Health 518-370-4793 AMB# 060606 NAIC# 10135	B- Rating Outlook: Negative FSC IX	'05	...	...	...	...	...	...	...	...	...	...	...	...	...	...	...	...
		'06	...	...	...	...	...	...	...	...	...	...	...	...	...	...	...	...
		'07	...	...	...	...	...	...	...	...	...	...	...	...	...	...	...	...
		'08	...	...	...	100.0	16,059	...	50.4	...	49.6	1,154	51,081	50,637	12,883	-4,096	-4,096	-4,096
		'09	25.5	...	...	74.5	27,936	...	83.3	...	16.7	7,213	100,415	100,103	11,446	-24,409	-24,409	-24,285
		Rating History: B- g, 06/11/10; B- gu, 11/19/09; B g, 06/11/09																
MVP HEALTH PLAN MVP Health Care Inc David W. Oliker President 625 State Street Schenectady, NY 12305 NY : 1983 : Non-Profit : Broker Medicare, Group A&H, Medicaid 518-370-4793 AMB# 068567 NAIC# 95521	B+ Rating Outlook: Negative FSC IX	'05	31.2	...	8.8	60.1	568,864	...	50.5	...	49.5	367,423	1,810,193	1,808,138	43,369	119,821	119,821	119,492
		'06	32.9	...	10.6	56.5	505,031	...	32.3	...	67.7	285,850	1,853,161	1,851,525	-67,978	80,656	79,540	80,003
		'07	39.8	...	11.1	49.1	553,406	...	35.4	...	64.6	322,054	1,956,607	1,955,312	39,784	76,815	77,026	80,822
		'08	43.8	...	6.8	49.4	583,254	...	40.0	...	60.0	288,519	2,276,112	2,274,746	-11,183	43,227	43,223	35,536
		'09	45.5	...	13.5	41.0	571,698	...	49.2	...	50.8	327,209	2,354,004	2,352,133	-36,843	128,227	128,624	122,452
		Rating History: B+, 06/11/10; B+ u, 11/19/09; B+ g, 06/11/09; B+ g, 03/05/08; B+ g, 02/15/07																
MVP HEALTH PLAN OF NH INC MVP Health Care Inc David Oliker President 625 State Street Schenectady, NY 12305 NH : 2005 : Other : Not Available Health 518-370-4793 AMB# 064829 NAIC# 10141	B- Rating Outlook: Negative FSC IX	'05	...	...	...	100.0	6,183	...	2.2	...	97.8	4,276	61	61	6,155	-1,722	-1,722	-1,722
		'06	...	...	14.4	85.6	7,540	...	15.7	...	84.3	6,359	1,703	1,701	1,181	-1,552	-1,552	-1,552
		'07	...	...	13.5	86.5	7,504	...	20.5	...	79.5	5,906	5,979	5,972	570	-280	-280	-280
		'08	...	...	18.1	81.9	6,381	...	33.2	...	66.8	5,314	4,221	4,216	1,812	-1,855	-1,855	-1,855
		'09	...	...	85.2	14.8	8,463	...	1.7	...	98.3	7,283	465	464	27,686	-802	-802	-802
		Rating History: B- g, 06/11/10; B- gu, 11/19/09; B g, 06/11/09; B+ g, 03/05/08; NR-2, 02/15/07																
MVP HEALTH SERVICES CORP MVP Health Care Inc David W. Oliker President 625 State Street Schenectady, NY 12305 NY : 1993 : Stock : Broker Dental 518-370-4793 AMB# 064648 NAIC# 47062	B+ Rating Outlook: Negative FSC III	'05	...	...	...	100.0	2,087	...	21.2	...	78.8	1,017	5,858	5,858	-2,192	199	-33	-41
		'06	...	...	...	100.0	2,520	...	29.8	...	70.2	1,814	5,578	5,578	102	1,258	812	812
		'07	...	...	...	100.0	3,276	...	28.1	...	71.9	2,738	4,766	4,766	1,053	1,351	886	886
		'08	13.0	...	...	87.0	4,726	...	5.7	...	94.3	3,231	3,993	3,993	279	835	490	490
		'09	...	...	...	100.0	4,461	...	12.0	...	88.0	3,352	3,544	3,544	824	91	118	123
		Rating History: B+, 06/11/10; B+ u, 11/19/09; B+, 06/11/09; NR-2, 03/05/08; NR-2, 02/15/07																

2010 BEST'S KEY RATING GUIDE — LIFE/HEALTH EDITION
BEST'S PROFITABILITY, LEVERAGE AND LIQUIDITY TESTS 2005 – 2009

Data in U.S. Dollars

—	Profitability Tests							Leverage Tests						Liquidity Tests					
Un-Realized Capital Gains ($000)	Benefits Paid to NPW & Dep (%)	Comm. & Expenses to NPW & Dep (%)	NOG to Total Assets (%)	NOG to Total Rev (%)	Operating Return on Equity (%)	Net Yield (%)	Total Return (%)	Change in NPW & Dep (%)	NPW & Dep to Capital (X)	Capital & Surplus to Liabilities (%)	Surplus Relief (%)	Reins Leverage (%)	Change in Capital (%)	Quick Liquidity (%)	Current Liquidity (%)	Non-Invest Grade Bonds to Capital (%)	Delinq. & Foreclosed Mortgages to Capital (%)	Mort. & Credit Tenant Loans & R.E. to Capital (%)	Affiliated Invest to Capital (%)
-20	48.5	16.0	0.1	0.4	3.9	5.76	5.76	-7.7	5.7	2.4	1.7	10.7	1.2	76.1	82.2	65.5	...	...	...
24	64.9	16.4	0.1	0.3	2.8	5.70	5.82	-3.6	5.3	2.4	2.7	12.7	5.3	77.3	82.7	82.5	...	...	...
4	95.7	21.7	0.0	0.3	2.5	5.82	5.88	-20.0	4.1	2.3	2.9	15.1	2.6	78.3	84.0	60.2	...	...	...
-198	105.7	20.1	0.2	1.1	8.6	5.76	5.36	7.5	5.0	2.0	2.3	19.5	-12.0	76.4	83.6	85.2	...	...	...
...	77.2	17.8	0.0	0.1	0.6	5.74	5.76	9.4	5.4	1.9	3.3	26.0	0.6	71.3	80.6	166.4	...	...	...
	Principal Lines of Business: IndAnn (84.3%), OrdLife (15.7%)													Principal States: PA (35.5%), NY (22.4%), NJ (18.3%), IL (16.4%)					
24,805	109.1	17.6	1.1	7.7	18.0	8.00	8.53	10.9	1.4	15.7	0.0	0.1	16.6	77.9	88.3	12.6	...	32.9	33.0
29,569	111.5	14.6	0.1	0.8	1.7	5.84	6.56	6.8	1.4	16.5	0.0	0.1	3.3	79.5	90.2	10.8	...	31.7	31.9
-14,458	104.9	13.9	-0.1	-0.8	-1.8	5.70	5.92	9.1	1.5	16.6	0.0	0.1	1.0	75.0	87.0	13.8	...	30.4	30.8
-22,795	103.7	14.4	0.0	0.1	0.2	5.64	4.51	-2.4	1.7	13.8	0.0	0.2	-11.2	77.7	89.3	12.7	...	33.2	33.8
14,559	75.7	14.8	0.0	0.2	0.4	5.71	5.96	5.9	1.7	13.9	0.0	0.2	2.9	77.4	87.8	31.0	...	31.3	31.8
	Principal Lines of Business: GrpAnn (74.8%), IndAnn (24.2%), GrpLife (0.6%), GrpA&H (0.3%), OrdLife (0.1%)													Principal States: NY (22.6%), CA (8.7%), TX (5.1%), FL (4.9%), PA (4.8%)					
-36,865	73.3	26.2	2.0	3.9	4.6	4.87	3.88	-0.4	1.1	74.9	0.4	4.8	0.0	51.6	72.0	5.8	...	4.1	79.1
8,916	73.0	25.6	1.9	3.6	4.4	4.43	4.91	16.8	1.0	84.2	0.1	4.4	22.3	65.8	88.4	3.1	...	7.2	66.2
7,676	81.8	29.6	1.3	2.9	2.8	3.52	4.43	-16.4	0.8	99.1	0.1	4.3	4.0	51.7	75.4	2.0	...	9.1	72.6
-214,520	65.6	30.2	4.0	9.9	8.5	6.05	0.53	-14.8	0.7	81.7	0.1	4.9	-6.5	33.0	52.8	3.4	...	13.2	86.8
63,290	69.5	29.0	1.7	4.6	3.8	3.33	3.56	4.3	0.7	90.8	0.1	4.8	6.5	33.8	53.5	4.9	...	12.1	84.5
	Principal Lines of Business: IndA&H (85.7%), GrpA&H (14.3%)													Principal States: TX (9.5%), NY (6.0%), NC (5.0%), FL (4.6%), IN (4.5%)					
-1,093	69.9	58.8	1.4	8.1	29.4	5.71	5.60	-6.0	2.4	5.4	1.5	35.6	-9.4	58.6	71.6	...	...	22.1	37.2
885	70.2	56.8	1.6	9.1	33.5	5.76	6.12	-2.3	2.1	6.0	1.8	36.4	10.0	59.2	72.1	...	...	19.0	36.6
860	66.5	58.0	1.6	9.5	31.2	5.70	6.47	-1.2	1.9	6.5	1.6	29.1	10.9	61.5	74.7	...	...	3.8	23.1
-558	70.7	60.5	1.5	9.3	28.4	5.70	4.40	-4.5	2.0	5.7	1.7	20.4	-12.2	68.2	79.0	0.6	...	4.1	25.3
757	80.8	52.1	1.7	11.0	26.6	5.78	6.00	-6.6	1.3	8.6	0.8	15.7	52.6	67.8	79.3	34.8	...	2.5	17.4
	Principal Lines of Business: OrdLife (81.6%), IndA&H (16.2%), IndLife (1.9%), IndAnn (0.2%)													Principal States: AL (83.1%), MS (10.3%), GA (4.3%)					
...	78.9	15.1	17.8	6.7	31.3	2.84	2.84	-20.8	4.3	166.8	...	1.1	15.5	363.0	376.8	...	...	...	...
...	79.0	18.3	8.6	4.6	12.7	4.63	4.63	-33.0	2.5	280.5	...	1.8	13.9	541.9	554.3	...	...	...	...
...	75.9	19.7	11.9	6.8	15.7	4.87	4.87	-2.9	2.1	349.4	...	1.4	16.7	586.7	602.8	...	...	...	...
...	85.7	18.0	-9.9	-2.7	-18.0	3.90	4.65	190.2	7.2	69.5	...	1.1	-15.0	182.7	186.2	...	...	...	...
-172	96.6	17.3	-69.9	-15.5	-99.9	1.99	2.99	210.3	7.6	64.1	...	1.2	191.9	220.0	232.0	...	...	...	...
	Principal Lines of Business: CompHosp/Med (100.0%)													Principal States: NY (81.2%), VT (18.8%)					
...	...	...	...	...	...	...	...	...	...	...	...	...	...	...	...	...	...	...	...
...	...	...	...	...	...	...	...	...	...	...	...	...	...	...	...	...	...	...	...
...	...	...	...	...	...	...	...	...	...	...	...	...	...	...	...	...	...	...	...
...	87.9	20.6	...	-8.1	...	...	...	...	43.9	7.7	...	17.2	...	184.4	194.5	...	...	...	...
...	104.2	17.7	-99.9	-24.3	-99.9	1.60	2.23	97.7	13.9	34.8	...	1.5	525.0	205.5	219.2	...	...	...	...
	Principal Lines of Business: CompHosp/Med (100.0%)													Principal States: NH (100.0%)					
...	85.2	9.2	22.7	6.6	39.2	3.61	3.54	9.8	4.9	182.4	...	3.6	50.9	280.7	293.2	...	...	...	10.2
...	87.7	9.2	14.8	4.2	24.4	5.55	5.66	2.4	6.5	130.4	...	3.7	-22.2	197.0	207.5	0.7	...	...	6.3
-459	87.5	9.5	14.6	3.9	25.3	4.66	5.49	5.6	6.1	139.2	...	3.7	12.7	210.4	223.6	0.3	...	...	5.6
-17,554	89.4	9.5	7.6	1.9	14.2	4.50	-1.53	16.3	7.9	97.9	...	4.3	-10.4	143.0	152.2	0.4	...	...	6.2
25,914	86.4	8.7	22.3	5.4	41.8	3.58	8.70	3.4	7.2	133.8	...	3.9	13.4	134.4	149.4	2.1	...	...	14.4
	Principal Lines of Business: Medicare (46.7%), CompHosp/Med (44.1%), Medicaid (3.9%), FEHBP (3.8%), OtherHlth (1.6%)													Principal States: NY (96.9%), VT (3.1%)					
...	122.5	999.9	...	-99.9	...	...	...	...	0.0	224.2	...	...	...	613.2	645.5	...	...	...	...
...	79.8	128.5	-22.6	-78.0	-29.2	4.52	4.52	999.9	0.3	538.0	...	...	48.7	944.1	994.2	...	...	...	17.1
...	71.7	38.1	-3.7	-4.5	-4.6	4.39	4.39	251.0	1.0	369.7	...	...	-7.1	760.7	801.3	...	...	...	17.2
-3,975	110.5	37.3	-26.7	-42.4	-33.1	2.62	-46.02	-29.4	0.8	498.3	...	...	-10.0	695.4	732.1	...	...	...	21.7
-24,391	69.3	206.0	-10.8	-99.9	-12.7	0.17	-99.90	-89.0	0.1	616.8	...	...	37.0	182.1	191.7	...	...	...	99.0
	Principal Lines of Business: CompHosp/Med (100.0%)													Principal States: NH (100.0%)					
...	79.5	17.7	-1.0	-0.6	-1.3	1.17	0.86	17.6	5.8	95.0	...	...	-74.3	238.8	248.2	...	...	...	...
...	63.1	15.8	35.3	14.3	57.4	5.08	5.08	-4.8	3.1	256.7	...	...	78.4	497.0	517.0	...	...	...	...
...	58.4	15.8	30.6	18.1	38.9	5.46	5.46	-14.6	1.7	509.2	...	...	51.0	999.9	999.9	...	...	...	...
...	63.0	18.2	12.2	12.0	16.4	3.01	3.01	-16.2	1.2	216.1	...	...	18.0	371.8	378.0	...	...	...	...
...	66.3	31.8	2.6	3.3	3.6	0.69	0.82	-11.2	1.1	302.2	...	...	3.7	688.0	707.2	...	...	...	...
	Principal Lines of Business: Dental (100.0%)													Principal States: NY (100.0%)					

Data in U.S. Dollars

COMPANY NAME Ultimate Parent Association Principal Officer Mailing Address Dom. : Began Bus. : Struct. : Mktg. Specialty Phone # AMB# NAIC#	Best's Financial Strength Rating FSC	Data Year	Balance Sheet Bonds (%)	Mort. Loans & R.E. (%)	Com & Pref. Stock (%)	All Other Assets (%)	Total Assets ($000)	Life Reserves (%)	Health Reserves (%)	Ann Res. & Dep. Liabilities (%)	All Other Liabilities (%)	Capital & Surplus ($000)	Operations Direct Premiums Written ($000)	Net Premiums Written & Deposits ($000)	Operating Cash Flow ($000)	NOG Before Taxes ($000)	NOG After Taxes ($000)	Net Income ($000)
NAP LIFE INS CO' George M. Wise III President 3755 Capital of Texas Highway South Austin, TX 78704-6600 TX : 1984 : Stock : Not Available 512-462-2728 AMB# 009485 NAIC# 66516	NR-1	'05	80.4	...	...	19.6	2,083	...	...	...	100.0	2,083	...	...	...	23	23	22
		'06	84.9	...	...	15.1	2,100	...	...	...	100.0	2,095	...	136	...	29	24	12
		'07	87.6	...	...	12.4	2,144	...	...	...	100.0	2,143	...	...	...	38	33	48
		'08	82.8	...	...	17.2	2,171	...	...	...	100.0	2,171	...	...	...	32	24	38
		'09	87.4	...	...	12.6	2,208	...	...	...	100.0	2,193	...	...	...	-1	-5	23
		Rating History: NR-1, 06/10/10; NR-5, 04/21/09; NR-5, 04/09/08; NR-5, 05/11/07; NR-5, 05/10/06																
NATIONAL BENEFIT LIFE INS CO Citigroup Inc. Raul Rivera Chairman, President & CEO One Court Square Long Island City, NY 11120-0001 NY : 1963 : Stock : Agency Dis inc, Term Life, Trad Life 718-248-8000 AMB# 006163 NAIC# 61409	A+ Rating Outlook: Negative FSC XIV	'05	84.4	...	1.9	13.7	809,556	79.1	3.5	3.4	13.9	324,148	155,720	296,642	18,531	57,349	37,202	36,720
		'06	84.2	...	1.3	14.5	834,142	80.5	3.3	3.6	12.5	329,519	162,244	311,179	29,119	52,827	36,938	36,333
		'07	88.2	...	0.7	11.1	691,213	80.1	4.7	4.8	10.4	304,949	169,321	233,404	-111,594	150,911	101,433	100,677
		'08	90.8	...	0.7	8.5	721,467	81.0	4.5	5.0	9.4	316,859	172,623	151,088	40,280	47,576	25,454	15,138
		'09	87.2	...	0.7	12.2	781,311	81.8	4.3	5.7	8.3	358,956	173,726	149,947	39,199	55,306	40,479	31,259
		Rating History: A+ g, 03/16/10; A+ gu, 11/09/09; A+ g, 05/15/09; A+ g, 05/15/08; A+ g, 11/02/06																
NATIONAL FAMILY CARE LIFE INS' Clyde W. Tullis President 13530 Inwood Road Dallas, TX 75244-5305 TX : 1977 : Stock : Not Available 972-387-8553 AMB# 008775 NAIC# 86959	NR-1	'05	73.6	...	...	26.4	17,791	...	...	...	100.0	7,300	9,758	9,758	...	801	681	681
		'06	76.1	...	...	23.9	17,164	...	...	...	100.0	7,550	9,822	9,822	...	300	198	198
		'07	79.9	...	...	20.1	16,361	...	...	...	100.0	8,164	9,367	9,367	...	416	411	411
		'08	83.2	...	...	16.8	15,132	...	...	...	100.0	8,229	9,138	9,138	...	403	283	283
		'09	83.2	...	...	16.8	15,111	...	...	...	100.0	8,444	9,057	9,057	...	131	131	131
		Rating History: NR-1, 06/10/10; NR-1, 06/12/09; NR-1, 06/12/08; NR-1, 06/08/07; NR-1, 06/07/06																
NATIONAL FARM LIFE INS CO National Farm Life Insurance Company Jerry D. Davis, Jr. President & CEO P.O. Box 1486 Fort Worth, TX 76101-1486 TX : 1946 : Stock : Agency Ann, Term Life, Whole life 817-451-9550 AMB# 006771 NAIC# 66532	B++ Rating Outlook: Stable FSC V	'05	79.1	6.3	1.9	12.7	231,254	64.4	...	30.7	4.9	21,550	18,922	23,430	11,385	764	532	434
		'06	77.5	6.6	3.0	12.9	243,362	64.4	...	30.7	4.9	22,057	21,115	24,934	11,408	665	405	459
		'07	75.9	7.8	4.2	12.2	252,805	65.6	...	29.7	4.6	22,300	21,677	24,704	8,293	682	499	499
		'08	74.3	6.7	4.0	15.1	259,486	66.9	...	29.9	3.1	20,244	23,849	27,208	8,349	2,541	2,113	-1,731
		'09	77.0	6.7	4.0	12.3	270,386	68.0	...	29.1	2.9	22,894	23,304	25,451	9,674	4,294	3,450	1,077
		Rating History: B++, 05/28/10; A-, 05/26/09; A-, 05/12/08; A-, 05/05/07; A-, 05/31/06																
NATIONAL FARMERS UNION LIFE Financial Holding Corporation Gary L. Muller CEO P.O. Box 410288 Kansas City, MO 64141-0288 TX : 1938 : Stock : Agency Ann, Ind Life, Univ Life 816-391-2000 AMB# 006772 NAIC# 66540	B+ Rating Outlook: Stable FSC VI	'05	59.4	11.7	3.1	25.8	291,610	88.2	0.0	7.3	4.5	40,606	11,276	9,183	-11,809	10,060	6,982	6,982
		'06	62.8	11.6	3.2	22.4	281,098	88.3	0.0	7.3	4.4	40,577	10,411	7,875	-8,996	8,376	5,574	5,501
		'07	62.2	10.8	6.2	20.7	272,705	87.5	0.0	7.3	5.2	42,957	9,722	7,566	-17,444	9,765	6,957	6,962
		'08	62.1	9.1	6.4	22.5	262,903	87.1	0.0	7.4	5.4	42,285	9,116	7,896	-514	8,769	6,203	6,918
		'09	68.0	8.1	3.3	20.6	251,770	88.6	0.0	7.7	3.7	43,631	8,465	6,654	-13,958	9,017	6,281	5,250
		Rating History: B+, 11/04/09; B+, 09/05/08; B+, 06/14/07; B+, 06/21/06; B+, 06/22/05																
NATIONAL FOUNDATION LIFE INS Credit Suisse Holdings (USA) Inc Benjamin M. Cutler Chairman, President & CEO 3100 Burnett Plaza, 801 Cherry Street Fort Worth, TX 76102 TX : 1983 : Stock : Agency A&H, Ind A&H, Med supp 817-878-3300 AMB# 006774 NAIC# 98205	B Rating Outlook: Negative FSC V	'05	93.4	...	...	6.6	46,984	8.7	80.7	1.1	9.5	9,611	34,256	52,245	-1,048	969	973	977
		'06	93.5	...	...	6.5	49,721	8.5	81.9	1.2	8.4	12,214	31,849	53,902	2,737	-257	-257	-282
		'07	85.8	...	...	14.2	50,040	8.2	82.8	1.2	7.9	12,257	32,505	53,910	-1,849	-2,725	-2,725	-2,725
		'08	87.2	...	...	12.8	42,910	0.2	69.9	...	29.9	8,164	29,347	48,087	-2,795	-4,038	-4,038	-4,380
		'09	70.0	...	...	30.0	40,833	0.3	68.0	...	31.8	7,899	28,098	55,494	-2,834	-133	-133	-217
		Rating History: B g, 02/08/10; B g, 02/04/09; B g, 04/01/08; B g, 05/31/07; B g, 05/22/06																
NATIONAL GUARDIAN LIFE INS CO National Guardian Life Insurance Company John D. Larson Chairman, President & CEO 2 East Gilman Street Madison, WI 53703-1494 WI : 1910 : Mutual : Agency Pre-need, Dental, Ordinary Life 608-257-5611 AMB# 006777 NAIC# 66583	A- Rating Outlook: Stable FSC VIII	'05	75.8	5.1	8.6	10.5	1,349,182	57.0	2.3	36.0	4.7	139,927	179,836	144,251	58,509	13,804	10,284	11,838
		'06	74.8	6.9	9.8	8.5	1,393,704	61.5	2.3	33.0	3.3	157,405	238,725	143,343	43,198	18,866	12,735	17,239
		'07	74.8	6.3	9.7	9.2	1,485,979	64.2	2.3	28.4	5.1	167,450	302,220	172,937	95,048	20,047	12,816	16,536
		'08	74.0	7.0	8.0	11.0	1,651,189	68.4	2.1	23.7	5.9	160,840	345,036	204,971	156,383	17,582	13,227	6,392
		'09	76.0	6.0	7.0	11.1	1,776,303	72.8	2.0	21.6	3.6	187,433	434,165	244,279	110,641	30,995	20,018	8,242
		Rating History: A- g, 03/15/10; A- g, 05/01/09; A- g, 06/11/08; A- g, 06/20/07; A-, 05/31/06																
NATIONAL HEALTH INSURANCE CO Southwest Insurance Partners, Inc. Charles W. Harris President & CEO P.O. Box 619999 Dallas, TX 75261-9999 TX : 1966 : Stock : Agency A&H, Dread dis 817-640-1900 AMB# 008392 NAIC# 82538	B++ Rating Outlook: Stable FSC V	'05	22.6	26.1	18.8	32.6	40,389	0.7	50.0	...	49.3	7,277	74,484	69,355	11,061	8,262	8,262	8,285
		'06	26.1	29.4	15.7	28.8	34,909	0.8	42.2	...	57.0	8,023	58,447	56,114	-1,987	3,247	3,247	3,247
		'07	22.1	28.8	...	49.1	36,655	0.9	44.4	...	54.7	17,449	44,522	42,976	-4,021	3,096	3,023	-1,199
		'08	29.7	2.9	23.2	44.2	25,798	1.7	79.6	...	18.7	16,861	33,767	32,757	-4,273	1,365	1,375	1,325
		'09	9.6	1.5	21.2	67.7	25,239	1.4	71.7	...	26.9	16,316	27,576	27,416	-554	-2,612	-1,927	-217
		Rating History: B++, 07/06/09; NR-5, 11/03/08; E, 03/03/04; C u, 05/16/03; B u, 03/18/03																
NATIONAL INCOME LIFE INSURANCE Torchmark Corporation Roger Smith President & CEO P.O. Box 5009 Syracuse, NY 13220 NY : 2000 : Stock : Agency Ind Life, Ind A&H 315-451-8180 AMB# 060343 NAIC# 10093	A+ Rating Outlook: Stable FSC X	'05	70.8	...	...	29.2	21,560	85.6	7.8	...	6.6	7,993	18,251	18,251	4,702	1,245	103	103
		'06	66.5	...	2.8	30.7	27,758	88.9	6.0	...	5.1	8,983	20,693	20,693	5,313	2,465	1,456	1,456
		'07	51.9	...	9.5	38.6	35,370	91.5	5.7	...	2.8	9,825	24,049	24,049	6,963	2,382	1,337	1,337
		'08	71.7	...	0.6	27.7	43,446	89.2	6.7	...	4.1	9,944	28,498	28,498	4,940	3,600	2,743	2,663
		'09	55.3	...	...	44.7	54,157	87.3	5.8	...	6.9	11,342	33,857	33,857	9,187	5,044	2,040	2,039
		Rating History: A+ g, 06/15/10; A+ g, 06/11/09; A+ g, 06/11/08; A+ g, 06/08/07; A+ g, 06/08/06																

Data in U.S. Dollars

—	Profitability Tests							Leverage Tests						Liquidity Tests					
Un-Realized Capital Gains ($000)	Benefits Paid to NPW & Dep (%)	Comm. & Expenses to NPW & Dep (%)	NOG to Total Assets (%)	NOG to Total Rev (%)	Operating Return on Equity (%)	Net Yield (%)	Total Return (%)	Change in NPW & Dep (%)	NPW & Dep to Capital (X)	Capital & Surplus to Liabilities (%)	Surplus Relief (%)	Reins Leverage (%)	Change in Capital (%)	Quick Liquidity (%)	Current Liquidity (%)	Non-Invest Grade Bonds to Capital (%)	Delinq. & Foreclosed Mortgages to Capital (%)	Mort. & Credit Tenant Loans & R.E. to Capital (%)	Affiliated Invest to Capital (%)
...	...	...	1.1	30.1	1.1	...	...	...	...	...	...	...	1.2	...	...	...	...	...	...
...	100.0	40.9	1.2	11.0	1.2	...	...	...	0.1	999.9	...	...	0.6	...	...	...	...	...	...
...	...	...	1.6	33.9	1.6	...	...	-99.9	...	999.9	...	...	2.3	...	...	...	...	...	...
...	...	...	1.1	25.0	1.1	...	...	...	...	...	...	...	1.3	...	...	...	...	...	...
...	...	...	-0.2	-6.8	-0.2	...	...	...	...	999.9	...	...	1.0	...	...	...	...	...	...
1,054	41.6	17.4	4.7	11.0	12.0	5.96	6.26	1.3	0.9	68.9	0.2	22.5	9.2	87.6	112.0	11.9	...	...	...
-421	40.9	17.5	4.5	10.8	11.3	6.06	6.11	4.9	0.9	67.3	0.2	22.2	1.6	107.7	126.1	11.0	...	...	...
-86	36.0	24.2	13.3	38.3	32.0	6.51	6.60	-25.0	0.8	81.8	0.2	25.2	-7.3	116.3	136.6	13.8	...	...	...
-242	32.3	37.0	3.6	14.8	8.2	5.74	4.40	-35.3	0.5	78.8	0.2	24.6	2.3	103.3	130.9	13.4	...	...	...
475	30.7	37.2	5.4	23.2	12.0	5.92	4.97	-0.8	0.4	85.3	0.2	22.5	13.1	109.9	139.1	12.2	...	...	...
	Principal Lines of Business: OrdLife (57.4%), GrpA&H (27.0%), IndAnn (13.6%), CrdLife (1.0%), GrpLife (0.5%)													Principal States: NY (76.4%), NJ (5.0%)					
...	18.9	76.0	3.9	6.6	9.7	...	...	-1.0	1.3	69.6	...	...	7.2	...	...	...	...	...	...
...	18.4	92.6	1.1	1.9	2.7	...	...	0.7	1.3	78.5	...	...	3.4	...	...	...	...	...	...
...	18.9	98.0	2.4	4.1	5.2	...	...	-4.6	1.1	99.6	...	...	8.1	...	...	...	...	...	...
...	18.7	96.5	1.8	2.9	3.5	...	...	-2.4	1.1	119.2	...	...	0.8	...	...	...	...	...	...
...	18.1	88.5	0.9	1.4	1.6	...	...	-0.9	1.1	126.7	...	...	2.6	...	...	...	...	...	...
	Principal Lines of Business: IndA&H (83.9%), OrdLife (16.1%)																		
187	43.4	32.1	0.2	1.7	2.5	6.11	6.27	3.1	1.0	11.2	1.0	10.4	3.1	56.7	64.8	50.0	...	62.9	8.0
176	46.6	32.8	0.2	1.2	1.9	6.01	6.22	6.4	1.0	10.9	0.8	8.8	3.1	57.1	65.3	45.7	...	67.4	7.7
26	48.9	35.3	0.2	1.4	2.3	6.09	6.19	-0.9	1.0	10.7	0.7	9.4	1.9	55.1	63.4	41.7	...	80.7	7.4
-3,173	41.2	34.5	0.8	5.7	9.9	6.09	3.36	10.1	1.3	8.5	0.8	9.7	-16.5	58.0	66.3	40.6	...	84.9	9.6
1,987	52.8	32.7	1.3	9.4	16.0	5.97	5.89	-6.5	1.1	9.4	0.7	9.9	14.6	53.8	62.5	55.9	...	78.1	8.3
	Principal Lines of Business: OrdLife (81.5%), IndAnn (10.3%), GrpAnn (8.2%)													Principal States: TX (94.8%)					
206	280.0	25.0	2.3	25.9	17.3	6.16	6.32	0.1	0.2	17.4	0.5	78.9	2.6	57.4	71.3	1.5	...	83.0	37.3
528	299.6	31.8	1.9	22.0	13.7	6.15	6.39	-14.2	0.2	18.1	0.3	70.0	-0.1	50.9	63.5	...	...	79.2	37.1
1,063	303.8	36.6	2.5	27.7	16.7	6.54	7.02	-3.9	0.2	20.4	0.5	68.9	7.0	49.7	63.3	6.5	...	67.1	2.1
-3,456	263.3	37.2	2.3	26.0	14.6	6.16	5.23	4.4	0.2	19.8	0.3	66.2	-5.8	56.5	70.7	1.0	...	58.0	2.6
1,460	268.0	39.1	2.4	28.4	14.6	6.11	6.42	-15.7	0.1	22.3	0.4	73.7	5.4	49.9	64.9	26.5	...	47.4	2.2
	Principal Lines of Business: OrdLife (96.8%), GrpLife (1.9%), IndAnn (1.2%), IndA&H (0.0%), GrpAnn (0.0%)													Principal States: CA (12.2%), TX (10.0%), FL (6.7%), ND (6.5%), MN (4.6%)					
-30	65.7	39.0	2.0	1.8	10.5	5.45	5.58	-9.6	5.3	26.6	0.0	4.3	6.0	90.4	100.1	14.1	...	...	...
...	68.8	39.7	-0.5	-0.4	-2.4	5.18	5.29	3.2	4.3	33.5	0.0	4.4	26.4	97.3	107.7	8.0	...	...	...
24	67.6	43.7	-5.5	-4.8	-22.3	5.39	5.58	0.0	4.3	33.4	0.0	7.1	0.4	96.3	106.0	9.9	...	...	...
...	58.2	48.7	-8.7	-7.9	-39.6	5.13	4.48	-10.8	5.9	23.6	12.8	20.2	-34.6	108.3	117.5	13.9	...	...	...
...	63.7	42.9	-0.3	-0.2	-1.7	4.64	4.65	15.4	7.0	24.1	1.4	14.7	-3.2	103.7	111.2	11.6	...	...	...
	Principal Lines of Business: GrpA&H (69.4%), IndA&H (30.4%), OrdLife (0.2%)													Principal States: TX (22.3%), CO (11.9%), MT (11.3%), AR (9.3%), NC (8.6%)					
-2,660	83.9	29.2	0.8	4.2	7.5	6.01	5.98	-12.9	0.9	13.0	6.8	10.1	2.7	63.6	74.5	40.4	0.0	47.6	37.6
145	94.6	25.4	0.9	5.0	8.6	6.04	6.44	-0.6	0.8	14.2	8.0	11.9	11.9	56.4	70.2	28.2	...	59.0	33.2
-2,369	90.1	24.2	0.9	4.4	7.9	5.98	6.14	20.6	0.9	14.2	10.4	11.2	6.5	56.7	71.8	29.5	...	54.4	31.9
-12,032	75.7	22.8	0.8	3.9	8.1	5.95	4.75	18.5	1.2	11.7	12.1	14.1	-5.8	54.7	68.8	47.2	...	71.9	34.7
4,646	62.7	24.1	1.2	4.9	11.5	6.37	5.98	19.2	1.2	12.6	14.4	13.9	14.7	55.0	69.8	35.5	2.2	60.3	30.5
	Principal Lines of Business: OrdLife (44.4%), GrpLife (38.1%), GrpA&H (9.6%), IndAnn (3.8%), GrpAnn (2.4%)													Principal States: WI (8.3%), NC (8.2%), PA (6.8%), CA (6.0%), TX (5.9%)					
-332	76.3	13.0	22.3	10.5	88.6	-2.60	-3.42	-27.1	8.8	24.3	131.0	341.1	-34.2	54.9	56.9	...	...	133.2	229.4
-2,102	74.0	20.4	8.6	5.8	42.4	-2.84	-9.30	-19.1	6.5	33.1	8.9	25.3	9.8	53.2	55.1	...	...	118.1	181.4
7,618	71.6	22.9	8.4	7.0	23.7	-1.35	15.30	-23.4	2.5	90.9	0.4	1.3	101.1	157.2	163.0	...	...	60.6	60.6
-1,330	71.3	24.8	4.4	4.2	8.0	-3.07	-7.65	-23.8	1.9	189.4	0.1	1.0	-3.2	195.5	225.8	...	...	4.5	4.5
864	78.2	30.5	-7.6	-7.1	-11.6	-3.03	8.56	-16.3	1.6	206.7	0.0	0.0	0.7	250.7	261.3	...	...	2.2	2.2
	Principal Lines of Business: GrpA&H (64.6%), IndA&H (35.2%), GrpLife (0.2%)													Principal States: TX (21.5%), OR (11.9%), CT (8.9%), NC (7.3%), SC (5.0%)					
...	20.6	49.7	0.6	0.5	1.4	5.04	5.08	17.8	2.3	59.5	...	...	11.3	102.4	113.0	1.5	...	...	...
...	17.6	49.4	5.9	6.7	17.1	5.44	5.47	13.4	2.3	48.4	...	...	12.6	88.0	104.2	1.3	...	...	...
...	19.4	47.9	4.2	5.2	14.2	5.75	5.75	16.2	2.4	39.1	...	...	9.7	93.2	112.2	3.6	...	...	...
...	17.7	51.8	7.0	9.1	27.8	5.46	5.22	18.5	2.8	30.2	...	...	1.4	58.2	74.7	...	...	...	...
...	15.2	52.2	4.2	5.7	19.2	5.01	4.99	18.8	2.9	27.0	...	...	14.2	90.4	102.7	2.5	...	...	...
	Principal Lines of Business: OrdLife (85.1%), IndA&H (14.6%), GrpA&H (0.4%)													Principal States: NY (99.5%)					

Data in U.S. Dollars

COMPANY NAME Ultimate Parent Association Principal Officer Mailing Address Dom. : Began Bus. : Struct. : Mkt. Specialty Phone # AMB# NAIC#	Best's Financial Strength Rating FSC	Data Year	Balance Sheet Bonds (%)	Mort. Loans & R.E. (%)	Com & Pref. Stock (%)	All Other Assets (%)	Total Assets ($000)	Life Reserves (%)	Health Reserves (%)	Ann Res. & Dep. Liabilities (%)	All Other Liabilities (%)	Capital & Surplus ($000)	Operations Direct Premiums Written ($000)	Net Premiums Written & Deposits ($000)	Operating Cash Flow ($000)	NOG Before Taxes ($000)	NOG After Taxes ($000)	Net Income ($000)
NATIONAL INSURANCE CO OF WI National Services Inc	**B++**	'05	36.4	0.5	3.8	59.2	35,989	...	96.1	...	3.9	13,238	4,604	12,162	881	1,363	900	1,013
Bruce A. Miller President		'06	38.2	0.5	3.7	57.7	39,377	...	96.4	...	3.6	13,654	4,961	12,923	822	1,255	916	893
250 South Executive Drive, Suite 300 Brookfield, WI 53005-4273	Rating Outlook: Stable	'07	37.5	0.4	3.8	58.3	43,727	...	90.6	...	9.4	15,886	5,526	13,678	1,796	3,516	2,321	2,322
WI : 1895 : Stock : Agency Dis inc		'08	35.1	0.0	3.2	61.6	44,201	...	91.5	...	8.5	14,595	5,765	12,697	268	1,390	942	809
262-785-9995		'09	37.6	2.6	3.9	56.0	47,287	...	89.9	...	10.1	16,808	5,065	12,426	2,896	3,317	2,156	2,235
AMB# 010794 NAIC# 30155	FSC V	**Rating History: B++, 05/20/10; B++, 06/11/09; B++, 06/10/08; B++, 06/06/07; B++, 06/21/06**																
NATIONAL INTEGRITY LIFE INS CO Western & Southern Mutual Holding Co	**A+**	'05	24.2	0.0	0.8	75.0	3,049,714	3.0	...	25.3	71.6	98,327	457,845	493,237	172,461	1,650	1,736	7,118
Jill T. McGruder President & CEO		'06	25.0	0.1	1.3	73.6	3,483,167	2.8	...	23.9	73.3	129,074	522,715	534,959	79,995	12,326	34,412	37,892
15 Matthews Street, Suite 200 Goshen, NY 10924	Rating Outlook: Stable	'07	27.0	0.1	1.0	71.9	3,677,509	2.9	...	25.1	72.0	142,135	517,677	532,561	119,419	10,401	9,385	5,115
NY : 1968 : Stock : Broker Ann, Var ann		'08	33.5	0.1	1.0	65.3	4,037,542	2.6	...	33.3	64.1	184,548	776,427	805,076	388,607	-46,741	-34,060	-56,756
845-615-2506		'09	39.3	0.6	0.3	59.7	4,432,445	2.4	...	38.7	58.9	225,590	552,695	575,690	333,650	16,765	15,205	1,130
AMB# 007798 NAIC# 75264	FSC XV	**Rating History: A+ g, 05/18/10; A+ g, 06/29/09; A++g, 07/09/08; A++g, 06/14/07; A++g, 06/21/06**																
NATIONAL LIFE INS CO National Life Holding Company	**A**	'05	58.9	12.1	4.2	24.7	7,901,244	58.3	7.2	16.4	18.2	623,465	636,120	619,086	206,611	137,535	125,532	91,566
Mehran Assadi President & CEO		'06	57.5	11.1	4.8	26.6	8,164,721	58.3	7.0	15.4	19.3	707,989	637,727	636,004	165,465	78,768	80,819	79,710
1 National Life Drive Montpelier, VT 05604	Rating Outlook: Stable	'07	58.2	10.8	4.9	26.1	8,275,646	59.1	7.2	14.8	18.8	826,783	586,322	584,098	20,258	57,854	62,476	65,012
VT : 1850 : Stock : Career Agent Ann, Term Life, Trad Life		'08	59.8	10.7	5.8	23.7	7,964,828	62.4	7.6	15.6	14.4	792,195	618,323	627,081	29,616	18,028	28,437	-4,911
802-229-3333		'09	60.3	9.3	6.1	24.3	8,501,197	60.8	7.3	16.2	15.7	1,134,203	618,754	617,037	275,353	32,414	30,396	-11,397
AMB# 006790 NAIC# 66680	FSC XII	**Rating History: A g, 09/21/09; A g, 11/12/08; A g, 06/15/07; A g, 06/21/06; A g, 05/06/05**																
NATIONAL LIFE INS CO National Promoters & Services Inc	**B+**	'05	63.0	5.4	9.2	22.5	128,007	55.5	14.9	24.7	4.9	26,684	64,856	58,158	18,212	2,447	2,447	2,846
Edgardo Van Rhyn President & CEO		'06	65.2	5.2	9.6	20.0	131,855	57.5	16.3	19.3	7.0	30,141	58,206	51,986	4,490	1,811	1,811	1,777
P.O. Box 366107 San Juan, PR 00936-6107	Rating Outlook: Negative	'07	66.8	5.0	6.6	21.7	134,975	59.0	17.3	18.0	5.6	26,270	63,052	60,277	5,044	1,893	1,893	1,477
PR : 1969 : Stock : Agency Credit Life, Group A&H, Ind A&H		'08	67.8	8.2	5.4	18.6	146,587	57.3	18.7	16.6	7.3	28,527	63,648	71,505	9,849	1,303	1,303	712
787-758-8080		'09	66.5	8.1	4.4	21.0	145,308	59.5	18.6	14.8	7.1	20,236	86,492	95,343	-8,164	1,516	1,516	1,438
AMB# 007447 NAIC# 72087	FSC V	**Rating History: B+, 06/15/10; B++, 06/22/09; A-, 01/07/09; A-, 10/15/07; A- u, 08/09/07**																
NATIONAL MASONIC PROVIDENT[1]	**NR-1**	'05	79.5	...	10.7	9.9	1,703	...	...	3.7	96.3	912	31	30	...	-46	-46	-46
Ronald A. Ives President		'06	79.7	...	9.8	10.5	1,594	...	...	3.6	96.4	834	30	29	...	-78	-78	-78
1801 Watermark Drive, Suite 100 Columbus, OH 43215		'07	83.1	...	6.9	10.0	1,485	...	...	3.9	96.1	786	26	26	...	-49	-49	-49
OH : 1890 : Mutual : Not Available		'08	73.1	...	6.1	20.8	1,318	...	...	4.3	95.7	732	20	19	...	-31	-31	-54
614-228-5130		'09	80.0	...	6.7	13.3	1,200	...	...	3.9	96.1	679	19	18	...	-53	-53	-53
AMB# 006793 NAIC# 66702		**Rating History: NR-1, 06/10/10; NR-1, 06/12/09; NR-1, 06/12/08; NR-1, 06/08/07; NR-1, 06/07/06**																
NATIONAL PACIFIC DENTAL INC UnitedHealth Group Inc	**NR-3**	'05	...	0.5	...	99.5	4,582	...	27.0	...	73.0	3,340	16,631	16,631	810	3,350	2,151	2,151
Diane D. Souza President		'06	2.5	0.4	...	97.1	4,063	...	71.6	...	28.4	3,448	16,180	16,180	-262	3,115	2,025	2,025
2300 Clayton Road, Suite 1000 Concord, CA 94520		'07	2.1	...	...	97.9	4,801	...	51.6	...	48.4	4,230	16,552	16,552	595	4,117	2,735	2,735
TX : 1989 : Stock : Not Available Dental		'08	2.0	...	...	98.0	5,046	...	48.7	...	51.3	4,553	14,046	14,046	203	3,458	2,281	2,281
713-803-8100		'09	2.1	...	...	97.9	4,736	...	59.8	...	40.2	4,152	14,536	14,536	-48	3,222	2,091	2,091
AMB# 068837 NAIC# 95251		**Rating History: NR-3, 06/15/09; NR-3, 01/29/08; NR-3, 11/21/07; NR-3, 11/20/06; NR-3, 06/16/06**																
NATIONAL SAFETY LIFE INS CO Columbian Mutual Life Insurance Company	**B+**	'05	98.9	...	...	1.1	5,107	9.7	82.1	...	8.2	2,875	1,689	1,689	-163	-890	-890	-890
Thomas E. Rattmann Chairman & CEO		'06	87.2	...	...	12.8	5,169	12.3	75.6	...	12.2	2,569	2,387	2,387	-582	-796	-534	-537
P.O. Box 1381 Binghamton, NY 13902-1381	Rating Outlook: Stable	'07	90.4	...	...	9.6	4,885	19.7	69.8	...	10.5	2,225	2,326	2,326	-12	-262	-299	-300
PA : 1963 : Stock : Agency A&H		'08	70.3	...	...	29.7	3,311	65.0	1.1	...	33.9	2,235	1,997	1,284	-1,636	3	52	51
610-684-2400		'09	74.4	...	...	25.6	3,114	70.7	0.8	...	28.5	2,024	523	523	-340	-290	-186	-186
AMB# 007850 NAIC# 75744	FSC III	**Rating History: B+, 06/10/10; B+, 06/12/09; B+, 06/11/08; B+, 06/18/07; B+, 06/20/06**																
NATIONAL SECURITY INS CO National Security Group, Inc	**B**	'05	75.0	2.9	12.0	10.1	42,252	82.4	2.5	4.2	10.9	9,931	6,280	6,320	289	-245	-201	-101
William L. Brunson, Jr. President		'06	75.2	3.2	14.1	7.5	41,941	83.7	3.4	4.0	9.0	9,343	6,592	6,671	-879	-2,476	-2,014	-1,581
661 East Davis Street Elba, AL 36323	Rating Outlook: Stable	'07	73.9	5.4	12.7	8.1	43,167	82.8	3.5	3.9	9.8	8,889	7,081	7,114	1,553	-510	-518	-351
AL : 1947 : Stock : Agency Ordinary Life, A&H, Dread dis		'08	71.5	6.0	8.8	13.7	41,368	87.9	3.8	4.1	4.1	8,205	7,003	7,028	-1,415	1,096	1,408	-442
334-897-2273		'09	75.3	6.7	9.3	8.6	43,884	86.2	3.7	3.9	6.1	9,126	7,247	7,273	2,935	1,323	1,250	1,314
AMB# 006802 NAIC# 66788	FSC IV	**Rating History: B, 04/16/10; B, 04/22/09; B, 03/24/08; B, 02/23/07; B, 03/17/06**																
NATIONAL SECURITY LF & ANNUITY Ohio National Mutual Holdings Inc	**A**	'05	55.1	1.4	...	43.5	60,247	...	...	35.1	64.9	20,735	8,522	4,216	202	-352	-352	-352
John J. Palmer President & CEO		'06	44.9	...	...	55.1	61,244	...	...	23.2	76.8	20,013	18,510	9,298	-15,246	-718	-718	-715
P.O. Box 1625 Binghamton, NY 13902-1625	Rating Outlook: Stable	'07	25.6	...	...	74.4	89,982	0.2	...	10.2	89.6	19,218	31,330	15,299	-3,278	-796	-796	-799
NY : 1975 : Stock : Other Direct Reins, Var ann, Var life		'08	29.3	...	...	70.7	81,703	0.2	...	17.0	82.8	16,748	22,523	10,892	1,689	-1,787	-1,787	-2,704
877-446-6060		'09	28.6	...	...	71.4	162,151	0.1	...	20.9	79.0	19,903	66,839	32,895	21,435	3,607	3,607	3,503
AMB# 008633 NAIC# 85472	FSC V	**Rating History: A, 05/21/10; A, 06/12/09; A, 06/06/08; A, 06/12/07; A, 04/12/06**																

BEST'S PROFITABILITY, LEVERAGE AND LIQUIDITY TESTS 2005 – 2009

Data in U.S. Dollars

—	Profitability Tests							Leverage Tests						Liquidity Tests					
Un-Realized Capital Gains ($000)	Benefits Paid to NPW & Dep (%)	Comm. & Expenses to NPW & Dep (%)	NOG to Total Assets (%)	NOG to Total Rev (%)	Operating Return on Equity (%)	Net Yield (%)	Total Return (%)	Change in NPW & Dep (%)	NPW & Dep to Capital (X)	Capital & Surplus to Liabilities (%)	Surplus Relief (%)	Reins Leverage (%)	Change in Capital (%)	Quick Liquidity (%)	Current Liquidity (%)	Non-Invest Grade Bonds to Capital (%)	Delinq. & Foreclosed Mortgages to Capital (%)	Mort. & Credit Tenant Loans & R.E. to Capital (%)	Affiliated Invest to Capital (%)
-177	67.3	32.8	2.6	6.5	7.1	3.97	3.59	8.7	0.9	58.2	1.7	20.4	8.4	56.9	59.7	10.9	...	1.4	...
123	73.1	27.7	2.4	6.2	6.8	4.26	4.84	6.3	0.9	53.1	3.6	21.4	3.1	56.4	58.6	4.4	...	1.4	...
-131	54.7	32.3	5.6	14.8	15.7	4.68	3.98	5.8	0.9	57.1	1.7	168.3	16.3	58.2	60.2	3.3	...	1.2	...
-605	70.8	31.8	2.1	6.4	6.2	4.30	0.58	-7.2	0.9	49.3	2.0	23.0	-8.1	51.8	56.3	2.0	...	0.1	...
592	54.2	33.4	4.7	14.9	13.7	4.14	7.45	-2.1	0.7	55.1	1.5	17.9	15.2	55.5	61.8	...	...	7.3	7.2
	Principal Lines of Business: GrpA&H (100.0%), IndA&H (0.0%)													Principal States: WI (64.1%), MN (17.2%), MI (10.0%), IN (3.8%), ND (3.3%)					
845	51.7	7.3	0.1	0.3	1.8	5.31	6.07	16.6	4.2	14.7	...	1.4	-0.4	86.1	100.8	14.4	...	0.3	...
...	59.2	7.3	1.1	5.8	30.3	5.71	6.03	8.5	3.5	17.9	...	0.5	28.2	70.3	88.6	12.7	...	2.3	...
...	88.5	7.7	0.3	1.6	6.9	5.53	5.02	-0.4	3.3	16.7	...	0.5	5.6	65.1	85.5	13.2	...	1.7	...
-7,049	50.8	6.7	-0.9	-3.9	-20.9	5.75	3.44	51.2	4.3	13.6	...	1.2	16.3	70.4	85.9	49.5	...	2.1	...
3,443	77.2	7.5	0.4	2.3	7.4	5.97	5.31	-28.5	2.5	13.7	...	1.1	25.0	64.1	79.7	71.6	...	11.9	3.5
	Principal Lines of Business: IndAnn (99.5%), GrpAnn (0.5%), OrdLife (0.0%)													Principal States: NY (94.5%)					
-6,464	83.5	25.0	1.6	11.9	21.5	7.67	7.12	-12.0	0.9	10.8	1.5	30.3	11.4	42.2	54.5	32.3	0.8	144.0	40.5
36,263	85.6	26.6	1.0	8.1	12.1	6.70	7.27	2.7	0.8	12.1	1.3	29.0	13.3	44.8	56.8	30.6	0.6	120.3	39.3
46,951	102.6	30.0	0.8	6.4	8.1	6.33	7.08	-8.2	0.6	14.2	1.0	25.6	15.8	42.0	54.0	27.1	0.3	102.4	41.5
-43,575	92.8	27.2	0.4	2.9	3.5	5.93	4.85	7.4	0.8	12.7	1.0	29.6	-8.5	41.2	53.0	25.4	0.4	106.6	52.1
74,792	91.2	30.8	0.4	3.2	3.2	5.75	6.26	-1.6	0.5	17.4	0.7	21.7	39.9	44.3	56.3	27.9	0.3	70.5	43.9
	Principal Lines of Business: OrdLife (65.4%), IndAnn (21.2%), GrpAnn (12.2%), IndA&H (1.2%)													Principal States: NY (15.0%), CA (7.1%), FL (6.1%), GA (5.0%), NJ (3.7%)					
-310	38.7	49.6	2.1	3.9	12.5	4.65	4.72	-1.6	2.1	27.7	...	32.0	99.7	76.4	82.9	...	...	24.9	60.0
955	57.5	52.3	1.4	3.1	6.4	4.77	5.54	-10.6	1.7	30.8	0.7	86.5	11.7	75.3	81.9	15.6	...	21.9	57.5
-2,745	45.2	48.1	1.4	2.8	6.7	4.76	2.14	15.9	2.2	25.4	0.0	93.4	-11.7	76.5	82.7	7.5	...	24.5	52.7
2,032	51.4	45.2	0.9	1.7	4.8	4.77	5.95	18.6	2.3	26.9	1.0	96.6	13.4	72.6	80.0	8.2	...	38.8	59.9
-1,493	62.6	37.1	1.0	1.5	6.2	4.63	3.47	33.3	4.2	18.3	...	98.2	-27.5	61.6	67.7	17.9	...	52.1	76.0
	Principal Lines of Business: GrpA&H (46.1%), IndA&H (21.8%), OrdLife (18.5%), GrpLife (7.9%), CrdLife (4.2%)													Principal States: PR (99.5%)					
...	261.9	386.2	-2.7	-40.7	-5.0	...	...	-30.7	0.0	115.9	...	...	-4.8	...	...	...	...	...	...
...	245.1	490.8	-4.7	-70.9	-8.9	...	...	-5.3	0.0	110.4	...	...	-8.5	...	...	...	...	...	...
...	294.3	394.2	-3.2	-47.8	-6.0	...	...	-10.0	0.0	113.0	...	...	-5.8	...	...	...	...	...	...
...	695.9	467.9	-2.2	-37.9	-4.1	...	...	-25.9	0.0	125.9	...	...	-6.8	...	...	...	...	...	...
...	446.1	542.9	-4.2	-73.5	-7.5	...	...	-3.4	0.0	131.3	...	...	-7.3	...	...	...	...	...	...
	Principal Lines of Business: IndA&H (58.8%), OrdLife (41.2%)																		
...	66.9	13.0	52.1	12.9	68.4	0.18	0.18	4.6	5.0	269.1	...	...	13.2	287.5	287.5	...	...	0.7	0.7
...	66.5	14.3	46.8	12.5	59.6	0.21	0.21	-2.7	4.7	561.1	...	...	3.2	589.7	592.8	...	...	0.5	0.5
...	61.1	14.8	61.7	16.4	71.2	3.43	3.43	2.3	3.9	740.3	...	...	22.7	999.9	999.9	...	...	...	...
...	61.4	14.4	46.3	16.2	51.9	1.70	1.70	-15.1	3.1	924.2	...	...	7.6	999.9	999.9	...	...	...	...
...	62.9	13.8	42.7	14.5	48.0	0.33	0.33	3.5	3.5	711.1	...	...	-8.8	916.8	938.8	...	...	...	...
	Principal Lines of Business: Dental (100.0%)													Principal States: TX (100.0%)					
...	53.7	73.9	-17.1	-45.5	-26.9	5.00	5.54	17.6	0.6	130.8	...	...	-23.5	175.5	189.8	6.9	...	...	...
...	38.0	98.3	-10.4	-20.0	-19.6	5.52	5.91	41.3	0.9	99.6	...	...	-10.9	144.1	155.4	...	...	...	...
...	52.5	76.1	-6.0	-10.9	-12.5	5.31	5.45	-2.6	1.0	84.3	...	...	-13.4	143.9	154.6	...	...	...	...
...	39.8	73.5	1.3	2.9	2.3	5.10	5.29	-44.8	0.6	209.9	12.8	3.1	0.4	282.5	299.7	...	...	...	...
...	36.4	165.1	-5.8	-21.5	-8.7	4.54	4.76	-59.3	0.3	187.8	...	...	-9.4	224.8	241.7	...	...	...	...
	Principal Lines of Business: OrdLife (94.1%), IndA&H (5.9%)													Principal States: PA (74.8%), MD (17.9%), DE (7.4%)					
91	51.1	71.6	-0.5	-2.4	-2.0	4.24	4.94	0.6	0.6	34.2	...	0.3	-5.9	106.1	112.0	2.3	...	11.6	40.4
161	51.4	72.5	-4.8	-23.3	-20.9	4.71	6.37	5.6	0.6	32.5	...	0.3	-4.4	97.4	104.2	2.4	...	12.9	8.0
-72	55.5	64.7	-1.2	-5.7	-5.7	4.87	5.25	6.6	0.7	29.8	...	0.3	-3.8	91.1	99.4	2.5	1.4	23.4	18.4
-1,489	57.2	53.3	3.3	14.3	16.5	5.71	-2.35	-1.2	0.8	25.5	...	0.4	-15.3	89.2	98.1	13.6	...	29.4	23.4
118	56.5	54.6	2.9	12.3	14.4	6.06	6.61	3.5	0.8	28.2	...	0.3	14.8	85.6	95.6	13.9	...	30.5	56.0
	Principal Lines of Business: OrdLife (69.0%), IndA&H (25.1%), IndLife (2.5%), GrpLife (1.2%), GrpA&H (1.2%)													Principal States: AL (57.1%), GA (21.4%), MS (10.1%), SC (7.0%)					
...	9.6	41.8	-0.6	-3.4	-1.7	3.89	3.98	55.1	0.2	84.1	2.0	30.8	-1.8	138.0	151.0	8.8	...	4.0	...
-18	53.5	24.5	-1.2	-4.5	-3.5	4.88	4.68	120.5	0.5	191.8	3.6	31.7	-3.4	197.6	222.5	9.8	...	...	...
-18	12.1	14.3	-1.1	-2.5	-4.1	4.52	4.73	64.5	0.8	258.4	5.8	27.6	-4.0	254.4	285.3	11.6	...	...	...
-18	20.8	17.9	-2.1	-7.7	-9.9	4.51	1.29	-28.8	0.7	141.7	5.6	122.9	-13.7	191.6	215.7	11.2	...	...	...
-18	9.1	8.4	3.0	5.4	19.7	4.80	4.58	202.0	1.6	66.4	11.5	55.8	19.1	124.1	144.4	8.4	...	...	...
	Principal Lines of Business: IndAnn (100.0%), OrdLife (0.0%)													Principal States: NY (99.7%)					

Data in U.S. Dollars

COMPANY NAME / Ultimate Parent Association / Principal Officer / Mailing Address / Dom. : Began Bus. : Struct. : Mktg. / Specialty / Phone # / AMB# / NAIC# — Best's Financial Strength Rating / FSC

Balance Sheet: Data Year, Bonds (%), Mort. Loans & R.E. (%), Com & Pref. Stock (%), All Other Assets (%), Total Assets ($000), Life Reserves (%), Health Reserves (%), Ann Res. & Dep. Liabilities (%), All Other Liabilities (%), Capital & Surplus ($000). Operations: Direct Premiums Written ($000), Net Premiums Written & Deposits ($000), Operating Cash Flow ($000), NOG Before Taxes ($000), NOG After Taxes ($000), Net Income ($000)

NATIONAL STATES INS CO[1]
Thomas R. Green
President
1830 Craig Park Court
St. Louis, MO 63146-4148
MO : 1964 : Stock : Not Available
In Rehabilitation
314-878-0101
AMB# 006071 NAIC# 60593

Rating: **E**

Data Year	Bonds (%)	Mort. Loans & R.E. (%)	Com & Pref. Stock (%)	All Other Assets (%)	Total Assets ($000)	Life Reserves (%)	Health Reserves (%)	Ann Res. & Dep. Liabilities (%)	All Other Liabilities (%)	Capital & Surplus ($000)	Direct Premiums Written ($000)	Net Premiums Written & Deposits ($000)	Operating Cash Flow ($000)	NOG Before Taxes ($000)	NOG After Taxes ($000)	Net Income ($000)
'05	74.5	2.6	...	22.9	91,962	...	...	...	100.0	15,616	100,216	82,725	...	-3,581	-3,460	-3,460
'06	70.3	3.0	...	26.7	77,990	...	...	...	100.0	15,729	94,581	65,181	...	763	748	748
'07	69.7	2.9	...	27.5	79,093	...	...	...	100.0	16,940	89,196	60,857	...	460	460	459
'08	68.4	2.8	...	28.8	78,281	...	...	...	100.0	11,768	84,779	57,976	...	-5,180	-5,193	-5,645
'09	61.8	3.2	0.1	34.8	64,302	...	...	...	100.0	5,785	93,628	64,072	...	-8,526	-8,506	-8,477

Rating History: E, 04/07/10; NR-4, 12/02/09; C-, 12/02/09; C++, 02/27/09; B-, 01/18/08

NATIONAL TEACHERS ASSOCIATES
Ellard Enterprises, Inc.
Raymond J. Martin, Jr.
President & CEO
4949 Keller Springs Road
Addison, TX 75001-5910
TX : 1938 : Stock : Agency
Dis inc, Dread dis, Ind Life
972-532-2100
AMB# 006588 NAIC# 87963

Rating: **B++** — Rating Outlook: Stable — FSC VI

Data Year	Bonds (%)	Mort. Loans & R.E. (%)	Com & Pref. Stock (%)	All Other Assets (%)	Total Assets ($000)	Life Reserves (%)	Health Reserves (%)	Ann Res. & Dep. Liabilities (%)	All Other Liabilities (%)	Capital & Surplus ($000)	Direct Premiums Written ($000)	Net Premiums Written & Deposits ($000)	Operating Cash Flow ($000)	NOG Before Taxes ($000)	NOG After Taxes ($000)	Net Income ($000)
'05	93.6	...	...	6.4	134,625	4.3	91.1	0.0	4.6	20,263	53,871	53,402	27,684	5,106	3,372	3,372
'06	93.8	...	...	6.2	166,316	3.7	92.6	0.0	3.7	24,396	60,849	60,439	30,107	5,645	3,862	3,862
'07	92.9	...	...	7.1	198,081	3.2	93.8	0.0	2.9	26,873	68,968	68,567	30,451	8,818	5,714	1,722
'08	93.2	...	...	6.8	229,363	2.9	93.7	0.0	3.4	27,520	78,284	77,886	30,490	11,764	7,712	-1,117
'09	93.7	...	0.1	6.2	272,944	2.7	94.2	0.0	3.1	35,270	83,788	83,412	40,670	10,170	6,224	4,661

Rating History: B++, 09/21/09; B++, 10/14/08; B++, 11/15/07; B++, 10/13/06; B++, 11/07/05

NATIONAL WESTERN LIFE INS CO
Ross R. Moody
President & COO
850 East Anderson Lane
Austin, TX 78752-1602
CO : 1957 : Stock : Agency
Ann, Trad Life, Univ Life
512-836-1010
AMB# 006811 NAIC# 66850

Rating: **A** — Rating Outlook: Stable — FSC XI

Data Year	Bonds (%)	Mort. Loans & R.E. (%)	Com & Pref. Stock (%)	All Other Assets (%)	Total Assets ($000)	Life Reserves (%)	Health Reserves (%)	Ann Res. & Dep. Liabilities (%)	All Other Liabilities (%)	Capital & Surplus ($000)	Direct Premiums Written ($000)	Net Premiums Written & Deposits ($000)	Operating Cash Flow ($000)	NOG Before Taxes ($000)	NOG After Taxes ($000)	Net Income ($000)
'05	92.0	2.1	1.9	4.0	5,655,249	13.4	0.0	84.7	1.9	598,468	685,468	724,693	341,431	89,571	59,356	60,074
'06	89.4	1.9	2.0	6.7	5,962,810	13.5	0.0	84.5	2.0	673,262	641,027	669,621	251,884	110,101	71,597	72,585
'07	90.9	1.8	2.1	5.2	6,078,774	14.3	0.0	84.0	1.7	710,935	623,625	636,011	148,181	37,369	29,075	32,290
'08	91.2	1.7	2.5	4.5	6,126,954	14.9	0.0	83.0	2.1	708,047	595,416	618,478	68,810	48,853	28,980	9,643
'09	89.1	1.7	2.8	6.5	6,726,515	14.3	0.0	83.0	2.7	817,042	1,007,234	1,041,366	472,045	140,226	80,155	72,944

Rating History: A, 06/03/10; A, 06/17/09; A-, 06/13/08; A-, 06/19/07; A-, 06/20/06

NATIONWIDE LIFE & ANNUITY INS
Nationwide Mutual Insurance Company
Kirt A. Walker
President & COO
One Nationwide Plaza 1-4-20
Columbus, OH 43215-2220
OH : 1981 : Stock : Broker
Ind Ann
800-882-2822
AMB# 009070 NAIC# 92657

Rating: **A+** — Rating Outlook: Negative — FSC XV

Data Year	Bonds (%)	Mort. Loans & R.E. (%)	Com & Pref. Stock (%)	All Other Assets (%)	Total Assets ($000)	Life Reserves (%)	Health Reserves (%)	Ann Res. & Dep. Liabilities (%)	All Other Liabilities (%)	Capital & Surplus ($000)	Direct Premiums Written ($000)	Net Premiums Written & Deposits ($000)	Operating Cash Flow ($000)	NOG Before Taxes ($000)	NOG After Taxes ($000)	Net Income ($000)
'05	53.2	14.4	0.1	32.4	8,688,074	3.6	...	64.1	32.3	272,711	302,902	147,735	-347,469	-11,896	-3,718	-7,072
'06	47.7	14.5	0.1	37.7	7,391,543	6.1	...	58.9	34.9	232,658	280,744	142,615	-1,115,678	-34,684	-33,004	-35,439
'07	46.6	14.3	0.1	39.0	6,103,538	8.8	...	51.9	39.3	256,534	319,664	187,453	-976,959	9,084	11,561	-3,909
'08	52.5	15.6	0.2	31.8	4,879,251	14.0	...	58.2	27.8	122,672	506,178	220,975	-288,726	-23,620	-8,839	-90,374
'09	56.0	12.6	0.0	31.3	5,243,361	17.8	...	53.7	28.4	213,512	608,659	295,751	282,990	-21,750	4,051	-61,089

Rating History: A+ g, 03/25/10; A+ g, 01/27/09; A+ g, 03/11/08; A+ g, 02/09/07; A+ g, 01/30/06

NATIONWIDE LIFE INS CO
Nationwide Mutual Insurance Company
Kirt A. Walker
President & COO
One Nationwide Plaza 1-4-20
Columbus, OH 43215-2220
OH : 1931 : Stock : Broker
Group pens, Ind Ann, Life
614-249-7111
AMB# 006812 NAIC# 66869

Rating: **A+** — Rating Outlook: Negative — FSC XV

Data Year	Bonds (%)	Mort. Loans & R.E. (%)	Com & Pref. Stock (%)	All Other Assets (%)	Total Assets ($000)	Life Reserves (%)	Health Reserves (%)	Ann Res. & Dep. Liabilities (%)	All Other Liabilities (%)	Capital & Surplus ($000)	Direct Premiums Written ($000)	Net Premiums Written & Deposits ($000)	Operating Cash Flow ($000)	NOG Before Taxes ($000)	NOG After Taxes ($000)	Net Income ($000)
'05	24.0	7.7	0.4	67.8	99,325,940	6.6	0.2	25.5	67.6	3,262,090	11,003,321	11,804,988	-145,307	692,520	607,617	575,190
'06	22.0	7.3	0.6	70.1	103,708,785	6.5	0.2	24.0	69.4	3,336,588	11,666,760	13,425,718	-506,459	568,794	621,415	632,788
'07	21.0	6.8	0.7	71.5	105,355,236	6.4	0.1	22.4	71.1	3,175,132	11,364,584	12,570,310	-1,354,858	590,625	483,985	400,633
'08	24.4	8.2	0.7	66.7	82,303,554	8.9	0.2	28.2	62.7	2,749,933	10,129,870	10,397,228	329,417	-685,164	-613,614	-870,538
'09	23.7	6.7	0.3	69.4	88,955,178	7.8	0.2	24.4	67.6	3,129,557	9,014,382	9,156,193	-2,561,956	1,486,271	1,342,666	397,293

Rating History: A+ g, 03/25/10; A+ g, 01/27/09; A+ g, 03/11/08; A+ g, 02/09/07; A+ g, 01/30/06

NEIGHBORHOOD HLTH PARTNERSHIP
UnitedHealth Group Inc
Daniel I. Rosenthal
President & CEO
P.O. Box 025680
Miami, FL 33102-5680
FL : 1993 : Stock : Broker
Group A&H
305-715-2200
AMB# 064001 NAIC# 95123

Rating: **A-** — Rating Outlook: Stable — FSC VI

Data Year	Bonds (%)	Mort. Loans & R.E. (%)	Com & Pref. Stock (%)	All Other Assets (%)	Total Assets ($000)	Life Reserves (%)	Health Reserves (%)	Ann Res. & Dep. Liabilities (%)	All Other Liabilities (%)	Capital & Surplus ($000)	Direct Premiums Written ($000)	Net Premiums Written & Deposits ($000)	Operating Cash Flow ($000)	NOG Before Taxes ($000)	NOG After Taxes ($000)	Net Income ($000)
'05	64.9	...	...	35.1	113,918	...	83.3	...	16.7	30,663	612,735	612,735	-19,234	12,374	7,414	7,333
'06	67.5	...	...	32.5	114,750	...	79.8	...	20.2	49,271	413,508	413,508	3,041	35,634	23,546	23,446
'07	73.4	...	...	26.6	135,645	...	67.4	...	32.6	54,344	422,300	422,300	24,407	31,392	21,308	21,588
'08	71.4	...	...	28.6	127,287	...	61.6	...	38.4	46,622	423,922	423,922	-6,322	13,495	9,257	9,236
'09	76.9	...	...	23.1	117,877	...	68.0	...	32.0	48,065	431,571	431,571	-5,108	22,106	14,679	14,891

Rating History: A-, 06/15/09; A-, 01/29/08; A-, 11/21/07; B++, 11/16/06; B++, 08/17/06

NEIGHBORHOOD HEALTH PLAN INC
Deborah Enos
President & CEO
253 Summer Street
Boston, MA 02210-1120
MA : 1988 : Non-Profit : Broker
Group A&H, Medicaid
617-772-5500
AMB# 068744 NAIC# 11109

Rating: **NR-5**

Data Year	Bonds (%)	Mort. Loans & R.E. (%)	Com & Pref. Stock (%)	All Other Assets (%)	Total Assets ($000)	Life Reserves (%)	Health Reserves (%)	Ann Res. & Dep. Liabilities (%)	All Other Liabilities (%)	Capital & Surplus ($000)	Direct Premiums Written ($000)	Net Premiums Written & Deposits ($000)	Operating Cash Flow ($000)	NOG Before Taxes ($000)	NOG After Taxes ($000)	Net Income ($000)
'05	68.8	...	...	31.2	147,852	...	75.5	...	24.5	69,824	441,172	439,871	26,847	12,568	12,568	12,222
'06	85.7	...	...	14.3	192,489	...	73.2	...	26.8	97,766	528,085	526,670	40,203	24,245	24,245	24,400
'07	79.5	...	...	20.5	248,292	...	89.4	...	10.6	132,823	671,329	667,983	43,236	36,035	36,035	36,230
'08	83.5	...	...	16.5	288,261	...	19.9	...	80.1	153,320	844,059	838,573	35,850	23,390	23,390	24,721
'09	88.5	...	...	11.5	261,304	...	28.0	...	72.0	121,965	930,697	923,914	-44,675	-34,251	-34,251	-30,974

Rating History: NR-5, 04/06/10; NR-5, 08/26/09; B pd, 07/01/08; B- pd, 06/19/07; B- pd, 07/17/06

NEIGHBORHOOD HLTH PLAN OF RI
Mark E. Reynolds
President & CEO
299 Promenade Street
Providence, RI 02908
RI : 1994 : Non-Profit : Broker
Medicaid
401-459-6000
AMB# 064293 NAIC# 95402

Rating: **NR-5**

Data Year	Bonds (%)	Mort. Loans & R.E. (%)	Com & Pref. Stock (%)	All Other Assets (%)	Total Assets ($000)	Life Reserves (%)	Health Reserves (%)	Ann Res. & Dep. Liabilities (%)	All Other Liabilities (%)	Capital & Surplus ($000)	Direct Premiums Written ($000)	Net Premiums Written & Deposits ($000)	Operating Cash Flow ($000)	NOG Before Taxes ($000)	NOG After Taxes ($000)	Net Income ($000)
'05	36.9	...	...	63.1	56,842	...	31.6	...	68.4	20,324	168,857	167,795	13,800	9,110	9,110	9,105
'06	34.6	...	...	65.4	74,557	...	38.1	...	61.9	28,063	182,488	180,925	18,718	7,939	7,939	7,881
'07	35.2	...	0.3	64.5	71,578	...	59.9	...	40.1	38,108	188,592	187,641	-5,285	10,697	10,697	10,701
'08	32.2	...	...	67.8	116,181	...	45.8	...	54.2	36,873	254,856	253,839	33,272	-1,018	-1,018	-1,007
'09	29.7	...	1.8	68.5	108,341	...	47.7	...	52.3	18,814	338,103	337,045	988	-19,844	-19,844	-19,728

Rating History: NR-5, 04/06/10; NR-5, 08/26/09; B- pd, 09/08/08; B- pd, 10/08/07; C++pd, 07/10/06

NETCARE LIFE & HEALTH INS CO[1]
Kurt S. Moylan
President
Julale Center, Suite 200
Hagatna, GU 96910-5015
GU : 1998 : Stock : Direct Response
671-477-7514
AMB# 060302 NAIC# 60246

Rating: **NR-1**

Data Year	Bonds (%)	Mort. Loans & R.E. (%)	Com & Pref. Stock (%)	All Other Assets (%)	Total Assets ($000)	Life Reserves (%)	Health Reserves (%)	Ann Res. & Dep. Liabilities (%)	All Other Liabilities (%)	Capital & Surplus ($000)	Direct Premiums Written ($000)	Net Premiums Written & Deposits ($000)	Operating Cash Flow ($000)	NOG Before Taxes ($000)	NOG After Taxes ($000)	Net Income ($000)
'05	...	...	...	...	...	...	...	...	...	...	...	...	...	...	...	...
'06	40.6	...	0.1	59.3	23,401	...	...	0.1	99.9	1,804	26,504	21,336	...	375	375	374
'07	52.4	...	0.1	47.5	22,167	...	...	0.0	100.0	1,562	25,135	19,627	...	999	999	1,000
'08	45.9	...	0.1	54.0	24,413	...	...	0.0	100.0	1,441	28,333	21,729	...	-657	-657	-870
'09	62.4	...	0.1	37.6	20,740	...	...	0.0	100.0	1,397	33,724	27,149	...	977	977	981

Rating History: NR-1, 06/10/10; NR-1, 06/12/09; NR-1, 06/12/08; NR-1, 06/08/07; NR-5, 10/08/04

BEST'S PROFITABILITY, LEVERAGE AND LIQUIDITY TESTS 2005 – 2009

Data in U.S. Dollars

—	Profitability Tests							Leverage Tests						Liquidity Tests					
Un-Realized Capital Gains ($000)	Benefits Paid to NPW & Dep (%)	Comm. & Expenses to NPW & Dep (%)	NOG to Total Assets (%)	NOG to Total Rev (%)	Operating Return on Equity (%)	Net Yield (%)	Total Return (%)	Change in NPW & Dep (%)	NPW & Dep to Capital (X)	Capital & Surplus to Liabilities (%)	Surplus Relief (%)	Reins Leverage (%)	Change in Capital (%)	Quick Liquidity (%)	Current Liquidity (%)	Non-Invest Grade Bonds to Capital (%)	Delinq. & Foreclosed Mortgages to Capital (%)	Mort. & Credit Tenant Loans & R.E. to Capital (%)	Affiliated Invest to Capital (%)
...	71.4	29.4	-3.3	-3.7	-23.4	...	...	-10.4	5.2	21.0	33.9	...	11.6	...	...	...	...	15.2	...
...	68.8	32.1	0.9	1.0	4.8	...	...	-21.2	4.1	25.9	45.7	...	0.3	...	...	...	...	14.4	...
...	65.3	30.6	0.6	0.6	2.8	...	...	-6.6	3.5	27.8	40.6	...	7.4	...	...	...	...	13.3	...
...	81.0	31.5	-6.6	-7.7	-36.2	...	...	-4.7	4.9	18.0	51.5	...	-30.7	...	...	...	...	18.2	...
...	79.0	33.4	-11.9	-11.6	-96.9	...	...	10.5	10.7	10.2	115.1	...	-50.0	...	...	...	...	34.6	...
	Principal Lines of Business: IndA&H (91.6%), OrdLife (8.4%)																		
...	13.4	42.8	2.8	5.7	18.1	4.85	4.92	14.9	2.6	18.0	0.6	6.1	19.9	83.9	95.9	14.2	...	...	...
...	17.8	41.6	2.6	5.7	17.3	5.01	5.02	13.2	2.4	17.5	0.5	5.1	20.9	80.9	94.2	14.0	...	...	...
...	17.2	41.6	3.1	7.4	22.3	5.27	3.02	13.4	2.6	15.7	0.4	4.9	8.5	80.8	93.3	24.6	...	...	...
-890	17.8	41.6	3.6	8.7	28.4	5.12	0.50	13.6	2.8	13.6	0.4	4.8	2.4	86.9	96.1	17.6	...	...	...
653	24.4	39.7	2.5	6.6	19.8	4.64	4.29	7.1	2.4	14.8	0.3	3.9	28.2	89.4	97.9	20.5	...	...	...
	Principal Lines of Business: IndA&H (98.3%), OrdLife (1.7%)													Principal States: CA (25.5%), TX (18.4%), NC (7.5%), VA (6.8%), SC (6.6%)					
16,669	68.7	19.3	1.1	5.9	10.6	5.64	6.00	-30.0	1.1	12.9	0.0	1.3	12.5	73.0	85.7	26.3	0.0	18.1	17.7
8,189	84.0	21.7	1.2	6.9	11.3	6.67	6.86	-7.6	0.9	13.6	0.0	2.2	11.0	75.6	88.1	21.7	1.0	15.5	17.3
-3,309	103.3	25.1	0.5	3.0	4.2	5.30	5.33	-5.0	0.8	14.1	0.0	1.1	5.0	75.8	88.8	15.0	0.5	14.5	17.2
-3,418	105.7	24.5	0.5	3.3	4.1	4.44	4.09	-2.8	0.8	14.0	0.0	0.9	0.2	76.5	90.8	13.7	0.6	14.2	23.2
29,385	61.5	19.3	1.2	5.6	10.5	6.16	6.52	68.4	1.2	14.9	0.0	1.3	15.5	73.8	88.9	21.3	0.6	13.2	23.6
	Principal Lines of Business: IndAnn (55.2%), GrpAnn (28.3%), OrdLife (16.4%), GrpA&H (0.1%), IndA&H (0.0%)													Principal States: FL (10.6%), TX (10.1%), CA (9.3%), MI (7.9%), OH (7.8%)					
190	367.8	47.3	0.0	4.2	-1.3	5.83	5.84	-29.1	0.5	5.4	16.5	315.4	-2.4	44.2	61.3	57.6	0.1	433.3	...
1,389	397.9	45.0	-0.4	4.0	-13.1	5.77	5.76	-3.5	0.5	5.8	15.8	362.5	-12.0	42.7	60.8	79.0	...	422.3	...
-3,150	319.6	49.9	0.2	-1.5	4.7	5.78	5.30	31.4	0.6	8.1	18.3	305.6	6.6	40.0	58.2	66.8	...	326.2	...
1,965	191.2	51.3	-0.2	-7.3	-4.7	5.65	3.45	17.9	1.7	3.8	31.3	577.4	-53.9	39.6	55.1	200.5	...	609.6	...
-11,003	95.4	47.3	0.1	1.0	2.4	5.65	3.52	33.8	1.3	6.1	17.8	330.6	69.6	47.9	63.1	87.8	0.0	312.6	4.4
	Principal Lines of Business: OrdLife (96.0%), IndAnn (3.6%), GrpAnn (0.5%), GrpA&H (0.0%), IndA&H (0.0%)													Principal States: CA (14.2%), OH (9.5%), PA (9.0%), FL (5.6%), TX (4.8%)					
-30,478	112.6	8.6	0.6	4.5	19.5	5.68	5.56	-1.9	3.3	11.6	4.5	21.7	9.5	40.4	56.6	43.9	0.8	232.0	9.4
-31,104	121.6	8.3	0.6	4.3	18.8	5.67	5.66	13.7	3.6	12.2	4.7	21.6	2.8	40.1	56.3	41.8	0.2	222.0	11.5
6,967	134.6	9.3	0.5	3.5	14.9	5.70	5.50	-6.4	3.6	12.1	4.0	21.4	-4.8	37.4	54.7	41.4	0.0	218.6	13.6
346,171	119.9	10.0	-0.7	-4.9	-20.7	5.23	5.55	-17.3	3.3	10.3	2.8	30.0	-11.4	39.7	53.8	61.2	0.4	232.3	6.5
-419,869	110.7	10.0	1.6	11.5	45.7	5.08	0.85	-11.9	2.8	11.6	2.6	22.0	3.9	40.1	54.0	73.5	0.3	198.2	11.3
	Principal Lines of Business: IndAnn (53.4%), GrpAnn (34.3%), OrdLife (9.1%), GrpLife (3.2%), GrpA&H (0.0%)													Principal States: CA (10.2%), NY (10.2%), FL (8.0%), TX (5.3%), PA (5.1%)					
...	83.5	20.4	6.0	1.1	28.0	3.27	3.20	-23.2	20.0	36.8	...	0.5	37.0	147.4	154.9	...	...	...	...
...	73.4	19.6	20.6	5.6	58.9	7.00	6.90	-32.5	8.4	75.2	...	...	60.7	184.0	194.3	...	...	...	...
...	77.6	17.0	17.0	5.0	41.1	6.65	6.90	2.1	7.8	66.8	...	...	10.3	182.2	191.5	...	...	...	...
...	83.1	17.2	7.0	2.2	18.3	3.87	3.86	0.4	9.1	57.8	...	...	-14.2	168.8	180.1	...	...	...	...
...	78.4	17.1	12.0	3.4	31.0	2.26	2.44	1.8	9.0	68.8	...	...	3.1	184.1	195.9	...	...	...	...
	Principal Lines of Business: CompHosp/Med (100.0%)													Principal States: FL (100.0%)					
...	89.4	8.6	9.3	2.8	19.6	2.62	2.36	13.5	6.3	89.5	...	0.4	19.3	166.8	173.2	...	...	...	...
...	88.0	8.6	14.2	4.6	28.9	3.67	3.76	19.7	5.4	103.2	...	0.6	40.0	171.3	179.2	...	...	...	...
...	86.9	9.1	16.4	5.3	31.3	4.56	4.66	26.8	5.0	115.0	...	4.3	35.9	186.8	196.1	...	...	...	...
...	89.8	8.5	8.7	2.8	16.3	3.83	4.37	25.5	5.5	113.6	...	7.8	15.4	179.1	187.4	...	...	...	...
...	95.6	7.5	-12.5	-3.7	-24.9	2.94	4.31	10.2	7.6	87.5	...	18.0	-20.5	135.4	142.8	...	...	...	...
	Principal Lines of Business: Medicaid (67.4%), CompHosp/Med (32.6%)													Principal States: MA (100.0%)					
...	89.2	7.5	18.0	5.3	55.8	2.63	2.62	25.0	8.3	55.7	...	1.1	64.8	170.3	172.0	...	...	...	...
...	89.5	8.7	12.1	4.3	32.8	3.82	3.73	7.8	6.4	60.4	...	0.4	38.1	96.8	96.8	...	...	...	...
...	88.2	9.0	14.6	5.5	32.3	4.60	4.60	3.7	4.9	113.9	...	1.3	35.8	241.3	242.1	...	...	...	...
...	93.0	9.4	-1.1	-0.4	-2.7	3.04	3.05	35.3	6.9	46.5	...	2.2	-3.2	138.3	139.5	...	...	...	...
2	93.0	10.2	-17.7	-5.8	-71.3	1.05	1.17	32.8	17.9	21.0	...	8.9	-49.0	165.6	171.5	...	...	...	...
	Principal Lines of Business: Medicaid (100.0%)													Principal States: RI (100.0%)					
...	...	...	...	...	...	...	...	...	...	...	...	...	...	...	...	...	...	...	...
2	88.9	19.3	...	1.6	...	...	...	...	11.5	8.6	-0.1	...	...	...	...	...	...	...	...
3	78.2	22.9	4.4	4.7	59.4	...	...	-8.0	12.1	7.9	...	...	-12.5	...	...	...	...	...	...
-158	85.6	20.5	-2.8	-2.8	-43.7	...	...	10.7	15.1	6.3	...	...	-11.1	...	...	...	...	...	...
32	101.5	18.2	4.3	3.4	68.9	...	...	24.9	19.0	7.4	...	...	-0.6	...	...	...	...	...	...
	Principal Lines of Business: GrpA&H (76.7%), GrpLife (13.8%), OrdLife (9.2%), CrdLife (0.2%), IndAnn (0.1%)																		

Column key: COMPANY NAME / Ultimate Parent Association / Principal Officer / Mailing Address / Dom. : Began Bus. : Struct. : Mktg. / Specialty / Phone # / AMB# / NAIC# — Best's Financial Strength Rating / FSC — Data Year — **Balance Sheet:** Bonds (%), Mort. Loans & R.E. (%), Com & Pref. Stock (%), All Other Assets (%), Total Assets ($000), Life Reserves (%), Health Reserves (%), Ann Res. & Dep. Liabilities (%), All Other Liabilities (%), Capital & Surplus ($000) — **Operations:** Direct Premiums Written ($000), Net Premiums Written & Deposits ($000), Operating Cash Flow ($000), NOG Before Taxes ($000), NOG After Taxes ($000), Net Income ($000)

NETWORK HEALTH INSURANCE CORP
Affinity Health System
Sheila A. Jenkins
President
P.O. Box 120
Menasha, WI 54952
WI : 2001 : Stock : Broker
Group A&H
920-720-1200
AMB# 064708 NAIC# 11137

Rating: **B++** — Rating Outlook: Stable — FSC VII

Data Year	Bonds (%)	Mort. Loans & R.E. (%)	Com & Pref. Stock (%)	All Other Assets (%)	Total Assets ($000)	Life Reserves (%)	Health Reserves (%)	Ann Res. & Dep. Liabilities (%)	All Other Liabilities (%)	Capital & Surplus ($000)	Direct Premiums Written ($000)	Net Premiums Written & Deposits ($000)	Operating Cash Flow ($000)	NOG Before Taxes ($000)	NOG After Taxes ($000)	Net Income ($000)
'05	52.7	...	...	47.3	6,777	...	90.0	...	10.0	3,203	10,108	10,068	2,214	-766	-766	-765
'06	41.8	...	...	58.2	15,307	...	57.2	...	42.8	5,410	43,966	43,859	8,123	3,047	1,907	1,899
'07	54.0	...	...	46.0	22,473	...	93.5	...	6.5	9,542	86,960	87,092	5,018	2,626	1,745	1,745
'08	64.0	...	...	36.0	35,259	...	90.9	...	9.1	20,063	131,280	131,408	13,933	14,181	9,532	9,598
'09	82.0	...	...	18.0	51,575	...	95.3	...	4.7	27,011	204,640	204,625	13,405	9,802	6,401	6,418

Rating History: B++g, 06/08/10; B++g, 06/18/09; B++g, 06/13/08; B++g, 05/22/07; B++g, 05/31/06

NETWORK HEALTH PLAN
Affinity Health System
Sheila A. Jenkins
President
P.O. Box 120
Menasha, WI 54952
WI : 1983 : Stock : Broker
Group A&H, Health
920-720-1200
AMB# 068627 NAIC# 95737

Rating: **B++** — Rating Outlook: Stable — FSC VII

Data Year	Bonds (%)	Mort. Loans & R.E. (%)	Com & Pref. Stock (%)	All Other Assets (%)	Total Assets ($000)	Life Reserves (%)	Health Reserves (%)	Ann Res. & Dep. Liabilities (%)	All Other Liabilities (%)	Capital & Surplus ($000)	Direct Premiums Written ($000)	Net Premiums Written & Deposits ($000)	Operating Cash Flow ($000)	NOG Before Taxes ($000)	NOG After Taxes ($000)	Net Income ($000)
'05	67.6	6.0	5.6	20.8	57,478	...	72.5	...	27.5	33,674	321,806	320,019	2,210	11,310	7,414	7,417
'06	61.9	6.0	10.0	22.2	56,822	...	72.3	...	27.7	29,494	350,472	349,235	-1,836	4,468	2,354	2,255
'07	56.6	5.0	14.2	24.2	67,398	...	18.2	...	81.8	30,316	349,935	348,644	4,454	-3,031	-1,694	-1,756
'08	47.8	4.3	25.0	22.9	80,299	...	19.2	...	80.8	53,437	354,579	352,992	7,721	7,605	-378	-338
'09	47.7	3.3	26.2	22.8	103,114	...	70.3	...	29.7	69,803	427,397	424,433	13,985	13,344	10,493	10,493

Rating History: B++g, 06/08/10; B++g, 06/18/09; B++g, 06/13/08; B++g, 05/22/07; B++g, 05/31/06

NEVADA PACIFIC DENTAL INC
UnitedHealth Group Inc
Diane D. Souza
President
6220 Old Dobbin Lane
Columbia, MD 21045
NV : 1987 : Stock : Broker
Dental
443-896-0634
AMB# 064826 NAIC# 95758

Rating: **NR-3**

Data Year	Bonds (%)	Mort. Loans & R.E. (%)	Com & Pref. Stock (%)	All Other Assets (%)	Total Assets ($000)	Life Reserves (%)	Health Reserves (%)	Ann Res. & Dep. Liabilities (%)	All Other Liabilities (%)	Capital & Surplus ($000)	Direct Premiums Written ($000)	Net Premiums Written & Deposits ($000)	Operating Cash Flow ($000)	NOG Before Taxes ($000)	NOG After Taxes ($000)	Net Income ($000)
'05	...	6.3	...	93.7	7,702	...	17.1	...	82.9	2,492	40,266	40,266	1,027	3,263	2,128	2,128
'06	...	4.1	...	95.9	7,929	...	82.0	...	18.0	3,093	45,960	45,960	664	4,039	2,625	2,625
'07	...	3.9	...	96.1	8,716	...	23.3	...	76.7	4,909	47,709	47,709	678	3,131	2,016	2,016
'08	...	...	...	100.0	11,142	...	19.8	...	80.2	7,056	46,907	46,907	2,067	3,471	2,338	2,338
'09	...	...	...	100.0	14,055	...	11.5	...	88.5	9,968	41,572	41,572	1,762	3,471	2,256	2,256

Rating History: NR-3, 06/15/09; NR-3, 01/29/08; NR-3, 11/21/07; NR-3, 11/20/06; NR-3, 06/16/06

NEW ENGLAND LIFE INS CO
MetLife Inc
Lisa M. Weber
Chairman, President & CEO
18210 Crane Nest Dr., 3rd Floor
Tampa, FL 33647
MA : 1980 : Stock : Career Agent
Var ann, Var life, Var Univ life
617-578-2000
AMB# 009043 NAIC# 91626

Rating: **A+ u** — Under Review Implication: Negative — FSC XV

Data Year	Bonds (%)	Mort. Loans & R.E. (%)	Com & Pref. Stock (%)	All Other Assets (%)	Total Assets ($000)	Life Reserves (%)	Health Reserves (%)	Ann Res. & Dep. Liabilities (%)	All Other Liabilities (%)	Capital & Surplus ($000)	Direct Premiums Written ($000)	Net Premiums Written & Deposits ($000)	Operating Cash Flow ($000)	NOG Before Taxes ($000)	NOG After Taxes ($000)	Net Income ($000)
'05	7.3	0.2	0.1	92.4	10,779,110	8.8	0.1	2.8	88.3	318,776	1,868,020	1,700,744	19,283	68,111	50,208	50,005
'06	6.8	0.0	0.6	92.6	12,015,453	8.7	0.1	2.3	89.0	434,812	1,899,522	1,774,824	165,461	105,699	109,030	109,416
'07	6.2	0.0	0.5	93.3	12,459,014	7.8	0.1	2.1	89.9	544,237	2,022,698	1,939,695	51,507	118,093	122,341	121,649
'08	10.4	0.6	0.7	88.3	8,966,118	11.5	0.1	5.0	83.5	469,364	1,733,500	1,664,565	226,107	23,595	29,350	27,936
'09	11.2	0.8	0.1	88.0	10,718,859	10.0	0.1	3.6	86.3	564,189	1,066,491	998,561	114,240	128,187	108,928	110,817

Rating History: A+ gu, 02/09/10; A+ g, 02/20/09; A+ g, 06/05/08; A+ g, 05/29/07; A+ g, 05/05/06

NEW ERA LIFE INS CO
New Era Enterprises Inc
Bill S. Chen
President, Treasurer & CEO
200 Westlake Park Boulevard
Houston, TX 77079-2663
TX : 1924 : Stock : Agency
Ind A&H, Ind Ann, Ind Life
281-368-7200
AMB# 007087 NAIC# 78743

Rating: **B+** — Rating Outlook: Negative — FSC VI

Data Year	Bonds (%)	Mort. Loans & R.E. (%)	Com & Pref. Stock (%)	All Other Assets (%)	Total Assets ($000)	Life Reserves (%)	Health Reserves (%)	Ann Res. & Dep. Liabilities (%)	All Other Liabilities (%)	Capital & Surplus ($000)	Direct Premiums Written ($000)	Net Premiums Written & Deposits ($000)	Operating Cash Flow ($000)	NOG Before Taxes ($000)	NOG After Taxes ($000)	Net Income ($000)
'05	69.0	9.7	10.6	10.6	228,981	10.9	9.6	70.4	9.1	35,251	91,571	99,489	19,015	1,213	1,004	362
'06	68.0	11.9	10.3	9.8	265,489	9.4	7.8	78.2	4.7	39,670	106,392	108,968	36,782	2,005	1,517	2,000
'07	63.9	13.4	13.8	9.0	299,809	8.1	6.5	83.6	1.8	44,659	115,808	117,590	34,721	2,466	1,719	-778
'08	59.4	18.4	14.4	7.8	301,819	8.0	6.2	80.9	4.9	44,597	75,975	77,566	233	940	971	-892
'09	63.8	16.3	11.9	8.0	320,052	4.8	5.6	82.1	7.5	45,225	107,779	71,430	12,378	1,198	831	-3,700

Rating History: B+ g, 12/04/09; B+ g, 12/04/08; B+ g, 10/12/07; B+ g, 09/19/06; B+ g, 06/15/06

NEW ERA LIFE INS CO MIDWEST
New Era Enterprises Inc
Bill S. Chen
President, Treasurer & CEO
200 Westlake Park Boulevard
Houston, TX 77079-2663
TX : 1961 : Stock : Agency
Ind A&H, Ind Ann, Ind Life
281-368-7200
AMB# 007148 NAIC# 69698

Rating: **B+** — Rating Outlook: Negative — FSC VI

Data Year	Bonds (%)	Mort. Loans & R.E. (%)	Com & Pref. Stock (%)	All Other Assets (%)	Total Assets ($000)	Life Reserves (%)	Health Reserves (%)	Ann Res. & Dep. Liabilities (%)	All Other Liabilities (%)	Capital & Surplus ($000)	Direct Premiums Written ($000)	Net Premiums Written & Deposits ($000)	Operating Cash Flow ($000)	NOG Before Taxes ($000)	NOG After Taxes ($000)	Net Income ($000)
'05	83.4	8.4	...	8.2	27,197	45.4	10.9	37.7	6.0	8,891	7,048	19,882	-1,324	1,250	1,005	877
'06	89.7	6.4	...	3.9	32,247	31.5	7.8	55.5	5.1	7,640	13,385	40,052	5,873	932	644	674
'07	83.7	4.9	5.0	6.4	40,052	22.5	6.0	68.0	3.5	8,428	14,500	42,963	7,662	1,176	838	575
'08	77.4	3.6	7.7	11.3	41,625	20.0	6.9	70.2	2.9	8,634	10,884	40,598	1,443	806	680	111
'09	80.4	4.1	4.3	11.2	46,752	16.5	7.8	71.5	4.3	8,642	17,300	36,386	4,063	238	-16	-773

Rating History: B+ g, 12/04/09; B+ g, 12/04/08; B+ g, 10/12/07; B+ g, 09/19/06; B+ g, 06/15/06

NEW FOUNDATION LIFE INSURANCE[1]
Eunice C. Reed
President
P.O. Box 164867
Little Rock, AR 72216-4867
AR : 1959 : Stock : Not Available
501-375-2403
AMB# 068212 NAIC# 83984

Rating: **NR-1**

Data Year	Bonds (%)	Mort. Loans & R.E. (%)	Com & Pref. Stock (%)	All Other Assets (%)	Total Assets ($000)	Life Reserves (%)	Health Reserves (%)	Ann Res. & Dep. Liabilities (%)	All Other Liabilities (%)	Capital & Surplus ($000)	Direct Premiums Written ($000)	Net Premiums Written & Deposits ($000)	Operating Cash Flow ($000)	NOG Before Taxes ($000)	NOG After Taxes ($000)	Net Income ($000)
'05	29.7	...	2.0	68.2	2,017	...	...	...	100.0	1,555	33	33	...	75	71	71
'06	19.4	...	1.7	78.9	2,062	...	...	...	100.0	1,590	38	38	...	31	29	36
'07	9.6	...	1.2	89.2	2,079	...	...	...	100.0	1,616	43	43	...	37	35	36
'08	4.8	...	0.3	94.8	2,061	...	...	...	100.0	1,591	43	43	...	-9	-8	-8
'09	4.9	...	0.6	94.5	2,043	...	...	...	100.0	1,631	16	16	...	39	36	36

Rating History: NR-1, 06/10/10; NR-1, 06/12/09; NR-1, 06/12/08; NR-1, 06/08/07; NR-1, 06/07/06

NEW WEST HEALTH SERVICES[2]
David C. Henry
President
130 Neill Avenue
Helena, MT 59601
MT : 1998 : Non-Profit : Agency
Group A&H, Medicare, Med supp
406-457-2200
AMB# 064398 NAIC# 95829

Rating: **NR-5**

Data Year	Bonds (%)	Mort. Loans & R.E. (%)	Com & Pref. Stock (%)	All Other Assets (%)	Total Assets ($000)	Life Reserves (%)	Health Reserves (%)	Ann Res. & Dep. Liabilities (%)	All Other Liabilities (%)	Capital & Surplus ($000)	Direct Premiums Written ($000)	Net Premiums Written & Deposits ($000)	Operating Cash Flow ($000)	NOG Before Taxes ($000)	NOG After Taxes ($000)	Net Income ($000)
'05	4.0	...	...	96.0	17,367	...	69.8	...	30.2	5,215	61,209	60,235	-679	-4,776	-4,776	-4,776
'06	...	...	...	100.0	25,187	...	47.2	...	52.8	12,830	69,804	68,675	7,854	5,292	5,186	5,177
'07	...	...	...	100.0	31,958	...	60.0	...	40.0	17,760	72,844	71,747	6,799	4,935	4,816	4,816
'08	...	...	...	100.0	34,876	...	47.5	...	52.5	20,035	82,003	80,651	1,533	3,316	3,261	3,261
'09	...	...	14.8	85.2	35,871	...	55.1	...	44.9	20,506	99,433	98,267	1,486	662	628	655

Rating History: NR-5, 04/09/10; NR-5, 08/26/09; C+ pd, 07/14/08; C+ pd, 06/05/07; C- pd, 06/20/06

NEW YORK LIFE INS & ANNUITY
New York Life Insurance Company
Theodore A. Mathas
Chairman & President
51 Madison Avenue
New York, NY 10010
DE : 1980 : Stock : Career Agent
Univ Life, Var ann
212-576-7000
AMB# 009054 NAIC# 91596

Rating: **A++** — Rating Outlook: Stable — FSC XV

Data Year	Bonds (%)	Mort. Loans & R.E. (%)	Com & Pref. Stock (%)	All Other Assets (%)	Total Assets ($000)	Life Reserves (%)	Health Reserves (%)	Ann Res. & Dep. Liabilities (%)	All Other Liabilities (%)	Capital & Surplus ($000)	Direct Premiums Written ($000)	Net Premiums Written & Deposits ($000)	Operating Cash Flow ($000)	NOG Before Taxes ($000)	NOG After Taxes ($000)	Net Income ($000)
'05	57.9	5.9	0.2	36.0	60,315,889	18.9	...	36.8	44.3	2,157,379	7,029,567	6,723,761	2,889,414	354,336	229,067	230,983
'06	55.7	6.2	0.3	37.9	66,967,145	18.0	...	36.9	45.1	2,323,868	7,858,867	7,590,174	3,482,834	339,389	248,002	251,606
'07	52.6	7.1	0.1	40.2	72,685,506	16.9	...	36.2	46.8	2,649,933	7,875,933	7,644,431	2,692,068	488,434	348,323	289,028
'08	58.3	7.4	1.6	32.7	74,943,575	17.2	...	44.6	38.3	3,595,817	11,231,728	11,129,393	6,297,493	-220,866	-128,745	-386,931
'09	61.4	6.4	0.0	32.2	88,832,647	15.4	...	47.1	37.5	4,997,629	12,562,182	12,587,616	9,646,190	601,871	351,029	225,227

Rating History: A++g, 06/14/10; A++g, 06/11/09; A++g, 03/11/08; A++g, 11/21/06; A++g, 12/23/04

BEST'S PROFITABILITY, LEVERAGE AND LIQUIDITY TESTS 2005 – 2009

Data in U.S. Dollars

—	Profitability Tests							Leverage Tests						Liquidity Tests					
Un-Realized Capital Gains ($000)	Benefits Paid to NPW & Dep (%)	Comm. & Expenses to NPW & Dep (%)	NOG to Total Assets (%)	NOG to Total Rev (%)	Operating Return on Equity (%)	Net Yield (%)	Total Return (%)	Change in NPW & Dep (%)	NPW & Dep to Capital (X)	Capital & Surplus to Liabilities (%)	Surplus Relief (%)	Reins Leverage (%)	Change in Capital (%)	Quick Liquidity (%)	Current Liquidity (%)	Non-Invest Grade Bonds to Capital (%)	Delinq. & Foreclosed Mortgages to Capital (%)	Mort. & Credit Tenant Loans & R.E. to Capital (%)	Affiliated Invest to Capital (%)
...	75.9	33.7	-13.9	-7.5	-21.8	3.93	3.95	242.8	3.1	89.6	...	...	-16.6	176.3	177.4	...	...	...	...
...	81.1	13.3	17.3	4.3	44.3	5.92	5.85	335.6	8.1	54.7	...	...	68.9	183.1	187.8	...	...	...	...
...	87.8	10.4	9.2	2.0	23.3	6.47	6.47	98.6	9.1	73.8	...	0.8	76.4	153.8	154.9	...	...	...	...
...	81.5	8.5	33.0	7.2	64.4	4.03	4.28	50.9	6.5	132.0	...	1.1	110.3	229.1	231.6	...	...	...	...
...	87.3	8.3	14.7	3.1	27.2	2.45	2.49	55.7	7.6	110.0	...	2.3	34.6	184.7	185.9	...	...	...	...
Principal Lines of Business: Medicare (97.4%), CompHosp/Med (2.6%)														Principal States: WI (100.0%)					
-765	86.2	11.0	13.1	2.3	23.5	4.79	3.32	7.2	9.5	141.5	...	0.5	14.4	185.7	186.7	...	...	10.3	19.8
2,022	88.4	11.1	4.1	0.7	7.5	5.23	9.00	9.1	11.8	107.9	...	0.5	-12.4	162.6	164.4	...	...	11.5	30.7
3,877	91.2	10.5	-2.7	-0.5	-5.7	5.37	12.41	-0.2	11.5	81.8	...	1.6	2.8	127.5	128.5	...	...	11.1	42.6
10,521	87.6	11.0	-0.5	-0.1	-0.9	3.84	20.35	1.2	6.6	198.9	...	1.5	76.3	199.0	199.9	...	...	6.5	44.0
6,948	88.5	8.9	11.4	2.5	17.0	2.56	10.74	20.2	6.1	209.5	...	1.2	30.6	199.5	200.5	...	...	4.8	43.5
Principal Lines of Business: CompHosp/Med (66.6%), Medicaid (33.4%)														Principal States: WI (100.0%)					
...	75.4	17.4	30.6	5.2	104.0	2.53	2.53	21.0	16.2	47.8	...	...	55.7	110.0	110.0	...	...	19.3	19.3
...	75.3	17.0	33.6	5.7	94.0	4.33	4.33	14.1	14.9	64.0	...	...	24.1	255.5	269.2	...	...	10.6	10.6
...	75.5	19.4	24.2	4.2	50.4	5.09	5.09	3.8	9.7	129.0	...	...	58.7	380.0	401.6	...	...	6.9	6.9
...	76.3	17.8	23.5	4.9	39.1	2.33	2.33	-1.7	6.6	172.7	...	...	43.7	453.8	477.5	...	...	...	...
...	74.5	17.4	17.9	5.4	26.5	0.34	0.34	-11.4	4.2	243.9	...	...	41.3	502.0	521.8	...	...	...	...
Principal Lines of Business: Dental (100.0%)														Principal States: NV (100.0%)					
57	74.8	15.7	0.5	2.7	14.5	5.48	5.50	-2.7	5.2	32.4	12.1	85.7	-13.9	43.8	57.8	6.9	...	5.5	18.6
-4,655	82.7	14.5	1.0	5.6	28.9	5.41	5.08	4.4	4.0	41.3	5.2	75.6	35.5	41.4	56.4	6.9	...	0.4	31.7
5,399	100.6	14.5	1.0	5.6	25.0	5.39	5.70	9.3	3.5	55.0	2.9	66.7	25.0	43.6	59.6	8.8	...	0.3	24.4
1,459	86.8	14.1	0.3	1.5	5.8	5.03	4.99	-14.2	3.5	35.4	2.9	123.7	-13.3	34.4	49.2	9.3	...	10.9	42.1
-8,620	106.8	27.3	1.1	8.5	21.1	5.40	4.97	-40.0	1.7	42.5	1.6	93.8	19.2	46.2	62.8	11.5	...	14.3	10.5
Principal Lines of Business: IndAnn (59.3%), OrdLife (36.8%), GrpAnn (3.7%), IndA&H (0.1%)														Principal States: FL (10.2%), MA (10.1%), NJ (9.5%), PA (9.1%), NY (8.2%)					
1,056	65.9	15.3	0.5	0.9	2.9	4.76	5.23	-9.6	2.7	19.3	0.2	37.2	5.6	60.3	73.7	12.1	...	60.3	59.9
3,758	70.4	14.2	0.6	1.3	4.1	4.85	6.85	9.5	2.6	18.9	0.1	0.9	14.0	64.6	77.8	9.5	...	75.0	57.2
3,780	66.1	13.5	0.6	1.3	4.1	5.13	5.83	7.9	2.6	18.1	0.1	0.4	9.2	60.7	74.6	16.2	...	87.2	60.8
477	107.0	18.7	0.3	1.1	2.2	5.13	4.75	-34.0	1.7	17.8	0.1	1.1	-0.9	50.1	63.2	42.5	...	121.9	62.7
965	91.9	10.8	0.3	1.0	1.9	4.43	3.48	-7.9	1.6	16.8	4.5	16.6	0.7	49.9	61.8	61.3	6.6	113.3	64.4
Principal Lines of Business: IndAnn (66.1%), IndA&H (40.2%), GrpA&H (1.5%), GrpAnn (0.0%), OrdLife (-7.8%)														Principal States: TX (74.7%), PA (8.3%), GA (6.3%), FL (3.2%)					
94	74.0	29.8	3.6	4.6	10.7	6.61	6.56	197.3	2.2	50.7	...	35.7	-10.4	89.6	104.3	3.9	...	24.9	...
6	66.3	21.4	2.2	1.5	7.8	7.14	7.34	101.4	5.1	32.5	...	39.1	-13.5	86.1	100.2	0.7	...	25.9	...
...	60.2	24.4	2.3	1.9	10.4	5.98	5.30	7.3	5.0	27.2	...	32.9	8.3	82.4	98.5	3.2	...	22.7	...
-1	83.2	18.1	1.7	1.6	8.0	6.15	4.80	-5.5	4.7	26.2	...	29.0	1.0	84.5	99.7	34.4	...	17.3	...
-1	77.8	17.3	0.0	0.0	-0.2	5.62	3.92	-10.4	4.2	22.7	...	28.7	0.0	76.9	90.7	55.2	...	22.4	...
Principal Lines of Business: IndA&H (85.4%), IndAnn (13.8%), OrdLife (0.8%), GrpAnn (0.0%)														Principal States: TX (74.6%), TN (22.3%)					
108	96.1	73.7	3.6	73.5	4.8	...	...	92.9	0.0	345.8	...	...	13.0	...	...	...	...	...	...
-7	84.7	110.8	1.4	25.0	1.9	...	...	14.1	0.0	340.4	...	...	1.9	...	...	...	...	...	...
-9	66.1	158.4	1.7	26.6	2.2	...	...	15.2	0.0	350.1	...	...	1.4	...	...	...	...	...	...
-18	72.0	144.8	-0.4	-9.3	-0.5	...	...	-1.8	0.0	339.3	...	...	-1.6	...	...	...	...	...	...
5	181.6	313.4	1.8	66.9	2.2	...	...	-62.7	0.0	400.1	...	...	2.7	...	...	...	...	...	...
Principal Lines of Business: OrdLife (100.0%)																			
36	86.3	22.2	-27.7	-7.9	-80.5	1.96	2.21	11.3	11.6	42.9	...	7.9	-21.7	122.3	122.3	...	...	...	...
...	74.8	18.9	24.4	7.4	57.5	4.86	4.82	14.0	5.4	103.8	...	0.2	146.0	184.0	184.0	...	...	...	...
...	76.4	17.1	16.9	6.7	31.5	0.74	0.74	4.5	4.0	125.1	...	0.3	38.4	208.0	208.0	...	...	...	...
...	78.1	17.7	9.8	4.0	17.3	-0.61	-0.61	12.4	4.0	135.0	...	...	12.8	351.8	351.8	...	...	...	...
373	81.7	16.9	1.8	0.6	3.1	-2.56	-1.30	21.8	4.8	133.5	...	0.6	2.4	339.3	344.4	...	...	...	...
Principal Lines of Business: CompHosp/Med (70.9%), Medicare (25.0%), FEHBP (3.6%), MedSup (0.5%)														Principal States: MT (100.0%)					
1,712	50.0	13.6	0.4	2.5	11.0	5.70	5.77	-11.8	2.6	6.0	7.2	243.7	8.2	46.8	60.6	123.2	...	137.0	16.7
-1,674	57.1	13.3	0.4	2.4	11.1	5.70	5.73	12.9	2.7	6.0	5.5	230.1	8.2	46.9	61.0	118.5	...	146.9	16.9
-11,313	70.2	12.8	0.5	3.3	14.0	5.64	5.49	0.7	2.4	6.4	4.6	206.9	11.4	49.0	62.5	105.2	0.0	164.1	8.1
33,807	46.4	10.0	-0.2	-0.9	-4.1	5.53	5.09	45.6	2.8	7.1	3.1	153.8	27.7	49.4	62.4	97.0	0.0	138.7	20.4
-28,992	38.3	10.0	0.4	2.2	8.2	5.41	5.16	13.1	2.3	8.5	2.1	111.4	37.7	49.6	63.5	86.5	0.1	103.1	21.0
Principal Lines of Business: IndAnn (87.1%), OrdLife (11.0%), GrpAnn (1.3%), GrpLife (0.6%)														Principal States: CA (10.4%), NY (10.1%), FL (7.1%), TX (5.4%), PA (4.9%)					

2010 BEST'S KEY RATING GUIDE — LIFE/HEALTH EDITION
ANNUAL STATEMENT DATA FOR YEARS 2005 – 2009

Data in U.S. Dollars

COMPANY NAME Ultimate Parent Association Principal Officer Mailing Address Dom. : Began Bus. : Struct. : Mktg. Specialty Phone # AMB# NAIC#	Best's Financial Strength Rating FSC	Data Year	Balance Sheet Bonds (%)	Mort. Loans & R.E. (%)	Com & Pref. Stock (%)	All Other Assets (%)	Total Assets ($000)	Life Reserves (%)	Health Reserves %)	Ann Res. & Dep. Liabilities (%)	All Other Liabilities (%)	Capital & Surplus ($000)	Operations Direct Premiums Written ($000)	Net Premiums Written & Deposits ($000)	Operating Cash Flow ($000)	NOG Before Taxes ($000)	NOG After Taxes ($000)	Net Income ($000)
NEW YORK LIFE INS CO New York Life Insurance Company Theodore A. Mathas Chairman, President & CEO 51 Madison Avenue New York, NY 10010 NY : 1845 : Mutual : Agency Ind Life, Ind Ann 212-576-7000 AMB# 006820 NAIC# 66915	**A++** Rating Outlook: Stable **FSC XV**	'05	56.8	7.6	7.4	28.2	107,881,619	46.7	1.9	33.9	17.6	10,549,095	8,928,060	17,178,956	5,625,126	618,137	719,436	1,198,299
		'06	56.6	7.6	7.3	28.5	113,703,802	46.5	1.9	34.4	17.2	11,300,273	8,955,177	17,294,895	4,372,996	735,852	493,508	794,264
		'07	54.3	7.8	7.2	30.7	122,753,467	45.1	1.8	33.9	19.3	11,959,230	9,423,877	17,696,573	6,590,756	693,480	577,230	856,435
		'08	55.7	8.7	5.6	30.0	117,305,625	49.4	2.0	34.1	14.6	11,793,474	11,027,870	19,879,201	-2,763,210	488,595	433,265	-564,359
		'09	55.4	8.5	6.0	30.2	117,835,521	52.0	2.1	30.8	15.1	13,686,268	10,889,632	16,094,452	-975,839	898,721	793,726	455,267
		Rating History: A++g, 06/14/10; A++g, 06/11/09; A++g, 03/11/08; A++g, 11/21/06; A++g, 12/23/04																
NHP OF INDIANA LLC Steven J. Bory President 101 S.E. Third Street Evansville, IN 47708 IN : 2006 : Stock : Broker Group A&H, Medicare 812-773-0353 AMB# 064857 NAIC# 12540	**NR-5**	'05	...	...	...	...	...	...	...	...	...	...	...	...	...	...	...	...
		'06	...	...	...	100.0	21,920	...	70.9	...	29.1	8,082	57,695	57,479	21,227	2,483	2,483	2,483
		'07	...	...	...	100.0	27,550	...	83.5	...	16.5	11,816	123,570	123,218	4,617	2,671	2,671	2,671
		'08	26.1	...	...	73.9	30,421	...	81.2	...	18.8	9,760	145,325	144,836	4,088	-1,436	-1,436	-1,436
		'09	9.5	...	...	90.5	37,868	...	86.3	...	13.7	14,497	174,260	173,189	3,127	3,618	3,618	3,618
		Rating History: NR-5, 04/07/10; NR-5, 04/08/09; NR-5, 03/18/08; NR-5, 04/09/07; NR-5, 11/07/06																
NIAGARA LIFE AND HEALTH INS CO Blue Cross&Blue Shield of South Carolina Trescott N. Hinton, Jr. President & COO 7909 Parklane Road, Suite 200 Columbia, SC 29223-5666 NY : 2005 : Stock : Agency Dental, Group A&H, Group Life 803-735-1251 AMB# 060566 NAIC# 12285	**NR-3**	'05	59.4	...	...	40.6	7,090	0.2	...	...	99.8	6,061	2	2	7,027	-165	-193	-193
		'06	75.8	...	3.1	21.1	6,359	2.2	...	...	97.8	6,144	7	7	-749	118	87	88
		'07	4.0	...	...	96.0	6,236	...	...	...	100.0	6,161	...	...	50	204	133	132
		'08	4.1	...	...	95.9	6,158	...	...	...	100.0	6,152	...	...	-27	-32	-32	-32
		'09	4.1	...	...	95.9	6,140	...	...	...	100.0	6,125	...	...	22	-9	-34	-34
		Rating History: NR-3, 12/16/09; NR-3, 05/13/09; NR-3, 02/25/08; NR-2, 12/13/06; NR-2, 12/15/05																
NIPPON LIFE INS CO OF AMER Nippon Life Insurance Company Toshihiro Nakashima President 521 Fifth Avenue New York, NY 10175 IA : 1973 : Stock : Agency Group A&H, Group Life 212-682-3000 AMB# 008419 NAIC# 81264	**A-** Rating Outlook: Stable **FSC VIII**	'05	86.3	6.9	0.0	6.7	162,854	10.4	67.7	...	21.8	111,196	213,956	211,134	5,956	6,893	4,597	4,984
		'06	86.5	4.3	0.9	8.2	168,671	9.9	67.2	1.9	21.0	116,711	215,854	214,113	6,316	7,682	5,214	5,265
		'07	88.2	2.5	2.1	7.2	169,464	11.9	62.1	1.9	24.1	117,980	231,431	229,497	747	1,397	1,257	1,260
		'08	87.8	2.1	1.8	8.3	159,640	14.4	65.1	2.2	18.4	113,898	225,798	223,098	-7,056	569	519	-3,982
		'09	92.3	1.4	0.7	5.6	157,904	16.3	62.8	2.4	18.5	114,720	215,345	211,475	-635	5,950	4,272	744
		Rating History: A-, 12/28/09; A-, 03/19/09; A-, 03/06/08; A-, 11/07/06; A-, 06/28/06																
NORIDIAN MUTUAL INSURANCE CO Noridian Mutual Insurance Company Michael B. Unhjem President & CEO 4510 13th Avenue South Fargo, ND 58121-0001 ND : 1940 : Non-Profit : Not Available Group A&H, FEHBP, Medicare 701-282-1100 AMB# 068581 NAIC# 55891	**NR-5**	'05	43.8	8.3	26.8	21.1	373,086	...	54.3	...	45.7	222,708	689,158	687,664	23,628	41,064	32,938	38,547
		'06	37.8	7.0	28.6	26.7	394,524	...	57.0	...	43.0	233,271	723,966	722,228	-8,183	-3,926	-2,047	3,927
		'07	34.5	7.3	27.4	30.8	399,180	...	59.7	...	40.3	236,335	795,240	793,409	10,445	9,985	9,329	18,012
		'08	34.6	7.6	20.3	37.6	373,025	...	60.9	...	39.1	195,803	851,887	850,080	-11,672	2,755	3,210	8,755
		'09	35.1	7.0	23.4	34.6	392,574	...	60.6	...	39.4	216,140	911,164	909,406	19,279	15,839	14,828	10,000
		Rating History: NR-5, 04/19/10; NR-5, 04/02/09; NR-5, 03/28/08; NR-5, 04/03/07; NR-5, 04/27/06																
NORTH AMERICAN CO FOR L&H Sammons Enterprises, Inc. Michael M. Masterson Chairman One Sammons Plaza Sioux Falls, SD 57193 IA : 1886 : Stock : Agency Univ Life, Ann, Term Life 312-648-7600 AMB# 006827 NAIC# 66974	**A+** Rating Outlook: Negative **FSC XIV**	'05	90.1	...	3.0	6.8	5,103,273	31.8	0.0	48.8	19.5	432,732	737,373	572,926	515,273	69,837	42,119	41,003
		'06	89.8	...	1.2	9.0	5,451,981	31.4	...	54.0	14.6	399,659	963,220	802,220	337,695	66,976	37,215	84,580
		'07	93.2	...	0.9	5.8	6,637,313	26.8	...	56.2	17.0	387,652	1,297,480	1,176,091	1,192,966	5,213	3,343	2,370
		'08	91.2	...	1.3	7.5	8,446,862	21.6	...	60.8	17.6	526,559	2,013,429	1,856,786	1,754,724	19,443	5,170	-18,257
		'09	88.6	...	1.3	10.1	9,117,526	20.0	...	64.1	15.8	647,389	1,671,852	1,506,731	568,995	64,547	28,674	-7,720
		Rating History: A+ g, 04/16/09; A+ g, 01/04/08; A+ g, 08/31/06; A, 06/16/05; A, 06/07/04																
NORTH AMERICAN INS CO AMERCO Mark A. Haydukovich President & CEO 2721 North Central Avenue Phoenix, AZ 85004-1172 WI : 1965 : Stock : Agency Med supp 608-662-1232 AMB# 060015 NAIC# 68349	**B+** Rating Outlook: Stable **FSC IV**	'05	80.8	...	0.1	19.1	34,807	45.8	37.9	2.4	13.9	16,150	12,268	14,556	1,292	4,774	3,105	3,076
		'06	85.4	...	0.1	14.4	31,949	52.3	31.7	3.0	13.0	17,432	3,267	6,189	-2,433	9,271	6,344	6,198
		'07	80.7	...	0.1	19.2	24,706	58.5	23.7	8.3	9.4	15,555	1,768	1,766	-6,886	9,205	6,098	6,105
		'08	88.2	...	0.8	10.9	16,180	70.7	20.5	8.1	0.6	10,340	1,577	1,575	-7,851	2,203	1,663	1,663
		'09	85.6	...	0.7	13.7	14,330	66.2	16.7	8.0	9.1	9,301	1,277	1,275	-1,875	1,228	837	847
		Rating History: B+, 03/31/10; B+, 03/20/09; B+, 01/31/08; B+, 11/29/06; B+, 10/19/05																
NORTH AMERICAN LIFE INS OF TX R D Tips Inc Clifton M. Mitchell President 4611 Bee Caves Road, Suite 201 Austin, TX 78746 TX : 1984 : Stock : Not Available Ordinary Life 512-347-1835 AMB# 068234 NAIC# 67580	**NR-5**	'05	2.9	14.1	11.1	71.8	74,829	45.7	0.0	43.1	11.1	2,870	2,658	-105	1,444	336	10	-9
		'06	2.2	12.6	10.2	75.1	84,921	61.3	0.0	34.8	3.9	2,199	3,442	21,491	-1,253	43	124	-111
		'07	26.4	16.9	8.0	48.7	119,821	73.0	0.0	22.9	4.1	4,724	7,237	8,692	13,545	1,022	967	1,304
		'08	18.5	23.8	9.8	47.8	104,493	69.2	0.0	24.7	6.0	4,233	8,582	-6,446	-13,216	1,021	1,093	1,082
		'09	33.1	24.6	10.3	32.0	106,840	71.1	0.0	22.8	6.1	1,399	12,921	12,967	24,224	-2,380	-2,183	-3,307
		Rating History: NR-5, 04/28/10; NR-5, 05/11/09; NR-5, 06/30/08; NR-5, 06/28/07; NR-5, 06/16/06																
NORTH AMERICAN NATL RE INS CO Gardiner Limited Partnership Gregory J. Palmquist President 8400 E. Prentice Avenue, Suite 645 Greenwood Village, CO 80111 AZ : 1998 : Stock : Not Available Ordinary Life 303-790-2090 AMB# 060310 NAIC# 60118	**NR-5**	'05	65.3	...	13.8	21.0	30,742	94.3	...	...	5.7	7,284	...	5,070	2,125	1,777	1,514	2,262
		'06	63.9	8.6	5.1	22.5	32,008	92.8	...	...	7.2	7,877	...	4,027	4,448	1,526	1,333	1,938
		'07	56.3	8.6	20.5	14.7	31,861	98.6	...	...	1.4	7,224	...	4,308	615	942	805	1,109
		'08	53.2	10.3	30.1	6.4	27,399	97.0	...	...	3.0	3,771	...	2,887	-3,436	922	836	-643
		'09	47.5	10.4	26.5	15.6	27,767	94.3	...	...	5.7	4,270	...	3,157	-2,482	999	954	579
		Rating History: NR-5, 03/31/10; NR-5, 04/27/09; NR-5, 04/22/08; NR-5, 04/25/07; NR-5, 05/11/06																

2010 BEST'S KEY RATING GUIDE — LIFE/HEALTH EDITION
BEST'S PROFITABILITY, LEVERAGE AND LIQUIDITY TESTS 2005 – 2009
Data in U.S. Dollars

—	Profitability Tests							Leverage Tests						Liquidity Tests					
Un-Realized Capital Gains ($000)	Benefits Paid to NPW & Dep (%)	Comm. & Expenses to NPW & Dep (%)	NOG to Total Assets (%)	NOG to Total Rev (%)	Operating Return on Equity (%)	Net Yield (%)	Total Return (%)	Change in NPW & Dep (%)	NPW & Dep to Capital (X)	Capital & Surplus to Liabilities (%)	Surplus Relief (%)	Reins Leverage (%)	Change in Capital (%)	Quick Liquidity (%)	Current Liquidity (%)	Non-Invest Grade Bonds to Capital (%)	Delinq. & Foreclosed Mortgages to Capital (%)	Mort. & Credit Tenant Loans & R.E. to Capital (%)	Affiliated Invest to Capital (%)
-43,738	49.7	10.4	0.7	4.9	7.1	5.57	6.16	8.0	1.3	13.9	0.3	48.8	8.4	43.1	56.3	36.1	0.4	64.3	70.2
423,356	51.2	11.2	0.4	3.2	4.5	5.82	6.64	0.7	1.3	14.2	0.2	46.2	7.7	42.4	56.1	34.5	0.3	62.8	64.8
362,861	54.5	11.1	0.5	3.7	5.0	5.80	6.50	2.3	1.2	13.9	-0.1	44.3	5.9	43.7	56.5	32.3	0.3	65.4	74.9
-2,613,213	48.9	10.2	0.4	2.6	3.6	5.23	1.73	12.3	1.5	12.6	0.2	45.8	-11.8	39.7	51.7	38.3	0.3	79.3	75.0
616,072	57.9	13.3	0.7	4.7	6.2	5.24	5.55	-19.0	1.1	15.0	0.1	39.5	16.2	37.9	49.8	39.1	0.4	66.9	72.2
Principal Lines of Business: GrpAnn (43.6%), OrdLife (35.6%), GrpLife (9.7%), IndAnn (8.1%), GrpA&H (2.0%)														Principal States: NY (26.8%), NH (13.2%), DE (7.2%), CA (6.0%)					
...	...	...	...	...	...	...	...	...	...	...	...	...	...	...	...	...	...	...	...
...	87.8	10.3	...	4.2	...	...	...	...	7.1	58.4	...	...	...	153.4	153.4	...	...	...	...
...	89.1	11.3	10.8	2.1	26.8	4.24	4.24	114.4	10.4	75.1	...	...	46.2	164.3	164.3	...	...	...	...
...	90.7	11.4	-5.0	-1.0	-13.3	-9.42	-9.42	17.5	14.8	47.2	...	...	-17.4	96.5	96.5	...	...	...	...
...	90.4	10.7	10.6	2.0	29.8	6.55	6.55	19.6	11.9	62.0	...	1.9	48.5	120.1	120.1	...	...	...	...
Principal Lines of Business: CompHosp/Med (82.1%), Medicare (17.9%)														Principal States: IN (98.1%)					
...	...	999.9	...	-99.9	...	...	...	...	0.0	591.1	...	...	...	814.0	874.1	...	...	...	...
...	34.1	999.9	1.3	27.5	1.4	4.68	4.72	205.2	0.0	999.9	...	...	1.4	999.9	999.9	...	...	...	...
...	...	...	2.1	42.2	2.2	5.23	5.17	-99.9	...	999.9	...	...	0.2	999.9	999.9	...	...	...	...
...	...	...	-0.5	-26.5	-0.5	2.06	2.00	...	...	999.9	...	...	-0.2	999.9	999.9	...	...	...	...
...	...	...	-0.6	-99.9	-0.6	0.19	0.14	...	...	999.9	...	...	-0.4	999.9	999.9	...	...	...	...
2	86.0	18.1	2.9	2.1	4.2	5.24	5.60	1.1	1.9	219.1	...	3.1	5.0	214.2	247.8	0.7	...	10.1	...
6	80.8	18.9	3.1	2.4	4.6	5.09	5.23	1.4	1.8	228.4	...	3.2	4.9	228.1	264.3	0.5	...	6.2	...
-2	84.3	19.1	0.7	0.5	1.1	4.95	5.05	7.2	1.9	232.8	...	2.2	1.1	234.8	274.6	...	...	3.5	...
-40	82.6	20.2	0.3	0.2	0.4	4.78	1.98	-2.8	2.0	249.3	...	2.6	-3.9	264.6	305.3	...	...	2.9	...
-252	80.2	20.6	2.7	2.0	3.7	4.55	2.06	-5.2	1.8	265.9	0.5	2.4	0.7	265.9	304.7	3.5	...	2.0	...
Principal Lines of Business: GrpA&H (97.2%), GrpLife (2.8%)														Principal States: NY (22.2%), CA (19.4%), IL (16.2%), NJ (9.2%), IN (8.2%)					
-4,920	86.9	8.7	9.2	4.7	15.6	2.73	2.97	8.3	3.1	148.1	1.0	...	11.0	146.2	164.1	...	...	13.9	15.6
8,229	93.4	9.0	-0.5	-0.3	-0.9	2.93	7.37	5.0	3.1	144.7	1.7	0.1	4.7	141.7	157.7	0.2	...	11.8	17.0
-2,689	91.5	8.9	2.4	1.2	4.0	3.29	5.17	9.9	3.4	145.1	0.0	0.8	1.3	144.5	160.6	...	...	12.3	15.3
-25,299	92.2	8.6	0.8	0.4	1.5	2.98	-3.12	7.1	4.3	110.5	0.0	0.2	-17.2	126.0	137.4	0.1	...	14.5	22.0
4,137	90.6	8.8	3.9	1.6	7.2	2.81	2.60	7.0	4.2	122.5	0.0	...	10.4	128.1	141.4	0.4	...	12.6	18.6
Principal Lines of Business: CompHosp/Med (74.3%), OtherHlth (9.3%), FEHBP (8.7%), MedSup (7.6%), Medicare (0.1%)														Principal States: ND (99.6%)					
5,148	56.9	24.7	0.9	4.8	10.1	7.32	7.41	-2.2	1.2	10.0	4.7	151.0	9.6	44.9	66.7	56.5	...	3.9	16.6
8,387	43.4	19.8	0.7	3.3	8.9	7.41	8.63	40.0	1.8	8.7	5.8	177.9	-5.1	54.4	72.0	61.1	...	6.7	...
16,079	37.5	16.1	0.1	0.2	0.8	6.68	6.99	46.6	2.7	7.1	5.8	194.6	0.0	51.5	69.1	86.2	...	6.5	...
-22,314	28.9	13.5	0.1	0.2	1.1	4.72	4.00	57.9	3.2	7.4	4.0	161.7	33.4	52.9	70.0	67.4	...	4.7	...
54,381	42.1	16.6	0.3	1.4	4.9	7.73	7.90	-18.9	2.2	8.3	2.9	220.6	19.6	49.0	65.9	66.8	...	6.8	...
Principal Lines of Business: IndAnn (76.3%), OrdLife (12.0%), GrpAnn (11.0%), GrpLife (0.7%), IndA&H (0.0%)														Principal States: CA (12.5%), TX (9.9%), PA (8.5%), FL (8.0%), NJ (6.5%)					
-5	34.1	83.9	9.1	13.9	20.3	4.64	4.67	-3.1	0.9	87.3	-8.3	63.8	11.4	157.8	169.8	1.9	...	...	...
70	58.1	84.2	19.0	47.3	37.8	5.63	5.51	-57.5	0.4	121.3	-10.9	22.0	7.9	164.0	185.0	4.6	...	...	...
-1	137.8	147.3	21.5	59.0	37.0	5.79	5.89	-71.5	0.1	171.2	0.2	19.4	-11.0	199.6	225.8	...	...	...	...
-27	141.8	183.1	8.1	32.5	12.8	5.54	5.47	-10.8	0.2	179.1	0.3	27.0	-33.4	189.7	221.0	...	...	...	...
...	132.2	208.2	5.5	18.8	8.5	4.53	4.61	-19.0	0.1	187.7	0.3	27.6	-10.0	209.7	236.0	1.2	...	...	...
Principal Lines of Business: IndA&H (83.8%), GrpA&H (17.0%), OrdLife (0.6%), CrdA&H (-0.4%), CrdLife (-0.9%)														Principal States: WI (57.0%), IN (12.2%), SC (7.4%), MO (5.2%), MI (3.1%)					
-557	-99.9	999.9	0.0	0.1	0.5	4.52	1.88	-99.9	0.0	4.3	342.7	999.9	85.2	2.0	2.6	...	...	346.0	257.1
558	17.9	-1.5	0.2	0.5	4.9	4.01	5.56	999.9	9.0	2.9	222.7	999.9	-21.4	1.4	1.9	...	...	444.1	345.1
49	88.1	27.9	0.9	7.8	27.9	6.40	7.34	-59.6	1.7	4.5	71.0	999.9	114.1	28.1	30.0	...	39.8	395.1	270.7
-787	-79.2	-79.3	1.0	-54.4	24.4	4.44	3.20	-99.9	-1.4	4.6	66.7	999.9	-11.1	16.8	19.0	2.2	3.0	544.9	382.9
2,527	37.5	66.8	-2.1	-12.5	-77.5	5.51	7.88	301.2	6.7	1.8	140.5	999.9	-57.5	43.9	48.1	...	189.7	999.9	973.1
Principal Lines of Business: OrdLife (99.7%), IndAnn (0.1%), GrpAnn (0.1%), IndA&H (0.0%)														Principal States: TX (100.0%)					
1,023	24.1	34.7	5.3	22.9	25.2	5.13	11.62	-12.9	0.6	37.0	1.6	9.8	52.8	88.2	99.4	24.2	...	...	...
-1,083	56.1	45.7	4.2	23.8	17.6	4.68	3.37	-20.6	0.5	35.5	1.3	11.3	1.0	93.7	102.7	21.1	...	32.8	...
-1,183	28.2	44.0	2.5	13.8	10.7	4.59	1.99	7.0	0.6	30.4	1.0	24.5	-11.3	80.0	90.5	28.6	...	36.8	...
-1,445	77.8	87.2	2.8	16.7	15.2	5.95	-3.64	-33.0	0.7	18.0	3.7	118.5	-43.8	63.9	76.6	19.7	...	67.8	...
866	97.0	42.7	3.5	20.1	23.7	5.31	7.48	9.4	0.6	24.6	1.8	120.0	31.2	59.7	71.8	24.4	...	52.6	...
Principal Lines of Business: OrdLife (100.0%)																			

2010 BEST'S KEY RATING GUIDE — LIFE/HEALTH EDITION
ANNUAL STATEMENT DATA FOR YEARS 2005 – 2009
Data in U.S. Dollars

COMPANY NAME / Ultimate Parent Association / Principal Officer / Mailing Address / Dom. : Began Bus. : Struct. : Mktg. / Specialty / Phone # / AMB# / NAIC# — Best's Financial Strength Rating / FSC

Balance Sheet: Data Year, Bonds (%), Mort. Loans & R.E. (%), Com & Pref. Stock (%), All Other Assets (%), Total Assets ($000), Life Reserves (%), Health Reserves %), Ann Res. & Dep. Liabilities (%), All Other Liabilities (%), Capital & Surplus ($000)

Operations: Direct Premiums Written ($000), Net Premiums Written & Deposits ($000), Operating Cash Flow ($000), NOG Before Taxes ($000), NOG After Taxes ($000), Net Income ($000)

NORTH CAROLINA MUTUAL LIFE INS
James H. Speed, Jr.
President & CEO
411 W. Chapel Hill Street
Durham, NC 27701-3616
NC : 1899 : Mutual : Agency
Group Life, Home serv, Univ Life
919-682-9201
AMB# 006835 NAIC# 67032

C+ u — Under Review Implication: Negative — FSC IV

Data Year	Bonds (%)	Mort. Loans & R.E. (%)	Com & Pref. Stock (%)	All Other Assets (%)	Total Assets ($000)	Life Reserves (%)	Health Reserves %)	Ann Res. & Dep. Liabilities (%)	All Other Liabilities (%)	Capital & Surplus ($000)	Direct Premiums Written ($000)	Net Premiums Written & Deposits ($000)	Operating Cash Flow ($000)	NOG Before Taxes ($000)	NOG After Taxes ($000)	Net Income ($000)
'05	54.2	11.1	2.6	32.1	144,306	80.5	3.0	3.9	12.6	12,569	68,794	70,861	-10,500	-3,016	-2,969	-2,614
'06	57.2	7.8	1.2	33.8	139,751	83.5	1.9	4.2	10.5	14,945	67,785	68,275	1,014	-4,594	-4,594	1,750
'07	63.3	8.8	0.7	27.2	132,733	84.9	1.1	4.2	9.8	12,971	48,555	46,864	-5,820	-4,294	-4,294	-2,838
'08	64.7	7.9	0.6	26.7	159,411	87.7	0.4	3.4	8.5	9,495	23,893	37,398	27,196	-4,534	-4,534	-4,410
'09	65.8	8.6	0.3	25.3	151,580	87.9	0.4	3.6	8.1	6,365	22,432	26,795	-3,320	-944	-944	-2,506

Rating History: C+ u, 09/01/09; B- u, 04/01/09; B, 12/03/08; B, 10/22/07; B, 07/26/06

NORTH COAST LIFE INS CO
R J Martin Mortgage Company
Robert J. Ogden
President
P.O. Box 1445
Spokane, WA 99210-1445
WA : 1965 : Stock : Agency
ISWL, Term Life, Ind Ann
509-838-4235
AMB# 006837 NAIC# 67059

C+ — Rating Outlook: Negative — FSC IV

Data Year	Bonds (%)	Mort. Loans & R.E. (%)	Com & Pref. Stock (%)	All Other Assets (%)	Total Assets ($000)	Life Reserves (%)	Health Reserves %)	Ann Res. & Dep. Liabilities (%)	All Other Liabilities (%)	Capital & Surplus ($000)	Direct Premiums Written ($000)	Net Premiums Written & Deposits ($000)	Operating Cash Flow ($000)	NOG Before Taxes ($000)	NOG After Taxes ($000)	Net Income ($000)
'05	74.1	0.4	7.6	17.8	126,259	54.8	0.0	42.6	2.6	6,151	11,439	10,995	7,489	739	678	180
'06	72.9	0.3	7.2	19.7	126,860	54.6	0.0	43.4	2.0	5,826	8,060	8,538	769	400	329	195
'07	71.4	0.3	8.9	19.3	123,165	58.1	0.0	39.9	2.0	5,728	7,796	8,540	-2,893	258	238	232
'08	72.4	0.2	8.2	19.2	121,081	59.2	0.0	39.7	1.1	5,737	7,679	7,116	-153	1,661	1,357	628
'09	70.8	0.2	5.4	23.7	124,665	57.4	0.0	40.5	2.1	5,539	8,602	9,061	2,360	569	475	-1,702

Rating History: C+, 04/30/10; C++, 04/17/09; C++u, 11/21/08; C++, 04/14/08; C++, 03/23/07

NORTHERN NATIONAL LIFE OF RI'
Brian J. Murphy
President
One Home Loan Plaza
Warwick, RI 02886-1764
RI : 1977 : Stock : Not Available
800-223-1700
AMB# 008788 NAIC# 87564

NR-1

Data Year	Bonds (%)	Mort. Loans & R.E. (%)	Com & Pref. Stock (%)	All Other Assets (%)	Total Assets ($000)	Life Reserves (%)	Health Reserves %)	Ann Res. & Dep. Liabilities (%)	All Other Liabilities (%)	Capital & Surplus ($000)	Direct Premiums Written ($000)	Net Premiums Written & Deposits ($000)	Operating Cash Flow ($000)	NOG Before Taxes ($000)	NOG After Taxes ($000)	Net Income ($000)
'05	...	...	...	100.0	3,751	...	...	...	100.0	3,623	...	17	...	69	52	52
'06	...	...	...	100.0	3,838	...	...	...	100.0	3,759	...	9	...	104	137	137
'07	...	...	...	100.0	3,923	...	...	...	100.0	3,833	...	5	...	98	74	74
'08	50.8	...	...	49.2	3,934	...	...	...	100.0	3,851	...	2	...	24	18	18
'09	54.2	...	...	45.8	3,693	...	...	...	100.0	3,687	...	1	...	-200	-164	-164

Rating History: NR-1, 06/10/10; NR-1, 06/12/09; NR-1, 06/12/08; NR-1, 06/08/07; NR-1, 06/07/06

NORTHWESTERN LONG TERM CARE
Northwestern Mutual Life Ins Co
John E. Schlifske
President & CEO
720 East Wisconsin Avenue
Milwaukee, WI 53202-4797
WI : 1953 : Stock : Agency
LTC
414-661-2510
AMB# 007067 NAIC# 69000

A++ — Rating Outlook: Stable — FSC XV

Data Year	Bonds (%)	Mort. Loans & R.E. (%)	Com & Pref. Stock (%)	All Other Assets (%)	Total Assets ($000)	Life Reserves (%)	Health Reserves %)	Ann Res. & Dep. Liabilities (%)	All Other Liabilities (%)	Capital & Surplus ($000)	Direct Premiums Written ($000)	Net Premiums Written & Deposits ($000)	Operating Cash Flow ($000)	NOG Before Taxes ($000)	NOG After Taxes ($000)	Net Income ($000)
'05	80.1	...	14.5	5.4	157,906	0.9	75.0	...	24.2	62,382	88,749	69,072	40,830	-3,470	-3,470	-2,547
'06	78.7	...	14.3	7.0	217,061	0.5	76.5	...	23.0	58,307	114,125	94,114	57,969	-9,237	-9,238	-8,842
'07	78.9	...	14.4	6.7	287,380	0.3	81.6	...	18.1	53,566	145,339	124,571	69,561	-6,400	-6,402	-3,763
'08	80.5	...	9.9	9.6	402,675	0.2	83.9	...	15.9	63,403	180,429	158,859	120,977	-7,548	-7,550	-17,643
'09	83.3	...	11.6	5.1	528,231	0.1	88.8	...	11.1	71,403	208,687	186,466	107,658	-16,215	-16,217	-17,112

Rating History: A++g, 03/01/10; A++g, 06/04/09; A++g, 03/21/08; A++g, 02/23/07; A++g, 05/23/06

NORTHWESTERN MUTUAL LIFE INS
Northwestern Mutual Life Ins Co
Edward J. Zore
Chairman & CEO
720 East Wisconsin Avenue
Milwaukee, WI 53202-4797
WI : 1858 : Mutual : Agency
Ind Life, Ann, Dis inc
414-271-1444
AMB# 006845 NAIC# 67091

A++ — Rating Outlook: Stable — FSC XV

Data Year	Bonds (%)	Mort. Loans & R.E. (%)	Com & Pref. Stock (%)	All Other Assets (%)	Total Assets ($000)	Life Reserves (%)	Health Reserves %)	Ann Res. & Dep. Liabilities (%)	All Other Liabilities (%)	Capital & Surplus ($000)	Direct Premiums Written ($000)	Net Premiums Written & Deposits ($000)	Operating Cash Flow ($000)	NOG Before Taxes ($000)	NOG After Taxes ($000)	Net Income ($000)
'05	49.5	14.8	6.1	29.6	132,972,532	69.0	3.5	3.9	23.6	10,380,535	11,952,574	12,452,415	6,429,091	674,698	617,351	926,389
'06	48.6	14.4	6.4	30.7	144,961,942	68.6	3.3	3.7	24.3	11,684,376	12,717,591	13,227,905	7,668,003	445,644	428,887	838,201
'07	49.0	14.3	6.1	30.6	156,332,490	68.8	3.1	3.6	24.5	12,105,970	13,809,492	14,552,855	8,150,773	407,897	387,380	1,003,784
'08	51.0	15.0	3.7	30.3	154,834,649	75.1	3.2	4.2	17.5	12,401,283	14,222,438	15,085,738	6,769,556	853,308	1,157,188	500,826
'09	54.3	13.6	3.6	28.6	166,746,624	73.2	3.1	4.3	19.4	12,402,560	13,764,621	15,684,088	8,604,989	533,187	491,130	338,147

Rating History: A++g, 03/01/10; A++g, 06/04/09; A++g, 03/21/08; A++g, 02/23/07; A++g, 05/23/06

NYLIFE INS CO OF ARIZONA
New York Life Insurance Company
Scott L. Berlin
Chairman & President
51 Madison Avenue
New York, NY 10010
AZ : 1987 : Stock : Agency
Term Life
212-576-7000
AMB# 068015 NAIC# 81353

A++ — Rating Outlook: Stable — FSC XV

Data Year	Bonds (%)	Mort. Loans & R.E. (%)	Com & Pref. Stock (%)	All Other Assets (%)	Total Assets ($000)	Life Reserves (%)	Health Reserves %)	Ann Res. & Dep. Liabilities (%)	All Other Liabilities (%)	Capital & Surplus ($000)	Direct Premiums Written ($000)	Net Premiums Written & Deposits ($000)	Operating Cash Flow ($000)	NOG Before Taxes ($000)	NOG After Taxes ($000)	Net Income ($000)
'05	58.6	...	...	41.4	140,267	84.8	...	9.2	6.0	29,820	68,654	59,998	14,675	-10,532	-7,692	-7,692
'06	59.7	...	...	40.3	155,489	87.0	...	7.0	5.9	31,296	71,514	63,935	14,404	594	-649	-649
'07	64.4	...	...	35.6	178,118	89.0	...	6.1	4.9	36,053	72,954	60,812	21,975	-5,049	-3,689	-3,689
'08	64.5	...	...	35.5	189,617	86.3	...	7.8	6.0	37,973	75,640	64,997	8,545	5,449	2,490	1,591
'09	63.6	...	...	36.4	193,204	87.3	...	7.5	5.2	54,514	75,467	64,826	732	4,602	2,767	2,896

Rating History: A++g, 06/14/10; A++g, 06/11/09; A++g, 03/11/08; A++g, 11/21/06; A++g, 12/23/04

OCCIDENTAL LIFE INS CO OF NC
Thoma Cressey Bravo Inc
S. Lanny Peavy
President & CEO
425 Austin Avenue
Waco, TX 76701
TX : 1906 : Stock : Agency
Trad Life, Univ Life, ISWL
254-297-2775
AMB# 006849 NAIC# 67148

A- — Rating Outlook: Stable — FSC VII

Data Year	Bonds (%)	Mort. Loans & R.E. (%)	Com & Pref. Stock (%)	All Other Assets (%)	Total Assets ($000)	Life Reserves (%)	Health Reserves %)	Ann Res. & Dep. Liabilities (%)	All Other Liabilities (%)	Capital & Surplus ($000)	Direct Premiums Written ($000)	Net Premiums Written & Deposits ($000)	Operating Cash Flow ($000)	NOG Before Taxes ($000)	NOG After Taxes ($000)	Net Income ($000)
'05	88.5	...	0.4	11.1	258,376	87.6	0.0	10.2	2.2	27,174	25,486	24,224	-3,473	5,263	5,098	4,587
'06	87.4	...	0.4	12.3	250,054	87.9	0.0	10.1	2.0	23,744	27,309	26,524	-6,587	3,327	3,614	3,614
'07	87.5	...	0.3	12.1	255,218	87.7	0.0	10.2	2.0	27,760	36,110	34,636	3,663	6,465	5,207	4,951
'08	88.3	...	0.1	11.5	259,021	85.7	0.0	10.1	4.2	29,003	33,070	31,966	5,033	5,184	3,536	3,094
'09	89.4	...	...	10.6	261,453	85.5	0.0	10.6	4.0	32,924	34,270	32,803	-1,313	5,992	3,785	3,017

Rating History: A- g, 03/02/10; B++g, 01/16/09; B++g, 01/17/08; B++g, 01/10/07; B++g, 02/13/06

ODS HEALTH PLAN INC
Oregon Dental Association
Robert G. Gootee
President & CEO
601 SW Second Avenue
Portland, OR 97204
OR : 1988 : Stock : Broker
Group A&H
503-228-6554
AMB# 011437 NAIC# 47098

B+ — Rating Outlook: Negative — FSC VII

Data Year	Bonds (%)	Mort. Loans & R.E. (%)	Com & Pref. Stock (%)	All Other Assets (%)	Total Assets ($000)	Life Reserves (%)	Health Reserves %)	Ann Res. & Dep. Liabilities (%)	All Other Liabilities (%)	Capital & Surplus ($000)	Direct Premiums Written ($000)	Net Premiums Written & Deposits ($000)	Operating Cash Flow ($000)	NOG Before Taxes ($000)	NOG After Taxes ($000)	Net Income ($000)
'05	46.1	...	37.2	16.7	132,335	...	12.7	...	87.3	36,610	135,836	134,004	9,274	6,654	3,973	4,913
'06	45.9	...	38.2	15.9	140,635	...	11.3	...	88.7	37,794	146,307	144,356	-1,065	5,384	5,104	5,119
'07	47.2	...	37.6	15.2	147,242	...	12.9	...	87.1	38,281	150,900	149,570	7,523	4,268	2,703	3,538
'08	43.1	...	13.9	43.1	178,793	...	18.2	...	81.8	39,846	183,702	182,592	11,460	2,199	5,617	1,329
'09	45.0	...	14.3	40.7	231,701	...	17.8	...	82.2	71,413	219,964	216,864	30,617	-16,338	-10,851	-9,979

Rating History: B+, 05/28/10; B+, 06/09/09; B+, 06/17/08; B+, 06/12/07; B+, 04/28/06

OHIO MOTORISTS LIFE INS CO
AAA East Central
Peter C. Ohlheiser
President
P.O. Box 6150
Cleveland, OH 44101
OH : 1991 : Stock : Not Available
Group A&H
216-606-6312
AMB# 068360 NAIC# 66005

NR-5

Data Year	Bonds (%)	Mort. Loans & R.E. (%)	Com & Pref. Stock (%)	All Other Assets (%)	Total Assets ($000)	Life Reserves (%)	Health Reserves %)	Ann Res. & Dep. Liabilities (%)	All Other Liabilities (%)	Capital & Surplus ($000)	Direct Premiums Written ($000)	Net Premiums Written & Deposits ($000)	Operating Cash Flow ($000)	NOG Before Taxes ($000)	NOG After Taxes ($000)	Net Income ($000)
'05	93.9	...	...	6.1	7,961	34.1	13.3	...	52.6	7,367	655	133	402	477	407	374
'06	95.7	...	...	4.3	7,954	66.7	8.7	...	24.6	7,650	399	102	39	353	283	283
'07	96.5	...	...	3.5	8,231	83.4	9.4	...	7.3	8,007	355	88	299	422	357	357
'08	96.4	...	...	3.6	8,563	84.6	8.5	...	7.0	8,327	325	79	346	386	320	320
'09	96.0	...	...	4.0	8,840	82.7	8.5	...	8.8	8,637	293	72	319	372	310	310

Rating History: NR-5, 04/21/10; NR-5, 04/23/09; NR-5, 04/10/08; NR-5, 05/11/07; NR-5, 05/10/06

BEST'S PROFITABILITY, LEVERAGE AND LIQUIDITY TESTS 2005 – 2009

Data in U.S. Dollars

	Profitability Tests							Leverage Tests						Liquidity Tests					
Un-Realized Capital Gains ($000)	Benefits Paid to NPW & Dep (%)	Comm. & Expenses to NPW & Dep (%)	NOG to Total Assets (%)	NOG to Total Rev (%)	Operating Return on Equity (%)	Net Yield (%)	Total Return (%)	Change in NPW & Dep (%)	NPW & Dep to Capital (X)	Capital & Surplus to Liabilities (%)	Surplus Relief (%)	Reins Leverage (%)	Change in Capital (%)	Quick Liquidity (%)	Current Liquidity (%)	Non-Invest Grade Bonds to Capital (%)	Delinq. & Foreclosed Mortgages to Capital (%)	Mort. & Credit Tenant Loans & R.E. to Capital (%)	Affiliated Invest to Capital (%)
-1,664	76.7	38.0	-1.9	-3.5	-18.2	4.20	3.91	4.0	4.3	10.8	43.8	420.1	-33.2	51.4	56.8	17.8	9.2	97.3	21.4
-192	74.6	39.0	-3.2	-5.5	-33.4	4.37	10.50	-3.6	4.1	12.9	48.7	345.7	2.6	61.3	66.7	26.4	8.2	64.7	...
-7	82.4	38.3	-3.2	-7.2	-30.8	5.43	7.07	-31.4	2.8	11.5	40.0	387.1	-1.2	60.1	65.4	5.6	9.8	69.9	...
251	75.3	41.0	-3.1	-5.6	-40.4	6.10	6.57	-20.2	2.9	6.8	127.9	587.8	-21.9	66.1	71.9	15.2	6.0	97.5	0.5
-600	75.2	50.8	-0.6	-2.4	-11.9	5.61	4.18	-28.4	2.8	4.6	90.9	869.8	-26.6	58.7	62.9	67.5	8.9	136.5	1.1
Principal Lines of Business: OrdLife (48.8%), GrpLife (44.4%), GrpA&H (3.3%), IndA&H (1.3%), IndLife (1.2%)														Principal States: NC (24.4%), IL (13.7%), GA (11.4%), CA (8.8%), PA (5.3%)					
-9	53.1	41.2	0.6	3.9	11.0	5.93	5.63	-56.7	1.7	5.5	6.2	4.7	-3.0	47.0	58.1	150.2	1.6	8.2	28.5
31	108.7	36.9	0.3	2.2	5.5	5.68	5.70	-22.3	1.3	5.3	0.5	5.7	-3.2	55.2	64.6	108.3	1.2	6.5	29.9
80	173.9	36.1	0.2	1.6	4.1	5.73	5.84	0.0	1.3	5.7	0.4	9.0	3.0	52.2	62.1	87.7	1.5	5.0	30.2
-1,313	152.6	31.0	1.1	9.0	23.7	6.20	4.52	-16.7	1.2	5.1	16.2	22.5	-10.7	50.1	60.1	122.3	...	3.9	35.4
1,006	102.8	30.9	0.4	3.1	8.4	6.15	5.13	27.3	1.6	4.9	0.4	23.7	-1.4	52.8	62.1	185.1	1.7	3.7	22.3
Principal Lines of Business: IndAnn (44.7%), OrdLife (44.6%), GrpAnn (10.7%), IndA&H (0.0%)														Principal States: CA (28.7%), OR (19.0%), WA (16.0%), ID (10.4%), AZ (8.6%)					
...	-14.2	449.5	1.4	42.6	1.4	...	...	-43.5	0.0	999.9	...	...	1.4	...	...	...	...	...	...
...	-7.1	941.2	3.6	76.9	3.7	...	...	-46.6	0.0	999.9	...	...	3.8	...	...	...	...	...	...
...	-15.3	999.9	1.9	44.3	1.9	...	...	-41.9	0.0	999.9	...	...	2.0	...	...	...	...	...	...
...	-20.8	999.9	0.5	21.4	0.5	...	...	-63.4	0.0	999.9	...	...	0.5	...	...	...	...	...	...
...	-25.7	999.9	-4.3	-99.9	-4.3	...	...	-67.5	0.0	999.9	...	...	-4.2	...	...	...	...	...	...
Principal Lines of Business: CrdLife (100.0%)																			
579	1.0	63.6	-2.5	-4.3	-5.9	4.41	5.94	45.9	1.0	71.8	8.0	162.8	11.7	128.2	143.0	2.2	...	...	...
1,003	1.6	62.7	-4.9	-8.5	-15.3	4.71	5.73	36.3	1.5	41.0	8.7	208.8	-4.3	107.2	119.8	0.5	...	...	...
488	1.9	54.5	-2.5	-4.5	-11.4	4.73	6.18	32.4	2.1	26.5	10.2	267.3	-4.7	95.3	106.5	0.8	...	...	...
-8,698	2.4	49.5	-2.2	-4.2	-12.9	4.41	-0.84	27.5	2.5	18.7	9.1	261.8	5.3	94.8	105.1	3.2	...	...	...
8,884	3.2	49.2	-3.5	-7.6	-24.1	4.46	6.34	17.4	2.3	17.8	8.2	265.5	26.0	85.6	97.8	4.5	...	...	...
Principal Lines of Business: IndA&H (100.0%)														Principal States: IL (8.1%), WI (6.6%), CA (5.9%), NY (5.5%), FL (5.1%)					
340,525	36.8	12.4	0.5	3.4	6.4	6.04	6.68	6.8	1.0	12.4	1.7	12.5	12.4	40.1	53.2	40.5	0.3	152.9	27.7
571,348	38.2	12.5	0.3	2.2	3.9	6.10	6.95	6.2	0.9	13.2	1.5	12.1	14.5	38.1	51.6	44.7	0.1	141.2	29.1
-17,370	38.7	12.1	0.3	1.8	3.3	6.05	6.54	10.0	0.9	13.1	1.5	12.4	6.9	36.5	50.5	53.1	0.1	141.5	29.0
-3,183,400	40.7	12.0	0.7	5.3	9.4	5.96	3.16	3.7	1.1	10.5	1.4	12.5	-14.0	38.3	50.6	65.9	0.1	170.9	41.5
307,073	43.7	12.1	0.3	2.3	4.0	5.64	5.77	4.0	1.1	10.5	1.5	12.4	4.8	38.8	51.5	62.5	0.1	158.8	44.2
Principal Lines of Business: OrdLife (66.9%), IndAnn (19.3%), GrpAnn (7.9%), IndA&H (5.4%), GrpA&H (0.4%)														Principal States: NY (5.9%), IL (5.7%), CA (5.3%), FL (4.4%), WI (4.1%)					
...	17.9	42.4	-5.8	-16.5	-23.3	4.29	4.40	-11.5	2.0	27.2	7.6	205.5	-17.4	82.3	94.7	...	...	...	5.1
...	17.0	31.9	-0.4	-1.3	-2.1	4.91	4.96	6.6	2.0	25.4	6.6	203.2	5.1	82.1	95.1	...	...	...	9.2
0	22.5	30.8	-2.2	-7.8	-11.0	4.82	4.81	-4.9	1.7	25.6	5.3	200.2	15.3	85.7	98.1	...	...	...	4.5
6	27.6	28.4	1.4	5.2	6.7	4.67	4.04	6.9	1.7	25.0	5.2	179.4	4.7	86.2	99.6	2.7	...	...	0.0
-2	28.3	30.7	1.4	5.9	6.0	4.32	4.43	-0.3	1.2	39.3	2.8	120.5	43.6	86.6	101.6	2.6	...	...	6.4
Principal Lines of Business: OrdLife (59.7%), IndAnn (40.3%)														Principal States: CA (19.9%), TX (9.0%), FL (5.9%), WA (4.3%), GA (3.6%)					
798	100.6	39.5	2.0	14.3	20.1	4.99	5.18	10.2	0.9	12.2	2.3	7.0	12.6	88.8	93.7	8.2	...	...	...
-1,349	91.3	41.1	1.4	9.6	14.2	5.11	4.67	9.5	1.1	10.5	2.5	7.8	-15.1	91.1	94.9	0.8	...	...	...
-200	68.3	42.7	2.1	11.3	20.2	5.14	5.07	30.6	1.2	12.2	2.4	5.8	16.8	92.9	97.0	4.0	...	...	...
-282	80.7	44.1	1.4	8.1	12.5	5.04	4.85	-7.7	1.1	12.6	1.8	6.8	4.2	86.3	94.6	1.6	...	...	...
832	74.2	42.1	1.5	8.6	12.2	4.83	4.94	2.6	1.0	14.6	1.7	6.9	14.7	91.0	97.6	...	...	...	...
Principal Lines of Business: OrdLife (90.2%), IndAnn (6.6%), GrpAnn (3.2%), IndA&H (0.0%), GrpLife (0.0%)														Principal States: NC (11.3%), PR (10.8%), CA (6.7%), SC (6.2%), FL (5.4%)					
2,564	85.5	11.6	3.1	2.9	11.5	2.49	5.68	33.3	3.7	38.2	...	1.3	12.9	83.7	91.7	...	...	...	49.2
1,476	83.8	15.2	3.7	3.4	13.7	3.57	4.84	7.7	3.8	36.8	...	0.2	3.2	67.9	78.3	...	...	...	47.2
767	83.9	15.8	1.9	1.8	7.1	3.15	4.44	3.6	3.9	35.1	...	0.5	1.3	71.5	80.6	...	...	...	48.0
-4,532	88.0	12.6	3.4	3.0	14.4	2.53	-4.04	22.1	4.6	28.7	...	0.5	4.1	96.3	101.0	1.1	...	...	42.4
2,487	101.0	8.3	-5.3	-4.9	-19.5	2.62	4.83	18.8	3.0	44.6	...	26.4	79.2	99.3	105.2	...	...	...	41.5
Principal Lines of Business: CompHosp/Med (89.5%), Medicare (8.2%), OtherHlth (2.3%)														Principal States: OR (94.5%), AK (5.5%)					
...	55.0	5.1	5.3	58.9	5.7	5.37	4.95	-47.1	0.0	999.9	2.0	2.6	5.3	999.9	999.9	3.0	...	...	...
...	69.9	93.5	3.6	51.3	3.8	5.27	5.27	-23.6	0.0	999.9	0.5	2.7	3.8	999.9	999.9	...	...	...	...
...	39.1	61.2	4.4	66.8	4.6	5.18	5.18	-13.6	0.0	999.9	0.4	2.3	4.7	999.9	999.9	...	...	...	...
...	68.3	58.0	3.8	63.0	3.9	4.84	4.84	-9.7	0.0	999.9	0.4	3.2	4.0	999.9	999.9	...	...	...	...
...	50.3	61.7	3.6	66.7	3.7	4.28	4.28	-9.1	0.0	999.9	0.3	1.9	3.7	999.9	999.9	...	...	...	...
Principal Lines of Business: GrpLife (51.9%), GrpA&H (48.1%)														Principal States: OH (100.0%)					

Data in U.S. Dollars

COMPANY NAME Ultimate Parent Association Principal Officer Mailing Address Dom. : Began Bus. : Struct. : Mktg. Specialty Phone # AMB# NAIC#	Best's Financial Strength Rating FSC	Data Year	Balance Sheet Bonds (%)	Mort. Loans & R.E. (%)	Com & Pref. Stock (%)	All Other Assets (%)	Total Assets ($000)	Life Reserves (%)	Health Reserves %)	Ann Res. & Dep. Liabilities (%)	All Other Liabilities (%)	Capital & Surplus ($000)	Operations Direct Premiums Written ($000)	Net Premiums Written & Deposits ($000)	Operating Cash Flow ($000)	NOG Before Taxes ($000)	NOG After Taxes ($000)	Net Income ($000)
OHIO NATIONAL LIFE ASSUR CORP Ohio National Mutual Holdings Inc David B. O'Maley Chairman, President & CEO One Financial Way Cincinnati, OH 45242 OH : 1979 : Stock : Agency Ind Life, Ind Ann, Dis inc 513-794-6100 AMB# 008930 NAIC# 89206	**A+** Rating Outlook: Stable **FSC XI**	**'05**	63.1	16.6	...	20.3	2,208,576	75.3	2.2	9.6	13.0	164,446	364,518	281,473	127,000	14,384	8,208	-20,249
		'06	63.1	16.6	0.7	19.5	2,475,117	78.4	1.8	7.2	12.5	169,415	465,081	356,330	235,425	22,922	2,288	-6,012
		'07	64.2	15.8	0.7	19.2	2,690,966	80.2	1.8	5.4	12.7	188,621	454,393	297,130	185,955	21,465	7,165	7,295
		'08	62.9	16.6	0.7	19.7	2,739,296	83.6	1.9	4.3	10.1	267,465	411,683	291,022	46,657	46,353	4,713	-43,407
		'09	63.4	14.5	0.0	22.1	2,886,948	84.7	1.8	3.7	9.8	277,844	411,031	267,446	150,624	24,041	9,524	-565
		Rating History: A+ g, 05/21/10; A+ g, 06/12/09; A+ g, 06/06/08; A+ g, 06/12/07; A+ g, 04/12/06																
OHIO NATIONAL LIFE INS CO Ohio National Mutual Holdings Inc David B. O'Maley President & CEO One Financial Way Cincinnati, OH 45242 OH : 1910 : Mutual : Agency Ind Life, Ann, Dis inc 513-794-6100 AMB# 006852 NAIC# 67172	**A+** Rating Outlook: Stable **FSC XI**	**'05**	52.5	8.8	2.0	36.7	10,361,575	9.3	0.8	52.3	37.6	749,816	1,445,895	1,388,428	-104,777	128,167	109,489	94,434
		'06	43.9	7.7	1.9	46.4	11,246,638	9.5	0.8	41.7	48.0	791,304	1,979,530	1,975,676	-538,888	110,310	86,666	76,111
		'07	35.2	6.8	1.8	56.2	13,004,213	9.3	0.7	32.2	57.7	794,948	2,684,698	2,861,493	-343,894	71,565	43,223	36,883
		'08	36.1	7.5	2.6	53.8	12,159,782	10.8	0.8	37.9	50.4	757,192	2,529,505	2,911,727	435,314	-61,071	-37,123	-129,622
		'09	27.3	5.4	2.1	65.2	15,785,004	8.9	0.6	28.7	61.8	816,716	2,889,983	3,127,631	-128,559	192,009	140,613	80,833
		Rating History: A+ g, 05/21/10; A+ g, 06/12/09; A+ g, 06/06/08; A+ g, 06/12/07; A+ g, 04/12/06																
OHIO STATE LIFE INS CO Financial Holding Corporation Gary L. Muller CEO P.O. Box 410288 Kansas City, MO 64141-0288 TX : 1906 : Stock : Agency Ind Ann, Term Life, Univ Life 816-391-2000 AMB# 006853 NAIC# 67180	**B+** Rating Outlook: Stable **FSC IV**	**'05**	55.0	...	0.1	44.9	10,678	...	...	...	100.0	6,501	53,449	1,423	-5,186	-535	-27	-27
		'06	72.5	...	10.7	16.8	9,493	...	...	...	100.0	6,881	50,072	1,032	155	83	445	445
		'07	75.1	...	0.2	24.7	9,326	...	...	...	100.0	6,709	47,358	660	676	-770	-186	-186
		'08	69.4	...	0.1	30.5	10,242	...	...	...	100.0	6,833	44,967	512	366	-217	125	125
		'09	58.0	...	0.1	41.9	12,174	...	...	...	100.0	8,282	42,605	419	2,249	496	848	848
		Rating History: B+, 11/04/09; B+, 09/05/08; B+, 06/14/07; B+, 06/21/06; B+, 06/22/05																
OLD AMERICAN INS CO Kansas City Life Insurance Company Walter E. Bixby President 3520 Broadway Kansas City, MO 64111-2565 MO : 1939 : Stock : Career Agent A&H, Ind Life 816-753-4900 AMB# 006854 NAIC# 67199	**B++** Rating Outlook: Positive **FSC V**	**'05**	70.6	13.5	0.8	15.1	246,206	92.4	0.4	0.1	7.1	23,579	70,105	65,060	-14,007	8,228	5,758	7,330
		'06	72.5	12.8	0.7	13.9	243,672	94.0	0.4	0.1	5.5	23,730	67,507	63,106	-2,367	8,561	6,708	6,766
		'07	70.2	12.3	0.7	16.8	245,542	93.4	0.4	0.1	6.1	22,091	66,242	62,346	2,654	7,211	5,704	5,214
		'08	73.2	11.7	1.0	14.2	239,865	93.5	0.3	0.1	6.1	18,065	64,818	61,523	-4,869	5,599	3,937	1,624
		'09	73.4	9.9	0.5	16.2	239,744	94.1	0.3	0.0	5.6	19,780	66,767	63,819	-3,887	4,575	3,799	1,077
		Rating History: B++, 06/04/10; B++, 06/02/09; B++, 12/07/07; B++, 11/14/06; B++, 12/21/05																
OLD RELIANCE INS CO[1] David G. Elmore President 1295 Kelly Johnson Blvd., #100 Colorado Springs, CO 80920 AZ : 1961 : Stock : Agency 719-457-7562 AMB# 006861 NAIC# 67253	**NR-1**	**'05**	63.5	...	23.2	13.2	3,340	...	...	4.3	95.7	1,653	1,909	992	...	-285	-285	-294
		'06	61.2	5.7	22.3	10.8	3,496	...	...	3.9	96.1	1,667	2,009	1,137	...	-425	-425	-441
		'07	58.5	22.7	9.5	9.2	3,691	...	...	3.6	96.4	1,652	2,084	1,254	...	-249	-249	-242
		'08	50.8	22.8	8.2	18.2	3,880	...	...	4.1	95.9	1,650	2,154	1,341	...	-213	-213	-219
		'09	45.6	32.5	7.4	14.5	4,403	...	...	4.3	95.7	1,934	2,228	1,466	...	-208	-208	-174
		Rating History: NR-1, 06/10/10; NR-1, 06/12/09; NR-1, 06/12/08; NR-1, 06/08/07; NR-1, 06/07/06																
OLD REPUBLIC LIFE INS CO Old Republic International Corporation Aldo C. Zucaro Chairman, President & CEO 307 North Michigan Avenue Chicago, IL 60601 IL : 1923 : Stock : Direct Response Group A&H, Credit Life, Ind Life 312-346-8100 AMB# 006863 NAIC# 67261	**A-** Rating Outlook: Stable **FSC VI**	**'05**	74.4	...	0.0	25.6	142,721	63.5	13.8	15.0	7.7	31,847	45,672	28,114	29,568	642	612	1,683
		'06	77.0	...	0.0	23.0	149,306	63.2	15.8	13.5	7.5	34,474	44,441	32,110	9,099	2,708	3,288	3,350
		'07	71.0	...	1.2	27.8	162,491	62.5	16.1	12.7	8.6	43,016	42,316	30,392	8,334	6,847	4,417	4,302
		'08	77.4	...	0.2	22.4	153,975	61.4	15.1	12.2	11.3	35,061	41,874	28,405	-5,680	3,554	3,228	750
		'09	76.5	...	0.3	23.2	151,874	64.4	14.3	12.4	8.8	41,039	39,439	25,492	2,225	6,777	4,921	5,142
		Rating History: A-, 09/29/09; A-, 12/09/08; A-, 06/24/08; A-, 06/07/07; A-, 06/23/06																
OLD SPARTAN LIFE INS CO INC[1] Albert R. Biggs President 181 Security Place Spartanburg, SC 29307 SC : 1984 : Stock : Not Available 864-237-6131 AMB# 007878 NAIC# 65480	**NR-1**	**'05**	8.0	...	36.9	55.1	24,532	...	...	...	100.0	18,410	5,155	7,942	...	2,464	2,050	2,347
		'06	9.3	...	44.3	46.4	28,962	...	...	...	100.0	22,670	5,929	8,640	...	3,992	3,512	3,591
		'07	7.7	...	56.5	35.8	32,273	...	...	...	100.0	26,444	6,261	8,098	...	4,846	3,594	4,387
		'08	...	...	59.3	40.7	27,954	...	...	...	100.0	24,042	6,648	7,072	...	3,518	2,890	2,701
		'09	9.6	...	63.6	26.8	28,822	...	...	...	100.0	22,992	7,109	7,705	...	3,173	2,485	1,734
		Rating History: NR-1, 06/10/10; NR-1, 06/12/09; NR-1, 06/12/08; NR-1, 06/08/07; NR-1, 06/07/06																
OLD SURETY LIFE INS CO[1] Dale L. Phillips President 5235 North Lincoln Boulevard Oklahoma City, OK 73105-1804 OK : 1932 : Stock : Broker 405-523-2112 AMB# 006867 NAIC# 67326	**NR-1**	**'05**	75.1	6.3	5.9	12.8	16,444	...	...	2.3	97.7	5,883	17,281	17,203	...	690	488	560
		'06	72.1	5.4	6.9	15.6	17,756	...	...	2.1	97.9	6,797	18,889	18,808	...	1,361	1,059	1,134
		'07	67.9	5.8	9.4	17.0	19,131	...	...	1.9	98.1	7,582	20,483	20,400	...	1,916	1,543	1,618
		'08	70.7	6.0	5.1	18.2	19,141	...	...	1.5	98.5	7,647	21,809	21,760	...	1,540	1,241	1,119
		'09	75.9	7.4	7.7	9.0	18,931	...	...	1.4	98.6	7,146	22,446	22,362	...	1,459	1,162	1,050
		Rating History: NR-1, 06/10/10; NR-1, 06/12/09; NR-1, 06/12/08; NR-1, 06/08/07; NR-1, 06/07/06																
OLD UNITED LIFE INS CO Van Enterprises Daniel K. Mattox President P.O. Box 795 Shawnee Mission, KS 66201 AZ : 1964 : Stock : Other Agency Credit A&H, Credit Life, Ann 913-432-6400 AMB# 007879 NAIC# 76007	**B++** Rating Outlook: Stable **FSC VI**	**'05**	86.8	...	9.2	4.0	62,322	51.4	41.5	3.7	3.4	33,969	14,220	3,555	-3,406	5,557	4,914	5,264
		'06	81.8	...	9.7	8.5	68,793	46.9	42.7	3.1	7.2	34,546	17,161	9,577	5,833	423	255	546
		'07	84.2	...	10.2	5.6	73,461	45.9	42.8	2.8	8.5	34,641	14,817	9,224	5,635	141	136	588
		'08	88.6	...	6.2	5.2	71,440	51.3	43.0	3.1	2.6	34,860	8,916	5,354	77	2,566	1,493	70
		'09	89.3	...	1.0	9.8	73,529	53.5	39.6	3.3	3.6	40,155	6,684	3,359	590	5,320	4,160	4,222
		Rating History: B++, 03/30/10; B++, 04/16/09; B++, 04/29/08; B++, 04/03/07; B++, 04/05/06																

BEST'S PROFITABILITY, LEVERAGE AND LIQUIDITY TESTS 2005 – 2009

Data in U.S. Dollars

Un-Realized Capital Gains ($000)	Benefits Paid to NPW & Dep (%)	Comm. & Expenses to NPW & Dep (%)	NOG to Total Assets (%)	NOG to Total Rev (%)	Operating Return on Equity (%)	Net Yield (%)	Total Return (%)	Change in NPW & Dep (%)	NPW & Dep to Capital (X)	Capital & Surplus to Liabilities (%)	Surplus Relief (%)	Reins Leverage (%)	Change in Capital (%)	Quick Liquidity (%)	Current Liquidity (%)	Non-Invest Grade Bonds to Capital (%)	Delinq. & Foreclosed Mortgages to Capital (%)	Mort. & Credit Tenant Loans & R.E. to Capital (%)	Affiliated Invest to Capital (%)
	Profitability Tests							Leverage Tests						Liquidity Tests					
16,604	48.6	22.8	0.4	1.9	5.4	7.06	6.40	18.9	1.7	9.4	11.0	221.2	17.1	39.2	50.8	79.5	...	216.5	...
3,121	48.2	17.8	0.1	0.4	1.4	6.97	6.70	26.6	2.0	8.6	9.7	262.8	3.1	36.9	50.8	74.3	...	241.7	...
4,580	66.2	22.9	0.3	1.5	4.0	6.70	6.92	-16.6	1.5	9.0	9.3	314.9	13.8	37.6	52.0	78.0	...	220.0	...
-5,299	65.9	13.1	0.2	0.9	2.1	6.72	4.42	-2.1	1.1	11.9	20.0	303.7	37.4	36.6	51.1	57.0	0.9	170.6	...
3,221	52.0	23.5	0.3	2.0	3.5	6.41	6.15	-8.1	0.9	11.9	14.2	337.2	3.5	46.2	60.9	66.9	...	152.1	...
Principal Lines of Business: OrdLife (97.6%), IndA&H (1.8%), IndAnn (0.6%)														Principal States: OH (10.0%), CA (9.1%), FL (7.4%), TX (7.0%), TN (5.3%)					
4,635	74.2	11.3	1.1	6.0	15.2	6.75	6.66	12.8	1.8	12.5	1.7	151.1	8.1	47.4	62.4	51.3	0.7	124.2	27.9
3,294	83.8	9.9	0.8	3.6	11.2	6.56	6.51	42.3	2.4	14.6	1.6	151.1	6.0	46.3	61.3	49.5	0.5	113.3	26.0
12,092	50.9	8.6	0.4	1.3	5.4	6.45	6.61	44.8	3.5	15.7	1.0	139.0	1.6	45.2	59.7	49.1	0.5	112.7	28.5
70,397	48.9	8.1	-0.3	-1.2	-4.8	6.10	5.82	1.8	3.8	12.9	0.9	144.1	-7.0	56.7	69.5	52.7	1.2	124.5	40.4
10,982	36.4	8.4	1.0	4.1	17.9	5.82	5.13	7.4	3.8	14.4	0.7	141.7	8.5	59.5	73.0	47.0	0.4	108.3	39.6
Principal Lines of Business: IndAnn (81.0%), GrpAnn (11.4%), OrdLife (7.1%), IndA&H (0.5%)														Principal States: OH (11.2%), FL (7.1%), PA (6.4%), NJ (5.6%), MD (5.5%)					
0	...	62.5	-0.2	-0.3	-0.4	4.39	4.88	-3.9	0.2	158.6	123.1	999.9	4.6	167.7	193.4	...	...	...	...
0	...	25.5	4.4	5.6	6.7	5.51	5.84	-27.5	0.1	270.8	108.1	999.9	5.9	268.5	304.7	...	...	...	...
1	...	-15.0	-2.0	-2.4	-2.7	6.62	7.23	-36.0	0.1	261.9	105.9	999.9	-2.6	326.3	344.7	...	...	...	...
-1	...	127.0	1.3	1.7	1.8	5.03	5.48	-22.5	0.1	204.2	99.8	999.9	1.9	251.5	264.8	...	...	...	...
1	...	-43.2	7.6	13.1	11.2	3.01	3.44	-18.1	0.1	216.4	74.4	999.9	21.1	323.1	348.1	...	...	...	...
Principal Lines of Business: GrpAnn (57.2%), OrdLife (25.7%), IndAnn (17.1%)														Principal States: NJ (12.0%), OH (10.5%), CA (8.5%), FL (8.5%), PA (7.9%)					
42	67.7	37.4	2.3	7.3	24.3	6.02	6.79	-3.6	2.5	11.6	3.1	237.1	-1.1	58.5	66.8	45.3	...	129.7	...
-36	67.4	38.1	2.7	8.7	28.4	6.15	6.17	-3.0	2.5	11.7	2.7	216.0	-0.8	57.9	66.7	39.1	...	122.9	...
...	66.8	41.6	2.3	7.5	24.9	6.16	5.93	-1.2	2.6	10.6	3.0	224.3	-7.4	61.7	70.2	42.0	...	128.4	...
0	71.3	41.9	1.6	5.3	19.6	5.88	4.87	-1.3	3.2	8.6	3.2	253.8	-19.2	50.5	63.4	34.7	...	147.2	...
0	63.8	48.8	1.6	4.9	20.1	6.02	4.79	3.7	2.9	9.9	2.6	265.0	13.6	52.7	65.0	45.9	...	113.9	...
Principal Lines of Business: OrdLife (99.2%), IndA&H (0.8%), GrpAnn (0.0%), IndAnn (0.0%)														Principal States: MO (7.6%), TX (5.9%), IL (5.5%), KS (5.3%), KY (4.9%)					
-8	34.3	97.9	-8.4	-25.7	-16.3	...	...	-51.5	0.6	98.4	...	...	-10.8	...	...	...	...	...	...
-9	43.0	95.1	-12.4	-33.7	-25.6	...	...	14.6	0.7	91.8	...	...	1.0	...	...	...	...	12.0	...
1	36.9	77.4	-6.9	-18.1	-15.0	...	...	10.3	0.8	82.8	...	...	-0.1	...	...	...	...	50.2	...
-8	33.2	78.4	-5.6	-14.8	-12.9	...	...	6.9	0.8	76.9	...	...	0.9	...	...	...	...	52.6	...
-37	34.0	74.9	-5.0	-13.0	-11.6	...	...	9.4	0.7	80.4	...	...	16.3	...	...	...	...	72.9	...
Principal Lines of Business: OrdLife (98.4%), IndA&H (1.6%)																			
-1,069	-5.1	27.6	0.5	1.6	2.2	4.52	4.59	-9.3	0.9	29.3	16.0	245.1	28.4	90.1	99.1	3.4	...	...	0.0
...	76.9	25.4	2.3	7.8	9.9	4.92	5.01	14.2	0.9	30.5	12.3	237.1	7.9	93.8	103.4	3.1	...	...	...
46	65.0	28.0	2.8	10.8	11.4	4.95	4.91	-5.4	0.7	36.7	9.5	200.2	24.8	103.4	113.2	1.3	...	...	...
-45	85.4	36.1	2.0	8.2	8.3	4.68	2.78	-6.5	0.8	29.9	13.5	256.6	-18.7	94.0	103.0	2.5	...	...	...
109	79.2	30.6	3.2	13.9	12.9	4.43	4.71	-10.3	0.6	37.7	10.8	218.4	17.2	104.7	114.4	2.9	...	...	...
Principal Lines of Business: OrdLife (67.0%), GrpA&H (33.7%), CrdLife (-0.2%), CrdA&H (-0.5%)														Principal States: TX (18.7%), CA (10.5%), TN (7.3%), IL (5.7%), IN (5.2%)					
-131	15.6	66.8	8.5	23.9	11.6	...	...	-6.4	0.4	383.2	...	...	7.2	...	...	...	...	...	...
591	11.9	50.5	13.1	36.6	17.1	...	...	8.8	0.4	510.3	...	...	24.5	...	...	...	...	...	...
-662	11.6	49.3	11.7	37.7	14.6	...	...	-6.3	0.3	635.9	...	...	15.2	...	...	...	...	...	...
-6,593	14.2	49.1	9.6	36.0	11.4	...	...	-12.7	0.3	614.6	...	...	-13.8	...	...	...	...	...	...
4,742	13.1	48.4	8.8	29.9	10.6	...	...	9.0	0.3	736.8	...	...	5.6	...	...	...	...	...	...
Principal Lines of Business: CrdA&H (61.3%), CrdLife (39.7%), OrdLife (-1.0%)																			
-29	70.6	29.5	3.0	2.7	8.4	...	...	9.1	2.8	58.1	0.2	...	2.3	...	...	...	...	17.1	...
79	68.9	27.8	6.2	5.4	16.7	...	...	9.3	2.7	65.0	0.2	...	15.7	...	...	...	...	13.7	...
-112	65.9	28.1	8.4	7.3	21.5	...	...	8.5	2.6	68.3	0.2	...	11.1	...	...	...	...	14.2	...
-673	69.2	27.7	6.5	5.5	16.3	...	...	6.7	2.8	66.9	0.1	...	-1.3	...	...	...	...	14.9	...
383	67.0	29.8	6.1	5.0	15.7	...	...	2.8	3.0	63.2	0.2	...	-4.4	...	...	...	...	19.1	...
Principal Lines of Business: IndA&H (99.2%), OrdLife (0.8%), IndAnn (0.0%)																			
-56	51.2	74.9	7.6	40.3	15.0	4.05	4.69	-29.6	0.1	130.8	17.6	45.7	7.4	180.3	198.8	2.7	...	...	...
231	18.9	58.7	0.4	1.5	0.7	4.14	5.12	169.4	0.3	110.2	13.4	43.9	2.1	166.7	182.3	3.0	...	...	...
-239	17.3	67.1	0.2	0.9	0.4	4.32	4.74	-3.7	0.3	97.7	10.8	36.8	0.7	158.3	172.0	3.0	...	...	...
-1,056	32.3	91.0	2.1	12.8	4.3	4.61	1.30	-42.0	0.2	95.3	8.4	27.2	-4.0	158.7	174.2	4.2	...	...	...
875	37.0	97.7	5.7	47.2	11.1	4.58	6.04	-37.3	0.1	121.5	5.3	16.5	16.2	193.9	212.7	5.2	...	...	...
Principal Lines of Business: CrdLife (82.2%), CrdA&H (17.4%), OrdLife (0.4%)														Principal States: TX (58.0%), MI (25.0%), GA (5.0%)					

Data in U.S. Dollars

COMPANY NAME Ultimate Parent Association Principal Officer Mailing Address Dom. : Began Bus. : Struct. : Mktg. Specialty Phone # AMB# NAIC#	Best's Financial Strength Rating FSC	Data Year	Balance Sheet Bonds (%)	Mort. Loans & R.E. (%)	Com & Pref. Stock (%)	All Other Assets (%)	Total Assets ($000)	Life Reserves (%)	Health Reserves (%)	Ann Res. & Dep. Liabilities (%)	All Other Liabilities (%)	Capital & Surplus ($000)	Operations Direct Premiums Written ($000)	Net Premiums Written & Deposits ($000)	Operating Cash Flow ($000)	NOG Before Taxes ($000)	NOG After Taxes ($000)	Net Income ($000)
OM FINANCIAL LIFE INS CO Old Mutual plc John A. Phelps President 1001 Fleet Street Baltimore, MD 21202 MD : 1960 : Stock : Agency Life, SPDA's, Struc Sett 410-895-0100 AMB# 006384 NAIC# 63274	**A- u** Under Review Implication: Developing **FSC XI**	'05	84.2	0.2	3.4	12.2	17,867,125	3.0	0.0	87.7	9.2	670,355	3,281,445	2,761,357	2,593,366	-176,851	-159,024	-157,886
		'06	76.6	0.1	7.4	15.9	19,507,667	3.6	0.0	88.2	8.2	647,364	2,792,486	2,734,706	1,955,743	-164,762	-164,691	-172,318
		'07	81.4	0.0	7.8	10.8	18,202,294	3.6	0.0	90.7	5.6	702,714	2,755,350	2,511,908	-1,149,211	-41,001	-40,675	-41,128
		'08	79.6	0.0	7.9	12.5	17,450,041	4.2	0.0	91.8	4.0	802,695	2,225,525	2,021,599	-591,580	65,170	67,217	-284,105
		'09	85.5	0.0	2.3	12.2	16,742,277	4.5	0.0	90.6	4.9	816,375	1,155,180	1,042,221	-718,066	60,578	59,354	-319,144
		Rating History: A- gu, 03/11/10; A- g, 03/17/09; A g, 01/09/09; A g, 09/11/08; A g, 09/25/07																
OM FINANCIAL LIFE INS CO OF NY Old Mutual plc John A. Phelps President 1001 Fleet Street Baltimore, MD 21202 NY : 1962 : Stock : Agency FPDA's, Life, Struc Sett 866-746-2624 AMB# 007122 NAIC# 69434	**A- u** Under Review Implication: Developing **FSC XI**	'05	92.4	...	3.7	3.8	493,177	5.9	...	90.3	3.8	36,809	13,386	14,473	-14,112	4,944	4,116	3,758
		'06	86.7	...	8.9	4.5	487,639	6.6	...	89.3	4.1	33,072	36,856	35,747	-5,027	-3,187	-3,283	-3,221
		'07	85.7	...	8.5	5.8	483,895	6.8	...	88.9	4.3	37,957	50,540	50,052	-1,580	5,682	4,917	4,918
		'08	88.4	...	7.9	3.7	472,553	6.8	...	90.6	2.6	34,843	58,172	56,928	-9,248	5,249	4,034	-5,920
		'09	90.6	...	2.0	7.4	461,820	6.9	...	90.2	2.9	39,371	18,980	19,389	-8,840	3,093	2,239	-3,544
		Rating History: A- gu, 03/11/10; A- g, 03/17/09; A g, 01/09/09; A g, 09/11/08; A g, 09/25/07																
OMAHA INSURANCE COMPANY Mutual of Omaha Insurance Company James T. Blackledge President Mutual of Omaha Plaza Omaha, NE 68175 NE : Stock : Not Available Inactive 402-342-7600 AMB# 060694 NAIC# 13100	**NR-2**	'05	...	...	...	...	...	...	...	...	...	...	...	...	...	...	...	...
		'06	...	...	...	...	...	...	...	...	...	...	...	...	...	...	...	...
		'07	...	...	...	...	...	...	...	...	...	...	...	...	...	...	...	...
		'08	15.7	...	...	84.3	10,448	...	...	...	100.0	10,391	...	...	168	247	161	161
		'09	16.3	...	...	83.7	10,491	...	...	...	100.0	10,470	...	...	72	111	73	73
		Rating History: NR-2, 03/15/10; NR-2, 06/12/09																
OMAHA LIFE INSURANCE COMPANY Mutual of Omaha Insurance Company James T. Blackledge President Mutual of Omaha Plaza Omaha, NE 68175 NE : Stock : Not Available Inactive 402-342-7600 AMB# 060695 NAIC# 13120	**NR-2**	'05	...	...	...	...	...	...	...	...	...	...	...	...	...	...	...	...
		'06	...	...	...	...	...	...	...	...	...	...	...	...	...	...	...	...
		'07	...	...	...	...	...	...	...	...	...	...	...	...	...	...	...	...
		'08	15.7	...	...	84.3	10,448	...	...	...	100.0	10,391	...	...	168	248	162	162
		'09	16.3	...	...	83.7	10,491	...	...	...	100.0	10,470	...	...	72	111	73	73
		Rating History: NR-2, 03/15/10; NR-2, 06/12/09																
OMNICARE HEALTH PLAN INC Coventry Health Care Inc Beverly A. Allen President & CEO 1333 Gratiot Detroit, MI 48207 MI : 2004 : Stock : Other Medicaid 313-465-1519 AMB# 064810 NAIC# 12193	**B+** Rating Outlook: Negative **FSC V**	'05	16.4	...	...	83.6	46,110	...	87.4	...	12.6	22,038	156,502	155,685	17,991	11,606	8,122	8,122
		'06	17.5	...	...	82.5	48,361	...	84.2	...	15.8	31,657	148,043	146,962	4,010	19,673	13,482	13,476
		'07	48.2	...	...	51.8	46,315	...	57.4	...	42.6	26,609	177,245	176,086	-3,685	12,299	8,454	8,446
		'08	48.3	...	...	51.7	38,594	...	59.7	...	40.3	20,822	178,697	177,558	-8,790	2,479	2,224	2,097
		'09	40.6	...	...	59.4	43,899	...	56.2	...	43.8	22,991	189,913	188,810	4,062	3,637	1,569	1,616
		Rating History: B+, 02/12/10; B+, 11/19/08; B+, 10/30/07; B+, 07/11/07; B+, 10/27/06																
ON LOK SENIOR HEALTH SERVICES Linda P. Towbridge President 1333 Bush Street San Francisco, CA 94109 CA : 1971 : Non-Profit : Not Available Medicaid, Medicare, Group A&H 415-292-8888 AMB# 064666	**NR-5**	'05	...	9.7	...	90.3	45,831	...	...	...	100.0	36,780	58,887	58,887	4,119	1,806	1,806	1,806
		'06	...	...	...	100.0	58,628	...	...	...	100.0	45,218	69,106	69,106	17,396	8,438	8,438	8,438
		'07	...	...	...	100.0	72,279	...	...	...	100.0	59,587	85,260	85,260	10,599	14,365	14,365	14,365
		'08	...	5.7	...	94.3	79,598	...	...	...	100.0	68,259	83,702	83,702	10,205	8,672	8,672	8,672
		'09	...	9.5	...	90.5	89,741	...	...	...	100.0	64,044	83,098	83,098	14,551	-4,215	-4,215	-4,215
		Rating History: NR-5, 03/23/10; NR-5, 04/08/09; NR-5, 03/11/08; NR-5, 05/07/07; NR-5, 05/22/06																
ONENATION INSURANCE COMPANY WellPoint Inc. Joan E. Herman President 120 Monument Circle Indianapolis, IN 46204 IN : 1975 : Stock : Broker Group A&H, Group Life, Maj med 317-488-6000 AMB# 008665 NAIC# 85286	**NR-3**	'05	81.3	...	0.2	18.5	95,801	0.5	11.4	...	88.1	85,272	451	3,045	2,061	15,145	8,716	8,839
		'06	88.0	...	0.2	11.7	91,464	...	49.6	...	50.4	90,584	351	117	-5,615	3,988	4,674	4,691
		'07	87.5	...	0.2	12.3	93,780	...	39.6	...	60.4	92,878	294	264	8,526	2,961	2,222	2,105
		'08	86.0	...	0.2	13.9	75,179	...	48.0	...	52.0	74,433	259	241	-17,823	2,685	1,420	946
		'09	6.7	...	...	93.3	78,313	...	68.4	...	31.6	77,921	243	814	4,610	3,846	2,374	2,890
		Rating History: NR-3, 04/27/10; NR-3, 01/23/09; NR-3, 03/20/08; A-, 11/06/06; A-, 12/29/05																
OPTIMA HEALTH INSURANCE CO Sentara Healthcare Michael M. Dudley President 4417 Corporation Lane Norfolk, VA 23462 VA : 1994 : Stock : Broker Group A&H, Medicare 757-552-7401 AMB# 068490 NAIC# 70715	**NR-5**	'05	31.4	...	...	68.6	29,908	...	46.3	...	53.7	19,817	49,150	50,574	4,799	36	311	281
		'06	31.4	...	...	68.6	33,867	...	56.6	...	43.4	22,058	74,437	75,778	300	232	-241	-261
		'07	28.6	...	...	71.4	37,931	...	58.7	...	41.3	24,464	88,258	89,830	7,656	4,344	2,673	2,755
		'08	25.9	...	...	74.1	43,700	...	61.3	...	38.7	22,286	118,237	119,889	5,885	101	344	384
		'09	60.7	...	6.1	33.3	46,241	...	58.8	...	41.2	23,027	153,346	155,142	2,214	2,219	1,252	1,413
		Rating History: NR-5, 04/19/10; NR-5, 04/08/09; NR-5, 03/11/08; NR-5, 04/02/07; NR-5, 04/21/06																
OPTIMA HEALTH PLAN Sentara Healthcare Michael M. Dudley President 4417 Corporation Lane Virginia Beach, VA 23462 VA : 1984 : Non-Profit : Broker Medicaid, Group A&H, FEHBP 757-552-7306 AMB# 068821 NAIC# 95281	**NR-5**	'05	13.1	...	...	86.9	233,599	...	62.7	...	37.3	161,436	697,379	695,956	27,669	82,440	82,438	82,335
		'06	13.5	...	...	86.5	257,608	...	69.8	...	30.2	182,892	782,147	780,626	21,887	80,089	79,857	79,793
		'07	12.7	...	...	87.3	264,820	...	73.7	...	26.3	188,093	792,929	791,164	13,974	74,345	74,253	74,496
		'08	13.2	...	...	86.8	256,298	...	67.7	...	32.3	153,378	867,473	865,477	-9,545	44,502	43,255	43,380
		'09	41.6	...	2.9	55.5	247,388	...	60.6	...	39.4	130,783	986,868	984,606	-48,906	18,184	17,442	18,304
		Rating History: NR-5, 04/20/10; NR-5, 08/26/09; B+ pd, 07/28/08; B+ pd, 07/31/07; B+ pd, 09/01/06																

BEST'S PROFITABILITY, LEVERAGE AND LIQUIDITY TESTS 2005 – 2009

Data in U.S. Dollars

—	Profitability Tests							Leverage Tests						Liquidity Tests					
Un-Realized Capital Gains ($000)	Benefits Paid to NPW & Dep (%)	Comm. & Expenses to NPW & Dep (%)	NOG to Total Assets (%)	NOG to Total Rev (%)	Operating Return on Equity (%)	Net Yield (%)	Total Return (%)	Change in NPW & Dep (%)	NPW & Dep to Capital (X)	Capital & Surplus to Liabilities (%)	Surplus Relief (%)	Reins Leverage (%)	Change in Capital (%)	Quick Liquidity (%)	Current Liquidity (%)	Non-Invest Grade Bonds to Capital (%)	Delinq. & Foreclosed Mortgages to Capital (%)	Mort. & Credit Tenant Loans & R.E. to Capital (%)	Affiliated Invest to Capital (%)
-11,294	37.5	20.5	-1.0	-4.0	-22.6	5.37	5.59	-16.8	3.7	4.5	20.5	224.2	-6.4	55.9	74.4	60.7	...	19.6	15.9
19,606	73.6	19.0	-0.9	-4.0	-25.0	5.48	7.15	-1.0	3.7	4.0	23.5	275.1	-0.7	64.9	83.4	15.0	...	18.4	18.5
-8,922	155.3	18.7	-0.2	-1.1	-6.0	5.80	5.32	-8.1	3.1	4.7	19.2	263.5	8.8	53.9	73.8	39.7	...	12.6	16.3
-147,435	118.0	26.6	0.4	2.8	8.9	5.95	1.58	-19.5	2.5	4.9	-7.5	283.2	0.8	54.0	72.7	60.0	...	12.5	15.7
173,223	216.4	11.4	0.3	3.5	7.3	5.64	3.82	-48.4	1.3	5.2	14.6	299.5	1.7	53.6	71.2	126.1	...	12.3	16.0

Principal Lines of Business: IndAnn (77.5%), OrdLife (22.4%), GrpAnn (0.1%), GrpA&H (0.0%), GrpLife (0.0%)
Principal States: CA (15.1%), TX (9.4%), FL (8.9%), PA (7.2%), NJ (5.1%)

1	296.4	42.8	0.8	9.1	11.8	6.16	6.53	-32.2	0.4	8.6	0.9	8.5	11.5	54.6	74.2	63.1	...	...	...
...	209.5	17.9	-0.7	-4.9	-9.4	6.02	6.42	147.0	1.0	8.0	1.0	42.1	-8.0	57.8	76.9	61.2	...	...	...
...	151.4	11.6	1.0	6.2	13.8	5.91	6.24	40.0	1.2	9.3	0.4	38.1	14.4	61.7	80.9	39.3	...	...	...
-247	129.1	10.0	0.8	4.6	11.1	6.18	4.36	13.7	1.6	8.0	0.4	35.9	-14.9	60.3	77.6	50.2	...	...	...
-838	276.5	26.8	0.5	4.8	6.0	5.97	4.83	-65.9	0.5	9.3	0.3	29.9	12.3	67.9	83.9	70.7	...	...	...

Principal Lines of Business: IndAnn (88.8%), OrdLife (11.2%)
Principal States: NY (99.9%)

...	...	...	...	...	...	...	...	...	...	...	...	...	...	...	...	...	...	...	...
...	...	...	...	...	...	...	...	...	...	...	...	...	...	...	...	...	...	...	...
...	...	...	...	...	...	...	...	...	...	...	...	...	...	...	...	...	...	...	...
...	...	...	...	57.8	...	...	...	...	...	999.9	...	...	...	999.9	999.9	...	...	...	...
...	...	...	0.7	53.6	0.7	1.30	1.30	...	...	999.9	...	...	0.7	999.9	999.9	...	...	...	83.3

...	...	...	...	...	...	...	...	...	...	...	...	...	...	...	...	...	...	...	...
...	...	...	...	...	...	...	...	...	...	...	...	...	...	...	...	...	...	...	...
...	...	...	...	...	...	...	...	...	...	...	...	...	...	...	...	...	...	...	...
...	...	...	...	57.9	...	...	...	...	...	999.9	...	...	...	999.9	999.9	...	...	...	...
...	...	...	0.7	53.6	0.7	1.30	1.30	...	...	999.9	...	...	0.7	999.9	999.9	...	...	...	83.3

...	78.0	9.3	20.5	5.5	44.8	3.55	3.55	294.8	7.1	91.5	...	2.3	54.7	314.1	330.5	...	...	...	...
...	73.2	8.9	28.5	9.6	50.2	5.27	5.26	-5.6	4.6	189.5	...	0.0	43.7	487.3	514.2	...	...	...	...
...	81.0	7.6	17.9	5.0	29.0	4.78	4.76	19.8	6.6	135.0	...	1.5	-15.9	304.3	324.9	...	...	...	...
...	85.6	8.3	5.2	1.3	9.4	3.50	3.17	0.8	8.5	117.2	...	2.3	-21.7	269.7	289.9	...	...	...	...
...	85.5	11.7	3.8	0.8	7.2	2.30	2.43	6.3	8.2	110.0	...	2.3	10.4	267.3	286.1	...	...	...	...

Principal Lines of Business: Medicaid (100.0%)
Principal States: MI (100.0%)

...	92.5	7.2	4.1	3.0	5.0	2.60	2.60	3.2	1.6	406.4	...	...	5.2	170.9	170.9	...	...	12.1	12.1
...	84.8	7.1	16.2	11.7	20.6	4.04	4.04	17.4	1.5	337.2	...	...	22.9	237.3	237.3	...	...	...	...
...	80.3	7.9	21.9	16.0	27.4	4.80	4.80	23.4	1.4	469.5	...	...	31.8	275.3	275.3	...	...	...	...
...	85.3	8.0	11.4	10.0	13.6	4.32	4.32	-1.8	1.2	602.0	...	...	14.6	176.8	176.8	...	...	6.6	6.6
...	90.5	8.3	-5.0	-5.4	-6.4	3.65	3.65	-0.7	1.3	249.2	...	...	-6.2	65.2	65.2	...	...	13.3	13.3

Principal Lines of Business: Medicaid (63.8%), Medicare (34.1%), CompHosp/Med (2.1%)

...	-9.1	-93.5	9.0	79.6	11.0	4.09	4.23	-96.2	0.0	809.9	0.3	27.0	15.8	802.8	868.8	...	...	...	...
...	36.5	591.3	5.0	55.7	5.3	4.30	4.33	-96.1	0.0	999.9	0.1	25.1	6.2	999.9	999.9	...	...	...	...
-8	21.0	544.6	2.4	49.5	2.4	4.54	4.40	125.0	0.0	999.9	0.0	23.4	2.5	999.9	999.9	...	...	...	...
14	33.6	343.9	1.7	39.4	1.7	4.12	3.58	-8.7	0.0	999.9	0.0	22.6	-19.9	999.9	999.9	0.2	...	...	...
-6	-7.7	23.1	3.1	59.8	3.1	1.05	1.72	237.2	0.0	999.9	0.0	20.9	4.7	999.9	999.9	...	...	...	...

Principal Lines of Business: Life (99.9%), Dental (0.1%)
Principal States: NM (53.4%), CO (18.9%), NV (15.7%), WY (6.5%), UT (4.1%)

...	82.1	19.5	1.1	0.6	1.8	3.13	3.02	-14.6	2.6	196.4	...	...	38.7	449.6	470.0	...	...	...	...
...	83.4	18.1	-0.8	-0.3	-1.1	4.82	4.75	49.8	3.4	186.8	...	...	11.3	376.9	393.0	...	...	...	...
...	79.8	17.1	7.4	2.9	11.5	4.84	5.09	18.5	3.7	181.7	...	...	10.9	428.5	449.0	...	...	...	...
...	84.9	15.7	0.8	0.3	1.5	2.29	2.39	33.5	5.4	104.1	...	...	-8.9	335.9	337.9	...	...	...	...
259	84.4	14.6	2.8	0.8	5.5	1.24	2.19	29.4	6.7	99.2	...	...	3.3	227.8	235.0	...	...	...	...

Principal Lines of Business: CompHosp/Med (66.5%), Medicare (32.3%), OtherHlth (1.2%)
Principal States: VA (100.0%)

...	82.0	7.2	37.5	11.7	54.8	3.10	3.06	18.7	4.3	223.7	...	...	15.8	524.4	541.7	...	...	...	...
...	83.2	8.0	32.5	10.1	46.4	4.85	4.82	12.2	4.3	244.8	...	...	13.3	549.7	575.1	...	...	...	...
...	83.7	8.5	28.4	9.2	40.0	4.99	5.09	1.3	4.2	245.1	...	...	2.8	553.0	578.3	...	...	...	...
...	86.8	8.8	16.6	5.0	25.3	2.16	2.21	9.4	5.6	149.0	...	...	-18.5	413.9	415.2	...	...	...	...
1,134	90.6	7.9	6.9	1.8	12.3	1.08	1.97	13.8	7.5	112.2	...	...	-14.7	202.0	206.8	...	...	...	...

Principal Lines of Business: Medicaid (47.9%), CompHosp/Med (44.8%), FEHBP (7.3%)
Principal States: VA (100.0%)

Data in U.S. Dollars

COMPANY NAME / Ultimate Parent Association / Principal Officer / Mailing Address / Dom. : Began Bus. : Struct. : Mktg. / Specialty / Phone # / AMB# / NAIC# — Best's Financial Strength Rating / FSC

Balance Sheet: Data Year; Bonds (%); Mort. Loans & R.E. (%); Com & Pref. Stock (%); All Other Assets (%); Total Assets ($000); Life Reserves (%); Health Reserves (%); Ann Res. & Dep. Liabilities (%); All Other Liabilities (%); Capital & Surplus ($000). Operations: Direct Premiums Written ($000); Net Premiums Written & Deposits ($000); Operating Cash Flow ($000); NOG Before Taxes ($000); NOG After Taxes ($000); Net Income ($000)

OPTIMUM CHOICE INC
UnitedHealth Group Inc
James P. Cronin, Jr.
President & CEO
4 Taft Court
Rockville, MD 20850
MD : 1988 : Stock : Broker
Group A&H
301-762-8205
AMB# 068764 NAIC# 96940

A — Rating Outlook: Stable — FSC VIII

Data Year	Bonds (%)	Mort. Loans & R.E. (%)	Com & Pref. Stock (%)	All Other Assets (%)	Total Assets ($000)	Life Reserves (%)	Health Reserves (%)	Ann Res. & Dep. Liabilities (%)	All Other Liabilities (%)	Capital & Surplus ($000)	Direct Premiums Written ($000)	Net Premiums Written & Deposits ($000)	Operating Cash Flow ($000)	NOG Before Taxes ($000)	NOG After Taxes ($000)	Net Income ($000)
'05	44.0	...	...	56.0	296,946	...	23.0	...	77.0	132,156	1,160,737	1,159,577	31,982	75,769	49,756	49,627
'06	53.3	...	...	46.7	268,388	...	55.4	...	44.6	126,125	1,177,969	1,176,887	-40,901	87,021	59,403	59,213
'07	53.7	...	...	46.3	335,097	...	47.8	...	52.2	190,981	901,030	900,154	80,588	119,909	80,417	80,451
'08	52.0	...	...	48.0	360,586	...	46.1	...	53.9	258,652	654,929	654,283	43,777	88,799	60,277	58,576
'09	63.4	...	...	36.6	162,255	...	56.0	...	44.0	102,676	460,049	459,591	-189,001	66,386	44,610	45,452

Rating History: A, 06/15/09; A, 01/29/08; A, 11/21/07; A, 11/16/06; A, 08/17/06

OPTIMUM RE INSURANCE COMPANY
Optimum Group Inc
Mario Georgiev
President
1345 River Bend Drive, Suite 100
Dallas, TX 75247
TX : 1978 : Stock : Other Direct
Reins
214-528-2020
AMB# 008863 NAIC# 88099

A- — Rating Outlook: Stable — FSC V

Data Year	Bonds (%)	Mort. Loans & R.E. (%)	Com & Pref. Stock (%)	All Other Assets (%)	Total Assets ($000)	Life Reserves (%)	Health Reserves (%)	Ann Res. & Dep. Liabilities (%)	All Other Liabilities (%)	Capital & Surplus ($000)	Direct Premiums Written ($000)	Net Premiums Written & Deposits ($000)	Operating Cash Flow ($000)	NOG Before Taxes ($000)	NOG After Taxes ($000)	Net Income ($000)
'05	79.2	7.5	2.7	10.6	55,125	82.1	...	...	17.9	21,741	...	26,185	9,450	474	255	320
'06	87.1	7.0	3.6	2.3	58,079	89.4	...	...	10.6	22,832	...	22,361	5,483	1,445	1,146	1,249
'07	84.0	6.1	4.2	5.8	65,528	88.8	...	...	11.2	23,511	...	24,175	13,656	2,109	1,556	1,556
'08	91.4	8.2	5.3	-4.9	71,864	90.2	0.5	...	9.4	24,081	...	26,898	221	5,269	4,465	4,465
'09	81.5	3.9	5.8	8.8	78,977	89.4	0.8	...	9.7	24,173	...	31,923	14,106	2,098	1,341	1,375

Rating History: A-, 05/11/10; A-, 06/01/09; A-, 06/10/08; A-, 06/14/07; A-, 06/19/06

ORANGE PREV & TRTMT INT MED AS
Michael D. Stephens
Chairman
1120 West La Veta Avenue
Orange, CA 92868
CA : 1995 : Non-Profit : Broker
Medicaid, Medicare
714-246-8400
AMB# 064713

NR-5

Data Year	Bonds (%)	Mort. Loans & R.E. (%)	Com & Pref. Stock (%)	All Other Assets (%)	Total Assets ($000)	Life Reserves (%)	Health Reserves (%)	Ann Res. & Dep. Liabilities (%)	All Other Liabilities (%)	Capital & Surplus ($000)	Direct Premiums Written ($000)	Net Premiums Written & Deposits ($000)	Operating Cash Flow ($000)	NOG Before Taxes ($000)	NOG After Taxes ($000)	Net Income ($000)
'05	...	...	...	100.0	244,701	...	...	...	100.0	105,031	811,410	811,410	-19,095	-24,374	-24,374	-24,374
'06	...	...	...	100.0	327,766	...	...	...	100.0	80,723	917,982	917,982	83,606	-24,308	-24,308	-24,308
'07	...	...	...	100.0	304,936	...	...	...	100.0	139,150	931,298	931,298	9,409	58,427	58,427	58,427
'08	...	...	...	100.0	303,799	...	...	...	100.0	148,840	979,399	979,399	-29,802	9,690	9,690	9,690
'09	...	...	...	100.0	327,383	...	...	...	100.0	131,350	1,078,195	1,078,195	4,603	-17,490	-17,490	-17,490

Rating History: NR-5, 03/23/10; NR-5, 04/08/09; NR-5, 03/11/08; NR-5, 08/07/07; NR-5, 04/07/06

OREGON DENTAL SERVICE
Oregon Dental Association
Robert G. Gootee
President & CEO
601 SW Second Avenue
Portland, OR 97204
OR : 1954 : Non-Profit : Broker
Dental
503-228-6554
AMB# 064364 NAIC# 54941

B++ — Rating Outlook: Negative — FSC VII

Data Year	Bonds (%)	Mort. Loans & R.E. (%)	Com & Pref. Stock (%)	All Other Assets (%)	Total Assets ($000)	Life Reserves (%)	Health Reserves (%)	Ann Res. & Dep. Liabilities (%)	All Other Liabilities (%)	Capital & Surplus ($000)	Direct Premiums Written ($000)	Net Premiums Written & Deposits ($000)	Operating Cash Flow ($000)	NOG Before Taxes ($000)	NOG After Taxes ($000)	Net Income ($000)
'05	15.0	2.6	66.4	16.1	138,123	...	12.8	...	87.2	85,517	130,127	130,410	6,656	4,328	4,328	5,796
'06	15.0	5.1	67.5	12.4	133,931	...	13.5	...	86.5	88,442	128,014	128,798	-5,219	2,167	2,167	4,891
'07	15.1	4.9	66.4	13.5	136,180	...	6.6	...	93.4	90,134	104,283	105,406	3,897	1,525	1,525	3,806
'08	22.0	5.7	60.2	12.0	114,436	...	54.1	...	45.9	64,236	102,875	104,418	-3,167	-2,951	-2,951	-4,676
'09	14.1	5.6	74.1	6.1	113,294	...	43.3	...	56.7	83,203	77,325	78,073	-23,992	-2,763	-2,763	-5,855

Rating History: B++, 05/28/10; B++, 06/09/09; B++, 06/17/08; B++, 06/12/07; B++, 04/28/06

ORKNEY RE INC
Scottish Re Group Limited
Meredith A. Ratajczak
President & CEO
13840 Ballantyne Corporate Place
Charlotte, NC 28277
DE : 2005 : Stock : Other
Annuity, Life, Reins
704-943-2085
AMB# 060559 NAIC# 12266

NR-4

Data Year	Bonds (%)	Mort. Loans & R.E. (%)	Com & Pref. Stock (%)	All Other Assets (%)	Total Assets ($000)	Life Reserves (%)	Health Reserves (%)	Ann Res. & Dep. Liabilities (%)	All Other Liabilities (%)	Capital & Surplus ($000)	Direct Premiums Written ($000)	Net Premiums Written & Deposits ($000)	Operating Cash Flow ($000)	NOG Before Taxes ($000)	NOG After Taxes ($000)	Net Income ($000)
'05	88.0	...	...	12.0	911,857	98.3	...	...	1.7	145,542	...	195,917	828,543	-562,809	-562,783	-562,783
'06	85.8	...	...	14.2	1,036,698	98.6	...	...	1.4	123,169	...	121,279	122,841	-68,584	-67,372	-67,372
'07	89.8	...	...	10.2	1,176,664	81.6	...	...	18.4	874,876	...	105,975	167,794	11,803	-23,499	-23,834
'08	85.4	...	...	14.6	1,019,690	93.2	...	...	6.8	727,890	...	99,400	-136,824	30,092	18,887	-185,630
'09	...	...	...	...	...	...	...	...	...	...	...	...	...	...	...	...

Rating History: NR-4, 06/12/09; D, 06/12/09; D, 02/05/09; C- g, 07/23/08; C+ gu, 06/12/08

OUACHITA LIFE INSURANCE CO
Munich Reinsurance Company
John W. Hayden
Chairman & CEO
P.O. Box 5323
Cincinnati, OH 45201-5323
AR : 1987 : Stock : Inactive
Inactive
513-943-7200
AMB# 068362 NAIC# 88820

NR-3

Data Year	Bonds (%)	Mort. Loans & R.E. (%)	Com & Pref. Stock (%)	All Other Assets (%)	Total Assets ($000)	Life Reserves (%)	Health Reserves (%)	Ann Res. & Dep. Liabilities (%)	All Other Liabilities (%)	Capital & Surplus ($000)	Direct Premiums Written ($000)	Net Premiums Written & Deposits ($000)	Operating Cash Flow ($000)	NOG Before Taxes ($000)	NOG After Taxes ($000)	Net Income ($000)
'05	...	...	...	100.0	215	71.3	1.4	...	27.3	201	...	4	2	-3	-3	-3
'06	...	...	...	100.0	210	...	...	...	100.0	119	...	...	-10	7	6	6
'07	...	...	...	100.0	120	...	...	...	100.0	120	...	...	-86	2	1	1
'08	...	...	...	100.0	124	...	...	...	100.0	122	...	...	4	3	2	2
'09	...	...	...	100.0	126	...	...	...	100.0	124	...	...	4	2	1	1

Rating History: NR-3, 03/10/10; NR-3, 05/15/09; NR-3, 04/09/08; NR-3, 10/18/07; NR-3, 05/31/07

OXFORD HEALTH INS INC
UnitedHealth Group Inc
William J. Golden
President & CEO
48 Monroe Turnpike
Trumbull, CT 06611
NY : 1987 : Stock : Not Available
A&H, Group A&H, Ind A&H
203-459-6000
AMB# 060022 NAIC# 78026

A — Rating Outlook: Stable — FSC IX

Data Year	Bonds (%)	Mort. Loans & R.E. (%)	Com & Pref. Stock (%)	All Other Assets (%)	Total Assets ($000)	Life Reserves (%)	Health Reserves (%)	Ann Res. & Dep. Liabilities (%)	All Other Liabilities (%)	Capital & Surplus ($000)	Direct Premiums Written ($000)	Net Premiums Written & Deposits ($000)	Operating Cash Flow ($000)	NOG Before Taxes ($000)	NOG After Taxes ($000)	Net Income ($000)
'05	60.1	...	...	39.9	1,043,319	...	45.4	...	54.6	456,423	2,632,759	2,638,683	290,041	336,799	218,386	219,016
'06	55.5	...	...	44.5	1,224,482	...	45.9	...	54.1	615,216	3,256,443	1,454,824	232,093	235,614	160,115	159,257
'07	48.1	...	...	51.9	1,448,755	...	27.1	...	72.9	725,949	3,734,468	1,869,156	211,263	203,872	133,814	134,363
'08	67.6	...	...	32.4	1,289,613	...	25.9	...	74.1	617,469	4,305,554	2,161,448	-230,272	212,731	141,980	140,524
'09	65.6	...	...	34.4	1,018,928	...	14.1	...	85.9	315,084	4,357,891	2,177,529	-211,141	98,804	72,362	75,121

Rating History: A, 06/15/09; A-, 01/29/08; A-, 11/21/07; A-, 11/16/06; A-, 08/17/06

OXFORD HEALTH PLANS (CT) INC
UnitedHealth Group Inc
Stephen J. Farrell
President & CEO
48 Monroe Turnpike
Trumbull, CT 06611
CT : 1993 : Stock : Broker
Group A&H, Health
203-459-6000
AMB# 068933 NAIC# 96798

A — Rating Outlook: Stable — FSC V

Data Year	Bonds (%)	Mort. Loans & R.E. (%)	Com & Pref. Stock (%)	All Other Assets (%)	Total Assets ($000)	Life Reserves (%)	Health Reserves (%)	Ann Res. & Dep. Liabilities (%)	All Other Liabilities (%)	Capital & Surplus ($000)	Direct Premiums Written ($000)	Net Premiums Written & Deposits ($000)	Operating Cash Flow ($000)	NOG Before Taxes ($000)	NOG After Taxes ($000)	Net Income ($000)
'05	85.0	...	...	15.0	90,902	...	53.3	...	46.7	43,940	256,479	255,534	-890	27,699	18,259	18,518
'06	56.2	...	...	43.8	84,211	...	47.1	...	52.9	44,108	243,595	243,155	-6,614	22,129	14,740	14,009
'07	66.8	...	...	33.2	79,664	...	67.3	...	32.7	47,695	204,564	203,960	-2,870	24,197	14,993	15,109
'08	65.1	...	...	34.9	76,567	...	55.6	...	44.4	42,002	177,970	177,206	1,227	13,503	9,479	9,643
'09	57.7	...	...	42.3	55,592	...	13.1	...	86.9	22,956	146,915	146,237	-16,869	-218	86	229

Rating History: A, 06/15/09; A-, 01/29/08; A-, 11/21/07; A-, 11/16/06; A-, 08/17/06

OXFORD HEALTH PLANS (NJ) INC
UnitedHealth Group Inc
Michael McGuire
President & CEO
48 Monroe Turnpike
Trumbull, CT 06611
NJ : 1985 : Stock : Broker
Group A&H, Health, Ind A&H
203-459-6000
AMB# 068934 NAIC# 95506

A — Rating Outlook: Stable — FSC VIII

Data Year	Bonds (%)	Mort. Loans & R.E. (%)	Com & Pref. Stock (%)	All Other Assets (%)	Total Assets ($000)	Life Reserves (%)	Health Reserves (%)	Ann Res. & Dep. Liabilities (%)	All Other Liabilities (%)	Capital & Surplus ($000)	Direct Premiums Written ($000)	Net Premiums Written & Deposits ($000)	Operating Cash Flow ($000)	NOG Before Taxes ($000)	NOG After Taxes ($000)	Net Income ($000)
'05	58.6	...	...	41.4	220,217	...	48.1	...	51.9	99,370	588,538	581,328	24,260	67,647	45,446	45,166
'06	59.5	...	...	40.5	216,873	...	48.6	...	51.4	108,839	557,013	552,034	1,037	80,380	51,327	51,314
'07	65.2	...	...	34.8	195,680	...	62.5	...	37.5	100,671	575,146	571,090	-21,314	71,920	47,340	47,515
'08	51.8	...	...	48.2	209,827	...	65.6	...	34.4	118,181	588,620	583,404	-5,185	65,016	51,600	51,613
'09	48.6	...	...	51.4	253,883	...	28.6	...	71.4	156,994	665,092	663,639	76,967	39,808	28,362	28,146

Rating History: A, 06/15/09; A-, 01/29/08; A-, 11/21/07; A-, 11/16/06; A-, 08/17/06

BEST'S PROFITABILITY, LEVERAGE AND LIQUIDITY TESTS 2005 – 2009

Data in U.S. Dollars

—	Profitability Tests							Leverage Tests						Liquidity Tests					
Un-Realized Capital Gains ($000)	Benefits Paid to NPW & Dep (%)	Comm. & Expenses to NPW & Dep (%)	NOG to Total Assets (%)	NOG to Total Rev (%)	Operating Return on Equity (%)	Net Yield (%)	Total Return (%)	Change in NPW & Dep (%)	NPW & Dep to Capital (X)	Capital & Surplus to Liabilities (%)	Surplus Relief (%)	Reins Leverage (%)	Change in Capital (%)	Quick Liquidity (%)	Current Liquidity (%)	Non-Invest Grade Bonds to Capital (%)	Delinq. & Foreclosed Mortgages to Capital (%)	Mort. & Credit Tenant Loans & R.E. to Capital (%)	Affiliated Invest to Capital (%)
...	85.7	8.6	17.8	4.2	38.1	4.11	4.06	4.0	8.8	80.2	...	...	2.5	195.3	207.7	...	...	...	...
...	85.4	8.0	21.0	5.0	46.0	4.60	4.52	1.5	9.3	88.7	...	...	-4.6	162.4	175.5	...	...	...	...
...	80.3	7.7	26.7	8.8	50.7	5.21	5.22	-23.5	4.7	132.5	...	...	51.4	245.1	264.4	...	...	...	...
-1	80.2	8.1	17.3	9.1	26.8	3.74	3.19	-27.3	2.5	253.7	...	...	35.4	416.2	444.1	0.5	...	...	...
1	78.8	8.1	17.1	9.6	24.7	2.81	3.17	-29.8	4.5	172.3	...	...	-60.3	252.1	270.8	...	...	...	...
	Principal Lines of Business: CompHosp/Med (100.0%)													Principal States: MD (53.8%), VA (24.5%), DC (16.2%), WV (3.1%)					
33	43.5	36.0	0.5	0.7	1.2	3.75	4.40	-6.0	1.2	67.3	39.6	391.2	-0.1	146.8	156.7	...	...	18.6	22.9
221	48.8	41.7	2.0	3.1	5.1	4.14	4.77	-14.6	1.0	67.2	48.9	437.9	5.2	149.9	161.7	...	...	17.4	22.0
236	50.7	33.5	2.5	3.8	6.7	4.42	4.57	8.1	1.0	58.1	58.0	502.2	3.2	176.2	187.5	...	...	16.6	22.5
-90	54.2	38.2	6.5	8.8	18.8	3.77	3.04	11.3	1.1	51.9	61.3	599.6	2.0	141.1	153.1	...	...	24.0	14.8
294	54.6	31.3	1.8	2.6	5.6	3.34	3.86	18.7	1.3	46.0	64.6	631.9	1.2	148.9	160.6	...	...	12.4	17.3
	Principal Lines of Business: OrdLife (76.2%), GrpA&H (13.2%), GrpLife (7.6%), IndA&H (2.9%)																		
...	99.9	3.8	-9.7	-3.0	-20.8	2.51	2.51	2.7	7.7	75.2	...	...	-18.8	17.3	17.3	...	...	...	...
...	100.3	2.9	-8.5	-2.6	-26.2	3.43	3.43	13.1	11.4	32.7	...	...	-23.1	45.5	45.5	...	...	...	...
...	90.5	4.7	18.5	6.2	53.1	8.04	8.04	1.5	6.7	83.9	...	...	72.4	68.8	68.8	...	...	...	...
...	96.0	4.3	3.2	1.0	6.7	5.67	5.67	5.2	6.6	96.1	...	...	7.0	47.3	47.3	...	...	...	...
...	98.1	4.3	-5.5	-1.6	-12.5	4.46	4.46	10.1	8.2	67.0	...	...	-11.8	35.5	35.5	...	...	...	...
	Principal Lines of Business: Medicaid (90.4%), Medicare (9.6%)																		
21,979	86.7	11.4	3.5	3.3	5.9	2.01	26.20	2.2	1.5	162.6	...	...	39.1	77.3	87.4	...	...	4.1	77.8
841	86.0	12.8	1.6	1.7	2.5	0.63	3.64	-1.2	1.5	194.4	...	...	3.4	53.1	64.5	...	...	7.8	83.9
-33	84.7	14.9	1.1	1.4	1.7	1.08	2.98	-18.2	1.2	195.7	...	...	1.9	75.6	85.9	...	...	7.4	83.7
-20,783	85.3	18.3	-2.4	-2.8	-3.8	0.91	-17.45	-0.9	1.6	128.0	...	...	-28.7	67.9	73.0	0.3	...	10.2	106.5
24,335	90.5	14.5	-2.4	-3.5	-3.7	1.30	24.70	-25.2	0.9	276.5	...	...	29.5	41.1	46.8	0.0	...	7.7	106.2
	Principal Lines of Business: Dental (100.0%)													Principal States: OR (98.0%)					
...	23.3	11.6	...	-99.9	...	...	...	...	1.3	19.1	...	...	...	85.1	97.9	...	...	...	...
...	53.0	21.0	-6.9	-40.4	-50.1	5.22	5.22	-38.1	1.0	13.6	...	...	-14.9	87.7	99.7	...	...	...	...
...	62.5	21.2	-2.1	-14.6	-4.7	5.47	5.42	-12.6	0.1	291.9	...	...	604.5	308.5	352.8	...	...	...	...
...	75.3	19.8	1.7	13.2	2.4	4.14	-13.71	-6.2	0.1	249.4	...	...	-16.9	269.6	306.2	4.3	...	...	...
...	...	...	...	...	...	...	...	...	...	...	...	...	...	...	...	...	...	...	...
...	100.1	141.5	-1.4	-50.0	-1.5	0.99	0.99	-81.0	0.0	999.9	...	...	-1.4	999.9	999.9	...	...	...	...
...	...	...	2.6	70.6	3.5	3.81	3.81	-99.9	...	130.6	...	...	-40.9	222.7	222.7	...	...	...	...
...	...	...	0.6	33.8	0.8	1.73	1.73	...	...	...	...	...	0.8	...	...	...	...	...	...
...	...	...	1.9	46.4	1.9	4.25	4.25	...	...	999.9	...	...	2.0	999.9	999.9	...	...	...	...
...	...	...	1.2	40.3	1.2	2.94	2.94	...	...	999.9	...	...	1.2	999.9	999.9	...	...	...	...
...	77.2	11.2	24.5	8.2	57.0	3.67	3.74	40.4	5.8	77.8	...	0.0	47.5	203.8	216.2	...	...	...	...
-90	73.6	12.3	14.1	10.8	29.9	2.65	2.57	-44.9	2.4	101.0	...	30.8	34.8	252.3	266.9	0.3	...	...	...
1,049	79.6	11.2	10.0	7.0	20.0	2.30	2.43	28.5	2.6	100.4	...	32.6	18.0	268.7	282.6	...	...	...	...
1,123	79.8	11.1	10.4	6.6	21.1	1.74	1.71	15.6	3.5	91.9	...	40.0	-14.9	196.0	209.8	...	...	...	...
-2,082	84.6	11.4	6.3	3.3	15.5	1.19	1.26	0.7	6.9	44.8	...	85.1	-49.0	157.9	168.3	...	...	...	...
	Principal Lines of Business: CompHosp/Med (100.0%)													Principal States: NY (79.1%), NJ (15.0%), CT (6.0%)					
...	77.0	13.4	20.2	7.1	45.2	3.80	4.12	-2.3	5.8	93.6	...	3.4	19.4	144.3	161.6	1.5	...	...	...
-7	78.7	13.5	16.8	6.0	33.5	4.12	3.17	-4.8	5.5	110.0	...	2.4	0.4	231.9	244.3	0.4	...	...	...
7	78.0	12.0	18.3	7.2	32.7	5.25	5.42	-16.1	4.3	149.2	...	3.4	8.1	262.3	273.7	...	...	...	...
...	81.5	12.2	12.1	5.3	21.1	3.46	3.69	-13.1	4.2	121.5	...	3.3	-11.9	252.3	265.9	...	...	...	...
...	88.4	12.6	0.1	0.1	0.3	1.92	2.15	-17.5	6.4	70.3	...	6.6	-45.3	217.8	231.4	...	...	...	...
	Principal Lines of Business: CompHosp/Med (88.5%), Medicare (11.5%)													Principal States: CT (100.0%)					
...	76.6	12.9	22.6	7.7	51.0	3.87	3.71	14.8	5.9	82.2	...	1.4	26.0	187.5	201.4	...	...	...	...
...	74.4	12.8	23.5	9.2	49.3	4.44	4.43	-5.0	5.1	100.7	...	1.5	9.5	217.1	231.8	...	...	...	...
...	76.9	12.2	22.9	8.2	45.2	5.26	5.36	3.5	5.7	106.0	...	1.0	-7.5	208.7	226.2	...	...	...	...
-15	80.0	9.7	25.4	8.8	47.2	4.01	4.01	2.2	4.9	129.0	...	0.8	17.4	223.3	241.1	0.0	...	...	...
15	82.5	11.4	12.2	4.3	20.6	2.36	2.26	13.8	4.2	162.0	...	0.1	32.8	342.6	366.4	...	...	...	...
	Principal Lines of Business: CompHosp/Med (60.2%), Medicare (39.8%)													Principal States: NJ (100.0%)					

Data in U.S. Dollars

COMPANY NAME / Ultimate Parent Association / Principal Officer / Mailing Address / Dom. : Began Bus. : Struct. : Mktg. / Specialty / Phone # / AMB# NAIC# — Best's Financial Strength Rating / FSC

Balance Sheet: Data Year | Bonds (%) | Mort. Loans & R.E. (%) | Com & Pref. Stock (%) | All Other Assets (%) | Total Assets ($000) | Life Reserves (%) | Health Reserves %) | Ann Res. & Dep. Liabilities (%) | All Other Liabilities (%) | Capital & Surplus ($000)

Operations: Direct Premiums Written ($000) | Net Premiums Written & Deposits ($000) | Operating Cash Flow ($000) | NOG Before Taxes ($000) | NOG After Taxes ($000) | Net Income ($000)

OXFORD HEALTH PLANS (NY) INC
UnitedHealth Group Inc
William J. Golden
President & CEO
48 Monroe Turnpike
Trumbull, CT 06611
NY : 1986 : Stock : Broker
Group A&H, Health, Ind A&H
203-459-6000
AMB# 068716 NAIC# 95479

Rating: **A** — Rating Outlook: Stable — FSC X

Data Year	Bonds (%)	Mort. Loans & R.E. (%)	Com & Pref. Stock (%)	All Other Assets (%)	Total Assets ($000)	Life Reserves (%)	Health Reserves %)	Ann Res. & Dep. Liabilities (%)	All Other Liabilities (%)	Capital & Surplus ($000)	Direct Premiums Written ($000)	Net Premiums Written & Deposits ($000)	Operating Cash Flow ($000)	NOG Before Taxes ($000)	NOG After Taxes ($000)	Net Income ($000)
'05	45.3	...	27.7	26.9	1,645,651	...	35.8	...	64.2	947,511	2,809,505	2,806,128	261,996	352,083	244,202	241,129
'06	49.2	...	38.6	12.2	1,589,779	...	45.3	...	54.7	1,064,006	2,692,271	2,692,271	-185,259	428,308	268,297	266,975
'07	43.6	...	39.7	16.7	1,828,977	...	43.1	...	56.9	1,419,694	2,455,733	2,455,733	125,130	349,445	240,389	240,171
'08	40.6	...	38.2	21.2	1,614,986	...	53.9	...	46.1	1,259,762	2,122,864	2,122,864	-231,523	530,365	435,768	436,204
'09	39.4	...	32.0	28.7	998,735	...	41.4	...	58.6	685,737	2,051,386	2,051,386	-227,431	567,475	495,176	498,927

Rating History: A, 06/15/09; A-, 01/29/08; A-, 11/21/07; A-, 11/16/06; A-, 08/17/06

OXFORD LIFE INS CO
AMERCO
Mark A. Haydukovich
President & CEO
2721 North Central Avenue
Phoenix, AZ 85004-1172
AZ : 1968 : Stock : Agency
Life, Ind Ann
602-263-6666
AMB# 007890 NAIC# 76112

Rating: **B++** — Rating Outlook: Stable — FSC VIII

Data Year	Bonds (%)	Mort. Loans & R.E. (%)	Com & Pref. Stock (%)	All Other Assets (%)	Total Assets ($000)	Life Reserves (%)	Health Reserves %)	Ann Res. & Dep. Liabilities (%)	All Other Liabilities (%)	Capital & Surplus ($000)	Direct Premiums Written ($000)	Net Premiums Written & Deposits ($000)	Operating Cash Flow ($000)	NOG Before Taxes ($000)	NOG After Taxes ($000)	Net Income ($000)
'05	77.8	7.0	7.8	7.3	633,180	10.1	3.8	82.0	4.1	101,467	25,936	41,160	-57,815	14,720	9,585	7,992
'06	76.9	8.2	8.2	6.6	576,320	10.1	3.1	82.5	4.3	112,998	22,550	33,232	-53,545	19,111	14,877	14,869
'07	74.4	9.7	8.9	7.1	535,777	10.8	3.3	82.0	4.0	124,178	24,888	38,770	-41,524	14,234	13,465	13,143
'08	70.9	11.5	10.2	7.3	502,891	11.3	1.7	81.5	5.5	129,702	22,899	38,018	-31,079	14,894	10,236	9,789
'09	66.5	10.8	10.8	11.9	501,599	20.2	1.4	74.0	4.3	133,867	57,396	69,109	-6,249	3,863	4,333	3,277

Rating History: B++g, 03/31/10; B++g, 03/20/09; B++g, 01/31/08; B++, 11/29/06; B+, 10/19/05

OZARK NATIONAL LIFE INS CO MO
Charles N. Sharpe Trust
Charles N. Sharpe
Chairman & President
P.O. Box 15688
Kansas City, MO 64106-0688
MO : 1964 : Stock : Exclusive Agent
Term Life, Trad Life, Whole life
816-842-6300
AMB# 006877 NAIC# 67393

Rating: **B++** — Rating Outlook: Stable — FSC VIII

Data Year	Bonds (%)	Mort. Loans & R.E. (%)	Com & Pref. Stock (%)	All Other Assets (%)	Total Assets ($000)	Life Reserves (%)	Health Reserves %)	Ann Res. & Dep. Liabilities (%)	All Other Liabilities (%)	Capital & Surplus ($000)	Direct Premiums Written ($000)	Net Premiums Written & Deposits ($000)	Operating Cash Flow ($000)	NOG Before Taxes ($000)	NOG After Taxes ($000)	Net Income ($000)
'05	85.9	2.0	0.2	11.9	522,259	93.8	0.5	2.5	3.2	70,381	97,179	94,742	29,755	28,236	17,312	17,312
'06	86.0	1.8	...	12.2	554,238	94.5	0.4	2.4	2.7	79,096	95,949	93,581	28,546	31,474	20,985	20,597
'07	86.8	1.7	...	11.5	586,247	94.8	0.4	2.2	2.6	87,126	95,700	93,194	34,562	33,895	21,196	21,196
'08	86.0	1.5	0.0	12.5	617,627	94.8	0.4	2.1	2.7	96,581	92,828	90,258	31,676	31,831	21,051	21,051
'09	87.7	1.4	...	10.9	642,878	95.7	0.3	2.0	1.9	107,302	88,914	86,219	25,779	33,710	23,150	23,172

Rating History: B++, 02/02/10; B++, 01/14/09; B++, 12/11/07; B++, 12/11/06; B++, 11/23/05

PACIFIC BEACON LIFE REASSUR
California State Auto Assn Inter-Ins Bur
Paula F. Downey
President
745 Fort Street, Suite 800
Honolulu, HI 96813
HI : 1999 : Stock : Agency
Reins
805-585-3533
AMB# 060326 NAIC# 84162

Rating: **A-** — Rating Outlook: Stable — FSC VII

Data Year	Bonds (%)	Mort. Loans & R.E. (%)	Com & Pref. Stock (%)	All Other Assets (%)	Total Assets ($000)	Life Reserves (%)	Health Reserves %)	Ann Res. & Dep. Liabilities (%)	All Other Liabilities (%)	Capital & Surplus ($000)	Direct Premiums Written ($000)	Net Premiums Written & Deposits ($000)	Operating Cash Flow ($000)	NOG Before Taxes ($000)	NOG After Taxes ($000)	Net Income ($000)
'05	93.7	...	0.2	6.0	225,815	12.5	0.7	84.1	2.7	14,909	...	35,393	23,286	-5,156	-4,139	-4,206
'06	89.0	...	0.1	10.9	248,523	17.9	0.7	78.7	2.7	20,954	...	36,521	22,558	-10,949	-8,696	-8,671
'07	88.2	...	1.1	10.7	257,472	23.1	0.8	73.9	2.2	23,191	...	37,978	9,092	-3,647	-3,154	-3,310
'08	79.3	...	0.4	20.3	284,549	27.4	0.9	71.1	0.6	40,274	...	45,121	29,327	-3,683	-4,484	-7,172
'09	89.5	...	0.2	10.4	303,513	30.0	1.0	68.1	0.9	44,559	...	57,766	15,274	-901	-2,315	-2,545

Rating History: A- g, 05/26/10; A- g, 05/29/09; A- g, 03/17/08; A- g, 01/16/07; A- g, 01/03/06

PACIFIC CENTURY LIFE INS CORP[1]
Jan Reiko Yamasaki
President
2700 North Third Street, Suite 3050
Phoenix, AZ 85004-4620
AZ : 1982 : Stock : Agency
602-200-6900
AMB# 060335 NAIC# 93815

Rating: **NR-1**

Data Year	Bonds (%)	Mort. Loans & R.E. (%)	Com & Pref. Stock (%)	All Other Assets (%)	Total Assets ($000)	Life Reserves (%)	Health Reserves %)	Ann Res. & Dep. Liabilities (%)	All Other Liabilities (%)	Capital & Surplus ($000)	Direct Premiums Written ($000)	Net Premiums Written & Deposits ($000)	Operating Cash Flow ($000)	NOG Before Taxes ($000)	NOG After Taxes ($000)	Net Income ($000)
'05	3.5	91.2	0.2	5.1	320,677	...	...	...	100.0	316,817	-64	1,136	...	14,970	9,779	9,779
'06	3.7	92.0	0.2	4.2	319,957	...	...	...	100.0	316,398	7	1,116	...	14,238	9,352	9,352
'07	3.6	89.8	0.3	6.4	331,091	...	...	...	100.0	326,973	123	1,075	...	16,125	10,573	10,573
'08	3.7	87.6	0.3	8.4	331,420	...	...	...	100.0	327,752	48	758	...	17,122	11,265	11,265
'09	2.7	80.6	1.6	15.1	330,354	...	...	...	100.0	326,535	39	451	...	15,422	10,105	10,204

Rating History: NR-1, 06/10/10; NR-1, 06/12/09; NR-1, 06/12/08; NR-1, 06/08/07; NR-1, 06/07/06

PACIFIC GUARDIAN LIFE CO LTD
Meiji Yasuda Life Insurance Company
Tsukasa Namiki
President & CEO
Pacific Guardian Tower
Honolulu, HI 96814-3698
HI : 1962 : Stock : Agency
Group A&H, Group Life, Ind Life
808-955-2236
AMB# 006883 NAIC# 64343

Rating: **A** — Rating Outlook: Stable — FSC VII

Data Year	Bonds (%)	Mort. Loans & R.E. (%)	Com & Pref. Stock (%)	All Other Assets (%)	Total Assets ($000)	Life Reserves (%)	Health Reserves %)	Ann Res. & Dep. Liabilities (%)	All Other Liabilities (%)	Capital & Surplus ($000)	Direct Premiums Written ($000)	Net Premiums Written & Deposits ($000)	Operating Cash Flow ($000)	NOG Before Taxes ($000)	NOG After Taxes ($000)	Net Income ($000)
'05	59.7	27.0	3.6	9.8	453,044	68.0	1.8	26.4	3.8	81,233	68,643	63,686	6,657	9,047	6,622	7,256
'06	55.5	28.8	4.0	11.7	448,668	72.7	2.0	21.6	3.7	85,187	73,569	68,712	-5,766	8,576	6,170	6,873
'07	52.8	32.0	4.3	10.9	436,674	77.9	2.3	14.9	4.9	90,377	77,951	71,708	-12,607	12,342	8,860	9,173
'08	49.8	34.3	2.7	13.2	426,779	82.4	2.2	11.9	3.6	83,279	83,606	76,690	579	12,694	8,739	6,106
'09	51.1	34.3	2.6	12.1	433,306	83.8	2.3	10.6	3.3	87,474	75,326	68,306	3,577	11,832	8,266	6,644

Rating History: A, 06/15/10; A, 04/30/09; A, 05/13/08; A, 01/31/07; A, 02/22/06

PACIFIC LIFE & ANNUITY CO
Pacific Mutual Holding Company
James T. Morris
Chairman, President & CEO
700 Newport Center Drive
Newport Beach, CA 92660-6397
AZ : 1983 : Stock : Broker
Ind Ann, Ind Life
949-219-3011
AMB# 009156 NAIC# 97268

Rating: **A+** — Rating Outlook: Negative — FSC XV

Data Year	Bonds (%)	Mort. Loans & R.E. (%)	Com & Pref. Stock (%)	All Other Assets (%)	Total Assets ($000)	Life Reserves (%)	Health Reserves %)	Ann Res. & Dep. Liabilities (%)	All Other Liabilities (%)	Capital & Surplus ($000)	Direct Premiums Written ($000)	Net Premiums Written & Deposits ($000)	Operating Cash Flow ($000)	NOG Before Taxes ($000)	NOG After Taxes ($000)	Net Income ($000)
'05	49.7	4.0	0.8	45.5	1,505,917	0.9	0.6	51.8	46.8	359,344	711,683	440,042	13,068	54,657	35,377	37,074
'06	47.7	2.2	0.9	49.1	1,851,759	0.9	0.1	46.0	53.0	364,532	459,479	425,027	56,167	9,128	5,360	5,763
'07	40.3	3.9	1.0	54.9	2,415,295	1.0	0.0	41.7	57.3	369,074	594,347	637,168	148,042	8,005	6,198	1,861
'08	42.6	6.2	0.7	50.5	2,503,717	1.2	...	54.4	44.4	287,817	518,214	610,383	217,582	-116,229	-105,894	-115,594
'09	46.6	6.4	0.3	46.7	3,539,136	0.9	...	53.8	45.3	370,986	801,618	882,095	619,927	120,789	111,894	117,537

Rating History: A+ g, 03/05/10; A+ g, 03/06/09; A++g, 06/16/08; A++g, 06/14/07; A++g, 06/21/06

PACIFIC LIFE INSURANCE COMPANY
Pacific Mutual Holding Company
James T. Morris
Chairman, President & CEO
700 Newport Center Drive
Newport Beach, CA 92660-6397
NE : 1868 : Stock : Agency
Ind Ann, Ind Life
949-219-3011
AMB# 006885 NAIC# 67466

Rating: **A+** — Rating Outlook: Negative — FSC XV

Data Year	Bonds (%)	Mort. Loans & R.E. (%)	Com & Pref. Stock (%)	All Other Assets (%)	Total Assets ($000)	Life Reserves (%)	Health Reserves %)	Ann Res. & Dep. Liabilities (%)	All Other Liabilities (%)	Capital & Surplus ($000)	Direct Premiums Written ($000)	Net Premiums Written & Deposits ($000)	Operating Cash Flow ($000)	NOG Before Taxes ($000)	NOG After Taxes ($000)	Net Income ($000)
'05	32.1	5.4	0.9	61.6	74,885,539	23.2	0.0	24.1	52.7	3,008,818	9,758,211	10,764,438	710,339	146,485	199,973	234,374
'06	27.5	4.3	1.3	67.0	86,141,889	21.0	...	21.5	57.5	3,217,930	11,681,771	11,337,007	421,202	431,615	316,755	362,100
'07	25.9	4.9	1.1	68.0	96,551,166	19.6	...	20.0	60.4	3,707,975	13,165,081	11,538,680	1,671,282	352,659	349,593	362,190
'08	28.2	6.9	1.1	63.8	83,652,571	23.9	...	26.2	49.9	3,135,787	11,371,823	8,868,641	2,705,815	-1,485,538	-1,239,550	-1,528,807
'09	26.1	7.2	1.3	65.4	94,738,487	21.5	...	21.8	56.7	5,005,942	9,900,016	8,671,854	34,827	623,010	629,010	651,829

Rating History: A+ g, 03/05/10; A+ g, 03/06/09; A++g, 06/16/08; A++g, 06/14/07; A++g, 06/21/06

PACIFIC VISIONCARE WA INC
Debbie J. Eldredge
President, Secretary & Treasurer
P.O. Box 1283
Chehalis, WA 98532
WA : 1999 : Stock : Broker
Vision
360-748-8632
AMB# 064628 NAIC# 47100

Rating: **NR-5**

Data Year	Bonds (%)	Mort. Loans & R.E. (%)	Com & Pref. Stock (%)	All Other Assets (%)	Total Assets ($000)	Life Reserves (%)	Health Reserves %)	Ann Res. & Dep. Liabilities (%)	All Other Liabilities (%)	Capital & Surplus ($000)	Direct Premiums Written ($000)	Net Premiums Written & Deposits ($000)	Operating Cash Flow ($000)	NOG Before Taxes ($000)	NOG After Taxes ($000)	Net Income ($000)
'05	...	...	...	100.0	378	...	44.7	...	55.3	335	309	309	16	-32	-32	-32
'06	...	...	...	100.0	346	...	48.2	...	51.8	311	281	281	-33	-24	-24	-24
'07	...	...	...	100.0	336	...	53.0	...	47.0	313	232	232	-9	3	2	2
'08	...	...	...	100.0	349	...	49.0	...	51.0	342	104	104	12	-9	-9	-9
'09	...	...	...	100.0	331	...	100.0	...	...	331	13	13	-18	-11	-11	-11

Rating History: NR-5, 03/23/10; NR-5, 03/20/09; NR-5, 03/18/08; NR-5, 04/02/07; NR-5, 04/26/06

BEST'S PROFITABILITY, LEVERAGE AND LIQUIDITY TESTS 2005 – 2009

Data in U.S. Dollars

—	Profitability Tests							Leverage Tests						Liquidity Tests					
Un-Realized Capital Gains ($000)	Benefits Paid to NPW & Dep (%)	Comm. & Expenses to NPW & Dep (%)	NOG to Total Assets (%)	NOG to Total Rev (%)	Operating Return on Equity (%)	Net Yield (%)	Total Return (%)	Change in NPW & Dep (%)	NPW & Dep to Capital (X)	Capital & Surplus to Liabilities (%)	Surplus Relief (%)	Reins Leverage (%)	Change in Capital (%)	Quick Liquidity (%)	Current Liquidity (%)	Non-Invest Grade Bonds to Capital (%)	Delinq. & Foreclosed Mortgages to Capital (%)	Mort. & Credit Tenant Loans & R.E. to Capital (%)	Affiliated Invest to Capital (%)
...	78.9	9.8	17.1	8.6	31.0	2.49	2.26	-8.9	3.0	135.7	...	...	51.4	186.5	197.2	...	...	...	48.2
...	77.7	8.1	16.6	9.8	26.7	2.82	2.73	-4.1	2.5	202.4	...	...	12.3	167.4	181.9	...	...	...	57.7
111,761	80.5	7.0	14.1	9.6	19.4	2.71	9.76	-8.8	1.7	346.9	...	...	33.4	271.0	290.6	...	...	...	51.1
-108,483	80.5	8.0	25.3	18.0	32.5	19.92	13.31	-13.6	1.7	354.6	...	...	-11.3	223.4	242.4	0.2	...	...	49.0
-298,332	81.9	8.7	37.9	20.4	50.9	39.35	16.59	-3.4	3.0	219.1	...	3.9	-45.6	210.2	223.2	...	...	...	46.5
Principal Lines of Business: CompHosp/Med (56.5%), Medicare (43.5%)														Principal States: NY (100.0%)					
3,051	254.7	46.0	1.4	11.8	10.2	5.54	5.83	-12.5	0.4	20.6	0.2	19.7	11.0	78.7	86.5	13.1	...	40.9	49.8
-1,201	309.6	58.6	2.5	20.0	13.9	6.37	6.23	-19.3	0.3	26.0	0.0	13.6	10.1	76.7	88.7	10.0	...	39.9	41.7
1,393	227.1	57.4	2.4	17.1	11.4	6.80	7.02	16.7	0.3	31.1	0.0	10.2	7.0	74.5	87.4	3.4	...	40.7	35.5
2,563	207.1	59.1	2.0	13.9	8.1	6.78	7.23	-1.9	0.3	37.0	0.0	12.0	6.8	78.5	91.2	3.2	...	42.7	35.3
3,656	96.1	46.8	0.9	4.2	3.3	6.26	6.86	81.8	0.5	38.6	0.0	10.8	2.9	86.0	98.8	3.0	1.7	38.8	36.9
Principal Lines of Business: OrdLife (78.8%), IndA&H (15.2%), IndAnn (5.2%), GrpA&H (0.8%), CrdLife (0.0%)														Principal States: MI (10.6%), OH (10.4%), TX (8.6%), PA (8.4%), NC (7.9%)					
-48	37.6	30.2	3.4	14.8	25.4	4.78	4.83	-0.9	1.3	16.0	0.4	50.9	6.9	78.7	85.9	...	...	14.6	7.0
344	38.8	28.0	3.9	17.7	28.1	5.14	5.18	-1.2	1.2	17.0	0.3	45.4	11.7	81.4	87.2	...	...	12.5	5.9
...	38.1	29.2	3.7	17.5	25.5	5.32	5.37	-0.4	1.1	17.8	0.3	41.0	10.0	91.1	97.4	...	...	11.0	5.1
13	44.2	29.9	3.5	17.5	22.9	5.38	5.45	-3.2	0.9	18.9	0.2	36.6	10.8	93.6	99.9	...	...	9.3	4.3
-13	47.7	27.1	3.7	20.0	22.7	5.08	5.14	-4.5	0.8	20.3	0.2	32.9	10.6	95.1	99.7	...	...	8.5	4.2
Principal Lines of Business: OrdLife (99.3%), IndA&H (0.4%), IndAnn (0.2%), GrpAnn (0.1%)														Principal States: MO (21.5%), IA (12.1%), MN (8.1%), KS (6.9%), NE (6.6%)					
12	51.0	40.3	-1.9	-8.9	-31.7	4.80	4.98	-32.4	2.3	7.3	...	6.7	33.0	74.9	84.6	27.5	...	...	...
11	74.4	48.9	-3.7	-17.2	-48.5	5.09	5.25	3.2	1.7	9.7	...	4.2	42.0	78.8	88.3	63.6	...	...	...
-33	93.3	45.9	-1.2	-5.8	-14.3	5.44	5.51	4.0	1.6	10.4	...	1.2	11.2	76.8	87.5	61.8	...	...	...
-215	71.9	40.0	-1.7	-7.4	-14.1	5.43	4.41	18.8	1.1	16.5	...	0.7	65.7	91.4	102.5	35.8	...	...	...
214	66.2	33.1	-0.8	-3.1	-5.5	5.70	5.70	28.0	1.3	17.3	...	3.9	11.3	73.8	85.6	37.8	...	...	...
Principal Lines of Business: OrdLife (46.1%), IndAnn (36.0%), GrpLife (9.3%), GrpA&H (8.1%), IndA&H (0.5%)																			
...	44.4	20.4	3.1	65.2	3.1	...	...	-33.7	0.0	999.9	...	...	0.1	...	...	...	...	92.0	...
...	92.0	25.4	2.9	60.8	3.0	...	...	-1.8	0.0	999.9	...	...	-0.1	...	...	...	...	92.6	...
...	40.0	24.0	3.2	62.6	3.3	...	...	-3.7	0.0	999.9	...	...	3.3	...	...	...	...	90.5	...
...	41.6	26.3	3.4	64.3	3.4	...	...	-29.5	0.0	999.9	...	...	0.2	...	...	...	...	88.3	...
-201	88.1	35.7	3.1	64.2	3.1	...	...	-40.5	0.0	999.9	...	...	-0.3	...	...	...	...	81.2	...
Principal Lines of Business: GrpLife (59.6%), CrdLife (34.7%), GrpA&H (3.2%), CrdA&H (2.5%)																			
-685	85.3	32.7	1.5	7.5	8.3	5.84	5.89	7.2	0.7	23.1	1.5	23.8	4.4	58.3	66.2	...	...	143.6	...
611	102.3	31.1	1.4	6.7	7.4	5.89	6.20	7.9	0.8	24.8	1.3	27.3	4.9	54.2	61.9	...	...	144.6	...
-60	112.0	30.2	2.0	9.3	10.1	5.90	5.91	4.4	0.8	27.6	1.6	30.4	5.9	51.2	58.8	...	...	147.7	-0.1
-4,854	83.1	27.1	2.0	8.7	10.1	5.97	4.09	6.9	0.9	24.7	1.5	37.1	-10.6	48.7	56.7	...	...	172.9	-0.1
4,061	81.7	29.6	1.9	9.1	9.7	5.98	6.45	-10.9	0.8	26.2	1.3	40.4	6.4	45.8	54.6	...	...	165.0	0.0
Principal Lines of Business: GrpA&H (42.3%), OrdLife (37.3%), GrpLife (17.2%), GrpAnn (2.2%), IndAnn (0.7%)														Principal States: HI (73.0%), CA (17.3%), GU (5.4%)					
5,471	47.7	19.7	2.5	6.9	10.6	5.97	6.86	-55.1	1.2	58.1	6.5	18.5	17.8	86.0	111.3	5.8	...	15.9	0.2
2,538	36.1	9.8	0.3	1.1	1.5	6.38	6.76	-3.4	1.1	54.6	1.7	9.6	1.3	72.3	99.3	4.1	...	10.9	0.2
2,474	20.3	8.7	0.3	0.9	1.7	6.44	6.32	49.9	1.7	45.1	0.3	8.4	1.4	60.3	85.0	12.4	...	24.5	0.3
2,059	23.2	9.4	-4.3	-16.8	-32.2	5.93	5.38	-4.2	2.0	25.1	0.3	9.0	-21.9	61.1	80.7	18.1	...	52.1	0.4
-4,532	15.5	7.4	3.7	11.9	34.0	5.77	5.85	44.5	2.3	22.5	0.1	6.5	27.8	55.1	76.4	18.8	...	59.0	0.3
Principal Lines of Business: IndAnn (97.1%), OrdLife (2.9%)														Principal States: NY (57.1%), CO (37.3%)					
37,850	54.1	13.1	0.3	1.7	6.9	6.04	6.28	4.3	3.2	10.0	2.0	12.0	8.3	33.6	51.5	35.7	0.0	118.9	22.6
-38,398	58.7	13.5	0.4	2.2	10.2	5.97	6.00	5.3	3.2	10.4	4.0	15.4	5.4	37.3	55.0	30.6	0.0	106.7	22.0
104,143	67.5	11.5	0.4	2.2	10.1	6.05	6.36	1.8	2.8	11.5	8.0	18.5	16.9	33.2	50.8	24.5	0.1	117.3	23.3
718,617	80.2	12.6	-1.4	-8.2	-36.2	7.96	9.04	-23.1	2.5	9.0	8.4	40.2	-14.8	38.8	53.3	44.5	0.1	165.2	24.4
-1,111,702	73.4	12.9	0.7	6.1	15.5	1.61	-0.92	-2.2	1.7	13.3	2.9	30.6	44.2	34.6	49.6	51.8	0.1	134.2	34.1
Principal Lines of Business: IndAnn (71.3%), OrdLife (14.5%), GrpAnn (14.2%), GrpLife (0.0%)														Principal States: CA (13.2%), FL (7.2%), IL (5.6%), MN (5.1%), TX (4.9%)					
...	65.6	47.4	-8.6	-10.0	-9.7	2.25	2.25	13.1	0.9	784.4	...	...	4.9	999.9	999.9	...	...	...	...
...	81.9	31.4	-6.6	-8.2	-7.4	3.74	3.74	-9.3	0.9	893.1	...	...	-7.2	999.9	999.9	...	...	...	...
...	76.3	28.6	0.5	0.6	0.5	4.15	4.15	-17.4	0.7	999.9	...	...	0.8	999.9	999.9	...	...	...	...
...	85.7	28.9	-2.7	-8.4	-2.8	1.76	1.76	-55.1	0.3	999.9	...	...	9.0	999.9	999.9	...	...	...	...
...	109.3	81.9	-3.3	-84.8	-3.3	0.13	0.13	-87.7	0.0	999.9	...	...	-3.2	999.9	999.9	...	...	...	...
Principal Lines of Business: Vision (100.0%)														Principal States: WA (100.0%)					

ANNUAL STATEMENT DATA FOR YEARS 2005 – 2009

Data in U.S. Dollars

COMPANY NAME / Ultimate Parent Association / Principal Officer / Mailing Address / Dom. : Began Bus. : Struct. : Mktg. / Specialty / Phone # / AMB# / NAIC#	Best's Financial Strength Rating / FSC	Data Year	Balance Sheet: Bonds (%)	Mort. Loans & R.E. (%)	Com & Pref. Stock (%)	All Other Assets (%)	Total Assets ($000)	Life Reserves (%)	Health Reserves (%)	Ann Res. & Dep. Liabilities (%)	All Other Liabilities (%)	Capital & Surplus ($000)	Operations: Direct Premiums Written ($000)	Net Premiums Written & Deposits ($000)	Operating Cash Flow ($000)	NOG Before Taxes ($000)	NOG After Taxes ($000)	Net Income ($000)
PACIFICARE BHVRL HEALTH OF CA UnitedHealth Group Inc	A-	'05	...	...	...	100.0	56,381	...	...	...	100.0	27,478	151,169	151,169	5,192	25,746	15,637	15,637
David Chenok, President		'06	...	...	...	100.0	79,996	...	...	...	100.0	49,188	166,572	166,572	27,781	50,054	29,657	29,657
5995 Plaza Drive, Mail Stop CY20-327, Cypress, CA 90630	Rating Outlook: Stable	'07	...	...	...	100.0	84,913	...	...	...	100.0	63,091	174,244	174,244	14,410	63,215	37,163	37,163
CA : 1988 : Stock : Broker		'08	...	...	...	100.0	81,726	...	...	...	100.0	61,252	152,577	152,577	-4,896	38,855	23,114	23,114
Group A&H, 714-445-0300		'09	...	...	...	100.0	74,981	...	...	...	100.0	59,704	129,081	129,081	-4,767	28,712	17,082	17,082
AMB# 064644	FSC VII	Rating History: A-, 06/15/09; A-, 01/29/08; A-, 11/21/07; A-, 11/16/06; A-, 08/17/06																
PACIFICARE DENTAL OF COLORADO UnitedHealth Group Inc	NR-2	'05	10.0	...	...	90.0	2,902	...	39.2	...	60.8	2,735	2,867	2,867	1,609	699	450	450
Kirk E. Andrews, President		'06	8.1	...	...	91.9	3,506	...	29.7	...	70.3	3,294	2,996	2,996	694	872	566	566
5995 Plaza Drive, Mail Stop CY20-469, Cypress, CA 90630		'07	7.1	...	...	92.9	4,011	...	20.8	...	79.2	3,821	2,563	2,563	498	796	516	516
CO : 1998 : Stock : Broker		'08	6.3	...	...	93.7	4,563	...	14.1	...	85.9	4,349	2,461	2,461	620	812	526	526
Dental, 714-226-3873		'09	6.0	...	...	94.0	4,840	...	35.3	...	64.7	4,724	2,412	2,412	263	673	442	442
AMB# 064840 NAIC# 11189		Rating History: NR-2, 06/15/09; NR-2, 01/29/08; NR-2, 11/21/07; NR-2, 11/20/06; NR-2, 06/16/06																
PACIFICARE LIFE AND HEALTH INS UnitedHealth Group Inc	A-	'05	52.6	...	0.1	47.4	375,732	0.8	62.6	0.7	35.9	147,212	528,864	678,742	89,058	235,022	149,219	149,219
Steven H. Nelson, Chairman, President & CEO		'06	22.3	...	...	77.7	983,618	0.3	76.5	0.2	23.0	338,974	2,751,769	2,793,203	506,635	270,410	176,739	176,739
5995 Plaza Drive, Cypress, CA 90630	Rating Outlook: Stable	'07	63.6	...	...	36.4	896,092	0.5	72.3	0.4	26.9	552,192	1,332,724	1,333,112	-35,735	406,607	278,816	278,816
IN : 1967 : Stock : Broker		'08	74.4	...	...	25.6	778,584	0.5	50.0	1.0	48.5	642,789	433,725	433,725	-11,145	237,427	154,075	148,920
Group A&H, Group Life, 714-226-3876		'09	68.8	...	...	31.2	745,709	0.8	76.6	1.7	20.9	680,457	322,107	322,107	-14,275	177,614	120,409	120,705
AMB# 007278 NAIC# 70785	FSC XI	Rating History: A- g, 06/15/09; A- g, 01/29/08; A- g, 11/21/07; A- g, 11/16/06; A- g, 08/17/06																
PACIFICARE LIFE ASSURANCE CO UnitedHealth Group Inc	A-	'05	69.4	...	0.1	30.5	278,269	1.8	62.4	...	35.8	113,417	704,314	701,176	53,318	73,748	47,766	47,766
Steven H. Nelson, President & CEO		'06	83.2	...	...	16.8	245,620	2.4	72.0	...	25.7	121,514	802,269	783,815	-27,573	80,135	55,322	55,617
5995 Plaza Drive, Cypress, CA 90630	Rating Outlook: Stable	'07	70.4	...	...	29.6	229,624	3.0	61.0	...	36.0	135,185	526,731	527,083	825	19,264	10,653	10,653
CO : 1973 : Stock : Broker		'08	49.8	...	...	50.2	199,728	3.6	64.7	...	31.6	143,978	303,660	305,149	-20,457	24,941	17,096	16,704
Group A&H, Group Life, 714-825-5379		'09	45.2	...	...	54.8	174,062	4.3	71.0	...	24.7	138,592	197,878	198,600	-20,155	12,653	9,004	8,916
AMB# 008428 NAIC# 84506	FSC VIII	Rating History: A-, 06/15/09; A-, 01/29/08; A-, 11/21/07; A-, 11/16/06; A-, 08/17/06																
PACIFICARE OF ARIZONA INC UnitedHealth Group Inc	A-	'05	87.3	...	...	12.7	258,573	...	59.3	...	40.7	115,732	1,276,084	1,274,313	28,352	16,668	11,893	12,971
Anthony H. Solem, President & CEO		'06	59.9	...	...	40.1	342,121	...	59.8	...	40.2	126,524	1,362,149	1,341,858	57,237	32,506	19,838	18,216
5995 Plaza Drive, Cypress, CA 90630	Rating Outlook: Stable	'07	68.9	...	...	31.1	308,948	...	56.1	...	43.9	169,682	1,251,082	1,200,207	-22,792	59,647	42,581	42,541
AZ : 1997 : Stock : Broker		'08	60.2	...	...	39.8	236,797	...	61.7	...	38.3	143,995	1,157,978	1,156,981	-66,680	66,138	45,743	45,829
Medicare, Group A&H, FEHBP, 602-244-8200		'09	63.9	...	...	36.1	190,735	...	66.1	...	33.9	106,224	1,160,436	1,159,277	-43,391	19,498	13,149	13,260
AMB# 064218 NAIC# 95617	FSC VIII	Rating History: A-, 06/15/09; A-, 01/29/08; A-, 11/21/07; A-, 11/16/06; A-, 08/17/06																
PACIFICARE OF CALIFORNIA UnitedHealth Group Inc	A-	'05	...	1.3	...	98.7	1,221,167	...	...	...	100.0	514,571	6,629,075	6,629,075	77,664	327,514	200,269	200,269
David M. Hansen, President		'06	...	2.7	...	97.3	1,542,906	...	...	...	100.0	669,309	7,251,112	7,251,112	309,279	493,824	291,035	291,035
5995 Plaza Drive, Mail Stop CY20-327, Cypress, CA 90630	Rating Outlook: Stable	'07	...	2.2	...	97.8	1,707,089	...	...	...	100.0	773,372	7,841,324	7,841,324	-183,758	530,038	332,093	332,093
CA : 1975 : Stock : Broker		'08	...	...	...	100.0	1,510,672	...	...	...	100.0	743,239	7,442,596	7,442,596	-87,847	448,603	244,891	244,891
Group A&H, Medicare, 714-952-1121		'09	...	...	...	100.0	1,668,154	...	...	...	100.0	891,112	6,967,812	6,967,812	69,899	536,576	320,015	320,015
AMB# 068705	FSC XI	Rating History: A- g, 06/15/09; A- g, 01/29/08; A- g, 11/21/07; A- g, 11/16/06; A- g, 08/17/06																
PACIFICARE OF COLORADO INC UnitedHealth Group Inc	A-	'05	71.7	...	2.8	25.5	240,894	...	49.5	...	50.5	132,086	958,076	956,346	37,877	54,422	36,502	37,716
Elizabeth K. Soberg, President & CEO		'06	54.2	...	...	45.8	312,043	...	46.3	...	53.7	163,260	1,033,290	1,021,511	63,093	99,475	65,924	64,057
6465 Greenwood Plaza Blvd., Suite 300, Centennial, CO 80111	Rating Outlook: Stable	'07	64.8	...	...	35.2	272,853	...	58.9	...	41.1	174,171	960,940	959,956	-28,079	111,098	74,820	74,765
CO : 1988 : Stock : Broker		'08	78.3	...	...	21.7	262,402	...	52.0	...	48.0	186,053	878,548	877,673	-20,004	134,672	90,089	88,600
Group A&H, Medicare, FEHBP, 303-220-5800		'09	65.5	...	...	34.5	190,870	...	63.3	...	36.7	120,213	849,260	848,413	-59,694	68,623	45,471	46,411
AMB# 068639 NAIC# 95434	FSC VIII	Rating History: A-, 06/15/09; A-, 01/29/08; A-, 11/21/07; A-, 11/16/06; A-, 08/17/06																
PACIFICARE OF NEVADA INC UnitedHealth Group Inc	A-	'05	74.4	...	...	25.6	74,963	...	73.5	...	26.5	40,374	316,404	316,186	8,460	437	437	731
Donald J. Giancursio, President & Chairman		'06	50.0	...	...	50.0	106,003	...	63.3	...	36.7	44,961	382,155	378,752	29,542	9,989	9,989	9,529
9900 Bren Road East, MN008-W345, Minnetonka, MN 55343	Rating Outlook: Stable	'07	48.4	...	...	51.6	122,286	...	45.8	...	54.2	66,556	403,291	400,343	2,992	25,222	20,124	20,124
NV : 1961 : Stock : Broker		'08	87.2	...	...	12.8	95,905	...	26.7	...	73.3	74,653	215,922	214,433	-5,179	199,276	130,534	130,387
Group A&H, Medicare, FEHBP, 702-269-7500		'09	43.6	...	...	56.4	77,138	...	55.9	...	44.1	66,579	74,949	74,227	-20,817	-417	39	547
AMB# 064219 NAIC# 95685	FSC VII	Rating History: A-, 06/15/09; A-, 01/29/08; A-, 11/21/07; A-, 11/16/06; A-, 08/17/06																
PACIFICARE OF OKLAHOMA INC UnitedHealth Group Inc	A-	'05	50.5	...	...	49.5	62,255	...	58.7	...	41.3	37,743	233,338	232,673	1,470	6,585	1,415	1,298
Thomas J. Quirk, President & CEO		'06	34.3	...	...	65.7	86,086	...	41.2	...	58.8	46,236	284,032	282,330	24,946	19,127	11,537	11,245
9900 Bren Road East, MN008-T380, Minnetonka, MN 55343	Rating Outlook: Stable	'07	44.3	...	...	55.7	80,614	...	60.2	...	39.8	46,268	309,229	309,229	-9,729	42,181	28,054	28,054
OK : 1985 : Stock : Broker		'08	60.3	...	...	39.7	76,027	...	59.1	...	40.9	48,939	312,534	312,534	-3,057	48,370	31,913	31,593
Group A&H, Medicare, FEHBP, 918-459-1100		'09	50.9	...	...	49.1	71,994	...	69.4	...	30.6	42,837	332,665	332,665	-8,129	34,468	22,524	22,752
AMB# 068582 NAIC# 96903	FSC VI	Rating History: A-, 06/15/09; A-, 01/29/08; A-, 11/21/07; A-, 11/16/06; A-, 08/17/06																

BEST'S PROFITABILITY, LEVERAGE AND LIQUIDITY TESTS 2005 – 2009

Data in U.S. Dollars

—	Profitability Tests							Leverage Tests						Liquidity Tests					
Un-Realized Capital Gains ($000)	Benefits Paid to NPW & Dep (%)	Comm. & Expenses to NPW & Dep (%)	NOG to Total Assets (%)	NOG to Total Rev (%)	Operating Return on Equity (%)	Net Yield (%)	Total Return (%)	Change in NPW & Dep (%)	NPW & Dep to Capital (X)	Capital & Surplus to Liabilities (%)	Surplus Relief (%)	Reins Leverage (%)	Change in Capital (%)	Quick Liquidity (%)	Current Liquidity (%)	Non-Invest Grade Bonds to Capital (%)	Delinq. & Foreclosed Mortgages to Capital (%)	Mort. & Credit Tenant Loans & R.E. to Capital (%)	Affiliated Invest to Capital (%)
...	60.0	28.3	27.9	9.8	57.3	1.84	1.84	3.5	5.5	95.1	...	...	1.3	130.3	130.3	...	...	...	...
...	53.9	21.5	43.5	16.9	77.4	4.33	4.33	10.2	3.4	159.7	...	...	79.0	208.6	208.6	...	...	...	...
...	47.3	22.1	45.1	20.1	66.2	4.81	4.81	4.6	2.8	289.1	...	...	28.3	209.2	209.2	...	...	...	...
...	60.1	20.6	27.7	14.3	37.2	2.91	2.91	-12.4	2.5	299.2	...	...	-2.9	220.2	220.2	...	...	...	...
...	54.3	24.9	21.8	13.0	28.2	2.32	2.32	-15.4	2.2	390.8	...	...	-2.5	142.6	142.6	...	...	...	...
Principal Lines of Business: CompHosp/Med (98.9%), Medicare (1.1%)																			
...	56.4	21.3	...	15.4	...	...	...	...	1.0	999.9	...	...	...	999.9	999.9	...	...	...	...
...	55.0	19.9	17.7	18.2	18.8	4.09	4.09	4.5	0.9	999.9	...	...	20.4	999.9	999.9	...	...	...	...
...	54.0	15.7	13.7	20.0	14.5	0.53	0.53	-14.5	0.7	999.9	...	...	16.0	999.9	999.9	...	...	...	...
...	53.2	18.1	12.3	20.5	12.9	2.61	2.61	-4.0	0.6	999.9	...	...	13.8	999.9	999.9	...	...	...	...
...	55.2	18.1	9.4	18.1	9.7	0.65	0.65	-2.0	0.5	999.9	...	...	8.6	999.9	999.9	...	...	...	...
Principal Lines of Business: Dental (100.0%)													Principal States: CO (100.0%)						
...	84.6	15.6	51.3	15.5	124.1	6.17	6.28	76.2	4.6	64.6	26.6	14.2	58.0	130.4	139.6	...	...	...	...
-1,513	90.7	10.0	26.0	5.7	72.7	8.15	7.90	311.5	8.2	52.7	3.5	2.6	130.2	205.5	211.0	...	...	...	...
...	70.8	10.6	29.7	18.8	62.6	4.67	4.69	-52.3	2.4	161.5	0.0	0.3	63.0	237.3	255.4	...	...	...	...
...	66.7	14.4	18.4	26.4	25.8	3.88	3.28	-67.5	0.7	479.9	...	0.2	16.4	585.6	636.4	0.0	...	...	...
...	78.6	15.6	15.8	25.1	18.2	3.37	3.57	-25.7	0.5	999.9	...	0.1	5.8	999.9	999.9	...	...	...	...
Principal Lines of Business: GrpA&H (81.8%), IndA&H (18.2%), GrpLife (0.0%)													Principal States: CA (82.9%), AZ (8.1%)						
...	77.8	13.1	19.6	6.7	52.5	3.90	3.90	31.1	6.2	68.8	...	4.7	65.7	153.6	165.6	...	...	...	...
...	76.7	14.8	21.1	6.9	47.1	5.16	5.29	11.8	6.5	97.9	...	5.6	7.1	155.8	170.2	...	...	...	...
...	84.9	13.9	4.5	2.0	8.3	5.08	5.08	-32.8	3.9	143.1	0.0	...	11.3	243.0	261.9	...	...	...	...
-7	81.3	13.5	8.0	5.4	12.2	3.81	3.61	-42.1	2.1	258.3	...	...	6.5	449.9	481.5	0.0	...	...	...
7	82.2	13.5	4.8	4.4	6.4	2.38	2.34	-34.9	1.4	390.7	...	...	-3.7	659.1	700.4	...	...	...	...
Principal Lines of Business: CompHosp/Med (94.5%), MedSup (4.0%), FEHBP (1.1%), Dental (0.4%), Vision (0.1%)													Principal States: TX (49.7%), CO (15.7%), AZ (13.6%), OK (8.8%), WA (4.5%)						
...	85.8	13.7	4.9	0.9	10.3	4.33	4.81	24.6	11.0	81.0	...	0.3	0.3	140.1	154.5	...	...	...	...
...	85.8	13.3	6.6	1.5	16.4	4.83	4.21	5.3	10.6	58.7	...	19.9	9.3	161.0	171.7	...	...	...	...
...	84.2	13.2	13.1	3.5	28.8	5.27	5.26	-10.6	7.1	121.8	...	1.2	34.1	204.7	221.8	...	...	...	...
...	82.1	13.2	16.8	3.9	29.2	4.12	4.16	-3.6	8.0	155.2	...	...	-15.1	248.7	269.6	...	...	...	...
...	85.6	13.2	6.2	1.1	10.5	3.19	3.25	0.2	10.9	125.7	...	...	-26.2	199.0	216.4	...	...	...	...
Principal Lines of Business: Medicare (86.9%), CompHosp/Med (9.2%), FEHBP (3.9%)													Principal States: AZ (100.0%)						
...	87.0	9.1	16.9	3.0	39.2	4.26	4.26	5.8	12.9	72.8	...	...	1.5	133.1	133.1	...	...	3.0	3.0
...	86.6	7.9	21.1	4.0	49.2	4.94	4.94	9.4	10.8	76.6	...	...	30.1	143.0	143.0	...	...	6.3	6.3
...	87.7	7.0	20.4	4.2	46.0	5.38	5.38	8.1	10.1	82.8	...	...	15.5	115.8	115.8	...	...	4.8	4.8
...	88.0	7.3	15.2	3.2	32.3	3.77	3.77	-5.1	10.0	96.8	...	...	-3.9	133.6	133.6	...	...	...	...
...	86.8	6.7	20.1	4.5	39.2	3.01	3.01	-6.4	7.8	114.7	...	...	19.9	143.8	143.8	...	...	...	...
Principal Lines of Business: Medicare (57.8%), CompHosp/Med (42.2%)																			
...	84.0	11.1	16.1	3.8	30.8	4.09	4.72	3.7	7.2	121.4	...	...	25.6	169.5	186.3	...	...	...	...
...	80.2	11.2	23.8	6.4	44.6	5.08	4.31	6.8	6.3	109.7	...	5.6	23.6	226.4	243.0	...	...	...	...
...	80.1	9.6	25.6	7.7	44.3	5.83	5.81	-6.0	5.5	176.5	...	...	6.7	275.1	297.8	...	...	...	...
-35	76.4	9.5	33.7	10.1	50.0	4.53	3.88	-8.6	4.7	243.7	...	...	6.8	269.5	294.9	0.6	...	...	...
35	83.2	9.3	20.1	5.3	29.7	2.71	3.22	-3.3	7.1	170.1	...	...	-35.4	247.7	270.8	...	...	...	...
Principal Lines of Business: Medicare (79.7%), CompHosp/Med (11.3%), FEHBP (9.0%)													Principal States: CO (100.0%)						
...	87.1	13.6	0.6	0.1	1.1	4.41	4.88	27.6	7.8	116.7	...	2.6	-0.4	179.0	195.4	...	...	...	...
...	84.1	14.3	11.0	2.6	23.4	4.82	4.25	19.8	8.4	73.7	...	...	11.4	214.5	229.2	...	...	...	...
...	79.2	15.7	17.6	5.1	36.1	5.76	5.76	5.7	6.0	119.4	...	0.4	48.0	230.5	244.0	...	...	...	...
0	80.2	16.0	119.7	32.1	184.9	5.25	5.09	-46.4	2.9	351.3	...	...	12.2	398.4	436.7	0.6	...	...	...
0	81.1	22.3	0.0	0.1	0.1	2.73	3.36	-65.4	1.1	630.6	...	0.7	-10.8	921.0	991.3	...	...	...	...
Principal Lines of Business: CompHosp/Med (67.4%), Medicare (19.3%), FEHBP (13.2%)													Principal States: NV (100.0%)						
...	84.9	13.1	2.1	0.6	4.1	3.91	3.69	-33.2	6.2	154.0	...	0.4	17.6	237.4	253.2	...	...	...	...
...	81.4	12.9	15.6	4.1	27.5	5.06	4.61	21.3	6.1	116.0	...	0.0	22.5	303.3	318.4	...	...	...	...
...	76.4	11.3	33.7	9.1	60.7	5.92	5.92	9.5	6.7	134.7	...	...	0.1	272.2	288.1	...	...	...	...
-7	74.0	11.6	40.7	10.1	67.0	4.31	3.81	1.1	6.4	180.7	...	...	5.8	275.7	299.7	0.5	...	...	...
7	78.8	11.3	30.4	6.8	49.1	2.97	3.36	6.4	7.8	146.9	...	...	-12.5	234.6	254.1	...	...	...	...
Principal Lines of Business: Medicare (68.6%), CompHosp/Med (26.9%), FEHBP (4.4%)													Principal States: OK (100.0%)						

Data in U.S. Dollars

COMPANY NAME / Ultimate Parent Association / Principal Officer / Mailing Address / Dom. : Began Bus. : Struct. : Mktg. / Specialty / Phone # / AMB# / NAIC# — Best's Financial Strength Rating / FSC

Column key: Balance Sheet — Data Year | Bonds (%) | Mort. Loans & R.E. (%) | Com & Pref. Stock (%) | All Other Assets (%) | Total Assets ($000) | Life Reserves (%) | Health Reserves %) | Ann Res. & Dep. Liabilities (%) | All Other Liabilities (%) | Capital & Surplus ($000); Operations — Direct Premiums Written ($000) | Net Premiums Written & Deposits ($000) | Operating Cash Flow ($000) | NOG Before Taxes ($000) | NOG After Taxes ($000) | Net Income ($000)

PACIFICARE OF OREGON INC
UnitedHealth Group Inc
Steven H. Nelson
President & CEO
9900 Bren Road East
Minnetonka, MN 55343
OR : 1987 : Stock : Broker
Group A&H, Medicare
503-603-7355
AMB# 068707 NAIC# 95893

A- — Rating Outlook: Stable — FSC VI

Data Year	Bonds (%)	Mort. Loans & R.E. (%)	Com & Pref. Stock (%)	All Other Assets (%)	Total Assets ($000)	Life Reserves (%)	Health Reserves %)	Ann Res. & Dep. Liabilities (%)	All Other Liabilities (%)	Capital & Surplus ($000)	Direct Premiums Written ($000)	Net Premiums Written & Deposits ($000)	Operating Cash Flow ($000)	NOG Before Taxes ($000)	NOG After Taxes ($000)	Net Income ($000)
'05	82.9	...	...	17.1	78,455	...	59.8	...	40.2	44,841	310,900	310,630	769	12,579	7,269	7,559
'06	57.7	...	...	42.3	103,659	...	48.4	...	51.6	50,919	326,012	324,688	24,352	23,443	13,779	13,439
'07	66.8	...	...	33.2	82,057	...	63.6	...	36.4	46,677	309,300	309,300	-19,840	30,412	21,429	21,376
'08	66.2	...	...	33.8	62,647	...	62.5	...	37.5	44,885	272,471	272,471	-15,069	43,878	29,253	29,245
'09	39.5	...	...	60.5	54,951	...	49.4	...	50.6	28,374	254,064	254,064	-8,282	19,288	12,551	12,651

Rating History: A-, 06/15/09; A-, 01/29/08; A-, 11/21/07; A-, 11/16/06; A-, 08/17/06

PACIFICARE OF TEXAS INC
UnitedHealth Group Inc
Thomas J. Quirk
President
9900 Bren Road East
Minnetonka, MN 55343
TX : 1986 : Stock : Broker
Group A&H, Medicare, FEHBP
972-866-2693
AMB# 068706 NAIC# 95174

A- — Rating Outlook: Stable — FSC VIII

Data Year	Bonds (%)	Mort. Loans & R.E. (%)	Com & Pref. Stock (%)	All Other Assets (%)	Total Assets ($000)	Life Reserves (%)	Health Reserves %)	Ann Res. & Dep. Liabilities (%)	All Other Liabilities (%)	Capital & Surplus ($000)	Direct Premiums Written ($000)	Net Premiums Written & Deposits ($000)	Operating Cash Flow ($000)	NOG Before Taxes ($000)	NOG After Taxes ($000)	Net Income ($000)
'05	76.2	...	...	23.8	167,403	...	63.1	...	36.9	78,260	948,700	943,942	26,811	15,838	15,838	16,003
'06	30.0	...	...	70.0	338,520	...	45.1	...	54.9	178,230	1,308,795	1,303,679	160,038	93,417	93,417	92,457
'07	29.5	...	...	70.5	400,690	...	33.5	...	66.5	187,672	1,522,398	1,520,708	52,105	201,240	137,915	137,915
'08	59.5	...	...	40.5	317,267	...	45.0	...	55.0	187,397	1,726,179	1,724,440	-91,707	215,820	140,481	142,584
'09	35.9	...	...	64.1	351,773	...	50.2	...	49.8	187,402	1,902,638	1,900,745	-20,090	145,007	95,594	96,846

Rating History: A-, 06/15/09; A-, 01/29/08; A-, 11/21/07; A-, 11/16/06; A-, 08/17/06

PACIFICARE OF WASHINGTON
UnitedHealth Group Inc
Steven H. Nelson
President & CEO
9900 Bren Road East
Minnetonka, MN 55343
WA : 1986 : Stock : Broker
Group A&H, Medicare
206-230-7400
AMB# 068591 NAIC# 48038

A- — Rating Outlook: Stable — FSC VII

Data Year	Bonds (%)	Mort. Loans & R.E. (%)	Com & Pref. Stock (%)	All Other Assets (%)	Total Assets ($000)	Life Reserves (%)	Health Reserves %)	Ann Res. & Dep. Liabilities (%)	All Other Liabilities (%)	Capital & Surplus ($000)	Direct Premiums Written ($000)	Net Premiums Written & Deposits ($000)	Operating Cash Flow ($000)	NOG Before Taxes ($000)	NOG After Taxes ($000)	Net Income ($000)
'05	62.9	...	1.3	35.8	153,841	...	48.3	...	51.7	99,971	494,845	493,573	13,927	46,165	42,273	42,710
'06	45.2	...	...	54.8	197,797	...	45.1	...	54.9	133,824	523,341	522,139	46,393	65,179	43,610	42,709
'07	36.6	...	...	63.4	296,697	...	36.3	...	63.7	228,602	474,459	474,454	25,996	81,092	54,017	54,016
'08	52.9	...	...	47.1	291,693	...	58.5	...	41.5	249,555	428,333	428,333	66,113	67,354	45,060	45,816
'09	38.0	...	...	62.0	128,730	...	61.9	...	38.1	81,114	417,931	417,931	-155,661	43,849	29,384	32,020

Rating History: A-, 06/15/09; A-, 01/29/08; A-, 11/21/07; A-, 11/16/06; A-, 08/17/06

PACIFICSOURCE HEALTH PLANS
Kenneth P. Provencher
President & CEO
110 International Way
Springfield, OR 97477
OR : 1939 : Non-Profit : Broker
Group A&H, Dental
541-686-1242
AMB# 064500 NAIC# 54976

B++ u — Under Review Implication: Developing — FSC VIII

Data Year	Bonds (%)	Mort. Loans & R.E. (%)	Com & Pref. Stock (%)	All Other Assets (%)	Total Assets ($000)	Life Reserves (%)	Health Reserves %)	Ann Res. & Dep. Liabilities (%)	All Other Liabilities (%)	Capital & Surplus ($000)	Direct Premiums Written ($000)	Net Premiums Written & Deposits ($000)	Operating Cash Flow ($000)	NOG Before Taxes ($000)	NOG After Taxes ($000)	Net Income ($000)
'05	27.3	4.6	32.1	36.0	178,264	...	54.7	...	45.3	115,765	437,756	436,967	30,777	33,474	27,086	30,217
'06	28.8	4.6	32.9	33.7	186,457	...	55.8	...	44.2	126,524	464,252	463,583	4,232	24,324	19,689	25,749
'07	35.5	4.4	41.5	18.6	197,761	...	53.1	...	46.9	127,484	502,032	501,455	521	-5,226	-1,017	9,902
'08	36.7	5.4	20.7	37.2	157,365	...	42.1	...	57.9	96,198	512,924	512,341	-26,281	1,649	5,162	-3,633
'09	30.8	4.6	24.9	39.7	177,024	...	32.6	...	67.4	110,482	521,915	520,645	14,747	7,534	7,242	4,290

Rating History: B++u, 03/17/10; B++, 05/15/09; B++, 06/13/08; B++, 06/05/07; B++, 06/09/06

PAN-AMERICAN ASSURANCE COMPANY
Pan-American Life Mutual Holding Company
Jose S. Suquet
President & CEO
Pan-American Life Center
New Orleans, LA 70130
LA : 1981 : Stock : Agency
Univ Life
504-566-1300
AMB# 009058 NAIC# 93459

A — Rating Outlook: Stable — FSC IX

Data Year	Bonds (%)	Mort. Loans & R.E. (%)	Com & Pref. Stock (%)	All Other Assets (%)	Total Assets ($000)	Life Reserves (%)	Health Reserves %)	Ann Res. & Dep. Liabilities (%)	All Other Liabilities (%)	Capital & Surplus ($000)	Direct Premiums Written ($000)	Net Premiums Written & Deposits ($000)	Operating Cash Flow ($000)	NOG Before Taxes ($000)	NOG After Taxes ($000)	Net Income ($000)
'05	85.7	...	...	14.3	21,955	16.4	...	31.1	52.5	14,159	60,264	273	-1,353	683	118	118
'06	87.0	...	...	13.0	24,113	14.9	...	32.6	52.5	15,490	59,444	851	4,463	1,419	1,183	1,183
'07	75.1	...	1.1	23.8	22,387	23.0	...	47.1	29.9	16,491	50,647	158	-5,325	3,833	3,554	3,554
'08	75.5	...	12.0	12.5	23,066	23.1	...	44.6	32.3	16,889	45,139	451	2,785	926	884	884
'09	72.6	...	11.6	15.8	23,772	22.2	...	39.6	38.2	17,305	44,130	65	2,316	888	717	741

Rating History: A r, 05/18/10; A- r, 01/30/09; A- r, 10/23/07; A- r, 08/07/06; A- r, 08/08/05

PAN-AMERICAN LIFE INS CO
Pan-American Life Mutual Holding Company
Jose S. Suquet
President & CEO
601 Poydras Street
New Orleans, LA 70130
LA : 1912 : Stock : Broker
Trad Life, Univ Life, Group Life
504-566-1300
AMB# 006893 NAIC# 67539

A — Rating Outlook: Stable — FSC IX

Data Year	Bonds (%)	Mort. Loans & R.E. (%)	Com & Pref. Stock (%)	All Other Assets (%)	Total Assets ($000)	Life Reserves (%)	Health Reserves %)	Ann Res. & Dep. Liabilities (%)	All Other Liabilities (%)	Capital & Surplus ($000)	Direct Premiums Written ($000)	Net Premiums Written & Deposits ($000)	Operating Cash Flow ($000)	NOG Before Taxes ($000)	NOG After Taxes ($000)	Net Income ($000)
'05	72.8	4.1	3.8	19.3	1,640,445	72.9	5.3	8.7	13.1	269,942	184,211	145,154	32,125	-6,678	-3,814	-5,178
'06	71.4	1.9	4.4	22.3	1,673,577	71.7	5.2	8.3	14.9	289,020	169,416	163,247	-6,865	7,329	3,453	-7,301
'07	77.8	1.6	6.4	14.2	1,582,708	76.8	6.6	7.2	9.5	306,483	189,924	167,233	-20,807	30,156	23,445	25,697
'08	75.1	1.5	5.9	17.5	1,527,542	76.6	7.1	7.1	9.2	267,189	218,068	192,828	-46,911	18,125	16,935	349
'09	78.7	1.4	2.6	17.3	1,515,358	74.9	7.6	6.9	10.6	259,446	230,265	190,717	-28,760	17,888	14,402	9,020

Rating History: A g, 05/18/10; A- g, 01/30/09; A- g, 10/23/07; A- g, 08/07/06; A- g, 08/08/05

PAN-AMERICAN LIFE INS CO OF PR
Pan-American Life Mutual Holding Company
Juan A. Ortega
President
P.O. Box 364865
San Juan, PR 00936-4865
PR : 2007 : Stock : Agency
Health, Group Life
787-620-1414
AMB# 088748 NAIC# 12952

NR-2

Data Year	Bonds (%)	Mort. Loans & R.E. (%)	Com & Pref. Stock (%)	All Other Assets (%)	Total Assets ($000)	Life Reserves (%)	Health Reserves %)	Ann Res. & Dep. Liabilities (%)	All Other Liabilities (%)	Capital & Surplus ($000)	Direct Premiums Written ($000)	Net Premiums Written & Deposits ($000)	Operating Cash Flow ($000)	NOG Before Taxes ($000)	NOG After Taxes ($000)	Net Income ($000)
'05	...	...	...	...	...	...	...	...	...	...	...	...	...	...	...	...
'06	...	...	...	...	...	...	...	...	...	...	...	...	...	...	...	...
'07	67.5	...	...	32.5	4,712	...	...	...	100.0	4,501	...	...	190	-5	-6	-3
'08	42.2	...	...	57.8	7,273	...	85.9	...	14.1	5,884	8,599	8,530	1,607	453	453	453
'09	59.2	...	...	40.8	8,392	3.6	61.9	...	34.6	3,763	23,167	22,942	1,658	-2,008	-2,149	-2,150

Rating History: NR-2, 05/18/10; NR-2, 01/30/09; NR-2, 06/19/08

PARAMOUNT ADVANTAGE
ProMedica Health System, Inc.
John C. Randolph
President
P.O. Box 928
Toledo, OH 43697-0928
OH : 2005 : Stock : Broker
Medicaid
419-887-2500
AMB# 064833 NAIC# 12353

NR-5

Data Year	Bonds (%)	Mort. Loans & R.E. (%)	Com & Pref. Stock (%)	All Other Assets (%)	Total Assets ($000)	Life Reserves (%)	Health Reserves %)	Ann Res. & Dep. Liabilities (%)	All Other Liabilities (%)	Capital & Surplus ($000)	Direct Premiums Written ($000)	Net Premiums Written & Deposits ($000)	Operating Cash Flow ($000)	NOG Before Taxes ($000)	NOG After Taxes ($000)	Net Income ($000)
'05	2.2	...	...	97.8	18,192	...	26.6	...	73.4	2,785	7,645	7,546	15,897	-398	-398	-398
'06	6.9	...	...	93.1	48,982	...	39.1	...	60.9	17,644	105,004	103,744	29,926	46	46	46
'07	7.1	...	...	92.9	51,323	...	46.8	...	53.2	21,032	141,828	140,099	1,458	3,251	3,251	3,253
'08	6.6	...	...	93.4	54,529	...	59.6	...	40.4	26,607	166,142	164,135	1,891	-3,738	-6,292	-6,292
'09	4.6	...	...	95.4	74,201	...	37.7	...	62.3	31,886	211,972	210,891	18,521	2,759	3,596	3,602

Rating History: NR-5, 03/23/10; NR-5, 08/26/09; C++pd, 08/11/08; NR-5, 06/27/08; NR-5, 05/03/07

PARAMOUNT CARE INC
ProMedica Health System, Inc.
John C. Randolph
President
1901 Indian Wood Circle
Maumee, OH 43537
OH : 1988 : Stock : Broker
Group A&H, Medicare, FEHBP
419-887-2500
AMB# 068579 NAIC# 95189

NR-5

Data Year	Bonds (%)	Mort. Loans & R.E. (%)	Com & Pref. Stock (%)	All Other Assets (%)	Total Assets ($000)	Life Reserves (%)	Health Reserves %)	Ann Res. & Dep. Liabilities (%)	All Other Liabilities (%)	Capital & Surplus ($000)	Direct Premiums Written ($000)	Net Premiums Written & Deposits ($000)	Operating Cash Flow ($000)	NOG Before Taxes ($000)	NOG After Taxes ($000)	Net Income ($000)
'05	60.5	...	15.4	24.1	128,525	...	44.4	...	55.6	59,194	477,605	475,377	21,044	9,737	6,068	8,177
'06	59.7	...	16.8	23.5	136,263	...	40.6	...	59.4	59,274	421,173	420,073	5,819	22,518	14,520	14,894
'07	62.4	...	18.1	19.5	142,374	...	36.9	...	63.1	64,499	393,717	392,562	3,693	10,620	4,478	7,345
'08	60.7	...	13.4	25.8	118,943	...	42.5	...	57.5	48,685	356,024	354,845	-23,437	14,802	9,452	2,816
'09	54.0	...	13.4	32.6	146,094	...	29.1	...	70.9	56,060	332,726	331,136	9,940	9,446	7,512	10,519

Rating History: NR-5, 03/23/10; NR-5, 08/26/09; B- pd, 08/11/08; B- pd, 08/22/07; NR-5, 07/03/07

BEST'S PROFITABILITY, LEVERAGE AND LIQUIDITY TESTS 2005 – 2009

Data in U.S. Dollars

	Profitability Tests							Leverage Tests						Liquidity Tests					
Un-Realized Capital Gains ($000)	Benefits Paid to NPW & Dep (%)	Comm. & Expenses to NPW & Dep (%)	NOG to Total Assets (%)	NOG to Total Rev (%)	Operating Return on Equity (%)	Net Yield (%)	Total Return (%)	Change in NPW & Dep (%)	NPW & Dep to Capital (X)	Capital & Surplus to Liabilities (%)	Surplus Relief (%)	Reins Leverage (%)	Change in Capital (%)	Quick Liquidity (%)	Current Liquidity (%)	Non-Invest Grade Bonds to Capital (%)	Delinq. & Foreclosed Mortgages to Capital (%)	Mort. & Credit Tenant Loans & R.E. to Capital (%)	Affiliated Invest to Capital (%)
...	82.8	14.1	9.5	2.3	17.2	4.34	4.77	-5.1	6.9	133.4	...	0.4	13.2	166.8	185.0	...	...	...	...
...	80.0	13.8	15.1	4.3	28.8	4.74	4.31	4.5	6.4	96.5	...	...	13.6	219.7	231.2	...	...	...	...
...	78.5	13.0	23.1	6.9	43.9	5.65	5.58	-4.7	6.6	131.9	...	...	-8.3	217.4	235.8	...	...	...	...
0	74.2	13.5	40.4	10.6	63.9	4.59	4.58	-11.9	6.1	252.7	...	...	-3.8	351.1	378.2	1.0	...	...	...
0	79.1	13.6	21.3	4.9	34.3	2.87	3.07	-6.8	9.0	106.8	...	...	-36.8	247.8	265.8	...	...	...	...

Principal Lines of Business: Medicare (87.7%), CompHosp/Med (12.3%)

Principal States: OR (100.0%)

...	87.7	11.2	10.0	1.7	20.8	4.25	4.37	29.6	12.1	87.8	...	0.1	6.1	191.4	203.0	...	...	...	...
...	83.4	10.1	36.9	7.2	72.8	4.84	4.43	38.1	7.3	111.2	...	1.1	127.7	320.0	332.7	...	...	...	...
...	77.4	10.5	37.3	9.1	75.4	6.28	6.28	16.6	8.1	88.1	...	...	5.3	271.4	286.3	...	...	...	...
-20	78.2	10.2	39.1	8.0	74.9	4.28	4.94	13.4	9.2	144.3	...	...	-0.1	251.0	269.5	0.1	...	...	...
20	82.8	9.9	28.6	5.0	51.0	2.58	3.07	10.2	10.1	114.0	...	...	0.0	212.9	227.7	...	...	...	...

Principal Lines of Business: Medicare (96.0%), CompHosp/Med (2.4%), FEHBP (1.6%)

Principal States: TX (100.0%)

...	80.9	10.7	29.2	8.5	45.3	3.68	4.02	-12.6	4.9	185.6	...	0.0	15.5	293.3	311.7	...	...	...	...
...	78.7	10.2	24.8	8.3	37.3	5.18	4.62	5.8	3.9	209.2	...	0.0	33.9	408.6	435.0	...	...	...	...
...	78.8	6.1	21.8	11.2	29.8	5.52	5.52	-9.1	2.1	335.7	...	...	70.8	416.8	444.5	...	...	...	...
-3	76.0	10.7	15.3	10.3	18.8	4.30	4.61	-9.7	1.7	592.2	...	...	9.2	851.2	899.0	0.0	...	...	...
3	79.3	11.2	14.0	7.0	17.8	2.12	3.47	-2.4	5.2	170.4	...	...	-67.5	350.0	368.2	...	...	...	...

Principal Lines of Business: Medicare (92.7%), CompHosp/Med (7.3%)

Principal States: WA (100.0%)

1,726	82.6	11.1	16.7	6.1	26.7	6.29	9.51	9.7	3.8	185.2	...	...	32.7	150.5	168.5	2.4	...	7.0	8.6
831	85.3	11.0	10.8	4.2	16.3	5.72	9.79	6.1	3.7	211.1	...	...	9.3	196.6	220.1	2.5	...	6.8	8.2
396	88.5	13.3	-0.5	-0.2	-0.8	2.85	9.41	8.2	3.9	181.4	...	0.7	0.8	160.0	183.9	1.7	...	6.8	8.0
-16,441	86.3	13.5	2.9	1.0	4.6	0.65	-14.69	2.2	5.3	157.3	...	0.0	-24.5	152.5	167.4	1.3	...	8.8	10.8
5,111	84.4	14.8	4.3	1.4	7.0	2.45	4.02	1.6	4.7	166.0	...	0.3	14.8	153.1	169.6	...	...	7.4	8.9

Principal Lines of Business: CompHosp/Med (98.7%), Dental (1.2%), MedSup (0.0%), OtherHlth (0.0%)

Principal States: OR (90.9%), ID (9.1%)

...	31.8	91.1	0.5	1.2	0.9	5.75	6.09	-82.6	0.0	183.6	58.3	999.9	15.2	151.5	195.5	...	...	...	...
...	15.7	-47.5	5.1	12.2	8.0	6.12	6.38	211.7	0.1	181.5	53.9	999.9	9.4	142.0	177.2	...	...	...	...
...	121.3	-99.9	15.3	35.3	22.2	5.90	6.11	-81.4	0.0	283.2	52.5	999.9	6.4	208.2	257.0	...	...	...	1.5
-66	42.0	-33.9	3.9	14.3	5.3	4.74	4.55	185.0	0.0	281.4	30.7	999.9	2.9	204.9	269.0	...	...	...	16.2
-5	230.1	-99.9	3.1	14.7	4.2	3.83	4.03	-85.6	0.0	278.9	22.8	999.9	2.8	260.5	282.5	...	...	...	15.7

Principal Lines of Business: OrdLife (56.5%), IndAnn (43.5%)

Principal States: IA (14.8%), FL (12.5%), CA (8.6%), TX (7.8%), IL (4.6%)

-5,956	109.9	59.8	-0.2	-1.6	-1.5	5.87	5.50	-29.9	0.5	22.1	4.7	32.9	17.4	58.0	73.8	33.7	0.3	38.7	18.3
20,885	92.1	56.9	0.2	1.3	1.2	5.85	6.61	12.5	0.5	24.4	4.6	34.3	9.9	68.1	84.4	29.8	0.1	23.4	18.1
93	94.2	49.9	1.4	8.5	7.9	5.91	6.14	2.4	0.5	26.5	4.4	40.2	5.9	64.7	79.6	32.6	0.0	17.6	17.2
-24,870	91.3	50.9	1.1	5.7	5.9	6.07	3.42	15.3	0.7	21.7	4.9	49.2	-17.8	60.0	73.4	56.5	0.1	17.3	20.0
9,765	99.2	46.3	0.9	4.9	5.5	5.89	6.32	-1.1	0.7	21.6	5.1	57.3	-1.2	58.4	74.5	42.5	0.1	16.9	14.3

Principal Lines of Business: GrpA&H (57.8%), OrdLife (32.3%), IndA&H (4.8%), GrpLife (3.1%), IndLife (1.6%)

Principal States: TX (10.0%), CA (7.8%), LA (4.0%), FL (3.3%)

...	...	...	...	...	...	...	...	...	...	...	...	...	...	...	...	...	...	...	...
...	...	...	...	...	...	...	...	...	...	...	...	...	...	...	...	...	...	...	...
...	...	...	...	-2.7	...	...	...	...	...	999.9	...	...	...	999.9	999.9	...	...	...	...
...	72.5	23.8	7.6	5.2	8.7	3.26	3.26	...	1.4	424.9	...	...	30.7	488.1	509.5	...	...	...	...
...	78.0	31.4	-27.4	-9.3	-44.6	2.56	2.55	169.0	6.1	81.6	...	6.1	-35.9	153.7	161.7	...	...	...	...

Principal Lines of Business: GrpA&H (91.8%), IndA&H (4.6%), GrpLife (3.6%)

Principal States: PR (100.0%)

...	94.4	10.8	...	-5.3	...	...	...	...	2.7	18.1	...	...	...	103.0	103.0	...	...	...	...
-37	86.4	13.3	0.1	0.0	0.4	4.55	4.43	999.9	5.9	56.3	...	3.4	533.5	191.8	194.2	...	...	...	...
147	87.0	12.3	6.5	2.3	16.8	5.14	5.46	35.0	6.7	69.4	...	0.6	19.2	206.0	206.7	...	...	...	...
-32	90.3	12.7	-11.9	-3.8	-26.4	2.46	2.39	17.2	6.2	95.3	...	0.5	26.5	320.4	328.4	...	...	...	...
-72	87.4	12.2	5.6	1.7	12.3	0.29	0.18	28.5	6.6	75.4	...	0.2	19.8	256.8	259.2	...	...	...	...

Principal Lines of Business: Medicaid (100.0%)

Principal States: OH (100.0%)

-360	90.9	7.7	5.1	1.3	10.8	3.05	4.70	2.3	8.0	85.4	...	0.6	12.4	139.3	156.9	...	...	...	...
912	87.8	8.1	11.0	3.4	24.5	4.54	5.61	-11.6	7.1	77.0	...	1.4	0.1	118.2	136.3	...	...	...	...
-57	88.7	9.9	3.2	1.1	7.2	4.38	6.61	-6.5	6.1	82.8	...	1.0	8.8	126.4	144.4	...	...	...	...
-1,568	88.5	8.4	7.2	2.6	16.7	3.34	-3.46	-9.6	7.3	69.3	...	0.3	-24.5	108.5	121.2	...	...	...	...
1,277	88.6	9.4	5.7	2.3	14.3	2.24	5.82	-6.7	5.9	62.3	...	1.1	15.1	104.0	114.7	...	...	...	...

Principal Lines of Business: Medicare (50.3%), CompHosp/Med (48.3%), FEHBP (1.4%)

Principal States: OH (100.0%)

ANNUAL STATEMENT DATA FOR YEARS 2005 – 2009

Data in U.S. Dollars

Column key — COMPANY NAME / Ultimate Parent Association / Principal Officer / Mailing Address / Dom. : Began Bus. : Struct. : Mktg. / Specialty / Phone # / AMB# / NAIC#; Best's Financial Strength Rating / FSC

Balance Sheet: Data Year; Bonds (%); Mort. Loans & R.E. (%); Com & Pref. Stock (%); All Other Assets (%); Total Assets ($000); Life Reserves (%); Health Reserves (%); Ann Res. & Dep. Liabilities (%); All Other Liabilities (%); Capital & Surplus ($000). Operations: Direct Premiums Written ($000); Net Premiums Written & Deposits ($000); Operating Cash Flow ($000); NOG Before Taxes ($000); NOG After Taxes ($000); Net Income ($000)

PARAMOUNT CARE OF MICHIGAN
ProMedica Health System, Inc.
John C. Randolph
Chairman & President
106 Park Place
Dundee, MI 48131
MI : 1996 : Stock : Broker
Group A&H, Medicare
734-529-7800
AMB# 064294 NAIC# 95566

Best's Financial Strength Rating: **NR-5**

Data Year	Bonds (%)	Mort. Loans & R.E. (%)	Com & Pref. Stock (%)	All Other Assets (%)	Total Assets ($000)	Life Reserves (%)	Health Reserves (%)	Ann Res. & Dep. Liabilities (%)	All Other Liabilities (%)	Capital & Surplus ($000)	Direct Premiums Written ($000)	Net Premiums Written & Deposits ($000)	Operating Cash Flow ($000)	NOG Before Taxes ($000)	NOG After Taxes ($000)	Net Income ($000)
'05	...	...	...	100.0	8,950	...	65.1	...	34.9	5,321	31,072	30,743	130	-192	-98	-98
'06	...	...	...	100.0	12,574	...	42.1	...	57.9	6,321	34,763	34,469	4,353	1,588	1,021	1,021
'07	...	...	...	100.0	16,522	...	64.6	...	35.4	8,738	35,835	35,543	3,792	627	369	369
'08	...	...	...	100.0	15,613	...	51.5	...	48.5	10,119	34,649	34,389	-594	2,164	1,373	1,373
'09	...	...	...	100.0	14,473	...	61.3	...	38.7	10,548	34,096	33,916	-629	640	490	490

Rating History: NR-5, 03/23/10; NR-5, 08/26/09; B- pd, 08/11/08; B- pd, 08/22/07; NR-5, 07/03/07

PARAMOUNT INSURANCE COMPANY
ProMedica Health System, Inc.
John C. Randolph
President
1901 Indian Wood Circle
Maumee, OH 43537
OH : 2002 : Stock : Broker
Group A&H, Med supp, FEHBP
419-887-2500
AMB# 064742 NAIC# 11518

Best's Financial Strength Rating: **NR-5**

Data Year	Bonds (%)	Mort. Loans & R.E. (%)	Com & Pref. Stock (%)	All Other Assets (%)	Total Assets ($000)	Life Reserves (%)	Health Reserves (%)	Ann Res. & Dep. Liabilities (%)	All Other Liabilities (%)	Capital & Surplus ($000)	Direct Premiums Written ($000)	Net Premiums Written & Deposits ($000)	Operating Cash Flow ($000)	NOG Before Taxes ($000)	NOG After Taxes ($000)	Net Income ($000)
'05	...	...	...	100.0	5,806	...	65.1	...	34.9	2,593	7,767	7,650	976	-2,250	-1,839	-1,839
'06	1.0	...	...	99.0	10,068	...	53.2	...	46.8	5,088	13,881	13,694	4,222	-2,124	-1,458	-1,458
'07	0.9	...	...	99.1	11,496	...	58.7	...	41.3	6,921	20,994	20,718	1,793	2,099	1,577	1,577
'08	0.5	...	...	99.5	21,048	...	45.3	...	54.7	8,670	36,269	35,950	2,655	-6,368	-4,220	-4,220
'09	1.9	...	...	98.1	18,163	...	72.9	...	27.1	6,072	34,967	34,306	117	-10,419	-7,883	-7,884

Rating History: NR-5, 03/23/10; NR-5, 04/08/09; NR-5, 03/11/08; NR-5, 04/03/07; NR-5, 04/25/06

PARK AVENUE LIFE INS CO
Guardian Life Ins Co of America
Armand M. de Palo
President & CEO
7 Hanover Square
New York, NY 10004-4025
DE : 1965 : Stock : Inactive
Ind Life
212-598-8829
AMB# 006000 NAIC# 60003

Best's Financial Strength Rating: **A**
Rating Outlook: Stable
FSC VIII

Data Year	Bonds (%)	Mort. Loans & R.E. (%)	Com & Pref. Stock (%)	All Other Assets (%)	Total Assets ($000)	Life Reserves (%)	Health Reserves (%)	Ann Res. & Dep. Liabilities (%)	All Other Liabilities (%)	Capital & Surplus ($000)	Direct Premiums Written ($000)	Net Premiums Written & Deposits ($000)	Operating Cash Flow ($000)	NOG Before Taxes ($000)	NOG After Taxes ($000)	Net Income ($000)
'05	73.5	...	21.6	5.0	485,303	73.7	...	21.3	4.9	167,038	3,012	11,187	-18,788	17,237	15,862	16,055
'06	72.8	...	23.1	4.1	444,536	74.9	...	21.2	3.9	152,171	2,563	9,498	-34,322	16,724	13,208	12,886
'07	73.7	...	22.7	3.7	434,886	75.0	...	21.1	3.9	150,531	2,334	8,494	-7,558	18,512	15,703	15,813
'08	74.5	...	21.7	3.8	417,794	74.9	...	21.3	3.7	144,337	2,032	6,556	-9,407	20,314	17,430	16,903
'09	67.5	...	23.0	9.5	419,366	74.9	...	21.5	3.6	156,228	1,767	4,818	-4,221	9,267	6,278	6,285

Rating History: A, 10/13/09; A, 11/26/08; A, 04/23/08; A, 11/10/06; A, 11/18/05

PARKER CENTENNIAL ASSURANCE CO
Sentry Insurance a Mutual Company
Mark R. Hackl
President
1800 North Point Drive
Stevens Point, WI 54481
WI : 1973 : Stock : Broker
Struc Sett, Ann
715-346-6000
AMB# 060403 NAIC# 71099

Best's Financial Strength Rating: **A+**
Rating Outlook: Stable
FSC XV

Data Year	Bonds (%)	Mort. Loans & R.E. (%)	Com & Pref. Stock (%)	All Other Assets (%)	Total Assets ($000)	Life Reserves (%)	Health Reserves (%)	Ann Res. & Dep. Liabilities (%)	All Other Liabilities (%)	Capital & Surplus ($000)	Direct Premiums Written ($000)	Net Premiums Written & Deposits ($000)	Operating Cash Flow ($000)	NOG Before Taxes ($000)	NOG After Taxes ($000)	Net Income ($000)
'05	50.0	...	...	50.0	49,059	...	...	90.1	9.9	37,722	10,224	10,243	10,145	925	599	600
'06	68.5	...	...	31.5	54,380	...	...	94.9	5.1	38,627	6,660	6,664	6,678	1,441	947	947
'07	86.8	...	...	13.2	63,876	...	...	89.1	10.9	39,498	8,579	8,580	9,387	1,430	992	992
'08	95.1	...	...	4.9	64,676	...	...	93.2	6.8	39,525	4,379	4,381	812	1,898	1,296	776
'09	90.2	...	...	9.8	68,625	...	...	91.4	8.6	41,065	2,824	2,824	3,822	2,057	1,422	1,510

Rating History: A+ g, 01/26/10; A+ g, 02/03/09; A+ g, 01/24/08; A+ g, 05/04/07; A+ g, 06/19/06

PARKLAND COMMUNITY HEALTH PLAN[2]
Ronnie J. Anderson, M.D.
President & CEO
2777 Stemmons Freeway, Suite 1750
Dallas, TX 75207
TX : 1998 : Non-Profit : Not Available
Group A&H, Medicaid
214-266-2100
AMB# 064461 NAIC# 95414

Best's Financial Strength Rating: **NR-5**

Data Year	Bonds (%)	Mort. Loans & R.E. (%)	Com & Pref. Stock (%)	All Other Assets (%)	Total Assets ($000)	Life Reserves (%)	Health Reserves (%)	Ann Res. & Dep. Liabilities (%)	All Other Liabilities (%)	Capital & Surplus ($000)	Direct Premiums Written ($000)	Net Premiums Written & Deposits ($000)	Operating Cash Flow ($000)	NOG Before Taxes ($000)	NOG After Taxes ($000)	Net Income ($000)
'05	10.4	...	85.5	4.1	38,329	...	54.1	...	45.9	11,936	193,832	192,596	4,279	6,325	6,325	6,325
'06	...	...	...	...	...	...	...	...	...	...	...	...	...	...	...	...
'07	...	...	...	...	...	...	...	...	...	...	...	...	...	...	...	...
'08	76.7	...	...	23.3	143,850	...	67.3	...	32.7	73,574	385,348	384,338	51,164	33,486	33,486	33,481
'09	62.3	...	...	37.7	135,610	...	71.5	...	28.5	79,776	401,528	399,507	-8,737	5,426	5,426	5,924

Rating History: NR-5, 04/07/10; NR-5, 05/08/09; NR-5, 09/19/07; C+ pd, 07/17/06; C- pd, 07/18/05

PARTNERS NATL HLTH PLNS OF NC[2]
Blue Cross & BS of NC
Robert J. Greczyn, Jr.
President
P.O. Box 17509
Winston-Salem, NC 27116-7509
NC : 1986 : Stock : Other Direct
Medicare
336-760-4822
AMB# 068822 NAIC# 95300

Best's Financial Strength Rating: **NR-5**

Data Year	Bonds (%)	Mort. Loans & R.E. (%)	Com & Pref. Stock (%)	All Other Assets (%)	Total Assets ($000)	Life Reserves (%)	Health Reserves (%)	Ann Res. & Dep. Liabilities (%)	All Other Liabilities (%)	Capital & Surplus ($000)	Direct Premiums Written ($000)	Net Premiums Written & Deposits ($000)	Operating Cash Flow ($000)	NOG Before Taxes ($000)	NOG After Taxes ($000)	Net Income ($000)
'05	74.8	...	3.4	21.9	190,256	...	61.5	...	38.5	146,491	326,312	326,030	23,274	30,278	21,716	21,692
'06	70.5	...	3.2	26.3	223,704	...	51.9	...	48.1	169,813	374,675	374,387	31,030	28,472	20,379	20,373
'07	82.8	...	3.7	13.4	219,770	...	75.6	...	24.4	178,598	389,697	389,389	-5,548	9,994	9,573	9,477
'08	81.0	...	3.9	15.1	233,430	...	4.2	...	95.8	193,287	421,594	210,284	13,809	17,931	13,845	13,515
'09	73.0	...	3.7	23.3	248,339	...	...	...	100.0	201,848	460,596	...	12,949	8,978	8,364	8,541

Rating History: NR-5, 05/03/10; NR-5, 08/26/09; B++pd, 09/19/08; B++pd, 08/27/07; B++pd, 09/21/06

PATRIOT LIFE INS CO
Frankenmuth Mutual Insurance Company
Lincoln J. Merrill, Jr.
President
P.O. Box 1776
Brunswick, ME 04011-1776
ME : 1995 : Stock : Not Available
Ordinary Life
207-725-1776
AMB# 008973 NAIC# 60099

Best's Financial Strength Rating: **NR-5**

Data Year	Bonds (%)	Mort. Loans & R.E. (%)	Com & Pref. Stock (%)	All Other Assets (%)	Total Assets ($000)	Life Reserves (%)	Health Reserves (%)	Ann Res. & Dep. Liabilities (%)	All Other Liabilities (%)	Capital & Surplus ($000)	Direct Premiums Written ($000)	Net Premiums Written & Deposits ($000)	Operating Cash Flow ($000)	NOG Before Taxes ($000)	NOG After Taxes ($000)	Net Income ($000)
'05	...	...	...	...	...	...	...	...	...	...	...	...	...	...	...	...
'06	...	...	...	...	...	...	...	...	...	...	...	...	...	...	...	...
'07	56.7	...	...	43.3	7,194	40.5	...	...	59.5	6,793	1	1	445	138	120	443
'08	90.3	...	...	9.7	7,149	49.3	...	...	50.7	6,825	2	2	-96	175	39	39
'09	75.3	...	...	24.7	7,259	33.7	...	...	66.3	6,806	1	1	119	17	26	26

Rating History: NR-5, 06/14/10; NR-5, 06/17/09; NR-1, 06/12/08; NR-1, 06/08/07; NR-1, 06/07/06

PAUL REVERE LIFE INS CO
Unum Group
Thomas R. Watjen
Chairman, President & CEO
1 Fountain Square
Chattanooga, TN 37402-1330
MA : 1930 : Stock : Broker
Disability
423-294-1011
AMB# 006899 NAIC# 67598

Best's Financial Strength Rating: **A-**
Rating Outlook: Positive
FSC XIV

Data Year	Bonds (%)	Mort. Loans & R.E. (%)	Com & Pref. Stock (%)	All Other Assets (%)	Total Assets ($000)	Life Reserves (%)	Health Reserves (%)	Ann Res. & Dep. Liabilities (%)	All Other Liabilities (%)	Capital & Surplus ($000)	Direct Premiums Written ($000)	Net Premiums Written & Deposits ($000)	Operating Cash Flow ($000)	NOG Before Taxes ($000)	NOG After Taxes ($000)	Net Income ($000)
'05	86.7	0.3	6.8	6.2	5,325,917	0.5	92.8	4.0	2.7	1,138,139	501,816	644,918	49,676	187,728	143,688	130,309
'06	87.5	0.8	7.3	4.4	5,286,378	0.4	93.0	3.8	2.8	1,034,609	473,826	606,960	18,438	138,200	113,344	95,874
'07	85.2	1.1	5.2	8.5	4,920,984	0.4	88.3	3.6	7.7	458,736	447,664	101,839	-392,485	367,611	191,086	194,208
'08	87.0	1.6	5.2	6.2	4,710,077	0.4	90.9	3.6	5.1	340,303	420,450	96,835	-244,225	134,509	110,881	78,561
'09	88.2	2.2	3.5	6.1	4,744,807	0.3	91.8	3.6	4.3	450,488	394,143	93,418	55,567	159,056	141,188	131,418

Rating History: A- g, 03/08/10; A- g, 03/13/09; A- g, 01/29/08; A- g, 11/07/06; A- g, 06/07/06

PAUL REVERE VARIABLE ANNUITY
Unum Group
Thomas R. Watjen
Chairman, President & CEO
1 Fountain Square
Chattanooga, TN 37402-1330
MA : 1966 : Stock : Broker
Ind Ann, Ind Life
423-294-1011
AMB# 006900 NAIC# 67601

Best's Financial Strength Rating: **B++**
Rating Outlook: Stable
FSC XIV

Data Year	Bonds (%)	Mort. Loans & R.E. (%)	Com & Pref. Stock (%)	All Other Assets (%)	Total Assets ($000)	Life Reserves (%)	Health Reserves (%)	Ann Res. & Dep. Liabilities (%)	All Other Liabilities (%)	Capital & Surplus ($000)	Direct Premiums Written ($000)	Net Premiums Written & Deposits ($000)	Operating Cash Flow ($000)	NOG Before Taxes ($000)	NOG After Taxes ($000)	Net Income ($000)
'05	88.1	...	...	11.9	140,558	...	...	24.3	75.7	114,868	6,169	20,668	-6,903	11,888	8,617	8,560
'06	75.2	...	...	24.8	145,720	...	...	16.8	83.2	109,480	5,679	15,258	5,914	11,041	7,967	8,360
'07	82.9	...	...	17.1	132,608	...	...	32.0	68.0	114,046	5,520	11,649	-7,786	8,778	5,932	5,911
'08	90.9	...	...	9.1	110,191	...	...	37.6	62.4	94,726	5,254	10,717	-20,165	7,878	5,573	1,760
'09	85.2	...	...	14.8	49,142	...	...	34.4	65.6	31,776	5,122	6,663	-61,460	8,240	5,940	7,085

Rating History: B++, 03/08/10; A-, 03/13/09; A-, 01/29/08; A-, 11/07/06; A-, 06/07/06

BEST'S PROFITABILITY, LEVERAGE AND LIQUIDITY TESTS 2005 – 2009

Data in U.S. Dollars

—	Profitability Tests							Leverage Tests						Liquidity Tests					
Un-Realized Capital Gains ($000)	Benefits Paid to NPW & Dep (%)	Comm. & Expenses to NPW & Dep (%)	NOG to Total Assets (%)	NOG to Total Rev (%)	Operating Return on Equity (%)	Net Yield (%)	Total Return (%)	Change in NPW & Dep (%)	NPW & Dep to Capital (X)	Capital & Surplus to Liabilities (%)	Surplus Relief (%)	Reins Leverage (%)	Change in Capital (%)	Quick Liquidity (%)	Current Liquidity (%)	Non-Invest Grade Bonds to Capital (%)	Delinq. & Foreclosed Mortgages to Capital (%)	Mort. & Credit Tenant Loans & R.E. to Capital (%)	Affiliated Invest to Capital (%)
…	91.5	10.7	-1.2	-0.3	-1.9	2.70	2.70	10.5	5.8	146.6	…	0.1	6.7	196.8	196.8	…	…	…	…
…	88.3	8.3	9.5	2.9	17.5	4.53	4.53	12.1	5.5	101.1	…	1.0	18.8	255.9	263.9	…	…	…	…
…	92.3	7.6	2.5	1.0	4.9	4.48	4.48	3.1	4.1	112.3	…	…	38.2	257.6	264.1	…	…	…	…
…	86.5	8.1	8.5	4.0	14.6	2.04	2.04	-3.2	3.4	184.2	…	0.1	15.8	422.0	439.2	…	…	…	…
…	91.7	6.5	3.3	1.4	4.7	0.21	0.21	-1.4	3.2	268.7	…	…	4.2	575.6	599.6	…	…	…	…
	Principal Lines of Business: CompHosp/Med (61.2%), Medicare (38.8%)													Principal States: MI (100.0%)					
…	97.5	21.2	-38.3	-23.8	-66.3	1.93	1.93	170.6	3.0	80.7	…	2.0	-12.2	139.8	139.8	…	…	…	…
-3	98.9	18.6	-18.4	-10.5	-38.0	4.03	3.99	79.0	2.7	102.1	…	…	96.2	265.3	275.4	…	…	…	…
2	80.7	15.9	14.6	7.4	26.3	5.18	5.20	51.3	3.0	151.3	…	0.5	36.0	334.0	345.0	…	…	…	…
…	102.3	16.2	-25.9	-11.7	-54.1	2.23	2.23	73.5	4.1	70.0	…	1.6	25.3	189.4	198.6	…	…	…	…
-4	103.0	16.4	-40.2	-23.0	-99.9	0.17	0.13	-4.6	5.6	50.2	…	…	-30.0	150.3	154.7	…	…	…	…
	Principal Lines of Business: CompHosp/Med (90.7%), MedSup (7.0%), OtherHlth (1.6%), FEHBP (0.7%)													Principal States: OH (100.0%)					
5,649	232.0	27.9	3.2	36.7	9.6	6.81	8.18	-6.2	0.1	54.0	1.8	7.3	2.8	75.2	85.6	11.7	…	…	61.0
-5,187	404.9	28.6	2.8	34.1	8.3	6.84	5.79	-15.1	0.1	53.4	0.5	5.3	-9.1	74.8	85.8	10.8	…	…	66.2
-3,840	280.1	43.8	3.6	40.8	10.4	7.41	6.71	-10.6	0.1	54.2	-0.1	5.2	-1.3	77.8	89.2	6.6	…	…	64.5
-7,756	389.9	44.1	4.1	44.5	11.8	7.91	6.08	-22.8	0.0	53.9	0.0	5.2	-4.3	79.6	90.4	8.8	…	…	62.1
5,766	500.5	49.6	1.5	24.2	4.2	5.14	6.62	-26.5	0.0	60.6	0.0	4.8	8.2	87.1	98.2	9.3	…	…	61.0
	Principal Lines of Business: OrdLife (98.5%), GrpLife (1.1%), IndAnn (0.3%)													Principal States: CA (41.4%), MA (12.2%), PA (11.0%), CT (5.6%), NJ (5.4%)					
…	1.2	3.4	1.4	5.2	1.6	3.30	3.30	…	0.3	334.1	-0.3	1.4	1.6	535.1	568.6	…	…	…	…
…	39.3	6.8	1.8	10.3	2.5	5.19	5.19	-34.9	0.2	246.7	0.0	0.8	2.5	356.6	389.5	…	…	…	…
…	33.7	5.8	1.7	8.5	2.5	5.27	5.26	28.8	0.2	163.2	0.0	0.5	2.4	198.6	230.8	…	…	…	…
…	84.3	8.1	2.0	16.9	3.3	5.23	4.42	-48.9	0.1	157.2	0.0	0.3	-0.2	165.4	197.6	0.2	…	…	…
…	78.8	9.9	2.1	22.6	3.5	5.38	5.51	-35.5	0.1	149.8	0.0	0.1	4.1	168.8	201.5	0.2	…	…	…
	Principal Lines of Business: GrpAnn (100.0%)													Principal States: WI (100.0%)					
…	80.3	17.0	17.5	3.3	69.7	3.73	3.73	7.9	16.1	45.2	…	5.3	92.2	74.5	93.1	…	…	…	…
…	…	…	…	…	…	…	…	…	…	…	…	…	…	…	…	…	…	…	…
…	…	…	…	…	…	…	…	…	…	…	…	…	…	…	…	…	…	…	…
…	81.3	11.0	…	8.6	…	…	…	…	5.2	104.7	…	1.7	…	181.5	181.5	…	…	…	…
…	88.7	10.7	3.9	1.4	7.1	2.47	2.86	3.9	5.0	142.9	…	3.0	8.4	209.6	209.6	…	…	…	…
	Principal Lines of Business: Medicaid (77.9%), CompHosp/Med (22.1%)													Principal States: TX (100.0%)					
161	82.3	10.5	12.2	6.5	15.9	4.26	4.34	19.2	2.2	334.7	…	0.0	15.8	304.5	337.5	…	…	…	5.4
501	84.1	10.9	9.8	5.3	12.9	4.87	5.13	14.8	2.2	315.1	…	…	15.9	292.1	321.4	…	…	…	5.0
828	89.7	10.3	4.3	2.4	5.5	5.03	5.39	4.0	2.2	433.8	…	…	5.2	381.6	429.5	…	…	…	5.2
536	87.7	8.2	6.1	6.3	7.4	4.50	4.59	-46.0	1.1	481.5	…	14.4	8.2	434.5	486.9	…	…	…	5.1
29	…	…	3.5	100.3	4.2	3.77	3.87	-99.9	…	434.2	…	21.6	4.4	447.6	496.1	…	…	…	4.9
														Principal States: NC (100.0%)					
…	…	…	…	…	…	…	…	…	…	…	…	…	…	…	…	…	…	…	…
…	…	…	…	…	…	…	…	…	…	…	…	…	…	…	…	…	…	…	…
-237	583.4	999.9	…	48.4	…	…	…	…	0.0	999.9	…	…	…	999.9	999.9	…	…	…	…
…	458.2	999.9	0.5	13.3	0.6	4.02	4.11	9.4	0.0	999.9	…	…	0.5	999.9	999.9	…	…	…	…
…	594.4	999.9	0.4	9.6	0.4	3.78	3.88	-13.5	0.0	999.9	…	…	-0.2	999.9	999.9	…	…	…	…
	Principal Lines of Business: OrdLife (100.0%)													Principal States: ME (100.0%)					
-14,292	112.8	22.0	2.7	12.9	12.7	7.55	7.10	11.2	0.6	27.9	1.1	102.9	2.2	53.6	72.7	33.6	…	1.2	21.5
-12,317	123.2	18.5	2.1	10.7	10.4	7.34	6.85	-5.9	0.6	25.4	0.9	110.3	-8.0	54.1	73.3	30.6	…	5.7	22.2
-64,564	91.0	148.2	3.7	23.4	25.6	8.07	6.94	-83.2	0.2	11.2	61.0	257.1	-53.7	53.1	69.8	54.0	…	14.8	35.3
-20,367	62.8	289.8	2.3	18.2	27.8	7.38	6.36	-4.9	0.3	8.5	33.8	325.9	-26.0	47.7	64.4	56.1	…	26.3	43.0
-48,711	64.2	331.6	3.0	24.7	35.7	8.45	7.28	-3.5	0.2	11.1	24.5	236.6	29.3	46.3	64.0	57.1	…	26.0	22.5
	Principal Lines of Business: IndA&H (88.6%), GrpA&H (5.4%), GrpLife (3.2%), GrpAnn (1.5%), OrdLife (1.3%)													Principal States: NY (13.5%), CA (9.5%), NJ (5.7%), FL (4.9%), PA (4.9%)					
-26	1.6	-10.3	6.0	64.0	7.3	7.48	7.61	0.8	0.2	826.6	2.9	88.5	-5.1	361.3	585.1	0.0	…	…	…
…	2.0	-14.6	5.6	60.7	7.1	6.82	7.33	-26.2	0.1	453.7	3.7	96.8	-4.4	328.0	447.6	4.7	…	…	…
…	3.1	-8.0	4.3	58.3	5.3	6.19	6.38	-23.7	0.1	878.9	1.7	90.3	4.3	494.4	702.2	7.0	…	…	…
14	2.8	-3.6	4.6	59.2	5.3	6.44	3.44	-8.0	0.1	739.6	1.7	106.4	-17.5	300.8	496.0	10.9	…	…	…
2	7.1	-12.3	7.5	63.2	9.4	9.01	11.20	-37.8	0.2	217.1	4.7	290.9	-66.1	167.6	207.1	10.8	…	…	…
	Principal Lines of Business: GrpAnn (100.0%)													Principal States: CA (49.4%), OH (9.0%), NJ (6.7%), MA (3.1%)					

Data in U.S. Dollars

Column key: COMPANY NAME; Ultimate Parent Association; Principal Officer; Mailing Address; Dom. : Began Bus. : Struct. : Mktg.; Specialty; Phone #; AMB#; NAIC# — Best's Financial Strength Rating; FSC — Balance Sheet; Operations

PEACH STATE HEALTH PLAN INC — B+

Centene Corporation
Michael A. Cadger
President & CEO
7711 Carondelet Avenue
St. Louis, MO 63105-3389
GA : 2006 : Stock : Broker
Medicaid
314-725-4477
AMB# 064831 NAIC# 12315

Rating Outlook: Stable
FSC VII

Data Year	Bonds (%)	Mort. Loans & R.E. (%)	Com & Pref. Stock (%)	All Other Assets (%)	Total Assets ($000)	Life Reserves (%)	Health Reserves (%)	Ann Res. & Dep. Liabilities (%)	All Other Liabilities (%)	Capital & Surplus ($000)	Direct Premiums Written ($000)	Net Premiums Written & Deposits ($000)	Operating Cash Flow ($000)	NOG Before Taxes ($000)	NOG After Taxes ($000)	Net Income ($000)
'05	2.3	...	...	97.7	4,380	...	...	...	100.0	3,455	...	...	4,038	-790	-513	-513
'06	0.1	...	...	99.9	101,908	...	90.8	...	9.2	32,692	349,545	344,842	54,355	-10,900	-7,485	-7,485
'07	0.1	...	...	99.9	132,443	...	85.7	...	14.3	60,711	707,545	697,824	16,558	-31,639	-17,441	-17,441
'08	...	...	...	100.0	134,959	...	83.6	...	16.4	59,753	742,048	730,147	18,983	-15,936	-14,737	-15,475
'09	58.2	...	0.3	41.5	158,497	...	74.8	...	25.2	63,029	763,492	751,986	48,415	-48,268	-36,342	-36,342

Rating History: B+, 02/19/10; B+, 02/10/09; NR-5, 03/20/08; NR-5, 04/03/07; NR-5, 07/18/06

PEARLE VISION MGD CR - HMO TX[2] — NR-5

Luxottica US Holdings Corporation
Liz DiGiandomerico
President & Secretary
2465 Joe Field Road
Dallas, TX 75229-3479
TX : 1996 : Stock : Not Available
Group A&H
972-277-6000
AMB# 064516 NAIC# 95522

Data Year	Bonds (%)	Mort. Loans & R.E. (%)	Com & Pref. Stock (%)	All Other Assets (%)	Total Assets ($000)	Life Reserves (%)	Health Reserves (%)	Ann Res. & Dep. Liabilities (%)	All Other Liabilities (%)	Capital & Surplus ($000)	Direct Premiums Written ($000)	Net Premiums Written & Deposits ($000)	Operating Cash Flow ($000)	NOG Before Taxes ($000)	NOG After Taxes ($000)	Net Income ($000)
'05	...	...	...	100.0	2,632	...	2.7	...	97.3	1,858	...	...	1,003	875	541	541
'06	...	...	...	100.0	3,368	...	1.4	...	98.6	2,326	...	...	-1	784	484	484
'07	...	...	...	100.0	2,401	...	0.5	...	99.5	2,081	...	...	-970	346	237	237
'08	...	...	...	100.0	1,327	...	0.8	...	99.2	1,086	...	...	-237	626	393	393
'09	...	...	...	100.0	1,346	...	0.9	...	99.1	1,048	...	...	30	557	349	349

Rating History: NR-5, 04/07/10; NR-5, 03/31/09; NR-5, 04/28/08; NR-5, 04/11/07; NR-5, 05/22/06

PEKIN FINANCIAL LIFE INS CO — NR-3

Farmers Automobile Insurance Assn
Scott A. Martin
President & COO
2505 Court Street
Pekin, IL 61558
AZ : 1985 : Stock : Inactive
Inactive
309-346-1161
AMB# 009525 NAIC# 72362

Data Year	Bonds (%)	Mort. Loans & R.E. (%)	Com & Pref. Stock (%)	All Other Assets (%)	Total Assets ($000)	Life Reserves (%)	Health Reserves (%)	Ann Res. & Dep. Liabilities (%)	All Other Liabilities (%)	Capital & Surplus ($000)	Direct Premiums Written ($000)	Net Premiums Written & Deposits ($000)	Operating Cash Flow ($000)	NOG Before Taxes ($000)	NOG After Taxes ($000)	Net Income ($000)
'05	43.5	...	...	56.5	581	...	...	...	100.0	416	...	...	-83	-4	-5	-5
'06	37.0	...	...	63.0	683	...	...	...	100.0	415	...	...	101	0	-2	-2
'07	37.2	...	...	62.8	679	...	...	...	100.0	403	...	...	-4	1	-1	-1
'08	31.6	...	...	68.4	798	...	...	...	100.0	401	...	...	120	0	-2	-2
'09	36.7	...	...	63.3	688	...	...	...	100.0	397	...	...	-109	-3	-4	-4

Rating History: NR-3, 06/26/09; NR-3, 06/20/08; NR-3, 06/13/07; NR-3, 06/26/06; NR-3, 06/14/05

PEKIN LIFE INS CO — A-

Farmers Automobile Insurance Assn
Scott A. Martin
President & COO
2505 Court Street
Pekin, IL 61558
IL : 1965 : Stock : Agency
Group A&H, Life, Maj med
309-346-1161
AMB# 006901 NAIC# 67628

Rating Outlook: Stable
FSC VIII

Data Year	Bonds (%)	Mort. Loans & R.E. (%)	Com & Pref. Stock (%)	All Other Assets (%)	Total Assets ($000)	Life Reserves (%)	Health Reserves (%)	Ann Res. & Dep. Liabilities (%)	All Other Liabilities (%)	Capital & Surplus ($000)	Direct Premiums Written ($000)	Net Premiums Written & Deposits ($000)	Operating Cash Flow ($000)	NOG Before Taxes ($000)	NOG After Taxes ($000)	Net Income ($000)
'05	92.3	0.2	1.8	5.8	761,846	40.2	7.8	48.3	3.7	108,921	195,599	196,335	38,515	16,152	9,997	11,246
'06	92.2	0.1	1.8	5.8	794,256	41.7	6.9	47.0	4.5	119,279	205,704	205,453	31,029	20,102	12,715	14,033
'07	91.9	0.1	1.5	6.5	818,304	43.9	6.5	45.1	4.5	120,349	215,856	218,445	22,613	5,787	3,219	5,559
'08	92.8	0.1	0.7	6.3	854,397	44.7	6.0	45.6	3.7	117,159	218,519	217,980	41,223	7,893	6,602	1,227
'09	92.3	0.1	0.9	6.7	925,953	44.4	5.7	46.4	3.6	111,824	252,453	252,288	67,364	-228	-435	-2,741

Rating History: A-, 06/17/09; A-, 06/20/08; A-, 06/13/07; A-, 06/22/06; A-, 06/14/05

PELLERIN LIFE INS CO[1] — NR-1

Frank E. Pellerin
President
600 Corporate Boulevard
Breaux Bridge, LA 70517
LA : 1966 : Stock : Not Available
337-332-2111
AMB# 007909 NAIC# 76317

Data Year	Bonds (%)	Mort. Loans & R.E. (%)	Com & Pref. Stock (%)	All Other Assets (%)	Total Assets ($000)	Life Reserves (%)	Health Reserves (%)	Ann Res. & Dep. Liabilities (%)	All Other Liabilities (%)	Capital & Surplus ($000)	Direct Premiums Written ($000)	Net Premiums Written & Deposits ($000)	Operating Cash Flow ($000)	NOG Before Taxes ($000)	NOG After Taxes ($000)	Net Income ($000)
'05	20.7	51.9	0.4	26.9	7,845	...	...	...	100.0	1,056	1,026	951	...	-21	-21	-29
'06	23.8	45.2	5.5	25.5	8,026	...	...	...	100.0	993	1,129	1,051	...	-38	-38	-38
'07	28.2	46.0	0.4	25.4	7,946	...	...	...	100.0	723	1,102	1,019	...	-125	-125	-226
'08	30.5	43.5	0.2	25.8	8,014	...	...	...	100.0	641	1,058	979	...	-64	-64	-63
'09	33.7	39.6	0.4	26.3	8,484	...	...	...	100.0	833	1,162	1,081	...	-50	-50	191

Rating History: NR-1, 06/10/10; NR-1, 06/12/09; NR-1, 06/12/08; NR-1, 06/08/07; NR-1, 06/07/06

PEMCO LIFE INS CO — B+

PEMCO Mutual Insurance Company
Stan W. McNaughton
President
P.O. Box 778
Seattle, WA 98109-0778
WA : 1968 : Stock : Direct Response
Ind Life
206-628-4000
AMB# 007420 NAIC# 71803

Rating Outlook: Stable
FSC III

Data Year	Bonds (%)	Mort. Loans & R.E. (%)	Com & Pref. Stock (%)	All Other Assets (%)	Total Assets ($000)	Life Reserves (%)	Health Reserves (%)	Ann Res. & Dep. Liabilities (%)	All Other Liabilities (%)	Capital & Surplus ($000)	Direct Premiums Written ($000)	Net Premiums Written & Deposits ($000)	Operating Cash Flow ($000)	NOG Before Taxes ($000)	NOG After Taxes ($000)	Net Income ($000)
'05	58.5	...	1.4	40.1	7,261	84.7	...	...	15.3	4,591	2,998	1,579	-703	-311	-281	-385
'06	69.1	...	1.5	29.4	6,889	85.6	...	...	14.4	3,753	3,210	1,523	-775	-734	-683	-670
'07	65.4	...	1.5	33.1	6,626	85.6	...	...	14.4	3,173	3,564	1,616	-642	-551	-545	-545
'08	59.8	...	1.4	38.8	7,221	88.6	...	...	11.4	3,208	4,072	1,706	724	-807	-834	-1,063
'09	66.8	...	1.3	32.0	8,213	87.4	...	...	12.6	2,794	4,471	1,901	719	-2,048	-2,048	-2,070

Rating History: B+, 12/11/09; B+, 02/20/09; B+, 06/19/08; B+, 05/16/07; B++, 05/31/06

PENINSULA HEALTH CARE INC — A

WellPoint Inc.
Thomas R. Byrd
President
11870 Merchants Walk, Suite 200
Newport News, VA 23606
VA : 1984 : Stock : Broker
Group A&H, Health
757-875-5760
AMB# 068745 NAIC# 95167

Rating Outlook: Stable
FSC X

Data Year	Bonds (%)	Mort. Loans & R.E. (%)	Com & Pref. Stock (%)	All Other Assets (%)	Total Assets ($000)	Life Reserves (%)	Health Reserves (%)	Ann Res. & Dep. Liabilities (%)	All Other Liabilities (%)	Capital & Surplus ($000)	Direct Premiums Written ($000)	Net Premiums Written & Deposits ($000)	Operating Cash Flow ($000)	NOG Before Taxes ($000)	NOG After Taxes ($000)	Net Income ($000)
'05	82.6	...	0.2	17.1	79,357	...	27.7	...	72.3	44,661	139,539	138,435	12,144	18,279	12,106	12,136
'06	70.6	...	0.2	29.2	82,724	...	26.3	...	73.7	44,242	151,425	149,883	3,252	17,921	12,202	12,144
'07	78.4	...	0.2	21.4	78,349	...	22.7	...	77.3	33,498	162,747	161,111	-6,157	16,553	10,476	10,445
'08	71.8	...	0.1	28.1	84,178	...	16.8	...	83.2	39,055	172,485	171,252	1,084	23,564	15,780	15,667
'09	62.7	...	...	37.3	80,402	...	18.2	...	81.8	37,419	156,415	155,569	-10,092	19,740	13,430	13,424

Rating History: A g, 04/27/10; A, 01/23/09; A, 03/20/08; A, 11/06/06; A, 12/29/05

PENN INS AND ANNUITY COMPANY — A+

Penn Mutual Life Insurance Company
Eileen McDonnell
President
600 Dresher Road
Horsham, PA 19044
DE : 1981 : Stock : Career Agent
Ind Ann, Univ Life, Var ann
215-956-8000
AMB# 009073 NAIC# 93262

Rating Outlook: Stable
FSC XIII

Data Year	Bonds (%)	Mort. Loans & R.E. (%)	Com & Pref. Stock (%)	All Other Assets (%)	Total Assets ($000)	Life Reserves (%)	Health Reserves (%)	Ann Res. & Dep. Liabilities (%)	All Other Liabilities (%)	Capital & Surplus ($000)	Direct Premiums Written ($000)	Net Premiums Written & Deposits ($000)	Operating Cash Flow ($000)	NOG Before Taxes ($000)	NOG After Taxes ($000)	Net Income ($000)
'05	52.3	...	...	47.7	1,176,408	68.6	...	11.8	19.6	110,245	32,265	41,009	-21,572	28,710	20,482	20,799
'06	51.1	...	0.0	48.9	1,142,982	70.1	...	10.9	19.0	106,451	30,191	34,702	-19,163	28,241	20,009	18,850
'07	49.6	...	0.1	50.3	1,117,456	72.8	...	10.1	17.1	117,262	37,980	42,177	-3,524	26,032	19,592	19,510
'08	53.5	...	0.1	46.4	1,047,715	78.6	...	11.3	10.2	107,510	59,926	65,832	3,274	7,291	3,035	2,954
'09	54.0	...	0.0	46.0	1,092,166	79.9	...	9.5	10.6	103,591	96,320	103,938	38,149	-4,013	-801	-2,052

Rating History: A+ g, 01/15/10; A+ g, 04/23/09; A+ g, 04/09/08; A+ g, 03/14/07; A+ g, 06/21/06

PENN MUTUAL LIFE INS CO — A+

Penn Mutual Life Insurance Company
Eileen McDonnell
President
600 Dresher Road
Horsham, PA 19044
PA : 1847 : Mutual : Career Agent
Ind Life, Ind Ann
215-956-8000
AMB# 006903 NAIC# 67644

Rating Outlook: Stable
FSC XIII

Data Year	Bonds (%)	Mort. Loans & R.E. (%)	Com & Pref. Stock (%)	All Other Assets (%)	Total Assets ($000)	Life Reserves (%)	Health Reserves (%)	Ann Res. & Dep. Liabilities (%)	All Other Liabilities (%)	Capital & Surplus ($000)	Direct Premiums Written ($000)	Net Premiums Written & Deposits ($000)	Operating Cash Flow ($000)	NOG Before Taxes ($000)	NOG After Taxes ($000)	Net Income ($000)
'05	51.7	0.2	1.8	46.3	9,152,632	32.6	0.1	25.7	41.5	1,248,230	971,785	1,002,139	281,556	183,742	188,628	184,590
'06	49.8	0.2	1.7	48.3	9,972,863	31.9	0.1	24.0	43.9	1,295,642	1,052,146	1,075,476	225,605	31,205	64,575	56,694
'07	49.3	0.2	1.8	48.8	10,546,348	32.4	0.1	21.9	45.6	1,302,211	1,192,272	1,226,008	107,076	4,763	6,601	-5,962
'08	52.9	0.2	2.4	44.6	9,688,538	36.6	0.1	25.8	37.5	1,285,720	1,026,048	1,069,700	281,383	-21,223	-2,272	-49,296
'09	48.7	0.1	1.6	49.6	10,939,523	34.0	0.1	24.8	41.1	1,364,335	1,403,482	1,478,457	224,165	67,176	72,310	70,756

Rating History: A+ g, 01/15/10; A+ g, 04/23/09; A+ g, 04/09/08; A+ g, 03/14/07; A+ g, 06/21/06

BEST'S PROFITABILITY, LEVERAGE AND LIQUIDITY TESTS 2005 – 2009

Data in U.S. Dollars

	Profitability Tests							Leverage Tests						Liquidity Tests					
Un-Realized Capital Gains ($000)	Benefits Paid to NPW & Dep (%)	Comm. & Expenses to NPW & Dep (%)	NOG to Total Assets (%)	NOG to Total Rev (%)	Operating Return on Equity (%)	Net Yield (%)	Total Return (%)	Change in NPW & Dep (%)	NPW & Dep to Capital (X)	Capital & Surplus to Liabilities (%)	Surplus Relief (%)	Reins Leverage (%)	Change in Capital (%)	Quick Liquidity (%)	Current Liquidity (%)	Non-Invest Grade Bonds to Capital (%)	Delinq. & Foreclosed Mortgages to Capital (%)	Mort. & Credit Tenant Loans & R.E. to Capital (%)	Affiliated Invest to Capital (%)
...	...	...	...	-99.9	...	...	...	...	...	373.4	...	...	...	728.3	760.7	...	...	...	...
...	84.4	19.4	-14.1	-2.2	-41.4	6.73	6.73	...	10.5	47.2	...	6.1	846.3	162.4	171.0	...	...	...	...
...	85.2	19.0	-14.9	-2.5	-37.3	6.06	6.06	102.4	11.5	84.6	...	4.6	85.7	197.5	207.9	...	...	...	...
...	84.5	18.1	-11.0	-2.0	-24.5	2.92	2.06	4.6	12.2	79.5	...	7.1	-1.6	238.7	251.2	...	...	...	...
...	88.0	16.7	-24.8	-4.8	-59.2	1.20	1.20	3.0	11.9	66.0	...	9.3	5.5	174.2	188.4	...	...	...	...

Principal Lines of Business: Medicaid (100.0%) Principal States: GA (100.0%)

...	53.8	17.4	25.9	19.0	34.8	1.17	1.17	...	...	240.1	...	...	48.2	326.0	326.0	...	...	...	...
...	52.3	18.8	16.1	18.5	23.1	1.60	1.60	...	...	223.2	...	...	25.2	241.9	241.9	...	...	...	...
...	15.3	11.3	8.2	52.0	10.8	2.20	2.20	...	...	648.4	...	...	-10.6	483.3	483.3	...	...	...	...
...	21.3	16.7	21.1	39.2	24.8	0.83	0.83	...	...	451.9	...	...	-47.8	546.5	546.5	...	...	...	...
...	32.3	18.2	26.1	31.2	32.7	0.55	0.55	...	...	351.3	...	...	-3.5	450.3	450.3	...	...	...	...

...	...	...	-0.9	-79.1	-1.3	1.62	1.62	...	...	252.1	...	...	-1.5	333.3	334.4	...	...	...	...
...	...	...	-0.3	-15.4	-0.4	2.68	2.68	...	...	154.3	...	...	-0.3	241.1	241.6	...	...	...	...
...	...	...	-0.1	-5.3	-0.2	3.01	3.01	...	...	145.8	...	...	-2.8	231.5	231.9	...	...	...	...
...	...	...	-0.3	-19.5	-0.5	2.61	2.61	...	...	101.0	...	...	-0.5	193.8	194.4	...	...	...	...
...	...	...	-0.6	-52.4	-1.1	1.99	1.99	...	...	136.2	...	...	-1.1	227.6	228.4	...	...	...	...

163	72.1	22.8	1.3	4.3	9.5	5.74	5.99	0.9	1.7	17.7	0.7	12.7	7.8	78.1	88.3	19.4	...	1.1	1.5
1,112	77.3	22.5	1.6	5.2	11.1	5.74	6.10	4.6	1.6	18.9	0.6	13.3	10.2	77.4	87.8	16.6	...	0.9	1.5
-959	84.1	21.5	0.4	1.3	2.7	5.62	5.83	6.3	1.7	18.4	0.6	16.4	0.9	77.7	88.0	12.8	...	0.8	1.4
-5,067	72.1	22.3	0.8	2.6	5.6	5.79	4.56	-0.2	1.8	16.2	0.7	15.2	-6.2	75.1	87.1	15.4	...	1.0	1.6
2,629	69.2	20.0	0.0	-0.1	-0.4	5.73	5.82	15.7	2.2	14.2	0.8	18.2	-3.6	73.2	86.6	2.7	...	1.0	1.5

Principal Lines of Business: GrpA&H (23.9%), IndA&H (22.6%), IndAnn (20.7%), OrdLife (17.7%), GrpLife (9.5%) Principal States: IL (57.5%), IN (18.8%), WI (13.0%), IA (6.8%)

-6	63.1	55.4	-0.3	-1.7	-2.1	...	...	-7.7	0.8	17.6	...	...	4.2	...	...	...	...	347.8	...
3	55.6	48.3	-0.5	-2.8	-3.7	...	...	10.5	0.9	16.3	...	...	-4.0	...	...	...	...	323.0	...
2	63.5	59.2	-1.6	-9.2	-14.6	...	...	-3.0	1.2	11.8	...	...	-25.1	...	...	...	...	434.6	...
-13	71.0	54.3	-0.8	-4.8	-9.3	...	...	-3.9	1.3	10.4	...	...	-10.7	...	...	...	...	463.1	...
6	58.7	47.7	-0.6	-3.5	-6.8	...	...	10.4	1.2	12.4	...	...	24.5	...	...	...	...	358.7	...

Principal Lines of Business: OrdLife (94.7%), IndLife (5.3%)

...	24.5	87.4	-3.8	-12.6	-5.7	4.27	2.65	3.1	0.3	171.9	8.5	41.6	-14.3	246.4	254.9	3.3	...	...	...
...	44.1	97.1	-9.7	-30.3	-16.4	4.98	5.23	-3.6	0.4	120.7	12.1	78.8	-17.9	150.7	160.2	...	...	...	...
...	41.0	87.4	-8.1	-22.6	-15.7	5.67	5.69	6.1	0.5	92.7	16.2	133.8	-15.4	112.5	120.7	...	...	...	...
...	32.0	98.0	-12.0	-32.0	-26.1	4.61	0.19	5.6	0.5	80.0	20.9	172.9	0.7	115.4	122.4	...	...	...	...
...	37.5	113.2	-26.5	-75.5	-68.3	3.25	2.78	11.4	0.7	51.7	22.7	250.9	-12.7	100.5	106.0	...	...	...	...

Principal Lines of Business: OrdLife (97.0%), GrpLife (3.0%), CrdLife (0.0%) Principal States: WA (100.0%)

5	77.4	10.8	16.5	8.6	30.1	3.23	3.29	17.6	3.1	128.7	...	1.4	25.0	196.8	214.9	...	...	...	...
4	80.3	9.4	15.1	8.0	27.4	3.38	3.31	8.3	3.4	115.0	...	0.2	-0.9	214.0	232.9	...	...	...	...
-15	81.6	9.4	13.0	6.4	27.0	4.87	4.81	7.5	4.8	74.7	...	1.9	-24.3	147.9	162.5	...	...	...	...
-12	82.1	6.4	19.4	9.1	43.5	4.32	4.14	6.3	4.4	86.6	...	1.4	16.6	152.7	168.0	0.4	...	...	...
-30	84.3	5.1	16.3	8.5	35.1	3.94	3.89	-9.2	4.2	87.1	...	0.3	-4.2	139.5	153.5	0.3	...	...	...

Principal Lines of Business: CompHosp/Med (50.2%), Medicaid (49.8%) Principal States: VA (100.0%)

-162	244.4	25.0	1.7	20.2	18.4	6.77	6.71	13.2	0.4	13.3	0.9	3.0	-2.1	49.4	58.2	21.8	...	...	...
-202	291.9	29.6	1.7	22.0	18.5	6.20	5.99	-15.4	0.3	13.1	0.9	4.0	-3.7	49.7	58.4	24.1	...	...	...
319	262.5	30.3	1.7	19.8	17.5	6.27	6.25	21.5	0.3	14.5	0.8	3.5	9.4	49.8	58.2	13.2	...	...	...
-775	140.4	41.1	0.3	2.6	2.7	5.78	5.66	56.1	0.6	12.9	0.9	2.2	-9.0	48.8	57.9	6.4	...	...	...
-721	89.3	40.2	-0.1	-0.5	-0.8	5.37	5.15	57.9	1.0	11.6	1.0	2.4	-4.3	45.2	55.3	6.1	...	...	...

Principal Lines of Business: OrdLife (93.4%), IndAnn (6.1%), GrpLife (0.5%) Principal States: PA (16.3%), TX (13.1%), CA (11.5%), IL (6.0%), FL (5.0%)

-104,903	74.4	23.7	2.1	12.7	15.7	8.22	6.36	1.3	0.8	26.5	0.1	46.7	5.7	78.0	89.6	22.2	...	1.4	33.6
7,044	74.0	23.9	0.7	4.3	5.1	6.48	6.46	7.3	0.8	26.7	0.1	46.2	5.6	76.5	88.3	16.2	...	1.3	30.3
23,389	74.2	25.7	0.1	0.4	0.5	6.30	6.41	14.0	0.9	26.3	0.1	47.1	2.0	71.3	82.6	16.1	0.0	1.2	29.7
30,692	80.6	24.4	0.0	-0.2	-0.2	5.95	5.72	-12.7	0.8	24.4	0.2	47.5	0.6	69.2	82.0	14.3	...	1.1	28.9
-100,634	53.4	18.9	0.7	4.0	5.5	5.31	3.84	38.2	1.1	23.8	0.8	43.4	1.6	64.1	77.5	14.5	...	1.1	28.2

Principal Lines of Business: IndAnn (66.8%), OrdLife (30.2%), GrpAnn (2.9%), IndA&H (0.0%), GrpLife (0.0%) Principal States: NY (13.2%), PA (10.8%), NJ (7.5%), TX (6.8%), FL (5.9%)

COMPANY NAME / Ultimate Parent Association / Principal Officer / Mailing Address / Dom. : Began Bus. : Struct. : Mktg. / Specialty / Phone # / AMB# NAIC# — Best's Financial Strength Rating / FSC

Balance Sheet: Data Year; Bonds (%); Mort. Loans & R.E. (%); Com & Pref. Stock (%); All Other Assets (%); Total Assets ($000); Life Reserves (%); Health Reserves (%); Ann Res. & Dep. Liabilities (%); All Other Liabilities (%); Capital & Surplus ($000). Operations: Direct Premiums Written ($000); Net Premiums Written & Deposits ($000); Operating Cash Flow ($000); NOG Before Taxes ($000); NOG After Taxes ($000); Net Income ($000)

PENN TREATY NETWORK AMERICA
Penn Treaty American Corporation
William W. Hunt, Jr.
President & CEO
3440 Lehigh Street
Allentown, PA 18103-7001
PA : 1954 : Stock : Agency
Life, LTC, Med supp
610-965-2222
AMB# 006385 NAIC# 63282

E

Data Year	Bonds (%)	Mort. Loans & R.E. (%)	Com & Pref. Stock (%)	All Other Assets (%)	Total Assets ($000)	Life Reserves (%)	Health Reserves (%)	Ann Res. & Dep. Liabilities (%)	All Other Liabilities (%)	Capital & Surplus ($000)	Direct Premiums Written ($000)	Net Premiums Written & Deposits ($000)	Operating Cash Flow ($000)	NOG Before Taxes ($000)	NOG After Taxes ($000)	Net Income ($000)
'05	89.0	0.4	1.8	8.8	1,029,267	1.0	3.8	0.0	95.2	35,876	288,398	9,511	890,320	1,631	-4,103	-4,228
'06	87.6	0.4	2.0	10.0	1,046,719	...	4.6	...	95.4	39,264	275,644	38,850	-5,161	1,433	5,503	4,641
'07	77.9	0.4	2.3	19.4	1,039,141	...	6.1	...	93.9	25,091	262,314	36,896	1,127	-18,710	-15,487	-15,482
'08	83.0	0.4	0.8	15.8	1,001,191	...	6.0	...	94.0	-224,038	252,655	32,400	-57,962	1,540	3,607	180
'09	...	...	...	...	...	...	...	...	...	...	...	...	...	...	...	...

Rating History: E, 01/08/09; D g, 10/03/08; B- g, 02/20/08; B gu, 07/06/06; B g, 12/19/05

PENNSYLVANIA LIFE INSURANCE CO
Universal American Corp.
Gary W. Bryant
President
P.O. Box 958465
Lake Mary, FL 32795-8465
PA : 1948 : Stock : Career Agent
Annuity, Ind A&H, Life
407-995-8007
AMB# 006905 NAIC# 67660

B++ — Rating Outlook: Stable — FSC IX

Data Year	Bonds (%)	Mort. Loans & R.E. (%)	Com & Pref. Stock (%)	All Other Assets (%)	Total Assets ($000)	Life Reserves (%)	Health Reserves (%)	Ann Res. & Dep. Liabilities (%)	All Other Liabilities (%)	Capital & Surplus ($000)	Direct Premiums Written ($000)	Net Premiums Written & Deposits ($000)	Operating Cash Flow ($000)	NOG Before Taxes ($000)	NOG After Taxes ($000)	Net Income ($000)
'05	82.1	...	8.3	9.7	579,326	21.1	46.5	29.3	3.1	74,390	256,915	174,183	25,427	8,631	9,791	9,789
'06	52.4	...	...	47.6	964,047	13.0	30.4	16.7	39.8	112,410	786,611	362,501	263,039	25,338	21,947	22,646
'07	40.4	...	...	59.6	1,180,290	10.9	53.9	11.9	23.3	136,824	1,207,456	678,098	-323,014	76,732	51,110	51,072
'08	25.1	...	...	74.9	1,102,685	11.8	38.3	11.1	38.8	125,491	2,182,494	1,796,433	-189,609	23,406	20,773	7,339
'09	16.3	...	...	83.7	901,412	0.2	44.4	...	55.4	261,001	1,955,545	1,725,826	414,499	165,128	119,823	94,647

Rating History: B++g, 04/16/10; B++g, 12/03/08; B++g, 08/21/07; B++g, 06/21/06; B++g, 06/09/05

PEOPLES SAVINGS LIFE INS CO[1]
Nathan W. Stark
President
P.O. Box 866
Alexander City, AL 35010
AL : 1950 : Stock : Not Available
904-234-5119
AMB# 068468 NAIC# 84255

NR-1

Data Year	Bonds (%)	Mort. Loans & R.E. (%)	Com & Pref. Stock (%)	All Other Assets (%)	Total Assets ($000)	Life Reserves (%)	Health Reserves (%)	Ann Res. & Dep. Liabilities (%)	All Other Liabilities (%)	Capital & Surplus ($000)	Direct Premiums Written ($000)	Net Premiums Written & Deposits ($000)	Operating Cash Flow ($000)	NOG Before Taxes ($000)	NOG After Taxes ($000)	Net Income ($000)
'05	...	...	...	100.0	737	...	...	...	100.0	702	282	282	...	16	13	13
'06	...	...	...	100.0	762	...	...	...	100.0	729	263	263	...	28	26	26
'07	...	...	...	100.0	878	...	...	...	100.0	834	422	422	...	112	104	104
'08	5.7	...	...	94.3	360	...	...	...	100.0	309	380	380	...	82	75	74
'09	3.8	...	...	96.2	553	...	...	...	100.0	512	302	302	...	-106	-99	-98

Rating History: NR-1, 06/10/10; NR-1, 06/12/09; NR-1, 06/12/08; NR-1, 06/08/07; NR-1, 06/07/06

PERFORMANCE LIFE OF AMERICA
Louisiana Dealer Services Insurance Inc
Dick S. Taylor
President
PO Box 83480
Baton Rouge, LA 70884-3480
LA : 1982 : Stock : Other Direct
Credit A&H, Credit Life, Reins
225-769-9923
AMB# 009325 NAIC# 97209

B++ — Rating Outlook: Stable — FSC V

Data Year	Bonds (%)	Mort. Loans & R.E. (%)	Com & Pref. Stock (%)	All Other Assets (%)	Total Assets ($000)	Life Reserves (%)	Health Reserves (%)	Ann Res. & Dep. Liabilities (%)	All Other Liabilities (%)	Capital & Surplus ($000)	Direct Premiums Written ($000)	Net Premiums Written & Deposits ($000)	Operating Cash Flow ($000)	NOG Before Taxes ($000)	NOG After Taxes ($000)	Net Income ($000)
'05	90.3	...	...	9.7	30,040	54.2	42.7	...	3.1	14,503	...	22,747	5,979	3,417	2,846	2,852
'06	90.8	...	...	9.2	30,959	50.4	46.6	...	3.0	13,915	...	16,111	1,206	2,916	2,416	2,569
'07	89.7	...	...	10.3	33,141	49.4	48.9	...	1.6	15,144	...	15,889	2,566	3,266	2,612	2,615
'08	84.4	...	...	15.6	29,496	50.2	48.0	...	1.8	13,094	...	9,532	-2,941	3,384	2,622	2,671
'09	96.3	...	...	3.7	26,717	55.0	40.6	...	4.4	13,992	...	4,202	-2,789	3,047	2,454	2,454

Rating History: B++g, 06/03/09; B++g, 06/16/08; B++g, 06/13/07; B++g, 06/15/06; B++g, 05/31/05

PERICO LIFE INSURANCE COMPANY
HCC Insurance Holdings, Inc
Jeffrey Petty
President & CEO
13358 Manchester Road
St. Louis, MO 63131
DE : 1975 : Stock : General Agent
Group Life, Medical, Stop Loss
314-965-5675
AMB# 008618 NAIC# 85561

A — Rating Outlook: Stable — FSC VI

Data Year	Bonds (%)	Mort. Loans & R.E. (%)	Com & Pref. Stock (%)	All Other Assets (%)	Total Assets ($000)	Life Reserves (%)	Health Reserves (%)	Ann Res. & Dep. Liabilities (%)	All Other Liabilities (%)	Capital & Surplus ($000)	Direct Premiums Written ($000)	Net Premiums Written & Deposits ($000)	Operating Cash Flow ($000)	NOG Before Taxes ($000)	NOG After Taxes ($000)	Net Income ($000)
'05	79.6	...	...	20.4	17,302	...	...	...	100.0	15,520	487	...	-583	898	281	281
'06	55.7	...	...	44.3	45,425	0.6	83.6	...	15.7	27,544	26,370	31,944	23,644	4,411	2,950	2,950
'07	76.7	...	...	23.3	50,960	1.2	85.2	...	13.6	31,606	45,912	46,803	7,746	5,794	4,031	4,031
'08	77.0	...	...	23.0	61,334	0.6	83.3	...	16.1	39,480	51,886	51,936	10,938	11,843	8,078	7,756
'09	83.5	...	...	16.5	78,626	0.6	82.2	...	17.3	49,780	82,941	83,744	16,303	15,420	10,308	10,308

Rating History: A, 08/27/09; A, 07/30/08; A, 04/15/08; A, 01/04/07; A u, 11/22/06

PERSONALCARE INSURANCE OF IL
Coventry Health Care Inc
Todd A. Petersen
President
2110 Fox Drive, Suite A
Champaign, IL 61820
IL : 1988 : Stock : Broker
Group A&H, Ind A&H
217-366-1226
AMB# 060028 NAIC# 74160

B++ — Rating Outlook: Stable — FSC VII

Data Year	Bonds (%)	Mort. Loans & R.E. (%)	Com & Pref. Stock (%)	All Other Assets (%)	Total Assets ($000)	Life Reserves (%)	Health Reserves (%)	Ann Res. & Dep. Liabilities (%)	All Other Liabilities (%)	Capital & Surplus ($000)	Direct Premiums Written ($000)	Net Premiums Written & Deposits ($000)	Operating Cash Flow ($000)	NOG Before Taxes ($000)	NOG After Taxes ($000)	Net Income ($000)
'05	60.1	...	...	39.9	72,785	...	66.6	...	33.4	43,604	235,566	232,645	15,102	28,052	18,315	18,315
'06	53.5	...	...	46.5	81,138	...	78.5	...	21.5	49,594	280,821	277,268	6,541	31,544	22,283	22,283
'07	69.2	...	...	30.8	85,972	...	72.8	...	27.2	53,474	289,924	286,904	4,809	37,708	25,466	25,458
'08	62.4	...	...	37.6	83,090	...	70.5	...	29.5	47,118	306,553	303,431	-606	26,734	17,928	17,608
'09	44.0	...	...	56.0	90,034	...	71.1	...	28.9	55,853	298,312	295,216	-37,403	28,831	18,707	19,235

Rating History: B++, 02/12/10; B++, 11/19/08; B++, 10/30/07; B++, 07/11/07; B++, 10/27/06

PHARMACISTS LIFE INS CO
Pharmacists Mutual Insurance Company
Edward T. Berg
President
P.O. Box 370
Algona, IA 50511
IA : 1979 : Stock : Direct Response
Ann, Ind Life, Term Life
515-295-2461
AMB# 008946 NAIC# 90247

B+ — Rating Outlook: Negative — FSC IV

Data Year	Bonds (%)	Mort. Loans & R.E. (%)	Com & Pref. Stock (%)	All Other Assets (%)	Total Assets ($000)	Life Reserves (%)	Health Reserves (%)	Ann Res. & Dep. Liabilities (%)	All Other Liabilities (%)	Capital & Surplus ($000)	Direct Premiums Written ($000)	Net Premiums Written & Deposits ($000)	Operating Cash Flow ($000)	NOG Before Taxes ($000)	NOG After Taxes ($000)	Net Income ($000)
'05	84.3	...	7.1	8.6	32,309	63.2	...	32.7	4.2	6,558	4,231	2,880	2,527	-195	-271	-315
'06	83.8	...	7.2	9.0	35,549	64.5	...	32.3	3.2	6,995	3,998	2,426	3,134	-455	-439	-393
'07	82.1	...	8.4	9.5	37,175	65.6	...	31.7	2.7	6,812	4,361	2,882	1,557	-71	-88	-215
'08	82.0	...	5.2	12.9	38,902	65.6	...	33.3	1.1	5,500	5,301	3,504	2,087	-335	-411	-1,621
'09	83.1	...	7.1	9.8	46,292	58.9	...	38.6	2.5	5,906	8,763	6,920	7,575	137	57	-318

Rating History: B+, 04/29/09; B++, 06/03/08; B++, 06/07/07; B++, 05/23/06; B++, 06/15/05

PHILADELPHIA AMERICAN LIFE INS
New Era Enterprises Inc
Bill S. Chen
President, Treasurer & CEO
200 Westlake Park Boulevard
Houston, TX 77079-2663
TX : 1978 : Stock : Agency
Group A&H
281-368-7200
AMB# 009166 NAIC# 67784

B+ — Rating Outlook: Negative — FSC VI

Data Year	Bonds (%)	Mort. Loans & R.E. (%)	Com & Pref. Stock (%)	All Other Assets (%)	Total Assets ($000)	Life Reserves (%)	Health Reserves (%)	Ann Res. & Dep. Liabilities (%)	All Other Liabilities (%)	Capital & Surplus ($000)	Direct Premiums Written ($000)	Net Premiums Written & Deposits ($000)	Operating Cash Flow ($000)	NOG Before Taxes ($000)	NOG After Taxes ($000)	Net Income ($000)
'05	59.8	1.5	...	38.8	147,317	9.4	78.3	7.5	4.8	13,263	70,927	68,971	25,935	1,082	-434	-711
'06	91.2	1.7	0.9	6.2	159,970	9.2	71.1	15.4	4.3	16,463	88,060	63,054	41,648	4,341	2,819	3,021
'07	77.2	3.8	4.3	14.7	187,709	8.0	57.9	31.2	2.9	19,547	87,457	56,251	27,640	3,571	3,876	2,621
'08	77.4	8.9	5.8	7.9	174,075	9.4	63.5	24.8	2.4	19,965	72,618	25,592	-14,635	2,327	2,203	-99
'09	82.9	8.3	2.8	6.0	175,184	9.4	58.8	28.6	3.2	20,933	72,429	51,339	-847	2,141	2,516	160

Rating History: B+ g, 12/04/09; B+ g, 12/04/08; B+ g, 10/12/07; B+ g, 09/19/06; B+ g, 06/15/06

PHILADELPHIA-UNITED LIFE INS
Philadelphia-United Life Insurance Co
Robert B. Ries
Treasurer & CEO
150 Monument Road, Suite 600
Bala Cynwyd, PA 19004
PA : 1940 : Stock : Agency
Life, Trad Life, Whole life
610-660-6600
AMB# 006919 NAIC# 67792

B+ — Rating Outlook: Stable — FSC IV

Data Year	Bonds (%)	Mort. Loans & R.E. (%)	Com & Pref. Stock (%)	All Other Assets (%)	Total Assets ($000)	Life Reserves (%)	Health Reserves (%)	Ann Res. & Dep. Liabilities (%)	All Other Liabilities (%)	Capital & Surplus ($000)	Direct Premiums Written ($000)	Net Premiums Written & Deposits ($000)	Operating Cash Flow ($000)	NOG Before Taxes ($000)	NOG After Taxes ($000)	Net Income ($000)
'05	72.4	...	7.4	20.2	49,033	95.2	0.0	0.1	4.7	16,743	8,650	8,575	1,844	142	106	175
'06	78.7	...	8.5	12.8	43,119	95.0	0.0	0.1	4.9	8,534	9,059	8,986	-6,296	-407	-305	280
'07	78.4	...	7.4	14.2	44,326	96.2	0.0	0.1	3.7	8,117	9,127	9,048	1,925	12	7	425
'08	81.6	...	4.6	13.7	43,721	98.5	0.0	0.1	1.5	6,487	9,255	9,165	-143	455	471	148
'09	77.1	...	3.7	19.2	45,914	98.1	0.0	0.1	1.8	6,777	8,834	8,737	1,752	815	721	489

Rating History: B+, 05/06/09; B+, 05/05/08; B+, 03/30/07; B++, 02/07/06; B++, 12/14/04

BEST'S PROFITABILITY, LEVERAGE AND LIQUIDITY TESTS 2005 – 2009

Data in U.S. Dollars

—	Profitability Tests							Leverage Tests						Liquidity Tests					
Un-Realized Capital Gains ($000)	Benefits Paid to NPW & Dep (%)	Comm. & Expenses to NPW & Dep (%)	NOG to Total Assets (%)	NOG to Total Rev (%)	Operating Return on Equity (%)	Net Yield (%)	Total Return (%)	Change in NPW & Dep (%)	NPW & Dep to Capital (X)	Capital & Surplus to Liabilities (%)	Surplus Relief (%)	Reins Leverage (%)	Change in Capital (%)	Quick Liquidity (%)	Current Liquidity (%)	Non-Invest Grade Bonds to Capital (%)	Delinq. & Foreclosed Mortgages to Capital (%)	Mort. & Credit Tenant Loans & R.E. to Capital (%)	Affiliated Invest to Capital (%)
9,307	272.6	-99.9	-0.7	-3.2	-13.7	1.10	2.94	-47.8	0.3	3.7	315.1	999.9	51.4	66.3	72.9	...	...	12.0	61.9
2,985	20.4	79.4	0.5	5.1	14.6	0.35	0.57	308.5	0.9	4.1	150.1	999.9	12.0	64.2	71.2	...	...	10.7	60.9
3,170	34.5	83.7	-1.5	-16.2	-48.1	0.30	0.63	-5.0	1.3	2.8	221.8	999.9	-31.4	76.4	83.3	...	...	15.7	100.2
-15,810	34.2	69.6	0.4	3.4	-3.6	1.85	-0.19	-12.2	-0.1	-18.2	-24.7	-99.9	-99.9	49.4	55.3	-3.2	...	-1.9	-5.6
...	...	...	...	...	...	...	...	...	...	...	...	...	...	...	...	...	...	...	...
2,008	64.7	36.7	1.7	1.8	14.4	4.81	4.66	0.4	2.3	16.1	6.8	36.0	21.8	77.8	86.9	10.7	...	...	66.0
-7,872	82.3	22.5	2.8	5.0	23.5	6.34	5.46	108.1	3.2	13.5	27.6	45.1	51.0	89.4	95.5	30.8	...	...	25.6
86	75.6	21.2	4.8	6.8	41.0	5.98	6.13	87.1	4.9	13.4	28.3	48.0	21.7	39.3	43.5	15.3	...	...	8.9
-2,947	85.9	14.7	1.8	1.1	15.8	5.90	2.22	164.9	14.3	12.8	30.1	24.3	-10.1	22.8	25.6	28.4	...	...	...
-1,349	90.1	13.8	12.0	6.8	62.0	1.33	-3.46	-3.9	6.6	40.8	6.6	85.6	108.0	186.8	194.0	4.3	...	...	...
Principal Lines of Business: IndA&H (111.7%), IndAnn (-5.6%), OrdLife (-6.1%)														Principal States: TX (9.7%), GA (7.6%), FL (6.0%), OH (5.2%), PA (5.1%)					
...	62.5	65.7	1.7	3.3	1.8	...	...	-19.8	0.4	999.9	...	...	2.2	...	...	...	...	...	...
...	40.0	66.8	3.4	8.4	3.6	...	...	-6.9	0.4	999.9	...	...	3.7	...	...	...	...	...	...
...	32.3	46.5	12.7	23.4	13.3	...	...	60.7	0.5	999.9	...	...	14.5	...	...	...	...	...	...
...	27.1	54.1	12.0	19.1	13.0	...	...	-9.9	1.2	602.0	...	...	-63.0	...	...	...	...	...	...
...	35.2	104.0	-21.6	-31.4	-24.1	...	...	-20.5	0.6	999.9	...	...	65.7	...	...	...	...	...	...
Principal Lines of Business: GrpLife (100.0%)																			
...	8.4	63.2	10.6	11.9	20.9	4.86	4.88	109.3	1.6	95.3	...	3.1	13.6	171.1	178.4	...	...	...	...
...	13.5	68.3	7.9	13.7	17.0	5.15	5.66	-29.2	1.1	83.1	...	1.7	-4.2	162.3	168.5	...	...	...	...
...	12.6	68.7	8.1	15.0	18.0	4.92	4.93	-1.4	1.0	85.3	...	1.3	8.6	168.4	173.6	...	...	...	...
...	25.2	72.7	8.4	23.9	18.6	4.70	4.86	-40.0	0.7	81.0	...	-2.1	-13.5	166.0	170.6	...	...	...	...
...	58.6	90.9	8.7	45.0	18.1	4.53	4.53	-55.9	0.3	111.5	...	-0.8	6.7	189.6	194.1	1.4	...	...	...
Principal Lines of Business: CrdLife (102.9%), CrdA&H (-2.9%)																			
...	...	...	1.6	31.7	1.9	4.18	5.16	...	...	874.8	...	1.7	4.8	999.9	999.9	...	...	...	...
0	68.8	22.1	9.4	8.8	13.7	4.76	5.28	...	1.2	154.5	...	1.0	77.6	226.6	232.3	...	...	...	...
...	73.7	18.5	8.4	8.2	13.6	4.64	4.94	46.5	1.5	164.3	...	0.7	14.9	232.5	244.9	...	...	...	...
...	64.8	16.4	14.4	15.0	22.7	3.62	3.30	11.0	1.3	180.6	...	0.5	24.6	255.4	274.1	...	...	...	...
...	69.1	15.6	14.7	11.9	23.1	3.62	3.90	61.2	1.7	173.1	0.0	0.4	26.2	242.7	261.4	0.8	...	...	...
Principal Lines of Business: GrpA&H (99.6%), GrpLife (0.4%)														Principal States: IN (23.4%), TX (15.7%), LA (6.4%), IL (5.4%), NE (4.5%)					
...	79.1	9.8	25.8	7.8	46.0	2.35	2.35	9.6	5.3	149.4	...	1.5	21.3	219.7	233.5	...	...	...	...
...	80.8	8.8	29.0	8.0	47.8	3.61	3.61	19.2	5.6	157.2	...	1.8	13.7	224.3	237.1	...	...	...	...
...	78.0	10.0	30.5	8.8	49.4	4.23	4.22	3.5	5.4	164.5	...	2.5	7.8	228.7	245.7	...	...	...	...
...	81.9	10.2	21.2	5.9	35.6	3.56	3.16	5.8	6.4	131.0	...	2.3	-11.9	240.7	253.8	...	...	...	...
...	80.2	10.8	21.6	6.3	36.3	3.40	4.26	-2.7	5.3	163.4	...	1.9	18.5	105.5	116.0	...	...	...	...
Principal Lines of Business: CompHosp/Med (92.6%), FEHBP (3.7%), Medicare (3.6%), MedSup (0.1%)														Principal States: IL (99.7%)					
47	15.0	28.4	-0.9	-5.7	-4.0	5.15	5.40	-13.3	0.4	27.3	6.2	63.4	-3.5	82.1	93.9	6.6	...	...	...
8	34.7	37.6	-1.3	-10.1	-6.5	5.18	5.55	-15.8	0.3	26.6	5.2	67.8	7.7	77.7	89.3	24.4	...	...	...
-88	61.7	36.7	-0.2	-1.8	-1.3	5.48	5.01	18.8	0.4	24.2	4.1	86.8	-3.1	71.8	83.4	39.6	...	...	...
-1,147	33.4	33.0	-1.1	-7.2	-6.7	5.56	-0.86	21.6	0.6	16.5	5.2	121.3	-24.0	63.8	74.8	68.0	...	...	...
388	24.6	15.5	0.1	0.6	1.0	5.64	5.82	97.5	1.1	15.8	5.1	130.4	14.6	65.5	76.3	78.0	...	...	...
Principal Lines of Business: IndAnn (72.7%), OrdLife (26.8%), GrpAnn (0.5%)														Principal States: IA (26.3%), TX (9.0%), PA (8.9%), CO (6.2%), MO (5.1%)					
...	43.9	26.7	-0.4	-0.5	-3.3	6.22	5.94	23.7	5.0	10.2	35.5	252.8	0.3	79.9	88.2	6.5	2.1	15.6	...
...	73.7	22.5	1.8	3.6	19.0	6.23	6.38	-8.6	3.7	11.9	43.8	27.2	24.3	73.7	87.4	1.5	1.7	16.1	...
...	72.7	20.8	2.2	5.1	21.5	5.66	4.92	-10.8	2.8	11.8	45.7	20.6	16.9	83.3	97.2	8.3	...	36.3	...
...	141.3	53.4	1.2	5.2	11.1	6.53	5.24	-54.5	1.3	13.1	26.4	92.4	1.4	62.1	76.1	66.6	...	77.0	...
-92	83.7	28.8	1.4	3.9	12.3	5.60	4.17	100.6	2.4	13.7	17.3	81.0	4.5	59.9	72.8	81.5	...	69.3	...
Principal Lines of Business: IndA&H (72.6%), IndAnn (14.6%), GrpA&H (10.9%), OrdLife (1.2%), GrpLife (0.7%)														Principal States: PA (23.1%), TX (17.1%), OH (8.7%), IL (8.3%), NC (8.3%)					
-99	39.5	61.7	0.2	1.0	0.6	4.59	4.71	1.3	0.5	54.6	...	0.5	0.0	127.1	137.0	2.6	...	...	4.4
-60	41.8	63.2	-0.7	-2.8	-2.4	4.79	6.13	4.8	1.0	26.8	...	1.0	-47.4	86.0	95.7	...	...	...	8.7
-564	44.6	56.2	0.0	0.1	0.1	4.97	4.76	0.7	1.0	24.4	...	1.3	-4.5	85.2	95.0	2.3	...	...	9.4
-673	45.6	51.7	1.1	4.2	6.5	5.07	2.72	1.3	1.4	17.4	...	1.7	-25.5	75.2	84.8	5.9	...	...	13.0
517	46.2	46.9	1.6	6.7	10.9	4.81	5.52	-4.7	1.2	18.2	...	1.7	8.8	74.7	83.3	17.3	...	...	12.3
Principal Lines of Business: OrdLife (98.9%), IndLife (1.0%), IndA&H (0.1%), IndAnn (0.0%)														Principal States: MD (37.1%), PA (31.7%), VA (8.5%), OH (6.3%), NJ (6.1%)					

Data in U.S. Dollars

COMPANY NAME Ultimate Parent Association Principal Officer Mailing Address Dom. : Began Bus. : Struct. : Mktg. Specialty Phone # AMB# NAIC#	Best's Financial Strength Rating FSC	Data Year	Balance Sheet: Bonds (%)	Mort. Loans & R.E. (%)	Com & Pref. Stock (%)	All Other Assets (%)	Total Assets ($000)	Life Reserves (%)	Health Reserves (%)	Ann Res. & Dep. Liabilities (%)	All Other Liabilities (%)	Capital & Surplus ($000)	Operations: Direct Premiums Written ($000)	Net Premiums Written & Deposits ($000)	Operating Cash Flow ($000)	NOG Before Taxes ($000)	NOG After Taxes ($000)	Net Income ($000)
PHL VARIABLE INS CO Phoenix Companies Inc Philip K. Polkinghorn President One American Row Hartford, CT 06115 CT : 1981 : Stock : Broker Ann, Var ann, Var Univ life 860-403-5000 AMB# 009332 NAIC# 93548	**B+** Rating Outlook: Negative **FSC X**	'05	45.5	...	0.1	54.4	5,465,587	7.2	...	37.8	55.0	264,825	614,025	569,863	-217,943	-313	12,251	12,749
		'06	37.9	...	0.9	61.2	5,133,820	9.1	...	29.7	61.1	220,342	798,818	725,354	-458,857	-54,057	-33,094	-33,994
		'07	31.0	...	0.9	68.0	5,342,708	11.6	...	21.7	66.7	167,436	1,148,538	1,052,624	-222,389	-142,203	-98,589	-102,297
		'08	31.5	...	1.1	67.3	4,428,521	16.7	...	21.6	61.7	273,028	1,187,096	1,044,711	-128,611	-141,006	-138,012	-187,032
		'09	28.0	...	0.2	71.7	4,586,303	17.8	...	15.7	66.5	235,696	519,458	365,653	-305,729	-26,172	-31,030	-87,546
		Rating History: B+ g, 01/13/10; B++g, 03/10/09; A g, 01/15/09; A g, 11/14/08; A g, 02/08/08																
PHOENIX LIFE AND ANNUITY CO Phoenix Companies Inc Philip K. Polkinghorn President One American Row Hartford, CT 06115 CT : 1981 : Stock : Agency Var life 860-403-5000 AMB# 009072 NAIC# 93734	**B+** Rating Outlook: Negative **FSC VI**	'05	58.3	...	...	41.7	53,064	63.4	...	...	36.6	14,520	19,807	5,865	2,105	2,895	2,169	2,169
		'06	52.1	...	4.4	43.5	60,119	63.3	...	...	36.7	17,598	18,089	5,679	7,082	2,753	3,102	3,102
		'07	46.7	...	3.3	50.1	65,294	62.4	...	...	37.6	20,059	17,230	4,812	4,204	3,059	2,132	2,125
		'08	55.7	...	3.5	40.7	60,167	65.4	...	...	34.6	20,494	14,897	3,258	-3,628	1,514	746	74
		'09	46.1	...	...	53.9	60,427	59.0	...	...	41.0	25,423	13,478	2,381	3,591	1,967	-297	-339
		Rating History: B+, 01/13/10; B++, 03/10/09; A-, 01/15/09; A-, 11/14/08; A-, 02/08/08																
PHOENIX LIFE AND REASSUR OF NY Phoenix Companies Inc John K. Hillman President One American Row Hartford, CT 06115 NY : 1988 : Stock : Other Direct Reins 860-403-5000 AMB# 068237 NAIC# 73059	**NR-3**	'05	79.7	...	...	20.3	12,388	0.5	...	...	99.5	12,265	4	3	272	564	371	371
		'06	67.6	...	...	32.4	12,885	0.4	...	...	99.6	12,694	6	3	520	626	412	426
		'07	64.9	...	...	35.1	13,257	0.4	...	...	99.6	13,101	5	2	402	620	409	409
		'08	74.9	...	...	25.1	13,537	0.6	...	...	99.4	13,434	4	4	405	572	376	373
		'09	70.1	...	...	29.9	13,807	0.6	...	...	99.4	13,701	4	-1	302	428	277	276
		Rating History: NR-3, 01/13/10; NR-3, 03/10/09; NR-3, 01/15/09; NR-3, 11/14/08; NR-3, 02/08/08																
PHOENIX LIFE INSURANCE COMPANY Phoenix Companies Inc James D. Wehr President & CEO One American Row Hartford, CT 06115 NY : 1851 : Stock : Other Var ann, Var Univ life, Univ Life 860-403-5000 AMB# 006922 NAIC# 67814	**B+** Rating Outlook: Negative **FSC X**	'05	60.7	1.0	3.7	34.5	16,736,034	74.2	0.5	5.8	19.5	885,511	1,150,808	1,336,781	114,844	116,263	106,239	61,024
		'06	58.4	0.8	5.6	35.2	16,753,006	74.7	0.6	5.3	19.4	932,449	1,040,453	1,266,657	-12,143	153,959	131,641	162,012
		'07	58.0	0.3	5.7	36.1	16,714,606	75.1	0.4	4.9	19.6	848,117	1,001,129	1,298,159	10,764	146,451	115,245	79,968
		'08	59.7	0.3	5.5	34.6	15,392,479	81.5	0.2	5.2	13.1	758,914	958,291	1,200,045	-323,352	43,189	53,419	-82,267
		'09	61.5	0.2	3.5	34.8	14,654,500	79.8	0.5	5.3	14.5	517,162	783,559	1,099,105	-631,376	22,099	29,155	-59,874
		Rating History: B+ g, 01/13/10; B++g, 03/10/09; A g, 01/15/09; A g, 11/14/08; A g, 02/08/08																
PHP INSURANCE COMPANY OF IN Physicians Health Pl of Northern IN Inc Jay M. Gilbert President 8101 West Jefferson Boulevard Fort Wayne, IN 46804 IN : 2006 : Stock : Broker Health, Dental 260-432-6690 AMB# 064832 NAIC# 12331	**NR-2**	'05	...	...	...	100.0	2,031	...	...	...	100.0	1,984	...	...	2,031	-16	-16	-16
		'06	53.6	...	...	46.4	2,062	...	0.4	...	99.6	2,018	14	14	13	49	34	34
		'07	51.9	...	...	48.1	2,124	...	19.4	...	80.6	2,075	105	105	48	62	58	58
		'08	73.6	...	12.8	13.6	2,038	...	18.9	...	81.1	1,984	247	247	69	21	22	58
		'09	64.6	...	15.3	20.0	2,183	...	18.7	...	81.3	2,065	310	310	-65	4	7	-121
		Rating History: NR-2, 04/29/10; NR-2, 06/02/09; NR-2, 06/10/08; NR-2, 05/03/07; NR-2, 04/25/06																
PHPMM INSURANCE COMPANY[1] Sparrow Health System Scott Wilkerson President 1400 East Michigan Avenue Lansing, MI 48912 MI : 2006 : Stock 517-364-8400 AMB# 060652 NAIC# 12816	**NR-1**	'05	...	...	...	...	...	...	...	...	...	...	...	...	...	...	...	...
		'06	90.5	...	...	9.5	8,461	...	...	...	100.0	8,371	...	...	...	-127	-127	-127
		'07	...	...	...	100.0	8,706	...	...	...	100.0	8,415	266	262	...	91	49	49
		'08	...	...	...	100.0	9,981	...	...	...	100.0	8,470	5,163	5,082	...	268	104	104
		'09	...	...	...	100.0	10,007	...	...	...	100.0	9,080	6,630	6,541	...	825	582	582
		Rating History: NR-1, 06/10/10; NR-1, 06/12/09; NR-1, 06/12/08; NR-1, 06/08/07																
PHYSICIANS BENEFITS TRUST LIFE ISMIE Mutual Insurance Company M. LeRoy Sprang, M.D. President 20 North Michigan Avenue, Suite 700 Chicago, IL 60602-4822 IL : 1910 : Stock : Not Available Group A&H 312-782-2023 AMB# 007004 NAIC# 68519	**NR-5**	'05	...	...	...	...	...	...	...	...	...	...	...	...	...	...	...	...
		'06	...	...	...	...	...	...	...	...	...	...	...	...	...	...	...	...
		'07	...	...	...	...	...	...	...	...	...	...	...	...	...	...	...	...
		'08	89.8	...	...	10.2	19,896	...	72.5	...	27.5	10,272	25,650	24,167	-1,571	354	405	163
		'09	91.2	...	...	8.8	18,508	...	77.1	...	22.9	9,672	28,179	26,654	-1,841	-1,073	-651	-713
		Rating History: NR-5, 06/14/10; NR-5, 06/08/09; NR-1, 06/12/08; NR-1, 06/08/07; NR-1, 06/07/06																
PHYSICIANS HEALTH CHOICE OF TX[2] Nancy Erickson Executive Director 8637 Fredericksburg, Suite 400 San Antonio, TX 78240 TX : 2002 : Other : Broker Medicare 866-550-4736 AMB# 064777 NAIC# 11494	**NR-5**	'05	...	...	...	100.0	3,998	...	46.6	...	53.4	2,994	1,655	1,644	1,113	-2,071	-1,314	-1,314
		'06	...	...	...	100.0	10,190	...	61.4	...	38.6	3,403	36,826	36,773	5,012	-5,883	-3,806	-3,806
		'07	...	...	...	100.0	17,323	...	49.6	...	50.4	7,565	82,394	82,323	5,894	-7,589	-4,867	-4,867
		'08	...	...	...	100.0	14,815	...	18.8	...	81.2	10,521	134,399	134,318	-3,982	-9,625	-6,350	-6,350
		'09	...	...	...	100.0	18,435	...	...	...	100.0	12,841	214,977	214,977	2,709	-3,395	-1,629	-1,629
		Rating History: NR-5, 04/19/10; NR-5, 08/26/09; C pd, 05/23/08; NR-5, 04/05/07; NR-5, 05/30/06																
PHYSICIANS HLTH PLAN OF MID-MI Sparrow Health System Scott Wilkerson President P.O. Box 30377 Lansing, MI 48909 MI : 1981 : Non-Profit : Broker Group A&H, Health 517-364-8400 AMB# 068943 NAIC# 95849	**NR-5**	'05	...	3.9	31.1	65.0	77,587	...	40.6	...	59.4	34,738	215,371	214,380	8,640	9,671	9,671	9,835
		'06	...	3.6	31.0	65.4	72,524	...	44.4	...	55.6	30,640	231,296	230,418	-5,617	7,262	7,262	7,562
		'07	...	2.6	20.5	76.9	86,681	...	53.9	...	46.1	38,306	209,802	207,452	9,177	6,673	6,673	6,919
		'08	...	3.1	19.1	77.8	69,146	...	54.0	...	46.0	33,151	177,452	175,298	-8,923	5,342	5,342	3,232
		'09	...	2.7	34.6	62.7	80,032	...	47.8	...	52.2	51,114	180,342	178,323	4,144	6,562	6,562	5,958
		Rating History: NR-5, 05/21/10; NR-5, 08/26/09; B- pd, 07/28/08; B- pd, 07/31/07; B pd, 09/01/06																

BEST'S PROFITABILITY, LEVERAGE AND LIQUIDITY TESTS 2005 – 2009

Data in U.S. Dollars

—	Profitability Tests							Leverage Tests						Liquidity Tests					
Un-Realized Capital Gains ($000)	Benefits Paid to NPW & Dep (%)	Comm. & Expenses to NPW & Dep (%)	NOG to Total Assets (%)	NOG to Total Rev (%)	Operating Return on Equity (%)	Net Yield (%)	Total Return (%)	Change in NPW & Dep (%)	NPW & Dep to Capital (X)	Capital & Surplus to Liabilities (%)	Surplus Relief (%)	Reins Leverage (%)	Change in Capital (%)	Quick Liquidity (%)	Current Liquidity (%)	Non-Invest Grade Bonds to Capital (%)	Delinq. & Foreclosed Mortgages to Capital (%)	Mort. & Credit Tenant Loans & R.E. to Capital (%)	Affiliated Invest to Capital (%)
95	167.3	33.9	0.2	1.6	4.8	5.19	5.23	-9.6	2.1	11.5	6.6	97.2	6.8	58.6	80.3	69.0	...	1.8	...
62	185.5	47.0	-0.6	-3.6	-13.6	5.16	5.09	27.3	3.1	12.4	9.1	162.6	-13.2	55.4	79.6	72.9	...	2.1	...
62	86.1	46.7	-1.9	-7.9	-50.8	5.42	5.17	45.1	5.8	10.5	13.2	281.0	-22.4	55.5	79.5	78.6	...	2.7	...
-939	79.2	42.2	-2.8	-10.7	-62.7	4.87	2.16	-0.8	3.8	16.5	33.4	256.5	50.0	63.5	83.4	62.6	...	1.8	...
-24,649	205.4	43.6	-0.7	-5.5	-12.2	4.53	-0.24	-65.0	1.5	16.8	13.1	303.2	-12.9	51.6	70.1	90.0	...	...	...
Principal Lines of Business: OrdLife (63.7%), IndAnn (35.3%), GrpAnn (1.0%)														Principal States: CA (11.7%), TX (9.3%), MN (7.2%), FL (6.0%), DE (4.8%)					
...	47.2	10.6	4.2	21.3	16.1	4.80	4.85	51.5	0.4	57.9	16.0	331.0	17.4	94.4	110.9	2.0	...	...	...
...	29.7	13.2	5.5	31.1	19.3	5.02	5.05	-3.2	0.3	64.5	11.9	270.0	21.2	110.3	128.7	1.6	...	...	...
...	31.1	24.2	3.4	22.6	11.3	5.13	5.13	-15.3	0.2	70.0	10.3	215.6	14.1	143.1	159.3	6.3	...	...	...
...	184.2	23.4	1.2	9.7	3.7	4.79	3.24	-32.3	0.2	70.7	9.1	218.0	1.4	106.5	120.8	9.1	...	...	...
...	374.6	-52.2	-0.5	-3.4	-1.3	4.17	4.03	-26.9	0.1	98.9	16.5	146.6	24.5	183.0	193.7	12.0	...	...	...
Principal Lines of Business: OrdLife (100.0%)														Principal States: TX (15.3%), FL (8.9%), IL (8.3%), PA (6.4%), MI (6.0%)					
...	...	999.9	3.0	60.9	3.1	4.97	5.06	-77.0	0.0	999.9	...	0.0	3.1	999.9	999.9	...	...	4.1	...
...	...	999.9	3.3	62.0	3.3	5.28	5.49	-20.0	0.0	999.9	...	0.0	3.5	999.9	999.9	...	...	3.9	...
...	...	999.9	3.1	60.6	3.2	5.17	5.28	-18.6	0.0	999.9	...	0.0	3.2	999.9	999.9	...	...	3.8	...
...	...	999.9	2.8	59.5	2.8	4.74	4.77	101.3	0.0	999.9	...	0.0	2.6	999.9	999.9	3.9	...	3.7	...
...	...	-99.9	2.0	55.7	2.0	3.75	3.70	-99.9	0.0	999.9	...	0.0	2.1	999.9	999.9	3.4	...	...	...
Principal Lines of Business: OrdLife (100.0%)														Principal States: NY (62.6%), CT (37.4%)					
38,021	98.2	18.7	0.6	5.1	12.5	6.56	6.52	-3.5	1.2	8.3	0.4	51.8	7.2	36.1	54.7	65.7	0.7	18.3	44.5
-14,342	107.5	15.3	0.8	7.0	14.5	6.29	6.41	-5.2	1.1	8.5	0.3	46.1	2.2	35.9	55.4	69.5	0.7	14.2	36.2
-63,196	97.2	15.9	0.7	6.2	12.9	6.39	5.69	2.5	1.2	7.8	0.5	48.6	-7.1	34.4	53.9	73.2	...	7.7	33.3
-47,547	105.9	19.2	0.3	3.0	6.6	6.05	4.74	-7.6	1.4	6.5	0.4	51.0	-18.0	32.9	50.6	108.0	...	8.8	47.0
-199,369	169.4	14.6	0.2	1.9	4.6	5.77	3.64	-8.4	1.9	4.6	0.4	54.6	-32.7	32.8	49.6	186.4	...	9.9	66.3
Principal Lines of Business: OrdLife (57.5%), GrpAnn (40.4%), IndAnn (1.1%), GrpLife (1.0%), IndA&H (0.0%)														Principal States: NY (13.6%), CA (6.8%), FL (5.6%), NJ (5.2%), PA (4.1%)					
...	...	...	...	-92.9	...	...	...	...	...	999.9	...	...	...	999.9	999.9	...	...	...	...
...	97.2	325.7	1.7	31.8	1.7	4.64	4.64	...	0.0	999.9	...	...	1.7	999.9	999.9	...	...	...	...
...	95.5	44.5	2.8	27.6	2.8	5.31	5.31	672.0	0.1	999.9	...	...	2.9	999.9	999.9	...	...	...	...
-144	92.7	28.0	1.1	6.9	1.1	3.58	-1.37	135.4	0.1	999.9	...	...	-4.4	999.9	999.9	...	...	...	...
253	97.0	24.7	0.4	2.0	0.4	3.46	10.33	25.3	0.1	999.9	...	...	4.1	999.9	999.9	...	...	...	...
Principal Lines of Business: Dental (100.0%)														Principal States: IN (100.0%)					
...	...	...	...	...	...	...	...	...	...	...	...	...	...	...	...	...	...	...	...
-2	...	...	...	-99.9	...	...	...	...	...	999.9	...	...	...	...	...	...	...	...	...
2	80.8	141.5	0.6	7.2	0.6	...	...	...	0.0	999.9	...	...	0.6	...	...	...	...	...	...
...	86.7	12.0	1.1	2.0	1.2	...	...	999.9	0.6	566.3	...	...	0.7	...	...	...	...	...	...
...	71.6	15.7	5.8	8.9	6.6	...	...	28.7	0.7	999.9	...	...	7.2	...	...	...	...	...	...
Principal Lines of Business: GrpA&H (100.0%)																			
...	...	...	...	...	...	...	...	...	...	...	...	...	...	...	...	...	...	...	...
...	...	...	...	...	...	...	...	...	...	...	...	...	...	...	...	...	...	...	...
...	...	...	...	...	...	...	...	...	...	...	...	...	...	...	...	...	...	...	...
...	85.1	16.8	...	1.6	...	...	...	...	2.3	108.0	...	3.7	...	183.5	202.2	...	...	...	...
...	86.7	21.2	-3.4	-2.4	-6.5	4.26	3.93	10.3	2.7	110.9	...	2.8	-5.8	171.5	189.7	...	...	...	...
Principal Lines of Business: GrpA&H (100.0%)														Principal States: IL (100.0%)					
...	90.2	138.0	-46.0	-78.2	-56.1	1.61	1.61	...	0.5	298.2	...	...	77.1	365.2	365.2	...	...	...	...
...	88.3	28.2	-53.7	-10.3	-99.9	3.56	3.56	999.9	10.8	50.1	...	...	13.6	128.5	128.5	...	...	...	...
...	87.6	22.1	-35.4	-5.9	-88.7	3.46	3.46	123.9	10.9	77.5	...	...	122.3	150.2	150.2	...	...	...	...
...	86.4	20.8	-39.5	-4.7	-70.2	1.08	1.08	63.2	12.8	245.0	...	...	39.1	226.9	226.9	...	...	...	...
...	88.9	12.7	-9.8	-0.8	-13.9	0.13	0.13	60.1	16.7	229.6	...	...	22.1	222.6	222.6	...	...	...	...
Principal Lines of Business: Medicare (100.0%)														Principal States: TX (100.0%)					
-1,217	89.3	8.8	13.2	4.4	28.7	2.71	1.22	8.2	6.2	81.1	...	...	6.3	218.7	237.4	...	...	8.7	26.5
96	89.3	8.8	9.7	3.1	22.2	4.20	4.77	7.5	7.5	73.2	...	2.5	-11.8	190.3	204.9	...	...	8.5	60.0
87	87.9	10.2	8.4	3.2	19.4	3.67	4.14	-10.0	5.4	79.2	...	5.9	25.0	210.2	224.1	...	...	5.8	48.0
-3,079	87.9	9.3	6.9	3.0	15.0	0.62	-6.78	-15.5	5.3	92.1	...	1.9	-13.5	243.5	255.1	...	...	6.4	51.3
2,879	87.9	8.6	8.8	3.7	15.6	0.47	3.87	1.7	3.5	176.8	...	1.4	54.2	119.8	119.8	...	...	4.2	17.1
Principal Lines of Business: CompHosp/Med (97.5%), FEHBP (2.5%)														Principal States: MI (100.0%)					

Data in U.S. Dollars

COMPANY NAME Ultimate Parent Association Principal Officer Mailing Address Dom. : Began Bus. : Struct. : Mktg. Specialty Phone # AMB# NAIC#	Best's Financial Strength Rating FSC	Data Year	Balance Sheet: Bonds (%)	Mort. Loans & R.E. (%)	Com & Pref. Stock (%)	All Other Assets (%)	Total Assets ($000)	Life Reserves (%)	Health Reserves %)	Ann Res. & Dep. Liabilities (%)	All Other Liabilities (%)	Capital & Surplus ($000)	Operations: Direct Premiums Written ($000)	Net Premiums Written & Deposits ($000)	Operating Cash Flow ($000)	NOG Before Taxes ($000)	NOG After Taxes ($000)	Net Income ($000)
PHYSICIANS H P MID-MI FAMCARE Sparrow Health System Scott Wilkerson President P.O. Box 30377 Lansing, MI 48909 MI : 2003 : Non-Profit : Broker Health 517-364-8400 AMB# 064740 NAIC# 11537	NR-5	'05	...	...	32.0	68.0	11,584	...	69.4	...	30.6	5,729	37,647	37,474	1,156	-409	-409	-409
		'06	...	...	29.3	70.7	13,298	...	63.4	...	36.6	6,104	35,880	35,740	1,781	359	359	359
		'07	...	...	25.2	74.8	16,476	...	52.9	...	47.1	6,646	42,173	41,977	668	529	529	544
		'08	...	...	34.9	65.1	11,363	...	72.3	...	27.7	5,866	46,549	46,314	-1,925	-70	-70	-16
		'09	...	...	32.6	67.4	14,308	...	59.6	...	40.4	6,632	54,254	54,158	2,043	158	158	62
		Rating History: NR-5, 05/21/10; NR-5, 08/26/09; C++pd, 07/28/08; C++pd, 07/31/07; C++pd, 09/01/06																
PHYSICIANS HLTH PL-NORTHERN IN Physicians Health Pl of Northern IN Inc Jay M. Gilbert President & CEO 8101 West Jefferson Boulevard Fort Wayne, IN 46804 IN : 1983 : Non-Profit : Broker Group A&H, Ind A&H, Dental 260-432-6690 AMB# 068743 NAIC# 95436	B+ Rating Outlook: Negative FSC VI	'05	59.3	3.6	16.0	21.1	58,496	...	30.5	...	69.5	37,487	116,560	116,187	9,787	10,499	10,499	10,475
		'06	63.0	3.7	17.7	15.6	59,251	...	29.7	...	70.3	40,236	117,810	117,378	-27	2,486	2,486	2,802
		'07	61.5	3.4	17.8	17.2	64,390	...	38.6	...	61.4	42,305	129,031	128,560	5,536	1,104	1,104	1,490
		'08	61.6	3.8	16.6	18.0	56,412	...	30.0	...	70.0	34,377	141,208	140,930	-5,796	-3,327	-3,327	-5,374
		'09	54.8	3.3	18.7	23.1	61,572	...	30.1	...	69.9	31,915	144,023	143,717	836	-4,737	-4,737	-7,243
		Rating History: B+, 04/29/10; B+, 06/02/09; B+, 06/10/08; B+, 05/03/07; B+, 04/25/06																
PHYSICIANS LIFE INS CO Physicians Mutual Insurance Company Robert A. Reed President & CEO 2600 Dodge Street Omaha, NE 68131 NE : 1970 : Stock : Direct Response Ann, Term Life, Whole life 402-633-1000 AMB# 007451 NAIC# 72125	A Rating Outlook: Stable FSC XI	'05	95.4	...	0.7	4.0	1,334,089	46.0	...	51.1	3.0	79,088	311,330	288,193	36,914	6,294	2,670	2,062
		'06	90.9	...	0.6	8.5	1,333,763	48.4	...	49.0	2.6	80,948	290,863	250,971	1,860	3,004	931	1,150
		'07	92.0	...	1.7	6.2	1,290,550	51.9	...	43.5	4.6	84,503	250,649	187,995	-43,052	8,972	5,531	6,426
		'08	92.3	...	2.2	5.5	1,263,422	54.1	...	42.1	3.7	87,607	266,274	293,887	-20,937	8,562	5,331	-1,495
		'09	90.9	...	2.1	7.0	1,252,706	56.1	...	40.9	3.0	101,506	280,676	196,658	-24,830	12,089	8,053	6,279
		Rating History: A g, 08/27/09; A g, 08/22/08; A g, 08/30/07; A g, 08/11/06; A g, 08/09/05																
PHYSICIANS MUTUAL INSURANCE CO Physicians Mutual Insurance Company Robert A. Reed President & CEO 2600 Dodge Street Omaha, NE 68131 NE : 1902 : Mutual : Direct Response Hosp Ind, Ind A&H, Med supp 402-633-1000 AMB# 007372 NAIC# 80578	A Rating Outlook: Stable FSC XI	'05	82.6	1.1	9.0	7.3	1,241,343	...	86.1	...	13.9	717,891	421,294	461,142	50,781	52,942	42,058	48,049
		'06	86.1	1.0	9.0	3.9	1,301,479	...	86.7	...	13.3	751,953	383,298	439,019	62,718	54,964	42,456	47,318
		'07	82.4	0.9	10.5	6.2	1,389,129	...	89.2	...	10.8	760,027	352,756	422,211	64,909	43,462	32,005	32,353
		'08	83.6	0.8	10.5	5.1	1,432,789	...	92.0	...	8.0	771,937	322,258	403,383	72,737	42,091	32,523	19,015
		'09	83.9	0.7	11.0	4.4	1,539,420	...	88.6	...	11.4	799,112	293,718	386,005	86,920	40,069	30,268	25,041
		Rating History: A g, 08/27/09; A g, 08/22/08; A g, 08/30/07; A g, 08/11/06; A g, 08/09/05																
PHYSICIANS PLUS INS CORP Meriter Health Services Inc Michael A. Mohoney Acting President 22 East Mifflin Street, Suite 200 Madison, WI 53703 WI : 1986 : Stock : Broker Group A&H, Medicaid, Med supp 608-282-8900 AMB# 068683 NAIC# 95341	NR-5	'05	49.9	...	16.9	33.2	60,236	...	40.6	...	59.4	35,882	268,673	268,083	2,997	10,163	6,756	6,744
		'06	55.4	...	16.3	28.4	64,281	...	34.3	...	65.7	39,963	296,500	295,820	9,586	6,090	4,122	4,084
		'07	45.0	...	15.4	39.5	72,039	...	33.1	...	66.9	40,443	349,327	348,066	339	4,444	2,713	2,916
		'08	45.1	...	12.2	42.7	74,004	...	49.6	...	50.4	40,790	364,841	363,480	763	8,136	5,744	2,606
		'09	38.6	...	13.8	47.7	80,986	...	51.2	...	48.8	46,384	394,958	393,469	8,475	5,395	3,717	3,174
		Rating History: NR-5, 04/07/10; NR-5, 08/26/09; B pd, 05/23/08; B pd, 05/30/07; B pd, 05/30/06																
PHYSICIANS UNITED PLAN INC James D. Kollefrath President & CEO 6220 S. Orange Blossom Trail Orlando, FL 32809 FL : 2006 : Stock : Other Medicare 866-571-0693 AMB# 064839 NAIC# 10775	NR-5	'05	...	...	...	100.0	3,623	...	...	...	100.0	3,492	...	...	3,623	-397	-397	-397
		'06	...	...	...	100.0	2,791	...	49.3	...	50.7	1,500	6,462	6,462	-1,058	-2,933	-2,933	-2,933
		'07	...	...	...	100.0	5,396	...	65.7	...	34.3	251	25,425	25,425	407	-4,126	-4,126	-4,126
		'08	2.2	...	...	97.8	16,719	...	80.1	...	19.9	-384	86,283	86,283	3,926	-10,706	-10,706	-10,706
		'09	10.5	...	...	89.5	24,565	...	36.9	...	63.1	3,138	154,592	154,592	6,369	-4,701	-4,701	-4,701
		Rating History: NR-5, 04/07/10; NR-5, 04/14/09; NR-5, 04/15/08; NR-5, 04/17/07; NR-5, 04/25/06																
PHYSICIANSPLUS BAPTIST&ST DOM[2] Sister Mary D. Sondgeroth President 969 Lakeland Drive Jackson, MS 39216 MS : 1996 : Non-Profit : Not Available Health 601-200-6844 AMB# 064503 NAIC# 95686	NR-5	'05	92.8	...	...	7.2	1,240	...	...	...	100.0	1,240	...	...	12	17	17	23
		'06	89.8	...	...	10.2	1,274	...	...	...	100.0	1,260	...	...	40	20	20	20
		'07	87.8	...	...	12.2	1,296	...	...	...	100.0	1,282	...	...	28	21	21	21
		'08	86.7	...	...	13.3	1,305	...	...	...	100.0	1,291	...	...	16	9	9	9
		'09	85.8	...	...	14.2	1,310	...	...	...	100.0	1,310	...	...	11	20	20	20
		Rating History: NR-5, 04/26/10; NR-5, 04/14/09; NR-5, 03/27/08; NR-5, 05/03/07; NR-5, 04/27/06																
PIEDMONT COMMUNITY HEALTHCARE[2] Alan J. Wood President 2512 Langhorne Road Lynchburg, VA 24501 VA : 1999 : Stock : Broker Group A&H, FEHBP 434-947-4463 AMB# 064390 NAIC# 95811	NR-5	'05	...	...	...	100.0	13,305	...	35.0	...	65.0	4,794	32,977	32,665	1,318	891	550	550
		'06	...	...	...	100.0	15,825	...	28.2	...	71.8	5,585	38,135	37,806	2,565	1,300	785	785
		'07	...	...	...	100.0	14,345	...	40.2	...	59.8	5,936	38,747	38,530	-1,326	550	349	349
		'08	...	...	...	100.0	15,026	...	39.8	...	60.2	6,030	42,070	41,805	372	140	87	87
		'09	...	...	...	100.0	17,188	...	43.7	...	56.3	6,033	46,970	46,621	-1,616	3	3	3
		Rating History: NR-5, 05/11/10; NR-5, 04/30/09; NR-5, 09/19/07; C++pd, 10/11/06; C+ pd, 07/08/05																
PINE BELT LIFE INSURANCE CO[1] Charlotte Pearce President 851 County Road 1519 Bay Springs, MS 39422 MS : 2008 : Stock 601-764-3151 AMB# 060697 NAIC# 13158	NR-1	'05	...	...	...	...	...	...	...	...	...	...	...	...	...	...	...	...
		'06	...	...	...	...	...	...	...	...	...	...	...	...	...	...	...	...
		'07	...	...	...	...	...	...	...	...	...	...	...	...	...	...	...	...
		'08	66.0	...	...	34.0	2,306	...	...	...	100.0	339	2,526	2,526	...	59	55	55
		'09	59.4	...	...	40.6	3,573	...	...	...	100.0	309	1,908	1,908	...	9	-46	-46
		Rating History: NR-1, 06/10/10; NR-1, 06/12/09																

BEST'S PROFITABILITY, LEVERAGE AND LIQUIDITY TESTS 2005 – 2009

Data in U.S. Dollars

	Profitability Tests							Leverage Tests						Liquidity Tests					
Un-Realized Capital Gains ($000)	Benefits Paid to NPW & Dep (%)	Comm. & Expenses to NPW & Dep (%)	NOG to Total Assets (%)	NOG to Total Rev (%)	Operating Return on Equity (%)	Net Yield (%)	Total Return (%)	Change in NPW & Dep (%)	NPW & Dep to Capital (X)	Capital & Surplus to Liabilities (%)	Surplus Relief (%)	Reins Leverage (%)	Change in Capital (%)	Quick Liquidity (%)	Current Liquidity (%)	Non-Invest Grade Bonds to Capital (%)	Delinq. & Foreclosed Mortgages to Capital (%)	Mort. & Credit Tenant Loans & R.E. to Capital (%)	Affiliated Invest to Capital (%)
-110	83.9	10.9	-3.6	-1.1	-6.8	3.76	2.64	6.8	6.5	97.9	...	...	-8.3	260.5	282.2	...	...	...	...
16	86.5	10.5	2.9	1.0	6.1	4.67	4.82	-4.6	5.9	84.9	...	...	6.5	252.5	272.1	...	...	...	...
12	84.5	9.2	3.6	1.3	8.3	4.20	4.42	17.4	6.3	67.6	...	...	8.9	204.1	220.4	...	...	...	...
-484	85.6	9.2	-0.5	-0.2	-1.1	0.97	-2.61	10.3	7.9	106.7	...	0.4	-11.7	284.0	308.4	...	...	...	...
606	85.6	13.4	1.2	0.3	2.5	1.66	6.13	16.9	8.2	86.4	...	...	13.1	109.6	109.6	...	...	...	...
Principal Lines of Business: Medicaid (100.0%)														Principal States: MI (100.0%)					
36	77.9	14.8	19.4	8.9	32.2	3.82	3.84	-10.1	3.1	178.4	...	0.4	35.0	209.4	225.7	...	...	5.6	10.9
643	83.2	16.8	4.2	2.1	6.4	4.31	6.00	1.0	2.9	211.6	...	0.4	7.3	234.7	253.8	...	...	5.4	10.6
19	84.9	16.2	1.8	0.8	2.7	4.31	4.99	9.5	3.0	191.6	...	1.1	5.1	221.4	239.3	...	...	5.2	10.3
-3,066	89.2	14.8	-5.5	-2.3	-8.7	4.15	-4.39	9.6	4.1	156.0	...	0.0	-18.7	206.8	223.8	0.3	...	6.2	12.3
4,068	89.9	14.6	-8.0	-3.3	-14.3	3.16	6.29	2.0	4.5	107.6	...	2.1	-7.2	165.0	179.0	2.9	...	6.4	13.3
Principal Lines of Business: CompHosp/Med (98.1%), FEHBP (1.4%), Dental (0.5%)														Principal States: IN (100.0%)					
-448	89.8	21.7	0.2	0.8	3.4	5.17	5.22	-25.3	3.5	6.6	2.4	22.0	2.4	61.0	77.0	68.5	...	...	...
107	101.2	25.7	0.1	0.3	1.2	5.30	5.43	-12.9	2.9	6.9	2.3	26.0	5.2	63.9	79.5	88.4	...	...	...
395	135.9	32.3	0.4	2.1	6.7	5.43	5.64	-25.1	2.0	7.7	2.4	30.4	7.2	60.8	77.5	84.9	...	...	...
15	104.1	20.8	0.4	2.0	6.2	5.44	5.00	56.3	3.2	7.9	2.4	34.8	-0.7	58.6	75.3	95.3	...	...	...
-432	104.5	31.8	0.6	2.9	8.5	5.47	5.36	-33.1	1.8	9.3	2.2	33.6	15.9	58.6	74.7	96.9	...	...	...
Principal Lines of Business: OrdLife (79.5%), IndAnn (20.5%)														Principal States: TX (10.2%), WI (9.5%), CA (5.8%), OH (5.7%), LA (5.1%)					
-5,100	62.3	33.5	3.4	8.2	6.1	4.30	4.48	-2.7	0.6	141.9	0.0	0.1	4.3	145.4	177.3	9.1	...	1.8	12.7
-4,468	58.2	34.4	3.3	8.5	5.8	4.87	4.96	-4.8	0.6	140.4	0.0	0.1	4.4	129.9	161.9	11.9	...	1.7	12.3
3,822	61.6	32.7	2.4	6.5	4.2	5.08	5.45	-3.8	0.5	124.5	0.0	0.2	1.3	120.3	150.8	11.9	...	1.5	12.5
-6,047	61.1	34.1	2.3	6.8	4.2	5.14	3.78	-4.5	0.5	117.3	0.0	0.2	0.4	113.8	142.4	12.8	...	1.4	13.4
22,916	61.7	33.2	2.0	6.5	3.9	5.14	6.39	-4.3	0.5	109.9	0.1	0.2	4.2	111.4	137.7	15.4	...	1.3	14.4
Principal Lines of Business: IndA&H (99.0%), GrpA&H (1.0%)														Principal States: TX (12.4%), WI (10.2%), LA (5.8%), OK (4.4%), CA (4.4%)					
-1,392	87.7	10.0	11.1	2.5	18.6	4.00	0.86	5.9	7.5	147.3	...	...	-2.7	152.7	171.0	...	...	...	...
747	90.0	9.5	6.6	1.4	10.9	4.45	5.87	10.3	7.4	164.3	...	0.1	11.4	194.1	213.1	...	...	...	...
-739	91.5	8.6	4.0	0.8	6.7	5.05	4.09	17.7	8.6	128.0	...	0.4	1.2	156.3	173.5	...	...	...	...
-2,812	90.6	8.1	7.9	1.6	14.1	4.73	-5.80	4.4	8.9	122.8	...	0.4	0.9	140.2	154.5	3.0	...	...	...
3,638	92.1	7.3	4.8	0.9	8.5	3.20	8.49	8.3	8.5	134.0	...	0.1	13.7	175.8	190.7	3.2	...	...	...
Principal Lines of Business: CompHosp/Med (96.2%), Medicaid (2.8%), MedSup (0.9%)														Principal States: WI (99.8%)					
...	...	...	...	-99.9	...	...	...	...	...	999.9	...	...	...	999.9	999.9	...	...	...	...
...	96.7	49.8	-91.4	-44.9	-99.9	2.45	2.45	...	4.3	116.2	...	...	-57.0	198.7	198.7	...	...	...	...
...	91.1	26.0	-99.9	-16.1	-99.9	9.04	9.04	293.5	101.4	4.9	...	32.5	-83.3	57.8	57.8	...	...	...	...
...	94.4	18.2	-96.8	-12.4	999.9	4.03	4.03	239.4	-99.9	-2.2	...	-80.9	-99.9	51.5	53.0	...	...	...	...
...	89.2	14.0	-22.8	-3.0	-99.9	2.24	2.24	79.2	49.3	14.6	...	11.0	917.5	66.4	68.3	...	...	...	...
Principal Lines of Business: Medicare (100.0%)														Principal States: FL (100.0%)					
-6	...	...	1.4	37.5	1.4	3.75	3.76	...	...	999.9	...	...	1.4	999.9	999.9	...	...	...	...
...	...	...	1.6	40.0	1.6	4.05	4.05	...	...	999.9	...	...	1.6	999.9	999.9	...	...	...	...
...	...	...	1.7	41.9	1.7	4.07	4.07	...	...	999.9	...	...	1.7	999.9	999.9	...	...	...	...
...	...	...	0.7	19.1	0.7	3.80	3.80	...	...	999.9	...	...	0.7	999.9	999.9	...	...	...	...
...	...	...	1.5	42.1	1.5	3.61	3.61	...	...	...	...	...	1.5	...	...	...	...	...	...
...	86.2	12.0	4.3	1.7	12.3	2.68	2.68	-3.3	6.8	56.3	...	1.1	16.2	311.0	311.0	...	...	...	...
...	86.4	11.9	5.4	2.0	15.1	4.64	4.64	15.7	6.8	54.5	...	1.7	16.5	302.8	302.8	...	...	...	...
...	88.4	11.7	2.3	0.9	6.1	4.36	4.36	1.9	6.5	70.6	...	...	6.3	336.2	336.2	...	...	...	...
...	87.9	12.2	0.6	0.2	1.5	1.26	1.26	8.5	6.9	67.0	...	...	1.6	308.9	308.9	...	...	...	...
...	84.0	13.6	0.0	0.0	0.0	0.22	0.22	11.5	7.7	54.1	...	0.2	0.0	207.7	207.7	...	...	...	...
Principal Lines of Business: CompHosp/Med (98.4%), FEHBP (1.6%)														Principal States: VA (100.0%)					
...	...	...	...	...	...	...	...	...	...	...	...	...	...	...	...	...	...	...	...
...	...	...	...	...	...	...	...	...	...	...	...	...	...	...	...	...	...	...	...
...	...	...	...	...	...	...	...	...	...	...	...	...	...	...	...	...	...	...	...
...	5.8	20.5	...	2.2	...	...	...	...	7.5	17.2	...	...	...	...	...	...	...	...	...
...	21.0	19.6	-1.6	-2.4	-14.3	...	...	-24.5	6.2	9.5	...	...	-8.8	...	...	...	...	...	...
Principal Lines of Business: IndLife (100.0%)																			

Data in U.S. Dollars

COMPANY NAME Ultimate Parent Association Principal Officer Mailing Address Dom. : Began Bus. : Struct. : Mktg. Specialty Phone # AMB# NAIC#	Best's Financial Strength Rating FSC	Data Year	Balance Sheet Bonds (%)	Mort. Loans & R.E. (%)	Com & Pref. Stock (%)	All Other Assets (%)	Total Assets ($000)	Life Reserves (%)	Health Reserves (%)	Ann Res. & Dep. Liabilities (%)	All Other Liabilities (%)	Capital & Surplus ($000)	Operations Direct Premiums Written ($000)	Net Premiums Written & Deposits ($000)	Operating Cash Flow ($000)	NOG Before Taxes ($000)	NOG After Taxes ($000)	Net Income ($000)
PIONEER AMERICAN INS CO Thoma Cressey Bravo Inc S. Lanny Peavy President & CEO 425 Austin Avenue Waco, TX 76701 TX : 1946 : Stock : Agency Trad Life, Univ Life, ISWL 254-297-2776 AMB# 006929 NAIC# 67873	**A-** Rating Outlook: Stable **FSC VII**	'05	83.9	...	...	16.1	42,895	55.8	...	42.3	1.9	10,956	5,932	9,412	3,187	934	729	729
		'06	86.2	...	...	13.8	43,816	55.5	...	42.9	1.6	10,499	5,330	8,182	858	142	283	283
		'07	84.1	...	...	15.9	47,129	54.7	...	42.6	2.7	10,862	5,873	8,360	2,743	347	536	536
		'08	87.7	...	...	12.3	48,013	55.5	...	42.8	1.8	9,672	6,786	8,848	1,725	-306	-14	-14
		'09	85.4	...	...	14.6	51,492	54.9	...	41.7	3.4	9,729	8,373	9,958	2,165	-474	-322	-334
		Rating History: A- g, 03/02/10; B++g, 01/16/09; B++g, 01/17/08; B++g, 01/10/07; B++g, 02/13/06																
PIONEER MILITARY INSURANCE CO[1] Joe B. Freeman President 4700 Belleview Avenue, Suite 300 Kansas City, MO 64112-1359 NV : 2006 : Stock 816-756-2020 AMB# 060651 NAIC# 12783	**NR-1**	'05	...	...	...	...	...	...	...	...	...	...	...	...	...	...	...	...
		'06	43.6	...	...	56.4	6,219	...	...	...	100.0	1,938	...	4,773	...	-568	-679	-679
		'07	18.4	...	...	81.6	11,636	...	...	...	100.0	4,795	...	6,313	...	2,491	1,644	1,644
		'08	43.9	...	...	56.1	15,258	...	...	...	100.0	6,457	...	7,949	...	3,224	2,096	2,096
		'09	63.4	...	...	36.6	11,703	...	...	...	100.0	4,146	...	7,777	...	4,157	2,719	2,719
		Rating History: NR-1, 06/10/10; NR-1, 06/12/09; NR-1, 06/12/08; NR-1, 06/08/07																
PIONEER MUTUAL LIFE INS CO American United Mutual Insurance Hldg Co Dayton H. Molendorp Chairman & CEO P.O. Box 368 Indianapolis, IN 46206 ND : 1948 : Stock : Agency Univ Life, Ann 701-277-2300 AMB# 006933 NAIC# 67911	**A** Rating Outlook: Positive **FSC XI**	'05	79.5	11.1	...	9.4	465,077	48.2	0.0	48.7	3.1	32,042	39,140	32,355	5,542	2,240	1,739	2,142
		'06	77.6	12.7	...	9.6	467,337	51.9	0.0	45.4	2.7	32,614	40,459	34,237	-661	-164	-467	597
		'07	76.3	15.7	...	8.0	458,569	57.1	0.0	40.2	2.6	29,432	39,172	32,932	-4,262	-894	-531	-531
		'08	75.2	15.5	0.8	8.5	457,217	61.1	0.0	36.3	2.5	29,073	41,206	34,930	-1,788	621	5	-1,097
		'09	76.1	13.9	...	9.9	476,310	63.2	0.0	33.3	3.5	31,506	42,786	36,778	14,185	2,101	1,007	958
		Rating History: A g, 06/10/10; A g, 06/17/09; A g, 06/09/08; A g, 06/07/07; A g, 02/08/06																
PIONEER SECURITY LIFE INS CO Thoma Cressey Bravo Inc S. Lanny Peavy President & CEO 425 Austin Avenue Waco, TX 76701 TX : 1956 : Stock : Agency Trad Life, Univ Life, ISWL 254-297-2778 AMB# 006935 NAIC# 67946	**A-** Rating Outlook: Stable **FSC VII**	'05	31.0	...	62.4	6.6	84,213	35.6	...	59.7	4.7	66,782	5,418	6,158	-6,646	1,019	1,787	1,787
		'06	34.0	...	59.7	6.3	78,906	39.9	...	55.0	5.1	59,746	6,504	7,020	-1,463	7,775	8,342	8,342
		'07	30.3	...	63.1	6.5	91,061	45.9	...	50.5	3.5	70,451	6,619	6,918	2,966	-653	-761	-761
		'08	35.4	...	60.7	3.9	95,060	51.1	...	47.3	1.6	73,638	5,898	6,138	3,937	2,808	2,794	2,794
		'09	37.9	...	57.7	4.4	99,962	52.4	...	43.5	4.0	76,477	5,321	5,545	4,749	3,220	3,079	3,079
		Rating History: A- g, 03/02/10; B++g, 01/16/09; B++g, 01/17/08; B++g, 01/10/07; B++g, 02/13/06																
PLATEAU INS CO Plateau Group Inc William D. Williams President 2701 North Main Street Crossville, TN 38555-5407 TN : 1981 : Stock : Broker Credit A&H, Credit Life 931-484-8411 AMB# 009348 NAIC# 97152	**B++** Rating Outlook: Stable **FSC IV**	'05	63.1	1.5	4.9	30.4	14,824	52.8	36.3	...	10.8	5,013	17,144	9,210	-5,779	671	514	516
		'06	56.2	1.3	4.6	37.9	16,506	52.1	36.1	...	11.9	5,979	18,235	9,635	1,689	954	806	806
		'07	62.1	1.1	2.8	33.9	18,420	53.4	36.0	...	10.6	6,175	23,061	12,358	2,247	695	539	539
		'08	53.4	1.0	2.2	43.3	19,411	54.5	35.7	...	9.9	6,674	21,293	11,500	1,034	710	594	591
		'09	59.3	1.0	2.6	37.0	19,434	51.4	33.1	...	15.5	9,174	17,693	9,597	-78	2,966	2,467	2,467
		Rating History: B++, 05/03/10; B+, 04/07/09; B+, 04/09/08; B+, 04/02/07; B+, 03/24/06																
POLISH ROMAN CATHOLIC UNION Wallace M. Ozog President 984 Milwaukee Avenue Chicago, IL 60622-4101 IL : 1887 : Fraternal : Career Agent Term Life, Trad Life, Whole life 773-782-2600 AMB# 006940 NAIC# 57630	**C++** Rating Outlook: Negative **FSC IV**	'05	60.6	11.6	19.1	8.7	143,572	66.2	...	29.7	4.0	13,440	14,817	14,736	9,481	-2,161	-2,161	-545
		'06	63.1	10.2	17.1	9.6	152,388	62.8	...	33.6	3.6	14,252	12,679	12,619	7,533	-1,422	-1,422	50
		'07	68.2	8.7	17.5	5.6	161,983	57.9	...	39.3	2.9	12,082	17,022	16,937	11,239	-2,078	-2,078	-945
		'08	64.2	8.0	14.5	13.4	169,538	53.0	...	45.8	1.2	6,182	24,850	24,764	12,095	-2,027	-2,027	-3,398
		'09	73.2	6.9	14.4	5.5	178,199	50.1	...	48.4	1.5	4,312	17,353	17,256	7,895	-1,600	-1,600	-1,595
		Rating History: C++, 03/25/10; B-, 03/27/09; B, 06/12/08; B+, 06/14/07; B+, 06/20/06																
POPULAR LIFE RE Popular Inc Ramon D. Lloveras President P.O. Box 70331 Guaynabo, PR 00936-8331 PR : 2003 : Stock : Not Available Credit Life, Credit A&H, Group A&H 787-706-4111 AMB# 060399 NAIC# 11876	**B** Rating Outlook: Negative **FSC VI**	'05	56.9	...	...	43.1	39,016	50.0	45.3	...	4.7	11,615	...	29,166	10,720	383	91	91
		'06	87.6	...	...	12.4	46,463	47.6	49.5	...	2.9	15,193	...	23,820	7,595	3,915	3,589	3,589
		'07	89.4	...	...	10.6	51,105	47.9	49.7	...	2.4	20,172	...	18,669	4,623	5,309	4,978	4,978
		'08	84.9	...	7.0	8.1	54,743	47.7	50.3	...	2.0	25,619	...	16,763	4,105	5,870	5,546	5,546
		'09	69.2	...	7.3	23.6	56,408	46.5	49.9	...	3.6	31,657	...	12,497	2,053	6,543	6,190	6,190
		Rating History: B, 08/04/09; B+, 06/11/09; B++, 08/14/08; B++, 02/21/07; B++, 03/28/06																
PORT-O-CALL LIFE INS CO[1] Henry F. Trotter, Jr. President 3131 Olive Street Pine Bluff, AR 71603-6048 AR : 1969 : Stock : Not Available 870-535-4321 AMB# 007929 NAIC# 76503	**NR-1**	'05	62.4	...	6.6	31.0	1,615	...	...	...	100.0	1,453	61	61	...	49	41	41
		'06	69.2	...	7.8	23.0	1,528	...	...	...	100.0	1,303	145	145	...	-23	-23	-23
		'07	65.7	...	7.1	27.2	1,608	...	...	...	100.0	1,351	135	135	...	55	50	50
		'08	63.6	...	3.5	32.9	1,661	...	...	...	100.0	1,395	130	130	...	105	88	88
		'09	53.5	...	7.9	38.6	940	...	...	...	100.0	695	101	101	...	44	37	35
		Rating History: NR-1, 06/10/10; NR-1, 06/12/09; NR-1, 06/12/08; NR-1, 06/08/07; NR-1, 06/07/06																
PREFERRED ASSURANCE COMPANY MVP Health Care Inc David Oliker President & CEO 625 State Street Schenectady, NY 12305 NY : 1998 : Other : Agency Group A&H, Health 585-325-3920 AMB# 064595 NAIC# 49964	**B** Rating Outlook: Negative **FSC IV**	'05	...	...	...	100.0	2,545	...	64.8	...	35.2	2,207	3,333	3,333	1,672	939	939	939
		'06	...	...	...	100.0	1,626	...	59.4	...	40.6	1,030	3,985	3,982	-834	38	27	27
		'07	...	...	...	100.0	2,535	...	35.8	...	64.2	1,423	4,362	4,358	675	394	394	400
		'08	...	...	...	100.0	25,687	...	62.8	...	37.2	9,414	54,080	53,987	18,146	-21,999	-16,635	-16,635
		'09	...	...	...	100.0	19,162	...	60.8	...	39.2	7,227	81,198	81,133	-5,343	-8,233	-8,233	-8,213
		Rating History: B, 06/11/10; B u, 11/19/09; B+ g, 06/11/09; NR-2, 03/05/08; NR-2, 02/15/07																

BEST'S PROFITABILITY, LEVERAGE AND LIQUIDITY TESTS 2005 – 2009

Data in U.S. Dollars

—	Profitability Tests							Leverage Tests						Liquidity Tests					
Un-Realized Capital Gains ($000)	Benefits Paid to NPW & Dep (%)	Comm. & Expenses to NPW & Dep (%)	NOG to Total Assets (%)	NOG to Total Rev (%)	Operating Return on Equity (%)	Net Yield (%)	Total Return (%)	Change in NPW & Dep (%)	NPW & Dep to Capital (X)	Capital & Surplus to Liabilities (%)	Surplus Relief (%)	Reins Leverage (%)	Change in Capital (%)	Quick Liquidity (%)	Current Liquidity (%)	Non-Invest Grade Bonds to Capital (%)	Delinq. & Foreclosed Mortgages to Capital (%)	Mort. & Credit Tenant Loans & R.E. to Capital (%)	Affiliated Invest to Capital (%)
...	31.2	29.2	1.8	9.5	6.9	4.76	4.82	5.3	0.9	34.5	1.1	2.4	7.0	114.3	118.8	...	...	...	...
...	25.3	31.4	0.7	3.9	2.6	4.98	5.06	-13.1	0.8	31.6	1.5	1.1	-4.3	109.2	112.3	...	...	...	...
...	38.7	34.3	1.2	6.8	5.0	5.05	5.14	2.2	0.8	30.1	1.8	1.7	3.5	106.5	110.3	...	...	...	...
...	43.1	44.8	0.0	-0.2	-0.1	5.02	5.10	5.8	0.9	25.4	2.9	3.2	-10.7	93.4	101.7	...	...	...	...
...	31.5	54.7	-0.6	-3.1	-3.3	4.94	4.97	12.5	1.0	23.5	4.1	5.1	0.6	92.7	100.8	...	...	...	...

Principal Lines of Business: OrdLife (72.0%), GrpAnn (23.6%), IndAnn (3.3%), GrpLife (1.2%)

Principal States: PR (28.9%), TX (7.4%), AL (7.2%), LA (5.3%), NC (4.9%)

...	...	...	...	...	...	...	...	...	...	...	...	...	...	...	...	...	...	...	...
...	10.9	40.8	...	-12.1	...	...	...	...	2.5	45.4	...	...	...	...	...	...	...	...	...
...	8.6	42.4	18.4	24.6	48.8	...	...	32.3	1.3	70.3	...	...	147.3	...	...	...	...	...	...
...	7.6	45.1	15.6	26.2	37.3	...	...	25.9	1.2	73.6	...	...	34.7	...	...	...	...	...	...
...	5.6	44.1	20.2	34.3	51.3	...	...	-2.2	1.9	55.2	...	...	-35.7	...	...	...	...	...	...

Principal Lines of Business: CrdA&H (72.3%), CrdLife (27.7%)

-3	125.2	42.0	0.4	3.0	5.5	5.89	6.06	8.7	0.9	8.2	1.7	139.8	3.7	49.3	67.8	23.6	...	146.5	5.2
-1	143.7	46.3	-0.1	-0.8	-1.4	5.89	6.20	5.8	1.0	8.2	1.6	120.6	0.2	47.5	65.6	21.5	...	168.2	4.8
-1	151.8	44.1	-0.1	-0.9	-1.7	5.77	5.82	-3.8	1.0	7.5	1.3	126.0	-9.0	45.2	62.8	23.8	...	223.9	4.9
-8	124.1	44.7	0.0	0.0	0.0	5.82	5.63	6.1	1.1	7.3	1.3	133.3	-2.9	45.0	62.9	31.4	...	226.8	...
-98	90.4	40.7	0.2	1.6	3.3	5.95	5.97	5.3	1.1	7.7	0.9	138.5	9.5	45.0	63.1	35.9	...	194.2	...

Principal Lines of Business: OrdLife (95.2%), IndAnn (3.8%), GrpAnn (1.0%), GrpA&H (0.0%), IndA&H (0.0%)

Principal States: CA (16.3%), OR (13.3%), ND (8.1%), CO (7.0%), MN (6.8%)

12,291	28.3	65.8	2.2	22.6	2.8	3.32	20.04	30.9	0.1	383.8	0.5	0.2	6.4	158.4	164.1	...	...	...	78.7
-5,479	28.8	63.9	10.2	50.9	13.2	13.68	6.93	14.0	0.1	312.2	0.5	0.6	-10.5	128.2	132.1	...	...	...	78.8
10,393	37.9	56.3	-0.9	-9.7	-1.2	1.76	15.29	-1.5	0.1	342.3	0.4	0.7	17.9	142.0	148.5	...	...	...	81.6
207	47.0	43.8	3.0	28.8	3.9	4.61	4.84	-11.3	0.1	344.5	0.3	0.9	4.5	131.8	145.2	...	...	...	78.3
18	58.2	32.0	3.2	32.6	4.1	4.79	4.81	-9.7	0.1	326.6	0.2	1.1	3.9	146.4	158.5	...	...	...	75.4

Principal Lines of Business: OrdLife (85.8%), GrpAnn (13.0%), GrpLife (0.9%), IndAnn (0.3%)

Principal States: AL (22.7%), MS (11.0%), GA (9.9%), FL (9.2%), TX (7.8%)

-11	32.9	65.2	2.9	3.6	6.9	3.00	2.96	7.2	1.8	51.7	91.4	200.9	-52.0	125.0	132.9	...	...	4.4	7.7
10	29.8	61.1	5.1	5.3	14.7	3.75	3.82	4.6	1.6	57.3	81.9	169.5	19.1	132.5	139.8	...	...	3.6	6.4
0	24.3	63.2	3.1	2.8	8.9	4.55	4.55	28.3	2.0	50.8	94.4	169.3	3.2	133.6	139.0	...	...	3.4	6.1
-78	27.4	68.3	3.1	3.3	9.2	4.13	3.70	-6.9	1.7	52.6	86.1	149.3	7.8	137.7	142.9	...	...	3.0	5.6
73	32.9	71.3	12.7	16.4	31.1	3.03	3.51	-16.6	1.0	90.0	53.4	83.1	37.6	171.6	176.8	...	...	2.2	4.0

Principal Lines of Business: CrdLife (56.7%), CrdA&H (37.3%), OrdLife (5.8%), GrpLife (0.2%)

Principal States: TN (41.0%), MS (18.4%), GA (14.6%), LA (9.7%), AL (9.5%)

-1,894	55.2	32.1	-1.6	-10.0	-14.8	5.39	5.22	-3.2	0.9	13.2	...	1.2	-11.9	55.1	68.1	23.1	0.3	99.4	16.3
1,399	68.3	34.1	-1.0	-7.0	-10.3	5.36	7.33	-14.4	0.7	12.9	...	1.2	4.3	56.9	69.9	16.8	1.1	89.6	15.8
-1,466	58.7	27.1	-1.3	-8.2	-15.8	5.39	5.20	34.2	1.1	10.2	...	1.6	-13.9	54.4	67.0	17.6	0.2	93.7	19.3
-4,648	62.0	19.4	-1.2	-6.0	-22.2	5.73	2.15	46.2	3.8	4.0	...	3.4	-56.0	54.6	65.3	25.9	2.2	205.0	42.4
1,101	77.4	24.4	-0.9	-6.2	-30.5	5.03	5.68	-30.3	3.0	3.3	...	5.0	-12.6	53.0	65.6	32.4	3.5	212.9	48.6

Principal Lines of Business: IndAnn (84.5%), OrdLife (15.5%)

Principal States: MI (26.1%), DE (19.4%), IL (15.0%), TX (7.5%), KS (7.0%)

...	9.2	59.5	0.3	0.3	0.8	3.12	3.12	25.3	2.5	42.4	...	...	0.8	166.3	178.9	...	...	...	...
...	15.9	58.9	8.4	14.0	26.8	4.39	4.39	-18.3	1.6	48.6	...	...	30.8	140.3	140.7	...	...	...	...
...	27.4	56.8	10.2	23.8	28.2	4.77	4.77	-21.6	0.9	65.3	...	...	32.8	153.9	154.4	...	...	...	...
...	32.5	54.9	10.5	29.3	24.2	4.24	4.24	-10.2	0.7	88.7	...	...	27.5	167.8	170.3	...	...	...	7.8
...	44.4	54.2	11.1	42.9	21.6	3.62	3.62	-25.4	0.4	130.4	...	...	24.0	195.3	206.7	...	...	...	6.3

Principal Lines of Business: CrdLife (36.3%), IndA&H (29.7%), CrdA&H (20.6%), GrpA&H (7.0%), GrpLife (6.4%)

-9	53.6	73.5	2.6	38.4	2.9	...	...	-3.5	0.0	999.9	...	...	2.2	...	...	...	...	...	...
6	60.8	48.2	-1.5	-11.9	-1.7	...	...	137.8	0.1	674.6	...	...	-10.0	...	...	...	...	...	...
-3	23.3	55.3	3.2	25.7	3.8	...	...	-6.9	0.1	596.9	...	...	3.5	...	...	...	...	...	...
-55	...	58.7	5.4	44.6	6.4	...	...	-3.3	0.1	560.5	...	...	2.3	...	...	...	...	...	...
17	56.9	67.7	2.8	24.3	3.5	...	...	-22.2	0.1	312.1	...	...	-49.5	...	...	...	...	...	...

Principal Lines of Business: CrdLife (100.0%)

...	58.5	14.2	62.6	27.9	73.2	2.47	2.47	239.6	1.5	652.8	...	...	514.2	700.9	709.2	...	...	...	...
...	83.9	16.4	1.3	0.7	1.7	3.13	3.13	19.5	3.9	172.8	...	...	-53.3	224.4	225.4	...	...	...	...
...	83.6	8.5	18.9	8.9	32.1	3.04	3.45	9.4	3.1	128.0	...	...	38.2	303.5	317.7	...	...	...	...
...	125.1	15.8	-99.9	-30.8	-99.9	0.61	0.61	999.9	5.7	57.8	...	1.9	561.5	247.8	255.9	...	...	...	...
...	94.9	15.4	-36.7	-10.1	-98.9	0.52	0.63	50.3	11.2	60.6	...	...	-23.2	254.4	262.2	...	...	...	...

Principal Lines of Business: CompHosp/Med (100.0%)

Principal States: NY (100.0%)

COMPANY NAME / Ultimate Parent Association / Principal Officer / Mailing Address / Dom. : Began Bus. : Struct. : Mktg. / Specialty / Phone # / AMB# NAIC#	Best's Financial Strength Rating / FSC	Data Year	Balance Sheet: Bonds (%)	Mort. Loans & R.E. (%)	Com & Pref. Stock (%)	All Other Assets (%)	Total Assets ($000)	Life Reserves (%)	Health Reserves (%)	Ann Res. & Dep. Liabilities (%)	All Other Liabilities (%)	Capital & Surplus ($000)	Operations: Direct Premiums Written ($000)	Net Premiums Written & Deposits ($000)	Operating Cash Flow ($000)	NOG Before Taxes ($000)	NOG After Taxes ($000)	Net Income ($000)
PREFERRED HLTH PARTNERSHIP Humana Inc Michael B. McCallister President & CEO 1420 Centerpoint Boulevard Knoxville, TN 37932 TN : 1994 : Stock : Broker Health 865-670-7282 AMB# 064302 NAIC# 95749	NR-3	'05	95.4	...	...	4.6	58,779	...	28.4	...	71.6	35,095	...	...	-256	8,829	8,829	8,874
		'06	98.5	...	...	1.5	55,713	...	30.9	...	69.1	33,553	...	...	-2,643	1,466	1,306	1,246
		'07	94.5	...	...	5.5	57,312	...	32.5	...	67.5	39,149	...	...	1,926	2,719	2,827	2,755
		'08	57.1	...	...	42.9	57,184	...	...	...	100.0	44,682	...	...	-1,203	6,389	7,915	5,184
		'09	79.2	...	...	20.8	24,967	...	...	...	100.0	24,958	...	...	-30,549	9,930	10,140	10,620
		Rating History: NR-3, 06/02/10; NR-3, 06/05/09; NR-5, 07/10/08; NR-5, 04/02/07; NR-5, 06/15/06																
PREFERRED HEALTH PLAN INC[2] Paul R. Stewart Chairman & President P.O. Box 9 Klamath Falls, OR 97601-0383 OR : 2001 : Stock : Broker Dental, Group A&H, Vision 541-882-1466 AMB# 064793 NAIC# 11161	NR-5	'05	3.5	...	60.9	35.7	7,299	...	44.2	...	55.8	4,213	19,143	18,316	1,045	399	399	792
		'06	4.0	...	46.6	49.4	6,407	...	51.1	...	48.9	3,828	22,247	21,368	-591	-1,570	-1,570	-1,294
		'07	3.9	...	40.5	55.6	6,903	...	56.9	...	43.1	3,985	17,135	16,271	738	130	130	326
		'08	4.6	...	29.1	66.3	5,975	...	48.8	...	51.2	2,349	16,010	14,871	-708	-1,766	-1,766	-2,043
		'09	14.3	...	...	85.7	1,901	...	16.5	...	83.5	1,447	6,379	5,943	-3,980	-813	-813	-1,380
		Rating History: NR-5, 05/21/10; NR-5, 09/11/09; NR-5, 07/14/08; NR-5, 06/29/07; NR-5, 05/11/06																
PREFERRED HEALTH SYSTEMS INS Coventry Health Care Inc Marlon R. Dauner President & CEO 8535 East 21st Street North Wichita, KS 67206 KS : 1996 : Stock : Broker Group A&H 316-609-2345 AMB# 060224 NAIC# 60110	NR-2	'05	28.5	...	35.0	36.5	44,509	...	62.2	...	37.8	25,441	128,101	126,112	5,930	5,979	4,026	4,019
		'06	30.1	...	40.1	29.8	45,665	...	75.9	...	24.1	23,574	130,312	128,607	1,349	-120	-777	-747
		'07	29.7	...	38.4	31.9	43,213	...	76.4	...	23.6	23,920	134,987	133,236	-2,834	3,590	3,152	3,328
		'08	36.0	...	29.8	34.2	34,765	...	71.1	...	28.9	16,149	127,873	126,667	-4,484	-4,369	-2,840	-3,041
		'09	35.8	...	31.6	32.6	32,825	...	78.2	...	21.8	11,441	132,744	131,885	-3,385	-11,365	-7,357	-7,357
		Rating History: NR-2, 02/12/10; NR-5, 04/08/09; NR-5, 03/12/08; NR-5, 04/03/07; NR-5, 04/07/06																
PREFERRED PLUS OF KANSAS INC Coventry Health Care Inc Marlon R. Dauner President 8535 East 21st Street North Wichita, KS 67206 KS : 1992 : Stock : Broker Group A&H, Health 316-609-2345 AMB# 068937 NAIC# 95390	NR-2	'05	27.3	...	33.1	39.6	80,535	...	48.9	...	51.1	36,755	262,721	262,721	11,359	14,809	9,971	9,947
		'06	29.3	...	39.8	30.9	77,733	...	55.7	...	44.3	40,624	230,084	230,084	-3,292	8,980	6,139	6,180
		'07	25.8	...	35.1	39.1	81,153	...	60.9	...	39.1	42,181	259,404	259,404	-1,027	8,741	5,914	5,961
		'08	30.9	...	27.3	41.8	68,052	...	68.8	...	31.2	30,837	284,381	284,381	-5,209	1,424	637	-166
		'09	27.8	...	28.9	43.3	74,113	...	65.5	...	34.5	37,166	297,630	296,726	2,045	4,192	3,394	3,301
		Rating History: NR-2, 02/12/10; NR-5, 08/26/09; B- pd, 06/06/08; B- pd, 06/12/07; B- pd, 06/20/06																
PREFERRED SECURITY LIFE INS[1] Rhonda Hughes President P.O. Box 5357 Dallas, TX 75208-9357 TX : 1966 : Stock : Not Available 214-946-5133 AMB# 068266 NAIC# 82341	NR-1	'05	93.4	...	...	6.6	4,392	...	...	...	100.0	162	112	112	...	10	10	11
		'06	75.7	...	...	24.3	4,360	...	...	...	100.0	199	88	88	...	33	33	33
		'07	42.8	...	...	57.2	4,208	...	...	...	100.0	196	66	66	...	-13	-13	-13
		'08	57.1	...	...	42.9	4,028	...	...	...	100.0	154	45	45	...	-43	-43	-43
		'09	87.2	...	...	12.8	3,440	...	...	...	100.0	211	38	37	...	57	57	58
		Rating History: NR-1, 06/10/10; NR-1, 06/12/09; NR-1, 06/12/08; NR-1, 06/08/07; NR-1, 06/07/06																
PREFERREDONE COMMUNITY HLTH PL Fairview Health Services Marcus A. Merz President 6105 Golden Hills Drive Golden Valley, MN 55416 MN : 1996 : Non-Profit : Broker Group A&H 763-847-4000 AMB# 064054 NAIC# 95724	NR-5	'05	62.2	...	17.9	20.0	47,909	...	56.6	...	43.4	26,512	125,737	124,979	2,056	68	68	674
		'06	75.9	...	23.1	1.0	40,122	...	69.7	...	30.3	21,984	135,712	134,803	-8,336	-4,322	-4,322	-4,177
		'07	74.6	...	18.9	6.5	40,575	...	60.3	...	39.7	19,136	154,473	153,182	1,651	-3,586	-3,586	-2,058
		'08	73.7	...	17.9	8.4	34,009	...	66.0	...	34.0	14,715	158,330	157,003	-7,551	-2,195	-2,195	-4,261
		'09	67.7	...	12.9	19.4	27,933	...	61.0	...	39.0	11,420	136,849	136,054	-5,264	-2,938	-2,938	-2,125
		Rating History: NR-5, 08/26/09; B- pd, 06/06/08; B pd, 06/05/07; B+ pd, 06/13/06; B+ pd, 06/17/05																
PREFERREDONE INSURANCE CO Fairview Health Services Marcus A. Merz President 6105 Golden Hills Drive Golden Valley, MN 55416-1023 MN : 2003 : Stock : Broker Group A&H 763-847-4000 AMB# 013851 NAIC# 11817	NR-5	'05	...	...	...	...	...	...	...	...	...	...	...	...	...	...	...	...
		'06	...	...	...	...	...	...	...	...	...	...	...	...	...	...	...	...
		'07	88.6	...	...	11.4	7,474	...	32.1	...	67.9	5,328	6,336	5,810	1,268	431	296	295
		'08	48.5	...	6.9	44.6	18,230	...	51.2	...	48.8	11,817	18,895	18,222	10,600	2,419	1,633	1,662
		'09	74.5	...	13.6	11.9	31,984	0.9	55.4	...	43.7	19,604	81,304	79,716	12,328	2,519	1,866	2,002
		Rating History: NR-5, 04/08/09; NR-5, 04/09/08																
PREMERA BLUE CROSS Premera Herbert R. B. Barlow President & CEO P.O. Box 327 Seattle, WA 98111-0327 WA : 1945 : Non-Profit : Broker Maj med 425-918-4000 AMB# 060076 NAIC# 47570	A- Rating Outlook: Stable FSC XI	'05	53.0	3.6	21.4	22.0	1,083,065	...	52.2	...	47.8	525,447	2,372,348	2,365,871	91,642	93,686	79,361	84,107
		'06	44.0	3.3	29.6	23.1	1,270,521	...	42.2	...	57.8	661,486	2,344,326	2,338,252	145,018	119,279	93,013	103,062
		'07	37.6	3.3	40.0	19.1	1,319,699	...	49.6	...	50.4	783,895	2,495,807	2,488,811	58,279	101,965	95,573	105,876
		'08	37.1	3.5	35.6	23.8	1,197,340	...	40.9	...	59.1	672,236	2,515,658	2,508,780	-61,396	92,987	85,386	34,930
		'09	34.4	3.1	33.7	28.9	1,287,470	...	40.5	...	59.5	789,956	2,453,668	2,446,292	24,519	59,160	44,840	21,049
		Rating History: A- g, 06/15/09; A- g, 06/06/08; A- g, 05/23/07; B++g, 06/21/06; B++g, 06/20/05																
PREMIER ACCESS INSURANCE CO Abbaszadeh Dental Group Inc Reza Abbaszadeh, D.D.S. President, Secretary & Treasurer 8890 Cal Center Drive Sacramento, CA 95826 CA : 1998 : Stock : Broker Dental 916-920-9500 AMB# 060375 NAIC# 60237	A- Rating Outlook: Stable FSC V	'05	51.5	9.5	...	38.9	22,593	...	58.3	...	41.7	13,847	53,543	53,543	2,618	4,570	3,117	3,137
		'06	60.1	7.8	...	32.1	27,951	...	32.4	...	67.6	17,298	65,036	65,036	5,446	4,157	2,337	2,337
		'07	44.1	5.8	2.7	47.5	32,877	...	35.2	...	64.8	22,185	70,246	70,246	5,292	6,518	3,951	3,961
		'08	39.3	4.7	6.3	49.7	36,264	...	36.3	...	63.7	25,718	74,139	74,139	2,217	6,956	4,551	2,687
		'09	69.3	2.8	6.8	21.1	42,230	...	33.3	...	66.7	30,670	78,800	78,800	6,275	7,162	4,707	4,566
		Rating History: A-, 07/14/09; A-, 06/06/08; A- g, 06/13/07; A- g, 06/20/06; A- g, 06/22/05																

Data in U.S. Dollars

	Profitability Tests							Leverage Tests						Liquidity Tests					
Un-Realized Capital Gains ($000)	Benefits Paid to NPW & Dep (%)	Comm. & Expenses to NPW & Dep (%)	NOG to Total Assets (%)	NOG to Total Rev (%)	Operating Return on Equity (%)	Net Yield (%)	Total Return (%)	Change in NPW & Dep (%)	NPW & Dep to Capital (X)	Capital & Surplus to Liabilities (%)	Surplus Relief (%)	Reins Leverage (%)	Change in Capital (%)	Quick Liquidity (%)	Current Liquidity (%)	Non-Invest Grade Bonds to Capital (%)	Delinq. & Foreclosed Mortgages to Capital (%)	Mort. & Credit Tenant Loans & R.E. to Capital (%)	Affiliated Invest to Capital (%)
...	...	...	14.6	124.6	28.8	3.91	3.98	...	...	148.2	...	...	33.6	219.7	229.8	1.9	...	...	...
...	...	...	2.3	54.4	3.8	4.29	4.18	...	...	151.4	...	...	-4.4	214.5	228.8	...	...	...	...
...	...	...	5.0	47.4	7.8	4.18	4.05	...	...	215.5	...	...	16.7	274.6	296.3	...	...	...	...
128	...	...	13.8	262.3	18.9	5.44	0.95	...	...	357.4	...	...	14.1	564.0	583.2	...	...	...	...
...	...	...	24.7	999.9	29.1	2.53	3.73	...	...	999.9	...	...	-44.1	999.9	999.9	...	...	...	...
40	86.2	11.8	0.1	2.2	10.0	...	7.10	1.5	4.0	136.5	...	22.2	27.2	204.3	226.0	...	...	...	...
-127	96.2	11.6	-22.9	-7.3	-39.0	1.34	3.76	16.7	5.6	148.4	...	8.0	-9.1	274.1	291.5	...	...	...	...
-171	87.3	12.8	2.0	0.8	3.3	...	0.48	-23.9	4.1	136.6	...	5.3	4.1	268.4	282.7	...	...	...	...
-613	94.6	14.1	-27.4	-11.8	-55.8	1.60	-12.56	-8.6	6.3	64.8	...	10.0	-41.1	122.7	129.9	...	...	...	...
463	97.5	26.3	-20.6	-13.6	-42.8	0.81	-0.05	-60.0	4.1	318.7	...	0.0	-38.4	744.2	744.2	...	...	...	...
	Principal Lines of Business: CompHosp/Med (91.1%), Dental (7.3%), Vision (1.7%)													Principal States: OR (100.0%)					
382	85.3	11.1	9.6	3.2	17.5	3.36	4.30	13.8	5.0	133.4	...	1.6	23.9	188.7	206.2	...	...	...	...
557	88.9	11.5	-1.7	-0.6	-3.2	6.55	7.90	2.0	5.5	106.7	...	1.0	-7.3	169.2	184.5	...	...	...	...
-594	90.0	11.3	7.1	2.3	13.3	7.59	6.63	3.6	5.6	124.0	...	0.2	1.5	190.8	207.0	...	...	...	...
-4,312	93.2	11.6	-7.3	-2.2	-14.2	3.12	-8.79	-4.9	7.8	86.8	...	1.7	-32.5	138.1	152.0	...	...	...	...
2,061	97.4	11.5	-21.8	-5.5	-53.3	2.39	9.52	4.1	11.5	53.5	...	1.6	-29.2	130.8	143.0	...	...	...	...
	Principal Lines of Business: CompHosp/Med (94.8%), MedSup (5.2%)													Principal States: KS (100.0%)					
635	85.7	9.6	13.1	3.8	30.2	3.51	4.41	2.0	7.1	84.0	...	...	25.4	144.2	157.9	...	...	...	...
812	88.4	9.7	7.8	2.6	15.9	6.39	7.57	-12.4	5.7	109.5	...	...	10.5	158.7	174.4	...	...	...	...
-799	89.2	9.5	7.4	2.2	14.3	7.81	6.75	12.7	6.1	108.2	...	...	3.8	158.9	173.1	...	...	...	...
-7,097	91.3	8.9	0.9	0.2	1.7	3.10	-9.02	9.6	9.2	82.9	...	...	-26.9	124.4	136.6	...	...	...	...
3,888	90.2	8.8	4.8	1.1	10.0	2.40	9.24	4.3	8.0	100.6	...	0.8	20.5	147.5	161.1	...	...	...	...
	Principal Lines of Business: CompHosp/Med (100.0%)													Principal States: KS (100.0%)					
...	282.3	71.7	0.2	3.4	6.1	...	...	-10.3	0.6	4.1	...	...	5.8	...	...	...	...	...	...
...	266.5	66.1	0.8	13.3	18.4	...	...	-21.2	0.4	5.0	...	...	20.2	...	...	...	...	...	...
...	352.4	173.1	-0.3	-5.7	-6.6	...	...	-24.9	0.3	4.9	...	...	-6.2	...	...	...	...	...	...
...	609.8	156.1	-1.0	-25.2	-24.3	...	...	-31.4	0.3	4.0	...	...	-21.7	...	...	...	...	...	...
...	999.9	202.0	1.5	43.4	31.0	...	...	-17.3	0.2	6.6	...	...	37.9	...	...	...	...	...	...
	Principal Lines of Business: IndAnn (94.1%), OrdLife (5.9%)																		
-170	85.4	15.9	0.1	0.1	0.3	4.05	5.00	3.7	4.7	123.9	...	0.2	1.9	205.4	223.3	...	...	...	...
634	90.6	13.9	-9.8	-3.2	-17.8	4.05	5.88	7.9	6.1	121.2	...	0.9	-17.1	176.0	194.3	...	...	...	...
-884	87.9	15.5	-8.9	-2.3	-17.4	4.43	6.16	13.6	8.0	89.3	...	1.8	-13.0	163.2	176.9	...	...	...	...
-840	87.2	15.1	-5.9	-1.4	-13.0	4.35	-3.62	2.5	10.7	76.3	...	8.7	-23.1	145.0	159.4	0.7	...	...	...
876	88.2	14.6	-9.5	-2.1	-22.5	3.15	9.06	-13.3	11.9	69.2	...	2.7	-22.4	154.0	165.3	6.3	...	...	...
	Principal Lines of Business: CompHosp/Med (100.0%)													Principal States: MN (100.0%)					
...	...	...	...	...	...	...	...	...	...	...	...	...	...	...	...	...	...	...	...
...	...	...	...	...	...	...	...	...	...	...	...	...	...	...	...	...	...	...	...
...	76.2	20.6	...	4.9	...	...	...	...	1.1	248.3	...	2.7	...	330.9	351.7	...	...	...	...
-114	72.6	16.4	12.7	8.8	19.1	3.20	2.52	213.6	1.5	184.3	...	3.1	121.8	329.2	355.6	...	...	...	...
695	83.4	14.3	7.4	2.3	11.9	2.91	6.34	337.5	4.1	158.4	...	1.4	65.9	227.5	255.0	...	...	...	...
	Principal Lines of Business: CompHosp/Med (90.4%), OtherHlth (9.6%)													Principal States: MN (100.0%)					
-672	82.9	14.2	7.0	3.3	16.3	4.09	4.58	1.7	4.5	94.2	0.0	4.4	17.8	88.8	101.4	20.3	...	7.4	31.7
32,526	82.0	14.4	7.9	3.9	15.7	3.68	8.22	-1.2	3.5	108.6	0.0	4.1	25.9	106.6	122.7	13.3	...	6.3	28.9
12,577	85.1	11.7	7.4	3.8	13.2	3.72	5.88	6.4	3.2	146.3	0.0	4.0	18.5	115.7	134.1	7.4	...	5.6	28.6
-127,164	86.1	11.7	6.8	3.3	11.7	3.46	-13.33	0.8	3.7	128.0	0.0	5.4	-14.2	100.7	115.2	7.3	...	6.3	31.4
116,625	86.8	12.5	3.6	1.8	6.1	3.45	13.80	-2.5	3.1	158.8	0.0	5.3	17.5	141.8	157.0	8.3	...	5.0	28.3
	Principal Lines of Business: CompHosp/Med (80.7%), FEHBP (16.3%), MedSup (3.0%)													Principal States: WA (82.6%), AK (17.4%)					
-41	67.2	27.1	15.0	5.7	24.1	3.88	3.76	11.9	3.9	158.3	...	...	15.5	205.2	209.9	...	...	15.6	...
...	68.8	28.0	9.2	3.5	15.0	4.62	4.62	21.5	3.8	162.4	...	...	24.9	212.1	218.4	...	...	12.6	...
-306	69.7	24.7	13.0	5.4	20.0	4.98	3.96	8.0	3.2	207.5	...	...	28.2	254.7	263.0	...	...	8.5	8.5
-169	71.2	22.3	13.2	6.0	19.0	3.93	-2.17	5.5	2.9	243.9	...	...	15.9	268.2	280.3	...	...	6.7	6.7
682	69.2	25.7	12.0	5.7	16.7	3.35	4.83	6.3	2.6	265.3	...	...	19.3	278.2	301.7	...	...	3.9	3.9
	Principal Lines of Business: Dental (100.0%)													Principal States: CA (93.5%), NV (3.6%)					

COMPANY NAME Ultimate Parent Association Principal Officer Mailing Address Dom. : Began Bus. : Struct. : Mktg. Specialty Phone # AMB# NAIC#	Best's Financial Strength Rating FSC	Data Year	Balance Sheet: Bonds (%)	Mort. Loans & R.E. (%)	Com & Pref. Stock (%)	All Other Assets (%)	Total Assets ($000)	Life Reserves (%)	Health Reserves (%)	Ann Res. & Dep. Liabilities (%)	All Other Liabilities (%)	Capital & Surplus ($000)	Operations: Direct Premiums Written ($000)	Net Premiums Written & Deposits ($000)	Operating Cash Flow ($000)	NOG Before Taxes ($000)	NOG After Taxes ($000)	Net Income ($000)
PREMIER BEHAVIORAL SYSTS OF TN Magellan Health Services Inc Russell C. Petrella President 222 Second Avenue North, Suite 220 Nashville, TN 37201 TN : 1996 : Stock : Broker Medicaid 615-313-4463 AMB# 064433	NR-5	'05	8.4	...	...	91.6	39,606	...	90.2	...	9.8	11,067	226,640	226,640	14,829	...	...	...
		'06	6.1	...	...	93.9	54,004	...	57.8	...	42.2	27,494	228,418	228,418	17,386	18,726	18,726	18,726
		'07	7.3	...	...	92.7	41,235	...	40.2	...	59.8	14,461	129,814	129,814	-10,684	10,968	10,968	10,968
		'08	6.1	...	...	93.9	32,120	...	27.3	...	72.7	8,583	87,736	87,736	-8,959	5,122	5,122	5,122
		'09	10.6	...	...	89.4	18,082	...	7.9	...	92.1	4,275	32,369	32,369	-13,135	-1,288	-1,288	-1,288
		Rating History: NR-5, 04/08/10; NR-5, 03/30/09; NR-5, 04/22/08; NR-5, 04/23/07; NR-5, 06/15/06																
PREMIER CHOICE DENTAL INC Premier Dental Services Inc Samuel H. Gruenbaum President P.O. Box 14227 Orange, CA 92863 AZ : 1996 : Stock : Not Available Dental 800-333-8866 AMB# 064821 NAIC# 95224	NR-2	'05	...	...	...	100.0	655	...	1.5	...	98.5	237	624	624	32	559	559	559
		'06	...	...	...	100.0	970	...	0.8	...	99.2	187	977	977	297	875	702	702
		'07	...	...	...	100.0	1,391	...	0.5	...	99.5	184	1,203	1,203	431	1,107	741	741
		'08	...	...	...	100.0	1,006	...	0.8	...	99.2	277	1,252	1,252	-419	1,123	774	774
		'09	...	...	...	100.0	988	...	0.9	...	99.1	305	1,225	1,225	-24	1,140	761	761
		Rating History: NR-2, 05/05/10; NR-2, 06/12/09; NR-2, 01/10/08; NR-2, 11/22/06; NR-2, 11/21/05																
PRENEED REINSURANCE CO OF AMER National Guardian Life Insurance Company John D. Larson Chairman, President & CEO P.O. Box 1191 Madison, WI 53701-1191 AZ : 2001 : Stock : Other Reins 608-257-5611 AMB# 060371 NAIC# 11155	NR-2	'05	39.3	...	...	60.7	4,283	20.7	...	...	79.3	3,323	...	36,951	1,493	1,296	978	977
		'06	40.2	...	...	59.8	5,863	24.5	...	0.1	75.4	4,629	...	44,858	941	1,721	1,155	1,155
		'07	29.0	...	...	71.0	8,399	25.2	...	0.1	74.7	7,280	...	59,688	1,718	2,908	2,419	2,417
		'08	39.7	...	...	60.3	10,352	31.1	...	0.7	68.2	9,341	...	64,052	1,876	2,114	1,743	1,743
		'09	55.8	...	...	44.2	11,961	28.2	...	0.1	71.7	10,749	...	83,944	1,438	1,975	1,648	1,648
		Rating History: NR-2, 03/15/10; NR-2, 05/01/09; NR-2, 06/11/08; NR-2, 06/20/07; NR-2, 05/31/06																
PRESBYTERIAN HEALTH PLAN INC Southwest Health Foundation Dennis A. Batey, M.D. President 2301 Buena Vista Drive SE Albuquerque, NM 87106 NM : 1987 : Non-Profit : Broker Group A&H, Health, Ind A&H 505-923-5700 AMB# 068930 NAIC# 95330	NR-5	'05	62.6	...	8.7	28.7	236,119	...	51.9	...	48.1	131,655	871,470	869,486	14,153	70,101	41,733	43,004
		'06	40.3	...	8.2	51.4	208,071	...	51.2	...	48.8	95,477	887,697	884,884	-31,481	42,747	33,785	34,867
		'07	61.2	...	8.6	30.2	251,926	...	48.2	...	51.8	110,710	973,516	969,693	40,761	50,042	25,394	25,936
		'08	53.0	...	6.3	40.7	280,878	...	50.0	...	50.0	134,318	1,098,258	1,092,469	45,825	68,961	41,011	35,056
		'09	26.9	...	16.0	57.1	291,590	...	44.1	...	55.9	138,592	1,136,691	1,125,604	-11,170	58,590	34,085	38,030
		Rating History: NR-5, 03/23/10; NR-5, 08/26/09; B- pd, 09/08/08; NR-5, 06/30/08; NR-5, 05/29/07																
PRESBYTERIAN INSURANCE COMPANY Southwest Health Foundation Dennis A. Batey President 2301 Buena Vista Drive SE Albuquerque, NM 87106 NM : 2002 : Stock : Broker Group A&H, Medicare, Med supp 505-923-8811 AMB# 064748 NAIC# 11504	NR-5	'05	26.1	...	...	73.9	12,130	...	38.8	...	61.2	4,696	26,249	25,183	4,133	2,592	1,558	1,556
		'06	11.5	...	...	88.5	27,169	...	52.2	...	47.8	3,997	85,064	82,050	11,913	-4,957	-3,959	-3,959
		'07	62.5	...	...	37.5	34,998	...	51.9	...	48.1	18,342	97,368	95,681	10,143	5,660	4,046	4,194
		'08	58.6	...	...	41.4	38,102	...	53.4	...	46.6	22,306	94,258	92,955	3,032	6,735	3,758	3,775
		'09	72.9	...	...	27.1	31,796	...	49.3	...	50.7	17,787	103,756	102,131	-7,887	3,166	2,065	2,178
		Rating History: NR-5, 03/23/10; NR-5, 04/08/09; NR-5, 03/11/08; NR-5, 05/29/07; NR-4, 04/11/06																
PRESERVATION LIFE INSURANCE CO PFHC Medical Management LLC John W. McCulloch President 3401 W. Truman Blvd., Suite 100A Jefferson City, MO 65109 MO : 1994 : Stock : Other Direct Ind Ann 573-635-8492 AMB# 068602 NAIC# 60048	NR-5	'05	94.7	...	...	5.3	7,024	99.6	...	...	0.4	2,228	2,516	2,516	2,377	152	137	137
		'06	96.0	...	...	4.0	8,549	99.4	...	...	0.6	2,366	1,519	1,519	1,490	122	123	123
		'07	98.1	...	...	1.9	9,740	99.6	...	...	0.4	2,426	1,282	1,282	1,182	88	85	83
		'08	88.2	...	...	11.8	9,334	100.0	...	...	0.0	2,358	-14	-14	-262	85	82	-15
		'09	...	...	...	100.0	2,310	...	...	...	100.0	2,310	...	...	-7,062	33	40	-125
		Rating History: NR-5, 03/31/10; NR-5, 04/24/09; NR-5, 04/10/08; NR-5, 04/24/07; NR-5, 04/27/06																
PRESIDENTIAL LIFE INS CO Presidential Life Corporation Donald Barnes President 69 Lydecker Street Nyack, NY 10960-2103 NY : 1966 : Stock : Broker Ann, Life 845-358-2300 AMB# 006948 NAIC# 68039	B+ Rating Outlook: Stable FSC IX	'05	80.9	0.0	4.0	15.1	4,460,798	5.4	0.0	92.1	2.5	291,338	152,260	192,640	48,190	106,663	90,410	101,963
		'06	68.3	0.0	3.7	28.1	4,277,307	5.8	0.0	90.7	3.5	330,104	177,167	215,191	-254,999	82,938	83,973	74,976
		'07	72.0	0.0	8.5	19.4	3,925,692	6.7	0.0	89.3	4.0	360,373	151,276	185,809	-417,785	76,627	56,168	59,141
		'08	73.0	0.0	8.1	18.9	3,706,636	7.0	0.1	90.1	2.8	329,039	172,008	197,228	-178,664	67,838	44,675	16,932
		'09	81.0	0.0	2.8	16.1	3,613,890	7.1	0.1	90.8	2.0	269,777	215,866	252,484	14,182	33,023	23,011	36,029
		Rating History: B+, 05/25/10; B+ u, 12/11/09; B+, 04/16/09; B+, 03/28/08; B+, 02/22/07																
PRESIDENTIAL LIFE INS CO' Jerry L. McPeters President 12770 Merit Drive, Floor 2 Dallas, TX 75251-1209 TX : 1955 : Stock : Not Available 972-744-2448 AMB# 007931 NAIC# 76538	NR-1	'05	51.8	...	...	48.2	2,443	...	...	...	100.0	1,233	412	397	...	103	103	103
		'06	36.5	...	...	63.5	3,209	...	...	...	100.0	1,578	816	775	...	325	325	325
		'07	29.4	...	...	70.6	3,508	...	...	...	100.0	1,930	1,349	1,528	...	488	488	504
		'08	19.5	4.1	14.9	61.6	4,345	...	...	...	100.0	1,845	1,796	3,598	...	202	172	172
		'09	19.5	4.1	29.8	46.6	4,314	...	...	...	100.0	2,183	2,151	4,114	...	258	220	216
		Rating History: NR-1, 06/10/10; NR-1, 06/12/09; NR-1, 06/12/08; NR-1, 06/08/07; NR-1, 06/07/06																
PRIMECARE MEDICAL NETWORK INC Aveta Inc Richard Shinto, M.D. President & CEO 3281 East Guasti Road, 7th Floor Ontario, CA 91761-7643 CA : 1994 : Stock : Not Available Medical 909-605-8000 AMB# 064659	NR-5	'05	...	...	...	100.0	44,359	...	...	...	100.0	11,372	101,731	101,731	7,757	2,797	1,669	1,669
		'06	...	...	...	100.0	62,434	...	...	...	100.0	12,315	308,098	308,098	19,688	13,267	7,857	7,857
		'07	...	...	...	100.0	80,743	...	...	...	100.0	16,199	336,468	336,468	18,761	12,749	7,549	7,549
		'08	...	...	...	100.0	99,642	...	...	...	100.0	27,147	409,538	409,538	18,946	27,726	16,423	16,423
		'09	...	...	...	100.0	88,662	...	...	...	100.0	19,430	...	...	-11,107	26,545	15,721	15,721
		Rating History: NR-5, 05/26/10; NR-5, 08/26/09; C+ pd, 07/21/08; C+ pd, 07/09/07; C+ pd, 08/28/06																

BEST'S PROFITABILITY, LEVERAGE AND LIQUIDITY TESTS 2005 – 2009

Data in U.S. Dollars

—	Profitability Tests							Leverage Tests						Liquidity Tests					
Un-Realized Capital Gains ($000)	Benefits Paid to NPW & Dep (%)	Comm. & Expenses to NPW & Dep (%)	NOG to Total Assets (%)	NOG to Total Rev (%)	Operating Return on Equity (%)	Net Yield (%)	Total Return (%)	Change in NPW & Dep (%)	NPW & Dep to Capital (X)	Capital & Surplus to Liabilities (%)	Surplus Relief (%)	Reins Leverage (%)	Change in Capital (%)	Quick Liquidity (%)	Current Liquidity (%)	Non-Invest Grade Bonds to Capital (%)	Delinq. & Foreclosed Mortgages to Capital (%)	Mort. & Credit Tenant Loans & R.E. to Capital (%)	Affiliated Invest to Capital (%)
...	87.2	11.8	...	...	...	2.90	2.90	-5.2	20.5	38.8	...	...	0.0	115.1	115.1	...	...	...	...
...	76.9	11.4	40.0	8.5	97.1	5.06	5.06	0.8	8.3	103.7	...	...	148.4	189.5	189.5	...	...	...	...
...	77.4	11.6	23.0	8.7	52.3	4.70	4.70	-43.2	9.0	54.0	...	...	-47.4	147.9	147.9	...	...	...	...
...	81.1	11.6	14.0	5.9	44.5	1.44	1.44	-32.4	10.2	36.5	...	...	-40.6	130.2	130.2	...	...	...	...
...	103.8	13.0	-5.1	-3.5	-20.0	0.25	0.25	-63.1	7.6	31.0	...	...	-50.2	126.6	126.6	...	...	...	...
Principal Lines of Business: Medicaid (100.0%)													Principal States: TN (100.0%)						
...	0.1	11.0	88.1	89.0	201.2	0.60	0.60	27.0	2.0	50.0	...	...	25.4	150.0	150.0	...	...	...	...
...	...	10.9	86.4	71.5	331.0	0.68	0.68	56.4	5.2	23.9	...	...	-21.2	119.9	119.9	...	...	...	...
...	...	8.6	62.8	61.3	399.7	0.63	0.63	23.2	6.5	15.2	...	...	-1.7	113.6	113.6	...	...	...	...
...	0.8	9.9	64.6	61.5	335.4	0.51	0.51	4.1	4.5	38.1	...	...	50.9	130.5	130.5	...	...	...	...
...	1.1	6.0	76.3	62.0	261.4	0.18	0.18	-2.1	4.0	44.6	...	...	9.8	135.6	135.6	...	...	...	...
Principal Lines of Business: Dental (100.0%)													Principal States: AZ (100.0%)						
...	23.2	23.6	30.5	2.7	41.4	-6.11	-5.94	19.2	11.1	346.4	...	14.7	137.9	214.3	214.3	...	...	...	...
...	25.5	21.8	22.8	2.6	29.1	-3.50	-3.38	21.4	9.7	375.0	...	15.5	39.3	232.7	232.7	...	...	...	...
...	26.5	21.8	33.9	4.1	40.6	-1.25	-1.21	33.1	8.2	650.2	...	18.0	57.3	417.8	417.8	...	...	...	...
...	34.2	20.6	18.6	2.7	21.0	-0.10	-0.03	7.3	6.9	923.8	...	6.4	28.3	623.8	623.8	...	...	...	...
...	30.3	23.3	14.8	2.0	16.4	-0.80	-0.75	31.1	7.8	890.3	...	7.2	15.1	492.0	538.4	...	...	...	...
Principal Lines of Business: GrpLife (68.4%), OrdLife (30.9%), GrpAnn (0.5%), IndAnn (0.3%)																			
1,175	83.0	9.7	18.6	4.8	36.1	3.37	4.66	-3.4	6.6	126.0	...	1.3	32.0	181.9	190.3	...	...	...	0.9
1,791	84.9	12.2	15.2	3.7	29.7	4.92	6.50	1.8	9.3	84.8	...	0.3	-27.5	156.8	163.3	...	...	...	2.5
-623	85.2	10.5	11.0	2.6	24.6	4.69	4.65	9.6	8.8	78.4	...	0.5	16.0	126.2	132.6	...	...	...	2.1
-1,809	84.1	10.4	15.4	3.7	33.5	3.86	0.45	12.7	8.1	91.6	...	0.3	21.3	155.4	161.3	...	...	...	2.2
747	85.5	9.9	11.9	3.0	25.0	2.52	4.51	3.0	8.1	90.6	...	0.7	3.2	161.2	170.8	...	...	...	0.0
Principal Lines of Business: Medicaid (58.5%), CompHosp/Med (20.1%), Medicare (16.6%), FEHBP (4.8%)													Principal States: NM (100.0%)						
9	65.8	24.6	16.6	6.1	39.9	2.23	2.32	79.1	5.4	63.2	...	10.7	50.6	136.2	139.3	...	...	...	...
...	90.2	16.9	-20.1	-4.8	-91.1	5.00	4.99	225.8	20.5	17.3	...	27.6	-14.9	95.6	96.7	...	...	...	...
...	81.8	13.9	13.0	4.2	36.2	5.61	6.15	16.6	5.2	110.1	...	0.9	358.9	183.3	189.1	...	...	...	...
...	80.1	13.7	10.3	4.0	18.5	2.89	2.94	-2.8	4.2	141.2	...	0.4	21.6	218.6	223.5	...	...	...	...
...	83.7	14.0	5.9	2.0	10.3	2.44	2.79	9.9	5.7	127.0	...	5.3	-20.3	191.9	196.9	...	...	...	...
Principal Lines of Business: CompHosp/Med (61.7%), Medicare (38.2%), MedSup (0.1%)													Principal States: NM (100.0%)						
...	10.7	4.2	2.4	4.9	6.3	5.02	5.02	90.8	1.1	46.8	...	...	5.3	111.7	115.0	19.7	...	...	...
...	22.2	3.6	1.6	6.5	5.4	4.80	4.80	-39.6	0.6	38.8	...	...	6.6	106.9	111.0	18.5	...	...	...
...	30.0	6.6	0.9	5.0	3.5	4.66	4.65	-15.6	0.5	33.7	...	...	2.8	105.4	109.8	18.0	...	...	...
...	-99.9	-99.9	0.9	19.5	3.4	4.68	3.66	-99.9	0.0	33.8	...	...	-4.0	108.0	110.4	18.7	...	...	...
...	...	...	0.7	59.9	1.7	1.15	-1.65	100.0	...	...	...	...	-2.0	...	...	...	...	...	...
31,454	159.4	12.3	2.1	18.6	35.7	7.97	9.00	-35.0	0.6	8.2	0.6	7.7	28.1	67.1	77.4	77.0	...	0.1	2.9
-4,952	298.4	12.1	1.9	17.6	27.0	7.14	6.89	11.7	0.6	9.8	0.5	6.6	12.4	87.2	97.5	56.1	...	0.1	2.6
10,105	371.0	14.3	1.4	13.0	16.3	7.16	7.55	-13.7	0.4	11.9	0.4	5.9	10.0	75.1	87.2	40.7	...	0.1	0.1
-29,206	225.0	12.0	1.2	10.4	13.0	7.01	5.60	6.1	0.5	11.1	0.9	6.8	-11.3	66.5	81.1	45.9	...	0.1	0.1
-52,467	128.9	10.6	0.6	5.8	7.7	5.10	4.12	28.0	0.9	8.4	1.1	8.0	-24.4	68.8	83.4	73.9	...	0.1	0.1
Principal Lines of Business: IndAnn (93.2%), OrdLife (4.3%), GrpA&H (2.0%), GrpLife (0.5%), IndA&H (0.0%)													Principal States: NY (51.3%), FL (9.9%), PA (9.1%), NJ (3.1%)						
...	106.1	149.6	4.6	7.6	8.7	...	...	84.8	0.3	102.1	...	...	9.1	...	...	...	...	...	...
...	69.9	154.7	11.5	15.4	23.2	...	...	95.2	0.5	98.6	...	...	29.1	...	...	...	...	...	...
...	75.0	56.2	14.5	19.7	27.8	...	...	97.1	0.8	124.6	...	...	22.1	...	...	...	...	...	...
-345	86.5	75.0	4.4	2.8	9.1	...	...	135.5	2.0	73.8	...	...	-5.2	...	...	...	...	9.6	...
118	85.9	69.4	5.1	3.3	10.9	...	...	14.3	1.9	102.5	...	...	18.3	...	...	...	...	8.1	...
Principal Lines of Business: GrpA&H (96.5%), OrdLife (2.3%), IndA&H (1.1%)																			
...	83.3	14.2	3.7	1.6	10.3	0.65	0.65	-61.3	8.9	34.5	...	...	-45.9	118.2	118.2	...	...	...	...
...	81.1	15.9	14.7	2.5	66.3	3.73	3.73	202.9	25.0	24.6	...	...	8.3	117.1	117.1	...	...	...	...
...	81.7	16.3	10.5	2.2	53.0	4.06	4.06	9.2	20.8	25.1	...	...	31.5	120.0	120.0	...	...	...	...
...	80.2	14.6	18.2	3.9	75.8	1.97	1.97	21.7	15.1	37.4	...	...	67.6	133.1	133.1	...	...	...	...
...	...	...	16.7	3.8	67.5	0.62	0.62	-99.9	...	28.1	...	...	-28.4	123.4	123.4	...	...	...	...

COMPANY NAME Ultimate Parent Association Principal Officer Mailing Address Dom. : Began Bus. : Struct. : Mktg. Specialty Phone # AMB# NAIC#	Best's Financial Strength Rating FSC	Data Year	Balance Sheet Bonds (%)	Mort. Loans & R.E. (%)	Com & Pref. Stock (%)	All Other Assets (%)	Total Assets ($000)	Life Reserves (%)	Health Reserves (%)	Ann Res. & Dep. Liabilities (%)	All Other Liabilities (%)	Capital & Surplus ($000)	Operations Direct Premiums Written ($000)	Net Premiums Written & Deposits ($000)	Operating Cash Flow ($000)	NOG Before Taxes ($000)	NOG After Taxes ($000)	Net Income ($000)
PRIMERICA LIFE INS CO Citigroup Inc. Jeffrey S. Fendler President & CEO 3120 Breckinridge Boulevard Duluth, GA 30099-0001 MA : 1903 : Stock : Agency Term Life 770-381-1000 AMB# 006693 NAIC# 65919	A+ Rating Outlook: Negative FSC XIV	'05	77.6	...	15.8	6.5	5,437,586	78.9	1.3	10.1	9.7	1,702,667	1,515,522	1,465,108	126,843	489,675	335,861	344,329
		'06	76.7	...	16.3	7.0	5,549,726	80.7	1.2	9.0	9.1	1,665,068	1,582,508	1,499,091	160,923	460,891	300,675	302,868
		'07	72.3	...	14.1	13.6	5,895,972	82.7	0.9	8.0	8.4	1,654,849	1,637,609	1,498,386	421,185	481,396	353,489	350,992
		'08	76.7	...	14.6	8.7	5,958,953	85.9	...	7.8	6.3	1,472,548	1,699,646	1,544,791	38,130	343,120	156,740	73,596
		'09	70.6	...	14.4	15.0	6,805,090	82.3	...	7.8	10.0	1,705,595	1,751,269	1,554,406	498,018	346,901	174,155	125,943
		Rating History: A+ g, 03/16/10; A+ gu, 11/09/09; A+ g, 05/15/09; A+ g, 05/15/08; A+ g, 11/02/06																
PRINCIPAL LIFE INSURANCE CO Principal Financial Group Inc Larry D. Zimpleman Chairman, President & CEO 711 High Street Des Moines, IA 50392-2300 IA : 1879 : Stock : Exclusive Agent Retirement Savings, Life, Health 515-247-5111 AMB# 006150 NAIC# 61271	A+ Rating Outlook: Negative FSC XV	'05	34.4	7.9	1.0	56.8	111,738,632	7.8	1.0	35.8	55.5	3,660,313	6,436,364	20,821,835	2,614,724	819,332	630,673	666,212
		'06	30.6	7.2	1.6	60.7	125,532,325	6.7	0.9	33.7	58.7	3,598,624	7,056,930	23,622,310	2,349,651	859,168	660,426	684,902
		'07	29.7	7.2	1.8	61.3	135,714,882	6.4	0.9	33.7	59.0	3,697,486	8,404,970	25,932,786	3,239,369	846,380	686,488	540,156
		'08	36.4	9.1	1.7	52.8	115,411,350	7.9	1.2	42.6	48.4	4,810,232	9,084,610	25,415,238	3,719,611	768,670	651,333	83,345
		'09	35.1	8.1	0.6	56.2	118,786,258	7.8	1.1	38.0	53.0	4,588,745	6,429,053	15,735,521	-2,517,605	725,393	608,723	42,053
		Rating History: A+ g, 11/25/09; A+, 02/27/09; A+, 01/24/08; A+ g, 11/02/06; A+ g, 10/31/05																
PRINCIPAL NATIONAL LIFE INS CO Principal Financial Group Inc Deanna D. Strable-Soethout President 711 High Street Des Moines, IA 50392-2300 IA : 1968 : Stock : Inactive Life Reins 515-247-5111 AMB# 007326 NAIC# 71161	A+ Rating Outlook: Negative FSC XV	'05	76.1	...	...	23.9	11,089	...	...	...	100.0	10,850	...	...	-227	-57	42	42
		'06	74.7	...	...	25.3	11,313	0.4	...	...	99.6	11,136	...	1	271	350	287	287
		'07	73.1	...	...	26.9	11,581	0.5	...	...	99.5	11,453	...	1	-326	400	326	326
		'08	71.8	...	...	28.2	11,775	0.5	...	...	99.5	11,644	...	1	3,137	214	196	196
		'09	66.8	...	...	33.2	12,663	0.1	...	...	99.9	11,889	4,350	1	695	211	168	168
		Rating History: A+ r, 11/25/09; A+ r, 07/08/09; NR-2, 02/27/09; NR-3, 01/24/08; NR-3, 11/02/06																
PRIORITY HEALTH Spectrum Health System Kimberly K. Horn President & CEO 1231 East Beltline NE Grand Rapids, MI 49525-4501 MI : 1986 : Non-Profit : Broker Health 616-464-8198 AMB# 068977 NAIC# 95561	A- Rating Outlook: Stable FSC VIII	'05	30.8	0.0	11.1	58.1	416,197	...	48.0	...	52.0	247,997	1,347,033	1,345,220	50,860	64,115	64,115	64,107
		'06	30.5	...	13.7	55.8	421,669	...	52.9	...	47.1	273,454	1,390,483	1,388,641	-12,939	24,238	24,238	24,190
		'07	34.3	...	15.9	49.8	391,849	...	43.2	...	56.8	215,449	1,376,077	1,375,182	35,164	25,771	25,771	25,596
		'08	34.3	...	15.9	49.8	402,717	...	47.6	...	52.4	221,121	1,257,663	1,256,591	28,363	12,967	12,967	13,056
		'09	34.5	...	18.2	47.3	426,476	...	35.8	...	64.2	234,906	1,324,753	1,323,383	16,778	19,025	19,025	17,822
		Rating History: A-, 06/12/09; A-, 06/13/08; A-, 03/04/08; A-, 06/12/07; A-, 04/20/06																
PRIORITY HEALTH CARE INC WellPoint Inc. Thomas R. Byrd Chairman & President 2015 Staples Mill Road Richmond, VA 23230 VA : 1984 : Stock : Broker Group A&H, Health 804-354-7000 AMB# 068916 NAIC# 96512	A Rating Outlook: Stable FSC X	'05	79.8	...	...	20.2	103,921	...	34.9	...	65.1	63,633	207,675	207,391	16,544	27,184	18,087	18,004
		'06	82.6	...	...	17.4	104,638	...	33.0	...	67.0	69,150	227,715	227,206	449	36,684	24,788	24,728
		'07	84.9	...	...	15.1	87,992	...	35.1	...	64.9	49,520	230,680	229,948	-15,696	30,530	20,377	20,214
		'08	83.4	...	...	16.6	88,430	...	23.8	...	76.2	47,042	221,767	221,193	-3,162	27,532	18,351	17,777
		'09	68.2	...	...	31.8	84,860	...	35.5	...	64.5	42,280	221,432	220,535	-13,655	19,337	12,392	11,495
		Rating History: A g, 04/27/10; A, 01/23/09; A, 03/20/08; A, 11/06/06; A, 12/29/05																
PRIORITY HEALTH GOVT PROGRAMS Spectrum Health System Kimberly K. Horn President & CEO 1231 East Beltline NE Grand Rapids, MI 49525-4501 MI : 2002 : Non-Profit : Broker Health 616-464-8198 AMB# 064739 NAIC# 11520	B Rating Outlook: Stable FSC V	'05	...	...	...	100.0	16,724	...	66.9	...	33.1	4,660	80,119	79,987	1,852	-2,879	-2,879	-2,879
		'06	...	...	...	100.0	18,892	...	51.9	...	48.1	9,411	91,424	91,267	1,559	811	811	811
		'07	4.2	...	...	95.8	24,717	...	66.2	...	33.8	11,445	119,820	119,654	5,710	2,083	2,083	2,083
		'08	3.2	...	...	96.8	34,208	...	61.7	...	38.3	18,058	139,277	139,088	9,635	6,639	6,639	6,640
		'09	3.1	...	...	96.9	34,244	...	67.0	...	33.0	16,662	174,559	174,351	-1,433	10,302	10,302	10,305
		Rating History: B, 06/12/09; B, 06/13/08; B, 03/04/08; B, 06/12/07; B, 04/20/06																
PRIORITY HEALTH INSURANCE CO Spectrum Health System Kimberly K. Horn Chief Executive Officer 1231 East Beltline NE Grand Rapids, MI 49525-4501 MI : 2004 : Stock : Broker Health 616-464-8198 AMB# 060564 NAIC# 12208	NR-2	'05	3.8	...	...	96.2	9,189	...	86.7	...	13.3	8,018	2,692	2,688	819	309	178	178
		'06	...	...	...	100.0	19,607	...	50.8	...	49.2	9,393	34,738	34,701	7,390	1,324	856	855
		'07	1.8	...	...	98.2	19,638	...	73.6	...	26.4	9,619	45,340	45,269	-5,979	-4,479	-3,913	-3,913
		'08	1.8	...	...	98.2	20,355	...	80.7	...	19.3	10,049	38,911	38,818	2,451	-3,469	-3,469	-3,469
		'09	0.8	...	...	99.2	41,936	...	81.2	...	18.8	16,160	130,817	130,426	12,376	-11,740	-11,740	-11,740
		Rating History: NR-2, 06/12/09; NR-2, 06/13/08; NR-2, 03/04/08; NR-2, 06/12/07; NR-2, 04/20/06																
PROCARE HEALTH PLAN Augustine Kole-James, M.D. President & CEO 3956 Mount Elliott Detroit, MI 48207 MI : 2000 : Stock : Other Health 313-925-4607 AMB# 064686 NAIC# 11081	NR-5	'05	...	32.3	22.3	45.4	2,013	...	...	...	100.0	1,956	...	-58	-233	-369	-369	-368
		'06	...	28.3	...	71.7	2,085	...	...	...	100.0	2,000	...	-30	183	-350	-350	-367
		'07	...	31.4	...	68.6	1,817	...	...	...	100.0	1,651	...	-32	-287	-360	-360	-360
		'08	...	...	...	100.0	2,447	...	83.1	...	16.9	1,596	1,818	1,776	614	-186	-186	-55
		'09	...	...	...	100.0	3,640	...	82.0	...	18.0	2,146	4,491	4,420	1,368	254	254	252
		Rating History: NR-5, 05/21/10; NR-5, 04/14/09; NR-5, 05/12/08; NR-5, 04/03/07; NR-5, 04/27/06																
PROFESSIONAL INS COMPANY Sun Life Financial Inc Robert C. Salipante President One Sun Life Executive Park Wellesley Hills, MA 02481 TX : 1937 : Stock : Agency Dis inc, Hosp Ind, Life 860-737-6833 AMB# 006950 NAIC# 68047	A Rating Outlook: Stable FSC VI	'05	65.9	6.4	...	27.8	70,561	46.5	40.9	2.0	10.6	15,550	46,904	46,902	2,721	-2,304	-2,313	-2,313
		'06	65.3	7.4	5.2	22.1	76,632	42.9	44.3	2.0	10.8	19,192	55,227	55,224	6,732	-2,363	-2,620	-2,620
		'07	60.7	...	4.1	35.1	97,315	36.6	46.3	1.5	15.7	30,395	65,352	65,352	21,433	-535	-1,710	-1,763
		'08	72.0	...	3.9	24.1	102,186	35.5	53.0	1.4	10.1	32,179	69,847	69,847	2,261	-1,659	-937	-3,608
		'09	64.6	...	...	35.4	111,215	31.9	52.8	1.3	13.9	33,632	71,490	71,490	7,782	632	-286	39
		Rating History: A, 02/27/09; A+, 06/19/08; A+, 06/12/07; A u, 01/11/07; A, 06/02/06																

Data in U.S. Dollars

—	Profitability Tests							Leverage Tests						Liquidity Tests					
Un-Realized Capital Gains ($000)	Benefits Paid to NPW & Dep (%)	Comm. & Expenses to NPW & Dep (%)	NOG to Total Assets (%)	NOG to Total Rev (%)	Operating Return on Equity (%)	Net Yield (%)	Total Return (%)	Change in NPW & Dep (%)	NPW & Dep to Capital (X)	Capital & Surplus to Liabilities (%)	Surplus Relief (%)	Reins Leverage (%)	Change in Capital (%)	Quick Liquidity (%)	Current Liquidity (%)	Non-Invest Grade Bonds to Capital (%)	Delinq. & Foreclosed Mortgages to Capital (%)	Mort. & Credit Tenant Loans & R.E. to Capital (%)	Affiliated Invest to Capital (%)
-289,084	26.9	30.7	6.1	21.2	19.1	7.36	2.36	2.0	0.8	47.0	3.2	58.3	-9.2	69.9	87.8	16.4	...	...	47.3
47,142	26.6	32.1	5.5	19.1	17.9	6.55	7.61	2.3	0.9	45.0	2.5	56.9	-1.0	84.0	97.6	16.6	...	...	53.0
-80,817	26.8	33.5	6.2	20.2	21.3	9.99	8.64	0.0	0.9	40.5	2.3	56.5	-1.3	95.3	107.8	18.3	...	...	50.1
176,061	25.8	34.9	2.6	9.7	10.0	6.41	8.20	3.1	1.0	33.3	1.3	60.9	-12.3	73.2	90.5	20.9	...	...	69.3
104,968	26.4	31.4	2.7	10.9	11.0	5.39	6.48	0.6	0.9	35.1	1.1	55.5	18.6	77.4	95.2	18.9	...	...	64.5
Principal Lines of Business: OrdLife (76.7%), IndAnn (23.3%)														Principal States: CA (16.4%), TX (7.7%), FL (6.8%), GA (4.3%), IL (4.0%)					
-21,739	25.3	8.6	0.6	6.2	18.8	6.17	6.14	4.3	4.8	8.7	0.9	13.3	18.2	41.1	59.0	51.0	0.2	227.1	60.8
96,293	25.3	9.2	0.6	6.1	18.2	6.13	6.29	13.4	5.4	8.3	-3.9	22.0	0.8	40.6	58.4	45.4	0.3	228.8	75.9
126,745	24.3	8.7	0.5	5.4	18.8	6.21	6.10	9.8	5.9	8.0	-2.1	28.6	1.9	38.1	56.0	49.1	0.0	237.2	82.6
-58,437	24.7	8.7	0.5	4.9	15.3	6.01	4.92	-2.0	5.1	8.4	-0.6	29.1	12.2	38.9	55.4	58.4	0.0	225.3	76.2
-209,452	38.5	11.4	0.5	6.0	13.0	5.41	4.08	-38.1	3.3	8.5	0.0	36.6	-3.9	39.0	54.9	81.9	0.0	214.2	82.6
Principal Lines of Business: GrpAnn (61.7%), GrpA&H (14.6%), IndAnn (13.3%), OrdLife (7.1%), GrpLife (2.1%)														Principal States: CA (9.2%), NY (8.0%), TX (6.5%), IA (6.2%), IL (5.0%)					
...	...	...	0.3	8.9	0.4	4.18	4.76	...	...	999.9	...	...	0.3	999.9	999.9	...	...	...	...
...	...	999.9	2.6	57.1	2.6	5.32	5.86	...	0.0	999.9	...	...	2.6	999.9	999.9	...	...	...	...
...	...	999.9	2.8	62.9	2.9	5.66	6.08	2.3	0.0	999.9	...	...	2.8	999.9	999.9	...	...	...	...
...	...	999.9	1.7	45.7	1.7	4.05	4.29	6.8	0.0	999.9	...	...	1.7	999.9	999.9	...	...	...	...
...	...	999.9	1.4	5.8	1.4	2.89	3.02	9.8	0.0	999.9	21.5	47.0	2.1	999.9	999.9	...	...	...	...
Principal Lines of Business: OrdLife (100.0%)														Principal States: IA (70.9%), MN (13.1%), GA (6.0%), KS (4.7%), IL (3.5%)					
-1,664	87.1	9.3	16.6	4.7	29.3	3.25	2.80	10.5	5.4	147.4	...	0.2	31.3	292.8	308.1	...	...	0.0	5.1
6,864	89.8	9.7	5.8	1.7	9.3	4.46	6.22	3.2	5.1	184.5	...	0.1	10.3	319.1	336.0	...	...	...	6.9
-161	90.1	9.4	6.3	1.9	10.5	4.61	4.52	-1.0	6.4	122.1	...	...	-21.2	268.0	284.4	...	...	...	10.2
-13,732	90.5	9.7	3.3	1.0	5.9	3.77	0.21	-8.6	5.7	121.8	...	...	2.6	270.6	285.6	...	...	...	13.1
-3,552	90.9	9.4	4.6	1.4	8.3	5.06	3.84	5.3	5.6	122.6	...	...	6.2	223.6	234.8	...	...	...	14.0
Principal Lines of Business: CompHosp/Med (88.9%), Medicare (11.1%)														Principal States: MI (100.0%)					
...	77.0	11.6	19.0	8.6	31.7	3.87	3.77	7.9	3.3	157.9	...	0.3	26.4	231.0	252.8	...	...	...	...
-3	75.7	9.8	23.8	10.7	37.3	4.01	3.95	9.6	3.3	194.9	...	...	8.7	246.1	271.8	0.2	...	...	...
-18	80.9	7.9	21.2	8.7	34.3	5.24	5.04	1.2	4.6	128.7	...	0.5	-28.4	180.5	203.1	0.3	...	...	...
21	82.7	6.6	20.8	8.2	38.0	4.68	4.00	-3.8	4.7	113.7	...	1.9	-5.0	162.2	180.9	0.1	...	...	...
-8	82.9	9.0	14.3	5.5	27.7	4.57	3.32	-0.3	5.2	99.3	...	1.0	-10.1	135.6	149.8	0.6	...	...	...
Principal Lines of Business: CompHosp/Med (54.2%), Medicaid (45.8%)														Principal States: VA (100.0%)					
...	87.6	8.5	-18.5	-3.8	-47.8	3.12	3.12	37.1	17.2	38.6	...	...	-36.9	197.4	197.4	...	...	...	...
...	87.6	9.1	4.6	0.9	11.5	4.73	4.73	14.1	9.7	99.3	...	...	101.9	270.9	270.9	...	...	...	...
...	86.5	6.6	9.6	1.8	20.0	5.30	5.30	31.1	10.5	86.2	...	...	21.6	232.1	232.1	...	...	...	...
...	82.2	8.0	22.5	5.0	45.0	2.60	2.61	16.2	7.7	111.8	...	...	57.8	320.4	320.4	...	...	...	...
...	81.2	11.8	30.1	6.0	59.3	1.09	1.10	25.4	10.5	94.8	...	...	-7.7	322.2	322.2	...	...	...	...
Principal Lines of Business: Medicaid (99.1%), CompHosp/Med (0.9%)														Principal States: MI (100.0%)					
...	88.9	7.5	...	6.2	...	...	...	...	0.3	684.6	...	...	...	999.9	999.9	...	...	...	...
...	82.7	15.3	5.9	2.4	9.8	5.20	5.20	999.9	3.7	92.0	...	...	17.2	232.7	232.7	...	...	...	...
...	96.0	14.8	-19.9	-8.5	-41.2	6.67	6.67	30.5	4.7	96.0	...	...	2.4	220.4	220.4	...	...	...	...
...	97.3	13.4	-17.3	-8.9	-35.3	2.58	2.58	-14.3	3.9	97.5	...	...	4.5	245.8	245.8	...	...	...	...
...	96.9	11.8	-37.7	-9.0	-89.6	0.63	0.63	236.0	8.1	62.7	...	1.1	60.8	197.1	206.1	...	...	...	...
Principal Lines of Business: GrpA&H (96.2%), IndA&H (3.8%)														Principal States: MI (100.0%)					
-25	...	-99.9	-17.5	-73.2	-18.0	6.05	4.84	-6.0	0.0	999.9	...	...	-9.0	999.9	999.9	...	...	33.2	...
12	...	-99.9	-17.1	-62.4	-17.7	-2.08	-2.35	47.9	0.0	999.9	...	...	2.3	999.9	999.9	...	...	29.5	...
...	...	-99.9	-18.4	999.9	-19.7	0.52	0.52	-4.1	0.0	997.6	...	...	-17.5	724.4	724.4	...	...	34.6	...
...	76.5	31.7	-8.7	-10.7	-11.4	2.19	8.97	999.9	1.1	187.7	...	...	-3.3	255.2	255.2	...	...	...	...
...	63.7	42.4	8.3	5.1	13.6	0.23	0.18	148.8	2.1	143.6	...	...	34.4	236.9	236.9	...	...	...	...
Principal Lines of Business: Medicaid (100.0%)														Principal States: MI (100.0%)					
...	54.2	51.9	-3.4	-4.6	-14.8	5.09	5.13	23.4	3.0	28.7	...	...	-0.5	73.2	90.5	14.2	...	28.6	...
...	56.3	50.4	-3.6	-4.5	-15.1	5.19	5.15	17.7	2.8	34.0	...	...	23.8	67.7	86.0	20.3	...	29.1	...
-8	59.3	43.5	-2.0	-2.4	-6.9	5.64	5.57	18.3	2.1	46.2	...	...	58.0	89.6	101.1	17.3	...	...	...
-1	62.2	40.2	-0.9	-1.3	-3.0	5.51	2.73	6.9	2.2	46.0	...	...	4.7	99.6	114.5	9.5	...	...	...
-1,081	64.5	36.0	-0.3	-0.4	-0.9	4.50	3.81	2.4	2.1	43.4	...	...	4.5	99.9	118.3	27.9	...	...	...
Principal Lines of Business: IndA&H (94.5%), OrdLife (5.5%), IndAnn (0.0%)														Principal States: FL (17.5%), NC (11.6%), GA (8.8%), TX (8.6%), PA (6.9%)					

Data in U.S. Dollars

COMPANY NAME / Ultimate Parent Association / Principal Officer / Mailing Address / Dom. : Began Bus. : Struct. : Mktg. / Specialty / Phone # / AMB# NAIC#

Best's Financial Strength Rating / FSC

Balance Sheet: Data Year; Bonds (%); Mort. Loans & R.E. (%); Com & Pref. Stock (%); All Other Assets (%); Total Assets ($000); Life Reserves (%); Health Reserves %); Ann Res. & Dep. Liabilities (%); All Other Liabilities (%); Capital & Surplus ($000)

Operations: Direct Premiums Written ($000); Net Premiums Written & Deposits ($000); Operating Cash Flow ($000); NOG Before Taxes ($000); NOG After Taxes ($000); Net Income ($000)

PROFESSIONAL LIFE & CASUALTY

Judith M. Majko
President
20 North Wacker Drive, Ste. 3110
Chicago, IL 60606
IL : 1957 : Stock : Direct Response
Ind A&H, Ind Ann, Ind Life
312-220-0655
AMB# 006952 NAIC# 68063

C+ — Rating Outlook: Stable — **FSC V**

Data Year	Bonds (%)	Mort. Loans & R.E. (%)	Com & Pref. Stock (%)	All Other Assets (%)	Total Assets ($000)	Life Reserves (%)	Health Reserves %)	Ann Res. & Dep. Liabilities (%)	All Other Liabilities (%)	Capital & Surplus ($000)	Direct Premiums Written ($000)	Net Premiums Written & Deposits ($000)	Operating Cash Flow ($000)	NOG Before Taxes ($000)	NOG After Taxes ($000)	Net Income ($000)
'05	68.9	...	21.2	9.9	57,216	4.2	...	78.7	17.1	6,053	5,523	5,489	846	2,825	2,824	1,286
'06	76.0	...	19.4	4.6	67,486	3.7	...	78.1	18.2	14,229	3,121	3,100	937	2,631	2,486	3,851
'07	77.8	...	19.7	2.5	69,745	3.6	...	78.7	17.8	14,063	3,122	3,097	-3,022	2,877	2,424	181
'08	84.3	...	14.0	1.7	65,466	3.4	...	86.9	9.8	12,410	4,242	4,226	-5,690	2,994	2,601	-2,298
'09	78.1	...	17.6	4.3	81,817	2.4	...	71.1	26.5	11,342	7,195	7,188	3,377	3,953	3,285	2,474

Rating History: C+, 05/11/10; C+, 04/29/09; C+, 04/22/08; C+, 03/30/07; C+, 03/08/06

PROGRAMMED LIFE INS CO
Gardiner Limited Partnership

Gregory J. Palmquist
President
8400 E. Prentice Avenue, Suite 645
Greenwood Village, CO 80111
AZ : 1984 : Stock : Other Direct
Reins
303-790-2090
AMB# 009426 NAIC# 64866

NR-5

Data Year	Bonds (%)	Mort. Loans & R.E. (%)	Com & Pref. Stock (%)	All Other Assets (%)	Total Assets ($000)	Life Reserves (%)	Health Reserves %)	Ann Res. & Dep. Liabilities (%)	All Other Liabilities (%)	Capital & Surplus ($000)	Direct Premiums Written ($000)	Net Premiums Written & Deposits ($000)	Operating Cash Flow ($000)	NOG Before Taxes ($000)	NOG After Taxes ($000)	Net Income ($000)
'05	...	...	...	100.0	171	100.0	...	...	...	164	...	0	8	-5	-7	-7
'06	...	...	...	100.0	161	99.9	...	...	0.1	154	...	...	-10	-12	-14	-14
'07	...	...	...	100.0	170	64.5	...	...	35.5	161	...	...	-88	-6	-7	-103
'08	...	...	...	100.0	166	65.7	...	...	34.3	157	...	...	-4	-7	-7	-7
'09	...	...	...	100.0	163	100.0	...	...	...	157	...	...	-2	-3	-3	-3

Rating History: NR-5, 03/31/10; NR-5, 04/27/09; NR-5, 04/22/08; NR-5, 04/25/07; NR-5, 05/11/06

PROTECTIVE LIFE & ANNUITY INS
Protective Life Corporation

Wayne E. Stuenkel
President & Chief Actuary
2801 Highway 280 South
Birmingham, AL 35223
AL : 1978 : Stock : Agency
Ind Ann, Ind Life
205-268-1000
AMB# 008860 NAIC# 88536

A+ — Rating Outlook: Negative — **FSC XV**

Data Year	Bonds (%)	Mort. Loans & R.E. (%)	Com & Pref. Stock (%)	All Other Assets (%)	Total Assets ($000)	Life Reserves (%)	Health Reserves %)	Ann Res. & Dep. Liabilities (%)	All Other Liabilities (%)	Capital & Surplus ($000)	Direct Premiums Written ($000)	Net Premiums Written & Deposits ($000)	Operating Cash Flow ($000)	NOG Before Taxes ($000)	NOG After Taxes ($000)	Net Income ($000)
'05	76.3	0.1	0.7	22.9	660,482	79.7	1.4	2.2	16.7	107,369	14,596	30,118	-7,247	21,457	16,660	16,407
'06	76.7	0.1	3.0	20.2	579,775	82.0	1.3	2.4	14.3	43,093	15,856	26,827	-72,174	19,942	12,828	12,845
'07	74.8	2.7	5.6	16.9	620,997	75.4	1.0	11.8	11.9	37,998	71,205	78,377	44,525	14,022	8,772	8,772
'08	65.8	5.3	5.3	23.6	754,487	61.4	0.8	28.9	8.8	44,233	158,671	163,710	147,825	8,272	5,702	5,702
'09	82.9	4.7	0.5	11.9	927,370	50.9	0.6	41.7	6.7	78,664	182,590	185,855	165,623	21,761	13,603	13,417

Rating History: A+ g, 10/09/09; A+ g, 02/11/09; A+ g, 06/02/08; A+ g, 04/02/07; A+ g, 02/08/06

PROTECTIVE LIFE INS CO
Protective Life Corporation

John D. Johns
Chairman, President & CEO
2801 Highway 280 South
Birmingham, AL 35223
TN : 1907 : Stock : Agency
Ann, GIC's, Ind Life
205-268-1000
AMB# 006962 NAIC# 68136

A+ — Rating Outlook: Negative — **FSC XV**

Data Year	Bonds (%)	Mort. Loans & R.E. (%)	Com & Pref. Stock (%)	All Other Assets (%)	Total Assets ($000)	Life Reserves (%)	Health Reserves %)	Ann Res. & Dep. Liabilities (%)	All Other Liabilities (%)	Capital & Surplus ($000)	Direct Premiums Written ($000)	Net Premiums Written & Deposits ($000)	Operating Cash Flow ($000)	NOG Before Taxes ($000)	NOG After Taxes ($000)	Net Income ($000)
'05	58.1	9.0	4.3	28.6	25,306,552	26.6	0.3	47.5	25.7	1,899,679	3,119,657	3,957,981	1,428,625	121,449	71,931	62,717
'06	53.6	10.7	4.7	30.9	25,613,527	27.2	0.3	45.8	26.8	1,388,425	3,298,330	3,027,695	149,847	390,783	346,622	322,982
'07	56.1	6.3	7.2	30.4	25,800,880	26.7	0.3	46.0	27.0	1,796,945	3,247,536	2,587,098	283,514	287,999	350,486	350,917
'08	55.0	5.9	9.9	29.2	25,929,543	26.0	0.2	47.5	26.3	1,767,703	3,904,892	5,501,204	757,883	-102,390	-92,125	-300,392
'09	55.3	6.0	6.1	32.5	26,654,688	26.9	0.2	43.9	29.0	2,616,531	3,419,606	3,036,227	-566,617	680,169	704,822	549,924

Rating History: A+ g, 10/09/09; A+ g, 02/11/09; A+ g, 06/02/08; A+ g, 04/02/07; A+ g, 02/08/06

PROTECTIVE LIFE INSURANCE NY
Protective Life Corporation

Wayne E. Stuenkel
President
300 Brookhollow Road
Melville, NY 11749
NY : 2000 : Stock : Other
Annuity
205-268-1000
AMB# 060340 NAIC# 89006

A — Rating Outlook: Negative — **FSC VIII**

Data Year	Bonds (%)	Mort. Loans & R.E. (%)	Com & Pref. Stock (%)	All Other Assets (%)	Total Assets ($000)	Life Reserves (%)	Health Reserves %)	Ann Res. & Dep. Liabilities (%)	All Other Liabilities (%)	Capital & Surplus ($000)	Direct Premiums Written ($000)	Net Premiums Written & Deposits ($000)	Operating Cash Flow ($000)	NOG Before Taxes ($000)	NOG After Taxes ($000)	Net Income ($000)
'05	95.2	...	...	4.8	1,308,025	0.9	...	96.6	2.5	174,242	222,465	214,393	180,821	2,954	-673	-535
'06	85.7	...	...	14.3	1,361,202	1.0	...	96.5	2.5	163,285	163,398	120,961	39,969	26,688	16,182	16,089
'07	96.3	...	0.3	3.4	1,119,494	1.1	...	97.5	1.3	127,527	23,259	7,618	-184,317	1,044	2,280	2,280
'08	93.0	...	0.6	6.4	833,324	1.5	...	97.5	1.1	99,784	13,382	2,708	-276,128	4,549	732	-6,589
'09	87.2	...	...	12.8	719,205	1.8	...	97.7	0.5	100,236	18,034	5,443	-104,739	9,734	2,399	-3,818

Rating History: A, 10/09/09; A, 02/11/09; A, 06/02/08; A, 04/02/07; A, 02/08/06

PROVIDENCE HEALTH PLAN
Providence Health & Services

Jack A. Friedman
CEO
3601 SW Murray Blvd., Suite 10
Beaverton, OR 97005
OR : 1985 : Non-Profit : Broker
Group A&H, Health
503-574-7500
AMB# 068651 NAIC# 95005

A — Rating Outlook: Stable — **FSC IX**

Data Year	Bonds (%)	Mort. Loans & R.E. (%)	Com & Pref. Stock (%)	All Other Assets (%)	Total Assets ($000)	Life Reserves (%)	Health Reserves %)	Ann Res. & Dep. Liabilities (%)	All Other Liabilities (%)	Capital & Surplus ($000)	Direct Premiums Written ($000)	Net Premiums Written & Deposits ($000)	Operating Cash Flow ($000)	NOG Before Taxes ($000)	NOG After Taxes ($000)	Net Income ($000)
'05	92.6	...	1.4	6.0	300,527	...	62.6	...	37.4	224,156	664,134	661,478	76,085	60,345	60,345	59,440
'06	86.6	...	6.3	7.1	393,771	...	53.4	...	46.6	285,602	756,480	753,623	92,249	64,048	64,068	61,855
'07	78.1	...	13.8	8.1	442,397	...	60.1	...	39.9	340,520	813,080	809,441	44,811	60,456	60,456	58,468
'08	72.3	...	15.9	11.8	455,825	...	64.3	...	35.7	343,050	896,453	894,251	8,754	47,122	47,122	-2,142
'09	74.4	...	1.2	24.4	505,499	...	54.0	...	46.0	373,505	969,338	967,530	-8,503	35,190	35,190	28,801

Rating History: A, 06/11/09; A, 05/20/08; A, 08/17/07; A, 04/13/07; A-, 04/20/06

PROVIDENT AMERICAN INS CO[1]

Mike Weaver
President
10501 N. Central Expressway, #313
Dallas, TX 75231-2200
TX : 1939 : Stock : Not Available

214-696-9091
AMB# 006966 NAIC# 68179

NR-1

Data Year	Bonds (%)	Mort. Loans & R.E. (%)	Com & Pref. Stock (%)	All Other Assets (%)	Total Assets ($000)	Life Reserves (%)	Health Reserves %)	Ann Res. & Dep. Liabilities (%)	All Other Liabilities (%)	Capital & Surplus ($000)	Direct Premiums Written ($000)	Net Premiums Written & Deposits ($000)	Operating Cash Flow ($000)	NOG Before Taxes ($000)	NOG After Taxes ($000)	Net Income ($000)
'05	6.1	21.3	0.1	72.5	19,726	...	...	0.3	99.7	2,902	2,993	2,769	...	-1,536	-1,536	-1,536
'06	6.5	20.4	0.1	73.0	18,376	...	...	0.3	99.7	2,403	3,486	3,183	...	-2,633	-2,633	-2,633
'07	7.5	23.4	0.1	69.0	16,045	...	...	0.3	99.7	1,975	3,845	4,028	...	-2,258	-2,258	-2,258
'08	5.4	...	0.0	94.5	22,400	...	...	0.3	99.7	3,024	3,632	9,538	...	-2,136	-2,136	-2,175
'09	70.5	...	0.1	29.4	21,457	...	...	0.3	99.7	3,458	2,515	32,161	...	639	639	458

Rating History: NR-1, 06/11/10; NR-5, 05/12/10; NR-4, 06/12/08; D, 06/12/08; D, 10/03/07

PROVIDENT AMERICAN LIFE & HLTH
American Financial Group, Inc

Billy B. Hill, Jr.
President
11200 Lakeline Blvd., Suite 100
Austin, TX 78717
OH : 1949 : Stock : Career Agent
Group Life, Ind A&H, Ordinary Life
512-451-2224
AMB# 006932 NAIC# 67903

B++ — Rating Outlook: Stable — **FSC V**

Data Year	Bonds (%)	Mort. Loans & R.E. (%)	Com & Pref. Stock (%)	All Other Assets (%)	Total Assets ($000)	Life Reserves (%)	Health Reserves %)	Ann Res. & Dep. Liabilities (%)	All Other Liabilities (%)	Capital & Surplus ($000)	Direct Premiums Written ($000)	Net Premiums Written & Deposits ($000)	Operating Cash Flow ($000)	NOG Before Taxes ($000)	NOG After Taxes ($000)	Net Income ($000)
'05	55.6	...	...	44.4	6,557	1.7	64.8	...	33.5	4,903	4,074	4,070	502	748	485	485
'06	68.2	...	...	31.8	8,991	2.1	61.3	...	36.6	6,551	14,526	9,860	2,292	-955	-1,005	-1,005
'07	34.3	...	...	65.7	10,588	2.7	50.8	...	46.5	3,097	26,613	19,628	311	-1,450	-1,666	-1,666
'08	42.6	...	...	57.4	16,944	7.1	73.3	...	19.6	7,295	49,480	43,490	6,686	-2,769	-2,974	-2,974
'09	34.5	...	16.1	49.4	19,393	16.7	71.7	...	11.6	12,166	45,261	40,628	-1,043	-2,502	-2,472	-2,472

Rating History: B++, 05/10/10; B++, 03/27/09; B++, 12/17/07; B++, 11/28/06; NR-2, 05/02/06

PROVIDENT LIFE AND ACCIDENT
Unum Group

Thomas R. Watjen
President & CEO
1 Fountain Square
Chattanooga, TN 37402-1330
TN : 1887 : Stock : Broker
Disability, Group Life
423-294-1011
AMB# 006968 NAIC# 68195

A- — Rating Outlook: Positive — **FSC XIV**

Data Year	Bonds (%)	Mort. Loans & R.E. (%)	Com & Pref. Stock (%)	All Other Assets (%)	Total Assets ($000)	Life Reserves (%)	Health Reserves %)	Ann Res. & Dep. Liabilities (%)	All Other Liabilities (%)	Capital & Surplus ($000)	Direct Premiums Written ($000)	Net Premiums Written & Deposits ($000)	Operating Cash Flow ($000)	NOG Before Taxes ($000)	NOG After Taxes ($000)	Net Income ($000)
'05	89.3	1.7	1.5	7.5	7,952,622	13.2	65.8	15.1	5.9	1,343,689	1,209,805	1,057,909	-56,499	115,231	123,849	122,934
'06	87.1	2.9	2.1	7.9	7,872,146	13.9	66.0	14.3	5.7	1,121,764	1,200,317	1,068,282	-131,456	117,890	81,098	70,920
'07	83.9	4.0	2.0	10.1	7,735,411	13.9	65.9	12.9	7.2	435,070	1,189,223	820,172	-472,432	-161,186	-5,947	-17,837
'08	85.2	4.6	2.0	8.2	7,741,375	14.6	66.3	12.4	6.7	428,410	1,170,324	830,348	181,468	174,920	125,267	118,222
'09	85.8	4.9	0.9	8.5	8,004,252	15.1	66.8	11.7	6.4	567,078	1,191,320	866,832	86,123	181,096	127,066	113,255

Rating History: A- g, 03/08/10; A- g, 03/13/09; A- g, 01/29/08; A- g, 11/07/06; A- g, 06/07/06

BEST'S PROFITABILITY, LEVERAGE AND LIQUIDITY TESTS 2005 – 2009

Data in U.S. Dollars

—	Profitability Tests							Leverage Tests						Liquidity Tests					
Un-Realized Capital Gains ($000)	Benefits Paid to NPW & Dep (%)	Comm. & Expenses to NPW & Dep (%)	NOG to Total Assets (%)	NOG to Total Rev (%)	Operating Return on Equity (%)	Net Yield (%)	Total Return (%)	Change in NPW & Dep (%)	NPW & Dep to Capital (X)	Capital & Surplus to Liabilities (%)	Surplus Relief (%)	Reins Leverage (%)	Change in Capital (%)	Quick Liquidity (%)	Current Liquidity (%)	Non-Invest Grade Bonds to Capital (%)	Delinq. & Foreclosed Mortgages to Capital (%)	Mort. & Credit Tenant Loans & R.E. to Capital (%)	Affiliated Invest to Capital (%)
219	41.1	9.7	5.0	25.7	37.8	7.94	7.76	25.3	0.8	14.2	...	0.5	-32.1	81.7	87.5	246.9	...	...	...
1,124	130.5	19.5	4.0	28.2	24.5	7.64	13.56	-43.5	0.2	32.0	...	0.2	129.5	79.3	84.6	121.4	...	...	...
60	100.2	18.4	3.5	26.6	17.1	7.57	5.92	-0.1	0.2	31.5	...	0.2	2.2	80.6	86.1	102.7	...	...	...
-4,515	98.2	14.0	3.8	25.8	19.6	7.63	-4.48	36.5	0.3	23.4	...	0.2	-25.7	75.7	80.2	101.2	...	...	...
3,858	77.4	8.7	4.5	23.0	27.7	9.26	14.29	70.1	0.5	19.6	...	0.2	8.2	65.4	75.9	118.5	...	...	...
	Principal Lines of Business: IndAnn (98.9%), OrdLife (1.1%)													Principal States: IL (99.9%)					
...	...	999.9	-4.0	-99.9	-4.1	2.01	1.20	...	0.0	000.0	...	0.1	6.0	000.0	000.0	...	...	...	...
...	...	...	-8.4	-99.9	-8.8	3.27	1.68	-99.9	...	999.9	...	...	-5.7	999.9	999.9	...	...	...	...
...	...	...	-4.3	-99.9	-4.5	3.11	-43.74	...	...	999.9	...	...	4.4	999.9	999.9	...	...	...	...
...	...	...	-4.4	-99.9	-4.7	2.37	0.55	...	...	999.9	...	...	-2.7	999.9	999.9	...	...	...	...
...	...	...	-1.6	-31.7	-1.7	2.33	0.31	...	...	999.9	...	...	0.4	999.9	999.9	...	...	...	...
0	139.4	34.8	2.5	24.8	15.7	6.32	6.36	-4.1	0.3	22.8	2.5	59.1	1.0	70.2	85.1	20.7	...	0.9	...
...	161.1	33.3	2.1	20.8	17.1	6.06	6.13	-10.9	0.6	9.6	5.6	152.0	-58.4	57.6	71.8	24.4	...	1.5	...
...	49.1	15.0	1.5	7.6	21.6	6.28	6.33	192.2	1.9	7.9	7.1	200.0	-9.3	50.4	65.1	66.4	...	40.0	...
...	27.6	10.4	0.8	2.9	13.9	5.90	5.95	108.9	3.5	7.0	5.5	200.1	11.3	67.8	79.6	69.4	...	84.9	...
-994	32.9	9.9	1.6	5.7	22.1	6.09	5.99	13.5	2.2	10.5	2.4	124.7	80.8	56.1	70.1	47.2	...	51.5	...
	Principal Lines of Business: IndAnn (89.1%), OrdLife (7.5%), GrpLife (2.8%), CrdA&H (0.3%), CrdLife (0.2%)													Principal States: NY (97.0%)					
37,783	51.1	11.1	0.3	1.9	3.9	5.73	6.01	7.5	1.9	11.4	20.8	214.3	2.2	55.8	65.8	51.9	0.4	110.7	48.6
321,493	66.2	5.6	1.4	8.4	21.1	6.63	8.30	-23.5	2.0	8.4	40.1	337.8	-24.7	56.2	66.7	11.0	0.7	178.5	55.1
-513,901	70.3	3.4	1.4	12.1	22.0	5.77	3.17	-14.6	1.3	11.4	26.6	316.4	31.6	53.1	67.7	29.3	0.3	79.9	52.4
-119,652	37.2	3.9	-0.4	-2.5	-5.2	5.58	3.81	112.6	2.8	10.5	16.8	351.2	-3.6	51.0	64.4	58.7	0.3	78.5	61.6
140,780	63.9	6.8	2.7	17.6	32.2	5.76	5.81	-44.8	1.1	16.0	10.3	253.1	41.5	49.6	63.5	63.8	0.2	58.1	52.2
	Principal Lines of Business: IndAnn (56.5%), GrpAnn (23.2%), OrdLife (19.3%), IndA&H (0.8%), GrpLife (0.2%)													Principal States: MO (13.9%), TX (7.7%), CA (7.5%), FL (6.4%), OH (4.7%)					
...	39.4	6.0	-0.1	-0.2	-0.4	4.55	4.59	44.2	1.2	16.0	1.9	18.6	-0.9	85.6	95.8	35.7	...	...	...
330	77.1	-15.5	1.2	8.2	9.6	4.93	4.95	-43.6	0.7	14.1	21.4	41.5	-6.9	102.1	113.4	5.9	...	...	...
-415	999.9	164.7	0.2	-4.1	1.6	5.28	5.07	-93.7	0.1	13.5	-4.3	48.7	-20.9	87.8	100.2	18.0	...	...	...
-162	999.9	50.9	0.1	-0.8	0.6	4.75	3.80	-64.5	0.0	13.7	2.5	73.4	-24.5	89.0	100.4	41.5	...	...	...
52	999.9	15.3	0.3	-10.1	2.4	4.16	3.13	101.0	0.1	16.2	2.1	86.2	-0.3	95.4	107.9	48.9	...	...	...
	Principal Lines of Business: IndAnn (67.7%), OrdLife (32.3%)													Principal States: NY (93.2%)					
894	82.8	9.4	23.0	9.0	31.1	3.51	3.50	13.6	3.0	293.5	...	0.1	36.8	317.2	335.5	3.3	...	...	1.9
-1,034	85.3	8.2	18.5	8.3	25.1	4.18	3.22	13.9	2.6	264.0	...	0.1	27.4	252.1	270.0	12.0	...	...	1.2
-3,035	87.5	8.0	14.5	7.3	19.3	6.00	4.76	7.4	2.4	334.2	...	0.3	19.2	305.0	329.7	6.1	...	...	1.1
6,475	89.1	7.9	10.5	5.1	13.8	4.73	-4.51	10.5	2.6	304.2	...	0.2	0.7	301.7	323.1	2.0	...	...	1.3
894	89.7	8.3	7.3	3.6	9.8	4.03	2.78	8.2	2.6	283.0	...	0.0	8.9	259.8	273.5	4.5	...	...	1.6
	Principal Lines of Business: CompHosp/Med (59.0%), Medicare (40.7%), MedSup (0.3%)													Principal States: OR (96.9%), WA (3.1%)					
9	78.5	-77.9	-8.8	-53.4	-53.9	...	...	5.8	0.9	18.9	...	...	4.3	...	...	...	...	134.2	...
-9	114.8	101.4	-13.8	-82.2	-99.3	...	...	15.0	1.2	16.8	...	...	-15.6	...	...	...	...	142.0	...
-5	80.4	80.2	-13.1	-54.3	-99.9	...	...	26.6	1.8	16.1	...	...	-15.9	...	...	...	...	168.7	...
30	33.6	31.1	-11.1	-22.1	-85.4	...	...	136.8	3.2	15.6	...	...	36.2	...	...	...	...	...	...
2	87.6	19.3	2.9	1.9	19.7	...	...	237.2	9.2	19.4	...	...	15.2	...	...	...	...	...	...
	Principal Lines of Business: IndA&H (98.4%), OrdLife (1.5%), GrpA&H (0.1%)																		
...	44.4	42.6	7.6	11.4	11.1	3.05	3.10	-15.7	0.8	296.7	0.0	0.1	27.1	330.0	330.0	...	...	...	...
...	56.1	52.0	-12.9	-9.0	-17.5	3.42	3.46	142.2	1.5	269.3	15.7	16.8	33.7	333.6	333.6	...	...	...	...
...	63.0	40.8	-17.0	-7.6	-34.5	3.27	3.28	99.1	6.3	41.5	60.9	81.5	-52.7	141.3	142.5	...	...	...	...
...	67.8	37.2	-21.6	-6.5	-57.2	3.80	3.80	121.6	6.0	75.8	22.1	27.6	135.3	220.6	224.3	...	...	...	...
6	75.2	31.9	-13.6	-5.9	-25.4	1.38	1.42	-6.6	3.3	168.8	9.6	12.8	66.7	297.0	301.5	...	...	...	25.7
	Principal Lines of Business: IndA&H (96.5%), OrdLife (3.2%), GrpLife (0.2%)													Principal States: TX (58.8%), SC (8.7%), OR (6.5%), OK (4.0%), IA (3.2%)					
14,932	89.1	38.8	1.6	7.4	9.0	7.52	7.82	-5.9	0.7	21.3	3.3	392.4	-4.0	51.6	70.1	54.4	...	9.6	3.3
4,611	86.9	37.0	1.0	4.8	6.6	7.34	7.38	1.0	0.9	17.8	4.4	489.4	-14.7	51.0	70.0	47.7	...	21.4	4.3
2,331	49.4	120.3	-0.1	-0.5	-0.8	7.65	7.64	-23.2	1.5	7.0	-56.8	999.9	-56.7	43.8	61.5	72.6	...	64.6	10.5
-6,052	48.8	75.9	1.6	9.2	29.0	7.12	7.07	1.2	1.6	6.8	22.7	999.9	-1.6	44.3	62.0	91.5	...	73.7	12.1
1,543	48.2	72.1	1.6	8.8	25.5	6.98	6.93	4.4	1.3	8.6	15.5	862.6	25.7	44.2	61.6	74.8	...	67.1	10.5
	Principal Lines of Business: IndA&H (69.8%), OrdLife (25.0%), GrpLife (3.3%), GrpA&H (1.3%), IndAnn (0.5%)													Principal States: CA (7.6%), FL (7.1%), TX (6.8%), PA (5.9%), GA (5.5%)					

ANNUAL STATEMENT DATA FOR YEARS 2005 – 2009

Data in U.S. Dollars

COMPANY NAME Ultimate Parent Association Principal Officer Mailing Address Dom. : Began Bus. : Struct. : Mktg. Specialty Phone # AMB# NAIC#	Best's Financial Strength Rating FSC	Data Year	Balance Sheet Bonds (%)	Mort. Loans & R.E. (%)	Com & Pref. Stock (%)	All Other Assets (%)	Total Assets ($000)	Life Reserves (%)	Health Reserves %)	Ann Res. & Dep. Liabilities (%)	All Other Liabilities (%)	Capital & Surplus ($000)	Operations Direct Premiums Written ($000)	Net Premiums Written & Deposits ($000)	Operating Cash Flow ($000)	NOG Before Taxes ($000)	NOG After Taxes ($000)	Net Income ($000)
PROVIDENT LIFE AND CASUALTY Unum Group Thomas R. Watjen President & CEO 1 Fountain Square Chattanooga, TN 37402-1330 TN : 1952 : Stock : Agency Disability, Group Life 423-294-1011 AMB# 006969 NAIC# 68209	**A-** Rating Outlook: Positive **FSC XIV**	'05	96.7	...	...	3.3	649,341	2.1	92.4	0.3	5.1	90,793	72,630	76,556	11,925	15,130	10,883	12,691
		'06	96.4	...	...	3.6	665,245	2.1	92.2	0.2	5.4	100,464	73,071	75,807	19,863	17,433	11,434	10,271
		'07	96.9	...	...	3.1	685,522	2.2	92.5	0.1	5.2	99,046	75,755	79,258	19,188	13,686	16,433	16,415
		'08	96.9	...	...	3.1	701,112	2.1	92.5	0.1	5.3	121,082	80,431	84,125	14,109	34,116	22,605	22,570
		'09	95.5	0.7	...	3.8	722,010	2.3	93.1	0.1	4.5	130,227	82,999	86,625	18,101	12,451	6,470	6,069
		Rating History: A- g, 03/08/10; A- g, 03/13/09; A- g, 01/29/08; A- g, 11/07/06; A- g, 06/07/06																
PRUCO LIFE INS CO Prudential Financial Inc Scott D. Kaplan President 213 Washington Street, 9th Floor Newark, NJ 07102-2992 AZ : 1971 : Stock : Agency SPDA's, Var life, Var Univ life 877-301-1212 AMB# 008240 NAIC# 79227	**A+** Rating Outlook: Stable **FSC XV**	'05	18.4	1.1	1.1	79.4	23,433,175	13.2	...	9.2	77.7	540,132	2,623,637	2,458,576	98,724	-48,737	-13,675	1,951
		'06	13.4	1.8	1.1	83.7	25,360,118	11.4	...	7.0	81.6	1,020,302	3,013,590	2,732,975	-297,578	607,026	500,144	499,153
		'07	11.9	2.4	1.0	84.8	27,253,774	11.4	...	5.6	83.0	772,860	3,617,543	3,160,534	-112,096	64,309	57,456	60,627
		'08	16.8	3.3	1.1	78.7	22,061,367	15.6	...	12.5	71.9	600,640	3,818,947	3,306,525	1,038,551	-666,029	-533,563	-566,189
		'09	15.3	2.9	0.9	80.9	29,252,495	12.8	...	9.9	77.3	874,836	5,736,704	5,029,431	558,184	284,994	172,185	106,372
		Rating History: A+ g, 06/04/10; A+ g, 05/27/09; A+ g, 12/10/08; A+ g, 01/25/08; A+ g, 05/02/07																
PRUCO LIFE INSURANCE CO OF NJ Prudential Financial Inc Scott D. Kaplan President 213 Washington Street, 9th Floor Newark, NJ 07102-2992 NJ : 1982 : Stock : Agency SPDA's, Var life, Var Univ life 973-802-6000 AMB# 009371 NAIC# 97195	**A+** Rating Outlook: Stable **FSC XV**	'05	26.7	0.6	0.0	72.7	3,592,185	17.9	...	10.2	71.9	141,798	324,562	261,645	91,619	2,360	-2,672	-592
		'06	22.9	1.3	0.1	75.7	3,865,953	18.4	...	8.4	73.1	137,180	398,621	326,866	-42,090	7,067	1,742	1,413
		'07	20.8	2.4	0.1	76.7	4,209,847	18.9	...	6.2	74.9	130,360	525,017	416,723	35,247	5,013	-7,030	-7,531
		'08	23.1	4.1	0.1	72.7	3,667,799	24.3	...	8.7	67.0	112,456	616,961	496,839	69,453	-16,376	-18,864	-22,240
		'09	20.7	3.5	0.2	75.6	4,801,456	21.2	...	7.2	71.7	153,406	807,244	683,618	154,510	24,085	2,461	-3,822
		Rating History: A+ g, 06/04/10; A+ g, 05/27/09; A+ g, 12/10/08; A+ g, 01/25/08; A+ g, 05/02/07																
PRUDENTIAL ANNUITIES LIFE ASSR Prudential Financial Inc Stephen Pelletier President & CEO P.O. Box 883 Shelton, CT 06484-0883 CT : 1988 : Stock : Broker Ann, Var ann, Var Univ life 800-628-6039 AMB# 008715 NAIC# 86630	**A+** Rating Outlook: Stable **FSC XV**	'05	1.4	...	0.1	98.5	31,596,838	0.0	...	1.1	98.9	367,300	5,301,093	5,285,882	-74,035	-32,775	-32,826	-31,405
		'06	0.9	...	0.1	99.1	36,963,081	0.0	...	1.0	99.0	327,227	6,720,689	6,695,832	-209,917	112,268	112,200	110,161
		'07	0.8	...	0.0	99.2	43,236,057	0.0	...	1.0	99.0	438,349	8,381,793	8,315,409	49,802	103,589	104,977	106,000
		'08	7.7	...	0.0	92.3	35,015,040	0.1	...	8.4	91.5	633,365	7,627,557	7,543,774	2,361,567	-321,317	-321,317	-322,639
		'09	4.3	0.2	0.0	95.5	49,615,991	0.0	...	7.1	92.9	880,978	11,725,442	11,609,216	-51,392	89,319	309,815	266,600
		Rating History: A+ g, 06/04/10; A+ g, 05/27/09; A+ g, 12/10/08; A+ g, 01/25/08; A+ g, 05/02/07																
PRUDENTIAL INS CO OF AMERICA Prudential Financial Inc John R. Strangfeld, Jr. Chairman, President & CEO 751 Broad Street, 23rd Floor Newark, NJ 07102 NJ : 1875 : Stock : Agency Ann, Group A&H, Life 973-802-6000 AMB# 006974 NAIC# 68241	**A+** Rating Outlook: Stable **FSC XV**	'05	45.3	6.8	4.0	43.9	221,916,063	26.0	1.1	22.1	50.8	7,065,246	18,609,399	22,847,939	7,336,558	1,511,871	1,845,465	2,169,955
		'06	42.4	6.8	4.4	46.4	245,816,675	24.0	1.1	22.1	52.8	5,972,509	23,070,603	32,741,859	7,275,114	629,337	262,928	443,913
		'07	41.2	7.4	3.6	47.9	252,761,435	24.0	1.1	22.0	52.9	6,980,795	20,353,124	23,991,247	-798,937	1,476,021	1,024,458	1,274,293
		'08	41.3	8.6	3.1	47.0	237,497,815	26.1	1.4	24.3	48.2	6,432,375	18,860,438	23,055,764	-764,252	474,888	497,770	-807,813
		'09	41.7	8.4	3.9	46.0	225,787,699	28.5	1.7	25.6	44.2	10,041,654	19,069,157	23,537,995	-3,918,143	2,390,819	2,424,181	1,100,605
		Rating History: A+ g, 06/04/10; A+ g, 05/27/09; A+ g, 12/10/08; A+ g, 01/25/08; A+ g, 05/02/07																
PRUDENTIAL RETIREMENT INS&ANN Prudential Financial Inc Christine C. Marcks President 213 Washington Street, 9th Floor Newark, NJ 07102-2992 CT : 1981 : Stock : Broker Whole life 215-761-1000 AMB# 009144 NAIC# 93629	**A+** Rating Outlook: Stable **FSC XV**	'05	25.6	7.5	0.0	67.0	52,660,476	...	...	30.0	70.0	989,778	4,155	5,028,129	379,779	194,377	210,384	203,830
		'06	25.5	6.4	0.6	67.5	59,441,286	...	...	29.8	70.2	1,041,471	18,515	2,865,113	496,678	164,063	163,512	224,931
		'07	24.2	6.7	0.4	68.6	61,437,059	...	...	28.9	71.1	945,615	12,053	2,730,509	312,513	98,931	100,669	118,011
		'08	28.4	8.9	0.3	62.4	51,851,791	...	...	37.4	62.6	1,208,403	112,005	3,428,003	971,206	100,606	120,141	-12,474
		'09	25.7	7.3	0.1	66.9	59,982,602	...	...	32.5	67.5	1,166,402	72,549	3,333,882	315,837	191,396	191,056	107,045
		Rating History: A+ g, 06/04/10; A+ g, 05/27/09; A+ g, 12/10/08; A+ g, 01/25/08; A+ g, 05/02/07																
PUERTO RICO HEALTH PLAN INC[1] Independence Blue Cross Ivan E. Colon President & CEO P.O. Box 366068 San Juan, PR 00936-6068 PR : 1998 : Non-Profit : Broker Group A&H 787-272-7879 AMB# 060163 NAIC# 53546	**NR-1**	'05	...	...	...	...	...	...	...	...	...	...	...	...	...	...	...	...
		'06	25.4	...	0.2	74.4	46,031	...	...	...	100.0	4,735	123,066	122,474	...	-33,771	-33,771	-33,771
		'07	20.8	...	0.2	78.9	44,958	...	...	...	100.0	373	88,419	87,938	...	-21,717	-21,717	-21,717
		'08	20.8	...	0.3	78.9	38,079	...	...	...	100.0	-8,802	74,141	73,968	...	-13,344	-13,344	-13,966
		'09	36.3	...	0.3	63.4	31,725	...	...	...	100.0	-17,466	35,257	34,994	...	-30,238	-30,238	-30,277
		Rating History: NR-1, 06/10/10; NR-5, 05/05/09; NR-5, 04/24/08; NR-5, 05/07/07; NR-5, 06/01/06																
PUPIL BENEFITS PLAN INC[2] Carol Rog Chairman & President 101 Dutch Meadows Lane Glenville, NY 12302 NY : 1941 : Other : Agency Group A&H 518-377-5144 AMB# 064598 NAIC# 55271	**NR-5**	'05	61.2	3.9	10.2	24.7	7,905	...	43.0	...	57.0	3,550	3,680	3,680	263	-156	-123	-112
		'06	56.3	3.6	10.4	29.7	8,355	...	42.6	...	57.4	2,916	4,096	4,096	583	-252	-247	-233
		'07	55.9	3.5	9.4	31.3	8,420	...	40.5	...	59.5	2,429	4,639	4,639	53	-495	-495	-419
		'08	72.7	3.4	5.0	18.9	8,312	...	44.4	...	55.6	1,628	5,039	5,039	425	-334	-334	-334
		'09	51.7	3.3	7.3	37.6	8,216	...	44.7	...	55.3	798	5,425	5,425	-243	-1,020	-1,004	-1,008
		Rating History: NR-5, 04/30/10; NR-5, 04/15/09; NR-5, 04/29/08; NR-5, 04/02/07; NR-5, 05/10/06																
PURITAN LIFE INSURANCE COMPANY Kenneth W. Phillips Chairman, President & CEO 16801 Addison Road, #400 Addison, TX 75001 TX : 1984 : Stock : Agency Credit A&H, Credit Life 800-513-3243 AMB# 068115 NAIC# 68071	**NR-5**	'05	91.5	...	...	8.5	1,774	49.6	...	...	50.4	1,737	...	-1	33	56	48	48
		'06	91.6	...	...	8.4	1,826	44.3	...	...	55.7	1,795	...	0	51	68	59	59
		'07	8.8	...	...	91.2	15,600	2.4	...	...	97.6	1,850	...	7,755	55	68	56	56
		'08	...	...	...	...	...	...	...	...	...	...	...	...	...	...	...	...
		'09	40.5	...	2.6	56.8	3,798	82.0	...	...	18.0	2,690	...	2,948	360	500	415	415
		Rating History: NR-5, 04/12/10; NR-1, 06/12/09; NR-5, 04/21/08; NR-5, 04/27/07; NR-5, 05/08/06																

Data in U.S. Dollars

—	Profitability Tests							Leverage Tests						Liquidity Tests					
Un-Realized Capital Gains ($000)	Benefits Paid to NPW & Dep (%)	Comm. & Expenses to NPW & Dep (%)	NOG to Total Assets (%)	NOG to Total Rev (%)	Operating Return on Equity (%)	Net Yield (%)	Total Return (%)	Change in NPW & Dep (%)	NPW & Dep to Capital (X)	Capital & Surplus to Liabilities (%)	Surplus Relief (%)	Reins Leverage (%)	Change in Capital (%)	Quick Liquidity (%)	Current Liquidity (%)	Non-Invest Grade Bonds to Capital (%)	Delinq. & Foreclosed Mortgages to Capital (%)	Mort. & Credit Tenant Loans & R.E. to Capital (%)	Affiliated Invest to Capital (%)
0	86.6	35.9	1.7	9.0	12.4	6.88	7.29	7.1	0.8	16.6	1.4	107.8	9.4	56.6	74.7	36.2	...	...	...
...	92.9	34.0	1.7	9.5	12.0	6.66	6.62	-1.0	0.7	18.1	1.3	96.8	10.5	57.8	76.2	36.1	...	4.9	...
...	94.4	34.5	2.4	13.2	16.5	6.66	6.79	4.6	0.8	17.5	1.2	102.6	-0.2	57.0	75.5	35.3	...	4.8	...
...	85.4	35.1	3.3	17.4	20.5	6.66	6.80	6.1	0.7	21.8	1.0	87.3	22.9	58.2	77.9	37.1	...	3.8	...
...	80.0	37.0	0.9	4.8	5.1	6.87	6.94	3.0	0.6	23.1	0.8	63.1	8.2	55.4	75.3	53.0	...	7.1	...
Principal Lines of Business: IndA&H (92.3%), OrdLife (4.5%), GrpA&H (2.8%), GrpLife (0.4%)														Principal States: NY (64.0%), NJ (9.2%), CT (4.2%)					
-5,937	63.5	20.5	-0.1	-0.5	-2.5	5.05	5.21	7.9	4.1	11.4	17.3	211.5	-3.0	47.0	61.7	79.7	...	42.1	45.9
-892	69.8	20.0	2.1	14.5	64.1	5.39	5.18	11.2	2.5	24.6	11.9	233.5	79.8	54.3	69.5	37.2	...	43.1	27.0
-8,437	62.7	20.8	0.2	1.4	6.4	5.59	5.33	15.6	3.8	18.6	22.3	451.0	-22.6	41.3	55.6	47.8	...	77.9	36.8
-8,171	56.7	18.1	-2.2	-13.1	-77.7	5.17	4.25	4.6	5.1	11.0	32.0	761.4	-22.4	51.0	63.0	69.6	...	113.6	45.2
21,892	31.9	13.9	0.7	2.9	23.3	5.79	4.98	52.1	5.4	15.1	34.5	614.5	43.4	46.7	60.6	47.3	...	92.4	43.1
Principal Lines of Business: IndAnn (83.0%), OrdLife (15.9%), GrpAnn (1.1%)														Principal States: CA (12.1%), PA (8.3%), FL (7.8%), TX (6.3%), IL (6.1%)					
-177	56.7	27.3	-0.1	-0.7	-1.8	4.99	5.07	-10.3	1.7	13.6	19.2	223.8	-1.6	68.3	81.0	65.1	...	13.5	2.7
539	60.4	18.8	0.0	0.4	1.2	5.51	5.23	24.9	2.2	14.0	23.1	338.9	-1.9	58.9	71.7	81.3	...	33.1	9.0
-352	58.8	18.2	-0.2	-1.2	-5.3	5.83	5.59	27.5	2.9	13.0	30.1	500.6	-3.3	51.1	64.0	79.2	...	71.4	15.9
1,917	38.5	13.2	-0.5	-3.0	-15.5	5.69	5.45	19.2	4.0	10.5	37.3	749.7	-12.3	49.8	62.2	88.5	...	118.6	20.3
-4,695	24.5	11.2	0.1	0.3	1.9	5.44	4.53	37.6	4.2	12.2	24.9	600.0	30.0	48.2	61.5	67.3	...	102.7	15.3
Principal Lines of Business: IndAnn (64.5%), OrdLife (34.7%), GrpAnn (0.7%)														Principal States: NY (72.4%), NJ (26.3%)					
-1,843	71.8	8.9	-0.1	-0.6	-8.6	5.60	5.80	29.0	14.2	263.0	1.7	12.0	-11.7	309.0	344.2	...	...	...	...
67	63.2	8.4	0.3	1.6	32.3	2.94	7.87	26.7	19.7	627.2	1.7	24.4	-8.8	385.5	448.3	0.8	...	...	...
-317	56.3	8.9	0.3	1.2	27.4	3.87	3.84	24.2	18.6	914.7	1.5	40.0	31.3	531.1	615.3	0.6	...	...	...
28,971	60.2	9.3	-0.8	-3.6	-60.0	3.81	7.03	-9.3	11.6	29.7	1.0	37.5	45.9	93.8	105.7	0.3	...	...	...
-38,278	33.9	8.6	0.7	2.5	40.9	6.72	3.19	53.9	12.5	40.6	0.5	79.9	42.4	104.9	119.7	7.3	...	9.3	3.9
Principal Lines of Business: GrpAnn (71.6%), IndAnn (28.4%), OrdLife (0.0%)														Principal States: CA (8.7%), NY (7.5%), FL (7.1%), MI (6.2%), PA (5.9%)					
-571,825	67.6	5.8	0.9	8.3	23.8	5.48	5.40	7.9	2.4	6.8	6.2	18.2	-11.8	49.6	63.4	107.1	0.1	162.2	84.1
986,900	60.8	6.5	0.1	0.9	4.0	5.35	6.26	43.3	4.0	5.7	7.7	22.2	-11.5	48.5	61.3	138.8	0.1	202.3	111.2
255,934	93.0	5.0	0.4	4.5	15.8	5.49	5.88	-26.7	2.6	6.5	6.3	20.4	13.6	46.6	60.0	118.1	0.1	198.3	79.2
-1,072,284	87.0	4.9	0.2	2.1	7.4	5.29	3.67	-3.9	3.0	5.4	6.7	23.4	-18.2	43.3	57.2	170.0	0.0	267.2	139.2
468,855	82.1	6.3	1.0	10.1	29.4	6.10	5.54	2.1	2.0	8.6	4.1	13.9	54.2	46.7	60.1	96.8	0.0	160.6	94.2
Principal Lines of Business: GrpAnn (61.3%), GrpLife (15.5%), OrdLife (12.9%), IndAnn (5.1%), GrpA&H (4.4%)														Principal States: CA (15.6%), NY (11.9%), NJ (11.1%), PA (3.2%)					
-28,772	26.1	7.9	0.6	14.5	20.9	4.75	5.79	637.7	4.6	6.5	0.0	0.0	-0.2	44.8	61.6	57.7	...	357.1	2.3
17,192	36.9	10.9	0.3	11.2	16.1	4.72	6.06	-43.0	2.3	6.6	0.0	0.0	12.5	48.2	64.9	60.4	...	308.8	5.7
54,263	41.7	16.0	0.2	6.7	10.1	4.84	5.91	-4.7	2.3	6.3	0.0	0.0	-4.2	45.5	61.9	116.4	...	349.8	2.1
130,543	32.7	12.3	0.2	7.4	11.2	5.12	5.63	25.5	2.4	7.2	0.0	1.5	20.9	47.8	62.8	128.0	...	321.9	2.0
-83,257	32.1	12.0	0.3	12.1	16.1	5.20	4.72	-2.7	2.5	6.5	0.0	0.2	-8.5	46.1	60.7	140.3	...	333.6	21.9
Principal Lines of Business: GrpAnn (99.8%), IndAnn (0.2%)														Principal States: CT (55.0%), NC (18.7%), NJ (6.7%), NY (4.4%), PA (4.0%)					
...	...	...	...	...	...	...	...	...	...	...	...	...	...	...	...	...	...	...	...
1,926	100.3	28.4	...	-27.3	...	...	...	...	25.9	11.5	...	...	...	...	...	...	...	...	...
-452	86.0	40.1	-47.7	-24.4	-99.9	...	...	-28.2	235.9	0.8	...	...	-92.1	...	...	...	...	...	...
-1,599	86.9	32.1	-32.1	-17.9	316.6	...	...	-15.9	-8.4	-18.8	...	...	-99.9	...	...	...	...	...	...
2,093	88.4	101.0	-86.6	-83.9	230.2	...	...	-52.7	-2.0	-35.2	...	...	-95.4	...	...	...	...	...	...
Principal Lines of Business: GrpA&H (100.0%)																			
-7	87.2	21.8	-1.6	-3.2	-3.4	1.90	1.95	9.8	1.0	81.5	...	...	-3.2	147.1	159.2	...	...	8.7	8.7
50	88.2	21.0	-3.0	-5.7	-7.6	2.32	3.12	11.3	1.4	53.6	...	...	-17.9	129.4	138.7	...	...	10.3	10.3
-53	93.3	23.6	-5.9	-10.0	-18.5	3.14	3.41	13.3	1.9	40.5	...	...	-16.7	115.3	123.7	...	...	12.0	12.0
-374	85.9	22.2	-4.0	-6.4	-16.4	1.52	-2.91	8.6	3.1	24.4	...	...	-33.0	104.1	112.6	...	...	17.4	17.4
156	97.7	24.3	-12.1	-18.0	-82.7	1.34	3.21	7.7	6.8	10.8	...	...	-51.0	93.4	97.8	...	...	34.3	34.3
Principal Lines of Business: OtherHlth (100.0%)														Principal States: NY (100.0%)					
...	...	-99.9	2.7	77.5	2.8	3.54	3.61	-99.9	0.0	999.9	...	0.0	2.8	999.9	999.9	...	...	...	...
...	...	999.9	3.3	82.3	3.3	3.93	4.01	182.6	0.0	999.9	...	0.0	3.4	999.9	999.9	...	...	...	...
...	1.4	13.5	0.6	0.7	3.1	4.13	4.22	999.9	4.2	13.5	...	741.6	3.1	12.7	12.7	...	...	...	...
...	...	...	...	...	...	...	...	...	...	...	...	...	...	...	...	...	...	...	...
...	78.2	27.0	...	8.3	...	...	...	...	1.1	244.4	...	53.6	...	151.3	168.3	...	...	...	...
Principal Lines of Business: IndAnn (64.1%), OrdLife (35.9%)																			

2010 BEST'S KEY RATING GUIDE — LIFE/HEALTH EDITION
ANNUAL STATEMENT DATA FOR YEARS 2005 – 2009

Data in U.S. Dollars

COMPANY NAME Ultimate Parent Association Principal Officer Mailing Address Dom. : Began Bus. : Struct. : Mktg. Specialty Phone # AMB# NAIC#	Best's Financial Strength Rating FSC	Data Year	Balance Sheet Bonds (%)	Mort. Loans & R.E. (%)	Com & Pref. Stock (%)	All Other Assets (%)	Total Assets ($000)	Life Reserves (%)	Health Reserves %)	Ann Res. & Dep. Liabilities (%)	All Other Liabilities (%)	Capital & Surplus ($000)	Operations Direct Premiums Written ($000)	Net Premiums Written & Deposits ($000)	Operating Cash Flow ($000)	NOG Before Taxes ($000)	NOG After Taxes ($000)	Net Income ($000)
PYRAMID LIFE INSURANCE COMPANY Universal American Corp. Gary W. Bryant President P.O. Box 958465 Lake Mary, FL 32795-8465 KS : 1914 : Stock : Agency Ind Life, LTC, Med supp 407-995-8001	B++	'05	85.2	...	0.5	14.3	149,356	34.5	38.8	20.9	5.7	41,939	140,880	137,748	19,536	2,311	1,235	1,159
		'06	78.6	...	0.2	21.2	162,081	29.2	40.1	18.6	12.2	29,053	148,631	144,815	8,350	-1,181	-1,629	-1,629
	Rating Outlook: Stable	'07	35.3	...	...	64.7	462,013	12.7	59.5	6.3	21.5	150,491	1,158,250	912,095	228,279	14,384	10,945	10,945
		'08	61.8	...	...	38.2	460,978	14.2	51.6	5.6	28.6	178,520	1,282,754	1,016,241	21,045	30,443	20,942	16,534
		'09	92.5	...	...	7.5	369,314	0.4	73.9	...	25.7	179,546	1,408,776	1,063,452	-65,410	55,383	31,803	24,369
AMB# 006977 NAIC# 68284	FSC IX	**Rating History: B++g, 04/16/10; B++g, 12/03/08; B++g, 08/21/07; B++g, 06/21/06; B++g, 06/09/05**																
QCA HEALTH PLAN INC QualChoice of Arkansas Inc Michael E. Stock President & CEO 12615 Chenal Parkway, Suite 300 Little Rock, AR 72211 AR : 1996 : Stock : Broker Group A&H 501-228-7111	B	'05	54.5	...	...	45.5	25,566	...	28.7	...	71.3	13,622	61,062	59,884	2,033	1,960	1,929	1,929
		'06	55.0	...	...	45.0	24,852	...	45.5	...	54.5	14,941	61,788	60,478	-638	937	924	924
	Rating Outlook: Stable	'07	44.1	...	...	55.9	30,510	...	39.0	...	61.0	17,469	59,764	58,273	4,763	2,314	2,280	2,280
		'08	35.9	...	...	64.1	34,554	...	51.1	...	48.9	19,636	101,862	99,735	4,516	2,600	2,508	2,513
		'09	34.2	...	...	65.8	39,939	...	55.3	...	44.7	21,712	126,741	124,222	5,210	2,433	2,391	2,394
AMB# 064050 NAIC# 95448	FSC V	**Rating History: B, 02/19/10; B, 05/08/09; B, 05/12/08; B, 05/14/07; C++, 06/15/06**																
QUALCHOICE LIFE & HEALTH INS QualChoice of Arkansas Inc Michael E. Stock President 12615 Chenal Parkway, Suite 300 Little Rock, AR 72211 AR : 1965 : Stock : Not Available Ordinary Life 501-219-5109	NR-2	'05	...	...	...	...	...	...	...	...	...	...	...	...	...	...	...	...
		'06	...	...	...	...	...	...	...	...	...	...	...	...	...	...	...	...
		'07	49.0	...	4.2	46.9	473	82.1	...	...	17.9	270	271	143	-16	-71	-71	-71
		'08	65.7	...	8.0	26.4	254	88.3	...	...	11.7	201	56	42	-210	-70	-70	-70
		'09	57.6	...	...	42.4	177	...	...	...	100.0	176	15	15	-156	-45	-45	-44
AMB# 007304 NAIC# 70998		**Rating History: NR-2, 02/19/10; NR-1, 06/12/09; NR-1, 06/12/08; NR-1, 06/08/07; NR-1, 06/07/06**																
RABENHORST LIFE INS CO[1] David L. Rabenhorst President 833 Government Street Baton Rouge, LA 70802-6091 LA : 1933 : Stock : Not Available 225-387-0171	NR-1	'05	65.8	6.3	12.4	15.5	26,018	...	...	...	100.0	3,253	2,728	2,671	...	-300	-300	124
		'06	63.3	6.2	14.2	16.3	26,317	...	...	...	100.0	3,271	2,689	2,614	...	-330	-330	-112
		'07	59.9	9.4	13.6	17.2	27,558	...	...	...	100.0	2,297	2,772	2,685	...	-271	-271	1,065
		'08	61.2	9.6	9.4	19.8	26,468	...	...	...	100.0	1,360	2,792	2,693	...	-157	-157	-241
		'09	59.0	9.2	9.3	22.5	27,438	...	...	...	100.0	1,813	3,025	2,915	...	196	198	340
AMB# 007954 NAIC# 76767		**Rating History: NR-1, 06/10/10; NR-1, 06/12/09; NR-1, 06/12/08; NR-1, 06/08/07; NR-1, 06/07/06**																
RAYANT INSURANCE COMPANY OF NY[2] Horizon Healthcare Services Inc Robert A. Marino President & CEO 3 Penn Plz E, Ste PP-15D Newark, NJ 07105-2248 NY : 1999 : Stock : Agency Dental 973-466-5954	NR-5	'05	...	...	...	...	...	...	...	...	...	...	...	...	...	...	...	...
		'06	...	...	...	...	...	...	...	...	...	...	...	...	...	...	...	...
		'07	...	...	...	...	...	...	...	...	...	...	...	...	...	...	...	...
		'08	71.9	...	0.2	27.9	34,921	...	81.7	...	18.3	29,312	7,565	7,565	882	-204	-202	-419
		'09	80.7	...	...	19.3	35,733	...	66.0	...	34.0	29,739	7,848	7,848	1,714	103	203	451
AMB# 060327 NAIC# 60024		**Rating History: NR-5, 04/29/10; NR-5, 05/01/09; NR-5, 06/05/02; NR-1, 06/13/01; NR-1, 06/22/00**																
REASSURE AMERICA LIFE INS CO Swiss Reinsurance Company Ltd Kenneth H. Stewart President 175 King Street Armonk, NY 10504-1606 IN : 1956 : Stock : Agency Univ Life, Term Life, Var ann 877-794-7773	A	'05	69.2	1.8	0.1	28.9	16,392,445	30.9	0.0	6.8	62.3	1,097,960	1,314,063	-291,925	56,233	245,034	227,926	247,153
		'06	62.2	1.3	1.1	35.4	15,904,816	30.4	0.0	6.1	63.5	799,436	1,251,537	799,206	-439,945	319,091	265,295	251,106
	Rating Outlook: Stable	'07	67.3	0.8	1.3	30.6	18,276,975	25.2	0.0	4.8	70.0	496,100	1,174,706	855,137	1,062,945	239,270	183,367	167,876
		'08	67.6	0.6	1.5	30.3	16,470,295	27.9	0.0	5.1	67.0	520,396	1,081,344	780,579	-601,398	157,483	153,428	-50,198
		'09	66.0	0.5	0.0	33.5	16,106,982	27.7	0.0	5.1	67.2	647,931	1,046,843	646,686	-421,756	280,591	264,659	83,974
AMB# 007207 NAIC# 70211	FSC XV	**Rating History: A g, 12/14/09; A g, 02/27/09; A+ gu, 02/05/09; A+ g, 12/19/08; A+ g, 03/20/08**																
REGAL LIFE OF AMERICA INS CO[1] Frank M. Croy President P.O. Box 982005 Fort Worth, TX 76182-8005 TX : 1973 : Stock : Not Available 817-284-4888	NR-1	'05	17.6	...	44.7	37.7	8,221	...	...	...	100.0	3,539	1,474	8,748	...	705	671	671
		'06	40.9	...	40.2	18.9	8,669	...	...	...	100.0	3,781	1,337	9,590	...	1,305	1,144	1,144
		'07	41.2	...	43.8	15.0	10,351	...	...	...	100.0	5,619	1,183	9,131	...	994	843	843
		'08	31.9	...	39.7	28.4	13,630	...	...	...	100.0	6,987	1,021	10,586	...	1,404	1,281	1,281
		'09	25.6	...	45.1	29.3	14,088	...	...	...	100.0	7,882	889	7,871	...	721	609	609
AMB# 068098 NAIC# 82392		**Rating History: NR-1, 06/10/10; NR-1, 06/12/09; NR-1, 06/12/08; NR-1, 06/08/07; NR-1, 06/07/06**																
REGAL REINSURANCE CO Kevin J. McAdoo President One Monarch Place Springfield, MA 01133 MA : 1992 : Stock : Inactive Reins 413-784-2000	NR-5	'05	15.8	...	82.8	1.4	14,037	...	...	...	100.0	13,564	...	...	13	27	27	27
		'06	16.9	...	82.3	0.7	13,689	...	...	...	100.0	13,230	...	...	11	25	25	25
		'07	17.2	...	82.0	0.8	13,445	...	...	...	100.0	13,004	...	...	8	24	24	24
		'08	19.4	...	79.6	1.0	11,929	...	...	...	100.0	11,493	...	...	10	18	18	18
		'09	37.0	...	61.2	1.8	6,253	...	...	...	100.0	5,848	...	...	9	26	26	26
AMB# 060045 NAIC# 74920		**Rating History: NR-5, 04/19/10; NR-5, 04/22/09; NR-5, 04/09/08; NR-5, 04/27/07; NR-5, 05/09/06**																
REGENCE BC/BS OF OREGON Regence Group Jared L. Short President 100 Southwest Market Street Portland, OR 97201 OR : 1942 : Non-Profit : Broker Group A&H, Medicare, Med supp 503-225-5221	A-	'05	49.6	2.9	18.5	29.0	904,571	...	60.0	...	40.0	466,860	1,782,495	1,917,728	158,905	113,184	107,671	108,654
		'06	52.3	2.6	19.2	25.9	965,768	...	61.4	...	38.6	533,543	1,903,478	2,060,612	7,925	62,198	71,476	79,849
	Rating Outlook: Stable	'07	56.8	2.3	20.7	20.2	1,034,489	...	56.1	...	43.9	552,188	2,140,641	2,259,181	70,087	17,911	11,130	20,851
		'08	60.4	2.6	17.0	20.0	905,394	...	65.9	...	34.1	486,124	2,517,101	2,589,065	-47,362	54,531	51,885	25,094
		'09	51.8	2.3	19.3	26.6	1,000,274	...	68.0	...	32.0	565,198	2,396,428	2,455,280	-30,243	35,966	29,824	21,885
AMB# 060074 NAIC# 54933	FSC X	**Rating History: A-, 06/11/10; A-, 06/17/09; A-, 11/19/08; A- g, 10/16/07; A- g, 08/28/06**																

Data in U.S. Dollars

	Profitability Tests							Leverage Tests						Liquidity Tests					
Un-Realized Capital Gains ($000)	Benefits Paid to NPW & Dep (%)	Comm. & Expenses to NPW & Dep (%)	NOG to Total Assets (%)	NOG to Total Rev (%)	Operating Return on Equity (%)	Net Yield (%)	Total Return (%)	Change in NPW & Dep (%)	NPW & Dep to Capital (X)	Capital & Surplus to Liabilities (%)	Surplus Relief (%)	Reins Leverage (%)	Change in Capital (%)	Quick Liquidity (%)	Current Liquidity (%)	Non-Invest Grade Bonds to Capital (%)	Delinq. & Foreclosed Mortgages to Capital (%)	Mort. & Credit Tenant Loans & R.E. to Capital (%)	Affiliated Invest to Capital (%)
...	72.6	25.7	0.9	0.9	3.6	5.14	5.21	1.1	3.3	39.4	0.6	59.0	52.3	108.1	119.1	5.6	...	...	...
...	73.4	29.6	-1.0	-1.1	-4.6	5.38	5.51	5.1	4.9	22.2	2.7	91.9	-30.3	105.1	114.8	4.5	...	...	...
...	83.4	17.4	3.5	1.2	12.2	7.81	7.88	529.8	6.0	48.6	1.2	57.5	412.9	187.7	193.0	1.6	...	...	...
...	81.2	17.4	4.5	2.0	12.7	4.23	3.14	11.4	5.7	63.2	1.7	38.5	18.2	163.5	179.0	6.2	...	...	...
-783	84.6	16.6	7.7	2.9	17.8	4.81	2.55	4.6	5.9	94.6	4.5	65.3	0.6	156.4	175.9	1.3	...	...	...
	Principal Lines of Business: IndA&H (104.7%), IndAnn (-1.3%), OrdLife (-3.5%)													Principal States: IN (12.0%), TX (9.9%), VA (9.0%), NC (8.9%), OH (5.0%)					
...	86.3	11.6	7.9	3.2	14.9	3.19	3.19	5.3	4.4	114.0	...	...	11.3	197.3	197.3	...	...	...	0.0
...	87.3	12.6	3.7	1.5	6.5	4.59	4.59	1.0	4.0	150.8	...	1.7	9.7	228.7	228.7	...	...	...	0.0
...	81.6	16.6	8.2	3.8	14.1	4.92	4.92	-3.6	3.3	134.0	...	2.3	16.9	210.6	210.6	...	...	...	0.0
...	83.8	14.6	7.7	2.5	13.5	3.46	3.47	71.2	5.1	131.6	...	3.0	12.4	214.2	214.8	...	...	...	0.0
...	84.2	14.2	6.4	1.9	11.6	1.31	1.32	24.6	5.7	119.1	...	1.4	10.6	203.2	203.7	...	...	...	0.0
	Principal Lines of Business: CompHosp/Med (100.0%)													Principal States: AR (100.0%)					
...	...	...	...	...	...	...	...	...	...	...	...	...	...	...	...	...	...	...	...
...	...	...	...	...	...	...	...	...	...	...	...	...	...	...	...	...	...	...	...
-5	19.0	129.1	...	-32.2	...	...	...	...	0.5	133.1	22.8	56.9	...	212.7	216.0	...	...	...	...
1	76.3	300.6	-19.2	-69.5	-29.7	2.80	2.95	-70.9	0.2	392.0	3.5	...	-25.1	450.3	463.4	...	...	...	...
-10	196.2	252.5	-21.0	-99.9	-24.0	3.59	-1.49	-63.8	0.1	999.9	...	...	-12.9	999.9	999.9	...	...	...	...
	Principal Lines of Business: OrdLife (100.0%)													Principal States: AR (100.0%)					
-421	85.4	69.2	-1.1	-7.5	-8.9	...	...	-0.4	0.7	16.9	...	...	-7.2	...	...	...	...	43.7	...
227	82.8	70.5	-1.3	-8.3	-10.1	...	...	-2.1	0.7	17.1	...	...	2.1	...	...	...	...	42.4	...
165	87.9	69.7	-1.0	-6.7	-9.7	...	...	2.7	0.9	11.6	...	...	-25.4	...	...	...	...	90.3	...
-1,166	82.4	66.2	-0.6	-3.8	-8.6	...	...	0.3	1.8	5.9	...	...	-48.8	...	...	...	...	174.2	...
375	81.3	54.5	0.7	4.4	12.5	...	...	8.3	1.3	8.7	...	...	50.0	...	...	...	...	114.5	...
	Principal Lines of Business: OrdLife (93.6%), IndLife (6.4%)																		
...	...	...	...	...	...	...	...	...	...	...	...	...	...	...	...	...	...	...	...
...	...	...	...	...	...	...	...	...	...	...	...	...	...	...	...	...	...	...	...
...	...	...	...	...	...	...	...	...	...	...	...	...	...	...	...	...	...	...	...
...	94.7	27.3	...	-2.2	...	...	...	...	0.3	522.6	...	...	...	627.6	674.3	0.1	...	...	...
...	77.1	36.0	0.6	2.3	0.7	3.39	4.12	3.7	0.3	496.2	...	...	1.5	595.6	642.4	...	...	...	...
	Principal Lines of Business: Dental (100.0%)													Principal States: NY (100.0%)					
915	-99.9	-99.9	1.4	25.0	19.0	7.01	7.25	-99.9	-0.3	7.9	19.6	999.9	-15.0	51.1	60.9	36.6	0.2	39.6	0.0
4,092	124.5	89.0	1.6	13.0	28.0	6.92	6.97	373.8	0.9	5.9	22.6	999.9	-26.0	52.6	63.7	33.6	0.0	41.3	0.0
194	110.3	96.5	1.1	8.9	28.3	6.79	6.79	7.0	1.5	3.2	45.2	999.9	-35.1	50.7	61.3	51.7	...	51.2	0.0
-6,619	123.9	51.7	0.9	9.4	30.2	6.27	4.99	-8.7	1.5	3.3	36.6	999.9	-6.4	50.8	60.2	49.8	1.0	38.6	0.0
-90,118	135.7	53.0	1.6	17.8	45.3	6.00	4.33	-17.2	1.0	4.2	27.4	999.9	24.0	54.1	62.5	37.7	1.9	25.8	0.0
	Principal Lines of Business: OrdLife (55.3%), IndAnn (43.9%), GrpLife (0.6%), IndA&H (0.2%), GrpA&H (0.0%)													Principal States: CA (11.9%), TX (8.7%), FL (6.5%), PA (5.3%), IL (4.8%)					
668	36.5	29.2	9.5	6.2	20.0	...	...	46.3	2.5	75.6	57.1	...	11.2	...	...	...	...	...	...
-832	41.4	46.4	13.5	11.6	31.3	...	...	9.6	2.5	77.4	2.9	...	6.9	...	...	...	...	...	...
1,046	43.2	48.6	8.9	9.0	17.9	...	...	-4.8	1.6	118.7	1.5	...	48.6	...	...	...	...	...	...
878	32.6	36.4	10.7	11.3	20.3	...	...	15.9	1.5	105.2	7.8	...	24.3	...	...	...	...	...	...
940	45.1	51.0	4.4	7.5	8.2	...	...	-25.6	1.0	127.0	0.1	...	12.8	...	...	...	...	...	...
	Principal Lines of Business: IndA&H (90.1%), OrdLife (9.9%)																		
-194	...	...	0.2	19.3	0.2	0.88	-0.38	...	...	999.9	...	...	-1.2	404.9	464.0	...	...	...	85.7
-358	...	...	0.2	18.0	0.2	0.88	-1.54	...	...	999.9	...	...	-2.5	379.6	451.7	...	...	...	85.2
-248	...	...	0.2	17.1	0.2	0.89	-0.79	...	...	999.9	...	...	-1.7	397.1	474.6	...	...	...	84.7
-1,528	...	...	0.1	13.4	0.1	0.94	-10.29	...	...	999.9	...	...	-11.6	419.1	499.6	...	...	...	82.6
-5,672	...	...	0.3	19.2	0.3	1.30	-46.08	...	...	999.9	...	...	-49.1	448.5	535.0	...	...	...	65.3
-902	85.4	10.5	12.9	5.6	25.8	4.20	4.21	9.2	4.1	106.7	...	0.4	27.4	105.2	118.4	6.7	...	5.6	37.8
-8,053	87.1	11.9	7.6	3.3	14.3	4.65	4.70	7.5	3.9	123.4	...	1.8	14.3	95.4	112.2	7.7	...	4.7	29.8
979	88.7	13.8	1.1	0.5	2.1	9.07	10.34	9.6	4.1	114.5	...	0.6	3.5	102.3	121.1	7.1	...	4.3	18.0
-66,373	90.0	11.2	5.3	1.9	10.0	10.56	-0.52	14.6	5.3	115.9	...	0.8	-12.0	112.6	131.5	6.3	...	4.9	7.4
33,678	87.3	12.8	3.1	1.2	5.7	5.05	8.64	-5.2	4.3	129.9	...	0.8	16.3	112.1	129.2	6.8	...	4.0	6.3
	Principal Lines of Business: CompHosp/Med (58.1%), Medicare (26.9%), FEHBP (11.6%), MedSup (1.2%), Dental (1.0%)													Principal States: OR (96.7%), WA (3.3%)					

ANNUAL STATEMENT DATA FOR YEARS 2005 – 2009

Data in U.S. Dollars

COMPANY NAME Ultimate Parent Association Principal Officer Mailing Address Dom. : Began Bus. : Struct. : Mktg. Specialty Phone # AMB# NAIC#	Best's Financial Strength Rating FSC	Data Year	Balance Sheet: Bonds (%)	Mort. Loans & R.E. (%)	Com & Pref. Stock (%)	All Other Assets (%)	Total Assets ($000)	Life Reserves (%)	Health Reserves %)	Ann Res. & Dep. Liabilities (%)	All Other Liabilities (%)	Capital & Surplus ($000)	Operations: Direct Premiums Written ($000)	Net Premiums Written & Deposits ($000)	Operating Cash Flow ($000)	NOG Before Taxes ($000)	NOG After Taxes ($000)	Net Income ($000)
REGENCE BLUECROSS BLUESH OF UT Regence Group D. Scott Ideson President P.O. Box 1271 Portland, OR 97207-1271 UT : 1945 : Non-Profit : Broker Group A&H, FEHBP, Medicare 801-333-2000 AMB# 064412 NAIC# 54550	**A-** Rating Outlook: Negative **FSC VIII**	**'05**	37.1	3.0	31.7	28.2	354,924	...	60.3	...	39.7	179,389	697,908	702,974	23,398	21,840	25,522	27,084
		'06	44.9	2.6	30.9	21.7	407,053	...	65.0	...	35.0	215,554	773,755	796,759	32,119	26,477	26,781	30,654
		'07	44.7	2.4	32.0	20.9	438,356	...	57.3	...	42.7	237,721	861,306	883,014	33,464	12,600	11,473	14,958
		'08	40.1	2.6	28.1	29.3	429,577	...	67.2	...	32.8	228,855	991,279	1,011,572	-21,544	9,800	9,740	2,852
		'09	34.3	1.6	27.2	36.9	486,514	...	64.5	...	35.5	215,528	1,094,981	1,111,148	3,733	-30,499	-24,190	-25,010
		Rating History: A- g, 06/11/10; A- g, 06/17/09; A- g, 11/19/08; A- g, 10/16/07; A- g, 08/28/06																
REGENCE BLUESHIELD Regence Group Murphy J. Hensley President P.O. Box 1271 Portland, OR 97207-1271 WA : 1933 : Non-Profit : Broker Group A&H, FEHBP, Medicare 206-464-3600 AMB# 060199 NAIC# 53902	**A** Rating Outlook: Stable **FSC XI**	**'05**	49.0	1.7	29.3	20.0	1,109,753	...	59.3	...	40.7	716,582	1,762,119	1,762,119	133,369	153,694	100,759	128,106
		'06	49.6	1.4	31.2	17.8	1,289,974	...	65.1	...	34.9	880,928	1,956,728	1,956,728	81,303	123,064	92,530	105,848
		'07	50.7	1.3	29.9	18.2	1,400,525	...	57.5	...	42.5	924,880	2,202,637	2,202,637	67,627	63,026	49,689	66,598
		'08	51.7	3.2	27.2	17.8	1,314,846	...	55.4	...	44.6	796,022	2,285,203	2,285,203	-129,237	47,832	36,418	-16,312
		'09	48.4	2.8	30.7	18.0	1,427,859	...	57.6	...	42.4	892,796	2,400,318	2,400,318	-26,638	21,607	20,218	10,463
		Rating History: A g, 06/11/10; A, 06/17/09; A, 11/19/08; A, 10/16/07; A-, 08/28/06																
REGENCE BLUESHIELD OF IDAHO Regence Group John M. Stellmon President P.O. Box 1106 Lewiston, ID 83501-4061 ID : 1946 : Mutual : Broker Group A&H, Ind A&H 800-632-2022 AMB# 060266 NAIC# 60131	**NR-5**	**'05**	62.4	3.3	11.5	22.8	196,300	...	38.9	...	61.1	98,394	361,150	296,281	62,738	40,545	31,943	31,929
		'06	65.7	2.5	14.8	16.9	217,565	...	67.4	...	32.6	125,066	377,489	379,570	28,790	24,747	18,329	18,314
		'07	60.8	5.3	17.5	16.5	250,510	...	58.1	...	41.9	125,506	419,648	425,003	28,067	1,586	-1,198	-902
		'08	59.9	2.8	19.5	17.8	247,264	...	49.9	...	50.1	108,327	499,672	503,633	-335	3,109	-1,414	-10,620
		'09	61.7	2.6	14.3	21.4	237,468	...	63.7	...	36.3	116,659	510,796	513,573	-19,451	-5,638	-2,880	-5,094
		Rating History: NR-5, 06/11/10; NR-5, 06/17/09; NR-5, 06/27/08; NR-5, 08/28/06; NR-5, 10/25/05																
REGENCE HEALTH MAINT OF OR Regence Group Jared L. Short President 100 Southwest Market Street Portland, OR 97201 OR : 1986 : Non-Profit : Inactive Inactive 503-225-5221 AMB# 068584 NAIC# 96250	**NR-3**	**'05**	95.5	...	...	4.5	23,867	...	7.9	...	92.1	23,157	4,145	4,115	-1,525	1,666	1,283	1,308
		'06	93.2	...	...	6.8	24,813	...	9.2	...	90.8	23,998	-19	-19	1,270	954	731	637
		'07	74.8	...	...	25.2	5,354	...	...	...	100.0	4,733	...	...	375	1,240	713	735
		'08	58.7	...	...	41.3	5,047	...	...	...	100.0	4,851	...	...	-1,819	118	87	115
		'09	59.6	...	...	40.4	4,960	...	...	...	100.0	4,912	...	...	-1	94	91	91
		Rating History: NR-3, 06/11/10; NR-3, 06/17/09; NR-3, 11/19/08; NR-3, 10/16/07; NR-3, 08/28/06																
REGENCE HMO OREGON Regence Group Jared L. Short President 100 Southwest Market Street Portland, OR 97201 OR : 1977 : Non-Profit : Inactive Inactive 503-225-5221 AMB# 068583 NAIC# 95699	**NR-3**	**'05**	48.8	2.5	35.3	13.4	125,594	...	0.2	...	99.8	124,334	-193	-193	-3,004	3,223	4,158	3,999
		'06	58.8	2.7	22.5	15.9	108,747	...	...	...	100.0	105,777	...	...	5,585	3,985	2,475	2,368
		'07	41.4	6.0	...	52.6	47,874	...	...	...	100.0	47,414	...	...	-20,490	-9,317	712	4,253
		'08	41.7	36.1	...	22.2	7,511	...	...	...	100.0	6,302	...	...	-25,516	2,021	1,426	461
		'09	45.9	38.4	...	15.8	6,649	...	...	...	100.0	6,611	...	...	-1,033	39	309	309
		Rating History: NR-3, 06/11/10; NR-3, 06/17/09; NR-3, 11/19/08; NR-3, 10/16/07; NR-3, 08/28/06																
REGENCE LIFE AND HEALTH INS CO Regence Group Joseph J. Wilds Chairman 100 Southwest Market Street Portland, OR 97201 OR : 1966 : Non-Profit : Broker Group A&H, Group Life, Ind A&H 503-721-7161 AMB# 009345 NAIC# 97985	**A-** Rating Outlook: Stable **FSC X**	**'05**	64.7	...	17.9	17.4	60,305	48.7	17.2	0.2	33.8	30,501	180,048	35,089	-311	4,974	2,684	2,573
		'06	50.6	...	17.5	31.9	83,982	29.6	10.5	0.2	59.6	34,120	205,562	38,138	16,607	4,310	2,838	2,865
		'07	58.3	...	15.1	26.6	84,937	30.8	12.9	0.2	56.0	37,811	190,124	42,347	3,611	5,381	4,296	4,420
		'08	59.7	...	12.8	27.5	81,579	32.9	15.2	0.7	51.3	37,548	143,120	44,874	-3,792	5,541	2,744	803
		'09	60.0	...	20.0	20.0	89,200	32.5	15.3	0.9	51.3	42,749	127,415	45,267	8,170	4,940	3,575	2,754
		Rating History: A-, 06/11/10; A-, 06/17/09; A-, 11/19/08; A- g, 10/16/07; A- g, 08/28/06																
REGION 6 RX CORPORATION[2] Independence Blue Cross Daniel C. Lyons, M.D. President 1901 Market Street Philadelphia, PA 19103-1480 PA : 2007 : Stock : Not Available Health 215-241-2400 AMB# 064944 NAIC# 12812	**NR-5**	**'05**	...	...	...	...	...	...	...	...	...	...	...	...	...	...	...	...
		'06	...	...	...	...	...	...	...	...	...	...	...	...	...	...	...	...
		'07	...	...	...	100.0	7,949	...	...	...	100.0	1,778	...	...	-511	103	83	83
		'08	...	...	...	100.0	1,865	...	...	...	100.0	1,782	...	...	52	29	4	4
		'09	...	...	...	100.0	1,876	...	...	...	100.0	1,776	...	...	10	-9	-6	-6
		Rating History: NR-5, 04/09/10; NR-5, 04/08/09; NR-5, 05/07/08																
REINSURANCE CO OF MISSOURI Reinsurance Group of America Inc David B. Atkinson President & CEO 1370 Timberlake Manor Parkway Chesterfield, MO 63017-6039 MO : 1998 : Stock : Other Direct Ordinary Life, Ind Ann 636-736-7300 AMB# 050061 NAIC# 89004	**NR-3**	**'05**	10.7	...	80.5	8.8	1,210,843	98.6	...	...	1.4	1,007,351	...	60,380	118,717	-139,505	-90,070	-90,070
		'06	6.7	...	92.4	0.9	1,137,855	64.0	...	...	36.0	1,045,611	...	-6,733	75,911	103,998	69,923	68,484
		'07	4.3	...	95.0	0.7	1,250,885	98.5	...	...	1.5	1,184,135	...	35,308	27,863	4,126	5,606	5,167
		'08	5.2	...	94.2	0.5	1,174,550	98.7	...	...	1.3	1,107,899	...	43,203	64,072	-973	-606	-2,276
		'09	5.0	...	94.0	1.0	1,506,999	71.1	...	28.6	0.3	1,412,945	...	73,818	86,282	-24,168	-15,786	-16,800
		Rating History: NR-3, 10/12/09; NR-3, 06/02/08; NR-3, 10/05/07; NR-2, 09/20/06; NR-2, 08/02/05																
RELIABLE LIFE INSURANCE CO Unitrin, Inc Don M. Royster, Sr. President 12115 Lackland Road St. Louis, MO 63146-4003 MO : 1912 : Stock : Career Agent Home serv, Ind Life, Ind A&H 314-819-4300 AMB# 006986 NAIC# 68357	**A-** Rating Outlook: Stable **FSC IX**	**'05**	80.8	1.6	1.1	16.5	691,764	93.6	0.3	0.8	5.3	54,242	114,061	117,347	5,325	18,723	12,126	14,508
		'06	67.1	1.4	1.6	29.9	713,775	94.5	0.3	0.8	4.5	55,931	112,111	115,146	21,642	20,321	12,745	13,315
		'07	65.8	1.8	1.6	30.8	730,596	95.2	0.3	0.7	3.8	58,301	110,384	113,192	17,314	25,344	15,511	15,115
		'08	73.1	1.8	5.8	19.3	741,847	95.6	0.3	0.6	3.5	56,363	109,801	112,255	12,221	26,092	12,557	10,275
		'09	55.1	...	...	44.9	21,877	...	...	...	100.0	10,656	110,141	-9,271	-668,750	15,702	13,711	10,387
		Rating History: A- r, 05/25/10; A- g, 04/10/09; A g, 05/05/08; A g, 04/06/07; A g, 04/28/06																

Data in U.S. Dollars

—	Profitability Tests							Leverage Tests						Liquidity Tests					
Un-Realized Capital Gains ($000)	Benefits Paid to NPW & Dep (%)	Comm. & Expenses to NPW & Dep (%)	NOG to Total Assets (%)	NOG to Total Rev (%)	Operating Return on Equity (%)	Net Yield (%)	Total Return (%)	Change in NPW & Dep (%)	NPW & Dep to Capital (X)	Capital & Surplus to Liabilities (%)	Surplus Relief (%)	Reins Leverage (%)	Change in Capital (%)	Quick Liquidity (%)	Current Liquidity (%)	Non-Invest Grade Bonds to Capital (%)	Delinq. & Foreclosed Mortgages to Capital (%)	Mort. & Credit Tenant Loans & R.E. to Capital (%)	Affiliated Invest to Capital (%)
8,235	82.8	15.3	7.3	3.8	15.1	2.89	6.65	11.1	3.9	102.2	...	...	12.5	83.4	94.1	6.6	...	5.9	40.4
11,021	83.5	14.7	7.0	3.3	13.6	3.27	8.40	13.3	3.7	112.6	...	0.9	20.2	87.9	102.9	5.0	...	4.8	37.1
10,220	84.0	16.1	2.7	1.2	5.1	3.60	7.68	10.8	3.7	118.5	...	1.1	10.3	91.8	108.2	4.1	...	4.3	38.4
-229	87.4	13.0	2.2	0.9	4.2	3.50	1.47	14.6	4.4	114.0	...	0.4	-3.7	82.2	94.8	5.2	...	4.9	43.1
19,645	89.5	14.4	-5.3	-2.2	-10.9	2.86	8.58	9.8	5.2	79.5	...	0.4	-5.8	62.3	74.1	7.5	...	3.7	47.5

Principal Lines of Business: CompHosp/Med (43.6%), FEHBP (31.1%), Medicare (19.2%), MedSup (3.0%), OtherHlth (1.7%) — Principal States: UT (100.0%)

-23,337	77.2	16.5	9.7	5.8	15.1	4.37	4.89	4.4	2.5	102.0	...	...	15.0	171.0	191.0	6.7	...	2.7	10.8
19,425	80.4	15.8	7.7	4.6	11.6	4.47	7.62	11.0	2.2	215.4	...	...	22.9	180.4	207.8	5.2	...	2.1	9.1
510	83.1	16.5	3.7	2.2	5.5	4.74	6.25	12.6	2.4	194.4	...	...	5.0	155.4	182.4	4.5	...	1.9	10.9
-68,169	85.3	15.8	2.7	1.5	4.2	6.26	-3.92	3.7	2.9	153.4	...	...	-13.9	148.1	172.7	5.4	...	5.3	14.9
45,693	85.3	16.0	1.5	0.8	2.4	4.98	8.27	5.0	2.7	166.9	...	...	12.2	140.2	165.3	6.7	...	4.5	14.6

Principal Lines of Business: CompHosp/Med (75.2%), Medicare (9.0%), FEHBP (8.1%), Medicaid (2.9%), MedSup (2.8%) — Principal States: WA (100.0%)

619	67.4	20.6	18.8	10.5	39.1	5.75	6.24	43.6	3.0	100.5	...	18.7	51.4	103.5	118.2	1.1	...	6.6	6.1
2,605	77.8	18.2	8.9	4.7	16.4	5.34	6.86	28.1	3.0	135.2	...	3.0	27.1	130.9	151.3	5.0	...	4.4	4.1
1,291	81.2	20.9	-0.5	-0.3	-1.0	5.26	6.04	12.0	3.4	100.4	...	0.7	0.4	103.5	120.8	7.2	...	10.6	10.9
-3,257	82.1	19.1	-0.6	-0.3	-1.2	4.64	-1.22	18.5	4.6	78.0	...	1.2	-13.7	96.9	112.4	6.6	...	6.5	7.2
9,065	82.8	20.0	-1.2	-0.6	-2.6	4.35	7.94	2.0	4.4	96.6	...	3.1	7.7	108.1	124.8	8.4	...	5.4	6.6

Principal Lines of Business: CompHosp/Med (79.6%), Medicare (11.2%), MedSup (3.5%), FEHBP (2.5%), OtherHlth (1.9%) — Principal States: ID (98.7%)

-147	62.9	23.2	5.0	24.6	5.7	4.65	4.14	-83.5	0.2	999.9	...	...	4.9	999.9	999.9	4.5	...	...	...
154	-99.9	381.9	3.0	64.7	3.1	4.95	5.20	-99.9	0.0	999.9	...	...	3.6	999.9	999.9	...	...	...	...
...	...	...	4.7	57.5	5.0	8.87	9.02	100.0	...	762.4	...	...	-80.3	621.5	711.1	...	...	...	...
...	...	...	1.7	69.6	1.8	3.27	3.98	...	...	999.9	...	...	2.5	999.9	999.9	...	...	...	...
...	...	...	1.8	94.1	1.9	3.31	3.31	...	...	999.9	...	...	1.3	999.9	999.9	...	...	...	...

1,425	-99.9	-99.9	3.2	92.7	3.4	3.85	4.88	-99.9	0.0	999.9	...	...	3.8	999.9	999.9	0.5	...	2.5	22.5
2,788	...	...	2.1	47.8	2.2	4.61	6.97	100.0	...	999.9	...	...	-14.9	999.9	999.9	0.8	...	2.8	27.1
-21,818	...	...	0.9	-8.0	0.9	-11.69	-33.10	...	...	999.9	...	...	-55.2	999.9	999.9	...	...	6.1	19.6
118	...	...	5.1	46.4	5.3	15.65	11.75	...	...	521.3	...	...	-86.7	332.2	332.2	...	...	43.0	146.9
61	...	...	4.4	16.9	4.8	34.27	35.26	...	...	999.9	...	...	4.9	999.9	999.9	...	...	38.6	138.6

376	56.8	34.3	4.4	7.0	8.9	4.27	4.87	-0.3	1.1	116.1	4.1	123.4	3.9	131.8	149.2	1.2	...	...	...
1,162	60.6	34.1	3.9	6.8	8.8	4.17	6.23	8.7	1.0	80.4	2.8	128.6	15.5	116.0	130.5	1.4	...	...	...
70	59.2	35.2	5.1	9.3	11.9	4.38	4.65	11.0	1.0	93.5	2.3	106.8	9.6	119.3	137.7	...	...	...	...
-1,979	58.2	34.2	3.3	5.7	7.3	4.27	-1.31	6.0	1.1	92.0	0.6	136.1	-4.8	122.8	138.5	0.0	...	...	...
1,938	57.3	36.5	4.2	7.4	8.9	3.71	5.39	0.9	1.0	102.8	1.6	114.6	15.7	136.4	154.3	0.7	...	...	...

Principal Lines of Business: GrpLife (51.1%), GrpA&H (37.1%), IndA&H (10.9%), IndAnn (0.8%), OrdLife (0.1%) — Principal States: OR (60.7%), WA (16.3%), UT (15.8%), ID (7.1%)

...	...	...	...	...	...	...	...	...	...	...	...	...	...	...	...	...	...	...	...
...	...	...	...	...	...	...	...	...	...	...	...	...	...	...	...	...	...	...	...
...	...	...	...	76.2	...	...	...	...	...	28.8	...	...	...	29.3	29.3	...	...	...	...
...	...	...	0.1	10.7	0.2	2.07	2.07	...	...	999.9	...	...	0.2	999.9	999.9	...	...	...	...
...	...	...	-0.3	-99.9	-0.3	0.14	0.14	...	...	999.9	...	...	-0.3	999.9	999.9	...	...	...	...

97,667	13.4	0.0	-8.5	-99.9	-9.5	0.11	10.41	398.1	0.1	495.4	...	5.1	13.5	46.5	53.3	...	...	...	96.8
-44,970	-99.9	-60.8	6.0	-99.9	6.8	0.48	-3.61	-99.9	0.0	999.9	...	0.1	3.8	75.9	83.6	...	...	...	100.5
85,288	88.1	0.6	0.5	14.1	0.5	0.41	7.76	624.4	0.0	999.9	...	0.1	13.3	71.3	82.2	...	...	...	100.0
-138,516	92.9	0.4	0.0	-1.5	-0.1	-0.15	-11.16	22.4	0.0	999.9	...	0.0	-6.5	62.8	79.3	0.2	...	...	99.6
234,797	91.2	0.6	-1.2	-22.7	-1.3	-0.30	18.89	70.9	0.1	999.9	...	0.3	27.5	56.7	66.2	0.0	...	...	100.3

Principal Lines of Business: OrdLife (59.8%), IndAnn (40.2%)

-149	47.8	49.9	1.8	7.9	18.2	5.71	6.08	1.0	2.1	8.9	0.1	7.9	-30.2	66.1	73.5	14.2	...	23.2	1.7
16	46.9	48.6	1.8	8.3	23.1	5.77	5.88	-1.9	2.0	8.9	0.1	7.9	3.3	68.2	74.3	12.6	...	19.7	1.7
89	50.0	46.8	2.1	10.1	27.2	5.96	5.94	-1.7	1.9	9.1	0.1	7.4	4.4	82.6	89.7	17.3	...	23.3	1.5
-505	50.8	47.2	1.7	8.2	21.9	5.87	5.50	-0.8	1.9	8.4	...	0.3	-5.8	59.7	69.5	34.8	...	23.6	2.6
-294	-99.9	27.5	3.6	153.9	40.9	5.00	4.04	-99.9	-0.9	95.0	0.0	999.9	-81.5	420.4	425.3	...	...	...	8.4

Principal Lines of Business: OrdLife (128.0%), GrpA&H (0.4%), GrpAnn (-0.1%), IndLife (-4.3%), IndA&H (-24.0%) — Principal States: TX (76.2%), MO (12.0%), AR (8.5%)

Data in U.S. Dollars

COMPANY NAME / Ultimate Parent Association / Principal Officer / Mailing Address / Dom. : Began Bus. : Struct. : Mktg. / Specialty / Phone # / AMB# / NAIC#	Best's Financial Strength Rating / FSC	Data Year	Balance Sheet: Bonds (%)	Mort. Loans & R.E. (%)	Com & Pref. Stock (%)	All Other Assets (%)	Total Assets ($000)	Life Reserves (%)	Health Reserves %)	Ann Res. & Dep. Liabilities (%)	All Other Liabilities (%)	Capital & Surplus ($000)	Operations: Direct Premiums Written ($000)	Net Premiums Written & Deposits ($000)	Operating Cash Flow ($000)	NOG Before Taxes ($000)	NOG After Taxes ($000)	Net Income ($000)
RELIANCE STANDARD LIFE INS CO R & Co Capital Management, L.L.C.	**A**	'05	81.6	4.8	1.6	12.0	2,613,493	7.0	29.8	45.9	17.3	369,099	790,345	769,601	189,437	69,861	46,729	54,155
Lawrence E. Daurelle, President & CEO		'06	72.4	4.8	1.9	20.9	2,939,389	6.6	32.4	44.3	16.7	416,253	889,496	973,784	279,093	75,679	44,730	44,607
2001 Market Street, Suite 1500, Philadelphia, PA 19103	Rating Outlook: Negative	'07	72.4	4.4	2.7	20.5	3,240,629	6.5	34.3	39.0	20.2	457,548	1,027,876	1,003,947	296,958	101,484	54,756	54,293
IL : 1907 : Stock : Broker		'08	76.8	3.7	3.1	16.4	3,508,998	6.3	36.5	45.5	11.7	511,718	1,259,108	1,239,100	329,363	120,703	78,243	23,285
Ann, Dis inc, Group Life, 267-256-3500		'09	78.3	1.9	2.8	16.9	3,821,310	5.8	36.0	45.2	13.1	541,009	1,254,990	1,226,725	206,091	131,567	105,237	-29,061
AMB# 006990 NAIC# 68381	FSC X	**Rating History: A g, 12/22/09; A g, 12/22/08; A g, 01/08/08; A g, 12/19/06; A g, 12/21/05**																
RELIANCE STANDARD LIFE OF TX R & Co Capital Management, L.L.C.	**NR-3**	'05	13.5	...	85.0	1.5	408,920	3.6	0.5	0.3	95.6	350,228	82	169	-24,616	334	382	382
Lawrence E. Daurelle, President & CEO		'06	12.1	...	86.4	1.6	456,283	3.2	0.5	0.3	96.1	397,863	80	629	429	523	486	486
2001 Market Street, Suite 1500, Philadelphia, PA 19103		'07	11.0	...	87.4	1.5	497,905	3.0	0.5	0.3	96.2	439,773	61	193	277	725	646	646
TX : 1984 : Stock : Broker		'08	10.7	...	87.7	1.5	512,427	2.8	0.5	0.3	96.4	454,373	40	166	546	419	430	430
Group Life, 267-256-3500		'09	9.8	...	80.7	9.4	560,350	2.8	0.5	0.3	96.4	502,267	52	117	50,350	44,989	45,052	45,052
AMB# 009480 NAIC# 66575		**Rating History: NR-3, 12/22/09; NR-3, 12/22/08; NR-3, 01/08/08; NR-3, 12/19/06; NR-3, 12/21/05**																
RELIASTAR LIFE INSURANCE CO ING Groep N.V.	**A**	'05	61.0	10.5	1.5	27.0	22,042,631	21.7	6.6	46.2	25.5	1,880,140	2,941,071	3,761,353	798,597	277,469	190,707	182,513
Donald W. Britton, President		'06	60.6	10.1	2.1	27.2	22,050,608	22.6	7.1	46.3	24.1	2,323,459	2,762,047	3,695,248	424,374	230,315	133,160	129,500
5780 Powers Ferry Road, NW, Atlanta, GA 30327-4390	Rating Outlook: Stable	'07	60.9	11.2	2.1	25.8	22,384,571	22.4	6.9	45.8	25.0	2,325,927	2,807,552	2,869,128	700,452	260,307	149,893	153,050
MN : 1885 : Stock : Agency		'08	65.4	12.3	2.2	20.2	20,473,880	23.7	6.5	48.7	21.2	2,079,413	2,986,610	3,002,293	6,233	-68,474	43,401	-125,207
Group Life, Life Reins, Employee Benefits, 612-372-5432		'09	57.7	10.9	2.1	29.4	20,673,305	24.1	5.3	49.5	21.1	2,190,310	2,963,426	1,356,126	83,134	223,958	104,562	-92,496
AMB# 006846 NAIC# 67105	FSC XIV	**Rating History: A g, 06/11/10; A g, 04/24/09; A+ g, 06/18/08; A+ g, 05/11/07; A+ g, 02/24/06**																
RELIASTAR LIFE INS CO OF NY ING Groep N.V.	**A**	'05	61.5	6.8	0.1	31.5	2,805,404	47.7	0.7	18.8	32.8	279,896	406,067	433,394	7,939	43,744	36,030	35,598
Donald W. Britton, President		'06	56.8	5.3	0.2	37.7	2,999,326	46.2	1.3	16.5	36.0	278,212	460,108	496,739	-21,126	18,479	18,691	17,880
5780 Powers Ferry Road, NW, Atlanta, GA 30327-4390	Rating Outlook: Stable	'07	53.8	4.2	0.2	41.8	3,251,995	43.6	1.3	13.9	41.2	286,950	536,200	523,413	17,623	8,652	-7,933	-12,771
NY : 1917 : Stock : Broker		'08	55.7	3.8	0.1	40.4	3,207,471	42.8	1.4	19.5	36.2	221,964	655,369	595,005	23,027	-190,526	-194,827	-196,907
Ind Life, Ann, 516-682-8700		'09	50.0	3.2	0.0	46.7	3,209,428	44.2	1.5	17.1	37.2	322,591	403,201	365,347	5,775	125,936	119,083	95,246
AMB# 006157 NAIC# 61360	FSC XIV	**Rating History: A g, 06/11/10; A g, 04/24/09; A+ g, 06/18/08; A+ g, 05/11/07; A+ g, 02/24/06**																
RENAISSANCE HEALTH INS CO NY Renaissance Health Service Corp	**NR-2**	'05	...	...	...	...	...	...	...	...	...	...	...	...	...	...	...	...
Thomas J. Fleszar, D.D.S., President		'06	43.0	...	6.0	51.0	702	...	17.8	...	82.2	667	3	3	33	-67	-67	-67
P.O. Box 30416, Lansing, MI 48909-7916		'07	32.0	...	0.9	67.1	942	...	69.9	...	30.1	880	63	63	260	-137	-137	-137
NY : 1979 : Stock : Direct Response		'08	34.3	...	2.3	63.5	878	...	26.9	...	73.1	863	60	60	-61	-17	-17	-17
Dental, 517-349-6000		'09	26.6	...	2.7	70.7	1,130	...	13.5	...	86.5	801	513	505	76	-60	-60	-60
AMB# 002682 NAIC# 15638		**Rating History: NR-2, 06/17/09; NR-2, 12/17/07; NR-5, 06/01/07; NR-5, 06/04/04; NR-1, 06/05/03**																
RENAISSANCE LF & HLTH OF AMER Renaissance Health Service Corp	**B++**	'05	38.9	...	9.0	52.1	26,369	...	48.7	...	51.3	20,217	52,822	54,951	2,058	1,647	609	697
Thomas J. Fleszar, D.D.S., President & CEO		'06	36.6	...	8.1	55.4	32,379	...	41.8	...	58.2	24,964	54,103	59,099	6,018	3,805	2,369	2,410
P.O. Box 30381, Lansing, MI 48909	Rating Outlook: Stable	'07	34.8	...	8.0	57.3	34,861	...	35.8	...	64.2	25,126	66,490	73,506	4,000	806	64	-667
IN : 1953 : Stock : Direct Response		'08	30.8	...	23.0	46.2	30,344	...	41.8	...	58.2	19,754	83,680	92,407	-4,758	-3,260	-3,021	-3,044
Dental, 517-349-6000		'09	22.2	...	13.0	64.8	38,859	...	39.0	...	61.0	19,023	94,549	102,733	5,363	-4,785	-4,840	-4,946
AMB# 006201 NAIC# 61700	FSC V	**Rating History: B++, 06/03/10; B++, 06/17/09; B++, 12/17/07; NR-3, 06/01/07; NR-3, 02/17/06**																
REQUIA LIFE INSURANCE CORP[1]	**NR-1**	'05	...	...	...	...	...	...	...	...	...	...	...	...	...	...	...	...
Scott W. Peterson, Chief Executive Officer		'06	...	...	...	...	...	...	...	...	...	...	...	...	...	...	...	...
22 E. Mifflin Street, Suite 1010, Madison, WI 53703		'07	...	...	...	...	...	...	...	...	...	...	...	...	...	...	...	...
WI : 2009 : Stock : Not Available		'08	...	...	...	...	...	...	...	...	...	...	...	...	...	...	...	...
877-221-8059		'09	...	...	...	100.0	2,736	...	...	...	100.0	2,697	...	...	...	-501	-501	-501
AMB# 060716 NAIC# 13696		**Rating History: NR-1, 06/10/10**																
RESERVE NATIONAL INS CO Unitrin, Inc	**A-**	'05	85.2	2.8	0.2	11.8	98,874	6.5	74.9	0.4	18.2	34,809	132,750	131,941	2,114	13,012	6,615	6,849
Orin Crossley, President		'06	68.9	16.6	2.2	12.3	104,918	7.1	76.9	0.4	15.7	44,321	127,369	127,260	5,115	12,034	6,423	18,040
6100 Northwest Grand Boulevard, Oklahoma City, OK 73118	Rating Outlook: Negative	'07	60.7	9.9	5.8	23.7	108,314	6.8	75.4	0.3	17.5	44,623	129,593	129,392	3,410	12,590	7,071	6,357
OK : 1956 : Stock : Agency		'08	66.2	10.2	10.8	12.8	104,133	7.3	78.1	0.3	14.3	45,153	128,840	128,581	-3,851	9,791	5,314	6,070
Group A&H, Ind A&H, Med supp, 405-848-7931		'09	66.5	6.6	7.4	19.4	107,905	7.2	78.6	0.3	13.9	47,308	128,142	128,013	-569	6,493	3,569	2,709
AMB# 006998 NAIC# 68462	FSC VI	**Rating History: A-, 05/25/10; A- u, 03/03/10; A-, 04/10/09; A-, 05/05/08; A-, 04/06/07**																
RESOURCE LIFE INSURANCE CO Onex Corporation	**NR-3**	'05	86.0	...	0.7	13.2	126,172	3.5	0.0	...	96.5	32,550	54,014	1,369	-17,569	-1,363	-728	-1,072
David L. Cole, Chairman & CEO		'06	79.9	...	...	20.1	125,312	2.7	0.4	...	96.9	30,346	48,496	1,835	-1,433	-3,274	-1,901	-1,275
175 W. Jackson Blvd., Chicago, IL 60604		'07	89.7	...	...	10.3	103,154	9.5	29.7	...	60.8	14,804	46,608	42,915	-21,541	-13,677	-13,677	-13,640
IL : 1963 : Stock : Agency		'08	77.2	...	...	22.8	70,691	12.3	35.6	...	52.1	13,028	1,902	1,629	-27,869	5,725	7,952	7,033
Credit A&H, Credit Life, 312-356-2499		'09	96.3	...	...	3.7	49,882	11.6	37.1	...	51.3	16,836	-5,514	-6,678	-19,695	3,738	3,670	3,696
AMB# 006176 NAIC# 61506		**Rating History: NR-3, 02/18/10; NR-3, 02/13/09; B+, 12/13/07; B++, 11/30/06; B++, 06/16/06**																

BEST'S PROFITABILITY, LEVERAGE AND LIQUIDITY TESTS 2005 – 2009

Data in U.S. Dollars

—	Profitability Tests							Leverage Tests						Liquidity Tests					
Un-Realized Capital Gains ($000)	Benefits Paid to NPW & Dep (%)	Comm. & Expenses to NPW & Dep (%)	NOG to Total Assets (%)	NOG to Total Rev (%)	Operating Return on Equity (%)	Net Yield (%)	Total Return (%)	Change in NPW & Dep (%)	NPW & Dep to Capital (X)	Capital & Surplus to Liabilities (%)	Surplus Relief (%)	Reins Leverage (%)	Change in Capital (%)	Quick Liquidity (%)	Current Liquidity (%)	Non-Invest Grade Bonds to Capital (%)	Delinq. & Foreclosed Mortgages to Capital (%)	Mort. & Credit Tenant Loans & R.E. to Capital (%)	Affiliated Invest to Capital (%)
8,007	71.8	24.2	1.9	5.2	13.5	6.05	6.81	11.3	1.9	19.1	1.0	80.6	15.7	68.7	78.6	54.3	0.1	31.1	16.3
16,094	67.3	21.2	1.6	4.4	11.4	5.65	6.36	26.5	2.1	19.5	0.7	71.1	14.3	78.6	89.4	39.3	0.4	33.4	20.3
1,668	77.6	23.6	1.8	4.7	12.5	6.17	6.28	3.1	2.0	19.6	0.9	60.9	10.8	72.2	80.7	47.9	0.8	28.3	21.6
-45,791	64.9	21.5	2.3	5.5	16.1	5.78	2.63	23.4	2.3	18.5	0.9	50.7	4.5	70.0	82.9	72.7	10.2	24.5	16.7
16,219	65.0	22.4	2.9	7.5	20.0	5.74	2.40	-1.0	2.2	17.8	0.5	44.9	5.1	74.3	84.4	72.7	5.5	13.0	17.5
	Principal Lines of Business: GrpA&H (49.2%), GrpLife (29.0%), IndAnn (16.4%), GrpAnn (5.3%), OrdLife (0.1%)													Principal States: CA (12.7%), TX (6.9%), FL (6.6%), PA (5.7%), NJ (5.2%)					
43,699	41.8	146.0	0.1	54.3	0.1	0.16	14.38	15.9	0.0	599.2	...	0.5	14.4	15.7	64.0	...	...	...	110.9
47,154	114.1	31.0	0.1	38.7	0.1	0.17	13.56	273.0	0.0	683.7	...	0.4	13.6	19.0	67.9	...	...	...	112.1
41,295	88.8	24.4	0.1	70.6	0.2	0.17	10.51	-69.4	0.0	759.4	...	0.4	10.5	20.3	69.4	...	...	...	110.8
14,170	137.2	58.8	0.1	64.8	0.1	0.11	3.32	-13.8	0.0	785.5	0.0	0.3	3.3	21.8	71.0	...	...	...	110.4
-47,154	79.8	78.2	8.4	99.7	9.4	9.86	0.49	-29.5	0.0	867.8	0.0	0.3	10.5	23.9	72.2	...	...	...	100.4
	Principal Lines of Business: OrdLife (58.1%), GrpLife (36.3%), GrpA&H (5.7%)													Principal States: TX (100.0%)					
7,191	89.8	17.1	0.9	4.5	11.2	5.80	5.87	-1.9	1.9	12.6	3.3	121.2	20.7	47.3	63.5	26.7	...	118.2	33.1
12,088	103.8	17.1	0.6	3.1	6.3	5.69	5.75	-1.8	1.5	15.5	4.3	111.2	25.2	52.4	67.8	17.9	0.0	90.4	33.6
-174,208	122.5	9.2	0.7	3.7	6.4	5.62	4.64	-22.4	1.1	15.1	24.9	132.0	0.5	47.1	61.9	31.7	...	99.9	30.8
-226,340	101.5	27.0	0.2	1.2	2.0	5.09	2.83	4.6	1.4	13.1	8.1	193.2	-13.7	45.2	60.2	41.0	0.1	115.7	31.9
15,678	115.6	0.0	0.5	3.9	4.9	4.98	3.88	-54.8	0.6	13.6	39.1	216.1	2.9	51.7	65.6	44.4	...	100.3	33.4
	Principal Lines of Business: IndAnn (92.9%), GrpAnn (24.2%), GrpLife (3.5%), IndA&H (0.3%), CrdA&H (0.0%)													Principal States: CA (12.6%), FL (9.7%), OH (7.7%), TX (7.5%), MI (5.1%)					
1,201	63.9	18.7	1.3	7.3	13.3	5.87	6.02	26.2	1.4	15.9	2.6	69.7	5.8	64.0	78.6	18.9	...	62.9	1.0
2,007	56.2	18.1	0.6	3.3	6.7	5.75	5.89	14.6	1.7	16.0	2.0	67.5	-2.2	69.7	82.5	13.8	...	52.8	0.8
2,389	57.9	18.5	-0.3	-1.2	-2.8	6.03	5.93	5.4	1.7	16.6	20.5	86.7	3.2	64.7	77.5	28.8	...	44.0	4.5
-842	52.2	14.9	-6.0	-25.9	-76.6	5.76	5.61	13.7	2.4	12.0	32.5	189.1	-21.5	57.3	69.6	37.3	...	50.3	5.6
-3,140	134.2	12.9	3.7	26.4	43.7	5.16	3.77	-38.6	1.1	17.9	10.8	139.8	35.3	75.0	88.5	33.8	...	31.1	3.5
	Principal Lines of Business: IndAnn (56.6%), OrdLife (26.8%), GrpAnn (7.1%), GrpLife (3.9%), GrpA&H (3.9%)													Principal States: NY (75.1%), NJ (3.8%)					
...	...	...	...	...	...	...	...	...	...	...	...	...	...	...	...	...	...	...	...
...	154.4	999.9	...	-99.9	...	...	...	...	0.0	999.9	...	...	...	999.9	999.9	...	...	...	...
...	77.7	223.0	-16.7	-99.9	-17.8	3.14	3.14	999.9	0.1	999.9	...	...	31.8	999.9	999.9	...	...	...	...
...	76.9	157.2	-1.9	-20.4	-1.9	2.57	2.57	-5.2	0.1	999.9	...	...	-1.9	999.9	999.9	...	...	...	...
...	88.3	26.1	-5.9	-11.5	-7.2	1.64	1.64	743.5	0.6	244.1	...	0.8	-7.1	283.1	284.5	...	...	...	...
	Principal Lines of Business: Dental (100.0%)													Principal States: NY (100.0%)					
-117	85.6	13.1	2.4	1.1	3.0	4.00	3.87	16.8	2.7	328.6	...	5.7	-2.5	457.7	475.5	...	...	...	...
-2,308	82.2	13.0	8.1	3.9	10.5	4.17	-3.93	7.5	2.4	336.7	...	2.9	23.5	489.2	504.5	...	...	...	...
2,397	81.8	19.3	0.2	0.1	0.3	4.72	10.27	24.4	2.9	258.1	...	1.9	0.7	488.5	499.0	...	...	...	...
-1,846	83.4	22.0	-9.3	-3.2	-13.5	4.94	-1.14	25.7	4.7	186.5	...	58.1	-21.4	284.5	303.6	...	...	...	...
1,246	84.7	18.6	-14.0	-4.7	-25.0	1.69	5.63	11.2	5.4	95.9	...	58.5	-3.7	155.5	161.8	...	...	...	...
	Principal Lines of Business: Dental (98.3%), Vision (1.7%)													Principal States: IN (55.0%), MI (22.1%), TN (4.1%), NC (4.1%), FL (3.1%)					
...	...	...	...	...	...	...	...	...	...	...	...	...	...	...	...	...	...	...	...
...	...	...	...	...	...	...	...	...	...	...	...	...	...	...	...	...	...	...	...
...	...	...	...	...	...	...	...	...	...	...	...	...	...	...	...	...	...	...	...
...	...	...	...	...	...	...	...	...	...	...	...	...	...	...	...	...	...	...	...
...	...	...	...	-99.9	...	...	...	...	...	999.9	...	...	...	...	...	...	...	...	...
-25	64.8	29.4	6.8	4.8	18.6	6.03	6.43	3.3	3.7	55.6	0.1	0.4	-4.0	99.2	109.0	1.1	...	7.9	2.9
0	66.4	30.7	6.3	4.8	16.2	6.01	18.85	-3.5	2.8	75.3	0.0	0.2	27.6	93.7	103.3	0.9	...	38.6	0.5
0	65.1	29.9	6.6	5.2	15.9	5.41	4.84	1.7	2.8	72.4	0.1	0.3	0.9	115.2	127.0	1.0	...	23.5	0.5
-3	66.6	30.7	5.0	3.9	11.8	5.84	6.67	-0.6	2.8	79.5	0.1	0.2	1.4	87.5	106.2	...	...	23.0	2.3
4	67.6	32.1	3.4	2.7	7.7	5.88	5.06	-0.4	2.7	81.0	0.1	0.2	4.7	93.3	114.0	2.1	...	14.9	2.1
	Principal Lines of Business: IndA&H (94.2%), GrpA&H (5.2%), OrdLife (0.6%), IndAnn (0.0%)													Principal States: TX (13.2%), OK (8.0%), IN (7.6%), IL (7.2%), OH (6.9%)					
112	36.7	440.9	-0.5	-2.2	-2.2	1.70	1.73	-28.3	0.0	35.5	88.0	487.4	-3.0	111.5	120.4	...	...	...	10.3
-924	29.0	426.7	-1.5	-6.8	-6.0	2.17	2.09	34.1	0.1	32.4	76.2	405.7	-7.3	122.2	132.1	...	...	...	...
...	4.4	65.7	-12.0	-28.0	-60.6	3.10	3.28	999.9	2.9	17.0	15.4	471.8	-51.0	99.3	107.8	...	...	...	...
...	171.6	255.3	9.1	205.1	57.1	2.57	1.64	-96.2	0.1	22.6	-1.1	271.6	-13.3	121.7	133.3	0.9	...	...	...
...	-34.0	-13.8	6.1	-79.7	24.6	3.06	3.35	-99.9	-0.4	51.2	0.7	96.6	29.7	122.5	135.9	1.3	...	...	...
	Principal Lines of Business: CrdA&H (80.4%), CrdLife (19.6%)																		

Data in U.S. Dollars

COMPANY NAME Ultimate Parent Association Principal Officer Mailing Address Dom. : Began Bus. : Struct. : Mktg. Specialty Phone # AMB# NAIC#	Best's Financial Strength Rating FSC	Data Year	Balance Sheet: Bonds (%)	Mort. Loans & R.E. (%)	Com & Pref. Stock (%)	All Other Assets (%)	Total Assets ($000)	Life Reserves (%)	Health Reserves %)	Ann Res. & Dep. Liabilities (%)	All Other Liabilities (%)	Capital & Surplus ($000)	Operations: Direct Premiums Written ($000)	Net Premiums Written & Deposits ($000)	Operating Cash Flow ($000)	NOG Before Taxes ($000)	NOG After Taxes ($000)	Net Income ($000)
RGA REINSURANCE COMPANY Reinsurance Group of America Inc David B. Atkinson Chairman, President & CEO 1370 Timberlake Manor Parkway Chesterfield, MO 63017-6039 MO : 1982 : Stock : Other Direct Reins 636-736-7300 AMB# 009080 NAIC# 93572	**A+** Rating Outlook: Stable **FSC XIII**	'05	37.6	6.6	3.0	52.8	9,778,217	39.6	1.0	32.2	27.2	975,110	2,162	3,556,677	107,544	-27,287	-65,784	-62,759
		'06	37.4	6.6	2.1	54.0	11,061,595	36.5	1.0	31.8	30.7	1,050,846	1,994	3,848,413	565,360	35,094	-58,515	-61,466
		'07	34.8	7.0	2.3	55.9	11,821,492	37.2	1.1	31.0	30.7	1,184,134	2,235	4,288,999	299,776	34,156	-33,477	-41,535
		'08	36.2	5.9	2.5	55.3	13,008,986	34.2	1.3	33.3	31.2	1,103,753	2,222	3,053,453	694,998	6,762	43,724	-41,750
		'09	40.1	5.3	1.1	53.5	14,893,433	33.8	3.4	32.2	30.7	1,416,550	2,259	2,489,593	1,201,785	366,097	146,595	63,189
		Rating History: A+ g, 10/12/09; A+ g, 06/02/08; A+ g, 10/05/07; A+ g, 09/19/06; A+ g, 08/02/05																
RHODES LIFE INS CO OF LA' Duplynn J. Brown President 2929 Scenic Highway Baton Rouge, LA 70805 LA : 1928 : Stock : Not Available 225-383-1678 AMB# 008092 NAIC# 78085	**NR-1**	'05	...	...	...	...	...	...	...	...	...	...	...	...	...	...	...	...
		'06	...	...	...	...	...	...	...	...	...	...	...	...	...	...	...	...
		'07	...	...	...	...	...	...	...	...	...	...	...	...	...	...	...	...
		'08	49.7	17.5	22.5	10.3	3,796	...	...	...	100.0	268	774	774	...	45	45	31
		'09	58.6	22.3	3.5	15.6	3,841	...	...	...	100.0	136	626	626	...	-172	-172	-216
		Rating History: NR-1, 06/10/10; NR-1, 06/12/09; NR-5, 06/03/05; NR-1, 06/02/04; NR-1, 06/03/03																
RIGHTCHOICE INSURANCE CO WellPoint Inc. Dennis A. Matheis President 1831 Chestnut Street St. Louis, MO 63103-2275 IL : 1987 : Stock : Not Available Group A&H, A&H, Ind A&H 414-226-6833 AMB# 060024 NAIC# 83640	**NR-2**	'05	56.0	...	...	44.0	10,979	...	...	...	100.0	9,535	4	4	388	520	362	362
		'06	66.5	...	...	33.5	11,450	...	...	...	100.0	10,026	...	...	465	650	487	487
		'07	60.0	...	...	40.0	11,664	...	...	...	100.0	10,401	...	...	269	586	382	382
		'08	13.6	...	...	86.4	11,718	...	...	...	100.0	10,620	...	...	110	335	218	218
		'09	14.3	...	...	85.7	11,887	...	...	...	100.0	10,818	...	...	194	257	205	205
		Rating History: NR-2, 04/27/10; NR-2, 01/23/09; NR-2, 03/24/08; NR-2, 11/06/06; NR-2, 05/08/06																
RIVERSOURCE LIFE INS CO OF NY Ameriprise Financial Inc Timothy V. Bechtold President & CEO 227 Ameriprise Financial Center Minneapolis, MN 55474 NY : 1972 : Stock : Agency Dis inc, Ind Ann, Ind Life 518-869-8613 AMB# 008345 NAIC# 80594	**A+** Rating Outlook: Negative **FSC XV**	'05	44.0	5.8	0.0	50.2	4,274,188	5.1	2.9	42.1	49.9	289,672	504,933	497,131	4,035	46,136	36,728	36,877
		'06	37.5	5.4	0.0	57.0	4,757,138	4.7	2.8	34.7	57.8	331,528	670,062	661,475	-103,834	75,753	61,735	63,001
		'07	28.3	4.5	0.0	67.1	5,025,037	4.4	2.8	29.3	63.6	274,277	701,871	692,070	-212,113	58,062	33,925	34,027
		'08	33.4	5.1	0.0	61.5	4,197,067	5.4	3.8	34.7	56.1	215,625	599,540	587,564	-14,343	-38,408	-36,116	-34,045
		'09	34.0	3.7	0.0	62.4	5,048,403	4.7	3.3	31.5	60.5	284,340	603,145	590,395	175,315	130,552	101,034	86,189
		Rating History: A+ g, 09/30/09; A+ g, 03/04/09; A+ g, 04/22/08; A+ g, 02/26/07; A+ g, 06/21/06																
RIVERSOURCE LIFE INS CO Ameriprise Financial Inc Timothy V. Bechtold President 227 Ameriprise Financial Center Minneapolis, MN 55474 MN : 1957 : Stock : Agency Ind Ann 612-671-3131 AMB# 006592 NAIC# 65005	**A+** Rating Outlook: Negative **FSC XV**	'05	38.5	4.0	0.4	57.1	66,609,228	5.5	2.3	37.1	55.1	2,942,153	8,398,692	8,259,094	-260,144	379,140	326,808	340,324
		'06	31.1	3.4	0.5	64.9	74,682,920	4.8	2.2	29.3	63.6	3,258,058	11,388,001	11,250,101	-2,763,919	485,920	468,748	513,766
		'07	24.3	3.4	0.4	72.0	79,870,147	4.5	2.3	23.8	69.5	2,820,441	11,894,184	11,724,277	-3,161,896	490,257	522,844	554,747
		'08	26.5	3.7	0.7	69.0	67,906,201	5.3	3.0	29.6	62.1	2,528,647	10,069,337	9,851,609	1,210,807	-1,166,280	-1,183,686	-1,407,175
		'09	28.5	3.1	0.7	67.8	81,313,114	4.6	2.7	27.4	65.4	3,370,671	10,012,400	9,777,962	2,851,772	2,053,728	1,793,496	1,886,563
		Rating History: A+ g, 09/30/09; A+ g, 03/04/09; A+ g, 04/22/08; A+ g, 02/26/07; A+ g, 06/21/06																
ROCKY MOUNTAIN HLTH MAINT ORG Rocky Mountain Health Maint Org Inc. Stephen K. ErkenBrack President & CEO P.O. Box 10600 Grand Junction, CO 81502-5600 CO : 1974 : Non-Profit : Broker Group A&H, Health 970-244-7760 AMB# 064312 NAIC# 95482	**B++** Rating Outlook: Stable **FSC VII**	'05	54.8	3.2	3.2	38.8	112,829	...	27.2	...	72.8	61,259	189,922	189,589	16,028	10,409	10,409	10,154
		'06	49.3	2.9	2.2	45.5	125,006	...	26.6	...	73.4	69,152	215,245	214,887	12,342	10,310	10,310	8,656
		'07	51.8	4.3	2.3	41.6	127,129	...	30.9	...	69.1	72,068	203,825	203,362	3,144	6,228	6,228	6,158
		'08	52.3	4.2	2.4	41.2	130,215	...	30.7	...	69.3	85,839	228,793	228,299	3,446	15,755	15,755	16,223
		'09	52.6	3.9	1.0	42.5	139,875	...	36.4	...	63.6	98,906	215,755	215,265	8,410	17,662	17,662	16,158
		Rating History: B++g, 03/30/10; B++g, 05/27/09; B++g, 06/18/08; B++g, 04/13/07; B++g, 05/09/06																
ROCKY MOUNTAIN HTHCARE OPTIONS Rocky Mountain Health Maint Org Inc. Stephen K. ErkenBrack President & CEO P.O. Box 10600 Grand Junction, CO 81502-5600 CO : 1993 : Non-Profit : Broker Group A&H, Health 970-244-7760 AMB# 064561 NAIC# 47004	**B++** Rating Outlook: Stable **FSC VII**	'05	88.4	...	...	11.6	22,169	...	54.7	...	45.3	8,006	99,305	99,084	2,819	2,814	1,889	1,795
		'06	77.8	...	...	22.2	26,457	...	56.7	...	43.3	7,722	118,366	118,028	3,320	-189	-80	-162
		'07	73.7	...	...	26.3	28,503	...	59.0	...	41.0	9,944	113,364	112,949	699	-1,741	-1,165	-1,158
		'08	84.3	...	...	15.7	26,005	...	66.2	...	33.8	9,288	110,456	109,960	-2,109	-1,101	-746	-689
		'09	82.4	...	...	17.6	27,460	...	63.0	...	37.0	11,180	104,404	103,914	1,752	-1,045	-853	-374
		Rating History: B++g, 03/30/10; B++g, 05/27/09; B++g, 06/18/08; B++g, 04/13/07; B++g, 05/09/06																
ROCKY MOUNTAIN HOSP & MED SVC WellPoint Inc. David S. Helwig President 700 Broadway Denver, CO 80273-0002 CO : 1978 : Non-Profit : Not Available Group A&H 303-831-2131 AMB# 068817 NAIC# 11011	**A** Rating Outlook: Stable **FSC IX**	'05	52.3	3.5	16.3	27.9	439,137	...	52.4	...	47.6	186,834	1,008,659	1,006,005	16,844	108,801	77,082	77,191
		'06	44.6	2.7	21.8	30.9	523,669	...	60.7	...	39.3	234,803	1,154,391	1,154,391	-28,950	148,885	109,655	108,347
		'07	42.1	2.2	19.6	36.1	588,194	...	56.1	...	43.9	242,021	1,289,383	1,289,383	55,492	87,355	62,334	61,814
		'08	44.9	1.9	18.0	35.2	649,764	...	67.0	...	33.0	324,793	1,553,769	1,552,708	17,102	140,518	118,855	114,581
		'09	48.2	1.9	17.8	32.1	662,928	...	60.4	...	39.6	315,038	1,640,843	1,640,712	21,748	133,085	102,191	102,065
		Rating History: A g, 04/27/10; A, 01/23/09; A, 03/20/08; A, 11/06/06; A, 12/29/05																
ROYAL BANK OF CANADA INS CO LT Royal Bank of Canada Tom Dalinda Managing Director & CEO Building No. 1, Chelston Park St. Michael, Barbados BB : 1987 : Stock : Not Available Life Reins, Annuity, Reins 246-467-3950 AMB# 086956	**A** Rating Outlook: Stable **FSC XI**	'05	79.7	...	...	20.3	880,893	15.6	...	...	84.4	524,357	...	363,401	247,838	70,954	70,954	70,954
		'06	80.1	...	...	19.9	827,168	22.1	...	...	77.9	541,937	...	417,033	136,820	226,855	226,855	226,855
		'07	64.9	...	...	35.1	830,461	30.9	...	...	69.2	607,355	...	615,622	272,223	340,649	340,649	340,649
		'08	61.5	...	...	38.5	780,292	22.4	...	...	77.6	574,772	...	695,926	295,432	318,050	318,050	318,050
		'09	71.8	...	...	28.2	1,211,859	15.7	...	...	84.3	946,785	...	1,034,696	415,382	410,599	410,599	410,599
		Rating History: A, 07/15/09; A, 10/07/08; A, 07/02/07; A, 05/11/06; A, 07/21/05																

BEST'S PROFITABILITY, LEVERAGE AND LIQUIDITY TESTS 2005 – 2009

Data in U.S. Dollars

	Profitability Tests							Leverage Tests						Liquidity Tests					
Un-Realized Capital Gains ($000)	Benefits Paid to NPW & Dep (%)	Comm. & Expenses to NPW & Dep (%)	NOG to Total Assets (%)	NOG to Total Rev (%)	Operating Return on Equity (%)	Net Yield (%)	Total Return (%)	Change in NPW & Dep (%)	NPW & Dep to Capital (X)	Capital & Surplus to Liabilities (%)	Surplus Relief (%)	Reins Leverage (%)	Change in Capital (%)	Quick Liquidity (%)	Current Liquidity (%)	Non-Invest Grade Bonds to Capital (%)	Delinq. & Foreclosed Mortgages to Capital (%)	Mort. & Credit Tenant Loans & R.E. to Capital (%)	Affiliated Invest to Capital (%)
-468	45.6	20.9	-0.7	-1.3	-7.1	5.76	5.99	106.5	3.6	11.4	73.6	842.4	12.9	24.0	33.2	17.3	...	68.6	1.3
-946	46.7	17.0	-0.6	-1.9	-5.8	5.73	5.77	8.2	3.6	10.8	48.9	927.9	8.3	28.7	34.9	20.1	...	69.6	1.1
-3,762	59.7	16.0	-0.3	-0.8	-3.0	6.02	5.90	11.4	3.5	11.5	40.8	882.4	12.8	26.3	33.3	20.0	...	68.3	0.4
466	102.4	19.5	0.4	1.0	3.8	6.13	4.93	-28.8	2.8	9.3	46.5	999.9	-9.1	23.3	31.4	31.3	0.1	70.1	0.1
-3,689	80.2	22.3	1.1	5.4	11.6	6.02	4.93	-18.5	1.7	10.6	32.4	917.0	29.3	26.1	34.2	40.6	0.9	55.9	2.9
Principal Lines of Business: OrdLife (65.0%), IndAnn (18.0%), GrpAnn (10.0%), IndA&H (5.8%), GrpLife (0.8%)														Principal States: IA (98.9%)					
...	...	...	...	...	...	...	...	...	...	...	...	...	...	...	...	...	...	...	...
...	...	...	...	...	...	...	...	...	...	...	...	...	...	...	...	...	...	...	...
...	...	...	...	...	...	...	...	...	...	...	...	...	...	...	...	...	...	...	...
0	43.2	53.4	...	5.2	...	...	...	...	2.7	8.3	...	...	...	...	...	...	...	227.8	...
...	54.9	75.2	-4.5	-22.5	-85.1	...	...	-19.0	3.6	4.7	...	...	-40.7	...	...	...	...	497.3	...
Principal Lines of Business: IndLife (70.7%), OrdLife (29.0%), GrpLife (0.3%)																			
...	279.6	-99.9	...	77.3	...	...	...	...	0.0	662.3	...	...	...	915.1	935.2	...	...	...	...
...	...	...	4.3	80.1	5.0	4.59	5.54	-99.9	...	707.9	...	...	5.2	999.9	999.9	...	...	...	...
...	...	...	3.3	69.6	3.7	4.87	4.87	...	...	828.7	...	...	3.7	999.9	999.9	...	...	...	...
...	...	...	1.9	60.4	2.1	3.13	3.14	...	...	980.8	...	...	2.2	999.9	999.9	...	...	...	...
...	...	...	1.7	73.7	1.9	2.37	2.38	...	...	999.9	...	...	1.9	999.9	999.9	...	...	...	...
-61	73.9	13.1	0.9	5.6	13.0	5.71	5.73	7.6	1.6	15.9	...	19.2	5.5	67.8	80.8	45.5	...	80.4	...
...	78.1	9.7	1.4	7.5	19.9	5.61	5.70	33.1	1.9	19.5	...	20.7	13.1	68.7	82.1	35.8	...	74.1	...
-115	81.5	9.8	0.7	3.9	11.2	5.60	5.66	4.6	2.4	17.5	...	28.6	-17.2	81.1	91.6	37.7	...	79.0	...
26,260	82.0	11.9	-0.8	-4.8	-14.7	5.06	6.63	-15.1	2.6	13.3	...	42.5	-20.5	71.3	83.3	43.2	...	92.5	...
-30,783	66.3	10.3	2.2	13.3	40.4	5.54	3.38	0.5	2.1	15.5	0.8	36.8	24.9	63.2	78.3	30.8	...	65.0	...
Principal Lines of Business: IndAnn (83.6%), OrdLife (10.0%), GrpAnn (3.7%), IndA&H (2.8%), GrpLife (0.0%)														Principal States: NY (94.2%)					
-2,739	80.0	15.5	0.5	3.1	12.5	5.60	5.62	23.2	2.5	11.9	0.0	48.9	23.4	62.7	75.6	53.7	...	81.1	10.4
6,847	79.3	12.6	0.7	3.4	15.1	5.49	5.66	36.2	3.2	14.4	0.0	49.6	7.4	63.5	76.6	43.9	...	73.5	10.3
-40,834	79.5	13.1	0.7	3.7	17.2	5.67	5.63	4.2	3.9	13.8	0.0	63.8	-14.1	65.3	76.0	42.4	...	89.3	9.1
944,906	75.4	12.4	-1.6	-9.7	-44.3	4.90	7.76	-16.0	3.6	10.6	0.0	80.2	-9.8	67.1	77.4	45.3	...	93.8	16.8
-1,138,427	60.4	10.6	2.4	14.6	60.8	4.95	1.38	-0.7	2.8	13.1	1.4	65.9	27.3	53.0	68.3	37.5	0.1	72.4	18.5
Principal Lines of Business: IndAnn (87.1%), OrdLife (8.8%), IndA&H (2.7%), GrpAnn (1.3%), GrpA&H (0.1%)														Principal States: CA (9.8%), FL (7.7%), MN (6.3%), TX (5.7%), PA (5.2%)					
...	89.0	19.6	9.7	4.8	18.8	3.10	2.81	-0.6	3.1	118.8	...	...	24.1	173.1	179.6	...	...	5.9	12.8
...	86.4	12.6	8.7	4.6	15.8	4.37	2.79	13.3	3.1	123.8	...	0.6	12.9	179.7	186.0	...	...	5.3	10.3
...	87.7	13.7	4.9	2.9	8.8	4.68	4.62	-5.4	2.8	130.9	...	0.1	4.2	170.1	176.3	...	...	7.6	17.2
...	84.5	11.8	12.2	6.7	20.0	3.86	4.28	12.3	2.7	193.4	...	0.1	19.1	219.5	231.0	...	...	6.3	14.6
-577	80.5	13.6	13.1	8.0	19.1	3.22	1.44	-5.7	2.2	241.4	...	0.0	15.2	234.3	247.0	...	...	5.5	11.0
Principal Lines of Business: CompHosp/Med (75.6%), Medicare (23.1%), OtherHlth (1.3%)														Principal States: CO (99.9%)					
...	82.6	15.4	9.0	1.9	26.8	4.50	4.05	50.2	12.4	56.5	...	...	31.4	133.5	140.8	...	...	...	...
...	86.3	14.8	-0.3	-0.1	-1.0	4.87	4.53	19.1	15.3	41.2	...	...	-3.5	117.6	123.1	...	...	...	...
...	86.8	15.8	-4.2	-1.0	-13.2	4.85	4.88	-4.3	11.4	53.6	...	6.7	28.8	121.8	128.5	...	...	...	...
...	85.7	16.3	-2.7	-0.7	-7.8	4.45	4.68	-2.6	11.8	55.6	...	1.6	-6.6	129.4	136.8	...	...	...	...
...	83.7	18.3	-3.2	-0.8	-8.3	4.23	6.19	-5.5	9.3	68.7	...	0.6	20.4	130.2	139.2	...	...	...	...
Principal Lines of Business: CompHosp/Med (98.6%), OtherHlth (1.2%), MedSup (0.2%)														Principal States: CO (100.0%)					
-6,127	80.1	12.7	17.9	7.4	40.9	11.98	10.07	15.3	5.4	74.1	0.4	0.1	-1.6	72.7	82.7	...	...	8.3	46.4
5,880	77.5	12.3	22.8	9.4	52.0	10.63	12.07	14.8	4.9	81.3	...	...	25.7	52.2	60.6	...	...	6.1	55.6
-9,128	85.5	10.3	11.2	4.6	26.1	9.74	7.02	11.7	5.3	69.9	...	...	3.1	67.2	76.1	...	...	5.4	53.5
4,654	81.4	10.4	19.2	7.8	41.9	12.88	12.99	20.4	4.8	99.9	0.0	0.0	34.2	63.5	72.9	0.1	...	3.8	39.5
487	83.2	12.3	15.6	6.1	31.9	13.77	13.86	5.7	5.2	90.6	...	0.0	-3.0	64.3	74.1	0.8	...	4.1	41.1
Principal Lines of Business: CompHosp/Med (64.2%), FEHBP (30.0%), MedSup (2.2%), Dental (1.3%), OtherHlth (1.0%)														Principal States: CO (73.8%), NV (26.2%)					
...	103.4	18.7	8.9	13.8	13.1	4.75	4.75	-24.5	69.3	147.1	...	...	-5.8	215.8	210.0	...	...	...	...
2,942	62.5	26.9	26.6	37.9	42.6	5.12	5.12	14.8	77.0	190.0	...	...	3.4	248.6	233.1	...	...	...	...
-4,414	41.8	30.1	41.1	43.5	59.3	0.86	0.86	47.6	101.4	272.2	...	...	12.1	319.0	256.5	...	...	...	...
3,767	59.0	21.8	39.5	36.1	53.8	5.03	5.03	13.0	121.1	279.7	...	...	-5.4	324.6	245.3	...	...	...	...
11,482	64.8	16.4	41.2	32.8	54.0	1.93	1.93	48.7	109.3	357.2	...	...	64.7	396.6	328.3	...	...	...	...

2010 BEST'S KEY RATING GUIDE — LIFE/HEALTH EDITION
ANNUAL STATEMENT DATA FOR YEARS 2005 – 2009
Data in U.S. Dollars

Column key: COMPANY NAME / Ultimate Parent Association / Principal Officer / Mailing Address / Dom. : Began Bus. : Struct. : Mktg. / Specialty / Phone # / AMB# / NAIC# — Best's Financial Strength Rating / FSC — Balance Sheet / Operations

---

ROYAL NEIGHBORS OF AMERICA
Cynthia A. Tidwell
President & CEO
230 Sixteenth Street
Rock Island, IL 61201
IL : 1895 : Fraternal : Agency
Ann, Trad Life, Univ Life
800-627-4762
AMB# 007010 NAIC# 57657

Best's Financial Strength Rating: **A-** — Rating Outlook: Stable — **FSC VIII**

Data Year	Bonds (%)	Mort. Loans & R.E. (%)	Com & Pref. Stock (%)	All Other Assets (%)	Total Assets ($000)	Life Reserves (%)	Health Reserves %)	Ann Res. & Dep. Liabilities (%)	All Other Liabilities (%)	Capital & Surplus ($000)	Direct Premiums Written ($000)	Net Premiums Written & Deposits ($000)	Operating Cash Flow ($000)	NOG Before Taxes ($000)	NOG After Taxes ($000)	Net Income ($000)
'05	63.5	19.8	11.2	5.4	629,201	65.2	1.6	24.4	8.8	182,287	44,102	44,167	6,546	1,492	1,492	2,849
'06	62.4	19.8	11.3	6.5	647,990	65.8	0.3	25.3	8.6	211,148	92,760	29,893	7,423	20,713	20,713	23,774
'07	66.0	19.2	9.4	5.4	683,224	64.3	0.4	29.2	6.2	244,359	127,353	51,329	42,798	22,119	22,119	35,316
'08	67.6	20.6	5.6	6.2	671,601	61.0	0.4	31.9	6.7	213,503	133,868	58,030	18,544	11,844	11,844	10,414
'09	68.6	18.0	6.8	6.5	719,165	56.1	0.3	38.5	5.1	221,546	153,597	83,423	33,418	2,365	2,365	99

Rating History: A-, 03/01/10; A-, 04/14/09; A-, 04/28/08; A-, 03/29/07; A-, 05/24/06

ROYAL STATE NATIONAL INS CO
Mutual Benefit Trust
Douglas Murata
President & CEO
819 South Beretania Street, Suite 100
Honolulu, HI 96813
HI : 1961 : Stock : Agency
Group A&H, Group Life
808-539-1600
AMB# 007012 NAIC# 68551

Best's Financial Strength Rating: **B+** — Rating Outlook: Stable — **FSC VI**

Data Year	Bonds (%)	Mort. Loans & R.E. (%)	Com & Pref. Stock (%)	All Other Assets (%)	Total Assets ($000)	Life Reserves (%)	Health Reserves %)	Ann Res. & Dep. Liabilities (%)	All Other Liabilities (%)	Capital & Surplus ($000)	Direct Premiums Written ($000)	Net Premiums Written & Deposits ($000)	Operating Cash Flow ($000)	NOG Before Taxes ($000)	NOG After Taxes ($000)	Net Income ($000)
'05	85.6	...	6.6	7.8	46,335	59.4	34.9	0.4	5.3	26,845	5,520	5,342	1,511	1,420	1,237	1,243
'06	85.1	...	9.7	5.1	47,086	60.5	32.1	0.5	7.0	28,010	5,230	5,057	434	1,776	1,528	1,525
'07	81.8	...	11.1	7.1	48,679	59.2	32.1	0.4	8.3	29,271	5,767	5,860	1,049	1,729	1,566	1,697
'08	70.9	...	9.0	20.1	47,145	56.8	37.8	0.5	4.9	27,152	6,285	6,363	78	189	51	-452
'09	81.4	...	9.8	8.8	48,077	55.6	34.8	0.4	9.2	27,786	6,173	6,023	718	815	774	641

Rating History: B+, 02/05/10; B+, 01/27/09; B+, 10/22/07; B+, 11/09/06; B+, 11/14/05

S.USA LIFE INSURANCE COMPANY
SBLI USA Mutual Life Insurance Co., Inc
Vikki L. Pryor
President & CEO
P.O. Box 1050
Newark, NJ 07101
AZ : 1995 : Stock : Not Available
Life, Group Life
877-725-4375
AMB# 060110 NAIC# 60183

Best's Financial Strength Rating: **B+** — Rating Outlook: Negative — **FSC VIII**

Data Year	Bonds (%)	Mort. Loans & R.E. (%)	Com & Pref. Stock (%)	All Other Assets (%)	Total Assets ($000)	Life Reserves (%)	Health Reserves %)	Ann Res. & Dep. Liabilities (%)	All Other Liabilities (%)	Capital & Surplus ($000)	Direct Premiums Written ($000)	Net Premiums Written & Deposits ($000)	Operating Cash Flow ($000)	NOG Before Taxes ($000)	NOG After Taxes ($000)	Net Income ($000)
'05	64.0	...	...	36.0	15,355	28.4	0.1	...	71.5	11,402	1,879	1,397	2,971	-3,148	-3,148	-3,148
'06	54.9	...	...	45.1	17,399	52.7	4.6	0.4	42.4	13,776	2,216	984	1,983	-4,626	-4,626	-4,626
'07	57.6	...	...	42.4	17,333	74.1	0.5	1.2	24.2	14,013	2,460	1,339	-7	-1,754	-1,754	-1,754
'08	61.7	...	...	38.3	16,053	70.9	0.4	1.1	27.7	11,364	2,404	1,115	-1,224	-2,655	-2,655	-2,655
'09	68.6	...	...	31.4	14,340	76.7	0.4	5.3	17.7	9,488	2,459	1,658	-1,288	-1,824	-1,824	-1,824

Rating History: B+ g, 06/08/10; B++g, 06/08/09; A- g, 05/01/08; A- g, 03/27/07; A- g, 05/11/06

SABINE LIFE INS CO'
Floyd J. Giblin
President
610 San Antonio Avenue
Many, LA 71449-0119
LA : 1939 : Stock : Not Available
318-256-2812
AMB# 007970 NAIC# 76937

Best's Financial Strength Rating: **NR-1**

Data Year	Bonds (%)	Mort. Loans & R.E. (%)	Com & Pref. Stock (%)	All Other Assets (%)	Total Assets ($000)	Life Reserves (%)	Health Reserves %)	Ann Res. & Dep. Liabilities (%)	All Other Liabilities (%)	Capital & Surplus ($000)	Direct Premiums Written ($000)	Net Premiums Written & Deposits ($000)	Operating Cash Flow ($000)	NOG Before Taxes ($000)	NOG After Taxes ($000)	Net Income ($000)
'05	56.0	11.9	9.6	22.5	1,690	...	...	...	100.0	343	91	91	...	-40	-40	-39
'06	75.0	11.6	...	13.4	1,660	...	...	...	100.0	336	89	89	...	-41	-41	-34
'07	58.1	7.4	...	34.6	1,627	...	...	...	100.0	312	76	76	...	-31	-31	-31
'08	60.1	8.1	...	31.8	1,664	...	...	...	100.0	303	161	161	...	-31	-31	-28
'09	65.7	7.9	...	26.3	1,643	...	...	...	100.0	251	124	124	...	-52	-52	-52

Rating History: NR-1, 06/10/10; NR-1, 06/12/09; NR-1, 06/12/08; NR-1, 06/08/07; NR-1, 06/07/06

SAFEGUARD HEALTH PLANS NV CORP
MetLife Inc
Michael H. Schwartz
President
18210 Crane Nest Drive, 3rd Floor
Tampa, FL 33647
NV : Stock : Not Available
Inactive
949-425-4300
AMB# 064900 NAIC# 95747

Best's Financial Strength Rating: **NR-3**

Data Year	Bonds (%)	Mort. Loans & R.E. (%)	Com & Pref. Stock (%)	All Other Assets (%)	Total Assets ($000)	Life Reserves (%)	Health Reserves %)	Ann Res. & Dep. Liabilities (%)	All Other Liabilities (%)	Capital & Surplus ($000)	Direct Premiums Written ($000)	Net Premiums Written & Deposits ($000)	Operating Cash Flow ($000)	NOG Before Taxes ($000)	NOG After Taxes ($000)	Net Income ($000)
'05	...	...	...	...	...	...	...	...	...	...	...	...	...	...	...	...
'06	...	...	...	...	...	...	...	...	...	...	...	...	...	...	...	...
'07	...	...	...	100.0	299	...	7.3	...	92.7	272	21	21	-920	-38	-20	-20
'08	...	...	...	100.0	288	...	...	...	100.0	244	...	...	-10	-43	-35	-35
'09	67.9	...	...	32.1	271	...	...	...	100.0	251	...	...	-22	-3	4	4

Rating History: NR-3, 05/28/09; NR-2, 02/20/09; NR-2, 06/05/08

SAFEGUARD HEALTH PLANS (CA)
MetLife Inc
Robin Muck
President
95 Enterprise
Aliso Viejo, CA 92656
CA : 1974 : Stock : Broker
Dental
949-425-4300
AMB# 068512

Best's Financial Strength Rating: **A u** — Under Review Implication: Negative — **FSC VII**

Data Year	Bonds (%)	Mort. Loans & R.E. (%)	Com & Pref. Stock (%)	All Other Assets (%)	Total Assets ($000)	Life Reserves (%)	Health Reserves %)	Ann Res. & Dep. Liabilities (%)	All Other Liabilities (%)	Capital & Surplus ($000)	Direct Premiums Written ($000)	Net Premiums Written & Deposits ($000)	Operating Cash Flow ($000)	NOG Before Taxes ($000)	NOG After Taxes ($000)	Net Income ($000)
'05	...	...	...	100.0	45,155	...	...	...	100.0	35,460	100,356	100,356	5,404	8,109	10,558	10,558
'06	...	...	...	100.0	40,035	...	...	...	100.0	27,610	105,891	105,891	-845	14,356	8,521	8,521
'07	...	...	...	100.0	38,464	...	...	...	100.0	27,892	101,767	101,767	47	15,085	8,938	8,938
'08	...	...	...	100.0	107,154	...	...	...	100.0	84,614	88,317	88,317	11,201	7,871	5,129	5,129
'09	...	...	...	100.0	103,073	...	...	...	100.0	88,504	100,362	100,362	-5,071	5,229	3,352	3,352

Rating History: A u, 02/09/10; A, 05/28/09; NR-2, 02/20/09; NR-2, 06/05/08; B- pd, 07/16/07

SAFEGUARD HEALTH PLANS (FL)
MetLife Inc
Michael H. Schwartz
President
95 Enterprise
Aliso Viejo, CA 92656
FL : 1990 : Stock : Broker
Dental
949-425-4300
AMB# 064671 NAIC# 52009

Best's Financial Strength Rating: **A u** — Under Review Implication: Negative — **FSC IV**

Data Year	Bonds (%)	Mort. Loans & R.E. (%)	Com & Pref. Stock (%)	All Other Assets (%)	Total Assets ($000)	Life Reserves (%)	Health Reserves %)	Ann Res. & Dep. Liabilities (%)	All Other Liabilities (%)	Capital & Surplus ($000)	Direct Premiums Written ($000)	Net Premiums Written & Deposits ($000)	Operating Cash Flow ($000)	NOG Before Taxes ($000)	NOG After Taxes ($000)	Net Income ($000)
'05	7.2	...	...	92.8	2,017	...	18.4	...	81.6	1,109	12,525	12,525	-81	1,901	1,264	1,264
'06	9.4	...	...	90.6	1,501	...	24.2	...	75.8	352	9,490	9,490	-402	-463	-292	-292
'07	3.5	...	...	96.5	2,937	...	36.8	...	63.2	1,411	10,543	10,543	1,343	-442	-304	-304
'08	10.0	...	...	90.0	5,550	...	20.4	...	79.6	2,864	13,317	13,317	2,124	2,011	1,301	1,301
'09	4.1	...	...	95.9	7,356	...	33.0	...	67.0	5,049	12,282	12,282	1,789	-2,971	-2,947	-2,947

Rating History: A u, 02/09/10; A, 05/28/09; NR-2, 02/20/09; NR-2, 06/05/08; NR-5, 06/21/07

SAFEGUARD HEALTH PLANS (TX)
MetLife Inc
Michael H. Schwartz
President
18210 Crane Nest Drive, 3rd Floor
Tampa, FL 33647
TX : 1987 : Stock : Broker
Dental
972-364-5000
AMB# 064460 NAIC# 95051

Best's Financial Strength Rating: **A u** — Under Review Implication: Negative — **FSC IV**

Data Year	Bonds (%)	Mort. Loans & R.E. (%)	Com & Pref. Stock (%)	All Other Assets (%)	Total Assets ($000)	Life Reserves (%)	Health Reserves %)	Ann Res. & Dep. Liabilities (%)	All Other Liabilities (%)	Capital & Surplus ($000)	Direct Premiums Written ($000)	Net Premiums Written & Deposits ($000)	Operating Cash Flow ($000)	NOG Before Taxes ($000)	NOG After Taxes ($000)	Net Income ($000)
'05	3.1	...	...	96.9	2,440	...	17.9	...	82.1	1,401	9,764	9,764	355	289	172	172
'06	2.8	...	...	97.2	2,796	...	14.9	...	85.1	1,386	11,168	11,168	303	140	53	53
'07	8.0	...	...	92.0	4,527	...	7.9	...	92.1	847	11,894	11,894	1,655	-654	-458	-458
'08	15.5	...	...	84.5	8,306	...	10.5	...	89.5	5,862	12,823	12,823	1,244	-290	-277	-277
'09	6.4	...	...	93.6	7,562	...	54.2	...	45.8	6,358	13,420	13,420	1,418	-188	-163	-163

Rating History: A u, 02/09/10; A, 05/28/09; NR-2, 02/20/09; NR-2, 06/05/08; NR-5, 04/17/07

SAFEHEALTH LIFE INS CO
MetLife Inc
Michael H. Schwartz
President & CEO
18210 Crane Nest Dr., 3rd Floor
Tampa, FL 33647
CA : 1971 : Stock : Not Available
Group A&H
949-425-4300
AMB# 008221 NAIC# 79014

Best's Financial Strength Rating: **NR-2**

Data Year	Bonds (%)	Mort. Loans & R.E. (%)	Com & Pref. Stock (%)	All Other Assets (%)	Total Assets ($000)	Life Reserves (%)	Health Reserves %)	Ann Res. & Dep. Liabilities (%)	All Other Liabilities (%)	Capital & Surplus ($000)	Direct Premiums Written ($000)	Net Premiums Written & Deposits ($000)	Operating Cash Flow ($000)	NOG Before Taxes ($000)	NOG After Taxes ($000)	Net Income ($000)
'05	56.2	...	...	43.8	24,789	...	65.0	...	35.0	16,206	68,095	68,095	209	2,897	2,030	1,984
'06	52.3	...	...	47.7	22,987	...	68.9	...	31.1	15,303	74,740	74,772	-2,447	1,993	1,422	1,418
'07	37.5	...	...	62.5	27,770	...	46.4	...	53.6	17,882	83,344	83,344	4,978	3,628	2,558	2,558
'08	56.5	...	0.1	43.4	29,988	...	59.7	...	40.3	21,075	85,674	85,674	1,454	2,488	1,790	1,789
'09	74.9	...	...	25.1	19,070	...	53.9	...	46.1	14,881	38,582	38,582	-9,233	-173	-210	-203

Rating History: NR-2, 05/28/09; NR-2, 02/20/09; NR-2, 06/05/08; NR-1, 06/08/07; NR-1, 06/07/06

BEST'S PROFITABILITY, LEVERAGE AND LIQUIDITY TESTS 2005 – 2009

Data in U.S. Dollars

	Profitability Tests							Leverage Tests						Liquidity Tests					
Un-Realized Capital Gains ($000)	Benefits Paid to NPW & Dep (%)	Comm. & Expenses to NPW & Dep (%)	NOG to Total Assets (%)	NOG to Total Rev (%)	Operating Return on Equity (%)	Net Yield (%)	Total Return (%)	Change in NPW & Dep (%)	NPW & Dep to Capital (X)	Capital & Surplus to Liabilities (%)	Surplus Relief (%)	Reins Leverage (%)	Change in Capital (%)	Quick Liquidity (%)	Current Liquidity (%)	Non-Invest Grade Bonds to Capital (%)	Delinq. & Foreclosed Mortgages to Capital (%)	Mort. & Credit Tenant Loans & R.E. to Capital (%)	Affiliated Invest to Capital (%)
1,756	89.5	72.7	0.2	1.9	0.8	5.79	6.36	118.0	0.2	45.1	0.1	0.6	1.9	84.3	94.8	7.1	...	63.7	3.3
4,486	106.4	33.4	3.2	22.3	10.5	5.58	6.84	-32.3	0.1	53.0	13.8	10.4	14.8	81.6	95.2	5.3	...	57.0	1.3
-4,344	68.2	29.8	3.3	18.9	9.7	5.76	7.19	71.7	0.2	60.4	12.1	9.0	14.6	87.3	101.5	2.6	...	50.9	1.0
-31,814	66.6	45.0	1.7	9.8	5.2	5.65	0.83	13.1	0.3	47.0	11.9	11.4	-16.6	76.5	90.0	5.1	...	64.5	1.2
11,550	37.4	46.4	0.3	1.7	1.1	5.47	6.86	43.8	0.4	47.8	10.1	11.2	8.3	82.8	97.0	3.8	...	55.6	1.1
Principal Lines of Business: IndAnn (55.3%), OrdLife (35.4%), IndA&H (9.3%)														Principal States: TX (17.7%), IL (11.3%), CA (10.9%), PA (7.7%), WI (5.9%)					
-61	60.0	46.1	2.7	10.5	4.0	4.08	4.01	9.7	0.2	140.0	...	1.6	0.1	106.3	202.3	...	...	...	6.9
301	63.2	52.8	3.3	21.3	5.6	4.47	5.39	-5.3	0.2	154.0	...	1.4	5.4	206.9	215.6	0.4	...	...	6.9
410	64.2	41.8	3.3	19.7	5.5	4.36	5.68	15.9	0.2	161.1	...	1.5	5.2	204.9	217.7	0.3	...	...	7.5
-1,219	56.5	43.2	0.1	0.6	0.2	4.02	0.43	8.6	0.2	136.8	...	1.1	-9.3	192.8	205.6	1.4	...	...	7.3
667	65.3	50.1	1.6	10.1	2.8	3.24	4.63	-5.3	0.2	143.5	...	0.8	4.0	186.2	204.7	5.4	...	...	5.9
Principal Lines of Business: GrpA&H (50.8%), GrpLife (39.4%), OrdLife (8.5%), IndA&H (1.2%)														Principal States: HI (99.9%)					
...	11.3	312.4	-22.8	-99.9	-27.4	3.14	3.15	28.4	0.1	288.7	0.5	5.0	-1.3	329.7	331.3	...	...	...	...
...	36.8	539.6	-28.2	-99.9	-36.7	2.82	2.82	-29.6	0.1	380.7	4.0	8.8	20.8	576.9	580.6	...	...	...	...
...	26.3	220.8	-10.1	-74.5	-12.6	3.90	3.91	36.2	0.1	424.0	1.6	8.6	1.8	559.7	571.3	...	...	...	...
...	72.6	287.6	-15.9	-99.9	-20.9	3.29	3.29	-16.7	0.1	242.6	1.9	16.0	-19.0	379.1	379.1	...	...	...	...
...	46.7	142.5	-12.0	-88.9	-17.5	2.97	2.97	48.7	0.2	195.8	2.2	27.1	-16.5	304.4	304.4	...	...	...	...
Principal Lines of Business: OrdLife (52.9%), GrpAnn (32.8%), GrpLife (12.3%), GrpA&H (1.5%), IndA&H (0.5%)														Principal States: OH (20.0%), PA (10.2%), MA (8.9%), CA (7.9%), FL (7.4%)					
0	60.0	165.8	-2.3	-23.6	-10.6	...	...	-9.3	0.3	27.6	...	...	-15.3	...	...	...	...	55.2	...
-1	73.9	165.4	-2.5	-24.0	-12.2	...	...	-2.2	0.3	25.5	...	...	-7.6	...	...	...	...	56.9	...
...	90.8	181.4	-1.9	-19.2	-9.7	...	...	-15.5	0.2	23.8	...	...	-7.2	...	...	...	...	38.2	...
...	47.0	86.5	-1.9	-13.5	-10.2	...	...	112.8	0.5	22.4	...	...	-2.8	...	...	...	...	44.2	...
...	69.3	97.8	-3.1	-27.7	-18.7	...	...	-22.9	0.5	18.1	...	...	-17.1	...	...	...	...	51.6	...
Principal Lines of Business: OrdLife (59.4%), IndLife (40.6%)																			
...	...	...	...	...	...	...	...	...	...	...	...	...	...	...	...	...	...	...	...
...	...	...	...	...	...	...	...	...	...	...	...	...	...	...	...	...	...	...	...
...	100.0	230.4	...	-63.2	...	...	...	...	0.1	993.2	...	...	...	999.9	999.9	...	...	...	...
...	...	...	-12.0	-99.9	-13.7	0.86	0.86	-99.9	...	556.2	...	...	-10.2	666.5	667.6	...	...	...	...
...	...	...	1.5	92.9	1.7	1.62	1.62	...	...	999.9	...	...	2.9	999.9	999.9	...	...	...	...
...	70.8	21.4	28.1	10.5	37.2	2.67	2.67	34.3	2.8	365.8	...	...	66.3	130.8	130.8	...	...	...	...
...	65.2	21.6	20.0	8.0	27.0	2.73	2.73	5.5	3.8	222.2	...	...	-22.1	94.4	94.4	...	...	...	...
...	58.0	27.6	22.8	8.7	32.2	3.30	3.30	-3.9	3.6	263.8	...	...	1.0	109.6	109.6	...	...	...	...
...	60.4	31.6	7.0	5.8	9.1	1.50	1.50	-13.2	1.0	375.4	...	...	203.4	91.1	91.1	...	...	...	...
...	69.9	24.9	3.2	3.3	3.9	1.16	1.16	13.6	1.1	607.5	...	...	4.6	93.7	93.7	...	...	...	...
Principal Lines of Business: CompHosp/Med (72.0%), Medicaid (28.0%)																			
...	55.4	29.7	60.9	10.0	130.0	0.40	0.40	-3.0	11.3	122.2	...	...	32.7	200.8	202.5	...	...	...	...
...	65.1	39.9	-16.6	-3.1	-39.9	0.27	0.27	-24.2	27.0	30.6	...	...	-68.3	123.2	124.5	...	...	...	...
...	79.8	24.5	-13.7	-2.9	-34.5	0.60	0.60	11.1	7.5	92.5	...	...	300.8	196.3	199.8	...	...	...	...
...	74.4	10.3	30.7	9.8	60.9	1.24	1.24	26.3	4.6	106.6	...	...	103.0	287.6	302.5	...	...	...	...
...	92.7	31.7	-45.7	-24.2	-74.5	0.08	0.08	-7.8	2.4	218.9	...	...	76.3	526.2	527.3	...	...	...	...
Principal Lines of Business: Dental (100.0%)														Principal States: FL (100.0%)					
...	57.0	40.2	7.6	1.8	14.6	0.75	0.75	8.9	7.0	134.9	...	...	45.9	240.2	244.0	...	...	...	...
...	68.4	30.5	2.0	0.5	3.8	0.85	0.85	14.4	8.1	98.2	...	...	-1.1	204.3	207.8	...	...	...	...
...	73.8	31.9	-12.5	-3.8	-41.1	0.90	0.90	6.5	14.0	23.0	...	...	-38.9	135.9	139.4	...	...	...	...
...	70.1	32.6	-4.3	-2.2	-8.3	0.80	0.80	7.8	2.2	239.8	...	...	592.2	310.2	327.4	...	...	...	...
...	72.9	28.6	-2.1	-1.2	-2.7	0.24	0.23	4.7	2.1	527.7	...	...	8.5	999.9	999.9	...	...	...	...
Principal Lines of Business: Dental (100.0%)														Principal States: TX (100.0%)					
...	83.6	13.4	7.7	2.9	13.0	1.80	1.61	11.9	4.2	190.6	...	...	7.3	309.2	329.9	...	...	...	...
...	79.4	19.1	6.0	1.9	9.0	2.59	2.57	9.8	4.9	201.3	...	...	-5.5	342.8	367.3	...	...	...	...
...	77.6	18.7	10.1	3.0	15.4	3.33	3.33	11.5	4.6	182.6	...	...	16.8	342.5	362.6	...	...	...	...
...	79.3	18.7	6.2	2.1	9.2	2.40	2.39	2.8	4.1	238.0	...	...	17.7	345.4	373.8	...	...	...	...
...	78.5	23.6	-0.9	-0.5	-1.2	2.52	2.56	-55.0	2.6	359.8	...	...	-29.3	530.0	559.9	0.2	...	...	...
Principal Lines of Business: GrpA&H (100.0%)														Principal States: CA (47.1%), TX (43.6%), FL (7.6%)					

Column headings: COMPANY NAME, Ultimate Parent Association, Principal Officer, Mailing Address, Dom. : Began Bus. : Struct. : Mktg., Specialty, Phone #, AMB#, NAIC# | Best's Financial Strength Rating, FSC | Balance Sheet | Operations

SAGICOR CAPITAL LIFE INS CO
Sagicor Financial Corporation
Dr. M. Patricia Downes-Grant
President & Chief Executive Officer
Sagicor Financial Centre
St. Michael, Barbados
BS : 1958 : Stock : Not Available
Life, Annuity, Health
242-322-4195
AMB# 086658

Best's Financial Strength Rating: **A** — Rating Outlook: Negative — **FSC IX**

Data Year	Bonds (%)	Mort. Loans & R.E. (%)	Com & Pref. Stock (%)	All Other Assets (%)	Total Assets ($000)	Life Reserves (%)	Health Reserves (%)	Ann Res. & Dep. Liabilities (%)	All Other Liabilities (%)	Capital & Surplus ($000)	Direct Premiums Written ($000)	Net Premiums Written & Deposits ($000)	Operating Cash Flow ($000)	NOG Before Taxes ($000)	NOG After Taxes ($000)	Net Income ($000)
'05	41.8	11.2	11.0	36.1	115,103	83.6	...	...	16.4	29,637	27,682	25,860	...	-4,607	-4,289	-4,289
'06	65.1	8.2	2.1	24.6	124,742	78.0	...	...	22.0	27,137	34,600	27,920	11,868	4,024	5,276	5,276
'07	67.4	9.6	1.1	21.9	137,256	66.1	...	...	33.9	41,347	37,474	28,721	2,645	19,609	15,929	15,929
'08	68.3	8.6	0.6	22.4	196,626	68.4	...	...	31.6	54,392	50,730	38,834	21,580	16,322	16,101	16,101
'09	67.9	9.2	0.5	22.4	216,586	66.0	...	...	34.0	67,176	47,825	35,972	-9,235	12,955	11,816	11,816

Rating History: A g, 05/04/09; A g, 02/19/08; A g, 06/18/07; A g, 05/08/06; A g, 10/21/05

SAGICOR LIFE INC.
Sagicor Financial Corporation
Dr. M. Patricia Downes-Grant
President & CEO
Sagicor Corporate Centre, Wildey
St. Michael, Barbados
BB : 1851 : Stock : Not Available
Life, Health, Annuity
246-467-7500
AMB# 086569

Best's Financial Strength Rating: **A** — Rating Outlook: Negative — **FSC IX**

Data Year	Bonds (%)	Mort. Loans & R.E. (%)	Com & Pref. Stock (%)	All Other Assets (%)	Total Assets ($000)	Life Reserves (%)	Health Reserves (%)	Ann Res. & Dep. Liabilities (%)	All Other Liabilities (%)	Capital & Surplus ($000)	Direct Premiums Written ($000)	Net Premiums Written & Deposits ($000)	Operating Cash Flow ($000)	NOG Before Taxes ($000)	NOG After Taxes ($000)	Net Income ($000)
'05	49.1	11.2	6.9	32.8	3,272,068	44.3	0.7	16.4	38.6	390,507	...	320,910	179,442	98,949	84,012	98,063
'06	48.2	15.2	6.9	29.7	2,532,036	34.4	1.1	19.8	44.6	429,426	...	366,651	63,183	113,645	95,278	95,278
'07	48.3	16.3	6.5	29.0	2,680,133	33.6	1.2	20.1	45.1	443,411	...	393,151	-2,495	123,217	103,074	103,074
'08	46.9	17.4	3.7	32.1	3,008,396	31.4	1.8	21.0	45.8	441,115	...	531,348	200,986	151,469	132,795	132,795
'09	49.4	16.3	3.2	31.1	3,139,728	30.8	1.6	23.2	44.4	510,529	...	456,675	90,513	112,618	95,966	95,966

Rating History: A g, 05/04/09; A g, 02/19/08; A g, 06/18/07; A g, 05/08/06; A g, 10/21/05

SAGICOR LIFE INSURANCE COMPANY
Sagicor Financial Corporation
Kendrick A. Marshall
President & CEO
4343 North Scottsdale Road, Suite 300
Scottsdale, AZ 85251-3347
TX : 1954 : Stock : Agency
Ann, Trad Life, Univ Life
480-425-5100
AMB# 006057 NAIC# 60445

Best's Financial Strength Rating: **A-** — Rating Outlook: Negative — **FSC VI**

Data Year	Bonds (%)	Mort. Loans & R.E. (%)	Com & Pref. Stock (%)	All Other Assets (%)	Total Assets ($000)	Life Reserves (%)	Health Reserves (%)	Ann Res. & Dep. Liabilities (%)	All Other Liabilities (%)	Capital & Surplus ($000)	Direct Premiums Written ($000)	Net Premiums Written & Deposits ($000)	Operating Cash Flow ($000)	NOG Before Taxes ($000)	NOG After Taxes ($000)	Net Income ($000)
'05	86.0	3.7	2.2	8.0	501,392	28.9	0.1	41.3	29.8	42,279	23,375	26,439	1,966	3,801	4,307	4,788
'06	85.4	4.5	2.6	7.5	479,441	29.4	0.1	41.3	29.2	33,906	16,251	18,288	-21,109	-1,414	-668	-1,208
'07	80.6	5.1	3.0	11.2	527,926	37.6	0.1	35.4	26.9	35,142	14,172	13,399	-5,700	-4,550	-3,689	-3,523
'08	80.9	5.4	3.2	10.5	538,779	39.0	0.1	34.8	26.1	29,188	35,032	36,729	15,688	-17,461	-19,058	-21,226
'09	82.4	4.1	2.0	11.5	676,694	38.3	0.0	40.2	21.4	38,643	154,269	154,662	133,087	-17,483	-17,628	-23,761

Rating History: A-, 05/04/09; A-, 02/19/08; B++, 06/18/07; B++, 05/08/06; B++, 10/21/05

SAGICOR LIFE JAMAICA LIMITED
Sagicor Financial Corporation
Richard O. Byles
President & CEO
28-48 Barbados Avenue
Kingston 5, Jamaica
JM : 1970 : Stock : Agency
Life, Personal Accident, Annuity
876-929-8920
AMB# 086086

Best's Financial Strength Rating: **A** — Rating Outlook: Negative — **FSC IX**

Data Year	Bonds (%)	Mort. Loans & R.E. (%)	Com & Pref. Stock (%)	All Other Assets (%)	Total Assets ($000)	Life Reserves (%)	Health Reserves (%)	Ann Res. & Dep. Liabilities (%)	All Other Liabilities (%)	Capital & Surplus ($000)	Direct Premiums Written ($000)	Net Premiums Written & Deposits ($000)	Operating Cash Flow ($000)	NOG Before Taxes ($000)	NOG After Taxes ($000)	Net Income ($000)
'05	32.0	19.1	...	48.9	441,208	30.5	...	...	69.5	169,524	...	116,842	15,955	49,228	38,151	44,871
'06	60.9	7.6	...	31.5	1,245,167	16.7	...	...	83.3	226,986	...	155,426	-6,062	59,746	48,089	48,089
'07	67.8	8.5	...	23.7	1,261,640	21.8	...	...	78.2	224,697	...	160,666	1,349	62,489	49,572	49,572
'08	57.0	3.1	1.6	38.2	1,570,160	5.7	...	10.2	84.1	207,199	...	270,193	129,625	69,023	46,973	52,361
'09	59.5	3.0	1.5	36.0	1,561,928	4.6	...	11.9	83.4	229,017	...	210,030	75,411	59,984	44,070	50,618

Rating History: A g, 05/04/09; A g, 02/19/08; A g, 06/18/07; A g, 05/08/06; NR-5, 04/28/05

SAGICOR LIFE CAYMAN ISLANDS
Sagicor Financial Corporation
PO Box 1087
Grand Cayman KY-1105, Cayman Islands
KY : Stock : Not Available
Life
345-949-8211
AMB# 078642

Best's Financial Strength Rating: **NR-5**

Data Year	Bonds (%)	Mort. Loans & R.E. (%)	Com & Pref. Stock (%)	All Other Assets (%)	Total Assets ($000)	Life Reserves (%)	Health Reserves (%)	Ann Res. & Dep. Liabilities (%)	All Other Liabilities (%)	Capital & Surplus ($000)	Direct Premiums Written ($000)	Net Premiums Written & Deposits ($000)	Operating Cash Flow ($000)	NOG Before Taxes ($000)	NOG After Taxes ($000)	Net Income ($000)
'05	38.8	4.0	2.5	54.6	132,583	29.8	...	3.7	66.5	30,395	...	9,339	...	630	430	2,062
'06	45.1	3.6	...	51.4	145,958	15.7	...	9.5	74.8	37,192	...	27,166	-2,310	4,464	4,464	5,615
'07	46.0	3.3	...	50.6	123,342	14.1	...	16.3	69.6	33,384	...	21,970	6,000	3,174	3,174	4,535
'08	46.8	2.1	...	51.1	204,852	9.2	...	35.9	54.9	31,575	...	26,198	8,170	3,411	3,411	2,553
'09	...	...	...	...	...	...	...	...	...	...	...	...	...	...	...	...

Rating History: NR-5, 07/08/09; NR-5, 05/12/08

SAMARITAN HEALTH PLANS INC[2]
Larry A. Mullins
President
815 NW 9th Street, Suite 103
Corvallis, OR 97330
OR : 2005 : Stock : Not Available
Health
541-768-5328
AMB# 064906 NAIC# 12257

Best's Financial Strength Rating: **NR-5**

Data Year	Bonds (%)	Mort. Loans & R.E. (%)	Com & Pref. Stock (%)	All Other Assets (%)	Total Assets ($000)	Life Reserves (%)	Health Reserves (%)	Ann Res. & Dep. Liabilities (%)	All Other Liabilities (%)	Capital & Surplus ($000)	Direct Premiums Written ($000)	Net Premiums Written & Deposits ($000)	Operating Cash Flow ($000)	NOG Before Taxes ($000)	NOG After Taxes ($000)	Net Income ($000)
'05	...	...	...	...	...	...	...	...	...	...	...	...	...	...	...	...
'06	51.0	...	...	49.0	10,465	...	86.8	...	13.2	3,952	29,172	29,172	5,902	1,459	1,204	1,204
'07	69.8	...	...	30.2	9,708	...	79.3	...	20.7	4,313	32,793	32,437	-1,720	-55	56	56
'08	40.8	...	...	59.2	13,440	...	86.8	...	13.2	6,490	46,690	46,690	1,271	1,263	816	834
'09	58.0	...	6.0	36.0	15,692	...	73.2	...	26.8	6,275	53,586	53,586	3,768	434	263	270

Rating History: NR-5, 05/20/10; NR-5, 09/11/09; NR-5, 07/14/08; NR-5, 06/29/07

SAN FRANCISCO HEALTH PLAN
John Grgurina, Jr.
President & CEO
201 Third Street, 7th Floor
San Francisco, CA 94103
CA : 1996 : Stock : Not Available
Medicaid
415-547-7818
AMB# 064582

Best's Financial Strength Rating: **NR-5**

Data Year	Bonds (%)	Mort. Loans & R.E. (%)	Com & Pref. Stock (%)	All Other Assets (%)	Total Assets ($000)	Life Reserves (%)	Health Reserves (%)	Ann Res. & Dep. Liabilities (%)	All Other Liabilities (%)	Capital & Surplus ($000)	Direct Premiums Written ($000)	Net Premiums Written & Deposits ($000)	Operating Cash Flow ($000)	NOG Before Taxes ($000)	NOG After Taxes ($000)	Net Income ($000)
'05	...	...	...	100.0	44,580	...	...	...	100.0	29,237	81,780	81,780	1,156	11,365	11,365	11,365
'06	...	...	...	100.0	46,698	...	...	...	100.0	31,730	87,924	87,924	3,202	2,493	2,493	2,493
'07	...	...	...	100.0	46,637	...	...	...	100.0	31,317	92,541	92,541	109	-413	-413	-413
'08	...	...	...	100.0	59,512	...	...	...	100.0	34,095	104,377	104,377	11,638	2,778	2,778	2,778
'09	...	...	...	100.0	77,827	...	...	...	100.0	30,971	109,758	109,758	17,878	-3,124	-3,124	-3,124

Rating History: NR-5, 03/23/10; NR-5, 04/08/09; NR-5, 03/11/08; NR-5, 04/03/07; NR-5, 04/07/06

SAN JOAQUIN HEALTH COMMISSION
John Hackworth
President
7751 Manthey
French Camp, CA 95231
CA : 1996 : Non-Profit : Broker
Group A&H, Medicaid
209-942-6300
AMB# 064006

Best's Financial Strength Rating: **NR-5**

Data Year	Bonds (%)	Mort. Loans & R.E. (%)	Com & Pref. Stock (%)	All Other Assets (%)	Total Assets ($000)	Life Reserves (%)	Health Reserves (%)	Ann Res. & Dep. Liabilities (%)	All Other Liabilities (%)	Capital & Surplus ($000)	Direct Premiums Written ($000)	Net Premiums Written & Deposits ($000)	Operating Cash Flow ($000)	NOG Before Taxes ($000)	NOG After Taxes ($000)	Net Income ($000)
'05	...	0.0	...	100.0	54,802	...	...	...	100.0	41,612	83,316	83,316	289	2,841	2,841	2,841
'06	...	...	...	100.0	57,965	...	...	...	100.0	43,143	84,203	84,203	1,946	1,531	1,531	1,531
'07	...	22.6	...	77.4	55,035	...	...	...	100.0	40,597	87,992	87,992	-2,954	-2,546	-2,546	-2,546
'08	...	24.7	...	75.3	49,100	...	...	...	100.0	34,243	98,752	98,752	-4,609	-6,354	-6,354	-6,354
'09	...	...	...	100.0	53,003	...	...	...	100.0	36,296	127,077	127,077	-7,223	2,053	2,053	2,053

Rating History: NR-5, 03/23/10; NR-5, 04/08/09; NR-5, 03/11/08; NR-5, 04/03/07; NR-5, 04/28/06

SAN MATEO HEALTH COMMISSION
Michael W. Murray
CEO
701 Gateway Boulevard, Suite 400
South San Francisco, CA 94080
CA : 1987 : Stock : Not Available
Health
650-616-0050
AMB# 064575

Best's Financial Strength Rating: **NR-5**

Data Year	Bonds (%)	Mort. Loans & R.E. (%)	Com & Pref. Stock (%)	All Other Assets (%)	Total Assets ($000)	Life Reserves (%)	Health Reserves (%)	Ann Res. & Dep. Liabilities (%)	All Other Liabilities (%)	Capital & Surplus ($000)	Direct Premiums Written ($000)	Net Premiums Written & Deposits ($000)	Operating Cash Flow ($000)	NOG Before Taxes ($000)	NOG After Taxes ($000)	Net Income ($000)
'05	...	0.1	...	99.9	41,958	...	...	...	100.0	13,835	123,792	123,792	1,978	-1,486	-1,486	-1,486
'06	...	...	...	100.0	69,684	...	...	...	100.0	16,422	229,733	229,733	26,811	2,587	2,587	2,587
'07	...	...	...	100.0	88,274	...	...	...	100.0	33,362	245,787	245,787	5,175	16,940	16,940	16,940
'08	...	...	...	100.0	98,116	...	...	...	100.0	42,453	282,599	282,599	10,632	9,092	9,092	9,092
'09	...	...	...	100.0	110,238	...	...	...	100.0	57,469	302,737	302,737	11,891	15,015	15,015	15,015

Rating History: NR-5, 05/07/10; NR-5, 05/13/09; NR-5, 05/06/08; NR-5, 05/04/07; NR-5, 06/08/06

—	Profitability Tests							Leverage Tests						Liquidity Tests					
Un-Realized Capital Gains ($000)	Benefits Paid to NPW & Dep (%)	Comm. & Expenses to NPW & Dep (%)	NOG to Total Assets (%)	NOG to Total Rev (%)	Operating Return on Equity (%)	Net Yield (%)	Total Return (%)	Change in NPW & Dep (%)	NPW & Dep to Capital (X)	Capital & Surplus to Liabilities (%)	Surplus Relief (%)	Reins Leverage (%)	Change in Capital (%)	Quick Liquidity (%)	Current Liquidity (%)	Non-Invest Grade Bonds to Capital (%)	Delinq. & Foreclosed Mortgages to Capital (%)	Mort. & Credit Tenant Loans & R.E. to Capital (%)	Affiliated Invest to Capital (%)
979	91.8	70.2	-3.7	-11.2	-13.1	5.61	5.61	-13.2	87.3	34.7	...	...	-17.3	98.5	93.1	...	...	43.3	...
-3	69.7	57.5	4.4	13.1	18.6	7.43	7.43	8.0	102.9	27.8	...	...	-8.4	96.0	102.2	...	...	37.9	...
-197	6.8	67.5	12.2	38.1	46.5	7.39	7.39	2.9	69.5	43.1	...	...	52.4	107.2	117.5	...	...	32.0	...
-2,522	44.2	56.6	9.6	28.6	33.6	6.21	6.21	35.2	71.4	38.2	...	...	31.6	109.6	113.4	...	...	31.2	...
920	51.1	47.1	5.7	24.1	19.4	5.71	5.71	-7.4	53.6	45.0	...	...	23.5	114.7	118.7	...	...	29.6	...
-27,464	70.8	52.5	3.5	14.4	22.0	10.22	10.92	10.0	82.2	14.3	...	...	12.2	69.2	95.1	...	...	93.9	6.5
-1,858	68.5	50.3	3.3	15.3	23.2	8.66	8.66	14.3	85.4	22.2	...	...	10.0	76.5	111.0	...	...	89.8	6.3
-22,921	70.1	52.2	4.0	15.2	23.6	10.17	10.17	7.2	88.7	21.4	...	...	3.3	74.2	110.9	...	...	98.5	7.0
-64,668	72.2	41.3	4.7	15.8	30.0	8.55	8.55	35.2	120.5	18.3	...	...	-0.5	67.5	106.4	...	...	118.6	7.3
13,323	75.9	50.3	3.1	12.2	20.2	9.56	9.56	-14.1	89.5	20.5	...	...	15.7	71.5	108.1	...	...	100.4	6.4
-273	132.5	27.1	0.9	9.5	11.8	5.14	5.32	-16.9	0.6	10.0	9.7	653.8	36.9	75.6	84.4	19.6	3.7	41.2	...
352	199.0	54.1	-0.1	-2.0	-1.8	5.01	5.08	-30.8	0.5	8.5	11.2	768.0	-17.7	73.3	82.7	9.2	0.7	57.8	...
-8	262.9	85.8	-0.7	-11.6	-10.7	4.56	4.72	-26.7	0.3	8.0	11.4	674.5	4.9	69.9	79.2	12.3	0.7	68.9	...
-519	99.2	52.1	-3.6	-33.7	-59.3	5.15	4.56	174.1	1.1	6.3	12.5	750.7	-18.3	67.8	77.4	34.3	...	90.1	...
131	25.5	20.5	-2.9	-9.7	-52.0	5.94	4.76	321.1	3.9	6.3	8.2	530.5	24.8	70.7	79.8	33.0	1.5	69.7	...
	Principal Lines of Business: IndAnn (62.7%), OrdLife (37.2%), GrpAnn (0.0%), GrpA&H (0.0%), IndA&H (0.0%)													Principal States: TX (16.8%), CA (11.6%), WA (8.9%), FL (8.0%), OH (6.1%)					
-12,432	54.8	59.1	9.9	20.1	28.2	24.16	27.54	38.3	68.9	62.4	...	...	68.2	53.5	85.0	...	...	49.7	0.0
16,390	52.9	58.1	5.7	20.7	24.3	9.93	9.93	33.0	68.5	24.0	...	...	33.9	83.5	92.4	...	...	41.5	0.0
-14,381	56.5	57.4	4.0	20.2	22.0	6.26	6.26	3.4	71.5	23.1	...	...	-1.0	90.8	100.6	...	...	47.9	0.0
-35,557	75.0	36.8	3.3	12.4	21.8	4.61	5.08	68.2	130.4	16.0	...	...	-7.8	77.0	94.0	...	...	23.6	0.0
13,669	67.7	52.6	2.8	13.7	20.2	5.57	6.09	-22.3	91.7	17.6	...	...	10.5	78.9	92.3	...	...	20.2	0.0
...	69.8	40.3	0.4	3.4	1.5	2.46	5.01	59.8	30.7	33.2	...	...	4.8	77.1	72.0	...	...	17.5	...
2,357	56.1	59.9	3.2	11.6	13.2	5.88	7.21	190.9	73.0	38.0	...	...	22.4	82.7	78.2	...	...	14.0	...
-796	62.1	70.3	2.4	9.1	9.0	5.79	7.40	-19.1	65.8	39.5	...	...	-10.2	81.2	77.4	...	...	12.3	...
-3,567	56.8	61.7	2.1	8.8	10.5	6.71	5.91	19.2	83.0	18.7	...	...	-5.4	65.3	73.0	...	...	13.7	...
...	...	...	...	...	...	...	...	...	...	...	...	...	...	...	...	...	...	...	...
...	...	...	...	...	...	...	...	...	...	...	...	...	...	...	...	...	...	...	...
...	88.9	7.3	...	4.1	...	...	...	...	7.4	60.7	...	15.4	...	138.2	138.2	...	...	...	...
...	94.3	7.2	0.6	0.2	1.4	5.39	5.39	11.2	7.5	80.0	...	5.2	9.2	136.1	136.1	...	...	...	...
...	92.4	5.6	7.1	1.7	15.1	4.11	4.32	43.9	7.2	93.4	...	0.9	50.4	47.6	47.6	...	...	...	...
36	92.7	6.5	1.8	0.5	4.1	0.21	0.61	14.8	8.5	66.6	...	7.6	-3.3	117.8	125.3	...	...	...	...
	Principal Lines of Business: Medicare (100.0%)													Principal States: OR (100.0%)					
...	79.1	9.2	27.3	13.6	48.2	1.68	1.68	17.1	2.8	190.6	...	...	63.6	243.4	243.4	...	...	...	...
...	91.5	9.3	5.5	2.7	8.2	2.72	2.72	7.5	2.8	212.0	...	...	8.5	225.9	225.9	...	...	...	...
...	95.0	10.8	-0.9	-0.4	-1.3	5.33	5.33	5.3	3.0	204.4	...	...	-1.3	215.0	215.0	...	...	...	...
...	94.0	12.3	5.2	2.4	8.5	4.25	4.25	12.8	3.1	134.1	...	...	8.9	160.9	160.9	...	...	...	...
...	95.6	15.2	-4.5	-2.6	-9.6	1.53	1.53	5.2	3.5	66.1	...	...	-9.2	123.7	123.7	...	...	...	...
	Principal Lines of Business: Medicaid (100.0%)																		
...	88.9	10.4	5.2	3.3	7.1	2.00	2.00	4.3	2.0	315.5	...	...	7.3	385.6	385.6	...	...	0.0	0.0
...	90.9	11.2	2.7	1.8	3.6	3.98	3.98	1.1	2.0	291.1	...	...	3.7	305.3	305.3	...	...	...	...
...	95.6	11.1	-4.5	-2.8	-6.1	4.32	4.32	4.5	2.2	281.2	...	...	-5.9	259.5	259.5	...	...	30.7	30.7
...	99.3	9.9	-12.2	-6.3	-17.0	3.10	3.10	12.2	2.9	230.5	...	...	-15.7	219.8	219.8	...	...	35.4	35.4
...	91.3	8.6	4.0	1.6	5.8	1.50	1.50	28.7	3.5	217.3	...	...	6.0	151.1	151.1	...	...	...	...
	Principal Lines of Business: Medicaid (89.9%), CompHosp/Med (10.1%)																		
...	99.5	9.3	-3.4	-1.1	-10.2	2.68	2.68	1.5	8.9	49.2	...	...	-9.7	104.5	104.5	...	...	0.4	0.4
...	101.3	7.1	4.6	1.0	17.1	7.10	7.10	85.6	14.0	30.8	...	...	18.7	104.7	104.7	...	...	...	...
...	91.9	7.9	21.4	6.5	68.1	5.49	5.49	7.0	7.4	60.8	...	...	103.2	110.6	110.6	...	...	...	...
...	90.9	6.6	9.8	3.2	24.0	2.97	2.97	15.0	6.7	76.3	...	...	27.3	120.8	120.8	...	...	...	...
...	89.6	6.6	14.4	4.9	30.1	0.58	0.58	7.1	5.3	108.9	...	...	35.4	147.7	147.7	...	...	...	...
	Principal Lines of Business: Medicaid (58.9%), Medicare (41.1%)																		

Data in U.S. Dollars

COMPANY NAME Ultimate Parent Association Principal Officer Mailing Address Dom. : Began Bus. : Struct. : Mktg. Specialty Phone # AMB# NAIC#	Best's Financial Strength Rating FSC	Data Year	Balance Sheet Bonds (%)	Mort. Loans & R.E. (%)	Com & Pref. Stock (%)	All Other Assets (%)	Total Assets ($000)	Life Reserves (%)	Health Reserves %)	Ann Res. & Dep. Liabilities (%)	All Other Liabilities (%)	Capital & Surplus ($000)	Operations Direct Premiums Written ($000)	Net Premiums Written & Deposits ($000)	Operating Cash Flow ($000)	NOG Before Taxes ($000)	NOG After Taxes ($000)	Net Income ($000)
SAN MIGUEL HEALTH PLAN Gerry Long President 100 West Broadway, Suite 4000 Long Beach, CA 90802 CA : 2007 : Stock : Not Available Medicare 562-435-3400 AMB# 064949	NR-5	'05	...	...	...	...	...	...	...	...	...	...	...	...	...	...	...	...
		'06	...	...	...	...	...	...	...	...	...	...	...	...	...	...	...	...
		'07	...	...	...	100.0	1,455	...	...	...	100.0	885	...	...	1,074	-2,130	-2,130	-2,130
		'08	...	74.5	...	25.5	5,144	...	...	...	100.0	1,735	16,060	16,060	3,639	-2,971	-2,971	-2,971
		'09	...	95.2	...	4.8	15,396	...	...	...	100.0	4,009	...	...	-73	-620	-620	-620
		Rating History: NR-5, 03/23/10; NR-5, 05/01/09; NR-5, 05/20/08																
SANFORD HEALTH PLAN Sanford Health Kelby Krabbenhoft CEO 300 Cherapa Place, Suite 201 Sioux Falls, SD 57103 SD : 1998 : Non-Profit : Agency Group A&H 605-328-6895 AMB# 064393 NAIC# 95683	NR-5	'05	55.0	...	...	45.0	19,837	...	57.3	...	42.7	9,040	66,916	65,815	835	3,464	3,394	3,394
		'06	41.0	...	...	59.0	25,760	...	59.0	...	41.0	12,511	79,909	78,595	5,963	3,368	3,307	3,307
		'07	34.9	...	...	65.1	25,317	...	59.7	...	40.3	9,703	94,335	92,659	-1,350	-1,636	-1,644	-1,644
		'08	42.8	...	...	57.2	24,396	...	61.8	...	38.2	10,228	97,976	96,702	46	204	196	196
		'09	80.5	...	...	19.5	24,420	...	55.7	...	44.3	9,524	106,403	105,044	-190	-506	-506	-506
		Rating History: NR-5, 04/20/10; NR-5, 08/26/09; C+ pd, 07/21/08; C++pd, 06/28/07; C++pd, 08/08/06																
SANFORD HEALTH PLAN OF MN Sanford Health Kelby Krabbenhoft CEO P.O. Box 91110 Sioux Falls, SD 57109-1110 MN : 1998 : Non-Profit : Not Available Health 605-328-6868 AMB# 064604 NAIC# 95725	NR-5	'05	25.1	...	...	74.9	2,194	...	55.0	...	45.0	1,916	2,123	2,091	260	413	404	404
		'06	22.7	...	...	77.3	2,428	...	50.7	...	49.3	2,151	1,625	1,601	239	216	211	211
		'07	13.9	...	...	86.1	2,889	...	20.3	...	79.7	2,391	1,590	1,563	452	329	224	224
		'08	5.9	...	...	94.1	2,525	...	44.2	...	55.8	2,020	2,493	2,462	-468	-470	-371	-371
		'09	4.4	...	...	95.6	2,269	...	40.6	...	59.4	1,706	3,070	3,035	-134	-313	-313	-313
		Rating History: NR-5, 04/20/10; NR-5, 04/08/09; NR-5, 03/26/08; NR-5, 04/20/07; NR-5, 06/20/06																
SANTA BARBARA REGIONAL H AUTH Richard L. Luman President 110 Castilian Drive Goleta, CA 93117-3028 CA : 1983 : Non-Profit : Broker Medicaid 805-685-9525 AMB# 064710	NR-5	'05	...	...	...	100.0	54,830	...	...	...	100.0	28,119	155,658	155,658	2,126	1,892	1,892	1,892
		'06	...	...	...	100.0	50,592	...	...	...	100.0	22,028	157,080	157,080	-2,164	-6,090	-6,090	-6,090
		'07	...	...	...	100.0	65,108	...	...	...	100.0	33,225	164,624	164,624	-6,283	11,197	11,197	11,197
		'08	...	...	...	100.0	79,439	...	...	...	100.0	15,507	199,084	199,084	25,446	-17,718	-17,718	-17,718
		'09	...	...	...	100.0	71,083	...	...	...	100.0	20,551	245,641	245,641	-3,630	5,045	5,045	5,045
		Rating History: NR-5, 03/23/10; NR-5, 04/08/09; NR-5, 03/11/08; NR-5, 04/03/07; NR-5, 04/07/06																
SANTA CLARA COUNTY Greg Price CEO 2325 Enborg Lane, Suite 290 San Jose, CA 95128 CA : 1985 : Non-Profit : Broker Health 408-885-4080 AMB# 064152	NR-5	'05	...	...	...	100.0	12,320	...	...	...	100.0	4,807	79,097	79,097	1,109	486	486	486
		'06	...	...	...	100.0	11,477	...	...	...	100.0	4,739	84,044	84,044	-1,809	11	11	11
		'07	...	...	...	100.0	9,789	...	...	...	100.0	2,430	92,384	92,384	-1,569	-2,310	-2,310	-2,310
		'08	...	...	...	100.0	12,202	...	...	...	100.0	3,142	103,701	103,701	485	713	713	713
		'09	...	...	...	100.0	17,510	...	...	...	100.0	3,400	62,505	62,505	7,279	257	257	257
		Rating History: NR-5, 03/23/10; NR-5, 08/26/09; C- pd, 05/23/08; C+ pd, 05/30/07; C+ pd, 05/30/06																
SANTA CLARA COUNTY HEALTH AUTH Leona M. Butler CEO 210 E. Hacienda Ave. Campbell, CA 95008-6617 CA : 1997 : Stock : Not Available Health 408-376-2000 AMB# 064576	NR-5	'05	...	...	...	100.0	36,733	...	...	...	100.0	25,584	118,507	118,507	-21,068	1,761	1,761	1,761
		'06	...	...	...	100.0	39,572	...	...	...	100.0	25,594	126,457	126,457	-10,071	11	11	11
		'07	...	...	...	100.0	30,608	...	...	...	100.0	21,153	134,491	134,491	-2,142	-4,441	-4,441	-4,441
		'08	...	...	...	100.0	33,354	...	...	...	100.0	13,625	168,359	168,359	2,301	-7,528	-7,528	-7,528
		'09	...	...	...	100.0	39,081	...	...	...	100.0	10,808	218,246	218,246	-5,455	-2,817	-2,817	-2,817
		Rating History: NR-5, 03/23/10; NR-5, 04/08/09; NR-5, 03/11/08; NR-5, 04/03/07; NR-5, 04/20/06																
SANTA CRUZ-MONTEREY MGD MED CR Alan McKay Executive Director 1600 Green Hills Road Scotts Valley, CA 95066 CA : Non-Profit : Not Available Health 831-430-5500 AMB# 064656	NR-5	'05	...	10.6	...	89.4	79,690	...	...	...	100.0	25,554	228,626	228,626	-10,609	-17,406	-17,406	-17,406
		'06	...	10.7	...	89.3	80,845	...	...	...	100.0	30,264	242,331	242,331	-15,002	4,710	4,710	4,710
		'07	...	7.1	...	92.9	118,427	...	...	...	100.0	62,801	288,939	288,939	27,948	32,537	32,537	32,537
		'08	...	5.8	...	94.2	141,214	...	...	...	100.0	84,621	294,131	294,131	9,289	21,820	21,820	21,820
		'09	...	5.4	...	94.6	182,855	...	...	...	100.0	89,535	385,503	385,503	19,142	13,866	4,914	4,914
		Rating History: NR-5, 05/06/10; NR-5, 05/05/09; NR-5, 05/06/08; NR-5, 05/07/07; NR-5, 06/21/06																
SAVINGS BANK LIFE INS CO OF MA Savings Bank Life Insurance Co of MA Robert K. Sheridan President & CEO One Linscott Road Woburn, MA 01801 MA : 1992 : Stock : Direct Response Ind Life, Ann 781-938-3500 AMB# 006696 NAIC# 70435	A+ Rating Outlook: Stable FSC VIII	'05	84.1	0.2	3.6	12.1	1,809,138	66.7	0.0	28.3	4.9	193,014	231,218	217,656	71,667	8,917	9,029	10,142
		'06	84.8	0.2	3.3	11.7	1,934,277	66.3	0.0	29.0	4.7	195,396	242,239	219,144	75,574	10,916	7,005	8,496
		'07	81.1	0.2	6.1	12.6	2,055,985	66.6	0.0	29.2	4.2	199,981	266,578	232,687	84,942	2,256	6,943	8,708
		'08	81.2	0.2	5.7	12.9	2,130,313	66.7	0.0	28.1	5.3	160,892	246,090	201,878	61,386	-6,934	-2,507	-28,594
		'09	83.0	0.1	3.4	13.5	2,203,667	64.7	0.0	30.8	4.5	162,938	327,161	230,152	66,876	-3,165	-12,819	-8,507
		Rating History: A+, 04/07/10; A+, 04/10/09; A+, 01/22/08; A+, 01/23/07; A+, 03/23/06																
SBLI USA MUTUAL LIFE INS CO SBLI USA Mutual Life Insurance Co., Inc Michael Akker President & CEO 460 West 34th Street, Suite 800 New York, NY 10001-2320 NY : 2000 : Mutual : Direct Response Ind Life, Group Life, Disability 212-356-0300 AMB# 006821 NAIC# 60176	B+ Rating Outlook: Negative FSC VIII	'05	81.3	1.4	3.5	13.9	1,515,654	77.8	0.1	15.8	6.3	119,225	106,342	134,702	8,545	7,442	7,444	8,216
		'06	80.3	2.5	3.7	13.4	1,525,082	77.9	0.1	15.6	6.5	123,738	140,597	128,969	23,201	11,116	10,875	11,463
		'07	83.0	2.0	2.7	12.3	1,526,361	78.4	0.1	15.6	6.0	129,484	132,998	122,872	13,216	4,972	4,962	4,542
		'08	79.5	1.5	4.0	14.9	1,486,061	80.8	0.1	15.5	3.7	122,816	102,649	114,487	-18,733	11,234	11,214	-7,168
		'09	79.8	1.2	2.0	17.0	1,502,754	78.5	0.1	18.1	3.3	113,065	194,604	161,610	40,332	20,244	20,195	6,989
		Rating History: B+ g, 06/08/10; B++g, 06/08/09; A- g, 05/01/08; A- g, 03/27/07; A- g, 05/11/06																

BEST'S PROFITABILITY, LEVERAGE AND LIQUIDITY TESTS 2005 – 2009

Data in U.S. Dollars

—	Profitability Tests							Leverage Tests						Liquidity Tests					
Un-Realized Capital Gains ($000)	Benefits Paid to NPW & Dep (%)	Comm. & Expenses to NPW & Dep (%)	NOG to Total Assets (%)	NOG to Total Rev (%)	Operating Return on Equity (%)	Net Yield (%)	Total Return (%)	Change in NPW & Dep (%)	NPW & Dep to Capital (X)	Capital & Surplus to Liabilities (%)	Surplus Relief (%)	Reins Leverage (%)	Change in Capital (%)	Quick Liquidity (%)	Current Liquidity (%)	Non-Invest Grade Bonds to Capital (%)	Delinq. & Foreclosed Mortgages to Capital (%)	Mort. & Credit Tenant Loans & R.E. to Capital (%)	Affiliated Invest to Capital (%)
...	...	...	...	...	...	...	...	...	...	...	...	...	...	...	...	...	...	...	...
...	...	...	...	...	...	...	...	...	...	...	...	...	...	...	...	...	...	...	...
...	...	...	...	999.9	...	...	...	...	...	155.4	...	...	...	155.8	155.8	...	...	...	...
...	80.2	38.1	-90.0	-18.5	-99.9	-3.78	-3.78	...	9.3	50.9	...	...	95.9	2.4	2.4	...	...	220.9	220.9
...	...	...	-6.0	-99.9	-21.6	-17.28	-17.28	-99.9	...	35.2	...	...	131.1	0.1	0.1	...	...	365.5	365.5
...	88.1	9.7	17.0	5.1	30.4	3.03	3.03	10.3	7.3	83.7	...	2.3	-6.0	178.1	178.9	...	...	...	...
...	88.2	9.0	14.5	4.1	30.7	4.54	4.54	19.4	6.3	94.4	...	1.0	38.4	196.9	197.3	...	...	...	...
...	92.8	9.6	-6.4	-1.8	-14.8	5.25	5.25	17.9	9.5	62.1	...	8.1	-22.4	220.1	220.6	...	...	...	...
...	92.0	8.7	0.8	0.2	2.0	3.54	3.54	4.4	9.5	72.2	...	0.3	5.4	236.9	239.9	...	...	...	...
...	92.6	8.7	-2.1	-0.5	-5.1	3.93	3.93	8.6	11.0	63.9	...	1.8	-6.9	144.7	150.6	...	...	...	...
Principal Lines of Business: CompHosp/Med (95.3%), MedSup (4.2%), FEHBP (0.4%)													Principal States: SD (98.0%)						
...	62.9	20.2	19.6	18.8	23.4	2.99	2.99	-37.4	1.1	688.7	...	...	24.1	999.9	999.9	...	...	...	...
...	73.8	19.0	9.1	12.4	10.4	4.41	4.41	-23.4	0.7	775.0	...	...	12.3	999.9	999.9	...	...	...	...
...	65.5	20.5	8.4	13.4	9.9	4.24	4.24	-2.4	0.7	480.7	...	...	11.2	750.5	750.5	...	...	...	...
...	101.0	19.9	-13.7	-14.8	-16.8	1.73	1.73	57.5	1.2	399.4	...	...	-15.5	698.2	698.2	...	...	...	...
...	91.2	19.5	-13.1	-10.3	-16.8	0.50	0.50	23.2	1.8	303.5	...	...	-15.5	613.8	613.8	...	...	...	...
Principal Lines of Business: CompHosp/Med (91.1%), MedSup (8.9%)													Principal States: MN (100.0%)						
...	92.8	6.7	3.6	1.2	7.0	2.70	2.70	2.2	5.5	105.3	...	...	7.2	121.3	121.3	...	...	...	...
...	95.0	6.9	-11.6	-4.0	-24.3	4.01	4.01	0.9	7.1	77.1	...	...	-21.7	105.0	105.0	...	...	...	...
...	88.8	7.1	19.4	6.6	40.5	6.29	6.29	4.8	5.0	104.2	...	...	50.8	73.0	73.0	...	...	...	...
...	96.4	6.9	-24.5	-9.4	-72.7	4.48	4.48	20.9	12.8	24.3	...	...	-53.3	75.4	75.4	...	...	...	...
...	101.0	7.3	6.7	1.9	28.0	2.14	2.14	23.4	12.0	40.7	...	...	32.5	87.8	87.8	...	...	...	...
Principal Lines of Business: Medicaid (98.7%), CompHosp/Med (1.3%)																			
...	103.1	8.8	4.1	0.5	10.6	4.06	4.06	12.2	16.5	64.0	...	...	11.2	158.0	158.0	...	...	...	...
...	101.7	11.0	0.1	0.0	0.2	7.41	7.41	6.3	17.7	70.3	...	...	-1.4	149.3	149.3	...	...	...	...
...	101.4	13.2	-21.7	-2.2	-64.4	11.34	11.34	9.9	38.0	33.0	...	...	-48.7	115.4	115.4	...	...	...	...
...	102.8	11.5	6.5	0.6	25.6	10.38	10.38	12.2	33.0	34.7	...	...	29.3	99.1	99.1	...	...	...	...
...	191.7	16.8	1.7	0.2	7.9	4.05	4.05	-39.7	18.4	24.1	...	...	8.2	115.2	115.2	...	...	...	...
Principal Lines of Business: CompHosp/Med (100.0%)																			
...	97.0	13.0	4.7	1.3	7.1	6.09	6.09	-7.2	4.6	229.5	...	...	7.4	38.0	38.0	...	...	...	...
...	98.0	13.6	0.0	0.0	0.0	14.34	14.34	6.7	4.9	183.1	...	...	0.0	91.5	91.5	...	...	...	...
...	97.8	16.3	-12.7	-3.0	-19.0	10.65	10.65	6.4	6.4	223.7	...	...	-17.4	117.2	117.2	...	...	...	...
...	97.4	14.8	-23.5	-4.1	-43.3	9.38	9.38	25.2	12.4	69.1	...	...	-35.6	67.8	67.8	...	...	...	...
...	91.2	15.5	-7.8	-1.2	-23.1	5.55	5.55	29.6	20.2	38.2	...	...	-20.7	48.5	48.5	...	...	...	...
Principal Lines of Business: Medicaid (79.5%), Medicare (20.5%)																			
...	102.6	6.8	-20.7	-7.5	-50.8	4.09	4.09	4.1	8.9	47.2	...	...	-40.5	55.9	55.9	...	...	33.1	33.1
...	93.8	5.7	5.9	1.9	16.9	6.08	6.08	6.0	8.0	59.8	...	...	18.4	30.6	30.6	...	...	28.6	28.6
...	85.6	5.2	32.7	11.0	69.9	7.19	7.19	19.2	4.6	112.9	...	...	107.5	79.0	79.0	...	...	13.4	13.4
...	89.8	5.1	16.8	7.2	29.6	5.65	5.65	1.8	3.5	149.5	...	...	34.7	94.9	94.9	...	...	9.7	9.7
...	92.1	5.3	3.0	1.3	5.6	2.78	2.78	31.1	4.3	95.9	...	...	5.8	68.0	68.0	...	...	11.0	11.0
Principal Lines of Business: Medicaid (92.7%), CompHosp/Med (7.3%)																			
-354	46.0	16.7	0.5	2.9	4.7	6.21	6.26	-3.3	1.1	12.5	5.3	44.4	2.1	84.0	87.2	2.6	...	2.1	1.1
3,345	48.3	16.3	0.4	2.2	3.6	6.16	6.43	0.7	1.1	12.0	6.0	65.5	3.5	84.1	87.1	2.9	...	1.8	1.1
-1,593	53.5	15.4	0.3	2.0	3.5	6.08	6.09	6.2	1.1	11.7	7.7	89.0	3.6	82.2	85.3	1.6	...	1.6	19.1
-17,618	68.2	19.6	-0.1	-0.8	-1.4	5.75	3.59	-13.2	1.2	8.2	11.9	153.4	-23.7	80.4	84.0	11.9	...	2.0	17.6
-26,081	60.4	1.7	-0.6	-3.2	-7.9	5.43	4.39	14.0	1.3	8.4	47.4	247.2	4.0	78.4	83.7	10.0	...	1.8	1.5
Principal Lines of Business: OrdLife (57.1%), IndAnn (42.9%), CrdA&H (0.0%), CrdLife (0.0%)													Principal States: MA (73.0%), NH (3.2%), NJ (3.1%)						
-3,023	71.5	43.5	0.5	4.1	6.2	5.34	5.50	-22.0	1.0	9.6	2.9	32.9	0.2	65.3	76.1	66.2	...	15.6	8.6
-4,670	71.2	47.9	0.7	5.6	9.0	5.77	5.73	-4.3	0.9	9.9	5.6	61.9	3.4	61.5	74.9	44.7	...	28.2	10.9
-2,481	76.2	50.7	0.3	2.6	3.9	5.65	5.62	-4.7	0.9	10.1	4.2	84.6	2.0	57.5	72.2	40.7	1.4	21.4	10.0
-8,309	85.1	45.6	0.7	6.5	8.9	5.51	3.80	-6.8	0.9	9.0	3.0	98.1	-12.3	59.3	73.5	45.3	9.6	18.6	9.3
-17,862	67.7	27.4	1.4	9.3	17.1	5.27	3.17	41.2	1.4	8.1	5.4	155.7	-7.9	63.4	74.2	140.3	13.1	15.7	8.4
Principal Lines of Business: IndAnn (35.1%), OrdLife (34.5%), GrpAnn (15.7%), GrpLife (14.1%), IndA&H (0.3%)													Principal States: NY (91.9%), NJ (4.2%)						

Data in U.S. Dollars

COMPANY NAME / Ultimate Parent Association / Principal Officer / Mailing Address / Dom. : Began Bus. : Struct. : Mktg. / Specialty / Phone # / AMB# / NAIC# — Best's Financial Strength Rating / FSC

SCAN HEALTH PLAN
SCAN Group
David Schmidt
President
P.O. Box 22616
Long Beach, CA 90802
CA : 1985 : Non-Profit : Broker
Ind A&H
562-989-5100
AMB# 060187

Best's Financial Strength Rating: NR-5

Data Year	Bonds (%)	Mort. Loans & R.E. (%)	Com & Pref. Stock (%)	All Other Assets (%)	Total Assets ($000)	Life Reserves (%)	Health Reserves (%)	Ann Res. & Dep. Liabilities (%)	All Other Liabilities (%)	Capital & Surplus ($000)	Direct Premiums Written ($000)	Net Premiums Written & Deposits ($000)	Operating Cash Flow ($000)	NOG Before Taxes ($000)	NOG After Taxes ($000)	Net Income ($000)
'05	...	...	...	100.0	543,596	...	...	...	100.0	451,591	975,285	975,285	89,470	141,681	141,681	141,681
'06	...	...	...	100.0	801,224	...	...	...	100.0	636,399	1,271,320	1,271,320	263,840	184,808	184,808	184,808
'07	...	...	...	100.0	734,420	...	...	...	100.0	588,915	1,456,913	1,456,913	-44,752	173,496	173,496	173,496
'08	...	...	...	100.0	766,577	...	...	...	100.0	598,858	1,535,133	1,535,133	134,738	54,942	54,942	54,942
'09	...	...	...	100.0	934,949	...	...	...	100.0	712,092	1,588,945	1,588,945	59,237	130,934	130,934	130,934

Rating History: NR-5, 05/07/10; NR-5, 08/26/09; B++pd, 07/21/08; B+ pd, 07/20/07; B pd, 08/29/06

SCAN HEALTH PLAN ARIZONA
SCAN Group
Henry Osowski
President
P.O. Box 22616
Long Beach, CA 90806
AZ : 2005 : Other : Broker
Medicare
562-989-5100
AMB# 064846 NAIC# 12279

Best's Financial Strength Rating: NR-5

Data Year	Bonds (%)	Mort. Loans & R.E. (%)	Com & Pref. Stock (%)	All Other Assets (%)	Total Assets ($000)	Life Reserves (%)	Health Reserves (%)	Ann Res. & Dep. Liabilities (%)	All Other Liabilities (%)	Capital & Surplus ($000)	Direct Premiums Written ($000)	Net Premiums Written & Deposits ($000)	Operating Cash Flow ($000)	NOG Before Taxes ($000)	NOG After Taxes ($000)	Net Income ($000)
'05	...	...	...	...	...	...	...	...	...	...	...	...	...	...	...	...
'06	...	...	...	100.0	7,344	...	...	...	100.0	6,215	...	...	3,365	-476	-476	-476
'07	9.3	...	...	90.7	6,453	...	75.0	...	25.0	4,049	5,892	5,892	860	-1,054	-1,054	-1,054
'08	11.0	...	...	89.0	8,876	...	81.1	...	18.9	3,070	18,035	17,858	545	-1,851	-1,851	-1,851
'09	7.7	...	...	92.3	20,589	...	81.6	...	18.4	7,635	31,583	31,314	10,737	-6,713	-6,713	-6,713

Rating History: NR-5, 04/07/10; NR-5, 05/14/09; NR-5, 04/22/08; NR-5, 05/23/07

SCOR GLOBAL LIFE RE INS CO TX
SCOR S.E.
Michael W. Pado
President & CEO
3900 Dallas Parkway
Plano, TX 75093
TX : 1977 : Stock : Other Direct
Reins
469-246-9500
AMB# 060212 NAIC# 87017

Best's Financial Strength Rating: A-
Rating Outlook: Positive
FSC XV

Data Year	Bonds (%)	Mort. Loans & R.E. (%)	Com & Pref. Stock (%)	All Other Assets (%)	Total Assets ($000)	Life Reserves (%)	Health Reserves (%)	Ann Res. & Dep. Liabilities (%)	All Other Liabilities (%)	Capital & Surplus ($000)	Direct Premiums Written ($000)	Net Premiums Written & Deposits ($000)	Operating Cash Flow ($000)	NOG Before Taxes ($000)	NOG After Taxes ($000)	Net Income ($000)
'05	56.0	...	...	44.0	340,828	53.8	6.8	...	39.4	61,353	...	25,272	11,649	2,256	2,723	3,707
'06	51.1	...	...	48.9	361,700	46.9	8.4	...	44.7	52,619	...	28,435	-4,266	-6,520	-7,067	-7,067
'07	43.8	...	...	56.2	376,592	48.8	6.1	...	45.0	42,618	...	45,246	-17,845	-7,165	-7,129	-7,121
'08	43.4	...	...	56.6	314,839	51.0	6.5	...	42.5	41,531	...	31,161	-97,033	-5,305	-5,089	-5,413
'09	55.9	...	1.9	42.2	320,955	45.9	4.1	...	50.0	19,891	...	27,211	53,807	-11,155	-9,373	-9,291

Rating History: A- g, 09/04/09; A- g, 11/14/08; A- g, 08/20/07; A- u, 05/14/07; A-, 09/08/06

SCOR GLOBAL LIFE REINS CO AMER
SCOR S.E.
Michael Pado
President
70 Seaview Avenue
Stamford, CT 06902-6040
DE : 1963 : Stock : Other
Reins
203-964-5200
AMB# 060575 NAIC# 80586

Best's Financial Strength Rating: A-
Rating Outlook: Positive
FSC XV

Data Year	Bonds (%)	Mort. Loans & R.E. (%)	Com & Pref. Stock (%)	All Other Assets (%)	Total Assets ($000)	Life Reserves (%)	Health Reserves (%)	Ann Res. & Dep. Liabilities (%)	All Other Liabilities (%)	Capital & Surplus ($000)	Direct Premiums Written ($000)	Net Premiums Written & Deposits ($000)	Operating Cash Flow ($000)	NOG Before Taxes ($000)	NOG After Taxes ($000)	Net Income ($000)
'05	...	...	...	...	...	...	...	...	...	...	...	...	...	...	...	...
'06	93.6	...	...	6.4	58,956	3.6	...	...	96.4	55,193	65	39	46,275	-990	-990	-1,017
'07	93.1	...	...	6.9	57,551	51.9	...	...	48.1	49,460	61	940	-1,705	-4,869	-4,869	-4,869
'08	96.5	...	...	3.5	55,522	84.8	...	...	15.2	32,909	62	5,570	494	-16,841	-16,841	-17,279
'09	71.9	...	...	28.1	65,130	74.2	...	...	25.8	31,947	52	7,407	2,243	-5,384	-5,384	-5,321

Rating History: A- g, 02/05/10; A-, 08/25/08; A- u, 07/29/08; A-, 01/25/08; A, 12/20/07

SCOR GLOBAL LIFE US RE INS CO
SCOR S.E.
Yves I. Corcos
President & CEO
3900 Dallas Parkway, Suite 200
Plano, TX 75093
TX : 1945 : Stock : Other Direct
Ann, Life Reins
469-246-9500
AMB# 006555 NAIC# 64688

Best's Financial Strength Rating: A-
Rating Outlook: Positive
FSC XV

Data Year	Bonds (%)	Mort. Loans & R.E. (%)	Com & Pref. Stock (%)	All Other Assets (%)	Total Assets ($000)	Life Reserves (%)	Health Reserves (%)	Ann Res. & Dep. Liabilities (%)	All Other Liabilities (%)	Capital & Surplus ($000)	Direct Premiums Written ($000)	Net Premiums Written & Deposits ($000)	Operating Cash Flow ($000)	NOG Before Taxes ($000)	NOG After Taxes ($000)	Net Income ($000)
'05	76.8	2.1	2.8	18.3	2,129,820	5.8	2.1	59.2	32.9	107,058	...	-60,366	217,970	17,519	17,254	22,998
'06	85.9	2.1	4.7	7.3	1,958,736	7.7	2.0	56.9	33.4	126,331	...	-17,842	-65,916	-9,949	-4,606	-4,613
'07	82.1	2.2	4.7	10.9	1,958,167	8.7	1.6	53.1	36.5	125,550	...	78,592	-4,774	34,509	25,954	25,954
'08	75.4	2.0	6.4	16.2	2,011,116	9.2	1.3	51.9	37.5	162,991	...	132,544	58,037	27,860	28,634	6,351
'09	83.3	1.6	3.8	11.3	2,307,874	8.3	1.0	59.4	31.3	126,158	...	499,094	254,522	-40,920	-41,763	-51,253

Rating History: A- g, 09/04/09; A- g, 11/14/08; A- g, 08/20/07; A- gu, 05/14/07; A- g, 09/08/06

SCOTIA INS (BARBADOS) LTD
Bank of Nova Scotia
Richard S. Tucker
Managing Director
3rd Floor, International Trading Centre
St. Michael BB22026, Barbados
BB : Stock : Not Available
Life, Non-Life
246-425-2164
AMB# 057051

Best's Financial Strength Rating: A
Rating Outlook: Stable
FSC VIII

Data Year	Bonds (%)	Mort. Loans & R.E. (%)	Com & Pref. Stock (%)	All Other Assets (%)	Total Assets ($000)	Life Reserves (%)	Health Reserves (%)	Ann Res. & Dep. Liabilities (%)	All Other Liabilities (%)	Capital & Surplus ($000)	Direct Premiums Written ($000)	Net Premiums Written & Deposits ($000)	Operating Cash Flow ($000)	NOG Before Taxes ($000)	NOG After Taxes ($000)	Net Income ($000)
'05	64.0	...	...	36.0	200,380	...	...	...	100.0	102,630	...	160,558	129,151	125,108	125,108	125,108
'06	61.4	...	...	38.6	268,181	...	...	...	100.0	135,781	...	155,384	146,112	140,152	140,152	140,152
'07	67.0	...	...	33.0	291,026	58.4	...	...	41.6	133,353	...	192,188	175,884	167,072	167,072	167,072
'08	54.9	...	...	45.1	336,692	38.5	...	...	61.5	123,587	...	257,895	184,477	187,734	187,734	187,734
'09	66.9	...	...	33.1	307,778	52.1	...	...	47.9	153,652	...	276,612	194,436	190,564	190,564	190,564

Rating History: A, 06/17/09; A, 08/28/08; A, 06/14/07; A, 05/10/06; A, 04/05/05

SCOTT & WHITE HEALTH PLAN
Scott & White Health Plan
Allan Einboden
CEO
2401 South 31st Street
Temple, TX 76508
TX : 1982 : Non-Profit : Exclusive Agent
Group A&H, Medicare
254-298-3000
AMB# 060161 NAIC# 95099

Best's Financial Strength Rating: A-
Rating Outlook: Negative
FSC VII

Data Year	Bonds (%)	Mort. Loans & R.E. (%)	Com & Pref. Stock (%)	All Other Assets (%)	Total Assets ($000)	Life Reserves (%)	Health Reserves (%)	Ann Res. & Dep. Liabilities (%)	All Other Liabilities (%)	Capital & Surplus ($000)	Direct Premiums Written ($000)	Net Premiums Written & Deposits ($000)	Operating Cash Flow ($000)	NOG Before Taxes ($000)	NOG After Taxes ($000)	Net Income ($000)
'05	29.6	...	13.0	57.4	90,932	...	24.9	...	75.1	49,737	437,530	437,530	12,747	3,792	3,516	3,943
'06	25.0	...	11.6	63.4	107,903	...	24.0	...	76.0	53,250	479,425	478,973	8,373	3,260	2,878	3,957
'07	25.6	...	11.7	62.7	114,313	...	57.1	...	42.9	60,463	508,446	507,714	11,064	7,807	7,133	7,664
'08	21.4	1.3	6.7	70.7	141,380	...	38.3	...	61.7	56,320	580,299	579,222	-20,412	956	384	-2,684
'09	14.2	2.9	6.9	76.0	152,720	...	23.3	...	76.7	69,888	616,221	614,431	-14,756	9,733	9,239	9,263

Rating History: A-, 07/10/09; A-, 01/18/08; A-, 11/30/06; A-, 11/18/05; A-, 01/20/05

SCOTTISH ANN&LF INS CO(CAYMAN)
Scottish Re Group Limited
Paul Goldean
President
P.O. Box 10657 APO
Grand Cayman, Cayman Islands
KY : Stock : Not Available
Var ann, Var life, Life Reins
345-949-2800
AMB# 086896

Best's Financial Strength Rating: NR-4

Data Year	Bonds (%)	Mort. Loans & R.E. (%)	Com & Pref. Stock (%)	All Other Assets (%)	Total Assets ($000)	Life Reserves (%)	Health Reserves (%)	Ann Res. & Dep. Liabilities (%)	All Other Liabilities (%)	Capital & Surplus ($000)	Direct Premiums Written ($000)	Net Premiums Written & Deposits ($000)	Operating Cash Flow ($000)	NOG Before Taxes ($000)	NOG After Taxes ($000)	Net Income ($000)
'05	47.5	...	...	52.5	10,915,542	75.3	...	...	24.7	1,304,682	...	1,840,197	308,138	123,420	135,910	139,092
'06	59.0	...	0.9	40.1	12,452,038	32.5	...	29.2	38.3	987,440	...	1,693,561	499,712	-62,946	-291,837	-317,463
'07	59.4	...	0.8	39.8	11,740,864	34.9	...	23.2	41.9	701,917	...	1,716,693	484,441	11,613	162,588	-768,253
'08	45.7	...	1.0	53.2	7,727,736	42.3	...	21.4	36.3	-1,761,965	...	1,596,817	-320,671	-558,865	-529,045	-2,440,135
'09	...	...	...	...	...	...	...	...	...	...	...	...	...	...	...	...

Rating History: NR-4, 06/12/09; D, 06/12/09; D, 02/05/09; C- g, 07/23/08; C+ gu, 06/12/08

SCOTTISH RE LIFE CORPORATION'
Scottish Re Group Limited
Meredith A. Ratajczak
President & CEO
14120 Ballantyne Corporate Place
Charlotte, NC 28277-2800
DE : 1979 : Stock : Other Direct
Reins
704-542-9192
AMB# 008928 NAIC# 90670

Best's Financial Strength Rating: NR-4

Data Year	Bonds (%)	Mort. Loans & R.E. (%)	Com & Pref. Stock (%)	All Other Assets (%)	Total Assets ($000)	Life Reserves (%)	Health Reserves (%)	Ann Res. & Dep. Liabilities (%)	All Other Liabilities (%)	Capital & Surplus ($000)	Direct Premiums Written ($000)	Net Premiums Written & Deposits ($000)	Operating Cash Flow ($000)	NOG Before Taxes ($000)	NOG After Taxes ($000)	Net Income ($000)
'05	48.7	...	8.1	43.2	614,660	...	...	1.1	98.9	74,332	...	114,286	...	7,917	8,757	8,757
'06	41.4	...	7.5	51.1	667,981	...	...	0.9	99.1	81,294	...	109,356	...	-3,618	-3,741	-3,741
'07	52.3	...	8.6	39.1	581,346	...	...	1.0	99.0	93,276	...	128,525	...	3,149	10,798	9,792
'08	47.0	...	9.6	43.4	521,439	...	...	1.0	99.0	66,445	...	123,026	...	2,199	3,931	-19,421
'09	50.0	...	8.7	41.4	576,484	...	...	0.9	99.1	72,808	...	126,920	...	-1,841	-932	-4,102

Rating History: NR-4, 06/12/09; D, 06/12/09; D, 02/05/09; C-, 07/23/08; C+ u, 06/12/08

BEST'S PROFITABILITY, LEVERAGE AND LIQUIDITY TESTS 2005 – 2009

Data in U.S. Dollars

—	Profitability Tests							Leverage Tests						Liquidity Tests					
Un-Realized Capital Gains ($000)	Benefits Paid to NPW & Dep (%)	Comm. & Expenses to NPW & Dep (%)	NOG to Total Assets (%)	NOG to Total Rev (%)	Operating Return on Equity (%)	Net Yield (%)	Total Return (%)	Change in NPW & Dep (%)	NPW & Dep to Capital (X)	Capital & Surplus to Liabilities (%)	Surplus Relief (%)	Reins Leverage (%)	Change in Capital (%)	Quick Liquidity (%)	Current Liquidity (%)	Non-Invest Grade Bonds to Capital (%)	Delinq. & Foreclosed Mortgages to Capital (%)	Mort. & Credit Tenant Loans & R.E. to Capital (%)	Affiliated Invest to Capital (%)
...	80.4	7.4	28.9	14.2	37.2	3.55	3.55	25.8	2.2	490.8	...	...	45.7	548.7	548.7	...	...	...	...
...	82.5	7.3	27.5	13.9	34.0	7.89	7.89	30.4	2.0	386.1	...	...	40.9	463.7	463.7	...	...	...	...
...	85.9	6.4	22.6	11.4	28.3	7.88	7.88	14.6	2.5	404.7	...	...	-7.5	475.1	475.1	...	...	...	...
...	86.3	5.8	7.3	3.7	9.3	-6.55	-6.55	5.4	2.6	357.1	...	...	1.7	431.6	431.6	...	...	...	...
...	92.8	5.6	15.4	7.7	20.0	2.66	2.66	3.5	2.2	319.5	...	...	18.9	385.7	385.7	...	...	...	...

Principal Lines of Business: Medicare (97.8%), Medicaid (2.2%)

...	...	...	...	...	...	...	...	...	...	...	...	...	...	...	...	...	...	...	...
...	...	...	...	-99.9	...	...	...	...	...	550.2	...	...	...	474.6	474.6	...	...	...	...
...	97.3	25.0	-15.3	-17.1	-20.5	4.61	4.61	...	1.5	168.4	...	...	-34.8	256.5	256.5	...	...	...	...
...	98.8	12.1	-24.2	-10.3	-52.0	1.58	1.58	203.1	5.8	52.9	...	...	-24.2	111.1	111.1	...	...	...	309.4
...	98.9	16.6	-45.6	-22.8	-99.9	0.96	0.96	75.3	4.1	58.9	...	...	148.6	131.5	131.5	...	...	...	45.8

Principal Lines of Business: Medicare (100.0%) Principal States: AZ (100.0%)

-1,302	112.1	67.3	0.8	3.5	5.5	4.74	4.83	-55.2	0.4	22.5	47.7	900.0	62.8	66.5	72.1	...	...	...	...
...	102.5	71.2	-2.0	-9.5	-12.4	4.80	4.95	12.5	0.5	17.3	60.6	999.9	-14.8	52.1	57.3	1.2	...	...	...
...	76.0	37.7	-1.9	-8.0	-15.0	3.79	3.93	59.1	1.0	13.0	77.5	999.9	-18.6	42.0	46.1	1.0	...	...	...
-3	144.7	62.3	-1.5	-8.2	-12.1	4.36	4.37	-31.1	0.7	15.4	49.3	999.9	-3.0	53.0	59.2	1.6	...	...	...
260	107.4	77.8	-2.9	-16.0	-30.5	2.41	2.73	-12.7	1.3	6.9	126.3	999.9	-50.8	57.1	63.4	6.3	...	...	...

Principal Lines of Business: OrdLife (51.1%), GrpLife (46.2%), IndA&H (2.6%)

...	...	...	...	...	...	...	...	...	...	...	...	...	...	...	...	...	...	...	...
...	34.1	999.9	...	-48.0	...	...	...	...	0.0	999.9	0.2	12.0	...	999.9	999.9	...	...	...	...
...	44.9	494.5	-8.4	-64.5	-9.3	5.29	5.30	999.9	0.0	617.3	7.4	45.2	-10.3	584.0	640.3	...	...	...	...
...	49.6	177.2	-29.8	-82.7	-40.9	4.97	4.25	492.2	0.2	145.5	36.5	227.8	-33.6	210.4	226.1	1.0	...	...	...
...	57.0	84.4	-8.9	-42.1	-16.6	4.59	4.86	33.0	0.2	96.4	8.4	290.7	-2.9	162.4	169.7	0.5	...	...	...

Principal Lines of Business: OrdLife (99.9%), IndAnn (0.1%) Principal States: NC (48.1%), WI (12.5%), GA (7.8%), MN (7.3%), DC (3.5%)

-2,366	-99.9	-24.6	0.8	21.8	22.2	4.79	5.05	-99.9	-0.5	5.5	42.6	869.2	116.0	63.3	72.7	15.1	...	40.5	50.4
9,712	-99.9	-60.8	-0.2	-3.9	-3.9	3.81	4.38	70.4	-0.1	7.2	39.7	716.5	18.3	65.1	76.5	2.6	...	30.5	44.7
-6,208	247.2	14.5	1.3	11.8	20.6	3.74	3.47	540.5	0.6	7.2	44.6	852.6	0.1	66.4	77.7	11.4	...	32.8	29.4
-3,718	132.1	18.9	1.4	9.7	19.8	3.50	2.19	68.6	0.8	8.8	31.9	703.3	23.6	71.7	83.6	13.8	...	25.1	40.5
-19,092	41.5	8.9	-1.9	-6.6	-28.9	2.98	1.66	276.6	4.0	5.8	57.2	982.5	-22.6	62.9	74.0	55.0	0.3	29.8	67.2

Principal Lines of Business: IndAnn (83.0%), OrdLife (13.3%), GrpLife (2.8%), IndA&H (1.0%), GrpA&H (0.0%)

...	39.6	13.3	44.5	59.6	77.7	2.70	2.70	-16.0	156.4	105.0	...	...	-53.3	185.0	131.1	...	...	...	...
...	42.1	12.7	59.8	62.2	117.6	3.93	3.93	-3.2	114.4	102.6	...	...	32.3	177.5	124.5	...	...	...	...
...	32.7	25.4	59.8	60.0	124.2	4.79	4.79	23.7	144.1	84.6	...	...	-1.8	160.7	123.7	...	...	...	...
...	36.8	22.6	59.8	55.0	146.1	4.34	4.34	34.2	208.7	58.0	...	...	-7.3	138.1	86.7	...	...	...	...
...	40.1	21.9	59.1	52.5	137.5	1.77	1.77	7.3	180.0	99.7	...	...	24.3	168.5	133.6	...	...	...	...

-641	93.6	7.9	4.0	0.8	7.4	3.99	3.66	2.8	8.8	120.7	...	1.5	9.4	153.6	167.9	...	...	...	4.6
-508	92.0	8.6	2.9	0.6	5.6	3.51	4.33	9.5	9.0	97.4	...	2.4	7.1	126.4	137.9	...	...	...	4.7
414	92.1	8.9	6.4	1.4	12.5	3.99	5.17	6.0	8.4	112.3	...	1.0	13.5	180.0	196.0	...	...	...	4.4
-1,343	94.9	7.5	0.3	0.1	0.7	3.63	-2.08	14.1	10.3	66.2	...	2.1	-6.9	78.7	86.9	...	...	3.2	7.9
1,539	90.9	8.4	6.3	1.5	14.6	3.63	6.31	6.1	8.8	84.4	...	0.1	24.1	50.3	55.6	...	...	6.4	10.3

Principal Lines of Business: CompHosp/Med (75.6%), Medicare (24.0%), OtherHlth (0.4%) Principal States: TX (100.0%)

-31,731	82.6	28.4	1.4	6.2	11.9	4.57	4.61	274.0	141.1	13.6	...	...	32.0	62.6	81.9	...	...	...	...
221	96.2	39.6	-2.5	-13.1	-25.5	6.11	5.84	-8.0	171.5	8.6	...	...	-24.3	69.6	82.7	...	...	...	...
42,165	91.4	40.7	1.3	12.0	19.3	5.54	-4.05	1.4	244.6	6.4	...	...	-28.9	70.4	79.1	...	...	...	...
-23,628	101.0	57.0	-5.4	-99.9	99.8	4.48	-20.11	-7.0	-90.6	-18.6	...	...	-99.9	45.8	56.8	...	...	...	...
...	...	...	...	...	...	...	...	...	...	...	...	...	...	...	...	...	...	...	...

...	139.6	26.1	1.4	5.4	11.7	...	...	400.6	1.5	13.9	5.8	...	-1.1	...	...	...	...	...	...
...	113.0	23.0	-0.6	-2.5	-4.8	...	...	-4.3	1.3	14.0	18.0	...	9.7	...	...	...	...	...	...
...	99.5	13.3	1.7	6.4	12.4	...	...	17.5	1.4	19.2	13.5	...	14.0	...	...	...	...	...	...
...	108.1	12.9	0.7	2.5	4.9	...	...	-4.3	1.9	14.6	18.7	...	-29.1	...	...	...	...	...	...
-251	117.3	-10.0	-0.2	-0.5	-1.3	...	...	3.2	1.7	14.5	49.2	...	9.6	...	...	...	...	...	...

Principal Lines of Business: OrdLife (99.8%), IndAnn (0.1%), GrpAnn (0.1%), GrpLife (0.0%)

COMPANY NAME / Ultimate Parent Association / Principal Officer / Mailing Address / Dom. : Began Bus. : Struct. : Mktg. / Specialty / Phone # / AMB# / NAIC# — Best's Financial Strength Rating / FSC

Balance Sheet: Data Year, Bonds (%), Mort. Loans & R.E. (%), Com & Pref. Stock (%), All Other Assets (%), Total Assets ($000), Life Reserves (%), Health Reserves (%), Ann Res. & Dep. Liabilities (%), All Other Liabilities (%), Capital & Surplus ($000). Operations: Direct Premiums Written ($000), Net Premiums Written & Deposits ($000), Operating Cash Flow ($000), NOG Before Taxes ($000), NOG After Taxes ($000), Net Income ($000)

SCOTTISH RE (US) INC.[1]
Scottish Re Group Limited
Meredith A. Ratajczak
President & CEO
13840 Ballantyne Corporate Place
Charlotte, NC 28277-2832
DE : 1977 : Stock : Not Available
704-542-9192
AMB# 008785 NAIC# 87572

Best's Financial Strength Rating: **E**

Data Year	Bonds (%)	Mort. Loans & R.E. (%)	Com & Pref. Stock (%)	All Other Assets (%)	Total Assets ($000)	Life Reserves (%)	Health Reserves (%)	Ann Res. & Dep. Liabilities (%)	All Other Liabilities (%)	Capital & Surplus ($000)	Direct Premiums Written ($000)	Net Premiums Written & Deposits ($000)	Operating Cash Flow ($000)	NOG Before Taxes ($000)	NOG After Taxes ($000)	Net Income ($000)
'05	61.0	...	14.4	24.7	3,042,647	...	...	0.0	100.0	491,105	...	636,375	...	-206,496	-207,503	-207,001
'06	63.5	...	5.2	31.3	3,090,604	...	...	0.0	100.0	306,699	...	74,764	...	-203,570	-207,097	-208,032
'07	59.6	...	4.9	35.5	2,950,563	...	...	0.0	100.0	248,558	...	764,770	...	-323,916	-327,707	-345,575
'08	64.2	...	5.2	30.7	2,238,840	...	...	0.0	100.0	197,366	...	-337,451	...	38,608	55,411	-114,767
'09	78.4	...	4.9	16.7	1,845,496	...	...	0.0	100.0	235,656	...	-149,300	...	106,742	126,766	119,134

Rating History: E, 02/05/09; C- g, 07/23/08; C+ gu, 06/12/08; B- gu, 04/11/08; B g, 02/27/08

SCRIPPS CLINIC HEALTH PLAN SVS
Marc A. Reynolds
President
10170 Sorrento Valley Road
San Diego, CA 92121
CA : 1999 : Non-Profit : Not Available
Group A&H
858-784-5961
AMB# 064661

Best's Financial Strength Rating: **NR-5**

Data Year	Bonds (%)	Mort. Loans & R.E. (%)	Com & Pref. Stock (%)	All Other Assets (%)	Total Assets ($000)	Life Reserves (%)	Health Reserves (%)	Ann Res. & Dep. Liabilities (%)	All Other Liabilities (%)	Capital & Surplus ($000)	Direct Premiums Written ($000)	Net Premiums Written & Deposits ($000)	Operating Cash Flow ($000)	NOG Before Taxes ($000)	NOG After Taxes ($000)	Net Income ($000)
'05	...	...	...	100.0	17,844	...	...	...	100.0	3,842	125,345	125,345	2,588	67	67	67
'06	...	...	...	100.0	18,313	...	...	...	100.0	3,591	134,011	134,011	-675	49	49	49
'07	...	...	...	100.0	25,810	...	...	...	100.0	3,792	164,666	164,666	7,039	201	201	201
'08	...	...	...	100.0	32,348	...	...	...	100.0	7,476	196,026	196,026	6,699	-906	-906	-906
'09	...	...	...	100.0	34,108	...	...	...	100.0	8,260	...	...	1,120	389	171	171

Rating History: NR-5, 03/23/10; NR-5, 08/26/09; C- pd, 06/06/08; C pd, 06/05/07; C pd, 06/13/06

SEARS LIFE INSURANCE COMPANY
Citigroup Inc.
Dava S. Carson
President & CEO
3001 Meacham Boulevard, Suite 100
Fort Worth, TX 76137
TX : 1956 : Stock : Direct Response
Group A&H, Group Life, Hosp Ind
800-316-5607
AMB# 007170 NAIC# 69914

Best's Financial Strength Rating: **A-**
Rating Outlook: Stable
FSC VII

Data Year	Bonds (%)	Mort. Loans & R.E. (%)	Com & Pref. Stock (%)	All Other Assets (%)	Total Assets ($000)	Life Reserves (%)	Health Reserves (%)	Ann Res. & Dep. Liabilities (%)	All Other Liabilities (%)	Capital & Surplus ($000)	Direct Premiums Written ($000)	Net Premiums Written & Deposits ($000)	Operating Cash Flow ($000)	NOG Before Taxes ($000)	NOG After Taxes ($000)	Net Income ($000)
'05	84.5	...	...	15.5	77,018	5.5	19.7	...	74.8	60,707	67,815	16,794	6,718	4,525	1,669	1,669
'06	79.3	...	...	20.7	75,743	8.4	25.0	...	66.5	54,151	66,187	23,257	-1,604	-6,412	-5,990	-5,990
'07	58.3	...	...	41.7	73,651	13.8	36.6	...	49.6	51,351	68,736	31,801	-202	-2,979	-2,860	-2,949
'08	53.1	...	...	46.9	73,633	12.0	50.1	...	37.9	51,010	64,358	31,944	-5,423	10,929	6,254	4,678
'09	53.3	...	0.2	46.5	83,297	17.2	56.6	...	26.2	59,247	52,867	24,245	12,947	10,934	7,080	6,651

Rating History: A-, 06/04/10; A-, 06/03/09; A g, 05/22/08; A g, 01/12/07; A g, 07/01/05

SEB TRYGG LIFE (USA) ASSUR LTD
Anders G. Mossberg
President
2999 North 44th Street, Suite 250
Phoenix, AZ 85018
AZ : 2001 : Stock : Inactive
Inactive
602-200-6900
AMB# 060372 NAIC# 89071

Best's Financial Strength Rating: **NR-5**

Data Year	Bonds (%)	Mort. Loans & R.E. (%)	Com & Pref. Stock (%)	All Other Assets (%)	Total Assets ($000)	Life Reserves (%)	Health Reserves (%)	Ann Res. & Dep. Liabilities (%)	All Other Liabilities (%)	Capital & Surplus ($000)	Direct Premiums Written ($000)	Net Premiums Written & Deposits ($000)	Operating Cash Flow ($000)	NOG Before Taxes ($000)	NOG After Taxes ($000)	Net Income ($000)
'05	...	...	...	100.0	629	...	...	...	100.0	475	...	...	6	-10	-10	-10
'06	...	...	...	100.0	639	...	...	...	100.0	461	...	...	9	-14	-14	-14
'07	...	...	...	100.0	649	...	...	...	100.0	453	...	...	10	-8	-8	-8
'08	...	...	...	100.0	656	...	...	...	100.0	442	...	...	7	-11	-11	-11
'09	...	...	...	100.0	659	...	...	...	100.0	427	...	...	3	-15	-15	-15

Rating History: NR-5, 04/26/10; NR-5, 04/27/09; NR-5, 04/22/08; NR-5, 04/25/07; NR-5, 05/03/06

SECURIAN LIFE INSURANCE CO
Minnesota Mutual Companies Inc
Robert L. Senkler
Chairman & CEO
400 Robert Street North
St. Paul, MN 55101-2098
MN : 1981 : Stock : Agency
Group Life, Group pens
651-665-3500
AMB# 009064 NAIC# 93742

Best's Financial Strength Rating: **A+**
Rating Outlook: Stable
FSC XIV

Data Year	Bonds (%)	Mort. Loans & R.E. (%)	Com & Pref. Stock (%)	All Other Assets (%)	Total Assets ($000)	Life Reserves (%)	Health Reserves (%)	Ann Res. & Dep. Liabilities (%)	All Other Liabilities (%)	Capital & Surplus ($000)	Direct Premiums Written ($000)	Net Premiums Written & Deposits ($000)	Operating Cash Flow ($000)	NOG Before Taxes ($000)	NOG After Taxes ($000)	Net Income ($000)
'05	11.7	...	...	88.3	116,560	32.9	26.1	6.7	34.3	113,138	6,903	6,872	100,823	100	105	105
'06	94.8	...	...	5.2	122,364	34.4	24.5	3.7	37.4	116,435	21,876	21,649	4,110	4,451	3,044	3,044
'07	93.9	...	...	6.1	141,543	54.3	15.1	0.6	30.1	118,950	40,487	38,099	17,635	5,816	2,933	2,323
'08	91.8	...	...	8.2	142,911	59.9	16.1	1.6	22.5	121,967	43,611	40,698	1,006	8,618	5,495	3,833
'09	92.9	...	...	7.1	149,667	64.6	14.8	1.3	19.3	126,512	42,729	44,638	5,698	7,237	4,720	3,922

Rating History: A+ g, 04/06/10; A+ g, 04/10/09; A+ g, 03/25/08; A+ g, 06/01/07; A, 06/14/06

SECURITAS FINANCIAL LIFE INS
Unity Mutual Life Insurance Company
Patrick A. Mannion
CEO
4964 University Parkway, Suite 203
Winston-Salem, NC 27106
NC : 1991 : Stock : Agency
Annuity
336-245-2238
AMB# 009068 NAIC# 94072

Best's Financial Strength Rating: **NR-3**

Data Year	Bonds (%)	Mort. Loans & R.E. (%)	Com & Pref. Stock (%)	All Other Assets (%)	Total Assets ($000)	Life Reserves (%)	Health Reserves (%)	Ann Res. & Dep. Liabilities (%)	All Other Liabilities (%)	Capital & Surplus ($000)	Direct Premiums Written ($000)	Net Premiums Written & Deposits ($000)	Operating Cash Flow ($000)	NOG Before Taxes ($000)	NOG After Taxes ($000)	Net Income ($000)
'05	30.9	...	...	69.1	9,189	...	...	...	100.0	8,521	...	...	187	282	298	298
'06	28.5	...	...	71.5	9,458	...	...	...	100.0	8,791	...	...	287	402	275	275
'07	27.5	...	...	72.5	9,764	...	...	...	100.0	9,115	...	...	315	480	328	328
'08	92.4	...	...	7.6	2,725	...	...	...	100.0	2,724	...	...	-7,163	646	583	583
'09	51.1	...	...	48.9	5,526	...	...	...	100.0	5,203	10	1	2,978	-433	-435	-435

Rating History: NR-3, 06/14/10; NR-2, 07/06/09; NR-3, 02/20/09; NR-3, 10/05/07; NR-3, 03/28/07

SECURITY BENEFIT LIFE INS CO
Security Benefit Mutual Holding Company
Kris A. Robbins
Chairman, President & CEO
One Security Benefit Place
Topeka, KS 66636-0001
KS : 1892 : Stock : Bank
Ann, Var ann
785-438-3000
AMB# 007025 NAIC# 68675

Best's Financial Strength Rating: **B u**
Under Review Implication: Positive
FSC IX

Data Year	Bonds (%)	Mort. Loans & R.E. (%)	Com & Pref. Stock (%)	All Other Assets (%)	Total Assets ($000)	Life Reserves (%)	Health Reserves (%)	Ann Res. & Dep. Liabilities (%)	All Other Liabilities (%)	Capital & Surplus ($000)	Direct Premiums Written ($000)	Net Premiums Written & Deposits ($000)	Operating Cash Flow ($000)	NOG Before Taxes ($000)	NOG After Taxes ($000)	Net Income ($000)
'05	41.0	0.0	1.2	57.8	11,509,560	0.1	0.0	44.0	55.9	588,211	1,276,686	1,579,273	180,366	37,133	36,369	36,079
'06	38.7	0.0	1.2	60.2	12,169,857	0.1	0.0	41.7	58.1	574,719	1,518,479	1,691,680	-6,975	27,485	34,970	38,890
'07	31.6	0.0	1.8	66.5	12,341,315	0.1	0.0	39.5	60.3	602,362	1,516,746	1,658,864	-135,009	17,393	31,846	19,138
'08	33.8	0.2	2.3	63.7	9,246,195	0.2	0.0	47.9	51.9	300,551	834,981	821,285	-538,610	-34,561	-21,880	-317,408
'09	30.4	0.2	0.9	68.5	9,862,138	0.2	0.0	44.0	55.8	427,351	528,302	519,948	-127,757	24,230	27,533	-21,098

Rating History: B gu, 02/19/10; B g, 02/27/09; B++gu, 10/13/08; A- g, 06/24/08; A g, 07/03/07

SECURITY HEALTH INS OF AMER NY
Safe Partners, LLC
Gilbert C. Rohde, Jr.
President
461 Clinton Street
Schenectady, NY 12305
NY : 2008 : Stock : Agency
Inactive
877-230-1024
AMB# 064979 NAIC# 13737

Best's Financial Strength Rating: **NR-2**

Data Year	Bonds (%)	Mort. Loans & R.E. (%)	Com & Pref. Stock (%)	All Other Assets (%)	Total Assets ($000)	Life Reserves (%)	Health Reserves (%)	Ann Res. & Dep. Liabilities (%)	All Other Liabilities (%)	Capital & Surplus ($000)	Direct Premiums Written ($000)	Net Premiums Written & Deposits ($000)	Operating Cash Flow ($000)	NOG Before Taxes ($000)	NOG After Taxes ($000)	Net Income ($000)
'05	...	...	...	...	...	...	...	...	...	...	...	...	...	...	...	...
'06	...	...	...	...	...	...	...	...	...	...	...	...	...	...	...	...
'07	...	...	...	...	...	...	...	...	...	...	...	...	...	...	...	...
'08	...	...	...	...	...	...	...	...	...	...	...	...	...	...	...	...
'09	31.9	...	...	68.1	1,103	...	...	...	100.0	1,096	...	...	1,098	-7	-4	-4

Rating History: NR-2, 05/04/10

SECURITY HEALTH PLAN OF WI
Marshfield Clinic
Karl J. Ulrich, M.D.
President
P.O. Box 8000
Marshfield, WI 54449
WI : 1986 : Non-Profit : Broker
Group A&H, Medicare, Medicaid
715-221-9555
AMB# 064207 NAIC# 96881

Best's Financial Strength Rating: **NR-5**

Data Year	Bonds (%)	Mort. Loans & R.E. (%)	Com & Pref. Stock (%)	All Other Assets (%)	Total Assets ($000)	Life Reserves (%)	Health Reserves (%)	Ann Res. & Dep. Liabilities (%)	All Other Liabilities (%)	Capital & Surplus ($000)	Direct Premiums Written ($000)	Net Premiums Written & Deposits ($000)	Operating Cash Flow ($000)	NOG Before Taxes ($000)	NOG After Taxes ($000)	Net Income ($000)
'05	66.7	0.1	...	33.2	125,996	...	28.9	...	71.1	53,848	385,590	385,590	24,409	13,850	13,850	13,823
'06	79.8	0.1	...	20.1	128,152	...	45.3	...	54.7	56,914	458,179	458,179	16,891	10,194	10,194	9,837
'07	70.5	0.3	...	29.2	148,942	...	43.5	...	56.5	64,673	595,015	595,015	13,797	10,616	10,616	10,711
'08	75.7	0.3	...	24.0	179,199	...	49.8	...	50.2	88,428	651,987	651,987	32,267	24,075	24,075	22,659
'09	68.5	0.3	...	31.2	214,044	...	42.1	...	57.9	124,870	804,094	804,094	31,734	36,700	36,700	37,041

Rating History: NR-5, 04/07/10; NR-5, 08/26/09; B- pd, 06/06/08; B- pd, 06/05/07; B- pd, 06/13/06

2010 BEST'S KEY RATING GUIDE — LIFE/HEALTH EDITION
BEST'S PROFITABILITY, LEVERAGE AND LIQUIDITY TESTS 2005 – 2009

Data in U.S. Dollars

—	Profitability Tests							Leverage Tests						Liquidity Tests					
Un-Realized Capital Gains ($000)	Benefits Paid to NPW & Dep (%)	Comm. & Expenses to NPW & Dep (%)	NOG to Total Assets (%)	NOG to Total Rev (%)	Operating Return on Equity (%)	Net Yield (%)	Total Return (%)	Change in NPW & Dep (%)	NPW & Dep to Capital (X)	Capital & Surplus to Liabilities (%)	Surplus Relief (%)	Reins Leverage (%)	Change in Capital (%)	Quick Liquidity (%)	Current Liquidity (%)	Non-Invest Grade Bonds to Capital (%)	Delinq. & Foreclosed Mortgages to Capital (%)	Mort. & Credit Tenant Loans & R.E. to Capital (%)	Affiliated Invest to Capital (%)
14,618	61.0	75.6	-7.8	-42.2	-55.7	...	...	-14.5	1.2	20.3	-25.2	...	99.7	...	...	...	...	...	...
8,321	424.5	207.7	-6.8	-44.2	-51.9	...	...	-88.3	0.2	11.4	81.3	...	-38.2	...	...	...	...	...	...
4,209	53.2	22.1	-10.8	-57.7	-99.9	...	...	922.9	3.1	9.2	60.1	...	-21.5	...	...	...	...	...	...
-23,080	-99.9	145.8	2.1	-19.0	24.9	...	...	-99.9	-1.7	9.7	34.1	...	-20.6	...	...	...	...	...	...
-142	-99.9	80.1	6.2	84.2	58.5	...	...	55.8	-0.6	14.6	93.1	...	19.2	...	...	...	...	...	...
Principal Lines of Business: OrdLife (127.0%), CrdLife (0.5%), CrdA&H (0.3%), IndA&H (0.0%), GrpAnn (-0.1%)																			
...	100.2	5.2	0.4	0.1	1.8	2.52	2.52	-3.0	32.0	27.4	...	...	1.7	124.6	124.6	...	...	...	...
...	100.6	5.5	0.3	0.0	1.3	4.42	4.42	6.9	37.3	24.4	...	...	-6.5	113.9	113.9	...	...	...	...
...	100.1	4.8	0.9	0.1	5.4	5.48	5.48	22.9	43.4	17.2	...	...	5.6	108.1	108.1	...	...	...	...
...	101.1	4.9	-3.1	-0.4	-16.1	3.77	3.77	19.0	26.2	30.1	...	...	97.1	122.7	122.7	...	...	...	...
...	...	...	0.5	0.1	2.2	1.15	1.15	-99.9	...	32.0	...	...	10.5	122.3	122.3	...	...	...	...
...	24.6	64.0	2.2	5.0	2.8	5.10	5.22	100.7	0.3	375.9	22.1	73.2	3.0	331.6	370.0	...	...	...	...
...	34.8	99.8	-7.8	-16.7	-10.4	4.78	4.95	38.5	0.4	253.4	17.4	88.8	-10.7	256.1	277.5	...	...	...	...
...	35.6	76.2	-3.8	-6.6	-5.4	4.89	4.90	36.7	0.6	232.0	15.8	96.0	-5.2	300.2	316.2	3.2	...	...	...
...	34.8	30.1	8.5	15.0	12.2	4.42	2.00	0.5	0.6	228.3	14.0	100.8	-0.5	266.0	294.7	4.4	...	...	...
-1	41.2	9.3	9.0	21.6	12.8	3.33	2.91	-24.1	0.4	249.3	10.6	86.4	16.1	298.2	326.3	1.4	...	...	...
Principal Lines of Business: GrpA&H (64.3%), GrpLife (21.9%), IndA&H (8.4%), OrdLife (5.4%)														Principal States: CA (13.3%), TX (11.4%), IL (6.2%), FL (4.0%), OH (4.0%)					
...	...	...	-1.6	-99.9	-2.2	0.97	0.97	...	...	307.5	...	...	-2.1	407.4	407.4	...	...	...	...
...	...	...	-2.3	-99.9	-3.1	1.52	1.52	...	...	258.3	...	...	-3.0	358.2	358.2	...	...	...	...
...	...	...	-1.2	-73.1	-1.7	1.62	1.62	...	...	230.9	...	...	-1.6	330.8	330.8	...	...	...	...
...	...	...	-1.7	-99.9	-2.5	1.03	1.03	...	...	206.7	...	...	-2.4	306.6	306.6	...	...	...	...
...	...	...	-2.2	-99.9	-3.3	0.47	0.47	...	...	184.7	...	...	-3.3	284.6	284.6	...	...	...	...
...	84.5	22.6	0.2	1.4	0.2	0.99	1.07	999.9	0.1	999.9	0.0	0.0	761.3	999.9	999.9	...	...	...	...
...	76.7	27.6	2.5	11.1	2.7	5.02	5.04	215.0	0.2	999.9	0.0	0.0	3.2	999.9	999.9	...	...	...	...
-1	68.7	30.6	2.2	6.3	2.5	5.57	5.10	76.0	0.3	537.9	0.6	0.4	2.2	490.6	565.1	...	...	...	...
2	69.9	24.8	3.9	11.3	4.6	5.28	4.07	6.8	0.3	602.1	0.6	1.6	2.5	551.9	627.9	...	...	...	...
-1	78.3	22.0	3.2	8.9	3.8	5.46	4.85	9.7	0.4	552.3	1.0	2.3	3.4	487.2	559.3	0.8	...	...	...
Principal Lines of Business: GrpA&H (67.1%), GrpLife (28.0%), CrdLife (3.0%), CrdA&H (1.4%), OrdLife (0.5%)														Principal States: NY (23.3%), NC (18.0%), ME (15.4%), OR (6.8%), SC (5.1%)					
...	...	...	3.3	105.7	3.6	2.78	3.14	...	...	999.9	...	...	3.7	999.9	999.9	...	...	...	...
...	...	...	2.9	68.3	3.2	4.02	4.39	...	...	999.9	...	...	3.2	999.9	999.9	...	...	...	...
...	...	...	3.4	68.2	3.7	4.71	5.11	...	...	999.9	...	...	3.7	999.9	999.9	...	...	...	...
...	...	...	9.3	90.3	9.9	2.79	10.70	...	...	999.9	...	...	-70.2	999.9	999.9	...	...	...	...
...	...	999.9	-10.5	-99.9	-11.0	2.70	2.70	...	0.0	999.9	1.2	0.1	91.0	999.9	999.9	...	...	...	...
Principal Lines of Business: IndAnn (100.0%)														Principal States: NY (100.0%)					
3,021	88.4	10.3	0.3	2.2	6.2	5.00	5.14	8.9	2.4	12.3	0.6	84.0	0.3	53.2	70.1	32.6	...	0.3	21.0
3,365	98.1	10.0	0.3	1.8	6.0	5.06	5.27	7.1	2.7	12.9	0.5	87.1	-1.6	53.8	73.3	29.9	...	0.5	21.1
-14,425	100.9	7.1	0.3	1.6	5.4	5.36	4.90	-1.9	2.7	13.4	0.5	85.9	-1.8	68.2	88.1	31.0	...	0.9	10.4
-13,710	171.8	14.9	-0.2	-1.8	-4.8	5.19	-1.07	-50.5	2.5	7.6	1.8	183.4	-47.8	46.1	61.2	44.3	...	5.3	232.2
-28,247	219.3	19.0	0.3	3.4	7.6	3.82	2.14	-36.7	1.1	11.3	0.9	131.0	44.4	48.4	60.2	69.9	...	3.4	161.7
Principal Lines of Business: IndAnn (67.5%), GrpAnn (31.4%), OrdLife (1.1%), IndA&H (0.0%), GrpA&H (0.0%)														Principal States: IN (23.1%), TX (10.2%), CA (9.3%), PA (8.2%), KS (4.1%)					
...	...	...	...	...	...	...	...	...	...	...	...	...	...	...	...	...	...	...	...
...	...	...	...	...	...	...	...	...	...	...	...	...	...	...	...	...	...	...	...
...	...	...	...	...	...	...	...	...	...	...	...	...	...	...	...	...	...	...	...
...	...	...	...	...	...	...	...	...	...	...	...	...	...	...	...	...	...	...	...
...	...	...	...	-99.9	...	...	...	...	...	999.9	...	...	...	999.9	999.9	...	...	...	...
...	89.6	7.5	12.3	3.6	29.5	4.51	4.48	4.3	7.2	74.6	...	...	34.1	112.6	119.4	...	...	0.2	0.2
-23	90.7	7.8	8.0	2.2	18.4	5.23	4.86	18.8	8.1	79.9	...	...	5.7	132.2	140.0	1.0	...	0.3	0.3
-202	92.5	6.7	7.7	1.8	17.5	5.45	5.35	29.9	9.2	76.7	...	...	13.6	125.0	131.8	1.0	...	0.7	0.7
18	90.1	7.2	14.7	3.7	31.4	4.69	3.69	9.6	7.4	97.4	...	...	36.7	146.3	154.1	1.3	...	0.6	0.6
-11	90.3	6.1	18.7	4.5	34.4	4.02	4.21	23.3	6.4	140.0	...	...	41.2	177.3	189.4	1.9	...	0.5	0.5
Principal Lines of Business: CompHosp/Med (58.4%), Medicare (28.4%), Medicaid (12.0%), MedSup (1.2%)														Principal States: WI (100.0%)					

Data in U.S. Dollars

COMPANY NAME Ultimate Parent Association Principal Officer Mailing Address Dom. : Began Bus. : Struct. : Mktg. Specialty Phone # AMB# NAIC#	Best's Financial Strength Rating FSC	Data Year	Balance Sheet: Bonds (%)	Mort. Loans & R.E. (%)	Com & Pref. Stock (%)	All Other Assets (%)	Total Assets ($000)	Life Reserves (%)	Health Reserves (%)	Ann Res. & Dep. Liabilities (%)	All Other Liabilities (%)	Capital & Surplus ($000)	Operations: Direct Premiums Written ($000)	Net Premiums Written & Deposits ($000)	Operating Cash Flow ($000)	NOG Before Taxes ($000)	NOG After Taxes ($000)	Net Income ($000)
SECURITY LIFE INS CO OF AMER Safe Partners, LLC Gil C. Rohde, Jr. President & CEO 10901 Red Circle Drive Minnetonka, MN 55343-9137 MN : 1956 : Stock : Agency Dental, Other A&H, Group Life 952-544-2121 AMB# 007030 NAIC# 68721	**B++ u** Under Review Implication: Developing **FSC V**	'05	57.2	13.2	...	29.5	83,064	38.2	7.4	16.3	38.1	12,359	75,621	105,878	8,269	3,242	2,821	2,796
		'06	62.9	12.1	...	25.0	79,093	41.6	7.8	17.2	33.4	14,858	66,812	111,166	-2,983	5,111	4,182	4,228
		'07	59.4	9.0	...	31.6	96,471	36.8	9.2	14.5	39.5	24,647	63,300	138,203	10,545	5,963	5,069	5,069
		'08	62.5	7.9	...	29.6	93,961	38.1	13.0	13.8	35.1	25,276	65,719	164,773	-4,688	4,695	3,671	3,135
		'09	67.1	8.1	...	24.8	79,206	47.6	14.8	16.4	21.1	24,450	63,896	75,821	-14,455	4,136	3,385	3,186
		Rating History: B++u, 05/04/10; B++, 04/16/09; B++, 04/29/08; B+, 04/20/07; B, 03/08/06																
SECURITY LIFE OF DENVER INS CO ING Groep N.V. Donald W. Britton President 5780 Powers Ferry Road, NW Atlanta, GA 30327-4390 CO : 1950 : Stock : Agency Corp Whole Life, Trad Life, Univ Life 303-860-1290 AMB# 007029 NAIC# 68713	**A** Rating Outlook: Stable **FSC XIV**	'05	69.4	12.5	0.8	17.3	23,814,540	40.5	0.0	43.2	16.3	1,529,862	1,235,128	6,316,538	2,903,916	288,317	122,993	139,428
		'06	72.6	10.4	1.4	15.7	23,761,829	39.8	...	45.9	14.2	1,595,344	962,060	3,615,211	433,695	160,054	130,102	135,443
		'07	71.9	8.2	1.7	18.2	24,221,950	38.4	...	46.8	14.8	1,305,671	984,976	5,922,229	375,889	45,532	27,325	20,224
		'08	68.3	7.7	1.5	22.5	24,264,720	38.9	1.1	43.0	17.0	1,438,954	1,446,645	4,217,593	-314,574	184,182	221,194	37,565
		'09	62.4	7.9	1.1	28.6	20,770,378	43.8	1.4	32.8	22.0	1,697,472	1,001,425	4,078,744	-2,996,122	261,858	221,748	23,735
		Rating History: A g, 06/11/10; A g, 04/24/09; A+ g, 06/18/08; A+ g, 05/11/07; A+ g, 02/24/06																
SECURITY MUTUAL LIFE OF NY Bruce W. Boyea Chairman, President & CEO P.O. Box 1625 Binghamton, NY 13902-1625 NY : 1887 : Mutual : Agency Group Life, Ind Ann, Ind Life 607-723-3551 AMB# 007034 NAIC# 68772	**A-** Rating Outlook: Stable **FSC VIII**	'05	76.6	5.3	0.7	17.5	1,958,418	70.6	0.2	22.6	6.6	99,751	361,304	277,293	100,134	12,663	7,446	7,348
		'06	75.8	5.4	1.4	17.5	2,041,281	71.1	0.2	22.1	6.6	106,828	342,005	257,823	82,310	11,538	6,580	7,029
		'07	73.6	7.1	0.4	18.8	2,116,279	71.6	0.1	21.5	6.8	114,730	346,345	255,510	64,219	13,476	7,120	5,717
		'08	69.8	9.0	0.4	20.9	2,220,992	69.6	0.1	24.4	5.9	107,896	426,090	328,644	123,697	5,239	4,051	-8,784
		'09	74.3	7.4	0.2	18.0	2,426,937	62.8	0.1	28.2	8.9	112,993	463,211	374,733	192,221	4,074	4,298	7,220
		Rating History: A-, 06/10/10; A, 05/26/09; A, 06/19/08; A, 06/02/07; A, 05/03/06																
SECURITY NATIONAL LIFE INS CO Security National Financial Scott M. Quist President 5300 South 360 West Salt Lake City, UT 84123 UT : 1967 : Stock : Agency Ann, Ind Ann, Reins 801-264-1060 AMB# 007127 NAIC# 69485	**NR-5**	'05	26.3	29.7	1.9	42.1	277,377	77.8	0.1	18.8	3.2	13,583	30,554	31,181	-728	506	504	622
		'06	33.1	30.6	2.9	33.3	297,098	78.4	0.1	18.2	3.3	19,780	32,718	35,918	41,747	282	282	566
		'07	35.2	31.2	3.5	30.2	329,294	75.5	0.1	19.3	5.1	17,875	33,973	37,291	34,843	2,662	2,496	2,637
		'08	35.3	41.9	3.7	19.1	342,913	75.9	0.1	20.1	3.9	16,432	39,911	44,665	19,655	-350	-350	-1,060
		'09	31.5	40.5	3.6	24.4	364,164	76.0	0.1	18.8	5.1	17,063	39,987	44,748	21,832	-1,019	-1,019	3,233
		Rating History: NR-5, 04/19/10; NR-5, 04/14/09; NR-5, 04/11/08; NR-5, 04/27/07; NR-5, 04/28/06																
SECURITY NATIONAL LIFE INS LA Scott M. Quist President P.O. Box 57220 Salt Lake City, UT 84157-0220 LA : 1957 : Stock : Not Available Life 601-346-2766 AMB# 007902 NAIC# 76244	**NR-5**	'05	52.0	7.1	13.4	27.5	3,280	89.5	0.0	...	10.5	1,242	432	434	-89	48	29	29
		'06	70.9	6.0	13.6	9.5	3,406	89.1	0.0	...	10.9	1,266	510	510	81	30	29	23
		'07	53.5	4.7	26.1	15.7	3,324	87.4	0.0	...	12.6	1,076	469	469	-469	31	31	24
		'08	64.6	4.5	8.9	21.9	2,757	95.6	...	...	4.4	653	516	516	44	105	100	102
		'09	...	...	...	100.0	...	...	...	...	100.0	...	554	553	-2,509	0	0	519
		Rating History: NR-5, 06/04/10; NR-5, 04/16/09; NR-5, 04/11/08; NR-5, 04/27/07; NR-5, 04/24/06																
SECURITY PLAN LIFE INS CO Citizens Inc Rick D. Riley Chairman, President & CEO P.O. Box 609 Donaldsonville, LA 70346-0609 LA : 1996 : Stock : Agency Home serv, Ind Life, Whole life 225-473-8654 AMB# 007450 NAIC# 60076	**NR-5**	'05	89.9	1.0	2.2	6.9	278,431	94.3	0.3	2.5	2.9	55,057	36,873	36,791	7,325	9,645	7,954	8,372
		'06	89.4	1.0	2.5	7.1	286,241	93.4	0.3	3.1	3.2	56,633	38,812	38,724	8,896	5,952	4,670	4,887
		'07	86.5	1.0	6.4	6.1	291,992	93.3	0.3	3.6	2.8	58,626	41,810	41,963	5,331	10,278	7,573	7,879
		'08	81.7	0.7	9.4	8.3	282,300	91.8	0.2	5.8	2.2	43,688	39,044	40,186	-10,058	1,332	1,611	-8,360
		'09	85.7	0.9	3.4	10.1	302,286	89.3	0.2	6.2	4.3	52,790	39,494	39,550	15,650	2,030	2,686	6,104
		Rating History: NR-5, 04/12/10; NR-5, 04/16/09; NR-5, 04/07/08; NR-5, 04/27/07; NR-5, 04/24/06																
SEECHANGE HEALTH INSURANCE CO[1] Martin Watson President 4079 Executive Parkway Westerville, OH 43081 OH : 1956 : Stock 614-797-5200 AMB# 060717 NAIC# 63541	**NR-1**	'05	...	...	...	...	...	...	...	...	...	...	...	...	...	...	...	...
		'06	...	...	...	...	...	...	...	...	...	...	...	...	...	...	...	...
		'07	...	...	...	...	...	...	...	...	...	...	...	...	...	...	...	...
		'08	...	...	...	...	...	...	...	...	...	...	...	...	...	...	...	...
		'09	36.6	...	...	63.4	5,806	...	...	...	100.0	5,770	...	...	...	-972	-972	-980
		Rating History: NR-1, 06/10/10																
SELECTCARE HEALTH PLANS INC Universal American Corp. Theodore M. Carpenter, Jr. President & CEO 4888 Loop Central Drive, Suite 700 Houston, TX 77081 TX : 2005 : Stock : Broker Health 713-965-9444 AMB# 064845 NAIC# 10768	**NR-2**	'05	...	...	...	100.0	1,859	...	...	...	100.0	1,853	...	...	1,859	3	3	3
		'06	...	...	...	100.0	1,907	...	...	...	100.0	1,885	...	...	37	48	32	32
		'07	45.3	...	...	54.7	3,389	...	57.5	...	42.5	2,152	5,131	5,112	1,223	426	274	274
		'08	11.7	...	...	88.3	13,022	...	48.6	...	51.4	4,065	28,657	28,578	9,399	1,647	1,025	1,025
		'09	51.5	...	...	48.5	15,376	...	116.3	...	-16.3	7,387	62,677	62,538	1,765	-1,065	-1,051	-1,051
		Rating History: NR-2, 04/16/10; NR-2, 12/03/08; NR-2, 08/21/07; NR-2, 05/30/06																
SELECTCARE OF MAINE Universal American Corp. Theodore M. Carpenter President 4888 Loop Central Drive, Suite 700 Houston, TX 77081 TX : 2009 : Stock : Broker Inactive 713-770-1111 AMB# 064975 NAIC# 13627	**NR-2**	'05	...	...	...	...	...	...	...	...	...	...	...	...	...	...	...	...
		'06	...	...	...	...	...	...	...	...	...	...	...	...	...	...	...	...
		'07	...	...	...	...	...	...	...	...	...	...	...	...	...	...	...	...
		'08	...	...	...	...	...	...	...	...	...	...	...	...	...	...	...	...
		'09	7.2	...	...	92.8	1,523	...	...	...	100.0	1,521	...	...	1,523	2	1	1
		Rating History: NR-2, 04/16/10																

Data in U.S. Dollars

—	Profitability Tests							Leverage Tests						Liquidity Tests					
Un-Realized Capital Gains ($000)	Benefits Paid to NPW & Dep (%)	Comm. & Expenses to NPW & Dep (%)	NOG to Total Assets (%)	NOG to Total Rev (%)	Operating Return on Equity (%)	Net Yield (%)	Total Return (%)	Change in NPW & Dep (%)	NPW & Dep to Capital (X)	Capital & Surplus to Liabilities (%)	Surplus Relief (%)	Reins Leverage (%)	Change in Capital (%)	Quick Liquidity (%)	Current Liquidity (%)	Non-Invest Grade Bonds to Capital (%)	Delinq. & Foreclosed Mortgages to Capital (%)	Mort. & Credit Tenant Loans & R.E. to Capital (%)	Affiliated Invest to Capital (%)
515	65.6	36.2	3.6	2.1	23.4	4.81	5.59	16.5	8.4	17.9	174.7	999.9	4.9	84.8	92.7	...	...	91.3	...
396	66.8	33.1	5.2	3.2	30.7	4.84	5.45	5.0	7.4	23.6	106.3	843.1	19.7	86.0	94.2	...	...	66.0	...
6,617	68.0	31.3	5.8	3.4	25.7	4.74	13.20	24.3	5.6	34.8	32.3	428.7	65.0	110.8	119.1	0.1	...	36.1	...
539	70.0	30.2	3.9	2.2	14.7	4.21	4.22	19.2	6.5	36.9	1.2	349.8	1.7	106.7	115.3	0.9	...	29.4	12.7
189	65.9	35.1	3.9	4.2	13.6	4.20	4.19	-54.0	3.1	44.8	0.8	319.5	-3.2	104.5	113.3	8.4	...	26.2	12.3
Principal Lines of Business: GrpA&H (94.4%), OrdLife (2.8%), GrpLife (2.1%), IndA&H (0.6%), IndAnn (0.2%)														Principal States: CA (26.8%), MN (9.9%), VA (6.3%), WA (5.6%), GA (5.2%)					
10,882	21.5	1.8	0.5	2.5	9.5	5.02	5.09	100.1	0.0	0.3	16.7	403.0	30.0	61.2	66.3	41.6	...	176.7	11.2
13,826	64.5	5.5	0.5	6.6	8.3	5.67	5.69	-42.8	2.1	8.5	14.5	453.3	3.5	55.4	68.9	34.3	...	141.5	32.4
-102,703	38.8	3.3	0.1	1.2	1.9	5.85	5.26	63.8	4.1	6.8	25.2	587.1	-17.3	54.9	67.9	50.0	...	138.4	60.2
-88,579	38.1	6.2	0.9	7.9	16.1	4.93	3.61	-28.8	2.8	6.9	17.0	578.2	3.2	52.7	65.5	80.1	...	126.3	26.3
-75,560	53.4	8.2	1.0	10.2	14.1	4.45	2.99	-3.3	2.4	9.7	12.1	535.9	15.4	48.9	60.5	101.0	...	95.4	50.8
Principal Lines of Business: GrpAnn (79.0%), OrdLife (12.0%), GrpA&H (5.1%), IndAnn (3.9%), GrpLife (0.0%)														Principal States: KS (37.8%), DE (16.2%), OH (8.0%), PA (4.9%), NJ (4.7%)					
-643	58.1	22.3	0.4	1.9	7.7	5.92	5.90	0.1	2.6	5.8	27.2	268.6	2.9	54.1	64.1	24.8	...	95.9	17.4
-634	63.5	24.5	0.3	1.8	6.4	5.93	5.91	-7.0	2.2	6.1	26.4	282.6	9.5	54.1	64.2	8.1	...	93.0	15.3
2,713	64.2	25.6	0.3	2.0	6.4	5.92	5.97	-0.9	2.0	6.4	25.5	291.8	8.2	53.5	63.2	12.9	...	117.9	8.5
-248	58.6	21.0	0.2	0.9	3.6	5.69	5.05	28.6	2.9	5.3	29.9	380.6	-10.9	58.2	67.0	9.2	...	174.9	8.6
1,071	46.4	34.2	0.2	0.9	3.9	5.40	5.65	14.0	3.0	5.2	30.6	424.2	9.1	53.8	63.7	18.6	...	145.2	8.2
Principal Lines of Business: IndAnn (40.4%), OrdLife (40.0%), GrpAnn (14.8%), GrpA&H (2.7%), GrpLife (2.1%)														Principal States: NY (61.4%), NJ (9.0%), PA (4.6%), FL (4.2%)					
24	68.5	68.3	0.2	0.4	3.4	6.56	6.66	-5.7	1.9	6.1	14.6	404.9	-12.3	43.2	46.6	15.0	6.8	515.4	75.1
2,320	69.2	62.0	0.1	0.5	1.7	7.11	8.12	15.2	1.6	8.4	6.9	4.2	44.3	50.9	55.7	4.3	7.1	394.4	49.6
-1,045	76.5	69.0	0.8	3.0	13.3	8.07	7.79	3.8	1.8	6.8	0.2	4.6	-9.4	49.1	54.0	15.6	22.4	491.1	60.5
-4,238	78.1	76.7	-0.1	-0.4	-2.0	5.97	4.48	19.8	2.3	6.0	0.6	63.3	-6.7	37.3	42.6	15.6	112.8	736.7	78.0
1,381	71.4	50.5	-0.3	-1.5	-6.1	4.86	6.51	0.2	1.8	7.5	0.7	33.5	31.0	41.0	46.0	31.0	69.2	576.5	41.4
Principal Lines of Business: OrdLife (66.7%), IndAnn (14.2%), IndLife (13.9%), GrpLife (3.2%), GrpAnn (1.7%)														Principal States: MS (29.3%), TX (17.2%), UT (11.7%), FL (6.8%), LA (5.4%)					
110	54.9	88.4	0.9	4.9	2.4	5.04	8.50	5.5	0.3	70.6	...	0.1	11.3	110.8	120.5	29.4	...	17.2	...
21	43.4	67.7	0.9	4.3	2.3	4.95	5.41	17.4	0.4	69.9	...	0.1	3.3	95.7	107.3	50.0	...	14.6	...
406	40.3	78.7	0.9	4.8	2.6	5.21	17.98	-8.1	0.4	58.7	...	0.0	-12.3	97.7	109.8	36.6	...	12.7	...
-622	34.3	62.5	3.3	15.7	11.6	4.21	-14.45	10.1	0.7	34.5	...	0.1	-42.5	87.0	94.9	63.7	...	17.6	...
...	24.1	453.0	0.0	0.0	0.0	...	...	7.3	...	...	...	...	-99.9	...	...	...	...	...	...
Principal Lines of Business: IndLife (80.8%), OrdLife (19.2%)														Principal States: LA (100.0%)					
-2,034	50.8	56.2	2.9	15.7	15.3	5.05	4.66	-3.4	0.7	25.2	0.0	4.0	10.9	81.7	91.0	2.7	0.0	5.1	7.2
-3,442	47.2	61.0	1.7	8.8	8.4	5.25	4.24	5.3	0.7	25.4	0.0	3.6	3.5	81.5	90.4	2.8	0.1	5.0	7.4
65	40.6	59.8	2.6	13.2	13.1	5.62	5.84	8.4	0.7	26.5	0.0	3.1	5.5	83.8	91.2	9.3	...	4.7	9.0
-2,137	47.8	71.8	0.6	3.0	3.2	5.19	0.99	-4.2	0.9	18.8	0.0	3.7	-26.9	77.4	84.7	12.9	0.1	4.2	9.5
2,787	46.8	69.4	0.9	5.0	5.6	4.91	7.24	-1.6	0.7	21.8	...	2.9	20.9	79.5	85.0	19.2	...	4.9	11.8
Principal Lines of Business: OrdLife (72.0%), IndLife (19.6%), IndAnn (6.6%), IndA&H (1.7%)														Principal States: LA (84.0%), AR (11.8%)					
...	...	...	...	...	...	...	...	...	...	...	...	...	...	...	...	...	...	...	...
...	...	...	...	...	...	...	...	...	...	...	...	...	...	...	...	...	...	...	...
...	...	...	...	...	...	...	...	...	...	...	...	...	...	...	...	...	...	...	...
...	...	...	...	...	...	...	...	...	...	...	...	...	...	...	...	...	...	...	...
...	...	...	...	-99.9	...	...	...	...	...	999.9	...	...	...	...	...	...	...	...	...
...	...	...	...	21.4	...	...	...	...	...	999.9	...	...	...	999.9	999.9	...	...	...	...
...	...	...	1.7	50.4	1.7	3.42	3.42	...	...	999.9	...	...	1.7	999.9	999.9	...	...	...	...
...	75.0	19.2	10.3	5.2	13.6	5.21	5.21	...	2.4	173.8	...	...	14.1	256.7	257.9	...	...	...	...
...	78.0	17.1	12.5	3.6	33.0	3.25	3.25	459.0	7.0	45.4	...	...	88.9	238.3	249.4	...	...	...	...
...	85.4	16.6	-7.4	-1.7	-18.3	1.23	1.23	118.8	8.5	92.5	...	...	81.7	226.3	233.6	...	...	...	...
Principal Lines of Business: Medicare (100.0%)														Principal States: TX (100.0%)					
...	...	...	...	...	...	...	...	...	...	...	...	...	...	...	...	...	...	...	...
...	...	...	...	...	...	...	...	...	...	...	...	...	...	...	...	...	...	...	...
...	...	...	...	...	...	...	...	...	...	...	...	...	...	...	...	...	...	...	...
...	...	...	...	...	...	...	...	...	...	...	...	...	...	...	...	...	...	...	...
...	...	...	...	45.3	...	...	...	...	...	999.9	...	...	...	999.9	999.9	...	...	...	...

COMPANY NAME / Ultimate Parent Association / Principal Officer / Mailing Address / Dom. : Began Bus. : Struct. : Mktg. / Specialty / Phone # / AMB# / NAIC#

Best's Financial Strength Rating / FSC

Balance Sheet: Data Year; Bonds (%); Mort. Loans & R.E. (%); Com & Pref. Stock (%); All Other Assets (%); Total Assets ($000); Life Reserves (%); Health Reserves (%); Ann Res. & Dep. Liabilities (%); All Other Liabilities (%); Capital & Surplus ($000)

Operations: Direct Premiums Written ($000); Net Premiums Written & Deposits ($000); Operating Cash Flow ($000); NOG Before Taxes ($000); NOG After Taxes ($000); Net Income ($000)

SELECTCARE OF OKLAHOMA INC
Universal American Corp.
Theodore M. Carpenter, Jr.
President
4888 Loop Central Drive, Suite 700
Houston, TX 77081
OK : 2004 : Stock : Broker
Medicare
713-965-9444
AMB# 064844 NAIC# 12284

NR-2

Data Year	Bonds (%)	Mort. Loans & R.E. (%)	Com & Pref. Stock (%)	All Other Assets (%)	Total Assets ($000)	Life Reserves (%)	Health Reserves (%)	Ann Res. & Dep. Liabilities (%)	All Other Liabilities (%)	Capital & Surplus ($000)	Direct Premiums Written ($000)	Net Premiums Written & Deposits ($000)	Operating Cash Flow ($000)	NOG Before Taxes ($000)	NOG After Taxes ($000)	Net Income ($000)
'05	24.7	...	...	75.3	2,021	...	62.2	...	37.8	1,779	500	498	1,665	-169	-169	-169
'06	20.8	...	...	79.2	2,401	...	41.4	...	58.6	1,726	2,318	2,306	362	-93	-93	-93
'07	21.4	...	...	78.6	2,340	...	64.9	...	35.1	1,515	3,153	3,141	-298	-221	-221	-221
'08	21.5	...	...	78.5	2,321	...	57.3	...	42.7	1,555	3,800	3,789	203	35	35	35
'09	21.9	...	...	78.1	2,514	...	55.3	...	44.7	1,501	3,536	3,528	56	-161	-156	-156

Rating History: NR-2, 04/16/10; NR-2, 12/03/08; NR-2, 08/21/07; NR-2, 05/30/06

SELECTCARE OF TEXAS LLC
Universal American Corp.
Theodore M. Carpenter, Jr.
President
4888 Loop Central Drive, Suite 700
Houston, TX 77081
TX : 2001 : Stock : Broker
Medicare
713-965-9444
AMB# 064744 NAIC# 10096

B+
Rating Outlook: Stable
FSC VII

Data Year	Bonds (%)	Mort. Loans & R.E. (%)	Com & Pref. Stock (%)	All Other Assets (%)	Total Assets ($000)	Life Reserves (%)	Health Reserves (%)	Ann Res. & Dep. Liabilities (%)	All Other Liabilities (%)	Capital & Surplus ($000)	Direct Premiums Written ($000)	Net Premiums Written & Deposits ($000)	Operating Cash Flow ($000)	NOG Before Taxes ($000)	NOG After Taxes ($000)	Net Income ($000)
'05	61.1	...	...	38.9	55,992	...	22.3	...	77.7	19,366	215,441	215,289	24,970	9,759	9,759	9,768
'06	38.3	...	...	61.7	101,827	...	24.8	...	75.2	35,513	326,000	325,709	40,716	17,277	17,277	17,326
'07	54.5	...	...	45.5	125,966	...	28.7	...	71.3	49,227	411,632	411,303	17,170	13,973	13,973	13,965
'08	51.8	...	...	48.2	159,496	...	23.0	...	77.0	74,128	502,626	502,328	29,520	27,208	27,208	26,303
'09	83.8	...	...	16.2	159,410	...	27.1	...	72.9	84,199	542,442	542,204	12,553	29,245	11,851	9,603

Rating History: B+, 04/16/10; B+, 12/03/08; B+, 08/21/07; B+, 06/21/06; B+, 06/09/05

SELECTED FUNERAL & LIFE INS CO[2]
Courtney C. Crouch, Jr.
President
P.O. Box 6040
Hot Springs, AR 71902-6040
AR : 1960 : Stock : Not Available
Ind Ann, Ordinary Life
501-624-2172
AMB# 068277 NAIC# 83836

NR-5

Data Year	Bonds (%)	Mort. Loans & R.E. (%)	Com & Pref. Stock (%)	All Other Assets (%)	Total Assets ($000)	Life Reserves (%)	Health Reserves (%)	Ann Res. & Dep. Liabilities (%)	All Other Liabilities (%)	Capital & Surplus ($000)	Direct Premiums Written ($000)	Net Premiums Written & Deposits ($000)	Operating Cash Flow ($000)	NOG Before Taxes ($000)	NOG After Taxes ($000)	Net Income ($000)
'05	90.9	1.3	3.6	4.2	127,508	43.3	...	54.2	2.5	19,813	13,724	13,700	4,609	734	604	598
'06	90.2	1.1	3.9	4.8	133,082	43.8	...	53.7	2.5	20,667	14,117	14,091	4,860	565	465	463
'07	90.6	1.0	3.7	4.7	137,891	44.9	...	52.8	2.3	21,054	13,546	13,523	5,074	656	531	682
'08	90.2	0.9	2.7	6.2	140,379	46.3	...	52.5	1.2	20,444	14,751	14,728	4,871	643	508	504
'09	92.3	0.8	3.0	3.8	146,319	47.3	...	51.0	1.7	20,916	14,742	14,718	4,813	542	442	280

Rating History: NR-5, 04/12/10; NR-5, 05/11/09; NR-5, 06/30/08; NR-5, 06/28/07; NR-5, 06/16/06

SENIOR AMERICAN LIFE INS CO
AF&L Holdings, LLC
Daniel G. Helle
Chairman
165 Veterans Way, Suite 300
Warminster, PA 18974
PA : 1962 : Stock : Agency
Ind A&H
215-918-0515
AMB# 060294 NAIC# 76759

D
Rating Outlook: Stable
FSC V

Data Year	Bonds (%)	Mort. Loans & R.E. (%)	Com & Pref. Stock (%)	All Other Assets (%)	Total Assets ($000)	Life Reserves (%)	Health Reserves (%)	Ann Res. & Dep. Liabilities (%)	All Other Liabilities (%)	Capital & Surplus ($000)	Direct Premiums Written ($000)	Net Premiums Written & Deposits ($000)	Operating Cash Flow ($000)	NOG Before Taxes ($000)	NOG After Taxes ($000)	Net Income ($000)
'05	96.1	...	...	3.9	14,526	...	95.5	...	4.5	5,339	6,468	6,078	3,326	1,831	1,831	1,831
'06	94.9	...	...	5.1	17,705	...	91.2	...	8.8	5,046	5,281	5,281	2,988	-502	-319	-319
'07	94.2	...	...	5.8	19,071	...	96.2	...	3.8	4,541	4,853	4,853	1,399	-494	-494	-519
'08	90.5	...	...	9.5	20,580	...	96.5	...	3.5	4,109	4,545	4,545	1,776	-353	-353	-353
'09	95.7	...	...	4.3	21,433	...	96.8	...	3.2	3,142	4,206	4,206	576	-739	-739	-739

Rating History: D g, 05/18/10; D g, 03/24/09; D g, 03/11/08; D g, 05/14/07; D g, 05/02/06

SENIOR HEALTH INS CO OF PA[1]
Holly C. Bakke
President & CEO
1289 West City Center Drive, Suite 200
Carmel, IN 46032
PA : 1965 : Stock : Agency
LTC
317-566-7500
AMB# 007910 NAIC# 76325

NR-4

Data Year	Bonds (%)	Mort. Loans & R.E. (%)	Com & Pref. Stock (%)	All Other Assets (%)	Total Assets ($000)	Life Reserves (%)	Health Reserves (%)	Ann Res. & Dep. Liabilities (%)	All Other Liabilities (%)	Capital & Surplus ($000)	Direct Premiums Written ($000)	Net Premiums Written & Deposits ($000)	Operating Cash Flow ($000)	NOG Before Taxes ($000)	NOG After Taxes ($000)	Net Income ($000)
'05	88.5	2.9	5.3	3.3	3,070,288	...	...	0.1	99.9	107,142	354,116	364,643	...	-52,607	-33,816	-36,659
'06	85.2	5.1	4.3	5.4	3,201,500	...	...	0.1	99.9	117,377	332,775	343,217	...	-118,324	-93,228	-98,188
'07	86.5	6.1	2.5	5.0	3,401,110	...	...	0.1	99.9	127,679	311,733	322,362	...	-212,229	-191,297	-190,671
'08	88.1	5.4	1.3	5.3	3,272,997	...	...	0.0	100.0	217,975	285,597	297,540	...	-37,948	-25,263	-52,450
'09	92.1	5.0	0.6	2.3	3,251,995	...	...	...	100.0	193,449	234,567	249,911	...	11,896	16,415	-17,457

Rating History: NR-4, 07/24/09; C, 07/24/09; C, 11/20/08; C++u, 08/12/08; C++, 08/07/07

SENIOR LIFE INSURANCE COMPANY[1]
Dale R. Powell, Jr.
President
1327 West Jackson Street
Thomasville, GA 31792-6366
GA : 1970 : Stock : Not Available
229-228-6936
AMB# 008148 NAIC# 78662

NR-1

Data Year	Bonds (%)	Mort. Loans & R.E. (%)	Com & Pref. Stock (%)	All Other Assets (%)	Total Assets ($000)	Life Reserves (%)	Health Reserves (%)	Ann Res. & Dep. Liabilities (%)	All Other Liabilities (%)	Capital & Surplus ($000)	Direct Premiums Written ($000)	Net Premiums Written & Deposits ($000)	Operating Cash Flow ($000)	NOG Before Taxes ($000)	NOG After Taxes ($000)	Net Income ($000)
'05	63.7	5.7	2.9	27.8	12,368	...	...	3.9	96.1	5,108	11,311	11,305	...	240	177	177
'06	43.4	6.8	3.0	46.8	17,394	...	...	2.9	97.1	7,291	12,786	12,781	...	526	385	694
'07	51.8	5.5	3.7	39.1	21,775	...	...	2.2	97.8	8,356	15,455	15,454	...	1,341	833	833
'08	48.1	4.5	2.2	45.2	26,652	...	...	1.8	98.2	9,580	17,505	17,502	...	1,838	1,330	1,302
'09	23.3	6.5	2.4	67.8	32,959	...	...	1.4	98.6	11,817	18,516	18,514	...	1,912	1,552	1,449

Rating History: NR-1, 06/10/10; NR-1, 06/12/09; NR-1, 06/12/08; NR-1, 06/08/07; NR-1, 06/07/06

SENIOR WHOLE HEALTH OF CT INC[2]
John Williamson Baaokes Jr.
President
58 Charles Street
Cambridge, MA 02141
CT : 2007 : Stock : Not Available
Medicare
617-494-5353
AMB# 064958 NAIC# 12809

NR-5

Data Year	Bonds (%)	Mort. Loans & R.E. (%)	Com & Pref. Stock (%)	All Other Assets (%)	Total Assets ($000)	Life Reserves (%)	Health Reserves (%)	Ann Res. & Dep. Liabilities (%)	All Other Liabilities (%)	Capital & Surplus ($000)	Direct Premiums Written ($000)	Net Premiums Written & Deposits ($000)	Operating Cash Flow ($000)	NOG Before Taxes ($000)	NOG After Taxes ($000)	Net Income ($000)
'05	...	...	...	...	...	...	...	...	...	...	...	...	...	...	...	...
'06	...	...	...	...	...	...	...	...	...	...	...	...	...	...	...	...
'07	...	...	...	100.0	3,470	...	61.9	...	38.1	2,120	1,847	1,847	-2,667	-3,219	-3,219	-3,219
'08	...	...	...	100.0	3,366	...	41.6	...	58.4	1,956	7,042	7,042	-225	-3,323	-3,323	-3,323
'09	...	...	...	100.0	1,979	...	...	...	100.0	1,978	600	600	-2,051	987	987	987

Rating History: NR-5, 04/15/10; NR-5, 03/30/09; NR-5, 07/29/08

SENIOR WHOLE HEALTH OF NY INC[2]
Senior Health Holdings LLC
John Baackes, Jr.
President
58 Charles Street
Cambridge, MA 02141
NY : 2007 : Stock : Not Available
Medicare, Medicaid
617-494-5353
AMB# 064947 NAIC# 12776

NR-5

Data Year	Bonds (%)	Mort. Loans & R.E. (%)	Com & Pref. Stock (%)	All Other Assets (%)	Total Assets ($000)	Life Reserves (%)	Health Reserves (%)	Ann Res. & Dep. Liabilities (%)	All Other Liabilities (%)	Capital & Surplus ($000)	Direct Premiums Written ($000)	Net Premiums Written & Deposits ($000)	Operating Cash Flow ($000)	NOG Before Taxes ($000)	NOG After Taxes ($000)	Net Income ($000)
'05	...	...	...	...	...	...	...	...	...	...	...	...	...	...	...	...
'06	...	...	...	...	...	...	...	...	...	...	...	...	...	...	...	...
'07	...	...	...	100.0	5,292	...	61.7	...	38.3	3,998	2,210	2,210	-2,912	-3,446	-3,446	-3,446
'08	...	...	...	100.0	6,434	...	81.2	...	18.8	1,083	9,059	9,059	349	-9,307	-9,316	-9,316
'09	...	...	...	100.0	8,302	...	67.0	...	33.0	4,836	18,143	18,143	1,997	-3,525	-3,525	-3,525

Rating History: NR-5, 04/30/10; NR-5, 04/15/09; NR-5, 05/07/08

SENTINEL AMERICAN LIFE INS CO
Guardian Life Ins Co of America
Armand M. de Palo
President & CEO
7 Hanover Square
New York, NY 10004-4025
TX : 1952 : Stock : Inactive
Ind Ann, Ind Life, Pre-need
800-538-6203
AMB# 007987 NAIC# 77119

A
Rating Outlook: Stable
FSC V

Data Year	Bonds (%)	Mort. Loans & R.E. (%)	Com & Pref. Stock (%)	All Other Assets (%)	Total Assets ($000)	Life Reserves (%)	Health Reserves (%)	Ann Res. & Dep. Liabilities (%)	All Other Liabilities (%)	Capital & Surplus ($000)	Direct Premiums Written ($000)	Net Premiums Written & Deposits ($000)	Operating Cash Flow ($000)	NOG Before Taxes ($000)	NOG After Taxes ($000)	Net Income ($000)
'05	85.0	...	...	15.0	47,464	61.0	...	36.7	2.3	15,093	99	99	-728	2,012	1,690	1,598
'06	89.7	...	...	10.3	46,999	60.5	...	36.8	2.8	15,705	79	79	-116	1,153	754	777
'07	84.4	...	...	15.6	46,876	60.7	...	36.9	2.4	16,882	75	75	88	1,698	1,112	1,160
'08	76.2	...	...	23.8	43,524	61.9	...	37.1	1.1	15,158	62	62	-2,678	997	513	-121
'09	90.0	...	...	10.0	43,461	61.5	...	36.7	1.7	15,746	56	56	434	881	568	568

Rating History: A, 10/13/09; A, 11/26/08; A, 04/23/08; A, 11/10/06; A, 11/18/05

2010 BEST'S KEY RATING GUIDE — LIFE/HEALTH EDITION
BEST'S PROFITABILITY, LEVERAGE AND LIQUIDITY TESTS 2005 – 2009

Data in U.S. Dollars

—	Profitability Tests							Leverage Tests						Liquidity Tests					
Un-Realized Capital Gains ($000)	Benefits Paid to NPW & Dep (%)	Comm. & Expenses to NPW & Dep (%)	NOG to Total Assets (%)	NOG to Total Rev (%)	Operating Return on Equity (%)	Net Yield (%)	Total Return (%)	Change in NPW & Dep (%)	NPW & Dep to Capital (X)	Capital & Surplus to Liabilities (%)	Surplus Relief (%)	Reins Leverage (%)	Change in Capital (%)	Quick Liquidity (%)	Current Liquidity (%)	Non-Invest Grade Bonds to Capital (%)	Delinq. & Foreclosed Mortgages to Capital (%)	Mort. & Credit Tenant Loans & R.E. to Capital (%)	Affiliated Invest to Capital (%)
...	60.5	75.5	...	-33.2	...	...	...	...	0.3	735.5	...	...	...	615.8	719.2	...	...	...	...
...	72.8	33.1	-4.2	-4.0	-5.3	2.07	2.07	363.4	1.3	255.7	...	...	-3.0	274.4	311.4	...	...	...	...
...	80.4	28.4	-9.3	-6.9	-13.6	2.56	2.56	36.3	2.1	183.7	...	...	-12.2	188.4	218.7	...	...	...	...
...	73.8	25.8	1.5	0.9	2.3	0.91	0.91	20.6	2.4	203.1	...	...	2.6	229.5	262.2	...	...	...	...
...	76.8	27.9	-6.4	-4.4	-10.2	0.25	0.25	-6.9	2.4	148.1	...	...	-3.5	226.4	226.5	...	...	...	...
	Principal Lines of Business: Medicare (100.0%)													Principal States: OK (100.0%)					
...	82.2	13.0	22.6	1.6	67.1	3.10	3.12	46.3	11.1	52.0	...	...	101.9	175.5	185.9	...	...	...	...
...	81.3	14.3	21.9	5.3	63.0	3.96	4.02	51.3	9.2	53.6	...	...	83.4	209.3	216.5	...	...	...	...
...	83.0	14.8	12.3	3.4	33.0	4.70	4.69	26.3	8.4	64.1	...	0.6	38.6	186.1	194.2	...	...	...	...
-2,416	81.3	14.3	19.1	5.4	44.1	3.98	1.38	22.1	6.8	86.8	...	...	50.6	214.6	230.2	0.4	...	...	...
0	82.1	13.5	7.4	2.2	15.0	3.76	2.23	7.9	6.4	111.9	...	0.0	13.6	196.9	216.7	0.1	...	...	...
	Principal Lines of Business: Medicare (100.0%)													Principal States: TX (100.0%)					
-67	69.6	32.4	0.5	3.1	3.1	4.59	4.56	6.4	0.7	19.7	...	0.1	1.6	95.9	102.6	11.0	...	8.2	3.4
627	73.5	33.0	0.4	2.3	2.3	4.69	5.19	2.9	0.6	19.8	...	0.0	4.9	94.9	101.3	9.7	...	6.6	3.1
-149	78.3	31.1	0.4	2.7	2.5	4.68	4.70	-4.0	0.6	19.4	...	0.0	1.9	86.3	92.4	10.1	...	6.2	2.9
-2,300	76.3	33.0	0.4	2.4	2.4	4.64	2.99	8.9	0.7	17.1	...	0.0	-8.4	81.2	87.8	8.4	...	6.4	3.0
847	76.2	32.0	0.3	2.1	2.1	4.79	5.28	-0.1	0.7	17.1	...	0.1	4.4	75.0	84.0	13.7	...	5.7	2.8
	Principal Lines of Business: OrdLife (54.1%), IndAnn (45.9%)													Principal States: AR (80.6%), OK (10.5%), LA (5.8%), MS (3.1%)					
...	22.8	27.0	14.2	26.7	42.0	5.07	5.21	-3.4	1.1	58.7	2.4	2.2	58.0	98.8	111.3	5.2	...	...	...
...	60.4	35.4	-2.0	-5.2	-6.1	5.16	5.24	-13.1	1.0	40.4	...	0.1	-5.1	84.4	96.0	5.5	...	...	...
...	74.2	32.5	-2.7	-8.4	-10.3	5.63	5.56	-8.1	1.1	31.7	...	...	-10.0	82.1	93.9	...	...	...	...
...	78.5	31.2	-1.8	-6.2	-8.2	5.76	5.80	-6.3	1.1	25.4	...	...	-9.1	83.9	95.5	...	...	...	...
...	115.2	30.0	-3.5	-13.2	-20.4	6.78	6.81	-7.5	1.3	17.7	...	...	-22.8	75.6	87.0	...	...	...	...
	Principal Lines of Business: IndA&H (100.0%)													Principal States: LA (28.3%), MS (23.8%), FL (21.0%), AZ (16.9%)					
-2,687	114.7	28.0	-1.1	-6.2	-29.0	...	...	-9.4	3.1	4.0	1.2	...	-12.6	...	...	...	...	76.1	...
-1,218	119.9	32.7	-3.0	-17.5	-83.0	...	...	-5.9	2.7	4.1	1.0	...	7.3	...	...	...	...	128.7	...
-3,962	138.0	31.0	-5.8	-36.8	-99.9	...	...	-6.1	2.3	4.3	0.9	...	9.8	...	...	...	...	149.0	...
5,320	125.1	149.0	-0.8	-4.0	-14.6	...	...	-7.7	1.4	7.2	0.2	...	58.5	...	...	...	...	79.8	...
388	165.1	25.1	0.5	3.6	8.0	...	...	-16.0	1.3	6.4	0.0	...	-11.3	...	...	...	...	84.0	...
	Principal Lines of Business: IndA&H (97.2%), GrpA&H (2.8%)																		
4	13.8	75.3	1.6	1.4	3.6	...	...	41.4	2.2	73.7	0.0	...	8.2	...	...	...	...	13.4	...
20	15.5	70.5	2.6	2.7	6.2	...	...	13.1	1.7	77.0	0.0	...	44.2	...	...	...	...	15.6	...
-23	18.9	63.2	4.3	4.8	10.6	...	...	20.9	1.8	65.7	0.0	...	14.1	...	...	...	...	13.9	...
-307	20.1	60.8	5.5	6.8	14.8	...	...	13.3	1.8	57.9	0.0	...	13.2	...	...	...	...	12.3	...
134	22.8	56.6	5.2	7.6	14.5	...	...	5.8	1.5	57.9	0.0	...	23.6	...	...	...	...	17.6	...
	Principal Lines of Business: OrdLife (100.0%), IndA&H (0.0%)																		
...	...	...	...	...	...	...	...	...	...	...	...	...	...	...	...	...	...	...	...
...	...	...	...	...	...	...	...	...	...	...	...	...	...	...	...	...	...	...	...
...	127.2	158.4	...	-99.9	...	...	...	...	0.9	157.1	...	...	...	247.0	247.0	...	...	...	...
...	102.2	46.7	-97.2	-46.4	-99.9	3.83	3.83	281.3	3.6	138.6	...	...	-7.8	220.4	220.4	...	...	...	...
...	11.1	-68.4	36.9	153.5	50.2	2.07	2.07	-91.5	0.3	999.9	...	...	1.1	999.9	999.9	...	...	...	...
	Principal Lines of Business: Medicare (100.0%)													Principal States: CT (100.0%)					
...	...	...	...	...	...	...	...	...	...	...	...	...	...	...	...	...	...	...	...
...	...	...	...	...	...	...	...	...	...	...	...	...	...	...	...	...	...	...	...
...	106.7	161.6	...	-99.9	...	...	...	...	0.6	309.1	...	...	...	397.2	397.2	...	...	...	...
...	127.9	45.7	-99.9	-99.9	-99.9	2.39	2.39	309.8	8.4	20.2	...	...	-72.9	102.6	102.6	...	...	...	...
...	102.6	27.2	-47.8	-19.4	-99.9	0.10	0.10	100.3	3.8	139.5	...	...	346.6	215.9	215.9	...	...	...	...
	Principal Lines of Business: Medicare (75.3%), Medicaid (24.7%)													Principal States: NY (100.0%)					
...	999.9	721.4	3.5	60.3	11.8	5.79	5.63	-20.1	0.0	47.9	...	...	11.4	125.5	136.7	9.8	...	...	...
...	999.9	404.7	1.6	27.2	4.9	5.84	5.93	-20.2	0.0	51.8	...	...	4.3	118.4	131.6	8.7	...	...	...
...	999.9	380.0	2.4	41.0	6.8	5.79	5.89	-5.5	0.0	57.6	...	...	6.8	140.1	153.4	...	...	...	...
...	999.9	398.8	1.1	21.5	3.2	5.41	3.93	-17.7	0.0	53.4	...	...	-11.5	119.7	130.6	2.8	...	...	...
...	999.9	782.3	1.3	24.5	3.7	5.53	5.38	-9.0	0.0	57.2	...	...	4.3	115.5	130.8	...	...	...	...
	Principal Lines of Business: OrdLife (99.8%), IndAnn (0.2%)													Principal States: TX (61.2%), OK (21.5%), LA (7.8%), AR (4.6%)					

Data in U.S. Dollars

COMPANY NAME Ultimate Parent Association Principal Officer Mailing Address Dom. : Began Bus. : Struct. : Mktg. Specialty Phone # AMB# NAIC#	Best's Financial Strength Rating FSC	Data Year	Balance Sheet Bonds (%)	Mort. Loans & R.E. (%)	Com & Pref. Stock (%)	All Other Assets (%)	Total Assets ($000)	Life Reserves (%)	Health Reserves (%)	Ann Res. & Dep. Liabilities (%)	All Other Liabilities (%)	Capital & Surplus ($000)	Operations Direct Premiums Written ($000)	Net Premiums Written & Deposits ($000)	Operating Cash Flow ($000)	NOG Before Taxes ($000)	NOG After Taxes ($000)	Net Income ($000)
SENTINEL SECURITY LIFE INS CO	**B++**	'05	27.1	4.6	59.8	8.5	50,626	88.2	...	1.1	10.7	21,108	5,445	5,444	216	934	1,001	994
Earl L. Tate President & CEO		'06	32.5	4.9	53.9	8.6	52,300	89.9	...	1.1	9.0	22,544	5,581	5,578	1,576	1,276	1,017	1,269
2121 South State Street Salt Lake City, UT 84115	Rating Outlook: Stable	'07	38.5	4.0	48.0	9.5	53,754	90.6	...	1.1	8.3	23,290	5,908	5,908	898	855	833	1,285
UT : 1948 : Stock : Agency Ind Life, Term Life, Whole life		'08	39.6	3.8	44.3	12.4	51,372	93.5	...	1.1	5.4	20,679	6,111	6,110	949	644	540	667
801-484-8514		'09	40.4	3.6	38.9	17.1	51,947	94.0	...	1.0	5.0	20,393	6,455	6,449	97	445	356	-135
AMB# 007040 NAIC# 68802	FSC V	**Rating History: B++, 05/11/10; B++, 05/13/09; B++, 06/04/08; B++, 06/07/07; B++, 06/08/06**																
SENTRY LIFE INS CO Sentry Insurance a Mutual Company	**A**	'05	55.5	...	0.3	44.2	2,817,409	10.4	1.2	42.7	45.8	233,522	313,820	297,591	75,638	32,281	27,143	27,248
Mark R. Hackl President		'06	52.9	...	0.2	46.9	3,096,615	9.4	1.1	40.3	49.3	249,821	338,940	317,490	51,335	29,997	23,808	24,258
1800 North Point Drive Stevens Point, WI 54481	Rating Outlook: Stable	'07	49.9	...	0.2	49.9	3,338,038	8.7	1.0	38.6	51.7	261,692	365,920	346,368	44,307	28,519	24,186	17,505
WI : 1958 : Stock : Exclusive Agent Group pens, Ind Ann, Ind Life		'08	60.5	...	0.4	39.2	2,882,466	10.0	0.9	48.7	40.4	262,501	323,025	319,615	78,524	29,702	25,161	15,445
715-346-6000		'09	55.2	...	0.3	44.5	3,340,602	8.4	0.8	45.3	45.4	275,113	359,871	343,055	114,794	30,635	23,827	18,516
AMB# 007041 NAIC# 68810	FSC IX	**Rating History: A g, 01/26/10; A g, 02/03/09; A g, 01/24/08; A g, 05/04/07; A g, 06/19/06**																
SENTRY LIFE INS CO OF NEW YORK Sentry Insurance a Mutual Company	**A**	'05	53.2	...	...	46.8	46,138	35.8	0.2	15.7	48.2	7,264	6,256	6,223	-439	1,510	1,032	1,034
Mark R. Hackl President & COO		'06	49.4	...	...	50.6	52,067	30.6	0.2	16.5	52.7	7,408	8,357	8,058	985	1,237	799	791
P.O. Box 4944 Syracuse, NY 13221	Rating Outlook: Stable	'07	46.4	...	...	53.6	54,952	28.0	0.2	15.2	56.7	7,402	7,857	7,569	126	980	700	607
NY : 1967 : Stock : Agency Group pens, Group Life, Ind Life		'08	56.3	...	...	43.7	50,063	33.7	0.2	21.1	45.0	10,124	7,001	6,691	3,668	801	517	466
315-453-6308		'09	52.0	...	...	48.0	58,248	26.8	0.2	20.1	52.9	10,268	7,691	7,461	1,385	890	589	579
AMB# 007042 NAIC# 68829	FSC IX	**Rating History: A g, 01/26/10; A g, 02/03/09; A g, 01/24/08; A g, 05/04/07; A g, 06/19/06**																
SERVCO LIFE INSURANCE COMPANY GS Administrators Inc	**B+**	'05	78.2	...	1.8	20.0	33,375	29.0	42.3	...	28.7	10,135	11,790	3,164	1,208	1,449	1,004	953
Stephen Lee Amos President		'06	54.9	...	2.3	42.8	30,391	28.2	42.4	...	29.4	6,052	12,330	3,581	-2,862	194	90	90
P.O. Box 441828 Houston, TX 77244-1828	Rating Outlook: Stable	'07	78.3	...	2.3	19.4	31,685	29.6	44.8	...	25.6	6,827	13,073	4,473	1,843	-266	-198	-198
TX : 1983 : Stock : Agency Credit A&H, Credit Life		'08	48.4	...	1.5	50.1	30,553	31.8	46.8	...	21.5	7,088	9,875	3,376	-220	941	631	275
713-580-3080		'09	92.9	...	2.1	5.0	28,244	30.2	43.9	...	25.9	9,776	3,238	-609	-873	3,924	2,721	2,741
AMB# 068023 NAIC# 99465	FSC IV	**Rating History: B+, 05/07/10; B+, 05/15/09; B+, 06/11/08; B+, 06/06/07; B+, 06/21/06**																
SERVICE LIFE & CASUALTY INS CO Gray Family	**B+**	'05	48.4	24.3	5.7	21.6	140,093	32.3	29.5	...	38.1	35,394	36,222	32,877	2,888	5,317	4,005	5,068
J. Kelly Gray Chairman, President & CEO		'06	51.1	22.7	5.1	21.1	139,579	33.0	26.6	...	40.4	35,421	35,942	30,575	2,155	589	226	1,733
P.O. Box 26800 Austin, TX 78755-0800	Rating Outlook: Stable	'07	55.9	17.6	5.1	21.5	149,449	32.4	26.2	...	41.5	34,206	42,292	24,460	13,184	3,080	1,279	2,846
TX : 1970 : Stock : Agency Credit A&H, Credit Life		'08	52.4	29.4	3.8	14.3	137,780	35.3	30.2	...	34.5	35,035	24,379	13,273	-264	6,663	5,950	4,632
512-343-0600		'09	35.0	43.5	2.7	18.8	127,675	33.9	26.2	...	40.0	34,335	12,451	3,073	-10,013	14,674	10,431	9,181
AMB# 007992 NAIC# 77151	FSC VI	**Rating History: B+, 09/28/09; B+, 09/23/08; B+, 12/06/07; B+, 11/20/06; B+, 11/04/05**																
SETON HEALTH PLAN INC[2] Ascension Health	**NR-5**	'05	...	...	...	100.0	8,422	...	56.4	...	43.6	4,645	15,435	15,244	1,474	1,296	1,279	1,261
John H. Evler, III President		'06	...	...	...	100.0	10,414	...	71.0	...	29.0	6,435	15,616	15,432	1,952	2,190	2,200	2,199
7715 Chevy Chase Drive, Building 4 Austin, TX 78752		'07	...	...	...	100.0	10,912	...	64.9	...	35.1	8,632	13,513	13,359	256	2,192	2,192	2,192
TX : 1995 : Stock : Broker Group A&H, Health, Ind A&H		'08	...	...	...	100.0	12,715	...	73.9	...	26.1	8,741	15,797	15,567	2,058	36	5	5
512-324-1953		'09	...	...	...	100.0	14,998	...	49.6	...	50.4	11,720	17,610	17,330	2,401	3,036	2,985	2,985
AMB# 064252 NAIC# 95240		**Rating History: NR-5, 04/06/10; NR-5, 08/26/09; B+ pd, 07/01/08; B pd, 06/19/07; B- pd, 07/17/06**																
SETTLERS LIFE INSURANCE CO National Guardian Life Insurance Company	**A-**	'05	90.1	1.4	2.5	6.1	368,075	96.7	0.4	0.6	2.4	46,407	36,682	35,373	1,803	7,339	5,728	4,931
John D. Larson Chairman & CEO		'06	88.0	1.2	4.8	6.0	373,479	96.7	0.4	0.5	2.5	46,998	36,092	34,998	5,628	7,157	5,371	5,354
2 East Gilman Street Madison, WI 53703-1494	Rating Outlook: Stable	'07	86.4	1.2	5.7	6.6	381,811	96.1	0.4	0.4	3.1	48,797	38,789	37,659	7,348	7,567	5,991	5,943
WI : 1982 : Stock : Broker Pre-need, Life		'08	86.3	1.1	4.3	8.3	414,231	96.3	0.3	1.4	2.0	53,011	41,030	39,786	-2,264	8,300	6,463	843
608-257-5611		'09	88.8	1.0	2.4	7.8	414,801	96.5	0.3	1.2	2.0	53,325	42,308	41,251	-744	11,204	8,137	6,861
AMB# 009322 NAIC# 97241	FSC VIII	**Rating History: A- g, 03/15/10; A- g, 05/01/09; A- g, 06/11/08; A- g, 06/20/07; B++, 05/31/06**																
SHA L L C St Joseph Health System	**B-**	'05	20.1	2.6	9.3	68.1	42,883	...	77.6	...	22.4	19,507	219,903	217,014	-1,236	-1,559	-1,559	-1,463
Clifford R. Frank President & CEO		'06	21.1	2.2	9.8	67.0	54,134	...	77.7	...	22.3	22,128	244,448	241,877	12,401	-2,219	-2,219	-2,225
12940 N. Highway 183 Austin, TX 78750-3203	Rating Outlook: Stable	'07	14.3	2.0	9.7	74.0	63,782	...	56.3	...	43.7	21,659	305,572	303,235	6,470	1,574	1,574	1,574
TX : 1994 : Other : Broker Group A&H, Medicaid, Medicare		'08	2.9	1.8	44.9	50.4	71,605	...	61.7	...	38.3	26,315	336,990	334,812	13,788	-9,743	-9,743	-8,339
512-257-6001		'09	2.3	2.1	56.9	38.7	68,295	...	63.0	...	37.0	35,757	324,246	322,370	3,556	-9,048	-9,048	-9,034
AMB# 060114 NAIC# 95138	FSC VI	**Rating History: B- g, 09/02/09; B g, 06/18/08; B g, 06/14/07; B g, 06/21/06; C+ pd, 08/13/04**																
SHARP HEALTH PLAN	**NR-5**	'05	...	...	...	100.0	31,422	...	...	...	100.0	18,527	132,401	132,401	2,645	23,182	23,182	23,182
Melissa Cook President & CEO		'06	...	...	...	100.0	32,732	...	...	...	100.0	18,535	144,911	144,911	-699	746	746	746
4305 University Avenue, Suite 200 San Diego, CA 92105		'07	...	...	...	100.0	33,569	...	...	...	100.0	21,165	144,038	144,038	3,527	2,586	2,586	2,586
CA : 1992 : Non-Profit : Broker Group A&H, Health		'08	...	...	...	100.0	34,632	...	...	...	100.0	22,922	151,517	151,517	1,780	1,874	1,874	1,874
619-228-2377		'09	...	...	...	100.0	38,409	...	...	...	100.0	26,039	171,252	171,252	6,167	3,372	3,372	3,372
AMB# 064064		**Rating History: NR-5, 03/23/10; NR-5, 08/26/09; C++pd, 06/06/08; C++pd, 06/12/07; B- pd, 06/20/06**																

BEST'S PROFITABILITY, LEVERAGE AND LIQUIDITY TESTS 2005 – 2009

Data in U.S. Dollars

—	Profitability Tests							Leverage Tests						Liquidity Tests					
Un-Realized Capital Gains ($000)	Benefits Paid to NPW & Dep (%)	Comm. & Expenses to NPW & Dep (%)	NOG to Total Assets (%)	NOG to Total Rev (%)	Operating Return on Equity (%)	Net Yield (%)	Total Return (%)	Change in NPW & Dep (%)	NPW & Dep to Capital (X)	Capital & Surplus to Liabilities (%)	Surplus Relief (%)	Reins Leverage (%)	Change in Capital (%)	Quick Liquidity (%)	Current Liquidity (%)	Non-Invest Grade Bonds to Capital (%)	Delinq. & Foreclosed Mortgages to Capital (%)	Mort. & Credit Tenant Loans & R.E. to Capital (%)	Affiliated Invest to Capital (%)
258	52.1	69.7	2.0	12.0	4.8	6.18	6.74	5.1	0.2	85.8	...	0.1	2.5	55.4	97.3	11.9	...	9.9	1.1
295	51.9	68.0	2.0	11.6	4.7	6.62	7.76	2.5	0.2	88.0	...	0.1	4.8	62.0	102.5	9.2	...	10.5	1.0
-101	51.2	72.8	1.6	9.2	3.6	6.20	6.91	5.9	0.2	87.6	...	0.0	2.5	71.1	103.5	8.8	...	8.6	0.9
-3,539	48.6	70.8	1.0	6.0	2.5	5.82	-0.64	3.4	0.3	72.9	...	0.1	-13.7	66.8	93.0	5.8	...	8.9	0.9
31	52.3	68.2	0.7	3.9	1.7	5.75	4.85	5.6	0.3	69.0	...	0.1	-2.1	62.6	91.3	14.4	...	8.7	0.9

Principal Lines of Business: OrdLife (100.0%), GrpAnn (0.0%)

Principal States: CA (47.3%), UT (15.0%), AZ (9.6%), NM (6.0%), ID (5.4%)

413	87.8	9.0	1.0	6.4	12.1	6.64	6.72	-3.0	1.2	16.7	3.0	62.8	8.6	70.4	83.9	11.0	...	...	3.0
130	83.8	9.1	0.8	5.3	9.9	6.54	6.61	6.7	1.2	17.6	3.5	54.3	7.5	68.1	82.9	7.1	...	...	2.9
26	80.9	9.1	0.8	5.1	9.5	6.41	6.06	9.1	1.3	17.8	3.3	48.0	4.0	68.3	83.8	12.6	...	...	2.8
-298	88.5	9.9	0.8	5.6	9.6	6.39	5.86	-7.7	1.2	16.7	2.8	40.3	-0.9	69.3	84.5	8.7	...	...	3.8
82	70.7	9.1	0.8	5.0	8.9	6.33	6.09	7.3	1.2	16.2	2.6	36.3	4.4	70.7	85.7	10.1	...	...	3.7

Principal Lines of Business: GrpAnn (89.4%), OrdLife (7.4%), GrpLife (1.8%), IndAnn (1.0%), GrpA&H (0.4%)

Principal States: WI (12.9%), TX (11.1%), IL (7.6%), CA (7.1%), GA (3.1%)

...	134.2	14.9	2.2	12.3	14.6	6.91	6.99	8.0	0.9	35.6	0.1	2.5	6.3	95.5	108.2	...	...	...	...
...	60.5	11.9	1.6	7.8	10.9	6.91	6.91	29.5	1.1	34.7	0.1	1.8	2.2	90.0	103.6	...	...	...	...
...	98.5	14.1	1.3	7.1	9.5	6.64	6.31	-6.1	1.0	34.8	0.0	1.7	-0.9	92.4	107.4	...	...	...	...
...	93.2	14.9	1.0	5.9	5.9	5.93	5.72	-11.6	0.7	45.2	0.0	1.1	37.1	107.1	120.5	...	...	...	...
...	74.4	14.1	1.1	6.1	5.8	5.98	5.89	11.5	0.7	43.8	0.0	0.7	1.6	103.0	117.8	...	...	...	...

Principal Lines of Business: GrpAnn (86.9%), OrdLife (7.7%), GrpA&H (3.2%), IndAnn (1.1%), GrpLife (0.7%)

Principal States: NY (97.0%)

17	38.1	77.0	3.1	8.1	9.5	4.17	4.05	-30.3	0.3	44.4	78.2	365.3	-7.8	124.3	136.5	...	...	...	...
84	25.7	78.0	0.3	0.7	1.1	4.60	4.90	13.2	0.6	25.6	136.8	742.5	-39.7	135.8	146.6	...	...	...	...
24	24.4	82.5	-0.6	-1.4	-3.1	4.60	4.68	24.9	0.6	28.1	123.0	717.5	12.4	100.8	111.2	...	...	...	...
-190	34.6	80.1	2.0	5.8	9.1	3.91	1.99	-24.5	0.5	30.2	88.0	675.0	1.9	110.1	116.5	0.8	...	...	...
74	-99.9	-99.9	9.3	74.6	32.3	4.53	4.77	-99.9	-0.1	53.9	29.8	364.1	39.6	106.1	120.2	...	...	...	...

Principal Lines of Business: CrdA&H (205.7%), CrdLife (-99.9%)

Principal States: TX (83.8%), LA (14.4%)

-2,149	40.7	69.3	2.8	7.5	11.4	4.52	3.66	53.4	0.8	38.2	40.2	123.6	0.1	87.0	91.9	0.3	0.6	87.9	5.3
-72	54.1	76.1	0.2	0.5	0.6	4.74	5.89	-7.0	0.8	38.8	34.8	125.5	0.7	78.1	82.9	0.3	0.6	81.3	5.5
-68	8.6	68.0	0.9	2.8	3.7	4.89	6.10	-20.0	0.6	34.2	37.6	124.8	-2.4	83.8	88.5	...	0.6	68.9	5.9
-4,285	34.5	74.3	4.1	20.8	17.2	4.75	0.72	-45.7	0.4	34.5	24.2	101.9	-7.2	67.7	73.3	...	0.7	114.7	6.3
-1,787	194.1	205.7	7.9	51.1	30.1	6.00	6.59	-76.9	0.1	46.4	15.4	72.2	14.5	54.2	58.4	2.2	0.6	137.2	5.3

Principal Lines of Business: CrdLife (144.5%), CrdA&H (-44.5%)

Principal States: TX (96.3%)

...	75.7	16.6	16.4	8.9	31.9	2.62	2.38	0.8	3.3	123.0	...	0.8	37.3	220.2	220.2	...	...	...	...
...	74.2	14.0	23.4	14.2	39.7	4.33	4.33	1.2	2.4	161.7	...	1.1	38.5	258.1	258.1	...	...	...	...
...	72.7	13.6	20.6	16.9	29.1	4.75	4.75	-13.4	1.5	378.6	...	...	34.1	461.7	461.7	...	...	...	...
...	86.0	11.7	0.0	0.0	0.1	2.13	2.13	16.5	1.8	219.9	...	0.9	1.3	316.7	316.7	...	...	...	...
...	76.2	9.9	21.5	17.2	29.2	0.37	0.37	11.3	1.5	357.5	...	...	34.1	457.1	457.1	...	...	...	...

Principal Lines of Business: CompHosp/Med (100.0%)

Principal States: TX (100.0%)

-198	82.7	50.2	1.6	10.0	12.7	6.17	6.02	-6.0	0.7	15.3	0.2	7.9	5.4	73.6	84.5	18.7	...	14.1	6.6
405	86.1	46.3	1.4	9.4	11.5	6.15	6.37	-1.1	0.7	15.5	0.2	8.9	2.6	66.3	81.2	17.8	...	14.5	6.2
-31	79.7	45.8	1.6	10.0	12.5	6.11	6.20	7.6	0.7	15.9	0.2	7.3	4.7	63.4	80.5	26.4	...	13.6	5.8
-1,083	93.3	45.5	1.6	10.2	12.7	6.20	4.62	5.6	0.7	14.8	0.2	6.8	1.9	63.8	79.6	40.7	...	17.0	5.5
506	85.1	42.5	2.0	12.4	15.3	6.15	6.06	3.7	0.8	15.0	0.2	7.4	1.4	61.3	77.8	36.7	...	17.8	5.2

Principal Lines of Business: OrdLife (79.8%), GrpLife (19.3%), IndA&H (0.7%), IndAnn (0.1%), GrpAnn (0.0%)

Principal States: VA (45.4%), NC (15.3%), TN (7.8%), SC (4.8%), GA (3.9%)

-2,928	91.9	9.8	-3.9	-0.7	-9.3	10.18	-1.75	4.1	11.1	83.4	...	4.3	39.5	65.8	66.1	...	...	5.8	26.5
-718	91.6	9.9	-4.6	-0.9	-10.7	6.01	3.39	11.5	10.9	69.1	...	2.0	13.4	108.5	108.7	...	...	5.3	30.3
-3,815	91.8	8.4	2.7	0.5	7.2	5.81	-3.82	25.4	14.0	51.4	...	2.9	-2.1	122.1	122.2	...	...	6.0	46.9
-11,518	94.0	9.2	-14.4	-2.9	-40.6	2.94	-18.13	10.4	12.7	58.1	...	0.8	21.5	71.8	80.1	...	...	4.8	49.8
5,577	91.7	11.3	-12.9	-2.8	-29.2	2.16	15.20	-3.7	9.0	109.9	...	0.7	35.9	111.9	125.8	...	...	4.0	40.4

Principal Lines of Business: CompHosp/Med (63.9%), Medicaid (20.9%), Medicare (9.4%), FEHBP (5.7%)

Principal States: TX (100.0%)

...	86.7	7.9	74.7	15.6	194.1	3.20	3.20	-34.2	7.1	143.7	...	...	245.8	120.3	120.3	...	...	...	...
...	91.0	9.3	2.3	0.5	4.0	3.95	3.95	9.4	7.8	130.5	...	...	0.0	104.3	104.3	...	...	...	...
...	88.2	11.4	7.8	1.8	13.0	-0.02	-0.02	-0.6	6.8	170.6	...	...	14.2	147.9	147.9	...	...	...	...
...	89.0	10.0	5.5	1.2	8.5	0.00	0.00	5.2	6.6	195.7	...	...	8.3	171.8	171.8	...	...	...	...
...	88.6	10.0	9.2	2.0	13.8	0.00	0.00	13.0	6.6	210.5	...	...	13.6	212.5	212.5	...	...	...	...

Principal Lines of Business: CompHosp/Med (100.0%)

2010 BEST'S KEY RATING GUIDE — LIFE/HEALTH EDITION
ANNUAL STATEMENT DATA FOR YEARS 2005 – 2009

Data in U.S. Dollars

COMPANY NAME Ultimate Parent Association Principal Officer Mailing Address Dom. : Began Bus. : Struct. : Mktg. Specialty Phone # AMB# NAIC#	Best's Financial Strength Rating FSC	Data Year	Balance Sheet: Bonds (%)	Mort. Loans & R.E. (%)	Com & Pref. Stock (%)	All Other Assets (%)	Total Assets ($000)	Life Reserves (%)	Health Reserves (%)	Ann Res. & Dep. Liabilities (%)	All Other Liabilities (%)	Capital & Surplus ($000)	Operations: Direct Premiums Written ($000)	Net Premiums Written & Deposits ($000)	Operating Cash Flow ($000)	NOG Before Taxes ($000)	NOG After Taxes ($000)	Net Income ($000)
SHELTER LIFE INS CO Shelter Mutual Insurance Company J. David Moore President & CEO 1817 West Broadway Columbia, MO 65218-0001 MO : 1959 : Stock : Exclusive Agent Ind Life, Ann 573-445-8441 AMB# 006675 NAIC# 65757	**A**	'05	83.1	...	6.3	10.5	877,780	55.4	2.7	27.1	14.8	149,196	109,465	106,523	14,276	14,782	9,589	11,393
		'06	83.7	0.6	7.0	8.7	898,253	58.3	2.4	27.5	11.8	162,077	118,804	113,410	16,667	15,549	10,186	12,118
	Rating Outlook: Stable	'07	82.9	0.7	8.3	8.2	915,427	61.0	2.7	27.2	9.1	171,799	125,546	119,388	9,881	16,458	10,881	11,890
		'08	82.7	0.7	4.6	12.0	920,220	64.3	2.7	28.0	5.1	169,482	135,617	128,624	8,138	16,191	9,041	-3,272
	FSC VIII	'09	86.8	0.6	0.8	11.7	940,409	65.6	1.8	29.4	3.2	176,650	138,100	130,455	50,089	28,298	19,544	44,106
		Rating History: A, 06/09/10; A, 06/02/09; A, 06/18/08; A, 06/12/07; A, 06/19/06																
SHENANDOAH LIFE INS CO Robert W. Clark President & CEO 2301 Brambleton Avenue, S.W. Roanoke, VA 24015 VA : 1916 : Mutual : Agency In Rehabilitation 540-985-4400 AMB# 007044 NAIC# 68845	**E**	'05	71.4	10.3	12.4	5.9	1,527,758	40.6	0.3	43.1	16.1	119,176	279,789	251,557	115,585	8,013	5,132	3,144
		'06	59.9	11.8	21.0	7.3	1,583,909	42.3	0.3	40.6	16.8	120,861	272,041	237,427	53,490	6,997	4,681	5,042
		'07	63.3	13.4	17.2	6.1	1,664,855	42.9	0.4	52.0	4.7	125,790	321,142	468,269	83,029	15,556	8,129	8,422
		'08	...	...	...	...	...	...	...	...	...	...	...	...	...	...	...	...
		'09	...	...	...	...	...	...	...	...	...	...	...	...	...	...	...	...
		Rating History: E, 02/12/09; B++u, 11/19/08; B++, 09/26/08; A-, 02/29/08; A-, 01/17/07																
SHERIDAN LIFE INS CO Wichita National Life Insurance Company Randall B. Gilliland President P.O. Box 1709 Lawton, OK 73502 OK : 1980 : Stock : Broker Credit A&H, Credit Life 580-353-5776 AMB# 009453 NAIC# 98868	**NR-2**	'05	...	...	...	100.0	1,684	80.0	19.0	...	1.0	1,454	44	98	29	67	56	56
		'06	...	...	...	100.0	1,774	81.5	18.2	...	0.2	1,473	192	187	85	16	15	15
		'07	...	...	...	100.0	1,874	81.9	14.6	...	3.5	1,583	109	98	103	125	112	112
		'08	...	...	...	100.0	1,940	79.4	18.8	...	1.7	1,681	156	106	68	127	106	106
		'09	...	...	...	100.0	1,987	83.6	15.3	...	1.1	1,744	75	85	45	76	63	63
		Rating History: NR-2, 11/24/09; NR-2, 10/22/08; NR-2, 11/15/07; NR-2, 01/09/07; NR-2, 02/07/06																
SIERRA HLTH & LF INS CO INC UnitedHealth Group Inc Jonathon W. Bunker President P.O. Box 14396 Las Vegas, NV 89114-4396 CA : 1906 : Stock : Broker Group A&H, Group Life, Med supp 702-243-8528 AMB# 007370 NAIC# 71420	**A-**	'05	57.3	6.1	...	36.6	77,163	0.6	77.3	...	22.1	45,173	109,490	109,049	4,655	10,291	6,514	6,510
		'06	37.7	5.5	...	56.8	152,841	0.2	37.3	...	62.5	63,752	325,444	324,942	-4,417	37,377	24,161	24,250
	Rating Outlook: Stable	'07	17.2	3.2	...	79.6	133,494	0.3	81.3	...	18.4	63,061	424,826	424,512	-34,714	-15,519	-11,171	-11,103
		'08	9.4	3.3	...	87.3	129,288	0.4	74.9	...	24.7	76,643	230,360	230,534	87,799	21,410	13,958	13,954
	FSC VIII	'09	31.0	3.3	...	65.7	121,425	0.7	82.3	...	17.0	70,350	215,240	215,571	-11,067	9,516	5,840	5,862
		Rating History: A- g, 06/15/09; A- g, 03/05/08; B++gu, 03/13/07; B++g, 06/08/06; B++g, 12/19/05																
SIGNIFICA INSURANCE GROUP INC Hospital Service Assn of Northeastern PA Lucille M. Connors President & CEO 19 North Main Street Wilkes-Barre, PA 18711 PA : 1910 : Stock : Agency Group A&H, Medicaid 717-581-1300 AMB# 006902 NAIC# 67636	**NR-5**	'05	62.7	...	...	37.3	5,947	...	...	...	100.0	5,859	9	...	57	2	2	2
		'06	43.1	...	...	56.9	8,392	...	42.6	...	57.4	8,014	412	358	511	-628	-402	-402
		'07	11.3	...	...	88.7	22,989	...	89.9	...	10.1	6,657	41,047	40,945	161	-1,827	-1,286	-1,286
		'08	9.3	...	...	90.7	31,023	...	62.8	...	37.2	7,689	87,657	87,171	6,014	-3,803	-2,473	-2,473
		'09	7.7	...	...	92.3	34,606	0.0	91.0	...	9.0	11,570	75,349	74,333	18,696	-24,917	-20,897	-20,897
		Rating History: NR-5, 03/24/10; NR-5, 04/09/09; NR-5, 03/25/08; NR-5, 06/27/07; NR-3, 06/21/06																
SILVERSCRIPT INSURANCE COMPANY CVS Caremark Corporation Lloyd D. McDonald President 211 Commerce Street Nashville, TN 37201 TN : 2008 : Stock : Not Available Medical 615-743-6600 AMB# 064967 NAIC# 12575	**NR-5**	'05	...	...	...	...	...	...	...	...	...	...	...	...	...	...	...	...
		'06	...	...	...	...	...	...	...	...	...	...	...	...	...	...	...	...
		'07	...	...	...	...	...	...	...	...	...	...	...	...	...	...	...	...
		'08	0.8	...	0.0	99.2	354,195	...	6.9	...	93.1	63,188	542,403	542,403	-126,938	-50,997	-33,153	-33,140
		'09	0.6	...	...	99.4	439,036	...	9.7	...	90.3	144,894	1,209,570	1,205,675	-54,985	18,765	12,126	12,126
		Rating History: NR-5, 04/06/10; NR-5, 04/14/09																
SISTEMAS MEDICOS NACIONALES Frank S. Carrillo President 303 H. Street, Suite 390 Chula Vista, CA 91910 CA : 1992 : Non-Profit : Broker Health 619-407-4082 AMB# 064711	**NR-5**	'05	...	5.8	...	94.2	2,634	...	...	...	100.0	1,443	14,586	14,586	327	-194	-136	-136
		'06	...	7.5	...	92.5	3,250	...	...	...	100.0	2,113	15,869	15,869	556	859	665	665
		'07	...	...	...	100.0	3,838	...	...	...	100.0	2,635	19,258	19,258	576	732	522	522
		'08	...	...	...	100.0	4,289	...	...	...	100.0	2,967	22,052	22,052	298	477	332	332
		'09	...	8.3	...	91.7	7,894	...	...	...	100.0	5,437	23,480	23,480	1,685	3,423	2,471	2,471
		Rating History: NR-5, 05/07/10; NR-5, 05/13/09; NR-5, 05/05/08; NR-5, 05/03/07; NR-5, 06/08/06																
SLOVENE NATIONAL BENEFIT SOC Joseph C. Evanish President 247 West Allegheny Road Imperial, PA 15126 PA : 1904 : Fraternal : Career Agent Ind Ann, Ind Life, ISWL 724-695-1100 AMB# 007046 NAIC# 57673	**NR-4**	'05	93.1	2.7	0.4	3.7	149,882	27.8	0.6	68.3	3.3	9,559	10,967	11,103	10,086	916	916	641
		'06	89.0	2.6	5.0	3.4	152,798	27.7	0.6	68.4	3.4	9,378	6,489	6,421	2,841	15	15	-68
		'07	90.3	2.4	5.0	2.3	156,724	27.3	0.5	68.1	4.1	9,293	7,161	7,367	3,529	170	170	151
		'08	90.4	2.3	4.8	2.5	156,684	27.1	0.5	69.1	3.4	6,309	10,361	10,266	1,260	334	334	-3,715
		'09	...	...	...	...	...	...	...	...	...	...	...	...	...	...	...	...
		Rating History: NR-4, 06/12/09; B, 06/12/09; B, 02/27/09; B+, 01/18/08; B+, 12/05/06																
SMITH BURIAL & LIFE INS CO[1] Virginia S. Stevens President 310 Church Street Stamps, AR 71860-2818 AR : 1961 : Stock : Not Available 870-533-2070 AMB# 068368 NAIC# 84069	**NR-1**	'05	81.3	...	8.0	10.7	4,593	...	...	...	100.0	651	475	475	...	95	95	84
		'06	84.9	...	5.8	9.3	4,664	...	...	...	100.0	631	471	471	...	41	35	104
		'07	84.8	...	7.3	7.9	4,708	...	...	...	100.0	656	470	470	...	60	52	84
		'08	83.9	...	4.7	11.4	4,698	...	...	...	100.0	613	464	464	...	8	8	3
		'09	61.7	...	2.5	35.8	4,772	...	...	...	100.0	668	469	469	...	62	62	-2
		Rating History: NR-1, 06/10/10; NR-1, 06/12/09; NR-1, 06/12/08; NR-1, 06/08/07; NR-1, 06/07/06																

BEST'S PROFITABILITY, LEVERAGE AND LIQUIDITY TESTS 2005 – 2009

Data in U.S. Dollars

	Profitability Tests							Leverage Tests						Liquidity Tests					
Un-Realized Capital Gains ($000)	Benefits Paid to NPW & Dep (%)	Comm. & Expenses to NPW & Dep (%)	NOG to Total Assets (%)	NOG to Total Rev (%)	Operating Return on Equity (%)	Net Yield (%)	Total Return (%)	Change in NPW & Dep (%)	NPW & Dep to Capital (X)	Capital & Surplus to Liabilities (%)	Surplus Relief (%)	Reins Leverage (%)	Change in Capital (%)	Quick Liquidity (%)	Current Liquidity (%)	Non-Invest Grade Bonds to Capital (%)	Delinq. & Foreclosed Mortgages to Capital (%)	Mort. & Credit Tenant Loans & R.E. to Capital (%)	Affiliated Invest to Capital (%)
-3,005	65.9	21.0	1.1	6.7	6.6	4.67	4.57	1.6	0.7	22.1	1.4	5.8	5.0	91.3	100.8	3.8	...	...	4.6
1,757	66.7	22.9	1.1	6.6	6.5	4.77	5.24	6.5	0.7	23.6	1.6	7.0	7.8	89.6	98.9	...	...	3.2	8.0
4,094	69.4	21.3	1.2	6.8	6.5	4.82	5.43	5.3	0.7	25.0	1.6	8.7	6.8	90.9	99.7	...	...	3.5	9.0
-10,199	65.7	19.7	1.0	5.2	5.3	5.05	2.58	7.7	0.8	22.6	1.6	9.8	-7.3	89.5	99.2	3.3	...	3.7	9.2
-9,854	64.5	19.5	2.1	11.3	11.3	5.01	6.78	1.4	0.7	23.5	1.7	14.6	5.5	84.4	94.2	2.2	...	3.4	8.7
Principal Lines of Business: OrdLife (64.5%), IndAnn (18.2%), GrpA&H (14.3%), IndA&H (1.4%), GrpLife (1.3%)														Principal States: MO (29.4%), AR (17.4%), OK (6.9%), KS (6.0%), TN (6.0%)					
29	70.9	30.9	0.3	1.5	4.0	6.00	6.20	5.0	2.0	0.0	9.2	70.0	1.9	45.4	04.0	15.9	...	100.2	3.0
-256	81.6	32.2	0.3	1.4	3.9	6.28	6.30	-5.6	1.9	8.8	11.5	85.2	3.9	42.2	62.6	15.9	...	174.5	3.3
-310	46.2	16.5	0.5	2.2	6.6	5.83	5.84	97.2	3.5	8.8	12.5	93.9	5.4	42.2	61.0	20.1	...	190.8	2.9
...	...	...	...	...	...	...	...	...	...	...	...	...	...	...	...	...	...	...	...
...	...	...	...	...	...	...	...	...	...	...	...	...	...	...	...	...	...	...	...
...	62.4	47.0	3.4	37.6	3.9	2.19	2.19	-11.2	0.1	632.0	1.0	3.2	4.8	730.9	730.9	...	...	...	...
...	42.3	44.5	0.9	4.8	1.0	3.67	3.67	91.5	0.1	490.4	4.4	8.2	1.3	587.9	587.9	...	...	...	...
...	16.6	49.4	6.2	52.1	7.4	4.15	4.15	-47.8	0.1	545.8	2.8	9.8	7.5	644.4	644.4	...	...	...	...
...	11.1	41.8	5.5	50.3	6.5	2.77	2.77	8.2	0.1	648.9	3.1	14.1	6.2	748.0	748.0	...	...	...	...
...	13.1	49.5	3.2	43.4	3.7	1.55	1.55	-19.6	0.0	716.3	1.7	10.6	3.7	814.3	814.3	...	...	...	...
Principal Lines of Business: CrdLife (87.8%), CrdA&H (12.2%)														Principal States: OK (100.0%)					
...	67.3	28.6	8.6	5.7	15.6	3.36	3.35	5.0	2.4	144.6	...	0.4	17.5	249.3	259.2	...	...	10.3	10.3
...	77.2	13.5	21.0	7.3	44.4	7.87	7.99	198.0	5.1	72.4	...	0.1	40.8	89.9	97.6	...	...	13.0	7.0
...	92.9	12.3	-7.8	-2.6	-17.6	10.53	10.73	30.6	6.7	90.7	...	90.1	-1.1	61.6	64.5	...	...	6.7	6.7
...	74.5	17.8	10.6	6.0	20.0	3.78	3.79	-45.7	3.0	147.7	...	5.5	21.4	412.4	422.1	...	...	5.5	5.5
...	80.7	14.1	4.7	2.7	7.9	1.39	1.39	-6.5	3.0	139.5	...	0.0	-8.3	275.8	282.3	...	...	5.7	5.7
Principal Lines of Business: GrpA&H (62.8%), IndA&H (36.5%), GrpLife (0.7%)														Principal States: NV (78.6%), UT (7.3%), TX (5.9%)					
...	...	...	0.0	1.3	0.0	2.68	2.68	...	...	999.9	...	0.3	0.0	999.9	999.9	...	...	...	...
...	96.9	261.3	-5.6	-61.5	-5.8	4.21	4.21	...	0.0	999.9	...	0.2	36.8	999.9	999.9	...	...	...	...
...	91.7	13.7	-8.2	-3.1	-17.5	4.66	4.66	999.9	6.2	40.8	...	0.0	-16.9	60.7	61.4	...	...	...	...
...	89.5	15.3	-9.2	-2.8	-34.5	3.03	3.03	112.9	11.3	33.0	...	1.0	15.5	68.7	69.6	...	...	...	...
...	103.6	19.4	-63.7	-28.0	-99.9	0.25	0.25	-14.7	6.4	50.2	...	0.6	50.5	253.1	265.4	...	...	...	...
Principal Lines of Business: CompHosp/Med (57.4%), Medicaid (42.6%), Life (0.0%)														Principal States: PA (59.9%), OH (26.7%), AZ (13.4%)					
...	...	...	...	...	...	...	...	...	...	...	...	...	...	...	...	...	...	...	...
...	...	...	...	...	...	...	...	...	...	...	...	...	...	...	...	...	...	...	...
...	...	...	...	...	...	...	...	...	...	...	...	...	...	...	...	...	...	...	...
...	103.0	5.5	...	-5.3	...	...	...	...	8.6	21.7	...	...	...	63.6	63.6	...	...	...	...
...	93.4	5.0	3.1	1.0	11.7	0.20	0.20	122.3	8.3	49.3	0.0	0.2	129.3	14.4	14.5	...	...	...	...
Principal Lines of Business: OtherHlth (100.0%)														Principal States: NY (8.4%), NJ (8.1%), OH (6.6%), MA (6.0%), NC (5.4%)					
...	75.6	25.8	-5.3	-0.9	-8.9	1.86	1.86	10.2	10.1	121.2	...	...	-10.7	70.4	70.4	...	...	10.6	10.6
...	69.2	26.9	22.6	4.0	37.4	1.65	1.65	8.8	7.5	185.8	...	...	46.4	104.1	104.1	...	...	11.5	11.5
...	82.3	16.8	14.7	2.6	22.0	1.49	1.49	21.4	7.3	219.0	...	...	24.7	127.8	127.8	...	...	...	...
...	70.0	28.1	8.2	1.5	11.8	...	...	14.5	7.4	224.4	...	...	12.6	115.5	115.5	...	...	...	...
...	55.9	30.4	40.6	10.1	58.8	1.30	1.30	6.5	4.3	221.3	...	...	83.3	61.4	61.4	...	...	12.0	12.0
Principal Lines of Business: CompHosp/Med (100.0%)																			
23	57.3	24.7	0.6	4.8	10.0	5.79	5.71	-7.9	1.1	7.6	...	1.2	5.8	72.5	82.1	22.2	3.2	39.0	11.1
45	139.8	46.5	0.0	0.1	0.2	5.64	5.75	-42.2	0.6	7.4	...	1.6	-0.5	69.2	81.0	25.9	3.2	38.2	10.9
15	137.2	37.3	0.1	1.1	1.8	5.56	5.73	14.7	0.7	7.1	...	1.2	-0.2	70.6	82.0	33.0	3.2	36.2	10.7
-188	113.9	26.2	0.2	1.8	4.3	5.53	3.06	39.4	1.6	4.4	...	1.9	-37.1	70.1	81.0	49.0	2.9	54.0	16.6
...	...	...	...	...	...	...	...	...	...	...	...	...	...	...	...	...	...	...	...
27	52.7	72.4	2.1	13.4	15.7	...	...	-1.0	0.7	17.7	...	...	14.8	...	...	...	...	...	...
-40	50.1	73.9	0.8	5.1	5.4	...	...	-0.8	0.7	16.8	...	...	-2.6	...	...	...	...	...	...
-22	52.6	74.3	1.1	7.6	8.1	...	...	-0.4	0.7	17.5	...	...	4.3	...	...	...	...	...	...
-52	66.3	69.7	0.2	1.2	1.2	...	...	-1.2	0.7	16.3	...	...	-6.3	...	...	...	...	...	...
52	53.5	64.1	1.3	9.6	9.8	...	...	1.1	0.7	17.4	...	...	7.3	...	...	...	...	...	...
Principal Lines of Business: OrdLife (100.0%)																			

Data in U.S. Dollars

COMPANY NAME Ultimate Parent Association Principal Officer Mailing Address Dom. : Began Bus. : Struct. : Mktg. Specialty Phone # AMB# NAIC#	Best's Financial Strength Rating FSC	Data Year	Balance Sheet Bonds (%)	Mort. Loans & R.E. (%)	Com & Pref. Stock (%)	All Other Assets (%)	Total Assets ($000)	Life Reserves (%)	Health Reserves (%)	Ann Res. & Dep. Liabilities (%)	All Other Liabilities (%)	Capital & Surplus ($000)	Operations Direct Premiums Written ($000)	Net Premiums Written & Deposits ($000)	Operating Cash Flow ($000)	NOG Before Taxes ($000)	NOG After Taxes ($000)	Net Income ($000)
SOLANO-NAPA-YOLO COMM MED CARE Jack Horn President 360 Campus Lane, Suite 100 Fairfield, CA 94534-4036 CA : 1994 : Non-Profit : Not Available Medicaid, Medicare, Group A&H 707-863-4100 AMB# 064877	NR-5	'05	...	...	...	...	...	...	...	...	...	...	...	...	...	...	...	...
		'06	...	...	...	100.0	94,198	...	...	...	100.0	27,438	258,221	258,221	-1,286	-13,607	-13,607	-13,607
		'07	...	...	...	100.0	91,040	...	...	...	100.0	27,324	276,875	276,875	-29,155	-114	-114	-114
		'08	...	...	...	100.0	87,771	...	...	...	100.0	23,859	323,584	323,584	21,282	-3,465	-3,465	-3,465
		'09	...	...	...	100.0	111,317	...	...	...	100.0	40,917	429,817	429,817	28,525	17,058	17,058	17,058
		Rating History: NR-5, 03/24/10; NR-5, 04/08/09; NR-5, 03/11/08; NR-5, 03/19/07																
SOMERS ISLES INS CO LTD Argus Group Holdings Limited Gerald D. E. Simons President & CEO Argus Building, 12 Wesley St Hamilton HM EX, Bermuda BM : 1950 : Stock : Not Available Health 441-295-2021 AMB# 086637	A- Rating Outlook: Negative FSC VIII	'05	...	6.9	0.0	93.1	28,054	77.1	...	...	22.9	15,096	...	76,291	...	6,809	6,809	6,809
		'06	...	4.5	87.4	8.1	56,652	30.9	...	...	69.1	20,409	...	84,054	...	5,260	5,260	5,260
		'07	...	6.8	...	93.2	42,373	69.9	...	...	30.1	23,059	...	96,452	...	7,486	7,486	7,486
		'08	...	6.2	...	93.8	47,720	56.0	...	...	44.0	27,601	...	107,034	...	11,543	11,543	11,543
		'09	...	7.2	...	92.8	42,184	70.4	...	...	29.6	22,000	...	113,083	...	9,861	9,861	9,861
		Rating History: A- g, 07/02/09; A g, 10/17/06; A g, 12/17/04; A g, 09/30/03; A gu, 09/08/03																
SONS OF HERMANN IN TEXAS Leroy P. Muehlstein President & CEO P.O. Box 1941 San Antonio, TX 78297 TX : 1890 : Fraternal : Career Agent Ann, Term Life, Whole life 210-226-9261 AMB# 068030 NAIC# 57444	NR-5	'05	81.2	7.1	6.6	5.1	161,666	60.6	...	34.9	4.5	17,572	10,015	9,874	6,620	263	263	227
		'06	81.1	7.6	6.5	4.8	167,009	60.4	...	34.3	5.3	18,479	8,476	8,296	4,514	655	655	904
		'07	81.7	7.3	6.0	5.0	169,517	61.9	...	33.1	4.9	19,633	8,031	7,861	2,761	288	288	432
		'08	84.6	6.7	3.9	4.8	172,225	61.1	...	36.5	2.4	14,855	15,769	15,581	10,562	-337	-337	-427
		'09	83.9	6.9	4.6	4.7	191,738	55.2	...	40.5	4.3	11,886	22,752	22,560	14,165	-522	-522	-3,966
		Rating History: NR-5, 04/14/10; NR-5, 04/23/09; NR-5, 04/21/08; NR-5, 05/08/07; NR-5, 05/10/06																
SOUTH DAKOTA STATE MED HLDG CO Stephen H. Gehring, M.D. President 2600 West 49th Street Sioux Falls, SD 57105 SD : 1985 : Stock : Broker Group A&H 605-334-4000 AMB# 068969 NAIC# 96598	B Rating Outlook: Negative FSC V	'05	17.1	8.6	8.1	66.2	28,867	...	47.5	...	52.5	11,685	84,806	84,178	1,049	4,709	3,267	3,267
		'06	14.4	7.7	8.7	69.2	31,374	...	52.1	...	47.9	15,073	85,341	84,738	842	4,841	3,303	3,303
		'07	15.1	6.8	7.5	70.7	34,763	...	59.9	...	40.1	15,180	93,060	92,229	956	305	226	206
		'08	11.5	6.1	8.4	74.0	37,626	...	61.7	...	38.3	13,521	150,650	148,721	1,946	-2,409	-1,651	-1,651
		'09	31.7	6.5	10.2	51.6	33,806	...	49.8	...	50.2	17,579	92,509	91,280	-4,449	795	551	553
		Rating History: B, 05/07/09; B, 05/21/08; B+, 04/24/07; B+, 04/28/06; B+, 02/22/05																
SOUTHEAST FAMILY LIFE INS CO Central States Health & Life Co of Omaha Richard T. Kizer Chairman & President 1212 North 96th Street Omaha, NE 68114 AZ : 1985 : Stock : Other Direct Credit A&H, Credit Life 402-397-1111 AMB# 009520 NAIC# 89281	B++ Rating Outlook: Stable FSC VIII	'05	91.2	...	0.0	8.8	23,500	71.1	18.6	...	10.3	9,391	...	7,425	-63	1,959	1,814	1,814
		'06	82.0	...	1.5	16.6	17,309	72.7	16.1	...	11.2	2,849	...	7,420	-6,163	948	896	878
		'07	93.5	...	...	6.5	16,227	69.5	19.1	...	11.4	5,321	...	4,773	-591	3,409	3,098	3,098
		'08	118.9	...	...	-18.9	10,944	67.5	20.6	...	11.9	3,095	...	341	-2,107	-173	-824	-1,344
		'09	89.0	...	...	11.0	10,199	58.4	24.4	...	17.3	5,279	...	1,829	-3,464	3,606	3,464	3,086
		Rating History: B++g, 05/27/10; B++g, 04/28/09; B++g, 04/18/08; B++g, 05/08/07; B++, 06/08/06																
SOUTHERN CAPITAL LIFE INS CO Southern Farm Bureau Life Insurance Co Larry B. Wooten Chairman & President P.O. Box 78 Jackson, MS 39205 MS : 1982 : Stock : Other Direct Reins 601-981-7422 AMB# 009118 NAIC# 94617	NR-3	'05	98.1	...	...	1.9	6,128	...	...	...	100.0	5,993	...	...	-128	298	194	194
		'06	98.8	...	...	1.2	6,443	...	...	...	100.0	6,199	...	...	-29	317	206	206
		'07	98.7	...	...	1.3	6,615	...	...	...	100.0	6,451	...	...	-221	370	252	252
		'08	99.1	...	...	0.9	6,864	...	...	...	100.0	6,702	...	...	-170	373	251	251
		'09	99.1	...	...	0.9	7,113	...	...	...	100.0	6,952	...	...	-172	376	250	250
		Rating History: NR-3, 03/30/10; NR-3, 05/26/09; NR-3, 06/17/08; NR-3, 06/18/07; NR-3, 06/06/06																
SOUTHERN FARM BUREAU LIFE INS Southern Farm Bureau Life Insurance Co Larry B. Wooten Chairman & President P.O. Box 78 Jackson, MS 39205 MS : 1946 : Stock : Agency Ind Ann, Term Life, Trad Life 601-981-7422 AMB# 007053 NAIC# 68896	A+ Rating Outlook: Stable FSC XIV	'05	65.9	13.2	6.2	14.7	9,269,977	42.2	0.6	51.3	5.9	1,292,284	767,291	783,317	445,355	164,578	132,518	194,085
		'06	66.3	13.0	5.7	15.0	9,680,833	43.3	0.7	50.3	5.7	1,483,227	746,741	774,828	305,510	155,403	115,040	164,960
		'07	65.0	12.8	5.1	17.1	9,949,156	44.7	0.8	49.0	5.6	1,587,191	709,791	743,720	275,950	172,766	124,519	143,728
		'08	65.3	13.9	4.0	16.8	10,019,877	46.7	0.8	49.0	3.5	1,570,638	825,394	839,622	275,011	157,677	123,119	63,093
		'09	65.2	12.5	4.3	18.0	10,545,745	47.0	0.9	47.3	4.8	1,669,157	846,961	914,564	246,426	107,148	79,517	10,439
		Rating History: A+, 03/30/10; A+, 05/26/09; A+, 06/17/08; A+, 06/14/07; A+, 06/06/06																
SOUTHERN FIDELITY LIFE INS CO' Martha S. Ford President 310 Church Street Stamps, AR 71860-2818 AR : 1959 : Stock : Not Available 870-533-2070 AMB# 068491 NAIC# 84077	NR-1	'05	...	...	8.9	91.1	79	...	...	...	100.0	68	1	1	...	0	0	4
		'06	...	...	9.1	90.9	81	...	...	...	100.0	69	1	1	...	1	1	1
		'07	...	...	9.1	90.9	81	...	...	...	100.0	70	1	1	...	1	1	1
		'08	...	...	9.1	90.9	80	...	...	...	100.0	69	1	1	...	0	0	0
		'09	...	...	9.1	90.9	81	...	...	...	100.0	70	1	1	...	0	0	0
		Rating History: NR-1, 06/10/10; NR-1, 06/12/09; NR-1, 06/12/08; NR-1, 06/08/07; NR-1, 06/07/06																
SOUTHERN FINANCIAL LIFE INS CO David N. Wakely Chairman, President, Treasurer & Actuary 516 Lakeview Road, Villa 2 Clearwater, FL 33756 LA : 1984 : Stock : Other Direct Credit A&H, Ordinary Life 727-442-4084 AMB# 060006 NAIC# 69418	NR-5	'05	56.3	0.1	30.0	13.6	57,924	70.7	15.9	5.9	7.5	11,873	985	11,630	6,222	814	647	802
		'06	48.6	0.1	32.8	18.5	62,972	69.9	15.9	5.3	8.9	12,886	522	9,838	2,661	-81	-47	260
		'07	49.4	0.1	34.6	15.9	63,816	70.9	16.1	5.2	7.8	14,325	445	8,602	3,539	1,981	1,676	2,566
		'08	57.3	0.1	26.4	16.2	66,188	81.1	13.0	4.4	1.5	10,117	399	18,925	7,718	45	-20	-1,441
		'09	67.8	0.1	17.1	15.0	69,734	79.4	10.9	4.1	5.6	11,827	350	9,338	1,664	2,218	2,189	2,066
		Rating History: NR-5, 04/22/10; NR-5, 04/22/09; NR-5, 04/09/08; NR-5, 04/24/07; NR-5, 05/09/06																

BEST'S PROFITABILITY, LEVERAGE AND LIQUIDITY TESTS 2005 – 2009

Data in U.S. Dollars

—	Profitability Tests							Leverage Tests						Liquidity Tests					
Un-Realized Capital Gains ($000)	Benefits Paid to NPW & Dep (%)	Comm. & Expenses to NPW & Dep (%)	NOG to Total Assets (%)	NOG to Total Rev (%)	Operating Return on Equity (%)	Net Yield (%)	Total Return (%)	Change in NPW & Dep (%)	NPW & Dep to Capital (X)	Capital & Surplus to Liabilities (%)	Surplus Relief (%)	Reins Leverage (%)	Change in Capital (%)	Quick Liquidity (%)	Current Liquidity (%)	Non-Invest Grade Bonds to Capital (%)	Delinq. & Foreclosed Mortgages to Capital (%)	Mort. & Credit Tenant Loans & R.E. to Capital (%)	Affiliated Invest to Capital (%)
...	...	...	...	...	...	...	...	...	...	...	...	...	...	...	...	...	...	...	...
...	104.0	5.8	...	-5.0	...	...	...	...	9.4	41.1	...	...	...	92.5	92.5	...	...	...	...
...	95.1	6.2	-0.1	0.0	-0.4	6.28	6.28	7.2	10.1	42.9	...	...	-0.4	50.8	50.8	...	...	...	...
...	96.1	6.1	-3.9	-1.1	-13.5	6.95	6.95	16.9	13.6	37.3	...	...	-12.7	83.3	83.3	...	...	...	...
...	90.6	5.8	17.1	4.0	52.7	2.01	2.01	32.8	10.5	58.1	...	...	71.5	115.8	115.8	...	...	...	...
	Principal Lines of Business: Medicaid (87.0%), Medicare (12.4%), CompHosp/Med (0.6%)																		
-107	82.5	10.3	24.5	8.8	43.0	2.85	2.85	59.9	505.1	116.5	...	...	-5.2	0.0	188.1	...	...	12.0	148.8
83	85.1	15.5	12.4	5.9	29.6	3.52	3.52	10.2	411.9	56.3	...	...	35.2	136.6	146.9	...	...	12.5	5.8
-80	83.0	12.0	15.1	7.6	34.5	2.17	2.17	14.8	418.3	119.4	...	...	13.0	...	200.4	...	...	12.5	155.3
50	80.8	10.8	25.6	10.5	45.6	3.58	3.58	11.0	387.8	137.2	...	...	19.7	...	214.2	...	...	10.7	145.4
-59	82.2	10.5	21.9	8.6	39.8	3.91	3.91	5.7	514.0	109.0	...	...	-20.3	...	180.8	...	...	13.8	152.1
68	64.1	61.4	0.2	1.3	1.5	6.16	6.20	-28.9	0.5	14.7	0.2	1.8	1.7	56.3	65.9	53.4	...	55.3	19.4
1,037	96.6	72.5	0.4	3.5	3.6	6.06	6.86	-16.0	0.4	15.4	0.2	1.9	7.5	58.2	68.0	38.7	...	56.8	17.4
50	123.8	75.3	0.2	1.6	1.5	6.12	6.25	-5.2	0.3	16.0	0.2	2.0	5.1	59.2	69.2	35.6	...	53.0	16.1
-7,714	55.3	40.9	-0.2	-1.3	-2.0	6.06	1.62	98.2	1.0	9.7	0.3	2.9	-34.6	56.1	67.0	37.0	...	75.0	23.9
5,262	37.8	28.7	-0.3	-1.5	-3.9	5.99	7.07	44.8	1.5	8.2	0.4	4.1	-4.7	54.6	65.3	56.8	...	90.6	24.6
	Principal Lines of Business: IndAnn (72.9%), OrdLife (27.1%)												Principal States: TX (97.8%)						
143	85.2	11.4	11.6	3.8	25.1	3.39	3.93	5.8	7.2	68.0	...	0.2	-18.8	123.8	126.4	...	...	21.4	39.9
383	85.0	12.6	11.0	3.8	24.7	4.66	6.04	0.7	5.6	92.5	...	3.6	29.0	137.2	139.7	...	...	16.1	33.1
199	90.4	13.2	0.7	0.2	1.5	4.47	5.08	8.8	6.1	77.5	...	6.0	0.7	119.6	122.1	...	...	15.5	31.6
547	94.6	9.2	-4.6	-1.1	-11.5	2.36	4.13	61.3	11.0	56.1	...	3.9	-10.9	106.6	108.5	...	...	16.9	39.0
273	88.3	12.6	1.5	0.6	3.5	1.71	2.63	-38.6	5.2	108.3	...	2.7	30.0	125.1	131.8	...	...	12.5	31.2
	Principal Lines of Business: CompHosp/Med (100.0%)												Principal States: SD (98.5%)						
...	49.2	51.3	7.8	21.4	20.7	4.26	4.73	-9.7	0.8	67.5	...	5.5	15.8	132.9	144.8	13.6	...	...	...
...	45.1	52.0	4.4	10.6	14.6	5.12	5.35	-0.1	2.6	20.2	...	33.4	-69.3	100.5	111.7	1.8	...	...	...
...	62.6	51.7	18.5	55.1	75.8	5.32	5.47	-35.7	0.9	49.8	...	11.8	85.5	108.8	122.0	14.1	...	...	...
...	717.6	519.6	-6.1	-70.0	-19.6	5.61	2.31	-92.9	0.1	39.4	...	11.1	-42.6	133.9	150.0	20.6	...	...	...
-260	80.4	-0.8	32.8	138.0	82.7	5.44	0.57	435.8	0.3	107.3	...	4.0	70.6	168.0	187.0	3.0	...	...	...
	Principal Lines of Business: CrdA&H (91.1%), CrdLife (8.9%)																		
...	...	...	3.2	62.7	3.3	5.27	5.27	...	...	999.9	...	...	3.3	999.9	999.9	...	...	...	...
...	...	...	3.3	63.2	3.4	5.32	5.32	...	...	999.9	...	...	3.4	999.9	999.9	...	...	...	...
...	...	...	3.9	66.2	4.0	5.49	5.97	...	...	999.9	...	...	4.1	999.9	999.9	...	...	...	...
...	...	...	3.7	65.9	3.8	5.43	5.81	...	...	999.9	...	...	3.9	999.9	999.9	...	...	...	...
...	...	...	3.6	64.4	3.7	5.46	5.70	...	...	999.9	...	...	3.7	999.9	999.9	...	...	...	...
-24,282	66.3	21.3	1.5	10.9	11.0	5.65	6.06	-3.8	0.5	19.0	0.8	9.6	13.0	60.5	74.1	7.8	0.1	83.4	2.0
56,828	80.7	22.3	1.2	9.5	8.3	5.57	6.71	-1.1	0.5	21.0	0.6	10.1	13.0	60.3	74.1	4.7	0.0	75.8	2.9
-32,930	91.5	23.8	1.3	10.4	8.1	5.69	5.53	-4.0	0.4	21.8	0.5	11.3	5.7	60.4	75.7	3.2	...	72.6	2.7
-115,225	71.0	21.8	1.2	9.5	7.8	5.40	3.58	12.9	0.5	19.5	0.4	13.2	-7.5	57.0	71.8	4.5	...	86.0	4.7
116,358	66.2	22.0	0.8	6.0	4.9	5.22	5.69	8.9	0.5	21.0	0.4	14.2	11.4	58.3	74.1	8.4	...	73.1	5.3
	Principal Lines of Business: OrdLife (58.8%), IndAnn (27.8%), GrpAnn (10.8%), IndA&H (1.2%), GrpLife (0.8%)												Principal States: TX (19.8%), NC (19.2%), MS (9.5%), GA (8.6%), AR (8.4%)						
0	139.9	295.8	-0.2	-5.9	-0.2	...	...	-9.4	0.0	696.8	...	...	7.9	...	...	...	...	...	...
2	...	256.6	0.7	17.6	0.8	...	...	15.9	0.0	677.2	...	...	1.2	...	...	...	...	...	...
2	132.3	261.4	1.0	22.7	1.1	...	...	-6.2	0.0	713.5	...	...	1.2	...	...	...	...	...	...
-2	105.0	391.6	-0.4	-10.3	-0.5	...	...	-2.1	0.0	723.1	...	...	-0.5	...	...	...	...	...	...
0	...	261.6	0.4	9.7	0.4	...	...	5.5	0.0	688.7	...	...	0.5	...	...	...	...	...	...
	Principal Lines of Business: OrdLife (100.0%)																		
342	34.0	37.0	1.2	4.4	5.7	6.57	7.72	122.6	0.8	31.9	...	42.1	9.3	60.1	74.2	34.3	...	0.4	0.4
1,322	43.5	64.9	-0.1	-0.4	-0.4	6.27	9.39	-15.4	0.6	32.4	...	45.1	10.0	54.1	68.9	33.1	...	0.3	0.3
-1,928	54.1	62.8	2.6	13.7	12.3	6.47	4.83	-12.6	0.5	34.5	...	34.2	6.2	48.2	64.4	45.9	...	0.3	0.3
-5,617	26.7	43.7	0.0	-0.1	-0.2	6.68	-4.63	120.0	1.9	18.0	...	44.0	-38.2	44.5	57.4	66.3	...	0.5	0.5
1,696	60.6	72.5	3.2	15.6	20.0	7.64	10.29	-50.7	0.7	24.1	...	33.3	33.8	50.1	62.3	79.6	...	0.3	0.3
	Principal Lines of Business: OrdLife (59.3%), CrdA&H (37.3%), CrdLife (3.7%), GrpLife (-0.3%)												Principal States: TX (68.7%), LA (6.2%), FL (3.3%)						

Data in U.S. Dollars

COMPANY NAME Ultimate Parent Association Principal Officer Mailing Address Dom. : Began Bus. : Struct. : Mktg. Specialty Phone # AMB# NAIC#	Best's Financial Strength Rating FSC	Data Year	Balance Sheet Bonds (%)	Mort. Loans & R.E. (%)	Com & Pref. Stock (%)	All Other Assets (%)	Total Assets ($000)	Life Reserves (%)	Health Reserves (%)	Ann Res. & Dep. Liabilities (%)	All Other Liabilities (%)	Capital & Surplus ($000)	Operations Direct Premiums Written ($000)	Net Premiums Written & Deposits ($000)	Operating Cash Flow ($000)	NOG Before Taxes ($000)	NOG After Taxes ($000)	Net Income ($000)
SOUTHERN FINANCIAL LIFE INS CO Summit Partners LP	B++	'05	76.6	...	11.5	11.9	4,900	31.9	16.0	...	52.1	3,613	10,928	649	-457	446	384	403
Richard S. Kahlbaugh Chief Executive Officer		'06	77.2	...	3.3	19.5	5,184	31.6	17.0	...	51.4	4,259	10,879	908	-73	646	525	571
100 West Bay Street Jacksonville, FL 32202-3806	Rating Outlook: Stable	'07	63.8	...	1.5	34.7	4,727	32.7	19.6	...	47.7	4,071	10,779	504	-32	350	286	298
KY : 1998 : Stock : Agency Credit A&H, Credit Life		'08	66.1	...	0.1	33.7	4,695	23.9	16.3	...	59.8	4,008	10,866	344	97	333	302	302
904-350-9660 AMB# 060271 NAIC# 60242	FSC V	'09	60.6	...	0.6	38.9	3,882	24.2	19.2	...	56.5	3,338	10,351	184	-777	138	114	86
		Rating History: B++g, 03/23/10; B++g, 02/03/09; B++g, 12/20/07; B++g, 11/01/06; B+ g, 08/05/05																
SOUTHERN HEALTH SERVICES Coventry Health Care Inc	B++	'05	71.6	2.7	...	25.7	92,641	...	74.8	...	25.2	46,218	342,690	338,028	7,099	25,280	19,188	19,170
Drew A. Joyce President & CEO		'06	66.6	2.3	...	31.1	102,840	...	69.7	...	30.3	61,353	366,929	362,708	9,661	44,989	31,429	31,420
9881 Mayland Drive Richmond, VA 23233	Rating Outlook: Stable	'07	74.1	2.3	...	23.6	106,789	...	64.8	...	35.2	57,225	392,178	387,874	5,440	39,080	27,703	27,705
VA : 1991 : Stock : Broker Group A&H, Medicaid		'08	78.4	2.3	...	19.3	102,867	...	59.9	...	40.1	60,603	341,652	337,625	-4,626	23,998	17,341	17,352
804-747-3700 AMB# 068607 NAIC# 96555	FSC VII	'09	87.5	2.3	...	10.2	98,074	...	52.0	...	48.0	60,532	279,278	276,041	-7,896	5,487	4,513	4,492
		Rating History: B++, 02/12/10; B++, 11/19/08; B++, 10/30/07; B++, 07/11/07; B++, 10/27/06																
SOUTHERN LIFE AND HEALTH INS Geneve Holdings, Inc.	NR-3	'05	49.5	...	37.5	13.0	123,774	33.2	0.0	57.1	9.7	37,787	2	482	-26,958	6,343	6,093	13,434
Larry R. Graber President		'06	50.8	...	40.6	8.6	117,122	35.3	0.0	55.2	9.5	36,941	3	92	2,180	1,343	1,632	7,417
600 University Park Place, Suite 300 Birmingham, AL 35209		'07	36.9	...	49.6	13.6	110,960	36.1	...	51.9	12.1	35,998	...	26	-3,002	1,676	1,418	2,398
WI : 1890 : Stock : Inactive Ind Ann, Ind Life, Reins		'08	38.9	...	37.6	23.5	96,599	41.8	...	53.5	4.8	32,810	...	56	-15,718	-65	368	-2,583
205-414-3000 AMB# 007055 NAIC# 88323		'09	45.1	...	40.0	14.9	94,667	41.3	...	50.1	8.6	31,264	0	28	-5,232	635	635	957
		Rating History: NR-3, 12/18/09; NR-3, 01/29/09; NR-3, 11/19/07; NR-3, 09/05/07; NR-3, 06/09/06																
SOUTHERN NATIONAL LIFE INS' Louisiana Health Service & Indemnity Co	NR-1	'05	51.9	...	24.2	24.0	16,261	...	...	...	100.0	10,280	11,605	9,759	...	551	389	407
Michael H. Reitz President & CEO		'06	53.9	...	31.6	14.6	15,631	...	...	...	100.0	11,010	11,573	9,652	...	-440	-353	-353
5525 Reitz Avenue Baton Rouge, LA 70809-3802		'07	52.2	...	31.4	16.4	16,969	...	...	...	100.0	12,282	12,020	9,978	...	1,200	948	1,053
LA : 1994 : Stock : Not Available		'08	56.5	...	25.6	17.9	16,875	...	...	...	100.0	12,416	12,716	10,801	...	767	484	462
225-295-2583 AMB# 060085 NAIC# 60009		'09	49.2	...	37.9	12.9	17,270	...	...	...	100.0	12,242	13,081	11,391	...	-618	-511	-666
		Rating History: NR-1, 06/10/10; NR-1, 06/12/09; NR-1, 06/12/08; NR-1, 06/08/07; NR-1, 06/07/06																
SOUTHERN PIONEER LIFE INS CO Munich Reinsurance Company	B++	'05	48.5	4.5	5.1	41.9	23,080	56.5	34.1	...	9.4	7,928	13,851	8,353	730	3,363	2,806	2,801
John W. Hayden Vice Chairman & CEO		'06	37.5	...	3.8	58.7	24,185	55.7	33.8	...	10.6	10,150	13,166	7,985	936	1,870	1,254	1,250
P.O. Box 5323 Cincinnati, OH 45201-5323	Rating Outlook: Stable	'07	47.9	...	3.6	48.5	25,027	53.5	35.7	...	10.8	11,823	12,367	7,549	932	1,912	1,515	1,540
AR : 1966 : Stock : Direct Response Credit A&H, Credit Life		'08	32.1	...	3.5	64.4	25,442	54.0	36.9	...	9.0	12,739	11,213	7,010	668	1,051	1,003	991
513-943-7200 AMB# 007521 NAIC# 74365	FSC V	'09	68.6	...	4.2	27.3	25,292	47.0	32.4	...	20.6	12,334	8,366	5,162	-339	-772	-488	-488
		Rating History: B++, 03/10/10; B++, 05/15/09; B++, 04/09/08; B++u, 10/18/07; B++, 05/31/07																
SOUTHERN SECURITY LIFE INS CO Security National Financial	NR-5	'05	...	...	...	...	...	...	...	...	...	...	...	...	...	...	...	...
Scott M. Quist President		'06	...	...	...	...	...	...	...	...	...	...	...	...	...	...	...	...
P.O. Box 57220 Salt Lake City, UT 84157-0220		'07	...	...	...	...	...	...	...	...	...	...	...	...	...	...	...	...
MS : 1973 : Stock : Not Available Life		'08	55.7	26.5	...	17.9	1,617	...	...	...	100.0	1,556	3,050	2,259	-22,393	1,242	1,242	1,282
801-264-1060 AMB# 068370 NAIC# 75531		'09	16.5	31.7	...	51.8	1,579	...	...	...	100.0	1,552	1,828	...	-61	2	2	2
		Rating History: NR-5, 04/19/10; NR-5, 03/06/09; NR-1, 06/12/08; NR-1, 06/08/07; NR-1, 06/07/06																
SOUTHLAND NATIONAL INS CORP Collateral Holdings Ltd	B+	'05	90.3	0.4	4.3	5.0	132,780	94.7	0.5	0.7	4.1	10,385	44,808	32,538	9,153	671	345	668
Jeffrey D. Wright President		'06	91.5	0.4	3.1	5.0	141,562	94.2	0.6	0.5	4.7	8,543	43,446	28,288	7,662	-2,156	-2,167	-2,225
P.O. Box 1520 Tuscaloosa, AL 35403	Rating Outlook: Negative	'07	89.3	0.2	3.8	6.7	151,221	95.2	0.6	0.4	3.8	10,696	37,977	27,619	7,498	1,206	1,571	1,486
AL : 1969 : Stock : Agency Life, Pre-need, Whole life		'08	86.3	0.2	3.4	10.1	154,913	97.0	0.5	0.4	2.1	8,722	35,150	28,073	4,747	815	545	-5,280
205-345-7410 AMB# 008225 NAIC# 79057	FSC V	'09	92.4	0.2	2.2	5.2	168,196	96.6	0.4	0.4	2.7	11,089	38,818	31,383	11,525	616	612	595
		Rating History: B+, 11/16/09; B+, 10/24/08; B+, 10/24/07; B+, 11/09/06; B+, 11/09/05																
SOUTHWEST CREDIT LIFE INC	NR-5	'05	85.6	...	...	14.4	2,485	97.5	...	...	2.5	2,257	154	154	-19	23	23	23
Patrick J. Gurley President		'06	72.5	...	...	27.5	2,454	98.0	...	...	2.0	2,228	150	150	-28	-29	-29	-29
P.O. Box 1377 Gallup, NM 87305-1377		'07	90.0	...	...	10.0	1,419	94.7	...	...	5.3	1,122	143	143	-1,013	-67	-67	-67
NM : 1979 : Stock : Not Available Credit Life		'08	80.0	...	...	20.0	1,385	96.5	...	...	3.5	935	185	185	-28	-187	-187	-187
505-722-6621 AMB# 068282 NAIC# 91448		'09	67.8	...	...	32.2	1,187	97.4	...	...	2.6	862	121	121	-186	-73	-73	-73
		Rating History: NR-5, 06/14/10; NR-5, 07/01/09; NR-1, 06/12/09; NR-1, 06/12/08; NR-1, 06/08/07																
SOUTHWEST LIFE & HEALTH INS CO St Joseph Health System	B-	'05	63.6	...	...	36.4	12,524	...	61.7	...	38.3	3,969	44,634	42,711	-4,296	-2,729	-1,754	-1,789
Clifford R. Frank President		'06	49.3	...	...	50.7	15,252	...	56.9	...	43.1	5,283	59,469	58,604	3,683	-1,676	-746	-746
12940 N. Highway 183 Austin, TX 78750-3203	Rating Outlook: Stable	'07	36.2	...	...	63.8	15,811	...	47.2	...	52.8	6,194	64,358	63,834	-2,565	-6,244	-6,244	-6,244
TX : 1962 : Stock : Broker Group A&H, Group Life		'08	43.8	...	...	56.2	18,136	...	57.7	...	42.3	7,245	61,800	61,281	4,262	-5,435	-5,435	-5,365
512-257-6001 AMB# 006719 NAIC# 66117	FSC VI	'09	52.2	...	...	47.8	15,806	0.1	56.4	...	43.5	8,831	54,267	53,697	1,156	1,822	1,808	1,813
		Rating History: B- g, 09/02/09; B g, 06/18/08; B g, 06/14/07; B g, 06/21/06; NR-5, 05/10/05																

BEST'S PROFITABILITY, LEVERAGE AND LIQUIDITY TESTS 2005 – 2009

Data in U.S. Dollars

	Profitability Tests							Leverage Tests						Liquidity Tests					
Un-Realized Capital Gains ($000)	Benefits Paid to NPW & Dep (%)	Comm. & Expenses to NPW & Dep (%)	NOG to Total Assets (%)	NOG to Total Rev (%)	Operating Return on Equity (%)	Net Yield (%)	Total Return (%)	Change in NPW & Dep (%)	NPW & Dep to Capital (X)	Capital & Surplus to Liabilities (%)	Surplus Relief (%)	Reins Leverage (%)	Change in Capital (%)	Quick Liquidity (%)	Current Liquidity (%)	Non-Invest Grade Bonds to Capital (%)	Delinq. & Foreclosed Mortgages to Capital (%)	Mort. & Credit Tenant Loans & R.E. to Capital (%)	Affiliated Invest to Capital (%)
-32	22.1	42.5	7.3	6.2	10.0	1.79	1.44	157.8	0.2	303.5	150.6	655.8	-10.4	341.9	348.8	...	...	...	...
14	23.1	38.8	10.4	8.6	13.3	2.90	4.06	39.8	0.2	474.9	118.9	462.5	16.2	485.0	487.9	...	...	...	...
4	27.3	56.2	5.8	5.2	6.9	3.62	4.04	-44.5	0.1	631.4	119.5	426.9	-4.7	780.5	795.6	...	...	...	...
-85	36.8	28.3	6.4	6.1	7.5	3.24	1.44	-31.6	0.1	583.3	111.2	426.0	-1.8	722.1	785.7	0.1	...	...	...
49	49.1	51.3	2.7	2.5	3.1	2.55	3.12	-46.7	0.1	624.4	126.8	509.6	-16.5	819.1	863.6	...	...	...	...
Principal Lines of Business: CrdLife (50.1%), CrdA&H (49.9%)														Principal States: KY (100.0%)					
...	84.4	9.0	21.4	5.6	43.5	3.42	3.39	8.8	7.3	99.6	...	1.1	10.2	212.9	228.8	...	...	5.4	5.4
...	80.4	8.1	32.2	8.6	58.4	3.98	3.97	7.3	5.9	147.9	...	2.0	32.7	278.4	301.9	...	...	3.9	3.9
...	82.4	8.8	26.4	7.1	46.7	4.81	4.81	6.9	6.8	115.5	...	1.2	-6.7	218.6	238.6	...	...	4.3	4.3
...	86.2	7.7	16.5	5.1	29.4	3.72	3.73	-13.0	5.6	143.4	...	0.1	5.9	228.6	249.5	...	...	3.9	3.9
...	89.1	9.7	4.5	1.6	7.5	2.84	2.82	-18.2	4.6	161.2	...	0.2	-0.1	195.2	218.0	...	...	3.7	3.7
Principal Lines of Business: CompHosp/Med (76.1%), Medicaid (23.9%)														Principal States: VA (100.0%)					
-7,583	999.9	-99.9	4.2	-45.3	13.2	5.34	5.46	-98.8	0.0	51.4	...	15.3	-27.9	65.5	74.5	6.0	...	...	74.2
-2,113	999.9	999.9	1.4	31.3	4.4	4.39	7.59	-81.0	0.0	56.7	...	13.3	0.9	71.0	81.6	4.4	...	...	73.2
9	999.9	999.9	1.2	35.1	3.9	3.74	4.53	-71.1	0.0	61.9	...	11.6	0.0	74.5	86.1	4.3	...	...	80.6
-2,924	999.9	999.9	0.4	11.5	1.1	3.16	-2.62	113.0	0.0	55.2	...	...	-19.0	70.7	78.3	...	...	...	93.1
872	999.9	999.9	0.7	17.3	2.0	4.03	5.15	-49.6	0.0	56.1	...	...	-0.9	61.6	70.5	8.2	...	...	91.5
Principal Lines of Business: IndAnn (100.0%)														Principal States: TX (100.0%)					
558	50.7	49.3	2.5	3.8	4.0	...	...	21.9	0.9	201.3	0.1	...	10.2	...	...	...	...	...	...
963	48.7	63.0	-2.2	-3.4	-3.3	...	...	-1.1	0.8	304.2	0.1	...	8.3	...	...	...	...	...	...
225	51.0	45.2	5.8	8.8	8.1	...	...	3.4	0.8	337.5	0.1	...	11.3	...	...	...	...	...	...
-776	54.1	44.9	2.9	4.2	3.9	...	...	8.3	0.9	299.5	0.1	...	-3.4	...	...	...	...	...	...
556	61.4	51.0	-3.0	-4.2	-4.1	...	...	5.5	0.9	299.8	0.1	...	2.4	...	...	...	...	...	...
Principal Lines of Business: GrpA&H (51.5%), GrpLife (47.8%), OrdLife (0.7%)																			
10	39.5	61.4	12.2	22.8	41.0	3.31	3.66	-6.5	1.0	54.6	35.3	87.9	36.0	126.9	131.3	...	...	12.7	4.8
-145	45.4	64.5	5.3	10.6	13.9	4.72	4.29	-4.4	0.8	74.0	26.6	75.5	26.2	180.6	184.4	...	...	...	8.6
-42	34.6	61.7	6.2	13.6	13.8	4.27	4.35	-5.5	0.6	91.5	21.9	57.6	16.3	184.5	191.2	...	...	...	7.5
-4	38.4	61.2	4.0	9.9	8.2	3.10	3.14	-7.1	0.5	102.3	18.2	51.2	7.6	249.7	254.8	...	...	...	6.9
114	43.5	100.7	-1.9	-6.8	-3.9	1.48	1.90	-26.4	0.4	97.2	13.8	45.7	-3.1	172.9	175.7	...	...	...	7.3
Principal Lines of Business: CrdLife (76.2%), CrdA&H (21.9%), OrdLife (1.9%)														Principal States: AR (61.0%), OK (23.8%), MS (14.4%)					
...	...	...	...	...	...	...	...	...	...	...	...	...	...	...	...	...	...	...	...
...	...	...	...	...	...	...	...	...	...	...	...	...	...	...	...	...	...	...	...
...	...	...	...	...	...	...	...	...	...	...	...	...	...	...	...	...	...	...	...
204	69.0	999.9	...	27.1	...	...	...	...	1.4	999.9	102.2	999.9	...	999.9	999.9	...	...	27.4	...
...	...	...	0.1	0.7	0.1	3.54	3.54	-99.9	...	999.9	15.0	999.9	-0.3	999.9	999.9	...	5.1	32.1	...
														Principal States: MS (100.0%)					
-853	54.0	25.6	0.3	0.8	3.5	5.61	5.32	-14.4	3.1	8.7	18.9	191.0	3.5	86.2	92.2	26.1	...	5.3	11.6
31	65.8	35.0	-1.6	-5.7	-22.9	5.49	5.58	-13.1	3.2	6.6	26.3	329.8	-17.1	82.4	89.4	35.6	...	6.2	14.2
-26	67.3	29.7	1.1	4.1	16.3	5.61	5.62	-2.4	2.4	7.7	17.8	298.2	33.1	83.1	91.0	8.9	...	2.9	8.8
-175	71.7	28.3	0.4	1.4	5.6	5.78	1.92	1.6	3.2	6.0	13.0	386.8	-25.3	81.0	89.7	28.4	...	3.7	1.3
618	66.0	28.4	0.4	1.5	6.2	5.39	5.89	11.8	2.8	7.2	9.0	326.2	29.0	78.8	88.1	25.2	0.3	2.4	9.2
Principal Lines of Business: GrpLife (54.7%), OrdLife (39.6%), GrpA&H (5.6%), IndAnn (0.0%), IndA&H (0.0%)														Principal States: TN (19.9%), AL (16.0%), GA (14.3%), VA (12.3%), TX (6.7%)					
...	21.1	121.6	...	9.9	...	...	...	...	0.1	998.9	...	...	...	999.9	999.9	...	...	...	...
...	46.7	127.2	-1.2	-12.2	-1.3	3.61	3.61	-2.8	0.1	996.7	...	...	-1.3	999.9	999.9	...	...	...	...
...	52.5	137.8	-3.4	-28.3	-4.0	4.83	4.90	-4.2	0.1	379.8	...	...	-49.6	487.3	497.4	...	...	...	...
...	57.2	101.5	-13.4	-81.2	-18.2	3.11	3.33	28.9	0.2	208.2	...	...	-16.7	336.2	345.0	...	...	...	...
...	67.4	171.3	-5.6	-46.5	-8.1	2.58	2.81	-34.7	0.1	266.6	...	...	-7.8	444.6	457.4	...	...	...	...
Principal Lines of Business: CrdLife (100.0%)														Principal States: NM (100.0%)					
...	80.7	25.1	-13.0	-4.0	-34.4	3.63	3.31	-24.6	10.8	46.4	...	5.2	-36.2	98.1	98.1	...	...	...	...
...	85.7	20.5	-5.4	-1.3	-16.1	4.09	4.09	37.2	11.1	53.0	...	18.2	33.1	131.3	131.3	...	...	...	...
...	91.8	18.8	-40.2	-9.7	-99.9	4.85	4.85	8.9	10.3	64.4	...	10.5	17.3	132.8	132.8	...	...	...	...
...	93.0	15.5	-32.0	-8.8	-80.9	3.04	3.64	-4.0	8.5	66.5	...	7.6	17.0	131.7	138.4	...	...	...	...
...	82.8	14.9	10.7	3.3	22.5	1.95	1.99	-12.4	6.1	126.6	...	1.3	21.9	221.5	232.4	...	...	...	...
Principal Lines of Business: CompHosp/Med (99.6%), Life (0.2%), Dental (0.2%)														Principal States: TX (99.9%)					

Data in U.S. Dollars

COMPANY NAME / Ultimate Parent Association / Principal Officer / Mailing Address / Dom. : Began Bus. : Struct. : Mktg. / Specialty / Phone # / AMB# NAIC#	Best's Financial Strength Rating / FSC	Data Year	Balance Sheet: Bonds (%)	Mort. Loans & R.E. (%)	Com & Pref. Stock (%)	All Other Assets (%)	Total Assets ($000)	Life Reserves (%)	Health Reserves (%)	Ann Res. & Dep. Liabilities (%)	All Other Liabilities (%)	Capital & Surplus ($000)	Operations: Direct Premiums Written ($000)	Net Premiums Written & Deposits ($000)	Operating Cash Flow ($000)	NOG Before Taxes ($000)	NOG After Taxes ($000)	Net Income ($000)
SOUTHWEST SERVICE LIFE INS CO[1]	NR-1	'05	46.7	...	29.8	23.5	6,847	...	...	...	100.0	3,674	20,088	8,500	...	1,349	1,174	1,174
Frank M. Croy, President		'06	52.7	...	25.4	22.0	9,107	...	...	...	100.0	3,486	20,473	11,128	...	796	827	827
P.O. Box 982005, Fort Worth, TX 76182-8005		'07	63.2	...	23.8	13.0	10,110	...	...	...	100.0	4,533	19,329	9,339	...	1,026	863	863
TX : 1963 : Stock : Not Available		'08	58.0	...	24.6	17.5	11,070	...	...	...	100.0	5,411	17,581	8,964	...	1,049	945	945
817-284-4888		'09	44.5	...	25.2	30.2	11,743	...	...	...	100.0	6,351	16,056	7,898	...	720	602	602
AMB# 068099 NAIC# 82430		Rating History: NR-1, 06/10/10; NR-1, 06/12/09; NR-1, 06/12/08; NR-1, 06/08/07; NR-1, 06/07/06																
SPJST	B	'05	70.8	17.2	8.7	3.3	185,322	41.7	...	54.1	4.3	25,376	10,754	10,553	7,011	1,224	1,224	1,493
Brian Vanicek, President		'06	69.9	16.0	10.4	3.7	190,661	41.6	...	54.3	4.0	25,743	11,755	11,335	5,839	689	689	1,827
P.O. Box 100, Temple, TX 76503	Rating Outlook: Negative	'07	65.3	16.0	13.5	5.1	192,059	42.3	...	54.5	3.2	24,261	9,408	10,018	4,508	-564	-564	455
TX : 1897 : Fraternal : Career Agent		'08	64.9	16.1	10.8	8.2	185,108	42.6	...	54.9	2.5	13,023	13,821	12,554	-2,065	-1,918	-1,918	-9,061
Term Life, Trad Life, Univ Life; 254-773-1575		'09	72.0	15.9	9.3	2.8	196,978	40.9	...	54.2	5.0	13,808	18,044	16,320	8,794	-492	-492	-1,245
AMB# 009606 NAIC# 57436	FSC V	Rating History: B, 05/10/10; B, 04/01/09; B+, 04/22/08; B++, 05/04/07; B++, 05/15/06																
STANDARD INSURANCE COMPANY; StanCorp Financial Group Inc	A	'05	41.0	27.8	...	31.2	10,810,753	7.3	33.0	25.3	34.3	944,536	2,941,053	3,115,818	479,209	312,137	205,573	205,550
Eric E. Parsons, President & CEO		'06	38.7	27.5	0.0	33.7	12,148,124	7.0	30.4	24.7	37.8	936,747	3,261,681	3,439,495	524,607	266,638	168,942	167,044
1100 S.W. Sixth Avenue, Portland, OR 97204-1093	Rating Outlook: Stable	'07	36.6	27.3	...	36.1	13,265,338	6.9	28.9	24.3	39.9	1,014,381	3,363,981	3,619,062	578,010	309,914	198,751	241,217
OR : 1906 : Stock : Not Available		'08	40.6	31.3	...	28.1	12,874,451	7.3	30.7	32.0	29.9	1,112,301	4,018,601	4,324,046	942,725	338,597	232,327	134,897
Dis inc, Group A&H, Group Life; 971-321-7000		'09	40.1	28.9	0.0	31.1	14,524,929	6.6	27.4	31.4	34.7	1,193,708	3,335,683	3,658,484	529,275	363,287	244,285	217,793
AMB# 007069 NAIC# 69019	FSC XIII	Rating History: A g, 06/15/10; A g, 06/10/09; A g, 05/22/08; A g, 07/05/07; A g, 07/05/06																
STANDARD LIFE AND ACCIDENT INS; American National Insurance Company	A	'05	76.0	7.8	11.0	5.2	513,541	38.5	29.0	25.9	6.6	198,392	213,619	214,146	29,772	30,380	19,894	21,505
G. R. Ferdinandtsen, Chairman, President & CEO		'06	75.0	5.9	13.8	5.2	528,743	38.4	25.6	28.2	7.8	211,568	173,118	173,201	11,677	26,116	17,767	21,132
One Moody Plaza, Galveston, TX 77550-7999	Rating Outlook: Stable	'07	73.1	5.4	15.6	5.9	531,349	37.7	24.8	27.5	9.9	210,946	146,219	145,217	2,344	11,600	8,668	9,377
TX : 1976 : Stock : Agency		'08	75.2	8.1	9.3	7.4	490,140	40.9	25.4	30.1	3.6	201,855	135,756	131,983	-21,091	20,909	16,584	2,259
Med supp, Whole life, Annuity; 409-763-4661		'09	69.7	10.0	11.0	9.3	505,917	40.2	23.3	30.2	6.3	217,655	128,760	121,438	-8,598	16,279	12,909	3,230
AMB# 007070 NAIC# 86355	FSC VIII	Rating History: A, 05/20/10; A, 06/09/09; A, 05/13/08; A, 04/26/07; A, 02/08/06																
STANDARD LIFE & CASUALTY INS; Fidelity Ventures Inc	B	'05	71.5	8.7	6.9	12.9	19,935	78.5	3.8	14.4	3.3	3,886	4,160	4,247	450	589	560	567
Brad Piercey, President		'06	76.1	6.5	6.0	11.3	20,647	77.7	5.1	14.0	3.3	4,305	4,115	4,200	128	949	981	1,188
P.O. Box 510690, Salt Lake City, UT 84151-0690	Rating Outlook: Stable	'07	79.2	1.4	7.5	12.0	21,468	77.7	5.7	13.7	3.0	4,611	4,683	4,760	557	715	712	708
UT : 1948 : Stock : Not Available		'08	78.0	1.4	6.4	14.3	21,922	77.3	6.9	13.0	2.8	4,644	6,609	6,670	65	853	823	189
A&S, Life; 801-538-0376		'09	85.1	1.5	1.2	12.2	22,427	76.4	8.1	12.2	3.3	4,692	8,396	8,330	763	983	769	509
AMB# 007408 NAIC# 71706	FSC III	Rating History: B, 11/03/09; B, 11/06/08; NR-1, 06/12/08; NR-1, 06/08/07; NR-1, 06/07/06																
STANDARD LIFE INS CO OF IN[1]; Capital Assurance Holdings LLC	E	'05	94.9	0.0	0.4	4.7	1,552,219	...	...	26.6	73.4	80,795	83,950	-6,292	...	19,089	17,307	15,831
Randolph D. Lamberjack, Special Deputy Rehabilitator		'06	91.3	0.0	2.0	6.7	1,643,066	...	...	34.3	65.7	92,466	75,354	65,530	...	12,002	8,847	8,760
10689 N. Pennsylvania Street, Indianapolis, IN 46280		'07	90.1	0.0	5.1	4.8	1,988,892	...	...	52.8	47.2	106,200	33,493	30,232	...	13,501	11,556	7,675
IN : 1935 : Stock : Agency		'08	92.3	...	3.4	4.2	2,088,894	...	...	61.4	38.6	44,377	26,921	24,256	...	13,789	9,819	-91,614
In Rehabilitation; 317-574-6201		'09	94.2	...	1.5	4.3	1,948,951	...	...	62.7	37.3	18,384	828	-409	...	31,681	28,576	-19,436
AMB# 007073 NAIC# 69051		Rating History: E, 12/22/08; B, 11/25/08; B++u, 10/15/08; B++, 07/03/08; B++, 05/18/07																
STANDARD LIFE INSURANCE OF NY; StanCorp Financial Group Inc	A	'05	50.3	29.9	...	19.8	71,108	10.8	68.1	1.3	19.7	24,152	57,957	38,458	32,906	1,822	1,960	1,955
J. Greg Ness, President & CEO		'06	41.5	46.1	...	12.4	99,013	12.1	76.5	1.6	9.8	30,747	67,748	45,127	28,802	4,496	3,864	3,827
1100 S.W. Sixth Avenue, Portland, OR 97204-1093	Rating Outlook: Stable	'07	47.0	44.9	...	8.1	141,485	12.6	71.4	1.6	14.5	33,426	77,768	51,926	42,261	-742	-1,505	-1,662
NY : 2001 : Stock : Not Available		'08	45.1	46.7	...	8.2	176,261	14.9	69.3	3.0	12.8	42,266	93,910	64,185	32,075	3,007	1,928	1,055
Dis inc, Group A&H; 914-989-4400		'09	44.5	47.6	...	8.0	196,168	17.6	63.4	4.3	14.7	49,453	92,853	66,315	17,907	11,617	7,127	6,715
AMB# 060342 NAIC# 89009	FSC XIII	Rating History: A g, 06/15/10; A g, 06/10/09; A g, 05/22/08; A g, 07/05/07; A g, 07/05/06																
STANDARD SECURITY LIFE OF NY; Geneve Holdings, Inc.	A-	'05	70.8	...	10.6	18.6	312,423	13.5	21.3	55.1	10.1	110,593	222,804	169,444	23,337	14,644	9,720	10,535
Rachel Lipari, President & COO		'06	61.6	...	9.8	28.6	344,283	8.3	22.0	54.3	15.4	107,918	265,013	190,161	32,138	15,275	10,637	11,416
485 Madison Avenue, 14th Floor, New York, NY 10022-5872	Rating Outlook: Negative	'07	57.2	...	16.5	26.3	367,199	7.9	26.8	52.7	12.6	109,648	305,915	212,698	17,791	6,920	4,583	4,617
NY : 1958 : Stock : General Agent		'08	56.2	...	15.7	28.2	369,681	8.2	25.9	55.1	10.8	114,274	278,977	205,507	-4,765	10,690	7,819	-3,803
Group A&H, Ind Life, Stop Loss; 212-355-4141		'09	63.6	...	14.6	21.7	370,831	8.2	21.9	57.7	12.2	115,055	247,227	189,351	12,258	10,270	8,519	8,783
AMB# 007075 NAIC# 69078	FSC VIII	Rating History: A- g, 12/18/09; A- g, 01/29/09; A- g, 11/19/07; A, 09/05/07; A, 06/09/06																
STARMOUNT LIFE INS CO; H & J Capital LLC	B++	'05	34.5	10.7	1.0	53.8	17,091	48.0	29.8	1.3	20.8	8,201	30,015	31,757	1,930	2,456	2,352	2,334
Erich Sternberg, President		'06	31.5	8.7	0.8	59.0	20,571	49.9	28.3	1.2	20.7	9,819	31,515	33,416	3,105	2,392	2,125	2,099
P.O. Box 98100, Baton Rouge, LA 70898-9100	Rating Outlook: Stable	'07	22.8	7.4	0.3	69.5	24,769	52.0	31.1	1.0	15.9	11,725	33,681	39,141	2,570	2,255	2,198	2,201
LA : 1983 : Stock : Direct Response		'08	18.5	6.7	0.2	74.5	32,957	43.6	21.4	0.6	34.4	13,914	37,116	44,620	7,910	2,651	2,557	2,557
A&H, Dental, Ind Life; 225-400-9100		'09	23.7	5.4	0.2	70.7	32,891	61.5	25.2	0.6	12.7	15,608	38,587	50,944	2,992	2,640	2,478	2,478
AMB# 009370 NAIC# 68985	FSC V	Rating History: B++, 03/05/10; B++, 04/23/09; B++, 01/21/08; B++, 01/08/07; B++, 12/19/05																

BEST'S PROFITABILITY, LEVERAGE AND LIQUIDITY TESTS 2005 – 2009

Data in U.S. Dollars

—	Profitability Tests							Leverage Tests						Liquidity Tests					
Un-Realized Capital Gains ($000)	Benefits Paid to NPW & Dep (%)	Comm. & Expenses to NPW & Dep (%)	NOG to Total Assets (%)	NOG to Total Rev (%)	Operating Return on Equity (%)	Net Yield (%)	Total Return (%)	Change in NPW & Dep (%)	NPW & Dep to Capital (X)	Capital & Surplus to Liabilities (%)	Surplus Relief (%)	Reins Leverage (%)	Change in Capital (%)	Quick Liquidity (%)	Current Liquidity (%)	Non-Invest Grade Bonds to Capital (%)	Delinq. & Foreclosed Mortgages to Capital (%)	Mort. & Credit Tenant Loans & R.E. to Capital (%)	Affiliated Invest to Capital (%)
-502	37.8	46.9	17.8	8.8	35.2	...	...	-16.8	2.3	115.8	130.8	...	22.2	...	...	...	...	...	...
-294	33.5	38.0	10.4	5.1	23.1	...	...	30.9	3.2	62.0	141.8	...	-5.1	...	...	...	...	...	...
93	41.0	50.6	9.0	6.1	21.5	...	...	-16.1	2.1	81.3	100.7	...	30.0	...	...	...	...	...	...
315	39.0	48.0	8.9	6.9	19.0	...	...	-4.0	1.7	95.6	83.2	...	19.4	...	...	...	...	...	...
243	41.9	52.6	5.3	4.9	10.2	...	...	-11.9	1.2	117.8	63.4	...	17.4	...	...	...	...	...	...
	Principal Lines of Business: IndA&H (88.2%), OrdLife (11.8%)																		
862	81.3	47.3	0.7	5.7	4.0	5.02	6.00	4.1	0.4	17.2	...	4.4	2.5	63.0	69.5	57.9	...	110.9	2.2
-607	93.4	48.4	0.4	3.1	2.7	5.51	6.10	7.4	0.4	17.5	...	4.9	4.4	64.0	70.2	62.0	...	107.5	3.7
-2,528	111.3	67.4	-0.3	-2.8	-2.3	5.83	5.31	-11.6	0.4	15.9	0.0	6.1	-7.2	62.0	68.8	69.6	...	116.8	10.1
-3,458	84.6	54.6	-1.0	-9.3	-10.3	4.27	-1.03	25.3	0.9	8.0	0.2	14.5	-47.8	59.2	65.5	100.1	...	216.9	20.1
4,695	85.2	34.5	-0.3	-1.9	-3.7	4.61	7.00	30.0	0.9	9.6	0.1	14.0	24.8	61.9	69.9	74.7	...	182.3	15.6
	Principal Lines of Business: IndAnn (62.2%), OrdLife (37.8%)													Principal States: TX (100.0%)					
-966	56.3	16.5	2.0	6.0	22.0	6.28	6.29	7.8	3.0	15.2	1.4	88.8	3.3	42.2	51.3	17.0	0.1	290.7	18.5
-410	60.6	15.6	1.5	4.5	18.0	6.00	5.98	10.4	3.3	14.2	1.5	92.1	0.0	43.9	52.6	14.8	0.5	323.6	3.7
-4,034	65.6	15.9	1.6	5.1	20.4	5.90	6.36	5.2	3.2	14.4	1.5	86.5	8.0	44.6	53.0	17.8	0.0	324.8	3.3
-5,281	55.9	14.4	1.8	5.0	21.8	5.88	4.76	19.5	3.6	13.8	1.5	80.6	6.7	45.7	54.2	22.3	0.1	338.3	3.1
3,534	65.8	16.4	1.8	6.2	21.2	5.79	5.56	-15.4	2.9	14.1	1.4	74.2	7.7	42.9	51.6	24.5	0.2	326.8	2.8
	Principal Lines of Business: GrpA&H (30.7%), GrpAnn (28.8%), GrpLife (19.4%), IndAnn (16.6%), IndA&H (4.5%)													Principal States: CA (14.7%), OR (10.2%), TX (9.8%), WA (5.9%), FL (5.2%)					
-1,456	66.9	25.2	4.0	7.9	10.3	5.73	5.83	1.0	1.0	69.7	4.4	20.5	5.9	94.3	112.1	13.8	...	19.1	1.6
1,691	74.3	27.6	3.4	8.4	8.7	5.79	6.84	-19.1	0.8	76.5	3.7	21.7	8.6	101.8	119.1	10.8	...	13.7	8.0
965	84.9	29.3	1.6	4.8	4.1	5.54	5.87	-16.2	0.6	76.4	3.2	17.0	0.5	104.2	121.7	7.8	...	12.6	11.0
-13,842	84.1	27.7	3.2	10.0	8.0	5.59	0.02	-9.1	0.7	70.5	2.9	18.8	-12.0	106.8	124.6	6.8	...	19.7	0.1
12,403	83.6	29.9	2.6	8.4	6.2	5.55	6.18	-8.0	0.5	81.1	2.1	11.4	11.8	108.7	126.9	7.7	...	22.4	0.0
	Principal Lines of Business: IndA&H (76.6%), OrdLife (11.7%), IndAnn (6.7%), GrpA&H (5.0%), GrpAnn (0.0%)													Principal States: TX (9.7%), OH (9.2%), IN (7.6%), FL (7.5%), TN (5.1%)					
26	50.2	57.9	2.8	10.6	15.4	5.64	5.88	8.6	1.1	24.9	0.0	1.0	12.6	72.7	79.2	14.5	...	43.7	1.7
-23	52.2	50.4	4.8	18.6	24.0	5.76	6.76	-1.1	0.9	27.3	0.0	1.0	11.6	77.2	83.0	21.7	...	30.5	1.7
-21	50.4	47.4	3.4	12.1	16.0	5.85	5.77	13.3	1.0	28.1	0.0	1.0	6.3	82.0	89.0	14.7	...	6.6	1.7
161	52.9	46.5	3.8	10.4	17.8	5.86	3.68	40.1	1.4	27.2	0.0	1.1	-0.5	83.9	90.3	5.6	...	6.5	1.9
-44	54.2	43.6	3.5	8.3	16.5	4.64	3.27	24.9	1.8	26.7	0.0	1.2	1.0	93.1	94.1	16.8	...	7.3	2.9
	Principal Lines of Business: IndA&H (74.9%), OrdLife (22.8%), GrpA&H (2.2%), IndAnn (0.1%), GrpAnn (0.0%)													Principal States: TX (47.0%), NC (31.9%), SC (14.3%), GA (3.8%)					
-1,703	-99.9	-99.9	1.1	20.3	23.0	...	...	-99.9	-0.1	6.0	15.8	...	14.6	...	...	...	...	0.2	...
14	285.9	33.0	0.6	5.7	10.2	...	...	999.9	0.7	6.5	0.6	...	15.0	...	...	...	...	0.1	...
-4,316	727.7	75.7	0.6	8.7	11.6	...	...	-53.9	0.3	5.8	0.2	...	9.1	...	...	...	...	0.0	...
9,014	772.5	129.8	0.5	7.6	13.0	...	...	-19.8	0.5	2.2	0.1	...	-59.3	...	...	...	...	...	...
-4,938	-99.9	-99.9	1.4	21.2	91.1	...	...	-99.9	0.0	1.0	0.4	...	-57.4	...	...	...	...	...	...
	Principal Lines of Business: IndAnn (113.5%), IndA&H (-1.0%), GrpAnn (-12.5%)																		
...	38.0	29.6	3.7	4.1	9.7	4.20	4.19	116.5	1.6	52.4	...	6.3	48.9	70.1	81.7	1.3	...	86.9	...
...	41.4	24.5	4.5	6.8	14.1	5.01	4.96	17.3	1.4	46.3	...	6.4	28.3	55.7	65.9	1.9	...	145.7	...
...	47.4	29.6	-1.3	-2.2	-4.7	5.54	5.40	15.1	1.5	31.9	...	7.4	9.1	50.8	60.5	2.3	...	185.9	...
...	57.7	27.0	1.2	2.5	5.1	5.69	5.12	23.6	1.5	32.3	...	7.5	25.9	50.9	59.4	0.6	...	191.0	...
...	51.0	29.2	3.8	10.0	15.5	5.76	5.51	3.3	1.3	34.5	...	6.2	16.9	46.2	55.3	...	...	185.4	...
	Principal Lines of Business: GrpA&H (53.8%), GrpLife (38.2%), GrpAnn (7.8%), OrdLife (0.2%)													Principal States: NY (99.9%)					
-1,495	57.7	24.0	3.3	5.1	9.0	4.39	4.00	35.0	1.5	58.7	24.7	55.0	4.4	71.4	85.2	12.2	...	...	25.0
-1,359	62.8	26.3	3.2	4.9	9.7	5.56	5.25	12.2	1.7	47.3	21.8	56.6	-4.4	73.9	85.9	2.6	...	...	16.7
-1,760	68.5	26.0	1.3	1.8	4.2	5.34	4.67	11.9	1.9	44.0	26.6	70.7	1.5	64.7	78.0	2.4	...	...	21.6
-7,730	71.5	28.3	2.1	3.3	7.0	5.07	-1.34	-3.4	1.8	44.9	20.2	63.1	2.1	60.4	72.1	2.6	...	...	30.5
-6,000	74.1	28.5	2.3	3.9	7.4	4.40	2.53	-7.9	1.6	45.3	19.1	54.5	0.9	59.5	73.4	12.7	...	...	28.7
	Principal Lines of Business: GrpA&H (93.1%), GrpAnn (3.0%), IndAnn (1.8%), GrpLife (1.7%), OrdLife (0.3%)													Principal States: NY (24.4%), TX (8.9%), AZ (4.9%), IL (4.4%), CA (3.9%)					
0	58.4	33.3	15.4	6.9	32.0	3.66	3.50	-5.8	3.8	94.5	25.6	23.9	25.6	113.6	121.1	...	...	22.1	22.1
...	60.5	32.7	11.3	5.9	23.6	3.62	3.44	5.2	3.4	93.0	15.5	21.0	19.4	145.8	155.0	...	...	18.1	18.1
-3	63.1	31.0	9.7	5.2	20.4	3.59	3.59	17.1	3.3	91.5	14.8	18.4	19.4	121.8	126.3	0.9	...	15.4	15.4
2	61.8	30.9	8.9	5.4	19.9	1.88	1.89	14.0	3.2	74.3	12.2	14.5	18.7	157.5	164.7	0.7	...	15.8	15.8
1	64.9	27.3	7.5	4.6	16.8	0.68	0.68	14.2	3.2	92.8	11.5	15.9	12.7	164.6	173.3	1.9	...	11.2	11.2
	Principal Lines of Business: GrpA&H (84.4%), OrdLife (15.0%), GrpLife (0.4%), IndA&H (0.2%), IndAnn (0.0%)													Principal States: LA (60.0%), MS (18.9%), TX (4.1%), FL (4.1%)					

2010 BEST'S KEY RATING GUIDE — LIFE/HEALTH EDITION
ANNUAL STATEMENT DATA FOR YEARS 2005 – 2009

Data in U.S. Dollars

COMPANY NAME Ultimate Parent Association Principal Officer Mailing Address Dom. : Began Bus. : Struct. : Mktg. Specialty Phone # AMB# NAIC#	Best's Financial Strength Rating FSC	Data Year	Balance Sheet Bonds (%)	Mort. Loans & R.E. (%)	Com & Pref. Stock (%)	All Other Assets (%)	Total Assets ($000)	Life Reserves (%)	Health Reserves %)	Ann Res. & Dep. Liabilities (%)	All Other Liabilities (%)	Capital & Surplus ($000)	Operations Direct Premiums Written ($000)	Net Premiums Written & Deposits ($000)	Operating Cash Flow ($000)	NOG Before Taxes ($000)	NOG After Taxes ($000)	Net Income ($000)
STATE FARM ANN & LIFE INS CO State Farm Mutual Automobile Ins Co Edward B. Rust, Jr. President One State Farm Plaza Bloomington, IL 61710 IL : Stock : Inactive 309-766-2311 AMB# 009158 NAIC# 94498	**NR-3**	'05	61.6	...	...	38.4	7,919	...	...	...	100.0	7,882	...	...	239	188	122	122
		'06	43.5	...	...	56.5	8,107	...	...	...	100.0	8,049	...	...	260	258	169	169
		'07	43.3	...	...	56.7	8,260	...	...	...	100.0	8,229	...	...	202	278	181	180
		'08	25.4	...	...	74.6	8,354	...	...	...	100.0	8,308	...	...	124	122	79	79
		'09	55.4	...	...	44.6	8,336	...	...	...	100.0	8,314	...	...	-16	7	5	5
		Rating History: NR-3, 04/23/10; NR-3, 06/17/09; NR-3, 06/12/08; NR-3, 06/11/07; NR-3, 06/15/06																
STATE FARM INTL LF INS CO LTD State Farm Mutual Automobile Ins Co Barbara Bellissimo President Richmond House, 12 Par-la-Ville Road Hamilton HM 08, Bermuda BM : Stock : Exclusive Agent Life 414-299-4994 AMB# 078618	**A+** Rating Outlook: Stable **FSC XV**	'05	...	...	...	...	...	...	...	...	...	...	...	...	...	...	...	...
		'06	...	...	...	100.0	4,586	...	...	...	100.0	4,571	...	...	...	44	29	29
		'07	87.6	...	...	12.5	957,693	83.8	...	...	16.2	195,399	...	...	...	35,946	17,231	17,231
		'08	87.6	...	...	12.4	878,440	83.9	...	...	16.1	162,672	...	...	...	-12,218	-10,507	-10,466
		'09	88.0	...	...	12.0	1,073,643	83.9	...	...	16.1	210,992	...	...	...	45,122	30,561	30,584
		Rating History: A+, 04/23/10; A+ g, 06/17/09; A+ g, 06/12/08; A+ g, 06/11/07																
STATE FARM LIFE & ACC ASSUR CO State Farm Mutual Automobile Ins Co Edward B. Rust, Jr. President One State Farm Plaza Bloomington, IL 61710 IL : 1961 : Stock : Exclusive Agent Ind Life, Ind Ann, Group Life 309-766-2311 AMB# 007079 NAIC# 69094	**A++** Rating Outlook: Stable **FSC XV**	'05	87.2	...	...	12.8	1,388,812	64.0	...	26.6	9.3	243,562	143,961	170,319	89,512	23,250	14,171	15,598
		'06	87.1	...	...	12.9	1,467,428	64.9	...	25.1	10.0	255,327	147,865	170,857	72,442	30,892	19,766	20,420
		'07	86.1	...	...	13.9	1,549,554	65.8	...	24.9	9.4	266,526	156,330	181,101	79,009	24,421	11,318	10,267
		'08	84.5	...	...	15.5	1,660,908	65.0	...	27.2	7.8	266,545	194,701	220,863	128,043	15,877	1,533	-3,402
		'09	86.9	...	...	13.1	1,792,629	64.4	...	27.5	8.2	289,151	183,703	215,837	123,602	39,064	25,435	25,661
		Rating History: A++g, 04/23/10; A++g, 06/17/09; A++g, 06/12/08; A++g, 06/11/07; A++g, 06/15/06																
STATE FARM LIFE INS CO State Farm Mutual Automobile Ins Co Edward B. Rust, Jr. Chairman & President One State Farm Plaza Bloomington, IL 61710 IL : 1929 : Stock : Exclusive Agent Ind Life, Ind Ann, Group Life 309-766-2311 AMB# 007080 NAIC# 69108	**A++** Rating Outlook: Stable **FSC XV**	'05	69.8	11.5	5.3	13.3	39,874,561	57.9	...	32.7	9.4	4,504,454	3,662,001	4,534,529	2,228,559	488,131	294,249	317,458
		'06	67.5	12.1	5.8	14.6	42,209,002	58.8	...	31.4	9.8	5,061,878	3,763,512	4,565,591	1,906,126	587,518	358,778	388,068
		'07	66.3	12.9	6.5	14.3	43,307,957	59.8	...	30.0	10.1	5,255,532	3,727,940	4,568,994	1,758,213	608,644	349,058	382,173
		'08	68.8	12.7	4.1	14.4	44,630,862	61.0	...	31.4	7.6	5,060,054	4,597,630	5,560,345	2,734,726	566,119	327,106	185,700
		'09	70.4	11.7	4.6	13.3	47,959,821	60.4	...	31.2	8.3	5,662,640	4,275,687	5,277,385	2,653,480	737,178	449,561	404,921
		Rating History: A++g, 04/23/10; A++g, 06/17/09; A++g, 06/12/08; A++g, 06/11/07; A++g, 06/15/06																
STATE LIFE INS CO American United Mutual Insurance Hldg Co Dayton H. Molendorp Chairman & CEO P.O. Box 406 Indianapolis, IN 46206-0406 IN : 1894 : Stock : Broker Ind Life, Ind Ann, LTC 317-285-1877 AMB# 007082 NAIC# 69116	**A** Rating Outlook: Positive **FSC XI**	'05	90.1	2.9	...	7.0	2,302,845	58.1	0.1	39.3	2.5	108,377	103,706	98,114	1,848,907	-47,082	-57,607	-57,293
		'06	89.4	4.3	0.1	6.2	2,386,103	60.2	0.1	37.8	2.0	131,651	83,245	208,314	88,602	33,797	25,818	25,607
		'07	88.7	6.1	0.1	5.1	2,504,181	60.7	0.0	37.0	2.3	150,799	133,443	233,671	120,056	27,285	21,416	19,515
		'08	88.0	6.4	0.9	4.7	2,840,070	56.0	0.0	42.4	1.6	177,887	189,124	450,426	328,017	40,472	30,744	20,498
		'09	87.7	6.6	0.4	5.4	3,162,483	53.6	0.0	44.4	2.0	210,204	381,928	391,131	308,657	42,812	28,558	27,612
		Rating History: A g, 06/10/10; A g, 06/17/09; A g, 06/09/08; A g, 06/07/07; A g, 02/08/06																
STATE LIFE INSURANCE FUND WI[1] Sean Dilweg President 125 S. Webster Madison, WI 53703 WI : 1913 : Stock : Direct Response Ind Life 608-266-0107 AMB# 007255 NAIC# 70599	**NR-1**	'05	90.7	...	...	9.3	82,964	...	...	21.4	78.6	3,828	2,224	2,184	...	1,887	1,887	1,887
		'06	90.6	...	...	9.4	84,830	...	...	21.2	78.8	4,910	2,141	2,100	...	1,230	1,230	1,230
		'07	91.4	...	...	8.6	87,024	...	...	21.3	78.7	6,209	2,041	2,001	...	1,366	1,366	1,366
		'08	92.2	...	...	7.8	87,847	...	...	21.4	78.6	6,441	1,935	1,896	...	540	540	540
		'09	91.7	...	...	8.3	89,602	...	...	21.7	78.3	7,349	1,948	1,907	...	1,210	1,210	920
		Rating History: NR-1, 06/10/10; NR-1, 06/12/09; NR-1, 06/12/08; NR-5, 04/27/07; NR-5, 05/09/06																
STATE MUTUAL INS CO State Mutual Insurance Company Delos H. Yancey, III Chairman, President & CEO P.O. Box 153 Rome, GA 30162-0153 GA : 1894 : Mutual : Agency Med supp 706-291-1054 AMB# 007085 NAIC# 69132	**B+** Rating Outlook: Negative **FSC VI**	'05	55.0	11.9	2.3	30.8	358,543	87.8	0.4	3.4	8.4	23,223	110,239	25,990	26,460	4,118	3,096	2,094
		'06	53.2	18.2	4.1	24.6	370,548	88.7	0.5	3.2	7.7	29,075	94,398	27,199	2,524	406	297	2,157
		'07	50.2	19.0	6.1	24.8	374,893	89.2	0.5	2.8	7.5	30,606	83,718	32,650	11,238	822	737	608
		'08	47.3	17.7	5.3	29.7	386,050	89.2	0.4	2.6	7.8	29,173	75,910	42,120	1,669	2,642	1,870	1,398
		'09	47.5	15.9	5.8	30.7	392,821	88.3	0.4	2.5	8.8	29,894	67,799	30,230	12,167	3,023	2,725	1,335
		Rating History: B+, 02/12/10; B+, 03/18/09; B+, 01/30/08; B+, 12/14/06; B+, 12/23/05																
STERLING INVESTORS LIFE INS CO Sterling Holdings, Inc. Delos H. Yancey, Jr. President 210 East Second Avenue, Suite 105 Rome, GA 30161 GA : 1978 : Stock : Mng Gen Agent Med supp, Life, Whole life 706-235-8154 AMB# 008841 NAIC# 89184	**B** Rating Outlook: Stable **FSC IV**	'05	54.2	15.9	...	29.9	22,321	50.7	7.8	24.8	16.7	5,500	15,239	3,028	1,464	-253	-253	-183
		'06	38.4	7.3	...	54.3	25,526	4.2	10.8	15.5	69.5	6,589	33,217	-1,495	-308	404	350	349
		'07	27.0	...	...	73.0	22,647	12.0	15.7	22.2	50.2	6,453	57,640	10,415	-2,531	159	56	56
		'08	34.7	...	...	65.3	22,038	11.9	16.7	22.8	48.6	6,680	67,409	11,703	-779	499	376	376
		'09	47.8	...	...	52.2	20,403	14.1	16.2	24.2	45.5	7,356	58,122	10,017	-568	251	104	104
		Rating History: B, 11/30/09; B, 01/07/09; B, 11/14/07; B, 11/21/06; B, 09/16/05																
STERLING LIFE INS CO Munich Reinsurance Company Michael A. Muchnicki President & CEO 2219 Rimland Drive Bellingham, WA 98226 IL : 1958 : Stock : Direct Response Med supp 360-647-9080 AMB# 008021 NAIC# 77399	**A-** Rating Outlook: Stable **FSC VIII**	'05	95.2	...	0.5	4.3	145,506	0.0	80.4	...	19.5	85,891	287,000	287,000	38,801	45,909	34,923	34,886
		'06	83.0	...	...	17.0	204,137	0.2	70.0	...	29.8	102,152	516,661	497,788	41,264	63,240	41,048	41,395
		'07	54.0	...	1.2	44.9	303,866	0.4	78.3	...	21.3	183,890	817,284	788,305	99,612	30,461	18,859	18,773
		'08	72.9	...	0.5	26.7	346,265	0.5	74.0	...	25.5	192,735	1,023,734	998,828	25,030	19,020	13,001	7,875
		'09	71.5	...	...	28.5	331,679	1.9	71.1	...	27.0	209,036	962,895	938,466	-32,675	13,962	13,297	12,279
		Rating History: A-, 03/12/10; A-, 12/29/08; A-, 04/11/08; A- u, 12/17/07; A- u, 08/01/07																

2010 BEST'S KEY RATING GUIDE — LIFE/HEALTH EDITION
BEST'S PROFITABILITY, LEVERAGE AND LIQUIDITY TESTS 2005 – 2009
Data in U.S. Dollars

—	Profitability Tests							Leverage Tests						Liquidity Tests					
Un-Realized Capital Gains ($000)	Benefits Paid to NPW & Dep (%)	Comm. & Expenses to NPW & Dep (%)	NOG to Total Assets (%)	NOG to Total Rev (%)	Operating Return on Equity (%)	Net Yield (%)	Total Return (%)	Change in NPW & Dep (%)	NPW & Dep to Capital (X)	Capital & Surplus to Liabilities (%)	Surplus Relief (%)	Reins Leverage (%)	Change in Capital (%)	Quick Liquidity (%)	Current Liquidity (%)	Non-Invest Grade Bonds to Capital (%)	Delinq. & Foreclosed Mortgages to Capital (%)	Mort. & Credit Tenant Loans & R.E. to Capital (%)	Affiliated Invest to Capital (%)
0	...	...	1.6	43.4	1.6	3.65	3.64	...	...	999.9	...	...	1.6	999.9	999.9	...	...	...	...
0	...	...	2.1	47.1	2.1	4.55	4.55	...	...	999.9	...	...	2.1	999.9	999.9	...	...	...	...
0	...	...	2.2	48.9	2.2	4.62	4.61	...	...	999.9	...	...	2.2	999.9	999.9	...	...	...	...
0	...	...	1.0	33.5	1.0	2.89	2.89	...	...	999.9	...	...	1.0	999.9	999.9	...	...	...	...
0	...	...	0.1	4.2	0.1	1.40	1.40	...	...	999.9	...	...	0.1	999.9	999.9	...	...	...	...

								...	...	...	...	...	...	...	...	...	...	...	...
...	...	...	...	58.0	...	...	...	...	...	999.9	...	...	...	999.9	999.9	...	...	...	...
495	...	...	3.6	2.3	17.2	9.92	9.92	...	...	25.6	...	...	999.9	112.9	117.2	...	...	...	...
10,388	...	...	-1.1	-7.9	-5.9	4.43	4.44	...	...	22.7	...	...	-16.8	111.0	114.4	...	...	...	...
-8,647	...	...	3.1	18.3	16.4	4.96	4.96	...	...	24.5	...	...	29.7	114.5	116.4	...	...	...	...

0	41.8	23.6	1.1	6.5	6.0	5.89	6.05	2.1	0.7	22.7	...	0.6	7.5	77.7	90.3	8.8	...	...	...
0	47.3	24.2	1.4	8.8	7.9	5.76	5.85	0.3	0.7	22.6	...	0.2	4.9	77.4	90.9	7.3	...	...	...
0	44.7	23.8	0.8	4.8	4.3	5.70	5.67	6.0	0.7	22.2	...	0.1	4.3	78.3	92.3	6.0	...	...	...
2	39.6	19.2	0.1	0.5	0.6	5.57	5.29	22.0	0.8	19.9	...	0.1	-0.7	78.9	92.3	6.5	...	...	...
-2	43.1	20.9	1.5	9.2	9.2	5.59	5.64	-2.3	0.7	20.1	...	0.1	8.8	78.2	92.1	4.0	...	0.6	...

Principal Lines of Business: OrdLife (74.6%), IndAnn (24.2%), GrpAnn (1.1%), GrpLife (0.1%), CrdLife (0.0%)
Principal States: NY (55.4%), WI (31.9%)

60,307	49.0	20.4	0.8	5.1	6.8	5.86	6.12	2.1	0.9	15.2	0.0	0.0	9.5	62.1	72.2	9.0	...	90.0	0.2
192,267	53.3	20.2	0.9	6.0	7.5	5.68	6.27	0.7	0.8	16.6	0.0	0.0	13.6	62.2	73.1	5.3	...	87.5	3.1
-81,000	56.2	20.0	0.8	5.8	6.8	5.60	5.49	0.1	0.7	17.3	0.0	0.0	6.4	59.0	71.6	4.6	...	90.6	4.9
-542,306	49.3	17.9	0.7	4.7	6.3	5.67	4.06	21.7	1.0	14.2	0.0	0.0	-12.1	59.6	71.7	6.9	...	104.0	6.6
271,670	50.3	17.9	1.0	6.6	8.4	5.69	6.21	-5.1	0.8	15.4	0.0	0.0	15.2	61.2	73.6	4.0	0.3	90.9	6.2

Principal Lines of Business: OrdLife (72.4%), IndAnn (25.7%), GrpLife (1.2%), GrpAnn (0.7%), CrdLife (0.0%)
Principal States: CA (9.3%), TX (8.1%), IL (6.3%), FL (5.6%), PA (4.6%)

...	66.0	84.0	-4.2	-36.3	-74.2	3.75	3.85	81.3	0.9	5.2	10.4	242.5	132.4	61.7	76.0	20.4	...	58.4	2.4
...	92.2	17.4	1.1	7.5	21.5	5.55	5.66	112.3	1.5	6.2	6.5	237.8	22.8	61.4	76.4	31.0	...	73.7	1.9
...	89.0	16.8	0.9	5.8	15.2	5.60	5.60	12.2	1.5	6.8	3.7	231.8	14.6	56.4	73.2	29.1	...	94.8	1.6
...	43.2	8.0	1.2	8.0	18.7	5.48	5.16	92.8	2.5	6.9	3.3	219.8	13.9	56.5	73.6	37.6	...	98.9	1.3
-184	46.8	11.9	1.0	5.2	14.7	5.77	5.78	-13.2	1.8	7.5	2.3	204.4	20.3	55.8	73.4	53.6	...	94.2	1.0

Principal Lines of Business: IndAnn (58.1%), OrdLife (37.9%), GrpAnn (4.0%), IndA&H (0.0%), GrpLife (0.0%)
Principal States: CA (10.7%), IN (7.5%), OH (7.4%), HI (6.3%), TX (5.9%)

...	93.4	27.5	2.3	25.5	49.7	...	...	-22.1	0.5	5.0	...	...	0.2	...	...	...	...	...	...
...	110.3	25.6	1.5	17.0	28.2	...	...	-3.9	0.4	6.4	...	...	28.5	...	...	...	...	...	...
...	114.9	27.3	1.6	18.9	24.6	...	...	-4.7	0.3	8.1	...	...	26.8	...	...	...	...	...	...
-1,202	127.1	31.7	0.6	7.4	8.5	...	...	-5.2	0.3	7.9	...	...	-0.7	...	...	...	...	...	...
...	125.4	37.4	1.4	16.8	17.5	...	...	0.6	0.3	8.9	...	...	14.1	...	...	...	...	...	...

Principal Lines of Business: OrdLife (100.0%)

-2,954	68.5	38.2	0.9	3.6	13.4	5.81	4.49	26.0	1.1	7.1	84.9	733.0	1.9	66.6	70.0	25.6	...	177.8	48.2
10,665	76.3	28.4	0.1	0.4	1.1	5.89	9.69	4.7	0.9	9.1	52.2	563.8	29.4	61.0	63.8	21.3	...	217.4	61.4
106	80.7	39.8	0.2	1.1	2.5	5.90	5.90	20.0	1.0	9.5	31.5	523.6	5.2	59.8	62.7	0.8	2.6	218.8	59.0
-1,952	68.8	23.0	0.5	2.5	6.3	6.05	5.36	29.0	1.4	8.6	26.0	568.7	-5.8	56.1	59.8	3.9	16.1	222.5	36.0
4,090	92.0	30.5	0.7	4.5	9.2	5.79	6.59	-28.2	0.9	9.5	20.5	498.5	10.8	62.2	67.8	11.5	23.6	183.9	40.2

Principal Lines of Business: OrdLife (93.9%), IndA&H (5.3%), IndAnn (0.7%), GrpAnn (0.2%)
Principal States: GA (14.0%), FL (11.4%), SC (8.5%), LA (7.8%), TX (7.4%)

-43	87.5	60.3	-1.1	-3.1	-4.6	4.97	5.16	160.7	0.5	33.0	80.8	999.9	-0.7	92.0	93.7	...	...	64.3	...
...	-99.9	-99.9	1.5	3.3	5.8	4.71	4.73	-99.9	-0.2	34.9	168.4	999.9	19.1	83.5	84.3	...	...	28.2	...
...	79.4	26.9	0.2	0.2	0.9	3.53	3.44	796.4	1.6	39.9	282.6	999.9	-2.1	115.4	118.0	...	...	...	...
0	82.2	18.3	1.7	1.2	5.7	3.03	3.00	12.4	1.8	43.5	291.1	999.9	3.5	99.9	101.1	...	...	...	...
0	81.7	20.3	0.5	0.4	1.5	1.87	1.93	-14.4	1.4	56.4	198.9	999.9	10.1	107.9	109.5	...	...	...	...

Principal Lines of Business: IndA&H (98.7%), OrdLife (1.1%), IndAnn (0.3%)
Principal States: MO (15.3%), OH (13.5%), MS (10.0%), IL (7.5%), TX (6.8%)

94	67.5	18.3	26.8	11.9	51.0	4.34	4.39	33.6	3.3	144.1	...	...	68.4	180.8	205.4	...	...	...	0.1
-616	70.7	17.7	23.5	8.1	43.7	5.62	5.46	73.4	4.9	100.2	...	4.6	18.9	156.9	178.4	0.5	...	...	...
...	83.9	14.4	7.4	2.3	13.2	5.98	5.94	58.4	4.3	153.3	0.0	2.1	80.0	284.2	313.4	0.4	...	...	...
-2	85.2	14.9	4.0	1.3	6.9	4.74	3.00	26.7	5.2	125.5	0.0	1.5	4.8	204.1	220.4	0.1	...	...	...
289	84.7	15.4	3.9	1.4	6.6	3.85	3.59	-6.0	4.5	170.4	0.0	1.4	8.5	212.0	237.2	0.1	...	...	2.2

Principal Lines of Business: Medicare (88.0%), OtherHlth (6.1%), MedSup (5.7%), Life (0.1%)
Principal States: WA (25.0%), TX (12.3%), LA (10.5%), MT (6.8%), ID (5.9%)

Data in U.S. Dollars

COMPANY NAME / Ultimate Parent Association / Principal Officer / Mailing Address / Dom. : Began Bus. : Struct. : Mkt. / Specialty / Phone # / AMB# NAIC# — Best's Financial Strength Rating / FSC

Balance Sheet: Data Year; Bonds (%); Mort. Loans & R.E. (%); Com & Pref. Stock (%); All Other Assets (%); Total Assets ($000); Life Reserves (%); Health Reserves (%); Ann Res. & Dep. Liabilities (%); All Other Liabilities (%); Capital & Surplus ($000). Operations: Direct Premiums Written ($000); Net Premiums Written & Deposits ($000); Operating Cash Flow ($000); NOG Before Taxes ($000); NOG After Taxes ($000); Net Income ($000)

STONEBRIDGE LIFE INSURANCE CO
AEGON N.V.
Marilyn Carp
President
4333 Edgewood Road N.E.
Cedar Rapids, IA 52499
VT : 1906 : Stock : Direct Response
Group A&H, Group Life, Whole life
319-355-8511
AMB# 006594 NAIC# 65021

A — Rating Outlook: Stable — FSC XV

Data Year	Bonds (%)	Mort. Loans & R.E. (%)	Com & Pref. Stock (%)	All Other Assets (%)	Total Assets ($000)	Life Reserves (%)	Health Reserves (%)	Ann Res. & Dep. Liabilities (%)	All Other Liabilities (%)	Capital & Surplus ($000)	Direct Premiums Written ($000)	Net Premiums Written & Deposits ($000)	Operating Cash Flow ($000)	NOG Before Taxes ($000)	NOG After Taxes ($000)	Net Income ($000)
'05	80.8	7.5	1.0	10.7	2,152,694	56.6	29.5	3.6	10.3	169,955	625,431	624,289	147,430	212,355	179,232	184,844
'06	74.9	10.1	3.5	11.5	2,176,089	56.3	29.7	2.9	11.0	180,254	605,243	607,055	24,112	224,061	144,239	144,843
'07	69.0	11.0	2.9	17.1	2,206,086	57.4	30.7	2.3	9.5	241,534	574,314	591,122	41,699	129,864	111,967	110,823
'08	73.1	11.1	3.0	12.8	2,138,240	56.3	30.9	1.6	11.2	172,446	563,232	525,117	-69,691	259,939	209,942	211,039
'09	68.9	10.6	0.0	20.6	2,024,829	59.8	32.1	1.5	6.6	182,141	510,619	515,675	-40,569	190,229	141,210	135,014

Rating History: A g, 04/23/09; A+ g, 06/18/08; A+ g, 05/30/07; A+ g, 06/21/06; A+ g, 05/13/05

SUMMA INSURANCE COMPANY
Summa Health System
Martin P. Hauser
President
P.O. Box 3620
Akron, OH 44309-3620
OH : 1996 : Stock : Broker
Group A&H
330-996-8410
AMB# 012024 NAIC# 10649

B++ — Rating Outlook: Stable — FSC VI

Data Year	Bonds (%)	Mort. Loans & R.E. (%)	Com & Pref. Stock (%)	All Other Assets (%)	Total Assets ($000)	Life Reserves (%)	Health Reserves (%)	Ann Res. & Dep. Liabilities (%)	All Other Liabilities (%)	Capital & Surplus ($000)	Direct Premiums Written ($000)	Net Premiums Written & Deposits ($000)	Operating Cash Flow ($000)	NOG Before Taxes ($000)	NOG After Taxes ($000)	Net Income ($000)
'05	10.0	...	72.5	17.5	45,571	...	...	...	100.0	37,091	49,588	49,412	1,271	1,607	899	899
'06	...	...	65.9	34.1	52,366	...	...	...	100.0	40,131	67,026	66,746	5,411	3,617	2,146	2,175
'07	...	...	56.4	43.6	61,208	...	...	...	100.0	40,836	97,789	97,414	7,645	3,719	2,260	2,260
'08	15.1	...	62.1	22.8	43,807	...	...	...	100.0	22,208	133,444	132,972	-6,557	-8,285	-6,807	-6,807
'09	30.4	...	40.0	29.6	69,369	...	...	...	100.0	40,767	146,481	145,849	22,746	-12,091	-7,358	-7,358

Rating History: B++g, 06/03/10; B++g, 12/12/08; B++g, 10/25/07; B++g, 09/12/06; NR-5, 04/26/06

SUMMACARE INC
Summa Health System
Martin P. Hauser
President
P.O. Box 3620
Akron, OH 44309-3620
OH : 1993 : Stock : Broker
Group A&H, Medicare
330-996-8410
AMB# 060143 NAIC# 95202

B++ — Rating Outlook: Stable — FSC VI

Data Year	Bonds (%)	Mort. Loans & R.E. (%)	Com & Pref. Stock (%)	All Other Assets (%)	Total Assets ($000)	Life Reserves (%)	Health Reserves (%)	Ann Res. & Dep. Liabilities (%)	All Other Liabilities (%)	Capital & Surplus ($000)	Direct Premiums Written ($000)	Net Premiums Written & Deposits ($000)	Operating Cash Flow ($000)	NOG Before Taxes ($000)	NOG After Taxes ($000)	Net Income ($000)
'05	73.5	...	...	26.5	47,105	...	41.7	...	58.3	33,038	193,496	193,334	-12,045	7,249	4,593	4,593
'06	74.7	...	...	25.3	53,352	...	64.3	...	35.7	34,507	173,211	173,082	4,038	946	472	472
'07	74.8	...	...	25.2	55,311	...	65.6	...	34.4	34,534	190,590	190,465	-1,367	1,714	1,058	1,067
'08	59.6	...	...	40.4	55,995	...	21.0	...	79.0	27,184	216,132	216,015	2,058	-9,013	-6,469	-6,160
'09	62.4	...	...	37.6	44,722	...	23.8	...	76.2	27,767	242,189	242,102	-9,000	3,079	2,401	2,943

Rating History: B++g, 06/03/10; B++g, 12/12/08; B++g, 10/25/07; B++g, 09/12/06; C++pd, 07/08/05

SUMMIT HEALTH PLAN INC
Coventry Health Care Inc
Christopher A. Ciano
CEO
1340 Concord Terrace
Sunrise, FL 33323
FL : 2006 : Stock : Broker
Medicare
954-858-3000
AMB# 064917 NAIC# 10771

B — Rating Outlook: Stable — FSC IV

Data Year	Bonds (%)	Mort. Loans & R.E. (%)	Com & Pref. Stock (%)	All Other Assets (%)	Total Assets ($000)	Life Reserves (%)	Health Reserves (%)	Ann Res. & Dep. Liabilities (%)	All Other Liabilities (%)	Capital & Surplus ($000)	Direct Premiums Written ($000)	Net Premiums Written & Deposits ($000)	Operating Cash Flow ($000)	NOG Before Taxes ($000)	NOG After Taxes ($000)	Net Income ($000)
'05	60.6	...	...	39.4	3,065	...	...	...	100.0	3,038	...	...	3,056	-61	-87	-87
'06	47.6	...	...	52.4	7,187	...	33.5	...	66.5	2,853	13,589	13,589	2,884	308	183	183
'07	46.2	...	...	53.8	21,314	...	44.2	...	55.8	5,313	98,892	98,892	14,111	4,097	2,289	2,276
'08	34.9	...	...	65.1	28,549	...	36.1	...	63.9	6,160	147,359	147,359	5,090	1,110	1,548	1,548
'09	50.3	...	...	49.7	57,551	...	28.2	...	71.8	8,489	266,383	266,383	31,457	1,912	-161	-161

Rating History: B, 02/12/10; B, 11/19/08; B, 10/30/07; NR-5, 06/21/07

SUN LIFE AND HEALTH INS CO US
Sun Life Financial Inc
Robert C. Salipante
President
One Sun Life Executive Park
Wellesley Hills, MA 02481
CT : 1975 : Stock : Broker
Group A&H, Group Life
860-737-1000
AMB# 008474 NAIC# 80926

A — Rating Outlook: Stable — FSC VI

Data Year	Bonds (%)	Mort. Loans & R.E. (%)	Com & Pref. Stock (%)	All Other Assets (%)	Total Assets ($000)	Life Reserves (%)	Health Reserves (%)	Ann Res. & Dep. Liabilities (%)	All Other Liabilities (%)	Capital & Surplus ($000)	Direct Premiums Written ($000)	Net Premiums Written & Deposits ($000)	Operating Cash Flow ($000)	NOG Before Taxes ($000)	NOG After Taxes ($000)	Net Income ($000)
'05	84.8	8.9	...	6.2	873,272	18.6	61.2	7.6	12.6	229,681	652,988	611,363	41,159	36,943	31,307	30,297
'06	77.0	14.8	4.0	4.1	868,137	20.2	63.6	7.3	8.9	254,126	664,969	680,088	17,879	52,569	41,643	41,914
'07	105.0	...	...	-5.0	119,235	...	...	41.3	58.7	35,290	670,321	-237,922	-709,099	351,900	342,444	338,787
'08	53.0	...	...	47.0	87,717	...	...	...	100.0	39,023	538,105	7,889	-38,422	21,526	22,349	19,475
'09	21.8	...	...	78.2	72,719	...	...	...	100.0	40,792	427,042	8,190	-11,716	1,212	-1,062	-1,145

Rating History: A, 02/27/09; A+, 06/19/08; A+, 06/12/07; A u, 01/11/07; A, 06/02/06

SUN LIFE ASSUR CO OF CA (US)
Sun Life Financial Inc
Robert C. Salipante
President
One Sun Life Executive Park
Wellesley Hills, MA 02481
DE : 1973 : Stock : Broker
Ann, Ind Life
781-237-6030
AMB# 008226 NAIC# 79065

A+ — Rating Outlook: Stable — FSC XV

Data Year	Bonds (%)	Mort. Loans & R.E. (%)	Com & Pref. Stock (%)	All Other Assets (%)	Total Assets ($000)	Life Reserves (%)	Health Reserves (%)	Ann Res. & Dep. Liabilities (%)	All Other Liabilities (%)	Capital & Surplus ($000)	Direct Premiums Written ($000)	Net Premiums Written & Deposits ($000)	Operating Cash Flow ($000)	NOG Before Taxes ($000)	NOG After Taxes ($000)	Net Income ($000)
'05	34.9	3.5	0.8	60.8	40,293,921	1.3	...	33.6	65.1	1,542,520	3,069,526	3,935,499	81,750	137,803	144,273	146,536
'06	33.0	4.5	1.0	61.5	42,552,002	1.4	...	33.4	65.2	1,426,474	3,895,051	5,662,281	702,523	207,903	171,205	171,854
'07	26.5	4.1	0.9	68.5	44,700,806	1.3	...	27.1	71.7	1,174,144	6,524,908	6,516,098	-2,128,000	22,970	-7,336	-55,000
'08	27.1	4.1	0.9	67.9	39,669,904	0.9	...	29.3	69.8	1,267,093	4,111,393	2,875,393	-591,524	-853,957	-734,450	-988,348
'09	20.9	3.4	0.7	75.0	42,453,649	0.8	...	26.1	73.0	1,749,838	4,420,191	4,223,392	-431,185	357,218	324,662	-44,014

Rating History: A+ g, 02/27/09; A++g, 06/19/08; A++g, 06/12/07; A++g, 07/10/06; A++g, 06/30/05

SUN LIFE INS & ANNUITY OF NY
Sun Life Financial Inc
Westley V. Thompson
President
One Sun Life Executive Park
Wellesley Hills, MA 02481
NY : 1985 : Stock : Broker
Ann, Group Life, Dis inc
781-237-6030
AMB# 009513 NAIC# 72664

A+ — Rating Outlook: Stable — FSC XV

Data Year	Bonds (%)	Mort. Loans & R.E. (%)	Com & Pref. Stock (%)	All Other Assets (%)	Total Assets ($000)	Life Reserves (%)	Health Reserves (%)	Ann Res. & Dep. Liabilities (%)	All Other Liabilities (%)	Capital & Surplus ($000)	Direct Premiums Written ($000)	Net Premiums Written & Deposits ($000)	Operating Cash Flow ($000)	NOG Before Taxes ($000)	NOG After Taxes ($000)	Net Income ($000)
'05	58.9	4.7	...	36.4	2,585,887	1.3	0.9	60.8	36.9	186,981	166,549	169,119	-115,016	-3,752	-3,267	-8,617
'06	48.9	5.5	0.5	45.1	2,567,345	5.9	1.1	48.7	44.3	132,693	278,619	279,374	-237,215	-49,958	-53,363	-51,183
'07	39.5	4.4	0.3	55.7	2,639,502	2.0	2.5	37.4	58.1	206,952	379,085	392,790	-171,715	-13,850	-21,295	-25,380
'08	35.7	4.1	0.2	59.9	2,587,732	2.3	2.4	34.5	60.9	207,348	476,760	508,909	117,247	-137,164	-123,801	-149,475
'09	34.5	3.2	0.0	62.3	3,071,403	2.4	2.1	34.9	60.6	232,392	720,545	733,512	-23,038	55,702	27,923	17,570

Rating History: A+ g, 02/27/09; A++g, 06/19/08; A++g, 06/12/07; A++g, 07/10/06; A++g, 06/30/05

SUNAMERICA ANNUITY & LIFE ASSR
American International Group, Inc
Jana W. Greer
President
1 SunAmerica Center
Los Angeles, CA 90067-6100
AZ : 1965 : Stock : Broker
Ind Ann, SPDA's, Var ann
310-772-6000
AMB# 006115 NAIC# 60941

A — Rating Outlook: Negative — FSC X

Data Year	Bonds (%)	Mort. Loans & R.E. (%)	Com & Pref. Stock (%)	All Other Assets (%)	Total Assets ($000)	Life Reserves (%)	Health Reserves (%)	Ann Res. & Dep. Liabilities (%)	All Other Liabilities (%)	Capital & Surplus ($000)	Direct Premiums Written ($000)	Net Premiums Written & Deposits ($000)	Operating Cash Flow ($000)	NOG Before Taxes ($000)	NOG After Taxes ($000)	Net Income ($000)
'05	14.4	1.5	0.5	83.6	31,514,716	5.3	...	10.8	83.9	950,636	3,282,873	3,227,423	-316,331	169,450	150,852	171,505
'06	11.1	1.6	0.6	86.7	32,726,522	4.9	...	8.4	86.7	788,854	4,210,413	4,157,148	-819,064	140,434	131,796	147,384
'07	9.5	1.2	0.6	88.6	35,072,377	4.4	...	7.2	88.4	1,154,680	4,383,219	4,333,712	-181,081	173,139	181,208	175,403
'08	8.9	1.7	0.6	88.8	24,396,263	6.2	...	11.0	82.9	1,274,742	3,353,943	3,309,131	-189,816	-514,117	-613,059	-782,331
'09	7.4	1.5	0.3	90.8	25,887,982	5.4	...	8.7	85.9	653,857	915,360	881,775	-981,479	222,170	190,739	122,616

Rating History: A, 12/16/09; A, 11/10/08; A gu, 09/15/08; A+ g, 06/17/08; A++g, 05/28/08

SUNAMERICA LIFE INS CO
American International Group, Inc
Jay S. Wintrob
CEO
1 SunAmerica Center
Los Angeles, CA 90067-6022
AZ : 1890 : Stock : Broker
GIC's, Ind Ann, SPDA's
310-772-6000
AMB# 007102 NAIC# 69256

A — Rating Outlook: Negative — FSC XV

Data Year	Bonds (%)	Mort. Loans & R.E. (%)	Com & Pref. Stock (%)	All Other Assets (%)	Total Assets ($000)	Life Reserves (%)	Health Reserves (%)	Ann Res. & Dep. Liabilities (%)	All Other Liabilities (%)	Capital & Surplus ($000)	Direct Premiums Written ($000)	Net Premiums Written & Deposits ($000)	Operating Cash Flow ($000)	NOG Before Taxes ($000)	NOG After Taxes ($000)	Net Income ($000)
'05	57.6	6.2	6.3	30.0	62,336,638	0.6	0.0	70.7	28.7	4,409,984	27,803	2,297,902	-6,524,667	452,732	349,417	259,003
'06	57.0	7.4	7.7	27.9	46,889,646	0.8	0.0	83.0	16.2	4,462,568	22,072	40,157	-4,559,719	808,376	498,263	538,746
'07	53.0	7.1	10.5	29.4	39,454,568	0.9	0.0	76.8	22.3	4,721,343	19,696	36,807	-9,091,398	936,391	746,963	353,964
'08	44.4	9.8	18.1	27.7	24,857,470	1.5	0.0	83.2	15.3	4,658,761	20,183	37,440	-13,934,887	451,350	502,780	-2,231,657
'09	37.6	10.9	18.2	33.3	17,549,131	2.2	0.0	78.6	19.2	4,023,612	17,112	31,353	-5,257,034	361,660	458,887	222,287

Rating History: A, 12/16/09; A, 11/10/08; A gu, 09/15/08; A+ g, 06/17/08; A++g, 05/28/08

2010 BEST'S KEY RATING GUIDE — LIFE/HEALTH EDITION
BEST'S PROFITABILITY, LEVERAGE AND LIQUIDITY TESTS 2005 – 2009

Data in U.S. Dollars

	Profitability Tests							Leverage Tests						Liquidity Tests					
Un-Realized Capital Gains ($000)	Benefits Paid to NPW & Dep (%)	Comm. & Expenses to NPW & Dep (%)	NOG to Total Assets (%)	NOG to Total Rev (%)	Operating Return on Equity (%)	Net Yield (%)	Total Return (%)	Change in NPW & Dep (%)	NPW & Dep to Capital (X)	Capital & Surplus to Liabilities (%)	Surplus Relief (%)	Reins Leverage (%)	Change in Capital (%)	Quick Liquidity (%)	Current Liquidity (%)	Non-Invest Grade Bonds to Capital (%)	Delinq. & Foreclosed Mortgages to Capital (%)	Mort. & Credit Tenant Loans & R.E. to Capital (%)	Affiliated Invest to Capital (%)
-88,437	34.9	32.2	8.3	25.3	103.0	5.48	1.61	-8.6	3.3	9.7	24.8	124.0	-3.0	60.9	72.6	62.8	...	84.9	26.1
-3,051	38.6	29.9	6.7	20.9	82.4	5.30	5.35	-2.8	3.1	10.0	18.7	113.6	3.9	57.6	69.9	52.2	1.9	110.8	21.5
-53,348	41.5	41.9	5.1	17.1	53.1	4.87	2.42	-2.6	2.3	13.4	3.9	91.8	32.0	62.6	74.2	35.6	1.0	93.0	27.7
-375	50.1	27.0	9.7	32.6	101.4	5.73	6.00	-11.2	2.7	9.8	8.8	144.3	-26.5	53.9	64.4	58.5	...	124.4	37.0
-126,274	48.4	34.7	6.8	22.6	79.6	5.00	-1.59	-1.8	2.6	10.7	7.6	123.3	2.3	55.0	67.3	49.1	...	109.0	49.3
Principal Lines of Business: GrpA&H (54.0%), GrpLife (23.9%), OrdLife (15.3%), IndA&H (4.6%), GrpAnn (1.1%)														Principal States: CA (12.7%), TX (11.1%), FL (5.7%), PA (5.2%), OH (4.9%)					
5,015	79.0	17.5	2.1	1.8	2.0	0.93	10.30	44.8	1.3	437.4	...	0.1	19.1	109.8	109.8	...	...	...	89.4
1,903	80.0	15.0	4.4	3.2	5.6	0.88	5.16	35.1	1.7	328.0	...	...	8.2	70.7	70.7	...	...	...	102.3
310	80.4	16.4	4.0	2.3	5.6	1.28	1.86	45.9	2.4	200.5	...	...	1.8	80.0	80.0	...	...	...	101.3
-7,462	90.7	15.9	-13.0	-5.1	-21.6	0.88	-13.61	36.5	6.0	102.8	...	0.8	-45.6	43.5	43.5	...	...	...	152.6
1,216	94.6	13.9	-13.0	-5.0	-23.4	0.73	3.17	9.7	3.6	142.5	...	0.0	83.6	114.1	114.1	...	...	...	86.1
Principal Lines of Business: CompHosp/Med (99.5%), Medicare (0.5%)														Principal States: OH (100.0%)					
...	87.6	21.9	8.5	2.1	15.0	3.05	3.05	-31.9	5.9	234.9	...	...	17.5	284.2	284.2	...	...	...	...
...	84.7	24.0	0.9	0.3	1.4	4.20	4.20	-10.5	5.0	183.1	...	0.1	4.4	240.7	240.7	...	...	...	...
...	85.5	25.0	1.9	0.5	3.1	5.49	5.51	10.0	5.5	166.2	...	...	0.1	198.3	198.3	...	...	...	...
...	89.0	27.2	-11.6	-2.7	-21.0	4.32	5.02	13.4	7.9	94.4	...	...	-21.3	169.4	169.4	...	...	...	...
...	85.5	23.2	4.8	0.9	8.7	2.21	3.53	12.1	8.7	163.8	...	...	2.1	222.5	222.5	...	...	...	...
Principal Lines of Business: Medicare (88.8%), CompHosp/Med (11.1%), MedSup (0.0%), FEHBP (0.0%)														Principal States: OH (100.0%)					
...	...	...	...	-99.9	...	...	...	...	...	999.9	...	...	...	999.9	999.9	...	...	...	...
...	77.3	19.7	3.6	1.3	6.2	4.94	4.94	...	4.8	65.8	...	...	-6.1	172.6	185.9	...	...	...	...
...	78.9	15.7	16.1	2.3	56.1	7.12	7.02	627.8	18.6	33.2	...	...	86.2	127.0	134.4	...	...	...	...
...	83.3	16.4	6.2	1.0	27.0	4.13	4.13	49.0	23.9	27.5	...	...	15.9	138.2	143.5	...	...	...	...
...	89.6	9.3	-0.4	-0.1	-2.2	1.61	1.61	80.8	31.4	17.3	...	8.0	37.8	149.1	155.5	...	...	...	...
Principal Lines of Business: Medicare (100.0%)														Principal States: FL (100.0%)					
...	68.4	30.9	3.6	4.7	14.1	5.69	5.83	4.4	2.6	36.8	1.1	316.6	7.8	69.2	88.8	8.1	...	33.2	...
...	62.9	25.5	4.8	6.1	17.2	5.71	5.93	11.2	2.6	42.8	1.2	310.0	10.8	69.7	89.4	12.7	...	49.5	...
...	-51.5	102.8	69.4	220.0	236.6	7.01	6.45	-99.9	-6.6	43.4	999.9	999.9	-86.1	50.0	86.7	15.5	...	...	...
...	...	-99.9	21.6	27.2	60.1	3.32	0.58	103.3	0.2	81.2	202.3	999.9	9.0	203.2	218.4	...	...	...	...
...	...	3.9	-1.3	-2.1	-2.7	2.04	2.14	3.8	0.2	128.8	120.6	999.9	4.1	350.8	360.3	...	...	...	...
Principal Lines of Business: IndAnn (100.0%)														Principal States: NY (12.8%), CA (7.8%), PA (7.1%), TX (5.7%), GA (5.1%)					
-1,665	116.6	10.5	0.4	3.5	9.2	4.23	4.37	-0.6	2.3	10.6	0.1	119.6	-2.2	45.8	59.7	42.9	0.1	81.3	22.0
-4,651	94.6	7.9	0.4	3.3	11.5	5.13	5.20	43.9	3.4	9.5	0.0	126.6	-4.7	45.7	58.2	40.3	...	114.5	19.6
-187,890	87.8	8.4	0.0	-0.1	-0.6	5.02	3.70	15.1	4.6	9.6	0.0	153.3	-14.4	48.5	61.1	34.7	...	129.5	24.4
-364,402	180.9	20.9	-1.7	-14.0	-60.2	5.23	1.18	-55.9	2.1	9.3	3.4	166.6	-5.5	50.6	64.8	48.7	...	119.4	25.7
-34,398	117.1	15.0	0.8	6.4	21.5	2.22	-0.80	46.9	2.4	13.8	1.5	125.7	32.3	69.2	81.4	70.0	...	86.4	20.7
Principal Lines of Business: GrpAnn (73.1%), IndAnn (27.6%), OrdLife (1.2%), GrpLife (-1.8%)														Principal States: CA (9.9%), FL (7.5%), PA (7.2%), NJ (6.6%), TX (6.5%)					
-486	203.4	19.3	-0.1	-1.2	-1.7	5.08	4.98	-30.3	0.9	12.9	0.0	4.1	-2.9	61.1	76.5	53.8	...	61.8	...
554	169.5	16.6	-2.1	-14.0	-33.4	5.58	5.88	65.2	1.9	10.4	0.0	7.6	-26.1	55.5	70.5	45.5	...	97.2	...
-72	130.8	40.5	-0.8	-3.9	-12.5	5.77	5.55	40.6	1.8	18.9	26.2	126.0	50.3	62.1	77.7	19.9	...	53.6	...
-2,479	95.0	15.5	-4.7	-20.7	-59.8	4.26	2.21	29.6	2.4	17.1	3.8	106.5	-4.4	92.3	106.9	35.8	...	51.3	...
555	47.9	12.4	1.0	3.4	12.7	3.35	2.68	44.1	3.0	20.7	3.6	115.4	18.8	80.3	96.3	25.5	...	40.4	...
Principal Lines of Business: IndAnn (81.7%), GrpA&H (11.7%), GrpLife (5.2%), OrdLife (1.3%)														Principal States: NY (99.5%)					
-18,711	116.2	12.2	0.5	3.7	16.8	5.58	5.60	-19.8	3.3	16.8	0.0	5.4	14.9	48.2	62.3	22.1	...	48.4	16.6
9,072	106.3	11.1	0.4	2.6	15.2	5.45	5.84	28.8	5.0	21.5	0.0	6.5	-15.6	63.6	80.2	13.8	...	62.8	13.8
38,057	108.2	11.5	0.5	3.5	18.6	5.85	6.49	4.2	3.5	33.8	0.0	4.6	47.4	69.9	85.8	6.4	...	35.6	9.8
559,363	146.0	14.0	-2.1	-15.0	-50.5	5.02	13.59	-23.6	2.5	34.4	0.0	6.3	7.8	97.5	110.3	5.1	...	31.4	7.9
-707,125	373.9	32.7	0.8	13.0	19.8	3.60	-13.20	-73.4	1.3	20.9	0.0	24.3	-48.1	72.6	84.0	17.7	...	55.2	12.7
Principal Lines of Business: GrpAnn (65.0%), IndAnn (34.6%), OrdLife (0.5%)														Principal States: NJ (11.0%), CA (9.1%), OH (7.5%), MO (6.4%), TX (5.6%)					
583,663	112.5	1.6	0.5	13.1	7.4	4.11	4.94	-78.6	0.4	9.8	...	14.2	-3.0	37.5	50.0	56.3	...	71.0	71.7
218,970	999.9	84.5	0.9	17.4	11.2	5.34	5.85	-98.3	0.0	14.1	...	13.6	3.5	48.4	61.8	36.1	...	61.7	64.6
940,971	999.9	115.2	1.7	28.9	16.3	6.20	7.52	-8.3	0.0	17.8	...	12.7	2.9	55.4	69.6	17.9	...	48.4	74.8
-3,043,000	999.9	56.1	1.6	30.4	10.7	5.43	-12.22	1.7	0.0	23.9	...	12.3	-19.4	34.6	47.9	19.7	...	52.7	103.9
-1,213,966	999.9	51.9	2.2	43.5	10.6	5.45	-1.75	-16.3	0.0	30.9	...	13.5	-14.0	34.5	44.8	41.4	0.5	48.5	100.2
Principal Lines of Business: IndAnn (105.4%), GrpAnn (1.3%), OrdLife (-6.7%)														Principal States: CA (45.3%), NJ (8.3%), FL (5.2%), TX (4.2%), IL (3.8%)					

Data in U.S. Dollars

COMPANY NAME / Ultimate Parent Association / Principal Officer / Mailing Address / Dom. : Began Bus. : Struct. : Mktg. / Specialty / Phone # / AMB# / NAIC#	Best's Financial Strength Rating / FSC	Data Year	Balance Sheet: Bonds (%)	Mort. Loans & R.E. (%)	Com & Pref. Stock (%)	All Other Assets (%)	Total Assets ($000)	Life Reserves (%)	Health Reserves (%)	Ann Res. & Dep. Liabilities (%)	All Other Liabilities (%)	Capital & Surplus ($000)	Operations: Direct Premiums Written ($000)	Net Premiums Written & Deposits ($000)	Operating Cash Flow ($000)	NOG Before Taxes ($000)	NOG After Taxes ($000)	Net Income ($000)
SUNSET LIFE INS CO OF AMERICA Kansas City Life Insurance Company	A	'05	84.3	8.4	0.3	7.0	479,322	55.2	0.0	41.5	3.3	38,010	36,531	23,550	-2,204	11,417	9,555	11,242
R. Philip Bixby, President		'06	83.4	9.5	0.5	6.6	456,697	56.9	0.0	40.1	3.0	37,758	31,178	17,526	-24,461	11,836	9,206	9,177
3520 Broadway, Kansas City, MO 64111-2565	Rating Outlook: Stable	'07	82.1	9.3	0.5	8.0	430,172	57.7	0.0	38.2	4.1	38,366	26,517	13,117	-21,644	12,479	9,466	9,353
MO : 1937 : Stock : Career Agent; Ind Ann, Term Life, Univ Life		'08	83.4	8.7	0.6	7.4	408,034	58.0	0.0	37.3	4.6	34,894	24,536	11,583	-19,974	10,629	8,213	5,186
816-753-7000		'09	81.1	8.3	0.3	10.2	402,377	56.5	0.0	37.9	5.5	34,931	26,733	13,903	-6,832	9,535	6,852	5,237
AMB# 007104 NAIC# 69272	FSC IX	Rating History: A g, 06/04/10; A g, 06/02/09; A g, 12/07/07; A g, 11/14/06; A g, 12/21/05																
SUNSHINE STATE HEALTH PLAN INC Centene Corporation	B+	'05	...	...	...	...	...	...	...	...	...	...	...	...	...	...	...	...
Jesse N. Hunter, President		'06	...	...	...	...	...	...	...	...	...	...	...	...	...	...	...	...
7711 Carondelet Avenue, St. Louis, MO 63105	Rating Outlook: Stable	'07	...	...	...	...	...	...	...	...	...	...	...	...	...	...	...	...
FL : 2008 : Stock : Other Direct; Medicaid		'08	...	...	...	100.0	3,062	...	...	...	100.0	3,042	...	...	48	51	37	37
314-725-4477		'09	27.5	...	...	72.5	64,850	...	33.6	...	66.4	13,560	107,354	106,777	49,718	-13,919	-10,827	-10,827
AMB# 064960 NAIC# 13148	FSC V	Rating History: B+, 02/19/10; NR-2, 02/10/09																
SUNTRUST INSURANCE CO[1]	NR-1	'05	92.1	...	...	7.9	18,066	...	...	...	100.0	13,316	...	-425	...	2,225	1,599	1,599
Steven H. Turtz, President		'06	93.4	...	...	6.6	16,910	...	...	...	100.0	13,776	...	-200	...	1,590	1,033	1,033
303 Peachtree Center Avenue, Atlanta, GA 30303		'07	87.4	...	...	12.6	15,427	...	...	...	100.0	13,412	...	-75	...	1,179	834	834
AZ : 1976 : Stock : Not Available		'08	86.1	...	...	13.9	16,296	...	...	...	100.0	15,026	...	-24	...	945	684	458
404-813-7446		'09	94.0	...	...	6.0	16,286	...	...	...	100.0	15,586	...	-9	...	772	542	542
AMB# 068107 NAIC# 85995		Rating History: NR-1, 06/10/10; NR-1, 06/12/09; NR-1, 06/12/08; NR-1, 06/08/07; NR-1, 06/07/06																
SUPERIOR DENTAL CARE INC	NR-5	'05	37.2	...	1.9	60.9	5,738	...	28.0	...	72.0	3,111	23,013	23,013	660	677	422	465
Richard W. Portune, D.D.S., Chairman		'06	35.4	...	1.9	62.6	5,845	...	21.0	...	79.0	3,380	26,230	26,230	714	928	599	599
6683 Centerville Business Parkway, Dayton, OH 45459		'07	30.0	...	1.9	68.1	6,245	...	32.4	...	67.6	3,704	27,511	27,511	134	641	422	422
OH : 1986 : Stock : Not Available; Dental		'08	74.1	...	...	25.9	5,909	...	36.5	...	63.5	3,860	28,205	28,205	-238	816	536	532
937-438-0283		'09	54.7	...	...	45.3	6,843	...	24.1	...	75.9	4,783	29,412	29,412	102	313	203	210
AMB# 065724 NAIC# 96280		Rating History: NR-5, 03/24/10; NR-5, 08/26/09; B- pd, 07/21/08; B- pd, 07/16/07; B- pd, 07/17/06																
SUPERIOR HEALTHPLAN INC Centene Corporation	B+	'05	54.5	...	...	45.5	48,634	...	60.4	...	39.6	20,045	264,538	228,843	-2,273	9,386	6,288	6,278
Thomas Wise, President & CEO		'06	43.3	...	...	56.7	60,500	...	66.9	...	33.1	20,506	322,215	269,903	-2,024	17	-3	-13
7711 Carondelet Avenue, Suite 800, St. Louis, MO 63105	Rating Outlook: Stable	'07	65.2	...	...	34.8	147,417	...	51.4	...	48.6	39,713	638,409	602,107	81,877	22,926	12,629	12,690
TX : 1997 : Stock : Broker; Medicaid, Medicare, Group A&H		'08	67.4	...	...	32.6	182,082	...	52.1	...	47.9	58,946	802,544	776,080	30,692	29,705	13,947	13,024
314-725-4477		'09	61.5	...	...	38.5	182,440	...	51.8	...	48.2	76,775	844,849	820,348	9,970	36,784	32,039	32,041
AMB# 064457 NAIC# 95647	FSC VII	Rating History: B+, 02/19/10; B+, 02/10/09; C pd, 07/09/07; C+ pd, 08/08/06; C pd, 09/29/05																
SUPREME COUNCIL ROYAL ARCANUM	NR-5	'05	63.1	0.9	25.4	10.5	63,379	77.8	0.0	11.3	10.9	13,353	3,311	3,316	1,444	-556	-556	-479
William J. Wire, Supreme Regent		'06	64.1	0.8	26.0	9.1	66,665	77.4	0.0	13.1	9.5	14,499	2,940	2,951	2,127	-434	-434	-331
61 Batterymarch Street, Boston, MA 02110		'07	73.2	0.5	16.1	10.1	67,057	79.4	0.0	14.1	6.4	15,449	2,216	2,215	1,095	-581	-581	-96
MA : 1877 : Fraternal : Direct Response; Ordinary Life, Ind Ann, Ind A&H		'08	74.2	0.5	15.6	9.7	60,000	83.8	0.0	14.0	2.2	10,649	3,223	3,201	619	68	68	-382
617-426-4135		'09	78.9	0.3	11.4	9.4	82,775	71.0	0.0	26.4	2.5	12,644	4,237	4,315	18,647	1,130	1,130	441
AMB# 007008 NAIC# 58181		Rating History: NR-5, 04/20/10; NR-5, 04/14/09; NR-5, 04/10/08; NR-5, 04/30/07; NR-5, 05/03/06																
SURENCY LIFE & HEALTH INS CO	NR-5	'05	...	...	...	...	...	...	...	...	...	...	...	...	...	...	...	...
Linda L. Brantner, President		'06	...	...	...	...	...	...	...	...	...	...	...	...	...	...	...	...
1619 N Waterfront Parkway, Wichita, KS 67206		'07	...	...	...	...	...	...	...	...	...	...	...	...	...	...	...	...
KS : 2008 : Stock : Not Available; Group A&H		'08	...	...	...	100.0	2,417	...	...	...	100.0	2,331	0	0	2,389	-511	-302	-302
316-219-5749		'09	...	...	...	100.0	4,260	...	4.0	...	96.0	3,817	98	98	1,736	-527	-737	-737
AMB# 060699 NAIC# 13175		Rating History: NR-5, 06/14/10; NR-5, 11/25/09; NR-1, 06/12/09																
SURETY LIFE & CASUALTY INS CO[1]	NR-1	'05	50.9	9.7	10.0	29.4	4,169	...	...	...	100.0	1,566	585	585	...	112	87	124
Duane A. Steffes, President		'06	43.5	34.6	7.6	14.3	4,470	...	...	...	100.0	1,626	856	856	...	83	78	82
827 28th Street SW, Unit C, Fargo, ND 58103-8727		'07	31.6	26.3	12.4	29.6	5,016	...	...	...	100.0	1,766	1,085	1,085	...	163	158	160
ND : 1936 : Stock : Not Available		'08	43.1	20.7	20.4	15.9	6,497	...	...	...	100.0	2,732	1,335	1,335	...	166	152	136
701-235-6653		'09	42.3	15.9	19.0	22.8	7,676	...	...	...	100.0	3,150	1,446	1,446	...	443	385	313
AMB# 007110 NAIC# 69329		Rating History: NR-1, 06/10/10; NR-1, 06/12/09; NR-1, 06/12/08; NR-1, 06/08/07; NR-1, 06/07/06																
SURETY LIFE INS CO Allstate Corporation	NR-3	'05	103.8	...	0.0	-3.8	31,326	...	...	...	100.0	11,456	61,459	-21,462	-4,318	1,065	1,004	1,004
Frederick F. Cripe, CEO		'06	80.3	...	1.6	18.1	13,326	...	...	...	100.0	12,238	57,509	91	-20,546	751	453	453
3075 Sanders Road, Suite H1A, Northbrook, IL 60062-7127		'07	83.9	...	0.0	16.0	12,600	...	...	...	100.0	11,607	54,870	70	-879	773	487	487
NE : 1936 : Stock : Agency; Life, Ann		'08	80.7	...	0.0	19.2	13,022	...	...	...	100.0	12,205	51,558	134	1,195	753	501	430
800-525-9287		'09	78.1	...	0.0	21.9	13,303	...	...	...	100.0	12,660	49,064	56	201	670	428	428
AMB# 007109 NAIC# 69310		Rating History: NR-3, 11/20/09; NR-3, 10/23/08; NR-3, 01/09/08; NR-3, 02/06/07; NR-3, 11/07/05																

Best's Member Center

Access All of Your A.M. Best Product Subscriptions

Joining the Member Center Is Easy...

1 Visit www.ambest.com and click on the Member Center Sign-Up link at the top right.

2 Click "New Member Sign Up" on the following page.

3 Enter your e-mail address, choose a password for your account, then click "Continue." Fill in the information on the page that follows to create your profile.

Now that you've created your profile, you can register your products.

4 To access the products to which you subscribe, register them by clicking the "Product Registration" link.

5 On the screen that follows, enter the registration number for the product you'd like to register. This number can be found on the product shipping label or in the registration reminder that was mailed or e-mailed to you by A.M. Best. If you cannot find or have not received your registration number, please call us at (908) 439-2200, ext 5742.

6 Locate the product on the list that appears, and check the box next to it. If your purchase includes *Best's Review*® or *BestWeek*, remember to check the boxes next to those as well.

1

2

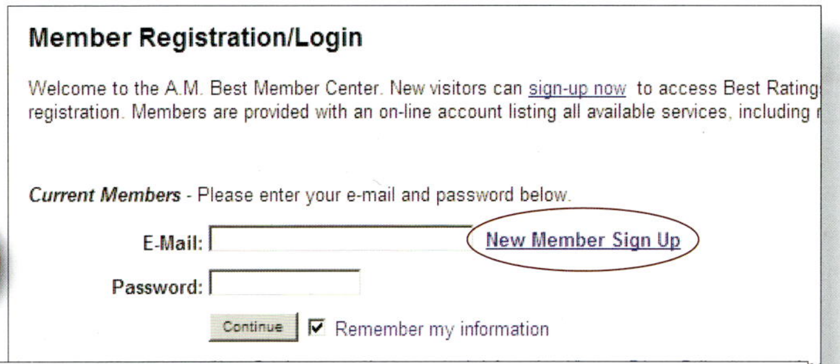

3

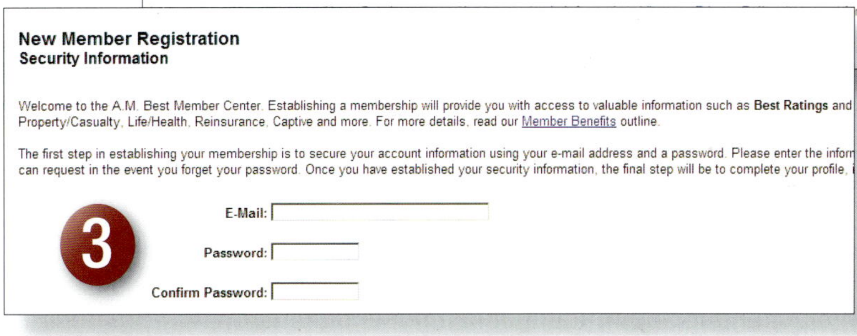

4

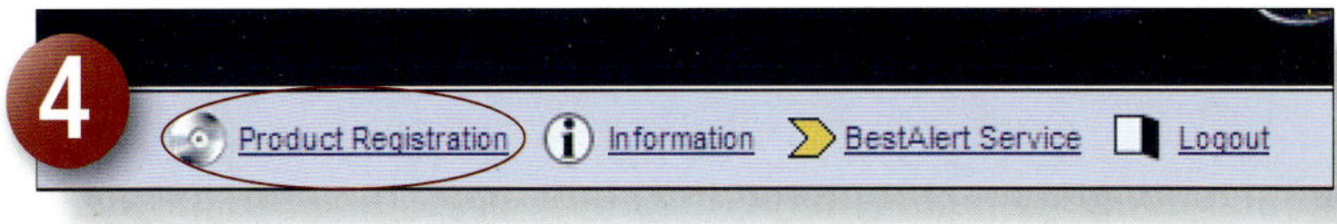

5

6

☑ Product Name

☑ Best's Review

Be sure to register all of your subscriptions so that you may access all of them from the Member Center link on the A.M. Best home page.

03424B

Your purchase of

Best's Key Rating Guide®

entitles all product users to a host of online features and services, accessible through the completion of our free registration process. See the reverse side for instructions. Benefits of registering include:

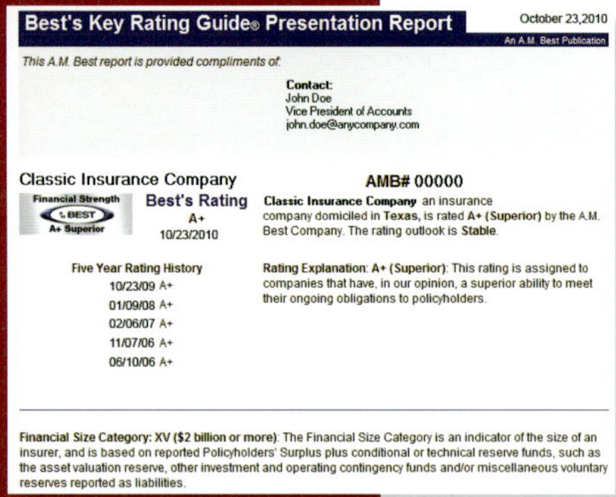
Best's Key Rating Guide® Presentation Report

October 23,2010

An A.M. Best Publication

This A.M. Best report is provided compliments of:

Contact:
John Doe
Vice President of Accounts
john.doe@anycompany.com

Classic Insurance Company

AMB# 00000

Financial Strength A+ Superior

Best's Rating A+ 10/23/2010

Classic Insurance Company an insurance company domiciled in Texas, is rated A+ (Superior) by the A.M. Best Company. The rating outlook is Stable.

Five Year Rating History
10/23/09 A+
01/09/08 A+
02/06/07 A+
11/07/06 A+
06/10/06 A+

Rating Explanation: A+ (Superior): This rating is assigned to companies that have, in our opinion, a superior ability to meet their ongoing obligations to policyholders.

Financial Size Category: XV ($2 billion or more): The Financial Size Category is an indicator of the size of an insurer, and is based on reported Policyholders' Surplus plus conditional or technical reserve funds, such as the asset valuation reserve, other investment and operating contingency funds and/or miscellaneous voluntary reserves reported as liabilities.

Access to customized **Presentation Reports**, which include the subscriber's name and business information followed by all of the data presented in a company's ***Best's Key Rating Guide*** entry.

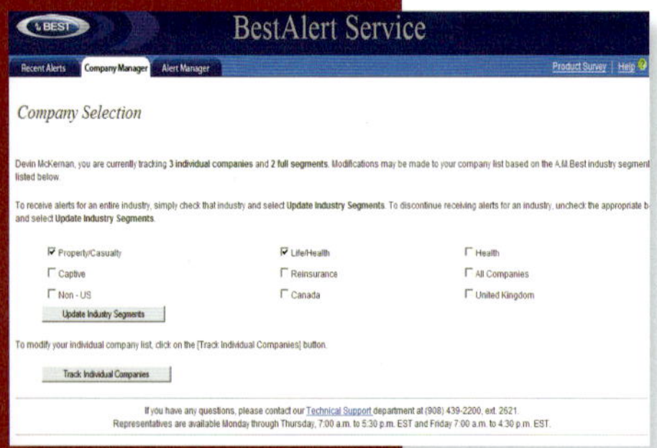

Access to ***BestAlert® Service***, A.M. Best's company-tracking and e-mail notification system, which lets you monitor the latest news, ratings and reports for the companies you select.

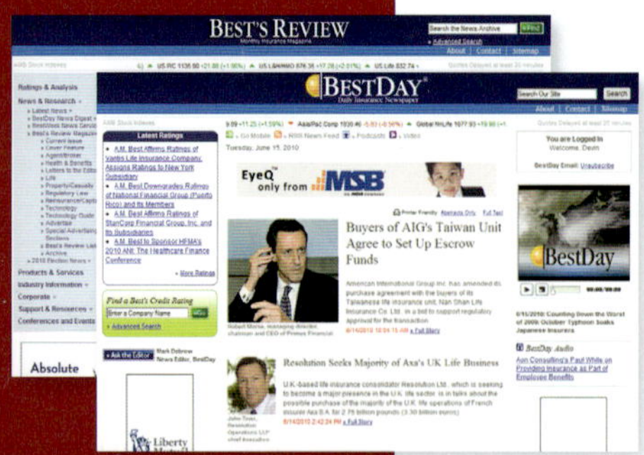

Access to the online edition of ***Best's Review***, as well as ***BestDay***®, A.M. Best's online insurance newspaper.

Access to ***BestWeek***®, A.M. Best's comprehensive news service featuring international coverage of three regions: U.S./Canada, Europe and Asia/Pacific. (Available to Full Service subscribers only.)

A.M. BEST®

www.ambest.com

Take full advantage of your subscription by registering today!
See the reverse side for instructions.

BEST'S PROFITABILITY, LEVERAGE AND LIQUIDITY TESTS 2005 – 2009

Data in U.S. Dollars

—	Profitability Tests							Leverage Tests						Liquidity Tests					
Un-Realized Capital Gains ($000)	Benefits Paid to NPW & Dep (%)	Comm. & Expenses to NPW & Dep (%)	NOG to Total Assets (%)	NOG to Total Rev (%)	Operating Return on Equity (%)	Net Yield (%)	Total Return (%)	Change in NPW & Dep (%)	NPW & Dep to Capital (X)	Capital & Surplus to Liabilities (%)	Surplus Relief (%)	Reins Leverage (%)	Change in Capital (%)	Quick Liquidity (%)	Current Liquidity (%)	Non-Invest Grade Bonds to Capital (%)	Delinq. & Foreclosed Mortgages to Capital (%)	Mort. & Credit Tenant Loans & R.E. to Capital (%)	Affiliated Invest to Capital (%)
66	168.2	25.0	2.0	19.0	25.9	5.90	6.31	-18.2	0.6	9.6	1.5	92.2	5.3	64.7	74.7	59.0	...	96.0	...
-47	269.8	24.2	2.0	20.7	24.3	5.90	5.92	-25.6	0.4	9.9	1.3	106.1	-2.0	63.1	73.3	48.1	...	104.5	...
...	389.2	33.0	2.1	24.5	24.9	5.97	5.97	-25.2	0.3	10.8	1.2	97.0	1.5	65.6	75.4	53.6	...	95.5	...
-29	339.2	33.7	2.0	24.0	22.4	5.64	4.94	-11.7	0.3	10.1	1.1	111.2	-10.8	57.5	71.6	59.0	...	94.6	...
29	224.8	29.9	1.7	18.4	19.6	5.72	5.39	20.0	0.4	10.3	1.0	107.2	0.6	61.3	75.1	66.4	...	95.7	...

Principal Lines of Business: OrdLife (51.9%), IndAnn (47.3%), GrpAnn (0.6%), GrpLife (0.2%), IndA&H (0.1%)
Principal States: WA (27.5%), CA (25.0%), TX (11.0%), HI (7.1%), OR (4.0%)

...	...	...	...	...	...	...	...	...	...	...	...	...	...	...	...	...	...	...	...
...	...	...	...	...	...	...	...	...	...	...	...	...	...	...	...	...	...	...	...
...	...	...	...	...	...	...	...	...	...	...	...	...	...	...	...	...	...	...	...
...	...	...	...	68.4	...	...	...	...	...	999.9	...	...	...	999.9	999.9	...	...	...	...
...	99.1	14.1	-31.9	-10.1	-99.9	0.53	0.53	...	7.9	26.4	...	3.2	345.8	113.3	118.5	...	...	...	...

Principal Lines of Business: Medicaid (100.0%)
Principal States: FL (100.0%)

...	-99.9	1.1	8.5	274.9	12.8	...	...	54.0	0.0	282.9	...	...	13.4	...	...	...	...	...	...
...	-99.9	-63.4	5.9	138.4	7.6	...	...	53.0	0.0	444.5	...	...	3.4	...	...	...	...	...	...
...	-99.9	-99.9	5.2	104.8	6.1	...	...	62.6	0.0	678.5	...	...	-2.6	...	...	...	...	...	...
...	-99.9	-99.9	4.3	105.5	4.8	...	...	68.0	0.0	999.9	...	...	11.9	...	...	...	...	...	...
...	-99.9	-41.6	3.3	119.2	3.5	...	...	63.5	0.0	999.9	...	...	3.7	...	...	...	...	...	...

Principal Lines of Business: CrdLife (81.4%), CrdA&H (18.6%)

-30	80.3	19.4	7.8	1.8	14.7	2.77	3.03	6.8	7.4	118.4	...	...	17.8	170.0	170.7	...	...	...	3.9
38	80.4	18.9	10.3	2.2	18.5	3.29	3.99	14.0	7.8	137.1	...	...	8.6	221.2	221.9	...	...	...	...
-2	80.9	19.8	7.0	1.5	11.9	3.70	3.65	4.9	7.4	145.8	...	...	9.6	220.5	221.2	...	...	...	...
1	79.2	18.3	8.8	1.9	14.2	1.95	1.90	2.5	7.3	188.3	...	...	4.2	261.1	261.1	...	...	...	...
...	79.6	19.6	3.2	0.7	4.7	1.27	1.40	4.3	6.1	232.3	...	...	23.9	263.9	265.3	...	...	...	...

Principal Lines of Business: Dental (100.0%)
Principal States: OH (98.9%)

...	79.0	17.4	12.9	2.7	37.2	3.37	3.34	8.2	11.4	70.1	...	48.6	45.3	151.1	163.8	...	...	...	...
...	82.4	18.1	0.0	0.0	0.0	4.01	3.98	17.9	13.2	51.3	...	89.5	2.3	112.3	121.8	...	...	...	...
...	81.3	15.5	12.1	2.1	41.9	4.96	5.04	123.1	15.2	36.9	...	45.2	93.7	102.6	112.8	...	...	...	...
...	81.3	14.8	8.5	1.8	28.3	3.00	2.31	28.9	13.2	47.9	...	13.9	48.4	117.3	129.2	7.9	...	...	...
...	81.9	14.5	17.6	3.9	47.2	2.20	2.20	5.7	10.7	72.7	...	10.7	30.2	157.2	171.5	5.2	...	...	...

Principal Lines of Business: Medicaid (91.4%), CompHosp/Med (8.3%), Medicare (0.3%)
Principal States: TX (100.0%)

-14	66.0	74.0	-0.9	-8.1	-4.1	5.55	5.87	-9.6	0.2	31.7	...	0.1	-1.7	74.5	88.4	23.2	...	3.9	3.9
1,746	66.4	81.5	-0.7	-6.6	-3.1	5.47	8.56	-11.0	0.2	34.0	...	0.1	11.0	80.9	94.2	20.2	...	3.3	3.3
-690	95.3	108.8	-0.9	-10.2	-3.9	5.13	4.97	-24.9	0.1	34.2	...	0.1	1.1	87.9	99.8	11.3	...	2.0	...
-4,855	106.9	79.5	0.1	1.0	0.5	5.68	-2.26	44.5	0.3	21.6	...	0.1	-37.6	76.0	88.6	8.5	...	2.7	...
2,457	179.4	76.7	1.6	13.5	9.7	6.04	8.66	34.8	0.3	20.0	...	1.5	29.4	79.7	90.9	14.9	...	1.9	...

Principal Lines of Business: OrdLife (78.8%), IndAnn (17.3%), IndA&H (3.8%)
Principal States: MA (21.7%), CT (10.6%), NY (7.8%), ME (7.6%), CA (7.5%)

...	...	...	...	...	...	...	...	...	...	...	...	...	...	...	...	...	...	...	...
...	...	...	...	...	...	...	...	...	...	...	...	...	...	...	...	...	...	...	...
...	...	...	...	...	...	...	...	...	...	...	...	...	...	...	...	...	...	...	...
...	...	999.9	...	-99.9	...	...	...	...	0.0	999.9	...	...	...	999.9	999.9	...	...	...	...
...	82.4	593.2	-22.1	-99.9	-24.0	1.45	1.45	999.9	0.0	863.4	...	...	63.8	979.0	979.0	...	...	...	...

Principal Lines of Business: GrpA&H (100.0%)
Principal States: KS (100.0%)

-44	30.4	53.4	2.2	11.1	5.8	...	...	7.9	0.4	63.6	...	...	6.7	...	...	...	...	25.0	...
0	23.7	67.2	1.8	7.1	4.9	...	...	46.3	0.5	60.5	...	...	4.0	...	...	...	...	91.8	...
-16	14.8	56.0	3.3	11.8	9.3	...	...	26.7	0.6	57.5	...	...	8.7	...	...	...	...	72.1	...
-272	30.9	48.7	2.6	8.9	6.8	...	...	23.0	0.5	74.6	...	...	51.6	...	...	...	...	48.4	...
300	24.5	45.1	5.4	20.4	13.1	...	...	8.3	0.4	79.2	...	...	22.3	...	...	...	...	36.0	...

Principal Lines of Business: OrdLife (60.2%), IndA&H (39.8%), GrpLife (0.0%)

...	-5.4	-0.2	2.9	-5.4	9.0	6.12	6.59	-99.9	-1.9	58.1	9.2	999.9	4.8	129.5	136.3	...	...	...	...
...	...	21.6	2.0	25.8	3.8	3.79	3.61	100.4	0.0	999.9	8.0	999.9	6.4	999.9	999.9	...	...	...	...
...	...	...	3.8	28.3	4.1	8.02	7.57	-22.7	0.0	999.9	8.2	999.9	-5.2	999.8	999.9	...	...	...	...
...	...	...	3.9	29.3	4.2	7.02	6.53	89.8	0.0	999.9	7.8	999.9	5.1	999.9	999.9	...	...	...	...
...	...	...	3.3	20.8	3.4	6.08	5.96	-58.0	0.0	999.9	10.9	999.9	3.8	999.9	999.9	...	...	...	...

Principal Lines of Business: GrpAnn (83.7%), OrdLife (16.3%)
Principal States: CA (35.3%), IL (5.4%), NJ (4.7%), TX (4.7%), FL (4.5%)

COMPANY NAME / Ultimate Parent Association / Principal Officer / Mailing Address / Dom. : Began Bus. : Struct. : Mktg. / Specialty / Phone # / AMB# NAIC#	Best's Financial Strength Rating FSC	Data Year	Balance Sheet: Bonds (%)	Mort. Loans & R.E. (%)	Com & Pref. Stock (%)	All Other Assets (%)	Total Assets ($000)	Life Reserves (%)	Health Reserves (%)	Ann Res. & Dep. Liabilities (%)	All Other Liabilities (%)	Capital & Surplus ($000)	Operations: Direct Premiums Written ($000)	Net Premiums Written & Deposits ($000)	Operating Cash Flow ($000)	NOG Before Taxes ($000)	NOG After Taxes ($000)	Net Income ($000)
SWISS RE LIFE & HEALTH AMERICA Swiss Reinsurance Company Ltd	A	'05	76.9	0.0	10.8	12.2	12,172,850	42.0	19.5	2.4	36.0	2,341,297	1,532	2,190,836	311,815	404,049	449,370	441,211
W. Weldon Wilson Chairman		'06	75.5	0.0	9.2	15.3	11,973,008	43.6	20.0	2.1	34.3	2,140,062	1,406	2,317,764	-308,786	288,169	247,529	233,300
175 King Street Armonk, NY 10504-1606	Rating Outlook: Stable	'07	78.0	...	6.4	15.6	11,925,550	45.8	18.4	1.9	33.9	1,640,179	1,293	2,422,785	-251,008	313,458	300,232	277,661
CT : 1967 : Stock : Other Direct Reins		'08	75.8	...	6.4	17.8	12,775,210	43.8	15.7	1.6	38.9	1,788,034	1,139	2,484,422	992,750	450,431	550,432	375,176
877-794-7773		'09	72.0	...	6.8	21.3	12,176,227	27.9	18.1	2.0	52.1	3,039,453	1,044	311,523	489,613	594,289	441,035	367,292
AMB# 007283 NAIC# 82627	FSC XV		**Rating History: A g, 12/14/09; A g, 02/27/09; A+ gu, 02/05/09; A+ g, 12/19/08; A+ g, 03/20/08**															
SWISSPARTNERS INS CO SPC LTD Liechtensteinische Landesbank AG	A-	'05	0.7	...	0.7	98.6	319,071	0.1	...	...	99.9	9,543	...	...	1,816	2,272	2,272	2,586
Martin P. Egli Chairman		'06	0.5	...	1.0	98.5	427,416	3.4	...	...	96.6	11,805	...	...	2,863	1,976	1,976	2,400
Buckingham Square, P.O. Box 1125 Grand Cayman, Cayman Islands KY1-1101	Rating Outlook: Stable	'07	0.1	...	0.2	99.7	2,266,186	0.9	...	...	99.1	13,362	...	...	2,219	2,124	2,124	2,470
KY : Stock : Not Available Var Univ life, Var ann, Life Reins		'08	0.3	...	...	99.7	2,088,226	1.6	...	...	98.4	12,467	...	...	4,265	210	210	-714
345-914-8914		'09	0.2	...	0.1	99.7	2,459,061	1.4	...	...	98.7	13,688	...	...	5,094	2,371	2,371	2,146
AMB# 072461	FSC V		**Rating History: A-, 02/18/10; A-, 02/05/09**															
SYMETRA LIFE INSURANCE COMPANY Symetra Financial Corporation	A	'05	73.0	4.1	1.0	21.9	18,824,483	10.6	0.7	66.4	22.3	1,260,136	967,521	1,003,213	-699,565	138,098	151,072	162,210
Randall H. Talbot President		'06	67.1	4.3	3.8	24.7	18,364,578	10.4	0.6	63.9	25.1	1,266,222	1,122,750	1,146,648	-855,474	196,586	166,415	145,020
P.O. Box 34690 Seattle, WA 98124-1690	Rating Outlook: Stable	'07	64.9	4.7	4.0	26.5	18,004,829	9.9	0.6	62.1	27.5	1,224,998	1,262,410	1,374,335	-676,154	164,958	135,216	134,105
WA : 1957 : Stock : Bank Ind Ann, Stop Loss, Univ Life		'08	66.0	5.3	3.9	24.8	18,646,103	9.4	0.7	65.1	24.8	1,178,975	2,343,550	2,376,433	959,599	114,169	99,220	36,708
425-256-8000		'09	69.6	5.7	1.4	23.3	20,799,084	7.9	0.5	67.3	24.2	1,415,435	2,889,784	2,941,463	1,641,534	160,209	129,467	43,052
AMB# 007017 NAIC# 68608	FSC XIV		**Rating History: A g, 09/17/09; A g, 06/13/08; A g, 06/11/07; A g, 05/05/06; A g, 05/10/05**															
SYMETRA NATIONAL LIFE INS CO Symetra Financial Corporation	NR-3	'05	84.6	...	3.0	12.4	16,496	95.5	...	0.0	4.5	9,815	409	409	-658	-651	-932	-936
Randall H. Talbot President		'06	85.2	...	3.0	11.8	16,175	96.7	...	...	3.3	10,223	398	398	-800	1,271	1,112	1,107
P.O. Box 34690 Seattle, WA 98124-1690		'07	90.1	...	2.9	7.0	16,808	96.8	...	...	3.2	10,504	374	374	1,103	670	454	453
WA : 1979 : Stock : Broker Ind Life, Term Life, Trad Life		'08	90.6	...	2.8	6.5	17,365	96.4	...	...	3.6	10,985	339	339	869	688	471	470
425-256-8000		'09	91.7	...	3.0	5.3	16,784	97.0	...	...	3.0	10,244	316	316	-556	422	242	241
AMB# 008934 NAIC# 90581			**Rating History: NR-3, 09/17/09; NR-3, 06/13/08; NR-3, 06/11/07; NR-2, 05/05/06; NR-2, 05/10/05**															
TANDY LIFE INSURANCE COMPANY[1]	NR-1	'05	...	...	...	100.0	74,444	...	...	...	100.0	4,774	2,167	734	...	2,459	1,564	1,564
James F. Gooch President		'06	...	...	...	100.0	75,451	...	...	...	100.0	4,725	2,099	744	...	2,883	1,862	1,862
300 Radioshack Circle, CF3.340.08 Fort Worth, TX 76102		'07	...	...	...	100.0	77,395	...	...	...	100.0	4,826	2,122	548	...	3,018	1,939	1,939
TX : 1980 : Stock : Not Available		'08	...	...	...	100.0	80,120	...	...	...	100.0	4,739	2,126	339	...	2,792	1,822	1,822
817-415-3700		'09	...	...	...	100.0	82,870	...	...	...	100.0	4,625	2,105	137	...	2,657	1,676	1,676
AMB# 009052 NAIC# 91790			**Rating History: NR-1, 06/10/10; NR-1, 06/12/09; NR-1, 06/12/08; NR-1, 06/08/07; NR-1, 06/07/06**															
TD REINSURANCE (BARBADOS) INC. Toronto-Dominion Bank	A	'05	72.5	...	...	27.5	218,184	46.3	...	...	53.7	181,688	...	306,345	192,679	196,596	196,596	196,651
Richard Bruce Chairman		'06	76.2	...	...	23.8	222,789	13.1	...	...	86.9	190,980	...	268,845	207,283	236,721	236,721	236,721
P.O. Box 1325 St. Michael, Barbados	Rating Outlook: Stable	'07	75.1	...	...	24.9	289,257	7.2	...	...	92.8	229,224	...	412,390	342,770	355,975	355,975	355,975
BB : Stock : Not Available Life Reins		'08	73.1	...	...	26.9	246,502	10.1	...	...	89.9	185,330	...	284,780	305,475	316,036	316,036	316,036
246-421-8755		'09	74.2	...	...	25.8	276,809	8.5	...	...	91.5	210,143	...	348,353	365,425	374,132	374,132	374,132
AMB# 056952	FSC VIII		**Rating History: A, 06/10/09; A, 09/23/08; A, 06/27/07; A, 05/19/06; A, 03/16/05**															
TEACHERS INS & ANNUITY ASSOC Teachers Insurance & Ann Assn of America	A++	'05	69.7	14.8	2.9	12.6	174,921,341	0.5	0.0	84.7	14.8	13,222,641	10,174,167	10,442,141	8,321,656	2,214,476	1,684,033	2,000,797
Roger W. Ferguson, Jr. President & CEO		'06	66.3	13.7	4.7	15.3	183,697,732	0.5	0.0	84.3	15.2	15,282,165	10,278,248	10,486,196	4,441,728	2,254,166	1,726,371	2,333,792
730 Third Avenue New York, NY 10017-3206	Rating Outlook: Stable	'07	67.1	11.3	4.4	17.2	196,409,275	0.4	0.0	82.2	17.3	17,827,120	9,508,377	9,658,254	7,992,094	1,932,246	1,565,606	1,428,746
NY : 1918 : Stock : Direct Response Ann		'08	69.5	10.9	3.2	16.4	195,236,800	0.4	0.0	89.5	10.0	17,754,167	13,378,525	13,592,827	7,753,475	1,122,696	1,167,479	-3,283,391
212-490-9000		'09	75.6	9.8	1.6	13.1	201,727,945	1.7	0.0	90.3	8.0	22,843,951	9,778,444	10,055,449	7,437,388	2,816,089	2,874,406	-452,061
AMB# 007112 NAIC# 69345	FSC XV		**Rating History: A++g, 12/18/09; A++g, 09/04/08; A++g, 06/15/07; A++g, 06/21/06; A++g, 05/31/05**															
TEACHERS PROTECTIVE MUTUAL	B-	'05	88.4	0.4	4.8	6.3	48,623	9.6	76.7	10.6	3.1	6,126	27,646	26,231	3,712	82	18	159
D. Edward Young President & CEO		'06	86.6	0.3	4.7	8.4	54,099	8.9	78.5	10.0	2.7	7,322	24,418	23,213	5,389	1,028	909	1,107
116-118 North Prince Street Lancaster, PA 17603-3526	Rating Outlook: Stable	'07	84.8	0.3	5.2	9.7	56,968	8.5	78.7	10.0	2.8	8,635	21,397	20,314	3,410	1,575	1,222	1,318
PA : 1912 : Mutual : Agency Accident, Dis Inc, Group A&H		'08	88.8	0.3	3.5	7.5	58,077	8.0	79.8	9.8	2.4	7,528	21,551	20,254	1,856	5	-6	-301
717-394-7156		'09	88.4	0.2	3.9	7.5	61,704	7.3	80.8	9.3	2.6	7,470	23,661	21,301	3,028	-588	-450	-587
AMB# 007114 NAIC# 69353	FSC IV		**Rating History: B-, 02/16/10; B-, 03/04/09; B-, 02/21/08; B-, 01/30/07; B-, 12/21/05**															
TENNESSEE BEHAVIORAL HEALTH Magellan Health Services Inc	NR-5	'05	...	...	...	...	...	...	...	...	...	...	...	...	...	...	...	...
Russell C. Petrella President		'06	5.4	...	...	94.6	47,807	...	57.6	...	42.4	19,291	194,478	194,478	-3,211	18,457	11,997	11,997
222 Second Avenue North, Suite 220 Nashville, TN 37201		'07	4.7	...	...	95.3	51,369	...	60.7	...	39.3	14,823	196,804	196,804	4,307	12,272	7,977	7,977
TN : 1996 : Stock : Not Available Medicaid		'08	4.1	...	...	95.9	57,911	...	47.8	...	52.2	19,469	198,518	198,518	7,062	24,532	15,946	15,946
615-313-4463		'09	13.0	...	...	87.0	18,404	...	4.7	...	95.3	7,560	-75	-75	-37,560	-1,384	-900	-900
AMB# 064880 NAIC# 95780			**Rating History: NR-5, 04/08/10; NR-5, 04/09/09; NR-5, 04/22/08; NR-5, 03/20/07**															

BEST'S PROFITABILITY, LEVERAGE AND LIQUIDITY TESTS 2005 – 2009

Data in U.S. Dollars

	Profitability Tests							Leverage Tests						Liquidity Tests					
Un-Realized Capital Gains ($000)	Benefits Paid to NPW & Dep (%)	Comm. & Expenses to NPW & Dep (%)	NOG to Total Assets (%)	NOG to Total Rev (%)	Operating Return on Equity (%)	Net Yield (%)	Total Return (%)	Change in NPW & Dep (%)	NPW & Dep to Capital (X)	Capital & Surplus to Liabilities (%)	Surplus Relief (%)	Reins Leverage (%)	Change in Capital (%)	Quick Liquidity (%)	Current Liquidity (%)	Non-Invest Grade Bonds to Capital (%)	Delinq. & Foreclosed Mortgages to Capital (%)	Mort. & Credit Tenant Loans & R.E. to Capital (%)	Affiliated Invest to Capital (%)
108,166	88.8	24.7	3.7	13.6	20.7	7.13	8.29	1.0	0.9	24.3	13.7	296.6	16.9	63.4	74.8	16.9	...	3.1	54.7
17,752	89.5	24.6	2.1	7.3	11.0	7.05	7.26	5.8	1.1	22.3	14.3	333.6	-8.4	63.5	77.9	12.6	...	3.7	45.4
-125,303	89.9	24.3	2.5	8.1	15.9	7.42	6.12	4.5	1.4	16.4	25.7	481.3	-23.0	59.6	73.5	14.3	...	3.6	38.7
-304,932	89.4	19.0	4.5	12.3	32.1	6.36	1.90	2.5	1.4	16.3	28.4	509.5	6.4	66.3	77.4	9.9	...	2.1	38.7
-38,680	654.0	49.8	3.5	28.7	18.3	4.40	3.45	-87.5	0.1	33.3	26.6	414.6	70.0	81.8	92.5	5.2	...	1.2	27.1
Principal Lines of Business: OrdLife (60.9%), IndA&H (30.5%), GrpLife (9.3%), GrpA&H (0.7%), GrpAnn (0.1%)														Principal States: NY (100.0%)					
...	...	...	0.8	43.5	24.7	1.00	4.46	...	...	3.1	...	...	7.9	2.4	2.1	...	...	...	...
...	...	...	0.5	30.4	18.5	1.34	5.20	...	...	2.8	...	...	23.7	2.4	2.2	...	...	...	...
...	...	...	0.2	26.4	16.9	1.66	4.21	...	...	0.6	...	...	13.2	0.5	0.5	...	...	...	...
...	...	...	0.0	3.1	1.6	1.60	-4.47	...	...	0.6	...	...	-6.7	0.5	0.5	...	...	...	...
...	...	...	0.1	26.6	18.1	1.18	-0.04	...	...	0.6	...	...	9.8	0.6	0.5	...	...	...	...
1,376	230.9	29.0	0.8	7.7	12.6	6.37	6.56	-1.6	0.7	10.0	0.8	20.5	12.4	56.6	71.3	55.5	...	54.8	2.4
12,903	193.7	24.6	0.9	8.1	13.2	6.26	6.33	14.3	0.8	10.8	0.8	27.3	1.7	56.7	73.0	47.9	...	55.5	2.6
1,235	153.5	21.8	0.7	6.3	10.9	6.25	6.39	19.9	1.0	11.1	1.0	30.7	-1.7	54.5	70.7	52.1	...	60.4	2.8
-72,916	69.8	14.0	0.5	3.1	8.3	6.09	5.28	72.9	1.8	9.5	1.1	34.0	-7.8	56.3	71.1	68.0	...	76.7	4.4
34,791	55.6	12.2	0.7	3.4	10.0	6.28	6.08	23.8	1.9	10.1	0.7	30.0	18.8	57.4	71.3	68.5	0.1	76.8	5.0
Principal Lines of Business: IndAnn (78.3%), GrpA&H (14.1%), OrdLife (3.6%), GrpAnn (2.8%), GrpLife (1.2%)														Principal States: CA (24.3%), WA (7.3%), FL (6.8%), TX (6.4%), IL (4.4%)					
...	50.7	92.1	-5.5	-72.4	-9.0	5.26	5.36	-9.0	0.0	148.7	...	...	-9.0	199.2	224.2	1.9	...	...	...
...	97.6	70.6	6.8	86.2	11.1	5.68	5.76	-2.7	0.0	173.8	...	...	4.1	209.4	233.0	0.6	...	...	...
...	68.9	78.3	2.8	35.7	4.4	5.67	5.74	-6.0	0.0	168.0	...	...	2.6	218.4	234.3	...	...	...	...
...	57.1	82.7	2.8	39.0	4.4	5.19	5.24	-9.4	0.0	173.9	...	...	4.6	229.4	243.1	4.5	...	...	...
...	81.7	85.5	1.4	21.2	2.3	4.96	4.99	-6.7	0.0	158.6	...	...	-6.6	213.8	226.2	4.9	...	...	...
Principal Lines of Business: OrdLife (100.0%)														Principal States: WA (15.6%), MO (9.6%), CA (9.2%), TN (6.9%), IL (5.2%)					
...	...	7.2	2.2	28.0	35.0	...	...	11.8	0.2	6.9	...	...	14.7	...	...	...	...	...	...
...	375.2	8.1	2.5	30.8	39.2	...	...	1.3	0.2	6.7	...	...	-1.0	...	...	...	...	...	...
...	...	11.6	2.5	32.9	40.6	...	...	-26.3	0.1	6.6	...	...	2.1	...	...	...	...	...	...
...	...	17.5	2.3	32.1	38.1	...	...	-38.2	0.1	6.3	...	...	-1.8	...	...	...	...	...	...
...	...	48.2	2.1	30.5	35.8	...	...	-59.5	0.0	5.9	...	...	-2.4	...	...	...	...	...	...
Principal Lines of Business: OrdLife (100.0%)																			
...	50.8	30.2	91.3	44.0	110.4	4.96	4.99	29.7	168.6	497.8	...	...	4.2	487.3	433.7	...	...	...	...
...	44.3	30.9	107.4	53.9	127.0	5.15	5.15	-12.2	140.8	600.4	...	...	5.1	566.5	533.9	...	...	...	...
...	47.8	21.9	139.0	55.0	169.4	5.32	5.32	53.4	179.9	381.8	...	...	20.0	400.8	361.8	...	...	...	...
...	58.5	31.2	118.0	55.3	152.5	4.17	4.17	-30.9	153.7	303.0	...	...	-19.2	317.7	294.5	...	...	...	...
...	58.6	35.9	143.0	53.2	189.2	3.96	3.96	22.3	165.8	315.2	...	...	13.4	330.5	308.2	...	...	...	...
519,138	76.4	4.3	1.0	7.3	13.8	6.46	7.08	15.5	0.6	11.1	0.1	6.8	16.9	42.5	57.9	46.5	0.7	159.6	42.6
308,744	93.8	5.6	1.0	7.3	12.1	6.39	7.03	0.4	0.6	12.7	0.1	6.1	16.9	42.1	59.6	35.5	...	132.6	35.6
831,925	105.1	7.6	0.8	6.5	9.5	6.46	6.94	-7.9	0.4	14.4	0.0	4.1	17.0	42.7	60.3	30.4	...	99.3	34.2
-2,318,657	100.4	6.2	0.6	4.1	6.6	6.08	2.35	40.7	0.8	11.0	...	3.9	-18.8	46.9	62.9	37.2	...	117.8	39.3
740,272	111.4	8.1	1.4	12.3	14.2	5.72	4.37	-26.0	0.4	13.8	...	2.6	29.7	47.2	61.9	46.8	...	85.9	33.7
Principal Lines of Business: IndAnn (61.1%), GrpAnn (35.1%), OrdLife (3.8%), IndA&H (0.0%)														Principal States: NY (17.2%), PA (7.0%), MA (6.3%), CA (6.2%), NJ (4.6%)					
-79	72.0	23.8	0.0	0.1	0.3	5.27	5.43	14.9	4.0	15.5	...	42.2	-7.0	87.0	95.8	3.8	...	3.2	2.2
127	67.3	24.7	1.8	3.5	13.5	5.13	5.80	-11.5	3.0	16.8	...	45.4	19.1	92.1	100.4	...	...	2.3	1.6
-30	71.5	27.3	2.2	5.2	15.3	5.21	5.36	-12.5	2.2	19.0	...	38.0	16.8	93.6	101.5	...	...	2.0	1.4
-933	73.6	26.7	0.0	0.0	-0.1	4.80	2.67	-0.3	2.6	15.7	0.8	43.1	-13.4	90.5	99.5	...	...	2.0	1.5
516	77.2	25.8	-0.8	-1.8	-6.0	4.63	5.35	5.2	2.7	14.7	4.2	55.5	0.1	88.9	98.0	...	...	1.6	1.2
Principal Lines of Business: GrpA&H (62.8%), IndA&H (34.1%), OrdLife (1.9%), GrpLife (1.2%)														Principal States: PA (76.7%), OH (11.7%), VA (6.0%)					
...	...	...	...	...	...	...	...	...	...	...	...	...	...	...	...	...	...	...	...
...	78.4	11.2	...	6.2	...	...	...	...	10.1	67.6	...	...	...	154.2	154.2	...	...	...	...
...	81.4	11.5	16.1	4.1	46.8	5.49	5.49	1.2	13.3	40.6	...	...	-23.2	132.1	132.1	...	...	...	...
...	76.0	11.2	29.2	8.1	93.0	1.99	1.99	0.9	10.2	50.6	...	...	31.3	144.0	144.0	...	...	...	...
...	-99.9	68.0	-2.4	-99.9	-6.7	0.11	0.11	-99.9	0.0	69.7	...	...	-61.2	165.2	165.2	...	...	...	...
Principal Lines of Business: Medicaid (100.0%)																			

Data in U.S. Dollars

COMPANY NAME Ultimate Parent Association Principal Officer Mailing Address Dom. : Began Bus. : Struct. : Mktg. Specialty Phone # AMB# NAIC#	Best's Financial Strength Rating FSC		Balance Sheet									Operations					
		Data Year	Bonds (%)	Mort. Loans & R.E. (%)	Com & Pref. Stock (%)	All Other Assets (%)	Total Assets ($000)	Life Reserves (%)	Health Reserves (%)	Ann Res. & Dep. Liabilities (%)	All Other Liabilities (%)	Capital & Surplus ($000)	Direct Premiums Written ($000)	Net Premiums Written & Deposits ($000)	Operating Cash Flow ($000)	NOG Before Taxes ($000)	NOG After Taxes ($000)	Net Income ($000)
TENNESSEE FARMERS LIFE INS CO	**A+**	'05	71.5	1.0	22.3	5.1	1,149,410	40.7	0.0	54.2	5.1	188,941	102,232	135,838	75,902	15,894	12,438	12,523
Lacy Upchurch President		'06	70.6	1.2	22.2	6.0	1,213,792	41.3	0.0	53.6	5.1	198,140	101,403	131,042	62,129	13,377	9,272	10,341
P.O. Box 307 Columbia, TN 38402-0307	Rating Outlook: Stable	'07	67.5	1.1	23.2	8.2	1,260,667	42.2	0.0	52.3	5.5	196,030	130,258	138,322	17,647	16,273	9,933	13,292
TN : 1973 : Stock : Exclusive Agent Ind Ann, Term Life, Univ Life		'08	67.2	1.2	22.5	9.1	1,295,963	44.3	0.0	53.9	1.8	202,245	142,552	153,182	231,699	13,992	10,990	-5,726
931-388-7872		'09	65.0	2.2	22.0	10.9	1,399,780	43.9	0.0	53.6	2.5	228,638	152,433	164,960	70,952	27,161	21,344	12,076
AMB# 008443 NAIC# 82759	**FSC VIII**	**Rating History: A+, 04/29/10; A+, 05/21/09; A+, 06/18/08; A+ g, 06/08/07; A+ g, 06/16/06**																
TENNESSEE LIFE INSURANCE CO Plateau Group Inc	**NR-3**	'05	44.4	...	...	55.6	1,127	97.7	...	...	2.3	701	...	1,007	34	247	211	211
William D. Williams Chairman & President		'06	50.3	...	...	49.7	1,032	99.7	...	...	0.3	598	...	1,070	-96	216	179	179
P.O. Box 7001 Crossville, TN 38557-7001		'07	52.9	...	...	47.1	982	99.9	...	...	0.1	556	...	999	-51	198	171	171
AZ : 1986 : Stock : Broker Credit A&H, Credit Life		'08	39.3	...	...	60.7	809	96.8	...	...	3.2	430	...	786	-18	214	186	186
931-484-8411		'09	38.5	...	...	61.5	778	99.8	...	...	0.2	540	...	587	-176	156	137	137
AMB# 068373 NAIC# 85502		**Rating History: NR-3, 05/03/10; NR-3, 04/07/09; NR-3, 04/09/08; NR-3, 04/02/07; NR-3, 03/24/06**																
TEXAS CHILDRENS HLTH PLAN[2] Texas Children's Hospital	**NR-5**	'05	1.2	...	1.0	97.9	57,506	...	69.3	...	30.7	33,568	170,053	164,705	-4,851	605	541	541
Christopher M. Born President		'06	2.7	...	0.8	96.5	71,600	...	81.1	...	18.9	42,832	206,731	203,299	17,628	10,092	10,064	10,064
P.O. Box 31011 Houston, TX 77030		'07	2.5	...	0.9	96.5	69,869	...	73.8	...	26.2	31,037	277,627	274,168	-4,275	-4,816	-4,890	-4,890
TX : 1995 : Non-Profit : Broker Medicaid, Group A&H		'08	2.3	...	0.5	97.2	88,709	...	80.0	...	20.0	41,884	354,307	349,433	17,243	9,835	9,702	9,702
832-828-1020		'09	...	...	0.5	99.5	100,426	...	79.6	...	20.4	50,324	424,352	417,848	13,575	7,885	7,765	7,765
AMB# 064244 NAIC# 95329		**Rating History: NR-5, 04/09/10; NR-5, 08/26/09; C++pd, 07/21/08; B pd, 07/20/07; B- pd, 08/29/06**																
TEXAS DIRECTORS LIFE INS CO Directors Investment Group Inc	**NR-2**	'05	93.4	...	3.5	3.1	8,789	97.5	...	...	2.5	2,693	635	632	408	337	282	287
B. Kris Seale President		'06	91.8	...	4.7	3.5	9,020	98.0	...	...	2.0	3,035	583	581	279	274	221	221
P.O. Box 5649 Abilene, TX 79606		'07	87.7	...	8.8	3.5	9,365	98.5	...	...	1.5	3,471	534	532	375	430	308	302
TX : 1981 : Stock : Not Available Ind Life, Life		'08	88.1	...	8.0	3.8	9,434	99.3	...	...	0.7	3,632	488	486	195	368	265	120
325-695-3412		'09	88.6	...	5.1	6.2	9,730	99.3	...	...	0.7	4,042	451	449	226	458	344	254
AMB# 068292 NAIC# 99546		**Rating History: NR-2, 07/01/09; NR-2, 06/05/08; NR-2, 05/16/07; NR-2, 06/19/06; NR-2, 06/21/05**																
TEXAS HEALTHSPRING LLC[2] HealthSpring, Inc.	**NR-5**	'05	21.3	...	...	78.7	59,971	...	81.4	...	18.6	40,450	245,429	245,429	30,913	25,103	15,608	15,608
Scott Huebner President		'06	11.3	...	...	88.7	90,253	...	39.5	...	60.5	35,486	363,154	363,154	27,588	46,934	31,111	31,111
2900 North Loop West, Suite 1300 Houston, TX 77092		'07	9.5	...	...	90.5	77,539	...	64.0	...	36.0	42,609	407,195	407,195	-28,396	44,796	29,282	29,282
TX : 2003 : Stock : Broker Medicare		'08	1.0	...	...	99.0	111,297	...	71.5	...	28.5	62,523	510,856	510,856	31,722	57,273	41,833	41,833
832-553-3300		'09	0.4	...	...	99.6	130,320	...	65.0	...	35.0	75,975	635,786	635,786	21,618	41,617	25,156	25,156
AMB# 064828 NAIC# 11593		**Rating History: NR-5, 04/07/10; NR-5, 08/26/09; C++pd, 10/10/08; C++pd, 08/22/07; NR-5, 07/03/07**																
TEXAS IMPERIAL LIFE INS CO[1]	**NR-1**	'05	96.9	0.3	...	2.8	25,162	...	...	...	100.0	2,409	3,886	3,234	...	690	680	630
Charlie R. Allison President		'06	95.4	0.3	...	4.3	26,266	...	...	...	100.0	2,762	3,770	3,183	...	450	438	414
351 S. Sherman Street, Suite 102 Richardson, TX 75081		'07	96.3	0.3	...	3.4	26,222	...	...	...	100.0	2,432	2,228	1,570	...	263	290	290
TX : 1980 : Stock : Not Available		'08	69.5	0.3	...	30.2	25,798	...	...	...	100.0	2,566	1,647	1,459	...	93	93	49
469-330-2200		'09	73.1	...	...	26.9	24,461	...	...	...	100.0	2,431	1,266	1,266	...	444	444	444
AMB# 068290 NAIC# 99449		**Rating History: NR-1, 06/10/10; NR-1, 06/12/09; NR-1, 06/12/08; NR-1, 06/08/07; NR-4, 03/23/07**																
TEXAS INTERNATIONAL LIFE INS[1]	**NR-1**	'05	91.6	...	2.1	6.3	32,126	...	...	0.2	99.8	6,844	...	24,859	...	-165	786	778
Larry J. Doze President & CEO		'06	81.6	...	1.8	16.6	27,010	...	...	0.0	100.0	4,552	...	12,037	...	-1,971	-1,439	-1,471
6300 Bridge Point Parkway Austin, TX 78730-5016		'07	78.3	...	...	21.7	7,998	...	...	0.0	100.0	1,451	...	8,138	...	-2,244	-1,837	-1,751
TX : 1976 : Stock : Other Direct		'08	82.1	...	...	17.9	6,991	...	...	...	100.0	1,433	...	7,472	...	28	28	-167
512-342-1912		'09	79.3	...	...	20.7	6,738	...	...	...	100.0	1,875	...	6,313	...	345	345	345
AMB# 008686 NAIC# 86169		**Rating History: NR-1, 06/10/10; NR-1, 06/12/09; NR-1, 06/12/08; NR-1, 06/08/07; NR-1, 06/07/06**																
TEXAS LIFE INS CO Wilton Re Holdings Limited	**A-**	'05	86.0	6.3	0.3	7.3	896,350	57.3	0.0	40.2	2.5	34,185	94,575	117,272	17,661	12,397	6,454	6,379
Steven T. Cates President & CEO		'06	37.7	2.7	2.6	57.0	1,910,465	27.6	0.0	1.4	71.0	39,696	104,845	125,805	26,826	124,621	6,540	6,439
P.O. Box 830 Waco, TX 76703-0830	Rating Outlook: Positive	'07	75.4	7.2	3.1	14.3	630,855	92.9	0.0	4.1	3.0	45,714	116,673	121,715	-306,311	22,532	14,367	13,247
TX : 1901 : Stock : Worksite Mktg Trad Life, Univ Life		'08	76.7	6.4	2.8	14.1	664,998	93.2	0.0	3.8	3.0	47,963	134,318	141,520	38,223	12,282	6,389	-3,437
254-752-6521		'09	84.5	0.2	0.5	14.9	727,016	90.3	0.0	3.4	6.4	48,359	146,986	104,712	47,562	23,821	17,362	18,080
AMB# 007118 NAIC# 69396	**FSC VIII**	**Rating History: A- g, 04/06/10; A-, 03/20/09; A-, 11/11/08; A, 06/05/08; A, 05/29/07**																
TEXAS MEMORIAL LIFE INS CO[1]	**E**	'05	45.3	...	...	54.7	796	...	...	...	100.0	696	134	134	...	-82	-82	-106
Forrest Roan President		'06	...	...	...	100.0	746	...	...	...	100.0	649	...	...	...	-53	-53	-52
8310 Capital of Texas Hwy North Austin, TX 78731-1011		'07	75.0	...	...	25.0	3,148	...	...	...	100.0	358	741	2,988	...	-287	-287	-290
TX : 1975 : Stock : Not Available In Rehabilitation		'08	33.3	...	...	66.7	3,981	...	...	...	100.0	-1,217	4,401	3,655	...	-2,322	-2,322	-2,323
512-338-1212		'09	...	...	...	...	...	...	...	...	...	...	...	...	...	...	...	...
AMB# 068258 NAIC# 85200		**Rating History: E, 06/10/09; NR-1, 06/12/08; NR-1, 06/08/07; NR-1, 06/07/06; NR-1, 06/07/05**																

2010 BEST'S KEY RATING GUIDE — LIFE/HEALTH EDITION
BEST'S PROFITABILITY, LEVERAGE AND LIQUIDITY TESTS 2005 – 2009
Data in U.S. Dollars

	Profitability Tests							Leverage Tests						Liquidity Tests					
Un-Realized Capital Gains ($000)	Benefits Paid to NPW & Dep (%)	Comm. & Expenses to NPW & Dep (%)	NOG to Total Assets (%)	NOG to Total Rev (%)	Operating Return on Equity (%)	Net Yield (%)	Total Return (%)	Change in NPW & Dep (%)	NPW & Dep to Capital (X)	Capital & Surplus to Liabilities (%)	Surplus Relief (%)	Reins Leverage (%)	Change in Capital (%)	Quick Liquidity (%)	Current Liquidity (%)	Non-Invest Grade Bonds to Capital (%)	Delinq. & Foreclosed Mortgages to Capital (%)	Mort. & Credit Tenant Loans & R.E. to Capital (%)	Affiliated Invest to Capital (%)
6,170	19.7	18.1	1.1	8.4	6.8	4.16	4.80	3.3	0.7	21.4	0.9	21.4	6.0	75.4	84.5	1.4	...	5.9	106.1
857	57.2	19.5	0.8	5.9	4.8	4.51	4.73	-3.5	0.6	21.5	1.1	20.7	6.0	74.8	83.3	1.8	...	6.7	104.6
3,045	-85.6	20.8	0.8	5.3	5.0	4.57	5.10	5.6	0.6	20.6	0.9	21.6	0.3	72.6	80.9	1.1	...	6.6	112.9
-9,071	63.6	19.0	0.9	5.4	5.5	4.66	2.53	10.7	0.7	19.4	0.4	7.3	-2.2	64.3	75.3	8.4	...	7.1	127.0
7,027	52.8	19.6	1.6	9.8	9.9	4.95	4.77	7.7	0.7	20.9	0.5	7.8	15.0	53.1	71.3	12.1	...	12.8	115.1
Principal Lines of Business: OrdLife (55.2%), IndAnn (41.7%), GrpA&H (2.1%), GrpAnn (0.9%)														Principal States: TN (99.1%)					
	25.8	54.1	18.7	20.3	30.7	2.77	2.77	2.5	1.4	165.0			4.3	256.6	256.6				
...	28.9	53.1	16.5	16.1	27.5	3.80	3.80	6.2	1.8	137.7	...	...	-14.7	228.5	228.5	...	...	...	...
...	32.0	53.0	17.0	16.5	29.7	4.09	4.09	-6.6	1.8	130.9	...	...	-6.9	224.2	224.2	...	...	...	...
...	30.9	53.1	20.8	22.7	37.8	3.88	3.88	-21.3	1.8	113.2	...	...	-22.8	239.9	239.9	...	...	...	...
...	44.6	53.7	17.2	22.6	28.2	2.31	2.32	-25.3	1.1	226.3	...	...	25.7	278.9	299.8	...	...	...	...
Principal Lines of Business: CrdA&H (50.3%), CrdLife (49.7%)																			
...	86.3	14.8	0.9	0.3	1.6	2.91	2.91	4.9	4.9	140.2	...	19.0	4.0	208.8	209.1	...	...	...	...
...	83.5	13.8	15.6	4.8	26.3	5.22	5.22	23.4	4.7	148.9	...	1.2	27.6	235.7	236.0	...	...	...	...
...	91.3	11.2	-6.9	-1.8	-13.2	2.55	2.55	34.9	8.8	79.9	...	8.8	-27.5	163.5	163.8	...	...	...	...
...	87.2	10.7	12.2	2.8	26.6	3.06	3.06	27.5	8.3	89.4	...	7.7	34.9	172.5	172.6	...	...	...	...
...	88.6	9.8	8.2	1.9	16.8	2.85	2.85	19.6	8.3	100.4	...	5.6	20.2	188.2	188.4	...	...	...	...
Principal Lines of Business: Medicaid (78.8%), CompHosp/Med (21.2%)														Principal States: TX (100.0%)					
0	92.6	37.4	3.3	25.4	11.3	5.67	5.80	-9.8	0.2	44.9	...	...	15.8	97.7	110.5	...	...	...	...
8	114.9	39.1	2.5	20.5	7.7	5.75	5.89	-8.1	0.2	51.7	...	...	12.9	107.6	120.7	...	...	...	...
-11	85.6	41.1	3.4	29.2	9.5	5.85	5.71	-8.5	0.2	59.7	...	...	13.9	104.1	120.2	...	...	...	...
-46	108.3	41.6	2.8	25.8	7.5	5.88	3.92	-8.6	0.1	62.6	...	...	3.7	101.6	118.6	4.9	...	...	...
30	108.1	29.9	3.6	35.2	9.0	5.60	5.06	-7.5	0.1	71.1	...	...	11.3	114.6	130.6	9.1	...	...	...
Principal Lines of Business: OrdLife (100.0%)														Principal States: TX (100.0%)					
...	78.8	11.5	35.0	6.3	55.6	2.99	2.99	55.3	6.1	207.2	...	...	157.7	293.0	299.5	...	...	...	...
...	77.3	10.6	41.4	8.5	81.9	4.55	4.55	48.0	10.2	64.8	...	...	-12.3	155.7	157.6	...	...	...	...
...	79.2	11.1	34.9	7.1	75.0	7.63	7.63	12.1	9.6	122.0	...	...	20.1	158.0	160.3	...	...	...	...
...	78.0	11.3	44.3	8.2	79.6	3.10	3.10	25.5	8.2	128.2	...	...	46.7	179.3	179.5	...	...	...	...
...	81.4	12.1	20.8	4.0	36.3	0.49	0.49	24.5	8.4	139.8	...	...	21.5	200.9	200.9	...	...	...	...
Principal Lines of Business: Medicare (100.0%)														Principal States: TX (100.0%)					
-17	46.9	18.9	2.7	15.0	27.4	...	...	13.6	1.3	10.6	31.3	...	-5.2	...	...	...	...	3.4	...
17	49.9	26.7	1.7	9.5	17.0	...	...	-1.6	1.1	12.0	26.9	...	16.3	...	...	...	...	2.9	...
...	88.0	25.3	1.1	9.6	11.2	...	...	-50.7	0.6	10.5	28.3	...	-11.0	...	...	...	...	3.1	...
...	127.3	53.7	0.4	3.5	3.7	...	...	-7.1	0.6	11.2	8.1	...	3.8	...	...	...	...	2.9	...
...	159.3	46.1	1.8	21.3	17.8	...	...	-13.2	0.5	11.2	...	...	-5.0	...	...	...	...	...	...
Principal Lines of Business: OrdLife (91.1%), IndAnn (8.9%)																			
...	85.0	282.5	1.1	2.8	11.2	...	...	-25.3	3.6	27.4	0.3	...	-5.0	...	...	...	...	...	...
-47	91.6	158.3	-4.9	-11.6	-25.2	...	...	-51.6	2.6	20.5	...	...	-33.6	...	...	...	...	...	...
-12	97.6	48.5	-10.5	-22.2	-61.2	...	...	-32.4	5.5	22.5	...	...	-68.0	...	...	...	...	...	...
...	65.9	46.7	0.4	0.4	2.0	...	...	-8.2	5.2	25.8	...	...	-2.4	...	...	...	...	...	...
...	65.4	42.7	5.0	5.2	20.9	...	...	-15.5	3.4	38.8	...	...	31.4	...	...	...	...	...	...
Principal Lines of Business: IndA&H (94.2%), GrpA&H (5.8%)																			
-161	60.6	30.7	0.7	4.5	19.4	6.34	6.33	11.6	2.9	4.7	...	999.9	7.2	55.2	67.6	61.0	...	140.4	0.1
173	62.0	34.8	0.5	4.1	17.7	6.25	6.26	7.3	2.8	2.4	...	999.9	11.4	27.1	33.7	47.6	...	114.9	...
-306	48.9	36.7	1.1	9.4	33.6	5.15	4.95	-3.3	2.5	8.4	...	8.7	9.6	61.3	74.2	34.6	...	93.1	...
582	49.8	35.7	1.0	3.8	13.6	5.93	4.46	16.3	2.9	7.9	...	7.5	-1.2	63.9	74.9	45.6	...	87.2	...
42	45.0	28.9	2.5	11.0	36.0	5.43	5.53	-26.0	2.1	7.3	36.2	26.0	2.2	62.7	77.2	6.1	...	3.0	...
Principal Lines of Business: OrdLife (98.3%), GrpAnn (1.1%), IndAnn (0.6%), IndA&H (0.0%), GrpLife (0.0%)														Principal States: TX (37.8%), CA (6.1%), LA (6.0%), NC (5.9%), OK (4.8%)					
...	150.0	999.9	-4.0	-30.0	-11.1	...	...	-27.8	0.2	740.1	...	...	-12.2	...	...	...	...	...	...
...	...	...	-6.8	-99.9	-7.8	...	...	-99.9	...	664.1	...	...	-7.5	...	...	...	...	...	...
...	11.1	15.2	-14.7	-7.8	-57.0	...	...	...	8.3	12.8	147.1	...	-44.7	...	...	...	...	...	...
...	11.5	107.5	-65.2	-48.9	541.3	...	...	22.3	-3.0	-23.4	-74.9	...	-99.9	...	...	...	...	...	...
...	...	...	...	...	...	...	...	...	...	...	...	...	...	...	...	...	...	...	...

COMPANY NAME / Ultimate Parent Association / Principal Officer / Mailing Address / Dom. : Began Bus. : Struct. : Mktg. / Specialty / Phone # / AMB# / NAIC#	Best's Financial Strength Rating / FSC	Data Year	Balance Sheet: Bonds (%)	Mort. Loans & R.E. (%)	Com & Pref. Stock (%)	All Other Assets (%)	Total Assets ($000)	Life Reserves (%)	Health Reserves (%)	Ann Res. & Dep. Liabilities (%)	All Other Liabilities (%)	Capital & Surplus ($000)	Operations: Direct Premiums Written ($000)	Net Premiums Written & Deposits ($000)	Operating Cash Flow ($000)	NOG Before Taxes ($000)	NOG After Taxes ($000)	Net Income ($000)
TEXAS SECURITY MUTUAL LIFE INS[1]	NR-1	'05	68.2	...	25.4	6.4	1,425	...	...	...	100.0	636	11	11	...	-30	-30	-47
Wendell A. Klein, President, P.O. Box 19647, Houston, TX 77224-9647		'06	67.4	...	21.5	11.2	1,269	...	...	...	100.0	542	10	10	...	-87	-87	-91
TX : 1950 : Mutual : Not Available		'07	63.3	...	30.3	6.3	1,212	...	...	...	100.0	511	10	10	...	-120	-120	-132
361-594-8520		'08	75.3	...	6.9	17.8	995	...	...	...	100.0	395	8	8	...	-23	-23	74
AMB# 068499 NAIC# 70745		'09	50.0	...	19.8	30.2	1,027	...	...	...	100.0	448	8	8	...	16	16	3
		Rating History: NR-1, 06/10/10; NR-1, 06/12/09; NR-1, 06/12/08; NR-1, 06/08/07; NR-1, 06/07/06																
TEXAS SERVICE LIFE INS CO[1]	NR-1	'05	32.7	10.7	9.4	47.2	6,296	...	...	...	100.0	804	3,934	2,919	...	183	168	168
Susan M. Thomas, President, P.O. Box 341899, Austin, TX 78734-0032		'06	50.8	11.6	4.8	32.8	5,912	...	...	...	100.0	849	5,729	443	...	188	173	170
TX : 1985 : Stock : Not Available		'07	44.1	9.9	1.9	44.1	7,968	...	...	...	100.0	1,233	10,198	3,335	...	439	354	354
512-263-6977		'08	40.9	9.0	0.8	49.3	10,167	...	...	...	100.0	1,349	10,930	4,263	...	287	209	209
AMB# 068291 NAIC# 83160		'09	39.1	7.5	0.9	52.4	11,862	...	...	...	100.0	1,928	13,475	5,098	...	257	48	48
		Rating History: NR-1, 06/10/10; NR-1, 06/12/09; NR-1, 06/12/08; NR-1, 06/08/07; NR-1, 06/07/06																
THRIVENT FINANCIAL LUTHERANS, Thrivent Financial for Lutherans	A++	'05	57.4	12.8	3.0	26.8	50,815,607	37.3	5.0	30.1	27.5	3,578,993	3,467,663	3,929,020	-197,383	455,694	455,694	522,028
Bradford L. Hewitt, Chairman, President & CEO, 625 Fourth Avenue South, Minneapolis, MN 55415-1624		'06	54.4	13.1	3.3	29.2	52,538,897	37.5	5.4	27.7	29.4	4,116,849	3,398,927	3,851,060	-43,534	416,493	416,493	523,804
WI : 1902 : Fraternal : Career Agent	Rating Outlook: Negative	'07	51.9	13.3	3.5	31.3	53,474,099	38.1	5.9	24.7	31.2	4,433,621	3,270,043	3,766,207	-354,526	348,285	348,285	391,031
Ann, Trad Life, Univ Life; 800-847-4836		'08	55.2	14.8	2.8	27.2	49,470,159	42.3	7.1	28.0	22.6	3,934,709	3,668,157	4,374,803	-246,983	101,803	101,803	-315,261
AMB# 006008 NAIC# 56014	FSC XV	'09	54.9	14.0	2.4	28.8	54,372,055	39.7	7.0	27.1	26.2	4,126,774	4,088,179	4,721,297	2,200,195	274,431	274,431	-18,270
		Rating History: A++g, 04/03/09; A++g, 06/19/08; A++g, 06/08/07; A++g, 06/14/06; A++g, 06/16/05																
THRIVENT LIFE INSURANCE CO, Thrivent Financial for Lutherans	A++	'05	29.6	...	...	70.4	3,922,480	1.2	0.0	26.3	72.5	163,358	146,611	167,122	80,394	36,298	34,491	34,490
Bradford L. Hewitt, Chairman, President & CEO, 625 Fourth Avenue South, Minneapolis, MN 55415-1624		'06	29.0	...	0.4	70.6	3,731,231	1.3	0.0	25.8	72.9	167,537	120,458	136,297	-145,693	43,951	34,072	34,036
MN : 1982 : Stock : Career Agent	Rating Outlook: Negative	'07	28.5	...	0.3	71.3	3,664,564	1.3	0.0	24.4	74.3	178,076	118,505	133,211	-39,455	62,391	50,253	49,385
Var ann, Var Univ life; 800-847-4836		'08	38.6	...	0.4	61.0	2,689,220	1.8	0.0	37.9	60.3	173,639	146,580	161,801	63,502	34,149	24,532	20,117
AMB# 009342 NAIC# 97721	FSC XV	'09	39.8	...	0.2	60.0	3,035,086	1.4	0.0	37.1	61.5	172,162	155,048	169,131	62,217	26,789	16,194	12,355
		Rating History: A++g, 04/03/09; A++g, 06/19/08; A++g, 06/08/07; A++g, 06/14/06; A++g, 06/16/05																
TIAA-CREF LIFE INS CO, Teachers Insurance & Ann Assn of America	A++	'05	80.9	4.1	0.3	14.7	3,326,952	1.1	...	83.8	15.1	324,430	171,235	371,392	-50,912	33,912	22,407	21,418
Eric Jones, Chairman, President & CEO, 730 Third Avenue, New York, NY 10017-3206		'06	72.2	3.4	1.1	23.3	3,208,373	1.6	...	76.5	21.9	340,553	173,821	313,540	-211,147	24,336	18,090	17,279
NY : 1996 : Stock : Other Direct	Rating Outlook: Stable	'07	69.5	2.8	2.0	25.7	3,115,350	2.0	...	71.4	26.6	332,130	214,507	296,551	-154,049	24,597	18,424	10,098
Ind Ann, Ind Life; 800-223-1200		'08	73.0	2.8	1.5	22.7	2,917,585	2.6	...	78.0	19.4	280,331	205,501	353,327	20,101	15,569	11,564	-61,476
AMB# 060222 NAIC# 60142	FSC XV	'09	71.9	1.9	0.2	26.1	3,319,088	3.3	...	73.1	23.7	353,313	269,786	475,507	222,433	24,358	12,436	-7,016
		Rating History: A++g, 12/18/09; A++g, 09/04/08; A++g, 06/15/07; A++g, 06/21/06; A++g, 05/31/05																
TIME INSURANCE COMPANY, Assurant Inc	A-	'05	72.0	8.6	4.4	15.0	879,226	0.3	55.2	11.6	33.0	262,296	1,471,337	1,361,864	-16,222	160,179	102,180	102,021
Donald G. Hamm, Jr., President & CEO, P.O. Box 3050, Milwaukee, WI 53201-3050		'06	72.9	10.4	6.1	10.5	820,779	0.3	57.4	13.3	29.0	238,563	1,474,779	1,365,808	9,861	158,214	99,611	99,887
WI : 1910 : Stock : Agency	Rating Outlook: Stable	'07	67.5	12.7	8.7	11.2	812,867	0.3	55.9	14.0	29.8	254,508	1,489,474	1,395,035	-5,807	162,494	114,491	112,515
Ind A&H, Life; 414-271-3011		'08	61.1	16.5	9.1	13.4	678,112	0.4	61.3	16.8	21.5	211,842	1,460,344	1,363,774	-132,500	114,805	73,230	39,042
AMB# 007126 NAIC# 69477	FSC VIII	'09	57.6	13.5	4.0	24.9	795,822	0.3	65.0	14.3	20.4	239,511	1,440,554	1,340,396	72,564	-65,104	-40,692	-43,507
		Rating History: A- g, 11/18/09; A- g, 11/25/08; A- g, 06/24/08; A- g, 07/17/07; A- g, 06/19/06																
TJM LIFE INSURANCE COMPANY[1]	NR-1	'05	92.4	...	...	7.6	9,684	...	...	...	100.0	2,110	1,006	1,006	...	262	237	237
Billy W. Turrentine, President, P.O. Box 1007, McKinney, TX 75070-8147		'06	90.4	...	...	9.6	10,416	...	...	...	100.0	2,197	1,127	1,127	...	215	193	193
TX : 1977 : Stock : Not Available		'07	88.5	...	...	11.5	11,046	...	...	...	100.0	2,239	1,027	1,027	...	166	153	153
972-542-2601		'08	74.1	...	...	25.9	11,914	...	...	...	100.0	2,272	1,237	1,237	...	182	166	166
AMB# 068286 NAIC# 87823		'09	60.8	5.2	...	34.0	12,297	...	...	...	100.0	2,023	1,151	1,151	...	62	59	59
		Rating History: NR-1, 06/10/10; NR-1, 06/12/09; NR-1, 06/12/08; NR-1, 06/08/07; NR-1, 06/07/06																
TOTAL HEALTH CARE INC, Total Health Care Inc	NR-5	'05	3.6	...	26.1	70.3	28,169	...	57.8	...	42.2	14,166	140,000	139,745	-1,277	-1,422	-1,422	-1,422
Lyle E. Algate, Executive Director, 3011 West Grand Boulevard, Suite 1600, Detroit, MI 48202		'06	2.7	...	25.9	71.4	36,947	...	71.7	...	28.3	20,714	122,907	122,692	7,036	4,028	4,028	4,029
MI : 1976 : Non-Profit : Broker		'07	1.9	...	30.4	67.7	53,177	...	81.9	...	18.1	31,360	163,095	162,846	10,608	7,432	7,432	7,432
Medicaid; 313-871-2000		'08	2.1	...	28.6	69.3	46,856	...	57.3	...	42.7	32,698	166,995	166,768	-6,121	5,749	5,749	5,749
AMB# 064297 NAIC# 95644		'09	...	...	20.9	79.1	39,810	...	57.7	...	42.3	21,560	182,649	182,506	-2,851	-5,289	-5,289	-5,289
		Rating History: NR-5, 05/21/10; NR-5, 08/26/09; C++pd, 11/24/08; C++pd, 08/08/07; C+ pd, 09/01/06																
TOTAL HEALTH CARE USA INC, Total Health Care Inc	NR-5	'05	7.2	...	...	92.8	4,352	...	54.5	...	45.5	2,608	4,309	4,292	2,968	990	990	990
Lyle E. Algate, Executive Director, 3011 West Grand Boulevard, Suite 1600, Detroit, MI 48202		'06	5.2	...	...	94.8	8,388	...	65.8	...	34.2	4,201	24,832	24,728	3,837	1,562	1,562	1,562
MI : 1994 : Non-Profit : Broker		'07	0.5	...	...	99.5	15,152	...	64.7	...	35.3	10,063	28,046	27,904	7,295	2,014	2,014	2,014
Group A&H; 313-871-2000		'08	13.9	...	...	86.1	15,267	...	67.7	...	32.3	6,489	41,643	41,425	-939	-4,281	-4,281	-4,281
AMB# 064866 NAIC# 12326		'09	...	...	...	100.0	17,862	...	67.4	...	32.6	8,306	55,026	54,830	1,592	2,095	2,095	2,095
		Rating History: NR-5, 05/21/10; NR-5, 05/15/09; NR-5, 06/30/08; NR-5, 05/04/07; NR-5, 12/06/06																

BEST'S PROFITABILITY, LEVERAGE AND LIQUIDITY TESTS 2005 – 2009

Data in U.S. Dollars

—	Profitability Tests							Leverage Tests						Liquidity Tests					
Un-Realized Capital Gains ($000)	Benefits Paid to NPW & Dep (%)	Comm. & Expenses to NPW & Dep (%)	NOG to Total Assets (%)	NOG to Total Rev (%)	Operating Return on Equity (%)	Net Yield (%)	Total Return (%)	Change in NPW & Dep (%)	NPW & Dep to Capital (X)	Capital & Surplus to Liabilities (%)	Surplus Relief (%)	Reins Leverage (%)	Change in Capital (%)	Quick Liquidity (%)	Current Liquidity (%)	Non-Invest Grade Bonds to Capital (%)	Delinq. & Foreclosed Mortgages to Capital (%)	Mort. & Credit Tenant Loans & R.E. to Capital (%)	Affiliated Invest to Capital (%)
20	562.1	999.9	-2.1	-23.4	-4.7	...	...	-10.1	0.0	88.7	...	...	-3.4	...	...	...	...	...	...
-7	597.4	999.9	-6.5	-99.9	-14.8	...	...	-10.7	0.0	81.6	...	...	-14.9	...	...	...	...	...	...
125	481.8	999.9	-9.6	-99.9	-22.7	...	...	-4.3	0.0	86.6	...	...	-1.4	...	...	...	...	...	...
-201	477.3	999.9	-2.1	-23.4	-5.1	...	...	-14.2	0.0	67.4	...	...	-28.8	...	...	...	...	...	...
81	470.5	999.9	1.6	10.9	3.8	...	...	-6.2	0.0	89.3	...	...	21.0	...	...	...	...	...	...
Principal Lines of Business: OrdLife (100.0%)																			
-16	10.0	35.8	3.2	3.2	22.3	...	...	305.6	3.5	15.5	216.1	...	14.5	...	...	...	...	79.8	...
-67	77.2	352.6	2.8	4.8	21.0	...	...	-84.8	0.5	17.7	264.1	...	5.3	...	...	...	...	77.3	...
-8	15.1	64.2	5.1	5.0	34.0	...	...	652.2	2.6	19.1	216.5	...	43.8	...	...	...	...	61.6	...
-66	12.3	62.9	2.3	2.5	16.2	...	...	27.8	3.0	16.1	218.6	...	9.9	...	...	...	...	65.1	...
18	14.4	66.5	0.4	0.5	2.9	...	...	19.6	2.6	20.2	149.2	...	41.8	...	...	...	...	44.8	...
Principal Lines of Business: OrdLife (100.0%), IndAnn (0.0%)																			
64,386	88.2	19.2	0.9	7.5	13.7	5.33	5.83	-5.8	1.0	10.7	0.3	3.0	16.5	56.1	68.6	44.2	0.2	161.3	54.4
34,422	104.2	21.3	0.8	6.8	10.8	5.44	5.91	-2.0	0.8	12.3	0.3	3.7	14.4	50.1	65.6	40.4	0.2	148.9	44.0
30,902	117.1	21.0	0.7	5.7	8.1	5.55	5.80	-2.2	0.7	13.7	0.3	4.3	8.7	52.5	66.6	34.9	0.1	141.2	40.7
-409,130	87.1	17.6	0.2	1.6	2.4	5.77	3.84	16.2	1.1	11.1	0.4	5.9	-18.2	51.2	63.9	51.8	0.3	177.2	45.1
240,442	71.7	16.2	0.5	4.1	6.8	5.51	5.45	7.9	1.1	11.3	0.4	6.9	8.0	51.5	63.0	64.1	0.6	172.9	32.9
Principal Lines of Business: IndAnn (64.9%), OrdLife (28.1%), IndA&H (7.0%)														Principal States: WI (10.9%), MN (10.8%), CA (7.2%), IL (5.9%), MI (5.3%)					
...	237.5	10.7	0.9	14.1	23.2	4.52	4.62	-19.9	1.0	14.1	0.0	...	22.5	82.5	99.6	35.0	...	...	89.5
6,573	337.6	11.5	0.9	14.9	20.6	5.68	6.23	-18.4	0.8	16.8	0.0	...	3.5	81.4	96.7	38.6	...	...	44.9
-4,223	325.6	11.4	1.4	21.0	29.1	7.45	7.01	-2.3	0.7	19.0	0.0	...	6.5	81.3	95.2	52.2	...	...	30.4
-1,209	228.3	11.6	0.8	9.7	13.9	6.69	6.18	21.5	0.9	17.1	0.0	...	-4.0	81.6	94.3	58.9	...	...	27.0
992	148.1	11.4	0.6	6.5	9.4	5.73	5.49	4.5	1.0	15.2	0.0	...	-1.2	70.5	82.7	88.2	...	...	6.4
Principal Lines of Business: IndAnn (93.4%), OrdLife (6.6%), IndA&H (0.0%)														Principal States: CA (20.0%), MN (11.7%), TX (9.9%), OH (6.7%), WI (6.6%)					
-214	90.9	11.3	0.7	7.5	7.2	5.17	5.20	-17.6	1.1	13.2	1.7	40.8	9.1	63.3	82.6	26.8	...	40.3	0.3
-292	135.0	13.0	0.6	6.3	5.4	5.24	5.24	-15.6	0.9	15.6	1.8	58.5	5.1	70.4	89.4	15.8	...	30.7	0.3
704	87.3	12.2	0.6	6.0	5.5	5.26	4.95	-5.4	0.9	16.5	1.9	66.2	-3.9	66.9	87.3	15.5	...	25.4	0.3
1,318	52.8	9.0	0.4	3.8	3.8	5.21	2.32	19.1	1.3	13.1	2.7	93.5	-17.9	71.6	89.4	15.8	...	28.7	0.4
-1,706	36.3	7.4	0.4	3.3	3.9	5.37	4.55	34.6	1.3	15.5	2.3	83.9	25.7	76.7	93.2	12.8	...	17.4	...
Principal Lines of Business: GrpAnn (49.8%), IndAnn (43.6%), OrdLife (6.6%)														Principal States: MI (16.1%), CT (12.9%), FL (7.8%), NY (6.5%), MN (6.0%)					
...	59.8	29.8	12.0	7.4	40.2	5.35	5.35	-6.2	5.1	44.1	6.7	525.8	6.8	63.9	85.0	18.8	0.1	28.0	6.5
...	61.9	28.7	11.7	7.0	39.8	5.52	5.50	0.3	5.6	42.8	14.3	617.3	-8.6	67.4	90.0	18.9	...	34.8	6.8
0	60.9	30.1	14.0	7.9	46.4	6.23	5.87	2.1	5.3	47.6	8.5	584.6	6.5	63.7	86.0	19.1	...	39.3	6.2
-55	63.6	30.5	9.8	5.2	31.4	6.52	1.54	-2.2	6.3	46.4	9.3	711.6	-17.9	54.4	72.9	27.2	...	51.9	7.2
-972	74.6	33.2	-5.5	-2.9	-18.0	5.78	5.06	-1.7	5.5	43.8	3.8	661.8	12.7	70.3	87.2	21.1	1.6	44.3	6.1
Principal Lines of Business: GrpA&H (64.3%), IndA&H (33.2%), GrpAnn (2.2%), GrpLife (0.2%), OrdLife (0.0%)														Principal States: TX (10.8%), IL (6.9%), FL (5.8%), CO (5.0%), GA (4.6%)					
...	40.8	23.7	2.5	15.8	11.6	...	...	3.7	0.5	28.1	...	...	6.6	...	...	...	...	...	...
...	40.0	26.2	1.9	11.8	9.0	...	...	12.1	0.5	27.0	...	...	4.4	...	...	...	...	...	...
...	48.4	27.2	1.4	9.7	6.9	...	...	-8.9	0.5	25.8	...	...	2.1	...	...	...	...	...	...
...	41.2	25.4	1.4	9.1	7.4	...	...	20.4	0.5	24.2	...	...	2.7	...	...	...	...	...	...
...	51.0	27.4	0.5	3.6	2.7	...	...	-7.0	0.6	20.5	...	...	-10.1	...	...	...	...	30.6	...
Principal Lines of Business: IndAnn (57.4%), OrdLife (42.6%)																			
898	80.9	14.6	-4.8	-1.1	-10.3	3.01	6.67	4.4	9.9	101.2	...	...	4.6	212.3	222.7	...	...	...	58.7
1,473	77.9	13.7	12.4	3.5	23.1	4.11	9.21	-12.2	5.9	127.6	...	...	46.2	230.2	239.6	...	...	...	46.1
2,809	79.3	11.2	16.5	4.8	28.5	4.05	10.83	32.7	5.2	143.7	...	...	51.4	223.1	230.5	...	...	...	51.6
-3,755	81.1	10.4	11.5	3.6	17.9	1.81	-5.80	2.4	5.1	230.9	...	...	4.3	310.4	322.1	...	...	...	40.9
-4,320	87.2	14.4	-12.2	-2.9	-19.5	0.37	-9.99	9.4	8.5	118.1	...	0.4	-34.1	149.2	149.2	...	...	...	...
Principal Lines of Business: Medicaid (99.9%), CompHosp/Med (0.1%)														Principal States: MI (100.0%)					
...	73.8	3.5	...	23.0	...	...	...	...	1.6	149.6	...	...	...	216.9	222.7	...	...	...	...
...	76.6	17.3	24.5	6.3	45.9	1.02	1.02	476.1	5.9	100.3	...	...	61.1	197.5	202.0	...	...	...	...
...	77.0	16.9	17.1	7.1	28.2	2.87	2.87	12.8	2.8	197.7	...	...	139.5	448.2	466.9	...	...	...	...
...	93.9	17.3	-28.1	-10.2	-51.7	2.54	2.54	48.5	6.4	73.9	...	2.8	-35.5	150.1	152.6	...	...	...	...
...	79.0	17.5	12.6	3.8	28.3	1.22	1.22	32.4	6.6	86.9	...	0.5	28.0	156.7	156.7	...	...	...	...
Principal Lines of Business: CompHosp/Med (100.0%)														Principal States: MI (100.0%)					

2010 BEST'S KEY RATING GUIDE — LIFE/HEALTH EDITION
ANNUAL STATEMENT DATA FOR YEARS 2005 – 2009

Data in U.S. Dollars

COMPANY NAME Ultimate Parent Association Principal Officer Mailing Address Dom. : Began Bus. : Struct. : Mktg. Specialty Phone # AMB# NAIC#	Best's Financial Strength Rating FSC		Balance Sheet										Operations					
		Data Year	Bonds (%)	Mort. Loans & R.E. (%)	Com & Pref. Stock (%)	All Other Assets (%)	Total Assets ($000)	Life Reserves (%)	Health Reserves %)	Ann Res. & Dep. Liabilities (%)	All Other Liabilities (%)	Capital & Surplus ($000)	Direct Premiums Written ($000)	Net Premiums Written & Deposits ($000)	Operating Cash Flow ($000)	NOG Before Taxes ($000)	NOG After Taxes ($000)	Net Income ($000)
TOWER LIFE INS CO James P. Zachry Chairman & President 310 South St. Mary's St. San Antonio, TX 78205 TX : 1955 : Stock : Agency A&H, Ann, Ind Life 210-554-4400 AMB# 007128 NAIC# 69493	**B++** Rating Outlook: Stable **FSC VI**	**'05**	34.3	13.6	0.9	51.2	79,401	80.4	0.3	12.2	7.0	37,621	2,300	2,685	1,019	487	411	512
		'06	44.4	13.4	0.7	41.5	78,950	81.2	0.4	12.1	6.3	39,071	2,400	2,291	386	1,537	1,381	1,503
		'07	42.7	13.8	0.4	43.2	78,649	80.0	0.3	12.6	7.1	40,137	2,222	2,335	486	1,396	1,163	1,171
		'08	59.5	13.8	0.5	26.2	75,399	78.5	0.3	12.6	8.7	36,684	1,946	1,899	-2,348	237	199	206
		'09	64.5	13.4	0.4	21.7	74,476	78.9	0.3	13.0	7.8	36,814	1,751	1,640	-204	11	-5	-28
		Rating History: B++, 06/15/09; B++, 06/11/08; B++, 06/13/07; B++, 02/21/06; B++, 02/18/05																
TOWN & COUNTRY LIFE INS CO Moreton & Company Scott C. Ulbrich President P.O. Box 58769 Salt Lake City, UT 84158-0769 UT : 1955 : Stock : Other Direct Ann, Life 801-715-7123 AMB# 008049 NAIC# 77674	**NR-5**	**'05**	38.9	14.5	2.1	44.5	5,236	2.6	...	89.4	8.0	2,807	9	139	7	-5	-4	-2
		'06	24.7	10.7	3.5	61.2	5,253	3.6	0.1	88.8	7.5	2,859	34	219	-7	40	40	40
		'07	67.0	11.2	3.7	18.1	5,212	0.8	4.3	87.5	7.4	2,899	757	790	-52	46	46	46
		'08	59.0	11.6	2.0	27.4	5,182	0.7	7.4	86.9	5.0	2,845	1,514	1,514	58	-4	-4	-4
		'09	60.5	5.2	6.7	27.7	5,480	1.6	5.6	75.2	17.6	2,856	1,796	1,796	66	52	52	52
		Rating History: NR-5, 04/22/10; NR-5, 04/27/09; NR-5, 04/18/08; NR-5, 04/25/07; NR-5, 05/11/06																
TRANS-CITY LIFE INS CO Trans-City Life Insurance Co Michael E. Jones President 7500 East McDonald Drive, Suite 700 Scottsdale, AZ 85250-6055 AZ : 1967 : Stock : Not Available Credit A&H, Credit Life 480-483-6500 AMB# 008051 NAIC# 77690	**B+** Rating Outlook: Stable **FSC IV**	**'05**	73.2	4.3	2.4	20.1	19,858	63.1	24.9	...	12.0	9,032	2,567	2,061	-235	2,171	1,960	1,960
		'06	60.0	4.5	2.7	32.7	18,519	63.2	23.9	...	12.9	7,797	2,750	2,258	-228	2,046	1,831	1,831
		'07	54.3	4.8	2.7	38.2	19,808	64.9	20.5	...	14.6	7,811	3,106	2,716	496	1,075	958	958
		'08	41.8	4.4	22.5	31.2	20,218	67.9	21.5	...	10.6	9,978	1,967	1,672	593	1,833	1,555	1,555
		'09	36.2	4.4	25.4	33.9	17,941	67.5	23.1	...	9.4	9,819	792	713	-2,112	1,435	1,223	1,223
		Rating History: B+, 11/10/09; B+, 10/29/08; B+, 10/17/07; B+, 11/02/06; B+, 08/10/05																
TRANS-OCEANIC LIFE INS CO Victory Insurance Corporation Nicolas Touma-Correa Chairman & President P.O. Box 363467 San Juan, PR 00936-3467 PR : 1959 : Stock : Agency Credit Life, Ind A&H, Ind Life 787-620-2680 AMB# 007132 NAIC# 69523	**B++** Rating Outlook: Stable **FSC IV**	**'05**	44.5	6.6	15.8	33.1	19,636	20.9	51.0	11.0	17.1	7,694	17,124	16,924	2,807	827	827	892
		'06	45.4	5.5	14.7	34.4	22,621	16.9	56.4	10.1	16.6	9,388	16,685	16,485	2,581	891	891	798
		'07	43.5	4.9	14.5	37.0	24,691	13.4	61.0	9.4	16.3	9,839	16,658	16,460	2,386	901	901	861
		'08	49.9	4.3	8.7	37.1	27,560	7.4	75.3	4.3	13.0	6,500	27,665	27,186	1,390	6,792	6,792	6,331
		'09	53.8	3.6	0.8	41.9	32,343	7.3	74.9	4.0	13.9	9,010	25,458	24,854	5,254	2,441	2,368	2,093
		Rating History: B++, 05/18/10; B++, 06/15/09; B++, 06/07/08; B++, 05/25/07; B+, 05/03/06																
TRANS-WESTERN LIFE INS CO R D Tips Inc Clifton M. Mitchell President 4611 Bee Cave Road, Suite 201 Austin, TX 78746 TX : 1983 : Stock : Not Available Life 512-347-1835 AMB# 068066 NAIC# 99473	**NR-5**	**'05**	...	...	...	...	...	...	...	...	...	...	...	...	...	...	...	...
		'06	...	...	...	...	...	...	...	...	...	...	...	...	...	...	...	...
		'07	...	...	...	...	...	...	...	...	...	...	...	...	...	...	...	...
		'08	...	...	...	100.0	725	...	...	...	100.0	489	1,450	...	-551	64	41	41
		'09	...	...	...	100.0	833	...	...	...	100.0	509	1,881	...	118	41	19	19
		Rating History: NR-5, 06/14/10; NR-5, 06/17/09; NR-1, 06/12/08; NR-1, 06/08/07; NR-1, 06/07/06																
TRANS WORLD ASSURANCE CO TWA Corporation Charles B. Royals President 885 South El Camino Real San Mateo, CA 94402 CA : 1963 : Stock : Agency Univ Life, Term Life, Whole life 650-348-2300 AMB# 007136 NAIC# 69566	**B++** Rating Outlook: Stable **FSC VII**	**'05**	79.7	3.8	12.2	4.3	311,412	21.8	...	74.2	4.0	64,754	13,674	35,751	13,271	7,361	6,656	6,703
		'06	77.9	5.2	12.4	4.6	323,901	21.4	...	74.6	4.0	66,593	14,613	36,859	11,727	1,787	1,266	904
		'07	76.5	8.1	11.7	3.7	331,959	21.1	...	75.3	3.7	67,120	13,632	35,369	10,206	1,368	1,026	1,026
		'08	77.1	8.0	11.0	3.9	334,900	20.8	...	76.1	3.1	67,232	11,334	32,173	6,439	1,843	1,337	1,337
		'09	74.6	10.2	10.6	4.6	338,375	20.8	...	76.3	2.8	70,012	10,867	30,355	5,684	4,610	3,953	3,953
		Rating History: B++, 12/16/09; B++, 03/20/09; B++, 01/16/08; B++, 11/09/06; B++, 12/15/05																
TRANSAM ASSURANCE COMPANY TWA Corporation Barbara J. Woodbury President 4060 Barrancas Avenue Pensacola, FL 32507 AZ : 1966 : Stock : Agency Ind Life, Term Life, Whole life 850-456-7406 AMB# 007437 NAIC# 71986	**B+** Rating Outlook: Stable **FSC III**	**'05**	72.4	...	19.6	8.0	4,006	7.0	...	68.1	24.8	3,014	7	26	69	52	44	44
		'06	68.7	...	19.6	11.6	4,081	6.9	...	67.7	25.4	3,077	6	23	69	55	47	47
		'07	56.8	...	19.3	23.9	4,236	6.7	...	68.8	24.4	3,170	7	22	130	95	84	84
		'08	46.8	...	19.4	33.8	4,361	6.5	...	69.4	24.1	3,297	6	20	72	108	88	88
		'09	46.2	...	19.8	34.0	4,409	6.6	...	67.5	25.9	3,344	5	21	51	38	31	31
		Rating History: B+, 12/16/09; B+, 03/20/09; B+, 01/16/08; B+, 11/09/06; B+, 12/15/05																
TRANSAMERICA FINANCIAL LIFE AEGON N.V. Mark W. Mullin Chairman & President 4333 Edgewood Road N.E. Cedar Rapids, IA 52499 NY : 1947 : Stock : Direct Response Group pens 319-355-8511 AMB# 007267 NAIC# 70688	**A** Rating Outlook: Stable **FSC XV**	**'05**	40.4	4.8	0.5	54.3	16,512,513	6.0	0.3	38.1	55.6	802,096	2,345,100	2,589,479	62,031	150,234	118,314	116,706
		'06	37.4	6.3	1.2	55.1	16,802,679	6.3	0.3	36.8	56.6	888,077	2,281,852	2,615,015	103,776	125,648	98,173	93,267
		'07	32.3	6.6	1.0	60.1	17,771,745	6.1	0.3	35.4	58.3	813,295	3,244,223	3,601,769	121,511	153,170	116,823	124,760
		'08	34.4	6.3	1.0	58.4	18,792,373	6.1	0.7	39.9	53.3	806,474	4,313,323	4,672,423	1,083,020	-400,162	-324,063	-296,851
		'09	38.0	4.6	0.1	57.3	20,937,072	5.8	0.6	35.4	58.2	911,627	4,051,555	4,333,008	238,675	551,351	459,902	274,899
		Rating History: A g, 04/23/09; A+ g, 06/18/08; A+ g, 05/30/07; A+ g, 06/21/06; A+ g, 05/13/05																
TRANSAMERICA LIFE INSURANCE CO AEGON N.V. Larry N. Norman Chairman & President 4333 Edgewood Road N.E. Cedar Rapids, IA 52499 IA : 1962 : Stock : Agency Ind Ann, Group A&H, Ind Life 319-355-8511 AMB# 006095 NAIC# 86231	**A** Rating Outlook: Stable **FSC XV**	**'05**	57.0	10.6	1.1	31.4	108,852,304	14.6	2.6	51.2	31.7	4,689,358	9,648,716	14,602,205	-1,979,095	105,997	-62,271	-5,285
		'06	50.0	10.0	3.2	36.8	113,414,585	14.2	2.7	43.8	39.3	4,403,590	10,503,241	13,698,265	-1,094,616	-14,104	-176,243	-26,856
		'07	46.1	10.5	2.5	41.0	112,802,514	14.5	3.0	38.9	43.6	4,324,562	11,455,634	14,630,178	-4,632,770	136,045	-51,160	262,639
		'08	49.5	10.6	2.7	37.1	103,871,552	15.6	3.4	37.8	43.2	4,926,874	13,280,814	3,322,669	738,874	-1,020,140	-894,689	-528,468
		'09	46.5	9.3	1.2	43.0	101,455,188	15.8	3.6	28.4	52.2	5,026,824	12,694,917	9,514,826	-7,219,894	589,154	601,050	-99,471
		Rating History: A g, 04/23/09; A+ g, 06/18/08; A+ g, 05/30/07; A+ g, 06/21/06; A+ g, 05/13/05																

BEST'S PROFITABILITY, LEVERAGE AND LIQUIDITY TESTS 2005 – 2009

Data in U.S. Dollars

	Profitability Tests							Leverage Tests						Liquidity Tests					
Un-Realized Capital Gains ($000)	Benefits Paid to NPW & Dep (%)	Comm. & Expenses to NPW & Dep (%)	NOG to Total Assets (%)	NOG to Total Rev (%)	Operating Return on Equity (%)	Net Yield (%)	Total Return (%)	Change in NPW & Dep (%)	NPW & Dep to Capital (X)	Capital & Surplus to Liabilities (%)	Surplus Relief (%)	Reins Leverage (%)	Change in Capital (%)	Quick Liquidity (%)	Current Liquidity (%)	Non-Invest Grade Bonds to Capital (%)	Delinq. & Foreclosed Mortgages to Capital (%)	Mort. & Credit Tenant Loans & R.E. to Capital (%)	Affiliated Invest to Capital (%)
-77	136.1	13.9	0.5	9.7	1.1	1.98	2.04	0.7	0.1	93.8	0.0	0.7	1.3	199.2	212.9	3.9	...	28.1	23.1
-53	201.2	-21.1	1.7	31.8	3.6	2.66	2.77	-14.7	0.1	102.1	0.0	0.7	3.8	191.8	206.3	...	...	26.5	22.1
-72	197.8	-9.0	1.5	25.7	2.9	2.83	2.77	1.9	0.1	108.5	0.0	1.0	2.6	193.5	208.5	4.5	...	26.5	21.9
-17	155.6	23.4	0.3	5.8	0.5	2.02	2.02	-18.7	0.1	99.0	0.0	0.7	-8.4	153.1	164.9	1.4	...	27.8	23.5
-12	173.7	47.3	0.0	-0.2	0.0	1.94	1.90	-13.6	0.0	102.3	0.0	0.7	0.4	144.8	157.3	3.2	...	26.5	22.6

Principal Lines of Business: OrdLife (39.5%), GrpLife (25.4%), GrpA&H (22.5%), IndA&H (10.9%), GrpAnn (0.9%)
Principal States: TX (95.1%)

8	232.2	84.8	-0.1	-1.5	-0.2	2.82	3.67	58.4	0.0	119.1	...	...	12.1	228.3	229.0		...	26.7	...
22	145.6	58.2	0.8	9.0	1.4	3.95	4.89	57.5	0.1	124.2	...	...	2.2	243.7	244.8	...	...	19.3	...
8	100.1	38.4	0.9	4.5	1.6	4.09	4.72	259.9	0.3	130.7	...	...	1.5	170.6	177.2	...	...	19.8	...
-84	79.2	31.6	-0.1	-0.2	-0.1	2.82	1.63	91.7	0.5	123.1	...	...	-3.2	176.0	180.5	...	...	21.0	...
10	76.3	28.9	1.0	2.7	1.8	1.23	1.79	18.6	0.6	114.2	...	...	2.2	173.9	186.5	...	...	9.8	...

Principal Lines of Business: GrpA&H (99.7%), IndAnn (0.3%)
Principal States: UT (91.6%), AZ (8.1%)

27	53.7	141.2	9.9	34.6	22.9	3.87	4.01	-28.5	0.2	86.2	3.0	19.5	11.2	177.7	183.1	...	...	9.2	7.0
27	48.7	140.0	9.5	28.9	21.8	5.26	5.41	9.6	0.3	75.6	3.3	23.6	-13.2	163.8	168.5	...	...	10.6	6.3
28	47.1	135.1	5.0	13.6	12.3	6.11	6.26	20.3	0.3	68.0	2.9	24.2	0.5	155.4	159.5	...	...	11.9	40.5
15	38.4	182.7	7.8	32.5	17.5	3.62	3.70	-38.5	0.2	100.6	1.3	16.9	26.5	178.0	185.1	...	...	8.9	44.9
4	117.7	319.4	6.4	45.2	12.4	1.71	1.73	-57.4	0.1	125.4	0.3	12.3	-1.6	205.6	211.0	...	...	8.0	45.7

Principal Lines of Business: CrdLife (72.8%), CrdA&H (27.2%)
Principal States: AZ (100.0%)

-20	32.2	61.2	4.5	4.8	11.6	1.68	2.29	5.6	2.2	66.1	...	1.7	18.0	113.2	120.4	...	0.4	16.6	16.6
338	29.1	62.8	4.2	5.2	10.4	3.59	5.01	-2.6	1.7	72.6	...	1.3	21.7	124.3	131.5	...	0.3	13.2	13.2
-110	35.3	60.9	3.8	5.2	9.4	4.10	3.42	-0.2	1.7	67.7	...	1.5	4.8	122.1	129.2	...	0.3	12.2	12.2
-276	31.2	55.4	26.0	24.3	83.1	3.45	0.37	65.2	4.1	31.5	...	1.4	-33.8	89.2	95.1	...	0.5	18.1	18.1
111	33.2	57.1	7.9	9.2	30.5	3.70	3.20	-8.6	2.7	39.3	...	1.4	38.2	106.1	109.9	...	0.3	12.7	12.7

Principal Lines of Business: IndA&H (89.0%), OrdLife (7.2%), GrpLife (3.1%), CrdLife (0.6%), IndAnn (0.1%)
Principal States: PR (99.7%)

...	...	...	...	...	...	...	...	...	...	...	...	...	...	...	...	...	...	...	...
...	...	...	...	...	...	...	...	...	...	...	...	...	...	...	...	...	...	...	...
...	...	...	...	...	...	...	...	...	...	...	...	...	...	...	...	...	...	...	...
...	...	...	...	12.1	...	...	...	...	...	206.8	65.2	999.9	...	270.4	270.4	...	...	...	...
...	...	...	2.4	7.8	3.8	1.63	1.63	...	...	157.0	45.3	999.9	4.1	233.5	233.5	...	...	...	...

Principal States: TX (100.0%)

3,829	40.1	24.1	2.2	24.2	10.9	4.02	5.32	-0.4	0.5	29.1	0.0	0.8	12.2	99.3	99.5	2.1	...	17.1	51.6
2,129	43.5	24.2	0.4	4.5	1.9	3.71	4.27	3.1	0.5	28.8	0.0	0.8	3.2	96.6	96.8	1.9	...	23.1	52.1
-1,097	47.1	25.2	0.3	3.7	1.5	3.82	3.48	-4.0	0.5	27.8	0.0	0.8	-0.5	92.7	92.8	1.8	...	37.1	55.7
-2,096	48.1	25.9	0.4	5.2	2.0	3.84	3.20	-9.0	0.5	26.8	0.0	0.8	-1.9	91.0	92.0	1.7	...	37.8	54.4
-1,054	45.4	22.6	1.2	15.4	5.8	3.92	3.61	-5.6	0.4	27.8	0.0	0.7	3.9	88.7	90.6	1.5	...	47.0	50.6

Principal Lines of Business: GrpAnn (58.8%), OrdLife (33.4%), GrpLife (4.6%), IndAnn (3.2%)
Principal States: CA (20.5%), TX (14.8%), FL (4.8%), NC (3.9%), VA (3.7%)

12	168.7	73.3	1.1	37.7	1.5	2.72	3.03	-2.9	0.0	364.6	0.0	0.3	1.7	392.5	401.8	...	...	...	19.9
18	296.9	162.4	1.2	34.0	1.5	3.25	3.69	-12.5	0.0	367.7	0.0	0.2	2.1	401.3	411.9	...	...	...	5.7
15	215.7	83.4	2.0	50.9	2.7	3.80	4.17	-1.9	0.0	355.0	0.0	0.2	3.0	380.5	388.2	...	...	...	12.3
31	229.2	112.2	2.1	50.2	2.7	3.98	4.71	-9.5	0.0	362.9	0.0	0.2	3.4	361.2	363.8	...	...	...	20.0
25	177.9	103.8	0.7	31.7	0.9	2.10	2.67	4.9	0.0	369.1	0.0	0.2	1.5	366.6	369.3	...	...	...	20.1

Principal Lines of Business: GrpAnn (63.1%), OrdLife (22.6%), GrpLife (14.2%)
Principal States: FL (27.2%), AZ (22.7%), GA (9.8%), NV (5.7%), MO (5.7%)

-5,505	90.8	5.7	0.7	3.8	15.9	5.50	5.60	14.9	2.9	12.2	14.2	119.1	16.3	60.2	75.6	55.0	...	89.3	1.8
-369	120.1	6.3	0.6	3.1	11.6	5.44	5.50	1.0	2.7	13.5	6.3	131.5	10.9	54.8	70.5	50.2	...	108.7	2.7
12,415	85.7	4.7	0.7	2.8	13.7	5.50	5.83	37.7	3.9	12.3	7.4	159.9	-6.5	57.6	74.7	41.3	...	128.4	20.1
134,817	67.4	5.1	-1.8	-6.2	-40.0	5.51	7.43	29.7	5.2	10.1	7.3	168.6	-2.6	60.3	73.9	60.4	0.6	132.5	19.0
-129,137	60.7	5.1	2.3	9.2	53.5	5.54	2.24	-7.3	4.3	11.5	6.2	161.8	12.4	57.5	71.7	64.1	...	96.6	16.5

Principal Lines of Business: GrpAnn (75.9%), IndAnn (13.6%), OrdLife (8.5%), GrpA&H (0.8%), IndA&H (0.7%)
Principal States: NY (32.2%), FL (15.8%), CA (7.6%), MO (6.0%), NC (5.5%)

43,922	73.2	12.9	-0.1	-0.5	-1.3	5.44	5.66	4.3	2.5	7.7	5.3	257.7	-2.2	47.4	61.7	70.2	0.8	196.2	15.4
5,620	95.2	14.2	-0.2	-1.2	-3.9	5.56	5.82	-6.2	2.3	7.7	-1.5	314.2	-0.8	45.1	60.2	68.9	0.7	195.1	34.7
281,150	94.9	18.1	0.0	-0.3	-1.2	5.68	6.51	6.8	2.5	8.3	3.1	395.1	0.4	42.8	57.6	56.7	0.5	202.7	63.6
-337,435	350.2	92.0	-0.8	-8.2	-19.3	5.39	5.47	-77.3	0.5	8.8	-6.6	462.0	5.6	44.9	58.3	78.0	1.3	179.0	76.7
-381,912	83.4	12.8	0.6	4.9	12.1	4.50	2.94	186.4	1.6	9.4	16.8	618.9	-4.9	48.1	61.7	99.3	0.1	164.0	52.1

Principal Lines of Business: GrpAnn (42.8%), IndAnn (35.2%), OrdLife (13.3%), IndA&H (4.8%), GrpA&H (2.3%)
Principal States: CA (11.1%), FL (7.5%), TX (7.3%), NC (6.7%), NJ (4.8%)

Data in U.S. Dollars

COMPANY NAME Ultimate Parent Association Principal Officer Mailing Address Dom. : Began Bus. : Struct. : Mktg. Specialty Phone # AMB# NAIC#	Best's Financial Strength Rating FSC	Data Year	Balance Sheet Bonds (%)	Mort. Loans & R.E. (%)	Com & Pref. Stock (%)	All Other Assets (%)	Total Assets ($000)	Life Reserves (%)	Health Reserves (%)	Ann Res. & Dep. Liabilities (%)	All Other Liabilities (%)	Capital & Surplus ($000)	Operations Direct Premiums Written ($000)	Net Premiums Written & Deposits ($000)	Operating Cash Flow ($000)	NOG Before Taxes ($000)	NOG After Taxes ($000)	Net Income ($000)
TRAVELERS PROTEC ASSOC OF AMER	NR-5	'05	86.1	0.0	...	13.9	11,201	...	80.7	...	19.3	9,332	1,841	1,841	180	127	127	127
George J. Kern President		'06	86.0	0.0	...	14.0	11,213	...	80.9	...	19.1	9,562	1,503	1,503	6	230	230	230
3755 Lindell Blvd. St. Louis, MO 63108-3476		'07	86.3	0.0	...	13.7	11,291	...	80.8	...	19.2	9,721	1,405	1,405	76	159	159	159
MO : 1890 : Fraternal : Career Agent Ind A&H		'08	77.1	0.0	...	22.9	11,154	...	85.3	...	14.7	9,733	1,269	1,269	-119	12	12	12
314-371-0533		'09	83.1	0.0	...	16.9	11,226	...	81.2	...	18.8	9,685	1,300	1,300	58	-47	-47	-47
AMB# 009769 NAIC# 56006		**Rating History: NR-5, 04/14/10; NR-5, 04/21/09; NR-5, 04/21/08; NR-5, 05/09/07; NR-5, 05/08/06**																
TRH HEALTH INSURANCE COMPANY TN Rural Health Improvement Association	NR-5	'05	...	...	...	...	...	...	...	...	...	...	...	...	...	...	...	...
Flavius A. Barker President		'06	...	...	...	...	...	...	...	...	...	...	...	...	...	...	...	...
P.O. Box 1801 Columbia, TN 38402-1801		'07	86.4	...	...	13.6	15,304	...	...	...	100.0	14,293	...	...	945	585	567	567
TN : 1999 : Stock : Not Available		'08	84.4	...	...	15.6	15,330	...	...	...	100.0	14,408	...	...	-75	596	568	72
931-388-7872		'09	79.9	...	10.8	9.3	16,094	...	...	...	100.0	14,890	...	...	593	619	623	541
AMB# 060354 NAIC# 89005		**Rating History: NR-5, 04/13/10; NR-5, 05/19/09; NR-5, 10/13/08; NR-1, 06/12/08; NR-1, 06/08/07**																
TRILLIUM COMMUNITY HEALTH PLAN[2]	NR-5	'05	...	...	...	...	...	...	...	...	...	...	...	...	...	...	...	...
Thomas K. Wuest President		'06	72.6	...	...	27.4	4,049	...	...	...	100.0	3,946	...	...	4,049	-1,054	-1,054	-1,054
1800 Millrace Drive Eugene, OR 97403		'07	2.7	...	...	97.3	9,700	...	61.9	...	38.1	4,122	26,408	26,235	1,955	874	586	586
OR : Stock : Not Available Medicare		'08	...	...	...	100.0	9,174	...	60.8	...	39.2	4,712	29,880	29,681	1,652	367	33	33
541-338-2938		'09	2.3	...	...	97.7	11,418	...	48.9	...	51.1	5,877	37,265	36,771	1,490	1,300	1,226	1,226
AMB# 064863 NAIC# 12559		**Rating History: NR-5, 04/07/10; NR-5, 09/11/09; NR-5, 08/07/08; NR-5, 05/04/07; NR-5, 11/08/06**																
TRINITY LIFE INSURANCE COMPANY[1]	NR-1	'05	80.1	9.8	2.3	7.8	18,849	...	...	0.9	99.1	2,725	8,080	7,667	...	-65	-65	-65
Gregg E. Zahn President & CEO		'06	63.5	20.3	1.1	15.1	24,516	...	...	0.5	99.5	3,966	7,954	7,372	...	194	194	216
7633 E 63rd Pl, Suite 230 Tulsa, OK 74133		'07	75.7	16.1	0.6	7.5	29,972	...	...	0.3	99.7	3,801	9,835	9,339	...	34	34	35
OK : 1998 : Stock : Broker		'08	76.4	13.0	0.7	9.9	32,500	...	...	0.2	99.8	2,700	7,016	6,608	...	-257	-285	-1,058
785-267-7077		'09	68.0	10.4	1.0	20.6	39,727	...	...	0.3	99.7	4,327	10,231	9,714	...	-489	-489	-882
AMB# 060252 NAIC# 60227		**Rating History: NR-1, 06/10/10; NR-1, 06/12/09; NR-1, 06/12/08; NR-1, 06/08/07; NR-5, 05/10/06**																
TRIPLE-S SALUD INC Triple-S Management Corporation	B++	'05	62.7	...	17.6	19.7	504,435	...	34.2	...	65.8	194,813	1,279,187	1,277,618	8,923	12,338	10,327	16,126
Socorro Rivas President & CEO		'06	54.6	...	16.8	28.6	553,903	...	30.0	...	70.0	191,420	1,337,839	1,335,673	22,450	37,322	24,231	24,723
1441 F.D. Roosevelt Avenue San Juan, PR 00920	Rating Outlook: Stable	'07	49.8	...	12.1	38.1	702,131	...	23.1	...	76.9	217,775	1,305,242	1,302,049	40,104	53,598	37,848	41,743
PR : 1960 : Stock : Agency Group A&H, Medicaid, FEHBP		'08	63.1	...	7.6	29.3	595,731	...	33.3	...	66.7	209,039	1,518,503	1,512,999	-54,060	44,281	33,877	21,838
787-749-4949		'09	56.6	...	8.1	35.3	661,752	...	34.4	...	65.6	257,259	1,685,475	1,678,289	8,614	62,162	42,811	42,598
AMB# 068130 NAIC# 55816	FSC IX	**Rating History: B++, 06/24/09; B++, 06/18/08; B++, 06/13/07; B++, 07/10/06; A- u, 12/22/05**																
TRIPLE-S VIDA, INC. Triple-S Management Corporation	B++	'05	58.6	...	1.8	39.5	407,298	43.8	5.2	14.2	36.9	32,262	118,123	108,240	-6,004	-50,293	-50,719	-42,350
Arturo Carrion Crespo President		'06	83.6	...	4.8	11.6	292,972	69.4	8.4	17.6	4.6	39,270	111,080	101,215	9,054	7,028	7,017	7,077
P.O. Box 363786 San Juan, PR 00936-3786	Rating Outlook: Stable	'07	85.0	...	5.1	9.9	309,465	70.3	8.6	17.2	3.9	45,105	109,505	100,666	19,675	7,676	7,603	8,280
PR : 1964 : Stock : Exclusive Agent Home serv, Cancer Life, Ordinary Life		'08	84.7	...	4.3	10.9	329,391	70.0	9.0	17.3	3.6	48,742	114,587	107,017	17,240	6,370	6,164	2,624
787-758-4888		'09	87.0	...	3.7	9.3	352,485	68.9	8.9	15.7	6.6	49,326	118,197	112,065	15,463	22	-194	-1,063
AMB# 007631 NAIC# 73814	FSC VI	**Rating History: B++, 06/24/09; B++, 06/18/08; B++, 06/13/07; B++, 07/10/06; A-, 12/20/05**																
TRUASSURE INSURANCE COMPANY[1]	NR-1	'05	78.9	...	...	21.1	2,735	...	...	...	100.0	2,692	0	0	...	-27	-27	-27
Thomas J. Colgan President & CEO		'06	79.9	...	...	20.1	2,702	...	...	...	100.0	2,635	97	37	...	-56	-56	-56
111 Shuman Boulevard Naperville, IL 60532-1337		'07	40.4	...	...	59.6	5,345	...	...	...	100.0	5,219	400	89	...	7	7	7
IL : 1991 : Stock : Agency		'08	57.3	...	...	42.7	5,319	...	...	...	100.0	5,153	1,298	188	...	-49	-49	-49
630-718-4700		'09	...	...	...	100.0	5,315	...	...	...	100.0	5,012	1,958	233	...	-130	-130	-130
AMB# 008957 NAIC# 92525		**Rating History: NR-1, 06/10/10; NR-1, 06/12/09; NR-5, 08/07/08; NR-1, 06/12/08; NR-1, 06/08/07**																
TRUSTMARK INSURANCE COMPANY Trustmark Mutual Holding Company	A-	'05	74.3	3.0	5.7	17.0	1,210,244	13.1	46.1	25.1	15.7	203,790	279,425	226,247	-73,528	30,365	21,438	26,214
David M. McDonough CEO		'06	75.7	3.1	8.4	12.9	1,282,004	12.6	41.9	25.4	20.1	239,808	270,356	220,955	98,140	40,067	39,918	42,494
400 Field Drive Lake Forest, IL 60045-2581	Rating Outlook: Stable	'07	74.5	4.1	7.6	13.9	1,236,856	28.8	36.6	21.6	12.9	236,391	258,238	197,593	-17,660	44,551	29,083	30,071
IL : 1913 : Stock : Broker Group A&H, Ind Life, Ind A&H		'08	75.2	5.2	6.8	12.7	1,168,327	32.5	35.4	18.2	14.0	212,236	254,082	246,582	-20,020	64,367	47,328	46,891
847-615-1500		'09	75.9	5.1	7.6	11.4	1,172,032	36.1	33.8	14.8	15.3	240,292	270,456	282,362	-8,452	42,007	29,286	26,153
AMB# 006165 NAIC# 61425	FSC IX	**Rating History: A- g, 01/18/10; A-, 01/21/09; A-, 11/06/07; B++, 12/07/06; B++, 08/31/06**																
TRUSTMARK LIFE INS CO Trustmark Mutual Holding Company	A-	'05	76.5	...	12.7	10.8	558,413	30.3	35.4	8.0	26.3	88,641	623,370	724,477	-30,576	22,374	21,019	17,746
David M. McDonough CEO		'06	79.7	...	13.1	7.3	564,631	38.5	32.3	6.8	22.3	140,446	540,821	623,492	-13,081	32,494	21,885	45,500
400 Field Drive Lake Forest, IL 60045-2581	Rating Outlook: Stable	'07	71.6	...	17.0	11.4	361,681	15.8	44.4	15.1	24.7	171,697	412,589	504,014	-195,086	42,716	36,109	35,014
IL : 1925 : Stock : Broker Group A&H, Group Life		'08	74.0	...	11.3	14.7	377,360	13.5	44.5	16.3	25.7	183,535	422,078	417,268	17,950	-11,381	-4,260	-14,491
847-615-1500		'09	75.6	...	9.8	14.7	362,207	14.1	44.4	18.2	23.3	184,619	384,605	389,037	-4,637	-799	1,989	2,110
AMB# 006335 NAIC# 62863	FSC VIII	**Rating History: A-, 01/18/10; A-, 01/21/09; A-, 11/06/07; B++, 12/07/06; B++, 08/31/06**																

BEST'S PROFITABILITY, LEVERAGE AND LIQUIDITY TESTS 2005 – 2009

Data in U.S. Dollars

—	Profitability Tests							Leverage Tests						Liquidity Tests					
Un-Realized Capital Gains ($000)	Benefits Paid to NPW & Dep (%)	Comm. & Expenses to NPW & Dep (%)	NOG to Total Assets (%)	NOG to Total Rev (%)	Operating Return on Equity (%)	Net Yield (%)	Total Return (%)	Change in NPW & Dep (%)	NPW & Dep to Capital (X)	Capital & Surplus to Liabilities (%)	Surplus Relief (%)	Reins Leverage (%)	Change in Capital (%)	Quick Liquidity (%)	Current Liquidity (%)	Non-Invest Grade Bonds to Capital (%)	Delinq. & Foreclosed Mortgages to Capital (%)	Mort. & Credit Tenant Loans & R.E. to Capital (%)	Affiliated Invest to Capital (%)
...	46.4	63.4	1.1	5.4	1.4	4.47	4.47	59.8	0.2	499.4	...	...	1.1	448.5	477.0	...	...	0.0	0.0
...	56.7	75.4	2.0	11.4	2.4	4.59	4.59	-18.3	0.2	579.2	...	...	2.5	512.6	544.9	...	...	0.0	0.0
...	50.7	81.3	1.4	8.1	1.6	4.96	4.96	-6.5	0.1	619.1	...	...	1.7	549.7	581.7	...	...	0.0	0.0
...	63.0	84.4	0.1	0.7	0.1	4.40	4.40	-9.7	0.1	684.6	...	...	0.1	652.9	667.5	...	...	0.0	0.0
...	50.2	87.2	-0.4	-2.6	-0.5	4.02	4.02	2.5	0.1	628.7	...	...	-0.5	540.1	576.0	...	...	0.0	0.0
Principal Lines of Business: IndA&H (40.1%)														Principal States: PA (15.9%), KY (11.6%), MI (11.1%), NC (10.2%), WI (7.6%)					
...	...	...	...	...	...	...	...	...	...	...	...	...	...	...	...	...	...	...	...
...	...	...	...	...	...	...	...	...	...	...	...	...	...	...	...	...	...	...	...
...	...	...	...	84.0	...	...	...	...	...	999.9	...	...	...	999.9	999.9	7.0	...	...	...
...	...	...	3.7	84.1	4.0	4.30	1.10	...	...	999.9	...	...	0.7	999.9	999.9	...	...	...	...
159	...	...	4.0	89.2	4.3	4.36	4.87	...	...	999.9	...	...	4.8	999.9	999.9	...	...	...	...
...	...	...	...	...	...	...	...	...	...	...	...	...	...	...	...	...	...	...	...
...	...	...	...	-99.9	...	...	...	...	...	999.9	...	...	...	999.9	999.9	...	...	...	...
...	83.4	14.7	8.5	2.2	14.5	7.66	7.66	...	6.4	73.9	...	15.6	4.5	156.1	156.1	...	...	...	...
...	81.4	18.0	0.4	0.1	0.8	2.46	2.46	13.1	6.3	105.6	...	2.3	14.3	171.7	171.7	...	...	...	...
...	78.9	17.9	11.9	3.3	23.2	1.47	1.47	23.9	6.3	106.1	...	4.2	24.7	214.7	214.7	...	...	...	...
Principal Lines of Business: Medicare (100.0%)														Principal States: OR (100.0%)					
-2	18.4	35.2	-0.4	-0.7	-2.5	...	...	35.5	2.7	17.5	18.1	...	9.2	...	...	...	...	65.5	...
26	24.8	31.3	0.9	2.1	5.8	...	...	-3.8	1.8	20.3	9.7	...	47.3	...	...	...	...	120.1	...
-73	27.6	27.7	0.1	0.3	0.9	...	...	26.7	2.3	15.7	2.6	...	-1.9	...	...	...	...	118.8	...
-403	50.2	30.8	-0.9	-3.4	-8.8	...	...	-29.2	2.3	9.6	1.5	...	-30.2	...	...	...	...	149.4	...
227	32.0	42.0	-1.4	-4.2	-13.9	...	...	47.0	2.1	12.9	0.7	...	60.5	...	...	...	...	90.6	...
Principal Lines of Business: OrdLife (61.9%), IndAnn (38.0%), IndA&H (0.0%)																			
-10,793	90.5	9.5	2.1	0.8	5.4	3.18	1.93	6.8	6.6	62.9	...	0.2	3.7	116.6	123.0	1.0	...	...	...
3,094	87.6	10.4	4.6	1.8	12.5	2.52	3.46	4.5	7.0	52.8	...	0.5	-1.7	101.6	108.0	8.1	...	...	...
-7,171	87.1	10.0	6.0	2.9	18.5	3.04	2.36	-2.5	6.0	45.0	...	0.1	13.8	103.6	108.8	6.0	...	...	...
-12,232	88.9	9.5	5.2	2.2	15.9	4.06	-1.05	16.2	7.2	54.1	...	0.9	-4.0	85.3	91.7	1.0	...	...	...
8,111	89.9	7.7	6.8	2.5	18.4	4.72	6.78	10.9	6.5	63.6	...	3.9	23.1	80.7	89.6	3.7	...	...	...
Principal Lines of Business: CompHosp/Med (40.6%), Medicare (29.5%), Medicaid (20.7%), FEHBP (7.5%), MedSup (0.9%)														Principal States: PR (99.9%)					
-11,365	38.3	100.9	-14.3	-40.9	-99.9	5.63	4.72	8.5	3.2	9.1	1.7	819.1	-51.6	56.5	59.0	2.1	...	...	0.6
595	53.8	50.9	2.0	6.0	19.6	5.70	6.02	-6.5	2.4	16.5	0.7	51.4	21.7	82.1	86.8	16.5	...	...	...
-1,604	44.4	51.5	2.5	6.5	18.0	5.83	5.54	-0.5	2.1	17.9	0.6	42.9	13.2	77.0	83.0	12.2	...	...	...
-210	43.9	53.3	1.9	4.9	13.1	6.11	4.93	6.3	2.2	17.4	0.6	44.2	3.8	75.4	81.9	10.5	...	...	...
1,009	44.2	61.9	-0.1	-0.1	-0.4	5.63	5.90	4.7	2.2	16.5	0.1	40.8	2.5	72.4	80.3	10.3	...	...	...
Principal Lines of Business: OrdLife (60.5%), IndA&H (27.7%), GrpA&H (4.5%), IndAnn (4.0%), GrpLife (3.4%)														Principal States: PR (100.0%)					
...	51.7	999.9	-1.1	-42.2	-1.1	...	...	49.5	0.0	999.9	...	...	13.6	...	...	...	...	...	...
...	81.0	481.0	-2.1	-37.3	-2.1	...	...	999.9	0.0	999.9	0.1	...	-2.1	...	...	...	...	...	...
...	81.2	361.1	0.2	1.7	0.2	...	...	144.0	0.0	999.9	0.1	...	98.0	...	...	...	...	...	...
...	86.1	550.5	-0.9	-4.2	-0.9	...	...	111.3	0.0	999.9	0.3	...	-1.3	...	...	...	...	...	...
...	153.1	622.0	-2.5	-7.7	-2.6	...	...	23.6	0.0	999.9	0.5	...	-2.7	...	...	...	...	...	...
Principal Lines of Business: GrpLife (80.6%), GrpA&H (19.2%), IndA&H (0.2%)																			
950	54.6	30.0	1.7	6.7	11.3	5.04	5.79	-48.1	1.0	21.7	18.4	252.6	16.8	71.7	86.4	13.5	...	21.6	26.3
4,411	53.8	32.8	3.2	18.3	18.0	5.18	6.02	-2.3	0.9	24.7	12.2	222.0	17.8	73.1	88.7	11.2	...	19.2	21.4
670	73.9	40.2	2.3	7.3	12.2	5.19	5.50	-10.6	0.8	25.4	8.6	147.6	-1.2	79.2	93.7	12.8	...	23.3	21.4
-22,242	58.2	46.3	3.9	15.8	21.1	5.31	3.50	24.8	1.2	22.5	1.0	140.7	-14.6	76.8	92.0	13.0	...	31.8	22.2
11,766	48.3	44.6	2.5	9.0	12.9	5.07	6.03	14.5	1.1	27.8	1.1	109.8	19.0	73.0	88.9	31.3	0.1	26.2	16.6
Principal Lines of Business: GrpLife (36.7%), GrpA&H (28.7%), IndA&H (21.4%), GrpAnn (6.5%), OrdLife (5.7%)														Principal States: IL (28.6%), FL (12.1%), NY (9.8%), CA (6.9%), MA (5.8%)					
-4,527	73.5	28.2	3.6	2.8	25.8	6.27	5.06	14.1	8.2	18.9	-0.1	7.8	16.7	70.9	89.5	13.7	...	...	10.1
4,083	69.2	27.5	3.9	3.4	19.1	4.91	10.47	-13.9	4.4	33.4	1.3	5.3	59.6	75.8	97.5	10.1	...	...	...
83	66.3	60.9	7.8	6.9	23.1	5.66	5.63	-19.2	2.9	91.8	-0.2	4.3	22.4	113.7	142.4	7.2	...	...	...
-1,587	76.5	28.9	-1.2	-1.0	-2.4	3.98	0.58	-17.2	2.3	94.7	2.0	7.1	6.0	127.0	149.5	6.7	...	...	...
1,649	74.3	27.8	0.5	0.5	1.1	3.94	4.57	-6.8	2.1	104.4	0.5	4.4	0.8	138.3	165.2	7.6	...	...	...
Principal Lines of Business: GrpA&H (93.8%), GrpLife (4.0%), GrpAnn (2.2%), OrdLife (0.0%), IndA&H (0.0%)														Principal States: IL (53.2%), TX (9.3%), KS (6.4%), WY (3.9%)					

Data in U.S. Dollars

COMPANY NAME Ultimate Parent Association Principal Officer Mailing Address Dom. : Began Bus. : Struct. : Mktg. Specialty Phone # AMB# NAIC#	Best's Financial Strength Rating FSC	Data Year	Balance Sheet Bonds (%)	Mort. Loans & R.E. (%)	Com & Pref. Stock (%)	All Other Assets (%)	Total Assets ($000)	Life Reserves (%)	Health Reserves (%)	Ann Res. & Dep. Liabilities (%)	All Other Liabilities (%)	Capital & Surplus ($000)	Operations Direct Premiums Written ($000)	Net Premiums Written & Deposits ($000)	Operating Cash Flow ($000)	NOG Before Taxes ($000)	NOG After Taxes ($000)	Net Income ($000)
TRUSTMARK LIFE INS CO OF NY Trustmark Mutual Holding Company David M. McDonough CEO 400 Field Drive Lake Forest, IL 60045 NY : 2009 : Mutual : Broker Life 847-615-1500 AMB# 060706 NAIC# 13653	A- Rating Outlook: Stable FSC IX	'05	...	...	...	...	...	...	...	...	...	...	...	...	...	...	...	...
		'06	...	...	...	...	...	...	...	...	...	...	...	...	...	...	...	...
		'07	...	...	...	...	...	...	...	...	...	...	...	...	...	...	...	...
		'08	...	...	...	...	...	...	...	...	...	...	...	...	...	...	...	...
		'09	94.6	...	...	5.4	6,140	...	...	...	100.0	6,081	...	...	6,091	125	82	82
		Rating History: A- g, 01/18/10																
TUFTS ASSOCIATED HMO INC Tufts Associated Health Maint Org Inc James Roosevelt, Jr. President & CEO 705 Mount Auburn Street Watertown, MA 02472-1508 MA : 1981 : Non-Profit : Broker Group A&H, Medicare 617-972-9400 AMB# 068684 NAIC# 95688	NR-5	'05	33.4	...	49.1	17.5	705,808	...	38.7	...	61.3	404,403	1,812,878	1,812,878	-2,860	64,349	64,349	74,375
		'06	32.2	...	45.1	22.7	842,872	...	26.6	...	73.4	481,199	1,699,296	1,699,296	142,554	79,402	79,402	82,834
		'07	30.9	10.6	42.4	16.1	884,136	...	38.4	...	61.6	536,153	2,007,105	2,007,105	48,273	60,284	60,284	76,431
		'08	34.7	12.4	37.4	15.5	738,548	...	42.0	...	58.0	446,326	2,242,061	2,242,061	-65,685	55,044	55,044	8,659
		'09	31.3	11.7	42.9	14.1	801,336	...	44.0	...	56.0	516,801	2,273,001	2,273,001	13,376	23,734	23,734	13,843
		Rating History: NR-5, 03/24/10; NR-5, 08/26/09; B pd, 07/01/08; B pd, 06/12/07; B pd, 07/10/06																
TUFTS INSURANCE CO Tufts Associated Health Maint Org Inc James Roosevelt, Jr. President & CEO 705 Mount Auburn Street Watertown, MA 02472-1508 MA : 1996 : Stock : Not Available Group A&H 617-972-9400 AMB# 060313 NAIC# 60117	NR-5	'05	...	...	...	100.0	21,076	...	59.2	...	40.8	15,590	44,008	32,910	3,780	407	354	354
		'06	...	...	...	100.0	18,940	...	64.1	...	35.9	10,666	54,123	37,927	-2,505	-4,374	-4,374	-4,374
		'07	19.4	...	...	80.6	25,723	...	74.3	...	25.7	16,109	43,589	38,520	6,025	-5,141	-5,141	-5,140
		'08	40.8	...	...	59.2	31,094	...	86.2	...	13.8	15,006	55,723	55,723	1,946	-8,098	-6,447	-7,872
		'09	28.2	...	...	71.8	48,903	...	84.6	...	15.4	23,652	100,940	100,940	17,816	-12,248	-10,502	-10,427
		Rating History: NR-5, 03/24/10; NR-5, 04/08/09; NR-5, 03/20/08; NR-5, 04/02/07; NR-5, 06/03/05																
UAHC HEALTH PLAN OF TN INC United American HealthCare Corp Stephanie Dowell CEO 6555 Quince, Suite 300A Memphis, TN 38119 TN : 1994 : Stock : Broker Medicare 901-348-2201 AMB# 064435	NR-5	'05	57.8	...	...	42.2	12,363	...	...	...	100.0	10,853	2	2	1,130	2,176	1,683	1,683
		'06	53.9	...	...	46.1	13,808	...	...	...	100.0	11,699	...	...	706	1,660	1,291	1,291
		'07	47.2	...	...	52.8	20,372	...	39.3	...	60.7	14,616	5,711	5,711	6,910	798	-179	-179
		'08	57.8	...	...	42.2	18,259	...	36.4	...	63.6	13,100	11,063	10,986	-1,148	1	-417	-417
		'09	22.4	...	...	77.6	10,362	...	64.4	...	35.6	8,111	8,976	8,910	-6,871	-5,648	-5,648	-5,648
		Rating History: NR-5, 03/24/10; NR-5, 03/20/09; NR-5, 04/15/08; NR-5, 05/04/07; NR-5, 07/18/06																
UBS LIFE INSURANCE COMPANY USA[1] David Peterson President 1001 State Street Erie, PA 16501-1834 CA : 1956 : Stock : Not Available Var ann 800-986-0088 AMB# 006882 NAIC# 67423	NR-1	'05	18.5	...	...	81.5	43,479	...	...	...	100.0	28,608	...	3,230	...	6,840	6,637	6,637
		'06	17.0	...	...	83.0	47,181	...	...	...	100.0	35,142	...	1,185	...	3,986	3,886	3,886
		'07	18.8	...	...	81.2	42,518	...	...	...	100.0	36,314	...	1,871	...	3,897	3,824	3,824
		'08	26.4	...	...	73.6	41,393	...	...	...	100.0	37,536	...	1,115	...	1,760	1,744	1,744
		'09	52.0	...	...	48.0	44,075	...	...	...	100.0	38,578	...	438	...	447	471	471
		Rating History: NR-1, 06/10/10; NR-1, 06/12/09; NR-1, 06/12/08; NR-5, 04/30/07; NR-5, 05/11/06																
UCARE MINNESOTA[2] UCare Minnesota Nancy J. Feldman President P.O. Box 52 Minneapolis, MN 55440-0052 MN : 1989 : Non-Profit : Career Agent Medicaid, Medicare 612-676-6500 AMB# 068935 NAIC# 52629	NR-5	'05	50.1	...	...	49.9	279,194	...	56.3	...	43.7	137,563	707,053	704,932	22,515	19,928	19,928	19,871
		'06	45.1	...	6.7	48.2	371,804	...	56.5	...	43.5	169,950	891,218	890,286	91,828	33,981	33,981	33,810
		'07	50.5	...	11.5	38.0	413,566	...	52.4	...	47.6	198,850	1,016,691	1,015,496	37,959	32,248	32,248	31,884
		'08	53.8	...	9.4	36.8	408,265	...	73.7	...	26.3	203,828	1,153,860	1,152,164	2,482	5,282	5,282	3,213
		'09	55.8	...	5.2	38.9	503,095	...	68.1	...	31.9	246,134	1,463,563	1,461,266	70,500	38,520	38,520	37,542
		Rating History: NR-5, 05/26/10; NR-5, 08/26/09; B pd, 10/10/08; B pd, 09/21/07; B pd, 07/10/06																
UDC DENTAL CALIFORNIA INC Assurant Inc Fred R. Cook President 2323 Grand Boulevard Kansas City, MO 64108 CA : 1989 : Stock : Broker Dental 619-236-9595 AMB# 064361 NAIC# 52031	A- Rating Outlook: Stable FSC III	'05	...	...	...	100.0	3,934	...	...	...	100.0	3,606	3,012	3,012	481	861	559	559
		'06	...	...	...	100.0	4,764	...	...	...	100.0	4,083	3,070	3,070	937	742	481	481
		'07	...	...	...	100.0	5,661	...	...	...	100.0	4,789	3,633	3,633	827	1,074	697	697
		'08	...	...	...	100.0	2,429	...	...	...	100.0	1,588	4,569	4,569	-3,313	1,181	767	767
		'09	...	...	...	100.0	3,473	...	...	...	100.0	2,451	5,293	5,293	691	1,359	883	883
		Rating History: A-, 11/18/09; A-, 11/25/08; A-, 06/24/08; A-, 07/17/07; A-, 06/19/06																
UDC OHIO INC Assurant Inc Stacia N. Almquist President 2323 Grand Boulevard Kansas City, MO 64108 OH : 1990 : Stock : Broker Dental 816-474-2345 AMB# 065707 NAIC# 52022	NR-3	'05	23.9	...	...	76.1	851	...	16.0	...	84.0	644	2,097	2,097	152	203	126	126
		'06	22.2	...	...	77.8	912	...	16.9	...	83.1	710	1,598	1,598	59	83	48	48
		'07	20.6	...	...	79.4	977	...	20.6	...	79.4	818	1,390	1,390	96	157	99	99
		'08	19.5	...	...	80.5	1,029	...	24.6	...	75.4	903	1,281	1,281	50	125	78	78
		'09	20.3	...	...	79.7	1,017	...	40.6	...	59.4	935	1,157	1,157	-23	52	36	36
		Rating History: NR-3, 11/18/09; NR-3, 11/25/08; NR-3, 06/24/08; A-, 07/17/07; A-, 06/19/06																
UKRAINIAN NATIONAL ASSOC Stefan Kaczaraj President 2200 Route 10 Parsippany, NJ 07054 NJ : 1894 : Fraternal : Career Agent Ind Life 973-292-9800 AMB# 009821 NAIC# 57215	NR-5	'05	75.5	10.5	6.4	7.7	64,876	61.0	0.0	34.4	4.6	4,263	3,534	3,500	278	-1,283	-1,283	-1,585
		'06	79.3	9.7	5.4	5.6	62,173	62.4	0.0	34.8	2.8	2,852	2,410	2,382	-2,627	-1,906	-1,906	-1,903
		'07	83.8	5.2	2.7	8.3	68,923	59.5	0.0	36.1	4.5	6,773	4,349	4,337	6,578	-1,257	-1,257	-1,206
		'08	88.5	4.4	1.7	5.4	76,798	50.7	0.0	44.4	4.9	4,454	12,774	12,817	8,661	-752	-752	-677
		'09	89.9	3.1	1.4	5.7	110,271	34.6	0.0	62.7	2.7	4,899	35,971	36,290	33,157	-369	-369	-469
		Rating History: NR-5, 04/15/10; NR-5, 04/21/09; NR-5, 04/18/08; NR-5, 05/08/07; NR-5, 04/25/06																

BEST'S PROFITABILITY, LEVERAGE AND LIQUIDITY TESTS 2005 – 2009

Data in U.S. Dollars

	Profitability Tests							Leverage Tests						Liquidity Tests					
Un-Realized Capital Gains ($000)	Benefits Paid to NPW & Dep (%)	Comm. & Expenses to NPW & Dep (%)	NOG to Total Assets (%)	NOG to Total Rev (%)	Operating Return on Equity (%)	Net Yield (%)	Total Return (%)	Change in NPW & Dep (%)	NPW & Dep to Capital (X)	Capital & Surplus to Liabilities (%)	Surplus Relief (%)	Reins Leverage (%)	Change in Capital (%)	Quick Liquidity (%)	Current Liquidity (%)	Non-Invest Grade Bonds to Capital (%)	Delinq. & Foreclosed Mortgages to Capital (%)	Mort. & Credit Tenant Loans & R.E. to Capital (%)	Affiliated Invest to Capital (%)
...	...	...	...	...	...	...	...	...	...	...	...	...	...	...	...	...	...	...	...
...	...	...	...	...	...	...	...	...	...	...	...	...	...	...	...	...	...	...	...
...	...	...	...	...	...	...	...	...	...	...	...	...	...	...	...	...	...	...	...
...	...	...	...	...	...	...	...	...	...	...	...	...	...	...	...	...	...	...	...
...	...	...	...	53.8	...	...	...	...	...	999.9	...	...	...	999.9	999.9	...	...	...	...
-7,974	86.6	11.0	9.1	3.5	17.4	3.17	3.49	11.9	4.5	134.2	...	...	20.0	153.4	173.1	6.2	...	...	4.7
11,214	85.0	11.9	10.3	4.6	17.9	3.68	5.64	-6.3	3.5	133.0	...	...	19.0	164.1	182.1	5.3	...	...	5.3
-13,710	86.6	12.0	7.0	3.0	11.9	3.98	4.30	18.1	3.7	154.1	...	...	11.4	153.5	171.9	3.9	...	17.5	24.1
...	88.4	10.6	6.8	2.4	11.2	4.11	-1.74	11.7	5.0	152.7	...	...	-16.8	143.2	161.7	3.2	...	20.6	29.9
65,836	90.3	9.5	3.1	1.0	4.9	2.66	10.83	1.4	4.4	181.6	...	...	15.8	161.1	183.4	2.3	...	18.1	29.1
	Principal Lines of Business: CompHosp/Med (54.4%), Medicare (44.4%), OtherHlth (1.2%)													Principal States: MA (99.9%)					
...	80.1	20.3	1.8	1.1	2.3	2.93	2.93	105.0	2.1	284.2	...	6.4	2.1	371.3	371.3	...	...	...	...
...	90.9	22.0	-21.9	-11.3	-33.3	4.75	4.75	15.2	3.6	128.9	...	18.9	-31.6	215.9	215.9	...	...	...	...
...	98.5	14.7	-23.0	-13.1	-38.4	4.04	4.04	1.6	2.4	167.6	...	1.1	51.0	196.5	196.5	...	...	...	...
...	95.9	15.3	-22.7	-11.4	-41.4	2.97	-2.59	44.7	3.7	93.3	...	...	-6.8	142.1	144.4	...	...	...	...
...	96.4	14.9	-26.3	-10.4	-54.3	0.82	1.03	81.1	4.3	93.7	...	...	57.6	165.5	167.0	...	...	...	...
	Principal Lines of Business: CompHosp/Med (100.0%)													Principal States: MA (87.7%), RI (12.3%)					
73	-99.9	-99.9	13.4	236.5	14.9	1.63	2.31	-98.4	0.0	718.8	...	...	-7.0	540.8	540.8	...	...	...	...
43	...	...	9.9	129.2	11.4	5.50	5.86	-99.9	...	554.8	...	...	7.8	421.8	421.8	...	...	...	...
122	91.0	-3.6	-1.0	-3.1	-1.4	5.21	5.99	...	0.4	253.9	...	...	24.9	315.7	315.7	...	...	...	...
-35	90.4	37.1	-2.2	-3.0	-3.0	3.72	3.52	92.4	0.8	253.9	...	...	-10.4	326.6	326.6	...	...	...	...
-76	93.6	75.3	-39.5	-59.4	-53.3	1.34	0.79	-18.9	1.1	360.4	...	...	-38.1	453.2	453.2	...	...	...	...
	Principal Lines of Business: Medicare (100.0%)													Principal States: TN (100.0%)					
...	999.9	260.0	16.3	4.3	26.4	...	...	-6.1	0.1	-99.9	0.4	...	31.6	...	...	...	...	...	...
...	999.9	507.9	8.6	2.8	12.2	...	...	-63.3	0.0	-99.9	0.4	...	22.8	...	...	...	...	...	...
...	999.9	492.9	8.5	2.1	10.7	...	...	57.9	0.1	-99.9	0.2	...	3.3	...	...	...	...	...	...
...	999.9	471.0	4.2	1.4	4.7	...	...	-40.4	0.0	-99.9	...	...	3.4	...	...	...	...	...	...
...	999.9	999.9	1.1	0.7	1.2	...	...	-60.8	0.0	999.9	...	...	2.8	...	...	...	...	...	...
	Principal Lines of Business: IndAnn (65.8%), GrpAnn (34.2%)																		
...	90.2	8.2	7.4	2.8	15.5	3.21	3.19	16.3	5.1	97.1	...	0.2	15.8	179.4	187.1	...	...	...	...
...	89.7	8.2	10.4	3.8	22.1	4.96	4.90	26.3	5.2	84.2	...	0.0	23.5	165.4	174.1	...	...	...	...
...	90.0	8.6	8.2	3.1	17.5	5.09	4.99	14.1	5.1	92.6	...	0.1	17.0	165.6	175.3	...	...	...	2.1
...	93.2	6.7	1.3	0.5	2.6	1.16	0.62	13.5	5.7	99.7	...	...	2.5	207.7	219.3	...	...	...	1.3
6,119	91.1	6.9	8.5	2.6	17.1	2.60	3.85	26.8	5.9	95.8	...	...	20.8	220.2	231.2	0.3	...	...	1.4
	Principal Lines of Business: Medicaid (59.7%), Medicare (40.3%), MedSup (0.0%)													Principal States: MN (100.0%)					
...	54.7	19.8	15.4	18.0	16.8	2.81	2.81	-0.1	0.8	999.9	...	...	18.3	806.0	806.0	...	...	...	...
...	61.6	19.8	11.1	14.9	12.5	4.42	4.42	1.9	0.8	599.3	...	...	13.2	525.8	525.8	...	...	...	...
...	56.5	19.7	13.4	18.2	15.7	4.36	4.36	18.4	0.8	549.3	...	...	17.3	505.8	505.8	...	...	...	...
...	56.8	19.8	19.0	16.4	24.1	3.10	3.10	25.8	2.9	189.0	...	...	-66.8	102.8	102.8	...	...	...	...
...	55.0	19.8	29.9	16.6	43.7	1.24	1.24	15.8	2.2	239.8	...	...	54.3	153.0	153.0	...	...	...	...
	Principal Lines of Business: Dental (100.0%)																		
...	58.1	33.2	16.0	6.0	22.0	2.82	2.82	-13.1	3.3	310.8	...	...	28.9	659.3	659.3	...	...	...	...
...	55.6	41.3	5.4	2.9	7.1	4.10	4.10	-23.8	2.2	352.1	...	...	10.4	738.1	738.1	...	...	...	...
...	56.4	34.8	10.5	6.9	12.9	3.94	3.94	-13.0	1.7	514.4	...	...	15.1	999.9	999.9	...	...	...	...
...	56.8	34.9	7.7	6.0	9.0	1.99	1.99	-7.8	1.4	717.6	...	...	10.4	999.9	999.9	...	...	...	...
...	61.0	35.0	3.5	3.1	3.9	0.59	0.59	-9.7	1.2	999.9	...	...	3.6	999.9	999.9	...	...	...	...
	Principal Lines of Business: Dental (100.0%)													Principal States: OH (100.0%)					
127	89.3	93.9	-2.0	-19.7	-26.9	4.74	4.50	-8.0	0.7	8.0	...	0.4	-16.6	76.1	83.1	16.6	...	141.6	73.4
240	182.1	135.1	-3.0	-35.0	-53.6	4.93	5.34	-31.9	0.7	5.8	...	0.5	-28.7	74.4	81.8	15.2	...	176.4	111.4
-131	96.7	68.5	-1.9	-16.1	-26.1	5.46	5.35	82.0	0.6	11.8	...	0.2	112.8	84.6	90.8	11.8	...	49.5	3.8
-537	40.1	24.8	-1.0	-4.5	-13.4	5.67	5.05	195.6	2.6	6.8	...	0.4	-32.4	80.2	86.6	26.9	...	68.6	1.1
179	12.1	9.3	-0.4	-0.9	-7.9	5.41	5.51	183.1	6.7	5.2	...	0.5	10.8	77.0	83.3	35.1	...	62.1	1.0
	Principal Lines of Business: IndAnn (96.5%), OrdLife (3.4%), IndA&H (0.0%)													Principal States: PA (35.8%), FL (29.0%), NJ (8.5%), OH (6.6%), NY (6.5%)					

Data in U.S. Dollars

COMPANY NAME Ultimate Parent Association Principal Officer Mailing Address Dom. : Began Bus. : Struct. : Mktg. Specialty Phone # AMB# NAIC#	Best's Financial Strength Rating FSC	Data Year	Balance Sheet: Bonds (%)	Mort. Loans & R.E. (%)	Com & Pref. Stock (%)	All Other Assets (%)	Total Assets ($000)	Life Reserves (%)	Health Reserves %)	Ann Res. & Dep. Liabilities (%)	All Other Liabilities (%)	Capital & Surplus ($000)	Operations: Direct Premiums Written ($000)	Net Premiums Written & Deposits ($000)	Operating Cash Flow ($000)	NOG Before Taxes ($000)	NOG After Taxes ($000)	Net Income ($000)
ULLICO LIFE INSURANCE COMPANY ULLICO Inc Gary L. Burke President 1625 Eye Street, N.W. Washington, DC 20006 TX : 1948 : Stock : Agency Ann, Univ Life 202-682-0900 AMB# 006316 NAIC# 86371	NR-3	'05	67.3	...	...	32.7	11,769	90.3	...	...	9.7	9,280	1,469	1,457	1,690	440	430	430
		'06	85.3	...	...	14.7	12,958	92.1	...	...	7.9	9,921	1,318	1,308	1,157	635	622	640
		'07	93.0	...	...	7.0	14,293	95.4	...	...	4.6	10,926	1,190	1,183	1,097	810	798	798
		'08	93.7	...	...	6.3	15,300	94.4	...	...	5.6	11,582	1,100	1,075	980	626	617	617
		'09	83.9	...	...	16.1	13,720	97.2	...	...	2.8	9,865	965	960	-1,668	-1,841	-1,820	-1,819
		Rating History: NR-3, 05/22/09; NR-3, 01/25/08; NR-3, 12/07/06; NR-3, 05/08/06; B, 06/16/05																
UNICARE HEALTH INS CO OF TX WellPoint Inc. David W. Fields President 233 South Wacker Drive, Suite 3900 Chicago, IL 60606 TX : 2001 : Stock : Broker Med supp 877-864-2273 AMB# 060368 NAIC# 10076	A- Rating Outlook: Stable FSC IX	'05	...	...	...	100.0	12,127	...	50.0	...	50.0	6,324	16,618	16,618	-1,017	-1,248	-792	-792
		'06	...	...	...	100.0	9,931	...	73.4	...	26.6	6,305	15,652	15,652	-1,670	-73	-40	-40
		'07	...	...	...	100.0	9,429	...	73.2	...	26.8	5,966	15,569	15,569	-662	-638	-471	-471
		'08	...	...	...	100.0	8,987	...	68.9	...	31.1	5,335	15,309	15,309	-481	-880	-659	-659
		'09	...	...	...	100.0	7,380	...	75.3	...	24.7	3,734	13,750	13,750	-2,273	-2,793	-1,835	-1,835
		Rating History: A- g, 04/27/10; A- g, 01/23/09; A- g, 03/20/08; NR-2, 11/06/06; NR-2, 01/03/06																
UNICARE HEALTH INS OF MIDWEST WellPoint Inc. David W. Fields President 233 South Wacker Drive, Suite 3900 Chicago, IL 60606 IL : 1993 : Stock : Broker Group A&H, Ind A&H, Group Life 877-864-2273 AMB# 009437 NAIC# 70700	A- Rating Outlook: Stable FSC IX	'05	78.9	...	...	21.1	136,464	0.2	67.4	...	32.3	32,476	451,552	451,539	-18,209	6,894	2,000	2,000
		'06	78.3	...	...	21.7	137,630	0.3	71.8	...	27.9	41,562	454,971	454,956	10,329	1,593	3,970	3,970
		'07	93.8	...	0.0	6.2	136,664	0.7	74.9	...	24.4	54,559	420,421	420,406	12,808	18,854	12,696	12,462
		'08	92.4	...	...	7.6	129,307	0.5	71.1	...	28.4	48,648	387,281	387,265	-6,120	8,700	5,328	5,329
		'09	111.1	...	...	-11.1	102,452	0.6	69.7	...	29.6	51,249	315,223	315,210	-30,020	11,950	9,256	9,462
		Rating History: A- g, 04/27/10; A- g, 01/23/09; A- g, 03/20/08; A- g, 11/06/06; A- g, 12/29/05																
UNICARE HEALTH PLAN OF KANSAS WellPoint Inc. John P. Monahan President 1 Wellpoint Way Thousand Oaks, CA 91362 KS : Stock : Not Available Health 877-864-2273 AMB# 064878 NAIC# 12805	A- Rating Outlook: Stable FSC IX	'05	...	...	...	...	...	...	...	...	...	...	...	...	...	...	...	...
		'06	...	...	...	100.0	10,135	...	...	...	100.0	9,808	...	...	9,800	13	8	8
		'07	0.8	...	...	99.2	39,602	...	80.5	...	19.5	18,945	114,736	114,736	21,948	15,493	9,949	9,949
		'08	0.6	...	...	99.4	47,906	...	82.1	...	17.9	24,471	125,716	125,716	7,422	8,966	5,002	5,002
		'09	100.2	...	...	-0.2	47,625	...	75.8	...	24.2	32,173	128,095	128,095	-1,916	18,402	12,877	12,883
		Rating History: A- g, 04/27/10; A- g, 01/23/09; A- g, 03/20/08; NR-2, 06/05/07																
UNICARE HEALTH PLAN OF WV WellPoint Inc. John Monahan Executive Director 1 Wellpoint Way Thousand Oaks, CA 91362 WV : 2003 : Stock : Broker Health 877-864-2273 AMB# 064776 NAIC# 11810	A- Rating Outlook: Stable FSC IX	'05	...	...	...	100.0	26,536	...	90.3	...	9.7	9,619	90,557	90,557	5,663	471	326	326
		'06	10.2	...	...	89.8	50,277	...	51.2	...	48.8	23,262	137,911	137,911	10,391	5,594	3,666	3,666
		'07	10.9	...	...	89.1	46,903	...	90.2	...	9.8	27,749	141,231	141,231	6,399	5,693	4,565	4,565
		'08	0.4	...	...	99.6	57,744	...	82.7	...	17.3	33,551	151,271	151,271	11,910	9,551	5,797	5,797
		'09	76.8	...	...	23.2	59,242	...	85.4	...	14.6	43,540	155,100	155,100	3,781	19,575	13,176	13,292
		Rating History: A- g, 04/27/10; A- g, 01/23/09; A- g, 03/20/08; NR-2, 11/06/06; NR-2, 01/03/06																
UNICARE HEALTH PLANS OF TX WellPoint Inc. David W. Fields President 233 S. Wacker Drive, Suite 3900 Chicago, IL 60606 TX : 1996 : Stock : Broker Group A&H, Health 877-864-2273 AMB# 064240 NAIC# 95420	A- Rating Outlook: Stable FSC IX	'05	47.8	...	...	52.2	38,382	...	65.9	...	34.1	28,319	66,100	66,100	6,771	4,186	3,300	3,300
		'06	39.8	...	...	60.2	46,303	...	68.0	...	32.0	33,823	69,852	69,852	5,252	6,622	4,736	4,736
		'07	36.5	...	...	63.5	50,426	...	80.4	...	19.6	31,612	102,911	102,911	3,428	-4,360	-2,959	-3,107
		'08	37.4	...	...	62.6	49,217	...	81.3	...	18.7	27,555	104,469	104,469	-2,641	-1,333	-1,067	-1,067
		'09	85.3	...	...	14.7	49,733	...	79.1	...	20.9	33,423	119,754	119,754	1,031	8,401	7,263	7,229
		Rating History: A- g, 04/27/10; A- g, 01/23/09; A- g, 03/20/08; A- g, 11/06/06; A- g, 12/29/05																
UNICARE HEALTH PLANS MIDWEST WellPoint Inc. David W. Fields President 233 South Wacker Drive, Suite 3900 Chicago, IL 60606 IL : 1993 : Stock : Broker Group A&H, Health 877-864-2273 AMB# 068895 NAIC# 95505	A- Rating Outlook: Stable FSC IX	'05	62.9	...	...	37.1	131,902	...	37.0	...	63.0	39,026	373,033	373,033	-21,167	304	2,400	2,000
		'06	51.5	...	...	48.5	159,383	...	36.6	...	63.4	52,454	377,770	377,770	3,845	11,205	10,083	10,097
		'07	56.9	...	0.0	43.1	150,144	...	50.4	...	49.6	69,445	361,475	361,475	9,050	24,253	16,679	16,676
		'08	61.0	...	...	39.0	136,758	...	53.6	...	46.4	58,203	334,474	334,474	-10,680	10,517	5,722	5,723
		'09	64.0	...	...	36.0	148,652	...	42.6	...	57.4	63,983	300,834	300,834	1,782	17,833	12,137	12,135
		Rating History: A- g, 04/27/10; A- g, 01/23/09; A- g, 03/20/08; A- g, 11/06/06; A- g, 12/29/05																
UNICARE LIFE & HEALTH INS CO WellPoint Inc. David W. Fields President & CEO 120 Monument Circle Indianapolis, IN 46204-4903 IN : 1980 : Stock : Not Available A&H 877-864-2273 AMB# 009233 NAIC# 80314	A- Rating Outlook: Stable FSC IX	'05	82.7	...	0.9	16.4	1,258,803	18.3	35.3	17.0	29.4	287,986	1,631,695	1,671,027	-13,030	27,851	16,366	16,243
		'06	71.4	...	0.4	28.2	1,491,396	13.9	33.1	12.3	40.7	278,102	2,376,612	2,425,701	27,741	158,656	117,628	116,215
		'07	73.7	...	0.7	25.6	1,725,805	12.1	28.5	10.2	49.2	344,935	2,593,165	2,645,980	242,218	136,498	116,759	111,596
		'08	78.1	...	0.6	21.4	1,636,272	12.1	33.7	11.0	43.2	361,461	2,855,967	2,928,177	-8,722	58,183	34,520	7,077
		'09	74.6	...	...	25.4	1,482,436	13.4	19.3	13.0	54.2	381,336	2,415,583	2,525,216	-240,532	253,045	181,710	156,488
		Rating History: A- g, 04/27/10; A- g, 01/23/09; A- g, 03/20/08; A- g, 11/06/06; A- g, 12/29/05																
UNIFIED LIFE INSURANCE COMPANY John E. Tiller, Jr. President 7201 West 129th Street, Suite 300 Overland Park, KS 66213 TX : 2001 : Stock : Agency Ind A&H, Group A&H, Ordinary Life 877-492-4678 AMB# 060366 NAIC# 11121	B++ Rating Outlook: Stable FSC V	'05	75.3	0.8	0.0	23.8	134,979	64.7	16.2	12.9	6.2	24,074	61,122	28,746	5,070	3,944	2,956	3,153
		'06	73.1	0.5	0.0	26.3	133,370	69.0	12.4	12.6	6.0	21,092	46,842	27,757	4,779	3,805	2,859	2,863
		'07	65.1	0.5	0.0	34.4	143,101	67.3	13.1	10.6	9.0	20,536	39,477	27,303	10,303	2,904	3,112	3,112
		'08	56.8	0.5	...	42.8	148,950	68.0	15.0	9.9	7.1	23,488	31,522	29,475	3,513	3,945	3,355	3,355
		'09	77.3	0.3	...	22.4	139,062	68.5	14.9	9.4	7.2	14,317	25,572	28,708	29,284	3,649	3,332	3,332
		Rating History: B++, 05/28/10; B++, 05/15/09; B++, 06/24/08; B++, 06/20/07; A-, 06/07/06																

BEST'S PROFITABILITY, LEVERAGE AND LIQUIDITY TESTS 2005 – 2009

Data in U.S. Dollars

	Profitability Tests							Leverage Tests						Liquidity Tests						
Un-Realized Capital Gains ($000)	Benefits Paid to NPW & Dep (%)	Comm. & Expenses to NPW & Dep (%)	NOG to Total Assets (%)	NOG to Total Rev (%)	Operating Return on Equity (%)	Net Yield (%)	Total Return (%)	Change in NPW & Dep (%)	NPW & Dep to Capital (X)	Capital & Surplus to Liabilities (%)	Surplus Relief (%)	Reins Leverage (%)	Change in Capital (%)	Quick Liquidity (%)	Current Liquidity (%)	Non-Invest Grade Bonds to Capital (%)	Delinq. & Foreclosed Mortgages to Capital (%)	Mort. & Credit Tenant Loans & R.E. to Capital (%)	Affiliated Invest to Capital (%)
...	22.5	28.0	3.8	24.3	4.7	2.50	2.50	25.6	0.2	372.9	0.0	196.0	4.9	576.2	589.4	...	...	...	...
...	18.6	27.1	5.0	34.6	6.5	3.84	4.03	-10.2	0.1	326.7	0.0	26.2	6.9	436.5	436.5	...	...	...	...
...	27.2	18.4	5.9	44.8	7.7	4.39	4.46	-9.5	0.1	324.9	0.0	22.2	10.2	383.4	386.5	...	...	...	...
...	28.2	42.2	4.2	36.9	5.5	4.08	4.15	-9.2	0.1	311.8	...	20.9	6.0	370.5	373.1	...	...	...	...
...	48.3	279.1	-12.5	-99.9	-17.0	3.69	3.75	-10.7	0.1	256.2	0.0	24.8	-14.8	348.6	351.1	...	...	...	...
Principal Lines of Business: OrdLife (100.0%)														Principal States: IL (23.6%), HI (8.9%), OH (7.6%), CA (6.6%), PA (6.4%)					
...	76.7	33.6	6.1	4.7	-11.7	2.77	2.77	19.4	2.6	109.0	...	...	-12.9	363.6	363.9	...	...	...	...
...	76.4	27.3	-0.4	-0.2	-0.6	5.25	5.25	-5.8	2.5	173.9	...	...	-0.3	493.5	497.0	...	...	...	...
...	82.7	24.0	-4.9	-3.0	-7.7	4.93	4.93	-0.5	2.6	172.3	...	...	-5.4	457.4	482.3	...	...	...	...
...	83.2	24.1	-7.2	-4.2	-11.7	3.07	3.07	-1.7	2.9	146.1	...	...	-10.6	384.2	403.7	...	...	...	...
...	99.7	19.1	-22.4	-13.3	-40.5	0.30	0.30	-10.2	3.7	102.4	...	...	-30.0	146.3	146.3	...	...	...	...
Principal Lines of Business: MedSup (100.0%)														Principal States: TX (100.0%)					
...	76.4	22.5	1.4	0.4	6.4	4.29	4.29	14.1	13.9	31.2	...	0.1	6.8	94.9	95.2	...	...	...	...
...	82.0	19.0	2.9	0.9	10.7	4.81	4.81	0.8	10.9	43.3	...	0.1	28.0	125.9	127.0	...	...	...	...
1	79.7	17.2	9.3	3.0	26.4	5.31	5.11	-7.6	7.7	66.4	0.0	0.1	31.3	149.7	150.1	...	...	...	...
-1	81.5	16.8	4.0	1.4	10.3	4.40	4.40	-7.9	8.0	60.3	0.0	0.1	-10.8	142.3	142.6	...	...	...	...
...	80.4	19.3	8.0	2.8	18.5	4.17	4.37	-18.6	6.2	100.1	0.0	0.1	5.3	175.1	176.5	...	...	...	...
Principal Lines of Business: CompHosp/Med (96.6%), MedSup (2.8%), Life (0.5%), OtherHlth (0.0%), FEHBP (0.0%)														Principal States: IL (98.9%)					
...	...	...	...	...	...	...	...	...	...	...	...	...	...	...	...	...	...	...	...
...	...	...	...	...	...	...	...	...	...	999.9	...	...	...	999.9	999.9	...	...	...	...
...	80.2	7.3	40.0	8.6	69.2	6.10	6.10	...	6.1	91.7	...	...	93.2	298.1	314.2	...	...	...	...
...	84.9	7.6	11.4	3.9	23.0	3.55	3.55	9.6	5.1	104.4	...	...	29.2	330.1	335.4	...	...	...	...
...	77.6	10.2	27.0	10.0	45.5	2.94	2.95	1.9	4.0	208.2	...	...	31.5	176.4	200.5	...	...	...	...
Principal Lines of Business: Medicaid (86.0%), CompHosp/Med (14.0%)														Principal States: KS (100.0%)					
...	87.0	12.8	1.5	0.4	4.7	3.04	3.04	83.8	9.4	56.9	...	...	124.9	160.8	164.0	...	...	...	...
...	83.3	12.0	9.5	2.7	22.3	4.70	4.70	52.3	5.9	86.1	...	...	141.8	165.2	165.3	...	...	...	...
...	86.9	9.1	9.4	3.2	17.9	4.86	4.86	2.4	5.1	144.9	...	...	19.3	283.6	298.1	...	...	...	...
...	86.3	8.2	11.1	3.8	18.9	3.50	3.50	7.1	4.5	138.7	...	...	20.9	312.4	316.6	...	...	...	...
...	77.9	10.1	22.5	8.4	34.2	2.17	2.44	2.5	3.6	277.3	...	...	29.8	228.2	251.6	...	...	...	...
Principal Lines of Business: Medicaid (100.0%)														Principal States: WV (100.0%)					
...	79.4	15.8	9.1	4.9	12.8	3.32	3.32	0.3	2.3	281.4	...	...	21.4	491.2	491.9	...	...	...	...
...	81.3	13.0	11.2	6.6	15.2	4.43	4.43	5.7	2.1	271.0	...	...	19.4	485.8	486.1	...	...	...	...
...	92.5	11.6	-6.1	-2.8	-9.0	5.01	4.65	47.3	3.3	168.0	...	...	-6.5	355.1	369.3	...	...	...	...
...	91.7	9.8	-2.1	-1.0	-3.6	3.78	3.78	1.5	3.8	127.2	...	...	-12.8	278.8	287.2	...	...	...	...
...	84.6	11.8	14.7	6.0	23.8	3.09	3.01	14.6	3.6	204.9	...	...	21.3	217.8	229.9	...	...	...	...
Principal Lines of Business: Medicaid (52.7%), CompHosp/Med (47.3%)														Principal States: TX (100.0%)					
...	85.5	16.2	1.7	0.6	5.9	4.52	4.11	-7.1	9.6	42.0	...	...	-6.3	98.3	98.7	...	...	...	...
...	87.4	10.8	6.9	2.6	22.0	4.69	4.70	1.3	7.2	49.1	...	...	34.4	90.1	91.2	...	...	...	...
1	86.1	8.4	10.8	4.6	27.4	4.54	4.54	-4.3	5.2	86.1	...	...	32.4	131.8	133.2	...	...	...	...
-1	89.0	9.0	4.0	1.7	9.0	3.92	3.92	-7.5	5.7	74.1	...	...	-16.2	109.0	109.3	...	...	...	...
...	84.8	11.3	8.5	4.0	19.9	3.90	3.90	-10.1	4.7	75.6	...	...	9.9	103.8	104.1	...	...	...	...
Principal Lines of Business: CompHosp/Med (86.0%), FEHBP (14.0%)														Principal States: IL (97.2%)					
-22	79.0	18.0	1.3	1.0	5.6	4.85	5.00	2.6	5.7	30.3	0.5	18.2	-3.8	87.7	99.3	23.9	...	...	...
222	78.6	14.5	8.6	4.9	41.6	5.58	5.57	45.2	8.6	23.5	0.4	19.4	-3.2	74.9	85.0	26.9	...	...	...
305	81.3	13.4	7.3	4.4	37.5	5.89	5.60	9.1	7.6	25.1	0.4	14.6	22.1	73.3	83.6	31.4	...	...	...
-1,828	85.9	11.9	2.1	1.2	9.8	5.76	3.70	10.7	8.1	28.4	0.4	14.6	4.4	76.3	87.1	29.6	...	...	...
1,344	77.8	13.2	11.7	7.3	48.9	5.82	4.07	-13.8	6.6	34.6	0.5	16.9	5.5	72.3	83.1	28.8	...	...	...
Principal Lines of Business: IndA&H (67.4%), GrpA&H (22.8%), GrpLife (5.9%), IndAnn (3.7%), GrpAnn (0.1%)														Principal States: TX (21.0%), IN (7.1%), FL (7.0%), MI (6.3%), MN (6.2%)					
...	92.7	15.6	2.2	6.4	11.8	5.11	5.35	-3.9	1.2	21.9	25.9	55.1	-7.8	95.9	99.4	0.3	...	4.6	...
120	96.1	30.2	2.1	6.7	12.7	5.25	5.42	-3.4	1.3	18.9	12.5	38.4	-12.6	102.3	104.9	...	...	3.4	...
...	89.2	37.3	2.3	7.9	15.0	4.99	5.04	-1.6	1.3	16.9	6.1	51.1	-2.6	100.6	102.9	...	...	3.4	...
...	95.3	37.3	2.3	8.1	15.2	4.48	4.51	8.0	1.2	18.8	5.9	33.3	14.3	113.8	117.5	2.0	...	2.9	...
...	96.2	37.9	2.3	7.9	17.6	5.51	5.55	-2.6	2.0	11.7	9.4	76.6	-38.5	67.1	74.1	28.0	...	2.6	...
Principal Lines of Business: IndA&H (43.9%), GrpA&H (31.4%), OrdLife (23.1%), GrpLife (0.9%), IndAnn (0.7%)														Principal States: TX (21.6%), NH (9.4%), IL (8.8%), MA (7.4%), CA (5.7%)					

Data in U.S. Dollars

Column key: COMPANY NAME; Ultimate Parent Association; Principal Officer; Mailing Address; Dom. : Began Bus. : Struct. : Mktg.; Specialty; Phone #; AMB#; NAIC#; Best's Financial Strength Rating; FSC. Balance Sheet: Bonds (%), Mort. Loans & R.E. (%), Com & Pref. Stock (%), All Other Assets (%), Total Assets ($000), Life Reserves (%), Health Reserves (%), Ann Res. & Dep. Liabilities (%), All Other Liabilities (%), Capital & Surplus ($000). Operations: Direct Premiums Written ($000), Net Premiums Written & Deposits ($000), Operating Cash Flow ($000), NOG Before Taxes ($000), NOG After Taxes ($000), Net Income ($000).

UNIMERICA INSURANCE COMPANY
UnitedHealth Group Inc
Diane D. Souza
President & CEO
3900 McCarty Lane, Suite 220
Lafayette, IN 47905-8701
WI : 1980 : Stock : Broker
Reins
952-936-3956
AMB# 009065 NAIC# 91529

Best's Financial Strength Rating: **A** — Rating Outlook: Stable — **FSC VIII**

Data Year	Bonds (%)	Mort. Loans & R.E. (%)	Com & Pref. Stock (%)	All Other Assets (%)	Total Assets ($000)	Life Reserves (%)	Health Reserves (%)	Ann Res. & Dep. Liabilities (%)	All Other Liabilities (%)	Capital & Surplus ($000)	Direct Premiums Written ($000)	Net Premiums Written & Deposits ($000)	Operating Cash Flow ($000)	NOG Before Taxes ($000)	NOG After Taxes ($000)	Net Income ($000)
'05	12.8	...	...	87.2	54,783	14.8	58.2	0.3	26.6	28,761	45,965	55,451	10,616	6,952	4,270	4,270
'06	7.7	...	...	92.3	94,298	13.0	47.4	2.6	37.0	37,716	64,072	89,779	42,323	13,053	8,428	8,428
'07	32.4	...	...	67.6	150,182	22.0	54.7	4.1	19.2	60,084	146,273	162,763	29,705	8,995	5,326	5,326
'08	73.4	...	...	26.6	244,431	24.9	60.9	0.9	13.3	104,728	258,929	262,510	109,926	-7,554	-5,096	-5,511
'09	77.9	...	...	22.1	262,067	26.4	50.2	1.9	21.5	112,957	241,108	237,422	23,492	7,834	5,075	5,235

Rating History: A g, 06/15/09; A g, 01/29/08; A g, 11/21/07; A g, 11/16/06; A, 08/17/06

UNIMERICA LIFE INS CO OF NY
UnitedHealth Group Inc
Diane D. Souza
President
48 Monroe Turnpike
Trumbull, CT 06611
NY : 2003 : Stock : Broker
Group A&H, Group Life
877-832-7734
AMB# 060392 NAIC# 11596

Best's Financial Strength Rating: **A** — Rating Outlook: Stable — **FSC VIII**

Data Year	Bonds (%)	Mort. Loans & R.E. (%)	Com & Pref. Stock (%)	All Other Assets (%)	Total Assets ($000)	Life Reserves (%)	Health Reserves (%)	Ann Res. & Dep. Liabilities (%)	All Other Liabilities (%)	Capital & Surplus ($000)	Direct Premiums Written ($000)	Net Premiums Written & Deposits ($000)	Operating Cash Flow ($000)	NOG Before Taxes ($000)	NOG After Taxes ($000)	Net Income ($000)
'05	90.2	...	...	9.8	7,252	...	84.7	...	15.3	6,701	914	876	184	160	104	104
'06	62.8	...	...	37.2	10,585	44.3	36.6	...	19.1	6,322	3,340	3,336	2,366	-574	-365	-365
'07	46.7	...	...	53.3	15,043	28.9	51.3	8.7	11.1	6,686	7,114	7,609	3,409	-1,822	-1,877	-1,877
'08	27.8	...	...	72.2	25,810	31.8	62.4	0.7	5.0	16,284	9,487	8,720	11,332	135	81	24
'09	58.4	...	...	41.6	29,936	17.0	55.8	0.4	26.8	17,606	8,150	7,068	3,782	2,078	1,748	1,758

Rating History: A g, 06/15/09; A g, 01/29/08; A g, 11/21/07; A g, 11/16/06; A g, 08/17/06

UNION BANKERS INS CO
Universal American Corp.
Gary W. Bryant
President & CEO
P.O. Box 958465
Lake Mary, FL 32795-8465
TX : 1953 : Stock : Agency
Ind A&H, Life
407-995-8000
AMB# 007149 NAIC# 69701

Best's Financial Strength Rating: **B+** — Rating Outlook: Stable — **FSC VI**

Data Year	Bonds (%)	Mort. Loans & R.E. (%)	Com & Pref. Stock (%)	All Other Assets (%)	Total Assets ($000)	Life Reserves (%)	Health Reserves (%)	Ann Res. & Dep. Liabilities (%)	All Other Liabilities (%)	Capital & Surplus ($000)	Direct Premiums Written ($000)	Net Premiums Written & Deposits ($000)	Operating Cash Flow ($000)	NOG Before Taxes ($000)	NOG After Taxes ($000)	Net Income ($000)
'05	79.0	...	...	21.0	98,462	55.6	28.7	7.9	7.7	9,676	53,185	18,573	3,333	-1,571	-1,165	-1,161
'06	78.9	...	...	21.1	99,578	57.6	27.7	7.7	7.0	13,071	59,743	22,172	501	2,389	2,707	3,292
'07	67.9	...	...	32.1	104,521	56.2	29.0	7.3	7.5	14,543	53,419	28,297	5,534	1,159	1,153	1,153
'08	67.2	...	...	32.8	107,233	56.7	30.1	7.2	6.0	18,494	48,343	45,716	3,924	4,452	4,431	3,767
'09	83.3	...	...	16.7	66,424	0.4	89.8	...	9.8	36,719	47,329	-8,870	-39,269	8,375	8,083	8,045

Rating History: B+, 04/16/10; B+, 12/03/08; B+, 08/21/07; B+, 06/21/06; B+, 06/09/05

UNION CENTRAL LIFE INS CO
UNIFI Mutual Holding Company
JoAnn M. Martin
Chair
P.O. Box 40888
Cincinnati, OH 45240
NE : 1867 : Stock : General Agent
Life, Disability, Ann
513-595-2200
AMB# 007150 NAIC# 80837

Best's Financial Strength Rating: **A** — Rating Outlook: Stable — **FSC XIII**

Data Year	Bonds (%)	Mort. Loans & R.E. (%)	Com & Pref. Stock (%)	All Other Assets (%)	Total Assets ($000)	Life Reserves (%)	Health Reserves (%)	Ann Res. & Dep. Liabilities (%)	All Other Liabilities (%)	Capital & Surplus ($000)	Direct Premiums Written ($000)	Net Premiums Written & Deposits ($000)	Operating Cash Flow ($000)	NOG Before Taxes ($000)	NOG After Taxes ($000)	Net Income ($000)
'05	52.4	8.0	0.6	39.0	6,685,105	26.4	3.8	31.9	37.9	336,939	954,752	974,099	128,519	16,538	12,340	18,332
'06	49.1	7.4	2.4	41.1	7,093,698	26.5	3.7	30.4	39.4	327,083	1,001,583	1,031,862	142,820	-12,818	-9,480	-9,075
'07	47.9	7.6	3.0	41.5	7,284,871	27.8	3.7	28.6	39.9	321,059	1,020,456	1,022,499	116,901	2,528	5,399	-105
'08	54.7	8.9	2.7	33.7	6,310,581	33.6	4.5	32.7	29.2	266,977	1,095,935	1,086,711	51,372	-19,782	-21,472	-156,271
'09	56.4	8.4	0.3	34.9	6,743,143	32.5	4.3	32.5	30.6	400,877	882,585	850,224	194,562	36,653	40,096	-119,780

Rating History: A g, 04/13/10; A g, 01/30/09; A g, 05/01/08; A g, 02/02/07; A, 01/04/06

UNION FIDELITY LIFE INS CO
General Electric Company
Michael Barnett
President
500 Virginia Drive
Fort Washington, PA 19034
IL : 1926 : Stock : Inactive
Credit Life, Group Life, Ind Life
215-542-4590
AMB# 006297 NAIC# 62596

Best's Financial Strength Rating: **A-** — Rating Outlook: Stable — **FSC X**

Data Year	Bonds (%)	Mort. Loans & R.E. (%)	Com & Pref. Stock (%)	All Other Assets (%)	Total Assets ($000)	Life Reserves (%)	Health Reserves (%)	Ann Res. & Dep. Liabilities (%)	All Other Liabilities (%)	Capital & Surplus ($000)	Direct Premiums Written ($000)	Net Premiums Written & Deposits ($000)	Operating Cash Flow ($000)	NOG Before Taxes ($000)	NOG After Taxes ($000)	Net Income ($000)
'05	88.2	5.5	0.4	5.8	19,119,732	1.5	12.4	79.1	6.9	891,265	106,985	439,154	-211,795	87,488	151,777	166,430
'06	84.8	6.2	4.0	5.0	18,253,645	1.4	14.2	78.0	6.5	772,796	93,580	394,765	-634,534	44,010	65,407	32,681
'07	84.9	6.7	3.6	4.9	18,204,149	1.4	15.4	74.7	8.5	414,434	83,159	362,614	-96,882	-83,471	-41,378	-41,027
'08	82.1	6.2	3.5	8.1	18,264,425	1.3	18.5	74.4	5.8	456,312	73,988	357,611	-336,936	-240,551	-195,449	-512,110
'09	89.4	5.6	0.5	4.5	18,377,842	1.3	20.8	72.3	5.6	611,682	65,888	344,692	524,723	-55,700	4,574	32,730

Rating History: A- g, 05/27/09; A- g, 06/09/08; A-, 06/13/07; A-, 06/12/06; A-, 06/23/05

UNION LABOR LIFE INS CO
ULLICO Inc
Gary L. Burke
President
1625 Eye Street, N.W.
Washington, DC 20006
MD : 1927 : Stock : Direct Response
Group A&H, Group Life, Group pens
202-682-0900
AMB# 007152 NAIC# 69744

Best's Financial Strength Rating: **B+** — Rating Outlook: Stable — **FSC VII**

Data Year	Bonds (%)	Mort. Loans & R.E. (%)	Com & Pref. Stock (%)	All Other Assets (%)	Total Assets ($000)	Life Reserves (%)	Health Reserves (%)	Ann Res. & Dep. Liabilities (%)	All Other Liabilities (%)	Capital & Surplus ($000)	Direct Premiums Written ($000)	Net Premiums Written & Deposits ($000)	Operating Cash Flow ($000)	NOG Before Taxes ($000)	NOG After Taxes ($000)	Net Income ($000)
'05	11.1	0.5	0.3	88.1	3,347,083	2.9	2.6	4.9	89.6	139,715	225,921	264,166	-3,566	53,733	52,327	47,224
'06	10.0	0.6	0.3	89.0	3,496,021	2.7	2.2	4.5	90.6	139,356	196,174	223,538	-11,478	-672	-685	-354
'07	7.9	0.4	0.3	91.4	4,058,035	2.4	1.8	3.8	92.0	126,204	161,211	200,777	-39,155	-16,880	-16,482	-16,482
'08	6.6	0.4	0.3	92.7	4,364,925	2.2	1.7	3.3	92.9	107,849	118,938	179,690	-51,874	5,784	5,719	4,147
'09	8.1	0.3	0.3	91.3	3,882,289	2.4	1.8	3.7	92.2	92,058	97,658	168,299	2,980	9,209	9,060	8,713

Rating History: B+, 05/22/09; B+, 01/25/08; B+, 12/07/06; B+, 05/08/06; B, 06/16/05

UNION LIFE INS CO
Munich Reinsurance Company
John W. Hayden
Chairman & CEO
P.O. Box 5323
Cincinnati, OH 45201-5323
AR : 1999 : Stock : Inactive
Credit A&H, Credit Life
513-943-7200
AMB# 009489 NAIC# 83909

Best's Financial Strength Rating: **NR-3**

Data Year	Bonds (%)	Mort. Loans & R.E. (%)	Com & Pref. Stock (%)	All Other Assets (%)	Total Assets ($000)	Life Reserves (%)	Health Reserves (%)	Ann Res. & Dep. Liabilities (%)	All Other Liabilities (%)	Capital & Surplus ($000)	Direct Premiums Written ($000)	Net Premiums Written & Deposits ($000)	Operating Cash Flow ($000)	NOG Before Taxes ($000)	NOG After Taxes ($000)	Net Income ($000)
'05	...	...	...	100.0	169	62.7	12.4	...	24.9	149	...	3	4	13	8	8
'06	...	...	...	100.0	163	...	...	...	100.0	120	...	...	-20	13	13	13
'07	...	...	...	100.0	118	...	...	...	100.0	118	...	...	-42	-2	-2	-2
'08	...	...	...	100.0	117	...	...	...	100.0	117	...	...	4	-2	-1	-1
'09	...	...	...	100.0	120	...	...	...	100.0	120	...	...	3	4	3	3

Rating History: NR-3, 03/10/10; NR-3, 05/15/09; NR-3, 04/09/08; NR-3, 10/18/07; NR-3, 05/31/07

UNION NATIONAL LIFE INS CO
Unitrin, Inc
Don M. Royster, Sr.
President
12115 Lackland Road
St. Louis, MO 63146-4003
LA : 1930 : Stock : Career Agent
Home serv, Ind A&H, Ind Life
314-819-4300
AMB# 007155 NAIC# 69779

Best's Financial Strength Rating: **A-** — Rating Outlook: Stable — **FSC IX**

Data Year	Bonds (%)	Mort. Loans & R.E. (%)	Com & Pref. Stock (%)	All Other Assets (%)	Total Assets ($000)	Life Reserves (%)	Health Reserves (%)	Ann Res. & Dep. Liabilities (%)	All Other Liabilities (%)	Capital & Surplus ($000)	Direct Premiums Written ($000)	Net Premiums Written & Deposits ($000)	Operating Cash Flow ($000)	NOG Before Taxes ($000)	NOG After Taxes ($000)	Net Income ($000)
'05	72.8	0.5	6.5	20.2	444,825	90.8	2.1	0.3	6.9	104,827	83,214	84,239	22,531	12,415	11,512	10,266
'06	67.5	1.1	1.1	30.4	414,120	92.2	2.2	...	5.6	56,056	87,774	87,756	-25,536	13,275	8,383	14,910
'07	68.5	1.0	0.4	30.1	429,710	93.0	2.3	...	4.7	62,336	81,921	81,907	15,007	18,818	11,948	11,485
'08	70.9	1.0	4.2	23.9	448,668	93.5	2.3	...	4.2	68,715	78,411	78,390	17,314	17,733	11,292	9,986
'09	86.9	0.2	...	12.9	15,371	...	...	...	100.0	10,144	79,681	-6,792	-402,284	13,328	13,149	12,864

Rating History: A- r, 05/25/10; A- g, 04/10/09; A g, 05/05/08; A g, 04/06/07; A g, 04/28/06

UNION SECURITY DENTALCARE NJ
Assurant Inc
Stacia N. Almquist
President
2323 Grand Boulevard
Kansas City, MO 64108-2670
NJ : 1984 : Stock : Broker
Dental
816-474-2345
AMB# 064677 NAIC# 11244

Best's Financial Strength Rating: **A-** — Rating Outlook: Stable — **FSC III**

Data Year	Bonds (%)	Mort. Loans & R.E. (%)	Com & Pref. Stock (%)	All Other Assets (%)	Total Assets ($000)	Life Reserves (%)	Health Reserves (%)	Ann Res. & Dep. Liabilities (%)	All Other Liabilities (%)	Capital & Surplus ($000)	Direct Premiums Written ($000)	Net Premiums Written & Deposits ($000)	Operating Cash Flow ($000)	NOG Before Taxes ($000)	NOG After Taxes ($000)	Net Income ($000)
'05	4.2	...	...	95.8	1,311	...	0.6	...	99.4	926	2,243	2,243	-104	33	0	0
'06	1.9	...	...	98.1	2,906	...	0.5	...	99.5	2,463	1,996	1,996	1,609	85	12	12
'07	1.8	...	...	98.2	3,112	...	0.6	...	99.4	2,610	1,789	1,789	177	120	58	59
'08	2.0	...	...	98.0	2,813	...	0.3	...	99.7	2,591	577	577	-177	47	110	110
'09	2.0	...	...	98.0	2,776	...	0.1	...	99.9	2,604	514	514	-39	9	9	9

Rating History: A-, 11/18/09; A-, 11/25/08; A-, 06/24/08; A-, 07/17/07; A-, 06/19/06

BEST'S PROFITABILITY, LEVERAGE AND LIQUIDITY TESTS 2005 – 2009

Data in U.S. Dollars

	Profitability Tests							Leverage Tests						Liquidity Tests					
Un-Realized Capital Gains ($000)	Benefits Paid to NPW & Dep (%)	Comm. & Expenses to NPW & Dep (%)	NOG to Total Assets (%)	NOG to Total Rev (%)	Operating Return on Equity (%)	Net Yield (%)	Total Return (%)	Change in NPW & Dep (%)	NPW & Dep to Capital (X)	Capital & Surplus to Liabilities (%)	Surplus Relief (%)	Reins Leverage (%)	Change in Capital (%)	Quick Liquidity (%)	Current Liquidity (%)	Non-Invest Grade Bonds to Capital (%)	Delinq. & Foreclosed Mortgages to Capital (%)	Mort. & Credit Tenant Loans & R.E. to Capital (%)	Affiliated Invest to Capital (%)
...	50.0	22.7	8.5	7.6	15.1	3.31	3.33	28.1	1.9	110.7	1.1	3.7	3.8	261.3	271.2	...	...	...	...
...	44.4	24.9	11.3	9.7	25.4	4.92	4.93	61.9	2.4	66.8	0.7	16.8	31.2	279.3	293.3	...	...	...	...
...	47.4	21.0	4.4	3.5	10.9	4.47	4.48	81.3	2.7	66.8	1.9	36.1	59.3	186.8	196.5	...	...	...	...
-8	65.7	20.1	-2.6	-1.9	-6.2	3.80	3.56	61.3	2.5	75.0	1.4	31.8	74.1	167.1	181.0	0.0	...	...	...
8	80.6	20.2	2.0	2.1	4.7	3.08	3.20	-9.6	2.1	76.0	1.9	42.9	8.0	162.4	177.4	...	...	...	...
Principal Lines of Business: GrpA&H (69.0%), GrpLife (28.7%), IndA&H (1.5%), IndAnn (0.7%), OrdLife (0.0%)														Principal States: TX (14.2%), CA (10.1%), AL (7.5%), IL (6.7%), PA (6.3%)					
...	36.4	30.1	1.4	0.3	1.6	3.32	3.33	613.0	0.1	000.0	0.0	0.8	1.6	000.0	000.0	...	...	...	...
...	7.8	30.8	-4.1	-10.1	-5.6	3.55	3.51	280.7	0.5	148.7	...	0.5	-5.6	269.5	280.7	...	...	...	...
...	27.7	26.0	-14.7	-26.8	-28.9	4.32	4.34	128.0	1.1	80.2	...	3.4	5.8	208.7	219.1	...	...	...	...
...	58.5	25.1	0.4	0.9	0.7	3.14	2.83	14.6	0.5	171.0	...	0.5	143.3	411.9	425.4	...	...	...	...
...	42.4	32.6	6.3	23.5	10.3	1.46	1.48	-18.9	0.4	142.8	...	1.8	8.1	214.0	217.3	...	...	...	...
Principal Lines of Business: GrpA&H (51.6%), GrpLife (48.3%), IndAnn (0.1%)														Principal States: NY (100.0%)					
-2	89.0	55.2	-1.2	-2.9	-13.4	4.88	5.09	-15.2	1.9	11.1	157.3	234.8	25.1	93.2	101.2	10.4	...	...	...
...	71.3	42.5	2.7	7.5	23.8	5.36	6.21	19.4	1.7	15.5	68.6	165.9	35.4	95.8	104.4	7.7	...	...	...
...	86.1	27.3	1.1	2.8	8.3	5.50	5.62	27.6	1.9	16.5	51.0	150.3	10.9	114.8	123.1	6.9	...	...	0.0
-95	85.2	16.2	4.2	8.0	26.8	4.69	3.99	61.6	2.5	20.8	32.0	113.3	25.1	120.6	129.7	5.3	...	...	...
95	-99.9	17.9	9.3	123.3	29.3	3.45	3.62	-99.9	-0.2	124.3	34.1	200.7	99.0	197.5	212.4	...	...	...	0.0
Principal Lines of Business: OrdLife (541.5%), IndAnn (39.8%), IndA&H (-99.9%)														Principal States: CA (12.3%), IN (9.7%), PA (8.6%), NC (6.6%), TX (6.5%)					
-1,705	75.8	21.3	0.2	1.0	3.7	5.95	6.27	27.2	2.7	8.9	5.8	90.9	2.0	55.1	67.6	35.6	2.7	147.8	11.4
10,197	82.2	19.7	-0.1	-0.8	-2.9	5.98	6.40	5.9	2.8	8.6	5.2	106.6	0.4	56.5	69.1	26.3	2.1	144.4	14.0
-4,086	90.3	23.6	0.1	0.4	1.7	5.89	5.79	-0.9	2.8	8.3	5.7	115.9	-1.6	56.0	69.0	24.4	1.1	154.9	14.4
-27,773	95.3	24.0	-0.3	-1.6	-7.3	5.87	2.35	6.3	4.0	6.2	8.2	155.6	-24.4	56.8	68.8	50.8	0.3	208.1	11.4
14,288	96.4	23.1	0.6	3.9	12.0	5.41	2.30	-21.8	2.1	9.1	6.0	126.1	50.4	58.7	70.8	31.9	0.2	138.8	5.2
Principal Lines of Business: GrpAnn (46.4%), OrdLife (23.0%), IndAnn (21.4%), IndA&H (7.9%), GrpA&H (1.2%)														Principal States: NY (12.6%), CA (11.0%), OH (9.9%), NE (9.0%), PA (6.1%)					
5,166	645.6	36.3	0.8	9.1	18.1	5.75	6.12	-32.2	0.4	5.5	0.6	14.1	18.1	49.7	65.9	110.4	...	107.0	...
563	761.1	38.5	0.4	4.0	7.9	5.94	6.05	-10.1	0.5	5.0	0.8	19.1	-12.2	49.7	66.0	98.7	...	129.1	...
-1,402	775.5	41.1	-0.2	-2.6	-7.0	6.23	6.52	-8.1	0.7	3.1	0.4	27.0	-38.0	48.6	63.4	197.6	...	226.7	...
-25	667.5	35.7	-1.1	-12.8	-44.9	6.00	4.55	-1.4	0.8	2.6	0.2	19.7	-14.1	49.3	63.1	153.0	1.4	243.7	...
1,995	542.9	35.3	0.0	0.3	0.9	6.11	6.60	-3.6	0.6	3.5	0.2	13.0	33.8	50.8	64.7	146.6	1.5	165.9	35.9
Principal Lines of Business: IndA&H (74.0%), GrpA&H (11.0%), GrpLife (6.6%), IndAnn (5.9%), OrdLife (2.3%)														Principal States: CA (13.0%), TX (9.4%), IL (6.0%), FL (5.5%), PA (5.4%)					
2,767	75.4	31.6	1.6	15.2	45.9	5.47	5.14	-9.9	1.9	30.1	2.5	89.7	50.5	90.4	94.0	0.5	...	10.9	7.3
706	81.3	37.5	0.0	-0.3	-0.5	5.87	6.26	-15.4	1.6	38.2	1.6	33.0	-0.1	113.8	116.9	0.4	...	16.2	7.6
760	81.6	51.7	-0.4	-6.7	-12.4	5.71	6.04	-10.2	1.6	36.0	1.2	35.8	-9.3	107.0	110.8	0.4	0.0	11.7	9.0
327	78.7	40.8	0.1	2.7	4.9	4.87	4.71	-10.5	1.7	33.3	1.1	49.2	-14.4	93.2	97.0	0.4	...	15.6	10.9
-1,916	78.0	40.4	0.2	4.5	9.1	4.61	4.18	-6.3	1.8	30.1	0.0	14.5	-13.6	88.3	94.1	14.4	...	13.6	10.5
Principal Lines of Business: GrpA&H (52.5%), GrpLife (33.0%), GrpAnn (10.7%), OrdLife (2.6%), IndA&H (1.1%)														Principal States: NJ (20.3%), NY (11.3%), CA (11.1%), PA (7.5%), DC (6.1%)					
...	44.0	164.0	5.0	157.1	5.9	1.20	1.20	-76.0	0.0	753.4	...	...	6.0	840.7	840.7	...	...	...	...
...	...	...	8.0	177.0	9.9	4.80	4.80	-99.9	...	280.0	...	...	-19.6	342.3	342.3	...	...	...	...
...	...	...	-1.1	-25.3	-1.3	4.89	4.89	...	...	...	...	...	-1.3	...	...	...	...	...	...
...	...	...	-1.0	431.8	-1.0	-0.26	-0.26	...	...	...	...	...	-1.0	...	...	...	...	...	...
...	...	...	2.1	48.6	2.1	4.70	4.70	...	...	...	...	...	2.1	...	...	...	...	...	...
855	46.0	51.3	2.7	10.8	12.1	5.75	5.74	-2.7	0.8	32.3	...	0.1	11.8	85.9	95.0	0.6	...	2.0	1.8
-4,267	42.0	49.1	2.0	7.5	10.4	5.91	6.55	4.2	1.5	16.0	...	0.2	-47.4	68.6	75.3	2.8	...	7.7	...
...	41.1	46.9	2.8	11.3	20.2	6.01	5.95	-6.7	1.3	17.2	...	0.2	10.6	70.5	76.6	3.5	...	7.0	...
...	46.3	43.0	2.6	11.1	17.2	5.75	5.49	-4.3	1.1	18.2	...	0.1	9.5	62.9	72.9	6.1	...	6.3	...
...	-44.6	45.6	5.7	365.6	33.3	4.72	4.62	-99.9	-0.7	194.1	0.0	999.9	-85.3	342.0	366.7	...	...	0.2	...
Principal Lines of Business: OrdLife (132.5%), IndLife (-4.5%), IndA&H (-28.0%)														Principal States: LA (72.2%), MS (26.9%)					
...	80.0	19.9	0.0	0.0	0.0	2.59	2.59	1.7	2.4	240.6	...	...	14.2	583.5	583.5	...	...	...	...
...	80.1	20.0	0.6	0.6	0.7	4.48	4.48	-11.0	0.8	556.2	...	...	165.9	999.9	999.9	...	...	...	...
...	80.0	19.9	1.9	3.0	2.3	4.22	4.25	-10.4	0.7	520.3	...	...	6.0	999.9	999.9	...	...	...	...
...	80.0	20.0	3.7	17.6	4.2	1.64	1.64	-67.7	0.2	999.9	...	...	-0.7	999.9	999.9	...	...	...	...
...	80.0	19.5	0.3	1.7	0.3	0.24	0.24	-10.9	0.2	999.9	...	...	0.5	999.9	999.9	...	...	...	...
Principal Lines of Business: Dental (100.0%)														Principal States: NJ (100.0%)					

Data in U.S. Dollars

COMPANY NAME / Ultimate Parent Association / Principal Officer / Mailing Address / Dom. : Began Bus. : Struct. : Mktg. / Specialty / Phone # / AMB# / NAIC#	Best's Financial Strength Rating / FSC	Data Year	Balance Sheet: Bonds (%)	Mort. Loans & R.E. (%)	Com & Pref. Stock (%)	All Other Assets (%)	Total Assets ($000)	Life Reserves (%)	Health Reserves (%)	Ann Res. & Dep. Liabilities (%)	All Other Liabilities (%)	Capital & Surplus ($000)	Operations: Direct Premiums Written ($000)	Net Premiums Written & Deposits ($000)	Operating Cash Flow ($000)	NOG Before Taxes ($000)	NOG After Taxes ($000)	Net Income ($000)
UNION SECURITY INSURANCE CO Assurant Inc	**A-**	'05	39.8	9.2	3.9	47.1	8,408,618	26.8	19.6	4.2	49.3	535,021	1,929,435	1,885,792	77,896	172,042	129,463	127,084
John S. Roberts, President & CEO		'06	35.3	10.0	6.3	48.4	7,494,681	26.1	22.1	2.0	49.7	515,105	1,490,612	1,042,918	-364,231	284,083	188,442	212,898
PO Box 419052, Kansas City, MO 64141-6052	Rating Outlook: Stable	'07	36.4	11.5	6.0	46.2	7,195,167	25.8	22.9	2.0	49.4	438,924	1,292,440	1,346,768	-176,321	198,779	171,100	138,496
KS : 1910 : Stock : Broker; Group A&H, Group Life, Pre-need		'08	41.9	15.2	5.4	37.4	5,523,783	33.0	28.6	2.5	36.0	350,383	1,248,226	1,289,005	-305,462	160,531	122,564	1,754
816-474-2345; AMB# 007232 NAIC# 70408	FSC IX	'09	44.3	13.8	2.4	39.5	5,653,173	31.3	27.4	2.2	39.2	418,397	1,157,939	1,133,009	-91,103	106,816	78,636	59,863
		Rating History: A- g, 11/18/09; A- g, 11/25/08; A g, 06/24/08; A g, 07/17/07; A g, 06/19/06																
UNION SECURITY LIFE INS NY Assurant Inc	**A-**	'05	64.3	7.8	5.0	22.9	181,839	16.5	54.6	0.0	28.9	49,026	74,394	58,992	-520	15,706	10,571	10,538
John S. Roberts, Chairman & CEO		'06	59.2	12.1	7.4	21.3	179,635	14.7	58.7	0.0	26.6	52,053	68,211	60,892	2,929	20,589	13,651	14,471
212 Highbridge Street, Suite D, Fayetteville, NY 13066	Rating Outlook: Stable	'07	56.3	17.3	6.5	19.9	178,564	13.9	60.0	0.0	26.1	45,034	66,635	59,906	-672	8,866	6,396	5,747
NY : 1974 : Stock : Direct Response; Group A&H, Life, Credit A&H		'08	55.8	16.6	6.1	21.5	171,983	14.1	66.3	...	19.6	45,986	65,751	64,750	5,887	14,281	9,615	4,270
315-451-0066; AMB# 008533 NAIC# 81477	FSC IX	'09	62.6	16.8	4.3	16.3	164,473	13.6	64.4	...	22.1	50,493	53,710	43,541	-7,430	12,781	9,361	9,565
		Rating History: A- g, 11/18/09; A- g, 11/25/08; A g, 06/24/08; A g, 07/17/07; A g, 06/19/06																
UNISON FAMILY HEALTH PLAN PA UnitedHealth Group Inc	**A-**	'05	...	...	...	...	...	...	...	...	...	...	...	...	...	...	...	...
John P. Blank, M.D., CEO		'06	0.8	...	...	99.2	12,611	...	43.1	...	56.9	7,759	29,170	29,118	4,340	7,827	4,628	4,628
Unison Plaza, 1001 Brinton Road, Pittsburgh, PA 15221	Rating Outlook: Stable	'07	0.6	...	...	99.4	15,983	...	45.9	...	54.1	11,556	30,410	30,381	3,296	6,020	3,799	3,799
PA : 2004 : Stock : Not Available; Group A&H		'08	0.5	...	...	99.5	22,419	...	29.0	...	71.0	15,935	34,793	34,767	6,046	6,227	4,431	4,431
412-858-4000; AMB# 064925 NAIC# 12012	FSC V	'09	0.5	...	...	99.5	21,109	...	32.7	...	67.3	15,927	37,420	37,386	179	4,990	3,229	3,229
		Rating History: A-, 06/15/09; NR-5, 04/01/08																
UNISON HEALTH PLAN OF OHIO INC UnitedHealth Group Inc	**A-**	'05	6.9	...	...	93.1	5,796	...	39.9	...	60.1	1,766	4,069	3,999	5,512	45	38	38
Scott A. Bowers, President		'06	9.8	...	...	90.2	34,621	...	26.8	...	73.2	9,931	51,194	50,694	25,093	755	195	195
Unison Plaza, 1001 Brinton Road, Pittsburgh, PA 15221	Rating Outlook: Stable	'07	4.2	...	...	95.8	80,935	...	31.5	...	68.5	26,279	216,556	215,390	40,323	8,798	5,385	5,385
OH : 2005 : Stock : Not Available; Medicaid		'08	4.0	...	...	96.0	84,950	...	39.6	...	60.4	41,257	320,443	318,128	-198	18,268	15,256	15,256
412-858-4000; AMB# 064874 NAIC# 12323	FSC VII	'09	2.2	...	...	97.8	168,561	...	25.8	...	74.2	60,526	409,541	405,399	77,924	28,167	15,219	15,219
		Rating History: A-, 06/15/09; NR-5, 04/30/08; NR-5, 06/14/07; NR-5, 02/15/07																
UNISON HEALTH PLAN OF PA INC UnitedHealth Group Inc	**A-**	'05	...	...	5.4	94.6	125,206	...	49.1	...	50.9	52,268	684,296	682,628	-5,876	-201	-1,921	-1,921
John Blank, M.D., CEO		'06	...	...	3.5	96.5	219,950	...	47.8	...	52.2	86,073	735,131	732,833	84,926	63,969	31,613	31,613
Unison Plaza, 1001 Brinton Road, Pittsburgh, PA 15221	Rating Outlook: Stable	'07	15.7	...	6.0	78.3	193,761	...	42.4	...	57.6	101,475	652,273	650,731	-21,534	63,466	42,079	42,079
PA : 1996 : Stock : Not Available; Medicaid, Medicare		'08	...	...	6.9	93.1	232,577	...	41.5	...	58.5	130,640	660,826	659,385	1,448	25,098	24,766	25,486
412-858-4000; AMB# 064104 NAIC# 95220	FSC VIII	'09	20.8	...	7.6	71.5	209,134	...	38.0	...	62.0	104,450	716,735	714,982	-38,814	18,342	12,915	12,873
		Rating History: A-, 06/15/09; C++pd, 05/30/07; C+ pd, 05/30/06; C++pd, 05/23/05; C++pd, 06/11/04																
UNISON HEALTH PLAN OF SC INC UnitedHealth Group Inc	**A-**	'05	...	...	...	...	...	...	...	...	...	...	...	...	...	...	...	...
Daniel T. Gallagher, President		'06	...	...	...	100.0	12,845	...	38.7	...	61.3	7,068	21,904	21,829	7,820	4,452	4,452	4,452
Unison Plaza, 1001 Brinton Road, Pittsburgh, PA 15221	Rating Outlook: Stable	'07	...	...	...	100.0	19,139	...	44.5	...	55.5	11,217	34,839	34,769	4,251	4,169	4,169	4,169
SC : 2004 : Stock : Not Available; Medicaid		'08	...	...	...	100.0	43,650	...	30.8	...	69.2	14,081	76,758	76,649	22,759	3,011	2,187	2,187
412-858-4000; AMB# 064886 NAIC# 11775	FSC V	'09	0.6	...	...	99.4	65,706	...	30.4	...	69.6	13,629	196,982	196,836	11,642	5,381	3,028	3,028
		Rating History: A-, 06/15/09; NR-5, 03/25/08; NR-5, 04/17/07																
UNISON HEALTH PLAN OF TN INC UnitedHealth Group Inc	**NR-5**	'05	...	...	...	...	...	...	...	...	...	...	...	...	...	...	...	...
John P. Blank, M.D., CEO		'06	46.2	...	...	53.8	6,700	...	19.5	...	80.5	5,452	...	...	452	728	480	480
Unison Plaza, 1001 Brinton Road, Pittsburgh, PA 15221		'07	38.0	...	...	62.0	12,047	...	52.1	...	47.9	6,828	7,135	7,114	4,488	2,072	1,435	1,435
TN : 2001 : Stock : Not Available; Medicare		'08	25.7	...	...	74.3	21,374	...	57.8	...	42.2	10,315	26,758	26,689	9,544	4,206	3,438	3,438
412-858-4000; AMB# 064879 NAIC# 11139		'09	22.9	...	...	77.1	28,190	...	39.7	...	60.3	13,516	55,798	55,633	4,597	9,049	5,861	5,860
		Rating History: NR-5, 06/15/09; NR-5, 03/25/08; NR-5, 03/20/07																
UNISON HEALTH PLAN OF CAP AREA UnitedHealth Group Inc	**NR-2**	'05	...	...	...	...	...	...	...	...	...	...	...	...	...	...	...	...
John P. Blank, M.D., President & CEO		'06	...	...	...	...	...	...	...	...	...	...	...	...	...	...	...	...
Unison Plaza, 1001 Brinton Road, Pittsburgh, PA 15221		'07	19.7	...	...	80.3	1,527	...	...	...	100.0	1,527	...	...	1,517	27	27	27
DC : Stock : Not Available; Group A&H, Medicaid		'08	...	...	...	100.0	14,641	...	55.9	...	44.1	-124	32,729	32,571	7,107	-6,628	-4,978	-4,978
412-858-4000; AMB# 064963 NAIC# 13032		'09	1.0	...	...	99.0	31,812	...	56.8	...	43.2	12,575	71,441	71,336	21,166	-9,343	-5,876	-5,876
		Rating History: NR-2, 06/15/09																
UNITED AMERICAN INS CO Torchmark Corporation	**A+**	'05	74.2	0.8	8.9	16.1	1,139,897	16.0	29.4	0.0	54.6	189,281	822,703	737,185	-5,755	76,051	84,765	83,373
Vern D. Herbel, CEO		'06	71.9	1.1	11.9	15.1	1,192,630	15.3	28.4	0.0	56.3	178,172	1,090,046	950,095	70,826	95,572	66,371	64,568
P.O. Box 8080, McKinney, TX 75070-8080	Rating Outlook: Stable	'07	75.9	0.0	8.4	15.7	1,309,632	13.7	26.6	0.0	59.7	168,471	1,135,688	953,035	132,279	80,495	61,913	61,487
NE : 1947 : Stock : Broker; Ind A&H, Med supp		'08	76.4	0.0	9.7	13.9	1,384,726	12.9	24.1	0.0	63.0	183,136	1,054,618	851,885	64,352	112,786	89,805	78,913
972-529-5085; AMB# 007161 NAIC# 92916	FSC X	'09	82.5	...	4.4	13.1	1,649,620	14.2	21.6	0.0	64.2	257,005	972,652	787,214	255,599	104,058	84,385	79,354
		Rating History: A+ g, 06/15/10; A+ g, 06/11/09; A+ g, 06/11/08; A+ g, 06/08/07; A+ g, 06/08/06																

BEST'S PROFITABILITY, LEVERAGE AND LIQUIDITY TESTS 2005 – 2009

Data in U.S. Dollars

—	Profitability Tests							Leverage Tests						Liquidity Tests					
Un-Realized Capital Gains ($000)	Benefits Paid to NPW & Dep (%)	Comm. & Expenses to NPW & Dep (%)	NOG to Total Assets (%)	NOG to Total Rev (%)	Operating Return on Equity (%)	Net Yield (%)	Total Return (%)	Change in NPW & Dep (%)	NPW & Dep to Capital (X)	Capital & Surplus to Liabilities (%)	Surplus Relief (%)	Reins Leverage (%)	Change in Capital (%)	Quick Liquidity (%)	Current Liquidity (%)	Non-Invest Grade Bonds to Capital (%)	Delinq. & Foreclosed Mortgages to Capital (%)	Mort. & Credit Tenant Loans & R.E. to Capital (%)	Affiliated Invest to Capital (%)
4,681	65.5	50.6	1.6	6.0	22.9	6.31	6.38	-3.0	3.3	12.5	9.5	245.4	-8.6	40.5	54.9	49.8	...	134.4	0.3
-1,113	103.9	85.6	2.4	13.6	35.9	6.34	6.85	-44.7	1.9	14.2	9.6	268.9	-3.5	45.9	62.3	52.7	...	135.2	0.2
-3,852	72.5	64.7	2.3	10.7	35.9	7.00	6.22	29.1	2.8	12.4	10.0	331.0	-14.1	39.9	55.3	57.6	...	172.5	0.1
-1,601	78.8	51.3	1.9	8.2	31.1	6.19	3.17	-4.3	3.5	10.3	11.5	436.1	-22.5	42.6	56.1	71.0	...	227.0	0.2
1,711	85.1	48.5	1.4	5.8	20.5	5.91	5.42	-12.1	2.6	12.7	7.9	391.9	18.9	42.1	55.6	69.9	1.2	176.8	0.3
Principal Lines of Business: GrpA&H (78.3%), GrpLife (17.0%), IndAnn (2.6%), OrdLife (1.5%), IndA&H (0.5%)														Principal States: CA (10.4%), TX (8.6%), FL (6.6%), MN (5.6%), PA (5.0%)					
...	63.0	44.0	5.7	14.8	23.0	0.14	0.17	-4.0	1.2	47.0	7.1	233.7	13.2	75.0	94.8	18.1	...	28.4	...
...	52.6	39.2	7.6	18.8	27.0	6.37	6.95	3.2	1.1	50.9	5.1	234.7	6.3	75.1	93.9	18.0	...	40.8	...
...	63.7	36.3	3.6	8.9	13.2	6.30	5.83	-1.6	1.3	41.0	6.9	291.0	-13.5	57.5	74.1	22.8	...	67.0	...
0	55.2	34.3	5.5	12.6	21.1	6.00	2.47	8.1	1.4	41.1	6.5	304.6	0.5	78.8	94.7	17.6	...	61.6	...
0	77.9	37.9	5.6	17.1	19.4	5.84	5.88	-32.8	0.9	50.6	5.1	358.5	10.2	71.6	89.5	14.8	...	54.3	...
Principal Lines of Business: GrpA&H (78.4%), GrpLife (15.2%), CrdA&H (3.5%), CrdLife (2.3%), OrdLife (0.6%)														Principal States: NY (99.6%)					
...	...	...	...	...	...	...	...	...	...	...	...	...	...	...	...	...	...	...	...
...	60.1	14.4	...	15.7	...	...	...	...	3.8	159.9	...	...	...	209.4	209.4	...	...	...	...
...	67.6	14.5	26.6	12.3	39.3	4.85	4.85	4.3	2.6	261.1	...	...	48.9	304.0	304.0	...	...	...	...
...	67.0	15.7	23.1	12.7	32.2	1.30	1.30	14.4	2.2	245.7	...	...	37.9	604.6	604.6	...	...	...	...
...	70.3	16.4	14.8	8.6	20.3	0.15	0.15	7.5	2.3	307.4	...	...	0.0	668.5	689.0	...	...	...	...
Principal Lines of Business: CompHosp/Med (100.0%)														Principal States: PA (100.0%)					
...	85.7	14.0	...	0.9	...	...	...	...	2.3	43.8	...	...	...	136.5	136.5	...	...	...	...
...	81.5	17.9	1.0	0.4	3.3	2.35	2.35	999.9	5.1	40.2	...	1.9	462.2	123.7	123.7	...	...	...	...
...	81.5	15.3	9.3	2.5	29.7	3.79	3.79	324.9	8.2	48.1	...	2.6	164.6	130.6	130.7	...	...	...	...
...	79.2	15.8	18.4	4.8	45.2	3.07	3.07	47.7	7.7	94.4	...	6.6	57.0	303.3	319.0	...	...	...	...
...	79.9	13.8	12.0	3.7	29.9	0.25	0.25	27.4	6.7	56.0	...	4.7	46.7	222.9	230.0	...	...	...	...
Principal Lines of Business: Medicaid (99.6%), Medicare (0.4%)														Principal States: OH (100.0%)					
863	82.1	18.3	-1.4	-0.3	-3.2	2.94	3.72	8.9	13.1	71.7	...	2.7	-24.7	205.2	207.4	...	...	...	6.0
4,626	75.2	17.4	18.3	4.3	45.7	5.55	8.60	7.4	8.5	64.3	...	1.3	64.7	227.8	227.8	...	...	...	9.0
3,797	73.9	18.1	20.3	6.4	44.9	5.05	7.06	-11.2	6.4	110.0	...	0.2	17.9	273.6	275.3	...	...	...	11.4
4,378	78.9	17.7	11.6	3.7	21.3	1.43	4.23	1.3	5.0	128.2	...	0.6	28.7	343.8	343.8	...	...	...	12.2
-7	81.2	16.5	5.8	1.8	11.0	2.61	2.58	8.4	6.8	99.8	...	1.6	-20.0	188.5	200.0	...	...	...	15.2
Principal Lines of Business: Medicaid (71.2%), Medicare (28.8%)														Principal States: PA (100.0%)					
...	...	...	...	...	...	...	...	...	...	...	...	...	...	...	...	...	...	...	...
...	68.5	12.8	...	20.1	...	...	...	...	3.1	122.4	...	0.2	...	213.3	213.3	...	...	...	...
...	77.2	12.8	26.1	11.8	45.6	5.05	5.05	59.3	3.1	141.6	...	0.1	58.7	209.2	209.2	...	...	...	...
...	84.1	12.8	7.0	2.8	17.3	2.37	2.37	120.4	5.4	47.6	...	...	25.5	260.6	274.7	...	...	...	...
...	85.1	12.2	5.5	1.5	21.9	0.18	0.18	156.8	14.4	26.2	...	...	-3.2	176.1	181.7	...	...	...	...
Principal Lines of Business: Medicaid (99.3%), CompHosp/Med (0.7%)														Principal States: SC (100.0%)					
...	...	...	...	...	...	...	...	...	...	...	...	...	...	...	...	...	...	...	...
...	...	...	...	218.2	...	...	...	...	...	436.6	...	...	...	484.1	484.1	...	...	...	...
...	70.3	5.8	15.3	19.2	23.4	4.52	4.52	...	1.0	130.9	...	...	25.3	200.6	200.6	...	...	...	...
...	75.3	10.5	20.6	12.9	40.1	3.38	3.38	275.2	2.6	93.3	...	0.4	51.1	304.3	318.8	...	...	...	...
...	68.9	15.1	23.7	10.5	49.2	0.78	0.78	108.5	4.1	92.1	...	0.9	31.0	230.8	234.1	...	...	...	...
Principal Lines of Business: Medicare (100.0%)														Principal States: TN (96.6%)					
...	...	...	...	...	...	...	...	...	...	...	...	...	...	...	...	...	...	...	...
...	...	...	...	...	...	...	...	...	...	...	...	...	...	...	...	...	...	...	...
...	...	...	...	100.0	...	...	...	...	...	...	...	...	...	...	...	...	...	...	...
...	100.3	15.3	-61.6	-15.2	-99.9	2.66	2.66	...	-99.9	-0.8	...	-99.9	-99.9	126.0	133.3	...	...	...	...
...	102.2	11.9	-25.3	-8.2	-94.4	0.21	0.21	119.0	5.7	65.4	...	...	999.9	237.2	243.2	...	...	...	...
Principal Lines of Business: CompHosp/Med (50.4%), Medicaid (49.6%)														Principal States: DC (100.0%)					
-2,651	64.0	30.5	7.6	10.3	46.5	6.41	6.25	-2.9	3.7	21.1	3.3	270.9	9.0	58.5	73.4	13.4	...	4.6	30.4
498	65.2	28.5	5.7	6.4	36.1	6.10	6.17	28.9	5.1	18.4	5.3	312.9	-6.7	56.0	70.3	15.0	...	6.9	37.9
5,785	67.9	27.3	4.9	5.9	35.7	5.55	6.16	0.3	5.4	15.6	8.2	385.9	-4.7	52.2	64.4	18.6	...	0.1	42.4
-2,827	66.5	25.1	6.7	9.4	51.1	6.19	5.23	-10.6	4.5	15.6	7.9	423.5	6.1	48.3	61.6	17.9	...	0.2	38.6
1,417	70.8	22.0	5.6	8.9	38.3	5.51	5.29	-7.6	3.0	18.9	4.5	329.3	40.1	51.6	66.7	19.6	...	...	22.2
Principal Lines of Business: IndA&H (86.1%), GrpA&H (8.6%), OrdLife (5.3%), GrpLife (0.1%), GrpAnn (0.0%)														Principal States: FL (12.5%), NC (10.9%), TX (6.0%), GA (5.9%), SC (5.3%)					

COMPANY NAME Ultimate Parent Association Principal Officer Mailing Address Dom. : Began Bus. : Struct. : Mktg. Specialty Phone # AMB# NAIC#	Best's Financial Strength Rating FSC	Data Year	Balance Sheet: Bonds (%)	Mort. Loans & R.E. (%)	Com & Pref. Stock (%)	All Other Assets (%)	Total Assets ($000)	Life Reserves (%)	Health Reserves (%)	Ann Res. & Dep. Liabilities (%)	All Other Liabilities (%)	Capital & Surplus ($000)	Operations: Direct Premiums Written ($000)	Net Premiums Written & Deposits ($000)	Operating Cash Flow ($000)	NOG Before Taxes ($000)	NOG After Taxes ($000)	Net Income ($000)
UNITED ASSURANCE LIFE INS CO' Frank M. Croy President P.O. Box 982005 Fort Worth, TX 76182-8005 TX : 1977 : Stock : Not Available 817-284-4888 AMB# 068091 NAIC# 90387	NR-1	'05	81.2	...	...	18.8	1,256	...	...	...	100.0	1,206	299	134	...	-5	-1	-1
		'06	78.0	...	...	22.0	1,309	...	...	...	100.0	1,189	357	200	...	0	-2	-2
		'07	76.0	...	...	24.0	1,406	...	...	...	100.0	1,196	413	292	...	11	8	8
		'08	51.8	...	...	48.2	1,539	...	...	...	100.0	1,240	427	322	...	31	24	24
		'09	43.5	...	...	56.5	1,629	...	...	...	100.0	1,252	453	361	...	11	7	7
		Rating History: NR-1, 06/10/10; NR-1, 06/12/09; NR-1, 06/12/08; NR-1, 06/08/07; NR-1, 06/07/06																
UNITED BENEFIT LIFE INS CO American Financial Group, Inc Billy B. Hill, Jr. President 11200 Lakeline Blvd., Suite 100 Austin, TX 78717 OH : 1957 : Stock : Inactive Med supp 512-451-2224 AMB# 006619 NAIC# 65269	NR-3	'05	66.9	...	...	33.1	3,045	...	...	...	100.0	2,919	...	...	-2,456	-65	-42	-42
		'06	79.6	...	...	20.4	3,177	...	...	...	100.0	3,061	...	...	986	-11	-7	-7
		'07	80.3	...	...	19.7	3,154	...	...	...	100.0	3,112	...	...	-4	98	67	67
		'08	53.5	...	...	46.5	3,195	...	...	...	100.0	3,130	...	...	53	21	23	23
		'09	53.8	...	...	46.2	3,194	...	...	...	100.0	3,132	...	...	26	-6	-3	-3
		Rating History: NR-3, 05/10/10; NR-3, 03/27/09; NR-3, 12/17/07; NR-3, 11/28/06; NR-3, 05/02/06																
UNITED CONCORDIA COMPANIES INC Highmark Inc. Frederick G. "Chip" Merkel President & CEO 4401 Deer Path Road Harrisburg, PA 17110 PA : 2001 : Stock : Not Available Dental 717-260-7081 AMB# 050692 NAIC# 89070	A-	'05	18.0	...	50.3	31.7	236,592	...	30.8	...	69.2	156,971	390,758	390,758	8,592	9,372	11,331	11,331
		'06	15.7	...	49.7	34.6	297,003	...	12.5	...	87.5	210,456	442,901	442,901	28,640	33,621	25,075	25,075
	Rating Outlook: Stable	'07	12.8	...	49.5	37.7	346,708	...	25.8	...	74.2	257,928	472,896	472,896	28,580	45,815	34,340	34,340
		'08	12.7	...	48.6	38.7	396,585	...	17.8	...	82.2	309,013	505,412	505,412	22,753	56,704	40,287	40,287
		'09	23.4	...	44.3	32.4	438,064	...	18.3	...	81.7	335,125	601,868	601,868	-381	66,711	48,433	48,558
	FSC IX	**Rating History: A-, 03/25/10; A-, 06/15/09; A-, 06/12/08; A-, 03/05/07; A-, 02/07/06**																
UNITED CONCORDIA DENTAL CP AL Highmark Inc. Frederick G. "Chip" Merkel President & CEO 400 Vestavia Parkway, Suite 205 Birmingham, AL 35216 AL : Stock : Broker Dental 205-824-1235 AMB# 064649 NAIC# 47038	NR-2	'05	...	...	...	...	3,122	...	...	...	...	1,233	...	6,372	...	...	...	748
		'06	...	...	...	...	2,107	...	...	...	...	1,095	...	5,173	...	...	...	-176
		'07	...	...	...	...	2,229	...	...	...	...	1,036	...	7,078	...	...	...	-49
		'08	...	...	...	...	2,005	...	...	...	...	842	...	8,788	...	...	...	-166
		'09	...	...	...	...	1,659	...	...	...	...	624	...	8,596	...	...	...	-238
		Rating History: NR-2, 03/25/10; NR-2, 06/15/09; NR-2, 06/13/08; NR-2, 03/05/07; NR-2, 03/09/06																
UNITED CONCORDIA DENTAL PLANS Highmark Inc. Frederick G. "Chip" Merkel Chairman, President & CEO 4401 Deer Path Road Harrisburg, PA 17110 MD : 1987 : Stock : Broker Dental 443-886-9500 AMB# 065705 NAIC# 95253	A-	'05	21.3	...	...	78.7	7,029	...	12.4	...	87.6	3,756	21,917	21,917	1,373	1,397	1,047	1,047
		'06	2.2	...	...	97.8	8,472	...	13.9	...	86.1	5,067	19,524	19,524	1,385	1,756	1,255	1,255
	Rating Outlook: Stable	'07	1.8	...	...	98.2	10,520	...	14.0	...	86.0	7,057	18,223	18,248	2,502	2,865	2,034	2,034
		'08	19.2	...	...	80.8	11,488	...	11.7	...	88.3	8,552	17,344	17,344	1,061	2,170	1,539	1,539
		'09	37.2	...	...	62.8	11,306	...	11.6	...	88.4	8,686	15,924	15,924	-254	204	246	246
	FSC IV	**Rating History: A-, 03/25/10; A-, 06/15/09; A-, 06/12/08; A-, 03/05/07; A-, 02/07/06**																
UNITED CONCORDIA DENTAL PLS CA Highmark Inc. Frederick G. "Chip" Merkel President & CEO 4401 Deer Path Road Harrisburg, PA 17110 CA : 1987 : Stock : Broker Dental 818-710-9400 AMB# 064008 NAIC# 95789	A-	'05	...	...	...	100.0	9,104	...	...	...	100.0	3,388	36,279	36,279	-43	1,316	765	765
		'06	...	...	...	100.0	10,547	...	...	...	100.0	3,616	37,546	37,546	1,291	1,275	728	728
	Rating Outlook: Stable	'07	...	...	...	100.0	11,271	...	...	...	100.0	4,761	37,412	37,412	1,115	1,981	1,145	1,145
		'08	...	...	...	100.0	11,215	...	...	...	100.0	5,442	35,956	35,956	840	1,140	681	681
		'09	...	...	...	100.0	9,853	...	...	...	100.0	5,553	26,779	26,779	-634	241	110	110
	FSC IV	**Rating History: A-, 03/25/10; A-, 06/15/09; A-, 06/12/08; A-, 03/05/07; A-, 02/07/06**																
UNITED CONCORDIA DENTAL PLS FL Highmark Inc. Frederick G. "Chip" Merkel President & CEO 4401 Deer Path Road Harrisburg, PA 17110 FL : 1991 : Stock : Broker Dental 727-441-8585 AMB# 065704 NAIC# 52020	NR-2	'05	15.6	...	...	84.4	333	...	11.6	...	88.4	314	86	86	-40	-68	-44	-44
		'06	18.3	...	...	81.7	285	...	7.4	...	92.6	270	16	16	-52	-67	-43	-43
		'07	21.8	...	...	78.2	240	...	21.2	...	78.8	229	10	10	-48	-64	-41	-41
		'08	27.4	...	...	72.6	190	...	22.9	...	77.1	178	6	6	-46	-79	-52	-52
		'09	31.8	...	...	68.2	169	...	15.9	...	84.1	151	3	3	-20	-46	-19	-19
		Rating History: NR-2, 03/25/10; NR-2, 06/15/09; NR-2, 06/12/08; NR-2, 03/05/07; NR-2, 02/07/06																
UNITED CONCORDIA DENTAL PLS KY Highmark Inc. Daniel J. Lebish Chairman & CEO 4401 Deer Path Road Harrisburg, PA 17110 KY : 1982 : Stock : Broker Dental 800-972-4191 AMB# 065702 NAIC# 52048	NR-2	'05	85.5	...	...	14.5	589	...	31.2	...	68.8	492	716	716	-10	-30	-19	-19
		'06	79.2	...	...	20.8	519	...	39.1	...	60.9	429	657	657	-74	-145	-94	-96
		'07	11.1	...	...	88.9	454	...	43.5	...	56.5	372	611	611	-56	-143	-93	-93
		'08	13.6	...	...	86.4	370	...	21.3	...	78.7	281	572	572	-102	-149	-96	-96
		'09	16.5	...	...	83.5	304	...	25.1	...	74.9	236	558	558	-48	-139	-91	-91
		Rating History: NR-2, 03/25/10; NR-2, 06/15/09; NR-2, 06/13/08; NR-2, 03/05/07; NR-2, 03/09/06																
UNITED CONCORDIA DENTAL PLS PA Highmark Inc. Frederick G. "Chip" Merkel President & CEO 4401 Deer Path Road Harrisburg, PA 17110 PA : 1990 : Stock : Agency Dental 800-972-4191 AMB# 064353 NAIC# 47089	A-	'05	...	...	...	100.0	7,040	...	16.4	...	83.6	3,091	35,324	35,324	2,031	1,851	1,198	1,198
		'06	...	...	...	100.0	7,468	...	22.6	...	77.4	3,777	33,557	33,557	511	375	241	241
	Rating Outlook: Stable	'07	...	...	...	100.0	8,281	...	26.7	...	73.3	4,497	33,331	33,331	613	584	403	403
		'08	...	...	...	100.0	8,582	...	19.1	...	80.9	4,670	32,884	32,884	1,365	277	180	180
		'09	47.9	...	...	52.1	6,807	...	25.0	...	75.0	3,941	30,518	30,518	-2,366	-1,145	-741	-741
	FSC III	**Rating History: A-, 03/25/10; A-, 06/15/09; A-, 06/12/08; A-, 03/05/07; A-, 02/07/06**																

BEST'S PROFITABILITY, LEVERAGE AND LIQUIDITY TESTS 2005 – 2009

Data in U.S. Dollars

—	Profitability Tests							Leverage Tests						Liquidity Tests					
Un-Realized Capital Gains ($000)	Benefits Paid to NPW & Dep (%)	Comm. & Expenses to NPW & Dep (%)	NOG to Total Assets (%)	NOG to Total Rev (%)	Operating Return on Equity (%)	Net Yield (%)	Total Return (%)	Change in NPW & Dep (%)	NPW & Dep to Capital (X)	Capital & Surplus to Liabilities (%)	Surplus Relief (%)	Reins Leverage (%)	Change in Capital (%)	Quick Liquidity (%)	Current Liquidity (%)	Non-Invest Grade Bonds to Capital (%)	Delinq. & Foreclosed Mortgages to Capital (%)	Mort. & Credit Tenant Loans & R.E. to Capital (%)	Affiliated Invest to Capital (%)
...	20.0	96.4	0.0	-0.2	-0.1	...	...	106.5	0.1	999.9	6.8	...	-0.4	...	...	...	...	...	...
...	19.2	76.5	-0.1	-0.6	-0.1	...	...	49.1	0.2	991.8	2.9	...	-1.4	...	...	...	...	...	...
...	25.7	63.0	0.6	2.2	0.7	...	...	45.8	0.2	567.4	2.5	...	0.6	...	...	...	...	...	...
...	23.0	51.0	1.6	6.1	2.0	...	...	10.3	0.3	415.1	2.0	...	3.7	...	...	...	...	...	...
...	40.6	45.1	0.4	1.6	0.5	...	...	12.0	0.3	331.8	1.7	...	0.9	...	...	...	...	...	...
Principal Lines of Business: OrdLife (100.0%)																			
...	...	...	1.0	53.5	-1.4	2.22	2.27	...	...	999.9	...	0.7	-2.1	999.9	999.9	...	...	...	...
...	...	...	-0.2	-5.5	-0.2	3.41	3.47	...	...	999.9	...	0.2	4.9	999.9	999.9	...	...	...	...
...	...	...	2.1	47.9	2.2	2.90	2.95	...	...	999.9	...	0.0	1.7	999.9	999.9	...	...	...	...
...	...	...	0.7	26.2	0.7	2.74	2.79	...	...	999.9	...	0.0	0.6	999.9	999.9	...	...	...	...
...	...	...	-0.1	-6.0	-0.1	1.41	1.46	...	...	999.9	...	...	0.0	999.9	999.9	...	...	...	...
21,253	92.9	10.3	5.2	2.7	8.2	14.60	28.82	4.3	2.5	197.1	...	...	30.4	75.5	75.5	...	...	...	76.6
27,684	86.5	9.4	9.4	5.5	13.6	7.65	21.86	13.3	2.1	243.2	...	...	34.1	105.9	105.9	...	...	...	70.7
25,274	85.9	7.8	10.7	7.0	14.7	6.26	16.32	6.8	1.8	290.5	...	...	22.6	132.9	132.9	...	...	...	67.6
20,742	83.8	7.8	10.8	7.8	14.2	4.67	11.55	6.9	1.6	352.9	...	...	19.8	273.7	293.7	...	...	...	63.1
4,321	83.5	8.2	11.6	7.8	15.0	5.17	6.51	19.1	1.8	325.6	...	...	8.5	167.7	185.9	...	...	...	59.5
Principal Lines of Business: Dental (100.0%)													Principal States: CO (100.0%)						
...	70.0	9.3	36.7	11.6	86.0	...	...	...	5.2	...	...	...	...	...	...	...	...	...	...
...	78.4	23.8	-6.7	-3.4	-15.1	...	...	...	4.7	...	...	...	...	...	...	...	...	...	...
...	81.6	17.5	-2.3	-0.7	-4.6	...	...	...	6.8	...	...	...	...	...	...	...	...	...	...
...	83.7	17.4	-7.8	-1.9	-17.7	...	...	...	10.4	...	...	...	...	...	...	...	...	...	...
...	85.7	17.3	-13.0	-2.8	-32.5	...	...	...	13.8	...	...	...	...	...	...	...	...	...	...
...	72.8	22.1	16.4	4.7	37.1	2.66	2.66	-32.0	5.8	114.7	...	...	98.7	176.1	176.1	...	...	...	...
...	70.8	22.5	16.2	6.3	28.5	4.69	4.69	-10.9	3.9	148.8	...	...	34.9	209.7	209.7	...	...	...	...
...	65.1	22.4	21.4	10.8	33.5	5.17	5.17	-6.5	2.6	203.8	...	...	39.3	278.6	278.6	...	...	...	...
...	69.9	20.1	14.0	8.7	19.7	2.69	2.69	-5.0	2.0	291.2	...	...	21.2	657.6	662.9	...	...	...	...
...	75.0	24.5	2.2	1.5	2.9	0.55	0.55	-8.2	1.8	331.4	...	...	1.6	614.7	617.4	...	...	...	...
Principal Lines of Business: Dental (100.0%)													Principal States: MD (94.4%), NJ (3.9%)						
...	70.5	34.1	8.3	1.9	25.5	2.72	2.72	-2.9	10.7	59.3	...	...	29.2	87.5	87.5	...	...	...	...
...	71.9	32.7	7.4	1.8	20.8	5.11	5.11	3.5	10.4	52.2	...	...	6.7	90.4	90.4	...	...	...	...
...	71.8	30.8	10.5	2.8	27.3	4.66	4.66	-0.4	7.9	73.1	...	...	31.7	113.2	113.2	...	...	...	...
...	73.6	30.8	6.1	1.8	13.4	1.89	1.89	-3.9	6.6	94.3	...	...	14.3	139.5	139.5	...	...	...	...
...	69.6	41.2	1.0	0.4	2.0	0.26	0.26	-25.5	4.8	129.1	...	...	2.0	172.0	172.0	...	...	...	...
Principal Lines of Business: Dental (100.0%)																			
...	80.4	72.6	-12.4	-69.6	-13.2	-6.27	-6.27	-25.2	0.3	999.9	...	...	-11.8	999.9	999.9	...	...	...	...
...	71.6	321.2	-14.1	999.9	-14.9	-6.21	-6.21	-81.0	0.1	999.9	...	...	-13.8	999.9	999.9	...	...	...	...
...	73.7	469.7	-15.7	567.3	-16.5	-7.96	-7.96	-36.4	0.0	999.9	...	...	-15.2	999.9	999.9	...	...	...	...
...	82.2	931.5	-24.0	250.3	-25.3	-12.36	-12.36	-44.0	0.0	999.9	...	...	-22.2	999.9	999.9	...	...	...	...
...	52.5	999.9	-10.6	-99.9	-11.5	0.96	0.96	-47.0	0.0	876.4	...	...	-15.1	999.9	999.9	...	...	...	...
Principal Lines of Business: Dental (100.0%)													Principal States: FL (100.0%)						
...	83.2	23.3	-3.2	-2.7	-3.9	2.97	2.97	-14.4	1.5	506.2	...	...	-3.6	542.1	542.1	...	...	...	...
...	98.3	26.2	-17.0	-14.0	-20.5	3.01	2.67	-8.3	1.5	477.4	...	...	-12.7	528.6	528.6	...	...	...	...
...	100.7	25.0	-19.0	-14.8	-23.1	3.36	3.34	-6.9	1.6	452.2	...	...	-13.3	505.7	505.7	...	...	...	...
...	102.9	25.2	-23.3	-16.5	-29.5	3.08	3.08	-6.4	2.0	315.6	...	...	-24.5	648.3	657.4	...	...	...	...
...	94.7	30.7	-27.0	-16.2	-35.2	0.88	0.88	-2.5	2.4	348.5	...	...	-15.9	694.0	700.0	...	...	...	...
Principal Lines of Business: Dental (100.0%)													Principal States: KY (100.0%)						
...	76.8	18.3	20.2	3.4	48.7	2.52	2.52	-1.2	11.4	78.3	...	...	68.9	139.7	139.7	...	...	...	...
...	80.2	19.5	3.3	0.7	7.0	4.68	4.68	-5.0	8.9	102.3	...	...	22.2	163.3	163.3	...	...	...	...
...	80.4	18.7	5.1	1.2	9.7	4.99	4.99	-0.7	7.4	118.9	...	...	19.1	175.5	175.5	...	...	...	...
...	82.8	16.8	2.1	0.5	3.9	2.12	2.12	-1.3	7.0	119.4	...	...	3.8	412.2	423.2	...	...	...	...
...	87.5	16.3	-9.6	-2.4	-17.2	0.26	0.26	-7.2	7.7	137.5	...	...	-15.6	299.0	301.1	...	...	...	...
Principal Lines of Business: Dental (100.0%)													Principal States: PA (100.0%)						

ANNUAL STATEMENT DATA FOR YEARS 2005 – 2009

Data in U.S. Dollars

Column key: COMPANY NAME; Ultimate Parent Association; Principal Officer; Mailing Address; Dom. : Began Bus. : Struct. : Mkt.; Specialty; Phone #; AMB#; NAIC#. Best's Financial Strength Rating; FSC.

UNITED CONCORDIA DENTAL PLS TX

Highmark Inc.
Frederick G. "Chip" Merkel, President & CEO
4401 Deer Path Road, Harrisburg, PA 17110
TX : 1988 : Stock : Broker
Dental
214-378-6410
AMB# 064351 NAIC# 95160

Best's Financial Strength Rating: NR-2

Data Year	Bonds (%)	Mort. Loans & R.E. (%)	Com & Pref. Stock (%)	All Other Assets (%)	Total Assets ($000)	Life Reserves (%)	Health Reserves (%)	Ann Res. & Dep. Liabilities (%)	All Other Liabilities (%)	Capital & Surplus ($000)	Direct Premiums Written ($000)	Net Premiums Written & Deposits ($000)	Operating Cash Flow ($000)	NOG Before Taxes ($000)	NOG After Taxes ($000)	Net Income ($000)
'05	18.5	...	...	81.5	568	...	20.3	...	79.7	505	639	639	-19	-122	-77	-77
'06	8.6	...	...	91.4	631	...	28.6	...	71.4	554	738	738	63	-78	-53	-53
'07	7.9	...	...	92.1	690	...	29.7	...	70.3	538	771	771	60	-25	-13	-13
'08	8.2	...	...	91.8	671	...	15.0	...	85.0	522	828	828	-57	-71	-43	-43
'09	7.7	...	...	92.3	716	...	16.7	...	83.3	597	781	781	27	-65	-39	-39

Rating History: NR-2, 03/25/10; NR-2, 06/15/09; NR-2, 06/12/08; NR-2, 03/05/07; NR-2, 02/07/06

UNITED CONCORDIA D PLS THE MW

Highmark Inc.
Frederick G. "Chip" Merkel, President & CEO
4401 Deer Path Road, Harrisburg, PA 17110
MI : 1980 : Stock : Broker
Dental
248-458-1580
AMB# 065700 NAIC# 96150

Best's Financial Strength Rating: NR-2

Data Year	Bonds (%)	Mort. Loans & R.E. (%)	Com & Pref. Stock (%)	All Other Assets (%)	Total Assets ($000)	Life Reserves (%)	Health Reserves (%)	Ann Res. & Dep. Liabilities (%)	All Other Liabilities (%)	Capital & Surplus ($000)	Direct Premiums Written ($000)	Net Premiums Written & Deposits ($000)	Operating Cash Flow ($000)	NOG Before Taxes ($000)	NOG After Taxes ($000)	Net Income ($000)
'05	15.7	...	...	84.3	4,366	...	32.9	...	67.1	3,277	19,603	19,603	-464	-578	-371	-371
'06	15.0	...	...	85.0	4,538	...	38.6	...	61.4	3,489	18,627	18,627	869	-761	-492	-492
'07	15.5	...	...	84.5	4,402	...	43.7	...	56.3	3,532	16,461	16,461	11	-426	-275	-275
'08	12.6	...	0.1	87.3	5,047	...	20.3	...	79.7	4,056	14,127	14,127	523	526	357	357
'09	13.2	...	...	86.8	4,802	...	17.4	...	82.6	4,068	11,645	11,645	-288	38	3	3

Rating History: NR-2, 03/25/10; NR-2, 06/15/09; NR-2, 06/13/08; NR-2, 03/05/07; NR-2, 03/09/06

UNITED CONCORDIA INSURANCE CO

Highmark Inc.
Frederick G. "Chip" Merkel, President & CEO
4401 Deer Path Road, Harrisburg, PA 17110
AZ : 1975 : Stock : Broker
Dental
717-260-7081
AMB# 008651 NAIC# 85766

Best's Financial Strength Rating: A-
Rating Outlook: Stable
FSC VI

Data Year	Bonds (%)	Mort. Loans & R.E. (%)	Com & Pref. Stock (%)	All Other Assets (%)	Total Assets ($000)	Life Reserves (%)	Health Reserves (%)	Ann Res. & Dep. Liabilities (%)	All Other Liabilities (%)	Capital & Surplus ($000)	Direct Premiums Written ($000)	Net Premiums Written & Deposits ($000)	Operating Cash Flow ($000)	NOG Before Taxes ($000)	NOG After Taxes ($000)	Net Income ($000)
'05	62.1	...	...	37.9	55,425	...	50.0	...	50.0	35,633	182,529	91,328	7,218	7,021	4,530	4,542
'06	50.3	...	...	49.7	65,837	...	34.9	...	65.1	40,824	238,376	119,184	8,306	7,971	5,111	5,111
'07	31.8	...	...	68.2	71,416	...	39.4	...	60.6	41,942	258,939	143,161	3,972	1,923	1,247	1,247
'08	44.2	...	...	55.8	64,941	...	30.0	...	70.0	42,307	269,010	134,664	-2,287	776	734	734
'09	61.6	...	...	38.4	59,003	...	27.4	...	72.6	40,103	286,093	142,831	-5,468	-2,886	-1,991	-1,991

Rating History: A-, 03/25/10; A-, 06/15/09; A-, 06/12/08; A-, 03/05/07; A-, 02/07/06

UNITED CONCORDIA INS CO OF NY

Highmark Inc.
Frederick G. "Chip" Merkel, Chairman & President
4401 Deer Path Road, Harrisburg, PA 17110
NY : 1990 : Stock : Broker
Dental
717-260-7081
AMB# 060255 NAIC# 60222

Best's Financial Strength Rating: A-
Rating Outlook: Stable
FSC VI

Data Year	Bonds (%)	Mort. Loans & R.E. (%)	Com & Pref. Stock (%)	All Other Assets (%)	Total Assets ($000)	Life Reserves (%)	Health Reserves (%)	Ann Res. & Dep. Liabilities (%)	All Other Liabilities (%)	Capital & Surplus ($000)	Direct Premiums Written ($000)	Net Premiums Written & Deposits ($000)	Operating Cash Flow ($000)	NOG Before Taxes ($000)	NOG After Taxes ($000)	Net Income ($000)
'05	59.5	...	...	40.5	3,574	...	47.7	...	52.3	2,258	7,880	7,860	130	191	120	120
'06	52.8	...	...	47.2	4,026	...	32.0	...	68.0	2,367	9,600	9,581	414	202	132	132
'07	60.6	...	...	39.4	4,361	...	40.2	...	59.8	2,768	10,038	9,976	347	628	413	413
'08	57.8	...	...	42.2	4,638	...	27.0	...	73.0	2,950	9,822	9,822	192	289	188	188
'09	25.4	...	...	74.6	4,252	...	31.3	...	68.7	2,942	9,558	9,558	-342	79	55	55

Rating History: A-, 03/25/10; A-, 06/15/09; A-, 06/12/08; A-, 03/05/07; A-, 02/07/06

UNITED CONCORDIA LIFE & HEALTH

Highmark Inc.
Frederick G. "Chip" Merkel, Chairman & President
4401 Deer Path Road, Harrisburg, PA 17110
PA : 1965 : Stock : Broker
Dental
717-260-7081
AMB# 006265 NAIC# 62294

Best's Financial Strength Rating: A-
Rating Outlook: Stable
FSC VIII

Data Year	Bonds (%)	Mort. Loans & R.E. (%)	Com & Pref. Stock (%)	All Other Assets (%)	Total Assets ($000)	Life Reserves (%)	Health Reserves (%)	Ann Res. & Dep. Liabilities (%)	All Other Liabilities (%)	Capital & Surplus ($000)	Direct Premiums Written ($000)	Net Premiums Written & Deposits ($000)	Operating Cash Flow ($000)	NOG Before Taxes ($000)	NOG After Taxes ($000)	Net Income ($000)
'05	54.4	...	21.3	24.3	167,016	...	40.2	...	59.8	102,623	332,737	416,581	20,638	50,661	33,094	33,103
'06	35.5	...	21.0	43.5	194,468	...	29.7	...	70.3	128,224	351,028	447,140	21,933	49,723	32,233	32,233
'07	28.2	...	19.3	52.5	217,243	...	44.7	...	55.3	148,489	408,766	510,057	15,009	44,369	28,880	28,879
'08	32.9	...	17.2	49.9	246,078	...	29.3	...	70.7	168,241	509,504	643,850	12,907	43,569	28,035	28,035
'09	48.8	...	16.1	35.2	249,514	...	24.8	...	75.2	171,415	501,447	644,715	12,266	31,119	20,234	20,390

Rating History: A-, 03/25/10; A-, 06/15/09; A-, 06/12/08; A-, 03/05/07; A-, 02/07/06

UNITED DENTAL CARE OF AZ INC

Assurant Inc
Stacia N. Almquist, President
2323 Grand Boulevard, Kansas City, MO 64108
AZ : 1985 : Stock : Broker
Dental
816-474-2345
AMB# 065711 NAIC# 47708

Best's Financial Strength Rating: A-
Rating Outlook: Stable
FSC III

Data Year	Bonds (%)	Mort. Loans & R.E. (%)	Com & Pref. Stock (%)	All Other Assets (%)	Total Assets ($000)	Life Reserves (%)	Health Reserves (%)	Ann Res. & Dep. Liabilities (%)	All Other Liabilities (%)	Capital & Surplus ($000)	Direct Premiums Written ($000)	Net Premiums Written & Deposits ($000)	Operating Cash Flow ($000)	NOG Before Taxes ($000)	NOG After Taxes ($000)	Net Income ($000)
'05	7.4	...	...	92.6	2,713	...	15.7	...	84.3	1,592	8,846	8,846	-5,562	1,517	1,076	1,076
'06	4.4	...	...	95.6	4,657	...	13.7	...	86.3	3,656	7,894	7,894	2,021	1,596	1,025	1,025
'07	3.6	...	...	96.4	5,682	...	14.2	...	85.8	4,679	7,260	7,260	1,071	1,561	1,006	1,006
'08	6.2	...	...	93.8	3,408	...	15.0	...	85.0	2,577	6,525	6,525	-2,041	1,301	816	816
'09	5.3	...	...	94.7	3,987	...	16.7	...	83.3	3,286	5,096	5,096	504	1,080	697	697

Rating History: A-, 11/18/09; A-, 11/25/08; A-, 06/24/08; A-, 07/17/07; A-, 06/19/06

UNITED DENTAL CARE OF CO INC

Assurant Inc
Stacia N. Almquist, President
2323 Grand Boulevard, Kansas City, MO 64108
CO : 1989 : Stock : Broker
Dental
816-474-2345
AMB# 064674 NAIC# 52032

Best's Financial Strength Rating: A-
Rating Outlook: Stable
FSC III

Data Year	Bonds (%)	Mort. Loans & R.E. (%)	Com & Pref. Stock (%)	All Other Assets (%)	Total Assets ($000)	Life Reserves (%)	Health Reserves (%)	Ann Res. & Dep. Liabilities (%)	All Other Liabilities (%)	Capital & Surplus ($000)	Direct Premiums Written ($000)	Net Premiums Written & Deposits ($000)	Operating Cash Flow ($000)	NOG Before Taxes ($000)	NOG After Taxes ($000)	Net Income ($000)
'05	24.6	...	...	75.4	1,777	...	26.1	...	73.9	1,559	3,730	3,730	-4,943	927	598	598
'06	13.2	...	...	86.8	3,330	...	23.6	...	76.4	3,090	3,508	3,508	1,565	818	534	534
'07	11.3	...	...	88.7	3,842	...	26.6	...	73.4	3,632	3,168	3,168	525	810	518	518
'08	13.2	...	...	86.8	3,283	...	23.4	...	76.6	3,077	2,934	2,934	-561	678	434	434
'09	12.2	...	...	87.8	3,531	...	41.9	...	58.1	3,393	2,705	2,705	196	486	315	315

Rating History: A-, 11/18/09; A-, 11/25/08; A-, 06/24/08; A-, 07/17/07; A-, 06/19/06

UNITED DENTAL CARE OF MI INC

Assurant Inc
Stacia N. Almquist, President
2323 Grand Boulevard, Kansas City, MO 64108
MI : 1989 : Stock : Broker
Dental
816-474-2345
AMB# 065709 NAIC# 11111

Best's Financial Strength Rating: NR-3

Data Year	Bonds (%)	Mort. Loans & R.E. (%)	Com & Pref. Stock (%)	All Other Assets (%)	Total Assets ($000)	Life Reserves (%)	Health Reserves (%)	Ann Res. & Dep. Liabilities (%)	All Other Liabilities (%)	Capital & Surplus ($000)	Direct Premiums Written ($000)	Net Premiums Written & Deposits ($000)	Operating Cash Flow ($000)	NOG Before Taxes ($000)	NOG After Taxes ($000)	Net Income ($000)
'05	19.2	...	...	80.8	678	...	7.9	...	92.1	640	461	461	12	41	26	26
'06	19.2	...	...	80.8	692	...	2.6	...	97.4	664	376	376	18	34	21	21
'07	19.0	...	...	81.0	702	...	4.4	...	95.6	675	366	366	12	18	12	12
'08	18.1	...	...	81.9	722	...	4.2	...	95.8	693	385	385	16	20	10	10
'09	18.3	...	...	81.7	740	...	10.7	...	89.3	726	422	422	23	62	44	44

Rating History: NR-3, 11/18/09; NR-3, 11/25/08; NR-3, 06/24/08; NR-3, 07/17/07; NR-3, 06/19/06

UNITED DENTAL CARE OF MO INC

Assurant Inc
Stacia N. Almquist, President
2323 Grand Boulevard, Kansas City, MO 64108-2670
MO : 1993 : Stock : Broker
Dental
816-474-2345
AMB# 065710 NAIC# 47044

Best's Financial Strength Rating: A-
Rating Outlook: Stable
FSC III

Data Year	Bonds (%)	Mort. Loans & R.E. (%)	Com & Pref. Stock (%)	All Other Assets (%)	Total Assets ($000)	Life Reserves (%)	Health Reserves (%)	Ann Res. & Dep. Liabilities (%)	All Other Liabilities (%)	Capital & Surplus ($000)	Direct Premiums Written ($000)	Net Premiums Written & Deposits ($000)	Operating Cash Flow ($000)	NOG Before Taxes ($000)	NOG After Taxes ($000)	Net Income ($000)
'05	31.1	...	...	68.9	836	...	29.3	...	70.7	478	3,392	3,392	-911	-4	-12	-12
'06	9.0	...	...	91.0	2,860	...	36.5	...	63.5	2,492	2,898	2,898	2,046	-23	-29	-29
'07	8.9	...	...	91.1	2,881	...	47.2	...	52.8	2,501	2,430	2,430	73	34	28	28
'08	9.1	...	...	90.9	2,836	...	44.4	...	55.6	2,542	2,223	2,223	-40	62	38	38
'09	5.9	...	...	94.1	2,690	...	54.3	...	45.7	2,528	2,014	2,014	-165	-28	-20	-20

Rating History: A-, 11/18/09; A-, 11/25/08; A-, 06/24/08; A-, 07/17/07; A-, 06/19/06

2010 BEST'S KEY RATING GUIDE — LIFE/HEALTH EDITION
BEST'S PROFITABILITY, LEVERAGE AND LIQUIDITY TESTS 2005 – 2009

Data in U.S. Dollars

—	Profitability Tests							Leverage Tests						Liquidity Tests					
Un-Realized Capital Gains ($000)	Benefits Paid to NPW & Dep (%)	Comm. & Expenses to NPW & Dep (%)	NOG to Total Assets (%)	NOG to Total Rev (%)	Operating Return on Equity (%)	Net Yield (%)	Total Return (%)	Change in NPW & Dep (%)	NPW & Dep to Capital (X)	Capital & Surplus to Liabilities (%)	Surplus Relief (%)	Reins Leverage (%)	Change in Capital (%)	Quick Liquidity (%)	Current Liquidity (%)	Non-Invest Grade Bonds to Capital (%)	Delinq. & Foreclosed Mortgages to Capital (%)	Mort. & Credit Tenant Loans & R.E. to Capital (%)	Affiliated Invest to Capital (%)
...	93.6	26.1	-13.1	-11.9	-14.8	0.74	0.74	11.5	1.3	803.1	...	...	-5.1	891.7	891.7	...	...	...	...
...	84.8	26.6	-8.8	-7.1	-10.0	1.03	1.03	15.5	1.3	724.3	...	...	9.6	813.0	813.0	...	...	...	...
...	81.3	25.4	-2.0	-1.6	-2.4	4.19	4.19	4.4	1.4	353.6	...	...	-2.9	448.7	448.7	...	...	...	...
...	71.7	38.1	-6.3	-5.1	-8.1	1.52	1.52	7.4	1.6	348.7	...	...	-3.0	420.0	420.0	...	...	...	...
...	78.2	30.2	-5.6	-4.9	-6.9	0.16	0.16	-5.6	1.3	504.1	...	...	14.5	999.9	999.9	...	...	...	...
	Principal Lines of Business: Dental (100.0%)													Principal States: TX (100.0%)					
...	94.4	9.0	0.0	1.0	11.6	2.81	2.81	1.0	6.0	301.0	...	...	4.7	318.4	318.4	...	...	...	...
...	96.2	8.7	-11.1	-2.6	-14.5	4.15	4.15	-5.0	5.3	332.7	...	...	6.5	411.0	411.0	...	...	...	...
...	94.6	9.0	-6.2	-1.7	-7.8	3.97	3.97	-11.6	4.7	406.2	...	...	1.2	498.2	498.2	...	...	...	...
...	87.7	9.4	7.6	2.5	9.4	2.42	2.42	-14.2	3.5	409.3	...	...	14.8	813.5	849.3	...	...	...	...
...	87.7	12.2	0.1	0.0	0.1	0.45	0.45	-17.6	2.9	554.3	...	...	0.3	999.9	999.9	...	...	...	...
	Principal Lines of Business: Dental (100.0%)													Principal States: MI (91.0%), OH (5.8%)					
...	77.7	16.4	9.0	4.9	13.6	3.47	3.50	26.1	2.6	180.0	40.3	20.7	14.5	251.1	252.7	...	...	...	...
...	78.1	17.5	8.4	4.2	13.4	5.08	5.08	30.5	2.9	163.2	45.2	18.7	14.6	229.8	229.9	...	...	...	...
...	82.3	18.7	1.8	0.9	3.0	5.45	5.45	20.1	3.4	142.3	0.0	19.3	2.7	217.4	217.5	...	...	...	...
...	82.2	18.9	1.1	0.5	1.7	3.64	3.64	-5.9	3.2	186.9	0.1	22.0	0.9	379.3	408.6	...	...	...	...
...	85.5	17.5	-3.2	-1.4	-4.8	2.35	2.35	6.1	3.6	212.2	0.1	21.1	-5.2	374.7	411.1	...	...	...	...
	Principal Lines of Business: Dental (100.0%)													Principal States: GA (22.2%), CA (19.0%), FL (9.4%), TX (8.7%), WA (8.2%)					
...	76.8	21.6	3.5	1.5	5.6	2.10	2.10	15.9	3.5	171.6	0.0	...	9.4	244.2	244.2	...	...	...	...
...	76.2	22.6	3.5	1.4	5.7	2.47	2.47	21.9	4.0	142.7	0.0	0.0	4.8	223.2	223.2	...	...	...	...
...	73.2	21.5	9.9	4.1	16.1	2.48	2.48	4.1	3.6	173.8	0.0	...	16.9	249.8	249.8	...	...	...	...
...	77.5	20.5	4.2	1.9	6.6	2.25	2.25	-1.5	3.3	174.8	...	...	6.6	280.3	280.3	...	...	...	...
...	79.9	20.1	1.2	0.6	1.9	1.77	1.77	-2.7	3.2	224.6	...	...	-0.3	456.4	456.4	...	...	...	...
	Principal Lines of Business: Dental (100.0%)													Principal States: NY (100.0%)					
4,512	74.6	14.1	21.3	7.9	35.2	2.65	5.83	7.4	4.1	159.4	0.1	...	20.3	199.2	200.4	...	...	...	34.7
5,191	75.7	14.5	17.8	7.1	27.9	3.50	6.59	7.3	3.5	193.6	0.2	...	24.9	222.2	222.6	...	...	...	31.8
1,118	78.3	14.6	14.0	5.6	20.9	4.12	4.70	14.1	3.4	216.0	0.0	...	15.8	230.7	231.1	...	...	...	28.2
402	79.9	14.2	12.1	4.3	17.7	2.86	3.05	26.2	3.8	216.1	...	...	13.3	316.3	336.5	...	...	...	25.2
-2,046	80.9	14.8	8.2	3.1	11.9	1.65	0.80	0.1	3.8	219.5	...	...	1.9	293.5	318.1	...	...	...	23.5
	Principal Lines of Business: Dental (100.0%)													Principal States: PA (66.9%), DC (15.3%), MD (7.6%), NC (7.5%)					
...	63.7	21.2	19.2	11.9	24.3	3.67	3.67	-16.3	5.6	142.0	...	...	-78.1	356.3	356.3	...	...	...	...
...	60.6	21.1	27.8	12.7	39.1	4.70	4.70	-10.8	2.2	365.1	...	...	129.7	800.7	800.7	...	...	...	...
...	61.5	19.9	19.5	13.5	24.1	4.55	4.55	-8.0	1.6	466.8	...	...	28.0	999.9	999.9	...	...	...	...
...	61.7	19.9	18.0	12.3	22.5	2.33	2.33	-10.1	2.5	309.8	...	...	-44.9	728.1	728.1	...	...	...	...
...	59.1	19.9	18.9	13.7	23.8	0.37	0.37	-21.9	1.6	468.4	...	...	27.5	999.9	999.9	...	...	...	...
	Principal Lines of Business: Dental (100.0%)													Principal States: AZ (100.0%)					
...	58.8	20.5	14.0	15.4	14.9	3.79	3.79	-9.2	2.4	713.2	...	...	-75.8	999.9	999.9	...	...	...	...
...	59.5	20.3	20.9	14.8	23.0	4.53	4.53	-6.0	1.1	999.9	...	...	98.3	999.9	999.9	...	...	...	...
...	59.4	19.9	14.5	15.6	15.4	4.51	4.51	-9.7	0.9	999.9	...	...	17.5	999.9	999.9	...	...	...	...
...	59.5	20.0	12.2	14.4	12.9	2.22	2.22	-7.4	1.0	999.9	...	...	-15.3	999.9	999.9	...	...	...	...
...	62.7	20.0	9.2	11.5	9.7	0.49	0.49	-7.8	0.8	999.9	...	...	10.3	999.9	999.9	...	...	...	...
	Principal Lines of Business: Dental (100.0%)													Principal States: CO (100.0%)					
...	61.8	33.5	3.8	5.2	4.1	2.86	2.86	-18.7	0.7	999.9	...	...	4.7	999.9	999.9	...	...	...	...
...	63.3	35.2	3.0	5.1	3.2	4.20	4.20	-18.3	0.6	999.9	...	...	3.8	999.9	999.9	...	...	...	...
...	68.1	34.9	1.7	3.0	1.7	4.33	4.33	-2.8	0.5	999.9	...	...	1.6	999.9	999.9	...	...	...	...
...	63.6	35.0	1.4	2.4	1.4	2.04	2.04	5.1	0.6	999.9	...	...	2.7	999.9	999.9	...	...	...	...
...	52.0	34.4	6.0	10.2	6.1	0.60	0.60	9.8	0.6	999.9	...	...	4.7	999.9	999.9	...	...	...	...
	Principal Lines of Business: Dental (100.0%)													Principal States: MI (100.0%)					
...	69.8	31.2	-0.9	-0.4	-1.2	2.51	2.51	-15.9	7.1	133.3	...	...	-67.4	310.0	310.0	...	...	...	...
...	70.8	32.7	-1.6	-1.0	-2.0	4.46	4.46	-14.6	1.2	677.2	...	...	421.7	999.9	999.9	...	...	...	...
...	69.3	34.3	1.0	1.1	1.1	4.31	4.31	-16.2	1.0	658.5	...	...	0.4	999.9	999.9	...	...	...	...
...	64.6	34.9	1.3	1.6	1.5	1.80	1.80	-8.5	0.9	865.2	...	...	1.6	999.9	999.9	...	...	...	...
...	66.8	35.0	-0.7	-0.9	-0.8	0.36	0.36	-9.4	0.8	999.9	...	...	-0.5	999.9	999.9	...	...	...	...
	Principal Lines of Business: Dental (100.0%)													Principal States: MO (88.0%), KS (12.0%)					

Data in U.S. Dollars

COMPANY NAME Ultimate Parent Association Principal Officer Mailing Address Dom. : Began Bus. : Struct. : Mktg. Specialty Phone # AMB# NAIC#	Best's Financial Strength Rating FSC	Data Year	Balance Sheet Bonds (%)	Mort. Loans & R.E. (%)	Com & Pref. Stock (%)	All Other Assets (%)	Total Assets ($000)	Life Reserves (%)	Health Reserves %)	Ann Res. & Dep. Liabilities (%)	All Other Liabilities (%)	Capital & Surplus ($000)	Operations Direct Premiums Written ($000)	Net Premiums Written & Deposits ($000)	Operating Cash Flow ($000)	NOG Before Taxes ($000)	NOG After Taxes ($000)	Net Income ($000)
UNITED DENTAL CARE OF NM INC Assurant Inc Stacia N. Almquist President 2323 Grand Boulevard Kansas City, MO 64108 NM : 1980 : Stock : Broker Dental 816-474-2345 AMB# 064360 NAIC# 47042	**A-** Rating Outlook: Stable **FSC III**	'05	13.7	...	...	86.3	1,539	...	31.6	...	68.4	1,445	968	968	227	386	249	249
		'06	7.7	...	...	92.3	2,739	...	30.6	...	69.4	2,673	709	709	1,253	347	225	225
		'07	7.2	...	...	92.8	2,935	...	30.4	...	69.6	2,881	544	544	197	316	204	204
		'08	6.8	...	...	93.2	3,077	...	29.8	...	70.2	3,027	472	472	147	223	145	145
		'09	6.9	...	...	93.1	3,167	...	41.6	...	58.4	3,132	420	420	88	159	103	103
		Rating History: A-, 11/18/09; A-, 11/25/08; A-, 06/24/08; A-, 07/17/07; A-, 06/19/06																
UNITED DENTAL CARE OF TX INC Assurant Inc Stacia N. Almquist President 2745 N Dallas Parkway, Suite 500 Plano, TX 75093 TX : 1985 : Stock : Broker Dental 800-262-5388 AMB# 064363 NAIC# 95142	**A-** Rating Outlook: Stable **FSC III**	'05	28.5	...	...	71.5	6,421	...	12.5	...	87.5	4,620	17,482	17,482	-1,921	2,830	1,847	1,847
		'06	46.2	...	...	53.8	7,580	...	10.5	...	89.5	5,844	13,926	13,926	994	1,848	1,221	1,222
		'07	61.4	...	...	38.6	5,701	...	10.8	...	89.2	4,251	9,993	9,993	-1,507	2,129	1,436	1,436
		'08	54.6	...	...	45.4	6,436	...	13.0	...	87.0	5,332	9,534	9,534	-855	1,633	1,040	1,040
		'09	78.1	...	...	21.9	4,498	...	16.6	...	83.4	3,541	8,986	8,986	-322	1,102	723	724
		Rating History: A-, 11/18/09; A-, 11/25/08; A-, 06/24/08; A-, 07/17/07; A-, 06/19/06																
UNITED DENTAL CARE OF UT INC Assurant Inc Stacia N. Almquist President 2323 Grand Boulevard Kansas City, MO 64108 UT : 1989 : Stock : Broker Dental 816-474-2345 AMB# 064362 NAIC# 95450	**NR-3**	'05	5.1	...	...	94.9	492	...	6.3	...	93.7	451	437	437	23	37	25	25
		'06	4.9	...	...	95.1	509	...	5.8	...	94.2	468	456	456	20	28	19	19
		'07	4.6	...	...	95.4	531	...	6.3	...	93.7	486	504	504	18	28	17	17
		'08	4.6	...	...	95.4	543	...	4.3	...	95.7	494	529	529	7	15	9	9
		'09	4.8	...	...	95.2	544	...	15.3	...	84.7	526	565	565	-3	52	35	35
		Rating History: NR-3, 11/18/09; NR-3, 11/25/08; NR-3, 06/24/08; NR-3, 07/17/07; NR-3, 06/19/06																
UNITED FARM FAMILY LIFE INS CO Indiana Farm Bureau Inc Donald B. Villwock Chairman & President 225 South East Street Indianapolis, IN 46202 IN : 1964 : Stock : Career Agent Ann, Term Life, Whole life 317-692-7200 AMB# 007168 NAIC# 69892	**A** Rating Outlook: Stable **FSC VIII**	'05	74.5	13.2	1.5	10.8	1,598,228	67.0	0.5	26.7	5.8	175,050	124,242	122,197	50,405	19,668	14,045	12,553
		'06	73.6	13.6	2.1	10.7	1,638,269	67.9	0.5	25.7	5.9	189,128	123,968	118,402	38,911	25,832	16,189	17,878
		'07	71.6	14.5	3.5	10.5	1,667,509	69.4	0.4	24.7	5.5	205,095	119,737	112,847	27,208	24,589	16,500	10,514
		'08	69.5	15.0	3.7	11.8	1,692,107	70.1	0.4	24.1	5.4	197,730	123,974	114,737	32,293	24,965	15,815	9,601
		'09	69.8	15.5	3.0	11.7	1,768,006	68.9	0.4	24.1	6.7	218,815	142,564	120,870	47,792	24,915	16,619	13,255
		Rating History: A, 04/26/10; A, 06/01/09; A, 05/30/08; A, 05/01/07; A, 06/05/06																
UNITED FIDELITY LIFE INS CO Financial Holding Corporation Gary L. Muller CEO P.O. Box 410288 Kansas City, MO 64141-0288 TX : 1977 : Stock : Agency Ann, ISWL, Term Life 816-391-2000 AMB# 007169 NAIC# 87645	**NR-3**	'05	25.8	8.3	48.6	17.3	610,349	52.5	0.0	14.4	33.1	200,987	15,791	30,587	-27,673	11,968	-34,872	-38,140
		'06	27.3	7.8	52.5	12.4	611,954	52.8	0.0	14.3	32.8	212,540	14,840	29,610	-8,960	-3,135	324	4,741
		'07	26.6	6.5	55.9	10.9	609,661	53.4	0.0	14.4	32.2	226,062	13,827	29,023	-18,831	-3,466	-73	212
		'08	26.1	8.4	47.5	17.9	572,103	71.0	0.0	14.4	14.5	196,474	13,033	25,621	15,360	6,478	9,088	8,949
		'09	24.8	6.5	60.2	8.5	690,452	71.0	0.0	14.6	14.4	328,441	12,188	11,898	17,435	-13,718	-7,412	-8,384
		Rating History: NR-3, 11/04/09; NR-3, 09/05/08; NR-3, 06/14/07; NR-3, 06/21/06; NR-2, 06/22/05																
UNITED FUNERAL BENEFIT LIFE[1] Charlie R. Allison President 351 South Sherman Street, Suite 102 Richardson, TX 75081 TX : 1972 : Stock : Agency 469-330-2200 AMB# 008301 NAIC# 79502	**NR-1**	'05	80.9	0.3	5.5	13.3	29,955	...	...	...	100.0	2,820	2,710	2,707	...	751	712	712
		'06	83.4	0.2	6.9	9.5	29,636	...	...	...	100.0	1,955	2,473	2,471	...	63	53	53
		'07	86.4	0.2	6.5	6.9	29,618	...	...	...	100.0	1,706	2,057	2,053	...	104	102	102
		'08	82.2	0.3	6.9	10.7	32,151	...	...	...	100.0	2,542	2,468	2,462	...	642	572	572
		'09	86.0	0.2	7.4	6.4	35,701	...	...	...	100.0	3,581	2,070	2,079	...	1,307	1,186	1,163
		Rating History: NR-1, 06/10/10; NR-1, 06/12/09; NR-1, 06/12/08; NR-1, 06/08/07; NR-1, 06/07/06																
UNITED FUNERAL DIR BENEFIT[1] Charlie Allison President P.O. Box 831670 Richardson, TX 75083-1670 TX : 1989 : Stock : Agency 469-330-2200 AMB# 068068 NAIC# 77194	**NR-1**	'05	83.9	...	2.2	13.9	17,088	...	...	...	100.0	1,001	1,547	765	...	250	217	217
		'06	80.8	...	4.9	14.3	24,931	...	...	...	100.0	1,358	1,673	1,171	...	164	104	104
		'07	88.7	1.3	5.0	5.0	26,325	...	...	...	100.0	1,200	2,462	1,723	...	-24	-18	-18
		'08	86.6	1.9	2.0	9.5	31,126	...	...	...	100.0	1,462	2,782	1,947	...	367	328	328
		'09	85.3	1.8	9.2	3.7	34,212	...	...	...	100.0	1,907	3,989	3,054	...	723	627	517
		Rating History: NR-1, 06/10/10; NR-1, 06/12/09; NR-1, 06/12/08; NR-1, 06/08/07; NR-1, 06/07/06																
UNITED HERITAGE LIFE INS CO United Heritage Mutual Holding Company Dennis L. Johnson President & CEO P.O. Box 7777 Meridian, ID 83680-7777 ID : 1935 : Stock : Agency Pre-need, Univ Life, Ann 208-493-6100 AMB# 006472 NAIC# 63983	**A-** Rating Outlook: Negative **FSC VI**	'05	79.3	11.4	3.8	5.4	410,038	40.6	0.1	56.9	2.4	40,969	47,138	47,785	12,123	2,204	2,301	2,006
		'06	77.8	11.3	5.0	5.9	409,752	42.8	0.1	54.5	2.5	41,228	54,978	55,716	-5,321	2,474	2,419	2,000
		'07	76.1	10.8	6.9	6.2	411,703	44.6	0.1	52.9	2.4	41,634	65,737	65,872	-2,465	2,276	2,061	1,704
		'08	77.1	10.4	4.7	7.8	420,525	45.4	0.1	53.0	1.5	40,022	60,587	59,267	1,720	4,499	2,907	-5,143
		'09	83.8	8.8	0.2	7.2	438,330	45.5	0.1	52.2	2.2	40,807	59,956	57,383	8,510	6,638	6,894	648
		Rating History: A-, 05/21/09; A-, 01/25/08; A-, 02/21/07; A-, 02/08/06; A-, 03/10/05																
UNITED HOME LIFE INS CO Indiana Farm Bureau Inc Donald B. Villwock Chairman & President 225 South East Street Indianapolis, IN 46202 IN : 1948 : Stock : Agency Term Life, Whole life 317-692-7979 AMB# 007172 NAIC# 69922	**A-** Rating Outlook: Stable **FSC V**	'05	77.5	2.1	3.8	16.6	46,156	74.6	1.0	19.2	5.2	8,235	12,401	8,055	-2,160	-1,847	-1,564	-1,564
		'06	77.6	0.5	4.0	17.8	48,850	75.3	1.0	18.1	5.5	9,965	15,444	10,520	1,378	-1,323	-1,200	-1,212
		'07	78.0	0.3	4.3	17.4	59,191	78.9	0.9	15.3	4.9	15,885	17,433	11,452	9,326	-445	-488	-476
		'08	78.3	0.2	2.9	18.5	60,014	80.9	0.6	13.8	4.7	16,033	18,183	11,878	1,454	-223	-209	-209
		'09	77.2	0.1	2.6	20.1	62,925	74.8	0.5	11.9	12.7	16,398	21,602	10,902	774	491	372	307
		Rating History: A-, 04/26/10; A-, 06/01/09; A-, 05/30/08; B++, 05/01/07; B++, 06/05/06																

BEST'S PROFITABILITY, LEVERAGE AND LIQUIDITY TESTS 2005 – 2009

Data in U.S. Dollars

	Profitability Tests							Leverage Tests						Liquidity Tests					
Un-Realized Capital Gains ($000)	Benefits Paid to NPW & Dep (%)	Comm. & Expenses to NPW & Dep (%)	NOG to Total Assets (%)	NOG to Total Rev (%)	Operating Return on Equity (%)	Net Yield (%)	Total Return (%)	Change in NPW & Dep (%)	NPW & Dep to Capital (X)	Capital & Surplus to Liabilities (%)	Surplus Relief (%)	Reins Leverage (%)	Change in Capital (%)	Quick Liquidity (%)	Current Liquidity (%)	Non-Invest Grade Bonds to Capital (%)	Delinq. & Foreclosed Mortgages to Capital (%)	Mort. & Credit Tenant Loans & R.E. to Capital (%)	Affiliated Invest to Capital (%)
...	41.9	22.7	17.6	24.5	18.9	2.97	2.97	-20.4	0.7	999.9	...	...	21.6	999.9	999.9	...	...	...	...
...	44.8	20.0	10.5	27.8	10.9	4.55	4.55	-26.8	0.3	999.9	...	...	85.1	999.9	999.9	...	...	...	...
...	45.1	20.0	7.2	30.3	7.3	4.50	4.50	-23.3	0.2	999.9	...	...	7.8	999.9	999.9	...	...	...	...
...	44.2	19.9	4.8	27.5	4.9	1.81	1.81	-13.2	0.2	999.9	...	...	5.1	999.9	999.9	...	...	...	...
...	44.8	19.9	3.3	23.8	3.3	0.34	0.34	-11.1	0.1	999.9	...	...	3.5	999.9	999.9	...	...	...	...

Principal Lines of Business: Dental (100.0%) Principal States: NM (100.0%)

...	55.2	20.7	24.0	10.4	36.8	2.86	2.86	-8.7	3.8	256.5	...	...	-18.8	302.1	302.1				
...	53.1	35.0	17.4	8.6	23.3	3.04	3.04	-20.3	2.4	336.5	...	...	26.5	527.1	527.1	...	...	...	...
...	47.7	34.1	21.6	13.9	28.5	5.70	5.70	-28.2	2.4	293.2	...	...	-27.2	434.6	434.6	...	...	...	...
...	49.7	34.8	17.1	10.7	21.7	3.03	3.03	-4.6	1.8	483.0	...	...	25.4	400.1	400.1	...	...	...	...
...	54.1	35.0	13.2	7.9	16.3	2.56	2.58	-5.7	2.5	370.0	...	...	-33.6	392.4	392.4	...	...	...	...

Principal Lines of Business: Dental (100.0%) Principal States: TX (100.0%)

...	63.9	30.2	5.2	5.5	5.7	2.53	2.53	4.9	1.0	999.9	...	...	5.4	999.9	999.9	...	...	...	...
...	67.0	31.1	3.7	3.9	4.0	3.88	3.88	4.4	1.0	999.9	...	...	3.8	999.9	999.9	...	...	...	...
...	64.1	34.9	3.4	3.3	3.7	4.48	4.48	10.5	1.0	999.9	...	...	3.7	999.9	999.9	...	...	...	...
...	64.2	34.8	1.8	1.8	1.9	1.80	1.80	5.0	1.1	999.9	...	...	1.7	999.9	999.9	...	...	...	...
...	56.0	35.0	6.5	6.2	6.9	0.33	0.33	6.7	1.1	999.9	...	...	6.4	999.9	999.9	...	...	...	...

Principal Lines of Business: Dental (100.0%) Principal States: UT (100.0%)

-944	74.7	26.8	0.9	6.7	8.2	5.44	5.53	-2.7	0.7	13.2	3.5	10.3	4.8	64.3	73.6	10.6	...	113.2	9.1
348	86.8	25.8	1.0	7.6	8.9	5.59	5.92	-3.1	0.6	14.2	3.7	13.1	9.0	65.4	74.3	5.5	...	109.8	7.3
4,174	91.0	25.7	1.0	7.9	8.4	5.60	5.61	-4.7	0.5	15.3	3.8	14.2	8.7	63.4	72.6	3.7	...	109.1	8.6
-10,829	83.6	25.1	0.9	7.5	7.9	5.70	4.75	1.7	0.6	13.9	4.4	17.2	-6.7	61.9	70.3	11.4	...	123.1	10.0
6,124	80.7	27.3	1.0	7.5	8.0	5.69	5.93	5.3	0.5	15.1	4.4	25.2	12.5	63.5	71.6	6.9	0.7	118.4	10.2

Principal Lines of Business: OrdLife (74.1%), IndAnn (24.4%), IndA&H (0.9%), GrpAnn (0.5%), GrpLife (0.1%) Principal States: IN (85.9%)

22,738	44.3	111.9	-5.8	-57.0	-18.6	6.06	9.47	-21.4	0.1	52.3	3.2	41.0	16.0	38.6	46.0	6.7	0.1	24.1	143.8
24,872	84.0	111.6	0.1	0.6	0.2	3.56	8.60	-3.2	0.1	56.2	2.7	37.2	5.0	34.4	41.3	5.6	0.1	21.7	143.9
16,371	75.0	92.1	0.0	-0.2	0.0	1.46	4.30	-2.0	0.1	62.6	1.3	33.4	6.5	32.8	40.3	3.3	0.0	16.9	140.5
-64,468	85.4	96.9	1.5	7.8	4.3	3.73	-6.83	-11.7	0.1	53.2	1.1	0.4	-15.3	38.8	45.9	6.1	0.1	24.2	137.0
120,591	247.4	135.5	-1.2	-33.9	-2.8	1.63	23.07	-53.6	0.0	93.1	0.0	0.2	67.6	29.2	39.0	4.2	...	13.6	125.0

Principal Lines of Business: OrdLife (94.7%), IndAnn (4.2%), GrpAnn (0.9%), GrpLife (0.1%), CrdLife (0.0%) Principal States: TX (15.8%), NC (9.2%), CA (6.4%), GA (6.2%), FL (4.3%)

-230	64.2	36.8	2.4	16.7	26.1	...	...	16.1	1.0	10.4	0.0	...	6.9	...	...	...	...	2.9	...
356	70.0	41.0	0.2	1.6	2.2	...	...	-8.7	1.3	7.1	0.0	...	-30.6	...	...	...	...	3.4	...
-158	89.1	37.9	0.3	3.5	5.6	...	...	-16.9	1.2	6.1	0.1	...	-12.7	...	...	...	...	3.0	...
262	70.3	30.0	1.9	15.0	26.9	...	...	19.9	1.0	8.6	0.1	...	48.8	...	...	...	...	3.3	...
446	79.7	39.9	3.5	27.3	38.7	...	...	-15.6	0.6	11.2	0.0	...	40.7	...	...	...	...	2.0	...

Principal Lines of Business: OrdLife (61.5%), IndAnn (38.5%)

-39	78.9	29.6	1.3	14.2	19.4	...	...	-10.5	0.8	6.3	16.9	...	-18.5	...	...	...	...	...	...
-91	91.7	42.5	0.5	1.7	8.9	...	...	53.0	0.9	5.8	7.7	...	36.2	...	...	...	...	...	...
-346	80.6	49.4	-0.1	-0.7	-1.4	...	...	47.2	1.4	4.9	11.7	...	-10.9	...	...	...	...	28.0	...
-971	72.7	74.4	1.1	6.1	24.7	...	...	13.0	1.3	4.9	14.3	...	19.7	...	...	...	...	39.7	...
163	48.3	42.7	1.9	12.4	37.2	...	...	56.9	1.6	6.0	8.2	...	31.1	...	...	...	...	31.8	...

Principal Lines of Business: OrdLife (54.6%), IndAnn (45.4%)

-307	90.4	33.1	0.6	3.4	6.1	6.28	6.13	-0.9	1.1	11.8	0.0	8.2	18.0	61.0	72.2	24.0	...	107.9	14.9
199	107.2	29.3	0.6	3.2	5.9	6.19	6.14	16.6	1.3	12.1	0.0	10.0	1.9	58.4	70.4	37.6	...	104.7	14.3
-2,032	100.6	24.7	0.5	2.4	5.0	6.21	5.62	18.2	1.5	11.9	0.0	10.0	-1.2	53.3	66.4	46.8	...	102.3	14.2
852	79.4	27.7	0.7	3.5	7.1	6.51	4.74	-10.0	1.5	10.7	0.0	11.0	-6.7	52.5	63.9	49.8	...	107.8	15.9
1,151	75.2	31.1	1.6	8.3	17.1	6.68	5.49	-3.2	1.4	10.5	0.0	12.2	1.9	57.5	68.1	53.2	...	93.2	15.2

Principal Lines of Business: OrdLife (63.7%), IndAnn (31.2%), GrpLife (2.3%), GrpAnn (1.5%), GrpA&H (1.3%) Principal States: ID (18.4%), MN (11.5%), OR (9.5%), WA (9.5%), CA (7.6%)

61	48.7	85.5	-3.4	-11.6	-17.2	5.10	5.44	49.5	0.9	22.8	38.7	95.1	-16.2	81.2	89.8	4.6	2.9	11.1	...
142	43.9	82.0	-2.5	-7.6	-13.2	5.31	5.76	30.6	1.0	26.9	29.4	113.1	20.7	82.8	91.9	4.8	0.3	2.3	...
54	29.6	68.8	-0.9	-2.9	-3.8	5.02	5.24	8.9	0.7	38.0	19.0	81.6	57.7	87.6	98.6	3.1	0.2	1.0	...
-506	42.8	69.6	-0.4	-1.2	-1.3	5.70	4.81	3.7	0.7	37.1	17.3	93.4	-0.4	88.9	99.7	3.1	0.4	0.9	...
241	47.8	88.4	0.6	1.9	2.3	5.64	6.04	-8.2	0.7	36.3	31.4	124.5	3.2	87.7	98.4	...	0.2	0.4	...

Principal Lines of Business: OrdLife (99.2%), IndA&H (0.5%), IndAnn (0.2%), GrpAnn (0.1%), GrpLife (0.0%) Principal States: TX (11.8%), CA (11.6%), GA (9.9%), FL (8.5%), AL (5.6%)

Data in U.S. Dollars

COMPANY NAME / Ultimate Parent Association / Principal Officer / Mailing Address / Dom. : Began Bus. : Struct. : Mktg. / Specialty / Phone # / AMB# / NAIC# — Best's Financial Strength Rating / FSC

Column key: Balance Sheet — Bonds (%), Mort. Loans & R.E. (%), Com & Pref. Stock (%), All Other Assets (%), Total Assets ($000), Life Reserves (%), Health Reserves (%), Ann Res. & Dep. Liabilities (%), All Other Liabilities (%), Capital & Surplus ($000); Operations — Direct Premiums Written ($000), Net Premiums Written & Deposits ($000), Operating Cash Flow ($000), NOG Before Taxes ($000), NOG After Taxes ($000), Net Income ($000)

UNITED INSURANCE CO OF AMERICA
Unitrin, Inc
Don M. Royster, Sr.
President
12115 Lackland Road
St. Louis, MO 63146
IL : 1928 : Stock : Career Agent
Home serv, Ind A&H, Ind Life
314-819-4300
AMB# 007174 NAIC# 69930

Best's Financial Strength Rating: **A-** — Rating Outlook: Stable — **FSC IX**

Data Year	Bonds (%)	Mort. Loans & R.E. (%)	Com & Pref. Stock (%)	All Other Assets (%)	Total Assets ($000)	Life Reserves (%)	Health Reserves (%)	Ann Res. & Dep. Liabilities (%)	All Other Liabilities (%)	Capital & Surplus ($000)	Direct Premiums Written ($000)	Net Premiums Written & Deposits ($000)	Operating Cash Flow ($000)	NOG Before Taxes ($000)	NOG After Taxes ($000)	Net Income ($000)
'05	60.3	7.1	3.5	29.2	1,959,226	92.1	1.3	0.0	6.6	179,830	243,167	234,259	-262,586	29,077	17,877	-38,601
'06	63.9	6.9	4.4	24.8	2,032,678	92.5	1.1	0.0	6.4	208,804	233,805	225,791	58,605	65,663	40,670	45,192
'07	56.6	7.5	7.9	28.1	2,055,249	92.1	1.0	0.0	6.8	204,197	220,995	213,786	26,991	90,312	35,951	31,893
'08	59.5	8.3	10.3	21.8	2,005,027	95.1	1.0	0.0	3.8	190,165	208,914	201,876	-31,080	92,188	70,626	-5,642
'09	61.7	5.7	10.2	22.4	3,238,886	95.9	1.0	0.1	2.9	303,513	205,848	407,372	1,105,776	85,726	61,981	52,046

Rating History: A- g, 05/25/10; A- g, 04/10/09; A g, 05/05/08; A g, 04/06/07; A g, 04/28/06

UNITED INTERNATIONAL LIFE INS
United International Corporation
James I. Dunham
President
3555 NW 58th Street, Suite 505
Oklahoma City, OK 73112-4703
OK : 2002 : Stock : Not Available
Ind Ann, Ordinary Life
405-942-3617
AMB# 060387 NAIC# 11262

Best's Financial Strength Rating: **NR-5**

Data Year	Bonds (%)	Mort. Loans & R.E. (%)	Com & Pref. Stock (%)	All Other Assets (%)	Total Assets ($000)	Life Reserves (%)	Health Reserves (%)	Ann Res. & Dep. Liabilities (%)	All Other Liabilities (%)	Capital & Surplus ($000)	Direct Premiums Written ($000)	Net Premiums Written & Deposits ($000)	Operating Cash Flow ($000)	NOG Before Taxes ($000)	NOG After Taxes ($000)	Net Income ($000)
'05	92.5	...	...	7.5	2,999	1.2	...	98.4	0.4	876	47	47	88	-40	-40	-40
'06	95.5	...	...	4.5	3,113	1.4	...	98.2	0.4	861	38	37	228	-54	-54	-54
'07	96.4	...	...	3.6	3,267	1.5	...	98.1	0.4	891	41	40	148	-5	-5	-5
'08	95.7	...	...	4.3	2,822	2.2	...	96.6	1.2	803	50	48	-434	-50	-50	-50
'09	87.5	...	...	12.5	2,458	3.0	...	96.5	0.5	748	48	48	-332	-89	-89	-89

Rating History: NR-5, 04/26/10; NR-5, 04/22/09; NR-5, 04/09/08; NR-5, 04/24/07; NR-5, 05/03/06

UNITED INVESTORS LIFE INS CO
Torchmark Corporation
Anthony L. McWhorter
President & CEO
P.O. Box 10207
Birmingham, AL 35202-0207
NE : 1981 : Stock : Agency
Term Life, Var ann, Var Univ life
205-325-4300
AMB# 007175 NAIC# 94099

Best's Financial Strength Rating: **A** — Rating Outlook: Stable — **FSC IX**

Data Year	Bonds (%)	Mort. Loans & R.E. (%)	Com & Pref. Stock (%)	All Other Assets (%)	Total Assets ($000)	Life Reserves (%)	Health Reserves (%)	Ann Res. & Dep. Liabilities (%)	All Other Liabilities (%)	Capital & Surplus ($000)	Direct Premiums Written ($000)	Net Premiums Written & Deposits ($000)	Operating Cash Flow ($000)	NOG Before Taxes ($000)	NOG After Taxes ($000)	Net Income ($000)
'05	27.0	...	4.8	68.2	3,047,361	22.2	...	22.0	55.8	298,649	117,287	147,167	27,434	90,375	74,456	72,653
'06	25.4	...	6.6	67.9	3,046,829	19.4	...	23.4	57.2	386,734	114,641	204,512	4,045	83,323	66,941	65,831
'07	24.9	...	7.0	68.1	3,058,372	19.8	...	25.9	54.3	389,642	105,226	239,574	-13,752	90,775	62,478	62,742
'08	27.8	...	8.5	63.7	2,543,231	25.7	...	38.3	36.0	420,956	95,741	255,181	-20,963	65,622	47,102	39,887
'09	27.1	...	6.8	66.0	2,753,457	23.2	...	41.8	35.0	466,771	92,481	279,519	-39,709	81,059	52,038	37,081

Rating History: A, 06/15/10; A, 06/11/09; A, 06/11/08; A, 06/08/07; A, 06/08/06

UNITED LIFE INS CO
United Fire & Casualty Company
Randy A. Ramlo
President & CEO
118 Second Avenue SE
Cedar Rapids, IA 52401-1212
IA : 1962 : Stock : Agency
SPDA's, Trad Life, Univ Life
319-399-5700
AMB# 007178 NAIC# 69973

Best's Financial Strength Rating: **A-** — Rating Outlook: Stable — **FSC VIII**

Data Year	Bonds (%)	Mort. Loans & R.E. (%)	Com & Pref. Stock (%)	All Other Assets (%)	Total Assets ($000)	Life Reserves (%)	Health Reserves (%)	Ann Res. & Dep. Liabilities (%)	All Other Liabilities (%)	Capital & Surplus ($000)	Direct Premiums Written ($000)	Net Premiums Written & Deposits ($000)	Operating Cash Flow ($000)	NOG Before Taxes ($000)	NOG After Taxes ($000)	Net Income ($000)
'05	92.0	1.4	0.7	5.9	1,433,114	16.2	0.9	80.9	2.0	135,362	101,806	148,643	34,214	22,786	17,265	17,640
'06	90.9	1.7	1.4	6.0	1,393,179	18.1	0.7	79.1	2.0	151,676	181,920	228,498	-40,222	18,881	16,185	18,006
'07	83.5	1.4	1.5	13.5	1,356,739	20.1	0.7	77.3	2.0	164,168	196,847	242,093	-38,718	19,234	13,634	15,115
'08	91.0	0.6	0.9	7.5	1,322,029	21.9	0.7	76.2	1.2	157,003	199,071	246,113	-16,853	16,414	6,575	646
'09	91.2	0.5	1.0	7.3	1,480,566	20.9	0.5	77.2	1.4	160,179	258,055	298,690	154,565	17,169	7,904	3,523

Rating History: A-, 05/03/10; A-, 04/08/09; A-, 02/26/08; A-, 02/22/07; A-, 05/02/06

UNITED NATIONAL LIFE OF AMER
Guarantee Trust Life Insurance Company
Arthur G. Fess
President
1275 Milwaukee Avenue
Glenview, IL 60025
IL : 1961 : Stock : Agency
A&H, Ind Life, Med supp
847-803-5252
AMB# 006236 NAIC# 92703

Best's Financial Strength Rating: **NR-2**

Data Year	Bonds (%)	Mort. Loans & R.E. (%)	Com & Pref. Stock (%)	All Other Assets (%)	Total Assets ($000)	Life Reserves (%)	Health Reserves (%)	Ann Res. & Dep. Liabilities (%)	All Other Liabilities (%)	Capital & Surplus ($000)	Direct Premiums Written ($000)	Net Premiums Written & Deposits ($000)	Operating Cash Flow ($000)	NOG Before Taxes ($000)	NOG After Taxes ($000)	Net Income ($000)
'05	65.9	3.0	...	31.2	8,116	77.6	6.2	12.8	3.3	1,846	3,249	2,327	569	-124	-124	-124
'06	77.5	...	...	22.5	7,374	62.8	8.8	18.1	10.4	2,853	3,348	1,950	-21	-135	-135	-135
'07	79.1	...	...	20.9	7,199	63.6	9.4	17.9	9.1	2,483	3,634	1,786	-188	-266	-280	-280
'08	74.6	9.0	...	16.5	6,939	64.7	12.0	17.2	6.1	2,093	4,038	2,531	-209	-253	-253	-357
'09	78.3	8.1	...	13.6	7,329	61.9	13.6	15.3	9.1	2,050	4,770	3,149	313	-33	-33	-33

Rating History: NR-2, 05/25/10; NR-3, 05/29/09; NR-3, 06/26/08; NR-3, 06/13/07; NR-3, 02/23/06

UNITED OF OMAHA LIFE INS CO
Mutual of Omaha Insurance Company
Daniel P. Neary
Chairman & CEO
Mutual of Omaha Plaza
Omaha, NE 68175
NE : 1926 : Stock : Agency
Group Life, Ind Life, Ind Ann
402-342-7600
AMB# 007164 NAIC# 69868

Best's Financial Strength Rating: **A+** — Rating Outlook: Stable — **FSC XIII**

Data Year	Bonds (%)	Mort. Loans & R.E. (%)	Com & Pref. Stock (%)	All Other Assets (%)	Total Assets ($000)	Life Reserves (%)	Health Reserves (%)	Ann Res. & Dep. Liabilities (%)	All Other Liabilities (%)	Capital & Surplus ($000)	Direct Premiums Written ($000)	Net Premiums Written & Deposits ($000)	Operating Cash Flow ($000)	NOG Before Taxes ($000)	NOG After Taxes ($000)	Net Income ($000)
'05	72.7	8.2	0.7	18.4	12,803,845	26.9	0.0	57.3	15.8	1,208,196	1,586,476	1,639,005	-223,561	83,683	109,298	3,059
'06	70.7	8.7	0.7	19.9	12,866,253	29.0	0.0	53.0	18.0	1,219,902	1,711,231	1,736,195	-102,550	38,625	23,194	11,265
'07	69.5	10.4	0.8	19.3	13,227,858	30.4	2.7	48.3	18.5	1,358,060	1,768,682	2,081,649	427,049	99,933	90,495	88,640
'08	68.5	13.2	1.1	17.2	12,879,237	32.3	3.2	49.8	14.7	1,196,272	1,929,618	3,002,229	125,498	-10,918	-8,706	-69,569
'09	64.7	14.2	1.1	20.0	14,037,295	30.9	3.3	48.5	17.3	1,245,139	2,497,891	3,425,476	591,563	14,441	34,904	-5,248

Rating History: A+ g, 01/20/10; A+ g, 04/08/09; A+ g, 06/09/08; A+ g, 06/06/07; A g, 06/07/06

UNITED SECURITY ASSUR CO OF PA
Coventry Resources Corp.
William J. Neugroschel
President & CEO
673 East Cherry Lane
Souderton, PA 18964
PA : 1983 : Stock : Agency
Health, LTC, Whole life
215-723-3044
AMB# 001850 NAIC# 42129

Best's Financial Strength Rating: **B+** — Rating Outlook: Negative — **FSC V**

Data Year	Bonds (%)	Mort. Loans & R.E. (%)	Com & Pref. Stock (%)	All Other Assets (%)	Total Assets ($000)	Life Reserves (%)	Health Reserves (%)	Ann Res. & Dep. Liabilities (%)	All Other Liabilities (%)	Capital & Surplus ($000)	Direct Premiums Written ($000)	Net Premiums Written & Deposits ($000)	Operating Cash Flow ($000)	NOG Before Taxes ($000)	NOG After Taxes ($000)	Net Income ($000)
'05	66.8	...	25.1	8.1	32,408	0.0	96.2	...	3.8	14,755	10,497	10,497	2,723	1,018	779	779
'06	67.3	...	24.0	8.7	37,338	0.1	95.5	...	4.5	18,016	11,019	11,019	3,494	2,333	1,850	1,850
'07	67.2	...	25.6	7.2	39,958	0.1	97.0	...	2.9	19,093	11,430	11,430	1,427	2,185	1,639	1,639
'08	67.0	...	7.0	26.0	65,138	1.4	95.9	...	2.6	21,035	11,290	11,653	19,284	8,308	8,185	7,741
'09	77.5	...	4.3	18.2	106,358	0.8	97.6	...	1.7	20,445	16,553	22,112	49,289	1,682	1,223	1,078

Rating History: B+, 03/17/10; B+, 10/30/08; B++, 10/18/07; B++, 11/02/06; B++, 09/14/05

UNITED SECURITY LF & H INS CO
J and P Holdings, Inc.
Sandra J. Horn
President
6640 S. Cicero Avenue
Bedford Park, IL 60638
IL : 1973 : Stock : Broker
Dis inc, Maj med, Whole life
708-475-6100
AMB# 008442 NAIC# 81108

Best's Financial Strength Rating: **D** — Rating Outlook: Negative — **FSC III**

Data Year	Bonds (%)	Mort. Loans & R.E. (%)	Com & Pref. Stock (%)	All Other Assets (%)	Total Assets ($000)	Life Reserves (%)	Health Reserves (%)	Ann Res. & Dep. Liabilities (%)	All Other Liabilities (%)	Capital & Surplus ($000)	Direct Premiums Written ($000)	Net Premiums Written & Deposits ($000)	Operating Cash Flow ($000)	NOG Before Taxes ($000)	NOG After Taxes ($000)	Net Income ($000)
'05	61.9	...	11.4	26.7	27,068	51.1	40.0	...	8.9	10,492	31,466	29,287	-152	2,696	1,938	1,955
'06	66.4	...	14.3	19.3	26,307	52.0	36.9	...	11.2	9,531	35,398	32,971	-797	424	346	318
'07	54.6	...	15.4	30.0	26,139	47.9	39.6	...	12.5	7,396	39,889	37,029	-565	-2,593	-2,251	-2,171
'08	59.0	...	15.9	25.1	22,838	49.6	41.2	...	9.2	4,644	42,216	38,861	-1,674	-2,897	-2,897	-3,221
'09	59.8	...	20.0	20.2	23,763	46.3	42.7	...	10.9	4,148	39,295	36,446	579	-172	-172	-559

Rating History: D, 05/10/10; C+, 05/27/09; C++, 02/09/09; B-, 06/11/08; B-, 05/24/07

UNITED STATES LIFE INS OF NY
American International Group, Inc
Mary Jane B. Fortin
President & CEO
3600 Route 66 P.O. Box 1580
Neptune, NJ 07754-1580
NY : 1850 : Stock : Bank
Life, Ann, A&H
212-709-6000
AMB# 007192 NAIC# 70106

Best's Financial Strength Rating: **A** — Rating Outlook: Negative — **FSC X**

Data Year	Bonds (%)	Mort. Loans & R.E. (%)	Com & Pref. Stock (%)	All Other Assets (%)	Total Assets ($000)	Life Reserves (%)	Health Reserves (%)	Ann Res. & Dep. Liabilities (%)	All Other Liabilities (%)	Capital & Surplus ($000)	Direct Premiums Written ($000)	Net Premiums Written & Deposits ($000)	Operating Cash Flow ($000)	NOG Before Taxes ($000)	NOG After Taxes ($000)	Net Income ($000)
'05	81.8	4.9	0.2	13.1	4,112,661	58.8	18.6	16.9	5.7	337,314	983,809	383,263	432,494	-261,293	-145,972	-140,659
'06	77.3	8.3	2.5	11.9	4,251,950	60.4	17.1	15.9	6.6	390,062	911,109	294,883	164,914	106,945	53,747	47,226
'07	79.3	7.1	2.1	11.6	5,314,659	53.9	25.3	11.9	8.9	472,399	817,576	821,489	964,925	178,880	103,530	72,287
'08	74.5	6.9	1.7	16.8	5,318,291	55.4	25.5	11.2	7.9	251,378	825,663	634,559	-527,847	-66,939	-89,588	-642,886
'09	73.8	6.5	0.7	19.0	5,318,059	54.7	24.7	11.6	9.0	488,892	679,246	496,019	133,377	286,434	260,210	193,876

Rating History: A, 12/16/09; A, 11/10/08; A gu, 09/15/08; A+ g, 06/17/08; A++g, 05/28/08

BEST'S PROFITABILITY, LEVERAGE AND LIQUIDITY TESTS 2005 – 2009

Data in U.S. Dollars

—	Profitability Tests							Leverage Tests						Liquidity Tests					
Un-Realized Capital Gains ($000)	Benefits Paid to NPW & Dep (%)	Comm. & Expenses to NPW & Dep (%)	NOG to Total Assets (%)	NOG to Total Rev (%)	Operating Return on Equity (%)	Net Yield (%)	Total Return (%)	Change in NPW & Dep (%)	NPW & Dep to Capital (X)	Capital & Surplus to Liabilities (%)	Surplus Relief (%)	Reins Leverage (%)	Change in Capital (%)	Quick Liquidity (%)	Current Liquidity (%)	Non-Invest Grade Bonds to Capital (%)	Delinq. & Foreclosed Mortgages to Capital (%)	Mort. & Credit Tenant Loans & R.E. to Capital (%)	Affiliated Invest to Capital (%)
143,302	51.0	52.2	0.9	5.5	7.1	5.14	10.05	-1.2	1.1	11.6	-1.5	49.6	-41.2	64.3	70.1	23.4	...	67.6	17.1
14,084	50.5	51.9	2.0	12.1	20.9	5.86	6.85	-3.6	0.9	13.8	0.5	42.8	20.8	56.5	63.1	53.3	...	57.1	18.0
5,705	52.4	49.6	1.8	10.8	17.4	6.17	6.27	-5.3	0.9	13.3	0.4	43.0	-2.2	58.5	65.9	45.0	...	63.6	18.6
-23,098	55.9	48.1	3.5	21.7	35.8	6.57	1.55	-5.6	1.1	10.5	0.4	45.8	-21.2	43.1	53.8	92.2	...	88.0	23.9
34,264	46.3	-99.9	2.4	11.3	25.1	5.90	6.95	101.8	1.2	11.2	0.2	17.3	72.1	41.3	53.2	60.6	...	56.2	47.0
Principal Lines of Business: OrdLife (93.2%), IndA&H (5.3%), IndLife (1.4%), GrpA&H (0.0%), IndAnn (0.0%)														Principal States: FL (10.7%), CA (10.2%), NC (9.6%), GA (8.6%), IL (8.1%)					
...	46.2	159.8		-21.2				...	0.1	41.3	...	...	...	114.9	114.9	...	...	...	...
...	14.7	330.0	-1.8	-27.3	-6.3	5.61	5.61	-21.9	0.0	38.2	...	...	-1.7	117.0	117.0	...	...	...	...
...	39.6	198.2	-0.2	-2.3	-0.6	5.61	5.61	10.0	0.0	37.5	...	...	3.5	116.2	116.2	...	...	...	...
...	999.9	241.1	-1.7	-24.2	-6.0	5.40	5.40	20.7	0.1	39.7	...	...	-9.9	118.4	118.4	...	...	...	...
...	893.1	247.2	-3.4	-55.4	-11.5	4.39	4.39	-1.8	0.1	43.8	...	...	-6.8	125.3	125.3	...	...	...	...
Principal Lines of Business: IndAnn (61.2%), OrdLife (38.5%), GrpAnn (0.3%)														Principal States: OK (99.5%)					
...	122.5	17.1	2.5	26.0	30.2	11.23	11.09	-16.5	0.5	25.6	0.0	139.8	52.6	39.6	49.6	25.3	...	...	45.3
...	100.2	4.0	2.2	19.7	19.5	10.11	10.05	39.0	0.5	33.9	0.0	119.0	29.4	37.9	49.6	17.3	...	...	37.9
...	85.9	10.7	2.0	16.5	16.1	10.47	10.55	17.1	0.6	32.1	0.0	142.4	1.3	32.1	42.6	18.9	...	...	39.0
-11,323	77.6	9.6	1.7	11.8	11.6	11.64	9.90	6.5	0.6	30.9	0.0	162.7	6.0	34.3	42.7	13.7	...	...	36.9
10,887	69.7	8.2	2.0	12.7	11.7	11.12	10.78	9.5	0.6	31.6	0.0	176.7	11.8	28.5	35.1	20.6	...	...	40.0
Principal Lines of Business: IndAnn (68.2%), OrdLife (28.7%), GrpLife (3.1%)														Principal States: CA (9.1%), TX (8.2%), AL (6.3%), IL (6.2%), FL (5.4%)					
722	95.5	9.4	1.2	9.2	13.3	6.14	6.32	22.6	1.0	11.8	0.3	1.6	10.1	77.0	89.6	72.6	...	23.2	...
1,574	127.5	7.7	1.1	6.1	11.3	5.98	6.30	53.7	1.4	13.6	0.2	1.4	10.5	79.1	92.6	53.8	...	24.6	...
1,108	119.1	7.4	1.0	4.9	8.6	5.94	6.21	6.0	1.4	15.2	0.2	1.4	7.5	91.4	105.4	39.2	...	19.6	...
-6,609	109.3	7.9	0.5	2.4	4.1	5.71	4.83	1.7	1.5	14.2	0.2	1.8	-8.1	84.5	98.6	43.5	...	13.9	...
5,152	49.8	7.4	0.6	2.4	5.0	5.48	5.58	21.4	1.7	13.1	0.2	2.0	4.5	79.9	94.7	43.5	...	14.2	...
Principal Lines of Business: IndAnn (86.9%), OrdLife (12.5%), IndA&H (0.5%), GrpLife (0.1%), CrdA&H (0.0%)														Principal States: IA (35.9%), NE (12.6%), MN (8.9%), WI (8.7%), IL (7.1%)					
...	47.0	50.6	-1.6	-3.8	-7.0	3.75	3.80	-12.8	1.2	29.8	36.0	70.6	9.4	105.4	110.9	5.4	...	12.9	...
...	44.0	66.3	-1.7	-4.7	-5.8	4.51	4.55	-16.2	0.7	63.9	20.9	139.8	54.3	142.8	151.9	...	...	...	...
...	44.7	74.6	-3.8	-10.4	-10.5	4.56	4.59	-8.4	0.7	53.5	23.9	180.5	-12.7	124.6	132.2	6.0	...	...	...
...	42.4	70.3	-3.6	-7.8	-11.1	4.48	2.98	41.7	1.2	43.3	19.6	233.1	-16.5	118.6	126.1	7.2	...	29.7	...
...	33.1	69.5	-0.5	-0.8	-1.6	4.45	4.51	24.4	1.5	39.4	26.3	265.0	-1.2	113.0	121.2	7.2	...	28.8	...
Principal Lines of Business: IndA&H (63.9%), OrdLife (19.5%), GrpA&H (16.1%), IndAnn (0.5%)														Principal States: IL (19.1%), WV (17.9%), TX (17.2%), NE (15.4%), MN (5.8%)					
894	93.0	23.0	0.8	5.6	9.0	6.45	5.56	3.0	1.3	12.1	3.9	58.1	-3.8	41.0	63.4	36.0	...	85.7	11.6
11,482	101.3	21.0	0.2	1.2	1.9	6.17	6.23	5.9	1.4	12.4	4.4	61.6	2.2	41.2	63.8	24.2	...	88.8	16.6
-6,992	77.1	22.9	0.7	4.0	7.0	6.52	6.50	19.9	1.5	13.9	3.0	29.2	13.0	40.5	63.3	22.5	0.0	96.4	23.6
18,872	61.9	20.0	-0.1	-0.3	-0.7	5.90	5.58	44.2	2.4	12.2	1.4	33.3	-10.3	35.1	56.2	45.1	0.5	133.3	37.6
-6,121	51.6	21.4	0.3	1.1	2.9	6.02	5.66	14.1	2.6	11.8	1.2	34.9	3.0	34.4	55.6	46.7	...	151.8	46.3
Principal Lines of Business: GrpAnn (37.4%), OrdLife (23.4%), IndAnn (15.6%), GrpA&H (10.1%), GrpLife (8.4%)														Principal States: KS (15.0%), CA (7.1%), TX (6.0%), NE (5.8%), FL (5.6%)					
1,056	31.1	50.5	2.6	6.8	5.6	3.36	6.89	13.8	0.7	83.6	...	...	14.0	128.9	129.4	...	...	...	55.2
803	31.5	45.8	5.3	15.1	11.3	3.52	5.88	5.0	0.6	93.3	...	...	22.1	134.4	134.7	...	...	...	49.7
1,290	28.2	48.1	4.2	12.8	8.8	3.64	7.09	3.7	0.6	91.6	...	...	6.0	127.9	130.7	...	...	...	53.6
-5,694	28.8	53.5	15.6	40.2	40.8	20.80	8.26	1.9	0.6	47.7	...	47.1	10.1	87.9	97.6	0.2	...	...	21.6
7	32.4	47.9	1.4	4.8	5.9	4.35	4.21	89.8	1.1	23.8	...	2.3	-2.8	97.3	107.0	1.7	...	...	22.3
Principal Lines of Business: IndA&H (98.6%), OrdLife (1.1%), GrpA&H (0.2%)														Principal States: PA (41.2%), FL (17.8%), TX (9.8%), OH (7.7%), MO (4.8%)					
99	60.3	31.0	7.3	6.3	20.7	2.87	3.45	-2.0	2.7	66.0	6.2	32.4	27.9	129.0	138.9	...	...	...	...
179	66.4	33.6	1.3	1.0	3.5	3.45	4.13	12.6	3.3	60.2	6.8	46.8	-8.1	118.3	130.5	...	...	...	...
227	74.9	33.5	-8.6	-5.8	-26.6	3.51	4.83	12.3	4.7	42.7	8.6	73.6	-20.9	98.3	107.4	...	...	...	...
-1,024	74.2	34.6	-11.8	-7.2	-48.1	3.51	-2.28	4.9	8.3	25.8	13.5	117.1	-40.1	86.5	95.7	...	...	...	...
831	73.0	30.0	-0.7	-0.5	-3.9	3.36	5.45	-6.2	7.6	25.4	12.1	128.2	2.6	85.9	96.7	...	...	...	...
Principal Lines of Business: GrpA&H (94.1%), OrdLife (4.2%), IndA&H (1.5%), GrpLife (0.2%)														Principal States: IN (29.4%), IL (23.2%), NE (19.3%), AZ (13.3%), AR (11.1%)					
-1,883	109.6	25.6	-3.7	-18.4	-39.5	7.15	7.36	-4.0	1.0	9.8	61.2	390.3	-12.7	41.0	57.8	76.6	...	62.3	35.9
884	148.6	35.5	1.3	6.9	14.8	6.80	6.75	-23.1	0.7	11.1	52.8	366.7	15.6	38.9	56.5	69.9	...	88.8	31.1
-218	20.3	29.7	2.2	8.6	24.0	7.22	6.57	178.6	1.6	10.6	10.5	155.8	19.9	41.2	59.9	63.3	...	79.8	27.5
-6,785	92.5	35.4	-1.7	-8.8	-24.8	6.79	-4.06	-22.8	2.1	6.1	22.5	275.1	-40.3	40.3	57.3	92.7	...	131.5	43.6
-4,393	112.0	38.4	4.9	30.2	70.3	6.39	4.82	-21.8	0.9	11.3	11.2	148.4	77.2	54.8	71.6	62.8	...	70.0	25.9
Principal Lines of Business: GrpA&H (42.8%), GrpLife (27.2%), OrdLife (24.8%), IndAnn (5.2%), CrdLife (0.1%)														Principal States: NY (43.5%), CA (6.9%), NJ (6.7%), FL (5.3%), TX (3.1%)					

ANNUAL STATEMENT DATA FOR YEARS 2005 – 2009

Data in U.S. Dollars

COMPANY NAME Ultimate Parent Association Principal Officer Mailing Address Dom. : Began Bus. : Struct. : Mktg. Specialty Phone # AMB# NAIC#	Best's Financial Strength Rating FSC	Data Year	Balance Sheet: Bonds (%)	Mort. Loans & R.E. (%)	Com & Pref. Stock (%)	All Other Assets (%)	Total Assets ($000)	Life Reserves (%)	Health Reserves (%)	Ann Res. & Dep. Liabilities (%)	All Other Liabilities (%)	Capital & Surplus ($000)	Operations: Direct Premiums Written ($000)	Net Premiums Written & Deposits ($000)	Operating Cash Flow ($000)	NOG Before Taxes ($000)	NOG After Taxes ($000)	Net Income ($000)
UNITED TEACHER ASSOCIATES INS American Financial Group, Inc Billy B. Hill, Jr. President P.O. Box 26580 Austin, TX 78755 TX : 1959 : Stock : Agency Ann, Med supp, LTC 512-451-2224 AMB# 006410 NAIC# 63479	B++ Rating Outlook: Stable FSC VII	'05	91.0	0.9	0.0	8.1	463,750	1.7	42.4	50.0	5.9	64,656	221,943	232,484	79,274	12,595	4,224	4,179
		'06	84.6	0.8	1.1	13.5	488,096	2.1	44.3	50.3	3.3	70,184	215,036	231,351	11,400	14,948	6,388	6,388
		'07	89.9	0.7	1.0	8.4	499,286	2.5	46.4	48.5	2.6	65,651	202,625	218,092	26,100	8,983	3,828	3,007
		'08	85.3	0.8	0.2	13.8	506,374	3.1	48.0	46.8	2.1	58,642	189,602	204,446	-3,071	8,003	5,110	-7,979
		'09	85.3	0.5	0.5	13.7	736,878	2.5	57.6	31.4	8.6	66,245	191,804	235,884	68,962	6,972	-5,265	-7,360
		Rating History: B++, 05/10/10; A-, 03/27/09; A-, 12/17/07; A-, 11/28/06; A-, 06/17/05																
UNITED TRANSPORTATION UNION Malcom B. Futhey, Jr. Chairman & President 14600 Detroit Avenue Cleveland, OH 44107-4250 OH : 1971 : Fraternal : Agency Ann, Dis inc, Life 216-228-9400 AMB# 008272 NAIC# 56413	NR-4	'05	84.9	1.2	6.0	7.8	226,390	41.3	3.5	49.3	5.8	26,454	17,096	18,433	-3,449	-2,220	-2,220	-2,235
		'06	85.5	1.2	7.6	5.7	222,288	43.0	4.5	47.2	5.4	28,381	14,195	14,990	-2,950	-303	-303	2,041
		'07	85.1	1.2	9.2	4.5	216,185	44.6	4.5	45.9	5.0	28,548	14,804	15,556	-3,013	-1,107	-1,107	2,401
		'08	85.6	1.3	7.0	6.1	205,539	46.8	4.6	46.4	2.3	23,964	14,889	15,112	-4,365	65	65	-2,280
		'09	...	...	...	...	...	...	...	...	...	...	...	...	...	...	...	...
		Rating History: NR-4, 06/12/09; B, 06/12/09; B, 05/04/09; B, 05/09/08; B, 05/04/07																
UNITED TRUST INS CO' Blue Cross and Blue Shield of Alabama Gary P. Pope President 450 Riverchase Parkway East Birmingham, AL 35298-0001 AL : 1964 : Stock : Not Available 205-220-2100 AMB# 007379 NAIC# 81531	NR-1	'05	51.8	...	...	48.2	4,982	...	...	...	100.0	4,726	315	385	...	707	562	562
		'06	39.5	...	...	60.5	6,535	...	...	...	100.0	5,428	344	411	...	1,053	709	699
		'07	57.6	...	...	42.4	7,146	...	...	...	100.0	6,404	206	275	...	1,529	987	987
		'08	63.1	...	...	36.9	5,252	...	...	...	100.0	4,013	166	236	...	2,489	1,615	1,610
		'09	41.9	...	...	58.1	6,688	...	...	...	100.0	5,908	140	211	...	2,398	1,895	1,895
		Rating History: NR-1, 06/10/10; NR-1, 06/12/09; NR-1, 06/12/08; NR-1, 06/08/07; NR-1, 06/07/06																
UNITED WORLD LIFE INS CO Mutual of Omaha Insurance Company Michael C. Weekly President Mutual of Omaha Plaza Omaha, NE 68175 NE : 1970 : Stock : Direct Response Ind Life, Med supp 402-342-7600 AMB# 007528 NAIC# 72850	A+ Rating Outlook: Stable FSC XIII	'05	85.3	...	...	14.7	69,138	84.3	...	1.0	14.7	17,687	28,583	2,972	2,637	3,315	2,235	2,222
		'06	82.1	...	...	17.9	79,650	74.4	...	0.7	24.9	19,989	93,944	2,766	7,406	3,682	2,421	2,421
		'07	68.3	...	...	31.7	91,904	65.5	...	0.4	34.2	22,557	237,287	2,575	10,054	3,661	2,424	2,412
		'08	79.8	...	...	20.2	90,578	82.8	...	0.5	16.7	34,839	397,087	2,491	4,754	3,743	2,343	1,897
		'09	79.2	...	...	20.8	92,756	94.8	...	0.7	4.6	43,172	499,934	2,286	4,737	3,710	2,270	2,270
		Rating History: A+ g, 01/20/10; A+ g, 04/08/09; A+ g, 06/09/08; A+ g, 06/06/07; A g, 06/07/06																
UNITEDHEALTHCARE INS CO UnitedHealth Group Inc Allen J. Sorbo President & CEO 450 Columbus Boulevard Hartford, CT 06103 CT : 1972 : Stock : Agency Group A&H, Maj med 877-832-7734 AMB# 008290 NAIC# 79413	A Rating Outlook: Stable FSC XV	'05	48.6	...	12.7	38.6	7,250,080	0.4	53.2	2.2	44.2	1,836,613	16,458,386	18,098,957	593,440	2,590,297	1,810,457	1,807,955
		'06	35.6	...	8.6	55.8	10,260,186	0.4	45.4	1.4	52.8	2,464,266	22,046,256	25,623,460	2,251,262	3,288,728	2,195,955	2,195,076
		'07	46.8	...	8.6	44.6	11,425,484	0.6	46.2	2.0	51.2	3,104,865	25,769,466	29,557,501	543,009	3,433,085	2,291,246	2,290,322
		'08	53.9	...	7.7	38.4	10,522,869	0.8	56.1	1.9	41.2	2,821,569	28,376,821	32,424,857	-1,149,351	2,779,954	1,896,040	1,867,011
		'09	49.9	...	7.3	42.8	11,899,664	0.6	56.7	1.0	41.7	3,425,789	31,806,941	35,966,584	1,136,552	2,982,239	2,012,898	1,993,882
		Rating History: A g, 06/15/09; A g, 01/29/08; A g, 11/21/07; A g, 11/16/06; A+ g, 08/17/06																
UNITEDHEALTHCARE INS CO OF IL UnitedHealth Group Inc Thomas P. Wiffler President & CEO 450 Columbus Boulevard, 4NB Hartford, CT 06103 IL : 1991 : Stock : Agency Dental, Group A&H, Group Life 312-424-4460 AMB# 060071 NAIC# 60318	A Rating Outlook: Stable FSC XV	'05	61.7	...	...	38.3	119,704	0.0	71.8	...	28.2	82,073	268,952	268,952	-15,580	55,048	36,779	36,779
		'06	73.0	...	...	27.0	110,840	0.0	71.9	...	28.0	73,428	256,556	256,556	-8,533	40,641	26,766	26,766
		'07	67.8	...	...	32.2	114,786	0.0	71.7	...	28.3	74,296	278,994	278,994	2,832	41,369	27,367	27,367
		'08	54.0	...	...	46.0	122,177	0.0	63.0	...	37.0	72,438	307,863	307,863	10,213	33,242	22,305	21,976
		'09	61.4	...	...	38.6	114,860	...	76.0	...	24.0	71,840	317,153	317,153	-21,801	40,941	26,208	26,060
		Rating History: A g, 06/15/09; A g, 01/29/08; A g, 11/21/07; A g, 11/16/06; A+ g, 08/17/06																
UNITEDHEALTHCARE INS CO OF NY UnitedHealth Group Inc Jeffrey D. Alter President & CEO 450 Columbus Boulevard, CT030-04NB Hartford, CT 06103-1809 NY : 1995 : Stock : Agency Group A&H, Med supp, Medicare 877-832-7734 AMB# 060108 NAIC# 60093	A Rating Outlook: Stable FSC XV	'05	47.0	...	...	53.0	1,140,013	...	11.7	...	88.3	273,611	3,012,757	966,465	73,946	63,751	43,243	42,992
		'06	39.7	...	...	60.3	1,403,521	...	18.5	...	81.5	299,704	3,196,492	1,006,996	246,213	67,891	42,640	41,622
		'07	35.9	...	...	64.1	1,629,972	...	24.4	...	75.6	349,854	3,563,912	1,129,798	98,841	47,684	39,676	39,423
		'08	29.5	...	...	70.5	2,338,711	...	18.8	...	81.2	422,507	5,028,354	1,361,324	433,518	90,510	63,299	64,468
		'09	35.0	...	...	65.0	1,984,117	...	17.0	...	83.0	436,954	5,516,852	1,519,693	-293,214	50,846	34,520	35,753
		Rating History: A g, 06/15/09; A g, 01/29/08; A g, 11/21/07; A g, 11/16/06; A+ g, 08/17/06																
UNITEDHEALTHCARE INS CO OF OH UnitedHealth Group Inc Robert C. Falkenberg Chairman, President & CEO 450 Columbus Boulevard 4NB Hartford, CT 06103 OH : 1991 : Stock : Agency Dental, Group A&H, Stop Loss 614-410-7000 AMB# 060046 NAIC# 73518	A Rating Outlook: Stable FSC XV	'05	48.0	...	...	52.0	110,057	0.1	66.7	...	33.2	53,056	357,434	357,434	-9,977	43,479	29,244	29,244
		'06	61.9	...	...	38.1	112,341	0.1	69.8	...	30.1	44,426	408,636	408,636	6,417	27,913	18,277	18,277
		'07	57.9	...	...	42.1	159,473	0.0	60.0	...	40.0	69,947	529,574	529,574	40,982	52,805	34,021	34,021
		'08	64.0	...	...	36.0	154,626	0.0	57.0	...	43.0	69,650	530,662	530,662	3,416	42,176	28,401	27,053
		'09	68.1	...	...	31.9	129,236	0.0	63.5	...	36.5	67,476	444,459	444,459	-25,418	49,030	32,987	33,375
		Rating History: A g, 06/15/09; A g, 01/29/08; A g, 11/21/07; A g, 11/16/06; A+ g, 08/17/06																
UNITEDHEALTHCARE INS RVR VALL UnitedHealth Group Inc Daniel R. Kueter President 1300 River Drive, Suite 200 Moline, IL 61265 IL : 2004 : Stock : Broker Health, Stop Loss 309-736-4600 AMB# 064827 NAIC# 12231	A- Rating Outlook: Stable FSC IV	'05	93.3	...	...	6.7	7,969	...	62.2	...	37.8	7,646	274	253	4,847	209	135	135
		'06	39.5	...	...	60.5	14,906	...	42.5	...	57.5	9,282	17,148	16,881	6,678	2,516	1,685	1,639
		'07	30.4	...	...	69.6	19,369	...	74.6	...	25.4	10,762	45,956	45,910	3,823	4,615	2,846	2,846
		'08	23.0	...	...	77.0	25,570	...	66.6	...	33.4	13,692	64,972	64,950	4,598	8,786	5,896	5,896
		'09	23.5	...	...	76.5	25,985	...	60.8	...	39.2	8,297	69,257	69,257	1,126	574	312	312
		Rating History: A-, 06/15/09; NR-3, 01/29/08; NR-3, 11/21/07; NR-3, 11/16/06; NR-3, 03/02/06																

BEST'S PROFITABILITY, LEVERAGE AND LIQUIDITY TESTS 2005 – 2009

Data in U.S. Dollars

	Profitability Tests							Leverage Tests						Liquidity Tests					
Un-Realized Capital Gains ($000)	Benefits Paid to NPW & Dep (%)	Comm. & Expenses to NPW & Dep (%)	NOG to Total Assets (%)	NOG to Total Rev (%)	Operating Return on Equity (%)	Net Yield (%)	Total Return (%)	Change in NPW & Dep (%)	NPW & Dep to Capital (X)	Capital & Surplus to Liabilities (%)	Surplus Relief (%)	Reins Leverage (%)	Change in Capital (%)	Quick Liquidity (%)	Current Liquidity (%)	Non-Invest Grade Bonds to Capital (%)	Delinq. & Foreclosed Mortgages to Capital (%)	Mort. & Credit Tenant Loans & R.E. to Capital (%)	Affiliated Invest to Capital (%)
45	64.7	27.5	1.0	1.6	6.7	5.71	5.79	2.1	3.5	16.7	2.0	41.7	7.7	79.3	88.8	23.2	...	6.0	6.2
52	67.8	28.4	1.3	2.4	9.5	5.68	5.77	-0.5	3.2	17.6	1.6	37.9	10.0	79.5	88.5	34.9	...	5.2	5.4
-937	71.5	28.4	0.8	1.6	5.6	6.07	5.77	-5.7	3.2	15.9	0.4	20.3	-6.1	78.5	87.9	32.5	...	5.3	5.5
4,731	69.8	31.4	1.0	2.2	8.2	6.00	4.38	-6.3	3.5	13.1	0.4	22.3	-14.4	77.4	85.8	41.7	...	6.5	0.3
1,714	58.7	30.5	-0.8	-1.9	-8.4	6.63	6.60	15.4	3.5	10.0	0.3	20.7	14.1	77.4	85.9	47.8	...	5.7	0.3

Principal Lines of Business: IndA&H (82.1%), GrpA&H (11.0%), OrdLife (3.7%), GrpAnn (2.8%), IndAnn (0.4%) — Principal States: TX (27.8%), KY (7.7%), FL (6.0%), NC (4.9%), LA (4.9%)

70	99.8	63.3	-1.0	-7.6	-8.0	4.97	5.41	4.3	0.6	15.0	...	1.1	-5.8	80.1	88.5	...	...	9.6	...
186	134.2	61.1	-0.1	-1.2	-1.1	4.90	6.35	-18.7	0.5	16.9	...	0.8	8.7	81.0	90.0	...	...	8.6	...
-1,714	138.9	59.4	-0.5	-4.2	-3.9	5.11	6.20	3.8	0.5	17.4	...	0.8	-0.4	81.1	90.8	...	...	8.4	...
-5,522	119.6	60.2	0.0	0.2	0.2	5.37	1.90	-2.9	0.6	13.3	...	1.0	-24.5	79.9	89.0	0.6	...	10.8	...
...	...	...	...	...	...	...	...	...	...	...	...	...	...	...	...	...	...	...	...

...	46.8	93.1	11.3	44.6	12.6	...	...	23.5	0.1	999.9	...	...	13.4	...	...	...	...	...	...
...	60.3	131.9	12.3	37.6	14.0	...	...	6.8	0.1	494.9	...	...	14.8	...	...	...	...	...	...
...	60.2	283.5	14.4	40.0	16.7	...	...	-33.1	0.0	878.1	...	...	18.0	...	...	...	...	...	...
...	55.4	398.9	26.1	45.4	31.0	...	...	-14.3	0.1	327.9	...	...	-37.3	...	...	...	...	...	...
...	95.9	622.4	31.7	48.3	38.2	...	...	-10.4	0.0	770.6	...	...	47.1	...	...	...	...	...	...

Principal Lines of Business: GrpA&H (100.0%)

40	73.6	17.1	3.4	14.3	12.7	6.09	6.20	-6.8	0.2	36.4	50.8	73.1	1.9	72.8	96.0	16.6	...	...	...
...	63.3	15.8	3.3	7.8	12.9	6.19	6.24	-6.9	0.1	35.1	122.0	134.7	12.3	71.4	92.1	13.7	...	...	...
...	76.1	5.9	2.8	4.6	11.4	5.21	5.25	-6.9	0.1	33.8	206.9	248.4	12.5	89.4	107.9	7.0	...	...	...
...	87.3	16.0	2.6	3.3	8.2	5.30	4.81	-3.3	0.1	63.6	182.5	325.2	52.4	100.9	124.6	7.2	...	...	...
...	75.3	21.6	2.5	2.9	5.8	5.11	5.14	-8.2	0.1	89.1	165.0	169.4	24.3	120.2	149.0	5.6	...	...	...

Principal Lines of Business: OrdLife (96.7%), IndAnn (3.3%), GrpAnn (0.0%) — Principal States: IN (13.4%), GA (7.4%), CA (5.7%), NC (5.5%), KS (4.7%)

138,798	81.4	9.4	26.7	9.5	116.2	9.81	12.29	24.1	9.3	36.8	0.1	14.2	42.5	121.3	130.7	0.5	...	...	51.1
-19,018	80.3	9.0	25.1	8.4	102.1	9.94	9.71	41.6	9.9	33.6	0.0	21.3	32.3	135.5	144.7	0.3	...	...	37.2
88,121	80.0	10.4	21.1	7.6	82.3	8.73	9.75	15.4	9.1	39.7	0.0	17.1	25.7	116.5	125.7	0.5	...	...	32.4
-110,066	82.0	10.8	17.3	5.8	64.0	6.78	5.17	9.7	11.3	37.5	0.0	23.0	-11.6	90.7	99.9	0.8	...	...	30.5
6,488	81.9	10.6	18.0	5.5	64.4	5.46	5.40	10.9	10.3	41.4	0.0	18.2	21.5	101.5	111.0	0.8	...	...	26.8

Principal Lines of Business: GrpA&H (70.7%), IndA&H (28.7%), GrpLife (0.3%), GrpAnn (0.3%), IndAnn (0.0%) — Principal States: FL (13.9%), TX (10.3%), CA (5.2%), OH (4.6%), WI (4.4%)

...	66.8	14.6	28.8	13.4	43.1	3.62	3.73	-16.6	3.3	220.8	...	...	-7.1	371.0	401.4	...	...	...	...
...	71.7	14.8	23.2	10.2	34.4	4.18	4.29	-4.6	3.5	198.9	...	...	-10.5	306.6	334.0	...	...	...	...
...	73.1	14.0	24.3	9.6	37.1	4.89	4.96	8.7	3.7	185.5	...	...	1.1	305.2	328.1	...	...	...	...
0	78.1	12.6	18.8	7.1	30.4	3.63	3.43	10.3	4.2	146.0	...	...	-2.8	317.5	332.3	0.0	...	...	...
0	74.8	13.2	22.1	8.2	36.3	2.74	2.74	3.0	4.4	167.0	...	...	-0.9	250.0	270.8	0.0	...	...	...

Principal Lines of Business: GrpA&H (100.0%) — Principal States: IL (100.0%)

...	83.9	12.4	4.0	4.3	17.3	4.37	4.33	7.7	3.5	31.6	80.1	163.8	21.2	105.0	112.7	...	...	...	...
0	85.4	12.0	3.4	4.1	14.9	5.00	4.88	4.2	3.4	27.2	72.4	205.2	9.5	121.4	127.1	...	...	...	...
...	86.7	13.1	2.6	3.4	12.2	4.53	4.51	12.2	3.2	27.3	0.1	240.8	16.7	117.0	123.1	0.1	...	...	...
-10	87.3	9.4	3.2	4.5	16.4	3.09	3.18	20.5	3.2	22.0	0.0	300.6	20.8	115.0	118.9	0.0	...	...	...
10	86.8	11.2	1.6	2.2	8.0	1.61	1.70	11.6	3.5	28.2	0.0	258.3	3.4	98.5	103.4	0.0	...	...	...

Principal Lines of Business: CompHosp/Med (64.4%), MedSup (18.5%), OtherHlth (10.4%), Medicare (5.9%), Dental (0.4%) — Principal States: NY (100.0%)

756	76.4	12.7	25.8	8.1	59.6	3.54	4.34	-15.6	6.7	93.9	...	...	17.7	234.4	250.8	...	...	...	...
97	82.4	12.0	16.4	4.4	37.5	4.94	5.09	14.3	9.1	66.1	...	...	-16.1	185.4	199.3	...	...	...	...
280	77.9	13.3	25.0	6.4	59.5	4.64	4.87	29.6	7.5	78.7	...	...	57.1	202.8	214.4	...	...	...	...
-737	81.6	11.7	18.1	5.3	40.7	3.82	2.53	0.2	7.6	82.0	...	...	-0.8	210.6	223.1	...	...	...	...
0	78.4	11.6	23.2	7.3	48.1	3.07	3.63	-16.2	6.6	110.3	...	...	-2.7	228.9	246.8	0.1	...	...	...

Principal Lines of Business: GrpA&H (100.0%) — Principal States: OH (100.0%)

...	93.4	19.3	2.5	27.3	2.5	4.52	4.52	...	0.0	999.9	...	...	153.9	999.9	999.9	...	...	...	...
...	74.1	13.6	14.7	9.7	19.9	4.11	3.70	999.9	1.8	165.0	...	1.4	21.4	383.1	398.1	...	...	...	...
...	72.2	19.4	16.6	6.1	28.4	4.73	4.73	172.0	4.3	125.0	...	...	15.9	333.1	346.5	...	...	...	...
...	70.3	17.0	26.2	9.0	48.2	2.93	2.93	41.5	4.7	115.3	...	...	27.2	325.0	331.5	...	...	...	...
...	83.0	16.6	1.2	0.4	2.8	1.09	1.09	6.6	8.3	46.9	...	...	-39.4	224.2	234.2	...	...	...	...

Principal Lines of Business: CompHosp/Med (98.4%), OtherHlth (1.6%) — Principal States: IL (97.7%)

Data in U.S. Dollars

COMPANY NAME Ultimate Parent Association Principal Officer Mailing Address Dom. : Began Bus. : Struct. : Mktg. Specialty Phone # AMB# NAIC#	Best's Financial Strength Rating FSC	Data Year	Balance Sheet: Bonds (%)	Mort. Loans & R.E. (%)	Com & Pref. Stock (%)	All Other Assets (%)	Total Assets ($000)	Life Reserves (%)	Health Reserves %)	Ann Res. & Dep. Liabilities (%)	All Other Liabilities (%)	Capital & Surplus ($000)	Operations: Direct Premiums Written ($000)	Net Premiums Written & Deposits ($000)	Operating Cash Flow ($000)	NOG Before Taxes ($000)	NOG After Taxes ($000)	Net Income ($000)
UNITEDHEALTHCARE OF ALABAMA UnitedHealth Group Inc Glen J. Golemi Chairman, President & CEO 33 Inverness Center Parkway Birmingham, AL 35242 AL : 1986 : Stock : Broker Medicare, Med supp 205-437-8500 AMB# 068500 NAIC# 95784	**A** Rating Outlook: Stable **FSC VII**	'05	40.8	...	...	59.2	81,135	...	62.6	...	37.4	35,572	312,323	312,011	-19,300	28,374	19,952	20,068
		'06	26.2	...	...	73.8	159,724	...	36.0	...	64.0	53,174	357,023	356,673	78,271	47,621	31,381	31,445
		'07	45.3	...	...	54.7	148,455	...	45.2	...	54.8	83,448	379,665	379,281	-19,799	88,359	57,980	57,990
		'08	81.7	...	...	18.3	103,602	...	65.8	...	34.2	55,295	377,867	377,456	-42,656	45,704	29,875	29,395
		'09	53.0	...	...	47.0	108,861	...	71.3	...	28.7	57,686	389,592	389,205	5,300	43,883	28,586	29,075
		Rating History: A, 06/15/09; A, 01/29/08; A, 11/21/07; A, 11/16/06; A, 08/17/06																
UNITEDHEALTHCARE OF ARIZONA UnitedHealth Group Inc Benton V. Davis President & CEO 5995 Plaza Drive Cypress, CA 90630 AZ : 1985 : Stock : Broker Group A&H, Medicare 602-954-3500 AMB# 068847 NAIC# 96016	**A-** Rating Outlook: Stable **FSC VIII**	'05	11.1	...	63.5	25.5	68,425	...	62.7	...	37.3	47,463	91,320	91,228	-8,059	-5,322	-3,566	-3,539
		'06	10.3	...	63.7	26.0	82,767	...	69.9	...	30.1	59,563	108,287	108,172	15,083	2,949	1,685	1,685
		'07	9.3	...	72.8	17.9	103,666	...	72.3	...	27.7	88,127	106,209	106,104	2,793	10,001	7,498	7,544
		'08	12.3	...	73.0	14.7	110,727	...	63.6	...	36.4	95,504	103,350	103,251	2,276	17,815	16,169	16,007
		'09	10.3	...	70.9	18.8	120,868	...	65.6	...	34.4	102,023	128,171	128,044	2,753	12,281	11,800	11,847
		Rating History: A-, 06/15/09; A-, 01/29/08; A-, 11/21/07; A-, 11/16/06; A-, 08/17/06																
UNITEDHEALTHCARE OF ARKANSAS UnitedHealth Group Inc Garland G. Scott III Chairman, President & CEO 10 Cadillac Drive, Suite 200 Brentwood, TN 37027 AR : 1992 : Stock : Broker Group A&H, Medicare 501-664-7700 AMB# 068914 NAIC# 95446	**A** Rating Outlook: Stable **FSC IV**	'05	36.6	...	...	63.4	17,351	...	45.5	...	54.5	12,025	49,218	49,169	-3,539	6,047	3,998	4,068
		'06	2.5	...	...	97.5	12,196	...	49.0	...	51.0	7,892	30,784	30,753	-4,804	5,770	3,882	3,969
		'07	2.9	...	...	97.1	10,469	-3.0	50.4	...	52.6	6,851	23,922	23,898	-1,651	4,555	2,855	2,863
		'08	3.4	...	...	96.6	8,819	...	60.3	...	39.7	4,805	19,989	19,968	-2,026	1,080	530	530
		'09	3.3	...	...	96.7	9,079	...	63.6	...	36.4	5,323	18,190	18,172	403	885	520	520
		Rating History: A, 06/15/09; A, 01/29/08; A, 11/21/07; A, 11/16/06; A, 08/17/06																
UNITEDHEALTHCARE OF COLORADO UnitedHealth Group Inc Elizabeth K. Soberg President & CEO 6465 S. Greenwood Plaza Blvd. Centennial, CO 80111-7101 CO : 1986 : Stock : Broker Group A&H, Health 303-267-3300 AMB# 068848 NAIC# 95090	**A-** Rating Outlook: Stable **FSC IV**	'05	45.7	...	...	54.3	25,452	...	49.9	...	50.1	15,848	75,378	75,301	-13,040	2,280	1,470	2,281
		'06	5.2	...	...	94.8	20,663	...	54.1	...	45.9	16,018	35,164	35,128	-5,445	-262	-344	-39
		'07	5.6	...	...	94.4	19,480	...	60.1	...	39.9	16,353	20,514	20,494	-1,019	489	417	417
		'08	6.2	...	...	93.8	17,696	...	62.8	...	37.2	16,555	4,605	4,601	-1,143	121	124	125
		'09	18.5	...	...	81.5	6,402	...	36.7	...	63.3	5,888	2,645	2,642	-11,454	312	200	200
		Rating History: A-, 06/15/09; A-, 01/29/08; A-, 11/21/07; A-, 11/16/06; A-, 08/17/06																
UNITEDHEALTHCARE OF FLORIDA UnitedHealth Group Inc Thomas D. Lewis President & CEO 495 North Keller Road, Suite 200 Maitland, FL 32751 FL : 1973 : Stock : Broker Group A&H, Medicaid, Medicare 407-659-7041 AMB# 068782 NAIC# 95264	**A** Rating Outlook: Stable **FSC VIII**	'05	68.4	...	...	31.6	412,335	...	53.4	...	46.6	147,826	1,912,552	1,910,613	-181,381	100,728	73,034	73,390
		'06	77.3	...	...	22.7	374,090	...	42.2	...	57.8	115,362	1,744,904	1,743,166	-17,867	84,634	59,475	59,401
		'07	84.7	...	...	15.3	326,270	...	49.3	...	50.7	129,881	1,471,552	1,470,070	-52,996	58,235	43,334	44,152
		'08	66.3	...	...	33.7	320,210	...	42.9	...	57.1	97,676	1,365,341	1,363,952	-13,305	-18,407	-16,927	-15,934
		'09	65.7	...	...	34.3	316,535	...	49.8	...	50.2	101,200	1,301,879	1,300,578	13,043	7,413	8,823	6,576
		Rating History: A, 06/15/09; A, 01/29/08; A, 11/21/07; A, 11/16/06; A, 08/17/06																
UNITEDHEALTHCARE OF GEORGIA UnitedHealth Group Inc Richard A. Elliot, Jr. Chairman, President & CEO 3720 DaVinci Court, Suite 300 Norcross, GA 30092 GA : 1986 : Stock : Broker Group A&H, Medicare 770-300-3501 AMB# 068893 NAIC# 95850	**A** Rating Outlook: Stable **FSC VI**	'05	63.1	...	...	36.9	40,808	...	52.6	...	47.4	23,076	150,657	150,506	-1,481	10,434	6,974	6,926
		'06	77.3	...	...	22.7	42,165	...	54.1	...	45.9	17,496	156,680	156,523	-1,930	5,391	3,613	3,712
		'07	68.8	...	...	31.2	51,350	...	59.2	...	40.8	17,955	185,270	185,085	7,515	-3,256	-3,479	-3,445
		'08	67.3	...	...	32.7	51,236	...	64.7	...	35.3	15,057	188,929	188,737	2,089	-17,434	-13,916	-13,941
		'09	69.0	...	...	31.0	48,782	...	64.7	...	35.3	26,497	157,677	157,519	-650	9,288	9,046	8,695
		Rating History: A, 06/15/09; A, 01/29/08; A, 11/21/07; A, 11/16/06; A, 08/17/06																
UNITEDHEALTHCARE OF ILLINOIS UnitedHealth Group Inc Thomas P. Wiffler President & CEO 233 North Michigan Avenue Chicago, IL 60601 IL : 1976 : Stock : Broker Group A&H, Health 312-424-4500 AMB# 068532 NAIC# 95776	**A** Rating Outlook: Stable **FSC V**	'05	55.8	...	...	44.2	40,011	...	38.8	...	61.2	17,390	149,393	149,244	-1,111	7,179	5,178	5,247
		'06	47.1	...	...	52.9	31,191	...	40.2	...	59.8	15,335	101,113	101,011	-7,480	1,217	1,202	1,354
		'07	46.6	...	...	53.4	31,076	...	28.8	...	71.2	17,055	73,504	73,431	-2,685	2,149	1,695	1,754
		'08	57.7	...	...	42.3	22,091	...	43.7	...	56.3	9,194	76,961	76,884	-5,469	-2,487	-2,121	-2,273
		'09	37.8	...	...	62.2	34,577	...	54.9	...	45.1	17,845	80,867	80,787	13,640	-7,479	-6,031	-5,983
		Rating History: A, 06/15/09; A, 01/29/08; A, 11/21/07; A, 11/16/06; A, 08/17/06																
UNITEDHEALTHCARE OF KY LTD UnitedHealth Group Inc Daniel Krajnovich President & CEO 9900 Bren Road East, MN008-W345 Minnetonka, MN 55343 KY : 1986 : Stock : Broker Group A&H, Health 859-260-3600 AMB# 068690 NAIC# 96644	**A-** Rating Outlook: Stable **FSC V**	'05	51.5	...	...	48.5	52,565	...	45.7	...	54.3	42,032	77,895	77,816	1,287	2,706	2,912	3,270
		'06	71.4	...	...	28.6	34,998	...	46.6	...	53.4	26,658	67,604	67,536	-17,876	1,671	1,988	2,164
		'07	2.7	...	...	97.3	17,938	...	43.1	...	56.9	10,889	52,606	52,553	-16,562	3,184	2,659	2,733
		'08	2.8	...	...	97.2	17,925	...	40.4	...	59.6	11,622	47,156	47,109	-19	1,674	1,770	1,786
		'09	2.9	...	...	97.1	18,783	...	44.4	...	55.6	10,137	48,996	48,947	1,199	-2,272	-1,304	-1,304
		Rating History: A-, 06/15/09; A-, 01/29/08; A-, 11/21/07; A-, 11/16/06; A-, 08/17/06																
UNITEDHEALTHCARE OF LOUISIANA UnitedHealth Group Inc Glen J. Golemi Chairman, President & CEO 3838 N. Causeway Blvd., Suite 2600 Metairie, LA 70002 LA : 1986 : Stock : Broker Group A&H, Health 504-849-1603 AMB# 068661 NAIC# 95833	**A-** Rating Outlook: Stable **FSC IV**	'05	...	...	...	100.0	20,248	...	37.9	...	62.1	12,950	45,448	45,400	-13,159	3,279	1,872	2,648
		'06	...	...	...	100.0	10,559	...	52.0	...	48.0	7,876	21,708	21,686	-9,925	3,572	2,428	2,428
		'07	...	...	...	100.0	8,015	...	27.4	...	72.6	6,277	10,417	10,406	-2,064	2,171	1,388	1,388
		'08	...	...	...	100.0	7,035	...	45.2	...	54.8	5,489	7,666	7,658	-1,466	1,114	700	700
		'09	...	...	...	100.0	15,256	...	59.1	...	40.9	7,538	29,186	29,156	1,490	-4,933	-4,267	-4,267
		Rating History: A-, 06/15/09; A-, 01/29/08; A-, 11/21/07; A-, 11/16/06; A-, 08/17/06																

—	Profitability Tests							Leverage Tests						Liquidity Tests					
Un-Realized Capital Gains ($000)	Benefits Paid to NPW & Dep (%)	Comm. & Expenses to NPW & Dep (%)	NOG to Total Assets (%)	NOG to Total Rev (%)	Operating Return on Equity (%)	Net Yield (%)	Total Return (%)	Change in NPW & Dep (%)	NPW & Dep to Capital (X)	Capital & Surplus to Liabilities (%)	Surplus Relief (%)	Reins Leverage (%)	Change in Capital (%)	Quick Liquidity (%)	Current Liquidity (%)	Non-Invest Grade Bonds to Capital (%)	Delinq. & Foreclosed Mortgages to Capital (%)	Mort. & Credit Tenant Loans & R.E. to Capital (%)	Affiliated Invest to Capital (%)
...	84.0	8.5	21.9	6.3	49.2	4.48	4.61	25.6	8.8	78.1	...	...	-21.8	263.8	273.5	...	...	...	...
...	78.4	10.3	26.1	8.8	70.7	6.12	6.17	14.3	6.7	49.9	...	...	49.5	251.8	256.7	...	...	...	...
...	71.2	8.6	37.6	14.7	84.9	6.69	6.69	6.3	4.5	128.4	...	...	56.9	306.4	319.5	...	...	...	...
-11	79.9	9.8	23.7	7.8	43.1	4.52	4.10	-0.5	6.8	114.5	...	...	-33.7	190.3	209.9	0.1	...	...	...
11	80.6	8.8	26.9	7.3	50.6	3.07	3.58	3.1	6.7	112.7	...	...	4.3	210.7	221.1	...	...	...	...
Principal Lines of Business: Medicare (98.9%), MedSup (1.0%), CompHosp/Med (0.1%)													Principal States: AL (100.0%)						
...	86.6	15.8	-5.0	-3.9	-6.6	1.44	1.48	41.5	1.9	226.4	...	...	-22.4	101.8	106.9	...	...	...	91.5
...	85.4	15.9	2.2	1.5	3.1	1.93	1.93	18.6	1.8	256.7	...	0.5	25.5	50.5	50.5	...	...	...	88.5
...	80.0	14.7	8.0	6.9	10.2	1.66	1.72	-1.9	1.2	567.1	...	0.0	48.0	218.5	228.5	...	...	...	85.6
-2	81.9	14.6	15.1	13.6	17.6	16.91	16.75	-2.7	1.1	627.4	...	...	8.4	236.6	252.9	0.0	...	...	84.6
4,926	85.4	14.1	10.2	8.6	11.9	9.66	14.28	24.0	1.3	541.4	...	...	6.8	226.4	239.1	0.1	...	...	84.0
Principal Lines of Business: CompHosp/Med (54.5%), Medicare (45.5%), MedSup (0.0%)													Principal States: AZ (100.0%)						
...	72.0	17.4	20.9	8.0	30.7	4.81	5.19	-18.0	4.1	225.8	...	...	-14.1	475.4	494.0	...	...	...	...
...	66.1	17.5	26.3	12.4	39.0	5.60	6.22	-37.5	3.9	183.3	...	...	-34.4	524.9	535.0	...	...	...	...
...	64.9	18.2	25.2	11.7	38.7	5.51	5.58	-22.3	3.5	189.3	...	...	-13.2	531.4	544.5	...	...	...	...
...	77.0	16.6	5.5	2.6	9.1	2.19	2.19	-16.4	4.2	119.7	...	...	-29.9	297.7	297.7	...	...	...	...
...	77.3	17.0	5.8	2.9	10.3	0.29	0.29	-9.0	3.4	141.7	...	...	10.8	260.4	264.7	...	...	...	...
Principal Lines of Business: CompHosp/Med (67.5%), Medicare (32.5%)													Principal States: AR (100.0%)						
...	82.1	15.7	4.5	1.9	7.0	4.58	7.16	-31.0	4.8	165.0	...	...	-39.2	370.1	387.9	...	...	...	...
...	88.8	16.6	-1.5	-0.9	-2.2	4.94	6.32	-53.4	2.2	344.9	...	...	1.1	774.3	813.9	...	...	...	...
...	87.4	15.3	2.1	1.9	2.6	4.90	4.91	-41.7	1.3	522.9	...	...	2.1	999.9	999.9	...	...	...	...
...	90.8	19.0	0.7	2.4	0.8	2.74	2.74	-77.6	0.3	999.9	...	...	1.2	999.9	999.9	...	...	...	...
...	63.5	26.7	1.7	8.1	1.8	0.44	0.44	-42.6	0.4	999.9	...	...	-64.4	999.9	999.9	...	...	...	...
Principal Lines of Business: CompHosp/Med (100.0%)													Principal States: CO (100.0%)						
...	81.0	14.4	14.6	3.8	42.8	3.81	3.89	-15.4	12.9	55.9	...	...	-23.6	166.5	179.6	...	...	...	...
...	82.7	14.3	15.1	3.4	45.2	4.94	4.92	-8.8	15.1	44.6	...	...	-22.0	147.6	161.7	...	...	...	...
...	84.6	13.8	12.4	2.9	35.3	5.36	5.60	-15.7	11.3	66.1	...	...	12.6	149.2	164.7	...	...	...	...
...	87.5	13.4	-5.2	-1.2	-14.9	4.34	4.67	-7.2	14.0	43.9	...	...	-24.8	147.5	161.1	...	...	...	...
0	87.2	13.4	2.8	0.7	8.9	3.14	2.39	-4.6	12.9	47.0	...	...	3.6	159.6	172.7	0.0	...	...	...
Principal Lines of Business: CompHosp/Med (50.3%), Medicaid (25.9%), Medicare (23.4%), FEHBP (0.4%)													Principal States: FL (100.0%)						
...	77.7	16.4	16.6	4.6	29.0	5.04	4.92	-2.7	6.5	130.1	...	...	-7.7	265.9	287.9	...	...	...	...
...	80.6	16.4	8.7	2.3	17.8	6.00	6.25	4.0	8.9	70.9	...	...	-24.2	146.1	158.9	...	...	...	...
...	85.0	16.4	-7.4	-1.9	-19.6	5.20	5.28	18.2	10.3	53.8	...	...	2.6	140.4	152.1	...	...	...	...
-16	89.6	18.1	-27.1	-7.3	-84.3	4.02	3.93	2.0	12.5	41.6	...	...	-16.1	139.0	151.9	2.7	...	...	...
16	83.9	16.2	18.1	5.7	43.5	3.37	2.65	-16.5	5.9	118.9	...	...	76.0	227.1	246.0	...	...	...	...
Principal Lines of Business: CompHosp/Med (87.6%), Medicare (12.5%), FEHBP (0.0%)													Principal States: GA (100.0%)						
...	79.7	17.3	11.9	3.4	28.9	4.91	5.10	-6.6	8.6	76.9	...	...	-5.5	195.2	209.7	...	...	...	...
...	81.6	18.7	3.4	1.2	7.3	4.95	5.42	-32.3	6.6	96.7	...	...	-11.8	248.0	265.2	...	...	...	...
...	80.0	19.0	5.4	2.3	10.5	5.61	5.84	-27.3	4.3	121.6	...	...	11.2	258.2	267.4	...	...	...	...
0	84.9	18.9	-8.0	-2.7	-16.2	3.94	3.25	4.7	8.4	71.3	...	...	-46.1	210.1	222.7	0.0	...	...	...
0	87.4	18.3	-21.3	-7.4	-44.6	2.10	2.28	5.1	4.5	106.6	...	...	94.1	252.1	263.4	...	...	...	...
Principal Lines of Business: CompHosp/Med (100.0%)													Principal States: IL (99.0%)						
...	81.7	17.9	5.6	3.6	7.2	4.43	5.13	-22.9	1.9	399.0	...	...	8.1	681.7	714.7	...	...	...	...
...	83.6	17.6	4.5	2.8	5.8	5.61	6.02	-13.2	2.5	319.7	...	...	-36.6	472.5	502.8	...	...	...	...
...	79.2	17.2	10.0	4.9	14.2	5.92	6.21	-22.2	4.8	154.5	...	...	-59.2	458.2	482.0	...	...	...	...
...	81.4	16.6	9.9	3.7	15.7	2.53	2.62	-10.4	4.1	184.4	...	...	6.7	520.1	538.3	...	...	...	...
...	85.7	17.5	-7.1	-2.7	-12.0	0.43	0.43	3.9	4.8	117.2	...	...	-12.8	401.3	418.8	...	...	...	...
Principal Lines of Business: CompHosp/Med (100.0%)													Principal States: KY (100.0%)						
...	73.4	20.6	6.9	4.0	9.8	3.32	6.29	-52.0	3.5	177.4	...	...	-48.6	523.8	536.7	...	...	...	...
...	62.6	22.2	15.8	10.9	23.3	4.53	4.53	-52.2	2.8	293.4	...	...	-39.2	720.3	734.9	...	...	...	...
...	62.0	26.0	14.9	12.8	19.6	4.82	4.82	-52.0	1.7	361.2	...	...	-20.3	842.1	860.5	...	...	...	...
...	65.3	21.1	9.3	8.9	11.9	2.59	2.59	-26.4	1.4	355.1	...	...	-12.6	734.2	751.1	...	...	...	...
...	90.0	16.8	-38.3	-14.6	-65.5	0.61	0.61	280.7	3.9	97.7	...	...	37.3	185.2	188.8	...	...	...	...
Principal Lines of Business: CompHosp/Med (100.0%)													Principal States: LA (100.0%)						

2010 BEST'S KEY RATING GUIDE — LIFE/HEALTH EDITION
ANNUAL STATEMENT DATA FOR YEARS 2005 – 2009

Data in U.S. Dollars

COMPANY NAME Ultimate Parent Association Principal Officer Mailing Address Dom. : Began Bus. : Struct. : Mktg. Specialty Phone # AMB# NAIC#	Best's Financial Strength Rating FSC	Data Year	Balance Sheet Bonds (%)	Mort. Loans & R.E. (%)	Com & Pref. Stock (%)	All Other Assets (%)	Total Assets ($000)	Life Reserves (%)	Health Reserves %)	Ann Res. & Dep. Liabilities (%)	All Other Liabilities (%)	Capital & Surplus ($000)	Operations Direct Premiums Written ($000)	Net Premiums Written & Deposits ($000)	Operating Cash Flow ($000)	NOG Before Taxes ($000)	NOG After Taxes ($000)	Net Income ($000)
UNITEDHEALTHCARE OF MS UnitedHealth Group Inc Glen J. Golemi President & CEO 800 Woodlands Parkway, Suite 102 Ridgeland, MS 39157 MS : 1993 : Stock : Broker Group A&H, Health 504-849-1603 AMB# 060118 NAIC# 95716	NR-3	'05	18.0	...	...	82.0	4,397	...	61.6	...	38.4	4,264	116	116	725	-298	516	516
		'06	14.2	...	...	85.8	4,211	...	60.8	...	39.2	4,141	1	1	-245	-192	-132	-132
		'07	15.1	...	...	84.9	4,094	...	89.8	...	10.2	4,048	-8	-8	-69	-140	-92	-92
		'08	14.6	...	...	85.4	4,206	...	86.7	...	13.3	4,076	...	...	46	39	26	26
		'09	14.5	...	...	85.5	4,180	...	93.4	...	6.6	4,167	13	13	49	140	92	92
		Rating History: NR-3, 06/15/09; NR-3, 01/29/08; NR-3, 11/21/07; A-, 11/16/06; A-, 08/17/06																
UNITEDHEALTHCARE OF NEW ENG UnitedHealth Group Inc Stephen J. Farrell President 48 Monroe Turnpike Trumbull, CT 06611 RI : 1984 : Stock : Broker Medicare, Medicaid, Group A&H 203-459-6000 AMB# 068891 NAIC# 95149	A Rating Outlook: Stable FSC VIII	'05	50.4	...	41.0	8.6	165,780	...	37.9	...	62.1	91,186	517,947	344,919	-1,070	24,483	17,230	17,078
		'06	51.3	...	13.7	35.0	171,039	...	34.6	...	65.4	91,347	516,802	364,791	5,521	26,160	18,025	17,944
		'07	81.6	...	5.3	13.1	183,727	...	41.6	...	58.4	119,297	510,309	378,117	14,599	36,369	25,059	25,081
		'08	78.1	...	6.9	15.0	200,517	...	36.6	...	63.4	127,051	491,221	381,501	10,368	28,359	18,818	18,191
		'09	83.2	...	1.7	15.1	190,628	...	42.9	...	57.1	117,686	474,750	401,763	-11,274	6,912	5,345	4,971
		Rating History: A, 06/15/09; A, 01/29/08; A, 11/21/07; A, 11/16/06; A, 08/17/06																
UNITEDHEALTHCARE OF NEW YORK UnitedHealth Group Inc Pasquale Celli CEO 48 Monroe Turnpike Trumbull, CT 06611 NY : 1987 : Stock : Broker Medicaid, Medicare, Group A&H 203-459-6000 AMB# 068856 NAIC# 95085	A Rating Outlook: Stable FSC VIII	'05	35.2	...	...	64.8	302,189	...	61.7	...	38.3	163,133	681,109	681,109	-4,113	57,806	40,566	40,562
		'06	32.7	...	...	67.3	332,418	...	62.9	...	37.1	182,069	667,495	667,495	64,738	27,683	20,304	20,225
		'07	34.8	...	...	65.2	337,873	...	66.0	...	34.0	193,973	666,090	666,090	28,445	13,211	10,922	10,917
		'08	73.7	...	...	26.3	358,845	...	47.0	...	53.0	219,034	730,679	730,679	29,006	34,420	23,287	24,719
		'09	73.8	...	...	26.2	306,945	...	49.7	...	50.3	167,156	824,312	824,312	-70,281	64,701	43,704	44,408
		Rating History: A, 06/15/09; A, 01/29/08; A, 11/21/07; A, 11/16/06; A, 08/17/06																
UNITEDHEALTHCARE OF NC UnitedHealth Group Inc Austin T. Pittman, Jr. Chairman, President & CEO 3803 North Elm Street Greensboro, NC 27455 NC : 1985 : Stock : Broker Medicare, Group A&H 336-282-0900 AMB# 068572 NAIC# 95103	A Rating Outlook: Stable FSC VIII	'05	54.9	...	...	45.1	262,099	...	47.2	...	52.8	148,110	890,575	884,631	5,219	54,118	37,050	36,916
		'06	65.6	...	...	34.4	300,229	...	37.5	...	62.5	159,137	882,781	877,160	42,863	37,996	27,210	27,091
		'07	69.0	...	...	31.0	331,621	...	36.2	...	63.8	217,155	780,196	776,051	27,363	83,405	55,419	55,418
		'08	80.0	...	...	20.0	291,963	...	65.8	...	34.2	176,795	737,802	735,040	-45,223	24,344	12,342	9,964
		'09	78.3	...	...	21.7	233,121	...	67.7	...	32.3	122,128	783,592	781,772	-66,115	56,423	43,648	42,934
		Rating History: A, 06/15/09; A, 01/29/08; A, 11/21/07; A, 11/16/06; A, 08/17/06																
UNITEDHEALTHCARE OF OHIO INC UnitedHealth Group Inc Robert C. Falkenberg Chairman, President & CEO 9200 Worthington Road Westerville, OH 43082-8823 OH : 1980 : Stock : Broker Medicare, FEHBP, Group A&H 614-410-7000 AMB# 068580 NAIC# 95186	A Rating Outlook: Stable FSC VII	'05	70.4	...	...	29.6	214,873	...	56.0	...	44.0	85,387	1,018,731	1,017,696	-72,825	8,771	5,073	5,246
		'06	76.8	...	...	23.2	248,854	...	47.5	...	52.5	92,728	919,858	918,949	36,788	25,070	22,015	22,048
		'07	69.4	...	...	30.6	244,768	...	56.5	...	43.5	116,846	778,493	777,717	-7,383	76,204	48,953	48,998
		'08	72.4	...	...	27.6	187,367	...	67.3	...	32.7	97,073	703,930	703,189	-62,214	36,989	27,104	27,654
		'09	62.8	...	...	37.2	191,900	...	67.7	...	32.3	78,818	752,999	752,250	4,162	13,403	8,958	8,768
		Rating History: A, 06/15/09; A, 01/29/08; A, 11/21/07; A, 11/16/06; A, 08/17/06																
UNITEDHEALTHCARE OF TN INC UnitedHealth Group Inc Garland G. Scott III Chairman, President & CEO 10 Cadillac Drive, Suite 200 Brentwood, TN 37027 TN : 1992 : Stock : Broker Medicare, Group A&H 615-372-3622 AMB# 068730 NAIC# 11147	A- Rating Outlook: Stable FSC V	'05	52.6	...	...	47.4	18,578	...	53.4	...	46.6	10,689	60,016	60,016	-5,864	6,495	4,356	4,527
		'06	9.8	...	...	90.2	18,014	...	50.2	...	49.8	9,453	50,629	50,629	-5,195	7,178	4,567	4,748
		'07	12.6	...	...	87.4	14,274	...	63.9	...	36.1	7,604	42,242	42,242	1,109	5,396	3,259	3,259
		'08	15.4	...	...	84.6	11,856	...	55.9	...	44.1	8,643	26,832	26,832	-2,475	6,492	4,567	4,567
		'09	14.3	...	...	85.7	13,334	...	66.6	...	33.4	10,434	24,439	24,439	1,413	3,312	2,143	2,143
		Rating History: A-, 06/15/09; A-, 01/29/08; A-, 11/21/07; A-, 11/16/06; A-, 08/17/06																
UNITEDHEALTHCARE OF TX INC UnitedHealth Group Inc Thomas J. Quirk Chairman, President & CEO 5800 Granite Parkway, Suite 900 Plano, TX 75024 TX : 1985 : Stock : Broker Group A&H, Health 512-347-2600 AMB# 068841 NAIC# 95765	A- Rating Outlook: Stable FSC IV	'05	28.0	...	...	72.0	37,398	...	52.8	...	47.2	19,533	136,773	136,636	-6,210	4,167	2,791	3,151
		'06	0.4	...	...	99.6	26,581	...	70.4	...	29.6	15,994	54,113	54,060	-12,100	-5,655	-4,747	-4,394
		'07	0.5	...	...	99.5	21,316	...	69.4	...	30.6	7,882	45,634	45,588	-4,111	-11,524	-8,606	-8,606
		'08	0.6	...	...	99.4	18,000	...	80.4	...	19.6	7,685	27,364	27,336	-3,367	-1,109	63	63
		'09	0.7	...	...	99.3	14,917	...	55.0	...	45.0	7,357	32,404	32,371	-1,289	534	1,858	1,858
		Rating History: A-, 06/15/09; A-, 01/29/08; A-, 11/21/07; A-, 11/16/06; A-, 08/17/06																
UNITEDHEALTHCARE OF MID-ATL UnitedHealth Group Inc Scott A. Bowers Chairman, President & CEO 4 Taft Court Rockville, MD 20850 MD : 1978 : Stock : Broker Medicaid, Group A&H 952-992-5739 AMB# 068987 NAIC# 95025	A- Rating Outlook: Stable FSC VII	'05	53.3	...	...	46.7	109,792	...	68.5	...	31.5	57,333	480,441	479,956	2,929	16,414	14,127	14,135
		'06	44.9	...	...	55.1	160,261	...	40.3	...	59.7	68,460	470,065	469,594	48,252	16,541	15,119	15,101
		'07	59.8	...	...	40.2	176,449	...	47.3	...	52.7	71,746	501,082	500,552	17,920	3,735	3,284	3,287
		'08	62.6	...	...	37.4	188,665	...	48.0	...	52.0	63,623	577,929	577,352	9,852	-16,942	-11,703	-9,917
		'09	59.5	...	...	40.5	196,132	...	55.1	...	44.9	56,095	680,482	679,804	14,902	-32,935	-25,892	-26,034
		Rating History: A-, 06/15/09; A-, 01/29/08; A-, 11/21/07; A-, 11/16/06; A-, 08/17/06																
UNITEDHEALTHCARE OF MIDLANDS UnitedHealth Group Inc William C. Tracy Chairman, President & CEO 2717 N. 118th Circle Omaha, NE 68164-9672 NE : 1984 : Stock : Broker Group A&H, Health 402-445-5000 AMB# 068892 NAIC# 95591	A Rating Outlook: Stable FSC V	'05	65.6	...	...	34.4	43,823	...	63.0	...	37.0	19,486	166,330	165,845	-7,608	10,252	7,159	7,135
		'06	61.9	...	...	38.1	48,761	...	51.5	...	48.5	15,705	169,153	168,483	27	4,763	3,304	3,256
		'07	60.6	...	...	39.4	51,790	...	64.9	...	35.1	23,499	174,548	173,854	-228	10,936	6,753	6,763
		'08	62.2	...	...	37.8	53,691	...	40.0	...	60.0	19,459	163,361	162,700	4,497	7,707	5,183	5,100
		'09	62.2	...	...	37.8	46,456	...	74.7	...	25.3	24,962	145,722	145,153	-5,264	7,917	5,811	5,624
		Rating History: A, 06/15/09; A, 01/29/08; A, 11/21/07; A, 11/16/06; A, 08/17/06																

2010 BEST'S KEY RATING GUIDE — LIFE/HEALTH EDITION
BEST'S PROFITABILITY, LEVERAGE AND LIQUIDITY TESTS 2005 – 2009

Data in U.S. Dollars

	Profitability Tests							Leverage Tests						Liquidity Tests					
Un-Realized Capital Gains ($000)	Benefits Paid to NPW & Dep (%)	Comm. & Expenses to NPW & Dep (%)	NOG to Total Assets (%)	NOG to Total Rev (%)	Operating Return on Equity (%)	Net Yield (%)	Total Return (%)	Change in NPW & Dep (%)	NPW & Dep to Capital (X)	Capital & Surplus to Liabilities (%)	Surplus Relief (%)	Reins Leverage (%)	Change in Capital (%)	Quick Liquidity (%)	Current Liquidity (%)	Non-Invest Grade Bonds to Capital (%)	Delinq. & Foreclosed Mortgages to Capital (%)	Mort. & Credit Tenant Loans & R.E. to Capital (%)	Affiliated Invest to Capital (%)
...	161.8	318.0	11.6	200.4	12.3	3.56	3.56	-98.3	0.0	999.9	...	...	3.0	999.9	999.9	...	...	...	...
...	999.9	999.9	-3.1	-67.2	-3.1	4.69	4.69	-99.4	0.0	999.9	...	...	-2.9	999.9	999.9	...	...	...	...
...	-99.9	-99.9	-2.2	-48.1	-2.2	4.94	4.94	-99.9	0.0	999.9	...	...	-2.3	999.9	999.9	...	...	...	...
...	...	...	0.6	22.7	0.6	2.82	2.82	100.0	...	999.9	...	...	0.7	999.9	999.9	...	...	...	...
...	-99.9	300.7	2.2	191.9	2.2	0.84	0.84	...	0.0	999.9	...	...	2.2	999.9	999.9	...	...	...	...
Principal Lines of Business: CompHosp/Med (100.0%)													Principal States: MS (100.0%)						
...	80.6	14.2	10.3	4.9	19.2	4.18	4.08	13.9	3.8	122.2	...	32.8	3.7	141.4	165.5	...	...	...	...
...	80.9	14.1	10.7	4.9	19.7	5.42	5.37	5.8	4.0	114.6	...	26.1	0.2	213.0	233.6	...	...	...	...
...	78.8	13.8	14.1	6.5	23.8	5.67	5.68	3.7	3.2	185.2	...	18.0	30.6	227.0	253.6	...	...	...	...
-1	81.6	13.2	9.8	4.8	15.3	4.54	4.18	0.9	3.0	172.9	...	14.8	6.5	206.4	232.1	0.9	...	...	...
1	86.0	14.0	2.7	1.3	4.4	4.02	3.81	5.3	3.4	161.3	...	10.1	-7.4	194.0	216.8	...	...	...	...
Principal Lines of Business: Medicare (48.4%), Medicaid (39.8%), CompHosp/Med (11.8%)													Principal States: RI (95.9%), MA (4.1%)						
...	79.5	13.9	14.2	5.9	27.8	3.99	3.99	4.0	4.2	117.3	...	...	26.5	230.2	238.1	...	...	...	...
...	85.4	12.5	6.4	3.0	11.8	5.01	4.98	-2.0	3.7	121.1	...	0.9	11.6	299.5	307.9	...	...	...	...
...	85.7	14.5	3.3	1.6	5.8	5.05	5.05	-0.2	3.4	134.8	...	2.3	6.5	346.4	355.0	0.1	...	...	...
...	84.9	11.9	6.7	3.1	11.3	3.54	3.98	9.7	3.3	156.7	...	0.9	12.9	226.5	243.0	...	...	...	...
...	80.6	12.8	13.1	5.2	22.6	3.45	3.69	12.8	4.9	119.6	...	0.1	-23.7	170.7	185.9	...	...	...	...
Principal Lines of Business: Medicaid (71.1%), Medicare (25.4%), CompHosp/Med (3.5%)													Principal States: NY (100.0%)						
...	78.1	17.0	14.3	4.1	27.9	3.92	3.87	1.8	6.0	129.9	...	...	26.2	283.2	300.0	...	...	...	...
...	81.1	16.1	9.7	3.1	17.7	5.08	5.04	-0.8	5.5	112.8	...	...	7.4	241.9	260.0	...	...	...	...
...	75.2	15.7	17.5	7.0	29.5	5.10	5.10	-11.5	3.6	189.7	...	...	36.5	311.8	338.1	...	...	...	...
-85	80.2	16.5	4.0	1.7	6.3	4.41	3.58	-5.3	4.2	153.5	...	...	-18.6	229.3	252.5	2.1	...	...	...
85	81.6	14.5	16.6	5.6	29.2	4.39	4.13	6.4	6.4	110.0	...	...	-30.9	157.1	174.3	...	...	...	...
Principal Lines of Business: Medicare (86.9%), CompHosp/Med (13.1%)													Principal States: NC (100.0%)						
-157	84.3	15.9	2.0	0.5	5.0	4.46	4.47	-10.6	11.9	65.9	...	...	-26.3	172.2	189.0	1.7	...	...	...
...	83.6	15.0	9.5	2.4	24.7	5.66	5.67	-9.7	9.9	59.4	...	...	8.6	157.7	172.9	...	...	...	...
...	77.1	13.9	19.8	6.2	46.7	6.15	6.17	-15.4	6.7	91.3	...	...	26.0	203.1	218.6	...	...	...	...
...	83.5	13.5	12.5	3.8	25.3	4.83	5.11	-9.6	7.2	107.5	...	...	-16.9	199.1	213.3	...	...	...	...
...	85.1	13.6	4.7	1.2	10.2	3.62	3.51	7.0	9.5	69.7	...	...	-18.8	172.1	185.4	...	...	...	...
Principal Lines of Business: Medicare (91.2%), FEHBP (5.4%), CompHosp/Med (3.3%)													Principal States: OH (99.2%)						
...	70.8	19.9	20.2	7.1	34.2	4.65	5.47	-25.3	5.6	135.5	...	...	-27.8	296.4	317.0	...	...	...	...
...	69.1	17.4	25.0	8.9	45.3	6.19	7.38	-15.6	5.4	110.4	...	...	-11.6	260.6	273.4	...	...	...	...
...	71.9	16.4	20.2	7.6	38.2	6.78	6.78	-16.6	5.6	114.0	...	...	-19.6	365.6	383.7	...	...	...	...
...	64.1	17.2	35.0	16.8	56.2	3.35	3.35	-36.5	3.1	269.0	...	...	13.7	615.0	644.8	...	...	...	...
...	69.1	17.6	17.0	8.8	22.5	0.60	0.60	-8.9	2.3	359.7	...	...	20.7	798.9	823.4	...	...	...	...
Principal Lines of Business: Medicare (66.2%), CompHosp/Med (33.8%)													Principal States: TN (100.0%)						
...	80.8	18.1	6.6	2.0	12.0	2.71	3.63	-18.6	7.0	109.3	...	...	-27.4	322.7	338.5	...	...	...	...
...	83.7	23.0	-14.8	-8.6	-26.7	4.51	5.71	-60.4	3.4	151.1	...	...	-18.1	424.7	447.1	...	...	...	...
...	100.3	23.0	-35.9	-18.4	-72.1	5.12	5.12	-15.7	5.8	58.7	...	...	-50.7	275.8	290.3	...	...	...	...
...	93.0	19.7	0.3	0.2	0.8	2.31	2.31	-40.0	3.6	74.5	...	...	-2.5	297.6	313.3	...	...	...	...
...	90.4	17.1	11.3	5.7	24.7	0.31	0.31	18.4	4.4	97.3	...	...	-4.3	372.5	392.0	...	...	...	...
Principal Lines of Business: CompHosp/Med (100.0%)													Principal States: TX (100.0%)						
...	82.4	15.0	11.9	2.9	28.4	4.34	4.35	-6.5	8.4	109.3	...	...	35.9	224.7	239.8	...	...	...	...
...	82.4	15.3	11.2	3.2	24.0	5.04	5.02	-2.2	6.9	74.6	...	...	19.4	189.5	199.7	...	...	...	...
...	85.1	15.4	2.0	0.6	4.7	4.61	4.61	6.6	7.0	68.5	...	...	4.8	183.0	195.7	...	...	...	...
0	88.3	15.2	-6.4	-2.0	-17.3	3.73	4.83	15.3	9.1	50.9	...	...	-11.3	156.5	169.2	0.6	...	...	...
0	88.4	15.2	-13.5	-3.8	-43.3	2.79	2.70	17.7	12.1	40.1	...	...	-11.8	162.4	174.1	...	...	...	...
Principal Lines of Business: Medicaid (65.6%), CompHosp/Med (34.4%)													Principal States: MD (78.3%), VA (20.1%)						
...	81.3	13.6	15.0	4.3	35.4	4.33	4.27	0.1	8.5	80.1	...	...	-7.2	180.2	192.8	...	...	...	...
...	85.2	13.2	7.1	2.0	18.8	6.29	6.16	1.6	10.7	47.5	...	...	-19.4	128.4	140.8	...	...	...	...
...	81.5	13.0	13.4	3.9	34.5	6.55	6.57	3.2	7.4	83.1	...	...	49.6	135.4	148.2	...	...	...	...
0	84.2	13.1	9.8	3.1	24.1	5.10	4.89	-6.4	8.4	56.8	...	...	-17.2	133.0	145.0	2.1	...	...	...
0	82.4	13.1	11.6	4.0	26.2	3.68	3.21	-10.8	5.8	116.1	...	...	28.3	182.7	199.3	...	...	...	...
Principal Lines of Business: Medicaid (64.8%), Medicare (34.8%), CompHosp/Med (0.4%)													Principal States: NE (92.0%), IA (8.0%)						

ANNUAL STATEMENT DATA FOR YEARS 2005 – 2009

Data in U.S. Dollars

COMPANY NAME Ultimate Parent Association Principal Officer Mailing Address Dom. : Began Bus. : Struct. : Mktg. Specialty Phone # AMB# NAIC#	Best's Financial Strength Rating FSC	Data Year	Balance Sheet: Bonds (%)	Mort. Loans & R.E. (%)	Com & Pref. Stock (%)	All Other Assets (%)	Total Assets ($000)	Life Reserves (%)	Health Reserves (%)	Ann Res. & Dep. Liabilities (%)	All Other Liabilities (%)	Capital & Surplus ($000)	Operations: Direct Premiums Written ($000)	Net Premiums Written & Deposits ($000)	Operating Cash Flow ($000)	NOG Before Taxes ($000)	NOG After Taxes ($000)	Net Income ($000)
UNITEDHEALTHCARE OF MIDWEST UnitedHealth Group Inc Steven C. Walli Chairman, President & CEO 9900 Bren Road East, MN008-W345 Minnetonka, MN 55343 MO : 1985 : Stock : Broker Medicare, FEHBP, Group A&H 314-592-7000 AMB# 068560 NAIC# 96385	**A** Rating Outlook: Stable FSC VII	'05	62.3	...	...	37.7	203,930	...	36.0	...	64.0	96,085	648,117	521,081	-43,033	45,341	32,649	32,550
		'06	52.6	...	...	47.4	217,510	...	31.9	...	68.1	71,323	655,929	554,516	13,840	41,757	31,149	31,134
		'07	69.2	...	...	30.8	224,171	...	27.3	...	72.7	96,581	645,927	564,110	13,791	76,707	51,018	51,019
		'08	79.5	...	...	20.5	177,509	...	39.1	...	60.9	84,782	544,307	500,292	-54,309	49,304	31,299	35,528
		'09	64.6	...	...	35.4	163,181	...	42.8	...	57.2	68,796	562,548	524,404	-11,720	54,469	36,582	36,961
		Rating History: A, 06/15/09; A, 01/29/08; A, 11/21/07; A, 11/16/06; A, 08/17/06																
UNITEDHEALTHCARE OF UTAH UnitedHealth Group Inc Christopher Lockett Hard President & CEO 2525 Lake Park Boulevard Salt Lake City, UT 84120 UT : 1984 : Stock : Broker Medicare, Group A&H 801-942-6200 AMB# 068770 NAIC# 95501	**A-** Rating Outlook: Stable FSC V	'05	38.4	...	...	61.6	39,059	...	67.8	...	32.2	31,335	37,783	37,744	4,435	4,084	3,056	3,290
		'06	48.3	...	...	51.7	50,984	...	44.7	...	55.3	39,253	50,380	50,330	11,746	11,725	7,691	7,687
		'07	60.4	...	...	39.6	54,690	...	68.3	...	31.7	45,960	46,135	46,089	3,382	10,076	6,778	6,775
		'08	82.7	...	...	17.3	45,533	...	74.5	...	25.5	31,057	62,159	62,094	-10,972	2,382	981	662
		'09	66.7	...	...	33.3	39,465	...	69.4	...	30.6	18,310	120,701	120,581	-5,874	11,628	8,841	8,912
		Rating History: A-, 06/15/09; A-, 01/29/08; A-, 11/21/07; A-, 11/16/06; A-, 08/17/06																
UNITEDHEALTHCARE OF WISCONSIN UnitedHealth Group Inc Wendy D. Amone President & CEO 9900 Bren Road East, MN008-T380 Minnetonka, MN 55343 WI : 1986 : Stock : Broker Medicaid, Medicare, Group A&H 414-443-4070 AMB# 068824 NAIC# 95710	**A** Rating Outlook: Stable FSC VII	'05	52.5	5.3	...	42.3	177,521	...	47.7	...	52.3	99,178	579,823	652,076	-40,141	59,832	42,107	42,130
		'06	62.0	5.5	...	32.5	163,796	...	52.2	...	47.8	78,200	650,763	647,876	-12,342	34,664	23,121	23,057
		'07	80.1	4.5	...	15.4	195,643	...	57.9	...	42.1	107,677	685,806	683,865	35,926	50,790	33,795	33,865
		'08	71.2	...	...	28.8	208,870	...	60.6	...	39.4	110,150	698,704	697,230	9,564	53,949	34,374	41,806
		'09	57.9	...	...	42.1	228,487	...	55.1	...	44.9	93,745	1,040,098	1,038,828	3,133	69,008	45,275	45,617
		Rating History: A, 06/15/09; A, 01/29/08; A, 11/21/07; A, 11/16/06; A, 08/17/06																
UNITEDHEALTHCARE PLAN RVR VALL UnitedHealth Group Inc Daniel R. Kueter President 1300 River Drive, Suite 200 Moline, IL 61265 IL : 1985 : Stock : Broker Medicaid, Medicare, Group A&H 309-736-4600 AMB# 068702 NAIC# 95378	**A-** Rating Outlook: Stable FSC IX	'05	86.7	...	...	13.3	223,441	...	57.3	...	42.7	115,392	664,962	664,290	8,214	34,082	22,254	22,431
		'06	43.0	...	...	57.0	387,465	...	27.8	...	72.2	157,938	736,407	735,716	154,894	69,521	45,926	41,528
		'07	59.5	...	...	40.5	397,082	...	66.8	...	33.2	168,499	1,110,812	1,110,200	-14,365	58,742	45,860	46,194
		'08	60.6	...	...	39.4	513,577	...	72.5	...	27.5	225,551	1,439,068	1,438,002	106,051	80,764	55,139	56,995
		'09	57.5	...	...	42.5	814,058	...	46.6	...	53.4	267,996	2,378,914	2,376,529	257,792	107,358	75,576	76,328
		Rating History: A-, 06/15/09; A-, 01/29/08; A-, 11/21/07; A-, 11/16/06; A-, 08/17/06																
UNITY DPO INC[2] Robert Dubman President 600 Lanidex Plaza, Second Floor Parsippany, NJ 07054 NJ : 1980 : Non-Profit : Broker Dental 973-439-8634 AMB# 064747 NAIC# 11159	**NR-5**	'05	...	...	...	100.0	172	...	...	...	100.0	172	164	164	32	-5	-5	-5
		'06	...	...	...	100.0	167	...	...	...	100.0	167	189	189	-12	-5	-5	-5
		'07	...	...	...	100.0	160	...	...	...	100.0	160	179	179	7	-7	-7	-7
		'08	...	...	...	100.0	165	...	...	...	100.0	162	100	100	-2	3	3	3
		'09	...	...	...	100.0	167	...	...	...	100.0	166	73	73	-7	3	3	3
		Rating History: NR-5, 04/19/10; NR-5, 05/29/09; NR-5, 05/20/08; NR-5, 06/20/07; NR-5, 05/11/06																
UNITY FINANCIAL LIFE INS CO Unity Financial Insurance Group LLC Tom Hardy President & CEO 4675 Cornell Road, Suite 160 Cincinnati, OH 45241 PA : 1964 : Stock : Agency Pre-need 513-247-0711 AMB# 006454 NAIC# 63819	**B+** Rating Outlook: Stable FSC IV	'05	95.5	...	...	4.5	36,828	96.3	...	...	3.7	5,939	30,773	16,343	8,011	246	206	206
		'06	93.5	...	...	6.5	45,709	96.3	...	...	3.7	6,038	38,990	18,162	8,488	341	290	290
		'07	94.0	...	...	6.0	57,747	94.9	...	...	5.1	6,747	44,742	21,284	11,437	733	476	476
		'08	90.4	...	...	9.6	74,619	94.1	...	...	5.9	6,751	46,175	23,122	16,420	481	278	278
		'09	95.8	...	...	4.2	87,263	96.7	...	...	3.3	8,113	52,742	28,690	12,778	1,531	1,441	1,380
		Rating History: B+, 06/03/09; B+, 06/18/08; B+, 06/14/07; B+, 06/15/06; B+, 06/10/05																
UNITY MUTUAL LIFE INS CO Unity Mutual Life Insurance Company Patrick A. Mannion President & CEO P.O. Box 5000 Syracuse, NY 13250-5000 NY : 1905 : Mutual : Agency Ordinary Life 315-448-7000 AMB# 007196 NAIC# 70114	**B-** Rating Outlook: Stable FSC V	'05	88.8	0.0	2.3	8.9	357,906	41.6	0.2	54.4	3.8	21,389	24,578	30,056	-17,457	3,208	3,193	2,175
		'06	85.1	0.0	4.2	10.7	333,444	44.6	0.2	51.1	4.2	17,051	21,473	31,572	-25,030	29	-71	-200
		'07	86.1	0.0	2.4	11.4	320,911	47.4	0.2	48.6	3.8	19,280	19,976	31,523	-13,594	-696	-814	-886
		'08	77.8	0.0	1.9	20.3	267,880	52.3	0.2	41.4	6.1	24,547	17,604	28,558	-56,963	1,744	1,431	1,434
		'09	83.4	0.0	1.9	14.6	277,027	50.3	0.2	36.8	12.7	17,041	14,801	30,806	13,380	-1,530	-1,475	-2,094
		Rating History: B-, 06/17/09; B-, 06/20/08; B-, 06/19/07; B-, 05/19/06; B-, 02/10/05																
UNIVANTAGE INSURANCE CO Workers Compensation Fund Ray D. Pickup President 392 East 6400 South Murray, UT 84107 UT : 1996 : Stock : Inactive Inactive 801-288-8000 AMB# 060210 NAIC# 60104	**NR-5**	'05	78.8	...	...	21.2	1,635	...	...	...	100.0	1,635	...	...	56	54	47	47
		'06	82.1	...	...	17.9	1,685	...	...	...	100.0	1,684	...	...	64	58	49	49
		'07	79.6	...	...	20.4	1,747	...	...	...	100.0	1,743	...	...	55	72	59	59
		'08	39.0	...	...	61.0	1,790	...	...	...	100.0	1,791	...	...	39	58	48	48
		'09	95.4	...	...	4.6	1,819	...	...	...	100.0	1,822	...	...	18	36	31	31
		Rating History: NR-5, 04/21/10; NR-5, 04/24/09; NR-5, 04/18/08; NR-5, 04/24/07; NR-5, 04/27/06																
UNIVERSAL CARE Howard E. Davis President 1600 E. Hill Street Signal Hill, CA 90806 CA : 1985 : Stock : Broker Group A&H, Health 562-424-6200 AMB# 068894	**NR-5**	'05	...	13.7	...	86.3	107,804	...	...	...	100.0	19,121	441,248	441,248	5,533	7,303	4,446	4,446
		'06	...	4.5	...	95.5	75,740	...	...	...	100.0	12,076	46,388	46,388	-60,984	32,160	19,396	19,396
		'07	...	...	...	100.0	28,752	...	...	...	100.0	6,392	7,975	7,975	-41,299	-9,608	-5,785	-5,785
		'08	...	...	...	100.0	15,842	...	...	...	100.0	-507	12,052	12,052	-7,117	-10,171	-6,899	-6,899
		'09	...	...	...	100.0	11,674	...	...	...	100.0	651	23,521	23,521	-1,329	2,327	1,158	1,158
		Rating History: NR-5, 03/24/10; NR-5, 06/01/09; NR-4, 06/16/08; NR-4, 05/21/07; NR-4, 04/20/06																

BEST'S PROFITABILITY, LEVERAGE AND LIQUIDITY TESTS 2005 – 2009

Data in U.S. Dollars

	Profitability Tests							Leverage Tests						Liquidity Tests					
Un-Realized Capital Gains ($000)	Benefits Paid to NPW & Dep (%)	Comm. & Expenses to NPW & Dep (%)	NOG to Total Assets (%)	NOG to Total Rev (%)	Operating Return on Equity (%)	Net Yield (%)	Total Return (%)	Change in NPW & Dep (%)	NPW & Dep to Capital (X)	Capital & Surplus to Liabilities (%)	Surplus Relief (%)	Reins Leverage (%)	Change in Capital (%)	Quick Liquidity (%)	Current Liquidity (%)	Non-Invest Grade Bonds to Capital (%)	Delinq. & Foreclosed Mortgages to Capital (%)	Mort. & Credit Tenant Loans & R.E. to Capital (%)	Affiliated Invest to Capital (%)
...	79.0	14.0	14.2	6.2	31.0	4.41	4.37	-6.2	5.4	89.1	...	24.3	-16.3	192.8	208.5	...	...	...	...
...	80.7	13.5	14.8	5.6	37.2	5.47	5.46	6.4	7.8	48.8	...	24.7	-25.8	174.4	185.9	...	...	...	...
...	74.8	13.6	23.1	9.0	60.8	5.87	5.87	1.7	5.8	75.7	...	9.9	35.4	191.6	205.2	...	...	...	...
...	76.7	14.0	15.6	6.2	34.5	4.35	6.68	-11.3	5.9	91.4	...	10.2	-12.2	163.6	178.4	...	...	...	...
...	77.5	13.5	21.5	6.9	47.6	3.35	3.61	4.8	7.6	72.9	...	12.1	-18.9	170.9	184.6	...	...	...	...
Principal Lines of Business: Medicare (95.3%), FEHBP (3.7%), CompHosp/Med (1.0%)													Principal States: MO (85.7%), IL (13.0%)						
...	74.1	19.5	8.2	7.8	10.3	4.40	5.04	-19.1	1.2	405.7	...	0.2	11.0	759.5	795.8	...	...	...	...
...	64.1	16.8	17.1	14.8	21.8	5.21	5.21	33.3	1.3	334.6	...	...	25.3	604.0	641.3	...	...	...	...
...	68.4	15.2	12.8	14.0	15.9	5.28	5.28	-8.4	1.0	526.5	...	...	17.1	776.1	831.5	...	...	...	...
-8	78.4	17.2	2.0	1.5	2.5	4.40	3.73	34.7	2.0	214.5	...	...	-32.4	288.2	314.4	1.6	...	...	...
8	77.8	15.9	20.8	7.3	35.8	3.66	3.86	94.2	6.6	86.6	...	...	-41.0	197.2	214.2	0.8	...	...	...
Principal Lines of Business: Medicare (97.3%), CompHosp/Med (2.7%)													Principal States: UT (100.0%)						
...	79.3	12.6	20.7	6.4	41.6	3.75	3.76	-20.8	6.6	126.6	...	2.9	-4.0	257.9	276.0	...	...	9.4	9.4
...	83.9	12.1	13.5	3.5	26.1	5.18	5.14	-0.6	8.3	91.4	...	1.6	-21.2	199.5	215.4	...	...	11.5	11.5
...	83.2	10.7	18.8	4.9	36.4	5.13	5.18	5.6	6.4	122.4	...	...	37.7	204.5	224.1	...	...	8.1	8.1
0	82.5	10.9	17.0	4.9	31.6	4.10	7.99	2.0	6.3	111.6	...	...	2.3	223.4	243.7	0.4	...	...	...
0	85.8	8.2	20.7	4.3	44.4	3.07	3.24	49.0	11.1	69.6	...	0.4	-14.9	182.1	196.0	...	...	...	...
Principal Lines of Business: Medicaid (60.2%), Medicare (28.3%), CompHosp/Med (11.5%)													Principal States: WI (100.0%)						
...	83.4	12.8	10.1	3.3	21.1	4.44	4.53	-8.5	5.8	106.8	...	0.1	20.9	187.4	201.3	...	...	...	...
...	82.9	9.6	15.0	6.1	33.6	4.80	3.33	10.8	4.7	68.8	...	...	36.9	241.4	249.6	...	...	...	...
...	83.7	12.5	11.7	4.1	28.1	4.78	4.87	50.9	6.6	73.7	...	0.3	6.7	198.0	205.5	...	...	...	...
...	83.3	12.1	12.1	3.8	28.0	3.51	3.95	29.5	6.4	78.3	...	0.4	33.9	195.6	205.0	...	...	...	...
...	82.9	13.1	11.4	3.2	30.6	2.43	2.56	65.3	8.9	49.1	...	...	18.8	157.0	168.6	...	...	...	...
Principal Lines of Business: Medicaid (62.5%), Medicare (21.4%), CompHosp/Med (15.5%), FEHBP (0.7%)													Principal States: TN (84.1%), IA (9.6%), VA (4.1%)						
...	89.5	15.3	-3.1	-3.2	-3.1	1.61	1.61	-89.8	1.0	...	...	...	-3.0	...	...	...	...	...	...
...	84.0	20.2	-2.7	-2.3	-2.7	2.09	2.09	15.1	1.1	...	...	...	-2.6	...	...	...	...	...	...
...	87.7	19.5	-4.6	-4.0	-4.6	3.53	3.53	-5.3	1.1	...	...	...	-4.5	...	...	...	...	...	...
...	82.0	20.3	1.6	2.5	1.7	3.29	3.29	-44.0	0.6	999.9	...	...	1.7	317.7	317.7	...	...	...	...
...	83.4	20.0	2.0	4.2	2.0	4.02	4.02	-27.2	0.4	999.9	...	...	2.1	82.3	82.3	...	...	...	...
Principal Lines of Business: Dental (100.0%)													Principal States: NJ (100.0%)						
...	31.7	27.9	0.6	0.8	3.5	4.86	5.30	41.4	2.7	19.5	128.6	352.9	4.4	77.7	88.0	...	...	...	...
...	34.7	28.7	0.7	1.0	4.8	5.07	5.29	11.1	3.0	15.5	166.6	454.1	2.0	75.3	84.9	...	...	...	...
...	34.6	26.0	0.9	1.3	7.5	5.14	5.17	17.2	3.1	13.5	184.9	526.9	12.1	72.6	83.0	...	...	...	...
...	39.6	5.9	0.4	0.8	4.1	4.91	4.91	8.6	3.3	10.2	106.3	579.4	0.7	73.9	83.7	...	...	...	...
...	38.6	26.5	1.8	3.6	19.4	5.22	5.14	24.1	3.5	10.5	96.6	585.4	19.6	73.1	83.2	...	...	...	...
Principal Lines of Business: GrpLife (80.5%), OrdLife (19.5%)													Principal States: TX (18.5%), NC (15.0%), FL (10.1%), OH (7.9%), MS (5.0%)						
-2,498	161.8	53.2	0.9	6.6	14.8	6.21	5.33	5.2	1.3	6.5	12.2	999.9	-3.4	63.2	77.4	7.1	...	0.6	18.5
-510	146.2	56.3	0.0	-0.2	-0.4	5.43	5.37	5.0	1.7	5.6	16.5	999.9	-20.1	61.0	75.9	7.6	...	0.8	16.8
3,491	122.3	57.1	-0.2	-1.7	-4.5	5.40	6.60	-0.2	1.5	6.7	14.4	913.1	13.2	61.7	75.4	20.5	...	0.7	16.6
-566	97.8	231.8	0.5	3.4	6.5	4.66	4.57	-9.4	1.1	10.6	21.9	899.9	29.3	66.3	79.3	18.4	...	0.5	13.6
-266	87.0	47.2	-0.5	-3.4	-7.1	5.36	5.15	7.9	1.7	7.1	25.1	999.9	-29.5	64.7	77.1	17.0	...	0.7	56.8
Principal Lines of Business: OrdLife (80.4%), GrpAnn (11.9%), IndAnn (6.9%), IndLife (0.7%), IndA&H (0.2%)													Principal States: NY (60.9%), NJ (16.2%), FL (3.3%)						
...	...	...	2.9	67.5	2.9	4.41	4.41	...	...	999.9	...	...	3.0	999.9	999.9	...	...	...	...
...	...	...	3.0	61.1	3.0	4.99	4.99	...	...	999.9	...	...	3.0	999.9	999.9	...	...	...	...
...	...	...	3.4	68.6	3.4	5.13	5.13	...	...	999.9	...	...	3.5	999.9	999.9	...	...	...	...
...	...	...	2.7	66.0	2.7	4.19	4.19	...	...	-99.9	...	...	2.7	-99.9	-99.9	...	...	...	...
...	...	...	1.7	64.2	1.7	2.64	2.64	...	...	-99.9	...	...	1.7	-99.9	-99.9	...	...	...	...
...	89.2	11.8	4.2	1.0	26.3	2.70	2.70	1.7	23.1	21.6	...	...	30.3	61.4	61.4	...	...	77.5	77.5
...	101.2	11.8	21.1	22.9	124.3	3.47	3.47	-89.5	3.8	19.0	...	...	-36.8	63.5	63.5	...	...	28.1	28.1
...	433.4	139.3	-11.1	-10.9	-62.6	3.77	3.77	-82.8	1.2	28.6	...	...	-47.1	29.5	29.5	...	...	...	...
...	343.8	75.1	-30.9	-11.1	-99.9	3.98	3.98	51.1	-23.8	-3.1	...	...	-99.9	0.0	0.0	...	...	...	...
...	162.3	-1.9	8.4	2.8	999.9	11.61	11.61	95.2	36.1	5.9	...	...	228.5	0.1	0.1	...	...	...	...
Principal Lines of Business: CompHosp/Med (100.0%)																			

Data in U.S. Dollars

COMPANY NAME Ultimate Parent Association Principal Officer Mailing Address Dom. : Began Bus. : Struct. : Mktg. Specialty Phone # AMB# NAIC#	Best's Financial Strength Rating FSC	Data Year	Balance Sheet: Bonds (%)	Mort. Loans & R.E. (%)	Com & Pref. Stock (%)	All Other Assets (%)	Total Assets ($000)	Life Reserves (%)	Health Reserves (%)	Ann Res. & Dep. Liabilities (%)	All Other Liabilities (%)	Capital & Surplus ($000)	Operations: Direct Premiums Written ($000)	Net Premiums Written & Deposits ($000)	Operating Cash Flow ($000)	NOG Before Taxes ($000)	NOG After Taxes ($000)	Net Income ($000)
UNIVERSAL FIDELITY LIFE INS CO Universal Fidelity Holding Company Inc Steven R. Hague President 13931 Quail Pointe Drive Oklahoma City, OK 73134 OK : 1935 : Stock : Agency Med supp, Trad Life, Reins 800-366-8354 AMB# 007198 NAIC# 70122	B+ Rating Outlook: Stable FSC III	'05	58.1	...	16.2	25.6	5,122	42.0	0.7	0.3	56.9	2,711	32,752	675	725	453	388	388
		'06	56.2	6.9	11.9	25.0	7,032	52.3	0.4	0.2	47.2	3,107	28,408	500	1,241	546	472	472
		'07	41.0	5.1	7.3	46.5	9,071	35.2	48.3	0.1	16.5	3,163	15,943	3,835	-762	-304	-287	-287
		'08	4.6	4.4	5.8	85.3	10,211	34.6	37.6	0.1	27.8	3,759	13,718	4,649	601	1,289	1,203	973
		'09	25.3	12.3	5.6	56.8	10,480	34.0	38.8	0.1	27.1	3,643	12,270	5,398	-341	269	137	106
		Rating History: B+, 04/16/10; B+, 05/08/09; B+, 05/30/08; B+, 05/31/07; B+, 06/15/06																
UNIVERSAL GUARANTY LIFE INS CO[1] James P. Rousey President 5250 S 6th Street Rd Springfield, IL 62703-5128 OH : 1966 : Stock : Agency Ordinary Life, Ind Ann, Group Life 217-241-6590 AMB# 007199 NAIC# 70130	NR-1	'05	51.8	15.3	14.8	18.1	259,754	...	...	4.4	95.6	25,646	15,563	13,061	...	2,773	2,703	5,114
		'06	59.1	13.3	13.8	13.8	262,745	...	...	4.3	95.7	31,210	14,267	11,753	...	1,838	1,643	5,162
		'07	44.9	19.8	18.6	16.7	263,088	...	...	4.3	95.7	30,131	13,632	11,248	...	3,882	3,040	4,662
		'08	44.6	19.4	17.9	18.2	256,890	...	...	4.6	95.4	27,483	12,961	9,444	...	913	708	4,825
		'09	39.0	24.1	14.1	22.8	265,010	...	...	4.4	95.6	27,350	11,856	8,955	...	-461	-453	204
		Rating History: NR-1, 06/10/10; NR-5, 06/24/09; NR-1, 06/12/08; NR-1, 06/08/07; NR-1, 06/07/06																
UNIVERSAL LIFE INS CO[1] Walter Howlett, Jr. Chairman & President 1728 3rd Avenue North Birmingham, AL 35203-2030 AL : 1923 : Stock : Agency In Rehabilitation 205-328-5454 AMB# 007201 NAIC# 70157	E	'05	28.8	10.1	9.1	52.0	19,494	...	...	0.4	99.6	3,165	1,363	1,332	...	276	276	274
		'06	24.7	8.7	9.9	56.7	19,516	...	...	0.4	99.6	2,604	2,066	1,826	...	210	210	293
		'07	61.2	6.3	9.7	22.8	19,989	...	...	0.3	99.7	-1,149	2,015	1,819	...	-4,078	-4,078	-4,266
		'08	53.7	8.3	12.1	25.9	13,145	...	...	...	100.0	560	-14	-177	...	459	459	573
		'09	...	...	...	...	...	...	...	...	...	...	...	...	...	...	...	...
		Rating History: E, 02/09/10; NR-1, 06/12/09; NR-1, 06/12/08; NR-1, 06/08/07; NR-1, 06/07/06																
UNIVERSAL LIFE INSURANCE CO Universal Group, Inc. Jose C. Benitez Ulmer President P.O. Box 2145 San Juan, PR 00922-2145 PR : 1994 : Stock : General Agent Ind Ann, Ind A&H, Credit Life 787-706-7337 AMB# 060097 NAIC# 60041	B++ Rating Outlook: Stable FSC V	'05	68.5	...	5.6	26.0	31,075	54.1	21.3	2.9	21.8	8,652	34,500	27,160	773	914	663	663
		'06	71.0	...	7.1	21.9	40,992	34.8	24.7	27.5	12.9	9,403	40,080	37,554	10,876	880	880	880
		'07	41.8	...	4.2	54.0	96,135	12.8	12.4	26.9	47.9	10,441	87,496	59,067	15,693	-890	-927	-927
		'08	38.8	...	3.5	57.8	128,097	9.2	2.5	31.9	56.4	20,261	92,534	49,544	15,803	6,600	6,760	6,760
		'09	42.1	...	1.7	56.2	216,953	4.4	1.1	35.0	59.5	22,108	99,753	64,365	37,581	1,874	1,874	1,231
		Rating History: B++, 06/16/09; B++, 07/09/08; B++, 06/08/07; B++, 06/06/06; B++, 05/16/05																
UNIVERSAL UNDERWRITERS LIFE Zurich Financial Services Ltd Lisa Ann Versch President 7045 College Boulevard Overland Park, KS 66211 KS : 1965 : Stock : Direct Response Term Life, Univ Life 913-339-1000 AMB# 007204 NAIC# 70173	A- Rating Outlook: Stable FSC VII	'05	93.5	...	...	6.5	287,569	69.1	12.9	1.6	16.4	40,195	68,244	51,462	-55,291	12,717	8,218	8,218
		'06	71.7	...	...	28.3	387,157	48.4	7.5	0.7	43.3	42,430	41,031	29,734	97,649	1,874	766	766
		'07	79.2	...	0.3	20.6	328,940	51.0	5.5	1.0	42.4	46,408	-7,783	-5,190	-60,471	19,444	8,826	8,826
		'08	89.0	...	0.2	10.8	253,961	65.6	4.5	1.2	28.7	59,617	13,818	10,722	-64,095	25,869	24,666	22,074
		'09	83.6	...	0.1	16.3	258,997	63.9	2.2	1.3	32.6	75,322	12,315	8,906	6,230	13,120	14,841	13,009
		Rating History: A-, 06/16/09; A-, 06/18/08; A-, 06/19/07; A-, 02/03/06; A-, 04/04/05																
UNIVERSITY HEALTH ALLIANCE[2] Max G. Botticelli, M.D. Chairman, President & CEO 700 Bishop Street, Suite 300 Honolulu, HI 96813 HI : 1988 : Mutual : Agency Group A&H 808-532-4000 AMB# 064548 NAIC# 47953	NR-5	'05	31.2	...	2.8	65.9	27,168	...	69.2	...	30.8	12,708	83,692	82,720	6,363	6,265	4,007	3,999
		'06	36.1	...	3.1	60.9	33,062	...	...	...	100.0	14,918	98,850	97,727	5,208	3,716	2,629	2,624
		'07	20.1	...	25.7	54.2	32,840	...	...	...	100.0	10,175	112,485	111,193	-532	-2,620	-1,990	-1,868
		'08	...	...	12.4	87.6	29,484	...	...	...	100.0	13,390	125,896	124,570	-2,697	5,197	3,465	3,247
		'09	5.1	...	18.5	76.4	30,669	...	...	...	100.0	16,045	104,412	103,418	556	5,494	3,585	3,710
		Rating History: NR-5, 05/13/10; NR-5, 04/16/09; NR-5, 03/13/08; NR-5, 04/03/07; NR-5, 05/08/06																
UNIVERSITY HEALTH PLANS INC Centene Corporation Mary Garcia President & CEO 7711 Carondelet Avenue, Suite 700 St. Louis, MO 63105 NJ : 1994 : Stock : Broker Medicaid 314-725-4477 AMB# 060157 NAIC# 95503	NR-3	'05	45.1	...	...	54.9	37,349	...	63.8	...	36.2	20,427	116,850	115,789	-1,080	3,141	3,149	3,149
		'06	41.4	...	...	58.6	45,549	...	45.2	...	54.8	17,019	139,125	137,058	7,652	-1,348	-1,859	-1,859
		'07	59.8	...	...	40.2	34,139	...	76.1	...	23.9	8,953	150,070	147,707	-16,638	-11,349	-6,827	-6,857
		'08	42.2	...	...	57.8	38,217	...	84.4	...	15.6	10,838	150,638	147,792	4,075	-6,034	-3,558	-4,256
		'09	70.6	...	1.4	28.0	30,632	...	87.6	...	12.4	11,013	145,097	142,322	-2,289	-10,212	-5,855	-5,855
		Rating History: NR-3, 03/16/10; B, 02/19/10; B, 02/10/09; C+ pd, 07/09/07; C++pd, 08/08/06																
UNUM LIFE INS CO OF AMER Unum Group Thomas R. Watjen Chairman, President & CEO 1 Fountain Square Chattanooga, TN 37402-1330 ME : 1966 : Stock : Broker Dis inc, Group Life 207-575-2211 AMB# 006256 NAIC# 62235	A- Rating Outlook: Positive FSC XIV	'05	88.4	4.6	1.5	5.4	15,074,438	6.9	53.5	5.4	34.2	1,354,600	4,153,046	3,440,705	2,307,025	269,030	255,053	249,159
		'06	86.3	4.5	2.0	7.1	16,025,917	6.5	61.4	4.5	27.6	1,580,144	4,090,275	3,972,073	877,898	-1,626	22,067	-14,856
		'07	88.4	4.3	1.4	5.9	16,438,519	6.4	61.3	4.1	28.1	1,490,503	3,894,578	3,407,403	297,477	241,401	249,364	194,995
		'08	86.4	4.6	1.5	7.5	16,890,055	6.2	59.7	3.9	30.2	1,353,250	3,800,125	3,307,140	398,726	420,623	268,769	190,940
		'09	87.7	4.9	0.2	7.1	17,214,784	6.2	58.3	4.1	31.4	1,541,119	3,684,207	3,153,784	160,883	431,835	302,493	249,419
		Rating History: A- g, 03/08/10; A- g, 03/13/09; A- g, 01/29/08; A- g, 11/07/06; A- g, 06/07/06																
UPMC FOR YOU INC University of Pittsburgh Medical Center John G. Lovelace CEO 112 Washington Place Pittsburgh, PA 15219 PA : 2004 : Stock : Direct Response Medicaid, Medicare 412-434-1200 AMB# 064807 NAIC# 11995	B++ Rating Outlook: Stable FSC VII	'05	14.6	...	5.3	80.1	94,666	...	45.6	...	54.4	37,270	420,759	418,232	-4,627	4,251	2,995	2,311
		'06	56.9	...	...	43.1	93,782	...	44.0	...	56.0	49,850	405,458	404,192	2,538	13,109	7,838	7,893
		'07	68.8	...	...	31.2	114,933	...	37.9	...	62.1	66,074	460,159	458,575	40,781	24,561	20,861	21,295
		'08	56.7	...	...	43.3	150,210	...	42.8	...	57.2	90,241	616,102	615,656	-7,066	28,866	28,862	28,289
		'09	43.7	...	0.4	55.9	185,448	...	43.4	...	56.6	91,695	794,286	793,558	19,951	3,727	3,727	2,715
		Rating History: B++, 01/29/10; B++, 02/26/09; B++, 08/24/07; B+, 01/12/07; B+, 02/17/06																

BEST'S PROFITABILITY, LEVERAGE AND LIQUIDITY TESTS 2005 – 2009

Data in U.S. Dollars

	Profitability Tests							Leverage Tests						Liquidity Tests					
Un-Realized Capital Gains ($000)	Benefits Paid to NPW & Dep (%)	Comm. & Expenses to NPW & Dep (%)	NOG to Total Assets (%)	NOG to Total Rev (%)	Operating Return on Equity (%)	Net Yield (%)	Total Return (%)	Change in NPW & Dep (%)	NPW & Dep to Capital (X)	Capital & Surplus to Liabilities (%)	Surplus Relief (%)	Reins Leverage (%)	Change in Capital (%)	Quick Liquidity (%)	Current Liquidity (%)	Non-Invest Grade Bonds to Capital (%)	Delinq. & Foreclosed Mortgages to Capital (%)	Mort. & Credit Tenant Loans & R.E. to Capital (%)	Affiliated Invest to Capital (%)
0	39.8	25.6	8.1	12.0	14.5	4.05	4.26	57.1	0.2	115.2	79.0	885.7	4.4	139.2	143.7	...	...	...	27.8
0	45.1	-30.8	7.8	13.2	16.2	4.06	4.06	-26.0	0.2	81.9	61.1	863.8	15.5	120.2	122.6	...	...	15.3	39.3
90	38.9	32.2	-3.6	-5.1	-9.2	2.15	3.53	666.9	1.2	55.8	37.0	935.4	2.6	71.6	73.8	...	...	14.4	32.6
-53	61.9	121.0	12.5	12.5	34.7	2.47	-2.43	21.2	1.2	60.2	17.0	831.2	18.2	149.8	151.5	...	...	11.7	20.8
55	59.4	119.2	1.3	1.3	3.7	0.89	1.21	16.1	1.4	55.5	14.7	842.5	-2.5	68.7	70.9	...	...	34.6	34.0
Principal Lines of Business: GrpA&H (92.6%), OrdLife (5.4%), IndA&H (2.0%)														Principal States: OK (48.8%), TX (46.0%), NM (5.2%)					
-395	128.9	37.4	1.0	10.9	11.4	...	...	-6.4	0.4	14.9	1.2	...	16.1	...	...	...	...	118.3	...
387	157.0	51.3	0.6	6.1	5.8	...	...	-10.0	0.3	16.8	1.0	...	12.1	...	...	...	...	92.6	...
525	168.8	32.8	1.2	11.4	9.9	...	...	-4.3	0.3	17.3	1.0	...	3.0	...	...	...	...	134.1	...
-6,510	202.6	38.1	0.3	3.0	2.5	...	...	-16.0	0.3	15.2	1.0	...	-12.4	...	...	...	...	146.5	...
-650	208.9	39.0	-0.2	-2.1	-1.7	...	...	-5.2	0.3	14.8	1.0	...	0.5	...	...	...	...	186.9	...
Principal Lines of Business: OrdLife (91.6%), IndAnn (5.0%), GrpLife (3.0%), IndA&H (0.2%), CrdLife (0.1%)																			
57	133.6	3.6	1.4	13.1	9.8	...	...	-40.5	0.4	21.7	...	...	20.4	...	...	...	...	56.6	...
...	82.4	43.4	1.1	7.9	7.3	...	...	37.1	0.6	18.6	...	...	-12.1	...	...	...	...	55.8	...
45	74.7	31.9	-20.6	-99.9	-99.9	...	...	-0.4	-2.1	-4.1	...	...	-99.9	...	...	...	...	-99.9	...
-513	-99.9	-92.9	2.8	61.0	-99.9	...	...	-99.9	-0.2	7.2	...	...	203.2	...	...	...	...	123.5	...
...	...	...	...	...	...	...	...	...	...	...	...	...	...	...	...	...	...	...	...
-184	20.9	61.6	2.3	2.4	6.9	3.98	3.21	35.0	3.1	38.9	...	82.7	-18.2	100.0	106.1	...	...	...	...
-77	29.5	48.9	2.4	2.3	9.7	4.51	4.28	38.3	4.0	29.9	...	55.1	8.4	103.5	107.2	...	...	...	...
-334	23.2	30.2	-1.4	-1.5	-9.3	4.79	4.02	57.3	5.7	22.4	...	66.2	10.7	100.9	104.2	9.6	...	...	...
159	34.5	21.7	6.0	7.7	44.0	4.26	4.53	-16.1	2.4	42.2	...	41.4	97.3	124.4	132.6	13.4	...	...	...
-10	21.1	14.8	1.1	2.1	8.8	5.15	4.22	29.9	2.9	26.0	...	84.5	7.9	99.0	105.7	18.1	...	...	...
Principal Lines of Business: IndAnn (85.0%), GrpLife (7.4%), CrdLife (3.6%), GrpA&H (3.2%), OrdLife (1.1%)														Principal States: PR (100.0%)					
...	44.3	59.9	2.6	11.2	11.6	4.18	4.65	-7.0	1.3	16.5	19.0	114.5	-60.1	92.4	99.0	...	...	...	...
...	59.6	123.9	0.2	1.5	1.9	4.31	4.53	-42.2	0.7	12.5	14.1	92.2	5.6	87.5	94.6	...	...	...	...
...	-99.9	-99.9	2.5	73.6	19.9	4.39	4.47	-99.9	-0.1	16.7	4.4	73.2	9.4	88.9	99.7	...	...	...	...
...	165.6	34.2	8.5	101.2	46.5	4.75	3.87	306.6	0.2	31.2	0.9	22.6	28.0	95.3	107.8	0.2	...	...	...
-8	177.0	74.7	5.8	64.8	22.0	4.85	4.18	-16.9	0.1	41.2	1.7	8.7	25.1	110.4	122.8	11.6	...	...	...
Principal Lines of Business: OrdLife (120.7%), IndA&H (0.5%), IndAnn (0.0%), CrdA&H (-7.8%), CrdLife (-13.4%)														Principal States: CA (13.8%), TX (8.4%), IL (6.4%), FL (6.4%), NJ (4.3%)					
19	81.6	11.1	16.9	4.8	38.1	3.04	3.09	25.9	6.5	87.9	...	2.2	52.5	230.7	232.7	...	...	...	...
112	86.3	10.8	8.7	2.7	19.0	4.29	4.67	18.1	6.6	82.2	...	...	17.4	212.5	214.3	...	...	...	...
-62	92.6	10.8	-6.0	-1.8	-15.9	5.25	5.44	13.8	10.9	44.9	...	2.3	-31.8	148.9	154.6	...	...	...	...
85	85.9	10.3	11.1	2.8	29.4	3.01	2.55	12.0	9.3	83.2	...	4.8	31.6	257.0	260.5	...	...	...	...
-133	81.4	13.3	11.9	3.5	24.4	1.03	1.01	-17.0	6.4	109.7	...	7.8	19.8	264.3	271.2	...	...	...	...
Principal Lines of Business: CompHosp/Med (80.0%), OtherHlth (16.0%), Dental (3.0%), Vision (1.0%)														Principal States: HI (100.0%)					
...	83.9	14.2	8.4	2.7	16.7	3.00	3.00	1.4	5.7	120.7	...	1.6	18.2	219.9	223.8	...	...	...	...
...	86.8	15.2	-4.5	-1.3	-9.9	3.80	3.80	18.4	8.1	59.7	...	2.7	-16.7	191.4	198.2	...	...	...	...
...	91.3	16.0	-17.1	-4.6	-52.6	4.01	3.91	7.8	16.5	35.6	...	4.5	-47.4	94.6	95.7	...	...	...	...
...	87.9	16.0	-9.8	-2.4	-36.0	4.07	1.28	0.1	13.6	39.6	...	6.6	21.0	134.9	139.0	...	...	...	...
...	93.3	15.1	-17.0	-4.1	-53.6	1.21	1.21	-3.7	12.9	56.1	...	4.4	1.6	132.6	134.0	...	...	...	...
Principal Lines of Business: Medicaid (100.0%)														Principal States: NJ (100.0%)					
-21,061	19.8	23.9	1.8	6.6	20.0	6.56	6.43	-5.3	2.4	10.7	17.0	388.1	13.5	50.5	66.1	55.2	...	51.9	20.2
-41,543	37.4	23.4	0.1	0.5	1.5	6.87	6.39	15.4	2.4	11.7	8.2	289.6	16.1	52.8	69.0	54.8	0.1	48.1	14.1
34,473	56.1	24.3	1.5	6.4	16.2	6.64	6.56	-14.2	2.1	11.0	13.1	303.8	-3.8	51.4	67.6	70.7	0.1	48.5	6.6
-7,840	48.3	37.8	1.6	7.1	18.9	6.38	5.87	-2.9	2.2	9.6	18.7	357.8	-8.5	50.5	67.8	82.6	0.5	58.1	7.1
9,673	49.0	44.1	1.8	8.6	20.9	6.37	6.11	-4.6	1.9	10.9	14.8	340.1	14.3	48.8	66.4	84.3	1.3	54.4	6.3
Principal Lines of Business: GrpA&H (64.8%), GrpLife (18.1%), IndAnn (16.3%), OrdLife (0.5%), IndA&H (0.2%)														Principal States: CA (10.3%), TX (9.7%), FL (4.9%), MA (4.8%), PA (4.5%)					
-46	87.1	12.3	3.4	0.7	8.8	3.39	2.11	134.6	11.2	64.9	...	3.1	22.1	119.4	133.4	...	...	...	8.0
-2	84.5	12.9	8.3	1.9	18.0	5.41	5.50	-3.4	8.1	113.5	...	1.3	33.8	102.9	112.9	...	...	...	6.0
...	81.8	14.1	20.0	4.5	36.0	4.58	5.14	13.5	6.9	135.2	...	1.1	32.5	178.3	194.2	...	...	...	4.5
...	84.3	11.7	21.8	4.7	36.9	4.34	3.75	34.3	6.8	150.5	...	...	36.6	117.5	128.0	...	...	...	5.5
-25	87.9	10.7	2.2	0.5	4.1	2.96	1.95	28.9	8.7	97.8	...	...	1.6	100.6	108.7	...	...	...	12.0
Principal Lines of Business: Medicaid (73.0%), Medicare (27.0%)														Principal States: PA (100.0%)					

Data in U.S. Dollars

COMPANY NAME Ultimate Parent Association Principal Officer Mailing Address Dom. : Began Bus. : Struct. : Mktg. Specialty Phone # AMB# NAIC#	Best's Financial Strength Rating FSC	Data Year	Balance Sheet: Bonds (%)	Mort. Loans & R.E. (%)	Com & Pref. Stock (%)	All Other Assets (%)	Total Assets ($000)	Life Reserves (%)	Health Reserves %)	Ann Res. & Dep. Liabilities (%)	All Other Liabilities (%)	Capital & Surplus ($000)	Operations: Direct Premiums Written ($000)	Net Premiums Written & Deposits ($000)	Operating Cash Flow ($000)	NOG Before Taxes ($000)	NOG After Taxes ($000)	Net Income ($000)
UPMC HEALTH BENEFITS INC University of Pittsburgh Medical Center Diane P. Holder CEO 112 Washington Place Pittsburgh, PA 15219 PA : 2000 : Stock : Broker Medicare, Med supp 412-434-1200 AMB# 012486 NAIC# 11018	NR-2	'05	69.5	...	...	30.5	6,852	...	22.4	...	77.6	3,958	376	376	-53,983	-921	-704	-896
		'06	58.4	...	...	41.6	7,342	...	53.5	...	46.5	6,945	1,639	1,639	-110	165	176	176
		'07	1.6	...	...	98.4	12,452	...	56.8	...	43.2	7,477	31,059	30,991	2,281	-2,153	-1,447	-1,482
		'08	0.2	...	...	99.8	54,152	...	63.5	...	36.5	28,153	115,237	115,135	40,818	-19,281	-15,320	-15,320
		'09	0.2	...	...	99.8	47,356	...	54.2	...	45.8	36,241	109,524	109,436	-3,335	8,977	8,349	8,348
		Rating History: NR-2, 01/29/10; NR-3, 02/26/09; NR-3, 08/24/07; NR-3, 01/12/07; NR-3, 02/17/06																
UPMC HEALTH NETWORK INC University of Pittsburgh Medical Center Diane P. Holder CEO 112 Washington Place Pittsburgh, PA 15219 PA : 2005 : Stock : Agency Medical 412-434-1200 AMB# 064808 NAIC# 11994	B++ Rating Outlook: Stable FSC VIII	'05	43.1	...	10.3	46.6	105,073	...	45.2	...	54.8	52,298	372,982	372,153	73,813	32,027	21,555	21,555
		'06	38.7	...	2.0	59.3	91,364	...	58.1	...	41.9	51,985	431,455	430,472	-4,013	14,752	9,380	9,342
		'07	76.3	...	3.0	20.7	104,784	...	55.1	...	44.9	58,728	482,826	481,595	11,614	10,233	6,492	6,736
		'08	56.8	...	1.0	42.2	104,886	...	41.5	...	58.5	55,807	570,536	569,022	1,732	17,041	11,732	8,325
		'09	67.9	...	0.7	31.3	121,658	...	36.7	...	63.3	66,986	606,138	604,371	17,617	8,764	5,934	3,168
		Rating History: B++g, 01/29/10; B++g, 02/26/09; B++g, 08/24/07; B++g, 01/12/07; B++g, 02/17/06																
UPMC HEALTH PLAN INC University of Pittsburgh Medical Center Diane P. Holder CEO 112 Washington Place Pittsburgh, PA 15219 PA : 1996 : Stock : Broker Medicare, FEHBP, Group A&H 412-434-1200 AMB# 064162 NAIC# 95216	B++ Rating Outlook: Stable FSC VIII	'05	56.6	...	0.6	42.8	171,410	...	28.2	...	71.8	61,357	472,925	471,298	-13,162	14,836	9,535	215
		'06	55.7	...	3.3	41.1	185,572	...	34.3	...	65.7	65,268	651,896	650,298	24,567	28,259	16,891	16,966
		'07	57.6	...	1.1	41.3	180,996	...	40.6	...	59.4	85,538	738,369	736,410	-22,876	28,417	18,032	18,259
		'08	50.7	...	...	49.3	171,309	...	37.7	...	62.3	99,114	790,641	789,681	-21,983	58,304	38,453	37,705
		'09	48.1	...	0.0	51.9	184,680	...	37.3	...	62.7	107,104	772,301	771,275	24,144	17,158	11,602	9,569
		Rating History: B++g, 01/29/10; B++g, 02/26/09; B++g, 08/24/07; B++g, 01/12/07; B++g, 02/17/06																
UPPER PENINSULA HEALTH PLAN Dennis H. Smith President & CEO 228 West Washington Street Marquette, MI 49855 MI : 1998 : Non-Profit : Not Available Group A&H 906-225-7500 AMB# 064619 NAIC# 52615	NR-5	'05	29.8	...	...	70.2	11,728	...	67.3	...	32.7	4,603	50,017	49,724	-778	809	1,168	1,168
		'06	23.6	...	...	76.4	14,818	...	76.5	...	23.5	7,384	48,781	48,498	3,492	2,858	2,858	2,858
		'07	7.3	...	...	92.7	22,630	...	85.8	...	14.2	13,218	66,951	66,798	6,841	5,959	5,959	5,959
		'08	...	...	...	100.0	28,417	...	69.2	...	30.8	18,125	83,029	82,890	6,701	4,919	4,919	4,919
		'09	...	...	...	100.0	35,705	...	76.3	...	23.7	23,890	93,147	92,980	7,336	5,828	5,828	5,828
		Rating History: NR-5, 05/21/10; NR-5, 08/26/09; B- pd, 07/14/08; C++pd, 06/26/07; C+ pd, 07/25/06																
U S BEHAVIORAL HEALTH PLAN CA UnitedHealth Group Inc James E. Davis President 9900 Bren Road East, MN008-T380 Minnetonka, MN 55343 CA : 1990 : Stock : Broker Health 415-547-5000 AMB# 064733	NR-2	'05	...	...	...	100.0	32,473	...	...	...	100.0	12,206	122,620	122,620	-5,104	36,372	21,582	21,582
		'06	...	...	...	100.0	28,982	...	...	...	100.0	7,532	126,465	126,465	-1,287	25,770	15,171	15,171
		'07	...	...	...	100.0	24,352	...	...	...	100.0	8,041	112,267	112,267	-5,192	16,569	9,731	9,731
		'08	...	...	...	100.0	26,067	...	...	...	100.0	9,413	115,401	115,401	111	9,185	5,334	5,334
		'09	...	...	...	100.0	29,290	...	...	...	100.0	13,045	113,884	113,884	4,610	6,897	4,107	4,107
		Rating History: NR-2, 06/15/09; NR-2, 01/29/08; NR-2, 11/21/07; NR-2, 11/16/06; NR-2, 08/17/06																
US FINANCIAL LIFE INS CO AXA S.A. Charles A. Marino President 1290 Avenue of the Americas New York, NY 10104 OH : 1974 : Stock : Broker Ind Ann, Term Life, Univ Life 212-554-1234 AMB# 008492 NAIC# 84530	A Rating Outlook: Stable FSC XV	'05	71.4	...	1.0	27.7	410,051	77.2	0.0	3.7	19.0	49,541	275,936	34,368	80,738	-47,827	-36,540	-36,291
		'06	81.0	...	1.2	17.9	503,890	85.0	0.0	2.8	12.3	39,802	293,199	84,868	102,058	-60,025	-48,315	-48,332
		'07	78.5	...	1.1	20.3	543,684	84.7	0.0	2.3	13.0	45,431	293,365	73,705	48,178	-36,542	-27,783	-27,794
		'08	77.9	...	1.1	21.0	567,974	85.8	0.0	2.1	12.1	48,411	266,939	65,372	920	14,011	5,606	-2,879
		'09	79.5	...	1.0	19.5	598,828	87.6	...	2.0	10.4	70,561	248,179	61,202	37,922	18,049	17,849	16,700
		Rating History: A, 06/04/10; A, 06/12/09; A, 05/29/08; A+ g, 01/25/07; A+ g, 08/12/05																
US HEALTH AND LIFE INS CO Daniel Gorczyca President & COO 8220 Irving Road Sterling Heights, MI 48312 MI : 1984 : Stock : Agency Group A&H, Group Life, Med supp 586-693-4300 AMB# 009184 NAIC# 97772	NR-5	'05	19.0	...	...	81.0	33,067	0.0	70.6	...	29.3	8,923	60,214	31,182	12,672	997	531	531
		'06	31.1	...	...	68.9	32,966	0.0	67.7	...	32.3	8,765	58,506	32,212	745	24	-50	-50
		'07	32.8	...	...	67.2	31,210	0.1	81.2	...	18.7	9,280	42,369	26,240	1,983	529	438	438
		'08	12.9	...	...	87.1	31,504	0.1	81.2	...	18.7	8,942	42,649	26,923	-1,113	96	56	56
		'09	43.7	...	...	56.3	30,332	0.2	77.2	...	22.6	9,393	44,163	28,519	189	960	648	648
		Rating History: NR-5, 03/31/10; NR-5, 04/09/09; NR-5, 04/21/08; NR-5, 04/30/07; NR-5, 04/20/06																
USA LIFE ONE INS CO OF IN' Roger W. Smith President 7735 Loma Court Fishers, IN 46038 IN : 1894 : Mutual : Broker 317-585-0541 AMB# 006161 NAIC# 70955	NR-1	'05	89.9	0.6	0.2	9.2	37,947	...	...	0.8	99.2	15,721	1,521	1,450	...	779	651	651
		'06	90.5	0.6	0.2	8.7	37,964	...	...	0.8	99.2	16,470	1,441	1,357	...	939	759	726
		'07	89.9	0.5	0.1	9.5	37,855	...	...	0.8	99.2	17,020	1,421	1,342	...	864	696	416
		'08	88.1	0.5	0.7	10.7	36,547	...	...	0.8	99.2	16,765	1,174	1,142	...	790	765	50
		'09	74.6	0.4	0.1	24.9	35,916	...	...	0.8	99.2	16,375	1,061	1,011	...	420	360	-12
		Rating History: NR-1, 06/10/10; NR-1, 06/12/09; NR-1, 06/12/08; NR-1, 06/08/07; NR-5, 05/03/06																
USAA DIRECT LIFE INSURANCE CO United Services Automobile Association Russell A. Evenson President & Chief Actuary 9800 Fredericksburg Road San Antonio, TX 78288 NE : 1969 : Stock : Agency Credit Life 210-498-8000 AMB# 060314 NAIC# 72613	NR-3	'05	14.2	...	...	85.8	9,650	2.1	10.7	...	87.2	9,408	-54	...	362	227	221	221
		'06	...	...	...	...	...	...	...	...	...	...	...	...	...	...	...	...
		'07	46.2	...	...	53.8	8,944	...	...	...	100.0	8,888	-6	...	244	173	120	120
		'08	44.9	...	...	55.1	9,168	...	...	...	100.0	9,153	1	...	-1,719	132	269	269
		'09	86.8	...	...	13.2	9,303	...	...	...	100.0	9,247	1	...	2,087	23	97	97
		Rating History: NR-3, 12/22/09; NR-3, 12/23/08; A++g, 12/11/07; NR-1, 06/08/07; NR-5, 04/27/06																

BEST'S PROFITABILITY, LEVERAGE AND LIQUIDITY TESTS 2005 – 2009

Data in U.S. Dollars

—	Profitability Tests							Leverage Tests						Liquidity Tests					
Un-Realized Capital Gains ($000)	Benefits Paid to NPW & Dep (%)	Comm. & Expenses to NPW & Dep (%)	NOG to Total Assets (%)	NOG to Total Rev (%)	Operating Return on Equity (%)	Net Yield (%)	Total Return (%)	Change in NPW & Dep (%)	NPW & Dep to Capital (X)	Capital & Surplus to Liabilities (%)	Surplus Relief (%)	Reins Leverage (%)	Change in Capital (%)	Quick Liquidity (%)	Current Liquidity (%)	Non-Invest Grade Bonds to Capital (%)	Delinq. & Foreclosed Mortgages to Capital (%)	Mort. & Credit Tenant Loans & R.E. to Capital (%)	Affiliated Invest to Capital (%)
-541	277.3	267.9	-1.7	-62.5	-4.0	2.33	0.10	-99.9	0.1	136.8	...	...	-87.5	167.6	184.7	...	...	...	...
335	83.5	15.8	2.5	9.8	3.2	2.91	9.39	336.5	0.2	999.9	...	...	75.5	999.9	999.9	...	...	...	...
...	97.1	10.8	-14.6	-4.6	-20.1	4.44	3.89	999.9	4.1	150.3	...	2.5	7.7	244.1	254.5	...	...	...	...
...	102.7	8.0	-46.0	-13.3	-86.0	0.78	0.78	271.5	4.1	108.3	...	...	276.5	351.2	369.6	...	...	...	...
-297	91.3	6.3	16.5	7.7	25.9	-1.81	-2.45	-5.0	3.0	326.1	...	...	28.7	748.3	753.7	...	...	...	...
	Principal Lines of Business: Medicare (95.2%), OtherHlth (4.6%), MedSup (0.2%)													Principal States: OH (42.8%), PA (33.8%), WV (23.4%)					
69	83.2	8.5	39.3	5.8	75.9	2.28	2.44	...	7.1	99.1	...	0.6	999.9	157.5	181.9	...	...	...	...
88	88.4	8.4	9.6	2.2	18.0	3.22	3.29	15.7	8.3	132.0	...	0.4	-0.6	256.2	277.1	...	...	...	4.8
-50	89.8	9.0	6.6	1.3	11.7	3.94	4.18	11.9	8.2	127.5	...	0.6	13.0	132.7	152.0	...	...	...	7.7
-2,434	89.1	8.4	11.2	2.1	20.5	3.77	-2.93	18.2	10.2	113.7	...	1.0	-5.0	181.4	195.5	2.7	...	...	8.1
2,825	90.5	8.4	5.2	1.0	9.7	2.07	2.22	6.2	9.0	122.5	...	0.1	20.0	162.0	172.3	1.1	...	...	6.7
	Principal Lines of Business: CompHosp/Med (96.3%), Medicare (3.7%)													Principal States: PA (100.0%)					
6,035	87.1	10.0	5.7	2.0	12.1	0.77	-1.37	-22.3	7.7	55.8	...	0.4	-36.6	108.9	120.1	1.2	...	...	9.8
1,043	86.5	9.1	9.5	2.6	26.7	-0.26	0.54	38.0	10.0	54.3	...	0.5	6.4	121.1	133.5	0.4	...	...	9.2
-100	87.8	8.8	9.8	2.4	23.9	2.17	2.26	13.2	8.6	89.6	...	0.4	31.1	108.4	119.3	0.3	...	...	7.0
-1,564	84.9	8.1	21.8	4.9	41.6	2.21	0.26	7.2	8.0	137.3	...	0.1	15.9	110.6	121.5	0.9	...	...	6.1
1,108	90.2	7.7	6.5	1.5	11.3	1.26	0.49	-2.3	7.2	138.1	...	0.2	8.1	139.9	147.2	3.2	...	...	5.6
	Principal Lines of Business: Medicare (82.0%), FEHBP (9.8%), CompHosp/Med (8.2%)													Principal States: PA (99.9%)					
...	84.3	14.8	9.8	2.3	24.0	3.15	3.15	2.5	10.8	64.6	...	...	-10.4	173.6	173.6	...	...	...	...
...	81.8	15.4	21.5	5.8	47.7	5.04	5.04	-2.5	6.6	99.3	...	...	60.4	191.2	191.2	...	...	...	...
...	78.7	13.6	31.8	8.8	57.8	4.82	4.82	37.7	5.1	140.4	...	...	79.0	224.0	224.0	...	...	...	...
...	81.0	13.6	19.3	5.9	31.4	2.05	2.05	24.1	4.6	176.1	...	...	37.1	269.9	269.9	...	...	...	...
...	80.5	13.3	18.2	6.3	27.7	0.14	0.14	12.2	3.9	202.2	...	...	31.8	297.2	297.2	...	...	...	...
	Principal Lines of Business: Medicaid (99.6%), CompHosp/Med (0.4%)													Principal States: MI (100.0%)					
...	64.4	7.2	62.6	17.2	175.8	3.90	3.90	8.0	10.0	60.2	...	...	-1.2	92.6	92.6	...	...	...	...
...	73.9	7.1	49.4	11.7	153.7	5.03	5.03	3.1	16.8	35.1	...	...	-38.3	69.2	69.2	...	...	...	...
...	79.3	7.3	36.5	8.4	125.0	4.72	4.72	-11.2	14.0	49.3	...	...	6.8	84.3	84.3	...	...	...	...
...	84.9	7.7	21.2	4.6	61.1	4.10	4.10	2.8	12.3	56.5	...	...	17.1	63.3	63.3	...	...	...	...
...	86.4	8.3	14.8	3.5	36.6	2.37	2.37	-1.3	8.7	80.3	...	...	38.6	97.6	97.6	...	...	...	...
	Principal Lines of Business: CompHosp/Med (100.0%)																		
-246	97.4	143.8	-10.2	-29.6	-85.4	5.18	5.37	-34.1	0.7	14.0	95.8	999.9	37.2	73.4	81.1	1.8	...	...	...
...	64.4	61.0	-10.6	-35.1	-99.9	5.08	5.19	146.9	2.0	8.9	81.6	999.9	-17.6	74.7	83.7	4.5	...	...	...
...	92.8	53.5	-5.3	-19.8	-65.2	5.51	5.58	-13.2	1.6	9.5	89.3	999.9	13.4	77.3	86.7	4.0	...	...	...
...	100.1	-17.5	1.0	4.3	11.9	5.27	3.60	-11.3	1.4	9.3	80.4	999.9	3.0	69.5	79.1	21.8	...	...	...
...	122.9	-34.7	3.1	14.1	30.0	5.26	5.01	-6.4	0.9	13.4	52.9	999.9	45.8	70.5	80.4	22.0	...	...	...
	Principal Lines of Business: OrdLife (100.0%), IndAnn (0.0%)													Principal States: TX (8.6%), CA (8.3%), FL (6.6%), OH (6.0%), PA (5.0%)					
...	74.3	25.2	1.9	1.4	6.7	2.29	2.29	12.3	3.5	37.2	64.2	158.6	31.0	172.3	173.6	...	...	...	...
...	75.5	26.6	-0.2	-0.1	-0.6	3.35	3.35	3.3	3.7	36.3	60.1	139.3	-2.1	168.1	170.2	...	...	...	...
...	73.6	27.8	1.4	1.4	4.9	4.41	4.41	-18.5	2.8	42.4	32.2	117.1	5.9	204.2	206.5	...	...	...	...
...	72.7	28.2	0.2	0.2	0.6	2.33	2.33	2.6	3.0	39.6	35.3	124.2	-3.8	219.0	219.0	...	...	...	...
...	70.2	25.9	2.1	2.0	7.1	0.60	0.60	5.9	3.0	45.4	33.2	83.9	5.9	173.0	175.8	...	...	...	...
	Principal Lines of Business: GrpA&H (99.3%), GrpLife (0.7%)													Principal States: MI (73.3%), TX (26.6%)					
-1	134.4	55.3	1.7	19.1	4.2	...	...	-7.0	0.1	72.0	0.0	...	2.6	...	...	...	...	1.5	...
30	178.6	58.8	2.0	22.7	4.7	...	...	-6.4	0.1	78.0	0.0	...	4.8	...	...	...	...	1.3	...
-5	160.1	50.4	1.8	20.9	4.2	...	...	-1.1	0.1	81.8	0.0	...	2.4	...	...	...	...	1.2	...
-17	172.5	68.4	2.1	24.5	4.5	...	...	-14.9	0.1	84.9	0.0	...	-1.5	...	...	...	...	1.1	...
17	229.0	84.3	1.0	12.7	2.2	...	...	-11.5	0.1	83.9	0.0	...	-2.3	...	...	...	...	0.9	...
	Principal Lines of Business: OrdLife (99.1%), IndAnn (0.9%)																		
...	...	...	2.3	70.7	2.4	3.34	3.34	100.0	...	999.9	...	3.2	2.5	999.9	999.9	...	...	...	...
...	...	...	...	...	...	...	...	...	...	...	...	...	...	...	...	...	...	...	...
...	...	...	...	46.0	...	...	...	...	...	999.9	...	1.1	...	999.9	999.9	...	...	...	...
...	...	...	3.0	101.3	3.0	2.94	2.94	...	...	999.9	...	0.6	3.0	999.9	999.9	...	...	...	...
...	...	...	1.0	62.1	1.0	1.58	1.58	...	...	999.9	...	0.2	1.1	999.9	999.9	...	...	...	...
														Principal States: CA (39.2%), IL (37.0%), IN (18.8%), WA (5.0%)					

Data in U.S. Dollars

COMPANY NAME Ultimate Parent Association Principal Officer Mailing Address Dom. : Began Bus. : Struct. : Mktg. Specialty Phone # AMB# NAIC#	Best's Financial Strength Rating FSC	Data Year	Balance Sheet: Bonds (%)	Mort. Loans & R.E. (%)	Com & Pref. Stock (%)	All Other Assets (%)	Total Assets ($000)	Life Reserves (%)	Health Reserves (%)	Ann Res. & Dep. Liabilities (%)	All Other Liabilities (%)	Capital & Surplus ($000)	Operations: Direct Premiums Written ($000)	Net Premiums Written & Deposits ($000)	Operating Cash Flow ($000)	NOG Before Taxes ($000)	NOG After Taxes ($000)	Net Income ($000)
USAA LIFE INS CO United Services Automobile Association Russell A. Evenson President 9800 Fredericksburg Road San Antonio, TX 78288 TX : 1963 : Stock : Direct Response Ind Ann, Ind Life, Ind A&H 210-498-8000 AMB# 007146 NAIC# 69663	**A++**	'05	80.6	0.0	4.7	14.7	10,501,303	30.4	0.6	56.6	12.4	875,942	1,089,984	948,169	459,066	201,820	133,977	133,011
		'06	87.4	0.0	7.2	5.4	10,177,338	31.8	0.8	63.8	3.7	925,313	1,206,285	1,049,773	661,605	180,572	118,933	117,835
	Rating Outlook: Stable	'07	80.7	0.0	13.7	5.7	10,862,262	31.2	0.8	65.0	3.0	965,126	1,411,159	1,199,418	677,752	216,742	136,284	103,029
		'08	81.7	0.0	12.2	6.1	12,583,746	28.5	0.6	68.8	2.1	1,105,518	2,264,904	2,020,762	1,776,423	216,937	126,592	23,678
		'09	92.7	0.0	1.8	5.6	14,780,134	25.6	0.5	72.3	1.6	1,295,124	2,604,260	2,336,001	2,080,012	310,018	165,869	41,961
	FSC XIII	**Rating History: A++g, 12/22/09; A++g, 12/23/08; A++g, 12/11/07; A++g, 12/20/06; A++g, 12/20/05**																
USAA LIFE INS CO OF NY United Services Automobile Association Russell A. Evenson President 9800 Fredericksburg Road San Antonio, TX 78288 NY : 1997 : Stock : Direct Response Ind Ann, Ind Life 210-498-8000 AMB# 060247 NAIC# 60228	**A++**	'05	90.4	...	3.1	6.5	296,304	32.4	...	65.9	1.8	46,373	27,345	22,113	14,174	8,511	5,464	5,389
		'06	90.6	...	3.9	5.5	306,802	32.8	...	64.0	3.2	43,414	28,131	22,775	12,403	4,759	3,008	2,958
	Rating Outlook: Stable	'07	85.5	...	10.3	4.3	321,906	33.3	...	63.9	2.8	40,342	30,900	23,086	14,444	5,130	2,636	2,636
		'08	85.5	...	8.5	6.0	377,216	30.0	...	66.1	3.9	40,097	66,344	57,280	54,840	6,793	3,460	1,590
		'09	90.9	...	1.5	7.6	436,581	26.7	...	70.1	3.2	42,024	70,002	60,831	56,676	6,964	3,506	823
	FSC XIII	**Rating History: A++g, 12/22/09; A++g, 12/23/08; A++g, 12/11/07; A++g, 12/20/06; A++g, 12/20/05**																
USABLE CORPORATION USAble Mutual Insurance Company Curtis E. Barnett President & CEO 601 South Gaines Little Rock, AR 72201 AR : Other : Other Life, A&H 501-378-2000 AMB# 050925	**A**	'05	...	...	...	...	175,800	...	...	...	...	142,951	...	49,723	...	...	...	-1,212
		'06	...	...	...	...	154,168	...	...	...	...	135,467	...	...	...	...	...	4,475
	Rating Outlook: Stable	'07	...	...	...	...	170,481	...	...	...	...	142,166	...	...	...	...	...	4,404
		'08	...	...	...	...	167,686	...	...	...	...	135,370	...	...	...	...	...	-4,032
		'09	...	...	...	...	156,602	...	...	...	...	115,697	...	...	...	...	...	-24,115
	FSC IX	**Rating History: A, 06/19/09; A, 05/13/08; A, 06/15/07; A, 05/16/06; A- g, 09/21/04**																
USABLE LIFE LSV Partners LLC Jason D. Mann President & CEO 400 West Capitol, Suite 1500 Little Rock, AR 72201 AR : 1980 : Stock : Affinity Grp Mktg A&H, Group Life, Dread dis 501-375-7200 AMB# 009350 NAIC# 94358	**A**	'05	45.8	...	17.6	36.6	180,138	36.1	38.7	...	25.2	82,154	122,713	116,889	19,193	14,193	8,192	8,461
		'06	48.2	...	16.4	35.4	204,997	37.9	37.2	...	24.9	97,725	143,006	155,738	14,961	22,891	15,108	16,890
	Rating Outlook: Stable	'07	41.4	...	16.6	41.9	239,530	41.9	33.0	...	25.0	99,308	163,316	205,318	20,128	16	21	4,319
		'08	47.2	...	11.3	41.6	286,748	40.9	39.7	...	19.3	117,607	184,305	366,679	42,828	4,860	3,120	351
		'09	46.3	...	9.6	44.1	305,878	39.9	41.3	...	18.8	122,286	194,675	384,004	17,770	-3,966	-2,265	2,672
	FSC VIII	**Rating History: A g, 05/22/09; A g, 04/08/08; A g, 06/18/07; A g, 03/03/06; A-, 09/21/04**																
USABLE MUTUAL INSURANCE CO USAble Mutual Insurance Company Robert L. Shoptaw CEO 601 South Gaines Little Rock, AR 72201 AR : 1949 : Mutual : Agency Group A&H, Ind A&H, Med supp 501-378-2000 AMB# 009586 NAIC# 83470	**A**	'05	32.6	5.6	25.0	36.8	765,025	...	46.5	...	53.5	428,675	863,748	916,510	33,606	84,339	48,933	51,555
		'06	28.4	4.8	29.7	37.1	891,799	...	41.9	...	58.1	495,046	929,793	961,884	91,000	70,241	38,106	43,240
	Rating Outlook: Stable	'07	26.9	4.6	29.8	38.7	957,742	...	35.5	...	64.5	511,331	945,312	981,830	45,982	31,348	14,289	28,279
		'08	26.3	4.9	28.3	40.5	891,778	...	39.0	...	61.0	463,397	1,008,659	1,070,657	21,060	44,668	25,037	22,192
		'09	25.2	4.5	27.5	42.7	951,873	...	38.8	...	61.2	482,504	1,081,432	1,148,299	18,532	28,411	16,383	24,051
	FSC IX	**Rating History: A, 06/19/09; A, 04/17/08; A, 06/15/07; A, 05/16/06; A, 11/10/05**																
USIC LIFE INSURANCE COMPANY USIC Group, Inc. Frederick Millan President P.O. Box 2111 San Juan, PR 00922-2111 PR : 2006 : Stock : General Agent Term Life, Credit Life, Group Life 787-273-1818 AMB# 060567 NAIC# 11067	**B+**	'05	93.3	...	...	6.7	3,013	...	...	...	100.0	3,004	...	...	2,993	4	4	4
		'06	95.7	...	...	4.3	3,110	34.7	...	...	65.3	3,057	36	30	96	72	72	72
	Rating Outlook: Stable	'07	95.3	...	...	4.7	3,191	26.6	0.6	...	72.8	3,071	87	65	68	25	25	25
		'08	95.0	...	...	5.0	3,328	27.7	48.0	...	24.3	3,126	117	230	139	-46	-46	-472
		'09	94.3	...	...	5.7	3,953	8.9	74.3	...	16.8	3,564	184	910	566	-9	-9	-62
	FSC III	**Rating History: B+, 05/14/10; B+, 04/02/09; B+, 12/17/07; B+, 12/08/06; B+, 12/15/05**																
UTMB HEALTH PLANS INC[2] UTMB Health Care Systems Inc David M. Connaughton President & CEO 301 University Boulevard, Route 0985 Galveston, TX 77555-0985 TX : 1994 : Stock : Agency Med supp 409-797-8000 AMB# 064511 NAIC# 95764	**NR-5**	'05	...	...	...	100.0	11,669	...	59.2	...	40.8	6,638	28,362	28,362	-1,379	1,071	1,071	1,071
		'06	...	...	...	100.0	12,453	...	60.6	...	39.4	7,756	25,430	25,430	1,560	2,118	2,118	2,118
		'07	...	...	...	100.0	10,286	...	25.2	...	74.8	7,535	8,479	8,479	-2,844	819	819	819
		'08	...	...	...	100.0	14,947	...	76.4	...	23.6	12,461	1,150	1,150	-1,203	-47	-47	-47
		'09	...	...	...	100.0	11,025	...	80.7	...	19.3	8,352	931	931	-1,995	-630	-630	-630
		Rating History: NR-5, 04/08/10; NR-5, 06/16/09; C++pd, 07/01/08; C++pd, 06/19/07; C+ pd, 07/17/06																
VALLEY BAPTIST INSURANCE CO Valley Baptist Health System James E. Eastham President 2005 Ed Carey Drive Harlingen, TX 78550 TX : 2006 : Stock : Broker Group A&H, Medicare 956-389-2273 AMB# 064852 NAIC# 12346	**B**	'05	40.5	...	...	59.5	13,806	...	38.9	...	61.1	7,418	37,352	36,773	-2,259	376	248	248
		'06	15.0	...	1.1	83.9	26,834	...	50.7	...	49.3	11,665	63,358	62,520	7,426	400	194	194
	Rating Outlook: Negative	'07	8.6	...	0.5	90.9	23,271	...	60.3	...	39.7	7,635	80,788	79,740	-6,356	-3,447	-3,437	-3,437
		'08	10.5	...	...	89.5	18,968	...	71.0	...	29.0	6,220	94,089	92,910	-8,626	-1,229	-1,229	-1,219
		'09	0.7	...	...	99.3	14,595	...	56.2	...	43.8	6,033	65,250	64,248	2,660	-2,878	-2,878	-2,878
	FSC IV	**Rating History: B, 02/09/10; B, 01/30/09; B+, 05/23/07; B+, 08/15/06**																
VALUE BEHAVIORAL HEALTH OF PA[2] FHC Health Systems Inc Ronald I. Dozoretz, M.D. President 240 Corporate Boulevard Norfolk, VA 23502 PA : 1999 : Stock : Broker Medicaid 757-459-5200 AMB# 064550 NAIC# 47025	**NR-5**	'05	...	...	16.1	83.9	29,646	...	45.2	...	54.8	11,302	116,758	116,615	-582	6,475	4,030	4,030
		'06	...	...	11.2	88.8	42,857	...	28.0	...	72.0	12,867	141,173	141,173	12,043	8,104	5,249	5,249
		'07	...	...	6.2	93.8	76,847	...	57.5	...	42.5	16,229	210,685	210,685	8,326	3,845	1,497	1,446
		'08	...	...	4.2	95.8	80,837	...	42.1	...	57.9	21,663	297,946	297,946	3,843	8,068	6,579	5,244
		'09	...	...	...	100.0	84,466	...	40.4	...	59.6	22,939	319,234	319,234	3,321	9,319	4,830	5,232
		Rating History: NR-5, 04/06/10; NR-5, 04/07/09; NR-5, 04/30/08; NR-5, 05/25/06; NR-5, 04/26/05																

BEST'S PROFITABILITY, LEVERAGE AND LIQUIDITY TESTS 2005 – 2009

Data in U.S. Dollars

—	Profitability Tests							Leverage Tests						Liquidity Tests					
Un-Realized Capital Gains ($000)	Benefits Paid to NPW & Dep (%)	Comm. & Expenses to NPW & Dep (%)	NOG to Total Assets (%)	NOG to Total Rev (%)	Operating Return on Equity (%)	Net Yield (%)	Total Return (%)	Change in NPW & Dep (%)	NPW & Dep to Capital (X)	Capital & Surplus to Liabilities (%)	Surplus Relief (%)	Reins Leverage (%)	Change in Capital (%)	Quick Liquidity (%)	Current Liquidity (%)	Non-Invest Grade Bonds to Capital (%)	Delinq. & Foreclosed Mortgages to Capital (%)	Mort. & Credit Tenant Loans & R.E. to Capital (%)	Affiliated Invest to Capital (%)
5,501	72.4	9.0	1.3	8.9	16.1	5.32	5.55	-6.5	1.0	10.2	10.6	109.9	11.2	70.5	82.5	5.6	...	0.2	5.0
6,254	97.5	9.7	1.2	7.2	13.2	5.54	5.70	10.7	1.1	10.8	11.1	126.8	5.9	72.3	86.0	1.2	...	0.2	4.4
-5,584	71.5	8.7	1.3	7.1	14.4	6.18	5.90	14.3	1.2	10.4	12.6	145.1	4.0	67.0	83.4	5.4	...	0.1	7.9
-22,804	37.4	5.0	1.1	4.5	12.2	6.27	5.26	68.5	1.8	9.7	11.6	153.8	8.5	58.4	75.4	13.2	...	0.1	16.5
11,044	31.3	5.2	1.2	5.0	13.8	6.74	5.97	15.6	1.8	9.6	10.2	153.1	16.9	60.9	78.3	46.1	...	0.1	14.5

Principal Lines of Business: IndAnn (78.7%), OrdLife (15.7%), IndA&H (5.6%), GrpA&H (0.0%), GrpAnn (0.0%) Principal States: TX (19.3%), CA (10.5%), FL (9.1%), VA (6.7%), GA (3.8%)

...	52.1	5.9	1.9	13.8	12.5	5.72	5.76	-8.2	0.5	19.3	4.0	16.7	13.5	84.3	96.8	5.1	...	...	...
...	94.9	17.4	1.0	7.0	6.7	5.78	5.80	3.0	0.5	17.2	5.4	29.1	-5.8	81.8	94.6	2.9	...	...	...
...	65.0	10.0	0.8	6.0	6.3	5.85	5.89	1.4	0.5	15.1	7.5	35.3	-6.2	73.9	90.2	4.8	...	...	...
-54	35.0	3.9	1.0	4.2	8.6	6.12	5.62	148.1	1.4	12.4	7.9	54.1	-2.0	62.7	80.3	11.1	...	...	...
-520	23.4	7.2	0.9	3.9	8.5	6.43	5.65	6.2	1.4	10.8	7.8	71.0	2.5	66.3	82.4	38.5	...	...	...

Principal Lines of Business: IndAnn (81.7%), OrdLife (18.3%) Principal States: NY (91.7%)

...	25.3	62.9	-0.5	-1.1	-0.9	...	...	...	0.3	...	...	...	...	...	...	...	...	...	...
...	...	85.9	2.7	7.8	3.2	...	...	...	...	...	...	...	...	...	...	...	...	...	...
...	...	90.0	2.7	6.2	3.2	...	...	...	...	...	...	...	...	...	...	...	...	...	...
...	...	108.5	-2.4	-5.1	-2.9	...	...	...	...	...	...	...	...	...	...	...	...	...	...
...	...	140.3	-14.9	-26.6	-19.2	...	...	...	...	...	...	...	...	...	...	...	...	...	...

2,344	58.4	30.5	5.0	6.6	10.6	3.84	5.58	42.5	1.3	103.5	2.3	33.7	13.9	208.9	221.6	3.4	...	...	3.2
1,767	57.4	29.7	7.8	9.1	16.8	4.27	6.32	33.2	1.4	111.3	2.3	39.0	17.9	203.7	217.4	2.0	...	...	1.4
3,026	62.1	38.1	0.0	0.0	0.0	4.63	8.51	31.8	1.8	87.0	3.0	46.7	3.2	187.5	198.3	1.7	...	...	1.3
-11,101	66.7	33.1	1.2	0.8	2.9	3.86	-2.34	78.6	2.9	76.5	3.8	32.5	11.6	152.3	161.8	1.8	...	...	0.2
2,468	68.4	32.8	-0.8	-0.6	-1.9	2.65	5.76	4.7	3.0	72.5	1.3	38.4	3.4	163.6	172.5	1.7	...	...	0.2

Principal Lines of Business: GrpA&H (64.6%), GrpLife (26.6%), IndA&H (7.3%), OrdLife (1.4%) Principal States: AR (28.5%), TN (20.0%), NC (13.4%), HI (8.3%), MN (6.5%)

14,136	78.9	12.0	6.7	5.4	12.1	2.70	5.76	0.9	2.1	127.4	...	1.9	12.2	127.5	135.6	1.7	...	10.0	37.4
3,691	80.3	13.9	4.6	3.9	8.3	2.83	4.24	5.0	1.9	124.8	...	2.9	15.5	104.7	111.0	0.8	...	8.7	55.8
10,297	84.1	14.4	1.5	1.4	2.8	2.34	5.71	2.1	1.9	114.5	...	7.5	3.3	110.9	117.0	0.6	...	8.6	55.5
-48,031	83.9	13.8	2.7	2.3	5.1	2.03	-4.64	9.0	2.3	108.2	...	0.9	-9.4	117.0	122.3	0.7	...	9.4	58.3
-1,421	83.6	14.8	1.8	1.4	3.5	1.54	2.39	7.3	2.4	102.8	...	0.8	4.1	119.3	125.6	0.2	...	9.0	54.1

Principal Lines of Business: CompHosp/Med (59.5%), FEHBP (19.0%), MedSup (17.2%), OtherHlth (3.9%), Medicare (0.4%) Principal States: AR (100.0%)

...	...	...	...	2.9	...	...	...	...	...	999.9	...	...	...	999.9	999.9	...	...	...	...
...	60.0	346.2	2.3	36.8	2.4	5.53	5.53	...	0.0	999.9	...	0.1	2.4	999.9	999.9	26.7	...	...	...
...	26.5	259.0	0.8	10.8	0.8	5.31	5.31	114.6	0.0	999.9	...	0.8	0.8	999.9	999.9	26.4	...	...	...
...	116.3	72.7	-1.4	-11.9	-1.5	4.94	-7.41	252.6	0.1	999.9	...	1.6	0.8	842.0	958.1	26.0	...	...	...
...	85.3	32.8	-0.2	-0.8	-0.3	4.44	2.96	296.3	0.3	915.1	...	0.6	14.0	584.8	663.8	18.3	...	...	...

Principal Lines of Business: GrpA&H (86.6%), GrpLife (12.8%), IndA&H (0.6%) Principal States: PR (100.0%)

...	73.6	23.4	8.5	3.9	14.0	2.47	2.47	-15.2	4.3	131.9	...	8.7	-23.4	205.0	205.0	...	...	...	...
...	71.6	21.9	17.6	8.2	29.4	4.17	4.17	-10.3	3.3	165.2	...	...	16.8	252.8	252.8	...	...	...	...
...	67.2	30.8	7.2	9.0	10.7	6.30	6.30	-66.7	1.1	273.9	...	...	-2.9	334.0	334.0	...	...	...	...
...	59.3	53.0	-0.4	-3.8	-0.5	0.85	0.85	-86.4	0.1	501.1	...	...	65.4	522.2	522.2	...	...	...	...
...	85.1	47.2	-4.9	-78.5	-6.1	-1.06	-1.06	-19.0	0.1	312.4	...	...	-33.0	411.2	411.2	...	...	...	...

Principal Lines of Business: MedSup (100.0%) Principal States: TX (100.0%)

...	73.5	26.3	1.7	0.7	3.4	2.45	2.45	15.1	5.0	116.1	...	0.0	3.7	285.3	285.3	...	...	...	...
...	77.9	23.3	1.0	0.3	2.0	4.88	4.88	70.0	5.4	76.9	...	8.0	57.3	150.4	150.4	...	...	...	2.5
45	87.1	18.7	-13.7	-4.2	-35.6	5.94	6.16	27.5	10.4	48.8	...	1.5	-34.5	105.3	105.3	...	...	...	3.7
-279	94.4	13.5	-5.8	-1.2	-17.7	3.37	1.22	16.5	14.9	48.8	...	7.6	-18.5	62.2	62.2	...	...	...	...
...	92.2	16.0	-17.2	-4.4	-47.0	0.85	0.85	-30.8	10.6	70.5	...	3.0	-3.0	123.5	123.7	...	...	...	...

Principal Lines of Business: CompHosp/Med (99.5%), Medicare (0.5%) Principal States: TX (100.0%)

...	86.4	9.1	14.0	3.4	37.3	0.82	0.82	15.7	10.3	61.6	...	...	9.4	185.0	197.7	...	...	...	...
...	86.4	8.9	14.5	3.7	43.4	1.50	1.50	21.1	11.0	42.9	...	...	13.8	190.6	202.5	...	...	...	...
-240	89.4	10.2	2.5	0.7	10.3	5.40	4.63	49.2	13.0	26.8	...	...	26.1	103.8	109.2	...	...	...	...
...	88.8	9.0	8.3	2.2	34.7	1.58	-1.39	41.4	13.8	36.6	...	...	33.5	140.1	147.1	...	...	...	...
...	88.5	8.9	5.8	1.5	21.7	0.23	1.07	7.1	13.9	37.3	...	...	5.9	151.5	151.5	...	...	...	...

Principal Lines of Business: Medicaid (100.0%) Principal States: PA (100.0%)

ANNUAL STATEMENT DATA FOR YEARS 2005 – 2009

Data in U.S. Dollars

COMPANY NAME Ultimate Parent Association Principal Officer Mailing Address Dom. : Began Bus. : Struct. : Mktg. Specialty Phone # AMB# NAIC#	Best's Financial Strength Rating FSC	Data Year	Balance Sheet: Bonds (%)	Mort. Loans & R.E. (%)	Com & Pref. Stock (%)	All Other Assets (%)	Total Assets ($000)	Life Reserves (%)	Health Reserves (%)	Ann Res. & Dep. Liabilities (%)	All Other Liabilities (%)	Capital & Surplus ($000)	Operations: Direct Premiums Written ($000)	Net Premiums Written & Deposits ($000)	Operating Cash Flow ($000)	NOG Before Taxes ($000)	NOG After Taxes ($000)	Net Income ($000)
VALUEOPTIONS OF CALIFORNIA INC Barbara Hill President 10805 Holder Street, Suite 300 Cypress, CA 90630 CA : 1991 : Stock : Not Available Group A&H 714-763-2427 AMB# 064653	NR-5	'05	...	0.0	...	100.0	2,938	...	...	...	100.0	1,087	6,389	6,389	-2,612	-80	-47	-47
		'06	...	4.2	...	95.8	2,496	...	...	...	100.0	590	5,401	5,401	350	1,030	213	213
		'07	...	2.3	...	97.7	4,131	...	...	...	100.0	1,359	5,919	5,919	1,864	1,302	769	769
		'08	...	1.7	...	98.3	4,092	...	...	...	100.0	1,367	5,779	5,779	261	2,562	1,508	1,508
		'09	...	0.9	...	99.1	5,149	...	...	...	100.0	2,670	5,187	5,187	1,260	2,181	1,303	1,303
		Rating History: NR-5, 05/05/10; NR-5, 05/01/09; NR-5, 05/09/08; NR-5, 05/04/07; NR-5, 09/06/06																
VALUEOPTIONS OF TEXAS INC[2] FHC Health Systems Inc Barbara B. Hill President 240 Corporate Boulevard Norfolk, VA 23502 TX : 1999 : Stock : Agency Medicaid 757-459-6200 AMB# 064514 NAIC# 95799	NR-5	'05	...	...	...	100.0	11,243	...	63.0	...	37.0	2,471	51,740	51,740	-1,949	98	-4	-4
		'06	...	...	...	100.0	10,560	...	40.8	...	59.2	2,781	49,911	49,911	-413	130	-14	-14
		'07	...	...	...	100.0	14,982	...	19.2	...	80.8	3,077	51,276	51,276	3,515	277	-28	-40
		'08	...	...	13.5	86.5	15,058	...	36.6	...	63.4	3,516	56,864	56,864	-818	37	608	-163
		'09	...	...	...	100.0	14,532	...	...	...	100.0	3,856	56,694	56,694	-40	-92	-407	-142
		Rating History: NR-5, 04/06/10; NR-5, 03/30/09; NR-5, 05/05/08; NR-5, 04/17/07; NR-5, 05/22/06																
VANTAGE HEALTH PLAN INC P. Gary Jones, M.D. President & CEO 130 DeSiard Street, Suite 300 Monroe, LA 71201 LA : 1994 : Stock : Broker Group A&H, Medicare, FEHBP 318-361-0900 AMB# 064282 NAIC# 95584	NR-5	'05	...	...	...	100.0	13,167	...	81.6	...	18.4	7,844	45,844	45,336	2,050	2,121	1,911	1,911
		'06	...	...	...	100.0	18,089	...	77.4	...	22.6	11,204	57,291	56,926	4,116	5,908	4,505	4,505
		'07	...	...	...	100.0	16,430	...	68.5	...	31.5	10,088	55,976	55,489	738	1,807	1,095	1,095
		'08	...	...	...	100.0	18,531	...	82.8	...	17.2	9,645	62,590	61,914	2,716	622	707	707
		'09	...	6.2	...	93.8	27,531	...	69.5	...	30.5	12,425	98,251	97,342	8,597	5,976	3,766	3,766
		Rating History: NR-5, 04/26/10; NR-5, 08/26/09; B- pd, 07/01/08; B- pd, 06/26/07; C++pd, 07/25/06																
VANTIS LIFE INSURANCE COMPANY Vantis Life Insurance Company Peter L. Tedone President & CEO 200 Day Hill Road Windsor, CT 06095 CT : 1964 : Stock : Bank Ann, Life 860-298-6000 AMB# 007021 NAIC# 68632	A-	'05	94.0	1.2	0.8	3.9	712,835	13.1	0.0	83.1	3.7	64,948	49,047	52,313	21,850	2,957	2,212	2,212
		'06	93.4	1.4	1.2	4.0	684,449	14.3	0.0	81.7	3.9	66,868	33,473	31,621	-26,319	3,279	2,195	2,195
	Rating Outlook: Stable	'07	93.2	1.3	0.8	4.6	649,526	15.6	0.0	80.4	4.0	67,314	35,728	33,612	-34,562	1,490	1,114	1,114
		'08	91.4	1.2	1.1	6.4	669,461	15.2	0.0	81.5	3.2	64,602	92,158	90,268	27,331	1,422	669	-4,683
	FSC VII	'09	89.4	0.8	1.0	8.7	870,801	11.9	0.0	85.4	2.7	71,078	242,083	240,862	180,235	4,966	3,529	345
		Rating History: A- g, 06/15/10; A-, 06/12/09; A-, 06/12/08; A-, 06/12/07; A-, 06/21/06																
VANTIS LIFE INSURANCE CO OF NY Vantis Life Insurance Company Peter L. Tedone President & CEO 200 Day Hill Road Windsor, CT 06095 NY : 2009 : Stock : Not Available 860-298-6000 AMB# 060691 NAIC# 13588	A-	'05	...	...	...	...	...	...	...	...	...	...	...	...	...	...	...	...
		'06	...	...	...	...	...	...	...	...	...	...	...	...	...	...	...	...
	Rating Outlook: Stable	'07	...	...	...	...	...	...	...	...	...	...	...	...	...	...	...	...
		'08	...	...	...	...	...	...	...	...	...	...	...	...	...	...	...	...
	FSC VII	'09	92.3	...	...	7.7	6,644	2.1	...	...	97.9	6,528	31	30	-129	186	137	137
		Rating History: A- g, 06/15/10																
VARIABLE ANNUITY LIFE INS CO American International Group, Inc Bruce R. Abrams President & CEO 70 Pine Street, 19th Floor New York, NY 10270 TX : 1969 : Stock : Career Agent Ann, Group pens, Ind Ann 713-522-1111 AMB# 007208 NAIC# 70238	A	'05	49.2	4.4	1.4	45.0	58,319,135	...	...	55.0	45.0	2,904,170	5,529,141	5,532,111	719,842	994,931	745,143	726,338
		'06	42.8	5.5	3.6	48.1	61,980,055	...	...	51.8	48.2	3,128,773	5,564,056	5,581,002	230,500	938,913	639,236	616,910
	Rating Outlook: Negative	'07	38.0	6.9	1.3	53.8	63,998,991	...	...	49.5	50.5	2,841,306	5,896,154	6,137,983	-661,752	800,012	553,025	302,504
		'08	43.0	8.1	1.3	47.5	53,699,125	...	...	62.2	37.8	2,844,336	6,089,552	6,454,351	-3,735,703	501,930	230,019	-4,497,616
	FSC XV	'09	39.0	6.9	0.4	53.7	59,451,514	...	...	57.6	42.4	3,625,701	5,231,079	5,247,196	1,952,262	907,630	831,992	129,605
		Rating History: A, 12/16/09; A, 11/10/08; A gu, 09/15/08; A+ g, 06/17/08; A++g, 05/28/08																
VERMONT HEALTH PLAN LLC Blue Cross and Blue Shield of Vermont Don C. George President P.O. Box 186 Montpelier, VT 05601-0186 VT : 1997 : Other : Agency Group A&H 802-223-6131 AMB# 064124 NAIC# 95696	B++	'05	73.0	...	...	27.0	49,276	...	55.2	...	44.8	28,320	80,258	78,443	4,240	3,181	3,180	3,279
		'06	81.1	...	...	18.9	49,038	...	65.8	...	34.2	20,445	86,293	84,515	333	-7,876	-7,876	-7,876
	Rating Outlook: Stable	'07	77.5	...	...	22.5	45,071	...	23.7	...	76.3	26,509	95,174	91,807	1,253	6,176	6,176	6,172
		'08	65.0	...	...	35.0	40,966	...	21.0	...	79.0	21,929	112,901	110,717	-5,260	3,881	3,881	3,899
	FSC VII	'09	79.7	...	2.1	18.2	42,397	...	24.8	...	75.2	21,665	120,422	117,528	512	885	885	407
		Rating History: B++g, 02/19/10; B++g, 02/03/09; B++g, 03/21/08; B++g, 02/22/07; B++g, 03/08/06																
VERSANT LIFE INSURANCE COMPANY Louisiana Dealer Services Insurance Inc Dick S. Taylor President P.O. Box 84410 Baton Rouge, LA 70884-4410 MS : 2000 : Stock : Broker Credit Life, Credit A&H 225-769-9923 AMB# 060339 NAIC# 93650	B+	'05	75.7	...	...	24.3	4,796	54.7	43.1	...	2.2	2,476	2,080	2,577	1,007	185	165	165
		'06	75.1	...	...	24.9	5,855	45.8	39.9	...	14.3	3,012	2,448	1,928	897	684	552	552
	Rating Outlook: Stable	'07	69.9	...	...	30.1	6,427	47.4	44.6	...	8.0	3,687	2,100	1,895	737	838	730	730
		'08	69.6	...	...	30.4	6,466	52.9	47.2	...	-0.1	4,256	1,334	1,126	85	690	628	628
	FSC III	'09	76.5	...	...	23.5	6,126	52.1	44.2	...	3.7	4,598	224	198	-315	469	432	432
		Rating History: B+, 06/03/09; B+, 06/16/08; B+, 06/13/07; B+, 06/15/06; B+, 05/31/05																
VIRGINIA PREMIER HEALTH PLAN[2] Virginia Commonwealth University H Systs Sheldon Retchin, M.D. President P.O. Box 5307 Richmond, VA 23220 VA : 1995 : Stock : Broker Health 804-819-5164 AMB# 064251 NAIC# 95612	NR-5	'05	26.5	...	...	73.5	68,146	...	85.2	...	14.8	32,848	293,681	292,715	8,286	18,867	12,223	12,223
		'06	4.8	0.4	...	94.8	83,117	...	70.2	...	29.8	45,776	335,491	334,504	14,595	22,538	13,659	13,659
		'07	...	0.3	...	99.7	87,648	...	81.9	...	18.1	44,276	363,928	362,889	-1,430	1,647	780	780
		'08	...	0.4	...	99.6	81,820	...	85.6	...	14.4	33,385	414,715	413,542	-10,686	-17,209	-10,265	-10,265
		'09	...	0.3	...	99.7	94,876	...	85.8	...	14.2	36,679	472,621	471,897	-28,078	-8,497	-3,974	-3,974
		Rating History: NR-5, 05/11/10; NR-5, 08/26/09; B- pd, 07/01/08; B- pd, 06/26/07; C++pd, 07/25/06																

2010 BEST'S KEY RATING GUIDE — LIFE/HEALTH EDITION
BEST'S PROFITABILITY, LEVERAGE AND LIQUIDITY TESTS 2005 – 2009
Data in U.S. Dollars

	Profitability Tests							Leverage Tests						Liquidity Tests					
Un-Realized Capital Gains ($000)	Benefits Paid to NPW & Dep (%)	Comm. & Expenses to NPW & Dep (%)	NOG to Total Assets (%)	NOG to Total Rev (%)	Operating Return on Equity (%)	Net Yield (%)	Total Return (%)	Change in NPW & Dep (%)	NPW & Dep to Capital (X)	Capital & Surplus to Liabilities (%)	Surplus Relief (%)	Reins Leverage (%)	Change in Capital (%)	Quick Liquidity (%)	Current Liquidity (%)	Non-Invest Grade Bonds to Capital (%)	Delinq. & Foreclosed Mortgages to Capital (%)	Mort. & Credit Tenant Loans & R.E. to Capital (%)	Affiliated Invest to Capital (%)
...	161.2	124.7	-1.0	-0.3	-3.0	2.14	2.14	-1.5	5.9	58.7	...	...	-48.3	63.5	63.5	...	...	0.1	0.1
...	80.8	196.5	7.9	1.3	25.4	4.79	4.79	-15.5	9.2	31.0	...	...	-45.7	54.7	54.7	...	...	17.7	17.7
...	76.3	167.9	23.2	4.9	78.9	4.10	4.10	9.6	4.4	49.1	...	...	130.3	102.0	102.0	...	...	6.9	6.9
...	72.3	170.5	36.7	9.1	110.6	3.15	3.15	-2.4	4.2	50.2	...	...	0.6	108.6	108.6	...	...	5.1	5.1
...	75.2	177.7	28.2	8.5	64.6	0.34	0.34	-10.2	1.9	107.7	...	...	95.3	167.7	167.7	...	...	1.7	1.7
	Principal Lines of Business: CompHosp/Med (100.0%)																		
...	216.7	18.2	0.0	0.0	-0.2	2.03	2.03	3.6	20.9	28.2	...	...	3.7	144.3	147.6	...	...	...	...
...	213.9	27.7	-0.1	0.0	-0.5	2.44	2.44	-3.5	17.9	35.8	...	...	12.6	135.7	136.9	...	...	...	...
-127	214.5	29.8	-0.2	0.0	-0.9	3.49	2.29	2.7	16.7	25.8	...	...	10.6	186.0	194.3	...	...	...	...
...	217.2	26.6	4.0	0.4	18.4	2.07	-3.75	10.9	16.2	30.5	...	...	14.3	100.4	103.1	...	...	...	...
...	243.8	27.2	-2.7	-0.3	-11.0	0.12	2.27	-0.3	14.7	36.1	...	...	9.7	115.8	115.8	...	...	...	...
	Principal Lines of Business: Medicaid (100.0%)												Principal States: TX (100.0%)						
37	84.0	11.7	15.8	4.2	27.0	1.61	1.98	4.3	5.8	147.4	...	3.6	24.1	188.3	188.3	...	...	...	50.4
-219	78.4	11.9	28.8	7.9	47.3	3.15	1.48	25.6	5.1	162.7	...	1.1	42.8	220.2	220.2	...	...	...	46.1
37	81.6	16.0	6.3	2.0	10.3	3.06	3.31	-2.5	5.5	159.1	...	2.8	-10.0	250.5	250.5	...	...	...	51.7
-1,173	82.9	16.1	4.0	1.1	7.2	1.00	-5.98	11.6	6.4	108.6	...	2.5	-4.4	200.0	200.0	...	...	...	51.4
-400	79.8	13.8	16.4	3.9	34.1	0.17	-1.72	57.2	7.8	82.2	...	4.5	28.8	158.9	158.9	...	...	13.7	55.2
	Principal Lines of Business: CompHosp/Med (49.7%), Medicare (49.0%), FEHBP (1.4%)												Principal States: LA (100.0%)						
...	101.6	30.2	0.3	2.6	3.4	5.40	5.40	-30.2	0.8	10.4	0.3	116.5	3.3	73.1	87.8	6.0	...	13.0	...
...	230.7	50.9	0.3	3.4	3.3	5.33	5.31	-39.6	0.5	11.3	0.7	117.0	3.7	70.3	86.0	7.0	...	13.4	8.9
...	235.4	45.1	0.2	1.7	1.7	5.41	5.40	6.3	0.5	12.2	0.8	120.6	1.4	67.4	84.4	16.7	...	12.0	8.6
-74	81.3	18.8	0.1	0.5	1.0	5.37	4.55	168.6	1.4	10.9	0.8	115.5	-6.9	65.1	82.6	24.2	...	12.0	18.8
-980	23.8	8.7	0.5	1.3	5.2	5.53	5.04	166.8	3.4	8.9	0.4	91.8	8.7	62.6	81.0	43.5	...	10.3	17.2
	Principal Lines of Business: IndAnn (92.9%), OrdLife (5.1%), GrpLife (1.9%), CrdA&H (0.0%), GrpA&H (0.0%)												Principal States: CT (92.5%)						
...	...	...	...	...	...	...	...	...	...	...	...	...	...	...	...	...	...	...	...
...	...	...	...	...	...	...	...	...	...	...	...	...	...	...	...	...	...	...	...
...	...	...	...	...	...	...	...	...	...	...	...	...	...	...	...	...	...	...	...
...	...	...	...	...	...	...	...	...	...	...	...	...	...	...	...	...	...	...	...
...	...	905.5	...	29.5	...	...	...	...	0.0	999.9	...	0.1	...	999.9	999.9	2.8	...	...	...
	Principal Lines of Business: OrdLife (100.0%)												Principal States: NY (100.0%)						
90,903	103.4	7.1	1.3	9.2	26.7	6.68	7.02	-0.4	1.7	10.8	...	0.2	11.3	44.1	62.4	72.5	0.2	81.1	38.8
207,866	111.6	6.9	1.1	7.9	21.2	6.38	6.99	0.9	1.5	12.1	...	0.2	11.4	40.8	59.3	58.7	...	98.1	45.6
73,495	107.0	6.9	0.9	6.4	18.5	6.21	5.75	10.0	1.7	11.8	...	0.2	-2.5	37.2	54.5	64.8	...	125.7	14.8
-348,979	109.3	6.1	0.4	2.6	8.1	6.24	-7.80	5.2	2.2	9.2	...	0.0	-19.0	43.5	59.7	76.4	...	153.7	19.4
-214,747	123.8	7.1	1.5	10.9	25.7	6.28	3.53	-18.7	1.4	11.2	...	0.0	24.2	63.8	80.5	68.3	...	116.9	14.6
	Principal Lines of Business: GrpAnn (59.0%), IndAnn (41.0%)												Principal States: FL (14.8%), CA (7.6%), TX (7.5%), NC (6.6%), GA (6.5%)						
...	84.5	13.0	6.8	4.0	11.9	3.41	3.67	2.0	2.8	135.1	...	3.0	13.3	189.4	201.9	...	...	...	...
...	90.3	13.2	-16.0	-9.1	-32.3	3.99	3.99	7.7	4.1	71.5	...	5.2	-27.8	124.1	133.0	...	...	...	...
...	87.0	14.5	13.1	6.2	26.3	4.35	4.34	8.6	3.5	142.8	...	7.3	29.7	225.7	239.3	...	...	...	...
...	82.5	16.0	9.0	3.5	16.0	4.30	4.34	20.6	5.0	115.2	...	11.5	-17.3	213.0	224.1	...	...	...	...
71	85.7	14.6	2.1	0.7	4.1	3.40	2.30	6.2	5.4	104.5	...	13.5	-1.2	161.1	170.3	4.6	...	...	...
	Principal Lines of Business: CompHosp/Med (100.0%)												Principal States: VT (100.0%)						
...	10.9	54.1	3.9	5.2	6.9	3.60	3.60	139.8	1.0	107.1	18.6	16.7	6.2	198.9	207.7	...	...	...	...
...	15.6	52.1	10.4	22.2	20.1	4.00	4.00	-25.2	0.6	106.3	11.7	15.5	21.6	186.9	194.5	...	...	...	...
...	13.2	52.2	11.9	31.7	21.8	4.55	4.55	-1.7	0.5	135.1	3.8	9.9	22.4	251.1	261.6	...	...	...	...
...	32.2	61.9	9.7	41.1	15.8	4.14	4.14	-40.6	0.3	193.5	3.3	8.2	15.4	269.4	282.4	...	...	...	...
...	200.9	126.2	6.9	103.6	9.8	3.27	3.27	-82.4	0.0	302.8	0.4	5.4	8.0	362.5	377.9	...	...	...	...
	Principal Lines of Business: CrdLife (96.9%), CrdA&H (3.1%)												Principal States: MS (100.0%)						
...	85.1	9.1	19.0	4.1	42.4	3.16	3.16	17.5	8.9	93.1	...	...	32.2	248.9	248.9	...	...	...	...
...	84.4	10.0	18.1	4.0	34.7	5.26	5.26	14.3	7.3	122.6	...	0.2	39.4	403.1	403.1	...	...	0.7	0.7
...	91.7	9.0	0.9	0.2	1.7	5.35	5.35	8.5	8.2	102.1	...	0.2	-3.3	375.0	375.0	...	...	0.7	...
...	97.8	6.7	-12.1	-2.5	-26.4	2.40	2.40	14.0	12.4	68.9	...	0.1	-24.6	233.6	233.6	...	...	0.9	...
...	95.0	7.0	-4.5	-0.8	-11.3	1.18	1.18	14.1	12.9	63.0	...	0.8	9.9	135.0	135.0	...	...	0.8	0.8
	Principal Lines of Business: Medicaid (98.9%), Medicare (1.1%)												Principal States: VA (100.0%)						

Data in U.S. Dollars

COMPANY NAME / Ultimate Parent Association / Principal Officer / Mailing Address / Dom. : Began Bus. : Struct. : Mktg. / Specialty / Phone # / AMB# NAIC#	Best's Financial Strength Rating / FSC	Data Year	Balance Sheet: Bonds (%)	Mort. Loans & R.E. (%)	Com & Pref. Stock (%)	All Other Assets (%)	Total Assets ($000)	Life Reserves (%)	Health Reserves (%)	Ann Res. & Dep. Liabilities (%)	All Other Liabilities (%)	Capital & Surplus ($000)	Operations: Direct Premiums Written ($000)	Net Premiums Written & Deposits ($000)	Operating Cash Flow ($000)	NOG Before Taxes ($000)	NOG After Taxes ($000)	Net Income ($000)
VISION BENEFITS OF AMERICA[2]	NR-5	'05	...	...	...	100.0	28,518	...	51.3	...	48.7	20,913	33,990	33,990	2,703	2,010	2,010	2,010
Michael S. Gissin, President & CEO		'06	...	...	...	100.0	31,284	...	47.7	...	52.3	23,319	34,896	34,896	2,588	2,670	2,670	2,670
300 Weyman Plaza, Suite 400, Pittsburgh, PA 15236-1588		'07	...	...	...	100.0	32,986	...	45.3	...	54.7	25,034	37,881	37,881	1,856	1,648	1,648	1,648
PA : 1965 : Non-Profit : Broker, Vision		'08	...	...	...	100.0	34,626	...	44.9	...	55.1	27,948	40,072	40,072	1,848	2,879	2,879	2,879
412-881-4900		'09	...	...	...	100.0	37,376	...	32.5	...	67.5	30,614	41,939	41,939	2,547	2,673	2,673	2,673
AMB# 064636 NAIC# 53953		**Rating History: NR-5, 04/06/10; NR-5, 04/07/09; NR-5, 04/02/08; NR-5, 05/22/06; NR-5, 04/27/05**																
VISION CARE NETWORK INS CORP[2]	NR-5	'05	...	...	...	100.0	29	...	...	...	100.0	29	62	62	-3	14	8	8
Bruce A. Savin, M.D., President		'06	...	...	...	100.0	28	...	...	...	100.0	28	45	45	-1	17	14	14
1421 Washington Avenue, Racine, WI 53403		'07	...	...	...	100.0	28	...	...	...	100.0	28	44	44	0	14	10	10
WI : 1990 : Stock : Broker, Health		'08	...	...	...	100.0	28	...	...	...	100.0	28	47	47	1	26	23	23
262-637-7494		'09	...	...	...	100.0	31	...	...	...	100.0	31	63	63	2	11	2	2
AMB# 064801 NAIC# 52613		**Rating History: NR-5, 05/21/10; NR-5, 07/13/09; NR-5, 05/19/08; NR-5, 06/20/07; NR-5, 07/10/06**																
VISION FIRST EYE CARE INC	NR-5	'05	...	...	...	100.0	1,556	...	...	...	100.0	535	138	138	145	-19	70	70
James Kim-Tzong Eu, President		'06	...	...	...	100.0	1,655	...	...	...	100.0	585	124	124	-37	100	50	50
1937-A Tully Road, San Jose, CA 95122		'07	...	...	...	100.0	1,563	...	...	...	100.0	618	129	129	139	61	33	33
CA : 1997 : Stock : Broker, Health		'08	...	...	...	100.0	1,503	...	...	...	100.0	655	105	105	27	52	37	37
408-923-0400		'09	...	...	...	100.0	1,441	...	...	...	100.0	627	88	88	51	-53	-28	-28
AMB# 064654		**Rating History: NR-5, 05/07/10; NR-5, 05/13/09; NR-5, 05/06/08; NR-5, 05/07/07; NR-5, 05/25/06**																
VISION INSURANCE PLAN AMERICA[2] Block Vision Holdings LLC	NR-5	'05	...	...	...	100.0	1,116	...	43.3	...	56.7	618	5,675	5,775	-451	1,073	699	699
Andrew Alcorn, President		'06	...	...	...	100.0	1,221	...	50.0	...	50.0	685	6,117	6,274	-11	1,239	805	805
P.O. Box 44077, West Allis, WI 53214		'07	...	...	...	100.0	2,575	...	20.5	...	79.5	778	7,238	7,558	1,337	1,429	966	966
WI : 1992 : Stock : Broker, Health		'08	...	...	...	100.0	1,568	...	45.2	...	54.8	706	8,552	8,967	-1,026	1,579	976	976
414-475-1875		'09	...	...	...	100.0	1,351	...	42.4	...	57.6	686	8,566	9,175	-283	1,701	1,219	1,219
AMB# 064800 NAIC# 52005		**Rating History: NR-5, 05/24/10; NR-5, 07/17/09; NR-5, 05/19/08; NR-5, 06/20/07; NR-5, 07/11/06**																
VISION PLAN OF AMERICA	NR-5	'05	...	...	...	100.0	290	...	...	...	100.0	83	1,527	1,527	-172	-30	-30	-30
S. W. Needleman, O.D., President		'06	...	...	...	100.0	321	...	...	...	100.0	172	1,525	1,525	3	89	89	89
3255 Wilshire Blvd., #1610, Los Angeles, CA 90010-1404		'07	...	...	...	100.0	287	...	...	...	100.0	157	1,324	1,324	-33	64	64	64
CA : 1987 : Non-Profit : Not Available, Group A&H		'08	...	...	...	100.0	246	...	...	...	100.0	104	1,190	1,190	-29	-3	-3	-3
213-384-2600		'09	...	...	...	100.0	295	...	...	...	100.0	143	1,069	1,069	52	39	39	39
AMB# 068816		**Rating History: NR-5, 03/24/10; NR-5, 04/08/09; NR-5, 03/11/08; NR-5, 04/02/07; NR-5, 05/30/06**																
VISION SERVICE PLAN Vision Service Plan	A	'05	...	0.6	...	99.4	547,857	...	...	...	100.0	330,901	614,385	614,385	10,473	31,075	17,113	17,113
James Robinson Lynch, President & CEO		'06	...	0.6	...	99.4	564,039	...	...	...	100.0	349,830	646,675	646,675	38,501	27,429	15,342	15,342
3333 Quality Drive, Rancho Cordova, CA 95670	Rating Outlook: Stable	'07	...	0.5	...	99.5	608,470	...	...	...	100.0	353,751	683,069	683,069	37,084	20,260	10,492	10,492
CA : 1955 : Other : Agency, Group A&H		'08	...	0.5	...	99.5	612,379	...	...	...	100.0	370,696	713,138	713,138	2,302	10,098	6,146	6,146
916-851-5000		'09	...	0.5	...	99.5	650,263	...	...	...	100.0	396,648	710,413	710,413	43,625	-76	12,160	12,160
AMB# 064607	FSC IX	**Rating History: A g, 02/09/10; A g, 11/24/08; A g, 11/30/07; A g, 10/12/06; A g, 11/10/05**																
VISION SERVICE PLAN INC Vision Service Plan	A	'05	42.5	...	22.8	34.7	16,431	...	41.1	...	58.9	15,294	8,928	8,928	1,284	1,957	1,631	2,267
James Robinson Lynch, President & CEO		'06	40.8	...	23.4	35.8	18,802	...	24.8	...	75.2	17,559	7,529	7,529	1,938	2,408	1,148	1,393
3333 Quality Drive, Rancho Cordova, CA 95670	Rating Outlook: Stable	'07	58.2	...	23.9	18.0	20,607	...	27.3	...	72.7	19,515	7,339	7,339	1,946	2,703	1,933	2,597
NV : 1987 : Other : Agency, Group A&H		'08	53.0	...	12.4	34.6	22,421	...	12.2	...	87.8	19,562	8,513	8,513	-74	1,985	1,440	447
916-851-5000		'09	60.9	...	16.4	22.7	22,404	...	19.8	...	80.2	21,158	8,190	8,190	2,075	1,726	1,484	1,579
AMB# 064474 NAIC# 48321	FSC IX	**Rating History: A g, 02/09/10; A g, 11/24/08; A g, 11/30/07; A g, 10/12/06; A g, 11/10/05**																
VISION SERVICE PLAN INS CO(CT) Vision Service Plan	A	'05	50.1	...	4.0	45.9	299,338	...	60.7	...	39.3	250,881	436,764	436,764	18,565	59,242	44,055	44,066
James Robinson Lynch, President & CEO		'06	68.4	...	5.3	26.4	340,046	...	54.2	...	45.8	289,214	478,938	478,938	58,806	64,158	41,716	42,061
3333 Quality Drive, Rancho Cordova, CA 95670	Rating Outlook: Stable	'07	37.6	...	25.1	37.3	387,965	...	63.0	...	37.0	319,899	557,209	557,209	43,486	41,384	25,196	26,897
CT : 1987 : Stock : Broker, Group A&H		'08	25.3	...	0.0	74.7	128,993	...	70.9	...	29.1	62,677	544,440	544,440	36,621	49,509	35,724	34,882
916-851-5000		'09	23.8	...	0.0	76.2	178,307	...	47.2	...	52.8	94,141	568,917	568,917	28,073	44,928	30,896	27,675
AMB# 011105 NAIC# 39616	FSC IX	**Rating History: A g, 02/09/10; A g, 11/24/08; A g, 11/30/07; A g, 10/12/06; A g, 11/10/05**																
VISION SERVICE PLAN INS CO(MO) Vision Service Plan	A	'05	51.2	...	2.7	46.0	56,954	...	51.0	...	49.0	50,227	47,872	47,872	5,240	10,239	6,416	6,630
James Robinson Lynch, President & CEO		'06	46.3	...	2.9	50.8	69,900	...	28.4	...	71.6	60,572	60,763	60,763	11,189	15,713	11,026	11,172
3333 Quality Drive, Rancho Cordova, CA 95670	Rating Outlook: Stable	'07	50.9	...	3.7	45.4	70,563	...	37.5	...	62.5	59,483	71,000	71,000	945	13,316	7,777	8,004
MO : 1987 : Other : Broker, Group A&H		'08	49.2	...	2.4	48.3	71,909	...	32.5	...	67.5	61,121	85,883	85,883	1,354	15,025	10,412	10,039
916-851-5000		'09	52.6	...	3.9	43.4	54,869	...	32.7	...	67.3	38,106	97,431	97,431	-14,812	10,255	5,695	5,505
AMB# 011496 NAIC# 32395	FSC IX	**Rating History: A g, 02/09/10; A g, 11/24/08; A g, 11/30/07; A g, 10/12/06; A g, 11/10/05**																

BEST'S PROFITABILITY, LEVERAGE AND LIQUIDITY TESTS 2005 – 2009

Data in U.S. Dollars

—	Profitability Tests							Leverage Tests						Liquidity Tests					
Un-Realized Capital Gains ($000)	Benefits Paid to NPW & Dep (%)	Comm. & Expenses to NPW & Dep (%)	NOG to Total Assets (%)	NOG to Total Rev (%)	Operating Return on Equity (%)	Net Yield (%)	Total Return (%)	Change in NPW & Dep (%)	NPW & Dep to Capital (X)	Capital & Surplus to Liabilities (%)	Surplus Relief (%)	Reins Leverage (%)	Change in Capital (%)	Quick Liquidity (%)	Current Liquidity (%)	Non-Invest Grade Bonds to Capital (%)	Delinq. & Foreclosed Mortgages to Capital (%)	Mort. & Credit Tenant Loans & R.E. to Capital (%)	Affiliated Invest to Capital (%)
...	76.2	17.4	7.3	5.8	10.1	3.06	3.06	2.6	1.6	275.0	...	...	11.4	348.2	348.2	...	...	...	...
...	79.6	16.3	8.9	7.4	12.1	4.16	4.16	2.7	1.5	292.8	...	...	11.5	365.0	365.0	...	...	...	...
...	83.6	16.3	5.1	4.2	6.8	4.78	4.78	8.6	1.5	314.8	...	...	7.4	388.9	388.9	...	...	...	...
...	81.3	15.6	8.5	7.0	10.9	4.25	4.25	5.8	1.4	418.5	...	...	11.6	490.7	490.7	...	...	...	...
...	83.1	14.9	7.4	6.2	9.1	3.30	3.30	4.7	1.4	452.8	...	...	9.5	522.4	522.4	...	...	...	...
Principal Lines of Business: Vision (100.0%)													Principal States: PA (76.1%), DE (9.3%), MO (5.7%)						
...	44.6	32.6	26.6	12.9	26.6	...	...	-6.0	2.2	...	...	...	-9.5	...	...	...	...	...	...
...	48.7	13.3	50.0	31.1	50.0	...	...	-27.4	1.6	...	...	...	-3.4	...	...	...	...	...	...
...	49.6	17.8	36.7	23.0	36.7	...	...	-2.1	1.6	...	...	...	0.5	...	...	...	...	...	...
...	39.9	5.7	82.8	49.4	82.8	...	...	6.6	1.7	...	...	...	2.7	...	...	...	...	...	...
...	55.1	27.1	7.8	3.7	7.8	...	...	33.3	2.0	...	...	...	8.1	...	...	...	...	...	...
Principal Lines of Business: FEHBP (100.0%)													Principal States: WI (100.0%)						
...	64.9	35.0	5.2	2.2	13.9	-3.22	-3.22	22.9	0.3	52.4	...	...	15.0	33.8	33.8	...	...	...	...
...	58.7	37.5	3.1	1.4	9.0	27.34	27.34	-10.4	0.2	54.7	...	...	9.4	32.1	32.1	...	...	...	...
...	64.3	33.5	2.1	0.8	5.5	61.57	61.57	4.2	0.2	65.4	...	...	5.7	31.5	31.5	...	...	...	...
...	999.9	999.9	2.4	0.9	5.8	-33.74	-33.74	-18.8	0.2	77.3	...	...	6.0	37.9	37.9	...	...	...	...
...	67.7	33.2	-1.9	-0.8	-4.4	-58.31	-58.31	-15.9	0.1	77.1	...	...	-4.3	42.5	42.5	...	...	...	...
Principal Lines of Business: Vision (100.0%)																			
...	48.6	35.5	53.8	11.6	112.9	3.57	3.57	10.8	9.3	124.3	...	...	-0.3	197.4	197.4	...	...	...	...
...	47.9	33.7	68.9	12.5	123.6	7.47	7.47	8.7	9.2	128.0	...	...	10.8	181.4	181.4	...	...	...	...
...	51.4	31.0	50.9	12.4	132.1	4.40	4.40	20.5	9.7	43.3	...	...	13.5	128.4	128.4	...	...	...	...
...	55.3	27.7	47.1	10.7	131.6	1.89	1.89	18.6	12.7	81.9	...	...	-9.2	148.7	148.7	...	...	...	...
...	56.8	25.0	83.5	13.0	175.1	0.60	0.60	2.3	13.4	103.1	...	...	-2.8	150.0	150.0	...	...	...	...
Principal Lines of Business: Vision (100.0%)													Principal States: WI (100.0%)						
...	32.6	72.6	-7.8	-1.9	-21.4	0.42	0.42	-24.9	18.3	40.3	...	...	-58.0	85.7	85.7	...	...	...	...
...	30.5	65.9	29.1	5.7	69.5	-1.36	-1.36	-0.2	8.8	115.6	...	...	106.6	155.3	155.3	...	...	...	...
...	32.3	64.9	20.9	4.7	38.7	-0.96	-0.96	-13.1	8.5	120.3	...	...	-9.1	150.0	150.0	...	...	...	...
...	32.7	67.4	-1.1	-0.3	-2.3	-2.95	-2.95	-10.1	11.5	72.7	...	...	-33.8	81.3	81.3	...	...	...	...
...	33.1	63.1	14.4	3.6	31.5	-1.96	-1.96	-10.2	7.5	94.0	...	...	37.7	111.0	111.0	...	...	...	...
Principal Lines of Business: Vision (100.0%)																			
...	96.0	14.6	3.2	2.4	5.2	3.04	3.04	4.5	1.9	152.5	...	...	-0.5	27.0	27.0	...	...	1.0	1.0
...	97.4	15.1	2.8	2.0	4.5	3.71	3.71	5.3	1.8	163.3	...	...	5.7	152.4	152.4	...	...	0.9	0.9
...	98.5	15.9	1.8	1.3	3.0	3.72	3.72	5.6	1.9	138.9	...	...	1.1	133.8	133.8	...	...	0.9	0.9
...	100.6	14.0	1.0	0.7	1.7	1.16	1.16	4.4	1.9	153.4	...	...	4.8	34.6	34.6	...	...	0.9	0.9
...	101.4	13.9	1.9	1.5	3.2	0.02	0.02	-0.4	1.8	156.4	...	...	7.0	38.6	38.6	...	...	0.8	0.8
Principal Lines of Business: Vision (100.0%)																			
-99	85.4	-3.9	10.3	17.5	11.3	2.13	6.11	2.1	0.6	999.9	...	...	13.0	999.9	999.9	...	...	...	...
510	69.0	8.0	6.5	13.7	7.0	3.21	8.08	-15.7	0.4	999.9	...	...	14.8	999.9	999.9	...	...	...	...
-180	63.9	10.2	9.8	21.9	10.4	3.32	6.10	-2.5	0.4	999.9	...	...	11.1	999.9	999.9	...	...	...	...
-747	73.8	9.7	6.7	15.4	7.4	2.75	-6.07	16.0	0.4	684.2	...	...	0.2	605.8	659.1	...	...	...	...
670	74.4	9.4	6.6	16.8	7.3	1.82	5.64	-3.8	0.4	999.9	...	...	8.2	999.9	999.9	3.5	...	...	...
Principal Lines of Business: Vision (100.0%)													Principal States: NV (100.0%)						
1,977	90.2	-1.6	15.8	9.9	19.6	2.85	3.76	9.4	1.7	517.7	...	...	25.7	502.3	532.4	...	...	...	2.3
1,246	80.1	9.8	13.0	8.3	15.4	4.37	4.99	9.7	1.7	569.0	...	...	15.3	572.5	599.5	...	...	...	2.0
3,344	81.2	11.3	6.9	4.3	8.3	4.02	5.68	16.3	1.7	470.0	...	...	10.6	523.8	574.3	...	...	...	2.8
-30,293	82.8	10.8	13.8	6.2	18.7	8.37	-6.12	-2.3	8.7	94.5	...	...	-80.4	145.2	154.2	2.5	...	...	422.5
18,918	82.7	10.9	20.1	5.2	39.4	2.86	23.28	4.5	6.0	111.9	...	...	50.2	171.3	180.2	...	...	...	319.3
Principal Lines of Business: Vision (100.0%)													Principal States: TX (21.1%), DC (11.1%), NJ (9.4%), CO (6.9%), NC (6.1%)						
-170	84.3	-2.6	12.0	12.7	13.9	2.96	3.05	-6.6	1.0	746.6	...	...	19.2	906.8	910.2	...	...	...	...
132	72.3	8.9	17.4	16.5	19.9	4.17	4.67	26.9	1.0	649.4	...	...	20.6	862.8	872.7	...	...	...	...
-130	72.7	11.3	11.1	10.0	13.0	4.96	5.12	16.8	1.2	536.8	...	...	-1.8	724.3	744.5	...	...	...	...
-351	75.5	11.0	14.6	11.3	17.3	3.01	1.84	21.0	1.4	566.6	...	...	2.8	730.4	773.1	...	...	...	...
400	77.7	10.9	9.0	5.6	11.5	1.61	2.00	13.4	2.6	227.3	...	...	-37.7	315.1	339.8	1.3	...	...	...
Principal Lines of Business: Vision (100.0%)													Principal States: MO (37.7%), FL (31.2%), GA (23.5%), NM (7.6%)						

Data in U.S. Dollars

COMPANY NAME Ultimate Parent Association Principal Officer Mailing Address Dom. : Began Bus. : Struct. : Mktg. Specialty Phone # AMB# NAIC#	Best's Financial Strength Rating FSC	Data Year	Balance Sheet Bonds (%)	Mort. Loans & R.E. (%)	Com & Pref. Stock (%)	All Other Assets (%)	Total Assets ($000)	Life Reserves (%)	Health Reserves (%)	Ann Res. & Dep. Liabilities (%)	All Other Liabilities (%)	Capital & Surplus ($000)	Operations Direct Premiums Written ($000)	Net Premiums Written & Deposits ($000)	Operating Cash Flow ($000)	NOG Before Taxes ($000)	NOG After Taxes ($000)	Net Income ($000)
VISION SERVICE PLAN OF IDAHO Vision Service Plan James Robinson Lynch President & CEO 3333 Quality Drive Rancho Cordova, CA 95670 ID : 1968 : Other : Agency Group A&H 916-851-5000 AMB# 064482 NAIC# 47783	**A**	'05	56.1	...	12.6	31.3	4,455	...	36.3	...	63.7	4,009	4,068	4,068	1,205	704	704	812
		'06	14.0	...	7.3	78.6	7,123	...	43.7	...	56.3	6,368	7,714	7,714	2,145	2,397	2,397	2,364
	Rating Outlook: Stable	'07	28.7	...	7.6	63.7	10,563	...	28.7	...	71.3	9,541	9,599	9,599	2,657	3,143	3,143	3,214
		'08	22.5	...	3.8	73.6	11,518	...	5.8	...	94.2	8,236	5,854	5,854	1,378	1,406	-1,191	-1,536
		'09	45.0	...	4.8	50.3	12,278	...	5.1	...	94.9	8,909	5,859	5,859	1,510	1,007	714	726
	FSC IX	**Rating History: A g, 02/09/10; A g, 11/24/08; A g, 11/30/07; A g, 10/12/06; A g, 11/10/05**																
VISION SERVICE PLAN OF IL NFP Vision Service Plan James Robinson Lynch President & CEO 3333 Quality Drive Rancho Cordova, CA 95670 IL : 2005 : Other : Agency Health 916-851-5000 AMB# 064834 NAIC# 12516	**NR-2**	'05	...	...	...	100.0	204	...	...	...	100.0	204	...	...	102	3	3	3
		'06	98.3	...	...	1.7	54	...	...	...	100.0	52	...	...	-149	4	1	1
		'07	30.1	...	...	69.9	360	...	...	...	100.0	360	...	...	305	3	2	2
		'08	1.1	...	...	98.9	10,116	...	45.7	...	54.3	3,100	75,968	75,968	4,107	5,255	2,951	2,951
		'09	10.4	...	...	89.6	11,574	...	46.5	...	53.5	3,073	77,235	77,235	2,155	4,833	2,968	2,968
		Rating History: NR-2, 02/09/10; NR-2, 11/24/08; NR-2, 12/03/07; NR-2, 10/12/06; NR-2, 04/07/06																
VISION SERVICE PLAN (OH) Vision Service Plan James Robinson Lynch President & CEO 3333 Quality Drive Rancho Cordova, CA 95670 OH : 1967 : Other : Agency Group A&H 916-851-5000 AMB# 064473 NAIC# 54380	**A**	'05	46.8	6.2	5.0	42.0	57,130	...	24.4	...	75.6	41,866	59,576	59,576	8,454	8,388	6,355	6,461
		'06	43.4	6.1	5.7	44.8	56,912	...	47.7	...	52.3	47,179	62,876	62,876	69	8,052	3,774	3,824
	Rating Outlook: Stable	'07	50.0	5.6	12.5	31.9	60,365	...	41.6	...	58.4	52,024	68,536	68,536	3,356	6,703	5,293	5,659
		'08	54.0	5.2	7.5	33.4	63,886	...	37.5	...	62.5	53,825	74,176	74,176	2,698	5,576	3,890	1,767
		'09	58.2	4.7	8.0	29.1	68,336	...	41.3	...	58.7	57,333	76,629	76,629	5,197	4,297	3,336	2,968
	FSC IX	**Rating History: A g, 02/09/10; A g, 11/24/08; A g, 11/30/07; A g, 10/12/06; A g, 11/10/05**																
VISION SERVICE PLAN (WA) Vision Service Plan James Robinson Lynch President & CEO 3333 Quality Drive Rancho Cordova, CA 95670 WA : 1959 : Other : Agency Group A&H 916-851-5000 AMB# 064475 NAIC# 47317	**A**	'05	58.2	...	...	41.8	47,234	...	53.4	...	46.6	45,208	21,028	21,028	3,108	5,976	5,976	5,976
		'06	55.9	...	...	44.1	54,518	...	44.1	...	55.9	52,121	22,994	22,994	8,692	6,915	6,915	6,915
	Rating Outlook: Stable	'07	71.4	...	...	28.6	62,030	...	32.6	...	67.4	59,050	23,317	23,317	6,925	6,945	6,945	6,945
		'08	65.6	...	...	34.4	69,347	...	10.4	...	89.6	59,080	25,216	25,216	2,909	7,467	-328	-363
		'09	56.5	...	...	43.5	76,519	...	11.6	...	88.4	63,351	26,281	26,281	11,785	6,554	4,119	4,292
	FSC IX	**Rating History: A g, 02/09/10; A g, 11/24/08; A g, 11/30/07; A g, 10/12/06; A g, 11/10/05**																
VISION SERVICES PLAN INC OK Vision Service Plan James Robinson Lynch President & CEO 3333 Quality Drive Rancho Cordova, CA 95670 OK : 1969 : Other : Agency Group A&H 916-851-5000 AMB# 064476 NAIC# 47097	**A**	'05	17.2	...	20.9	61.9	8,728	...	49.1	...	50.9	7,421	15,238	15,238	794	1,877	1,037	1,064
		'06	20.0	...	19.6	60.4	9,989	...	56.0	...	44.0	8,702	16,763	16,763	1,733	1,879	1,351	1,642
	Rating Outlook: Stable	'07	20.2	...	17.5	62.3	11,655	...	48.4	...	51.6	10,252	19,288	19,288	1,414	2,518	1,499	1,595
		'08	43.3	...	8.9	47.9	14,083	...	25.5	...	74.5	11,412	22,039	22,039	1,022	2,372	1,624	1,098
		'09	67.7	...	14.9	17.4	12,115	...	26.0	...	74.0	9,512	25,424	25,424	-1,011	3,195	2,292	2,303
	FSC IX	**Rating History: A g, 02/09/10; A g, 11/24/08; A g, 11/30/07; A g, 10/12/06; A g, 11/10/05**																
VISIONCARE OF CALIFORNIA Nick Shashati, O.D. President 9625 Black Mountain Drive, Suite 311 San Diego, CA 92126 CA : 1989 : Non-Profit : Not Available Health 858-831-9322 AMB# 064660	**NR-5**	'05	...	...	...	100.0	791	...	...	...	100.0	567	3,398	3,398	64	76	75	75
		'06	...	...	...	100.0	839	...	...	...	100.0	613	3,382	3,382	106	45	45	45
		'07	...	...	...	100.0	864	...	...	...	100.0	631	3,513	3,513	-55	38	29	29
		'08	...	7.0	...	93.0	909	...	...	...	100.0	671	3,551	3,551	-14	50	39	39
		'09	...	...	...	100.0	945	...	...	...	100.0	697	3,521	3,521	53	33	27	27
		Rating History: NR-5, 05/07/10; NR-5, 05/13/09; NR-5, 05/09/08; NR-5, 04/23/07; NR-5, 06/08/06																
VISTA HEALTH PLAN INC[2] Independence Blue Cross John A. Daddis President 1901 Market Street Philadelphia, PA 19101 PA : 1986 : Stock : Broker Medicaid 215-241-2193 AMB# 064191 NAIC# 96660	**NR-5**	'05	13.9	...	6.9	79.2	130,852	...	...	...	100.0	104,068	1,633,254	1,633,254	69,613	3,000	2,169	2,304
		'06	14.1	...	8.5	77.4	131,649	...	...	...	100.0	107,858	1,475,136	1,475,136	-227	5,204	3,616	3,637
		'07	13.5	...	7.7	78.8	139,159	...	...	...	100.0	110,951	1,769,526	1,769,526	8,005	5,748	3,995	4,020
		'08	29.7	...	2.8	67.5	311,031	...	...	...	100.0	115,870	1,945,000	1,945,000	1,406	1,412	1,193	-1,581
		'09	15.6	...	2.1	82.4	475,045	...	...	...	100.0	137,442	2,107,247	2,107,247	26,455	582	372	1,665
		Rating History: NR-5, 04/12/10; NR-5, 08/26/09; C++pd, 10/10/08; NR-5, 06/30/08; NR-5, 05/30/06																
VISTA HEALTH PLAN INC[2] Vista Service Corporation Paul Tovar President 1701 E. 77th Street Austin, TX 78702-2712 TX : 1996 : Stock : Broker Health 512-433-1000 AMB# 064245 NAIC# 95313	**NR-5**	'05	...	...	...	100.0	1,668	...	21.5	...	78.5	1,575	...	...	-21	-54	-54	-54
		'06	...	...	...	100.0	1,687	...	21.6	...	78.4	1,595	...	...	26	-6	-6	-6
		'07	...	...	...	100.0	1,753	...	21.6	...	78.4	1,661	...	...	73	22	22	22
		'08	...	...	...	100.0	1,744	...	35.1	...	64.9	1,687	...	...	-4	4	4	4
		'09	...	...	...	100.0	1,731	...	46.7	...	53.3	1,688	...	...	-13	-7	-7	-7
		Rating History: NR-5, 04/06/10; NR-5, 03/25/09; NR-5, 03/28/08; NR-5, 04/10/07; NR-5, 06/06/06																
VISTA HEALTHPLAN INC Coventry Health Care Inc Christopher A. Ciano CEO 1340 Concord Terrace Sunrise, FL 33323 FL : 1985 : Non-Profit : Broker Group A&H, Medicaid, Medicare 954-858-3000 AMB# 064066 NAIC# 95114	**B**	'05	58.3	6.1	...	35.6	103,442	...	20.4	...	79.6	17,619	641,400	641,400	3,790	57,039	55,984	55,984
		'06	60.3	6.4	...	33.4	104,544	...	31.5	...	68.5	15,136	674,940	674,940	-546	22,495	22,495	22,495
	Rating Outlook: Stable	'07	65.0	7.2	...	27.8	100,559	...	38.0	...	62.0	23,708	700,207	700,207	-10,103	-44	6,952	6,935
		'08	57.9	7.5	...	34.6	123,934	...	30.8	...	69.2	22,079	696,802	696,802	30,836	-776	-955	-1,083
		'09	54.1	6.0	...	39.9	151,163	...	29.5	...	70.5	33,863	771,418	771,418	30,845	-3,852	-3,398	-3,398
	FSC IX	**Rating History: B, 02/12/10; B, 11/19/08; B, 10/30/07; C+ pd, 09/15/06; C- pd, 10/06/05**																

BEST'S PROFITABILITY, LEVERAGE AND LIQUIDITY TESTS 2005 – 2009

Data in U.S. Dollars

	Profitability Tests							Leverage Tests						Liquidity Tests					
Un-Realized Capital Gains ($000)	Benefits Paid to NPW & Dep (%)	Comm. & Expenses to NPW & Dep (%)	NOG to Total Assets (%)	NOG to Total Rev (%)	Operating Return on Equity (%)	Net Yield (%)	Total Return (%)	Change in NPW & Dep (%)	NPW & Dep to Capital (X)	Capital & Surplus to Liabilities (%)	Surplus Relief (%)	Reins Leverage (%)	Change in Capital (%)	Quick Liquidity (%)	Current Liquidity (%)	Non-Invest Grade Bonds to Capital (%)	Delinq. & Foreclosed Mortgages to Capital (%)	Mort. & Credit Tenant Loans & R.E. to Capital (%)	Affiliated Invest to Capital (%)
-39	85.1	-1.7	17.4	17.1	19.8	1.82	4.07	-1.2	1.0	899.2	...	...	28.7	754.8	773.6	...	...	...	...
-3	64.4	7.7	41.4	30.0	46.2	3.22	2.48	89.7	1.2	843.0	...	...	58.8	999.9	999.9	...	...	...	...
38	62.1	8.6	35.5	31.4	39.5	4.20	5.73	24.4	1.0	933.8	...	...	49.8	999.9	999.9	...	...	...	...
-25	72.8	8.7	-10.8	-18.7	-13.4	3.21	-0.76	-39.0	0.7	251.0	...	...	-13.7	363.1	369.8	...	...	...	...
81	76.5	9.0	6.0	11.5	8.3	1.18	2.06	0.1	0.7	264.4	...	...	8.2	291.2	307.9	8.4	...	...	...
Principal Lines of Business: Vision (100.0%)													Principal States: ID (100.0%)						
...	...	...	...	100.0	...	...	...	...	...	...	...	...	...	...	...	...	...	...	...
...	...	...	0.6	17.3	0.6	3.36	3.36	...	...	999.9	...	...	-74.5	999.9	999.9	...	...	...	...
...	...	...	1.0	59.2	1.0	1.68	1.68	...	...	999.9	...	...	589.2	999.9	999.9	...	...	...	...
...	83.7	9.7	56.3	3.8	170.6	-0.44	-0.44	...	24.5	44.2	...	...	761.9	103.9	108.4	...	...	...	...
...	83.5	9.5	27.4	3.8	96.2	-0.08	-0.08	1.7	25.1	36.1	...	...	-0.9	153.0	161.4	...	...	...	...
Principal Lines of Business: Vision (100.0%)													Principal States: IL (100.0%)						
-33	88.2	-4.9	12.2	10.9	15.7	2.59	2.75	9.7	1.4	274.3	...	...	7.0	368.9	371.7	...	...	8.5	8.5
298	78.0	7.6	6.6	5.9	8.5	3.63	4.33	5.5	1.3	484.8	...	...	12.7	589.7	598.9	...	...	7.4	7.4
-295	83.9	10.1	9.0	7.4	10.7	4.16	4.30	9.0	1.3	623.8	...	...	10.3	629.6	659.6	...	...	6.5	6.5
-575	83.8	9.4	6.3	5.1	7.3	2.93	-2.00	8.2	1.4	535.0	...	...	3.5	518.6	553.4	...	...	6.1	6.1
644	84.5	9.4	5.0	4.2	6.0	1.81	2.29	3.3	1.3	521.1	...	...	6.5	493.2	538.9	1.3	...	5.6	5.6
Principal Lines of Business: Vision (100.0%)													Principal States: OH (100.0%)						
...	80.5	1.6	13.3	26.1	14.3	2.89	2.89	4.2	0.5	999.9	...	...	17.6	999.9	999.9	...	...	...	...
...	73.2	6.8	13.6	26.4	14.2	4.37	4.37	9.3	0.4	999.9	...	...	15.3	999.9	999.9	...	...	...	...
...	73.8	8.9	11.9	25.2	12.5	4.97	4.97	1.4	0.4	999.9	...	...	13.3	999.9	999.9	...	...	...	...
...	73.9	6.5	-0.5	-1.1	-0.6	4.04	3.98	8.1	0.4	575.4	...	...	0.1	639.7	670.3	...	...	...	...
...	74.1	7.1	5.6	14.2	6.7	2.09	2.35	4.2	0.4	481.1	...	...	7.2	503.9	533.6	1.2	...	...	...
Principal Lines of Business: Vision (100.0%)													Principal States: WA (100.0%)						
165	92.0	-3.1	13.0	6.8	15.5	1.55	4.66	13.0	2.1	567.7	...	...	25.4	601.4	622.3	...	...	...	...
-131	81.6	8.8	14.4	7.9	16.8	3.05	5.28	10.0	1.9	676.2	...	...	17.3	771.1	793.9	...	...	...	...
-32	79.3	9.5	13.8	7.6	15.8	3.63	4.35	15.1	1.9	730.9	...	...	17.8	930.4	961.9	...	...	...	...
-158	81.3	9.3	12.6	7.2	15.0	2.44	-3.78	14.3	1.9	427.2	...	...	11.3	427.3	453.3	...	...	...	...
333	79.0	9.4	17.5	8.8	21.9	1.73	4.92	15.4	2.7	365.5	...	...	-16.7	298.1	338.1	5.3	...	...	...
Principal Lines of Business: Vision (100.0%)													Principal States: OK (100.0%)						
...	82.0	16.3	10.0	2.2	14.2	0.36	0.36	-8.0	6.0	253.8	...	...	15.3	128.1	128.1	...	...	...	...
...	86.7	13.3	5.5	1.3	7.7	1.23	1.23	-0.5	5.5	271.7	...	...	8.1	164.9	164.9	...	...	...	...
...	87.4	12.3	3.4	0.8	4.7	1.66	1.66	3.9	5.6	270.5	...	...	2.9	77.8	77.8	...	...	...	...
...	79.8	19.0	4.5	1.1	6.1	0.81	0.81	1.1	5.3	281.5	...	...	6.3	69.5	69.5	...	...	9.5	9.5
...	78.7	21.3	2.9	0.8	3.9	0.44	0.44	-0.8	5.0	281.4	...	...	4.0	88.3	88.3	...	...	...	...
Principal Lines of Business: Vision (100.0%)																			
-107	91.5	8.5	2.3	0.1	2.7	3.70	3.73	141.0	15.7	388.5	...	...	82.9	768.7	828.3	...	...	...	...
153	94.0	6.1	2.8	0.2	3.4	4.99	5.12	-9.7	13.7	453.4	...	...	3.6	845.8	916.1	...	...	...	...
-927	94.0	6.1	3.0	0.2	3.7	5.46	4.78	20.0	15.9	393.3	...	...	2.9	759.1	820.1	...	...	...	...
-687	95.0	5.0	0.5	0.1	1.1	4.17	1.64	9.9	16.8	59.4	...	...	4.4	69.8	77.6	0.7	...	...	...
1,094	95.5	4.5	0.1	0.0	0.3	3.66	5.26	8.3	15.3	40.7	...	...	18.6	61.9	67.5	0.4	...	...	...
Principal Lines of Business: Medicaid (100.0%)													Principal States: PA (100.0%)						
...	...	...	-3.2	-27.0	-3.4	1.86	1.86	...	...	999.9	...	...	-1.4	999.9	999.9	...	...	...	...
...	...	...	-0.4	-3.8	-0.4	1.46	1.46	...	...	999.9	...	...	1.3	999.9	999.9	...	...	...	...
...	...	...	1.3	25.1	1.4	2.90	2.90	...	...	999.9	...	...	4.1	999.9	999.9	...	...	...	...
...	...	...	0.2	8.3	0.2	2.27	2.27	...	...	999.9	...	...	1.6	999.9	999.9	...	...	...	...
...	...	...	-0.4	-17.5	-0.4	0.78	0.78	...	...	999.9	...	...	0.1	999.9	999.9	...	...	...	...
...	82.3	9.4	55.3	8.7	369.1	4.30	4.30	3.6	36.4	20.5	...	12.6	38.5	106.2	115.7	...	...	36.0	36.0
...	81.7	15.5	21.6	3.3	137.3	5.67	5.67	5.2	44.6	16.9	...	7.0	-14.1	104.2	113.4	...	...	44.0	44.0
...	84.5	16.1	6.8	1.0	35.8	5.75	5.73	3.7	29.5	30.8	...	7.2	56.6	85.9	94.9	...	...	30.4	...
...	86.7	14.2	-0.9	-0.1	-4.2	4.78	4.65	-0.5	31.6	21.7	...	0.0	-6.9	86.8	93.3	...	...	41.9	...
...	89.0	12.1	-2.5	-0.4	-12.1	2.82	2.82	10.7	22.8	28.9	...	7.1	53.4	121.1	129.3	...	...	26.7	...
Principal Lines of Business: CompHosp/Med (82.5%), Medicaid (10.2%), Medicare (7.3%)													Principal States: FL (100.0%)						

Data in U.S. Dollars

COMPANY NAME Ultimate Parent Association Principal Officer Mailing Address Dom. : Began Bus. : Struct. : Mktg. Specialty Phone # AMB# NAIC#	Best's Financial Strength Rating FSC	Data Year	Balance Sheet										Operations					
			Bonds (%)	Mort. Loans & R.E. (%)	Com & Pref. Stock (%)	All Other Assets (%)	Total Assets ($000)	Life Reserves (%)	Health Reserves %)	Ann Res. & Dep. Liabilities (%)	All Other Liabilities (%)	Capital & Surplus ($000)	Direct Premiums Written ($000)	Net Premiums Written & Deposits ($000)	Operating Cash Flow ($000)	NOG Before Taxes ($000)	NOG After Taxes ($000)	Net Income ($000)
VISTA HEALTHPLAN OF SOUTH FL Coventry Health Care Inc Christopher A. Ciano CEO 1340 Concord Terrace Sunrise, FL 33323 FL : 1994 : Stock : Broker Group A&H, Medicare, Medicaid 954-858-3000 AMB# 064102 NAIC# 95266	**B** Rating Outlook: Stable **FSC VI**	'05	52.8	...	...	47.2	68,089	...	21.9	...	78.1	9,878	342,524	342,524	5,822	5,541	5,466	5,462
		'06	63.3	...	...	36.7	60,668	...	27.0	...	73.0	9,746	392,305	392,305	-10,266	5,963	4,529	4,529
		'07	69.5	...	...	30.5	54,427	...	34.3	...	65.7	16,866	364,647	364,647	-8,465	4,236	5,304	5,304
		'08	52.1	...	...	47.9	77,332	...	28.6	...	71.4	24,625	326,480	326,480	25,775	11,829	7,568	7,440
		'09	54.3	...	...	45.7	88,290	...	22.5	...	77.5	30,096	313,277	313,277	12,540	11,695	5,611	5,612
		Rating History: B, 02/12/10; B, 11/19/08; B, 10/30/07; C+ pd, 09/15/06; C- pd, 10/06/05																
VISTA LIFE INS CO Ford Motor Company Clifford G. Rager President One American Road Dearborn, MI 48126-2701 MI : 1974 : Stock : Other Reins 313-594-1914 AMB# 008549 NAIC# 84549	**NR-3**	'05	86.7	...	...	13.3	27,157	3.8	10.0	...	86.3	18,841	91	-373	-795	3,630	2,397	2,397
		'06	88.1	...	...	11.9	22,586	4.0	9.5	...	86.5	19,648	88	-3	-4,661	1,121	824	824
		'07	94.4	...	...	5.6	40,796	1.4	10.7	...	88.0	34,646	78	-3,664	12,293	-2,280	-1,455	10,067
		'08	89.9	...	...	10.1	39,571	0.7	27.7	...	71.5	37,827	69	-2	-144	4,975	3,262	3,152
		'09	90.7	...	...	9.3	40,139	2.6	9.7	...	87.8	39,362	58	...	-372	2,075	1,586	1,586
		Rating History: NR-3, 09/15/09; NR-3, 10/17/08; NR-3, 10/10/07; NR-3, 10/30/06; NR-3, 10/21/05																
VIVA HEALTH INC[2] University of Alabama Board of Trustees Arthur B. Rollow President 1222 14th Avenue South Birmingham, AL 35205 AL : 1996 : Stock : Broker Medicare, Group A&H 205-939-1718 AMB# 064257 NAIC# 95322	**NR-5**	'05	54.2	...	...	45.8	23,347	...	24.0	...	76.0	13,163	201,956	201,180	-1,668	1,453	937	936
		'06	18.5	...	...	81.5	51,934	...	19.4	...	80.6	15,641	273,026	272,067	26,966	4,854	3,453	3,469
		'07	9.2	...	...	90.8	44,200	...	27.6	...	72.4	18,355	330,381	329,228	-9,049	2,381	1,161	1,139
		'08	...	...	...	100.0	44,236	...	51.8	...	48.2	23,051	361,852	360,401	-3,234	7,615	4,965	4,977
		'09	...	...	...	100.0	77,198	...	29.1	...	70.9	31,205	382,607	380,914	33,264	12,944	8,490	8,496
		Rating History: NR-5, 04/21/10; NR-5, 08/26/09; C++pd, 07/01/08; C++pd, 06/26/07; C++pd, 07/17/06																
VOLUNTEER STATE HEALTH PLAN BlueCross BlueShield of Tennessee Inc Vicky Gregg Chairman 801 Pine Street Chattanooga, TN 37402-2555 TN : 1996 : Stock : Not Available Medicaid 423-535-5600 AMB# 064304	**NR-5**	'05	71.0	...	...	29.0	41,099	...	...	...	100.0	30,421	-185	-185	1,845	-946	-570	-596
		'06	61.1	...	...	38.9	46,712	...	...	...	100.0	30,758	-103	-103	-804	384	313	337
		'07	60.5	...	...	39.5	43,670	...	...	...	100.0	31,363	-86	-86	-1,405	924	608	605
		'08	18.2	...	...	81.8	151,643	...	82.2	...	17.8	26,856	77,924	77,924	58,557	-69,105	-61,776	-61,776
		'09	34.5	...	...	65.5	270,183	...	73.0	...	27.0	86,912	1,197,311	1,197,311	86,635	-95,651	-64,438	-64,416
		Rating History: NR-5, 03/24/10; NR-5, 04/09/09; NR-5, 03/28/08; NR-5, 04/13/07; NR-5, 06/15/06																
WASHINGTON DENTAL SERVICE James D. Dwyer President & CEO P.O. Box 75688 Seattle, WA 98125 WA : 1954 : Non-Profit : Agency Dental 206-522-1300 AMB# 064410 NAIC# 47341	**A-** Rating Outlook: Stable **FSC VIII**	'05	27.5	5.1	32.5	34.8	137,847	...	54.6	...	45.4	97,433	341,327	341,327	22,124	13,812	13,812	16,879
		'06	27.1	3.8	38.6	30.5	170,168	...	63.5	...	36.5	117,883	357,624	357,624	31,422	18,542	18,542	24,240
		'07	30.5	3.5	42.8	23.1	178,216	...	64.3	...	35.7	122,009	380,971	380,971	25,189	11,552	11,552	15,762
		'08	32.1	3.8	28.8	35.3	158,246	...	43.8	...	56.2	104,331	407,194	407,194	-4,671	26,117	26,117	20,090
		'09	28.5	3.0	17.0	51.5	186,853	...	40.5	...	59.5	130,318	424,102	424,102	23,001	9,478	9,478	13,013
		Rating History: A-, 01/20/10; A-, 05/07/09; A-, 01/22/08; A-, 01/08/07; A-, 12/08/05																
WASHINGTON NATIONAL INS CO CNO Financial Group, Inc. Steven M. Stecher President 11825 N. Pennsylvania Street Carmel, IN 46032 IL : 1923 : Stock : Agency Dis inc, Group A&H, Ind A&H 317-817-6100 AMB# 007218 NAIC# 70319	**B** Rating Outlook: Stable **FSC X**	'05	61.1	5.0	25.6	8.3	2,657,760	40.5	18.6	34.5	6.4	762,013	245,322	271,784	-76,917	58,867	58,857	48,115
		'06	63.9	6.0	20.7	9.4	2,609,705	36.7	17.4	40.1	5.8	585,767	439,066	465,043	106,636	1,413	7,425	4,249
		'07	65.8	8.1	17.6	8.5	2,473,581	32.9	17.9	41.0	8.2	435,586	425,439	451,949	-78,524	-40,611	-42,749	-45,206
		'08	64.6	8.7	17.3	9.4	2,348,189	34.2	17.8	43.3	4.7	457,013	261,192	283,820	-97,972	10,847	25,734	13,480
		'09	61.9	10.1	16.2	11.9	1,926,723	24.5	23.0	47.0	5.5	400,130	201,602	212,788	-389,672	-38,773	-22,808	-43,315
		Rating History: B g, 03/23/10; B g, 10/16/09; B gu, 03/04/09; B+ g, 11/20/08; B+ gu, 08/12/08																
WATEREE LIFE INSURANCE COMPANY[1] Craig L. Nix President P.O. Box 29 Columbia, SC 29202-0029 SC : 1989 : Stock : Not Available 803-931-1720 AMB# 068303 NAIC# 92053	**NR-1**	'05	95.0	...	...	5.0	9,997	...	...	...	100.0	6,187	431	443	...	1,818	1,208	1,208
		'06	91.7	...	...	8.3	10,082	...	...	...	100.0	7,053	955	835	...	1,314	866	866
		'07	91.9	...	...	8.1	10,078	...	...	...	100.0	7,803	1,312	1,038	...	1,144	750	750
		'08	90.6	...	...	9.4	10,303	...	...	...	100.0	8,545	1,506	1,091	...	1,148	746	746
		'09	92.7	...	...	7.3	10,181	...	...	...	100.0	8,825	1,400	983	...	393	253	278
		Rating History: NR-1, 06/10/10; NR-1, 06/12/09; NR-1, 06/12/08; NR-1, 06/08/07; NR-1, 06/07/06																
WEA INSURANCE CORPORATION WEA Insurance Trust Fred Evert President P.O. Box 7338 Madison, WI 53707-7338 WI : 1985 : Stock : Not Available Group A&H 608-276-4000 AMB# 009506 NAIC# 72273	**NR-5**	'05	57.4	...	18.2	24.4	478,568	...	68.8	...	31.2	202,042	885,526	885,526	21,181	-2,036	-2,036	334
		'06	60.8	...	19.3	19.8	516,790	...	70.0	...	30.0	218,952	909,895	909,895	34,227	12,573	12,573	17,501
		'07	62.4	...	19.1	18.5	559,113	...	69.1	...	30.9	243,346	897,723	897,723	48,483	19,473	19,473	23,407
		'08	66.6	...	12.2	21.2	540,989	...	74.0	...	26.0	223,926	856,331	856,331	17,306	14,959	14,959	5,410
		'09	66.6	...	16.2	17.2	596,588	...	73.7	...	26.3	240,176	863,435	863,435	26,366	1,890	1,890	2,688
		Rating History: NR-5, 03/31/10; NR-5, 03/27/09; NR-5, 04/14/08; NR-5, 04/30/07; NR-5, 04/05/06																
WELLCARE OF OHIO INC WellCare Health Plans, Inc. Heath G. Scheisser President & CEO P.O. Box 31391 Tampa, FL 33631-3391 OH : 2007 : Stock : Broker Medicaid, Medicare 813-243-2974 AMB# 051406 NAIC# 12749	**NR-5**	'05	...	...	...	...	...	...	...	...	...	...	...	...	...	...	...	...
		'06	...	...	...	...	...	...	...	...	...	...	...	...	...	...	...	...
		'07	0.6	...	...	99.4	68,204	...	42.8	...	57.2	15,768	171,074	161,662	50,378	-6,398	-5,271	-5,271
		'08	0.5	...	...	99.5	88,683	...	71.9	...	28.1	39,088	295,692	286,040	18,397	-11,819	-7,046	-7,046
		'09	0.3	...	...	99.7	115,922	...	26.0	...	74.0	57,232	271,458	252,875	25,911	19,398	11,530	11,530
		Rating History: NR-5, 03/24/10; NR-5, 04/15/09																

	Profitability Tests							Leverage Tests						Liquidity Tests					
Un-Realized Capital Gains ($000)	Benefits Paid to NPW & Dep (%)	Comm. & Expenses to NPW & Dep (%)	NOG to Total Assets (%)	NOG to Total Rev (%)	Operating Return on Equity (%)	Net Yield (%)	Total Return (%)	Change in NPW & Dep (%)	NPW & Dep to Capital (X)	Capital & Surplus to Liabilities (%)	Surplus Relief (%)	Reins Leverage (%)	Change in Capital (%)	Quick Liquidity (%)	Current Liquidity (%)	Non-Invest Grade Bonds to Capital (%)	Delinq. & Foreclosed Mortgages to Capital (%)	Mort. & Credit Tenant Loans & R.E. to Capital (%)	Affiliated Invest to Capital (%)
...	82.9	15.8	8.3	1.6	65.2	3.63	3.62	14.2	34.7	17.0	...	2.1	43.3	140.4	150.5	...	...	...	...
...	83.2	16.6	7.0	1.1	46.2	5.84	5.84	14.5	40.3	19.1	...	10.4	-1.3	122.6	132.4	...	...	...	...
...	83.1	16.3	9.2	1.4	39.9	6.00	6.00	-7.0	21.6	44.9	...	0.9	73.1	113.7	123.8	...	...	...	...
...	82.6	14.3	11.5	2.3	36.5	4.17	3.95	-10.5	13.3	46.7	...	...	46.0	158.4	166.0	...	...	...	...
...	83.1	13.5	6.8	1.8	20.5	2.17	2.18	-4.0	10.4	51.7	...	1.1	22.2	161.2	170.2	...	...	...	...
Principal Lines of Business: Medicare (44.2%), CompHosp/Med (35.8%), Medicaid (17.2%), FEHBP (2.8%)														Principal States: FL (100.0%)					
...	-46.5	-89.0	8.8	87.2	13.6	4.07	4.46	58.5	0.0	227.4	-1.0	58.3	14.2	310.4	318.8	...	...	...	...
...	-99.9	-99.9	3.3	64.1	4.3	5.23	5.52	99.2	0.0	675.2	-0.2	14.8	4.3	688.9	721.8	...	...	...	...
...	-2.3	-22.7	-4.6	98.6	-5.4	3.96	50.34	-99.9	-0.1	573.2	0.0	0.4	76.6	498.9	558.6	...	...	...	...
...	-99.9	999.9	8.1	68.8	9.0	4.91	4.81	100.0	0.0	999.9	...	0.3	9.1	999.9	999.9	0.0	...	...	...
0	...	...	4.0	81.2	4.1	4.86	5.08	100.0	...	999.9	...	0.4	4.1	999.9	999.9	0.0	...	...	...
														Principal States: MI (100.0%)					
...	87.7	12.0	3.8	0.5	7.2	4.68	4.67	12.3	15.3	129.2	...	...	3.4	326.6	326.6	...	...	...	...
...	88.7	10.4	9.2	1.3	24.0	7.03	7.07	35.2	17.4	43.1	...	...	18.8	240.1	240.1	...	...	...	...
...	88.9	11.3	2.4	0.3	6.8	7.38	7.33	21.0	17.9	71.0	...	...	17.4	237.2	237.2	...	...	...	...
...	87.4	10.8	11.2	1.4	24.0	3.16	3.19	9.5	15.6	108.8	...	...	25.6	308.3	308.3	...	...	...	...
...	86.2	10.4	14.0	2.2	31.3	0.39	0.40	5.7	12.2	67.8	...	...	35.4	149.1	149.1	...	...	...	...
Principal Lines of Business: Medicare (78.4%), CompHosp/Med (21.6%)														Principal States: AL (100.0%)					
...	-99.9	-99.9	-1.5	-57.8	-1.9	3.13	3.06	-99.9	0.0	284.9	...	...	-1.9	595.4	607.3	...	...	...	...
...	423.5	-99.9	0.7	18.6	1.0	4.75	4.82	44.4	0.0	192.8	...	...	1.1	234.5	243.0	...	...	...	...
...	999.9	-99.9	1.3	34.0	2.0	5.18	5.17	16.5	0.0	254.8	...	...	2.0	299.9	311.9	...	...	...	...
...	97.7	38.2	-63.3	-77.7	-99.9	2.36	2.36	999.9	2.9	21.5	...	...	-14.4	109.7	114.2	...	...	...	...
-39	94.4	13.8	-30.6	-5.4	-99.9	1.78	1.76	999.9	13.8	47.4	...	...	223.6	132.2	139.9	...	...	...	...
Principal Lines of Business: Medicaid (100.0%)														Principal States: TN (100.0%)					
-3,947	88.3	8.5	10.6	4.0	15.4	2.94	2.24	5.3	3.5	241.1	...	...	19.0	199.6	221.0	0.3	...	7.3	10.8
-3,777	87.6	8.5	12.0	5.1	17.2	3.34	4.93	4.8	3.0	225.5	...	...	21.0	187.9	212.8	0.1	...	5.5	9.8
-4,965	88.0	9.7	6.6	3.0	9.6	3.54	3.14	6.5	3.1	217.1	...	...	3.5	196.9	225.0	0.1	...	5.2	10.1
-30,947	87.9	8.3	15.5	6.3	23.1	3.65	-20.25	6.9	3.9	193.5	...	...	-14.5	137.4	158.0	0.2	...	5.7	24.4
13,543	89.5	9.3	5.5	2.2	8.1	2.94	16.16	4.2	3.3	230.5	...	...	24.9	184.2	199.0	0.1	...	4.3	19.2
Principal Lines of Business: Dental (100.0%)														Principal States: WA (100.0%)					
33,510	79.1	21.3	2.2	15.7	7.7	5.75	6.86	-13.7	0.3	41.9	0.4	22.2	-2.4	53.8	66.8	9.5	...	17.9	85.5
-168,538	59.6	18.3	0.3	1.3	1.1	5.55	-0.76	71.1	0.8	31.0	0.5	28.1	-21.4	52.4	65.8	14.7	...	27.2	88.0
-46,733	60.4	18.8	-1.7	-8.0	-8.4	5.27	3.42	-2.8	1.0	22.9	1.1	86.0	-25.2	46.8	61.0	21.9	...	49.2	95.4
-25,336	111.2	24.0	1.1	7.5	5.8	4.13	2.63	-37.2	0.6	25.2	0.5	74.3	2.7	43.8	59.2	33.8	...	48.6	80.3
-73,534	150.3	13.9	-1.1	-7.9	-5.3	4.81	0.25	-25.0	0.5	26.7	5.0	142.4	-14.0	40.4	57.1	23.9	1.7	53.1	74.0
Principal Lines of Business: IndA&H (45.8%), IndAnn (28.0%), GrpAnn (15.5%), OrdLife (7.8%), GrpA&H (2.9%)														Principal States: PA (11.9%), FL (11.6%), CA (8.8%), TX (7.9%), NJ (5.1%)					
...	18.4	54.2	11.9	165.7	21.6	...	...	275.0	0.1	162.4	0.1	...	24.2	...	...	...	...	...	...
...	35.7	52.0	8.6	68.7	13.1	...	...	88.7	0.1	232.8	1.0	...	14.0	...	...	...	...	...	...
...	55.2	46.5	7.4	45.8	10.1	...	...	24.3	0.1	343.1	1.9	...	10.6	...	...	...	...	...	...
...	34.3	44.8	7.3	42.3	9.1	...	...	5.1	0.1	486.0	2.6	...	9.5	...	...	...	...	...	...
...	80.4	45.9	2.5	17.7	2.9	...	...	-9.9	0.1	651.1	2.6	...	3.3	...	...	...	...	...	...
Principal Lines of Business: CrdLife (100.0%)																			
796	92.8	7.4	-0.4	-0.2	-1.0	3.21	4.12	7.2	4.0	85.2	...	...	0.4	166.8	180.9	...	...	...	...
3,290	89.2	9.3	2.5	1.4	6.0	3.68	5.46	2.8	3.8	86.5	...	...	8.9	158.3	173.2	...	...	...	...
1,663	88.1	9.5	3.6	2.1	8.4	3.94	5.04	-1.3	3.4	90.5	...	...	10.9	163.5	179.4	...	...	...	...
-33,614	89.8	8.1	2.7	1.7	6.4	3.71	-4.33	-4.6	3.6	78.6	...	...	-10.4	160.7	175.3	0.0	...	...	...
19,574	91.0	7.6	0.3	0.2	0.8	3.33	7.31	0.8	3.3	77.6	...	...	9.4	152.0	166.0	0.2	...	...	...
Principal Lines of Business: GrpA&H (100.0%)														Principal States: WI (100.0%)					
...	...	...	...	...	...	...	...	...	...	...	...	...	...	...	...	...	...	...	...
...	...	...	...	...	...	...	...	...	...	...	...	...	...	...	...	...	...	...	...
...	87.4	17.5	...	-3.2	...	...	...	...	10.3	30.1	...	49.8	...	107.9	107.9	...	...	...	...
...	87.0	17.6	-9.0	-2.5	-25.7	2.02	2.02	76.9	7.3	78.8	...	13.1	147.9	151.1	151.1	...	...	...	...
...	73.2	19.2	11.3	4.6	23.9	0.21	0.21	-11.6	4.4	97.5	...	25.4	46.4	171.9	171.9	...	...	...	...
Principal Lines of Business: Medicaid (90.1%), Medicare (9.9%)														Principal States: OH (100.0%)					

Data in U.S. Dollars

COMPANY NAME Ultimate Parent Association Principal Officer Mailing Address Dom. : Began Bus. : Struct. : Mktg. Specialty Phone # AMB# NAIC#	Best's Financial Strength Rating FSC	Data Year	Balance Sheet: Bonds (%)	Mort. Loans & R.E. (%)	Com & Pref. Stock (%)	All Other Assets (%)	Total Assets ($000)	Life Reserves (%)	Health Reserves (%)	Ann Res. & Dep. Liabilities (%)	All Other Liabilities (%)	Capital & Surplus ($000)	Operations: Direct Premiums Written ($000)	Net Premiums Written & Deposits ($000)	Operating Cash Flow ($000)	NOG Before Taxes ($000)	NOG After Taxes ($000)	Net Income ($000)
WELLCARE OF TEXAS INC[2] WellCare Health Plans, Inc. Heath G. Schiesser President & CEO P.O. Box 31391 Tampa, FL 33631-3391 TX : 2008 : Stock : Not Available Medicare 813-243-2974 AMB# 064954 NAIC# 12964	NR-5	'05	...	...	...	...	...	...	...	...	...	...	...	...	...	...	...	...
		'06	...	...	...	...	...	...	...	...	...	...	...	...	...	...	...	...
		'07	41.4	...	...	58.6	4,088	...	...	...	100.0	4,054	...	...	4,072	98	64	64
		'08	11.6	...	...	88.4	14,664	...	88.5	...	11.5	1,513	40,505	40,254	8,194	-7,992	-5,206	-5,206
		'09	6.0	...	...	94.0	28,403	...	83.7	...	16.3	11,759	77,626	76,267	13,069	3,482	2,037	2,037
		Rating History: NR-5, 03/25/10; NR-5, 03/27/09; NR-5, 07/02/08																
WELLMARK HEALTH PLAN OF IOWA Wellmark Inc Timothy R. Weber President 636 Grand Avenue Des Moines, IA 50309-2565 IA : 1997 : Stock : Broker Group A&H 515-245-4500 AMB# 064385 NAIC# 95531	A Rating Outlook: Negative FSC XI	'05	52.5	...	14.9	32.6	81,745	...	51.5	...	48.5	45,292	275,951	273,741	4,674	10,300	6,761	6,924
		'06	51.9	...	16.4	31.8	106,175	...	45.2	...	54.8	55,294	270,037	267,847	25,114	15,497	10,061	10,001
		'07	53.5	...	15.7	30.8	160,255	...	33.9	...	66.1	75,152	362,458	359,558	57,885	28,381	17,117	18,882
		'08	66.9	...	13.6	19.5	150,440	...	47.1	...	52.9	79,536	403,673	403,673	-14,294	22,823	14,771	7,199
		'09	56.0	...	16.4	27.6	154,763	...	40.9	...	59.1	97,289	295,275	295,275	-7,860	18,825	12,134	13,975
		Rating History: A g, 05/19/09; A g, 06/16/08; A g, 06/01/07; A g, 06/20/06; A g, 06/21/05																
WELLMARK INC Wellmark Inc John D. Forsyth Chairman, President & CEO 636 Grand Avenue Des Moines, IA 50309-2565 IA : 1939 : Mutual : Broker Group A&H, Med supp, FEHBP 515-245-4500 AMB# 068347 NAIC# 88848	A Rating Outlook: Negative FSC XI	'05	31.1	0.9	58.3	9.7	1,399,098	...	36.9	...	63.1	919,600	1,796,835	1,799,045	66,356	121,196	80,067	102,938
		'06	27.9	0.8	58.1	13.2	1,612,922	...	35.3	...	64.7	1,073,457	1,959,714	1,961,904	106,630	93,657	91,196	136,583
		'07	28.4	0.7	56.9	14.0	1,634,309	...	32.4	...	67.6	1,059,765	2,068,727	2,071,627	-28,289	5,921	4,908	14,086
		'08	25.0	3.1	48.9	23.1	1,338,628	...	39.3	...	60.7	809,257	2,022,522	2,022,522	-198,413	-26,690	-11,241	-177,927
		'09	24.3	1.7	50.9	23.1	1,452,723	...	38.8	...	61.2	880,454	2,124,967	2,124,967	85,233	-81,544	-56,561	-146
		Rating History: A g, 05/19/09; A g, 06/16/08; A g, 06/01/07; A g, 06/20/06; A g, 06/21/05																
WELLMARK OF SOUTH DAKOTA INC Wellmark Inc Philip M. Davis President & COO 1601 West Madison Street Sioux Falls, SD 57104 SD : 1996 : Stock : Broker Group A&H, FEHBP, Med supp 605-373-7200 AMB# 060207 NAIC# 60128	A Rating Outlook: Negative FSC XI	'05	50.1	0.7	29.8	19.4	230,804	...	43.3	...	56.7	121,791	416,493	416,493	25,751	23,582	17,791	21,619
		'06	49.6	0.6	30.0	19.9	265,919	...	41.6	...	58.4	149,975	471,848	471,848	18,359	24,963	19,507	23,668
		'07	47.8	0.5	28.5	23.2	278,046	...	39.7	...	60.3	157,247	503,077	503,077	5,860	796	4,176	6,771
		'08	45.5	0.6	24.4	29.5	243,339	...	44.9	...	55.1	124,663	544,816	544,816	-36,220	-5,159	-3,233	-26,918
		'09	38.5	0.5	27.0	34.0	277,427	...	43.5	...	56.5	119,466	579,101	579,101	21,712	-26,724	-17,252	-12,676
		Rating History: A g, 05/19/09; A g, 06/16/08; A g, 06/01/07; A g, 06/20/06; A g, 06/21/05																
WELLPATH OF SOUTH CAROLINA Coventry Health Care Inc Beverly Allen CEO 1333 Gratiot, Brewery Park One Detroit, MI 48207 SC : 2006 : Stock : Broker Medicaid 313-465-1519 AMB# 064871 NAIC# 12604	NR-2	'05	...	...	...	...	...	...	...	...	...	...	...	...	...	...	...	...
		'06	...	...	...	100.0	629	...	...	...	100.0	413	...	...	610	-282	-187	-187
		'07	11.4	...	...	88.6	2,628	...	1.5	...	98.5	1,708	15	15	1,985	-828	-546	-546
		'08	5.0	...	...	95.0	5,959	...	48.4	...	51.6	865	5,646	5,506	2,427	-2,701	-2,147	-2,147
		'09	6.9	...	...	93.1	4,327	...	94.6	...	5.4	3,060	13,436	13,200	-1,030	-1,949	-892	-892
		Rating History: NR-2, 02/12/10; NR-2, 06/23/09; NR-2, 03/24/08; NR-2, 11/30/06																
WELLPATH SELECT INC Coventry Health Care Inc Tracy H. Baker President & CEO 2801 Slater Road, Suite 200 Morrisville, NC 27560 NC : 1996 : Stock : Broker Group A&H, Health 919-337-1800 AMB# 064274 NAIC# 95321	B++ Rating Outlook: Stable FSC VI	'05	68.7	...	...	31.3	53,967	...	69.8	...	30.2	30,441	213,325	209,282	2,982	19,890	13,982	14,095
		'06	66.8	...	...	33.2	58,308	...	59.6	...	40.4	39,410	210,143	206,114	4,881	26,866	18,967	18,972
		'07	78.3	...	...	21.7	51,462	...	64.8	...	35.2	29,727	222,691	217,672	-6,418	21,622	15,903	15,903
		'08	76.1	...	...	23.9	54,238	...	57.0	...	43.0	24,519	256,414	250,686	1,873	13,690	9,101	8,153
		'09	70.0	...	...	30.0	54,336	...	72.5	...	27.5	29,550	232,074	227,752	-3,867	6,405	4,862	5,215
		Rating History: B++, 02/12/10; B++, 11/19/08; B++, 10/30/07; B++, 07/11/07; B++, 10/27/06																
WEST COAST LIFE INS CO Protective Life Corporation Carolyn Johnson President 2801 Highway 280 South Birmingham, AL 35223 NE : 1915 : Stock : Agency ISWL, Term Life, Univ Life 415-591-8200 AMB# 007222 NAIC# 70335	A+ Rating Outlook: Negative FSC XV	'05	82.5	11.2	0.0	6.3	2,752,463	94.0	0.0	1.0	4.9	260,455	560,203	203,544	233,267	38,365	30,114	27,503
		'06	72.0	16.4	8.8	2.9	3,004,311	93.9	0.0	0.9	5.1	337,993	609,834	202,401	229,970	13,784	8,263	12,956
		'07	70.7	16.0	9.4	3.8	3,130,421	95.0	0.0	0.9	4.1	299,377	759,475	230,703	130,197	-59,538	-49,175	-49,682
		'08	63.5	21.2	8.4	6.9	3,400,574	93.6	0.0	2.1	4.3	333,302	761,648	373,077	200,835	-86,833	-71,697	-121,083
		'09	66.7	20.9	3.9	8.5	3,529,519	93.3	0.0	3.7	3.0	525,617	773,864	449,651	74,628	-35,503	-36,760	-95,921
		Rating History: A+ g, 10/09/09; A+ g, 02/11/09; A+ g, 06/02/08; A+ g, 04/02/07; A+ g, 02/08/06																
WESTERN AMERICAN LIFE INS CO Maximum Corporation William H. Lewis, Jr. Chairman & President P.O. Box 833879 Richardson, TX 75083-3879 TX : 1966 : Stock : Agency Pre-need, Trad Life, Whole life 972-699-2770 AMB# 007404 NAIC# 80993	NR-5	'05	92.0	...	2.2	5.8	32,544	90.3	0.2	0.2	9.2	1,550	3,934	3,726	3,200	1,014	843	842
		'06	93.8	...	1.5	4.7	32,949	89.9	0.2	0.2	9.7	2,084	3,887	3,727	292	1,453	1,099	1,081
		'07	94.6	...	1.3	4.1	33,106	89.9	0.2	0.3	9.6	2,489	3,726	3,576	40	1,161	1,105	1,146
		'08	92.5	...	1.9	5.6	32,648	90.1	0.2	0.3	9.4	2,335	3,532	3,392	-334	959	797	605
		'09	84.3	...	0.9	14.8	32,854	89.9	0.2	0.3	9.7	2,585	3,414	3,283	89	898	754	644
		Rating History: NR-5, 04/14/10; NR-5, 04/16/09; NR-5, 04/10/08; NR-5, 04/24/07; NR-5, 05/10/06																
WESTERN AND SOUTHERN LIFE INS Western & Southern Mutual Holding Co John F. Barrett Chairman, President & CEO 400 Broadway Cincinnati, OH 45202 OH : 1888 : Stock : Career Agent Life, Term Life, Trad Life 513-629-1800 AMB# 007243 NAIC# 70483	A+ Rating Outlook: Stable FSC XV	'05	36.1	2.2	40.1	21.6	8,308,135	48.6	4.6	5.3	41.4	3,070,525	298,083	406,361	99,607	144,124	124,863	144,008
		'06	36.7	1.5	43.4	18.3	9,097,602	46.0	4.7	4.9	44.4	3,515,012	297,287	393,560	492,194	97,216	64,938	154,049
		'07	35.0	1.4	42.8	20.8	8,832,318	50.7	5.3	5.3	38.7	3,705,965	296,303	381,504	47,547	210,741	210,456	264,345
		'08	39.8	1.4	35.6	23.1	7,727,827	59.0	6.0	6.0	29.0	3,301,984	292,949	374,376	83,805	253,828	233,327	295,051
		'09	44.1	1.0	32.0	22.9	7,955,404	58.8	5.4	6.2	29.7	3,464,875	292,220	329,946	-52,933	51,568	51,434	78,838
		Rating History: A+ g, 05/18/10; A+ g, 06/29/09; A++g, 07/09/08; A++g, 06/14/07; A++g, 06/21/06																

BEST'S PROFITABILITY, LEVERAGE AND LIQUIDITY TESTS 2005 – 2009

Data in U.S. Dollars

	Profitability Tests							Leverage Tests						Liquidity Tests					
Un-Realized Capital Gains ($000)	Benefits Paid to NPW & Dep (%)	Comm. & Expenses to NPW & Dep (%)	NOG to Total Assets (%)	NOG to Total Rev (%)	Operating Return on Equity (%)	Net Yield (%)	Total Return (%)	Change in NPW & Dep (%)	NPW & Dep to Capital (X)	Capital & Surplus to Liabilities (%)	Surplus Relief (%)	Reins Leverage (%)	Change in Capital (%)	Quick Liquidity (%)	Current Liquidity (%)	Non-Invest Grade Bonds to Capital (%)	Delinq. & Foreclosed Mortgages to Capital (%)	Mort. & Credit Tenant Loans & R.E. to Capital (%)	Affiliated Invest to Capital (%)
...	...	...	...	...	...	...	...	...	...	...	...	...	...	...	...	...	...	...	...
...	...	...	...	...	...	...	...	...	...	...	...	...	...	...	...	...	...	...	...
...	...	...	...	62.4	...	...	...	...	...	999.9	...	...	...	999.9	999.9	...	...	...	...
...	82.6	37.8	-55.5	-12.9	-99.9	2.69	2.69	...	26.6	11.5	...	...	-62.7	93.3	93.3	...	...	...	...
...	73.8	21.8	9.5	2.7	30.7	0.83	0.83	89.5	6.5	70.7	...	0.3	677.1	151.8	151.8	...	...	...	...

Principal Lines of Business: Medicare (100.0%) | Principal States: TX (100.0%)

211	87.6	9.5	8.8	2.4	16.0	3.93	4.55	24.8	6.0	124.2	...	...	14.9	143.6	159.2	1.6	...	...	...
1,284	86.5	8.9	10.7	3.7	20.0	4.01	5.63	-2.2	4.8	108.7	...	...	22.1	160.7	176.1	0.6	...	...	...
-773	84.9	8.5	12.8	4.7	26.2	4.01	4.86	34.2	4.8	88.3	...	...	35.9	168.2	183.3	...	...	...	...
-3,243	88.3	7.5	9.5	3.6	19.1	4.43	-3.27	12.3	5.1	112.2	...	...	5.8	135.3	151.4	0.0	...	...	...
3,104	87.4	8.2	8.0	4.0	13.7	4.51	8.47	-26.9	3.0	169.3	...	...	22.3	179.1	199.2	0.0	...	...	...

Principal Lines of Business: CompHosp/Med (100.0%) | Principal States: IA (100.0%)

44,488	82.6	11.3	6.0	4.4	10.2	1.97	7.54	3.2	2.0	191.8	...	...	42.0	158.5	187.8	0.6	...	1.4	21.9
35,917	83.3	13.7	6.1	4.6	9.2	2.34	8.42	9.1	1.8	199.0	...	...	16.7	150.2	178.4	0.7	...	1.2	22.6
15,305	86.4	15.3	0.3	0.2	0.5	2.75	4.47	5.6	2.0	184.5	...	0.0	-1.3	135.3	162.5	0.8	...	1.1	24.9
-91,865	87.1	16.0	-0.8	-0.5	-1.2	2.99	-16.56	-2.4	2.5	152.9	...	...	-23.6	111.6	132.1	0.7	...	5.0	33.2
63,059	89.7	14.5	-4.1	-2.7	-6.7	2.10	12.85	5.1	2.4	153.9	...	...	8.8	136.1	158.2	0.3	...	2.8	27.8

Principal Lines of Business: CompHosp/Med (64.4%), MedSup (14.5%), FEHBP (9.5%), OtherHlth (9.0%), Medicare (1.4%) | Principal States: IA (99.5%)

361	84.6	11.0	8.2	4.1	17.1	3.35	5.50	13.0	3.4	111.7	...	...	40.3	150.3	168.9	3.8	...	1.4	1.4
4,096	84.6	12.0	7.9	4.1	14.4	3.93	7.64	13.3	3.1	129.4	...	...	23.1	149.9	169.8	5.8	...	1.1	1.1
-610	89.1	12.8	1.5	0.8	2.7	4.15	4.97	6.6	3.2	130.2	...	0.2	4.8	149.1	170.5	5.8	...	1.0	1.0
-11,060	89.8	12.9	-1.2	-0.6	-2.3	4.59	-10.72	8.3	4.4	105.0	...	...	-20.7	109.1	126.2	6.3	...	1.2	1.2
9,287	93.4	12.0	-6.6	-3.0	-14.1	4.18	11.04	6.3	4.8	75.6	...	...	-4.2	124.6	137.2	3.0	...	1.2	1.2

Principal Lines of Business: CompHosp/Med (65.6%), FEHBP (20.1%), MedSup (9.4%), OtherHlth (3.5%), Medicare (1.4%) | Principal States: SD (100.0%)

...	...	...	...	...	...	...	...	...	...	...	...	...	...	...	...	...	...	...	...
...	...	...	...	-99.9	...	...	...	...	...	191.6	...	...	...	537.3	565.5	...	...	...	...
...	107.4	999.9	-33.5	-99.9	-51.4	5.73	5.73	...	0.0	185.8	...	...	313.3	504.9	529.8	...	...	...	...
...	96.5	39.0	-50.0	-38.5	-99.9	1.88	1.88	999.9	6.4	17.0	...	8.2	-49.4	187.9	197.9	...	...	...	...
...	103.1	15.6	-17.3	-6.9	-45.5	0.63	0.63	139.7	4.3	241.6	...	3.2	253.7	582.6	612.5	...	...	...	...

Principal Lines of Business: Medicaid (100.0%) | Principal States: SC (100.0%)

...	79.1	12.3	26.8	6.6	49.0	4.20	4.43	1.3	6.9	129.4	...	3.5	14.5	240.2	261.2	...	...	...	...
...	74.5	13.6	33.8	9.1	54.3	4.82	4.83	-1.5	5.2	208.6	...	2.7	29.5	305.1	331.2	...	...	...	...
...	72.6	18.8	29.0	7.2	46.0	5.49	5.49	5.6	7.3	136.8	...	6.1	-24.6	242.7	266.1	...	...	...	...
...	78.5	16.8	17.2	3.6	33.6	4.35	2.47	15.2	10.2	82.5	...	13.4	-17.5	186.3	203.3	...	...	...	...
...	79.8	17.9	9.0	2.1	18.0	3.36	4.08	-9.1	7.7	119.2	...	4.4	20.5	211.3	229.5	...	...	...	...

Principal Lines of Business: CompHosp/Med (100.0%) | Principal States: NC (87.7%), SC (12.3%)

765	35.2	22.4	1.1	6.3	13.5	6.09	6.06	2.1	0.7	11.4	46.6	703.3	34.8	62.0	74.6	30.1	1.5	108.9	...
35,241	63.4	29.9	0.3	1.7	2.8	5.87	7.33	-0.6	0.6	13.9	36.2	651.6	29.5	51.6	64.7	11.0	0.3	134.2	51.4
-6,073	64.4	54.3	-1.6	-8.8	-15.4	5.77	5.58	14.0	0.7	12.1	54.3	913.6	-7.6	51.2	64.7	23.7	0.3	148.2	43.0
-24,036	40.5	32.8	-2.2	-15.3	-22.7	5.65	3.42	61.7	1.1	11.1	32.2	957.5	0.5	47.6	58.7	47.5	0.2	211.9	35.4
8,666	69.0	33.5	-1.1	-7.5	-8.6	5.59	4.16	20.5	0.8	17.7	16.0	668.0	55.7	50.7	63.7	33.8	0.1	139.2	24.6

Principal Lines of Business: GrpAnn (50.8%), OrdLife (47.8%), IndAnn (1.4%), IndA&H (0.0%) | Principal States: CA (17.4%), TX (6.5%), FL (6.1%), PA (4.8%), IL (4.5%)

6	78.2	35.9	2.7	16.6	53.9	4.77	4.78	7.7	2.3	5.2	...	58.1	-1.3	78.0	88.4	...	...	...	...
9	68.8	35.4	3.4	21.2	60.5	4.82	4.93	0.0	1.7	7.0	...	41.7	32.8	77.8	88.4	8.1	...	...	...
10	76.4	37.2	3.3	21.8	48.3	4.87	5.20	-4.1	1.4	8.4	...	35.3	19.8	81.6	92.1	12.5	...	...	...
-103	78.0	38.4	2.4	16.6	33.1	4.61	3.83	-5.1	1.5	7.7	...	36.7	-9.2	71.9	82.6	4.2	...	...	...
109	78.2	38.8	2.3	16.2	30.7	4.47	4.69	-3.2	1.3	8.6	...	32.7	11.7	93.3	104.2	2.5	...	...	...

Principal Lines of Business: OrdLife (99.5%), IndA&H (0.5%), IndAnn (0.0%) | Principal States: TX (100.0%)

725	123.6	12.5	1.5	16.6	4.2	4.95	5.37	1.9	0.1	81.8	0.0	24.8	4.2	78.7	97.6	4.7	0.2	5.4	36.1
341,062	136.3	6.2	0.7	8.7	2.0	4.67	10.50	-3.2	0.1	87.9	0.0	20.9	14.2	84.5	105.1	3.4	0.0	3.6	44.9
-212,413	159.8	63.5	2.3	24.8	5.8	6.02	4.17	-3.1	0.1	94.6	0.0	19.2	0.7	79.6	99.9	2.1	0.0	3.3	53.0
-835,287	123.3	59.6	2.8	14.5	6.7	5.33	-4.46	-1.9	0.1	87.6	0.0	20.7	-14.5	74.3	90.5	3.0	0.0	3.4	64.9
100,604	119.2	63.5	0.7	9.2	1.5	3.88	5.79	-11.9	0.1	97.5	0.0	20.1	7.7	74.2	89.1	8.5	0.0	2.3	67.4

Principal Lines of Business: OrdLife (74.1%), GrpAnn (10.4%), IndA&H (9.8%), IndLife (4.5%), GrpLife (1.1%) | Principal States: OH (23.7%), NC (9.1%), IL (8.1%), IN (7.5%), PA (4.5%)

Data in U.S. Dollars

COMPANY NAME / Ultimate Parent Association / Principal Officer / Mailing Address / Dom. : Began Bus. : Struct. : Mktg. / Specialty / Phone # / AMB# NAIC#	Best's Financial Strength Rating / FSC	Data Year	Balance Sheet: Bonds (%)	Mort. Loans & R.E. (%)	Com & Pref. Stock (%)	All Other Assets (%)	Total Assets ($000)	Life Reserves (%)	Health Reserves (%)	Ann Res. & Dep. Liabilities (%)	All Other Liabilities (%)	Capital & Surplus ($000)	Operations: Direct Premiums Written ($000)	Net Premiums Written & Deposits ($000)	Operating Cash Flow ($000)	NOG Before Taxes ($000)	NOG After Taxes ($000)	Net Income ($000)
WESTERN DENTAL SERVICES INC Premier Dental Services Inc	B++	'05	...	...	...	100.0	120,476	...	...	...	100.0	47,109	103,172	103,172	11,517	722	932	932
Samuel H. Gruenbaum, President		'06	...	...	...	100.0	432,764	...	...	...	100.0	391,119	112,347	112,347	11,669	-16,741	-26,672	-26,672
P.O. Box 14227, Orange, CA 92868	Rating Outlook: Stable	'07	...	...	...	100.0	437,183	...	...	...	100.0	383,496	128,428	128,428	12,091	41,864	24,427	24,427
CA : 1985 : Stock : Not Available; Dental		'08	...	...	...	100.0	376,664	...	...	...	100.0	321,776	146,013	146,013	15,922	-37,448	-27,535	-27,535
714-480-3000		'09	...	...	...	100.0	390,329	...	...	...	100.0	350,266	154,803	154,803	34,888	48,075	28,835	28,835
AMB# 064651	FSC IX	**Rating History: B++, 05/05/10; B++, 06/12/09; B++, 01/10/08; B++, 11/22/06; A-, 11/21/05**																
WESTERN HEALTH ADVANTAGE	B+	'05	...	...	...	100.0	17,946	...	...	...	100.0	8,207	201,318	201,318	1,832	4,392	3,355	3,355
Garry Maisel, President & CEO		'06	...	...	...	100.0	21,691	...	...	...	100.0	8,814	235,145	235,145	5,995	1,126	608	608
2349 Gateway Oaks Drive, Suite 100, Sacramento, CA 95833	Rating Outlook: Stable	'07	...	...	...	100.0	27,989	...	...	...	100.0	10,383	276,893	276,893	7,046	2,451	1,582	1,582
CA : 1997 : Non-Profit : Not Available; Group A&H, Health		'08	...	...	...	100.0	27,221	...	...	...	100.0	11,572	280,266	280,266	2,950	2,065	1,182	1,182
916-563-2200		'09	...	...	...	100.0	30,204	...	...	...	100.0	13,250	276,291	276,291	1,649	2,906	1,669	1,669
AMB# 064577	FSC V	**Rating History: B+, 04/01/10; B+, 03/13/09; B+, 12/07/07; B, 11/21/06; C pd, 06/17/05**																
WESTERN MUTUAL INS CO	NR-5	'05	75.2	...	14.8	10.0	9,594	...	64.0	...	36.0	4,429	18,271	17,815	860	563	403	402
David T. Leo, President & CEO		'06	81.6	...	15.8	2.6	10,436	0.2	85.1	...	14.7	5,039	19,473	19,117	656	408	296	295
P.O. Box 572450, Murray, UT 84157-2450		'07	77.1	...	16.7	6.2	10,081	0.2	85.1	...	14.7	5,147	19,184	18,832	-231	108	88	235
UT : 1987 : Mutual : Other Direct; Group A&H		'08	76.7	...	12.2	11.1	10,888	0.2	63.8	...	36.0	5,585	18,871	18,498	854	648	704	462
801-263-8000		'09	79.1	...	12.1	8.7	11,663	0.2	68.5	...	31.4	5,821	20,149	19,754	483	348	187	56
AMB# 068150 NAIC# 68420		**Rating History: NR-5, 03/29/10; NR-5, 03/27/09; NR-5, 04/03/08; NR-5, 05/08/07; NR-5, 03/01/06**																
WESTERN NATIONAL LIFE INS CO American International Group, Inc	A	'05	90.5	2.9	2.6	4.0	54,002,929	0.3	...	96.3	3.4	3,934,817	5,906,354	220,231	3,093,359	708,995	488,493	431,441
Bruce R. Abrams, President & CEO		'06	86.4	3.7	5.1	4.8	53,107,957	0.3	...	96.2	3.5	4,211,921	4,201,291	-225,248	-873,017	737,872	372,604	416,533
P.O. Box 3206, A6-20, Houston, TX 77253-3206	Rating Outlook: Negative	'07	81.3	4.9	1.8	12.0	50,552,568	0.3	...	95.1	4.6	3,731,275	3,933,559	1,350,537	-2,885,145	653,172	375,907	-104,377
TX : 1944 : Stock : Agency; FPDA's, SPDA's, Struc Sett		'08	77.9	5.5	1.6	15.0	45,803,022	0.3	...	97.9	1.8	3,047,157	5,697,154	5,711,484	-12,023,845	372,962	231,207	-7,900,969
806-345-7400		'09	73.8	5.2	0.8	20.2	43,440,973	0.3	...	98.1	1.5	3,185,303	3,571,382	3,602,617	-1,849,903	317,543	317,938	-228,590
AMB# 007235 NAIC# 70432	FSC XV	**Rating History: A, 12/16/09; A, 11/10/08; A gu, 09/15/08; A+ g, 06/17/08; A++g, 05/28/08**																
WESTERN RESERVE LF ASSUR OF OH AEGON N.V.	A	'05	6.4	0.5	0.5	92.6	10,697,715	4.8	...	6.9	88.3	391,449	1,200,410	1,163,932	43,362	145,084	105,129	104,546
Timmy L. Stonehocker, Chairman of the Board		'06	5.4	0.6	0.2	93.8	11,528,514	9.0	...	5.9	85.1	467,098	1,229,016	1,177,910	103,860	179,622	111,644	111,989
4333 Edgewood Road N.E., Cedar Rapids, IA 52499	Rating Outlook: Stable	'07	5.9	0.5	0.2	93.3	11,768,905	9.5	...	5.4	85.1	488,703	1,083,730	1,024,545	72,629	196,241	134,278	131,655
OH : 1980 : Stock : Agency; Var life, Var ann		'08	7.6	0.6	0.4	91.4	8,127,643	14.4	0.0	8.1	77.4	280,092	989,727	794,378	137,610	-114,141	-59,497	-59,128
319-355-8511		'09	8.9	0.6	0.4	90.2	8,821,381	13.3	0.0	7.4	79.3	363,146	768,173	668,110	-25,980	180,671	139,919	115,655
AMB# 007239 NAIC# 91413	FSC XV	**Rating History: A g, 04/23/09; A+ g, 06/18/08; A+ g, 05/30/07; A+ g, 06/21/06; A+ g, 05/13/05**																
WESTERN-SOUTHERN LIFE ASSUR Western & Southern Mutual Holding Co	A+	'05	83.6	4.4	2.5	9.6	9,132,725	12.4	...	79.3	8.3	578,102	958,422	886,562	63,734	127,479	92,385	96,402
John F. Barrett, Chairman, President & CEO		'06	84.5	4.1	5.1	6.3	8,732,436	13.3	...	80.6	6.0	631,420	925,464	1,083,169	-97,083	105,916	77,657	91,161
400 Broadway, Cincinnati, OH 45202	Rating Outlook: Stable	'07	82.7	4.7	5.0	7.5	9,294,094	12.7	...	82.4	5.0	693,651	815,432	1,724,905	536,656	118,674	83,154	40,147
OH : 1981 : Stock : Career Agent; Ind Ann, Ind Life, Var ann		'08	83.7	5.9	4.7	5.8	10,031,439	12.1	...	85.0	3.0	868,681	1,388,981	1,480,105	588,886	7,837	7,686	-109,123
513-629-1800		'09	86.2	6.4	1.2	6.2	10,884,697	11.3	...	84.9	3.8	1,005,041	1,206,278	1,218,942	714,272	104,123	92,607	-57,389
AMB# 009071 NAIC# 92622	FSC XV	**Rating History: A+ g, 05/18/10; A+ g, 06/29/09; A++g, 07/09/08; A++g, 06/14/07; A++g, 06/21/06**																
WESTERN UNITED LIFE ASSUR CO[2] Global Life Acquisition LLC	NR-5	'05	57.6	22.8	1.2	18.4	1,159,580	0.0	...	95.3	4.7	41,664	72,728	24,144	-217,435	-12,785	-12,785	-29,271
Wayne C. Metcalf, III, Chief Deputy Receiver		'06	75.5	8.8	1.3	14.4	1,011,611	0.0	...	93.9	6.1	47,680	72,664	84,550	-159,661	-7,756	-7,756	-4,927
P.O. Box 2290, Spokane, WA 99210-2217		'07	76.2	6.2	1.6	16.0	812,526	...	...	95.4	4.6	45,557	66,206	73,977	-203,912	-3,386	-3,386	-48
WA : 1963 : Stock : Broker; Ind Ann, ISWL, Whole life		'08	77.5	4.0	2.4	16.1	713,965	...	...	96.8	3.2	26,144	77,429	110,501	-104,040	-4,236	-4,236	-10,997
800-247-2045		'09	88.1	3.6	1.4	6.9	764,475	0.6	...	85.3	14.1	27,249	155,666	80,821	50,578	-4,233	-4,233	-10,018
AMB# 008077 NAIC# 77925		**Rating History: NR-5, 04/26/10; NR-5, 04/24/09; NR-5, 12/17/08; E, 03/04/04; C, 01/14/04**																
WESTPORT LIFE INS CO IAC Group Inc	B+	'05	85.7	...	...	14.3	18,338	72.8	20.4	...	6.8	8,642	...	9,187	-962	1,299	1,107	1,107
Robert E. Stroud, President		'06	83.6	...	...	16.4	18,047	72.2	20.5	...	7.2	9,416	...	7,231	-376	1,899	1,602	1,602
2400 West 75th Street, Prairie Village, KS 66208-3509	Rating Outlook: Stable	'07	87.5	...	...	12.5	16,052	72.8	19.7	...	7.4	8,208	...	6,462	-1,351	1,873	1,591	1,591
AZ : 1984 : Stock : Other Direct; Credit A&H, Credit Life		'08	90.8	...	...	9.2	14,570	68.2	20.0	...	11.8	7,888	...	4,510	-1,058	1,020	860	860
913-432-1451		'09	90.3	...	...	9.7	14,736	64.4	17.3	...	18.3	8,108	...	2,656	172	1,138	949	949
AMB# 068070 NAIC# 62332	FSC V	**Rating History: B+ g, 04/30/10; B+ g, 05/01/09; B+ g, 06/02/08; B+, 04/20/07; B+, 03/27/06**																
WESTWARD LIFE INS CO MF Salta Company Inc	B+	'05	81.5	...	13.3	5.1	47,143	13.2	23.4	17.7	45.7	41,582	2,987	827	-1,808	2,349	1,957	2,494
Michele F. Salta, Chairman & President		'06	76.0	...	17.2	6.7	24,225	7.0	15.6	17.1	60.3	19,227	3,576	1,138	-23,373	2,579	2,273	2,308
9 Executive Circle, Suite 200, Irvine, CA 92614	Rating Outlook: Stable	'07	72.0	...	17.2	10.8	23,666	4.3	15.1	7.2	73.4	19,958	3,013	946	-644	863	730	730
AZ : 1965 : Stock : Agency; Ann, Credit A&H, Credit Life		'08	48.3	...	...	51.7	23,622	0.2	1.0	2.2	96.7	11,137	1,383	456	2,983	2,027	2,006	3,351
949-250-8627		'09	95.1	...	...	4.9	10,373	0.1	1.9	13.3	84.7	8,300	181	90	-13,223	-53	-33	48
AMB# 008115 NAIC# 78301	FSC IV	**Rating History: B+, 10/05/09; B+, 09/18/08; B+, 10/15/07; B+, 03/19/07; B+, 01/20/06**																

BEST'S PROFITABILITY, LEVERAGE AND LIQUIDITY TESTS 2005 – 2009

Data in U.S. Dollars

—	Profitability Tests							Leverage Tests						Liquidity Tests					
Un-Realized Capital Gains ($000)	Benefits Paid to NPW & Dep (%)	Comm. & Expenses to NPW & Dep (%)	NOG to Total Assets (%)	NOG to Total Rev (%)	Operating Return on Equity (%)	Net Yield (%)	Total Return (%)	Change in NPW & Dep (%)	NPW & Dep to Capital (X)	Capital & Surplus to Liabilities (%)	Surplus Relief (%)	Reins Leverage (%)	Change in Capital (%)	Quick Liquidity (%)	Current Liquidity (%)	Non-Invest Grade Bonds to Capital (%)	Delinq. & Foreclosed Mortgages to Capital (%)	Mort. & Credit Tenant Loans & R.E. to Capital (%)	Affiliated Invest to Capital (%)
...	222.8	62.1	0.9	0.3	1.7	43.14	43.14	10.8	2.2	64.2	...	...	-25.0	3.1	3.1	...	...	...	...
...	257.1	60.3	-9.6	-7.8	-12.2	25.13	25.13	8.9	0.3	939.2	...	...	730.2	4.3	4.3	...	...	...	...
...	225.1	23.0	5.6	6.8	6.3	28.42	28.42	14.3	0.3	714.3	...	...	-1.9	7.0	7.0	...	...	...	...
...	220.1	18.7	-6.8	-8.8	-7.8	5.75	5.75	13.7	0.5	586.2	...	...	-16.1	5.3	5.3	...	...	...	...
...	215.5	17.5	7.5	7.1	8.6	0.02	0.02	6.0	0.4	874.3	...	...	8.9	52.3	52.3	...	...	...	...
	Principal Lines of Business: Dental (100.0%)																		
...	88.9	9.0	15.5	1.7	51.4	-0.04	-0.04	25.2	24.5	84.3	...	...	69.2	90.1	90.1	...	...	...	...
...	90.5	9.2	3.1	0.3	7.1	0.44	0.44	16.8	26.7	68.4	...	...	7.4	113.6	113.6	...	...	...	...
...	90.7	8.7	6.4	0.6	16.5	2.25	2.25	17.8	26.7	59.0	...	...	17.8	117.0	117.0	...	...	...	...
...	90.4	9.1	4.3	0.4	10.8	2.11	2.11	1.2	24.2	73.9	...	...	11.5	146.1	146.1	...	...	...	...
...	89.7	9.5	5.8	0.6	13.4	0.80	0.80	-1.4	20.9	78.2	...	...	14.5	144.0	144.0	...	...	...	...
	Principal Lines of Business: CompHosp/Med (85.2%), Medicaid (10.3%), Medicare (4.5%)																		
60	79.8	18.2	4.4	2.2	9.5	1.37	1.94	2.6	3.8	96.4	...	0.7	10.5	158.1	177.3	...	...	...	4.0
228	82.5	17.5	3.0	1.5	6.2	2.84	5.09	7.3	3.6	102.0	...	6.7	11.9	157.7	178.9	...	...	...	4.3
-159	82.7	18.7	0.9	0.5	1.7	2.78	2.58	-1.5	3.5	114.0	...	0.1	1.9	166.9	188.4	...	...	...	4.8
-165	79.0	19.7	6.7	3.7	13.1	3.02	-1.01	-1.8	3.3	106.5	...	...	4.6	164.7	183.8	...	...	...	5.0
180	81.6	18.4	1.7	0.9	3.3	2.32	2.67	6.8	3.3	103.2	...	3.8	5.5	158.0	176.5	...	...	...	5.0
	Principal Lines of Business: GrpA&H (99.6%), GrpLife (0.4%)													Principal States: MT (57.2%), UT (16.9%), NV (10.9%), ID (8.1%), AZ (5.0%)					
158,574	999.9	29.4	0.9	6.6	13.1	6.07	6.32	-72.8	0.0	9.2	8.9	5.1	15.2	59.2	74.1	84.6	0.2	38.4	46.4
282,300	-99.9	-17.5	0.7	7.4	9.1	6.09	6.71	-99.9	0.0	10.6	6.9	1.7	11.8	58.3	73.5	75.9	0.1	42.5	48.8
34,313	448.1	9.7	0.7	8.6	9.5	6.05	5.14	699.6	0.3	10.8	5.2	0.7	-3.2	57.5	72.5	76.5	...	53.2	15.0
-544,996	91.1	5.7	0.5	7.1	6.8	6.19	-10.91	322.9	1.8	7.7	2.0	0.0	-33.5	56.7	71.9	102.4	...	82.1	20.8
-188,302	95.8	5.6	0.7	21.2	10.2	5.83	3.79	-36.9	1.1	8.3	1.5	0.0	2.1	57.8	79.0	89.9	2.4	71.2	19.7
	Principal Lines of Business: IndAnn (100.0%), GrpAnn (0.0%), OrdLife (0.0%)													Principal States: CA (16.6%), OH (12.7%), TX (10.4%), FL (6.2%), NJ (6.2%)					
17,411	93.4	22.5	1.0	7.7	31.4	8.12	9.65	0.6	2.9	47.8	0.9	21.3	40.4	58.6	69.6	12.7	...	14.4	22.2
-28,376	98.7	23.5	1.0	7.9	26.0	5.71	3.27	1.2	2.5	55.0	2.0	21.9	17.0	74.8	85.1	6.8	...	13.7	13.2
639	130.0	28.9	1.2	10.4	28.1	5.81	5.61	-13.0	2.1	55.1	2.4	27.8	4.8	59.4	70.8	5.9	...	12.7	14.6
1,738	158.2	290.7	-0.6	-2.0	-15.5	5.46	5.58	-22.5	2.8	18.1	-4.0	103.4	-42.6	45.5	58.7	15.5	...	17.8	22.5
161	121.3	29.6	1.7	12.8	43.5	3.47	1.77	-15.9	1.8	28.9	12.1	92.8	30.6	53.9	65.9	14.6	...	13.3	25.9
	Principal Lines of Business: OrdLife (74.9%), IndAnn (14.1%), GrpAnn (10.6%), GrpA&H (0.2%), GrpLife (0.2%)													Principal States: CA (32.6%), IL (9.9%), TX (8.3%), FL (3.7%)					
-1,033	119.2	11.2	1.0	6.9	17.3	5.83	5.92	-13.4	1.4	7.8	4.3	3.4	18.8	63.4	76.6	89.0	...	63.7	2.9
-6,219	142.8	10.3	0.9	6.0	12.8	5.94	6.05	22.2	1.5	9.0	3.6	2.9	9.9	60.5	76.4	86.3	...	52.2	13.6
31,000	80.0	5.9	0.9	7.0	12.6	5.84	5.71	59.2	2.3	8.9	3.2	2.9	5.2	61.9	78.1	71.5	...	59.9	13.3
-32,066	57.4	12.9	0.1	0.4	1.0	6.01	4.43	-14.2	1.7	9.6	2.3	1.9	16.2	60.5	74.3	93.2	...	68.9	10.4
35,272	75.5	12.2	0.9	5.2	9.9	5.85	4.73	-17.6	1.2	10.4	...	1.6	16.9	61.7	75.5	114.3	2.6	69.2	8.7
	Principal Lines of Business: IndAnn (87.0%), OrdLife (12.2%), GrpAnn (0.8%)													Principal States: OH (16.6%), MI (9.0%), PA (7.5%), WI (7.0%), IL (6.6%)					
6,524	653.3	36.5	-1.0	-20.1	-24.4	4.57	3.88	-75.4	0.5	4.8	0.2	356.1	-25.8	53.8	71.1	23.3	341.4	496.1	9.0
9,843	281.6	8.5	-0.7	-6.8	-17.4	3.74	5.13	250.2	1.5	6.1	4.2	276.2	8.3	61.9	81.1	12.3	122.9	153.9	...
-195	328.3	24.8	-0.4	-3.2	-7.3	4.57	5.09	-12.5	1.4	7.0	0.0	204.9	-7.8	66.6	85.9	5.4	63.9	94.0	...
-1,604	168.8	11.3	-0.6	-3.0	-11.8	4.49	3.51	49.4	3.8	4.2	0.6	203.5	-45.6	63.1	83.6	27.2	78.0	99.1	9.3
2,583	141.4	15.1	-0.6	-3.8	-15.9	4.67	4.46	-26.9	2.7	4.0	4.5	389.7	4.0	57.0	77.5	22.0	71.8	91.4	2.2
	Principal Lines of Business: IndAnn (100.0%), GrpAnn (0.0%)													Principal States: WA (36.9%), OR (30.2%), UT (11.2%), ND (7.3%), ID (6.4%)					
...	85.9	21.6	5.9	11.3	12.7	3.77	3.77	160.8	1.1	89.5	...	14.1	-1.3	154.4	160.6	...	...	...	...
...	67.7	26.0	8.8	20.4	17.7	3.86	3.87	-21.3	0.8	109.6	...	13.2	8.9	162.9	174.0	...	...	...	...
...	64.2	27.8	9.3	22.2	18.1	4.52	4.51	-10.6	0.8	105.2	...	7.9	-12.8	156.3	168.7	...	...	...	...
...	67.8	35.4	5.6	16.5	10.7	4.87	4.85	-30.2	0.6	118.8	...	3.0	-3.9	166.2	179.4	...	...	...	...
...	40.1	58.7	6.5	28.4	11.9	4.91	4.89	-41.1	0.3	123.1	...	2.8	2.8	170.9	183.8	...	...	...	...
	Principal Lines of Business: CrdLife (84.3%), CrdA&H (15.2%), GrpLife (0.5%)																		
-508	82.8	139.6	4.0	49.2	4.7	4.12	4.29	6.0	0.0	864.6	2.8	3.0	-3.3	701.9	784.0	2.4	...	...	10.0
-397	44.0	118.5	6.4	47.6	7.5	6.52	5.69	37.5	0.1	406.0	6.2	7.5	-54.0	386.7	412.1	...	...	...	20.5
-28	65.9	115.4	3.0	25.1	3.7	4.18	4.41	-16.9	0.0	584.6	4.5	6.9	4.0	561.5	587.7	...	...	...	20.1
-3,083	55.1	208.1	8.5	58.1	12.9	11.05	5.00	-51.8	0.0	89.4	3.6	0.4	-44.8	267.9	272.2	...	...	...	...
-102	108.1	606.0	-0.2	-6.0	-0.3	2.03	2.40	-80.2	0.0	403.3	0.3	0.5	-25.5	473.7	489.0	0.9	...	...	...
	Principal Lines of Business: GrpA&H (100.1%), OrdLife (0.4%), CrdLife (-0.2%), CrdA&H (-0.3%)													Principal States: AZ (54.6%), TX (38.3%), CA (7.4%)					

COMPANY NAME Ultimate Parent Association Principal Officer Mailing Address Dom. : Began Bus. : Struct. : Mktg. Specialty Phone # AMB# NAIC#	Best's Financial Strength Rating FSC	Data Year	Balance Sheet Bonds (%)	Mort. Loans & R.E. (%)	Com & Pref. Stock (%)	All Other Assets (%)	Total Assets ($000)	Life Reserves (%)	Health Reserves (%)	Ann Res. & Dep. Liabilities (%)	All Other Liabilities (%)	Capital & Surplus ($000)	Operations Direct Premiums Written ($000)	Net Premiums Written & Deposits ($000)	Operating Cash Flow ($000)	NOG Before Taxes ($000)	NOG After Taxes ($000)	Net Income ($000)
WICHITA NATIONAL LIFE INS CO Wichita National Life Insurance Company	B+	'05	4.0	2.6	8.0	85.5	18,271	72.6	20.7	...	6.7	6,604	7,013	5,615	-2,938	94	78	78
Randall B. Gilliland Chairman & President		'06	4.1	2.3	7.8	85.7	18,868	72.4	20.0	...	7.5	6,751	7,988	5,982	529	396	313	366
P.O. Box 1709 Lawton, OK 73502	Rating Outlook: Stable	'07	4.5	3.1	8.2	84.1	19,247	73.7	19.5	...	6.8	6,968	7,989	5,575	369	707	611	611
OK : 1957 : Stock : Broker Credit A&H, Credit Life, Trad Life		'08	4.9	3.0	8.8	83.2	19,001	74.1	19.1	...	6.8	7,016	6,887	5,069	-270	537	457	457
580-353-5776		'09	5.0	2.9	9.4	82.7	18,547	74.4	18.1	...	7.5	7,295	5,672	4,024	-471	518	448	448
AMB# 007248 NAIC# 70548	FSC IV	Rating History: B+, 11/24/09; B+, 10/22/08; B+, 11/15/07; B+, 01/09/07; B+, 02/07/06																
WILLAMETTE DENTAL INSURANCE[2] Willamette Dental of Idaho Inc	NR-5	'05	...	...	8.4	91.6	3,593	...	...	...	100.0	2,256	16,736	16,736	564	703	452	455
Eugene C. Skourtes, D.M.D. President & Secretary		'06	...	...	8.9	91.1	3,875	...	...	...	100.0	2,784	17,770	17,770	-64	735	442	590
6950 NE Campus Way Hillsboro, OR 97124-5611		'07	...	...	9.7	90.3	3,654	...	...	...	100.0	2,661	19,961	19,961	-724	-43	-20	6
OR : 1999 : Stock : Agency Dental		'08	...	...	5.9	94.1	3,501	...	...	...	100.0	2,698	23,698	23,698	855	204	204	95
503-952-2000		'09	...	...	6.8	93.2	4,012	...	...	...	100.0	3,102	26,359	26,359	533	513	332	374
AMB# 064497 NAIC# 52555		Rating History: NR-5, 04/08/10; NR-5, 09/11/09; NR-5, 07/14/08; NR-5, 07/02/07; NR-5, 05/03/06																
WILLAMETTE DENTAL OF IDAHO INC[2] Willamette Dental of Idaho Inc	NR-5	'05	...	...	78.0	22.0	6,936	...	6.0	...	94.0	6,577	3,872	3,872	361	183	125	125
Eugene C. Skourtes, D.M.D. President & Secretary		'06	...	...	78.4	21.6	8,546	...	3.4	...	96.6	7,900	5,638	5,638	611	364	248	248
6950 NE Campus Way Hillsboro, OR 97124-5611		'07	...	...	83.8	16.2	8,506	...	18.1	...	81.9	8,337	7,051	7,051	-695	397	262	262
ID : 1997 : Stock : Not Available Dental		'08	...	...	90.2	9.8	8,323	...	15.4	...	84.6	8,070	7,482	7,482	-233	173	118	118
503-952-2000		'09	...	...	92.9	7.1	8,660	...	23.0	...	77.0	8,485	7,411	7,411	-237	106	72	72
AMB# 064402 NAIC# 95819		Rating History: NR-5, 04/15/10; NR-5, 03/26/09; NR-5, 05/05/08; NR-5, 04/23/07; NR-5, 07/17/06																
WILLAMETTE DENTAL OF WA INC Willamette Dental of Idaho Inc	NR-5	'05	...	...	21.9	78.1	3,818	...	0.5	...	99.5	3,152	21,285	21,285	1,095	875	511	513
Eugene C. Skourtes, D.M.D. President & Secretary		'06	...	...	22.3	77.7	4,157	...	...	...	100.0	3,915	22,681	22,681	235	1,012	692	692
6950 NE Campus Way Hillsboro, OR 97124-5611		'07	...	...	32.8	67.2	4,767	...	...	...	100.0	4,467	23,240	23,240	746	939	616	662
WA : 1996 : Stock : Not Available Dental		'08	...	...	22.2	77.8	5,184	...	...	...	100.0	4,810	39,743	39,743	214	968	657	654
503-952-2000		'09	...	...	16.5	83.5	5,410	...	...	...	100.0	4,943	42,316	42,316	911	1,098	739	739
AMB# 064529 NAIC# 47050		Rating History: NR-5, 03/24/10; NR-5, 03/16/09; NR-5, 04/30/08; NR-5, 04/23/07; NR-5, 07/17/06																
WILLIAM PENN ASSOCIATION	B++	'05	90.3	0.6	4.7	4.3	193,105	23.6	0.1	72.2	4.2	25,036	23,671	24,179	11,881	150	150	419
George S. Charles, Jr. National President		'06	92.4	0.6	3.7	3.3	192,031	24.0	0.1	72.0	3.9	26,330	9,966	10,244	-671	380	380	874
709 Brighton Road Pittsburgh, PA 15233-1821	Rating Outlook: Negative	'07	91.9	0.6	4.4	3.2	188,435	24.8	0.0	71.3	3.8	26,555	8,566	8,837	-3,114	421	421	613
PA : 1886 : Fraternal : Career Agent Ind Ann, Ind Life		'08	87.1	0.9	4.9	7.1	186,748	24.2	0.0	72.7	3.0	21,609	13,315	13,652	923	90	90	-3,704
412-231-2979		'09	92.7	0.8	3.2	3.2	199,480	22.2	0.0	74.7	3.1	19,894	20,116	20,332	12,016	-31	-31	-1,181
AMB# 007249 NAIC# 57010	FSC V	Rating History: B++, 06/04/10; B++, 06/03/09; B++, 06/06/08; B++, 06/13/07; B++, 06/06/06																
WILLIAM PENN LIFE INS CO OF NY Legal & General Group plc	A+	'05	87.5	...	...	12.5	999,518	68.4	0.0	29.1	2.5	118,868	163,298	57,460	-47,824	21,885	21,754	21,768
James D. Atkins President		'06	90.3	...	...	9.7	989,171	70.7	0.0	27.6	1.7	120,700	166,797	56,435	21,207	18,674	17,356	17,356
1701 Research Boulevard Rockville, MD 20850	Rating Outlook: Stable	'07	89.0	...	0.8	10.2	976,986	72.3	0.0	25.9	1.8	110,476	172,151	52,987	-16,502	-3,237	290	-535
NY : 1963 : Stock : Broker Ind Life, Ind Ann		'08	89.5	...	0.8	9.7	965,647	73.3	0.0	24.2	2.5	96,013	175,560	30,511	2,444	-14,834	-13,521	-28,443
516-794-3700		'09	89.0	...	...	11.0	988,968	71.7	0.0	24.0	4.2	124,065	177,247	53,940	5,127	2,416	1,813	1,527
AMB# 006734 NAIC# 66230	FSC IX	Rating History: A+ g, 05/03/10; A+ g, 03/25/09; A+ g, 01/25/08; A+ g, 02/02/07; A+ g, 12/02/05																
WILLIAMS PROGRESSIVE L & A INS[1]	NR-1	'05	51.0	20.2	25.0	3.8	10,405	...	...	...	100.0	1,581	1,257	1,256	...	-199	-198	-87
Patrick Fontenot President & CEO		'06	48.7	19.7	27.6	4.0	11,060	...	...	...	100.0	1,983	1,263	1,262	...	-14	-15	320
323 South Academy Street Opelousas, LA 70570-7301		'07	45.4	24.0	26.4	4.2	11,246	...	...	...	100.0	2,251	1,320	1,318	...	288	262	478
LA : 1947 : Stock : Not Available		'08	45.5	28.6	19.8	6.2	10,539	...	...	...	100.0	1,671	1,469	1,469	...	-85	-85	-292
337-948-8238		'09	39.1	30.9	22.6	7.4	11,078	...	...	...	100.0	1,647	1,521	1,516	...	-22	-15	-47
AMB# 008118 NAIC# 78344		Rating History: NR-1, 06/10/10; NR-1, 06/12/09; NR-1, 06/12/08; NR-1, 06/08/07; NR-1, 06/07/06																
WILTON REASSURANCE COMPANY Wilton Re Holdings Limited	A-	'05	4.6	...	...	95.4	151,472	70.6	...	...	29.4	54,362	...	49,052	74,957	-23,941	-23,941	-23,941
Chris C. Stroup Chairman, President & CEO		'06	25.8	...	30.8	43.4	333,670	78.6	...	...	21.4	202,377	...	69,544	253,930	-123,435	-123,435	-123,529
187 Danbury Road, Riverview Building Wilton, CT 06897	Rating Outlook: Positive	'07	24.8	...	25.6	49.6	433,471	58.2	...	...	41.8	116,832	...	105,625	43,445	-82,490	-79,946	-79,942
MN : 1901 : Stock : Broker Reins		'08	29.2	...	12.1	58.6	668,443	81.3	...	12.5	6.2	126,425	...	406,109	361,466	8,551	9,565	5,062
203-762-4400		'09	60.4	...	13.5	26.1	1,179,640	83.2	0.6	7.4	8.8	258,305	...	31,341	351,201	-58,057	5,822	1,636
AMB# 060560 NAIC# 66133	FSC IX	Rating History: A- g, 04/06/10; A- g, 03/20/09; A- g, 01/18/08; A- g, 10/04/06; A- g, 02/08/06																
WILTON REASSURANCE LIFE CO NY Wilton Re Holdings Limited	A-	'05	92.6	...	0.7	6.8	1,338,489	36.5	0.0	58.2	5.3	125,889	115,117	65,481	-30,913	15,015	6,449	4,710
Chris C. Stroup Chairman, President & CEO		'06	90.3	...	1.3	8.4	1,264,263	37.4	0.0	58.6	4.0	100,808	96,147	57,994	-65,395	15,546	13,938	16,073
187 Danbury Road Wilton, CT 06897	Rating Outlook: Positive	'07	87.8	...	4.2	8.0	1,219,486	42.1	0.0	55.4	2.5	93,361	95,356	61,311	-46,061	-12,228	-14,554	-15,293
NY : 1956 : Stock : Direct Response Life, Ann		'08	85.2	...	7.5	7.3	1,184,341	46.5	0.0	50.9	2.6	70,632	85,249	64,674	-35,954	274	-717	-26,150
203-762-4400		'09	88.9	...	1.4	9.7	1,182,496	46.5	0.0	50.3	3.2	95,258	82,594	54,381	1,548	52,230	45,917	28,017
AMB# 006084 NAIC# 60704	FSC VIII	Rating History: A- g, 04/06/10; A- g, 03/20/09; A- g, 01/18/08; A- g, 10/04/06; B g, 01/19/06																

BEST'S PROFITABILITY, LEVERAGE AND LIQUIDITY TESTS 2005 – 2009

Data in U.S. Dollars

—	Profitability Tests							Leverage Tests						Liquidity Tests					
Un-Realized Capital Gains ($000)	Benefits Paid to NPW & Dep (%)	Comm. & Expenses to NPW & Dep (%)	NOG to Total Assets (%)	NOG to Total Rev (%)	Operating Return on Equity (%)	Net Yield (%)	Total Return (%)	Change in NPW & Dep (%)	NPW & Dep to Capital (X)	Capital & Surplus to Liabilities (%)	Surplus Relief (%)	Reins Leverage (%)	Change in Capital (%)	Quick Liquidity (%)	Current Liquidity (%)	Non-Invest Grade Bonds to Capital (%)	Delinq. & Foreclosed Mortgages to Capital (%)	Mort. & Credit Tenant Loans & R.E. to Capital (%)	Affiliated Invest to Capital (%)
67	49.8	70.0	0.4	1.0	1.2	3.12	3.47	-16.0	0.8	57.1	15.3	61.9	2.9	127.0	127.0	...	...	7.2	26.7
19	33.6	70.0	1.7	3.8	4.7	3.57	3.98	6.5	0.9	56.1	17.5	69.2	2.2	127.7	127.7	...	...	6.5	26.1
110	30.5	72.0	3.2	7.5	8.9	4.33	4.93	-6.8	0.8	57.3	19.6	70.7	3.3	127.1	127.1	...	...	8.6	26.6
98	40.4	75.2	2.4	6.2	6.5	4.08	4.60	-9.1	0.7	59.2	15.7	71.5	0.8	128.2	128.2	...	...	8.1	27.6
63	41.1	82.3	2.4	7.5	6.3	3.38	3.73	-20.6	0.5	65.7	12.6	63.8	4.0	132.5	132.5	...	...	7.4	27.3
	Principal Lines of Business: CrdLife (62.3%), OrdLife (19.5%), CrdA&H (18.1%), IndA&H (0.1%)													Principal States: OK (76.9%), AR (23.1%)					
17	90.2	6.4	13.2	2.7	19.9	1.15	1.93	24.2	7.4	168.6	...	...	-0.9	206.7	210.1	...	...	...	...
36	90.4	6.3	11.8	2.5	17.5	2.19	8.96	6.2	6.4	255.1	...	...	23.4	235.1	239.8	...	...	...	...
-37	88.7	12.0	-0.5	-0.1	-0.7	3.33	2.86	12.3	7.5	268.2	...	...	-4.4	179.5	184.8	...	...	...	...
-94	86.9	12.4	5.7	0.9	7.6	1.53	-7.03	18.7	8.8	335.9	...	...	1.4	329.9	333.8	...	...	...	...
43	91.3	6.9	8.9	1.3	11.5	0.11	2.93	11.2	8.5	341.0	...	...	15.0	349.4	353.9	...	...	...	...
	Principal Lines of Business: Dental (100.0%)													Principal States: OR (100.0%)					
861	81.9	11.9	2.0	3.3	2.0	0.02	15.71	38.6	0.6	999.9	...	...	16.0	261.4	261.4	...	...	...	82.2
1,291	81.9	10.1	3.2	4.5	3.4	0.02	19.43	45.6	0.7	999.9	...	...	20.1	239.9	239.9	...	...	...	84.8
430	82.0	10.7	3.1	3.8	3.2	0.04	5.48	25.1	0.8	999.9	...	...	5.5	505.4	505.4	...	...	...	85.5
379	83.9	9.0	1.4	1.7	1.4	0.03	4.85	6.1	0.9	999.9	...	...	-3.2	246.6	246.6	...	...	...	93.0
537	88.1	9.2	0.8	1.0	0.9	0.01	6.72	-1.0	0.9	999.9	...	...	5.1	220.0	220.0	...	...	...	94.8
	Principal Lines of Business: Dental (100.0%)													Principal States: ID (100.0%)					
15	89.9	6.2	15.4	2.4	17.7	0.93	1.52	12.4	6.8	473.6	...	...	20.0	465.1	484.0	...	...	...	...
59	90.1	5.8	17.4	3.0	19.6	2.67	4.34	6.6	5.8	999.9	...	...	24.2	999.9	999.9	...	...	...	...
-67	89.9	6.6	13.8	2.6	14.7	3.28	2.78	2.5	5.2	999.9	...	...	14.1	999.9	999.9	...	...	...	...
-144	92.1	5.7	13.2	1.6	14.2	2.06	-1.37	71.0	8.3	999.9	...	...	7.7	972.9	999.9	...	...	...	...
172	91.8	5.7	14.0	1.7	15.2	0.91	4.88	6.5	8.6	999.9	...	...	2.8	999.9	999.9	...	...	...	...
	Principal Lines of Business: Dental (100.0%)													Principal States: WA (100.0%)					
-189	73.0	20.8	0.1	0.4	0.6	5.93	6.08	-4.1	0.9	16.0	...	...	0.7	82.4	90.8	2.7	...	4.5	5.8
-249	173.6	45.7	0.2	1.8	1.5	5.96	6.18	-57.6	0.4	16.6	...	...	2.7	81.2	89.7	0.9	...	4.3	5.6
-345	202.2	53.7	0.2	2.1	1.6	6.02	6.03	-13.7	0.3	17.1	...	...	0.6	81.1	89.5	...	...	3.9	5.9
-2,161	107.6	35.0	0.0	0.4	0.4	6.00	2.94	54.5	0.6	13.1	...	...	-21.3	79.1	88.5	4.1	...	7.8	7.6
635	64.0	24.2	0.0	-0.1	-0.2	5.88	5.70	48.9	1.0	11.5	...	...	-4.7	70.8	81.5	6.5	...	8.1	8.9
	Principal Lines of Business: IndAnn (88.2%), OrdLife (11.8%), IndA&H (0.0%)													Principal States: PA (46.9%), OH (17.2%), IN (6.6%), MI (5.5%), FL (5.2%)					
392	132.1	49.3	2.2	17.3	19.2	5.93	6.13	-26.2	0.5	14.0	9.9	456.3	9.7	75.6	87.4	...	...	...	...
228	147.0	49.6	1.7	14.0	14.5	5.99	6.11	-1.8	0.5	14.4	9.4	518.0	1.6	79.4	90.4	7.9	...	...	...
-682	164.9	66.7	0.0	0.2	0.3	5.88	5.74	-6.1	0.5	13.1	11.0	660.6	-9.0	75.8	87.1	5.2	...	...	...
-195	267.7	55.2	-1.4	-12.5	-13.1	5.91	4.22	-42.4	0.3	11.0	26.2	832.7	-15.4	75.6	86.7	6.6	...	...	...
195	153.0	49.7	0.2	1.5	1.6	5.97	5.99	76.8	0.4	14.5	12.8	652.7	30.7	74.4	85.3	22.6	...	...	...
	Principal Lines of Business: OrdLife (88.4%), IndAnn (11.5%), IndA&H (0.1%)													Principal States: NY (78.9%), NJ (6.6%), FL (4.6%)					
58	64.7	85.4	-1.9	-11.1	-12.2	...	...	-4.4	0.6	23.7	...	...	-4.5	...	...	...	...	105.6	...
6	51.8	80.1	-0.1	-0.8	-0.8	...	...	0.4	0.5	29.0	...	...	24.6	...	...	...	...	87.7	...
-228	49.6	81.3	2.4	11.6	12.4	...	...	4.5	0.5	31.7	...	...	8.9	...	...	...	...	99.9	...
-634	53.9	68.7	-0.8	-4.2	-4.4	...	...	11.4	0.8	19.8	...	...	-35.8	...	...	...	...	173.2	...
333	55.9	66.1	-0.1	-0.7	-0.9	...	...	3.2	0.8	22.0	...	...	15.0	...	...	...	...	171.5	...
	Principal Lines of Business: OrdLife (90.6%), IndLife (9.4%)																		
...	14.2	39.3	-29.8	-30.6	-75.2	3.69	3.69	...	0.9	56.0	23.0	129.9	481.5	142.9	142.9	...	...	...	...
-56,070	88.8	237.5	-50.9	-65.8	-96.2	5.23	-22.44	41.8	0.3	154.1	31.7	107.5	272.2	136.8	145.8	...	...	...	50.7
-9,023	108.8	86.3	-20.8	-30.0	-50.1	5.37	2.24	51.9	0.9	36.9	58.2	308.8	-42.2	72.0	75.5	0.4	...	...	94.8
-47,731	27.9	13.9	1.7	1.6	7.9	4.28	-6.54	284.5	3.2	23.3	90.5	378.9	8.1	139.7	145.1	1.1	...	...	62.6
101,661	448.9	-99.9	0.6	1.0	3.0	12.40	25.31	-92.3	0.1	28.0	164.1	307.9	104.3	65.0	76.2	0.5	...	...	60.8
	Principal Lines of Business: OrdLife (90.0%), IndAnn (7.1%), IndA&H (2.8%)													Principal States: VA (91.5%), TN (8.5%)					
2,197	179.2	41.7	0.5	4.2	5.1	6.28	6.49	-23.2	0.5	10.6	7.4	113.4	-0.6	64.8	80.1	25.8	...	49.6	...
116	270.1	11.7	1.1	9.5	12.3	6.02	6.33	-11.4	0.5	9.1	5.7	160.8	-17.4	70.4	83.6	18.7	...	37.2	...
-2,075	251.7	18.5	-1.2	-10.4	-15.0	6.31	6.15	5.7	0.6	8.8	4.8	164.1	-7.1	70.3	81.9	19.8	...	...	...
-126	196.8	30.3	-0.1	-0.5	-0.9	5.99	3.90	5.5	0.9	6.4	6.9	211.9	-27.7	57.7	72.8	35.8	...	42.4	...
-113	175.2	12.8	3.9	36.2	55.4	6.16	4.64	-15.9	0.6	8.8	4.6	170.9	34.2	64.9	80.1	36.4	...	29.3	...
	Principal Lines of Business: OrdLife (82.2%), IndAnn (17.7%), IndA&H (0.1%), GrpLife (0.0%), GrpA&H (0.0%)													Principal States: NY (74.9%), FL (4.3%), PA (3.7%), NJ (3.5%)					

Data in U.S. Dollars

COMPANY NAME / Ultimate Parent Association / Principal Officer / Mailing Address / Dom. : Began Bus. : Struct. : Mktg. / Specialty / Phone # / AMB# NAIC#	Best's Financial Strength Rating / FSC	Data Year	Balance Sheet: Bonds (%)	Mort. Loans & R.E. (%)	Com & Pref. Stock (%)	All Other Assets (%)	Total Assets ($000)	Life Reserves (%)	Health Reserves (%)	Ann Res. & Dep. Liabilities (%)	All Other Liabilities (%)	Capital & Surplus ($000)	Operations: Direct Premiums Written ($000)	Net Premiums Written & Deposits ($000)	Operating Cash Flow ($000)	NOG Before Taxes ($000)	NOG After Taxes ($000)	Net Income ($000)
WILTON REINSURANCE BERMUDA LTD Wilton Re Holdings Limited	A-	'05	...	...	...	100.0	139,863	77.6	...	...	22.5	19,696	...	17,527	...	-304	-304	-304
Michael N. Smith, Chief Executive Officer		'06	5.2	...	...	94.8	2,373,762	99.4	...	...	0.6	290,900	...	31,660	...	24,851	24,851	24,820
Parlaville Place, 14 Par-la-Ville Road, Hamilton HM 08, Bermuda	Rating Outlook: Positive	'07	6.0	...	...	94.0	2,281,671	93.8	...	...	6.2	270,750	...	40,728	...	21,142	21,142	19,851
BM : Stock : Not Available; Life Reins		'08	3.9	...	...	96.1	2,197,653	94.6	...	...	5.4	240,829	...	86,525	...	-105,293	-105,293	-108,422
441-295-6752		'09	11.5	...	0.1	88.5	2,823,955	94.4	...	...	5.6	420,791	...	229,595	...	182,450	182,450	179,962
AMB# 077621	FSC VIII	Rating History: A- g, 04/06/10; A- g, 03/20/09; A- g, 01/18/08; A- g, 10/04/06; A- g, 02/08/06																
WINDSOR LIFE INSURANCE COMPANY Optimum Group Inc	NR-2	'05	82.2	...	...	17.8	2,860	64.9	...	...	35.1	2,638	913	234	58	6	6	6
Mario Georgiev, President		'06	91.2	...	...	8.8	2,927	66.0	...	...	34.0	2,699	860	251	90	23	21	33
1345 River Bend Drive, Suite 100, Dallas, TX 75247		'07	96.0	...	...	4.0	2,931	78.7	...	...	21.3	2,707	719	188	-6	4	2	2
TX : 1984 : Stock : Mng Gen Agent; Life		'08	95.6	...	...	4.4	2,794	31.5	...	...	68.5	2,721	115	37	-61	10	14	14
214-559-0850		'09	54.5	...	...	45.5	2,804	15.7	...	...	84.3	2,726	85	29	55	7	5	5
AMB# 068306 NAIC# 65960		Rating History: NR-2, 05/17/10; NR-2, 06/01/09; NR-2, 06/16/08; NR-2, 06/14/07; NR-2, 06/19/06																
WINNFIELD LIFE INS CO Realty Advisors Inc	NR-2	'05	55.0	23.1	0.9	21.0	33,173	85.1	...	11.9	3.1	3,898	1,890	1,890	18,067	362	186	214
Bradford A. Phillips, President & CEO		'06	60.1	10.8	2.7	26.4	39,412	77.5	...	10.8	11.7	7,487	2,115	2,115	6,178	360	-22	31
1010 RR 620 South, Suite 200, Austin, TX 78734		'07	70.6	10.7	5.1	13.7	38,745	78.7	...	11.3	10.0	7,957	1,923	1,923	-604	596	532	536
LA : 1936 : Stock : Agency; Ordinary Life, Ind Life, Ind Ann		'08	70.5	18.4	5.9	5.2	37,969	76.3	...	11.0	12.8	6,634	1,783	1,783	-275	477	381	-462
512-263-6977		'09	74.9	17.5	3.0	4.6	38,872	74.5	...	11.0	14.4	7,945	1,784	1,784	581	1,634	1,144	1,043
AMB# 008119 NAIC# 78352		Rating History: NR-2, 11/24/09; NR-2, 06/18/09; NR-2, 05/23/08; NR-2, 11/17/06; NR-2, 06/06/06																
WISCONSIN PHYSICIANS SRVC INS Wisconsin Physicians Service Ins Corp	NR-5	'05	26.5	14.3	25.1	34.0	226,193	...	41.6	...	58.4	95,077	416,522	414,516	2,730	18,953	19,103	20,519
James R. Riordan, President		'06	21.9	12.7	29.0	36.4	248,067	...	36.5	...	63.5	117,893	476,726	471,449	6,028	15,114	10,911	11,581
1717 West Broadway, Madison, WI 53713-1895		'07	17.3	12.0	28.7	41.9	286,418	...	35.6	...	64.4	141,520	480,705	476,104	33,968	26,420	15,125	17,155
WI : 1977 : Non-Profit : Not Available; Group A&H, Med supp, Dental		'08	27.2	12.3	23.2	37.4	277,459	...	31.7	...	68.3	136,624	454,806	450,379	11,185	23,243	17,000	15,926
608-221-4711		'09	24.0	10.8	29.0	36.2	303,346	...	32.1	...	67.9	167,082	435,660	430,814	19,591	3,226	7,180	5,575
AMB# 060073 NAIC# 53139		Rating History: NR-5, 03/24/10; NR-5, 03/16/09; NR-5, 03/11/08; NR-5, 05/03/07; NR-5, 05/22/06																
WISCONSIN VISION SERVICE PLAN Vision Service Plan	A	'05	40.5	...	...	59.5	7,645	...	71.4	...	28.6	6,683	11,477	11,618	1,656	2,068	2,068	2,068
James Robinson Lynch, President & CEO		'06	33.4	...	...	66.6	9,295	...	50.8	...	49.2	7,991	12,063	12,182	1,490	1,308	1,308	1,308
3333 Quality Drive, Rancho Cordova, CA 95670	Rating Outlook: Stable	'07	50.7	...	4.4	44.9	10,811	...	52.5	...	47.5	9,655	12,041	12,670	2,032	1,655	1,655	1,703
WI : 1958 : Other : Agency; Group A&H		'08	69.8	...	...	30.2	11,797	...	30.9	...	69.1	9,230	12,050	12,369	799	907	-497	-579
916-851-5000		'09	41.8	...	...	58.2	12,536	...	36.5	...	63.5	9,285	11,407	11,655	1,116	347	71	71
AMB# 064477 NAIC# 54682	FSC IX	Rating History: A g, 02/09/10; A g, 11/24/08; A g, 11/30/07; A g, 10/12/06; A g, 11/10/05																
WOMAN'S LIFE INS SOCIETY	A-	'05	90.3	0.4	...	9.3	180,951	56.9	...	34.8	8.4	30,904	10,753	10,962	5,658	915	915	897
Janice U. Whipple, Chairman & National President		'06	91.0	0.4	...	8.6	183,101	55.5	...	36.1	8.4	31,571	9,633	9,840	2,079	797	797	761
P.O. Box 5020, Port Huron, MI 48061-5020	Rating Outlook: Negative	'07	91.5	0.4	...	8.1	184,371	55.5	...	36.3	8.2	32,840	8,468	8,693	1,361	1,049	1,049	969
MI : 1892 : Fraternal : Agency; Ann, Univ Life, Whole life		'08	90.1	0.4	...	9.5	182,739	54.5	...	37.2	8.4	28,693	10,023	10,172	-1,982	933	933	-3,401
810-985-5191		'09	90.6	0.3	...	9.1	185,701	52.9	...	39.6	7.5	29,237	9,991	10,254	4,106	230	230	855
AMB# 006826 NAIC# 56170	FSC VI	Rating History: A-, 06/04/10; A-, 05/29/09; A-, 06/17/08; A-, 06/07/07; A-, 06/14/06																
WONDER STATE LIFE INS CO[1]	F	'05	17.1	3.0	60.0	19.9	2,426	...	...	36.6	63.4	409	48	48	...	-135	-135	138
Ralph G. Olsen II, President		'06	22.2	3.2	41.9	32.7	2,275	...	...	34.3	65.7	349	104	104	...	-164	-164	23
400 Hardin Road, Suite 110, Little Rock, AR 72211-3501		'07	20.3	4.2	42.8	32.8	1,901	...	...	33.7	66.3	238	41	41	...	-81	-81	-41
AR : 1950 : Stock : Not Available; In Liquidation		'08	...	...	...	...	...	...	...	...	...	...	...	...	...	...	...	...
877-219-9775		'09	...	...	...	...	...	...	...	...	...	...	...	...	...	...	...	...
AMB# 068529 NAIC# 84131		Rating History: F, 02/09/10; NR-5, 06/08/09; NR-1, 06/12/08; NR-1, 06/08/07; NR-1, 06/07/06																
WOODMEN OF THE WORLD LIFE SOC	A+	'05	69.0	18.3	4.7	7.9	7,213,404	57.3	0.3	34.2	8.1	753,473	588,184	673,194	308,214	65,942	65,942	71,468
Danny E. Cummins, President & CEO		'06	68.4	18.0	5.4	8.2	7,465,154	57.7	0.3	33.8	8.1	875,526	548,328	638,336	186,096	67,705	67,705	76,816
1700 Farnam Street, Omaha, NE 68102	Rating Outlook: Stable	'07	67.9	17.4	6.1	8.6	7,647,374	57.5	0.3	33.4	8.7	916,734	528,466	643,358	162,756	76,001	76,001	125,984
NE : 1890 : Fraternal : Exclusive Agent; Univ Life, Ind Ann, Trad Life		'08	69.5	19.0	4.1	7.4	7,582,357	58.3	0.4	34.1	7.2	756,614	833,560	910,095	154,593	68,612	68,612	-27,808
402-342-1890		'09	69.5	17.2	4.6	8.6	8,074,593	56.4	0.4	35.3	7.9	823,308	811,637	892,855	346,845	42,913	42,913	7,991
AMB# 007259 NAIC# 57320	FSC XI	Rating History: A+, 01/20/10; A+, 04/08/09; A+, 03/13/08; A+, 02/02/07; A+, 01/23/06																
WORKMEN'S LIFE INS CO Workmen's Holding Company	NR-5	'05	84.4	...	...	15.6	604	...	...	...	100.0	603	...	...	-1,696	21	13	16
Nicholas J. Lannutti, President & CEO		'06	87.4	...	...	12.6	584	...	...	...	100.0	580	...	...	-19	-39	-28	-28
P.O. Box 54845, Los Angeles, CA 90054-0845		'07	90.0	...	...	10.0	558	...	...	...	100.0	554	...	...	-28	-43	-30	-30
AZ : 1966 : Stock : Inactive; Inactive		'08	95.0	...	0.8	4.1	533	...	...	...	100.0	520	...	...	-21	-55	-38	-38
213-747-6492		'09	98.1	...	...	1.9	515	...	...	...	100.0	504	...	...	-15	-28	-19	-19
AMB# 008125 NAIC# 78409		Rating History: NR-5, 04/19/10; NR-5, 04/20/09; NR-5, 04/07/08; NR-5, 04/30/07; NR-5, 04/25/06																

BEST'S PROFITABILITY, LEVERAGE AND LIQUIDITY TESTS 2005 – 2009

Data in U.S. Dollars

	Profitability Tests							Leverage Tests						Liquidity Tests					
Un-Realized Capital Gains ($000)	Benefits Paid to NPW & Dep (%)	Comm. & Expenses to NPW & Dep (%)	NOG to Total Assets (%)	NOG to Total Rev (%)	Operating Return on Equity (%)	Net Yield (%)	Total Return (%)	Change in NPW & Dep (%)	NPW & Dep to Capital (X)	Capital & Surplus to Liabilities (%)	Surplus Relief (%)	Reins Leverage (%)	Change in Capital (%)	Quick Liquidity (%)	Current Liquidity (%)	Non-Invest Grade Bonds to Capital (%)	Delinq. & Foreclosed Mortgages to Capital (%)	Mort. & Credit Tenant Loans & R.E. to Capital (%)	Affiliated Invest to Capital (%)
...	71.3	35.0	...	-1.7	...	...	...	...	89.0	16.4	...	...	...	21.2	...	...	...	...	...
...	65.7	231.9	2.0	20.9	16.0	59.33	59.30	80.6	10.9	14.0	...	...	999.9	9.2	5.9	...	...	...	...
...	54.3	263.1	0.9	14.2	7.5	68.59	67.85	28.6	15.0	13.5	...	...	-6.9	7.7	6.8	...	...	...	...
...	75.3	11.2	-4.7	313.6	-41.2	39.16	37.31	112.5	35.9	12.3	...	...	-11.1	8.8	5.0	...	...	...	...
...	53.5	105.2	7.3	33.5	55.2	41.83	41.04	165.4	54.6	17.5	...	...	74.7	16.4	15.6	...	...	...	...
...	18.1	94.6	0.2	1.1	0.2	2.82	2.85	-13.7	0.1	999.9	8.4	33.7	0.5	999.9	999.9	...	...	...	...
...	13.8	101.0	0.7	4.3	0.8	3.42	3.79	7.0	0.1	999.9	5.3	37.3	2.3	999.9	999.9	...	...	...	...
...	16.9	129.8	0.1	0.6	0.1	4.07	3.78	-24.9	0.1	999.9	4.8	39.3	0.3	999.9	999.9	...	...	...	...
...	36.8	655.4	0.5	6.7	0.5	2.91	3.05	-80.4	0.0	999.9	3.1	3.5	0.5	999.9	999.9	...	...	...	...
...	-9.7	208.9	0.2	6.0	0.2	1.70	1.77	-22.2	0.0	999.9	0.2	0.7	0.2	999.9	999.9	...	...	...	...
	Principal Lines of Business: OrdLife (100.0%)												Principal States: TX (98.2%)						
14	115.6	58.3	0.8	5.0	4.6	7.55	7.75	35.4	0.5	14.3	...	0.0	-1.9	53.9	58.7	15.2	12.0	184.0	...
-54	122.1	67.1	-0.1	-0.5	-0.4	7.47	7.49	11.9	0.3	24.1	...	...	84.2	81.2	88.9	5.1	0.0	55.5	...
...	121.9	87.9	1.4	12.6	6.9	6.66	6.69	-9.1	0.2	26.7	...	...	6.7	72.1	81.8	22.5	...	50.6	...
-259	134.8	71.7	1.0	9.9	5.2	6.15	3.01	-7.3	0.3	21.8	...	...	-16.7	56.4	66.7	23.4	48.5	102.8	...
392	120.8	72.9	3.0	26.6	15.7	7.57	8.44	0.1	0.2	27.0	...	...	21.6	62.4	75.9	35.9	...	82.3	...
	Principal Lines of Business: OrdLife (48.4%), IndLife (34.4%), IndAnn (17.3%)												Principal States: LA (100.0%)						
-3,567	81.4	16.9	8.8	4.5	20.4	3.34	2.11	10.1	4.4	72.5	...	2.4	3.4	82.1	89.5	0.8	...	34.1	70.2
3,228	81.4	21.0	4.6	2.2	10.2	4.60	6.80	13.7	4.0	90.6	...	4.0	24.0	84.1	92.7	0.7	...	26.8	57.2
980	82.1	21.2	5.7	2.9	11.7	5.03	6.55	1.0	3.4	97.7	...	3.1	20.0	114.9	126.8	0.7	...	24.4	48.5
-11,882	81.4	21.3	6.0	3.5	12.2	4.04	-1.91	-5.4	3.3	97.0	...	5.3	-3.5	98.3	109.4	0.9	...	24.9	48.1
8,089	81.3	20.8	2.5	1.6	4.7	4.25	7.25	-4.3	2.6	122.6	...	5.0	22.3	89.6	99.8	0.5	...	19.7	45.3
	Principal Lines of Business: CompHosp/Med (68.9%), MedSup (19.4%), OtherHlth (10.5%), Dental (1.3%)												Principal States: WI (100.0%)						
...	83.5	0.1	31.5	17.6	37.3	2.89	2.89	3.4	1.7	695.0	...	...	51.7	919.0	920.1	...	...	...	...
...	82.6	10.1	15.4	10.2	17.8	4.91	4.91	4.9	1.5	612.8	...	...	19.6	986.7	987.5	...	...	...	...
-8	80.8	9.7	16.5	12.4	18.8	5.08	5.52	4.0	1.3	835.6	...	...	20.8	999.9	999.9	...	...	...	...
8	84.5	9.6	-4.4	-3.8	-5.3	3.31	2.61	-2.4	1.3	359.6	...	...	-4.4	488.5	510.9	...	...	...	...
...	85.3	9.2	0.6	0.6	0.8	1.69	1.69	-5.8	1.3	285.7	...	...	0.6	507.3	535.2	...	...	...	...
	Principal Lines of Business: Vision (100.0%)												Principal States: WI (100.0%)						
...	78.9	56.9	0.5	4.2	3.0	6.41	6.52	-10.1	0.3	21.3	...	0.7	2.8	79.4	86.9	25.9	...	2.4	2.3
...	119.6	64.1	0.4	3.9	2.6	6.21	6.31	-10.2	0.3	21.7	...	0.7	2.8	81.1	88.7	20.1	...	2.3	2.3
...	124.7	67.8	0.6	5.3	3.3	6.20	6.31	-11.7	0.3	22.5	...	0.6	3.9	82.3	90.1	17.5	...	2.1	2.1
...	105.2	61.4	0.5	4.4	3.0	6.22	4.05	17.0	0.4	18.8	...	0.7	-14.8	80.7	88.8	9.0	...	2.3	2.3
...	94.9	62.4	0.1	1.1	0.8	6.04	6.52	0.8	0.3	19.3	...	0.8	3.9	79.5	89.3	11.2	...	2.1	2.1
	Principal Lines of Business: IndAnn (57.6%), OrdLife (42.4%)												Principal States: MI (37.3%), IN (25.0%), NY (8.2%), OH (6.1%), IL (4.8%)						
-1	203.5	243.5	-5.6	-88.4	-37.8	...	...	-16.5	0.1	25.7	...	...	42.3	...	...	...	...	14.8	...
-122	129.7	195.0	-7.0	-78.5	-43.2	...	...	114.5	0.3	21.3	...	...	-19.5	...	...	...	...	18.4	...
-200	382.0	499.0	-3.9	-67.1	-27.5	...	...	-60.3	0.2	16.5	...	...	-32.6	...	...	...	...	29.4	...
...	...	...	...	...	...	...	...	...	...	...	...	...	...	...	...	...	...	...	...
...	...	...	...	...	...	...	...	...	...	...	...	...	...	...	...	...	...	...	...
8,485	64.5	24.1	0.9	6.5	9.1	6.19	6.52	-10.2	0.8	13.6	0.0	3.7	8.8	58.7	68.8	23.6	7.9	159.6	2.7
25,480	77.8	24.3	0.9	6.9	8.3	6.08	6.68	-5.2	0.7	15.4	0.0	3.8	15.3	61.1	71.8	14.0	6.6	140.4	2.3
-27,011	82.8	23.6	1.0	8.0	8.5	5.92	6.35	0.8	0.6	16.2	0.0	4.3	6.5	62.5	73.0	13.1	5.3	130.5	2.0
-144,908	74.5	18.4	0.9	5.4	8.2	5.70	2.60	41.5	1.1	12.1	0.0	5.9	-22.5	62.2	71.4	16.3	6.2	182.7	3.7
75,618	61.9	21.6	0.5	3.5	5.4	5.41	6.06	-1.9	1.0	13.2	0.0	6.2	14.6	64.7	73.9	19.1	5.6	155.3	4.4
	Principal Lines of Business: IndAnn (50.5%), OrdLife (48.5%), IndA&H (1.0%)												Principal States: NC (12.0%), GA (11.5%), TN (7.4%), AL (6.3%), LA (5.8%)						
-5	...	...	0.9	20.2	0.9	4.67	4.43	...	...	999.9	...	...	-74.5	999.9	999.9	...	...	...	...
...	...	...	-4.6	-99.9	-4.7	2.36	1.60	...	...	999.9	...	...	-3.8	999.9	999.9	...	...	...	...
...	...	...	-5.3	-99.9	-5.3	2.80	2.00	...	...	999.9	...	...	-4.4	999.9	999.9	...	...	...	...
...	...	...	-6.9	-99.9	-7.0	2.63	1.92	...	...	999.9	...	...	-6.1	999.9	999.9	...	...	...	...
...	...	...	-3.7	-99.9	-3.8	0.80	0.24	...	...	999.9	...	...	-3.2	999.9	999.9	...	...	...	...

Data in U.S. Dollars

COMPANY NAME / Ultimate Parent Association / Principal Officer / Mailing Address / Dom. : Began Bus. : Struct. : Mktg. / Specialty / Phone # / AMB# / NAIC# — Best's Financial Strength Rating / FSC

Balance Sheet: Data Year, Bonds (%), Mort. Loans & R.E. (%), Com & Pref. Stock (%), All Other Assets (%), Total Assets ($000), Life Reserves (%), Health Reserves (%), Ann Res. & Dep. Liabilities (%), All Other Liabilities (%), Capital & Surplus ($000). Operations: Direct Premiums Written ($000), Net Premiums Written & Deposits ($000), Operating Cash Flow ($000), NOG Before Taxes ($000), NOG After Taxes ($000), Net Income ($000)

WORLD CORP INSURANCE COMPANY
American Enterprise Mutual Holding Co
Michael E. Abbott
President & CEO
P.O. Box 3160
Omaha, NE 68103-0160
NE : 1960 : Stock : Agency
Ind A&H
402-496-8000
AMB# 008350 NAIC# 79987

A- Rating Outlook: Stable — FSC VIII

Data Year	Bonds (%)	Mort. Loans & R.E. (%)	Com & Pref. Stock (%)	All Other Assets (%)	Total Assets ($000)	Life Reserves (%)	Health Reserves (%)	Ann Res. & Dep. Liabilities (%)	All Other Liabilities (%)	Capital & Surplus ($000)	Direct Premiums Written ($000)	Net Premiums Written & Deposits ($000)	Operating Cash Flow ($000)	NOG Before Taxes ($000)	NOG After Taxes ($000)	Net Income ($000)
'05	91.7	...	...	8.3	23,033	...	53.6	...	46.4	21,384	3,034	3,033	799	1,494	904	904
'06	97.0	...	...	3.0	23,695	...	48.9	...	51.1	22,339	2,068	2,067	753	1,331	857	857
'07	91.0	...	...	9.0	23,198	...	51.8	...	48.2	22,236	1,656	1,655	-524	-241	-157	-157
'08	93.5	...	...	6.5	23,327	...	51.5	...	48.5	22,328	1,857	1,950	183	166	80	60
'09	94.8	...	...	5.2	22,984	...	52.9	...	47.1	22,164	1,658	1,658	-266	80	19	-185

Rating History: A- r, 04/14/10; B++, 01/13/09; B++, 01/08/08; B++, 01/12/07; B+, 02/23/06

WORLD INSURANCE COMPANY
American Enterprise Mutual Holding Co
Michael E. Abbott
President
P.O. Box 3160
Omaha, NE 68103-0160
NE : 1903 : Stock : Agency
A&H, Hosp Ind, Ind Life
402-496-8000
AMB# 007262 NAIC# 70629

A- Rating Outlook: Stable — FSC VIII

Data Year	Bonds (%)	Mort. Loans & R.E. (%)	Com & Pref. Stock (%)	All Other Assets (%)	Total Assets ($000)	Life Reserves (%)	Health Reserves (%)	Ann Res. & Dep. Liabilities (%)	All Other Liabilities (%)	Capital & Surplus ($000)	Direct Premiums Written ($000)	Net Premiums Written & Deposits ($000)	Operating Cash Flow ($000)	NOG Before Taxes ($000)	NOG After Taxes ($000)	Net Income ($000)
'05	67.1	0.0	19.8	13.1	222,527	36.2	26.9	8.2	28.7	96,572	164,062	163,988	19,512	28,896	18,739	18,940
'06	69.5	0.0	20.1	10.4	228,911	37.0	27.4	7.9	27.8	108,342	175,218	173,845	-828	13,688	9,535	9,567
'07	68.3	0.0	18.9	12.8	231,501	37.7	27.1	7.8	27.3	116,376	174,077	172,418	2,230	10,559	7,298	7,906
'08	75.0	...	14.3	10.7	210,260	40.0	23.8	8.4	27.8	104,115	158,200	156,158	-13,991	2,854	1,638	-913
'09	67.7	...	12.6	19.6	251,900	28.9	33.6	5.9	31.7	107,101	137,223	211,653	19,454	3,994	3,792	2,594

Rating History: A- g, 04/14/10; A- g, 01/13/09; A- g, 01/08/08; A- g, 01/12/07; A- g, 02/23/06

WPS HEALTH PLAN INC
Wisconsin Physicians Service Ins Corp
James R. Riordan
President
P.O. Box 14540
Madison, WI 53708
WI : 2005 : Other : Not Available
Group A&H, Med supp
920-490-6900
AMB# 064830 NAIC# 10159

NR-5

Data Year	Bonds (%)	Mort. Loans & R.E. (%)	Com & Pref. Stock (%)	All Other Assets (%)	Total Assets ($000)	Life Reserves (%)	Health Reserves (%)	Ann Res. & Dep. Liabilities (%)	All Other Liabilities (%)	Capital & Surplus ($000)	Direct Premiums Written ($000)	Net Premiums Written & Deposits ($000)	Operating Cash Flow ($000)	NOG Before Taxes ($000)	NOG After Taxes ($000)	Net Income ($000)
'05	77.6	...	0.1	22.4	20,345	...	67.3	...	32.7	6,062	56,610	55,598	17,279	-2,703	-2,703	-2,842
'06	76.8	...	0.7	22.5	19,478	...	58.7	...	41.3	6,723	84,214	82,532	260	1,357	1,124	962
'07	74.5	...	0.8	24.7	24,741	...	56.2	...	43.8	10,819	80,742	78,651	5,876	1,555	1,037	1,110
'08	78.9	...	...	21.1	25,489	...	53.2	...	46.8	10,581	84,746	82,305	-493	1,188	756	-138
'09	87.1	...	...	12.9	24,511	...	48.7	...	51.3	10,856	95,170	92,057	676	-1,041	-698	-1,214

Rating History: NR-5, 03/24/10; NR-5, 08/26/09; B- pd, 05/23/08; NR-5, 04/03/07; NR-5, 03/14/06

WYSSTA INSURANCE COMPANY INC
Delta Dental of Wisconsin Inc
Dennis L. Brown
President
P.O. Box 828
Stevens Point, WI 54481
WI : 2005 : Stock : Direct Response
Vision
715-344-6087
AMB# 064836 NAIC# 12352

NR-2

Data Year	Bonds (%)	Mort. Loans & R.E. (%)	Com & Pref. Stock (%)	All Other Assets (%)	Total Assets ($000)	Life Reserves (%)	Health Reserves (%)	Ann Res. & Dep. Liabilities (%)	All Other Liabilities (%)	Capital & Surplus ($000)	Direct Premiums Written ($000)	Net Premiums Written & Deposits ($000)	Operating Cash Flow ($000)	NOG Before Taxes ($000)	NOG After Taxes ($000)	Net Income ($000)
'05	...	...	...	100.0	4,025	...	...	...	100.0	3,837	...	...	4,025	-163	-163	-163
'06	70.1	...	...	29.9	3,576	...	...	...	100.0	3,498	82	82	-446	-340	-340	-339
'07	78.1	...	...	21.9	3,377	...	...	...	100.0	3,258	1,383	1,383	-236	-247	-247	-240
'08	85.3	...	...	14.7	3,271	...	...	...	100.0	2,975	2,292	2,292	-243	-330	-330	-282
'09	56.8	...	...	43.2	5,144	...	...	...	100.0	4,647	3,544	3,544	1,806	-346	-346	-329

Rating History: NR-2, 10/02/09; NR-2, 11/21/08; NR-2, 11/12/07; NR-2, 11/06/06; NR-2, 04/07/06

XL LIFE INS AND ANNUITY CO
XL Capital Ltd
Steven D. Powell
Senior Vice President & Actuary
20 N. Martingale Road, Suite 200
Schaumburg, IL 60173
IL : 1978 : Stock : Direct Response
Ann
847-517-2990
AMB# 060395 NAIC# 88080

A- Rating Outlook: Stable — FSC V

Data Year	Bonds (%)	Mort. Loans & R.E. (%)	Com & Pref. Stock (%)	All Other Assets (%)	Total Assets ($000)	Life Reserves (%)	Health Reserves (%)	Ann Res. & Dep. Liabilities (%)	All Other Liabilities (%)	Capital & Surplus ($000)	Direct Premiums Written ($000)	Net Premiums Written & Deposits ($000)	Operating Cash Flow ($000)	NOG Before Taxes ($000)	NOG After Taxes ($000)	Net Income ($000)
'05	31.9	...	...	68.1	834,978	...	...	25.5	74.5	86,882	1,324,457	1,325,000	129,835	4,602	5,019	4,822
'06	28.4	...	...	71.6	810,810	...	...	21.9	78.1	92,325	-118	...	-36,133	-2,816	-4,345	-4,159
'07	21.4	...	...	78.6	736,669	...	...	21.7	78.3	26,051	16	...	-73,206	-15,222	-17,373	-18,238
'08	78.0	...	...	22.0	82,503	...	...	98.0	2.0	16,019	-2	...	-78,842	14,924	13,243	-14,871
'09	72.0	...	...	28.0	67,032	...	...	98.9	1.1	19,353	-570	...	-8,457	-956	2,793	2,185

Rating History: A-, 01/18/10; A-, 08/25/08; A- u, 07/29/08; A-, 01/25/08; A, 12/20/07

XL LIFE LTD
XL Capital Ltd
Simon Rich
Resident Director
One Bermudiana Road
Hamilton HM 11, Bermuda
BM : Stock : Not Available
Reins, Group pens, Ordinary Life
441-292-8515
AMB# 073313

A- Rating Outlook: Stable — FSC I

Data Year	Bonds (%)	Mort. Loans & R.E. (%)	Com & Pref. Stock (%)	All Other Assets (%)	Total Assets ($000)	Life Reserves (%)	Health Reserves (%)	Ann Res. & Dep. Liabilities (%)	All Other Liabilities (%)	Capital & Surplus ($000)	Direct Premiums Written ($000)	Net Premiums Written & Deposits ($000)	Operating Cash Flow ($000)	NOG Before Taxes ($000)	NOG After Taxes ($000)	Net Income ($000)
'05	37.4	...	...	62.6	5,163,269	98.2	...	...	1.8	237,471	...	...	...	70,567	70,567	89,063
'06	33.9	...	...	66.1	5,137,156	98.0	...	...	2.0	207,407	...	...	...	-132,681	-132,681	-100,063
'07	29.4	...	...	70.6	4,900,695	95.6	...	...	4.4	171,373	...	...	...	54,090	54,090	-117,306
'08	30.9	...	...	69.1	3,067,066	94.4	...	...	5.6	-51,059	...	...	...	-19,212	-19,212	-200,917
'09	...	...	...	...	...	...	...	...	...	...	...	...	...	...	...	...

Rating History: A-, 01/18/10; A-, 10/16/08; A, 08/25/08; A u, 07/29/08; A, 01/25/08

ZALE LIFE INS CO
Zale Corporation
Stephen C. Massanelli
Chairman & President
P.O. Box 152762, M.S. 5A-9
Irving, TX 75015-2762
AZ : 1964 : Stock : Agency
Credit A&H, Credit Life, Group Life
972-580-4039
AMB# 007349 NAIC# 71323

B+ Rating Outlook: Stable — FSC IV

Data Year	Bonds (%)	Mort. Loans & R.E. (%)	Com & Pref. Stock (%)	All Other Assets (%)	Total Assets ($000)	Life Reserves (%)	Health Reserves (%)	Ann Res. & Dep. Liabilities (%)	All Other Liabilities (%)	Capital & Surplus ($000)	Direct Premiums Written ($000)	Net Premiums Written & Deposits ($000)	Operating Cash Flow ($000)	NOG Before Taxes ($000)	NOG After Taxes ($000)	Net Income ($000)
'05	64.8	...	16.5	18.6	12,591	54.5	9.5	...	35.9	9,341	2,613	1,907	625	1,026	674	787
'06	89.1	...	3.4	7.5	12,345	65.7	10.8	...	23.6	9,589	2,430	1,719	-288	751	497	599
'07	87.1	...	4.1	8.8	12,128	66.2	12.0	...	21.8	9,645	2,445	1,719	47	642	438	438
'08	80.7	...	7.4	11.9	11,935	69.7	13.3	...	17.1	9,691	2,577	1,848	165	935	635	635
'09	77.5	...	13.5	8.9	11,006	61.5	12.9	...	25.6	8,604	2,610	1,879	-1,202	791	538	538

Rating History: B+, 01/12/10; B+, 01/12/09; B+, 11/13/07; B+, 11/20/06; B++, 10/14/05

BEST'S PROFITABILITY, LEVERAGE AND LIQUIDITY TESTS 2005 – 2009

Data in U.S. Dollars

—	Profitability Tests							Leverage Tests						Liquidity Tests					
Un-Realized Capital Gains ($000)	Benefits Paid to NPW & Dep (%)	Comm. & Expenses to NPW & Dep (%)	NOG to Total Assets (%)	NOG to Total Rev (%)	Operating Return on Equity (%)	Net Yield (%)	Total Return (%)	Change in NPW & Dep (%)	NPW & Dep to Capital (X)	Capital & Surplus to Liabilities (%)	Surplus Relief (%)	Reins Leverage (%)	Change in Capital (%)	Quick Liquidity (%)	Current Liquidity (%)	Non-Invest Grade Bonds to Capital (%)	Delinq. & Foreclosed Mortgages to Capital (%)	Mort. & Credit Tenant Loans & R.E. to Capital (%)	Affiliated Invest to Capital (%)
...	69.3	8.5	4.0	23.7	4.3	4.16	3.54	-35.2	0.1	999.9	...	16.5	5.1	999.9	999.9	...	...	...	...
...	68.4	17.6	3.7	27.9	3.9	4.93	4.45	-31.9	0.1	999.9	...	13.7	4.5	999.9	999.9	...	...	...	...
...	66.6	114.1	-0.7	-5.8	-0.7	4.98	4.56	-19.9	0.1	999.9	...	2.5	-0.4	999.9	999.9	0.4	...	...	...
...	85.6	60.3	0.3	2.7	0.4	4.97	4.51	17.9	0.1	999.9	...	2.8	0.8	999.9	999.9	2.1	...	...	...
...	96.2	63.7	0.1	0.7	0.1	4.95	3.75	-15.0	0.1	999.9	...	2.8	-0.8	999.9	999.9	1.3	...	...	...
	Principal Lines of Business: IndA&H (100.0%)													Principal States: NC (29.3%), MO (19.7%), TN (9.7%), GA (9.5%), CO (7.1%)					
1,335	57.6	32.6	8.6	10.7	21.5	3.98	5.07	5.9	1.6	81.4	0.3	21.6	26.9	92.8	115.4	2.8	...	0.0	28.7
1,246	66.2	34.0	4.2	5.1	9.3	4.70	5.63	6.0	1.5	96.3	0.3	18.5	12.5	94.9	120.9	...	...	0.0	26.1
-603	65.3	36.2	3.2	4.0	6.5	4.70	4.93	-0.8	1.4	107.6	0.4	17.1	6.8	94.2	124.1	0.6	...	0.0	24.4
-643	67.6	38.7	0.7	1.0	1.5	4.63	3.26	-9.4	1.5	103.4	0.4	18.4	-10.9	88.8	121.9	2.8	...	...	20.4
1,450	72.8	31.2	1.6	1.7	3.6	4.74	5.02	35.5	1.9	77.5	0.4	34.3	2.9	84.1	108.0	4.2	...	...	20.0
	Principal Lines of Business: IndA&H (69.0%), GrpA&H (29.4%), OrdLife (1.6%), GrpAnn (0.0%), IndAnn (0.0%)													Principal States: CO (14.9%), TX (13.1%), MT (7.0%), NC (6.3%), MI (5.7%)					
-3	94.0	11.7	...	-4.8	...	...	...	...	9.2	42.4	...	12.7	...	95.8	105.3	1.6	...	...	...
3	87.6	11.8	5.6	1.3	17.6	5.10	4.20	48.4	12.3	52.7	...	14.4	10.9	119.7	131.8	0.3	...	...	...
-14	86.9	12.5	4.7	1.3	11.8	5.33	5.62	-4.7	7.3	77.7	...	8.1	60.9	169.5	184.2	0.2	...	...	...
-43	88.3	11.7	3.0	0.9	7.1	4.94	0.98	4.6	7.8	71.0	...	17.3	-2.2	145.7	160.3	1.1	...	...	...
-128	89.9	12.3	-2.8	-0.8	-6.5	4.43	1.64	11.8	8.5	79.5	...	11.6	2.6	137.4	149.2	1.1	...	...	...
	Principal Lines of Business: CompHosp/Med (99.2%), MedSup (0.8%)													Principal States: WI (100.0%)					
...	...	...	...	-99.9	...	...	...	...	...	999.9	...	...	...	999.9	999.9	...	...	...	...
...	70.3	610.0	-9.0	-99.9	-9.3	3.70	3.72	...	0.0	999.9	...	...	-8.8	999.9	999.9	...	...	...	...
...	83.9	43.4	-7.1	-16.3	-7.3	3.81	4.01	999.9	0.4	999.9	...	...	-6.9	999.9	999.9	...	...	...	...
...	81.8	36.2	-9.9	-13.9	-10.6	2.60	4.11	65.8	0.8	999.9	...	...	-8.7	947.0	999.9	...	...	...	...
...	82.3	29.2	-8.2	-9.6	-9.1	1.58	2.01	54.7	0.8	935.1	...	...	56.2	928.9	964.1	...	...	...	...
	Principal Lines of Business: Vision (100.0%)													Principal States: WI (100.0%)					
-16	0.1	0.3	0.7	39.4	5.8	4.65	4.50	130.4	14.7	46.8	2.6	11.6	1.8	110.9	127.5	1.7	...	...	...
16	...	...	-0.5	-23.8	-4.8	5.18	5.10	-99.9	...	59.2	1.2	3.5	6.5	103.3	125.4	0.4	...	...	...
...	...	...	-2.2	-99.9	-29.4	5.43	4.84	...	...	16.7	4.2	4.1	-72.5	71.7	87.6	4.3	...	...	...
...	...	...	3.2	-99.9	63.0	4.50	-18.87	...	...	24.1	4.9	3.3	-39.2	92.7	102.7	14.0	...	...	...
...	...	...	3.7	-99.9	15.8	4.40	-2.64	...	...	40.6	1.8	1.4	20.8	133.1	145.3	3.2	...	...	...
...	...	...	1.8	3.7	37.3	13.65	14.97	...	...	4.8	...	...	67.9	40.7	39.6	...	...	...	7.7
...	...	...	-2.6	-27.7	-59.7	13.67	15.37	...	...	4.2	...	...	-12.7	36.2	35.5	...	...	...	4.7
-83,730	...	...	1.1	15.3	28.6	15.28	5.64	...	...	3.6	...	...	-17.4	37.0	30.7	...	...	...	5.7
-204,516	...	...	-0.5	-5.7	-31.9	16.06	3.07	...	...	-1.6	...	...	-99.9	33.3	30.4	...	...	...	...
...	...	...	...	...	...	...	...	...	...	...	...	...	...	...	...	...	...	...	...
-98	37.3	40.2	5.4	26.8	7.3	3.05	3.37	14.9	0.2	345.8	...	8.5	2.0	405.8	430.8	...	...	...	...
-60	37.8	43.6	4.0	23.5	5.3	3.20	3.67	-9.9	0.2	363.7	...	11.2	-0.9	380.7	397.9	...	...	...	...
9	44.0	46.5	3.6	21.3	4.6	2.83	2.96	0.0	0.2	404.3	...	8.1	0.4	417.2	436.6	...	...	...	...
-229	29.7	43.4	5.3	29.5	6.6	2.64	0.70	7.5	0.2	434.3	...	8.6	-0.2	436.3	454.5	...	...	...	...
196	31.1	43.0	4.7	25.4	5.9	2.15	3.94	1.6	0.2	399.6	...	10.4	-9.3	408.4	425.3	...	...	...	...
	Principal Lines of Business: CrdA&H (47.5%), CrdLife (39.8%), GrpLife (10.8%), OrdLife (1.9%)													Principal States: TX (56.1%), FL (6.1%), CA (5.9%), LA (3.6%)					

Canadian Companies
Financial and Operating Exhibits
of
LICENSED INSURANCE CARRIERS
WRITING LIFE/HEALTH INSURANCE
with
KEY RATINGS

Notes to Canadian Section

The general rating methodologies followed for Canadian life and health companies align very closely with those for U.S. companies. Therefore, the Overview of Best's Credit Rating Methodology included in the Preface of this publication generally applies to our analysis of Canadian companies.

The data contained in the following tables was obtained from the Annual Return (Life-1 or Life-2) for Canadian Life and Health Insurers. These financial statements have been prepared in accordance with Canadian generally accepted accounting principles (Canadian GAAP) except as otherwise specified by the Office of the Superintendent of Financial Institutions, Canada (OSFI), or by the provincial governing body having regulatory authority over the company.

On January 1, 2007, Canadian insurers adopted a number of new accounting standards that were issued by The Canadian Institute of Chartered Accountants (CICA). The adoption of these standards resulted in changes in the accounting for financial instruments and the recognition of certain transitional adjustments recorded in the opening balances for retained earnings and accumulated other comprehensive income. The most significant change relates to the establishment of standards for recognizing and measuring financial assets and liabilities and non-financial derivatives. The presentation of most financial instruments on the 2007 balance sheet is now at fair market value as reported by the company. Prior period balances before 2007 were not restated in company filings. As such, a comparison of 2007 data and ratios to prior years may not be appropriate.

Notice

[1] Where financial information for companies was obtained by A.M. Best from Beyond 20/20 Inc., Ottawa, Canada, a superscript "1" will appear next to the company name in the first column of the table. The company's management has not reviewed the data reflected herein.

Canadian Companies — Data in Canadian Dollars

COMPANY NAME Ultimate Parent Association Principal Officer Mailing Address Dom. : Began Bus. : Struct. : Mktg. Specialty Phone # AMB#	Best's Financial Strength Rating FSC	Data Year	Balance Sheet Bonds (%)	Mort. Loans & R.E. (%)	Com & Pref. Shares (%)	All Other Assets (%)	Total Assets ($000)	Life Reserves (%)	Health Reserves (%)	Ann Res. Liabilities (%)	All Other Liabilities (%)	Capital & Surplus ($000)	Operations Direct Premiums Written ($000)	Net Premiums Written ($000)	Operating Cash Flow ($000)	NOG Before Taxes ($000)	NOG After Taxes ($000)	Net Income ($000)
ACE INA LIFE INSURANCE ACE Limited Karen L. Barkley President & CEO 25 York Street, Suite 1400 Toronto, ON, Canada M5J 2V5 CA : 2003 : Other : Not Available Group A&S, Ind A&S, Group Life 416-368-2911 AMB# 066873	NR-5	'05	75.2	...	...	24.8	52,497	31.1	27.5	...	41.4	20,176	79,412	43,208	-2,619	5,721	3,670	3,670
		'06	76.7	...	...	23.3	61,236	31.6	18.7	...	49.7	25,758	85,342	39,142	9,008	8,652	5,582	5,582
		'07	78.9	...	...	21.1	79,652	19.9	35.8	...	44.3	32,106	102,148	64,659	12,483	14,409	9,295	9,295
		'08	83.6	...	...	16.4	99,166	20.3	36.4	...	43.3	45,274	109,129	68,040	14,062	17,182	11,381	11,381
		'09	86.4	...	...	13.6	112,267	22.7	33.2	...	44.1	58,143	100,426	59,767	9,160	20,162	13,406	13,406
		Rating History: NR-5, 04/26/10; NR-5, 03/12/09; NR-2, 11/26/07; NR-2, 10/16/06; NR-5, 05/16/06																
AETNA LIFE INS CO CAB Aetna Inc Colleen Sexsmith Chief Agent in Canada 1145 Nicholson Road, Unit 2 Newmarket, ON, Canada L3Y 9C3 CA : 1850 : Stock : Not Available A&S 905-853-0858 AMB# 069358	A Rating Outlook: Stable FSC XV	'05	87.6	...	...	12.4	51,771	53.8	33.5	0.2	12.4	34,815	3,003	5,871	1,975	3,082	2,385	2,385
		'06	87.0	...	...	13.0	53,129	55.3	33.7	0.2	10.9	37,127	1,993	4,403	1,234	2,556	2,162	2,162
		'07	86.7	...	...	13.3	56,029	54.3	30.9	0.1	14.7	39,548	2,060	2,392	3,172	3,316	2,669	2,669
		'08	86.3	...	...	13.7	58,213	53.1	35.3	0.1	11.5	40,674	1,635	2,193	1,620	549	976	976
		'09	75.2	...	...	24.8	59,997	55.6	32.3	0.1	12.0	42,364	1,982	-1,332	1,564	1,524	1,540	1,540
		Rating History: A g, 06/17/09; A g, 06/16/08; A g, 06/11/07; A g, 01/20/06; A g, 03/04/05																
ALLIANZ LIFE INS OF NA CAB Allianz Societas Europaea Gary C. Bhojwani President & CEO 2005 Sheppard Avenue East, Suite 700 Willowdale, ON, Canada M2J 5B4 CA : 1981 : Stock : Not Available A&S 416-502-2500 AMB# 069312	A Rating Outlook: Stable FSC XV	'05	92.4	...	...	7.6	73,555	55.5	0.2	0.1	44.2	48,856	4,700	4,621	6,789	10,496	8,001	8,001
		'06	91.4	...	...	8.6	75,944	52.7	10.7	0.1	36.4	53,837	5,352	5,291	4,529	6,909	5,380	5,380
		'07	46.4	...	...	53.6	158,309	59.5	14.1	0.2	26.2	60,197	5,599	5,562	3,430	4,946	3,654	3,654
		'08	59.3	...	...	40.7	135,791	77.7	11.5	...	10.8	59,182	5,493	5,448	-1,051	-4,457	-1,906	-1,906
		'09	31.0	...	...	69.0	139,841	60.7	10.9	...	28.4	66,169	6,407	3,281	7,658	8,054	6,393	6,393
		Rating History: A g, 02/12/10; A g, 12/15/08; A g, 10/04/07; A g, 10/10/06; A g, 09/16/05																
ALLSTATE LIFE INS CO OF CANADA' Allstate Corporation Michael J. Donoghue President & CEO 10 Allstate Parkway Markham, ON, Canada L3R 5P8 CA : 1963 : Stock : Inactive Life 905-477-6900 AMB# 006028	NR-5	'05	98.3	...	...	1.7	3,386	...	...	...	100.0	3,370	...	...	...	57	36	36
		'06	95.9	...	...	4.1	3,447	...	...	...	100.0	3,420	...	...	...	79	50	50
		'07	93.9	...	...	6.1	3,520	...	...	...	100.0	3,485	...	...	...	102	65	65
		'08	97.6	...	...	2.4	3,688	...	...	...	100.0	3,623	...	...	...	91	60	60
		'09	97.1	...	...	2.9	3,719	...	...	...	100.0	3,697	...	...	...	88	58	58
		Rating History: NR-5, 04/26/10; NR-5, 05/21/09; NR-5, 05/12/08; NR-5, 05/14/07; NR-5, 05/17/06																
AMERICAN BANKERS LF ASSR CAB Assurant Inc S. Craig Lemasters CEO 5160 Yonge Street, Suite 500 North York, ON, Canada M2N 7C7 CA : 1971 : Stock : Not Available A&S 416-733-3360 AMB# 069313	A- Rating Outlook: Stable FSC VIII	'05	87.5	...	...	12.5	218,704	24.4	41.0	...	34.6	88,333	210,111	69,264	7,375	11,677	8,281	8,281
		'06	89.1	...	...	10.9	206,684	18.3	41.9	...	39.8	94,233	179,865	56,608	-13,938	4,780	3,798	3,798
		'07	88.7	...	...	11.3	215,115	14.6	38.8	...	46.6	104,752	245,439	48,852	19,922	13,700	10,159	10,159
		'08	93.0	...	...	7.0	214,188	14.6	40.8	...	44.5	117,472	271,618	49,591	-3,985	15,285	11,841	11,841
		'09	92.2	...	...	7.8	236,296	14.0	36.2	...	49.7	132,644	310,255	36,248	13,749	21,078	15,807	15,807
		Rating History: A- g, 11/18/09; A- g, 11/25/08; A- g, 06/24/08; A g, 07/17/07; A g, 06/19/06																
AMERICAN HEALTH & LIFE INS CAB Citigroup Inc. Dava S. Carson President & CEO 355 Wellington Street London, ON, Canada N6A 3N7 CA : 2000 : Stock : Not Available Group Life, Ind Life 519-680-4738 AMB# 066870	A Rating Outlook: Stable FSC X	'05	89.7	...	...	10.3	130,359	80.7	...	...	19.3	82,490	29,688	9,508	14,240	18,973	13,387	13,387
		'06	93.7	...	...	6.3	138,829	78.4	...	...	21.6	96,141	22,999	3,680	8,786	19,278	13,651	13,651
		'07	91.9	...	...	8.1	154,357	78.0	...	...	22.0	110,591	30,697	10,249	15,692	21,491	15,123	15,123
		'08	92.9	...	...	7.1	153,222	75.4	...	...	24.6	102,603	37,187	12,926	19,777	22,417	16,391	16,391
		'09	93.6	...	...	6.4	115,065	92.8	...	...	7.2	84,748	18,537	-1,399	-7,302	20,835	15,493	15,493
		Rating History: A, 06/04/10; A, 06/03/09; A g, 05/22/08; A g, 01/12/07; A g, 07/01/05																
AMERICAN INCOME LIFE INS CAB Torchmark Corporation Robin B. Cumine Chief Agent 130 Adelaide Street West, Suite 2800 Toronto, ON, Canada M5H 3P5 CA : 1988 : Stock : Not Available A&S 416-364-5371 AMB# 069314	A+ Rating Outlook: Stable FSC X	'05	72.2	...	...	27.8	149,300	27.5	10.9	...	61.6	82,902	51,938	51,916	27,392	15,430	10,438	10,438
		'06	60.3	...	...	39.7	174,716	33.1	12.8	...	54.1	108,041	57,845	57,838	20,527	23,170	20,411	20,411
		'07	71.9	...	...	28.1	138,835	41.7	15.9	...	42.4	74,167	64,361	64,339	8,730	30,059	15,543	15,543
		'08	45.0	...	...	55.0	198,742	41.9	28.6	...	29.5	170,285	71,215	71,190	39,985	61,337	117,262	117,262
		'09	79.4	...	...	20.6	167,686	50.2	24.1	...	25.7	110,558	77,644	77,618	82,996	23,776	23,776	23,776
		Rating History: A+ g, 06/15/10; A+ g, 06/11/09; A+ g, 06/11/08; A+ g, 06/08/07; A+ g, 06/08/06																
AMEX ASSURANCE COMPANY CAB American Express Company Kenneth J. Ciak President 36 King St. E, # 500 Toronto, ON, Canada M5C 1E5 CA : 1997 : Stock : Not Available Group A&S 416-361-1728 AMB# 066865	NR-5	'05	79.5	...	...	20.5	6,357	...	-71.5	...	171.5	6,234	2,169	1,443	781	1,170	1,017	1,017
		'06	76.2	...	...	23.8	6,622	...	-75.4	...	175.4	6,496	2,287	1,474	769	799	615	615
		'07	71.6	...	...	28.4	7,050	...	-99.9	...	199.9	6,992	2,160	1,536	633	955	698	698
		'08	80.9	...	...	19.1	6,312	...	...	...	100.0	6,213	1,511	849	-588	405	315	315
		'09	81.2	...	...	18.8	6,148	...	...	...	100.0	6,111	...	34	902	58	67	67
		Rating History: NR-5, 05/04/10; NR-5, 05/20/09; NR-5, 05/09/08; NR-5, 04/27/07; NR-5, 05/16/06																
ASSUMPTION MUTUAL LIFE INS CO Denis Losier President & CEO P.O. Box 160 Moncton, NB, Canada E1C 8L1 CA : 1907 : Mutual : Agency Group Life, Ind Ann, Ind Life 506-853-6040 AMB# 008074	A- Rating Outlook: Stable FSC VII	'05	55.9	28.6	3.1	12.4	455,177	46.9	0.3	42.8	10.1	65,333	80,565	57,788	12,217	4,384	3,334	6,075
		'06	56.0	26.5	3.4	14.0	473,157	47.1	0.2	41.7	10.9	70,434	79,637	56,548	5,437	7,159	4,879	5,101
		'07	61.3	21.2	3.2	14.3	556,559	54.1	0.2	37.2	8.6	77,914	83,397	59,952	6,355	5,829	4,011	4,011
		'08	61.3	22.9	3.6	12.3	547,322	53.2	0.1	37.4	9.3	81,085	85,638	62,445	-5,076	6,072	4,308	4,308
		'09	61.2	22.6	3.8	12.4	567,259	53.1	0.0	36.7	10.1	88,001	89,122	67,100	2,126	9,375	6,346	6,346
		Rating History: A-, 02/24/10; A-, 04/23/09; A-, 04/03/08; A-, 03/19/07; A-, 02/22/06																

BEST'S PROFITABILITY, LEVERAGE AND LIQUIDITY TESTS 2005 – 2009

Canadian Companies — Data in Canadian Dollars

	Profitability Tests							Leverage Tests						Liquidity Tests					
AOCI ($000)	Benefits Paid to NPW (%)	Comm. & Expenses to NPW (%)	NOG to Total Assets (%)	NOG to Total Rev (%)	Operating Return on Equity (%)	Yield on Invested Assets (%)	Total Return (%)	Change in NPW (%)	NPW to Capital (X)	Capital & Surplus to Liabilities (%)	Surplus Relief (%)	Reins Leverage (%)	Change in Capital (%)	Quick Liquidity (%)	Current Liquidity (%)	Non-Invest Grade Bonds to Capital (%)	Delinq. & Foreclosed Mortgages to Capital (%)	Mort. & Credit Tenant Loans & R.E. to Capital (%)	Affiliated Invest to Capital (%)
...	20.8	62.7	7.0	8.1	20.0	4.08	3.79	26.9	2.1	62.4	...	15.8	22.2	11.3	160.3	...	...	...	...
...	26.4	59.4	9.8	13.6	24.3	4.23	4.29	-9.4	1.5	72.6	...	12.3	27.7	13.9	170.6	...	...	...	...
386	31.0	52.8	13.2	12.9	32.1	4.01	4.64	65.2	2.0	67.5	...	5.8	24.6	12.1	165.7	...	...	...	...
2,173	26.7	47.0	12.7	15.9	29.4	4.09	6.36	5.2	1.5	84.0	...	6.3	41.0	5.5	179.8	...	...	...	...
1,636	27.5	46.5	12.7	20.9	25.9	4.72	4.14	-12.2	1.0	107.4	...	7.1	28.4	0.8	202.9	...	...	...	...
...	97.8	23.0	4.7	27.6	7.1	5.76	5.37	7.0	0.2	205.3	...	...	7.9	25.8	294.7	...	...	...	...
...	90.1	26.5	4.1	30.3	6.0	5.45	5.27	-25.0	0.1	232.0	...	...	6.6	28.9	321.7	...	...	...	...
328	88.6	31.2	4.9	52.6	7.0	5.13	5.74	-45.7	0.1	244.8	...	...	6.5	36.6	338.4	...	...	...	...
904	97.8	50.9	1.7	20.6	2.4	4.64	5.66	-8.3	0.1	244.5	...	...	2.8	37.4	340.3	...	...	...	...
1,306	63.4	-30.6	2.6	171.7	3.7	3.90	4.59	-99.9	0.0	259.5	...	...	4.2	82.4	359.9	...	...	...	...
...	36.1	52.4	7.7	63.9	10.0	7.45	10.38	9.3	0.1	197.8	...	9.1	-56.0	16.9	293.6	...	...	...	...
...	11.6	50.3	7.2	51.3	10.5	6.64	2.39	14.5	0.1	243.5	...	8.2	10.2	23.0	340.0	...	...	...	...
821	41.7	50.1	4.7	37.9	6.4	4.53	5.59	5.1	0.1	321.3	...	7.3	11.8	26.5	422.1	...	...	...	...
4,150	47.7	85.9	-2.3	-20.9	-3.2	4.25	8.21	-2.0	0.1	228.4	...	6.5	-1.7	16.6	329.1	...	...	...	...
2,223	96.1	105.2	7.0	63.7	10.2	6.27	4.09	-39.8	0.0	259.7	...	5.6	11.8	194.2	366.4	...	...	...	...
...	...	...	1.1	34.3	1.1	3.19	3.19	...	...	999.9	...	...	1.1	187.5	999.9	...	...	...	...
...	...	...	1.5	41.0	1.5	3.64	3.64	...	...	999.9	...	...	1.5	437.0	999.9	...	...	...	...
...	...	...	1.9	48.1	1.9	3.95	3.95	...	...	999.9	...	...	1.9	551.4	999.9	...	...	...	...
78	...	...	1.7	45.5	1.7	3.73	5.87	...	...	999.9	...	...	4.0	89.2	999.9	...	...	...	...
94	...	...	1.6	44.3	1.6	3.62	4.05	...	...	999.9	...	...	2.0	204.5	999.9	...	...	...	...
...	10.2	84.6	3.8	10.5	9.8	4.78	4.91	11.8	0.8	67.8	...	59.0	8.7	12.4	162.9	...	...	...	...
...	22.0	118.6	1.8	5.7	4.2	5.10	4.98	-18.3	0.6	83.8	...	43.7	6.7	9.7	178.6	...	...	...	...
-1,377	17.9	90.6	4.8	17.5	10.2	4.55	3.88	-13.7	0.5	93.7	...	33.2	11.2	18.6	190.9	...	...	...	...
-2,303	13.4	86.2	5.5	19.8	10.7	4.99	4.56	1.5	0.4	118.6	...	34.2	12.1	8.5	213.6	...	...	...	...
7,775	7.8	81.5	7.0	33.9	12.6	4.81	9.23	-26.9	0.3	138.3	60.4	33.5	12.9	15.7	244.3	...	...	...	...
...	15.6	-62.8	10.9	86.2	17.7	5.09	5.09	-29.9	0.1	172.3	...	...	19.4	22.9	267.2	...	...	...	...
...	51.7	-99.9	10.1	138.0	15.3	4.76	4.76	-61.3	0.0	225.2	...	...	16.5	14.9	319.8	...	...	...	...
1,144	19.5	-63.0	10.3	90.0	14.6	4.59	5.37	178.4	0.1	259.5	...	...	15.0	24.6	357.6	...	...	...	...
3,793	15.2	-43.2	10.7	78.5	15.4	5.32	7.03	26.1	0.1	219.1	...	...	-7.2	19.5	323.5	...	...	...	...
3,162	-99.9	396.1	11.5	217.2	16.5	6.63	6.15	-99.9	0.0	312.1	9.8	...	-17.4	16.7	413.8	...	...	...	...
...	19.6	43.1	7.6	17.7	13.1	5.76	6.06	11.4	0.6	124.9	...	0.0	8.4	44.5	220.1	...	...	...	...
...	17.8	43.6	12.6	31.1	21.4	5.27	5.23	11.4	0.5	162.0	...	0.0	30.3	84.9	256.9	...	...	...	...
2,431	16.7	42.0	9.9	21.5	17.1	5.52	7.16	11.2	0.9	119.2	...	0.0	-31.4	39.5	217.5	...	...	...	...
-11,463	18.5	42.4	69.5	120.9	95.9	22.08	10.82	10.6	0.4	426.6	...	0.0	129.6	95.1	349.8	...	...	...	...
3,454	18.8	44.8	13.0	28.0	16.9	5.38	15.59	9.0	0.7	206.0	...	0.0	-35.1	14.4	291.0	...	...	...	...
...	-31.2	73.0	16.4	57.7	17.2	5.31	5.31	37.0	0.2	999.9	...	2.0	11.4	921.1	999.9	...	...	...	...
...	...	61.5	9.5	36.2	9.7	3.53	3.53	2.1	0.2	999.9	...	2.4	4.2	999.9	999.9	...	...	...	...
-4	...	53.5	10.2	39.3	10.3	3.60	3.55	4.2	0.2	999.9	...	2.2	7.6	999.9	999.9	...	...	...	...
57	...	67.4	4.7	29.4	4.8	3.62	4.59	-44.7	0.1	999.9	...	1.2	-11.1	714.3	999.9	...	...	...	...
...	...	450.0	1.1	53.2	1.1	1.62	0.62	-96.0	0.0	999.9	...	...	-1.6	999.9	999.9	...	...	...	...
...	89.3	36.5	1.3	6.5	9.8	6.45	6.43	2.9	0.9	16.8	6.8	78.2	10.3	3.1	73.9	0.9	3.6	199.3	27.6
...	83.0	42.9	1.1	5.8	7.5	6.63	6.70	-2.1	0.8	17.5	5.1	75.4	7.8	3.2	75.4	...	...	178.3	28.2
38,592	79.7	43.8	0.8	4.7	5.4	4.75	5.32	6.0	0.8	16.3	4.5	78.4	10.6	5.1	81.7	...	...	151.2	27.4
38,992	81.6	44.4	0.8	6.0	5.4	1.63	1.31	4.2	0.8	17.4	4.2	70.5	4.1	2.2	79.0	...	...	154.7	28.8
2,328	73.9	45.8	1.1	6.2	7.5	6.60	6.27	7.5	0.8	18.4	...	69.6	8.5	1.9	80.0	...	...	145.4	29.3

2010 BEST'S KEY RATING GUIDE — LIFE/HEALTH EDITION
ANNUAL STATEMENT DATA FOR YEARS 2005 – 2009
Canadian Companies — Data in Canadian Dollars

COMPANY NAME Ultimate Parent Association Principal Officer Mailing Address Dom. : Began Bus. : Struct. : Mktg. Specialty Phone # AMB#	Best's Financial Strength Rating FSC	Data Year	Balance Sheet: Bonds (%)	Mort. Loans & R.E. (%)	Com & Pref. Shares (%)	All Other Assets (%)	Total Assets ($000)	Life Reserves (%)	Health Reserves (%)	Ann Res. Liabilities (%)	All Other Liabilities (%)	Capital & Surplus ($000)	Operations: Direct Premiums Written ($000)	Net Premiums Written ($000)	Operating Cash Flow ($000)	NOG Before Taxes ($000)	NOG After Taxes ($000)	Net Income ($000)
ASSURANT LIFE OF CANADA Assurant Inc Francois Genest President 5160 Yonge Street, Suite 500 Toronto, ON, Canada M2N 7C7 CA : 2006 : Stock : Agency Pre-need 416-733-3360 AMB# 066882	A- Rating Outlook: Stable FSC VII	'05	...	...	...	...	...	...	...	...	...	...	...	...	...	...	...	...
		'06	91.7	4.6	...	3.6	543,917	42.1	...	53.6	4.3	39,404	98,746	98,746	62,184	8,694	4,819	4,819
		'07	90.6	4.2	...	5.1	635,457	40.3	...	57.2	2.5	48,633	135,253	135,253	79,354	35,356	24,053	24,053
		'08	90.1	4.1	...	5.7	659,982	37.5	...	60.1	2.5	56,457	140,629	140,629	81,308	72,836	48,968	48,968
		'09	93.5	3.2	...	3.2	812,834	37.7	...	60.3	2.0	70,497	148,708	148,708	86,112	-47,332	-31,970	-31,970
		Rating History: A-, 11/18/09; A-, 11/25/08; A-, 06/24/08; A-, 07/17/07; A-, 06/19/06																
AURIGEN REINSURANCE COMPANY Aurigen Capital Limited Alan Ryder President & CEO 18 King Street East, 2nd Floor Toronto, ON, Canada M5C 1C4 CA : Stock : Not Available Life Reins 416-847-0192 AMB# 066889	A- Rating Outlook: Stable FSC VII	'05	...	...	...	...	...	...	...	...	...	...	...	...	...	...	...	...
		'06	...	...	...	...	...	...	...	...	...	...	...	...	...	...	...	...
		'07	...	...	...	...	...	...	...	...	...	...	...	...	...	...	...	...
		'08	35.2	...	...	64.8	100,917	91.1	...	...	8.9	74,139	...	14,664	-5,621	-9,649	-10,126	-10,126
		'09	90.6	...	...	9.4	98,453	40.0	...	...	60.0	73,523	...	17,618	7,609	-1,546	-2,025	-2,025
		Rating History: A- g, 10/27/09; A- g, 08/19/08																
AXA EQUITABLE LIFE INS CO CAB AXA S.A. Christopher M. Condron President & CEO 55 Town Centre Court, Suite 606 Scarborough, ON, Canada M1P 4X4 CA : 1968 : Stock : Not Available A&S 416-290-6666 AMB# 066819	A+ Rating Outlook: Stable FSC XV	'05	75.9	...	...	24.1	33,257	60.2	...	1.1	38.7	16,601	234	5,359	-2,393	-1,059	-125	-125
		'06	87.6	...	...	12.4	33,473	50.5	...	0.7	48.7	11,948	198	7,206	7,064	-2,034	-1,587	-1,587
		'07	88.9	...	...	11.1	38,408	56.8	...	0.9	42.3	16,838	166	7,896	1,062	1,753	862	862
		'08	97.0	...	...	3.0	75,824	16.3	...	0.8	82.9	40,282	178	8,076	6,823	-4,482	-3,373	-3,373
		'09	97.3	...	...	2.7	89,110	21.0	...	0.5	78.4	63,670	183	9,084	2,544	15,802	10,422	10,422
		Rating History: A+ g, 06/04/10; A+ g, 06/12/09; A+ g, 05/29/08; A+ g, 01/25/07; A+ g, 08/12/05																
BLUE CROSS LIFE INS CO OF CA James K. Gilligan President & CEO P.O. Box 220 Moncton, NB, Canada E1C 8L3 CA : 1972 : Stock : Not Available Group A&S, Group Life, Ind A&S 506-853-1811 AMB# 068557	A- Rating Outlook: Stable FSC VII	'05	61.1	...	18.8	20.1	213,747	27.8	39.8	...	32.4	48,522	134,222	86,887	22,331	4,033	3,046	3,046
		'06	62.2	...	17.2	20.6	249,094	26.4	44.6	...	29.0	56,402	139,275	101,626	27,817	5,473	3,881	3,881
		'07	66.2	...	16.8	16.9	289,200	27.8	50.0	...	22.2	69,742	158,717	119,575	29,460	7,666	5,380	5,380
		'08	66.7	...	14.3	19.0	316,604	26.7	50.4	...	22.8	72,114	171,823	132,674	31,329	5,640	4,243	4,243
		'09	67.0	...	14.0	19.0	367,165	26.8	50.8	...	22.4	84,340	181,716	139,281	32,692	6,371	4,719	4,719
		Rating History: A-, 02/24/10; A-, 04/30/09; A-, 03/14/08; A-, 03/07/07; A-, 02/06/06																
BMO LIFE ASSURANCE COMPANY Bank of Montreal Peter McCarthy President & CEO 60 Yonge Street Toronto, ON, Canada M5E 1H5 CA : 1994 : Stock : Broker Accident, Sickness, Life 416-596-3900 AMB# 066835	A Rating Outlook: Stable FSC IX	'05	61.0	2.2	...	36.8	1,346,836	44.5	0.0	38.2	17.2	177,866	462,257	374,559	274,471	20,415	18,071	18,071
		'06	60.7	1.5	...	37.8	1,703,069	45.8	0.2	40.2	13.7	224,724	517,540	424,744	291,385	43,233	40,858	40,858
		'07	63.1	1.0	28.0	7.8	2,097,632	43.9	0.3	43.5	12.3	302,017	644,579	541,259	405,000	77,183	48,817	48,817
		'08	67.8	2.0	15.0	15.2	3,101,347	40.3	-0.1	51.0	8.8	335,927	1,135,674	251,399	779,289	-12,697	-45,777	-45,777
		'09	72.4	1.1	14.0	12.5	3,897,106	39.9	0.2	54.4	5.5	368,745	633,326	379,644	341,759	19,312	7,976	7,976
		Rating History: A, 10/30/09; A u, 01/14/09; A, 11/10/08; A gu, 09/15/08; A+ g, 06/17/08																
BMO LIFE INSURANCE COMPANY[1] Bank of Montreal Gordon J. Henderson President & CEO 55 Bloor Street West, 15th Floor Toronto, ON, Canada M4W 3N5 CA : Other : Not Available Group A&S, Group Life, Ind Life AMB# 066874	NR-5	'05	22.2	...	1.6	76.1	46,377	5.2	11.2	...	83.5	35,957	46,035	43,433	...	18,775	12,226	12,226
		'06	20.1	...	1.3	78.5	59,047	-27.2	-99.9	...	227.1	55,085	51,887	48,175	...	29,257	19,128	19,128
		'07	26.1	...	1.4	72.5	70,729	96.9	166.4	...	-99.9	74,644	58,758	54,326	...	29,407	19,307	19,307
		'08	37.7	...	0.9	61.4	82,672	75.0	209.0	...	-99.9	86,683	65,758	60,711	...	34,318	23,140	23,140
		'09	6.3	1.0	70.6	22.2	436,991	5.6	...	-30.4	124.8	405,507	71,261	66,377	...	48,314	39,824	39,824
		Rating History: NR-5, 04/28/10; NR-5, 05/20/09; NR-5, 05/12/08; NR-5, 05/14/07; NR-5, 05/16/06																
CANADA LIFE ASSURANCE CO Power Corporation of Canada D. Allen Loney President & CEO 330 University Avenue Toronto, ON, Canada M5G 1R8 CA : 1847 : Stock : Agency A&S, Ann, Life 416-597-1456 AMB# 006183	A+ Rating Outlook: Stable FSC XV	'05	42.4	20.4	20.9	16.3	14,682,236	5.7	3.0	44.1	47.2	3,121,380	2,784,499	485,207	18,000	540,315	551,463	551,463
		'06	40.7	18.0	27.5	13.7	15,952,258	5.7	3.3	45.3	45.7	4,085,839	3,124,769	1,285,269	2,617,000	696,751	643,317	643,317
		'07	43.0	14.9	28.0	14.1	18,350,105	6.4	3.4	43.8	46.3	4,314,900	3,373,995	993,113	2,508,239	657,592	776,001	776,001
		'08	43.6	14.9	28.7	12.9	18,924,724	5.4	3.6	42.7	48.2	4,982,611	3,354,034	1,079,647	2,138,220	1,142,963	1,047,113	1,047,113
		'09	36.5	11.6	24.7	27.3	22,397,733	6.6	4.0	43.9	45.6	8,172,555	3,627,962	1,306,859	1,185,372	1,090,632	1,052,122	1,052,122
		Rating History: A+ g, 01/22/09; A+ g, 06/22/07; A+ gu, 02/01/07; A+ g, 06/19/06; A+ g, 03/09/05																
CANADA LIFE INS CO OF CANADA Power Corporation of Canada D. Allen Loney President & CEO 330 University Avenue Toronto, ON, Canada M5G 1R8 CA : 1997 : Stock : Not Available Ind Life 416-597-1440 AMB# 066839	NR-3	'05	54.5	20.8	5.0	19.7	4,233,631	82.7	...	...	17.3	181,857	...	303,382	130,713	17,954	5,944	5,944
		'06	57.3	21.5	6.3	15.0	4,302,173	85.7	...	...	14.3	188,033	...	312,033	175,692	22,173	6,176	6,176
		'07	46.4	19.4	6.5	27.7	8,826,602	63.7	9.1	20.8	6.4	685,032	...	4,347,492	...	60,718	48,720	48,720
		'08	44.7	17.4	4.7	33.2	8,739,878	61.9	8.7	18.7	10.8	743,477	...	982,907	...	89,490	64,543	64,543
		'09	40.2	16.0	10.4	33.4	8,835,176	64.3	8.5	19.6	7.7	790,396	...	1,013,506	99,191	199,872	143,027	143,027
		Rating History: NR-3, 01/22/09; NR-3, 06/22/07; NR-3, 02/01/07; NR-3, 06/19/06; NR-3, 03/09/05																
CANADIAN PREMIER LIFE INS CO AEGON N.V. Isaac Sananes President & CEO 80 Tiverton Court, 5th Floor Markham, ON, Canada L3R 0G4 CA : 1955 : Stock : Direct Response A&S, Credit A&S, Credit Life 905-479-3122 AMB# 066801	A- Rating Outlook: Stable FSC VIII	'05	82.2	...	...	17.8	129,201	52.3	-76.3	...	124.1	95,634	168,799	123,537	13,514	16,137	10,438	10,438
		'06	84.5	...	...	15.5	124,083	64.5	-94.5	...	130.0	91,555	185,061	130,515	17,219	29,001	18,921	18,921
		'07	83.2	...	...	16.8	133,398	105.2	-99.9	...	94.7	113,151	204,276	140,022	13,553	32,403	21,261	21,261
		'08	74.9	...	...	25.1	215,760	44.1	-35.0	...	90.9	132,713	260,276	174,400	81,741	37,663	24,522	24,522
		'09	73.4	...	...	26.6	176,176	50.5	-35.9	...	85.4	103,676	294,644	168,874	10,891	32,771	22,375	22,375
		Rating History: A-, 04/23/09; A-, 06/18/08; A-, 05/30/07; A-, 06/21/06; A-, 05/13/05																

BEST'S PROFITABILITY, LEVERAGE AND LIQUIDITY TESTS 2005 – 2009

Canadian Companies — Data in Canadian Dollars

—	Profitability Tests							Leverage Tests						Liquidity Tests					
AOCI ($000)	Benefits Paid to NPW (%)	Comm. & Expenses to NPW (%)	NOG to Total Assets (%)	NOG to Total Rev (%)	Operating Return on Equity (%)	Yield on Invested Assets (%)	Total Return (%)	Change in NPW (%)	NPW to Capital (X)	Capital & Surplus to Liabilities (%)	Surplus Relief (%)	Reins Leverage (%)	Change in Capital (%)	Quick Liquidity (%)	Current Liquidity (%)	Non-Invest Grade Bonds to Capital (%)	Delinq. & Foreclosed Mortgages to Capital (%)	Mort. & Credit Tenant Loans & R.E. to Capital (%)	Affiliated Invest to Capital (%)
...	...	...	...	...	...	...	...	...	...	...	...	...	...	...	...	...	...	...	...
...	30.9	23.3	...	4.0	...	...	...	...	2.5	7.8	...	...	...	2.0	101.0	...	...	63.8	...
5,557	34.9	24.0	4.1	14.5	54.6	5.37	6.32	37.0	2.8	8.3	...	...	23.4	3.6	101.9	...	...	55.5	...
-35,587	36.5	22.5	7.6	28.4	93.2	5.06	-1.56	4.0	2.5	9.4	...	...	16.1	3.9	102.6	...	...	48.3	...
10,423	37.7	26.8	-4.3	-17.1	-50.4	5.43	11.52	5.7	2.1	9.5	...	...	24.9	1.9	104.5	...	...	37.4	...
...	...	...	...	...	...	...	...	...	...	...	...	...	...	...	...	...	...	...	...
...	...	...	...	...	...	...	...	...	...	...	...	...	...	...	...	...	...	...	...
...	...	...	...	...	...	...	...	...	...	...	...	...	...	...	...	...	...	...	...
151	...	14.9	...	-59.5	...	...	...	...	0.2	276.9	...	24.5	...	167.0	366.9	...	...	...	...
372	168.4	40.2	-2.0	-9.6	-2.7	4.24	4.50	20.1	0.2	294.9	0.7	55.4	-0.8	4.4	385.3	...	...	...	...
...	109.3	11.0	-0.4	-1.9	-0.7	4.48	4.48	-11.4	0.3	99.7	...	0.9	-2.9	1.9	181.7	...	...	...	...
...	121.1	8.9	-4.8	-18.6	-11.1	4.47	4.47	34.4	0.6	55.5	...	1.2	-28.0	1.6	142.6	...	...	...	...
352	73.9	8.8	2.4	9.0	6.0	4.48	5.55	9.6	0.5	79.4	...	0.3	40.9	0.8	165.2	...	...	...	...
2,761	109.8	10.1	-5.9	-32.7	-11.8	4.04	8.33	2.3	0.2	122.9	...	0.1	139.2	1.5	228.8	...	...	...	...
1,612	12.4	9.2	12.6	85.2	20.1	3.41	1.99	12.5	0.1	267.2	...	0.0	58.1	0.9	370.6	...	...	...	...
...	44.2	33.6	1.6	3.1	6.9	5.63	11.89	24.1	1.8	29.4	0.3	239.5	20.4	11.4	115.7	...	...	...	...
...	44.7	36.9	1.7	3.4	7.4	5.35	5.64	17.0	1.8	29.3	0.3	222.8	16.2	12.6	116.4	...	...	...	...
5,616	46.0	40.2	2.0	4.0	8.5	4.79	7.17	17.7	1.7	31.8	0.2	197.1	23.7	9.7	120.2	...	...	...	...
1,110	46.5	42.7	1.4	3.0	6.0	2.41	0.68	11.0	1.8	29.5	0.2	200.1	3.4	10.7	119.1	...	...	...	...
5,206	46.6	42.6	1.4	2.9	6.0	6.81	8.15	5.0	1.7	29.8	...	184.4	17.0	16.1	121.5	...	...	...	...
...	17.5	32.0	1.5	4.0	11.2	7.34	7.67	7.2	2.1	15.2	...	307.6	22.0	2.0	103.5	3.4	...	16.5	...
...	16.0	29.5	2.7	7.5	20.3	8.66	8.43	13.4	1.9	15.2	1.0	247.0	26.3	2.8	104.1	2.6	...	11.5	...
-178	15.4	25.4	2.6	8.9	18.5	0.42	0.41	27.4	1.8	16.8	1.5	212.4	34.4	3.6	80.2	1.9	...	7.2	193.1
-738	66.4	46.1	-1.8	-8.1	-14.4	-15.62	-15.64	-53.6	0.7	12.1	...	187.4	11.2	21.4	101.2	...	...	18.3	...
2,700	40.9	20.6	0.2	0.7	2.3	18.49	18.59	51.0	1.0	10.5	...	194.8	9.8	19.0	102.4	...	...	11.8	...
...	6.6	53.5	30.1	27.6	41.0	2.18	2.41	30.8	1.2	345.1	...	15.2	51.5	334.0	436.7	...	...	...	...
...	7.6	50.5	36.3	38.3	42.0	3.30	3.47	10.9	0.9	999.9	...	14.0	53.2	999.9	999.9	...	...	...	...
94	10.5	47.6	29.8	34.0	29.8	3.93	4.08	12.8	0.7	-99.9	...	14.9	35.5	-99.9	-99.9	...	...	...	...
-100	4.7	44.3	30.2	36.6	28.7	3.29	3.03	11.8	0.7	-99.9	...	41.3	16.1	-99.9	-99.9	...	...	...	...
-12	7.6	52.9	15.3	45.8	16.2	-0.66	-0.53	9.3	0.2	999.9	...	9.5	367.8	95.8	372.2	...	...	1.0	75.8
...	471.0	84.3	3.5	27.6	18.3	8.03	8.32	603.4	0.2	27.0	...	178.9	6.9	7.0	66.4	4.7	0.1	96.2	108.8
...	90.9	31.5	4.2	23.8	17.9	7.53	7.54	164.9	0.3	34.4	...	137.8	30.9	8.6	68.7	2.5	...	70.4	108.5
-554,923	131.7	15.7	4.5	33.5	18.5	4.35	1.38	-22.7	0.2	30.7	...	151.9	5.6	9.4	71.6	2.4	...	63.6	109.4
-611,767	113.9	31.2	5.6	46.1	22.5	1.66	1.22	8.7	0.2	35.7	...	122.8	15.5	6.6	72.1	1.1	...	56.4	101.9
-1,062,663	83.2	25.6	5.1	34.9	16.0	7.19	3.61	21.0	0.2	57.5	...	80.8	64.0	7.1	69.9	1.3	...	31.7	104.9
...	53.3	15.5	0.1	1.1	3.3	6.99	10.29	-2.9	1.7	4.5	...	47.5	1.9	3.8	69.5	6.4	...	485.0	25.0
...	56.5	18.7	0.1	1.1	3.3	7.03	8.18	2.9	1.7	4.6	...	25.5	3.4	4.6	68.0	5.4	...	491.0	24.0
165	15.4	1.5	0.7	1.1	11.2	7.50	7.50	999.9	6.3	8.4	...	8.4	264.3	3.9	70.8	1.5	...	249.4	97.3
-5,933	96.0	8.5	0.7	7.4	9.0	2.75	2.66	-77.4	1.3	9.3	...	7.3	8.5	4.0	75.4	0.1	...	204.6	73.0
-1,932	85.2	9.2	1.6	8.5	18.6	7.42	7.48	3.1	1.3	9.8	...	7.3	6.3	5.7	54.1	...	...	179.1	300.7
...	29.4	65.5	8.5	7.7	11.5	4.28	4.21	11.0	1.3	284.9	...	1.0	12.3	39.0	380.9	...	...	...	...
...	22.3	63.4	14.9	13.6	20.2	5.10	5.98	5.6	1.4	281.5	...	1.1	-4.3	29.7	377.7	...	...	...	...
-1,500	20.3	69.3	16.5	14.3	20.8	3.68	2.43	7.3	1.2	558.9	...	1.0	23.6	68.6	653.8	...	...	...	...
-1,957	24.1	77.6	14.0	12.9	19.9	4.96	4.68	24.6	1.3	159.8	...	2.2	17.3	49.3	258.0	...	...	...	...
-869	22.4	46.7	11.4	11.9	18.9	6.56	7.15	-3.2	1.6	143.0	...	2.7	-21.9	52.1	241.8	...	...	...	...

ANNUAL STATEMENT DATA FOR YEARS 2005 – 2009

Canadian Companies — Data in Canadian Dollars

COMPANY NAME Ultimate Parent Association Principal Officer Mailing Address Dom. : Began Bus. : Struct. : Mktg. Specialty Phone # AMB#	Best's Financial Strength Rating FSC	Data Year	Balance Sheet: Bonds (%)	Mort. Loans & R.E. (%)	Com & Pref. Shares (%)	All Other Assets (%)	Total Assets ($000)	Life Reserves (%)	Health Reserves (%)	Ann Res. Liabilities (%)	All Other Liabilities (%)	Capital & Surplus ($000)	Operations: Direct Premiums Written ($000)	Net Premiums Written ($000)	Operating Cash Flow ($000)	NOG Before Taxes ($000)	NOG After Taxes ($000)	Net Income ($000)
CANASSURANCE HOSP SVC ASSN Canassurance Hospital Service Assn Claude Boivin President & CEO 550 Sherbrooke Street West Montreal, QC, Canada H3A 3S3 CA : 1942 : Non-Profit : Broker Ind A&S, Group A&S 514-286-8400 AMB# 066881	**A** Rating Outlook: Stable **FSC IX**	'05	51.7	...	5.1	43.2	223,955	...	25.6	...	74.4	172,152	123,025	121,975	...	19,511	19,511	19,511
		'06	54.9	...	5.4	39.6	241,994	...	26.5	...	73.5	191,567	123,958	123,442	21,219	19,415	19,415	19,415
		'07	74.9	...	18.8	6.4	266,869	...	27.8	...	72.2	218,150	124,450	124,034	20,426	20,511	20,511	20,511
		'08	61.2	...	28.8	10.0	261,691	...	30.2	...	69.8	214,456	126,446	125,994	13,625	11,094	11,094	11,094
		'09	61.0	...	20.8	18.2	295,040	...	29.9	...	70.1	246,275	131,615	131,199	14,909	17,469	17,469	17,469
		Rating History: A g, 05/25/10; A- g, 06/16/09; A- g, 05/16/08; A- g, 03/30/07; A- g, 02/08/06																
CANASSURANCE INSURANCE COMPANY Canassurance Hospital Service Assn Claude Boivin President & CEO 550 Sherbrooke Street West Montreal, QC, Canada H3A 3S3 CA : 1987 : Stock : Agency Ind A&S, Group A&S, Group Life 514-286-8400 AMB# 066878	**A** Rating Outlook: Stable **FSC IX**	'05	49.7	0.5	...	49.8	78,450	13.3	56.0	...	30.7	31,200	22,147	23,881	...	4,104	2,913	2,913
		'06	40.2	0.5	...	59.3	74,971	14.9	59.7	...	25.4	31,387	24,098	25,104	-4,496	282	187	187
		'07	57.8	1.1	3.2	38.0	80,519	16.6	60.8	...	22.6	32,764	29,547	29,064	1,654	808	546	546
		'08	73.1	...	2.3	24.6	86,015	18.3	56.2	...	25.5	31,186	33,870	32,699	3,127	-677	-476	-476
		'09	72.4	...	2.5	25.1	86,863	21.5	60.3	...	18.3	32,706	36,484	35,750	-3,855	603	385	385
		Rating History: A g, 05/25/10; A- g, 06/16/09; A- g, 05/16/08; A- g, 03/30/07; A- g, 02/08/06																
CIBC LIFE INSURANCE CO LTD' Canadian Imperial Bank of Commerce Rick W. Lancaster President & CEO Box 3020, Mississauga Station A Mississauga, ON, Canada L5A 4M2 CA : 1993 : Stock : Not Available A&S 905-306-4903 AMB# 066838	**NR-5**	'05	80.6	...	...	19.4	30,527	-6.8	111.1	...	-4.4	50,784	27,240	13,742	...	8,669	5,351	5,351
		'06	84.2	...	...	15.8	30,167	-4.1	112.9	...	-8.8	57,801	28,611	14,913	...	10,814	7,017	7,017
		'07	77.7	...	...	22.3	29,459	-1.6	111.5	...	-9.9	68,311	32,809	18,549	...	15,856	10,338	10,338
		'08	80.1	...	...	19.9	28,856	-0.9	108.8	...	-7.9	83,408	36,866	22,322	...	22,475	15,080	15,080
		'09	71.3	...	...	28.7	30,599	-0.4	105.8	...	-5.5	98,881	40,350	26,057	...	21,725	14,864	14,864
		Rating History: NR-5, 05/04/10; NR-5, 05/20/09; NR-5, 05/12/08; NR-5, 05/14/07; NR-5, 05/16/06																
CIGNA LIFE INS CO OF CANADA CIGNA Corporation M. Eman Hassan President & CEO 55 Town Centre Court, Suite 606 Scarborough, ON, Canada M1P 4X4 CA : 1979 : Stock : Direct Response A&S, Credit A&S, Credit Life 416-290-6666 AMB# 068625	**NR-5**	'05	81.1	...	...	18.9	42,222	0.7	60.0	7.6	31.6	7,798	9,398	3,024	-1,522	1,294	666	666
		'06	79.3	...	...	20.7	40,683	0.8	56.9	8.3	34.0	9,359	9,385	6,980	-1,467	3,479	2,161	2,161
		'07	76.6	...	...	23.4	37,740	0.8	71.7	12.8	14.7	11,391	10,206	9,894	524	3,329	2,315	2,315
		'08	66.7	...	0.6	32.6	41,084	0.9	67.4	14.0	17.8	14,403	11,894	11,337	4,667	5,124	3,209	3,209
		'09	59.6	...	0.7	39.6	41,272	0.6	67.4	14.0	18.0	15,599	12,662	11,985	-1,524	3,813	2,379	2,379
		Rating History: NR-5, 01/08/10; NR-5, 11/14/08; NR-5, 02/11/08; NR-5, 12/14/06; NR-5, 12/21/05																
CO-OPERATORS LIFE INS CO The Co-operators Group Limited Kathy Bardswick Chief Agent, President & CEO 1920 College Avenue Regina, SK, Canada S4P 1C4 CA : 1981 : Stock : Exclusive Agent Group A&H, Ind Life, Ann 306-347-6200 AMB# 006290	**A** Rating Outlook: Stable **FSC X**	'05	46.0	25.8	15.1	13.1	2,310,572	46.4	18.2	11.0	24.4	440,074	494,039	508,060	53,103	66,628	43,980	43,980
		'06	46.2	24.5	15.8	13.5	2,464,175	44.0	18.3	13.6	24.2	496,735	572,630	610,382	75,325	74,012	53,010	53,010
		'07	47.6	24.4	15.5	12.5	2,636,979	45.5	19.3	14.4	20.8	606,923	534,466	599,998	38,880	72,382	52,827	52,827
		'08	48.7	25.7	12.1	13.5	2,478,426	48.2	20.7	14.7	16.3	582,406	572,584	634,231	49,314	67,522	46,950	46,950
		'09	46.0	23.8	17.1	13.1	2,630,383	48.6	19.8	14.2	17.4	676,197	569,295	631,608	4,528	45,571	33,696	33,696
		Rating History: A, 03/16/10; A, 02/25/09; A, 12/21/07; A, 12/20/06; A, 11/21/05																
COLISEE RE CAB AXA S.A. Philippe Donnet President 1800 McGill College Avenue, Suite 2000 Montreal, QC, Canada H3A 3J6 CA : 1982 : Stock : Not Available Reins 514-842-9262 AMB# 066868	**NR-4**	'05	87.6	...	...	12.4	30,239	78.9	2.4	...	18.7	15,540	...	3,051	1,779	970	870	870
		'06	90.3	...	...	9.7	32,155	81.1	1.6	...	17.3	16,892	...	2,809	1,565	1,665	1,352	1,352
		'07	94.8	...	...	5.2	31,545	91.0	1.3	...	7.8	12,238	...	2,637	1,145	1,859	1,497	1,497
		'08	92.4	...	...	7.6	30,789	89.2	1.4	...	9.4	13,452	...	2,631	18	2,081	1,214	1,214
		'09	90.6	...	...	9.4	33,538	91.3	2.5	...	6.2	15,061	...	2,564	...	1,050	1,609	1,609
		Rating History: NR-4, 07/07/08; A- g, 07/07/08; A- g, 07/03/07; A g, 07/06/05; A- g, 06/21/04																
COMBINED INS CO OF AMER CAB ACE Limited Douglas R. Wendt President & CEO 300 - 7300 Warden Avenue Markham, ON, Canada L3R 0X3 CA : 1956 : Stock : Not Available A&S 905-305-1922 AMB# 069320	**A** Rating Outlook: Stable **FSC X**	'05	89.9	...	1.8	8.3	548,984	20.6	58.0	0.0	21.4	241,850	210,416	210,367	48,613	76,623	51,168	51,168
		'06	85.7	...	6.0	8.3	565,233	20.2	62.1	0.0	17.7	241,538	219,553	219,490	57,833	60,641	42,021	42,021
		'07	84.5	...	5.0	10.5	615,753	20.3	56.0	0.1	23.7	306,293	226,283	226,186	80,762	123,970	81,567	81,567
		'08	88.8	...	4.3	6.9	590,144	21.6	51.4	0.1	26.9	353,884	229,676	218,076	-42,894	72,914	51,621	51,621
		'09	95.4	...	...	4.6	543,011	25.1	56.4	0.1	18.4	325,739	232,407	185,608	59,222	96,805	61,938	61,938
		Rating History: A g, 05/03/10; A g, 03/20/09; A g, 04/11/08; A gu, 12/17/07; A gu, 08/01/07																
COMPCORP LIFE INSURANCE CO' Gordon M. Dunning President & CEO 1 Queen Street East Toronto, ON, Canada M5C 2X9 CA : Stock : Not Available Life, A&S 416-359-2001 AMB# 066880	**NR-5**	'05	...	...	...	100.0	10,000	...	...	...	100.0	9,845	...	...	...	...	...	...
		'06	...	...	...	100.0	10,000	...	...	...	100.0	9,799	...	...	...	-46	-46	-46
		'07	...	...	...	100.0	10,000	...	...	...	100.0	9,754	...	...	...	-45	-45	-45
		'08	...	...	...	100.0	10,000	...	...	...	100.0	9,694	...	...	...	-60	-60	-60
		'09	...	...	...	100.0	10,000	...	...	...	100.0	9,646	...	...	...	-48	-48	-48
		Rating History: NR-5, 05/04/10; NR-5, 05/20/09; NR-5, 05/09/08; NR-5, 05/14/07; NR-5, 05/17/06																
CONNECTICUT GENERAL LIFE CAB' CIGNA Corporation Eman Hassan Chief Agent in Canada 55 Town Centre Court, Suite 606 Scarborough, ON, Canada M1P 4X4 CA : 1946 : Stock : Not Available A&S 416-290-0789 AMB# 069322	**A** Rating Outlook: Negative **FSC XV**	'05	91.0	...	...	9.0	69,603	90.5	3.2	3.0	3.3	10,741	4,917	4,859	1,934	-3,072	-2,658	-2,658
		'06	26.1	...	...	73.9	72,950	87.1	2.5	3.1	7.2	11,793	5,622	5,560	6,780	5,068	3,358	3,358
		'07	93.0	...	...	7.0	76,620	90.2	3.1	3.8	2.9	19,449	4,895	4,826	-8,947	-873	-1,804	-1,804
		'08	91.7	...	...	8.3	100,166	92.6	1.8	3.2	2.4	18,691	4,043	3,963	7,519	-6,241	-5,004	-5,004
		'09	96.9	...	...	3.1	98,506	91.3	2.3	3.7	2.7	29,698	4,074	3,846	3,929	19,817	13,795	13,795
		Rating History: A g, 01/08/10; A g, 11/14/08; A g, 02/11/08; A g, 12/14/06; A- g, 12/21/05																

BEST'S PROFITABILITY, LEVERAGE AND LIQUIDITY TESTS 2005 – 2009

Canadian Companies — Data in Canadian Dollars

—	Profitability Tests							Leverage Tests						Liquidity Tests					
AOCI ($000)	Benefits Paid to NPW (%)	Comm. & Expenses to NPW (%)	NOG to Total Assets (%)	NOG to Total Rev (%)	Operating Return on Equity (%)	Yield on Invested Assets (%)	Total Return (%)	Change in NPW (%)	NPW to Capital (X)	Capital & Surplus to Liabilities (%)	Surplus Relief (%)	Reins Leverage (%)	Change in Capital (%)	Quick Liquidity (%)	Current Liquidity (%)	Non-Invest Grade Bonds to Capital (%)	Delinq. & Foreclosed Mortgages to Capital (%)	Mort. & Credit Tenant Loans & R.E. to Capital (%)	Affiliated Invest to Capital (%)
...	67.2	24.8	9.3	14.8	12.0	4.55	5.97	4.8	0.7	332.3	...	...	12.8	35.3	331.9	...	...	...	21.7
...	64.1	25.9	8.3	14.7	10.7	4.42	4.48	1.2	0.6	379.9	...	...	11.3	34.1	383.5	...	...	...	16.4
218,150	63.3	28.6	8.1	15.2	10.0	5.16	6.23	0.5	0.6	447.8	...	...	13.9	39.6	462.6	...	...	...	15.0
214,456	64.0	30.1	4.2	8.5	5.1	2.53	-2.12	1.6	0.6	454.0	...	...	-1.7	86.8	458.4	...	...	...	14.5
1,890	66.0	30.7	6.3	12.0	7.6	5.92	5.92	4.1	0.5	505.0	...	...	14.8	102.9	500.2	...	...	...	13.2
...	53.6	54.2	3.9	10.4	9.8	6.17	7.06	25.0	0.8	66.0	...	100.2	10.3	2.5	140.3	...	...	1.2	1.1
...	49.8	62.3	0.2	0.6	0.6	5.67	5.56	5.1	0.8	72.0	0.7	93.3	0.6	1.6	138.7	...	...	1.2	1.1
-139	43.0	63.1	0.7	1.7	1.7	5.84	5.63	15.8	0.9	68.6	0.4	94.3	4.4	4.9	148.6	...	...	2.6	1.1
-1,241	36.8	63.7	-0.6	-1.3	-1.5	5.73	4.15	12.5	1.0	56.9	...	90.2	-4.8	12.4	133.0	...	...	...	1.2
-106	40.7	54.5	0.4	1.0	1.2	3.69	5.32	9.3	1.1	60.4	...	79.1	4.9	4.6	131.8	...	...	...	1.2
...	49.4	58.7	14.3	33.8	10.2	5.71	6.03	14.9	0.3	-99.9	...	36.2	-6.7	-12.3	-99.9	...	...	...	...
...	40.8	61.0	23.1	42.8	12.9	5.20	4.99	8.5	0.3	-99.9	...	39.7	13.8	-11.0	-99.9	...	...	...	...
20	29.3	66.9	34.7	52.1	16.4	4.65	4.72	24.4	0.3	-99.9	...	37.4	18.2	-12.8	-74.8	...	...	...	...
37	20.1	56.6	51.7	63.4	19.9	4.74	4.80	20.3	0.3	-99.9	...	33.3	22.1	-6.9	-52.1	...	...	...	...
646	16.9	58.4	50.0	53.0	16.3	3.54	5.66	16.7	0.3	-99.9	...	33.7	18.6	-11.0	-43.4	...	...	...	...
...	119.7	78.2	1.5	12.0	7.4	6.22	5.41	5.5	0.4	22.7	...	128.4	-23.0	10.2	113.2	...	...	...	...
...	84.6	43.3	5.2	22.7	25.2	6.08	5.24	130.8	0.7	29.9	...	76.6	20.0	9.9	119.2	...	...	...	...
1,950	75.8	20.4	5.9	21.1	22.3	4.98	10.40	41.7	0.9	43.2	...	25.5	21.7	18.9	134.5	...	...	...	...
2,152	61.5	34.1	8.1	20.8	24.9	3.07	3.63	14.6	0.8	54.0	...	21.4	26.4	37.4	151.9	...	...	...	...
1,969	50.9	35.6	5.8	15.7	15.9	3.85	3.35	5.7	0.8	60.8	...	18.2	8.3	39.5	154.4	...	...	...	...
...	66.9	40.1	2.0	6.6	10.5	7.40	7.34	3.5	1.2	23.5	...	42.2	11.0	13.1	80.7	...	0.1	135.3	9.0
...	60.3	37.5	2.2	6.8	11.3	7.06	7.66	20.1	1.2	25.2	...	41.6	12.9	14.1	83.3	...	...	121.8	8.4
17,518	63.7	44.8	2.1	7.2	9.6	5.31	6.04	-1.7	1.0	29.9	...	46.0	22.2	15.3	88.7	0.3	...	105.8	1.6
-53,557	60.3	44.9	1.8	6.3	7.9	4.03	1.02	5.7	1.1	30.7	...	56.1	-4.0	12.1	83.8	0.2	...	109.6	2.3
6,762	58.2	48.1	1.3	4.3	5.4	5.78	8.35	-0.4	0.9	34.6	...	48.8	16.1	11.9	83.6	0.2	...	92.6	17.9
...	45.7	27.6	3.0	17.7	5.8	6.72	7.05	2.1	0.2	105.7	...	...	5.9	22.9	204.3	...	...	...	...
...	53.0	32.4	4.3	28.6	8.3	6.37	5.21	-7.9	0.2	110.7	...	...	8.7	19.0	209.5	...	...	...	...
2,311	48.1	29.9	4.7	37.1	10.3	4.51	11.51	-6.1	0.2	72.0	...	...	-27.6	8.3	184.7	...	...	...	...
606	75.2	27.2	3.9	28.5	9.5	5.37	-0.28	-0.2	0.2	80.4	...	...	9.9	12.0	183.2	...	...	...	...
1,334	62.4	26.6	5.0	37.8	11.3	5.42	7.66	-2.5	0.2	87.9	...	...	12.0	17.6	194.9	...	...	...	...
...	35.9	35.8	9.5	21.7	22.4	4.63	4.84	3.8	0.9	78.7	...	0.1	12.1	11.3	172.8	...	...	...	...
...	33.4	36.0	7.5	17.6	17.4	3.60	3.03	4.3	0.9	74.6	...	0.1	-0.1	14.3	167.3	...	...	...	...
-441	33.3	36.9	13.8	32.4	29.8	4.38	4.31	3.1	0.7	98.8	...	0.1	26.8	22.3	191.9	...	...	...	...
10,669	81.6	33.7	8.6	20.7	15.6	5.47	7.35	-3.6	0.6	156.9	...	29.6	15.5	9.9	244.9	...	...	...	...
13,090	29.1	30.0	10.9	29.2	18.2	4.76	5.20	-14.9	0.6	159.5	5.5	36.0	-8.0	6.0	260.6	...	...	...	...
...	...	...	...	...	...	...	...	...	...	999.9	...	...	-0.4	...	999.9	...	...	...	...
...	...	...	-0.5	...	-0.5	...	...	...	...	999.9	...	...	-0.5	...	999.9	...	...	...	...
...	...	...	-0.5	...	-0.5	...	...	...	...	999.9	...	...	-0.5	...	999.9	...	...	...	...
...	...	...	-0.6	...	-0.6	...	...	...	...	999.9	...	...	-0.6	...	999.9	...	...	...	...
...	...	...	-0.5	...	-0.5	...	...	...	...	999.9	...	...	-0.5	...	999.9	...	...	...	...
...	15.0	12.6	-3.8	-32.3	-21.0	5.32	4.94	3.8	0.5	18.2	...	59.1	-26.6	1.5	109.2	...	...	...	...
...	57.8	12.3	4.7	38.1	29.8	4.92	5.27	14.4	0.5	19.3	...	47.4	9.8	81.4	113.0	...	...	...	...
1,625	89.2	13.5	-2.4	-20.9	-11.5	5.12	7.38	-13.2	0.2	35.0	...	45.0	64.9	0.7	129.7	...	...	...	...
2,697	65.8	15.3	-5.7	-25.1	-26.2	20.96	22.21	-17.9	0.2	23.7	...	53.3	-3.9	3.4	120.4	...	...	...	...
5,303	76.2	17.1	13.9	162.2	57.0	4.94	7.60	-3.0	0.1	46.8	...	28.8	58.9	1.7	152.3	...	...	...	...

2010 BEST'S KEY RATING GUIDE — LIFE/HEALTH EDITION
ANNUAL STATEMENT DATA FOR YEARS 2005 – 2009

Canadian Companies — Data in Canadian Dollars

COMPANY NAME Ultimate Parent Association Principal Officer Mailing Address Dom. : Began Bus. : Struct. : Mktg. Specialty Phone # AMB#	Best's Financial Strength Rating FSC	Data Year	Balance Sheet: Bonds (%)	Mort. Loans & R.E. (%)	Com & Pref. Shares (%)	All Other Assets (%)	Total Assets ($000)	Life Reserves (%)	Health Reserves (%)	Ann Res. Liabilities (%)	All Other Liabilities (%)	Capital & Surplus ($000)	Operations: Direct Premiums Written ($000)	Net Premiums Written ($000)	Operating Cash Flow ($000)	NOG Before Taxes ($000)	NOG After Taxes ($000)	Net Income ($000)
CROWN LIFE INSURANCE COMPANY[1] Power Corporation of Canada D. Allen Loney President & CEO 1874 Scarth Street, Suite 1900 Regina, SK, Canada S4P 4B3 CA : 1901 : Stock : Agency A&S, Ann, Life 306-546-8000 AMB# 006300	NR-5	'05	50.4	4.0	3.6	41.9	701,092	...	...	...	100.0	201,669	85,632	23,365	9,906	11,798	13,720	13,720
		'06	58.0	1.9	3.8	36.4	691,623	...	...	...	100.0	218,522	102,826	20,555	4,287	17,228	16,545	16,545
		'07	83.1	...	...	16.9	454,812	...	...	...	100.0	101,103	93,258	19,134	...	32,719	6,762	6,762
		'08	84.7	...	...	15.3	463,724	...	...	...	100.0	81,742	92,630	16,873	...	13,907	11,097	11,097
		'09	78.4	...	...	21.6	448,064	...	...	...	100.0	80,778	87,218	17,246	...	12,892	5,879	5,879
		Rating History: NR-5, 06/15/10; NR-4, 01/22/09; NR-4, 12/06/07; A-, 12/06/07; A-, 12/22/06																
CUMIS LIFE INSURANCE COMPANY The Co-operators Group Limited Kathy Bardswick CEO PO Box 5065 Burlington, ON, Canada L7R 4C2 CA : 1977 : Stock : Not Available Group Life 905-632-1221 AMB# 008815	NR-3	'05	82.3	1.8	6.7	9.2	602,614	8.2	14.3	47.0	30.5	91,573	256,978	151,080	30,586	20,567	14,247	14,247
		'06	81.7	1.8	7.1	9.4	600,880	7.1	13.9	45.8	33.2	80,341	259,233	154,481	-2,247	22,628	15,368	15,368
		'07	78.4	2.7	5.6	13.3	601,821	7.0	15.0	50.2	27.9	109,368	274,587	167,027	5,620	42,681	32,281	32,281
		'08	76.4	5.1	3.7	14.9	537,683	6.9	15.0	50.6	27.5	79,371	271,526	161,746	-20,796	18,719	12,597	12,597
		'09	71.6	4.9	0.7	22.8	596,235	6.7	12.6	46.1	34.7	66,784	286,484	170,311	74,915	6,155	4,566	4,566
		Rating History: NR-3, 06/14/10; NR-5, 04/10/09; NR-5, 01/30/08; NR-5, 01/05/07; NR-5, 11/23/05																
CUNA MUTUAL INS SOCIETY CAB CUNA Mutual Insurance Society Jeff H. Post President & CEO 151 North Service Road Burlington, ON, Canada L7R 4C2 CA : 1942 : Mutual : Not Available Life 905-632-1221 AMB# 069318	A Rating Outlook: Negative FSC XII	'05	81.6	...	0.4	18.0	22,779	83.8	...	...	16.2	5,064	297	150	-424	-660	-466	-466
		'06	84.3	...	0.5	15.2	21,745	80.0	...	...	20.0	6,035	275	137	93	2,254	1,104	1,104
		'07	84.5	...	0.5	15.1	21,624	79.1	...	...	20.9	6,226	262	119	180	658	285	285
		'08	87.5	...	0.5	12.1	21,596	79.4	...	...	20.6	6,002	255	126	229	-66	-29	-29
		'09	85.4	...	0.5	14.1	21,248	78.8	...	...	21.2	6,638	236	117	443	637	636	636
		Rating History: A, 04/06/10; A, 03/24/09; A, 01/30/08; A g, 01/05/07; A g, 11/23/05																
EMPIRE LIFE INS CO E-L Financial Corp Ltd Les Herr President & CEO 259 King Street East Kingston, ON, Canada K7L 3A8 CA : 1923 : Stock : Agency Group A&S, Ind Ann, Ind Life 613-548-1881 AMB# 006329	A Rating Outlook: Stable FSC XI	'05	49.8	8.0	19.5	22.7	2,961,186	48.5	2.9	36.1	12.5	457,604	585,056	538,552	5,884	43,232	35,464	35,464
		'06	55.7	7.5	19.7	17.1	3,252,862	50.1	3.0	32.4	14.4	519,758	650,155	601,873	79,928	95,130	62,154	62,154
		'07	59.6	6.8	19.1	14.5	3,867,411	62.9	3.4	27.9	5.8	707,922	685,699	631,326	65,164	68,563	50,712	50,712
		'08	61.4	6.9	16.5	15.2	3,758,853	60.1	4.0	26.6	9.3	645,826	745,559	686,178	106,831	73,757	45,088	45,088
		'09	63.4	5.4	21.2	10.0	4,411,783	58.0	3.3	27.9	10.8	811,866	927,163	839,876	329,514	69,648	64,926	64,926
		Rating History: A, 06/10/10; A, 06/12/09; A, 06/02/08; A, 06/15/07; A, 04/26/06																
EMPLOYERS REASSURANCE CAB[1] General Electric Company 123 Front Street West, Suite 800 Toronto, ON, Canada M5J 2M2 CA : 1999 : Stock : Not Available Life Reins 416-217-5500 AMB# 066867	A- Rating Outlook: Stable FSC X	'05	85.9	...	...	14.1	725,682	66.6	6.9	...	26.5	389,039	...	163,625	20,848	99,648	70,810	70,810
		'06	82.2	...	...	17.8	898,869	44.0	34.0	...	22.0	385,053	...	259,704	124,894	-25,700	-17,946	-17,946
		'07	90.2	...	...	9.8	1,022,980	59.0	28.1	...	12.9	396,043	...	173,660	91,688	103,257	79,518	79,518
		'08	91.0	...	...	9.0	1,058,732	49.3	33.6	...	17.0	497,271	...	169,288	66,210	129,787	88,530	88,530
		'09	91.9	...	...	8.1	1,086,490	48.9	34.8	...	16.3	507,824	...	174,185	65,809	89,392	67,744	67,744
		Rating History: A- g, 05/27/09; A- g, 06/09/08; A-, 06/13/07; B++g, 06/12/06; B++g, 03/31/05																
EQUITABLE LIFE INS CO OF CA Ronald E. Beettam President & CEO PO Box 1603, Stn. Waterloo Waterloo, ON, Canada N2J 4C7 CA : 1920 : Mutual : Broker Ann, Life, Health 519-886-5110 AMB# 006343	NR-5	'05	40.4	26.4	23.2	9.9	1,025,152	43.5	3.5	33.3	19.7	167,042	341,846	244,696	35,113	17,790	14,366	14,366
		'06	37.5	24.0	27.7	10.8	1,094,317	44.1	3.7	31.3	20.9	183,189	367,992	267,210	16,595	19,148	16,147	16,147
		'07	42.2	21.5	25.4	10.9	1,189,288	48.9	3.5	29.9	17.7	207,391	391,150	288,047	22,037	26,790	21,420	21,420
		'08	44.9	21.4	22.6	11.1	1,132,407	48.2	3.0	29.6	19.2	236,044	398,982	294,132	16,654	29,228	21,952	21,952
		'09	47.1	18.0	23.9	11.0	1,317,606	45.2	2.3	36.5	16.0	269,643	520,887	414,119	139,488	36,695	29,648	29,648
		Rating History: NR-5, 04/26/10; NR-5, 05/21/09; NR-5, 05/12/08; NR-5, 04/27/07; NR-5, 05/16/06																
EXCELLENCE LIFE INSURANCE CO Industrial Alliance Ins & Financial Svcs Antoine Ponce President 5055, boul Metropolitain est Montreal, QC, Canada H1R 1Z7 CA Life, A&S 514-327-0020 AMB# 066890	NR-3	'05	...	...	...	...	...	...	...	...	...	...	...	...	...	...	...	...
		'06	...	...	...	...	...	...	...	...	...	...	...	...	...	...	...	...
		'07	80.0	3.7	...	16.2	86,094	15.1	63.7	...	21.2	21,314	85,079	44,799	597	5,061	3,417	3,417
		'08	80.7	3.5	...	15.7	93,844	12.4	67.3	...	20.3	24,977	89,607	48,044	5,406	5,288	3,663	3,663
		'09	81.8	3.4	...	14.8	100,817	10.6	71.7	...	17.7	27,020	93,290	50,285	6,077	5,571	3,821	3,821
		Rating History: NR-3, 03/12/10; NR-5, 02/12/09; NR-5, 06/18/08																
FIRST ALLMERICA FINL LF CAB Goldman Sachs Group Inc Michael A. Reardon President & CEO 40 King Street West Toronto, ON, Canada M5H 3C2 CA : 1960 : Stock : Not Available In Run Off 416-869-5300 AMB# 069349	A- Rating Outlook: Stable FSC I	'05	89.1	...	...	10.9	2,280	88.6	...	...	11.4	934	36	36	-37	-45	-45	-45
		'06	88.9	...	...	11.1	2,271	90.3	...	...	9.7	781	32	32	-4	-148	-148	-148
		'07	91.2	...	...	8.8	2,201	90.0	...	...	10.0	1,036	17	17	-409	-103	-103	-103
		'08	91.2	...	...	8.8	2,240	90.5	...	...	9.5	781	15	15	256	-59	-59	-59
		'09	92.1	...	...	7.9	2,217	82.7	...	...	17.3	933	17	17	-123	97	97	97
		Rating History: A- g, 08/24/09; A- g, 01/19/09; B+ u, 07/31/08; B+, 06/12/08; B+, 05/23/07																
GAN VIE CO FRANCAISE ASSR CAB[1] Groupama S.A. Eric L. Clark Chief Agent 1155 Metcalfe Street, Suite 1470 Montreal, QC, Canada H3B 2V6 CA : 1979 : Stock : Not Available Ind Life 514-288-1900 AMB# 066861	NR-5	'05	88.1	...	...	11.9	19,992	84.1	...	...	15.9	8,550	342	-22	488	312	488	488
		'06	88.4	...	...	11.6	20,002	85.7	...	...	14.3	8,825	331	-61	328	448	275	275
		'07	91.0	...	...	9.0	19,971	99.6	...	...	0.4	9,409	326	-45	238	377	234	234
		'08	88.4	...	...	11.6	15,544	99.2	...	...	0.8	4,542	299	-80	344	9	133	133
		'09	94.6	...	...	5.4	15,096	99.4	...	...	0.6	4,780	301	-102	-95	1,186	238	238
		Rating History: NR-5, 04/28/10; NR-5, 05/20/09; NR-5, 05/09/08; NR-5, 05/14/07; NR-5, 05/16/06																

BEST'S PROFITABILITY, LEVERAGE AND LIQUIDITY TESTS 2005 – 2009

Canadian Companies — Data in Canadian Dollars

—	Profitability Tests							Leverage Tests						Liquidity Tests					
AOCI ($000)	Benefits Paid to NPW (%)	Comm. & Expenses to NPW (%)	NOG to Total Assets (%)	NOG to Total Rev (%)	Operating Return on Equity (%)	Yield on Invested Assets (%)	Total Return (%)	Change in NPW (%)	NPW to Capital (X)	Capital & Surplus to Liabilities (%)	Surplus Relief (%)	Reins Leverage (%)	Change in Capital (%)	Quick Liquidity (%)	Current Liquidity (%)	Non-Invest Grade Bonds to Capital (%)	Delinq. & Foreclosed Mortgages to Capital (%)	Mort. & Credit Tenant Loans & R.E. to Capital (%)	Affiliated Invest to Capital (%)
...	154.1	48.4	2.0	22.3	7.0	6.19	5.45	-9.0	0.1	40.4	...	2.6	7.2	49.1	126.9	...	...	14.0	...
...	199.9	38.1	2.4	27.0	7.9	6.30	6.04	-12.0	0.1	46.2	...	2.4	8.4	44.5	135.6	...	...	5.9	...
3,646	202.7	86.3	1.2	7.9	4.2	12.95	11.18	-6.9	0.2	28.6	...	...	-53.7	15.7	127.3	...	...	...	...
13,203	223.9	12.4	2.4	51.5	12.1	0.92	3.05	-11.8	0.2	21.4	...	...	-19.1	13.8	119.6	...	...	...	...
6,360	198.9	0.6	1.3	8.5	7.2	12.56	10.98	2.2	0.2	22.0	...	...	-1.2	16.9	120.8	...	...	...	...
...	50.2	43.3	2.4	7.9	16.6	5.39	5.38	3.9	1.6	17.9	...	96.9	14.0	8.6	112.9	...	...	11.9	...
...	59.4	44.5	2.6	8.2	17.9	5.55	5.32	2.3	1.9	15.4	...	105.9	-12.3	8.4	110.3	...	...	13.1	...
165	56.9	42.1	5.4	15.7	34.0	6.62	6.65	8.1	1.5	22.2	...	78.1	36.1	12.4	116.2	...	...	14.7	...
-8,929	62.6	44.3	2.2	7.0	13.3	3.27	1.55	-3.2	2.0	17.3	...	95.3	-27.4	9.7	108.5	...	...	34.2	...
-82	52.5	42.7	0.8	2.3	6.2	5.00	6.67	5.3	2.6	12.6	...	123.5	-15.9	17.6	105.9	...	...	43.3	...
...	160.7	214.0	-2.0	-74.4	-8.4	2.32	2.37	-3.8	0.0	28.6	...	...	-15.5	4.2	109.6	...	...	...	...
...	192.7	192.7	5.0	188.4	19.9	2.26	2.27	-8.7	0.0	38.4	...	...	19.2	4.9	122.4	...	...	...	...
...	195.8	34.5	1.3	72.9	4.6	1.37	1.37	-13.1	0.0	40.4	...	...	3.2	5.5	125.7	...	...	...	...
...	200.8	358.7	-0.1	-3.0	-0.5	4.20	4.20	5.9	0.0	38.5	...	...	-3.6	2.8	124.0	...	...	...	...
...	252.1	268.4	3.0	145.5	10.1	1.60	1.60	-7.1	0.0	45.4	...	...	10.6	8.9	133.5	...	...	...	...
...	73.9	39.5	1.2	4.4	8.0	7.92	9.16	14.1	1.2	18.3	...	25.3	5.9	18.3	93.7	6.1	...	51.8	...
...	70.7	40.7	2.0	6.8	12.7	8.24	10.48	11.8	1.2	19.0	0.4	20.5	13.6	17.1	96.2	...	...	47.1	...
42,513	71.9	44.6	1.4	5.6	8.3	5.18	6.41	4.9	0.9	22.4	0.3	17.0	36.2	19.7	103.4	0.7	...	37.1	...
-64,671	68.9	38.9	1.2	6.6	6.7	-2.90	-5.84	8.7	1.1	20.7	0.3	6.8	-8.8	17.0	105.9	0.7	...	40.0	...
36,443	56.8	30.0	1.6	5.3	8.9	7.18	9.66	22.4	1.0	22.6	...	3.6	25.7	16.2	111.5	...	...	29.5	...
...	58.4	30.9	8.6	30.8	14.9	9.30	11.09	1.8	0.4	115.6	...	1.4	-30.7	7.8	200.9	...	...	...	...
...	47.1	22.1	-2.2	-5.8	-4.6	6.60	7.48	58.7	0.7	74.9	...	1.9	-1.0	14.3	164.7	...	...	...	...
80,865	75.9	12.0	8.3	32.3	20.4	8.40	17.03	-33.1	0.4	72.5	...	3.8	2.9	7.4	182.5	...	...	...	...
44,367	76.1	9.2	8.5	38.9	19.8	5.96	2.23	-2.5	0.3	96.2	...	4.5	25.6	9.6	201.8	...	...	...	...
58,809	69.6	7.8	6.3	29.4	13.5	5.53	6.91	2.9	0.3	97.7	0.0	4.4	2.1	9.0	207.6	...	...	...	...
...	77.3	33.7	1.4	4.5	9.0	6.19	7.61	7.8	1.5	19.5	...	122.1	9.4	9.7	69.7	...	...	162.2	0.1
...	72.1	37.2	1.5	4.5	9.2	7.36	7.22	9.2	1.5	20.1	...	127.2	9.7	12.6	72.0	...	...	143.4	0.1
159,195	71.1	44.7	1.9	6.3	11.0	2.96	16.39	7.8	1.4	21.1	...	150.9	13.2	13.5	80.5	...	...	123.3	0.1
190,332	67.2	46.4	1.9	7.5	9.9	-1.92	0.81	2.1	1.2	26.3	...	129.9	13.8	12.9	86.3	...	...	102.4	3.4
207,773	47.1	32.7	2.4	5.6	11.7	8.38	-8.08	40.8	1.5	25.7	...	107.9	14.2	13.1	91.4	...	...	87.8	0.3
...	...	...	...	...	...	...	...	...	...	...	...	...	...	...	...	...	...	...	...
...	...	...	...	...	...	...	...	...	...	...	...	...	...	...	...	...	...	...	...
191	43.4	49.9	...	7.1	...	...	...	...	2.1	32.9	...	211.4	...	1.8	125.9	...	...	15.1	...
...	40.5	48.3	4.1	7.1	15.8	5.11	4.86	7.2	1.9	36.3	...	181.5	17.2	0.9	129.7	...	...	13.2	...
76	39.0	50.8	3.9	7.1	14.7	4.46	4.55	4.7	1.9	36.6	...	205.3	8.2	0.0	129.1	...	...	12.5	...
...	144.4	258.3	-2.0	-36.3	-4.7	3.90	3.90	-10.0	0.0	69.4	...	...	-4.1	1.9	152.7	...	...	...	...
...	37.5	243.8	-6.5	-99.9	-17.3	3.81	3.81	-11.1	0.0	52.4	...	...	-16.4	1.3	136.9	...	...	...	...
...	999.9	999.9	-4.6	-99.9	-11.3	3.23	3.23	-46.9	0.0	88.9	...	...	32.7	1.6	174.0	...	...	...	...
...	6.7	-99.9	-2.7	-64.8	-6.5	3.48	3.48	-11.8	0.0	53.5	...	...	-24.6	1.3	141.3	...	...	...	...
...	-36.4	999.9	4.4	115.5	11.3	3.33	3.33	-26.7	0.0	72.7	...	...	19.5	2.6	161.7	...	...	...	...
...	-99.9	-99.9	2.5	62.3	5.9	4.70	6.98	-99.9	0.0	74.7	...	15.2	6.1	1.6	156.5	...	...	...	...
...	-99.9	-99.9	1.4	37.1	3.2	4.52	4.43	-99.9	0.0	79.0	...	17.1	3.2	3.9	162.5	...	...	...	...
...	-99.9	-99.9	1.2	32.6	2.6	4.22	4.22	27.9	0.0	89.1	...	18.9	6.6	1.8	174.4	...	...	...	...
...	-43.8	-99.9	0.7	18.3	1.9	5.08	5.08	-81.8	0.0	41.3	...	41.9	-51.7	1.3	126.5	...	...	...	...
...	-99.9	-99.9	1.6	24.1	5.1	7.92	7.92	-27.5	0.0	46.3	0.4	42.0	5.2	1.3	140.2	...	...	...	...

Canadian Companies — Data in Canadian Dollars

COMPANY NAME / Ultimate Parent Association / Principal Officer / Mailing Address / Dom. : Began Bus. : Struct. : Mktg. / Specialty / Phone # / AMB#	Best's Financial Strength Rating / FSC	Data Year	Balance Sheet: Bonds (%)	Mort. Loans & R.E. (%)	Com & Pref. Shares (%)	All Other Assets (%)	Total Assets ($000)	Life Reserves (%)	Health Reserves (%)	Ann Res. Liabilities (%)	All Other Liabilities (%)	Capital & Surplus ($000)	Operations: Direct Premiums Written ($000)	Net Premiums Written ($000)	Operating Cash Flow ($000)	NOG Before Taxes ($000)	NOG After Taxes ($000)	Net Income ($000)
GENERAL AMERICAN LIFE CAB MetLife Inc	A+ u	'05	87.3	...	...	12.7	1,161,270	85.1	...	...	14.9	553,400	...	176,466	54,669	170,358	127,141	127,141
Kevin C. Eichner President & CEO		'06	85.7	...	...	14.3	1,225,877	85.8	...	...	14.2	715,644	...	189,809	-17,074	163,810	112,922	112,922
1255 Peel Street, Suite 1000 Montreal, QC, Canada H3B 2T9	Under Review Implication: Negative	'07	95.8	...	...	4.2	1,409,158	83.4	...	...	16.6	844,565	...	196,498	6,938	191,945	114,866	114,866
CA : 1963 : Stock : Not Available A&S		'08	92.0	...	...	8.0	1,201,185	82.2	...	...	17.8	770,903	...	204,334	-21,823	158,143	119,509	119,509
514-985-5260		'09	90.8	...	...	9.2	1,256,211	84.9	...	...	15.1	760,391	...	205,832	3,967	-3,847	-10,512	-10,512
AMB# 066822	FSC XV	**Rating History: A+ gu, 02/09/10; A+ g, 02/20/09; A+ g, 06/05/08; A+ g, 05/29/07; A+ g, 05/05/06**																
GENERAL RE LIFE CORP CAB Berkshire Hathaway Inc	A++	'05	48.2	...	...	51.8	9,066	81.7	...	...	18.3	6,565	...	1,826	1,372	1,445	1,445	1,445
Christopher Walton Chief Agent		'06	2.4	...	...	97.6	8,467	93.5	...	...	6.5	6,475	...	2,081	-547	-124	-124	-124
1 First Canadian Place, Suite 5705 Toronto, ON, Canada M5X 1E4	Rating Outlook: Stable	'07	2.0	...	...	98.0	10,888	65.8	...	...	34.2	8,004	...	1,836	559	287	287	287
CA : 1975 : Stock : Other Direct Life, Reins		'08	0.9	...	...	99.1	12,605	74.3	...	...	25.7	10,162	...	2,064	1,180	1,917	1,917	1,917
416-360-2006		'09	0.9	...	...	99.1	12,231	72.9	...	...	27.1	9,766	...	2,071	-833	-866	-866	-866
AMB# 069319	FSC XV	**Rating History: A++g, 05/06/10; A++gu, 11/06/09; A++g, 10/02/09; A++g, 08/26/08; A++g, 08/07/07**																
GERBER LIFE INSURANCE CO CAB Nestle S A	A	'05	89.3	...	...	10.7	15,881	97.2	...	...	2.8	12,152	1,937	1,933	1,432	-486	-488	-488
Wesley D. Protheroe President & CEO		'06	96.0	...	...	4.0	17,863	95.7	...	...	4.3	13,338	2,206	2,189	1,605	864	864	864
1145 Nicholson Road, Unit 2 Newmarket, ON, Canada L3Y 9C3	Rating Outlook: Negative	'07	96.7	...	...	3.3	20,365	95.4	...	...	4.6	14,570	2,506	2,464	1,804	402	402	402
CA : 2001 : Stock : Direct Response Ind Life		'08	97.1	...	...	2.9	22,902	98.1	...	...	1.9	14,511	2,701	2,684	2,197	190	189	189
914-272-4031		'09	94.3	...	...	5.7	24,933	96.6	...	...	3.4	15,709	2,809	2,835	2,549	1,091	1,034	1,034
AMB# 066871	FSC VIII	**Rating History: A, 06/01/10; A, 05/04/09; A, 04/30/08; A g, 03/05/07; A g, 04/10/06**																
GREAT-WEST LIFE ASSURANCE CO Power Corporation of Canada	A+	'05	32.3	12.0	49.7	6.0	22,134,447	30.5	7.4	15.2	46.9	9,298,363	4,005,344	3,340,149	2,889,000	1,402,710	1,335,698	1,335,698
D. Allen Loney President & CEO		'06	28.3	12.7	53.1	5.8	23,701,205	...	...	...	100.0	10,660,868	4,131,441	3,952,795	3,597,000	1,714,719	1,568,445	1,568,445
100 Osborne Street North Winnipeg, MB, Canada R3C 3A5	Rating Outlook: Stable	'07	18.4	11.8	63.6	6.2	20,288,822	42.4	24.0	4.5	29.2	10,781,955	4,361,554	538,641	3,418,456	1,764,387	1,648,973	1,648,973
CA : 1892 : Stock : Agency Group A&S, Group Life, Var ann		'08	17.9	11.7	63.1	7.2	21,686,983	40.5	23.3	4.2	32.0	11,748,960	4,727,060	3,568,026	3,835,614	2,029,111	1,909,299	1,909,299
204-946-1190		'09	17.9	9.4	66.1	6.6	26,958,975	28.1	16.4	4.0	51.5	11,704,649	5,001,646	3,859,259	3,264,871	1,765,345	1,761,453	1,761,453
AMB# 006493	FSC XV	**Rating History: A+ g, 01/22/09; A+ g, 06/22/07; A+ gu, 02/01/07; A+ g, 06/19/06; A+ g, 03/09/05**																
HARTFORD LIFE INS CO CAB Hartford Financial Services Group Inc	A	'05	84.5	...	...	15.5	50,099	...	77.1	5.9	17.0	19,179	...	11,222	1,822	5,723	5,723	5,723
Colleen Sexsmith Chief Agent		'06	90.5	...	...	9.5	53,180	...	82.8	2.1	15.1	22,795	...	7,886	3,610	3,608	3,608	3,608
1145 Nicholson Road, Unit 2 Newmarket, ON, Canada L3Y 9C3	Rating Outlook: Stable	'07	48.2	...	...	51.8	29,405	...	60.3	32.4	7.3	20,135	...	5,104	-28,003	-2,829	-2,830	-2,830
CA : 1979 : Stock : Not Available A&S		'08	64.1	...	...	35.9	23,981	...	58.0	36.9	5.1	19,263	...	383	158	-871	-872	-872
416-204-9916		'09	67.9	...	...	32.1	24,561	...	67.7	26.5	5.8	20,050	...	74	168	788	787	787
AMB# 069326	FSC XV	**Rating History: A g, 03/24/10; A g, 02/27/09; A+ g, 12/23/08; A+ gu, 10/06/08; A+ g, 05/23/08**																
HOUSEHOLD LIFE INS CO CAB HSBC Holdings plc	A	'05	81.6	...	...	18.4	135,676	10.2	68.9	...	20.9	91,517	42,174	42,174	30,757	20,157	14,616	14,616
Patrick A. Cozza President & CEO		'06	85.2	...	...	14.8	165,694	29.7	70.0	...	0.3	106,208	52,251	52,251	19,561	9,031	5,476	5,476
3381 Steeles Avenue East, Suite 300 Toronto, ON, Canada M2H 3S7	Rating Outlook: Stable	'07	94.4	...	...	5.6	174,348	27.4	59.1	...	13.6	111,374	42,821	42,821	11,482	10,957	5,112	5,112
CA : 1997 : Stock : Other Credit		'08	96.9	...	...	3.1	172,454	32.2	56.3	...	11.6	114,866	33,198	33,198	-3,808	2,961	3,539	3,539
416-443-0499		'09	94.8	...	...	5.2	181,830	31.8	44.2	...	24.0	129,381	36,114	35,774	6,749	20,391	14,522	14,522
AMB# 066830	FSC IX	**Rating History: A g, 06/05/09; A+ g, 06/12/08; A+ g, 06/06/07; A+ g, 06/21/06; A+ g, 06/22/05**																
INDEPENDENT ORDER OF FORESTERS Independent Order of Foresters	A	'05	71.9	1.6	18.0	8.5	4,755,515	13.9	...	...	86.1	1,155,828	241,148	239,746	-25,776	61,100	65,797	65,797
George Mohacsi President & CEO		'06	72.2	1.4	19.6	6.8	4,867,355	13.5	...	...	86.5	1,196,343	290,059	287,604	100,044	36,240	33,233	33,233
789 Don Mills Road Toronto, ON, Canada M3C 1T9	Rating Outlook: Stable	'07	69.5	1.1	19.9	9.5	4,540,982	17.6	...	...	82.4	1,416,331	204,293	202,197	53,743	144,191	138,835	138,835
CA : 1881 : Fraternal : Career Agent Ann, Univ Life, Whole life		'08	75.5	0.9	15.3	8.4	4,886,986	15.1	...	...	84.9	1,243,335	222,058	220,690	90,491	-192,282	-197,126	-197,126
416-429-3000		'09	74.7	0.8	14.5	10.0	4,408,911	17.2	...	...	82.8	1,357,316	250,353	250,593	39,157	99,798	95,658	95,658
AMB# 060132	FSC XIII	**Rating History: A, 05/07/10; A, 05/08/09; A, 04/03/08; A, 01/09/08; A, 09/20/06**																
INDUSTRIAL ALLIANCE INS & FINL Industrial Alliance Ins & Financial Svcs	A	'05	55.3	21.9	14.4	8.3	10,078,640	41.9	5.4	36.8	15.9	1,374,292	1,621,301	1,511,036	-489,500	175,690	129,217	129,217
Yvon Charest President & CEO		'06	54.8	20.1	15.6	9.5	11,144,183	43.9	5.7	34.3	16.1	1,626,966	2,038,476	1,896,385	641,100	289,093	230,045	230,045
1080 Grande Allee West, P.O. Box 1907 Quebec City, QC, Canada G1K 7M3	Rating Outlook: Stable	'07	53.5	21.0	16.0	9.5	13,000,781	51.8	5.4	32.5	10.3	1,811,066	2,275,431	2,099,001	675,000	289,633	250,026	250,026
CA : 1892 : Stock : Agency Ind Life, Ind Ann, Group pens		'08	50.3	26.0	13.7	10.0	12,968,659	50.8	5.8	33.8	9.5	1,873,983	2,592,977	2,427,616	676,000	72,666	75,308	75,308
418-684-5000		'09	51.3	22.3	14.6	11.8	15,007,920	52.8	5.5	31.0	10.7	2,167,253	2,451,763	2,288,589	891,000	254,461	214,110	214,110
AMB# 006554	FSC XV	**Rating History: A g, 03/12/10; A g, 02/12/09; A g, 06/18/08; A g, 05/31/07; A g, 02/15/06**																
INDUSTRIAL ALLIANCE PAC I&F SV Industrial Alliance Ins & Financial Svcs	A	'05	46.2	31.3	14.5	8.0	2,025,797	32.5	4.5	21.5	41.5	253,699	494,872	421,847	108,372	60,181	45,917	45,917
Gerald Bouwers President & COO		'06	45.6	29.8	15.5	9.0	2,155,169	35.1	4.6	19.1	41.2	281,021	548,090	481,108	110,477	59,536	52,686	52,686
2165 West Broadway, PO Box 5900 Vancouver, BC, Canada V6B 5H6	Rating Outlook: Stable	'07	46.0	28.1	16.3	9.6	2,339,236	42.7	4.6	18.7	34.1	303,432	614,672	551,839	274,943	61,019	52,881	52,881
CA : 1967 : Stock : Agency Ind Ann, ISWL, Univ Life		'08	47.6	29.7	11.2	11.4	2,518,211	39.6	4.3	16.5	39.6	325,185	621,898	546,926	134,545	68,405	57,650	57,650
604-734-1667		'09	50.3	25.6	11.2	12.9	2,689,876	42.2	4.2	16.5	37.0	394,479	612,101	537,560	158,034	65,495	52,643	52,643
AMB# 006838	FSC XV	**Rating History: A g, 03/12/10; A g, 02/12/09; A g, 06/18/08; A g, 05/31/07; A g, 02/15/06**																

2010 BEST'S KEY RATING GUIDE — LIFE/HEALTH EDITION
BEST'S PROFITABILITY, LEVERAGE AND LIQUIDITY TESTS 2005 – 2009

Canadian Companies — Data in Canadian Dollars

	Profitability Tests							Leverage Tests						Liquidity Tests					
AOCI ($000)	Benefits Paid to NPW (%)	Comm. & Expenses to NPW (%)	NOG to Total Assets (%)	NOG to Total Rev (%)	Operating Return on Equity (%)	Yield on Invested Assets (%)	Total Return (%)	Change in NPW (%)	NPW to Capital (X)	Capital & Surplus to Liabilities (%)	Surplus Relief (%)	Reins Leverage (%)	Change in Capital (%)	Quick Liquidity (%)	Current Liquidity (%)	Non-Invest Grade Bonds to Capital (%)	Delinq. & Foreclosed Mortgages to Capital (%)	Mort. & Credit Tenant Loans & R.E. to Capital (%)	Affiliated Invest to Capital (%)
...	71.9	15.4	11.1	51.8	26.1	7.19	7.54	17.0	0.3	91.0	...	55.4	31.4	7.0	189.6	...	...	...	...
...	75.2	18.1	9.5	43.2	17.8	6.95	6.80	7.6	0.3	140.3	...	44.2	29.3	14.4	238.5	...	...	...	...
...	69.1	16.7	8.7	60.1	14.7	3.72	3.72	3.5	0.2	149.6	...	61.4	18.0	1.3	243.5	...	...	...	...
...	67.2	17.0	9.2	56.2	14.8	-1.28	-1.28	4.0	0.3	179.2	...	67.6	-8.7	3.1	264.3	...	...	...	...
...	85.0	16.7	-0.9	-3.9	-1.4	7.73	7.73	0.7	0.3	153.4	0.3	68.8	-1.4	3.7	239.8	...	...	...	...
...	52.0	13.6	16.7	71.2	24.3	2.94	2.94	2.0	0.3	202.5	...	4.0	20.5	100.5	357.0	...	...	...	...
...	120.0	10.2	-1.4	-5.2	-1.9	3.95	3.95	14.0	0.3	325.1	...	4.0	-1.4	400.4	422.7	...	...	...	...
21	88.0	17.2	3.0	13.0	4.0	4.05	4.28	-11.8	0.2	279.6	...	3.3	23.6	353.3	379.9	...	...	...	...
18	18.7	9.9	16.3	79.1	21.1	3.25	3.22	12.4	0.2	419.1	...	3.3	27.0	493.0	519.5	...	...	...	...
10	135.2	12.2	-7.0	-39.9	-8.7	0.86	0.79	0.3	0.2	397.8	0.0	2.9	-3.9	475.8	498.0	...	...	...	...
...	4.0	61.3	-3.3	-18.6	-4.0	4.74	4.74	25.6	0.2	325.9	...	0.1	-0.2	41.7	422.2	...	...	...	...
...	7.2	51.6	5.1	30.2	6.8	4.04	4.67	13.2	0.2	294.8	...	0.1	9.8	11.9	391.2	...	...	...	...
-9	9.5	53.8	2.1	12.8	2.9	3.61	3.56	12.6	0.2	251.0	...	0.1	9.2	7.3	347.5	...	...	...	...
702	6.4	41.1	0.9	5.5	1.3	3.68	6.91	8.9	0.2	188.7	...	0.1	-0.4	4.9	294.7	...	...	...	...
211	10.2	37.9	4.3	28.5	6.8	3.29	1.21	5.6	0.2	174.3	0.4	0.1	8.3	12.3	273.5	...	...	...	...
...	62.2	25.6	6.3	24.9	14.8	7.71	9.05	-5.7	0.4	72.4	...	27.2	6.6	4.3	64.8	0.4	0.0	28.6	113.8
...	58.4	22.2	6.8	25.9	15.7	7.25	8.33	18.3	0.4	81.8	...	...	14.7	5.2	61.3	0.1	...	28.3	112.9
-565,523	394.9	176.6	7.5	63.6	15.4	5.21	0.82	-86.4	0.0	113.4	...	39.8	1.1	5.3	53.1	0.6	...	22.2	113.6
-539,072	67.7	26.3	9.1	33.4	16.9	2.36	2.71	562.4	0.3	118.2	...	33.7	9.0	7.4	53.8	0.1	...	21.7	112.1
-1,060,699	65.2	23.5	7.2	27.8	15.0	9.80	3.29	8.2	0.3	76.7	...	34.6	-0.4	3.9	40.7	0.2	...	21.6	148.8
...	63.2	8.7	11.7	42.3	34.3	4.64	5.75	0.8	0.6	62.0	...	...	35.1	20.0	160.1	...	...	...	...
...	68.5	15.1	7.0	34.9	17.2	4.85	4.64	-29.7	0.3	75.0	...	15.2	18.9	12.6	173.1	...	...	...	...
-659	105.3	16.0	-7.4	-37.3	-13.2	6.70	4.94	-35.3	0.3	526.3	...	15.9	-11.7	230.7	604.1	...	...	...	...
-158	101.0	154.8	-3.7	-99.9	-4.4	0.59	2.73	-92.5	0.0	459.5	...	19.8	-4.3	182.3	551.4	...	...	...	...
86	400.0	655.4	3.3	81.1	4.0	3.85	4.89	-80.7	0.0	558.8	...	9.7	4.1	188.1	656.3	...	...	...	...
...	24.2	16.4	12.0	32.1	17.0	2.82	2.42	30.2	0.5	207.2	...	...	13.5	45.4	304.3	...	...	...	...
...	23.9	16.9	3.6	10.0	5.5	1.71	1.39	23.9	0.5	178.5	...	...	16.1	33.1	275.8	...	...	...	...
-943	34.0	67.3	3.0	10.2	4.7	4.57	3.87	-18.0	0.4	174.2	...	...	4.9	8.8	268.6	...	...	...	...
1,962	44.5	87.4	2.0	8.7	3.1	4.46	6.13	-22.5	0.3	206.5	...	...	3.1	6.9	307.7	...	...	...	...
4,791	37.9	60.1	8.2	34.2	11.9	3.86	5.45	7.8	0.3	271.5	0.1	1.1	12.6	15.8	377.8	...	...	...	...
...	112.3	78.3	1.4	11.2	5.8	7.08	7.82	10.1	0.2	32.1	...	...	3.0	17.1	115.9	...	...	6.7	5.3
...	119.4	64.9	0.7	5.3	2.8	6.86	7.42	20.0	0.2	32.6	...	...	3.5	17.1	117.0	...	...	5.6	6.6
-143,400	123.0	82.2	3.0	25.3	10.6	7.37	3.51	-29.7	0.1	45.3	...	...	18.4	18.1	128.6	...	...	3.5	7.5
-119,270	108.9	84.6	-4.2	-85.9	-14.8	0.01	0.54	9.1	0.2	34.1	...	...	-12.2	11.1	118.3	0.2	...	3.5	14.1
-100,947	102.5	80.2	2.1	24.1	7.4	2.87	3.28	13.5	0.2	44.5	...	...	9.2	11.4	126.7	2.7	...	2.7	14.8
...	70.6	27.0	1.5	6.0	10.0	6.59	7.83	34.7	1.1	15.8	...	20.2	12.5	9.2	78.9	1.7	1.0	160.6	58.2
...	69.4	24.7	2.2	8.1	15.3	8.28	9.49	25.5	1.2	17.1	...	17.3	18.4	10.7	81.1	1.4	...	137.8	56.7
-3,603	69.5	23.1	2.1	8.8	14.5	4.78	4.75	10.7	1.2	16.2	...	11.1	11.3	4.1	71.2	0.5	...	150.5	119.8
-54,056	67.4	20.6	0.6	3.0	4.1	1.37	0.89	15.7	1.3	16.9	...	10.7	3.5	1.8	66.7	1.0	...	179.9	106.8
11,031	70.7	23.1	1.5	5.9	10.6	7.96	8.53	-5.7	1.1	16.9	...	8.5	15.6	3.1	69.4	...	...	154.4	115.6
...	45.9	48.6	2.3	8.1	19.0	6.62	6.66	7.0	1.7	14.3	0.3	31.0	10.7	8.3	73.2	0.0	...	249.8	7.8
...	41.3	51.0	2.5	8.1	19.7	7.09	7.01	14.0	1.7	15.0	1.0	25.7	10.8	10.4	74.5	0.0	...	228.8	7.7
-16,102	36.9	48.1	2.4	7.7	18.1	4.97	4.20	14.7	1.8	14.9	...	3.2	8.0	5.9	69.1	...	...	216.4	60.8
-24,030	37.2	49.1	2.4	9.5	18.3	2.91	2.55	-0.9	1.7	14.8	...	10.5	7.2	4.5	73.0	...	...	230.0	42.8
-7,379	37.5	47.7	2.0	7.0	14.6	6.15	6.85	-1.7	1.4	17.2	...	-0.9	21.3	4.1	78.0	0.1	...	174.6	45.0

2010 BEST'S KEY RATING GUIDE — LIFE/HEALTH EDITION
ANNUAL STATEMENT DATA FOR YEARS 2005 – 2009
Canadian Companies — Data in Canadian Dollars

COMPANY NAME / Ultimate Parent Association / Principal Officer / Mailing Address / Dom. : Began Bus. : Struct. : Mktg. / Specialty / Phone # / AMB#	Best's Financial Strength Rating / FSC	Data Year	Balance Sheet: Bonds (%)	Mort. Loans & R.E. (%)	Com & Pref. Shares (%)	All Other Assets (%)	Total Assets ($000)	Life Reserves (%)	Health Reserves (%)	Ann Res. Liabilities (%)	All Other Liabilities (%)	Capital & Surplus ($000)	Operations: Direct Premiums Written ($000)	Net Premiums Written ($000)	Operating Cash Flow ($000)	NOG Before Taxes ($000)	NOG After Taxes ($000)	Net Income ($000)
KNIGHTS OF COLUMBUS CAB	A++	'05	90.2	0.2	2.2	7.4	1,441,139	59.6	0.1	35.2	5.2	242,151	173,648	173,635	105,421	46,460	46,454	52,865
Carl A. Andersen, CEO		'06	88.4	0.1	2.3	9.2	1,553,209	60.6	0.1	34.6	4.7	264,448	165,345	165,284	105,495	22,302	22,297	28,453
139 Front Street, Suite 100, Belleville, ON, Canada K8N 5B5	Rating Outlook: Stable	'07	87.7	0.1	2.2	10.0	1,689,192	62.1	0.2	34.6	3.1	330,836	167,740	167,745	101,000	33,400	33,396	40,060
CA : 1897 : Fraternal : Career Agent		'08	87.7	0.1	1.3	10.9	1,781,007	62.2	0.3	34.8	2.7	253,835	188,719	188,678	121,238	-76,984	-76,987	-70,272
Whole life, Term Life, FPDA's; 613-962-5347		'09	90.0	0.0	1.8	8.2	2,002,759	58.7	0.3	38.0	2.9	354,448	242,365	242,392	179,665	100,627	100,627	109,826
AMB# 066815	FSC XIV	Rating History: A++, 06/17/09; A++, 06/20/08; A++, 06/12/07; A++, 06/13/06; A++, 06/14/05																
LIBERTY LIFE ASSR BOSTON CAB; Liberty Mutual Holding Company Inc.	A	'05	89.0	...	...	11.0	13,348	...	88.2	...	11.8	10,012	169	169	-1,151	485	491	491
Edmund F. Kelly, Chairman, President & CEO		'06	83.8	...	...	16.2	13,974	...	87.8	...	12.2	10,832	162	162	555	745	820	820
100 Liberty Way, Dover, NH 03820-1525	Rating Outlook: Negative	'07	89.1	...	...	10.9	13,960	...	97.1	...	2.9	11,626	203	203	-193	773	794	794
CA : 1987 : Stock : Other Agency		'08	83.3	...	...	16.7	15,397	...	97.0	...	3.0	12,074	269	269	611	447	448	448
A&S; 416-365-7587		'09	90.0	...	...	10.0	15,395	...	95.9	...	4.1	12,469	288	288	533	366	395	395
AMB# 069357	FSC X	Rating History: A, 06/11/10; A, 04/09/09; A, 03/05/08; A g, 02/28/07; A g, 01/25/06																
LIFE INS CO OF NORTH AMER CAB; CIGNA Corporation	A	'05	91.6	...	...	8.4	39,229	0.0	97.7	0.1	2.1	17,186	1,596	1,604	-150	-3,674	-3,742	-3,742
Eman Hassan, Chief Agent in Canada		'06	93.0	...	...	7.0	39,885	0.0	97.9	0.2	1.9	16,416	2,431	2,429	248	-978	-1,115	-1,115
55 Town Centre Court, Suite 606, Scarborough, ON, Canada M1P 4X4	Rating Outlook: Negative	'07	91.4	...	...	8.6	41,490	0.0	97.7	0.1	2.1	17,894	3,214	3,162	1,007	1,715	1,825	1,825
CA : 1963 : Stock : Not Available		'08	90.9	...	...	9.1	43,103	0.0	97.9	0.1	2.0	17,456	3,131	3,082	1,594	-627	-823	-823
A&S; 416-290-6666		'09	92.6	...	...	7.4	44,976	0.0	98.3	0.1	1.6	19,398	3,187	3,188	1,000	1,688	1,639	1,639
AMB# 069330	FSC XV	Rating History: A g, 01/08/10; A g, 11/14/08; A g, 02/11/08; A g, 12/14/06; A- g, 12/21/05																
LONDON LIFE INSURANCE COMPANY; Power Corporation of Canada	A+	'05	50.7	28.5	9.1	11.6	21,180,087	58.8	0.0	21.9	19.2	1,674,557	2,924,037	3,108,770	1,471,778	516,246	416,549	416,549
D. Allen Loney, President & CEO		'06	47.0	26.7	8.2	18.1	22,387,616	60.6	2.1	20.1	17.1	2,328,374	2,039,864	2,707,135	608,944	633,441	522,342	522,342
255 Dufferin Avenue, London, ON, Canada N6A 4K1	Rating Outlook: Stable	'07	43.1	27.3	14.6	14.9	23,426,934	65.2	4.2	19.0	11.7	2,486,445	2,136,815	2,866,688	516,667	693,589	488,975	488,975
CA : 1874 : Stock : Career Agent		'08	41.1	30.3	13.4	15.3	23,160,968	64.6	3.9	19.0	12.5	2,839,069	2,295,054	2,636,622	910,529	642,004	540,633	540,633
Ind Life; 519-435-5281		'09	40.7	27.4	15.8	16.1	24,835,435	66.3	3.5	18.8	11.5	2,812,617	2,499,601	2,950,429	1,148,097	484,916	389,985	389,985
AMB# 006667	FSC XV	Rating History: A+ g, 01/22/09; A+ g, 06/22/07; A+ gu, 02/01/07; A+ g, 06/19/06; A+ g, 03/09/05																
MANUFACTURERS LIFE INS CO; Manulife Financial Corporation	A+	'05	37.8	20.7	6.3	35.2	50,896,006	28.9	9.3	32.9	29.0	12,139,989	6,321,066	4,045,350	...	2,228,484	2,074,826	2,074,826
Donald A. Guloien, President & CEO		'06	36.2	19.4	27.2	17.2	53,390,780	31.9	9.7	31.7	26.7	14,576,575	6,590,066	6,186,275	5,106,000	2,876,225	2,781,264	2,781,264
250 Bloor Street East, Main C-28, Toronto, ON, Canada M4W 1E5	Rating Outlook: Stable	'07	37.5	18.1	7.8	36.6	55,181,168	36.5	10.1	33.4	20.0	15,473,877	7,001,829	6,661,562	...	3,918,048	3,579,626	3,579,626
CA : 1887 : Stock : Agency		'08	30.3	15.7	3.7	50.3	62,258,689	35.7	10.5	30.2	23.6	20,450,793	7,600,054	9,259,850	...	404,540	-99,208	-99,208
Life, Annuity, Group pens; 416-926-3000		'09	29.3	12.2	3.4	55.1	80,452,512	37.2	9.6	27.4	25.9	31,431,193	9,001,387	7,116,787	...	2,079,241	2,743,522	2,743,522
AMB# 006688	FSC XV	Rating History: A+ g, 01/19/10; A+ g, 07/17/09; A++g, 02/04/09; A++g, 06/06/08; A++g, 06/07/07																
MANULIFE CANADA LTD[1]; Manulife Financial Corporation	NR-3	'05	57.6	11.2	20.4	10.7	3,596,478	88.2	0.0	...	11.8	295,385	91,958	2,214,149	...	89,913	63,367	63,367
Paul Rooney, Senior Executive Vice President & General Manager,		'06	62.8	11.4	15.8	10.0	4,205,803	88.4	0.0	...	11.6	563,437	92,499	145,944	341,532	-3,769	17,347	17,347
500 King Street North, Waterloo, ON, Canada N2J 4C6		'07	62.0	11.5	15.6	10.9	4,478,258	93.5	0.0	...	6.5	571,888	92,561	120,930	195,499	-27,812	6,346	6,346
CA : 1887 : Stock : Not Available		'08	71.0	8.2	5.4	15.4	2,267,716	93.0	0.0	0.1	6.9	238,456	92,408	-1,743,030	...	-200,379	-146,033	-146,033
Ind Life, Ind A&S; 519-747-7000		'09	65.9	7.4	7.3	19.4	1,401,356	86.9	0.0	0.2	12.9	272,486	94,165	-904,231	...	75,453	57,889	57,889
AMB# 066879		Rating History: NR-3, 01/19/10; NR-3, 07/17/09; NR-3, 02/04/09; NR-3, 06/07/08; NR-3, 06/07/07																
MASSACHUSETTS MUTUAL LF CAB; Massachusetts Mutual Life Insurance Co	A++	'05	94.8	...	...	5.2	23,260	91.1	...	...	8.9	15,070	798	798	1,904	-730	-730	-730
J. Brian Reeve, Chief Agent in Canada		'06	94.6	...	...	5.4	23,198	56.9	0.1	33.5	9.5	14,737	884	884	2,162	1,695	1,695	1,695
40 King Street West, Toronto, ON, Canada M5H 3C2	Rating Outlook: Negative	'07	96.2	...	...	3.8	46,139	67.1	0.1	26.9	5.8	35,496	774	774	2,341	2,151	2,151	2,151
CA : 1949 : Mutual : General Agent		'08	94.8	...	...	5.2	62,693	75.2	0.1	21.0	3.7	33,495	1,553	1,553	12,957	-2,099	-2,099	-2,099
Life, Accident, Sickness; 416-869-5745		'09	93.6	...	...	6.4	48,928	58.5	0.1	20.9	20.5	23,490	2,055	2,055	2,160	2,594	2,594	2,594
AMB# 069335	FSC XV	Rating History: A++g, 06/04/10; A++g, 06/11/09; A++g, 03/25/08; A++g, 05/25/07; A++g, 05/02/06																
MD LIFE INSURANCE COMPANY[1]	NR-5	'05	43.4	2.3	6.3	48.0	208,560	93.5	...	...	6.5	30,293	46,626	38,779	...	5,904	3,727	3,727
Charles K. Hamilton, President & CEO		'06	29.4	1.8	24.2	44.6	276,593	94.9	...	...	5.1	34,390	52,494	46,955	...	5,878	4,097	4,097
1870 Alta Vista Drive, Ottawa, ON, Canada K1G 6R7		'07	30.5	2.0	22.8	44.8	331,075	95.8	...	...	4.2	41,030	61,143	55,085	...	7,287	4,918	4,918
CA : Other : Not Available		'08	54.7	2.6	19.2	23.4	358,338	93.8	...	...	6.2	32,318	68,967	62,362	...	-23,644	-16,034	-16,034
Ind Life; 613-731-8610		'09	30.0	...	18.4	51.6	70,427	...	...	...	100.0	43,359	...	...	...	8,326	6,004	9,705
AMB# 066875		Rating History: NR-5, 05/04/10; NR-5, 05/21/09; NR-5, 05/09/08; NR-5, 05/14/07; NR-5, 05/16/06																
METLIFE CANADA; MetLife Inc	NR-5	'05	...	...	...	...	...	...	...	...	...	...	...	...	...	...	...	...
Karen J. Sauve, President & CEO		'06	89.8	...	...	10.2	367,887	36.8	0.8	59.3	3.1	44,564	6,478	5,054	...	7,640	4,824	4,824
Constitution Square, 360 Albert Street, Ottawa, ON, Canada K1R 7X7		'07	95.0	...	...	5.0	368,551	34.7	0.7	61.8	2.8	37,740	2,523	800	...	4,780	-6,730	-6,730
CA : Stock : Not Available		'08	92.5	...	...	7.5	342,110	33.6	0.7	62.7	3.0	33,540	3,620	1,061	...	3,329	2,313	2,313
In Run Off		'09	59.9	...	...	40.1	47,205	91.8	...	...	8.2	34,022	2,020	-106	-16,030	-6,031	-7,371	-7,371
AMB# 066883		Rating History: NR-5, 02/20/09; NR-5, 06/10/08; NR-5, 07/03/07																

BEST'S PROFITABILITY, LEVERAGE AND LIQUIDITY TESTS 2005 – 2009

Canadian Companies — Data in Canadian Dollars

—	Profitability Tests							Leverage Tests						Liquidity Tests					
AOCI ($000)	Benefits Paid to NPW (%)	Comm. & Expenses to NPW (%)	NOG to Total Assets (%)	NOG to Total Rev (%)	Operating Return on Equity (%)	Yield on Invested Assets (%)	Total Return (%)	Change in NPW (%)	NPW to Capital (X)	Capital & Surplus to Liabilities (%)	Surplus Relief (%)	Reins Leverage (%)	Change in Capital (%)	Quick Liquidity (%)	Current Liquidity (%)	Non-Invest Grade Bonds to Capital (%)	Delinq. & Foreclosed Mortgages to Capital (%)	Mort. & Credit Tenant Loans & R.E. to Capital (%)	Affiliated Invest to Capital (%)
...	32.6	21.5	3.8	20.6	24.1	6.01	4.80	11.3	0.7	20.2	...	...	23.7	3.1	112.3	...	...	1.3	...
...	39.1	22.8	1.9	11.3	11.2	5.86	5.86	-4.8	0.6	20.5	...	...	9.2	4.3	111.6	...	...	0.5	...
-737	42.8	25.8	2.5	18.4	13.5	3.09	3.02	1.5	0.5	24.3	...	...	25.1	5.5	115.2	...	...	0.3	...
-16,083	37.7	23.3	-4.1	-26.9	-24.0	4.28	3.38	12.5	0.7	16.4	...	...	-23.3	6.4	108.1	...	...	0.4	...
5,081	32.1	19.7	5.8	31.1	36.1	5.92	7.04	28.5	0.7	21.6	...	...	39.6	4.6	114.8	...	...	0.2	...
...	168.6	75.1	3.5	45.9	5.0	5.27	4.85	-13.3	0.0	300.1	...	...	5.2	39.2	395.3	...	...	...	...
...	156.2	60.5	6.0	89.8	7.9	5.71	4.95	-4.1	0.0	344.7	...	...	8.2	63.0	436.0	...	...	...	...
270	183.3	10.3	5.7	193.2	7.1	5.45	7.38	25.3	0.0	563.3	...	...	7.3	63.2	670.1	...	...	...	...
1,178	84.4	34.2	3.1	53.2	3.8	3.94	9.97	32.5	0.0	562.9	...	...	3.9	112.6	710.8	...	...	...	...
674	94.1	38.9	2.6	47.7	3.2	3.55	0.20	7.1	0.0	553.7	...	...	3.3	61.6	676.9	...	...	...	...
...	208.1	19.4	-9.5	-99.9	-19.9	4.91	4.55	5.9	0.1	78.0	...	9.9	-16.0	13.1	176.4	...	...	...	...
...	140.5	17.2	-2.8	-26.0	-6.6	4.85	4.68	51.4	0.1	69.9	...	7.3	-4.5	9.4	168.2	...	...	...	...
199	112.0	14.7	4.5	36.4	10.6	4.65	5.14	30.2	0.2	76.5	...	7.5	9.0	12.5	175.4	...	...	...	...
1,073	105.0	15.9	-1.9	-19.2	-4.7	2.21	4.26	-2.5	0.2	71.0	...	9.7	-2.4	13.9	174.0	...	...	...	...
1,691	100.6	15.3	3.7	32.7	8.9	4.24	5.64	3.4	0.2	81.2	...	8.2	11.1	11.6	186.6	...	...	...	...
...	51.2	21.6	2.0	8.7	26.7	6.75	7.14	11.5	1.9	8.6	...	108.3	16.2	5.5	62.4	7.8	0.1	361.1	51.1
...	64.7	24.7	2.4	11.6	26.1	6.56	6.66	-12.9	1.2	11.6	...	57.4	39.0	9.1	65.7	4.1	...	256.6	40.0
-258,364	65.2	24.2	2.1	10.8	20.3	5.05	4.69	5.9	1.2	11.9	...	40.7	6.8	9.6	63.4	0.5	...	257.7	37.9
-159,459	67.8	25.0	2.3	17.1	20.3	-0.39	0.08	-8.0	0.9	14.0	...	34.9	14.2	8.5	59.9	0.8	...	247.2	42.9
-268,242	62.2	22.8	1.6	7.2	13.8	9.38	8.88	11.9	1.0	12.8	...	34.8	-0.9	12.1	61.2	3.9	...	241.8	52.3
...	126.5	46.7	4.0	24.0	16.8	7.16	7.53	...	0.3	31.3	...	37.3	-3.1	11.4	66.4	2.3	0.1	86.6	93.1
...	81.5	32.9	5.3	24.4	20.8	7.54	7.58	52.9	0.4	37.6	...	36.3	20.1	10.0	66.4	...	...	71.1	93.0
-1,142,915	81.3	32.0	6.6	29.7	23.8	5.69	6.23	7.7	0.4	39.0	...	39.1	6.2	9.5	68.1	...	...	64.7	92.4
-919,536	58.5	24.4	-0.2	-1.0	-0.6	4.01	4.61	39.0	0.5	48.9	...	13.7	32.2	13.6	64.0	...	...	47.9	103.7
-4,666,996	47.6	32.3	3.8	22.5	10.6	6.08	-4.18	-23.1	0.2	64.1	...	7.5	53.7	10.7	64.6	1.9	...	31.2	112.0
...	2.3	2.1	2.7	2.5	24.1	15.73	16.24	999.9	7.5	8.9	...	19.7	28.3	17.6	92.0	...	...	136.8	...
...	29.3	25.1	0.4	4.3	4.0	6.97	7.85	-93.4	0.3	15.5	...	12.4	90.7	19.1	99.7	...	...	85.1	...
9,572	43.2	33.3	0.1	2.1	1.1	4.28	4.50	-17.1	0.2	14.6	...	14.9	1.5	19.9	98.5	...	...	90.3	...
-86,762	-3.1	-1.8	-4.3	7.8	-36.0	-3.99	-6.99	-99.9	-7.3	11.8	...	14.4	-58.3	5.9	97.8	...	...	78.1	...
-11,471	-2.7	0.6	3.2	-7.2	22.7	6.10	10.42	48.1	-3.3	24.1	...	11.2	14.3	10.1	107.8	...	...	38.0	...
...	55.0	24.3	-2.4	-23.7	-3.2	7.94	7.55	224.4	0.1	184.0	...	...	-51.7	2.1	271.3	...	...	...	...
...	57.1	20.1	7.3	61.7	11.4	8.35	8.23	10.8	0.1	174.2	...	...	-2.2	1.1	260.6	...	...	...	...
-1,067	49.5	23.6	6.2	53.8	8.6	9.76	6.39	-12.4	0.0	303.1	...	...	140.9	3.5	382.4	...	...	...	...
10,212	22.6	12.8	-3.9	-36.0	-6.1	8.22	26.95	100.5	0.0	176.4	...	...	-5.6	6.9	319.9	...	...	...	...
6,781	182.6	9.1	4.6	45.1	9.1	6.90	0.52	32.4	0.1	125.9	...	...	-29.9	6.4	251.7	...	...	...	...
...	5.2	66.6	2.0	4.6	13.1	8.68	9.66	12.1	1.3	17.0	...	300.3	14.0	28.3	102.3	...	...	15.8	...
...	5.3	57.9	1.7	4.1	12.7	11.02	11.28	21.1	1.4	14.2	...	267.8	13.5	60.5	101.8	...	...	14.7	...
-220	4.6	46.4	1.6	6.1	13.0	0.50	0.43	17.3	1.3	14.1	...	245.7	19.3	52.9	102.6	...	...	16.0	...
-1,898	3.0	37.8	-4.7	-53.1	-43.7	-14.67	-15.16	13.2	1.9	9.9	...	251.9	-21.2	25.6	100.2	...	...	29.3	...
-562	...	...	4.5	37.8	25.6	2.35	3.01	-99.9	...	160.2	...	...	34.2	127.0	324.2	...	...	...	...
...	...	...	...	...	...	...	...	...	...	...	...	...	...	...	...	...	...	...	...
...	469.4	47.5	...	19.7	...	...	...	...	0.1	13.8	...	10.1	...	4.5	106.8	...	...	...	...
-1,340	999.9	281.3	-1.8	-61.0	-16.4	2.93	2.55	-84.2	0.0	11.4	...	11.1	-15.3	1.8	107.7	...	...	...	...
-7,853	999.9	200.5	0.7	36.7	6.5	1.48	-0.41	32.6	0.0	10.9	...	15.5	-11.1	3.9	106.7	...	...	...	...
...	-99.9	-99.9	-3.8	-29.8	-21.8	14.06	18.11	-99.9	0.0	258.1	...	0.7	1.4	127.5	353.6	...	...	...	...

Canadian Companies — Data in Canadian Dollars

COMPANY NAME Ultimate Parent Association Principal Officer Mailing Address Dom. : Began Bus. : Struct. : Mktg. Specialty Phone # AMB#	Best's Financial Strength Rating FSC	Data Year	Balance Sheet: Bonds (%)	Mort. Loans & R.E. (%)	Com & Pref. Shares (%)	All Other Assets (%)	Total Assets ($000)	Life Reserves (%)	Health Reserves (%)	Ann Res. Liabilities (%)	All Other Liabilities (%)	Capital & Surplus ($000)	Operations: Direct Premiums Written ($000)	Net Premiums Written ($000)	Operating Cash Flow ($000)	NOG Before Taxes ($000)	NOG After Taxes ($000)	Net Income ($000)
METROPOLITAN LIFE INS CO CAB MetLife Inc Robert H. Benmosche Chairman & CEO Constitution Square, 360 Albert Street Ottawa, ON, Canada K1R 7X7 CA : 1872 : Stock : Career Agent A&S, Life 613-237-7171 AMB# 069336	**A+ u** Under Review Implication: Negative **FSC XV**	'05	90.6	2.9	0.0	6.5	1,695,090	31.6	...	38.9	29.6	1,232,536	5,997	5,997	41,589	84,547	63,783	63,575
		'06	87.8	3.1	0.0	9.1	1,399,793	1.3	0.7	...	97.9	1,275,230	...	1,424	-275,605	64,099	42,444	42,444
		'07	87.8	3.2	0.0	9.0	1,249,397	1.9	0.9	...	97.2	1,159,456	...	1,723	45,056	43,165	41,812	47,264
		'08	81.6	3.8	0.0	14.6	799,983	3.5	1.3	...	95.2	756,814	...	2,559	38,411	62,521	42,358	42,358
		'09	56.3	...	0.1	43.6	220,016	0.4	1.1	...	98.6	150,077	...	2,126	14,150	-9,142	-18,309	-18,309
		Rating History: A+ gu, 02/09/10; A+ g, 02/20/09; A+ g, 06/05/08; A+ g, 05/29/07; A+ g, 05/05/06																
MINNESOTA LIFE INS CO CAB Minnesota Mutual Companies Inc Robin B. Cumine Chief Agent in Canada 130 Adelaide Street West, Suite 2800 Toronto, ON, Canada M5H 3P5 CA : 1952 : Stock : Not Available A&S 416-364-5371 AMB# 069337	**NR-5**	'05	80.6	...	...	19.4	2,537	46.7	...	5.6	47.7	2,430	29	29	89	22	43	43
		'06	76.8	...	...	23.2	2,662	35.7	...	2.3	62.0	2,396	52	52	-6	-164	-110	-110
		'07	87.8	...	...	12.2	5,984	30.2	...	3.8	66.0	5,788	62	62	29	123	123	123
		'08	85.9	...	...	14.1	6,700	24.2	...	3.9	71.9	5,972	42	42	149	111	111	111
		'09	89.2	...	...	10.8	6,148	...	...	...	100.0	5,765	38	38	78	153	153	153
		Rating History: NR-5, 04/06/10; NR-5, 06/03/09; A+ g, 04/10/09; A+ g, 03/25/08; A+ g, 06/01/07																
MUNICH REINSURANCE CO CAB Munich Reinsurance Company Mary Forrest Chief Agent 390 Bay Street, 26th Floor Toronto, ON, Canada M5H 2Y2 CA : Stock : Not Available Life Reins 416-359-2200 AMB# 066862	**A+** Rating Outlook: Stable **FSC XV**	'05	42.4	...	...	57.6	7,003,537	22.3	60.8	...	17.0	1,128,789	...	2,385,897	371,970	19,508	9,208	9,208
		'06	55.6	...	...	44.4	6,001,734	27.5	52.8	...	19.7	1,302,034	...	2,161,766	385,484	85,094	86,838	86,838
		'07	92.7	...	...	7.3	5,022,864	45.5	41.0	...	13.5	1,331,806	...	1,650,860	342,830	-17,952	10,778	10,778
		'08	92.5	...	...	7.5	5,534,079	42.9	42.7	...	14.4	1,626,402	...	1,135,999	381,080	181,377	143,274	143,274
		'09	95.9	...	...	4.1	5,602,360	40.9	45.7	...	13.4	1,762,516	...	3,897,551	300,775	397,165	244,253	244,253
		Rating History: A+ g, 07/20/09; A+ g, 09/25/08; A+ g, 09/07/07; A+ g, 11/07/06; A+ g, 11/03/05																
NEW YORK LIFE INS CO CAB New York Life Insurance Company Seymour Sternberg Chairman & CEO Scotia Plaza Toronto, ON, Canada M5H 3C2 CA : 1858 : Mutual : Not Available Group Life 416-869-5745 AMB# 069340	**A++** Rating Outlook: Stable **FSC XV**	'05	94.9	1.7	...	3.5	263,999	55.9	1.8	13.1	29.2	170,651	29,805	30,334	15,561	14,104	12,049	12,049
		'06	94.7	1.4	...	3.8	283,814	54.7	2.2	11.2	31.9	180,223	30,444	30,847	18,205	9,843	9,572	9,572
		'07	95.9	1.2	...	2.9	302,576	58.7	1.6	11.1	28.6	191,392	30,725	31,160	9,933	10,061	11,334	11,334
		'08	95.8	1.0	...	3.2	324,244	60.5	1.7	9.9	28.0	199,620	33,526	34,005	14,463	8,853	8,228	8,228
		'09	92.9	0.9	...	6.2	339,898	57.5	1.5	8.7	32.4	211,446	35,109	35,346	14,220	10,212	11,826	11,826
		Rating History: A++g, 06/14/10; A++g, 06/11/09; A++g, 03/11/08; A++g, 11/21/06; A++g, 12/23/04																
OPTIMUM REASSURANCE INC Optimum Group Inc Mario Georgiev President 425 De Maisonneuve Blvd. West Montreal, QC, Canada H3A 3G5 CA : 1957 : Stock : Other Direct Reins 514-288-1900 AMB# 066827	**A-** Rating Outlook: Stable **FSC VII**	'05	70.3	...	4.6	25.2	266,494	53.2	13.2	0.3	33.3	29,968	20	34,019	3,806	5,081	3,319	3,319
		'06	72.2	...	4.4	23.4	273,296	55.3	14.6	0.3	29.7	33,161	17	39,795	5,153	8,090	5,936	5,936
		'07	74.4	...	4.2	21.5	316,364	67.1	14.7	0.1	18.0	47,725	-413	35,495	9,625	8,581	6,309	6,309
		'08	76.8	...	2.9	20.3	317,363	65.8	15.5	0.1	18.5	51,646	...	37,914	10,389	7,403	7,356	7,356
		'09	76.9	...	3.3	19.8	347,807	64.6	15.4	0.1	19.9	57,565	...	41,589	9,953	8,214	6,938	6,938
		Rating History: A-, 05/11/10; A-, 06/01/09; A-, 06/10/08; A-, 06/14/07; A-, 06/19/06																
PARTNER REINSURANCE CO LTD CAB[1] PartnerRe Ltd Francis Blumberg Chief Agent 130 King Street West, Suite 2300 Toronto, ON, Canada M5X 1C7 CA : Stock Reins 416-861-0033 AMB# 066891	**A+** Rating Outlook: Stable **FSC XV**	'05	...	...	...	...	...	...	...	...	...	...	...	...	...	...	...	...
		'06	...	...	...	...	...	...	...	...	...	...	...	...	...	...	...	...
		'07	...	...	...	...	...	...	...	...	...	...	...	...	...	...	...	...
		'08	92.8	...	...	7.2	265,409	70.2	14.8	...	15.0	95,267	...	45,925	169,179	22,290	14,427	14,427
		'09	92.7	...	...	7.3	262,414	70.7	18.9	...	10.4	98,081	...	52,309	438	15,761	9,795	9,795
		Rating History: A+ g, 12/16/09																
PENNCORP LIFE INSURANCE CO La Capitale Civil Service Mutual Lynn C. M. Grenier-Lew EVP & CFO 55 Superior Boulevard Mississauga, ON, Canada L5T 2X9 CA : 1993 : Stock : Career Agent Ind A&S, Annuity, Health 905-795-2300 AMB# 060155	**NR-5**	'05	94.6	...	...	5.4	236,791	19.7	70.2	1.8	8.3	62,307	78,272	76,560	21,942	16,015	11,259	11,259
		'06	94.2	...	...	5.8	261,938	18.5	68.8	1.5	11.3	62,733	77,716	76,145	...	19,290	12,335	12,335
		'07	95.9	...	...	4.1	326,422	17.4	76.8	1.2	4.7	81,753	76,346	74,843	10,192	19,132	12,996	12,996
		'08	92.1	...	1.2	6.7	333,555	13.0	81.1	1.2	4.7	88,303	74,854	74,202	16,799	18,418	12,225	12,225
		'09	88.1	2.4	4.6	4.8	353,270	8.8	88.0	1.0	2.2	93,744	74,131	74,812	21,345	13,086	7,957	7,957
		Rating History: NR-5, 05/18/10; NR-5, 05/19/09; NR-5, 06/16/08; NR-4, 01/04/07; B++, 01/04/07																
PHOENIX LIFE INSURANCE CO CAB Phoenix Companies Inc J. Brian Reeve Chief Agent 40 King Street West Toronto, ON, Canada M5H 3C2 CA : 1974 : Stock : Other A&S 416-869-5300 AMB# 069343	**NR-5**	'05	98.1	...	...	1.9	2,184	67.0	25.4	...	7.6	1,618	...	1	-16	39	35	35
		'06	89.5	...	...	10.5	2,385	...	100.0	...	...	1,907	...	...	-114	-50	-50	-50
		'07	90.7	...	...	9.3	2,357	...	93.8	...	6.2	1,987	...	...	-83	41	41	41
		'08	92.2	...	...	7.8	2,508	...	93.6	...	6.4	1,906	...	...	-70	-122	-126	-126
		'09	93.9	...	...	6.1	2,230	...	94.4	...	5.6	1,937	...	...	-114	-18	-14	-14
		Rating History: NR-5, 01/13/10; NR-5, 03/10/09; NR-5, 01/15/09; NR-5, 11/14/08; NR-5, 02/08/08																
PRIMERICA LIFE INS CO OF CA Citigroup Inc. John A. Adams CEO 2000 Argentia Road, Plaza V, Suite 300 Mississauga, ON, Canada L5N 2R7 CA : 1991 : Stock : Exclusive Agent Term Life, Var ann, Ind A&S 905-812-2900 AMB# 060156	**A+** Rating Outlook: Negative **FSC XIV**	'05	91.5	...	0.7	7.7	411,805	-99.9	3.8	6.8	189.3	405,638	167,591	151,606	61,981	66,460	43,457	43,457
		'06	92.5	...	0.4	7.1	482,675	-99.9	4.6	8.8	186.5	477,689	180,433	163,634	69,399	103,265	72,034	72,034
		'07	89.3	...	0.5	10.2	455,593	-99.9	1.3	2.3	196.3	436,488	194,614	176,631	60,986	77,899	55,809	55,809
		'08	88.5	...	0.7	10.8	531,131	-99.9	0.8	1.3	197.8	499,062	210,764	191,717	73,578	90,201	63,071	63,071
		'09	94.2	...	0.7	5.1	627,217	-99.9	1.7	2.1	196.0	608,374	223,386	202,836	99,095	153,530	101,437	101,437
		Rating History: A+ g, 03/16/10; A+ gu, 11/09/09; A+ g, 05/15/09; A+ g, 05/15/08; A+ g, 11/02/06																

BEST'S PROFITABILITY, LEVERAGE AND LIQUIDITY TESTS 2005 – 2009

Canadian Companies — Data in Canadian Dollars

	Profitability Tests							Leverage Tests						Liquidity Tests					
AOCI ($000)	Benefits Paid to NPW (%)	Comm. & Expenses to NPW (%)	NOG to Total Assets (%)	NOG to Total Rev (%)	Operating Return on Equity (%)	Yield on Invested Assets (%)	Total Return (%)	Change in NPW (%)	NPW to Capital (X)	Capital & Surplus to Liabilities (%)	Surplus Relief (%)	Reins Leverage (%)	Change in Capital (%)	Quick Liquidity (%)	Current Liquidity (%)	Non-Invest Grade Bonds to Capital (%)	Delinq. & Foreclosed Mortgages to Capital (%)	Mort. & Credit Tenant Loans & R.E. to Capital (%)	Affiliated Invest to Capital (%)
...	778.0	42.1	3.8	62.7	5.3	6.16	6.25	-28.1	0.0	266.5	...	...	5.4	5.2	337.5	...	...	4.0	...
...	148.1	78.9	2.7	64.3	3.4	4.16	4.19	-49.3	0.0	999.9	...	...	3.5	20.3	999.9	...	...	3.4	...
5,418	50.3	28.3	3.6	104.0	3.9	3.80	4.24	21.0	0.0	999.9	...	...	-9.1	35.3	999.9	...	...	3.5	...
-31,170	127.9	3.6	4.1	63.8	4.4	6.42	2.52	48.5	0.0	999.9	...	...	-34.7	49.2	931.1	...	...	4.0	...
2,522	75.9	768.3	-3.6	-99.9	-4.0	2.25	9.42	-16.9	0.0	222.6	...	...	-80.2	74.2	266.7	...	...	...	...
...	60.7	250.0	1.7	40.2	1.8	3.29	3.29	-9.4	0.0	999.9	...	...	3.5	416.8	999.9	...	...	...	...
...	30.2	339.6	-4.2	-76.9	-4.6	3.62	3.62	89.3	0.0	900.8	...	...	-1.4	193.6	963.9	...	...	...	...
37	116.1	203.2	2.8	48.0	3.0	4.65	5.51	17.0	0.0	999.9	...	...	141.6	439.6	999.9	...	...	...	...
575	21.4	352.4	1.8	42.7	1.9	3.50	11.64	-32.3	0.0	999.9	...	...	3.2	602.0	999.9	...	...	...	...
345	26.3	315.8	2.4	61.0	2.6	3.37	-0.27	-9.5	0.0	999.9	...	...	-3.5	999.9	999.9	...	...	...	...
...	68.8	17.7	0.1	0.3	0.8	12.26	12.14	3.7	2.1	19.2	...	-0.4	6.3	1.8	117.9	...	...	...	...
...	65.5	16.5	1.3	3.4	7.1	11.80	11.79	-9.4	1.7	27.7	...	-1.8	15.3	5.6	125.7	...	...	...	...
45,634	60.2	17.2	0.2	0.6	0.8	4.75	5.79	-23.6	1.2	36.5	...	-14.0	2.3	2.7	135.0	...	...	...	...
67,672	61.3	17.4	2.7	11.3	9.7	2.60	3.03	-31.2	0.7	42.4	...	-19.4	22.1	4.4	141.2	...	...	...	...
38,033	71.9	12.7	4.4	6.0	14.4	3.81	3.26	243.1	2.2	46.4	1.0	-18.8	8.4	2.5	146.3	...	...	...	...
...	33.7	6.0	4.7	27.1	7.3	5.70	5.66	7.8	0.2	182.8	...	0.2	7.6	3.2	271.7	...	...	2.6	...
...	31.1	7.7	3.5	20.9	5.5	5.64	6.22	1.7	0.2	174.0	...	0.2	5.6	3.8	263.9	...	...	2.3	...
9,459	43.1	9.6	3.9	24.4	6.1	5.40	8.61	1.0	0.2	188.1	...	0.1	6.2	2.1	287.6	...	...	2.0	...
16,714	30.2	8.1	2.6	16.7	4.2	4.98	7.28	9.1	0.2	185.0	...	0.1	4.3	4.5	292.7	...	...	1.7	...
18,042	34.3	8.7	3.6	23.4	5.8	4.73	5.13	3.9	0.2	191.5	...	0.1	5.9	12.4	298.5	...	...	1.4	...
...	56.2	31.4	1.3	7.2	12.4	5.73	6.92	-20.1	1.1	12.7	...	999.9	27.8	8.2	105.0	...	...	...	16.1
...	50.5	38.3	2.2	10.8	18.8	7.02	5.90	17.0	1.2	13.8	...	999.9	10.7	5.8	104.4	...	...	...	14.9
-1,622	56.9	36.3	2.1	13.9	15.6	4.13	3.87	-10.8	0.7	17.8	30.5	999.9	43.9	6.1	109.9	0.0	...	...	5.7
-1,757	59.9	33.2	2.3	18.2	14.8	0.85	0.80	6.8	0.7	19.4	...	999.9	8.2	5.3	111.8	...	...	...	6.6
224	64.3	32.1	2.1	11.0	12.7	7.88	8.58	9.7	0.7	19.8	...	999.9	11.5	4.2	113.9	...	...	...	5.1
...	...	...	...	...	...	...	...	...	...	...	...	...	...	...	...	...	...	...	...
...	...	...	...	...	...	...	...	...	...	...	...	...	...	...	...	...	...	...	...
...	...	...	...	...	...	...	...	...	...	...	...	...	...	...	...	...	...	...	...
4,096	60.7	27.5	...	28.9	...	...	...	...	0.5	57.4	...	...	...	3.8	158.8	...	...	...	...
1,267	58.9	20.8	3.7	15.4	10.1	4.54	3.41	13.9	0.5	60.1	...	...	3.0	4.3	160.6	...	...	...	...
...	34.2	38.6	5.0	12.4	18.8	6.81	6.40	1.1	1.2	35.7	...	11.3	8.6	1.3	131.7	...	...	...	...
...	33.4	38.7	4.9	13.5	19.7	6.40	6.12	-0.5	1.2	31.5	...	20.9	0.7	2.5	128.0	...	...	...	...
1,074	36.2	36.4	4.4	14.4	18.0	5.49	5.87	-1.7	0.9	33.4	...	23.9	30.3	0.4	129.6	...	...	...	...
-513	36.4	39.1	3.7	15.9	14.4	0.74	0.23	-0.9	0.8	36.0	...	22.3	8.0	2.1	128.9	...	...	...	...
1,386	37.1	43.0	2.3	8.5	8.7	5.82	6.40	0.8	0.8	36.1	...	17.2	6.2	4.5	127.6	...	...	9.2	...
...	999.9	999.9	1.7	38.0	2.6	4.62	4.62	...	0.0	285.9	...	...	45.1	7.4	385.9	...	...	...	...
...	...	...	-2.2	-56.2	-2.8	3.97	3.97	-99.9	...	399.0	...	...	17.9	50.6	497.3	...	...	...	...
13	...	...	1.7	46.1	2.1	3.83	4.37	...	...	556.6	...	...	4.2	59.1	658.0	...	...	...	...
197	...	...	-5.2	-99.9	-6.5	3.68	10.97	...	...	470.6	...	...	-4.1	46.2	617.3	...	...	...	...
-8	...	...	-0.6	-15.9	-0.7	3.79	-5.28	...	...	643.5	...	...	1.6	39.2	734.9	...	...	...	...
...	27.8	47.7	11.4	22.1	11.3	5.67	5.65	8.0	0.4	999.9	...	6.8	12.0	63.9	999.9	1.4	...	...	0.7
...	23.7	52.7	16.1	32.8	16.3	4.97	4.95	7.9	0.3	999.9	0.1	-6.0	17.8	73.5	999.9	1.1	...	...	0.4
2,416	32.1	54.6	11.9	22.6	12.2	5.67	6.22	7.9	0.4	999.9	...	-8.2	-8.6	37.9	999.9	0.7	...	...	0.5
1,902	27.7	53.3	12.8	24.1	13.5	4.08	3.96	8.5	0.4	999.9	0.1	-16.0	14.3	37.5	999.9	0.4	...	...	0.7
9,755	27.9	45.0	17.5	36.6	18.3	4.52	5.96	5.8	0.3	999.9	0.1	-16.3	21.9	0.8	999.9	0.4	...	...	0.7

2010 BEST'S KEY RATING GUIDE — LIFE/HEALTH EDITION
ANNUAL STATEMENT DATA FOR YEARS 2005 – 2009

Canadian Companies — Data in Canadian Dollars

COMPANY NAME Ultimate Parent Association Principal Officer Mailing Address Dom. : Began Bus. : Struct. : Mktg. Specialty Phone # AMB#	Best's Financial Strength Rating FSC	Data Year	Balance Sheet Bonds (%)	Mort. Loans & R.E. (%)	Com & Pref. Shares (%)	All Other Assets (%)	Total Assets ($000)	Life Reserves (%)	Health Reserves (%)	Ann Res. Liabilities (%)	All Other Liabilities (%)	Capital & Surplus ($000)	Operations Direct Premiums Written ($000)	Net Premiums Written ($000)	Operating Cash Flow ($000)	NOG Before Taxes ($000)	NOG After Taxes ($000)	Net Income ($000)
PRINCIPAL LIFE INS CO CAB Principal Financial Group Inc John R. Milnes Chief Agent 1300 Bay Street, 4th Floor Toronto, ON, Canada M5R 3K8 CA : 1951 : Stock : Not Available Ann, A&S, Life 416-964-0067	**A+** Rating Outlook: Negative	'05	86.4	...	...	13.6	9,505	5.4	5.2	86.4	3.0	3,327	136	136	-103	247	247	247
		'06	89.9	...	...	10.1	9,150	5.7	5.4	88.9	0.1	3,150	351	351	185	172	172	172
		'07	89.5	...	...	10.5	8,475	5.9	6.4	86.8	0.9	3,445	1	1	-84	247	247	247
		'08	91.8	...	...	8.2	9,296	4.4	5.3	89.3	1.0	3,123	362	362	83	-59	-59	-59
		'09	93.7	...	...	6.3	8,374	3.3	5.6	90.1	0.9	2,678	473	473	318	20	20	20
AMB# 069355	**FSC XV**	**Rating History: A+ g, 11/25/09; A+, 02/27/09; A+, 01/24/08; A+ g, 11/02/06; A+ g, 10/31/05**																
RBC LIFE INSURANCE COMPANY Royal Bank of Canada Neil D. Skelding Chairman 6880 Financial Drive, West Tower Mississauga, ON, Canada L5N 7Y5 CA : 1989 : Stock : Career Agent Life 905-606-1000	**A** Rating Outlook: Stable	'05	80.6	2.0	8.2	9.2	4,201,750	47.6	43.6	1.5	7.4	898,148	1,007,675	895,861	195,323	110,767	70,214	70,214
		'06	71.7	2.9	8.3	17.1	4,804,394	50.3	41.5	1.1	7.1	1,252,970	1,077,340	979,682	341,901	169,416	104,822	104,822
		'07	74.2	4.9	8.7	12.2	5,470,822	57.3	37.5	0.8	4.4	1,305,134	1,137,488	1,005,568	354,597	106,114	59,054	59,054
		'08	67.6	7.3	6.9	18.2	5,205,006	56.7	36.7	0.9	5.7	1,400,882	986,188	895,785	306,551	151,150	110,008	110,008
		'09	68.8	6.7	6.5	17.9	6,149,892	61.5	33.5	0.7	4.3	1,527,221	1,204,264	1,084,119	431,493	174,184	118,908	118,908
AMB# 066806	**FSC XIV**	**Rating History: A, 12/08/09; A, 07/02/09; A, 07/09/08; A, 06/20/07; A, 04/27/06**																
REASSURE AMERICA LIFE INS CAB Swiss Reinsurance Company Ltd Jean-Jacques Henchoz Chief Agent 150 King Street West, Suite 1000 Toronto, ON, Canada M5H 1J9 CA : 1883 : Stock : Not Available Life Reins 416-947-3800	**A** Rating Outlook: Stable	'05	87.1	...	...	12.9	13,957	64.9	...	...	35.1	8,981	41	41	74	697	697	697
		'06	83.1	...	...	16.9	14,615	63.3	...	...	36.7	9,838	38	38	364	597	597	597
		'07	60.7	...	...	39.3	8,294	62.0	...	...	38.0	3,509	33	33	176	483	483	483
		'08	58.5	...	...	41.5	9,031	58.8	...	...	41.2	3,568	35	35	137	-204	-204	-204
		'09	71.9	...	...	28.1	6,633	60.8	...	...	39.2	1,055	31	31	134	-85	-85	-85
AMB# 069347	**FSC XV**	**Rating History: A g, 12/14/09; A g, 02/27/09; A+ gu, 02/05/09; A+ g, 12/19/08; A+ g, 03/20/08**																
RELIABLE LIFE INS CO[1] Old Republic International Corporation Paul M. Field CEO & CFO P.O. Box 557 Hamilton, ON, Canada L8N 3K9 CA : 1963 : Stock : Not Available Life, Group A&H 905-523-5587	**NR-5**	'05	63.4	...	1.0	35.6	47,272	-2.6	53.0	...	49.6	21,273	65,568	46,007	4,706	3,102	1,947	1,947
		'06	67.1	...	1.0	31.9	49,170	-3.8	50.3	...	53.4	23,519	65,528	46,350	3,273	3,561	2,246	2,246
		'07	66.5	...	0.6	32.9	54,432	-6.5	52.7	...	53.7	26,426	70,151	50,904	...	4,607	2,907	2,907
		'08	63.1	...	0.2	36.7	54,033	-8.1	54.4	...	53.7	28,407	67,149	51,434	...	3,706	2,481	2,481
		'09	59.3	...	0.2	40.5	52,891	-9.8	62.5	...	47.4	29,363	72,629	53,671	...	1,511	956	956
AMB# 009049		**Rating History: NR-5, 04/26/10; NR-5, 05/21/09; NR-5, 05/12/08; NR-5, 04/27/07; NR-5, 05/16/06**																
RELIASTAR LIFE INS CO CAB ING Groep N.V. V. Lorraine Williams Chief Agent 3650 Victoria Park Avenue, Suite 201 Toronto, ON, Canada M2H 3P7 CA : 1984 : Stock : Not Available Group Life, Life Reins, Employee Benefits 416-496-1148	**A** Rating Outlook: Stable	'05	83.9	...	...	16.1	127,535	0.6	71.7	...	27.7	58,627	...	17,430	1,227	9,458	6,708	6,708
		'06	82.4	...	...	17.6	117,490	0.5	77.1	...	22.4	47,741	...	17,175	8,187	5,975	4,928	4,928
		'07	84.5	...	...	15.5	111,569	0.9	82.9	...	16.2	48,834	...	15,234	1,068	10,637	7,389	7,389
		'08	88.2	...	...	11.8	121,889	1.0	84.1	...	14.9	46,799	...	13,407	3,214	-178	-581	-581
		'09	43.4	...	...	56.6	116,729	0.9	87.8	...	11.3	47,474	...	13,712	4,647	6,180	4,696	4,696
AMB# 066843	**FSC XIV**	**Rating History: A g, 06/11/10; A g, 04/24/09; A+ g, 06/18/08; A+ g, 05/11/07; A+ g, 02/24/06**																
RGA LIFE REINSURANCE OF CANADA Reinsurance Group of America Inc Alain Neemeh President & CEO 55 University Avenue, Suite 1100 Toronto, ON, Canada M5J 2H7 CA : 1992 : Stock : Other Direct Reins 416-682-0000	**A+** Rating Outlook: Stable	'05	69.2	...	0.2	30.6	2,186,822	82.6	1.1	1.3	15.0	402,127	...	120,369	78,022	-6,832	-6,156	-6,156
		'06	69.3	...	0.2	30.4	2,354,225	84.3	1.0	1.1	13.6	378,687	...	113,832	73,952	13,425	14,519	14,519
		'07	75.2	...	...	24.8	3,208,338	89.7	0.7	0.7	8.9	412,693	...	136,786	99,729	18,583	13,094	13,094
		'08	75.6	...	...	24.4	3,358,640	87.6	2.2	0.4	9.8	453,931	...	119,902	98,275	15,068	10,511	10,511
		'09	75.1	...	...	24.9	3,622,393	87.1	2.4	0.1	10.5	451,586	...	115,645	88,528	1,115	-2,976	-2,976
AMB# 066817	**FSC XIII**	**Rating History: A+ g, 10/12/09; A+ g, 06/02/08; A+ g, 10/05/07; A+ g, 09/19/06; A+ g, 08/02/05**																
SCOR GLOBAL LIFE CAB SCOR S.E. Francois Lemieux Executive Vice President 1250 Rene-Levesque, Blvd West Montreal, QC, Canada H3B 4W8 CA : 1991 : Stock : Not Available Reins, Life, A&S 514-933-6994	**A-** Rating Outlook: Positive	'05	86.7	...	...	13.3	240,141	31.9	62.5	...	5.6	69,150	...	76,631	13,165	1,800	2,665	2,665
		'06	82.7	...	...	17.3	258,657	37.7	58.2	...	4.1	65,705	...	74,180	18,044	-5,782	-3,671	-3,671
		'07	83.5	...	...	16.5	303,748	37.7	56.4	...	6.0	85,514	...	74,650	13,342	11,308	8,637	8,637
		'08	84.9	...	...	15.1	314,894	41.6	52.6	...	5.8	95,449	...	85,890	10,776	11,529	7,478	7,478
		'09	85.3	...	...	14.7	344,920	42.6	51.0	...	6.4	107,172	...	92,980	18,101	1,127	1,083	1,083
AMB# 066849	**FSC XV**	**Rating History: A- g, 09/04/09; A- g, 11/14/08; A- g, 08/20/07; A- gu, 05/14/07; A- g, 09/08/06**																
SCOTIA LIFE INSURANCE COMPANY[1] Bank of Nova Scotia Oscar Zimmerman President & CEO 44 King Street West Toronto, ON, Canada M5H 1H1 CA : 1959 : Stock : Not Available Term Life 416-866-7075	**NR-5**	'05	69.4	...	12.5	18.0	52,803	...	152.5	...	-52.5	70,848	18,677	13,660	...	17,795	11,501	11,501
		'06	71.5	...	11.3	17.2	59,005	6.9	135.1	...	-42.0	84,594	21,759	17,275	...	21,182	13,746	13,746
		'07	64.8	...	21.3	13.9	64,684	2.8	123.5	...	-26.3	100,668	25,380	21,633	...	18,057	12,199	12,199
		'08	63.6	...	13.6	22.8	68,443	1.6	123.7	...	-25.4	115,368	30,773	27,326	...	25,324	17,720	17,720
		'09	62.5	...	14.2	23.3	76,622	20.8	999.9	...	-99.9	79,702	35,843	32,436	...	17,386	12,041	12,041
AMB# 066845		**Rating History: NR-5, 05/04/10; NR-5, 05/20/09; NR-5, 05/09/08; NR-5, 05/14/07; NR-5, 05/16/06**																
STANDARD LIFE ASSURANCE CO[1] Joseph Iannicelli President & CEO 1245 Sherbrooke Street West Montreal, QC, Canada H3G 1G3 CA : Stock : Agency Ind Ann, Ann, Group A&S 514-499-4107	**NR-5**	'05	58.6	25.9	2.5	12.9	14,697,281	7.6	3.3	79.3	9.8	1,149,020	1,758,461	1,799,207	...	201,697	177,504	177,504
		'06	57.9	25.4	4.2	12.5	15,903,769	12.4	3.4	72.8	11.3	1,160,715	1,511,112	1,431,921	...	236,981	207,524	207,524
		'07	58.9	23.4	4.8	12.9	16,576,887	16.3	3.6	73.4	6.7	1,350,088	1,365,700	1,352,873	...	255,177	196,201	196,201
		'08	55.4	27.9	3.6	13.1	16,193,714	16.8	3.8	72.3	7.1	1,271,588	1,289,834	1,267,592	...	-82,122	-247	-247
		'09	53.8	27.8	4.1	14.3	17,209,995	15.2	4.0	74.0	6.7	1,383,897	1,627,523	1,605,640	...	172,494	110,397	110,397
AMB# 066846		**Rating History: NR-5, 04/28/10; NR-5, 05/20/09; NR-5, 05/12/08; NR-5, 05/14/07; NR-5, 05/16/06**																

2010 BEST'S KEY RATING GUIDE — LIFE/HEALTH EDITION
BEST'S PROFITABILITY, LEVERAGE AND LIQUIDITY TESTS 2005 – 2009
Canadian Companies — Data in Canadian Dollars

	Profitability Tests							Leverage Tests						Liquidity Tests					
AOCI ($000)	Benefits Paid to NPW (%)	Comm. & Expenses to NPW (%)	NOG to Total Assets (%)	NOG to Total Rev (%)	Operating Return on Equity (%)	Yield on Invested Assets (%)	Total Return (%)	Change in NPW (%)	NPW to Capital (X)	Capital & Surplus to Liabilities (%)	Surplus Relief (%)	Reins Leverage (%)	Change in Capital (%)	Quick Liquidity (%)	Current Liquidity (%)	Non-Invest Grade Bonds to Capital (%)	Delinq. & Foreclosed Mortgages to Capital (%)	Mort. & Credit Tenant Loans & R.E. to Capital (%)	Affiliated Invest to Capital (%)
...	363.2	122.8	2.6	44.3	7.7	4.84	4.84	-70.8	0.0	53.9	...	...	8.1	16.6	149.6	...	...	...	...
...	133.0	41.3	1.8	21.9	5.3	4.84	4.84	158.1	0.1	52.5	...	...	-5.3	14.3	151.4	...	...	...	...
...	999.9	999.9	2.8	77.4	7.5	5.20	5.20	-99.7	0.0	68.5	...	...	9.4	16.4	167.2	...	...	...	...
...	145.6	32.0	-0.7	-6.0	-1.8	4.62	4.62	999.9	0.1	50.6	...	...	-9.3	10.1	148.2	...	...	...	...
...	99.4	23.5	0.2	3.0	0.7	4.70	4.70	30.7	0.2	47.0	...	...	-14.2	8.3	146.1	...	...	...	...
...	47.9	41.4	1.7	6.1	8.4	6.22	6.68	29.9	1.0	27.2	0.9	76.2	15.5	9.9	119.1	0.6	...	9.5	...
...	44.3	41.9	2.3	8.3	9.7	6.38	6.84	9.4	0.8	35.3	0.1	62.1	39.5	18.9	125.6	...	...	11.1	...
-10,278	44.8	37.9	1.1	4.9	4.6	4.00	3.79	2.6	0.8	31.3	0.7	69.7	4.2	8.3	119.6	...	...	20.6	...
-24,538	44.4	38.2	2.1	21.7	8.1	-7.33	-7.61	-10.9	0.6	36.8	...	33.3	7.3	8.8	119.8	...	...	27.1	...
-17,107	44.9	38.4	2.1	6.2	8.1	16.10	16.24	21.0	0.7	33.0	...	36.7	9.0	6.3	117.2	1.0	...	27.1	...
...	573.2	146.3	5.1	115.8	8.2	4.18	4.18	-6.8	0.0	180.5	...	...	11.5	21.5	266.1	...	...	...	...
...	507.9	152.6	4.2	87.3	6.3	4.63	4.63	-7.3	0.0	205.9	...	...	9.5	36.6	291.1	...	...	...	...
122	869.7	166.7	4.2	71.4	7.2	5.78	6.84	-13.2	0.0	75.3	...	...	-64.3	56.9	165.0	...	...	...	...
366	999.9	88.6	-2.4	-55.1	-5.8	3.95	6.73	6.1	0.0	70.0	...	...	1.7	59.3	163.1	...	...	...	...
329	367.7	251.6	-1.1	-25.5	-3.7	3.94	3.46	-11.4	0.0	20.1	...	...	-70.4	24.6	115.6	...	...	...	...
...	35.3	61.0	4.3	4.1	9.6	3.96	3.81	13.0	2.2	81.8	...	126.9	10.1	23.6	147.9	...	...	...	...
...	32.9	64.8	4.7	4.7	10.0	3.83	4.41	0.7	2.0	91.7	...	100.9	10.6	23.6	161.6	...	...	...	...
...	29.1	62.9	5.6	5.5	11.6	4.09	4.09	9.8	1.9	94.4	...	77.3	12.4	28.5	164.4	...	...	...	...
...	30.4	67.8	4.6	4.7	9.0	4.24	4.24	1.0	1.8	110.9	...	66.2	7.5	27.3	164.8	...	...	...	...
...	33.5	65.0	1.8	1.7	3.3	3.32	3.32	4.3	1.8	124.8	...	26.7	3.4	38.6	176.8	...	...	...	...
...	15.7	29.5	5.3	28.8	12.1	4.93	4.85	55.4	0.3	85.1	...	12.5	12.4	19.7	182.9	...	...	...	...
...	44.7	27.0	4.0	21.2	9.3	5.32	5.05	-1.5	0.4	68.4	...	10.5	-18.6	22.0	166.4	...	...	...	...
-4,060	55.9	27.3	6.5	36.2	15.3	4.80	1.05	-11.3	0.3	73.1	...	15.7	2.3	18.0	164.7	...	...	...	...
5,937	69.5	31.0	-0.5	-3.6	-1.2	2.56	11.03	-12.0	0.3	67.7	...	15.1	-4.2	15.8	174.2	...	...	...	...
1,350	78.7	25.3	3.9	21.4	10.0	7.46	3.39	2.3	0.3	69.9	0.0	10.1	1.4	87.9	166.5	...	...	...	...
...	49.8	42.5	-0.3	-2.4	-1.7	9.97	10.00	-1.0	0.3	22.5	11.8	194.8	20.8	0.4	121.4	...	...	...	...
...	35.5	29.1	0.6	5.6	3.7	9.68	9.80	-5.4	0.3	19.2	18.0	218.6	-5.8	0.4	118.2	...	...	...	...
...	40.4	24.8	0.5	4.7	3.3	7.30	7.30	20.2	0.3	14.8	28.4	247.2	9.0	1.4	114.1	2.9	...	...	...
...	56.0	30.4	0.3	7.2	2.4	1.02	1.02	-12.3	0.3	15.6	29.0	203.1	10.0	0.4	115.0	2.5	...	...	...
...	63.4	27.2	-0.1	-1.1	-0.7	6.20	6.20	-3.6	0.3	14.2	31.9	213.6	-0.5	0.2	113.6	...	...	...	...
...	62.9	32.4	1.1	3.0	3.9	5.70	5.80	-1.5	1.1	40.4	...	5.4	4.3	8.6	134.0	...	...	...	...
...	58.4	34.9	-1.5	-4.2	-5.4	5.58	5.71	-3.2	1.1	34.1	...	5.2	-5.0	13.5	127.8	...	...	...	...
9,458	73.7	41.3	3.1	9.4	11.4	5.87	9.36	0.6	0.9	41.0	...	57.2	30.1	15.2	141.2	...	...	...	...
7,894	65.0	36.7	2.4	7.3	8.3	5.62	5.08	15.1	0.9	45.1	...	42.4	11.6	14.5	145.4	...	...	...	...
7,497	58.8	34.6	0.3	1.0	1.1	3.76	3.63	8.3	0.9	46.5	0.1	34.9	12.3	13.3	145.9	...	...	...	...
...	11.4	114.6	23.4	40.0	17.7	5.61	8.12	26.8	0.2	-99.9	...	-9.9	19.4	-73.7	-99.9	...	...	...	...
...	21.5	91.9	24.6	43.0	17.7	5.82	6.27	26.5	0.2	-99.9	...	-5.1	19.4	-55.2	-99.9	...	...	...	...
1,624	23.1	74.5	19.7	40.4	13.2	5.45	8.16	25.2	0.2	-99.9	...	-3.1	19.0	-38.1	-99.9	...	...	...	4.5
-1,396	13.2	70.0	26.6	51.0	16.4	5.97	0.94	26.3	0.2	-99.9	...	-1.8	14.6	-38.4	-99.9	...	...	...	3.9
898	17.1	61.0	16.6	31.9	12.3	3.76	7.11	18.7	0.4	-99.9	...	-1.3	-30.9	-99.9	-99.9	...	...	...	5.7
...	103.2	23.8	1.2	6.1	16.7	7.29	8.01	...	1.6	8.5	...	58.8	18.3	6.2	76.3	...	...	331.7	3.3
...	131.0	25.7	1.4	7.9	18.0	7.18	8.17	-20.4	1.2	7.9	...	67.7	1.0	6.8	75.3	...	...	347.4	9.7
107	134.7	25.6	1.2	8.4	15.6	5.04	5.04	-5.5	1.0	8.9	...	32.2	16.3	8.1	78.3	...	...	286.8	10.9
-146	135.8	27.5	0.0	0.0	-0.0	1.71	1.71	-6.3	1.0	8.5	...	47.0	-5.8	6.1	73.9	...	...	355.3	11.9
274	108.6	22.5	0.7	3.4	8.3	9.23	9.24	26.7	1.2	8.7	...	46.5	8.8	8.4	74.4	...	...	345.2	11.3

Canadian Companies — Data in Canadian Dollars

COMPANY NAME / Ultimate Parent Association / Principal Officer / Mailing Address / Dom. : Began Bus. : Struct. : Mktg. / Specialty / Phone # / AMB#	Best's Financial Strength Rating / FSC	Data Year	Balance Sheet: Bonds (%)	Mort. Loans & R.E. (%)	Com & Pref. Shares (%)	All Other Assets (%)	Total Assets ($000)	Life Reserves (%)	Health Reserves (%)	Ann Res. Liabilities (%)	All Other Liabilities (%)	Capital & Surplus ($000)	Operations: Direct Premiums Written ($000)	Net Premiums Written ($000)	Operating Cash Flow ($000)	NOG Before Taxes ($000)	NOG After Taxes ($000)	Net Income ($000)
STANDARD LIFE ASSUR LTD CAB[1] Standard Life Plc	NR-5	'05	...	...	...	...	...	...	...	...	...	...	...	...	...	...	...	...
		'06	93.7	...	...	6.3	5,226	...	...	...	100.0	5,188	27,056	...	196	188	188	188
1245 Sherbrooke Street West, 2nd Floor, Montreal, QC, Canada H3G 1G3		'07	8.2	...	...	91.8	60,569	...	...	100.0	...	5,479	31,390	...	28	263	263	263
CA : Other : Not Available		'08	8.5	...	...	91.5	58,776	...	...	100.0	...	5,779	35,041	...	-1,829	300	300	300
Ind Ann, Annuity; AMB# 066887		'09	9.2	...	...	90.8	56,374	...	...	100.0	...	5,838	37,512	...	-2,244	59	59	59
		Rating History: NR-5, 05/04/10; NR-5, 05/20/09; NR-5, 05/09/08; NR-5, 06/08/07																
STATE FARM INTL LF INS CO CAB State Farm Mutual Automobile Ins Co	A+	'05	...	...	...	...	...	...	...	...	...	...	...	...	...	...	...	...
Barbara Bellissimo, President & Chief Agent		'06	...	...	...	100.0	5,046	...	...	...	100.0	5,028	...	...	...	46	28	28
333 First Commerce Drive, Aurora, ON, Canada L4G 8A4	Rating Outlook: Stable	'07	87.6	...	...	12.4	997,734	83.5	...	...	16.5	197,710	106,027	106,018	47,164	37,318	17,816	17,816
CA : 2007 : Stock : Exclusive Agent; Life, Ann		'08	87.7	...	...	12.3	1,099,026	83.5	...	...	16.5	181,314	116,449	116,425	78,558	-15,248	-13,107	-13,107
905-750-4620; AMB# 066884	FSC XV	'09	88.0	...	...	12.0	1,155,588	83.7	...	...	16.3	214,240	126,050	125,992	87,725	48,603	32,926	32,926
		Rating History: A+, 04/23/10; A+ g, 06/17/09; A+ g, 06/12/08; A+ g, 06/11/07																
SUN LIFE ASSUR CO OF CANADA Sun Life Financial Inc	A+	'05	48.8	21.1	10.4	19.8	68,738,349	24.0	7.6	23.7	44.8	8,890,043	8,792,919	8,294,156	3,028,000	1,697,020	1,327,544	1,327,544
Donald A. Stewart, CEO		'06	46.2	22.0	13.0	18.9	72,115,483	24.4	7.7	22.0	45.9	9,756,092	9,647,398	8,898,773	3,297,000	1,586,994	1,418,745	1,418,745
150 King Street West, Toronto, ON, Canada M5H 1J9	Rating Outlook: Stable	'07	44.1	22.9	15.1	17.9	64,842,854	33.1	9.8	12.7	44.4	9,882,939	9,671,718	112,645	6,484,859	1,496,680	1,391,410	1,391,410
CA : 1871 : Stock : Career Agent; A&S, Ann, Life		'08	40.2	22.0	14.1	23.7	73,253,625	27.5	8.7	11.9	51.8	10,399,170	9,926,217	12,954,206	4,306,361	1,488,165	1,508,289	1,508,289
416-979-9966; AMB# 007101	FSC XV	'09	42.0	19.4	15.5	23.1	73,419,938	30.1	9.4	11.4	49.2	10,512,067	11,075,457	9,494,829	2,542,000	522,142	723,528	723,528
		Rating History: A+ g, 02/27/09; A++g, 06/19/08; A++g, 06/12/07; A++g, 07/10/06; A++g, 06/30/05																
SUN LIFE INS (CANADA) LTD[1] Sun Life Financial Inc	NR-5	'05	...	...	...	...	...	...	...	...	...	...	...	...	...	...	...	...
Dikran Ohannessian, President & CEO		'06	88.5	...	...	11.5	195,271	...	...	100.0	0.0	175,808	19,486	168,250	17,253	-300	-192	-192
150 King Street West, 6th Floor, Toronto, ON, Canada M5H 1J9		'07	52.1	12.8	30.7	4.4	10,885,010	0.8	...	81.6	17.6	859,250	70,308	8,821,914	...	103,284	89,301	89,301
CA : Other : Not Available; Ann		'08	54.7	12.5	29.0	3.8	10,330,224	0.7	...	79.9	19.4	712,416	42,759	808,790	...	246,191	157,036	157,036
416-979-4188; AMB# 066886		'09	52.0	11.2	28.8	8.0	11,137,092	0.7	...	89.6	9.8	1,322,048	119,759	1,249,175	...	221,060	272,294	272,294
		Rating History: NR-5, 02/27/09; NR-5, 06/19/08; NR-5, 06/12/07																
SWISS RE LIFE & HEALTH CANADA Swiss Reinsurance Company Ltd	NR-5	'05	82.3	0.0	...	17.7	2,733,765	45.6	4.0	1.8	48.6	279,550	...	51,449	38,679	106,317	90,242	90,242
Jean-Jacques Henchoz, President & CEO		'06	75.6	0.0	...	24.4	2,760,096	47.5	3.8	1.5	47.2	273,657	...	166,054	-30,516	84,759	79,107	79,107
150 King Street West, Suite 1000, Toronto, ON, Canada M5H 1J9		'07	82.2	...	...	17.8	3,302,777	63.2	5.0	1.2	30.6	345,750	...	232,010	47,950	22,085	22,265	22,265
CA : 1960 : Stock : Other Direct; A&S, Life, Reins		'08	84.9	...	...	15.1	3,401,628	65.2	4.9	1.4	28.5	350,047	...	244,531	133,284	1,474	8,052	8,052
416-947-3800; AMB# 066803		'09	69.5	...	...	30.5	3,484,003	62.5	4.6	1.8	31.1	373,402	...	75,336	75,327	35,309	22,039	22,039
		Rating History: NR-5, 04/12/10; A g, 12/14/09; A g, 02/27/09; A+ gu, 02/05/09; A+ g, 12/19/08																
SWISS REINSURANCE CO CAB Swiss Reinsurance Company Ltd	A	'05	83.1	...	...	16.9	1,924,900	68.3	-2.2	...	33.9	813,141	...	-23,577	45,480	72,693	63,245	63,245
Jean-Jacques Henchoz, Chief Agent		'06	70.8	...	...	29.2	1,857,687	67.4	-2.0	...	34.7	838,754	...	-37,482	865	71,952	65,613	65,613
150 King Street West, Suite 1000, Toronto, ON, Canada M5H 1J9	Rating Outlook: Stable	'07	92.3	...	...	7.7	1,937,389	91.1	-2.3	...	11.3	912,293	...	153,459	35,843	43,719	34,911	34,911
CA : 1959 : Stock : Not Available; A&S		'08	83.6	...	...	16.4	2,036,776	65.1	-2.5	...	37.4	940,652	...	-150,106	128,482	70,477	28,359	28,359
416-947-3800; AMB# 066833	FSC XV	'09	42.3	...	...	57.7	2,135,142	71.9	-2.6	...	30.7	1,081,381	...	104,788	-123,068	86,358	60,729	60,729
		Rating History: A g, 12/14/09; A g, 02/27/09; A+ gu, 02/05/09; A+ g, 12/19/08; A+ g, 03/20/08																
TD LIFE INSURANCE COMPANY[1] Toronto-Dominion Bank	NR-5	'05	63.1	...	...	36.9	22,524	77.3	267.5	...	-99.9	26,025	30,762	15,038	...	1,989	1,166	1,166
Dunbar Russel		'06	59.0	...	...	41.0	23,580	34.1	215.3	...	-99.9	27,330	36,070	16,910	...	2,082	1,305	1,305
P.O. Box 1, Toronto, ON, Canada M5K 1A2		'07	56.3	...	...	43.7	27,487	71.0	611.5	...	-99.9	28,626	39,857	23,139	...	2,187	1,448	1,448
CA : 1996 : Stock : Direct Response; Group A&S, Ind Life, Group Life		'08	59.6	...	...	40.4	43,942	-73.8	-96.6	...	270.4	40,163	55,253	37,646	...	2,290	1,542	1,542
416-982-6743; AMB# 066831		'09	54.7	...	...	45.3	50,624	-32.0	-29.8	...	161.8	42,435	65,043	46,270	...	3,213	2,090	2,090
		Rating History: NR-5, 04/28/10; NR-5, 05/20/09; NR-5, 05/09/08; NR-5, 05/14/07; NR-5, 05/16/06																
TRANSAMERICA LIFE CANADA AEGON N.V.	B++	'05	69.3	1.6	18.2	10.9	4,599,920	40.0	0.2	27.4	32.4	1,097,182	686,309	470,974	189,236	-142,940	-83,858	-83,858
Doug Brooks, President & CEO		'06	67.6	1.0	19.6	11.8	5,121,228	43.4	0.2	25.2	31.1	1,220,731	707,553	476,360	111,119	10,961	23,549	23,549
5000 Yonge Street, Toronto, ON, Canada M2N 7J8	Rating Outlook: Stable	'07	67.4	0.3	18.6	13.7	5,907,994	56.7	0.2	25.8	17.3	964,275	706,156	464,001	171,171	-446,145	-307,213	-307,213
CA : 1971 : Stock : Agency; Term Life, Var ann, Univ Life		'08	54.1	0.2	11.2	34.4	6,460,035	49.4	0.2	33.2	17.2	803,067	704,761	428,810	193,029	-747,124	-583,368	-583,368
416-883-5000; AMB# 066805	FSC XI	'09	53.2	0.2	16.6	30.0	6,440,120	56.6	0.3	26.6	16.4	892,576	708,126	390,327	-22,190	104,162	87,201	87,201
		Rating History: B++, 05/29/09; A-, 04/16/08; A, 05/30/07; A, 06/21/06; A, 05/13/05																
UKRAINIAN NATIONAL ASSOC CAB	NR-5	'05	96.7	...	...	3.3	10,415	95.9	0.1	...	4.0	4,135	93	93	229	241	241	257
Stefan Kaczaraj, President		'06	...	...	...	...	...	...	...	...	...	...	...	...	...	...	...	...
2200 Route 10, Parsippany, NJ 07054-0280		'07	95.9	...	...	4.1	11,015	96.5	...	...	3.5	4,904	100	100	187	423	423	430
CA : 1938 : Fraternal : Not Available; Ind Life, Ind A&S		'08	95.7	...	...	4.3	11,454	97.7	0.0	...	2.3	5,237	76	76	127	68	68	77
416-495-1755; AMB# 066825		'09	92.5	...	...	7.5	10,697	97.2	0.0	...	2.7	4,469	77	77	217	159	159	169
		Rating History: NR-5, 06/15/10; NR-5, 05/16/06; NR-5, 04/26/05; NR-5, 05/06/04; NR-5, 12/31/98																

BEST'S PROFITABILITY, LEVERAGE AND LIQUIDITY TESTS 2005 – 2009

Canadian Companies — Data in Canadian Dollars

—	Profitability Tests							Leverage Tests						Liquidity Tests					
AOCI ($000)	Benefits Paid to NPW (%)	Comm. & Expenses to NPW (%)	NOG to Total Assets (%)	NOG to Total Rev (%)	Operating Return on Equity (%)	Yield on Invested Assets (%)	Total Return (%)	Change in NPW (%)	NPW to Capital (X)	Capital & Surplus to Liabilities (%)	Surplus Relief (%)	Reins Leverage (%)	Change in Capital (%)	Quick Liquidity (%)	Current Liquidity (%)	Non-Invest Grade Bonds to Capital (%)	Delinq. & Foreclosed Mortgages to Capital (%)	Mort. & Credit Tenant Loans & R.E. to Capital (%)	Affiliated Invest to Capital (%)
...	...	...	...	...	...	...	...	...	...	...	...	...	...	...	...	...	...	...	...
...	...	...	...	100.0	...	...	...	...	...	999.9	...	999.9	...	747.4	999.9	...	...	...	...
...	...	...	0.8	375.7	4.9	6.66	6.66	...	...	9.9	...	999.9	5.6	0.9	109.9	...	...	...	...
...	...	...	0.5	-16.7	5.3	4.67	4.67	...	...	10.9	...	999.9	5.5	1.4	110.8	...	...	...	...
...	...	...	0.1	-2.5	1.0	4.34	4.34	...	...	11.6	...	999.9	1.0	1.3	111.5	...	...	...	...
...	...	...	...	...	...	...	...	...	...	...	...	...	...	...	...	...	...	...	...
...	...	...	...	60.9	...	...	...	...	...	999.9	...	...	...	999.9	999.9	...	...	...	...
5,637	46.7	32.9	3.6	11.6	17.6	10.32	11.47	...	0.5	24.9	...	0.0	999.9	2.9	113.0	...	...	...	...
21,927	40.8	32.4	-1.3	-7.9	-6.9	4.93	6.52	9.8	0.6	20.2	...	0.0	-8.3	3.4	111.0	...	...	...	...
12,618	42.7	29.1	2.9	18.3	16.6	4.69	3.85	8.2	0.6	23.1	...	0.3	18.2	4.9	114.5	...	...	...	...
...	82.3	31.1	1.9	10.0	13.8	7.30	8.13	0.3	0.9	14.9	...	10.0	-13.6	7.6	72.4	9.6	0.0	163.0	75.0
...	77.4	30.2	2.0	10.0	15.2	7.26	7.18	7.3	0.9	15.6	...	10.3	9.7	8.9	70.1	...	...	162.7	79.1
-1,521,075	999.9	999.9	2.0	31.1	14.2	5.54	4.38	-98.7	0.0	18.0	...	92.5	1.3	8.3	68.8	2.9	...	150.5	77.2
-1,365,473	55.5	12.9	2.2	9.9	14.9	3.74	4.02	999.9	1.2	16.5	...	80.9	5.2	8.4	69.7	...	...	155.2	79.5
-1,467,429	80.4	20.1	1.0	4.8	6.9	8.61	8.43	-26.7	0.9	16.7	...	92.2	1.1	10.9	72.9	...	...	135.8	79.9
...	...	...	...	...	...	...	...	...	...	...	...	...	...	...	...	...	...	...	...
...	0.0	0.4	...	-0.1	...	...	...	...	1.0	903.3	...	...	...	4.6	992.9	...	...	...	...
-114,884	6.2	3.0	1.6	1.0	17.3	6.74	3.71	999.9	10.3	8.6	...	...	388.7	2.0	60.4	...	...	161.9	388.3
-413,754	110.9	29.4	1.5	19.7	20.0	0.22	-3.92	-90.8	1.1	7.4	...	...	-17.1	0.6	62.0	...	...	181.1	419.7
-1,205	72.9	19.5	2.5	11.4	26.8	10.70	16.06	54.4	0.9	13.5	...	...	85.6	2.8	66.4	...	...	94.4	242.2
...	210.7	88.2	3.3	39.6	35.8	7.21	7.24	-71.4	0.2	11.4	...	72.0	24.6	4.3	110.8	...	...	0.0	...
...	84.7	28.4	2.9	23.7	28.6	7.04	9.33	222.8	0.6	11.0	...	79.5	-2.1	12.3	110.4	...	...	0.0	...
-3,266	51.9	20.1	0.7	6.5	7.2	3.92	3.80	39.7	0.7	11.7	...	62.0	26.3	7.3	111.2	...	...	...	...
-6,798	46.5	15.0	0.2	2.8	2.3	1.95	1.83	5.4	0.7	11.5	...	61.7	1.2	5.7	111.1	...	...	...	...
-5,482	160.7	45.3	0.6	13.2	6.1	3.57	3.61	-69.2	0.2	12.0	...	58.4	6.7	23.2	111.6	...	...	...	...
...	-56.7	-36.3	3.4	111.0	8.1	4.88	4.73	-99.9	0.0	73.1	...	-4.2	8.4	9.7	171.9	...	...	...	...
...	-87.1	-33.3	3.5	129.8	7.9	5.25	6.54	-59.0	0.0	82.3	...	-2.7	3.1	38.6	180.3	...	...	...	...
924	27.1	5.2	1.8	15.8	4.0	3.81	3.86	509.4	0.2	89.1	...	-1.8	8.8	3.6	187.2	...	...	...	...
22,554	-30.2	-6.7	1.4	-26.6	3.1	2.34	3.47	-99.9	-0.2	87.6	...	-1.9	3.1	23.8	188.7	...	...	...	...
3,075	43.5	7.6	2.9	30.8	6.0	4.87	3.87	169.8	0.1	102.9	3.6	-1.4	15.0	97.6	202.5	...	...	...	...
...	22.6	111.4	5.2	5.0	4.6	3.58	3.97	36.8	0.6	-99.9	...	-14.7	4.7	-99.9	-99.9	...	...	...	...
...	22.9	105.4	5.7	4.8	4.9	4.15	3.86	12.4	0.6	-99.9	...	7.1	5.0	-99.9	-99.9	...	...	...	...
-94	19.1	126.1	5.7	3.8	5.2	4.92	4.53	36.8	0.8	-99.9	...	17.9	4.7	-99.9	-99.9	...	...	...	...
401	20.4	113.2	4.3	2.8	4.5	3.16	4.59	62.7	0.9	999.9	...	14.1	40.3	422.1	999.9	...	...	...	...
583	22.8	102.0	4.4	3.2	5.1	2.91	3.31	22.9	1.1	518.2	...	10.4	5.7	246.3	610.4	...	...	...	...
...	55.7	56.1	-1.9	-9.6	-7.7	6.98	8.65	2.4	0.4	31.3	...	129.8	1.5	21.8	118.4	1.4	...	6.6	...
...	53.7	55.1	0.5	2.6	2.0	6.67	8.12	1.1	0.4	31.3	0.6	116.1	11.3	22.3	118.4	0.8	...	4.0	...
1,927	59.0	79.8	-5.6	-50.4	-28.1	0.34	0.38	-2.6	0.5	19.5	...	148.1	-21.0	20.0	106.1	...	...	1.9	...
-5,913	64.6	57.9	-9.4	-99.9	-66.0	-1.88	-2.02	-7.6	0.5	14.2	...	179.8	-16.7	14.4	101.4	...	...	1.6	...
-3,605	121.7	67.9	1.4	10.1	10.3	6.74	6.78	-9.0	0.4	16.1	...	141.9	11.1	19.1	102.1	...	...	1.1	...
...	190.3	345.2	2.3	36.2	5.3	5.68	5.68	-9.7	0.0	65.8	...	...	-25.6	2.5	162.8	...	...	...	...
...	...	...	...	...	...	...	...	...	...	...	...	...	...	...	...	...	...	...	...
...	181.0	288.0	...	61.0	...	...	...	...	0.0	80.2	...	...	...	4.2	177.1	...	...	...	...
...	193.4	409.2	0.7	11.0	1.5	5.67	5.67	-24.0	0.0	84.2	...	...	6.8	4.1	180.5	...	...	...	...
...	207.8	396.1	1.5	27.8	3.5	4.88	4.88	1.3	0.0	71.8	...	...	-14.7	9.9	168.8	...	...	...	...

Canadian Companies — Data in Canadian Dollars

COMPANY NAME Ultimate Parent Association Principal Officer Mailing Address Dom. : Began Bus. : Struct. : Mktg. Specialty Phone # AMB#	Best's Financial Strength Rating FSC	Data Year	Balance Sheet Bonds (%)	Mort. Loans & R.E. (%)	Com & Pref. Shares (%)	All Other Assets (%)	Total Assets ($000)	Life Reserves (%)	Health Reserves (%)	Ann Res. Liabilities (%)	All Other Liabilities (%)	Capital & Surplus ($000)	Operations Direct Premiums Written ($000)	Net Premiums Written ($000)	Operating Cash Flow ($000)	NOG Before Taxes ($000)	NOG After Taxes ($000)	Net Income ($000)
UNITED AMERICAN INS CO CAB Torchmark Corporation	A+	'05	86.8	...	...	13.2	10,837	92.2	0.0	...	7.7	5,286	734	734	103	563	458	458
Robin B. Cumine Chief Agent		'06	85.4	...	...	14.6	11,001	92.6	0.0	...	7.4	5,462	666	666	51	170	176	176
130 Adelaide Street West, Suite 2800 Toronto, ON, Canada M5H 3P5	Rating Outlook: Stable	'07	84.1	...	...	15.9	11,308	94.2	0.0	...	5.8	5,867	588	588	257	482	395	395
CA : 1967 : Stock : Not Available A&S		'08	89.2	...	...	10.8	10,144	91.0	0.0	...	9.0	6,453	534	534	153	830	586	586
416-366-0800		'09	91.1	...	...	8.9	11,495	93.9	0.0	...	6.1	6,650	467	467	146	-7	197	197
AMB# 069354	FSC X	**Rating History: A+ g, 06/15/10; A+ g, 06/11/09; A+ g, 06/11/08; A+ g, 06/08/07; A+ g, 06/08/06**																
UNITY LIFE OF CANADA Independent Order of Foresters	A-	'05	79.9	...	11.3	8.8	276,729	46.0	1.2	31.8	21.1	34,480	93,411	69,659	26,114	444	526	4,509
Anthony W. Poole President		'06	81.0	0.9	10.3	7.9	471,632	62.0	1.2	24.0	12.8	44,147	105,643	82,788	190,653	12,106	9,667	9,667
100 Milverton Drive, Suite 400 Mississauga, ON, Canada L5R 4H1	Rating Outlook: Stable	'07	77.9	0.7	14.1	7.3	566,373	63.3	1.1	25.4	10.2	50,848	110,871	86,154	23,884	3,631	4,227	4,227
CA : 1934 : Stock : Not Available Term Life		'08	80.2	0.6	10.4	8.7	637,346	55.7	0.9	32.7	10.7	61,381	111,839	86,593	13,053	9,047	6,831	6,831
905-219-8040		'09	85.3	...	7.8	6.8	992,373	46.4	1.0	45.5	7.2	82,870	118,773	90,573	1,538	11,889	9,019	9,019
AMB# 066847	FSC VII	**Rating History: A-, 05/07/10; A-, 05/08/09; A-, 04/03/08; NR-5, 05/14/07; NR-5, 05/16/06**																
WAWANESA LIFE INS CO Wawanesa Mutual Insurance Company	A	'05	68.0	5.9	11.2	14.9	418,426	64.5	3.1	23.8	8.6	70,380	83,317	76,454	20,438	10,553	7,080	7,080
Kenneth E. McCrea President & CEO		'06	65.4	6.5	11.4	16.8	446,663	65.1	3.4	22.8	8.7	76,203	86,326	78,587	19,406	8,252	5,823	5,823
400 - 200 Main Street Winnipeg, MB, Canada R3C 1A8	Rating Outlook: Stable	'07	72.1	5.7	13.6	8.6	496,704	69.8	3.1	21.7	5.3	91,689	92,103	83,344	25,733	9,522	7,302	7,302
CA : 1960 : Stock : Agency Life, Ind Ann, Group A&S		'08	77.2	5.7	8.9	8.2	493,230	68.7	3.3	23.4	4.5	100,485	96,390	85,675	26,950	3,947	3,598	3,598
204-985-3940		'09	79.8	4.4	10.9	4.9	546,934	71.5	3.5	21.5	3.5	111,987	98,465	86,359	17,099	8,611	5,079	5,079
AMB# 060079	FSC VIII	**Rating History: A, 10/19/09; A, 10/23/08; A, 10/25/07; A, 09/25/06; A, 08/02/05**																
WESTERN LIFE ASSURANCE COMPANY Western Financial Group Inc	B++	'05	71.1	...	10.2	18.7	57,355	58.1	4.3	2.8	34.7	16,892	25,885	19,912	859	2,143	1,485	1,485
Dominique Gregoire President & CEO		'06	73.9	...	10.2	15.9	61,951	57.5	5.0	2.5	35.0	18,949	33,124	23,562	3,347	2,830	2,057	2,057
1010 - 24 Street SE High River, AB, Canada T1V 2A7	Rating Outlook: Stable	'07	68.8	...	16.6	14.6	73,221	67.7	5.6	2.1	24.6	22,774	41,416	28,242	3,178	4,454	3,333	3,333
CA : 1988 : Stock : Other Agency Group A&H, A&S, Term Life		'08	72.5	...	13.2	14.3	74,892	67.0	5.9	1.8	25.3	23,685	47,270	32,527	5,237	2,093	1,009	1,009
403-652-2663		'09	83.4	...	4.5	12.1	80,318	65.4	4.9	1.6	28.1	24,639	51,538	38,670	5,325	5,398	4,041	4,041
AMB# 066802	FSC VI	**Rating History: B++, 06/25/09; B++, 06/05/08; B++, 06/13/07; B++, 05/10/06; B++, 03/29/05**																
WOMAN'S LIFE INS SOCIETY CAB	A-	'05	84.5	...	...	15.5	10,348	80.0	...	1.7	18.3	2,025	227	223	492	337	337	337
Janice U. Whipple President		'06	83.0	...	...	17.0	10,169	78.5	...	1.5	20.0	1,672	219	216	538	426	426	426
1455 Lakeshore Road Sarnia, ON, Canada N7S 2M4	Rating Outlook: Negative	'07	81.7	...	...	18.3	10,326	79.5	...	1.7	18.8	1,992	219	217	336	431	431	431
CA : 1895 : Fraternal : Not Available Ann, Univ Life, Whole life		'08	80.1	...	...	19.9	10,903	80.3	...	1.4	18.3	2,422	216	212	481	339	339	339
519-542-2826		'09	75.1	...	...	24.9	11,085	76.7	...	1.6	21.6	2,842	202	199	411	648	648	648
AMB# 066813	FSC VI	**Rating History: A-, 06/04/10; A-, 05/29/09; A-, 06/17/08; A-, 06/07/07; A-, 06/14/06**																

BEST'S PROFITABILITY, LEVERAGE AND LIQUIDITY TESTS 2005 – 2009

Canadian Companies — Data in Canadian Dollars

	Profitability Tests							Leverage Tests						Liquidity Tests					
AOCI ($000)	Benefits Paid to NPW (%)	Comm. & Expenses to NPW (%)	NOG to Total Assets (%)	NOG to Total Rev (%)	Operating Return on Equity (%)	Yield on Invested Assets (%)	Total Return (%)	Change in NPW (%)	NPW to Capital (X)	Capital & Surplus to Liabilities (%)	Surplus Relief (%)	Reins Leverage (%)	Change in Capital (%)	Quick Liquidity (%)	Current Liquidity (%)	Non-Invest Grade Bonds to Capital (%)	Delinq. & Foreclosed Mortgages to Capital (%)	Mort. & Credit Tenant Loans & R.E. to Capital (%)	Affiliated Invest to Capital (%)
...	105.3	37.5	4.3	33.0	9.1	6.26	7.13	-7.7	0.1	95.2	...	...	9.5	22.5	192.0	...	...	...	...
...	117.3	44.6	1.6	14.0	3.3	5.58	5.40	-9.3	0.1	98.6	...	...	3.3	23.3	193.0	...	...	...	...
105	119.2	41.7	3.5	34.1	7.0	5.28	6.22	-11.7	0.1	110.0	...	...	7.4	29.2	207.5	...	...	...	...
-1,088	130.1	47.0	5.5	53.4	9.5	5.39	-6.41	-9.2	0.1	135.0	...	...	10.0	17.4	207.0	...	...	...	...
185	170.2	45.2	1.8	19.2	3.0	5.30	16.37	-12.5	0.1	142.7	...	...	3.1	17.7	242.5	...	...	...	...
...	30.9	52.4	1.7	5.3	14.0	6.17	5.71	-3.4	2.0	14.2	...	287.6	15.0	3.2	102.7	...	...	...	12.0
...	34.2	48.2	2.6	9.4	24.6	5.57	5.70	18.8	1.9	10.3	...	221.1	28.0	4.3	99.3	...	...	9.1	10.4
19,862	42.6	49.9	0.8	4.2	8.9	2.79	3.04	4.1	1.7	9.9	...	244.0	15.2	3.5	97.7	...	...	7.9	9.6
980	43.4	56.4	1.1	10.0	12.2	-3.09	-3.09	0.5	1.4	10.7	...	190.9	20.7	4.4	100.2	...	...	6.5	7.9
1,650	55.0	54.4	1.1	5.8	12.5	8.36	8.44	4.6	1.1	9.1	...	151.8	35.0	2.1	101.7	...	...	...	5.9
...	61.8	24.3	1.7	6.9	10.6	6.29	6.94	6.9	1.1	20.2	...	45.9	11.2	21.2	105.9	...	0.2	35.3	...
...	61.3	25.7	1.3	5.4	7.9	6.38	6.41	2.8	1.0	20.6	...	51.7	8.3	23.1	105.1	...	...	37.9	...
7,065	60.2	26.9	1.5	7.1	8.7	3.77	5.28	6.1	0.9	22.6	...	50.3	20.3	15.8	107.6	...	...	30.9	...
-2,737	53.6	29.4	0.7	4.7	3.7	-2.29	-4.32	2.8	0.9	25.6	...	44.0	9.6	11.6	111.1	...	...	28.0	...
3,686	52.9	29.8	1.0	3.6	4.8	10.37	11.60	0.8	0.8	25.7	...	36.4	11.4	9.8	113.0	4.2	...	21.4	...
...	56.6	41.7	2.6	6.6	9.2	5.22	6.76	9.1	1.2	41.7	8.5	35.8	9.4	25.7	130.3	...	...	...	...
...	51.2	41.6	3.4	7.8	11.5	4.94	4.87	18.3	1.2	44.1	...	34.0	12.2	22.3	133.1	...	...	...	0.1
192	46.6	44.1	4.9	10.8	16.0	4.30	4.60	19.9	1.2	45.1	29.6	58.2	20.2	23.9	132.2	...	...	...	0.1
94	44.8	44.9	1.4	3.2	4.3	-1.29	-1.43	15.2	1.4	46.3	31.4	70.5	4.0	22.3	135.3	...	...	...	...
7	47.5	42.3	5.2	9.6	16.7	4.55	4.43	18.9	1.6	44.3	17.7	79.7	4.0	8.5	136.9	...	...	...	...
...	131.8	70.0	3.3	31.1	15.9	8.66	8.66	-10.4	0.1	24.3	...	...	-8.9	2.5	107.5	...	...	...	...
...	175.5	74.1	4.2	39.8	23.0	8.69	8.69	-3.1	0.1	19.7	...	...	-17.4	3.9	103.2	...	...	...	...
...	180.2	65.4	4.2	41.0	23.5	8.49	8.47	0.5	0.1	23.9	...	...	19.1	6.5	107.7	...	...	...	...
...	136.8	68.9	3.2	32.1	15.4	8.27	8.27	-2.3	0.1	28.6	...	...	21.6	9.7	112.7	...	...	...	...
...	268.3	80.9	5.9	66.5	24.6	7.31	7.31	-6.1	0.1	34.5	...	...	17.3	17.8	118.9	...	...	...	...

BEST'S
AGENT'S GUIDE®
Life/Health

2010 Edition

Best's Financial Strength Ratings
are as of publication date
June 15, 2010

For Current Ratings and Reports access www.ambest.com

A.M. BEST COMPANY
Oldwick, New Jersey 08858 USA • (908) 439-2200 • Fax: (908) 439-3296
www.ambest.com

AAA LIFE INSURANCE COMPANY

17900 N. Laurel Park Drive
Livonia, Michigan 48152
Tel: 800-624-1662

AMB#: 007424
Began Business: 07/24/1969
Agency Off: Paul Schechter

Best's Financial Strength Rating: A- g
FSC: VII

• NET PREMIUMS AND DEPOSITS ($000 omitted)

Year	Individual Life	Individual & Group Annuities	Group Life & A&H	Credit Life & A&H	Individual A&H	Total
2007	18,920	11,015	47,722	...	2,098	79,756
2008	81,246	16,323	50,424	...	2,270	150,262
2009	32,624	22,499	52,669	...	2,650	110,442

• NET OPERATING GAIN ($000 omitted)

Year	Individual Life	Individual & Group Annuities	Group Life & A&H	Credit Life & A&H	Individual A&H	Total
2007	-3,592	2,653	6,457	...	1,338	6,856
2008	-2,522	117	278	...	-572	-2,699
2009	430	1,099	1,474	...	-299	2,704

• COMPARATIVE FINANCIALS ($000 omitted)

Year	Assets	Capital & Surplus	Net Invest Income	Benefits Paid	Realized Cap Gains	Policyholder Dividends	Contract Lns (% of assets)
2007	296,328	68,738	13,938	48,707	-208	...	0.2
2008	369,389	71,888	14,826	48,150	-3,508	...	0.6
2009	402,849	84,242	18,893	57,035	-544	...	0.7

• ORDINARY LIFE STATISTICS

Year	Av. Ord. Policy Issued ($)	Av. Ord. Policy In Force ($)	Avg. Prem ($/M)	1st Yr Prem/ Total Prem	Ord. Lapse Ratio
2007	215,720	188,960	3.29	25.8	7.6
2008	205,291	194,555	3.27	21.3	7.0
2009	221,557	201,870	3.21	18.5	7.4

• NEW LIFE BUSINESS ISSUED ($000 omitted)

Year	Whole Life	Term	Credit	Group	Industrial	Total
2007	951,243	9,138,429	...	1,844,785	...	11,934,457
2008	881,696	8,082,322	...	4,206,796	...	13,170,814
2009	935,487	8,304,550	...	4,725,921	...	13,965,957

• LIFE INSURANCE IN FORCE ($000 omitted)

Year	Whole Life	Term	Credit	Group	Industrial	Total
2007	4,500,062	35,789,078	...	13,525,671	...	53,814,811
2008	4,817,322	40,763,403	...	15,649,961	...	61,230,686
2009	5,163,491	45,447,021	...	17,630,673	...	68,241,186

ACACIA LIFE INSURANCE COMPANY

P.O. Box 81889
Lincoln, Nebraska 68501-1889
Tel: 800-444-1889

AMB#: 006002
Began Business: 03/03/1869
Agency Off: Arnold D. Henkel

Best's Financial Strength Rating: A g
FSC: XIII

• NET PREMIUMS AND DEPOSITS ($000 omitted)

Year	Individual Life	Individual & Group Annuities	Group Life & A&H	Credit Life & A&H	Individual A&H	Total
2007	26,783	56,011	...	...	28	82,822
2008	30,308	63,779	...	...	22	94,110
2009	60,852	58,826	...	...	19	119,696

• NET OPERATING GAIN ($000 omitted)

Year	Individual Life	Individual & Group Annuities	Group Life & A&H	Credit Life & A&H	Individual A&H	Total
2007	11,222	1,894	...	...	98	14,853
2008	5,796	2,136	...	...	21	28,657
2009	-8,242	2,276	...	...	42	35,946

• COMPARATIVE FINANCIALS ($000 omitted)

Year	Assets	Capital & Surplus	Net Invest Income	Benefits Paid	Realized Cap Gains	Policyholder Dividends	Contract Lns (% of assets)
2007	1,647,280	341,355	83,166	128,814	6,532	10,082	3.2
2008	1,544,345	322,405	94,838	129,390	-29,416	9,930	3.4
2009	1,517,203	321,553	110,725	93,816	-2,127	7,783	3.5

• ORDINARY LIFE STATISTICS

Year	Av. Ord. Policy Issued ($)	Av. Ord. Policy In Force ($)	Avg. Prem ($/M)	1st Yr Prem/ Total Prem	Ord. Lapse Ratio
2007	244,451	70,377	9.15	3.2	6.8
2008	557,155	82,812	8.30	8.9	5.4
2009	402,952	94,735	7.70	17.3	3.8

• NEW LIFE BUSINESS ISSUED ($000 omitted)

Year	Whole Life	Term	Credit	Group	Industrial	Total
2007	20,530	64,539	...	...	...	85,069
2008	66,245	195,618	...	...	...	261,863
2009	481,000	193,945	...	...	...	674,945

• LIFE INSURANCE IN FORCE ($000 omitted)

Year	Whole Life	Term	Credit	Group	Industrial	Total
2007	5,510,916	952,145	...	...	...	6,463,061
2008	6,232,476	1,060,151	...	...	...	7,292,627
2009	5,143,860	6,880,933	...	...	...	12,024,794

ABILITY INSURANCE COMPANY

PO Box 3735
Omaha, Nebraska 68103
Tel: 402-391-6900

AMB#: 007378
Began Business: 06/10/1968
Agency Off: None

Best's Financial Strength Rating: B+ g
FSC: V

• NET PREMIUMS AND DEPOSITS ($000 omitted)

Year	Individual Life	Individual & Group Annuities	Group Life & A&H	Credit Life & A&H	Individual A&H	Total
2007	-55,679	16	...	...	107,035	51,372
2008	...	...	...	...	24,301	24,301
2009	...	...	...	...	22,899	22,899

• NET OPERATING GAIN ($000 omitted)

Year	Individual Life	Individual & Group Annuities	Group Life & A&H	Credit Life & A&H	Individual A&H	Total
2007	-373	1,523	...	...	-8,418	-7,268
2008	15	3	...	...	-21,902	-21,884
2009	15	3	...	...	-7,737	-7,718

• COMPARATIVE FINANCIALS ($000 omitted)

Year	Assets	Capital & Surplus	Net Invest Income	Benefits Paid	Realized Cap Gains	Policyholder Dividends	Contract Lns (% of assets)
2007	185,155	38,679	6,483	25,855	562	-473	...
2008	512,339	25,917	17,041	19,882	15,589	...	...
2009	195,279	21,720	18,509	20,381	233	...	...

• ORDINARY LIFE STATISTICS

Year	Av. Ord. Policy Issued ($)	Av. Ord. Policy In Force ($)	Avg. Prem ($/M)	1st Yr Prem/ Total Prem	Ord. Lapse Ratio
2007	...	...	...	...	...
2008	...	...	...	...	...
2009	...	...	...	...	...

• NEW LIFE BUSINESS ISSUED ($000 omitted)

Year	Whole Life	Term	Credit	Group	Industrial	Total
2007	27	...	...	...	...	27
2008	...	...	...	...	...	...
2009	...	...	...	...	...	...

• LIFE INSURANCE IN FORCE ($000 omitted)

Year	Whole Life	Term	Credit	Group	Industrial	Total
2007	99,912	13,735	...	...	...	113,647
2008	91,487	12,727	...	...	...	104,214
2009	50,353	5,950	...	...	...	56,303

ACE LIFE INSURANCE COMPANY

436 Walnut Street, P.O. Box 1000
Philadelphia, Pennsylvania 19106
Tel: 203-352-6602

AMB#: 060599
Began Business: 08/31/1965
Agency Off: None

Best's Financial Strength Rating: A-
FSC: V

• NET PREMIUMS AND DEPOSITS ($000 omitted)

Year	Individual Life	Individual & Group Annuities	Group Life & A&H	Credit Life & A&H	Individual A&H	Total
2007	2,597	...	36	566	...	3,199
2008	3,982	...	40	623	...	4,645
2009	4,268	...	-2	289	...	4,555

• NET OPERATING GAIN ($000 omitted)

Year	Individual Life	Individual & Group Annuities	Group Life & A&H	Credit Life & A&H	Individual A&H	Total
2007	-6,840	...	2	-120	935	-6,024
2008	-7,611	...	14	-137	...	-6,896
2009	-6,230	...	-94	47	...	-6,277

• COMPARATIVE FINANCIALS ($000 omitted)

Year	Assets	Capital & Surplus	Net Invest Income	Benefits Paid	Realized Cap Gains	Policyholder Dividends	Contract Lns (% of assets)
2007	19,663	13,663	931	524	-22	...	...
2008	34,324	19,977	837	1,702	165	...	...
2009	40,242	19,055	415	2,338	...	...	...

• ORDINARY LIFE STATISTICS

Year	Av. Ord. Policy Issued ($)	Av. Ord. Policy In Force ($)	Avg. Prem ($/M)	1st Yr Prem/ Total Prem	Ord. Lapse Ratio
2007	...	...	...	...	...
2008	...	...	...	...	...
2009	...	...	...	...	...

• NEW LIFE BUSINESS ISSUED ($000 omitted)

Year	Whole Life	Term	Credit	Group	Industrial	Total
2007	2,839	1,406	...	...	...	4,245
2008	...	514,401	...	...	...	514,401
2009	...	...	...	...	...	...

• LIFE INSURANCE IN FORCE ($000 omitted)

Year	Whole Life	Term	Credit	Group	Industrial	Total
2007	...	4,695,967	40,474	3,105	...	4,739,546
2008	...	12,250,295	85,748	8,178	...	12,344,221
2009	...	17,553,217	92,554	7,483	...	17,653,254

ADVANCE INSURANCE CO OF KANSAS

1133 SW Topeka Boulevard
Topeka, Kansas 66629-0001
Tel: 785-273-9804

AMB#: 060404
Began Business: 07/22/2004
Agency Off: Jennifer Rose-Long

Best's Financial Strength Rating: A g
FSC: X

• **NET PREMIUMS AND DEPOSITS ($000 omitted)**

Year	Individual Life	Individual & Group Annuities	Group Life & A&H	Credit Life & A&H	Individual A&H	Total
2007	1,219	...	9,975	...	...	11,194
2008	1,272	...	9,800	...	...	11,072
2009	1,285	...	9,434	...	...	10,719

• **NET OPERATING GAIN ($000 omitted)**

Year	Individual Life	Individual & Group Annuities	Group Life & A&H	Credit Life & A&H	Individual A&H	Total
2007	410	...	1,736	...	10	2,156
2008	589	...	1,583	...	...	2,173
2009	475	...	1,379	...	...	1,854

• **COMPARATIVE FINANCIALS ($000 omitted)**

Year	Assets	Capital & Surplus	Net Invest Income	Benefits Paid	Realized Cap Gains	Policyholder Dividends	Contract Lns (% of assets)
2007	39,040	32,413	1,725	6,561	531	...	0.0
2008	38,056	33,292	1,520	6,369	-1,815	...	...
2009	41,221	35,454	1,490	5,530	-115	...	...

• **ORDINARY LIFE STATISTICS**

Year	Av. Ord. Policy Issued ($)	Av. Ord. Policy In Force ($)	Avg. Prem ($/M)	1st Yr Prem/ Total Prem	Ord. Lapse Ratio
2007	...	...	...	...	...
2008	...	...	...	...	...
2009	...	...	...	...	...

• **NEW LIFE BUSINESS ISSUED ($000 omitted)**

Year	Whole Life	Term	Credit	Group	Industrial	Total
2007	224	47,970	...	217,130	...	265,324
2008	60	49,155	...	137,498	...	186,713
2009	30	36,250	...	151,571	...	187,851

• **LIFE INSURANCE IN FORCE ($000 omitted)**

Year	Whole Life	Term	Credit	Group	Industrial	Total
2007	584	217,545	...	2,514,633	...	2,732,762
2008	474	234,735	...	2,448,729	...	2,683,938
2009	474	239,310	...	2,404,555	...	2,644,339

AGC LIFE INSURANCE COMPANY

2727-A Allen Parkway
Houston, Texas 77019
Tel: 713-522-1111

AMB#: 009199
Began Business: 09/10/1982
Agency Off: None

Best's Financial Strength Rating: A
FSC: XV

• **NET PREMIUMS AND DEPOSITS ($000 omitted)**

Year	Individual Life	Individual & Group Annuities	Group Life & A&H	Credit Life & A&H	Individual A&H	Total
2007	2,701	...	1	...	...	2,702
2008	1,484	...	1	...	...	1,484
2009	2,878	...	0	...	...	2,878

• **NET OPERATING GAIN ($000 omitted)**

Year	Individual Life	Individual & Group Annuities	Group Life & A&H	Credit Life & A&H	Individual A&H	Total
2007	9,459	-186	3	...	...	1,256,307
2008	7,834	-1,087	4	...	...	-10,803
2009	8,989	-100	2	...	...	-162,823

• **COMPARATIVE FINANCIALS ($000 omitted)**

Year	Assets	Capital & Surplus	Net Invest Income	Benefits Paid	Realized Cap Gains	Policyholder Dividends	Contract Lns (% of assets)
2007	12,330,227	7,743,406	1,204,002	4,947	1,426	5	0.0
2008	11,339,434	5,901,925	-75,339	3,499	3,038	3	...
2009	11,801,538	8,154,648	-242,845	1,205	42,026	...	...

• **ORDINARY LIFE STATISTICS**

Year	Av. Ord. Policy Issued ($)	Av. Ord. Policy In Force ($)	Avg. Prem ($/M)	1st Yr Prem/ Total Prem	Ord. Lapse Ratio
2007	...	...	...	...	...
2008	...	...	...	...	...
2009	...	...	...	...	...

• **NEW LIFE BUSINESS ISSUED ($000 omitted)**

Year	Whole Life	Term	Credit	Group	Industrial	Total
2007	...	...	...	...	...	...
2008	...	...	...	...	...	...
2009	...	...	...	...	...	...

• **LIFE INSURANCE IN FORCE ($000 omitted)**

Year	Whole Life	Term	Credit	Group	Industrial	Total
2007	134,282	...	...	610	...	134,892
2008	116,672	...	...	310	...	116,982
2009	107,871	...	...	...	...	107,871

AETNA LIFE INS CO

151 Farmington Avenue, RT21
Hartford, Connecticut 06156
Tel: 860-273-0123

AMB#: 006006
Began Business: 12/31/1850
Agency Off: None

Best's Financial Strength Rating: A g
FSC: XV

• **NET PREMIUMS AND DEPOSITS ($000 omitted)**

Year	Individual Life	Individual & Group Annuities	Group Life & A&H	Credit Life & A&H	Individual A&H	Total
2007	13,815	1,010,758	8,882,629	...	1,615,072	11,522,274
2008	13,223	871,862	9,755,162	...	3,685,953	14,326,199
2009	13,432	769,527	10,556,191	...	4,686,756	16,025,905

• **NET OPERATING GAIN ($000 omitted)**

Year	Individual Life	Individual & Group Annuities	Group Life & A&H	Credit Life & A&H	Individual A&H	Total
2007	-4,700	79,651	874,340	0	86,015	1,194,588
2008	-4,969	-28,785	735,888	0	246,901	1,079,060
2009	1,751	-32,073	396,425	0	347,674	916,521

• **COMPARATIVE FINANCIALS ($000 omitted)**

Year	Assets	Capital & Surplus	Net Invest Income	Benefits Paid	Realized Cap Gains	Policyholder Dividends	Contract Lns (% of assets)
2007	33,471,046	3,239,164	704,573	9,417,515	-31,401	23	0.0
2008	20,880,604	3,743,547	596,090	11,875,281	-127,860	24	0.0
2009	22,490,327	4,858,175	763,490	13,729,132	-33,903	25	0.0

• **ORDINARY LIFE STATISTICS**

Year	Av. Ord. Policy Issued ($)	Av. Ord. Policy In Force ($)	Avg. Prem ($/M)	1st Yr Prem/ Total Prem	Ord. Lapse Ratio
2007	42,281	25,531	20.33	2.7	5.7
2008	49,969	25,540	21.16	2.9	5.5
2009	43,790	17,811	22.10	3.7	6.2

• **NEW LIFE BUSINESS ISSUED ($000 omitted)**

Year	Whole Life	Term	Credit	Group	Industrial	Total
2007	40,985	5,862	...	63,514,967	...	63,561,814
2008	51,111	4,355	...	76,378,737	...	76,434,203
2009	51,126	5,056	...	87,033,186	...	87,089,368

• **LIFE INSURANCE IN FORCE ($000 omitted)**

Year	Whole Life	Term	Credit	Group	Industrial	Total
2007	1,245,744	1,282,062	6,880	461,550,161	...	464,084,847
2008	1,086,816	1,284,415	4,383	440,914,385	...	443,289,999
2009	1,115,392	1,107,437	2,926	467,457,253	...	469,683,008

AGL LIFE ASSURANCE COMPANY

One American Row
Hartford, Connecticut 06115
Tel: 484-530-4800

AMB#: 007142
Began Business: 09/27/1960
Agency Off: None

Best's Financial Strength Rating: B+ u
FSC: X

• **NET PREMIUMS AND DEPOSITS ($000 omitted)**

Year	Individual Life	Individual & Group Annuities	Group Life & A&H	Credit Life & A&H	Individual A&H	Total
2007	54,700	406,754	...	...	...	461,453
2008	98,209	198,241	...	...	...	296,450
2009	24,503	129,038	...	...	...	153,541

• **NET OPERATING GAIN ($000 omitted)**

Year	Individual Life	Individual & Group Annuities	Group Life & A&H	Credit Life & A&H	Individual A&H	Total
2007	-2,680	-1,652	...	...	...	-4,331
2008	776	1,125	...	...	...	1,901
2009	231	209	...	...	...	440

• **COMPARATIVE FINANCIALS ($000 omitted)**

Year	Assets	Capital & Surplus	Net Invest Income	Benefits Paid	Realized Cap Gains	Policyholder Dividends	Contract Lns (% of assets)
2007	5,091,051	11,382	2,012	185,466	...	...	0.7
2008	4,143,050	13,762	2,782	596,770	153	...	1.4
2009	3,776,960	21,212	3,389	593,539	1	...	2.0

• **ORDINARY LIFE STATISTICS**

Year	Av. Ord. Policy Issued ($)	Av. Ord. Policy In Force ($)	Avg. Prem ($/M)	1st Yr Prem/ Total Prem	Ord. Lapse Ratio
2007	22,420,667	3,917,298	12.96	73.3	1.2
2008	14,272,706	4,494,304	21.01	78.3	2.6
2009	17,703,250	4,762,463	6.71	18.2	2.4

• **NEW LIFE BUSINESS ISSUED ($000 omitted)**

Year	Whole Life	Term	Credit	Group	Industrial	Total
2007	403,572	...	...	...	...	403,572
2008	485,272	...	...	...	...	485,272
2009	70,813	...	...	...	...	70,813

• **LIFE INSURANCE IN FORCE ($000 omitted)**

Year	Whole Life	Term	Credit	Group	Industrial	Total
2007	4,499,283	134,881	...	...	...	4,634,164
2008	4,894,646	116,503	...	...	...	5,011,149
2009	4,793,168	102,644	...	...	...	4,895,812

ALFA LIFE INS CORP

P.O. Box 11000
Montgomery, Alabama 36191-0001
Tel: 334-288-3900

AMB#: 006293
Began Business: 03/03/1955
Agency Off: None

Best's Financial Strength Rating: A+ **FSC:** VIII

• **NET PREMIUMS AND DEPOSITS ($000 omitted)**

Year	Individual Life	Individual & Group Annuities	Group Life & A&H	Credit Life & A&H	Individual A&H	Total
2007	121,450	2,064	475	126	531	124,647
2008	126,295	2,536	437	47	569	129,885
2009	116,848	6,053	471	-23	527	123,875

• **NET OPERATING GAIN ($000 omitted)**

Year	Individual Life	Individual & Group Annuities	Group Life & A&H	Credit Life & A&H	Individual A&H	Total
2007	12,211	-202	99	25	99	12,232
2008	-1,326	33	-12	-5	-33	-1,342
2009	22,233	-1,439	326	-9	437	21,548

• **COMPARATIVE FINANCIALS ($000 omitted)**

Year	Assets	Capital & Surplus	Net Invest Income	Benefits Paid	Realized Cap Gains	Policyholder Dividends	Contract Lns (% of assets)
2007	1,100,150	210,814	58,631	61,850	-1,900	4,287	6.2
2008	1,073,397	148,059	54,353	67,154	-51,840	4,421	6.7
2009	1,141,858	182,988	49,280	66,434	-3,237	4,492	6.6

• **ORDINARY LIFE STATISTICS**

Year	Av. Ord. Policy Issued ($)	Av. Ord. Policy In Force ($)	Avg. Prem ($/M)	1st Yr Prem/ Total Prem	Ord. Lapse Ratio
2007	128,100	95,331	5.58	12.1	7.1
2008	130,003	97,822	5.57	10.9	7.2
2009	129,398	100,053	4.92	12.1	7.3

• **NEW LIFE BUSINESS ISSUED ($000 omitted)**

Year	Whole Life	Term	Credit	Group	Industrial	Total
2007	647,695	2,743,241	5,109	3,687	...	3,399,732
2008	611,054	2,560,365	3,120	5,230	...	3,179,769
2009	635,871	2,665,590	294	2,596	...	3,304,352

• **LIFE INSURANCE IN FORCE ($000 omitted)**

Year	Whole Life	Term	Credit	Group	Industrial	Total
2007	8,180,504	14,641,705	10,620	48,425	...	22,881,254
2008	8,219,805	15,647,517	8,462	49,189	...	23,924,973
2009	8,272,765	16,669,280	5,492	48,836	...	24,996,374

ALLIANZ LIFE INS CO N AMERICA

P.O. Box 1344
Minneapolis, Minnesota 55440-1344
Tel: 763-765-6500

AMB#: 006830
Began Business: 12/27/1979
Agency Off: Thomas P. Burns

Best's Financial Strength Rating: A g **FSC:** XV

• **NET PREMIUMS AND DEPOSITS ($000 omitted)**

Year	Individual Life	Individual & Group Annuities	Group Life & A&H	Credit Life & A&H	Individual A&H	Total
2007	144,481	8,764,772	6,664	...	115,929	9,031,846
2008	199,059	8,025,435	8,094	...	118,855	8,351,443
2009	-9,087	8,350,350	4,837	...	130,057	8,476,157

• **NET OPERATING GAIN ($000 omitted)**

Year	Individual Life	Individual & Group Annuities	Group Life & A&H	Credit Life & A&H	Individual A&H	Total
2007	-27,397	120,505	34,705	...	-10,848	116,966
2008	-22,995	294,743	-3,014	...	-6,376	262,359
2009	136,382	179,481	2,785	...	-1,397	317,251

• **COMPARATIVE FINANCIALS ($000 omitted)**

Year	Assets	Capital & Surplus	Net Invest Income	Benefits Paid	Realized Cap Gains	Policyholder Dividends	Contract Lns (% of assets)
2007	68,688,474	2,441,338	2,436,290	5,119,531	-38,889	...	0.2
2008	66,374,757	2,009,309	2,751,827	5,536,952	-1,158,184	...	0.3
2009	75,453,862	3,923,209	3,066,104	5,875,624	-347,956	...	0.2

• **ORDINARY LIFE STATISTICS**

Year	Av. Ord. Policy Issued ($)	Av. Ord. Policy In Force ($)	Avg. Prem ($/M)	1st Yr Prem/ Total Prem	Ord. Lapse Ratio
2007	...	...	...	...	...
2008	...	...	...	...	...
2009	...	...	...	...	...

• **NEW LIFE BUSINESS ISSUED ($000 omitted)**

Year	Whole Life	Term	Credit	Group	Industrial	Total
2007	2,186,989	826,522	...	...	...	3,013,511
2008	2,754,821	1,167,200	...	...	...	3,922,021
2009	1,315,934	1,192,108	...	45,295	...	2,553,337

• **LIFE INSURANCE IN FORCE ($000 omitted)**

Year	Whole Life	Term	Credit	Group	Industrial	Total
2007	16,425,188	13,113,709	...	1,399,921	...	30,938,818
2008	17,924,964	13,229,633	...	1,208,405	...	32,363,002
2009	17,452,340	13,209,138	...	1,394,917	...	32,056,394

ALLIANZ LIFE INS CO OF NY

5701 Golden Hills Drive
Minneapolis, Minnesota 55416-1297
Tel: 212-586-7733

AMB#: 009417
Began Business: 04/11/1984
Agency Off: Vince Vitiello

Best's Financial Strength Rating: A g **FSC:** XV

• **NET PREMIUMS AND DEPOSITS ($000 omitted)**

Year	Individual Life	Individual & Group Annuities	Group Life & A&H	Credit Life & A&H	Individual A&H	Total
2007	318	157,254	267	...	1,727	159,567
2008	931	232,117	257	...	2,535	235,840
2009	424	187,944	236	...	3,095	191,699

• **NET OPERATING GAIN ($000 omitted)**

Year	Individual Life	Individual & Group Annuities	Group Life & A&H	Credit Life & A&H	Individual A&H	Total
2007	-2,659	-13,194	18,679	...	-341	2,485
2008	38	-44,999	506	...	-385	-44,838
2009	126	23,045	140	...	-74	23,238

• **COMPARATIVE FINANCIALS ($000 omitted)**

Year	Assets	Capital & Surplus	Net Invest Income	Benefits Paid	Realized Cap Gains	Policyholder Dividends	Contract Lns (% of assets)
2007	874,371	50,337	16,015	141,939	-313	...	0.0
2008	881,465	29,201	18,640	69,945	-2,662	...	0.0
2009	1,139,490	64,830	24,584	59,543	-6,536	...	0.0

• **ORDINARY LIFE STATISTICS**

Year	Av. Ord. Policy Issued ($)	Av. Ord. Policy In Force ($)	Avg. Prem ($/M)	1st Yr Prem/ Total Prem	Ord. Lapse Ratio
2007	...	...	...	...	...
2008	...	...	...	...	...
2009	...	...	...	...	...

• **NEW LIFE BUSINESS ISSUED ($000 omitted)**

Year	Whole Life	Term	Credit	Group	Industrial	Total
2007	11,712	...	...	...	...	11,712
2008	23,631	15,100	...	...	...	38,731
2009	641	3,100	...	...	...	3,741

• **LIFE INSURANCE IN FORCE ($000 omitted)**

Year	Whole Life	Term	Credit	Group	Industrial	Total
2007	13,681	...	...	81,175	...	94,856
2008	36,469	15,100	...	75,415	...	126,984
2009	34,404	18,200	...	67,558	...	120,162

ALLSTATE LIFE INS CO

3100 Sanders Road
Northbrook, Illinois 60062-7154
Tel: 847-402-5000

AMB#: 006027
Began Business: 09/03/1957
Agency Off: None

Best's Financial Strength Rating: A+ g **FSC:** XV

• **NET PREMIUMS AND DEPOSITS ($000 omitted)**

Year	Individual Life	Individual & Group Annuities	Group Life & A&H	Credit Life & A&H	Individual A&H	Total
2007	1,423,147	6,319,817	36,672	...	28,769	7,808,405
2008	1,424,263	7,525,568	40,910	...	91,878	9,082,618
2009	1,457,246	1,838,138	29,230	...	79,552	3,404,166

• **NET OPERATING GAIN ($000 omitted)**

Year	Individual Life	Individual & Group Annuities	Group Life & A&H	Credit Life & A&H	Individual A&H	Total
2007	159,531	15,745	-4,057	17	786	172,023
2008	102,864	-1,187,834	-5,855	7	1,663	-1,089,156
2009	72	-453	8	0	1	-373

• **COMPARATIVE FINANCIALS ($000 omitted)**

Year	Assets	Capital & Surplus	Net Invest Income	Benefits Paid	Realized Cap Gains	Policyholder Dividends	Contract Lns (% of assets)
2007	77,027,929	2,622,499	3,296,002	7,654,683	-30,290	58	1.0
2008	67,552,094	3,248,888	2,617,010	6,780,234	-858,038	60	1.1
2009	63,008,532	3,467,413	2,299,055	6,200,029	-895,523	63	1.2

• **ORDINARY LIFE STATISTICS**

Year	Av. Ord. Policy Issued ($)	Av. Ord. Policy In Force ($)	Avg. Prem ($/M)	1st Yr Prem/ Total Prem	Ord. Lapse Ratio
2007	2,535	120,787	5.97	-0.1	6.3
2008	53,684	115,757	5.66	0.0	9.1
2009	73,684	117,335	5.88	0.0	9.1

• **NEW LIFE BUSINESS ISSUED ($000 omitted)**

Year	Whole Life	Term	Credit	Group	Industrial	Total
2007	218,435	161,800	...	1,703	...	381,938
2008	94,763	10,619	...	406	...	105,788
2009	193,090	8,362	...	...	...	201,452

• **LIFE INSURANCE IN FORCE ($000 omitted)**

Year	Whole Life	Term	Credit	Group	Industrial	Total
2007	108,280,520	165,059,849	...	7,829,139	...	281,169,508
2008	130,489,736	159,511,800	...	7,260,926	...	297,262,462
2009	116,353,111	172,394,249	...	6,762,175	...	295,509,535

ALLSTATE LIFE INS CO OF NY

100 Motor Parkway, Suite 132
Hauppauge, New York 11788-5107
Tel: 516-451-5300

AMB#: 007291
Began Business: 12/15/1967
Agency Off: None

Best's Financial Strength Rating: A+ g   **FSC:** XV

• NET PREMIUMS AND DEPOSITS ($000 omitted)

Year	Individual Life	Individual & Group Annuities	Group Life & A&H	Credit Life & A&H	Individual A&H	Total
2007	134,246	466,072	...	...	6,530	606,848
2008	132,488	527,271	...	...	8,246	668,005
2009	125,822	194,855	...	...	9,485	330,161

• NET OPERATING GAIN ($000 omitted)

Year	Individual Life	Individual & Group Annuities	Group Life & A&H	Credit Life & A&H	Individual A&H	Total
2007	15,398	16,208	-5	...	-957	30,644
2008	3,795	-26,857	-4	...	-15	-23,081
2009	2,484	21,854	-6	...	684	25,015

• COMPARATIVE FINANCIALS ($000 omitted)

Year	Assets	Capital & Surplus	Net Invest Income	Benefits Paid	Realized Cap Gains	Policyholder Dividends	Contract Lns (% of assets)
2007	7,785,832	462,440	395,032	583,939	7,591	130	0.5
2008	7,627,457	410,472	402,068	617,420	4,204	243	0.5
2009	7,875,950	506,286	367,735	552,291	-33,633	113	0.5

• ORDINARY LIFE STATISTICS

Year	Av. Ord. Policy Issued ($)	Av. Ord. Policy In Force ($)	Avg. Prem ($/M)	1st Yr Prem/ Total Prem	Ord. Lapse Ratio
2007	320,634	205,108	4.82	12.0	5.7
2008	319,681	214,670	4.53	10.7	6.0
2009	289,895	221,138	4.83	9.3	6.1

• NEW LIFE BUSINESS ISSUED ($000 omitted)

Year	Whole Life	Term	Credit	Group	Industrial	Total
2007	999,646	3,312,562	...	...	...	4,312,208
2008	1,053,006	3,012,698	...	...	...	4,065,704
2009	939,368	2,587,200	...	...	...	3,526,568

• LIFE INSURANCE IN FORCE ($000 omitted)

Year	Whole Life	Term	Credit	Group	Industrial	Total
2007	8,700,861	22,876,504	...	...	...	31,577,365
2008	8,163,653	25,278,095	...	...	...	33,441,748
2009	8,301,463	26,319,017	...	...	...	34,620,480

AMERICAN-AMICABLE LIFE INS TX

425 Austin Avenue
Waco, Texas 76701
Tel: 254-297-2777

AMB#: 009122
Began Business: 12/14/1981
Agency Off: S. Lanny Peavy

Best's Financial Strength Rating: A- g   **FSC:** VII

• NET PREMIUMS AND DEPOSITS ($000 omitted)

Year	Individual Life	Individual & Group Annuities	Group Life & A&H	Credit Life & A&H	Individual A&H	Total
2007	36,207	22,682	4,450	...	...	63,338
2008	34,288	20,860	4,225	...	...	59,373
2009	38,144	20,246	4,059	...	...	62,448

• NET OPERATING GAIN ($000 omitted)

Year	Individual Life	Individual & Group Annuities	Group Life & A&H	Credit Life & A&H	Individual A&H	Total
2007	5,140	158	67	...	...	5,366
2008	4,026	268	469	...	...	4,762
2009	-155	167	565	...	...	577

• COMPARATIVE FINANCIALS ($000 omitted)

Year	Assets	Capital & Surplus	Net Invest Income	Benefits Paid	Realized Cap Gains	Policyholder Dividends	Contract Lns (% of assets)
2007	335,744	57,471	14,171	25,046	...	129	5.0
2008	353,383	57,678	14,943	24,426	...	129	4.7
2009	374,417	57,697	15,819	25,785	-239	120	4.3

• ORDINARY LIFE STATISTICS

Year	Av. Ord. Policy Issued ($)	Av. Ord. Policy In Force ($)	Avg. Prem ($/M)	1st Yr Prem/ Total Prem	Ord. Lapse Ratio
2007	43,867	31,519	13.18	21.9	15.6
2008	49,767	32,666	12.14	18.3	17.1
2009	54,138	34,705	11.91	26.8	18.1

• NEW LIFE BUSINESS ISSUED ($000 omitted)

Year	Whole Life	Term	Credit	Group	Industrial	Total
2007	129,564	548,533	...	765	...	678,862
2008	109,964	520,936	...	6,034	...	636,934
2009	213,375	796,683	...	17,250	...	1,027,308

• LIFE INSURANCE IN FORCE ($000 omitted)

Year	Whole Life	Term	Credit	Group	Industrial	Total
2007	1,254,392	1,510,017	...	557,356	...	3,321,765
2008	1,227,446	1,616,558	...	489,310	...	3,333,314
2009	1,278,909	1,951,181	...	454,886	...	3,684,976

AMALGAMATED LIFE INS CO

333 Westchester Avenue
White Plains, New York 10604
Tel: 914-367-5000

AMB#: 006031
Began Business: 02/01/1944
Agency Off: Paul Mallen

Best's Financial Strength Rating: A   **FSC:** VI

• NET PREMIUMS AND DEPOSITS ($000 omitted)

Year	Individual Life	Individual & Group Annuities	Group Life & A&H	Credit Life & A&H	Individual A&H	Total
2007	850	...	35,848	...	...	36,698
2008	1,235	...	36,857	...	...	38,093
2009	1,495	...	42,967	...	...	44,462

• NET OPERATING GAIN ($000 omitted)

Year	Individual Life	Individual & Group Annuities	Group Life & A&H	Credit Life & A&H	Individual A&H	Total
2007	67	...	4,069	...	...	4,135
2008	280	...	2,322	...	...	2,556
2009	253	...	2,263	...	...	2,516

• COMPARATIVE FINANCIALS ($000 omitted)

Year	Assets	Capital & Surplus	Net Invest Income	Benefits Paid	Realized Cap Gains	Policyholder Dividends	Contract Lns (% of assets)
2007	57,375	30,019	2,235	30,773	...	...	0.1
2008	62,441	30,861	2,484	31,933	-431	...	0.1
2009	65,764	33,536	2,292	38,014	-33	...	0.1

• ORDINARY LIFE STATISTICS

Year	Av. Ord. Policy Issued ($)	Av. Ord. Policy In Force ($)	Avg. Prem ($/M)	1st Yr Prem/ Total Prem	Ord. Lapse Ratio
2007	...	...	...	...	...
2008	...	...	...	...	...
2009	...	...	...	...	...

• NEW LIFE BUSINESS ISSUED ($000 omitted)

Year	Whole Life	Term	Credit	Group	Industrial	Total
2007	29,500	8	...	2,912,658	...	2,942,166
2008	30,078	...	...	1,087,236	...	1,117,314
2009	36,629	40	...	521,576	...	558,245

• LIFE INSURANCE IN FORCE ($000 omitted)

Year	Whole Life	Term	Credit	Group	Industrial	Total
2007	50,682	4,966	...	15,656,155	...	15,711,803
2008	66,645	5,373	...	16,215,526	...	16,287,544
2009	80,112	4,503	...	15,811,172	...	15,895,787

AMERICAN BANKERS LIFE ASSUR CO

11222 Quail Roost Drive
Miami, Florida 33157
Tel: 305-253-2244

AMB#: 006040
Began Business: 04/08/1952
Agency Off: None

Best's Financial Strength Rating: A- g   **FSC:** VIII

• NET PREMIUMS AND DEPOSITS ($000 omitted)

Year	Individual Life	Individual & Group Annuities	Group Life & A&H	Credit Life & A&H	Individual A&H	Total
2007	21,727	1,862	27,789	110,504	2,460	164,342
2008	18,143	2,503	20,326	88,083	2,913	131,969
2009	15,728	2,617	18,647	63,324	2,753	103,069

• NET OPERATING GAIN ($000 omitted)

Year	Individual Life	Individual & Group Annuities	Group Life & A&H	Credit Life & A&H	Individual A&H	Total
2007	7,116	1,387	2,123	264	2,641	13,532
2008	8,175	1,810	-954	5,861	2,588	17,480
2009	12,013	2,195	3,692	8,326	1,822	28,048

• COMPARATIVE FINANCIALS ($000 omitted)

Year	Assets	Capital & Surplus	Net Invest Income	Benefits Paid	Realized Cap Gains	Policyholder Dividends	Contract Lns (% of assets)
2007	789,738	127,417	42,344	84,437	994	...	0.9
2008	653,077	106,707	33,644	66,779	-15,796	...	1.0
2009	671,086	116,618	36,072	74,640	-1,051	...	1.0

• ORDINARY LIFE STATISTICS

Year	Av. Ord. Policy Issued ($)	Av. Ord. Policy In Force ($)	Avg. Prem ($/M)	1st Yr Prem/ Total Prem	Ord. Lapse Ratio
2007	85,584	82,549	7.75	3.5	10.0
2008	90,053	77,346	7.46	4.1	10.2
2009	69,209	77,428	7.45	4.1	10.1

• NEW LIFE BUSINESS ISSUED ($000 omitted)

Year	Whole Life	Term	Credit	Group	Industrial	Total
2007	195	42,854	16,350,453	3,575,107	...	19,968,609
2008	187	15,212	5,340,352	93,743	...	5,449,494
2009	126	7,487	4,067,009	29,005	...	4,103,627

• LIFE INSURANCE IN FORCE ($000 omitted)

Year	Whole Life	Term	Credit	Group	Industrial	Total
2007	2,520,184	910,702	26,932,784	1,358,752	...	31,722,422
2008	2,308,811	740,927	19,812,343	1,153,574	...	24,015,655
2009	2,054,875	641,320	16,617,540	966,456	...	20,280,190

AMERICAN BENEFIT LIFE

1605 LBJ Freeway, Suite 710
Dallas, Texas 75234
Tel: 972-484-6063

AMB#: 060382
Began Business: 05/15/1909
Agency Off: None

Best's Financial Strength Rating: B- **FSC:** III

• NET PREMIUMS AND DEPOSITS ($000 omitted)

Year	Individual Life	Individual & Group Annuities	Group Life & A&H	Credit Life & A&H	Individual A&H	Total
2007	5,435	...	...	...	...	5,435
2008	6,722	...	...	...	...	6,722
2009	10,454	...	...	...	...	10,454

• NET OPERATING GAIN ($000 omitted)

Year	Individual Life	Individual & Group Annuities	Group Life & A&H	Credit Life & A&H	Individual A&H	Total
2007	-32	...	...	...	...	-32
2008	407	...	...	...	...	407
2009	-227	...	...	...	...	-227

• COMPARATIVE FINANCIALS ($000 omitted)

Year	Assets	Capital & Surplus	Net Invest Income	Benefits Paid	Realized Cap Gains	Policyholder Dividends	Contract Lns (% of assets)
2007	11,513	3,435	655	608	...	27	...
2008	14,288	3,225	775	763	-557	-27	...
2009	21,565	3,966	1,061	1,366	-23	...	...

• ORDINARY LIFE STATISTICS

Year	Av. Ord. Policy Issued ($)	Av. Ord. Policy In Force ($)	Avg. Prem ($/M)	1st Yr Prem/ Total Prem	Ord. Lapse Ratio
2007	...	2,287	68.65	...	12.1
2008	...	2,154	73.00	...	0.3
2009	...	2,285	88.08	...	10.9

• NEW LIFE BUSINESS ISSUED ($000 omitted)

Year	Whole Life	Term	Credit	Group	Industrial	Total
2007	...	...	...	...	...	...
2008	...	...	...	...	...	...
2009	...	...	...	...	...	...

• LIFE INSURANCE IN FORCE ($000 omitted)

Year	Whole Life	Term	Credit	Group	Industrial	Total
2007	79,169	...	...	...	...	79,169
2008	92,086	...	...	...	...	92,086
2009	118,688	...	...	...	...	118,689

AMERICAN EQUITY INVEST LIFE NY

5000 Westown Parkway, Suite 440
West Des Moines, Iowa 50266
Tel: 866-233-6660

AMB#: 060367
Began Business: 07/01/2001
Agency Off: Ronald J. Grensteiner

Best's Financial Strength Rating: A- g **FSC:** XII

• NET PREMIUMS AND DEPOSITS ($000 omitted)

Year	Individual Life	Individual & Group Annuities	Group Life & A&H	Credit Life & A&H	Individual A&H	Total
2007	...	12,587	...	...	...	12,587
2008	...	3,749	...	...	...	3,749
2009	...	11,873	...	...	...	11,873

• NET OPERATING GAIN ($000 omitted)

Year	Individual Life	Individual & Group Annuities	Group Life & A&H	Credit Life & A&H	Individual A&H	Total
2007	...	1,152	...	...	...	1,152
2008	...	1,337	...	...	...	1,337
2009	...	-5,236	...	...	...	-5,236

• COMPARATIVE FINANCIALS ($000 omitted)

Year	Assets	Capital & Surplus	Net Invest Income	Benefits Paid	Realized Cap Gains	Policyholder Dividends	Contract Lns (% of assets)
2007	119,243	33,487	6,381	6,316	...	...	...
2008	117,102	33,412	6,528	8,603	-1,633	...	...
2009	124,842	26,568	6,542	7,108	-2,132	...	...

• ORDINARY LIFE STATISTICS

Year	Av. Ord. Policy Issued ($)	Av. Ord. Policy In Force ($)	Avg. Prem ($/M)	1st Yr Prem/ Total Prem	Ord. Lapse Ratio
2007	...	...	...	...	...
2008	...	...	...	...	...
2009	...	...	...	...	...

• NEW LIFE BUSINESS ISSUED ($000 omitted)

Year	Whole Life	Term	Credit	Group	Industrial	Total
2007	...	...	...	...	...	...
2008	...	...	...	...	...	...
2009	...	...	...	...	...	...

• LIFE INSURANCE IN FORCE ($000 omitted)

Year	Whole Life	Term	Credit	Group	Industrial	Total
2007	...	...	...	...	...	...
2008	...	...	...	...	...	...
2009	...	...	...	...	...	...

AMERICAN EQUITY INVEST LIFE

6000 Westown Parkway
West Des Moines, Iowa 50266
Tel: 515-221-0002

AMB#: 009024
Began Business: 01/01/1981
Agency Off: Kevin R. Wingert

Best's Financial Strength Rating: A- g **FSC:** XII

• NET PREMIUMS AND DEPOSITS ($000 omitted)

Year	Individual Life	Individual & Group Annuities	Group Life & A&H	Credit Life & A&H	Individual A&H	Total
2007	2,498	2,077,693	10,007	...	64	2,090,262
2008	2,717	2,268,935	10,478	...	7	2,282,137
2009	2,966	2,859,638	10,132	...	119	2,872,854

• NET OPERATING GAIN ($000 omitted)

Year	Individual Life	Individual & Group Annuities	Group Life & A&H	Credit Life & A&H	Individual A&H	Total
2007	26	18,961	1,640	...	47	20,674
2008	99	108,592	1,424	...	-157	109,958
2009	202	166,750	655	...	-58	167,549

• COMPARATIVE FINANCIALS ($000 omitted)

Year	Assets	Capital & Surplus	Net Invest Income	Benefits Paid	Realized Cap Gains	Policyholder Dividends	Contract Lns (% of assets)
2007	12,697,227	990,801	619,635	1,103,495	-4,816	...	0.0
2008	13,593,940	983,325	483,439	1,150,046	-116,712	...	0.0
2009	16,697,568	1,193,130	769,248	1,214,386	-42,913	...	0.0

• ORDINARY LIFE STATISTICS

Year	Av. Ord. Policy Issued ($)	Av. Ord. Policy In Force ($)	Avg. Prem ($/M)	1st Yr Prem/ Total Prem	Ord. Lapse Ratio
2007	...	...	...	...	...
2008	...	...	...	...	...
2009	...	...	...	...	...

• NEW LIFE BUSINESS ISSUED ($000 omitted)

Year	Whole Life	Term	Credit	Group	Industrial	Total
2007	6,203	300	...	20,914	...	27,417
2008	6,437	1,225	...	123,359	...	131,021
2009	8,513	2,400	...	61,396	...	72,309

• LIFE INSURANCE IN FORCE ($000 omitted)

Year	Whole Life	Term	Credit	Group	Industrial	Total
2007	90,988	27,796	...	2,460,008	...	2,578,792
2008	90,090	26,683	...	2,480,209	...	2,596,982
2009	89,735	24,623	...	2,464,196	...	2,578,554

AMERICAN FAM ASSUR COLUMBUS

1932 Wynnton Road
Columbus, Georgia 31999
Tel: 706-323-3431

AMB#: 006051
Began Business: 04/01/1956
Agency Off: Ronald E. Kirkland

Best's Financial Strength Rating: A+ g **FSC:** XV

• NET PREMIUMS AND DEPOSITS ($000 omitted)

Year	Individual Life	Individual & Group Annuities	Group Life & A&H	Credit Life & A&H	Individual A&H	Total
2007	1,319,404	309,860	10,015	...	11,496,957	13,136,236
2008	1,584,703	386,166	9,454	...	13,193,129	15,173,452
2009	1,887,539	444,986	9,120	...	14,537,239	16,878,884

• NET OPERATING GAIN ($000 omitted)

Year	Individual Life	Individual & Group Annuities	Group Life & A&H	Credit Life & A&H	Individual A&H	Total
2007	186,375	22,877	-5,050	...	1,428,306	1,807,768
2008	260,005	26,008	-1,160	...	1,359,607	1,789,318
2009	196,375	30,312	620	...	1,756,827	2,140,827

• COMPARATIVE FINANCIALS ($000 omitted)

Year	Assets	Capital & Surplus	Net Invest Income	Benefits Paid	Realized Cap Gains	Policyholder Dividends	Contract Lns (% of assets)
2007	55,667,865	4,208,297	2,287,981	5,988,290	-17,610	7	0.1
2008	71,782,958	4,601,314	2,536,905	7,388,865	-580,670	7	0.1
2009	75,798,442	5,767,939	2,732,104	8,402,162	-726,691	7	0.1

• ORDINARY LIFE STATISTICS

Year	Av. Ord. Policy Issued ($)	Av. Ord. Policy In Force ($)	Avg. Prem ($/M)	1st Yr Prem/ Total Prem	Ord. Lapse Ratio
2007	76,400	77,911	13.68	19.1	14.0
2008	77,867	89,112	13.08	17.8	14.9
2009	65,819	83,453	15.04	19.4	13.6

• NEW LIFE BUSINESS ISSUED ($000 omitted)

Year	Whole Life	Term	Credit	Group	Industrial	Total
2007	4,740,585	18,152,501	...	88	...	22,893,174
2008	5,948,942	19,802,060	...	17,330	...	25,768,332
2009	7,153,071	18,515,789	...	7,671	...	25,676,530

• LIFE INSURANCE IN FORCE ($000 omitted)

Year	Whole Life	Term	Credit	Group	Industrial	Total
2007	22,074,797	75,206,912	...	543,779	...	97,825,488
2008	30,242,782	91,910,745	...	500,419	...	122,653,946
2009	33,657,233	92,692,756	...	447,244	...	126,797,233

AMERICAN FAMILY LIFE ASSUR NY

1932 Wynnton Road
Columbus, Georgia 31999
Tel: 518-438-0764

AMB#: 006063
Began Business: 12/18/1964
Agency Off: Ronald E. Kirkland

Best's Financial Strength Rating: A+ g **FSC:** XV

• **NET PREMIUMS AND DEPOSITS ($000 omitted)**

Year	Individual Life	Individual & Group Annuities	Group Life & A&H	Credit Life & A&H	Individual A&H	Total
2007	316	1	10,571	...	163,773	174,661
2008	2,656	3	9,428	...	181,975	194,062
2009	4,263	68	8,311	...	199,342	211,985

• **NET OPERATING GAIN ($000 omitted)**

Year	Individual Life	Individual & Group Annuities	Group Life & A&H	Credit Life & A&H	Individual A&H	Total
2007	86	-19	1,595	...	8,821	11,862
2008	111	-1	1,057	...	10,798	13,915
2009	510	16	1,667	...	11,614	16,141

• **COMPARATIVE FINANCIALS ($000 omitted)**

Year	Assets	Capital & Surplus	Net Invest Income	Benefits Paid	Realized Cap Gains	Policyholder Dividends	Contract Lns (% of assets)
2007	227,891	51,479	11,372	83,854	...	...	0.1
2008	266,525	59,335	13,654	94,979	-2,322	...	0.1
2009	322,556	77,042	16,734	99,870	-3,273	...	0.0

• **ORDINARY LIFE STATISTICS**

Year	Av. Ord. Policy Issued ($)	Av. Ord. Policy In Force ($)	Avg. Prem ($/M)	1st Yr Prem/ Total Prem	Ord. Lapse Ratio
2007	...	...	...	...	...
2008	...	...	...	...	...
2009	...	...	...	...	...

• **NEW LIFE BUSINESS ISSUED ($000 omitted)**

Year	Whole Life	Term	Credit	Group	Industrial	Total
2007	20,355	165,778	...	...	...	186,133
2008	57,390	402,375	...	...	...	459,765
2009	75,160	282,305	...	...	...	357,465

• **LIFE INSURANCE IN FORCE ($000 omitted)**

Year	Whole Life	Term	Credit	Group	Industrial	Total
2007	32,995	168,054	...	...	...	201,049
2008	74,573	475,370	...	...	...	549,943
2009	114,129	609,192	...	...	...	723,320

AMERICAN FAMILY LIFE INS CO

6000 American Parkway
Madison, Wisconsin 53783-0001
Tel: 608-249-2111

AMB#: 006052
Began Business: 12/30/1957
Agency Off: Alan E. Meyer

Best's Financial Strength Rating: A **FSC:** X

• **NET PREMIUMS AND DEPOSITS ($000 omitted)**

Year	Individual Life	Individual & Group Annuities	Group Life & A&H	Credit Life & A&H	Individual A&H	Total
2007	359,189	78,023	3,821	...	...	441,033
2008	354,737	69,697	4,080	...	...	428,514
2009	354,564	58,259	4,047	...	...	416,870

• **NET OPERATING GAIN ($000 omitted)**

Year	Individual Life	Individual & Group Annuities	Group Life & A&H	Credit Life & A&H	Individual A&H	Total
2007	55,896	3,692	368	...	...	66,268
2008	49,322	-8,402	278	...	...	46,879
2009	53,824	-37	354	...	...	61,921

• **COMPARATIVE FINANCIALS ($000 omitted)**

Year	Assets	Capital & Surplus	Net Invest Income	Benefits Paid	Realized Cap Gains	Policyholder Dividends	Contract Lns (% of assets)
2007	3,893,876	501,515	199,859	236,943	-870	40,934	5.4
2008	3,860,797	446,822	205,659	240,208	-128,727	42,290	5.7
2009	4,153,238	556,480	209,799	248,146	15,001	41,395	5.5

• **ORDINARY LIFE STATISTICS**

Year	Av. Ord. Policy Issued ($)	Av. Ord. Policy In Force ($)	Avg. Prem ($/M)	1st Yr Prem/ Total Prem	Ord. Lapse Ratio
2007	204,048	103,606	4.91	12.5	8.3
2008	192,209	107,772	4.78	10.6	7.6
2009	182,241	110,525	4.64	8.6	7.7

• **NEW LIFE BUSINESS ISSUED ($000 omitted)**

Year	Whole Life	Term	Credit	Group	Industrial	Total
2007	2,011,253	11,478,752	...	103,925	...	13,593,930
2008	1,637,497	9,170,195	...	35,371	...	10,843,063
2009	1,197,281	8,160,775	...	31,228	...	9,389,284

• **LIFE INSURANCE IN FORCE ($000 omitted)**

Year	Whole Life	Term	Credit	Group	Industrial	Total
2007	22,286,310	58,892,637	...	1,009,689	...	82,188,636
2008	22,015,557	62,010,093	...	1,006,016	...	85,031,666
2009	21,410,763	63,992,717	...	1,017,878	...	86,421,358

AMERICAN FEDERATED LIFE INS

P.O. Box 321422
Flowood, Mississippi 39232
Tel: 601-992-6886

AMB#: 068071
Began Business: 03/01/1983
Agency Off: None

Best's Financial Strength Rating: B+ **FSC:** IV

• **NET PREMIUMS AND DEPOSITS ($000 omitted)**

Year	Individual Life	Individual & Group Annuities	Group Life & A&H	Credit Life & A&H	Individual A&H	Total
2007	...	...	...	9,931	...	9,931
2008	...	...	...	9,329	...	9,329
2009	...	...	...	10,401	...	10,401

• **NET OPERATING GAIN ($000 omitted)**

Year	Individual Life	Individual & Group Annuities	Group Life & A&H	Credit Life & A&H	Individual A&H	Total
2007	...	...	...	4,711	...	4,711
2008	...	...	...	4,859	...	4,859
2009	...	...	...	4,976	...	4,976

• **COMPARATIVE FINANCIALS ($000 omitted)**

Year	Assets	Capital & Surplus	Net Invest Income	Benefits Paid	Realized Cap Gains	Policyholder Dividends	Contract Lns (% of assets)
2007	18,111	5,967	662	2,381	8	...	...
2008	17,701	5,843	711	2,872	4	...	...
2009	18,964	6,057	690	2,706	8	...	...

• **ORDINARY LIFE STATISTICS**

Year	Av. Ord. Policy Issued ($)	Av. Ord. Policy In Force ($)	Avg. Prem ($/M)	1st Yr Prem/ Total Prem	Ord. Lapse Ratio
2007	...	...	...	...	...
2008	...	...	...	...	...
2009	...	...	...	...	...

• **NEW LIFE BUSINESS ISSUED ($000 omitted)**

Year	Whole Life	Term	Credit	Group	Industrial	Total
2007	...	...	251,680	...	...	251,680
2008	...	...	232,531	...	...	232,531
2009	...	...	255,859	...	...	255,859

• **LIFE INSURANCE IN FORCE ($000 omitted)**

Year	Whole Life	Term	Credit	Group	Industrial	Total
2007	...	...	291,192	...	...	291,192
2008	...	...	291,785	...	...	291,785
2009	...	...	311,993	...	...	311,993

AMERICAN FIDELITY ASSURANCE CO

2000 N. Classen Boulevard, Suite 10E
Oklahoma City, Oklahoma 73106
Tel: 405-523-2000

AMB#: 006054
Began Business: 12/01/1960
Agency Off: Cobern D. Hinton

Best's Financial Strength Rating: A+ **FSC:** IX

• **NET PREMIUMS AND DEPOSITS ($000 omitted)**

Year	Individual Life	Individual & Group Annuities	Group Life & A&H	Credit Life & A&H	Individual A&H	Total
2007	41,732	93,916	303,292	...	139,004	577,943
2008	51,275	106,026	339,724	...	155,130	652,155
2009	60,691	104,325	298,800	...	155,916	619,732

• **NET OPERATING GAIN ($000 omitted)**

Year	Individual Life	Individual & Group Annuities	Group Life & A&H	Credit Life & A&H	Individual A&H	Total
2007	3,827	3,090	13,383	...	1,306	21,607
2008	11,150	6,101	36,145	...	10,697	64,094
2009	5,220	4,005	33,316	...	16,891	59,432

• **COMPARATIVE FINANCIALS ($000 omitted)**

Year	Assets	Capital & Surplus	Net Invest Income	Benefits Paid	Realized Cap Gains	Policyholder Dividends	Contract Lns (% of assets)
2007	3,211,690	213,644	128,543	348,101	1,399	48	0.9
2008	3,311,754	239,134	138,028	358,162	-25,960	92	0.9
2009	3,567,593	282,119	143,995	318,705	-9,943	132	0.8

• **ORDINARY LIFE STATISTICS**

Year	Av. Ord. Policy Issued ($)	Av. Ord. Policy In Force ($)	Avg. Prem ($/M)	1st Yr Prem/ Total Prem	Ord. Lapse Ratio
2007	80,122	66,419	6.70	15.3	7.2
2008	78,821	68,234	6.52	12.5	7.9
2009	73,321	68,944	6.23	13.3	5.1

• **NEW LIFE BUSINESS ISSUED ($000 omitted)**

Year	Whole Life	Term	Credit	Group	Industrial	Total
2007	190,883	1,364,044	...	55,331	...	1,610,258
2008	280,267	2,565,488	...	9,838	...	2,855,593
2009	426,048	2,484,354	...	14,921	...	2,925,323

• **LIFE INSURANCE IN FORCE ($000 omitted)**

Year	Whole Life	Term	Credit	Group	Industrial	Total
2007	3,351,983	14,156,282	...	1,090,256	...	18,598,521
2008	3,410,667	15,334,967	...	701,791	...	19,447,425
2009	4,173,240	16,303,091	...	506,225	...	20,982,557

AMERICAN FIDELITY LIFE INS CO

4060 Barrancas Avenue
Pensacola, Florida 32507
Tel: 850-456-7401

AMB#: 006055
Began Business: 09/05/1956
Agency Off: Leonard B. Southerland

Best's Financial Strength Rating: B++ **FSC:** VII

• NET PREMIUMS AND DEPOSITS ($000 omitted)

Year	Individual Life	Individual & Group Annuities	Group Life & A&H	Credit Life & A&H	Individual A&H	Total
2007	13,403	20,239	1,524	...	...	35,167
2008	12,545	19,974	1,220	...	...	33,739
2009	11,515	18,802	1,416	...	...	31,733

• NET OPERATING GAIN ($000 omitted)

Year	Individual Life	Individual & Group Annuities	Group Life & A&H	Credit Life & A&H	Individual A&H	Total
2007	1,101	464	3	...	...	1,568
2008	788	361	3	...	...	1,152
2009	1,470	605	3	...	...	2,078

• COMPARATIVE FINANCIALS ($000 omitted)

Year	Assets	Capital & Surplus	Net Invest Income	Benefits Paid	Realized Cap Gains	Policyholder Dividends	Contract Lns (% of assets)
2007	477,240	77,055	20,123	25,177	342	69	1.4
2008	469,805	73,209	17,924	22,528	2	73	1.3
2009	460,907	71,489	16,861	20,001	-2,956	64	1.3

• ORDINARY LIFE STATISTICS

Year	Av. Ord. Policy Issued ($)	Av. Ord. Policy In Force ($)	Avg. Prem ($/M)	1st Yr Prem/ Total Prem	Ord. Lapse Ratio
2007	15,700	15,708	11.79	25.0	12.5
2008	15,721	15,732	11.57	22.8	12.7
2009	15,771	15,817	11.05	20.5	13.1

• NEW LIFE BUSINESS ISSUED ($000 omitted)

Year	Whole Life	Term	Credit	Group	Industrial	Total
2007	124,878	122	...	...	...	125,000
2008	112,967	33	...	...	...	113,000
2009	119,980	20	...	...	...	120,000

• LIFE INSURANCE IN FORCE ($000 omitted)

Year	Whole Life	Term	Credit	Group	Industrial	Total
2007	889,180	263,333	...	1,169,130	...	2,321,643
2008	849,638	250,025	...	1,128,204	...	2,227,867
2009	816,256	241,154	...	1,311,380	...	2,368,790

AMERICAN GENERAL LF & ACCIDENT

American General Center
Nashville, Tennessee 37250
Tel: 615-749-1000

AMB#: 006788
Began Business: 02/28/1900
Agency Off: None

Best's Financial Strength Rating: A **FSC:** XI

• NET PREMIUMS AND DEPOSITS ($000 omitted)

Year	Individual Life	Individual & Group Annuities	Group Life & A&H	Credit Life & A&H	Individual A&H	Total
2007	681,717	116,497	619	...	88,704	887,536
2008	678,242	194,154	436	...	85,465	958,296
2009	653,363	175,449	320	...	77,776	906,908

• NET OPERATING GAIN ($000 omitted)

Year	Individual Life	Individual & Group Annuities	Group Life & A&H	Credit Life & A&H	Individual A&H	Total
2007	255,415	22,498	1,102	...	-3,393	275,621
2008	214,079	-9,333	830	...	1,268	206,843
2009	136,003	23,991	451	...	5,390	165,836

• COMPARATIVE FINANCIALS ($000 omitted)

Year	Assets	Capital & Surplus	Net Invest Income	Benefits Paid	Realized Cap Gains	Policyholder Dividends	Contract Lns (% of assets)
2007	9,134,161	546,887	658,990	737,661	-71,804	1,427	4.7
2008	9,134,531	563,502	637,839	823,011	-1,023,791	1,343	4.7
2009	9,359,041	751,345	636,942	814,826	-56,876	1,161	4.6

• ORDINARY LIFE STATISTICS

Year	Av. Ord. Policy Issued ($)	Av. Ord. Policy In Force ($)	Avg. Prem ($/M)	1st Yr Prem/ Total Prem	Ord. Lapse Ratio
2007	77,270	15,615	11.64	10.2	9.7
2008	94,277	16,656	11.29	11.0	9.7
2009	99,290	17,636	10.73	10.8	10.3

• NEW LIFE BUSINESS ISSUED ($000 omitted)

Year	Whole Life	Term	Credit	Group	Industrial	Total
2007	4,846,701	3,332,435	...	...	...	8,179,136
2008	4,743,024	4,559,441	...	...	...	9,302,465
2009	4,141,682	5,368,369	...	...	...	9,510,051

• LIFE INSURANCE IN FORCE ($000 omitted)

Year	Whole Life	Term	Credit	Group	Industrial	Total
2007	42,013,197	21,092,745	...	41,415	1,453,483	64,600,840
2008	42,294,849	22,164,849	...	35,558	1,395,200	65,890,456
2009	41,603,805	23,851,045	...	31,298	1,339,816	66,825,964

AMERICAN GENERAL ASSURANCE CO

3600 Route 66
Neptune, New Jersey 07754-1580
Tel: 847-517-6000

AMB#: 006989
Began Business: 02/01/1930
Agency Off: None

Best's Financial Strength Rating: A **FSC:** VII

• NET PREMIUMS AND DEPOSITS ($000 omitted)

Year	Individual Life	Individual & Group Annuities	Group Life & A&H	Credit Life & A&H	Individual A&H	Total
2007	1,740	...	-109,448	3,373	-69	-104,405
2008	153	9	70,671	8,582	...	79,416
2009	137	...	67,017	200	...	67,354

• NET OPERATING GAIN ($000 omitted)

Year	Individual Life	Individual & Group Annuities	Group Life & A&H	Credit Life & A&H	Individual A&H	Total
2007	-1,586	...	37,982	-240	290	36,446
2008	160	0	-1,992	3,759	...	1,750
2009	87	1	13,292	-324	...	12,178

• COMPARATIVE FINANCIALS ($000 omitted)

Year	Assets	Capital & Surplus	Net Invest Income	Benefits Paid	Realized Cap Gains	Policyholder Dividends	Contract Lns (% of assets)
2007	287,681	144,673	25,237	411,870	-7,985	...	0.1
2008	193,923	74,867	13,592	44,630	-8,289	...	0.1
2009	184,651	91,453	10,881	27,808	-1,530	...	0.1

• ORDINARY LIFE STATISTICS

Year	Av. Ord. Policy Issued ($)	Av. Ord. Policy In Force ($)	Avg. Prem ($/M)	1st Yr Prem/ Total Prem	Ord. Lapse Ratio
2007	...	...	...	...	...
2008	...	...	...	...	...
2009	...	...	...	...	...

• NEW LIFE BUSINESS ISSUED ($000 omitted)

Year	Whole Life	Term	Credit	Group	Industrial	Total
2007	...	141,271	1,667,160	1,236,141	...	3,044,572
2008	...	53,316	1,887,717	509,243	...	2,450,276
2009	...	12,947	887,095	194,294	...	1,094,336

• LIFE INSURANCE IN FORCE ($000 omitted)

Year	Whole Life	Term	Credit	Group	Industrial	Total
2007	3,573	422,911	6,053,563	10,942,338	...	17,422,385
2008	3,221	344,365	5,210,997	8,870,745	...	14,429,328
2009	2,577	332,270	3,171,081	8,582,662	...	12,088,589

AMERICAN GENERAL LIFE INS CO

2727-A Allen Parkway
Houston, Texas 77019-2115
Tel: 713-522-1111

AMB#: 006058
Began Business: 08/01/1960
Agency Off: None

Best's Financial Strength Rating: A **FSC:** XV

• NET PREMIUMS AND DEPOSITS ($000 omitted)

Year	Individual Life	Individual & Group Annuities	Group Life & A&H	Credit Life & A&H	Individual A&H	Total
2007	961,890	2,041,478	-17,699	16	26,720	3,012,405
2008	891,547	3,248,845	57,297	...	27,776	4,225,466
2009	622,013	1,621,752	-29,021	...	29,127	2,243,871

• NET OPERATING GAIN ($000 omitted)

Year	Individual Life	Individual & Group Annuities	Group Life & A&H	Credit Life & A&H	Individual A&H	Total
2007	119,237	79,696	-14,961	62	-5,902	1,084,913
2008	11,525	-77,492	-5,339	-3	-174	58,505
2009	104,406	79,537	7,751	...	1,936	128,789

• COMPARATIVE FINANCIALS ($000 omitted)

Year	Assets	Capital & Surplus	Net Invest Income	Benefits Paid	Realized Cap Gains	Policyholder Dividends	Contract Lns (% of assets)
2007	36,717,239	5,780,109	2,574,546	2,351,737	-219,892	46,475	2.3
2008	38,668,102	5,214,869	1,987,785	2,500,406	-4,161,733	44,431	2.5
2009	39,653,080	5,954,032	1,996,244	2,719,893	-229,291	41,137	2.3

• ORDINARY LIFE STATISTICS

Year	Av. Ord. Policy Issued ($)	Av. Ord. Policy In Force ($)	Avg. Prem ($/M)	1st Yr Prem/ Total Prem	Ord. Lapse Ratio
2007	514,056	257,253	3.96	22.5	4.7
2008	538,965	276,922	3.80	14.4	5.4
2009	429,026	280,431	3.44	9.3	6.5

• NEW LIFE BUSINESS ISSUED ($000 omitted)

Year	Whole Life	Term	Credit	Group	Industrial	Total
2007	3,926,409	92,744,318	...	11,061	...	96,681,788
2008	4,603,976	92,697,596	...	2,404	...	97,303,976
2009	2,344,281	27,942,347	...	1,679	...	30,288,306

• LIFE INSURANCE IN FORCE ($000 omitted)

Year	Whole Life	Term	Credit	Group	Industrial	Total
2007	105,151,196	533,744,558	63	15,522,319	...	654,418,136
2008	105,711,072	588,723,791	33	14,843,114	...	709,278,010
2009	101,006,601	570,652,806	7	12,620,855	...	684,280,270

AMERICAN GENERAL LIFE INS DE

2727-A Allen Parkway
Houston, Texas 77019-2115
Tel: 713-522-1111

AMB#: 006809
Began Business: 09/04/1962
Agency Off: None

Best's Financial Strength Rating: A **FSC:** X

• NET PREMIUMS AND DEPOSITS ($000 omitted)

Year	Individual Life	Individual & Group Annuities	Group Life & A&H	Credit Life & A&H	Individual A&H	Total
2007	98,180	282,178	91,415	...	23,947	495,721
2008	38,688	236,882	98,894	...	23,927	398,392
2009	22,252	76,833	95,932	...	23,194	218,210

• NET OPERATING GAIN ($000 omitted)

Year	Individual Life	Individual & Group Annuities	Group Life & A&H	Credit Life & A&H	Individual A&H	Total
2007	49,700	52,872	-8,232	36	-1,741	92,633
2008	30,877	19,555	-646	11	-2,679	46,498
2009	18,991	34,304	-3,129	-297	-3,179	32,932

• COMPARATIVE FINANCIALS ($000 omitted)

Year	Assets	Capital & Surplus	Net Invest Income	Benefits Paid	Realized Cap Gains	Policyholder Dividends	Contract Lns (% of assets)
2007	10,790,222	444,806	533,237	1,320,051	-43,971	...	1.7
2008	9,429,399	364,387	499,242	1,198,482	-922,050	...	2.5
2009	9,357,652	454,784	455,117	929,250	-56,109	...	2.7

• ORDINARY LIFE STATISTICS

Year	Av. Ord. Policy Issued ($)	Av. Ord. Policy In Force ($)	Avg. Prem ($/M)	1st Yr Prem/ Total Prem	Ord. Lapse Ratio
2007	308,615	284,818	6.46	39.6	3.3
2008	320,647	289,420	4.46	13.9	3.9
2009	495,199	281,155	4.03	12.0	5.2

• NEW LIFE BUSINESS ISSUED ($000 omitted)

Year	Whole Life	Term	Credit	Group	Industrial	Total
2007	322,268	1,778	...	4,083,727	...	4,407,773
2008	327,643	700	...	3,035,381	...	3,363,724
2009	138,476	675	...	972,672	...	1,111,823

• LIFE INSURANCE IN FORCE ($000 omitted)

Year	Whole Life	Term	Credit	Group	Industrial	Total
2007	18,366,199	5,739,068	475	22,480,186	...	46,585,928
2008	17,982,947	5,410,873	190	21,948,370	...	45,342,380
2009	17,121,854	5,152,679	1	18,539,368	...	40,813,902

AMERICAN HEALTH AND LIFE INS

3001 Meacham Boulevard, Suite 100
Fort Worth, Texas 76137-4697
Tel: 800-316-5607

AMB#: 006062
Began Business: 06/23/1954
Agency Off: None

Best's Financial Strength Rating: A **FSC:** X

• NET PREMIUMS AND DEPOSITS ($000 omitted)

Year	Individual Life	Individual & Group Annuities	Group Life & A&H	Credit Life & A&H	Individual A&H	Total
2007	2,925	174	52,327	237,041	129	292,597
2008	2,694	219	51,092	228,205	128	282,337
2009	2,520	219	45,623	100,373	117	148,851

• NET OPERATING GAIN ($000 omitted)

Year	Individual Life	Individual & Group Annuities	Group Life & A&H	Credit Life & A&H	Individual A&H	Total
2007	643	2	7,437	90,333	4,182	102,597
2008	1,782	...	15,926	98,680	4,026	120,414
2009	369	-16	9,551	95,153	2,802	107,861

• COMPARATIVE FINANCIALS ($000 omitted)

Year	Assets	Capital & Surplus	Net Invest Income	Benefits Paid	Realized Cap Gains	Policyholder Dividends	Contract Lns (% of assets)
2007	1,676,168	886,185	88,048	134,892	-1,584	...	...
2008	1,519,632	656,795	81,735	127,206	-24,106	...	...
2009	1,360,547	623,730	73,822	131,458	-7,846	...	...

• ORDINARY LIFE STATISTICS

Year	Av. Ord. Policy Issued ($)	Av. Ord. Policy In Force ($)	Avg. Prem ($/M)	1st Yr Prem/ Total Prem	Ord. Lapse Ratio
2007	...	...	...	...	...
2008	...	...	...	...	...
2009	...	...	...	...	...

• NEW LIFE BUSINESS ISSUED ($000 omitted)

Year	Whole Life	Term	Credit	Group	Industrial	Total
2007	...	325	8,324,423	1,056,181	...	9,380,929
2008	...	1,273	12,918,459	2,096,391	...	15,016,123
2009	...	1,503	6,269,725	574,105	...	6,845,333

• LIFE INSURANCE IN FORCE ($000 omitted)

Year	Whole Life	Term	Credit	Group	Industrial	Total
2007	151,189	370,020	10,044,254	3,544,064	180	14,109,707
2008	145,068	315,932	10,420,002	3,180,527	174	14,061,703
2009	139,183	267,878	8,388,985	2,896,229	151	11,692,427

AMERICAN HERITAGE LIFE INS CO

1776 American Heritage Life Drive
Jacksonville, Florida 32224-6688
Tel: 904-992-1776

AMB#: 006064
Began Business: 12/27/1956
Agency Off: David A. Bird

Best's Financial Strength Rating: A+ g **FSC:** XV

• NET PREMIUMS AND DEPOSITS ($000 omitted)

Year	Individual Life	Individual & Group Annuities	Group Life & A&H	Credit Life & A&H	Individual A&H	Total
2007	94,555	516	86,471	23,403	255,778	460,723
2008	79,797	425	103,203	22,693	208,466	414,583
2009	67,988	400	144,562	16,343	229,058	458,349

• NET OPERATING GAIN ($000 omitted)

Year	Individual Life	Individual & Group Annuities	Group Life & A&H	Credit Life & A&H	Individual A&H	Total
2007	6,418	518	3,720	-2,628	644	8,672
2008	6,437	-14	3,632	-1,889	-3,346	4,820
2009	15,886	-260	7,238	-2,476	3,515	23,902

• COMPARATIVE FINANCIALS ($000 omitted)

Year	Assets	Capital & Surplus	Net Invest Income	Benefits Paid	Realized Cap Gains	Policyholder Dividends	Contract Lns (% of assets)
2007	1,376,587	203,963	62,602	229,878	3,814	1	21.9
2008	1,326,474	192,142	62,778	236,109	-4,541	2	24.6
2009	1,404,488	240,911	61,403	252,320	-5,705	2	21.9

• ORDINARY LIFE STATISTICS

Year	Av. Ord. Policy Issued ($)	Av. Ord. Policy In Force ($)	Avg. Prem ($/M)	1st Yr Prem/ Total Prem	Ord. Lapse Ratio
2007	47,280	40,120	8.04	18.3	15.2
2008	44,392	40,680	8.04	18.4	15.0
2009	43,130	41,661	8.08	17.8	14.9

• NEW LIFE BUSINESS ISSUED ($000 omitted)

Year	Whole Life	Term	Credit	Group	Industrial	Total
2007	1,376,027	1,519,435	1,010,764	517,136	...	4,423,362
2008	1,319,196	1,567,156	704,808	296,668	...	3,887,828
2009	1,087,374	1,802,103	431,255	659,420	...	3,980,152

• LIFE INSURANCE IN FORCE ($000 omitted)

Year	Whole Life	Term	Credit	Group	Industrial	Total
2007	9,843,863	4,631,247	2,070,074	2,304,015	...	18,849,199
2008	9,816,250	4,885,713	1,652,263	2,551,638	...	18,905,864
2009	9,588,520	5,287,360	1,276,418	2,777,070	...	18,929,368

AMERICAN HOME LIFE INS CO

P.O. Box 1497
Topeka, Kansas 66601-1497
Tel: 785-235-6276

AMB#: 006065
Began Business: 07/10/1909
Agency Off: Roger H. Prather

Best's Financial Strength Rating: B++ **FSC:** V

• NET PREMIUMS AND DEPOSITS ($000 omitted)

Year	Individual Life	Individual & Group Annuities	Group Life & A&H	Credit Life & A&H	Individual A&H	Total
2007	17,915	1,922	...	...	12	19,849
2008	17,385	1,996	...	...	9	19,390
2009	18,598	8,546	...	...	8	27,153

• NET OPERATING GAIN ($000 omitted)

Year	Individual Life	Individual & Group Annuities	Group Life & A&H	Credit Life & A&H	Individual A&H	Total
2007	879	147	0	...	7	1,032
2008	2,381	113	2	...	2	2,498
2009	509	503	1	...	-11	1,002

• COMPARATIVE FINANCIALS ($000 omitted)

Year	Assets	Capital & Surplus	Net Invest Income	Benefits Paid	Realized Cap Gains	Policyholder Dividends	Contract Lns (% of assets)
2007	164,090	14,637	8,863	12,757	-24	537	4.1
2008	165,548	14,258	9,491	16,417	-2,348	574	4.3
2009	176,385	14,390	9,083	15,380	-1,147	612	4.5

• ORDINARY LIFE STATISTICS

Year	Av. Ord. Policy Issued ($)	Av. Ord. Policy In Force ($)	Avg. Prem ($/M)	1st Yr Prem/ Total Prem	Ord. Lapse Ratio
2007	37,391	35,810	11.65	8.0	8.9
2008	41,220	36,087	11.54	7.5	8.8
2009	35,147	35,250	12.52	8.7	10.0

• NEW LIFE BUSINESS ISSUED ($000 omitted)

Year	Whole Life	Term	Credit	Group	Industrial	Total
2007	50,990	87,843	...	...	...	138,833
2008	48,253	89,422	...	...	...	137,675
2009	58,601	74,360	...	...	...	132,961

• LIFE INSURANCE IN FORCE ($000 omitted)

Year	Whole Life	Term	Credit	Group	Industrial	Total
2007	640,588	1,003,369	...	15	...	1,643,972
2008	644,967	992,532	...	14	...	1,637,513
2009	633,748	971,056	...	13	...	1,604,817

AMERICAN INCOME LIFE INS CO

P.O. Box 2608
Waco, Texas 76797
Tel: 254-761-6400

AMB#: 006069
Began Business: 08/01/1954
Agency Off: Debbie Gamble

Best's Financial Strength Rating: A+ g **FSC:** X

• NET PREMIUMS AND DEPOSITS ($000 omitted)

Year	Individual Life	Individual & Group Annuities	Group Life & A&H	Credit Life & A&H	Individual A&H	Total
2007	439,145	5,920	7,206	...	60,736	513,007
2008	461,331	6,189	8,105	...	62,510	538,135
2009	505,824	6,087	8,478	...	63,519	583,908

• NET OPERATING GAIN ($000 omitted)

Year	Individual Life	Individual & Group Annuities	Group Life & A&H	Credit Life & A&H	Individual A&H	Total
2007	65,926	10	803	...	16,884	83,624
2008	107,243	-33	760	...	20,700	128,670
2009	67,870	28	930	...	16,313	85,141

• COMPARATIVE FINANCIALS ($000 omitted)

Year	Assets	Capital & Surplus	Net Invest Income	Benefits Paid	Realized Cap Gains	Policyholder Dividends	Contract Lns (% of assets)
2007	1,705,887	221,186	82,551	133,395	12,698	37	3.3
2008	1,828,070	228,066	93,093	144,896	-29,892	31	3.5
2009	1,932,816	188,073	92,649	156,908	322	21	4.0

• ORDINARY LIFE STATISTICS

Year	Av. Ord. Policy Issued ($)	Av. Ord. Policy In Force ($)	Avg. Prem ($/M)	1st Yr Prem/ Total Prem	Ord. Lapse Ratio
2007	36,801	21,619	16.52	16.4	15.0
2008	36,823	21,795	16.59	17.6	20.0
2009	34,056	22,609	16.56	19.2	17.4

• NEW LIFE BUSINESS ISSUED ($000 omitted)

Year	Whole Life	Term	Credit	Group	Industrial	Total
2007	3,589,250	3,285,698	...	438	...	6,875,386
2008	4,390,408	3,625,514	...	462	...	8,016,384
2009	5,082,163	3,962,421	...	276	...	9,044,860

• LIFE INSURANCE IN FORCE ($000 omitted)

Year	Whole Life	Term	Credit	Group	Industrial	Total
2007	16,864,883	9,732,926	...	124,009	...	26,721,818
2008	17,769,257	10,056,114	...	160,870	...	27,986,241
2009	19,889,327	10,674,632	...	203,626	...	30,767,585

AMERICAN LIFE INS CO DE

600 King Street
Wilmington, Delaware 19801
Tel: 302-594-2000

AMB#: 006081
Began Business: 08/18/1921
Agency Off: Ralph Gaudio

Best's Financial Strength Rating: A u **FSC:** XV

• NET PREMIUMS AND DEPOSITS ($000 omitted)

Year	Individual Life	Individual & Group Annuities	Group Life & A&H	Credit Life & A&H	Individual A&H	Total
2007	25,844,847	4,808,771	423,519	91,182	2,655,635	33,823,954
2008	20,302,506	6,221,619	503,691	126,988	3,212,660	30,367,464
2009	4,895,185	4,612,422	493,620	121,335	3,441,692	13,564,255

• NET OPERATING GAIN ($000 omitted)

Year	Individual Life	Individual & Group Annuities	Group Life & A&H	Credit Life & A&H	Individual A&H	Total
2007	457,501	209,727	39,535	2,375	253,654	962,792
2008	305,455	482,248	51,026	9,715	399,049	1,247,493
2009	-27,449	78,838	32,020	-26,473	680,547	737,482

• COMPARATIVE FINANCIALS ($000 omitted)

Year	Assets	Capital & Surplus	Net Invest Income	Benefits Paid	Realized Cap Gains	Policyholder Dividends	Contract Lns (% of assets)
2007	101,632,307	6,720,961	2,678,828	19,450,196	-225,874	23,681	1.0
2008	86,338,053	3,902,904	2,932,244	31,423,893	-1,611,197	27,954	1.5
2009	91,042,803	4,146,527	2,792,060	11,625,350	-68,878	17,378	1.5

• ORDINARY LIFE STATISTICS

Year	Av. Ord. Policy Issued ($)	Av. Ord. Policy In Force ($)	Avg. Prem ($/M)	1st Yr Prem/ Total Prem	Ord. Lapse Ratio
2007	69,934	62,939	130.23	2.6	8.1
2008	79,418	69,186	90.34	3.2	13.1
2009	79,912	75,643	21.50	11.6	12.9

• NEW LIFE BUSINESS ISSUED ($000 omitted)

Year	Whole Life	Term	Credit	Group	Industrial	Total
2007	14,662,563	17,449,914	5,962,865	13,375,593	...	51,450,935
2008	16,893,452	19,787,160	13,062,241	10,905,639	...	60,648,492
2009	12,566,576	18,745,060	2,075,309	7,270,700	...	40,657,644

• LIFE INSURANCE IN FORCE ($000 omitted)

Year	Whole Life	Term	Credit	Group	Industrial	Total
2007	92,720,734	106,385,017	26,194,419	107,067,369	...	332,367,539
2008	101,950,721	123,483,538	38,319,859	100,331,345	...	364,085,463
2009	108,295,632	133,654,743	35,664,384	103,439,193	...	381,053,952

AMERICAN INTERN LIFE ASSUR NY

70 Pine Street, 19th Floor
New York, New York 10270
Tel: 212-770-7000

AMB#: 006072
Began Business: 11/28/1962
Agency Off: None

Best's Financial Strength Rating: A **FSC:** XV

• NET PREMIUMS AND DEPOSITS ($000 omitted)

Year	Individual Life	Individual & Group Annuities	Group Life & A&H	Credit Life & A&H	Individual A&H	Total
2007	12,003	426,178	48,141	...	1,633	487,955
2008	11,449	398,253	42,598	...	1,512	453,813
2009	10,525	122,409	62,617	...	1,426	196,976

• NET OPERATING GAIN ($000 omitted)

Year	Individual Life	Individual & Group Annuities	Group Life & A&H	Credit Life & A&H	Individual A&H	Total
2007	5,281	74,275	10,409	15	-62	89,918
2008	-22,999	-126,969	3,112	13	619	-146,594
2009	26,997	200,679	8,285	-573	-1,003	233,000

• COMPARATIVE FINANCIALS ($000 omitted)

Year	Assets	Capital & Surplus	Net Invest Income	Benefits Paid	Realized Cap Gains	Policyholder Dividends	Contract Lns (% of assets)
2007	7,092,807	552,637	488,896	1,460,417	-11,605	...	0.1
2008	6,660,685	370,537	449,369	985,823	-882,320	...	0.2
2009	6,543,627	523,626	402,705	658,412	-54,765	...	0.1

• ORDINARY LIFE STATISTICS

Year	Av. Ord. Policy Issued ($)	Av. Ord. Policy In Force ($)	Avg. Prem ($/M)	1st Yr Prem/ Total Prem	Ord. Lapse Ratio
2007	15,558	2,548	6.71	2.2	6.9
2008	18,761	2,837	7.00	0.8	6.0
2009	81,966	2,622	7.12	0.6	8.5

• NEW LIFE BUSINESS ISSUED ($000 omitted)

Year	Whole Life	Term	Credit	Group	Industrial	Total
2007	9,564	3,598	...	234,980	...	248,142
2008	12,599	3,648	...	131,498	...	147,745
2009	2,037	340	...	243,468	...	245,845

• LIFE INSURANCE IN FORCE ($000 omitted)

Year	Whole Life	Term	Credit	Group	Industrial	Total
2007	893,067	1,124,066	1,019	2,971,580	...	4,989,732
2008	824,000	1,026,665	180	2,857,548	...	4,708,393
2009	751,310	926,417	...	2,960,940	...	4,638,667

AMERICAN MEDICAL AND LIFE INS

8 West 38th Street, Suite 1002
New York, New York 10018
Tel: 646-223-9300

AMB#: 008304
Began Business: 02/17/1966
Agency Off: John Ollis

Best's Financial Strength Rating: B- **FSC:** IV

• NET PREMIUMS AND DEPOSITS ($000 omitted)

Year	Individual Life	Individual & Group Annuities	Group Life & A&H	Credit Life & A&H	Individual A&H	Total
2007	2	...	19,351	...	...	19,353
2008	4	...	28,496	...	...	28,500
2009	4	...	44,860	...	1	44,865

• NET OPERATING GAIN ($000 omitted)

Year	Individual Life	Individual & Group Annuities	Group Life & A&H	Credit Life & A&H	Individual A&H	Total
2007	2	...	1,453	...	...	785
2008	2	...	2,184	...	...	1,327
2009	4	...	-4,774	...	1	-6,130

• COMPARATIVE FINANCIALS ($000 omitted)

Year	Assets	Capital & Surplus	Net Invest Income	Benefits Paid	Realized Cap Gains	Policyholder Dividends	Contract Lns (% of assets)
2007	21,691	12,706	523	12,384	197	...	...
2008	32,050	12,100	624	17,653	...	...	...
2009	27,084	7,569	466	35,371	...	...	...

• ORDINARY LIFE STATISTICS

Year	Av. Ord. Policy Issued ($)	Av. Ord. Policy In Force ($)	Avg. Prem ($/M)	1st Yr Prem/ Total Prem	Ord. Lapse Ratio
2007	...	...	...	...	...
2008	...	...	...	...	...
2009	...	...	...	...	...

• NEW LIFE BUSINESS ISSUED ($000 omitted)

Year	Whole Life	Term	Credit	Group	Industrial	Total
2007	...	...	...	...	...	...
2008	...	...	...	...	...	...
2009	...	...	...	...	...	...

• LIFE INSURANCE IN FORCE ($000 omitted)

Year	Whole Life	Term	Credit	Group	Industrial	Total
2007	...	235	...	324,335	...	324,570
2008	...	235	...	293,250	...	293,485
2009	...	235	...	352,736	...	352,971

AMERICAN MEDICAL SECURITY LIFE

P.O. Box 19032
Green Bay, Wisconsin 54307-9032
Tel: 800-232-5432

AMB#: 007771
Began Business: 12/10/1982
Agency Off: None

Best's Financial Strength Rating: A-   **FSC:** VI

• NET PREMIUMS AND DEPOSITS ($000 omitted)

Year	Individual Life	Individual & Group Annuities	Group Life & A&H	Credit Life & A&H	Individual A&H	Total
2007	1	...	254,273	...	28,209	282,484
2008	1	...	174,275	...	24,191	198,468
2009	1	...	145,129	...	21,216	166,346

• NET OPERATING GAIN ($000 omitted)

Year	Individual Life	Individual & Group Annuities	Group Life & A&H	Credit Life & A&H	Individual A&H	Total
2007	1	...	54,543	...	3,170	57,713
2008	0	...	33,340	...	573	33,913
2009	0	...	20,656	...	-2,143	18,513

• COMPARATIVE FINANCIALS ($000 omitted)

Year	Assets	Capital & Surplus	Net Invest Income	Benefits Paid	Realized Cap Gains	Policyholder Dividends	Contract Lns (% of assets)
2007	237,916	153,420	16,961	160,492	...	...	...
2008	129,773	70,517	6,305	119,731	22,372	...	...
2009	79,638	39,919	2,024	113,686	-242	...	...

• ORDINARY LIFE STATISTICS

Year	Av. Ord. Policy Issued ($)	Av. Ord. Policy In Force ($)	Avg. Prem ($/M)	1st Yr Prem/ Total Prem	Ord. Lapse Ratio
2007	...	...	...	...	...
2008	...	...	...	...	...
2009	...	...	...	...	...

• NEW LIFE BUSINESS ISSUED ($000 omitted)

Year	Whole Life	Term	Credit	Group	Industrial	Total
2007	...	...	...	43,986	...	43,986
2008	...	...	...	18,936	...	18,936
2009	...	...	...	14,298	...	14,298

• LIFE INSURANCE IN FORCE ($000 omitted)

Year	Whole Life	Term	Credit	Group	Industrial	Total
2007	35	...	...	339,506	...	339,541
2008	35	...	...	252,559	...	252,594
2009	35	...	...	193,951	...	193,986

AMERICAN MEMORIAL LIFE INS CO

P.O. Box 2730
Rapid City, South Dakota 57709-2730
Tel: 605-719-0999

AMB#: 006942
Began Business: 10/01/1959
Agency Off: Tammy Schultz

Best's Financial Strength Rating: A-   **FSC:** VIII

• NET PREMIUMS AND DEPOSITS ($000 omitted)

Year	Individual Life	Individual & Group Annuities	Group Life & A&H	Credit Life & A&H	Individual A&H	Total
2007	83,985	7,705	201,592	...	15	293,297
2008	73,867	5,562	204,200	...	12	283,641
2009	79,951	6,891	203,659	...	11	290,512

• NET OPERATING GAIN ($000 omitted)

Year	Individual Life	Individual & Group Annuities	Group Life & A&H	Credit Life & A&H	Individual A&H	Total
2007	17,525	2,925	16,328	...	7	36,785
2008	11,517	3,327	14,712	...	-8	29,548
2009	8,105	2,764	11,898	...	37	22,804

• COMPARATIVE FINANCIALS ($000 omitted)

Year	Assets	Capital & Surplus	Net Invest Income	Benefits Paid	Realized Cap Gains	Policyholder Dividends	Contract Lns (% of assets)
2007	1,935,452	86,428	111,506	211,708	-8,451	871	0.7
2008	1,996,141	86,055	110,103	222,138	-52,526	844	0.6
2009	2,067,829	109,717	110,387	218,869	-4,564	799	0.6

• ORDINARY LIFE STATISTICS

Year	Av. Ord. Policy Issued ($)	Av. Ord. Policy In Force ($)	Avg. Prem ($/M)	1st Yr Prem/ Total Prem	Ord. Lapse Ratio
2007	5,022	4,425	72.68	6.1	1.4
2008	5,340	4,517	64.61	5.0	-0.3
2009	6,048	4,647	69.09	7.2	-0.1

• NEW LIFE BUSINESS ISSUED ($000 omitted)

Year	Whole Life	Term	Credit	Group	Industrial	Total
2007	66,154	...	...	190,963	2	257,119
2008	64,761	...	...	192,361	...	257,122
2009	90,909	...	...	205,031	...	295,940

• LIFE INSURANCE IN FORCE ($000 omitted)

Year	Whole Life	Term	Credit	Group	Industrial	Total
2007	1,068,551	88,162	...	1,397,384	6,977	2,561,074
2008	1,062,373	81,757	...	1,496,711	6,686	2,647,527
2009	1,081,609	76,750	...	1,602,760	6,395	2,767,514

AMERICAN MODERN LIFE INS CO

7000 Midland Blvd.
Amelia, Ohio 45102-2607
Tel: 513-943-7200

AMB#: 006680
Began Business: 01/03/1957
Agency Off: Frank J. May

Best's Financial Strength Rating: A-   **FSC:** V

• NET PREMIUMS AND DEPOSITS ($000 omitted)

Year	Individual Life	Individual & Group Annuities	Group Life & A&H	Credit Life & A&H	Individual A&H	Total
2007	...	...	...	12,313	...	12,313
2008	...	...	...	13,197	...	13,197
2009	...	...	...	11,052	...	11,052

• NET OPERATING GAIN ($000 omitted)

Year	Individual Life	Individual & Group Annuities	Group Life & A&H	Credit Life & A&H	Individual A&H	Total
2007	...	...	...	-934	...	-934
2008	...	...	...	-2,654	...	-2,654
2009	...	...	...	2,829	...	2,829

• COMPARATIVE FINANCIALS ($000 omitted)

Year	Assets	Capital & Surplus	Net Invest Income	Benefits Paid	Realized Cap Gains	Policyholder Dividends	Contract Lns (% of assets)
2007	63,526	22,068	2,058	5,657	...	...	...
2008	64,198	18,348	2,051	5,609	-33	...	...
2009	63,389	20,823	1,050	5,568	-37	...	...

• ORDINARY LIFE STATISTICS

Year	Av. Ord. Policy Issued ($)	Av. Ord. Policy In Force ($)	Avg. Prem ($/M)	1st Yr Prem/ Total Prem	Ord. Lapse Ratio
2007	...	...	...	...	...
2008	...	...	...	...	...
2009	...	...	...	...	...

• NEW LIFE BUSINESS ISSUED ($000 omitted)

Year	Whole Life	Term	Credit	Group	Industrial	Total
2007	...	...	857,171	...	...	857,171
2008	...	...	771,442	...	...	771,442
2009	...	...	787,729	...	...	787,729

• LIFE INSURANCE IN FORCE ($000 omitted)

Year	Whole Life	Term	Credit	Group	Industrial	Total
2007	...	...	2,561,699	...	...	2,561,699
2008	...	...	2,416,044	...	...	2,416,044
2009	...	...	2,019,612	...	...	2,019,612

AMERICAN NATIONAL INS CO

One Moody Plaza
Galveston, Texas 77550-7999
Tel: 409-763-4661

AMB#: 006087
Began Business: 03/17/1905
Agency Off: None

Best's Financial Strength Rating: A   **FSC:** XV

• NET PREMIUMS AND DEPOSITS ($000 omitted)

Year	Individual Life	Individual & Group Annuities	Group Life & A&H	Credit Life & A&H	Individual A&H	Total
2007	350,693	1,250,866	92,968	48,245	16,577	1,759,349
2008	367,173	1,881,819	73,384	44,714	15,347	2,382,436
2009	342,375	2,305,958	92,723	27,573	14,124	2,782,754

• NET OPERATING GAIN ($000 omitted)

Year	Individual Life	Individual & Group Annuities	Group Life & A&H	Credit Life & A&H	Individual A&H	Total
2007	23,090	40,046	-10,656	10,854	-1,309	62,602
2008	3,830	12,126	-2,204	-933	-597	11,392
2009	15,789	46,067	18,484	22,505	60	111,782

• COMPARATIVE FINANCIALS ($000 omitted)

Year	Assets	Capital & Surplus	Net Invest Income	Benefits Paid	Realized Cap Gains	Policyholder Dividends	Contract Lns (% of assets)
2007	13,839,936	2,164,812	646,748	1,381,276	-3,484	3,694	2.1
2008	13,586,041	1,805,670	670,853	1,655,803	-134,464	2,802	2.2
2009	15,359,313	1,892,467	699,934	1,450,659	-57,894	2,122	2.0

• ORDINARY LIFE STATISTICS

Year	Av. Ord. Policy Issued ($)	Av. Ord. Policy In Force ($)	Avg. Prem ($/M)	1st Yr Prem/ Total Prem	Ord. Lapse Ratio
2007	86,088	28,712	8.80	19.7	7.7
2008	88,758	30,739	9.09	21.7	8.2
2009	75,919	32,062	8.46	11.1	8.7

• NEW LIFE BUSINESS ISSUED ($000 omitted)

Year	Whole Life	Term	Credit	Group	Industrial	Total
2007	3,212,639	3,143,250	2,917,840	877,340	...	10,151,069
2008	2,971,685	3,413,996	2,613,518	355,862	...	9,355,061
2009	2,071,385	3,626,019	2,297,227	87,966	...	8,082,597

• LIFE INSURANCE IN FORCE ($000 omitted)

Year	Whole Life	Term	Credit	Group	Industrial	Total
2007	27,807,332	15,657,362	4,805,468	6,897,763	233,103	55,401,028
2008	28,389,704	17,041,650	4,447,066	6,944,319	225,041	57,047,780
2009	27,858,406	18,486,148	3,766,543	6,593,478	217,318	56,921,893

AMERICAN NATIONAL LIFE INS NY

One Moody Plaza
Galveston, Texas 77550
Tel: 409-766-6448

AMB#: 060708
Began Business: …
Agency Off: None

Best's Financial Strength Rating: A
FSC: V

• NET PREMIUMS AND DEPOSITS ($000 omitted)

Year	Individual Life	Individual & Group Annuities	Group Life & A&H	Credit Life & A&H	Individual A&H	Total
2007	…	…	…	…	…	…
2008	…	…	…	…	…	…
2009	…	…	…	…	…	…

• NET OPERATING GAIN ($000 omitted)

Year	Individual Life	Individual & Group Annuities	Group Life & A&H	Credit Life & A&H	Individual A&H	Total
2007	…	…	…	…	…	…
2008	…	…	…	…	…	…
2009	…	…	…	…	…	…

• COMPARATIVE FINANCIALS ($000 omitted)

Year	Assets	Capital & Surplus	Net Invest Income	Benefits Paid	Realized Cap Gains	Policyholder Dividends	Contract Lns (% of assets)
2007	…	…	…	…	…	…	…
2008	…	…	…	…	…	…	…
2009	…	…	…	…	…	…	…

• ORDINARY LIFE STATISTICS

Year	Av. Ord. Policy Issued ($)	Av. Ord. Policy In Force ($)	Avg. Prem ($/M)	1st Yr Prem/ Total Prem	Ord. Lapse Ratio
2007	…	…	…	…	…
2008	…	…	…	…	…
2009	…	…	…	…	…

• NEW LIFE BUSINESS ISSUED ($000 omitted)

Year	Whole Life	Term	Credit	Group	Industrial	Total
2007	…	…	…	…	…	…
2008	…	…	…	…	…	…
2009	…	…	…	…	…	…

• LIFE INSURANCE IN FORCE ($000 omitted)

Year	Whole Life	Term	Credit	Group	Industrial	Total
2007	…	…	…	…	…	…
2008	…	…	…	…	…	…
2009	…	…	…	…	…	…

AMERICAN PHOENIX LIFE&REASSUR

One American Row
Hartford, Connecticut 06115
Tel: 860-403-5000

AMB#: 068152
Began Business: 12/30/1994
Agency Off: None

Best's Financial Strength Rating: B+
FSC: V

• NET PREMIUMS AND DEPOSITS ($000 omitted)

Year	Individual Life	Individual & Group Annuities	Group Life & A&H	Credit Life & A&H	Individual A&H	Total
2007	…	…	299	…	…	299
2008	…	…	2,090	…	…	2,090
2009	…	…	16	…	…	16

• NET OPERATING GAIN ($000 omitted)

Year	Individual Life	Individual & Group Annuities	Group Life & A&H	Credit Life & A&H	Individual A&H	Total
2007	…	…	-652	…	…	-652
2008	…	…	-153	…	…	-153
2009	…	…	-950	…	…	-950

• COMPARATIVE FINANCIALS ($000 omitted)

Year	Assets	Capital & Surplus	Net Invest Income	Benefits Paid	Realized Cap Gains	Policyholder Dividends	Contract Lns (% of assets)
2007	69,903	58,566	2,299	3,461	-25	…	…
2008	26,375	17,628	1,327	3,714	1	…	…
2009	22,766	16,658	746	1,521	1	…	…

• ORDINARY LIFE STATISTICS

Year	Av. Ord. Policy Issued ($)	Av. Ord. Policy In Force ($)	Avg. Prem ($/M)	1st Yr Prem/ Total Prem	Ord. Lapse Ratio
2007	…	…	…	…	…
2008	…	…	…	…	…
2009	…	…	…	…	…

• NEW LIFE BUSINESS ISSUED ($000 omitted)

Year	Whole Life	Term	Credit	Group	Industrial	Total
2007	…	…	…	…	…	…
2008	…	…	…	…	…	…
2009	…	…	…	…	…	…

• LIFE INSURANCE IN FORCE ($000 omitted)

Year	Whole Life	Term	Credit	Group	Industrial	Total
2007	…	…	…	…	…	…
2008	…	…	…	…	…	…
2009	…	…	…	…	…	…

AMERICAN NAT'L LIFE INS TEXAS

One Moody Plaza
Galveston, Texas 77550-7999
Tel: 409-763-4661

AMB#: 007417
Began Business: 12/20/1954
Agency Off: None

Best's Financial Strength Rating: A
FSC: VI

• NET PREMIUMS AND DEPOSITS ($000 omitted)

Year	Individual Life	Individual & Group Annuities	Group Life & A&H	Credit Life & A&H	Individual A&H	Total
2007	1,461	18	61,151	…	13,013	75,642
2008	1,302	15	79,502	…	13,075	93,894
2009	1,204	20	89,937	…	13,937	105,097

• NET OPERATING GAIN ($000 omitted)

Year	Individual Life	Individual & Group Annuities	Group Life & A&H	Credit Life & A&H	Individual A&H	Total
2007	233	81	971	…	-2,713	-1,428
2008	-45	56	-5,370	…	-486	-5,845
2009	-277	97	-11,379	…	-1,819	-13,378

• COMPARATIVE FINANCIALS ($000 omitted)

Year	Assets	Capital & Surplus	Net Invest Income	Benefits Paid	Realized Cap Gains	Policyholder Dividends	Contract Lns (% of assets)
2007	140,309	44,191	7,425	58,890	…	…	2.5
2008	137,691	36,095	7,101	72,740	-2,545	1	2.8
2009	125,415	26,668	6,338	85,614	-1,088	…	3.6

• ORDINARY LIFE STATISTICS

Year	Av. Ord. Policy Issued ($)	Av. Ord. Policy In Force ($)	Avg. Prem ($/M)	1st Yr Prem/ Total Prem	Ord. Lapse Ratio
2007	…	…	…	…	…
2008	…	…	…	…	…
2009	…	…	…	…	…

• NEW LIFE BUSINESS ISSUED ($000 omitted)

Year	Whole Life	Term	Credit	Group	Industrial	Total
2007	…	…	…	1,214	…	1,214
2008	…	…	…	720	…	720
2009	…	…	…	1,420	…	1,420

• LIFE INSURANCE IN FORCE ($000 omitted)

Year	Whole Life	Term	Credit	Group	Industrial	Total
2007	492,346	86,290	…	5,969	…	584,605
2008	480,000	79,107	…	5,523	…	564,630
2009	466,482	73,185	…	5,720	…	545,387

AMERICAN PIONEER LIFE INS CO

P.O. Box 958465
Lake Mary, Florida 32795-8465
Tel: 407-995-8000

AMB#: 006090
Began Business: 03/01/1962
Agency Off: Harold W. Jenkins

Best's Financial Strength Rating: B+
FSC: V

• NET PREMIUMS AND DEPOSITS ($000 omitted)

Year	Individual Life	Individual & Group Annuities	Group Life & A&H	Credit Life & A&H	Individual A&H	Total
2007	5,927	570	14,895	…	78,048	99,440
2008	5,542	687	15,278	…	67,965	89,471
2009	-39,331	-24,287	15,569	…	58,584	10,535

• NET OPERATING GAIN ($000 omitted)

Year	Individual Life	Individual & Group Annuities	Group Life & A&H	Credit Life & A&H	Individual A&H	Total
2007	738	40	490	…	-5,042	-3,774
2008	206	339	-212	…	-3,907	-3,575
2009	-52	225	-991	…	-311	-1,129

• COMPARATIVE FINANCIALS ($000 omitted)

Year	Assets	Capital & Surplus	Net Invest Income	Benefits Paid	Realized Cap Gains	Policyholder Dividends	Contract Lns (% of assets)
2007	174,097	29,494	8,499	89,908	1,641	…	3.6
2008	160,573	21,076	7,660	84,638	-1,506	…	3.8
2009	86,465	20,898	3,502	70,226	-1,812	…	0.0

• ORDINARY LIFE STATISTICS

Year	Av. Ord. Policy Issued ($)	Av. Ord. Policy In Force ($)	Avg. Prem ($/M)	1st Yr Prem/ Total Prem	Ord. Lapse Ratio
2007	…	…	…	…	…
2008	…	…	…	…	…
2009	…	…	…	…	…

• NEW LIFE BUSINESS ISSUED ($000 omitted)

Year	Whole Life	Term	Credit	Group	Industrial	Total
2007	6,560	7	…	…	…	6,567
2008	6,413	20	…	…	…	6,433
2009	6,730	…	…	…	…	6,730

• LIFE INSURANCE IN FORCE ($000 omitted)

Year	Whole Life	Term	Credit	Group	Industrial	Total
2007	402,201	56,480	…	2,498	…	461,179
2008	377,213	54,370	…	1,403	…	432,986
2009	342,299	24,400	…	655	…	367,354

AMERICAN PROGRESSIVE L&H NY

P.O. Box 958465
Lake Mary, Florida 32795-8465
Tel: 914-934-8300

AMB#: 008411
Began Business: 03/26/1946
Agency Off: William Daly

Best's Financial Strength Rating: B++g **FSC:** IX

• NET PREMIUMS AND DEPOSITS ($000 omitted)

Year	Individual Life	Individual & Group Annuities	Group Life & A&H	Credit Life & A&H	Individual A&H	Total
2007	10,939	313	930	...	439,237	451,420
2008	10,775	344	838	...	594,844	606,801
2009	-31,341	-82,118	762	...	670,000	557,303

• NET OPERATING GAIN ($000 omitted)

Year	Individual Life	Individual & Group Annuities	Group Life & A&H	Credit Life & A&H	Individual A&H	Total
2007	1,279	1,978	257	...	10,900	14,414
2008	76	341	-67	...	14,758	15,108
2009	7	130	386	...	31,781	32,303

• COMPARATIVE FINANCIALS ($000 omitted)

Year	Assets	Capital & Surplus	Net Invest Income	Benefits Paid	Realized Cap Gains	Policyholder Dividends	Contract Lns (% of assets)
2007	419,907	93,146	15,818	385,912	...	...	0.4
2008	368,567	105,456	13,298	530,880	-3,873	...	0.5
2009	244,823	129,461	8,600	557,819	-7,239	...	0.0

• ORDINARY LIFE STATISTICS

Year	Av. Ord. Policy Issued ($)	Av. Ord. Policy In Force ($)	Avg. Prem ($/M)	1st Yr Prem/ Total Prem	Ord. Lapse Ratio
2007	...	...	...	...	...
2008	...	...	...	...	...
2009	...	...	...	...	...

• NEW LIFE BUSINESS ISSUED ($000 omitted)

Year	Whole Life	Term	Credit	Group	Industrial	Total
2007	40,358	...	...	...	...	40,358
2008	33,138	...	...	...	...	33,138
2009	41,117	...	...	...	...	41,117

• LIFE INSURANCE IN FORCE ($000 omitted)

Year	Whole Life	Term	Credit	Group	Industrial	Total
2007	340,067	51,129	...	...	...	391,196
2008	355,337	47,148	...	...	...	402,485
2009	378,607	46,499	...	...	...	425,106

AMERICAN REPUBLIC INS CO

P.O. Box 1
Des Moines, Iowa 50301
Tel: 515-245-2000

AMB#: 006096
Began Business: 05/10/1929
Agency Off: Mark L. Stadler

Best's Financial Strength Rating: A- g **FSC:** VIII

• NET PREMIUMS AND DEPOSITS ($000 omitted)

Year	Individual Life	Individual & Group Annuities	Group Life & A&H	Credit Life & A&H	Individual A&H	Total
2007	7,472	195	349,249	...	177,165	534,081
2008	7,097	41	274,254	...	178,237	459,629
2009	6,557	...	232,311	...	161,000	399,868

• NET OPERATING GAIN ($000 omitted)

Year	Individual Life	Individual & Group Annuities	Group Life & A&H	Credit Life & A&H	Individual A&H	Total
2007	472	94	27,446	1,099	812	29,923
2008	489	48	8,940	582	9,561	19,620
2009	850	7	11,780	508	7,984	21,129

• COMPARATIVE FINANCIALS ($000 omitted)

Year	Assets	Capital & Surplus	Net Invest Income	Benefits Paid	Realized Cap Gains	Policyholder Dividends	Contract Lns (% of assets)
2007	475,303	215,831	25,291	392,330	-232	456	1.3
2008	475,460	235,924	24,736	341,180	-1,826	426	1.3
2009	521,456	240,953	23,922	283,150	-2,120	441	1.1

• ORDINARY LIFE STATISTICS

Year	Av. Ord. Policy Issued ($)	Av. Ord. Policy In Force ($)	Avg. Prem ($/M)	1st Yr Prem/ Total Prem	Ord. Lapse Ratio
2007	...	...	...	...	...
2008	...	...	...	...	...
2009	...	...	...	...	...

• NEW LIFE BUSINESS ISSUED ($000 omitted)

Year	Whole Life	Term	Credit	Group	Industrial	Total
2007	619	1,442	183,577	1,584	...	187,222
2008	2,679	1,282	150,994	2,058	...	157,013
2009	1,036	2,087	108,327	546	...	111,996

• LIFE INSURANCE IN FORCE ($000 omitted)

Year	Whole Life	Term	Credit	Group	Industrial	Total
2007	485,512	2,258,345	...	8,733	...	2,752,590
2008	458,313	2,111,593	...	9,691	...	2,579,597
2009	427,866	1,997,751	...	4,738	...	2,430,355

AMERICAN PUBLIC LIFE INS CO

2305 Lakeland Drive
Jackson, Mississippi 39232
Tel: 601-936-6600

AMB#: 006094
Began Business: 03/01/1946
Agency Off: Cobern D. Hinton

Best's Financial Strength Rating: A- **FSC:** V

• NET PREMIUMS AND DEPOSITS ($000 omitted)

Year	Individual Life	Individual & Group Annuities	Group Life & A&H	Credit Life & A&H	Individual A&H	Total
2007	2,815	...	20,867	...	22,709	46,391
2008	2,884	...	18,970	...	22,240	44,094
2009	3,007	...	17,970	...	20,481	41,458

• NET OPERATING GAIN ($000 omitted)

Year	Individual Life	Individual & Group Annuities	Group Life & A&H	Credit Life & A&H	Individual A&H	Total
2007	382	...	1,182	...	465	2,030
2008	265	7	727	...	-3,458	-2,458
2009	432	2	1,397	...	1,665	3,497

• COMPARATIVE FINANCIALS ($000 omitted)

Year	Assets	Capital & Surplus	Net Invest Income	Benefits Paid	Realized Cap Gains	Policyholder Dividends	Contract Lns (% of assets)
2007	77,027	15,052	2,694	27,468	0	...	0.9
2008	74,494	12,861	2,851	30,909	-43	...	0.9
2009	77,202	17,582	2,860	19,833	20	...	0.9

• ORDINARY LIFE STATISTICS

Year	Av. Ord. Policy Issued ($)	Av. Ord. Policy In Force ($)	Avg. Prem ($/M)	1st Yr Prem/ Total Prem	Ord. Lapse Ratio
2007	...	...	...	...	...
2008	...	...	...	...	...
2009	...	...	...	...	...

• NEW LIFE BUSINESS ISSUED ($000 omitted)

Year	Whole Life	Term	Credit	Group	Industrial	Total
2007	7,029	6,740	...	...	...	13,769
2008	8,788	25,360	...	...	...	34,148
2009	6,354	29,945	...	...	...	36,299

• LIFE INSURANCE IN FORCE ($000 omitted)

Year	Whole Life	Term	Credit	Group	Industrial	Total
2007	59,202	864,828	...	...	...	924,030
2008	58,297	784,756	...	...	...	843,053
2009	66,770	736,311	...	...	...	803,082

AMERICAN UNDERWRITERS LIFE INS

P.O. Box 9510
Wichita, Kansas 67277-0510
Tel: 316-794-2200

AMB#: 008795
Began Business: 12/22/1977
Agency Off: R. Kell Hawkins

Best's Financial Strength Rating: B- g **FSC:** V

• NET PREMIUMS AND DEPOSITS ($000 omitted)

Year	Individual Life	Individual & Group Annuities	Group Life & A&H	Credit Life & A&H	Individual A&H	Total
2007	383	5,114	1,206	749	59	7,510
2008	329	30,146	898	449	49	31,871
2009	295	13,750	774	104	41	14,964

• NET OPERATING GAIN ($000 omitted)

Year	Individual Life	Individual & Group Annuities	Group Life & A&H	Credit Life & A&H	Individual A&H	Total
2007	112	-412	304	95	17	116
2008	249	65	-33	232	-28	485
2009	-242	608	-448	254	13	186

• COMPARATIVE FINANCIALS ($000 omitted)

Year	Assets	Capital & Surplus	Net Invest Income	Benefits Paid	Realized Cap Gains	Policyholder Dividends	Contract Lns (% of assets)
2007	56,072	12,456	2,633	16,309	3,334	...	1.2
2008	77,140	13,896	4,014	13,719	-1,521	...	0.7
2009	78,988	12,409	4,087	13,581	-2,306	...	0.5

• ORDINARY LIFE STATISTICS

Year	Av. Ord. Policy Issued ($)	Av. Ord. Policy In Force ($)	Avg. Prem ($/M)	1st Yr Prem/ Total Prem	Ord. Lapse Ratio
2007	...	...	...	...	...
2008	...	...	...	...	...
2009	...	...	...	...	...

• NEW LIFE BUSINESS ISSUED ($000 omitted)

Year	Whole Life	Term	Credit	Group	Industrial	Total
2007	35	1,675	15,702	1,035	...	18,447
2008	...	1,112	10,102	440	...	11,654
2009	85	638	5,227	1,926	...	7,876

• LIFE INSURANCE IN FORCE ($000 omitted)

Year	Whole Life	Term	Credit	Group	Industrial	Total
2007	92,657	355,735	27,085	5,679	...	481,156
2008	91,007	317,532	21,755	5,665	...	435,959
2009	82,472	290,691	15,470	6,824	...	395,457

AMERICAN UNITED LIFE INS CO

P.O. Box 368
Indianapolis, Indiana 46206-0368
Tel: 317-285-1877

AMB#: 006109
Began Business: 11/07/1877
Agency Off: B. Douglas Gritton

Best's Financial Strength Rating: A g **FSC:** XI

• NET PREMIUMS AND DEPOSITS ($000 omitted)

Year	Individual Life	Individual & Group Annuities	Group Life & A&H	Credit Life & A&H	Individual A&H	Total
2007	126,158	1,710,296	211,043	...	637	2,048,134
2008	122,809	2,502,040	216,074	...	331	2,841,254
2009	129,412	2,053,485	230,089	...	294	2,413,280

• NET OPERATING GAIN ($000 omitted)

Year	Individual Life	Individual & Group Annuities	Group Life & A&H	Credit Life & A&H	Individual A&H	Total
2007	11,905	23,306	7,049	2,917	7,894	59,731
2008	10,433	-1,098	2,917	1,301	2,212	23,338
2009	11,931	50,941	961	364	1,360	61,933

• COMPARATIVE FINANCIALS ($000 omitted)

Year	Assets	Capital & Surplus	Net Invest Income	Benefits Paid	Realized Cap Gains	Policyholder Dividends	Contract Lns (% of assets)
2007	14,032,818	677,927	363,468	2,157,341	-2,670	23,958	1.3
2008	12,526,176	656,212	403,511	1,830,204	-13,932	26,156	1.5
2009	14,839,168	758,847	431,669	1,681,280	-588	23,173	1.3

• ORDINARY LIFE STATISTICS

Year	Av. Ord. Policy Issued ($)	Av. Ord. Policy In Force ($)	Avg. Prem ($/M)	1st Yr Prem/ Total Prem	Ord. Lapse Ratio
2007	331,313	55,086	2.74	11.2	5.6
2008	390,608	55,264	2.85	10.1	7.2
2009	402,503	55,788	3.04	11.5	7.9

• NEW LIFE BUSINESS ISSUED ($000 omitted)

Year	Whole Life	Term	Credit	Group	Industrial	Total
2007	469,560	1,359,288	571,073	2,366,871	...	4,766,792
2008	427,012	1,494,779	424,238	3,220,871	...	5,566,900
2009	546,581	1,717,498	120,787	6,329,116	...	8,713,982

• LIFE INSURANCE IN FORCE ($000 omitted)

Year	Whole Life	Term	Credit	Group	Industrial	Total
2007	7,715,430	149,932,370	1,371,573	30,883,702	...	189,903,075
2008	7,646,165	140,121,106	1,083,510	28,606,135	...	177,456,916
2009	7,645,397	130,393,351	417,749	34,734,456	...	173,190,953

AMERITAS LIFE INSURANCE CORP.

P.O. Box 81889
Lincoln, Nebraska 68501-1889
Tel: 402-467-1122

AMB#: 006152
Began Business: 05/06/1887
Agency Off: Arnold D. Henkel

Best's Financial Strength Rating: A g **FSC:** XIII

• NET PREMIUMS AND DEPOSITS ($000 omitted)

Year	Individual Life	Individual & Group Annuities	Group Life & A&H	Credit Life & A&H	Individual A&H	Total
2007	113,454	539,757	507,650	...	...	1,160,861
2008	102,656	809,248	535,826	...	...	1,447,730
2009	113,870	604,228	568,358	...	...	1,286,456

• NET OPERATING GAIN ($000 omitted)

Year	Individual Life	Individual & Group Annuities	Group Life & A&H	Credit Life & A&H	Individual A&H	Total
2007	17,044	6,924	21,083	...	16	54,978
2008	-859	-39,974	24,004	...	15	816
2009	12,305	25,097	11,956	...	9	51,861

• COMPARATIVE FINANCIALS ($000 omitted)

Year	Assets	Capital & Surplus	Net Invest Income	Benefits Paid	Realized Cap Gains	Policyholder Dividends	Contract Lns (% of assets)
2007	6,398,880	878,120	137,341	922,203	22,217	10,157	1.7
2008	5,142,388	710,625	139,353	1,043,267	-72,798	9,995	2.1
2009	6,529,456	1,248,997	119,619	932,671	-1,934	8,245	1.5

• ORDINARY LIFE STATISTICS

Year	Av. Ord. Policy Issued ($)	Av. Ord. Policy In Force ($)	Avg. Prem ($/M)	1st Yr Prem/ Total Prem	Ord. Lapse Ratio
2007	301,517	171,190	6.69	16.0	5.5
2008	264,169	170,042	6.64	13.9	7.6
2009	345,729	170,209	7.31	25.1	8.8

• NEW LIFE BUSINESS ISSUED ($000 omitted)

Year	Whole Life	Term	Credit	Group	Industrial	Total
2007	780,891	214,717	...	1,425	...	997,033
2008	662,916	47,434	...	...	...	710,350
2009	919,941	15,256	...	...	...	935,196

• LIFE INSURANCE IN FORCE ($000 omitted)

Year	Whole Life	Term	Credit	Group	Industrial	Total
2007	14,233,624	6,512,438	...	550	...	20,746,612
2008	14,827,440	4,863,771	...	...	...	19,691,211
2009	13,232,433	5,457,677	...	...	...	18,690,110

AMERICO FINANCIAL LF & ANNUITY

P.O. Box 410288
Kansas City, Missouri 64141-0288
Tel: 816-391-2000

AMB#: 006233
Began Business: 07/25/1946
Agency Off: Rodney K. Foster

Best's Financial Strength Rating: A- **FSC:** IX

• NET PREMIUMS AND DEPOSITS ($000 omitted)

Year	Individual Life	Individual & Group Annuities	Group Life & A&H	Credit Life & A&H	Individual A&H	Total
2007	101,713	220,045	35,263	0	265	358,525
2008	119,520	150,747	38,080	...	250	309,326
2009	142,852	158,508	32,581	...	314	334,965

• NET OPERATING GAIN ($000 omitted)

Year	Individual Life	Individual & Group Annuities	Group Life & A&H	Credit Life & A&H	Individual A&H	Total
2007	-4,047	21,115	-8,434	0	18	9,196
2008	-2,309	50,884	-6,294	0	79	42,359
2009	24,843	26,465	1,776	0	23	53,107

• COMPARATIVE FINANCIALS ($000 omitted)

Year	Assets	Capital & Surplus	Net Invest Income	Benefits Paid	Realized Cap Gains	Policyholder Dividends	Contract Lns (% of assets)
2007	3,735,648	225,448	187,502	252,380	-578	369	2.4
2008	3,439,012	171,039	176,819	234,899	-63,130	309	1.1
2009	3,557,790	311,287	171,873	240,416	964	268	1.0

• ORDINARY LIFE STATISTICS

Year	Av. Ord. Policy Issued ($)	Av. Ord. Policy In Force ($)	Avg. Prem ($/M)	1st Yr Prem/ Total Prem	Ord. Lapse Ratio
2007	95,246	64,075	7.56	33.3	10.1
2008	88,045	61,838	7.18	32.4	10.6
2009	67,400	61,152	8.34	28.5	9.0

• NEW LIFE BUSINESS ISSUED ($000 omitted)

Year	Whole Life	Term	Credit	Group	Industrial	Total
2007	480,661	3,174,577	...	2,995,753	...	6,650,991
2008	611,187	2,955,961	...	1,966,539	...	5,533,687
2009	472,667	1,723,354	...	709,141	...	2,905,162

• LIFE INSURANCE IN FORCE ($000 omitted)

Year	Whole Life	Term	Credit	Group	Industrial	Total
2007	12,457,606	13,281,685	20	5,621,033	...	31,360,344
2008	14,840,294	14,727,288	11	5,970,688	1,835	35,540,116
2009	13,887,914	14,387,848	4	5,142,126	1,776	33,419,668

AMICA LIFE INS CO

P.O. Box 6008
Providence, Rhode Island 02940-6008
Tel: 800-652-6422

AMB#: 007464
Began Business: 05/06/1970
Agency Off: James E. McDermott, Jr.

Best's Financial Strength Rating: A+ **FSC:** VIII

• NET PREMIUMS AND DEPOSITS ($000 omitted)

Year	Individual Life	Individual & Group Annuities	Group Life & A&H	Credit Life & A&H	Individual A&H	Total
2007	41,284	31,119	2,606	...	...	75,009
2008	42,398	35,623	1,933	...	...	79,953
2009	44,833	56,632	1,992	...	...	103,457

• NET OPERATING GAIN ($000 omitted)

Year	Individual Life	Individual & Group Annuities	Group Life & A&H	Credit Life & A&H	Individual A&H	Total
2007	5,420	3,254	829	...	...	9,503
2008	2,694	5,325	791	...	...	8,809
2009	2,353	6,841	665	...	...	9,858

• COMPARATIVE FINANCIALS ($000 omitted)

Year	Assets	Capital & Surplus	Net Invest Income	Benefits Paid	Realized Cap Gains	Policyholder Dividends	Contract Lns (% of assets)
2007	923,146	158,641	45,087	55,729	548	...	0.5
2008	940,142	156,354	47,329	55,474	-87	...	0.6
2009	989,219	167,748	48,037	74,649	-1,008	...	0.6

• ORDINARY LIFE STATISTICS

Year	Av. Ord. Policy Issued ($)	Av. Ord. Policy In Force ($)	Avg. Prem ($/M)	1st Yr Prem/ Total Prem	Ord. Lapse Ratio
2007	421,435	290,948	2.75	10.1	3.5
2008	396,052	304,999	2.67	8.8	3.2
2009	398,581	316,384	2.64	8.6	3.4

• NEW LIFE BUSINESS ISSUED ($000 omitted)

Year	Whole Life	Term	Credit	Group	Industrial	Total
2007	43,372	2,970,730	...	...	...	3,014,102
2008	33,596	2,714,214	...	...	...	2,747,810
2009	42,707	2,485,491	...	...	...	2,528,198

• LIFE INSURANCE IN FORCE ($000 omitted)

Year	Whole Life	Term	Credit	Group	Industrial	Total
2007	986,235	21,004,451	...	555,180	...	22,545,866
2008	969,089	22,946,793	...	564,158	...	24,480,040
2009	971,001	24,543,154	...	584,760	...	26,098,915

ANNUITY INVESTORS LIFE INS CO

P.O. Box 5423
Cincinnati, Ohio 45201-5423
Tel: 513-357-3300

AMB#: 009088
Began Business: 12/21/1981
Agency Off: Charles R. Schepер

Best's Financial Strength Rating: A g **FSC:** XI

• NET PREMIUMS AND DEPOSITS ($000 omitted)

Year	Individual Life	Individual & Group Annuities	Group Life & A&H	Credit Life & A&H	Individual A&H	Total
2007	…	319,271	…	…	…	319,271
2008	…	418,514	…	…	…	418,514
2009	…	422,449	…	…	…	422,449

• NET OPERATING GAIN ($000 omitted)

Year	Individual Life	Individual & Group Annuities	Group Life & A&H	Credit Life & A&H	Individual A&H	Total
2007	…	290	…	…	…	290
2008	…	-3,031	…	…	…	-3,031
2009	…	11,632	…	…	…	11,632

• COMPARATIVE FINANCIALS ($000 omitted)

Year	Assets	Capital & Surplus	Net Invest Income	Benefits Paid	Realized Cap Gains	Policyholder Dividends	Contract Lns (% of assets)
2007	1,739,485	65,936	55,485	251,574	-1,492	…	2.2
2008	1,746,239	82,408	65,278	224,224	-18,828	…	2.9
2009	2,167,233	129,596	81,173	190,443	-14,626	…	2.5

• ORDINARY LIFE STATISTICS

Year	Av. Ord. Policy Issued ($)	Av. Ord. Policy In Force ($)	Avg. Prem ($/M)	1st Yr Prem/ Total Prem	Ord. Lapse Ratio
2007	…	…	…	…	…
2008	…	…	…	…	…
2009	…	…	…	…	…

• NEW LIFE BUSINESS ISSUED ($000 omitted)

Year	Whole Life	Term	Credit	Group	Industrial	Total
2007	…	…	…	…	…	…
2008	…	…	…	…	…	…
2009	…	…	…	…	…	…

• LIFE INSURANCE IN FORCE ($000 omitted)

Year	Whole Life	Term	Credit	Group	Industrial	Total
2007	…	…	…	…	…	…
2008	…	…	…	…	…	…
2009	…	…	…	…	…	…

ANTHEM LIFE INSURANCE COMPANY

PO Box 182361
Columbus, Ohio 43218
Tel: 614-433-8800

AMB#: 006126
Began Business: 06/07/1956
Agency Off: John M. Murphy

Best's Financial Strength Rating: A g **FSC:** VII

• NET PREMIUMS AND DEPOSITS ($000 omitted)

Year	Individual Life	Individual & Group Annuities	Group Life & A&H	Credit Life & A&H	Individual A&H	Total
2007	1,152	45,570	158,967	…	352	206,041
2008	1,767	52,453	171,380	…	120	225,719
2009	2,030	34,706	163,023	…	7	199,766

• NET OPERATING GAIN ($000 omitted)

Year	Individual Life	Individual & Group Annuities	Group Life & A&H	Credit Life & A&H	Individual A&H	Total
2007	-395	441	21,978	…	-94	21,929
2008	-378	301	24,841	…	2,651	27,415
2009	-168	849	19,317	…	-4	19,994

• COMPARATIVE FINANCIALS ($000 omitted)

Year	Assets	Capital & Surplus	Net Invest Income	Benefits Paid	Realized Cap Gains	Policyholder Dividends	Contract Lns (% of assets)
2007	276,394	64,145	13,654	91,882	-1,525	…	0.1
2008	288,278	65,434	14,151	101,393	-3,645	…	0.1
2009	285,246	60,796	14,044	96,690	-1,699	…	0.1

• ORDINARY LIFE STATISTICS

Year	Av. Ord. Policy Issued ($)	Av. Ord. Policy In Force ($)	Avg. Prem ($/M)	1st Yr Prem/ Total Prem	Ord. Lapse Ratio
2007	…	…	…	…	…
2008	…	…	…	…	…
2009	…	…	…	…	…

• NEW LIFE BUSINESS ISSUED ($000 omitted)

Year	Whole Life	Term	Credit	Group	Industrial	Total
2007	4,495	248,645	…	13,182,332	…	13,435,472
2008	4,479	175,860	…	5,625,542	…	5,805,881
2009	3,149	186,540	…	6,118,257	…	6,307,946

• LIFE INSURANCE IN FORCE ($000 omitted)

Year	Whole Life	Term	Credit	Group	Industrial	Total
2007	81,998	269,724	…	44,309,499	…	44,661,221
2008	77,538	325,569	…	44,525,974	…	44,929,081
2009	71,519	373,717	…	44,324,201	…	44,769,437

ANTHEM LF & DISABILITY INS CO

One Liberty Plaza, 1665 Broadway
New York, New York 10006
Tel: 212-476-6666

AMB#: 060687
Began Business: 01/01/2009
Agency Off: None

Best's Financial Strength Rating: A g **FSC:** VII

• NET PREMIUMS AND DEPOSITS ($000 omitted)

Year	Individual Life	Individual & Group Annuities	Group Life & A&H	Credit Life & A&H	Individual A&H	Total
2007	…	…	…	…	…	…
2008	…	…	…	…	…	…
2009	…	…	107	…	…	107

• NET OPERATING GAIN ($000 omitted)

Year	Individual Life	Individual & Group Annuities	Group Life & A&H	Credit Life & A&H	Individual A&H	Total
2007	…	…	…	…	…	…
2008	…	…	…	…	…	…
2009	…	…	229	…	…	229

• COMPARATIVE FINANCIALS ($000 omitted)

Year	Assets	Capital & Surplus	Net Invest Income	Benefits Paid	Realized Cap Gains	Policyholder Dividends	Contract Lns (% of assets)
2007	…	…	…	…	…	…	…
2008	…	…	…	…	…	…	…
2009	18,582	18,344	233	41	…	…	…

• ORDINARY LIFE STATISTICS

Year	Av. Ord. Policy Issued ($)	Av. Ord. Policy In Force ($)	Avg. Prem ($/M)	1st Yr Prem/ Total Prem	Ord. Lapse Ratio
2007	…	…	…	…	…
2008	…	…	…	…	…
2009	…	…	…	…	…

• NEW LIFE BUSINESS ISSUED ($000 omitted)

Year	Whole Life	Term	Credit	Group	Industrial	Total
2007	…	…	…	…	…	…
2008	…	…	…	…	…	…
2009	…	…	…	132,477	…	132,477

• LIFE INSURANCE IN FORCE ($000 omitted)

Year	Whole Life	Term	Credit	Group	Industrial	Total
2007	…	…	…	…	…	…
2008	…	…	…	…	…	…
2009	…	…	…	132,452	…	132,452

ASSURITY LIFE INS CO

P.O. Box 82533
Lincoln, Nebraska 68501-2533
Tel: 402-476-6500

AMB#: 007374
Began Business: 03/20/1964
Agency Off: Todd Reimers

Best's Financial Strength Rating: A- **FSC:** IX

• NET PREMIUMS AND DEPOSITS ($000 omitted)

Year	Individual Life	Individual & Group Annuities	Group Life & A&H	Credit Life & A&H	Individual A&H	Total
2007	114,087	29,065	29,326	…	71,207	243,685
2008	113,358	24,824	32,692	…	68,917	239,790
2009	132,580	47,029	30,074	…	66,521	276,204

• NET OPERATING GAIN ($000 omitted)

Year	Individual Life	Individual & Group Annuities	Group Life & A&H	Credit Life & A&H	Individual A&H	Total
2007	656	10,181	3,657	…	-1,322	13,172
2008	3,792	5,670	4,190	…	4,988	18,640
2009	2,635	3,372	2,691	…	-3,287	5,412

• COMPARATIVE FINANCIALS ($000 omitted)

Year	Assets	Capital & Surplus	Net Invest Income	Benefits Paid	Realized Cap Gains	Policyholder Dividends	Contract Lns (% of assets)
2007	2,189,168	245,521	122,264	206,442	1,465	24,398	4.6
2008	2,161,105	223,151	121,300	204,943	-16,693	24,875	4.7
2009	2,237,619	248,678	119,873	208,078	-11,254	24,345	4.7

• ORDINARY LIFE STATISTICS

Year	Av. Ord. Policy Issued ($)	Av. Ord. Policy In Force ($)	Avg. Prem ($/M)	1st Yr Prem/ Total Prem	Ord. Lapse Ratio
2007	40,093	41,218	15.43	7.3	9.7
2008	70,717	41,414	15.80	6.8	16.8
2009	86,103	45,699	15.33	10.5	4.0

• NEW LIFE BUSINESS ISSUED ($000 omitted)

Year	Whole Life	Term	Credit	Group	Industrial	Total
2007	350,267	506,766	…	49,484	…	906,517
2008	353,686	926,296	…	17,935	…	1,297,917
2009	232,056	1,428,433	…	4,737	…	1,665,227

• LIFE INSURANCE IN FORCE ($000 omitted)

Year	Whole Life	Term	Credit	Group	Industrial	Total
2007	5,760,312	2,654,195	…	2,560,046	…	10,974,553
2008	4,163,766	3,942,954	…	2,377,662	…	10,484,382
2009	6,207,032	2,659,253	…	2,056,452	…	10,922,738

ATLANTA LIFE INS CO

100 Auburn Avenue, N.E.
Atlanta, Georgia 30303-2599
Tel: 404-659-2100

AMB#: 006130
Began Business: 11/08/1916
Agency Off: Leonard Grimes

Best's Financial Strength Rating: C+ **FSC:** V

• NET PREMIUMS AND DEPOSITS ($000 omitted)

Year	Individual Life	Individual & Group Annuities	Group Life & A&H	Credit Life & A&H	Individual A&H	Total
2007	752	89	51,988	...	...	52,830
2008	615	53	61,840	...	...	62,508
2009	347	11	57,684	...	...	58,042

• NET OPERATING GAIN ($000 omitted)

Year	Individual Life	Individual & Group Annuities	Group Life & A&H	Credit Life & A&H	Individual A&H	Total
2007	-2,777	158	2,912	...	...	293
2008	-2,436	1,883	224	...	...	-330
2009	-2,017	554	-1,141	...	...	-2,604

• COMPARATIVE FINANCIALS ($000 omitted)

Year	Assets	Capital & Surplus	Net Invest Income	Benefits Paid	Realized Cap Gains	Policyholder Dividends	Contract Lns (% of assets)
2007	75,639	19,375	623	44,064	258	...	0.1
2008	75,434	17,341	259	54,781	-365	...	0.1
2009	74,928	11,152	-334	56,054	-238	...	0.1

• ORDINARY LIFE STATISTICS

Year	Av. Ord. Policy Issued ($)	Av. Ord. Policy In Force ($)	Avg. Prem ($/M)	1st Yr Prem/ Total Prem	Ord. Lapse Ratio
2007	...	...	...	...	...
2008	...	...	...	...	...
2009	...	...	...	...	...

• NEW LIFE BUSINESS ISSUED ($000 omitted)

Year	Whole Life	Term	Credit	Group	Industrial	Total
2007	1,817	...	...	1,225,629	...	1,227,446
2008	1,125	...	...	...	...	1,125
2009	...	...	...	...	...	...

• LIFE INSURANCE IN FORCE ($000 omitted)

Year	Whole Life	Term	Credit	Group	Industrial	Total
2007	128,592	134,871	...	20,828,844	97,278	21,189,585
2008	125,675	121,057	...	20,775,864	92,610	21,115,206
2009	109,849	118,829	...	18,220,291	87,614	18,536,583

ATLANTIC SOUTHERN INS CO

P.O. Box 362889
San Juan, Puerto Rico 00936-2889
Tel: 787-767-9750

AMB#: 006135
Began Business: 01/31/1947
Agency Off: Angel M. Rivera-Bretana

Best's Financial Strength Rating: C++ **FSC:** IV

• NET PREMIUMS AND DEPOSITS ($000 omitted)

Year	Individual Life	Individual & Group Annuities	Group Life & A&H	Credit Life & A&H	Individual A&H	Total
2007	828	189	4,605	683	4,645	10,951
2008	1,150	224	4,740	479	5,078	11,672
2009	1,431	97	4,875	188	5,567	12,159

• NET OPERATING GAIN ($000 omitted)

Year	Individual Life	Individual & Group Annuities	Group Life & A&H	Credit Life & A&H	Individual A&H	Total
2007	377	-2	154	292	-608	211
2008	512	49	-127	390	-360	463
2009	443	23	222	202	-419	523

• COMPARATIVE FINANCIALS ($000 omitted)

Year	Assets	Capital & Surplus	Net Invest Income	Benefits Paid	Realized Cap Gains	Policyholder Dividends	Contract Lns (% of assets)
2007	18,133	8,207	692	6,789	-79	72	0.5
2008	18,502	8,530	808	7,170	-154	67	0.6
2009	19,311	8,729	979	7,925	-122	66	0.7

• ORDINARY LIFE STATISTICS

Year	Av. Ord. Policy Issued ($)	Av. Ord. Policy In Force ($)	Avg. Prem ($/M)	1st Yr Prem/ Total Prem	Ord. Lapse Ratio
2007	...	...	...	...	...
2008	...	...	...	...	...
2009	...	...	...	...	...

• NEW LIFE BUSINESS ISSUED ($000 omitted)

Year	Whole Life	Term	Credit	Group	Industrial	Total
2007	18,678	...	13,569	717	...	32,964
2008	23,528	3,399	8,727	700	...	36,354
2009	21,126	2,143	3,638	130	...	27,037

• LIFE INSURANCE IN FORCE ($000 omitted)

Year	Whole Life	Term	Credit	Group	Industrial	Total
2007	106,908	...	30,073	47,925	796	185,702
2008	102,902	4,579	30,013	42,768	657	180,919
2009	99,449	4,827	23,028	40,008	621	167,934

ATLANTIC COAST LIFE INS CO

P.O. Box 20010
Charleston, South Carolina 29413-0010
Tel: 843-763-8680

AMB#: 006132
Began Business: 03/01/1925
Agency Off: None

Best's Financial Strength Rating: B+ **FSC:** V

• NET PREMIUMS AND DEPOSITS ($000 omitted)

Year	Individual Life	Individual & Group Annuities	Group Life & A&H	Credit Life & A&H	Individual A&H	Total
2007	7,620	509	...	...	301	8,431
2008	9,080	511	229	...	271	10,090
2009	11,456	1,046	1,396	...	238	14,135

• NET OPERATING GAIN ($000 omitted)

Year	Individual Life	Individual & Group Annuities	Group Life & A&H	Credit Life & A&H	Individual A&H	Total
2007	155	-9	0	...	15	162
2008	356	-77	-78	...	34	236
2009	-78	2	-97	...	13	-159

• COMPARATIVE FINANCIALS ($000 omitted)

Year	Assets	Capital & Surplus	Net Invest Income	Benefits Paid	Realized Cap Gains	Policyholder Dividends	Contract Lns (% of assets)
2007	67,521	15,712	3,603	3,794	49	...	2.1
2008	69,018	14,075	3,483	4,242	583	...	2.0
2009	75,505	13,755	3,495	5,531	674	...	1.8

• ORDINARY LIFE STATISTICS

Year	Av. Ord. Policy Issued ($)	Av. Ord. Policy In Force ($)	Avg. Prem ($/M)	1st Yr Prem/ Total Prem	Ord. Lapse Ratio
2007	10,702	6,054	44.11	14.7	13.3
2008	9,189	6,203	50.46	13.0	8.9
2009	8,310	6,112	63.57	12.7	13.0

• NEW LIFE BUSINESS ISSUED ($000 omitted)

Year	Whole Life	Term	Credit	Group	Industrial	Total
2007	27,806	951	...	...	...	28,757
2008	26,750	1,138	...	240	...	28,128
2009	30,396	1,297	...	1,838	...	33,530

• LIFE INSURANCE IN FORCE ($000 omitted)

Year	Whole Life	Term	Credit	Group	Industrial	Total
2007	143,135	29,627	...	20	24,531	197,313
2008	150,587	29,115	...	258	23,579	203,539
2009	152,935	27,388	...	1,921	22,677	204,922

AUTO CLUB LIFE INSURANCE CO

17900 N. Laurel Park Drive
Livonia, Michigan 48152
Tel: 734-779-2600

AMB#: 008525
Began Business: 08/05/1974
Agency Off: Gary S. Dick

Best's Financial Strength Rating: A- g **FSC:** VII

• NET PREMIUMS AND DEPOSITS ($000 omitted)

Year	Individual Life	Individual & Group Annuities	Group Life & A&H	Credit Life & A&H	Individual A&H	Total
2007	24,527	10,009	10,125	...	1,161	45,822
2008	25,655	17,599	10,937	...	1,092	55,282
2009	26,846	25,039	11,284	...	1,160	64,329

• NET OPERATING GAIN ($000 omitted)

Year	Individual Life	Individual & Group Annuities	Group Life & A&H	Credit Life & A&H	Individual A&H	Total
2007	204	2,219	1,624	...	286	4,333
2008	-103	-182	-785	...	-37	-1,107
2009	1,899	2,633	98	...	232	4,862

• COMPARATIVE FINANCIALS ($000 omitted)

Year	Assets	Capital & Surplus	Net Invest Income	Benefits Paid	Realized Cap Gains	Policyholder Dividends	Contract Lns (% of assets)
2007	430,009	58,039	22,025	47,645	-64	...	1.7
2008	423,260	48,803	21,394	45,134	-2,441	...	1.8
2009	450,264	62,962	22,133	45,405	-252	...	1.8

• ORDINARY LIFE STATISTICS

Year	Av. Ord. Policy Issued ($)	Av. Ord. Policy In Force ($)	Avg. Prem ($/M)	1st Yr Prem/ Total Prem	Ord. Lapse Ratio
2007	...	66,478	5.58	0.0	9.3
2008	...	67,404	5.55	0.0	8.8
2009	...	63,593	6.01	0.0	8.7

• NEW LIFE BUSINESS ISSUED ($000 omitted)

Year	Whole Life	Term	Credit	Group	Industrial	Total
2007	...	...	...	...	...	...
2008	...	...	...	...	...	...
2009	...	...	...	...	...	...

• LIFE INSURANCE IN FORCE ($000 omitted)

Year	Whole Life	Term	Credit	Group	Industrial	Total
2007	1,572,290	3,733,285	...	1,243,280	...	6,548,855
2008	1,540,646	3,931,435	...	1,424,450	...	6,896,531
2009	1,459,222	3,715,943	...	1,544,798	...	6,719,964

AUTO-OWNERS LIFE INS CO

P.O. Box 30660
Lansing, Michigan 48909-8160
Tel: 517-323-1200

AMB#: 006140
Began Business: 01/01/1966
Agency Off: Jeffrey F. Harrold

Best's Financial Strength Rating: A+ **FSC:** IX

• NET PREMIUMS AND DEPOSITS ($000 omitted)

Year	Individual Life	Individual & Group Annuities	Group Life & A&H	Credit Life & A&H	Individual A&H	Total
2007	69,961	142,777	2,654	...	11,264	226,657
2008	75,003	150,303	3,564	...	11,878	240,749
2009	80,187	188,359	3,162	...	11,768	283,475

• NET OPERATING GAIN ($000 omitted)

Year	Individual Life	Individual & Group Annuities	Group Life & A&H	Credit Life & A&H	Individual A&H	Total
2007	6,783	8,154	1,449	...	3,026	19,413
2008	3,632	6,431	341	...	2,572	16,759
2009	5,434	1,473	672	...	1,640	13,203

• COMPARATIVE FINANCIALS ($000 omitted)

Year	Assets	Capital & Surplus	Net Invest Income	Benefits Paid	Realized Cap Gains	Policyholder Dividends	Contract Lns (% of assets)
2007	2,009,921	224,668	105,105	116,211	752	...	0.5
2008	2,110,939	229,577	111,271	129,212	-3,315	...	0.5
2009	2,338,753	240,547	112,008	307,966	-4,015	...	0.4

• ORDINARY LIFE STATISTICS

Year	Av. Ord. Policy Issued ($)	Av. Ord. Policy In Force ($)	Avg. Prem ($/M)	1st Yr Prem/ Total Prem	Ord. Lapse Ratio
2007	103,015	89,908	3.54	15.7	6.4
2008	98,421	92,129	3.45	14.3	6.2
2009	106,676	94,977	3.36	14.4	6.3

• NEW LIFE BUSINESS ISSUED ($000 omitted)

Year	Whole Life	Term	Credit	Group	Industrial	Total
2007	328,872	3,177,967	...	1,031	...	3,507,870
2008	345,715	3,251,661	...	215	...	3,597,591
2009	428,303	3,398,929	...	...	...	3,827,232

• LIFE INSURANCE IN FORCE ($000 omitted)

Year	Whole Life	Term	Credit	Group	Industrial	Total
2007	3,139,355	17,067,725	...	476,461	...	20,683,541
2008	3,302,320	18,979,663	...	495,494	...	22,777,477
2009	3,518,071	20,910,650	...	516,734	...	24,945,454

AUTOMOBILE CLUB OF STHRN CA LF

17900 N. Laurel Park Drive
Livonia, Michigan 48152
Tel: 714-850-5111

AMB#: 060325
Began Business: 12/22/1999
Agency Off: None

Best's Financial Strength Rating: A- g **FSC:** VII

• NET PREMIUMS AND DEPOSITS ($000 omitted)

Year	Individual Life	Individual & Group Annuities	Group Life & A&H	Credit Life & A&H	Individual A&H	Total
2007	23,562	32,142	13,742	...	410	69,855
2008	28,207	70,389	15,862	...	586	115,044
2009	33,783	91,804	19,170	...	817	145,573

• NET OPERATING GAIN ($000 omitted)

Year	Individual Life	Individual & Group Annuities	Group Life & A&H	Credit Life & A&H	Individual A&H	Total
2007	-10,706	2,702	3,591	...	-53	-4,466
2008	-11,448	1,816	-34	...	-1	-9,666
2009	-5,787	4,830	-1,571	...	39	-2,489

• COMPARATIVE FINANCIALS ($000 omitted)

Year	Assets	Capital & Surplus	Net Invest Income	Benefits Paid	Realized Cap Gains	Policyholder Dividends	Contract Lns (% of assets)
2007	349,410	32,200	16,786	51,194	-302	...	0.2
2008	410,669	37,560	18,641	56,762	-3,850	...	0.2
2009	501,153	48,163	23,308	55,155	-595	...	0.3

• ORDINARY LIFE STATISTICS

Year	Av. Ord. Policy Issued ($)	Av. Ord. Policy In Force ($)	Avg. Prem ($/M)	1st Yr Prem/ Total Prem	Ord. Lapse Ratio
2007	...	90,770	4.82	...	9.7
2008	...	91,994	4.98	...	8.8
2009	...	81,131	6.08	...	8.7

• NEW LIFE BUSINESS ISSUED ($000 omitted)

Year	Whole Life	Term	Credit	Group	Industrial	Total
2007	...	...	...	...	...	...
2008	...	...	...	...	...	...
2009	...	...	...	...	...	...

• LIFE INSURANCE IN FORCE ($000 omitted)

Year	Whole Life	Term	Credit	Group	Industrial	Total
2007	1,195,090	3,694,600	...	2,548,353	...	7,438,043
2008	1,286,274	4,372,356	...	3,193,744	...	8,852,374
2009	1,226,443	4,330,653	...	3,954,657	...	9,511,752

AVIVA LIFE AND ANNUITY COMPANY

P.O. Box 1555, Mailstop H73
Des Moines, Iowa 50306-1555
Tel: 800-800-9882

AMB#: 006199
Began Business: 02/20/1896
Agency Off: Mark V. Heitz

Best's Financial Strength Rating: A g **FSC:** XV

• NET PREMIUMS AND DEPOSITS ($000 omitted)

Year	Individual Life	Individual & Group Annuities	Group Life & A&H	Credit Life & A&H	Individual A&H	Total
2007	438,220	5,301,715	3,806	...	938	5,744,679
2008	629,899	8,321,401	3,010	...	1,688	8,955,998
2009	727,653	-793,878	2,586	...	901	-62,738

• NET OPERATING GAIN ($000 omitted)

Year	Individual Life	Individual & Group Annuities	Group Life & A&H	Credit Life & A&H	Individual A&H	Total
2007	-7,177	-7,032	-151	...	1,044	55,649
2008	12,994	-179,978	-23,271	...	1,362	-130,842
2009	-150,339	194,967	18,705	...	137	169,081

• COMPARATIVE FINANCIALS ($000 omitted)

Year	Assets	Capital & Surplus	Net Invest Income	Benefits Paid	Realized Cap Gains	Policyholder Dividends	Contract Lns (% of assets)
2007	32,533,890	1,780,634	1,543,996	2,893,634	31,511	65,557	2.0
2008	39,019,896	2,196,563	1,106,650	3,044,038	-380,218	65,742	1.7
2009	41,990,392	2,282,876	1,764,702	4,000,594	-264,949	43,319	1.6

• ORDINARY LIFE STATISTICS

Year	Av. Ord. Policy Issued ($)	Av. Ord. Policy In Force ($)	Avg. Prem ($/M)	1st Yr Prem/ Total Prem	Ord. Lapse Ratio
2007	332,052	152,719	11.54	40.4	7.0
2008	317,840	158,411	10.80	34.3	7.8
2009	375,701	167,073	10.15	30.6	8.9

• NEW LIFE BUSINESS ISSUED ($000 omitted)

Year	Whole Life	Term	Credit	Group	Industrial	Total
2007	7,444,090	2,563,947	...	27,000	...	10,035,037
2008	7,229,277	2,318,640	...	15,328	...	9,563,245
2009	7,949,441	4,919,460	...	17,435	...	12,886,336

• LIFE INSURANCE IN FORCE ($000 omitted)

Year	Whole Life	Term	Credit	Group	Industrial	Total
2007	51,840,100	38,651,697	...	813,857	...	91,305,654
2008	55,254,617	36,479,455	...	651,754	...	92,385,826
2009	57,388,046	37,621,436	...	571,351	...	95,580,833

AVIVA LIFE & ANNUITY CO OF NY

P.O. Box 1555, Mailstop H73
Des Moines, Iowa 50306-1555
Tel: 800-252-4467

AMB#: 006467
Began Business: 11/25/1958
Agency Off: Mark V. Heitz

Best's Financial Strength Rating: A g **FSC:** XV

• NET PREMIUMS AND DEPOSITS ($000 omitted)

Year	Individual Life	Individual & Group Annuities	Group Life & A&H	Credit Life & A&H	Individual A&H	Total
2007	33,962	162,094	4,407	...	229	200,693
2008	69,732	94,964	4,173	...	209	169,077
2009	79,641	33,589	3,831	...	256	117,317

• NET OPERATING GAIN ($000 omitted)

Year	Individual Life	Individual & Group Annuities	Group Life & A&H	Credit Life & A&H	Individual A&H	Total
2007	10,467	-24,198	-13,343	...	-1,651	-17,472
2008	5,035	-4,589	-960	...	-24	-538
2009	-3,210	-3,376	-3,367	...	-559	-10,512

• COMPARATIVE FINANCIALS ($000 omitted)

Year	Assets	Capital & Surplus	Net Invest Income	Benefits Paid	Realized Cap Gains	Policyholder Dividends	Contract Lns (% of assets)
2007	1,335,950	90,425	72,997	141,856	-914	808	1.8
2008	1,394,307	80,410	72,574	111,462	-22,336	622	1.8
2009	1,474,773	98,156	77,688	98,668	-8,323	614	1.8

• ORDINARY LIFE STATISTICS

Year	Av. Ord. Policy Issued ($)	Av. Ord. Policy In Force ($)	Avg. Prem ($/M)	1st Yr Prem/ Total Prem	Ord. Lapse Ratio
2007	257,235	243,772	5.99	36.3	4.7
2008	411,857	250,217	5.48	25.5	4.7
2009	541,329	259,909	5.39	22.2	5.4

• NEW LIFE BUSINESS ISSUED ($000 omitted)

Year	Whole Life	Term	Credit	Group	Industrial	Total
2007	771,531	274,131	...	...	...	1,045,662
2008	672,054	246,388	...	...	...	918,442
2009	688,998	896,555	...	...	...	1,585,553

• LIFE INSURANCE IN FORCE ($000 omitted)

Year	Whole Life	Term	Credit	Group	Industrial	Total
2007	7,079,730	17,636,844	...	847,975	...	25,564,549
2008	7,299,172	17,039,186	...	761,091	...	25,099,449
2009	7,590,822	16,880,629	...	749,322	...	25,220,773

AXA CORPORATE SOLUTIONS LF RE

1290 Avenue of the Americas, 12th Floor
New York, New York 10104
Tel: 212-314-4168

AMB#: 009083
Began Business: 01/05/1983
Agency Off: None

Best's Financial Strength Rating: B++ **FSC:** IX

• NET PREMIUMS AND DEPOSITS ($000 omitted)

Year	Individual Life	Individual & Group Annuities	Group Life & A&H	Credit Life & A&H	Individual A&H	Total
2007	5,702	96,283	-64	...	...	101,921
2008	5,121	93,691	-102	...	...	98,711
2009	2,063	86,186	4	-3	...	88,251

• NET OPERATING GAIN ($000 omitted)

Year	Individual Life	Individual & Group Annuities	Group Life & A&H	Credit Life & A&H	Individual A&H	Total
2007	-10,685	33,667	2,528	...	...	25,509
2008	1,306	-755,524	687	...	...	-753,530
2009	-3,177	266,359	-306	-3	...	262,874

• COMPARATIVE FINANCIALS ($000 omitted)

Year	Assets	Capital & Surplus	Net Invest Income	Benefits Paid	Realized Cap Gains	Policyholder Dividends	Contract Lns (% of assets)
2007	817,071	487,875	32,341	61,786	-5,671	...	...
2008	1,540,933	254,539	33,089	104,157	234,896	...	...
2009	1,433,393	401,438	25,681	142,433	-271,180	...	...

• ORDINARY LIFE STATISTICS

Year	Av. Ord. Policy Issued ($)	Av. Ord. Policy In Force ($)	Avg. Prem ($/M)	1st Yr Prem/ Total Prem	Ord. Lapse Ratio
2007	...	...	...	...	...
2008	...	...	...	...	...
2009	...	...	...	...	...

• NEW LIFE BUSINESS ISSUED ($000 omitted)

Year	Whole Life	Term	Credit	Group	Industrial	Total
2007	...	...	...	...	...	...
2008	...	...	...	...	...	...
2009	...	...	...	...	...	...

• LIFE INSURANCE IN FORCE ($000 omitted)

Year	Whole Life	Term	Credit	Group	Industrial	Total
2007	...	4,741,247	...	...	...	4,741,247
2008	...	4,441,920	...	...	...	4,441,920
2009	...	4,071,210	...	277	...	4,071,487

AXA EQUITABLE LIFE INS CO

1290 Avenue of the Americas, 16th Floor
New York, New York 10104
Tel: 212-554-1234

AMB#: 006341
Began Business: 07/28/1859
Agency Off: Robert S. Jones, Jr.

Best's Financial Strength Rating: A+ g **FSC:** XV

• NET PREMIUMS AND DEPOSITS ($000 omitted)

Year	Individual Life	Individual & Group Annuities	Group Life & A&H	Credit Life & A&H	Individual A&H	Total
2007	2,591,586	16,925,882	...	...	61,476	19,578,800
2008	2,362,836	12,396,576	...	...	59,454	14,818,692
2009	2,280,328	8,132,592	...	...	52,893	10,465,809

• NET OPERATING GAIN ($000 omitted)

Year	Individual Life	Individual & Group Annuities	Group Life & A&H	Credit Life & A&H	Individual A&H	Total
2007	184,862	727,064	116	...	-295,575	641,776
2008	26,733	-2,707,878	-133	...	-112,235	-2,763,000
2009	707,473	1,784,269	33	...	-80,593	2,420,956

• COMPARATIVE FINANCIALS ($000 omitted)

Year	Assets	Capital & Surplus	Net Invest Income	Benefits Paid	Realized Cap Gains	Policyholder Dividends	Contract Lns (% of assets)
2007	142,433,163	6,569,263	2,820,951	13,511,866	-43,198	338,600	2.6
2008	111,795,878	3,155,026	2,627,133	11,500,143	1,688,216	349,137	3.3
2009	126,783,596	3,115,942	2,055,266	9,514,211	-638,054	346,261	2.8

• ORDINARY LIFE STATISTICS

Year	Av. Ord. Policy Issued ($)	Av. Ord. Policy In Force ($)	Avg. Prem ($/M)	1st Yr Prem/ Total Prem	Ord. Lapse Ratio
2007	937,273	52,314	8.23	29.3	4.0
2008	871,751	61,771	7.33	20.2	6.7
2009	903,305	63,992	6.70	16.1	5.6

• NEW LIFE BUSINESS ISSUED ($000 omitted)

Year	Whole Life	Term	Credit	Group	Industrial	Total
2007	17,968,971	17,885,454	...	...	...	35,854,425
2008	13,931,913	25,478,187	...	...	...	39,410,100
2009	10,368,663	35,829,956	...	...	...	46,198,619

• LIFE INSURANCE IN FORCE ($000 omitted)

Year	Whole Life	Term	Credit	Group	Industrial	Total
2007	213,880,005	138,203,243	...	1,421,120	...	353,504,368
2008	212,378,311	156,500,916	...	1,203,761	...	370,082,988
2009	211,720,655	181,253,692	...	1,022,573	...	393,996,920

AXA EQUITABLE LIFE & ANNUITY

10840 Ballantyne Commons Parkway
Charlotte, North Carolina 28277
Tel: 212-554-1234

AMB#: 009516
Began Business: 06/01/1984
Agency Off: None

Best's Financial Strength Rating: A **FSC:** VII

• NET PREMIUMS AND DEPOSITS ($000 omitted)

Year	Individual Life	Individual & Group Annuities	Group Life & A&H	Credit Life & A&H	Individual A&H	Total
2007	10,520	...	...	...	...	10,520
2008	7,830	...	...	...	...	7,830
2009	4,630	...	...	...	...	4,630

• NET OPERATING GAIN ($000 omitted)

Year	Individual Life	Individual & Group Annuities	Group Life & A&H	Credit Life & A&H	Individual A&H	Total
2007	7,247	-2	...	...	...	7,245
2008	9,744	...	...	...	...	9,744
2009	4,979	...	...	...	...	4,979

• COMPARATIVE FINANCIALS ($000 omitted)

Year	Assets	Capital & Surplus	Net Invest Income	Benefits Paid	Realized Cap Gains	Policyholder Dividends	Contract Lns (% of assets)
2007	554,701	105,245	31,152	22,880	...	...	44.4
2008	512,844	48,771	30,271	29,553	-1,105	...	47.6
2009	517,713	55,487	28,691	28,714	463	...	51.5

• ORDINARY LIFE STATISTICS

Year	Av. Ord. Policy Issued ($)	Av. Ord. Policy In Force ($)	Avg. Prem ($/M)	1st Yr Prem/ Total Prem	Ord. Lapse Ratio
2007	...	...	...	...	...
2008	...	...	...	...	...
2009	...	...	...	...	...

• NEW LIFE BUSINESS ISSUED ($000 omitted)

Year	Whole Life	Term	Credit	Group	Industrial	Total
2007	...	...	...	...	...	...
2008	...	2,300	...	...	...	2,300
2009	...	4,200	...	...	...	4,200

• LIFE INSURANCE IN FORCE ($000 omitted)

Year	Whole Life	Term	Credit	Group	Industrial	Total
2007	2,458,029	6,142,329	...	...	...	8,600,358
2008	2,430,343	5,167,209	...	...	...	7,597,552
2009	2,455,476	4,470,890	...	...	...	6,926,366

BALBOA LIFE INSURANCE COMPANY

3349 Michelson Drive, Suite 200
Irvine, California 92612-1627
Tel: 949-222-8000

AMB#: 006965
Began Business: 01/02/1969
Agency Off: None

Best's Financial Strength Rating: A- g **FSC:** VI

• NET PREMIUMS AND DEPOSITS ($000 omitted)

Year	Individual Life	Individual & Group Annuities	Group Life & A&H	Credit Life & A&H	Individual A&H	Total
2007	1,256	...	6,992	7,271	2	15,522
2008	1,159	...	8,259	6,737	2	16,156
2009	1,056	...	8,050	4,459	1,212	14,778

• NET OPERATING GAIN ($000 omitted)

Year	Individual Life	Individual & Group Annuities	Group Life & A&H	Credit Life & A&H	Individual A&H	Total
2007	231	-268	2,941	2,485	-30	5,360
2008	98	-56	3,360	566	-10	3,958
2009	107	51	4,020	911	638	5,727

• COMPARATIVE FINANCIALS ($000 omitted)

Year	Assets	Capital & Surplus	Net Invest Income	Benefits Paid	Realized Cap Gains	Policyholder Dividends	Contract Lns (% of assets)
2007	41,329	27,888	1,115	4,439	0	...	...
2008	43,255	30,692	902	5,297	...	...	...
2009	48,100	37,077	879	4,012	-162	...	...

• ORDINARY LIFE STATISTICS

Year	Av. Ord. Policy Issued ($)	Av. Ord. Policy In Force ($)	Avg. Prem ($/M)	1st Yr Prem/ Total Prem	Ord. Lapse Ratio
2007	...	...	...	...	...
2008	...	...	...	...	...
2009	...	...	...	...	...

• NEW LIFE BUSINESS ISSUED ($000 omitted)

Year	Whole Life	Term	Credit	Group	Industrial	Total
2007	...	194,316	789	...	...	195,105
2008	...	59,323	748	...	...	60,071
2009	...	30,671	1,710	...	...	32,381

• LIFE INSURANCE IN FORCE ($000 omitted)

Year	Whole Life	Term	Credit	Group	Industrial	Total
2007	91,169	583,570	308,367	46,633	...	1,029,739
2008	86,063	493,964	237,317	38,812	...	856,156
2009	80,309	430,681	175,161	33,520	...	719,671

BALBOA LIFE INSURANCE CO OF NY

3349 Michelson Drive, Suite 200
Irvine, California 92612-1627
Tel: 949-222-8000

AMB#: 060347
Began Business: 01/01/2001
Agency Off: None

Best's Financial Strength Rating: A- g
FSC: VI

• **NET PREMIUMS AND DEPOSITS ($000 omitted)**

Year	Individual Life	Individual & Group Annuities	Group Life & A&H	Credit Life & A&H	Individual A&H	Total
2007	123	...	7	1,581	...	1,711
2008	124	...	42	1,536	...	1,702
2009	134	...	53	671	...	858

• **NET OPERATING GAIN ($000 omitted)**

Year	Individual Life	Individual & Group Annuities	Group Life & A&H	Credit Life & A&H	Individual A&H	Total
2007	31	...	5	660	...	696
2008	25	...	23	1,022	...	1,069
2009	190	...	77	1,144	...	1,411

• **COMPARATIVE FINANCIALS ($000 omitted)**

Year	Assets	Capital & Surplus	Net Invest Income	Benefits Paid	Realized Cap Gains	Policyholder Dividends	Contract Lns (% of assets)
2007	17,595	16,291	845	725	...	...	...
2008	18,088	17,318	691	266	...	...	...
2009	18,390	17,834	635	232	-172	...	...

• **ORDINARY LIFE STATISTICS**

Year	Av. Ord. Policy Issued ($)	Av. Ord. Policy In Force ($)	Avg. Prem ($/M)	1st Yr Prem/ Total Prem	Ord. Lapse Ratio
2007	...	...	...	...	...
2008	...	...	...	...	...
2009	...	...	...	...	...

• **NEW LIFE BUSINESS ISSUED ($000 omitted)**

Year	Whole Life	Term	Credit	Group	Industrial	Total
2007	...	34,020	197	...	...	34,217
2008	...	15,050	79	...	...	15,129
2009	...	19,100	37	...	...	19,137

• **LIFE INSURANCE IN FORCE ($000 omitted)**

Year	Whole Life	Term	Credit	Group	Industrial	Total
2007	...	63,197	56,403	...	...	119,600
2008	...	56,528	50,817	...	...	107,345
2009	...	61,695	40,079	...	...	101,774

BANKERS CONSECO LIFE INSURANCE

11825 N. Pennsylvania Street
Carmel, Indiana 46032
Tel: 317-817-6100

AMB#: 060002
Began Business: 07/13/1987
Agency Off: Steven M. Stecher

Best's Financial Strength Rating: B g
FSC: X

• **NET PREMIUMS AND DEPOSITS ($000 omitted)**

Year	Individual Life	Individual & Group Annuities	Group Life & A&H	Credit Life & A&H	Individual A&H	Total
2007	14,671	1,373	19	...	9,800	25,863
2008	15,711	3,394	13	...	10,094	29,212
2009	17,053	7,773	12	...	9,995	34,834

• **NET OPERATING GAIN ($000 omitted)**

Year	Individual Life	Individual & Group Annuities	Group Life & A&H	Credit Life & A&H	Individual A&H	Total
2007	1,567	15	8	...	-18,718	-16,614
2008	1,980	-54	8	...	4,594	7,853
2009	1,505	50	1	...	-5,828	-3,273

• **COMPARATIVE FINANCIALS ($000 omitted)**

Year	Assets	Capital & Surplus	Net Invest Income	Benefits Paid	Realized Cap Gains	Policyholder Dividends	Contract Lns (% of assets)
2007	241,205	21,389	11,853	20,724	-659	...	1.0
2008	254,306	27,818	13,810	21,858	-2,237	...	1.0
2009	277,107	24,984	14,585	23,592	-865	...	0.9

• **ORDINARY LIFE STATISTICS**

Year	Av. Ord. Policy Issued ($)	Av. Ord. Policy In Force ($)	Avg. Prem ($/M)	1st Yr Prem/ Total Prem	Ord. Lapse Ratio
2007	1,596	2,745	76.68	13.9	-2.7
2008	2,475	2,933	76.19	18.0	-1.6
2009	6,415	3,540	68.03	19.1	0.6

• **NEW LIFE BUSINESS ISSUED ($000 omitted)**

Year	Whole Life	Term	Credit	Group	Industrial	Total
2007	9,767	...	...	...	...	9,767
2008	20,339	...	...	...	...	20,339
2009	54,806	...	...	...	...	54,806

• **LIFE INSURANCE IN FORCE ($000 omitted)**

Year	Whole Life	Term	Credit	Group	Industrial	Total
2007	178,026	13,294	...	564	...	191,884
2008	192,013	14,207	...	427	...	206,647
2009	236,710	13,965	...	384	...	251,058

BALTIMORE LIFE INS CO

10075 Red Run Boulevard
Owings Mills, Maryland 21117-6050
Tel: 410-581-6600

AMB#: 006143
Began Business: 03/22/1882
Agency Off: John V. Fleming

Best's Financial Strength Rating: B++
FSC: VII

• **NET PREMIUMS AND DEPOSITS ($000 omitted)**

Year	Individual Life	Individual & Group Annuities	Group Life & A&H	Credit Life & A&H	Individual A&H	Total
2007	67,537	10,922	2,555	...	296	81,310
2008	74,636	12,389	13,482	...	286	100,794
2009	87,679	21,139	4,636	...	306	113,759

• **NET OPERATING GAIN ($000 omitted)**

Year	Individual Life	Individual & Group Annuities	Group Life & A&H	Credit Life & A&H	Individual A&H	Total
2007	2,868	3,252	-47	-296	-179	5,599
2008	2,889	2,461	1,299	-153	-251	6,244
2009	3,328	1,355	722	-55	-292	5,058

• **COMPARATIVE FINANCIALS ($000 omitted)**

Year	Assets	Capital & Surplus	Net Invest Income	Benefits Paid	Realized Cap Gains	Policyholder Dividends	Contract Lns (% of assets)
2007	810,287	72,389	48,546	84,231	2,867	12,016	2.5
2008	834,794	71,538	46,823	74,982	-5,135	13,386	2.5
2009	856,828	80,274	47,618	85,722	-3,724	14,455	2.7

• **ORDINARY LIFE STATISTICS**

Year	Av. Ord. Policy Issued ($)	Av. Ord. Policy In Force ($)	Avg. Prem ($/M)	1st Yr Prem/ Total Prem	Ord. Lapse Ratio
2007	44,166	27,781	12.18	10.0	6.4
2008	38,778	28,285	13.61	10.1	8.0
2009	31,619	26,024	17.46	6.9	16.6

• **NEW LIFE BUSINESS ISSUED ($000 omitted)**

Year	Whole Life	Term	Credit	Group	Industrial	Total
2007	282,080	184,134	53	17,640	...	483,907
2008	380,580	180,854	...	11,148	...	572,582
2009	180,311	165,194	...	3,482	...	348,987

• **LIFE INSURANCE IN FORCE ($000 omitted)**

Year	Whole Life	Term	Credit	Group	Industrial	Total
2007	3,783,691	1,390,781	20,161	1,083,898	40,368	6,318,899
2008	3,793,502	1,459,046	5,629	810,597	38,606	6,107,380
2009	3,175,577	1,431,929	1,794	896,540	36,930	5,542,770

BANKERS FIDELITY LIFE INS CO

P.O. Box 105185
Atlanta, Georgia 30348
Tel: 404-266-5600

AMB#: 006145
Began Business: 11/22/1955
Agency Off: Robert Hines

Best's Financial Strength Rating: B++
FSC: VI

• **NET PREMIUMS AND DEPOSITS ($000 omitted)**

Year	Individual Life	Individual & Group Annuities	Group Life & A&H	Credit Life & A&H	Individual A&H	Total
2007	10,209	300	747	...	44,668	55,924
2008	10,165	238	146	...	44,608	55,157
2009	10,396	220	457	...	46,089	57,162

• **NET OPERATING GAIN ($000 omitted)**

Year	Individual Life	Individual & Group Annuities	Group Life & A&H	Credit Life & A&H	Individual A&H	Total
2007	2,641	-84	45	...	1,448	4,049
2008	1,403	143	113	...	1,275	2,934
2009	1,341	102	-37	...	973	2,379

• **COMPARATIVE FINANCIALS ($000 omitted)**

Year	Assets	Capital & Surplus	Net Invest Income	Benefits Paid	Realized Cap Gains	Policyholder Dividends	Contract Lns (% of assets)
2007	119,805	33,810	6,180	36,607	7,912	...	1.6
2008	110,664	29,876	6,051	38,776	-1,665	...	1.8
2009	116,032	31,493	5,561	39,820	91	...	1.8

• **ORDINARY LIFE STATISTICS**

Year	Av. Ord. Policy Issued ($)	Av. Ord. Policy In Force ($)	Avg. Prem ($/M)	1st Yr Prem/ Total Prem	Ord. Lapse Ratio
2007	15,963	6,943	37.93	7.2	7.9
2008	14,528	7,272	36.60	11.4	9.5
2009	12,456	7,493	36.75	14.7	10.8

• **NEW LIFE BUSINESS ISSUED ($000 omitted)**

Year	Whole Life	Term	Credit	Group	Industrial	Total
2007	23,661	7,722	...	210	...	31,593
2008	38,605	5,125	...	255	...	43,985
2009	47,051	383	...	75	...	47,509

• **LIFE INSURANCE IN FORCE ($000 omitted)**

Year	Whole Life	Term	Credit	Group	Industrial	Total
2007	206,049	64,666	...	1,593	...	272,308
2008	219,894	59,392	...	1,623	...	280,909
2009	232,767	52,802	...	1,487	...	287,056

BANKERS LIFE AND CASUALTY CO

11825 N. Pennsylvania Street
Carmel, Indiana 46032
Tel: 312-396-6000

AMB#: 006149
Began Business: 01/17/1879
Agency Off: Scott Goldberg

Best's Financial Strength Rating: B g
FSC: X

• **NET PREMIUMS AND DEPOSITS ($000 omitted)**

Year	Individual Life	Individual & Group Annuities	Group Life & A&H	Credit Life & A&H	Individual A&H	Total
2007	209,385	940,744	80,204	...	1,459,292	2,689,625
2008	214,925	1,280,908	6,462	...	1,484,572	2,986,868
2009	229,413	1,141,704	38,165	...	1,300,841	2,710,123

• **NET OPERATING GAIN ($000 omitted)**

Year	Individual Life	Individual & Group Annuities	Group Life & A&H	Credit Life & A&H	Individual A&H	Total
2007	213	28,136	5,691	...	65,706	125,578
2008	1,848	17,807	2,454	...	38,756	80,226
2009	4,492	57,898	2,169	...	101,925	189,613

• **COMPARATIVE FINANCIALS ($000 omitted)**

Year	Assets	Capital & Surplus	Net Invest Income	Benefits Paid	Realized Cap Gains	Policyholder Dividends	Contract Lns (% of assets)
2007	10,612,763	685,899	574,492	1,970,002	-11,848	292	0.3
2008	11,442,369	607,131	552,180	2,091,521	-107,541	237	0.3
2009	12,318,840	730,238	686,270	1,891,398	-102,917	200	0.3

• **ORDINARY LIFE STATISTICS**

Year	Av. Ord. Policy Issued ($)	Av. Ord. Policy In Force ($)	Avg. Prem ($/M)	1st Yr Prem/ Total Prem	Ord. Lapse Ratio
2007	32,023	22,721	20.27	20.6	10.6
2008	28,482	22,893	19.92	19.2	12.7
2009	31,243	23,107	20.68	18.0	14.1

• **NEW LIFE BUSINESS ISSUED ($000 omitted)**

Year	Whole Life	Term	Credit	Group	Industrial	Total
2007	2,088,813	464,252	...	...	...	2,553,065
2008	1,925,681	438,685	...	...	...	2,364,366
2009	2,103,284	540,843	...	...	...	2,644,127

• **LIFE INSURANCE IN FORCE ($000 omitted)**

Year	Whole Life	Term	Credit	Group	Industrial	Total
2007	10,094,331	2,502,677	...	19,698	...	12,616,706
2008	10,345,332	2,586,616	...	20,511	...	12,952,459
2009	10,365,129	2,947,797	...	19,768	...	13,332,694

BANKERS LIFE OF LOUISIANA

P.O. Box 44130
Jacksonville, Florida 32231-4130
Tel: 904-350-9660

AMB#: 006151
Began Business: 08/01/1959
Agency Off: None

Best's Financial Strength Rating: B++g
FSC: V

• **NET PREMIUMS AND DEPOSITS ($000 omitted)**

Year	Individual Life	Individual & Group Annuities	Group Life & A&H	Credit Life & A&H	Individual A&H	Total
2007	0	...	...	6,639	2,728	9,367
2008	1	...	...	11,370	3,897	15,268
2009	1	...	...	9,192	3,201	12,393

• **NET OPERATING GAIN ($000 omitted)**

Year	Individual Life	Individual & Group Annuities	Group Life & A&H	Credit Life & A&H	Individual A&H	Total
2007	8	...	...	1,283	389	1,680
2008	-2	...	...	1,337	2,413	3,748
2009	1	...	...	435	169	605

• **COMPARATIVE FINANCIALS ($000 omitted)**

Year	Assets	Capital & Surplus	Net Invest Income	Benefits Paid	Realized Cap Gains	Policyholder Dividends	Contract Lns (% of assets)
2007	29,389	14,070	1,119	1,769	12	...	0.0
2008	13,578	4,902	695	2,442	9	...	0.0
2009	11,541	3,228	415	2,352	-116	...	0.0

• **ORDINARY LIFE STATISTICS**

Year	Av. Ord. Policy Issued ($)	Av. Ord. Policy In Force ($)	Avg. Prem ($/M)	1st Yr Prem/ Total Prem	Ord. Lapse Ratio
2007	...	...	...	...	...
2008	...	...	...	...	...
2009	...	...	...	...	...

• **NEW LIFE BUSINESS ISSUED ($000 omitted)**

Year	Whole Life	Term	Credit	Group	Industrial	Total
2007	...	...	545,946	...	...	545,946
2008	...	...	439,824	...	...	439,824
2009	...	...	495,151	...	...	495,151

• **LIFE INSURANCE IN FORCE ($000 omitted)**

Year	Whole Life	Term	Credit	Group	Industrial	Total
2007	32	...	553,012	...	...	553,044
2008	34	...	532,757	...	...	532,791
2009	24	...	508,054	...	...	508,078

BANKERS LIFE INSURANCE CO

11101 Roosevelt Blvd N
St. Petersburg, Florida 33716
Tel: 727-823-4000

AMB#: 008448
Began Business: 05/09/1973
Agency Off: Melvin C. Parker

Best's Financial Strength Rating: B-
FSC: V

• **NET PREMIUMS AND DEPOSITS ($000 omitted)**

Year	Individual Life	Individual & Group Annuities	Group Life & A&H	Credit Life & A&H	Individual A&H	Total
2007	3	58,633	1	...	12	58,649
2008	2	43,817	0	...	12	43,831
2009	1	22,888	...	...	112	23,001

• **NET OPERATING GAIN ($000 omitted)**

Year	Individual Life	Individual & Group Annuities	Group Life & A&H	Credit Life & A&H	Individual A&H	Total
2007	232	-319	-2	-6	7	-88
2008	186	2,283	-2	-9	6	2,464
2009	186	3,416	0	-47	-564	2,992

• **COMPARATIVE FINANCIALS ($000 omitted)**

Year	Assets	Capital & Surplus	Net Invest Income	Benefits Paid	Realized Cap Gains	Policyholder Dividends	Contract Lns (% of assets)
2007	179,893	8,616	10,477	34,310	257	...	0.5
2008	213,300	8,993	14,191	17,964	-1,163	...	0.3
2009	209,953	11,479	15,591	36,839	-4,687	...	0.2

• **ORDINARY LIFE STATISTICS**

Year	Av. Ord. Policy Issued ($)	Av. Ord. Policy In Force ($)	Avg. Prem ($/M)	1st Yr Prem/ Total Prem	Ord. Lapse Ratio
2007	...	...	...	...	...
2008	...	...	...	...	...
2009	...	...	...	...	...

• **NEW LIFE BUSINESS ISSUED ($000 omitted)**

Year	Whole Life	Term	Credit	Group	Industrial	Total
2007	...	...	...	...	...	...
2008	...	...	76	...	...	76
2009	...	...	...	...	...	...

• **LIFE INSURANCE IN FORCE ($000 omitted)**

Year	Whole Life	Term	Credit	Group	Industrial	Total
2007	...	...	6,905	...	...	6,905
2008	3,136	...	2,369	...	...	5,505
2009	2,040	565	1,129	...	...	3,734

BANNER LIFE INS CO

1701 Research Boulevard
Rockville, Maryland 20850
Tel: 301-279-4800

AMB#: 006468
Began Business: 10/01/1981
Agency Off: Hank Cushard

Best's Financial Strength Rating: A+ g
FSC: IX

• **NET PREMIUMS AND DEPOSITS ($000 omitted)**

Year	Individual Life	Individual & Group Annuities	Group Life & A&H	Credit Life & A&H	Individual A&H	Total
2007	106,162	471	163	...	17	106,812
2008	194,149	601	177	...	13	194,940
2009	205,384	1,365	182	...	11	206,942

• **NET OPERATING GAIN ($000 omitted)**

Year	Individual Life	Individual & Group Annuities	Group Life & A&H	Credit Life & A&H	Individual A&H	Total
2007	-476,392	737	92	...	-1	-475,565
2008	-645	722	92	...	3	173
2009	101,117	882	97	...	0	102,096

• **COMPARATIVE FINANCIALS ($000 omitted)**

Year	Assets	Capital & Surplus	Net Invest Income	Benefits Paid	Realized Cap Gains	Policyholder Dividends	Contract Lns (% of assets)
2007	1,293,366	225,446	48,706	155,308	-1,041	3,499	2.7
2008	1,335,175	211,272	47,757	131,231	-16,253	2,556	2.5
2009	1,414,139	311,310	73,207	105,194	-835	2,252	2.3

• **ORDINARY LIFE STATISTICS**

Year	Av. Ord. Policy Issued ($)	Av. Ord. Policy In Force ($)	Avg. Prem ($/M)	1st Yr Prem/ Total Prem	Ord. Lapse Ratio
2007	630,899	463,177	1.87	14.2	3.9
2008	613,543	478,951	1.82	13.4	4.2
2009	542,739	483,513	1.83	10.9	5.0

• **NEW LIFE BUSINESS ISSUED ($000 omitted)**

Year	Whole Life	Term	Credit	Group	Industrial	Total
2007	351,687	44,850,328	...	9,871	...	45,211,886
2008	421,783	46,248,629	...	6,369	...	46,676,781
2009	346,344	33,850,540	...	7,979	...	34,204,863

• **LIFE INSURANCE IN FORCE ($000 omitted)**

Year	Whole Life	Term	Credit	Group	Industrial	Total
2007	4,887,103	277,506,415	...	55,098	...	282,448,616
2008	5,009,741	309,572,328	...	60,180	...	314,642,249
2009	4,988,132	325,074,021	...	65,853	...	330,128,005

BCS LIFE INSURANCE CO

2 Mid America Plaza, Suite 200
Oakbrook Terrace, Illinois 60181
Tel: 630-472-7700

AMB#: 007363
Began Business: 11/17/1949
Agency Off: Robert J. Krueger

Best's Financial Strength Rating: A-
FSC: VII

• NET PREMIUMS AND DEPOSITS ($000 omitted)

Year	Individual Life	Individual & Group Annuities	Group Life & A&H	Credit Life & A&H	Individual A&H	Total
2007	19	...	207,599	...	...	207,618
2008	20	...	200,922	...	...	200,941
2009	40	...	188,512	...	...	188,551

• NET OPERATING GAIN ($000 omitted)

Year	Individual Life	Individual & Group Annuities	Group Life & A&H	Credit Life & A&H	Individual A&H	Total
2007	15	...	5,308	...	...	7,629
2008	8	...	662	...	...	3,668
2009	35	...	99	...	...	2,907

• COMPARATIVE FINANCIALS ($000 omitted)

Year	Assets	Capital & Surplus	Net Invest Income	Benefits Paid	Realized Cap Gains	Policyholder Dividends	Contract Lns (% of assets)
2007	196,902	80,547	6,527	147,637	-303	...	0.1
2008	180,558	79,727	6,231	169,614	-2,554	...	0.1
2009	181,394	80,566	6,379	160,634	-472	...	0.0

• ORDINARY LIFE STATISTICS

Year	Av. Ord. Policy Issued ($)	Av. Ord. Policy In Force ($)	Avg. Prem ($/M)	1st Yr Prem/ Total Prem	Ord. Lapse Ratio
2007	...	...	...	...	...
2008	...	...	...	...	...
2009	...	...	...	...	...

• NEW LIFE BUSINESS ISSUED ($000 omitted)

Year	Whole Life	Term	Credit	Group	Industrial	Total
2007	...	...	...	192,650	...	192,650
2008	...	...	...	156,080	...	156,080
2009	302	...	...	29,609	...	29,911

• LIFE INSURANCE IN FORCE ($000 omitted)

Year	Whole Life	Term	Credit	Group	Industrial	Total
2007	906	...	...	4,827,932	...	4,828,838
2008	856	...	...	5,075,661	...	5,076,517
2009	1,128	...	...	4,904,697	...	4,905,825

BENEFICIAL LIFE INS CO

150 E. Social Hall Avenue, Suite 500
Salt Lake City, Utah 84111-1578
Tel: 801-933-1100

AMB#: 006162
Began Business: 05/10/1905
Agency Off: Tyler Norton

Best's Financial Strength Rating: A-
FSC: IX

• NET PREMIUMS AND DEPOSITS ($000 omitted)

Year	Individual Life	Individual & Group Annuities	Group Life & A&H	Credit Life & A&H	Individual A&H	Total
2007	-20,493	356,406	2,859	...	4	338,777
2008	61,884	308,863	4,872	...	8	375,629
2009	63,854	243,868	3,535	...	7	311,263

• NET OPERATING GAIN ($000 omitted)

Year	Individual Life	Individual & Group Annuities	Group Life & A&H	Credit Life & A&H	Individual A&H	Total
2007	15,134	23,584	5,067	...	121	43,905
2008	39,958	49,155	2,129	...	-84	91,159
2009	18,380	14,531	635	...	-52	33,493

• COMPARATIVE FINANCIALS ($000 omitted)

Year	Assets	Capital & Surplus	Net Invest Income	Benefits Paid	Realized Cap Gains	Policyholder Dividends	Contract Lns (% of assets)
2007	3,559,646	341,146	223,965	432,400	-218,372	2,917	3.3
2008	3,437,234	451,321	218,073	458,655	-330,892	2,823	3.4
2009	3,446,437	478,068	205,200	451,170	-23,013	2,661	3.4

• ORDINARY LIFE STATISTICS

Year	Av. Ord. Policy Issued ($)	Av. Ord. Policy In Force ($)	Avg. Prem ($/M)	1st Yr Prem/ Total Prem	Ord. Lapse Ratio
2007	482,842	152,654	5.72	33.5	4.0
2008	469,488	166,186	5.50	29.9	5.2
2009	405,778	169,888	4.91	19.8	7.0

• NEW LIFE BUSINESS ISSUED ($000 omitted)

Year	Whole Life	Term	Credit	Group	Industrial	Total
2007	1,006,192	2,792,325	...	650	...	3,799,167
2008	911,806	2,651,607	...	4,300	...	3,567,713
2009	498,312	1,596,719	...	125	...	2,095,156

• LIFE INSURANCE IN FORCE ($000 omitted)

Year	Whole Life	Term	Credit	Group	Industrial	Total
2007	9,637,832	14,159,403	...	5,722,261	...	29,519,496
2008	10,070,668	15,464,478	...	2,584,487	...	28,119,633
2009	9,934,356	15,280,311	...	2,722,452	...	27,937,119

BERKSHIRE HATHAWAY LIFE OF NE

3024 Harney Street
Omaha, Nebraska 68131-3580
Tel: 402-916-3000

AMB#: 060060
Began Business: 06/11/1993
Agency Off: None

Best's Financial Strength Rating: A++
FSC: XV

• NET PREMIUMS AND DEPOSITS ($000 omitted)

Year	Individual Life	Individual & Group Annuities	Group Life & A&H	Credit Life & A&H	Individual A&H	Total
2007	96,199	3,020	...	...	...	99,218
2008	52,980	510	4,365	...	...	57,855
2009	2,338,418	519	...	...	...	2,338,938

• NET OPERATING GAIN ($000 omitted)

Year	Individual Life	Individual & Group Annuities	Group Life & A&H	Credit Life & A&H	Individual A&H	Total
2007	44,705	1,883	...	...	...	55,597
2008	49,186	11,579	184	...	...	70,144
2009	-952,846	46,429	1,101	...	...	-876,628

• COMPARATIVE FINANCIALS ($000 omitted)

Year	Assets	Capital & Surplus	Net Invest Income	Benefits Paid	Realized Cap Gains	Policyholder Dividends	Contract Lns (% of assets)
2007	3,658,554	858,078	181,600	277,026	1,146	...	...
2008	3,528,028	810,409	182,059	238,187	...	...	...
2009	7,624,963	1,032,640	279,275	590,228	-1,948	...	...

• ORDINARY LIFE STATISTICS

Year	Av. Ord. Policy Issued ($)	Av. Ord. Policy In Force ($)	Avg. Prem ($/M)	1st Yr Prem/ Total Prem	Ord. Lapse Ratio
2007	...	8,093	4.98	...	53.4
2008	...	...	...	...	99.7
2009	...	46,790	6.78	...	...

• NEW LIFE BUSINESS ISSUED ($000 omitted)

Year	Whole Life	Term	Credit	Group	Industrial	Total
2007	...	...	...	...	...	...
2008	...	...	...	...	...	...
2009	...	...	...	...	...	...

• LIFE INSURANCE IN FORCE ($000 omitted)

Year	Whole Life	Term	Credit	Group	Industrial	Total
2007	...	19,306,062	...	...	...	19,306,062
2008	...	...	...	...	...	...
2009	...	346,560,666	...	...	...	346,560,665

BERKSHIRE LIFE INS CO OF AMER

700 South Street
Pittsfield, Massachusetts 01201
Tel: 413-499-4321

AMB#: 007409
Began Business: 07/01/2001
Agency Off: Mark Haydon

Best's Financial Strength Rating: A++g
FSC: XV

• NET PREMIUMS AND DEPOSITS ($000 omitted)

Year	Individual Life	Individual & Group Annuities	Group Life & A&H	Credit Life & A&H	Individual A&H	Total
2007	269	...	...	...	402,121	402,390
2008	1,987	...	...	...	417,312	419,299
2009	1,805	...	...	...	443,748	445,553

• NET OPERATING GAIN ($000 omitted)

Year	Individual Life	Individual & Group Annuities	Group Life & A&H	Credit Life & A&H	Individual A&H	Total
2007	-12	...	...	...	62,106	62,095
2008	1,671	...	...	...	34,803	36,474
2009	2,132	...	...	...	35,658	37,790

• COMPARATIVE FINANCIALS ($000 omitted)

Year	Assets	Capital & Surplus	Net Invest Income	Benefits Paid	Realized Cap Gains	Policyholder Dividends	Contract Lns (% of assets)
2007	2,292,683	386,608	133,419	165,292	-86	3,549	0.0
2008	2,455,455	423,850	140,750	175,313	-7,821	4,338	0.0
2009	2,626,861	452,274	149,138	194,714	-3,803	4,934	0.0

• ORDINARY LIFE STATISTICS

Year	Av. Ord. Policy Issued ($)	Av. Ord. Policy In Force ($)	Avg. Prem ($/M)	1st Yr Prem/ Total Prem	Ord. Lapse Ratio
2007	...	...	...	...	...
2008	...	...	...	...	...
2009	...	...	...	...	...

• NEW LIFE BUSINESS ISSUED ($000 omitted)

Year	Whole Life	Term	Credit	Group	Industrial	Total
2007	173,280	...	...	...	...	173,280
2008	12,003	...	...	...	...	12,003
2009	...	1,500	...	...	...	1,500

• LIFE INSURANCE IN FORCE ($000 omitted)

Year	Whole Life	Term	Credit	Group	Industrial	Total
2007	465,243	8,415,899	...	...	...	8,881,142
2008	434,219	7,967,453	...	...	...	8,401,672
2009	410,292	7,360,309	...	...	...	7,770,601

BEST LIFE AND HEALTH INS CO

P.O. Box 19721
Irvine, California 92623-9721
Tel: 949-253-4080

AMB#: 007246
Began Business: 11/17/1964
Agency Off: Paul Peatross

Best's Financial Strength Rating: B **FSC:** IV

• **NET PREMIUMS AND DEPOSITS ($000 omitted)**

Year	Individual Life	Individual & Group Annuities	Group Life & A&H	Credit Life & A&H	Individual A&H	Total
2007	3	...	41,830	...	...	41,833
2008	2	...	48,403	...	...	48,405
2009	3	...	46,683	...	...	46,687

• **NET OPERATING GAIN ($000 omitted)**

Year	Individual Life	Individual & Group Annuities	Group Life & A&H	Credit Life & A&H	Individual A&H	Total
2007	-2	...	406	-1	...	404
2008	-51	...	-619	0	...	-670
2009	-9	...	-1,604	...	...	-1,613

• **COMPARATIVE FINANCIALS ($000 omitted)**

Year	Assets	Capital & Surplus	Net Invest Income	Benefits Paid	Realized Cap Gains	Policyholder Dividends	Contract Lns (% of assets)
2007	16,881	10,703	655	27,903	...	...	...
2008	16,671	9,814	524	35,298	...	...	...
2009	14,731	8,198	547	36,065	-122	...	...

• **ORDINARY LIFE STATISTICS**

Year	Av. Ord. Policy Issued ($)	Av. Ord. Policy In Force ($)	Avg. Prem ($/M)	1st Yr Prem/ Total Prem	Ord. Lapse Ratio
2007	...	...	...	...	...
2008	...	...	...	...	...
2009	...	...	...	...	...

• **NEW LIFE BUSINESS ISSUED ($000 omitted)**

Year	Whole Life	Term	Credit	Group	Industrial	Total
2007	...	...	...	52,407	...	52,407
2008	...	...	...	64,771	...	64,771
2009	...	...	...	81,215	...	81,215

• **LIFE INSURANCE IN FORCE ($000 omitted)**

Year	Whole Life	Term	Credit	Group	Industrial	Total
2007	183	8,314	...	124,475	...	132,972
2008	184	8,273	...	156,792	...	165,249
2009	...	9,063	...	166,574	...	175,637

BLUE SHIELD OF CA LIFE & HLTH

50 Beale Street
San Francisco, California 94105
Tel: 888-800-2742

AMB#: 006181
Began Business: 07/01/1954
Agency Off: None

Best's Financial Strength Rating: A g **FSC:** XV

• **NET PREMIUMS AND DEPOSITS ($000 omitted)**

Year	Individual Life	Individual & Group Annuities	Group Life & A&H	Credit Life & A&H	Individual A&H	Total
2007	1,235	30	233,281	...	236,389	470,935
2008	1,426	...	442,632	...	306,468	750,525
2009	1,444	...	785,658	...	427,077	1,214,179

• **NET OPERATING GAIN ($000 omitted)**

Year	Individual Life	Individual & Group Annuities	Group Life & A&H	Credit Life & A&H	Individual A&H	Total
2007	151	...	22,227	...	219	22,597
2008	631	...	2,625	...	1,435	4,690
2009	552	...	-70,204	...	6,760	-62,892

• **COMPARATIVE FINANCIALS ($000 omitted)**

Year	Assets	Capital & Surplus	Net Invest Income	Benefits Paid	Realized Cap Gains	Policyholder Dividends	Contract Lns (% of assets)
2007	218,807	105,444	11,943	321,775	...	...	0.0
2008	324,328	138,487	11,181	566,089	-1,723	...	0.0
2009	521,027	247,857	14,741	1,034,350	-343	...	0.0

• **ORDINARY LIFE STATISTICS**

Year	Av. Ord. Policy Issued ($)	Av. Ord. Policy In Force ($)	Avg. Prem ($/M)	1st Yr Prem/ Total Prem	Ord. Lapse Ratio
2007	...	...	...	...	...
2008	...	...	...	...	...
2009	...	...	...	...	...

• **NEW LIFE BUSINESS ISSUED ($000 omitted)**

Year	Whole Life	Term	Credit	Group	Industrial	Total
2007	...	...	...	...	...	...
2008	...	...	...	...	...	...
2009	...	...	...	...	...	...

• **LIFE INSURANCE IN FORCE ($000 omitted)**

Year	Whole Life	Term	Credit	Group	Industrial	Total
2007	1,222	104,910	...	2,934,371	...	3,040,503
2008	1,197	372,070	...	2,815,177	...	3,188,444
2009	1,203	381,495	...	2,899,388	...	3,282,086

BEST MERIDIAN INS CO

1320 S. Dixie Highway, 6th Floor
Coral Gables, Florida 33146
Tel: 305-443-2898

AMB#: 060007
Began Business: 08/01/1987
Agency Off: Anthony F. Sierra

Best's Financial Strength Rating: B++ **FSC:** VI

• **NET PREMIUMS AND DEPOSITS ($000 omitted)**

Year	Individual Life	Individual & Group Annuities	Group Life & A&H	Credit Life & A&H	Individual A&H	Total
2007	14,554	...	1,473	...	30,846	46,873
2008	37,445	...	1,957	...	34,099	73,501
2009	20,168	...	1,843	...	38,656	60,667

• **NET OPERATING GAIN ($000 omitted)**

Year	Individual Life	Individual & Group Annuities	Group Life & A&H	Credit Life & A&H	Individual A&H	Total
2007	2,234	0	382	...	929	3,545
2008	5	...	509	...	6,507	7,021
2009	1,153	-2	395	...	4,762	6,309

• **COMPARATIVE FINANCIALS ($000 omitted)**

Year	Assets	Capital & Surplus	Net Invest Income	Benefits Paid	Realized Cap Gains	Policyholder Dividends	Contract Lns (% of assets)
2007	153,192	22,964	7,339	21,615	-29	...	4.4
2008	164,787	27,541	7,895	26,466	-3,303	...	3.9
2009	181,776	32,864	8,495	25,745	-501	...	3.5

• **ORDINARY LIFE STATISTICS**

Year	Av. Ord. Policy Issued ($)	Av. Ord. Policy In Force ($)	Avg. Prem ($/M)	1st Yr Prem/ Total Prem	Ord. Lapse Ratio
2007	221,567	248,051	7.23	17.6	6.0
2008	217,780	246,209	7.38	15.5	5.7
2009	220,358	239,871	7.36	14.0	5.7

• **NEW LIFE BUSINESS ISSUED ($000 omitted)**

Year	Whole Life	Term	Credit	Group	Industrial	Total
2007	343,208	...	...	22,150	...	365,358
2008	275,760	22,598	...	7,904	...	306,262
2009	182,519	30,347	...	3,237	...	216,103

• **LIFE INSURANCE IN FORCE ($000 omitted)**

Year	Whole Life	Term	Credit	Group	Industrial	Total
2007	3,469,507	36,943	...	129,655	...	3,636,105
2008	3,592,135	73,425	...	115,159	...	3,780,719
2009	3,710,711	93,888	...	108,696	...	3,913,295

BLUEBONNET LIFE INS CO

3545 Lakeland Drive
Flowood, Mississippi 39232-9799
Tel: 601-664-4218

AMB#: 068175
Began Business: 06/11/1984
Agency Off: None

Best's Financial Strength Rating: A g **FSC:** X

• **NET PREMIUMS AND DEPOSITS ($000 omitted)**

Year	Individual Life	Individual & Group Annuities	Group Life & A&H	Credit Life & A&H	Individual A&H	Total
2007	82	...	7,602	...	1	7,685
2008	77	...	7,323	...	1	7,401
2009	77	...	6,833	...	1	6,912

• **NET OPERATING GAIN ($000 omitted)**

Year	Individual Life	Individual & Group Annuities	Group Life & A&H	Credit Life & A&H	Individual A&H	Total
2007	-16	...	3,459	...	2	3,444
2008	16	...	3,645	...	1	3,662
2009	-134	...	3,196	...	1	3,062

• **COMPARATIVE FINANCIALS ($000 omitted)**

Year	Assets	Capital & Surplus	Net Invest Income	Benefits Paid	Realized Cap Gains	Policyholder Dividends	Contract Lns (% of assets)
2007	34,637	30,282	1,539	2,599	...	...	...
2008	38,395	33,719	1,536	2,163	...	...	...
2009	40,771	36,898	1,563	2,226	...	...	...

• **ORDINARY LIFE STATISTICS**

Year	Av. Ord. Policy Issued ($)	Av. Ord. Policy In Force ($)	Avg. Prem ($/M)	1st Yr Prem/ Total Prem	Ord. Lapse Ratio
2007	...	...	...	...	...
2008	...	...	...	...	...
2009	...	...	...	...	...

• **NEW LIFE BUSINESS ISSUED ($000 omitted)**

Year	Whole Life	Term	Credit	Group	Industrial	Total
2007	...	...	...	60,306	...	60,306
2008	...	...	...	56,295	...	56,295
2009	...	...	...	29,012	...	29,012

• **LIFE INSURANCE IN FORCE ($000 omitted)**

Year	Whole Life	Term	Credit	Group	Industrial	Total
2007	...	6,243	...	1,205,905	...	1,212,148
2008	...	5,738	...	1,137,186	...	1,142,924
2009	...	5,107	...	983,999	...	989,106

BOSTON MUTUAL LIFE INS CO

120 Royall Street
Canton, Massachusetts 02021-1098
Tel: 781-828-7000

AMB#: 006170
Began Business: 02/15/1892
Agency Off: Timothy E. Flannigan

Best's Financial Strength Rating: A- g **FSC:** VIII

• NET PREMIUMS AND DEPOSITS ($000 omitted)

Year	Individual Life	Individual & Group Annuities	Group Life & A&H	Credit Life & A&H	Individual A&H	Total
2007	120,673	556	47,840	22	1,282	170,372
2008	121,363	560	46,409	2	3,251	171,585
2009	121,886	673	44,250	0	4,695	171,505

• NET OPERATING GAIN ($000 omitted)

Year	Individual Life	Individual & Group Annuities	Group Life & A&H	Credit Life & A&H	Individual A&H	Total
2007	9,828	-6	1,242	-38	-476	10,550
2008	12,235	-30	-850	10	-220	11,145
2009	12,016	-25	-1,493	-4	-109	10,384

• COMPARATIVE FINANCIALS ($000 omitted)

Year	Assets	Capital & Surplus	Net Invest Income	Benefits Paid	Realized Cap Gains	Policyholder Dividends	Contract Lns (% of assets)
2007	893,465	102,139	44,435	94,817	-215	656	9.2
2008	929,127	77,722	46,727	96,907	-1,540	736	9.9
2009	995,277	108,146	46,987	97,165	-398	1,072	10.2

• ORDINARY LIFE STATISTICS

Year	Av. Ord. Policy Issued ($)	Av. Ord. Policy In Force ($)	Avg. Prem ($/M)	1st Yr Prem/ Total Prem	Ord. Lapse Ratio
2007	21,331	19,510	12.12	10.2	11.1
2008	22,160	19,395	12.29	10.3	13.9
2009	22,857	19,094	12.47	10.6	16.8

• NEW LIFE BUSINESS ISSUED ($000 omitted)

Year	Whole Life	Term	Credit	Group	Industrial	Total
2007	1,093,915	248,824	...	594,395	...	1,937,134
2008	1,352,245	222,981	...	645,916	...	2,221,142
2009	1,759,890	190,879	...	512,306	...	2,463,075

• LIFE INSURANCE IN FORCE ($000 omitted)

Year	Whole Life	Term	Credit	Group	Industrial	Total
2007	8,724,057	2,065,114	257	9,000,557	1,219	19,791,204
2008	8,774,924	1,873,534	194	8,142,053	1,119	18,791,824
2009	8,875,879	1,643,040	259	7,368,226	1,032	17,888,435

BROOKE LIFE INSURANCE CO

1 Corporate Way
Lansing, Michigan 48951
Tel: 517-381-5500

AMB#: 068117
Began Business: 08/26/1987
Agency Off: Clifford J. Jack

Best's Financial Strength Rating: A+ gu **FSC:** XV

• NET PREMIUMS AND DEPOSITS ($000 omitted)

Year	Individual Life	Individual & Group Annuities	Group Life & A&H	Credit Life & A&H	Individual A&H	Total
2007	-252	20,456	675	...	...	20,879
2008	294	217,585	755	...	...	218,634
2009	216	20,175	797	...	...	21,188

• NET OPERATING GAIN ($000 omitted)

Year	Individual Life	Individual & Group Annuities	Group Life & A&H	Credit Life & A&H	Individual A&H	Total
2007	31,383	127,715	1,090	...	...	160,189
2008	26,770	188,834	1,144	...	...	216,748
2009	21,315	159,097	906	...	...	181,317

• COMPARATIVE FINANCIALS ($000 omitted)

Year	Assets	Capital & Surplus	Net Invest Income	Benefits Paid	Realized Cap Gains	Policyholder Dividends	Contract Lns (% of assets)
2007	4,210,876	2,508,309	167,008	26,351	...	41	0.1
2008	4,128,859	2,244,925	239,765	25,639	-721	37	0.1
2009	4,365,025	2,674,214	200,607	31,192	-657	37	0.1

• ORDINARY LIFE STATISTICS

Year	Av. Ord. Policy Issued ($)	Av. Ord. Policy In Force ($)	Avg. Prem ($/M)	1st Yr Prem/ Total Prem	Ord. Lapse Ratio
2007	...	...	...	...	...
2008	...	...	...	...	...
2009	...	...	...	...	...

• NEW LIFE BUSINESS ISSUED ($000 omitted)

Year	Whole Life	Term	Credit	Group	Industrial	Total
2007	...	...	...	61,958	...	61,958
2008	...	...	...	60,827	...	60,827
2009	...	...	...	49,218	...	49,218

• LIFE INSURANCE IN FORCE ($000 omitted)

Year	Whole Life	Term	Credit	Group	Industrial	Total
2007	117,691	52,730	...	389,229	...	559,650
2008	107,900	45,130	...	431,480	...	584,510
2009	99,954	40,364	...	442,394	...	582,711

BROKERS NATIONAL LIFE ASSUR

P.O. Box 92529
Austin, Texas 78709-2529
Tel: 512-383-0220

AMB#: 006023
Began Business: 07/08/1964
Agency Off: Barry Shamas

Best's Financial Strength Rating: B+ **FSC:** V

• NET PREMIUMS AND DEPOSITS ($000 omitted)

Year	Individual Life	Individual & Group Annuities	Group Life & A&H	Credit Life & A&H	Individual A&H	Total
2007	218	61	42,317	...	1,996	44,592
2008	192	101	41,469	...	1,776	43,539
2009	142	70	39,811	...	1,613	41,635

• NET OPERATING GAIN ($000 omitted)

Year	Individual Life	Individual & Group Annuities	Group Life & A&H	Credit Life & A&H	Individual A&H	Total
2007	227	93	2,665	...	355	3,339
2008	260	76	2,392	...	189	2,918
2009	200	138	2,323	...	100	2,761

• COMPARATIVE FINANCIALS ($000 omitted)

Year	Assets	Capital & Surplus	Net Invest Income	Benefits Paid	Realized Cap Gains	Policyholder Dividends	Contract Lns (% of assets)
2007	26,976	15,834	1,124	27,625	11	15	0.6
2008	26,577	16,965	961	26,993	-288	15	0.7
2009	28,383	19,130	924	26,011	-28	15	0.6

• ORDINARY LIFE STATISTICS

Year	Av. Ord. Policy Issued ($)	Av. Ord. Policy In Force ($)	Avg. Prem ($/M)	1st Yr Prem/ Total Prem	Ord. Lapse Ratio
2007	...	...	...	...	...
2008	...	...	...	...	...
2009	...	...	...	...	...

• NEW LIFE BUSINESS ISSUED ($000 omitted)

Year	Whole Life	Term	Credit	Group	Industrial	Total
2007	...	7,556	...	2,425	...	9,981
2008	...	3,488	...	995	...	4,483
2009	...	460	...	2,370	...	2,830

• LIFE INSURANCE IN FORCE ($000 omitted)

Year	Whole Life	Term	Credit	Group	Industrial	Total
2007	7,443	27,241	...	9,195	...	43,879
2008	7,151	21,027	...	5,518	...	33,696
2009	6,646	17,536	...	6,475	...	30,657

BUPA INSURANCE COMPANY

7001 S.W. 97th Avenue
Miami, Florida 33173
Tel: 305-275-1400

AMB#: 008449
Began Business: 07/16/1973
Agency Off: Michael Carricarte

Best's Financial Strength Rating: B++ **FSC:** VI

• NET PREMIUMS AND DEPOSITS ($000 omitted)

Year	Individual Life	Individual & Group Annuities	Group Life & A&H	Credit Life & A&H	Individual A&H	Total
2007	59	2	4,492	...	100,032	104,585
2008	128	5	3,731	...	108,118	111,981
2009	38	9	3,027	...	126,671	129,745

• NET OPERATING GAIN ($000 omitted)

Year	Individual Life	Individual & Group Annuities	Group Life & A&H	Credit Life & A&H	Individual A&H	Total
2007	106	19	583	...	-2,659	-1,952
2008	163	16	230	...	1,193	1,602
2009	-20	5	1,090	...	1,522	2,596

• COMPARATIVE FINANCIALS ($000 omitted)

Year	Assets	Capital & Surplus	Net Invest Income	Benefits Paid	Realized Cap Gains	Policyholder Dividends	Contract Lns (% of assets)
2007	91,286	19,128	3,245	63,698	...	...	0.6
2008	101,521	23,141	2,180	73,190	...	0	0.5
2009	111,272	27,709	1,040	75,556	...	...	0.4

• ORDINARY LIFE STATISTICS

Year	Av. Ord. Policy Issued ($)	Av. Ord. Policy In Force ($)	Avg. Prem ($/M)	1st Yr Prem/ Total Prem	Ord. Lapse Ratio
2007	...	...	...	...	...
2008	...	...	...	...	...
2009	...	...	...	...	...

• NEW LIFE BUSINESS ISSUED ($000 omitted)

Year	Whole Life	Term	Credit	Group	Industrial	Total
2007	...	...	...	...	...	...
2008	...	...	...	1,892	...	1,892
2009	...	100	...	1,803	...	1,903

• LIFE INSURANCE IN FORCE ($000 omitted)

Year	Whole Life	Term	Credit	Group	Industrial	Total
2007	10,068	26,160	...	9,006	...	45,234
2008	8,782	19,946	...	10,370	...	39,098
2009	8,172	18,035	...	11,973	...	38,180

C M LIFE INSURANCE COMPANY

1295 State Street
Springfield, Massachusetts 01111
Tel: 413-788-8411

AMB#: 009062
Began Business: 05/12/1981
Agency Off: Alan Taylor

Best's Financial Strength Rating: A++g **FSC:** XV

• **NET PREMIUMS AND DEPOSITS ($000 omitted)**

Year	Individual Life	Individual & Group Annuities	Group Life & A&H	Credit Life & A&H	Individual A&H	Total
2007	183,546	356,214	1,557	...	...	541,318
2008	170,339	611,497	1,523	...	...	783,359
2009	140,671	742,685	1,468	...	...	884,824

• **NET OPERATING GAIN ($000 omitted)**

Year	Individual Life	Individual & Group Annuities	Group Life & A&H	Credit Life & A&H	Individual A&H	Total
2007	70,924	36,145	97	...	...	107,165
2008	19,692	-35,902	1,296	...	...	-14,915
2009	60,312	30,639	2,525	...	...	93,476

• **COMPARATIVE FINANCIALS ($000 omitted)**

Year	Assets	Capital & Surplus	Net Invest Income	Benefits Paid	Realized Cap Gains	Policyholder Dividends	Contract Lns (% of assets)
2007	8,625,435	607,849	348,371	1,530,123	-21,449	...	1.9
2008	7,539,867	707,773	296,088	1,219,253	-61,677	...	2.3
2009	8,170,601	717,528	327,070	911,558	-49,724	...	2.3

• **ORDINARY LIFE STATISTICS**

Year	Av. Ord. Policy Issued ($)	Av. Ord. Policy In Force ($)	Avg. Prem ($/M)	1st Yr Prem/ Total Prem	Ord. Lapse Ratio
2007	772,314	352,623	6.26	1.5	5.9
2008	769,799	349,507	6.47	2.0	6.5
2009	1,279,533	343,962	6.22	0.6	6.8

• **NEW LIFE BUSINESS ISSUED ($000 omitted)**

Year	Whole Life	Term	Credit	Group	Industrial	Total
2007	402,796	20,432	...	...	...	423,228
2008	339,578	16,069	...	...	...	355,647
2009	19,193	...	...	...	...	19,193

• **LIFE INSURANCE IN FORCE ($000 omitted)**

Year	Whole Life	Term	Credit	Group	Industrial	Total
2007	51,620,535	3,244,762	...	122,983	...	54,988,280
2008	48,855,868	2,436,338	...	115,136	...	51,407,342
2009	45,670,252	1,870,125	...	114,639	...	47,655,016

CARDIF LIFE INSURANCE COMPANY

12485 SW 137th Avenue, Suite 300
Miami, Florida 33186
Tel: 305-234-1771

AMB#: 007376
Began Business: 06/14/1964
Agency Off: Michael J. Casale

Best's Financial Strength Rating: B++u **FSC:** V

• **NET PREMIUMS AND DEPOSITS ($000 omitted)**

Year	Individual Life	Individual & Group Annuities	Group Life & A&H	Credit Life & A&H	Individual A&H	Total
2007	...	...	...	12,233	...	12,233
2008	...	...	...	10,193	...	10,193
2009	...	...	...	5,359	...	5,359

• **NET OPERATING GAIN ($000 omitted)**

Year	Individual Life	Individual & Group Annuities	Group Life & A&H	Credit Life & A&H	Individual A&H	Total
2007	...	...	...	-3,453	...	-3,453
2008	...	...	...	-971	...	-971
2009	...	...	...	747	...	747

• **COMPARATIVE FINANCIALS ($000 omitted)**

Year	Assets	Capital & Surplus	Net Invest Income	Benefits Paid	Realized Cap Gains	Policyholder Dividends	Contract Lns (% of assets)
2007	62,019	10,833	1,907	3,020	-7	...	...
2008	61,054	14,219	2,455	2,936	-955	...	...
2009	54,227	17,468	2,275	2,102	-65	...	...

• **ORDINARY LIFE STATISTICS**

Year	Av. Ord. Policy Issued ($)	Av. Ord. Policy In Force ($)	Avg. Prem ($/M)	1st Yr Prem/ Total Prem	Ord. Lapse Ratio
2007	...	...	...	...	...
2008	...	...	...	...	...
2009	...	...	...	...	...

• **NEW LIFE BUSINESS ISSUED ($000 omitted)**

Year	Whole Life	Term	Credit	Group	Industrial	Total
2007	...	...	964,605	...	...	964,605
2008	...	...	868,605	...	...	868,605
2009	...	...	622,808	...	...	622,808

• **LIFE INSURANCE IN FORCE ($000 omitted)**

Year	Whole Life	Term	Credit	Group	Industrial	Total
2007	...	...	1,601,303	...	...	1,601,303
2008	...	...	1,745,227	...	...	1,745,227
2009	...	...	1,627,869	...	...	1,627,869

CAMBRIDGE LIFE INS CO

3200 Highland Avenue
Downers Grove, Illinois 60515
Tel: 630-737-5750

AMB#: 008545
Began Business: 01/01/1974
Agency Off: None

Best's Financial Strength Rating: B++ **FSC:** VI

• **NET PREMIUMS AND DEPOSITS ($000 omitted)**

Year	Individual Life	Individual & Group Annuities	Group Life & A&H	Credit Life & A&H	Individual A&H	Total
2007	...	...	1,586	...	54,040	55,625
2008	...	...	1,381	...	55,283	56,664
2009	...	...	684	...	55,869	56,553

• **NET OPERATING GAIN ($000 omitted)**

Year	Individual Life	Individual & Group Annuities	Group Life & A&H	Credit Life & A&H	Individual A&H	Total
2007	...	...	365	...	-6,423	-6,057
2008	...	...	158	...	-12,745	-12,587
2009	...	...	51	...	-636	-562

• **COMPARATIVE FINANCIALS ($000 omitted)**

Year	Assets	Capital & Surplus	Net Invest Income	Benefits Paid	Realized Cap Gains	Policyholder Dividends	Contract Lns (% of assets)
2007	45,706	26,164	667	56,646	...	...	0.0
2008	80,361	41,953	581	63,371	-174	...	0.0
2009	74,670	47,988	426	66,656	10	...	0.0

• **ORDINARY LIFE STATISTICS**

Year	Av. Ord. Policy Issued ($)	Av. Ord. Policy In Force ($)	Avg. Prem ($/M)	1st Yr Prem/ Total Prem	Ord. Lapse Ratio
2007	...	...	...	...	...
2008	...	...	...	...	...
2009	...	...	...	...	...

• **NEW LIFE BUSINESS ISSUED ($000 omitted)**

Year	Whole Life	Term	Credit	Group	Industrial	Total
2007	...	...	...	...	...	...
2008	...	...	...	...	...	...
2009	...	...	...	...	...	...

• **LIFE INSURANCE IN FORCE ($000 omitted)**

Year	Whole Life	Term	Credit	Group	Industrial	Total
2007	6	...	...	853	...	859
2008	6	...	...	10	...	16
2009	5	...	...	10	...	15

CAREAMERICA LIFE INS CO

50 Beale Street
San Francisco, California 94105
Tel: 888-646-0789

AMB#: 007351
Began Business: 08/23/1968
Agency Off: None

Best's Financial Strength Rating: A- **FSC:** XV

• **NET PREMIUMS AND DEPOSITS ($000 omitted)**

Year	Individual Life	Individual & Group Annuities	Group Life & A&H	Credit Life & A&H	Individual A&H	Total
2007	324	...	3,223	...	13	3,560
2008	277	...	3,348	...	7	3,632
2009	232	...	3,207	...	4	3,443

• **NET OPERATING GAIN ($000 omitted)**

Year	Individual Life	Individual & Group Annuities	Group Life & A&H	Credit Life & A&H	Individual A&H	Total
2007	109	...	1,069	...	-21	1,157
2008	126	...	1,831	...	13	1,971
2009	129	...	1,804	...	7	1,940

• **COMPARATIVE FINANCIALS ($000 omitted)**

Year	Assets	Capital & Surplus	Net Invest Income	Benefits Paid	Realized Cap Gains	Policyholder Dividends	Contract Lns (% of assets)
2007	25,533	22,201	1,360	2,214	...	...	0.1
2008	27,900	24,123	1,151	1,047	-107	...	0.1
2009	26,949	23,547	1,105	1,010	-76	...	0.1

• **ORDINARY LIFE STATISTICS**

Year	Av. Ord. Policy Issued ($)	Av. Ord. Policy In Force ($)	Avg. Prem ($/M)	1st Yr Prem/ Total Prem	Ord. Lapse Ratio
2007	...	...	...	...	...
2008	...	...	...	...	...
2009	...	...	...	...	...

• **NEW LIFE BUSINESS ISSUED ($000 omitted)**

Year	Whole Life	Term	Credit	Group	Industrial	Total
2007	...	...	...	...	...	...
2008	...	...	...	...	...	...
2009	...	...	...	...	...	...

• **LIFE INSURANCE IN FORCE ($000 omitted)**

Year	Whole Life	Term	Credit	Group	Industrial	Total
2007	...	45,678	...	380,810	...	426,488
2008	...	35,251	...	388,186	...	423,437
2009	...	32,123	...	365,568	...	397,691

CARIBBEAN AMERICAN LIFE ASSUR

273 Ponce de Leon Avenue, Suite 1300
San Juan, Puerto Rico 00917-1838
Tel: 787-250-6470

AMB#: 068045
Began Business: 12/15/1988
Agency Off: None

Best's Financial Strength Rating: A- g **FSC:** VIII

• **NET PREMIUMS AND DEPOSITS ($000 omitted)**

Year	Individual Life	Individual & Group Annuities	Group Life & A&H	Credit Life & A&H	Individual A&H	Total
2007	...	...	2,590	29,059	...	31,649
2008	...	...	2,164	12,755	...	14,919
2009	...	...	952	11,884	...	12,836

• **NET OPERATING GAIN ($000 omitted)**

Year	Individual Life	Individual & Group Annuities	Group Life & A&H	Credit Life & A&H	Individual A&H	Total
2007	2	...	585	2,688	...	3,275
2008	0	...	602	7,106	...	7,709
2009	1	...	822	4,904	...	5,728

• **COMPARATIVE FINANCIALS ($000 omitted)**

Year	Assets	Capital & Surplus	Net Invest Income	Benefits Paid	Realized Cap Gains	Policyholder Dividends	Contract Lns (% of assets)
2007	69,296	13,848	3,406	12,307	127	...	...
2008	64,001	18,725	4,942	10,462	61	...	...
2009	54,001	16,669	4,353	8,185	24	...	...

• **ORDINARY LIFE STATISTICS**

Year	Av. Ord. Policy Issued ($)	Av. Ord. Policy In Force ($)	Avg. Prem ($/M)	1st Yr Prem/ Total Prem	Ord. Lapse Ratio
2007	...	...	...	...	...
2008	...	...	...	...	...
2009	...	...	...	...	...

• **NEW LIFE BUSINESS ISSUED ($000 omitted)**

Year	Whole Life	Term	Credit	Group	Industrial	Total
2007	...	...	1,932,902	3,308	...	1,936,210
2008	...	...	1,835,793	41,645	...	1,877,438
2009	...	...	1,212,673	8,342	...	1,221,015

• **LIFE INSURANCE IN FORCE ($000 omitted)**

Year	Whole Life	Term	Credit	Group	Industrial	Total
2007	...	277	2,080,410	420,574	...	2,501,261
2008	...	130	1,888,984	298,167	...	2,187,281
2009	...	53	1,565,391	297,141	...	1,862,585

CATHOLIC LIFE INSURANCE

1635 N.E. Loop 410
San Antonio, Texas 78209-1694
Tel: 210-828-9921

AMB#: 008827
Began Business: 01/01/1902
Agency Off: Dennis R. Best

Best's Financial Strength Rating: A- **FSC:** VII

• **NET PREMIUMS AND DEPOSITS ($000 omitted)**

Year	Individual Life	Individual & Group Annuities	Group Life & A&H	Credit Life & A&H	Individual A&H	Total
2007	10,775	...	...	...	...	34,917
2008	11,411	...	...	...	...	53,056
2009	12,766	...	...	...	...	71,636

• **NET OPERATING GAIN ($000 omitted)**

Year	Individual Life	Individual & Group Annuities	Group Life & A&H	Credit Life & A&H	Individual A&H	Total
2007	1,121	3,795	...	...	1	3,784
2008	431	3,640	...	...	...	2,900
2009	794	5,550	...	...	...	5,092

• **COMPARATIVE FINANCIALS ($000 omitted)**

Year	Assets	Capital & Surplus	Net Invest Income	Benefits Paid	Realized Cap Gains	Policyholder Dividends	Contract Lns (% of assets)
2007	671,496	51,279	36,381	42,543	264	937	1.0
2008	704,237	50,909	37,710	38,624	-4,915	960	1.0
2009	770,595	54,072	40,014	33,512	-1,953	989	0.9

• **ORDINARY LIFE STATISTICS**

Year	Av. Ord. Policy Issued ($)	Av. Ord. Policy In Force ($)	Avg. Prem ($/M)	1st Yr Prem/ Total Prem	Ord. Lapse Ratio
2007	49,398	31,209	6.26	12.7	2.9
2008	52,409	31,960	6.37	12.6	3.4
2009	51,082	32,702	6.91	14.4	3.2

• **NEW LIFE BUSINESS ISSUED ($000 omitted)**

Year	Whole Life	Term	Credit	Group	Industrial	Total
2007	90,151	...	...	...	...	90,151
2008	136,683	...	...	...	...	136,683
2009	121,064	...	...	...	...	121,064

• **LIFE INSURANCE IN FORCE ($000 omitted)**

Year	Whole Life	Term	Credit	Group	Industrial	Total
2007	1,740,367	...	...	...	...	1,740,367
2008	1,809,050	...	...	...	...	1,809,050
2009	1,864,057	...	...	...	...	1,864,057

CATHOLIC KNIGHTS

1100 West Wells Street
Milwaukee, Wisconsin 53233-2316
Tel: 414-273-6266

AMB#: 008188
Began Business: 02/24/1885
Agency Off: William H. Thompson

Best's Financial Strength Rating: B u **FSC:** VI

• **NET PREMIUMS AND DEPOSITS ($000 omitted)**

Year	Individual Life	Individual & Group Annuities	Group Life & A&H	Credit Life & A&H	Individual A&H	Total
2007	25,481	...	...	...	31	43,162
2008	25,941	...	...	...	28	58,344
2009	27,464	...	...	...	24	70,234

• **NET OPERATING GAIN ($000 omitted)**

Year	Individual Life	Individual & Group Annuities	Group Life & A&H	Credit Life & A&H	Individual A&H	Total
2007	487	1,482	...	...	104	2,073
2008	1,181	1,379	...	...	46	2,606
2009	598	2,549	...	...	48	3,194

• **COMPARATIVE FINANCIALS ($000 omitted)**

Year	Assets	Capital & Surplus	Net Invest Income	Benefits Paid	Realized Cap Gains	Policyholder Dividends	Contract Lns (% of assets)
2007	817,567	51,873	45,370	50,366	7,208	3,573	2.4
2008	831,150	36,284	47,051	47,499	-9,845	3,672	2.3
2009	873,716	32,058	48,415	45,379	-15,461	3,345	2.3

• **ORDINARY LIFE STATISTICS**

Year	Av. Ord. Policy Issued ($)	Av. Ord. Policy In Force ($)	Avg. Prem ($/M)	1st Yr Prem/ Total Prem	Ord. Lapse Ratio
2007	114,161	40,530	7.87	4.9	3.6
2008	101,114	42,166	7.77	5.4	4.0
2009	94,048	43,407	8.10	7.5	4.7

• **NEW LIFE BUSINESS ISSUED ($000 omitted)**

Year	Whole Life	Term	Credit	Group	Industrial	Total
2007	198,869	...	...	...	...	198,869
2008	274,018	...	...	...	...	274,018
2009	268,131	...	...	...	...	268,131

• **LIFE INSURANCE IN FORCE ($000 omitted)**

Year	Whole Life	Term	Credit	Group	Industrial	Total
2007	3,281,300	...	...	...	...	3,281,300
2008	3,398,315	...	...	...	...	3,398,315
2009	3,476,778	...	...	...	...	3,476,778

CATHOLIC ORDER OF FORESTERS

P.O. Box 3012
Naperville, Illinois 60566-7012
Tel: 630-983-4900

AMB#: 006191
Began Business: 05/24/1883
Agency Off: Thomas E. Adamson

Best's Financial Strength Rating: B++ **FSC:** VI

• **NET PREMIUMS AND DEPOSITS ($000 omitted)**

Year	Individual Life	Individual & Group Annuities	Group Life & A&H	Credit Life & A&H	Individual A&H	Total
2007	29,506	...	...	...	1,461	55,206
2008	31,473	...	...	...	1,028	76,970
2009	30,428	...	...	...	1,011	111,627

• **NET OPERATING GAIN ($000 omitted)**

Year	Individual Life	Individual & Group Annuities	Group Life & A&H	Credit Life & A&H	Individual A&H	Total
2007	1,110	-264	...	...	88	228
2008	1,276	2,033	...	...	-650	1,908
2009	2,588	2,286	...	...	396	4,071

• **COMPARATIVE FINANCIALS ($000 omitted)**

Year	Assets	Capital & Surplus	Net Invest Income	Benefits Paid	Realized Cap Gains	Policyholder Dividends	Contract Lns (% of assets)
2007	618,796	39,053	32,474	48,563	493	6,807	1.4
2008	632,921	35,673	33,451	59,505	-3,635	6,369	1.5
2009	685,405	38,125	35,990	75,032	-1,291	7,184	1.5

• **ORDINARY LIFE STATISTICS**

Year	Av. Ord. Policy Issued ($)	Av. Ord. Policy In Force ($)	Avg. Prem ($/M)	1st Yr Prem/ Total Prem	Ord. Lapse Ratio
2007	21,226	19,126	10.48	4.8	5.3
2008	40,254	19,752	10.95	4.3	4.5
2009	71,004	20,137	10.50	3.1	5.4

• **NEW LIFE BUSINESS ISSUED ($000 omitted)**

Year	Whole Life	Term	Credit	Group	Industrial	Total
2007	201,813	...	...	...	...	201,813
2008	151,114	...	...	...	...	151,114
2009	146,836	...	...	...	...	146,836

• **LIFE INSURANCE IN FORCE ($000 omitted)**

Year	Whole Life	Term	Credit	Group	Industrial	Total
2007	2,751,964	...	...	...	...	2,751,964
2008	2,777,335	...	...	...	...	2,777,335
2009	2,750,536	...	...	...	...	2,750,536

CELTIC INSURANCE COMPANY

233 South Wacker Drive, Suite 700
Chicago, Illinois 60606-6393
Tel: 312-332-5401

AMB#: 006999
Began Business: 01/20/1950
Agency Off: Blake A. Westerfield

Best's Financial Strength Rating: B++ **FSC:** V

• NET PREMIUMS AND DEPOSITS ($000 omitted)

Year	Individual Life	Individual & Group Annuities	Group Life & A&H	Credit Life & A&H	Individual A&H	Total
2007	0	...	52,550	...	40,530	93,080
2008	0	...	42,945	...	40,264	83,210
2009	0	...	39,051	...	40,312	79,363

• NET OPERATING GAIN ($000 omitted)

Year	Individual Life	Individual & Group Annuities	Group Life & A&H	Credit Life & A&H	Individual A&H	Total
2007	-5	...	2,004	...	3,079	5,079
2008	-7	...	2,400	...	3,403	5,796
2009	-5	...	318	...	2,019	2,332

• COMPARATIVE FINANCIALS ($000 omitted)

Year	Assets	Capital & Surplus	Net Invest Income	Benefits Paid	Realized Cap Gains	Policyholder Dividends	Contract Lns (% of assets)
2007	99,645	49,055	5,014	58,869	...	...	...
2008	66,800	22,378	3,867	53,631	-1,091	...	...
2009	58,158	19,797	1,697	51,122	...	...	...

• ORDINARY LIFE STATISTICS

Year	Av. Ord. Policy Issued ($)	Av. Ord. Policy In Force ($)	Avg. Prem ($/M)	1st Yr Prem/ Total Prem	Ord. Lapse Ratio
2007	...	...	...	...	...
2008	...	...	...	...	...
2009	...	...	...	...	...

• NEW LIFE BUSINESS ISSUED ($000 omitted)

Year	Whole Life	Term	Credit	Group	Industrial	Total
2007	...	300	...	895	...	1,195
2008	...	...	...	1,650	...	1,650
2009	...	...	...	1,700	...	1,700

• LIFE INSURANCE IN FORCE ($000 omitted)

Year	Whole Life	Term	Credit	Group	Industrial	Total
2007	2,562	29,302	...	1,481	...	33,345
2008	2,315	24,173	...	3,114	...	29,602
2009	2,174	20,823	...	2,808	...	25,805

CENTRAL RESERVE LIFE

11200 Lakeline Blvd., Suite 100
Austin, Texas 78717
Tel: 512-451-2224

AMB#: 006203
Began Business: 05/12/1965
Agency Off: None

Best's Financial Strength Rating: B++ **FSC:** V

• NET PREMIUMS AND DEPOSITS ($000 omitted)

Year	Individual Life	Individual & Group Annuities	Group Life & A&H	Credit Life & A&H	Individual A&H	Total
2007	573	138	178	...	18,866	19,755
2008	894	126	261	...	19,026	20,307
2009	653	95	104	...	14,642	15,494

• NET OPERATING GAIN ($000 omitted)

Year	Individual Life	Individual & Group Annuities	Group Life & A&H	Credit Life & A&H	Individual A&H	Total
2007	14	219	-153	-498	529	112
2008	9	6	406	...	375	796
2009	-216	-57	-33	...	-226	-532

• COMPARATIVE FINANCIALS ($000 omitted)

Year	Assets	Capital & Surplus	Net Invest Income	Benefits Paid	Realized Cap Gains	Policyholder Dividends	Contract Lns (% of assets)
2007	31,942	17,389	921	14,717	-20	5	0.1
2008	25,029	14,622	478	14,308	-4	3	0.2
2009	26,121	16,716	326	11,056	...	3	0.2

• ORDINARY LIFE STATISTICS

Year	Av. Ord. Policy Issued ($)	Av. Ord. Policy In Force ($)	Avg. Prem ($/M)	1st Yr Prem/ Total Prem	Ord. Lapse Ratio
2007	...	...	...	...	...
2008	...	...	...	...	...
2009	...	...	...	...	...

• NEW LIFE BUSINESS ISSUED ($000 omitted)

Year	Whole Life	Term	Credit	Group	Industrial	Total
2007	5,590	440	...	...	...	6,030
2008	2,831	...	...	...	...	2,831
2009	1,403	...	...	...	...	1,403

• LIFE INSURANCE IN FORCE ($000 omitted)

Year	Whole Life	Term	Credit	Group	Industrial	Total
2007	15,159	56,136	...	168,636	...	239,931
2008	14,911	50,145	...	...	...	65,056
2009	13,927	46,604	...	...	...	60,530

CENSTAT LIFE ASSURANCE COMPANY

P.O. Box 34350
Omaha, Nebraska 68134-0350
Tel: 402-397-1111

AMB#: 060246
Began Business: 01/27/1987
Agency Off: T. Edward Kizer

Best's Financial Strength Rating: B++g **FSC:** VIII

• NET PREMIUMS AND DEPOSITS ($000 omitted)

Year	Individual Life	Individual & Group Annuities	Group Life & A&H	Credit Life & A&H	Individual A&H	Total
2007	...	...	...	2,383	...	2,383
2008	...	...	...	2,364	...	2,364
2009	...	...	...	2,277	...	2,277

• NET OPERATING GAIN ($000 omitted)

Year	Individual Life	Individual & Group Annuities	Group Life & A&H	Credit Life & A&H	Individual A&H	Total
2007	...	...	...	699	...	699
2008	...	...	...	429	...	429
2009	...	...	...	604	...	604

• COMPARATIVE FINANCIALS ($000 omitted)

Year	Assets	Capital & Surplus	Net Invest Income	Benefits Paid	Realized Cap Gains	Policyholder Dividends	Contract Lns (% of assets)
2007	4,735	3,094	189	568	...	...	...
2008	4,819	3,223	184	710	...	...	...
2009	5,064	3,493	174	537	...	...	...

• ORDINARY LIFE STATISTICS

Year	Av. Ord. Policy Issued ($)	Av. Ord. Policy In Force ($)	Avg. Prem ($/M)	1st Yr Prem/ Total Prem	Ord. Lapse Ratio
2007	...	...	...	...	...
2008	...	...	...	...	...
2009	...	...	...	...	...

• NEW LIFE BUSINESS ISSUED ($000 omitted)

Year	Whole Life	Term	Credit	Group	Industrial	Total
2007	...	...	...	...	...	...
2008	...	...	...	...	...	...
2009	...	...	...	...	...	...

• LIFE INSURANCE IN FORCE ($000 omitted)

Year	Whole Life	Term	Credit	Group	Industrial	Total
2007	...	...	84,711	...	...	84,711
2008	...	...	84,678	...	...	84,678
2009	...	...	85,585	...	...	85,585

CENTRAL STATES H&L CO OF OMAHA

1212 North 96th Street
Omaha, Nebraska 68114
Tel: 402-397-1111

AMB#: 006206
Began Business: 06/02/1932
Agency Off: Jeffrey Wanning

Best's Financial Strength Rating: B++g **FSC:** VIII

• NET PREMIUMS AND DEPOSITS ($000 omitted)

Year	Individual Life	Individual & Group Annuities	Group Life & A&H	Credit Life & A&H	Individual A&H	Total
2007	3,377	1	571	76,770	-4	80,714
2008	3,189	7	228	82,179	-40	85,565
2009	2,824	1	71	54,882	-10	57,767

• NET OPERATING GAIN ($000 omitted)

Year	Individual Life	Individual & Group Annuities	Group Life & A&H	Credit Life & A&H	Individual A&H	Total
2007	3,511	0	1,058	51	4,971	5,606
2008	1,367	-1	635	82	4,794	1,812
2009	1,742	-1	-220	7,158	1,189	5,627

• COMPARATIVE FINANCIALS ($000 omitted)

Year	Assets	Capital & Surplus	Net Invest Income	Benefits Paid	Realized Cap Gains	Policyholder Dividends	Contract Lns (% of assets)
2007	290,811	99,050	16,327	20,356	0	104	1.2
2008	320,030	85,145	13,387	21,784	-2,572	97	0.9
2009	329,652	98,105	13,893	22,150	-1,473	91	0.9

• ORDINARY LIFE STATISTICS

Year	Av. Ord. Policy Issued ($)	Av. Ord. Policy In Force ($)	Avg. Prem ($/M)	1st Yr Prem/ Total Prem	Ord. Lapse Ratio
2007	...	...	...	...	...
2008	...	...	...	...	...
2009	...	...	...	...	...

• NEW LIFE BUSINESS ISSUED ($000 omitted)

Year	Whole Life	Term	Credit	Group	Industrial	Total
2007	16	1,087	2,605,143	11,090	...	2,617,336
2008	...	612	2,906,190	6,465	...	2,913,267
2009	...	992	2,556,450	7,360	...	2,564,802

• LIFE INSURANCE IN FORCE ($000 omitted)

Year	Whole Life	Term	Credit	Group	Industrial	Total
2007	146,225	84,126	4,377,413	86,781	...	4,694,545
2008	138,088	76,836	4,985,929	64,760	...	5,265,613
2009	130,298	70,759	5,069,507	56,682	...	5,327,245

CENTRAL UNITED LIFE INS CO

2727 Allen Parkway Wortham Tower, Suite 500
Houston, Texas 77019
Tel: 713-529-0045

AMB#: 006222
Began Business: 09/03/1963
Agency Off: Thomas Luchetta

Best's Financial Strength Rating: B+ **FSC:** VI

• NET PREMIUMS AND DEPOSITS ($000 omitted)

Year	Individual Life	Individual & Group Annuities	Group Life & A&H	Credit Life & A&H	Individual A&H	Total
2007	7,248	1,539	5,383	...	88,172	102,341
2008	6,631	1,401	4,660	...	81,218	93,911
2009	5,833	1,484	4,439	...	87,916	99,672

• NET OPERATING GAIN ($000 omitted)

Year	Individual Life	Individual & Group Annuities	Group Life & A&H	Credit Life & A&H	Individual A&H	Total
2007	764	443	86	...	3,888	5,182
2008	1,184	162	235	...	670	2,252
2009	1,749	289	20	...	2,453	4,510

• COMPARATIVE FINANCIALS ($000 omitted)

Year	Assets	Capital & Surplus	Net Invest Income	Benefits Paid	Realized Cap Gains	Policyholder Dividends	Contract Lns (% of assets)
2007	332,548	37,018	10,195	102,017	8	402	2.4
2008	321,381	38,090	8,190	93,606	...	335	2.4
2009	332,629	44,620	6,046	90,141	-307	389	2.2

• ORDINARY LIFE STATISTICS

Year	Av. Ord. Policy Issued ($)	Av. Ord. Policy In Force ($)	Avg. Prem ($/M)	1st Yr Prem/ Total Prem	Ord. Lapse Ratio
2007	...	...	...	...	...
2008	...	...	...	...	...
2009	...	...	...	...	...

• NEW LIFE BUSINESS ISSUED ($000 omitted)

Year	Whole Life	Term	Credit	Group	Industrial	Total
2007	4,796	4,226	...	...	...	9,022
2008	12,276	3,921	...	...	...	16,197
2009	4,642	9,615	...	...	...	14,257

• LIFE INSURANCE IN FORCE ($000 omitted)

Year	Whole Life	Term	Credit	Group	Industrial	Total
2007	569,350	527,485	...	4,736	...	1,101,571
2008	625,265	521,388	...	4,112	...	1,150,765
2009	684,919	600,237	...	3,594	...	1,288,752

CENTURY LIFE ASSUR CO

P.O. Box 9510
Wichita, Kansas 67277
Tel: 316-794-2200

AMB#: 009124
Began Business: 05/01/1980
Agency Off: Bruce Welner

Best's Financial Strength Rating: B- g **FSC:** V

• NET PREMIUMS AND DEPOSITS ($000 omitted)

Year	Individual Life	Individual & Group Annuities	Group Life & A&H	Credit Life & A&H	Individual A&H	Total
2007	398	33	2	1,598	22	2,053
2008	291	120	0	1,226	25	1,663
2009	349	238	...	535	28	1,150

• NET OPERATING GAIN ($000 omitted)

Year	Individual Life	Individual & Group Annuities	Group Life & A&H	Credit Life & A&H	Individual A&H	Total
2007	53	...	0	-86	64	31
2008	441	9	0	472	56	978
2009	16	18	...	350	51	436

• COMPARATIVE FINANCIALS ($000 omitted)

Year	Assets	Capital & Surplus	Net Invest Income	Benefits Paid	Realized Cap Gains	Policyholder Dividends	Contract Lns (% of assets)
2007	10,027	4,208	301	1,013	5	...	0.1
2008	9,376	4,761	434	647	-458	...	0.1
2009	9,736	5,109	413	776	-8	...	0.1

• ORDINARY LIFE STATISTICS

Year	Av. Ord. Policy Issued ($)	Av. Ord. Policy In Force ($)	Avg. Prem ($/M)	1st Yr Prem/ Total Prem	Ord. Lapse Ratio
2007	...	...	...	...	...
2008	...	...	...	...	...
2009	...	...	...	...	...

• NEW LIFE BUSINESS ISSUED ($000 omitted)

Year	Whole Life	Term	Credit	Group	Industrial	Total
2007	...	4,543	75,315	...	...	79,858
2008	...	2,515	61,672	...	...	64,187
2009	37	1,761	34,533	...	...	36,331

• LIFE INSURANCE IN FORCE ($000 omitted)

Year	Whole Life	Term	Credit	Group	Industrial	Total
2007	4,621	89,542	125,649	...	...	219,812
2008	4,311	79,029	116,055	...	...	199,395
2009	3,988	69,219	89,904	...	...	163,110

CENTURION LIFE INS CO

800 Walnut Street
Des Moines, Iowa 50309
Tel: 515-557-2131

AMB#: 006276
Began Business: 07/01/1956
Agency Off: None

Best's Financial Strength Rating: A **FSC:** XII

• NET PREMIUMS AND DEPOSITS ($000 omitted)

Year	Individual Life	Individual & Group Annuities	Group Life & A&H	Credit Life & A&H	Individual A&H	Total
2007	...	45,361	...	48,757	...	94,118
2008	...	81,274	...	54,045	...	135,319
2009	...	151,262	3,763	47,548	...	202,573

• NET OPERATING GAIN ($000 omitted)

Year	Individual Life	Individual & Group Annuities	Group Life & A&H	Credit Life & A&H	Individual A&H	Total
2007	21	2,021	...	40,845	...	42,888
2008	23	4,378	...	45,557	...	49,957
2009	21	5,849	758	34,297	...	40,871

• COMPARATIVE FINANCIALS ($000 omitted)

Year	Assets	Capital & Surplus	Net Invest Income	Benefits Paid	Realized Cap Gains	Policyholder Dividends	Contract Lns (% of assets)
2007	1,521,634	949,939	47,235	28,951	2,137	...	...
2008	1,620,996	993,314	43,851	35,330	-2,176	...	...
2009	1,887,808	1,023,395	59,794	37,844	-3,408	...	...

• ORDINARY LIFE STATISTICS

Year	Av. Ord. Policy Issued ($)	Av. Ord. Policy In Force ($)	Avg. Prem ($/M)	1st Yr Prem/ Total Prem	Ord. Lapse Ratio
2007	...	...	...	...	...
2008	...	...	...	...	...
2009	...	...	...	...	...

• NEW LIFE BUSINESS ISSUED ($000 omitted)

Year	Whole Life	Term	Credit	Group	Industrial	Total
2007	...	...	718,924	...	...	718,924
2008	...	...	446,727	...	...	446,727
2009	...	...	86,645	...	...	86,645

• LIFE INSURANCE IN FORCE ($000 omitted)

Year	Whole Life	Term	Credit	Group	Industrial	Total
2007	59	56	2,743,960	...	...	2,744,075
2008	59	440	2,285,151	...	...	2,285,650
2009	59	56	1,855,291	...	...	1,855,406

CHARLESTON CAPITAL RE LLC

132 Turnpike Road, Suite 210
Southborough, Massachusetts 01772
Tel: 843-577-1030

AMB#: 076825
Began Business: 12/15/2004
Agency Off: None

Best's Financial Strength Rating: A- g **FSC:** IX

• NET PREMIUMS AND DEPOSITS ($000 omitted)

Year	Individual Life	Individual & Group Annuities	Group Life & A&H	Credit Life & A&H	Individual A&H	Total
2007	...	787	...	...	...	787
2008	19,205	483	84	...	...	19,772
2009	16,110	842	38	...	...	16,990

• NET OPERATING GAIN ($000 omitted)

Year	Individual Life	Individual & Group Annuities	Group Life & A&H	Credit Life & A&H	Individual A&H	Total
2007	...	-950	...	...	...	-950
2008	-3,182	95	-23	...	...	-3,110
2009	2,635	892	47	...	...	7,323

• COMPARATIVE FINANCIALS ($000 omitted)

Year	Assets	Capital & Surplus	Net Invest Income	Benefits Paid	Realized Cap Gains	Policyholder Dividends	Contract Lns (% of assets)
2007	61,803	9,157	2,656	7,025	-29	...	0.2
2008	724,220	54,520	33,033	82,634	-9,567	12,892	17.4
2009	690,742	70,748	42,202	88,392	-145	12,634	15.1

• ORDINARY LIFE STATISTICS

Year	Av. Ord. Policy Issued ($)	Av. Ord. Policy In Force ($)	Avg. Prem ($/M)	1st Yr Prem/ Total Prem	Ord. Lapse Ratio
2007	...	...	...	...	...
2008	...	34,671	14.74	...	...
2009	...	33,300	13.82	...	...

• NEW LIFE BUSINESS ISSUED ($000 omitted)

Year	Whole Life	Term	Credit	Group	Industrial	Total
2007	...	...	...	...	...	...
2008	...	...	...	...	...	...
2009	...	...	...	...	...	...

• LIFE INSURANCE IN FORCE ($000 omitted)

Year	Whole Life	Term	Credit	Group	Industrial	Total
2007	...	...	...	...	...	...
2008	1,269,747	33,443	...	1,372	...	1,304,562
2009	1,135,997	30,003	...	1,163	...	1,167,163

CHARTER NATIONAL LIFE INS CO

3100 Sanders Road
Northbrook, Illinois 60062-7154
Tel: 847-402-5000

AMB#: 006211
Began Business: 12/18/1955
Agency Off: None

Best's Financial Strength Rating: B++ **FSC:** V

• NET PREMIUMS AND DEPOSITS ($000 omitted)

Year	Individual Life	Individual & Group Annuities	Group Life & A&H	Credit Life & A&H	Individual A&H	Total
2007	...	4	...	...	...	4
2008	...	11	...	...	...	11
2009	...	7	...	...	...	7

• NET OPERATING GAIN ($000 omitted)

Year	Individual Life	Individual & Group Annuities	Group Life & A&H	Credit Life & A&H	Individual A&H	Total
2007	...	...	...	...	...	364
2008	...	...	...	...	...	334
2009	...	...	...	...	...	294

• COMPARATIVE FINANCIALS ($000 omitted)

Year	Assets	Capital & Surplus	Net Invest Income	Benefits Paid	Realized Cap Gains	Policyholder Dividends	Contract Lns (% of assets)
2007	254,443	9,693	508	...	...	...	...
2008	150,135	10,024	469	...	...	...	...
2009	158,196	10,317	412	...	...	...	...

• ORDINARY LIFE STATISTICS

Year	Av. Ord. Policy Issued ($)	Av. Ord. Policy In Force ($)	Avg. Prem ($/M)	1st Yr Prem/ Total Prem	Ord. Lapse Ratio
2007	...	...	...	...	...
2008	...	...	...	...	...
2009	...	...	...	...	...

• NEW LIFE BUSINESS ISSUED ($000 omitted)

Year	Whole Life	Term	Credit	Group	Industrial	Total
2007	...	...	...	...	...	...
2008	...	...	...	...	...	...
2009	...	...	...	...	...	...

• LIFE INSURANCE IN FORCE ($000 omitted)

Year	Whole Life	Term	Credit	Group	Industrial	Total
2007	62,406	...	...	5,178	...	67,584
2008	56,086	...	...	5,117	...	61,203
2009	55,509	...	...	5,027	...	60,537

CHESAPEAKE LIFE INS CO

9151 Boulevard 26
North Richland Hills, Texas 76180
Tel: 817-255-3100

AMB#: 006215
Began Business: 10/01/1956
Agency Off: None

Best's Financial Strength Rating: B++g **FSC:** VIII

• NET PREMIUMS AND DEPOSITS ($000 omitted)

Year	Individual Life	Individual & Group Annuities	Group Life & A&H	Credit Life & A&H	Individual A&H	Total
2007	1,090	500	20,603	...	5,189	27,382
2008	160	429	104,174	...	12,778	117,540
2009	53	402	7,193	...	10,431	18,079

• NET OPERATING GAIN ($000 omitted)

Year	Individual Life	Individual & Group Annuities	Group Life & A&H	Credit Life & A&H	Individual A&H	Total
2007	2,052	437	1,838	...	-6,238	-1,910
2008	-5,134	4,246	-5,979	...	553	-6,314
2009	-1	8	-507	...	22	-478

• COMPARATIVE FINANCIALS ($000 omitted)

Year	Assets	Capital & Surplus	Net Invest Income	Benefits Paid	Realized Cap Gains	Policyholder Dividends	Contract Lns (% of assets)
2007	96,029	48,300	4,715	18,003	641	27	2.7
2008	83,771	42,461	4,087	90,830	-2,470	-21	...
2009	73,365	42,256	2,167	14,658	-658	...	...

• ORDINARY LIFE STATISTICS

Year	Av. Ord. Policy Issued ($)	Av. Ord. Policy In Force ($)	Avg. Prem ($/M)	1st Yr Prem/ Total Prem	Ord. Lapse Ratio
2007	...	...	...	...	...
2008	...	...	...	...	...
2009	...	...	...	...	...

• NEW LIFE BUSINESS ISSUED ($000 omitted)

Year	Whole Life	Term	Credit	Group	Industrial	Total
2007	312,369	900,075	...	...	...	1,212,444
2008	303,696	543,103	...	...	...	846,799
2009	65,907	500	...	...	...	66,407

• LIFE INSURANCE IN FORCE ($000 omitted)

Year	Whole Life	Term	Credit	Group	Industrial	Total
2007	1,390,609	3,796,386	...	39	8,278	5,195,312
2008	1,492,347	3,536,534	...	39	7,905	5,036,825
2009	1,351,567	3,127,414	...	...	7,657	4,486,638

CHEROKEE NATIONAL LIFE INS CO

P.O. Box 6097
Macon, Georgia 31208-6097
Tel: 478-477-0400

AMB#: 006214
Began Business: 04/01/1956
Agency Off: None

Best's Financial Strength Rating: A- **FSC:** V

• NET PREMIUMS AND DEPOSITS ($000 omitted)

Year	Individual Life	Individual & Group Annuities	Group Life & A&H	Credit Life & A&H	Individual A&H	Total
2007	...	...	...	14,316	103	14,419
2008	...	...	...	11,975	46	12,022
2009	...	...	...	8,656	29	8,685

• NET OPERATING GAIN ($000 omitted)

Year	Individual Life	Individual & Group Annuities	Group Life & A&H	Credit Life & A&H	Individual A&H	Total
2007	...	...	...	1,320	-75	1,245
2008	...	...	...	813	-23	791
2009	...	...	...	1,271	-19	1,252

• COMPARATIVE FINANCIALS ($000 omitted)

Year	Assets	Capital & Surplus	Net Invest Income	Benefits Paid	Realized Cap Gains	Policyholder Dividends	Contract Lns (% of assets)
2007	34,699	11,860	1,585	6,961	-5	...	...
2008	30,991	11,506	1,278	6,227	-970	...	...
2009	28,445	13,244	1,363	5,423	189	...	...

• ORDINARY LIFE STATISTICS

Year	Av. Ord. Policy Issued ($)	Av. Ord. Policy In Force ($)	Avg. Prem ($/M)	1st Yr Prem/ Total Prem	Ord. Lapse Ratio
2007	...	...	...	...	...
2008	...	...	...	...	...
2009	...	...	...	...	...

• NEW LIFE BUSINESS ISSUED ($000 omitted)

Year	Whole Life	Term	Credit	Group	Industrial	Total
2007	...	...	777,069	...	...	777,069
2008	...	...	665,450	...	...	665,450
2009	...	...	525,379	...	...	525,379

• LIFE INSURANCE IN FORCE ($000 omitted)

Year	Whole Life	Term	Credit	Group	Industrial	Total
2007	925	717	956,518	...	...	958,160
2008	865	745	825,657	...	...	827,267
2009	798	745	732,518	...	...	734,062

CHRISTIAN FIDELITY LIFE INS CO

2721 North Central Avenue
Phoenix, Arizona 85004-1172
Tel: 800-527-6797

AMB#: 006217
Began Business: 12/01/1935
Agency Off: Don C. Smith

Best's Financial Strength Rating: B++g **FSC:** VIII

• NET PREMIUMS AND DEPOSITS ($000 omitted)

Year	Individual Life	Individual & Group Annuities	Group Life & A&H	Credit Life & A&H	Individual A&H	Total
2007	884	83	8	...	57,465	58,439
2008	644	134	6	...	55,339	56,122
2009	1,111	28	0	...	52,754	53,893

• NET OPERATING GAIN ($000 omitted)

Year	Individual Life	Individual & Group Annuities	Group Life & A&H	Credit Life & A&H	Individual A&H	Total
2007	145	139	-6	...	3,084	4,189
2008	-13	92	2	...	3,529	4,342
2009	47	149	7	...	6,244	6,588

• COMPARATIVE FINANCIALS ($000 omitted)

Year	Assets	Capital & Surplus	Net Invest Income	Benefits Paid	Realized Cap Gains	Policyholder Dividends	Contract Lns (% of assets)
2007	79,114	25,414	3,865	45,250	...	...	0.4
2008	86,902	34,357	4,011	44,298	...	...	0.4
2009	88,089	39,784	3,719	43,159	-149	...	0.4

• ORDINARY LIFE STATISTICS

Year	Av. Ord. Policy Issued ($)	Av. Ord. Policy In Force ($)	Avg. Prem ($/M)	1st Yr Prem/ Total Prem	Ord. Lapse Ratio
2007	...	...	...	...	...
2008	...	...	...	...	...
2009	...	...	...	...	...

• NEW LIFE BUSINESS ISSUED ($000 omitted)

Year	Whole Life	Term	Credit	Group	Industrial	Total
2007	5,031	...	...	...	...	5,031
2008	5,192	...	...	...	...	5,192
2009	4,354	...	...	...	...	4,354

• LIFE INSURANCE IN FORCE ($000 omitted)

Year	Whole Life	Term	Credit	Group	Industrial	Total
2007	22,464	737	...	...	...	23,201
2008	24,819	517	...	...	...	25,336
2009	26,536	714	...	...	...	27,250

CHURCH LIFE INS CORPORATION

445 Fifth Avenue
New York, New York 10016
Tel: 212-592-1800

AMB#: 006221
Began Business: 07/01/1922
Agency Off: None

Best's Financial Strength Rating: A- **FSC:** VI

• **NET PREMIUMS AND DEPOSITS** ($000 omitted)

Year	Individual Life	Individual & Group Annuities	Group Life & A&H	Credit Life & A&H	Individual A&H	Total
2007	884	19,442	10,994	...	...	31,321
2008	874	16,079	11,555	...	...	28,508
2009	855	19,686	18,052	...	...	38,593

• **NET OPERATING GAIN** ($000 omitted)

Year	Individual Life	Individual & Group Annuities	Group Life & A&H	Credit Life & A&H	Individual A&H	Total
2007	-439	876	1,960	...	...	2,397
2008	-399	446	3,039	...	...	3,086
2009	-530	306	4,033	...	...	3,809

• **COMPARATIVE FINANCIALS** ($000 omitted)

Year	Assets	Capital & Surplus	Net Invest Income	Benefits Paid	Realized Cap Gains	Policyholder Dividends	Contract Lns (% of assets)
2007	201,279	37,456	9,639	29,321	...	...	0.2
2008	205,902	31,476	10,070	23,092	-6,204	...	0.2
2009	219,533	35,308	10,049	24,257	-1,528	...	0.2

• **ORDINARY LIFE STATISTICS**

Year	Av. Ord. Policy Issued ($)	Av. Ord. Policy In Force ($)	Avg. Prem ($/M)	1st Yr Prem/ Total Prem	Ord. Lapse Ratio
2007	...	...	...	...	...
2008	...	...	...	...	...
2009	...	...	...	...	...

• **NEW LIFE BUSINESS ISSUED** ($000 omitted)

Year	Whole Life	Term	Credit	Group	Industrial	Total
2007	581	2,085	...	87,933	...	90,599
2008	340	3,090	...	118,168	...	121,598
2009	657	6,550	...	88,328	...	95,535

• **LIFE INSURANCE IN FORCE** ($000 omitted)

Year	Whole Life	Term	Credit	Group	Industrial	Total
2007	24,933	28,539	...	922,503	...	975,975
2008	23,757	29,837	...	987,096	...	1,040,690
2009	22,942	35,353	...	1,409,022	...	1,467,316

CIGNA WORLDWIDE INSURANCE CO

P.O. Box 15050
Wilmington, Delaware
Tel: 215-761-6244

AMB#: 008944
Began Business: 05/17/1979
Agency Off: Virginia W. Hollis

Best's Financial Strength Rating: A- **FSC:** IV

• **NET PREMIUMS AND DEPOSITS** ($000 omitted)

Year	Individual Life	Individual & Group Annuities	Group Life & A&H	Credit Life & A&H	Individual A&H	Total
2007	...	...	57,368	...	...	57,368
2008	17	...	37,150	...	...	37,167
2009	20	...	17,457	...	-6	17,470

• **NET OPERATING GAIN** ($000 omitted)

Year	Individual Life	Individual & Group Annuities	Group Life & A&H	Credit Life & A&H	Individual A&H	Total
2007	-2	-88	9,144	...	41	9,095
2008	10	-94	9,559	...	...	9,475
2009	-105	-86	4,354	...	-6	4,157

• **COMPARATIVE FINANCIALS** ($000 omitted)

Year	Assets	Capital & Surplus	Net Invest Income	Benefits Paid	Realized Cap Gains	Policyholder Dividends	Contract Lns (% of assets)
2007	60,733	17,427	2,257	38,674	...	...	...
2008	53,377	16,412	2,103	18,188	-34	...	...
2009	48,188	8,965	1,231	7,966	...	...	...

• **ORDINARY LIFE STATISTICS**

Year	Av. Ord. Policy Issued ($)	Av. Ord. Policy In Force ($)	Avg. Prem ($/M)	1st Yr Prem/ Total Prem	Ord. Lapse Ratio
2007	...	...	...	...	...
2008	...	...	...	...	...
2009	...	...	...	...	...

• **NEW LIFE BUSINESS ISSUED** ($000 omitted)

Year	Whole Life	Term	Credit	Group	Industrial	Total
2007	...	...	...	99,438	...	99,438
2008	...	...	...	216	...	216
2009	...	...	...	...	...	...

• **LIFE INSURANCE IN FORCE** ($000 omitted)

Year	Whole Life	Term	Credit	Group	Industrial	Total
2007	...	...	...	717,619	...	717,619
2008	...	706,737	...	654,682	...	1,361,419
2009	...	859,640	...	864,026	...	1,723,666

CIGNA LIFE INS CO OF NEW YORK

Two Liberty Place, 1601 Chestnut Street, TL14A
Philadelphia, Pennsylvania 19192-2362
Tel: 215-761-1000

AMB#: 006538
Began Business: 12/28/1965
Agency Off: None

Best's Financial Strength Rating: A g **FSC:** XV

• **NET PREMIUMS AND DEPOSITS** ($000 omitted)

Year	Individual Life	Individual & Group Annuities	Group Life & A&H	Credit Life & A&H	Individual A&H	Total
2007	...	...	115,657	...	89	115,746
2008	...	...	122,942	...	92	123,034
2009	...	...	123,721	...	422	124,143

• **NET OPERATING GAIN** ($000 omitted)

Year	Individual Life	Individual & Group Annuities	Group Life & A&H	Credit Life & A&H	Individual A&H	Total
2007	...	-135	15,454	...	-1	15,318
2008	...	-57	32,572	...	1,177	33,692
2009	...	73	15,151	...	500	15,725

• **COMPARATIVE FINANCIALS** ($000 omitted)

Year	Assets	Capital & Surplus	Net Invest Income	Benefits Paid	Realized Cap Gains	Policyholder Dividends	Contract Lns (% of assets)
2007	381,697	85,420	21,069	80,019	1,027	...	...
2008	401,175	100,020	23,725	77,124	-7,940	...	...
2009	388,041	97,194	21,132	88,579	-203	...	...

• **ORDINARY LIFE STATISTICS**

Year	Av. Ord. Policy Issued ($)	Av. Ord. Policy In Force ($)	Avg. Prem ($/M)	1st Yr Prem/ Total Prem	Ord. Lapse Ratio
2007	...	...	...	...	...
2008	...	...	...	...	...
2009	...	...	...	...	...

• **NEW LIFE BUSINESS ISSUED** ($000 omitted)

Year	Whole Life	Term	Credit	Group	Industrial	Total
2007	...	...	...	4,632,656	...	4,632,656
2008	...	...	...	2,198,871	...	2,198,871
2009	...	...	...	2,666,296	...	2,666,296

• **LIFE INSURANCE IN FORCE** ($000 omitted)

Year	Whole Life	Term	Credit	Group	Industrial	Total
2007	675	129	...	13,534,825	...	13,535,629
2008	664	121	...	15,911,844	...	15,912,629
2009	630	158	...	14,250,162	...	14,250,950

CINCINNATI EQUITABLE LIFE

P.O. Box 3428
Cincinnati, Ohio 45201-3428
Tel: 513-621-1826

AMB#: 006757
Began Business: 07/11/1978
Agency Off: Gregory A. Baker

Best's Financial Strength Rating: B+ **FSC:** IV

• **NET PREMIUMS AND DEPOSITS** ($000 omitted)

Year	Individual Life	Individual & Group Annuities	Group Life & A&H	Credit Life & A&H	Individual A&H	Total
2007	5,219	0	...	...	185	5,404
2008	7,872	0	...	...	159	8,031
2009	9,932	0	...	...	154	10,086

• **NET OPERATING GAIN** ($000 omitted)

Year	Individual Life	Individual & Group Annuities	Group Life & A&H	Credit Life & A&H	Individual A&H	Total
2007	-532	0	-5	...	6	-531
2008	-204	-3	...	...	17	-189
2009	-270	0	...	...	12	-258

• **COMPARATIVE FINANCIALS** ($000 omitted)

Year	Assets	Capital & Surplus	Net Invest Income	Benefits Paid	Realized Cap Gains	Policyholder Dividends	Contract Lns (% of assets)
2007	15,558	9,524	284	567	3	1	0.5
2008	19,753	8,904	895	1,451	-129	1	0.3
2009	25,016	8,651	1,413	2,633	-25	2	0.2

• **ORDINARY LIFE STATISTICS**

Year	Av. Ord. Policy Issued ($)	Av. Ord. Policy In Force ($)	Avg. Prem ($/M)	1st Yr Prem/ Total Prem	Ord. Lapse Ratio
2007	...	...	...	...	...
2008	...	...	...	...	...
2009	...	...	...	...	...

• **NEW LIFE BUSINESS ISSUED** ($000 omitted)

Year	Whole Life	Term	Credit	Group	Industrial	Total
2007	8,843	40	...	...	...	8,883
2008	10,564	...	...	...	...	10,564
2009	12,995	...	...	...	...	12,995

• **LIFE INSURANCE IN FORCE** ($000 omitted)

Year	Whole Life	Term	Credit	Group	Industrial	Total
2007	9,706	1,235	...	...	...	10,941
2008	18,273	1,225	...	...	...	19,498
2009	27,716	1,171	...	...	...	28,887

CINCINNATI LIFE INSURANCE CO

P.O. Box 145496
Cincinnati, Ohio 45250-5496
Tel: 513-870-2000

AMB#: 006568
Began Business: 02/01/1988
Agency Off: J. F. Scherer, Jr.

Best's Financial Strength Rating: A **FSC:** IX

• **NET PREMIUMS AND DEPOSITS ($000 omitted)**

Year	Individual Life	Individual & Group Annuities	Group Life & A&H	Credit Life & A&H	Individual A&H	Total
2007	130,663	37,294	2,793	...	2,278	173,028
2008	138,562	41,986	2,565	...	2,208	185,321
2009	152,120	190,581	2,371	...	2,241	347,314

• **NET OPERATING GAIN ($000 omitted)**

Year	Individual Life	Individual & Group Annuities	Group Life & A&H	Credit Life & A&H	Individual A&H	Total
2007	-22,749	3,175	3,625	...	143	6,884
2008	-12,769	3,136	3,112	...	-118	-17,561
2009	7,179	-3,668	477	...	38	10,879

• **COMPARATIVE FINANCIALS ($000 omitted)**

Year	Assets	Capital & Surplus	Net Invest Income	Benefits Paid	Realized Cap Gains	Policyholder Dividends	Contract Lns (% of assets)
2007	2,549,965	476,935	114,430	107,517	32,401	0	1.2
2008	2,477,627	290,089	119,545	117,827	-52,560	0	1.5
2009	2,830,559	300,245	126,204	117,115	4,211	0	1.4

• **ORDINARY LIFE STATISTICS**

Year	Av. Ord. Policy Issued ($)	Av. Ord. Policy In Force ($)	Avg. Prem ($/M)	1st Yr Prem/ Total Prem	Ord. Lapse Ratio
2007	210,647	170,159	2.99	16.5	4.5
2008	216,751	178,187	2.94	14.8	4.9
2009	209,168	184,549	2.95	15.3	5.0

• **NEW LIFE BUSINESS ISSUED ($000 omitted)**

Year	Whole Life	Term	Credit	Group	Industrial	Total
2007	701,485	7,124,911	...	19,788	...	7,846,184
2008	609,285	6,822,250	...	20,020	...	7,451,555
2009	612,492	7,007,725	...	14,829	...	7,635,046

• **LIFE INSURANCE IN FORCE ($000 omitted)**

Year	Whole Life	Term	Credit	Group	Industrial	Total
2007	6,675,321	53,369,233	...	1,797,427	32,970	61,874,951
2008	6,791,787	57,210,317	...	1,854,511	31,611	65,888,226
2009	6,856,271	61,022,986	...	1,905,317	30,279	69,814,854

CITIZENS SECURITY LIFE INS CO

12910 Shelbyville Road, Suite 300
Louisville, Kentucky 40243
Tel: 502-244-2420

AMB#: 006227
Began Business: 10/02/1965
Agency Off: Michael S. Williams

Best's Financial Strength Rating: C++ **FSC:** IV

• **NET PREMIUMS AND DEPOSITS ($000 omitted)**

Year	Individual Life	Individual & Group Annuities	Group Life & A&H	Credit Life & A&H	Individual A&H	Total
2007	10,787	330	9,960	...	700	21,777
2008	10,257	50	13,547	...	664	24,517
2009	8,387	98	18,976	...	1,709	29,170

• **NET OPERATING GAIN ($000 omitted)**

Year	Individual Life	Individual & Group Annuities	Group Life & A&H	Credit Life & A&H	Individual A&H	Total
2007	937	-30	-1,812	...	-141	-1,046
2008	19	-370	-939	...	-161	-1,451
2009	-724	-86	-2,437	...	352	-2,895

• **COMPARATIVE FINANCIALS ($000 omitted)**

Year	Assets	Capital & Surplus	Net Invest Income	Benefits Paid	Realized Cap Gains	Policyholder Dividends	Contract Lns (% of assets)
2007	134,969	10,684	6,473	18,565	1,925	-8	3.4
2008	127,482	6,115	5,779	21,030	-8,008	21	3.7
2009	108,411	8,014	3,427	25,259	1,811	20	4.1

• **ORDINARY LIFE STATISTICS**

Year	Av. Ord. Policy Issued ($)	Av. Ord. Policy In Force ($)	Avg. Prem ($/M)	1st Yr Prem/ Total Prem	Ord. Lapse Ratio
2007	...	...	...	...	...
2008	...	...	...	...	...
2009	...	...	...	...	...

• **NEW LIFE BUSINESS ISSUED ($000 omitted)**

Year	Whole Life	Term	Credit	Group	Industrial	Total
2007	72,076	1,911	...	12,955	...	86,942
2008	53,917	2,599	...	47,892	...	104,408
2009	31,110	1,158	...	41,798	...	74,066

• **LIFE INSURANCE IN FORCE ($000 omitted)**

Year	Whole Life	Term	Credit	Group	Industrial	Total
2007	493,844	95,159	79	83,515	11,647	684,244
2008	482,750	93,561	40	128,297	13,781	718,429
2009	450,748	92,860	17	130,825	12,970	687,419

COLONIAL LIFE & ACCIDENT INS

1200 Colonial Life Blvd.
Columbia, South Carolina 29210
Tel: 803-798-7000

AMB#: 006238
Began Business: 09/22/1939
Agency Off: Tom Gilligan

Best's Financial Strength Rating: A- g **FSC:** XIV

• **NET PREMIUMS AND DEPOSITS ($000 omitted)**

Year	Individual Life	Individual & Group Annuities	Group Life & A&H	Credit Life & A&H	Individual A&H	Total
2007	176,688	...	32,465	...	736,393	945,545
2008	188,988	...	35,394	...	787,305	1,011,687
2009	194,876	...	35,427	...	812,657	1,042,960

• **NET OPERATING GAIN ($000 omitted)**

Year	Individual Life	Individual & Group Annuities	Group Life & A&H	Credit Life & A&H	Individual A&H	Total
2007	10,729	11	4,574	...	99,107	114,421
2008	14,641	-1	4,592	...	104,893	124,125
2009	19,730	12	8,736	...	103,490	131,969

• **COMPARATIVE FINANCIALS ($000 omitted)**

Year	Assets	Capital & Surplus	Net Invest Income	Benefits Paid	Realized Cap Gains	Policyholder Dividends	Contract Lns (% of assets)
2007	1,902,121	369,259	111,965	389,542	2,015	...	1.9
2008	1,988,846	379,589	116,579	417,765	-14,831	...	1.8
2009	2,141,799	459,733	124,591	447,764	-7,603	...	1.8

• **ORDINARY LIFE STATISTICS**

Year	Av. Ord. Policy Issued ($)	Av. Ord. Policy In Force ($)	Avg. Prem ($/M)	1st Yr Prem/ Total Prem	Ord. Lapse Ratio
2007	58,798	43,220	6.68	22.7	17.3
2008	60,942	44,611	6.61	20.4	16.3
2009	61,248	45,644	6.53	18.5	15.9

• **NEW LIFE BUSINESS ISSUED ($000 omitted)**

Year	Whole Life	Term	Credit	Group	Industrial	Total
2007	1,998,164	6,354,805	...	607,627	...	8,960,596
2008	1,766,206	6,456,855	...	573,271	...	8,796,332
2009	1,936,696	5,701,430	...	430,185	...	8,068,311

• **LIFE INSURANCE IN FORCE ($000 omitted)**

Year	Whole Life	Term	Credit	Group	Industrial	Total
2007	14,592,420	15,933,033	...	1,900,565	...	32,426,018
2008	14,571,845	17,779,876	...	1,818,425	...	34,170,146
2009	14,751,257	18,728,882	...	1,745,956	...	35,226,095

COLONIAL PENN LIFE INSURANCE

11825 N. Pennsylvania Street
Carmel, Indiana 46032
Tel: 215-928-8000

AMB#: 006240
Began Business: 09/02/1959
Agency Off: Gaetano J. Fiordimondo

Best's Financial Strength Rating: B g **FSC:** X

• **NET PREMIUMS AND DEPOSITS ($000 omitted)**

Year	Individual Life	Individual & Group Annuities	Group Life & A&H	Credit Life & A&H	Individual A&H	Total
2007	61,932	4	54,102	...	8,746	124,785
2008	89,647	11	77,216	...	7,672	174,546
2009	97,203	190	78,301	...	6,583	182,276

• **NET OPERATING GAIN ($000 omitted)**

Year	Individual Life	Individual & Group Annuities	Group Life & A&H	Credit Life & A&H	Individual A&H	Total
2007	-28,289	-866	-23,801	...	-4,443	-55,332
2008	331	-26	-220	...	194	2,094
2009	7,093	-808	3,039	...	977	-239

• **COMPARATIVE FINANCIALS ($000 omitted)**

Year	Assets	Capital & Surplus	Net Invest Income	Benefits Paid	Realized Cap Gains	Policyholder Dividends	Contract Lns (% of assets)
2007	710,859	47,226	40,926	86,132	-56	...	2.3
2008	692,246	37,575	40,255	132,229	-2,447	...	2.5
2009	683,579	32,651	23,255	133,623	-3,538	...	2.4

• **ORDINARY LIFE STATISTICS**

Year	Av. Ord. Policy Issued ($)	Av. Ord. Policy In Force ($)	Avg. Prem ($/M)	1st Yr Prem/ Total Prem	Ord. Lapse Ratio
2007	3,739	2,750	55.78	22.0	5.3
2008	4,347	2,971	56.60	22.9	7.0
2009	3,858	3,134	57.27	17.9	5.1

• **NEW LIFE BUSINESS ISSUED ($000 omitted)**

Year	Whole Life	Term	Credit	Group	Industrial	Total
2007	63,740	159,595	...	175,893	...	399,228
2008	94,436	206,678	...	226,245	...	527,359
2009	50,244	158,426	...	161,858	...	370,528

• **LIFE INSURANCE IN FORCE ($000 omitted)**

Year	Whole Life	Term	Credit	Group	Industrial	Total
2007	933,832	567,956	...	1,518,214	27,235	3,047,237
2008	978,030	643,119	...	1,893,536	26,257	3,540,942
2009	1,000,063	671,403	...	1,229,745	25,522	2,926,733

COLORADO BANKERS LIFE INS CO

5990 Greenwood Plaza Blvd., #325
Greenwood Village, Colorado 80111
Tel: 303-220-8500

AMB#: 008502
Began Business: 11/07/1974
Agency Off: Robert Schmitz

Best's Financial Strength Rating: A **FSC:** V

• **NET PREMIUMS AND DEPOSITS ($000 omitted)**

Year	Individual Life	Individual & Group Annuities	Group Life & A&H	Credit Life & A&H	Individual A&H	Total
2007	32,151	14,422	1,437	...	1,967	49,977
2008	37,797	16,690	1,305	...	2,338	58,130
2009	47,814	19,132	1,029	...	2,684	70,659

• **NET OPERATING GAIN ($000 omitted)**

Year	Individual Life	Individual & Group Annuities	Group Life & A&H	Credit Life & A&H	Individual A&H	Total
2007	1,057	487	104	...	-14	1,635
2008	0	-43	-11	...	6	-48
2009	-4,026	1,188	342	...	79	-2,417

• **COMPARATIVE FINANCIALS ($000 omitted)**

Year	Assets	Capital & Surplus	Net Invest Income	Benefits Paid	Realized Cap Gains	Policyholder Dividends	Contract Lns (% of assets)
2007	140,920	21,263	6,829	22,258	-138	...	1.2
2008	144,871	17,484	7,183	24,748	-708	...	1.3
2009	154,632	14,172	7,051	25,426	-1,775	...	1.3

• **ORDINARY LIFE STATISTICS**

Year	Av. Ord. Policy Issued ($)	Av. Ord. Policy In Force ($)	Avg. Prem ($/M)	1st Yr Prem/ Total Prem	Ord. Lapse Ratio
2007	47,216	28,098	14.11	33.3	48.6
2008	45,297	27,842	15.15	38.4	29.8
2009	35,249	26,043	17.21	43.3	30.1

• **NEW LIFE BUSINESS ISSUED ($000 omitted)**

Year	Whole Life	Term	Credit	Group	Industrial	Total
2007	237,584	742,046	...	7,543	...	987,173
2008	342,679	905,655	...	17,124	...	1,265,458
2009	544,712	916,355	...	3,989	...	1,465,056

• **LIFE INSURANCE IN FORCE ($000 omitted)**

Year	Whole Life	Term	Credit	Group	Industrial	Total
2007	834,404	1,591,230	...	4,838	...	2,430,472
2008	990,985	1,655,037	...	12,313	...	2,658,335
2009	1,281,508	1,642,638	...	9,647	...	2,933,793

COLUMBIAN MUTUAL LIFE INS CO

4704 Vestal Parkway East
Binghamton, New York 13902-1381
Tel: 607-724-2472

AMB#: 006243
Began Business: 02/01/1883
Agency Off: August S. Dittemore

Best's Financial Strength Rating: A- g **FSC:** VII

• **NET PREMIUMS AND DEPOSITS ($000 omitted)**

Year	Individual Life	Individual & Group Annuities	Group Life & A&H	Credit Life & A&H	Individual A&H	Total
2007	113,004	8,199	17,823	...	452	139,477
2008	120,627	5,103	18,654	...	395	144,786
2009	125,999	1,307	19,467	...	351	147,123

• **NET OPERATING GAIN ($000 omitted)**

Year	Individual Life	Individual & Group Annuities	Group Life & A&H	Credit Life & A&H	Individual A&H	Total
2007	2,080	472	-243	...	162	2,472
2008	8,136	1,166	-291	...	162	9,172
2009	5,952	1,183	-85	...	655	7,704

• **COMPARATIVE FINANCIALS ($000 omitted)**

Year	Assets	Capital & Surplus	Net Invest Income	Benefits Paid	Realized Cap Gains	Policyholder Dividends	Contract Lns (% of assets)
2007	969,050	92,033	49,476	97,601	-86	7,186	6.2
2008	846,269	79,424	51,874	92,757	-3,089	6,926	7.0
2009	872,777	86,529	46,546	84,353	-1,053	6,621	6.4

• **ORDINARY LIFE STATISTICS**

Year	Av. Ord. Policy Issued ($)	Av. Ord. Policy In Force ($)	Avg. Prem ($/M)	1st Yr Prem/ Total Prem	Ord. Lapse Ratio
2007	21,842	13,494	23.46	8.8	8.5
2008	18,520	12,828	24.79	8.5	8.4
2009	14,989	12,283	26.38	8.2	8.7

• **NEW LIFE BUSINESS ISSUED ($000 omitted)**

Year	Whole Life	Term	Credit	Group	Industrial	Total
2007	242,175	68,500	...	362	...	311,037
2008	219,826	57,660	...	...	...	277,486
2009	152,855	42,483	...	...	...	195,339

• **LIFE INSURANCE IN FORCE ($000 omitted)**

Year	Whole Life	Term	Credit	Group	Industrial	Total
2007	4,215,357	1,020,046	...	55,456	87,516	5,378,375
2008	4,214,343	980,834	...	67,451	84,139	5,346,767
2009	4,177,129	912,537	...	78,297	80,509	5,248,473

COLUMBIAN LIFE INSURANCE CO

P.O. Box 1381
Binghamton, New York 13902-1381
Tel: 607-724-2472

AMB#: 068009
Began Business: 06/01/1988
Agency Off: August S. Dittemore

Best's Financial Strength Rating: A- g **FSC:** VII

• **NET PREMIUMS AND DEPOSITS ($000 omitted)**

Year	Individual Life	Individual & Group Annuities	Group Life & A&H	Credit Life & A&H	Individual A&H	Total
2007	28,532	...	11,334	...	1	39,866
2008	27,702	...	10,882	...	2	38,587
2009	30,562	10	11,968	...	2	42,543

• **NET OPERATING GAIN ($000 omitted)**

Year	Individual Life	Individual & Group Annuities	Group Life & A&H	Credit Life & A&H	Individual A&H	Total
2007	-3,855	-99	570	...	-14	-2,457
2008	-5,261	-57	1,203	...	-4	-3,481
2009	-3,713	-45	1,432	...	-4	-1,661

• **COMPARATIVE FINANCIALS ($000 omitted)**

Year	Assets	Capital & Surplus	Net Invest Income	Benefits Paid	Realized Cap Gains	Policyholder Dividends	Contract Lns (% of assets)
2007	242,456	22,260	11,709	35,086	-9	49	1.4
2008	245,170	19,228	12,161	33,854	-2,187	48	1.8
2009	248,445	19,024	12,696	32,570	936	49	2.3

• **ORDINARY LIFE STATISTICS**

Year	Av. Ord. Policy Issued ($)	Av. Ord. Policy In Force ($)	Avg. Prem ($/M)	1st Yr Prem/ Total Prem	Ord. Lapse Ratio
2007	13,284	13,268	38.16	19.3	15.0
2008	14,608	13,247	38.59	18.2	15.6
2009	12,575	12,788	40.46	21.6	15.2

• **NEW LIFE BUSINESS ISSUED ($000 omitted)**

Year	Whole Life	Term	Credit	Group	Industrial	Total
2007	442,052	118,481	...	104,790	...	665,323
2008	494,808	152,186	...	53,961	...	700,955
2009	556,850	114,606	...	27,807	...	699,263

• **LIFE INSURANCE IN FORCE ($000 omitted)**

Year	Whole Life	Term	Credit	Group	Industrial	Total
2007	1,317,740	635,881	...	582,807	...	2,536,428
2008	1,483,301	675,555	...	530,222	...	2,689,078
2009	1,683,657	668,420	...	487,991	...	2,840,068

COLUMBUS LIFE INSURANCE CO

400 East 4th Street
Cincinnati, Ohio 45202-3302
Tel: 513-361-6700

AMB#: 006244
Began Business: 07/01/1988
Agency Off: Charles W. Wood, Jr.

Best's Financial Strength Rating: A+ g **FSC:** XV

• **NET PREMIUMS AND DEPOSITS ($000 omitted)**

Year	Individual Life	Individual & Group Annuities	Group Life & A&H	Credit Life & A&H	Individual A&H	Total
2007	136,128	34,959	...	...	393	171,480
2008	128,539	82,421	...	...	343	211,303
2009	116,733	276,076	...	...	293	393,102

• **NET OPERATING GAIN ($000 omitted)**

Year	Individual Life	Individual & Group Annuities	Group Life & A&H	Credit Life & A&H	Individual A&H	Total
2007	11,196	11,600	...	...	230	23,026
2008	15,555	12,628	...	...	451	28,633
2009	8,081	11,450	...	...	398	19,929

• **COMPARATIVE FINANCIALS ($000 omitted)**

Year	Assets	Capital & Surplus	Net Invest Income	Benefits Paid	Realized Cap Gains	Policyholder Dividends	Contract Lns (% of assets)
2007	2,507,354	229,061	147,807	206,315	-7,121	11,897	2.9
2008	2,500,566	208,958	142,339	182,018	-11,670	11,901	2.9
2009	2,719,124	271,591	138,309	207,702	-16,072	12,048	2.8

• **ORDINARY LIFE STATISTICS**

Year	Av. Ord. Policy Issued ($)	Av. Ord. Policy In Force ($)	Avg. Prem ($/M)	1st Yr Prem/ Total Prem	Ord. Lapse Ratio
2007	460,254	108,710	12.13	20.5	5.0
2008	451,655	114,587	11.60	18.5	4.9
2009	378,319	118,685	10.82	14.3	5.3

• **NEW LIFE BUSINESS ISSUED ($000 omitted)**

Year	Whole Life	Term	Credit	Group	Industrial	Total
2007	607,253	602,295	...	...	...	1,209,548
2008	561,604	532,757	...	...	...	1,094,361
2009	343,354	652,382	...	...	...	995,736

• **LIFE INSURANCE IN FORCE ($000 omitted)**

Year	Whole Life	Term	Credit	Group	Industrial	Total
2007	10,203,371	3,404,455	...	...	...	13,607,826
2008	10,191,853	3,679,689	...	...	...	13,871,542
2009	9,866,115	4,072,356	...	...	...	13,938,471

COMBINED INS CO OF AMERICA

1000 North Milwaukee Avenue
Glenview, Illinois 60025
Tel: 847-953-2025

AMB#: 006246
Began Business: 01/01/1922
Agency Off: None

Best's Financial Strength Rating: A g **FSC:** X

• NET PREMIUMS AND DEPOSITS ($000 omitted)

Year	Individual Life	Individual & Group Annuities	Group Life & A&H	Credit Life & A&H	Individual A&H	Total
2007	77,740	2,929	44,651	-5,069	1,126,422	1,246,673
2008	-25,045	1,192	47,745	...	671,164	695,056
2009	67,929	1,341	114,039	-10	687,180	870,479

• NET OPERATING GAIN ($000 omitted)

Year	Individual Life	Individual & Group Annuities	Group Life & A&H	Credit Life & A&H	Individual A&H	Total
2007	18,731	-63	9,387	460	208,962	237,478
2008	-15,814	-2	10,358	4	173,245	167,791
2009	18,619	303	-13,118	34	194,448	200,287

• COMPARATIVE FINANCIALS ($000 omitted)

Year	Assets	Capital & Surplus	Net Invest Income	Benefits Paid	Realized Cap Gains	Policyholder Dividends	Contract Lns (% of assets)
2007	3,214,961	933,732	166,024	506,796	-4,507	1,141	1.4
2008	2,382,484	593,513	150,295	407,932	215,682	1,346	1.8
2009	2,508,210	642,729	173,404	401,406	-21,397	-3,359	1.7

• ORDINARY LIFE STATISTICS

Year	Av. Ord. Policy Issued ($)	Av. Ord. Policy In Force ($)	Avg. Prem ($/M)	1st Yr Prem/ Total Prem	Ord. Lapse Ratio
2007	30,136	14,030	11.27	9.3	9.7
2008	24,530	13,380	12.08	9.3	13.9
2009	20,981	13,494	11.03	-0.5	10.3

• NEW LIFE BUSINESS ISSUED ($000 omitted)

Year	Whole Life	Term	Credit	Group	Industrial	Total
2007	568,322	502,155	32,108	16,644	...	1,119,229
2008	368,685	272,870	524	13,169	...	655,248
2009	336,430	228,054	...	30,972	...	595,456

• LIFE INSURANCE IN FORCE ($000 omitted)

Year	Whole Life	Term	Credit	Group	Industrial	Total
2007	4,420,709	2,615,187	1,013,006	1,018,030	...	9,066,932
2008	4,085,945	2,414,633	547,916	201,648	...	7,250,142
2009	4,007,035	2,270,164	278,128	160,802	...	6,716,128

COMBINED LIFE INS CO OF NY

1000 North Milwaukee Avenue
Glenview, Illinois 60025
Tel: 518-220-9333

AMB#: 008187
Began Business: 06/14/1971
Agency Off: None

Best's Financial Strength Rating: A g **FSC:** X

• NET PREMIUMS AND DEPOSITS ($000 omitted)

Year	Individual Life	Individual & Group Annuities	Group Life & A&H	Credit Life & A&H	Individual A&H	Total
2007	18,632	...	20,394	...	106,007	145,033
2008	18,187	...	18,709	...	108,533	145,429
2009	17,684	...	17,688	...	102,641	138,014

• NET OPERATING GAIN ($000 omitted)

Year	Individual Life	Individual & Group Annuities	Group Life & A&H	Credit Life & A&H	Individual A&H	Total
2007	5,087	...	1,961	...	10,129	17,177
2008	6,147	...	3,539	...	18,894	28,580
2009	5,561	...	2,039	...	14,250	21,851

• COMPARATIVE FINANCIALS ($000 omitted)

Year	Assets	Capital & Surplus	Net Invest Income	Benefits Paid	Realized Cap Gains	Policyholder Dividends	Contract Lns (% of assets)
2007	359,855	60,071	16,877	44,183	-321	0	2.1
2008	375,950	59,122	17,453	72,553	-2,210	0	2.0
2009	391,081	61,635	16,929	77,995	-1,320	1	1.9

• ORDINARY LIFE STATISTICS

Year	Av. Ord. Policy Issued ($)	Av. Ord. Policy In Force ($)	Avg. Prem ($/M)	1st Yr Prem/ Total Prem	Ord. Lapse Ratio
2007	18,728	10,555	20.78	12.4	11.0
2008	18,919	11,030	19.98	14.9	11.3
2009	19,066	11,437	18.86	16.0	12.3

• NEW LIFE BUSINESS ISSUED ($000 omitted)

Year	Whole Life	Term	Credit	Group	Industrial	Total
2007	113,239	17,353	...	...	...	130,592
2008	122,216	15,571	...	...	...	137,787
2009	141,218	21,148	...	...	...	162,366

• LIFE INSURANCE IN FORCE ($000 omitted)

Year	Whole Life	Term	Credit	Group	Industrial	Total
2007	750,991	165,957	...	...	...	916,948
2008	753,545	176,830	...	...	...	930,375
2009	783,516	172,340	...	...	...	955,856

COMMERCIAL TRAVELERS MUTUAL

70 Genesee Street
Utica, New York 13502-3502
Tel: 315-797-5200

AMB#: 007361
Began Business: 03/20/1883
Agency Off: Richard A. Lang

Best's Financial Strength Rating: B+ **FSC:** IV

• NET PREMIUMS AND DEPOSITS ($000 omitted)

Year	Individual Life	Individual & Group Annuities	Group Life & A&H	Credit Life & A&H	Individual A&H	Total
2007	...	...	35,940	...	592	36,532
2008	...	...	32,871	...	533	33,404
2009	...	...	34,326	...	471	34,797

• NET OPERATING GAIN ($000 omitted)

Year	Individual Life	Individual & Group Annuities	Group Life & A&H	Credit Life & A&H	Individual A&H	Total
2007	...	...	1,357	...	95	1,452
2008	...	...	1,238	...	21	1,259
2009	...	...	-2,677	...	9	-2,668

• COMPARATIVE FINANCIALS ($000 omitted)

Year	Assets	Capital & Surplus	Net Invest Income	Benefits Paid	Realized Cap Gains	Policyholder Dividends	Contract Lns (% of assets)
2007	37,617	12,829	759	21,783	88	...	...
2008	35,203	12,418	664	20,636	-271	...	...
2009	33,773	8,780	263	23,292	13	...	...

• ORDINARY LIFE STATISTICS

Year	Av. Ord. Policy Issued ($)	Av. Ord. Policy In Force ($)	Avg. Prem ($/M)	1st Yr Prem/ Total Prem	Ord. Lapse Ratio
2007	...	...	...	...	...
2008	...	...	...	...	...
2009	...	...	...	...	...

• NEW LIFE BUSINESS ISSUED ($000 omitted)

Year	Whole Life	Term	Credit	Group	Industrial	Total
2007	...	...	...	...	...	...
2008	...	...	...	...	...	...
2009	...	...	...	...	...	...

• LIFE INSURANCE IN FORCE ($000 omitted)

Year	Whole Life	Term	Credit	Group	Industrial	Total
2007	...	...	...	...	...	...
2008	...	...	...	...	...	...
2009	...	...	...	...	...	...

COMMONWEALTH ANNUITY AND LIFE

132 Turnpike Road, Suite 210
Southborough, Massachusetts 01772
Tel: 508-460-2400

AMB#: 008491
Began Business: 01/31/1967
Agency Off: None

Best's Financial Strength Rating: A- g **FSC:** IX

• NET PREMIUMS AND DEPOSITS ($000 omitted)

Year	Individual Life	Individual & Group Annuities	Group Life & A&H	Credit Life & A&H	Individual A&H	Total
2007	9,126	607,828	59	...	...	617,013
2008	28,847	160,623	373	...	2	189,846
2009	1,341,004	217,926	400	...	103	1,559,433

• NET OPERATING GAIN ($000 omitted)

Year	Individual Life	Individual & Group Annuities	Group Life & A&H	Credit Life & A&H	Individual A&H	Total
2007	28,020	26,176	-175	...	...	72,475
2008	36,119	-279,012	-31,649	...	-343	-253,872
2009	-159,588	25,656	2,933	...	-42	-104,899

• COMPARATIVE FINANCIALS ($000 omitted)

Year	Assets	Capital & Surplus	Net Invest Income	Benefits Paid	Realized Cap Gains	Policyholder Dividends	Contract Lns (% of assets)
2007	9,653,746	461,351	63,128	2,217,727	-14,313	...	1.1
2008	5,334,786	390,622	61,681	1,629,568	6,782	...	1.7
2009	6,929,434	455,862	144,750	1,345,013	-35,654	11	3.1

• ORDINARY LIFE STATISTICS

Year	Av. Ord. Policy Issued ($)	Av. Ord. Policy In Force ($)	Avg. Prem ($/M)	1st Yr Prem/ Total Prem	Ord. Lapse Ratio
2007	44,625	187,699	5.17	...	8.1
2008	476,880	135,577	8.40	0.9	9.6
2009	...	82,220	50.14	-0.2	8.7

• NEW LIFE BUSINESS ISSUED ($000 omitted)

Year	Whole Life	Term	Credit	Group	Industrial	Total
2007	1,071	...	...	...	...	1,071
2008	11,922	...	...	...	...	11,922
2009	28	...	...	...	...	28

• LIFE INSURANCE IN FORCE ($000 omitted)

Year	Whole Life	Term	Credit	Group	Industrial	Total
2007	13,500,955	1,160,974	...	375,310	...	15,037,239
2008	13,762,301	1,048,506	...	315,007	...	15,125,814
2009	27,602,624	1,329,541	...	296,650	...	29,228,815

COMMONWEALTH DEALERS LIFE INS

8001 W. Broad Street
Richmond, Virginia 23294
Tel: 800-229-0121

AMB#: 068105
Began Business: 02/28/1989
Agency Off: Mark Albert

Best's Financial Strength Rating: B+ **FSC:** IV

• NET PREMIUMS AND DEPOSITS ($000 omitted)

Year	Individual Life	Individual & Group Annuities	Group Life & A&H	Credit Life & A&H	Individual A&H	Total
2007	...	...	...	3,042	...	3,042
2008	...	...	...	476	...	476
2009	...	...	...	200	...	200

• NET OPERATING GAIN ($000 omitted)

Year	Individual Life	Individual & Group Annuities	Group Life & A&H	Credit Life & A&H	Individual A&H	Total
2007	...	...	...	490	...	490
2008	...	...	...	2,094	...	2,094
2009	...	...	...	993	...	993

• COMPARATIVE FINANCIALS ($000 omitted)

Year	Assets	Capital & Surplus	Net Invest Income	Benefits Paid	Realized Cap Gains	Policyholder Dividends	Contract Lns (% of assets)
2007	16,452	5,545	568	1,723	-74	...	...
2008	13,878	7,411	518	1,466	-322	...	...
2009	11,861	7,328	361	1,249	-24	...	...

• ORDINARY LIFE STATISTICS

Year	Av. Ord. Policy Issued ($)	Av. Ord. Policy In Force ($)	Avg. Prem ($/M)	1st Yr Prem/ Total Prem	Ord. Lapse Ratio
2007	...	...	...	...	...
2008	...	...	...	...	...
2009	...	...	...	...	...

• NEW LIFE BUSINESS ISSUED ($000 omitted)

Year	Whole Life	Term	Credit	Group	Industrial	Total
2007	...	...	9,768	...	...	9,768
2008	...	...	503	...	...	503
2009	...	...	...	...	...	...

• LIFE INSURANCE IN FORCE ($000 omitted)

Year	Whole Life	Term	Credit	Group	Industrial	Total
2007	...	...	228,628	...	...	228,628
2008	...	...	134,874	...	...	134,874
2009	...	...	71,377	...	...	71,377

COMPANION LIFE INSURANCE CO

P.O. Box 100102
Columbia, South Carolina 29202-3102
Tel: 803-735-1251

AMB#: 008064
Began Business: 07/01/1970
Agency Off: Trescott N. Hinton, Jr.

Best's Financial Strength Rating: A+ g **FSC:** XIV

• NET PREMIUMS AND DEPOSITS ($000 omitted)

Year	Individual Life	Individual & Group Annuities	Group Life & A&H	Credit Life & A&H	Individual A&H	Total
2007	...	14	135,508	...	9	135,530
2008	...	115	137,749	...	8	137,872
2009	...	132	152,041	...	38	152,212

• NET OPERATING GAIN ($000 omitted)

Year	Individual Life	Individual & Group Annuities	Group Life & A&H	Credit Life & A&H	Individual A&H	Total
2007	...	27	9,153	...	14	9,194
2008	...	17	7,910	...	13	7,940
2009	...	7	7,518	...	24	7,549

• COMPARATIVE FINANCIALS ($000 omitted)

Year	Assets	Capital & Surplus	Net Invest Income	Benefits Paid	Realized Cap Gains	Policyholder Dividends	Contract Lns (% of assets)
2007	122,047	63,045	4,669	83,661	284	...	...
2008	130,402	67,499	4,612	83,666	-1,244	...	...
2009	140,246	84,831	3,810	95,366	-557	...	...

• ORDINARY LIFE STATISTICS

Year	Av. Ord. Policy Issued ($)	Av. Ord. Policy In Force ($)	Avg. Prem ($/M)	1st Yr Prem/ Total Prem	Ord. Lapse Ratio
2007	...	...	...	...	...
2008	...	...	...	...	...
2009	...	...	...	...	...

• NEW LIFE BUSINESS ISSUED ($000 omitted)

Year	Whole Life	Term	Credit	Group	Industrial	Total
2007	879	...	...	1,165,331	...	1,166,210
2008	1,077	...	...	1,246,456	...	1,247,533
2009	...	...	...	1,469,360	...	1,469,360

• LIFE INSURANCE IN FORCE ($000 omitted)

Year	Whole Life	Term	Credit	Group	Industrial	Total
2007	27,920	2,310	...	7,017,738	...	7,047,968
2008	26,666	2,076	...	7,250,325	...	7,279,067
2009	24,021	1,850	...	7,627,836	...	7,653,707

COMPANION LIFE INS COMPANY

Mutual of Omaha Plaza
Omaha, Nebraska 68175
Tel: 402-342-7600

AMB#: 006258
Began Business: 07/18/1949
Agency Off: None

Best's Financial Strength Rating: A+ g **FSC:** XIII

• NET PREMIUMS AND DEPOSITS ($000 omitted)

Year	Individual Life	Individual & Group Annuities	Group Life & A&H	Credit Life & A&H	Individual A&H	Total
2007	62,452	11,336	512	...	9	74,308
2008	62,504	17,490	708	...	8	80,711
2009	63,210	30,866	851	...	9	94,935

• NET OPERATING GAIN ($000 omitted)

Year	Individual Life	Individual & Group Annuities	Group Life & A&H	Credit Life & A&H	Individual A&H	Total
2007	2,149	1,875	-70	...	-19	3,934
2008	2,840	1,047	-60	...	1	3,829
2009	1,129	1,659	-775	...	-12	2,001

• COMPARATIVE FINANCIALS ($000 omitted)

Year	Assets	Capital & Surplus	Net Invest Income	Benefits Paid	Realized Cap Gains	Policyholder Dividends	Contract Lns (% of assets)
2007	672,853	58,047	35,874	-6,117	-2	36	2.2
2008	699,427	61,471	37,471	57,351	-888	35	2.4
2009	751,040	65,407	37,694	53,883	-1,250	36	2.6

• ORDINARY LIFE STATISTICS

Year	Av. Ord. Policy Issued ($)	Av. Ord. Policy In Force ($)	Avg. Prem ($/M)	1st Yr Prem/ Total Prem	Ord. Lapse Ratio
2007	47,954	71,066	8.48	13.0	6.1
2008	51,694	68,755	8.68	10.7	7.1
2009	58,881	67,676	8.75	12.5	6.8

• NEW LIFE BUSINESS ISSUED ($000 omitted)

Year	Whole Life	Term	Credit	Group	Industrial	Total
2007	368,503	371,372	...	906,890	...	1,646,765
2008	342,435	384,893	...	807,465	...	1,534,793
2009	355,714	420,215	...	2,033,781	...	2,809,710

• LIFE INSURANCE IN FORCE ($000 omitted)

Year	Whole Life	Term	Credit	Group	Industrial	Total
2007	4,689,825	4,313,897	...	2,783,478	...	11,787,200
2008	4,697,595	4,200,313	...	3,335,589	...	12,233,497
2009	4,738,517	4,144,596	...	4,470,143	...	13,353,256

CONNECTICUT GENERAL LIFE INS

Two Liberty Plaza, 1601 Chestnut Street
Philadelphia, Pennsylvania 19192-2362
Tel: 860-226-6000

AMB#: 006266
Began Business: 10/01/1865
Agency Off: Shelley Hayes

Best's Financial Strength Rating: A g **FSC:** XV

• NET PREMIUMS AND DEPOSITS ($000 omitted)

Year	Individual Life	Individual & Group Annuities	Group Life & A&H	Credit Life & A&H	Individual A&H	Total
2007	136,064	752,087	5,440,506	...	326,403	6,655,060
2008	136,289	862,993	6,517,977	...	324,601	7,841,861
2009	80,018	934,903	6,171,891	...	552,536	7,739,348

• NET OPERATING GAIN ($000 omitted)

Year	Individual Life	Individual & Group Annuities	Group Life & A&H	Credit Life & A&H	Individual A&H	Total
2007	79,329	-116,028	660,248	...	7,300	636,669
2008	-206,437	-265,466	432,672	...	7,662	3,702
2009	-168,594	181,400	667,184	...	-5,130	669,565

• COMPARATIVE FINANCIALS ($000 omitted)

Year	Assets	Capital & Surplus	Net Invest Income	Benefits Paid	Realized Cap Gains	Policyholder Dividends	Contract Lns (% of assets)
2007	16,582,319	1,897,090	719,543	5,786,283	31,567	2,579	8.4
2008	17,733,121	2,030,228	678,266	6,419,647	-2,724	1,651	8.4
2009	19,036,994	2,919,212	673,067	6,342,272	-22,477	2,865	7.8

• ORDINARY LIFE STATISTICS

Year	Av. Ord. Policy Issued ($)	Av. Ord. Policy In Force ($)	Avg. Prem ($/M)	1st Yr Prem/ Total Prem	Ord. Lapse Ratio
2007	277,817	46,085	11.57	0.4	6.3
2008	203,070	58,397	10.16	0.2	-11.7
2009	264,319	55,249	9.84	0.1	13.3

• NEW LIFE BUSINESS ISSUED ($000 omitted)

Year	Whole Life	Term	Credit	Group	Industrial	Total
2007	76,905	56,447	...	3,561,551	...	3,694,903
2008	17,740	109,788	...	3,201,032	...	3,328,560
2009	127,266	44,277	...	3,133,593	...	3,305,136

• LIFE INSURANCE IN FORCE ($000 omitted)

Year	Whole Life	Term	Credit	Group	Industrial	Total
2007	40,730,500	1,194,634	...	93,879,988	...	135,805,122
2008	45,869,321	937,538	...	88,708,212	...	135,515,071
2009	39,455,206	754,406	...	75,131,887	...	115,341,500

CONSECO HEALTH INS CO

11825 N. Pennsylvania Street
Carmel, Indiana 46032
Tel: 317-817-4300

AMB#: 008101
Began Business: 12/01/1970
Agency Off: Steven M. Stecher

Best's Financial Strength Rating: B g
FSC: VIII

- **NET PREMIUMS AND DEPOSITS ($000 omitted)**

Year	Individual Life	Individual & Group Annuities	Group Life & A&H	Credit Life & A&H	Individual A&H	Total
2007	1,950	95,179	63,705	...	228,231	389,065
2008	1,839	121,947	70,836	...	220,447	415,070
2009	1,683	140,154	77,595	...	219,071	438,503

- **NET OPERATING GAIN ($000 omitted)**

Year	Individual Life	Individual & Group Annuities	Group Life & A&H	Credit Life & A&H	Individual A&H	Total
2007	95	788	-2,968	...	10,269	11,257
2008	451	2,192	-6,344	...	19,978	21,149
2009	-79	2,869	-6,476	...	12,452	13,607

- **COMPARATIVE FINANCIALS ($000 omitted)**

Year	Assets	Capital & Surplus	Net Invest Income	Benefits Paid	Realized Cap Gains	Policyholder Dividends	Contract Lns (% of assets)
2007	2,361,268	108,497	134,777	159,156	-1,314	...	0.0
2008	2,472,317	128,610	141,763	160,092	-19,773	...	0.0
2009	2,558,880	150,574	144,419	164,388	-20,075	...	0.0

- **ORDINARY LIFE STATISTICS**

Year	Av. Ord. Policy Issued ($)	Av. Ord. Policy In Force ($)	Avg. Prem ($/M)	1st Yr Prem/ Total Prem	Ord. Lapse Ratio
2007	...	...	...	...	...
2008	...	...	...	...	...
2009	...	...	...	...	...

- **NEW LIFE BUSINESS ISSUED ($000 omitted)**

Year	Whole Life	Term	Credit	Group	Industrial	Total
2007	82	...	...	...	...	82
2008	...	...	...	...	...	...
2009	...	...	...	...	...	...

- **LIFE INSURANCE IN FORCE ($000 omitted)**

Year	Whole Life	Term	Credit	Group	Industrial	Total
2007	47,452	15,987	...	...	...	63,439
2008	43,591	14,884	...	...	...	58,475
2009	40,764	14,464	...	...	...	55,228

CONSECO LIFE INSURANCE COMPANY

11825 N. Pennsylvania Street
Carmel, Indiana 46032
Tel: 317-817-6400

AMB#: 006692
Began Business: 05/03/1962
Agency Off: Steven M. Stecher

Best's Financial Strength Rating: B-
FSC: VIII

- **NET PREMIUMS AND DEPOSITS ($000 omitted)**

Year	Individual Life	Individual & Group Annuities	Group Life & A&H	Credit Life & A&H	Individual A&H	Total
2007	223,901	627,641	27,993	...	66,360	945,896
2008	213,010	152,933	26,864	...	72,117	464,925
2009	194,674	159,233	26,410	...	95,765	476,083

- **NET OPERATING GAIN ($000 omitted)**

Year	Individual Life	Individual & Group Annuities	Group Life & A&H	Credit Life & A&H	Individual A&H	Total
2007	-42,966	3,512	-8,373	...	12,841	-31,364
2008	-12,528	1,072	-2,253	...	-19,106	-27,293
2009	-6,470	5,768	-1,007	...	5,245	7,329

- **COMPARATIVE FINANCIALS ($000 omitted)**

Year	Assets	Capital & Surplus	Net Invest Income	Benefits Paid	Realized Cap Gains	Policyholder Dividends	Contract Lns (% of assets)
2007	4,256,095	148,160	247,011	529,840	-22,965	782	4.8
2008	4,529,499	162,350	247,698	569,179	-40,907	797	4.6
2009	4,382,162	111,499	255,921	675,677	-28,505	778	4.6

- **ORDINARY LIFE STATISTICS**

Year	Av. Ord. Policy Issued ($)	Av. Ord. Policy In Force ($)	Avg. Prem ($/M)	1st Yr Prem/ Total Prem	Ord. Lapse Ratio
2007	749,222	89,940	6.10	0.1	5.2
2008	4,803,824	86,513	6.07	0.0	5.4
2009	181,000	85,184	6.20	0.0	7.1

- **NEW LIFE BUSINESS ISSUED ($000 omitted)**

Year	Whole Life	Term	Credit	Group	Industrial	Total
2007	28,520	25,424	...	11	...	53,955
2008	2,014	79,651	...	461	...	82,126
2009	238	848	...	13	...	1,099

- **LIFE INSURANCE IN FORCE ($000 omitted)**

Year	Whole Life	Term	Credit	Group	Industrial	Total
2007	42,168,496	5,057,469	...	162,226	...	47,388,191
2008	39,937,221	4,691,527	3	144,457	...	44,773,208
2009	36,846,357	4,266,311	...	131,444	...	41,244,112

CONSECO INSURANCE COMPANY

11825 N. Pennsylvania Street
Carmel, Indiana 46032
Tel: 317-817-4000

AMB#: 006080
Began Business: 12/31/1951
Agency Off: Steven M. Stecher

Best's Financial Strength Rating: B g
FSC: VIII

- **NET PREMIUMS AND DEPOSITS ($000 omitted)**

Year	Individual Life	Individual & Group Annuities	Group Life & A&H	Credit Life & A&H	Individual A&H	Total
2007	13,944	176,729	1,189	...	56,647	248,510
2008	14,307	52,389	1,293	...	65,909	133,898
2009	5,257	40,495	1,461	...	73,054	120,266

- **NET OPERATING GAIN ($000 omitted)**

Year	Individual Life	Individual & Group Annuities	Group Life & A&H	Credit Life & A&H	Individual A&H	Total
2007	-19,106	-1,370	167	...	-4,004	-10,923
2008	-244	31,887	11	...	-4,917	31,189
2009	21,878	-9,172	-1,548	...	-15,691	2,941

- **COMPARATIVE FINANCIALS ($000 omitted)**

Year	Assets	Capital & Surplus	Net Invest Income	Benefits Paid	Realized Cap Gains	Policyholder Dividends	Contract Lns (% of assets)
2007	1,242,277	232,968	76,172	135,687	135	41	3.1
2008	1,044,458	159,078	49,262	151,472	-12,525	42	3.4
2009	759,442	137,694	48,131	147,483	-9,874	...	0.1

- **ORDINARY LIFE STATISTICS**

Year	Av. Ord. Policy Issued ($)	Av. Ord. Policy In Force ($)	Avg. Prem ($/M)	1st Yr Prem/ Total Prem	Ord. Lapse Ratio
2007	...	...	...	...	...
2008	...	...	...	...	...
2009	...	...	...	...	...

- **NEW LIFE BUSINESS ISSUED ($000 omitted)**

Year	Whole Life	Term	Credit	Group	Industrial	Total
2007	247,846	185,069	...	22,579	...	455,494
2008	152,880	129,858	...	15,060	...	297,798
2009	252,418	142,117	...	889	...	395,424

- **LIFE INSURANCE IN FORCE ($000 omitted)**

Year	Whole Life	Term	Credit	Group	Industrial	Total
2007	1,416,752	495,586	...	104,789	...	2,017,127
2008	1,377,127	537,428	...	109,328	...	2,023,883
2009	1,447,085	559,107	...	96,673	...	2,102,866

CONSTITUTION LIFE INS CO

1001 Heathrow Park Lane, Suite 5001
Lake Mary, Florida 32746
Tel: 407-995-8000

AMB#: 006273
Began Business: 06/11/1929
Agency Off: David Donaghy

Best's Financial Strength Rating: B+
FSC: VI

- **NET PREMIUMS AND DEPOSITS ($000 omitted)**

Year	Individual Life	Individual & Group Annuities	Group Life & A&H	Credit Life & A&H	Individual A&H	Total
2007	2,407	3	...	...	33,124	35,534
2008	2,344	366	...	...	28,889	31,599
2009	-41,121	-4,187	...	...	41,545	-3,763

- **NET OPERATING GAIN ($000 omitted)**

Year	Individual Life	Individual & Group Annuities	Group Life & A&H	Credit Life & A&H	Individual A&H	Total
2007	293	61	...	...	721	1,075
2008	418	22	...	...	1,161	1,601
2009	-652	60	...	...	4,520	3,928

- **COMPARATIVE FINANCIALS ($000 omitted)**

Year	Assets	Capital & Surplus	Net Invest Income	Benefits Paid	Realized Cap Gains	Policyholder Dividends	Contract Lns (% of assets)
2007	87,691	17,469	4,359	29,538	-841	...	4.6
2008	87,358	19,055	4,038	26,030	-276	...	5.0
2009	54,702	27,507	1,736	24,346	-194	...	0.0

- **ORDINARY LIFE STATISTICS**

Year	Av. Ord. Policy Issued ($)	Av. Ord. Policy In Force ($)	Avg. Prem ($/M)	1st Yr Prem/ Total Prem	Ord. Lapse Ratio
2007	...	...	...	...	...
2008	...	...	...	...	...
2009	...	...	...	...	...

- **NEW LIFE BUSINESS ISSUED ($000 omitted)**

Year	Whole Life	Term	Credit	Group	Industrial	Total
2007	8,100	...	...	...	...	8,100
2008	6,476	...	...	...	...	6,476
2009	11,921	...	...	...	...	11,921

- **LIFE INSURANCE IN FORCE ($000 omitted)**

Year	Whole Life	Term	Credit	Group	Industrial	Total
2007	247,415	21,172	...	...	...	268,587
2008	236,759	20,071	...	...	...	256,830
2009	224,075	19,074	...	...	...	243,148

CONTINENTAL AMERICAN INS CO

P.O. Box 427
Columbia, South Carolina 29202
Tel: 803-256-6265

AMB#: 007411
Began Business: 01/03/1969
Agency Off: Leon S. Goodall

Best's Financial Strength Rating: A+ g
FSC: XV

• **NET PREMIUMS AND DEPOSITS** ($000 omitted)

Year	Individual Life	Individual & Group Annuities	Group Life & A&H	Credit Life & A&H	Individual A&H	Total
2007	119	…	63,569	…	1,240	64,928
2008	393	…	67,850	…	885	69,127
2009	486	3	83,147	…	3,709	87,345

• **NET OPERATING GAIN** ($000 omitted)

Year	Individual Life	Individual & Group Annuities	Group Life & A&H	Credit Life & A&H	Individual A&H	Total
2007	39	…	4,595	…	528	5,163
2008	-203	…	7,605	…	223	7,626
2009	-291	-6	5,193	…	1,017	6,498

• **COMPARATIVE FINANCIALS** ($000 omitted)

Year	Assets	Capital & Surplus	Net Invest Income	Benefits Paid	Realized Cap Gains	Policyholder Dividends	Contract Lns (% of assets)
2007	102,769	26,959	3,498	24,389	-33	…	1.1
2008	104,027	32,646	2,951	23,341	-708	…	1.2
2009	117,984	38,471	2,746	27,833	-696	…	1.4

• **ORDINARY LIFE STATISTICS**

Year	Av. Ord. Policy Issued ($)	Av. Ord. Policy In Force ($)	Avg. Prem ($/M)	1st Yr Prem/ Total Prem	Ord. Lapse Ratio
2007	…	…	…	…	…
2008	…	…	…	…	…
2009	…	…	…	…	…

• **NEW LIFE BUSINESS ISSUED** ($000 omitted)

Year	Whole Life	Term	Credit	Group	Industrial	Total
2007	24,868	…	…	165,014	…	189,882
2008	50,308	…	…	228,396	…	278,704
2009	…	…	…	191,100	…	191,100

• **LIFE INSURANCE IN FORCE** ($000 omitted)

Year	Whole Life	Term	Credit	Group	Industrial	Total
2007	54,604	8,443	…	839,522	…	902,569
2008	104,111	8,345	…	922,030	…	1,034,486
2009	20,110	8,102	…	1,108,638	…	1,136,850

CONTINENTAL GENERAL INS CO

11200 Lakeline Blvd., Suite 100
Austin, Texas 78717
Tel: 512-451-2224

AMB#: 007360
Began Business: 07/11/1961
Agency Off: None

Best's Financial Strength Rating: B++
FSC: VI

• **NET PREMIUMS AND DEPOSITS** ($000 omitted)

Year	Individual Life	Individual & Group Annuities	Group Life & A&H	Credit Life & A&H	Individual A&H	Total
2007	9,896	8,004	1,501	…	70,916	90,317
2008	7,996	2,473	-1,183	…	69,496	78,783
2009	7,454	465	275	…	58,950	67,144

• **NET OPERATING GAIN** ($000 omitted)

Year	Individual Life	Individual & Group Annuities	Group Life & A&H	Credit Life & A&H	Individual A&H	Total
2007	1,719	1,689	-135	…	6,400	9,674
2008	-1,014	221	-396	…	6,526	5,337
2009	501	563	39	…	4,436	5,538

• **COMPARATIVE FINANCIALS** ($000 omitted)

Year	Assets	Capital & Surplus	Net Invest Income	Benefits Paid	Realized Cap Gains	Policyholder Dividends	Contract Lns (% of assets)
2007	262,038	51,310	12,978	71,020	2,096	7	1.1
2008	227,247	44,577	11,043	66,452	-1,485	15	1.3
2009	214,082	32,144	10,930	57,178	-8,422	12	1.4

• **ORDINARY LIFE STATISTICS**

Year	Av. Ord. Policy Issued ($)	Av. Ord. Policy In Force ($)	Avg. Prem ($/M)	1st Yr Prem/ Total Prem	Ord. Lapse Ratio
2007	…	…	…	…	…
2008	…	…	…	…	…
2009	…	…	…	…	…

• **NEW LIFE BUSINESS ISSUED** ($000 omitted)

Year	Whole Life	Term	Credit	Group	Industrial	Total
2007	44,343	4,107	…	970	…	49,420
2008	18,888	242	…	195	…	19,325
2009	10,554	…	…	…	…	10,554

• **LIFE INSURANCE IN FORCE** ($000 omitted)

Year	Whole Life	Term	Credit	Group	Industrial	Total
2007	981,368	312,367	…	1,077,258	…	2,370,993
2008	928,276	291,822	…	150	…	1,220,248
2009	924,290	221,346	…	150	…	1,145,785

CONTINENTAL ASSURANCE CO

333 S. Wabash Avenue
Chicago, Illinois 60604
Tel: 312-822-5000

AMB#: 006280
Began Business: 08/15/1911
Agency Off: None

Best's Financial Strength Rating: A-
FSC: IX

• **NET PREMIUMS AND DEPOSITS** ($000 omitted)

Year	Individual Life	Individual & Group Annuities	Group Life & A&H	Credit Life & A&H	Individual A&H	Total
2007	316	16,704	2,204	…	98	19,323
2008	…	17,010	468	…	395	17,873
2009	1,183	15,884	245	…	357	17,669

• **NET OPERATING GAIN** ($000 omitted)

Year	Individual Life	Individual & Group Annuities	Group Life & A&H	Credit Life & A&H	Individual A&H	Total
2007	12,879	3,776	-7,377	…	57	49,265
2008	4,397	-28,076	787	…	-590	-2,239
2009	-165	-64,486	3,387	…	-9,842	-46,982

• **COMPARATIVE FINANCIALS** ($000 omitted)

Year	Assets	Capital & Surplus	Net Invest Income	Benefits Paid	Realized Cap Gains	Policyholder Dividends	Contract Lns (% of assets)
2007	4,120,081	471,190	147,191	153,927	-22,005	-4,202	0.0
2008	3,333,560	487,288	139,831	177,835	-48,501	-2,274	0.0
2009	3,208,225	447,634	148,126	171,830	-18,104	1,163	0.0

• **ORDINARY LIFE STATISTICS**

Year	Av. Ord. Policy Issued ($)	Av. Ord. Policy In Force ($)	Avg. Prem ($/M)	1st Yr Prem/ Total Prem	Ord. Lapse Ratio
2007	…	…	…	…	…
2008	…	…	…	…	…
2009	…	…	…	…	…

• **NEW LIFE BUSINESS ISSUED** ($000 omitted)

Year	Whole Life	Term	Credit	Group	Industrial	Total
2007	322	…	…	21,380	…	21,702
2008	1,385	…	…	3,081	…	4,466
2009	545	…	…	1,940	…	2,485

• **LIFE INSURANCE IN FORCE** ($000 omitted)

Year	Whole Life	Term	Credit	Group	Industrial	Total
2007	2,658,256	6,545,920	…	4,885,817	…	14,089,993
2008	2,521,625	5,982,002	…	2,301,570	…	10,805,197
2009	2,355,487	5,398,299	…	1,405,282	…	9,159,068

CONTINENTAL LIFE BRENTWOOD TN

P.O. Box 1188
Brentwood, Tennessee 37024
Tel: 800-264-4000

AMB#: 009502
Began Business: 12/16/1983
Agency Off: None

Best's Financial Strength Rating: A-
FSC: VII

• **NET PREMIUMS AND DEPOSITS** ($000 omitted)

Year	Individual Life	Individual & Group Annuities	Group Life & A&H	Credit Life & A&H	Individual A&H	Total
2007	6,350	…	7,981	…	161,273	175,604
2008	6,321	…	10,231	…	154,561	171,113
2009	5,999	…	11,813	…	134,381	152,193

• **NET OPERATING GAIN** ($000 omitted)

Year	Individual Life	Individual & Group Annuities	Group Life & A&H	Credit Life & A&H	Individual A&H	Total
2007	149	…	2,238	…	4,672	7,058
2008	-295	…	1,665	…	11,172	12,542
2009	147	…	1,318	…	9,850	11,315

• **COMPARATIVE FINANCIALS** ($000 omitted)

Year	Assets	Capital & Surplus	Net Invest Income	Benefits Paid	Realized Cap Gains	Policyholder Dividends	Contract Lns (% of assets)
2007	155,922	60,108	7,470	122,937	-3	…	0.2
2008	152,963	59,993	7,164	117,930	-649	…	0.2
2009	146,042	61,387	5,533	113,713	-184	…	0.3

• **ORDINARY LIFE STATISTICS**

Year	Av. Ord. Policy Issued ($)	Av. Ord. Policy In Force ($)	Avg. Prem ($/M)	1st Yr Prem/ Total Prem	Ord. Lapse Ratio
2007	…	…	…	…	…
2008	…	…	…	…	…
2009	…	…	…	…	…

• **NEW LIFE BUSINESS ISSUED** ($000 omitted)

Year	Whole Life	Term	Credit	Group	Industrial	Total
2007	33,844	4,992	…	…	…	38,836
2008	25,235	1,849	…	…	…	27,084
2009	5,672	…	…	…	…	5,672

• **LIFE INSURANCE IN FORCE** ($000 omitted)

Year	Whole Life	Term	Credit	Group	Industrial	Total
2007	207,490	27,469	…	…	…	234,959
2008	208,202	25,287	…	…	…	233,489
2009	198,516	23,251	…	…	…	221,768

COOPERATIVA DE SEGUROS DE VIDA

400 Americo Miranda Avenue
San Juan, Puerto Rico 00936-3428
Tel: 787-751-5656

AMB#: 007607
Began Business: 09/11/1960
Agency Off: Margarita Olivella

Best's Financial Strength Rating: B-   **FSC:** VI

• NET PREMIUMS AND DEPOSITS ($000 omitted)

Year	Individual Life	Individual & Group Annuities	Group Life & A&H	Credit Life & A&H	Individual A&H	Total
2007	8,374	26,628	106,699	14,565	10,066	166,332
2008	9,211	34,818	147,238	12,030	11,382	214,678
2009	8,662	46,858	61,563	11,167	12,725	140,975

• NET OPERATING GAIN ($000 omitted)

Year	Individual Life	Individual & Group Annuities	Group Life & A&H	Credit Life & A&H	Individual A&H	Total
2007	1,509	-472	-1,232	1,251	-1,422	-365
2008	539	-1,131	-13,321	-1,254	-1,464	-16,632
2009	1,437	-1,163	-2,159	472	1,183	-230

• COMPARATIVE FINANCIALS ($000 omitted)

Year	Assets	Capital & Surplus	Net Invest Income	Benefits Paid	Realized Cap Gains	Policyholder Dividends	Contract Lns (% of assets)
2007	327,243	38,786	14,495	119,408	-139	455	1.3
2008	316,367	19,175	16,362	169,063	-12,066	202	1.3
2009	379,819	23,721	16,323	89,125	1,526	...	1.1

• ORDINARY LIFE STATISTICS

Year	Av. Ord. Policy Issued ($)	Av. Ord. Policy In Force ($)	Avg. Prem ($/M)	1st Yr Prem/ Total Prem	Ord. Lapse Ratio
2007	...	...	...	...	...
2008	...	...	...	...	...
2009	...	...	...	...	...

• NEW LIFE BUSINESS ISSUED ($000 omitted)

Year	Whole Life	Term	Credit	Group	Industrial	Total
2007	16,155	125,818	...	200,612	...	342,585
2008	38,038	219,968	17,647	138,530	...	414,183
2009	39,144	222,634	4,119	208,133	...	474,030

• LIFE INSURANCE IN FORCE ($000 omitted)

Year	Whole Life	Term	Credit	Group	Industrial	Total
2007	229,231	961,915	158,385	5,900,121	...	7,249,652
2008	346,357	922,276	149,972	5,368,727	...	6,787,332
2009	209,002	988,649	107,801	5,002,347	...	6,307,799

COUNTRY INVESTORS LIFE ASSUR

1701 N. Towanda Avenue
Bloomington, Illinois 61701-2090
Tel: 309-821-3000

AMB#: 009084
Began Business: 11/13/1981
Agency Off: Doyle J. Williams

Best's Financial Strength Rating: A+ r   **FSC:** XI

• NET PREMIUMS AND DEPOSITS ($000 omitted)

Year	Individual Life	Individual & Group Annuities	Group Life & A&H	Credit Life & A&H	Individual A&H	Total
2007	...	13,192	...	...	...	13,192
2008	...	14,604	...	...	...	14,604
2009	...	15,272	...	...	...	15,272

• NET OPERATING GAIN ($000 omitted)

Year	Individual Life	Individual & Group Annuities	Group Life & A&H	Credit Life & A&H	Individual A&H	Total
2007	51	-1,408	...	...	...	-1,357
2008	1,141	2,665	...	...	...	3,806
2009	514	1,254	...	...	...	1,768

• COMPARATIVE FINANCIALS ($000 omitted)

Year	Assets	Capital & Surplus	Net Invest Income	Benefits Paid	Realized Cap Gains	Policyholder Dividends	Contract Lns (% of assets)
2007	167,570	132,395	6,792	...	...	...	0.1
2008	199,151	152,157	6,741	...	252	...	0.1
2009	205,383	154,947	6,807	...	30	...	0.1

• ORDINARY LIFE STATISTICS

Year	Av. Ord. Policy Issued ($)	Av. Ord. Policy In Force ($)	Avg. Prem ($/M)	1st Yr Prem/ Total Prem	Ord. Lapse Ratio
2007	...	...	...	...	...
2008	...	...	...	...	...
2009	...	...	...	...	...

• NEW LIFE BUSINESS ISSUED ($000 omitted)

Year	Whole Life	Term	Credit	Group	Industrial	Total
2007	315,695	...	...	...	...	315,695
2008	209,548	...	...	...	...	209,548
2009	205,541	...	...	...	...	205,541

• LIFE INSURANCE IN FORCE ($000 omitted)

Year	Whole Life	Term	Credit	Group	Industrial	Total
2007	3,718,628	6,505	...	...	...	3,725,133
2008	3,655,702	5,900	...	...	...	3,661,602
2009	3,603,167	5,331	...	...	...	3,608,498

COTTON STATES LIFE INS CO

P.O. Box 2000
Bloomington, Illinois 61702-2000
Tel: 770-391-8789

AMB#: 006292
Began Business: 12/22/1955
Agency Off: Doyle J. Williams

Best's Financial Strength Rating: A-   **FSC:** VI

• NET PREMIUMS AND DEPOSITS ($000 omitted)

Year	Individual Life	Individual & Group Annuities	Group Life & A&H	Credit Life & A&H	Individual A&H	Total
2007	45,653	95	2,321	...	37	48,105
2008	44,881	240	533	...	32	45,686
2009	41,734	205	11	...	32	41,982

• NET OPERATING GAIN ($000 omitted)

Year	Individual Life	Individual & Group Annuities	Group Life & A&H	Credit Life & A&H	Individual A&H	Total
2007	2,103	200	18	...	-227	2,094
2008	2,873	131	5	...	-212	2,796
2009	2,988	56	11	...	-356	2,699

• COMPARATIVE FINANCIALS ($000 omitted)

Year	Assets	Capital & Surplus	Net Invest Income	Benefits Paid	Realized Cap Gains	Policyholder Dividends	Contract Lns (% of assets)
2007	273,720	31,059	13,627	33,622	297	338	4.7
2008	281,158	31,691	13,977	34,375	-1,426	358	5.0
2009	291,707	34,820	14,358	34,474	-3,760	393	5.0

• ORDINARY LIFE STATISTICS

Year	Av. Ord. Policy Issued ($)	Av. Ord. Policy In Force ($)	Avg. Prem ($/M)	1st Yr Prem/ Total Prem	Ord. Lapse Ratio
2007	102,247	60,041	8.02	8.9	8.5
2008	129,569	64,026	7.54	7.5	8.6
2009	155,509	67,495	7.16	5.9	9.2

• NEW LIFE BUSINESS ISSUED ($000 omitted)

Year	Whole Life	Term	Credit	Group	Industrial	Total
2007	267,353	657,267	...	...	...	924,620
2008	167,474	640,646	...	...	...	808,120
2009	50,619	641,084	...	...	...	691,703

• LIFE INSURANCE IN FORCE ($000 omitted)

Year	Whole Life	Term	Credit	Group	Industrial	Total
2007	2,912,812	3,634,621	...	1,756,049	...	8,303,482
2008	2,790,780	3,847,126	...	1,477	...	6,639,383
2009	2,579,723	4,023,889	...	1,426	...	6,605,037

COUNTRY LIFE INS CO

1701 N. Towanda Avenue
Bloomington, Illinois 61701-2090
Tel: 309-821-3000

AMB#: 006294
Began Business: 12/29/1928
Agency Off: Doyle J. Williams

Best's Financial Strength Rating: A+ g   **FSC:** XI

• NET PREMIUMS AND DEPOSITS ($000 omitted)

Year	Individual Life	Individual & Group Annuities	Group Life & A&H	Credit Life & A&H	Individual A&H	Total
2007	327,651	210,989	41,447	12	82,650	662,749
2008	337,311	262,111	44,842	12	86,164	730,439
2009	349,176	440,099	47,255	11	83,929	920,470

• NET OPERATING GAIN ($000 omitted)

Year	Individual Life	Individual & Group Annuities	Group Life & A&H	Credit Life & A&H	Individual A&H	Total
2007	15,843	13,629	5,133	-8	4,309	38,906
2008	7,135	6,924	6,081	-8	11,869	32,002
2009	22,138	959	4,616	-9	7,455	35,160

• COMPARATIVE FINANCIALS ($000 omitted)

Year	Assets	Capital & Surplus	Net Invest Income	Benefits Paid	Realized Cap Gains	Policyholder Dividends	Contract Lns (% of assets)
2007	7,356,243	980,992	357,659	360,665	-2,876	94,797	4.1
2008	7,270,651	944,900	354,253	376,563	-41,747	97,780	4.3
2009	7,895,262	918,023	360,788	376,297	-73,946	80,425	4.1

• ORDINARY LIFE STATISTICS

Year	Av. Ord. Policy Issued ($)	Av. Ord. Policy In Force ($)	Avg. Prem ($/M)	1st Yr Prem/ Total Prem	Ord. Lapse Ratio
2007	199,020	87,831	6.68	7.2	7.0
2008	199,167	92,890	6.48	6.8	7.0
2009	188,882	96,730	6.44	6.8	7.2

• NEW LIFE BUSINESS ISSUED ($000 omitted)

Year	Whole Life	Term	Credit	Group	Industrial	Total
2007	729,167	6,512,169	...	...	...	7,241,336
2008	782,785	6,176,322	...	...	...	6,959,107
2009	841,512	5,857,764	...	...	...	6,699,276

• LIFE INSURANCE IN FORCE ($000 omitted)

Year	Whole Life	Term	Credit	Group	Industrial	Total
2007	15,815,492	36,888,745	2,249	2,541,714	...	55,248,200
2008	15,987,918	39,972,819	2,032	1,380,841	...	57,343,610
2009	16,279,100	42,355,846	1,986	1,450,823	...	60,087,754

CUNA MUTUAL INS SOCIETY

PO Box 391
Madison, Wisconsin 53701-0391
Tel: 608-238-5851

AMB#: 006302
Began Business: 08/13/1935
Agency Off: Robert Trunzo

Best's Financial Strength Rating: A **FSC:** XII

• NET PREMIUMS AND DEPOSITS ($000 omitted)

Year	Individual Life	Individual & Group Annuities	Group Life & A&H	Credit Life & A&H	Individual A&H	Total
2007	233,674	1,658,103	387,556	571,366	21,392	2,872,091
2008	145,915	1,348,801	394,808	563,981	29,413	2,482,919
2009	144,459	1,493,511	370,758	551,741	36,062	2,596,531

• NET OPERATING GAIN ($000 omitted)

Year	Individual Life	Individual & Group Annuities	Group Life & A&H	Credit Life & A&H	Individual A&H	Total
2007	-12,427	-4,385	36,219	22,471	-12,408	50,751
2008	-2,639	-6,452	41,020	48,886	-10,386	251,936
2009	11,488	48,370	46,514	-1,581	-20,286	432,270

• COMPARATIVE FINANCIALS ($000 omitted)

Year	Assets	Capital & Surplus	Net Invest Income	Benefits Paid	Realized Cap Gains	Policyholder Dividends	Contract Lns (% of assets)
2007	12,215,107	1,035,435	346,090	1,976,256	-40,147	30,498	0.8
2008	11,002,454	985,178	518,749	1,817,949	-289,764	29,150	0.9
2009	12,441,231	1,201,075	696,468	1,607,707	-150,626	30,110	0.8

• ORDINARY LIFE STATISTICS

Year	Av. Ord. Policy Issued ($)	Av. Ord. Policy In Force ($)	Avg. Prem ($/M)	1st Yr Prem/ Total Prem	Ord. Lapse Ratio
2007	41,520	42,302	8.98	11.9	6.0
2008	37,066	42,002	9.08	9.5	6.9
2009	35,476	41,753	9.56	10.6	6.4

• NEW LIFE BUSINESS ISSUED ($000 omitted)

Year	Whole Life	Term	Credit	Group	Industrial	Total
2007	251,951	1,219,214	17,482,263	2,863,731	...	21,817,159
2008	227,996	926,127	17,159,885	2,385,334	...	20,699,342
2009	268,323	925,237	14,302,398	2,279,581	...	17,775,539

• LIFE INSURANCE IN FORCE ($000 omitted)

Year	Whole Life	Term	Credit	Group	Industrial	Total
2007	7,737,245	9,045,225	35,561,734	26,533,120	...	78,877,324
2008	7,501,127	9,118,341	34,459,775	25,403,399	...	76,482,642
2009	7,300,119	9,295,250	28,733,009	24,988,498	...	70,316,876

DIRECT GENERAL LIFE INSURANCE

1281 Murfreesboro Road
Nashville, Tennessee 37217
Tel: 615-399-4700

AMB#: 009373
Began Business: 12/30/1982
Agency Off: None

Best's Financial Strength Rating: B **FSC:** V

• NET PREMIUMS AND DEPOSITS ($000 omitted)

Year	Individual Life	Individual & Group Annuities	Group Life & A&H	Credit Life & A&H	Individual A&H	Total
2007	19,964	...	...	...	...	19,964
2008	23,345	...	...	...	...	23,345
2009	21,386	...	...	...	...	21,386

• NET OPERATING GAIN ($000 omitted)

Year	Individual Life	Individual & Group Annuities	Group Life & A&H	Credit Life & A&H	Individual A&H	Total
2007	5,657	...	...	...	...	5,657
2008	6,404	...	...	...	...	6,404
2009	6,566	...	...	...	...	6,566

• COMPARATIVE FINANCIALS ($000 omitted)

Year	Assets	Capital & Surplus	Net Invest Income	Benefits Paid	Realized Cap Gains	Policyholder Dividends	Contract Lns (% of assets)
2007	26,949	15,501	824	2,376	...	...	...
2008	35,468	22,009	720	3,427	...	...	...
2009	29,433	17,065	570	3,257	-11	...	...

• ORDINARY LIFE STATISTICS

Year	Av. Ord. Policy Issued ($)	Av. Ord. Policy In Force ($)	Avg. Prem ($/M)	1st Yr Prem/ Total Prem	Ord. Lapse Ratio
2007	11,571	11,422	13.48	75.4	82.3
2008	11,755	11,638	13.67	71.7	57.4
2009	11,174	11,158	13.48	66.6	59.1

• NEW LIFE BUSINESS ISSUED ($000 omitted)

Year	Whole Life	Term	Credit	Group	Industrial	Total
2007	...	3,349,355	...	...	...	3,349,355
2008	...	2,999,365	...	...	...	2,999,365
2009	...	2,660,510	...	...	...	2,660,510

• LIFE INSURANCE IN FORCE ($000 omitted)

Year	Whole Life	Term	Credit	Group	Industrial	Total
2007	...	1,481,030	...	...	...	1,481,030
2008	...	1,707,790	...	...	...	1,707,790
2009	...	1,586,140	...	...	...	1,586,140

DELAWARE AMERICAN LIFE INS CO

P.O. Box 1591
Houston, Texas 77251
Tel: 713-522-1111

AMB#: 006305
Began Business: 08/01/1966
Agency Off: None

Best's Financial Strength Rating: A **FSC:** VI

• NET PREMIUMS AND DEPOSITS ($000 omitted)

Year	Individual Life	Individual & Group Annuities	Group Life & A&H	Credit Life & A&H	Individual A&H	Total
2007	1,689	536	15,327	...	...	17,553
2008	1,511	221	25,076	...	...	26,809
2009	-17,259	-9,877	20,755	...	723	-5,659

• NET OPERATING GAIN ($000 omitted)

Year	Individual Life	Individual & Group Annuities	Group Life & A&H	Credit Life & A&H	Individual A&H	Total
2007	-528	0	1,941	...	...	1,414
2008	-696	57	3,686	...	...	3,044
2009	370	-143	2,049	...	229	2,505

• COMPARATIVE FINANCIALS ($000 omitted)

Year	Assets	Capital & Surplus	Net Invest Income	Benefits Paid	Realized Cap Gains	Policyholder Dividends	Contract Lns (% of assets)
2007	76,362	26,317	3,893	12,882	-530	0	1.8
2008	83,876	27,313	3,814	17,842	-763	0	1.7
2009	65,311	25,880	3,410	17,500	178	0	...

• ORDINARY LIFE STATISTICS

Year	Av. Ord. Policy Issued ($)	Av. Ord. Policy In Force ($)	Avg. Prem ($/M)	1st Yr Prem/ Total Prem	Ord. Lapse Ratio
2007	...	...	...	...	...
2008	...	...	...	...	...
2009	...	...	...	...	...

• NEW LIFE BUSINESS ISSUED ($000 omitted)

Year	Whole Life	Term	Credit	Group	Industrial	Total
2007	1,556	...	...	275,389	...	276,945
2008	20	...	...	127,059	...	127,079
2009	200	...	...	2,181,110	...	2,181,310

• LIFE INSURANCE IN FORCE ($000 omitted)

Year	Whole Life	Term	Credit	Group	Industrial	Total
2007	71,146	333,053	...	1,414,619	...	1,818,818
2008	66,004	296,500	...	894,333	...	1,256,837
2009	56,120	95,260	42,062	5,076,784	...	5,270,225

EASTERN LIFE AND HEALTH INS CO

P.O. Box 83149
Lancaster, Pennsylvania 17608-3149
Tel: 717-391-5767

AMB#: 006325
Began Business: 01/30/1911
Agency Off: M. Christine Gimber

Best's Financial Strength Rating: A- u **FSC:** VI

• NET PREMIUMS AND DEPOSITS ($000 omitted)

Year	Individual Life	Individual & Group Annuities	Group Life & A&H	Credit Life & A&H	Individual A&H	Total
2007	...	...	35,863	...	...	35,863
2008	...	...	36,723	...	...	36,723
2009	...	...	35,937	...	...	35,937

• NET OPERATING GAIN ($000 omitted)

Year	Individual Life	Individual & Group Annuities	Group Life & A&H	Credit Life & A&H	Individual A&H	Total
2007	...	...	4,258	...	...	4,258
2008	...	...	1,699	...	...	1,699
2009	...	...	2,239	...	...	2,239

• COMPARATIVE FINANCIALS ($000 omitted)

Year	Assets	Capital & Surplus	Net Invest Income	Benefits Paid	Realized Cap Gains	Policyholder Dividends	Contract Lns (% of assets)
2007	85,667	60,679	3,278	24,650	323	...	...
2008	58,541	37,817	2,578	26,000	-2,409	...	...
2009	48,709	28,676	1,591	25,714	-117	...	...

• ORDINARY LIFE STATISTICS

Year	Av. Ord. Policy Issued ($)	Av. Ord. Policy In Force ($)	Avg. Prem ($/M)	1st Yr Prem/ Total Prem	Ord. Lapse Ratio
2007	...	...	...	...	...
2008	...	...	...	...	...
2009	...	...	...	...	...

• NEW LIFE BUSINESS ISSUED ($000 omitted)

Year	Whole Life	Term	Credit	Group	Industrial	Total
2007	...	...	...	375,611	...	375,611
2008	...	...	...	473,627	...	473,627
2009	...	...	...	356,335	...	356,335

• LIFE INSURANCE IN FORCE ($000 omitted)

Year	Whole Life	Term	Credit	Group	Industrial	Total
2007	...	...	...	1,782,647	...	1,782,647
2008	...	...	...	1,758,863	...	1,758,863
2009	...	...	...	1,742,954	...	1,742,954

EMC NATIONAL LIFE COMPANY

P.O. Box 9202
Des Moines, Iowa 50306-9202
Tel: 515-237-2000

AMB#: 006339
Began Business: 04/01/1963
Agency Off: Alan D. Huisinga

Best's Financial Strength Rating: B++ **FSC:** VII

• NET PREMIUMS AND DEPOSITS ($000 omitted)

Year	Individual Life	Individual & Group Annuities	Group Life & A&H	Credit Life & A&H	Individual A&H	Total
2007	25,971	60,480	6,407	3	38,336	131,197
2008	22,826	61,369	5,866	3	35,123	125,187
2009	26,332	84,852	6,143	3	16,745	134,075

• NET OPERATING GAIN ($000 omitted)

Year	Individual Life	Individual & Group Annuities	Group Life & A&H	Credit Life & A&H	Individual A&H	Total
2007	1,806	3,152	787	3	-6,957	-1,210
2008	-821	2,448	-806	2	-18,696	-17,873
2009	-25,812	-601	-423	2	-1,454	-28,289

• COMPARATIVE FINANCIALS ($000 omitted)

Year	Assets	Capital & Surplus	Net Invest Income	Benefits Paid	Realized Cap Gains	Policyholder Dividends	Contract Lns (% of assets)
2007	663,411	52,982	35,810	148,776	21	259	1.2
2008	682,705	41,271	35,624	106,789	-4,119	258	1.2
2009	958,729	55,011	40,531	87,999	6,326	466	2.7

• ORDINARY LIFE STATISTICS

Year	Av. Ord. Policy Issued ($)	Av. Ord. Policy In Force ($)	Avg. Prem ($/M)	1st Yr Prem/ Total Prem	Ord. Lapse Ratio
2007	112,504	72,697	6.21	14.8	7.0
2008	157,785	78,418	5.60	10.1	6.4
2009	136,354	83,689	5.37	10.5	6.7

• NEW LIFE BUSINESS ISSUED ($000 omitted)

Year	Whole Life	Term	Credit	Group	Industrial	Total
2007	100,395	914,733	...	126,374	...	1,141,502
2008	68,957	878,383	...	108,695	...	1,056,035
2009	112,715	793,359	...	131,904	...	1,037,977

• LIFE INSURANCE IN FORCE ($000 omitted)

Year	Whole Life	Term	Credit	Group	Industrial	Total
2007	2,460,695	5,051,318	250	3,749,714	...	11,261,977
2008	2,263,401	5,605,489	267	3,654,889	...	11,524,046
2009	2,235,060	5,900,329	241	4,046,959	...	12,182,589

EMPLOYEES LIFE CO (MUTUAL)

916 Sherwood Drive
Lake Bluff, Illinois 60044-2285
Tel: 847-295-6000

AMB#: 008005
Began Business: 05/31/1946
Agency Off: R. P. Leach

Best's Financial Strength Rating: B+ **FSC:** V

• NET PREMIUMS AND DEPOSITS ($000 omitted)

Year	Individual Life	Individual & Group Annuities	Group Life & A&H	Credit Life & A&H	Individual A&H	Total
2007	15,469	36,021	3,781	...	...	55,271
2008	10,983	99,770	4,024	...	...	114,777
2009	12,223	289,609	4,036	...	...	305,868

• NET OPERATING GAIN ($000 omitted)

Year	Individual Life	Individual & Group Annuities	Group Life & A&H	Credit Life & A&H	Individual A&H	Total
2007	440	214	64	...	...	2,300
2008	95	-275	132	...	...	732
2009	326	223	72	...	...	1,325

• COMPARATIVE FINANCIALS ($000 omitted)

Year	Assets	Capital & Surplus	Net Invest Income	Benefits Paid	Realized Cap Gains	Policyholder Dividends	Contract Lns (% of assets)
2007	266,335	23,123	14,994	26,711	-195	186	0.2
2008	290,663	18,100	14,857	30,886	4	256	0.1
2009	477,181	18,554	17,375	37,226	-727	208	0.1

• ORDINARY LIFE STATISTICS

Year	Av. Ord. Policy Issued ($)	Av. Ord. Policy In Force ($)	Avg. Prem ($/M)	1st Yr Prem/ Total Prem	Ord. Lapse Ratio
2007	8,478	6,626	151.87	0.5	2.5
2008	6,414	6,621	103.56	10.6	0.9
2009	9,881	6,603	110.51	1.4	8.9

• NEW LIFE BUSINESS ISSUED ($000 omitted)

Year	Whole Life	Term	Credit	Group	Industrial	Total
2007	17,625	...	...	...	...	17,625
2008	11,367	30	...	36,188	...	47,585
2009	20,612	...	...	...	...	20,612

• LIFE INSURANCE IN FORCE ($000 omitted)

Year	Whole Life	Term	Credit	Group	Industrial	Total
2007	80,414	21,447	...	1,681,822	...	1,783,683
2008	86,700	19,313	...	1,707,411	...	1,813,424
2009	90,641	19,883	...	1,904,059	...	2,014,583

EMPIRE FIDELITY INVESTMENTS LF

82 Devonshire Street, V5A
Boston, Massachusetts 02109-3605
Tel: 212-335-5082

AMB#: 060055
Began Business: 06/01/1992
Agency Off: Jeff Cimini

Best's Financial Strength Rating: A+ g **FSC:** X

• NET PREMIUMS AND DEPOSITS ($000 omitted)

Year	Individual Life	Individual & Group Annuities	Group Life & A&H	Credit Life & A&H	Individual A&H	Total
2007	452	250,584	...	...	...	251,036
2008	389	204,271	...	...	...	204,660
2009	356	138,497	...	...	...	138,853

• NET OPERATING GAIN ($000 omitted)

Year	Individual Life	Individual & Group Annuities	Group Life & A&H	Credit Life & A&H	Individual A&H	Total
2007	211	2,757	...	...	...	2,967
2008	-49	789	...	...	...	740
2009	24	1,742	...	...	...	1,766

• COMPARATIVE FINANCIALS ($000 omitted)

Year	Assets	Capital & Surplus	Net Invest Income	Benefits Paid	Realized Cap Gains	Policyholder Dividends	Contract Lns (% of assets)
2007	1,613,193	51,161	2,885	122,257	-180	...	...
2008	1,197,658	52,056	1,934	128,930	-475	...	...
2009	1,451,050	54,461	1,197	146,716	91	...	0.0

• ORDINARY LIFE STATISTICS

Year	Av. Ord. Policy Issued ($)	Av. Ord. Policy In Force ($)	Avg. Prem ($/M)	1st Yr Prem/ Total Prem	Ord. Lapse Ratio
2007	...	...	...	...	...
2008	...	...	...	...	...
2009	...	...	...	...	...

• NEW LIFE BUSINESS ISSUED ($000 omitted)

Year	Whole Life	Term	Credit	Group	Industrial	Total
2007	4,980	85,824	...	...	...	90,804
2008	6,200	82,800	...	...	...	89,000
2009	...	65,200	...	...	...	65,200

• LIFE INSURANCE IN FORCE ($000 omitted)

Year	Whole Life	Term	Credit	Group	Industrial	Total
2007	10,680	944,794	...	...	...	955,474
2008	16,880	994,019	...	...	...	1,010,899
2009	16,608	1,003,019	...	...	...	1,019,626

EMPLOYEES LIFE INSURANCE CO

9311 San Pedro, Suite 550
San Antonio, Texas 78216
Tel: 210-321-7361

AMB#: 009027
Began Business: 12/31/1980
Agency Off: Charles E. Amato

Best's Financial Strength Rating: B+ **FSC:** V

• NET PREMIUMS AND DEPOSITS ($000 omitted)

Year	Individual Life	Individual & Group Annuities	Group Life & A&H	Credit Life & A&H	Individual A&H	Total
2007	156	...	18	7,119	2	7,295
2008	154	...	19	7,141	2	7,317
2009	174	...	16	7,108	1	7,300

• NET OPERATING GAIN ($000 omitted)

Year	Individual Life	Individual & Group Annuities	Group Life & A&H	Credit Life & A&H	Individual A&H	Total
2007	23	...	14	1,149	-3	1,183
2008	42	...	15	1,657	1	1,715
2009	-16	...	10	1,826	1	1,821

• COMPARATIVE FINANCIALS ($000 omitted)

Year	Assets	Capital & Surplus	Net Invest Income	Benefits Paid	Realized Cap Gains	Policyholder Dividends	Contract Lns (% of assets)
2007	14,066	7,684	685	2,086	0	...	...
2008	15,631	8,969	715	1,822	-119	...	...
2009	17,331	10,755	664	2,122	-144	...	...

• ORDINARY LIFE STATISTICS

Year	Av. Ord. Policy Issued ($)	Av. Ord. Policy In Force ($)	Avg. Prem ($/M)	1st Yr Prem/ Total Prem	Ord. Lapse Ratio
2007	...	...	...	...	...
2008	...	...	...	...	...
2009	...	...	...	...	...

• NEW LIFE BUSINESS ISSUED ($000 omitted)

Year	Whole Life	Term	Credit	Group	Industrial	Total
2007	...	...	47,888	659	...	48,547
2008	...	...	36,974	655	...	37,629
2009	...	...	26,353	654	...	27,007

• LIFE INSURANCE IN FORCE ($000 omitted)

Year	Whole Life	Term	Credit	Group	Industrial	Total
2007	...	29,043	394,585	5,773	...	429,401
2008	...	28,976	398,912	5,426	...	433,314
2009	...	29,682	388,764	5,103	...	423,549

EMPLOYERS REASSURANCE CORP

5700 Broadmoor, Suite 1000
Mission, Kansas 66201
Tel: 913-982-3700

AMB#: 006976
Began Business: 11/12/1907
Agency Off: None

Best's Financial Strength Rating: A- g
FSC: X

• **NET PREMIUMS AND DEPOSITS ($000 omitted)**

Year	Individual Life	Individual & Group Annuities	Group Life & A&H	Credit Life & A&H	Individual A&H	Total
2007	708,875	22,330	-7,609	37	350,351	1,073,985
2008	363,929	3,438	-1,031	505	320,067	686,908
2009	368,838	2,526	27,114	57	272,842	671,377

• **NET OPERATING GAIN ($000 omitted)**

Year	Individual Life	Individual & Group Annuities	Group Life & A&H	Credit Life & A&H	Individual A&H	Total
2007	-16,648	33,068	-17,251	-55	-329,800	-330,686
2008	-138,977	13,925	6,179	464	-465,741	-584,150
2009	-375,333	18,743	20,763	-363	249,386	-86,803

• **COMPARATIVE FINANCIALS ($000 omitted)**

Year	Assets	Capital & Surplus	Net Invest Income	Benefits Paid	Realized Cap Gains	Policyholder Dividends	Contract Lns (% of assets)
2007	8,666,442	780,301	650,110	1,224,633	-851	...	0.5
2008	9,697,674	681,200	443,906	748,754	-34,900	...	0.4
2009	9,604,673	724,509	485,643	763,294	-43,029	...	0.4

• **ORDINARY LIFE STATISTICS**

Year	Av. Ord. Policy Issued ($)	Av. Ord. Policy In Force ($)	Avg. Prem ($/M)	1st Yr Prem/ Total Prem	Ord. Lapse Ratio
2007	...	51,355	2.40	...	4.6
2008	...	49,100	2.63	...	9.5
2009	...	50,055	2.72	...	6.0

• **NEW LIFE BUSINESS ISSUED ($000 omitted)**

Year	Whole Life	Term	Credit	Group	Industrial	Total
2007	...	...	...	...	...	...
2008	...	...	...	...	...	...
2009	...	...	...	...	...	...

• **LIFE INSURANCE IN FORCE ($000 omitted)**

Year	Whole Life	Term	Credit	Group	Industrial	Total
2007	34,008,383	367,463,382	76,254	590,479	...	402,138,498
2008	27,721,029	334,222,446	32,026	426,259	...	362,401,760
2009	28,321,423	295,888,677	31,016	185,314	...	324,426,429

EQUITRUST LIFE INSURANCE CO

5400 University Avenue
West Des Moines, Iowa 50266-5997
Tel: 877-249-3694

AMB#: 060315
Began Business: 07/07/1967
Agency Off: Tom May

Best's Financial Strength Rating: B+
FSC: IX

• **NET PREMIUMS AND DEPOSITS ($000 omitted)**

Year	Individual Life	Individual & Group Annuities	Group Life & A&H	Credit Life & A&H	Individual A&H	Total
2007	15,646	1,608,663	...	...	...	1,624,310
2008	14,185	1,588,589	...	...	...	1,602,774
2009	10,426	664,533	...	...	...	674,959

• **NET OPERATING GAIN ($000 omitted)**

Year	Individual Life	Individual & Group Annuities	Group Life & A&H	Credit Life & A&H	Individual A&H	Total
2007	4,920	17,548	...	...	...	25,168
2008	3,929	-42,639	...	...	...	-37,060
2009	25,428	25,361	...	...	...	53,227

• **COMPARATIVE FINANCIALS ($000 omitted)**

Year	Assets	Capital & Surplus	Net Invest Income	Benefits Paid	Realized Cap Gains	Policyholder Dividends	Contract Lns (% of assets)
2007	6,841,531	391,638	321,926	449,352	-2,883	865	0.3
2008	7,779,919	416,978	291,488	725,661	-79,871	821	0.2
2009	7,163,793	434,967	347,607	1,342,580	3,997	589	0.0

• **ORDINARY LIFE STATISTICS**

Year	Av. Ord. Policy Issued ($)	Av. Ord. Policy In Force ($)	Avg. Prem ($/M)	1st Yr Prem/ Total Prem	Ord. Lapse Ratio
2007	224,221	438,108	8.45	28.2	4.3
2008	300,757	442,881	7.89	15.5	4.6
2009	349,257	150,679	18.81	16.1	3.6

• **NEW LIFE BUSINESS ISSUED ($000 omitted)**

Year	Whole Life	Term	Credit	Group	Industrial	Total
2007	33,449	-40	...	...	...	33,409
2008	30,383	595	...	...	...	30,978
2009	23,208	1,240	...	...	...	24,448

• **LIFE INSURANCE IN FORCE ($000 omitted)**

Year	Whole Life	Term	Credit	Group	Industrial	Total
2007	1,853,170	322,035	...	...	...	2,175,205
2008	1,684,880	408,177	...	...	...	2,093,057
2009	608,470	62,354	...	...	...	670,825

EQUITABLE LIFE & CASUALTY

P.O. Box 2460
Salt Lake City, Utah 84110-2460
Tel: 801-579-3400

AMB#: 006342
Began Business: 06/25/1935
Agency Off: Larry A. Thomas

Best's Financial Strength Rating: B+
FSC: VI

• **NET PREMIUMS AND DEPOSITS ($000 omitted)**

Year	Individual Life	Individual & Group Annuities	Group Life & A&H	Credit Life & A&H	Individual A&H	Total
2007	9,002	...	...	...	98,929	107,931
2008	9,520	...	...	...	94,653	104,173
2009	11,467	...	...	...	97,624	109,091

• **NET OPERATING GAIN ($000 omitted)**

Year	Individual Life	Individual & Group Annuities	Group Life & A&H	Credit Life & A&H	Individual A&H	Total
2007	-590	...	...	...	3,748	3,158
2008	-1,720	...	...	...	2,337	616
2009	-1,970	...	...	...	1,786	85

• **COMPARATIVE FINANCIALS ($000 omitted)**

Year	Assets	Capital & Surplus	Net Invest Income	Benefits Paid	Realized Cap Gains	Policyholder Dividends	Contract Lns (% of assets)
2007	207,246	40,223	9,547	62,733	...	0	0.4
2008	214,517	38,078	10,119	66,701	-1,535	0	0.5
2009	233,120	30,040	9,967	68,964	-1,556	0	0.5

• **ORDINARY LIFE STATISTICS**

Year	Av. Ord. Policy Issued ($)	Av. Ord. Policy In Force ($)	Avg. Prem ($/M)	1st Yr Prem/ Total Prem	Ord. Lapse Ratio
2007	7,412	5,834	57.54	9.7	4.6
2008	10,003	6,131	57.36	15.7	3.8
2009	13,095	7,215	56.85	33.2	4.9

• **NEW LIFE BUSINESS ISSUED ($000 omitted)**

Year	Whole Life	Term	Credit	Group	Industrial	Total
2007	10,367	1,670	...	...	...	12,037
2008	20,671	2,636	...	...	...	23,307
2009	65,590	2,975	...	...	...	68,565

• **LIFE INSURANCE IN FORCE ($000 omitted)**

Year	Whole Life	Term	Credit	Group	Industrial	Total
2007	140,488	17,745	...	...	...	158,233
2008	149,329	18,643	...	...	...	167,972
2009	199,489	19,393	...	...	...	218,882

ERIE FAMILY LIFE INS CO

100 Erie Insurance Place
Erie, Pennsylvania 16530
Tel: 814-870-2000

AMB#: 007276
Began Business: 09/01/1967
Agency Off: Kevin Marti

Best's Financial Strength Rating: A
FSC: VIII

• **NET PREMIUMS AND DEPOSITS ($000 omitted)**

Year	Individual Life	Individual & Group Annuities	Group Life & A&H	Credit Life & A&H	Individual A&H	Total
2007	67,586	63,817	2,967	...	261	134,631
2008	74,334	142,832	2,749	...	237	220,152
2009	90,845	134,559	2,648	...	241	228,294

• **NET OPERATING GAIN ($000 omitted)**

Year	Individual Life	Individual & Group Annuities	Group Life & A&H	Credit Life & A&H	Individual A&H	Total
2007	7,536	14,759	1,383	...	115	23,793
2008	8,109	10,138	513	...	42	18,802
2009	16,339	11,328	4,189	...	-44	31,812

• **COMPARATIVE FINANCIALS ($000 omitted)**

Year	Assets	Capital & Surplus	Net Invest Income	Benefits Paid	Realized Cap Gains	Policyholder Dividends	Contract Lns (% of assets)
2007	1,563,947	183,521	91,346	158,419	-11,328	...	0.9
2008	1,533,697	105,817	91,188	169,217	-85,203	...	1.0
2009	1,665,915	173,543	96,488	181,989	-28,567	...	0.9

• **ORDINARY LIFE STATISTICS**

Year	Av. Ord. Policy Issued ($)	Av. Ord. Policy In Force ($)	Avg. Prem ($/M)	1st Yr Prem/ Total Prem	Ord. Lapse Ratio
2007	171,373	125,388	2.95	9.9	9.1
2008	196,040	131,800	2.97	11.8	4.2
2009	175,145	136,490	3.39	24.9	5.0

• **NEW LIFE BUSINESS ISSUED ($000 omitted)**

Year	Whole Life	Term	Credit	Group	Industrial	Total
2007	291,969	3,373,007	...	72,802	...	3,737,778
2008	304,119	4,064,826	...	66,543	...	4,435,488
2009	599,694	3,307,626	...	79,425	...	3,986,745

• **LIFE INSURANCE IN FORCE ($000 omitted)**

Year	Whole Life	Term	Credit	Group	Industrial	Total
2007	4,393,268	29,812,356	...	825,411	...	35,031,035
2008	4,227,511	32,721,098	...	748,399	...	37,697,008
2009	4,133,475	34,124,387	...	703,206	...	38,961,068

FAMILY HERITAGE LIFE OF AMER

P.O. Box 470608
Cleveland, Ohio 44147
Tel: 440-922-5200

AMB#: 068197
Began Business: 11/17/1989
Agency Off: Howard L. Lewis

Best's Financial Strength Rating: B++
FSC: VI

• NET PREMIUMS AND DEPOSITS ($000 omitted)

Year	Individual Life	Individual & Group Annuities	Group Life & A&H	Credit Life & A&H	Individual A&H	Total
2007	179	...	...	...	104,459	104,638
2008	509	...	...	...	119,475	119,984
2009	560	...	...	...	131,390	131,950

• NET OPERATING GAIN ($000 omitted)

Year	Individual Life	Individual & Group Annuities	Group Life & A&H	Credit Life & A&H	Individual A&H	Total
2007	-75	...	...	...	7,224	7,149
2008	-65	...	...	...	12,780	12,714
2009	12	...	...	...	13,322	13,334

• COMPARATIVE FINANCIALS ($000 omitted)

Year	Assets	Capital & Surplus	Net Invest Income	Benefits Paid	Realized Cap Gains	Policyholder Dividends	Contract Lns (% of assets)
2007	262,362	27,090	15,832	18,688	...	...	...
2008	309,399	34,025	18,262	22,724	2	...	...
2009	365,394	41,694	20,205	26,456	...	...	...

• ORDINARY LIFE STATISTICS

Year	Av. Ord. Policy Issued ($)	Av. Ord. Policy In Force ($)	Avg. Prem ($/M)	1st Yr Prem/ Total Prem	Ord. Lapse Ratio
2007	...	...	...	...	...
2008	...	...	...	...	...
2009	...	...	...	...	...

• NEW LIFE BUSINESS ISSUED ($000 omitted)

Year	Whole Life	Term	Credit	Group	Industrial	Total
2007	8,801	...	...	...	...	8,801
2008	34,385	...	...	...	...	34,385
2009	20,726	...	...	...	...	20,726

• LIFE INSURANCE IN FORCE ($000 omitted)

Year	Whole Life	Term	Credit	Group	Industrial	Total
2007	8,791	...	...	...	...	8,791
2008	30,170	...	...	...	...	30,170
2009	36,143	...	...	...	...	36,143

FAMILY SERVICE LIFE INS CO

7 Hanover Square
New York, New York 10004-2616
Tel: 800-538-6203

AMB#: 007650
Began Business: 11/02/1955
Agency Off: None

Best's Financial Strength Rating: A
FSC: VII

• NET PREMIUMS AND DEPOSITS ($000 omitted)

Year	Individual Life	Individual & Group Annuities	Group Life & A&H	Credit Life & A&H	Individual A&H	Total
2007	16	1	...	...	...	18
2008	21	0	...	...	...	21
2009	15	...	...	...	...	15

• NET OPERATING GAIN ($000 omitted)

Year	Individual Life	Individual & Group Annuities	Group Life & A&H	Credit Life & A&H	Individual A&H	Total
2007	5,293	4,855	...	...	...	10,149
2008	3,646	5,235	...	...	...	8,881
2009	2,242	3,948	...	...	...	6,190

• COMPARATIVE FINANCIALS ($000 omitted)

Year	Assets	Capital & Surplus	Net Invest Income	Benefits Paid	Realized Cap Gains	Policyholder Dividends	Contract Lns (% of assets)
2007	560,761	94,499	33,328	40,820	990	...	0.1
2008	530,615	90,769	32,565	43,259	-2,276	...	0.1
2009	519,558	96,540	29,550	38,524	1,775	...	0.1

• ORDINARY LIFE STATISTICS

Year	Av. Ord. Policy Issued ($)	Av. Ord. Policy In Force ($)	Avg. Prem ($/M)	1st Yr Prem/ Total Prem	Ord. Lapse Ratio
2007	...	...	...	...	...
2008	...	...	...	...	...
2009	...	...	...	...	...

• NEW LIFE BUSINESS ISSUED ($000 omitted)

Year	Whole Life	Term	Credit	Group	Industrial	Total
2007	...	...	...	...	...	...
2008	...	...	...	...	...	...
2009	...	...	...	...	...	...

• LIFE INSURANCE IN FORCE ($000 omitted)

Year	Whole Life	Term	Credit	Group	Industrial	Total
2007	227,815	6,006	...	...	...	233,821
2008	216,460	2,729	...	...	...	219,189
2009	203,966	2,532	...	...	...	206,498

FAMILY LIFE INS CO

10700 Northwest Freeway
Houston, Texas 77092
Tel: 713-529-0045

AMB#: 006360
Began Business: 06/16/1949
Agency Off: Thomas Luchetta

Best's Financial Strength Rating: B+
FSC: VI

• NET PREMIUMS AND DEPOSITS ($000 omitted)

Year	Individual Life	Individual & Group Annuities	Group Life & A&H	Credit Life & A&H	Individual A&H	Total
2007	19,996	133	...	...	...	20,129
2008	15,802	195	...	...	...	15,997
2009	15,168	170	...	...	1,002	16,341

• NET OPERATING GAIN ($000 omitted)

Year	Individual Life	Individual & Group Annuities	Group Life & A&H	Credit Life & A&H	Individual A&H	Total
2007	6,389	122	...	...	...	6,512
2008	5,135	696	...	...	...	5,831
2009	3,974	220	...	...	177	4,370

• COMPARATIVE FINANCIALS ($000 omitted)

Year	Assets	Capital & Surplus	Net Invest Income	Benefits Paid	Realized Cap Gains	Policyholder Dividends	Contract Lns (% of assets)
2007	127,816	22,514	5,756	14,004	-4	...	3.7
2008	126,179	25,371	5,093	13,092	-916	...	3.8
2009	122,349	25,987	4,394	11,192	...	...	3.7

• ORDINARY LIFE STATISTICS

Year	Av. Ord. Policy Issued ($)	Av. Ord. Policy In Force ($)	Avg. Prem ($/M)	1st Yr Prem/ Total Prem	Ord. Lapse Ratio
2007	181,896	74,480	5.87	0.0	11.8
2008	170,733	75,832	5.42	1.6	14.8
2009	179,852	77,865	5.74	2.3	13.9

• NEW LIFE BUSINESS ISSUED ($000 omitted)

Year	Whole Life	Term	Credit	Group	Industrial	Total
2007	201	11,986	...	...	...	12,187
2008	2,750	114,202	...	...	...	116,952
2009	2,625	163,199	...	...	...	165,824

• LIFE INSURANCE IN FORCE ($000 omitted)

Year	Whole Life	Term	Credit	Group	Industrial	Total
2007	766,383	2,846,571	...	...	...	3,612,954
2008	711,323	2,457,072	...	...	...	3,168,395
2009	659,503	2,203,516	...	...	...	2,863,019

FARM BUREAU LIFE INS CO

5400 University Avenue
West Des Moines, Iowa 50266-5997
Tel: 515-225-5400

AMB#: 006362
Began Business: 01/25/1945
Agency Off: David T. Sebastian

Best's Financial Strength Rating: B++
FSC: IX

• NET PREMIUMS AND DEPOSITS ($000 omitted)

Year	Individual Life	Individual & Group Annuities	Group Life & A&H	Credit Life & A&H	Individual A&H	Total
2007	240,878	381,359	749	0	...	622,986
2008	246,809	479,516	812	0	...	727,138
2009	252,559	494,509	1,368	...	...	748,437

• NET OPERATING GAIN ($000 omitted)

Year	Individual Life	Individual & Group Annuities	Group Life & A&H	Credit Life & A&H	Individual A&H	Total
2007	26,233	19,282	98	0	874	51,706
2008	19,021	11,227	-331	-1	2,071	38,182
2009	52,118	20,351	624	0	496	78,747

• COMPARATIVE FINANCIALS ($000 omitted)

Year	Assets	Capital & Surplus	Net Invest Income	Benefits Paid	Realized Cap Gains	Policyholder Dividends	Contract Lns (% of assets)
2007	5,633,103	364,915	296,890	449,563	3,447	21,154	2.8
2008	5,591,863	385,372	290,598	436,691	-66,894	19,066	2.9
2009	5,983,345	428,458	299,994	416,757	-33,229	19,000	2.8

• ORDINARY LIFE STATISTICS

Year	Av. Ord. Policy Issued ($)	Av. Ord. Policy In Force ($)	Avg. Prem ($/M)	1st Yr Prem/ Total Prem	Ord. Lapse Ratio
2007	188,555	89,904	6.35	11.2	4.6
2008	193,898	95,076	6.17	11.4	5.2
2009	186,071	99,553	5.97	11.2	5.7

• NEW LIFE BUSINESS ISSUED ($000 omitted)

Year	Whole Life	Term	Credit	Group	Industrial	Total
2007	964,995	4,266,655	...	...	...	5,231,650
2008	916,502	4,369,537	...	...	...	5,286,039
2009	889,510	5,042,065	...	...	...	5,931,575

• LIFE INSURANCE IN FORCE ($000 omitted)

Year	Whole Life	Term	Credit	Group	Industrial	Total
2007	17,451,778	22,749,844	99	482,439	...	40,684,160
2008	17,516,547	25,093,293	100	512,399	...	43,122,339
2009	17,411,578	27,725,434	50	494,253	...	45,631,315

FARM BUREAU LIFE INS CO OF MI

P.O. Box 30200
Lansing, Michigan 48909
Tel: 517-323-7000

AMB#: 006363
Began Business: 09/20/1951
Agency Off: Victor Verchereau

Best's Financial Strength Rating: A
FSC: IX

• NET PREMIUMS AND DEPOSITS ($000 omitted)

Year	Individual Life	Individual & Group Annuities	Group Life & A&H	Credit Life & A&H	Individual A&H	Total
2007	51,586	51,556	525	...	...	103,666
2008	58,542	78,646	545	...	...	137,733
2009	63,880	102,334	563	...	...	166,778

• NET OPERATING GAIN ($000 omitted)

Year	Individual Life	Individual & Group Annuities	Group Life & A&H	Credit Life & A&H	Individual A&H	Total
2007	12,406	8,794	1	...	...	21,201
2008	7,079	3,276	14	...	...	10,368
2009	6,941	9,076	21	...	...	16,039

• COMPARATIVE FINANCIALS ($000 omitted)

Year	Assets	Capital & Surplus	Net Invest Income	Benefits Paid	Realized Cap Gains	Policyholder Dividends	Contract Lns (% of assets)
2007	1,695,448	298,980	93,726	129,838	-231	4,570	1.4
2008	1,740,878	283,724	94,234	113,704	-16,831	4,645	1.3
2009	1,884,159	300,480	98,514	114,361	2,861	4,682	1.3

• ORDINARY LIFE STATISTICS

Year	Av. Ord. Policy Issued ($)	Av. Ord. Policy In Force ($)	Avg. Prem ($/M)	1st Yr Prem/ Total Prem	Ord. Lapse Ratio
2007	194,004	114,735	5.54	12.2	7.1
2008	173,907	118,951	6.01	12.1	6.9
2009	182,251	124,108	6.17	11.0	6.5

• NEW LIFE BUSINESS ISSUED ($000 omitted)

Year	Whole Life	Term	Credit	Group	Industrial	Total
2007	209,268	1,155,743	...	...	...	1,365,011
2008	227,809	1,126,581	...	...	...	1,354,390
2009	196,763	1,296,054	...	...	...	1,492,817

• LIFE INSURANCE IN FORCE ($000 omitted)

Year	Whole Life	Term	Credit	Group	Industrial	Total
2007	3,449,063	6,509,158	...	126,204	...	10,084,425
2008	3,435,448	6,986,654	...	133,357	...	10,555,459
2009	3,419,562	7,647,433	...	132,732	...	11,199,727

FARM FAMILY LIFE INS CO

P.O. Box 656
Albany, New York 12201-0656
Tel: 518-431-5000

AMB#: 006365
Began Business: 01/20/1954
Agency Off: Lewis E. Dufort

Best's Financial Strength Rating: A
FSC: VIII

• NET PREMIUMS AND DEPOSITS ($000 omitted)

Year	Individual Life	Individual & Group Annuities	Group Life & A&H	Credit Life & A&H	Individual A&H	Total
2007	47,016	23,031	387	...	4,699	75,132
2008	46,048	38,664	399	...	4,564	89,675
2009	45,980	42,237	424	...	4,469	93,109

• NET OPERATING GAIN ($000 omitted)

Year	Individual Life	Individual & Group Annuities	Group Life & A&H	Credit Life & A&H	Individual A&H	Total
2007	5,395	3,547	58	...	104	9,104
2008	6,245	3,223	172	...	588	10,228
2009	6,295	3,322	168	...	-230	9,556

• COMPARATIVE FINANCIALS ($000 omitted)

Year	Assets	Capital & Surplus	Net Invest Income	Benefits Paid	Realized Cap Gains	Policyholder Dividends	Contract Lns (% of assets)
2007	1,014,955	125,127	56,323	66,915	2,435	8,550	3.7
2008	990,963	91,290	55,971	68,711	-22,745	7,509	4.0
2009	1,055,361	108,683	55,680	64,636	-7,650	7,617	3.9

• ORDINARY LIFE STATISTICS

Year	Av. Ord. Policy Issued ($)	Av. Ord. Policy In Force ($)	Avg. Prem ($/M)	1st Yr Prem/ Total Prem	Ord. Lapse Ratio
2007	218,062	79,648	8.57	9.9	5.5
2008	252,723	84,086	8.15	8.2	6.4
2009	231,737	87,639	8.02	8.1	6.5

• NEW LIFE BUSINESS ISSUED ($000 omitted)

Year	Whole Life	Term	Credit	Group	Industrial	Total
2007	157,103	582,782	...	9,602	...	749,487
2008	133,150	565,377	...	8,546	...	707,073
2009	134,616	514,247	...	4,584	...	653,447

• LIFE INSURANCE IN FORCE ($000 omitted)

Year	Whole Life	Term	Credit	Group	Industrial	Total
2007	2,717,299	3,084,418	...	66,153	...	5,867,870
2008	2,709,800	3,336,966	...	72,099	...	6,118,865
2009	2,699,555	3,521,081	...	70,933	...	6,291,569

FARM BUREAU LIFE INS CO OF MO

P.O. Box 658
Jefferson City, Missouri 65102-0658
Tel: 573-893-1400

AMB#: 006364
Began Business: 07/27/1950
Agency Off: Ray Mabury

Best's Financial Strength Rating: A-
FSC: VI

• NET PREMIUMS AND DEPOSITS ($000 omitted)

Year	Individual Life	Individual & Group Annuities	Group Life & A&H	Credit Life & A&H	Individual A&H	Total
2007	24,516	5,957	105	...	6	30,584
2008	25,025	8,697	118	...	9	33,848
2009	25,443	18,255	121	...	4	43,824

• NET OPERATING GAIN ($000 omitted)

Year	Individual Life	Individual & Group Annuities	Group Life & A&H	Credit Life & A&H	Individual A&H	Total
2007	-492	-109	51	...	-12	1,418
2008	1,298	-267	-20	...	-18	2,541
2009	666	-551	45	...	2	2,254

• COMPARATIVE FINANCIALS ($000 omitted)

Year	Assets	Capital & Surplus	Net Invest Income	Benefits Paid	Realized Cap Gains	Policyholder Dividends	Contract Lns (% of assets)
2007	363,501	52,529	19,766	23,223	...	3,139	4.5
2008	367,925	45,307	20,327	20,191	-2,779	3,024	4.7
2009	391,118	45,267	20,753	22,914	-616	3,034	4.8

• ORDINARY LIFE STATISTICS

Year	Av. Ord. Policy Issued ($)	Av. Ord. Policy In Force ($)	Avg. Prem ($/M)	1st Yr Prem/ Total Prem	Ord. Lapse Ratio
2007	120,473	64,817	8.49	8.5	6.6
2008	79,869	66,071	7.48	9.8	7.0
2009	95,666	68,385	7.22	8.9	7.0

• NEW LIFE BUSINESS ISSUED ($000 omitted)

Year	Whole Life	Term	Credit	Group	Industrial	Total
2007	113,788	327,746	...	...	...	441,534
2008	105,467	794,661	...	...	...	900,128
2009	102,785	556,926	...	...	...	659,711

• LIFE INSURANCE IN FORCE ($000 omitted)

Year	Whole Life	Term	Credit	Group	Industrial	Total
2007	1,401,301	1,989,281	...	42,731	...	3,433,313
2008	1,406,415	2,568,056	...	44,998	...	4,019,469
2009	1,443,038	2,799,568	...	45,997	...	4,288,603

FARMERS NEW WORLD LIFE INS CO

3003 77th Avenue Southeast
Mercer Island, Washington 98040-2837
Tel: 206-232-8400

AMB#: 006373
Began Business: 05/23/1911
Agency Off: Jerry J. Carnahan

Best's Financial Strength Rating: A
FSC: X

• NET PREMIUMS AND DEPOSITS ($000 omitted)

Year	Individual Life	Individual & Group Annuities	Group Life & A&H	Credit Life & A&H	Individual A&H	Total
2007	508,480	245,609	25,932	...	3,101	783,122
2008	500,632	252,406	20,852	...	4,519	778,409
2009	481,137	266,023	23,873	...	6,650	777,682

• NET OPERATING GAIN ($000 omitted)

Year	Individual Life	Individual & Group Annuities	Group Life & A&H	Credit Life & A&H	Individual A&H	Total
2007	78,440	8,863	385	...	2,116	89,804
2008	103,161	22,899	858	...	1,016	127,934
2009	123,695	6,378	849	...	125	131,048

• COMPARATIVE FINANCIALS ($000 omitted)

Year	Assets	Capital & Surplus	Net Invest Income	Benefits Paid	Realized Cap Gains	Policyholder Dividends	Contract Lns (% of assets)
2007	6,987,510	641,255	325,614	515,841	8,142	...	3.8
2008	6,443,866	551,476	310,566	527,488	-108,728	...	4.3
2009	6,739,594	674,128	316,902	480,030	-144,357	...	4.3

• ORDINARY LIFE STATISTICS

Year	Av. Ord. Policy Issued ($)	Av. Ord. Policy In Force ($)	Avg. Prem ($/M)	1st Yr Prem/ Total Prem	Ord. Lapse Ratio
2007	150,224	141,467	3.55	12.8	7.2
2008	153,334	144,578	3.48	10.5	7.8
2009	163,868	148,016	3.39	9.7	8.1

• NEW LIFE BUSINESS ISSUED ($000 omitted)

Year	Whole Life	Term	Credit	Group	Industrial	Total
2007	5,753,871	25,487,090	...	...	...	31,240,961
2008	4,111,227	21,916,683	...	...	...	26,027,910
2009	3,572,579	22,424,406	...	...	...	25,996,985

• LIFE INSURANCE IN FORCE ($000 omitted)

Year	Whole Life	Term	Credit	Group	Industrial	Total
2007	75,584,393	138,250,634	...	20,006,251	...	233,841,278
2008	74,380,614	145,790,011	...	19,271,258	...	239,441,883
2009	72,486,819	153,116,899	...	21,996,995	...	247,600,713

FEDERATED LIFE INS CO

121 East Park Square
Owatonna, Minnesota 55060-3046
Tel: 507-455-5200

AMB#: 006381
Began Business: 01/05/1959
Agency Off: Jeffrey Fetters

Best's Financial Strength Rating: A+ **FSC:** VIII

• NET PREMIUMS AND DEPOSITS ($000 omitted)

Year	Individual Life	Individual & Group Annuities	Group Life & A&H	Credit Life & A&H	Individual A&H	Total
2007	82,806	5,933	7,213	...	22,521	118,474
2008	85,008	9,084	6,319	...	23,207	123,618
2009	94,318	12,763	6,133	...	23,217	136,431

• NET OPERATING GAIN ($000 omitted)

Year	Individual Life	Individual & Group Annuities	Group Life & A&H	Credit Life & A&H	Individual A&H	Total
2007	5,523	551	1,873	...	5,791	21,077
2008	5,037	721	1,949	...	6,294	19,860
2009	9,410	1,073	2,088	...	7,218	26,532

• COMPARATIVE FINANCIALS ($000 omitted)

Year	Assets	Capital & Surplus	Net Invest Income	Benefits Paid	Realized Cap Gains	Policyholder Dividends	Contract Lns (% of assets)
2007	919,053	216,977	52,288	56,730	-6	...	1.6
2008	954,854	217,960	54,568	56,346	-7,611	...	1.6
2009	1,018,531	234,536	59,010	66,742	-7,356	...	1.6

• ORDINARY LIFE STATISTICS

Year	Av. Ord. Policy Issued ($)	Av. Ord. Policy In Force ($)	Avg. Prem ($/M)	1st Yr Prem/ Total Prem	Ord. Lapse Ratio
2007	479,632	289,389	5.77	21.0	5.5
2008	483,810	301,383	5.72	21.0	6.3
2009	462,752	311,484	6.12	27.5	7.0

• NEW LIFE BUSINESS ISSUED ($000 omitted)

Year	Whole Life	Term	Credit	Group	Industrial	Total
2007	692,089	1,530,524	...	210,638	...	2,433,251
2008	809,131	1,324,953	...	178,391	...	2,312,475
2009	922,723	1,312,370	...	138,840	...	2,373,933

• LIFE INSURANCE IN FORCE ($000 omitted)

Year	Whole Life	Term	Credit	Group	Industrial	Total
2007	7,244,751	8,201,975	...	1,432,084	...	16,878,810
2008	7,476,153	8,687,616	...	1,357,414	...	17,521,183
2009	7,711,650	9,001,942	...	1,418,476	...	18,132,068

FIDELITY LIFE ASSOCIATION

1211 W. 22nd Street, Suite 209
Oak Brook, Illinois 60523
Tel: 630-522-0392

AMB#: 006386
Began Business: 02/24/1896
Agency Off: None

Best's Financial Strength Rating: A- **FSC:** VIII

• NET PREMIUMS AND DEPOSITS ($000 omitted)

Year	Individual Life	Individual & Group Annuities	Group Life & A&H	Credit Life & A&H	Individual A&H	Total
2007	20,827	38,107	255	...	1	59,190
2008	32,600	27,471	1,979	...	33	62,083
2009	34,299	20,966	7,748	...	85	63,098

• NET OPERATING GAIN ($000 omitted)

Year	Individual Life	Individual & Group Annuities	Group Life & A&H	Credit Life & A&H	Individual A&H	Total
2007	-6,993	5,659	-37	...	0	-1,371
2008	-5,691	4,635	-1,179	...	-13	-2,248
2009	-3,417	1,844	-2,084	...	-11	-3,667

• COMPARATIVE FINANCIALS ($000 omitted)

Year	Assets	Capital & Surplus	Net Invest Income	Benefits Paid	Realized Cap Gains	Policyholder Dividends	Contract Lns (% of assets)
2007	538,268	275,248	24,537	36,594	1,295	1,311	2.8
2008	514,697	256,820	22,217	32,260	-11,856	1,326	2.8
2009	484,842	220,503	22,076	31,478	-16,013	1,292	2.8

• ORDINARY LIFE STATISTICS

Year	Av. Ord. Policy Issued ($)	Av. Ord. Policy In Force ($)	Avg. Prem ($/M)	1st Yr Prem/ Total Prem	Ord. Lapse Ratio
2007	147,986	304,500	2.31	14.3	6.2
2008	139,496	274,240	2.59	22.2	10.6
2009	121,946	256,854	3.01	19.8	9.1

• NEW LIFE BUSINESS ISSUED ($000 omitted)

Year	Whole Life	Term	Credit	Group	Industrial	Total
2007	22,624	1,846,292	...	16,250	...	1,885,166
2008	30,771	2,348,759	...	259,574	...	2,639,104
2009	34,826	1,716,925	...	428,793	...	2,180,544

• LIFE INSURANCE IN FORCE ($000 omitted)

Year	Whole Life	Term	Credit	Group	Industrial	Total
2007	709,075	21,987,174	...	16,250	...	22,712,499
2008	674,892	21,753,017	...	262,865	...	22,690,774
2009	644,445	21,231,851	...	641,368	...	22,517,664

FIDELITY INVESTMENTS LIFE INS

82 Devonshire Street, V5A
Boston, Massachusetts 02109-3605
Tel: 801-537-2070

AMB#: 009138
Began Business: 12/21/1981
Agency Off: Jeff Cimini

Best's Financial Strength Rating: A+ g **FSC:** X

• NET PREMIUMS AND DEPOSITS ($000 omitted)

Year	Individual Life	Individual & Group Annuities	Group Life & A&H	Credit Life & A&H	Individual A&H	Total
2007	18,814	2,147,361	...	...	...	2,166,176
2008	12,575	2,174,015	...	...	...	2,186,590
2009	5,822	1,188,176	...	...	...	1,193,998

• NET OPERATING GAIN ($000 omitted)

Year	Individual Life	Individual & Group Annuities	Group Life & A&H	Credit Life & A&H	Individual A&H	Total
2007	2,254	45,907	...	...	...	48,160
2008	-1,106	1,744	...	...	...	638
2009	-1,067	12,570	...	...	...	11,504

• COMPARATIVE FINANCIALS ($000 omitted)

Year	Assets	Capital & Surplus	Net Invest Income	Benefits Paid	Realized Cap Gains	Policyholder Dividends	Contract Lns (% of assets)
2007	16,033,979	645,223	33,060	1,059,118	-726	...	0.0
2008	11,892,930	648,121	25,756	1,304,679	-8,643	...	0.0
2009	14,513,448	669,319	17,319	1,224,436	1,799	...	0.0

• ORDINARY LIFE STATISTICS

Year	Av. Ord. Policy Issued ($)	Av. Ord. Policy In Force ($)	Avg. Prem ($/M)	1st Yr Prem/ Total Prem	Ord. Lapse Ratio
2007	...	...	...	...	...
2008	...	...	...	...	...
2009	...	...	...	...	...

• NEW LIFE BUSINESS ISSUED ($000 omitted)

Year	Whole Life	Term	Credit	Group	Industrial	Total
2007	123,360	843,050	...	...	...	966,410
2008	124,748	740,455	...	...	...	865,203
2009	1,000	542,940	...	...	...	543,940

• LIFE INSURANCE IN FORCE ($000 omitted)

Year	Whole Life	Term	Credit	Group	Industrial	Total
2007	368,461	9,404,786	...	...	...	9,773,247
2008	441,565	9,751,565	...	...	...	10,193,130
2009	425,822	9,772,325	...	...	...	10,198,148

FIDELITY SECURITY LIFE INS CO

3130 Broadway
Kansas City, Missouri 64111-2452
Tel: 816-756-1060

AMB#: 007426
Began Business: 07/01/1969
Agency Off: David J. Smith

Best's Financial Strength Rating: A- **FSC:** VII

• NET PREMIUMS AND DEPOSITS ($000 omitted)

Year	Individual Life	Individual & Group Annuities	Group Life & A&H	Credit Life & A&H	Individual A&H	Total
2007	3,365	13,506	295,300	107	1,400	313,679
2008	3,224	22,417	272,517	78	1,335	299,572
2009	8,944	25,938	324,224	75	3,433	362,614

• NET OPERATING GAIN ($000 omitted)

Year	Individual Life	Individual & Group Annuities	Group Life & A&H	Credit Life & A&H	Individual A&H	Total
2007	61	3,524	5,347	5	273	9,294
2008	313	1,623	5,810	35	240	8,085
2009	18	3,162	6,835	25	223	10,452

• COMPARATIVE FINANCIALS ($000 omitted)

Year	Assets	Capital & Surplus	Net Invest Income	Benefits Paid	Realized Cap Gains	Policyholder Dividends	Contract Lns (% of assets)
2007	488,087	77,276	23,662	245,038	286	...	1.5
2008	538,362	84,615	23,925	227,790	208	...	1.3
2009	608,514	93,875	26,442	269,222	-64	...	1.2

• ORDINARY LIFE STATISTICS

Year	Av. Ord. Policy Issued ($)	Av. Ord. Policy In Force ($)	Avg. Prem ($/M)	1st Yr Prem/ Total Prem	Ord. Lapse Ratio
2007	...	...	...	...	...
2008	...	...	...	...	...
2009	...	...	...	...	...

• NEW LIFE BUSINESS ISSUED ($000 omitted)

Year	Whole Life	Term	Credit	Group	Industrial	Total
2007	4,679	11,717	6,613	442,968	...	465,977
2008	2,785	6,457	5,404	227,373	...	242,019
2009	11,564	9,107	3,538	303,274	...	327,483

• LIFE INSURANCE IN FORCE ($000 omitted)

Year	Whole Life	Term	Credit	Group	Industrial	Total
2007	83,784	208,719	43,934	2,909,243	...	3,245,680
2008	78,911	180,417	35,581	2,722,723	...	3,017,632
2009	76,917	169,038	28,409	2,610,868	...	2,885,232

FIRST ALLMERICA FINANCIAL LIFE

132 Turnpike Road, Suite 210
Southborough, Massachusetts 01772
Tel: 508-460-2400

AMB#: 007086
Began Business: 06/01/1845
Agency Off: None

Best's Financial Strength Rating: A- g
FSC: IX

• NET PREMIUMS AND DEPOSITS ($000 omitted)

Year	Individual Life	Individual & Group Annuities	Group Life & A&H	Credit Life & A&H	Individual A&H	Total
2007	32,081	4,298	4,600	...	78	41,056
2008	28,053	5,734	4,051	...	67	37,905
2009	66,086	89,031	...	...	0	155,117

• NET OPERATING GAIN ($000 omitted)

Year	Individual Life	Individual & Group Annuities	Group Life & A&H	Credit Life & A&H	Individual A&H	Total
2007	12,421	5,810	-1,373	...	-564	16,407
2008	3,130	51,621	-5,232	...	3,212	52,414
2009	-2,328	-6,478	-1,823	14,603	53	12,666

• COMPARATIVE FINANCIALS ($000 omitted)

Year	Assets	Capital & Surplus	Net Invest Income	Benefits Paid	Realized Cap Gains	Policyholder Dividends	Contract Lns (% of assets)
2007	2,155,843	163,729	76,354	155,276	556	18,345	5.4
2008	1,714,062	113,697	63,379	137,622	-19,290	15,200	6.5
2009	1,580,619	156,923	71,353	114,557	-1,854	12,218	6.6

• ORDINARY LIFE STATISTICS

Year	Av. Ord. Policy Issued ($)	Av. Ord. Policy In Force ($)	Avg. Prem ($/M)	1st Yr Prem/ Total Prem	Ord. Lapse Ratio
2007	...	32,315	14.34	0.0	4.8
2008	...	32,290	14.63	...	5.4
2009	...	25,734	34.99	...	6.0

• NEW LIFE BUSINESS ISSUED ($000 omitted)

Year	Whole Life	Term	Credit	Group	Industrial	Total
2007	...	...	...	...	...	...
2008	...	...	...	...	...	...
2009	...	...	...	...	...	...

• LIFE INSURANCE IN FORCE ($000 omitted)

Year	Whole Life	Term	Credit	Group	Industrial	Total
2007	1,978,325	71,568	...	262,269	...	2,312,162
2008	1,852,565	68,600	...	242,902	...	2,164,067
2009	1,829,849	75,672	...	233,429	...	2,138,950

FIRST ASSUR LIFE OF AMERICA

PO Box 83480
Baton Rouge, Louisiana 70884-3480
Tel: 225-769-9923

AMB#: 009125
Began Business: 09/01/1981
Agency Off: Dick S. Taylor

Best's Financial Strength Rating: B++g
FSC: V

• NET PREMIUMS AND DEPOSITS ($000 omitted)

Year	Individual Life	Individual & Group Annuities	Group Life & A&H	Credit Life & A&H	Individual A&H	Total
2007	...	...	...	4,355	...	4,355
2008	...	...	...	4,715	...	4,715
2009	...	...	...	4,274	...	4,274

• NET OPERATING GAIN ($000 omitted)

Year	Individual Life	Individual & Group Annuities	Group Life & A&H	Credit Life & A&H	Individual A&H	Total
2007	...	...	...	1,597	...	1,597
2008	...	...	...	1,101	...	1,101
2009	...	...	...	1,054	...	1,054

• COMPARATIVE FINANCIALS ($000 omitted)

Year	Assets	Capital & Surplus	Net Invest Income	Benefits Paid	Realized Cap Gains	Policyholder Dividends	Contract Lns (% of assets)
2007	27,103	21,368	1,104	671	-11	...	...
2008	28,967	22,916	1,098	806	8	...	...
2009	30,698	24,310	1,064	775	-156	...	...

• ORDINARY LIFE STATISTICS

Year	Av. Ord. Policy Issued ($)	Av. Ord. Policy In Force ($)	Avg. Prem ($/M)	1st Yr Prem/ Total Prem	Ord. Lapse Ratio
2007	...	...	...	...	...
2008	...	...	...	...	...
2009	...	...	...	...	...

• NEW LIFE BUSINESS ISSUED ($000 omitted)

Year	Whole Life	Term	Credit	Group	Industrial	Total
2007	...	...	401,924	...	...	401,924
2008	...	...	306,795	...	...	306,795
2009	...	...	210,595	...	...	210,595

• LIFE INSURANCE IN FORCE ($000 omitted)

Year	Whole Life	Term	Credit	Group	Industrial	Total
2007	...	...	729,795	...	...	729,795
2008	...	...	698,898	...	...	698,898
2009	...	...	597,328	...	...	597,328

FIRST AMERITAS LIFE OF NY

P.O. Box 81889
Lincoln, Nebraska 68510-1889
Tel: 800-628-8889

AMB#: 068545
Began Business: 05/17/1994
Agency Off: Arnold D. Henkel

Best's Financial Strength Rating: A g
FSC: XIII

• NET PREMIUMS AND DEPOSITS ($000 omitted)

Year	Individual Life	Individual & Group Annuities	Group Life & A&H	Credit Life & A&H	Individual A&H	Total
2007	3,124	412	23,263	...	...	26,799
2008	3,808	1,040	22,508	...	...	27,357
2009	6,639	474	23,080	...	...	30,193

• NET OPERATING GAIN ($000 omitted)

Year	Individual Life	Individual & Group Annuities	Group Life & A&H	Credit Life & A&H	Individual A&H	Total
2007	-575	-93	1,117	...	...	707
2008	-1,522	-38	739	...	...	-555
2009	-1,520	-26	767	...	...	-368

• COMPARATIVE FINANCIALS ($000 omitted)

Year	Assets	Capital & Surplus	Net Invest Income	Benefits Paid	Realized Cap Gains	Policyholder Dividends	Contract Lns (% of assets)
2007	37,557	20,679	1,503	18,423	16	35	0.8
2008	37,809	19,832	1,600	20,172	...	109	1.0
2009	40,493	19,261	1,668	18,511	-57	189	0.8

• ORDINARY LIFE STATISTICS

Year	Av. Ord. Policy Issued ($)	Av. Ord. Policy In Force ($)	Avg. Prem ($/M)	1st Yr Prem/ Total Prem	Ord. Lapse Ratio
2007	...	...	...	...	...
2008	...	...	...	...	...
2009	...	...	...	...	...

• NEW LIFE BUSINESS ISSUED ($000 omitted)

Year	Whole Life	Term	Credit	Group	Industrial	Total
2007	54,482	3,778	...	...	...	58,260
2008	128,955	2,035	...	...	...	130,990
2009	176,086	2,732	...	...	...	178,818

• LIFE INSURANCE IN FORCE ($000 omitted)

Year	Whole Life	Term	Credit	Group	Industrial	Total
2007	128,387	254,383	...	...	...	382,770
2008	226,280	252,840	...	...	...	479,120
2009	330,814	227,126	...	...	...	557,939

FIRST CATHOLIC SLOVAK LADIES

24950 Chagrin Boulevard
Beachwood, Ohio 44122-5634
Tel: 800-464-4642

AMB#: 009869
Began Business: 01/01/1892
Agency Off: None

Best's Financial Strength Rating: A-
FSC: VII

• NET PREMIUMS AND DEPOSITS ($000 omitted)

Year	Individual Life	Individual & Group Annuities	Group Life & A&H	Credit Life & A&H	Individual A&H	Total
2007	12,919	...	...	...	...	21,288
2008	5,777	...	...	...	...	21,586
2009	9,103	...	...	...	...	43,658

• NET OPERATING GAIN ($000 omitted)

Year	Individual Life	Individual & Group Annuities	Group Life & A&H	Credit Life & A&H	Individual A&H	Total
2007	3,686	4,063	...	...	...	1,468
2008	1,616	3,520	...	...	...	2,378
2009	958	4,459	...	...	...	2,225

• COMPARATIVE FINANCIALS ($000 omitted)

Year	Assets	Capital & Surplus	Net Invest Income	Benefits Paid	Realized Cap Gains	Policyholder Dividends	Contract Lns (% of assets)
2007	529,123	90,735	30,796	20,509	-736	1,950	0.2
2008	544,660	84,502	31,218	19,679	-6,954	1,798	0.2
2009	590,102	86,527	31,816	21,311	-607	2,004	0.3

• ORDINARY LIFE STATISTICS

Year	Av. Ord. Policy Issued ($)	Av. Ord. Policy In Force ($)	Avg. Prem ($/M)	1st Yr Prem/ Total Prem	Ord. Lapse Ratio
2007	...	...	...	...	...
2008	...	...	...	...	...
2009	...	...	...	...	...

• NEW LIFE BUSINESS ISSUED ($000 omitted)

Year	Whole Life	Term	Credit	Group	Industrial	Total
2007	40,108	...	...	...	...	40,108
2008	21,745	...	...	...	...	21,745
2009	32,016	...	...	...	...	32,016

• LIFE INSURANCE IN FORCE ($000 omitted)

Year	Whole Life	Term	Credit	Group	Industrial	Total
2007	725,991	...	...	...	...	725,991
2008	743,910	...	...	...	...	743,910
2009	766,386	...	...	...	...	766,386

FIRST CENTRAL NAT LIFE OF NY

200 Somerset Corporate Blvd., Suite 100
Bridgewater, New Jersey 08807
Tel: 800-443-7187

AMB#: 008256
Began Business: 11/30/1971
Agency Off: None

Best's Financial Strength Rating: A g
FSC: IX

• NET PREMIUMS AND DEPOSITS ($000 omitted)

Year	Individual Life	Individual & Group Annuities	Group Life & A&H	Credit Life & A&H	Individual A&H	Total
2007	496	0	...	11,774	796	13,065
2008	3,634	0	...	10,656	714	15,004
2009	4,310	1	...	8,103	689	13,103

• NET OPERATING GAIN ($000 omitted)

Year	Individual Life	Individual & Group Annuities	Group Life & A&H	Credit Life & A&H	Individual A&H	Total
2007	-811	-1	...	5,939	7	5,135
2008	681	2	...	-1,029	178	-168
2009	-2,055	-10	...	1,783	15	-267

• COMPARATIVE FINANCIALS ($000 omitted)

Year	Assets	Capital & Surplus	Net Invest Income	Benefits Paid	Realized Cap Gains	Policyholder Dividends	Contract Lns (% of assets)
2007	55,096	33,775	2,814	8,462	...	...	...
2008	52,533	25,257	2,402	7,779	-4,086	...	...
2009	53,986	23,588	2,286	9,897	131	...	...

• ORDINARY LIFE STATISTICS

Year	Av. Ord. Policy Issued ($)	Av. Ord. Policy In Force ($)	Avg. Prem ($/M)	1st Yr Prem/ Total Prem	Ord. Lapse Ratio
2007	...	...	...	...	...
2008	...	...	...	...	...
2009	...	...	...	...	...

• NEW LIFE BUSINESS ISSUED ($000 omitted)

Year	Whole Life	Term	Credit	Group	Industrial	Total
2007	...	303,450	284,214	...	...	587,664
2008	...	689,250	120,036	...	...	809,286
2009	...	864,054	14,726	...	...	878,780

• LIFE INSURANCE IN FORCE ($000 omitted)

Year	Whole Life	Term	Credit	Group	Industrial	Total
2007	1,642	296,185	920,866	...	...	1,218,693
2008	1,544	915,296	744,789	...	...	1,661,629
2009	1,552	1,416,749	546,967	...	...	1,965,268

FIRST GREAT-WEST LF & ANNUITY

8515 East Orchard Road
Greenwood Village, Colorado 80111
Tel: 914-682-3611

AMB#: 008257
Began Business: 01/01/1972
Agency Off: None

Best's Financial Strength Rating: A+ g
FSC: XV

• NET PREMIUMS AND DEPOSITS ($000 omitted)

Year	Individual Life	Individual & Group Annuities	Group Life & A&H	Credit Life & A&H	Individual A&H	Total
2007	16,148	69,849	7,084	...	16	93,097
2008	14,889	113,601	-582	...	15	127,923
2009	14,542	102,422	238	...	14	117,216

• NET OPERATING GAIN ($000 omitted)

Year	Individual Life	Individual & Group Annuities	Group Life & A&H	Credit Life & A&H	Individual A&H	Total
2007	2,131	141	2,925	...	-6	5,191
2008	5,025	1,863	1,745	...	-12	8,621
2009	6,529	1,437	996	...	-22	8,940

• COMPARATIVE FINANCIALS ($000 omitted)

Year	Assets	Capital & Surplus	Net Invest Income	Benefits Paid	Realized Cap Gains	Policyholder Dividends	Contract Lns (% of assets)
2007	650,423	47,783	30,044	57,015	13	2,050	1.9
2008	656,304	53,410	33,068	129,313	-3,679	1,296	2.0
2009	889,492	65,871	32,801	67,525	0	1,462	1.5

• ORDINARY LIFE STATISTICS

Year	Av. Ord. Policy Issued ($)	Av. Ord. Policy In Force ($)	Avg. Prem ($/M)	1st Yr Prem/ Total Prem	Ord. Lapse Ratio
2007	73,859	134,289	4.53	6.8	10.7
2008	75,579	132,630	4.94	4.8	14.5
2009	74,749	137,059	4.84	13.1	10.7

• NEW LIFE BUSINESS ISSUED ($000 omitted)

Year	Whole Life	Term	Credit	Group	Industrial	Total
2007	9,756	517,375	...	...	...	527,131
2008	10,481	297,200	...	...	...	307,681
2009	8,412	129,275	...	...	...	137,687

• LIFE INSURANCE IN FORCE ($000 omitted)

Year	Whole Life	Term	Credit	Group	Industrial	Total
2007	1,499,511	4,323,928	...	226,952	...	6,050,391
2008	1,232,004	3,964,457	...	214,894	...	5,411,355
2009	1,161,786	3,573,326	...	266,138	...	5,001,250

FIRST HEALTH LIFE & HEALTH INS

3200 Highland Avenue
Downers Grove, Illinois 60515-1282
Tel: 630-737-7900

AMB#: 008951
Began Business: 06/19/1979
Agency Off: None

Best's Financial Strength Rating: B++
FSC: IX

• NET PREMIUMS AND DEPOSITS ($000 omitted)

Year	Individual Life	Individual & Group Annuities	Group Life & A&H	Credit Life & A&H	Individual A&H	Total
2007	...	0	226,083	...	1,227,435	1,453,518
2008	0	63	416,093	...	1,618,027	2,034,183
2009	...	0	601,492	...	2,127,720	2,729,212

• NET OPERATING GAIN ($000 omitted)

Year	Individual Life	Individual & Group Annuities	Group Life & A&H	Credit Life & A&H	Individual A&H	Total
2007	...	...	12,640	...	29,461	47,620
2008	...	...	3,432	...	-79,486	-69,658
2009	...	...	6,485	...	-64,699	-49,445

• COMPARATIVE FINANCIALS ($000 omitted)

Year	Assets	Capital & Surplus	Net Invest Income	Benefits Paid	Realized Cap Gains	Policyholder Dividends	Contract Lns (% of assets)
2007	488,450	137,061	27,636	1,262,786	...	...	...
2008	682,069	214,661	18,301	1,997,592	-7,145	...	...
2009	811,138	269,529	11,202	2,615,503	30	...	...

• ORDINARY LIFE STATISTICS

Year	Av. Ord. Policy Issued ($)	Av. Ord. Policy In Force ($)	Avg. Prem ($/M)	1st Yr Prem/ Total Prem	Ord. Lapse Ratio
2007	...	...	...	...	...
2008	...	...	...	...	...
2009	...	...	...	...	...

• NEW LIFE BUSINESS ISSUED ($000 omitted)

Year	Whole Life	Term	Credit	Group	Industrial	Total
2007	...	...	...	...	...	...
2008	...	...	...	...	...	...
2009	...	...	...	...	...	...

• LIFE INSURANCE IN FORCE ($000 omitted)

Year	Whole Life	Term	Credit	Group	Industrial	Total
2007	95,589	18,835	...	166,636	...	281,060
2008	90,229	17,266	...	145,200	...	252,695
2009	85,524	15,764	...	21,342	...	122,630

FIRST INVESTORS LIFE INS CO

Raritan Plaza 1, P.O. Box 7836
Edison, New Jersey 08818-7836
Tel: 212-858-8200

AMB#: 006413
Began Business: 12/13/1962
Agency Off: Ronald Ruderman

Best's Financial Strength Rating: A-
FSC: VIII

• NET PREMIUMS AND DEPOSITS ($000 omitted)

Year	Individual Life	Individual & Group Annuities	Group Life & A&H	Credit Life & A&H	Individual A&H	Total
2007	66,522	20,642	2,205	...	13	89,382
2008	63,550	15,756	1,829	...	9	81,145
2009	61,817	18,800	2,126	...	11	82,755

• NET OPERATING GAIN ($000 omitted)

Year	Individual Life	Individual & Group Annuities	Group Life & A&H	Credit Life & A&H	Individual A&H	Total
2007	8,080	3,760	28	...	1	11,869
2008	8,280	2,827	133	...	13	11,253
2009	8,086	2,603	3	...	5	10,696

• COMPARATIVE FINANCIALS ($000 omitted)

Year	Assets	Capital & Surplus	Net Invest Income	Benefits Paid	Realized Cap Gains	Policyholder Dividends	Contract Lns (% of assets)
2007	1,370,125	113,027	16,241	111,736	305	1,104	4.4
2008	1,011,132	119,664	17,269	112,438	-2,496	991	6.1
2009	1,139,212	120,027	16,736	83,142	-959	736	5.6

• ORDINARY LIFE STATISTICS

Year	Av. Ord. Policy Issued ($)	Av. Ord. Policy In Force ($)	Avg. Prem ($/M)	1st Yr Prem/ Total Prem	Ord. Lapse Ratio
2007	139,863	87,352	9.07	12.2	5.7
2008	147,138	87,355	8.55	10.5	10.9
2009	176,706	91,767	7.88	10.9	9.3

• NEW LIFE BUSINESS ISSUED ($000 omitted)

Year	Whole Life	Term	Credit	Group	Industrial	Total
2007	320,779	954,495	...	...	...	1,275,274
2008	273,955	809,865	...	...	...	1,083,820
2009	292,468	1,043,782	...	...	...	1,336,250

• LIFE INSURANCE IN FORCE ($000 omitted)

Year	Whole Life	Term	Credit	Group	Industrial	Total
2007	3,685,810	4,055,955	...	1,702,059	...	9,443,824
2008	3,466,100	4,367,384	...	1,711,556	...	9,545,040
2009	3,402,229	4,925,599	...	1,961,953	...	10,289,781

FIRST METLIFE INVESTORS INS CO

18210 Crane Nest Dr., 3rd Floor
Tampa, Florida 33647
Tel: 949-717-6536

AMB#: 006119
Began Business: 03/12/1993
Agency Off: None

Best's Financial Strength Rating: A+ gu   **FSC:** XV

• NET PREMIUMS AND DEPOSITS ($000 omitted)

Year	Individual Life	Individual & Group Annuities	Group Life & A&H	Credit Life & A&H	Individual A&H	Total
2007	18,244	582,786	...	...	...	601,030
2008	26,196	522,618	...	...	...	548,814
2009	-42,649	685,523	...	...	...	642,874

• NET OPERATING GAIN ($000 omitted)

Year	Individual Life	Individual & Group Annuities	Group Life & A&H	Credit Life & A&H	Individual A&H	Total
2007	-35,403	-6,513	...	...	...	-41,916
2008	-39,174	-16,935	...	...	...	-56,109
2009	-30,707	23,263	...	...	...	-7,444

• COMPARATIVE FINANCIALS ($000 omitted)

Year	Assets	Capital & Surplus	Net Invest Income	Benefits Paid	Realized Cap Gains	Policyholder Dividends	Contract Lns (% of assets)
2007	2,025,534	58,867	7,742	116,601	-337	...	...
2008	2,067,211	73,978	9,622	120,135	-805	...	...
2009	3,013,344	225,876	20,100	92,318	-726	...	...

• ORDINARY LIFE STATISTICS

Year	Av. Ord. Policy Issued ($)	Av. Ord. Policy In Force ($)	Avg. Prem ($/M)	1st Yr Prem/ Total Prem	Ord. Lapse Ratio
2007	...	...	...	...	...
2008	...	...	...	...	...
2009	...	...	...	...	...

• NEW LIFE BUSINESS ISSUED ($000 omitted)

Year	Whole Life	Term	Credit	Group	Industrial	Total
2007	...	6,492,139	...	...	...	6,492,139
2008	...	7,726,075	...	...	...	7,726,075
2009	...	11,213,877	...	...	...	11,213,877

• LIFE INSURANCE IN FORCE ($000 omitted)

Year	Whole Life	Term	Credit	Group	Industrial	Total
2007	22,604	13,108,150	...	...	...	13,130,754
2008	22,588	20,094,799	...	...	...	20,117,387
2009	22,036	29,832,929	...	...	...	29,854,965

FIRST REHABILITATION LF OF AM

600 Northern Boulevard
Great Neck, New York 11021-5202
Tel: 516-829-8100

AMB#: 009877
Began Business: 11/01/1972
Agency Off: David Epstein

Best's Financial Strength Rating: A-   **FSC:** VI

• NET PREMIUMS AND DEPOSITS ($000 omitted)

Year	Individual Life	Individual & Group Annuities	Group Life & A&H	Credit Life & A&H	Individual A&H	Total
2007	...	...	79,494	...	...	79,494
2008	...	...	83,717	...	...	83,717
2009	...	...	95,330	...	...	95,330

• NET OPERATING GAIN ($000 omitted)

Year	Individual Life	Individual & Group Annuities	Group Life & A&H	Credit Life & A&H	Individual A&H	Total
2007	...	...	4,855	...	...	4,855
2008	...	...	8,145	...	...	8,145
2009	...	...	2,508	...	...	2,508

• COMPARATIVE FINANCIALS ($000 omitted)

Year	Assets	Capital & Surplus	Net Invest Income	Benefits Paid	Realized Cap Gains	Policyholder Dividends	Contract Lns (% of assets)
2007	95,199	35,512	3,758	52,047	4	...	...
2008	90,701	42,850	3,329	55,174	-407	...	...
2009	93,461	42,011	3,321	57,977	-150	...	...

• ORDINARY LIFE STATISTICS

Year	Av. Ord. Policy Issued ($)	Av. Ord. Policy In Force ($)	Avg. Prem ($/M)	1st Yr Prem/ Total Prem	Ord. Lapse Ratio
2007	...	...	...	...	...
2008	...	...	...	...	...
2009	...	...	...	...	...

• NEW LIFE BUSINESS ISSUED ($000 omitted)

Year	Whole Life	Term	Credit	Group	Industrial	Total
2007	...	...	...	5,045	...	5,045
2008	...	...	...	3,760	...	3,760
2009	...	...	...	5,527	...	5,527

• LIFE INSURANCE IN FORCE ($000 omitted)

Year	Whole Life	Term	Credit	Group	Industrial	Total
2007	...	...	...	46,327	...	46,327
2008	...	...	...	39,875	...	39,875
2009	...	...	...	39,804	...	39,804

FIRST PENN-PACIFIC LIFE INS CO

1300 South Clinton Street
Fort Wayne, Indiana 46802-3518
Tel: 260-455-2000

AMB#: 006904
Began Business: 06/10/1964
Agency Off: Bob Dineen

Best's Financial Strength Rating: A+ g   **FSC:** XV

• NET PREMIUMS AND DEPOSITS ($000 omitted)

Year	Individual Life	Individual & Group Annuities	Group Life & A&H	Credit Life & A&H	Individual A&H	Total
2007	59,810	846	427	...	...	61,083
2008	55,931	539	391	...	...	56,861
2009	1,983	131	357	...	...	2,471

• NET OPERATING GAIN ($000 omitted)

Year	Individual Life	Individual & Group Annuities	Group Life & A&H	Credit Life & A&H	Individual A&H	Total
2007	62,082	255	-53	...	...	62,284
2008	49,927	650	-113	...	...	50,463
2009	44,963	1,007	-49	...	...	45,921

• COMPARATIVE FINANCIALS ($000 omitted)

Year	Assets	Capital & Surplus	Net Invest Income	Benefits Paid	Realized Cap Gains	Policyholder Dividends	Contract Lns (% of assets)
2007	1,921,633	186,713	116,473	126,273	-3,643	...	1.7
2008	1,890,903	192,458	110,594	130,187	-23,138	...	1.8
2009	1,857,132	205,404	107,829	146,580	-14,303	...	1.8

• ORDINARY LIFE STATISTICS

Year	Av. Ord. Policy Issued ($)	Av. Ord. Policy In Force ($)	Avg. Prem ($/M)	1st Yr Prem/ Total Prem	Ord. Lapse Ratio
2007	...	...	...	...	...
2008	...	...	...	...	...
2009	...	...	...	...	...

• NEW LIFE BUSINESS ISSUED ($000 omitted)

Year	Whole Life	Term	Credit	Group	Industrial	Total
2007	26,368	4,953	...	25	...	31,346
2008	2,319	850	...	...	...	3,169
2009	242	...	...	...	...	242

• LIFE INSURANCE IN FORCE ($000 omitted)

Year	Whole Life	Term	Credit	Group	Industrial	Total
2007	6,066,009	103,483,637	...	57,117	...	109,606,763
2008	5,959,692	97,990,922	...	53,382	...	104,003,996
2009	19,850,932	92,534,256	...	49,195	...	112,434,383

FIRST RELIANCE STANDARD LIFE

2001 Market Street, Suite 1500
Philadelphia, Pennsylvania 19103
Tel: 212-303-8400

AMB#: 009418
Began Business: 10/01/1984
Agency Off: Christopher A. Fazzini

Best's Financial Strength Rating: A g   **FSC:** X

• NET PREMIUMS AND DEPOSITS ($000 omitted)

Year	Individual Life	Individual & Group Annuities	Group Life & A&H	Credit Life & A&H	Individual A&H	Total
2007	91	489	61,356	...	6	61,941
2008	66	147	61,446	...	5	61,663
2009	82	360	58,020	...	5	58,467

• NET OPERATING GAIN ($000 omitted)

Year	Individual Life	Individual & Group Annuities	Group Life & A&H	Credit Life & A&H	Individual A&H	Total
2007	-57	106	9,510	...	4	9,564
2008	39	125	9,512	...	4	9,680
2009	-6	217	8,902	...	4	9,116

• COMPARATIVE FINANCIALS ($000 omitted)

Year	Assets	Capital & Surplus	Net Invest Income	Benefits Paid	Realized Cap Gains	Policyholder Dividends	Contract Lns (% of assets)
2007	128,066	44,398	4,912	34,948	...	...	0.0
2008	133,393	48,501	5,472	36,910	-376	...	0.0
2009	147,708	56,760	6,232	32,936	-3,059	...	0.0

• ORDINARY LIFE STATISTICS

Year	Av. Ord. Policy Issued ($)	Av. Ord. Policy In Force ($)	Avg. Prem ($/M)	1st Yr Prem/ Total Prem	Ord. Lapse Ratio
2007	...	...	...	...	...
2008	...	...	...	...	...
2009	...	...	...	...	...

• NEW LIFE BUSINESS ISSUED ($000 omitted)

Year	Whole Life	Term	Credit	Group	Industrial	Total
2007	275	...	...	1,847,729	...	1,848,004
2008	107	...	...	607,597	...	607,704
2009	40	862	...	1,982,622	...	1,983,524

• LIFE INSURANCE IN FORCE ($000 omitted)

Year	Whole Life	Term	Credit	Group	Industrial	Total
2007	2,873	52	...	10,844,377	...	10,847,302
2008	2,650	52	...	10,192,346	...	10,195,048
2009	2,605	907	...	10,073,951	...	10,077,463

FIRST SECURITY BENEFIT L&A NY

One Security Benefit Place
Topeka, Kansas 66636-0001
Tel: 914-697-4748

AMB#: 060104
Began Business: 07/31/1995
Agency Off: Peggy S. Avey

Best's Financial Strength Rating: B gu
FSC: IX

• NET PREMIUMS AND DEPOSITS ($000 omitted)

Year	Individual Life	Individual & Group Annuities	Group Life & A&H	Credit Life & A&H	Individual A&H	Total
2007	...	42,633	...	...	...	42,633
2008	...	27,391	...	...	...	27,391
2009	...	15,555	...	...	...	15,555

• NET OPERATING GAIN ($000 omitted)

Year	Individual Life	Individual & Group Annuities	Group Life & A&H	Credit Life & A&H	Individual A&H	Total
2007	...	-197	...	...	...	-197
2008	...	-1,371	...	...	...	-1,371
2009	...	819	...	...	...	819

• COMPARATIVE FINANCIALS ($000 omitted)

Year	Assets	Capital & Surplus	Net Invest Income	Benefits Paid	Realized Cap Gains	Policyholder Dividends	Contract Lns (% of assets)
2007	188,472	11,034	581	17,411	...	...	0.1
2008	151,809	9,758	594	16,975	0	...	0.1
2009	180,192	10,708	612	15,669	...	...	0.1

• ORDINARY LIFE STATISTICS

Year	Av. Ord. Policy Issued ($)	Av. Ord. Policy In Force ($)	Avg. Prem ($/M)	1st Yr Prem/ Total Prem	Ord. Lapse Ratio
2007	...	...	...	...	...
2008	...	...	...	...	...
2009	...	...	...	...	...

• NEW LIFE BUSINESS ISSUED ($000 omitted)

Year	Whole Life	Term	Credit	Group	Industrial	Total
2007	...	...	...	...	...	...
2008	...	...	...	...	...	...
2009	...	...	...	...	...	...

• LIFE INSURANCE IN FORCE ($000 omitted)

Year	Whole Life	Term	Credit	Group	Industrial	Total
2007	206	18	...	...	...	224
2008	192	17	...	...	...	209
2009	188	17	...	...	...	205

FIRST SYMETRA NAT LIFE INS NY

P.O. Box 34690
Seattle, Washington 98124-1690
Tel: 425-256-8000

AMB#: 068147
Began Business: 01/02/1990
Agency Off: Linda C. Mahaffey

Best's Financial Strength Rating: A g
FSC: XIV

• NET PREMIUMS AND DEPOSITS ($000 omitted)

Year	Individual Life	Individual & Group Annuities	Group Life & A&H	Credit Life & A&H	Individual A&H	Total
2007	111	13,080	5,561	...	...	18,752
2008	595	174,901	7,642	...	...	183,138
2009	2,607	221,297	10,179	...	...	234,083

• NET OPERATING GAIN ($000 omitted)

Year	Individual Life	Individual & Group Annuities	Group Life & A&H	Credit Life & A&H	Individual A&H	Total
2007	-421	2,111	741	...	...	2,431
2008	-270	-2,043	148	...	...	-2,165
2009	-243	-94	231	...	...	-107

• COMPARATIVE FINANCIALS ($000 omitted)

Year	Assets	Capital & Surplus	Net Invest Income	Benefits Paid	Realized Cap Gains	Policyholder Dividends	Contract Lns (% of assets)
2007	123,377	25,085	6,823	52,691	-60	...	0.0
2008	306,671	42,673	8,578	23,240	-4	...	0.0
2009	537,957	62,010	23,156	27,508	-491	...	0.0

• ORDINARY LIFE STATISTICS

Year	Av. Ord. Policy Issued ($)	Av. Ord. Policy In Force ($)	Avg. Prem ($/M)	1st Yr Prem/ Total Prem	Ord. Lapse Ratio
2007	...	...	...	...	...
2008	...	...	...	...	...
2009	...	...	...	...	...

• NEW LIFE BUSINESS ISSUED ($000 omitted)

Year	Whole Life	Term	Credit	Group	Industrial	Total
2007	68	18,945	...	...	...	19,013
2008	785	30,890	...	...	...	31,675
2009	4,064	8,750	...	...	...	12,814

• LIFE INSURANCE IN FORCE ($000 omitted)

Year	Whole Life	Term	Credit	Group	Industrial	Total
2007	68	38,869	...	...	...	38,937
2008	855	59,144	...	...	...	59,999
2009	4,524	56,864	...	...	...	61,389

FIRST SUNAMERICA LIFE INS CO

70 Pine Street, 19th Floor
New York, New York 10270
Tel: 310-772-6000

AMB#: 009023
Began Business: 09/30/1980
Agency Off: Jana W. Greer

Best's Financial Strength Rating: A
FSC: XI

• NET PREMIUMS AND DEPOSITS ($000 omitted)

Year	Individual Life	Individual & Group Annuities	Group Life & A&H	Credit Life & A&H	Individual A&H	Total
2007	780	1,156,149	...	...	...	1,156,929
2008	783	1,594,114	...	...	...	1,594,898
2009	804	1,802,416	...	...	...	1,803,220

• NET OPERATING GAIN ($000 omitted)

Year	Individual Life	Individual & Group Annuities	Group Life & A&H	Credit Life & A&H	Individual A&H	Total
2007	3,527	58,847	...	...	...	62,374
2008	2,485	-152,134	...	...	...	-149,649
2009	-8,938	135,267	...	...	...	126,329

• COMPARATIVE FINANCIALS ($000 omitted)

Year	Assets	Capital & Surplus	Net Invest Income	Benefits Paid	Realized Cap Gains	Policyholder Dividends	Contract Lns (% of assets)
2007	6,479,345	503,904	299,346	614,386	-69,511	...	0.4
2008	7,445,660	547,171	335,299	779,685	-983,150	...	0.3
2009	8,949,760	775,623	344,514	800,978	-83,205	...	0.2

• ORDINARY LIFE STATISTICS

Year	Av. Ord. Policy Issued ($)	Av. Ord. Policy In Force ($)	Avg. Prem ($/M)	1st Yr Prem/ Total Prem	Ord. Lapse Ratio
2007	...	...	...	...	...
2008	...	...	...	...	...
2009	...	...	...	...	...

• NEW LIFE BUSINESS ISSUED ($000 omitted)

Year	Whole Life	Term	Credit	Group	Industrial	Total
2007	500	...	...	...	...	500
2008	...	...	...	...	...	...
2009	...	...	...	...	...	...

• LIFE INSURANCE IN FORCE ($000 omitted)

Year	Whole Life	Term	Credit	Group	Industrial	Total
2007	831,997	25,336	...	...	...	857,333
2008	775,954	22,180	...	...	...	798,134
2009	714,988	19,540	...	...	...	734,529

FIRST UNITED AMERICAN LIFE INS

P.O. Box 3125
Syracuse, New York 13220
Tel: 315-451-2544

AMB#: 009412
Began Business: 12/10/1984
Agency Off: None

Best's Financial Strength Rating: A+ g
FSC: X

• NET PREMIUMS AND DEPOSITS ($000 omitted)

Year	Individual Life	Individual & Group Annuities	Group Life & A&H	Credit Life & A&H	Individual A&H	Total
2007	20,266	128	1,291	...	47,580	69,264
2008	20,606	479	1,409	...	42,585	65,079
2009	20,528	142	1,500	...	42,283	64,453

• NET OPERATING GAIN ($000 omitted)

Year	Individual Life	Individual & Group Annuities	Group Life & A&H	Credit Life & A&H	Individual A&H	Total
2007	1,805	416	177	...	6,224	8,623
2008	2,165	300	16	...	4,832	7,312
2009	2,529	275	96	...	4,484	7,384

• COMPARATIVE FINANCIALS ($000 omitted)

Year	Assets	Capital & Surplus	Net Invest Income	Benefits Paid	Realized Cap Gains	Policyholder Dividends	Contract Lns (% of assets)
2007	120,976	42,460	6,967	42,481	...	...	1.8
2008	125,418	37,806	7,285	40,515	-807	...	2.2
2009	126,774	38,374	6,626	40,071	-2,491	...	2.7

• ORDINARY LIFE STATISTICS

Year	Av. Ord. Policy Issued ($)	Av. Ord. Policy In Force ($)	Avg. Prem ($/M)	1st Yr Prem/ Total Prem	Ord. Lapse Ratio
2007	16,830	11,735	12.63	18.0	36.1
2008	18,224	13,497	10.40	15.8	25.8
2009	17,998	12,053	11.93	12.6	37.3

• NEW LIFE BUSINESS ISSUED ($000 omitted)

Year	Whole Life	Term	Credit	Group	Industrial	Total
2007	966,685	40,060	...	...	...	1,006,745
2008	517,476	540,606	...	...	...	1,058,082
2009	403,609	477,535	...	...	...	881,144

• LIFE INSURANCE IN FORCE ($000 omitted)

Year	Whole Life	Term	Credit	Group	Industrial	Total
2007	1,564,878	39,181	...	...	...	1,604,059
2008	1,476,306	505,152	...	...	...	1,981,458
2009	1,153,283	567,346	...	...	...	1,720,629

FIRST UNUM LIFE INS CO

1 Fountain Square
Chattanooga, Tennessee 37402-1330
Tel: 212-953-1130

AMB#: 006514
Began Business: 01/22/1960
Agency Off: Stephen Meahl

Best's Financial Strength Rating: A- g
FSC: XIV

• NET PREMIUMS AND DEPOSITS ($000 omitted)

Year	Individual Life	Individual & Group Annuities	Group Life & A&H	Credit Life & A&H	Individual A&H	Total
2007	3,586	37,870	314,683	...	90,198	446,336
2008	3,372	43,241	317,642	...	92,325	456,580
2009	3,835	45,122	304,773	...	93,115	446,844

• NET OPERATING GAIN ($000 omitted)

Year	Individual Life	Individual & Group Annuities	Group Life & A&H	Credit Life & A&H	Individual A&H	Total
2007	1,670	1,167	26,847	...	-11,889	17,796
2008	1,525	1,104	31,770	...	-9,571	24,828
2009	1,161	1,280	37,430	...	-13,831	26,039

• COMPARATIVE FINANCIALS ($000 omitted)

Year	Assets	Capital & Surplus	Net Invest Income	Benefits Paid	Realized Cap Gains	Policyholder Dividends	Contract Lns (% of assets)
2007	1,779,790	184,025	103,053	263,221	2,905	...	0.6
2008	1,933,234	193,793	111,373	291,645	-5,355	...	0.5
2009	2,012,186	218,301	120,050	291,148	-18,500	...	0.4

• ORDINARY LIFE STATISTICS

Year	Av. Ord. Policy Issued ($)	Av. Ord. Policy In Force ($)	Avg. Prem ($/M)	1st Yr Prem/ Total Prem	Ord. Lapse Ratio
2007	...	...	...	...	...
2008	...	...	...	...	...
2009	...	...	...	...	...

• NEW LIFE BUSINESS ISSUED ($000 omitted)

Year	Whole Life	Term	Credit	Group	Industrial	Total
2007	11,048	343	...	3,275,016	...	3,286,407
2008	9,515	405	...	5,236,087	...	5,246,007
2009	129,678	1,128	...	3,170,075	...	3,300,881

• LIFE INSURANCE IN FORCE ($000 omitted)

Year	Whole Life	Term	Credit	Group	Industrial	Total
2007	441,660	18,399	...	28,270,026	...	28,730,085
2008	415,603	9,015	...	33,242,293	...	33,666,911
2009	500,438	9,592	...	33,757,755	...	34,267,785

FLORIDA COMBINED LIFE INS CO

4800 Deerwood Campus Parkway, Bldg. 200
Jacksonville, Florida 32256
Tel: 904-828-7800

AMB#: 060033
Began Business: 05/11/1988
Agency Off: Terri A. Schmidt

Best's Financial Strength Rating: A g
FSC: V

• NET PREMIUMS AND DEPOSITS ($000 omitted)

Year	Individual Life	Individual & Group Annuities	Group Life & A&H	Credit Life & A&H	Individual A&H	Total
2007	...	...	47,566	...	10,067	57,633
2008	...	...	192	...	8,100	8,293
2009	...	...	...	...	...	...

• NET OPERATING GAIN ($000 omitted)

Year	Individual Life	Individual & Group Annuities	Group Life & A&H	Credit Life & A&H	Individual A&H	Total
2007	...	...	-895	...	-4,637	-5,531
2008	...	...	1,191	...	1,068	2,259
2009	120	...	512	...	...	663

• COMPARATIVE FINANCIALS ($000 omitted)

Year	Assets	Capital & Surplus	Net Invest Income	Benefits Paid	Realized Cap Gains	Policyholder Dividends	Contract Lns (% of assets)
2007	94,213	30,034	3,120	30,285	-30	...	...
2008	32,270	18,701	1,739	1,369	-409	...	...
2009	31,985	20,339	997	...	...	...	...

• ORDINARY LIFE STATISTICS

Year	Av. Ord. Policy Issued ($)	Av. Ord. Policy In Force ($)	Avg. Prem ($/M)	1st Yr Prem/ Total Prem	Ord. Lapse Ratio
2007	...	...	...	...	...
2008	...	...	...	...	...
2009	...	...	...	...	...

• NEW LIFE BUSINESS ISSUED ($000 omitted)

Year	Whole Life	Term	Credit	Group	Industrial	Total
2007	4,300	53,504	...	1,546,100	...	1,603,904
2008	1,979	47,457	...	1,180,118	...	1,229,554
2009	7,251	47,075	...	1,031,696	...	1,086,022

• LIFE INSURANCE IN FORCE ($000 omitted)

Year	Whole Life	Term	Credit	Group	Industrial	Total
2007	22,008	208,955	...	11,135,037	...	11,366,000
2008	17,270	215,170	...	10,657,240	...	10,889,680
2009	9,329	214,523	...	11,129,122	...	11,352,974

5 STAR LIFE INSURANCE CO

909 N. Washington Street
Alexandria, Virginia 22314
Tel: 800-776-2322

AMB#: 008069
Began Business: 05/24/1943
Agency Off: Craig S. Piers

Best's Financial Strength Rating: A-
FSC: VII

• NET PREMIUMS AND DEPOSITS ($000 omitted)

Year	Individual Life	Individual & Group Annuities	Group Life & A&H	Credit Life & A&H	Individual A&H	Total
2007	7,682	...	84,074	...	...	91,756
2008	10,477	...	84,019	...	...	94,497
2009	11,845	...	87,036	...	...	98,881

• NET OPERATING GAIN ($000 omitted)

Year	Individual Life	Individual & Group Annuities	Group Life & A&H	Credit Life & A&H	Individual A&H	Total
2007	-2,894	...	4,134	...	...	1,241
2008	-1,431	...	1,262	...	...	-169
2009	-2,008	...	6,005	...	...	3,998

• COMPARATIVE FINANCIALS ($000 omitted)

Year	Assets	Capital & Surplus	Net Invest Income	Benefits Paid	Realized Cap Gains	Policyholder Dividends	Contract Lns (% of assets)
2007	165,974	52,275	7,379	73,278	-139	...	3.3
2008	174,786	48,407	8,108	73,627	-4,910	...	3.2
2009	188,378	50,997	9,045	75,233	-3,498	...	3.2

• ORDINARY LIFE STATISTICS

Year	Av. Ord. Policy Issued ($)	Av. Ord. Policy In Force ($)	Avg. Prem ($/M)	1st Yr Prem/ Total Prem	Ord. Lapse Ratio
2007	20,156	65,837	4.85	37.5	7.9
2008	37,610	61,572	5.48	35.2	10.6
2009	39,838	61,398	5.95	24.8	14.1

• NEW LIFE BUSINESS ISSUED ($000 omitted)

Year	Whole Life	Term	Credit	Group	Industrial	Total
2007	45,537	443,549	...	3,249,929	...	3,739,015
2008	34,701	541,711	...	3,851,585	...	4,427,997
2009	35,228	462,861	...	3,720,312	...	4,218,401

• LIFE INSURANCE IN FORCE ($000 omitted)

Year	Whole Life	Term	Credit	Group	Industrial	Total
2007	100,615	1,839,282	...	35,592,928	...	37,532,825
2008	119,586	2,136,058	...	36,611,805	...	38,867,449
2009	132,085	2,217,252	...	35,945,651	...	38,294,989

FORETHOUGHT LIFE INS CO

300 North Meridian Street, Suite 1800
Indianapolis, Indiana 46204
Tel: 317-223-2700

AMB#: 009053
Began Business: 09/29/1980
Agency Off: Ronald Townsend

Best's Financial Strength Rating: A-
FSC: IX

• NET PREMIUMS AND DEPOSITS ($000 omitted)

Year	Individual Life	Individual & Group Annuities	Group Life & A&H	Credit Life & A&H	Individual A&H	Total
2007	48,351	86,058	382,438	...	...	516,847
2008	46,747	379,420	350,193	...	...	776,361
2009	39,003	570,247	313,623	...	...	922,874

• NET OPERATING GAIN ($000 omitted)

Year	Individual Life	Individual & Group Annuities	Group Life & A&H	Credit Life & A&H	Individual A&H	Total
2007	8,591	-757	25,729	1	...	33,564
2008	-11,030	-17,575	12,839	...	...	-15,767
2009	7,066	9,159	44,040	...	...	60,265

• COMPARATIVE FINANCIALS ($000 omitted)

Year	Assets	Capital & Surplus	Net Invest Income	Benefits Paid	Realized Cap Gains	Policyholder Dividends	Contract Lns (% of assets)
2007	3,689,002	226,718	193,275	385,096	-10,983	...	0.1
2008	3,870,190	189,717	182,425	416,899	-55,819	...	0.1
2009	4,543,351	346,778	234,395	426,236	8,013	...	0.1

• ORDINARY LIFE STATISTICS

Year	Av. Ord. Policy Issued ($)	Av. Ord. Policy In Force ($)	Avg. Prem ($/M)	1st Yr Prem/ Total Prem	Ord. Lapse Ratio
2007	4,197	4,067	32.98	38.2	-1.4
2008	7,342	4,417	52.08	44.3	0.0
2009	7,885	4,516	40.89	39.4	5.4

• NEW LIFE BUSINESS ISSUED ($000 omitted)

Year	Whole Life	Term	Credit	Group	Industrial	Total
2007	54,587	...	...	409,023	...	463,610
2008	134,637	...	...	377,361	...	511,998
2009	152,418	...	...	320,559	...	472,977

• LIFE INSURANCE IN FORCE ($000 omitted)

Year	Whole Life	Term	Credit	Group	Industrial	Total
2007	1,669,682	1,455	72	7,133,251	...	8,804,460
2008	896,129	1,425	...	3,934,596	...	4,832,150
2009	952,460	1,417	...	3,945,779	...	4,899,656

FORT DEARBORN LIFE INS CO

1020 31st Street
Downers Grove, Illinois 60515-5591
Tel: 800-633-3696

AMB#: 007322
Began Business: 04/01/1969
Agency Off: Bradley S. Gary

Best's Financial Strength Rating: A+ **FSC:** IX

• **NET PREMIUMS AND DEPOSITS ($000 omitted)**

Year	Individual Life	Individual & Group Annuities	Group Life & A&H	Credit Life & A&H	Individual A&H	Total
2007	17,413	308,013	648,610	...	24	974,060
2008	17,392	603,048	638,223	...	138	1,258,801
2009	15,593	501,098	631,674	...	116	1,148,482

• **NET OPERATING GAIN ($000 omitted)**

Year	Individual Life	Individual & Group Annuities	Group Life & A&H	Credit Life & A&H	Individual A&H	Total
2007	5,391	14,147	1,889	...	120	41,097
2008	6,806	-54,562	9,402	...	45	-21,683
2009	3,616	-9,048	140	...	35	12,203

• **COMPARATIVE FINANCIALS ($000 omitted)**

Year	Assets	Capital & Surplus	Net Invest Income	Benefits Paid	Realized Cap Gains	Policyholder Dividends	Contract Lns (% of assets)
2007	2,238,646	468,463	61,261	768,238	1,654	...	0.3
2008	2,616,352	290,336	67,907	720,900	-16,787	...	0.3
2009	3,093,100	457,396	108,010	700,683	-52,011	...	0.2

• **ORDINARY LIFE STATISTICS**

Year	Av. Ord. Policy Issued ($)	Av. Ord. Policy In Force ($)	Avg. Prem ($/M)	1st Yr Prem/ Total Prem	Ord. Lapse Ratio
2007	26,745	12,959	11.82	4.1	14.0
2008	19,355	12,846	12.77	3.2	15.3
2009	35,544	13,168	12.01	6.2	15.2

• **NEW LIFE BUSINESS ISSUED ($000 omitted)**

Year	Whole Life	Term	Credit	Group	Industrial	Total
2007	22,068	178,088	...	14,064,815	...	14,264,971
2008	19,413	154,531	...	11,666,434	...	11,840,378
2009	22,966	162,645	...	12,452,127	...	12,637,738

• **LIFE INSURANCE IN FORCE ($000 omitted)**

Year	Whole Life	Term	Credit	Group	Industrial	Total
2007	291,610	1,186,806	...	151,291,256	...	152,769,672
2008	283,657	1,098,727	...	160,059,018	...	161,441,402
2009	280,638	1,038,503	...	163,210,864	...	164,530,004

FORT DEARBORN LIFE INS CO NY

1020 31st Street
Downers Grove, Illinois 60515-5591
Tel: 866-406-3356

AMB#: 068158
Began Business: 01/09/1991
Agency Off: None

Best's Financial Strength Rating: A **FSC:** V

• **NET PREMIUMS AND DEPOSITS ($000 omitted)**

Year	Individual Life	Individual & Group Annuities	Group Life & A&H	Credit Life & A&H	Individual A&H	Total
2007	...	...	808	539	...	1,347
2008	33	3,882	16,623	...	...	20,538
2009	3	30,683	5,460	...	...	36,146

• **NET OPERATING GAIN ($000 omitted)**

Year	Individual Life	Individual & Group Annuities	Group Life & A&H	Credit Life & A&H	Individual A&H	Total
2007	...	...	2,536	105	...	1,723
2008	2	-206	-1,186	...	...	-1,305
2009	-29	-1,199	-846	0	...	-2,075

• **COMPARATIVE FINANCIALS ($000 omitted)**

Year	Assets	Capital & Surplus	Net Invest Income	Benefits Paid	Realized Cap Gains	Policyholder Dividends	Contract Lns (% of assets)
2007	25,966	25,004	1,856	1,085	...	...	...
2008	44,252	24,748	1,814	4,498	-112	...	...
2009	69,920	22,523	3,368	6,547	-243	...	...

• **ORDINARY LIFE STATISTICS**

Year	Av. Ord. Policy Issued ($)	Av. Ord. Policy In Force ($)	Avg. Prem ($/M)	1st Yr Prem/ Total Prem	Ord. Lapse Ratio
2007	...	...	...	...	...
2008	...	...	...	...	...
2009	...	...	...	...	...

• **NEW LIFE BUSINESS ISSUED ($000 omitted)**

Year	Whole Life	Term	Credit	Group	Industrial	Total
2007	...	...	5,745	7,873	...	13,618
2008	...	...	...	115,608	...	115,608
2009	20	...	...	286,074	...	286,094

• **LIFE INSURANCE IN FORCE ($000 omitted)**

Year	Whole Life	Term	Credit	Group	Industrial	Total
2007	...	...	1,825	15,162	...	16,987
2008	135	...	119	1,193,899	...	1,194,153
2009	110	5	300	1,320,878	...	1,321,293

FREEDOM LIFE INS CO OF AMER

3100 Burnett Plaza, 801 Cherry Street
Fort Worth, Texas 76102
Tel: 817-878-3300

AMB#: 006269
Began Business: 06/01/1956
Agency Off: James R. White, Jr.

Best's Financial Strength Rating: B g **FSC:** V

• **NET PREMIUMS AND DEPOSITS ($000 omitted)**

Year	Individual Life	Individual & Group Annuities	Group Life & A&H	Credit Life & A&H	Individual A&H	Total
2007	421	...	16,342	...	6,704	23,466
2008	1,005	...	21,422	...	6,812	29,238
2009	1,573	...	24,405	...	-6,327	19,651

• **NET OPERATING GAIN ($000 omitted)**

Year	Individual Life	Individual & Group Annuities	Group Life & A&H	Credit Life & A&H	Individual A&H	Total
2007	23	...	-1,465	...	321	-1,122
2008	-123	...	-4,205	...	2,617	-1,711
2009	-51	...	-7,560	...	791	-6,820

• **COMPARATIVE FINANCIALS ($000 omitted)**

Year	Assets	Capital & Surplus	Net Invest Income	Benefits Paid	Realized Cap Gains	Policyholder Dividends	Contract Lns (% of assets)
2007	33,054	8,890	1,817	14,430	...	...	...
2008	38,305	15,001	1,714	17,737	-110	...	...
2009	31,844	17,825	1,589	19,849	-23	...	...

• **ORDINARY LIFE STATISTICS**

Year	Av. Ord. Policy Issued ($)	Av. Ord. Policy In Force ($)	Avg. Prem ($/M)	1st Yr Prem/ Total Prem	Ord. Lapse Ratio
2007	...	...	...	...	...
2008	...	...	...	...	...
2009	...	...	...	...	...

• **NEW LIFE BUSINESS ISSUED ($000 omitted)**

Year	Whole Life	Term	Credit	Group	Industrial	Total
2007	...	62,245	...	...	...	62,245
2008	...	90,964	...	...	...	90,964
2009	...	119,895	...	...	...	119,895

• **LIFE INSURANCE IN FORCE ($000 omitted)**

Year	Whole Life	Term	Credit	Group	Industrial	Total
2007	...	74,703	...	...	...	74,703
2008	...	118,000	...	...	...	118,000
2009	...	168,905	...	...	...	168,905

FUNERAL DIRECTORS LIFE INS CO

P.O. Box 5649
Abilene, Texas 79606
Tel: 325-695-3412

AMB#: 009492
Began Business: 04/01/1981
Agency Off: B. Kris Seale

Best's Financial Strength Rating: A- **FSC:** VII

• **NET PREMIUMS AND DEPOSITS ($000 omitted)**

Year	Individual Life	Individual & Group Annuities	Group Life & A&H	Credit Life & A&H	Individual A&H	Total
2007	19,925	59,955	19,679	...	...	99,559
2008	23,434	78,697	22,155	...	...	124,285
2009	30,845	85,473	27,308	...	...	143,626

• **NET OPERATING GAIN ($000 omitted)**

Year	Individual Life	Individual & Group Annuities	Group Life & A&H	Credit Life & A&H	Individual A&H	Total
2007	1,123	728	1,241	...	...	3,092
2008	1,572	664	1,866	...	...	4,101
2009	1,774	3,001	2,385	...	...	7,160

• **COMPARATIVE FINANCIALS ($000 omitted)**

Year	Assets	Capital & Surplus	Net Invest Income	Benefits Paid	Realized Cap Gains	Policyholder Dividends	Contract Lns (% of assets)
2007	500,389	48,511	28,152	53,697	739	2,876	0.0
2008	556,606	48,561	32,745	63,676	-3,074	3,202	0.0
2009	632,477	57,766	36,118	72,299	-1,153	2,829	0.0

• **ORDINARY LIFE STATISTICS**

Year	Av. Ord. Policy Issued ($)	Av. Ord. Policy In Force ($)	Avg. Prem ($/M)	1st Yr Prem/ Total Prem	Ord. Lapse Ratio
2007	4,973	3,940	108.16	15.9	0.0
2008	4,845	4,042	117.53	18.5	0.0
2009	4,712	4,141	139.00	16.8	0.0

• **NEW LIFE BUSINESS ISSUED ($000 omitted)**

Year	Whole Life	Term	Credit	Group	Industrial	Total
2007	18,027	...	...	23,245	...	41,272
2008	23,907	...	...	27,256	...	51,163
2009	32,552	1	...	30,764	...	63,317

• **LIFE INSURANCE IN FORCE ($000 omitted)**

Year	Whole Life	Term	Credit	Group	Industrial	Total
2007	182,620	1,573	...	157,329	625	342,147
2008	197,818	1,525	...	177,191	583	377,117
2009	220,434	1,480	...	200,102	554	422,570

GARDEN STATE LIFE INS CO

One Moody Plaza
Galveston, Texas 77550-7999
Tel: 281-538-1037

AMB#: 006436
Began Business: 11/01/1956
Agency Off: None

Best's Financial Strength Rating: A **FSC:** V

• **NET PREMIUMS AND DEPOSITS ($000 omitted)**

Year	Individual Life	Individual & Group Annuities	Group Life & A&H	Credit Life & A&H	Individual A&H	Total
2007	40,905	172	87	...	67	41,232
2008	39,175	283	80	...	59	39,597
2009	36,240	70	77	...	58	36,445

• **NET OPERATING GAIN ($000 omitted)**

Year	Individual Life	Individual & Group Annuities	Group Life & A&H	Credit Life & A&H	Individual A&H	Total
2007	-988	80	70	...	43	-795
2008	-200	12	63	...	54	-71
2009	-660	-117	108	...	20	-649

• **COMPARATIVE FINANCIALS ($000 omitted)**

Year	Assets	Capital & Surplus	Net Invest Income	Benefits Paid	Realized Cap Gains	Policyholder Dividends	Contract Lns (% of assets)
2007	92,179	17,269	3,964	19,547	74	...	2.3
2008	91,014	17,678	3,923	21,514	-1,501	...	2.7
2009	93,243	18,690	3,441	22,218	-75	...	2.9

• **ORDINARY LIFE STATISTICS**

Year	Av. Ord. Policy Issued ($)	Av. Ord. Policy In Force ($)	Avg. Prem ($/M)	1st Yr Prem/ Total Prem	Ord. Lapse Ratio
2007	77,677	75,785	7.27	13.1	18.1
2008	77,453	74,967	7.50	10.2	19.1
2009	86,135	75,043	7.57	7.1	16.8

• **NEW LIFE BUSINESS ISSUED ($000 omitted)**

Year	Whole Life	Term	Credit	Group	Industrial	Total
2007	13,932	1,349,541	...	...	...	1,363,473
2008	12,463	1,075,436	...	...	...	1,087,899
2009	10,164	735,246	...	...	...	745,410

• **LIFE INSURANCE IN FORCE ($000 omitted)**

Year	Whole Life	Term	Credit	Group	Industrial	Total
2007	165,246	5,962,459	...	301	...	6,128,006
2008	159,841	5,595,484	...	209	...	5,755,534
2009	152,684	5,169,225	...	196	...	5,322,105

GENERAL FIDELITY LIFE INS CO

3349 Michelson Drive, Suite 200
Irvine, California 92612
Tel: 980-386-3640

AMB#: 006441
Began Business: 07/10/1981
Agency Off: None

Best's Financial Strength Rating: A- **FSC:** VIII

• **NET PREMIUMS AND DEPOSITS ($000 omitted)**

Year	Individual Life	Individual & Group Annuities	Group Life & A&H	Credit Life & A&H	Individual A&H	Total
2007	...	...	-1,147	41,756	...	40,609
2008	...	...	-577	49,235	...	48,659
2009	...	...	-313	56,050	...	55,737

• **NET OPERATING GAIN ($000 omitted)**

Year	Individual Life	Individual & Group Annuities	Group Life & A&H	Credit Life & A&H	Individual A&H	Total
2007	...	-119	3,841	9,323	...	13,045
2008	...	-281	5,861	7,112	...	12,692
2009	...	-320	4,767	3,128	...	7,574

• **COMPARATIVE FINANCIALS ($000 omitted)**

Year	Assets	Capital & Surplus	Net Invest Income	Benefits Paid	Realized Cap Gains	Policyholder Dividends	Contract Lns (% of assets)
2007	250,147	161,953	8,785	12,770	602	...	...
2008	210,242	164,414	8,331	10,545	-4,752	...	...
2009	214,902	170,548	7,717	13,102	-4,764	...	...

• **ORDINARY LIFE STATISTICS**

Year	Av. Ord. Policy Issued ($)	Av. Ord. Policy In Force ($)	Avg. Prem ($/M)	1st Yr Prem/ Total Prem	Ord. Lapse Ratio
2007	...	...	...	...	...
2008	...	...	...	...	...
2009	...	...	...	...	...

• **NEW LIFE BUSINESS ISSUED ($000 omitted)**

Year	Whole Life	Term	Credit	Group	Industrial	Total
2007	...	...	6,848	95	...	6,943
2008	...	...	50,268	22	...	50,290
2009	...	...	14,435	107	...	14,542

• **LIFE INSURANCE IN FORCE ($000 omitted)**

Year	Whole Life	Term	Credit	Group	Industrial	Total
2007	...	...	470,634	274,702	...	745,336
2008	...	...	468,831	215,694	...	684,525
2009	...	...	738,830	160,239	...	899,069

GENERAL AMERICAN LIFE INS CO

18210 Crane Nest Dr., 3rd Floor
Tampa, Florida 33647
Tel: 314-843-8700

AMB#: 006439
Began Business: 09/05/1933
Agency Off: None

Best's Financial Strength Rating: A+ gu **FSC:** XV

• **NET PREMIUMS AND DEPOSITS ($000 omitted)**

Year	Individual Life	Individual & Group Annuities	Group Life & A&H	Credit Life & A&H	Individual A&H	Total
2007	453,261	195,202	2	...	38	648,503
2008	431,179	181,270	1	...	-579	611,871
2009	372,808	151,172	...	...	-138	523,842

• **NET OPERATING GAIN ($000 omitted)**

Year	Individual Life	Individual & Group Annuities	Group Life & A&H	Credit Life & A&H	Individual A&H	Total
2007	196,065	21,251	-2,600	...	-3,164	211,551
2008	37,658	8,764	-2,170	...	4,068	48,320
2009	152,367	-3,275	-2,271	...	2,414	149,235

• **COMPARATIVE FINANCIALS ($000 omitted)**

Year	Assets	Capital & Surplus	Net Invest Income	Benefits Paid	Realized Cap Gains	Policyholder Dividends	Contract Lns (% of assets)
2007	14,122,917	2,279,712	523,837	930,912	-105,528	157,155	11.7
2008	11,734,937	1,079,457	538,262	781,971	1,128,746	165,680	14.4
2009	11,049,153	995,160	485,457	737,173	-83,736	157,532	16.1

• **ORDINARY LIFE STATISTICS**

Year	Av. Ord. Policy Issued ($)	Av. Ord. Policy In Force ($)	Avg. Prem ($/M)	1st Yr Prem/ Total Prem	Ord. Lapse Ratio
2007	412,781	438,225	6.76	1.3	0.6
2008	783,945	411,901	7.54	4.6	10.6
2009	...	430,947	6.77	0.2	1.1

• **NEW LIFE BUSINESS ISSUED ($000 omitted)**

Year	Whole Life	Term	Credit	Group	Industrial	Total
2007	224,553	...	...	...	...	224,553
2008	395,892	...	...	...	...	395,892
2009	...	...	...	...	...	...

• **LIFE INSURANCE IN FORCE ($000 omitted)**

Year	Whole Life	Term	Credit	Group	Industrial	Total
2007	46,189,115	93,289,228	...	8,286	...	139,486,629
2008	46,275,232	77,921,465	...	8,152	...	124,204,849
2009	43,371,568	78,862,153	...	7,925	...	122,241,647

GENERAL RE LIFE CORPORATION

120 Long Ridge Road
Stamford, Connecticut 06902
Tel: 203-352-3000

AMB#: 006234
Began Business: 08/01/1967
Agency Off: None

Best's Financial Strength Rating: A++g **FSC:** XV

• **NET PREMIUMS AND DEPOSITS ($000 omitted)**

Year	Individual Life	Individual & Group Annuities	Group Life & A&H	Credit Life & A&H	Individual A&H	Total
2007	441,143	16	104,398	-3	510,239	1,055,794
2008	485,890	15	78,209	-2	521,958	1,086,070
2009	504,831	...	47,028	0	520,968	1,072,826

• **NET OPERATING GAIN ($000 omitted)**

Year	Individual Life	Individual & Group Annuities	Group Life & A&H	Credit Life & A&H	Individual A&H	Total
2007	27,872	153	-33,210	90	-14,666	-19,762
2008	26,711	-71	10,549	59	-7,606	29,641
2009	53,502	-25	21,825	35	25,764	101,102

• **COMPARATIVE FINANCIALS ($000 omitted)**

Year	Assets	Capital & Surplus	Net Invest Income	Benefits Paid	Realized Cap Gains	Policyholder Dividends	Contract Lns (% of assets)
2007	2,637,601	440,229	116,735	837,137	4,239	...	0.1
2008	2,615,078	466,576	76,255	814,198	2,308	...	0.1
2009	2,780,942	560,763	154,917	807,710	-1,973	...	0.1

• **ORDINARY LIFE STATISTICS**

Year	Av. Ord. Policy Issued ($)	Av. Ord. Policy In Force ($)	Avg. Prem ($/M)	1st Yr Prem/ Total Prem	Ord. Lapse Ratio
2007	...	36,757	3.11	...	5.5
2008	...	37,966	3.31	...	5.4
2009	...	39,530	3.52	...	7.2

• **NEW LIFE BUSINESS ISSUED ($000 omitted)**

Year	Whole Life	Term	Credit	Group	Industrial	Total
2007	...	...	...	...	...	...
2008	...	...	...	...	...	...
2009	...	...	...	...	...	...

• **LIFE INSURANCE IN FORCE ($000 omitted)**

Year	Whole Life	Term	Credit	Group	Industrial	Total
2007	228,241	150,768,036	...	5,226,175	...	156,222,452
2008	220,021	155,533,699	...	5,772,145	...	161,525,865
2009	213,178	153,130,035	...	6,569,286	...	159,912,499

GENERALI USA LIFE REASSURANCE

P.O. Box 419076
Kansas City, Missouri 64141-6076
Tel: 913-901-4600

AMB#: 009189
Began Business: 10/14/1982
Agency Off: None

Best's Financial Strength Rating: A
FSC: IX

• NET PREMIUMS AND DEPOSITS ($000 omitted)

Year	Individual Life	Individual & Group Annuities	Group Life & A&H	Credit Life & A&H	Individual A&H	Total
2007	220,062	...	20,888	...	4,395	245,344
2008	254,140	...	19,893	...	4,022	278,055
2009	265,530	...	23,728	...	3,752	293,010

• NET OPERATING GAIN ($000 omitted)

Year	Individual Life	Individual & Group Annuities	Group Life & A&H	Credit Life & A&H	Individual A&H	Total
2007	-2,629	...	1,906	...	1,885	3,523
2008	6,451	...	2,111	...	1,384	4,734
2009	17,849	...	2,981	...	-80	19,900

• COMPARATIVE FINANCIALS ($000 omitted)

Year	Assets	Capital & Surplus	Net Invest Income	Benefits Paid	Realized Cap Gains	Policyholder Dividends	Contract Lns (% of assets)
2007	801,290	256,201	32,251	167,950	5	132	...
2008	831,112	259,547	33,562	212,447	-4,039	62	...
2009	913,098	311,423	33,800	203,257	-7,529	34	...

• ORDINARY LIFE STATISTICS

Year	Av. Ord. Policy Issued ($)	Av. Ord. Policy In Force ($)	Avg. Prem ($/M)	1st Yr Prem/ Total Prem	Ord. Lapse Ratio
2007	...	55,310	1.71	...	5.2
2008	...	61,766	1.64	...	6.2
2009	...	66,492	1.67	...	6.2

• NEW LIFE BUSINESS ISSUED ($000 omitted)

Year	Whole Life	Term	Credit	Group	Industrial	Total
2007	...	...	...	...	...	...
2008	...	...	...	...	...	...
2009	...	...	...	...	...	...

• LIFE INSURANCE IN FORCE ($000 omitted)

Year	Whole Life	Term	Credit	Group	Industrial	Total
2007	179,077,299	179,408,200	...	3,896,642	...	362,382,141
2008	189,884,725	219,497,947	...	30,665,306	...	440,047,978
2009	203,029,613	245,421,093	...	37,037,224	...	485,487,930

GENWORTH LIFE INSURANCE CO

6604 West Broad Street
Richmond, Virginia 23230
Tel: 888-322-4629

AMB#: 007183
Began Business: 10/01/1956
Agency Off: None

Best's Financial Strength Rating: A g
FSC: XV

• NET PREMIUMS AND DEPOSITS ($000 omitted)

Year	Individual Life	Individual & Group Annuities	Group Life & A&H	Credit Life & A&H	Individual A&H	Total
2007	174,758	652,912	88,201	32	902,502	1,818,406
2008	133,345	2,152,957	89,202	29	-65,108	2,310,425
2009	69,846	438,856	69,568	430	829,036	1,407,737

• NET OPERATING GAIN ($000 omitted)

Year	Individual Life	Individual & Group Annuities	Group Life & A&H	Credit Life & A&H	Individual A&H	Total
2007	23,583	90,583	37,000	-57	148,614	299,722
2008	49,357	175,723	-28,112	19	101,726	298,712
2009	-84,361	40,802	138,549	232	112,682	207,903

• COMPARATIVE FINANCIALS ($000 omitted)

Year	Assets	Capital & Surplus	Net Invest Income	Benefits Paid	Realized Cap Gains	Policyholder Dividends	Contract Lns (% of assets)
2007	34,571,591	3,142,794	1,962,243	4,879,732	-117,515	...	3.3
2008	34,733,533	3,326,835	1,713,245	4,831,446	-647,876	...	3.7
2009	32,974,558	3,164,850	1,525,387	4,589,640	-407,255	...	2.6

• ORDINARY LIFE STATISTICS

Year	Av. Ord. Policy Issued ($)	Av. Ord. Policy In Force ($)	Avg. Prem ($/M)	1st Yr Prem/ Total Prem	Ord. Lapse Ratio
2007	387,671	372,754	2.47	44.9	3.2
2008	330,101	367,703	2.37	43.8	3.4
2009	279,858	362,263	2.28	35.0	4.3

• NEW LIFE BUSINESS ISSUED ($000 omitted)

Year	Whole Life	Term	Credit	Group	Industrial	Total
2007	3,199,846	15,013,695	...	18,898	...	18,232,439
2008	2,067,021	10,130,221	...	...	...	12,197,242
2009	751,482	10,165,210	...	1,097	...	10,917,789

• LIFE INSURANCE IN FORCE ($000 omitted)

Year	Whole Life	Term	Credit	Group	Industrial	Total
2007	4,061,621	134,674,232	...	3,176,271	...	141,912,124
2008	4,859,205	141,780,663	...	3,289,627	...	149,929,495
2009	5,226,362	145,122,997	...	2,027,975	...	152,377,334

GENWORTH LIFE AND ANNUITY INS

6610 West Broad Street
Richmond, Virginia 23230
Tel: 804-662-2400

AMB#: 006648
Began Business: 04/01/1871
Agency Off: None

Best's Financial Strength Rating: A g
FSC: XV

• NET PREMIUMS AND DEPOSITS ($000 omitted)

Year	Individual Life	Individual & Group Annuities	Group Life & A&H	Credit Life & A&H	Individual A&H	Total
2007	231,405	4,195,876	9,112	...	79,109	4,515,502
2008	132,036	3,242,651	9,406	...	72,765	3,456,859
2009	-680,020	784,700	8,416	...	68,971	182,067

• NET OPERATING GAIN ($000 omitted)

Year	Individual Life	Individual & Group Annuities	Group Life & A&H	Credit Life & A&H	Individual A&H	Total
2007	247,605	94,978	-4,027	-75	2,262	440,923
2008	586,996	-711,561	2,798	...	4,770	-116,996
2009	79,512	527,569	771	...	5,785	613,637

• COMPARATIVE FINANCIALS ($000 omitted)

Year	Assets	Capital & Surplus	Net Invest Income	Benefits Paid	Realized Cap Gains	Policyholder Dividends	Contract Lns (% of assets)
2007	29,146,511	1,414,244	1,040,998	2,298,555	-20,216	0	1.6
2008	25,963,876	1,930,920	816,178	2,310,016	-125,052	0	1.9
2009	25,113,007	1,935,719	643,446	1,784,295	-362,760	0	2.0

• ORDINARY LIFE STATISTICS

Year	Av. Ord. Policy Issued ($)	Av. Ord. Policy In Force ($)	Avg. Prem ($/M)	1st Yr Prem/ Total Prem	Ord. Lapse Ratio
2007	...	...	...	...	...
2008	...	...	...	...	...
2009	...	...	...	...	...

• NEW LIFE BUSINESS ISSUED ($000 omitted)

Year	Whole Life	Term	Credit	Group	Industrial	Total
2007	3,740,913	35,585,876	...	1,045	...	39,327,834
2008	2,971,826	26,599,566	...	1,205	...	29,572,597
2009	1,847,788	23,250,754	...	1,144	...	25,099,686

• LIFE INSURANCE IN FORCE ($000 omitted)

Year	Whole Life	Term	Credit	Group	Industrial	Total
2007	122,670,679	520,503,362	230	87,870	74,376	643,336,517
2008	113,998,761	537,910,890	20	87,690	70,311	652,067,672
2009	108,809,288	541,351,206	20	84,325	66,321	650,311,159

GENWORTH LIFE INSURANCE CO NY

666 Third Avenue, 9th Floor
New York, New York 10017
Tel: 212-895-4137

AMB#: 060026
Began Business: 10/31/1988
Agency Off: None

Best's Financial Strength Rating: A g
FSC: XV

• NET PREMIUMS AND DEPOSITS ($000 omitted)

Year	Individual Life	Individual & Group Annuities	Group Life & A&H	Credit Life & A&H	Individual A&H	Total
2007	27,160	706,858	3,477	...	141,472	878,967
2008	36,733	1,018,909	3,506	...	151,953	1,211,101
2009	33,126	176,446	3,821	...	151,904	365,298

• NET OPERATING GAIN ($000 omitted)

Year	Individual Life	Individual & Group Annuities	Group Life & A&H	Credit Life & A&H	Individual A&H	Total
2007	-2,506	17,606	-132	...	97,917	112,885
2008	1,546	-97,998	7,569	...	-22,501	-111,384
2009	-6,594	111,671	-7,609	...	7,403	104,870

• COMPARATIVE FINANCIALS ($000 omitted)

Year	Assets	Capital & Surplus	Net Invest Income	Benefits Paid	Realized Cap Gains	Policyholder Dividends	Contract Lns (% of assets)
2007	6,465,058	408,841	296,025	761,017	-2,171	10	0.5
2008	6,999,427	434,358	304,523	716,191	-147,463	10	0.5
2009	7,218,410	429,513	309,781	555,715	-64,000	29	0.4

• ORDINARY LIFE STATISTICS

Year	Av. Ord. Policy Issued ($)	Av. Ord. Policy In Force ($)	Avg. Prem ($/M)	1st Yr Prem/ Total Prem	Ord. Lapse Ratio
2007	500,728	320,528	2.53	22.4	4.6
2008	422,844	328,475	2.81	19.8	4.6
2009	312,893	330,733	2.73	13.2	5.3

• NEW LIFE BUSINESS ISSUED ($000 omitted)

Year	Whole Life	Term	Credit	Group	Industrial	Total
2007	217,483	3,106,847	...	...	...	3,324,330
2008	205,302	2,138,099	...	...	...	2,343,401
2009	130,847	1,355,395	...	...	...	1,486,242

• LIFE INSURANCE IN FORCE ($000 omitted)

Year	Whole Life	Term	Credit	Group	Industrial	Total
2007	4,394,826	23,452,316	...	1,015	...	27,848,157
2008	4,106,668	24,546,538	...	1,015	...	28,654,221
2009	3,792,693	24,636,754	...	1,015	...	28,430,462

GERBER LIFE INS CO

1311 Mamaroneck Ave
White Plains, New York 10605
Tel: 914-272-4000

AMB#: 007299
Began Business: 09/30/1968
Agency Off: Robert J. Lodewick

Best's Financial Strength Rating: A **FSC:** VIII

• NET PREMIUMS AND DEPOSITS ($000 omitted)

Year	Individual Life	Individual & Group Annuities	Group Life & A&H	Credit Life & A&H	Individual A&H	Total
2007	235,313	...	101,106	...	9,857	346,276
2008	249,199	...	109,182	...	9,747	368,128
2009	250,825	...	118,529	...	9,668	379,022

• NET OPERATING GAIN ($000 omitted)

Year	Individual Life	Individual & Group Annuities	Group Life & A&H	Credit Life & A&H	Individual A&H	Total
2007	4,202	...	7,042	...	1,025	12,269
2008	895	...	8,744	...	202	9,841
2009	3,696	...	11,349	...	1,125	16,171

• COMPARATIVE FINANCIALS ($000 omitted)

Year	Assets	Capital & Surplus	Net Invest Income	Benefits Paid	Realized Cap Gains	Policyholder Dividends	Contract Lns (% of assets)
2007	1,422,128	201,154	65,543	123,448	1,795	...	2.5
2008	1,567,859	160,419	72,578	129,414	-51,930	...	2.8
2009	1,712,613	194,251	80,126	141,693	1,415	...	3.2

• ORDINARY LIFE STATISTICS

Year	Av. Ord. Policy Issued ($)	Av. Ord. Policy In Force ($)	Avg. Prem ($/M)	1st Yr Prem/ Total Prem	Ord. Lapse Ratio
2007	10,865	11,582	7.15	17.6	10.3
2008	11,276	11,919	7.08	15.7	9.8
2009	11,781	12,188	6.89	12.3	9.0

• NEW LIFE BUSINESS ISSUED ($000 omitted)

Year	Whole Life	Term	Credit	Group	Industrial	Total
2007	5,378,052	1,196,072	...	22,174	...	6,596,298
2008	5,173,103	1,061,683	...	14,408	...	6,249,194
2009	4,494,748	799,515	...	14,203	...	5,308,466

• LIFE INSURANCE IN FORCE ($000 omitted)

Year	Whole Life	Term	Credit	Group	Industrial	Total
2007	24,735,018	8,787,068	...	158,821	...	33,680,907
2008	26,173,714	9,601,960	...	117,258	...	35,892,932
2009	27,021,191	10,249,275	...	99,494	...	37,369,959

GLEANER LIFE INS SOCIETY

5200 West U.S. Hwy. 223
Adrian, Michigan 49221-7894
Tel: 517-263-2244

AMB#: 006459
Began Business: 10/19/1894
Agency Off: Larry Gordon

Best's Financial Strength Rating: A- **FSC:** VII

• NET PREMIUMS AND DEPOSITS ($000 omitted)

Year	Individual Life	Individual & Group Annuities	Group Life & A&H	Credit Life & A&H	Individual A&H	Total
2007	6,661	...	...	...	35	63,629
2008	6,348	...	...	...	32	64,821
2009	7,282	...	...	...	23	95,857

• NET OPERATING GAIN ($000 omitted)

Year	Individual Life	Individual & Group Annuities	Group Life & A&H	Credit Life & A&H	Individual A&H	Total
2007	1,444	5,185	...	...	-207	2,512
2008	1,707	5,006	...	...	-134	2,799
2009	2,218	6,854	...	...	-28	5,282

• COMPARATIVE FINANCIALS ($000 omitted)

Year	Assets	Capital & Surplus	Net Invest Income	Benefits Paid	Realized Cap Gains	Policyholder Dividends	Contract Lns (% of assets)
2007	1,148,018	92,938	64,654	183,891	-510	238	2.0
2008	1,103,005	80,600	61,921	138,912	-15,710	219	2.1
2009	1,143,428	81,142	60,076	94,163	-4,902	233	2.2

• ORDINARY LIFE STATISTICS

Year	Av. Ord. Policy Issued ($)	Av. Ord. Policy In Force ($)	Avg. Prem ($/M)	1st Yr Prem/ Total Prem	Ord. Lapse Ratio
2007	...	...	...	...	...
2008	...	...	...	...	...
2009	...	...	...	...	...

• NEW LIFE BUSINESS ISSUED ($000 omitted)

Year	Whole Life	Term	Credit	Group	Industrial	Total
2007	121,051	...	...	...	...	121,051
2008	143,155	...	...	...	...	143,155
2009	138,411	...	...	...	...	138,411

• LIFE INSURANCE IN FORCE ($000 omitted)

Year	Whole Life	Term	Credit	Group	Industrial	Total
2007	1,886,932	...	...	...	...	1,886,932
2008	1,909,962	...	...	...	...	1,909,962
2009	1,936,027	...	...	...	...	1,936,027

GERMANIA LIFE INS CO

P.O. Box 645
Brenham, Texas 77834-0645
Tel: 979-836-5224

AMB#: 009530
Began Business: 12/29/1983
Agency Off: Rodney Foerster

Best's Financial Strength Rating: B++ **FSC:** V

• NET PREMIUMS AND DEPOSITS ($000 omitted)

Year	Individual Life	Individual & Group Annuities	Group Life & A&H	Credit Life & A&H	Individual A&H	Total
2007	3,517	641	214	...	...	4,372
2008	3,883	1,073	220	...	...	5,177
2009	4,620	1,041	227	...	...	5,888

• NET OPERATING GAIN ($000 omitted)

Year	Individual Life	Individual & Group Annuities	Group Life & A&H	Credit Life & A&H	Individual A&H	Total
2007	-438	-35	212	...	...	-261
2008	-660	127	217	...	...	-316
2009	-331	130	185	...	...	-16

• COMPARATIVE FINANCIALS ($000 omitted)

Year	Assets	Capital & Surplus	Net Invest Income	Benefits Paid	Realized Cap Gains	Policyholder Dividends	Contract Lns (% of assets)
2007	41,244	11,374	1,775	3,940	65	46	1.5
2008	43,306	10,850	2,011	2,962	-165	50	1.5
2009	47,455	10,759	2,237	1,815	-33	71	1.5

• ORDINARY LIFE STATISTICS

Year	Av. Ord. Policy Issued ($)	Av. Ord. Policy In Force ($)	Avg. Prem ($/M)	1st Yr Prem/ Total Prem	Ord. Lapse Ratio
2007	...	...	...	...	...
2008	...	...	...	...	...
2009	...	...	...	...	...

• NEW LIFE BUSINESS ISSUED ($000 omitted)

Year	Whole Life	Term	Credit	Group	Industrial	Total
2007	19,882	137,689	...	1,620	...	159,191
2008	18,504	166,370	...	2,025	...	186,899
2009	22,495	225,810	...	1,700	...	250,005

• LIFE INSURANCE IN FORCE ($000 omitted)

Year	Whole Life	Term	Credit	Group	Industrial	Total
2007	134,081	866,752	...	41,470	...	1,042,303
2008	146,392	987,368	...	42,215	...	1,175,975
2009	161,812	1,153,274	...	44,025	...	1,359,111

GLOBE LIFE AND ACCIDENT INS CO

204 North Robinson Avenue
Oklahoma City, Oklahoma 73102
Tel: 405-270-1400

AMB#: 006462
Began Business: 04/09/1951
Agency Off: None

Best's Financial Strength Rating: A+ g **FSC:** X

• NET PREMIUMS AND DEPOSITS ($000 omitted)

Year	Individual Life	Individual & Group Annuities	Group Life & A&H	Credit Life & A&H	Individual A&H	Total
2007	231,083	140	236,112	...	57,528	524,864
2008	199,519	123	256,497	...	55,541	511,680
2009	184,601	73	282,421	...	31,037	498,132

• NET OPERATING GAIN ($000 omitted)

Year	Individual Life	Individual & Group Annuities	Group Life & A&H	Credit Life & A&H	Individual A&H	Total
2007	87,754	735	27,866	...	14,078	130,434
2008	121,439	68	6,298	...	26,412	154,217
2009	153,403	656	84,851	...	8,179	247,089

• COMPARATIVE FINANCIALS ($000 omitted)

Year	Assets	Capital & Surplus	Net Invest Income	Benefits Paid	Realized Cap Gains	Policyholder Dividends	Contract Lns (% of assets)
2007	2,554,739	324,521	197,948	225,712	-345	235	2.0
2008	2,736,764	392,687	211,025	224,538	-20,508	47	2.0
2009	2,899,403	479,548	294,366	200,795	-21,981	34	1.9

• ORDINARY LIFE STATISTICS

Year	Av. Ord. Policy Issued ($)	Av. Ord. Policy In Force ($)	Avg. Prem ($/M)	1st Yr Prem/ Total Prem	Ord. Lapse Ratio
2007	12,819	8,869	8.36	5.0	18.5
2008	14,257	8,986	8.32	6.2	22.8
2009	13,960	9,123	7.84	7.3	19.8

• NEW LIFE BUSINESS ISSUED ($000 omitted)

Year	Whole Life	Term	Credit	Group	Industrial	Total
2007	6,252,836	1,621,077	...	17,014,235	...	24,888,148
2008	7,358,760	1,658,001	...	19,010,957	...	28,027,718
2009	7,492,997	1,560,673	...	20,047,233	...	29,100,903

• LIFE INSURANCE IN FORCE ($000 omitted)

Year	Whole Life	Term	Credit	Group	Industrial	Total
2007	27,500,538	7,600,478	...	17,312,560	...	52,413,576
2008	26,695,029	8,078,895	...	20,283,393	...	55,057,317
2009	26,358,884	7,916,409	...	23,505,149	...	57,780,442

GOLDEN RULE INS CO

7440 Woodland Drive
Indianapolis, Indiana 46278-1719
Tel: 618-943-8000

AMB#: 006263
Began Business: 06/23/1961
Agency Off: None

Best's Financial Strength Rating: A **FSC:** VIII

• **NET PREMIUMS AND DEPOSITS ($000 omitted)**

Year	Individual Life	Individual & Group Annuities	Group Life & A&H	Credit Life & A&H	Individual A&H	Total
2007	268	99	960,414	...	167,471	1,128,252
2008	374	...	1,076,713	...	183,734	1,260,822
2009	316	...	1,117,134	...	206,964	1,324,415

• **NET OPERATING GAIN ($000 omitted)**

Year	Individual Life	Individual & Group Annuities	Group Life & A&H	Credit Life & A&H	Individual A&H	Total
2007	1,674	1,111	147,266	...	12,492	162,543
2008	976	640	125,627	...	12,617	139,860
2009	1,111	720	141,614	...	12,354	155,798

• **COMPARATIVE FINANCIALS ($000 omitted)**

Year	Assets	Capital & Surplus	Net Invest Income	Benefits Paid	Realized Cap Gains	Policyholder Dividends	Contract Lns (% of assets)
2007	590,141	263,874	29,822	685,660	17	...	...
2008	613,699	267,811	22,380	794,013	4,881	...	...
2009	524,422	175,793	16,828	838,721	455	...	...

• **ORDINARY LIFE STATISTICS**

Year	Av. Ord. Policy Issued ($)	Av. Ord. Policy In Force ($)	Avg. Prem ($/M)	1st Yr Prem/ Total Prem	Ord. Lapse Ratio
2007	...	...	...	...	...
2008	...	...	...	...	...
2009	...	...	...	...	...

• **NEW LIFE BUSINESS ISSUED ($000 omitted)**

Year	Whole Life	Term	Credit	Group	Industrial	Total
2007	...	163,903	...	242,089	...	405,992
2008	62,662	60,723	...	348,245	...	471,630
2009	...	172,814	...	632,640	...	805,454

• **LIFE INSURANCE IN FORCE ($000 omitted)**

Year	Whole Life	Term	Credit	Group	Industrial	Total
2007	2,241,069	6,741,691	...	362,737	...	9,345,497
2008	2,268,736	6,234,336	...	439,166	...	8,942,238
2009	2,145,217	5,943,266	...	763,497	...	8,851,980

GRANGE LIFE INS CO

P.O. Box 1218
Columbus, Ohio 43216-1218
Tel: 614-445-2900

AMB#: 007332
Began Business: 07/01/1968
Agency Off: Doug Sharp

Best's Financial Strength Rating: A- **FSC:** VI

• **NET PREMIUMS AND DEPOSITS ($000 omitted)**

Year	Individual Life	Individual & Group Annuities	Group Life & A&H	Credit Life & A&H	Individual A&H	Total
2007	34,212	4,570	1,082	...	284	40,149
2008	36,805	3,568	1,142	...	268	41,783
2009	39,358	4,096	1,186	...	141	44,781

• **NET OPERATING GAIN ($000 omitted)**

Year	Individual Life	Individual & Group Annuities	Group Life & A&H	Credit Life & A&H	Individual A&H	Total
2007	2,371	436	536	...	-29	3,314
2008	389	339	1,140	...	-105	1,763
2009	2,197	642	628	...	99	3,566

• **COMPARATIVE FINANCIALS ($000 omitted)**

Year	Assets	Capital & Surplus	Net Invest Income	Benefits Paid	Realized Cap Gains	Policyholder Dividends	Contract Lns (% of assets)
2007	245,496	34,163	11,407	24,708	...	456	3.4
2008	254,933	33,571	11,778	30,110	-2,975	385	3.3
2009	271,857	37,911	12,163	27,770	-670	170	3.2

• **ORDINARY LIFE STATISTICS**

Year	Av. Ord. Policy Issued ($)	Av. Ord. Policy In Force ($)	Avg. Prem ($/M)	1st Yr Prem/ Total Prem	Ord. Lapse Ratio
2007	159,517	156,239	3.42	18.6	4.5
2008	163,792	144,104	3.78	15.6	4.7
2009	153,231	147,010	3.80	14.3	4.5

• **NEW LIFE BUSINESS ISSUED ($000 omitted)**

Year	Whole Life	Term	Credit	Group	Industrial	Total
2007	155,150	2,103,606	...	10,465	...	2,269,221
2008	192,297	1,927,336	...	20,815	...	2,140,448
2009	171,682	1,579,744	...	13,316	...	1,764,742

• **LIFE INSURANCE IN FORCE ($000 omitted)**

Year	Whole Life	Term	Credit	Group	Industrial	Total
2007	2,220,695	14,850,145	...	244,292	...	17,315,132
2008	2,240,536	14,302,336	...	256,695	...	16,799,567
2009	2,270,764	15,146,699	...	263,875	...	17,681,338

GOVERNMENT PERSONNEL MUTUAL

P.O. Box 659567
San Antonio, Texas 78265-9567
Tel: 210-357-2222

AMB#: 006470
Began Business: 10/09/1934
Agency Off: Peter J. Hennessey IV

Best's Financial Strength Rating: A- **FSC:** VII

• **NET PREMIUMS AND DEPOSITS ($000 omitted)**

Year	Individual Life	Individual & Group Annuities	Group Life & A&H	Credit Life & A&H	Individual A&H	Total
2007	45,869	5,061	7,035	...	1	57,965
2008	45,795	5,243	6,399	...	1	57,438
2009	44,025	12,060	6,014	...	0	62,099

• **NET OPERATING GAIN ($000 omitted)**

Year	Individual Life	Individual & Group Annuities	Group Life & A&H	Credit Life & A&H	Individual A&H	Total
2007	5,140	835	418	...	3	6,397
2008	3,881	178	253	...	-5	4,308
2009	4,990	624	246	...	0	5,861

• **COMPARATIVE FINANCIALS ($000 omitted)**

Year	Assets	Capital & Surplus	Net Invest Income	Benefits Paid	Realized Cap Gains	Policyholder Dividends	Contract Lns (% of assets)
2007	786,599	87,957	42,388	55,809	-1,263	6,562	9.1
2008	787,153	83,559	44,002	58,761	-7,446	6,656	9.3
2009	801,887	87,788	42,528	52,704	-5,230	6,704	9.3

• **ORDINARY LIFE STATISTICS**

Year	Av. Ord. Policy Issued ($)	Av. Ord. Policy In Force ($)	Avg. Prem ($/M)	1st Yr Prem/ Total Prem	Ord. Lapse Ratio
2007	80,973	49,259	11.44	5.7	5.3
2008	81,378	47,502	11.30	6.1	5.9
2009	74,134	48,843	10.96	7.1	5.4

• **NEW LIFE BUSINESS ISSUED ($000 omitted)**

Year	Whole Life	Term	Credit	Group	Industrial	Total
2007	130,770	144,782	...	1,360,538	...	1,636,090
2008	139,990	119,851	...	779,510	...	1,039,351
2009	158,360	131,725	...	585,652	...	875,737

• **LIFE INSURANCE IN FORCE ($000 omitted)**

Year	Whole Life	Term	Credit	Group	Industrial	Total
2007	2,680,355	1,546,195	...	12,154,423	...	16,380,973
2008	2,729,283	1,552,204	...	11,464,960	...	15,746,447
2009	2,735,995	1,567,124	...	10,838,706	...	15,141,825

GREAT AMERICAN LIFE ASSUR CO

P.O. Box 26580
Austin, Texas 78755
Tel: 512-451-2224

AMB#: 006253
Began Business: 09/30/1967
Agency Off: Charles R. Scheper

Best's Financial Strength Rating: B++ **FSC:** IV

• **NET PREMIUMS AND DEPOSITS ($000 omitted)**

Year	Individual Life	Individual & Group Annuities	Group Life & A&H	Credit Life & A&H	Individual A&H	Total
2007	...	624	...	...	...	624
2008	...	8	...	...	...	8
2009	...	22	...	...	...	22

• **NET OPERATING GAIN ($000 omitted)**

Year	Individual Life	Individual & Group Annuities	Group Life & A&H	Credit Life & A&H	Individual A&H	Total
2007	211	121	...	...	...	332
2008	103	165	...	...	...	268
2009	84	-506	...	...	...	-422

• **COMPARATIVE FINANCIALS ($000 omitted)**

Year	Assets	Capital & Surplus	Net Invest Income	Benefits Paid	Realized Cap Gains	Policyholder Dividends	Contract Lns (% of assets)
2007	21,374	8,646	1,185	2,237	...	...	8.6
2008	20,204	8,288	1,036	636	...	...	9.5
2009	19,762	7,798	826	1,590	-166	...	10.3

• **ORDINARY LIFE STATISTICS**

Year	Av. Ord. Policy Issued ($)	Av. Ord. Policy In Force ($)	Avg. Prem ($/M)	1st Yr Prem/ Total Prem	Ord. Lapse Ratio
2007	...	...	...	...	...
2008	...	...	...	...	...
2009	...	...	...	...	...

• **NEW LIFE BUSINESS ISSUED ($000 omitted)**

Year	Whole Life	Term	Credit	Group	Industrial	Total
2007	...	...	...	...	...	...
2008	...	...	...	...	...	...
2009	...	...	...	...	...	...

• **LIFE INSURANCE IN FORCE ($000 omitted)**

Year	Whole Life	Term	Credit	Group	Industrial	Total
2007	6,376	...	...	...	...	6,376
2008	6,451	...	...	...	...	6,451
2009	5,818	...	...	...	...	5,818

GREAT AMERICAN LIFE INS CO

P.O. Box 5420
Cincinnati, Ohio 45201-5420
Tel: 513-357-3300

AMB#: 006474
Began Business: 08/13/1963
Agency Off: Charles R. Scheper

Best's Financial Strength Rating: A g
FSC: XI

• **NET PREMIUMS AND DEPOSITS** ($000 omitted)

Year	Individual Life	Individual & Group Annuities	Group Life & A&H	Credit Life & A&H	Individual A&H	Total
2007	36,851	1,200,887	747	...	30,293	1,268,778
2008	10,241	1,165,526	523	...	38,143	1,214,433
2009	20,809	1,000,235	-6,060	...	-89,682	925,302

• **NET OPERATING GAIN** ($000 omitted)

Year	Individual Life	Individual & Group Annuities	Group Life & A&H	Credit Life & A&H	Individual A&H	Total
2007	12,120	77,445	-2,677	...	-6,471	80,416
2008	14,763	141,187	-2,669	...	7,150	160,431
2009	6,544	76,185	90	...	-1,017	81,802

• **COMPARATIVE FINANCIALS** ($000 omitted)

Year	Assets	Capital & Surplus	Net Invest Income	Benefits Paid	Realized Cap Gains	Policyholder Dividends	Contract Lns (% of assets)
2007	9,295,574	732,328	523,026	1,105,734	-36,438	...	2.0
2008	9,648,623	794,257	557,453	1,129,175	-164,411	...	1.9
2009	9,962,026	874,636	551,266	976,420	-136,242	...	1.7

• **ORDINARY LIFE STATISTICS**

Year	Av. Ord. Policy Issued ($)	Av. Ord. Policy In Force ($)	Avg. Prem ($/M)	1st Yr Prem/ Total Prem	Ord. Lapse Ratio
2007	147,484	193,453	3.62	1.0	5.2
2008	25,381	191,523	3.73	1.5	6.9
2009	12,717	187,143	3.75	1.4	8.0

• **NEW LIFE BUSINESS ISSUED** ($000 omitted)

Year	Whole Life	Term	Credit	Group	Industrial	Total
2007	20,212	3,238	...	...	...	23,450
2008	17,697	2,151	...	...	...	19,848
2009	23,172	3,522	...	...	...	26,694

• **LIFE INSURANCE IN FORCE** ($000 omitted)

Year	Whole Life	Term	Credit	Group	Industrial	Total
2007	1,961,581	19,011,629	...	35,056	...	21,008,266
2008	1,889,336	17,577,432	...	33,143	...	19,499,911
2009	1,800,831	16,065,107	...	31,162	...	17,897,100

GREAT SOUTHERN LIFE INS CO

P.O. Box 410288
Kansas City, Missouri 64141-0288
Tel: 816-391-2000

AMB#: 006491
Began Business: 11/01/1909
Agency Off: Rodney K. Foster

Best's Financial Strength Rating: B+
FSC: VI

• **NET PREMIUMS AND DEPOSITS** ($000 omitted)

Year	Individual Life	Individual & Group Annuities	Group Life & A&H	Credit Life & A&H	Individual A&H	Total
2007	881	3,735	...	...	...	4,616
2008	272	2,598	...	...	...	2,871
2009	386	1,643	...	...	...	2,029

• **NET OPERATING GAIN** ($000 omitted)

Year	Individual Life	Individual & Group Annuities	Group Life & A&H	Credit Life & A&H	Individual A&H	Total
2007	-429	302	-207	0	28	-307
2008	942	760	-220	0	31	1,513
2009	2,334	-10	-238	0	32	2,117

• **COMPARATIVE FINANCIALS** ($000 omitted)

Year	Assets	Capital & Surplus	Net Invest Income	Benefits Paid	Realized Cap Gains	Policyholder Dividends	Contract Lns (% of assets)
2007	289,242	31,058	17,146	1,429	-27	6	0.2
2008	274,057	34,181	15,215	1,764	-2,630	5	0.3
2009	254,776	34,292	14,856	1,357	-2,139	5	0.3

• **ORDINARY LIFE STATISTICS**

Year	Av. Ord. Policy Issued ($)	Av. Ord. Policy In Force ($)	Avg. Prem ($/M)	1st Yr Prem/ Total Prem	Ord. Lapse Ratio
2007	...	...	...	...	...
2008	...	...	...	...	...
2009	...	...	...	...	...

• **NEW LIFE BUSINESS ISSUED** ($000 omitted)

Year	Whole Life	Term	Credit	Group	Industrial	Total
2007	225	299	...	495,879	...	496,403
2008	513	106	...	203,212	...	203,831
2009	...	...	...	4,525	...	4,525

• **LIFE INSURANCE IN FORCE** ($000 omitted)

Year	Whole Life	Term	Credit	Group	Industrial	Total
2007	8,832,679	2,488,784	21	1,484,241	...	12,805,725
2008	8,231,955	2,332,124	11	1,444,429	...	12,008,519
2009	7,697,807	2,142,798	4	1,230,274	...	11,070,883

GREAT AMERICAN LIFE INS OF NY

P.O. Box 21029
New York, New York 10129
Tel: 212-885-1544

AMB#: 006864
Began Business: 04/30/1964
Agency Off: Charles R. Scheper

Best's Financial Strength Rating: A-
FSC: IV

• **NET PREMIUMS AND DEPOSITS** ($000 omitted)

Year	Individual Life	Individual & Group Annuities	Group Life & A&H	Credit Life & A&H	Individual A&H	Total
2007	0	4	...	...	...	4
2008	0	5	...	...	...	5
2009	0	26	...	...	...	26

• **NET OPERATING GAIN** ($000 omitted)

Year	Individual Life	Individual & Group Annuities	Group Life & A&H	Credit Life & A&H	Individual A&H	Total
2007	0	673	...	...	0	673
2008	0	123	...	...	0	123
2009	0	1,003	...	...	0	1,003

• **COMPARATIVE FINANCIALS** ($000 omitted)

Year	Assets	Capital & Surplus	Net Invest Income	Benefits Paid	Realized Cap Gains	Policyholder Dividends	Contract Lns (% of assets)
2007	52,573	10,980	3,054	3,778	0	...	...
2008	46,882	7,093	2,773	3,439	-73	...	...
2009	45,035	8,011	2,380	3,239	-221	...	...

• **ORDINARY LIFE STATISTICS**

Year	Av. Ord. Policy Issued ($)	Av. Ord. Policy In Force ($)	Avg. Prem ($/M)	1st Yr Prem/ Total Prem	Ord. Lapse Ratio
2007	...	...	...	...	...
2008	...	...	...	...	...
2009	...	...	...	...	...

• **NEW LIFE BUSINESS ISSUED** ($000 omitted)

Year	Whole Life	Term	Credit	Group	Industrial	Total
2007	...	...	...	...	...	...
2008	...	...	...	...	...	...
2009	...	...	...	...	...	...

• **LIFE INSURANCE IN FORCE** ($000 omitted)

Year	Whole Life	Term	Credit	Group	Industrial	Total
2007	18	...	...	...	...	18
2008	12	...	...	...	...	12
2009	12	...	...	...	...	12

GREAT-WEST LIFE & ANN

8515 East Orchard Road
Greenwood Village, Colorado 80111
Tel: 303-737-3000

AMB#: 006981
Began Business: 04/24/1907
Agency Off: Marc Neely

Best's Financial Strength Rating: A+ g
FSC: XV

• **NET PREMIUMS AND DEPOSITS** ($000 omitted)

Year	Individual Life	Individual & Group Annuities	Group Life & A&H	Credit Life & A&H	Individual A&H	Total
2007	-1,028,509	3,320,756	717,434	...	-18,226	2,991,456
2008	1,097,565	3,003,603	161,589	...	-344	4,262,413
2009	944,368	5,019,280	112,574	...	...	6,076,222

• **NET OPERATING GAIN** ($000 omitted)

Year	Individual Life	Individual & Group Annuities	Group Life & A&H	Credit Life & A&H	Individual A&H	Total
2007	290,877	140,684	140,577	...	-240	547,477
2008	111,244	139,848	61,799	...	-6,946	296,152
2009	48,289	88,352	194,702	...	-113	337,553

• **COMPARATIVE FINANCIALS** ($000 omitted)

Year	Assets	Capital & Surplus	Net Invest Income	Benefits Paid	Realized Cap Gains	Policyholder Dividends	Contract Lns (% of assets)
2007	38,409,183	1,846,171	1,082,257	4,809,735	2,993	94,976	9.8
2008	34,960,361	901,429	1,047,584	3,285,618	-36,803	70,484	11.3
2009	40,039,587	1,375,267	1,067,393	3,797,865	-55,520	71,358	9.9

• **ORDINARY LIFE STATISTICS**

Year	Av. Ord. Policy Issued ($)	Av. Ord. Policy In Force ($)	Avg. Prem ($/M)	1st Yr Prem/ Total Prem	Ord. Lapse Ratio
2007	81,076	117,554	-18.09	22.3	4.4
2008	152,772	115,697	20.22	13.4	5.1
2009	134,422	111,997	17.71	26.1	6.7

• **NEW LIFE BUSINESS ISSUED** ($000 omitted)

Year	Whole Life	Term	Credit	Group	Industrial	Total
2007	388,495	1,606,388	...	341,921	...	2,336,804
2008	1,875,068	1,325,501	...	1,179,258	...	4,379,827
2009	1,256,143	1,537,150	...	1,343,917	...	4,137,211

• **LIFE INSURANCE IN FORCE** ($000 omitted)

Year	Whole Life	Term	Credit	Group	Industrial	Total
2007	28,865,479	25,899,476	...	41,452,233	...	96,217,188
2008	30,550,891	25,437,454	...	38,785,606	...	94,773,951
2009	31,071,159	24,474,332	...	39,484,465	...	95,029,955

GREAT WESTERN INS CO

3434 Washington Boulevard, Suite 300
Ogden, Utah 84401-4108
Tel: 801-689-1415

AMB#: 009362
Began Business: 05/01/1983
Agency Off: Shelly Payan

Best's Financial Strength Rating: B+ **FSC:** VI

• NET PREMIUMS AND DEPOSITS ($000 omitted)

Year	Individual Life	Individual & Group Annuities	Group Life & A&H	Credit Life & A&H	Individual A&H	Total
2007	40,161	2,516	105,614	25	...	148,315
2008	-2,746	1,924	-13,194	26	...	-13,990
2009	33,642	1,887	85,401	21	...	120,951

• NET OPERATING GAIN ($000 omitted)

Year	Individual Life	Individual & Group Annuities	Group Life & A&H	Credit Life & A&H	Individual A&H	Total
2007	2,032	68	3,629	8	...	5,737
2008	11,812	-48	15,408	10	...	27,182
2009	-894	-67	-156	-2	...	-1,119

• COMPARATIVE FINANCIALS ($000 omitted)

Year	Assets	Capital & Surplus	Net Invest Income	Benefits Paid	Realized Cap Gains	Policyholder Dividends	Contract Lns (% of assets)
2007	499,842	33,824	26,144	55,991	-9,163	4,259	0.1
2008	403,032	32,426	28,558	65,090	-20,830	1,866	0.1
2009	462,148	34,308	24,905	47,392	-2,948	...	0.1

• ORDINARY LIFE STATISTICS

Year	Av. Ord. Policy Issued ($)	Av. Ord. Policy In Force ($)	Avg. Prem ($/M)	1st Yr Prem/ Total Prem	Ord. Lapse Ratio
2007	5,032	4,668	183.86	2.2	0.0
2008	4,901	4,791	166.38	5.8	-0.8
2009	4,153	4,755	156.91	5.3	-0.7

• NEW LIFE BUSINESS ISSUED ($000 omitted)

Year	Whole Life	Term	Credit	Group	Industrial	Total
2007	34,845	...	472	112,842	...	148,159
2008	28,008	...	267	119,562	...	147,837
2009	29,670	...	267	106,437	...	136,374

• LIFE INSURANCE IN FORCE ($000 omitted)

Year	Whole Life	Term	Credit	Group	Industrial	Total
2007	218,437	...	2,310	494,961	...	715,708
2008	232,761	...	1,077	577,254	...	811,092
2009	245,883	...	1,092	640,376	...	887,351

GREATER GEORGIA LIFE INS CO

2 Gannett Drive
South Portland, Maine 04106
Tel: 678-443-5200

AMB#: 009177
Began Business: 05/06/1982
Agency Off: Robert J. Matz, Jr.

Best's Financial Strength Rating: A g **FSC:** IX

• NET PREMIUMS AND DEPOSITS ($000 omitted)

Year	Individual Life	Individual & Group Annuities	Group Life & A&H	Credit Life & A&H	Individual A&H	Total
2007	474	9,551	28,176	...	...	38,202
2008	535	9,247	30,100	...	...	39,882
2009	634	10,604	27,729	...	...	38,968

• NET OPERATING GAIN ($000 omitted)

Year	Individual Life	Individual & Group Annuities	Group Life & A&H	Credit Life & A&H	Individual A&H	Total
2007	289	...	1,722	...	...	2,011
2008	156	...	2,235	...	...	2,392
2009	367	...	972	...	...	1,339

• COMPARATIVE FINANCIALS ($000 omitted)

Year	Assets	Capital & Surplus	Net Invest Income	Benefits Paid	Realized Cap Gains	Policyholder Dividends	Contract Lns (% of assets)
2007	43,176	22,166	1,788	18,098	-55	...	0.1
2008	44,758	22,687	1,963	18,927	-161	...	0.1
2009	45,601	20,645	2,014	17,907	-476	...	0.1

• ORDINARY LIFE STATISTICS

Year	Av. Ord. Policy Issued ($)	Av. Ord. Policy In Force ($)	Avg. Prem ($/M)	1st Yr Prem/ Total Prem	Ord. Lapse Ratio
2007	...	...	...	...	...
2008	...	...	...	...	...
2009	...	...	...	...	...

• NEW LIFE BUSINESS ISSUED ($000 omitted)

Year	Whole Life	Term	Credit	Group	Industrial	Total
2007	...	35,430	...	913,714	...	949,144
2008	...	39,315	...	1,673,675	...	1,712,990
2009	...	50,475	...	1,239,621	...	1,290,096

• LIFE INSURANCE IN FORCE ($000 omitted)

Year	Whole Life	Term	Credit	Group	Industrial	Total
2007	...	70,461	...	7,251,100	...	7,321,561
2008	...	111,875	...	7,742,020	...	7,853,895
2009	...	107,360	...	7,585,120	...	7,692,480

GREATER BENEFICIAL UNION

4254 Clairton Boulevard
Pittsburgh, Pennsylvania 15227-3394
Tel: 800-765-4428

AMB#: 008161
Began Business: 04/13/1892
Agency Off: James S. Laick

Best's Financial Strength Rating: B++ **FSC:** VI

• NET PREMIUMS AND DEPOSITS ($000 omitted)

Year	Individual Life	Individual & Group Annuities	Group Life & A&H	Credit Life & A&H	Individual A&H	Total
2007	3,191	...	...	...	...	55,769
2008	2,943	...	...	...	...	63,376
2009	1,614	...	...	...	...	120,286

• NET OPERATING GAIN ($000 omitted)

Year	Individual Life	Individual & Group Annuities	Group Life & A&H	Credit Life & A&H	Individual A&H	Total
2007	1,591	2,974	...	...	...	3,576
2008	1,276	4,172	...	...	...	4,676
2009	1,401	3,753	...	...	...	4,489

• COMPARATIVE FINANCIALS ($000 omitted)

Year	Assets	Capital & Surplus	Net Invest Income	Benefits Paid	Realized Cap Gains	Policyholder Dividends	Contract Lns (% of assets)
2007	464,485	31,868	27,593	53,843	47	277	0.2
2008	498,869	27,675	29,794	42,141	-6,430	291	0.2
2009	602,550	31,005	33,869	43,366	-2,385	294	0.1

• ORDINARY LIFE STATISTICS

Year	Av. Ord. Policy Issued ($)	Av. Ord. Policy In Force ($)	Avg. Prem ($/M)	1st Yr Prem/ Total Prem	Ord. Lapse Ratio
2007	...	...	...	...	...
2008	...	...	...	...	...
2009	...	...	...	...	...

• NEW LIFE BUSINESS ISSUED ($000 omitted)

Year	Whole Life	Term	Credit	Group	Industrial	Total
2007	25,075	...	...	...	...	25,075
2008	22,258	...	...	...	...	22,258
2009	26,867	...	...	...	...	26,867

• LIFE INSURANCE IN FORCE ($000 omitted)

Year	Whole Life	Term	Credit	Group	Industrial	Total
2007	251,410	...	...	...	...	251,410
2008	259,901	...	...	...	...	259,901
2009	271,499	...	...	...	...	271,499

GUARANTEE TRUST LIFE INS CO

1275 Milwaukee Avenue
Glenview, Illinois 60025
Tel: 847-699-0600

AMB#: 006503
Began Business: 06/16/1936
Agency Off: Richard S. Holson III

Best's Financial Strength Rating: B+ **FSC:** VI

• NET PREMIUMS AND DEPOSITS ($000 omitted)

Year	Individual Life	Individual & Group Annuities	Group Life & A&H	Credit Life & A&H	Individual A&H	Total
2007	17,457	79	54,343	5,496	53,365	130,741
2008	17,712	34	72,540	6,040	64,106	160,432
2009	16,377	33	65,293	4,493	78,391	164,588

• NET OPERATING GAIN ($000 omitted)

Year	Individual Life	Individual & Group Annuities	Group Life & A&H	Credit Life & A&H	Individual A&H	Total
2007	82	-7	191	-212	956	1,012
2008	3,039	-7	1,597	-384	-3,697	547
2009	2,318	-10	1,122	-604	200	3,026

• COMPARATIVE FINANCIALS ($000 omitted)

Year	Assets	Capital & Surplus	Net Invest Income	Benefits Paid	Realized Cap Gains	Policyholder Dividends	Contract Lns (% of assets)
2007	207,663	43,517	8,525	70,942	...	...	1.1
2008	218,660	42,048	8,879	87,855	-1,808	...	1.0
2009	232,502	40,358	9,792	82,110	-1,442	...	0.9

• ORDINARY LIFE STATISTICS

Year	Av. Ord. Policy Issued ($)	Av. Ord. Policy In Force ($)	Avg. Prem ($/M)	1st Yr Prem/ Total Prem	Ord. Lapse Ratio
2007	37,592	13,261	11.76	10.7	18.8
2008	39,843	13,162	11.71	11.4	18.8
2009	49,089	13,265	11.65	11.7	19.1

• NEW LIFE BUSINESS ISSUED ($000 omitted)

Year	Whole Life	Term	Credit	Group	Industrial	Total
2007	112,705	618,577	1,639,922	39,284	...	2,410,488
2008	123,090	449,931	2,499,259	19,698	...	3,091,978
2009	26,820	513,208	2,663,652	15,595	...	3,219,275

• LIFE INSURANCE IN FORCE ($000 omitted)

Year	Whole Life	Term	Credit	Group	Industrial	Total
2007	1,426,742	1,785,326	1,142,662	376,687	...	4,731,417
2008	1,377,638	1,650,580	1,034,363	253,543	...	4,316,124
2009	1,222,074	1,645,843	897,104	145,350	...	3,910,371

GUARANTY INCOME LIFE INS CO

P.O. Box 2231
Baton Rouge, Louisiana 70821-2231
Tel: 800-535-8110

AMB#: 006504
Began Business: 02/11/1926
Agency Off: None

Best's Financial Strength Rating: B
FSC: V

• **NET PREMIUMS AND DEPOSITS ($000 omitted)**

Year	Individual Life	Individual & Group Annuities	Group Life & A&H	Credit Life & A&H	Individual A&H	Total
2007	2,186	54,345	...	...	2,613	59,143
2008	2,018	65,710	...	...	2,803	70,531
2009	1,934	78,222	...	...	2,939	83,095

• **NET OPERATING GAIN ($000 omitted)**

Year	Individual Life	Individual & Group Annuities	Group Life & A&H	Credit Life & A&H	Individual A&H	Total
2007	-826	1,383	...	...	265	822
2008	73	743	...	...	126	942
2009	46	818	...	...	207	1,071

• **COMPARATIVE FINANCIALS ($000 omitted)**

Year	Assets	Capital & Surplus	Net Invest Income	Benefits Paid	Realized Cap Gains	Policyholder Dividends	Contract Lns (% of assets)
2007	373,694	23,597	18,865	49,303	92	...	0.4
2008	407,337	22,716	20,858	44,073	-1,839	...	0.4
2009	457,793	21,573	20,472	39,012	-2,701	...	0.3

• **ORDINARY LIFE STATISTICS**

Year	Av. Ord. Policy Issued ($)	Av. Ord. Policy In Force ($)	Avg. Prem ($/M)	1st Yr Prem/ Total Prem	Ord. Lapse Ratio
2007	...	...	...	...	...
2008	...	...	...	...	...
2009	...	...	...	...	...

• **NEW LIFE BUSINESS ISSUED ($000 omitted)**

Year	Whole Life	Term	Credit	Group	Industrial	Total
2007	972	...	...	...	...	972
2008	743	...	...	...	...	743
2009	391	...	...	...	...	391

• **LIFE INSURANCE IN FORCE ($000 omitted)**

Year	Whole Life	Term	Credit	Group	Industrial	Total
2007	263,239	36,149	...	...	...	299,388
2008	251,119	33,349	...	...	...	284,468
2009	235,579	30,683	...	...	...	266,262

GUARDIAN INS & ANNUITY CO INC

7 Hanover Square
New York, New York 10004-4025
Tel: 212-598-8000

AMB#: 008197
Began Business: 12/27/1971
Agency Off: None

Best's Financial Strength Rating: A++g
FSC: XV

• **NET PREMIUMS AND DEPOSITS ($000 omitted)**

Year	Individual Life	Individual & Group Annuities	Group Life & A&H	Credit Life & A&H	Individual A&H	Total
2007	7,367	1,182,381	368	...	...	1,190,117
2008	6,747	934,051	335	...	...	941,133
2009	8,770	1,301,508	299	...	...	1,310,577

• **NET OPERATING GAIN ($000 omitted)**

Year	Individual Life	Individual & Group Annuities	Group Life & A&H	Credit Life & A&H	Individual A&H	Total
2007	-73	17,730	66	...	...	17,723
2008	1,714	-34,840	-284	...	...	-33,411
2009	4,044	33,126	-1,162	...	...	36,008

• **COMPARATIVE FINANCIALS ($000 omitted)**

Year	Assets	Capital & Surplus	Net Invest Income	Benefits Paid	Realized Cap Gains	Policyholder Dividends	Contract Lns (% of assets)
2007	10,402,935	244,674	111,225	1,908,140	2,270	...	0.9
2008	7,502,709	212,558	101,387	1,466,253	-1,687	...	1.3
2009	9,022,922	236,201	98,078	1,046,093	-26,109	...	1.1

• **ORDINARY LIFE STATISTICS**

Year	Av. Ord. Policy Issued ($)	Av. Ord. Policy In Force ($)	Avg. Prem ($/M)	1st Yr Prem/ Total Prem	Ord. Lapse Ratio
2007	...	...	...	...	...
2008	...	...	...	...	...
2009	...	...	...	...	...

• **NEW LIFE BUSINESS ISSUED ($000 omitted)**

Year	Whole Life	Term	Credit	Group	Industrial	Total
2007	174,073	3,092	...	89,727	...	266,892
2008	312,485	2,750	...	59,398	...	374,633
2009	572,179	950	...	29,437	...	602,566

• **LIFE INSURANCE IN FORCE ($000 omitted)**

Year	Whole Life	Term	Credit	Group	Industrial	Total
2007	6,125,702	339,010	...	566,627	...	7,031,339
2008	5,768,847	262,284	...	520,366	...	6,551,497
2009	5,736,022	227,397	...	456,758	...	6,420,177

GUARDIAN LIFE INS CO OF AMER

7 Hanover Square
New York, New York 10004-4025
Tel: 212-598-8000

AMB#: 006508
Began Business: 07/16/1860
Agency Off: Donald P. Sullivan

Best's Financial Strength Rating: A++g
FSC: XV

• **NET PREMIUMS AND DEPOSITS ($000 omitted)**

Year	Individual Life	Individual & Group Annuities	Group Life & A&H	Credit Life & A&H	Individual A&H	Total
2007	2,569,950	174,751	3,317,486	0	4,204	6,066,338
2008	2,690,473	154,262	3,205,020	...	5,012	6,054,735
2009	2,967,234	156,327	2,933,857	...	2,145	6,059,565

• **NET OPERATING GAIN ($000 omitted)**

Year	Individual Life	Individual & Group Annuities	Group Life & A&H	Credit Life & A&H	Individual A&H	Total
2007	60,498	1,120	157,853	-1,889	-71	218,614
2008	22,318	89,612	198,967	4,433	-2,254	311,513
2009	29,942	-10,494	109,596	-1,761	-3,706	124,193

• **COMPARATIVE FINANCIALS ($000 omitted)**

Year	Assets	Capital & Surplus	Net Invest Income	Benefits Paid	Realized Cap Gains	Policyholder Dividends	Contract Lns (% of assets)
2007	28,328,340	3,750,545	1,438,393	3,734,638	73,412	651,401	7.3
2008	28,973,450	3,658,868	1,466,926	3,729,389	125,797	714,168	7.9
2009	30,895,175	4,187,965	1,551,424	3,768,615	-96,460	708,415	8.0

• **ORDINARY LIFE STATISTICS**

Year	Av. Ord. Policy Issued ($)	Av. Ord. Policy In Force ($)	Avg. Prem ($/M)	1st Yr Prem/ Total Prem	Ord. Lapse Ratio
2007	638,029	76,578	12.61	7.3	5.6
2008	667,112	92,399	12.58	7.1	5.8
2009	661,490	102,261	13.16	6.7	6.0

• **NEW LIFE BUSINESS ISSUED ($000 omitted)**

Year	Whole Life	Term	Credit	Group	Industrial	Total
2007	10,350,900	14,929,737	...	15,636,842	...	40,917,479
2008	10,993,489	14,351,442	...	15,682,538	...	41,027,469
2009	11,382,041	16,612,887	...	14,505,516	...	42,500,444

• **LIFE INSURANCE IN FORCE ($000 omitted)**

Year	Whole Life	Term	Credit	Group	Industrial	Total
2007	156,483,731	60,455,876	191	124,559,028	...	341,498,826
2008	155,992,279	71,655,291	51	127,604,083	...	355,251,704
2009	161,529,147	77,888,650	15	118,346,591	...	357,764,403

GULF GUARANTY LIFE INS CO

4785 I-55 North, Suite 200
Jackson, Mississippi 39206
Tel: 601-981-4920

AMB#: 008081
Began Business: 07/08/1970
Agency Off: None

Best's Financial Strength Rating: B-
FSC: IV

• **NET PREMIUMS AND DEPOSITS ($000 omitted)**

Year	Individual Life	Individual & Group Annuities	Group Life & A&H	Credit Life & A&H	Individual A&H	Total
2007	442	101	129	5,727	...	6,400
2008	510	201	103	6,105	...	6,919
2009	590	190	88	5,251	...	6,119

• **NET OPERATING GAIN ($000 omitted)**

Year	Individual Life	Individual & Group Annuities	Group Life & A&H	Credit Life & A&H	Individual A&H	Total
2007	-153	390	72	-796	...	-487
2008	-137	-2	47	-425	...	-517
2009	-69	-2	10	106	...	45

• **COMPARATIVE FINANCIALS ($000 omitted)**

Year	Assets	Capital & Surplus	Net Invest Income	Benefits Paid	Realized Cap Gains	Policyholder Dividends	Contract Lns (% of assets)
2007	16,245	7,524	316	1,444	312	...	...
2008	17,799	8,438	387	1,653	1,074	...	...
2009	17,827	8,466	354	1,486	-91	...	...

• **ORDINARY LIFE STATISTICS**

Year	Av. Ord. Policy Issued ($)	Av. Ord. Policy In Force ($)	Avg. Prem ($/M)	1st Yr Prem/ Total Prem	Ord. Lapse Ratio
2007	...	...	...	...	...
2008	...	...	...	...	...
2009	...	...	...	...	...

• **NEW LIFE BUSINESS ISSUED ($000 omitted)**

Year	Whole Life	Term	Credit	Group	Industrial	Total
2007	380	...	262,187	...	5,667	268,234
2008	420	...	283,282	...	4,651	288,353
2009	2,890	...	260,357	...	6,381	269,628

• **LIFE INSURANCE IN FORCE ($000 omitted)**

Year	Whole Life	Term	Credit	Group	Industrial	Total
2007	4,435	10	365,380	...	9,397	379,222
2008	3,695	150	392,377	...	10,438	406,660
2009	4,850	345	397,756	...	13,638	416,589

HANNOVER LIFE REASSURANCE AMER

800 N. Magnolia Avenue, Suite 1400
Orlando, Florida 32803-3268
Tel: 407-649-8411

AMB#: 068031
Began Business: 10/01/1988
Agency Off: None

Best's Financial Strength Rating: A g
FSC: XV

• NET PREMIUMS AND DEPOSITS ($000 omitted)

Year	Individual Life	Individual & Group Annuities	Group Life & A&H	Credit Life & A&H	Individual A&H	Total
2007	158,256	11,242	34,750	...	91,224	295,472
2008	605,481	8,914	45,217	...	128,732	788,343
2009	168,108	35,508	53,274	5,784	140,332	403,006

• NET OPERATING GAIN ($000 omitted)

Year	Individual Life	Individual & Group Annuities	Group Life & A&H	Credit Life & A&H	Individual A&H	Total
2007	-7,918	1,569	36,971	...	-5,225	28,379
2008	-6,104	-842	2,404	...	-1,705	-4,805
2009	-6,029	736	3,946	-1,679	-1,132	-4,142

• COMPARATIVE FINANCIALS ($000 omitted)

Year	Assets	Capital & Surplus	Net Invest Income	Benefits Paid	Realized Cap Gains	Policyholder Dividends	Contract Lns (% of assets)
2007	1,710,630	136,570	51,875	271,236	1,940	-248	0.2
2008	3,572,590	128,073	48,922	312,725	-6,552	252	0.1
2009	3,499,867	140,766	60,584	340,746	-1,915	219	0.8

• ORDINARY LIFE STATISTICS

Year	Av. Ord. Policy Issued ($)	Av. Ord. Policy In Force ($)	Avg. Prem ($/M)	1st Yr Prem/ Total Prem	Ord. Lapse Ratio
2007	...	...	101.87	...	5.4
2008	...	...	22.20	...	5.5
2009	...	...	10.79	...	8.9

• NEW LIFE BUSINESS ISSUED ($000 omitted)

Year	Whole Life	Term	Credit	Group	Industrial	Total
2007	...	...	...	...	...	...
2008	...	...	...	...	...	...
2009	...	...	...	...	...	...

• LIFE INSURANCE IN FORCE ($000 omitted)

Year	Whole Life	Term	Credit	Group	Industrial	Total
2007	15,901,079	77,690,497	...	798,607	...	94,390,183
2008	46,674,751	228,046,448	...	10,559,288	...	285,280,487
2009	46,708,347	445,302,067	73,726	217,378,201	...	709,462,341

HARTFORD INTERNAT LIFE REASSUR

200 Hopmeadow Street
Simsbury, Connecticut 06089
Tel: 860-525-8555

AMB#: 009117
Began Business: 09/23/1987
Agency Off: None

Best's Financial Strength Rating: A-
FSC: VII

• NET PREMIUMS AND DEPOSITS ($000 omitted)

Year	Individual Life	Individual & Group Annuities	Group Life & A&H	Credit Life & A&H	Individual A&H	Total
2007	9,943	...	2,680	...	...	12,623
2008	7,204	...	2,576	...	...	9,780
2009	9,502	...	2,490	...	...	11,993

• NET OPERATING GAIN ($000 omitted)

Year	Individual Life	Individual & Group Annuities	Group Life & A&H	Credit Life & A&H	Individual A&H	Total
2007	1,271	...	1,771	...	...	4,086
2008	1,948	...	1,928	...	...	4,721
2009	1,858	...	1,521	...	...	4,182

• COMPARATIVE FINANCIALS ($000 omitted)

Year	Assets	Capital & Surplus	Net Invest Income	Benefits Paid	Realized Cap Gains	Policyholder Dividends	Contract Lns (% of assets)
2007	1,135,919	106,354	65,192	53,250	-368	6,580	58.9
2008	1,115,772	102,380	67,325	55,579	-366	7,554	63.8
2009	1,129,423	91,849	66,652	58,718	-7,481	7,932	63.2

• ORDINARY LIFE STATISTICS

Year	Av. Ord. Policy Issued ($)	Av. Ord. Policy In Force ($)	Avg. Prem ($/M)	1st Yr Prem/ Total Prem	Ord. Lapse Ratio
2007	...	...	...	...	...
2008	...	...	...	...	...
2009	...	...	...	...	...

• NEW LIFE BUSINESS ISSUED ($000 omitted)

Year	Whole Life	Term	Credit	Group	Industrial	Total
2007	...	...	...	...	...	...
2008	...	...	...	...	...	...
2009	...	...	...	...	...	...

• LIFE INSURANCE IN FORCE ($000 omitted)

Year	Whole Life	Term	Credit	Group	Industrial	Total
2007	244,597	8,247,805	...	761,860	...	9,254,262
2008	293,460	7,275,804	...	779,922	...	8,349,186
2009	290,810	6,928,810	...	789,223	...	8,008,843

HARLEYSVILLE LIFE INS CO

355 Maple Avenue
Harleysville, Pennsylvania 19438-2297
Tel: 215-513-6400

AMB#: 006517
Began Business: 06/12/1961
Agency Off: William J. Tevlin

Best's Financial Strength Rating: A-
FSC: V

• NET PREMIUMS AND DEPOSITS ($000 omitted)

Year	Individual Life	Individual & Group Annuities	Group Life & A&H	Credit Life & A&H	Individual A&H	Total
2007	15,358	16,751	20,535	...	58	52,702
2008	14,130	15,950	21,591	...	40	51,711
2009	15,995	16,825	20,429	...	41	53,291

• NET OPERATING GAIN ($000 omitted)

Year	Individual Life	Individual & Group Annuities	Group Life & A&H	Credit Life & A&H	Individual A&H	Total
2007	-1,841	211	-419	...	34	-2,015
2008	-1,896	-100	710	...	-18	-1,304
2009	-2,397	358	-954	...	-10	-3,003

• COMPARATIVE FINANCIALS ($000 omitted)

Year	Assets	Capital & Surplus	Net Invest Income	Benefits Paid	Realized Cap Gains	Policyholder Dividends	Contract Lns (% of assets)
2007	374,093	21,197	17,145	44,290	...	...	1.3
2008	341,303	20,319	17,258	41,918	-3,643	...	1.5
2009	356,484	18,967	17,203	39,815	231	...	1.7

• ORDINARY LIFE STATISTICS

Year	Av. Ord. Policy Issued ($)	Av. Ord. Policy In Force ($)	Avg. Prem ($/M)	1st Yr Prem/ Total Prem	Ord. Lapse Ratio
2007	346,065	208,767	3.64	14.4	2.2
2008	373,018	220,122	3.42	12.0	3.7
2009	331,666	227,743	3.39	12.8	4.2

• NEW LIFE BUSINESS ISSUED ($000 omitted)

Year	Whole Life	Term	Credit	Group	Industrial	Total
2007	65,794	1,019,120	...	958,007	...	2,042,921
2008	49,523	1,074,007	...	400,883	...	1,524,413
2009	63,061	995,618	...	470,106	...	1,528,785

• LIFE INSURANCE IN FORCE ($000 omitted)

Year	Whole Life	Term	Credit	Group	Industrial	Total
2007	1,321,056	7,615,006	...	5,008,891	...	13,944,953
2008	1,309,455	8,291,597	...	4,972,663	...	14,573,715
2009	1,412,516	8,674,445	...	4,226,079	...	14,313,040

HARTFORD LIFE & ACCIDENT INS

200 Hopmeadow Street
Simsbury, Connecticut 06089
Tel: 860-525-8555

AMB#: 007285
Began Business: 02/14/1967
Agency Off: None

Best's Financial Strength Rating: A g
FSC: XV

• NET PREMIUMS AND DEPOSITS ($000 omitted)

Year	Individual Life	Individual & Group Annuities	Group Life & A&H	Credit Life & A&H	Individual A&H	Total
2007	30,176	630,447	4,016,923	...	525	4,678,071
2008	31,299	757,785	4,004,258	...	7	4,793,349
2009	31,240	605,694	3,319,522	...	4	3,956,461

• NET OPERATING GAIN ($000 omitted)

Year	Individual Life	Individual & Group Annuities	Group Life & A&H	Credit Life & A&H	Individual A&H	Total
2007	15,567	206,843	317,226	...	-1,652	784,440
2008	13,286	196,223	348,253	...	-847	613,783
2009	5,517	43,124	253,605	...	-1,432	234,976

• COMPARATIVE FINANCIALS ($000 omitted)

Year	Assets	Capital & Surplus	Net Invest Income	Benefits Paid	Realized Cap Gains	Policyholder Dividends	Contract Lns (% of assets)
2007	14,187,519	5,786,073	945,556	2,769,235	-7,687	213	0.3
2008	14,413,998	6,045,731	741,066	2,799,881	-350,405	246	0.3
2009	14,254,524	6,005,261	424,951	2,296,426	-164,526	23	0.3

• ORDINARY LIFE STATISTICS

Year	Av. Ord. Policy Issued ($)	Av. Ord. Policy In Force ($)	Avg. Prem ($/M)	1st Yr Prem/ Total Prem	Ord. Lapse Ratio
2007	...	158,107	11.10	...	6.7
2008	...	130,221	12.03	...	6.0
2009	10,000	126,461	12.79	...	6.9

• NEW LIFE BUSINESS ISSUED ($000 omitted)

Year	Whole Life	Term	Credit	Group	Industrial	Total
2007	...	...	...	63,805,015	...	63,805,015
2008	...	...	...	95,131,318	...	95,131,318
2009	...	40	...	77,671,034	...	77,671,074

• LIFE INSURANCE IN FORCE ($000 omitted)

Year	Whole Life	Term	Credit	Group	Industrial	Total
2007	3,750,246	213,972	...	525,844,733	...	529,808,951
2008	3,415,881	213,759	...	621,065,817	...	624,695,457
2009	3,141,377	186,067	...	663,200,218	...	666,527,662

HARTFORD LIFE AND ANNUITY INS

200 Hopmeadow Street
Simsbury, Connecticut 06089
Tel: 860-525-8555

AMB#: 007325
Began Business: 07/01/1965
Agency Off: None

Best's Financial Strength Rating: A g **FSC:** XV

• **NET PREMIUMS AND DEPOSITS ($000 omitted)**

Year	Individual Life	Individual & Group Annuities	Group Life & A&H	Credit Life & A&H	Individual A&H	Total
2007	856,271	9,599,426	2,484	...	1,144	10,459,324
2008	998,422	8,454,475	-6	...	1,047	9,453,938
2009	778,872	-55,839,611	-46	...	951	-55,059,834

• **NET OPERATING GAIN ($000 omitted)**

Year	Individual Life	Individual & Group Annuities	Group Life & A&H	Credit Life & A&H	Individual A&H	Total
2007	43,391	321,485	1,164	...	135	366,275
2008	65,020	-3,048,107	1,233	...	418	-2,944,267
2009	163,804	2,465,821	826	...	716	2,678,682

• **COMPARATIVE FINANCIALS ($000 omitted)**

Year	Assets	Capital & Surplus	Net Invest Income	Benefits Paid	Realized Cap Gains	Policyholder Dividends	Contract Lns (% of assets)
2007	89,347,777	2,556,588	348,437	9,893,235	-81,759	2,025	0.4
2008	65,460,546	2,177,858	376,034	10,638,911	961,162	1,555	0.5
2009	73,406,512	4,085,601	507,049	6,034,949	-270,071	945	0.5

• **ORDINARY LIFE STATISTICS**

Year	Av. Ord. Policy Issued ($)	Av. Ord. Policy In Force ($)	Avg. Prem ($/M)	1st Yr Prem/ Total Prem	Ord. Lapse Ratio
2007	478,683	258,525	10.89	47.5	4.3
2008	516,253	281,088	10.02	46.3	5.2
2009	443,701	298,800	8.59	38.8	4.9

• **NEW LIFE BUSINESS ISSUED ($000 omitted)**

Year	Whole Life	Term	Credit	Group	Industrial	Total
2007	13,287,107	10,711,207	...	...	...	23,998,314
2008	12,977,760	14,007,291	...	...	...	26,985,051
2009	9,128,264	10,781,037	...	...	...	19,909,301

• **LIFE INSURANCE IN FORCE ($000 omitted)**

Year	Whole Life	Term	Credit	Group	Industrial	Total
2007	107,030,890	46,346,612	...	291,583	...	153,669,085
2008	112,160,241	56,919,137	...	254,563	...	169,333,941
2009	115,860,554	63,598,157	...	233,360	...	179,692,071

HCC LIFE INSURANCE COMPANY

225 TownPark Drive, Suite 145
Kennesaw, Georgia 30144
Tel: 770-973-9851

AMB#: 009081
Began Business: 03/12/1981
Agency Off: Craig J. Kelbel

Best's Financial Strength Rating: A+ **FSC:** IX

• **NET PREMIUMS AND DEPOSITS ($000 omitted)**

Year	Individual Life	Individual & Group Annuities	Group Life & A&H	Credit Life & A&H	Individual A&H	Total
2007	...	...	645,447	...	4,082	649,529
2008	...	...	662,012	...	1,417	663,429
2009	...	...	650,564	...	1,274	651,838

• **NET OPERATING GAIN ($000 omitted)**

Year	Individual Life	Individual & Group Annuities	Group Life & A&H	Credit Life & A&H	Individual A&H	Total
2007	466	...	59,180	...	661	60,307
2008	448	...	63,396	...	1,832	65,677
2009	444	...	65,119	...	392	65,955

• **COMPARATIVE FINANCIALS ($000 omitted)**

Year	Assets	Capital & Surplus	Net Invest Income	Benefits Paid	Realized Cap Gains	Policyholder Dividends	Contract Lns (% of assets)
2007	623,203	336,165	23,513	500,150	3,926	...	...
2008	584,804	345,370	22,666	506,268	-5,381	...	...
2009	598,019	367,721	20,215	496,348	...	...	...

• **ORDINARY LIFE STATISTICS**

Year	Av. Ord. Policy Issued ($)	Av. Ord. Policy In Force ($)	Avg. Prem ($/M)	1st Yr Prem/ Total Prem	Ord. Lapse Ratio
2007	...	...	...	...	...
2008	...	...	...	...	...
2009	...	...	...	...	...

• **NEW LIFE BUSINESS ISSUED ($000 omitted)**

Year	Whole Life	Term	Credit	Group	Industrial	Total
2007	...	...	...	95,097	...	95,097
2008	...	...	...	425,396	...	425,396
2009	...	...	...	278,717	...	278,717

• **LIFE INSURANCE IN FORCE ($000 omitted)**

Year	Whole Life	Term	Credit	Group	Industrial	Total
2007	191,495	154,012	...	821,687	...	1,167,194
2008	177,694	143,526	...	931,448	...	1,252,668
2009	166,122	134,248	...	909,232	...	1,209,602

HARTFORD LIFE INS CO

200 Hopmeadow Street
Simsbury, Connecticut 06089
Tel: 860-525-8555

AMB#: 006518
Began Business: 01/01/1979
Agency Off: None

Best's Financial Strength Rating: A g **FSC:** XV

• **NET PREMIUMS AND DEPOSITS ($000 omitted)**

Year	Individual Life	Individual & Group Annuities	Group Life & A&H	Credit Life & A&H	Individual A&H	Total
2007	311,212	13,497,135	5,247,587	...	73	19,056,008
2008	217,731	10,880,541	229,234	...	73	11,327,579
2009	171,705	7,768,756	175,228	...	75	8,115,763

• **NET OPERATING GAIN ($000 omitted)**

Year	Individual Life	Individual & Group Annuities	Group Life & A&H	Credit Life & A&H	Individual A&H	Total
2007	55,163	27,278	-24,782	...	2	282,972
2008	12,947	-2,305,739	25,221	...	3	-2,179,124
2009	20,261	1,050,011	61,485	...	11	1,194,155

• **COMPARATIVE FINANCIALS ($000 omitted)**

Year	Assets	Capital & Surplus	Net Invest Income	Benefits Paid	Realized Cap Gains	Policyholder Dividends	Contract Lns (% of assets)
2007	165,997,882	4,448,474	2,061,543	12,913,433	-91,489	2,555	0.6
2008	133,562,466	4,071,384	1,838,924	11,888,095	-354,194	4,235	0.7
2009	140,231,960	5,365,015	1,388,954	10,046,723	-1,732,989	3,795	0.7

• **ORDINARY LIFE STATISTICS**

Year	Av. Ord. Policy Issued ($)	Av. Ord. Policy In Force ($)	Avg. Prem ($/M)	1st Yr Prem/ Total Prem	Ord. Lapse Ratio
2007	513,517	184,416	5.09	51.2	30.5
2008	669,597	187,297	3.70	34.8	2.9
2009	524,632	189,692	3.27	20.3	2.2

• **NEW LIFE BUSINESS ISSUED ($000 omitted)**

Year	Whole Life	Term	Credit	Group	Industrial	Total
2007	1,525,785	841,529	...	25,239,373	...	27,606,687
2008	1,261,740	1,025,602	...	5,035,663	...	7,323,005
2009	656,590	901,568	...	7,581,578	...	9,139,736

• **LIFE INSURANCE IN FORCE ($000 omitted)**

Year	Whole Life	Term	Credit	Group	Industrial	Total
2007	59,058,746	16,429,526	...	118,063,167	...	193,551,439
2008	59,549,449	15,618,648	...	109,475,015	...	184,643,112
2009	58,780,457	15,909,417	...	103,746,435	...	178,436,310

HEALTH NET LIFE INSURANCE CO

21281 Burbank Blvd., B3
Woodland Hills, California 91367-6607
Tel: 818-676-8256

AMB#: 006722
Began Business: 01/01/1987
Agency Off: Jerry V. Coil

Best's Financial Strength Rating: B+ g **FSC:** XIII

• **NET PREMIUMS AND DEPOSITS ($000 omitted)**

Year	Individual Life	Individual & Group Annuities	Group Life & A&H	Credit Life & A&H	Individual A&H	Total
2007	90	...	589,276	...	475,610	1,064,976
2008	82	...	632,328	...	608,813	1,241,223
2009	188	...	581,312	...	580,066	1,161,565

• **NET OPERATING GAIN ($000 omitted)**

Year	Individual Life	Individual & Group Annuities	Group Life & A&H	Credit Life & A&H	Individual A&H	Total
2007	-5	...	27,240	...	-47,189	-19,954
2008	-29	...	-7,094	...	22,690	15,568
2009	83	...	10,654	...	47,427	58,165

• **COMPARATIVE FINANCIALS ($000 omitted)**

Year	Assets	Capital & Surplus	Net Invest Income	Benefits Paid	Realized Cap Gains	Policyholder Dividends	Contract Lns (% of assets)
2007	656,005	233,580	18,236	838,241	...	...	0.0
2008	650,111	368,802	22,606	1,052,959	-1,481	...	0.0
2009	643,099	383,551	16,081	934,013	0	...	0.0

• **ORDINARY LIFE STATISTICS**

Year	Av. Ord. Policy Issued ($)	Av. Ord. Policy In Force ($)	Avg. Prem ($/M)	1st Yr Prem/ Total Prem	Ord. Lapse Ratio
2007	...	...	...	...	...
2008	...	...	...	...	...
2009	...	...	...	...	...

• **NEW LIFE BUSINESS ISSUED ($000 omitted)**

Year	Whole Life	Term	Credit	Group	Industrial	Total
2007	...	16,195	...	239,016	...	255,211
2008	...	5,320	...	165,304	...	170,624
2009	...	4,515	...	98,632	...	103,147

• **LIFE INSURANCE IN FORCE ($000 omitted)**

Year	Whole Life	Term	Credit	Group	Industrial	Total
2007	...	46,980	...	859,394	...	906,374
2008	...	41,065	...	836,490	...	877,555
2009	...	38,095	...	703,060	...	741,155

HEALTHY ALLIANCE LIFE INS CO

6775 W Washington Street
Milwaukee, Wisconsin 53214
Tel: 314-923-4444

AMB#: 008217
Began Business: 06/09/1971
Agency Off: John A. O'Rourke

Best's Financial Strength Rating: A g
FSC: IX

• NET PREMIUMS AND DEPOSITS ($000 omitted)

Year	Individual Life	Individual & Group Annuities	Group Life & A&H	Credit Life & A&H	Individual A&H	Total
2007	-1	1,868	1,193,837	...	285,219	1,480,923
2008	...	70	1,229,414	...	324,004	1,553,489
2009	...	...	1,266,083	...	325,081	1,591,164

• NET OPERATING GAIN ($000 omitted)

Year	Individual Life	Individual & Group Annuities	Group Life & A&H	Credit Life & A&H	Individual A&H	Total
2007	-9	...	69,949	...	14,979	84,918
2008	...	...	90,036	...	26,299	116,334
2009	...	...	87,866	...	26,853	114,719

• COMPARATIVE FINANCIALS ($000 omitted)

Year	Assets	Capital & Surplus	Net Invest Income	Benefits Paid	Realized Cap Gains	Policyholder Dividends	Contract Lns (% of assets)
2007	541,529	213,983	20,752	1,188,714	-1,889	...	...
2008	598,258	268,945	21,915	1,230,518	-8,799	...	...
2009	624,295	252,111	25,008	1,263,824	-8,054	...	...

• ORDINARY LIFE STATISTICS

Year	Av. Ord. Policy Issued ($)	Av. Ord. Policy In Force ($)	Avg. Prem ($/M)	1st Yr Prem/ Total Prem	Ord. Lapse Ratio
2007	...	...	...	...	...
2008	...	...	...	...	...
2009	...	...	...	...	...

• NEW LIFE BUSINESS ISSUED ($000 omitted)

Year	Whole Life	Term	Credit	Group	Industrial	Total
2007	...	...	...	...	...	...
2008	...	...	...	...	...	...
2009	...	...	...	...	...	...

• LIFE INSURANCE IN FORCE ($000 omitted)

Year	Whole Life	Term	Credit	Group	Industrial	Total
2007	...	...	...	3,191	...	3,191
2008	...	...	...	...	...	...
2009	...	...	...	...	...	...

HM LIFE INSURANCE COMPANY NY

P.O. Box 535061
Pittsburgh, Pennsylvania 15253-5061
Tel: 800-235-6753

AMB#: 060209
Began Business: 03/26/1997
Agency Off: Mark Lancellotti

Best's Financial Strength Rating: A- g
FSC: VIII

• NET PREMIUMS AND DEPOSITS ($000 omitted)

Year	Individual Life	Individual & Group Annuities	Group Life & A&H	Credit Life & A&H	Individual A&H	Total
2007	8	...	53,658	...	...	53,666
2008	-9	...	53,298	...	...	53,289
2009	...	...	61,236	...	...	61,236

• NET OPERATING GAIN ($000 omitted)

Year	Individual Life	Individual & Group Annuities	Group Life & A&H	Credit Life & A&H	Individual A&H	Total
2007	13	...	59	...	...	72
2008	-1	...	2,033	...	...	2,032
2009	...	...	-1,121	...	...	-1,121

• COMPARATIVE FINANCIALS ($000 omitted)

Year	Assets	Capital & Surplus	Net Invest Income	Benefits Paid	Realized Cap Gains	Policyholder Dividends	Contract Lns (% of assets)
2007	50,989	19,574	1,965	43,468	-21	...	...
2008	41,849	21,550	1,527	39,372	0	...	...
2009	41,082	20,592	1,329	50,035	...	...	...

• ORDINARY LIFE STATISTICS

Year	Av. Ord. Policy Issued ($)	Av. Ord. Policy In Force ($)	Avg. Prem ($/M)	1st Yr Prem/ Total Prem	Ord. Lapse Ratio
2007	...	...	...	...	...
2008	...	...	...	...	...
2009	...	...	...	...	...

• NEW LIFE BUSINESS ISSUED ($000 omitted)

Year	Whole Life	Term	Credit	Group	Industrial	Total
2007	270	...	...	6,011	...	6,281
2008	...	...	...	...	...	...
2009	...	...	...	...	...	...

• LIFE INSURANCE IN FORCE ($000 omitted)

Year	Whole Life	Term	Credit	Group	Industrial	Total
2007	155	...	...	3,072,046	...	3,072,201
2008	...	...	...	...	...	...
2009	...	...	...	...	...	...

HM LIFE INSURANCE COMPANY

P.O. Box 535061
Pittsburgh, Pennsylvania 15253-5061
Tel: 800-328-5433

AMB#: 009063
Began Business: 05/12/1981
Agency Off: Mark Lancellotti

Best's Financial Strength Rating: A- g
FSC: VIII

• NET PREMIUMS AND DEPOSITS ($000 omitted)

Year	Individual Life	Individual & Group Annuities	Group Life & A&H	Credit Life & A&H	Individual A&H	Total
2007	203	...	315,683	...	...	315,886
2008	327	...	383,619	...	...	383,947
2009	311	...	393,789	...	...	394,099

• NET OPERATING GAIN ($000 omitted)

Year	Individual Life	Individual & Group Annuities	Group Life & A&H	Credit Life & A&H	Individual A&H	Total
2007	22	...	4,598	...	...	4,620
2008	-145	...	2,263	...	...	2,119
2009	23	...	12,695	...	...	12,718

• COMPARATIVE FINANCIALS ($000 omitted)

Year	Assets	Capital & Surplus	Net Invest Income	Benefits Paid	Realized Cap Gains	Policyholder Dividends	Contract Lns (% of assets)
2007	317,951	141,816	12,968	234,916	-174	...	...
2008	350,111	148,492	12,032	299,111	-2,152	...	...
2009	346,167	157,802	10,812	282,300	0	...	...

• ORDINARY LIFE STATISTICS

Year	Av. Ord. Policy Issued ($)	Av. Ord. Policy In Force ($)	Avg. Prem ($/M)	1st Yr Prem/ Total Prem	Ord. Lapse Ratio
2007	...	...	...	...	...
2008	...	...	...	...	...
2009	...	...	...	...	...

• NEW LIFE BUSINESS ISSUED ($000 omitted)

Year	Whole Life	Term	Credit	Group	Industrial	Total
2007	10,858	...	...	12,972	...	23,830
2008	30,971	...	...	...	...	30,971
2009	2,122	...	...	...	...	2,122

• LIFE INSURANCE IN FORCE ($000 omitted)

Year	Whole Life	Term	Credit	Group	Industrial	Total
2007	15,371	...	...	27,699	...	43,070
2008	46,308	...	...	17,672	...	63,980
2009	46,519	...	...	8,973	...	55,492

HOMESTEADERS LIFE CO

P.O. Box 1756
Des Moines, Iowa 50306-1756
Tel: 515-440-7777

AMB#: 006534
Began Business: 02/13/1906
Agency Off: Stephen R. Lang

Best's Financial Strength Rating: B++
FSC: VIII

• NET PREMIUMS AND DEPOSITS ($000 omitted)

Year	Individual Life	Individual & Group Annuities	Group Life & A&H	Credit Life & A&H	Individual A&H	Total
2007	16,575	8,247	307,735	...	...	332,558
2008	12,958	9,103	321,782	...	...	343,843
2009	13,496	9,161	339,604	...	...	362,261

• NET OPERATING GAIN ($000 omitted)

Year	Individual Life	Individual & Group Annuities	Group Life & A&H	Credit Life & A&H	Individual A&H	Total
2007	4,004	57	4,520	...	...	8,581
2008	386	59	7,877	...	...	8,322
2009	499	52	9,861	...	...	10,412

• COMPARATIVE FINANCIALS ($000 omitted)

Year	Assets	Capital & Surplus	Net Invest Income	Benefits Paid	Realized Cap Gains	Policyholder Dividends	Contract Lns (% of assets)
2007	1,473,812	74,720	78,566	190,279	-815	...	0.1
2008	1,602,425	79,208	84,702	213,918	-8,162	...	0.1
2009	1,762,231	94,432	91,548	217,968	-86	...	0.1

• ORDINARY LIFE STATISTICS

Year	Av. Ord. Policy Issued ($)	Av. Ord. Policy In Force ($)	Avg. Prem ($/M)	1st Yr Prem/ Total Prem	Ord. Lapse Ratio
2007	4,230	3,112	60.03	5.0	-1.5
2008	5,732	3,198	48.08	1.2	-1.3
2009	6,226	3,296	50.85	3.0	-1.1

• NEW LIFE BUSINESS ISSUED ($000 omitted)

Year	Whole Life	Term	Credit	Group	Industrial	Total
2007	11,993	...	...	318,542	...	330,535
2008	8,650	...	...	321,927	...	330,577
2009	10,404	...	...	339,140	...	349,544

• LIFE INSURANCE IN FORCE ($000 omitted)

Year	Whole Life	Term	Credit	Group	Industrial	Total
2007	266,335	9,782	...	1,864,077	...	2,140,194
2008	260,434	9,092	...	2,034,059	...	2,303,585
2009	256,764	8,682	...	2,216,937	...	2,482,383

HORACE MANN LIFE INS CO

One Horace Mann Plaza
Springfield, Illinois 62715
Tel: 217-789-2500

AMB#: 006535
Began Business: 09/19/1949
Agency Off: Daniel M. Jensen

Best's Financial Strength Rating: A-
FSC: IX

• NET PREMIUMS AND DEPOSITS ($000 omitted)

Year	Individual Life	Individual & Group Annuities	Group Life & A&H	Credit Life & A&H	Individual A&H	Total
2007	93,730	365,062	5,299	...	1,833	465,924
2008	93,734	334,215	5,475	...	1,738	435,162
2009	92,520	369,296	4,767	...	1,596	468,179

• NET OPERATING GAIN ($000 omitted)

Year	Individual Life	Individual & Group Annuities	Group Life & A&H	Credit Life & A&H	Individual A&H	Total
2007	15,291	14,546	792	...	231	30,860
2008	17,173	13,692	308	...	4	31,178
2009	16,463	21,052	140	...	172	37,827

• COMPARATIVE FINANCIALS ($000 omitted)

Year	Assets	Capital & Surplus	Net Invest Income	Benefits Paid	Realized Cap Gains	Policyholder Dividends	Contract Lns (% of assets)
2007	5,069,884	276,611	185,049	431,123	-4,791	...	2.0
2008	4,540,834	270,433	194,700	346,854	-41,921	...	2.3
2009	5,087,047	307,550	212,795	314,131	1,666	...	2.2

• ORDINARY LIFE STATISTICS

Year	Av. Ord. Policy Issued ($)	Av. Ord. Policy In Force ($)	Avg. Prem ($/M)	1st Yr Prem/ Total Prem	Ord. Lapse Ratio
2007	164,708	70,971	8.03	4.9	5.9
2008	164,243	73,332	7.95	4.1	5.5
2009	165,901	75,845	7.70	4.4	5.6

• NEW LIFE BUSINESS ISSUED ($000 omitted)

Year	Whole Life	Term	Credit	Group	Industrial	Total
2007	177,348	917,465	...	16,774	...	1,111,587
2008	154,665	861,668	...	18,139	...	1,034,472
2009	159,456	915,418	...	7,438	...	1,082,312

• LIFE INSURANCE IN FORCE ($000 omitted)

Year	Whole Life	Term	Credit	Group	Industrial	Total
2007	4,660,287	7,432,281	...	1,483,970	...	13,576,538
2008	4,578,749	7,714,398	...	1,378,698	...	13,671,845
2009	4,508,754	8,032,267	...	1,220,231	...	13,761,252

HUMANA INSURANCE COMPANY

P.O. Box 740036
Louisville, Kentucky 40201-7436
Tel: 920-336-1100

AMB#: 007574
Began Business: 12/31/1968
Agency Off: Michael B. McCallister

Best's Financial Strength Rating: A- g
FSC: XV

• NET PREMIUMS AND DEPOSITS ($000 omitted)

Year	Individual Life	Individual & Group Annuities	Group Life & A&H	Credit Life & A&H	Individual A&H	Total
2007	937	28	3,220,292	...	8,978,308	12,199,565
2008	1,452	68	3,686,310	...	10,380,108	14,067,938
2009	1,502	225	3,961,144	...	10,281,290	14,244,161

• NET OPERATING GAIN ($000 omitted)

Year	Individual Life	Individual & Group Annuities	Group Life & A&H	Credit Life & A&H	Individual A&H	Total
2007	-937	-122	174,008	...	315,899	488,848
2008	-1,474	-58	109,182	...	236,496	344,146
2009	-675	-265	18,893	...	306,960	324,914

• COMPARATIVE FINANCIALS ($000 omitted)

Year	Assets	Capital & Surplus	Net Invest Income	Benefits Paid	Realized Cap Gains	Policyholder Dividends	Contract Lns (% of assets)
2007	3,836,602	1,879,192	265,958	9,959,175	3,309	...	...
2008	4,063,225	2,189,471	216,329	11,882,890	-23,263	...	...
2009	4,373,948	2,182,713	136,326	11,627,188	-16,850	...	...

• ORDINARY LIFE STATISTICS

Year	Av. Ord. Policy Issued ($)	Av. Ord. Policy In Force ($)	Avg. Prem ($/M)	1st Yr Prem/ Total Prem	Ord. Lapse Ratio
2007	...	...	...	...	...
2008	...	...	...	...	...
2009	...	...	...	...	...

• NEW LIFE BUSINESS ISSUED ($000 omitted)

Year	Whole Life	Term	Credit	Group	Industrial	Total
2007	...	295,321	...	2,166,601	...	2,461,922
2008	...	296,662	...	2,320,726	...	2,617,388
2009	...	181,084	...	1,686,253	...	1,867,337

• LIFE INSURANCE IN FORCE ($000 omitted)

Year	Whole Life	Term	Credit	Group	Industrial	Total
2007	...	674,091	...	8,162,030	...	8,836,121
2008	...	828,255	...	8,276,473	...	9,104,728
2009	45	818,064	...	7,810,511	...	8,628,620

HOUSEHOLD LIFE INS CO

200 Somerset Corporate Blvd., Suite 100
Bridgewater, New Jersey 08807
Tel: 800-443-7187

AMB#: 009129
Began Business: 01/21/1981
Agency Off: None

Best's Financial Strength Rating: A g
FSC: IX

• NET PREMIUMS AND DEPOSITS ($000 omitted)

Year	Individual Life	Individual & Group Annuities	Group Life & A&H	Credit Life & A&H	Individual A&H	Total
2007	46,651	...	42,190	174,363	2,403	265,606
2008	65,095	3	38,312	140,889	2,684	246,982
2009	58,360	3	32,096	114,366	2,291	207,116

• NET OPERATING GAIN ($000 omitted)

Year	Individual Life	Individual & Group Annuities	Group Life & A&H	Credit Life & A&H	Individual A&H	Total
2007	-4,017	0	11,819	49,453	2,327	59,583
2008	-23,697	...	9,383	40,860	2,067	28,614
2009	-26,121	0	10,180	31,682	1,536	17,278

• COMPARATIVE FINANCIALS ($000 omitted)

Year	Assets	Capital & Surplus	Net Invest Income	Benefits Paid	Realized Cap Gains	Policyholder Dividends	Contract Lns (% of assets)
2007	943,406	424,004	54,025	140,433	6	...	5.3
2008	829,108	329,513	43,805	132,204	-15,907	...	5.5
2009	797,433	351,666	35,440	101,878	1,395	...	4.9

• ORDINARY LIFE STATISTICS

Year	Av. Ord. Policy Issued ($)	Av. Ord. Policy In Force ($)	Avg. Prem ($/M)	1st Yr Prem/ Total Prem	Ord. Lapse Ratio
2007	132,090	45,076	5.10	99.9	15.3
2008	169,616	58,941	5.28	10.0	27.5
2009	179,889	71,474	4.51	60.3	20.7

• NEW LIFE BUSINESS ISSUED ($000 omitted)

Year	Whole Life	Term	Credit	Group	Industrial	Total
2007	...	1,785,325	4,317,862	1,247,437	...	7,350,624
2008	...	5,851,750	2,465,224	301,436	...	8,618,410
2009	...	5,891,005	1,738,146	21,890	...	7,651,041

• LIFE INSURANCE IN FORCE ($000 omitted)

Year	Whole Life	Term	Credit	Group	Industrial	Total
2007	14,434	9,184,039	14,058,298	7,909,482	...	31,166,253
2008	13,217	13,017,743	11,857,022	6,564,901	...	31,452,883
2009	12,403	14,624,731	10,031,782	5,562,275	...	30,231,191

HUMANA INSURANCE COMPANY OF KY

500 West Main Street
Louisville, Kentucky 40202
Tel: 502-580-1000

AMB#: 060248
Began Business: 01/01/2001
Agency Off: Michael B. McCallister

Best's Financial Strength Rating: A- g
FSC: XV

• NET PREMIUMS AND DEPOSITS ($000 omitted)

Year	Individual Life	Individual & Group Annuities	Group Life & A&H	Credit Life & A&H	Individual A&H	Total
2007	60	...	19,770	...	817	20,647
2008	99	...	24,427	...	1,702	26,229
2009	116	...	30,915	...	2,660	33,691

• NET OPERATING GAIN ($000 omitted)

Year	Individual Life	Individual & Group Annuities	Group Life & A&H	Credit Life & A&H	Individual A&H	Total
2007	-40	...	874	...	-147	686
2008	-53	...	8,280	...	-1,188	7,039
2009	-98	...	704	...	-458	148

• COMPARATIVE FINANCIALS ($000 omitted)

Year	Assets	Capital & Surplus	Net Invest Income	Benefits Paid	Realized Cap Gains	Policyholder Dividends	Contract Lns (% of assets)
2007	22,608	13,271	818	16,986	...	...	...
2008	29,640	18,978	377	13,210	1	...	...
2009	34,240	19,574	157	29,495	0	...	...

• ORDINARY LIFE STATISTICS

Year	Av. Ord. Policy Issued ($)	Av. Ord. Policy In Force ($)	Avg. Prem ($/M)	1st Yr Prem/ Total Prem	Ord. Lapse Ratio
2007	...	...	...	...	...
2008	...	...	...	...	...
2009	...	...	...	...	...

• NEW LIFE BUSINESS ISSUED ($000 omitted)

Year	Whole Life	Term	Credit	Group	Industrial	Total
2007	...	18,010	...	152,453	...	170,463
2008	...	18,449	...	187,147	...	205,596
2009	...	12,850	...	138,957	...	151,807

• LIFE INSURANCE IN FORCE ($000 omitted)

Year	Whole Life	Term	Credit	Group	Industrial	Total
2007	...	45,245	...	5,039,850	...	5,085,095
2008	...	54,649	...	5,820,563	...	5,875,212
2009	...	57,869	...	6,153,695	...	6,211,564

HUMANA INS OF PUERTO RICO INC

383 F.D. Roosevelt Avenue, 3rd Floor
San Juan, Puerto Rico 00918-2131
Tel: 787-282-7900

AMB#: 008265
Began Business: 09/27/1970
Agency Off: David M. Krebs

Best's Financial Strength Rating: B+ **FSC:** VI

• NET PREMIUMS AND DEPOSITS ($000 omitted)

Year	Individual Life	Individual & Group Annuities	Group Life & A&H	Credit Life & A&H	Individual A&H	Total
2007	12	...	65,555	...	...	65,567
2008	7	...	77,201	...	...	77,208
2009	4	...	80,578	...	...	80,582

• NET OPERATING GAIN ($000 omitted)

Year	Individual Life	Individual & Group Annuities	Group Life & A&H	Credit Life & A&H	Individual A&H	Total
2007	8	...	5,995	11	...	6,014
2008	2	...	7,183	...	...	7,186
2009	-6	...	1,289	...	...	1,283

• COMPARATIVE FINANCIALS ($000 omitted)

Year	Assets	Capital & Surplus	Net Invest Income	Benefits Paid	Realized Cap Gains	Policyholder Dividends	Contract Lns (% of assets)
2007	36,236	23,608	1,134	52,497	-2	...	...
2008	44,129	31,098	582	60,524	10	...	...
2009	49,793	32,751	264	69,183	-1	...	...

• ORDINARY LIFE STATISTICS

Year	Av. Ord. Policy Issued ($)	Av. Ord. Policy In Force ($)	Avg. Prem ($/M)	1st Yr Prem/ Total Prem	Ord. Lapse Ratio
2007	...	...	...	...	...
2008	...	...	...	...	...
2009	...	...	...	...	...

• NEW LIFE BUSINESS ISSUED ($000 omitted)

Year	Whole Life	Term	Credit	Group	Industrial	Total
2007	...	...	...	...	...	...
2008	...	...	...	28,134	...	28,134
2009	...	99	...	-15,474	...	-15,375

• LIFE INSURANCE IN FORCE ($000 omitted)

Year	Whole Life	Term	Credit	Group	Industrial	Total
2007	2,289	...	...	121,585	...	123,874
2008	2,290	...	...	149,560	...	151,850
2009	2,383	...	...	133,839	...	136,222

IA AMERICAN LIFE INSURANCE CO

P.O. Box 26900
Scottsdale, Arizona 85255
Tel: 480-473-5540

AMB#: 060682
Began Business: 05/30/1980
Agency Off: None

Best's Financial Strength Rating: A- **FSC:** V

• NET PREMIUMS AND DEPOSITS ($000 omitted)

Year	Individual Life	Individual & Group Annuities	Group Life & A&H	Credit Life & A&H	Individual A&H	Total
2007	15	729	...	...	...	744
2008	-33,771	4	-3,900	...	-691	-38,357
2009	530	0	...	...	12,402	12,933

• NET OPERATING GAIN ($000 omitted)

Year	Individual Life	Individual & Group Annuities	Group Life & A&H	Credit Life & A&H	Individual A&H	Total
2007	123	60	...	...	...	183
2008	3,050	43	1,048	...	283	4,424
2009	82	1,103	...	...	-10,000	-8,815

• COMPARATIVE FINANCIALS ($000 omitted)

Year	Assets	Capital & Surplus	Net Invest Income	Benefits Paid	Realized Cap Gains	Policyholder Dividends	Contract Lns (% of assets)
2007	9,180	2,228	376	321	...	11	3.6
2008	39,999	30,827	1,783	745	-18	-476	0.8
2009	37,856	16,866	958	368	93	42	0.8

• ORDINARY LIFE STATISTICS

Year	Av. Ord. Policy Issued ($)	Av. Ord. Policy In Force ($)	Avg. Prem ($/M)	1st Yr Prem/ Total Prem	Ord. Lapse Ratio
2007	...	...	...	...	...
2008	...	...	...	...	...
2009	...	...	...	...	...

• NEW LIFE BUSINESS ISSUED ($000 omitted)

Year	Whole Life	Term	Credit	Group	Industrial	Total
2007	...	...	...	...	...	...
2008	...	...	...	...	...	...
2009	...	...	...	...	...	...

• LIFE INSURANCE IN FORCE ($000 omitted)

Year	Whole Life	Term	Credit	Group	Industrial	Total
2007	7,028	61	...	...	...	7,089
2008	591,654	106,362	...	213,655	...	911,671
2009	557,984	100,476	...	199,692	...	858,152

HUMANADENTAL INSURANCE COMPANY

P.O. Box 740036
Louisville, Kentucky 40201-7436
Tel: 920-336-1100

AMB#: 007254
Began Business: 10/12/1908
Agency Off: Gerald L. Ganoni

Best's Financial Strength Rating: A- g **FSC:** XV

• NET PREMIUMS AND DEPOSITS ($000 omitted)

Year	Individual Life	Individual & Group Annuities	Group Life & A&H	Credit Life & A&H	Individual A&H	Total
2007	36	686	291,931	...	9,794	302,447
2008	46	478	280,983	...	15,445	296,952
2009	28	346	277,759	...	17,457	295,591

• NET OPERATING GAIN ($000 omitted)

Year	Individual Life	Individual & Group Annuities	Group Life & A&H	Credit Life & A&H	Individual A&H	Total
2007	...	...	20,435	...	2,066	22,502
2008	...	...	21,230	...	2,508	23,738
2009	...	...	15,136	...	285	15,421

• COMPARATIVE FINANCIALS ($000 omitted)

Year	Assets	Capital & Surplus	Net Invest Income	Benefits Paid	Realized Cap Gains	Policyholder Dividends	Contract Lns (% of assets)
2007	96,611	65,630	3,957	205,947	-13	...	...
2008	93,909	63,790	3,960	198,822	-1,073	...	...
2009	92,293	58,408	2,820	199,946	161	...	...

• ORDINARY LIFE STATISTICS

Year	Av. Ord. Policy Issued ($)	Av. Ord. Policy In Force ($)	Avg. Prem ($/M)	1st Yr Prem/ Total Prem	Ord. Lapse Ratio
2007	...	...	...	...	...
2008	...	...	...	...	...
2009	...	...	...	...	...

• NEW LIFE BUSINESS ISSUED ($000 omitted)

Year	Whole Life	Term	Credit	Group	Industrial	Total
2007	...	...	...	...	...	...
2008	...	...	...	...	...	...
2009	...	...	...	...	...	...

• LIFE INSURANCE IN FORCE ($000 omitted)

Year	Whole Life	Term	Credit	Group	Industrial	Total
2007	601,488	210,299	...	...	...	811,787
2008	569,343	190,898	...	...	...	760,241
2009	537,761	174,835	...	...	...	712,597

IDEALIFE INS CO

120 Long Ridge Road
Stamford, Connecticut 06902
Tel: 203-352-3000

AMB#: 009326
Began Business: 01/01/1983
Agency Off: None

Best's Financial Strength Rating: A- **FSC:** V

• NET PREMIUMS AND DEPOSITS ($000 omitted)

Year	Individual Life	Individual & Group Annuities	Group Life & A&H	Credit Life & A&H	Individual A&H	Total
2007	1,385	29	...	...	316	1,730
2008	1,622	32	...	...	277	1,931
2009	1,617	35	...	...	234	1,886

• NET OPERATING GAIN ($000 omitted)

Year	Individual Life	Individual & Group Annuities	Group Life & A&H	Credit Life & A&H	Individual A&H	Total
2007	903	139	...	...	3	1,045
2008	743	66	...	...	1	811
2009	-365	81	...	...	-3	-287

• COMPARATIVE FINANCIALS ($000 omitted)

Year	Assets	Capital & Surplus	Net Invest Income	Benefits Paid	Realized Cap Gains	Policyholder Dividends	Contract Lns (% of assets)
2007	21,185	13,795	919	2,009	4	...	21.4
2008	21,067	14,618	618	1,839	0	...	18.7
2009	19,853	14,347	243	2,872	0	...	18.4

• ORDINARY LIFE STATISTICS

Year	Av. Ord. Policy Issued ($)	Av. Ord. Policy In Force ($)	Avg. Prem ($/M)	1st Yr Prem/ Total Prem	Ord. Lapse Ratio
2007	...	...	...	...	...
2008	...	...	...	...	...
2009	...	...	...	...	...

• NEW LIFE BUSINESS ISSUED ($000 omitted)

Year	Whole Life	Term	Credit	Group	Industrial	Total
2007	...	...	...	...	...	...
2008	...	...	...	...	...	...
2009	...	...	...	...	...	...

• LIFE INSURANCE IN FORCE ($000 omitted)

Year	Whole Life	Term	Credit	Group	Industrial	Total
2007	130,911	534,196	...	225	...	665,332
2008	122,646	474,046	...	225	...	596,917
2009	113,088	443,355	...	225	...	556,668

ILLINOIS MUTUAL LIFE INS CO

300 S.W. Adams Street
Peoria, Illinois 61634
Tel: 309-674-8255

AMB#: 006542
Began Business: 07/09/1912
Agency Off: Stephen J. Kershaw

Best's Financial Strength Rating: B++ **FSC:** VIII

• **NET PREMIUMS AND DEPOSITS ($000 omitted)**

Year	Individual Life	Individual & Group Annuities	Group Life & A&H	Credit Life & A&H	Individual A&H	Total
2007	34,639	60,995	1,605	…	60,556	157,795
2008	37,811	49,388	1,792	…	60,588	149,578
2009	38,124	42,443	1,869	…	59,198	141,633

• **NET OPERATING GAIN ($000 omitted)**

Year	Individual Life	Individual & Group Annuities	Group Life & A&H	Credit Life & A&H	Individual A&H	Total
2007	-4,246	2,944	406	…	12,228	11,331
2008	-1,741	4,266	287	…	3,808	6,620
2009	-557	510	649	…	17,332	17,933

• **COMPARATIVE FINANCIALS ($000 omitted)**

Year	Assets	Capital & Surplus	Net Invest Income	Benefits Paid	Realized Cap Gains	Policyholder Dividends	Contract Lns (% of assets)
2007	1,253,563	145,648	70,025	131,512	5,936	639	1.3
2008	1,268,230	132,399	71,092	115,660	-15,760	504	1.3
2009	1,248,028	136,360	65,358	139,268	-16,896	699	1.4

• **ORDINARY LIFE STATISTICS**

Year	Av. Ord. Policy Issued ($)	Av. Ord. Policy In Force ($)	Avg. Prem ($/M)	1st Yr Prem/ Total Prem	Ord. Lapse Ratio
2007	84,677	87,308	6.48	16.8	7.5
2008	104,356	89,353	6.59	14.8	6.7
2009	93,999	89,236	6.44	11.5	8.0

• **NEW LIFE BUSINESS ISSUED ($000 omitted)**

Year	Whole Life	Term	Credit	Group	Industrial	Total
2007	149,390	785,531	…	5	…	934,926
2008	173,771	767,627	…	1,442	…	942,840
2009	196,786	726,759	…	1,900	…	925,444

• **LIFE INSURANCE IN FORCE ($000 omitted)**

Year	Whole Life	Term	Credit	Group	Industrial	Total
2007	2,300,226	4,497,081	…	28,702	…	6,826,009
2008	2,344,185	4,827,364	…	30,113	…	7,201,662
2009	2,331,931	5,067,756	…	29,818	…	7,429,505

INDEPENDENCE LIFE & ANNUITY CO

One Sun Life Executive Park
Wellesley Hills, Massachusetts 02481-5699
Tel: 781-237-6030

AMB#: 006547
Began Business: 11/23/1945
Agency Off: None

Best's Financial Strength Rating: A **FSC:** VII

• **NET PREMIUMS AND DEPOSITS ($000 omitted)**

Year	Individual Life	Individual & Group Annuities	Group Life & A&H	Credit Life & A&H	Individual A&H	Total
2007	-758	…	…	…	…	-758
2008	-780	…	…	…	…	-780
2009	-550	35	…	…	…	-515

• **NET OPERATING GAIN ($000 omitted)**

Year	Individual Life	Individual & Group Annuities	Group Life & A&H	Credit Life & A&H	Individual A&H	Total
2007	2,262	38	…	…	…	2,300
2008	2,766	42	…	…	…	2,808
2009	2,705	44	…	…	…	2,749

• **COMPARATIVE FINANCIALS ($000 omitted)**

Year	Assets	Capital & Surplus	Net Invest Income	Benefits Paid	Realized Cap Gains	Policyholder Dividends	Contract Lns (% of assets)
2007	162,387	53,251	4,617	19,101	-533	…	16.3
2008	131,607	52,709	4,618	14,786	-3,417	…	18.8
2009	125,888	55,431	4,304	16,528	-183	…	17.0

• **ORDINARY LIFE STATISTICS**

Year	Av. Ord. Policy Issued ($)	Av. Ord. Policy In Force ($)	Avg. Prem ($/M)	1st Yr Prem/ Total Prem	Ord. Lapse Ratio
2007	…	…	…	…	…
2008	…	…	…	…	…
2009	…	…	…	…	…

• **NEW LIFE BUSINESS ISSUED ($000 omitted)**

Year	Whole Life	Term	Credit	Group	Industrial	Total
2007	…	…	…	…	…	…
2008	…	…	…	…	…	…
2009	…	…	…	…	…	…

• **LIFE INSURANCE IN FORCE ($000 omitted)**

Year	Whole Life	Term	Credit	Group	Industrial	Total
2007	190,796	…	…	…	…	190,796
2008	155,655	…	…	…	…	155,655
2009	121,590	…	…	…	…	121,590

INDIVIDUAL ASSUR LF HLTH & ACC

2400 West 75th Street
Prairie Village, Kansas 66208-3509
Tel: 913-432-1451

AMB#: 008437
Began Business: 01/01/1974
Agency Off: Michael M. Strickland

Best's Financial Strength Rating: B+ g **FSC:** V

• **NET PREMIUMS AND DEPOSITS ($000 omitted)**

Year	Individual Life	Individual & Group Annuities	Group Life & A&H	Credit Life & A&H	Individual A&H	Total
2007	5,932	1,031	11,503	9,756	0	28,222
2008	5,813	789	9,621	8,525	0	24,749
2009	5,653	812	7,300	7,270	1	21,037

• **NET OPERATING GAIN ($000 omitted)**

Year	Individual Life	Individual & Group Annuities	Group Life & A&H	Credit Life & A&H	Individual A&H	Total
2007	-862	213	211	1,069	-1	157
2008	-240	117	26	448	-1	-121
2009	298	71	-299	186	0	46

• **COMPARATIVE FINANCIALS ($000 omitted)**

Year	Assets	Capital & Surplus	Net Invest Income	Benefits Paid	Realized Cap Gains	Policyholder Dividends	Contract Lns (% of assets)
2007	45,308	11,137	1,851	15,947	…	6	5.1
2008	45,695	11,329	1,837	14,286	…	5	5.7
2009	44,823	12,131	1,830	11,887	…	3	6.1

• **ORDINARY LIFE STATISTICS**

Year	Av. Ord. Policy Issued ($)	Av. Ord. Policy In Force ($)	Avg. Prem ($/M)	1st Yr Prem/ Total Prem	Ord. Lapse Ratio
2007	…	…	…	…	…
2008	…	…	…	…	…
2009	…	…	…	…	…

• **NEW LIFE BUSINESS ISSUED ($000 omitted)**

Year	Whole Life	Term	Credit	Group	Industrial	Total
2007	53,176	24,410	631,629	93,723	…	802,938
2008	38,551	20,365	717,873	63,897	…	840,686
2009	754	14,945	720,628	104,938	…	841,265

• **LIFE INSURANCE IN FORCE ($000 omitted)**

Year	Whole Life	Term	Credit	Group	Industrial	Total
2007	938,106	219,083	991,977	4,492,298	…	6,641,464
2008	904,630	213,464	1,070,112	3,507,284	…	5,695,490
2009	835,773	199,642	1,024,193	1,995,214	…	4,054,822

ING LIFE INSURANCE AND ANNUITY

5780 Powers Ferry Road, NW
Atlanta, Georgia 30327-4390
Tel: 860-580-4646

AMB#: 006895
Began Business: 04/06/1976
Agency Off: None

Best's Financial Strength Rating: A g **FSC:** XIV

• **NET PREMIUMS AND DEPOSITS ($000 omitted)**

Year	Individual Life	Individual & Group Annuities	Group Life & A&H	Credit Life & A&H	Individual A&H	Total
2007	…	10,239,944	…	…	…	10,239,944
2008	…	10,591,290	…	…	…	10,591,290
2009	…	8,390,204	…	…	…	8,390,204

• **NET OPERATING GAIN ($000 omitted)**

Year	Individual Life	Individual & Group Annuities	Group Life & A&H	Credit Life & A&H	Individual A&H	Total
2007	30,775	219,566	0	…	-7	250,334
2008	25,537	-209,710	…	…	-6	-188,012
2009	27,562	415,843	…	…	-9	458,315

• **COMPARATIVE FINANCIALS ($000 omitted)**

Year	Assets	Capital & Surplus	Net Invest Income	Benefits Paid	Realized Cap Gains	Policyholder Dividends	Contract Lns (% of assets)
2007	67,000,403	1,388,018	1,036,487	10,479,288	-4,829	…	0.4
2008	57,306,158	1,524,556	1,053,307	8,629,256	-240,341	…	0.5
2009	62,474,626	1,762,126	1,007,967	8,388,929	-186,667	…	0.4

• **ORDINARY LIFE STATISTICS**

Year	Av. Ord. Policy Issued ($)	Av. Ord. Policy In Force ($)	Avg. Prem ($/M)	1st Yr Prem/ Total Prem	Ord. Lapse Ratio
2007	…	…	…	…	…
2008	…	…	…	…	…
2009	…	…	…	…	…

• **NEW LIFE BUSINESS ISSUED ($000 omitted)**

Year	Whole Life	Term	Credit	Group	Industrial	Total
2007	…	…	…	…	…	…
2008	…	…	…	…	…	…
2009	…	…	…	…	…	…

• **LIFE INSURANCE IN FORCE ($000 omitted)**

Year	Whole Life	Term	Credit	Group	Industrial	Total
2007	18,843,497	479,851	…	1,615,520	…	20,938,868
2008	17,689,140	426,321	…	1,487,748	…	19,603,209
2009	16,847,627	400,187	…	1,384,793	…	18,632,607

ING USA ANNUITY & LIFE INS CO

5780 Powers Ferry Road, NW
Atlanta, Georgia 30327-4390
Tel: 515-698-7000

AMB#: 008388
Began Business: 10/01/1973
Agency Off: None

Best's Financial Strength Rating: A g **FSC:** XIV

• NET PREMIUMS AND DEPOSITS ($000 omitted)

Year	Individual Life	Individual & Group Annuities	Group Life & A&H	Credit Life & A&H	Individual A&H	Total
2007	53,523	18,526,209	-77	...	...	18,579,655
2008	66,453	16,252,504	285,478	...	...	16,604,434
2009	200,244	7,484,526	512,460	...	...	8,197,230

• NET OPERATING GAIN ($000 omitted)

Year	Individual Life	Individual & Group Annuities	Group Life & A&H	Credit Life & A&H	Individual A&H	Total
2007	9,186	28,634	208	...	...	38,028
2008	-19,492	-624,777	-6,282	...	...	-652,671
2009	24,201	811,487	-6,787	...	...	828,935

• COMPARATIVE FINANCIALS ($000 omitted)

Year	Assets	Capital & Surplus	Net Invest Income	Benefits Paid	Realized Cap Gains	Policyholder Dividends	Contract Lns (% of assets)
2007	74,257,086	2,552,616	1,171,960	7,080,709	-78,169	14,782	0.2
2008	64,089,977	1,872,666	897,430	7,731,464	-178,760	13,711	0.2
2009	71,917,082	1,485,056	781,516	5,974,422	-1,467,214	13,082	0.2

• ORDINARY LIFE STATISTICS

Year	Av. Ord. Policy Issued ($)	Av. Ord. Policy In Force ($)	Avg. Prem ($/M)	1st Yr Prem/ Total Prem	Ord. Lapse Ratio
2007	...	63,301	7.21	0.0	5.5
2008	...	150,649	1.96	0.0	3.3
2009	...	140,401	5.84	0.0	2.7

• NEW LIFE BUSINESS ISSUED ($000 omitted)

Year	Whole Life	Term	Credit	Group	Industrial	Total
2007	...	...	...	...	...	...
2008	...	...	...	...	...	...
2009	...	...	...	...	...	...

• LIFE INSURANCE IN FORCE ($000 omitted)

Year	Whole Life	Term	Credit	Group	Industrial	Total
2007	7,581,279	689,653	58	80,543	...	8,351,533
2008	35,936,595	618,870	...	164,428,717	...	200,984,182
2009	34,654,127	478,510	...	233,117,674	...	268,250,310

INTRAMERICA LIFE INS CO

100 Motor Parkway, Suite 132
Hauppauge, New York 11788-5107
Tel: 847-402-5000

AMB#: 006572
Began Business: 03/24/1966
Agency Off: None

Best's Financial Strength Rating: B++ **FSC:** IV

• NET PREMIUMS AND DEPOSITS ($000 omitted)

Year	Individual Life	Individual & Group Annuities	Group Life & A&H	Credit Life & A&H	Individual A&H	Total
2007	...	56	...	...	...	56
2008	...	13	...	...	...	13
2009	...	25	...	...	...	25

• NET OPERATING GAIN ($000 omitted)

Year	Individual Life	Individual & Group Annuities	Group Life & A&H	Credit Life & A&H	Individual A&H	Total
2007	...	486	...	...	...	486
2008	...	334	...	...	...	334
2009	...	203	...	...	...	203

• COMPARATIVE FINANCIALS ($000 omitted)

Year	Assets	Capital & Surplus	Net Invest Income	Benefits Paid	Realized Cap Gains	Policyholder Dividends	Contract Lns (% of assets)
2007	42,651	8,496	579	2,227	...	...	...
2008	28,640	8,810	440	4,008	...	...	...
2009	31,509	8,992	330	1,618	...	...	...

• ORDINARY LIFE STATISTICS

Year	Av. Ord. Policy Issued ($)	Av. Ord. Policy In Force ($)	Avg. Prem ($/M)	1st Yr Prem/ Total Prem	Ord. Lapse Ratio
2007	...	...	...	...	...
2008	...	...	...	...	...
2009	...	...	...	...	...

• NEW LIFE BUSINESS ISSUED ($000 omitted)

Year	Whole Life	Term	Credit	Group	Industrial	Total
2007	...	...	...	...	...	...
2008	...	...	...	...	...	...
2009	...	...	...	...	...	...

• LIFE INSURANCE IN FORCE ($000 omitted)

Year	Whole Life	Term	Credit	Group	Industrial	Total
2007	30,205	1,885	...	810	...	32,900
2008	27,132	1,729	...	760	...	29,621
2009	24,347	1,506	...	693	...	26,546

INTEGRITY LIFE INS CO

400 Broadway
Cincinnati, Ohio 45202
Tel: 513-629-1800

AMB#: 007739
Began Business: 05/25/1966
Agency Off: Mark Caner

Best's Financial Strength Rating: A+ g **FSC:** XV

• NET PREMIUMS AND DEPOSITS ($000 omitted)

Year	Individual Life	Individual & Group Annuities	Group Life & A&H	Credit Life & A&H	Individual A&H	Total
2007	199	560,776	...	...	...	560,975
2008	647	821,974	...	...	...	822,620
2009	637	639,905	...	...	...	640,543

• NET OPERATING GAIN ($000 omitted)

Year	Individual Life	Individual & Group Annuities	Group Life & A&H	Credit Life & A&H	Individual A&H	Total
2007	11,561	-2,073	25	...	...	9,514
2008	8,868	1,639	273	...	...	-11,658
2009	4,098	4,560	-5	...	...	-3,298

• COMPARATIVE FINANCIALS ($000 omitted)

Year	Assets	Capital & Surplus	Net Invest Income	Benefits Paid	Realized Cap Gains	Policyholder Dividends	Contract Lns (% of assets)
2007	4,692,412	355,341	103,599	433,887	20,992	...	2.5
2008	4,850,848	375,422	123,912	392,845	-15,752	...	2.4
2009	5,414,032	501,528	135,468	382,187	-9,099	...	2.2

• ORDINARY LIFE STATISTICS

Year	Av. Ord. Policy Issued ($)	Av. Ord. Policy In Force ($)	Avg. Prem ($/M)	1st Yr Prem/ Total Prem	Ord. Lapse Ratio
2007	...	...	...	...	...
2008	...	...	...	...	...
2009	...	...	...	...	...

• NEW LIFE BUSINESS ISSUED ($000 omitted)

Year	Whole Life	Term	Credit	Group	Industrial	Total
2007	...	...	...	...	...	...
2008	...	...	...	...	...	...
2009	...	...	...	...	...	...

• LIFE INSURANCE IN FORCE ($000 omitted)

Year	Whole Life	Term	Credit	Group	Industrial	Total
2007	550,747	11,062	...	45,420	...	607,229
2008	527,915	10,465	...	42,058	...	580,438
2009	500,000	9,069	...	33,929	...	542,998

INVESTORS CONSOLIDATED INS CO

2727 Allen Parkway Wortham Tower, Suite 500
Houston, Texas 77019-2115
Tel: 713-529-0045

AMB#: 008588
Began Business: 02/15/1975
Agency Off: Thomas Luchetta

Best's Financial Strength Rating: B+ **FSC:** IV

• NET PREMIUMS AND DEPOSITS ($000 omitted)

Year	Individual Life	Individual & Group Annuities	Group Life & A&H	Credit Life & A&H	Individual A&H	Total
2007	23	1	697	...	1,129	1,849
2008	4	1	626	...	1,038	1,669
2009	12	1	561	...	747	1,321

• NET OPERATING GAIN ($000 omitted)

Year	Individual Life	Individual & Group Annuities	Group Life & A&H	Credit Life & A&H	Individual A&H	Total
2007	29	2	337	...	113	482
2008	8	5	98	...	99	211
2009	40	5	201	...	683	929

• COMPARATIVE FINANCIALS ($000 omitted)

Year	Assets	Capital & Surplus	Net Invest Income	Benefits Paid	Realized Cap Gains	Policyholder Dividends	Contract Lns (% of assets)
2007	15,606	6,645	646	1,014	...	...	...
2008	15,746	6,900	523	849	...	...	...
2009	16,173	8,170	316	686	...	...	...

• ORDINARY LIFE STATISTICS

Year	Av. Ord. Policy Issued ($)	Av. Ord. Policy In Force ($)	Avg. Prem ($/M)	1st Yr Prem/ Total Prem	Ord. Lapse Ratio
2007	...	...	...	...	...
2008	...	...	...	...	...
2009	...	...	...	...	...

• NEW LIFE BUSINESS ISSUED ($000 omitted)

Year	Whole Life	Term	Credit	Group	Industrial	Total
2007	...	...	...	10	...	10
2008	...	...	...	...	...	...
2009	...	...	...	...	...	...

• LIFE INSURANCE IN FORCE ($000 omitted)

Year	Whole Life	Term	Credit	Group	Industrial	Total
2007	787	...	...	36,949	...	37,736
2008	769	...	...	34,774	...	35,543
2009	756	...	...	32,929	...	33,685

INVESTORS HERITAGE LIFE INS CO

P.O. Box 717
Frankfort, Kentucky 40602-0717
Tel: 502-223-2361

AMB#: 006580
Began Business: 03/01/1961
Agency Off: Donald R. Philpot

Best's Financial Strength Rating: B+ **FSC:** V

• NET PREMIUMS AND DEPOSITS ($000 omitted)

Year	Individual Life	Individual & Group Annuities	Group Life & A&H	Credit Life & A&H	Individual A&H	Total
2007	26,321	8,603	4,821	0	2	39,747
2008	27,483	6,787	3,978	...	2	38,250
2009	28,047	6,112	4,351	...	1	38,512

• NET OPERATING GAIN ($000 omitted)

Year	Individual Life	Individual & Group Annuities	Group Life & A&H	Credit Life & A&H	Individual A&H	Total
2007	1,022	124	58	-176	0	1,028
2008	971	142	17	40	1	1,170
2009	1,090	120	104	15	0	1,329

• COMPARATIVE FINANCIALS ($000 omitted)

Year	Assets	Capital & Surplus	Net Invest Income	Benefits Paid	Realized Cap Gains	Policyholder Dividends	Contract Lns (% of assets)
2007	341,832	19,083	17,953	42,393	107	539	2.0
2008	338,042	16,588	17,713	40,495	-4,692	519	2.1
2009	340,960	17,911	17,329	41,180	-741	302	2.0

• ORDINARY LIFE STATISTICS

Year	Av. Ord. Policy Issued ($)	Av. Ord. Policy In Force ($)	Avg. Prem ($/M)	1st Yr Prem/ Total Prem	Ord. Lapse Ratio
2007	9,498	5,722	26.47	4.9	5.5
2008	8,186	5,774	28.25	4.3	6.2
2009	6,629	5,723	29.57	3.5	5.8

• NEW LIFE BUSINESS ISSUED ($000 omitted)

Year	Whole Life	Term	Credit	Group	Industrial	Total
2007	49,505	33,271	228,218	8,738	...	319,732
2008	44,668	26,755	209,243	5,847	...	286,513
2009	31,785	19,010	165,752	102	...	216,649

• LIFE INSURANCE IN FORCE ($000 omitted)

Year	Whole Life	Term	Credit	Group	Industrial	Total
2007	770,158	368,417	396,135	1,762,746	...	3,297,456
2008	770,939	344,999	377,667	1,727,159	...	3,220,764
2009	743,488	324,848	313,632	2,060,327	...	3,442,295

INVESTORS INSURANCE CORP

P.O. Box 56050
Jacksonville, Florida 32241-6050
Tel: 904-260-6990

AMB#: 006583
Began Business: 07/16/1987
Agency Off: Susan F. Powell

Best's Financial Strength Rating: A- **FSC:** VI

• NET PREMIUMS AND DEPOSITS ($000 omitted)

Year	Individual Life	Individual & Group Annuities	Group Life & A&H	Credit Life & A&H	Individual A&H	Total
2007	8	39,129	...	...	...	39,137
2008	6	42,840	...	...	...	42,846
2009	7	116,138	...	...	...	116,145

• NET OPERATING GAIN ($000 omitted)

Year	Individual Life	Individual & Group Annuities	Group Life & A&H	Credit Life & A&H	Individual A&H	Total
2007	-189	3,951	...	...	...	3,762
2008	-195	4,501	...	...	12	4,318
2009	19	-9,873	...	...	...	-9,853

• COMPARATIVE FINANCIALS ($000 omitted)

Year	Assets	Capital & Surplus	Net Invest Income	Benefits Paid	Realized Cap Gains	Policyholder Dividends	Contract Lns (% of assets)
2007	245,173	31,699	11,430	29,774	...	56	0.2
2008	246,924	28,351	11,540	26,302	-3,692	59	0.2
2009	353,125	33,010	12,701	29,967	-2,520	52	0.1

• ORDINARY LIFE STATISTICS

Year	Av. Ord. Policy Issued ($)	Av. Ord. Policy In Force ($)	Avg. Prem ($/M)	1st Yr Prem/ Total Prem	Ord. Lapse Ratio
2007	...	...	...	...	...
2008	...	...	...	...	...
2009	...	...	...	...	...

• NEW LIFE BUSINESS ISSUED ($000 omitted)

Year	Whole Life	Term	Credit	Group	Industrial	Total
2007	...	...	...	...	...	...
2008	...	...	...	...	...	...
2009	...	...	...	...	...	...

• LIFE INSURANCE IN FORCE ($000 omitted)

Year	Whole Life	Term	Credit	Group	Industrial	Total
2007	3,885	...	...	...	...	3,885
2008	3,676	...	...	...	...	3,676
2009	3,338	...	...	...	...	3,339

INVESTORS LIFE OF NORTH AMER

P.O. Box 410288
Kansas City, Missouri 64141-0288
Tel: 816-391-2000

AMB#: 006412
Began Business: 12/27/1963
Agency Off: Wayne P. Whitmire

Best's Financial Strength Rating: B+ **FSC:** VI

• NET PREMIUMS AND DEPOSITS ($000 omitted)

Year	Individual Life	Individual & Group Annuities	Group Life & A&H	Credit Life & A&H	Individual A&H	Total
2007	30,277	1,176	82	...	70	31,605
2008	20,972	1,142	75	...	36	22,225
2009	-18	913	-2	...	-3	890

• NET OPERATING GAIN ($000 omitted)

Year	Individual Life	Individual & Group Annuities	Group Life & A&H	Credit Life & A&H	Individual A&H	Total
2007	357	3,650	-180	...	24	3,851
2008	816	1,565	-2,859	...	-32	-510
2009	487	1,813	178	...	0	2,478

• COMPARATIVE FINANCIALS ($000 omitted)

Year	Assets	Capital & Surplus	Net Invest Income	Benefits Paid	Realized Cap Gains	Policyholder Dividends	Contract Lns (% of assets)
2007	936,375	47,755	28,740	98,263	21	88	3.0
2008	754,802	34,193	26,244	134,708	...	32	3.4
2009	746,067	39,481	29,738	11,673	-609	-5	3.2

• ORDINARY LIFE STATISTICS

Year	Av. Ord. Policy Issued ($)	Av. Ord. Policy In Force ($)	Avg. Prem ($/M)	1st Yr Prem/ Total Prem	Ord. Lapse Ratio
2007	...	...	...	...	...
2008	...	...	...	...	...
2009	...	...	...	...	...

• NEW LIFE BUSINESS ISSUED ($000 omitted)

Year	Whole Life	Term	Credit	Group	Industrial	Total
2007	32,220	212,658	...	...	...	244,878
2008	4,312	1,443	...	...	...	5,755
2009	...	...	...	...	...	...

• LIFE INSURANCE IN FORCE ($000 omitted)

Year	Whole Life	Term	Credit	Group	Industrial	Total
2007	2,787,546	691,305	...	3,271	1,931	3,484,053
2008	2,950,104	869,007	...	5,450	1,835	3,826,396
2009	2,752,275	753,873	...	5,077	1,776	3,513,001

JACKSON NATIONAL LIFE INS CO

1 Corporate Way
Lansing, Michigan 48951
Tel: 517-381-5500

AMB#: 006596
Began Business: 08/30/1961
Agency Off: Clifford J. Jack

Best's Financial Strength Rating: A+ gu **FSC:** XV

• NET PREMIUMS AND DEPOSITS ($000 omitted)

Year	Individual Life	Individual & Group Annuities	Group Life & A&H	Credit Life & A&H	Individual A&H	Total
2007	482,046	13,314,857	2,260	...	...	13,799,164
2008	462,659	13,314,305	2,286	...	...	13,779,251
2009	431,100	13,069,327	2,389	...	...	13,502,817

• NET OPERATING GAIN ($000 omitted)

Year	Individual Life	Individual & Group Annuities	Group Life & A&H	Credit Life & A&H	Individual A&H	Total
2007	102,715	436,348	-1,177	...	...	537,885
2008	52,717	-337,223	-980	...	...	-285,486
2009	43,254	1,355,188	-1,048	...	...	1,397,394

• COMPARATIVE FINANCIALS ($000 omitted)

Year	Assets	Capital & Surplus	Net Invest Income	Benefits Paid	Realized Cap Gains	Policyholder Dividends	Contract Lns (% of assets)
2007	73,963,867	4,024,057	2,797,053	7,545,926	-47,875	335	1.1
2008	68,327,271	3,745,686	2,654,808	6,902,893	-337,909	274	1.2
2009	77,789,118	3,972,694	2,475,805	6,403,653	-1,023,800	265	1.1

• ORDINARY LIFE STATISTICS

Year	Av. Ord. Policy Issued ($)	Av. Ord. Policy In Force ($)	Avg. Prem ($/M)	1st Yr Prem/ Total Prem	Ord. Lapse Ratio
2007	203,234	93,018	5.38	8.6	5.8
2008	187,350	92,796	5.55	10.0	7.6
2009	176,255	91,855	5.58	9.6	8.1

• NEW LIFE BUSINESS ISSUED ($000 omitted)

Year	Whole Life	Term	Credit	Group	Industrial	Total
2007	978,622	2,230,855	...	21,843	...	3,231,320
2008	1,189,954	1,963,713	...	30,165	...	3,183,832
2009	1,106,969	1,769,681	...	22,763	...	2,899,413

• LIFE INSURANCE IN FORCE ($000 omitted)

Year	Whole Life	Term	Credit	Group	Industrial	Total
2007	27,487,534	85,388,949	...	1,229,010	469,249	114,574,742
2008	26,934,910	79,204,903	...	1,223,424	450,905	107,814,142
2009	26,438,057	72,693,576	...	1,198,727	434,106	100,764,466

JACKSON NATIONAL LF INS OF NY

1 Corporate Way
Lansing, Michigan 48951
Tel: 517-381-5500

AMB#: 060216
Began Business: 08/16/1996
Agency Off: Clifford J. Jack

Best's Financial Strength Rating: A+ gu **FSC:** XV

• **NET PREMIUMS AND DEPOSITS ($000 omitted)**

Year	Individual Life	Individual & Group Annuities	Group Life & A&H	Credit Life & A&H	Individual A&H	Total
2007	1,076	556,472	...	...	...	557,548
2008	983	215,535	...	...	...	216,518
2009	885	783,732	...	...	...	784,617

• **NET OPERATING GAIN ($000 omitted)**

Year	Individual Life	Individual & Group Annuities	Group Life & A&H	Credit Life & A&H	Individual A&H	Total
2007	-37	-2,327	...	...	...	-2,364
2008	310	-285,197	...	...	...	-284,887
2009	28	53,773	...	...	...	53,801

• **COMPARATIVE FINANCIALS ($000 omitted)**

Year	Assets	Capital & Surplus	Net Invest Income	Benefits Paid	Realized Cap Gains	Policyholder Dividends	Contract Lns (% of assets)
2007	3,039,695	132,086	83,314	286,122	-1,776	...	0.0
2008	2,681,811	94,662	78,247	355,647	-24,484	...	0.0
2009	3,398,281	212,409	79,764	383,930	-9,065	...	0.0

• **ORDINARY LIFE STATISTICS**

Year	Av. Ord. Policy Issued ($)	Av. Ord. Policy In Force ($)	Avg. Prem ($/M)	1st Yr Prem/ Total Prem	Ord. Lapse Ratio
2007	...	...	...	...	...
2008	...	...	...	...	...
2009	...	...	...	...	...

• **NEW LIFE BUSINESS ISSUED ($000 omitted)**

Year	Whole Life	Term	Credit	Group	Industrial	Total
2007	900	425	...	...	...	1,325
2008	825	...	...	...	...	825
2009	...	...	...	...	...	...

• **LIFE INSURANCE IN FORCE ($000 omitted)**

Year	Whole Life	Term	Credit	Group	Industrial	Total
2007	68,648	380,317	...	...	...	448,965
2008	67,795	355,055	...	...	...	422,850
2009	64,633	317,874	...	...	...	382,508

JOHN ALDEN LIFE INS CO

P.O. Box 3050
Milwaukee, Wisconsin 53201-3050
Tel: 414-271-3011

AMB#: 006600
Began Business: 01/01/1974
Agency Off: Laura Hohing

Best's Financial Strength Rating: A- g **FSC:** VIII

• **NET PREMIUMS AND DEPOSITS ($000 omitted)**

Year	Individual Life	Individual & Group Annuities	Group Life & A&H	Credit Life & A&H	Individual A&H	Total
2007	201	252	488,741	...	54,996	544,190
2008	199	197	458,968	-4	51,549	510,909
2009	80	202	435,710	0	51,000	486,993

• **NET OPERATING GAIN ($000 omitted)**

Year	Individual Life	Individual & Group Annuities	Group Life & A&H	Credit Life & A&H	Individual A&H	Total
2007	-3,518	3,337	32,653	4	6,764	39,239
2008	-2,225	2,019	33,250	-18	4,129	37,154
2009	-2,515	4,019	2,698	-1	-207	3,994

• **COMPARATIVE FINANCIALS ($000 omitted)**

Year	Assets	Capital & Surplus	Net Invest Income	Benefits Paid	Realized Cap Gains	Policyholder Dividends	Contract Lns (% of assets)
2007	526,043	93,111	32,452	373,725	-1,654	...	3.9
2008	490,584	94,328	29,752	335,455	-9,105	...	4.7
2009	462,740	85,197	26,550	373,727	-2,170	...	4.7

• **ORDINARY LIFE STATISTICS**

Year	Av. Ord. Policy Issued ($)	Av. Ord. Policy In Force ($)	Avg. Prem ($/M)	1st Yr Prem/ Total Prem	Ord. Lapse Ratio
2007	...	...	...	...	...
2008	...	...	...	...	...
2009	...	...	...	...	...

• **NEW LIFE BUSINESS ISSUED ($000 omitted)**

Year	Whole Life	Term	Credit	Group	Industrial	Total
2007	...	6,940	...	458,310	...	465,250
2008	...	7,859	...	438,347	...	446,206
2009	...	4,832	...	451,615	...	456,447

• **LIFE INSURANCE IN FORCE ($000 omitted)**

Year	Whole Life	Term	Credit	Group	Industrial	Total
2007	1,610,709	233,357	139	1,004,638	...	2,848,843
2008	1,538,201	216,856	47	897,530	...	2,652,634
2009	1,579,180	161,575	...	913,305	...	2,654,060

JEFFERSON NATIONAL LIFE INS CO

9920 Corporate Campus Drive, Suite 1000
Louisville, Kentucky 40223
Tel: 212-741-9311

AMB#: 006475
Began Business: 02/16/1937
Agency Off: David Lau

Best's Financial Strength Rating: B- **FSC:** VI

• **NET PREMIUMS AND DEPOSITS ($000 omitted)**

Year	Individual Life	Individual & Group Annuities	Group Life & A&H	Credit Life & A&H	Individual A&H	Total
2007	276	242,525	...	...	...	242,802
2008	258	183,031	...	...	...	183,289
2009	233	150,513	...	...	...	150,745

• **NET OPERATING GAIN ($000 omitted)**

Year	Individual Life	Individual & Group Annuities	Group Life & A&H	Credit Life & A&H	Individual A&H	Total
2007	858	-1,443	...	...	472	-112
2008	971	-9,895	...	...	472	-8,452
2009	1,006	2,892	...	...	472	4,370

• **COMPARATIVE FINANCIALS ($000 omitted)**

Year	Assets	Capital & Surplus	Net Invest Income	Benefits Paid	Realized Cap Gains	Policyholder Dividends	Contract Lns (% of assets)
2007	1,727,626	41,081	26,661	258,787	-108	...	1.0
2008	1,325,645	23,340	24,605	206,450	-6,391	...	1.2
2009	1,572,584	25,905	25,012	167,032	-2,991	...	0.9

• **ORDINARY LIFE STATISTICS**

Year	Av. Ord. Policy Issued ($)	Av. Ord. Policy In Force ($)	Avg. Prem ($/M)	1st Yr Prem/ Total Prem	Ord. Lapse Ratio
2007	...	...	...	...	...
2008	...	...	...	...	...
2009	...	...	...	...	...

• **NEW LIFE BUSINESS ISSUED ($000 omitted)**

Year	Whole Life	Term	Credit	Group	Industrial	Total
2007	...	...	...	...	...	...
2008	...	...	...	...	...	...
2009	...	...	...	...	...	...

• **LIFE INSURANCE IN FORCE ($000 omitted)**

Year	Whole Life	Term	Credit	Group	Industrial	Total
2007	1,733,968	1,449,989	...	60,272	186	3,244,415
2008	1,616,084	1,266,386	...	57,707	183	2,940,360
2009	1,506,198	1,092,906	...	54,437	176	2,653,717

JOHN HANCOCK LIFE & HEALTH INS

P.O. Box 717
Boston, Massachusetts 02117-0717
Tel: 617-572-6000

AMB#: 009074
Began Business: 10/26/1981
Agency Off: None

Best's Financial Strength Rating: A+ g **FSC:** XV

• **NET PREMIUMS AND DEPOSITS ($000 omitted)**

Year	Individual Life	Individual & Group Annuities	Group Life & A&H	Credit Life & A&H	Individual A&H	Total
2007	313	10,036	866	...	...	11,216
2008	-632	14,248	816	...	...	14,432
2009	1,003	18,602	1,110,052	...	29,138	1,158,795

• **NET OPERATING GAIN ($000 omitted)**

Year	Individual Life	Individual & Group Annuities	Group Life & A&H	Credit Life & A&H	Individual A&H	Total
2007	10,117	...	33	...	...	10,150
2008	1,330	...	116	...	...	7,910
2009	1,085	1,745	-129	...	-7,632	-1,952

• **COMPARATIVE FINANCIALS ($000 omitted)**

Year	Assets	Capital & Surplus	Net Invest Income	Benefits Paid	Realized Cap Gains	Policyholder Dividends	Contract Lns (% of assets)
2007	538,935	126,270	30,381	31,840	3,067	...	18.2
2008	2,573,744	193,247	28,154	41,601	-1,552	...	3.5
2009	6,443,031	350,912	46,747	101,377	529	...	1.3

• **ORDINARY LIFE STATISTICS**

Year	Av. Ord. Policy Issued ($)	Av. Ord. Policy In Force ($)	Avg. Prem ($/M)	1st Yr Prem/ Total Prem	Ord. Lapse Ratio
2007	...	...	...	...	...
2008	...	...	...	...	...
2009	...	...	...	...	...

• **NEW LIFE BUSINESS ISSUED ($000 omitted)**

Year	Whole Life	Term	Credit	Group	Industrial	Total
2007	...	...	...	...	...	...
2008	...	...	...	...	...	...
2009	...	...	...	...	...	...

• **LIFE INSURANCE IN FORCE ($000 omitted)**

Year	Whole Life	Term	Credit	Group	Industrial	Total
2007	483,251	1,208,418	...	...	...	1,691,669
2008	1,004,542	1,155,618	...	...	...	2,160,160
2009	987,745	12,408,182	...	...	...	13,395,927

JOHN HANCOCK LIFE INS CO NY

100 Summit Lake Drive, 2nd Floor
Valhalla, New York 10595
Tel: 914-773-0708

AMB#: 060056
Began Business: 07/22/1992
Agency Off: None

Best's Financial Strength Rating: A+ g
FSC: XV

• NET PREMIUMS AND DEPOSITS ($000 omitted)

Year	Individual Life	Individual & Group Annuities	Group Life & A&H	Credit Life & A&H	Individual A&H	Total
2007	107,525	1,392,204	...	...	...	1,499,729
2008	179,893	1,217,309	...	...	...	1,397,202
2009	251,951	924,393	...	...	...	1,176,344

• NET OPERATING GAIN ($000 omitted)

Year	Individual Life	Individual & Group Annuities	Group Life & A&H	Credit Life & A&H	Individual A&H	Total
2007	-28,254	94,605	...	...	...	66,351
2008	-69,845	-228,968	...	...	...	-328,077
2009	-33,864	196,565	...	...	...	309,504

• COMPARATIVE FINANCIALS ($000 omitted)

Year	Assets	Capital & Surplus	Net Invest Income	Benefits Paid	Realized Cap Gains	Policyholder Dividends	Contract Lns (% of assets)
2007	7,320,515	223,048	170,533	653,745	...	...	0.5
2008	6,221,292	218,287	170,992	647,317	21	...	0.7
2009	8,770,571	1,016,982	171,247	628,960	...	...	0.6

• ORDINARY LIFE STATISTICS

Year	Av. Ord. Policy Issued ($)	Av. Ord. Policy In Force ($)	Avg. Prem ($/M)	1st Yr Prem/ Total Prem	Ord. Lapse Ratio
2007	1,303,731	1,325,338	12.06	64.8	3.2
2008	1,538,247	1,391,726	10.90	57.3	4.2
2009	1,351,533	1,408,479	11.30	53.5	2.5

• NEW LIFE BUSINESS ISSUED ($000 omitted)

Year	Whole Life	Term	Credit	Group	Industrial	Total
2007	2,492,374	3,130,619	...	...	...	5,622,993
2008	2,986,514	5,615,361	...	...	...	8,601,875
2009	3,228,467	4,476,620	...	...	...	7,705,087

• LIFE INSURANCE IN FORCE ($000 omitted)

Year	Whole Life	Term	Credit	Group	Industrial	Total
2007	6,522,656	8,737,288	...	...	...	15,259,944
2008	9,158,298	13,795,444	...	...	...	22,953,742
2009	12,584,571	17,235,753	...	...	...	29,820,324

JOHN HANCOCK LIFE INS CO USA

601 Congress Street
Boston, Massachusetts 02210
Tel: 617-854-4300

AMB#: 006681
Began Business: 01/31/1956
Agency Off: None

Best's Financial Strength Rating: A+ g
FSC: XV

• NET PREMIUMS AND DEPOSITS ($000 omitted)

Year	Individual Life	Individual & Group Annuities	Group Life & A&H	Credit Life & A&H	Individual A&H	Total
2007	2,534,299	16,299,127	444,900	...	638,227	19,916,553
2008	2,418,748	9,942,712	391,758	...	716,779	13,469,998
2009	2,237,009	10,862,137	235,216	...	782,556	14,116,918

• NET OPERATING GAIN ($000 omitted)

Year	Individual Life	Individual & Group Annuities	Group Life & A&H	Credit Life & A&H	Individual A&H	Total
2007	45,891	203,698	28,721	-82	-36,428	919,376
2008	-271,540	-1,428,147	94,144	-5	-125,234	-1,869,686
2009	40,235	672,284	-18,061	0	-155,056	605,509

• COMPARATIVE FINANCIALS ($000 omitted)

Year	Assets	Capital & Surplus	Net Invest Income	Benefits Paid	Realized Cap Gains	Policyholder Dividends	Contract Lns (% of assets)
2007	210,291,317	5,840,788	5,267,198	18,685,819	212,286	207,550	2.1
2008	178,632,131	4,474,155	4,727,004	15,894,117	-569,757	199,504	2.7
2009	203,396,347	5,018,613	4,263,934	8,272,971	-677,109	123,639	2.4

• ORDINARY LIFE STATISTICS

Year	Av. Ord. Policy Issued ($)	Av. Ord. Policy In Force ($)	Avg. Prem ($/M)	1st Yr Prem/ Total Prem	Ord. Lapse Ratio
2007	1,328,991	73,135	9.84	30.1	6.3
2008	763,333	83,075	9.97	29.8	6.8
2009	1,339,549	100,463	9.90	32.4	5.5

• NEW LIFE BUSINESS ISSUED ($000 omitted)

Year	Whole Life	Term	Credit	Group	Industrial	Total
2007	30,758,005	19,820,747	...	...	...	50,578,752
2008	33,097,376	46,729,691	...	355,533	...	80,182,600
2009	30,796,770	25,642,459	...	...	...	56,439,229

• LIFE INSURANCE IN FORCE ($000 omitted)

Year	Whole Life	Term	Credit	Group	Industrial	Total
2007	276,916,844	302,159,264	3,273	63,300,253	...	642,379,634
2008	291,832,535	321,920,698	2,152	60,254,171	...	674,009,556
2009	308,380,712	312,094,777	...	63,601,356	...	684,076,845

KANAWHA INSURANCE COMPANY

P.O. Box 740036
Louisville, Kentucky 40201-7436
Tel: 803-283-5300

AMB#: 006604
Began Business: 12/01/1958
Agency Off: Stanley D. Johnson

Best's Financial Strength Rating: B++
FSC: VII

• NET PREMIUMS AND DEPOSITS ($000 omitted)

Year	Individual Life	Individual & Group Annuities	Group Life & A&H	Credit Life & A&H	Individual A&H	Total
2007	8,121	-1	74,737	...	79,946	162,803
2008	11,053	11	58,760	...	78,573	148,397
2009	14,445	2	60,625	...	82,156	157,228

• NET OPERATING GAIN ($000 omitted)

Year	Individual Life	Individual & Group Annuities	Group Life & A&H	Credit Life & A&H	Individual A&H	Total
2007	-1,320	-117	-10,574	1	-16,540	-30,332
2008	-2,262	-1,036	-14,891	4	-30,690	-53,807
2009	26,162	792	-11,855	0	-85,907	-70,195

• COMPARATIVE FINANCIALS ($000 omitted)

Year	Assets	Capital & Surplus	Net Invest Income	Benefits Paid	Realized Cap Gains	Policyholder Dividends	Contract Lns (% of assets)
2007	664,720	65,916	33,812	127,280	265	1,847	2.7
2008	823,103	59,571	34,653	122,767	-19,891	1,732	1.9
2009	926,380	92,684	42,878	120,718	-6,918	1,869	1.7

• ORDINARY LIFE STATISTICS

Year	Av. Ord. Policy Issued ($)	Av. Ord. Policy In Force ($)	Avg. Prem ($/M)	1st Yr Prem/ Total Prem	Ord. Lapse Ratio
2007	37,218	15,236	5.96	17.0	14.8
2008	34,256	16,145	6.98	22.0	12.9
2009	19,402	16,176	8.15	29.6	12.1

• NEW LIFE BUSINESS ISSUED ($000 omitted)

Year	Whole Life	Term	Credit	Group	Industrial	Total
2007	122,135	155,251	...	1,452,806	...	1,730,192
2008	190,521	137,375	...	1,228,809	...	1,556,705
2009	217,609	187,861	...	3,111,477	...	3,516,946

• LIFE INSURANCE IN FORCE ($000 omitted)

Year	Whole Life	Term	Credit	Group	Industrial	Total
2007	696,695	891,435	174	5,879,457	...	7,467,761
2008	790,426	873,791	...	7,155,101	...	8,819,318
2009	887,185	930,823	...	10,729,123	...	12,547,131

KANSAS CITY LIFE INS CO

3520 Broadway
Kansas City, Missouri 64111-2565
Tel: 816-753-7000

AMB#: 006605
Began Business: 06/00/1895
Agency Off: Donald E. Krebs

Best's Financial Strength Rating: A g
FSC: IX

• NET PREMIUMS AND DEPOSITS ($000 omitted)

Year	Individual Life	Individual & Group Annuities	Group Life & A&H	Credit Life & A&H	Individual A&H	Total
2007	118,300	101,035	46,009	...	441	265,786
2008	115,699	102,735	48,913	...	379	267,725
2009	110,583	152,495	48,212	...	334	311,624

• NET OPERATING GAIN ($000 omitted)

Year	Individual Life	Individual & Group Annuities	Group Life & A&H	Credit Life & A&H	Individual A&H	Total
2007	25,120	9,900	-1,896	...	-75	50,141
2008	8,817	4,803	-1,491	...	7	27,301
2009	6,686	20,202	-2,167	...	258	24,979

• COMPARATIVE FINANCIALS ($000 omitted)

Year	Assets	Capital & Surplus	Net Invest Income	Benefits Paid	Realized Cap Gains	Policyholder Dividends	Contract Lns (% of assets)
2007	3,258,283	357,332	183,022	370,727	-2,423	3,669	2.2
2008	2,998,063	306,247	170,969	344,582	-47,416	3,484	2.3
2009	3,152,631	336,615	167,449	308,859	-5,524	3,362	2.1

• ORDINARY LIFE STATISTICS

Year	Av. Ord. Policy Issued ($)	Av. Ord. Policy In Force ($)	Avg. Prem ($/M)	1st Yr Prem/ Total Prem	Ord. Lapse Ratio
2007	256,211	78,161	6.22	13.1	6.1
2008	241,980	80,827	6.20	10.9	7.2
2009	241,567	83,358	6.09	11.4	7.5

• NEW LIFE BUSINESS ISSUED ($000 omitted)

Year	Whole Life	Term	Credit	Group	Industrial	Total
2007	673,028	1,455,573	...	708,795	...	2,837,396
2008	535,550	1,273,731	...	614,475	...	2,423,756
2009	500,808	1,225,185	...	722,695	...	2,448,688

• LIFE INSURANCE IN FORCE ($000 omitted)

Year	Whole Life	Term	Credit	Group	Industrial	Total
2007	11,169,621	11,736,645	...	3,514,840	...	26,421,106
2008	10,771,891	11,862,902	...	3,304,822	...	25,939,615
2009	10,360,050	11,940,426	...	4,322,384	...	26,622,860

KEMPER INVESTORS LIFE INS CO

15375 SE 30th Place, Suite 310
Bellevue, Washington 98007
Tel: 425-577-5100

AMB#: 006225
Began Business: 09/22/1947
Agency Off: None

Best's Financial Strength Rating: A-
FSC: VIII

• **NET PREMIUMS AND DEPOSITS** ($000 omitted)

Year	Individual Life	Individual & Group Annuities	Group Life & A&H	Credit Life & A&H	Individual A&H	Total
2007	5,227	141,559	-120,749	...	...	26,037
2008	2	83,627	-162,667	...	...	-79,038
2009	0	84,070	-185,668	...	...	-101,598

• **NET OPERATING GAIN** ($000 omitted)

Year	Individual Life	Individual & Group Annuities	Group Life & A&H	Credit Life & A&H	Individual A&H	Total
2007	-11	-15,938	-3,700	...	...	-19,649
2008	-138	-3,551	-8,003	...	...	-11,692
2009	-273	25,122	-4,905	...	...	19,945

• **COMPARATIVE FINANCIALS** ($000 omitted)

Year	Assets	Capital & Surplus	Net Invest Income	Benefits Paid	Realized Cap Gains	Policyholder Dividends	Contract Lns (% of assets)
2007	16,700,205	186,926	16,414	896,071	-212	...	0.3
2008	13,886,167	166,863	24,127	919,535	-4,003	...	0.5
2009	13,324,913	187,496	25,263	1,416,927	-2,540	...	0.4

• **ORDINARY LIFE STATISTICS**

Year	Av. Ord. Policy Issued ($)	Av. Ord. Policy In Force ($)	Avg. Prem ($/M)	1st Yr Prem/ Total Prem	Ord. Lapse Ratio
2007	...	...	...	...	...
2008	...	...	...	...	...
2009	...	...	...	...	...

• **NEW LIFE BUSINESS ISSUED** ($000 omitted)

Year	Whole Life	Term	Credit	Group	Industrial	Total
2007	...	...	...	414,363	...	414,363
2008	...	...	...	614,063	...	614,063
2009	335	...	...	380,682	...	381,017

• **LIFE INSURANCE IN FORCE** ($000 omitted)

Year	Whole Life	Term	Credit	Group	Industrial	Total
2007	2,080,874	90,985	...	60,894,609	...	63,066,468
2008	1,986,223	83,394	...	61,020,910	...	63,090,527
2009	1,865,573	75,930	...	59,516,228	...	61,457,731

KNIGHTS OF COLUMBUS

P.O. Box 1670
New Haven, Connecticut 06507-0901
Tel: 203-752-4000

AMB#: 006616
Began Business: 02/02/1882
Agency Off: Thomas P. Smith

Best's Financial Strength Rating: A++
FSC: XIV

• **NET PREMIUMS AND DEPOSITS** ($000 omitted)

Year	Individual Life	Individual & Group Annuities	Group Life & A&H	Credit Life & A&H	Individual A&H	Total
2007	904,063	...	...	...	29,142	1,149,034
2008	945,300	...	...	...	33,039	1,328,979
2009	919,518	...	...	...	36,115	1,479,116

• **NET OPERATING GAIN** ($000 omitted)

Year	Individual Life	Individual & Group Annuities	Group Life & A&H	Credit Life & A&H	Individual A&H	Total
2007	73,528	38,246	...	...	10,149	54,585
2008	137,364	39,147	...	...	5,891	113,511
2009	119,268	40,248	...	...	8,068	85,622

• **COMPARATIVE FINANCIALS** ($000 omitted)

Year	Assets	Capital & Surplus	Net Invest Income	Benefits Paid	Realized Cap Gains	Policyholder Dividends	Contract Lns (% of assets)
2007	14,013,813	1,751,216	748,657	496,587	33,786	364,399	4.9
2008	14,051,335	1,618,816	781,158	521,225	-102,316	311,713	5.1
2009	15,548,928	1,647,504	799,662	558,164	-63,106	318,010	5.0

• **ORDINARY LIFE STATISTICS**

Year	Av. Ord. Policy Issued ($)	Av. Ord. Policy In Force ($)	Avg. Prem ($/M)	1st Yr Prem/ Total Prem	Ord. Lapse Ratio
2007	84,028	40,168	13.59	5.1	3.7
2008	90,629	40,791	13.85	4.9	3.7
2009	108,808	43,992	12.44	5.0	4.0

• **NEW LIFE BUSINESS ISSUED** ($000 omitted)

Year	Whole Life	Term	Credit	Group	Industrial	Total
2007	2,076,213	4,401,399	...	...	...	6,477,612
2008	2,015,052	4,611,640	...	...	...	6,626,692
2009	1,883,683	5,509,275	...	...	...	7,392,958

• **LIFE INSURANCE IN FORCE** ($000 omitted)

Year	Whole Life	Term	Credit	Group	Industrial	Total
2007	35,742,746	30,581,494	...	...	...	66,324,240
2008	35,971,979	32,074,017	...	...	...	68,045,996
2009	38,102,361	35,669,472	...	...	...	73,771,833

KENTUCKY FUNERAL DIRECTORS LF

P.O. Box 5649
Abilene, Texas 79606
Tel: 800-692-5976

AMB#: 060365
Began Business: 05/31/2001
Agency Off: B. Kris Seale

Best's Financial Strength Rating: B+
FSC: III

• **NET PREMIUMS AND DEPOSITS** ($000 omitted)

Year	Individual Life	Individual & Group Annuities	Group Life & A&H	Credit Life & A&H	Individual A&H	Total
2007	373	647	...	...	...	1,021
2008	623	606	...	...	...	1,228
2009	666	482	...	...	...	1,148

• **NET OPERATING GAIN** ($000 omitted)

Year	Individual Life	Individual & Group Annuities	Group Life & A&H	Credit Life & A&H	Individual A&H	Total
2007	63	106	...	...	...	169
2008	62	103	...	...	...	165
2009	100	130	...	...	...	230

• **COMPARATIVE FINANCIALS** ($000 omitted)

Year	Assets	Capital & Surplus	Net Invest Income	Benefits Paid	Realized Cap Gains	Policyholder Dividends	Contract Lns (% of assets)
2007	11,574	3,744	595	833	-2	...	0.0
2008	12,073	3,842	653	826	-45	...	...
2009	12,559	4,033	684	911	-34	...	0.0

• **ORDINARY LIFE STATISTICS**

Year	Av. Ord. Policy Issued ($)	Av. Ord. Policy In Force ($)	Avg. Prem ($/M)	1st Yr Prem/ Total Prem	Ord. Lapse Ratio
2007	...	...	...	...	...
2008	...	...	...	...	...
2009	...	...	...	...	...

• **NEW LIFE BUSINESS ISSUED** ($000 omitted)

Year	Whole Life	Term	Credit	Group	Industrial	Total
2007	467	...	...	...	...	467
2008	868	...	...	...	...	868
2009	702	...	...	...	...	702

• **LIFE INSURANCE IN FORCE** ($000 omitted)

Year	Whole Life	Term	Credit	Group	Industrial	Total
2007	5,128	...	...	...	...	5,128
2008	5,863	...	...	...	...	5,863
2009	6,374	...	...	...	...	6,374

LAFAYETTE LIFE INS CO

P.O. Box 7007
Lafayette, Indiana 47903-7007
Tel: 765-477-7411

AMB#: 006617
Began Business: 12/26/1905
Agency Off: Jerry B. Stillwell

Best's Financial Strength Rating: A+ g
FSC: XV

• **NET PREMIUMS AND DEPOSITS** ($000 omitted)

Year	Individual Life	Individual & Group Annuities	Group Life & A&H	Credit Life & A&H	Individual A&H	Total
2007	199,490	180,654	31,352	...	...	411,495
2008	211,870	184,303	30,681	...	...	426,854
2009	239,645	205,505	834	...	...	445,984

• **NET OPERATING GAIN** ($000 omitted)

Year	Individual Life	Individual & Group Annuities	Group Life & A&H	Credit Life & A&H	Individual A&H	Total
2007	2,070	2,184	-813	...	18	3,460
2008	2,840	669	-1,115	...	9	2,404
2009	7,059	1,054	34	...	11	8,158

• **COMPARATIVE FINANCIALS** ($000 omitted)

Year	Assets	Capital & Surplus	Net Invest Income	Benefits Paid	Realized Cap Gains	Policyholder Dividends	Contract Lns (% of assets)
2007	1,937,269	118,208	100,502	211,904	-4,100	31,664	6.3
2008	2,017,159	102,895	99,989	251,637	-12,031	34,066	7.3
2009	2,268,230	115,750	124,148	209,034	-7,937	37,328	7.7

• **ORDINARY LIFE STATISTICS**

Year	Av. Ord. Policy Issued ($)	Av. Ord. Policy In Force ($)	Avg. Prem ($/M)	1st Yr Prem/ Total Prem	Ord. Lapse Ratio
2007	347,333	127,490	20.39	16.1	6.7
2008	364,708	136,145	20.55	17.4	9.7
2009	352,986	146,733	21.31	15.2	9.2

• **NEW LIFE BUSINESS ISSUED** ($000 omitted)

Year	Whole Life	Term	Credit	Group	Industrial	Total
2007	964,257	479,257	...	3,296,116	...	4,739,630
2008	1,009,140	748,386	...	1,568,551	...	3,326,077
2009	1,024,042	1,037,399	...	...	...	2,061,441

• **LIFE INSURANCE IN FORCE** ($000 omitted)

Year	Whole Life	Term	Credit	Group	Industrial	Total
2007	7,938,050	2,991,641	...	12,380,556	...	23,310,247
2008	8,132,529	3,353,328	...	7,215,435	...	18,701,292
2009	8,365,119	3,982,427	...	768,530	...	13,116,076

LEWER LIFE INS CO

P.O. Box 32395
Kansas City, Missouri 64171-5395
Tel: 816-753-4390

AMB#: 007393
Began Business: 10/01/1987
Agency Off: Michael L. Dlugolecki

Best's Financial Strength Rating: B **FSC:** IV

• NET PREMIUMS AND DEPOSITS ($000 omitted)

Year	Individual Life	Individual & Group Annuities	Group Life & A&H	Credit Life & A&H	Individual A&H	Total
2007	438	287	4,361	...	...	5,085
2008	434	287	5,152	...	...	5,872
2009	373	227	4,733	...	...	5,332

• NET OPERATING GAIN ($000 omitted)

Year	Individual Life	Individual & Group Annuities	Group Life & A&H	Credit Life & A&H	Individual A&H	Total
2007	135	53	536	...	...	724
2008	199	57	304	...	...	561
2009	73	139	575	...	...	787

• COMPARATIVE FINANCIALS ($000 omitted)

Year	Assets	Capital & Surplus	Net Invest Income	Benefits Paid	Realized Cap Gains	Policyholder Dividends	Contract Lns (% of assets)
2007	27,493	7,896	1,425	3,738	...	...	2.1
2008	27,564	7,973	1,394	4,335	-116	...	2.2
2009	27,498	8,556	1,436	3,761	-35	...	2.1

• ORDINARY LIFE STATISTICS

Year	Av. Ord. Policy Issued ($)	Av. Ord. Policy In Force ($)	Avg. Prem ($/M)	1st Yr Prem/ Total Prem	Ord. Lapse Ratio
2007	...	...	...	...	...
2008	...	...	...	...	...
2009	...	...	...	...	...

• NEW LIFE BUSINESS ISSUED ($000 omitted)

Year	Whole Life	Term	Credit	Group	Industrial	Total
2007	...	...	...	...	...	...
2008	652	...	...	...	...	652
2009	1,265	...	...	...	...	1,265

• LIFE INSURANCE IN FORCE ($000 omitted)

Year	Whole Life	Term	Credit	Group	Industrial	Total
2007	39,811	...	...	...	...	39,811
2008	38,358	...	...	...	...	38,358
2009	36,340	...	...	...	...	36,340

LIBERTY LIFE ASSUR OF BOSTON

100 Liberty Way
Dover, New Hampshire 03820-1525
Tel: 617-357-9500

AMB#: 006627
Began Business: 01/15/1964
Agency Off: Stephen M. Batza

Best's Financial Strength Rating: A **FSC:** X

• NET PREMIUMS AND DEPOSITS ($000 omitted)

Year	Individual Life	Individual & Group Annuities	Group Life & A&H	Credit Life & A&H	Individual A&H	Total
2007	229,059	303,986	505,602	...	137	1,038,783
2008	245,051	339,333	596,097	...	156	1,180,637
2009	348,963	330,902	611,590	...	193	1,291,648

• NET OPERATING GAIN ($000 omitted)

Year	Individual Life	Individual & Group Annuities	Group Life & A&H	Credit Life & A&H	Individual A&H	Total
2007	7,185	-1,595	15,746	...	136	21,471
2008	8,513	-21,708	20,110	...	90	7,005
2009	-18	-4,355	-1,483	...	141	-5,715

• COMPARATIVE FINANCIALS ($000 omitted)

Year	Assets	Capital & Surplus	Net Invest Income	Benefits Paid	Realized Cap Gains	Policyholder Dividends	Contract Lns (% of assets)
2007	11,185,421	482,667	445,825	800,147	14,059	10,867	0.8
2008	11,605,062	460,448	469,364	835,259	-34,570	11,300	0.8
2009	12,983,175	597,543	494,457	916,742	-17,761	11,694	0.8

• ORDINARY LIFE STATISTICS

Year	Av. Ord. Policy Issued ($)	Av. Ord. Policy In Force ($)	Avg. Prem ($/M)	1st Yr Prem/ Total Prem	Ord. Lapse Ratio
2007	171,386	117,805	8.41	7.7	4.2
2008	169,650	121,133	8.61	6.9	7.1
2009	155,525	125,390	11.11	5.5	5.4

• NEW LIFE BUSINESS ISSUED ($000 omitted)

Year	Whole Life	Term	Credit	Group	Industrial	Total
2007	720,361	4,026,528	...	16,950,344	...	21,697,233
2008	788,120	4,267,788	...	10,939,556	...	15,995,464
2009	1,139,034	4,367,334	...	9,570,609	...	15,076,977

• LIFE INSURANCE IN FORCE ($000 omitted)

Year	Whole Life	Term	Credit	Group	Industrial	Total
2007	8,689,202	22,107,114	...	53,894,148	...	84,690,464
2008	8,588,320	24,540,490	...	66,303,792	...	99,432,602
2009	9,391,088	26,931,841	...	80,345,076	...	116,668,006

LIBERTY BANKERS LIFE INS CO

1605 LBJ Freeway, Suite 710
Dallas, Texas 75234
Tel: 972-484-6063

AMB#: 007011
Began Business: 02/07/1958
Agency Off: None

Best's Financial Strength Rating: B- **FSC:** VIII

• NET PREMIUMS AND DEPOSITS ($000 omitted)

Year	Individual Life	Individual & Group Annuities	Group Life & A&H	Credit Life & A&H	Individual A&H	Total
2007	8,698	176,034	...	...	...	184,732
2008	7,251	194,453	...	...	...	201,704
2009	9,538	295,246	...	...	...	304,783

• NET OPERATING GAIN ($000 omitted)

Year	Individual Life	Individual & Group Annuities	Group Life & A&H	Credit Life & A&H	Individual A&H	Total
2007	1,379	3,718	...	...	...	5,097
2008	2,262	12,118	...	...	...	14,380
2009	1,849	9,184	...	...	...	11,034

• COMPARATIVE FINANCIALS ($000 omitted)

Year	Assets	Capital & Surplus	Net Invest Income	Benefits Paid	Realized Cap Gains	Policyholder Dividends	Contract Lns (% of assets)
2007	666,011	60,937	41,708	67,601	4,430	9	0.3
2008	807,084	63,206	57,164	81,219	-12,393	9	0.2
2009	1,040,432	96,011	61,129	107,688	-6,799	10	0.2

• ORDINARY LIFE STATISTICS

Year	Av. Ord. Policy Issued ($)	Av. Ord. Policy In Force ($)	Avg. Prem ($/M)	1st Yr Prem/ Total Prem	Ord. Lapse Ratio
2007	...	...	...	...	...
2008	...	...	...	...	...
2009	...	...	...	...	...

• NEW LIFE BUSINESS ISSUED ($000 omitted)

Year	Whole Life	Term	Credit	Group	Industrial	Total
2007	31,394	7,562	...	...	...	38,956
2008	55,786	25,168	...	...	...	80,954
2009	247,751	4,616	...	...	...	252,367

• LIFE INSURANCE IN FORCE ($000 omitted)

Year	Whole Life	Term	Credit	Group	Industrial	Total
2007	196,309	45,089	...	...	29,854	271,252
2008	213,306	64,203	...	...	28,457	305,966
2009	394,355	36,700	...	...	27,301	458,356

LIBERTY LIFE INSURANCE COMPANY

P.O. Box 1389
Greenville, South Carolina 29602-1389
Tel: 800-551-8354

AMB#: 006175
Began Business: 07/01/1909
Agency Off: F. Erik Bugge

Best's Financial Strength Rating: A **FSC:** IX

• NET PREMIUMS AND DEPOSITS ($000 omitted)

Year	Individual Life	Individual & Group Annuities	Group Life & A&H	Credit Life & A&H	Individual A&H	Total
2007	133,459	131,685	43,527	25	11,505	320,200
2008	134,516	109,029	41,387	12	11,476	296,421
2009	126,419	820,268	37,856	9	11,072	995,623

• NET OPERATING GAIN ($000 omitted)

Year	Individual Life	Individual & Group Annuities	Group Life & A&H	Credit Life & A&H	Individual A&H	Total
2007	12,303	14,358	-3,594	-22	1,945	24,991
2008	7,484	9,852	-3,664	7	2,688	16,368
2009	9,726	-20,185	-1,760	12	2,332	-9,875

• COMPARATIVE FINANCIALS ($000 omitted)

Year	Assets	Capital & Surplus	Net Invest Income	Benefits Paid	Realized Cap Gains	Policyholder Dividends	Contract Lns (% of assets)
2007	3,722,392	261,542	200,190	425,552	14,268	1,089	2.8
2008	3,597,209	234,251	197,748	401,201	-35,479	1,099	2.9
2009	4,326,571	274,963	207,650	383,198	-21,981	1,072	2.4

• ORDINARY LIFE STATISTICS

Year	Av. Ord. Policy Issued ($)	Av. Ord. Policy In Force ($)	Avg. Prem ($/M)	1st Yr Prem/ Total Prem	Ord. Lapse Ratio
2007	149,405	35,563	5.97	11.2	7.8
2008	155,617	36,633	5.89	10.1	8.4
2009	147,031	38,086	5.81	8.3	8.2

• NEW LIFE BUSINESS ISSUED ($000 omitted)

Year	Whole Life	Term	Credit	Group	Industrial	Total
2007	271,244	4,303,692	...	367,083	...	4,942,019
2008	212,823	3,308,789	...	336,048	...	3,857,660
2009	139,101	2,904,725	...	255,528	...	3,299,354

• LIFE INSURANCE IN FORCE ($000 omitted)

Year	Whole Life	Term	Credit	Group	Industrial	Total
2007	17,987,825	13,852,566	1,507	2,781,752	249,403	34,873,053
2008	16,809,872	14,617,485	1,150	2,804,928	239,648	34,473,083
2009	15,928,336	15,537,227	872	2,665,762	229,998	34,362,195

LIBERTY NATIONAL LIFE INS CO

P.O. Box 2612
Birmingham, Alabama 35202
Tel: 205-325-2722

AMB#: 006629
Began Business: 07/01/1929
Agency Off: None

Best's Financial Strength Rating: A+ g **FSC:** X

• NET PREMIUMS AND DEPOSITS ($000 omitted)

Year	Individual Life	Individual & Group Annuities	Group Life & A&H	Credit Life & A&H	Individual A&H	Total
2007	379,168	4,871	16,782	...	139,218	540,039
2008	336,460	5,267	2,308	...	133,778	477,814
2009	319,137	146,875	1,895	...	130,419	598,326

• NET OPERATING GAIN ($000 omitted)

Year	Individual Life	Individual & Group Annuities	Group Life & A&H	Credit Life & A&H	Individual A&H	Total
2007	100,265	740	1,502	...	48,481	221,132
2008	93,283	1,028	3,145	...	48,241	217,586
2009	76,509	-3,819	-2,053	...	39,292	168,656

• COMPARATIVE FINANCIALS ($000 omitted)

Year	Assets	Capital & Surplus	Net Invest Income	Benefits Paid	Realized Cap Gains	Policyholder Dividends	Contract Lns (% of assets)
2007	4,981,019	607,030	354,228	305,753	-3,685	30	3.9
2008	5,149,123	674,133	360,684	295,368	-62,335	24	3.9
2009	5,514,587	721,609	341,212	300,931	-105,988	23	3.8

• ORDINARY LIFE STATISTICS

Year	Av. Ord. Policy Issued ($)	Av. Ord. Policy In Force ($)	Avg. Prem ($/M)	1st Yr Prem/ Total Prem	Ord. Lapse Ratio
2007	38,534	28,859	10.83	7.3	8.5
2008	38,167	29,144	10.69	7.3	9.5
2009	37,696	29,279	10.75	7.7	10.4

• NEW LIFE BUSINESS ISSUED ($000 omitted)

Year	Whole Life	Term	Credit	Group	Industrial	Total
2007	2,256,837	1,299,915	...	675,690	...	4,232,442
2008	2,668,661	1,646,289	...	676,960	...	4,991,910
2009	2,332,593	1,601,258	...	1,381,361	...	5,315,211

• LIFE INSURANCE IN FORCE ($000 omitted)

Year	Whole Life	Term	Credit	Group	Industrial	Total
2007	31,049,971	11,324,170	...	1,916,792	739,031	45,029,964
2008	30,979,028	11,191,158	...	1,973,069	718,350	44,861,605
2009	30,291,098	10,768,458	...	2,758,256	699,039	44,516,851

LIFE INSURANCE CO OF ALABAMA

P.O. Box 349
Gadsden, Alabama 35901
Tel: 256-543-2022

AMB#: 006637
Began Business: 08/13/1952
Agency Off: Clarence W. Bracewell, Jr.

Best's Financial Strength Rating: B+ **FSC:** V

• NET PREMIUMS AND DEPOSITS ($000 omitted)

Year	Individual Life	Individual & Group Annuities	Group Life & A&H	Credit Life & A&H	Individual A&H	Total
2007	4,427	79	2,728	...	30,038	37,272
2008	4,978	43	2,658	...	31,568	39,248
2009	5,118	38	2,674	...	32,909	40,739

• NET OPERATING GAIN ($000 omitted)

Year	Individual Life	Individual & Group Annuities	Group Life & A&H	Credit Life & A&H	Individual A&H	Total
2007	507	11	-6	...	1,914	2,425
2008	602	19	82	...	1,475	2,178
2009	359	-23	124	...	3,054	3,514

• COMPARATIVE FINANCIALS ($000 omitted)

Year	Assets	Capital & Surplus	Net Invest Income	Benefits Paid	Realized Cap Gains	Policyholder Dividends	Contract Lns (% of assets)
2007	79,199	16,632	4,067	20,003	0	19	3.3
2008	81,803	16,138	4,254	20,553	-811	18	3.3
2009	88,751	18,922	4,191	20,497	-202	17	3.1

• ORDINARY LIFE STATISTICS

Year	Av. Ord. Policy Issued ($)	Av. Ord. Policy In Force ($)	Avg. Prem ($/M)	1st Yr Prem/ Total Prem	Ord. Lapse Ratio
2007	...	...	...	...	...
2008	...	...	...	...	...
2009	...	...	...	...	...

• NEW LIFE BUSINESS ISSUED ($000 omitted)

Year	Whole Life	Term	Credit	Group	Industrial	Total
2007	65,281	78,063	...	...	...	143,344
2008	76,547	54,974	...	...	...	131,521
2009	65,046	65,083	...	...	...	130,129

• LIFE INSURANCE IN FORCE ($000 omitted)

Year	Whole Life	Term	Credit	Group	Industrial	Total
2007	280,177	389,703	...	1,204,834	...	1,874,714
2008	302,727	387,386	...	1,040,480	...	1,730,593
2009	342,104	373,153	...	1,190,105	...	1,905,362

LIBERTY UNION LIFE ASSURANCE

30775 Barrington Street
Madison Heights, Michigan 48071
Tel: 248-583-7123

AMB#: 006799
Began Business: 06/05/1964
Agency Off: None

Best's Financial Strength Rating: B **FSC:** III

• NET PREMIUMS AND DEPOSITS ($000 omitted)

Year	Individual Life	Individual & Group Annuities	Group Life & A&H	Credit Life & A&H	Individual A&H	Total
2007	1	...	30,270	...	...	30,271
2008	1	...	25,190	...	...	25,191
2009	1	...	21,058	...	103	21,162

• NET OPERATING GAIN ($000 omitted)

Year	Individual Life	Individual & Group Annuities	Group Life & A&H	Credit Life & A&H	Individual A&H	Total
2007	-1	...	203	...	...	202
2008	-2	...	-218	...	...	-219
2009	0	...	289	...	-28	261

• COMPARATIVE FINANCIALS ($000 omitted)

Year	Assets	Capital & Surplus	Net Invest Income	Benefits Paid	Realized Cap Gains	Policyholder Dividends	Contract Lns (% of assets)
2007	11,495	4,462	305	21,932	-96	...	0.1
2008	10,021	4,124	357	18,911	-695	...	0.1
2009	10,591	4,289	303	14,873	-1	...	0.1

• ORDINARY LIFE STATISTICS

Year	Av. Ord. Policy Issued ($)	Av. Ord. Policy In Force ($)	Avg. Prem ($/M)	1st Yr Prem/ Total Prem	Ord. Lapse Ratio
2007	...	...	...	...	...
2008	...	...	...	...	...
2009	...	...	...	...	...

• NEW LIFE BUSINESS ISSUED ($000 omitted)

Year	Whole Life	Term	Credit	Group	Industrial	Total
2007	...	...	...	20,568	...	20,568
2008	...	...	...	19,216	...	19,216
2009	...	...	...	21,306	...	21,306

• LIFE INSURANCE IN FORCE ($000 omitted)

Year	Whole Life	Term	Credit	Group	Industrial	Total
2007	15	20	...	124,703	...	124,738
2008	15	20	...	93,984	...	94,019
2009	15	20	...	76,696	...	76,731

LIFE INS CO OF BOSTON & NY

120 Royall Street
Canton, Massachusetts 02021-1098
Tel: 914-712-0610

AMB#: 068126
Began Business: 03/07/1990
Agency Off: Peter S. Tillson

Best's Financial Strength Rating: A- g **FSC:** VIII

• NET PREMIUMS AND DEPOSITS ($000 omitted)

Year	Individual Life	Individual & Group Annuities	Group Life & A&H	Credit Life & A&H	Individual A&H	Total
2007	10,021	...	1,206	...	7	11,233
2008	11,830	...	1,044	...	318	13,192
2009	12,813	...	925	...	925	14,663

• NET OPERATING GAIN ($000 omitted)

Year	Individual Life	Individual & Group Annuities	Group Life & A&H	Credit Life & A&H	Individual A&H	Total
2007	783	...	21	...	-13	791
2008	2,383	...	206	...	-29	2,559
2009	925	...	116	...	27	1,068

• COMPARATIVE FINANCIALS ($000 omitted)

Year	Assets	Capital & Surplus	Net Invest Income	Benefits Paid	Realized Cap Gains	Policyholder Dividends	Contract Lns (% of assets)
2007	62,967	9,591	3,246	4,554	-27	...	19.2
2008	68,395	11,544	3,527	4,878	-318	...	20.5
2009	77,271	13,225	3,733	5,291	-44	...	20.4

• ORDINARY LIFE STATISTICS

Year	Av. Ord. Policy Issued ($)	Av. Ord. Policy In Force ($)	Avg. Prem ($/M)	1st Yr Prem/ Total Prem	Ord. Lapse Ratio
2007	32,950	23,476	12.09	13.2	9.3
2008	38,850	23,790	13.25	18.8	18.6
2009	38,568	24,866	13.01	15.4	11.6

• NEW LIFE BUSINESS ISSUED ($000 omitted)

Year	Whole Life	Term	Credit	Group	Industrial	Total
2007	124,990	5,031	...	45,249	...	175,270
2008	239,285	8,811	...	92	...	248,188
2009	227,894	3,594	...	...	...	231,488

• LIFE INSURANCE IN FORCE ($000 omitted)

Year	Whole Life	Term	Credit	Group	Industrial	Total
2007	787,668	50,117	...	180,112	...	1,017,897
2008	851,634	52,251	...	116,130	...	1,020,015
2009	948,474	51,392	...	101,477	...	1,101,342

LIFE INSURANCE CO OF LOUISIANA

P.O. Box 1803
Shreveport, Louisiana 71166
Tel: 318-221-0646

AMB#: 007775
Began Business: 04/01/1964
Agency Off: None

Best's Financial Strength Rating: B
FSC: III

• NET PREMIUMS AND DEPOSITS ($000 omitted)

Year	Individual Life	Individual & Group Annuities	Group Life & A&H	Credit Life & A&H	Individual A&H	Total
2007	5	1	...	214	...	220
2008	9	2	...	139	...	151
2009	11	1	...	78	...	90

• NET OPERATING GAIN ($000 omitted)

Year	Individual Life	Individual & Group Annuities	Group Life & A&H	Credit Life & A&H	Individual A&H	Total
2007	-52	-3	...	201	...	146
2008	-13	1	...	152	...	140
2009	-31	-4	...	121	...	86

• COMPARATIVE FINANCIALS ($000 omitted)

Year	Assets	Capital & Surplus	Net Invest Income	Benefits Paid	Realized Cap Gains	Policyholder Dividends	Contract Lns (% of assets)
2007	7,894	3,582	282	140	136	...	0.1
2008	6,987	3,515	288	126	105	...	0.1
2009	7,246	3,716	256	81	30	...	0.1

• ORDINARY LIFE STATISTICS

Year	Av. Ord. Policy Issued ($)	Av. Ord. Policy In Force ($)	Avg. Prem ($/M)	1st Yr Prem/ Total Prem	Ord. Lapse Ratio
2007	...	...	...	...	...
2008	...	...	...	...	...
2009	...	...	...	...	...

• NEW LIFE BUSINESS ISSUED ($000 omitted)

Year	Whole Life	Term	Credit	Group	Industrial	Total
2007	...	...	12,468	...	...	12,468
2008	...	300	9,651	...	...	9,951
2009	500	...	5,342	...	...	5,842

• LIFE INSURANCE IN FORCE ($000 omitted)

Year	Whole Life	Term	Credit	Group	Industrial	Total
2007	2,983	105	29,013	...	...	32,101
2008	3,235	105	22,722	...	...	26,062
2009	3,745	71	17,111	...	...	20,927

LIFE INSURANCE CO OF SOUTHWEST

1300 West Mockingbird Lane
Dallas, Texas 75247-4921
Tel: 214-638-7100

AMB#: 006647
Began Business: 01/02/1956
Agency Off: None

Best's Financial Strength Rating: A g
FSC: XII

• NET PREMIUMS AND DEPOSITS ($000 omitted)

Year	Individual Life	Individual & Group Annuities	Group Life & A&H	Credit Life & A&H	Individual A&H	Total
2007	132,061	809,316	42	...	110	941,529
2008	166,886	1,091,553	37	...	101	1,258,577
2009	184,336	1,434,907	41	...	98	1,619,383

• NET OPERATING GAIN ($000 omitted)

Year	Individual Life	Individual & Group Annuities	Group Life & A&H	Credit Life & A&H	Individual A&H	Total
2007	9,969	40,656	244	...	86	51,363
2008	176	324	83	...	20	3,206
2009	15,289	63,901	428	...	72	92,359

• COMPARATIVE FINANCIALS ($000 omitted)

Year	Assets	Capital & Surplus	Net Invest Income	Benefits Paid	Realized Cap Gains	Policyholder Dividends	Contract Lns (% of assets)
2007	5,849,880	364,627	317,136	493,380	-7,869	20	2.4
2008	6,525,364	420,121	161,415	572,772	-40,212	21	2.3
2009	8,209,832	492,310	528,978	545,669	-40,585	37	1.9

• ORDINARY LIFE STATISTICS

Year	Av. Ord. Policy Issued ($)	Av. Ord. Policy In Force ($)	Avg. Prem ($/M)	1st Yr Prem/ Total Prem	Ord. Lapse Ratio
2007	219,621	139,598	9.58	33.2	11.9
2008	225,373	150,923	10.45	35.1	11.4
2009	202,526	155,581	10.54	29.1	12.4

• NEW LIFE BUSINESS ISSUED ($000 omitted)

Year	Whole Life	Term	Credit	Group	Industrial	Total
2007	3,244,765	540,621	...	...	...	3,785,386
2008	3,796,103	618,053	...	...	...	4,414,156
2009	3,734,304	614,737	...	...	...	4,349,041

• LIFE INSURANCE IN FORCE ($000 omitted)

Year	Whole Life	Term	Credit	Group	Industrial	Total
2007	11,923,324	2,608,114	...	18,388	...	14,549,826
2008	13,978,886	2,786,052	...	17,724	...	16,782,662
2009	15,527,418	2,826,358	...	17,390	...	18,371,166

LIFE INSURANCE OF NORTH AMER

1601 Chestnut Street, 2 Liberty Place
Philadelphia, Pennsylvania 19192-2362
Tel: 215-761-1000

AMB#: 006645
Began Business: 09/05/1957
Agency Off: None

Best's Financial Strength Rating: A g
FSC: XV

• NET PREMIUMS AND DEPOSITS ($000 omitted)

Year	Individual Life	Individual & Group Annuities	Group Life & A&H	Credit Life & A&H	Individual A&H	Total
2007	7,164	177	2,041,679	...	2,543	2,051,563
2008	7,249	379	2,246,902	...	1,315	2,255,845
2009	6,262	193	2,294,560	...	3,646	2,304,661

• NET OPERATING GAIN ($000 omitted)

Year	Individual Life	Individual & Group Annuities	Group Life & A&H	Credit Life & A&H	Individual A&H	Total
2007	-6,379	1,540	184,460	...	138	179,759
2008	-5,080	-44,513	203,398	...	540	154,345
2009	-5,821	29,362	197,397	...	1,037	221,975

• COMPARATIVE FINANCIALS ($000 omitted)

Year	Assets	Capital & Surplus	Net Invest Income	Benefits Paid	Realized Cap Gains	Policyholder Dividends	Contract Lns (% of assets)
2007	5,880,600	641,254	177,728	1,461,982	-6,803	...	0.0
2008	5,464,298	628,615	184,867	1,662,552	-29,322	...	0.0
2009	5,732,662	769,441	165,912	1,669,587	-6,347	...	0.0

• ORDINARY LIFE STATISTICS

Year	Av. Ord. Policy Issued ($)	Av. Ord. Policy In Force ($)	Avg. Prem ($/M)	1st Yr Prem/ Total Prem	Ord. Lapse Ratio
2007	...	...	...	...	...
2008	...	...	...	...	...
2009	...	...	...	...	...

• NEW LIFE BUSINESS ISSUED ($000 omitted)

Year	Whole Life	Term	Credit	Group	Industrial	Total
2007	41,721		...	56,452,920	...	56,494,641
2008	47,737	727	...	48,319,357	...	48,367,821
2009	65,467	778	...	68,641,152	...	68,707,397

• LIFE INSURANCE IN FORCE ($000 omitted)

Year	Whole Life	Term	Credit	Group	Industrial	Total
2007	190,847	120,055	...	188,869,047	...	189,179,949
2008	202,085	20,002	...	220,037,996	...	220,260,083
2009	217,351	16,790	...	354,296,385	...	354,530,527

LIFE OF THE SOUTH INSURANCE CO

P.O. Box 44130
Jacksonville, Florida 32231-4130
Tel: 904-350-9660

AMB#: 008921
Began Business: 01/15/1982
Agency Off: None

Best's Financial Strength Rating: B++g
FSC: V

• NET PREMIUMS AND DEPOSITS ($000 omitted)

Year	Individual Life	Individual & Group Annuities	Group Life & A&H	Credit Life & A&H	Individual A&H	Total
2007	18	...	...	36,039	19,704	55,761
2008	3	...	...	48,985	19,549	68,538
2009	8	...	...	30,338	19,126	49,473

• NET OPERATING GAIN ($000 omitted)

Year	Individual Life	Individual & Group Annuities	Group Life & A&H	Credit Life & A&H	Individual A&H	Total
2007	9	...	13	2,454	-1,027	1,449
2008	2	...	...	4,437	1,240	5,679
2009	6	-23	...	6,871	1,407	8,261

• COMPARATIVE FINANCIALS ($000 omitted)

Year	Assets	Capital & Surplus	Net Invest Income	Benefits Paid	Realized Cap Gains	Policyholder Dividends	Contract Lns (% of assets)
2007	68,105	23,802	2,145	10,393	-87	...	...
2008	70,462	19,216	2,691	15,434	0	...	...
2009	62,970	17,865	6,361	15,266	-374	...	...

• ORDINARY LIFE STATISTICS

Year	Av. Ord. Policy Issued ($)	Av. Ord. Policy In Force ($)	Avg. Prem ($/M)	1st Yr Prem/ Total Prem	Ord. Lapse Ratio
2007	...	...	...	...	...
2008	...	...	...	...	...
2009	...	...	...	...	...

• NEW LIFE BUSINESS ISSUED ($000 omitted)

Year	Whole Life	Term	Credit	Group	Industrial	Total
2007	...	20	5,417,282	...	...	5,417,302
2008	...	322	5,332,039	...	...	5,332,361
2009	...	80	4,720,396	...	...	4,720,476

• LIFE INSURANCE IN FORCE ($000 omitted)

Year	Whole Life	Term	Credit	Group	Industrial	Total
2007	...	859	2,812,759	5,349	...	2,818,967
2008	...	178	2,987,737	26	...	2,987,941
2009	...	736	2,634,295	5,345	...	2,640,375

LIFESHIELD NATIONAL INS CO

P.O. Box 18223
Oklahoma City, Oklahoma 73154-0223
Tel: 405-236-2640

AMB#: 009458
Began Business: 05/06/1982
Agency Off: Gary R. Peterson

Best's Financial Strength Rating: B++ **FSC:** V

• NET PREMIUMS AND DEPOSITS ($000 omitted)

Year	Individual Life	Individual & Group Annuities	Group Life & A&H	Credit Life & A&H	Individual A&H	Total
2007	2,523	8	2,138	-6	76	4,740
2008	2,309	69	2,052	-2	5,502	9,931
2009	2,050	180	2,340	-5	10,003	14,568

• NET OPERATING GAIN ($000 omitted)

Year	Individual Life	Individual & Group Annuities	Group Life & A&H	Credit Life & A&H	Individual A&H	Total
2007	92	902	2,057	14	96	3,161
2008	-161	230	2,601	27	-4,819	-2,123
2009	-537	-633	2,853	11	-2,404	-710

• COMPARATIVE FINANCIALS ($000 omitted)

Year	Assets	Capital & Surplus	Net Invest Income	Benefits Paid	Realized Cap Gains	Policyholder Dividends	Contract Lns (% of assets)
2007	63,324	25,345	3,520	5,916	1	313	3.1
2008	67,109	22,038	2,260	8,862	-17	148	2.8
2009	60,537	14,978	185	8,902	-4,069	195	3.2

• ORDINARY LIFE STATISTICS

Year	Av. Ord. Policy Issued ($)	Av. Ord. Policy In Force ($)	Avg. Prem ($/M)	1st Yr Prem/ Total Prem	Ord. Lapse Ratio
2007	...	...	...	...	...
2008	...	...	...	...	...
2009	...	...	...	...	...

• NEW LIFE BUSINESS ISSUED ($000 omitted)

Year	Whole Life	Term	Credit	Group	Industrial	Total
2007	...	...	...	...	...	...
2008	...	...	...	91	...	91
2009	...	620	...	1,735	...	2,355

• LIFE INSURANCE IN FORCE ($000 omitted)

Year	Whole Life	Term	Credit	Group	Industrial	Total
2007	63,130	399,539	799	98,701	...	562,169
2008	62,535	324,469	546	83,347	...	470,897
2009	58,958	297,096	340	78,294	...	434,688

LIFEWISE ASSURANCE COMPANY

7001 220th Street S.W.
Mountlake Terrace, Washington 98043-2124
Tel: 425-918-4575

AMB#: 009086
Began Business: 11/18/1981
Agency Off: Stephen D. Melton

Best's Financial Strength Rating: A- g **FSC:** XI

• NET PREMIUMS AND DEPOSITS ($000 omitted)

Year	Individual Life	Individual & Group Annuities	Group Life & A&H	Credit Life & A&H	Individual A&H	Total
2007	29	...	39,168	...	...	39,196
2008	35	...	47,026	...	...	47,061
2009	30	...	51,543	...	...	51,574

• NET OPERATING GAIN ($000 omitted)

Year	Individual Life	Individual & Group Annuities	Group Life & A&H	Credit Life & A&H	Individual A&H	Total
2007	-80	...	5,737	...	...	5,657
2008	-34	...	3,406	...	...	3,372
2009	-41	...	4,713	...	...	4,672

• COMPARATIVE FINANCIALS ($000 omitted)

Year	Assets	Capital & Surplus	Net Invest Income	Benefits Paid	Realized Cap Gains	Policyholder Dividends	Contract Lns (% of assets)
2007	67,073	39,395	3,148	20,396	-106	...	0.0
2008	70,387	41,225	3,463	28,579	-1,864	...	0.0
2009	76,427	45,418	3,492	31,869	-260	...	0.0

• ORDINARY LIFE STATISTICS

Year	Av. Ord. Policy Issued ($)	Av. Ord. Policy In Force ($)	Avg. Prem ($/M)	1st Yr Prem/ Total Prem	Ord. Lapse Ratio
2007	...	...	...	...	...
2008	...	...	...	...	...
2009	...	...	...	...	...

• NEW LIFE BUSINESS ISSUED ($000 omitted)

Year	Whole Life	Term	Credit	Group	Industrial	Total
2007	165	...	...	587,221	...	587,386
2008	115	...	...	1,159,034	...	1,159,149
2009	149	...	...	1,314,413	...	1,314,562

• LIFE INSURANCE IN FORCE ($000 omitted)

Year	Whole Life	Term	Credit	Group	Industrial	Total
2007	1,010	...	...	6,043,849	...	6,044,859
2008	814	...	...	13,121,443	...	13,122,257
2009	868	...	...	12,381,942	...	12,382,810

LINCOLN BENEFIT LIFE CO

2940 South 84th Street
Lincoln, Nebraska 68506-4142
Tel: 800-525-9287

AMB#: 006657
Began Business: 10/19/1938
Agency Off: None

Best's Financial Strength Rating: A+ r **FSC:** XV

• NET PREMIUMS AND DEPOSITS ($000 omitted)

Year	Individual Life	Individual & Group Annuities	Group Life & A&H	Credit Life & A&H	Individual A&H	Total
2007	77	50,324	...	...	...	50,401
2008	105	37,129	...	...	...	37,234
2009	12	31,235	...	...	...	31,246

• NET OPERATING GAIN ($000 omitted)

Year	Individual Life	Individual & Group Annuities	Group Life & A&H	Credit Life & A&H	Individual A&H	Total
2007	...	...	...	...	...	9,087
2008	...	...	...	...	...	9,000
2009	...	...	...	...	...	8,525

• COMPARATIVE FINANCIALS ($000 omitted)

Year	Assets	Capital & Surplus	Net Invest Income	Benefits Paid	Realized Cap Gains	Policyholder Dividends	Contract Lns (% of assets)
2007	3,442,530	282,931	13,975	...	...	...	...
2008	2,184,805	278,816	13,687	...	-1,200	...	...
2009	2,418,532	305,997	11,528	...	0	...	...

• ORDINARY LIFE STATISTICS

Year	Av. Ord. Policy Issued ($)	Av. Ord. Policy In Force ($)	Avg. Prem ($/M)	1st Yr Prem/ Total Prem	Ord. Lapse Ratio
2007	...	...	...	...	...
2008	...	...	...	...	...
2009	...	...	...	...	...

• NEW LIFE BUSINESS ISSUED ($000 omitted)

Year	Whole Life	Term	Credit	Group	Industrial	Total
2007	11,226,420	40,964,618	...	547,253	...	52,738,291
2008	8,000,420	38,561,852	...	1,127,442	...	47,689,714
2009	6,446,445	35,000,035	...	2,027	...	41,448,507

• LIFE INSURANCE IN FORCE ($000 omitted)

Year	Whole Life	Term	Credit	Group	Industrial	Total
2007	69,985,776	247,387,097	5	5,262,538	...	322,635,416
2008	75,959,483	262,944,783	...	5,345,763	...	344,250,029
2009	82,480,753	268,487,149	...	5,613,350	...	356,581,252

LINCOLN HERITAGE LIFE INS CO

4343 East Camelback Road
Phoenix, Arizona 85018
Tel: 602-957-1650

AMB#: 006694
Began Business: 10/19/1963
Agency Off: Thomas A. Londen

Best's Financial Strength Rating: A- **FSC:** VIII

• NET PREMIUMS AND DEPOSITS ($000 omitted)

Year	Individual Life	Individual & Group Annuities	Group Life & A&H	Credit Life & A&H	Individual A&H	Total
2007	148,376	2,348	18,400	...	13,196	182,319
2008	163,344	4,264	20,699	...	13,297	201,604
2009	179,399	5,610	22,409	...	12,571	219,990

• NET OPERATING GAIN ($000 omitted)

Year	Individual Life	Individual & Group Annuities	Group Life & A&H	Credit Life & A&H	Individual A&H	Total
2007	4,298	59	564	...	-905	4,016
2008	4,623	381	1,119	...	466	6,589
2009	9,934	353	252	...	331	10,870

• COMPARATIVE FINANCIALS ($000 omitted)

Year	Assets	Capital & Surplus	Net Invest Income	Benefits Paid	Realized Cap Gains	Policyholder Dividends	Contract Lns (% of assets)
2007	587,072	88,947	27,954	80,904	172	416	4.6
2008	621,699	86,064	28,901	88,131	-4,264	409	4.5
2009	697,715	109,752	30,859	96,017	-10,704	384	4.4

• ORDINARY LIFE STATISTICS

Year	Av. Ord. Policy Issued ($)	Av. Ord. Policy In Force ($)	Avg. Prem ($/M)	1st Yr Prem/ Total Prem	Ord. Lapse Ratio
2007	8,412	7,215	61.51	20.0	12.0
2008	8,186	7,161	65.87	21.8	9.4
2009	7,856	7,135	68.15	25.3	8.3

• NEW LIFE BUSINESS ISSUED ($000 omitted)

Year	Whole Life	Term	Credit	Group	Industrial	Total
2007	443,046	...	...	23,160	...	466,206
2008	537,941	16,492	...	26,058	...	580,491
2009	694,876	20,086	...	26,037	...	740,999

• LIFE INSURANCE IN FORCE ($000 omitted)

Year	Whole Life	Term	Credit	Group	Industrial	Total
2007	2,319,434	99,523	...	66,226	...	2,485,183
2008	2,487,512	110,077	...	77,050	...	2,674,639
2009	2,872,204	117,177	...	105,903	...	3,095,285

LINCOLN LIFE & ANNUITY CO NY

100 North Greene Street
Greensboro, North Carolina 27401
Tel: 603-226-5000

AMB#: 006239
Began Business: 12/31/1897
Agency Off: Warren H. May

Best's Financial Strength Rating: A+ g **FSC:** XV

• NET PREMIUMS AND DEPOSITS ($000 omitted)

Year	Individual Life	Individual & Group Annuities	Group Life & A&H	Credit Life & A&H	Individual A&H	Total
2007	320,449	849,357	26,971	...	717	1,197,494
2008	347,931	886,690	36,277	...	653	1,271,552
2009	338,270	788,254	44,267	...	505	1,171,296

• NET OPERATING GAIN ($000 omitted)

Year	Individual Life	Individual & Group Annuities	Group Life & A&H	Credit Life & A&H	Individual A&H	Total
2007	-204,152	42,342	-944	...	714	-162,040
2008	15,315	-3,222	974	...	-287	12,780
2009	64,419	43,657	-1,680	...	992	107,387

• COMPARATIVE FINANCIALS ($000 omitted)

Year	Assets	Capital & Surplus	Net Invest Income	Benefits Paid	Realized Cap Gains	Policyholder Dividends	Contract Lns (% of assets)
2007	9,000,554	832,793	361,384	730,575	-25,784	24,834	4.3
2008	8,440,912	795,171	393,320	752,078	-107,801	28,611	4.6
2009	9,375,138	818,994	406,252	680,002	-94,211	28,880	4.3

• ORDINARY LIFE STATISTICS

Year	Av. Ord. Policy Issued ($)	Av. Ord. Policy In Force ($)	Avg. Prem ($/M)	1st Yr Prem/ Total Prem	Ord. Lapse Ratio
2007	1,209,708	121,804	9.48	53.2	7.2
2008	1,471,518	129,961	10.24	41.4	3.7
2009	1,196,326	126,083	9.99	28.9	4.2

• NEW LIFE BUSINESS ISSUED ($000 omitted)

Year	Whole Life	Term	Credit	Group	Industrial	Total
2007	2,244,570	1,601,093	...	2,199,350	...	6,045,013
2008	2,328,244	1,063,605	...	1,662,110	...	5,053,959
2009	1,372,326	2,329,107	...	3,357,821	...	7,059,253

• LIFE INSURANCE IN FORCE ($000 omitted)

Year	Whole Life	Term	Credit	Group	Industrial	Total
2007	32,425,721	12,320,354	...	6,671,726	20,759	51,438,560
2008	32,482,042	12,860,017	...	7,883,822	19,835	53,245,716
2009	32,254,673	14,427,389	...	10,055,824	19,001	56,756,886

LINCOLN NATIONAL LIFE INS CO

1300 South Clinton Street
Fort Wayne, Indiana 46802-3518
Tel: 260-455-2000

AMB#: 006664
Began Business: 09/01/1905
Agency Off: Bob Dineen

Best's Financial Strength Rating: A+ g **FSC:** XV

• NET PREMIUMS AND DEPOSITS ($000 omitted)

Year	Individual Life	Individual & Group Annuities	Group Life & A&H	Credit Life & A&H	Individual A&H	Total
2007	3,207,900	16,559,551	1,353,557	...	9,890	21,130,899
2008	2,790,999	16,450,794	1,479,182	...	14,721	20,735,695
2009	2,016,410	15,489,353	1,538,132	...	14,638	19,058,533

• NET OPERATING GAIN ($000 omitted)

Year	Individual Life	Individual & Group Annuities	Group Life & A&H	Credit Life & A&H	Individual A&H	Total
2007	350,134	405,047	90,834	...	-4,731	895,906
2008	107,538	217,741	95,746	...	3,266	505,212
2009	3,925	646,694	86,579	...	5,477	684,902

• COMPARATIVE FINANCIALS ($000 omitted)

Year	Assets	Capital & Surplus	Net Invest Income	Benefits Paid	Realized Cap Gains	Policyholder Dividends	Contract Lns (% of assets)
2007	144,609,572	4,957,875	3,564,222	16,611,374	308,902	60,657	1.6
2008	119,849,817	4,585,435	3,406,781	15,109,776	-650,005	63,885	2.0
2009	143,345,609	6,245,064	3,368,878	12,967,534	-801,097	60,449	1.6

• ORDINARY LIFE STATISTICS

Year	Av. Ord. Policy Issued ($)	Av. Ord. Policy In Force ($)	Avg. Prem ($/M)	1st Yr Prem/ Total Prem	Ord. Lapse Ratio
2007	818,280	114,711	6.84	38.8	8.6
2008	1,008,869	119,590	7.04	32.5	6.0
2009	918,320	126,290	7.10	29.8	6.5

• NEW LIFE BUSINESS ISSUED ($000 omitted)

Year	Whole Life	Term	Credit	Group	Industrial	Total
2007	17,992,718	23,016,202	...	44,701,933	...	85,710,853
2008	17,976,332	20,738,012	...	48,964,153	...	87,678,497
2009	20,527,744	26,604,137	...	49,249,779	...	96,381,660

• LIFE INSURANCE IN FORCE ($000 omitted)

Year	Whole Life	Term	Credit	Group	Industrial	Total
2007	258,322,981	547,948,722	2,000,160	192,142,281	49,012	1,000,463,156
2008	268,133,146	525,162,156	1,088,037	221,719,869	47,403	1,016,150,611
2009	271,961,547	514,867,883	528,775	239,520,915	45,958	1,026,925,077

LONDON LIFE REINSURANCE CO

P.O. Box 1120
Blue Bell, Pennsylvania 19422-0319
Tel: 215-542-7200

AMB#: 060237
Began Business: 12/22/1969
Agency Off: None

Best's Financial Strength Rating: A **FSC:** VII

• NET PREMIUMS AND DEPOSITS ($000 omitted)

Year	Individual Life	Individual & Group Annuities	Group Life & A&H	Credit Life & A&H	Individual A&H	Total
2007	3,063	-253	17,281	114	...	20,206
2008	6,480	640	30,494	137	...	37,752
2009	4,997	226	45,656	174	...	51,054

• NET OPERATING GAIN ($000 omitted)

Year	Individual Life	Individual & Group Annuities	Group Life & A&H	Credit Life & A&H	Individual A&H	Total
2007	789	3,679	-1,268	220	78	3,497
2008	-1,951	1,087	4,328	178	72	3,715
2009	5,317	1,861	-367	122	6	6,939

• COMPARATIVE FINANCIALS ($000 omitted)

Year	Assets	Capital & Surplus	Net Invest Income	Benefits Paid	Realized Cap Gains	Policyholder Dividends	Contract Lns (% of assets)
2007	1,502,478	75,030	18,696	44,294	9	...	...
2008	713,239	70,409	17,556	45,026	-330	...	...
2009	704,488	73,996	13,946	55,900	-171	...	...

• ORDINARY LIFE STATISTICS

Year	Av. Ord. Policy Issued ($)	Av. Ord. Policy In Force ($)	Avg. Prem ($/M)	1st Yr Prem/ Total Prem	Ord. Lapse Ratio
2007	...	...	...	...	...
2008	...	...	...	...	...
2009	...	...	...	...	...

• NEW LIFE BUSINESS ISSUED ($000 omitted)

Year	Whole Life	Term	Credit	Group	Industrial	Total
2007	...	...	...	...	...	...
2008	...	...	...	...	...	...
2009	...	...	...	...	...	...

• LIFE INSURANCE IN FORCE ($000 omitted)

Year	Whole Life	Term	Credit	Group	Industrial	Total
2007	155,611,623	...	912,427	9,650	8,409	156,542,109
2008	195,587,758	...	988,657	...	...	196,576,415
2009	59,248,163	...	972,832	134,307	...	60,355,302

LOYAL AMERICAN LIFE INS CO

P.O. Box 26580
Austin, Texas 78755
Tel: 800-633-6752

AMB#: 006671
Began Business: 07/04/1955
Agency Off: None

Best's Financial Strength Rating: A- **FSC:** VII

• NET PREMIUMS AND DEPOSITS ($000 omitted)

Year	Individual Life	Individual & Group Annuities	Group Life & A&H	Credit Life & A&H	Individual A&H	Total
2007	1,682	30,535	588	1	27,118	59,924
2008	1,684	81,166	442	1	27,192	110,485
2009	2,574	1,988	313	...	48,640	53,515

• NET OPERATING GAIN ($000 omitted)

Year	Individual Life	Individual & Group Annuities	Group Life & A&H	Credit Life & A&H	Individual A&H	Total
2007	4,456	431	153	1	-79	4,962
2008	928	1,529	76	1	-490	2,044
2009	171	3,068	79	1	-131	3,188

• COMPARATIVE FINANCIALS ($000 omitted)

Year	Assets	Capital & Surplus	Net Invest Income	Benefits Paid	Realized Cap Gains	Policyholder Dividends	Contract Lns (% of assets)
2007	438,980	41,795	23,983	51,377	-58	-32	4.8
2008	483,899	37,698	26,523	54,388	-6,765	40	4.4
2009	465,849	33,330	24,399	55,338	-2,227	38	4.5

• ORDINARY LIFE STATISTICS

Year	Av. Ord. Policy Issued ($)	Av. Ord. Policy In Force ($)	Avg. Prem ($/M)	1st Yr Prem/ Total Prem	Ord. Lapse Ratio
2007	...	...	...	...	...
2008	...	...	...	...	...
2009	...	...	...	...	...

• NEW LIFE BUSINESS ISSUED ($000 omitted)

Year	Whole Life	Term	Credit	Group	Industrial	Total
2007	8,094	3,674	166	403	...	12,337
2008	4,578	558	76	155	...	5,367
2009	22,615	31	...	30	...	22,676

• LIFE INSURANCE IN FORCE ($000 omitted)

Year	Whole Life	Term	Credit	Group	Industrial	Total
2007	688,220	219,089	924	22,109	...	930,342
2008	637,788	199,168	...	19,997	...	856,953
2009	598,382	178,543	...	18,797	...	795,722

MADISON NATL LIFE INS CO INC

P.O. Box 5008
Madison, Wisconsin 53705-0008
Tel: 608-830-2000

AMB#: 006678
Began Business: 03/21/1962
Agency Off: None

Best's Financial Strength Rating: A- g
FSC: VIII

• **NET PREMIUMS AND DEPOSITS ($000 omitted)**

Year	Individual Life	Individual & Group Annuities	Group Life & A&H	Credit Life & A&H	Individual A&H	Total
2007	21,045	10,553	81,835	21,192	411	135,036
2008	24,778	11,864	92,818	653	399	130,513
2009	20,280	9,518	91,034	...	470	121,303

• **NET OPERATING GAIN ($000 omitted)**

Year	Individual Life	Individual & Group Annuities	Group Life & A&H	Credit Life & A&H	Individual A&H	Total
2007	5,544	1,503	1,581	-2,060	255	6,823
2008	271	2,068	8,610	2,884	-26	13,808
2009	14,361	2,245	1,285	1,140	51	19,081

• **COMPARATIVE FINANCIALS ($000 omitted)**

Year	Assets	Capital & Surplus	Net Invest Income	Benefits Paid	Realized Cap Gains	Policyholder Dividends	Contract Lns (% of assets)
2007	757,894	136,569	33,158	120,848	534	582	3.2
2008	799,124	138,243	34,688	114,804	-18,631	402	3.0
2009	784,366	169,301	32,410	114,120	2,341	416	2.9

• **ORDINARY LIFE STATISTICS**

Year	Av. Ord. Policy Issued ($)	Av. Ord. Policy In Force ($)	Avg. Prem ($/M)	1st Yr Prem/ Total Prem	Ord. Lapse Ratio
2007	38,537	11,841	11.76	16.1	11.0
2008	24,276	6,619	12.41	4.5	8.0
2009	8,645	7,034	13.14	9.6	-0.4

• **NEW LIFE BUSINESS ISSUED ($000 omitted)**

Year	Whole Life	Term	Credit	Group	Industrial	Total
2007	147,597	232	748,201	395,344	...	1,291,374
2008	64,796	482	1,517,141	206,494	...	1,788,913
2009	96,000	215	185,378	3,699,530	53	3,981,176

• **LIFE INSURANCE IN FORCE ($000 omitted)**

Year	Whole Life	Term	Credit	Group	Industrial	Total
2007	1,420,495	491,299	930,254	5,924,581	...	8,766,629
2008	1,447,915	457,223	405,448	5,462,715	54,642	7,827,943
2009	1,414,887	514,922	326,405	9,471,146	13,038	11,740,398

MANHATTAN NATIONAL LIFE INS CO

P.O. Box 5420
Cincinnati, Ohio 45201-5420
Tel: 513-357-3300

AMB#: 006842
Began Business: 01/04/1957
Agency Off: Adrienne S. Kessling

Best's Financial Strength Rating: A-
FSC: V

• **NET PREMIUMS AND DEPOSITS ($000 omitted)**

Year	Individual Life	Individual & Group Annuities	Group Life & A&H	Credit Life & A&H	Individual A&H	Total
2007	1,349	356	...	...	7	1,711
2008	1,312	386	...	...	7	1,704
2009	2,135	339	...	...	7	2,481

• **NET OPERATING GAIN ($000 omitted)**

Year	Individual Life	Individual & Group Annuities	Group Life & A&H	Credit Life & A&H	Individual A&H	Total
2007	4,291	1,058	0	...	26	5,376
2008	1,247	427	0	...	19	1,692
2009	1,274	-123	...	...	30	1,181

• **COMPARATIVE FINANCIALS ($000 omitted)**

Year	Assets	Capital & Surplus	Net Invest Income	Benefits Paid	Realized Cap Gains	Policyholder Dividends	Contract Lns (% of assets)
2007	265,320	48,503	4,133	4,950	146	6	3.3
2008	213,681	7,878	3,238	2,441	-1,773	6	3.9
2009	210,736	9,523	1,474	2,904	-63	6	3.9

• **ORDINARY LIFE STATISTICS**

Year	Av. Ord. Policy Issued ($)	Av. Ord. Policy In Force ($)	Avg. Prem ($/M)	1st Yr Prem/ Total Prem	Ord. Lapse Ratio
2007	...	...	...	...	...
2008	...	...	...	...	...
2009	...	...	...	...	...

• **NEW LIFE BUSINESS ISSUED ($000 omitted)**

Year	Whole Life	Term	Credit	Group	Industrial	Total
2007	53	4,958	...	...	...	5,011
2008	13	861	...	...	...	874
2009	66	143	...	...	...	209

• **LIFE INSURANCE IN FORCE ($000 omitted)**

Year	Whole Life	Term	Credit	Group	Industrial	Total
2007	914,399	5,630,223	...	...	...	6,544,622
2008	853,711	5,009,381	...	...	...	5,863,092
2009	800,213	4,451,546	...	...	...	5,251,758

MANHATTAN LIFE INS CO

2727 Allen Parkway Wortham Tower, Suite 500
Houston, Texas 77019-2115
Tel: 888-222-0843

AMB#: 006686
Began Business: 08/01/1850
Agency Off: Thomas Luchetta

Best's Financial Strength Rating: B+
FSC: VI

• **NET PREMIUMS AND DEPOSITS ($000 omitted)**

Year	Individual Life	Individual & Group Annuities	Group Life & A&H	Credit Life & A&H	Individual A&H	Total
2007	16,715	19,426	154	...	...	36,295
2008	14,850	14,433	72	...	...	29,355
2009	14,061	8,290	93	...	...	22,443

• **NET OPERATING GAIN ($000 omitted)**

Year	Individual Life	Individual & Group Annuities	Group Life & A&H	Credit Life & A&H	Individual A&H	Total
2007	1,097	-728	35	...	...	404
2008	26	672	-98	...	...	599
2009	2,250	233	...	...	...	2,484

• **COMPARATIVE FINANCIALS ($000 omitted)**

Year	Assets	Capital & Surplus	Net Invest Income	Benefits Paid	Realized Cap Gains	Policyholder Dividends	Contract Lns (% of assets)
2007	363,058	35,742	18,472	47,586	74	1,389	10.6
2008	354,152	32,017	18,590	42,705	-1,628	1,058	10.5
2009	345,166	34,226	15,209	39,451	...	469	9.8

• **ORDINARY LIFE STATISTICS**

Year	Av. Ord. Policy Issued ($)	Av. Ord. Policy In Force ($)	Avg. Prem ($/M)	1st Yr Prem/ Total Prem	Ord. Lapse Ratio
2007	379,454	58,602	12.52	7.2	12.3
2008	389,776	63,016	11.22	8.3	6.5
2009	412,217	69,305	10.38	13.4	8.9

• **NEW LIFE BUSINESS ISSUED ($000 omitted)**

Year	Whole Life	Term	Credit	Group	Industrial	Total
2007	67,911	124,472	...	393	...	192,776
2008	74,081	137,957	...	2,136	...	214,174
2009	138,634	134,666	...	2,560	...	275,860

• **LIFE INSURANCE IN FORCE ($000 omitted)**

Year	Whole Life	Term	Credit	Group	Industrial	Total
2007	973,568	721,082	...	18,183	...	1,712,833
2008	990,594	758,532	...	8,945	...	1,758,071
2009	1,065,102	795,102	...	6,845	...	1,867,049

MASSACHUSETTS MUTUAL LIFE INS

1295 State Street
Springfield, Massachusetts 01111
Tel: 413-788-8411

AMB#: 006695
Began Business: 08/01/1851
Agency Off: Alan Taylor

Best's Financial Strength Rating: A++g
FSC: XV

• **NET PREMIUMS AND DEPOSITS ($000 omitted)**

Year	Individual Life	Individual & Group Annuities	Group Life & A&H	Credit Life & A&H	Individual A&H	Total
2007	3,705,528	10,129,095	883,027	...	440,753	15,158,403
2008	3,820,493	9,928,106	262,176	...	458,589	14,469,364
2009	3,838,934	8,846,260	102,932	...	463,464	13,251,589

• **NET OPERATING GAIN ($000 omitted)**

Year	Individual Life	Individual & Group Annuities	Group Life & A&H	Credit Life & A&H	Individual A&H	Total
2007	222,537	265,883	50,193	...	32,090	570,703
2008	575,879	-448,926	78,502	...	34,964	240,419
2009	-34,919	494,312	76,993	...	35,597	571,982

• **COMPARATIVE FINANCIALS ($000 omitted)**

Year	Assets	Capital & Surplus	Net Invest Income	Benefits Paid	Realized Cap Gains	Policyholder Dividends	Contract Lns (% of assets)
2007	119,085,813	8,008,148	4,633,506	10,551,116	-430,697	1,372,522	7.0
2008	114,294,059	8,462,931	4,897,438	11,075,812	-1,233,887	1,331,650	7.8
2009	121,329,281	9,258,844	4,043,752	11,326,571	-861,348	1,211,616	7.0

• **ORDINARY LIFE STATISTICS**

Year	Av. Ord. Policy Issued ($)	Av. Ord. Policy In Force ($)	Avg. Prem ($/M)	1st Yr Prem/ Total Prem	Ord. Lapse Ratio
2007	599,909	190,000	13.25	13.3	4.7
2008	581,245	202,612	13.03	9.2	5.2
2009	520,803	213,347	12.63	9.3	5.8

• **NEW LIFE BUSINESS ISSUED ($000 omitted)**

Year	Whole Life	Term	Credit	Group	Industrial	Total
2007	16,210,269	20,890,507	...	5,308,453	...	42,409,229
2008	15,072,676	21,252,238	...	3,929,016	...	40,253,930
2009	14,757,075	22,717,853	...	2,034,496	...	39,509,424

• **LIFE INSURANCE IN FORCE ($000 omitted)**

Year	Whole Life	Term	Credit	Group	Industrial	Total
2007	170,467,474	134,244,438	...	58,363,163	...	363,075,075
2008	176,313,257	145,169,611	...	58,307,416	...	379,790,284
2009	180,283,046	155,649,931	...	51,839,272	...	387,772,249

MEDAMERICA INSURANCE CO

165 Court Street
Rochester, New York 14647
Tel: 800-544-0327

AMB#: 007131
Began Business: 08/30/1966
Agency Off: William L. Naylon

Best's Financial Strength Rating: B++g **FSC:** VI

• NET PREMIUMS AND DEPOSITS ($000 omitted)

Year	Individual Life	Individual & Group Annuities	Group Life & A&H	Credit Life & A&H	Individual A&H	Total
2007	...	...	11,349	...	-4,270	7,079
2008	...	...	5,523	...	88,438	93,961
2009	...	...	9,717	...	33,068	42,785

• NET OPERATING GAIN ($000 omitted)

Year	Individual Life	Individual & Group Annuities	Group Life & A&H	Credit Life & A&H	Individual A&H	Total
2007	...	...	3,024	...	-7,463	-4,439
2008	...	...	-24,731	...	17,505	-7,226
2009	...	...	4,590	...	1,908	6,497

• COMPARATIVE FINANCIALS ($000 omitted)

Year	Assets	Capital & Surplus	Net Invest Income	Benefits Paid	Realized Cap Gains	Policyholder Dividends	Contract Lns (% of assets)
2007	365,275	27,066	12,155	23,211	558	...	...
2008	451,588	17,830	10,745	25,292	-527	...	...
2009	497,148	33,132	18,488	28,562	-2,014	...	...

• ORDINARY LIFE STATISTICS

Year	Av. Ord. Policy Issued ($)	Av. Ord. Policy In Force ($)	Avg. Prem ($/M)	1st Yr Prem/ Total Prem	Ord. Lapse Ratio
2007	...	...	...	...	...
2008	...	...	...	...	...
2009	...	...	...	...	...

• NEW LIFE BUSINESS ISSUED ($000 omitted)

Year	Whole Life	Term	Credit	Group	Industrial	Total
2007	...	...	...	...	...	...
2008	...	...	...	...	...	...
2009	...	...	...	...	...	...

• LIFE INSURANCE IN FORCE ($000 omitted)

Year	Whole Life	Term	Credit	Group	Industrial	Total
2007	...	...	...	...	...	...
2008	...	...	...	...	...	...
2009	...	...	...	...	...	...

MEDAMERICA INS CO OF NEW YORK

165 Court Street
Rochester, New York 14647
Tel: 800-544-0327

AMB#: 060021
Began Business: 11/02/1987
Agency Off: William L. Naylon

Best's Financial Strength Rating: B++g **FSC:** XI

• NET PREMIUMS AND DEPOSITS ($000 omitted)

Year	Individual Life	Individual & Group Annuities	Group Life & A&H	Credit Life & A&H	Individual A&H	Total
2007	...	...	8,870	...	29,295	38,165
2008	...	...	9,271	...	31,587	40,858
2009	...	...	9,420	...	30,116	39,536

• NET OPERATING GAIN ($000 omitted)

Year	Individual Life	Individual & Group Annuities	Group Life & A&H	Credit Life & A&H	Individual A&H	Total
2007	...	...	-1,917	...	-5,111	-7,028
2008	...	...	274	...	-6,616	-6,343
2009	...	...	-1,419	...	-7,162	-8,580

• COMPARATIVE FINANCIALS ($000 omitted)

Year	Assets	Capital & Surplus	Net Invest Income	Benefits Paid	Realized Cap Gains	Policyholder Dividends	Contract Lns (% of assets)
2007	250,363	17,986	8,346	14,836	358	...	...
2008	280,520	14,673	8,371	15,557	-442	...	...
2009	328,970	18,739	11,551	17,819	-584	...	...

• ORDINARY LIFE STATISTICS

Year	Av. Ord. Policy Issued ($)	Av. Ord. Policy In Force ($)	Avg. Prem ($/M)	1st Yr Prem/ Total Prem	Ord. Lapse Ratio
2007	...	...	...	...	...
2008	...	...	...	...	...
2009	...	...	...	...	...

• NEW LIFE BUSINESS ISSUED ($000 omitted)

Year	Whole Life	Term	Credit	Group	Industrial	Total
2007	...	...	...	...	...	...
2008	...	...	...	...	...	...
2009	...	...	...	...	...	...

• LIFE INSURANCE IN FORCE ($000 omitted)

Year	Whole Life	Term	Credit	Group	Industrial	Total
2007	...	...	...	...	...	...
2008	...	...	...	...	...	...
2009	...	...	...	...	...	...

MEDAMERICA INS CO OF FLORIDA

165 Court Street
Rochester, New York 14647
Tel: 800-544-0327

AMB#: 060658
Began Business: 10/01/2007
Agency Off: None

Best's Financial Strength Rating: B++g **FSC:** XI

• NET PREMIUMS AND DEPOSITS ($000 omitted)

Year	Individual Life	Individual & Group Annuities	Group Life & A&H	Credit Life & A&H	Individual A&H	Total
2007	...	...	105	...	2,204	2,309
2008	...	...	72	...	4,120	4,193
2009	...	...	74	...	2,584	2,658

• NET OPERATING GAIN ($000 omitted)

Year	Individual Life	Individual & Group Annuities	Group Life & A&H	Credit Life & A&H	Individual A&H	Total
2007	...	...	-343	...	86	-257
2008	...	...	-4	...	-819	-823
2009	...	...	37	...	272	310

• COMPARATIVE FINANCIALS ($000 omitted)

Year	Assets	Capital & Surplus	Net Invest Income	Benefits Paid	Realized Cap Gains	Policyholder Dividends	Contract Lns (% of assets)
2007	5,862	2,725	102	36	...	...	...
2008	8,628	1,791	149	113	...	...	...
2009	11,906	3,755	250	413	0	...	...

• ORDINARY LIFE STATISTICS

Year	Av. Ord. Policy Issued ($)	Av. Ord. Policy In Force ($)	Avg. Prem ($/M)	1st Yr Prem/ Total Prem	Ord. Lapse Ratio
2007	...	...	...	...	...
2008	...	...	...	...	...
2009	...	...	...	...	...

• NEW LIFE BUSINESS ISSUED ($000 omitted)

Year	Whole Life	Term	Credit	Group	Industrial	Total
2007	...	...	...	...	...	...
2008	...	...	...	...	...	...
2009	...	...	...	...	...	...

• LIFE INSURANCE IN FORCE ($000 omitted)

Year	Whole Life	Term	Credit	Group	Industrial	Total
2007	...	...	...	...	...	...
2008	...	...	...	...	...	...
2009	...	...	...	...	...	...

MEDICAL BENEFITS MUTUAL LIFE

P.O. Box 1009
Newark, Ohio 43058-1009
Tel: 740-522-7324

AMB#: 068036
Began Business: 04/04/1938
Agency Off: Kurt J. Harden

Best's Financial Strength Rating: B+ **FSC:** V

• NET PREMIUMS AND DEPOSITS ($000 omitted)

Year	Individual Life	Individual & Group Annuities	Group Life & A&H	Credit Life & A&H	Individual A&H	Total
2007	...	...	6,877	...	...	6,877
2008	...	...	6,488	...	...	6,488
2009	...	...	13,974	...	...	13,974

• NET OPERATING GAIN ($000 omitted)

Year	Individual Life	Individual & Group Annuities	Group Life & A&H	Credit Life & A&H	Individual A&H	Total
2007	...	...	321	...	...	321
2008	...	...	431	...	...	431
2009	...	0	799	...	...	799

• COMPARATIVE FINANCIALS ($000 omitted)

Year	Assets	Capital & Surplus	Net Invest Income	Benefits Paid	Realized Cap Gains	Policyholder Dividends	Contract Lns (% of assets)
2007	20,642	13,496	396	4,882	14	...	...
2008	19,986	13,380	195	4,579	-28	...	...
2009	23,249	13,997	77	11,523	-62	...	...

• ORDINARY LIFE STATISTICS

Year	Av. Ord. Policy Issued ($)	Av. Ord. Policy In Force ($)	Avg. Prem ($/M)	1st Yr Prem/ Total Prem	Ord. Lapse Ratio
2007	...	...	...	...	...
2008	...	...	...	...	...
2009	...	...	...	...	...

• NEW LIFE BUSINESS ISSUED ($000 omitted)

Year	Whole Life	Term	Credit	Group	Industrial	Total
2007	...	...	...	53,340	...	53,340
2008	...	...	...	54,990	...	54,990
2009	...	...	...	20,258	...	20,258

• LIFE INSURANCE IN FORCE ($000 omitted)

Year	Whole Life	Term	Credit	Group	Industrial	Total
2007	...	...	...	117,538	...	117,538
2008	...	...	...	117,829	...	117,829
2009	...	...	...	85,449	...	85,449

MEDICO INSURANCE COMPANY

P.O. Box 3477
Omaha, Nebraska 68103
Tel: 402-391-6900

AMB#: 003150
Began Business: 04/26/1930
Agency Off: Randy Boldt

Best's Financial Strength Rating: B- **FSC:** VI

• NET PREMIUMS AND DEPOSITS ($000 omitted)

Year	Individual Life	Individual & Group Annuities	Group Life & A&H	Credit Life & A&H	Individual A&H	Total
2007	60,104	...	...	...	-191,238	-131,133
2008	4,060	14	224	...	11,242	15,539
2009	3,727	12	3,420	...	11,424	18,583

• NET OPERATING GAIN ($000 omitted)

Year	Individual Life	Individual & Group Annuities	Group Life & A&H	Credit Life & A&H	Individual A&H	Total
2007	2,720	-1,612	...	...	18,864	19,973
2008	399	21	33	...	-3,967	-3,514
2009	866	37	-724	...	-3,934	-3,755

• COMPARATIVE FINANCIALS ($000 omitted)

Year	Assets	Capital & Surplus	Net Invest Income	Benefits Paid	Realized Cap Gains	Policyholder Dividends	Contract Lns (% of assets)
2007	127,945	49,306	11,178	44,335	12,726	2,006	0.4
2008	117,816	45,528	3,964	17,205	-1,458	1,476	0.4
2009	113,109	44,669	4,298	18,578	-217	1,410	0.5

• ORDINARY LIFE STATISTICS

Year	Av. Ord. Policy Issued ($)	Av. Ord. Policy In Force ($)	Avg. Prem ($/M)	1st Yr Prem/ Total Prem	Ord. Lapse Ratio
2007	...	...	...	...	...
2008	...	...	...	...	...
2009	...	...	...	...	...

• NEW LIFE BUSINESS ISSUED ($000 omitted)

Year	Whole Life	Term	Credit	Group	Industrial	Total
2007	1	...	...	...	...	1
2008	138	...	...	...	...	138
2009	215	...	...	...	...	215

• LIFE INSURANCE IN FORCE ($000 omitted)

Year	Whole Life	Term	Credit	Group	Industrial	Total
2007	99,913	13,735	...	...	...	113,648
2008	91,627	12,727	...	...	...	104,354
2009	83,922	11,573	...	...	...	95,495

MEMBERS LIFE INS CO

P.O. Box 391
Madison, Wisconsin 53701-0391
Tel: 608-238-5851

AMB#: 008719
Began Business: 03/19/1976
Agency Off: Robert N. Trunzo

Best's Financial Strength Rating: B++ **FSC:** V

• NET PREMIUMS AND DEPOSITS ($000 omitted)

Year	Individual Life	Individual & Group Annuities	Group Life & A&H	Credit Life & A&H	Individual A&H	Total
2007	-83,027	-491,469	3,179	...	0	-571,316
2008	2,216	1	2,754	...	...	4,971
2009	2,054	6	2,497	...	...	4,557

• NET OPERATING GAIN ($000 omitted)

Year	Individual Life	Individual & Group Annuities	Group Life & A&H	Credit Life & A&H	Individual A&H	Total
2007	1,220	19,991	565	1	-54	22,742
2008	-13,016	...	6,355	1	...	-7,059
2009	-2,354	-11	-507	0	...	-2,822

• COMPARATIVE FINANCIALS ($000 omitted)

Year	Assets	Capital & Surplus	Net Invest Income	Benefits Paid	Realized Cap Gains	Policyholder Dividends	Contract Lns (% of assets)
2007	66,612	30,887	45,092	147,965	-31,379	-194	4.2
2008	45,950	12,231	2,066	4,388	1,559	...	5.9
2009	54,337	21,565	1,903	4,012	7,353	...	4.7

• ORDINARY LIFE STATISTICS

Year	Av. Ord. Policy Issued ($)	Av. Ord. Policy In Force ($)	Avg. Prem ($/M)	1st Yr Prem/ Total Prem	Ord. Lapse Ratio
2007	...	...	...	...	...
2008	...	...	...	...	...
2009	...	...	...	...	...

• NEW LIFE BUSINESS ISSUED ($000 omitted)

Year	Whole Life	Term	Credit	Group	Industrial	Total
2007	...	...	...	...	...	...
2008	...	...	...	...	...	...
2009	...	...	...	...	...	...

• LIFE INSURANCE IN FORCE ($000 omitted)

Year	Whole Life	Term	Credit	Group	Industrial	Total
2007	95,614	102,403	...	109,075	...	307,092
2008	89,380	86,197	...	92,734	...	268,311
2009	84,586	73,754	...	79,216	...	237,556

MEGA LIFE AND HEALTH INS CO

9151 Boulevard 26
North Richland Hills, Texas 76180
Tel: 817-255-3100

AMB#: 009190
Began Business: 06/15/1982
Agency Off: None

Best's Financial Strength Rating: B++g **FSC:** VIII

• NET PREMIUMS AND DEPOSITS ($000 omitted)

Year	Individual Life	Individual & Group Annuities	Group Life & A&H	Credit Life & A&H	Individual A&H	Total
2007	52,725	1,006	815,256	981	89,830	959,797
2008	-1,217	673	748,971	592	100,789	849,808
2009	430	94	582,048	...	105,981	688,554

• NET OPERATING GAIN ($000 omitted)

Year	Individual Life	Individual & Group Annuities	Group Life & A&H	Credit Life & A&H	Individual A&H	Total
2007	-13,222	2,865	43,138	808	-3,457	30,133
2008	-12,374	-5,495	-350	2,412	9,849	-5,957
2009	9,153	446	60,346	...	-1,049	68,897

• COMPARATIVE FINANCIALS ($000 omitted)

Year	Assets	Capital & Surplus	Net Invest Income	Benefits Paid	Realized Cap Gains	Policyholder Dividends	Contract Lns (% of assets)
2007	1,061,133	274,935	64,413	524,303	1,187	67	0.8
2008	708,328	190,990	42,012	531,849	-6,856	-49	...
2009	651,185	239,119	29,037	380,931	-1,318	...	...

• ORDINARY LIFE STATISTICS

Year	Av. Ord. Policy Issued ($)	Av. Ord. Policy In Force ($)	Avg. Prem ($/M)	1st Yr Prem/ Total Prem	Ord. Lapse Ratio
2007	...	...	...	...	...
2008	...	...	...	...	...
2009	...	...	...	...	...

• NEW LIFE BUSINESS ISSUED ($000 omitted)

Year	Whole Life	Term	Credit	Group	Industrial	Total
2007	61,286	402,010	5,465	164,812	...	633,573
2008	26,183	228,245	188	104,197	...	358,813
2009	238	6,210	...	4,400	...	10,848

• LIFE INSURANCE IN FORCE ($000 omitted)

Year	Whole Life	Term	Credit	Group	Industrial	Total
2007	2,082,695	4,154,716	76,763	496,046	1,711	6,811,931
2008	2,122,936	4,458,222	59,782	438,331	1,624	7,080,895
2009	592,325	1,161,848	8,007	296,098	1,560	2,059,838

MERIT LIFE INSURANCE CO

601 N.W. Second Street
Evansville, Indiana 47708-1013
Tel: 812-424-8031

AMB#: 006703
Began Business: 10/28/1957
Agency Off: None

Best's Financial Strength Rating: A- **FSC:** IX

• NET PREMIUMS AND DEPOSITS ($000 omitted)

Year	Individual Life	Individual & Group Annuities	Group Life & A&H	Credit Life & A&H	Individual A&H	Total
2007	20,927	26	2,664	69,090	13,844	106,552
2008	15,567	35	3,030	60,503	10,149	89,284
2009	9,484	17	3,513	38,088	5,757	56,858

• NET OPERATING GAIN ($000 omitted)

Year	Individual Life	Individual & Group Annuities	Group Life & A&H	Credit Life & A&H	Individual A&H	Total
2007	15,648	5,818	304	14,600	6,029	42,399
2008	14,838	6,222	-359	14,053	8,379	43,132
2009	11,529	3,944	84	12,196	7,041	34,792

• COMPARATIVE FINANCIALS ($000 omitted)

Year	Assets	Capital & Surplus	Net Invest Income	Benefits Paid	Realized Cap Gains	Policyholder Dividends	Contract Lns (% of assets)
2007	1,096,282	707,006	65,755	51,046	3,561	15	0.2
2008	776,733	408,194	62,619	54,343	-59,841	17	0.2
2009	659,563	316,091	39,713	50,793	-6,777	19	0.3

• ORDINARY LIFE STATISTICS

Year	Av. Ord. Policy Issued ($)	Av. Ord. Policy In Force ($)	Avg. Prem ($/M)	1st Yr Prem/ Total Prem	Ord. Lapse Ratio
2007	...	...	...	...	...
2008	...	...	...	...	...
2009	...	...	...	...	...

• NEW LIFE BUSINESS ISSUED ($000 omitted)

Year	Whole Life	Term	Credit	Group	Industrial	Total
2007	...	494,552	2,360,427	65,040	...	2,920,019
2008	...	397,543	2,027,656	85,880	...	2,511,079
2009	...	268,968	1,363,116	93,200	...	1,725,284

• LIFE INSURANCE IN FORCE ($000 omitted)

Year	Whole Life	Term	Credit	Group	Industrial	Total
2007	77,935	1,812,157	2,718,538	150,743	...	4,759,373
2008	73,818	1,599,500	2,666,569	212,354	...	4,552,241
2009	70,170	1,316,893	2,166,654	205,277	...	3,758,994

MERRILL LYNCH LIFE INS CO

4333 Edgewood Road NE
Cedar Rapids, Iowa 52499
Tel: 319-355-8511

AMB#: 009537
Began Business: 12/23/1986
Agency Off: None

Best's Financial Strength Rating: A g **FSC:** XV

• NET PREMIUMS AND DEPOSITS ($000 omitted)

Year	Individual Life	Individual & Group Annuities	Group Life & A&H	Credit Life & A&H	Individual A&H	Total
2007	-6,125	751,567	...	...	...	745,442
2008	801	454,381	...	...	...	455,182
2009	6,268	290,535	...	...	...	296,802

• NET OPERATING GAIN ($000 omitted)

Year	Individual Life	Individual & Group Annuities	Group Life & A&H	Credit Life & A&H	Individual A&H	Total
2007	35,934	71,561	...	...	...	107,494
2008	78,535	-373,146	...	...	...	-294,611
2009	42,999	239,664	...	...	...	282,663

• COMPARATIVE FINANCIALS ($000 omitted)

Year	Assets	Capital & Surplus	Net Invest Income	Benefits Paid	Realized Cap Gains	Policyholder Dividends	Contract Lns (% of assets)
2007	13,911,027	366,011	121,104	1,969,791	1,296	...	6.8
2008	10,341,871	356,135	124,693	1,447,086	34,749	...	8.8
2009	11,102,780	599,014	115,835	1,120,488	-57,376	...	7.8

• ORDINARY LIFE STATISTICS

Year	Av. Ord. Policy Issued ($)	Av. Ord. Policy In Force ($)	Avg. Prem ($/M)	1st Yr Prem/ Total Prem	Ord. Lapse Ratio
2007	...	...	...	...	...
2008	...	...	...	...	...
2009	...	...	...	...	...

• NEW LIFE BUSINESS ISSUED ($000 omitted)

Year	Whole Life	Term	Credit	Group	Industrial	Total
2007	1,184	...	...	...	...	1,184
2008	1,807	...	...	...	...	1,807
2009	988	...	...	...	...	988

• LIFE INSURANCE IN FORCE ($000 omitted)

Year	Whole Life	Term	Credit	Group	Industrial	Total
2007	9,376,330	5,706	...	...	...	9,382,036
2008	7,953,359	5,452	...	...	...	7,958,811
2009	7,251,048	5,157	...	...	...	7,256,206

METLIFE INSURANCE CO OF CT

18210 Crane Nest Drive, 3rd Floor
Tampa, Florida 33647
Tel: 860-308-1000

AMB#: 007330
Began Business: 04/01/1864
Agency Off: None

Best's Financial Strength Rating: A+ gu **FSC:** XV

• NET PREMIUMS AND DEPOSITS ($000 omitted)

Year	Individual Life	Individual & Group Annuities	Group Life & A&H	Credit Life & A&H	Individual A&H	Total
2007	465,202	3,184,582	278	...	32,917	3,682,980
2008	403,181	5,690,592	635	...	19,622	6,114,029
2009	272,186	17,160,003	348	...	7,411	17,439,949

• NET OPERATING GAIN ($000 omitted)

Year	Individual Life	Individual & Group Annuities	Group Life & A&H	Credit Life & A&H	Individual A&H	Total
2007	459,521	559,542	20,830	-2	45,345	1,026,252
2008	208,469	160,599	3,486	...	81,408	714,726
2009	112,393	392,610	2,005	...	14,061	659,680

• COMPARATIVE FINANCIALS ($000 omitted)

Year	Assets	Capital & Surplus	Net Invest Income	Benefits Paid	Realized Cap Gains	Policyholder Dividends	Contract Lns (% of assets)
2007	83,221,523	4,208,400	2,551,030	8,444,691	74,374	...	1.1
2008	69,829,133	5,471,465	2,236,656	7,124,120	-472,383	...	1.6
2009	67,232,743	4,928,675	1,800,476	5,027,222	-579,155	...	1.7

• ORDINARY LIFE STATISTICS

Year	Av. Ord. Policy Issued ($)	Av. Ord. Policy In Force ($)	Avg. Prem ($/M)	1st Yr Prem/ Total Prem	Ord. Lapse Ratio
2007	771,978	251,556	7.82	3.5	4.2
2008	555,161	253,378	7.36	2.6	5.5
2009	235,784	251,211	6.44	0.8	6.2

• NEW LIFE BUSINESS ISSUED ($000 omitted)

Year	Whole Life	Term	Credit	Group	Industrial	Total
2007	1,540,836	169,096	...	...	...	1,709,932
2008	650,746	26,550	...	...	...	677,296
2009	11,995	30	...	...	...	12,025

• LIFE INSURANCE IN FORCE ($000 omitted)

Year	Whole Life	Term	Credit	Group	Industrial	Total
2007	70,847,915	32,636,892	...	849,068	...	104,333,875
2008	67,256,744	30,523,689	...	848,421	...	98,628,854
2009	63,216,922	27,771,282	...	847,786	...	91,835,990

METLIFE INVESTORS INSURANCE CO

18210 Crane Nest Dr., 3rd Floor
Tampa, Florida 33647
Tel: 949-717-6536

AMB#: 009075
Began Business: 09/08/1981
Agency Off: None

Best's Financial Strength Rating: A+ gu **FSC:** XV

• NET PREMIUMS AND DEPOSITS ($000 omitted)

Year	Individual Life	Individual & Group Annuities	Group Life & A&H	Credit Life & A&H	Individual A&H	Total
2007	10,355	1,439,532	-22	...	-1	1,449,864
2008	5,323	1,498,710	-16	...	0	1,504,016
2009	3,245	1,388,441	-20	...	1	1,391,667

• NET OPERATING GAIN ($000 omitted)

Year	Individual Life	Individual & Group Annuities	Group Life & A&H	Credit Life & A&H	Individual A&H	Total
2007	-19	37,473	1,916	...	2	39,372
2008	3,839	-34,122	128	...	0	-30,154
2009	-750	61,262	4,151	...	0	64,663

• COMPARATIVE FINANCIALS ($000 omitted)

Year	Assets	Capital & Surplus	Net Invest Income	Benefits Paid	Realized Cap Gains	Policyholder Dividends	Contract Lns (% of assets)
2007	11,882,623	328,563	103,627	1,329,600	314	...	0.2
2008	9,523,373	397,632	107,708	983,691	-4,795	...	0.3
2009	11,670,931	410,754	106,352	669,335	-15,621	...	0.2

• ORDINARY LIFE STATISTICS

Year	Av. Ord. Policy Issued ($)	Av. Ord. Policy In Force ($)	Avg. Prem ($/M)	1st Yr Prem/ Total Prem	Ord. Lapse Ratio
2007	...	...	...	...	...
2008	...	...	...	...	...
2009	...	...	...	...	...

• NEW LIFE BUSINESS ISSUED ($000 omitted)

Year	Whole Life	Term	Credit	Group	Industrial	Total
2007	120,729	...	...	...	...	120,729
2008	51,272	...	...	...	...	51,272
2009	750	...	...	...	...	750

• LIFE INSURANCE IN FORCE ($000 omitted)

Year	Whole Life	Term	Credit	Group	Industrial	Total
2007	743,155	434,926	...	86,377	...	1,264,458
2008	758,763	401,885	...	80,402	...	1,241,050
2009	698,736	376,175	...	79,840	...	1,154,752

METLIFE INVESTORS USA INS CO

18210 Crane Nest Dr., 3rd Floor
Tampa, Florida 33647
Tel: 949-717-6536

AMB#: 006125
Began Business: 03/10/1961
Agency Off: None

Best's Financial Strength Rating: A+ gu **FSC:** XV

• NET PREMIUMS AND DEPOSITS ($000 omitted)

Year	Individual Life	Individual & Group Annuities	Group Life & A&H	Credit Life & A&H	Individual A&H	Total
2007	538,548	6,808,158	...	...	...	7,346,706
2008	542,828	6,376,871	...	...	...	6,919,699
2009	590,549	8,441,268	...	...	...	9,031,817

• NET OPERATING GAIN ($000 omitted)

Year	Individual Life	Individual & Group Annuities	Group Life & A&H	Credit Life & A&H	Individual A&H	Total
2007	-1,107,286	15,008	...	...	...	-1,092,279
2008	-139,328	-305,254	...	...	...	-444,582
2009	-171,469	182,966	...	...	...	11,497

• COMPARATIVE FINANCIALS ($000 omitted)

Year	Assets	Capital & Surplus	Net Invest Income	Benefits Paid	Realized Cap Gains	Policyholder Dividends	Contract Lns (% of assets)
2007	29,684,128	584,168	216,284	2,614,984	-14,219	...	0.1
2008	26,939,324	760,534	264,165	2,222,759	-37,683	...	0.2
2009	40,666,152	1,406,057	363,933	1,808,529	-35,718	...	0.1

• ORDINARY LIFE STATISTICS

Year	Av. Ord. Policy Issued ($)	Av. Ord. Policy In Force ($)	Avg. Prem ($/M)	1st Yr Prem/ Total Prem	Ord. Lapse Ratio
2007	590,193	373,939	8.71	84.5	2.9
2008	565,131	485,964	7.21	70.7	6.7
2009	595,437	596,487	6.17	62.6	4.3

• NEW LIFE BUSINESS ISSUED ($000 omitted)

Year	Whole Life	Term	Credit	Group	Industrial	Total
2007	9,449,629	32,137,134	...	...	...	41,586,763
2008	11,390,927	35,674,873	...	...	...	47,065,800
2009	12,898,950	54,276,457	...	...	...	67,175,408

• LIFE INSURANCE IN FORCE ($000 omitted)

Year	Whole Life	Term	Credit	Group	Industrial	Total
2007	26,655,845	72,574,088	...	...	...	99,229,933
2008	32,946,696	103,641,634	...	...	...	136,588,330
2009	45,008,218	150,535,008	...	...	...	195,543,227

METROPOLITAN LIFE INS CO

18210 Crane Nest Drive, 3rd Floor
Tampa, Florida 33647
Tel: 212-579-2211

AMB#: 006704
Began Business: 03/25/1868
Agency Off: None

Best's Financial Strength Rating: A+ gu
FSC: XV

• NET PREMIUMS AND DEPOSITS ($000 omitted)

Year	Individual Life	Individual & Group Annuities	Group Life & A&H	Credit Life & A&H	Individual A&H	Total
2007	-13,959,836	31,723,841	12,400,347	...	669,081	46,867,774
2008	2,985,955	61,150,328	11,972,997	...	729,381	76,747,602
2009	2,703,197	53,342,335	7,357,047	-1	764,719	63,434,916

• NET OPERATING GAIN ($000 omitted)

Year	Individual Life	Individual & Group Annuities	Group Life & A&H	Credit Life & A&H	Individual A&H	Total
2007	-79,133	1,196,397	551,236	...	-50,700	2,069,704
2008	-138,923	-965,618	264,100	-300	-77,749	552,499
2009	-103,085	1,308,448	216,603	-2,609	-142,108	1,872,172

• COMPARATIVE FINANCIALS ($000 omitted)

Year	Assets	Capital & Surplus	Net Invest Income	Benefits Paid	Realized Cap Gains	Policyholder Dividends	Contract Lns (% of assets)
2007	297,465,527	13,003,979	11,507,524	27,891,604	53,391	-399,153	1.9
2008	289,578,009	11,592,263	11,975,928	27,455,510	-890,142	192,724	2.0
2009	289,575,344	12,633,855	9,865,902	27,169,381	-650,750	245,723	2.0

• ORDINARY LIFE STATISTICS

Year	Av. Ord. Policy Issued ($)	Av. Ord. Policy In Force ($)	Avg. Prem ($/M)	1st Yr Prem/ Total Prem	Ord. Lapse Ratio
2007	341,732	74,369	9.54	7.5	4.3
2008	303,647	109,900	7.59	6.3	4.9
2009	158,332	117,886	7.07	6.0	3.2

• NEW LIFE BUSINESS ISSUED ($000 omitted)

Year	Whole Life	Term	Credit	Group	Industrial	Total
2007	13,109,244	16,508,695	...	183,930,031	...	213,547,970
2008	10,612,980	11,450,299	...	192,600,266	...	214,663,545
2009	10,282,282	77,711	...	175,246,802	...	185,606,795

• LIFE INSURANCE IN FORCE ($000 omitted)

Year	Whole Life	Term	Credit	Group	Industrial	Total
2007	287,543,020	211,484,201	55,514	2,475,080,963	2,623,288	2,976,786,986
2008	284,961,945	402,325,870	51,178	2,838,819,038	2,555,920	3,528,713,951
2009	284,014,631	416,566,921	39,712	2,993,450,758	2,478,134	3,696,550,156

METROPOLITAN TOWER LIFE INS CO

18210 Crane Nest Dr., 3rd Floor
Tampa, Florida 33647
Tel: 212-578-2211

AMB#: 009165
Began Business: 02/15/1983
Agency Off: None

Best's Financial Strength Rating: A+ gu
FSC: XV

• NET PREMIUMS AND DEPOSITS ($000 omitted)

Year	Individual Life	Individual & Group Annuities	Group Life & A&H	Credit Life & A&H	Individual A&H	Total
2007	51,411	140,011	...	...	...	191,422
2008	54,233	145,614	...	...	...	199,847
2009	49,556	173,477	...	...	...	223,033

• NET OPERATING GAIN ($000 omitted)

Year	Individual Life	Individual & Group Annuities	Group Life & A&H	Credit Life & A&H	Individual A&H	Total
2007	103,629	642	...	...	...	104,271
2008	76,714	3,316	...	...	...	80,030
2009	91,390	2,534	...	...	...	93,924

• COMPARATIVE FINANCIALS ($000 omitted)

Year	Assets	Capital & Surplus	Net Invest Income	Benefits Paid	Realized Cap Gains	Policyholder Dividends	Contract Lns (% of assets)
2007	6,179,138	1,137,780	310,458	297,056	-1,056	...	5.7
2008	5,511,567	884,826	283,412	304,579	132,166	...	6.3
2009	5,000,315	866,623	265,328	271,923	-36,743	...	6.8

• ORDINARY LIFE STATISTICS

Year	Av. Ord. Policy Issued ($)	Av. Ord. Policy In Force ($)	Avg. Prem ($/M)	1st Yr Prem/ Total Prem	Ord. Lapse Ratio
2007	...	82,576	6.32	0.1	5.8
2008	1,035,500	81,680	6.44	0.0	6.3
2009	-796,500	81,077	6.73	0.0	5.9

• NEW LIFE BUSINESS ISSUED ($000 omitted)

Year	Whole Life	Term	Credit	Group	Industrial	Total
2007	...	...	...	...	...	...
2008	2,071	...	...	...	...	2,071
2009	1,593	...	...	...	...	1,593

• LIFE INSURANCE IN FORCE ($000 omitted)

Year	Whole Life	Term	Credit	Group	Industrial	Total
2007	26,880,776	22,958	...	...	...	26,903,734
2008	23,887,483	1,092,201	...	...	...	24,979,684
2009	22,239,942	984,934	...	...	...	23,224,876

MID-WEST NATIONAL LIFE OF TN

9151 Boulevard 26
North Richland Hills, Texas 76180
Tel: 817-255-3100

AMB#: 006715
Began Business: 05/21/1965
Agency Off: None

Best's Financial Strength Rating: B++g
FSC: VIII

• NET PREMIUMS AND DEPOSITS ($000 omitted)

Year	Individual Life	Individual & Group Annuities	Group Life & A&H	Credit Life & A&H	Individual A&H	Total
2007	8,596	802	320,624	148	33,931	364,101
2008	926	334	247,152	-45	24,626	272,994
2009	160	36	221,960	...	25,452	247,608

• NET OPERATING GAIN ($000 omitted)

Year	Individual Life	Individual & Group Annuities	Group Life & A&H	Credit Life & A&H	Individual A&H	Total
2007	2,513	971	58,493	666	8,663	71,305
2008	1,471	824	42,236	445	5,500	49,823
2009	891	...	25,042	-550	2,773	28,157

• COMPARATIVE FINANCIALS ($000 omitted)

Year	Assets	Capital & Surplus	Net Invest Income	Benefits Paid	Realized Cap Gains	Policyholder Dividends	Contract Lns (% of assets)
2007	374,848	145,267	20,970	174,278	868	23	0.8
2008	218,508	98,335	15,485	142,343	-11,355	-14	0.1
2009	197,285	77,820	8,805	136,212	3,712	...	0.1

• ORDINARY LIFE STATISTICS

Year	Av. Ord. Policy Issued ($)	Av. Ord. Policy In Force ($)	Avg. Prem ($/M)	1st Yr Prem/ Total Prem	Ord. Lapse Ratio
2007	...	...	...	...	...
2008	...	...	...	...	...
2009	...	...	...	...	...

• NEW LIFE BUSINESS ISSUED ($000 omitted)

Year	Whole Life	Term	Credit	Group	Industrial	Total
2007	21,673	122,623	7,367	9,020	...	160,683
2008	12,777	76,754	2,936	7,620	...	100,087
2009	148	1,553	...	620	...	2,321

• LIFE INSURANCE IN FORCE ($000 omitted)

Year	Whole Life	Term	Credit	Group	Industrial	Total
2007	445,061	628,734	44,568	107,510	...	1,225,873
2008	388,932	578,791	24,231	84,411	...	1,076,365
2009	302,227	528,396	14,717	62,720	...	908,060

MIDLAND NATIONAL LIFE INS CO

One Sammons Plaza
Sioux Falls, South Dakota 57193
Tel: 605-335-5700

AMB#: 006711
Began Business: 09/04/1906
Agency Off: Steven C. Palmitier

Best's Financial Strength Rating: A+ g
FSC: XIV

• NET PREMIUMS AND DEPOSITS ($000 omitted)

Year	Individual Life	Individual & Group Annuities	Group Life & A&H	Credit Life & A&H	Individual A&H	Total
2007	616,978	1,468,412	1,892	...	0	2,087,281
2008	541,619	1,718,930	3,765	...	1	2,264,315
2009	640,754	1,683,497	4,572	...	1	2,328,823

• NET OPERATING GAIN ($000 omitted)

Year	Individual Life	Individual & Group Annuities	Group Life & A&H	Credit Life & A&H	Individual A&H	Total
2007	90,172	17,443	1,141	...	-59	108,697
2008	65,147	101,032	2,405	...	-74	168,510
2009	49,212	38,182	-4,050	...	-18	83,327

• COMPARATIVE FINANCIALS ($000 omitted)

Year	Assets	Capital & Surplus	Net Invest Income	Benefits Paid	Realized Cap Gains	Policyholder Dividends	Contract Lns (% of assets)
2007	23,518,176	1,109,422	976,068	1,553,411	3,469	1,080	1.3
2008	25,408,812	1,240,344	857,692	1,549,510	-57,901	1,038	1.2
2009	26,496,854	1,391,869	1,087,136	1,580,458	-114,580	981	1.2

• ORDINARY LIFE STATISTICS

Year	Av. Ord. Policy Issued ($)	Av. Ord. Policy In Force ($)	Avg. Prem ($/M)	1st Yr Prem/ Total Prem	Ord. Lapse Ratio
2007	310,163	151,945	6.56	34.9	5.4
2008	307,881	157,928	5.93	27.9	5.8
2009	306,655	163,430	6.77	36.8	7.0

• NEW LIFE BUSINESS ISSUED ($000 omitted)

Year	Whole Life	Term	Credit	Group	Industrial	Total
2007	3,749,135	7,158,056	...	...	...	10,907,191
2008	3,597,916	7,366,955	...	...	...	10,964,871
2009	3,992,931	7,261,631	...	75,826	...	11,330,388

• LIFE INSURANCE IN FORCE ($000 omitted)

Year	Whole Life	Term	Credit	Group	Industrial	Total
2007	51,541,240	65,430,438	...	4,256	...	116,975,934
2008	51,755,002	67,937,127	...	3,983	...	119,696,112
2009	51,775,800	69,414,742	...	462,873	...	121,653,415

MIDWEST SECURITY LIFE INS CO

2700 Midwest Drive
Onalaska, Wisconsin 54650-8764
Tel: 608-783-7130

AMB#: 008297
Began Business: 03/15/1973
Agency Off: None

Best's Financial Strength Rating: A- **FSC:** V

• NET PREMIUMS AND DEPOSITS ($000 omitted)

Year	Individual Life	Individual & Group Annuities	Group Life & A&H	Credit Life & A&H	Individual A&H	Total
2007	5	...	127,685	...	...	127,690
2008	5	...	118,718	...	...	118,723
2009	6	...	90,056	...	...	90,061

• NET OPERATING GAIN ($000 omitted)

Year	Individual Life	Individual & Group Annuities	Group Life & A&H	Credit Life & A&H	Individual A&H	Total
2007	4	...	4,589	...	...	4,593
2008	2	...	1,143	...	...	1,146
2009	-6	...	5,936	...	...	5,930

• COMPARATIVE FINANCIALS ($000 omitted)

Year	Assets	Capital & Surplus	Net Invest Income	Benefits Paid	Realized Cap Gains	Policyholder Dividends	Contract Lns (% of assets)
2007	64,083	34,843	3,679	108,572	...	...	...
2008	50,291	24,359	2,575	101,762	1,845	...	...
2009	39,759	20,906	1,389	73,205	-111	...	...

• ORDINARY LIFE STATISTICS

Year	Av. Ord. Policy Issued ($)	Av. Ord. Policy In Force ($)	Avg. Prem ($/M)	1st Yr Prem/ Total Prem	Ord. Lapse Ratio
2007	...	...	...	...	...
2008	...	...	...	...	...
2009	...	...	...	...	...

• NEW LIFE BUSINESS ISSUED ($000 omitted)

Year	Whole Life	Term	Credit	Group	Industrial	Total
2007	...	...	...	108,806	...	108,806
2008	15	...	...	53,828	...	53,843
2009	20	...	...	11,392	...	11,412

• LIFE INSURANCE IN FORCE ($000 omitted)

Year	Whole Life	Term	Credit	Group	Industrial	Total
2007	140	...	...	300,384	...	300,524
2008	155	...	...	237,739	...	237,894
2009	160	...	...	148,359	...	148,519

MII LIFE INC

3535 Blue Cross Road
St. Paul, Minnesota 55122
Tel: 651-662-8000

AMB#: 009495
Began Business: 09/29/1959
Agency Off: None

Best's Financial Strength Rating: B++ **FSC:** IV

• NET PREMIUMS AND DEPOSITS ($000 omitted)

Year	Individual Life	Individual & Group Annuities	Group Life & A&H	Credit Life & A&H	Individual A&H	Total
2007	41	107,835	21,161	...	1	129,038
2008	...	118,631	496	...	...	119,127
2009	...	136,929	465	...	...	137,395

• NET OPERATING GAIN ($000 omitted)

Year	Individual Life	Individual & Group Annuities	Group Life & A&H	Credit Life & A&H	Individual A&H	Total
2007	598	...	-382	...	1	-8,023
2008	150	...	1,579	...	2	-757
2009	715	...	1,813	...	...	2,493

• COMPARATIVE FINANCIALS ($000 omitted)

Year	Assets	Capital & Surplus	Net Invest Income	Benefits Paid	Realized Cap Gains	Policyholder Dividends	Contract Lns (% of assets)
2007	111,169	13,011	3,656	23,679	-59	12	...
2008	139,420	10,437	5,284	2,241	-4,547	-11	...
2009	164,376	6,497	4,975	1,914	-3,427	...	...

• ORDINARY LIFE STATISTICS

Year	Av. Ord. Policy Issued ($)	Av. Ord. Policy In Force ($)	Avg. Prem ($/M)	1st Yr Prem/ Total Prem	Ord. Lapse Ratio
2007	...	...	...	...	...
2008	...	...	...	...	...
2009	...	...	...	...	...

• NEW LIFE BUSINESS ISSUED ($000 omitted)

Year	Whole Life	Term	Credit	Group	Industrial	Total
2007	636	720	...	38,892	...	40,248
2008	...	...	...	...	...	...
2009	...	...	...	...	...	...

• LIFE INSURANCE IN FORCE ($000 omitted)

Year	Whole Life	Term	Credit	Group	Industrial	Total
2007	12,448	187,850	...	4,356,655	...	4,556,953
2008	4,020	64,125	...	614,288	...	682,433
2009	2,802	36,613	...	...	...	39,415

MIDWESTERN UNITED LIFE INS CO

5780 Powers Ferry Road, NW
Atlanta, Georgia 30327-4390
Tel: 770-980-5100

AMB#: 006718
Began Business: 08/05/1948
Agency Off: None

Best's Financial Strength Rating: A- **FSC:** VIII

• NET PREMIUMS AND DEPOSITS ($000 omitted)

Year	Individual Life	Individual & Group Annuities	Group Life & A&H	Credit Life & A&H	Individual A&H	Total
2007	4,865	4,392	...	...	...	9,257
2008	4,724	4,542	...	...	...	9,266
2009	4,361	5,370	...	...	...	9,732

• NET OPERATING GAIN ($000 omitted)

Year	Individual Life	Individual & Group Annuities	Group Life & A&H	Credit Life & A&H	Individual A&H	Total
2007	786	31	...	...	...	817
2008	2,511	210	...	...	...	2,721
2009	8,197	-166	...	...	...	8,031

• COMPARATIVE FINANCIALS ($000 omitted)

Year	Assets	Capital & Surplus	Net Invest Income	Benefits Paid	Realized Cap Gains	Policyholder Dividends	Contract Lns (% of assets)
2007	250,388	96,143	13,501	13,781	639	616	4.9
2008	244,724	96,123	13,227	15,354	-1,990	555	4.8
2009	243,674	102,865	11,123	14,279	-558	556	4.5

• ORDINARY LIFE STATISTICS

Year	Av. Ord. Policy Issued ($)	Av. Ord. Policy In Force ($)	Avg. Prem ($/M)	1st Yr Prem/ Total Prem	Ord. Lapse Ratio
2007	...	...	...	...	...
2008	...	...	...	...	...
2009	...	...	...	...	...

• NEW LIFE BUSINESS ISSUED ($000 omitted)

Year	Whole Life	Term	Credit	Group	Industrial	Total
2007	...	...	...	...	...	...
2008	...	...	...	...	...	...
2009	...	...	...	...	...	...

• LIFE INSURANCE IN FORCE ($000 omitted)

Year	Whole Life	Term	Credit	Group	Industrial	Total
2007	530,760	56,876	...	...	...	587,636
2008	497,472	52,088	...	...	...	549,560
2009	466,464	48,858	...	...	...	515,322

MINNESOTA LIFE INS COMPANY

400 Robert Street North
St. Paul, Minnesota 55101-2098
Tel: 651-665-3500

AMB#: 006724
Began Business: 08/06/1880
Agency Off: Wilford J. Kavanaugh

Best's Financial Strength Rating: A+ g **FSC:** XIV

• NET PREMIUMS AND DEPOSITS ($000 omitted)

Year	Individual Life	Individual & Group Annuities	Group Life & A&H	Credit Life & A&H	Individual A&H	Total
2007	667,952	2,072,183	1,336,649	127,612	59	4,204,455
2008	665,611	2,432,348	1,475,448	123,078	58	4,696,543
2009	719,552	2,145,377	1,511,419	106,519	56	4,482,922

• NET OPERATING GAIN ($000 omitted)

Year	Individual Life	Individual & Group Annuities	Group Life & A&H	Credit Life & A&H	Individual A&H	Total
2007	30,669	41,022	50,649	10,750	8,441	141,531
2008	-5,110	-52,485	30,916	6,953	-775	-20,501
2009	7,067	40,420	18,069	5,669	-1,445	69,781

• COMPARATIVE FINANCIALS ($000 omitted)

Year	Assets	Capital & Surplus	Net Invest Income	Benefits Paid	Realized Cap Gains	Policyholder Dividends	Contract Lns (% of assets)
2007	23,829,005	1,818,067	510,515	3,540,989	40,229	103,959	1.3
2008	19,697,080	1,431,990	514,483	3,751,222	-215,598	102,468	1.7
2009	22,800,080	1,741,622	512,193	3,583,316	-9,067	94,019	1.5

• ORDINARY LIFE STATISTICS

Year	Av. Ord. Policy Issued ($)	Av. Ord. Policy In Force ($)	Avg. Prem ($/M)	1st Yr Prem/ Total Prem	Ord. Lapse Ratio
2007	669,301	306,946	7.74	9.5	6.4
2008	691,520	327,435	7.31	9.9	7.4
2009	707,028	349,497	7.44	17.3	7.7

• NEW LIFE BUSINESS ISSUED ($000 omitted)

Year	Whole Life	Term	Credit	Group	Industrial	Total
2007	4,672,399	8,255,811	3,608,296	47,577,765	...	64,114,271
2008	4,343,393	10,506,304	3,250,769	67,754,396	...	85,854,862
2009	5,208,638	11,405,109	3,148,135	76,486,241	...	96,248,123

• LIFE INSURANCE IN FORCE ($000 omitted)

Year	Whole Life	Term	Credit	Group	Industrial	Total
2007	54,588,903	40,249,563	9,064,356	525,674,957	...	629,577,779
2008	54,194,049	46,721,517	8,443,940	616,854,477	...	726,213,983
2009	54,008,248	53,612,445	7,745,371	488,595,494	...	603,961,558

ML LIFE INS CO OF NY

4333 Edgewood Road NE
Cedar Rapid, Iowa 52499
Tel: 319-355-8511

AMB#: 008487
Began Business: 03/27/1974
Agency Off: None

Best's Financial Strength Rating: A g
FSC: XV

• **NET PREMIUMS AND DEPOSITS ($000 omitted)**

Year	Individual Life	Individual & Group Annuities	Group Life & A&H	Credit Life & A&H	Individual A&H	Total
2007	-1,261	36,110	...	...	...	34,849
2008	-102	11,766	...	...	...	11,664
2009	-1,569	4,554	...	...	...	2,985

• **NET OPERATING GAIN ($000 omitted)**

Year	Individual Life	Individual & Group Annuities	Group Life & A&H	Credit Life & A&H	Individual A&H	Total
2007	3,676	16,293	...	...	...	19,969
2008	445	-14,189	...	...	...	-13,744
2009	4,703	19,237	...	...	...	23,940

• **COMPARATIVE FINANCIALS ($000 omitted)**

Year	Assets	Capital & Surplus	Net Invest Income	Benefits Paid	Realized Cap Gains	Policyholder Dividends	Contract Lns (% of assets)
2007	1,169,230	76,871	8,260	161,420	0	...	5.9
2008	835,362	51,928	8,155	105,367	632	...	8.1
2009	882,568	81,728	7,570	82,384	-1,683	...	7.1

• **ORDINARY LIFE STATISTICS**

Year	Av. Ord. Policy Issued ($)	Av. Ord. Policy In Force ($)	Avg. Prem ($/M)	1st Yr Prem/ Total Prem	Ord. Lapse Ratio
2007	...	...	...	...	...
2008	...	...	...	...	...
2009	...	...	...	...	...

• **NEW LIFE BUSINESS ISSUED ($000 omitted)**

Year	Whole Life	Term	Credit	Group	Industrial	Total
2007	...	...	...	...	...	...
2008	...	...	...	...	...	...
2009	...	...	...	...	...	...

• **LIFE INSURANCE IN FORCE ($000 omitted)**

Year	Whole Life	Term	Credit	Group	Industrial	Total
2007	562,829	297	...	...	...	563,126
2008	453,281	297	...	...	...	453,578
2009	429,889	297	...	...	...	430,186

MODERN WOODMEN OF AMERICA

1701 First Avenue
Rock Island, Illinois 61201-8779
Tel: 309-786-6481

AMB#: 006737
Began Business: 01/05/1883
Agency Off: George R. Worley

Best's Financial Strength Rating: A+
FSC: XII

• **NET PREMIUMS AND DEPOSITS ($000 omitted)**

Year	Individual Life	Individual & Group Annuities	Group Life & A&H	Credit Life & A&H	Individual A&H	Total
2007	228,238	...	...	...	159	663,050
2008	234,061	...	...	...	140	843,997
2009	227,792	...	...	...	121	1,028,385

• **NET OPERATING GAIN ($000 omitted)**

Year	Individual Life	Individual & Group Annuities	Group Life & A&H	Credit Life & A&H	Individual A&H	Total
2007	53,242	39,688	...	...	159	66,472
2008	63,202	29,500	...	...	-40	62,263
2009	58,723	38,742	...	...	32	66,562

• **COMPARATIVE FINANCIALS ($000 omitted)**

Year	Assets	Capital & Surplus	Net Invest Income	Benefits Paid	Realized Cap Gains	Policyholder Dividends	Contract Lns (% of assets)
2007	8,318,153	1,170,475	434,957	563,018	30,091	23,690	2.3
2008	8,479,198	1,104,955	458,928	568,659	-69,687	24,206	2.3
2009	9,266,005	1,136,447	487,079	577,670	-36,731	24,930	2.1

• **ORDINARY LIFE STATISTICS**

Year	Av. Ord. Policy Issued ($)	Av. Ord. Policy In Force ($)	Avg. Prem ($/M)	1st Yr Prem/ Total Prem	Ord. Lapse Ratio
2007	82,083	45,067	7.28	10.7	7.1
2008	84,316	46,353	7.33	10.5	7.3
2009	82,872	47,299	7.15	11.4	7.5

• **NEW LIFE BUSINESS ISSUED ($000 omitted)**

Year	Whole Life	Term	Credit	Group	Industrial	Total
2007	3,551,149	...	...	...	...	3,551,149
2008	3,262,505	...	...	...	...	3,262,505
2009	3,005,505	...	...	...	...	3,005,505

• **LIFE INSURANCE IN FORCE ($000 omitted)**

Year	Whole Life	Term	Credit	Group	Industrial	Total
2007	33,080,688	...	...	...	...	33,080,688
2008	33,540,038	...	...	...	...	33,540,038
2009	33,680,120	...	...	...	...	33,680,120

MML BAY STATE LIFE INS CO

1295 State Street
Springfield, Massachusetts 01111
Tel: 413-788-8411

AMB#: 007233
Began Business: 07/01/1894
Agency Off: Alan Taylor

Best's Financial Strength Rating: A++g
FSC: XV

• **NET PREMIUMS AND DEPOSITS ($000 omitted)**

Year	Individual Life	Individual & Group Annuities	Group Life & A&H	Credit Life & A&H	Individual A&H	Total
2007	53,983	1,090	-3,812	...	...	51,260
2008	45,642	889	2,071	...	...	48,603
2009	38,663	1,081	-760	...	...	38,984

• **NET OPERATING GAIN ($000 omitted)**

Year	Individual Life	Individual & Group Annuities	Group Life & A&H	Credit Life & A&H	Individual A&H	Total
2007	14,322	7,327	-7,980	...	...	13,668
2008	22,457	-1,505	-7,569	...	...	13,383
2009	18,196	455	-8,946	...	...	9,705

• **COMPARATIVE FINANCIALS ($000 omitted)**

Year	Assets	Capital & Surplus	Net Invest Income	Benefits Paid	Realized Cap Gains	Policyholder Dividends	Contract Lns (% of assets)
2007	4,636,984	183,358	16,328	124,843	-2,856	...	1.9
2008	4,176,228	191,776	14,724	104,609	-3,714	...	2.3
2009	4,345,097	158,093	13,926	90,555	-1,980	...	2.3

• **ORDINARY LIFE STATISTICS**

Year	Av. Ord. Policy Issued ($)	Av. Ord. Policy In Force ($)	Avg. Prem ($/M)	1st Yr Prem/ Total Prem	Ord. Lapse Ratio
2007	...	213,346	7.04	0.0	6.4
2008	...	209,549	6.97	...	7.9
2009	...	206,090	6.90	...	8.9

• **NEW LIFE BUSINESS ISSUED ($000 omitted)**

Year	Whole Life	Term	Credit	Group	Industrial	Total
2007	17,240	...	...	320	...	17,560
2008	11,993	...	...	...	...	11,993
2009	3,926	...	...	...	...	3,926

• **LIFE INSURANCE IN FORCE ($000 omitted)**

Year	Whole Life	Term	Credit	Group	Industrial	Total
2007	10,895,684	6,522	...	8,266,142	...	19,168,348
2008	10,027,569	5,644	...	8,106,881	...	18,140,094
2009	9,119,773	5,872	...	7,963,254	...	17,088,899

MONITOR LIFE INSURANCE CO

70 Genesee Street
Utica, New York 13502-3502
Tel: 315-797-5200

AMB#: 008664
Began Business: 06/01/1972
Agency Off: Richard Lang

Best's Financial Strength Rating: B+
FSC: III

• **NET PREMIUMS AND DEPOSITS ($000 omitted)**

Year	Individual Life	Individual & Group Annuities	Group Life & A&H	Credit Life & A&H	Individual A&H	Total
2007	5	0	1,242	...	7	1,254
2008	-51	59	1,267	...	5	1,281
2009	6	0	1,254	...	5	1,265

• **NET OPERATING GAIN ($000 omitted)**

Year	Individual Life	Individual & Group Annuities	Group Life & A&H	Credit Life & A&H	Individual A&H	Total
2007	333	91	-433	...	5	-4
2008	214	49	-378	...	3	-112
2009	156	20	-319	...	3	-139

• **COMPARATIVE FINANCIALS ($000 omitted)**

Year	Assets	Capital & Surplus	Net Invest Income	Benefits Paid	Realized Cap Gains	Policyholder Dividends	Contract Lns (% of assets)
2007	9,128	5,321	326	931	...	...	0.3
2008	8,724	5,056	266	984	...	...	0.3
2009	8,487	4,723	214	819	...	...	0.3

• **ORDINARY LIFE STATISTICS**

Year	Av. Ord. Policy Issued ($)	Av. Ord. Policy In Force ($)	Avg. Prem ($/M)	1st Yr Prem/ Total Prem	Ord. Lapse Ratio
2007	...	...	...	...	...
2008	...	...	...	...	...
2009	...	...	...	...	...

• **NEW LIFE BUSINESS ISSUED ($000 omitted)**

Year	Whole Life	Term	Credit	Group	Industrial	Total
2007	64	200	...	51,971	...	52,235
2008	235	228	...	30,387	...	30,850
2009	151	76	...	35,213	...	35,440

• **LIFE INSURANCE IN FORCE ($000 omitted)**

Year	Whole Life	Term	Credit	Group	Industrial	Total
2007	24,296	6,657	...	435,552	...	466,505
2008	21,119	5,458	...	444,193	...	470,770
2009	19,097	4,841	...	387,294	...	411,232

MONUMENTAL LIFE INS CO

4333 Edgewood Road N.E.
Cedar Rapids, Iowa 52499
Tel: 319-355-8511

AMB#: 006742
Began Business: 05/22/1860
Agency Off: None

Best's Financial Strength Rating: A g
FSC: XV

• NET PREMIUMS AND DEPOSITS ($000 omitted)

Year	Individual Life	Individual & Group Annuities	Group Life & A&H	Credit Life & A&H	Individual A&H	Total
2007	606,334	7,105,727	500,379	37,485	236,390	8,486,316
2008	-4,048,551	4,764,365	491,418	33,784	259,037	1,500,054
2009	340,818	-2,849,849	491,908	17,677	190,964	-1,808,482

• NET OPERATING GAIN ($000 omitted)

Year	Individual Life	Individual & Group Annuities	Group Life & A&H	Credit Life & A&H	Individual A&H	Total
2007	135,979	61,071	81,000	39,671	-32,693	285,028
2008	243,122	116,328	82,794	43,513	43,035	528,792
2009	202,564	130,962	49,252	23,858	29,200	435,836

• COMPARATIVE FINANCIALS ($000 omitted)

Year	Assets	Capital & Surplus	Net Invest Income	Benefits Paid	Realized Cap Gains	Policyholder Dividends	Contract Lns (% of assets)
2007	37,935,163	731,779	1,465,481	2,566,057	76,354	1,492	1.3
2008	35,531,178	1,236,153	1,322,769	2,529,044	-185,128	1,484	1.4
2009	34,727,978	1,436,586	1,093,285	2,073,291	-244,158	1,444	1.4

• ORDINARY LIFE STATISTICS

Year	Av. Ord. Policy Issued ($)	Av. Ord. Policy In Force ($)	Avg. Prem ($/M)	1st Yr Prem/ Total Prem	Ord. Lapse Ratio
2007	30,855	20,289	11.50	8.4	4.8
2008	29,706	20,317	11.43	7.2	9.1
2009	32,100	20,559	11.44	6.6	7.9

• NEW LIFE BUSINESS ISSUED ($000 omitted)

Year	Whole Life	Term	Credit	Group	Industrial	Total
2007	2,464,733	2,637,825	1,010,539	795,462	...	6,908,559
2008	2,077,812	1,936,043	2,244,399	445,558	...	6,703,812
2009	1,842,101	1,783,465	607,534	366,206	...	4,599,305

• LIFE INSURANCE IN FORCE ($000 omitted)

Year	Whole Life	Term	Credit	Group	Industrial	Total
2007	39,482,983	23,370,775	5,968,719	9,636,023	856,804	79,315,304
2008	39,069,494	21,887,163	5,302,910	8,368,577	821,593	75,449,737
2009	38,188,134	21,063,919	3,579,243	7,426,929	788,996	71,047,222

MONY LIFE INSURANCE CO OF AMER

1290 Avenue of the Americas, 16th Floor
New York, New York 10104
Tel: 212-554-1234

AMB#: 008091
Began Business: 06/26/1969
Agency Off: Robert S. Jones, Jr.

Best's Financial Strength Rating: A+ g
FSC: XV

• NET PREMIUMS AND DEPOSITS ($000 omitted)

Year	Individual Life	Individual & Group Annuities	Group Life & A&H	Credit Life & A&H	Individual A&H	Total
2007	190,945	101,519	12,591	...	...	305,055
2008	198,268	97,706	10,797	...	64	306,835
2009	176,755	86,610	7,709	...	4	271,078

• NET OPERATING GAIN ($000 omitted)

Year	Individual Life	Individual & Group Annuities	Group Life & A&H	Credit Life & A&H	Individual A&H	Total
2007	1,846	23,333	-705	...	...	24,474
2008	-31,206	-8,057	-1,122	...	42	-40,343
2009	19,637	18,341	-104	...	3	37,877

• COMPARATIVE FINANCIALS ($000 omitted)

Year	Assets	Capital & Surplus	Net Invest Income	Benefits Paid	Realized Cap Gains	Policyholder Dividends	Contract Lns (% of assets)
2007	5,594,467	291,315	124,547	931,211	-17,201	...	2.1
2008	4,198,940	191,705	114,663	790,358	-27,869	...	2.9
2009	4,276,906	273,755	108,647	552,101	-26,215	...	2.9

• ORDINARY LIFE STATISTICS

Year	Av. Ord. Policy Issued ($)	Av. Ord. Policy In Force ($)	Avg. Prem ($/M)	1st Yr Prem/ Total Prem	Ord. Lapse Ratio
2007	406,500	368,254	4.72	16.7	6.8
2008	391,672	367,449	4.92	19.3	6.2
2009	359,287	359,723	4.62	13.3	7.0

• NEW LIFE BUSINESS ISSUED ($000 omitted)

Year	Whole Life	Term	Credit	Group	Industrial	Total
2007	3,496,509	4,270	...	48,086	...	3,548,865
2008	2,655,989	1,894	...	6,000	...	2,663,883
2009	1,539,903	...	...	2,524	...	1,542,427

• LIFE INSURANCE IN FORCE ($000 omitted)

Year	Whole Life	Term	Credit	Group	Industrial	Total
2007	21,169,727	33,443,130	...	1,101,838	...	55,714,695
2008	22,030,837	31,421,617	...	973,746	...	54,426,200
2009	21,703,654	29,403,240	...	868,384	...	51,975,278

MONY LIFE INS CO

1290 Avenue of the Americas, 16th Floor
New York, New York 10104
Tel: 212-554-1234

AMB#: 006751
Began Business: 02/01/1843
Agency Off: Andrew McMahon

Best's Financial Strength Rating: A+ g
FSC: XV

• NET PREMIUMS AND DEPOSITS ($000 omitted)

Year	Individual Life	Individual & Group Annuities	Group Life & A&H	Credit Life & A&H	Individual A&H	Total
2007	419,104	132,661	14,564	...	7,442	573,788
2008	412,907	137,733	3,389	...	13,125	567,150
2009	384,880	133,638	2,943	...	16,272	537,736

• NET OPERATING GAIN ($000 omitted)

Year	Individual Life	Individual & Group Annuities	Group Life & A&H	Credit Life & A&H	Individual A&H	Total
2007	135,423	3,787	6,218	...	-3,130	142,570
2008	114,471	-35,457	4,710	...	-3,120	80,760
2009	81,727	31,296	3,731	...	-1,050	115,590

• COMPARATIVE FINANCIALS ($000 omitted)

Year	Assets	Capital & Surplus	Net Invest Income	Benefits Paid	Realized Cap Gains	Policyholder Dividends	Contract Lns (% of assets)
2007	9,917,633	961,274	551,123	817,651	-12,151	154,018	9.8
2008	9,161,876	520,732	516,839	790,535	-77,882	160,987	10.5
2009	9,181,461	728,706	456,845	712,852	-71,025	161,043	10.3

• ORDINARY LIFE STATISTICS

Year	Av. Ord. Policy Issued ($)	Av. Ord. Policy In Force ($)	Avg. Prem ($/M)	1st Yr Prem/ Total Prem	Ord. Lapse Ratio
2007	896,306	68,409	11.52	0.4	5.9
2008	950,424	68,270	11.90	0.4	6.1
2009	...	67,956	11.89	0.4	6.2

• NEW LIFE BUSINESS ISSUED ($000 omitted)

Year	Whole Life	Term	Credit	Group	Industrial	Total
2007	29,947	2,320	...	468	...	32,735
2008	21,499	9,865	...	...	...	31,364
2009	8,397	10	...	75	...	8,482

• LIFE INSURANCE IN FORCE ($000 omitted)

Year	Whole Life	Term	Credit	Group	Industrial	Total
2007	21,543,354	16,818,827	...	195,122	...	38,557,303
2008	19,314,914	16,654,524	...	172,785	...	36,142,223
2009	18,052,210	15,599,138	...	156,414	...	33,807,762

MOTORISTS LIFE INS CO

471 East Broad Street
Columbus, Ohio 43215-3861
Tel: 614-225-8358

AMB#: 006744
Began Business: 01/24/1967
Agency Off: Charles A. Wickert

Best's Financial Strength Rating: A-
FSC: VI

• NET PREMIUMS AND DEPOSITS ($000 omitted)

Year	Individual Life	Individual & Group Annuities	Group Life & A&H	Credit Life & A&H	Individual A&H	Total
2007	34,185	8,501	377	...	...	43,063
2008	36,001	9,659	369	...	...	46,029
2009	38,986	18,698	405	...	...	58,088

• NET OPERATING GAIN ($000 omitted)

Year	Individual Life	Individual & Group Annuities	Group Life & A&H	Credit Life & A&H	Individual A&H	Total
2007	-1,061	1,362	299	...	...	600
2008	-2,256	1,424	84	...	...	-748
2009	-2,422	1,100	142	...	...	-1,180

• COMPARATIVE FINANCIALS ($000 omitted)

Year	Assets	Capital & Surplus	Net Invest Income	Benefits Paid	Realized Cap Gains	Policyholder Dividends	Contract Lns (% of assets)
2007	333,633	50,806	15,190	31,959	63	945	2.1
2008	334,026	43,109	15,372	34,375	-7,580	1,084	2.4
2009	359,305	44,497	15,387	34,249	124	1,152	2.5

• ORDINARY LIFE STATISTICS

Year	Av. Ord. Policy Issued ($)	Av. Ord. Policy In Force ($)	Avg. Prem ($/M)	1st Yr Prem/ Total Prem	Ord. Lapse Ratio
2007	68,397	67,692	7.63	15.2	5.9
2008	69,054	68,418	7.58	15.0	6.4
2009	58,249	67,844	7.82	16.0	5.9

• NEW LIFE BUSINESS ISSUED ($000 omitted)

Year	Whole Life	Term	Credit	Group	Industrial	Total
2007	152,027	566,007	...	...	...	718,034
2008	162,197	590,082	...	...	...	752,279
2009	179,693	571,544	...	...	...	751,237

• LIFE INSURANCE IN FORCE ($000 omitted)

Year	Whole Life	Term	Credit	Group	Industrial	Total
2007	1,290,102	4,332,878	...	144,730	...	5,767,710
2008	1,342,944	4,602,983	...	158,447	...	6,104,374
2009	1,408,668	4,864,751	...	166,422	...	6,439,841

MOUNTAIN LIFE INS CO

P.O. Box 240
Alcoa, Tennessee 37701-0240
Tel: 865-970-2800

AMB#: 008354
Began Business: 10/04/1972
Agency Off: David E. Line

Best's Financial Strength Rating: B+ **FSC:** III

• NET PREMIUMS AND DEPOSITS ($000 omitted)

Year	Individual Life	Individual & Group Annuities	Group Life & A&H	Credit Life & A&H	Individual A&H	Total
2007	587	...	125	1,584	...	2,296
2008	551	...	113	1,221	...	1,886
2009	502	...	80	1,152	...	1,734

• NET OPERATING GAIN ($000 omitted)

Year	Individual Life	Individual & Group Annuities	Group Life & A&H	Credit Life & A&H	Individual A&H	Total
2007	238	...	27	39	...	303
2008	211	...	58	-135	...	134
2009	100	...	8	-76	...	33

• COMPARATIVE FINANCIALS ($000 omitted)

Year	Assets	Capital & Surplus	Net Invest Income	Benefits Paid	Realized Cap Gains	Policyholder Dividends	Contract Lns (% of assets)
2007	10,502	3,495	361	785	...	...	...
2008	9,390	3,362	274	793	5	...	...
2009	8,635	3,337	189	847	...	...	...

• ORDINARY LIFE STATISTICS

Year	Av. Ord. Policy Issued ($)	Av. Ord. Policy In Force ($)	Avg. Prem ($/M)	1st Yr Prem/ Total Prem	Ord. Lapse Ratio
2007	...	...	...	...	...
2008	...	...	...	...	...
2009	...	...	...	...	...

• NEW LIFE BUSINESS ISSUED ($000 omitted)

Year	Whole Life	Term	Credit	Group	Industrial	Total
2007	...	13,637	333,187	...	...	346,824
2008	...	9,844	279,896	...	...	289,740
2009	...	5,323	212,810	...	...	218,133

• LIFE INSURANCE IN FORCE ($000 omitted)

Year	Whole Life	Term	Credit	Group	Industrial	Total
2007	...	165,383	427,729	...	...	593,112
2008	...	143,789	374,413	...	...	518,202
2009	...	122,538	324,004	...	...	446,542

MUNICH AMERICAN REASSURANCE CO

P.O. Box 3210
Atlanta, Georgia 30302-3210
Tel: 770-350-3200

AMB#: 006746
Began Business: 11/27/1959
Agency Off: None

Best's Financial Strength Rating: A+ g **FSC:** XV

• NET PREMIUMS AND DEPOSITS ($000 omitted)

Year	Individual Life	Individual & Group Annuities	Group Life & A&H	Credit Life & A&H	Individual A&H	Total
2007	824,081	44,700	75,368	16,547	203,803	1,164,498
2008	885,813	14,543	88,380	59,687	229,622	1,278,046
2009	663,046	53,551	96,698	2,003	257,950	1,073,248

• NET OPERATING GAIN ($000 omitted)

Year	Individual Life	Individual & Group Annuities	Group Life & A&H	Credit Life & A&H	Individual A&H	Total
2007	24,425	10,991	6,618	3,152	7,615	52,801
2008	-59,213	-384	6,642	5,689	3,330	-43,937
2009	39,470	-10,188	3,161	5,434	11,167	49,045

• COMPARATIVE FINANCIALS ($000 omitted)

Year	Assets	Capital & Surplus	Net Invest Income	Benefits Paid	Realized Cap Gains	Policyholder Dividends	Contract Lns (% of assets)
2007	5,029,518	673,037	222,827	924,740	9,789	...	0.1
2008	5,506,150	649,235	241,734	1,095,271	-14,657	...	0.1
2009	5,984,409	609,661	225,380	1,096,270	-2,936	...	0.1

• ORDINARY LIFE STATISTICS

Year	Av. Ord. Policy Issued ($)	Av. Ord. Policy In Force ($)	Avg. Prem ($/M)	1st Yr Prem/ Total Prem	Ord. Lapse Ratio
2007	...	36,422	2.35	...	6.8
2008	...	38,161	2.17	...	6.1
2009	...	40,416	2.34	...	6.8

• NEW LIFE BUSINESS ISSUED ($000 omitted)

Year	Whole Life	Term	Credit	Group	Industrial	Total
2007	...	...	...	...	...	...
2008	...	...	...	...	...	...
2009	...	...	...	...	...	...

• LIFE INSURANCE IN FORCE ($000 omitted)

Year	Whole Life	Term	Credit	Group	Industrial	Total
2007	16,630,048	690,707,748	1,433,739	20,260,313	...	729,031,848
2008	15,493,590	703,629,171	1,415,320	24,125,262	...	744,663,343
2009	14,524,717	731,517,782	2,177,522	23,216,644	...	771,436,666

MTL INSURANCE COMPANY

1200 Jorie Boulevard
Oak Brook, Illinois 60523-2218
Tel: 630-990-1000

AMB#: 006756
Began Business: 04/14/1905
Agency Off: Charles F. McAleer

Best's Financial Strength Rating: A- **FSC:** VIII

• NET PREMIUMS AND DEPOSITS ($000 omitted)

Year	Individual Life	Individual & Group Annuities	Group Life & A&H	Credit Life & A&H	Individual A&H	Total
2007	122,386	15,102	...	...	...	137,489
2008	138,229	19,477	...	...	...	157,706
2009	145,694	17,428	...	...	...	163,122

• NET OPERATING GAIN ($000 omitted)

Year	Individual Life	Individual & Group Annuities	Group Life & A&H	Credit Life & A&H	Individual A&H	Total
2007	-1,669	756	...	...	...	-913
2008	-6,610	1,636	...	...	...	-4,974
2009	-510	1,234	...	...	...	723

• COMPARATIVE FINANCIALS ($000 omitted)

Year	Assets	Capital & Surplus	Net Invest Income	Benefits Paid	Realized Cap Gains	Policyholder Dividends	Contract Lns (% of assets)
2007	1,273,967	105,276	69,905	107,640	101	16,611	9.0
2008	1,319,361	89,225	71,237	92,246	-6,294	16,874	10.7
2009	1,398,474	92,138	73,745	88,174	-2,948	17,155	12.0

• ORDINARY LIFE STATISTICS

Year	Av. Ord. Policy Issued ($)	Av. Ord. Policy In Force ($)	Avg. Prem ($/M)	1st Yr Prem/ Total Prem	Ord. Lapse Ratio
2007	307,423	92,740	14.39	16.5	5.2
2008	292,766	100,830	15.07	16.3	5.4
2009	290,917	106,390	15.29	13.0	6.4

• NEW LIFE BUSINESS ISSUED ($000 omitted)

Year	Whole Life	Term	Credit	Group	Industrial	Total
2007	824,740	686,553	...	...	...	1,511,293
2008	829,581	568,668	...	...	...	1,398,249
2009	715,629	512,330	...	...	...	1,227,959

• LIFE INSURANCE IN FORCE ($000 omitted)

Year	Whole Life	Term	Credit	Group	Industrial	Total
2007	5,526,489	4,037,247	...	...	...	9,563,736
2008	6,005,183	4,279,440	...	...	...	10,284,623
2009	6,259,455	4,400,067	...	...	...	10,659,522

MUTUAL OF AMERICA LIFE INS CO

320 Park Avenue
New York, New York 10022
Tel: 212-224-1600

AMB#: 008851
Began Business: 10/01/1945
Agency Off: William S. Conway

Best's Financial Strength Rating: A+ **FSC:** XI

• NET PREMIUMS AND DEPOSITS ($000 omitted)

Year	Individual Life	Individual & Group Annuities	Group Life & A&H	Credit Life & A&H	Individual A&H	Total
2007	1,740	1,389,872	15,170	...	...	1,406,782
2008	1,615	1,356,235	14,732	...	...	1,372,582
2009	1,442	1,438,435	13,363	...	...	1,453,241

• NET OPERATING GAIN ($000 omitted)

Year	Individual Life	Individual & Group Annuities	Group Life & A&H	Credit Life & A&H	Individual A&H	Total
2007	-1,887	-15,934	3,041	...	...	-14,780
2008	719	-6,158	6,683	...	...	1,244
2009	847	-6,943	9,406	...	...	3,310

• COMPARATIVE FINANCIALS ($000 omitted)

Year	Assets	Capital & Surplus	Net Invest Income	Benefits Paid	Realized Cap Gains	Policyholder Dividends	Contract Lns (% of assets)
2007	13,016,898	831,510	345,442	1,475,678	22,066	1,311	0.8
2008	10,971,697	783,832	349,880	1,423,582	-55,289	1,111	0.8
2009	12,427,574	796,924	365,968	1,099,798	-6,040	293	0.7

• ORDINARY LIFE STATISTICS

Year	Av. Ord. Policy Issued ($)	Av. Ord. Policy In Force ($)	Avg. Prem ($/M)	1st Yr Prem/ Total Prem	Ord. Lapse Ratio
2007	...	...	...	...	...
2008	...	...	...	...	...
2009	...	...	...	...	...

• NEW LIFE BUSINESS ISSUED ($000 omitted)

Year	Whole Life	Term	Credit	Group	Industrial	Total
2007	1,299	...	...	357,951	...	359,250
2008	820	...	...	497,262	...	498,082
2009	875	...	...	166,961	...	167,836

• LIFE INSURANCE IN FORCE ($000 omitted)

Year	Whole Life	Term	Credit	Group	Industrial	Total
2007	241,995	761	...	1,266,956	...	1,509,712
2008	231,812	634	...	1,494,299	...	1,726,745
2009	217,024	618	...	1,122,309	...	1,339,951

MUTUAL OF OMAHA INS CO

Mutual of Omaha Plaza
Omaha, Nebraska 68175
Tel: 402-342-7600

AMB#: 007369
Began Business: 01/10/1910
Agency Off: John Haver

Best's Financial Strength Rating: A+ g
FSC: XIII

• NET PREMIUMS AND DEPOSITS ($000 omitted)

Year	Individual Life	Individual & Group Annuities	Group Life & A&H	Credit Life & A&H	Individual A&H	Total
2007	...	6,138	658,477	...	1,160,207	1,824,822
2008	...	0	244,103	...	1,310,151	1,554,254
2009	...	...	231,308	...	1,389,084	1,620,392

• NET OPERATING GAIN ($000 omitted)

Year	Individual Life	Individual & Group Annuities	Group Life & A&H	Credit Life & A&H	Individual A&H	Total
2007	...	...	13,524	...	36,250	60,083
2008	...	...	46,787	...	60,489	182,560
2009	...	...	43,116	...	41,825	82,217

• COMPARATIVE FINANCIALS ($000 omitted)

Year	Assets	Capital & Surplus	Net Invest Income	Benefits Paid	Realized Cap Gains	Policyholder Dividends	Contract Lns (% of assets)
2007	4,541,725	2,217,383	151,203	1,492,485	29,542	34	...
2008	4,700,084	2,098,578	252,499	1,019,457	-30,526	35	...
2009	4,730,154	2,237,934	142,694	1,126,495	-56,183	41	...

• ORDINARY LIFE STATISTICS

Year	Av. Ord. Policy Issued ($)	Av. Ord. Policy In Force ($)	Avg. Prem ($/M)	1st Yr Prem/ Total Prem	Ord. Lapse Ratio
2007	...	...	...	...	...
2008	...	...	...	...	...
2009	...	...	...	...	...

• NEW LIFE BUSINESS ISSUED ($000 omitted)

Year	Whole Life	Term	Credit	Group	Industrial	Total
2007	...	...	...	...	...	...
2008	...	...	...	...	...	...
2009	...	...	...	...	...	...

• LIFE INSURANCE IN FORCE ($000 omitted)

Year	Whole Life	Term	Credit	Group	Industrial	Total
2007	...	...	...	...	...	...
2008	...	...	...	...	...	...
2009	...	...	...	...	...	...

NATIONAL BENEFIT LIFE INS CO

One Court Square
Long Island City, New York 11120-0001
Tel: 718-248-8000

AMB#: 006163
Began Business: 05/14/1963
Agency Off: Sheila R. Wyse

Best's Financial Strength Rating: A+ g
FSC: XIV

• NET PREMIUMS AND DEPOSITS ($000 omitted)

Year	Individual Life	Individual & Group Annuities	Group Life & A&H	Credit Life & A&H	Individual A&H	Total
2007	169,991	17,999	42,451	2,741	221	233,404
2008	86,757	20,110	41,377	2,641	203	151,088
2009	86,018	20,328	41,215	2,206	179	149,947

• NET OPERATING GAIN ($000 omitted)

Year	Individual Life	Individual & Group Annuities	Group Life & A&H	Credit Life & A&H	Individual A&H	Total
2007	97,766	138	2,929	717	-117	101,433
2008	22,735	2	2,211	549	-43	25,454
2009	36,983	92	2,224	765	415	40,479

• COMPARATIVE FINANCIALS ($000 omitted)

Year	Assets	Capital & Surplus	Net Invest Income	Benefits Paid	Realized Cap Gains	Policyholder Dividends	Contract Lns (% of assets)
2007	691,213	304,949	44,980	84,073	-756	...	3.1
2008	721,467	316,859	37,840	48,744	-10,316	...	2.5
2009	781,311	358,956	41,502	46,016	-9,220	...	2.1

• ORDINARY LIFE STATISTICS

Year	Av. Ord. Policy Issued ($)	Av. Ord. Policy In Force ($)	Avg. Prem ($/M)	1st Yr Prem/ Total Prem	Ord. Lapse Ratio
2007	87,705	80,853	6.09	15.7	36.5
2008	95,008	88,683	3.53	15.2	11.1
2009	100,096	95,982	3.48	14.2	11.1

• NEW LIFE BUSINESS ISSUED ($000 omitted)

Year	Whole Life	Term	Credit	Group	Industrial	Total
2007	481,022	5,848,267	77,862	...	...	6,407,151
2008	414,968	5,927,654	184,518	...	...	6,527,140
2009	362,281	5,528,050	38,811	...	...	5,929,142

• LIFE INSURANCE IN FORCE ($000 omitted)

Year	Whole Life	Term	Credit	Group	Industrial	Total
2007	2,526,516	31,639,383	181,658	97,634	...	34,445,191
2008	2,512,337	33,310,215	158,448	84,487	...	36,065,487
2009	2,477,887	34,372,482	117,694	72,978	...	37,041,041

MUTUAL SAVINGS LIFE INS CO

12115 Lackland Road
St. Louis, Missouri 63146-4003
Tel: 256-552-7011

AMB#: 006753
Began Business: 01/10/1927
Agency Off: Richard J. Miller

Best's Financial Strength Rating: A- g
FSC: IX

• NET PREMIUMS AND DEPOSITS ($000 omitted)

Year	Individual Life	Individual & Group Annuities	Group Life & A&H	Credit Life & A&H	Individual A&H	Total
2007	40,780	385	...	...	7,858	49,023
2008	39,313	113	...	...	7,373	46,799
2009	36,533	83	...	...	7,104	43,720

• NET OPERATING GAIN ($000 omitted)

Year	Individual Life	Individual & Group Annuities	Group Life & A&H	Credit Life & A&H	Individual A&H	Total
2007	6,574	361	...	...	11	6,946
2008	6,463	428	...	...	-334	6,557
2009	7,210	329	...	...	-44	7,494

• COMPARATIVE FINANCIALS ($000 omitted)

Year	Assets	Capital & Surplus	Net Invest Income	Benefits Paid	Realized Cap Gains	Policyholder Dividends	Contract Lns (% of assets)
2007	425,913	23,596	22,750	32,612	1,734	...	3.1
2008	424,531	22,624	22,899	33,110	-5,277	3	3.3
2009	439,467	33,824	23,472	35,314	-311	0	3.3

• ORDINARY LIFE STATISTICS

Year	Av. Ord. Policy Issued ($)	Av. Ord. Policy In Force ($)	Avg. Prem ($/M)	1st Yr Prem/ Total Prem	Ord. Lapse Ratio
2007	13,813	6,474	19.25	12.3	11.5
2008	14,043	7,775	21.37	11.5	12.6
2009	11,237	7,563	20.94	8.7	10.9

• NEW LIFE BUSINESS ISSUED ($000 omitted)

Year	Whole Life	Term	Credit	Group	Industrial	Total
2007	240,039	72,553	...	...	...	312,592
2008	225,862	67,596	...	...	...	293,458
2009	108,257	47,376	...	...	...	155,633

• LIFE INSURANCE IN FORCE ($000 omitted)

Year	Whole Life	Term	Credit	Group	Industrial	Total
2007	1,585,518	583,972	...	...	337,831	2,507,321
2008	1,418,043	477,049	...	...	233,786	2,128,878
2009	1,251,024	544,182	...	...	227,492	2,022,698

NATIONAL FARM LIFE INS CO

P.O. Box 1486
Fort Worth, Texas 76101-1486
Tel: 817-451-9550

AMB#: 006771
Began Business: 05/01/1946
Agency Off: Cary L. Wright

Best's Financial Strength Rating: B++
FSC: V

• NET PREMIUMS AND DEPOSITS ($000 omitted)

Year	Individual Life	Individual & Group Annuities	Group Life & A&H	Credit Life & A&H	Individual A&H	Total
2007	21,325	3,379	...	...	...	24,704
2008	22,040	5,169	...	...	...	27,208
2009	20,739	4,712	...	...	...	25,451

• NET OPERATING GAIN ($000 omitted)

Year	Individual Life	Individual & Group Annuities	Group Life & A&H	Credit Life & A&H	Individual A&H	Total
2007	284	215	...	...	...	499
2008	1,930	184	...	...	...	2,113
2009	3,165	284	...	...	...	3,450

• COMPARATIVE FINANCIALS ($000 omitted)

Year	Assets	Capital & Surplus	Net Invest Income	Benefits Paid	Realized Cap Gains	Policyholder Dividends	Contract Lns (% of assets)
2007	252,805	22,300	14,248	12,081	...	4,075	7.8
2008	259,486	20,244	14,713	11,204	-3,844	2,293	7.7
2009	270,386	22,894	14,905	13,445	-2,372	2,221	7.6

• ORDINARY LIFE STATISTICS

Year	Av. Ord. Policy Issued ($)	Av. Ord. Policy In Force ($)	Avg. Prem ($/M)	1st Yr Prem/ Total Prem	Ord. Lapse Ratio
2007	47,066	45,696	9.69	12.8	7.9
2008	47,035	45,886	9.78	10.5	8.1
2009	48,952	45,973	9.55	8.9	8.0

• NEW LIFE BUSINESS ISSUED ($000 omitted)

Year	Whole Life	Term	Credit	Group	Industrial	Total
2007	155,745	166,044	...	...	...	321,789
2008	150,404	145,495	...	...	...	295,899
2009	114,953	146,351	...	...	...	261,304

• LIFE INSURANCE IN FORCE ($000 omitted)

Year	Whole Life	Term	Credit	Group	Industrial	Total
2007	1,210,248	899,529	...	...	...	2,109,777
2008	1,264,289	922,487	...	...	...	2,186,776
2009	1,279,550	951,247	...	...	...	2,230,797

NATIONAL FARMERS UNION LIFE

P.O. Box 410288
Kansas City, Missouri 64141-0288
Tel: 816-391-2000

AMB#: 006772
Began Business: 04/18/1938
Agency Off: None

Best's Financial Strength Rating: B+ **FSC:** VI

• NET PREMIUMS AND DEPOSITS ($000 omitted)

Year	Individual Life	Individual & Group Annuities	Group Life & A&H	Credit Life & A&H	Individual A&H	Total
2007	7,367	57	141	…	1	7,566
2008	7,449	316	130	…	1	7,896
2009	6,442	83	128	…	1	6,654

• NET OPERATING GAIN ($000 omitted)

Year	Individual Life	Individual & Group Annuities	Group Life & A&H	Credit Life & A&H	Individual A&H	Total
2007	6,777	105	86	…	-11	6,957
2008	5,939	91	180	…	-8	6,203
2009	6,025	153	110	…	-6	6,281

• COMPARATIVE FINANCIALS ($000 omitted)

Year	Assets	Capital & Surplus	Net Invest Income	Benefits Paid	Realized Cap Gains	Policyholder Dividends	Contract Lns (% of assets)
2007	272,705	42,957	16,301	22,988	5	128	7.3
2008	262,903	42,285	14,787	20,793	716	114	6.5
2009	251,770	43,631	13,936	17,833	-1,032	90	6.3

• ORDINARY LIFE STATISTICS

Year	Av. Ord. Policy Issued ($)	Av. Ord. Policy In Force ($)	Avg. Prem ($/M)	1st Yr Prem/ Total Prem	Ord. Lapse Ratio
2007	…	…	…	…	…
2008	…	…	…	…	…
2009	…	…	…	…	…

• NEW LIFE BUSINESS ISSUED ($000 omitted)

Year	Whole Life	Term	Credit	Group	Industrial	Total
2007	…	…	…	…	…	…
2008	…	…	…	…	…	…
2009	…	…	…	…	…	…

• LIFE INSURANCE IN FORCE ($000 omitted)

Year	Whole Life	Term	Credit	Group	Industrial	Total
2007	1,059,235	163,867	…	16,014	…	1,239,116
2008	978,705	151,099	…	14,967	…	1,144,771
2009	910,014	137,980	…	14,402	…	1,062,396

NATIONAL FOUNDATION LIFE INS

3100 Burnett Plaza, 801 Cherry Street
Fort Worth, Texas 76102
Tel: 817-878-3300

AMB#: 006774
Began Business: 11/02/1983
Agency Off: James R. White, Jr.

Best's Financial Strength Rating: B g **FSC:** V

• NET PREMIUMS AND DEPOSITS ($000 omitted)

Year	Individual Life	Individual & Group Annuities	Group Life & A&H	Credit Life & A&H	Individual A&H	Total
2007	242	…	32,117	…	21,550	53,910
2008	-2,935	…	34,825	…	16,197	48,087
2009	93	…	38,511	…	16,891	55,494

• NET OPERATING GAIN ($000 omitted)

Year	Individual Life	Individual & Group Annuities	Group Life & A&H	Credit Life & A&H	Individual A&H	Total
2007	50	…	-1,074	…	-1,701	-2,725
2008	101	…	-3,728	…	-411	-4,038
2009	32	…	-2,099	…	1,933	-133

• COMPARATIVE FINANCIALS ($000 omitted)

Year	Assets	Capital & Surplus	Net Invest Income	Benefits Paid	Realized Cap Gains	Policyholder Dividends	Contract Lns (% of assets)
2007	50,040	12,257	2,405	36,464	…	2	0.4
2008	42,910	8,164	2,162	27,996	-341	…	…
2009	40,833	7,899	1,825	35,337	-84	…	…

• ORDINARY LIFE STATISTICS

Year	Av. Ord. Policy Issued ($)	Av. Ord. Policy In Force ($)	Avg. Prem ($/M)	1st Yr Prem/ Total Prem	Ord. Lapse Ratio
2007	…	…	…	…	…
2008	…	…	…	…	…
2009	…	…	…	…	…

• NEW LIFE BUSINESS ISSUED ($000 omitted)

Year	Whole Life	Term	Credit	Group	Industrial	Total
2007	…	4,426	…	…	…	4,426
2008	…	5,691	…	…	…	5,691
2009	…	5,536	…	…	…	5,536

• LIFE INSURANCE IN FORCE ($000 omitted)

Year	Whole Life	Term	Credit	Group	Industrial	Total
2007	9,861	9,938	…	…	…	19,799
2008	2,919	8,347	…	…	…	11,266
2009	1,559	9,138	…	…	…	10,697

NATIONAL GUARDIAN LIFE INS CO

2 East Gilman Street
Madison, Wisconsin 53703-1494
Tel: 608-257-5611

AMB#: 006777
Began Business: 10/11/1910
Agency Off: None

Best's Financial Strength Rating: A- g **FSC:** VIII

• NET PREMIUMS AND DEPOSITS ($000 omitted)

Year	Individual Life	Individual & Group Annuities	Group Life & A&H	Credit Life & A&H	Individual A&H	Total
2007	71,228	15,433	81,835	…	4,441	172,937
2008	94,894	11,829	94,252	…	3,995	204,971
2009	109,067	14,983	116,320	…	3,908	244,279

• NET OPERATING GAIN ($000 omitted)

Year	Individual Life	Individual & Group Annuities	Group Life & A&H	Credit Life & A&H	Individual A&H	Total
2007	7,401	2,512	212	…	-746	12,816
2008	3,951	3,396	2,417	…	-394	13,227
2009	6,128	1,440	4,615	…	-230	20,018

• COMPARATIVE FINANCIALS ($000 omitted)

Year	Assets	Capital & Surplus	Net Invest Income	Benefits Paid	Realized Cap Gains	Policyholder Dividends	Contract Lns (% of assets)
2007	1,485,979	167,450	81,444	155,849	3,720	4,332	2.2
2008	1,651,189	160,840	86,508	155,189	-6,836	4,770	2.0
2009	1,776,303	187,433	100,423	153,211	-11,776	4,834	1.9

• ORDINARY LIFE STATISTICS

Year	Av. Ord. Policy Issued ($)	Av. Ord. Policy In Force ($)	Avg. Prem ($/M)	1st Yr Prem/ Total Prem	Ord. Lapse Ratio
2007	4,285	28,439	19.78	4.0	4.2
2008	4,882	22,274	25.20	5.0	4.8
2009	4,524	20,937	31.09	5.8	3.8

• NEW LIFE BUSINESS ISSUED ($000 omitted)

Year	Whole Life	Term	Credit	Group	Industrial	Total
2007	41,797	…	…	110,113	…	151,910
2008	55,611	…	…	118,048	…	173,659
2009	78,824	…	…	280,757	…	359,581

• LIFE INSURANCE IN FORCE ($000 omitted)

Year	Whole Life	Term	Credit	Group	Industrial	Total
2007	3,041,944	1,458,549	…	457,405	…	4,957,898
2008	3,150,538	1,433,230	…	539,653	44,174	5,167,595
2009	3,100,185	1,318,531	…	780,125	43,444	5,242,285

NATIONAL INCOME LIFE INSURANCE

P.O. Box 5009
Syracuse, New York 13220
Tel: 315-451-8180

AMB#: 060343
Began Business: 11/16/2000
Agency Off: Debbie Gamble

Best's Financial Strength Rating: A+ g **FSC:** X

• NET PREMIUMS AND DEPOSITS ($000 omitted)

Year	Individual Life	Individual & Group Annuities	Group Life & A&H	Credit Life & A&H	Individual A&H	Total
2007	19,405	…	83	…	4,561	24,049
2008	23,757	…	88	…	4,654	28,498
2009	28,808	…	121	…	4,928	33,857

• NET OPERATING GAIN ($000 omitted)

Year	Individual Life	Individual & Group Annuities	Group Life & A&H	Credit Life & A&H	Individual A&H	Total
2007	1,264	…	-173	…	246	1,337
2008	2,644	…	-274	…	374	2,743
2009	1,718	…	-104	…	426	2,040

• COMPARATIVE FINANCIALS ($000 omitted)

Year	Assets	Capital & Surplus	Net Invest Income	Benefits Paid	Realized Cap Gains	Policyholder Dividends	Contract Lns (% of assets)
2007	35,370	9,825	1,429	4,669	…	…	0.6
2008	43,446	9,944	1,739	5,038	-80	…	0.9
2009	54,157	11,342	1,950	5,151	-1	…	1.3

• ORDINARY LIFE STATISTICS

Year	Av. Ord. Policy Issued ($)	Av. Ord. Policy In Force ($)	Avg. Prem ($/M)	1st Yr Prem/ Total Prem	Ord. Lapse Ratio
2007	40,904	32,198	14.53	26.1	22.5
2008	40,536	32,975	14.69	30.2	22.2
2009	42,575	33,956	14.30	31.8	25.7

• NEW LIFE BUSINESS ISSUED ($000 omitted)

Year	Whole Life	Term	Credit	Group	Industrial	Total
2007	311,583	217,913	…	…	…	529,496
2008	468,960	228,171	…	…	…	697,131
2009	638,036	356,483	…	…	…	994,519

• LIFE INSURANCE IN FORCE ($000 omitted)

Year	Whole Life	Term	Credit	Group	Industrial	Total
2007	775,722	559,353	…	…	…	1,335,075
2008	1,008,010	609,395	…	…	…	1,617,405
2009	1,281,120	734,109	…	…	…	2,015,229

NATIONAL INTEGRITY LIFE INS CO

15 Matthews Street, Suite 200
Goshen, New York 10924
Tel: 845-615-2506

AMB#: 007798
Began Business: 12/30/1968
Agency Off: None

Best's Financial Strength Rating: A+ g **FSC:** XV

• NET PREMIUMS AND DEPOSITS ($000 omitted)

Year	Individual Life	Individual & Group Annuities	Group Life & A&H	Credit Life & A&H	Individual A&H	Total
2007	5,743	526,817	...	...	...	532,561
2008	1,290	803,786	...	...	...	805,076
2009	-39	575,729	...	...	...	575,690

• NET OPERATING GAIN ($000 omitted)

Year	Individual Life	Individual & Group Annuities	Group Life & A&H	Credit Life & A&H	Individual A&H	Total
2007	416	6,345	...	...	...	9,385
2008	331	-5,100	...	...	...	-34,060
2009	377	20,031	...	...	...	15,205

• COMPARATIVE FINANCIALS ($000 omitted)

Year	Assets	Capital & Surplus	Net Invest Income	Benefits Paid	Realized Cap Gains	Policyholder Dividends	Contract Lns (% of assets)
2007	3,677,509	142,135	55,251	471,256	-4,271	...	1.2
2008	4,037,542	184,548	73,689	408,802	-22,696	...	1.0
2009	4,432,445	225,590	99,757	444,145	-14,074	...	0.9

• ORDINARY LIFE STATISTICS

Year	Av. Ord. Policy Issued ($)	Av. Ord. Policy In Force ($)	Avg. Prem ($/M)	1st Yr Prem/ Total Prem	Ord. Lapse Ratio
2007	...	...	...	...	...
2008	...	...	...	...	...
2009	...	...	...	...	...

• NEW LIFE BUSINESS ISSUED ($000 omitted)

Year	Whole Life	Term	Credit	Group	Industrial	Total
2007	...	...	...	...	...	...
2008	...	...	...	...	...	...
2009	...	...	...	...	...	...

• LIFE INSURANCE IN FORCE ($000 omitted)

Year	Whole Life	Term	Credit	Group	Industrial	Total
2007	356,671	88	...	...	...	356,759
2008	122,323	85	...	...	...	122,408
2009	116,641	88	...	...	...	116,729

NATIONAL LIFE INS CO

P.O. Box 366107
San Juan, Puerto Rico 00936-6107
Tel: 787-758-8080

AMB#: 007447
Began Business: 07/03/1969
Agency Off: Carlos M. Benitez, Jr.

Best's Financial Strength Rating: B+ **FSC:** V

• NET PREMIUMS AND DEPOSITS ($000 omitted)

Year	Individual Life	Individual & Group Annuities	Group Life & A&H	Credit Life & A&H	Individual A&H	Total
2007	19,025	1,112	21,939	6,696	11,505	60,277
2008	20,123	947	24,863	5,535	20,036	71,505
2009	17,678	967	51,494	4,377	20,828	95,343

• NET OPERATING GAIN ($000 omitted)

Year	Individual Life	Individual & Group Annuities	Group Life & A&H	Credit Life & A&H	Individual A&H	Total
2007	-1,540	-27	2,068	960	432	1,893
2008	896	-137	-548	319	773	1,303
2009	-3,080	-511	2,988	851	1,268	1,516

• COMPARATIVE FINANCIALS ($000 omitted)

Year	Assets	Capital & Surplus	Net Invest Income	Benefits Paid	Realized Cap Gains	Policyholder Dividends	Contract Lns (% of assets)
2007	134,975	26,270	5,587	27,221	-416	...	2.8
2008	146,587	28,527	5,873	36,752	-590	...	2.6
2009	145,308	20,236	5,705	59,702	-78	...	2.3

• ORDINARY LIFE STATISTICS

Year	Av. Ord. Policy Issued ($)	Av. Ord. Policy In Force ($)	Avg. Prem ($/M)	1st Yr Prem/ Total Prem	Ord. Lapse Ratio
2007	271,706	109,303	5.18	13.3	21.4
2008	43,792	75,530	3.76	7.7	15.9
2009	42,648	71,607	3.60	8.4	15.1

• NEW LIFE BUSINESS ISSUED ($000 omitted)

Year	Whole Life	Term	Credit	Group	Industrial	Total
2007	...	1,405,535	8,577	125,940	...	1,540,052
2008	...	743,889	8,327	236,952	...	989,168
2009	...	653,201	...	16,013	...	669,214

• LIFE INSURANCE IN FORCE ($000 omitted)

Year	Whole Life	Term	Credit	Group	Industrial	Total
2007	...	4,043,667	123,000	706,251	...	4,872,918
2008	...	5,664,179	147,051	910,805	...	6,722,035
2009	...	5,344,506	130,592	1,325,572	...	6,800,670

NATIONAL LIFE INS CO

1 National Life Drive
Montpelier, Vermont 05604
Tel: 802-229-3333

AMB#: 006790
Began Business: 01/17/1850
Agency Off: None

Best's Financial Strength Rating: A g **FSC:** XII

• NET PREMIUMS AND DEPOSITS ($000 omitted)

Year	Individual Life	Individual & Group Annuities	Group Life & A&H	Credit Life & A&H	Individual A&H	Total
2007	429,986	146,194	...	...	7,919	584,098
2008	439,660	179,880	...	...	7,540	627,081
2009	403,693	206,205	...	...	7,140	617,037

• NET OPERATING GAIN ($000 omitted)

Year	Individual Life	Individual & Group Annuities	Group Life & A&H	Credit Life & A&H	Individual A&H	Total
2007	34,511	11,233	...	...	16,733	62,476
2008	12,668	9,831	...	...	5,938	28,437
2009	6,248	17,412	...	...	6,736	30,396

• COMPARATIVE FINANCIALS ($000 omitted)

Year	Assets	Capital & Surplus	Net Invest Income	Benefits Paid	Realized Cap Gains	Policyholder Dividends	Contract Lns (% of assets)
2007	8,275,646	826,783	426,858	599,150	2,536	126,066	6.8
2008	7,964,828	792,195	402,144	581,976	-33,348	128,399	7.1
2009	8,501,197	1,134,203	400,615	562,453	-41,793	129,801	6.6

• ORDINARY LIFE STATISTICS

Year	Av. Ord. Policy Issued ($)	Av. Ord. Policy In Force ($)	Avg. Prem ($/M)	1st Yr Prem/ Total Prem	Ord. Lapse Ratio
2007	472,744	191,043	10.82	7.6	6.3
2008	461,553	196,044	11.17	7.7	7.0
2009	445,641	198,734	10.61	5.7	7.6

• NEW LIFE BUSINESS ISSUED ($000 omitted)

Year	Whole Life	Term	Credit	Group	Industrial	Total
2007	1,849,415	1,851,698	...	...	...	3,701,113
2008	1,670,881	1,667,529	...	...	...	3,338,410
2009	1,280,807	1,486,175	...	...	...	2,766,982

• LIFE INSURANCE IN FORCE ($000 omitted)

Year	Whole Life	Term	Credit	Group	Industrial	Total
2007	26,185,052	17,313,481	...	...	...	43,498,533
2008	25,951,312	17,215,579	...	...	...	43,166,891
2009	25,241,601	16,949,994	...	...	...	42,191,595

NATIONAL SAFETY LIFE INS CO

P.O. Box 1381
Binghamton, New York 13902-1381
Tel: 610-684-2400

AMB#: 007850
Began Business: 01/14/1963
Agency Off: A. Scott Dittemore

Best's Financial Strength Rating: B+ **FSC:** III

• NET PREMIUMS AND DEPOSITS ($000 omitted)

Year	Individual Life	Individual & Group Annuities	Group Life & A&H	Credit Life & A&H	Individual A&H	Total
2007	682	...	...	...	1,644	2,326
2008	537	...	...	...	747	1,284
2009	493	...	...	...	31	523

• NET OPERATING GAIN ($000 omitted)

Year	Individual Life	Individual & Group Annuities	Group Life & A&H	Credit Life & A&H	Individual A&H	Total
2007	-107	...	...	...	-192	-299
2008	26	...	...	...	27	52
2009	-340	...	...	...	154	-186

• COMPARATIVE FINANCIALS ($000 omitted)

Year	Assets	Capital & Surplus	Net Invest Income	Benefits Paid	Realized Cap Gains	Policyholder Dividends	Contract Lns (% of assets)
2007	4,885	2,225	238	1,220	-1	...	0.0
2008	3,311	2,235	189	511	-2	...	0.0
2009	3,114	2,024	126	190	...	...	0.0

• ORDINARY LIFE STATISTICS

Year	Av. Ord. Policy Issued ($)	Av. Ord. Policy In Force ($)	Avg. Prem ($/M)	1st Yr Prem/ Total Prem	Ord. Lapse Ratio
2007	...	...	...	...	...
2008	...	...	...	...	...
2009	...	...	...	...	...

• NEW LIFE BUSINESS ISSUED ($000 omitted)

Year	Whole Life	Term	Credit	Group	Industrial	Total
2007	16,346	...	...	...	...	16,346
2008	1,179	...	...	...	...	1,179
2009	...	...	...	...	...	...

• LIFE INSURANCE IN FORCE ($000 omitted)

Year	Whole Life	Term	Credit	Group	Industrial	Total
2007	23,134	1,170	...	...	...	24,304
2008	17,215	528	...	...	...	17,743
2009	14,750	797	...	...	...	15,547

NATIONAL SECURITY INS CO

661 East Davis Street
Elba, Alabama 36323
Tel: 334-897-2273

AMB#: 006802
Began Business: 02/05/1947
Agency Off: Eddie C. Vaughan

Best's Financial Strength Rating: B **FSC:** IV

• NET PREMIUMS AND DEPOSITS ($000 omitted)

Year	Individual Life	Individual & Group Annuities	Group Life & A&H	Credit Life & A&H	Individual A&H	Total
2007	5,390	81	199	...	1,445	7,114
2008	5,295	69	178	...	1,486	7,028
2009	5,198	72	176	...	1,827	7,273

• NET OPERATING GAIN ($000 omitted)

Year	Individual Life	Individual & Group Annuities	Group Life & A&H	Credit Life & A&H	Individual A&H	Total
2007	-601	1	-18	0	67	-518
2008	740	-4	60	...	96	1,408
2009	263	1	82	...	368	1,250

• COMPARATIVE FINANCIALS ($000 omitted)

Year	Assets	Capital & Surplus	Net Invest Income	Benefits Paid	Realized Cap Gains	Policyholder Dividends	Contract Lns (% of assets)
2007	43,167	8,889	1,925	3,946	167	4	2.1
2008	41,368	8,205	2,219	4,020	-1,849	6	2.3
2009	43,884	9,126	2,398	4,108	64	3	2.3

• ORDINARY LIFE STATISTICS

Year	Av. Ord. Policy Issued ($)	Av. Ord. Policy In Force ($)	Avg. Prem ($/M)	1st Yr Prem/ Total Prem	Ord. Lapse Ratio
2007	...	...	...	...	...
2008	...	...	...	...	...
2009	...	...	...	...	...

• NEW LIFE BUSINESS ISSUED ($000 omitted)

Year	Whole Life	Term	Credit	Group	Industrial	Total
2007	36,674	2,819	...	6,620	...	46,113
2008	39,962	201	...	4,148	...	44,311
2009	36,967	...	...	2,220	...	39,187

• LIFE INSURANCE IN FORCE ($000 omitted)

Year	Whole Life	Term	Credit	Group	Industrial	Total
2007	164,466	17,611	...	29,752	28,862	240,691
2008	156,879	17,737	...	17,300	22,244	214,160
2009	162,466	14,912	...	16,064	21,586	215,028

NATIONAL SECURITY LF & ANNUITY

P.O. Box 1625
Binghamton, New York 13902-1625
Tel: 877-446-6060

AMB#: 008633
Began Business: 07/25/1975
Agency Off: None

Best's Financial Strength Rating: A **FSC:** V

• NET PREMIUMS AND DEPOSITS ($000 omitted)

Year	Individual Life	Individual & Group Annuities	Group Life & A&H	Credit Life & A&H	Individual A&H	Total
2007	3	15,296	...	...	...	15,299
2008	3	10,890	...	...	...	10,892
2009	3	32,893	...	...	...	32,895

• NET OPERATING GAIN ($000 omitted)

Year	Individual Life	Individual & Group Annuities	Group Life & A&H	Credit Life & A&H	Individual A&H	Total
2007	-125	-671	...	...	...	-796
2008	62	-1,849	...	...	...	-1,787
2009	637	2,970	...	...	...	3,607

• COMPARATIVE FINANCIALS ($000 omitted)

Year	Assets	Capital & Surplus	Net Invest Income	Benefits Paid	Realized Cap Gains	Policyholder Dividends	Contract Lns (% of assets)
2007	89,982	19,218	1,228	1,858	-3	...	...
2008	81,703	16,748	1,190	2,260	-917	...	...
2009	162,151	19,903	1,813	2,987	-104	...	...

• ORDINARY LIFE STATISTICS

Year	Av. Ord. Policy Issued ($)	Av. Ord. Policy In Force ($)	Avg. Prem ($/M)	1st Yr Prem/ Total Prem	Ord. Lapse Ratio
2007	...	...	...	...	...
2008	...	...	...	...	...
2009	...	...	...	...	...

• NEW LIFE BUSINESS ISSUED ($000 omitted)

Year	Whole Life	Term	Credit	Group	Industrial	Total
2007	...	...	...	...	...	...
2008	...	...	...	...	...	...
2009	...	...	...	...	...	...

• LIFE INSURANCE IN FORCE ($000 omitted)

Year	Whole Life	Term	Credit	Group	Industrial	Total
2007	70,980	99,627	...	...	...	170,607
2008	64,225	86,655	...	...	...	150,880
2009	44,592	75,777	...	...	...	120,369

NATIONAL TEACHERS ASSOCIATES

4949 Keller Springs Road
Addison, Texas 75001-5910
Tel: 972-532-2100

AMB#: 006588
Began Business: 07/14/1938
Agency Off: Bill J. Ellard

Best's Financial Strength Rating: B++ **FSC:** VI

• NET PREMIUMS AND DEPOSITS ($000 omitted)

Year	Individual Life	Individual & Group Annuities	Group Life & A&H	Credit Life & A&H	Individual A&H	Total
2007	1,368	...	...	...	67,198	68,567
2008	1,390	...	...	...	76,496	77,886
2009	1,388	...	...	...	82,024	83,412

• NET OPERATING GAIN ($000 omitted)

Year	Individual Life	Individual & Group Annuities	Group Life & A&H	Credit Life & A&H	Individual A&H	Total
2007	375	...	...	...	5,339	5,714
2008	371	...	...	...	7,341	7,712
2009	188	...	...	...	6,036	6,224

• COMPARATIVE FINANCIALS ($000 omitted)

Year	Assets	Capital & Surplus	Net Invest Income	Benefits Paid	Realized Cap Gains	Policyholder Dividends	Contract Lns (% of assets)
2007	198,081	26,873	9,033	11,781	-3,991	...	0.1
2008	229,363	27,520	10,295	13,894	-8,829	...	0.1
2009	272,944	35,270	10,960	20,354	-1,563	...	0.1

• ORDINARY LIFE STATISTICS

Year	Av. Ord. Policy Issued ($)	Av. Ord. Policy In Force ($)	Avg. Prem ($/M)	1st Yr Prem/ Total Prem	Ord. Lapse Ratio
2007	...	...	...	...	...
2008	...	...	...	...	...
2009	...	...	...	...	...

• NEW LIFE BUSINESS ISSUED ($000 omitted)

Year	Whole Life	Term	Credit	Group	Industrial	Total
2007	2,981	21,625	...	...	...	24,606
2008	2,917	22,345	...	...	...	25,262
2009	2,748	19,700	...	...	...	22,448

• LIFE INSURANCE IN FORCE ($000 omitted)

Year	Whole Life	Term	Credit	Group	Industrial	Total
2007	67,308	211,718	...	...	...	279,026
2008	66,644	212,601	...	...	...	279,245
2009	64,689	212,346	...	...	...	277,035

NATIONAL WESTERN LIFE INS CO

850 East Anderson Lane
Austin, Texas 78752-1602
Tel: 512-836-1010

AMB#: 006811
Began Business: 06/28/1957
Agency Off: S. Christopher Johnson

Best's Financial Strength Rating: A **FSC:** XI

• NET PREMIUMS AND DEPOSITS ($000 omitted)

Year	Individual Life	Individual & Group Annuities	Group Life & A&H	Credit Life & A&H	Individual A&H	Total
2007	173,284	461,754	968	...	4	636,011
2008	170,000	447,300	1,174	...	4	618,478
2009	171,022	869,041	1,300	...	4	1,041,366

• NET OPERATING GAIN ($000 omitted)

Year	Individual Life	Individual & Group Annuities	Group Life & A&H	Credit Life & A&H	Individual A&H	Total
2007	2,230	1,986	18	...	-6	29,075
2008	4,977	4,817	14	...	-3	28,980
2009	31,685	28,247	16	...	-8	80,155

• COMPARATIVE FINANCIALS ($000 omitted)

Year	Assets	Capital & Surplus	Net Invest Income	Benefits Paid	Realized Cap Gains	Policyholder Dividends	Contract Lns (% of assets)
2007	6,078,774	710,935	309,860	656,927	3,215	88	1.4
2008	6,126,954	708,047	264,374	653,530	-19,337	83	1.3
2009	6,726,515	817,042	382,247	640,928	-7,211	77	1.2

• ORDINARY LIFE STATISTICS

Year	Av. Ord. Policy Issued ($)	Av. Ord. Policy In Force ($)	Avg. Prem ($/M)	1st Yr Prem/ Total Prem	Ord. Lapse Ratio
2007	264,950	117,344	10.75	34.7	9.6
2008	290,601	127,038	10.10	30.4	10.6
2009	307,779	132,059	10.24	27.4	13.3

• NEW LIFE BUSINESS ISSUED ($000 omitted)

Year	Whole Life	Term	Credit	Group	Industrial	Total
2007	3,412,051	259,091	...	...	...	3,671,142
2008	3,032,472	493,102	...	...	...	3,525,574
2009	2,401,104	494,790	...	...	...	2,895,894

• LIFE INSURANCE IN FORCE ($000 omitted)

Year	Whole Life	Term	Credit	Group	Industrial	Total
2007	16,301,418	1,332,894	...	...	...	17,634,312
2008	17,186,201	1,658,094	...	...	...	18,844,295
2009	16,741,601	1,970,260	...	...	...	18,711,861

NATIONWIDE LIFE & ANNUITY INS

One Nationwide Plaza 1-4-20
Columbus, Ohio 43215-2220
Tel: 800-882-2822

AMB#: 009070
Began Business: 05/06/1981
Agency Off: None

Best's Financial Strength Rating: A+ g
FSC: XV

• NET PREMIUMS AND DEPOSITS ($000 omitted)

Year	Individual Life	Individual & Group Annuities	Group Life & A&H	Credit Life & A&H	Individual A&H	Total
2007	156,637	30,815	0	...	2	187,453
2008	203,299	17,391	283	...	2	220,975
2009	283,815	11,935	0	...	1	295,751

• NET OPERATING GAIN ($000 omitted)

Year	Individual Life	Individual & Group Annuities	Group Life & A&H	Credit Life & A&H	Individual A&H	Total
2007	-22,036	17,165	2	...	1	11,561
2008	-32,751	6,631	168	...	1	-8,839
2009	-35,582	12,922	17	...	-1	4,051

• COMPARATIVE FINANCIALS ($000 omitted)

Year	Assets	Capital & Surplus	Net Invest Income	Benefits Paid	Realized Cap Gains	Policyholder Dividends	Contract Lns (% of assets)
2007	6,103,538	256,534	243,090	599,032	-15,470	1,144	0.4
2008	4,879,251	122,672	202,293	422,506	-81,535	1,109	0.4
2009	5,243,361	213,512	202,614	282,012	-65,141	1,039	0.4

• ORDINARY LIFE STATISTICS

Year	Av. Ord. Policy Issued ($)	Av. Ord. Policy In Force ($)	Avg. Prem ($/M)	1st Yr Prem/ Total Prem	Ord. Lapse Ratio
2007	366,633	383,058	6.54	22.5	7.2
2008	294,828	356,647	6.51	54.5	7.8
2009	258,174	338,781	7.29	45.8	7.1

• NEW LIFE BUSINESS ISSUED ($000 omitted)

Year	Whole Life	Term	Credit	Group	Industrial	Total
2007	1,785,554	8,418,948	...	...	...	10,204,502
2008	2,665,054	8,483,849	...	...	...	11,148,903
2009	3,605,400	8,211,745	...	...	...	11,817,145

• LIFE INSURANCE IN FORCE ($000 omitted)

Year	Whole Life	Term	Credit	Group	Industrial	Total
2007	9,139,077	22,747,039	...	...	...	31,886,116
2008	10,700,721	29,014,398	...	411	...	39,715,530
2009	13,483,866	34,383,575	...	170	...	47,867,611

NATIONWIDE LIFE INS CO

One Nationwide Plaza 1-4-20
Columbus, Ohio 43215-2220
Tel: 614-249-7111

AMB#: 006812
Began Business: 01/10/1931
Agency Off: Michael C. Butler

Best's Financial Strength Rating: A+ g
FSC: XV

• NET PREMIUMS AND DEPOSITS ($000 omitted)

Year	Individual Life	Individual & Group Annuities	Group Life & A&H	Credit Life & A&H	Individual A&H	Total
2007	1,101,892	10,998,549	469,709	...	160	12,570,310
2008	975,219	8,902,220	519,640	...	149	10,397,228
2009	831,924	8,030,410	293,717	...	142	9,156,193

• NET OPERATING GAIN ($000 omitted)

Year	Individual Life	Individual & Group Annuities	Group Life & A&H	Credit Life & A&H	Individual A&H	Total
2007	213,009	171,098	-60,036	...	43	483,985
2008	74,228	-806,914	6,507	...	58	-613,614
2009	272,672	861,182	7,788	...	63	1,342,666

• COMPARATIVE FINANCIALS ($000 omitted)

Year	Assets	Capital & Surplus	Net Invest Income	Benefits Paid	Realized Cap Gains	Policyholder Dividends	Contract Lns (% of assets)
2007	105,355,236	3,175,132	1,809,162	16,919,978	-83,352	87,173	0.9
2008	82,303,554	2,749,933	1,646,086	12,464,204	-256,925	89,347	1.3
2009	88,955,178	3,129,557	1,556,324	10,132,052	-945,372	78,884	1.2

• ORDINARY LIFE STATISTICS

Year	Av. Ord. Policy Issued ($)	Av. Ord. Policy In Force ($)	Avg. Prem ($/M)	1st Yr Prem/ Total Prem	Ord. Lapse Ratio
2007	393,474	139,872	8.39	13.1	5.8
2008	460,560	140,344	7.92	15.0	6.8
2009	361,695	138,076	7.38	8.5	8.6

• NEW LIFE BUSINESS ISSUED ($000 omitted)

Year	Whole Life	Term	Credit	Group	Industrial	Total
2007	4,537,272	610,542	...	1,265,735	...	6,413,549
2008	3,549,979	473,014	...	3,334,782	...	7,357,775
2009	1,037,733	436,536	...	675,508	...	2,149,777

• LIFE INSURANCE IN FORCE ($000 omitted)

Year	Whole Life	Term	Credit	Group	Industrial	Total
2007	107,669,090	34,963,249	...	29,016,866	...	171,649,205
2008	103,724,081	32,526,828	...	35,331,517	...	171,582,426
2009	95,458,185	29,969,789	...	33,069,640	...	158,497,615

NEW ENGLAND LIFE INS CO

18210 Crane Nest Dr., 3rd Floor
Tampa, Florida 33647
Tel: 617-578-2000

AMB#: 009043
Began Business: 12/30/1980
Agency Off: None

Best's Financial Strength Rating: A+ gu
FSC: XV

• NET PREMIUMS AND DEPOSITS ($000 omitted)

Year	Individual Life	Individual & Group Annuities	Group Life & A&H	Credit Life & A&H	Individual A&H	Total
2007	553,507	1,384,602	...	...	1,586	1,939,695
2008	503,014	1,159,916	...	...	1,635	1,664,565
2009	367,907	629,373	...	...	1,281	998,561

• NET OPERATING GAIN ($000 omitted)

Year	Individual Life	Individual & Group Annuities	Group Life & A&H	Credit Life & A&H	Individual A&H	Total
2007	105,822	13,390	1,944	...	1,185	122,341
2008	67,115	-47,135	4,733	...	4,636	29,350
2009	82,200	24,421	-1,940	...	4,248	108,928

• COMPARATIVE FINANCIALS ($000 omitted)

Year	Assets	Capital & Surplus	Net Invest Income	Benefits Paid	Realized Cap Gains	Policyholder Dividends	Contract Lns (% of assets)
2007	12,459,014	544,237	73,838	1,950,450	-692	7,201	3.3
2008	8,966,118	469,364	75,917	1,444,221	-1,414	4,439	4.5
2009	10,718,859	564,189	90,061	1,066,020	1,888	3,789	3.7

• ORDINARY LIFE STATISTICS

Year	Av. Ord. Policy Issued ($)	Av. Ord. Policy In Force ($)	Avg. Prem ($/M)	1st Yr Prem/ Total Prem	Ord. Lapse Ratio
2007	635,901	342,872	7.21	21.8	6.7
2008	665,533	344,866	7.02	21.2	8.8
2009	1,781,065	342,913	5.90	5.5	8.7

• NEW LIFE BUSINESS ISSUED ($000 omitted)

Year	Whole Life	Term	Credit	Group	Industrial	Total
2007	2,571,491	3,980,192	...	16,888	...	6,568,571
2008	1,779,309	2,526,021	...	6,733	...	4,312,063
2009	101,849	8,577	...	...	...	110,426

• LIFE INSURANCE IN FORCE ($000 omitted)

Year	Whole Life	Term	Credit	Group	Industrial	Total
2007	52,433,088	36,002,930	...	297,727	...	88,733,745
2008	48,471,194	35,621,885	...	217,203	...	84,310,282
2009	44,143,478	32,164,017	...	154,023	...	76,461,518

NEW ERA LIFE INS CO

200 Westlake Park Boulevard, Suite 1200
Houston, Texas 77079-2663
Tel: 281-368-7200

AMB#: 007087
Began Business: 06/01/1924
Agency Off: None

Best's Financial Strength Rating: B+ g
FSC: VI

• NET PREMIUMS AND DEPOSITS ($000 omitted)

Year	Individual Life	Individual & Group Annuities	Group Life & A&H	Credit Life & A&H	Individual A&H	Total
2007	1,806	58,379	1,607	...	55,798	117,590
2008	1,976	16,872	1,326	...	57,392	77,566
2009	-5,590	47,198	1,079	...	28,743	71,430

• NET OPERATING GAIN ($000 omitted)

Year	Individual Life	Individual & Group Annuities	Group Life & A&H	Credit Life & A&H	Individual A&H	Total
2007	235	583	49	...	851	1,719
2008	24	247	8	...	693	971
2009	48	242	2	...	538	831

• COMPARATIVE FINANCIALS ($000 omitted)

Year	Assets	Capital & Surplus	Net Invest Income	Benefits Paid	Realized Cap Gains	Policyholder Dividends	Contract Lns (% of assets)
2007	299,809	44,659	13,640	77,681	-2,497	...	0.2
2008	301,819	44,597	14,486	82,975	-1,863	...	0.3
2009	320,052	45,225	12,677	65,675	-4,531	...	0.2

• ORDINARY LIFE STATISTICS

Year	Av. Ord. Policy Issued ($)	Av. Ord. Policy In Force ($)	Avg. Prem ($/M)	1st Yr Prem/ Total Prem	Ord. Lapse Ratio
2007	...	...	...	...	...
2008	...	...	...	...	...
2009	...	...	...	...	...

• NEW LIFE BUSINESS ISSUED ($000 omitted)

Year	Whole Life	Term	Credit	Group	Industrial	Total
2007	3,837	...	...	...	...	3,837
2008	4,597	...	...	...	...	4,597
2009	3,777	...	...	...	...	3,777

• LIFE INSURANCE IN FORCE ($000 omitted)

Year	Whole Life	Term	Credit	Group	Industrial	Total
2007	83,530	16,061	...	...	...	99,591
2008	75,516	22,356	...	...	...	97,872
2009	69,598	20,348	...	...	...	89,946

NEW ERA LIFE INS CO MIDWEST

200 Westlake Park Boulevard, Suite 1200
Houston, Texas 77079-2663
Tel: 281-368-7200

AMB#: 007148
Began Business: 05/13/1961
Agency Off: None

Best's Financial Strength Rating: B+ g
FSC: VI

• NET PREMIUMS AND DEPOSITS ($000 omitted)

Year	Individual Life	Individual & Group Annuities	Group Life & A&H	Credit Life & A&H	Individual A&H	Total
2007	282	8,291	...	...	34,391	42,963
2008	318	1,916	...	...	38,364	40,598
2009	286	5,020	...	...	31,081	36,386

• NET OPERATING GAIN ($000 omitted)

Year	Individual Life	Individual & Group Annuities	Group Life & A&H	Credit Life & A&H	Individual A&H	Total
2007	139	144	...	...	555	838
2008	190	362	...	...	129	680
2009	-2	-7	...	...	-7	-16

• COMPARATIVE FINANCIALS ($000 omitted)

Year	Assets	Capital & Surplus	Net Invest Income	Benefits Paid	Realized Cap Gains	Policyholder Dividends	Contract Lns (% of assets)
2007	40,052	8,428	2,076	25,854	-263	...	0.2
2008	41,625	8,634	2,413	33,781	-569	...	0.3
2009	46,752	8,642	2,370	28,319	-757	...	0.3

• ORDINARY LIFE STATISTICS

Year	Av. Ord. Policy Issued ($)	Av. Ord. Policy In Force ($)	Avg. Prem ($/M)	1st Yr Prem/ Total Prem	Ord. Lapse Ratio
2007	...	...	...	...	...
2008	...	...	...	...	...
2009	...	...	...	...	...

• NEW LIFE BUSINESS ISSUED ($000 omitted)

Year	Whole Life	Term	Credit	Group	Industrial	Total
2007	346	...	...	...	...	346
2008	820	...	...	...	...	820
2009	1,189	...	...	...	...	1,189

• LIFE INSURANCE IN FORCE ($000 omitted)

Year	Whole Life	Term	Credit	Group	Industrial	Total
2007	17,920	161	...	...	...	18,081
2008	17,288	170	...	...	...	17,458
2009	16,778	120	...	...	...	16,898

NEW YORK LIFE INS CO

51 Madison Avenue
New York, New York 10010
Tel: 212-576-7000

AMB#: 006820
Began Business: 04/12/1845
Agency Off: Mark W. Pfaff

Best's Financial Strength Rating: A++g
FSC: XV

• NET PREMIUMS AND DEPOSITS ($000 omitted)

Year	Individual Life	Individual & Group Annuities	Group Life & A&H	Credit Life & A&H	Individual A&H	Total
2007	5,523,237	10,403,858	1,623,955	...	145,522	17,696,573
2008	5,747,950	12,262,477	1,708,691	...	160,083	19,879,201
2009	5,730,640	8,309,507	1,880,691	...	173,614	16,094,452

• NET OPERATING GAIN ($000 omitted)

Year	Individual Life	Individual & Group Annuities	Group Life & A&H	Credit Life & A&H	Individual A&H	Total
2007	425,885	179,902	61,858	...	-94,976	577,230
2008	233,377	127,555	68,631	...	-2,160	433,265
2009	552,320	185,302	65,723	...	-12,255	793,726

• COMPARATIVE FINANCIALS ($000 omitted)

Year	Assets	Capital & Surplus	Net Invest Income	Benefits Paid	Realized Cap Gains	Policyholder Dividends	Contract Lns (% of assets)
2007	122,753,467	11,959,230	5,594,843	9,651,848	279,204	1,644,148	5.4
2008	117,305,625	11,793,474	5,148,919	9,728,846	-997,623	1,420,697	6.0
2009	117,835,521	13,686,268	5,035,365	9,316,223	-338,459	1,332,767	6.4

• ORDINARY LIFE STATISTICS

Year	Av. Ord. Policy Issued ($)	Av. Ord. Policy In Force ($)	Avg. Prem ($/M)	1st Yr Prem/ Total Prem	Ord. Lapse Ratio
2007	287,695	126,044	10.91	6.3	5.8
2008	289,385	132,754	10.76	6.2	6.2
2009	273,442	138,524	10.27	6.3	6.9

• NEW LIFE BUSINESS ISSUED ($000 omitted)

Year	Whole Life	Term	Credit	Group	Industrial	Total
2007	19,088,799	45,694,329	...	13,791,203	...	78,574,331
2008	19,228,833	46,163,737	...	14,341,253	...	79,733,823
2009	20,476,226	51,784,138	...	19,658,063	...	91,918,427

• LIFE INSURANCE IN FORCE ($000 omitted)

Year	Whole Life	Term	Credit	Group	Industrial	Total
2007	267,418,535	254,615,748	...	258,135,964	...	780,170,247
2008	272,935,538	277,203,597	...	265,931,200	...	816,070,335
2009	229,517,252	346,315,260	...	316,445,108	...	892,277,620

NEW YORK LIFE INS & ANNUITY

51 Madison Avenue
New York, New York 10010
Tel: 212-576-7000

AMB#: 009054
Began Business: 12/26/1980
Agency Off: Mark W. Pfaff

Best's Financial Strength Rating: A++g
FSC: XV

• NET PREMIUMS AND DEPOSITS ($000 omitted)

Year	Individual Life	Individual & Group Annuities	Group Life & A&H	Credit Life & A&H	Individual A&H	Total
2007	1,226,194	6,122,198	296,039	...	...	7,644,431
2008	1,192,427	9,857,735	79,231	...	...	11,129,393
2009	1,390,478	11,127,813	69,325	...	...	12,587,616

• NET OPERATING GAIN ($000 omitted)

Year	Individual Life	Individual & Group Annuities	Group Life & A&H	Credit Life & A&H	Individual A&H	Total
2007	165,728	161,870	-10,242	...	...	348,323
2008	85,641	-243,505	-7,032	...	...	-128,745
2009	55,466	225,339	15,925	...	...	351,029

• COMPARATIVE FINANCIALS ($000 omitted)

Year	Assets	Capital & Surplus	Net Invest Income	Benefits Paid	Realized Cap Gains	Policyholder Dividends	Contract Lns (% of assets)
2007	72,685,506	2,649,933	2,489,889	5,362,976	-59,294	...	1.0
2008	74,943,575	3,595,817	2,714,950	5,169,592	-258,186	...	1.0
2009	88,832,647	4,997,629	3,100,017	4,820,580	-125,802	...	0.9

• ORDINARY LIFE STATISTICS

Year	Av. Ord. Policy Issued ($)	Av. Ord. Policy In Force ($)	Avg. Prem ($/M)	1st Yr Prem/ Total Prem	Ord. Lapse Ratio
2007	480,058	276,576	11.60	20.8	3.5
2008	431,842	282,689	11.30	7.4	5.4
2009	360,555	288,503	12.33	9.2	4.7

• NEW LIFE BUSINESS ISSUED ($000 omitted)

Year	Whole Life	Term	Credit	Group	Industrial	Total
2007	12,577,315	238,785	...	3,015,921	...	15,832,021
2008	9,538,560	239,632	...	484,380	...	10,262,572
2009	9,409,556	51,418	...	238,328	...	9,699,302

• LIFE INSURANCE IN FORCE ($000 omitted)

Year	Whole Life	Term	Credit	Group	Industrial	Total
2007	148,075,084	5,686,708	...	6,802,882	...	160,564,674
2008	148,428,482	5,583,308	...	6,817,879	...	160,829,669
2009	150,468,883	4,883,149	...	6,174,113	...	161,526,144

NIPPON LIFE INS CO OF AMER

521 Fifth Avenue
New York, New York 10175
Tel: 212-682-3000

AMB#: 008419
Began Business: 07/24/1973
Agency Off: Richard J. Kuhn

Best's Financial Strength Rating: A-
FSC: VIII

• NET PREMIUMS AND DEPOSITS ($000 omitted)

Year	Individual Life	Individual & Group Annuities	Group Life & A&H	Credit Life & A&H	Individual A&H	Total
2007	...	37	229,460	...	...	229,497
2008	...	...	223,098	...	...	223,098
2009	...	...	211,475	...	...	211,475

• NET OPERATING GAIN ($000 omitted)

Year	Individual Life	Individual & Group Annuities	Group Life & A&H	Credit Life & A&H	Individual A&H	Total
2007	...	...	-1,552	...	...	1,257
2008	...	...	-1,973	...	...	519
2009	...	...	1,996	...	...	4,272

• COMPARATIVE FINANCIALS ($000 omitted)

Year	Assets	Capital & Surplus	Net Invest Income	Benefits Paid	Realized Cap Gains	Policyholder Dividends	Contract Lns (% of assets)
2007	169,464	117,980	7,852	193,371	4	...	...
2008	159,640	113,898	7,399	184,270	-4,501	...	...
2009	157,904	114,720	6,830	169,599	-3,529	...	...

• ORDINARY LIFE STATISTICS

Year	Av. Ord. Policy Issued ($)	Av. Ord. Policy In Force ($)	Avg. Prem ($/M)	1st Yr Prem/ Total Prem	Ord. Lapse Ratio
2007	...	...	...	...	...
2008	...	...	...	...	...
2009	...	...	...	...	...

• NEW LIFE BUSINESS ISSUED ($000 omitted)

Year	Whole Life	Term	Credit	Group	Industrial	Total
2007	...	...	...	190,309	...	190,309
2008	...	...	...	206,546	...	206,546
2009	...	...	...	73,754	...	73,754

• LIFE INSURANCE IN FORCE ($000 omitted)

Year	Whole Life	Term	Credit	Group	Industrial	Total
2007	...	...	...	2,557,152	...	2,557,152
2008	...	...	...	2,763,785	...	2,763,785
2009	...	...	...	2,767,739	...	2,767,739

NORTH AMERICAN CO FOR L&H

One Sammons Plaza
Sioux Falls, South Dakota 57193
Tel: 312-648-7600

AMB#: 006827
Began Business: 06/15/1886
Agency Off: Garth A. Garlock

Best's Financial Strength Rating: A+ g
FSC: XIV

• **NET PREMIUMS AND DEPOSITS ($000 omitted)**

Year	Individual Life	Individual & Group Annuities	Group Life & A&H	Credit Life & A&H	Individual A&H	Total
2007	256,399	915,714	3,974	...	4	1,176,091
2008	215,955	1,638,771	2,064	...	-3	1,856,786
2009	180,741	1,315,660	10,325	...	4	1,506,731

• **NET OPERATING GAIN ($000 omitted)**

Year	Individual Life	Individual & Group Annuities	Group Life & A&H	Credit Life & A&H	Individual A&H	Total
2007	16,352	-12,345	-665	...	2	3,343
2008	3,272	2,290	-386	...	-6	5,170
2009	4,414	23,251	1,007	...	1	28,674

• **COMPARATIVE FINANCIALS ($000 omitted)**

Year	Assets	Capital & Surplus	Net Invest Income	Benefits Paid	Realized Cap Gains	Policyholder Dividends	Contract Lns (% of assets)
2007	6,637,313	387,652	342,699	440,840	-973	...	1.2
2008	8,446,862	526,559	299,393	536,139	-23,428	...	1.0
2009	9,117,526	647,389	565,229	634,635	-36,394	...	0.9

• **ORDINARY LIFE STATISTICS**

Year	Av. Ord. Policy Issued ($)	Av. Ord. Policy In Force ($)	Avg. Prem ($/M)	1st Yr Prem/ Total Prem	Ord. Lapse Ratio
2007	406,813	268,365	4.28	26.7	5.5
2008	408,228	271,950	4.05	20.9	5.6
2009	392,683	275,435	3.96	20.0	6.2

• **NEW LIFE BUSINESS ISSUED ($000 omitted)**

Year	Whole Life	Term	Credit	Group	Industrial	Total
2007	1,343,356	3,410,254	...	260,443	...	5,014,053
2008	1,141,667	3,749,310	...	287,266	...	5,178,243
2009	1,519,226	4,343,536	...	270,693	...	6,133,454

• **LIFE INSURANCE IN FORCE ($000 omitted)**

Year	Whole Life	Term	Credit	Group	Industrial	Total
2007	23,008,572	79,650,535	...	5,027,657	...	107,686,764
2008	23,087,724	77,497,675	...	4,819,181	...	105,404,580
2009	23,013,524	75,847,103	...	4,768,706	...	103,629,334

NORTH AMERICAN INS CO

2721 North Central Avenue
Phoenix, Arizona 85004-1172
Tel: 608-662-1232

AMB#: 060015
Began Business: 12/31/1965
Agency Off: Don C. Smith

Best's Financial Strength Rating: B+
FSC: IV

• **NET PREMIUMS AND DEPOSITS ($000 omitted)**

Year	Individual Life	Individual & Group Annuities	Group Life & A&H	Credit Life & A&H	Individual A&H	Total
2007	9	...	269	-312	1,800	1,766
2008	9	...	259	-56	1,363	1,575
2009	7	...	216	-17	1,068	1,275

• **NET OPERATING GAIN ($000 omitted)**

Year	Individual Life	Individual & Group Annuities	Group Life & A&H	Credit Life & A&H	Individual A&H	Total
2007	121	6	299	3,328	1,717	6,098
2008	117	206	133	419	266	1,663
2009	53	10	7	301	32	837

• **COMPARATIVE FINANCIALS ($000 omitted)**

Year	Assets	Capital & Surplus	Net Invest Income	Benefits Paid	Realized Cap Gains	Policyholder Dividends	Contract Lns (% of assets)
2007	24,706	15,555	1,528	2,435	8	...	0.0
2008	16,180	10,340	1,058	2,233	...	...	0.0
2009	14,330	9,301	651	1,686	9	...	0.0

• **ORDINARY LIFE STATISTICS**

Year	Av. Ord. Policy Issued ($)	Av. Ord. Policy In Force ($)	Avg. Prem ($/M)	1st Yr Prem/ Total Prem	Ord. Lapse Ratio
2007	...	...	...	...	...
2008	...	...	...	...	...
2009	...	...	...	...	...

• **NEW LIFE BUSINESS ISSUED ($000 omitted)**

Year	Whole Life	Term	Credit	Group	Industrial	Total
2007	...	...	515	...	...	515
2008	...	...	143	...	...	143
2009	...	...	...	...	...	...

• **LIFE INSURANCE IN FORCE ($000 omitted)**

Year	Whole Life	Term	Credit	Group	Industrial	Total
2007	8,317	305	72,709	...	...	81,331
2008	7,749	267	33,461	...	...	41,477
2009	7,106	259	14,657	...	...	22,022

NORTH CAROLINA MUTUAL LIFE INS

411 W. Chapel Hill Street
Durham, North Carolina 27701-3616
Tel: 919-682-9201

AMB#: 006835
Began Business: 04/01/1899
Agency Off: Ron Corlew

Best's Financial Strength Rating: C+ u
FSC: IV

• **NET PREMIUMS AND DEPOSITS ($000 omitted)**

Year	Individual Life	Individual & Group Annuities	Group Life & A&H	Credit Life & A&H	Individual A&H	Total
2007	13,127	340	32,965	...	431	46,864
2008	16,258	388	20,366	...	386	37,398
2009	13,395	261	12,799	...	340	26,795

• **NET OPERATING GAIN ($000 omitted)**

Year	Individual Life	Individual & Group Annuities	Group Life & A&H	Credit Life & A&H	Individual A&H	Total
2007	-2,212	0	-1,783	...	-291	-4,294
2008	-870	-142	-3,303	...	-219	-4,534
2009	3,910	-489	-3,914	4	-456	-944

• **COMPARATIVE FINANCIALS ($000 omitted)**

Year	Assets	Capital & Surplus	Net Invest Income	Benefits Paid	Realized Cap Gains	Policyholder Dividends	Contract Lns (% of assets)
2007	132,733	12,971	5,992	38,634	1,456	430	3.7
2008	159,411	9,495	7,326	28,160	124	523	4.0
2009	151,580	6,365	7,405	20,162	-1,562	-97	4.3

• **ORDINARY LIFE STATISTICS**

Year	Av. Ord. Policy Issued ($)	Av. Ord. Policy In Force ($)	Avg. Prem ($/M)	1st Yr Prem/ Total Prem	Ord. Lapse Ratio
2007	21,886	7,515	17.82	20.1	15.8
2008	18,582	6,351	48.17	11.6	15.1
2009	14,887	7,086	19.36	14.0	11.2

• **NEW LIFE BUSINESS ISSUED ($000 omitted)**

Year	Whole Life	Term	Credit	Group	Industrial	Total
2007	134,728	52,115	...	818,753	...	1,005,596
2008	86,753	39,008	...	2,970,093	...	3,095,854
2009	93,007	16,128	...	1,469,849	...	1,578,984

• **LIFE INSURANCE IN FORCE ($000 omitted)**

Year	Whole Life	Term	Credit	Group	Industrial	Total
2007	631,524	251,212	...	8,663,878	79,962	9,626,576
2008	745,474	267,461	...	8,710,316	75,892	9,799,143
2009	719,939	246,964	...	7,602,103	85,695	8,654,701

NORTH COAST LIFE INS CO

P.O. Box 1445
Spokane, Washington 99210-1445
Tel: 509-838-4235

AMB#: 006837
Began Business: 05/03/1965
Agency Off: Bonnie L. Patey

Best's Financial Strength Rating: C+
FSC: IV

• **NET PREMIUMS AND DEPOSITS ($000 omitted)**

Year	Individual Life	Individual & Group Annuities	Group Life & A&H	Credit Life & A&H	Individual A&H	Total
2007	4,807	3,732	...	...	1	8,540
2008	3,807	3,309	...	...	1	7,116
2009	4,037	5,022	...	...	1	9,061

• **NET OPERATING GAIN ($000 omitted)**

Year	Individual Life	Individual & Group Annuities	Group Life & A&H	Credit Life & A&H	Individual A&H	Total
2007	292	-55	...	...	1	238
2008	1,230	122	...	...	4	1,357
2009	-31	504	...	...	1	475

• **COMPARATIVE FINANCIALS ($000 omitted)**

Year	Assets	Capital & Surplus	Net Invest Income	Benefits Paid	Realized Cap Gains	Policyholder Dividends	Contract Lns (% of assets)
2007	123,165	5,728	6,831	14,851	-6	6	12.6
2008	121,081	5,737	7,213	10,856	-729	5	12.8
2009	124,665	5,539	7,198	9,316	-2,177	4	12.7

• **ORDINARY LIFE STATISTICS**

Year	Av. Ord. Policy Issued ($)	Av. Ord. Policy In Force ($)	Avg. Prem ($/M)	1st Yr Prem/ Total Prem	Ord. Lapse Ratio
2007	...	...	...	...	...
2008	...	...	...	...	...
2009	...	...	...	...	...

• **NEW LIFE BUSINESS ISSUED ($000 omitted)**

Year	Whole Life	Term	Credit	Group	Industrial	Total
2007	21,275	14,844	...	...	...	36,119
2008	22,301	20,861	...	...	...	43,162
2009	12,003	15,742	...	...	...	27,745

• **LIFE INSURANCE IN FORCE ($000 omitted)**

Year	Whole Life	Term	Credit	Group	Industrial	Total
2007	338,560	122,081	...	...	...	460,641
2008	325,954	125,817	...	...	...	451,771
2009	302,941	124,594	...	...	...	427,535

NORTHWESTERN LONG TERM CARE

720 East Wisconsin Avenue
Milwaukee, Wisconsin 53202-4797
Tel: 414-661-2510

AMB#: 007067
Began Business: 10/07/1953
Agency Off: Todd M. Schoon

Best's Financial Strength Rating: A++g **FSC:** XV

• NET PREMIUMS AND DEPOSITS ($000 omitted)

Year	Individual Life	Individual & Group Annuities	Group Life & A&H	Credit Life & A&H	Individual A&H	Total
2007	...	...	...	...	124,571	124,571
2008	...	...	...	...	158,859	158,859
2009	...	...	...	...	186,466	186,466

• NET OPERATING GAIN ($000 omitted)

Year	Individual Life	Individual & Group Annuities	Group Life & A&H	Credit Life & A&H	Individual A&H	Total
2007	...	-12	...	...	-6,389	-6,402
2008	...	-29	...	...	-7,521	-7,550
2009	...	9	...	...	-16,225	-16,217

• COMPARATIVE FINANCIALS ($000 omitted)

Year	Assets	Capital & Surplus	Net Invest Income	Benefits Paid	Realized Cap Gains	Policyholder Dividends	Contract Lns (% of assets)
2007	287,380	53,566	11,557	2,392	2,639	3,589	...
2008	402,675	63,403	14,777	3,773	-10,094	5,530	...
2009	528,231	71,403	20,153	5,967	-895	5,077	...

• ORDINARY LIFE STATISTICS

Year	Av. Ord. Policy Issued ($)	Av. Ord. Policy In Force ($)	Avg. Prem ($/M)	1st Yr Prem/ Total Prem	Ord. Lapse Ratio
2007	...	...	...	...	...
2008	...	...	...	...	...
2009	...	...	...	...	...

• NEW LIFE BUSINESS ISSUED ($000 omitted)

Year	Whole Life	Term	Credit	Group	Industrial	Total
2007	...	...	...	...	...	...
2008	...	...	...	...	...	...
2009	...	...	...	...	...	...

• LIFE INSURANCE IN FORCE ($000 omitted)

Year	Whole Life	Term	Credit	Group	Industrial	Total
2007	...	...	...	...	...	...
2008	...	...	...	...	...	...
2009	...	...	...	...	...	...

NYLIFE INS CO OF ARIZONA

51 Madison Avenue
New York, New York 10010
Tel: 212-576-7000

AMB#: 068015
Began Business: 12/30/1987
Agency Off: None

Best's Financial Strength Rating: A++g **FSC:** XV

• NET PREMIUMS AND DEPOSITS ($000 omitted)

Year	Individual Life	Individual & Group Annuities	Group Life & A&H	Credit Life & A&H	Individual A&H	Total
2007	39,560	21,251	...	...	...	60,812
2008	39,308	25,689	...	...	...	64,997
2009	38,714	26,112	...	...	...	64,826

• NET OPERATING GAIN ($000 omitted)

Year	Individual Life	Individual & Group Annuities	Group Life & A&H	Credit Life & A&H	Individual A&H	Total
2007	-3,734	45	...	...	...	-3,689
2008	2,273	217	...	...	...	2,490
2009	2,471	296	...	...	...	2,767

• COMPARATIVE FINANCIALS ($000 omitted)

Year	Assets	Capital & Surplus	Net Invest Income	Benefits Paid	Realized Cap Gains	Policyholder Dividends	Contract Lns (% of assets)
2007	178,118	36,053	6,018	13,668	...	...	...
2008	189,617	37,973	6,538	17,924	-900	...	...
2009	193,204	54,514	6,241	18,348	128	...	...

• ORDINARY LIFE STATISTICS

Year	Av. Ord. Policy Issued ($)	Av. Ord. Policy In Force ($)	Avg. Prem ($/M)	1st Yr Prem/ Total Prem	Ord. Lapse Ratio
2007	585,159	490,404	1.91	10.5	5.2
2008	568,922	492,420	1.99	10.5	7.3
2009	551,717	493,590	2.04	11.9	9.2

• NEW LIFE BUSINESS ISSUED ($000 omitted)

Year	Whole Life	Term	Credit	Group	Industrial	Total
2007	...	3,573,564	...	...	...	3,573,564
2008	...	3,521,625	...	...	...	3,521,625
2009	...	3,888,503	...	...	...	3,888,503

• LIFE INSURANCE IN FORCE ($000 omitted)

Year	Whole Life	Term	Credit	Group	Industrial	Total
2007	...	38,456,046	...	...	...	38,456,046
2008	...	38,156,614	...	...	...	38,156,614
2009	...	37,271,965	...	...	...	37,271,965

NORTHWESTERN MUTUAL LIFE INS

720 East Wisconsin Avenue
Milwaukee, Wisconsin 53202-4797
Tel: 414-271-1444

AMB#: 006845
Began Business: 11/25/1858
Agency Off: Todd M. Schoon

Best's Financial Strength Rating: A++g **FSC:** XV

• NET PREMIUMS AND DEPOSITS ($000 omitted)

Year	Individual Life	Individual & Group Annuities	Group Life & A&H	Credit Life & A&H	Individual A&H	Total
2007	10,824,898	2,909,106	65,014	...	753,836	14,552,855
2008	11,095,046	3,102,985	86,258	...	800,909	15,085,738
2009	10,494,366	4,267,386	82,826	...	839,194	15,684,088

• NET OPERATING GAIN ($000 omitted)

Year	Individual Life	Individual & Group Annuities	Group Life & A&H	Credit Life & A&H	Individual A&H	Total
2007	102,893	43,882	12,295	...	228,310	387,380
2008	952,101	26,714	12,848	...	165,526	1,157,188
2009	341,191	58,994	8,357	...	82,588	491,130

• COMPARATIVE FINANCIALS ($000 omitted)

Year	Assets	Capital & Surplus	Net Invest Income	Benefits Paid	Realized Cap Gains	Policyholder Dividends	Contract Lns (% of assets)
2007	156,332,490	12,105,970	7,527,550	5,638,448	616,403	5,008,470	7.5
2008	154,834,649	12,401,283	7,786,018	6,136,293	-656,363	4,541,223	8.3
2009	166,746,624	12,402,560	7,712,821	6,849,484	-152,983	4,709,458	8.2

• ORDINARY LIFE STATISTICS

Year	Av. Ord. Policy Issued ($)	Av. Ord. Policy In Force ($)	Avg. Prem ($/M)	1st Yr Prem/ Total Prem	Ord. Lapse Ratio
2007	437,384	213,422	10.82	5.6	3.7
2008	435,004	223,143	10.46	5.5	4.2
2009	409,693	231,090	9.51	5.9	4.7

• NEW LIFE BUSINESS ISSUED ($000 omitted)

Year	Whole Life	Term	Credit	Group	Industrial	Total
2007	32,895,264	78,180,960	...	...	...	111,076,224
2008	33,499,932	77,797,206	...	...	...	111,297,138
2009	30,350,391	82,782,310	...	...	...	113,132,701

• LIFE INSURANCE IN FORCE ($000 omitted)

Year	Whole Life	Term	Credit	Group	Industrial	Total
2007	475,149,632	588,632,247	...	987,901	...	1,064,769,780
2008	494,390,000	629,757,411	...	1,071,762	...	1,125,219,173
2009	505,944,352	670,901,082	...	1,101,000	...	1,177,946,433

OCCIDENTAL LIFE INS CO OF NC

425 Austin Avenue
Waco, Texas 76701
Tel: 254-297-2775

AMB#: 006849
Began Business: 11/01/1906
Agency Off: S. Lanny Peavy

Best's Financial Strength Rating: A- g **FSC:** VII

• NET PREMIUMS AND DEPOSITS ($000 omitted)

Year	Individual Life	Individual & Group Annuities	Group Life & A&H	Credit Life & A&H	Individual A&H	Total
2007	31,955	2,672	6	...	2	34,636
2008	28,926	3,033	6	...	1	31,966
2009	29,587	3,209	6	...	1	32,803

• NET OPERATING GAIN ($000 omitted)

Year	Individual Life	Individual & Group Annuities	Group Life & A&H	Credit Life & A&H	Individual A&H	Total
2007	5,030	177	-2	...	2	5,207
2008	3,400	133	3	...	0	3,536
2009	3,639	147	2	...	-3	3,785

• COMPARATIVE FINANCIALS ($000 omitted)

Year	Assets	Capital & Surplus	Net Invest Income	Benefits Paid	Realized Cap Gains	Policyholder Dividends	Contract Lns (% of assets)
2007	255,218	27,760	12,318	23,653	-255	273	5.4
2008	259,021	29,003	12,267	25,807	-442	262	5.1
2009	261,453	32,924	11,891	24,355	-768	248	5.0

• ORDINARY LIFE STATISTICS

Year	Av. Ord. Policy Issued ($)	Av. Ord. Policy In Force ($)	Avg. Prem ($/M)	1st Yr Prem/ Total Prem	Ord. Lapse Ratio
2007	34,216	37,914	13.49	22.4	12.6
2008	35,927	37,603	12.02	17.6	13.8
2009	37,937	37,674	12.11	18.1	12.6

• NEW LIFE BUSINESS ISSUED ($000 omitted)

Year	Whole Life	Term	Credit	Group	Industrial	Total
2007	169,952	381,746	...	...	...	551,698
2008	159,767	314,107	...	...	...	473,874
2009	138,013	311,962	...	1,700	...	451,675

• LIFE INSURANCE IN FORCE ($000 omitted)

Year	Whole Life	Term	Credit	Group	Industrial	Total
2007	1,671,886	900,795	...	156	...	2,572,837
2008	1,654,048	942,930	...	156	...	2,597,134
2009	1,610,385	1,033,483	...	1,856	...	2,645,724

OHIO NATIONAL LIFE ASSUR CORP

One Financial Way
Cincinnati, Ohio 45242
Tel: 513-794-6100

AMB#: 008930
Began Business: 08/22/1979
Agency Off: Larry J. Adams

Best's Financial Strength Rating: A+ g
FSC: XI

• NET PREMIUMS AND DEPOSITS ($000 omitted)

Year	Individual Life	Individual & Group Annuities	Group Life & A&H	Credit Life & A&H	Individual A&H	Total
2007	290,572	126	...	...	6,433	297,130
2008	285,374	148	...	...	5,500	291,022
2009	260,909	1,704	...	...	4,833	267,446

• NET OPERATING GAIN ($000 omitted)

Year	Individual Life	Individual & Group Annuities	Group Life & A&H	Credit Life & A&H	Individual A&H	Total
2007	5,261	1,264	...	...	641	7,165
2008	1,483	1,968	...	...	1,261	4,713
2009	6,374	1,566	...	...	1,584	9,524

• COMPARATIVE FINANCIALS ($000 omitted)

Year	Assets	Capital & Surplus	Net Invest Income	Benefits Paid	Realized Cap Gains	Policyholder Dividends	Contract Lns (% of assets)
2007	2,690,966	188,621	140,690	196,838	130	...	2.4
2008	2,739,296	267,465	148,916	191,925	-48,119	...	2.5
2009	2,886,948	277,844	148,474	139,182	-10,089	...	2.7

• ORDINARY LIFE STATISTICS

Year	Av. Ord. Policy Issued ($)	Av. Ord. Policy In Force ($)	Avg. Prem ($/M)	1st Yr Prem/ Total Prem	Ord. Lapse Ratio
2007	606,470	448,270	4.68	9.1	4.9
2008	644,904	468,607	3.86	11.0	5.4
2009	651,034	488,088	3.51	12.3	5.7

• NEW LIFE BUSINESS ISSUED ($000 omitted)

Year	Whole Life	Term	Credit	Group	Industrial	Total
2007	1,277,179	13,017,327	...	...	...	14,294,506
2008	1,203,489	13,797,619	...	...	...	15,001,108
2009	1,120,279	15,553,347	...	...	...	16,673,626

• LIFE INSURANCE IN FORCE ($000 omitted)

Year	Whole Life	Term	Credit	Group	Industrial	Total
2007	15,661,321	76,905,439	...	...	...	92,566,760
2008	15,893,492	85,545,416	...	...	...	101,438,908
2009	16,175,233	94,894,569	...	...	...	111,069,802

OHIO NATIONAL LIFE INS CO

One Financial Way
Cincinnati, Ohio 45242
Tel: 513-794-6100

AMB#: 006852
Began Business: 10/10/1910
Agency Off: Larry J. Adams

Best's Financial Strength Rating: A+ g
FSC: XI

• NET PREMIUMS AND DEPOSITS ($000 omitted)

Year	Individual Life	Individual & Group Annuities	Group Life & A&H	Credit Life & A&H	Individual A&H	Total
2007	246,624	2,601,379	...	...	13,491	2,861,493
2008	217,670	2,679,726	...	...	14,330	2,911,727
2009	221,477	2,891,612	...	...	14,542	3,127,631

• NET OPERATING GAIN ($000 omitted)

Year	Individual Life	Individual & Group Annuities	Group Life & A&H	Credit Life & A&H	Individual A&H	Total
2007	2,580	40,812	245	...	-414	43,223
2008	14,202	-52,890	692	...	873	-37,123
2009	17,120	119,248	498	...	3,748	140,613

• COMPARATIVE FINANCIALS ($000 omitted)

Year	Assets	Capital & Surplus	Net Invest Income	Benefits Paid	Realized Cap Gains	Policyholder Dividends	Contract Lns (% of assets)
2007	13,004,213	794,948	384,200	1,457,233	-6,340	38,620	1.4
2008	12,159,782	757,192	369,119	1,422,868	-92,498	40,736	1.6
2009	15,785,004	816,716	365,440	1,138,859	-59,781	39,589	1.4

• ORDINARY LIFE STATISTICS

Year	Av. Ord. Policy Issued ($)	Av. Ord. Policy In Force ($)	Avg. Prem ($/M)	1st Yr Prem/ Total Prem	Ord. Lapse Ratio
2007	295,243	99,500	29.02	12.1	4.6
2008	255,151	197,214	10.49	9.6	6.2
2009	251,943	286,265	7.26	9.8	5.3

• NEW LIFE BUSINESS ISSUED ($000 omitted)

Year	Whole Life	Term	Credit	Group	Industrial	Total
2007	1,056,923	176,896	...	...	...	1,233,819
2008	866,635	80,484	...	...	...	947,119
2009	925,507	81,509	...	...	...	1,007,016

• LIFE INSURANCE IN FORCE ($000 omitted)

Year	Whole Life	Term	Credit	Group	Industrial	Total
2007	7,777,569	815,075	...	20,041	...	8,612,685
2008	8,193,448	13,370,305	...	18,936	...	21,582,689
2009	8,684,378	25,140,642	...	17,468	...	33,842,488

OHIO STATE LIFE INS CO

P.O. Box 410288
Kansas City, Missouri 64141-0288
Tel: 816-391-2000

AMB#: 006853
Began Business: 07/25/1906
Agency Off: Rodney K. Foster

Best's Financial Strength Rating: B+
FSC: IV

• NET PREMIUMS AND DEPOSITS ($000 omitted)

Year	Individual Life	Individual & Group Annuities	Group Life & A&H	Credit Life & A&H	Individual A&H	Total
2007	134	526	...	...	...	660
2008	184	328	...	...	...	512
2009	108	311	...	...	...	419

• NET OPERATING GAIN ($000 omitted)

Year	Individual Life	Individual & Group Annuities	Group Life & A&H	Credit Life & A&H	Individual A&H	Total
2007	-207	22	-1	...	0	-186
2008	120	7	-1	...	0	125
2009	835	15	-2	...	0	848

• COMPARATIVE FINANCIALS ($000 omitted)

Year	Assets	Capital & Surplus	Net Invest Income	Benefits Paid	Realized Cap Gains	Policyholder Dividends	Contract Lns (% of assets)
2007	9,326	6,709	486	...	...	...	...
2008	10,242	6,833	396	...	...	...	...
2009	12,174	8,282	275	...	...	...	...

• ORDINARY LIFE STATISTICS

Year	Av. Ord. Policy Issued ($)	Av. Ord. Policy In Force ($)	Avg. Prem ($/M)	1st Yr Prem/ Total Prem	Ord. Lapse Ratio
2007	...	...	...	...	...
2008	...	...	...	...	...
2009	...	...	...	...	...

• NEW LIFE BUSINESS ISSUED ($000 omitted)

Year	Whole Life	Term	Credit	Group	Industrial	Total
2007	...	...	...	...	...	...
2008	...	...	...	...	...	...
2009	...	...	...	...	...	...

• LIFE INSURANCE IN FORCE ($000 omitted)

Year	Whole Life	Term	Credit	Group	Industrial	Total
2007	5,218,757	2,443,084	...	11,225	...	7,673,066
2008	4,845,031	2,245,017	...	11,220	...	7,101,268
2009	4,478,542	2,043,408	...	10,890	...	6,532,840

OLD AMERICAN INS CO

3520 Broadway
Kansas City, Missouri 64111-2565
Tel: 816-753-4900

AMB#: 006854
Began Business: 12/30/1939
Agency Off: John Alderton

Best's Financial Strength Rating: B++
FSC: V

• NET PREMIUMS AND DEPOSITS ($000 omitted)

Year	Individual Life	Individual & Group Annuities	Group Life & A&H	Credit Life & A&H	Individual A&H	Total
2007	61,625	0	...	...	721	62,346
2008	60,842	37	...	...	644	61,523
2009	63,288	0	...	...	530	63,819

• NET OPERATING GAIN ($000 omitted)

Year	Individual Life	Individual & Group Annuities	Group Life & A&H	Credit Life & A&H	Individual A&H	Total
2007	5,500	3	...	...	202	5,704
2008	3,724	0	...	...	214	3,937
2009	3,723	3	...	...	74	3,799

• COMPARATIVE FINANCIALS ($000 omitted)

Year	Assets	Capital & Surplus	Net Invest Income	Benefits Paid	Realized Cap Gains	Policyholder Dividends	Contract Lns (% of assets)
2007	245,542	22,091	13,312	41,659	-490	...	3.6
2008	239,865	18,065	12,651	43,864	-2,313	...	3.7
2009	239,744	19,780	12,760	40,743	-2,723	...	3.8

• ORDINARY LIFE STATISTICS

Year	Av. Ord. Policy Issued ($)	Av. Ord. Policy In Force ($)	Avg. Prem ($/M)	1st Yr Prem/ Total Prem	Ord. Lapse Ratio
2007	6,378	4,461	72.99	11.1	7.5
2008	6,673	4,646	72.68	12.1	7.9
2009	6,975	4,855	73.11	15.8	7.9

• NEW LIFE BUSINESS ISSUED ($000 omitted)

Year	Whole Life	Term	Credit	Group	Industrial	Total
2007	95,199	1,044	...	...	...	96,243
2008	103,952	1,549	...	...	...	105,501
2009	139,833	2,414	...	...	...	142,247

• LIFE INSURANCE IN FORCE ($000 omitted)

Year	Whole Life	Term	Credit	Group	Industrial	Total
2007	846,819	32,353	...	...	...	879,172
2008	836,541	31,065	...	...	...	867,606
2009	861,955	30,049	...	...	...	892,004

OLD REPUBLIC LIFE INS CO

307 North Michigan Avenue
Chicago, Illinois 60601
Tel: 312-346-8100

AMB#: 006863
Began Business: 04/17/1923
Agency Off: Spencer LeRoy III

Best's Financial Strength Rating: A- **FSC:** VI

• NET PREMIUMS AND DEPOSITS ($000 omitted)

Year	Individual Life	Individual & Group Annuities	Group Life & A&H	Credit Life & A&H	Individual A&H	Total
2007	17,914	...	10,745	1,733	...	30,392
2008	18,079	...	10,405	-80	...	28,405
2009	17,067	...	8,597	-172	...	25,492

• NET OPERATING GAIN ($000 omitted)

Year	Individual Life	Individual & Group Annuities	Group Life & A&H	Credit Life & A&H	Individual A&H	Total
2007	2,486	-125	2,033	-102	125	4,417
2008	205	65	1,381	1,381	196	3,228
2009	3,139	-66	1,160	522	167	4,921

• COMPARATIVE FINANCIALS ($000 omitted)

Year	Assets	Capital & Surplus	Net Invest Income	Benefits Paid	Realized Cap Gains	Policyholder Dividends	Contract Lns (% of assets)
2007	162,491	43,016	6,264	19,768	-115	...	0.8
2008	153,975	35,061	5,971	24,261	-2,478	...	0.7
2009	151,874	41,039	5,559	20,181	221	...	0.8

• ORDINARY LIFE STATISTICS

Year	Av. Ord. Policy Issued ($)	Av. Ord. Policy In Force ($)	Avg. Prem ($/M)	1st Yr Prem/ Total Prem	Ord. Lapse Ratio
2007	...	133,496	2.35	0.0	4.5
2008	...	125,990	2.64	...	9.8
2009	...	119,512	2.66	...	9.0

• NEW LIFE BUSINESS ISSUED ($000 omitted)

Year	Whole Life	Term	Credit	Group	Industrial	Total
2007	...	...	47,494	...	...	47,494
2008	...	...	5,538	...	...	5,538
2009	...	...	...	...	...	...

• LIFE INSURANCE IN FORCE ($000 omitted)

Year	Whole Life	Term	Credit	Group	Industrial	Total
2007	102,490	13,222,842	128,673	564	42	13,454,611
2008	92,965	11,907,949	81,812	498	39	12,083,263
2009	88,047	10,811,684	46,305	480	38	10,946,554

OM FINANCIAL LIFE INS CO

1001 Fleet Street
Baltimore, Maryland 21202
Tel: 410-895-0100

AMB#: 006384
Began Business: 11/01/1960
Agency Off: Richard C. Pretty

Best's Financial Strength Rating: A- gu **FSC:** XI

• NET PREMIUMS AND DEPOSITS ($000 omitted)

Year	Individual Life	Individual & Group Annuities	Group Life & A&H	Credit Life & A&H	Individual A&H	Total
2007	197,696	2,313,991	221	...	...	2,511,908
2008	238,603	1,782,877	118	...	...	2,021,599
2009	233,917	808,136	168	...	...	1,042,221

• NET OPERATING GAIN ($000 omitted)

Year	Individual Life	Individual & Group Annuities	Group Life & A&H	Credit Life & A&H	Individual A&H	Total
2007	-32,668	-7,138	-801	...	-67	-40,675
2008	21,657	46,041	-125	...	-355	67,217
2009	84,359	-25,081	108	...	-31	59,354

• COMPARATIVE FINANCIALS ($000 omitted)

Year	Assets	Capital & Surplus	Net Invest Income	Benefits Paid	Realized Cap Gains	Policyholder Dividends	Contract Lns (% of assets)
2007	18,202,294	702,714	1,015,844	3,899,763	-453	257	0.4
2008	17,450,041	802,695	982,508	2,385,508	-351,322	233	0.5
2009	16,742,277	816,375	897,174	2,255,851	-378,499	232	0.5

• ORDINARY LIFE STATISTICS

Year	Av. Ord. Policy Issued ($)	Av. Ord. Policy In Force ($)	Avg. Prem ($/M)	1st Yr Prem/ Total Prem	Ord. Lapse Ratio
2007	148,058	195,248	5.68	26.9	19.2
2008	136,297	192,522	5.84	21.8	13.3
2009	185,095	195,181	5.50	6.6	9.8

• NEW LIFE BUSINESS ISSUED ($000 omitted)

Year	Whole Life	Term	Credit	Group	Industrial	Total
2007	5,159,916	17,029,318	...	...	...	22,189,234
2008	5,410,395	9,333,238	...	...	...	14,743,633
2009	2,115,472	166,748	...	...	...	2,282,220

• LIFE INSURANCE IN FORCE ($000 omitted)

Year	Whole Life	Term	Credit	Group	Industrial	Total
2007	16,087,781	109,491,460	...	585	...	125,579,826
2008	18,056,860	102,128,737	...	566	...	120,186,163
2009	17,245,629	90,970,366	...	546	...	108,216,541

OLD UNITED LIFE INS CO

P.O. Box 795
Shawnee Mission, Kansas 66201
Tel: 913-432-6400

AMB#: 007879
Began Business: 01/02/1964
Agency Off: Daniel K. Mattox

Best's Financial Strength Rating: B++ **FSC:** VI

• NET PREMIUMS AND DEPOSITS ($000 omitted)

Year	Individual Life	Individual & Group Annuities	Group Life & A&H	Credit Life & A&H	Individual A&H	Total
2007	16	...	...	9,207	...	9,224
2008	15	...	...	5,339	...	5,354
2009	14	...	...	3,345	...	3,359

• NET OPERATING GAIN ($000 omitted)

Year	Individual Life	Individual & Group Annuities	Group Life & A&H	Credit Life & A&H	Individual A&H	Total
2007	8	62	...	66	...	136
2008	21	29	...	1,443	...	1,493
2009	15	42	...	4,102	...	4,160

• COMPARATIVE FINANCIALS ($000 omitted)

Year	Assets	Capital & Surplus	Net Invest Income	Benefits Paid	Realized Cap Gains	Policyholder Dividends	Contract Lns (% of assets)
2007	73,461	34,641	2,952	1,600	452	...	0.0
2008	71,440	34,860	3,212	1,727	-1,423	...	0.0
2009	73,529	40,155	3,193	1,242	63	...	0.0

• ORDINARY LIFE STATISTICS

Year	Av. Ord. Policy Issued ($)	Av. Ord. Policy In Force ($)	Avg. Prem ($/M)	1st Yr Prem/ Total Prem	Ord. Lapse Ratio
2007	...	...	...	...	...
2008	...	...	...	...	...
2009	...	...	...	...	...

• NEW LIFE BUSINESS ISSUED ($000 omitted)

Year	Whole Life	Term	Credit	Group	Industrial	Total
2007	...	...	530,504	...	...	530,504
2008	...	...	425,480	...	...	425,480
2009	...	...	289,931	...	...	289,931

• LIFE INSURANCE IN FORCE ($000 omitted)

Year	Whole Life	Term	Credit	Group	Industrial	Total
2007	1,200	340	969,363	...	...	970,903
2008	1,110	340	900,733	...	...	902,183
2009	1,050	340	777,647	...	...	779,037

OM FINANCIAL LIFE INS CO OF NY

1001 Fleet Street
Baltimore, Maryland 21202
Tel: 866-746-2624

AMB#: 007122
Began Business: 11/26/1962
Agency Off: Alan M. Harrington

Best's Financial Strength Rating: A- gu **FSC:** XI

• NET PREMIUMS AND DEPOSITS ($000 omitted)

Year	Individual Life	Individual & Group Annuities	Group Life & A&H	Credit Life & A&H	Individual A&H	Total
2007	2,584	47,468	...	...	...	50,052
2008	1,948	54,980	...	...	...	56,928
2009	2,163	17,226	...	...	...	19,389

• NET OPERATING GAIN ($000 omitted)

Year	Individual Life	Individual & Group Annuities	Group Life & A&H	Credit Life & A&H	Individual A&H	Total
2007	-132	5,043	7	...	...	4,917
2008	863	3,165	6	...	...	4,034
2009	672	1,562	6	...	...	2,239

• COMPARATIVE FINANCIALS ($000 omitted)

Year	Assets	Capital & Surplus	Net Invest Income	Benefits Paid	Realized Cap Gains	Policyholder Dividends	Contract Lns (% of assets)
2007	483,895	37,957	27,819	75,765	1	12	0.5
2008	472,553	34,843	28,607	73,491	-9,954	11	0.5
2009	461,820	39,371	27,007	53,621	-5,783	11	0.5

• ORDINARY LIFE STATISTICS

Year	Av. Ord. Policy Issued ($)	Av. Ord. Policy In Force ($)	Avg. Prem ($/M)	1st Yr Prem/ Total Prem	Ord. Lapse Ratio
2007	...	...	...	...	...
2008	...	...	...	...	...
2009	...	...	...	...	...

• NEW LIFE BUSINESS ISSUED ($000 omitted)

Year	Whole Life	Term	Credit	Group	Industrial	Total
2007	...	81,926	...	...	...	81,926
2008	...	17,949	...	...	...	17,949
2009	...	...	...	...	...	...

• LIFE INSURANCE IN FORCE ($000 omitted)

Year	Whole Life	Term	Credit	Group	Industrial	Total
2007	201,028	636,037	...	...	...	837,065
2008	187,760	561,628	...	...	...	749,388
2009	174,837	496,140	...	...	...	670,977

OPTIMUM RE INSURANCE COMPANY

1345 River Bend Drive, Suite 100
Dallas, Texas 75247
Tel: 214-528-2020

AMB#: 008863
Began Business: 06/19/1978
Agency Off: None

Best's Financial Strength Rating: A-
FSC: V

• NET PREMIUMS AND DEPOSITS ($000 omitted)

Year	Individual Life	Individual & Group Annuities	Group Life & A&H	Credit Life & A&H	Individual A&H	Total
2007	24,175	...	...	...	...	24,175
2008	24,795	...	1,504	...	599	26,898
2009	24,320	...	6,663	...	940	31,923

• NET OPERATING GAIN ($000 omitted)

Year	Individual Life	Individual & Group Annuities	Group Life & A&H	Credit Life & A&H	Individual A&H	Total
2007	1,556	...	...	...	...	1,556
2008	4,081	...	202	...	181	4,465
2009	1,019	...	190	...	133	1,341

• COMPARATIVE FINANCIALS ($000 omitted)

Year	Assets	Capital & Surplus	Net Invest Income	Benefits Paid	Realized Cap Gains	Policyholder Dividends	Contract Lns (% of assets)
2007	65,528	23,511	3,015	12,269	...	...	...
2008	71,864	24,081	2,957	14,591	...	...	...
2009	78,977	24,173	2,968	17,443	34	...	...

• ORDINARY LIFE STATISTICS

Year	Av. Ord. Policy Issued ($)	Av. Ord. Policy In Force ($)	Avg. Prem ($/M)	1st Yr Prem/ Total Prem	Ord. Lapse Ratio
2007	...	52,636	3.88	...	7.9
2008	...	57,669	3.76	...	7.3
2009	...	61,364	3.89	...	6.7

• NEW LIFE BUSINESS ISSUED ($000 omitted)

Year	Whole Life	Term	Credit	Group	Industrial	Total
2007	...	...	...	...	...	...
2008	...	...	...	...	...	...
2009	...	...	...	...	...	...

• LIFE INSURANCE IN FORCE ($000 omitted)

Year	Whole Life	Term	Credit	Group	Industrial	Total
2007	327,069	24,214,552	...	931,383	...	25,473,004
2008	332,045	28,710,204	...	1,011,400	...	30,053,649
2009	342,788	30,978,337	...	1,031,652	...	32,352,777

OZARK NATIONAL LIFE INS CO MO

P.O. Box 15688
Kansas City, Missouri 64106-0688
Tel: 816-842-6300

AMB#: 006877
Began Business: 06/24/1964
Agency Off: Charles N. Sharpe

Best's Financial Strength Rating: B++
FSC: VIII

• NET PREMIUMS AND DEPOSITS ($000 omitted)

Year	Individual Life	Individual & Group Annuities	Group Life & A&H	Credit Life & A&H	Individual A&H	Total
2007	92,693	89	...	...	413	93,194
2008	89,627	237	...	...	394	90,258
2009	85,606	240	...	...	373	86,219

• NET OPERATING GAIN ($000 omitted)

Year	Individual Life	Individual & Group Annuities	Group Life & A&H	Credit Life & A&H	Individual A&H	Total
2007	18,459	39	...	...	52	21,196
2008	17,679	31	...	...	190	21,051
2009	19,563	-2	...	...	164	23,150

• COMPARATIVE FINANCIALS ($000 omitted)

Year	Assets	Capital & Surplus	Net Invest Income	Benefits Paid	Realized Cap Gains	Policyholder Dividends	Contract Lns (% of assets)
2007	586,247	87,126	27,597	35,526	...	175	2.9
2008	617,627	96,581	29,648	39,918	...	168	3.0
2009	642,878	107,302	29,423	41,139	22	162	3.1

• ORDINARY LIFE STATISTICS

Year	Av. Ord. Policy Issued ($)	Av. Ord. Policy In Force ($)	Avg. Prem ($/M)	1st Yr Prem/ Total Prem	Ord. Lapse Ratio
2007	53,664	38,036	11.06	10.3	7.7
2008	53,017	37,803	11.04	8.3	8.2
2009	49,748	37,314	11.06	6.8	8.2

• NEW LIFE BUSINESS ISSUED ($000 omitted)

Year	Whole Life	Term	Credit	Group	Industrial	Total
2007	447,537	221,978	...	...	...	669,515
2008	377,143	183,835	...	...	...	560,978
2009	266,436	145,927	...	...	...	412,363

• LIFE INSURANCE IN FORCE ($000 omitted)

Year	Whole Life	Term	Credit	Group	Industrial	Total
2007	6,500,223	2,156,252	...	...	...	8,656,475
2008	6,283,646	2,123,381	...	...	...	8,407,027
2009	5,964,482	2,074,979	...	...	...	8,039,461

OXFORD LIFE INS CO

2721 North Central Avenue
Phoenix, Arizona 85004-1172
Tel: 602-263-6666

AMB#: 007890
Began Business: 06/24/1968
Agency Off: Don C. Smith

Best's Financial Strength Rating: B++g
FSC: VIII

• NET PREMIUMS AND DEPOSITS ($000 omitted)

Year	Individual Life	Individual & Group Annuities	Group Life & A&H	Credit Life & A&H	Individual A&H	Total
2007	15,238	7,574	1,516	-110	14,552	38,770
2008	16,019	9,022	621	-43	12,399	38,018
2009	54,471	3,586	587	-13	10,478	69,109

• NET OPERATING GAIN ($000 omitted)

Year	Individual Life	Individual & Group Annuities	Group Life & A&H	Credit Life & A&H	Individual A&H	Total
2007	-180	2,733	-1,377	194	1,177	13,465
2008	-1,597	1,356	772	-125	1,653	10,236
2009	-7,445	3,625	-57	-88	893	4,333

• COMPARATIVE FINANCIALS ($000 omitted)

Year	Assets	Capital & Surplus	Net Invest Income	Benefits Paid	Realized Cap Gains	Policyholder Dividends	Contract Lns (% of assets)
2007	535,777	124,178	36,165	88,049	-322	...	0.8
2008	502,891	129,702	33,771	78,731	-448	...	0.8
2009	501,599	133,867	30,282	66,391	-1,056	...	0.8

• ORDINARY LIFE STATISTICS

Year	Av. Ord. Policy Issued ($)	Av. Ord. Policy In Force ($)	Avg. Prem ($/M)	1st Yr Prem/ Total Prem	Ord. Lapse Ratio
2007	10,560	2,834	9.31	48.6	5.6
2008	10,465	3,609	10.97	39.4	24.4
2009	12,692	4,050	38.01	18.8	24.5

• NEW LIFE BUSINESS ISSUED ($000 omitted)

Year	Whole Life	Term	Credit	Group	Industrial	Total
2007	86,204	...	...	...	...	86,204
2008	146,892	...	...	...	...	146,892
2009	191,715	...	...	...	...	191,715

• LIFE INSURANCE IN FORCE ($000 omitted)

Year	Whole Life	Term	Credit	Group	Industrial	Total
2007	208,944	1,430,435	10,885	5,497	...	1,655,761
2008	330,238	1,132,145	4,400	4,726	...	1,471,509
2009	504,860	928,887	1,628	4,295	...	1,439,669

PACIFIC BEACON LIFE REASSUR

745 Fort Street, Suite 800
Honolulu, Hawaii 96813
Tel: 805-585-3533

AMB#: 060326
Began Business: 07/01/1999
Agency Off: None

Best's Financial Strength Rating: A- g
FSC: VII

• NET PREMIUMS AND DEPOSITS ($000 omitted)

Year	Individual Life	Individual & Group Annuities	Group Life & A&H	Credit Life & A&H	Individual A&H	Total
2007	20,304	10,033	7,482	...	158	37,978
2008	22,836	12,824	9,221	...	240	45,121
2009	26,626	20,801	10,033	...	306	57,766

• NET OPERATING GAIN ($000 omitted)

Year	Individual Life	Individual & Group Annuities	Group Life & A&H	Credit Life & A&H	Individual A&H	Total
2007	-5,064	1,378	551	...	-18	-3,154
2008	-4,847	1,116	-733	...	-20	-4,484
2009	-3,944	1,530	75	...	24	-2,315

• COMPARATIVE FINANCIALS ($000 omitted)

Year	Assets	Capital & Surplus	Net Invest Income	Benefits Paid	Realized Cap Gains	Policyholder Dividends	Contract Lns (% of assets)
2007	257,472	23,191	12,818	35,428	-156	...	0.3
2008	284,549	40,274	13,632	32,434	-2,688	...	0.4
2009	303,513	44,559	15,346	38,243	-230	...	0.5

• ORDINARY LIFE STATISTICS

Year	Av. Ord. Policy Issued ($)	Av. Ord. Policy In Force ($)	Avg. Prem ($/M)	1st Yr Prem/ Total Prem	Ord. Lapse Ratio
2007	...	91,954	4.54	...	9.7
2008	...	93,092	4.49	...	8.4
2009	...	84,042	5.34	...	7.9

• NEW LIFE BUSINESS ISSUED ($000 omitted)

Year	Whole Life	Term	Credit	Group	Industrial	Total
2007	...	...	...	...	...	...
2008	...	...	...	...	...	...
2009	...	...	...	...	...	...

• LIFE INSURANCE IN FORCE ($000 omitted)

Year	Whole Life	Term	Credit	Group	Industrial	Total
2007	1,123,667	3,380,780	...	1,111,928	...	5,616,375
2008	1,191,951	3,924,225	...	1,403,575	...	6,519,751
2009	1,142,348	3,840,776	...	1,529,097	...	6,512,221

PACIFIC GUARDIAN LIFE CO LTD

Pacific Guardian Tower, 1440 Kapiolani Blvd
Honolulu, Hawaii 96814-3698
Tel: 808-955-2236

AMB#: 006883
Began Business: 06/13/1962
Agency Off: Carol Shimomura

Best's Financial Strength Rating: A **FSC:** VII

- **NET PREMIUMS AND DEPOSITS ($000 omitted)**

Year	Individual Life	Individual & Group Annuities	Group Life & A&H	Credit Life & A&H	Individual A&H	Total
2007	27,958	2,514	40,986	...	250	71,708
2008	33,211	1,976	41,272	...	231	76,690
2009	25,465	1,939	40,672	...	229	68,306

- **NET OPERATING GAIN ($000 omitted)**

Year	Individual Life	Individual & Group Annuities	Group Life & A&H	Credit Life & A&H	Individual A&H	Total
2007	4,609	311	3,988	...	-48	8,860
2008	4,425	381	3,969	...	-36	8,739
2009	5,138	204	2,952	...	-28	8,266

- **COMPARATIVE FINANCIALS ($000 omitted)**

Year	Assets	Capital & Surplus	Net Invest Income	Benefits Paid	Realized Cap Gains	Policyholder Dividends	Contract Lns (% of assets)
2007	436,674	90,377	24,384	80,286	313	130	5.3
2008	426,779	83,279	23,969	63,733	-2,633	132	5.7
2009	433,306	87,474	23,879	55,824	-1,623	138	5.8

- **ORDINARY LIFE STATISTICS**

Year	Av. Ord. Policy Issued ($)	Av. Ord. Policy In Force ($)	Avg. Prem ($/M)	1st Yr Prem/ Total Prem	Ord. Lapse Ratio
2007	172,585	80,843	8.57	12.8	5.7
2008	168,089	84,512	9.75	25.2	5.7
2009	157,243	87,763	7.80	11.8	5.6

- **NEW LIFE BUSINESS ISSUED ($000 omitted)**

Year	Whole Life	Term	Credit	Group	Industrial	Total
2007	119,963	294,240	...	207,795	...	621,998
2008	117,361	225,036	...	134,778	...	477,175
2009	100,391	179,187	...	78,027	...	357,605

- **LIFE INSURANCE IN FORCE ($000 omitted)**

Year	Whole Life	Term	Credit	Group	Industrial	Total
2007	2,205,712	1,667,579	...	7,960,120	...	11,833,411
2008	2,190,296	1,758,363	...	7,378,443	...	11,327,102
2009	2,147,506	1,811,151	...	7,334,763	...	11,293,421

PACIFIC LIFE INSURANCE COMPANY

700 Newport Center Drive
Newport Beach, California 92660-6397
Tel: 949-219-3011

AMB#: 006885
Began Business: 05/01/1868
Agency Off: Richard J. Schindler

Best's Financial Strength Rating: A+ g **FSC:** XV

- **NET PREMIUMS AND DEPOSITS ($000 omitted)**

Year	Individual Life	Individual & Group Annuities	Group Life & A&H	Credit Life & A&H	Individual A&H	Total
2007	1,905,112	9,633,578	-10	...	...	11,538,680
2008	1,935,091	6,933,534	15	...	...	8,868,641
2009	1,253,943	7,417,949	-37	...	...	8,671,854

- **NET OPERATING GAIN ($000 omitted)**

Year	Individual Life	Individual & Group Annuities	Group Life & A&H	Credit Life & A&H	Individual A&H	Total
2007	128,269	195,853	1,799	...	...	349,593
2008	113,363	-1,517,445	146	...	...	-1,239,550
2009	145,072	721,832	237	...	...	629,010

- **COMPARATIVE FINANCIALS ($000 omitted)**

Year	Assets	Capital & Surplus	Net Invest Income	Benefits Paid	Realized Cap Gains	Policyholder Dividends	Contract Lns (% of assets)
2007	96,551,166	3,707,975	2,250,412	7,788,332	12,597	20,041	6.6
2008	83,652,571	3,135,787	3,115,813	7,108,544	-289,257	21,931	8.3
2009	94,738,487	5,005,942	674,413	6,369,055	22,819	22,414	6.9

- **ORDINARY LIFE STATISTICS**

Year	Av. Ord. Policy Issued ($)	Av. Ord. Policy In Force ($)	Avg. Prem ($/M)	1st Yr Prem/ Total Prem	Ord. Lapse Ratio
2007	1,136,845	388,660	11.85	35.4	3.5
2008	1,356,704	417,864	11.47	36.9	4.6
2009	1,259,166	457,602	10.84	36.9	6.8

- **NEW LIFE BUSINESS ISSUED ($000 omitted)**

Year	Whole Life	Term	Credit	Group	Industrial	Total
2007	8,710,996	10,185,646	...	...	...	18,896,642
2008	10,125,118	12,876,450	...	...	...	23,001,568
2009	6,443,531	11,747,636	...	...	...	18,191,167

- **LIFE INSURANCE IN FORCE ($000 omitted)**

Year	Whole Life	Term	Credit	Group	Industrial	Total
2007	111,731,085	91,322,236	...	18,199	...	203,071,520
2008	115,464,560	99,357,988	...	18,568	...	214,841,116
2009	114,931,291	99,933,788	...	18,546	...	214,883,625

PACIFIC LIFE & ANNUITY CO

700 Newport Center Drive
Newport Beach, California 92660-6397
Tel: 949-219-3011

AMB#: 009156
Began Business: 07/01/1983
Agency Off: Richard J. Schindler

Best's Financial Strength Rating: A+ g **FSC:** XV

- **NET PREMIUMS AND DEPOSITS ($000 omitted)**

Year	Individual Life	Individual & Group Annuities	Group Life & A&H	Credit Life & A&H	Individual A&H	Total
2007	67,365	569,856	-53	...	...	637,168
2008	36,686	573,697	...	...	...	610,383
2009	25,279	856,816	...	...	...	882,095

- **NET OPERATING GAIN ($000 omitted)**

Year	Individual Life	Individual & Group Annuities	Group Life & A&H	Credit Life & A&H	Individual A&H	Total
2007	-3,891	10,207	-118	...	...	6,198
2008	-2,402	-105,185	1,692	...	...	-105,894
2009	6,280	105,057	557	...	...	111,894

- **COMPARATIVE FINANCIALS ($000 omitted)**

Year	Assets	Capital & Surplus	Net Invest Income	Benefits Paid	Realized Cap Gains	Policyholder Dividends	Contract Lns (% of assets)
2007	2,415,295	369,074	71,164	129,637	-4,337	...	0.1
2008	2,503,717	287,817	76,682	141,466	-9,699	...	0.1
2009	3,539,136	370,986	98,540	137,121	5,642	...	0.1

- **ORDINARY LIFE STATISTICS**

Year	Av. Ord. Policy Issued ($)	Av. Ord. Policy In Force ($)	Avg. Prem ($/M)	1st Yr Prem/ Total Prem	Ord. Lapse Ratio
2007	1,875,566	251,037	15.91	84.2	3.1
2008	1,706,864	289,738	6.69	70.9	3.8
2009	1,649,575	284,312	4.81	26.2	5.5

- **NEW LIFE BUSINESS ISSUED ($000 omitted)**

Year	Whole Life	Term	Credit	Group	Industrial	Total
2007	567,212	1,122,673	...	...	...	1,689,885
2008	337,008	1,265,737	...	...	...	1,602,745
2009	88,042	486,010	...	...	...	574,052

- **LIFE INSURANCE IN FORCE ($000 omitted)**

Year	Whole Life	Term	Credit	Group	Industrial	Total
2007	1,135,650	3,340,845	...	638	...	4,477,133
2008	1,401,681	4,578,806	...	635	...	5,981,122
2009	1,392,473	4,658,256	...	635	...	6,051,364

PACIFICARE LIFE AND HEALTH INS

5995 Plaza Drive
Cypress, California 90630
Tel: 714-226-3876

AMB#: 007278
Began Business: 09/01/1967
Agency Off: None

Best's Financial Strength Rating: A- g **FSC:** XI

- **NET PREMIUMS AND DEPOSITS ($000 omitted)**

Year	Individual Life	Individual & Group Annuities	Group Life & A&H	Credit Life & A&H	Individual A&H	Total
2007	...	...	561,135	...	771,977	1,333,112
2008	...	...	382,251	...	51,474	433,725
2009	...	...	263,527	...	58,580	322,107

- **NET OPERATING GAIN ($000 omitted)**

Year	Individual Life	Individual & Group Annuities	Group Life & A&H	Credit Life & A&H	Individual A&H	Total
2007	...	...	101,362	...	98,521	278,816
2008	...	...	31,776	...	43,350	154,075
2009	...	0	37,621	3,627	-10,923	120,409

- **COMPARATIVE FINANCIALS ($000 omitted)**

Year	Assets	Capital & Surplus	Net Invest Income	Benefits Paid	Realized Cap Gains	Policyholder Dividends	Contract Lns (% of assets)
2007	896,092	552,192	34,798	943,691	...	...	0.0
2008	778,584	642,789	28,197	289,406	-5,155	...	...
2009	745,709	680,457	24,161	253,124	296	...	...

- **ORDINARY LIFE STATISTICS**

Year	Av. Ord. Policy Issued ($)	Av. Ord. Policy In Force ($)	Avg. Prem ($/M)	1st Yr Prem/ Total Prem	Ord. Lapse Ratio
2007	...	...	...	...	...
2008	...	...	...	...	...
2009	...	...	...	...	...

- **NEW LIFE BUSINESS ISSUED ($000 omitted)**

Year	Whole Life	Term	Credit	Group	Industrial	Total
2007	...	...	...	...	...	...
2008	...	...	...	...	...	...
2009	...	...	...	...	...	...

- **LIFE INSURANCE IN FORCE ($000 omitted)**

Year	Whole Life	Term	Credit	Group	Industrial	Total
2007	...	219	...	48	...	267
2008	...	194	...	...	...	194
2009	...	194	...	...	...	194

PAN-AMERICAN ASSURANCE COMPANY

Pan-American Life Center, 601 Poydras Street
New Orleans, Louisiana 70130
Tel: 504-566-1300

AMB#: 009058
Began Business: 06/04/1981
Agency Off: Eugenio Magdalena

Best's Financial Strength Rating: A r
FSC: IX

• **NET PREMIUMS AND DEPOSITS** ($000 omitted)

Year	Individual Life	Individual & Group Annuities	Group Life & A&H	Credit Life & A&H	Individual A&H	Total
2007	31	127	...	...	...	158
2008	33	418	...	...	...	451
2009	37	28	...	...	...	65

• **NET OPERATING GAIN** ($000 omitted)

Year	Individual Life	Individual & Group Annuities	Group Life & A&H	Credit Life & A&H	Individual A&H	Total
2007	3,732	-178	...	...	...	3,554
2008	1,035	-150	...	...	...	884
2009	851	-134	...	...	...	717

• **COMPARATIVE FINANCIALS** ($000 omitted)

Year	Assets	Capital & Surplus	Net Invest Income	Benefits Paid	Realized Cap Gains	Policyholder Dividends	Contract Lns (% of assets)
2007	22,387	16,491	1,209	192	0	...	...
2008	23,066	16,889	915	189	...	...	...
2009	23,772	17,305	838	149	24	...	...

• **ORDINARY LIFE STATISTICS**

Year	Av. Ord. Policy Issued ($)	Av. Ord. Policy In Force ($)	Avg. Prem ($/M)	1st Yr Prem/ Total Prem	Ord. Lapse Ratio
2007	...	...	...	...	...
2008	...	...	...	...	...
2009	...	...	...	...	...

• **NEW LIFE BUSINESS ISSUED** ($000 omitted)

Year	Whole Life	Term	Credit	Group	Industrial	Total
2007	96,442	11,687	...	...	...	108,129
2008	36,425	4,018	...	...	...	40,443
2009	23,429	5,040	...	...	...	28,469

• **LIFE INSURANCE IN FORCE** ($000 omitted)

Year	Whole Life	Term	Credit	Group	Industrial	Total
2007	7,163,718	424,820	...	...	...	7,588,538
2008	6,719,999	389,112	...	...	...	7,109,111
2009	6,285,052	354,362	...	...	...	6,639,414

PAN-AMERICAN LIFE INS CO

601 Poydras Street
New Orleans, Louisiana 70130
Tel: 504-566-1300

AMB#: 006893
Began Business: 03/28/1912
Agency Off: Eugenio Magdalena

Best's Financial Strength Rating: A g
FSC: IX

• **NET PREMIUMS AND DEPOSITS** ($000 omitted)

Year	Individual Life	Individual & Group Annuities	Group Life & A&H	Credit Life & A&H	Individual A&H	Total
2007	63,951	2,753	90,413	...	10,116	167,233
2008	65,079	1,275	117,110	...	9,364	192,828
2009	64,656	714	116,251	...	9,096	190,717

• **NET OPERATING GAIN** ($000 omitted)

Year	Individual Life	Individual & Group Annuities	Group Life & A&H	Credit Life & A&H	Individual A&H	Total
2007	20,224	2,607	407	...	208	23,445
2008	21,909	-445	-4,019	...	-510	16,935
2009	22,113	356	-4,186	...	-3,881	14,402

• **COMPARATIVE FINANCIALS** ($000 omitted)

Year	Assets	Capital & Surplus	Net Invest Income	Benefits Paid	Realized Cap Gains	Policyholder Dividends	Contract Lns (% of assets)
2007	1,582,708	306,483	89,567	157,564	2,252	5,153	5.9
2008	1,527,542	267,189	89,207	175,976	-16,587	5,175	6.3
2009	1,515,358	259,446	83,859	189,177	-5,382	4,952	6.1

• **ORDINARY LIFE STATISTICS**

Year	Av. Ord. Policy Issued ($)	Av. Ord. Policy In Force ($)	Avg. Prem ($/M)	1st Yr Prem/ Total Prem	Ord. Lapse Ratio
2007	133,492	124,104	7.68	21.1	7.3
2008	120,238	126,019	7.71	19.5	5.8
2009	119,329	144,791	7.16	19.6	7.5

• **NEW LIFE BUSINESS ISSUED** ($000 omitted)

Year	Whole Life	Term	Credit	Group	Industrial	Total
2007	507,979	35,199	...	460,466	...	1,003,644
2008	370,088	119,161	...	362,523	...	851,772
2009	312,893	89,963	...	557,010	...	959,866

• **LIFE INSURANCE IN FORCE** ($000 omitted)

Year	Whole Life	Term	Credit	Group	Industrial	Total
2007	11,039,906	1,373,229	...	1,544,122	210,220	14,167,477
2008	10,838,310	1,301,871	...	1,586,005	205,356	13,931,542
2009	11,295,238	1,734,647	...	1,434,805	198,987	14,663,677

PARK AVENUE LIFE INS CO

7 Hanover Square
New York, New York 10004-4025
Tel: 212-598-8829

AMB#: 006000
Began Business: 04/09/1965
Agency Off: None

Best's Financial Strength Rating: A
FSC: VIII

• **NET PREMIUMS AND DEPOSITS** ($000 omitted)

Year	Individual Life	Individual & Group Annuities	Group Life & A&H	Credit Life & A&H	Individual A&H	Total
2007	8,497	17	-20	...	...	8,494
2008	6,472	20	64	...	...	6,556
2009	4,748	16	54	...	...	4,818

• **NET OPERATING GAIN** ($000 omitted)

Year	Individual Life	Individual & Group Annuities	Group Life & A&H	Credit Life & A&H	Individual A&H	Total
2007	11,707	4,013	-17	...	...	15,703
2008	12,864	4,102	463	...	...	17,430
2009	4,404	1,890	-16	...	...	6,278

• **COMPARATIVE FINANCIALS** ($000 omitted)

Year	Assets	Capital & Surplus	Net Invest Income	Benefits Paid	Realized Cap Gains	Policyholder Dividends	Contract Lns (% of assets)
2007	434,886	150,531	31,118	23,793	110	...	1.0
2008	417,794	144,337	32,131	25,562	-526	...	1.0
2009	419,366	156,228	20,827	24,114	7	...	0.9

• **ORDINARY LIFE STATISTICS**

Year	Av. Ord. Policy Issued ($)	Av. Ord. Policy In Force ($)	Avg. Prem ($/M)	1st Yr Prem/ Total Prem	Ord. Lapse Ratio
2007	...	...	...	...	...
2008	...	...	...	...	...
2009	...	...	...	...	...

• **NEW LIFE BUSINESS ISSUED** ($000 omitted)

Year	Whole Life	Term	Credit	Group	Industrial	Total
2007	...	...	...	...	...	...
2008	...	...	...	...	...	...
2009	...	...	...	...	...	...

• **LIFE INSURANCE IN FORCE** ($000 omitted)

Year	Whole Life	Term	Credit	Group	Industrial	Total
2007	391,583	148,268	...	22,470	...	562,321
2008	362,615	130,137	...	15,130	...	507,882
2009	335,934	112,848	...	4,067	...	452,849

PARKER CENTENNIAL ASSURANCE CO

1800 North Point Drive
Stevens Point, Wisconsin 54481
Tel: 715-346-6000

AMB#: 060403
Began Business: 08/31/1973
Agency Off: None

Best's Financial Strength Rating: A+ g
FSC: XV

• **NET PREMIUMS AND DEPOSITS** ($000 omitted)

Year	Individual Life	Individual & Group Annuities	Group Life & A&H	Credit Life & A&H	Individual A&H	Total
2007	...	8,580	...	...	...	8,580
2008	...	4,381	...	...	...	4,381
2009	...	2,824	...	...	...	2,824

• **NET OPERATING GAIN** ($000 omitted)

Year	Individual Life	Individual & Group Annuities	Group Life & A&H	Credit Life & A&H	Individual A&H	Total
2007	...	992	...	...	...	992
2008	...	1,296	...	...	...	1,296
2009	...	1,422	...	...	...	1,422

• **COMPARATIVE FINANCIALS** ($000 omitted)

Year	Assets	Capital & Surplus	Net Invest Income	Benefits Paid	Realized Cap Gains	Policyholder Dividends	Contract Lns (% of assets)
2007	63,876	39,498	3,029	2,894	0	...	...
2008	64,676	39,525	3,271	3,694	-520	...	...
2009	68,625	41,065	3,485	2,226	88	...	...

• **ORDINARY LIFE STATISTICS**

Year	Av. Ord. Policy Issued ($)	Av. Ord. Policy In Force ($)	Avg. Prem ($/M)	1st Yr Prem/ Total Prem	Ord. Lapse Ratio
2007	...	...	...	...	...
2008	...	...	...	...	...
2009	...	...	...	...	...

• **NEW LIFE BUSINESS ISSUED** ($000 omitted)

Year	Whole Life	Term	Credit	Group	Industrial	Total
2007	...	...	...	...	...	...
2008	...	...	...	...	...	...
2009	...	...	...	...	...	...

• **LIFE INSURANCE IN FORCE** ($000 omitted)

Year	Whole Life	Term	Credit	Group	Industrial	Total
2007	...	...	2,581	...	...	2,581
2008	...	...	1,475	...	...	1,475
2009	...	...	678	...	...	678

PAUL REVERE LIFE INS CO

1 Fountain Square
Chattanooga, Tennessee 37402-1330
Tel: 423-294-1011

AMB#: 006899
Began Business: 07/10/1930
Agency Off: Stephen Meahl

Best's Financial Strength Rating: A- g
FSC: XIV

• NET PREMIUMS AND DEPOSITS ($000 omitted)

Year	Individual Life	Individual & Group Annuities	Group Life & A&H	Credit Life & A&H	Individual A&H	Total
2007	596	2,150	11,502	...	87,591	101,839
2008	998	1,911	9,867	...	84,059	96,835
2009	1,225	1,372	8,057	...	82,764	93,418

• NET OPERATING GAIN ($000 omitted)

Year	Individual Life	Individual & Group Annuities	Group Life & A&H	Credit Life & A&H	Individual A&H	Total
2007	3,082	-931	2,478	...	186,456	191,086
2008	3,094	-5,391	2,804	...	110,374	110,881
2009	4,500	3,414	1,576	...	131,698	141,188

• COMPARATIVE FINANCIALS ($000 omitted)

Year	Assets	Capital & Surplus	Net Invest Income	Benefits Paid	Realized Cap Gains	Policyholder Dividends	Contract Lns (% of assets)
2007	4,920,984	458,736	387,593	92,712	3,122	...	...
2008	4,710,077	340,303	332,507	60,815	-32,320	...	...
2009	4,744,807	450,488	369,939	59,981	-9,769	...	...

• ORDINARY LIFE STATISTICS

Year	Av. Ord. Policy Issued ($)	Av. Ord. Policy In Force ($)	Avg. Prem ($/M)	1st Yr Prem/ Total Prem	Ord. Lapse Ratio
2007	...	...	...	...	...
2008	...	...	...	...	...
2009	...	...	...	...	...

• NEW LIFE BUSINESS ISSUED ($000 omitted)

Year	Whole Life	Term	Credit	Group	Industrial	Total
2007	...	79,614	...	440	...	80,054
2008	...	114,736	...	1,433	...	116,169
2009	634	110,098	...	463	...	111,195

• LIFE INSURANCE IN FORCE ($000 omitted)

Year	Whole Life	Term	Credit	Group	Industrial	Total
2007	858,524	500,614	...	999,651	...	2,358,789
2008	793,681	532,007	...	872,797	...	2,198,485
2009	705,508	543,703	...	662,513	...	1,911,724

PEKIN LIFE INS CO

2505 Court Street
Pekin, Illinois 61558
Tel: 309-346-1161

AMB#: 006901
Began Business: 09/13/1965
Agency Off: David A. Jones

Best's Financial Strength Rating: A-
FSC: VIII

• NET PREMIUMS AND DEPOSITS ($000 omitted)

Year	Individual Life	Individual & Group Annuities	Group Life & A&H	Credit Life & A&H	Individual A&H	Total
2007	41,266	41,872	72,427	11,558	51,321	218,445
2008	41,588	39,000	74,678	10,153	52,561	217,980
2009	44,683	58,102	84,446	7,975	57,082	252,288

• NET OPERATING GAIN ($000 omitted)

Year	Individual Life	Individual & Group Annuities	Group Life & A&H	Credit Life & A&H	Individual A&H	Total
2007	1,517	2,112	-2,052	1,711	-670	3,219
2008	2,439	1,571	-200	1,019	1,137	6,602
2009	1,743	3,005	-1,137	388	-5,134	-435

• COMPARATIVE FINANCIALS ($000 omitted)

Year	Assets	Capital & Surplus	Net Invest Income	Benefits Paid	Realized Cap Gains	Policyholder Dividends	Contract Lns (% of assets)
2007	818,304	120,349	43,204	183,810	2,340	22	1.7
2008	854,397	117,159	46,106	157,074	-5,375	26	1.7
2009	925,953	111,824	48,614	174,618	-2,307	19	1.6

• ORDINARY LIFE STATISTICS

Year	Av. Ord. Policy Issued ($)	Av. Ord. Policy In Force ($)	Avg. Prem ($/M)	1st Yr Prem/ Total Prem	Ord. Lapse Ratio
2007	172,661	120,808	4.78	21.7	6.0
2008	183,920	124,553	4.54	18.0	7.9
2009	160,960	128,851	4.52	23.6	5.6

• NEW LIFE BUSINESS ISSUED ($000 omitted)

Year	Whole Life	Term	Credit	Group	Industrial	Total
2007	267,266	1,112,294	443,222	76,714	...	1,899,496
2008	324,299	1,257,600	397,444	83,191	...	2,062,534
2009	284,611	1,243,868	348,439	79,784	...	1,956,702

• LIFE INSURANCE IN FORCE ($000 omitted)

Year	Whole Life	Term	Credit	Group	Industrial	Total
2007	2,643,580	6,912,061	530,312	322,187	...	10,408,140
2008	2,730,942	7,522,879	504,342	352,853	...	11,111,016
2009	2,914,721	8,098,554	464,767	383,460	...	11,861,502

PAUL REVERE VARIABLE ANNUITY

1 Fountain Square
Chattanooga, Tennessee 37402-1330
Tel: 423-294-1011

AMB#: 006900
Began Business: 02/18/1966
Agency Off: Stephen Meahl

Best's Financial Strength Rating: B++
FSC: XIV

• NET PREMIUMS AND DEPOSITS ($000 omitted)

Year	Individual Life	Individual & Group Annuities	Group Life & A&H	Credit Life & A&H	Individual A&H	Total
2007	...	11,649	...	...	...	11,649
2008	...	10,717	...	...	...	10,717
2009	...	6,663	...	...	...	6,663

• NET OPERATING GAIN ($000 omitted)

Year	Individual Life	Individual & Group Annuities	Group Life & A&H	Credit Life & A&H	Individual A&H	Total
2007	848	5,084	...	...	...	5,932
2008	638	4,934	...	...	...	5,573
2009	749	5,191	...	...	...	5,940

• COMPARATIVE FINANCIALS ($000 omitted)

Year	Assets	Capital & Surplus	Net Invest Income	Benefits Paid	Realized Cap Gains	Policyholder Dividends	Contract Lns (% of assets)
2007	132,608	114,046	7,788	356	-21	...	...
2008	110,191	94,726	7,216	301	-3,813	...	...
2009	49,142	31,776	6,498	474	1,145	...	...

• ORDINARY LIFE STATISTICS

Year	Av. Ord. Policy Issued ($)	Av. Ord. Policy In Force ($)	Avg. Prem ($/M)	1st Yr Prem/ Total Prem	Ord. Lapse Ratio
2007	...	...	...	...	...
2008	...	...	...	...	...
2009	...	...	...	...	...

• NEW LIFE BUSINESS ISSUED ($000 omitted)

Year	Whole Life	Term	Credit	Group	Industrial	Total
2007	...	...	...	...	...	...
2008	...	...	...	...	...	...
2009	...	...	...	...	...	...

• LIFE INSURANCE IN FORCE ($000 omitted)

Year	Whole Life	Term	Credit	Group	Industrial	Total
2007	439,798	138,673	...	...	...	578,471
2008	398,293	128,375	...	...	...	526,668
2009	325,030	114,224	...	...	...	439,254

PEMCO LIFE INS CO

P.O. Box 778
Seattle, Washington 98109-0778
Tel: 206-628-4000

AMB#: 007420
Began Business: 05/01/1968
Agency Off: Stan W. McNaughton

Best's Financial Strength Rating: B+
FSC: III

• NET PREMIUMS AND DEPOSITS ($000 omitted)

Year	Individual Life	Individual & Group Annuities	Group Life & A&H	Credit Life & A&H	Individual A&H	Total
2007	1,547	...	68	0	...	1,616
2008	1,644	...	62	0	...	1,706
2009	1,844	...	57	0	...	1,901

• NET OPERATING GAIN ($000 omitted)

Year	Individual Life	Individual & Group Annuities	Group Life & A&H	Credit Life & A&H	Individual A&H	Total
2007	-549	...	17	-13	...	-545
2008	-838	...	5	-2	...	-834
2009	-2,031	...	-15	-3	...	-2,048

• COMPARATIVE FINANCIALS ($000 omitted)

Year	Assets	Capital & Surplus	Net Invest Income	Benefits Paid	Realized Cap Gains	Policyholder Dividends	Contract Lns (% of assets)
2007	6,626	3,173	279	662	...	...	0.5
2008	7,221	3,208	228	545	-229	...	0.6
2009	8,213	2,794	184	712	-21	...	1.2

• ORDINARY LIFE STATISTICS

Year	Av. Ord. Policy Issued ($)	Av. Ord. Policy In Force ($)	Avg. Prem ($/M)	1st Yr Prem/ Total Prem	Ord. Lapse Ratio
2007	...	...	...	...	...
2008	...	...	...	...	...
2009	...	...	...	...	...

• NEW LIFE BUSINESS ISSUED ($000 omitted)

Year	Whole Life	Term	Credit	Group	Industrial	Total
2007	2,412	250,303	...	...	...	252,715
2008	3,608	316,263	15	...	...	319,886
2009	3,040	292,878	...	...	...	295,918

• LIFE INSURANCE IN FORCE ($000 omitted)

Year	Whole Life	Term	Credit	Group	Industrial	Total
2007	12,695	1,519,634	25	18,059	...	1,550,413
2008	15,901	1,780,532	15	16,965	...	1,813,413
2009	18,356	2,005,729	10	15,748	...	2,039,843

PENN INS AND ANNUITY COMPANY

600 Dresher Road
Horsham, Pennsylvania 19044
Tel: 215-956-8000

AMB#: 009073
Began Business: 04/09/1981
Agency Off: Eileen McDonnell

Best's Financial Strength Rating: A+ g
FSC: XIII

• NET PREMIUMS AND DEPOSITS ($000 omitted)

Year	Individual Life	Individual & Group Annuities	Group Life & A&H	Credit Life & A&H	Individual A&H	Total
2007	32,903	8,743	531	...	...	42,177
2008	59,774	5,536	522	...	...	65,832
2009	97,126	6,305	507	...	...	103,938

• NET OPERATING GAIN ($000 omitted)

Year	Individual Life	Individual & Group Annuities	Group Life & A&H	Credit Life & A&H	Individual A&H	Total
2007	15,857	3,615	120	...	...	19,592
2008	7,496	-4,569	109	...	...	3,035
2009	-6,792	5,862	129	...	...	-801

• COMPARATIVE FINANCIALS ($000 omitted)

Year	Assets	Capital & Surplus	Net Invest Income	Benefits Paid	Realized Cap Gains	Policyholder Dividends	Contract Lns (% of assets)
2007	1,117,456	117,262	58,102	110,723	-82	...	31.7
2008	1,047,715	107,510	53,864	92,421	-81	...	33.6
2009	1,092,166	103,591	51,252	92,841	-1,250	...	32.8

• ORDINARY LIFE STATISTICS

Year	Av. Ord. Policy Issued ($)	Av. Ord. Policy In Force ($)	Avg. Prem ($/M)	1st Yr Prem/ Total Prem	Ord. Lapse Ratio
2007	1,029,975	203,174	12.64	17.5	4.2
2008	732,608	240,888	16.50	53.6	5.3
2009	787,329	303,575	19.74	65.9	3.9

• NEW LIFE BUSINESS ISSUED ($000 omitted)

Year	Whole Life	Term	Credit	Group	Industrial	Total
2007	162,736	...	...	...	...	162,736
2008	952,391	...	...	...	...	952,391
2009	1,621,110	...	...	...	...	1,621,110

• LIFE INSURANCE IN FORCE ($000 omitted)

Year	Whole Life	Term	Credit	Group	Industrial	Total
2007	3,584,402	...	...	36,133	...	3,620,535
2008	4,304,426	...	...	34,319	...	4,338,745
2009	5,676,860	...	...	32,623	...	5,709,483

PENN MUTUAL LIFE INS CO

600 Dresher Road
Horsham, Pennsylvania 19044
Tel: 215-956-8000

AMB#: 006903
Began Business: 05/25/1847
Agency Off: Eileen McDonnell

Best's Financial Strength Rating: A+ g
FSC: XIII

• NET PREMIUMS AND DEPOSITS ($000 omitted)

Year	Individual Life	Individual & Group Annuities	Group Life & A&H	Credit Life & A&H	Individual A&H	Total
2007	517,573	707,153	585	...	698	1,226,008
2008	404,887	662,341	527	...	1,946	1,069,700
2009	446,628	1,030,689	524	...	617	1,478,457

• NET OPERATING GAIN ($000 omitted)

Year	Individual Life	Individual & Group Annuities	Group Life & A&H	Credit Life & A&H	Individual A&H	Total
2007	-9,423	16,581	171	...	-728	6,601
2008	62,559	-65,291	-108	...	568	-2,272
2009	5,997	61,721	109	...	4,483	72,310

• COMPARATIVE FINANCIALS ($000 omitted)

Year	Assets	Capital & Surplus	Net Invest Income	Benefits Paid	Realized Cap Gains	Policyholder Dividends	Contract Lns (% of assets)
2007	10,546,348	1,302,211	384,910	909,381	-12,563	32,475	3.0
2008	9,688,538	1,285,720	380,054	862,292	-47,024	30,657	3.3
2009	10,939,523	1,364,335	354,513	789,780	-1,554	30,863	3.0

• ORDINARY LIFE STATISTICS

Year	Av. Ord. Policy Issued ($)	Av. Ord. Policy In Force ($)	Avg. Prem ($/M)	1st Yr Prem/ Total Prem	Ord. Lapse Ratio
2007	711,611	187,232	9.39	37.7	5.7
2008	634,219	198,679	7.64	22.3	7.3
2009	611,349	213,405	8.00	26.5	7.3

• NEW LIFE BUSINESS ISSUED ($000 omitted)

Year	Whole Life	Term	Credit	Group	Industrial	Total
2007	4,205,915	3,855,213	...	...	...	8,061,128
2008	2,507,509	4,289,412	...	...	...	6,796,921
2009	2,826,427	4,899,802	...	...	...	7,726,229

• LIFE INSURANCE IN FORCE ($000 omitted)

Year	Whole Life	Term	Credit	Group	Industrial	Total
2007	39,791,138	20,582,037	...	151,815	...	60,524,990
2008	38,991,979	22,814,714	...	157,559	...	61,964,252
2009	38,531,960	26,194,307	...	169,201	...	64,895,467

PENNSYLVANIA LIFE INSURANCE CO

P.O. Box 958465
Lake Mary, Florida 32795-8465
Tel: 407-995-8007

AMB#: 006905
Began Business: 01/12/1948
Agency Off: Peter English

Best's Financial Strength Rating: B++g
FSC: IX

• NET PREMIUMS AND DEPOSITS ($000 omitted)

Year	Individual Life	Individual & Group Annuities	Group Life & A&H	Credit Life & A&H	Individual A&H	Total
2007	18,048	2,042	-6	...	658,013	678,098
2008	16,718	1,360	...	...	1,778,355	1,796,433
2009	-105,256	-97,318	...	...	1,928,400	1,725,826

• NET OPERATING GAIN ($000 omitted)

Year	Individual Life	Individual & Group Annuities	Group Life & A&H	Credit Life & A&H	Individual A&H	Total
2007	-475	-340	-1	...	51,926	51,110
2008	-2,732	1,461	1	...	22,043	20,773
2009	-4,859	2,209	8	...	122,465	119,823

• COMPARATIVE FINANCIALS ($000 omitted)

Year	Assets	Capital & Surplus	Net Invest Income	Benefits Paid	Realized Cap Gains	Policyholder Dividends	Contract Lns (% of assets)
2007	1,180,290	136,824	39,052	512,977	-38	...	0.4
2008	1,102,685	125,491	23,556	1,543,561	-13,434	...	0.4
2009	901,412	261,001	6,730	1,554,486	-25,176	...	0.0

• ORDINARY LIFE STATISTICS

Year	Av. Ord. Policy Issued ($)	Av. Ord. Policy In Force ($)	Avg. Prem ($/M)	1st Yr Prem/ Total Prem	Ord. Lapse Ratio
2007	...	...	...	...	...
2008	...	...	...	...	...
2009	...	...	...	...	...

• NEW LIFE BUSINESS ISSUED ($000 omitted)

Year	Whole Life	Term	Credit	Group	Industrial	Total
2007	51,000	26,724	...	...	...	77,724
2008	50,948	52,109	...	...	...	103,057
2009	81,525	...	...	...	...	81,525

• LIFE INSURANCE IN FORCE ($000 omitted)

Year	Whole Life	Term	Credit	Group	Industrial	Total
2007	634,554	369,079	...	240	17	1,003,890
2008	621,238	368,952	...	220	17	990,427
2009	571,670	272,769	...	216	17	844,671

PERFORMANCE LIFE OF AMERICA

PO Box 83480
Baton Rouge, Louisiana 70884-3480
Tel: 225-769-9923

AMB#: 009325
Began Business: 12/15/1982
Agency Off: Dick S. Taylor

Best's Financial Strength Rating: B++g
FSC: V

• NET PREMIUMS AND DEPOSITS ($000 omitted)

Year	Individual Life	Individual & Group Annuities	Group Life & A&H	Credit Life & A&H	Individual A&H	Total
2007	...	...	...	15,889	...	15,889
2008	...	...	...	9,532	...	9,532
2009	...	...	...	4,202	...	4,202

• NET OPERATING GAIN ($000 omitted)

Year	Individual Life	Individual & Group Annuities	Group Life & A&H	Credit Life & A&H	Individual A&H	Total
2007	...	...	...	2,612	...	2,612
2008	...	...	...	2,622	...	2,622
2009	...	...	...	2,454	...	2,454

• COMPARATIVE FINANCIALS ($000 omitted)

Year	Assets	Capital & Surplus	Net Invest Income	Benefits Paid	Realized Cap Gains	Policyholder Dividends	Contract Lns (% of assets)
2007	33,141	15,144	1,520	1,997	3	...	...
2008	29,496	13,094	1,436	2,401	49	...	...
2009	26,717	13,992	1,251	2,461	...	...	...

• ORDINARY LIFE STATISTICS

Year	Av. Ord. Policy Issued ($)	Av. Ord. Policy In Force ($)	Avg. Prem ($/M)	1st Yr Prem/ Total Prem	Ord. Lapse Ratio
2007	...	...	...	...	...
2008	...	...	...	...	...
2009	...	...	...	...	...

• NEW LIFE BUSINESS ISSUED ($000 omitted)

Year	Whole Life	Term	Credit	Group	Industrial	Total
2007	...	...	...	...	...	...
2008	...	...	...	...	...	...
2009	...	...	...	...	...	...

• LIFE INSURANCE IN FORCE ($000 omitted)

Year	Whole Life	Term	Credit	Group	Industrial	Total
2007	...	...	448,050	...	...	448,050
2008	...	...	418,347	...	...	418,347
2009	...	...	358,832	...	...	358,832

PERICO LIFE INSURANCE COMPANY

13358 Manchester Road
St. Louis, Missouri 63131
Tel: 314-965-5675

AMB#: 008618
Began Business: 10/09/1975
Agency Off: Carl J. Petty, Jr.

Best's Financial Strength Rating: A **FSC:** VI

• NET PREMIUMS AND DEPOSITS ($000 omitted)

Year	Individual Life	Individual & Group Annuities	Group Life & A&H	Credit Life & A&H	Individual A&H	Total
2007	...	...	46,803	...	...	46,803
2008	...	...	51,936	...	...	51,936
2009	...	...	83,744	...	...	83,744

• NET OPERATING GAIN ($000 omitted)

Year	Individual Life	Individual & Group Annuities	Group Life & A&H	Credit Life & A&H	Individual A&H	Total
2007	0	...	4,033	-2	1	4,031
2008	0	...	8,076	...	1	8,078
2009	0	...	10,307	...	1	10,308

• COMPARATIVE FINANCIALS ($000 omitted)

Year	Assets	Capital & Surplus	Net Invest Income	Benefits Paid	Realized Cap Gains	Policyholder Dividends	Contract Lns (% of assets)
2007	50,960	31,606	2,034	34,510	...	...	...
2008	61,334	39,480	1,933	33,655	-322	...	...
2009	78,626	49,780	2,423	57,861	...	...	...

• ORDINARY LIFE STATISTICS

Year	Av. Ord. Policy Issued ($)	Av. Ord. Policy In Force ($)	Avg. Prem ($/M)	1st Yr Prem/ Total Prem	Ord. Lapse Ratio
2007	...	...	...	...	...
2008	...	...	...	...	...
2009	...	...	...	...	...

• NEW LIFE BUSINESS ISSUED ($000 omitted)

Year	Whole Life	Term	Credit	Group	Industrial	Total
2007	...	...	...	42,245	...	42,245
2008	...	...	...	27,375	...	27,375
2009	...	...	...	4,629	...	4,629

• LIFE INSURANCE IN FORCE ($000 omitted)

Year	Whole Life	Term	Credit	Group	Industrial	Total
2007	...	882	...	99,471	...	100,353
2008	...	768	...	94,921	...	95,689
2009	...	645	...	60,722	...	61,367

PHILADELPHIA AMERICAN LIFE INS

200 Westlake Park Boulevard, Suite 1200
Houston, Texas 77079-2663
Tel: 281-368-7200

AMB#: 009166
Began Business: 03/01/1978
Agency Off: None

Best's Financial Strength Rating: B+ g **FSC:** VI

• NET PREMIUMS AND DEPOSITS ($000 omitted)

Year	Individual Life	Individual & Group Annuities	Group Life & A&H	Credit Life & A&H	Individual A&H	Total
2007	989	14,339	10,144	...	30,779	56,251
2008	1,355	-11,895	7,820	...	28,313	25,592
2009	629	7,496	5,962	...	37,251	51,339

• NET OPERATING GAIN ($000 omitted)

Year	Individual Life	Individual & Group Annuities	Group Life & A&H	Credit Life & A&H	Individual A&H	Total
2007	500	792	717	...	1,867	3,876
2008	524	609	383	...	687	2,203
2009	349	614	836	...	716	2,516

• COMPARATIVE FINANCIALS ($000 omitted)

Year	Assets	Capital & Surplus	Net Invest Income	Benefits Paid	Realized Cap Gains	Policyholder Dividends	Contract Lns (% of assets)
2007	187,709	19,547	9,341	40,880	-1,255	...	0.0
2008	174,075	19,965	11,170	36,158	-2,301	...	0.1
2009	175,184	20,933	9,208	42,971	-2,357	...	0.1

• ORDINARY LIFE STATISTICS

Year	Av. Ord. Policy Issued ($)	Av. Ord. Policy In Force ($)	Avg. Prem ($/M)	1st Yr Prem/ Total Prem	Ord. Lapse Ratio
2007	...	...	...	...	...
2008	...	...	...	...	...
2009	...	...	...	...	...

• NEW LIFE BUSINESS ISSUED ($000 omitted)

Year	Whole Life	Term	Credit	Group	Industrial	Total
2007	1,000	...	...	...	...	1,000
2008	3,440	...	...	...	...	3,440
2009	2,276	...	...	...	...	2,276

• LIFE INSURANCE IN FORCE ($000 omitted)

Year	Whole Life	Term	Credit	Group	Industrial	Total
2007	13,111	9,208	...	31,231	...	53,550
2008	21,539	2,412	...	21,061	...	45,012
2009	22,873	2,182	...	19,017	...	44,072

PHARMACISTS LIFE INS CO

P.O. Box 370
Algona, Iowa 50511
Tel: 515-295-2461

AMB#: 008946
Began Business: 07/17/1979
Agency Off: Steven M. Hoskins

Best's Financial Strength Rating: B+ **FSC:** IV

• NET PREMIUMS AND DEPOSITS ($000 omitted)

Year	Individual Life	Individual & Group Annuities	Group Life & A&H	Credit Life & A&H	Individual A&H	Total
2007	2,006	876	...	...	...	2,882
2008	2,069	1,435	...	...	...	3,504
2009	1,854	5,066	...	...	...	6,920

• NET OPERATING GAIN ($000 omitted)

Year	Individual Life	Individual & Group Annuities	Group Life & A&H	Credit Life & A&H	Individual A&H	Total
2007	-156	69	...	...	...	-88
2008	-432	21	...	...	...	-411
2009	-41	99	...	...	...	57

• COMPARATIVE FINANCIALS ($000 omitted)

Year	Assets	Capital & Surplus	Net Invest Income	Benefits Paid	Realized Cap Gains	Policyholder Dividends	Contract Lns (% of assets)
2007	37,175	6,812	1,844	1,777	-127	8	1.9
2008	38,902	5,500	1,920	1,172	-1,209	8	1.8
2009	46,292	5,906	2,181	1,705	-376	9	1.7

• ORDINARY LIFE STATISTICS

Year	Av. Ord. Policy Issued ($)	Av. Ord. Policy In Force ($)	Avg. Prem ($/M)	1st Yr Prem/ Total Prem	Ord. Lapse Ratio
2007	...	...	...	...	...
2008	...	...	...	...	...
2009	...	...	...	...	...

• NEW LIFE BUSINESS ISSUED ($000 omitted)

Year	Whole Life	Term	Credit	Group	Industrial	Total
2007	10,689	168,375	...	...	...	179,064
2008	8,045	195,710	...	...	...	203,755
2009	7,773	121,188	...	...	...	128,961

• LIFE INSURANCE IN FORCE ($000 omitted)

Year	Whole Life	Term	Credit	Group	Industrial	Total
2007	118,971	1,175,981	...	...	...	1,294,952
2008	122,653	1,279,677	...	...	...	1,402,330
2009	125,477	1,302,338	...	...	...	1,427,815

PHILADELPHIA-UNITED LIFE INS

150 Monument Road, Suite 600
Bala Cynwyd, Pennsylvania 19004
Tel: 610-660-6600

AMB#: 006919
Began Business: 07/11/1940
Agency Off: Robert B. Ries

Best's Financial Strength Rating: B+ **FSC:** IV

• NET PREMIUMS AND DEPOSITS ($000 omitted)

Year	Individual Life	Individual & Group Annuities	Group Life & A&H	Credit Life & A&H	Individual A&H	Total
2007	9,039	1	...	...	8	9,048
2008	9,157	2	...	...	7	9,165
2009	8,729	2	...	...	6	8,737

• NET OPERATING GAIN ($000 omitted)

Year	Individual Life	Individual & Group Annuities	Group Life & A&H	Credit Life & A&H	Individual A&H	Total
2007	5	0	...	...	2	7
2008	467	0	...	...	4	471
2009	717	0	...	...	3	721

• COMPARATIVE FINANCIALS ($000 omitted)

Year	Assets	Capital & Surplus	Net Invest Income	Benefits Paid	Realized Cap Gains	Policyholder Dividends	Contract Lns (% of assets)
2007	44,326	8,117	1,978	4,031	418	...	4.0
2008	43,721	6,487	2,021	4,177	-323	...	4.2
2009	45,914	6,777	1,939	4,036	-231	...	4.6

• ORDINARY LIFE STATISTICS

Year	Av. Ord. Policy Issued ($)	Av. Ord. Policy In Force ($)	Avg. Prem ($/M)	1st Yr Prem/ Total Prem	Ord. Lapse Ratio
2007	...	...	...	...	...
2008	...	...	...	...	...
2009	...	...	...	...	...

• NEW LIFE BUSINESS ISSUED ($000 omitted)

Year	Whole Life	Term	Credit	Group	Industrial	Total
2007	43,891	38,525	...	...	...	82,416
2008	45,462	26,437	...	...	...	71,899
2009	27,130	17,375	...	...	...	44,505

• LIFE INSURANCE IN FORCE ($000 omitted)

Year	Whole Life	Term	Credit	Group	Industrial	Total
2007	212,724	112,274	...	...	23,620	348,618
2008	214,256	125,454	...	...	22,570	362,280
2009	206,954	128,587	...	...	21,635	357,175

PHL VARIABLE INS CO

One American Row
Hartford, Connecticut 06115
Tel: 860-403-5000

AMB#: 009332
Began Business: 07/15/1981
Agency Off: None

Best's Financial Strength Rating: B+ g **FSC:** X

• NET PREMIUMS AND DEPOSITS ($000 omitted)

Year	Individual Life	Individual & Group Annuities	Group Life & A&H	Credit Life & A&H	Individual A&H	Total
2007	445,837	606,787	...	...	...	1,052,624
2008	461,756	582,955	...	...	...	1,044,711
2009	233,047	132,606	...	...	...	365,653

• NET OPERATING GAIN ($000 omitted)

Year	Individual Life	Individual & Group Annuities	Group Life & A&H	Credit Life & A&H	Individual A&H	Total
2007	-89,227	-9,362	...	...	...	-98,589
2008	17,446	-155,458	...	...	...	-138,012
2009	-51,398	20,368	...	...	...	-31,030

• COMPARATIVE FINANCIALS ($000 omitted)

Year	Assets	Capital & Surplus	Net Invest Income	Benefits Paid	Realized Cap Gains	Policyholder Dividends	Contract Lns (% of assets)
2007	5,342,708	167,436	104,767	906,449	-3,708	...	0.4
2008	4,428,521	273,028	88,170	827,250	-49,020	...	0.8
2009	4,586,303	235,696	74,884	751,187	-56,516	...	1.1

• ORDINARY LIFE STATISTICS

Year	Av. Ord. Policy Issued ($)	Av. Ord. Policy In Force ($)	Avg. Prem ($/M)	1st Yr Prem/ Total Prem	Ord. Lapse Ratio
2007	1,311,454	1,048,223	7.69	63.3	4.0
2008	1,134,730	1,068,624	7.17	50.5	4.9
2009	897,997	1,061,368	4.75	17.5	6.2

• NEW LIFE BUSINESS ISSUED ($000 omitted)

Year	Whole Life	Term	Credit	Group	Industrial	Total
2007	7,492,951	11,077,235	...	...	...	18,570,186
2008	7,064,152	11,510,246	...	...	...	18,574,398
2009	1,343,543	2,279,874	...	...	...	3,623,417

• LIFE INSURANCE IN FORCE ($000 omitted)

Year	Whole Life	Term	Credit	Group	Industrial	Total
2007	20,410,031	50,213,967	...	...	...	70,623,998
2008	26,863,931	57,456,898	...	...	...	84,320,829
2009	26,682,861	54,504,359	...	...	...	81,187,219

PHOENIX LIFE INSURANCE COMPANY

One American Row
Hartford, Connecticut 06115
Tel: 860-403-5000

AMB#: 006922
Began Business: 05/01/1851
Agency Off: None

Best's Financial Strength Rating: B+ g **FSC:** X

• NET PREMIUMS AND DEPOSITS ($000 omitted)

Year	Individual Life	Individual & Group Annuities	Group Life & A&H	Credit Life & A&H	Individual A&H	Total
2007	801,070	483,555	13,475	...	59	1,298,159
2008	773,865	408,853	17,279	...	48	1,200,045
2009	632,250	456,051	10,766	...	38	1,099,105

• NET OPERATING GAIN ($000 omitted)

Year	Individual Life	Individual & Group Annuities	Group Life & A&H	Credit Life & A&H	Individual A&H	Total
2007	91,810	-5,633	29,694	...	-625	115,245
2008	39,984	-35,226	49,034	...	-374	53,419
2009	73,719	-5,781	-38,809	...	26	29,155

• COMPARATIVE FINANCIALS ($000 omitted)

Year	Assets	Capital & Surplus	Net Invest Income	Benefits Paid	Realized Cap Gains	Policyholder Dividends	Contract Lns (% of assets)
2007	16,714,606	848,117	869,321	1,261,546	-35,277	345,062	13.9
2008	15,392,479	758,914	816,204	1,270,588	-135,685	315,740	15.9
2009	14,654,500	517,162	746,473	1,861,815	-89,029	306,939	15.5

• ORDINARY LIFE STATISTICS

Year	Av. Ord. Policy Issued ($)	Av. Ord. Policy In Force ($)	Avg. Prem ($/M)	1st Yr Prem/ Total Prem	Ord. Lapse Ratio
2007	798,597	179,972	13.48	5.5	6.0
2008	675,183	190,817	13.15	5.0	6.8
2009	772,551	183,831	12.33	1.2	9.2

• NEW LIFE BUSINESS ISSUED ($000 omitted)

Year	Whole Life	Term	Credit	Group	Industrial	Total
2007	1,303,717	645,659	...	...	...	1,949,376
2008	1,080,559	525,026	...	...	...	1,605,585
2009	78,804	95,020	...	...	...	173,824

• LIFE INSURANCE IN FORCE ($000 omitted)

Year	Whole Life	Term	Credit	Group	Industrial	Total
2007	53,182,480	17,808,169	...	1,582,124	...	72,572,773
2008	54,045,156	17,139,350	...	1,729,531	...	72,914,037
2009	48,369,711	15,520,474	...	1,287,771	...	65,177,956

PHOENIX LIFE AND ANNUITY CO

One American Row
Hartford, Connecticut 06115
Tel: 860-403-5000

AMB#: 009072
Began Business: 12/28/1981
Agency Off: None

Best's Financial Strength Rating: B+ **FSC:** VI

• NET PREMIUMS AND DEPOSITS ($000 omitted)

Year	Individual Life	Individual & Group Annuities	Group Life & A&H	Credit Life & A&H	Individual A&H	Total
2007	4,812	...	...	...	...	4,812
2008	3,258	...	...	...	...	3,258
2009	2,381	...	...	...	...	2,381

• NET OPERATING GAIN ($000 omitted)

Year	Individual Life	Individual & Group Annuities	Group Life & A&H	Credit Life & A&H	Individual A&H	Total
2007	2,132	...	...	...	...	2,132
2008	746	...	...	...	...	746
2009	-297	...	...	...	...	-297

• COMPARATIVE FINANCIALS ($000 omitted)

Year	Assets	Capital & Surplus	Net Invest Income	Benefits Paid	Realized Cap Gains	Policyholder Dividends	Contract Lns (% of assets)
2007	65,294	20,059	2,130	1,497	-7	...	1.8
2008	60,167	20,494	2,002	6,003	-672	...	3.0
2009	60,427	25,423	1,746	8,920	-42	...	3.6

• ORDINARY LIFE STATISTICS

Year	Av. Ord. Policy Issued ($)	Av. Ord. Policy In Force ($)	Avg. Prem ($/M)	1st Yr Prem/ Total Prem	Ord. Lapse Ratio
2007	...	...	...	...	...
2008	...	...	...	...	...
2009	...	...	...	...	...

• NEW LIFE BUSINESS ISSUED ($000 omitted)

Year	Whole Life	Term	Credit	Group	Industrial	Total
2007	...	...	...	...	...	...
2008	...	...	...	...	...	...
2009	...	...	...	...	...	...

• LIFE INSURANCE IN FORCE ($000 omitted)

Year	Whole Life	Term	Credit	Group	Industrial	Total
2007	296,561	9,671,103	...	...	...	9,967,664
2008	247,500	9,143,517	...	...	...	9,391,017
2009	195,871	8,562,379	...	...	...	8,758,250

PHYSICIANS LIFE INS CO

2600 Dodge Street
Omaha, Nebraska 68131
Tel: 402-633-1000

AMB#: 007451
Began Business: 01/28/1970
Agency Off: Ben Baldwin

Best's Financial Strength Rating: A g **FSC:** XI

• NET PREMIUMS AND DEPOSITS ($000 omitted)

Year	Individual Life	Individual & Group Annuities	Group Life & A&H	Credit Life & A&H	Individual A&H	Total
2007	165,727	22,268	...	...	...	187,995
2008	160,811	133,076	...	...	...	293,887
2009	156,334	40,323	...	...	...	196,658

• NET OPERATING GAIN ($000 omitted)

Year	Individual Life	Individual & Group Annuities	Group Life & A&H	Credit Life & A&H	Individual A&H	Total
2007	3,827	1,373	...	...	331	5,531
2008	2,472	2,382	...	...	476	5,331
2009	5,139	2,283	...	...	631	8,053

• COMPARATIVE FINANCIALS ($000 omitted)

Year	Assets	Capital & Surplus	Net Invest Income	Benefits Paid	Realized Cap Gains	Policyholder Dividends	Contract Lns (% of assets)
2007	1,290,550	84,503	68,643	255,474	895	...	1.7
2008	1,263,422	87,607	66,516	305,859	-6,826	...	1.8
2009	1,252,706	101,506	65,720	205,454	-1,774	...	2.0

• ORDINARY LIFE STATISTICS

Year	Av. Ord. Policy Issued ($)	Av. Ord. Policy In Force ($)	Avg. Prem ($/M)	1st Yr Prem/ Total Prem	Ord. Lapse Ratio
2007	3,974	6,962	44.18	10.5	2.6
2008	3,593	7,682	41.53	9.8	-0.7
2009	2,753	7,893	40.85	10.0	2.9

• NEW LIFE BUSINESS ISSUED ($000 omitted)

Year	Whole Life	Term	Credit	Group	Industrial	Total
2007	103,792	189,381	...	...	...	293,173
2008	74,092	157,153	...	...	...	231,245
2009	59,510	127,711	...	...	...	187,221

• LIFE INSURANCE IN FORCE ($000 omitted)

Year	Whole Life	Term	Credit	Group	Industrial	Total
2007	2,382,663	1,425,082	...	...	...	3,807,745
2008	2,298,741	1,633,756	...	...	...	3,932,497
2009	2,176,595	1,711,238	...	...	...	3,887,833

PHYSICIANS MUTUAL INSURANCE CO

2600 Dodge Street
Omaha, Nebraska 68131
Tel: 402-633-1000

AMB#: 007372
Began Business: 02/10/1902
Agency Off: Ben Baldwin

Best's Financial Strength Rating: A g
FSC: XI

• NET PREMIUMS AND DEPOSITS ($000 omitted)

Year	Individual Life	Individual & Group Annuities	Group Life & A&H	Credit Life & A&H	Individual A&H	Total
2007	...	...	2,568	...	419,643	422,211
2008	...	...	2,837	...	400,546	403,383
2009	...	...	3,927	...	382,077	386,005

• NET OPERATING GAIN ($000 omitted)

Year	Individual Life	Individual & Group Annuities	Group Life & A&H	Credit Life & A&H	Individual A&H	Total
2007	...	...	1,082	...	30,923	32,005
2008	...	...	580	...	31,943	32,523
2009	...	...	-1,027	...	31,295	30,268

• COMPARATIVE FINANCIALS ($000 omitted)

Year	Assets	Capital & Surplus	Net Invest Income	Benefits Paid	Realized Cap Gains	Policyholder Dividends	Contract Lns (% of assets)
2007	1,389,129	760,027	65,677	260,129	348	...	...
2008	1,432,789	771,937	69,600	246,409	-13,508	...	...
2009	1,539,420	799,112	73,541	238,200	-5,227	...	...

• ORDINARY LIFE STATISTICS

Year	Av. Ord. Policy Issued ($)	Av. Ord. Policy In Force ($)	Avg. Prem ($/M)	1st Yr Prem/ Total Prem	Ord. Lapse Ratio
2007	...	...	...	...	...
2008	...	...	...	...	...
2009	...	...	...	...	...

• NEW LIFE BUSINESS ISSUED ($000 omitted)

Year	Whole Life	Term	Credit	Group	Industrial	Total
2007	...	...	...	...	...	...
2008	...	...	...	...	...	...
2009	...	...	...	...	...	...

• LIFE INSURANCE IN FORCE ($000 omitted)

Year	Whole Life	Term	Credit	Group	Industrial	Total
2007	...	...	...	...	...	...
2008	...	...	...	...	...	...
2009	...	...	...	...	...	...

PIONEER MUTUAL LIFE INS CO

P.O. Box 368
Indianapolis, Indiana 46206
Tel: 701-277-2300

AMB#: 006933
Began Business: 02/02/1948
Agency Off: B. Douglas Gritton

Best's Financial Strength Rating: A g
FSC: XI

• NET PREMIUMS AND DEPOSITS ($000 omitted)

Year	Individual Life	Individual & Group Annuities	Group Life & A&H	Credit Life & A&H	Individual A&H	Total
2007	31,512	1,397	19	...	4	32,932
2008	32,683	2,213	31	...	3	34,930
2009	35,001	1,757	17	...	3	36,778

• NET OPERATING GAIN ($000 omitted)

Year	Individual Life	Individual & Group Annuities	Group Life & A&H	Credit Life & A&H	Individual A&H	Total
2007	-2,407	1,873	3	...	0	-531
2008	-975	977	0	...	3	5
2009	-278	1,277	6	...	2	1,007

• COMPARATIVE FINANCIALS ($000 omitted)

Year	Assets	Capital & Surplus	Net Invest Income	Benefits Paid	Realized Cap Gains	Policyholder Dividends	Contract Lns (% of assets)
2007	458,569	29,432	25,519	49,996	1	594	4.4
2008	457,217	29,073	25,555	43,331	-1,102	538	4.6
2009	476,310	31,506	26,475	33,238	-48	536	4.8

• ORDINARY LIFE STATISTICS

Year	Av. Ord. Policy Issued ($)	Av. Ord. Policy In Force ($)	Avg. Prem ($/M)	1st Yr Prem/ Total Prem	Ord. Lapse Ratio
2007	152,863	84,171	11.13	31.0	4.8
2008	196,869	85,629	11.57	33.0	6.5
2009	196,267	86,178	12.60	39.5	6.8

• NEW LIFE BUSINESS ISSUED ($000 omitted)

Year	Whole Life	Term	Credit	Group	Industrial	Total
2007	206,212	...	...	1,830	...	208,042
2008	217,934	...	...	240	...	218,174
2009	174,678	...	...	925	...	175,603

• LIFE INSURANCE IN FORCE ($000 omitted)

Year	Whole Life	Term	Credit	Group	Industrial	Total
2007	2,650,856	752,865	...	74,476	...	3,478,197
2008	2,672,448	693,878	...	72,938	...	3,439,264
2009	2,644,601	630,096	...	43,888	...	3,318,584

PIONEER AMERICAN INS CO

425 Austin Avenue
Waco, Texas 76701
Tel: 254-297-2776

AMB#: 006929
Began Business: 05/01/1946
Agency Off: S. Lanny Peavy

Best's Financial Strength Rating: A- g
FSC: VII

• NET PREMIUMS AND DEPOSITS ($000 omitted)

Year	Individual Life	Individual & Group Annuities	Group Life & A&H	Credit Life & A&H	Individual A&H	Total
2007	5,143	3,095	122	...	...	8,360
2008	5,794	2,939	116	...	...	8,848
2009	7,169	2,674	115	...	...	9,958

• NET OPERATING GAIN ($000 omitted)

Year	Individual Life	Individual & Group Annuities	Group Life & A&H	Credit Life & A&H	Individual A&H	Total
2007	560	14	-39	...	...	536
2008	-108	11	83	...	...	-14
2009	-295	5	-31	...	...	-322

• COMPARATIVE FINANCIALS ($000 omitted)

Year	Assets	Capital & Surplus	Net Invest Income	Benefits Paid	Realized Cap Gains	Policyholder Dividends	Contract Lns (% of assets)
2007	47,129	10,862	2,160	3,237	...	...	7.2
2008	48,013	9,672	2,253	3,812	...	...	7.6
2009	51,492	9,729	2,316	3,137	-13	...	7.5

• ORDINARY LIFE STATISTICS

Year	Av. Ord. Policy Issued ($)	Av. Ord. Policy In Force ($)	Avg. Prem ($/M)	1st Yr Prem/ Total Prem	Ord. Lapse Ratio
2007	...	...	...	...	...
2008	...	...	...	...	...
2009	...	...	...	...	...

• NEW LIFE BUSINESS ISSUED ($000 omitted)

Year	Whole Life	Term	Credit	Group	Industrial	Total
2007	47,448	130,249	...	...	...	177,697
2008	43,644	181,147	...	...	...	224,791
2009	64,366	199,472	...	7,072	...	270,910

• LIFE INSURANCE IN FORCE ($000 omitted)

Year	Whole Life	Term	Credit	Group	Industrial	Total
2007	180,667	303,543	...	34,199	...	518,409
2008	142,725	417,143	...	29,577	...	589,445
2009	212,297	440,403	...	32,484	...	685,184

PIONEER SECURITY LIFE INS CO

425 Austin Avenue
Waco, Texas 76701
Tel: 254-297-2778

AMB#: 006935
Began Business: 11/20/1956
Agency Off: S. Lanny Peavy

Best's Financial Strength Rating: A- g
FSC: VII

• NET PREMIUMS AND DEPOSITS ($000 omitted)

Year	Individual Life	Individual & Group Annuities	Group Life & A&H	Credit Life & A&H	Individual A&H	Total
2007	5,951	911	56	...	...	6,918
2008	5,283	803	52	...	...	6,138
2009	4,756	737	51	...	...	5,545

• NET OPERATING GAIN ($000 omitted)

Year	Individual Life	Individual & Group Annuities	Group Life & A&H	Credit Life & A&H	Individual A&H	Total
2007	-558	8	32	...	...	-761
2008	148	145	1	...	...	2,794
2009	298	-38	19	...	...	3,079

• COMPARATIVE FINANCIALS ($000 omitted)

Year	Assets	Capital & Surplus	Net Invest Income	Benefits Paid	Realized Cap Gains	Policyholder Dividends	Contract Lns (% of assets)
2007	91,061	70,451	1,431	2,619	...	...	1.1
2008	95,060	73,638	4,108	2,883	...	...	1.0
2009	99,962	76,477	4,476	3,226	...	...	1.0

• ORDINARY LIFE STATISTICS

Year	Av. Ord. Policy Issued ($)	Av. Ord. Policy In Force ($)	Avg. Prem ($/M)	1st Yr Prem/ Total Prem	Ord. Lapse Ratio
2007	...	...	...	...	...
2008	...	...	...	...	...
2009	...	...	...	...	...

• NEW LIFE BUSINESS ISSUED ($000 omitted)

Year	Whole Life	Term	Credit	Group	Industrial	Total
2007	38,855	53,750	...	...	...	92,605
2008	20,280	34,677	...	...	...	54,957
2009	8,191	12,428	...	...	...	20,619

• LIFE INSURANCE IN FORCE ($000 omitted)

Year	Whole Life	Term	Credit	Group	Industrial	Total
2007	162,462	107,223	...	20,389	...	290,074
2008	142,483	102,941	...	18,262	...	263,686
2009	129,018	91,159	...	17,213	...	237,390

PLATEAU INS CO

2701 North Main Street
Crossville, Tennessee 38555-5407
Tel: 931-484-8411

AMB#: 009348
Began Business: 03/23/1981
Agency Off: William D. Williams

Best's Financial Strength Rating: B++ **FSC:** IV

• NET PREMIUMS AND DEPOSITS ($000 omitted)

Year	Individual Life	Individual & Group Annuities	Group Life & A&H	Credit Life & A&H	Individual A&H	Total
2007	721	...	...	11,637	...	12,358
2008	657	...	34	10,809	...	11,500
2009	561	...	15	9,021	...	9,597

• NET OPERATING GAIN ($000 omitted)

Year	Individual Life	Individual & Group Annuities	Group Life & A&H	Credit Life & A&H	Individual A&H	Total
2007	113	...	...	426	...	539
2008	49	...	-3	548	...	594
2009	136	...	...	2,331	...	2,467

• COMPARATIVE FINANCIALS ($000 omitted)

Year	Assets	Capital & Surplus	Net Invest Income	Benefits Paid	Realized Cap Gains	Policyholder Dividends	Contract Lns (% of assets)
2007	18,420	6,175	745	2,997	...	...	...
2008	19,411	6,674	737	3,156	-3	...	...
2009	19,434	9,174	556	3,160	0	...	...

• ORDINARY LIFE STATISTICS

Year	Av. Ord. Policy Issued ($)	Av. Ord. Policy In Force ($)	Avg. Prem ($/M)	1st Yr Prem/ Total Prem	Ord. Lapse Ratio
2007	...	...	...	...	...
2008	...	...	...	...	...
2009	...	...	...	...	...

• NEW LIFE BUSINESS ISSUED ($000 omitted)

Year	Whole Life	Term	Credit	Group	Industrial	Total
2007	...	242,893	904,659	...	...	1,147,552
2008	...	152,759	1,147,546	714	...	1,301,019
2009	...	108,649	969,939	720	...	1,079,308

• LIFE INSURANCE IN FORCE ($000 omitted)

Year	Whole Life	Term	Credit	Group	Industrial	Total
2007	...	70,814	866,026	...	...	936,840
2008	...	84,679	865,401	712	...	950,792
2009	...	78,405	803,149	1,294	...	882,848

POPULAR LIFE RE

P.O. Box 70331
Guaynabo, Puerto Rico 00936-8331
Tel: 787-706-4111

AMB#: 060399
Began Business: 12/10/2003
Agency Off: Ramon D. Lloveras

Best's Financial Strength Rating: B **FSC:** VI

• NET PREMIUMS AND DEPOSITS ($000 omitted)

Year	Individual Life	Individual & Group Annuities	Group Life & A&H	Credit Life & A&H	Individual A&H	Total
2007	...	...	567	13,924	4,177	18,669
2008	...	...	562	12,028	4,173	16,763
2009	...	...	1,674	7,113	3,710	12,497

• NET OPERATING GAIN ($000 omitted)

Year	Individual Life	Individual & Group Annuities	Group Life & A&H	Credit Life & A&H	Individual A&H	Total
2007	...	...	273	2,899	1,806	4,978
2008	...	...	306	3,434	1,805	5,546
2009	...	...	462	4,286	1,443	6,190

• COMPARATIVE FINANCIALS ($000 omitted)

Year	Assets	Capital & Surplus	Net Invest Income	Benefits Paid	Realized Cap Gains	Policyholder Dividends	Contract Lns (% of assets)
2007	51,105	20,172	2,211	5,110	...	...	...
2008	54,743	25,619	2,157	5,449	...	...	...
2009	56,408	31,657	1,942	5,553	...	...	...

• ORDINARY LIFE STATISTICS

Year	Av. Ord. Policy Issued ($)	Av. Ord. Policy In Force ($)	Avg. Prem ($/M)	1st Yr Prem/ Total Prem	Ord. Lapse Ratio
2007	...	...	...	...	...
2008	...	...	...	...	...
2009	...	...	...	...	...

• NEW LIFE BUSINESS ISSUED ($000 omitted)

Year	Whole Life	Term	Credit	Group	Industrial	Total
2007	...	...	312,191	-119,071	...	193,120
2008	...	...	293,227	9,618	...	302,845
2009	...	...	107,575	113,651	...	221,226

• LIFE INSURANCE IN FORCE ($000 omitted)

Year	Whole Life	Term	Credit	Group	Industrial	Total
2007	...	...	716,856	18,996	...	735,852
2008	...	...	690,302	28,614	...	718,916
2009	...	...	580,414	141,902	...	722,316

POLISH ROMAN CATHOLIC UNION

984 Milwaukee Avenue
Chicago, Illinois 60622-4101
Tel: 773-782-2600

AMB#: 006940
Began Business: 12/16/1887
Agency Off: Wallace M. Ozog

Best's Financial Strength Rating: C++ **FSC:** IV

• NET PREMIUMS AND DEPOSITS ($000 omitted)

Year	Individual Life	Individual & Group Annuities	Group Life & A&H	Credit Life & A&H	Individual A&H	Total
2007	2,461	...	...	...	...	16,937
2008	2,330	...	...	...	...	24,764
2009	2,672	...	...	...	...	17,256

• NET OPERATING GAIN ($000 omitted)

Year	Individual Life	Individual & Group Annuities	Group Life & A&H	Credit Life & A&H	Individual A&H	Total
2007	-1,028	-1,056	...	...	...	-2,078
2008	-259	-751	...	...	...	-2,027
2009	-760	23	...	...	...	-1,600

• COMPARATIVE FINANCIALS ($000 omitted)

Year	Assets	Capital & Surplus	Net Invest Income	Benefits Paid	Realized Cap Gains	Policyholder Dividends	Contract Lns (% of assets)
2007	161,983	12,082	8,246	9,946	1,134	324	0.7
2008	169,538	6,182	9,230	15,351	-1,370	458	0.7
2009	178,199	4,312	8,521	13,361	5	169	0.7

• ORDINARY LIFE STATISTICS

Year	Av. Ord. Policy Issued ($)	Av. Ord. Policy In Force ($)	Avg. Prem ($/M)	1st Yr Prem/ Total Prem	Ord. Lapse Ratio
2007	...	...	...	...	...
2008	...	...	...	...	...
2009	...	...	...	...	...

• NEW LIFE BUSINESS ISSUED ($000 omitted)

Year	Whole Life	Term	Credit	Group	Industrial	Total
2007	8,288	...	...	...	...	8,288
2008	5,906	...	...	...	...	5,906
2009	5,173	...	...	...	...	5,173

• LIFE INSURANCE IN FORCE ($000 omitted)

Year	Whole Life	Term	Credit	Group	Industrial	Total
2007	372,970	...	...	...	...	372,970
2008	365,658	...	...	...	...	365,658
2009	360,277	...	...	...	...	360,277

PRESIDENTIAL LIFE INS CO

69 Lydecker Street
Nyack, New York 10960-2103
Tel: 845-358-2300

AMB#: 006948
Began Business: 10/20/1966
Agency Off: Donald Barnes

Best's Financial Strength Rating: B+ **FSC:** IX

• NET PREMIUMS AND DEPOSITS ($000 omitted)

Year	Individual Life	Individual & Group Annuities	Group Life & A&H	Credit Life & A&H	Individual A&H	Total
2007	11,292	168,686	5,829	...	1	185,809
2008	11,039	180,065	6,106	...	18	197,228
2009	10,731	235,261	6,457	...	36	252,484

• NET OPERATING GAIN ($000 omitted)

Year	Individual Life	Individual & Group Annuities	Group Life & A&H	Credit Life & A&H	Individual A&H	Total
2007	-1,237	57,341	63	...	1	56,168
2008	6,790	37,920	-35	...	0	44,675
2009	1,330	21,288	377	...	15	23,011

• COMPARATIVE FINANCIALS ($000 omitted)

Year	Assets	Capital & Surplus	Net Invest Income	Benefits Paid	Realized Cap Gains	Policyholder Dividends	Contract Lns (% of assets)
2007	3,925,692	360,373	280,320	689,355	2,973	...	0.5
2008	3,706,636	329,039	255,153	443,729	-27,743	...	0.5
2009	3,613,890	269,777	179,704	325,343	13,018	...	0.5

• ORDINARY LIFE STATISTICS

Year	Av. Ord. Policy Issued ($)	Av. Ord. Policy In Force ($)	Avg. Prem ($/M)	1st Yr Prem/ Total Prem	Ord. Lapse Ratio
2007	16,073	47,854	13.08	31.0	5.1
2008	13,075	44,666	14.43	20.7	5.9
2009	11,729	41,916	15.36	17.4	6.3

• NEW LIFE BUSINESS ISSUED ($000 omitted)

Year	Whole Life	Term	Credit	Group	Industrial	Total
2007	63,715	...	...	...	...	63,715
2008	45,215	...	...	3,649	...	48,864
2009	38,200	1	...	...	...	38,200

• LIFE INSURANCE IN FORCE ($000 omitted)

Year	Whole Life	Term	Credit	Group	Industrial	Total
2007	615,391	612,506	...	1,033,701	...	2,261,598
2008	603,302	575,704	...	1,010,767	...	2,189,773
2009	585,133	536,203	...	1,185,296	...	2,306,632

PRIMERICA LIFE INS CO

3120 Breckinridge Boulevard
Duluth, Georgia 30099-0001
Tel: 770-381-1000

AMB#: 006693
Began Business: 01/01/1903
Agency Off: Glenn J. Williams

Best's Financial Strength Rating: A+ g
FSC: XIV

• **NET PREMIUMS AND DEPOSITS** ($000 omitted)

Year	Individual Life	Individual & Group Annuities	Group Life & A&H	Credit Life & A&H	Individual A&H	Total
2007	1,156,740	346,062	...	-4,417	...	1,498,386
2008	1,188,898	355,893	...	...	...	1,544,791
2009	1,191,743	362,663	...	...	...	1,554,406

• **NET OPERATING GAIN** ($000 omitted)

Year	Individual Life	Individual & Group Annuities	Group Life & A&H	Credit Life & A&H	Individual A&H	Total
2007	347,719	4,820	6	913	31	353,489
2008	132,517	3,691	8	20,485	38	156,740
2009	169,233	4,887	6	...	29	174,155

• **COMPARATIVE FINANCIALS** ($000 omitted)

Year	Assets	Capital & Surplus	Net Invest Income	Benefits Paid	Realized Cap Gains	Policyholder Dividends	Contract Lns (% of assets)
2007	5,895,972	1,654,849	530,631	401,912	-2,496	...	...
2008	5,958,953	1,472,548	359,563	397,797	-83,144	...	...
2009	6,805,090	1,705,595	322,556	409,828	-48,212	...	...

• **ORDINARY LIFE STATISTICS**

Year	Av. Ord. Policy Issued ($)	Av. Ord. Policy In Force ($)	Avg. Prem ($/M)	1st Yr Prem/ Total Prem	Ord. Lapse Ratio
2007	354,542	254,858	3.12	14.1	9.1
2008	359,134	263,611	3.16	14.3	9.7
2009	341,666	269,246	3.25	13.4	9.9

• **NEW LIFE BUSINESS ISSUED** ($000 omitted)

Year	Whole Life	Term	Credit	Group	Industrial	Total
2007	...	71,851,862	...	...	...	71,851,862
2008	...	70,413,665	...	...	...	70,413,665
2009	...	65,855,185	...	...	...	65,855,185

• **LIFE INSURANCE IN FORCE** ($000 omitted)

Year	Whole Life	Term	Credit	Group	Industrial	Total
2007	...	528,135,828	930,000	...	...	529,065,828
2008	...	536,175,956	...	...	...	536,175,956
2009	...	537,282,214	...	...	...	537,282,214

PRINCIPAL LIFE INSURANCE CO

711 High Street
Des Moines, Iowa 50392-2300
Tel: 515-247-5111

AMB#: 006150
Began Business: 09/02/1879
Agency Off: Nick Cecere

Best's Financial Strength Rating: A+ g
FSC: XV

• **NET PREMIUMS AND DEPOSITS** ($000 omitted)

Year	Individual Life	Individual & Group Annuities	Group Life & A&H	Credit Life & A&H	Individual A&H	Total
2007	1,338,724	21,466,287	2,967,882	...	159,893	25,932,786
2008	1,259,927	21,185,623	2,797,128	...	172,560	25,415,238
2009	1,114,826	11,812,554	2,626,601	...	181,540	15,735,521

• **NET OPERATING GAIN** ($000 omitted)

Year	Individual Life	Individual & Group Annuities	Group Life & A&H	Credit Life & A&H	Individual A&H	Total
2007	-21,055	430,650	85,090	...	16,189	686,488
2008	-37,194	340,426	135,913	...	29,656	651,333
2009	-12,228	399,643	121,667	...	25,786	608,723

• **COMPARATIVE FINANCIALS** ($000 omitted)

Year	Assets	Capital & Surplus	Net Invest Income	Benefits Paid	Realized Cap Gains	Policyholder Dividends	Contract Lns (% of assets)
2007	135,714,882	3,697,486	3,461,070	6,306,310	-146,331	291,589	0.6
2008	115,411,350	4,810,232	3,550,851	6,287,671	-567,988	250,303	0.8
2009	118,786,258	4,588,745	3,210,475	6,051,300	-566,670	228,610	0.7

• **ORDINARY LIFE STATISTICS**

Year	Av. Ord. Policy Issued ($)	Av. Ord. Policy In Force ($)	Avg. Prem ($/M)	1st Yr Prem/ Total Prem	Ord. Lapse Ratio
2007	698,889	188,818	12.40	11.5	5.1
2008	730,651	207,874	12.35	13.7	5.8
2009	612,116	223,031	10.81	9.0	5.9

• **NEW LIFE BUSINESS ISSUED** ($000 omitted)

Year	Whole Life	Term	Credit	Group	Industrial	Total
2007	7,945,528	6,090,269	...	16,197,961	...	30,233,758
2008	9,301,992	7,013,436	...	9,511,792	...	25,827,220
2009	5,328,109	8,202,707	...	12,895,399	...	26,426,215

• **LIFE INSURANCE IN FORCE** ($000 omitted)

Year	Whole Life	Term	Credit	Group	Industrial	Total
2007	85,579,101	27,628,564	...	125,250,231	...	238,457,896
2008	89,436,723	31,865,895	...	121,105,069	...	242,407,687
2009	86,960,926	39,319,090	...	109,772,227	...	236,052,243

PROFESSIONAL INS COMPANY

One Sun Life Executive Park
Wellesley Hills, Massachusetts 02481
Tel: 860-737-6833

AMB#: 006950
Began Business: 09/09/1937
Agency Off: None

Best's Financial Strength Rating: A
FSC: VI

• **NET PREMIUMS AND DEPOSITS** ($000 omitted)

Year	Individual Life	Individual & Group Annuities	Group Life & A&H	Credit Life & A&H	Individual A&H	Total
2007	5,168	14	...	...	60,170	65,352
2008	2,911	11	...	...	66,925	69,847
2009	3,909	12	...	...	67,570	71,490

• **NET OPERATING GAIN** ($000 omitted)

Year	Individual Life	Individual & Group Annuities	Group Life & A&H	Credit Life & A&H	Individual A&H	Total
2007	842	45	...	...	-2,598	-1,710
2008	143	28	...	...	-1,108	-937
2009	-238	3	...	...	-50	-286

• **COMPARATIVE FINANCIALS** ($000 omitted)

Year	Assets	Capital & Surplus	Net Invest Income	Benefits Paid	Realized Cap Gains	Policyholder Dividends	Contract Lns (% of assets)
2007	97,315	30,395	4,491	38,731	-52	...	5.1
2008	102,186	32,179	5,038	43,418	-2,671	...	5.1
2009	111,215	33,632	4,335	46,090	325	...	4.6

• **ORDINARY LIFE STATISTICS**

Year	Av. Ord. Policy Issued ($)	Av. Ord. Policy In Force ($)	Avg. Prem ($/M)	1st Yr Prem/ Total Prem	Ord. Lapse Ratio
2007	...	...	...	...	...
2008	...	...	...	...	...
2009	...	...	...	...	...

• **NEW LIFE BUSINESS ISSUED** ($000 omitted)

Year	Whole Life	Term	Credit	Group	Industrial	Total
2007	...	120,144	...	...	...	120,144
2008	...	100,392	...	...	...	100,392
2009	...	100,511	...	...	...	100,511

• **LIFE INSURANCE IN FORCE** ($000 omitted)

Year	Whole Life	Term	Credit	Group	Industrial	Total
2007	76,717	474,950	...	...	...	551,667
2008	75,132	429,210	...	...	...	504,342
2009	78,580	406,928	...	...	...	485,508

PROFESSIONAL LIFE & CASUALTY

20 North Wacker Drive, Ste. 3110
Chicago, Illinois 60606
Tel: 312-220-0655

AMB#: 006952
Began Business: 09/24/1957
Agency Off: None

Best's Financial Strength Rating: C+
FSC: V

• **NET PREMIUMS AND DEPOSITS** ($000 omitted)

Year	Individual Life	Individual & Group Annuities	Group Life & A&H	Credit Life & A&H	Individual A&H	Total
2007	89	3,008	...	...	...	3,097
2008	93	4,133	...	...	...	4,226
2009	77	7,110	...	...	...	7,188

• **NET OPERATING GAIN** ($000 omitted)

Year	Individual Life	Individual & Group Annuities	Group Life & A&H	Credit Life & A&H	Individual A&H	Total
2007	139	2,285	...	...	...	2,424
2008	141	2,460	...	...	...	2,601
2009	88	3,197	...	...	...	3,285

• **COMPARATIVE FINANCIALS** ($000 omitted)

Year	Assets	Capital & Surplus	Net Invest Income	Benefits Paid	Realized Cap Gains	Policyholder Dividends	Contract Lns (% of assets)
2007	69,745	14,063	5,006	3,103	-2,243	47	0.1
2008	65,466	12,410	4,968	4,149	-4,899	41	0.1
2009	81,817	11,342	6,512	5,565	-811	46	0.1

• **ORDINARY LIFE STATISTICS**

Year	Av. Ord. Policy Issued ($)	Av. Ord. Policy In Force ($)	Avg. Prem ($/M)	1st Yr Prem/ Total Prem	Ord. Lapse Ratio
2007	...	...	...	...	...
2008	...	...	...	...	...
2009	...	...	...	...	...

• **NEW LIFE BUSINESS ISSUED** ($000 omitted)

Year	Whole Life	Term	Credit	Group	Industrial	Total
2007	150	...	...	...	...	150
2008	...	...	...	...	...	...
2009	15	...	...	...	...	15

• **LIFE INSURANCE IN FORCE** ($000 omitted)

Year	Whole Life	Term	Credit	Group	Industrial	Total
2007	2,617	2,975	...	...	...	5,592
2008	2,549	2,503	...	...	...	5,052
2009	2,378	2,120	...	...	...	4,498

PROTECTIVE LIFE & ANNUITY INS

2801 Highway 280 South
Birmingham, Alabama 35223
Tel: 205-268-1000

AMB#: 008860
Began Business: 12/08/1978
Agency Off: Carolyn Johnson

Best's Financial Strength Rating: A+ g
FSC: XV

• NET PREMIUMS AND DEPOSITS ($000 omitted)

Year	Individual Life	Individual & Group Annuities	Group Life & A&H	Credit Life & A&H	Individual A&H	Total
2007	14,888	55,452	6,585	1,338	113	78,377
2008	13,356	143,156	5,724	1,384	91	163,710
2009	14,009	165,607	5,207	935	98	185,855

• NET OPERATING GAIN ($000 omitted)

Year	Individual Life	Individual & Group Annuities	Group Life & A&H	Credit Life & A&H	Individual A&H	Total
2007	-2,002	9,587	86	461	-194	8,772
2008	7,868	-5,450	2,767	458	-95	5,702
2009	8,933	1,547	2,644	445	118	13,603

• COMPARATIVE FINANCIALS ($000 omitted)

Year	Assets	Capital & Surplus	Net Invest Income	Benefits Paid	Realized Cap Gains	Policyholder Dividends	Contract Lns (% of assets)
2007	620,997	37,998	33,594	38,481	...	95	8.1
2008	754,487	44,233	37,241	45,197	...	92	6.5
2009	927,370	78,664	47,800	61,222	-186	88	5.2

• ORDINARY LIFE STATISTICS

Year	Av. Ord. Policy Issued ($)	Av. Ord. Policy In Force ($)	Avg. Prem ($/M)	1st Yr Prem/ Total Prem	Ord. Lapse Ratio
2007	522,390	71,567	4.73	22.6	4.1
2008	473,546	74,901	4.59	16.4	4.0
2009	456,987	78,207	4.72	20.3	3.8

• NEW LIFE BUSINESS ISSUED ($000 omitted)

Year	Whole Life	Term	Credit	Group	Industrial	Total
2007	23,859	558,084	33,535	...	...	615,478
2008	14,195	338,123	33,013	...	...	385,331
2009	10,113	274,133	25,301	...	...	309,547

• LIFE INSURANCE IN FORCE ($000 omitted)

Year	Whole Life	Term	Credit	Group	Industrial	Total
2007	2,602,856	5,192,037	94,705	1,615,095	...	9,504,693
2008	2,474,045	5,303,795	79,157	1,487,757	...	9,344,754
2009	2,338,646	5,375,812	66,116	1,384,842	...	9,165,417

PROTECTIVE LIFE INSURANCE NY

300 Brookhollow Road
Melville, New York 11749
Tel: 205-268-1000

AMB#: 060340
Began Business: 08/31/2000
Agency Off: None

Best's Financial Strength Rating: A
FSC: VIII

• NET PREMIUMS AND DEPOSITS ($000 omitted)

Year	Individual Life	Individual & Group Annuities	Group Life & A&H	Credit Life & A&H	Individual A&H	Total
2007	564	7,054	...	...	...	7,618
2008	1,728	980	...	...	...	2,708
2009	1,756	3,687	...	...	...	5,443

• NET OPERATING GAIN ($000 omitted)

Year	Individual Life	Individual & Group Annuities	Group Life & A&H	Credit Life & A&H	Individual A&H	Total
2007	-794	1,418	...	...	...	2,280
2008	1,282	-2,697	...	...	...	732
2009	158	2,356	...	...	...	2,399

• COMPARATIVE FINANCIALS ($000 omitted)

Year	Assets	Capital & Surplus	Net Invest Income	Benefits Paid	Realized Cap Gains	Policyholder Dividends	Contract Lns (% of assets)
2007	1,119,494	127,527	62,499	127,840	...	...	0.0
2008	833,324	99,784	44,550	151,192	-7,321	...	0.0
2009	719,205	100,236	31,078	71,469	-6,217	...	...

• ORDINARY LIFE STATISTICS

Year	Av. Ord. Policy Issued ($)	Av. Ord. Policy In Force ($)	Avg. Prem ($/M)	1st Yr Prem/ Total Prem	Ord. Lapse Ratio
2007	...	...	...	...	...
2008	...	...	...	...	...
2009	...	...	...	...	...

• NEW LIFE BUSINESS ISSUED ($000 omitted)

Year	Whole Life	Term	Credit	Group	Industrial	Total
2007	464	7,443	...	...	...	7,907
2008	933	100	...	...	...	1,033
2009	300	...	...	...	...	300

• LIFE INSURANCE IN FORCE ($000 omitted)

Year	Whole Life	Term	Credit	Group	Industrial	Total
2007	14,201	6,158,121	...	...	...	6,172,322
2008	14,296	5,873,063	...	...	...	5,887,359
2009	13,740	5,619,815	...	...	...	5,633,554

PROTECTIVE LIFE INS CO

2801 Highway 280 South
Birmingham, Alabama 35223
Tel: 205-268-1000

AMB#: 006962
Began Business: 09/01/1907
Agency Off: Carolyn Johnson

Best's Financial Strength Rating: A+ g
FSC: XV

• NET PREMIUMS AND DEPOSITS ($000 omitted)

Year	Individual Life	Individual & Group Annuities	Group Life & A&H	Credit Life & A&H	Individual A&H	Total
2007	-38,324	2,596,107	-9,245	10,609	27,949	2,587,098
2008	467,600	4,998,184	7,124	1,617	26,680	5,501,204
2009	586,736	2,422,335	6,167	-3,224	24,214	3,036,227

• NET OPERATING GAIN ($000 omitted)

Year	Individual Life	Individual & Group Annuities	Group Life & A&H	Credit Life & A&H	Individual A&H	Total
2007	301,491	38,751	280	-540	-966	350,486
2008	115,058	-158,412	374	7,166	-3,725	-92,125
2009	267,095	409,758	-770	3,688	-5,499	704,822

• COMPARATIVE FINANCIALS ($000 omitted)

Year	Assets	Capital & Surplus	Net Invest Income	Benefits Paid	Realized Cap Gains	Policyholder Dividends	Contract Lns (% of assets)
2007	25,800,880	1,796,945	1,078,389	1,818,504	431	30,590	2.9
2008	25,929,543	1,767,703	1,065,162	2,047,585	-208,267	31,194	2.8
2009	26,654,688	2,616,531	1,105,208	1,940,035	-154,898	31,477	2.7

• ORDINARY LIFE STATISTICS

Year	Av. Ord. Policy Issued ($)	Av. Ord. Policy In Force ($)	Avg. Prem ($/M)	1st Yr Prem/ Total Prem	Ord. Lapse Ratio
2007	363,063	225,107	3.68	11.8	5.1
2008	366,493	294,916	2.63	9.5	5.3
2009	372,001	297,577	3.03	8.4	4.4

• NEW LIFE BUSINESS ISSUED ($000 omitted)

Year	Whole Life	Term	Credit	Group	Industrial	Total
2007	16,000,483	500,734	10,135,698	485,236	...	27,122,151
2008	13,730,101	408,098	8,093,496	402,939	...	22,634,634
2009	13,808,149	365,818	6,087,634	363,092	...	20,624,692

• LIFE INSURANCE IN FORCE ($000 omitted)

Year	Whole Life	Term	Credit	Group	Industrial	Total
2007	185,706,819	282,986,706	3,972,049	1,652,145	...	474,317,719
2008	187,292,126	400,809,513	3,537,589	2,256,988	...	593,896,216
2009	190,524,235	376,764,824	2,920,898	2,482,351	...	572,692,307

PROVIDENT AMERICAN LIFE & HLTH

11200 Lakeline Blvd., Suite 100
Austin, Texas 78717
Tel: 512-451-2224

AMB#: 006932
Began Business: 09/30/1949
Agency Off: None

Best's Financial Strength Rating: B++
FSC: V

• NET PREMIUMS AND DEPOSITS ($000 omitted)

Year	Individual Life	Individual & Group Annuities	Group Life & A&H	Credit Life & A&H	Individual A&H	Total
2007	594	...	335	...	18,699	19,628
2008	1,685	...	72	...	41,733	43,490
2009	1,320	...	82	...	39,226	40,628

• NET OPERATING GAIN ($000 omitted)

Year	Individual Life	Individual & Group Annuities	Group Life & A&H	Credit Life & A&H	Individual A&H	Total
2007	-86	...	-22	...	-1,558	-1,666
2008	-313	...	68	...	-2,728	-2,974
2009	-101	...	74	...	-2,445	-2,472

• COMPARATIVE FINANCIALS ($000 omitted)

Year	Assets	Capital & Surplus	Net Invest Income	Benefits Paid	Realized Cap Gains	Policyholder Dividends	Contract Lns (% of assets)
2007	10,588	3,097	267	12,364	...	...	...
2008	16,944	7,295	441	29,493	...	...	...
2009	19,393	12,166	222	30,542	...	...	0.0

• ORDINARY LIFE STATISTICS

Year	Av. Ord. Policy Issued ($)	Av. Ord. Policy In Force ($)	Avg. Prem ($/M)	1st Yr Prem/ Total Prem	Ord. Lapse Ratio
2007	...	...	...	...	...
2008	...	...	...	...	...
2009	...	...	...	...	...

• NEW LIFE BUSINESS ISSUED ($000 omitted)

Year	Whole Life	Term	Credit	Group	Industrial	Total
2007	10,083	...	...	372	...	10,455
2008	9,279	...	...	...	...	9,279
2009	5,460	...	...	...	...	5,460

• LIFE INSURANCE IN FORCE ($000 omitted)

Year	Whole Life	Term	Credit	Group	Industrial	Total
2007	10,692	...	...	5,072	...	15,764
2008	15,424	...	...	...	...	15,424
2009	16,851	...	...	3,029	...	19,879

PROVIDENT LIFE AND ACCIDENT

1 Fountain Square
Chattanooga, Tennessee 37402-1330
Tel: 423-294-1011

AMB#: 006968
Began Business: 05/24/1887
Agency Off: Stephen Meahl

Best's Financial Strength Rating: A- g **FSC:** XIV

• NET PREMIUMS AND DEPOSITS ($000 omitted)

Year	Individual Life	Individual & Group Annuities	Group Life & A&H	Credit Life & A&H	Individual A&H	Total
2007	217,686	9,825	63,919	1	528,741	820,172
2008	206,284	10,156	41,788	1	572,118	830,348
2009	217,056	4,269	40,059	1	605,448	866,832

• NET OPERATING GAIN ($000 omitted)

Year	Individual Life	Individual & Group Annuities	Group Life & A&H	Credit Life & A&H	Individual A&H	Total
2007	-7,988	3,990	4,594	-13	-6,529	-5,947
2008	42,188	8,905	20,551	-4	53,629	125,267
2009	52,883	7,523	9,958	-3	56,705	127,066

• COMPARATIVE FINANCIALS ($000 omitted)

Year	Assets	Capital & Surplus	Net Invest Income	Benefits Paid	Realized Cap Gains	Policyholder Dividends	Contract Lns (% of assets)
2007	7,735,411	435,070	545,677	404,872	-11,890	...	1.0
2008	7,741,375	428,410	501,904	404,978	-7,045	...	1.0
2009	8,004,252	567,078	502,905	417,704	-13,811	...	1.1

• ORDINARY LIFE STATISTICS

Year	Av. Ord. Policy Issued ($)	Av. Ord. Policy In Force ($)	Avg. Prem ($/M)	1st Yr Prem/ Total Prem	Ord. Lapse Ratio
2007	24,020	30,703	9.35	16.0	15.3
2008	24,543	29,850	9.22	10.1	13.8
2009	22,040	28,756	9.17	10.6	11.8

• NEW LIFE BUSINESS ISSUED ($000 omitted)

Year	Whole Life	Term	Credit	Group	Industrial	Total
2007	5,263,610	541,244	...	725	...	5,805,579
2008	2,864,866	433,238	...	250	...	3,298,354
2009	4,835,221	426,525	...	180	...	5,261,926

• LIFE INSURANCE IN FORCE ($000 omitted)

Year	Whole Life	Term	Credit	Group	Industrial	Total
2007	27,144,444	7,371,195	153	8,261,480	...	42,777,272
2008	25,897,264	6,156,056	142	7,364,920	...	39,418,382
2009	27,162,765	5,800,998	119	7,016,068	...	39,979,951

PROVIDENT LIFE AND CASUALTY

1 Fountain Square
Chattanooga, Tennessee 37402-1330
Tel: 423-294-1011

AMB#: 006969
Began Business: 01/01/1952
Agency Off: Stephen Meahl

Best's Financial Strength Rating: A- g **FSC:** XIV

• NET PREMIUMS AND DEPOSITS ($000 omitted)

Year	Individual Life	Individual & Group Annuities	Group Life & A&H	Credit Life & A&H	Individual A&H	Total
2007	2,552	221	973	...	75,512	79,258
2008	3,547	685	774	...	79,119	84,125
2009	3,860	...	2,803	...	79,962	86,625

• NET OPERATING GAIN ($000 omitted)

Year	Individual Life	Individual & Group Annuities	Group Life & A&H	Credit Life & A&H	Individual A&H	Total
2007	40	31	657	...	15,706	16,433
2008	201	22	2,669	...	19,713	22,605
2009	163	18	2,425	...	3,864	6,470

• COMPARATIVE FINANCIALS ($000 omitted)

Year	Assets	Capital & Surplus	Net Invest Income	Benefits Paid	Realized Cap Gains	Policyholder Dividends	Contract Lns (% of assets)
2007	685,522	99,046	43,161	74,806	-18	...	0.0
2008	701,112	121,082	44,307	71,811	-34	...	0.0
2009	722,010	130,227	46,712	69,329	-401	...	0.0

• ORDINARY LIFE STATISTICS

Year	Av. Ord. Policy Issued ($)	Av. Ord. Policy In Force ($)	Avg. Prem ($/M)	1st Yr Prem/ Total Prem	Ord. Lapse Ratio
2007	...	...	...	...	...
2008	...	...	...	...	...
2009	...	...	...	...	...

• NEW LIFE BUSINESS ISSUED ($000 omitted)

Year	Whole Life	Term	Credit	Group	Industrial	Total
2007	121,466	3,743	...	...	...	125,209
2008	153,664	2,519	...	...	...	156,183
2009	...	...	...	...	...	...

• LIFE INSURANCE IN FORCE ($000 omitted)

Year	Whole Life	Term	Credit	Group	Industrial	Total
2007	379,530	11,027	...	196,121	...	586,678
2008	476,339	11,946	...	135,856	...	624,141
2009	394,825	10,362	...	130,233	...	535,420

PRUCO LIFE INS CO

213 Washington Street, 9th Floor
Newark, New Jersey 07102-2992
Tel: 877-301-1212

AMB#: 008240
Began Business: 12/27/1971
Agency Off: Clifford E. Kirsch

Best's Financial Strength Rating: A+ g **FSC:** XV

• NET PREMIUMS AND DEPOSITS ($000 omitted)

Year	Individual Life	Individual & Group Annuities	Group Life & A&H	Credit Life & A&H	Individual A&H	Total
2007	753,109	2,407,425	...	...	...	3,160,534
2008	841,978	2,464,547	...	...	...	3,306,525
2009	798,901	4,230,531	...	...	...	5,029,431

• NET OPERATING GAIN ($000 omitted)

Year	Individual Life	Individual & Group Annuities	Group Life & A&H	Credit Life & A&H	Individual A&H	Total
2007	-10,630	63,816	...	...	...	57,456
2008	3,194	-526,388	...	...	...	-533,563
2009	26,895	109,374	...	...	...	172,185

• COMPARATIVE FINANCIALS ($000 omitted)

Year	Assets	Capital & Surplus	Net Invest Income	Benefits Paid	Realized Cap Gains	Policyholder Dividends	Contract Lns (% of assets)
2007	27,253,774	772,860	283,987	1,982,697	3,171	...	2.9
2008	22,061,367	600,640	286,207	1,874,289	-32,626	...	3.8
2009	29,252,495	874,836	366,501	1,605,825	-65,813	...	2.9

• ORDINARY LIFE STATISTICS

Year	Av. Ord. Policy Issued ($)	Av. Ord. Policy In Force ($)	Avg. Prem ($/M)	1st Yr Prem/ Total Prem	Ord. Lapse Ratio
2007	661,876	329,683	4.58	29.0	4.3
2008	658,400	363,515	4.49	25.7	5.3
2009	657,076	397,261	4.27	28.0	5.0

• NEW LIFE BUSINESS ISSUED ($000 omitted)

Year	Whole Life	Term	Credit	Group	Industrial	Total
2007	7,626,816	72,259,668	...	...	...	79,886,484
2008	7,071,197	66,210,682	...	...	...	73,281,879
2009	8,338,223	75,005,934	...	...	...	83,344,157

• LIFE INSURANCE IN FORCE ($000 omitted)

Year	Whole Life	Term	Credit	Group	Industrial	Total
2007	77,271,823	226,955,905	...	...	...	304,227,728
2008	78,679,477	277,934,234	...	...	...	356,613,711
2009	82,893,394	333,625,662	...	...	...	416,519,057

PRUCO LIFE INSURANCE CO OF NJ

213 Washington Street, 9th Floor
Newark, New Jersey 07102-2992
Tel: 973-802-6000

AMB#: 009371
Began Business: 12/27/1982
Agency Off: Clifford E. Kirsch

Best's Financial Strength Rating: A+ g **FSC:** XV

• NET PREMIUMS AND DEPOSITS ($000 omitted)

Year	Individual Life	Individual & Group Annuities	Group Life & A&H	Credit Life & A&H	Individual A&H	Total
2007	230,332	186,391	...	...	...	416,723
2008	237,712	259,127	...	...	...	496,839
2009	237,446	446,172	...	...	...	683,618

• NET OPERATING GAIN ($000 omitted)

Year	Individual Life	Individual & Group Annuities	Group Life & A&H	Credit Life & A&H	Individual A&H	Total
2007	-21,882	4,682	...	...	...	-7,030
2008	-9,013	-10,849	...	...	...	-18,864
2009	-40	686	...	...	...	2,461

• COMPARATIVE FINANCIALS ($000 omitted)

Year	Assets	Capital & Surplus	Net Invest Income	Benefits Paid	Realized Cap Gains	Policyholder Dividends	Contract Lns (% of assets)
2007	4,209,847	130,360	65,794	244,964	-502	...	4.0
2008	3,667,799	112,456	67,645	191,424	-3,376	...	4.6
2009	4,801,456	153,406	72,069	167,715	-6,283	...	3.5

• ORDINARY LIFE STATISTICS

Year	Av. Ord. Policy Issued ($)	Av. Ord. Policy In Force ($)	Avg. Prem ($/M)	1st Yr Prem/ Total Prem	Ord. Lapse Ratio
2007	737,578	348,387	4.73	39.8	3.9
2008	720,953	380,200	4.55	12.5	4.7
2009	664,467	402,076	4.35	10.1	3.9

• NEW LIFE BUSINESS ISSUED ($000 omitted)

Year	Whole Life	Term	Credit	Group	Industrial	Total
2007	2,534,780	16,201,925	...	...	...	18,736,705
2008	671,955	14,760,038	...	...	...	15,431,993
2009	401,664	10,425,831	...	...	...	10,827,496

• LIFE INSURANCE IN FORCE ($000 omitted)

Year	Whole Life	Term	Credit	Group	Industrial	Total
2007	14,531,190	64,085,749	...	...	...	78,616,939
2008	14,014,481	74,994,497	...	...	...	89,008,978
2009	14,295,148	81,105,316	...	...	...	95,400,465

PRUDENTIAL ANNUITIES LIFE ASSR

P.O. Box 883
Shelton, Connecticut 06484-0883
Tel: 800-628-6039

AMB#: 008715
Began Business: 05/25/1988
Agency Off: Wade A. Dokken

Best's Financial Strength Rating: A+ g **FSC:** XV

• NET PREMIUMS AND DEPOSITS ($000 omitted)

Year	Individual Life	Individual & Group Annuities	Group Life & A&H	Credit Life & A&H	Individual A&H	Total
2007	1,681	8,313,728	...	...	...	8,315,409
2008	1,357	7,542,417	...	...	...	7,543,774
2009	906	11,608,310	...	...	...	11,609,216

• NET OPERATING GAIN ($000 omitted)

Year	Individual Life	Individual & Group Annuities	Group Life & A&H	Credit Life & A&H	Individual A&H	Total
2007	646	115,133	...	...	...	104,977
2008	651	-314,617	...	...	...	-321,317
2009	-672	305,412	...	0	...	309,815

• COMPARATIVE FINANCIALS ($000 omitted)

Year	Assets	Capital & Surplus	Net Invest Income	Benefits Paid	Realized Cap Gains	Policyholder Dividends	Contract Lns (% of assets)
2007	43,236,057	438,349	-15,911	4,683,442	1,022	...	0.0
2008	35,015,040	633,365	34,101	4,541,773	-1,322	...	0.0
2009	49,615,991	880,978	139,737	3,935,510	-43,215	...	0.0

• ORDINARY LIFE STATISTICS

Year	Av. Ord. Policy Issued ($)	Av. Ord. Policy In Force ($)	Avg. Prem ($/M)	1st Yr Prem/ Total Prem	Ord. Lapse Ratio
2007	...	...	...	...	...
2008	...	...	...	...	...
2009	...	...	...	...	...

• NEW LIFE BUSINESS ISSUED ($000 omitted)

Year	Whole Life	Term	Credit	Group	Industrial	Total
2007	...	...	...	...	...	...
2008	...	...	...	...	...	...
2009	...	...	...	...	...	...

• LIFE INSURANCE IN FORCE ($000 omitted)

Year	Whole Life	Term	Credit	Group	Industrial	Total
2007	797,869	...	...	...	...	797,869
2008	699,750	...	...	...	...	699,750
2009	659,790	...	...	...	...	659,790

PRUDENTIAL INS CO OF AMERICA

751 Broad Street, 23rd Floor
Newark, New Jersey 07102
Tel: 973-802-6000

AMB#: 006974
Began Business: 10/13/1875
Agency Off: None

Best's Financial Strength Rating: A+ g **FSC:** XV

• NET PREMIUMS AND DEPOSITS ($000 omitted)

Year	Individual Life	Individual & Group Annuities	Group Life & A&H	Credit Life & A&H	Individual A&H	Total
2007	3,095,018	15,866,429	4,894,394	-23	135,429	23,991,247
2008	2,864,009	15,827,570	4,217,365	-3	146,823	23,055,764
2009	3,060,259	15,624,956	4,696,981	-7	155,806	23,537,995

• NET OPERATING GAIN ($000 omitted)

Year	Individual Life	Individual & Group Annuities	Group Life & A&H	Credit Life & A&H	Individual A&H	Total
2007	159,254	677,778	178,337	907	-43,610	1,024,458
2008	503,123	-426,543	222,983	363	-64,642	497,770
2009	561,804	393,719	151,428	-19	-82,787	2,424,181

• COMPARATIVE FINANCIALS ($000 omitted)

Year	Assets	Capital & Surplus	Net Invest Income	Benefits Paid	Realized Cap Gains	Policyholder Dividends	Contract Lns (% of assets)
2007	252,761,435	6,980,795	7,592,965	22,309,558	249,835	769,598	2.7
2008	237,497,815	6,432,375	7,363,724	20,047,564	-1,305,583	1,130,110	2.9
2009	225,787,699	10,041,654	8,357,871	19,333,157	-1,323,576	544,271	3.1

• ORDINARY LIFE STATISTICS

Year	Av. Ord. Policy Issued ($)	Av. Ord. Policy In Force ($)	Avg. Prem ($/M)	1st Yr Prem/ Total Prem	Ord. Lapse Ratio
2007	46,718	72,188	8.85	0.2	5.6
2008	50,831	80,719	8.72	0.1	6.7
2009	58,638	88,576	7.41	0.1	5.8

• NEW LIFE BUSINESS ISSUED ($000 omitted)

Year	Whole Life	Term	Credit	Group	Industrial	Total
2007	348,780	41,455	10,200	39,180,867	...	39,581,302
2008	203,675	38,381	5,234	63,804,240	...	64,051,530
2009	223,159	30,159	1,985	110,695,401	...	110,950,704

• LIFE INSURANCE IN FORCE ($000 omitted)

Year	Whole Life	Term	Credit	Group	Industrial	Total
2007	251,615,864	397,051,837	15,771	1,548,117,895	3,152,830	2,199,954,197
2008	241,117,323	453,324,081	9,373	1,555,407,072	3,134,185	2,252,992,034
2009	236,339,444	495,479,785	5,047	1,678,718,814	3,074,260	2,413,617,350

PRUDENTIAL RETIREMENT INS&ANN

213 Washington Street, 9th Floor
Newark, New Jersey 07102-2992
Tel: 215-761-1000

AMB#: 009144
Began Business: 10/01/1981
Agency Off: None

Best's Financial Strength Rating: A+ g **FSC:** XV

• NET PREMIUMS AND DEPOSITS ($000 omitted)

Year	Individual Life	Individual & Group Annuities	Group Life & A&H	Credit Life & A&H	Individual A&H	Total
2007	...	2,730,509	...	...	...	2,730,509
2008	...	3,428,003	...	...	...	3,428,003
2009	...	3,333,882	...	...	...	3,333,882

• NET OPERATING GAIN ($000 omitted)

Year	Individual Life	Individual & Group Annuities	Group Life & A&H	Credit Life & A&H	Individual A&H	Total
2007	...	118,143	...	...	...	100,669
2008	...	137,753	...	...	...	120,141
2009	...	207,739	...	...	...	191,056

• COMPARATIVE FINANCIALS ($000 omitted)

Year	Assets	Capital & Surplus	Net Invest Income	Benefits Paid	Realized Cap Gains	Policyholder Dividends	Contract Lns (% of assets)
2007	61,437,059	945,615	936,760	1,138,321	17,342	...	...
2008	51,851,791	1,208,403	1,025,408	1,120,437	-132,615	...	...
2009	59,982,602	1,166,402	1,076,719	1,070,760	-84,011	...	...

• ORDINARY LIFE STATISTICS

Year	Av. Ord. Policy Issued ($)	Av. Ord. Policy In Force ($)	Avg. Prem ($/M)	1st Yr Prem/ Total Prem	Ord. Lapse Ratio
2007	...	...	...	...	...
2008	...	...	...	...	...
2009	...	...	...	...	...

• NEW LIFE BUSINESS ISSUED ($000 omitted)

Year	Whole Life	Term	Credit	Group	Industrial	Total
2007	...	...	...	...	...	...
2008	...	...	...	...	...	...
2009	...	...	...	...	...	...

• LIFE INSURANCE IN FORCE ($000 omitted)

Year	Whole Life	Term	Credit	Group	Industrial	Total
2007	...	...	...	...	...	...
2008	...	...	...	...	...	...
2009	...	...	...	...	...	...

PYRAMID LIFE INSURANCE COMPANY

P.O. Box 958465
Lake Mary, Florida 32795-8465
Tel: 407-995-8001

AMB#: 006977
Began Business: 08/10/1914
Agency Off: Glenn W. Parker

Best's Financial Strength Rating: B++g **FSC:** IX

• NET PREMIUMS AND DEPOSITS ($000 omitted)

Year	Individual Life	Individual & Group Annuities	Group Life & A&H	Credit Life & A&H	Individual A&H	Total
2007	7,961	705	...	...	903,430	912,095
2008	7,851	104	...	...	1,008,286	1,016,241
2009	-36,746	-13,667	...	...	1,113,865	1,063,452

• NET OPERATING GAIN ($000 omitted)

Year	Individual Life	Individual & Group Annuities	Group Life & A&H	Credit Life & A&H	Individual A&H	Total
2007	2,111	310	-1	...	8,524	10,945
2008	1,536	739	-1	...	18,668	20,942
2009	-1,424	-30	0	...	33,256	31,803

• COMPARATIVE FINANCIALS ($000 omitted)

Year	Assets	Capital & Surplus	Net Invest Income	Benefits Paid	Realized Cap Gains	Policyholder Dividends	Contract Lns (% of assets)
2007	462,013	150,491	19,927	761,024	...	49	0.4
2008	460,978	178,520	16,126	825,410	-4,408	23	0.4
2009	369,314	179,546	16,992	900,125	-7,434	...	0.0

• ORDINARY LIFE STATISTICS

Year	Av. Ord. Policy Issued ($)	Av. Ord. Policy In Force ($)	Avg. Prem ($/M)	1st Yr Prem/ Total Prem	Ord. Lapse Ratio
2007	...	...	...	...	...
2008	...	...	...	...	...
2009	...	...	...	...	...

• NEW LIFE BUSINESS ISSUED ($000 omitted)

Year	Whole Life	Term	Credit	Group	Industrial	Total
2007	37,256	15,470	...	...	...	52,726
2008	66,400	12,560	...	...	...	78,960
2009	45	...	...	...	...	45

• LIFE INSURANCE IN FORCE ($000 omitted)

Year	Whole Life	Term	Credit	Group	Industrial	Total
2007	326,555	163,416	...	...	...	489,971
2008	357,735	159,674	...	...	...	517,409
2009	290,903	147,011	...	...	...	437,914

REASSURE AMERICA LIFE INS CO

175 King Street
Armonk, New York 10504-1606
Tel: 877-794-7773

AMB#: 007207
Began Business: 12/01/1956
Agency Off: None

Best's Financial Strength Rating: A g
FSC: XV

• **NET PREMIUMS AND DEPOSITS ($000 omitted)**

Year	Individual Life	Individual & Group Annuities	Group Life & A&H	Credit Life & A&H	Individual A&H	Total
2007	420,462	428,061	5,561	...	1,052	855,137
2008	431,817	342,658	4,676	...	1,428	780,579
2009	357,430	283,804	4,189	...	1,263	646,686

• **NET OPERATING GAIN ($000 omitted)**

Year	Individual Life	Individual & Group Annuities	Group Life & A&H	Credit Life & A&H	Individual A&H	Total
2007	172,387	8,032	2,080	...	868	183,367
2008	204,619	-57,417	5,371	...	856	153,428
2009	340,281	-80,642	4,123	...	896	264,659

• **COMPARATIVE FINANCIALS ($000 omitted)**

Year	Assets	Capital & Surplus	Net Invest Income	Benefits Paid	Realized Cap Gains	Policyholder Dividends	Contract Lns (% of assets)
2007	18,276,975	496,100	1,040,528	942,977	-15,491	15,483	16.4
2008	16,470,295	520,396	979,796	966,988	-203,626	13,384	18.9
2009	16,106,982	647,931	913,724	877,817	-180,685	12,819	20.1

• **ORDINARY LIFE STATISTICS**

Year	Av. Ord. Policy Issued ($)	Av. Ord. Policy In Force ($)	Avg. Prem ($/M)	1st Yr Prem/ Total Prem	Ord. Lapse Ratio
2007	204,701	132,411	3.29	0.4	7.0
2008	264,976	130,362	4.03	0.3	8.1
2009	192,054	128,637	4.10	0.2	8.3

• **NEW LIFE BUSINESS ISSUED ($000 omitted)**

Year	Whole Life	Term	Credit	Group	Industrial	Total
2007	91,769	64,418	...	...	...	156,187
2008	118,485	47,920	...	...	...	166,405
2009	84,285	39,782	...	...	...	124,067

• **LIFE INSURANCE IN FORCE ($000 omitted)**

Year	Whole Life	Term	Credit	Group	Industrial	Total
2007	53,569,814	279,617,217	...	2,533,632	5,972	335,726,635
2008	53,205,209	257,544,824	...	2,287,612	5,808	313,043,453
2009	53,511,058	233,577,552	...	2,062,540	5,626	289,156,776

RELIABLE LIFE INSURANCE CO

12115 Lackland Road
St. Louis, Missouri 63146-4003
Tel: 314-819-4300

AMB#: 006986
Began Business: 01/22/1912
Agency Off: Richard J. Miller

Best's Financial Strength Rating: A- r
FSC: IX

• **NET PREMIUMS AND DEPOSITS ($000 omitted)**

Year	Individual Life	Individual & Group Annuities	Group Life & A&H	Credit Life & A&H	Individual A&H	Total
2007	106,353	14	31	...	6,794	113,192
2008	105,459	14	26	...	6,757	112,255
2009	-11,466	5	-38	...	2,228	-9,271

• **NET OPERATING GAIN ($000 omitted)**

Year	Individual Life	Individual & Group Annuities	Group Life & A&H	Credit Life & A&H	Individual A&H	Total
2007	15,285	158	36	...	31	15,511
2008	12,239	84	17	...	218	12,557
2009	14,416	-159	-11	...	-536	13,711

• **COMPARATIVE FINANCIALS ($000 omitted)**

Year	Assets	Capital & Surplus	Net Invest Income	Benefits Paid	Realized Cap Gains	Policyholder Dividends	Contract Lns (% of assets)
2007	730,596	58,301	39,902	56,551	-396	5	7.7
2008	741,847	56,363	40,128	57,037	-2,282	5	7.8
2009	21,877	10,656	18,075	9,430	-3,324	2	...

• **ORDINARY LIFE STATISTICS**

Year	Av. Ord. Policy Issued ($)	Av. Ord. Policy In Force ($)	Avg. Prem ($/M)	1st Yr Prem/ Total Prem	Ord. Lapse Ratio
2007	...	...	...	...	...
2008	...	...	...	...	...
2009	...	...	...	...	...

• **NEW LIFE BUSINESS ISSUED ($000 omitted)**

Year	Whole Life	Term	Credit	Group	Industrial	Total
2007	271,427	254,271	...	...	...	525,698
2008	235,189	186,268	...	...	...	421,457
2009	332,720	221,022	...	...	...	553,742

• **LIFE INSURANCE IN FORCE ($000 omitted)**

Year	Whole Life	Term	Credit	Group	Industrial	Total
2007	3,263,935	1,910,032	...	354	207,263	5,381,584
2008	3,172,746	1,884,583	...	129	199,261	5,256,719
2009	3,187,525	1,892,884	...	122	191,551	5,272,082

REGENCE LIFE AND HEALTH INS CO

100 Southwest Market Street
Portland, Oregon 97201
Tel: 503-721-7161

AMB#: 009345
Began Business: 07/01/1966
Agency Off: None

Best's Financial Strength Rating: A-
FSC: X

• **NET PREMIUMS AND DEPOSITS ($000 omitted)**

Year	Individual Life	Individual & Group Annuities	Group Life & A&H	Credit Life & A&H	Individual A&H	Total
2007	63	...	39,603	...	2,681	42,347
2008	54	186	41,497	...	3,137	44,874
2009	54	371	39,902	...	4,940	45,267

• **NET OPERATING GAIN ($000 omitted)**

Year	Individual Life	Individual & Group Annuities	Group Life & A&H	Credit Life & A&H	Individual A&H	Total
2007	-174	...	3,451	...	1,020	4,296
2008	-43	-92	2,455	...	424	2,744
2009	129	-275	2,858	...	863	3,575

• **COMPARATIVE FINANCIALS ($000 omitted)**

Year	Assets	Capital & Surplus	Net Invest Income	Benefits Paid	Realized Cap Gains	Policyholder Dividends	Contract Lns (% of assets)
2007	84,937	37,811	3,030	25,075	123	...	...
2008	81,579	37,548	2,900	26,131	-1,941	...	...
2009	89,200	42,749	2,595	25,948	-821	...	...

• **ORDINARY LIFE STATISTICS**

Year	Av. Ord. Policy Issued ($)	Av. Ord. Policy In Force ($)	Avg. Prem ($/M)	1st Yr Prem/ Total Prem	Ord. Lapse Ratio
2007	...	...	...	...	...
2008	...	...	...	...	...
2009	...	...	...	...	...

• **NEW LIFE BUSINESS ISSUED ($000 omitted)**

Year	Whole Life	Term	Credit	Group	Industrial	Total
2007	208	...	...	1,925,694	...	1,925,902
2008	35	...	...	421,792	...	421,827
2009	21	...	...	1,361,911	...	1,361,932

• **LIFE INSURANCE IN FORCE ($000 omitted)**

Year	Whole Life	Term	Credit	Group	Industrial	Total
2007	1,480	...	...	8,964,213	...	8,965,693
2008	1,182	...	...	9,753,656	...	9,754,838
2009	1,028	...	...	9,715,295	...	9,716,323

RELIANCE STANDARD LIFE INS CO

2001 Market Street, Suite 1500
Philadelphia, Pennsylvania 19103
Tel: 267-256-3500

AMB#: 006990
Began Business: 04/15/1907
Agency Off: Christopher A. Fazzini

Best's Financial Strength Rating: A g
FSC: X

• **NET PREMIUMS AND DEPOSITS ($000 omitted)**

Year	Individual Life	Individual & Group Annuities	Group Life & A&H	Credit Life & A&H	Individual A&H	Total
2007	276	115,937	887,585	...	148	1,003,947
2008	939	252,548	985,443	...	169	1,239,100
2009	647	266,723	959,197	...	158	1,226,725

• **NET OPERATING GAIN ($000 omitted)**

Year	Individual Life	Individual & Group Annuities	Group Life & A&H	Credit Life & A&H	Individual A&H	Total
2007	-259	14,495	39,246	...	6	54,756
2008	300	17,765	59,603	...	-41	78,243
2009	-581	16,797	92,178	...	15	105,237

• **COMPARATIVE FINANCIALS ($000 omitted)**

Year	Assets	Capital & Surplus	Net Invest Income	Benefits Paid	Realized Cap Gains	Policyholder Dividends	Contract Lns (% of assets)
2007	3,240,629	457,548	168,432	779,256	-463	...	0.0
2008	3,508,998	511,718	175,297	804,769	-54,958	...	0.0
2009	3,821,310	541,009	190,405	797,466	-134,298	...	0.0

• **ORDINARY LIFE STATISTICS**

Year	Av. Ord. Policy Issued ($)	Av. Ord. Policy In Force ($)	Avg. Prem ($/M)	1st Yr Prem/ Total Prem	Ord. Lapse Ratio
2007	...	...	...	...	...
2008	...	...	...	...	...
2009	...	...	...	...	...

• **NEW LIFE BUSINESS ISSUED ($000 omitted)**

Year	Whole Life	Term	Credit	Group	Industrial	Total
2007	3,181	...	...	28,436,664	...	28,439,845
2008	4,894	...	...	26,585,833	...	26,590,727
2009	5,966	...	...	28,133,017	...	28,138,983

• **LIFE INSURANCE IN FORCE ($000 omitted)**

Year	Whole Life	Term	Credit	Group	Industrial	Total
2007	382,055	278,356	...	147,867,694	5,053	148,533,158
2008	363,682	256,558	...	153,082,178	4,908	153,707,326
2009	345,709	235,760	...	143,373,364	4,731	143,959,564

RELIASTAR LIFE INSURANCE CO

5780 Powers Ferry Road, NW
Atlanta, Georgia 30327-4390
Tel: 612-372-5432

AMB#: 006846
Began Business: 09/15/1885
Agency Off: None

Best's Financial Strength Rating: A g
FSC: XIV

• NET PREMIUMS AND DEPOSITS ($000 omitted)

Year	Individual Life	Individual & Group Annuities	Group Life & A&H	Credit Life & A&H	Individual A&H	Total
2007	-193,674	1,732,147	1,327,667	-56	3,044	2,869,128
2008	569,518	1,516,498	912,288	-26	4,015	3,002,293
2009	-200,488	1,587,561	-34,593	0	3,646	1,356,126

• NET OPERATING GAIN ($000 omitted)

Year	Individual Life	Individual & Group Annuities	Group Life & A&H	Credit Life & A&H	Individual A&H	Total
2007	13,862	64,961	70,447	176	446	149,893
2008	14,291	29,116	-13,061	-56	188	43,401
2009	72,937	37,727	-6,013	287	-431	104,562

• COMPARATIVE FINANCIALS ($000 omitted)

Year	Assets	Capital & Surplus	Net Invest Income	Benefits Paid	Realized Cap Gains	Policyholder Dividends	Contract Lns (% of assets)
2007	22,384,571	2,325,927	958,240	3,515,634	3,156	18,500	3.1
2008	20,473,880	2,079,413	880,893	3,046,833	-168,608	17,316	3.4
2009	20,673,305	2,190,310	866,422	1,567,886	-197,058	14,704	3.3

• ORDINARY LIFE STATISTICS

Year	Av. Ord. Policy Issued ($)	Av. Ord. Policy In Force ($)	Avg. Prem ($/M)	1st Yr Prem/ Total Prem	Ord. Lapse Ratio
2007	...	...	...	...	...
2008	...	...	...	...	...
2009	...	...	...	...	...

• NEW LIFE BUSINESS ISSUED ($000 omitted)

Year	Whole Life	Term	Credit	Group	Industrial	Total
2007	3,087,217	47,172,719	...	35,454,257	...	85,714,193
2008	2,535,384	86,809,594	...	43,867,490	...	133,212,468
2009	1,554,158	87,648,340	...	26,176,065	...	115,378,562

• LIFE INSURANCE IN FORCE ($000 omitted)

Year	Whole Life	Term	Credit	Group	Industrial	Total
2007	53,838,450	154,269,655	5,965	435,609,861	...	643,723,931
2008	52,519,684	236,285,350	2,549	358,101,518	...	646,909,101
2009	50,275,695	310,047,173	989	253,089,810	...	613,413,667

RESERVE NATIONAL INS CO

6100 Northwest Grand Boulevard
Oklahoma City, Oklahoma 73118
Tel: 405-848-7931

AMB#: 006998
Began Business: 09/19/1956
Agency Off: Kempner Joe Cole, Jr.

Best's Financial Strength Rating: A-
FSC: VI

• NET PREMIUMS AND DEPOSITS ($000 omitted)

Year	Individual Life	Individual & Group Annuities	Group Life & A&H	Credit Life & A&H	Individual A&H	Total
2007	728	8	11,130	...	117,526	129,392
2008	734	8	8,605	...	119,234	128,581
2009	747	8	6,637	...	120,621	128,013

• NET OPERATING GAIN ($000 omitted)

Year	Individual Life	Individual & Group Annuities	Group Life & A&H	Credit Life & A&H	Individual A&H	Total
2007	257	9	1,391	...	5,414	7,071
2008	260	13	662	...	4,379	5,314
2009	268	12	1,224	...	2,065	3,569

• COMPARATIVE FINANCIALS ($000 omitted)

Year	Assets	Capital & Surplus	Net Invest Income	Benefits Paid	Realized Cap Gains	Policyholder Dividends	Contract Lns (% of assets)
2007	108,314	44,623	5,358	84,297	-714	22	0.1
2008	104,133	45,153	5,739	85,698	757	19	0.1
2009	107,905	47,308	5,635	86,473	-860	21	0.1

• ORDINARY LIFE STATISTICS

Year	Av. Ord. Policy Issued ($)	Av. Ord. Policy In Force ($)	Avg. Prem ($/M)	1st Yr Prem/ Total Prem	Ord. Lapse Ratio
2007	...	...	...	...	...
2008	...	...	...	...	...
2009	...	...	...	...	...

• NEW LIFE BUSINESS ISSUED ($000 omitted)

Year	Whole Life	Term	Credit	Group	Industrial	Total
2007	1,258	...	...	...	...	1,258
2008	1,323	...	...	...	...	1,323
2009	1,615	...	...	...	...	1,615

• LIFE INSURANCE IN FORCE ($000 omitted)

Year	Whole Life	Term	Credit	Group	Industrial	Total
2007	14,105	10,844	...	...	...	24,949
2008	13,584	9,887	...	...	...	23,471
2009	13,430	8,540	...	...	...	21,970

RELIASTAR LIFE INS CO OF NY

5780 Powers Ferry Road, NW
Atlanta, Georgia 30327-4390
Tel: 516-682-8700

AMB#: 006157
Began Business: 09/18/1917
Agency Off: None

Best's Financial Strength Rating: A g
FSC: XIV

• NET PREMIUMS AND DEPOSITS ($000 omitted)

Year	Individual Life	Individual & Group Annuities	Group Life & A&H	Credit Life & A&H	Individual A&H	Total
2007	117,105	354,898	40,409	...	11,001	523,413
2008	80,300	467,820	40,735	...	6,150	595,005
2009	97,902	232,641	28,430	...	6,374	365,347

• NET OPERATING GAIN ($000 omitted)

Year	Individual Life	Individual & Group Annuities	Group Life & A&H	Credit Life & A&H	Individual A&H	Total
2007	-10,727	9,194	-1,716	...	-4,684	-7,933
2008	16,681	-200,409	-8,236	...	-2,612	-194,827
2009	34,863	86,444	749	...	-2,970	119,083

• COMPARATIVE FINANCIALS ($000 omitted)

Year	Assets	Capital & Surplus	Net Invest Income	Benefits Paid	Realized Cap Gains	Policyholder Dividends	Contract Lns (% of assets)
2007	3,251,995	286,950	117,963	303,121	-4,839	915	3.1
2008	3,207,471	221,964	112,999	310,605	-2,080	844	3.2
2009	3,209,428	322,591	103,303	490,293	-23,837	937	3.4

• ORDINARY LIFE STATISTICS

Year	Av. Ord. Policy Issued ($)	Av. Ord. Policy In Force ($)	Avg. Prem ($/M)	1st Yr Prem/ Total Prem	Ord. Lapse Ratio
2007	588,763	103,932	5.81	16.7	5.9
2008	701,374	132,217	4.81	17.2	5.4
2009	682,816	158,380	4.21	15.8	4.8

• NEW LIFE BUSINESS ISSUED ($000 omitted)

Year	Whole Life	Term	Credit	Group	Industrial	Total
2007	589,070	6,379,526	...	189,538	...	7,158,134
2008	479,457	10,464,083	...	488,479	...	11,432,019
2009	410,335	10,032,647	...	86,926	...	10,529,909

• LIFE INSURANCE IN FORCE ($000 omitted)

Year	Whole Life	Term	Credit	Group	Industrial	Total
2007	14,451,378	20,992,187	...	9,091,871	...	44,535,436
2008	14,016,145	29,929,213	...	8,523,647	...	52,469,005
2009	13,534,666	38,058,004	...	4,293,052	...	55,885,723

RGA REINSURANCE COMPANY

1370 Timberlake Manor Parkway
Chesterfield, Missouri 63017-6039
Tel: 636-736-7300

AMB#: 009080
Began Business: 10/01/1982
Agency Off: None

Best's Financial Strength Rating: A+ g
FSC: XIII

• NET PREMIUMS AND DEPOSITS ($000 omitted)

Year	Individual Life	Individual & Group Annuities	Group Life & A&H	Credit Life & A&H	Individual A&H	Total
2007	1,675,780	2,533,316	28,707	-3,732	54,928	4,288,999
2008	1,195,399	1,710,222	31,730	9,195	106,907	3,053,453
2009	1,619,079	697,916	21,866	6,312	144,419	2,489,593

• NET OPERATING GAIN ($000 omitted)

Year	Individual Life	Individual & Group Annuities	Group Life & A&H	Credit Life & A&H	Individual A&H	Total
2007	-54,611	1,633	-4,152	-64	-3,499	-33,477
2008	43,154	-17,031	-10,666	-1,510	-12,860	43,724
2009	61,031	53,163	-2,239	-273	50	146,595

• COMPARATIVE FINANCIALS ($000 omitted)

Year	Assets	Capital & Surplus	Net Invest Income	Benefits Paid	Realized Cap Gains	Policyholder Dividends	Contract Lns (% of assets)
2007	11,821,492	1,184,134	374,946	2,562,393	-8,058	9,023	9.0
2008	13,008,986	1,103,753	410,621	3,127,264	-85,474	9,397	8.4
2009	14,893,433	1,416,550	456,845	1,995,533	-83,406	6,752	7.6

• ORDINARY LIFE STATISTICS

Year	Av. Ord. Policy Issued ($)	Av. Ord. Policy In Force ($)	Avg. Prem ($/M)	1st Yr Prem/ Total Prem	Ord. Lapse Ratio
2007	...	47,935	2.52	...	13.9
2008	...	53,235	2.58	...	7.6
2009	...	53,016	2.53	...	6.8

• NEW LIFE BUSINESS ISSUED ($000 omitted)

Year	Whole Life	Term	Credit	Group	Industrial	Total
2007	...	...	...	...	...	...
2008	...	...	...	...	...	...
2009	...	...	...	...	...	...

• LIFE INSURANCE IN FORCE ($000 omitted)

Year	Whole Life	Term	Credit	Group	Industrial	Total
2007	15,204,523	1,380,476,852	7,222,165	43,837,859	...	1,446,741,399
2008	15,503,792	1,407,515,146	10,276,648	27,139,604	...	1,460,435,190
2009	54,445,066	1,444,351,418	5,380,053	18,832,281	...	1,523,008,818

RIVERSOURCE LIFE INS CO OF NY

227 Ameriprise Financial Center
Minneapolis, Minnesota 55474
Tel: 518-869-8613

AMB#: 008345
Began Business: 10/25/1972
Agency Off: Maureen A. Buckley

Best's Financial Strength Rating: A+ g **FSC:** XV

• NET PREMIUMS AND DEPOSITS ($000 omitted)

Year	Individual Life	Individual & Group Annuities	Group Life & A&H	Credit Life & A&H	Individual A&H	Total
2007	60,997	613,410	...	...	17,663	692,070
2008	64,148	507,112	...	...	16,304	587,564
2009	58,751	515,295	0	...	16,349	590,395

• NET OPERATING GAIN ($000 omitted)

Year	Individual Life	Individual & Group Annuities	Group Life & A&H	Credit Life & A&H	Individual A&H	Total
2007	5,692	20,412	2,126	...	5,696	33,925
2008	7,727	-40,946	833	...	-3,731	-36,116
2009	14,400	79,537	-1,105	...	7,664	101,034

• COMPARATIVE FINANCIALS ($000 omitted)

Year	Assets	Capital & Surplus	Net Invest Income	Benefits Paid	Realized Cap Gains	Policyholder Dividends	Contract Lns (% of assets)
2007	5,025,037	274,277	110,178	563,748	102	...	0.7
2008	4,197,067	215,625	94,667	481,679	2,071	...	0.9
2009	5,048,403	284,340	107,922	391,553	-14,845	...	0.7

• ORDINARY LIFE STATISTICS

Year	Av. Ord. Policy Issued ($)	Av. Ord. Policy In Force ($)	Avg. Prem ($/M)	1st Yr Prem/ Total Prem	Ord. Lapse Ratio
2007	607,937	167,717	6.54	17.0	5.0
2008	577,238	183,221	6.61	22.1	4.7
2009	526,906	194,292	6.22	16.7	4.8

• NEW LIFE BUSINESS ISSUED ($000 omitted)

Year	Whole Life	Term	Credit	Group	Industrial	Total
2007	676,091	569,571	...	21	...	1,245,683
2008	493,035	530,986	...	73	...	1,024,094
2009	274,745	399,695	...	...	...	674,440

• LIFE INSURANCE IN FORCE ($000 omitted)

Year	Whole Life	Term	Credit	Group	Industrial	Total
2007	6,169,722	4,097,265	...	63,087	...	10,330,074
2008	6,261,624	4,472,187	...	64,134	...	10,797,945
2009	6,087,194	4,740,299	...	61,728	...	10,889,220

RIVERSOURCE LIFE INS CO

227 Ameriprise Financial Center
Minneapolis, Minnesota 55474
Tel: 612-671-3131

AMB#: 006592
Began Business: 10/31/1957
Agency Off: Douglas Lennick

Best's Financial Strength Rating: A+ g **FSC:** XV

• NET PREMIUMS AND DEPOSITS ($000 omitted)

Year	Individual Life	Individual & Group Annuities	Group Life & A&H	Credit Life & A&H	Individual A&H	Total
2007	996,166	10,436,261	11,552	...	280,298	11,724,277
2008	961,091	8,626,382	7,144	...	256,991	9,851,609
2009	862,932	8,641,049	6,317	...	267,664	9,777,962

• NET OPERATING GAIN ($000 omitted)

Year	Individual Life	Individual & Group Annuities	Group Life & A&H	Credit Life & A&H	Individual A&H	Total
2007	179,726	279,534	14,241	...	49,342	522,844
2008	29,044	-1,317,759	41,482	...	57,426	-1,183,686
2009	193,962	1,502,770	-2,454	...	95,182	1,793,496

• COMPARATIVE FINANCIALS ($000 omitted)

Year	Assets	Capital & Surplus	Net Invest Income	Benefits Paid	Realized Cap Gains	Policyholder Dividends	Contract Lns (% of assets)
2007	79,870,147	2,820,441	1,432,693	9,323,821	31,904	...	0.8
2008	67,906,201	2,528,647	1,243,887	7,425,865	-223,489	...	1.0
2009	81,313,114	3,370,671	1,360,057	5,903,264	93,067	...	0.8

• ORDINARY LIFE STATISTICS

Year	Av. Ord. Policy Issued ($)	Av. Ord. Policy In Force ($)	Avg. Prem ($/M)	1st Yr Prem/ Total Prem	Ord. Lapse Ratio
2007	481,698	295,826	6.23	21.3	4.5
2008	486,051	306,101	5.95	20.2	6.1
2009	475,954	314,255	5.57	16.8	6.0

• NEW LIFE BUSINESS ISSUED ($000 omitted)

Year	Whole Life	Term	Credit	Group	Industrial	Total
2007	12,307,689	9,361,482	...	19	...	21,669,190
2008	6,994,058	9,945,779	...	...	...	16,939,837
2009	4,682,371	7,940,404	...	171	...	12,622,946

• LIFE INSURANCE IN FORCE ($000 omitted)

Year	Whole Life	Term	Credit	Group	Industrial	Total
2007	111,446,195	64,731,767	...	767,025	...	176,944,987
2008	109,717,070	71,038,031	...	738,731	...	181,493,832
2009	106,084,311	75,159,069	...	716,543	...	181,959,923

ROYAL NEIGHBORS OF AMERICA

230 Sixteenth Street
Rock Island, Illinois 61201
Tel: 800-627-4762

AMB#: 007010
Began Business: 03/21/1895
Agency Off: Chris T. Seistrup

Best's Financial Strength Rating: A- **FSC:** VIII

• NET PREMIUMS AND DEPOSITS ($000 omitted)

Year	Individual Life	Individual & Group Annuities	Group Life & A&H	Credit Life & A&H	Individual A&H	Total
2007	13,626	...	...	...	8,459	51,329
2008	20,508	...	...	...	8,415	58,030
2009	29,525	...	...	...	7,735	83,423

• NET OPERATING GAIN ($000 omitted)

Year	Individual Life	Individual & Group Annuities	Group Life & A&H	Credit Life & A&H	Individual A&H	Total
2007	19,791	1,952	...	...	-849	22,119
2008	10,954	200	...	...	-431	11,844
2009	4,119	-1,575	...	...	-1,257	2,365

• COMPARATIVE FINANCIALS ($000 omitted)

Year	Assets	Capital & Surplus	Net Invest Income	Benefits Paid	Realized Cap Gains	Policyholder Dividends	Contract Lns (% of assets)
2007	683,224	244,359	36,732	35,021	13,197	1,604	2.1
2008	671,601	213,503	36,727	38,627	-1,429	1,467	2.1
2009	719,165	221,546	36,398	31,227	-2,266	1,436	1.9

• ORDINARY LIFE STATISTICS

Year	Av. Ord. Policy Issued ($)	Av. Ord. Policy In Force ($)	Avg. Prem ($/M)	1st Yr Prem/ Total Prem	Ord. Lapse Ratio
2007	15,693	11,357	7.21	3.2	5.7
2008	33,038	12,435	9.75	32.8	6.3
2009	59,862	15,453	11.50	40.2	8.8

• NEW LIFE BUSINESS ISSUED ($000 omitted)

Year	Whole Life	Term	Credit	Group	Industrial	Total
2007	28,467	...	...	...	...	28,467
2008	341,047	...	...	...	...	341,047
2009	893,439	...	...	...	...	893,439

• LIFE INSURANCE IN FORCE ($000 omitted)

Year	Whole Life	Term	Credit	Group	Industrial	Total
2007	1,980,227	...	...	...	...	1,980,227
2008	2,183,517	...	...	...	...	2,183,517
2009	2,750,221	...	...	...	...	2,750,221

ROYAL STATE NATIONAL INS CO

819 South Beretania Street, Suite 100
Honolulu, Hawaii 96813
Tel: 808-539-1600

AMB#: 007012
Began Business: 08/14/1961
Agency Off: Lilia Yu-Lum

Best's Financial Strength Rating: B+ **FSC:** VI

• NET PREMIUMS AND DEPOSITS ($000 omitted)

Year	Individual Life	Individual & Group Annuities	Group Life & A&H	Credit Life & A&H	Individual A&H	Total
2007	553	...	5,036	...	271	5,860
2008	537	...	5,600	...	226	6,363
2009	514	...	5,438	...	71	6,023

• NET OPERATING GAIN ($000 omitted)

Year	Individual Life	Individual & Group Annuities	Group Life & A&H	Credit Life & A&H	Individual A&H	Total
2007	413	...	1,116	...	37	1,566
2008	64	...	-25	...	12	51
2009	115	...	757	...	-98	774

• COMPARATIVE FINANCIALS ($000 omitted)

Year	Assets	Capital & Surplus	Net Invest Income	Benefits Paid	Realized Cap Gains	Policyholder Dividends	Contract Lns (% of assets)
2007	48,679	29,271	2,002	3,761	131	17	0.4
2008	47,145	27,152	1,853	3,593	-504	9	0.4
2009	48,077	27,786	1,495	3,935	-133	11	0.5

• ORDINARY LIFE STATISTICS

Year	Av. Ord. Policy Issued ($)	Av. Ord. Policy In Force ($)	Avg. Prem ($/M)	1st Yr Prem/ Total Prem	Ord. Lapse Ratio
2007	...	...	...	...	...
2008	...	...	...	...	...
2009	...	...	...	...	...

• NEW LIFE BUSINESS ISSUED ($000 omitted)

Year	Whole Life	Term	Credit	Group	Industrial	Total
2007	749	...	...	...	...	749
2008	641	...	...	...	...	641
2009	689	...	...	...	...	689

• LIFE INSURANCE IN FORCE ($000 omitted)

Year	Whole Life	Term	Credit	Group	Industrial	Total
2007	16,864	7,510	...	507,561	...	531,935
2008	16,699	6,654	...	482,316	...	505,669
2009	16,846	5,755	...	466,747	...	489,348

S.USA LIFE INSURANCE COMPANY

P.O. Box 1050
Newark, New Jersey 07101
Tel: 877-725-4375

AMB#: 060110
Began Business: 07/14/1995
Agency Off: James Machovsky

Best's Financial Strength Rating: B+ g
FSC: VIII

• **NET PREMIUMS AND DEPOSITS** (\$000 omitted)

Year	Individual Life	Individual & Group Annuities	Group Life & A&H	Credit Life & A&H	Individual A&H	Total
2007	728	306	299	...	6	1,339
2008	757	104	247	...	7	1,115
2009	877	544	229	...	8	1,658

• **NET OPERATING GAIN** (\$000 omitted)

Year	Individual Life	Individual & Group Annuities	Group Life & A&H	Credit Life & A&H	Individual A&H	Total
2007	-1,539	2	-235	...	18	-1,754
2008	-2,344	3	-319	...	4	-2,655
2009	-1,340	1	-338	...	-146	-1,824

• **COMPARATIVE FINANCIALS** (\$000 omitted)

Year	Assets	Capital & Surplus	Net Invest Income	Benefits Paid	Realized Cap Gains	Policyholder Dividends	Contract Lns (% of assets)
2007	17,333	14,013	611	353	...	...	0.2
2008	16,053	11,364	493	810	...	...	0.4
2009	14,340	9,488	407	775	...	...	0.9

• **ORDINARY LIFE STATISTICS**

Year	Av. Ord. Policy Issued (\$)	Av. Ord. Policy In Force (\$)	Avg. Prem (\$/M)	1st Yr Prem/ Total Prem	Ord. Lapse Ratio
2007	...	...	...	...	...
2008	...	...	...	...	...
2009	...	...	...	...	...

• **NEW LIFE BUSINESS ISSUED** (\$000 omitted)

Year	Whole Life	Term	Credit	Group	Industrial	Total
2007	7,966	92,075	...	504	...	100,545
2008	4,290	113,982	...	4,982	...	123,254
2009	8,244	71,535	...	10,940	...	90,719

• **LIFE INSURANCE IN FORCE** (\$000 omitted)

Year	Whole Life	Term	Credit	Group	Industrial	Total
2007	19,876	156,494	...	19,686	...	196,056
2008	22,583	241,400	...	24,870	...	288,853
2009	23,582	287,348	...	32,782	...	343,713

SAGICOR LIFE INSURANCE COMPANY

4343 North Scottsdale Road, Suite 300
Scottsdale, Arizona 85251-3347
Tel: 480-425-5100

AMB#: 006057
Began Business: 04/05/1954
Agency Off: Bart F. Catmull

Best's Financial Strength Rating: A-
FSC: VI

• **NET PREMIUMS AND DEPOSITS** (\$000 omitted)

Year	Individual Life	Individual & Group Annuities	Group Life & A&H	Credit Life & A&H	Individual A&H	Total
2007	8,409	4,899	30	...	62	13,399
2008	25,100	11,539	45	...	44	36,729
2009	57,599	97,004	23	...	37	154,662

• **NET OPERATING GAIN** (\$000 omitted)

Year	Individual Life	Individual & Group Annuities	Group Life & A&H	Credit Life & A&H	Individual A&H	Total
2007	-3,498	-369	144	...	34	-3,689
2008	-12,010	-7,239	119	...	72	-19,058
2009	-15,164	-2,615	90	...	61	-17,628

• **COMPARATIVE FINANCIALS** (\$000 omitted)

Year	Assets	Capital & Surplus	Net Invest Income	Benefits Paid	Realized Cap Gains	Policyholder Dividends	Contract Lns (% of assets)
2007	527,926	35,142	16,679	35,229	165	150	6.5
2008	538,779	29,188	20,355	36,431	-2,168	143	6.1
2009	676,694	38,643	27,558	39,376	-6,132	144	4.6

• **ORDINARY LIFE STATISTICS**

Year	Av. Ord. Policy Issued (\$)	Av. Ord. Policy In Force (\$)	Avg. Prem (\$/M)	1st Yr Prem/ Total Prem	Ord. Lapse Ratio
2007	336,987	23,855	13.56	0.8	6.7
2008	240,594	28,100	21.51	63.8	8.2
2009	106,184	30,933	38.93	2.5	7.8

• **NEW LIFE BUSINESS ISSUED** (\$000 omitted)

Year	Whole Life	Term	Credit	Group	Industrial	Total
2007	35	52,872	...	5,179	...	58,086
2008	2,848	307,759	...	4,170	...	314,777
2009	19,787	269,245	...	2,239	...	291,271

• **LIFE INSURANCE IN FORCE** (\$000 omitted)

Year	Whole Life	Term	Credit	Group	Industrial	Total
2007	863,844	515,421	...	101,721	7,220	1,488,206
2008	1,142,720	414,612	...	85,510	6,826	1,649,668
2009	846,833	835,906	...	74,008	6,462	1,763,209

SAVINGS BANK LIFE INS CO OF MA

One Linscott Road
Woburn, Massachusetts 01801
Tel: 781-938-3500

AMB#: 006696
Began Business: 01/01/1992
Agency Off: William J. Gaffney, Jr.

Best's Financial Strength Rating: A+
FSC: VIII

• **NET PREMIUMS AND DEPOSITS** (\$000 omitted)

Year	Individual Life	Individual & Group Annuities	Group Life & A&H	Credit Life & A&H	Individual A&H	Total
2007	179,171	53,346	...	171	...	232,687
2008	168,702	33,052	...	124	...	201,878
2009	131,457	98,627	...	68	...	230,152

• **NET OPERATING GAIN** (\$000 omitted)

Year	Individual Life	Individual & Group Annuities	Group Life & A&H	Credit Life & A&H	Individual A&H	Total
2007	7,457	130	-304	-340	...	6,943
2008	-2,653	929	-347	-436	...	-2,507
2009	-12,930	1,125	-595	-420	...	-12,819

• **COMPARATIVE FINANCIALS** (\$000 omitted)

Year	Assets	Capital & Surplus	Net Invest Income	Benefits Paid	Realized Cap Gains	Policyholder Dividends	Contract Lns (% of assets)
2007	2,055,985	199,981	110,752	124,573	1,765	44,637	3.7
2008	2,130,313	160,892	109,978	137,684	-26,087	43,161	3.5
2009	2,203,667	162,938	107,409	139,054	4,312	48,467	3.5

• **ORDINARY LIFE STATISTICS**

Year	Av. Ord. Policy Issued (\$)	Av. Ord. Policy In Force (\$)	Avg. Prem (\$/M)	1st Yr Prem/ Total Prem	Ord. Lapse Ratio
2007	475,004	159,209	2.83	7.6	2.4
2008	472,199	173,749	2.66	7.3	2.3
2009	529,667	197,862	2.48	11.4	2.6

• **NEW LIFE BUSINESS ISSUED** (\$000 omitted)

Year	Whole Life	Term	Credit	Group	Industrial	Total
2007	103,346	9,280,352	1,781	...	...	9,385,479
2008	83,577	8,594,974	1,148	...	...	8,679,699
2009	78,098	16,142,414	397	...	...	16,220,909

• **LIFE INSURANCE IN FORCE** (\$000 omitted)

Year	Whole Life	Term	Credit	Group	Industrial	Total
2007	2,466,879	74,309,821	10,774	3,592	...	76,791,066
2008	2,447,924	80,457,103	8,305	3,249	...	82,916,581
2009	2,410,993	93,664,967	5,122	2,672	...	96,083,754

SBLI USA MUTUAL LIFE INS CO

460 West 34th Street, Suite 800
New York, New York 10001-2320
Tel: 212-356-0300

AMB#: 006821
Began Business: 01/01/2000
Agency Off: James Machovsky

Best's Financial Strength Rating: B+ g
FSC: VIII

• **NET PREMIUMS AND DEPOSITS** (\$000 omitted)

Year	Individual Life	Individual & Group Annuities	Group Life & A&H	Credit Life & A&H	Individual A&H	Total
2007	58,882	35,221	28,279	6	484	122,872
2008	56,778	30,493	26,736	5	475	114,487
2009	55,830	82,201	23,099	2	477	161,610

• **NET OPERATING GAIN** (\$000 omitted)

Year	Individual Life	Individual & Group Annuities	Group Life & A&H	Credit Life & A&H	Individual A&H	Total
2007	3,418	-1,822	3,231	1	134	4,962
2008	8,546	242	2,364	1	62	11,214
2009	9,633	432	9,610	2	517	20,195

• **COMPARATIVE FINANCIALS** (\$000 omitted)

Year	Assets	Capital & Surplus	Net Invest Income	Benefits Paid	Realized Cap Gains	Policyholder Dividends	Contract Lns (% of assets)
2007	1,526,361	129,484	83,008	93,642	-420	8,948	7.7
2008	1,486,061	122,816	79,944	97,459	-18,382	8,720	7.7
2009	1,502,754	113,065	75,913	109,452	-13,205	8,814	7.5

• **ORDINARY LIFE STATISTICS**

Year	Av. Ord. Policy Issued (\$)	Av. Ord. Policy In Force (\$)	Avg. Prem (\$/M)	1st Yr Prem/ Total Prem	Ord. Lapse Ratio
2007	98,681	24,386	9.86	4.2	5.1
2008	94,871	25,825	9.43	4.7	5.2
2009	79,437	26,915	9.34	4.9	5.2

• **NEW LIFE BUSINESS ISSUED** (\$000 omitted)

Year	Whole Life	Term	Credit	Group	Industrial	Total
2007	65,483	443,712	...	110,187	...	619,382
2008	75,213	453,880	...	65,279	...	594,372
2009	81,996	337,033	...	57,016	...	476,044

• **LIFE INSURANCE IN FORCE** (\$000 omitted)

Year	Whole Life	Term	Credit	Group	Industrial	Total
2007	3,212,539	3,514,929	895	9,012,099	...	15,740,462
2008	3,142,019	3,707,841	821	8,316,655	...	15,167,336
2009	3,058,106	3,785,135	455	8,078,216	...	14,921,912

SCOR GLOBAL LIFE RE INS CO TX

3900 Dallas Parkway
Plano, Texas 75093
Tel: 469-246-9500

AMB#: 060212
Began Business: 05/16/1977
Agency Off: None

Best's Financial Strength Rating: A- g **FSC:** XV

• NET PREMIUMS AND DEPOSITS ($000 omitted)

Year	Individual Life	Individual & Group Annuities	Group Life & A&H	Credit Life & A&H	Individual A&H	Total
2007	17,495	...	27,181	...	569	45,246
2008	29,908	...	-208	...	1,461	31,161
2009	13,917	...	12,575	...	719	27,211

• NET OPERATING GAIN ($000 omitted)

Year	Individual Life	Individual & Group Annuities	Group Life & A&H	Credit Life & A&H	Individual A&H	Total
2007	-15,127	...	10,444	...	-2,446	-7,129
2008	-16,633	...	11,794	...	-250	-5,089
2009	-17,714	...	8,935	...	-594	-9,373

• COMPARATIVE FINANCIALS ($000 omitted)

Year	Assets	Capital & Surplus	Net Invest Income	Benefits Paid	Realized Cap Gains	Policyholder Dividends	Contract Lns (% of assets)
2007	376,592	42,618	10,050	34,381	8	...	...
2008	314,839	41,531	10,400	45,084	-324	...	...
2009	320,955	19,891	5,290	29,236	82	...	...

• ORDINARY LIFE STATISTICS

Year	Av. Ord. Policy Issued ($)	Av. Ord. Policy In Force ($)	Avg. Prem ($/M)	1st Yr Prem/ Total Prem	Ord. Lapse Ratio
2007	...	30,466	2.13	...	5.7
2008	...	32,111	2.09	...	8.2
2009	...	32,777	2.54	...	9.9

• NEW LIFE BUSINESS ISSUED ($000 omitted)

Year	Whole Life	Term	Credit	Group	Industrial	Total
2007	...	...	...	...	...	...
2008	...	...	...	...	...	...
2009	...	...	...	...	...	...

• LIFE INSURANCE IN FORCE ($000 omitted)

Year	Whole Life	Term	Credit	Group	Industrial	Total
2007	46,699,233	86,727,148	...	8,782,722	...	142,209,103
2008	43,113,275	80,067,512	...	7,876,026	...	131,056,813
2009	38,999,485	72,427,616	...	6,751,264	...	118,178,365

SCOR GLOBAL LIFE US RE INS CO

3900 Dallas Parkway, Suite 200
Plano, Texas 75093
Tel: 469-246-9500

AMB#: 006555
Began Business: 04/04/1945
Agency Off: None

Best's Financial Strength Rating: A- g **FSC:** XV

• NET PREMIUMS AND DEPOSITS ($000 omitted)

Year	Individual Life	Individual & Group Annuities	Group Life & A&H	Credit Life & A&H	Individual A&H	Total
2007	54,843	22,902	67	...	779	78,592
2008	20,489	111,821	-600	...	834	132,544
2009	66,348	414,068	13,712	...	4,965	499,094

• NET OPERATING GAIN ($000 omitted)

Year	Individual Life	Individual & Group Annuities	Group Life & A&H	Credit Life & A&H	Individual A&H	Total
2007	773	25,614	-69	...	-364	25,954
2008	276	31,428	-3,746	...	676	28,634
2009	13,288	-51,931	1,229	...	-4,348	-41,763

• COMPARATIVE FINANCIALS ($000 omitted)

Year	Assets	Capital & Surplus	Net Invest Income	Benefits Paid	Realized Cap Gains	Policyholder Dividends	Contract Lns (% of assets)
2007	1,958,167	125,550	69,241	194,255	0	...	0.4
2008	2,011,116	162,991	64,658	175,077	-22,284	...	0.4
2009	2,307,874	126,158	59,565	206,986	-9,490	...	0.3

• ORDINARY LIFE STATISTICS

Year	Av. Ord. Policy Issued ($)	Av. Ord. Policy In Force ($)	Avg. Prem ($/M)	1st Yr Prem/ Total Prem	Ord. Lapse Ratio
2007	...	49,980	2.74	...	6.3
2008	...	48,617	2.17	...	5.0
2009	...	49,476	2.57	...	2.2

• NEW LIFE BUSINESS ISSUED ($000 omitted)

Year	Whole Life	Term	Credit	Group	Industrial	Total
2007	...	...	...	...	...	...
2008	...	...	...	...	...	...
2009	...	...	...	...	...	...

• LIFE INSURANCE IN FORCE ($000 omitted)

Year	Whole Life	Term	Credit	Group	Industrial	Total
2007	47,615,004	87,349,631	...	286	...	134,964,921
2008	49,223,379	91,414,848	...	286	...	140,638,513
2009	52,179,474	96,904,738	...	1,857	...	149,086,069

SCOR GLOBAL LIFE REINS CO AMER

70 Seaview Avenue
Stamford, Connecticut 06902-6040
Tel: 203-964-5200

AMB#: 060575
Began Business: 09/18/1963
Agency Off: None

Best's Financial Strength Rating: A- g **FSC:** XV

• NET PREMIUMS AND DEPOSITS ($000 omitted)

Year	Individual Life	Individual & Group Annuities	Group Life & A&H	Credit Life & A&H	Individual A&H	Total
2007	900	40	...	...	...	940
2008	5,570	...	...	...	...	5,570
2009	7,402	4	...	...	...	7,407

• NET OPERATING GAIN ($000 omitted)

Year	Individual Life	Individual & Group Annuities	Group Life & A&H	Credit Life & A&H	Individual A&H	Total
2007	-7,830	...	...	...	...	-4,869
2008	-19,040	...	...	...	...	-16,841
2009	-7,068	...	...	...	...	-5,384

• COMPARATIVE FINANCIALS ($000 omitted)

Year	Assets	Capital & Surplus	Net Invest Income	Benefits Paid	Realized Cap Gains	Policyholder Dividends	Contract Lns (% of assets)
2007	57,551	49,460	2,979	422	...	...	...
2008	55,522	32,909	2,750	2,762	-438	...	...
2009	65,130	31,947	2,615	4,218	64	...	...

• ORDINARY LIFE STATISTICS

Year	Av. Ord. Policy Issued ($)	Av. Ord. Policy In Force ($)	Avg. Prem ($/M)	1st Yr Prem/ Total Prem	Ord. Lapse Ratio
2007	...	...	...	...	...
2008	...	...	...	...	...
2009	...	...	...	...	...

• NEW LIFE BUSINESS ISSUED ($000 omitted)

Year	Whole Life	Term	Credit	Group	Industrial	Total
2007	...	...	...	...	...	...
2008	...	...	...	...	...	...
2009	...	...	...	...	...	...

• LIFE INSURANCE IN FORCE ($000 omitted)

Year	Whole Life	Term	Credit	Group	Industrial	Total
2007	2,654,863	1,472,421	...	...	...	4,127,284
2008	8,080,125	7,158,365	...	...	...	15,238,490
2009	10,075,198	7,851,032	...	...	...	17,926,230

SEARS LIFE INSURANCE COMPANY

3001 Meacham Boulevard, Suite 100
Fort Worth, Texas 76137
Tel: 800-316-5607

AMB#: 007170
Began Business: 05/04/1956
Agency Off: None

Best's Financial Strength Rating: A- **FSC:** VII

• NET PREMIUMS AND DEPOSITS ($000 omitted)

Year	Individual Life	Individual & Group Annuities	Group Life & A&H	Credit Life & A&H	Individual A&H	Total
2007	1,927	...	27,411	...	2,464	31,801
2008	1,682	...	27,627	...	2,636	31,944
2009	1,301	...	20,908	...	2,035	24,245

• NET OPERATING GAIN ($000 omitted)

Year	Individual Life	Individual & Group Annuities	Group Life & A&H	Credit Life & A&H	Individual A&H	Total
2007	-1,009	...	-1,665	...	-186	-2,860
2008	331	...	5,578	...	346	6,254
2009	50	...	6,435	...	596	7,080

• COMPARATIVE FINANCIALS ($000 omitted)

Year	Assets	Capital & Surplus	Net Invest Income	Benefits Paid	Realized Cap Gains	Policyholder Dividends	Contract Lns (% of assets)
2007	73,651	51,351	3,074	11,312	-89	...	...
2008	73,633	51,010	2,627	11,118	-1,576	...	...
2009	83,297	59,247	2,094	9,989	-430	...	...

• ORDINARY LIFE STATISTICS

Year	Av. Ord. Policy Issued ($)	Av. Ord. Policy In Force ($)	Avg. Prem ($/M)	1st Yr Prem/ Total Prem	Ord. Lapse Ratio
2007	...	...	...	...	...
2008	...	...	...	...	...
2009	...	...	...	...	...

• NEW LIFE BUSINESS ISSUED ($000 omitted)

Year	Whole Life	Term	Credit	Group	Industrial	Total
2007	...	164,075	...	796,765	...	960,840
2008	...	17,220	...	98,170	...	115,390
2009	...	...	...	...	...	...

• LIFE INSURANCE IN FORCE ($000 omitted)

Year	Whole Life	Term	Credit	Group	Industrial	Total
2007	...	377,210	...	1,813,095	...	2,190,305
2008	...	288,975	...	1,430,800	...	1,719,775
2009	...	225,270	...	1,117,031	...	1,342,301

SECURIAN LIFE INSURANCE CO

400 Robert Street North
St. Paul, Minnesota 55101-2098
Tel: 651-665-3500

AMB#: 009064
Began Business: 12/29/1981
Agency Off: Wilford J. Kavanaugh

Best's Financial Strength Rating: A+ g **FSC:** XIV

• NET PREMIUMS AND DEPOSITS ($000 omitted)

Year	Individual Life	Individual & Group Annuities	Group Life & A&H	Credit Life & A&H	Individual A&H	Total
2007	241	2	37,106	750	...	38,099
2008	232	189	38,403	1,874	...	40,698
2009	219	10	42,442	1,967	...	44,638

• NET OPERATING GAIN ($000 omitted)

Year	Individual Life	Individual & Group Annuities	Group Life & A&H	Credit Life & A&H	Individual A&H	Total
2007	233	40	2,204	456	...	2,933
2008	282	62	4,590	560	...	5,495
2009	-81	62	4,168	571	...	4,720

• COMPARATIVE FINANCIALS ($000 omitted)

Year	Assets	Capital & Surplus	Net Invest Income	Benefits Paid	Realized Cap Gains	Policyholder Dividends	Contract Lns (% of assets)
2007	141,543	118,950	6,757	26,183	-610	102	0.1
2008	142,911	121,967	7,167	28,449	-1,662	102	0.1
2009	149,667	126,512	7,210	34,967	-798	86	0.1

• ORDINARY LIFE STATISTICS

Year	Av. Ord. Policy Issued ($)	Av. Ord. Policy In Force ($)	Avg. Prem ($/M)	1st Yr Prem/ Total Prem	Ord. Lapse Ratio
2007	...	...	...	...	...
2008	...	...	...	...	...
2009	...	...	...	...	...

• NEW LIFE BUSINESS ISSUED ($000 omitted)

Year	Whole Life	Term	Credit	Group	Industrial	Total
2007	387	...	11,141	1,670,431	...	1,681,959
2008	287	...	16,299	295,208	...	311,794
2009	298	...	59,719	211,765	...	271,782

• LIFE INSURANCE IN FORCE ($000 omitted)

Year	Whole Life	Term	Credit	Group	Industrial	Total
2007	13,909	2,557	300,533	3,911,947	...	4,228,946
2008	13,661	2,267	276,872	4,086,364	...	4,379,164
2009	12,264	1,652	435,718	8,498,564	...	8,948,198

SECURITY BENEFIT LIFE INS CO

One Security Benefit Place
Topeka, Kansas 66636-0001
Tel: 785-438-3000

AMB#: 007025
Began Business: 02/22/1892
Agency Off: Kalman Bakk, Jr.

Best's Financial Strength Rating: B gu **FSC:** IX

• NET PREMIUMS AND DEPOSITS ($000 omitted)

Year	Individual Life	Individual & Group Annuities	Group Life & A&H	Credit Life & A&H	Individual A&H	Total
2007	9,455	1,643,798	5,608	...	3	1,658,864
2008	7,185	811,942	2,154	...	4	821,285
2009	5,824	514,123	-2	...	3	519,948

• NET OPERATING GAIN ($000 omitted)

Year	Individual Life	Individual & Group Annuities	Group Life & A&H	Credit Life & A&H	Individual A&H	Total
2007	1,436	30,581	-119	...	-52	31,846
2008	-409	-22,476	993	...	11	-21,880
2009	1,992	24,777	701	...	63	27,533

• COMPARATIVE FINANCIALS ($000 omitted)

Year	Assets	Capital & Surplus	Net Invest Income	Benefits Paid	Realized Cap Gains	Policyholder Dividends	Contract Lns (% of assets)
2007	12,341,315	602,362	268,911	1,673,962	-12,708	-5	0.8
2008	9,246,195	300,551	241,298	1,411,277	-295,528	0	1.1
2009	9,862,138	427,351	165,147	1,140,288	-48,632	0	0.9

• ORDINARY LIFE STATISTICS

Year	Av. Ord. Policy Issued ($)	Av. Ord. Policy In Force ($)	Avg. Prem ($/M)	1st Yr Prem/ Total Prem	Ord. Lapse Ratio
2007	...	...	...	...	...
2008	...	...	...	...	...
2009	...	...	...	...	...

• NEW LIFE BUSINESS ISSUED ($000 omitted)

Year	Whole Life	Term	Credit	Group	Industrial	Total
2007	3,449	59	...	...	...	3,508
2008	...	81	...	...	...	81
2009	3	69	...	...	...	72

• LIFE INSURANCE IN FORCE ($000 omitted)

Year	Whole Life	Term	Credit	Group	Industrial	Total
2007	3,174,101	704,159	...	571,081	...	4,449,341
2008	3,002,379	649,549	...	451,751	...	4,103,679
2009	2,873,528	590,891	...	481,581	...	3,946,000

SECURITY LIFE INS CO OF AMER

10901 Red Circle Drive
Minnetonka, Minnesota 55343-9137
Tel: 952-544-2121

AMB#: 007030
Began Business: 07/20/1956
Agency Off: Ted Williams

Best's Financial Strength Rating: B++u **FSC:** V

• NET PREMIUMS AND DEPOSITS ($000 omitted)

Year	Individual Life	Individual & Group Annuities	Group Life & A&H	Credit Life & A&H	Individual A&H	Total
2007	2,233	193	135,261	...	516	138,203
2008	2,207	268	161,826	...	472	164,773
2009	2,085	130	73,173	...	432	75,821

• NET OPERATING GAIN ($000 omitted)

Year	Individual Life	Individual & Group Annuities	Group Life & A&H	Credit Life & A&H	Individual A&H	Total
2007	-43	414	4,571	...	128	5,069
2008	74	338	3,112	...	148	3,671
2009	-24	227	2,987	...	195	3,385

• COMPARATIVE FINANCIALS ($000 omitted)

Year	Assets	Capital & Surplus	Net Invest Income	Benefits Paid	Realized Cap Gains	Policyholder Dividends	Contract Lns (% of assets)
2007	96,471	24,647	3,783	93,964	...	...	1.0
2008	93,961	25,276	3,634	115,267	-537	...	1.1
2009	79,206	24,450	3,252	49,946	-199	...	1.4

• ORDINARY LIFE STATISTICS

Year	Av. Ord. Policy Issued ($)	Av. Ord. Policy In Force ($)	Avg. Prem ($/M)	1st Yr Prem/ Total Prem	Ord. Lapse Ratio
2007	...	...	...	...	...
2008	...	...	...	...	...
2009	...	...	...	...	...

• NEW LIFE BUSINESS ISSUED ($000 omitted)

Year	Whole Life	Term	Credit	Group	Industrial	Total
2007	20	...	...	...	...	20
2008	...	...	...	...	...	...
2009	20	...	...	...	...	20

• LIFE INSURANCE IN FORCE ($000 omitted)

Year	Whole Life	Term	Credit	Group	Industrial	Total
2007	168,130	18,928	...	408,541	1,601	597,200
2008	154,652	18,926	...	399,451	1,558	574,587
2009	144,640	17,194	...	393,688	1,511	557,033

SECURITY LIFE OF DENVER INS CO

5780 Powers Ferry Road, NW
Atlanta, Georgia 30327-4390
Tel: 303-860-1290

AMB#: 007029
Began Business: 05/12/1950
Agency Off: None

Best's Financial Strength Rating: A g **FSC:** XIV

• NET PREMIUMS AND DEPOSITS ($000 omitted)

Year	Individual Life	Individual & Group Annuities	Group Life & A&H	Credit Life & A&H	Individual A&H	Total
2007	423,249	5,498,012	968	...	...	5,922,229
2008	558,549	3,412,027	247,017	...	...	4,217,593
2009	488,494	3,381,411	208,839	...	...	4,078,744

• NET OPERATING GAIN ($000 omitted)

Year	Individual Life	Individual & Group Annuities	Group Life & A&H	Credit Life & A&H	Individual A&H	Total
2007	57,828	-30,047	-456	...	...	27,325
2008	-63,672	285,252	1,176	...	11	221,194
2009	277,784	-65,428	9,243	...	137	221,748

• COMPARATIVE FINANCIALS ($000 omitted)

Year	Assets	Capital & Surplus	Net Invest Income	Benefits Paid	Realized Cap Gains	Policyholder Dividends	Contract Lns (% of assets)
2007	24,221,950	1,305,671	1,217,930	2,299,394	-7,101	8,761	5.6
2008	24,264,720	1,438,954	1,037,074	1,607,098	-183,629	2,597	5.7
2009	20,770,378	1,697,472	841,867	2,179,194	-198,013	2,196	6.2

• ORDINARY LIFE STATISTICS

Year	Av. Ord. Policy Issued ($)	Av. Ord. Policy In Force ($)	Avg. Prem ($/M)	1st Yr Prem/ Total Prem	Ord. Lapse Ratio
2007	1,204,661	100,713	3.51	26.8	0.8
2008	1,103,963	103,527	3.60	26.2	0.8
2009	793,811	101,441	3.61	17.1	1.1

• NEW LIFE BUSINESS ISSUED ($000 omitted)

Year	Whole Life	Term	Credit	Group	Industrial	Total
2007	7,040,745	500	...	...	...	7,041,245
2008	6,787,167	1,100	...	...	...	6,788,267
2009	4,565,292	1,500	...	...	...	4,566,792

• LIFE INSURANCE IN FORCE ($000 omitted)

Year	Whole Life	Term	Credit	Group	Industrial	Total
2007	67,316,199	585,605,496	...	76,841	174,272	653,172,808
2008	70,237,025	548,507,533	...	93,700	168,916	619,007,174
2009	68,537,074	509,413,265	...	89,816	163,962	578,204,116

SECURITY MUTUAL LIFE OF NY

P.O. Box 1625
Binghamton, New York 13902-1625
Tel: 607-723-3551

AMB#: 007034
Began Business: 01/03/1887
Agency Off: None

Best's Financial Strength Rating: A- **FSC:** VIII

• NET PREMIUMS AND DEPOSITS ($000 omitted)

Year	Individual Life	Individual & Group Annuities	Group Life & A&H	Credit Life & A&H	Individual A&H	Total
2007	168,174	67,611	19,701	1	23	255,510
2008	161,537	148,785	18,302	...	20	328,644
2009	149,859	206,929	17,925	...	20	374,733

• NET OPERATING GAIN ($000 omitted)

Year	Individual Life	Individual & Group Annuities	Group Life & A&H	Credit Life & A&H	Individual A&H	Total
2007	5,155	955	812	0	197	7,120
2008	4,792	-896	-2	-3	161	4,051
2009	4,714	-681	141	-4	128	4,298

• COMPARATIVE FINANCIALS ($000 omitted)

Year	Assets	Capital & Surplus	Net Invest Income	Benefits Paid	Realized Cap Gains	Policyholder Dividends	Contract Lns (% of assets)
2007	2,116,279	114,730	113,867	164,161	-1,403	23,490	9.9
2008	2,220,992	107,896	114,631	192,671	-12,835	22,372	9.9
2009	2,426,937	112,993	117,364	174,035	2,922	20,187	9.9

• ORDINARY LIFE STATISTICS

Year	Av. Ord. Policy Issued ($)	Av. Ord. Policy In Force ($)	Avg. Prem ($/M)	1st Yr Prem/ Total Prem	Ord. Lapse Ratio
2007	59,944	87,482	10.14	18.4	7.6
2008	53,264	83,397	10.03	18.0	7.4
2009	46,026	78,606	9.75	15.1	7.9

• NEW LIFE BUSINESS ISSUED ($000 omitted)

Year	Whole Life	Term	Credit	Group	Industrial	Total
2007	2,311,335	971,268	...	239,559	...	3,522,162
2008	2,302,752	968,323	...	592,190	...	3,863,265
2009	2,227,151	797,830	...	163,486	...	3,188,467

• LIFE INSURANCE IN FORCE ($000 omitted)

Year	Whole Life	Term	Credit	Group	Industrial	Total
2007	15,395,337	11,322,107	...	4,018,706	...	30,736,150
2008	16,120,119	11,397,260	...	2,630,835	...	30,148,214
2009	16,743,358	11,126,795	...	2,524,994	...	30,395,147

SENIOR AMERICAN LIFE INS CO

165 Veterans Way, Suite 300
Warminster, Pennsylvania 18974
Tel: 215-918-0515

AMB#: 060294
Began Business: 11/15/1962
Agency Off: James P. McDermott

Best's Financial Strength Rating: D g **FSC:** V

• NET PREMIUMS AND DEPOSITS ($000 omitted)

Year	Individual Life	Individual & Group Annuities	Group Life & A&H	Credit Life & A&H	Individual A&H	Total
2007	...	...	...	...	4,853	4,853
2008	...	...	...	...	4,545	4,545
2009	...	...	...	...	4,206	4,206

• NET OPERATING GAIN ($000 omitted)

Year	Individual Life	Individual & Group Annuities	Group Life & A&H	Credit Life & A&H	Individual A&H	Total
2007	...	...	...	...	-494	-494
2008	...	...	...	...	-353	-353
2009	...	...	...	...	-739	-739

• COMPARATIVE FINANCIALS ($000 omitted)

Year	Assets	Capital & Surplus	Net Invest Income	Benefits Paid	Realized Cap Gains	Policyholder Dividends	Contract Lns (% of assets)
2007	19,071	4,541	995	3,599	-25	...	...
2008	20,580	4,109	1,099	3,568	...	...	...
2009	21,433	3,142	1,366	4,848	...	...	...

• ORDINARY LIFE STATISTICS

Year	Av. Ord. Policy Issued ($)	Av. Ord. Policy In Force ($)	Avg. Prem ($/M)	1st Yr Prem/ Total Prem	Ord. Lapse Ratio
2007	...	...	...	...	...
2008	...	...	...	...	...
2009	...	...	...	...	...

• NEW LIFE BUSINESS ISSUED ($000 omitted)

Year	Whole Life	Term	Credit	Group	Industrial	Total
2007	...	...	...	...	...	...
2008	...	...	...	...	...	...
2009	...	...	...	...	...	...

• LIFE INSURANCE IN FORCE ($000 omitted)

Year	Whole Life	Term	Credit	Group	Industrial	Total
2007	...	...	...	...	...	...
2008	...	...	...	...	...	...
2009	...	...	...	...	...	...

SENTINEL AMERICAN LIFE INS CO

7 Hanover Square
New York, New York 10004-4025
Tel: 800-538-6203

AMB#: 007987
Began Business: 11/12/1952
Agency Off: None

Best's Financial Strength Rating: A **FSC:** V

• NET PREMIUMS AND DEPOSITS ($000 omitted)

Year	Individual Life	Individual & Group Annuities	Group Life & A&H	Credit Life & A&H	Individual A&H	Total
2007	74	1	...	...	...	75
2008	61	0	...	...	...	62
2009	56	0	...	...	...	56

• NET OPERATING GAIN ($000 omitted)

Year	Individual Life	Individual & Group Annuities	Group Life & A&H	Credit Life & A&H	Individual A&H	Total
2007	704	408	...	...	...	1,112
2008	375	137	...	...	...	513
2009	459	108	...	...	...	568

• COMPARATIVE FINANCIALS ($000 omitted)

Year	Assets	Capital & Surplus	Net Invest Income	Benefits Paid	Realized Cap Gains	Policyholder Dividends	Contract Lns (% of assets)
2007	46,876	16,882	2,637	1,900	48	...	0.3
2008	43,524	15,158	2,364	2,353	-634	...	0.3
2009	43,461	15,746	2,325	1,837	...	...	0.3

• ORDINARY LIFE STATISTICS

Year	Av. Ord. Policy Issued ($)	Av. Ord. Policy In Force ($)	Avg. Prem ($/M)	1st Yr Prem/ Total Prem	Ord. Lapse Ratio
2007	...	...	...	...	...
2008	...	...	...	...	...
2009	...	...	...	...	...

• NEW LIFE BUSINESS ISSUED ($000 omitted)

Year	Whole Life	Term	Credit	Group	Industrial	Total
2007	...	...	...	...	...	...
2008	...	...	...	...	...	...
2009	...	...	...	...	...	...

• LIFE INSURANCE IN FORCE ($000 omitted)

Year	Whole Life	Term	Credit	Group	Industrial	Total
2007	21,058	3,672	...	...	...	24,730
2008	21,788	1,763	...	...	...	23,551
2009	20,883	1,696	...	...	...	22,579

SENTINEL SECURITY LIFE INS CO

2121 South State Street
Salt Lake City, Utah 84115
Tel: 801-484-8514

AMB#: 007040
Began Business: 09/01/1948
Agency Off: Vern T. Neilson

Best's Financial Strength Rating: B++ **FSC:** V

• NET PREMIUMS AND DEPOSITS ($000 omitted)

Year	Individual Life	Individual & Group Annuities	Group Life & A&H	Credit Life & A&H	Individual A&H	Total
2007	5,907	1	...	...	...	5,908
2008	6,109	1	...	...	...	6,110
2009	6,448	1	...	...	...	6,449

• NET OPERATING GAIN ($000 omitted)

Year	Individual Life	Individual & Group Annuities	Group Life & A&H	Credit Life & A&H	Individual A&H	Total
2007	828	5	...	...	...	833
2008	546	-5	...	...	...	540
2009	354	2	...	...	...	356

• COMPARATIVE FINANCIALS ($000 omitted)

Year	Assets	Capital & Surplus	Net Invest Income	Benefits Paid	Realized Cap Gains	Policyholder Dividends	Contract Lns (% of assets)
2007	53,754	23,290	3,081	3,025	452	20	1.6
2008	51,372	20,679	2,869	2,971	126	20	1.8
2009	51,947	20,393	2,769	3,370	-491	19	2.0

• ORDINARY LIFE STATISTICS

Year	Av. Ord. Policy Issued ($)	Av. Ord. Policy In Force ($)	Avg. Prem ($/M)	1st Yr Prem/ Total Prem	Ord. Lapse Ratio
2007	...	...	...	...	...
2008	...	...	...	...	...
2009	...	...	...	...	...

• NEW LIFE BUSINESS ISSUED ($000 omitted)

Year	Whole Life	Term	Credit	Group	Industrial	Total
2007	18,473	2,563	...	...	...	21,036
2008	17,289	3,260	...	...	...	20,549
2009	17,527	2,273	...	...	...	19,800

• LIFE INSURANCE IN FORCE ($000 omitted)

Year	Whole Life	Term	Credit	Group	Industrial	Total
2007	113,341	18,546	...	...	...	131,887
2008	116,613	18,297	...	...	...	134,910
2009	120,225	17,903	...	...	...	138,129

SENTRY LIFE INS CO

1800 North Point Drive
Stevens Point, Wisconsin 54481
Tel: 715-346-6000

AMB#: 007041
Began Business: 11/11/1958
Agency Off: None

Best's Financial Strength Rating: A g **FSC:** IX

• NET PREMIUMS AND DEPOSITS ($000 omitted)

Year	Individual Life	Individual & Group Annuities	Group Life & A&H	Credit Life & A&H	Individual A&H	Total
2007	26,584	312,349	7,404	...	31	346,368
2008	26,397	290,902	2,289	...	27	319,615
2009	25,312	310,217	7,505	...	22	343,055

• NET OPERATING GAIN ($000 omitted)

Year	Individual Life	Individual & Group Annuities	Group Life & A&H	Credit Life & A&H	Individual A&H	Total
2007	10,825	12,292	1,123	...	-55	24,186
2008	10,291	13,386	1,463	...	21	25,161
2009	10,241	12,887	675	...	24	23,827

• COMPARATIVE FINANCIALS ($000 omitted)

Year	Assets	Capital & Surplus	Net Invest Income	Benefits Paid	Realized Cap Gains	Policyholder Dividends	Contract Lns (% of assets)
2007	3,338,038	261,692	107,592	280,347	-6,681	238	0.5
2008	2,882,466	262,501	111,064	282,899	-9,715	221	0.6
2009	3,340,602	275,113	116,101	242,591	-5,311	245	0.5

• ORDINARY LIFE STATISTICS

Year	Av. Ord. Policy Issued ($)	Av. Ord. Policy In Force ($)	Avg. Prem ($/M)	1st Yr Prem/ Total Prem	Ord. Lapse Ratio
2007	160,183	90,597	5.52	5.3	7.1
2008	132,103	93,093	5.40	6.3	7.5
2009	131,012	95,241	5.26	6.5	8.6

• NEW LIFE BUSINESS ISSUED ($000 omitted)

Year	Whole Life	Term	Credit	Group	Industrial	Total
2007	54,797	476,689	...	109,841	...	641,327
2008	84,736	543,017	...	...	...	627,753
2009	89,550	529,615	...	115,924	...	735,088

• LIFE INSURANCE IN FORCE ($000 omitted)

Year	Whole Life	Term	Credit	Group	Industrial	Total
2007	2,193,390	3,625,811	...	1,683,378	...	7,502,579
2008	2,110,671	3,836,420	...	1,679,211	...	7,626,302
2009	2,006,646	3,973,087	...	1,604,138	...	7,583,872

SENTRY LIFE INS CO OF NEW YORK

P.O. Box 4944
Syracuse, New York 13221
Tel: 315-453-6308

AMB#: 007042
Began Business: 01/27/1967
Agency Off: None

Best's Financial Strength Rating: A g **FSC:** IX

• NET PREMIUMS AND DEPOSITS ($000 omitted)

Year	Individual Life	Individual & Group Annuities	Group Life & A&H	Credit Life & A&H	Individual A&H	Total
2007	617	6,535	394	...	23	7,569
2008	601	5,708	360	...	23	6,691
2009	573	6,568	294	...	26	7,461

• NET OPERATING GAIN ($000 omitted)

Year	Individual Life	Individual & Group Annuities	Group Life & A&H	Credit Life & A&H	Individual A&H	Total
2007	624	-139	217	...	-2	700
2008	498	-146	173	...	-8	517
2009	552	-125	181	...	-20	589

• COMPARATIVE FINANCIALS ($000 omitted)

Year	Assets	Capital & Surplus	Net Invest Income	Benefits Paid	Realized Cap Gains	Policyholder Dividends	Contract Lns (% of assets)
2007	54,952	7,402	1,843	7,455	-93	0	2.3
2008	50,063	10,124	1,765	6,236	-52	0	2.4
2009	58,248	10,268	1,927	5,550	-10	0	1.8

• ORDINARY LIFE STATISTICS

Year	Av. Ord. Policy Issued ($)	Av. Ord. Policy In Force ($)	Avg. Prem ($/M)	1st Yr Prem/ Total Prem	Ord. Lapse Ratio
2007	...	...	...	...	...
2008	...	...	...	...	...
2009	...	...	...	...	...

• NEW LIFE BUSINESS ISSUED ($000 omitted)

Year	Whole Life	Term	Credit	Group	Industrial	Total
2007	671	...	...	1,607	...	2,278
2008	775	50	...	...	...	825
2009	410	66	...	2,971	...	3,447

• LIFE INSURANCE IN FORCE ($000 omitted)

Year	Whole Life	Term	Credit	Group	Industrial	Total
2007	69,708	8,707	...	18,435	...	96,850
2008	65,574	7,741	...	18,552	...	91,867
2009	60,728	7,143	...	18,024	...	85,894

SERVCO LIFE INSURANCE COMPANY

P.O. Box 441828
Houston, Texas 77244-1828
Tel: 713-580-3080

AMB#: 068023
Began Business: 03/09/1983
Agency Off: None

Best's Financial Strength Rating: B+ **FSC:** IV

• NET PREMIUMS AND DEPOSITS ($000 omitted)

Year	Individual Life	Individual & Group Annuities	Group Life & A&H	Credit Life & A&H	Individual A&H	Total
2007	...	...	...	4,473	...	4,473
2008	...	...	...	3,376	...	3,376
2009	...	...	...	-609	...	-609

• NET OPERATING GAIN ($000 omitted)

Year	Individual Life	Individual & Group Annuities	Group Life & A&H	Credit Life & A&H	Individual A&H	Total
2007	...	...	...	-198	...	-198
2008	...	...	...	631	...	631
2009	...	...	...	2,721	...	2,721

• COMPARATIVE FINANCIALS ($000 omitted)

Year	Assets	Capital & Surplus	Net Invest Income	Benefits Paid	Realized Cap Gains	Policyholder Dividends	Contract Lns (% of assets)
2007	31,685	6,827	1,256	1,093	...	...	...
2008	30,553	7,088	1,087	1,167	-356	...	...
2009	28,244	9,776	1,218	835	20	...	...

• ORDINARY LIFE STATISTICS

Year	Av. Ord. Policy Issued ($)	Av. Ord. Policy In Force ($)	Avg. Prem ($/M)	1st Yr Prem/ Total Prem	Ord. Lapse Ratio
2007	...	...	...	...	...
2008	...	...	...	...	...
2009	...	...	...	...	...

• NEW LIFE BUSINESS ISSUED ($000 omitted)

Year	Whole Life	Term	Credit	Group	Industrial	Total
2007	...	...	497,037	...	...	497,037
2008	...	...	460,309	...	...	460,309
2009	...	...	190,206	...	...	190,206

• LIFE INSURANCE IN FORCE ($000 omitted)

Year	Whole Life	Term	Credit	Group	Industrial	Total
2007	...	...	1,564,585	...	...	1,564,585
2008	...	...	1,604,085	...	...	1,604,085
2009	...	...	1,272,349	...	...	1,272,349

SERVICE LIFE & CASUALTY INS CO

P.O. Box 26800
Austin, Texas 78755-0800
Tel: 512-343-0600

AMB#: 007992
Began Business: 01/01/1970
Agency Off: J. Kelly Gray

Best's Financial Strength Rating: B+ **FSC:** VI

• NET PREMIUMS AND DEPOSITS ($000 omitted)

Year	Individual Life	Individual & Group Annuities	Group Life & A&H	Credit Life & A&H	Individual A&H	Total
2007	...	...	1,555	22,905	...	24,460
2008	...	...	...	13,273	...	13,273
2009	...	...	...	3,073	...	3,073

• NET OPERATING GAIN ($000 omitted)

Year	Individual Life	Individual & Group Annuities	Group Life & A&H	Credit Life & A&H	Individual A&H	Total
2007	-8	...	1,086	201	...	1,279
2008	0	...	223	5,727	...	5,950
2009	12	...	...	10,418	...	10,431

• COMPARATIVE FINANCIALS ($000 omitted)

Year	Assets	Capital & Surplus	Net Invest Income	Benefits Paid	Realized Cap Gains	Policyholder Dividends	Contract Lns (% of assets)
2007	149,449	34,206	6,260	2,094	1,567	...	...
2008	137,780	35,035	6,191	4,585	-1,318	...	...
2009	127,675	34,335	7,380	5,964	-1,250	...	...

• ORDINARY LIFE STATISTICS

Year	Av. Ord. Policy Issued ($)	Av. Ord. Policy In Force ($)	Avg. Prem ($/M)	1st Yr Prem/ Total Prem	Ord. Lapse Ratio
2007	...	...	...	...	...
2008	...	...	...	...	...
2009	...	...	...	...	...

• NEW LIFE BUSINESS ISSUED ($000 omitted)

Year	Whole Life	Term	Credit	Group	Industrial	Total
2007	...	...	1,779,233	...	...	1,779,233
2008	...	...	1,534,234	...	...	1,534,234
2009	...	...	746,143	...	...	746,143

• LIFE INSURANCE IN FORCE ($000 omitted)

Year	Whole Life	Term	Credit	Group	Industrial	Total
2007	431	...	3,304,766	...	...	3,305,197
2008	421	...	3,270,780	...	...	3,271,201
2009	399	...	2,637,459	...	...	2,637,858

SETTLERS LIFE INSURANCE CO

2 East Gilman Street
Madison, Wisconsin 53703-1494
Tel: 608-257-5611

AMB#: 009322
Began Business: 09/07/1982
Agency Off: None

Best's Financial Strength Rating: A- g
FSC: VIII

• **NET PREMIUMS AND DEPOSITS** ($000 omitted)

Year	Individual Life	Individual & Group Annuities	Group Life & A&H	Credit Life & A&H	Individual A&H	Total
2007	28,585	5	8,700	...	369	37,659
2008	30,640	122	8,678	...	346	39,786
2009	32,902	70	7,976	...	304	41,251

• **NET OPERATING GAIN** ($000 omitted)

Year	Individual Life	Individual & Group Annuities	Group Life & A&H	Credit Life & A&H	Individual A&H	Total
2007	-244	-23	5,785	...	213	5,991
2008	1,226	69	5,026	...	365	6,463
2009	2,458	75	6,301	...	84	8,137

• **COMPARATIVE FINANCIALS** ($000 omitted)

Year	Assets	Capital & Surplus	Net Invest Income	Benefits Paid	Realized Cap Gains	Policyholder Dividends	Contract Lns (% of assets)
2007	381,811	48,797	22,070	30,004	-48	371	1.0
2008	414,231	53,011	23,570	37,125	-5,620	373	1.1
2009	414,801	53,325	24,221	35,108	-1,276	371	1.2

• **ORDINARY LIFE STATISTICS**

Year	Av. Ord. Policy Issued ($)	Av. Ord. Policy In Force ($)	Avg. Prem ($/M)	1st Yr Prem/ Total Prem	Ord. Lapse Ratio
2007	8,622	12,005	22.77	20.2	10.1
2008	11,022	11,419	24.16	17.4	12.3
2009	12,052	11,216	25.87	15.5	10.5

• **NEW LIFE BUSINESS ISSUED** ($000 omitted)

Year	Whole Life	Term	Credit	Group	Industrial	Total
2007	168,333	852	...	64	...	169,249
2008	182,100	2,093	...	50	...	184,243
2009	179,480	954	...	17	...	180,451

• **LIFE INSURANCE IN FORCE** ($000 omitted)

Year	Whole Life	Term	Credit	Group	Industrial	Total
2007	841,738	454,094	...	585,895	...	1,881,727
2008	883,954	426,725	...	610,911	...	1,921,590
2009	906,996	397,308	...	591,544	...	1,895,848

SIERRA HLTH & LF INS CO INC

P.O. Box 14396
Las Vegas, Nevada 89114-4396
Tel: 702-243-8528

AMB#: 007370
Began Business: 08/16/1906
Agency Off: None

Best's Financial Strength Rating: A- g
FSC: VIII

• **NET PREMIUMS AND DEPOSITS** ($000 omitted)

Year	Individual Life	Individual & Group Annuities	Group Life & A&H	Credit Life & A&H	Individual A&H	Total
2007	...	...	111,086	...	313,426	424,512
2008	...	...	129,658	...	100,876	230,534
2009	...	...	136,943	...	78,628	215,571

• **NET OPERATING GAIN** ($000 omitted)

Year	Individual Life	Individual & Group Annuities	Group Life & A&H	Credit Life & A&H	Individual A&H	Total
2007	...	...	8,711	...	-19,882	-11,171
2008	...	...	10,729	...	3,229	13,958
2009	...	...	7,482	...	-1,642	5,840

• **COMPARATIVE FINANCIALS** ($000 omitted)

Year	Assets	Capital & Surplus	Net Invest Income	Benefits Paid	Realized Cap Gains	Policyholder Dividends	Contract Lns (% of assets)
2007	133,494	63,061	5,210	394,498	68	...	...
2008	129,288	76,643	2,801	171,795	-4	...	...
2009	121,425	70,350	1,567	173,902	22	...	...

• **ORDINARY LIFE STATISTICS**

Year	Av. Ord. Policy Issued ($)	Av. Ord. Policy In Force ($)	Avg. Prem ($/M)	1st Yr Prem/ Total Prem	Ord. Lapse Ratio
2007	...	...	...	...	...
2008	...	...	...	...	...
2009	...	...	...	...	...

• **NEW LIFE BUSINESS ISSUED** ($000 omitted)

Year	Whole Life	Term	Credit	Group	Industrial	Total
2007	...	...	...	29,022	...	29,022
2008	...	...	...	,85,110	...	85,110
2009	...	...	...	38,655	...	38,655

• **LIFE INSURANCE IN FORCE** ($000 omitted)

Year	Whole Life	Term	Credit	Group	Industrial	Total
2007	...	...	...	108,391	...	108,391
2008	...	...	...	763,339	...	763,339
2009	...	...	...	721,872	...	721,872

SHELTER LIFE INS CO

1817 West Broadway
Columbia, Missouri 65218-0001
Tel: 573-445-8441

AMB#: 006675
Began Business: 03/02/1959
Agency Off: C. Tyler Bailey

Best's Financial Strength Rating: A
FSC: VIII

• **NET PREMIUMS AND DEPOSITS** ($000 omitted)

Year	Individual Life	Individual & Group Annuities	Group Life & A&H	Credit Life & A&H	Individual A&H	Total
2007	86,458	13,726	16,694	323	2,186	119,388
2008	88,303	17,753	20,234	321	2,013	128,624
2009	84,139	23,906	20,365	215	1,829	130,455

• **NET OPERATING GAIN** ($000 omitted)

Year	Individual Life	Individual & Group Annuities	Group Life & A&H	Credit Life & A&H	Individual A&H	Total
2007	10,130	1,513	-576	111	-298	10,881
2008	6,870	820	1,266	122	-37	9,041
2009	13,576	928	5,608	34	-604	19,544

• **COMPARATIVE FINANCIALS** ($000 omitted)

Year	Assets	Capital & Surplus	Net Invest Income	Benefits Paid	Realized Cap Gains	Policyholder Dividends	Contract Lns (% of assets)
2007	915,427	171,799	41,595	82,809	1,010	5,822	2.9
2008	920,220	169,482	43,772	84,561	-12,313	6,312	2.9
2009	940,409	176,650	43,731	84,086	24,562	4,892	2.8

• **ORDINARY LIFE STATISTICS**

Year	Av. Ord. Policy Issued ($)	Av. Ord. Policy In Force ($)	Avg. Prem ($/M)	1st Yr Prem/ Total Prem	Ord. Lapse Ratio
2007	104,125	71,883	5.65	21.1	5.8
2008	105,241	74,554	5.41	19.1	5.6
2009	105,606	77,044	5.00	11.9	6.4

• **NEW LIFE BUSINESS ISSUED** ($000 omitted)

Year	Whole Life	Term	Credit	Group	Industrial	Total
2007	289,533	2,122,844	6,345	37,856	...	2,456,578
2008	294,984	2,107,464	6,052	25,948	...	2,434,448
2009	162,253	2,129,918	4,182	16,111	...	2,312,464

• **LIFE INSURANCE IN FORCE** ($000 omitted)

Year	Whole Life	Term	Credit	Group	Industrial	Total
2007	4,988,845	11,764,252	23,769	378,449	...	17,155,315
2008	5,024,647	12,856,708	22,326	370,389	...	18,274,070
2009	4,972,811	13,918,317	20,102	366,366	...	19,277,597

SOUTHEAST FAMILY LIFE INS CO

1212 North 96th Street
Omaha, Nebraska 68114
Tel: 402-397-1111

AMB#: 009520
Began Business: 12/31/1985
Agency Off: Jeffrey Wanning

Best's Financial Strength Rating: B++g
FSC: VIII

• **NET PREMIUMS AND DEPOSITS** ($000 omitted)

Year	Individual Life	Individual & Group Annuities	Group Life & A&H	Credit Life & A&H	Individual A&H	Total
2007	...	...	...	4,773	...	4,773
2008	...	...	...	341	...	341
2009	...	...	...	1,829	...	1,829

• **NET OPERATING GAIN** ($000 omitted)

Year	Individual Life	Individual & Group Annuities	Group Life & A&H	Credit Life & A&H	Individual A&H	Total
2007	...	...	...	3,098	...	3,098
2008	...	...	...	-824	...	-824
2009	...	...	...	3,464	...	3,464

• **COMPARATIVE FINANCIALS** ($000 omitted)

Year	Assets	Capital & Surplus	Net Invest Income	Benefits Paid	Realized Cap Gains	Policyholder Dividends	Contract Lns (% of assets)
2007	16,227	5,321	825	2,988	0	...	...
2008	10,944	3,095	791	2,449	-520	...	...
2009	10,199	5,279	613	1,469	-378	...	...

• **ORDINARY LIFE STATISTICS**

Year	Av. Ord. Policy Issued ($)	Av. Ord. Policy In Force ($)	Avg. Prem ($/M)	1st Yr Prem/ Total Prem	Ord. Lapse Ratio
2007	...	...	...	...	...
2008	...	...	...	...	...
2009	...	...	...	...	...

• **NEW LIFE BUSINESS ISSUED** ($000 omitted)

Year	Whole Life	Term	Credit	Group	Industrial	Total
2007	...	...	...	...	...	...
2008	...	...	...	...	...	...
2009	...	...	...	...	...	...

• **LIFE INSURANCE IN FORCE** ($000 omitted)

Year	Whole Life	Term	Credit	Group	Industrial	Total
2007	...	...	303,446	...	...	303,446
2008	...	...	238,057	...	...	238,057
2009	...	...	155,334	...	...	155,334

SOUTHERN FARM BUREAU LIFE INS

P.O. Box 78
Jackson, Mississippi 39205
Tel: 601-981-7422

AMB#: 007053
Began Business: 12/18/1946
Agency Off: Mark G. Gianfrancesco

Best's Financial Strength Rating: A+ **FSC:** XIV

• NET PREMIUMS AND DEPOSITS ($000 omitted)

Year	Individual Life	Individual & Group Annuities	Group Life & A&H	Credit Life & A&H	Individual A&H	Total
2007	504,690	216,370	11,169	...	11,490	743,720
2008	519,112	299,604	9,888	...	11,017	839,622
2009	537,547	353,261	13,202	...	10,554	914,564

• NET OPERATING GAIN ($000 omitted)

Year	Individual Life	Individual & Group Annuities	Group Life & A&H	Credit Life & A&H	Individual A&H	Total
2007	76,815	43,935	2,196	...	1,573	124,519
2008	73,826	45,379	2,468	...	1,446	123,119
2009	37,283	38,778	3,054	...	401	79,517

• COMPARATIVE FINANCIALS ($000 omitted)

Year	Assets	Capital & Surplus	Net Invest Income	Benefits Paid	Realized Cap Gains	Policyholder Dividends	Contract Lns (% of assets)
2007	9,949,156	1,587,191	524,619	680,343	19,209	47,385	3.8
2008	10,019,877	1,570,638	507,737	596,218	-60,026	48,348	4.0
2009	10,545,745	1,669,157	504,924	605,561	-69,077	49,009	4.0

• ORDINARY LIFE STATISTICS

Year	Av. Ord. Policy Issued ($)	Av. Ord. Policy In Force ($)	Avg. Prem ($/M)	1st Yr Prem/ Total Prem	Ord. Lapse Ratio
2007	152,361	85,108	5.85	10.4	6.2
2008	141,021	87,725	5.78	9.8	6.3
2009	163,045	92,006	5.62	9.9	6.7

• NEW LIFE BUSINESS ISSUED ($000 omitted)

Year	Whole Life	Term	Credit	Group	Industrial	Total
2007	2,088,898	8,788,127	...	81,392	...	10,958,417
2008	1,951,181	8,522,602	...	84,318	...	10,558,101
2009	1,901,282	10,931,493	...	80,034	...	12,912,808

• LIFE INSURANCE IN FORCE ($000 omitted)

Year	Whole Life	Term	Credit	Group	Industrial	Total
2007	27,779,937	57,912,274	...	1,900,924	...	87,593,135
2008	28,208,134	61,457,091	...	1,965,930	...	91,631,155
2009	28,481,700	66,990,800	...	2,028,540	...	97,501,040

SOUTHERN PIONEER LIFE INS CO

P.O. Box 5323
Cincinnati, Ohio 45201-5323
Tel: 513-943-7200

AMB#: 007521
Began Business: 07/12/1966
Agency Off: Frank J. May

Best's Financial Strength Rating: B++ **FSC:** V

• NET PREMIUMS AND DEPOSITS ($000 omitted)

Year	Individual Life	Individual & Group Annuities	Group Life & A&H	Credit Life & A&H	Individual A&H	Total
2007	119	...	...	7,430	...	7,549
2008	159	...	...	6,851	...	7,010
2009	100	...	...	5,062	...	5,162

• NET OPERATING GAIN ($000 omitted)

Year	Individual Life	Individual & Group Annuities	Group Life & A&H	Credit Life & A&H	Individual A&H	Total
2007	159	...	...	1,356	...	1,515
2008	155	...	...	848	...	1,003
2009	66	...	...	-554	...	-488

• COMPARATIVE FINANCIALS ($000 omitted)

Year	Assets	Capital & Surplus	Net Invest Income	Benefits Paid	Realized Cap Gains	Policyholder Dividends	Contract Lns (% of assets)
2007	25,027	11,823	987	2,609	25	...	...
2008	25,442	12,739	740	2,690	-12	...	...
2009	25,292	12,334	357	2,247	...	...	...

• ORDINARY LIFE STATISTICS

Year	Av. Ord. Policy Issued ($)	Av. Ord. Policy In Force ($)	Avg. Prem ($/M)	1st Yr Prem/ Total Prem	Ord. Lapse Ratio
2007	...	...	...	...	...
2008	...	...	...	...	...
2009	...	...	...	...	...

• NEW LIFE BUSINESS ISSUED ($000 omitted)

Year	Whole Life	Term	Credit	Group	Industrial	Total
2007	...	320	683,736	...	...	684,056
2008	...	...	610,703	...	...	610,703
2009	...	...	473,637	...	...	473,637

• LIFE INSURANCE IN FORCE ($000 omitted)

Year	Whole Life	Term	Credit	Group	Industrial	Total
2007	...	30,761	880,452	...	...	911,213
2008	...	28,819	828,566	...	...	857,385
2009	...	27,063	709,070	...	...	736,133

SOUTHERN FINANCIAL LIFE INS CO

100 West Bay Street
Jacksonville, Florida 32202-3806
Tel: 904-350-9660

AMB#: 060271
Began Business: 08/03/1998
Agency Off: None

Best's Financial Strength Rating: B++g **FSC:** V

• NET PREMIUMS AND DEPOSITS ($000 omitted)

Year	Individual Life	Individual & Group Annuities	Group Life & A&H	Credit Life & A&H	Individual A&H	Total
2007	...	...	...	504	...	504
2008	...	...	...	344	...	344
2009	...	...	...	184	...	184

• NET OPERATING GAIN ($000 omitted)

Year	Individual Life	Individual & Group Annuities	Group Life & A&H	Credit Life & A&H	Individual A&H	Total
2007	56	...	...	229	...	286
2008	-13	...	...	315	...	302
2009	-15	...	...	129	...	114

• COMPARATIVE FINANCIALS ($000 omitted)

Year	Assets	Capital & Surplus	Net Invest Income	Benefits Paid	Realized Cap Gains	Policyholder Dividends	Contract Lns (% of assets)
2007	4,727	4,071	162	137	12	...	...
2008	4,695	4,008	145	127	...	...	...
2009	3,882	3,338	104	90	-28	...	...

• ORDINARY LIFE STATISTICS

Year	Av. Ord. Policy Issued ($)	Av. Ord. Policy In Force ($)	Avg. Prem ($/M)	1st Yr Prem/ Total Prem	Ord. Lapse Ratio
2007	...	...	...	...	...
2008	...	...	...	...	...
2009	...	...	...	...	...

• NEW LIFE BUSINESS ISSUED ($000 omitted)

Year	Whole Life	Term	Credit	Group	Industrial	Total
2007	...	2,665	1,023,904	...	...	1,026,569
2008	...	3,316	656,153	...	...	659,469
2009	...	3,355	651,165	...	...	654,520

• LIFE INSURANCE IN FORCE ($000 omitted)

Year	Whole Life	Term	Credit	Group	Industrial	Total
2007	...	9,208	460,131	...	...	469,339
2008	...	11,121	413,610	...	...	424,731
2009	...	13,248	304,875	...	...	318,123

SOUTHLAND NATIONAL INS CORP

P.O. Box 1520
Tuscaloosa, Alabama 35403
Tel: 205-345-7410

AMB#: 008225
Began Business: 01/21/1969
Agency Off: Virginia H. Hardy

Best's Financial Strength Rating: B+ **FSC:** V

• NET PREMIUMS AND DEPOSITS ($000 omitted)

Year	Individual Life	Individual & Group Annuities	Group Life & A&H	Credit Life & A&H	Individual A&H	Total
2007	13,021	1	14,595	0	2	27,619
2008	11,733	10	16,329	0	2	28,073
2009	12,434	7	18,941	...	1	31,383

• NET OPERATING GAIN ($000 omitted)

Year	Individual Life	Individual & Group Annuities	Group Life & A&H	Credit Life & A&H	Individual A&H	Total
2007	816	7	85	0	663	1,571
2008	1,283	33	-1,336	1	564	545
2009	-89	-2	686	1	17	612

• COMPARATIVE FINANCIALS ($000 omitted)

Year	Assets	Capital & Surplus	Net Invest Income	Benefits Paid	Realized Cap Gains	Policyholder Dividends	Contract Lns (% of assets)
2007	151,221	10,696	7,851	18,577	-86	...	0.1
2008	154,913	8,722	8,446	20,123	-5,825	...	0.1
2009	168,196	11,089	8,356	20,705	-17	...	0.1

• ORDINARY LIFE STATISTICS

Year	Av. Ord. Policy Issued ($)	Av. Ord. Policy In Force ($)	Avg. Prem ($/M)	1st Yr Prem/ Total Prem	Ord. Lapse Ratio
2007	7,366	4,541	65.50	4.3	3.9
2008	5,141	4,684	52.12	1.5	0.2
2009	4,417	4,904	54.43	4.3	-1.8

• NEW LIFE BUSINESS ISSUED ($000 omitted)

Year	Whole Life	Term	Credit	Group	Industrial	Total
2007	35,848	...	...	35,293	...	71,141
2008	16,682	...	...	31,894	...	48,576
2009	15,302	...	...	25,938	...	41,240

• LIFE INSURANCE IN FORCE ($000 omitted)

Year	Whole Life	Term	Credit	Group	Industrial	Total
2007	300,187	5,063	277	74,508	...	380,035
2008	297,530	5,802	171	101,276	...	404,779
2009	301,482	6,425	23	128,404	...	436,334

SPJST

P.O. Box 100
Temple, Texas 76503
Tel: 254-773-1575

AMB#: 009606
Began Business: 07/01/1897
Agency Off: Gene McBride

Best's Financial Strength Rating: B
FSC: V

• NET PREMIUMS AND DEPOSITS (\$000 omitted)

Year	Individual Life	Individual & Group Annuities	Group Life & A&H	Credit Life & A&H	Individual A&H	Total
2007	5,387	...	...	...	...	10,018
2008	6,127	...	...	...	...	12,554
2009	6,173	...	...	...	...	16,320

• NET OPERATING GAIN (\$000 omitted)

Year	Individual Life	Individual & Group Annuities	Group Life & A&H	Credit Life & A&H	Individual A&H	Total
2007	1,742	-241	...	...	3	-564
2008	-564	874	...	...	30	-1,918
2009	225	1,257	...	...	17	-492

• COMPARATIVE FINANCIALS (\$000 omitted)

Year	Assets	Capital & Surplus	Net Invest Income	Benefits Paid	Realized Cap Gains	Policyholder Dividends	Contract Lns (% of assets)
2007	192,059	24,261	10,841	11,151	1,019	7	1.2
2008	185,108	13,023	7,890	10,617	-7,143	6	1.2
2009	196,978	13,808	8,600	13,912	-753	-1	1.1

• ORDINARY LIFE STATISTICS

Year	Av. Ord. Policy Issued (\$)	Av. Ord. Policy In Force (\$)	Avg. Prem (\$/M)	1st Yr Prem/ Total Prem	Ord. Lapse Ratio
2007	...	...	...	...	...
2008	...	...	...	...	...
2009	...	...	...	...	...

• NEW LIFE BUSINESS ISSUED (\$000 omitted)

Year	Whole Life	Term	Credit	Group	Industrial	Total
2007	219,679	...	...	...	...	219,679
2008	161,304	...	...	...	...	161,304
2009	91,306	...	...	...	...	91,306

• LIFE INSURANCE IN FORCE (\$000 omitted)

Year	Whole Life	Term	Credit	Group	Industrial	Total
2007	889,817	...	...	...	...	889,817
2008	932,827	...	...	...	...	932,827
2009	919,818	...	...	...	...	919,818

STANDARD LIFE AND ACCIDENT INS

One Moody Plaza
Galveston, Texas 77550-7999
Tel: 409-763-4661

AMB#: 007070
Began Business: 06/01/1976
Agency Off: None

Best's Financial Strength Rating: A
FSC: VIII

• NET PREMIUMS AND DEPOSITS (\$000 omitted)

Year	Individual Life	Individual & Group Annuities	Group Life & A&H	Credit Life & A&H	Individual A&H	Total
2007	16,383	11,263	4,275	...	113,296	145,217
2008	14,160	10,527	5,751	...	101,545	131,983
2009	14,202	8,116	6,130	...	92,990	121,438

• NET OPERATING GAIN (\$000 omitted)

Year	Individual Life	Individual & Group Annuities	Group Life & A&H	Credit Life & A&H	Individual A&H	Total
2007	4,302	2,679	205	...	1,482	8,668
2008	5,423	3,283	-362	...	8,239	16,584
2009	5,487	2,796	-1,372	...	5,998	12,909

• COMPARATIVE FINANCIALS (\$000 omitted)

Year	Assets	Capital & Surplus	Net Invest Income	Benefits Paid	Realized Cap Gains	Policyholder Dividends	Contract Lns (% of assets)
2007	531,349	210,946	27,782	123,301	708	404	1.3
2008	490,140	201,855	26,955	111,004	-14,325	270	1.4
2009	505,917	217,655	25,901	101,545	-9,679	291	1.3

• ORDINARY LIFE STATISTICS

Year	Av. Ord. Policy Issued (\$)	Av. Ord. Policy In Force (\$)	Avg. Prem (\$/M)	1st Yr Prem/ Total Prem	Ord. Lapse Ratio
2007	19,152	5,812	39.06	4.0	7.4
2008	15,152	5,756	36.53	1.9	8.1
2009	14,124	5,854	38.30	4.9	7.1

• NEW LIFE BUSINESS ISSUED (\$000 omitted)

Year	Whole Life	Term	Credit	Group	Industrial	Total
2007	27,799	125	...	...	...	27,924
2008	15,272	1	...	...	...	15,273
2009	22,330	...	...	...	...	22,330

• LIFE INSURANCE IN FORCE (\$000 omitted)

Year	Whole Life	Term	Credit	Group	Industrial	Total
2007	377,186	40,302	...	...	...	417,488
2008	346,761	37,287	...	...	...	384,048
2009	332,573	34,723	...	...	...	367,296

STANDARD INSURANCE COMPANY

1100 S.W. Sixth Avenue
Portland, Oregon 97204-1093
Tel: 971-321-7000

AMB#: 007069
Began Business: 04/12/1906
Agency Off: None

Best's Financial Strength Rating: A g
FSC: XIII

• NET PREMIUMS AND DEPOSITS (\$000 omitted)

Year	Individual Life	Individual & Group Annuities	Group Life & A&H	Credit Life & A&H	Individual A&H	Total
2007	2,508	1,611,617	1,882,455	...	122,482	3,619,062
2008	2,291	2,281,970	1,902,414	...	137,371	4,324,046
2009	2,540	1,658,812	1,833,066	...	164,065	3,658,484

• NET OPERATING GAIN (\$000 omitted)

Year	Individual Life	Individual & Group Annuities	Group Life & A&H	Credit Life & A&H	Individual A&H	Total
2007	3,727	18,941	151,479	...	16,461	198,751
2008	202	2,342	211,316	...	8,063	232,327
2009	694	12,451	191,250	...	25,473	244,285

• COMPARATIVE FINANCIALS (\$000 omitted)

Year	Assets	Capital & Surplus	Net Invest Income	Benefits Paid	Realized Cap Gains	Policyholder Dividends	Contract Lns (% of assets)
2007	13,265,338	1,014,381	483,968	2,374,634	42,466	87	0.0
2008	12,874,451	1,112,301	523,444	2,417,537	-97,431	92	0.0
2009	14,524,929	1,193,708	556,490	2,406,661	-26,492	102	0.0

• ORDINARY LIFE STATISTICS

Year	Av. Ord. Policy Issued (\$)	Av. Ord. Policy In Force (\$)	Avg. Prem (\$/M)	1st Yr Prem/ Total Prem	Ord. Lapse Ratio
2007	...	...	...	...	...
2008	...	...	...	...	...
2009	...	...	...	...	...

• NEW LIFE BUSINESS ISSUED (\$000 omitted)

Year	Whole Life	Term	Credit	Group	Industrial	Total
2007	8,085	1	...	59,815,493	...	59,823,579
2008	5,388	...	...	45,657,445	...	45,662,833
2009	8,284	...	...	41,835,766	...	41,844,050

• LIFE INSURANCE IN FORCE (\$000 omitted)

Year	Whole Life	Term	Credit	Group	Industrial	Total
2007	2,615,029	1,263,696	...	302,749,672	...	306,628,397
2008	2,450,469	1,128,899	...	298,107,263	...	301,686,631
2009	2,284,620	1,039,128	...	292,724,810	...	296,048,559

STANDARD LIFE INSURANCE OF NY

1100 S.W. Sixth Avenue
Portland, Oregon 97204-1093
Tel: 914-989-4400

AMB#: 060342
Began Business: 01/01/2001
Agency Off: None

Best's Financial Strength Rating: A g
FSC: XIII

• NET PREMIUMS AND DEPOSITS (\$000 omitted)

Year	Individual Life	Individual & Group Annuities	Group Life & A&H	Credit Life & A&H	Individual A&H	Total
2007	96	517	51,313	...	...	51,926
2008	142	2,354	61,689	...	...	64,185
2009	162	5,152	61,000	...	...	66,315

• NET OPERATING GAIN (\$000 omitted)

Year	Individual Life	Individual & Group Annuities	Group Life & A&H	Credit Life & A&H	Individual A&H	Total
2007	-251	...	-1,254	...	...	-1,505
2008	-246	...	2,174	...	...	1,928
2009	18	...	7,127	...	...	7,127

• COMPARATIVE FINANCIALS (\$000 omitted)

Year	Assets	Capital & Surplus	Net Invest Income	Benefits Paid	Realized Cap Gains	Policyholder Dividends	Contract Lns (% of assets)
2007	141,485	33,426	6,163	24,636	-156	...	...
2008	176,261	42,266	8,400	37,012	-873	...	...
2009	196,168	49,453	9,869	33,843	-412	...	0.0

• ORDINARY LIFE STATISTICS

Year	Av. Ord. Policy Issued (\$)	Av. Ord. Policy In Force (\$)	Avg. Prem (\$/M)	1st Yr Prem/ Total Prem	Ord. Lapse Ratio
2007	...	...	...	...	...
2008	...	...	...	...	...
2009	...	...	...	...	...

• NEW LIFE BUSINESS ISSUED (\$000 omitted)

Year	Whole Life	Term	Credit	Group	Industrial	Total
2007	975	8,242	...	4,678,024	...	4,687,241
2008	2,378	4,767	...	3,749,136	...	3,756,281
2009	1,312	4,830	...	2,681,848	...	2,687,990

• LIFE INSURANCE IN FORCE (\$000 omitted)

Year	Whole Life	Term	Credit	Group	Industrial	Total
2007	1,749	4,720	...	11,836,841	...	11,843,310
2008	3,485	4,922	...	14,755,276	...	14,763,683
2009	4,063	3,959	...	15,816,772	...	15,824,795

STANDARD SECURITY LIFE OF NY

485 Madison Avenue, 14th Floor
New York, New York 10022-5872
Tel: 212-355-4141

AMB#: 007075
Began Business: 12/22/1958
Agency Off: David T. Kettig

Best's Financial Strength Rating: A- g **FSC:** VIII

• NET PREMIUMS AND DEPOSITS ($000 omitted)

Year	Individual Life	Individual & Group Annuities	Group Life & A&H	Credit Life & A&H	Individual A&H	Total
2007	725	8,064	203,708	...	201	212,698
2008	725	7,928	196,748	...	106	205,507
2009	612	9,174	179,469	...	95	189,351

• NET OPERATING GAIN ($000 omitted)

Year	Individual Life	Individual & Group Annuities	Group Life & A&H	Credit Life & A&H	Individual A&H	Total
2007	1,643	1,479	1,586	...	-124	4,583
2008	169	949	6,749	...	-48	7,819
2009	217	738	7,633	...	-68	8,519

• COMPARATIVE FINANCIALS ($000 omitted)

Year	Assets	Capital & Surplus	Net Invest Income	Benefits Paid	Realized Cap Gains	Policyholder Dividends	Contract Lns (% of assets)
2007	367,199	109,648	15,431	145,789	34	20	0.3
2008	369,681	114,274	14,851	146,954	-11,622	18	0.2
2009	370,831	115,055	13,291	140,397	263	16	0.2

• ORDINARY LIFE STATISTICS

Year	Av. Ord. Policy Issued ($)	Av. Ord. Policy In Force ($)	Avg. Prem ($/M)	1st Yr Prem/ Total Prem	Ord. Lapse Ratio
2007	...	...	...	...	...
2008	...	...	...	...	...
2009	...	...	...	...	...

• NEW LIFE BUSINESS ISSUED ($000 omitted)

Year	Whole Life	Term	Credit	Group	Industrial	Total
2007	...	...	...	23,545	...	23,545
2008	2	...	...	16,051	...	16,053
2009	2	...	...	120,988	...	120,990

• LIFE INSURANCE IN FORCE ($000 omitted)

Year	Whole Life	Term	Credit	Group	Industrial	Total
2007	54,330	20,243	...	301,861	...	376,434
2008	50,975	18,379	...	286,515	...	355,869
2009	47,239	16,932	...	329,630	...	393,802

STATE FARM LIFE & ACC ASSUR CO

One State Farm Plaza
Bloomington, Illinois 61710
Tel: 309-766-2311

AMB#: 007079
Began Business: 07/01/1961
Agency Off: Michael C. Davidson

Best's Financial Strength Rating: A++g **FSC:** XV

• NET PREMIUMS AND DEPOSITS ($000 omitted)

Year	Individual Life	Individual & Group Annuities	Group Life & A&H	Credit Life & A&H	Individual A&H	Total
2007	145,601	35,307	173	20	...	181,101
2008	152,917	67,741	217	-12	...	220,863
2009	161,106	54,526	209	-4	...	215,837

• NET OPERATING GAIN ($000 omitted)

Year	Individual Life	Individual & Group Annuities	Group Life & A&H	Credit Life & A&H	Individual A&H	Total
2007	17,722	-6,473	67	2	...	11,318
2008	20,147	-18,704	74	16	...	1,533
2009	20,014	5,333	80	9	...	25,435

• COMPARATIVE FINANCIALS ($000 omitted)

Year	Assets	Capital & Surplus	Net Invest Income	Benefits Paid	Realized Cap Gains	Policyholder Dividends	Contract Lns (% of assets)
2007	1,549,554	266,526	79,962	81,003	-1,051	18,816	7.1
2008	1,660,908	266,545	83,824	87,379	-4,935	19,719	7.1
2009	1,792,629	289,151	91,118	93,129	226	20,664	6.9

• ORDINARY LIFE STATISTICS

Year	Av. Ord. Policy Issued ($)	Av. Ord. Policy In Force ($)	Avg. Prem ($/M)	1st Yr Prem/ Total Prem	Ord. Lapse Ratio
2007	129,615	93,045	4.89	12.5	7.4
2008	121,492	95,798	4.86	12.1	7.4
2009	122,075	98,503	4.86	13.1	7.9

• NEW LIFE BUSINESS ISSUED ($000 omitted)

Year	Whole Life	Term	Credit	Group	Industrial	Total
2007	688,346	3,549,557	2,432	12,656	...	4,252,991
2008	679,614	3,590,720	...	7,066	...	4,277,400
2009	770,337	3,864,722	...	5,055	...	4,640,114

• LIFE INSURANCE IN FORCE ($000 omitted)

Year	Whole Life	Term	Credit	Group	Industrial	Total
2007	8,494,057	19,941,166	7,092	51,957	...	28,494,272
2008	8,695,584	21,398,561	3,727	60,271	...	30,158,143
2009	8,947,654	22,817,309	1,833	56,576	...	31,823,372

STARMOUNT LIFE INS CO

P.O. Box 98100
Baton Rouge, Louisiana 70898-9100
Tel: 225-400-9100

AMB#: 009370
Began Business: 08/25/1983
Agency Off: None

Best's Financial Strength Rating: B++ **FSC:** V

• NET PREMIUMS AND DEPOSITS ($000 omitted)

Year	Individual Life	Individual & Group Annuities	Group Life & A&H	Credit Life & A&H	Individual A&H	Total
2007	6,551	0	32,518	...	71	39,141
2008	7,032	0	37,509	...	79	44,620
2009	7,662	0	43,197	...	85	50,944

• NET OPERATING GAIN ($000 omitted)

Year	Individual Life	Individual & Group Annuities	Group Life & A&H	Credit Life & A&H	Individual A&H	Total
2007	25	1	2,133	...	39	2,198
2008	73	-2	2,478	...	9	2,557
2009	5	-4	2,468	...	8	2,478

• COMPARATIVE FINANCIALS ($000 omitted)

Year	Assets	Capital & Surplus	Net Invest Income	Benefits Paid	Realized Cap Gains	Policyholder Dividends	Contract Lns (% of assets)
2007	24,769	11,725	585	24,696	4	...	0.2
2008	32,957	13,914	366	27,556	...	...	0.2
2009	32,891	15,608	154	33,053	...	...	0.3

• ORDINARY LIFE STATISTICS

Year	Av. Ord. Policy Issued ($)	Av. Ord. Policy In Force ($)	Avg. Prem ($/M)	1st Yr Prem/ Total Prem	Ord. Lapse Ratio
2007	...	...	...	...	...
2008	...	...	...	...	...
2009	...	...	...	...	...

• NEW LIFE BUSINESS ISSUED ($000 omitted)

Year	Whole Life	Term	Credit	Group	Industrial	Total
2007	8,859	142,165	...	...	...	151,024
2008	8,799	143,455	...	...	...	152,254
2009	8,289	141,754	...	...	...	150,043

• LIFE INSURANCE IN FORCE ($000 omitted)

Year	Whole Life	Term	Credit	Group	Industrial	Total
2007	32,048	514,311	...	3,790	...	550,149
2008	33,822	551,438	...	3,604	...	588,864
2009	33,641	575,254	...	30,113	...	639,008

STATE FARM LIFE INS CO

One State Farm Plaza
Bloomington, Illinois 61710
Tel: 309-766-2311

AMB#: 007080
Began Business: 04/19/1929
Agency Off: Michael C. Davidson

Best's Financial Strength Rating: A++g **FSC:** XV

• NET PREMIUMS AND DEPOSITS ($000 omitted)

Year	Individual Life	Individual & Group Annuities	Group Life & A&H	Credit Life & A&H	Individual A&H	Total
2007	3,560,071	950,893	57,171	859	...	4,568,994
2008	3,693,404	1,807,231	60,169	-459	...	5,560,345
2009	3,818,416	1,394,948	64,190	-169	...	5,277,385

• NET OPERATING GAIN ($000 omitted)

Year	Individual Life	Individual & Group Annuities	Group Life & A&H	Credit Life & A&H	Individual A&H	Total
2007	284,226	57,777	5,999	1,055	...	349,058
2008	284,973	16,873	23,768	1,493	...	327,106
2009	366,561	75,414	6,605	981	...	449,561

• COMPARATIVE FINANCIALS ($000 omitted)

Year	Assets	Capital & Surplus	Net Invest Income	Benefits Paid	Realized Cap Gains	Policyholder Dividends	Contract Lns (% of assets)
2007	43,307,957	5,255,532	2,223,644	2,567,164	33,115	579,041	7.5
2008	44,630,862	5,060,054	2,331,570	2,741,301	-141,406	595,458	7.7
2009	47,959,821	5,662,640	2,477,356	2,655,907	-44,639	613,384	7.6

• ORDINARY LIFE STATISTICS

Year	Av. Ord. Policy Issued ($)	Av. Ord. Policy In Force ($)	Avg. Prem ($/M)	1st Yr Prem/ Total Prem	Ord. Lapse Ratio
2007	141,410	91,055	5.32	11.4	6.8
2008	133,092	93,536	5.32	11.0	7.5
2009	132,019	95,823	5.33	11.3	7.8

• NEW LIFE BUSINESS ISSUED ($000 omitted)

Year	Whole Life	Term	Credit	Group	Industrial	Total
2007	14,007,247	68,578,312	157,608	188,155	...	82,931,322
2008	13,337,927	66,784,881	41	145,104	...	80,267,953
2009	14,098,965	67,570,273	...	87,924	...	81,757,162

• LIFE INSURANCE IN FORCE ($000 omitted)

Year	Whole Life	Term	Credit	Group	Industrial	Total
2007	203,782,758	414,320,556	268,826	12,896,179	...	631,268,319
2008	206,119,417	435,706,830	141,669	13,116,121	...	655,084,037
2009	209,138,401	453,598,977	66,125	13,378,097	...	676,181,600

STATE LIFE INS CO

P.O. Box 406
Indianapolis, Indiana 46206-0406
Tel: 317-285-1877

AMB#: 007082
Began Business: 09/24/1894
Agency Off: None

Best's Financial Strength Rating: A g   **FSC:** XI

- **NET PREMIUMS AND DEPOSITS ($000 omitted)**

Year	Individual Life	Individual & Group Annuities	Group Life & A&H	Credit Life & A&H	Individual A&H	Total
2007	123,381	110,212	41	...	38	233,671
2008	118,310	332,046	37	...	33	450,426
2009	148,074	243,000	40	...	17	391,131

- **NET OPERATING GAIN ($000 omitted)**

Year	Individual Life	Individual & Group Annuities	Group Life & A&H	Credit Life & A&H	Individual A&H	Total
2007	16,053	5,284	8	...	-488	21,416
2008	23,663	5,659	20	...	159	30,744
2009	21,450	6,900	22	...	-38	28,558

- **COMPARATIVE FINANCIALS ($000 omitted)**

Year	Assets	Capital & Surplus	Net Invest Income	Benefits Paid	Realized Cap Gains	Policyholder Dividends	Contract Lns (% of assets)
2007	2,504,181	150,799	131,486	207,987	-1,901	2,395	1.2
2008	2,840,070	177,887	140,994	194,658	-10,246	2,498	1.0
2009	3,162,483	210,204	166,225	183,239	-945	2,450	1.0

- **ORDINARY LIFE STATISTICS**

Year	Av. Ord. Policy Issued ($)	Av. Ord. Policy In Force ($)	Avg. Prem ($/M)	1st Yr Prem/ Total Prem	Ord. Lapse Ratio
2007	161,477	63,830	10.83	3.0	2.4
2008	157,226	63,552	11.22	5.5	2.4
2009	142,246	63,334	13.88	5.5	2.6

- **NEW LIFE BUSINESS ISSUED ($000 omitted)**

Year	Whole Life	Term	Credit	Group	Industrial	Total
2007	49,412	...	...	...	...	49,412
2008	89,776	...	...	...	...	89,776
2009	205,403	...	...	...	...	205,403

- **LIFE INSURANCE IN FORCE ($000 omitted)**

Year	Whole Life	Term	Credit	Group	Industrial	Total
2007	3,449,432	10,607,861	...	735	...	14,058,028
2008	3,434,196	9,760,522	...	682	...	13,195,400
2009	3,511,255	8,949,204	...	518	...	12,460,976

STATE MUTUAL INS CO

P.O. Box 153
Rome, Georgia 30162-0153
Tel: 706-291-1054

AMB#: 007085
Began Business: 02/14/1894
Agency Off: None

Best's Financial Strength Rating: B+   **FSC:** VI

- **NET PREMIUMS AND DEPOSITS ($000 omitted)**

Year	Individual Life	Individual & Group Annuities	Group Life & A&H	Credit Life & A&H	Individual A&H	Total
2007	30,146	406	...	...	2,098	32,650
2008	39,871	431	0	...	1,818	42,120
2009	28,386	253	...	...	1,590	30,230

- **NET OPERATING GAIN ($000 omitted)**

Year	Individual Life	Individual & Group Annuities	Group Life & A&H	Credit Life & A&H	Individual A&H	Total
2007	588	41	0	...	108	737
2008	1,631	34	0	...	205	1,870
2009	2,284	235	...	...	206	2,725

- **COMPARATIVE FINANCIALS ($000 omitted)**

Year	Assets	Capital & Surplus	Net Invest Income	Benefits Paid	Realized Cap Gains	Policyholder Dividends	Contract Lns (% of assets)
2007	374,893	30,606	19,809	26,333	-129	13,158	9.2
2008	386,050	29,173	20,504	28,964	-472	14,307	9.0
2009	392,821	29,894	20,040	27,808	-1,391	11,641	9.1

- **ORDINARY LIFE STATISTICS**

Year	Av. Ord. Policy Issued ($)	Av. Ord. Policy In Force ($)	Avg. Prem ($/M)	1st Yr Prem/ Total Prem	Ord. Lapse Ratio
2007	11,525	34,412	15.78	0.4	4.3
2008	29,522	29,311	20.43	0.0	4.4
2009	21,325	33,259	16.93	0.1	8.9

- **NEW LIFE BUSINESS ISSUED ($000 omitted)**

Year	Whole Life	Term	Credit	Group	Industrial	Total
2007	4,541	...	...	...	...	4,541
2008	1,978	...	...	...	...	1,978
2009	853	...	...	...	...	853

- **LIFE INSURANCE IN FORCE ($000 omitted)**

Year	Whole Life	Term	Credit	Group	Industrial	Total
2007	1,786,426	835,275	...	...	4,027	2,625,728
2008	1,721,234	795,315	...	...	3,945	2,520,494
2009	1,612,981	661,872	...	...	3,841	2,278,695

STERLING INVESTORS LIFE INS CO

210 East Second Avenue, Suite 105
Rome, Georgia 30161
Tel: 706-235-8154

AMB#: 008841
Began Business: 08/15/1978
Agency Off: Alison M. Huffman

Best's Financial Strength Rating: B   **FSC:** IV

- **NET PREMIUMS AND DEPOSITS ($000 omitted)**

Year	Individual Life	Individual & Group Annuities	Group Life & A&H	Credit Life & A&H	Individual A&H	Total
2007	87	83	...	...	10,245	10,415
2008	63	127	...	...	11,513	11,703
2009	106	27	...	...	9,884	10,017

- **NET OPERATING GAIN ($000 omitted)**

Year	Individual Life	Individual & Group Annuities	Group Life & A&H	Credit Life & A&H	Individual A&H	Total
2007	8	1	0	...	44	56
2008	5	0	-117	...	487	376
2009	8	2	1	...	93	104

- **COMPARATIVE FINANCIALS ($000 omitted)**

Year	Assets	Capital & Surplus	Net Invest Income	Benefits Paid	Realized Cap Gains	Policyholder Dividends	Contract Lns (% of assets)
2007	22,647	6,453	599	8,271	...	2	0.2
2008	22,038	6,680	466	9,623	...	-5	0.2
2009	20,403	7,356	277	8,181	...	2	0.2

- **ORDINARY LIFE STATISTICS**

Year	Av. Ord. Policy Issued ($)	Av. Ord. Policy In Force ($)	Avg. Prem ($/M)	1st Yr Prem/ Total Prem	Ord. Lapse Ratio
2007	...	...	...	...	...
2008	...	...	...	...	...
2009	...	...	...	...	...

- **NEW LIFE BUSINESS ISSUED ($000 omitted)**

Year	Whole Life	Term	Credit	Group	Industrial	Total
2007	3,782	...	...	...	...	3,782
2008	1,232	...	...	...	...	1,232
2009	1,718	...	...	...	...	1,718

- **LIFE INSURANCE IN FORCE ($000 omitted)**

Year	Whole Life	Term	Credit	Group	Industrial	Total
2007	358,647	22,438	...	...	...	381,085
2008	338,561	17,279	...	...	...	355,840
2009	316,700	15,356	...	...	...	332,056

STONEBRIDGE LIFE INSURANCE CO

4333 Edgewood Road N.E.
Cedar Rapids, Iowa 52499
Tel: 319-355-8511

AMB#: 006594
Began Business: 05/07/1906
Agency Off: None

Best's Financial Strength Rating: A g   **FSC:** XV

- **NET PREMIUMS AND DEPOSITS ($000 omitted)**

Year	Individual Life	Individual & Group Annuities	Group Life & A&H	Credit Life & A&H	Individual A&H	Total
2007	78,336	56,127	424,443	7,963	24,252	591,122
2008	81,483	6,403	405,436	7,319	24,476	525,117
2009	78,784	5,775	401,329	6,031	23,757	515,675

- **NET OPERATING GAIN ($000 omitted)**

Year	Individual Life	Individual & Group Annuities	Group Life & A&H	Credit Life & A&H	Individual A&H	Total
2007	-22,232	1,744	124,127	1,929	6,399	111,967
2008	43,122	1,305	161,176	1,498	2,841	209,942
2009	12,639	777	103,595	1,277	22,922	141,210

- **COMPARATIVE FINANCIALS ($000 omitted)**

Year	Assets	Capital & Surplus	Net Invest Income	Benefits Paid	Realized Cap Gains	Policyholder Dividends	Contract Lns (% of assets)
2007	2,206,086	241,534	96,976	245,534	-1,144	...	1.6
2008	2,138,240	172,446	110,218	263,218	1,096	...	1.5
2009	2,024,829	182,141	91,037	249,827	-6,196	...	1.6

- **ORDINARY LIFE STATISTICS**

Year	Av. Ord. Policy Issued ($)	Av. Ord. Policy In Force ($)	Avg. Prem ($/M)	1st Yr Prem/ Total Prem	Ord. Lapse Ratio
2007	14,945	9,265	27.19	8.0	8.1
2008	32,723	11,378	23.08	9.0	13.6
2009	28,798	13,874	19.64	14.5	14.5

- **NEW LIFE BUSINESS ISSUED ($000 omitted)**

Year	Whole Life	Term	Credit	Group	Industrial	Total
2007	39,132	321,247	3,755	1,372,843	...	1,736,977
2008	182,856	818,193	3,554	1,047,436	...	2,052,039
2009	262,554	1,131,255	2,791	762,715	...	2,159,314

- **LIFE INSURANCE IN FORCE ($000 omitted)**

Year	Whole Life	Term	Credit	Group	Industrial	Total
2007	1,589,327	1,651,447	331,208	7,592,389	...	11,164,371
2008	1,454,139	2,161,288	287,399	7,091,102	...	10,993,928
2009	1,483,850	2,778,660	237,870	6,594,891	...	11,095,270

SUN LIFE AND HEALTH INS CO US

One Sun Life Executive Park
Wellesley Hills, Massachusetts 02481
Tel: 860-737-1000

AMB#: 008474
Began Business: 01/01/1975
Agency Off: None

Best's Financial Strength Rating: A **FSC:** VI

• **NET PREMIUMS AND DEPOSITS ($000 omitted)**

Year	Individual Life	Individual & Group Annuities	Group Life & A&H	Credit Life & A&H	Individual A&H	Total
2007	...	19,571	-257,493	...	...	-237,922
2008	...	7,889	...	...	...	7,889
2009	...	8,190	...	...	...	8,190

• **NET OPERATING GAIN ($000 omitted)**

Year	Individual Life	Individual & Group Annuities	Group Life & A&H	Credit Life & A&H	Individual A&H	Total
2007	...	...	342,444	...	...	342,444
2008	...	...	22,349	...	...	22,349
2009	...	...	-1,062	...	...	-1,062

• **COMPARATIVE FINANCIALS ($000 omitted)**

Year	Assets	Capital & Surplus	Net Invest Income	Benefits Paid	Realized Cap Gains	Policyholder Dividends	Contract Lns (% of assets)
2007	119,235	35,290	31,992	122,457	-3,657	...	...
2008	87,717	39,023	3,039	...	-2,874	...	...
2009	72,719	40,792	1,377	...	-83	...	...

• **ORDINARY LIFE STATISTICS**

Year	Av. Ord. Policy Issued ($)	Av. Ord. Policy In Force ($)	Avg. Prem ($/M)	1st Yr Prem/ Total Prem	Ord. Lapse Ratio
2007	...	...	...	...	...
2008	...	...	...	...	...
2009	...	...	...	...	...

• **NEW LIFE BUSINESS ISSUED ($000 omitted)**

Year	Whole Life	Term	Credit	Group	Industrial	Total
2007	...	...	...	9,502,452	...	9,502,452
2008	...	...	...	1,591,614	...	1,591,614
2009	...	...	...	2,722,841	...	2,722,841

• **LIFE INSURANCE IN FORCE ($000 omitted)**

Year	Whole Life	Term	Credit	Group	Industrial	Total
2007	...	...	...	55,525,176	...	55,525,176
2008	...	...	...	44,551,565	...	44,551,565
2009	...	...	...	34,701,961	...	34,701,961

SUN LIFE INS & ANNUITY OF NY

One Sun Life Executive Park
Wellesley Hills, Massachusetts 02481
Tel: 781-237-6030

AMB#: 009513
Began Business: 08/15/1985
Agency Off: None

Best's Financial Strength Rating: A+ g **FSC:** XV

• **NET PREMIUMS AND DEPOSITS ($000 omitted)**

Year	Individual Life	Individual & Group Annuities	Group Life & A&H	Credit Life & A&H	Individual A&H	Total
2007	-40,473	304,410	128,853	...	...	392,790
2008	2,760	384,755	121,393	...	...	508,909
2009	9,896	599,575	124,041	...	...	733,512

• **NET OPERATING GAIN ($000 omitted)**

Year	Individual Life	Individual & Group Annuities	Group Life & A&H	Credit Life & A&H	Individual A&H	Total
2007	2,499	5,009	-28,811	...	7	-21,295
2008	-6,137	-121,393	3,724	...	5	-123,801
2009	-237	20,292	4,768	...	...	27,923

• **COMPARATIVE FINANCIALS ($000 omitted)**

Year	Assets	Capital & Surplus	Net Invest Income	Benefits Paid	Realized Cap Gains	Policyholder Dividends	Contract Lns (% of assets)
2007	2,639,502	206,952	77,952	513,663	-4,085	...	0.0
2008	2,587,732	207,348	55,146	483,540	-25,674	...	0.0
2009	3,071,403	232,392	44,876	351,482	-10,353	...	0.0

• **ORDINARY LIFE STATISTICS**

Year	Av. Ord. Policy Issued ($)	Av. Ord. Policy In Force ($)	Avg. Prem ($/M)	1st Yr Prem/ Total Prem	Ord. Lapse Ratio
2007	...	...	...	...	...
2008	...	...	...	...	...
2009	...	...	...	...	...

• **NEW LIFE BUSINESS ISSUED ($000 omitted)**

Year	Whole Life	Term	Credit	Group	Industrial	Total
2007	421,729	257	...	3,018,935	...	3,440,921
2008	226,320	11,000	...	1,558,931	...	1,796,251
2009	310,194	367	...	1,627,033	...	1,937,594

• **LIFE INSURANCE IN FORCE ($000 omitted)**

Year	Whole Life	Term	Credit	Group	Industrial	Total
2007	1,467,640	257	...	17,451,195	...	18,919,092
2008	1,648,613	14,150	...	16,925,038	...	18,587,801
2009	1,943,354	16,746	...	16,028,759	...	17,988,859

SUN LIFE ASSUR CO OF CA (US)

One Sun Life Executive Park
Wellesley Hills, Massachusetts 02481
Tel: 781-237-6030

AMB#: 008226
Began Business: 01/01/1973
Agency Off: None

Best's Financial Strength Rating: A+ g **FSC:** XV

• **NET PREMIUMS AND DEPOSITS ($000 omitted)**

Year	Individual Life	Individual & Group Annuities	Group Life & A&H	Credit Life & A&H	Individual A&H	Total
2007	378,860	4,015,770	2,121,468	...	...	6,516,098
2008	-863,497	3,231,602	507,288	...	...	2,875,393
2009	48,603	4,252,869	-78,080	...	...	4,223,392

• **NET OPERATING GAIN ($000 omitted)**

Year	Individual Life	Individual & Group Annuities	Group Life & A&H	Credit Life & A&H	Individual A&H	Total
2007	-39,211	38,024	-6,148	...	...	-7,336
2008	-11,692	-710,644	-12,114	...	...	-734,450
2009	-51,601	369,215	7,048	...	...	324,662

• **COMPARATIVE FINANCIALS ($000 omitted)**

Year	Assets	Capital & Surplus	Net Invest Income	Benefits Paid	Realized Cap Gains	Policyholder Dividends	Contract Lns (% of assets)
2007	44,700,806	1,174,144	831,424	5,722,803	-47,664	...	1.5
2008	39,669,904	1,267,093	766,670	5,200,776	-253,898	...	1.8
2009	42,453,649	1,749,838	310,338	4,945,052	-368,676	...	1.7

• **ORDINARY LIFE STATISTICS**

Year	Av. Ord. Policy Issued ($)	Av. Ord. Policy In Force ($)	Avg. Prem ($/M)	1st Yr Prem/ Total Prem	Ord. Lapse Ratio
2007	881,933	361,136	36.78	3.0	4.3
2008	1,108,218	419,918	32.43	2.9	4.1
2009	1,135,682	465,004	20.05	28.3	4.8

• **NEW LIFE BUSINESS ISSUED ($000 omitted)**

Year	Whole Life	Term	Credit	Group	Industrial	Total
2007	1,392,967	22,536	...	6,524,562	...	7,940,065
2008	2,422,057	10,481	...	2,032,857	...	4,465,395
2009	1,891,543	87,950	...	82,708	...	2,062,201

• **LIFE INSURANCE IN FORCE ($000 omitted)**

Year	Whole Life	Term	Credit	Group	Industrial	Total
2007	9,499,900	1,215,009	...	28,120,038	...	38,834,947
2008	11,230,954	1,297,711	...	30,019,354	...	42,548,019
2009	12,200,996	1,472,439	...	26,128,224	...	39,801,659

SUNAMERICA ANNUITY & LIFE ASSR

1 SunAmerica Center
Los Angeles, California 90067-6100
Tel: 310-772-6000

AMB#: 006115
Began Business: 08/06/1965
Agency Off: Jana W. Greer

Best's Financial Strength Rating: A **FSC:** X

• **NET PREMIUMS AND DEPOSITS ($000 omitted)**

Year	Individual Life	Individual & Group Annuities	Group Life & A&H	Credit Life & A&H	Individual A&H	Total
2007	7,646	4,326,066	...	...	...	4,333,712
2008	4,866	3,304,265	...	...	...	3,309,131
2009	3,987	877,789	...	...	...	881,775

• **NET OPERATING GAIN ($000 omitted)**

Year	Individual Life	Individual & Group Annuities	Group Life & A&H	Credit Life & A&H	Individual A&H	Total
2007	21,613	159,595	...	...	...	181,208
2008	12,725	-625,784	...	...	...	-613,059
2009	-326	191,065	...	...	...	190,739

• **COMPARATIVE FINANCIALS ($000 omitted)**

Year	Assets	Capital & Surplus	Net Invest Income	Benefits Paid	Realized Cap Gains	Policyholder Dividends	Contract Lns (% of assets)
2007	35,072,377	1,154,680	267,115	4,688,912	-5,805	...	0.4
2008	24,396,263	1,274,742	241,781	4,832,580	-169,272	...	0.6
2009	25,887,982	653,857	153,785	3,296,531	-68,122	...	0.5

• **ORDINARY LIFE STATISTICS**

Year	Av. Ord. Policy Issued ($)	Av. Ord. Policy In Force ($)	Avg. Prem ($/M)	1st Yr Prem/ Total Prem	Ord. Lapse Ratio
2007	...	...	...	...	...
2008	...	...	...	...	...
2009	...	...	...	...	...

• **NEW LIFE BUSINESS ISSUED ($000 omitted)**

Year	Whole Life	Term	Credit	Group	Industrial	Total
2007	...	...	...	...	...	...
2008	...	...	...	...	...	...
2009	...	...	...	...	...	...

• **LIFE INSURANCE IN FORCE ($000 omitted)**

Year	Whole Life	Term	Credit	Group	Industrial	Total
2007	4,425,440	126,297	...	...	...	4,551,737
2008	4,086,194	118,185	...	...	...	4,204,379
2009	3,738,205	108,886	...	...	...	3,847,091

SUNAMERICA LIFE INS CO

1 SunAmerica Center
Los Angeles, California 90067-6022
Tel: 310-772-6000

AMB#: 007102
Began Business: 06/05/1890
Agency Off: Jana W. Greer

Best's Financial Strength Rating: A
FSC: XV

• **NET PREMIUMS AND DEPOSITS ($000 omitted)**

Year	Individual Life	Individual & Group Annuities	Group Life & A&H	Credit Life & A&H	Individual A&H	Total
2007	-2,167	38,973	...	...	...	36,807
2008	-1,980	39,420	...	...	...	37,440
2009	-2,114	33,467	...	...	...	31,353

• **NET OPERATING GAIN ($000 omitted)**

Year	Individual Life	Individual & Group Annuities	Group Life & A&H	Credit Life & A&H	Individual A&H	Total
2007	5,834	741,129	0	...	...	746,963
2008	5,052	497,728	0	...	...	502,780
2009	7,349	451,538	1	...	...	458,887

• **COMPARATIVE FINANCIALS ($000 omitted)**

Year	Assets	Capital & Surplus	Net Invest Income	Benefits Paid	Realized Cap Gains	Policyholder Dividends	Contract Lns (% of assets)
2007	39,454,568	4,721,343	2,566,335	2,066,937	-392,999	...	0.1
2008	24,857,470	4,658,761	1,664,267	1,597,925	-2,734,437	...	0.2
2009	17,549,131	4,023,612	1,088,158	965,975	-236,600	...	0.3

• **ORDINARY LIFE STATISTICS**

Year	Av. Ord. Policy Issued ($)	Av. Ord. Policy In Force ($)	Avg. Prem ($/M)	1st Yr Prem/ Total Prem	Ord. Lapse Ratio
2007	...	...	...	...	...
2008	...	...	...	...	...
2009	...	...	...	...	...

• **NEW LIFE BUSINESS ISSUED ($000 omitted)**

Year	Whole Life	Term	Credit	Group	Industrial	Total
2007	147	...	...	...	...	147
2008	500	...	...	...	...	500
2009	...	...	...	...	...	...

• **LIFE INSURANCE IN FORCE ($000 omitted)**

Year	Whole Life	Term	Credit	Group	Industrial	Total
2007	1,441,467	206,971	...	...	...	1,648,438
2008	1,354,231	188,524	...	...	...	1,542,755
2009	1,264,536	174,648	...	...	...	1,439,184

SWISS RE LIFE & HEALTH AMERICA

175 King Street
Armonk, New York 10504-1606
Tel: 877-794-7773

AMB#: 007283
Began Business: 09/29/1967
Agency Off: None

Best's Financial Strength Rating: A g
FSC: XV

• **NET PREMIUMS AND DEPOSITS ($000 omitted)**

Year	Individual Life	Individual & Group Annuities	Group Life & A&H	Credit Life & A&H	Individual A&H	Total
2007	2,326,865	-56,069	39,762	17	112,210	2,422,785
2008	2,356,779	129	9,614	21	117,880	2,484,422
2009	189,766	-4,463	31,172	10	95,038	311,523

• **NET OPERATING GAIN ($000 omitted)**

Year	Individual Life	Individual & Group Annuities	Group Life & A&H	Credit Life & A&H	Individual A&H	Total
2007	257,334	14,193	23,143	-16	5,579	300,232
2008	364,379	16,008	84,319	92	85,633	550,432
2009	371,345	2,041	61,085	-38	6,602	441,035

• **COMPARATIVE FINANCIALS ($000 omitted)**

Year	Assets	Capital & Surplus	Net Invest Income	Benefits Paid	Realized Cap Gains	Policyholder Dividends	Contract Lns (% of assets)
2007	11,925,550	1,640,179	718,677	2,177,515	-22,571	4,589	0.8
2008	12,775,210	1,788,034	642,108	2,220,375	-175,256	4,873	0.7
2009	12,176,227	3,039,453	488,611	2,037,274	-73,743	3,924	0.7

• **ORDINARY LIFE STATISTICS**

Year	Av. Ord. Policy Issued ($)	Av. Ord. Policy In Force ($)	Avg. Prem ($/M)	1st Yr Prem/ Total Prem	Ord. Lapse Ratio
2007	...	50,567	2.99	...	7.6
2008	...	54,371	2.99	...	6.1
2009	...	57,266	3.01	...	6.8

• **NEW LIFE BUSINESS ISSUED ($000 omitted)**

Year	Whole Life	Term	Credit	Group	Industrial	Total
2007	...	...	...	...	...	...
2008	...	...	...	...	...	...
2009	...	...	...	...	...	...

• **LIFE INSURANCE IN FORCE ($000 omitted)**

Year	Whole Life	Term	Credit	Group	Industrial	Total
2007	4,830,273	1,089,474,278	7,561	48,436,428	...	1,142,748,540
2008	5,603,522	1,146,928,914	5,790	41,623,734	...	1,194,161,960
2009	5,565,726	1,166,185,111	5,628	64,770,218	...	1,236,526,683

SUNSET LIFE INS CO OF AMERICA

3520 Broadway
Kansas City, Missouri 64111-2565
Tel: 816-753-7000

AMB#: 007104
Began Business: 05/12/1937
Agency Off: Donald E. Krebs

Best's Financial Strength Rating: A g
FSC: IX

• **NET PREMIUMS AND DEPOSITS ($000 omitted)**

Year	Individual Life	Individual & Group Annuities	Group Life & A&H	Credit Life & A&H	Individual A&H	Total
2007	10,212	2,888	7	...	10	13,117
2008	8,463	3,105	6	...	9	11,583
2009	7,213	6,660	23	...	7	13,903

• **NET OPERATING GAIN ($000 omitted)**

Year	Individual Life	Individual & Group Annuities	Group Life & A&H	Credit Life & A&H	Individual A&H	Total
2007	7,225	2,206	25	...	10	9,466
2008	6,232	1,920	54	...	8	8,213
2009	4,978	1,684	185	...	5	6,852

• **COMPARATIVE FINANCIALS ($000 omitted)**

Year	Assets	Capital & Surplus	Net Invest Income	Benefits Paid	Realized Cap Gains	Policyholder Dividends	Contract Lns (% of assets)
2007	430,172	38,366	25,182	51,053	-113	61	2.7
2008	408,034	34,894	22,637	39,293	-3,027	40	2.8
2009	402,377	34,931	22,155	31,254	-1,614	84	2.6

• **ORDINARY LIFE STATISTICS**

Year	Av. Ord. Policy Issued ($)	Av. Ord. Policy In Force ($)	Avg. Prem ($/M)	1st Yr Prem/ Total Prem	Ord. Lapse Ratio
2007	...	...	...	...	...
2008	...	...	...	...	...
2009	...	...	...	...	...

• **NEW LIFE BUSINESS ISSUED ($000 omitted)**

Year	Whole Life	Term	Credit	Group	Industrial	Total
2007	100	535	...	...	...	635
2008	...	333	...	...	...	333
2009	11	619	...	...	...	630

• **LIFE INSURANCE IN FORCE ($000 omitted)**

Year	Whole Life	Term	Credit	Group	Industrial	Total
2007	2,531,186	1,401,660	...	2,264	...	3,935,110
2008	2,323,582	1,254,685	...	2,164	...	3,580,431
2009	2,136,854	1,105,707	...	1,966	...	3,244,527

SYMETRA LIFE INSURANCE COMPANY

P.O. Box 34690
Seattle, Washington 98124-1690
Tel: 425-256-8000

AMB#: 007017
Began Business: 04/05/1957
Agency Off: Linda C. Mahaffey

Best's Financial Strength Rating: A g
FSC: XIV

• **NET PREMIUMS AND DEPOSITS ($000 omitted)**

Year	Individual Life	Individual & Group Annuities	Group Life & A&H	Credit Life & A&H	Individual A&H	Total
2007	121,390	834,237	417,488	...	1,221	1,374,335
2008	109,133	1,803,104	463,076	...	1,120	2,376,433
2009	107,241	2,385,542	447,667	...	1,012	2,941,463

• **NET OPERATING GAIN ($000 omitted)**

Year	Individual Life	Individual & Group Annuities	Group Life & A&H	Credit Life & A&H	Individual A&H	Total
2007	33,553	53,352	47,479	...	832	135,216
2008	31,139	32,386	35,220	...	475	99,220
2009	35,945	63,344	30,146	...	32	129,467

• **COMPARATIVE FINANCIALS ($000 omitted)**

Year	Assets	Capital & Surplus	Net Invest Income	Benefits Paid	Realized Cap Gains	Policyholder Dividends	Contract Lns (% of assets)
2007	18,004,829	1,224,998	855,779	2,109,071	-1,110	6	0.4
2008	18,646,103	1,178,975	842,866	1,659,369	-62,512	4	0.4
2009	20,799,084	1,415,435	947,509	1,634,297	-86,415	5	0.4

• **ORDINARY LIFE STATISTICS**

Year	Av. Ord. Policy Issued ($)	Av. Ord. Policy In Force ($)	Avg. Prem ($/M)	1st Yr Prem/ Total Prem	Ord. Lapse Ratio
2007	238,595	192,167	3.21	5.6	5.1
2008	229,993	197,178	3.10	5.0	5.0
2009	196,587	199,082	3.05	7.8	6.5

• **NEW LIFE BUSINESS ISSUED ($000 omitted)**

Year	Whole Life	Term	Credit	Group	Industrial	Total
2007	282,651	2,257,194	...	1,368,876	...	3,908,721
2008	215,298	1,807,259	...	671,428	...	2,693,985
2009	225,733	2,039,543	...	754,430	...	3,019,705

• **LIFE INSURANCE IN FORCE ($000 omitted)**

Year	Whole Life	Term	Credit	Group	Industrial	Total
2007	19,963,985	31,999,877	...	4,418,558	...	56,382,420
2008	19,733,924	31,403,831	...	4,564,425	...	55,702,180
2009	19,020,471	30,771,622	...	5,123,578	...	54,915,671

TEACHERS INS & ANNUITY ASSOC

730 Third Avenue
New York, New York 10017-3206
Tel: 212-490-9000

AMB#: 007112
Began Business: 05/17/1918
Agency Off: None

Best's Financial Strength Rating: A++g **FSC:** XV

• **NET PREMIUMS AND DEPOSITS ($000 omitted)**

Year	Individual Life	Individual & Group Annuities	Group Life & A&H	Credit Life & A&H	Individual A&H	Total
2007	369,205	9,309,538	...	-20,496	7	9,658,254
2008	375,482	13,217,340	...	...	5	13,592,827
2009	382,297	9,673,147	...	...	5	10,055,449

• **NET OPERATING GAIN ($000 omitted)**

Year	Individual Life	Individual & Group Annuities	Group Life & A&H	Credit Life & A&H	Individual A&H	Total
2007	78,004	540,287	-340	6,542	773	1,565,606
2008	30,573	43,352	-375	...	2,359	1,167,479
2009	40,972	1,697,158	-260	...	2,322	2,874,406

• **COMPARATIVE FINANCIALS ($000 omitted)**

Year	Assets	Capital & Surplus	Net Invest Income	Benefits Paid	Realized Cap Gains	Policyholder Dividends	Contract Lns (% of assets)
2007	196,409,275	17,827,120	10,705,120	10,151,834	-136,860	4,578,061	0.4
2008	195,236,800	17,754,167	10,498,388	13,642,177	-4,450,869	4,573,806	0.5
2009	201,727,945	22,843,951	10,272,127	11,197,845	-3,326,468	2,645,809	0.5

• **ORDINARY LIFE STATISTICS**

Year	Av. Ord. Policy Issued ($)	Av. Ord. Policy In Force ($)	Avg. Prem ($/M)	1st Yr Prem/ Total Prem	Ord. Lapse Ratio
2007	76,987	74,912	11.47	0.2	13.9
2008	74,145	74,794	12.34	0.4	5.3
2009	66,066	75,336	13.12	0.4	4.2

• **NEW LIFE BUSINESS ISSUED ($000 omitted)**

Year	Whole Life	Term	Credit	Group	Industrial	Total
2007	23,789	...	...	...	...	23,789
2008	38,481	...	...	...	...	38,481
2009	39,751	-5,925	...	...	...	33,826

• **LIFE INSURANCE IN FORCE ($000 omitted)**

Year	Whole Life	Term	Credit	Group	Industrial	Total
2007	1,710,441	30,540,471	...	102,343	...	32,353,255
2008	1,671,583	28,781,361	...	94,137	...	30,547,081
2009	1,636,474	27,441,060	...	87,897	...	29,165,431

TENNESSEE FARMERS LIFE INS CO

P.O. Box 307
Columbia, Tennessee 38402-0307
Tel: 931-388-7872

AMB#: 008443
Began Business: 09/01/1973
Agency Off: Neal Townsend

Best's Financial Strength Rating: A+ **FSC:** VIII

• **NET PREMIUMS AND DEPOSITS ($000 omitted)**

Year	Individual Life	Individual & Group Annuities	Group Life & A&H	Credit Life & A&H	Individual A&H	Total
2007	80,378	54,574	3,370	...	...	138,322
2008	86,711	63,040	3,431	...	...	153,182
2009	91,085	70,372	3,503	...	...	164,960

• **NET OPERATING GAIN ($000 omitted)**

Year	Individual Life	Individual & Group Annuities	Group Life & A&H	Credit Life & A&H	Individual A&H	Total
2007	12,199	-3,900	1,634	...	...	9,933
2008	5,461	3,673	1,856	...	...	10,990
2009	9,594	9,685	2,065	...	...	21,344

• **COMPARATIVE FINANCIALS ($000 omitted)**

Year	Assets	Capital & Surplus	Net Invest Income	Benefits Paid	Realized Cap Gains	Policyholder Dividends	Contract Lns (% of assets)
2007	1,260,667	196,030	53,882	-118,379	3,359	2,900	1.1
2008	1,295,963	202,245	56,325	97,449	-16,716	2,996	1.1
2009	1,399,780	228,638	62,893	87,110	-9,268	3,047	1.1

• **ORDINARY LIFE STATISTICS**

Year	Av. Ord. Policy Issued ($)	Av. Ord. Policy In Force ($)	Avg. Prem ($/M)	1st Yr Prem/ Total Prem	Ord. Lapse Ratio
2007	127,634	94,913	4.11	17.7	5.7
2008	125,495	100,933	3.98	17.0	6.2
2009	119,034	103,563	3.93	16.6	5.6

• **NEW LIFE BUSINESS ISSUED ($000 omitted)**

Year	Whole Life	Term	Credit	Group	Industrial	Total
2007	396,784	3,226,096	...	...	...	3,622,880
2008	497,035	3,101,400	...	...	...	3,598,435
2009	388,510	3,238,820	...	...	...	3,627,330

• **LIFE INSURANCE IN FORCE ($000 omitted)**

Year	Whole Life	Term	Credit	Group	Industrial	Total
2007	5,171,102	16,674,823	...	...	...	21,845,925
2008	5,287,163	18,046,696	...	...	...	23,333,859
2009	5,446,495	19,640,261	...	...	...	25,086,756

TEACHERS PROTECTIVE MUTUAL

116-118 North Prince Street
Lancaster, Pennsylvania 17603-3526
Tel: 717-394-7156

AMB#: 007114
Began Business: 05/11/1912
Agency Off: James Godfrey

Best's Financial Strength Rating: B- **FSC:** IV

• **NET PREMIUMS AND DEPOSITS ($000 omitted)**

Year	Individual Life	Individual & Group Annuities	Group Life & A&H	Credit Life & A&H	Individual A&H	Total
2007	497	...	11,651	...	8,166	20,314
2008	454	...	11,984	...	7,816	20,254
2009	412	...	13,629	...	7,261	21,301

• **NET OPERATING GAIN ($000 omitted)**

Year	Individual Life	Individual & Group Annuities	Group Life & A&H	Credit Life & A&H	Individual A&H	Total
2007	95	-30	382	...	774	1,222
2008	176	-43	56	...	-195	-6
2009	127	-64	107	...	-620	-450

• **COMPARATIVE FINANCIALS ($000 omitted)**

Year	Assets	Capital & Surplus	Net Invest Income	Benefits Paid	Realized Cap Gains	Policyholder Dividends	Contract Lns (% of assets)
2007	56,968	8,635	2,791	14,517	96	36	0.5
2008	58,077	7,528	2,674	14,904	-295	30	0.5
2009	61,704	7,470	2,677	16,444	-137	23	0.4

• **ORDINARY LIFE STATISTICS**

Year	Av. Ord. Policy Issued ($)	Av. Ord. Policy In Force ($)	Avg. Prem ($/M)	1st Yr Prem/ Total Prem	Ord. Lapse Ratio
2007	...	...	...	...	...
2008	...	...	...	...	...
2009	...	...	...	...	...

• **NEW LIFE BUSINESS ISSUED ($000 omitted)**

Year	Whole Life	Term	Credit	Group	Industrial	Total
2007	...	...	...	6,994	...	6,994
2008	...	...	...	6,306	...	6,306
2009	...	...	...	3,442	...	3,442

• **LIFE INSURANCE IN FORCE ($000 omitted)**

Year	Whole Life	Term	Credit	Group	Industrial	Total
2007	8,980	508	...	40,134	...	49,622
2008	8,416	396	...	33,322	...	42,134
2009	7,756	367	...	28,203	...	36,326

TEXAS LIFE INS CO

P.O. Box 830
Waco, Texas 76703-0830
Tel: 254-752-6521

AMB#: 007118
Began Business: 04/01/1901
Agency Off: Steven R. Worley

Best's Financial Strength Rating: A- g **FSC:** VIII

• **NET PREMIUMS AND DEPOSITS ($000 omitted)**

Year	Individual Life	Individual & Group Annuities	Group Life & A&H	Credit Life & A&H	Individual A&H	Total
2007	111,876	9,798	34	...	6	121,715
2008	129,470	12,008	36	...	6	141,520
2009	102,910	1,757	40	...	5	104,712

• **NET OPERATING GAIN ($000 omitted)**

Year	Individual Life	Individual & Group Annuities	Group Life & A&H	Credit Life & A&H	Individual A&H	Total
2007	12,980	1,573	-179	...	-7	14,367
2008	6,288	175	-78	...	4	6,389
2009	17,006	444	-88	...	0	17,362

• **COMPARATIVE FINANCIALS ($000 omitted)**

Year	Assets	Capital & Surplus	Net Invest Income	Benefits Paid	Realized Cap Gains	Policyholder Dividends	Contract Lns (% of assets)
2007	630,855	45,714	38,298	59,568	-1,120	3,174	5.4
2008	664,998	47,963	36,349	70,483	-9,825	3,796	5.3
2009	727,016	48,359	35,525	47,165	719	3,435	4.8

• **ORDINARY LIFE STATISTICS**

Year	Av. Ord. Policy Issued ($)	Av. Ord. Policy In Force ($)	Avg. Prem ($/M)	1st Yr Prem/ Total Prem	Ord. Lapse Ratio
2007	38,129	43,352	7.74	18.7	9.0
2008	39,192	42,636	8.14	19.5	8.5
2009	37,772	41,885	8.22	15.4	7.6

• **NEW LIFE BUSINESS ISSUED ($000 omitted)**

Year	Whole Life	Term	Credit	Group	Industrial	Total
2007	2,858,725	91	...	...	...	2,858,816
2008	3,021,554	...	...	...	...	3,021,554
2009	2,885,662	...	...	...	...	2,885,662

• **LIFE INSURANCE IN FORCE ($000 omitted)**

Year	Whole Life	Term	Credit	Group	Industrial	Total
2007	14,607,760	412,829	...	...	...	15,020,589
2008	16,077,472	384,709	...	10,099	...	16,472,280
2009	17,468,555	354,880	...	11,440	...	17,834,875

THRIVENT FINANCIAL LUTHERANS

625 Fourth Avenue South
Minneapolis, Minnesota 55415-1624
Tel: 800-847-4836

AMB#: 006008
Began Business: 08/15/1902
Agency Off: James A. Thomsen

Best's Financial Strength Rating: A++g
FSC: XV

• NET PREMIUMS AND DEPOSITS ($000 omitted)

Year	Individual Life	Individual & Group Annuities	Group Life & A&H	Credit Life & A&H	Individual A&H	Total
2007	1,197,400	...	...	...	327,893	3,766,207
2008	1,298,275	...	...	...	333,154	4,374,803
2009	1,327,548	...	...	...	329,298	4,721,297

• NET OPERATING GAIN ($000 omitted)

Year	Individual Life	Individual & Group Annuities	Group Life & A&H	Credit Life & A&H	Individual A&H	Total
2007	130,864	115,908	...	...	-21,943	348,285
2008	104,922	13,322	...	...	-36,520	101,803
2009	94,068	149,323	...	...	-9,063	274,431

• COMPARATIVE FINANCIALS ($000 omitted)

Year	Assets	Capital & Surplus	Net Invest Income	Benefits Paid	Realized Cap Gains	Policyholder Dividends	Contract Lns (% of assets)
2007	53,474,099	4,433,621	2,261,896	4,410,152	42,746	322,781	2.3
2008	49,470,159	3,934,709	2,322,268	3,809,628	-417,065	336,112	2.5
2009	54,372,055	4,126,774	2,272,436	3,385,534	-292,701	322,142	2.3

• ORDINARY LIFE STATISTICS

Year	Av. Ord. Policy Issued ($)	Av. Ord. Policy In Force ($)	Avg. Prem ($/M)	1st Yr Prem/ Total Prem	Ord. Lapse Ratio
2007	201,671	68,114	7.84	6.8	3.6
2008	198,159	70,462	8.40	6.0	3.3
2009	184,925	72,751	8.48	5.2	3.2

• NEW LIFE BUSINESS ISSUED ($000 omitted)

Year	Whole Life	Term	Credit	Group	Industrial	Total
2007	8,440,938	...	...	...	...	8,440,938
2008	2,364,535	5,929,397	...	...	...	8,293,932
2009	2,436,867	5,945,244	...	...	...	8,382,111

• LIFE INSURANCE IN FORCE ($000 omitted)

Year	Whole Life	Term	Credit	Group	Industrial	Total
2007	159,646,693	...	...	...	...	159,646,693
2008	109,666,878	52,121,197	...	...	...	161,788,075
2009	109,679,431	54,614,686	...	...	...	164,294,117

TIAA-CREF LIFE INS CO

730 Third Avenue
New York, New York 10017-3206
Tel: 800-223-1200

AMB#: 060222
Began Business: 12/18/1996
Agency Off: None

Best's Financial Strength Rating: A++g
FSC: XV

• NET PREMIUMS AND DEPOSITS ($000 omitted)

Year	Individual Life	Individual & Group Annuities	Group Life & A&H	Credit Life & A&H	Individual A&H	Total
2007	27,254	269,297	...	...	...	296,551
2008	25,884	327,443	...	...	...	353,327
2009	31,361	444,145	...	...	...	475,507

• NET OPERATING GAIN ($000 omitted)

Year	Individual Life	Individual & Group Annuities	Group Life & A&H	Credit Life & A&H	Individual A&H	Total
2007	-9,662	13,173	...	...	-102	18,424
2008	-14,048	11,844	...	...	104	11,564
2009	-8,682	-12,771	23,528	...	41	12,436

• COMPARATIVE FINANCIALS ($000 omitted)

Year	Assets	Capital & Surplus	Net Invest Income	Benefits Paid	Realized Cap Gains	Policyholder Dividends	Contract Lns (% of assets)
2007	3,115,350	332,130	128,587	258,760	-8,326	...	0.0
2008	2,917,585	280,331	121,767	186,492	-73,040	...	0.0
2009	3,319,088	353,313	130,321	172,804	-19,452	...	0.1

• ORDINARY LIFE STATISTICS

Year	Av. Ord. Policy Issued ($)	Av. Ord. Policy In Force ($)	Avg. Prem ($/M)	1st Yr Prem/ Total Prem	Ord. Lapse Ratio
2007	563,905	434,768	2.34	28.2	2.0
2008	585,281	444,263	2.45	27.2	2.9
2009	557,245	452,962	2.59	27.3	1.6

• NEW LIFE BUSINESS ISSUED ($000 omitted)

Year	Whole Life	Term	Credit	Group	Industrial	Total
2007	203,329	1,523,912	...	...	...	1,727,241
2008	254,839	1,033,950	...	...	...	1,288,789
2009	220,440	1,046,734	...	...	...	1,267,174

• LIFE INSURANCE IN FORCE ($000 omitted)

Year	Whole Life	Term	Credit	Group	Industrial	Total
2007	708,183	21,769,768	...	...	...	22,477,951
2008	941,708	22,110,236	...	...	...	23,051,944
2009	1,126,666	22,786,580	...	...	...	23,913,246

THRIVENT LIFE INSURANCE CO

625 Fourth Avenue South
Minneapolis, Minnesota 55415-1624
Tel: 800-847-4836

AMB#: 009342
Began Business: 12/01/1982
Agency Off: James A. Thomsen

Best's Financial Strength Rating: A++g
FSC: XV

• NET PREMIUMS AND DEPOSITS ($000 omitted)

Year	Individual Life	Individual & Group Annuities	Group Life & A&H	Credit Life & A&H	Individual A&H	Total
2007	12,496	120,714	...	...	1	133,211
2008	12,013	149,787	...	...	1	161,801
2009	11,094	158,036	...	...	1	169,131

• NET OPERATING GAIN ($000 omitted)

Year	Individual Life	Individual & Group Annuities	Group Life & A&H	Credit Life & A&H	Individual A&H	Total
2007	4,921	23,108	...	...	-1	50,253
2008	558	9,895	...	...	1	24,532
2009	2,605	9,983	...	...	0	16,194

• COMPARATIVE FINANCIALS ($000 omitted)

Year	Assets	Capital & Surplus	Net Invest Income	Benefits Paid	Realized Cap Gains	Policyholder Dividends	Contract Lns (% of assets)
2007	3,664,564	178,076	84,936	433,794	-868	...	0.4
2008	2,689,220	173,639	76,809	369,384	-4,415	...	0.5
2009	3,035,086	172,162	70,703	250,466	-3,839	...	0.4

• ORDINARY LIFE STATISTICS

Year	Av. Ord. Policy Issued ($)	Av. Ord. Policy In Force ($)	Avg. Prem ($/M)	1st Yr Prem/ Total Prem	Ord. Lapse Ratio
2007	...	153,576	6.95	...	3.1
2008	...	150,731	7.21	...	6.2
2009	...	152,222	6.97	...	3.1

• NEW LIFE BUSINESS ISSUED ($000 omitted)

Year	Whole Life	Term	Credit	Group	Industrial	Total
2007	6,189	30	...	...	...	6,219
2008	6,194	10	...	...	...	6,204
2009	2,276	...	...	...	...	2,276

• LIFE INSURANCE IN FORCE ($000 omitted)

Year	Whole Life	Term	Credit	Group	Industrial	Total
2007	1,802,393	44,515	...	...	...	1,846,908
2008	1,673,680	41,640	...	...	...	1,715,320
2009	1,606,586	38,633	...	...	...	1,645,218

TIME INSURANCE COMPANY

P.O. Box 3050
Milwaukee, Wisconsin 53201-3050
Tel: 414-271-3011

AMB#: 007126
Began Business: 03/06/1910
Agency Off: Laura Hohing

Best's Financial Strength Rating: A- g
FSC: VIII

• NET PREMIUMS AND DEPOSITS ($000 omitted)

Year	Individual Life	Individual & Group Annuities	Group Life & A&H	Credit Life & A&H	Individual A&H	Total
2007	267	44,392	899,742	...	450,635	1,395,035
2008	545	37,766	897,172	...	428,290	1,363,774
2009	623	29,582	864,882	...	445,308	1,340,396

• NET OPERATING GAIN ($000 omitted)

Year	Individual Life	Individual & Group Annuities	Group Life & A&H	Credit Life & A&H	Individual A&H	Total
2007	9,604	324	59,610	0	44,953	114,491
2008	4,456	458	37,198	...	31,118	73,230
2009	4,881	440	-7,348	...	-38,665	-40,692

• COMPARATIVE FINANCIALS ($000 omitted)

Year	Assets	Capital & Surplus	Net Invest Income	Benefits Paid	Realized Cap Gains	Policyholder Dividends	Contract Lns (% of assets)
2007	812,867	254,508	45,528	849,440	-1,976	...	0.0
2008	678,112	211,842	42,954	867,138	-34,188	...	0.0
2009	795,822	239,511	36,299	999,398	-2,815	...	0.0

• ORDINARY LIFE STATISTICS

Year	Av. Ord. Policy Issued ($)	Av. Ord. Policy In Force ($)	Avg. Prem ($/M)	1st Yr Prem/ Total Prem	Ord. Lapse Ratio
2007	...	...	...	...	...
2008	...	...	...	...	...
2009	...	...	...	...	...

• NEW LIFE BUSINESS ISSUED ($000 omitted)

Year	Whole Life	Term	Credit	Group	Industrial	Total
2007	...	115,310	2,368	197,927	...	315,605
2008	...	138,064	1,266	330,989	...	470,319
2009	...	91,116	...	408,240	...	499,356

• LIFE INSURANCE IN FORCE ($000 omitted)

Year	Whole Life	Term	Credit	Group	Industrial	Total
2007	5,620,833	1,178,353	74,080	424,970	...	7,298,236
2008	5,245,669	1,122,625	64,197	497,437	...	6,929,928
2009	5,511,820	1,027,263	52,004	618,084	...	7,209,171

TOWER LIFE INS CO

310 South St. Mary's St.
San Antonio, Texas 78205
Tel: 210-554-4400

AMB#: 007128
Began Business: 03/29/1955
Agency Off: James P. Zachry

Best's Financial Strength Rating: B++
FSC: VI

• NET PREMIUMS AND DEPOSITS ($000 omitted)

Year	Individual Life	Individual & Group Annuities	Group Life & A&H	Credit Life & A&H	Individual A&H	Total
2007	771	135	1,237	...	192	2,335
2008	704	103	916	...	176	1,899
2009	648	27	785	...	179	1,640

• NET OPERATING GAIN ($000 omitted)

Year	Individual Life	Individual & Group Annuities	Group Life & A&H	Credit Life & A&H	Individual A&H	Total
2007	462	39	671	...	-9	1,163
2008	62	-35	151	...	20	199
2009	81	5	-110	...	19	-5

• COMPARATIVE FINANCIALS ($000 omitted)

Year	Assets	Capital & Surplus	Net Invest Income	Benefits Paid	Realized Cap Gains	Policyholder Dividends	Contract Lns (% of assets)
2007	78,649	40,137	2,170	4,620	8	90	8.9
2008	75,399	36,684	1,514	2,954	7	90	9.3
2009	74,476	36,814	1,418	2,848	-23	28	9.5

• ORDINARY LIFE STATISTICS

Year	Av. Ord. Policy Issued ($)	Av. Ord. Policy In Force ($)	Avg. Prem ($/M)	1st Yr Prem/ Total Prem	Ord. Lapse Ratio
2007	...	...	...	...	...
2008	...	...	...	...	...
2009	...	...	...	...	...

• NEW LIFE BUSINESS ISSUED ($000 omitted)

Year	Whole Life	Term	Credit	Group	Industrial	Total
2007	305	...	...	...	...	305
2008	456	...	...	...	...	456
2009	52	...	...	...	...	52

• LIFE INSURANCE IN FORCE ($000 omitted)

Year	Whole Life	Term	Credit	Group	Industrial	Total
2007	112,955	9,955	...	505,975	...	628,885
2008	106,439	7,559	...	451,978	...	565,976
2009	99,373	6,577	...	387,710	...	493,660

TRANS-CITY LIFE INS CO

7500 East McDonald Drive, Suite 700
Scottsdale, Arizona 85250-6055
Tel: 480-483-6500

AMB#: 008051
Began Business: 12/04/1967
Agency Off: Michael E. Jones

Best's Financial Strength Rating: B+
FSC: IV

• NET PREMIUMS AND DEPOSITS ($000 omitted)

Year	Individual Life	Individual & Group Annuities	Group Life & A&H	Credit Life & A&H	Individual A&H	Total
2007	...	...	...	2,716	...	2,716
2008	...	...	...	1,672	...	1,672
2009	...	...	...	713	...	713

• NET OPERATING GAIN ($000 omitted)

Year	Individual Life	Individual & Group Annuities	Group Life & A&H	Credit Life & A&H	Individual A&H	Total
2007	...	...	...	958	...	958
2008	...	...	...	1,555	...	1,555
2009	...	...	...	1,223	...	1,223

• COMPARATIVE FINANCIALS ($000 omitted)

Year	Assets	Capital & Surplus	Net Invest Income	Benefits Paid	Realized Cap Gains	Policyholder Dividends	Contract Lns (% of assets)
2007	19,808	7,811	1,046	1,280	...	...	...
2008	20,218	9,978	672	642	...	...	...
2009	17,941	9,819	313	839	...	...	...

• ORDINARY LIFE STATISTICS

Year	Av. Ord. Policy Issued ($)	Av. Ord. Policy In Force ($)	Avg. Prem ($/M)	1st Yr Prem/ Total Prem	Ord. Lapse Ratio
2007	...	...	...	...	...
2008	...	...	...	...	...
2009	...	...	...	...	...

• NEW LIFE BUSINESS ISSUED ($000 omitted)

Year	Whole Life	Term	Credit	Group	Industrial	Total
2007	...	...	152,390	...	...	152,390
2008	...	...	91,805	...	...	91,805
2009	...	...	51,704	...	...	51,704

• LIFE INSURANCE IN FORCE ($000 omitted)

Year	Whole Life	Term	Credit	Group	Industrial	Total
2007	...	...	558,846	...	...	558,846
2008	...	...	542,299	...	...	542,299
2009	...	...	472,656	...	...	472,656

TRANS-OCEANIC LIFE INS CO

P.O. Box 363467
San Juan, Puerto Rico 00936-3467
Tel: 787-620-2680

AMB#: 007132
Began Business: 12/22/1959
Agency Off: Humberto Tapia

Best's Financial Strength Rating: B++
FSC: IV

• NET PREMIUMS AND DEPOSITS ($000 omitted)

Year	Individual Life	Individual & Group Annuities	Group Life & A&H	Credit Life & A&H	Individual A&H	Total
2007	728	43	292	112	15,286	16,460
2008	550	34	204	178	26,220	27,186
2009	1,798	28	764	148	22,116	24,854

• NET OPERATING GAIN ($000 omitted)

Year	Individual Life	Individual & Group Annuities	Group Life & A&H	Credit Life & A&H	Individual A&H	Total
2007	173	43	27	51	607	901
2008	196	8	6	11	6,571	6,792
2009	359	17	44	17	1,931	2,368

• COMPARATIVE FINANCIALS ($000 omitted)

Year	Assets	Capital & Surplus	Net Invest Income	Benefits Paid	Realized Cap Gains	Policyholder Dividends	Contract Lns (% of assets)
2007	24,691	9,839	893	5,809	-40	...	1.0
2008	27,560	6,500	809	8,495	-460	...	0.3
2009	32,343	9,010	984	8,253	-275	...	0.3

• ORDINARY LIFE STATISTICS

Year	Av. Ord. Policy Issued ($)	Av. Ord. Policy In Force ($)	Avg. Prem ($/M)	1st Yr Prem/ Total Prem	Ord. Lapse Ratio
2007	...	...	...	...	...
2008	...	...	...	...	...
2009	...	...	...	...	...

• NEW LIFE BUSINESS ISSUED ($000 omitted)

Year	Whole Life	Term	Credit	Group	Industrial	Total
2007	5,575	...	1,528	...	...	7,103
2008	4,300	...	250	7,120	...	11,670
2009	6,450	...	3,245	137,305	...	147,000

• LIFE INSURANCE IN FORCE ($000 omitted)

Year	Whole Life	Term	Credit	Group	Industrial	Total
2007	709,309	16,079	49,400	30,397	...	805,185
2008	686,020	13,916	34,915	26,308	...	761,159
2009	809,885	11,300	28,315	147,611	...	997,111

TRANS WORLD ASSURANCE CO

885 South El Camino Real
San Mateo, California 94402
Tel: 650-348-2300

AMB#: 007136
Began Business: 12/19/1963
Agency Off: Charles B. Royals

Best's Financial Strength Rating: B++
FSC: VII

• NET PREMIUMS AND DEPOSITS ($000 omitted)

Year	Individual Life	Individual & Group Annuities	Group Life & A&H	Credit Life & A&H	Individual A&H	Total
2007	13,322	20,537	1,510	...	...	35,369
2008	11,145	19,813	1,214	...	...	32,173
2009	10,151	18,799	1,405	...	...	30,355

• NET OPERATING GAIN ($000 omitted)

Year	Individual Life	Individual & Group Annuities	Group Life & A&H	Credit Life & A&H	Individual A&H	Total
2007	964	59	3	...	...	1,026
2008	1,227	108	3	...	...	1,337
2009	3,518	433	3	...	...	3,953

• COMPARATIVE FINANCIALS ($000 omitted)

Year	Assets	Capital & Surplus	Net Invest Income	Benefits Paid	Realized Cap Gains	Policyholder Dividends	Contract Lns (% of assets)
2007	331,959	67,120	12,168	16,676	...	8	0.3
2008	334,900	67,232	12,436	15,459	...	7	0.3
2009	338,375	70,012	12,853	13,787	...	7	0.3

• ORDINARY LIFE STATISTICS

Year	Av. Ord. Policy Issued ($)	Av. Ord. Policy In Force ($)	Avg. Prem ($/M)	1st Yr Prem/ Total Prem	Ord. Lapse Ratio
2007	15,744	20,133	11.62	36.6	11.3
2008	14,638	19,819	10.54	27.2	14.6
2009	50,124	20,485	9.79	24.1	12.8

• NEW LIFE BUSINESS ISSUED ($000 omitted)

Year	Whole Life	Term	Credit	Group	Industrial	Total
2007	124,600	...	...	...	...	124,600
2008	100,532	...	...	...	...	100,532
2009	128,818	...	...	...	...	128,818

• LIFE INSURANCE IN FORCE ($000 omitted)

Year	Whole Life	Term	Credit	Group	Industrial	Total
2007	906,544	242,958	...	1,160,416	...	2,309,918
2008	821,408	240,492	...	1,124,094	...	2,185,994
2009	805,418	235,491	...	1,298,751	...	2,339,660

TRANSAM ASSURANCE COMPANY

4060 Barrancas Avenue
Pensacola, Florida 32507
Tel: 850-456-7406

AMB#: 007437
Began Business: 09/16/1966
Agency Off: Barbara J. Woodbury

Best's Financial Strength Rating: B+ **FSC:** III

• NET PREMIUMS AND DEPOSITS ($000 omitted)

Year	Individual Life	Individual & Group Annuities	Group Life & A&H	Credit Life & A&H	Individual A&H	Total
2007	6	13	3	...	...	22
2008	5	12	3	...	...	20
2009	5	13	3	...	...	21

• NET OPERATING GAIN ($000 omitted)

Year	Individual Life	Individual & Group Annuities	Group Life & A&H	Credit Life & A&H	Individual A&H	Total
2007	84	...	0	...	...	84
2008	88	...	0	...	...	88
2009	31	...	0	...	...	31

• COMPARATIVE FINANCIALS ($000 omitted)

Year	Assets	Capital & Surplus	Net Invest Income	Benefits Paid	Realized Cap Gains	Policyholder Dividends	Contract Lns (% of assets)
2007	4,236	3,170	155	48	...	...	0.2
2008	4,361	3,297	168	46	...	...	0.2
2009	4,409	3,344	91	38	...	...	0.1

• ORDINARY LIFE STATISTICS

Year	Av. Ord. Policy Issued ($)	Av. Ord. Policy In Force ($)	Avg. Prem ($/M)	1st Yr Prem/ Total Prem	Ord. Lapse Ratio
2007	...	...	...	...	...
2008	...	...	...	...	...
2009	...	...	...	...	...

• NEW LIFE BUSINESS ISSUED ($000 omitted)

Year	Whole Life	Term	Credit	Group	Industrial	Total
2007	...	...	...	...	...	...
2008	...	...	...	...	...	...
2009	...	...	...	...	...	...

• LIFE INSURANCE IN FORCE ($000 omitted)

Year	Whole Life	Term	Credit	Group	Industrial	Total
2007	477	279	...	2,582	...	3,338
2008	422	305	...	2,596	...	3,323
2009	384	308	...	2,722	...	3,414

TRANSAMERICA LIFE INSURANCE CO

4333 Edgewood Road N.E.
Cedar Rapids, Iowa 52499
Tel: 319-355-8511

AMB#: 006095
Began Business: 03/19/1962
Agency Off: None

Best's Financial Strength Rating: A g **FSC:** XV

• NET PREMIUMS AND DEPOSITS ($000 omitted)

Year	Individual Life	Individual & Group Annuities	Group Life & A&H	Credit Life & A&H	Individual A&H	Total
2007	1,743,745	11,970,394	378,440	34,226	503,372	14,630,178
2008	-1,425,673	3,866,193	370,648	-90	511,590	3,322,669
2009	1,261,888	7,424,513	344,829	25,623	457,972	9,514,826

• NET OPERATING GAIN ($000 omitted)

Year	Individual Life	Individual & Group Annuities	Group Life & A&H	Credit Life & A&H	Individual A&H	Total
2007	-275,205	154,549	21,101	93	48,302	-51,160
2008	-97,057	-1,325,799	386,983	5,978	135,205	-894,689
2009	191,694	227,315	45,973	14,139	121,928	601,050

• COMPARATIVE FINANCIALS ($000 omitted)

Year	Assets	Capital & Surplus	Net Invest Income	Benefits Paid	Realized Cap Gains	Policyholder Dividends	Contract Lns (% of assets)
2007	112,802,514	4,324,562	4,212,323	13,885,420	313,799	17,417	0.6
2008	103,871,552	4,926,874	3,886,850	11,634,549	366,221	12,166	0.7
2009	101,455,188	5,026,824	3,073,157	7,939,237	-700,521	11,010	0.7

• ORDINARY LIFE STATISTICS

Year	Av. Ord. Policy Issued ($)	Av. Ord. Policy In Force ($)	Avg. Prem ($/M)	1st Yr Prem/ Total Prem	Ord. Lapse Ratio
2007	291,534	108,888	5.26	8.8	4.2
2008	276,945	94,913	3.65	14.3	6.1
2009	301,814	84,570	3.58	13.4	7.3

• NEW LIFE BUSINESS ISSUED ($000 omitted)

Year	Whole Life	Term	Credit	Group	Industrial	Total
2007	7,783,173	20,870,831	4,094,240	3,165,077	...	35,913,321
2008	6,509,168	18,939,856	3,019,916	2,117,190	...	30,586,130
2009	7,461,124	34,798,889	2,607,775	1,701,272	...	46,569,060

• LIFE INSURANCE IN FORCE ($000 omitted)

Year	Whole Life	Term	Credit	Group	Industrial	Total
2007	146,211,644	873,499,276	5,136,354	28,644,394	...	1,053,491,668
2008	146,038,599	934,143,809	3,874,130	23,227,017	...	1,107,283,555
2009	145,649,164	985,780,800	3,480,140	20,913,513	...	1,155,823,618

TRANSAMERICA FINANCIAL LIFE

4333 Edgewood Road N.E.
Cedar Rapids, Iowa 52499
Tel: 319-355-8511

AMB#: 007267
Began Business: 10/17/1947
Agency Off: None

Best's Financial Strength Rating: A g **FSC:** XV

• NET PREMIUMS AND DEPOSITS ($000 omitted)

Year	Individual Life	Individual & Group Annuities	Group Life & A&H	Credit Life & A&H	Individual A&H	Total
2007	357,641	3,172,344	33,415	7,284	31,086	3,601,769
2008	357,758	4,239,606	36,309	8,068	30,681	4,672,423
2009	366,696	3,877,291	49,459	7,456	32,107	4,333,008

• NET OPERATING GAIN ($000 omitted)

Year	Individual Life	Individual & Group Annuities	Group Life & A&H	Credit Life & A&H	Individual A&H	Total
2007	28,657	83,151	4,109	-761	1,667	116,823
2008	8,921	-307,153	-31,611	6,918	-1,138	-324,063
2009	22,724	415,932	8,837	7,595	4,813	459,902

• COMPARATIVE FINANCIALS ($000 omitted)

Year	Assets	Capital & Surplus	Net Invest Income	Benefits Paid	Realized Cap Gains	Policyholder Dividends	Contract Lns (% of assets)
2007	17,771,745	813,295	427,355	3,086,631	7,937	6	0.3
2008	18,792,373	806,474	465,217	3,149,309	27,212	3	0.3
2009	20,937,072	911,627	505,584	2,632,096	-185,003	17	0.3

• ORDINARY LIFE STATISTICS

Year	Av. Ord. Policy Issued ($)	Av. Ord. Policy In Force ($)	Avg. Prem ($/M)	1st Yr Prem/ Total Prem	Ord. Lapse Ratio
2007	131,002	57,692	2.51	21.6	8.0
2008	177,821	63,063	2.44	21.1	8.6
2009	217,881	65,975	2.58	16.4	7.2

• NEW LIFE BUSINESS ISSUED ($000 omitted)

Year	Whole Life	Term	Credit	Group	Industrial	Total
2007	785,377	722,325	163,251	44,512	...	1,715,465
2008	779,759	764,440	306,912	31,229	...	1,882,340
2009	767,571	1,783,811	534,277	59,161	...	3,144,820

• LIFE INSURANCE IN FORCE ($000 omitted)

Year	Whole Life	Term	Credit	Group	Industrial	Total
2007	6,441,627	284,650,860	900,563	1,090,842	...	293,083,892
2008	7,004,802	287,382,527	890,279	1,139,596	...	296,417,204
2009	7,380,209	287,768,952	883,066	1,071,279	...	297,103,506

TRIPLE-S VIDA, INC.

P.O. Box 363786
San Juan, Puerto Rico 00936-3786
Tel: 787-758-4888

AMB#: 007631
Began Business: 09/15/1964
Agency Off: Edgardo A. Diaz Usero

Best's Financial Strength Rating: B++ **FSC:** VI

• NET PREMIUMS AND DEPOSITS ($000 omitted)

Year	Individual Life	Individual & Group Annuities	Group Life & A&H	Credit Life & A&H	Individual A&H	Total
2007	61,097	6,151	11,304	14	22,101	100,666
2008	62,832	8,018	10,454	14	25,699	107,017
2009	67,813	4,434	8,806	11	31,002	112,065

• NET OPERATING GAIN ($000 omitted)

Year	Individual Life	Individual & Group Annuities	Group Life & A&H	Credit Life & A&H	Individual A&H	Total
2007	6,323	-126	305	-3	1,104	7,603
2008	5,525	-191	-478	22	1,287	6,164
2009	381	111	-428	6	-264	-194

• COMPARATIVE FINANCIALS ($000 omitted)

Year	Assets	Capital & Surplus	Net Invest Income	Benefits Paid	Realized Cap Gains	Policyholder Dividends	Contract Lns (% of assets)
2007	309,465	45,105	15,943	44,664	677	...	1.8
2008	329,391	48,742	17,793	46,958	-3,541	...	1.7
2009	352,485	49,326	17,547	49,529	-869	...	1.7

• ORDINARY LIFE STATISTICS

Year	Av. Ord. Policy Issued ($)	Av. Ord. Policy In Force ($)	Avg. Prem ($/M)	1st Yr Prem/ Total Prem	Ord. Lapse Ratio
2007	27,755	23,780	11.13	31.0	14.2
2008	28,659	24,074	11.15	33.4	15.3
2009	25,665	23,914	11.68	37.0	19.6

• NEW LIFE BUSINESS ISSUED ($000 omitted)

Year	Whole Life	Term	Credit	Group	Industrial	Total
2007	81,130	1,030,184	...	213,268	...	1,324,582
2008	272,659	966,084	...	625,918	8	1,864,669
2009	372,936	931,537	...	245,822	1	1,550,296

• LIFE INSURANCE IN FORCE ($000 omitted)

Year	Whole Life	Term	Credit	Group	Industrial	Total
2007	1,237,351	4,443,531	233	4,639,221	1,414	10,321,750
2008	1,383,888	4,455,965	143	5,068,237	1,367	10,909,600
2009	1,538,206	4,491,389	75	3,249,696	1,324	9,280,690

TRUSTMARK INSURANCE COMPANY

400 Field Drive
Lake Forest, Illinois 60045-2581
Tel: 847-615-1500

AMB#: 006165
Began Business: 01/18/1913
Agency Off: None

Best's Financial Strength Rating: A- g **FSC:** IX

• NET PREMIUMS AND DEPOSITS ($000 omitted)

Year	Individual Life	Individual & Group Annuities	Group Life & A&H	Credit Life & A&H	Individual A&H	Total
2007	5,533	33,052	100,855	...	58,152	197,593
2008	16,275	15,617	155,563	...	59,126	246,582
2009	16,011	21,163	184,682	...	60,505	282,362

• NET OPERATING GAIN ($000 omitted)

Year	Individual Life	Individual & Group Annuities	Group Life & A&H	Credit Life & A&H	Individual A&H	Total
2007	278	1,188	15,841	...	11,776	29,083
2008	1,725	1,398	24,921	...	19,284	47,328
2009	2,113	1,276	13,711	...	12,186	29,286

• COMPARATIVE FINANCIALS ($000 omitted)

Year	Assets	Capital & Surplus	Net Invest Income	Benefits Paid	Realized Cap Gains	Policyholder Dividends	Contract Lns (% of assets)
2007	1,236,856	236,391	59,455	146,107	987	570	0.9
2008	1,168,327	212,236	58,793	143,405	-438	555	1.1
2009	1,172,032	240,292	55,062	136,396	-3,133	570	1.1

• ORDINARY LIFE STATISTICS

Year	Av. Ord. Policy Issued ($)	Av. Ord. Policy In Force ($)	Avg. Prem ($/M)	1st Yr Prem/ Total Prem	Ord. Lapse Ratio
2007	77,249	37,645	9.01	9.7	12.0
2008	74,605	40,252	8.85	12.6	14.0
2009	56,715	41,203	9.19	9.7	12.7

• NEW LIFE BUSINESS ISSUED ($000 omitted)

Year	Whole Life	Term	Credit	Group	Industrial	Total
2007	437,227	...	...	1,470,013	...	1,907,240
2008	437,784	...	...	1,645,344	...	2,083,128
2009	224,593	...	...	2,036,370	...	2,260,963

• LIFE INSURANCE IN FORCE ($000 omitted)

Year	Whole Life	Term	Credit	Group	Industrial	Total
2007	2,282,470	356,378	...	10,575,862	...	13,214,710
2008	2,307,545	326,481	...	11,088,415	...	13,722,441
2009	2,160,387	295,497	...	11,949,100	...	14,404,984

TRUSTMARK LIFE INS CO OF NY

400 Field Drive
Lake Forest, Illinois 60045
Tel: 847-615-1500

AMB#: 060706
Began Business: 06/17/2009
Agency Off: None

Best's Financial Strength Rating: A- g **FSC:** IX

• NET PREMIUMS AND DEPOSITS ($000 omitted)

Year	Individual Life	Individual & Group Annuities	Group Life & A&H	Credit Life & A&H	Individual A&H	Total
2007	...	...	...	...	...	...
2008	...	...	...	...	...	...
2009	...	...	...	...	...	...

• NET OPERATING GAIN ($000 omitted)

Year	Individual Life	Individual & Group Annuities	Group Life & A&H	Credit Life & A&H	Individual A&H	Total
2007	...	...	...	...	...	...
2008	...	...	...	...	...	...
2009	...	...	...	...	...	82

• COMPARATIVE FINANCIALS ($000 omitted)

Year	Assets	Capital & Surplus	Net Invest Income	Benefits Paid	Realized Cap Gains	Policyholder Dividends	Contract Lns (% of assets)
2007	...	...	...	...	...	...	...
2008	...	...	...	...	...	...	...
2009	6,140	6,081	152	...	...	...	...

• ORDINARY LIFE STATISTICS

Year	Av. Ord. Policy Issued ($)	Av. Ord. Policy In Force ($)	Avg. Prem ($/M)	1st Yr Prem/ Total Prem	Ord. Lapse Ratio
2007	...	...	...	...	...
2008	...	...	...	...	...
2009	...	...	...	...	...

• NEW LIFE BUSINESS ISSUED ($000 omitted)

Year	Whole Life	Term	Credit	Group	Industrial	Total
2007	...	...	...	...	...	...
2008	...	...	...	...	...	...
2009	...	...	...	...	...	...

• LIFE INSURANCE IN FORCE ($000 omitted)

Year	Whole Life	Term	Credit	Group	Industrial	Total
2007	...	...	...	...	...	...
2008	...	...	...	...	...	...
2009	...	...	...	...	...	...

TRUSTMARK LIFE INS CO

400 Field Drive
Lake Forest, Illinois 60045-2581
Tel: 847-615-1500

AMB#: 006335
Began Business: 02/27/1925
Agency Off: None

Best's Financial Strength Rating: A- **FSC:** VIII

• NET PREMIUMS AND DEPOSITS ($000 omitted)

Year	Individual Life	Individual & Group Annuities	Group Life & A&H	Credit Life & A&H	Individual A&H	Total
2007	10,307	8,519	485,105	...	82	504,014
2008	0	9,315	407,931	...	23	417,268
2009	0	8,399	380,627	...	10	389,037

• NET OPERATING GAIN ($000 omitted)

Year	Individual Life	Individual & Group Annuities	Group Life & A&H	Credit Life & A&H	Individual A&H	Total
2007	2,758	...	33,352	...	-2	36,109
2008	-2	...	-4,254	...	-3	-4,260
2009	-1	...	1,994	...	-4	1,989

• COMPARATIVE FINANCIALS ($000 omitted)

Year	Assets	Capital & Surplus	Net Invest Income	Benefits Paid	Realized Cap Gains	Policyholder Dividends	Contract Lns (% of assets)
2007	361,681	171,697	24,135	333,934	-1,095	28	...
2008	377,360	183,535	13,411	319,069	-10,232	41	...
2009	362,207	184,619	13,235	289,132	121	47	...

• ORDINARY LIFE STATISTICS

Year	Av. Ord. Policy Issued ($)	Av. Ord. Policy In Force ($)	Avg. Prem ($/M)	1st Yr Prem/ Total Prem	Ord. Lapse Ratio
2007	...	...	...	...	...
2008	...	...	...	...	...
2009	...	...	...	...	...

• NEW LIFE BUSINESS ISSUED ($000 omitted)

Year	Whole Life	Term	Credit	Group	Industrial	Total
2007	...	...	...	125,735	...	125,735
2008	...	...	...	204,746	...	204,746
2009	...	...	...	144,459	...	144,459

• LIFE INSURANCE IN FORCE ($000 omitted)

Year	Whole Life	Term	Credit	Group	Industrial	Total
2007	20	...	...	4,329,757	...	4,329,777
2008	15	...	...	4,318,474	...	4,318,489
2009	10	...	...	3,979,598	...	3,979,608

UNICARE LIFE & HEALTH INS CO

120 Monument Circle
Indianapolis, Indiana 46204-4903
Tel: 877-864-2273

AMB#: 009233
Began Business: 12/16/1980
Agency Off: Louis R. Raspa

Best's Financial Strength Rating: A- g **FSC:** IX

• NET PREMIUMS AND DEPOSITS ($000 omitted)

Year	Individual Life	Individual & Group Annuities	Group Life & A&H	Credit Life & A&H	Individual A&H	Total
2007	1,393	91,297	1,000,940	...	1,552,349	2,645,980
2008	1,302	95,998	903,248	...	1,927,630	2,928,177
2009	1,001	96,020	725,571	...	1,702,624	2,525,216

• NET OPERATING GAIN ($000 omitted)

Year	Individual Life	Individual & Group Annuities	Group Life & A&H	Credit Life & A&H	Individual A&H	Total
2007	11,716	1,822	35,236	...	67,985	116,759
2008	8,174	5,476	19,851	...	1,019	34,520
2009	9,759	5,736	56,404	...	109,811	181,710

• COMPARATIVE FINANCIALS ($000 omitted)

Year	Assets	Capital & Surplus	Net Invest Income	Benefits Paid	Realized Cap Gains	Policyholder Dividends	Contract Lns (% of assets)
2007	1,725,805	344,935	72,489	2,151,661	-5,163	...	0.0
2008	1,636,272	361,461	76,965	2,515,581	-27,443	...	0.0
2009	1,482,436	381,336	69,986	1,965,450	-25,222	...	0.0

• ORDINARY LIFE STATISTICS

Year	Av. Ord. Policy Issued ($)	Av. Ord. Policy In Force ($)	Avg. Prem ($/M)	1st Yr Prem/ Total Prem	Ord. Lapse Ratio
2007	...	...	...	...	...
2008	...	...	...	...	...
2009	...	...	...	...	...

• NEW LIFE BUSINESS ISSUED ($000 omitted)

Year	Whole Life	Term	Credit	Group	Industrial	Total
2007	...	62,838	...	2,040,989	...	2,103,827
2008	...	47,970	...	2,338,003	...	2,385,973
2009	...	18,465	...	541,283	...	559,748

• LIFE INSURANCE IN FORCE ($000 omitted)

Year	Whole Life	Term	Credit	Group	Industrial	Total
2007	...	171,136	...	37,299,223	...	37,470,359
2008	...	170,160	...	33,692,569	...	33,862,729
2009	...	132,150	...	33,603,086	...	33,735,236

UNIFIED LIFE INSURANCE COMPANY

7201 West 129th Street, Suite 300
Overland Park, Kansas 66213
Tel: 877-492-4678

AMB#: 060366
Began Business: 05/15/2001
Agency Off: John E. Tiller, Jr.

Best's Financial Strength Rating: B++ **FSC:** V

• NET PREMIUMS AND DEPOSITS ($000 omitted)

Year	Individual Life	Individual & Group Annuities	Group Life & A&H	Credit Life & A&H	Individual A&H	Total
2007	7,377	229	8,826	0	10,871	27,303
2008	6,852	198	7,490	0	14,934	29,475
2009	6,629	198	9,267	0	12,613	28,708

• NET OPERATING GAIN ($000 omitted)

Year	Individual Life	Individual & Group Annuities	Group Life & A&H	Credit Life & A&H	Individual A&H	Total
2007	2,477	346	-239	17	512	3,112
2008	1,066	132	1,235	17	904	3,355
2009	1,052	860	304	6	1,110	3,332

• COMPARATIVE FINANCIALS ($000 omitted)

Year	Assets	Capital & Surplus	Net Invest Income	Benefits Paid	Realized Cap Gains	Policyholder Dividends	Contract Lns (% of assets)
2007	143,101	20,536	6,284	24,364	...	18	5.8
2008	148,950	23,488	5,866	28,104	...	4	5.8
2009	139,062	14,317	6,915	27,611	...	19	6.3

• ORDINARY LIFE STATISTICS

Year	Av. Ord. Policy Issued ($)	Av. Ord. Policy In Force ($)	Avg. Prem ($/M)	1st Yr Prem/ Total Prem	Ord. Lapse Ratio
2007	...	...	...	...	...
2008	...	...	...	...	...
2009	...	...	...	...	...

• NEW LIFE BUSINESS ISSUED ($000 omitted)

Year	Whole Life	Term	Credit	Group	Industrial	Total
2007	13,822	...	...	223	...	14,045
2008	2,162	...	...	37	...	2,199
2009	151	...	...	563	...	714

• LIFE INSURANCE IN FORCE ($000 omitted)

Year	Whole Life	Term	Credit	Group	Industrial	Total
2007	512,184	221,296	1,858	140,836	...	876,174
2008	482,205	198,168	454	4,975	...	685,802
2009	456,949	175,947	10	5,104	...	638,010

UNION BANKERS INS CO

P.O. Box 958465
Lake Mary, Florida 32795-8465
Tel: 407-995-8000

AMB#: 007149
Began Business: 07/16/1953
Agency Off: Ken Hall

Best's Financial Strength Rating: B+ **FSC:** VI

• NET PREMIUMS AND DEPOSITS ($000 omitted)

Year	Individual Life	Individual & Group Annuities	Group Life & A&H	Credit Life & A&H	Individual A&H	Total
2007	10,720	416	...	...	17,162	28,297
2008	9,780	1,025	...	...	34,911	45,716
2009	-48,036	-3,532	...	...	42,697	-8,870

• NET OPERATING GAIN ($000 omitted)

Year	Individual Life	Individual & Group Annuities	Group Life & A&H	Credit Life & A&H	Individual A&H	Total
2007	2,432	11	...	...	-1,290	1,153
2008	2,627	-62	...	...	1,867	4,431
2009	6,971	475	...	...	636	8,083

• COMPARATIVE FINANCIALS ($000 omitted)

Year	Assets	Capital & Surplus	Net Invest Income	Benefits Paid	Realized Cap Gains	Policyholder Dividends	Contract Lns (% of assets)
2007	104,521	14,543	5,132	24,362	...	...	3.1
2008	107,233	18,494	4,598	38,966	-664	...	3.1
2009	66,424	36,719	2,784	40,214	-37	...	0.0

• ORDINARY LIFE STATISTICS

Year	Av. Ord. Policy Issued ($)	Av. Ord. Policy In Force ($)	Avg. Prem ($/M)	1st Yr Prem/ Total Prem	Ord. Lapse Ratio
2007	...	...	...	...	...
2008	...	...	...	...	...
2009	...	...	...	...	...

• NEW LIFE BUSINESS ISSUED ($000 omitted)

Year	Whole Life	Term	Credit	Group	Industrial	Total
2007	20,960	1,487	...	...	...	22,447
2008	11,237	467	...	...	...	11,704
2009	1,489	...	...	...	...	1,489

• LIFE INSURANCE IN FORCE ($000 omitted)

Year	Whole Life	Term	Credit	Group	Industrial	Total
2007	275,994	92,960	...	...	...	368,954
2008	248,198	85,734	...	...	...	333,932
2009	235,517	67,060	...	...	...	302,576

UNIMERICA INSURANCE COMPANY

3900 McCarty Lane, Suite 220
Lafayette, Indiana 47905-8701
Tel: 952-936-3956

AMB#: 009065
Began Business: 12/18/1980
Agency Off: None

Best's Financial Strength Rating: A g **FSC:** VIII

• NET PREMIUMS AND DEPOSITS ($000 omitted)

Year	Individual Life	Individual & Group Annuities	Group Life & A&H	Credit Life & A&H	Individual A&H	Total
2007	258	16,457	129,602	...	16,446	162,763
2008	106	6,660	244,578	...	11,166	262,510
2009	100	1,766	232,031	...	3,525	237,422

• NET OPERATING GAIN ($000 omitted)

Year	Individual Life	Individual & Group Annuities	Group Life & A&H	Credit Life & A&H	Individual A&H	Total
2007	208	...	4,588	...	530	5,326
2008	-135	...	-4,975	...	14	-5,096
2009	124	...	3,851	...	1,100	5,075

• COMPARATIVE FINANCIALS ($000 omitted)

Year	Assets	Capital & Surplus	Net Invest Income	Benefits Paid	Realized Cap Gains	Policyholder Dividends	Contract Lns (% of assets)
2007	150,182	60,084	4,478	77,128	...	...	...
2008	244,431	104,728	6,430	172,383	-415	...	...
2009	262,067	112,957	7,236	191,270	160	...	...

• ORDINARY LIFE STATISTICS

Year	Av. Ord. Policy Issued ($)	Av. Ord. Policy In Force ($)	Avg. Prem ($/M)	1st Yr Prem/ Total Prem	Ord. Lapse Ratio
2007	...	...	...	...	...
2008	...	...	...	...	...
2009	...	...	...	...	...

• NEW LIFE BUSINESS ISSUED ($000 omitted)

Year	Whole Life	Term	Credit	Group	Industrial	Total
2007	...	...	...	26,945,347	...	26,945,347
2008	...	...	...	18,949,653	...	18,949,653
2009	...	...	...	11,776,472	...	11,776,472

• LIFE INSURANCE IN FORCE ($000 omitted)

Year	Whole Life	Term	Credit	Group	Industrial	Total
2007	...	106,934	...	39,294,433	...	39,401,367
2008	...	95,843	...	46,100,338	...	46,196,181
2009	...	43,227	...	44,979,587	...	45,022,814

UNION CENTRAL LIFE INS CO

P.O. Box 40888
Cincinnati, Ohio 45240
Tel: 513-595-2200

AMB#: 007150
Began Business: 04/14/1867
Agency Off: Arnold D. Henkel

Best's Financial Strength Rating: A g **FSC:** XIII

• NET PREMIUMS AND DEPOSITS ($000 omitted)

Year	Individual Life	Individual & Group Annuities	Group Life & A&H	Credit Life & A&H	Individual A&H	Total
2007	302,984	645,681	16,037	...	57,796	1,022,499
2008	278,687	732,399	12,913	...	62,711	1,086,711
2009	195,683	577,048	10,422	...	67,071	850,224

• NET OPERATING GAIN ($000 omitted)

Year	Individual Life	Individual & Group Annuities	Group Life & A&H	Credit Life & A&H	Individual A&H	Total
2007	-22,268	16,457	3,971	...	3,032	5,399
2008	-45,575	-2,810	1,951	...	4,279	-21,472
2009	5,630	-1,622	5,434	...	1,503	40,096

• COMPARATIVE FINANCIALS ($000 omitted)

Year	Assets	Capital & Surplus	Net Invest Income	Benefits Paid	Realized Cap Gains	Policyholder Dividends	Contract Lns (% of assets)
2007	7,284,871	321,059	256,624	922,914	-5,503	11,860	2.1
2008	6,310,581	266,977	257,836	1,035,703	-134,799	12,249	2.4
2009	6,743,143	400,877	243,586	819,990	-159,876	11,018	2.5

• ORDINARY LIFE STATISTICS

Year	Av. Ord. Policy Issued ($)	Av. Ord. Policy In Force ($)	Avg. Prem ($/M)	1st Yr Prem/ Total Prem	Ord. Lapse Ratio
2007	565,690	231,749	8.03	40.1	5.3
2008	533,788	249,429	7.18	33.3	6.9
2009	478,087	258,971	6.06	17.4	7.3

• NEW LIFE BUSINESS ISSUED ($000 omitted)

Year	Whole Life	Term	Credit	Group	Industrial	Total
2007	2,941,706	5,539,689	...	5,735	...	8,487,130
2008	2,810,394	5,089,132	...	3,119	...	7,902,645
2009	1,259,233	5,187,287	...	1,785	...	6,448,305

• LIFE INSURANCE IN FORCE ($000 omitted)

Year	Whole Life	Term	Credit	Group	Industrial	Total
2007	21,816,973	25,789,577	...	37,112	...	47,643,662
2008	23,067,164	28,255,810	...	35,902	...	51,358,876
2009	22,618,060	30,474,963	...	32,527	...	53,125,550

UNION FIDELITY LIFE INS CO

500 Virginia Drive
Fort Washington, Pennsylvania 19034
Tel: 215-542-4590

AMB#: 006297
Began Business: 02/01/1926
Agency Off: None

Best's Financial Strength Rating: A- g **FSC:** X

• **NET PREMIUMS AND DEPOSITS ($000 omitted)**

Year	Individual Life	Individual & Group Annuities	Group Life & A&H	Credit Life & A&H	Individual A&H	Total
2007	9,594	22,325	75,502	805	254,389	362,614
2008	8,587	29,672	68,810	822	249,721	357,611
2009	8,076	20,451	60,832	302	255,030	344,692

• **NET OPERATING GAIN ($000 omitted)**

Year	Individual Life	Individual & Group Annuities	Group Life & A&H	Credit Life & A&H	Individual A&H	Total
2007	749	-29,201	28,515	4,619	-46,060	-41,378
2008	288	-173,042	24,303	1,107	-48,106	-195,449
2009	-537	-7,979	-4,039	-118	17,246	4,574

• **COMPARATIVE FINANCIALS ($000 omitted)**

Year	Assets	Capital & Surplus	Net Invest Income	Benefits Paid	Realized Cap Gains	Policyholder Dividends	Contract Lns (% of assets)
2007	18,204,149	414,434	1,095,044	2,812,136	351	...	0.0
2008	18,264,425	456,312	1,044,371	2,386,888	-316,660	...	0.0
2009	18,377,842	611,682	1,065,694	1,871,346	28,157	...	0.0

• **ORDINARY LIFE STATISTICS**

Year	Av. Ord. Policy Issued ($)	Av. Ord. Policy In Force ($)	Avg. Prem ($/M)	1st Yr Prem/ Total Prem	Ord. Lapse Ratio
2007	...	...	...	...	...
2008	...	...	...	...	...
2009	...	...	...	...	...

• **NEW LIFE BUSINESS ISSUED ($000 omitted)**

Year	Whole Life	Term	Credit	Group	Industrial	Total
2007	332	...	...	...	...	332
2008	356	...	...	...	...	356
2009	1,085	...	...	...	...	1,085

• **LIFE INSURANCE IN FORCE ($000 omitted)**

Year	Whole Life	Term	Credit	Group	Industrial	Total
2007	243,122	330,090	159,425	1,167,207	...	1,899,844
2008	226,158	299,915	115,525	1,064,006	...	1,705,604
2009	209,492	267,624	21,714	954,506	...	1,453,336

UNION LABOR LIFE INS CO

1625 Eye Street, N.W.
Washington, District of Columbia 20006
Tel: 202-682-0900

AMB#: 007152
Began Business: 05/01/1927
Agency Off: None

Best's Financial Strength Rating: B+ **FSC:** VII

• **NET PREMIUMS AND DEPOSITS ($000 omitted)**

Year	Individual Life	Individual & Group Annuities	Group Life & A&H	Credit Life & A&H	Individual A&H	Total
2007	5,749	7,380	185,281	...	2,368	200,777
2008	4,918	25,174	147,418	...	2,180	179,690
2009	4,339	18,135	143,936	...	1,889	168,299

• **NET OPERATING GAIN ($000 omitted)**

Year	Individual Life	Individual & Group Annuities	Group Life & A&H	Credit Life & A&H	Individual A&H	Total
2007	-3,224	-6,407	3,101	...	-3,021	-16,482
2008	-1,829	13,092	-1,122	...	-396	5,719
2009	121	6,509	5,085	...	-494	9,060

• **COMPARATIVE FINANCIALS ($000 omitted)**

Year	Assets	Capital & Surplus	Net Invest Income	Benefits Paid	Realized Cap Gains	Policyholder Dividends	Contract Lns (% of assets)
2007	4,058,035	126,204	23,299	163,751	0	4,862	0.0
2008	4,364,925	107,849	17,823	141,479	-1,572	3,021	0.0
2009	3,882,289	92,058	15,802	131,203	-347	744	0.0

• **ORDINARY LIFE STATISTICS**

Year	Av. Ord. Policy Issued ($)	Av. Ord. Policy In Force ($)	Avg. Prem ($/M)	1st Yr Prem/ Total Prem	Ord. Lapse Ratio
2007	...	...	...	...	...
2008	...	...	...	...	...
2009	...	...	...	...	...

• **NEW LIFE BUSINESS ISSUED ($000 omitted)**

Year	Whole Life	Term	Credit	Group	Industrial	Total
2007	525	25	...	1,745,904	...	1,746,454
2008	325	...	...	1,065,187	...	1,065,512
2009	175	50	...	520,150	...	520,375

• **LIFE INSURANCE IN FORCE ($000 omitted)**

Year	Whole Life	Term	Credit	Group	Industrial	Total
2007	35,266	1,409,217	...	12,444,680	...	13,889,163
2008	30,686	1,336,928	...	12,354,663	...	13,722,277
2009	26,539	953,671	...	12,755,103	...	13,735,314

UNION NATIONAL LIFE INS CO

12115 Lackland Road
St. Louis, Missouri 63146-4003
Tel: 314-819-4300

AMB#: 007155
Began Business: 07/30/1930
Agency Off: Richard Miller

Best's Financial Strength Rating: A- r **FSC:** IX

• **NET PREMIUMS AND DEPOSITS ($000 omitted)**

Year	Individual Life	Individual & Group Annuities	Group Life & A&H	Credit Life & A&H	Individual A&H	Total
2007	75,157	...	...	...	6,750	81,907
2008	72,138	...	...	...	6,252	78,390
2009	-8,695	...	...	...	1,904	-6,792

• **NET OPERATING GAIN ($000 omitted)**

Year	Individual Life	Individual & Group Annuities	Group Life & A&H	Credit Life & A&H	Individual A&H	Total
2007	10,969	...	...	...	980	11,948
2008	10,303	...	...	...	989	11,292
2009	12,080	...	...	...	1,068	13,149

• **COMPARATIVE FINANCIALS ($000 omitted)**

Year	Assets	Capital & Surplus	Net Invest Income	Benefits Paid	Realized Cap Gains	Policyholder Dividends	Contract Lns (% of assets)
2007	429,710	62,336	23,372	33,703	-464	...	8.3
2008	448,668	68,715	23,316	36,303	-1,306	...	8.2
2009	15,371	10,144	10,322	3,027	-285	...	...

• **ORDINARY LIFE STATISTICS**

Year	Av. Ord. Policy Issued ($)	Av. Ord. Policy In Force ($)	Avg. Prem ($/M)	1st Yr Prem/ Total Prem	Ord. Lapse Ratio
2007	...	...	...	...	...
2008	...	...	...	...	...
2009	...	...	...	...	...

• **NEW LIFE BUSINESS ISSUED ($000 omitted)**

Year	Whole Life	Term	Credit	Group	Industrial	Total
2007	243,349	198,597	...	...	...	441,946
2008	320,943	147,525	...	...	...	468,468
2009	365,564	182,650	...	...	...	548,214

• **LIFE INSURANCE IN FORCE ($000 omitted)**

Year	Whole Life	Term	Credit	Group	Industrial	Total
2007	2,466,195	1,721,159	...	...	44,426	4,231,780
2008	2,535,393	1,690,095	...	...	42,255	4,267,743
2009	2,559,623	1,693,302	...	...	40,125	4,293,050

UNION SECURITY INSURANCE CO

PO Box 419052
Kansas City, Missouri 64141-6052
Tel: 816-474-2345

AMB#: 007232
Began Business: 09/10/1910
Agency Off: None

Best's Financial Strength Rating: A- g **FSC:** IX

• **NET PREMIUMS AND DEPOSITS ($000 omitted)**

Year	Individual Life	Individual & Group Annuities	Group Life & A&H	Credit Life & A&H	Individual A&H	Total
2007	22,688	91,413	1,226,224	...	6,443	1,346,768
2008	56,293	75,724	1,150,704	...	6,283	1,289,005
2009	17,320	29,877	1,079,943	...	5,869	1,133,009

• **NET OPERATING GAIN ($000 omitted)**

Year	Individual Life	Individual & Group Annuities	Group Life & A&H	Credit Life & A&H	Individual A&H	Total
2007	50,515	20,768	96,938	...	2,880	171,100
2008	20,261	11,009	90,032	...	1,262	122,564
2009	26,093	9,226	44,180	...	-863	78,636

• **COMPARATIVE FINANCIALS ($000 omitted)**

Year	Assets	Capital & Surplus	Net Invest Income	Benefits Paid	Realized Cap Gains	Policyholder Dividends	Contract Lns (% of assets)
2007	7,195,167	438,924	285,940	976,527	-32,604	274	0.1
2008	5,523,783	350,383	239,780	1,016,065	-120,810	1,423	0.3
2009	5,653,173	418,397	217,858	964,657	-18,773	742	0.2

• **ORDINARY LIFE STATISTICS**

Year	Av. Ord. Policy Issued ($)	Av. Ord. Policy In Force ($)	Avg. Prem ($/M)	1st Yr Prem/ Total Prem	Ord. Lapse Ratio
2007	36,565	21,911	8.07	4.0	5.8
2008	34,717	21,229	10.18	4.0	7.5
2009	34,540	22,537	6.89	-0.1	-0.5

• **NEW LIFE BUSINESS ISSUED ($000 omitted)**

Year	Whole Life	Term	Credit	Group	Industrial	Total
2007	10,165	...	...	10,893,767	...	10,903,932
2008	8,714	...	...	9,600,314	...	9,609,028
2009	7,812	1,721	...	9,063,038	...	9,072,571

• **LIFE INSURANCE IN FORCE ($000 omitted)**

Year	Whole Life	Term	Credit	Group	Industrial	Total
2007	16,284,568	256,337	...	69,975,775	36,818	86,553,498
2008	15,035,900	263,907	...	66,691,376	35,450	82,026,633
2009	14,720,159	537,043	...	67,847,879	34,330	83,139,411

UNION SECURITY LIFE INS NY

212 Highbridge Street, Suite D
Fayetteville, New York 13066
Tel: 315-451-0066

AMB#: 008533
Began Business: 04/05/1974
Agency Off: Terry J. Kryshak

Best's Financial Strength Rating: A- g
FSC: IX

• **NET PREMIUMS AND DEPOSITS** ($000 omitted)

Year	Individual Life	Individual & Group Annuities	Group Life & A&H	Credit Life & A&H	Individual A&H	Total
2007	362	...	55,519	4,021	4	59,906
2008	309	...	60,686	3,749	6	64,750
2009	277	...	40,752	2,503	10	43,541

• **NET OPERATING GAIN** ($000 omitted)

Year	Individual Life	Individual & Group Annuities	Group Life & A&H	Credit Life & A&H	Individual A&H	Total
2007	168	593	5,159	402	75	6,396
2008	-190	544	8,712	420	129	9,615
2009	-318	446	8,773	521	-61	9,361

• **COMPARATIVE FINANCIALS** ($000 omitted)

Year	Assets	Capital & Surplus	Net Invest Income	Benefits Paid	Realized Cap Gains	Policyholder Dividends	Contract Lns (% of assets)
2007	178,564	45,034	9,086	38,145	-649	...	0.1
2008	171,983	45,986	8,802	35,728	-5,345	...	0.0
2009	164,473	50,493	8,190	33,926	204	...	0.0

• **ORDINARY LIFE STATISTICS**

Year	Av. Ord. Policy Issued ($)	Av. Ord. Policy In Force ($)	Avg. Prem ($/M)	1st Yr Prem/ Total Prem	Ord. Lapse Ratio
2007	...	...	...	...	...
2008	...	...	...	...	...
2009	...	...	...	...	...

• **NEW LIFE BUSINESS ISSUED** ($000 omitted)

Year	Whole Life	Term	Credit	Group	Industrial	Total
2007	593	...	2,313,944	474,111	...	2,788,648
2008	1,238	...	113,610	388,920	...	503,768
2009	1,303	...	101,989	205,010	...	308,302

• **LIFE INSURANCE IN FORCE** ($000 omitted)

Year	Whole Life	Term	Credit	Group	Industrial	Total
2007	14,288	152	850,990	2,715,240	...	3,580,670
2008	13,756	152	727,882	2,671,989	...	3,413,779
2009	12,439	152	600,395	1,979,942	...	2,592,928

UNITED FARM FAMILY LIFE INS CO

225 South East Street
Indianapolis, Indiana 46202
Tel: 317-692-7200

AMB#: 007168
Began Business: 05/01/1964
Agency Off: Patricia A. Poehler

Best's Financial Strength Rating: A
FSC: VIII

• **NET PREMIUMS AND DEPOSITS** ($000 omitted)

Year	Individual Life	Individual & Group Annuities	Group Life & A&H	Credit Life & A&H	Individual A&H	Total
2007	96,640	14,878	54	...	1,275	112,847
2008	97,339	16,153	81	...	1,164	114,737
2009	89,575	30,163	70	...	1,062	120,870

• **NET OPERATING GAIN** ($000 omitted)

Year	Individual Life	Individual & Group Annuities	Group Life & A&H	Credit Life & A&H	Individual A&H	Total
2007	12,938	2,992	61	...	509	16,500
2008	12,708	2,654	13	...	440	15,815
2009	13,362	3,086	32	...	139	16,619

• **COMPARATIVE FINANCIALS** ($000 omitted)

Year	Assets	Capital & Surplus	Net Invest Income	Benefits Paid	Realized Cap Gains	Policyholder Dividends	Contract Lns (% of assets)
2007	1,667,509	205,095	88,317	102,659	-5,986	15,952	5.7
2008	1,692,107	197,730	91,232	95,934	-6,214	17,219	5.7
2009	1,768,006	218,815	93,272	97,497	-3,364	18,710	5.4

• **ORDINARY LIFE STATISTICS**

Year	Av. Ord. Policy Issued ($)	Av. Ord. Policy In Force ($)	Avg. Prem ($/M)	1st Yr Prem/ Total Prem	Ord. Lapse Ratio
2007	131,902	65,981	8.21	7.2	8.5
2008	139,949	69,910	7.97	7.6	6.0
2009	132,150	74,338	7.89	8.1	5.5

• **NEW LIFE BUSINESS ISSUED** ($000 omitted)

Year	Whole Life	Term	Credit	Group	Industrial	Total
2007	268,936	1,170,252	...	...	...	1,439,188
2008	278,372	1,232,375	...	...	...	1,510,747
2009	272,279	1,324,491	...	...	...	1,596,770

• **LIFE INSURANCE IN FORCE** ($000 omitted)

Year	Whole Life	Term	Credit	Group	Industrial	Total
2007	6,550,658	7,324,795	...	828	...	13,876,281
2008	6,980,367	7,714,065	...	183	...	14,694,615
2009	7,719,950	8,197,490	...	295	...	15,917,735

UNITED AMERICAN INS CO

P.O. Box 8080
McKinney, Texas 75070-8080
Tel: 972-529-5085

AMB#: 007161
Began Business: 08/13/1947
Agency Off: None

Best's Financial Strength Rating: A+ g
FSC: X

• **NET PREMIUMS AND DEPOSITS** ($000 omitted)

Year	Individual Life	Individual & Group Annuities	Group Life & A&H	Credit Life & A&H	Individual A&H	Total
2007	30,915	66	52,586	...	869,468	953,035
2008	28,005	84	60,489	...	763,308	851,885
2009	41,874	42	67,810	...	677,488	787,214

• **NET OPERATING GAIN** ($000 omitted)

Year	Individual Life	Individual & Group Annuities	Group Life & A&H	Credit Life & A&H	Individual A&H	Total
2007	8,318	...	5,284	...	48,311	61,913
2008	3,486	...	3,300	...	83,018	89,805
2009	2,015	...	2,004	...	80,366	84,385

• **COMPARATIVE FINANCIALS** ($000 omitted)

Year	Assets	Capital & Surplus	Net Invest Income	Benefits Paid	Realized Cap Gains	Policyholder Dividends	Contract Lns (% of assets)
2007	1,309,632	168,471	63,734	647,531	-426	...	0.4
2008	1,384,726	183,136	76,136	566,217	-10,892	...	0.4
2009	1,649,620	257,005	75,874	557,161	-5,031	...	0.4

• **ORDINARY LIFE STATISTICS**

Year	Av. Ord. Policy Issued ($)	Av. Ord. Policy In Force ($)	Avg. Prem ($/M)	1st Yr Prem/ Total Prem	Ord. Lapse Ratio
2007	11,892	8,177	35.16	7.6	13.4
2008	28,755	9,673	29.70	7.3	25.5
2009	21,503	9,199	29.84	-0.6	12.7

• **NEW LIFE BUSINESS ISSUED** ($000 omitted)

Year	Whole Life	Term	Credit	Group	Industrial	Total
2007	137,800	89,059	...	86,730	...	313,589
2008	148,578	394,811	...	45,387	...	588,776
2009	7,397	32,061	...	8,578	...	48,036

• **LIFE INSURANCE IN FORCE** ($000 omitted)

Year	Whole Life	Term	Credit	Group	Industrial	Total
2007	832,793	447,598	...	95,026	...	1,375,417
2008	765,299	645,786	...	40,891	...	1,451,976
2009	666,972	509,849	...	25,978	...	1,202,799

UNITED HERITAGE LIFE INS CO

P.O. Box 7777
Meridian, Idaho 83680-7777
Tel: 208-493-6100

AMB#: 006472
Began Business: 09/10/1935
Agency Off: Robert J. McCarvel

Best's Financial Strength Rating: A-
FSC: VI

• **NET PREMIUMS AND DEPOSITS** ($000 omitted)

Year	Individual Life	Individual & Group Annuities	Group Life & A&H	Credit Life & A&H	Individual A&H	Total
2007	31,122	32,577	2,124	...	50	65,872
2008	33,057	23,862	2,309	...	39	59,267
2009	36,530	18,747	2,070	...	36	57,383

• **NET OPERATING GAIN** ($000 omitted)

Year	Individual Life	Individual & Group Annuities	Group Life & A&H	Credit Life & A&H	Individual A&H	Total
2007	1,616	956	-536	...	24	2,061
2008	2,230	1,242	-584	...	19	2,907
2009	3,395	3,626	-72	...	-55	6,894

• **COMPARATIVE FINANCIALS** ($000 omitted)

Year	Assets	Capital & Surplus	Net Invest Income	Benefits Paid	Realized Cap Gains	Policyholder Dividends	Contract Lns (% of assets)
2007	411,703	41,634	24,152	66,260	-356	870	1.3
2008	420,525	40,022	25,472	47,034	-8,050	899	1.3
2009	438,330	40,807	26,901	43,168	-6,246	917	1.3

• **ORDINARY LIFE STATISTICS**

Year	Av. Ord. Policy Issued ($)	Av. Ord. Policy In Force ($)	Avg. Prem ($/M)	1st Yr Prem/ Total Prem	Ord. Lapse Ratio
2007	19,611	20,283	25.32	10.1	6.3
2008	14,338	19,801	27.16	10.5	6.3
2009	13,170	19,082	29.95	12.3	6.8

• **NEW LIFE BUSINESS ISSUED** ($000 omitted)

Year	Whole Life	Term	Credit	Group	Industrial	Total
2007	91,436	26,641	...	116,691	...	234,768
2008	73,662	20,952	...	134,016	...	228,630
2009	94,811	14,845	...	158,364	...	268,020

• **LIFE INSURANCE IN FORCE** ($000 omitted)

Year	Whole Life	Term	Credit	Group	Industrial	Total
2007	837,112	418,900	...	1,235,146	...	2,491,158
2008	839,777	403,118	...	1,205,318	...	2,448,213
2009	860,609	381,452	...	1,267,292	...	2,509,352

UNITED HOME LIFE INS CO

225 South East Street
Indianapolis, Indiana 46202
Tel: 317-692-7979

AMB#: 007172
Began Business: 12/17/1948
Agency Off: Gerry Danielson

Best's Financial Strength Rating: A-
FSC: V

• NET PREMIUMS AND DEPOSITS ($000 omitted)

Year	Individual Life	Individual & Group Annuities	Group Life & A&H	Credit Life & A&H	Individual A&H	Total
2007	11,370	25	1	...	56	11,452
2008	11,802	20	1	...	56	11,878
2009	10,819	28	1	...	54	10,902

• NET OPERATING GAIN ($000 omitted)

Year	Individual Life	Individual & Group Annuities	Group Life & A&H	Credit Life & A&H	Individual A&H	Total
2007	-669	150	1	...	30	-488
2008	-472	171	-1	...	93	-209
2009	161	194	1	...	16	372

• COMPARATIVE FINANCIALS ($000 omitted)

Year	Assets	Capital & Surplus	Net Invest Income	Benefits Paid	Realized Cap Gains	Policyholder Dividends	Contract Lns (% of assets)
2007	59,191	15,885	2,358	3,388	12	15	3.4
2008	60,014	16,033	2,957	5,090	...	14	3.3
2009	62,925	16,398	2,992	5,207	-65	7	3.2

• ORDINARY LIFE STATISTICS

Year	Av. Ord. Policy Issued ($)	Av. Ord. Policy In Force ($)	Avg. Prem ($/M)	1st Yr Prem/ Total Prem	Ord. Lapse Ratio
2007	58,034	41,587	12.61	27.8	18.3
2008	56,337	42,224	12.56	25.1	20.4
2009	54,580	42,203	13.30	31.9	23.1

• NEW LIFE BUSINESS ISSUED ($000 omitted)

Year	Whole Life	Term	Credit	Group	Industrial	Total
2007	230,097	271,552	...	...	...	501,649
2008	214,116	247,170	...	...	...	461,286
2009	353,890	277,109	...	...	...	630,999

• LIFE INSURANCE IN FORCE ($000 omitted)

Year	Whole Life	Term	Credit	Group	Industrial	Total
2007	371,713	1,011,923	...	2,742	...	1,386,378
2008	431,985	1,021,904	...	2,536	...	1,456,425
2009	563,326	1,069,854	...	2,235	...	1,635,415

UNITED INVESTORS LIFE INS CO

P.O. Box 10207
Birmingham, Alabama 35202-0207
Tel: 205-325-4300

AMB#: 007175
Began Business: 10/01/1981
Agency Off: None

Best's Financial Strength Rating: A
FSC: IX

• NET PREMIUMS AND DEPOSITS ($000 omitted)

Year	Individual Life	Individual & Group Annuities	Group Life & A&H	Credit Life & A&H	Individual A&H	Total
2007	92,258	138,306	9,010	...	...	239,574
2008	83,282	163,094	8,804	...	...	255,181
2009	80,253	190,668	8,599	...	...	279,519

• NET OPERATING GAIN ($000 omitted)

Year	Individual Life	Individual & Group Annuities	Group Life & A&H	Credit Life & A&H	Individual A&H	Total
2007	42,741	10,565	9,173	...	...	62,478
2008	24,134	12,311	10,656	...	...	47,102
2009	33,701	6,970	11,367	...	...	52,038

• COMPARATIVE FINANCIALS ($000 omitted)

Year	Assets	Capital & Surplus	Net Invest Income	Benefits Paid	Realized Cap Gains	Policyholder Dividends	Contract Lns (% of assets)
2007	3,058,372	389,642	102,824	205,880	263	...	0.9
2008	2,543,231	420,956	113,592	198,130	-7,214	...	1.1
2009	2,753,457	466,771	109,344	194,842	-14,957	...	1.1

• ORDINARY LIFE STATISTICS

Year	Av. Ord. Policy Issued ($)	Av. Ord. Policy In Force ($)	Avg. Prem ($/M)	1st Yr Prem/ Total Prem	Ord. Lapse Ratio
2007	121,928	115,132	6.01	24.4	8.6
2008	139,766	112,937	6.02	21.9	9.9
2009	157,943	111,217	6.36	19.2	9.0

• NEW LIFE BUSINESS ISSUED ($000 omitted)

Year	Whole Life	Term	Credit	Group	Industrial	Total
2007	154,263	169,579	...	7,000	...	330,842
2008	66,441	62,004	...	6,945	...	135,390
2009	807	63,002	...	5,655	...	69,464

• LIFE INSURANCE IN FORCE ($000 omitted)

Year	Whole Life	Term	Credit	Group	Industrial	Total
2007	3,247,933	12,615,111	...	1,442,416	...	17,305,460
2008	2,841,140	11,486,705	...	1,409,296	...	15,737,141
2009	2,540,430	10,503,713	...	1,377,256	...	14,421,399

UNITED INSURANCE CO OF AMERICA

12115 Lackland Road
St. Louis, Missouri 63146
Tel: 314-819-4300

AMB#: 007174
Began Business: 04/25/1928
Agency Off: Richard J. Miller

Best's Financial Strength Rating: A- g
FSC: IX

• NET PREMIUMS AND DEPOSITS ($000 omitted)

Year	Individual Life	Individual & Group Annuities	Group Life & A&H	Credit Life & A&H	Individual A&H	Total
2007	198,391	...	16	...	15,379	213,786
2008	187,972	81	...	...	13,823	201,876
2009	385,687	1	53	...	21,631	407,372

• NET OPERATING GAIN ($000 omitted)

Year	Individual Life	Individual & Group Annuities	Group Life & A&H	Credit Life & A&H	Individual A&H	Total
2007	35,673	-2	174	...	1,628	35,951
2008	68,656	-5	830	...	2,708	70,626
2009	44,356	-97	243	...	2,212	61,981

• COMPARATIVE FINANCIALS ($000 omitted)

Year	Assets	Capital & Surplus	Net Invest Income	Benefits Paid	Realized Cap Gains	Policyholder Dividends	Contract Lns (% of assets)
2007	2,055,249	204,197	117,110	111,917	-4,058	...	4.9
2008	2,005,027	190,165	123,125	112,766	-76,269	...	5.0
2009	3,238,886	303,513	140,803	188,633	-9,935	2	6.5

• ORDINARY LIFE STATISTICS

Year	Av. Ord. Policy Issued ($)	Av. Ord. Policy In Force ($)	Avg. Prem ($/M)	1st Yr Prem/ Total Prem	Ord. Lapse Ratio
2007	14,916	7,277	19.54	8.6	10.2
2008	12,457	7,284	19.15	8.3	8.7
2009	14,718	7,396	38.99	9.7	8.3

• NEW LIFE BUSINESS ISSUED ($000 omitted)

Year	Whole Life	Term	Credit	Group	Industrial	Total
2007	450,393	499,889	...	...	...	950,282
2008	329,005	410,742	...	...	...	739,747
2009	442,869	464,914	...	...	...	907,783

• LIFE INSURANCE IN FORCE ($000 omitted)

Year	Whole Life	Term	Credit	Group	Industrial	Total
2007	7,218,645	2,977,479	...	12,610	494,873	10,703,607
2008	6,914,353	2,974,989	...	11,717	472,883	10,373,942
2009	6,824,697	3,016,790	...	10,642	452,257	10,304,386

UNITED LIFE INS CO

118 Second Avenue SE
Cedar Rapids, Iowa 52401-1212
Tel: 319-399-5700

AMB#: 007178
Began Business: 10/15/1962
Agency Off: Robert J. Celichowski

Best's Financial Strength Rating: A-
FSC: VIII

• NET PREMIUMS AND DEPOSITS ($000 omitted)

Year	Individual Life	Individual & Group Annuities	Group Life & A&H	Credit Life & A&H	Individual A&H	Total
2007	31,488	208,808	264	-87	1,621	242,093
2008	33,993	210,204	367	-25	1,574	246,113
2009	37,371	259,474	352	-14	1,507	298,690

• NET OPERATING GAIN ($000 omitted)

Year	Individual Life	Individual & Group Annuities	Group Life & A&H	Credit Life & A&H	Individual A&H	Total
2007	1,593	10,602	-194	862	772	13,634
2008	818	5,813	59	248	-364	6,575
2009	13	6,921	113	142	715	7,904

• COMPARATIVE FINANCIALS ($000 omitted)

Year	Assets	Capital & Surplus	Net Invest Income	Benefits Paid	Realized Cap Gains	Policyholder Dividends	Contract Lns (% of assets)
2007	1,356,739	164,168	78,986	288,424	1,481	...	0.6
2008	1,322,029	157,003	74,037	269,008	-5,929	...	0.6
2009	1,480,566	160,179	74,437	148,867	-4,381	...	0.5

• ORDINARY LIFE STATISTICS

Year	Av. Ord. Policy Issued ($)	Av. Ord. Policy In Force ($)	Avg. Prem ($/M)	1st Yr Prem/ Total Prem	Ord. Lapse Ratio
2007	109,555	80,511	7.73	9.4	5.1
2008	114,405	82,514	8.08	8.8	5.7
2009	103,867	83,910	8.63	9.4	5.1

• NEW LIFE BUSINESS ISSUED ($000 omitted)

Year	Whole Life	Term	Credit	Group	Industrial	Total
2007	126,529	294,710	...	11,198	...	432,437
2008	128,757	308,614	...	13,759	...	451,130
2009	120,023	295,133	...	6,687	...	421,843

• LIFE INSURANCE IN FORCE ($000 omitted)

Year	Whole Life	Term	Credit	Group	Industrial	Total
2007	1,768,377	2,536,249	36,416	126,165	...	4,467,207
2008	1,758,955	2,683,772	15,780	130,503	...	4,589,010
2009	1,773,337	2,804,033	8,435	129,453	...	4,715,258

UNITED OF OMAHA LIFE INS CO

Mutual of Omaha Plaza
Omaha, Nebraska 68175
Tel: 402-342-7600

AMB#: 007164
Began Business: 11/26/1926
Agency Off: John L. Haver

Best's Financial Strength Rating: A+ g **FSC:** XIII

• NET PREMIUMS AND DEPOSITS ($000 omitted)

Year	Individual Life	Individual & Group Annuities	Group Life & A&H	Credit Life & A&H	Individual A&H	Total
2007	695,990	929,626	455,902	...	132	2,081,649
2008	738,881	1,588,078	657,260	...	18,010	3,002,229
2009	801,450	1,816,582	633,361	...	174,084	3,425,476

• NET OPERATING GAIN ($000 omitted)

Year	Individual Life	Individual & Group Annuities	Group Life & A&H	Credit Life & A&H	Individual A&H	Total
2007	21,360	25,259	5,648	...	-1,600	90,495
2008	22,830	20,215	-18,624	...	-12,501	-8,706
2009	34,771	41,352	4,768	...	-32,285	34,904

• COMPARATIVE FINANCIALS ($000 omitted)

Year	Assets	Capital & Surplus	Net Invest Income	Benefits Paid	Realized Cap Gains	Policyholder Dividends	Contract Lns (% of assets)
2007	13,227,858	1,358,060	685,727	1,605,831	-1,855	19	1.2
2008	12,879,237	1,196,272	638,309	1,857,141	-60,863	17	1.3
2009	14,037,295	1,245,139	671,145	1,767,021	-40,152	17	1.2

• ORDINARY LIFE STATISTICS

Year	Av. Ord. Policy Issued ($)	Av. Ord. Policy In Force ($)	Avg. Prem ($/M)	1st Yr Prem/ Total Prem	Ord. Lapse Ratio
2007	41,460	50,043	9.08	13.7	7.0
2008	38,476	49,852	9.42	14.0	7.6
2009	45,161	49,690	9.75	16.6	8.1

• NEW LIFE BUSINESS ISSUED ($000 omitted)

Year	Whole Life	Term	Credit	Group	Industrial	Total
2007	4,112,969	3,794,570	...	22,148,764	...	30,056,303
2008	4,399,547	3,806,961	...	16,694,413	...	24,900,921
2009	5,544,689	6,413,788	...	21,423,972	...	33,382,449

• LIFE INSURANCE IN FORCE ($000 omitted)

Year	Whole Life	Term	Credit	Group	Industrial	Total
2007	38,409,232	48,402,385	...	108,269,852	...	195,081,469
2008	39,008,530	47,698,694	...	118,519,897	...	205,227,121
2009	40,436,558	49,395,573	...	117,732,611	...	207,564,742

UNITED SECURITY LF & H INS CO

6640 S. Cicero Avenue
Bedford Park, Illinois 60638
Tel: 708-475-6100

AMB#: 008442
Began Business: 12/17/1973
Agency Off: Peter J. Harmon

Best's Financial Strength Rating: D **FSC:** III

• NET PREMIUMS AND DEPOSITS ($000 omitted)

Year	Individual Life	Individual & Group Annuities	Group Life & A&H	Credit Life & A&H	Individual A&H	Total
2007	1,894	...	34,517	...	617	37,029
2008	1,707	...	36,586	...	568	38,861
2009	1,542	...	34,372	...	532	36,446

• NET OPERATING GAIN ($000 omitted)

Year	Individual Life	Individual & Group Annuities	Group Life & A&H	Credit Life & A&H	Individual A&H	Total
2007	-161	...	-2,332	...	242	-2,251
2008	-346	...	-2,602	...	51	-2,897
2009	-311	...	-128	...	267	-172

• COMPARATIVE FINANCIALS ($000 omitted)

Year	Assets	Capital & Surplus	Net Invest Income	Benefits Paid	Realized Cap Gains	Policyholder Dividends	Contract Lns (% of assets)
2007	26,139	7,396	832	27,720	80	...	2.0
2008	22,838	4,644	784	28,841	-324	...	2.7
2009	23,763	4,148	735	26,617	-387	...	3.2

• ORDINARY LIFE STATISTICS

Year	Av. Ord. Policy Issued ($)	Av. Ord. Policy In Force ($)	Avg. Prem ($/M)	1st Yr Prem/ Total Prem	Ord. Lapse Ratio
2007	...	...	...	...	...
2008	...	...	...	...	...
2009	...	...	...	...	...

• NEW LIFE BUSINESS ISSUED ($000 omitted)

Year	Whole Life	Term	Credit	Group	Industrial	Total
2007	8,046	...	...	6,195	...	14,241
2008	7,016	...	...	3,760	...	10,776
2009	4,625	...	...	1,270	...	5,895

• LIFE INSURANCE IN FORCE ($000 omitted)

Year	Whole Life	Term	Credit	Group	Industrial	Total
2007	74,974	4,338	...	19,925	...	99,237
2008	70,891	4,747	...	16,180	...	91,818
2009	65,997	4,771	...	10,740	...	81,508

UNITED SECURITY ASSUR CO OF PA

673 East Cherry Lane
Souderton, Pennsylvania 18964
Tel: 215-723-3044

AMB#: 001850
Began Business: 08/05/1983
Agency Off: Christopher F. Coady

Best's Financial Strength Rating: B+ **FSC:** V

• NET PREMIUMS AND DEPOSITS ($000 omitted)

Year	Individual Life	Individual & Group Annuities	Group Life & A&H	Credit Life & A&H	Individual A&H	Total
2007	16	...	74	...	11,340	11,430
2008	45	...	57	...	11,551	11,653
2009	248	...	54	...	21,810	22,112

• NET OPERATING GAIN ($000 omitted)

Year	Individual Life	Individual & Group Annuities	Group Life & A&H	Credit Life & A&H	Individual A&H	Total
2007	1	...	-109	...	1,747	1,639
2008	16	...	22	...	8,147	8,185
2009	32	...	-135	...	1,326	1,223

• COMPARATIVE FINANCIALS ($000 omitted)

Year	Assets	Capital & Surplus	Net Invest Income	Benefits Paid	Realized Cap Gains	Policyholder Dividends	Contract Lns (% of assets)
2007	39,958	19,093	1,357	3,220	-1	...	...
2008	65,138	21,035	8,719	3,359	-444	...	0.0
2009	106,358	20,445	3,322	7,165	-145	...	0.0

• ORDINARY LIFE STATISTICS

Year	Av. Ord. Policy Issued ($)	Av. Ord. Policy In Force ($)	Avg. Prem ($/M)	1st Yr Prem/ Total Prem	Ord. Lapse Ratio
2007	...	...	...	...	...
2008	...	...	...	...	...
2009	...	...	...	...	...

• NEW LIFE BUSINESS ISSUED ($000 omitted)

Year	Whole Life	Term	Credit	Group	Industrial	Total
2007	96	...	...	...	...	96
2008	196	...	...	...	...	196
2009	181	...	...	...	...	181

• LIFE INSURANCE IN FORCE ($000 omitted)

Year	Whole Life	Term	Credit	Group	Industrial	Total
2007	262	10	...	...	...	272
2008	3,626	...	...	...	...	3,626
2009	3,398	...	...	...	...	3,398

UNITED STATES LIFE INS OF NY

3600 Route 66 P.O. Box 1580
Neptune, New Jersey 07754-1580
Tel: 212-709-6000

AMB#: 007192
Began Business: 03/04/1850
Agency Off: Matthew E. Winter

Best's Financial Strength Rating: A **FSC:** X

• NET PREMIUMS AND DEPOSITS ($000 omitted)

Year	Individual Life	Individual & Group Annuities	Group Life & A&H	Credit Life & A&H	Individual A&H	Total
2007	166,753	18,493	639,989	-4,189	444	821,489
2008	157,992	12,986	469,533	-6,248	296	634,559
2009	122,792	25,255	347,428	299	244	496,019

• NET OPERATING GAIN ($000 omitted)

Year	Individual Life	Individual & Group Annuities	Group Life & A&H	Credit Life & A&H	Individual A&H	Total
2007	43,376	3,996	33,518	5,751	-559	103,530
2008	-46,185	-2,453	-52,605	-4,090	-213	-89,588
2009	236,981	6,412	10,341	80	-320	260,210

• COMPARATIVE FINANCIALS ($000 omitted)

Year	Assets	Capital & Surplus	Net Invest Income	Benefits Paid	Realized Cap Gains	Policyholder Dividends	Contract Lns (% of assets)
2007	5,314,659	472,399	314,334	166,723	-31,243	3,205	3.8
2008	5,318,291	251,378	323,069	586,751	-553,298	3,423	3.9
2009	5,318,059	488,892	305,006	555,379	-66,334	2,557	4.0

• ORDINARY LIFE STATISTICS

Year	Av. Ord. Policy Issued ($)	Av. Ord. Policy In Force ($)	Avg. Prem ($/M)	1st Yr Prem/ Total Prem	Ord. Lapse Ratio
2007	829,944	253,778	3.98	13.5	3.3
2008	774,631	269,255	3.97	10.7	4.5
2009	567,649	271,515	3.78	3.6	6.1

• NEW LIFE BUSINESS ISSUED ($000 omitted)

Year	Whole Life	Term	Credit	Group	Industrial	Total
2007	650,776	6,556,458	178,898	3,146,468	...	10,532,600
2008	413,130	5,920,257	231,917	1,689,102	...	8,254,406
2009	177,861	1,686,865	86,363	2,364,440	...	4,315,529

• LIFE INSURANCE IN FORCE ($000 omitted)

Year	Whole Life	Term	Credit	Group	Industrial	Total
2007	18,674,852	59,149,487	960,896	56,755,102	...	135,540,337
2008	17,973,617	62,047,862	651,751	52,942,247	...	133,615,477
2009	17,028,390	59,295,626	493,941	50,398,161	...	127,216,118

UNITED TEACHER ASSOCIATES INS

P.O. Box 26580
Austin, Texas 78755
Tel: 512-451-2224

AMB#: 006410
Began Business: 01/01/1959
Agency Off: None

Best's Financial Strength Rating: B++ **FSC:** VII

• **NET PREMIUMS AND DEPOSITS ($000 omitted)**

Year	Individual Life	Individual & Group Annuities	Group Life & A&H	Credit Life & A&H	Individual A&H	Total
2007	6,390	14,894	26,391	...	170,417	218,092
2008	7,389	10,277	25,400	...	161,380	204,446
2009	8,636	7,667	25,987	...	193,594	235,884

• **NET OPERATING GAIN ($000 omitted)**

Year	Individual Life	Individual & Group Annuities	Group Life & A&H	Credit Life & A&H	Individual A&H	Total
2007	-506	1,018	807	...	2,509	3,828
2008	-791	833	799	...	4,268	5,110
2009	-1,208	1,261	-4	...	-5,314	-5,265

• **COMPARATIVE FINANCIALS ($000 omitted)**

Year	Assets	Capital & Surplus	Net Invest Income	Benefits Paid	Realized Cap Gains	Policyholder Dividends	Contract Lns (% of assets)
2007	499,286	65,651	28,081	155,970	-822	...	3.7
2008	506,374	58,642	28,397	142,800	-13,089	...	3.7
2009	736,878	66,245	38,304	138,469	-2,094	...	2.5

• **ORDINARY LIFE STATISTICS**

Year	Av. Ord. Policy Issued ($)	Av. Ord. Policy In Force ($)	Avg. Prem ($/M)	1st Yr Prem/ Total Prem	Ord. Lapse Ratio
2007	...	...	...	...	...
2008	...	...	...	...	...
2009	...	...	...	...	...

• **NEW LIFE BUSINESS ISSUED ($000 omitted)**

Year	Whole Life	Term	Credit	Group	Industrial	Total
2007	21,900	...	...	...	...	21,900
2008	25,757	...	...	...	...	25,757
2009	38,199	...	...	...	...	38,199

• **LIFE INSURANCE IN FORCE ($000 omitted)**

Year	Whole Life	Term	Credit	Group	Industrial	Total
2007	96,158	764	...	...	...	96,922
2008	110,662	871	...	...	...	111,533
2009	129,673	803	...	...	...	130,476

UNITEDHEALTHCARE INS CO

450 Columbus Boulevard
Hartford, Connecticut 06103
Tel: 877-832-7734

AMB#: 008290
Began Business: 04/11/1972
Agency Off: None

Best's Financial Strength Rating: A g **FSC:** XV

• **NET PREMIUMS AND DEPOSITS ($000 omitted)**

Year	Individual Life	Individual & Group Annuities	Group Life & A&H	Credit Life & A&H	Individual A&H	Total
2007	...	178,856	22,793,270	...	6,585,375	29,557,501
2008	...	98,849	24,597,923	...	7,728,084	32,424,857
2009	...	120,538	25,533,692	...	10,312,354	35,966,584

• **NET OPERATING GAIN ($000 omitted)**

Year	Individual Life	Individual & Group Annuities	Group Life & A&H	Credit Life & A&H	Individual A&H	Total
2007	...	...	1,876,672	...	414,574	2,291,246
2008	...	...	1,451,037	...	445,004	1,896,040
2009	...	...	1,619,753	...	393,145	2,012,898

• **COMPARATIVE FINANCIALS ($000 omitted)**

Year	Assets	Capital & Surplus	Net Invest Income	Benefits Paid	Realized Cap Gains	Policyholder Dividends	Contract Lns (% of assets)
2007	11,425,484	3,104,865	726,823	23,655,707	-925	...	...
2008	10,522,869	2,821,569	550,295	26,582,247	-29,029	...	...
2009	11,899,664	3,425,789	441,437	29,461,568	-19,016	...	...

• **ORDINARY LIFE STATISTICS**

Year	Av. Ord. Policy Issued ($)	Av. Ord. Policy In Force ($)	Avg. Prem ($/M)	1st Yr Prem/ Total Prem	Ord. Lapse Ratio
2007	...	...	...	...	...
2008	...	...	...	...	...
2009	...	...	...	...	...

• **NEW LIFE BUSINESS ISSUED ($000 omitted)**

Year	Whole Life	Term	Credit	Group	Industrial	Total
2007	...	100	...	50,961,917	...	50,962,017
2008	...	...	...	28,974,061	...	28,974,061
2009	...	...	...	41,606,845	...	41,606,845

• **LIFE INSURANCE IN FORCE ($000 omitted)**

Year	Whole Life	Term	Credit	Group	Industrial	Total
2007	...	220	...	98,554,290	...	98,554,510
2008	...	220	...	99,967,039	...	99,967,259
2009	...	220	...	112,625,599	...	112,625,819

UNITED WORLD LIFE INS CO

Mutual of Omaha Plaza
Omaha, Nebraska 68175
Tel: 402-342-7600

AMB#: 007528
Began Business: 04/29/1970
Agency Off: None

Best's Financial Strength Rating: A+ g **FSC:** XIII

• **NET PREMIUMS AND DEPOSITS ($000 omitted)**

Year	Individual Life	Individual & Group Annuities	Group Life & A&H	Credit Life & A&H	Individual A&H	Total
2007	2,575	...	...	...	...	2,575
2008	2,372	119	...	...	...	2,491
2009	2,212	74	...	...	...	2,286

• **NET OPERATING GAIN ($000 omitted)**

Year	Individual Life	Individual & Group Annuities	Group Life & A&H	Credit Life & A&H	Individual A&H	Total
2007	2,303	115	7	...	...	2,424
2008	2,317	25	2	...	...	2,343
2009	2,274	-6	2	...	...	2,270

• **COMPARATIVE FINANCIALS ($000 omitted)**

Year	Assets	Capital & Surplus	Net Invest Income	Benefits Paid	Realized Cap Gains	Policyholder Dividends	Contract Lns (% of assets)
2007	91,904	22,557	3,856	1,959	-12	...	0.6
2008	90,578	34,839	4,312	2,174	-446	...	0.7
2009	92,756	43,172	4,404	1,721	...	...	0.7

• **ORDINARY LIFE STATISTICS**

Year	Av. Ord. Policy Issued ($)	Av. Ord. Policy In Force ($)	Avg. Prem ($/M)	1st Yr Prem/ Total Prem	Ord. Lapse Ratio
2007	...	...	...	...	...
2008	...	...	...	...	...
2009	...	...	...	...	...

• **NEW LIFE BUSINESS ISSUED ($000 omitted)**

Year	Whole Life	Term	Credit	Group	Industrial	Total
2007	40	...	...	...	...	40
2008	70	...	...	...	...	70
2009	23	...	...	...	...	23

• **LIFE INSURANCE IN FORCE ($000 omitted)**

Year	Whole Life	Term	Credit	Group	Industrial	Total
2007	184,949	76,235	...	37	...	261,221
2008	174,211	75,170	...	21	...	249,402
2009	165,839	74,196	...	20	...	240,055

UNITY FINANCIAL LIFE INS CO

4675 Cornell Road, Suite 160
Cincinnati, Ohio 45241
Tel: 513-247-0711

AMB#: 006454
Began Business: 05/06/1964
Agency Off: Leslie A. Thompson

Best's Financial Strength Rating: B+ **FSC:** IV

• **NET PREMIUMS AND DEPOSITS ($000 omitted)**

Year	Individual Life	Individual & Group Annuities	Group Life & A&H	Credit Life & A&H	Individual A&H	Total
2007	13,295	...	7,988	...	...	21,284
2008	11,261	...	11,861	...	...	23,122
2009	5,607	...	23,083	...	...	28,690

• **NET OPERATING GAIN ($000 omitted)**

Year	Individual Life	Individual & Group Annuities	Group Life & A&H	Credit Life & A&H	Individual A&H	Total
2007	168	...	308	...	...	476
2008	48	...	230	...	...	278
2009	824	...	617	...	...	1,441

• **COMPARATIVE FINANCIALS ($000 omitted)**

Year	Assets	Capital & Surplus	Net Invest Income	Benefits Paid	Realized Cap Gains	Policyholder Dividends	Contract Lns (% of assets)
2007	57,747	6,747	2,510	7,359	...	...	0.0
2008	74,619	6,751	3,073	9,156	...	...	0.0
2009	87,263	8,113	4,012	11,066	-61	...	0.0

• **ORDINARY LIFE STATISTICS**

Year	Av. Ord. Policy Issued ($)	Av. Ord. Policy In Force ($)	Avg. Prem ($/M)	1st Yr Prem/ Total Prem	Ord. Lapse Ratio
2007	...	...	...	...	...
2008	...	...	...	...	...
2009	...	...	...	...	...

• **NEW LIFE BUSINESS ISSUED ($000 omitted)**

Year	Whole Life	Term	Credit	Group	Industrial	Total
2007	165,129	120	...	7,734	...	172,983
2008	80,424	714	...	12,301	...	93,439
2009	109,599	141	...	27,046	...	136,786

• **LIFE INSURANCE IN FORCE ($000 omitted)**

Year	Whole Life	Term	Credit	Group	Industrial	Total
2007	487,023	12,035	2,692	34,636	...	536,386
2008	491,648	12,951	1,780	44,251	...	550,630
2009	511,727	13,359	1,092	65,824	...	592,002

UNITY MUTUAL LIFE INS CO

P.O. Box 5000
Syracuse, New York 13250-5000
Tel: 315-448-7000

AMB#: 007196
Began Business: 01/01/1905
Agency Off: Jeanne Clarke

Best's Financial Strength Rating: B- **FSC:** V

• NET PREMIUMS AND DEPOSITS ($000 omitted)

Year	Individual Life	Individual & Group Annuities	Group Life & A&H	Credit Life & A&H	Individual A&H	Total
2007	22,804	8,566	66	...	86	31,523
2008	21,682	6,774	27	...	74	28,558
2009	24,956	5,764	27	...	57	30,806

• NET OPERATING GAIN ($000 omitted)

Year	Individual Life	Individual & Group Annuities	Group Life & A&H	Credit Life & A&H	Individual A&H	Total
2007	-1,605	1,103	-149	...	-163	-814
2008	400	1,287	-115	...	-140	1,431
2009	-1,956	865	-131	...	-252	-1,475

• COMPARATIVE FINANCIALS ($000 omitted)

Year	Assets	Capital & Surplus	Net Invest Income	Benefits Paid	Realized Cap Gains	Policyholder Dividends	Contract Lns (% of assets)
2007	320,911	19,280	16,650	38,561	-73	450	4.1
2008	267,880	24,547	12,803	27,923	3	288	3.6
2009	277,027	17,041	12,969	26,816	-619	295	3.2

• ORDINARY LIFE STATISTICS

Year	Av. Ord. Policy Issued ($)	Av. Ord. Policy In Force ($)	Avg. Prem ($/M)	1st Yr Prem/ Total Prem	Ord. Lapse Ratio
2007	11,148	6,600	28.69	2.0	4.8
2008	11,791	7,740	29.38	0.9	4.2
2009	12,789	7,370	33.05	1.5	4.2

• NEW LIFE BUSINESS ISSUED ($000 omitted)

Year	Whole Life	Term	Credit	Group	Industrial	Total
2007	11,895	1,538	...	...	...	13,433
2008	3,587	410	...	...	...	3,997
2009	4,910	308	...	...	...	5,218

• LIFE INSURANCE IN FORCE ($000 omitted)

Year	Whole Life	Term	Credit	Group	Industrial	Total
2007	853,865	90,847	...	2,467	56,710	1,003,889
2008	983,172	86,309	...	2,185	54,273	1,125,939
2009	914,681	83,584	...	1,905	51,663	1,051,833

UNIVERSAL FIDELITY LIFE INS CO

13931 Quail Pointe Drive
Oklahoma City, Oklahoma 73134
Tel: 800-366-8354

AMB#: 007198
Began Business: 07/01/1935
Agency Off: Michael A. McLemore

Best's Financial Strength Rating: B+ **FSC:** III

• NET PREMIUMS AND DEPOSITS ($000 omitted)

Year	Individual Life	Individual & Group Annuities	Group Life & A&H	Credit Life & A&H	Individual A&H	Total
2007	436	...	3,399	...	...	3,835
2008	408	...	4,240	...	...	4,649
2009	294	...	4,998	...	106	5,398

• NET OPERATING GAIN ($000 omitted)

Year	Individual Life	Individual & Group Annuities	Group Life & A&H	Credit Life & A&H	Individual A&H	Total
2007	-5	...	-130	...	-152	-287
2008	18	...	631	...	553	1,203
2009	-137	...	404	...	-130	137

• COMPARATIVE FINANCIALS ($000 omitted)

Year	Assets	Capital & Surplus	Net Invest Income	Benefits Paid	Realized Cap Gains	Policyholder Dividends	Contract Lns (% of assets)
2007	9,071	3,163	120	1,493	...	1	0.5
2008	10,211	3,759	145	2,877	-230	1	0.5
2009	10,480	3,643	51	3,204	-30	1	0.7

• ORDINARY LIFE STATISTICS

Year	Av. Ord. Policy Issued ($)	Av. Ord. Policy In Force ($)	Avg. Prem ($/M)	1st Yr Prem/ Total Prem	Ord. Lapse Ratio
2007	...	...	...	...	...
2008	...	...	...	...	...
2009	...	...	...	...	...

• NEW LIFE BUSINESS ISSUED ($000 omitted)

Year	Whole Life	Term	Credit	Group	Industrial	Total
2007	...	...	...	...	...	...
2008	95	...	...	...	...	95
2009	290	...	...	...	...	290

• LIFE INSURANCE IN FORCE ($000 omitted)

Year	Whole Life	Term	Credit	Group	Industrial	Total
2007	26,619	2,929	...	...	...	29,548
2008	32,656	2,912	...	...	...	35,568
2009	30,791	2,591	...	...	...	33,382

UNIVERSAL LIFE INSURANCE CO

P.O. Box 2145
San Juan, Puerto Rico 00922-2145
Tel: 787-706-7337

AMB#: 060097
Began Business: 09/14/1994
Agency Off: None

Best's Financial Strength Rating: B++ **FSC:** V

• NET PREMIUMS AND DEPOSITS ($000 omitted)

Year	Individual Life	Individual & Group Annuities	Group Life & A&H	Credit Life & A&H	Individual A&H	Total
2007	557	30,973	5,526	7,044	14,967	59,067
2008	646	37,795	7,471	3,632	...	49,544
2009	712	54,718	6,821	2,114	...	64,365

• NET OPERATING GAIN ($000 omitted)

Year	Individual Life	Individual & Group Annuities	Group Life & A&H	Credit Life & A&H	Individual A&H	Total
2007	-519	494	-931	414	-386	-927
2008	28	28	-365	676	6,393	6,760
2009	-60	1,245	72	616	...	1,874

• COMPARATIVE FINANCIALS ($000 omitted)

Year	Assets	Capital & Surplus	Net Invest Income	Benefits Paid	Realized Cap Gains	Policyholder Dividends	Contract Lns (% of assets)
2007	96,135	10,441	2,010	13,698	...	...	...
2008	128,097	20,261	2,432	17,075	...	...	...
2009	216,953	22,108	4,282	13,584	-643	...	...

• ORDINARY LIFE STATISTICS

Year	Av. Ord. Policy Issued ($)	Av. Ord. Policy In Force ($)	Avg. Prem ($/M)	1st Yr Prem/ Total Prem	Ord. Lapse Ratio
2007	...	...	...	...	...
2008	...	...	...	...	...
2009	...	...	...	...	...

• NEW LIFE BUSINESS ISSUED ($000 omitted)

Year	Whole Life	Term	Credit	Group	Industrial	Total
2007	...	75,954	186,994	261,780	...	524,728
2008	637	36,541	107,254	425,414	...	569,846
2009	1,600	58,932	68,691	628,801	...	758,024

• LIFE INSURANCE IN FORCE ($000 omitted)

Year	Whole Life	Term	Credit	Group	Industrial	Total
2007	...	115,257	599,272	1,854,804	...	2,569,333
2008	2,763	111,825	500,329	2,127,759	...	2,742,676
2009	3,746	135,383	344,564	2,452,144	...	2,935,837

UNIVERSAL UNDERWRITERS LIFE

7045 College Boulevard
Overland Park, Kansas 66211
Tel: 913-339-1000

AMB#: 007204
Began Business: 10/01/1965
Agency Off: Lisa Ann Versch

Best's Financial Strength Rating: A- **FSC:** VII

• NET PREMIUMS AND DEPOSITS ($000 omitted)

Year	Individual Life	Individual & Group Annuities	Group Life & A&H	Credit Life & A&H	Individual A&H	Total
2007	14,182	0	...	-19,373	0	-5,190
2008	12,811	0	...	-2,089	0	10,722
2009	10,745	1	...	-1,887	46	8,906

• NET OPERATING GAIN ($000 omitted)

Year	Individual Life	Individual & Group Annuities	Group Life & A&H	Credit Life & A&H	Individual A&H	Total
2007	2,943	-79	1	5,960	1	8,826
2008	5,021	204	2	19,437	2	24,666
2009	4,009	155	2	10,638	37	14,841

• COMPARATIVE FINANCIALS ($000 omitted)

Year	Assets	Capital & Surplus	Net Invest Income	Benefits Paid	Realized Cap Gains	Policyholder Dividends	Contract Lns (% of assets)
2007	328,940	46,408	14,581	16,945	...	59	1.6
2008	253,961	59,617	12,795	17,752	-2,592	6	2.2
2009	258,997	75,322	11,643	15,767	-1,832	24	2.5

• ORDINARY LIFE STATISTICS

Year	Av. Ord. Policy Issued ($)	Av. Ord. Policy In Force ($)	Avg. Prem ($/M)	1st Yr Prem/ Total Prem	Ord. Lapse Ratio
2007	602,484	374,585	5.26	1.4	8.7
2008	493,346	374,406	5.27	1.5	9.5
2009	681,783	368,211	5.15	2.6	12.5

• NEW LIFE BUSINESS ISSUED ($000 omitted)

Year	Whole Life	Term	Credit	Group	Industrial	Total
2007	4,665	52,571	128,592	...	...	185,828
2008	8,975	55,160	3,551	...	...	67,686
2009	10,325	68,080	2,469	...	...	80,874

• LIFE INSURANCE IN FORCE ($000 omitted)

Year	Whole Life	Term	Credit	Group	Industrial	Total
2007	599,527	2,936,179	1,599,813	36	...	5,135,555
2008	536,253	2,712,841	858,254	36	...	4,107,384
2009	463,546	2,431,694	388,884	36	...	3,284,160

UNUM LIFE INS CO OF AMER

1 Fountain Square
Chattanooga, Tennessee 37402-1330
Tel: 207-575-2211

AMB#: 006256
Began Business: 09/03/1966
Agency Off: Stephen Mealh

Best's Financial Strength Rating: A- g **FSC:** XIV

• NET PREMIUMS AND DEPOSITS ($000 omitted)

Year	Individual Life	Individual & Group Annuities	Group Life & A&H	Credit Life & A&H	Individual A&H	Total
2007	15,124	618,794	2,763,901	...	10,072	3,407,403
2008	14,283	584,526	2,703,984	...	4,345	3,307,140
2009	14,998	516,137	2,615,280	...	6,638	3,153,784

• NET OPERATING GAIN ($000 omitted)

Year	Individual Life	Individual & Group Annuities	Group Life & A&H	Credit Life & A&H	Individual A&H	Total
2007	-15,304	20,882	172,547	...	78,108	249,364
2008	1,075	14,427	210,876	...	45,187	268,769
2009	-1,813	20,552	251,192	...	30,943	302,493

• COMPARATIVE FINANCIALS ($000 omitted)

Year	Assets	Capital & Surplus	Net Invest Income	Benefits Paid	Realized Cap Gains	Policyholder Dividends	Contract Lns (% of assets)
2007	16,438,519	1,490,503	1,009,136	1,910,346	-54,368	13,642	0.4
2008	16,890,055	1,353,250	997,414	1,596,024	-77,829	12,966	0.4
2009	17,214,784	1,541,119	1,017,968	1,545,338	-53,074	14,335	0.4

• ORDINARY LIFE STATISTICS

Year	Av. Ord. Policy Issued ($)	Av. Ord. Policy In Force ($)	Avg. Prem ($/M)	1st Yr Prem/ Total Prem	Ord. Lapse Ratio
2007	51,171	28,305	19.85	2.6	2.1
2008	44,749	28,310	19.98	2.0	5.5
2009	47,597	26,961	21.91	4.0	9.9

• NEW LIFE BUSINESS ISSUED ($000 omitted)

Year	Whole Life	Term	Credit	Group	Industrial	Total
2007	51,478	...	...	47,567,731	...	47,619,209
2008	38,887	...	...	45,428,895	...	45,467,782
2009	36,412	...	...	74,257,329	...	74,293,741

• LIFE INSURANCE IN FORCE ($000 omitted)

Year	Whole Life	Term	Credit	Group	Industrial	Total
2007	1,105,046	131,525	...	427,817,191	...	429,053,762
2008	1,050,411	127,049	...	418,452,093	...	419,629,553
2009	993,064	73,242	...	427,936,571	...	429,002,877

US FINANCIAL LIFE INS CO

1290 Avenue of the Americas, 16th Floor
New York, New York 10104
Tel: 212-554-1234

AMB#: 008492
Began Business: 09/30/1974
Agency Off: David J. Murphy

Best's Financial Strength Rating: A **FSC:** XV

• NET PREMIUMS AND DEPOSITS ($000 omitted)

Year	Individual Life	Individual & Group Annuities	Group Life & A&H	Credit Life & A&H	Individual A&H	Total
2007	73,668	37	...	...	...	73,705
2008	65,344	29	...	...	...	65,372
2009	61,179	23	...	...	...	61,202

• NET OPERATING GAIN ($000 omitted)

Year	Individual Life	Individual & Group Annuities	Group Life & A&H	Credit Life & A&H	Individual A&H	Total
2007	-27,726	-62	5	...	...	-27,783
2008	5,900	-293	-2	...	...	5,606
2009	18,159	-304	-5	...	...	17,849

• COMPARATIVE FINANCIALS ($000 omitted)

Year	Assets	Capital & Surplus	Net Invest Income	Benefits Paid	Realized Cap Gains	Policyholder Dividends	Contract Lns (% of assets)
2007	543,684	45,431	25,396	68,393	-11	...	1.9
2008	567,974	48,411	25,508	65,466	-8,484	...	2.5
2009	598,828	70,561	26,370	75,205	-1,149	...	3.2

• ORDINARY LIFE STATISTICS

Year	Av. Ord. Policy Issued ($)	Av. Ord. Policy In Force ($)	Avg. Prem ($/M)	1st Yr Prem/ Total Prem	Ord. Lapse Ratio
2007	592,632	339,125	4.90	10.4	5.5
2008	561,250	335,553	4.80	1.0	6.1
2009	...	331,489	4.84	0.1	7.4

• NEW LIFE BUSINESS ISSUED ($000 omitted)

Year	Whole Life	Term	Credit	Group	Industrial	Total
2007	254,220	5,857,592	...	...	...	6,111,812
2008	7,300	6,170	...	...	...	13,470
2009	...	...	...	...	...	...

• LIFE INSURANCE IN FORCE ($000 omitted)

Year	Whole Life	Term	Credit	Group	Industrial	Total
2007	4,238,014	55,579,885	...	...	...	59,817,899
2008	3,955,283	51,632,732	...	...	...	55,588,015
2009	3,650,094	47,575,957	...	...	...	51,226,051

USAA LIFE INS CO

9800 Fredericksburg Road
San Antonio, Texas 78288
Tel: 210-498-8000

AMB#: 007146
Began Business: 08/21/1963
Agency Off: None

Best's Financial Strength Rating: A++g **FSC:** XIII

• NET PREMIUMS AND DEPOSITS ($000 omitted)

Year	Individual Life	Individual & Group Annuities	Group Life & A&H	Credit Life & A&H	Individual A&H	Total
2007	339,729	733,642	363	...	125,683	1,199,418
2008	352,658	1,541,271	563	...	126,270	2,020,762
2009	367,275	1,838,351	531	...	129,844	2,336,001

• NET OPERATING GAIN ($000 omitted)

Year	Individual Life	Individual & Group Annuities	Group Life & A&H	Credit Life & A&H	Individual A&H	Total
2007	81,845	42,566	121	-9	11,759	136,284
2008	60,304	49,132	-322	...	17,478	126,592
2009	61,568	98,794	-179	...	5,687	165,869

• COMPARATIVE FINANCIALS ($000 omitted)

Year	Assets	Capital & Surplus	Net Invest Income	Benefits Paid	Realized Cap Gains	Policyholder Dividends	Contract Lns (% of assets)
2007	10,862,262	965,126	620,712	857,666	-33,254	43,074	1.3
2008	12,583,746	1,105,518	704,194	755,385	-102,914	42,562	1.2
2009	14,780,134	1,295,124	880,849	731,249	-123,909	42,681	1.1

• ORDINARY LIFE STATISTICS

Year	Av. Ord. Policy Issued ($)	Av. Ord. Policy In Force ($)	Avg. Prem ($/M)	1st Yr Prem/ Total Prem	Ord. Lapse Ratio
2007	300,759	277,658	2.56	11.2	2.6
2008	310,829	284,755	2.50	11.3	2.6
2009	368,696	294,121	2.48	10.6	2.5

• NEW LIFE BUSINESS ISSUED ($000 omitted)

Year	Whole Life	Term	Credit	Group	Industrial	Total
2007	1,359,758	41,044,584	...	...	...	42,404,342
2008	1,451,716	37,191,175	...	...	...	38,642,891
2009	1,882,483	31,004,118	...	...	...	32,886,601

• LIFE INSURANCE IN FORCE ($000 omitted)

Year	Whole Life	Term	Credit	Group	Industrial	Total
2007	18,384,198	230,874,786	...	31,497	...	249,290,481
2008	18,829,453	257,222,388	...	30,946	...	276,082,787
2009	19,965,748	277,426,898	...	30,865	...	297,423,512

USAA LIFE INS CO OF NY

9800 Fredericksburg Road
San Antonio, Texas 78288
Tel: 210-498-8000

AMB#: 060247
Began Business: 11/14/1997
Agency Off: None

Best's Financial Strength Rating: A++g **FSC:** XIII

• NET PREMIUMS AND DEPOSITS ($000 omitted)

Year	Individual Life	Individual & Group Annuities	Group Life & A&H	Credit Life & A&H	Individual A&H	Total
2007	10,070	13,016	...	...	...	23,086
2008	10,598	46,682	...	...	...	57,280
2009	11,154	49,678	...	...	...	60,831

• NET OPERATING GAIN ($000 omitted)

Year	Individual Life	Individual & Group Annuities	Group Life & A&H	Credit Life & A&H	Individual A&H	Total
2007	1,101	1,535	...	...	...	2,636
2008	1,562	1,897	...	...	...	3,460
2009	1,201	2,304	...	...	...	3,506

• COMPARATIVE FINANCIALS ($000 omitted)

Year	Assets	Capital & Surplus	Net Invest Income	Benefits Paid	Realized Cap Gains	Policyholder Dividends	Contract Lns (% of assets)
2007	321,906	40,342	17,600	15,003	0	1,593	1.1
2008	377,216	40,097	20,481	20,022	-1,870	1,603	1.1
2009	436,581	42,024	24,997	14,244	-2,683	1,636	1.1

• ORDINARY LIFE STATISTICS

Year	Av. Ord. Policy Issued ($)	Av. Ord. Policy In Force ($)	Avg. Prem ($/M)	1st Yr Prem/ Total Prem	Ord. Lapse Ratio
2007	570,303	345,975	2.92	10.9	2.6
2008	539,454	370,236	2.77	10.4	2.7
2009	531,532	388,349	2.57	10.1	2.4

• NEW LIFE BUSINESS ISSUED ($000 omitted)

Year	Whole Life	Term	Credit	Group	Industrial	Total
2007	25,335	1,301,761	...	...	...	1,327,096
2008	27,862	1,240,394	...	...	...	1,268,256
2009	38,766	1,166,216	...	...	...	1,204,982

• LIFE INSURANCE IN FORCE ($000 omitted)

Year	Whole Life	Term	Credit	Group	Industrial	Total
2007	610,598	5,712,447	...	...	...	6,323,045
2008	619,566	6,660,764	...	...	...	7,280,330
2009	629,456	7,537,527	...	...	...	8,166,983

USABLE LIFE

400 West Capitol, Suite 1500
Little Rock, Arkansas 72201
Tel: 501-375-7200

AMB#: 009350
Began Business: 12/22/1980
Agency Off: Terri Schmidt

Best's Financial Strength Rating: A g
FSC: VIII

• **NET PREMIUMS AND DEPOSITS ($000 omitted)**

Year	Individual Life	Individual & Group Annuities	Group Life & A&H	Credit Life & A&H	Individual A&H	Total
2007	5,604	...	173,243	...	26,470	205,318
2008	6,831	...	331,874	...	27,974	366,679
2009	5,351	...	350,516	...	28,137	384,004

• **NET OPERATING GAIN ($000 omitted)**

Year	Individual Life	Individual & Group Annuities	Group Life & A&H	Credit Life & A&H	Individual A&H	Total
2007	1,622	...	-4,133	...	2,532	21
2008	50	...	1,648	...	245	3,120
2009	-1,422	...	5,432	...	-3,637	-2,265

• **COMPARATIVE FINANCIALS ($000 omitted)**

Year	Assets	Capital & Surplus	Net Invest Income	Benefits Paid	Realized Cap Gains	Policyholder Dividends	Contract Lns (% of assets)
2007	239,530	99,308	8,857	127,604	4,297	...	1.2
2008	286,748	117,607	8,277	244,755	-2,770	...	1.1
2009	305,878	122,286	6,300	262,579	4,937	...	1.2

• **ORDINARY LIFE STATISTICS**

Year	Av. Ord. Policy Issued ($)	Av. Ord. Policy In Force ($)	Avg. Prem ($/M)	1st Yr Prem/ Total Prem	Ord. Lapse Ratio
2007	...	...	...	...	...
2008	...	...	...	...	...
2009	...	...	...	...	...

• **NEW LIFE BUSINESS ISSUED ($000 omitted)**

Year	Whole Life	Term	Credit	Group	Industrial	Total
2007	250,685	...	...	5,275,535	...	5,526,220
2008	389,240	...	...	3,491,551	...	3,880,791
2009	218,874	...	...	4,392,635	...	4,611,509

• **LIFE INSURANCE IN FORCE ($000 omitted)**

Year	Whole Life	Term	Credit	Group	Industrial	Total
2007	1,042,563	...	...	38,926,393	...	39,968,956
2008	1,119,847	...	...	37,029,842	...	38,149,689
2009	1,301,776	...	...	38,020,018	...	39,321,794

USIC LIFE INSURANCE COMPANY

P.O. Box 2111
San Juan, Puerto Rico 00922-2111
Tel: 787-273-1818

AMB#: 060567
Began Business: 05/01/2006
Agency Off: None

Best's Financial Strength Rating: B+
FSC: III

• **NET PREMIUMS AND DEPOSITS ($000 omitted)**

Year	Individual Life	Individual & Group Annuities	Group Life & A&H	Credit Life & A&H	Individual A&H	Total
2007	...	...	64	...	1	65
2008	...	...	226	...	4	230
2009	...	...	904	...	6	910

• **NET OPERATING GAIN ($000 omitted)**

Year	Individual Life	Individual & Group Annuities	Group Life & A&H	Credit Life & A&H	Individual A&H	Total
2007	...	...	24	...	1	25
2008	...	...	-47	...	1	-46
2009	...	...	-12	...	3	-9

• **COMPARATIVE FINANCIALS ($000 omitted)**

Year	Assets	Capital & Surplus	Net Invest Income	Benefits Paid	Realized Cap Gains	Policyholder Dividends	Contract Lns (% of assets)
2007	3,191	3,071	162	17	...	...	...
2008	3,328	3,126	156	267	-426	...	...
2009	3,953	3,564	156	776	-53	...	...

• **ORDINARY LIFE STATISTICS**

Year	Av. Ord. Policy Issued ($)	Av. Ord. Policy In Force ($)	Avg. Prem ($/M)	1st Yr Prem/ Total Prem	Ord. Lapse Ratio
2007	...	...	...	...	...
2008	...	...	...	...	...
2009	...	...	...	...	...

• **NEW LIFE BUSINESS ISSUED ($000 omitted)**

Year	Whole Life	Term	Credit	Group	Industrial	Total
2007	...	...	...	38,442	...	38,442
2008	...	...	...	47,703	...	47,703
2009	...	...	...	55,149	...	55,149

• **LIFE INSURANCE IN FORCE ($000 omitted)**

Year	Whole Life	Term	Credit	Group	Industrial	Total
2007	...	...	...	45,964	...	45,964
2008	...	...	...	93,667	...	93,667
2009	...	...	...	130,873	...	130,873

VANTIS LIFE INSURANCE COMPANY

200 Day Hill Road
Windsor, Connecticut 06095
Tel: 860-298-6000

AMB#: 007021
Began Business: 01/01/1964
Agency Off: Craig D. Simms

Best's Financial Strength Rating: A- g
FSC: VII

• **NET PREMIUMS AND DEPOSITS ($000 omitted)**

Year	Individual Life	Individual & Group Annuities	Group Life & A&H	Credit Life & A&H	Individual A&H	Total
2007	12,472	15,565	5,516	59	...	33,612
2008	12,302	72,829	5,115	22	...	90,268
2009	12,336	223,830	4,710	-14	...	240,862

• **NET OPERATING GAIN ($000 omitted)**

Year	Individual Life	Individual & Group Annuities	Group Life & A&H	Credit Life & A&H	Individual A&H	Total
2007	331	1,055	-324	52	...	1,114
2008	219	700	-298	48	...	669
2009	449	2,128	902	50	...	3,529

• **COMPARATIVE FINANCIALS ($000 omitted)**

Year	Assets	Capital & Surplus	Net Invest Income	Benefits Paid	Realized Cap Gains	Policyholder Dividends	Contract Lns (% of assets)
2007	649,526	67,314	34,108	79,112	...	1,655	1.0
2008	669,461	64,602	33,407	73,361	-5,351	1,128	1.0
2009	870,801	71,078	39,722	57,374	-3,184	1,029	0.8

• **ORDINARY LIFE STATISTICS**

Year	Av. Ord. Policy Issued ($)	Av. Ord. Policy In Force ($)	Avg. Prem ($/M)	1st Yr Prem/ Total Prem	Ord. Lapse Ratio
2007	122,837	56,735	4.00	12.2	6.8
2008	115,450	59,496	3.99	11.2	6.7
2009	94,731	61,210	4.03	12.3	6.8

• **NEW LIFE BUSINESS ISSUED ($000 omitted)**

Year	Whole Life	Term	Credit	Group	Industrial	Total
2007	27,388	509,286	2,199	2,672	...	541,545
2008	27,179	439,931	1,232	636	...	468,978
2009	28,240	417,090	534	1,306	...	447,170

• **LIFE INSURANCE IN FORCE ($000 omitted)**

Year	Whole Life	Term	Credit	Group	Industrial	Total
2007	281,900	3,332,712	5,982	1,148,830	...	4,769,424
2008	290,539	3,506,944	4,327	1,021,115	...	4,822,925
2009	300,848	3,642,867	2,660	904,187	...	4,850,562

VANTIS LIFE INSURANCE CO OF NY

200 Day Hill Road
Windsor, Connecticut 06095
Tel: 860-298-6000

AMB#: 060691
Began Business: 01/23/2009
Agency Off: None

Best's Financial Strength Rating: A- g
FSC: VII

• **NET PREMIUMS AND DEPOSITS ($000 omitted)**

Year	Individual Life	Individual & Group Annuities	Group Life & A&H	Credit Life & A&H	Individual A&H	Total
2007	...	...	...	...	...	...
2008	...	...	...	...	...	...
2009	30	...	...	...	...	30

• **NET OPERATING GAIN ($000 omitted)**

Year	Individual Life	Individual & Group Annuities	Group Life & A&H	Credit Life & A&H	Individual A&H	Total
2007	...	...	...	...	...	...
2008	...	...	...	...	...	...
2009	137	...	...	...	...	137

• **COMPARATIVE FINANCIALS ($000 omitted)**

Year	Assets	Capital & Surplus	Net Invest Income	Benefits Paid	Realized Cap Gains	Policyholder Dividends	Contract Lns (% of assets)
2007	...	...	...	...	...	...	...
2008	...	...	...	...	...	...	...
2009	6,644	6,528	433	...	...	...	...

• **ORDINARY LIFE STATISTICS**

Year	Av. Ord. Policy Issued ($)	Av. Ord. Policy In Force ($)	Avg. Prem ($/M)	1st Yr Prem/ Total Prem	Ord. Lapse Ratio
2007	...	...	...	...	...
2008	...	...	...	...	...
2009	...	...	...	...	...

• **NEW LIFE BUSINESS ISSUED ($000 omitted)**

Year	Whole Life	Term	Credit	Group	Industrial	Total
2007	...	...	...	...	...	...
2008	...	...	...	...	...	...
2009	190	4,860	...	...	...	5,050

• **LIFE INSURANCE IN FORCE ($000 omitted)**

Year	Whole Life	Term	Credit	Group	Industrial	Total
2007	...	...	...	...	...	...
2008	...	...	...	...	...	...
2009	175	4,535	...	...	...	4,710

VARIABLE ANNUITY LIFE INS CO

70 Pine Street, 19th Floor
New York, New York 10270
Tel: 713-522-1111

AMB#: 007208
Began Business: 05/01/1969
Agency Off: None

Best's Financial Strength Rating: A **FSC:** XV

• NET PREMIUMS AND DEPOSITS ($000 omitted)

Year	Individual Life	Individual & Group Annuities	Group Life & A&H	Credit Life & A&H	Individual A&H	Total
2007	...	6,137,983	...	...	...	6,137,983
2008	...	6,454,351	...	...	...	6,454,351
2009	...	5,247,196	...	...	...	5,247,196

• NET OPERATING GAIN ($000 omitted)

Year	Individual Life	Individual & Group Annuities	Group Life & A&H	Credit Life & A&H	Individual A&H	Total
2007	...	427,400	...	...	...	553,025
2008	-2	138,023	...	...	...	230,019
2009	...	657,512	...	...	...	831,992

• COMPARATIVE FINANCIALS ($000 omitted)

Year	Assets	Capital & Surplus	Net Invest Income	Benefits Paid	Realized Cap Gains	Policyholder Dividends	Contract Lns (% of assets)
2007	63,998,991	2,841,306	2,071,702	6,565,399	-250,521	...	1.6
2008	53,699,125	2,844,336	2,058,544	7,051,664	-4,727,636	...	1.9
2009	59,451,514	3,625,701	2,107,976	6,495,454	-702,387	...	1.6

• ORDINARY LIFE STATISTICS

Year	Av. Ord. Policy Issued ($)	Av. Ord. Policy In Force ($)	Avg. Prem ($/M)	1st Yr Prem/ Total Prem	Ord. Lapse Ratio
2007	...	...	...	...	...
2008	...	...	...	...	...
2009	...	...	...	...	...

• NEW LIFE BUSINESS ISSUED ($000 omitted)

Year	Whole Life	Term	Credit	Group	Industrial	Total
2007	...	...	...	...	...	...
2008	...	...	...	...	...	...
2009	...	...	...	...	...	...

• LIFE INSURANCE IN FORCE ($000 omitted)

Year	Whole Life	Term	Credit	Group	Industrial	Total
2007	87	...	...	...	...	87
2008	83	...	...	...	...	83
2009	83	...	...	...	...	83

VERSANT LIFE INSURANCE COMPANY

P.O. Box 84410
Baton Rouge, Louisiana 70884-4410
Tel: 225-769-9923

AMB#: 060339
Began Business: 06/20/2000
Agency Off: Dick S. Taylor

Best's Financial Strength Rating: B+ **FSC:** III

• NET PREMIUMS AND DEPOSITS ($000 omitted)

Year	Individual Life	Individual & Group Annuities	Group Life & A&H	Credit Life & A&H	Individual A&H	Total
2007	...	...	...	1,895	...	1,895
2008	...	...	...	1,126	...	1,126
2009	...	...	...	198	...	198

• NET OPERATING GAIN ($000 omitted)

Year	Individual Life	Individual & Group Annuities	Group Life & A&H	Credit Life & A&H	Individual A&H	Total
2007	...	...	...	730	...	730
2008	...	...	...	628	...	628
2009	...	...	...	432	...	432

• COMPARATIVE FINANCIALS ($000 omitted)

Year	Assets	Capital & Surplus	Net Invest Income	Benefits Paid	Realized Cap Gains	Policyholder Dividends	Contract Lns (% of assets)
2007	6,427	3,687	272	250	...	...	...
2008	6,466	4,256	261	363	...	...	...
2009	6,126	4,598	202	398	...	...	...

• ORDINARY LIFE STATISTICS

Year	Av. Ord. Policy Issued ($)	Av. Ord. Policy In Force ($)	Avg. Prem ($/M)	1st Yr Prem/ Total Prem	Ord. Lapse Ratio
2007	...	...	...	...	...
2008	...	...	...	...	...
2009	...	...	...	...	...

• NEW LIFE BUSINESS ISSUED ($000 omitted)

Year	Whole Life	Term	Credit	Group	Industrial	Total
2007	...	...	36,920	...	...	36,920
2008	...	...	27,017	...	...	27,017
2009	...	...	9,410	...	...	9,410

• LIFE INSURANCE IN FORCE ($000 omitted)

Year	Whole Life	Term	Credit	Group	Industrial	Total
2007	...	...	80,126	...	...	80,126
2008	...	...	71,640	...	...	71,640
2009	...	...	51,313	...	...	51,313

WASHINGTON NATIONAL INS CO

11825 N. Pennsylvania Street
Carmel, Indiana 46032
Tel: 317-817-6100

AMB#: 007218
Began Business: 09/07/1923
Agency Off: Steven M. Stecher

Best's Financial Strength Rating: B g **FSC:** X

• NET PREMIUMS AND DEPOSITS ($000 omitted)

Year	Individual Life	Individual & Group Annuities	Group Life & A&H	Credit Life & A&H	Individual A&H	Total
2007	38,681	277,023	8,308	...	127,937	451,949
2008	35,285	130,162	7,323	...	111,051	283,820
2009	16,616	92,575	6,188	...	97,408	212,788

• NET OPERATING GAIN ($000 omitted)

Year	Individual Life	Individual & Group Annuities	Group Life & A&H	Credit Life & A&H	Individual A&H	Total
2007	-7,941	-19,758	-10,885	...	-15,000	-42,749
2008	5,660	-5,252	-2,663	...	22,753	25,734
2009	12,382	-2,976	-14,451	...	-25,600	-22,808

• COMPARATIVE FINANCIALS ($000 omitted)

Year	Assets	Capital & Surplus	Net Invest Income	Benefits Paid	Realized Cap Gains	Policyholder Dividends	Contract Lns (% of assets)
2007	2,473,581	435,586	126,456	273,010	-2,457	3,459	2.6
2008	2,348,189	457,013	94,466	315,610	-12,254	3,086	2.6
2009	1,926,723	400,130	95,887	319,827	-20,506	583	2.0

• ORDINARY LIFE STATISTICS

Year	Av. Ord. Policy Issued ($)	Av. Ord. Policy In Force ($)	Avg. Prem ($/M)	1st Yr Prem/ Total Prem	Ord. Lapse Ratio
2007	...	18,002	16.50	0.0	7.2
2008	...	17,312	16.63	0.0	7.6
2009	10,000	16,764	16.48	0.0	7.0

• NEW LIFE BUSINESS ISSUED ($000 omitted)

Year	Whole Life	Term	Credit	Group	Industrial	Total
2007	...	...	...	...	...	...
2008	...	...	...	...	...	...
2009	10	...	...	...	...	10

• LIFE INSURANCE IN FORCE ($000 omitted)

Year	Whole Life	Term	Credit	Group	Industrial	Total
2007	2,230,942	1,017,084	...	88,117	22	3,336,165
2008	2,036,357	889,846	...	76,646	22	3,002,871
2009	1,886,692	768,001	...	72,868	22	2,727,583

WEST COAST LIFE INS CO

2801 Highway 280 South
Birmingham, Alabama 35223
Tel: 415-591-8200

AMB#: 007222
Began Business: 02/08/1915
Agency Off: Mark S. Rush

Best's Financial Strength Rating: A+ g **FSC:** XV

• NET PREMIUMS AND DEPOSITS ($000 omitted)

Year	Individual Life	Individual & Group Annuities	Group Life & A&H	Credit Life & A&H	Individual A&H	Total
2007	227,560	3,046	...	...	97	230,703
2008	181,653	191,338	...	...	86	373,077
2009	214,884	234,690	...	...	78	449,651

• NET OPERATING GAIN ($000 omitted)

Year	Individual Life	Individual & Group Annuities	Group Life & A&H	Credit Life & A&H	Individual A&H	Total
2007	-51,641	354	31	...	6	-49,175
2008	-71,993	7	24	...	277	-71,697
2009	-36,753	172	36	...	56	-36,760

• COMPARATIVE FINANCIALS ($000 omitted)

Year	Assets	Capital & Surplus	Net Invest Income	Benefits Paid	Realized Cap Gains	Policyholder Dividends	Contract Lns (% of assets)
2007	3,130,421	299,377	170,103	148,638	-507	2,705	1.0
2008	3,400,574	333,302	177,335	151,196	-49,387	485	1.1
2009	3,529,519	525,617	184,942	310,107	-59,161	1,620	1.0

• ORDINARY LIFE STATISTICS

Year	Av. Ord. Policy Issued ($)	Av. Ord. Policy In Force ($)	Avg. Prem ($/M)	1st Yr Prem/ Total Prem	Ord. Lapse Ratio
2007	577,600	446,788	2.65	18.4	3.6
2008	519,568	459,477	2.28	16.5	2.7
2009	486,498	460,765	2.30	18.2	4.4

• NEW LIFE BUSINESS ISSUED ($000 omitted)

Year	Whole Life	Term	Credit	Group	Industrial	Total
2007	1,279,876	63,000,097	...	9	...	64,279,982
2008	907,249	35,646,984	...	...	...	36,554,233
2009	1,441,957	29,620,909	...	286	...	31,063,152

• LIFE INSURANCE IN FORCE ($000 omitted)

Year	Whole Life	Term	Credit	Group	Industrial	Total
2007	15,267,100	259,680,629	...	5,246	...	274,952,975
2008	18,781,661	282,050,428	...	4,670	...	300,836,759
2009	18,987,019	296,327,062	...	5,040	...	315,319,120

WESTERN AND SOUTHERN LIFE INS

400 Broadway
Cincinnati, Ohio 45202
Tel: 513-629-1800

AMB#: 007243
Began Business: 04/30/1888
Agency Off: Bryan C. Dunn

Best's Financial Strength Rating: A+ g
FSC: XV

• NET PREMIUMS AND DEPOSITS ($000 omitted)

Year	Individual Life	Individual & Group Annuities	Group Life & A&H	Credit Life & A&H	Individual A&H	Total
2007	341,640	2,751	3,128	...	33,986	381,504
2008	332,517	4,975	3,135	...	33,748	374,376
2009	259,106	34,615	3,757	...	32,469	329,946

• NET OPERATING GAIN ($000 omitted)

Year	Individual Life	Individual & Group Annuities	Group Life & A&H	Credit Life & A&H	Individual A&H	Total
2007	44,150	-13,204	...	...	-1,471	210,456
2008	116,096	-15,140	...	...	18,231	233,327
2009	14,208	10,025	...	...	25,102	51,434

• COMPARATIVE FINANCIALS ($000 omitted)

Year	Assets	Capital & Surplus	Net Invest Income	Benefits Paid	Realized Cap Gains	Policyholder Dividends	Contract Lns (% of assets)
2007	8,832,318	3,705,965	469,515	609,629	53,889	58,729	1.8
2008	7,727,827	3,301,984	384,162	461,774	61,724	58,336	2.1
2009	7,955,404	3,464,875	264,658	393,301	27,404	57,883	2.1

• ORDINARY LIFE STATISTICS

Year	Av. Ord. Policy Issued ($)	Av. Ord. Policy In Force ($)	Avg. Prem ($/M)	1st Yr Prem/ Total Prem	Ord. Lapse Ratio
2007	22,741	19,108	10.43	8.2	5.9
2008	23,138	12,505	18.81	7.6	6.0
2009	23,124	12,835	14.48	8.9	6.7

• NEW LIFE BUSINESS ISSUED ($000 omitted)

Year	Whole Life	Term	Credit	Group	Industrial	Total
2007	903,522	258,242	...	...	...	1,161,764
2008	853,905	202,384	...	...	...	1,056,289
2009	1,032,950	188,702	...	...	...	1,221,652

• LIFE INSURANCE IN FORCE ($000 omitted)

Year	Whole Life	Term	Credit	Group	Industrial	Total
2007	25,170,418	5,737,247	...	633,935	561,325	32,102,925
2008	12,088,205	4,562,908	...	624,172	548,839	17,824,124
2009	12,115,071	4,292,976	...	656,393	537,300	17,601,740

WESTERN NATIONAL LIFE INS CO

P.O. Box 3206, A6-20
Houston, Texas 77253-3206
Tel: 806-345-7400

AMB#: 007235
Began Business: 07/05/1944
Agency Off: None

Best's Financial Strength Rating: A
FSC: XV

• NET PREMIUMS AND DEPOSITS ($000 omitted)

Year	Individual Life	Individual & Group Annuities	Group Life & A&H	Credit Life & A&H	Individual A&H	Total
2007	1,322	1,349,215	...	...	...	1,350,537
2008	1,316	5,710,168	...	...	...	5,711,484
2009	1,127	3,601,490	...	...	...	3,602,617

• NET OPERATING GAIN ($000 omitted)

Year	Individual Life	Individual & Group Annuities	Group Life & A&H	Credit Life & A&H	Individual A&H	Total
2007	1,066	206,202	...	...	...	375,907
2008	650	79,004	...	...	...	231,207
2009	1,164	131,112	...	...	...	317,938

• COMPARATIVE FINANCIALS ($000 omitted)

Year	Assets	Capital & Surplus	Net Invest Income	Benefits Paid	Realized Cap Gains	Policyholder Dividends	Contract Lns (% of assets)
2007	50,552,568	3,731,275	3,005,385	6,052,350	-480,284	0	0.1
2008	45,803,022	3,047,157	2,852,650	5,202,439	-8,132,176	0	0.1
2009	43,440,973	3,185,303	2,495,717	3,450,525	-546,528	0	0.1

• ORDINARY LIFE STATISTICS

Year	Av. Ord. Policy Issued ($)	Av. Ord. Policy In Force ($)	Avg. Prem ($/M)	1st Yr Prem/ Total Prem	Ord. Lapse Ratio
2007	...	...	...	...	...
2008	...	...	...	...	...
2009	...	...	...	...	...

• NEW LIFE BUSINESS ISSUED ($000 omitted)

Year	Whole Life	Term	Credit	Group	Industrial	Total
2007	...	...	...	...	...	...
2008	...	...	...	...	...	...
2009	...	...	...	...	...	...

• LIFE INSURANCE IN FORCE ($000 omitted)

Year	Whole Life	Term	Credit	Group	Industrial	Total
2007	95,928	101,703	...	...	...	197,631
2008	92,336	86,944	...	...	...	179,280
2009	86,715	73,970	...	...	...	160,684

WESTERN RESERVE LF ASSUR OF OH

4333 Edgewood Road N.E.
Cedar Rapids, Iowa 52499
Tel: 319-355-8511

AMB#: 007239
Began Business: 06/17/1980
Agency Off: None

Best's Financial Strength Rating: A g
FSC: XV

• NET PREMIUMS AND DEPOSITS ($000 omitted)

Year	Individual Life	Individual & Group Annuities	Group Life & A&H	Credit Life & A&H	Individual A&H	Total
2007	583,143	441,357	46	...	...	1,024,545
2008	573,661	220,341	375	...	...	794,378
2009	500,627	164,898	2,585	...	...	668,110

• NET OPERATING GAIN ($000 omitted)

Year	Individual Life	Individual & Group Annuities	Group Life & A&H	Credit Life & A&H	Individual A&H	Total
2007	106,442	28,441	-605	...	...	134,278
2008	41,001	-100,590	92	...	...	-59,497
2009	101,086	39,507	-674	...	...	139,919

• COMPARATIVE FINANCIALS ($000 omitted)

Year	Assets	Capital & Surplus	Net Invest Income	Benefits Paid	Realized Cap Gains	Policyholder Dividends	Contract Lns (% of assets)
2007	11,768,905	488,703	68,832	1,332,169	-2,623	27	3.5
2008	8,127,643	280,092	71,623	1,256,749	368	27	5.1
2009	8,821,381	363,146	48,371	810,649	-24,264	26	4.3

• ORDINARY LIFE STATISTICS

Year	Av. Ord. Policy Issued ($)	Av. Ord. Policy In Force ($)	Avg. Prem ($/M)	1st Yr Prem/ Total Prem	Ord. Lapse Ratio
2007	310,161	302,282	5.53	22.5	5.6
2008	316,124	302,309	5.44	20.0	10.4
2009	312,725	305,443	4.80	16.3	8.7

• NEW LIFE BUSINESS ISSUED ($000 omitted)

Year	Whole Life	Term	Credit	Group	Industrial	Total
2007	10,150,929	6,707,228	...	...	...	16,858,157
2008	8,525,869	8,593,834	...	27,549	...	17,147,252
2009	6,285,059	8,357,329	...	165,262	...	14,807,650

• LIFE INSURANCE IN FORCE ($000 omitted)

Year	Whole Life	Term	Credit	Group	Industrial	Total
2007	94,816,771	22,767,470	...	102,130	...	117,686,371
2008	91,662,223	28,135,299	...	125,181	...	119,922,703
2009	89,560,581	32,945,177	...	277,665	...	122,783,422

WESTERN-SOUTHERN LIFE ASSUR

400 Broadway
Cincinnati, Ohio 45202
Tel: 513-629-1800

AMB#: 009071
Began Business: 03/05/1981
Agency Off: Bryan C. Dunn

Best's Financial Strength Rating: A+ g
FSC: XV

• NET PREMIUMS AND DEPOSITS ($000 omitted)

Year	Individual Life	Individual & Group Annuities	Group Life & A&H	Credit Life & A&H	Individual A&H	Total
2007	56,905	1,668,000	...	...	...	1,724,905
2008	62,113	1,417,992	...	...	...	1,480,105
2009	148,463	1,070,480	...	...	...	1,218,942

• NET OPERATING GAIN ($000 omitted)

Year	Individual Life	Individual & Group Annuities	Group Life & A&H	Credit Life & A&H	Individual A&H	Total
2007	17,318	67,478	...	...	...	83,154
2008	-51,303	56,731	...	...	...	7,686
2009	19,597	68,118	...	...	...	92,607

• COMPARATIVE FINANCIALS ($000 omitted)

Year	Assets	Capital & Surplus	Net Invest Income	Benefits Paid	Realized Cap Gains	Policyholder Dividends	Contract Lns (% of assets)
2007	9,294,094	693,651	499,760	1,380,723	-43,007	...	0.5
2008	10,031,439	868,681	551,016	849,965	-116,808	...	0.5
2009	10,884,697	1,005,041	584,333	920,410	-149,996	...	0.4

• ORDINARY LIFE STATISTICS

Year	Av. Ord. Policy Issued ($)	Av. Ord. Policy In Force ($)	Avg. Prem ($/M)	1st Yr Prem/ Total Prem	Ord. Lapse Ratio
2007	112,293	88,901	5.20	3.8	6.5
2008	110,183	89,940	5.31	3.9	6.9
2009	91,808	90,280	5.85	8.1	7.2

• NEW LIFE BUSINESS ISSUED ($000 omitted)

Year	Whole Life	Term	Credit	Group	Industrial	Total
2007	83,693	1,411,370	...	...	...	1,495,063
2008	174,880	1,388,070	...	...	...	1,562,950
2009	503,901	1,660,483	...	...	...	2,164,384

• LIFE INSURANCE IN FORCE ($000 omitted)

Year	Whole Life	Term	Credit	Group	Industrial	Total
2007	13,456,542	14,368,477	...	...	...	27,825,019
2008	12,733,274	14,446,157	...	...	...	27,179,431
2009	12,280,007	14,759,084	...	...	...	27,039,091

WESTPORT LIFE INS CO

2400 West 75th Street
Prairie Village, Kansas 66208-3509
Tel: 913-432-1451

AMB#: 068070
Began Business: 04/17/1984
Agency Off: Robert E. Stroud

Best's Financial Strength Rating: B+ g
FSC: V

• **NET PREMIUMS AND DEPOSITS** ($000 omitted)

Year	Individual Life	Individual & Group Annuities	Group Life & A&H	Credit Life & A&H	Individual A&H	Total
2007	...	...	3,392	3,070	...	6,462
2008	...	...	1,750	2,760	...	4,510
2009	...	...	13	2,643	...	2,656

• **NET OPERATING GAIN** ($000 omitted)

Year	Individual Life	Individual & Group Annuities	Group Life & A&H	Credit Life & A&H	Individual A&H	Total
2007	...	...	467	1,124	...	1,591
2008	...	...	134	727	...	860
2009	...	...	96	853	...	949

• **COMPARATIVE FINANCIALS** ($000 omitted)

Year	Assets	Capital & Surplus	Net Invest Income	Benefits Paid	Realized Cap Gains	Policyholder Dividends	Contract Lns (% of assets)
2007	16,052	8,208	705	4,146	...	...	...
2008	14,570	7,888	702	3,060	...	...	...
2009	14,736	8,108	687	1,065	...	...	...

• **ORDINARY LIFE STATISTICS**

Year	Av. Ord. Policy Issued ($)	Av. Ord. Policy In Force ($)	Avg. Prem ($/M)	1st Yr Prem/ Total Prem	Ord. Lapse Ratio
2007	...	...	...	...	...
2008	...	...	...	...	...
2009	...	...	...	...	...

• **NEW LIFE BUSINESS ISSUED** ($000 omitted)

Year	Whole Life	Term	Credit	Group	Industrial	Total
2007	...	...	...	...	...	...
2008	...	...	...	...	...	...
2009	...	...	...	...	...	...

• **LIFE INSURANCE IN FORCE** ($000 omitted)

Year	Whole Life	Term	Credit	Group	Industrial	Total
2007	...	...	227,209	849,525	...	1,076,734
2008	...	...	207,571	2,081	...	209,652
2009	...	...	193,791	...	...	193,791

WICHITA NATIONAL LIFE INS CO

P.O. Box 1709
Lawton, Oklahoma 73502
Tel: 580-353-5776

AMB#: 007248
Began Business: 04/01/1957
Agency Off: Toby W. Osborne

Best's Financial Strength Rating: B+
FSC: IV

• **NET PREMIUMS AND DEPOSITS** ($000 omitted)

Year	Individual Life	Individual & Group Annuities	Group Life & A&H	Credit Life & A&H	Individual A&H	Total
2007	865	...	...	4,704	6	5,575
2008	870	...	...	4,194	6	5,069
2009	785	...	...	3,234	5	4,024

• **NET OPERATING GAIN** ($000 omitted)

Year	Individual Life	Individual & Group Annuities	Group Life & A&H	Credit Life & A&H	Individual A&H	Total
2007	-6	...	...	613	5	611
2008	-111	...	...	564	3	457
2009	-22	...	...	466	3	448

• **COMPARATIVE FINANCIALS** ($000 omitted)

Year	Assets	Capital & Surplus	Net Invest Income	Benefits Paid	Realized Cap Gains	Policyholder Dividends	Contract Lns (% of assets)
2007	19,247	6,968	787	1,700	...	...	2.3
2008	19,001	7,016	748	2,047	...	...	2.2
2009	18,547	7,295	612	1,655	...	...	2.2

• **ORDINARY LIFE STATISTICS**

Year	Av. Ord. Policy Issued ($)	Av. Ord. Policy In Force ($)	Avg. Prem ($/M)	1st Yr Prem/ Total Prem	Ord. Lapse Ratio
2007	...	...	...	...	...
2008	...	...	...	...	...
2009	...	...	...	...	...

• **NEW LIFE BUSINESS ISSUED** ($000 omitted)

Year	Whole Life	Term	Credit	Group	Industrial	Total
2007	443	13,468	259,074	...	...	272,985
2008	254	13,227	224,897	...	...	238,378
2009	176	8,310	188,164	...	...	196,650

• **LIFE INSURANCE IN FORCE** ($000 omitted)

Year	Whole Life	Term	Credit	Group	Industrial	Total
2007	18,553	126,282	316,376	...	...	461,211
2008	17,074	121,702	303,568	...	...	442,344
2009	15,880	114,600	276,503	...	...	406,983

WESTWARD LIFE INS CO

9 Executive Circle, Suite 200
Irvine, California 92614
Tel: 949-250-8627

AMB#: 008115
Began Business: 12/10/1965
Agency Off: None

Best's Financial Strength Rating: B+
FSC: IV

• **NET PREMIUMS AND DEPOSITS** ($000 omitted)

Year	Individual Life	Individual & Group Annuities	Group Life & A&H	Credit Life & A&H	Individual A&H	Total
2007	32	...	243	-38	709	946
2008	3	...	144	-4	313	456
2009	0	...	90	0	...	90

• **NET OPERATING GAIN** ($000 omitted)

Year	Individual Life	Individual & Group Annuities	Group Life & A&H	Credit Life & A&H	Individual A&H	Total
2007	383	-350	-19	292	424	730
2008	167	174	144	1,312	209	2,006
2009	2	1	-34	-2	...	-33

• **COMPARATIVE FINANCIALS** ($000 omitted)

Year	Assets	Capital & Surplus	Net Invest Income	Benefits Paid	Realized Cap Gains	Policyholder Dividends	Contract Lns (% of assets)
2007	23,666	19,958	977	623	...	...	...
2008	23,622	11,137	2,472	251	1,345	...	...
2009	10,373	8,300	340	98	81	...	...

• **ORDINARY LIFE STATISTICS**

Year	Av. Ord. Policy Issued ($)	Av. Ord. Policy In Force ($)	Avg. Prem ($/M)	1st Yr Prem/ Total Prem	Ord. Lapse Ratio
2007	...	...	...	...	...
2008	...	...	...	...	...
2009	...	...	...	...	...

• **NEW LIFE BUSINESS ISSUED** ($000 omitted)

Year	Whole Life	Term	Credit	Group	Industrial	Total
2007	...	...	17	...	...	17
2008	...	...	...	...	...	...
2009	...	...	...	...	...	...

• **LIFE INSURANCE IN FORCE** ($000 omitted)

Year	Whole Life	Term	Credit	Group	Industrial	Total
2007	3,168	53	7,611	...	...	10,832
2008	...	52	1,936	...	...	1,988
2009	...	21	186	...	...	207

WILLIAM PENN ASSOCIATION

709 Brighton Road
Pittsburgh, Pennsylvania 15233-1821
Tel: 412-231-2979

AMB#: 007249
Began Business: 02/21/1886
Agency Off: George S. Charles, Jr.

Best's Financial Strength Rating: B++
FSC: V

• **NET PREMIUMS AND DEPOSITS** ($000 omitted)

Year	Individual Life	Individual & Group Annuities	Group Life & A&H	Credit Life & A&H	Individual A&H	Total
2007	2,277	...	...	...	9	8,837
2008	2,108	...	...	...	8	13,652
2009	2,401	...	...	...	7	20,332

• **NET OPERATING GAIN** ($000 omitted)

Year	Individual Life	Individual & Group Annuities	Group Life & A&H	Credit Life & A&H	Individual A&H	Total
2007	600	1,174	...	...	16	421
2008	675	814	...	...	2	90
2009	347	935	...	...	-5	-31

• **COMPARATIVE FINANCIALS** ($000 omitted)

Year	Assets	Capital & Surplus	Net Invest Income	Benefits Paid	Realized Cap Gains	Policyholder Dividends	Contract Lns (% of assets)
2007	188,435	26,555	11,109	17,873	192	340	0.5
2008	186,748	21,609	10,918	14,683	-3,795	332	0.5
2009	199,480	19,894	11,024	13,005	-1,149	290	0.5

• **ORDINARY LIFE STATISTICS**

Year	Av. Ord. Policy Issued ($)	Av. Ord. Policy In Force ($)	Avg. Prem ($/M)	1st Yr Prem/ Total Prem	Ord. Lapse Ratio
2007	...	...	...	...	...
2008	...	...	...	...	...
2009	...	...	...	...	...

• **NEW LIFE BUSINESS ISSUED** ($000 omitted)

Year	Whole Life	Term	Credit	Group	Industrial	Total
2007	30,599	...	...	...	...	30,599
2008	24,597	...	...	...	...	24,597
2009	23,150	...	...	...	...	23,150

• **LIFE INSURANCE IN FORCE** ($000 omitted)

Year	Whole Life	Term	Credit	Group	Industrial	Total
2007	267,884	...	...	...	...	267,884
2008	274,053	...	...	...	...	274,053
2009	278,699	...	...	...	...	278,699

WILLIAM PENN LIFE INS CO OF NY

1701 Research Boulevard
Rockville, Maryland 20850
Tel: 516-794-3700

AMB#: 006734
Began Business: 02/23/1963
Agency Off: Kevin A. Harty

Best's Financial Strength Rating: A+ g
FSC: IX

• NET PREMIUMS AND DEPOSITS ($000 omitted)

Year	Individual Life	Individual & Group Annuities	Group Life & A&H	Credit Life & A&H	Individual A&H	Total
2007	51,337	1,606	...	...	43	52,987
2008	28,392	2,082	...	...	37	30,511
2009	47,683	6,218	...	...	39	53,940

• NET OPERATING GAIN ($000 omitted)

Year	Individual Life	Individual & Group Annuities	Group Life & A&H	Credit Life & A&H	Individual A&H	Total
2007	-3,366	3,718	...	...	-62	290
2008	-17,146	3,660	...	...	-35	-13,521
2009	-329	2,218	2	...	-79	1,813

• COMPARATIVE FINANCIALS ($000 omitted)

Year	Assets	Capital & Surplus	Net Invest Income	Benefits Paid	Realized Cap Gains	Policyholder Dividends	Contract Lns (% of assets)
2007	976,986	110,476	54,153	87,400	-825	1,067	4.5
2008	965,647	96,013	53,808	81,684	-14,922	764	4.5
2009	988,968	124,065	54,650	82,536	-286	848	4.3

• ORDINARY LIFE STATISTICS

Year	Av. Ord. Policy Issued ($)	Av. Ord. Policy In Force ($)	Avg. Prem ($/M)	1st Yr Prem/ Total Prem	Ord. Lapse Ratio
2007	700,244	428,005	2.80	9.0	4.2
2008	666,276	446,139	2.69	8.8	4.0
2009	588,149	456,729	2.62	7.7	4.8

• NEW LIFE BUSINESS ISSUED ($000 omitted)

Year	Whole Life	Term	Credit	Group	Industrial	Total
2007	191,396	7,601,619	...	...	...	7,793,015
2008	192,065	6,560,638	...	...	...	6,752,703
2009	103,958	5,538,154	...	...	...	5,642,112

• LIFE INSURANCE IN FORCE ($000 omitted)

Year	Whole Life	Term	Credit	Group	Industrial	Total
2007	6,579,147	54,439,771	...	180	...	61,019,098
2008	6,422,325	58,323,997	...	180	...	64,746,502
2009	6,090,235	60,607,761	...	74	...	66,698,070

WILTON REASSURANCE LIFE CO NY

187 Danbury Road, Riverview Bldg., 3rd Fl
Wilton, Connecticut 06897
Tel: 203-762-4400

AMB#: 006084
Began Business: 11/09/1956
Agency Off: None

Best's Financial Strength Rating: A- g
FSC: VIII

• NET PREMIUMS AND DEPOSITS ($000 omitted)

Year	Individual Life	Individual & Group Annuities	Group Life & A&H	Credit Life & A&H	Individual A&H	Total
2007	50,053	11,218	32	...	7	61,311
2008	54,047	10,593	26	...	8	64,674
2009	44,717	9,601	23	...	40	54,381

• NET OPERATING GAIN ($000 omitted)

Year	Individual Life	Individual & Group Annuities	Group Life & A&H	Credit Life & A&H	Individual A&H	Total
2007	-19,744	5,225	-24	...	-11	-14,554
2008	-32,215	31,499	-5	...	4	-717
2009	29,861	15,979	6	...	71	45,917

• COMPARATIVE FINANCIALS ($000 omitted)

Year	Assets	Capital & Surplus	Net Invest Income	Benefits Paid	Realized Cap Gains	Policyholder Dividends	Contract Lns (% of assets)
2007	1,219,486	93,361	74,810	154,290	-739	...	2.5
2008	1,184,341	70,632	68,879	127,260	-25,434	...	2.6
2009	1,182,496	95,258	69,792	95,299	-17,900	...	2.7

• ORDINARY LIFE STATISTICS

Year	Av. Ord. Policy Issued ($)	Av. Ord. Policy In Force ($)	Avg. Prem ($/M)	1st Yr Prem/ Total Prem	Ord. Lapse Ratio
2007	573,273	173,789	3.70	0.9	6.5
2008	269,754	155,086	3.88	0.5	6.4
2009	358,554	154,808	3.69	0.4	7.1

• NEW LIFE BUSINESS ISSUED ($000 omitted)

Year	Whole Life	Term	Credit	Group	Industrial	Total
2007	95,594	21,927	...	...	...	117,521
2008	2,269	52,491	...	...	...	54,760
2009	...	40,158	...	...	...	40,158

• LIFE INSURANCE IN FORCE ($000 omitted)

Year	Whole Life	Term	Credit	Group	Industrial	Total
2007	6,273,942	16,943,939	...	662	...	23,218,543
2008	5,801,821	16,336,186	...	574	...	22,138,581
2009	5,780,355	14,706,352	...	562	...	20,487,269

WILTON REASSURANCE COMPANY

187 Danbury Road, Riverview Building
Wilton, Connecticut 06897
Tel: 203-762-4400

AMB#: 060560
Began Business: 02/15/1901
Agency Off: Michael E. Fleitz

Best's Financial Strength Rating: A- g
FSC: IX

• NET PREMIUMS AND DEPOSITS ($000 omitted)

Year	Individual Life	Individual & Group Annuities	Group Life & A&H	Credit Life & A&H	Individual A&H	Total
2007	105,625	...	...	...	...	105,625
2008	337,503	68,606	...	...	...	406,109
2009	28,216	2,232	...	...	893	31,341

• NET OPERATING GAIN ($000 omitted)

Year	Individual Life	Individual & Group Annuities	Group Life & A&H	Credit Life & A&H	Individual A&H	Total
2007	-56,621	-23,325	...	...	...	-79,946
2008	9,328	237	...	...	...	9,565
2009	7,666	-2,688	...	...	844	5,822

• COMPARATIVE FINANCIALS ($000 omitted)

Year	Assets	Capital & Surplus	Net Invest Income	Benefits Paid	Realized Cap Gains	Policyholder Dividends	Contract Lns (% of assets)
2007	433,471	116,832	14,936	114,960	4	...	0.4
2008	668,443	126,425	19,288	113,121	-4,503	...	0.4
2009	1,179,640	258,305	94,581	140,703	-4,187	...	1.7

• ORDINARY LIFE STATISTICS

Year	Av. Ord. Policy Issued ($)	Av. Ord. Policy In Force ($)	Avg. Prem ($/M)	1st Yr Prem/ Total Prem	Ord. Lapse Ratio
2007	61,592	35,321	4.84	...	4.9
2008	663,900	34,047	8.93	...	9.0
2009	...	31,539	14.29	...	9.5

• NEW LIFE BUSINESS ISSUED ($000 omitted)

Year	Whole Life	Term	Credit	Group	Industrial	Total
2007	110,654	7,106,401	...	...	...	7,217,055
2008	...	6,639	...	...	...	6,639
2009	...	...	...	...	...	...

• LIFE INSURANCE IN FORCE ($000 omitted)

Year	Whole Life	Term	Credit	Group	Industrial	Total
2007	4,196,714	49,605,404	...	...	...	53,802,118
2008	7,942,091	54,719,717	...	...	...	62,661,808
2009	9,142,080	54,758,221	...	...	...	63,900,301

WOMAN'S LIFE INS SOCIETY

P.O. Box 5020
Port Huron, Michigan 48061-5020
Tel: 810-985-5191

AMB#: 006826
Began Business: 10/01/1892
Agency Off: Janice U. Whipple

Best's Financial Strength Rating: A-
FSC: VI

• NET PREMIUMS AND DEPOSITS ($000 omitted)

Year	Individual Life	Individual & Group Annuities	Group Life & A&H	Credit Life & A&H	Individual A&H	Total
2007	4,866	...	...	...	...	8,693
2008	5,012	...	...	...	...	10,172
2009	4,348	...	...	...	...	10,254

• NET OPERATING GAIN ($000 omitted)

Year	Individual Life	Individual & Group Annuities	Group Life & A&H	Credit Life & A&H	Individual A&H	Total
2007	594	455	...	...	...	1,049
2008	513	421	...	...	...	933
2009	9	222	...	...	...	230

• COMPARATIVE FINANCIALS ($000 omitted)

Year	Assets	Capital & Surplus	Net Invest Income	Benefits Paid	Realized Cap Gains	Policyholder Dividends	Contract Lns (% of assets)
2007	184,371	32,840	11,039	10,841	-80	949	5.3
2008	182,739	28,693	11,048	10,696	-4,334	940	5.0
2009	185,701	29,237	10,769	9,727	625	865	4.9

• ORDINARY LIFE STATISTICS

Year	Av. Ord. Policy Issued ($)	Av. Ord. Policy In Force ($)	Avg. Prem ($/M)	1st Yr Prem/ Total Prem	Ord. Lapse Ratio
2007	...	...	...	...	...
2008	...	...	...	...	...
2009	...	...	...	...	...

• NEW LIFE BUSINESS ISSUED ($000 omitted)

Year	Whole Life	Term	Credit	Group	Industrial	Total
2007	20,184	...	...	...	...	20,184
2008	16,683	...	...	...	...	16,683
2009	12,181	...	...	...	...	12,181

• LIFE INSURANCE IN FORCE ($000 omitted)

Year	Whole Life	Term	Credit	Group	Industrial	Total
2007	611,395	...	...	...	...	611,395
2008	595,052	...	...	...	...	595,052
2009	574,815	...	...	...	...	574,815

WOODMEN OF THE WORLD LIFE SOC

1700 Farnam Street
Omaha, Nebraska 68102
Tel: 402-342-1890

AMB#: 007259
Began Business: 12/31/1890
Agency Off: Pat Dees

Best's Financial Strength Rating: A+ **FSC:** XI

• NET PREMIUMS AND DEPOSITS ($000 omitted)

Year	Individual Life	Individual & Group Annuities	Group Life & A&H	Credit Life & A&H	Individual A&H	Total
2007	385,781	...	...	...	9,408	643,358
2008	417,738	...	...	...	9,254	910,095
2009	433,045	...	...	...	9,008	892,855

• NET OPERATING GAIN ($000 omitted)

Year	Individual Life	Individual & Group Annuities	Group Life & A&H	Credit Life & A&H	Individual A&H	Total
2007	65,681	12,917	...	...	-2,597	76,001
2008	55,775	16,957	...	...	-4,119	68,612
2009	39,473	5,193	...	...	-1,753	42,913

• COMPARATIVE FINANCIALS ($000 omitted)

Year	Assets	Capital & Surplus	Net Invest Income	Benefits Paid	Realized Cap Gains	Policyholder Dividends	Contract Lns (% of assets)
2007	7,647,374	916,734	423,816	532,511	49,983	133,003	2.2
2008	7,582,357	756,614	412,157	677,986	-96,420	131,014	2.2
2009	8,074,593	823,308	403,274	552,365	-34,923	108,782	2.1

• ORDINARY LIFE STATISTICS

Year	Av. Ord. Policy Issued ($)	Av. Ord. Policy In Force ($)	Avg. Prem ($/M)	1st Yr Prem/ Total Prem	Ord. Lapse Ratio
2007	77,109	42,185	11.01	18.8	5.7
2008	82,353	43,280	11.91	24.9	5.5
2009	85,727	44,395	12.33	26.9	5.7

• NEW LIFE BUSINESS ISSUED ($000 omitted)

Year	Whole Life	Term	Credit	Group	Industrial	Total
2007	2,622,154	...	...	...	...	2,622,154
2008	2,517,701	...	...	...	...	2,517,701
2009	2,736,054	...	...	...	...	2,736,054

• LIFE INSURANCE IN FORCE ($000 omitted)

Year	Whole Life	Term	Credit	Group	Industrial	Total
2007	34,654,733	...	...	...	...	34,654,733
2008	34,712,381	...	...	...	...	34,712,381
2009	34,890,092	...	...	...	...	34,890,092

WORLD INSURANCE COMPANY

P.O. Box 3160
Omaha, Nebraska 68103-0160
Tel: 402-496-8000

AMB#: 007262
Began Business: 11/17/1903
Agency Off: Mark L. Stadler

Best's Financial Strength Rating: A- g **FSC:** VIII

• NET PREMIUMS AND DEPOSITS ($000 omitted)

Year	Individual Life	Individual & Group Annuities	Group Life & A&H	Credit Life & A&H	Individual A&H	Total
2007	3,695	121	78,875	...	89,728	172,418
2008	3,463	54	69,072	...	83,569	156,158
2009	3,301	86	62,142	...	146,124	211,653

• NET OPERATING GAIN ($000 omitted)

Year	Individual Life	Individual & Group Annuities	Group Life & A&H	Credit Life & A&H	Individual A&H	Total
2007	1,914	690	4,995	...	-301	7,298
2008	1,575	590	1,345	...	-1,872	1,638
2009	2,800	147	6,670	...	-5,826	3,792

• COMPARATIVE FINANCIALS ($000 omitted)

Year	Assets	Capital & Surplus	Net Invest Income	Benefits Paid	Realized Cap Gains	Policyholder Dividends	Contract Lns (% of assets)
2007	231,501	116,376	9,714	112,505	608	378	2.3
2008	210,260	104,115	9,226	105,596	-2,551	406	2.5
2009	251,900	107,101	9,522	154,169	-1,198	407	2.1

• ORDINARY LIFE STATISTICS

Year	Av. Ord. Policy Issued ($)	Av. Ord. Policy In Force ($)	Avg. Prem ($/M)	1st Yr Prem/ Total Prem	Ord. Lapse Ratio
2007	...	...	...	...	...
2008	...	...	...	...	...
2009	...	...	...	...	...

• NEW LIFE BUSINESS ISSUED ($000 omitted)

Year	Whole Life	Term	Credit	Group	Industrial	Total
2007	84	...	...	...	...	84
2008	18	...	...	...	...	18
2009	...	60	...	...	...	60

• LIFE INSURANCE IN FORCE ($000 omitted)

Year	Whole Life	Term	Credit	Group	Industrial	Total
2007	283,946	101,731	...	...	...	385,677
2008	267,540	95,485	...	...	...	363,025
2009	252,451	88,395	...	...	...	340,846

WORLD CORP INSURANCE COMPANY

P.O. Box 3160
Omaha, Nebraska 68103-0160
Tel: 402-496-8000

AMB#: 008350
Began Business: 05/09/1960
Agency Off: Mark L. Stadler

Best's Financial Strength Rating: A- r **FSC:** VIII

• NET PREMIUMS AND DEPOSITS ($000 omitted)

Year	Individual Life	Individual & Group Annuities	Group Life & A&H	Credit Life & A&H	Individual A&H	Total
2007	...	...	...	...	1,655	1,655
2008	...	...	...	...	1,950	1,950
2009	...	...	...	...	1,658	1,658

• NET OPERATING GAIN ($000 omitted)

Year	Individual Life	Individual & Group Annuities	Group Life & A&H	Credit Life & A&H	Individual A&H	Total
2007	...	...	...	...	-157	-157
2008	...	...	...	...	80	80
2009	...	...	...	...	19	19

• COMPARATIVE FINANCIALS ($000 omitted)

Year	Assets	Capital & Surplus	Net Invest Income	Benefits Paid	Realized Cap Gains	Policyholder Dividends	Contract Lns (% of assets)
2007	23,198	22,236	1,135	1,102	...	...	...
2008	23,327	22,328	1,124	1,669	-19	...	...
2009	22,984	22,164	1,116	1,594	-204	...	...

• ORDINARY LIFE STATISTICS

Year	Av. Ord. Policy Issued ($)	Av. Ord. Policy In Force ($)	Avg. Prem ($/M)	1st Yr Prem/ Total Prem	Ord. Lapse Ratio
2007	...	...	...	...	...
2008	...	...	...	...	...
2009	...	...	...	...	...

• NEW LIFE BUSINESS ISSUED ($000 omitted)

Year	Whole Life	Term	Credit	Group	Industrial	Total
2007	...	...	...	...	...	...
2008	...	...	...	...	...	...
2009	...	...	...	...	...	...

• LIFE INSURANCE IN FORCE ($000 omitted)

Year	Whole Life	Term	Credit	Group	Industrial	Total
2007	...	...	...	...	...	...
2008	...	...	...	...	...	...
2009	...	...	...	...	...	...

XL LIFE INS AND ANNUITY CO

20 N. Martingale Road, Suite 200
Schaumburg, Illinois 60173
Tel: 847-517-2990

AMB#: 060395
Began Business: 08/01/1978
Agency Off: None

Best's Financial Strength Rating: A- **FSC:** V

• NET PREMIUMS AND DEPOSITS ($000 omitted)

Year	Individual Life	Individual & Group Annuities	Group Life & A&H	Credit Life & A&H	Individual A&H	Total
2007	...	...	...	...	...	...
2008	...	...	...	...	...	...
2009	...	...	...	...	...	...

• NET OPERATING GAIN ($000 omitted)

Year	Individual Life	Individual & Group Annuities	Group Life & A&H	Credit Life & A&H	Individual A&H	Total
2007	...	...	...	...	...	-17,373
2008	...	...	...	...	...	13,243
2009	...	...	...	...	...	2,793

• COMPARATIVE FINANCIALS ($000 omitted)

Year	Assets	Capital & Surplus	Net Invest Income	Benefits Paid	Realized Cap Gains	Policyholder Dividends	Contract Lns (% of assets)
2007	736,669	26,051	10,655	26,356	-865	...	...
2008	82,503	16,019	5,157	-20,035	-28,114	...	...
2009	67,032	19,353	2,856	-2,258	-608	...	...

• ORDINARY LIFE STATISTICS

Year	Av. Ord. Policy Issued ($)	Av. Ord. Policy In Force ($)	Avg. Prem ($/M)	1st Yr Prem/ Total Prem	Ord. Lapse Ratio
2007	...	...	...	...	...
2008	...	...	...	...	...
2009	...	...	...	...	...

• NEW LIFE BUSINESS ISSUED ($000 omitted)

Year	Whole Life	Term	Credit	Group	Industrial	Total
2007	...	...	869	...	...	869
2008	...	...	...	...	...	...
2009	...	...	...	...	...	...

• LIFE INSURANCE IN FORCE ($000 omitted)

Year	Whole Life	Term	Credit	Group	Industrial	Total
2007	...	...	12,606	...	...	12,606
2008	...	...	6,987	...	...	6,987
2009	...	...	3,500	...	...	3,500

ZALE LIFE INS CO

P.O. Box 152762, M.S. 5A-9
Irving, Texas 75015-2762
Tel: 972-580-4039

AMB#: 007349
Began Business: 06/05/1964
Agency Off: Michael R. Sabin

Best's Financial Strength Rating: B+

FSC: IV

• NET PREMIUMS AND DEPOSITS ($000 omitted)

Year	Individual Life	Individual & Group Annuities	Group Life & A&H	Credit Life & A&H	Individual A&H	Total
2007	45	...	288	1,385	...	1,719
2008	41	...	227	1,581	...	1,848
2009	36	...	203	1,640	...	1,879

• NET OPERATING GAIN ($000 omitted)

Year	Individual Life	Individual & Group Annuities	Group Life & A&H	Credit Life & A&H	Individual A&H	Total
2007	13	...	-1	425	...	438
2008	104	...	89	443	...	635
2009	21	...	-17	534	...	538

• COMPARATIVE FINANCIALS ($000 omitted)

Year	Assets	Capital & Surplus	Net Invest Income	Benefits Paid	Realized Cap Gains	Policyholder Dividends	Contract Lns (% of assets)
2007	12,128	9,645	334	755	0	0	2.0
2008	11,935	9,691	307	549	...	0	1.6
2009	11,006	8,604	238	585	...	0	1.7

• ORDINARY LIFE STATISTICS

Year	Av. Ord. Policy Issued ($)	Av. Ord. Policy In Force ($)	Avg. Prem ($/M)	1st Yr Prem/ Total Prem	Ord. Lapse Ratio
2007	...	...	...	...	...
2008	...	...	...	...	...
2009	...	...	...	...	...

• NEW LIFE BUSINESS ISSUED ($000 omitted)

Year	Whole Life	Term	Credit	Group	Industrial	Total
2007	...	...	53,285	...	...	53,285
2008	...	...	62,261	...	...	62,261
2009	...	...	58,724	...	...	58,724

• LIFE INSURANCE IN FORCE ($000 omitted)

Year	Whole Life	Term	Credit	Group	Industrial	Total
2007	2,582	932	71,846	417,918	...	493,278
2008	2,313	822	92,243	452,873	...	548,251
2009	2,088	742	82,437	391,301	...	476,568

Appendix A
United States and Caribbean

U.S. State Officials Having Charge of Insurance Affairs

Address	Name	Official Title	Telephone
Alabama, Montgomery 36104	Jim L. Ridling	Insurance Commissioner	334-269-3550
Alaska, Anchorage 99503-5948	Linda S. Hall	Director of Insurance	907-269-7900
Arizona, Phoenix 85018-7269	Christina Urias	Director of Insurance	602-364-3471
Arkansas, Little Rock 72201-1904	Jay Bradford	Insurance Commissioner	501-371-2600
California, Sacramento 95814	Steve Poizner	Insurance Commissioner	916-492-3500
Colorado, Denver 80202	Marcy Morrison	Insurance Commissioner	303-894-7499
Connecticut, Hartford 06103	Thomas R. Sullivan	Insurance Commissioner	860-297-3800
Delaware, Dover 19904	Karen Weldin-Stewart	Insurance Commissioner	302-674-7300
D.C., Washington 20002	Gennet Purcell	Insurance Commissioner	202-727-8000
Florida, Tallahassee 32399-0300	Kevin M. McCarty	Insurance Commissioner	850-413-3140
Georgia, Atlanta 30334	John Oxendine	Insurance Commissioner	404-656-2056
Hawaii, Honolulu 96813	Jeffrey P. Schmidt	Insurance Commissioner	808-586-2790
Idaho, Boise 83720-0043	William W. Deal	Director of Insurance	208-334-4250
Illinois, Springfield 62767-0001	Michael T. McRaith	Director of Insurance	217-785-4515
Indiana, Indianapolis 46204-2787	Carol Cutter	Insurance Commissioner	317-232-2385
Iowa, Des Moines 50319-0065	Susan E. Voss	Insurance Commissioner	515-281-5705
Kansas, Topeka 66612-1678	Sandy Praeger	Insurance Commissioner	785-296-3071
Kentucky, Frankfort 40601	Sharon P. Clark	Insurance Commissioner	502-564-6026
Louisiana, Baton Rouge 70802	James J. Donelon	Insurance Commissioner	225-342-5900
Maine, Augusta 04333-0034	Mila Kofman	Superintendent of Insurance	207-624-8475
Maryland, Baltimore 21202	Elizabeth "Beth" Sammis	Acting Insurance Commissioner	410-468-2090
Massachusetts, Boston 02110	Joseph G. Murphy	Acting Insurance Commissioner	617-521-7301
Michigan, Lansing 48933	Ken Ross	Insurance Commissioner	517-373-0220
Minnesota, St. Paul 55101	Glenn Wilson	Insurance Commissioner	651-296-4026
Mississippi, Jackson 39201	Mike Chaney	Insurance Commissioner	601-359-3569
Missouri, Jefferson City 65101	John M. Huff	Director of Insurance	573-751-4126
Montana, Helena 59601	Monica J. Lindeen	Insurance Commissioner	406-444-2040
Nebraska, Lincoln 68508-3639	Ann Frohman	Director of Insurance	402-471-2201
Nevada, Carson City 89706-5753	Brett Barratt	Acting Insurance Commissioner	775-687-4270
New Hampshire, Concord 03301	Roger A. Sevigny	Insurance Commissioner	603-271-2261
New Jersey, Trenton 08625-0325	Tom Considine	Insurance Commissioner	609-292-7272
New Mexico, Sante Fe 87501	Johnny L. Montoya	Acting Superintendent of Insurance	505-827-4601
New York, New York 10004	James J. Wrynn	Superintendent of Insurance	212-480-2301
North Carolina, Raleigh 27699-1201	Wayne Goodwin	Insurance Commissioner	919-733-3058
North Dakota, Bismarck 58505-0320	Adam Hamm	Insurance Commissioner	701-328-2440
Ohio, Columbus 43215	Mary Jo Hudson	Director of Insurance	614-644-2658
Oklahoma, Oklahoma City 73107	Kim Holland	Insurance Commissioner	405-521-2828
Oregon, Salem 97310-3883	Teresa Miller	Insurance Administrator	503-947-7980
Pennsylvania, Harrisburg 17120	Joel S. Ario	Insurance Commissioner	717-783-0442
Puerto Rico, Guaynabo 00968-3029	Ramon Cruz-Colon	Insurance Commissioner	787-304-8686
Rhode Island, Providence 02903-4233	Joseph Torti, III	Superintendent of Insurance	401-462-9520
South Carolina, Columbia 29201	Scott H. Richardson	Director of Insurance	803-737-6160
South Dakota, Pierre 57501-3185	Merle D. Scheiber	Director of Insurance	605-773-3563
Tennessee, Nashville 37243-0565	Leslie A. Newman	Insurance Commissioner	615-741-2241
Texas, Austin 78701	Mike Geeslin	Insurance Commissioner	512-463-6464
Utah, Salt Lake City 84114-6901	Neal Gooch	Acting Insurance Commissioner	801-538-3800
Vermont, Montpelier 05620-3101	Mike Bertrand	Insurance Commissioner	802-828-3301
Virginia, Richmond 23219	Alfred W. Gross	Insurance Commissioner	804-371-9741
Virgin Islands, St. Thomas 00802	Gregory R. Francis	Insurance Commissioner	340-774-7166
Washington, Tumwater 98501	Mike B. Kreidler	Insurance Commissioner	360-725-7000
West Virginia, Charleston 25301	Jane L. Cline	Insurance Commissioner	304-558-3354
Wisconsin, Madison 53703-3474	Sean Dilweg	Insurance Commissioner	608-266-3585
Wyoming, Cheyenne 82002-0440	Ken Vines	Insurance Commissioner	307-777-7401

U.S. State Officials Having Charge of HMO Affairs

Address	Name	Official Title	Telephone
Alabama, Montgomery 36130-3351	Kathleen Healey	Associate Counsel	334-240-4437
Alaska, Anchorage 99501-3567	Gloria G. Glover	Chief Financial Examiner	907-269-7900
Arizona, Phoenix 85018	Norman Brisker	Senior Financial Analyst	602-364-3991
Arkansas, Little Rock 72201-1904	Mel A. Anderson	Deputy Commissioner of Financial Regulation/Audit	501-683-0231
California, Sacramento 95814	Ed Heifig	Chief Deputy Director	916-324-8176
Colorado, Denver 80202	Scott Lloyd	Chief of Financial Affairs	303-894-7537
Connecticut, Hartford 06142-0816	Kathryn Belfi	CPA, Chief Examiner, Fin. Analysis & Compliance	860-297-3818
D.C., Washington 20002	Kathy Willis	Health Insurance Policy Advisor	202-442-7758
Delaware, Dover 19904	Charles Santana	Senior Financial Analyst	302-674-7341
Florida, Tallahassee 32399-0327	Robert A. Willis	Director, Life and Health Financial Oversight	850-413-5050
Georgia, Atlanta 30334	Scott A. Sanders	Life & Health Supervisor	404-657-7742
Hawaii, Honolulu 96813	J. P. Schmidt	Insurance Commissioner	808-586-2804
Idaho, Boise 83720-0043	Bill Deal	Director	208-334-4250
Illinois, Springfield 62767-0001	Alesia Pierce	Supervisor, HMO Financial Analysis Unit	217-782-1777
Indiana, Indianapolis 46204-2787	Amanda Denton	Supervising Life & Health Analysis	317-232-1369
Iowa, Des Moines 50319-0065	Tom O'Meara	Deputy Bureau Chief	515-281-4222
Kansas, Topeka 66612	Jay J. Rogers	Policy Examiner, A&H Division	785-296-7848
Kentucky, Frankfort 40602-0517	Bill Clark	Chief Financial Analyst	502-564-6082
Louisiana, Baton Rouge 70804	Stewart Guerin	Chief Examiner	225-219-3929
Maine, Augusta 04333-0034	Kendra Godbout	Director of Financial Analysis	207-624-8495
Maryland, Baltimore 21202	Lester C. Schott	Associate Commissioner	410-468-2119
Massachusetts, Boston 02210-2223	Robert G. Dynan	Deputy Commissioner, Financial Analysis	617-521-7420
Michigan, Lansing 48933	Linda Watters	Commissioner of Financial & Ins. Services	877-999-6442
Minnesota, St. Paul 55164-0882	Irene Goldman	Manager, Managed Care Systems	651-201-5166
Mississippi, Jackson 39215-1700	Vickey Maddox	Office Director, Office of Licensure	601-364-1104
Missouri, Jefferson City 65101	Debbie Doggett	Insurance Financial Analysis	573-526-2944
Montana, Helena 59604	Steve Matthews	Chief Examiner	406-444-2040
Nebraska, Lincoln 68508	Jim Nixon	Chief Financial Examiner	402-471-4734
Nevada, Carson City 89706-0661	Cliff King, CPCU, ARM	Chief Insurance Examiner	775-687-4270
New Hampshire, Concord 03301	Thomas Burke	Chief Financial Examiner	603-271-2241
New Jersey, Trenton 08625-0325	Frank J. Cipriani	Mgr. Office of Solvency Regulation	609-292-5350
New Mexico, Santa Fe 87504-1269	Michael Batte	Chief Life & Health Actuary	505-827-4625
New York, Albany 12237	Vallencia Lloyd	Director, Division of Managed Care	518-474-5737
North Carolina, Raleigh 27604	Raymond Martinez	Senior Deputy Commissioner	919-424-6482
North Dakota, Bismarck 58505	Yvonne Keniston	Company Administrator	701-328-3328
Ohio, Columbus 43215-1067	William Preston	Chief, Office of Life, Health & Managed Care Division	614-644-2661
Oklahoma, Oklahoma City 73107	Kelly Brown	Financial Analyst	405-521-3966
Oregon, Salem 97310	Russell Latham	Manager, Financial Regulation	503-947-7220
Pennsylvania, Harrisburg 17120	Stephen J. Johnson	Deputy Insurance Commissioner	717-783-2142
Puerto Rico, San Juan 00910-8330	Aurea E. Lopez Martinez	Examinations Director	787-722-8686
Rhode Island, Providence 02903	Christopher Koller	Health Insurance Commissioner	401-462-9645
South Carolina, Columbia 29202	Tim Campbell	Chief Financial Analyst	803-737-6109
South Dakota, Pierre 57501	Seth Doyle	Financial Analyst	605-773-3563
Tennessee, Nashville 37243-1135	Robert J. Ribe	CPA, CFE, CWCP	615-741-5072
Texas, Austin 78714-9104	Debra Diaz-Lara	Deputy Commissioner HWCN	512-305-7240
Utah, Salt Lake City 84114	Jake Garn	Chief Financial Examiner	801-538-3811
Vermont, Montpelier 05620-3101	Kenneth L. McGuckin		802-828-4849
Virginia, Richmond 23218	Andy R. Delbridge	Supervisor, Company Licensing	804-371-9636
Washington, Olympia 98504-0259	Dennis E. Julnes	Chief Financial Analyst	360-725-7209
West Virginia, Charleston 25305	Jane L. Cline	Insurance Commissioner	304-558-3354
Wisconsin, Madison 53707-7873	Sean Dilweg	Commissioner	608-266-3585
Wyoming, Cheyenne 82002	Brenda K. Patch, APRI	Insurance Standards Consultant	307-777-2447

Life/Health Guaranty Funds

Guaranty funds have been established by the states for the purpose of paying the claims of insurance companies which become insolvent or financially impaired. When needed, a guaranty fund will assess its association members — all financially sound insurers authorized to conduct business in the state — to meet the obligations of a failed insurer, subject to provisions established by state laws. These rules specify lines of insurance covered by the funds and limits payable on each line and in the aggregate on one life. Only 26 state funds specifically cover unallocated annuities (often in the form of pension funds invested in guaranteed investment contracts or GICs), the others specifically exclude this coverage or have no provision.

Solvent insurers operating in a state are assessed a percentage of applicable premiums to fund claims payments, and in most states can partially or fully recoup these assessments by premium tax offsets or other means.

Most states prohibit insurance companies or agents from advertising the funds' availability. The table below, based on information provided by the National Organization of Life and Health Insurance Guaranty Associations, provides a simplified view of various state fund provisions as of May 1, 2010. Because this is subject to change, exceptions and detailed provisions, care in using this information is urged. NOLHGA can be contacted at 13873 Park Center Road, Suite 329, Herndon, Virginia 20171, or on their website, www.NOLHGA.com, for more complete and specific information.

Guaranty Fund Provisions by State

State	Fund	Year Estab.	Maximum Benefits per Individual: Death	Cash Value	Annuities	Health and Disability	Aggregate Limit (1)	Coverage for Unallocated Annuities (2)	Assess-ments (3)	Recoup-ment (4)
Alabama	Al Life/Dis Ins Gnty Assoc Six Office Park Circle, Suite 200 Birmingham, AL 35223	1983	$300,000	$100,000	$100,000	$300,000	$300,000	Excluded	1%	PTO
Alaska	Ak Life/Hlth Ins Gnty Assoc 1007 W. 3rd Ave., Ste. 400 Anchorage, AK 99501	1990	$300,000	$100,000	$100,000	$100,000*	$300,000	$5 mil. per Contractholder	2%	NONE
Arizona	Az Life/Dis Ins Gnty Fund 1110 W. Washington, Ste. 270 Phoenix, AZ 85007	1977	$300,000	$100,000	$100,000	$300,000	$300,000	Not Specified	2%	PTO
Arkansas	Ar Life/Dis Ins Gnty Assoc 425 W. Capitol, Ste. 3700 Little Rock, AR 72201	1989	$300,000	$300,000	$300,000	$300,000	$300,000	$1 mil. per Contractholder	2%	PTO
California	Ca L/H Ins Guarantee Assoc 10780 Santa Monica Blvd, Ste. 401 Los Angeles, CA 90025	1991	$250,000	$100,000	$100,000	$200,000	$250,000	Excluded	1%	SURCH
Colorado	Co Lf/Hlth Ins Protec Assoc P.O. Box 36009 Denver, CO 80236	1991	$300,000	$250,000	$250,000	$100,000*	$500,000	Excluded	1%	PTO
Connecticut	Ct Lf/Hlth Ins Gnty Assoc 11 Round Hill Road Westerly, RI 02891-5170	1972	$500,000	$500,000	$500,000	$500,000	$500,000	$5 mil. per Contractholder	2%	PTO
Delaware	De Lf/Hlth Ins Gnty Assoc Christiana Executive Campus 220 Continental Drive, Ste. 309 Newark, DE 19713	1982	$300,000	$250,000	$250,000	$100,000*	$500,000	$1 mil. per Contractholder	2%	PTO
D. of C.	D.C. Lf/Hlth Ins. Gnty Assoc 1200 G Street, N.W., Suite 800 Washington, D.C. 20005	1992	$300,000	$100,000	$300,000	$100,000	$300,000	Excluded	2%	PTO
Florida	Fl Lf/Hlth Ins Gnty Assoc 3740 Beach Blvd, Ste. 201-A Jacksonville, FL 32207-3877	1979	$300,000	$100,000	$300,000	$300,000	$300,000	Not Specified	1%	PTO
Georgia	Ga Lf/Hlth Ins Gnty Assoc 2177 Flintstone Drive, Suite R Tucker, GA 30084	1981	$300,000	$100,000	$300,000	$300,000	$300,000	$5 mil. per Contractholder	2%	PTO
Hawaii	Hi Lf/Dis Ins Gnty Assoc 1132 Bishop St., Suite 1590 Honolulu, HI 96813	1979	$300,000	$100,000	$100,000	$100,000	$300,000	Excluded	2%	PTO

Footnotes:
(1) Maximum recoverable on any single life, regardless of the number of policies or coverages.
(2) Often applies to pension fund investments in guaranteed investment contracts (GICs).
(3) The maximum percentage of premiums that solvent insurers can be assessed in any one year to fund claims payments.
(4) Method of recouping assessments: premium tax offset (PTO); premium surcharge (SURCH); or by increasing rates and premiums (R&P).
* Guaranty association provides $100,000 for health coverage not defined as disability insurance or basic hospital, medical, and surgical insurance or major medical insurance, $300,000 for disability insurance and $500,000 for basic hospital, medical, and surgical insurance or major medical insurance.
** The $500,000 limit is for individual health policies issued by life companies; there is no coverage for policies issued by non-life companies, and unlimited coverage for group or blanket health insurance issued by a life company.

Guaranty Fund Provisions by State – *Continued*

State	Fund	Year Estab.	Maximum Benefits per Individual: Death	Cash Value	Annuities	Health and Disability	Aggregate Limit (1)	Coverage for Unallocated Annuities (2)	Assess-ments (3)	Recoup-ment (4)
Idaho	Id Lf/Hlth Ins Gnty Assoc 4700 N. Cloverdale Rd., Suite 204 Boise, ID 83713-1068	1977	$300,000	$100,000	$250,000	$300,000	$300,000	Excluded	2%	PTO
Illinois	Il Lf/Hlth Ins Gnty Assoc 8420 W. Bryn Mawr Ave, Ste. 550 Chicago, IL 60631-3404	1980	$300,000	$100,000	$100,000	$300,000	$300,000	$5 mil. per Contractholder	2%	None Expired in 2003
Indiana	In Lf/Hlth Ins Gnty Assoc 251 E. Ohio St, Ste. 1070 Indianapolis, IN 46204-2143	1978	$300,000	$100,000	$100,000	$300,000	$300,000	$5 mil. per Contractholder	2%	PTO
Iowa	Ia Lf/Hlth Ins Gnty Assoc 700 Walnut Street, Suite 1600 Des Moines, IA 50309-3899	1987	$300,000	$100,000	$250,000	$300,000	$350,000	$5 mil. per Contractholder	2%	PTO
Kansas	Ks Lf/Hlth Ins Gnty Assoc 2909 S.W. Maupin Lane Topeka, KS 66614-5335	1972	$300,000	$100,000	$100,000	$100,000	$300,000	Excluded	2%	PTO
Kentucky	Ky Lf/Hlth Ins Gnty Assoc 4010 Dupont Circle, Suite 232 Louisville, KY 40207	1978	$300,000	$100,000	$250,000	$300,000	$500,000	$5 mil. per Contractholder	2%	PTO
Louisiana	La Lf/Hlth Ins Gnty Assoc 450 Laurel Street, Ste. 1400 Baton Rouge, LA 70801	1991	$300,000	$100,000	$250,000	$500,000	$500,000	Excluded	2%	PTO
Maine	Me Lf/Hlth Ins Gnty Assoc P.O. Box 881 Boothbay Harbor, ME 04538	1984	$300,000	$100,000	$250,000	$300,000	$500,000	Not Specified	2%	PTO
Maryland	Md Lf/Hlth Ins Gnty Corp P.O. Box 671 Owings Mills, MD 21117-0671	1971	$300,000	$100,000	$100,000	$300,000		Excluded	2%	NONE
Massachusetts	Ma Lf/Hlth Ins Gnty Assoc P.O. Box 3171 Springfield, MA 01101-3171	1986	$300,000	$100,000	$100,000	$100,000	$300,000	Excluded	2%	PTO
Michigan	Mi Lf/Hlth Ins Gnty Assoc 1640 Haslett Rd., Ste. 160 Haslett, MI 48840-8683	1982	$300,000	$100,000	$100,000	$300,000	$300,000	$5 mil. per Contractholder	2%	PTO
Minnesota	Mn Lf/Hlth Ins Gnty Assoc 4760 White Bear Parkway Ste. 101 White Bear Lake, MN 55110	1977	$500,000	$130,000	$250,000 ($410,000 for structured settlements)	$500,000	$500,000	$10 mil. per plan	2%	PTO
Mississippi	Ms Lf/Hlth Ins Gnty Assoc P.O. Box 4562 Jackson, MS 39296	1985	$300,000	$100,000	$100,000	$100,000*	$500,000	$5 mil. per Contractholder	2%	PTO
Missouri	Mo Lf/Hlth Ins Gnty Assoc 994 Diamond Ridge, Ste. 102 Jefferson City, MO 65109	1988	$300,000	$100,000	$100,000	$100,000	$300,000	Excluded	2%	PTO
Montana	Mt Lf/Hlth Ins Gnty Assoc 39845 Cedar Lane Oconomowoc, WI 53066	1974	$300,000	$100,000	$100,000	$100,000*	$300,000	$5 mil. per Contractholder	2%	PTO
Nebraska	Ne Lf/Hlth Ins Gnty Assoc 1900 U.S. Bank Bldg.. 233 So. 13th St. Lincoln, NE 68508	1975	$300,000	$100,000	$100,000	$500,000	$300,000	Not Specified	2%	PTO
Nevada	Nv Lf/Hlth Ins Gnty Assoc One East First St, Ste. 605 Reno, NV 89501	1973	$300,000	$100,000	$100,000	$100,000*	$300,000	Excluded	2%	PTO

Footnotes:

(1) Maximum recoverable on any single life, regardless of the number of policies or coverages.
(2) Often applies to pension fund investments in guaranteed investment contracts (GICs).
(3) The maximum percentage of premiums that solvent insurers can be assessed in any one year to fund claims payments.
(4) Method of recouping assessments: premium tax offset (PTO); premium surcharge (SURCH); or by increasing rates and premiums (R&P).
* Guaranty association provides $100,000 for health coverage not defined as disability insurance or basic hospital, medical, and surgical insurance or major medical insurance, $300,000 for disability insurance and $500,000 for basic hospital, medical, and surgical insurance or major medical insurance.
** The $500,000 limit is for individual health policies issued by life companies; there is no coverage for policies issued by non-life companies, and unlimited coverage for group or blanket health insurance issued by a life company.

Guaranty Fund Provisions by State – *Continued*

State	Fund	Year Estab.	Maximum Benefits per Individual: Death	Cash Value	Annuities	Health and Disability	Aggregate Limit (1)	Coverage for Unallocated Annuities (2)	Assess-ments (3)	Recoup-ment (4)
New Hampshire	NH Lf/Hlth Ins Gnty Assoc 47 Hall Street, Ste. 2 Concord, NH 03301	1971	$300,000	$100,000	$100,000	$100,000	$300,000	$5 mil. per Contractholder	2%	PTO
New Jersey	NJ Lf/Hlth Ins Gnty Assoc One Gateway Center, 9th Fl Newark, NJ 07102	1991	$500,000	$100,000	$500,000 ($100,000 in cash val.)	No Limit	$500,000	$2 mil. per Contractholder	2%	PTO
New Mexico	NM Life Ins Guaranty Assoc P.O. Box 2880 Santa Fe, NM 87504-2880	1975	$300,000	$100,000	$300,000	$300,000	$300,000	Not Specified	2%	NONE
New York	Life Ins Co Gnty Corp/NY c/o NY Ins Dept Life Bureau 25 Beaver Street New York, NY 10004	1941	$500,000	$500,000**	$500,000	$500,000	$500,000	$1 mil. per Contractholder	2%	PTO
North Carolina	NC Lf/Hlth Ins Gnty Assoc P.O. Box 10218 Raleigh, NC 27605-0218	1974	$300,000	$300,000	$300,000	$300,000	$300,000	$5 mil. per Contractholder	2%	PTO
North Dakota	ND Lf/Hlth Ins Gnty Assoc P.O. Box 2422 Fargo, ND 58108-2422	1983	$300,000	$100,000	$100,000	$100,000	$300,000	$5 mil. per Contractholder	2%	PTO
Ohio	Oh Lf/Hlth Ins Gnty Assoc 1840 Mackenzie Drive Columbus, OH 43220	1989	$300,000	$100,000	$250,000	$100,000	$300,000	$1 mil. per Contractholder	2%	PTO
Oklahoma	Ok Lf/Hlth Ins Gnty Assoc 201 Robert S. Kerr Ave, Ste. 600 Oklahoma City, OK 73102	1981	$300,000	$100,000	$300,000	$300,000	$300,000	Excluded	2%	PTO
Oregon	Or Lf/Hlth Ins Gnty Assoc 3541 Elderberry Drive, South Salem, OR 97302-8520	1975	$300,000	$100,000	$250,000	$100,000	$250,000	Not Specified	2%	PTO
Pennsylvania	Pa Lf/Hlth Ins Gnty Assoc Radnor Station Bldg #2, Ste. 218 290 King of Prussia Rd. Radnor, PA 19087	1979	$300,000	$100,000	$300,000 ($100,000 in cash value, incl.)	$300,000	$300,000	$5 mil. per Contractholder	2%	PTO
Puerto Rico	Puerto Rico Life & Disability Ins Gnty Assoc c/o Scherrer Hernandez & Co. Attn: Cecilia Castro P.O. Box 363436 San Juan, PR 00936-3436	1974	$300,000	$100,000	$100,000	$100,000	$300,000	Excluded	2%	NONE
Rhode Island	RI Lf/Hlth Ins Gnty Assoc The Foundry, Ste. 426 235 Promenade Street Providence, RI 02908	1985	$300,000	$100,000	$100,000	$100,000	$300,000	$5 mil. per Contractholder	3%	PTO
South Carolina	SC Lf/Acc/Hlth Ins Gnty Assoc P.O. Box 6 Silverstreet, SC 29145	1972	$300,000	$300,000	$300,000	$300,000	$300,000	Not Specified	4%	PTO
South Dakota	SD Lf/Hlth Ins Gnty Assoc P.O. Box 1030 Sioux Falls, SD 57101-1030	1989	$300,000	$100,000	$100,000	$100,000*	$300,000	Excluded	2%	PTO
Tennessee	Tn Lf/Hlth Ins Gnty Assoc 150 4th Ave No, 1200 One Nashville Place Nashville, TN 37219-2433	1989	$300,000	$100,000	$250,000	$300,000	$300,000	Excluded	2%	PTO
Texas	Tx Lf. Ins Gnty Assoc 6504 Bridge Point Parkway, Ste. 450 Austin, TX 78730	1973	$300,000	$100,000	$100,000 (per contract-holder)	$300,000	$500,000	$5 mil. per Contractholder	2%	PTO

Footnotes:
(1) Maximum recoverable on any single life, regardless of the number of policies or coverages.
(2) Often applies to pension fund investments in guaranteed investment contracts (GICs).
(3) The maximum percentage of premiums that solvent insurers can be assessed in any one year to fund claims payments.
(4) Method of recouping assessments: premium tax offset (PTO); premium surcharge (SURCH); or by increasing rates and premiums (R&P).
* Guaranty association provides $100,000 for health coverage not defined as disability insurance or basic hospital, medical, and surgical insurance or major medical insurance, $300,000 for disability insurance and $500,000 for basic hospital, medical, and surgical insurance or major medical insurance.
** The $500,000 limit is for individual health policies issued by life companies; there is no coverage for policies issued by non-life companies, and unlimited coverage for group or blanket health insurance issued by a life company.

Guaranty Fund Provisions by State – *Continued*

State	Fund	Year Estab.	Maximum Benefits per Individual: Death	Cash Value	Annuities	Health and Disability	Aggregate Limit (1)	Coverage for Unallocated Annuities (2)	Assess-ments (3)	Recoup-ment (4)
Utah	Ut Lf/Dis Ins Gnty Assoc 136 So Main Street, Ste. 325 Salt Lake City, UT 84101	1979	$500,000	$200,000	$500,000	$500,000	$500,000	$5 mil. per Contractholder	2%	PTO
Vermont	Vt Lf/Hlth Ins Gnty Assoc c/o National Life Insurance Company, M-230 One National Life Drive Montpelier, VT 05604	1972	$300,000	$100,000	$250,000	$300,000	$500,000	$5 mil. per Contractholder	2%	PTO
Virginia	Va Lf Ins Gnty Assoc c/o APM Management Services, Inc. 8001 Franklin Farms Drive, Ste. 238 Richmond, VA 23229	1976	$300,000	$100,000	$250,000	$300,000	$350,000	$5 mil. per Contractholder	2%	PTO
Washington	Wa Lf/Dis Ins Gnty Assoc P.O. Box 2292 Shelton, WA 98584	1971	$500,000	$500,000	$500,000	$500,000	$500,000	$5 mil. per Contractholder	2%	PTO
West Virginia	WV Lf/Hlth Ins Gnty Assoc P.O. Box 816 Huntington, WV 25712	1977	$300,000	$100,000	$250,000	$300,000	$300,000 ($150,000 per indiv.)	$1 mil. per Contractholder	2%	NONE
Wisconsin	Wi Ins Security Fund 2820 Walton Commons West, Ste. 135 Madison, WI 53718-6797	1969	$300,000	$300,000	$300,000	$300,000	$300,000	Not Specified	2%	PTO
Wyoming	Wy Lf/Hlth Ins Gnty Assoc P.O. Box 36009 Denver, CO 80236	1990	$300,000	$100,000	$100,000	$100,000	$300,000	Excluded	2%	PTO

Footnotes:
(1) Maximum recoverable on any single life, regardless of the number of policies or coverages.
(2) Often applies to pension fund investments in guaranteed investment contracts (GICs).
(3) The maximum percentage of premiums that solvent insurers can be assessed in any one year to fund claims payments.
(4) Method of recouping assessments: premium tax offset (PTO); premium surcharge (SURCH); or by increasing rates and premiums (R&P).
* Guaranty association provides $100,000 for health coverage not defined as disability insurance or basic hospital, medical, and surgical insurance or major medical insurance, $300,000 for disability insurance and $500,000 for basic hospital, medical, and surgical insurance or major medical insurance.
** The $500,000 limit is for individual health policies issued by life companies; there is no coverage for policies issued by non-life companies, and unlimited coverage for group or blanket health insurance issued by a life company.

Corporate Structures

This section presents an alphabetical listing of insurance groups, displaying their organizational structure. Companies in italics are non-insurance entities. The effective date of this listing is as of June 15, 2010.

AMB#	COMPANY	DOMICILE	% OWN
055764	**A F HOLDINGS LTD**		
055763	*Colina Holdings Bahamas Ltd*	Bahamas	58.10
089077	Colina Insurance Limited	Bahamas	100.00
055377	**AAA EAST CENTRAL**		
055378	*Ohio Motorists Holding Company*	OH	100.00
068360	Ohio Motorists Life Ins Co	OH	100.00
052010	**ABBASZADEH DENTAL GROUP INC**		
064655	Access Dental Plan	CA	100.00
060375	Premier Access Insurance Co	CA	72.50
055921	**ABILITY REINSURANCE HLDGS LTD**		
071193	Ability Reins (Bermuda) Ltd	Bermuda	100.00
055920	*Ability Resources, Inc.*	DE	100.00
007378	Ability Insurance Company	NE	100.00
058303	**ACE LIMITED**		
050096	*ACE Group Holdings, Inc.*	DE	100.00
050095	*ACE INA Holdings Inc*	DE	80.00
006246	Combined Ins Co of America	IL	100.00
052296	*Chiewchanwit Company Limited*	Thailand	49.00
052297	*S.E.O.S. Limited*	Thailand	51.00
084380	Combined Ins Co of Europe Ltd	Ireland	100.00
084379	Combined Ins Co of New Zealand	New Zealand	100.00
084382	Combined Life Ins Co Australia	Australia	100.00
008187	Combined Life Ins Co of NY	NY	100.00
050160	*INA Corporation*	PA	100.00
050161	*ACE INA International Holdings*	DE	100.00
090897	ACE Arabia Cooperative Ins	Saudi Arabia	30.00
078420	ACE Arabia Ins Co Ltd BSC	Bahrain	50.00
051712	*ACE Australia Holdings Pty Ltd*	Australia	100.00
083313	ACE Insurance Limited	Australia	100.00
051713	*ACE INA Intl Hldgs Ltd.*	Chile	100.00
078411	ACE Seguros de Vida S.A.	Chile	99.50
050163	*ACE INA Overseas Holdings Inc*	DE	100.00
051714	*ACE European Holdings Ltd*	United Kingdom	100.00
051720	*ACE European Holdings No 2 Ltd*	United Kingdom	100.00
085979	ACE Insurance S.A.-N.V.	Belgium	99.90
086485	ACE European Group Limited	United Kingdom	69.10
078406	CJSC ACE Insurance Company	Russia	100.00
078828	CJSC ACE Life Insurance	Russia	100.00
073132	ACE INA Overseas Ins Co Ltd	Bermuda	100.00
051295	*ACE Canada Holdings Inc*	DE	100.00
050165	*INACAN Holdings Ltd*	Canada	100.00
085760	ACE INA Insurance	Canada	100.00
066873	ACE INA Life Insurance	Canada	100.00
090827	ACE Insurance Company Ltd	Japan	100.00
089425	ACE Insurance Limited	Singapore	100.00
010652	ACE Insurance Company (PR)	PR	100.00
078831	ACE Insurance Co Ltd	Vietnam	100.00
078413	ACE Insurance Co Egypt S.A.E.	Egypt	96.90
084399	ACE Insurance Limited (HK)	Hong Kong	100.00
086353	ACE Insurance Limited	New Zealand	100.00
078419	ACE Insurance Limited	Pakistan	100.00
078423	ACE Insurance Limited	South Africa	100.00
078414	ACE Life Insurance Co Ltd	Vietnam	100.00
078410	ACE Life Insurance Co S.A.E.	Egypt	98.30
052609	*ACE Participacoes Ltda.*	Brazil	99.00
090898	ACE Resseguradora S.A.	Brazil	99.90
078412	ACE Seguradora S.A.	Macau	99.90
077853	ACE Seguradora S.A.	Brazil	99.90
077345	ACE Seguros S.A.	Argentina	94.60
077016	ACE Seguros S.A.	Chile	78.33
084400	ACE Seguros S.A.	Colombia	99.90
077217	ACE Seguros S.A.	Ecuador	100.00
077981	ACE Seguros S.A.	Mexico	99.90
090179	ACE Seguros S.A.	Panama	100.00
077316	ACE Seguros S.A.	Peru	99.90
089102	ACE Synergy Insurance Berhad	Malaysia	51.00
050164	*AFIA Finance Corporation*	DE	100.00
086727	ACE INA Insurance, PT	Indonesia	95.30
013963	Pembroke Reinsurance, Inc.	DE	100.00
056487	RIYAD Insurance Co Ltd	Bermuda	80.00
051715	*Eksupsiri Company Ltd*	Thailand	49.00
078417	ACE Life Assurance Company Ltd	Thailand	75.00
090896	PT. ACE Life Assurance	Indonesia	93.50
050166	*INA Financial Corp*	DE	100.00
050167	*Brandywine Holdings Corp*	DE	100.00
004047	Century Indemnity Company	PA	100.00
072483	Century Intern Reins Co Ltd	Bermuda	100.00
050168	*INA Holdings Corporation*	DE	100.00
002257	ACE American Insurance Company	PA	100.00
002262	Pacific Employers Ins Co	PA	100.00
003510	Illinois Union Insurance Co	IL	100.00
001996	ACE Property & Casualty Ins Co	PA	100.00
002109	ACE Fire Underwriters Ins Co	PA	100.00
004854	ACE Insurance Co of the Mdwst	IN	100.00
002670	Atlantic Employers Ins Co	NJ	100.00
004333	Bankers Standard Ins Co	PA	100.00
002353	Bankers Standard Fire & Mar Co	PA	100.00
001793	Indemnity Insurance Co of NA	PA	100.00
003368	ACE Indemnity Insurance Co	PA	100.00
072895	INA Reinsurance Co Ltd	Bermuda	100.00
002259	Insurance Co of North America	PA	100.00
060599	ACE Life Insurance Company	CT	100.00
050170	*ACE US Holdings Inc*	DE	100.00
002137	Westchester Fire Ins Co	NY	100.00
004433	Westchester Surplus Lines Ins	GA	100.00
052295	*ACE Group Management & Hldgs*	Bermuda	100.00
086361	ACE Bermuda Insurance Ltd	Bermuda	100.00
086834	ACE Bermuda Intl Re (IE) Ltd	Ireland	100.00
086833	ACE Bermuda Intl Ins (IE) Ltd	Ireland	100.00
012641	ACE Capital Title Reins Co	NY	100.00
086156	Corp Officers & Directors Assr	Bermuda	100.00
078422	Freisenbruch-Meyer Ins Limited	Bermuda	40.00
073741	Paget Reinsurance Int'l Ltd	Bermuda	100.00
090180	Paget Reinsurance Ltd.	Bermuda	100.00
077030	ACE Tempest Life Reins Ltd	Bermuda	100.00
078826	ACE Europe Life Limited	United Kingdom	100.00
086198	ACE Tempest Reins Ltd	Bermuda	100.00
090770	ACE Ins (Switzerland) Ltd	Switzerland	100.00
090769	ACE Reins (Switzerland) Ltd	Switzerland	100.00
050296	**ACLI ACQUISITION COMPANY**		
007424	AAA Life Insurance Company	MI	100.00
060709	Life Alliance Reassurance Corp	HI	100.00
051723	**AEGIS INSURANCE HLDGS CO LP**		
051725	*American Southwest Hldg Co LLC*	DE	100.00
051726	*Directors Independent Svce Co*	OK	99.55
007616	Directors Life Assur Co	OK	100.00
060596	Shield Life Insurance Company	DE	100.00
085244	**AEGON N.V.**		
050645	*AEGON International BV*	Netherlands	100.00
052896	*AEGON Canada Holdings B.V.*	Netherlands	100.00
052897	*AEGON Canada ULC*	Canada	100.00
066805	Transamerica Life Canada	Canada	100.00
051253	*AEGON DMS Holding BV*	Netherlands	100.00
051349	*Canadian Premier Holdings Ltd*	Canada	100.00
066801	Canadian Premier Life Ins Co	Canada	100.00
087059	Legacy General Insurance Co	Canada	100.00
051346	*Cornerstone Internat Hldgs Ltd*	United Kingdom	100.00
087967	Stonebridge Intl Insurance Ltd	United Kingdom	100.00
052250	*AEGON Espana S.A.*	Spain	99.90
077794	Aegon Salud, S.A.	Spain	100.00
083156	Aegon Seguros de Vida Ahorro	Spain	100.00
083106	Aegon Union Aseguradora S.A.	Spain	100.00
052251	*AEGON Holdings (UK) Limited*	United Kingdom	100.00
086478	Aegon Insurance Co UK Ltd	United Kingdom	100.00
051913	*AEGON UK plc*	United Kingdom	100.00
085649	Guardian Assurance plc	United Kingdom	100.00
085207	Guardian Linked Life Assur Ltd	United Kingdom	100.00
085209	Guardian Pensions Mgmt Ltd	United Kingdom	100.00
051917	*Scottish Equitable Holdings*	United Kingdom	100.00
086884	Scottish Equitable plc	United Kingdom	100.00
087579	Scottish Equitable (Mgd Fds)	United Kingdom	100.00
052255	*AEGON Ireland Holding B.V.*	Netherlands	100.00
090161	AEGON Financial Assur IE Ltd	Ireland	100.00
077712	Aegon Ireland plc	Ireland	100.00
052895	*Scottish Equitable Int'l Svces*	Ireland	100.00
073744	Transamerica Life Intl BM Ltd	Bermuda	100.00
090160	Transamerica Intl Re Ie Ltd	Ireland	100.00
090162	AEGON Life Ins (Taiwan) Inc	Taiwan	100.00
083916	AEGON Magyarorszag Altalanos	Hungary	100.00
090163	AEGON Pojist'ovna a.s.	Czech Republic	100.00
051199	*AEGON Trust*	DE	100.00
058104	*Transamerica Corporation*	DE	100.00
050638	*AEGON U.S. Holding Corporation*	DE	100.00
032623	*AEGON Management Company*	IN	100.00
076273	River Ridge Insurance Company	VT	100.00
051200	*AEGON US Corporation*	IA	100.00
050646	*AEGON USA, LLC*	IA	100.00
051345	*AUSA Holding Company*	MD	100.00
051348	*AEGON Asset Management Srvcs*	DE	100.00
051347	*World Financial Group Inc*	DE	100.00
071192	WFG Reinsurance Limited	Bermuda	100.00
051915	*Creditor Resources, Inc.*	MI	100.00
078558	Academy Alliance Insurance Inc	Canada	100.00
072375	Global Preferred Re Limited	Bermuda	100.00
008487	ML Life Ins Co of NY	NY	100.00
009537	Merrill Lynch Life Ins Co	AR	100.00
060362	Southwest Equity Life Ins Co	AZ	100.00
000323	Stonebridge Casualty Ins Co	OH	100.00
007267	Transamerica Financial Life	NY	100.00
050635	*Transamerica Intern Hldngs Inc*	DE	100.00
006095	Transamerica Life Insurance Co	IA	100.00

Corporate Structures – *Continued*

AMB#	COMPANY	DOMICILE	% OWN
078557	Transamerica Life (BM) Ltd	Bermuda	100.00
052256	*LIICA Holdings, LLC*	DE	100.00
060654	LIICA RE I	VT	100.00
060655	LIICA RE II	VT	100.00
073451	Transamerica Int'l Re(Bermuda)	Bermuda	100.00
007239	Western Reserve Lf Assur of OH	OH	100.00
050647	*Commonwealth General Corp*	DE	100.00
050641	*Capital General Development Cp*	DE	100.00
006742	Monumental Life Ins Co	IA	100.00
073527	Global Premier Reins Co Ltd	British Virgin Islands	100.00
006594	Stonebridge Life Insurance Co	VT	100.00
060712	MLIC Re I Inc	VT	100.00
060665	Pine Falls Re Inc	VT	100.00
071188	Stonebridge Reinsurance Co	VT	100.00
073344	Transamerica Pac Ins Co Ltd	HI	100.00
057706	ARC Reinsurance Corp	HI	100.00
057740	Pyramid Insurance Co Ltd	HI	100.00
090164	AEGON TU na Zycie SA	Poland	100.00
051912	*AEGON Nederland N.V.*	Netherlands	100.00
086204	AEGON Levensverzekering N.V.	Netherlands	100.00
089633	AEGON NabestaandenZorg N.V.	Netherlands	100.00
089805	LPU Verzekeringen N.V.	Netherlands	100.00
077124	Aegon Spaarkas N.V.	Netherlands	100.00
051914	*AXENT/AEGON N.V.*	Netherlands	100.00
083710	AXENT/AEGON Leven N.V.	Netherlands	100.00
089666	AXENT/AEGON Schade N.V.	Netherlands	100.00
083712	AXENT/AEGON Sparen	Netherlands	100.00
089668	AXENT/AEGON Uitvaartverzek	Netherlands	100.00
086203	AEGON Schadeverzekering N.V.	Netherlands	100.00
088609	Seguros Banamex AEGON S.A.	Mexico	100.00
058700	**AETNA INC**		
051208	*Aetna International Inc*	CT	100.00
077031	Aetna Life & Casualty (BM) Ltd	Bermuda	100.00
008189	Aetna Health and Life Ins Co	CT	100.00
051141	*Aetna Health Holdings LLC*	DE	100.00
064964	Aetna Better Health Inc (CT)	CT	100.00
064709	Aetna Dental Inc (a NJ corp)	NJ	100.00
064718	Aetna Dental Inc (a TX corp)	TX	100.00
064634	Aetna Dental of CA	CA	100.00
064071	Aetna Health Inc (a CO corp)	CO	100.00
068698	Aetna Health Inc (a CT corp)	CT	100.00
068697	Aetna Health Inc (a DE corp)	DE	100.00
060120	Aetna Health Inc (a FL corp)	FL	100.00
068701	Aetna Health Inc (a GA corp)	GA	100.00
064366	Aetna Health Inc (a MI corp)	MI	100.00
068695	Aetna Health Inc (a NJ corp)	NJ	100.00
068696	Aetna Health Inc (a NY corp)	NY	100.00
068700	Aetna Health Inc (a PA corp)	PA	100.00
068913	Aetna Health Inc (a TX corp)	TX	100.00
060119	Aetna Health of CA	CA	100.00
050850	*NYLCARE Health Plans Inc*	DE	100.00
064155	Aetna Health Inc (a ME corp)	ME	100.00
068609	Aetna Health Inc (a WA corp)	WA	100.00
055361	*Schaller Anderson Incorporated*	AZ	100.00
064921	Missouri Care Incorporated	MO	100.00
009541	Aetna Health Ins Co of NY	NY	100.00
006006	Aetna Life Ins Co	CT	100.00
050848	*AHP Holdings Inc*	CT	100.00
011023	Aetna Insurance Company of CT	CT	100.00
072518	Aetna Risk Indemnity Co Ltd	Bermuda	100.00
007443	Aetna Health Insurance Company	PA	100.00
052876	**AF&L HOLDINGS, LLC**		
050909	*AF&L Inc*	PA	75.33
011131	AF&L Insurance Company	PA	100.00
060294	Senior American Life Ins Co	PA	100.00
034015	**AFFINITY HEALTH SYSTEM**		
050978	*Network Health System*	WI	100.00
068627	Network Health Plan	WI	100.00
064708	Network Health Insurance Corp	WI	100.00
058003	**AFLAC INCORPORATED**		
006051	American Fam Assur Columbus	NE	100.00
006063	American Family Life Assur NY	NY	100.00
055424	*Continental American Ins Group*	SC	100.00
007411	Continental American Ins Co	SC	100.00
052800	**AHN ACQUISITION LLC**		
055806	*American Health Network Inc*	DE	100.00
068815	American Health Network of IN	IN	100.00
064632	American Health Network IN LLC	IN	99.00
064632	American Health Network IN LLC	IN	1.00
002005	**ALFA MUTUAL INSURANCE COMPANY**		
058307	*Alfa Corporation*	AL	65.00
000954	Alfa Alliance Insurance Corp	VA	100.00
001724	Alfa General Insurance Corp	AL	100.00
002227	Alfa Insurance Corporation	AL	100.00
006293	Alfa Life Ins Corp	AL	100.00
010042	Alfa Vision Insurance Corp	AL	100.00
012333	Alfa Specialty Insurance Corp	AL	100.00
002006	Alfa Mutual Fire Insurance Co	AL	
058307	*Alfa Corporation*	AL	35.00
003314	Alfa Mutual General Ins Co	AL	
052501	**ALLEGIANCE HEALTH SYSTEM**		
064621	Physicians Health Plan of S MI	MI	100.00
085014	**ALLIANZ SOCIETAS EUROPAEA**		
052395	*A.C.I.F. SpA*	Italy	100.00
085307	Allianz S.p.A.	Italy	74.40
077704	Antoniana Veneta Popolare	Italy	50.00
084891	Antoniana Veneta Popolare Vita	Italy	50.00
086255	Assicuratrice Italiana Danni	Italy	100.00
086080	Assicuratrice Italiana Vita	Italy	100.00
089243	Bernese Assicurazioni S.p.A.	Italy	99.80
089244	Bernese Vita S.p.A.	Italy	100.00
086031	CreditRas Assicurazioni S.p.A.	Italy	50.00
086625	CreditRas Vita S.p.A.	Italy	50.00
078823	Darta Saving Life Assur Ltd	Ireland	100.00
085929	Genialloyd S.p.A.	Italy	99.90
089582	L.A. Vita S.p.A.	Italy	100.00
085969	R B Vita S.p.A.	Italy	100.00
085129	*Assurances Generales de France*	France	100.00
055302	*AGF Allianz South America*	Brazil	100.00
078143	Adriatica de Seguros, C.A.	Venezuela	98.28
077346	Allianz Argentina Cia de Seg	Argentina	100.00
086213	Allianz Seguros S.A.	Brazil	85.97
055287	*AGF Holding S.A.*	France	99.90
086019	*AGF International S.A.*	France	100.00
083208	Allianz Belgium s.a.	Belgium	100.00
078807	AGF Life Luxembourg S.A.	Luxembourg	100.00
077278	*Allianz Nederland Groep N.V.*	Netherlands	100.00
078481	Allianz Nederland Levensverz	Netherlands	100.00
078487	Allianz Nederland Schade	Netherlands	100.00
078520	London Verzekeringen N.V.	Netherlands	100.00
083517	Universal Leven N.V.	Netherlands	100.00
086303	*AGF Holdings (UK) Limited*	United Kingdom	100.00
086248	AGF Insurance Limited	United Kingdom	100.00
083067	Arcalis	France	79.37
089921	AVIP	France	100.00
085174	Allianz IARD	France	99.98
085109	Allianz Vie	France	99.99
078811	Calypso	France	99.98
083076	Coparc	France	99.98
055143	*Euler Hermes S.A.*	France	68.20
052670	*Euler Hermes ACI Holding Inc*	DE	100.00
002097	Euler Hermes Amer Credit Ind	MD	100.00
086444	Euler Hermes Credit SA Belgium	Belgium	100.00
086368	*Euler Hermes Holdings*	United Kingdom	100.00
087302	Euler Hermes Guarantee plc	United Kingdom	100.00
084119	Euler & Hermes Internatl Ltd	United Kingdom	100.00
087336	Euler Hermes UK plc	United Kingdom	100.00
086531	Euler Hermes Kreditvers	Germany	100.00
083510	Euler Hermes Interborg N.V.	Netherlands	95.00
077044	Euler Hermes Kreditforsakring	Sweden	100.00
089193	EULER-HERMES Magyar	Hungary	74.89
057467	Euler Hermes Re	Luxembourg	100.00
088920	Euler Hermes Kredietverz	Netherlands	100.00
078006	Euler Hermes Seg de Credito SA	Mexico	100.00
077878	Euler Hermes Seguros Credito	Brazil	100.00
086442	Euler Hermes SFAC S.A.	France	100.00
084209	Euler Hermes SIAC S.p.A.	Italy	100.00
086024	Rurale	France	99.76
050631	*Allianz of America Inc*	DE	100.00
000407	Allianz Global Risks US Ins Co	CA	100.00
002618	Allianz Underwriters Ins Co	CA	100.00
002179	Fireman's Fund Insurance Co	CA	100.00
002176	American Automobile Ins Co	MO	100.00
002178	Associated Indemnity Corp	CA	100.00
002177	American Insurance Company	OH	100.00
002717	Fireman's Fund Ins Co of HI	HI	100.00
002824	Fireman's Fund Ins Co of LA	LA	100.00
002843	Fireman's Fund Ins Co of OH	OH	100.00
001892	Fireman's Fund Indemnity Corp	NJ	100.00
050632	*Interstate National Corp*	IL	100.00
002267	Interstate Fire & Casualty Co	IL	100.00
002266	Chicago Insurance Company	IL	100.00
002268	AGCS Marine Insurance Company	IL	100.00
002182	National Surety Corporation	IL	100.00
002181	San Francisco Reinsurance Co	CA	100.00
054000	*Standard General Agency*	TX	100.00
003586	American Standard Lloyds	TX	
003682	Fireman's Fund Cnty Mut Ins Co	TX	
011672	Vintage Insurance Company	CA	100.00
004001	Jefferson Insurance Company	NY	100.00
006830	Allianz Life Ins Co N America	MN	100.00
009417	Allianz Life Ins Co of NY	NY	100.00
068026	Allianz Life and Annuity Co	MN	100.00
086517	Allianz Mexico SA	Mexico	99.90
055301	*Allianz of Asia-Pacific*	Germany	100.00
089588	Allianz Life ID, PT Asuransi	Indonesia	99.80
086726	Allianz Utama ID, PT Asuransi	Indonesia	75.40
086635	*Allianz Australia Ltd*	Australia	100.00

AMB#	COMPANY	DOMICILE	% OWN
078808	Allianz Australia Advantage	Australia	100.00
077889	Allianz Australia Ins Ltd	Australia	100.00
077161	Allianz New Zealand Limited	New Zealand	100.00
077902	CIC Allianz Insurance Limited	Australia	100.00
078813	FAI Allianz Limited	Australia	100.00
089147	*Allianz Bulgaria Holding AD*	Bulgaria	100.00
078809	Allianz Bulgaria Ins & Reins	Bulgaria	100.00
078810	Allianz Bulgaria Life Ins Co	Bulgaria	100.00
078814	Allianz China Life Ins Co Ltd	China	51.00
084145	Allianz Cia Seg Reaseguros	Spain	99.90
055288	*Allianz Deutschland AG*	Germany	100.00
085942	Allianz Private Krankenvers-AG	Germany	94.90
085473	Allianz Versicherungs-Aktieng	Germany	94.90
084038	Muenchener und Magdeburger	Germany	59.90
084667	Vereinte Spezial Kranken AG	Germany	100.00
084668	Vereinte Spezial Versicherung	Germany	100.00
055289	*Jota-Vermoegensverwaltungs*	Germany	94.90
078774	Allianz Lebensvers-AG	Germany	91.00
089636	Allianz Pensionsfonds AG	Germany	100.00
089079	Allianz Pensionskasse Aktieng	Germany	100.00
084488	Deutsche Lebensversicherungs	Germany	100.00
085968	Allianz Egypt Insurance Co SAE	Egypt	85.00
078815	Allianz Egypt Life Co SAE	Egypt	99.40
086744	Allianz Fire Marine Ins Japan	Japan	100.00
078816	Allianz Greece Ins Co Ltd	Greece	100.00
087997	Allianz Global Corp & Spec AG	Germany	100.00
086992	Allianz Global Corp & Spec FR	France	99.90
090660	Allianz Hayat ve Emeklilik	Turkey	89.00
055291	*Allianz Holdings plc*	United Kingdom	100.00
086373	Allianz Insurance plc	United Kingdom	100.00
087260	British Reserve Ins Co Ltd	United Kingdom	100.00
087311	DBI Insurance Company Ltd	United Kingdom	100.00
087635	Trafalgar Insurance Pub Ltd Co	United Kingdom	100.00
083918	Allianz Hungaria Biztosito Rt	Hungary	100.00
078817	Allianz Insurance (HK) Ltd	Hong Kong	100.00
089427	Allianz Ins Co of SG Pte Ltd	Singapore	100.00
085971	Allianz Life Insurance Co Ltd	South Korea	100.00
078818	Allianz Life Ins Co SA	Greece	100.00
052364	*Allianz Malaysia Berhad*	Malaysia	98.70
089124	Allianz Life Ins Malaysia Bhd	Malaysia	100.00
090299	Allianz General Ins Co MY Bhd	Malaysia	100.00
089127	Bright Mission BErhad	Malaysia	100.00
083776	Allianz pojist'ovna, a.s.	Czech Republic	100.00
078819	Allianz Taiwan Life Ins Co Ltd	Taiwan	50.20
078820	Allianz Re Ireland Limited	Ireland	100.00
077703	Allianz Risk Transfer	Switzerland	100.00
083297	Allianz Risk Transfer N.V.	Netherlands	100.00
084964	Allianz Sigorta A.S.	Turkey	84.20
083849	Allianz-Slovenska poist'ovna	Slovakia	84.60
089021	Allianz Worldwide Care Limited	Ireland	100.00
090595	Allianz Zagreb d.d.	Croatia	80.10
055290	*AZ-Argos 31 Vermoegens*	Germany	100.00
086225	*Allianz Irish Life Hldgs plc*	Ireland	100.00
085683	Allianz Public Limited Co	Ireland	66.40
086075	Burlco p.l.c.	Ireland	100.00
085617	NEM Insurance Ireland Limited	Ireland	100.00
089082	Cia Seg Allianz Portugal	Portugal	64.90
078025	Mondial Assistance Intl SA	France	100.00
083435	Mondial Assistance Seg Y Reas	Spain	100.00
089733	Mondial Assistance Europe NV	Netherlands	100.00
078821	Mondial Assistance B.V.	Netherlands	100.00
084907	Mondial Assistance Italia	Italy	100.00
083388	Eurovida Compania Seg y Reas	Spain	51.00
078824	Ins Joint Stock Co 'Allianz'	Russia	100.00
055286	*Ras International III B.V.*	Netherlands	100.00
086994	Allianz-Elementar Versicherung	Austria	50.10
086995	Allianz-Elementar Lebensvers	Austria	90.00
086462	Allianz Suisse Versicherungs	Switzerland	69.79
086840	Alba Allgemeine Versicherungs	Switzerland	100.00
086461	Allianz Suisse Lebensversich	Switzerland	99.99
083147	Amaya Compania Seg y Reaseg	Spain	100.00
083972	CAP Rechtsschutz-Versicherungs	Switzerland	100.00
083766	Phenix compagnie d'assurances	Switzerland	100.00
083765	Phenix cie d'assur sur la vie	Switzerland	100.00
083848	SC Allianz Tiriac Asigurari SA	Romania	51.60
077307	T.U. Allianz Polska S.A.	Poland	100.00
077308	T.U. Allianz Zycie Polska S.A.	Poland	100.00
058312	**ALLSTATE CORPORATION**		
620788	*Allstate Bank*	IL	100.00
052284	*Allstate Insurance Hldgs LLC*	DE	100.00
002017	Allstate Insurance Company	IL	100.00
000764	Allstate County Mutual Ins Co	TX	100.00
003652	Allstate Fire & Cas Ins Co	IL	100.00
002018	Allstate Indemnity Company	IL	100.00
085704	Allstate Insurance Co Canada	Canada	100.00
006028	Allstate Life Ins Co of Canada	Canada	100.00
003440	Pafco Insurance Company Ltd	Canada	100.00
085774	Pembridge Insurance Company	Canada	100.00
006027	Allstate Life Ins Co	IL	100.00
076727	ALIC Reinsurance Co	SC	100.00
007289	Allstate Assurance Company	IL	100.00
007291	Allstate Life Ins Co of NY	NY	100.00
006211	Charter National Life Ins Co	IL	100.00
006572	Intramerica Life Ins Co	NY	100.00
006657	Lincoln Benefit Life Co	NE	100.00
007109	Surety Life Ins Co	NE	100.00
012106	Allstate New Jersey Insurance	IL	100.00
013080	Allstate New Jersey P&C Ins Co	IL	100.00
012612	Encompass Insurance Co of NJ	IL	100.00
013082	Encompass Prop&Cas Ins Co NJ	IL	100.00
012482	Allstate North American Ins Co	IL	100.00
001978	Allstate Prop & Cas Ins Co	IL	100.00
050042	*Allstate Texas Lloyd's Inc.*		100.00
010678	Allstate Texas Lloyd's	TX	
010648	Castle Key Insurance Company	IL	100.00
012128	Castle Key Indemnity Company	IL	100.00
012711	Encompass Floridian Indemnity	IL	100.00
012710	Encompass Floridian Ins Co	IL	100.00
011559	Deerbrook Insurance Company	IL	100.00
012535	Encompass Home and Auto Ins Co	IL	100.00
000542	Encompass Indemnity Company	IL	100.00
012536	Encompass Independent Ins Co	IL	100.00
011794	Encompass Insurance Company	IL	100.00
011703	Encompass Ins Co of America	IL	100.00
010130	Encompass Insurance Co of MA	MA	100.00
011702	Encompass Prop & Cas Company	IL	100.00
003791	Northbrook Indemnity Company	IL	100.00
013927	North Light Specialty Ins Co	IL	100.00
058007	*American Heritage Life Inv Cp*	FL	100.00
006064	American Heritage Life Ins Co	FL	100.00
000201	First Colonial Insurance Co	FL	100.00
051436	**ALPHA INVESTMENT PARTNERSHIP**		
051311	*Cincinnati Equitable Cos Inc*	OH	89.60
006757	Cincinnati Equitable Life	OH	100.00
003228	Cincinnati Equitable Ins Co	OH	100.00
004874	Southern Michigan Insurance Co	MI	100.00
051477	**AMALGAMATED SOCIAL BEN ASSOC**		
006030	Amalgamated Life and Health	IL	100.00
058314	**AMERCO**		
007890	Oxford Life Ins Co	AZ	100.00
006217	Christian Fidelity Life Ins Co	TX	100.00
009442	Dallas General Life Ins Co	TX	100.00
060015	North American Ins Co	WI	100.00
003597	Republic Western Insurance Co	AZ	100.00
011685	North American Fire & Cas Ins	LA	100.00
013975	ARCOA Risk Retention Grp, Inc.	NV	100.00
055173	**AMERICAN AUTOMOBILE ASSN INC**		
087158	AAA Life Re, Ltd.	Bermuda	100.00
051497	**AMERICAN ENTERPRISE MUT HLDG**		
051496	*American Enterprise Group, Inc*		100.00
006096	American Republic Ins Co	IA	100.00
006906	American Republic Corp Ins Co	NE	100.00
007262	World Insurance Company	NE	100.00
008350	World Corp Insurance Company	NE	100.00
050750	**AMERICAN EQUITY INVEST LF HLDG**		
059222	*Amer Equity Capital Trust I*	IA	100.00
059223	*Amer Equity Capital Trust II*	IA	100.00
059316	*Amer Equity Capital Trust III*	IA	100.00
059317	*Amer Equity Capital Trust IV*	IA	100.00
059195	*Amer Equity Capital Trust V*	IA	100.00
059196	*Amer Equity Capital Trust VI*	IA	100.00
059318	*Amer Equity Capital Trust VII*	IA	100.00
059319	*Amer Equity Capital Trust VIII*	IA	100.00
059320	*Amer Equity Capital Trust IX*	IA	100.00
059321	*Amer Equity Capital Trust X*	IA	100.00
059322	*Amer Equity Capital Trust XI*	IA	100.00
059323	*Amer Equity Capital Trust XII*	IA	100.00
009024	American Equity Invest Life	IA	100.00
060367	American Equity Invest Life NY	NY	100.00
060690	Eagle Life Insurance Company	IA	100.00
002022	**AMERICAN FAMILY MUTUAL INS CO**		
050172	*AMFAM Inc*	WI	100.00
011789	American Family Insurance Co	OH	100.00
006052	American Family Life Ins Co	WI	100.00
011790	American Standard Ins Co of OH	OH	100.00
002023	American Standard Ins Co of WI	WI	100.00
001726	**AMER FARMERS & RANCHERS MUT**		
060341	American Farmers & Ranchers Lf	OK	100.00
001917	American Farmers & Ranchers	ID	100.00
058317	**AMERICAN FINANCIAL GROUP, INC**		
051163	*APU Holding Company*	OH	100.00
058319	*American Premier Undrs Inc*	PA	100.00
083534	GAI Insurance Company Ltd	Bermuda	100.00
000800	Republic Indemnity Co of Amer	CA	100.00
001856	Republic Indemnity Co of CA	CA	100.00
058004	*Great American Finl Resources*	OH	100.00
050333	*AAG Holding Company Inc*	OH	100.00
006474	Great American Life Ins Co	OH	100.00

AMB#	COMPANY	DOMICILE	% OWN
009088	Annuity Investors Life Ins Co	OH	100.00
006864	Great American Life Ins of NY	NY	100.00
052404	*Manhattan National Hldg Corp*	OH	100.00
006842	Manhattan National Life Ins Co	IL	100.00
051336	*Loyal American Holding Corp*	OH	100.00
006671	Loyal American Life Ins Co	OH	100.00
008831	American Retirement Life Ins	OH	100.00
006253	Great American Life Assur Co	OH	100.00
050334	*United Teacher Associates Ltd*	TX	100.00
006410	United Teacher Associates Ins	TX	100.00
058025	*Ceres Group Inc*	OH	100.00
006203	Central Reserve Life	OH	100.00
006932	Provident American Life & Hlth	OH	100.00
006619	United Benefit Life Ins Co	OH	100.00
055140	*Continental General Corp*		100.00
007360	Continental General Ins Co	OH	100.00
051081	*Great American Holding, Inc*	OH	100.00
003735	American Empire Surplus Lines	DE	100.00
002603	American Empire Insurance Co	OH	100.00
078385	Great American Intl Insur Ltd	Ireland	100.00
000606	Mid-Continent Casualty Co	OH	100.00
011321	Mid-Continent Assurance Co	OH	100.00
004038	Oklahoma Surety Company	OH	100.00
090942	Premier International Ins Co	Turks And Caicos Islands	100.00
002213	Great American Insurance Co	OH	100.00
083535	Aguila Cia de Seg SA de CV	Mexico	100.00
003521	Great American Alliance Ins Co	OH	100.00
002004	Great American Assurance Co	OH	100.00
002828	Great American Casualty Ins Co	OH	100.00
011873	Great Amer Contemporary Ins Co	OH	100.00
003837	Great American E&S Ins Co	DE	100.00
003293	Great American Fidelity Ins Co	DE	100.00
002210	Great American Insurance Co NY	NY	100.00
003839	Great American Lloyd's Ins Co	TX	
010937	Great Amer Protection Ins Co	OH	100.00
000173	Great American Security Ins Co	OH	100.00
010618	Great American Spirit Ins Co	OH	100.00
050332	*National Interstate Corp*	OH	52.60
072519	Hudson Indemnity Ltd	Cayman Islands	100.00
010829	National Interstate Ins Co	OH	100.00
012423	National Interstate Ins Co HI	OH	100.00
002810	Triumphe Casualty Company	PA	100.00
050335	*Penn Central UK Ltd*	United Kingdom	100.00
087405	Insurance (GB) Ltd	United Kingdom	100.00
058702	**AMERICAN INTL GROUP INC**		
055721	*AIG Capital Corporation*	DE	100.00
050385	*American General Finance Inc*	IN	100.00
050386	*American General Finance Corp*	IN	100.00
006703	Merit Life Insurance Co	IN	100.00
003222	Yosemite Insurance Company	IN	100.00
078792	AIG Israel Insurance Co Ltd	Israel	50.01
078801	AIG Kazakhstan Insurance Co SA	Kazakhstan	60.00
055314	*AIG Life Holdings (Intl) LLC*	DE	100.00
085459	AIG Star Life Insurance Co Ltd	Japan	100.00
085197	American Intern Reins Co Ltd	Bermuda	100.00
052598	*AIA Aurora LLC*	DE	99.00
052599	*AIA Group Limited*	Hong Kong	100.00
085102	American Intern Assur Co Ltd	Hong Kong	100.00
090247	AIA Australia Limited	Australia	100.00
090866	American International Asr Bhd	Malaysia	100.00
090867	AIA Takaful International Bhd.	Malaysia	100.00
085386	American Intern Assur Bermuda	Bermuda	100.00
088808	AIA Financial, PT	Indonesia	80.00
088796	AIA (Vietnam) Life Ins Co Ltd	Vietnam	100.00
090169	Tata AIG Life Insurance Co Ltd	India	26.00
084311	Philippine Amer Life & Gen Ins	Philippines	99.78
089273	BPI-Philam Life Assurance	Philippines	51.00
089324	Philam Equitable Life Assur	Philippines	95.00
088825	AIG Life International Ltd.	Isle Of Man	100.00
085862	AIG Mexico Seguros Interamer	Mexico	100.00
086003	Nan Shan Life Insurance Co.Ltd	Taiwan	97.57
058006	*AIG Life Holdings (US) Inc*	TX	100.00
009199	AGC Life Insurance Company	MO	100.00
073340	AIG Life of Bermuda	Bermuda	100.00
088794	American Gen Life Ins BM	Bermuda	100.00
006989	American General Assurance Co	IL	100.00
010687	American General Indemnity Co	IL	100.00
006788	American General Lf & Accident	TN	100.00
002103	American General Property Ins	TN	100.00
006058	American General Life Ins Co	TX	100.00
007208	Variable Annuity Life Ins Co	TX	100.00
006809	American General Life Ins DE	DE	100.00
006072	American Intern Life Assur NY	NY	100.00
007192	United States Life Ins of NY	NY	100.00
007235	Western National Life Ins Co	TX	100.00
078067	AIG Life Ins Co (Switzerland)	Switzerland	100.00
058101	*AIG Retirement Services, Inc.*	DE	100.00
007102	SunAmerica Life Ins Co	AZ	100.00
009023	First SunAmerica Life Ins Co	NY	100.00
006115	SunAmerica Annuity & Life Assr	AZ	100.00

AMB#	COMPANY	DOMICILE	% OWN
052600	*ALICO Holdings, LLC*	DE	100.00
006081	American Life Ins Co DE	DE	100.00
083917	AHICO Elso Amerikai-Magyar	Hungary	100.00
088791	ALICO Asigurari Romania S.A.	Romania	98.00
088790	ALICO Bulgaria Life Ins Co	Bulgaria	100.00
088788	ALICO Colombia Seg de Vida	Colombia	94.99
077646	Alico Compania de Seguros SA	Argentina	90.00
077561	Alico Cia de Seg de Retiro SA	Argentina	90.00
090846	ALICO European Holdings Ltd	Ireland	100.00
055276	*ZAO Master D*	Russia	100.00
078799	ALICO Insurance Company, CJSC	Russia	51.00
084794	ALICO Italia S.p.A.	Italy	100.00
073154	ALICO Life International Ltd	Ireland	100.00
078001	ALICO Mexico Cia Seg Vida	Mexico	99.99
083091	Alico S.A.	France	100.00
088797	American Life & Gen Ins Co TT	Trinidad And Tobago	80.92
078837	American Life Ins Co Pakistan	Pakistan	61.84
088798	American Life Sigorta A.S.	Turkey	100.00
088800	AMSLICO AIG Life poistovna a.s	Slovenia	100.00
089169	Amcico Pojist'ovna a.s.	Czech Republic	100.00
088795	First American Polish Life	Poland	100.00
055707	*Inversiones Interamericana SA*	Chile	99.99
077080	Interamericana Cia Seg Vida SA	Chile	100.00
055703	*Inversiones Inversegven, C.A.*	Venezuela	50.00
078153	Seguros Venezuela C.A.	Venezuela	92.79
088806	Pharaonic Amer Life Ins Co	Egypt	74.88
088836	UBB - ALICO Life Ins Co AD	Bulgaria	40.00
088799	American Security Life Ins Co	Liechtenstein	100.00
055702	*Caravan Investment, Inc.*		100.00
078832	AIG Caspian Insurance Company	Azerbaijan	51.00
052443	*Chartis Inc*	DE	100.00
055711	*Chartis U S Inc*	DE	100.00
002034	American Home Assurance Co	NY	100.00
000180	Audubon Insurance Company	LA	100.00
004121	Audubon Indemnity Company	MS	100.00
085727	Chartis Insurance Co of Canada	Canada	100.00
002349	Chartis Property Casualty Co	PA	100.00
004000	Commerce and Industry Ins Co	NY	100.00
083833	AIG Polska TU SA	Poland	99.25
002035	Insurance Co of the State PA	PA	100.00
003756	Landmark Insurance Company	CA	100.00
002351	National Union Fire Ins Co PA	PA	100.00
012244	Chartis Select Insurance Co	DE	100.00
087105	Chartis Excess Limited	Ireland	100.00
003535	Chartis Specialty Insurance Co	IL	70.00
002350	Lexington Insurance Company	DE	70.00
085863	JI Accident & Fire Ins Co Ltd	Japan	50.00
010725	National Union Fire Ins of LA	LA	100.00
075521	National Union Fire Ins Co VT	VT	100.00
050479	*United Guaranty Corporation*	NC	45.88
055274	*AIG Mortgage Hldgs Israel Ltd*	Israel	100.00
078805	EMI - Ezer Mortgage Ins Co Ltd	Israel	100.00
078789	AIG United Guar Ins (Asia) Ltd	Hong Kong	100.00
088830	AIG United Guaranty Mexico SA	Mexico	100.00
088793	AIG United Guaranty Re Ltd	Ireland	100.00
011344	United Guaranty Insurance Co	NC	100.00
011345	United Guaranty Mtge Ins Co	NC	100.00
011346	United Guaranty Mtge Ins Co NC	NC	100.00
073354	United Guar Partners Ins Co	VT	100.00
004817	United Guaranty Residential	NC	75.03
004821	United Guaranty Comm Ins Co NC	NC	100.00
001721	United Guaranty Credit Ins Co	NC	100.00
003587	United Guaranty Mtge Indem Co	NC	100.00
004816	United Guaranty Residential NC	NC	100.00
014124	First Mortgage Insurance Co	NC	100.00
002363	New Hampshire Insurance Co	PA	100.00
002833	Chartis Casualty Company	PA	100.00
002360	Granite State Insurance Co	PA	100.00
002361	Illinois National Insurance Co	IL	100.00
055280	*Chartis International LLC*	DE	100.00
078793	AIG Egypt Insurance Company SA	Egypt	95.02
011984	AIG Global Trade & Pol. Risk	NJ	100.00
002389	AIU Insurance Company	NY	100.00
088824	Chartis Insurance Co China Ltd	China	100.00
088822	Chartis Taiwan Ins Co Ltd	Taiwan	100.00
055275	*Chartis Africa Holdings Inc*	DE	100.00
078798	Chartis Kenya Insurance Co Ltd	Kenya	66.67
055277	*Chartis Central Eur & CIS Hldg*	DE	100.00
088829	CJSC Chartis Ukraine Ins Co	Ukraine	74.08
088835	UBB AIG Insurance and Rein Co	Bulgaria	40.00
055279	*Chartis Memsa Holdings Inc*	DE	100.00
055278	*AIG Hayleys Invmt Hldgs (Priv)*	Sri Lanka	100.00
078795	CHARTIS Insurance Ltd	Sri Lanka	100.00
078797	Chartis Lebanon S.A.L.	Lebanon	100.00
088792	CHARTIS Sigorta AS	Turkey	100.00
090168	Tata AIG General Ins Co Ltd	India	26.00
085111	Chartis Overseas, Ltd.	Bermuda	100.00
077218	AIG Metropolitana Cia Seg Reas	Ecuador	32.06
088801	Arabian American Ins Co (BH)	Bahrain	100.00
089999	Chartis Chile Compania de Seg	Chile	100.00
003536	Chartis Ins Co-Puerto Rico	PR	100.00

AMB#	COMPANY	DOMICILE	% OWN
090881	Chartis Insurance (GG) PCC Ltd	Guernsey	100.00
089587	Chartis Ins Indonesia, PT	Indonesia	61.01
089020	Charitis Ins Ireland Ltd	Ireland	100.00
088823	Chartis Insurance (TH) Ltd	Thailand	100.00
088826	Chartis MEMSA Ins Co Ltd	United Arab Emirates	100.00
052581	*Chartis Overseas Association*	Bermuda	67.00
052582	*Chartis Europe Holding Limited*	Ireland	63.92
078333	Chartis Europe S.A.	France	91.32
078804	Chartis Insurance Company CJSC	Russia	100.00
088821	Chartis Malaysia Ins Bhd	Malaysia	100.00
078800	Chartis Romania Ins Co SA	Romania	100.00
055715	*Chartis UK Holdings Limited*	United Kingdom	100.00
055714	*Chartis UK Financing Limited*	United Kingdom	100.00
055716	*Chartis Sub Holdings Limited*	United Kingdom	100.00
087416	Chartis Insurance UK Limited	United Kingdom	100.00
084309	Chartis Philippines Ins Inc	Philippines	100.00
087981	Chartis Seguros Brasil	Brazil	100.00
088789	Chartis Seguros Colombia S.A.	Colombia	100.00
077957	Chartis Seguros El Salvador	El Salvador	99.99
077958	Chartis, Vida Seguros Personas	El Salvador	99.99
078171	Chartis Seguros Guatemala, S A	Guatemala	100.00
089994	Chartis Seguros Uruguay	Uruguay	100.00
088828	CHARTIS Takaful -Enaya B.S.C.	Bahrain	100.00
078835	Chartis Uganda Ins Co Ltd	Uganda	100.00
078794	Chartis Uzbekistan Ins Co	Uzbekistan	51.00
078833	Chartis Vietnam Ins Co Ltd	Vietnam	100.00
088805	Hellas Insurance Co S.A.	Greece	50.00
055704	*Inversiones Segucasaj C.A.*	Venezuela	50.00
078145	C.A. de Seguros American Intl	Venezuela	93.72
055705	*Johannesburg Ins Hldgs (Pty)*	South Africa	100.00
078836	Chartis Life South Africa Ltd	South Africa	100.00
086785	Chartis South Africa Limited	South Africa	100.00
077411	Meridional Cia AR de Seg SA	Argentina	95.00
056753	Richmond Insurance Co Ltd	Bermuda	100.00
072836	Richmond Ins Co (Barbados) Ltd	Barbados	100.00
090880	AIU Insurance Company (TT) Ltd	Trinidad And Tobago	100.00
006305	Delaware American Life Ins Co	DE	100.00
055717	*Equitable Investment Co (HK)*	Hong Kong	100.00
088833	SEA Insurance Co. Limited	Papua New Guinea	100.00
088834	SEA Insurance Sdn. Bhd.	Brunei Darussalam	100.00
073274	MG Reinsurance Limited	VT	100.00
088827	Poistovna AIG Slovakia a.s.	Slovakia	100.00
006087	**AMERICAN NATIONAL INS CO**		
010255	American National County Mut	TX	
051072	*American Nat Life Hold, Inc.*	NV	100.00
060708	American National Life Ins NY	TX	100.00
007417	American Nat'l Life Ins Texas	TX	100.00
006436	Garden State Life Ins Co	TX	100.00
007070	Standard Life and Accident Ins	TX	100.00
058905	*American Natl Prop & Cas Hldgs*	NY	100.00
003533	Amer Nat Prop & Cas Co	MO	100.00
002803	American Natl General Ins Co	MO	100.00
050237	*ANPAC Lloyds Ins Mgmt Inc*	TX	100.00
011700	American Nat'l Lloyds Ins Co	TX	
012472	ANPAC Louisiana Insurance Co	LA	100.00
012411	Pacific Property & Casualty Co	CA	100.00
000362	Farm Family Casualty Ins Co	NY	100.00
006365	Farm Family Life Ins Co	NY	100.00
010701	United Farm Family Ins Co	NY	100.00
055413	**AMERICAN UNITED MUT INS HLDG**		
050881	*OneAmerica Financial Partners*	IN	100.00
006109	American United Life Ins Co	IN	100.00
006933	Pioneer Mutual Life Ins Co	ND	100.00
007082	State Life Ins Co	IN	100.00
051102	**AMERIGROUP CORPORATION**		
064890	AMGP Georgia Managed Care Co	GA	100.00
064926	AMERIGROUP Community Care NM	NM	100.00
064612	AMERIGROUP MD a Mgd Care Org	DC	100.00
064896	AMERIGROUP Nevada Inc	NV	100.00
064209	AMERIGROUP New Jersey Inc	NJ	100.00
064873	AMERIGROUP Ohio Inc	OH	100.00
064887	AMERIGROUP South Carolina Inc	SC	100.00
064927	AMERIGROUP Tennessee Inc	TN	100.00
064238	AMERIGROUP Texas Inc	TX	100.00
064899	AMERIGROUP Virginia Inc	VA	100.00
055613	*Physicians Healthcare Pl Hldgs*		100.00
068979	AMERIGROUP Florida Inc	FL	100.00
050542	**AMERIPRISE FINANCIAL INC**		
621925	*Ameriprise Bank, FSB*	NY	100.00
071300	Ameriprise Captive Ins Co	VT	100.00
003563	IDS Property Casualty Ins Co	WI	100.00
013104	Ameriprise Insurance Co	WI	100.00
006592	RiverSource Life Ins Co	MN	100.00
008345	RiverSource Life Ins Co of NY	NY	100.00
055925	*Threadneedle Asset Mgmt Hldgs*	United Kingdom	100.00
087631	Threadneedle Pension Limited	United Kingdom	100.00

AMB#	COMPANY	DOMICILE	% OWN
052026	**AMFI CORPORATION**		
006055	American Fidelity Life Ins Co	FL	100.00
052656	**AMFIRST HOLDINGS, INC.**		
012998	AmFirst Insurance Co	OK	100.00
052657	*OIC Holdings, Inc.*		100.00
076691	Amfirst Insurance Co Ltd	Bermuda	100.00
090943	America First Ins Co, S.A.	Uruguay	100.00
090944	MorganWhite Insurance Co SA	Uruguay	100.00
002162	**AMICA MUTUAL INSURANCE CO**		
007464	Amica Life Ins Co	RI	100.00
012269	Amica Lloyd's of Texas	TX	
011610	Amica P&C Insurance Company	RI	100.00
051657	**ARCADIAN MANAGEMENT SVCS**		
064812	Arcadian Health Plan Inc	WA	100.00
064868	Arkansas Community Care Inc	AR	100.00
064888	Arcadian Health Plan of GA Inc	GA	100.00
064945	Arcadian Health Plan of LA Inc	LA	100.00
064985	Arcadian Health Plan of NY	NY	100.00
064946	Arcadian Health Plan of NC Inc	NC	100.00
055793	**ARDENT HEALTH SERVICES LLC**		
055792	*Ardent Medical Services Inc*	DE	100.00
055794	*AHS New Mexico Holdings Inc*	NM	100.00
068562	Lovelace Health System Inc	NM	100.00
064943	Lovelace Insurance Company	NM	100.00
078393	**ARGUS GROUP HOLDINGS LIMITED**		
078343	Argus Ins Co (Europe) Ltd	Gibraltar	100.00
090076	Argus Insurance Company Ltd	Bermuda	100.00
073016	Argus Intl Life Bermuda Ltd	Bermuda	100.00
090638	Argus Intl Life Ins Ltd	Bermuda	74.00
086636	Bermuda Life Ins Co Ltd	Bermuda	100.00
084137	Bermuda Life Worldwide Limited	Bermuda	100.00
086638	St Martins Reinsurance Co Ltd	Bermuda	100.00
086637	Somers Isles Ins Co Ltd	Bermuda	100.00
055422	**ARMED FORCES BEN ASSN INV TR**		
051530	*5 Star Financial, LLC*		100.00
615212	*5 Star Bank*	CO	100.00
008069	5 Star Life Insurance Co	LA	100.00
030133	**ASCENSION HEALTH**		
052508	*Seton Healthcare*	TX	100.00
064252	Seton Health Plan Inc	TX	100.00
085124	**ASSICURAZIONI GENERALI S.P.A.**		
090864	Alleanza Toro S.p.A.	Italy	100.00
084406	Augusta Assicurazioni S.p.A.	Italy	100.00
084407	Augusta Vita S.p.A	Italy	100.00
086918	DAS Difesa Auto Sinistr S.p.A.	Italy	50.01
077101	Intesa Vita S.p.A.	Italy	50.00
078162	Aseguradora General, S.A.	Guatemala	58.08
055160	*Caja de Ahorro y Seguro S.A.*	Argentina	62.50
086957	Caja de Seguros S.A.	Argentina	99.00
077528	Caja ART ART SA	Argentina	50.00
077655	Caja de Seg de Retiro SA	Argentina	95.00
077659	Estrella SA Cia Seg Retiro	Argentina	50.00
077549	Instituto del Seguro Misiones	Argentina	94.95
078678	Fata Assicurazioni Danni SpA	Italy	99.88
088995	Fata Asigurari Agricole S.A.	Romania	100.00
090935	ZAD Victoria AD	Bulgaria	67.00
078679	Fata Vita S.p.A.	Italy	99.88
055155	*Generali Beteiligung-GmbH*	Germany	100.00
085756	Generali Deutschland Hldg	Germany	80.19
085761	AachenMuenchener Lebens	Germany	100.00
085302	AachenMuenchener Vers AG	Germany	100.00
085303	Central Krankenversicherung AG	Germany	100.00
085304	COSMOS Lebensversicherungs-AG	Germany	100.00
085382	COSMOS Versicherung AG	Germany	100.00
086246	ENVIVAS Krankenversicherung AG	Germany	100.00
086168	Generali Beteiligungs	Germany	98.78
084046	Dialog Lebensversicherungs AG	Germany	100.00
085074	Generali Lebensversicherung AG	Germany	100.00
085076	Generali Versicherung AG	Germany	100.00
084430	AdvoCard Rechtsschutzversich	Germany	70.71
077188	Generali DE Pensor Pensions	Germany	100.00
077831	Volksfuersorge Pensionskasse	Germany	100.00
083885	Generali Deutschland Pensions	Germany	100.00
087806	Generali Brasil Nacional Seg	Brazil	74.37
088996	Generali China Ins Co Ltd	China	49.00
078680	Generali China Life Ins Co Ltd	China	50.00
086549	Generali Colombia Seg General	Colombia	81.83
086050	Generali Colombia Vida-Cia Se	Colombia	68.28
077488	Generali Corporate Cia AR Seg	Argentina	100.00
077234	Generali Ecuador Cia de Seg	Ecuador	51.74
055153	*Generali Espana Holding S.A.*	Spain	100.00
086178	Banco Vitalicio de Espana	Spain	90.32
090937	Cajamar Seguros Generales SA	Spain	50.00
078672	Cajamar Vida SA Seg Reas	Spain	50.00
085903	Estrella SA de Seg y Reas	Spain	99.83
083077	*Generali France S.A.*	France	67.15
055396	Europ Assistance Holding	France	43.92

Corporate Structures – *Continued*

AMB#	COMPANY	DOMICILE	% OWN
083131	Europ Assistance (Belgium) SA	Belgium	100.00
083132	Europ Assistance Espana SA	Spain	95.00
077301	Europ Assistance France	France	100.00
055708	*Europ Assistance Holdings Ltd*	United Kingdom	100.00
087338	Europ Assistance Ins Ltd	United Kingdom	100.00
084909	Europ Assistance Italia SpA	Italy	61.03
078675	Europe Assistance Portugal	Portugal	53.00
078676	Europ Assistance S.A.	France	100.00
055158	*Europ Assistance (CH) Holding*	Switzerland	75.00
078677	Europ Assistance (CH) Asr	Switzerland	100.00
084500	EUROP ASSISTANCE Vers-AG	Germany	75.00
055148	*Icare S.A.*	France	100.00
078668	Icare Assurance S.A.	France	100.00
078671	*Generali France Asr SA*	France	100.00
090675	E-Cie Vie S.A.	France	100.00
084093	L'Equite	France	99.98
084409	L'Europeenne de Protection Jur	France	99.99
084095	Generali Iard	France	100.00
085695	Generali Vie	France	99.98
089927	GFA Caraibes	France	100.00
084799	PRUDENCE CREOLE	France	93.13
078670	Generali Hellas A.E.A.Z.	Greece	99.22
078657	Generali Life A.E.	Greece	99.97
052530	*Generali PPF Holding B.V.*	Netherlands	51.00
052532	*CZI Holdings N.V.*	Netherlands	100.00
090246	Ceska pojist'ovna, a.s.	Czech Republic	100.00
083780	Ceska pojist'ovna ZDRAVI a.s.	Czech Republic	100.00
090671	Generali Foreign Ins Co	Belarus	35.00
090885	Generali Life, Life Ins JSC	Kazakhstan	100.00
078881	Generali PPF Life Insurance	Russia	100.00
090672	Generali Life Ins CJSC IC	Ukraine	100.00
090939	Generali PPF General Ins LLC	Russia	100.00
078673	Delta Generali Osiguranje a.d.	Serbia, Republic Of	50.02
052531	*Delta Generali Holding d.o.o.*	Montenegro	36.59
090670	Delta Generali Osiguranje a.d.	Montenegro	100.00
088994	Delta Generali Reosiguranje	Serbia, Republic Of	99.99
090669	Delta Generali Zivotna Osig	Montenegro	100.00
055154	*Generali Bulgaria Holding AD*	Bulgaria	100.00
078655	Generali Insurance AD	Bulgaria	99.92
078659	Generali Life Insurance AD	Bulgaria	99.69
078665	Generali Zakrila Health Ins	Bulgaria	97.47
078660	Generali Osiguranje d.d.	Croatia	100.00
083785	Generali Pojist'ovna a.s.	Czech Republic	100.00
083923	Generali Providencia Biztosito	Hungary	100.00
083922	Europai Utazasi Biztosito rt	Hungary	61.00
090668	Genertel Biztosito Zrt	Hungary	100.00
077628	Generali Slovensko poist'ovna	Slovakia	100.00
083838	Generali T.U. S.A.	Poland	100.00
078666	Generali Zavarovalnica dd	Slovenia	99.84
083839	Generali Zycie T.U. S.A.	Poland	100.00
090667	GP Reinsurance EAD	Bulgaria	100.00
052650	*Iberian Structured Investments*	Netherlands	100.00
090940	S.C. Roumanie Asr Intl SA	Romania	100.00
083257	Generali Rueckversicherung AG	Austria	100.00
085943	*Generali (Schweiz) Holding*	Switzerland	58.95
087149	Fortuna Lebens Versicherungs	Liechtenstein	100.00
087156	Fortuna Rechtsschutz	Switzerland	100.00
085393	GENERALI General Ins	Switzerland	99.92
077641	Generali Personenversicherung	Switzerland	100.00
055146	*Generali U.S. Holdings Inc.*	DE	100.00
075764	Generali Reassurance (BM) Ltd	Bermuda	100.00
009189	Generali USA Life Reassurance	KS	100.00
087827	Generali Vida Cia Seguros SA	Portugal	99.99
078320	Genertel S.p.A.	Italy	100.00
084412	Genertellife S.p.A.	Italy	100.00
055147	*Genervest S.A.*	Belgium	64.96
086554	INA Assitalia S.p.A.	Italy	100.00
083129	Generali Belgium S.A.	Belgium	32.29
052651	*Generali Belgium Invest S.A.*	Belgium	100.00
078684	Generali Luxembourg S.A.	Luxembourg	100.00
055151	*Participatie Mij Graafschap*	Netherlands	71.20
090666	Future Generali India Ins Co	India	25.50
090647	Future Generali India Life Ins	India	25.50
055157	*Generali Asia N.V.*	Netherlands	60.00
090936	Asuransi Jiwa Generali ID	Indonesia	87.69
078662	*Generali Pilipinas Holding Co*	Philippines	60.00
078663	Generali Pilipinas Ins Co Inc	Philippines	100.00
078664	Generali Pilipinas Life	Philippines	100.00
055149	*IWF Holding Company Limited*	Thailand	58.10
055150	*KAG Holding Company Limited*	Thailand	100.00
078654	Generali Insurance (TH) Co Ltd	Thailand	50.00
078658	Generali Life Asr (TH) Co Ltd	Thailand	50.00
078656	*Generali Turkey Holding B.V.*	Netherlands	100.00
085902	Generali Sigorta A.S.	Turkey	99.67
083488	*GENERALI verzekeringsgroep nv*	Netherlands	36.46
089735	GENERALI levensverzekering mij	Netherlands	100.00
089694	GENERALI schadeverzekering mij	Netherlands	100.00
090664	NV Schade Mij de NL van Nu	Netherlands	100.00
075360	Generali Worldwide Ins Co Ltd	Guernsey	100.00
075359	Generali International Limited	Guernsey	100.00
089045	Generali PanEurope Limited	Ireland	39.09
077810	*Migdal Ins & Financial Hldgs*	Israel	42.85

AMB#	COMPANY	DOMICILE	% OWN
087817	Migdal Insurance Company Ltd	Israel	100.00
078075	Pensiones Banorte Generali SA	Mexico	24.50
078007	Seguros Banorte Generali	Mexico	21.85
078669	Solida Banorte Generali Afore	Mexico	24.50
084918	Risparmio Assicurazioni S.p.A.	Italy	100.00
055152	*Transocean Holding Corporation*	NY	100.00
084082	Generali Holding Vienna AG	Austria	37.81
084928	BAWAG P.S.K. Versicherung AG	Austria	50.01
084081	Europaeische Reiseversicherung	Austria	74.99
090662	Europaeische Reisevers	Ukraine	69.90
090663	Europaeische Reisevers	Russia	100.00
077720	Generali Asigurari S.A.	Romania	83.79
078681	Generali Garant Insurance JCS	Ukraine	52.39
078682	Generali Garant Life Ins JCS	Ukraine	35.85
078661	Generali Pensionskasse AG	Austria	100.00
084084	Generali Versicherung AG	Austria	92.19
051156	**ASSURANT INC**		
055469	*Insureco, Inc.*	CA	100.00
088612	Assurant Reins Turks & Caicos	Turks And Caicos Islands	100.00
005862	Interfinancial Incorporated		100.00
051302	*ALOC Holdings ULC*	Canada	100.00
066882	Assurant Life of Canada	Canada	100.00
058701	*American Bankers Ins Grp, Inc*	FL	100.00
055460	*ABI International*	Cayman Islands	100.00
050101	*Assurant Group Ltd*	United Kingdom	100.00
087227	Assurant General Ins Ltd	United Kingdom	100.00
087963	Assurant Life Limited	United Kingdom	100.00
050100	*American Bankers Intern Div*	PR	100.00
050680	*ABIG Holding de Espana S.L.*	Spain	100.00
084385	Assurant Argentina Compania	Argentina	99.99
055462	*Assurant Holding de PR, Inc.*	PR	100.00
078093	Assurant Danos Mexico, S.A.	Mexico	51.00
078094	Assurant Vida Mexico, S.A.	Mexico	51.00
077855	Assurant Seguradora S/A	Brazil	99.00
078093	Assurant Danos Mexico, S.A.	Mexico	49.00
077855	Assurant Seguradora S/A	Brazil	1.00
078094	Assurant Vida Mexico, S.A.	Mexico	49.00
068045	Caribbean American Life Assur	PR	100.00
011355	Caribbean American Prop Ins Co	PR	26.00
011355	Caribbean American Prop Ins Co	PR	74.00
084288	American Bankers Dominicana SA	Dominican Republic	100.00
000120	American Bankers Ins Co of FL	FL	100.00
055461	*American Bankers Gen Agency*	TX	100.00
011071	Reliable Lloyds Insurance Co	TX	
006040	American Bankers Life Assur Co	FL	100.00
000150	American Reliable Ins Co	AZ	100.00
084383	Bankers Atlantic Reins Company	Turks And Caicos Islands	100.00
050679	*Voyager Group Inc*	FL	100.00
002861	Voyager Indemnity Ins Co	GA	100.00
006942	American Memorial Life Ins Co	SD	100.00
002049	American Security Insurance Co	DE	100.00
002050	Standard Guaranty Ins Co	DE	100.00
060660	Denticare of Alabama Inc	AL	100.00
058059	*John Alden Financial Corp*	DE	100.00
006600	John Alden Life Ins Co	WI	100.00
075182	Mortgage Group Reinsurance Ltd	Bermuda	100.00
007126	Time Insurance Company	WI	100.00
064361	UDC Dental California Inc	CA	100.00
065707	UDC Ohio Inc	OH	100.00
064677	Union Security DentalCare NJ	NJ	100.00
007232	Union Security Insurance Co	KS	100.00
065711	United Dental Care of AZ Inc	AZ	100.00
064674	United Dental Care of CO Inc	CO	100.00
065709	United Dental Care of MI Inc	MI	100.00
065710	United Dental Care of MO Inc	MO	100.00
064360	United Dental Care of NM Inc	NM	100.00
064363	United Dental Care of TX Inc	TX	100.00
064362	United Dental Care of UT Inc	UT	100.00
008533	Union Security Life Ins NY	NY	100.00
051403	**ASSURITY SECURITY GROUP**		
050809	*Security Financial Inc*	NE	100.00
007374	Assurity Life Ins Co	NE	100.00
052467	**ATHENS REGIONAL HEALTH SRVCS**		
064556	Athens Area Health Plan Select	GA	100.00
051572	**ATLANTA LIFE FINANCIAL GROUP**		
006130	Atlanta Life Ins Co	GA	100.00
034018	**AULTMAN HEALTH FOUNDATION**		
038424	*Aultman Hospital*	OH	100.00
068111	McKinley Life Ins Co	OH	100.00
088597	**AURIGEN CAPITAL LIMITED**		
052455	*Aurigen Europe Holdings B V*	Netherlands	100.00
066889	Aurigen Reinsurance Company	Canada	100.00
088598	Aurigen Reinsurance Ltd	Bermuda	100.00
002139	**AUTO CLUB INSURANCE ASSN**		
004089	Auto Club Group Insurance Co	MI	100.00

AMB#	COMPANY	DOMICILE	% OWN
008525	Auto Club Life Insurance Co	MI	81.90
000650	Auto Club PC Insurance Co	IA	100.00
004435	MEEMIC Insurance Company	MI	100.00
002140	MemberSelect Insurance Company	MI	100.00
000188	**AUTO-OWNERS INSURANCE CO**		
006140	Auto-Owners Life Ins Co	MI	100.00
004373	Home-Owners Ins Co	MI	100.00
003628	Owners Insurance Company	OH	99.97
003648	Property-Owners Insurance Co	IN	100.00
011676	Southern-Owners Insurance Co	MI	100.00
051510	**AUTOMOBILE CLUB OF SOUTHERN CA**		
051670	*Auto Club Enterprises*	CA	100.00
050591	*Automobile Club of Missouri*	MO	100.00
060325	Automobile Club of Sthrn CA Lf	CA	50.00
000185	Automobile Club Inter-Ins Exch	MO	
010789	Auto Club Family Insurance Co	MO	100.00
000186	Interins Exch of the Auto Club	CA	
012338	Auto Club Casualty Company	TX	100.00
012339	Auto Club Indemnity Company	TX	100.00
060325	Automobile Club of Sthrn CA Lf	CA	50.00
001758	AAA Texas County Mutual Ins Co	TX	
051469	**AVATAR PARTNERS, LLC**		
064811	Abri Health Plan Inc	WI	100.00
052468	**AVERA HEALTH**		
064515	Avera Health Plans Inc	SD	100.00
055185	**AVETA INC**		
055183	*MMM Holdings Inc*		100.00
064707	MMM Healthcare Inc	PR	100.00
055182	*NAMM Holdings Inc*		100.00
055184	*North American Medical Mgmt IL*		100.00
064895	Aveta Health Illinois Inc	IL	100.00
064659	PrimeCare Medical Network Inc	CA	100.00
085909	**AVIVA PLC**		
055322	*Aviva Australia Holdings Ltd*	Australia	100.00
055324	*Aviva Group Limited*	Australia	100.00
077906	Norwich Union Life Australia	Australia	100.00
078843	AVIVA-COFCO Life Ins Co Ltd	China	50.00
051984	*Aviva Group Holdings Limited*	United Kingdom	100.00
085047	Aviva International Ins Ltd	United Kingdom	100.00
078773	Aviva Insurance Limited	United Kingdom	100.00
051983	*Aviva International Hldgs Ltd*	United Kingdom	100.00
058145	*Aviva USA Corporation*	IA	100.00
006199	Aviva Life and Annuity Company	IA	100.00
006467	Aviva Life & Annuity Co of NY	NY	100.00
060668	Aviva Re USA Inc	VT	100.00
083161	Aseguradora Valenciana Seg	Spain	50.00
078842	Aviva Asigurari de Viata S.A.	Romania	99.90
051986	*Aviva Canada Inc*	Canada	100.00
085748	Aviva Insurance Co of Canada	Canada	100.00
085742	Elite Insurance Company	Canada	100.00
085779	Pilot Insurance Company	Canada	100.00
085788	Scottish & York Ins Co Ltd	Canada	100.00
085795	Traders General Insurance Co	Canada	100.00
078844	Aviva Eletbiztosito Rt.	Hungary	100.00
078845	Aviva Hayat ve Emeklilik AS	Turkey	100.00
090242	AVIVA Italia Holding S.p.A.	Italy	100.00
089006	Area Life Internatl Assur Ltd	Ireland	55.00
084896	Aviva Assicurazioni S.p.A.	Italy	50.00
084897	Aviva Italia S.p.A.	Italy	100.00
084898	Aviva Life S.p.A.	Italy	50.00
084899	Aviva Previdencia S.p.A.	Italy	50.00
084900	Aviva S.p.A.	Italy	50.00
084756	AVIVA Vita S.p.A.	Italy	50.00
078846	Aviva Life Insurance Co Ltd	Hong Kong	100.00
085455	Aviva Ltd	Singapore	100.00
055325	*Aviva Participations S.A.*	France	100.00
085004	*Aviva France S.A.*	France	100.00
085256	Aviva Assurances	France	100.00
083049	La Paix Protection Juridique	France	100.00
087816	Aviva Courtage	France	100.00
085552	Aviva Vie	France	100.00
089965	Societe d'Epargne Viagere	France	100.00
083038	Eurofil	France	100.00
084963	Aviva Sigorta A.S.	Turkey	98.60
083198	Aviva Vida y Pensiones SA Seg	Spain	100.00
083860	Aviva zivotni pojist'ovna as	Czech Republic	100.00
083554	CXG Aviva Corp Caixa Galicia	Spain	50.00
083211	Caja Espana Vida Cia Seg Reas	Spain	50.00
055342	*CGU Special Investments Ltd*	United Kingdom	100.00
057117	Aviva Re Limited	Bermuda	100.00
078851	Curelife Limited	Bermuda	75.00
085907	*Aviva Group Ireland PLC*	Ireland	100.00
089027	Aviva Ins (Europe) PLC	Ireland	100.00
055331	*Aviva Life Holdings IE Ltd*	Ireland	100.00
089025	Ark Life Assurance Company Ltd	Ireland	100.00
089028	Aviva Life & Pensions Ireland	Ireland	100.00
055334	*NBD Finance Lanka (Pvt) Ltd*	Sri Lanka	58.40
078847	Aviva NDB	Sri Lanka	87.30

AMB#	COMPANY	DOMICILE	% OWN
089011	Aviva Life International Ltd	Ireland	100.00
083674	Unicorp Vida Cia de Seg y Reas	Spain	50.00
087357	CGU Bonus Limited	United Kingdom	100.00
078521	Scottish Boiler & Gen Insur Co	United Kingdom	100.00
087290	CGU Underwriting Limited	United Kingdom	100.00
077607	Aviva TU Ogolnych SA	Poland	90.00
089083	Aviva TU na Zycie SA	Poland	90.00
087371	Gresham Insurance Company Ltd	United Kingdom	100.00
083323	North British & Mercantile Ins	United Kingdom	100.00
086252	Northern Assurance Co Ltd	United Kingdom	100.00
086294	Ocean Marine Ins Co Ltd	United Kingdom	100.00
032905	*RAC plc*	United Kingdom	100.00
055344	*RAC Holdings Limited*	United Kingdom	100.00
055343	*RAC Acquisitions*	United Kingdom	100.00
055339	*RAC Recovery*	United Kingdom	100.00
055338	*RAC Motoring Services*	United Kingdom	100.00
055337	*RAC Investments Limited*	United Kingdom	100.00
087548	RAC Insurance Limited	United Kingdom	100.00
078841	World Auxiliary Ins Corp Ltd	United Kingdom	100.00
055326	*CGNU Investment Holdings Ltd*	United Kingdom	100.00
055332	*Morley Fund Management Grp Ltd*	United Kingdom	100.00
087494	Aviva Investors Pensions Ltd	United Kingdom	100.00
085250	Aviva Insurance UK Limited	United Kingdom	100.00
085643	London and Edinburgh Ins Ltd	United Kingdom	100.00
085361	London & Edinburgh Ins Grp Ltd	United Kingdom	100.00
055335	*Norwich Union Life Hldgs Ltd*	United Kingdom	100.00
085266	CGNU Life Assurance Limited	United Kingdom	100.00
087873	Commercial Union Life Assur Co	United Kingdom	100.00
086852	Norwich Union Life (RBS) Ltd	United Kingdom	100.00
087346	Fidelity Life Assurance Ltd	United Kingdom	100.00
086143	Hamilton Life Assurance Co Ltd	United Kingdom	100.00
085644	London and Edinburgh Life Assr	United Kingdom	100.00
086137	Aviva Life & Pensions UK Ltd	United Kingdom	100.00
087492	Aviva Annuity UK Limited	United Kingdom	100.00
087497	Norwich Union Life Ins Co Ltd	United Kingdom	100.00
087953	TPFL Limited	United Kingdom	100.00
085265	Undershaft (NULLA) Limited	United Kingdom	100.00
055958	*Undershaft Limited*	United Kingdom	100.00
087591	Undershaft (No. 6) Limited	United Kingdom	100.00
086169	Yorkshire Insurance Co Ltd	United Kingdom	100.00
055327	*CGU International Holdings BV*	Netherlands	100.00
087830	Delta Lloyd NV	Netherlands	100.00
055341	*Delta Lloyd 2000 N.V.*	Belgium	100.00
077711	Ohra Belgium	Belgium	100.00
055328	*Delta Lloyd ABN AMRO Verz Hldg*	Netherlands	51.00
083296	ABN AMRO Levensverzekering NV	Netherlands	100.00
083521	ABN AMRO Schadeverzekering NV	Netherlands	100.00
083347	*Delta Lloyd Deutschland AG*	Germany	100.00
086528	Delta Lloyd Lebensversicherung	Germany	99.70
086527	Hamburger Lebensversicherung	Germany	100.00
077729	Delta Lloyd Pensionskasse AG	Germany	100.00
084469	Delta Lloyd Rueckvericherung	Germany	100.00
055329	*Delta Lloyd Houdstermij Belgie*	Belgium	100.00
089464	Delta Lloyd Life N.V.	Belgium	99.00
055330	*Delta Lloyd Verzekeringen N.V.*	Netherlands	100.00
083305	Delta Lloyd Levensverzekering	Netherlands	100.00
083361	Delta Lloyd Schadeverzekering	Netherlands	100.00
083363	Delta Lloyd Zorgverzekering NV	Netherlands	100.00
055333	*Nationaal Spaarfonds Hldg BV*	Netherlands	100.00
089820	Nationaal Spaarfonds Verz	Netherlands	100.00
089812	N.V. Nationaal Spaarfonds	Netherlands	100.00
055336	*OHRA N.V.*	Netherlands	100.00
083422	OHRA Levensverzekeringen N.V.	Netherlands	100.00
083421	Delta Lloyd Groep Particuliere	Netherlands	100.00
083424	OHRA Ziektekostenverzekeringen	Netherlands	100.00
083809	Aviva Lietuva UAB	Lithuania	100.00
086001	*General Accident plc*	United Kingdom	100.00
050832	**AWARE INTEGRATED INC**		
060077	Blue Cross & Blue Shield of MN	MN	100.00
068646	HMO Minnesota	MN	100.00
050839	*MII Inc*		100.00
009495	MII Life Inc	MN	100.00
085085	**AXA S.A.**		
051925	*ASM Holdings Limited*	Thailand	48.80
089376	AXA Insurance Public Co Ltd	Thailand	37.43
086749	AXA AFFIN General Ins Berhad	Malaysia	50.50
086639	*AXA Asia Pacific Holdings Ltd*	Australia	49.65
051949	*National Mutual Intl Pty Ltd*	Australia	100.00
090267	AXA AFFIN Life Ins Bhd	Malaysia	49.00
051931	*AXA China Region Limited*	Bermuda	72.97
056781	AXA China Region Ins Co (BM)	Bermuda	100.00
078569	AXA China Region Ins Co Ltd	Hong Kong	100.00
052760	*AXA Financial Serv Hldgs Ltd*	Bermuda	100.00
078839	AXA (HK) Life Ins Co Ltd	Hong Kong	100.00
051932	*AXA Financial Serv (SG) Pte*	Singapore	100.00
078574	AXA Life Singapore Pte Ltd	Singapore	100.00
057501	NM Insurance (S) Pte Ltd	Singapore	100.00
078519	Nat Mut Life Association	Australia	100.00
078578	AXA Life Indonesia, PT	Indonesia	80.00
089229	Philippine AXA Life Ins Corp	Philippines	45.00
051928	*AXA Asssistance SA*	France	100.00

Corporate Structures – *Continued*

AMB#	COMPANY	DOMICILE	% OWN
051927	*AXA Assistance France*	France	100.00
078563	AXA Assistance France Assur	France	100.00
089154	Inter Partner Assistance	Belgium	100.00
083286	Inter Partner AssistanceEspana	Spain	100.00
078565	AXA Assurances Cameroun	Cameroon	99.90
078566	AXA Assurances Cote d'Ivoire	Cote D'Ivoire	75.83
078567	AXA Assurances Gabon	Gabon	86.49
078568	AXA Assurances Senegal	Senegal	51.52
055126	*AXA Beteiligungs-Gesellschaft*	Germany	100.00
055124	*WinCom Versicherungs-Hldg AG*	Germany	100.00
087187	*DBV Holding Aktiengesellschaft*	Germany	97.12
086810	AXA Krankenversicherung AG	Germany	56.33
087776	DBV Deutsche Beamten-Vers	Germany	100.00
087777	DBV Deutsche Beamtenvers	Germany	94.90
089187	winsecura Pensionskasse AG	Germany	100.00
089649	Rheinisch-Westfaelische Sterbe	Germany	100.00
055194	*AXA Canada Inc.*	Canada	100.00
085798	AXA Assurances Inc	Canada	100.00
078560	Anthony Insurance Inc.	Canada	100.00
086334	AXA Assurances agricoles inc	Canada	100.00
085705	AXA General Insurance	Canada	100.00
086239	AXA Insurance (Canada)	Canada	100.00
086185	AXA Pacific Insurance Company	Canada	100.00
084225	InnovAssur, assur generales	Canada	90.00
084358	AXA Cessions	France	100.00
051930	*AXA China*	France	51.00
078575	AXA-Minmetals Assurance Co Ltd	China	51.00
058039	*AXA Financial Inc*	DE	100.00
050842	*AXA Equitable Financial Svcs*		100.00
009516	AXA Equitable Life & Annuity	CO	100.00
006341	AXA Equitable Life Ins Co	NY	100.00
051413	*Equitable Holdings, LLC*		100.00
073555	Equitable Casualty Ins Co	VT	100.00
006751	MONY Life Ins Co	NY	100.00
051410	*MONY International Hldgs LLC*		100.00
078397	MONY Life Ins Co of Americas	Cayman Islands	100.00
008091	MONY Life Insurance Co of Amer	AZ	100.00
008492	US Financial Life Ins Co	OH	100.00
051933	*AXA France Assurance S.A.S.*	France	100.00
086096	Avanssur	France	100.00
086926	AXA Corporate Solutions Assur	France	98.75
086022	AXA France IARD	France	99.92
090243	AXA Assurcredit	France	50.00
090244	AXA Caraibes	Martinique	91.22
089262	Natio Assurance	France	50.00
086023	AXA France Vie	France	98.34
078561	Argovie	France	95.23
090812	AXA Caraibes Reseau Vie	Martinique	88.99
084147	AXA Portugal, Cia Seguros Vida	Portugal	87.63
086211	Direct Assurance Vie	France	100.00
083079	Juridica	France	98.51
086503	AXA General Ins Hong Kong Ltd	Hong Kong	100.00
051943	*AXA Holding A.S.*	Turkey	50.00
083739	AXA Hayat Sigorta A.S.	Turkey	100.00
083738	AXA Sigorta A.S.	Turkey	72.55
051924	*AXA Holdings Belgium*	Belgium	100.00
085604	AXA Belgium	Belgium	96.91
089417	Les Assures Reunis S.A.	Belgium	99.93
089503	Servis	Belgium	88.45
089512	Touring Assurances	Belgium	99.87
051940	*AXA Luxembourg SA*	Luxembourg	51.00
085614	AXA Assurances Luxembourg S.A.	Luxembourg	99.99
086865	AXA Assurances Vie Luxembourg	Luxembourg	99.99
083221	L'Ardenne Prevoyante	Belgium	100.00
089504	Servis-Life	Belgium	100.00
051934	*AXA Holding Maroc*	Morocco	100.00
078564	AXA Assurance Maroc	Morocco	100.00
090816	AXA Insurance	Ukraine	50.00
078570	AXA Insurance EC	Bahrain	90.00
090814	AXA Insurance (Gulf) B.S.C. c	Bahrain	50.00
090815	AXA Insurance (Saudi Arabia)	Saudi Arabia	50.00
089428	AXA Insurance SG Pte Ltd	Singapore	100.00
051938	*AXA Italia S.p.A.*	Italy	98.24
086897	AXA Assicurazioni S.p.A.	Italy	98.10
084208	AXA Interlife SpA	Italy	100.00
088879	Quixa S.p.A.	Italy	99.00
051939	*AXA Japan Holdings Co., Ltd.*	Japan	78.29
084747	AXA Financial Life Ins Co Ltd	Japan	100.00
086891	AXA Life Insurance Co Ltd	Japan	100.00
084182	AXA Non-Life Insurance Co Ltd	Japan	100.00
090818	SBI AXA Life Ins Co Ltd	Japan	40.00
078572	AXA Life Europe Limited	Ireland	100.00
078573	AXA Life Insurance Company Ltd	Hong Kong	100.00
051929	*AXA Mediterraenan Holding SA*	Spain	100.00
085526	AXA Insurance S.A.	Greece	100.00
084831	AXA MPS Assicurazioni Danni	Italy	50.00
084825	AXA MPS Assicurazioni Vita SpA	Italy	50.00
084790	Quadrifoglio Vita S.p.A.	Italy	100.00
083678	AXA Seg Generales SA Seg Reas	Spain	99.89
085571	AXA Seguros, S.A. de C.V.	Mexico	99.94
083654	AXA Vida S.A. Seg Reas Sobre	Spain	99.80
084420	AXA Aurora Vida SA Seg y Reas	Spain	99.96

AMB#	COMPANY	DOMICILE	% OWN
083603	AXA Winterthur Salud SA Seg	Spain	100.00
083395	Hilo Direct Seg y Reas SA	Spain	99.99
078580	Seguro Directo Gere Cia de Seg	Portugal	100.00
052761	*AXA pojist'ovna a.s.*	Czech Republic	100.00
084146	AXA Portugal, Cia Seguros SA	Portugal	83.02
051945	*Portman Holdings UK Limited*	United Kingdom	
086164	Portman Insurance Limited	United Kingdom	78.90
051946	*AXA UK Plc*	United Kingdom	78.30
051944	*AXA Sun Life Holdings PLC*	United Kingdom	100.00
087250	AXA Equity & Law Lf Assur Soc	United Kingdom	100.00
087249	AXA Sun Life plc	United Kingdom	100.00
088758	AXA Annuity Company Limited	United Kingdom	100.00
087615	Sun Life Assur Society plc	United Kingdom	100.00
087611	Sun Life Pensions Mgmt Ltd	United Kingdom	100.00
087616	Sun Life Unit Assurance Ltd	United Kingdom	100.00
055128	*Winterthur UK Financial Serv*	United Kingdom	100.00
055127	*Winterthur Life UK Hldgs Ltd*	United Kingdom	100.00
087287	Winterthur Life UK Limited	United Kingdom	100.00
087805	Winterthur Pension Funds UK	United Kingdom	100.00
087675	WLUK Limited	United Kingdom	100.00
085371	*Guardian Royal Exchange plc*	United Kingdom	100.00
085203	AXA Insurance plc	United Kingdom	100.00
051935	*AXA Holdings Ireland Limited*	Ireland	100.00
051937	*AXA Ireland Limited*	Ireland	100.00
086499	AXA Insurance Limited	Ireland	100.00
086845	AXA Insurance UK plc	United Kingdom	100.00
085550	AXA General Insurance Limited	United Kingdom	100.00
085547	Atlas Assurance Co Ltd	United Kingdom	100.00
086505	AXA Direct Insurance Limited	United Kingdom	100.00
087530	AXA PPP Healthcare Limited	United Kingdom	100.00
086507	Guardian Health Limited	United Kingdom	100.00
086501	Orion Personal Insurances Ltd	United Kingdom	100.00
087258	British Equitable Assur Co Ltd	United Kingdom	100.00
087375	Guardian Eastern Ins Co Ltd	United Kingdom	100.00
087531	PPP Lifetime Care Plc	United Kingdom	100.00
085549	Royal Exchange Assurance	United Kingdom	100.00
084834	State Assurance Company Ltd	United Kingdom	100.00
090817	AXA Ukraine	Ukraine	50.00
085341	AXA Versicherungen AG	Switzerland	100.00
078063	AXA-ARAG Rechtsschutz AG	Switzerland	66.67
090813	AXA General Ins China Ltd	China	100.00
085343	AXA Leben AG	Switzerland	100.00
083921	AXA Biztosito Zrt.	Hungary	65.00
052762	*AXA Powszechne TE SA*	Poland	70.00
078619	AXA Zycie TU S.A.	Poland	24.36
078621	*AXA Wealth Management (HK) Ltd*	Hong Kong	100.00
090811	Winterthur Lf ID, PT Asuransi	Indonesia	60.00
090245	AXA Towarzystwo Ubezpieczen SA	Poland	100.00
083781	AXA zivotni pojist'ovna, a.s.	Czech Republic	65.00
078622	AXA zivotni pojist'ovna a.s.	Slovakia	
085219	Colisee Re	France	100.00
084359	Colisee Re Finance	France	100.00
078495	Kyobo Axa Auto Ins Co. Ltd.	South Korea	92.36
051950	*Oudinot Participations*	France	100.00
051409	*AXA America Holdings, Inc.*		100.00
050578	*AXA America Corp Solutions Inc*	DE	100.00
003811	Coliseum Reinsurance Company	DE	100.00
009083	AXA Corporate Solutions Lf Re	DE	100.00
051412	*AXA Delaware LLC*		100.00
003718	AXA Insurance Company	NY	100.00
004779	AXA Re Prop & Cas Ins Co	DE	100.00
089204	AXA Indonesia, PT Asuransi	Indonesia	80.00
078579	Saint-Georges Re	France	100.00
051948	*Vinci B.V.*	Netherlands	100.00
085161	*AXA Konzern Aktiengesellschaft*	Germany	39.73
087927	AXA Art Versicherung AG	Germany	88.80
051926	*AXA Art Holdings Inc.*	NY	100.00
010599	AXA Art Insurance Corporation	NY	100.00
087490	AXA Art Insurance Limited	United Kingdom	100.00
084201	AXA ART Versicherung AG	Switzerland	100.00
085160	AXA Lebensversicherung AG	Germany	100.00
085159	AXA Versicherung AG	Germany	81.99
051942	*AXA Nordstern France S.A.*	France	100.00
078562	AXA Art d'Assurances S.A.	France	100.00
084717	ROLAND Rechtsschutz-Vers-AG	Germany	39.88
052447	*ROLAND Beteiligungsverwaltung*	Germany	100.00
087813	Jurpartner Rechtsschutz-Vers	Germany	100.00
084628	ROLAND Schutzbrief-Vers AG	Germany	100.00
086811	Deutsche Aerzteversicherung AG	Germany	100.00
084487	Deutsche Aerzte-Versicherung	Germany	70.37
089646	Pro bAV Pensionskasse AG	Germany	100.00
051526	**BALTIMORE LIFE HOLDINGS INC**		
050737	*Baltimore Financial Group Inc*	MD	100.00
006143	Baltimore Life Ins Co	MD	100.00
058018	**BANK OF AMERICA CORPORATION**		
050047	*Countrywide Financial Corp*	DE	100.00
050048	*CW Insurance Group LLC*	CA	100.00
072724	CW Reinsurance Company	VT	100.00
031174	*Merrill Lynch & Co Inc*	DE	100.00
051733	*Merrill Lynch Grp, Inc.*	DE	100.00

AMB#	COMPANY	DOMICILE	% OWN
056834	Investor Protection Ins Co	VT	100.00
050132	*NB Holdings Corporation*		100.00
603423	*BAC North America Holding Co*	NC	100.00
602690	*BANA Holding Corp*	NC	100.00
615439	*Bank of America NA*	NC	100.00
072286	Bank of America Reins Corp	VT	100.00
068229	Independence One Life Ins Co	AZ	100.00
050134	*BA Insurance Group, Inc.*	DE	100.00
000195	Balboa Insurance Company	CA	100.00
002260	Meritplan Insurance Company	CA	100.00
002068	Newport Insurance Company	AZ	100.00
006965	Balboa Life Insurance Company	CA	100.00
060347	Balboa Life Insurance Co of NY	NY	100.00
006441	General Fidelity Life Ins Co	NC	100.00
000247	General Fidelity Insurance Co	SC	100.00
068271	RIHT Life Insurance Company	AZ	100.00
008632	Summit Credit Life Ins	AZ	100.00
057845	Tryon Assurance Co	Bermuda	100.00
030194	**BANK OF MONTREAL**		
055770	*Bank of Montreal Holdings Inc*	Canada	100.00
055771	*BMO Investments Limited*	Bermuda	100.00
056229	Bank of Montreal Ins (BB) Ltd	Barbados	100.00
066874	BMO Life Insurance Company	Canada	100.00
052792	*BMO Life Holdings (CA) ULC*	Canada	100.00
066835	BMO Life Assurance Company	Canada	100.00
055772	*Harris Financial Corp.*	DE	100.00
055773	*Harris Bankcorp, Inc.*	IL	100.00
068220	Harris Life Insurance Company	AZ	100.00
030195	**BANK OF NOVA SCOTIA**		
055868	*Bank of Nova Scotia Intl Ltd*	Bahamas	100.00
057051	Scotia Ins (Barbados) Ltd	Barbados	100.00
066845	Scotia Life Insurance Company	Canada	100.00
050571	**BANKERS INTERN FIN CORP LTD**		
050572	*Bankers Intern Fin Corp*	FL	100.00
050573	*Bankers Financial Corporation*	FL	100.00
050574	*Bankers Insurance Group Inc*	FL	100.00
003683	Bankers Insurance Company	FL	100.00
008448	Bankers Life Insurance Co	FL	100.00
013845	Bankers Specialty Insurance Co	LA	80.00
011572	First Community Insurance Co	FL	50.00
011572	First Community Insurance Co	FL	50.00
013845	Bankers Specialty Insurance Co	LA	20.00
034020	**BAPTIST HEALTHCARE SYSTEM, INC**		
052523	*Baptist Healthcare Affiliates*		100.00
036385	*Baptist Hospital Northeast*	KY	100.00
036382	*Baptist Hospital East*	KY	100.00
036355	*Baptist Regional Medical Ctr*	KY	100.00
068747	Bluegrass Family Health Inc	KY	100.00
036365	*Central Baptist Hospital*	KY	100.00
036366	*Western Baptist Hospital*	KY	100.00
034013	**BAYSTATE HEALTH INC.**		
068553	Health New England Inc	MA	96.85
050703	**BCS FINANCIAL CORPORATION**		
003251	BCS Insurance Company	OH	100.00
010597	Plans' Liability Ins Co	OH	6.64
007363	BCS Life Insurance Co	IL	100.00
058334	**BERKSHIRE HATHAWAY INC**		
051688	*AU Holding Company, Inc.*	DE	100.00
051689	*Applied Group Ins Holdings Inc*	HI	100.00
073373	Commercial General Indem Inc	HI	100.00
051322	*Applied Underwriters, Inc.*	NE	100.00
075267	Applied Underwriters Capt Risk	British Virgin Islands	100.00
071253	Applied Undrwrtrs Capt Rsk Asr	AZ	100.00
013776	North American Casualty Co	NE	100.00
002637	California Insurance Company	CA	100.00
013065	Continental Indemnity Company	IA	100.00
058383	*General Re Corporation*	DE	100.00
002198	General Reinsurance Corp	DE	100.00
003676	Cologne Reinsurance Co of Amer	CT	100.00
084334	General Re Cia de Reaseguros	Uruguay	100.00
086345	General & Cologne RE Cia Re	Argentina	100.00
006234	General Re Life Corporation	CT	100.00
057173	GeneralCologne Re Barbados Ltd	Barbados	100.00
009326	IdeaLife Ins Co	CT	100.00
086052	General Reins Australia Ltd	Australia	100.00
003806	General Star Indemnity Co	CT	100.00
087931	General Star Intl Indemnity	United Kingdom	100.00
000646	General Star National Ins Co	OH	100.00
010757	Genesis Indemnity Ins Co	ND	100.00
010758	Genesis Insurance Company	CT	100.00
051690	*General Re Holdings Limited*	United Kingdom	100.00
050513	*Reinsurance Undrg Services Ltd*	United Kingdom	100.00
086483	General Reinsurance UK Limited	United Kingdom	100.00
086540	Koelnische Rueckversicherungs	Germany	80.00
086624	Cologne Re Co (Dublin) Ltd	Ireland	100.00
051136	*Cologne Reins Finance Hldgs BV*	Netherlands	100.00

AMB#	COMPANY	DOMICILE	% OWN
084336	General Cologne Re (BM) Ltd	Bermuda	100.00
084322	Gen Re Mexico, S.A.	Mexico	100.00
086651	General Reinsurance Africa Ltd	South Africa	100.00
086652	General Reins Life Australia	Australia	100.00
084325	Gen Reins Scandinavia A/S	Denmark	100.00
051692	Gen Re Warsaw Sp.z.o.o.	Poland	100.00
086628	Faraday Reinsurance Co Ltd	United Kingdom	100.00
084323	SIA Gen Re Riga	Latvia	100.00
002124	National Reinsurance Corp	DE	100.00
011242	Fairfield Insurance Company	CT	100.00
052347	*Railsplitter Holdings Corp*	DE	100.00
010634	Commercial Casualty Ins Co	CA	100.00
051182	*International America Grp Inc*	DE	100.00
004784	American Centennial Ins Co	DE	
073005	British Insurance Co of Cayman	Cayman Islands	100.00
002199	North Star Reinsurance Corp	DE	100.00
050517	*OBH Inc*	DE	100.00
050518	*BH Columbia Inc*	NE	100.00
004330	Columbia Insurance Company	NE	100.00
013867	Berkshire Hathaway Assr Corp	NY	51.00
050411	*Medical Protective Corporation*	IN	100.00
000591	Medical Protective Company	IN	100.00
014013	MedPro RRG Risk Retention Grp	DC	100.00
055440	*Nederlandse Reassurantie Grp*	Netherlands	100.00
055441	*NRG America Holding Company*	DE	100.00
003113	Philadelphia Reinsurance Corp	PA	100.00
052346	*NRG Victory Holdings Limited*	United Kingdom	100.00
087503	NRG Victory Reins Ltd	United Kingdom	100.00
050519	*Blue Chip Stamps*	CA	100.00
050520	*Wesco Financial Corporation*	DE	82.10
050521	*Wesco Holdings Midwest Inc*	NE	100.00
002026	Wesco-Financial Insurance Co	NE	100.00
000533	Kansas Bankers Surety Company	KS	100.00
012334	Brookwood Insurance Company	IA	100.00
050522	*Central States of Omaha Cos*	NE	82.00
002660	Central States Indemnity Co.	NE	100.00
008488	CSI Life Insurance Company	NE	100.00
000308	Cypress Insurance Company (CA)	CA	100.00
002428	National Fire & Marine Ins Co	NE	100.00
004329	Redwood Fire & Cas Ins Co	NE	100.00
002429	National Indemnity Company	NE	100.00
002126	Atlanta International Ins Co	NY	100.00
013867	Berkshire Hathaway Assr Corp	NY	49.00
087960	Berkshire Hathaway Intl Ins	United Kingdom	100.00
060060	Berkshire Hathaway Life of NE	NE	100.00
004207	Cornhusker Casualty Company	NE	100.00
060389	First Berkshire Hathaway Life	NY	100.00
003722	Oak River Insurance Company	NE	100.00
051402	*Boat America Corporation*	VA	100.00
011390	Seaworthy Insurance Company	MD	100.00
004068	Citadel Insurance Company	TX	100.00
003770	Continental Divide Ins Co	CO	100.00
011110	FFG Insurance Company	TX	100.00
059024	*Finial Holdings, Inc.*	DE	100.00
002696	Finial Reinsurance Company	CT	100.00
058381	*GEICO Corporation*	DE	100.00
002204	GEICO Indemnity Company	MD	100.00
001737	GEICO Casualty Company	MD	100.00
002205	Government Employees Ins Co	MD	100.00
001852	GEICO General Insurance Co	MD	100.00
004406	National Indem Co of Mid-Amer	IA	100.00
001824	National Indem Co of the South	FL	100.00
086491	Tenecom Limited	United Kingdom	100.00
087414	Kyoei F&M Ins Co (UK) Ltd	United Kingdom	100.00
078713	Transfercom Limited	United Kingdom	100.00
003775	Unione Italiana Reins of Amer	NY	100.00
000481	National Liab & Fire Ins Co	CT	100.00
050523	*U S Investment Corporation*	PA	100.00
002541	United States Liability Ins Co	PA	100.00
002540	Mount Vernon Fire Ins Co	PA	100.00
003736	U S Underwriters Insurance Co	ND	100.00
034069	**BEXAR COUNTY HOSPITAL DISTRICT**		
064787	Community First Grp Hosp Svc	TX	100.00
064049	Community First Health Plans	TX	100.00
084104	**BF&M LIMITED**		
071194	Bermuda Intl Ins Services Ltd	Bermuda	100.00
090184	Bermuda Intl Re Serv Ltd	Bermuda	100.00
084739	BF&M General Insurance Co Ltd	Bermuda	100.00
084740	BF&M Life Insurance Co Ltd	Bermuda	100.00
055593	*Hamilton Financial Limited*	Saint Lucia	100.00
086555	Ins Corp of Barbados Ltd	Barbados	51.70
088685	Hamilton Reinsurance Co Ltd	Bermuda	100.00
072839	Marchmont Insurance Co Ltd	Bermuda	100.00
052802	**BLACKSTONE INVESTOR GROUP**		
058107	*HealthMarkets, Inc.*	DE	54.60
051523	*HealthMarkets, LLC*	DE	100.00
009066	HealthMarkets Insurance Co	OK	100.00
009190	MEGA Life and Health Ins Co	OK	100.00
011963	Fidelity First Insurance Co	TX	100.00
006215	Chesapeake Life Ins Co	OK	100.00

AMB#	COMPANY	DOMICILE	% OWN
006715	Mid-West National Life of TN	TX	100.00
084840	United Group Reins Inc	Turks And Caicos Islands	100.00
051829	**BLOCK VISION HOLDINGS LLC**		
051830	*Block Vision Holdings Corp*	DE	100.00
051827	*BBC-COA Inc*	DE	100.00
051828	*Block Vision Inc*	NJ	100.00
064510	Block Vision of Texas Inc	TX	100.00
051826	*Vision Twenty-One of Wisconsin*	WI	100.00
064800	Vision Insurance Plan America	WI	100.00
060080	**BLUE CROSS & BLUE SHIELD OF AL**		
052471	*Alabama Industries Financial C*	AL	100.00
007379	United Trust Ins Co	AL	100.00
068174	**BLUE CROSS & BLUE SHIELD OF FL**		
064116	Capital Health Plan Inc	FL	
050851	*Diversified Health Services*	FL	100.00
012095	Comp Options Insurance Co	FL	100.00
064968	Florida Health Care Plan Inc	FL	100.00
068672	Health Options Inc	FL	100.00
064015	**BLUE CROSS&BLUE SHIELD OF K C**		
064824	Blue Advantage Plus of KC Inc	MO	100.00
068956	Good Health HMO Inc	MO	100.00
068244	Missouri Valley Life & Health	MO	100.00
060070	**BLUE CROSS AND BLUE SHIELD KS**		
060404	Advance Insurance Co of Kansas	KS	100.00
064562	**BLUE CROSS & BLUE SHIELD OF MA**		
064847	Blue Cr & Blue Sh of MA HMO Bl	MA	100.00
060217	**BLUE CROSS & BLUE SHIELD OF MS**		
068175	Bluebonnet Life Ins Co	MS	100.00
050875	*Capstone Corporation*	MS	100.00
064129	HMO of Mississippi Inc	MS	100.00
064338	**BLUE CROSS & BLUE SHIELD OF MT**		
052051	*Combined Benefits Management*		100.00
011784	Combined Benefits Insurance Co	MT	100.00
064070	**BLUE CROSS & BLUE SHIELD OF NC**		
068822	PARTNERS Natl Hlth Plns of NC	NC	100.00
001727	**BLUE CROSS & BLUE SHIELD OF SC**		
068593	BlueChoice HealthPlan of SC	SC	100.00
008064	Companion Life Insurance Co	SC	100.00
060566	Niagara Life and Health Ins Co	NY	100.00
001979	Companion Prop and Cas Ins Co	SC	100.00
012499	AmFed National Insurance Co	MS	100.00
012698	AmFed Casualty Insurance Co	MS	100.00
012069	Companion Commercial Ins Co	SC	100.00
013915	Companion Specialty Ins Co	DC	100.00
076603	Companion Captive Insurance Co	SC	75.00
013586	InStil Health Insurance Co	SC	100.00
064541	**BLUE CROSS & BLUE SHIELD OF VT**		
064124	Vermont Health Plan LLC	VT	100.00
060081	**BLUE CROSS BLUE SHIELD OF MI**		
052564	*Accident Fund Holdings Inc*	MI	100.00
011770	Accident Fund Ins Co of Amer	MI	100.00
013044	Accident Fund General Ins Co	MI	100.00
013043	Accident Fund National Ins Co	MI	100.00
055796	*CWI Holdings Inc*	DE	100.00
010134	CompWest Insurance Company	CA	100.00
011876	Third Coast Insurance Company	IL	100.00
001932	United Wisconsin Insurance Co	WI	100.00
068741	Blue Care Network of Michigan	MI	100.00
064738	BlueCaid of Michigan	MI	100.00
064870	Blue Care of Michigan Inc	MI	100.00
055130	*LifeSecure Holdings*	AZ	100.00
060645	LifeSecure Insurance Company	MI	100.00
064002	**BLUECROSS BLUESHIELD OF TN**		
051051	*Southern Diversified Business*	TN	100.00
009420	Golden Security Ins Co	TN	100.00
064304	Volunteer State Health Plan	TN	100.00
051318	**BMI FINANCIAL GROUP, INC.**		
090969	ARS BMI, S.A.	Dominican Republic	100.00
060007	Best Meridian Ins Co	FL	100.00
086911	Best Meridian Intl Ins Co SPC	Cayman Islands	100.00
090970	BMI Compania de Seg, SA	Dominican Republic	100.00
077222	BMI del Ecuador Cia Seg Vida	Ecuador	100.00
090971	BMI Igualas Medicas del Ecuado	Ecuador	100.00
051559	**BNL FINANCIAL CORPORATION**		
006023	Brokers National Life Assur	AR	100.00
055445	**BNP PARIBAS SA**		
052773	*BNP Paribas Assurance B.V.*	Netherlands	100.00
089670	Cardif Levensverzekeringen NV	Netherlands	100.00
089677	Cardif Schadeverzekeringen NV	Netherlands	100.00
086317	*BNP Paribas Assurance S.A.*	France	100.00

AMB#	COMPANY	DOMICILE	% OWN
086318	Cardif Assurances Vie	France	100.00
077296	Cardif Assurances Risques	France	100.00
055446	*Cardif Holdings, Incorporated*	DE	99.60
007376	Cardif Life Insurance Company	KS	100.00
013059	Cardif Prop & Cas Ins Co	TX	100.00
090798	Cardif Mexico Seg Generales	Mexico	100.00
090790	Cardif Mexico Seg de Vida	Mexico	100.00
052755	*Cardif Nordic AB*	Sweden	100.00
090795	Cardif Livforsakring AB	Sweden	100.00
090792	Cardif Forsakring AB	Sweden	100.00
052757	*CB (UK) Limited*	United Kingdom	100.00
052756	*Cardif Pinnacle Ins Hldgs plc*	United Kingdom	53.02
052754	*Archway Reinsurance Co Ltd*	Turks And Caicos Islands	88.33
075865	European Reinsurance Limited	Guernsey	100.00
087802	Pinnacle Insurance plc	United Kingdom	100.00
090802	Pocztylion-Arka Powszechne	Poland	33.30
036800	**BOSTON MEDICAL CENTER**		
064973	Boston Medical Center Hth Plan	MA	100.00
006170	**BOSTON MUTUAL LIFE INS CO**		
068126	Life Ins Co of Boston & NY	NY	100.00
051859	**BRAVO HEALTH INC**		
064697	Bravo Health Mid-Atlantic Inc	MD	100.00
064743	Bravo Health Pennsylvania Inc	PA	100.00
060649	Bravo Health Insurance Company	DE	100.00
064838	Bravo Health Texas Inc	TX	100.00
085572	**BRITISH UNITED PROVIDENT ASSN**		
051545	*BUPA Finance PLC*	United Kingdom	99.90
084804	BUPA Insurance Limited	United Kingdom	100.00
055691	*BUPA Investments Limited*	United Kingdom	100.00
087262	BUPA Health Assurance Ltd	United Kingdom	100.00
055692	*BUPA International Limited*	Hong Kong	100.00
083752	BUPA (Asia) Limited	Hong Kong	100.00
051328	*BUPA Overseas Investments Ltd*	United Kingdom	100.00
073172	Amedex Insurance Co (Bermuda)	Bermuda	100.00
088774	Amedex Ins Co Dominicana SA	Dominican Republic	37.00
088775	BUPA Egypt Insurance Company	Egypt	99.90
051548	*BUPA Iberia S.L.*	Spain	100.00
008449	Bupa Insurance Company	FL	100.00
078090	Bupa Mexico Cia de Seg SA CV	Mexico	99.90
051546	*BUPA Investment Holdings, Ltd.*	United Kingdom	100.00
051547	*BUPA U.S. Holdings Inc.*	FL	100.00
051549	*Amedex Investment Corp Inc.*	FL	100.00
077757	Bupa S.A. Cia de Seguros Reas	Ecuador	100.00
055693	*IHI Holdings A/S*	Denmark	100.00
056944	International Hlth Ins danmark	Denmark	100.00
083267	Sanitas SA de Seguros	Spain	99.90
055131	**BURLEN CORPORATION**		
007603	Continental Life Ins Co PA	PA	100.00
004893	Continental Mutual Ins Co	PA	
087844	**C L FINANCIAL LIMITED**		
088886	British American Ins Co Ltd	Bermuda	82.00
055752	*Clico Holdings (Barbados) Ltd*	Barbados	100.00
087843	CLICO (Bahamas) Limited	Bahamas	100.00
089458	Clico Intl General Ins Ltd	Barbados	100.00
084742	Clico International Life Ins	Barbados	100.00
088885	Clico Life & Gen Ins Co SA Ltd	Guyana	100.00
088890	Colonial Fire & Gen Ins Co Ltd	Trinidad And Tobago	94.00
084414	Colonial Life Ins Co Trinidad	Trinidad And Tobago	100.00
064012	**CALIFORNIA PHYSICIANS' SERVICE**		
006181	Blue Shield of CA Life & Hlth	CA	100.00
007351	CareAmerica Life Ins Co	CA	100.00
000228	**CALIFORNIA STATE AUTO ASSN IIB**		
012211	ACA Insurance Company	IN	100.00
050665	*CSAA Life & Financial Serv Inc*	CA	100.00
060326	Pacific Beacon Life Reassur	HI	100.00
011042	Western United Insurance Co	IN	100.00
052054	**CAMERON ASSOCIATES INC**		
052055	*Cameron Enterprises Ltd Ptrshp*	OK	100.00
050796	*American Fidelity Corporation*	NV	94.00
006054	American Fidelity Assurance Co	OK	100.00
006094	American Public Life Ins Co	OK	100.00
030325	**CANADIAN IMPERIAL BANK OF COMM**		
066838	CIBC Life Insurance Co Ltd	Canada	100.00
055769	*CIBC Holdings (Cayman) Limited*	Cayman Islands	100.00
072561	CIBC Reinsurance Co Limited	Barbados	100.00
066881	**CANASSURANCE HOSP SVC ASSN**		
051317	*Canassurance Financial Corp*	Canada	100.00
066878	Canassurance Insurance Company	Canada	100.00
055423	**CAPITAL ASSURANCE HOLDINGS LLC**		
051485	*Capital Assurance Corp*	DE	
007073	Standard Life Ins Co of IN	IN	100.00

Corporate Structures – *Continued*

AMB#	COMPANY	DOMICILE	% OWN
064554	**CAPITAL BLUE CROSS**		
001783	Capital Advantage Insurance Co	PA	100.00
064854	Avalon Insurance Company	PA	100.00
064051	Keystone Health Plan Central	PA	100.00
051862	*Dominion Dental USA, Inc.*	DE	100.00
064638	Dominion Dental Services Inc	VA	100.00
068563	**CAPITAL DISTRICT PHYS' HLTH PL**		
076318	Carter Insurance Co, Ltd	Bermuda	100.00
064596	CDPHP Universal Benefits Inc	NY	100.00
052591	**LA CAPITALE CIVIL SVCE MUTUAL**		
060155	PennCorp Life Insurance Co	Canada	100.00
085721	Capitale, Compagnie d'Assur	Canada	100.00
087101	Unique Compagnie DAssur Gen	Canada	100.00
086516	York Fire & Casualty Ins Co	Canada	100.00
051641	**CAREFIRST INC**		
064470	CareFirst of Maryland Inc	MD	100.00
050940	*CFS Health Group Inc*		100.00
068605	CareFirst BlueChoice Inc	DC	60.00
064862	CapitalCare Inc	VA	100.00
060307	FirstCare Inc	MD	100.00
064471	Group Hospital & Medical Svcs	DC	100.00
050941	*GHMSI Companies Inc*		100.00
068605	CareFirst BlueChoice Inc	DC	40.00
051850	**CARESOURCE MGMT GROUP CO**		
060598	CareSource	IN	100.00
068574	CareSource	OH	100.00
064042	CareSource Michigan	MI	100.00
051431	**CARLE CLINIC ASSOCIATION PC**		
068039	Health Alliance Medical Plans	IL	100.00
064392	Health Alliance-Midwest Inc	IL	100.00
030348	**CATERPILLAR INC**		
052701	*Caterpillar Ins Holdings Inc*	DE	100.00
012406	Caterpillar Insurance Company	MO	100.00
056201	Caterpillar Insurance Co Ltd	Bermuda	100.00
060402	Caterpillar Life Insurance Co	MO	100.00
051149	**CENTENE CORPORATION**		
064922	Absolute Total Care Inc	SC	100.00
060401	Bankers Reserve Life Ins of WI	WI	100.00
064768	Buckeye Community Health Plan	OH	100.00
051455	*Celtic Group Inc*		100.00
064978	CeltiCare Health Plan of MA	MA	100.00
006999	Celtic Insurance Company	IL	100.00
055636	*CenCorp Health Solutions Inc*	DE	100.00
052373	*Cenpatico Behavioral Hlth, LLC*	CA	100.00
064889	Cenpatico Behavioral Hlth TX	TX	100.00
055637	*OptiCare Managed Vision Inc*	DE	100.00
064512	AECC Total Vision Hth Pl of TX	TX	100.00
064266	Coordinated Care Corp Indiana	IN	100.00
060297	Hallmark Life Insurance Co	AZ	100.00
064205	Managed Health Services Ins Cp	WI	100.00
064831	Peach State Health Plan Inc	GA	100.00
052050	*Sunshine Health Holding Co*	FL	100.00
064960	Sunshine State Health Plan Inc	FL	100.00
064457	Superior HealthPlan Inc	TX	100.00
060157	University Health Plans Inc	NJ	100.00
006206	**CENTRAL STATES H&L CO OF OMAHA**		
012550	Censtat Casualty Company	NE	100.00
060246	Censtat Life Assurance Company	AZ	78.00
009520	Southeast Family Life Ins Co	AZ	74.20
055437	**CHARLES N. SHARPE TRUST**		
051363	*CNS Corporation*	MO	100.00
006877	Ozark National Life Ins Co MO	MO	100.00
034021	**CHILDREN'S MERCY HOSPITAL**		
064183	Children's Mercy's Fam H Prtnr	MO	100.00
051417	**CHURCH PENSION FUND**		
006221	Church Life Ins Corporation	NY	100.00
003042	Church Insurance Company	NY	100.00
073619	Church Insurance Company of VT	VT	100.00
052516	**CICO HOLDING CORP**		
055489	*Casualty Holdings, Inc.*		100.00
001788	Colonial Lloyds	TX	100.00
008864	Colonial Life Ins Co of Texas	TX	100.00
010080	Colonial Mortgage Insurance Co	TX	100.00
058703	**CIGNA CORPORATION**		
050828	*CIGNA Holdings Inc*	DE	100.00
050923	*CIGNA Global Holdings Inc*	DE	100.00
073722	CIGNA Global Reins Co Ltd	Bermuda	100.00
055224	*CIGNA Holdings Overseas, Inc.*	DE	100.00
055225	*CIGNA Apac Holdings Limited*	New Zealand	100.00
055227	*CIGNA Hong Kong Hldgs Co Ltd*	Hong Kong	100.00
078718	CIGNA Worldwide Gen Ins Co	Hong Kong	100.00
078719	CIGNA Worldwide Life Ins Co	Hong Kong	100.00
086363	CIGNA Life Ins New Zealand Ltd	New Zealand	100.00
078717	CIGNA Taiwan Life Ins Co Ltd	New Zealand	100.00
089527	CIGNA Europe Ins Co S.A.-N.V.	Belgium	100.00
076979	CIGNA Global Insurance Co Ltd	Guernsey	100.00
083121	CIGNA Life Ins Co of Europe	Belgium	100.00
078722	CIGNA Insurance Public Co Ltd	Thailand	25.00
078721	CIGNA Non-Life Ins Brokerage	Thailand	25.00
055229	*RHP (Thailand) Limited*	Thailand	100.00
078721	CIGNA Non-Life Ins Brokerage	Thailand	74.98
055230	*KDM (Thailand) Limited*	Thailand	99.99
078722	CIGNA Insurance Public Co Ltd	Thailand	75.00
008944	CIGNA Worldwide Insurance Co	DE	100.00
078720	CIGNA, PT Asuransi	Indonesia	80.00
050829	*Connecticut General Corp*	CT	100.00
055601	*Benefit Management Corp.*	MT	100.00
066335	Allegiance L & H Ins Co Inc	MT	100.00
066336	Allegiance Re, Inc.	MT	100.00
060710	CIGNA Arbor Life Ins Co	CT	100.00
055226	*CIGNA Behavioral Health, Inc.*	MN	100.00
064789	CIGNA Behavioral Health of CA	CA	100.00
050918	*CIGNA Dental Health Inc*	FL	100.00
060171	CIGNA Dental Health of CA Inc	CA	100.00
060196	CIGNA Dental Health of CO Inc	CO	100.00
060172	CIGNA Dental Health of DE Inc	DE	100.00
060173	CIGNA Dental Health of FL Inc	FL	100.00
064980	CIGNA Dental Health of IL	IL	100.00
060174	CIGNA Dental Health of KS Inc	KS	100.00
060175	CIGNA Dental Health of KY Inc	KY	100.00
060176	CIGNA Dental Health of MD Inc	MD	100.00
064702	CIGNA Dental Health of MO Inc	MO	100.00
060184	CIGNA Dental Health of NJ Inc	NJ	100.00
060178	CIGNA Dental Health of NC Inc	NC	100.00
060179	CIGNA Dental Health of OH Inc	OH	100.00
060180	CIGNA Dental Health of PA Inc	PA	100.00
060181	CIGNA Dental Health of TX Inc	TX	100.00
064706	CIGNA Dental Health of VA Inc	VA	100.00
060170	CIGNA Dental Health Pln AZ Inc	AZ	100.00
052553	*CIGNA Healthcare Holdings Inc*		100.00
064024	CIGNA Hthcare-Centennial State	CO	100.00
064023	CIGNA Healthcare - Pacific Inc	CA	100.00
064026	Great-West Healthcare of IL	IL	100.00
050841	*CIGNA Health Corporation*	DE	100.00
058049	*Healthsource Inc*	NH	100.00
068871	CIGNA HealthCare Mid-Atl Inc	MD	100.00
068726	CIGNA HealthCare of AZ Inc	AZ	100.00
068912	CIGNA HealthCare of CA Inc	CA	100.00
068864	CIGNA HealthCare of CO Inc	CO	100.00
068865	CIGNA HealthCare of CT Inc	CT	100.00
068866	CIGNA HealthCare of DE Inc	DE	100.00
068860	CIGNA HealthCare of FL Inc	FL	100.00
068753	CIGNA HealthCare of GA Inc	GA	100.00
068867	CIGNA HealthCare of IL Inc	IL	100.00
068536	CIGNA HealthCare of IN Inc	IN	100.00
068549	CIGNA HealthCare of ME Inc	ME	100.00
060201	CIGNA HealthCare of MA Inc	MA	100.00
068675	CIGNA HealthCare of NH Inc	NH	100.00
068862	CIGNA HealthCare of NJ Inc	NJ	100.00
068872	CIGNA HealthCare of NY Inc	NJ	100.00
068570	CIGNA HealthCare of NC Inc	NC	100.00
068788	CIGNA HealthCare of OH Inc	OH	100.00
068876	CIGNA HealthCare of PA Inc	PA	100.00
068877	CIGNA HealthCare of St Lou Inc	MO	100.00
068594	CIGNA HealthCare of SC Inc	SC	100.00
068878	CIGNA HealthCare of TN Inc	TN	100.00
068828	CIGNA HealthCare of TX Inc	TX	100.00
068881	CIGNA HealthCare of UT Inc	UT	100.00
068124	CIGNA Insurance Group Inc	NH	100.00
057220	Temple Insurance Co Ltd	Bermuda	100.00
068625	CIGNA Life Ins Co of Canada	Canada	100.00
006538	CIGNA Life Ins Co of New York	NY	100.00
006266	Connecticut General Life Ins	CT	100.00
006871	CIGNA Health & Life Insurance	CT	100.00
006645	Life Insurance of North Amer	PA	100.00
078714	CIGNA & CMC Life Ins Co Ltd	China	50.00
078716	LINA Life Ins Co of Korea	South Korea	100.00
058704	**CINCINNATI FINANCIAL CORP**		
000258	Cincinnati Insurance Company	OH	100.00
004289	Cincinnati Casualty Company	OH	100.00
010650	Cincinnati Indemnity Company	OH	100.00
006568	Cincinnati Life Insurance Co	OH	100.00
013843	Cincinnati Specialty Undrs Ins	DE	100.00
050281	**CITIGROUP INC.**		
073166	AAMBG Reinsurance Inc	VT	100.00
050282	*Associated Madison Cos Inc*	DE	100.00
050283	*Citigroup Ins Hldgs Corp.*	GA	100.00
006693	Primerica Life Ins Co	MA	100.00
089032	CitiLife Financial Limited	Ireland	100.00
006163	National Benefit Life Ins Co	NY	100.00
050291	*Primerica Fin Serv (Canada) Ltd*	Canada	100.00
060156	Primerica Life Ins Co of CA	Canada	100.00
084345	SL&H Reinsurance Ltd	Saint Kitts And Nevis	100.00

AMB#	COMPANY	DOMICILE	% OWN
050287	*Citicorp Banking Corporation*	DE	100.00
058509	*Associates First Capital Corp*	DE	100.00
056733	Atlantic General Invest Ltd	Bermuda	100.00
050288	*CitiFinancial Credit Company*	DE	100.00
006062	American Health and Life Ins	TX	100.00
007170	Sears Life Insurance Company	TX	100.00
055232	*Chesapeake Appr & Settlement*	MD	100.00
075979	Chesapeake Title Reins Co, Inc	VT	100.00
003298	Triton Insurance Company	TX	100.00
072361	Financial Reassurance Co Ltd	Bermuda	100.00
056217	Citicorp Insurance USA Inc	VT	100.00
073212	Copelco Reinsurance Co Ltd	Bermuda	100.00
052881	*Positive Capital Corp.*	British Virgin Islands	100.00
090964	Balboa Reinsurance, Ltd.	British Virgin Islands	100.00
055233	*Citicorp Holdings Inc.*	DE	100.00
051140	*Citibank, N.A.*		100.00
073473	Citibank Mortgage Reins Co	VT	100.00
055234	*Citicorp (Mexico) Hldgs LLC*	DE	100.00
055231	*Grupo Finan Banamex SA de CV*	Mexico	100.00
078074	Pensiones Banamex, SA de CV	Mexico	100.00
078644	Seguros Banamex, S.A. de C.V.	Mexico	100.00
073608	Principal Mortgage Reins Co	VT	100.00
050867	**CITIZENS FINANCIAL CORPORATION**		
006227	Citizens Security Life Ins Co	KY	100.00
000544	Citizens Insurance Company	KY	100.00
050794	**CITIZENS INC**		
006228	CICA Life Ins Co of America	CO	100.00
008947	Citizens National Life Ins Co	TX	100.00
052515	*Integrity Capital Corporation*		13.00
007450	Security Plan Life Ins Co	LA	100.00
011988	Security Plan Fire Ins Co	LA	100.00
052515	*Integrity Capital Corporation*		87.00
060398	Integrity Capital Insurance Co	IN	100.00
055955	**CLARIAN HEALTH PARTNERS, INC.**		
064984	Clarian Health Plans Inc	IN	100.00
060142	M-Plan Inc	IN	100.00
064386	MDwise Inc	IN	100.00
058030	**CNO FINANCIAL GROUP, INC.**		
051173	*CDOC Inc*	DE	100.00
007218	Washington National Ins Co	IL	100.00
006080	Conseco Insurance Company	IL	100.00
006692	Conseco Life Insurance Company	IN	100.00
008101	Conseco Health Ins Co	AZ	100.00
068083	Conseco Life Ins Co of Texas	TX	100.00
060002	Bankers Conseco Life Insurance	NY	100.00
006149	Bankers Life and Casualty Co	IL	100.00
006240	Colonial Penn Life Insurance	PA	100.00
051401	**COLLATERAL HOLDINGS LTD**		
008225	Southland National Ins Corp	AL	100.00
006243	**COLUMBIAN MUTUAL LIFE INS CO**		
051052	*Columbian Life Holdings Inc*		100.00
068009	Columbian Life Insurance Co	IL	100.00
007850	National Safety Life Ins Co	PA	100.00
007361	**COMMERCIAL TRAVELERS MUTUAL**		
008664	Monitor Life Insurance Co	NY	100.00
055804	**COMMUNITY HEALTH NETWORK OF WA**		
064472	Community Health Plan of WA	WA	100.00
051822	**COOK CHILDREN'S HEALTH CR SYST**		
064508	Cook Children's Health Plan	TX	100.00
086844	**THE CO-OPERATORS GROUP LIMITED**		
051263	*Co-operators Fin'l Serv Ltd*	Canada	100.00
085735	Co-operators General Ins Co	Canada	100.00
086567	COSECO Insurance Company	Canada	100.00
085743	Equitable General Insurance Co	Canada	100.00
085791	Sovereign General Ins Co	Canada	100.00
087721	Union Canadienne Cie D'Assur	Canada	100.00
006290	Co-operators Life Ins Co	Canada	99.00
050302	*CUMIS Group Ltd*	Canada	50.01
085737	CUMIS General Insurance Co	Canada	100.00
008815	CUMIS Life Insurance Company	Canada	100.00
058035	**COVENTRY HEALTH CARE INC**		
068616	Altius Health Plans	UT	100.00
064186	Carelink Health Plans Inc	WV	100.00
075711	CHC Casualty RRG, Inc.	VT	100.00
008812	Coventry Hlth and Life Ins Co	DE	100.00
068687	Coventry Health Care of DE	DE	100.00
068980	Coventry Health Care of GA Inc	GA	100.00
068541	Coventry Health Care of Iowa	IA	100.00
064126	Coventry Health Care of Kansas	KS	100.00
068689	Coventry Health Care of LA	LA	100.00
068544	Coventry Health Care of NE	NE	100.00
064429	Coventry Health Care of PA Inc	PA	100.00
050834	*First Health Group Corp*	DE	100.00

AMB#	COMPANY	DOMICILE	% OWN
008545	Cambridge Life Ins Co	MO	100.00
008951	First Health Life & Health Ins	TX	100.00
051842	*Florida Health Plan Admin LLC*		100.00
064917	Summit Health Plan Inc	FL	100.00
064066	Vista Healthplan Inc	FL	100.00
064102	Vista Healthplan of South FL	FL	100.00
055398	*Group Dental Service Inc*	MD	71.38
064791	Group Dental Service of MD Inc	MD	100.00
068534	Group Health Plan Inc	MO	100.00
068590	HealthAmerica Pennsylvania	PA	100.00
064719	HealthAssurance Pennsylvania	PA	100.00
064077	HealthCare USA of Missouri LLC	MO	100.00
052546	*MHNet Specialty Services LLC*	MD	100.00
060707	MHNet Life and Health Ins Co	TX	100.00
064810	OmniCare Health Plan Inc	MI	100.00
060028	PersonalCare Insurance of IL	IL	100.00
055171	*Preferred Health Systems, Inc.*	KS	100.00
060224	Preferred Health Systems Ins	KS	100.00
068937	Preferred Plus of Kansas Inc	KS	100.00
068607	Southern Health Services	VA	100.00
064871	WellPath of South Carolina	SC	100.00
064274	WellPath Select Inc	NC	100.00
052785	**COVENTRY RESOURCES CORP.**		
055621	*CMS Financial Services Corp*	MD	100.00
052786	*Coventry CareLink Holding Corp*	MD	100.00
060338	Coventry CareLink Ins Co of MD	MD	100.00
050906	*United Security Assurance Inc*	PA	100.00
001850	United Security Assur Co of PA	PA	100.00
007578	Colonial American Life Ins Co	PA	100.00
052491	**COX HEALTH**		
064421	Cox Health Systems HMO	MO	100.00
060096	Cox Health Systems Ins Co	MO	100.00
055400	**CREDIT SUISSE HLDGS (USA) INC**		
030493	Credit Suisse First Boston P E	Switzerland	100.00
055402	*Credit Suisse Legacy Hldgs, LP*		100.00
058117	*USHEALTH Group Inc*	TX	75.20
006269	Freedom Life Ins Co of Amer	TX	100.00
006774	National Foundation Life Ins	TX	100.00
073708	Pacific Casualty Co, Inc	HI	100.00
006302	**CUNA MUTUAL INS SOCIETY**		
084230	CUNA Caribbean Ins Society Ltd	Trinidad And Tobago	100.00
050316	*CUNA Mutual Australia Hldg Co*	Australia	100.00
084227	CUNA Mutual Life Australia Ltd	Australia	100.00
051738	*CUNA Mutual Grp Hldgs Europe*	Ireland	100.00
078469	CUNA Mut Life Assur Europe Ltd	Ireland	100.00
090489	CUNA Mut Ins (Europe) Ltd.	Ireland	100.00
050301	*CUNA Mutual Investment Corp*	WI	100.00
090694	CUMIS Bermuda Limited	Bermuda	100.00
003049	CUMIS Insurance Society Inc	IA	100.00
013757	CUMIS Specialty Ins Co Inc	IA	100.00
008719	MEMBERS Life Ins Co	IA	100.00
051292	*Producers AG Ins Grp, Inc.*	TX	100.00
012485	Producers Agriculture Ins Co	TX	100.00
002729	Producers Lloyds Insurance Co	TX	100.00
052060	**CVS CAREMARK CORPORATION**		
052451	*CVS Pharmacy Inc*	RI	100.00
052452	*Caremark Rx LLC*	DE	100.00
055885	*Rx America LLC*	DE	100.00
055888	*Accendo Holding Company Inc*	DE	100.00
060681	Accendo Insurance Company	UT	100.00
052453	*SilverScript LLC*	DE	100.00
064967	SilverScript Insurance Company	TN	100.00
055617	**DAVITA INC**		
055618	*DaVita VillageHealth Inc*	DE	100.00
064941	DaVita VillageHealth Ins of AL	AL	100.00
064938	DaVita VillageHealth of GA Inc	GA	100.00
064939	DaVita VillageHealth of OH Inc	OH	100.00
064940	DaVita VillageHealth of VA Inc	VA	100.00
051841	**DC HEALTHCARE SYSTEMS INC**		
064625	DC Chartered Health Plan Inc	DC	100.00
055805	**DCP HOLDING COMPANY**		
064687	Adenta Inc	KY	100.00
064698	Dental Care Plus Inc	OH	100.00
034028	**DEAN HEALTH SYSTEMS, INC.**		
060218	Dean Health Insurance Inc	WI	52.63
064203	Dean Health Plan Inc	WI	100.00
051848	**DECARE INTERNATIONAL**		
064440	Delta Dental of MN	MN	100.00
064540	Health Ventures Network	MN	100.00
060194	**DELTA DENTAL OF NEW JERSEY INC**		
030528	*DDPNJ Corp*	NJ	100.00
072006	Dental Reinsurance Co Ltd	Bermuda	100.00
068631	Flagship Health Systems Inc	NJ	100.00

AMB#	COMPANY	DOMICILE	% OWN
064571	**DELTA DENTAL OF RHODE ISLAND**		
055208	*Altus Group Inc*		100.00
060349	Altus Dental Insurance Company	RI	100.00
064409	**DELTA DENTAL OF WISCONSIN INC**		
051852	*Wyssta, Inc.*		100.00
064836	Wyssta Insurance Company Inc	WI	100.00
055222	**DENTAL ECONOMICS L P**		
055223	*Dental Economics L L C*	DE	100.00
006557	First Continental L & A Ins Co	TX	100.00
065731	Dental Source of Missouri & KS	MO	100.00
064513	MNM-1997 Inc	TX	10.00
008617	Guaranty Assurance Company	LA	100.00
064513	MNM-1997 Inc	TX	27.00
064513	MNM-1997 Inc	TX	63.00
052025	**DENTAL HEALTH SERVICES OF AMER**		
064730	Dental Health Services (CA)	CA	100.00
064527	Dental Health Services (WA)	WA	100.00
060193	**DENTAL SERVICE OF MA**		
051853	*DentalQuest Group Inc*		100.00
051854	*DentaQuest Management, Inc.*		100.00
051855	*D Q Massachusetts Business Tr*		100.00
051856	*DentaQuest Ventures, LLC.*		100.00
051857	*DentaQuest LLC*		100.00
051858	*D Q V Limited Partnership*		100.00
064799	DentaQuest Dental Plan of WI	WI	100.00
060597	DentaQuest USA Insurance Co	TX	100.00
064544	DentaQuest Mid-Atlantic Inc	MD	100.00
064637	DentaQuest Virginia Inc	VA	100.00
051028	**DENTEGRA GROUP INC**		
068800	Delta Dental of CA	CA	100.00
064883	Alpha Dental of Alabama Inc	AL	100.00
064881	Alpha Dental of Arizona Inc	AZ	100.00
064858	Alpha Dental of Nevada Inc	NV	100.00
064535	Alpha Dental of New Mexico Inc	NM	100.00
064859	Alpha Dental of Utah Inc	UT	100.00
064509	Alpha Dental Programs Inc	TX	100.00
009147	Delta Dental Insurance Co	DE	88.14
060383	Dentegra Insurance Company	DE	80.00
010110	Dentegra Ins Co of New England	MA	100.00
064557	Delta Dental of Pennsylvania	PA	100.00
064642	Delta Dental of Delaware	DE	100.00
064594	Delta Dental of New York	NY	
064643	Delta Dental of West Virginia	WV	100.00
056634	Delta Reinsurance Corp	Barbados	88.76
064884	Delta Vision of West Virginia	WV	
060383	Dentegra Insurance Company	DE	20.00
050818	**DIRECTORS INVESTMENT GROUP INC**		
055376	*Directors Holding Corporation*	NV	100.00
009492	Funeral Directors Life Ins Co	TX	100.00
060365	Kentucky Funeral Directors Lf	KY	100.00
068292	Texas Directors Life Ins Co	TX	100.00
055759	**DMC RESERVE TRUST**		
055758	*Deseret Management Corp*		100.00
006162	Beneficial Life Ins Co	UT	100.00
060669	Beneficial Reinsurance Company	UT	100.00
009490	Deseret Mutual Insurance Co	UT	
051486	**DNIC INSURANCE HLDGS, INC.**		
001790	Dallas National Insurance Co	TX	100.00
009521	Jefferson Life Insurance Co	TX	100.00
003686	**DOCTORS COMPANY INTERINS EXCH**		
009026	Doctors Life Insurance Co	CA	100.00
003778	OHIC Insurance Company	OH	100.00
010763	Professional Undrw Liab	UT	100.00
058713	*SCPIE Holdings Inc*	CA	100.00
011800	SCPIE Indemnity Company	CA	100.00
011856	American Healthcare Indemn Co	DE	100.00
090094	SCPIE Underwriting Limited	United Kingdom	100.00
011091	Underwriter for Professions	CO	100.00
010352	Northwest Physicians Ins Co	OR	100.00
051329	**EASTERN INSURANCE HLDGS, INC.**		
006325	Eastern Life and Health Ins Co	PA	100.00
072142	Eastern Re Ltd S.P.C.	Cayman Islands	100.00
051015	*Global Alliance Holdings, Ltd*	PA	100.00
012527	Allied Eastern Indemnity Co	PA	100.00
013861	Eastern Advantage Assurance Co	PA	100.00
012115	Eastern Alliance Insurance Co	PA	100.00
011404	Employers Security Ins Co	IN	100.00
052394	**EDMUND GIBBONS LIMITED**		
623779	*Capital G Limited*	Bermuda	100.00
623780	*Capital G Bank Limited*	Bermuda	100.00
052393	*Colonial Group Intl Ltd*	Bermuda	100.00
086819	Atlantic Medical Insurance Ltd	Bahamas	100.00
055199	*British Caymanian Holdings Ltd*	Cayman Islands	75.00
086808	British Caymanian Ins Company	Cayman Islands	100.00

AMB#	COMPANY	DOMICILE	% OWN
083012	Colonial Insurance (BVI) Ltd	British Virgin Islands	50.00
086816	Colonial Insurance Company Ltd	Bermuda	100.00
086817	Colonial Life Assurance Co Ltd	Bermuda	100.00
086818	Colonial Medical Ins Co Ltd	Bermuda	100.00
084348	Colonial Re Ltd	Bermuda	100.00
086820	Security & General Ins Co Ltd	Bahamas	75.00
009123	**EDUCATORS MUTUAL INS ASSOC**		
068603	Educators Health Care	UT	100.00
064914	Educators Health Plans Health	UT	100.00
060648	Educators Hth Plans Lf Acc Hth	UT	100.00
085498	**E-L FINANCIAL CORP LTD**		
085739	Dominion of Canada General Ins	Canada	100.00
055957	*E-L Financial Services Limited*	Canada	81.00
006329	Empire Life Ins Co	Canada	98.30
055399	**ELARA HOLDINGS, INC.**		
051147	*Direct General Corporation*	TN	100.00
012040	Direct General Insurance Co	IN	100.00
012130	Direct General Ins Co of MS	MS	100.00
009373	Direct General Life Insurance	SC	100.00
007430	Direct Life Insurance Company	GA	100.00
011947	Direct General Insurance Co LA	LA	100.00
011320	Direct Insurance Company	TN	100.00
000681	Direct National Insurance Co	AR	100.00
055439	**ELLARD ENTERPRISES, INC.**		
006588	National Teachers Associates	TX	100.00
051016	**EMBLEMHEALTH INC**		
064601	Group Health Incorporated	NY	100.00
052492	*GHI Services LLC*	NY	100.00
064564	GHI HMO Select Inc	NY	100.00
068985	Health Ins Plan of Greater NY	NY	100.00
051017	*HIP Holdings Inc*	DE	100.00
051234	*ConnectiCare Holding Company*	CT	100.00
051233	*ConnectiCare Capital LLC*	CT	100.00
068517	ConnectiCare Inc	CT	100.00
064784	ConnectiCare Insurance Co Inc	CT	100.00
064464	ConnectiCare of Massachusetts	MA	100.00
064450	ConnectiCare of New York Inc	NY	100.00
008034	HIP Insurance Co of New York	NY	100.00
051383	**EMPIRE INSURANCE AGENCY, INC.**		
006888	Great Republic Life Ins Co	WA	100.00
002161	**EMPLOYERS MUTUAL CASUALTY CO**		
058358	*EMC Insurance Group Inc*	IA	59.80
000311	Dakota Fire Insurance Co	ND	100.00
002808	EMC Reinsurance Company	IA	100.00
002160	EMCASCO Insurance Company	IA	100.00
003638	Illinois EMCASCO Insurance Co	IA	100.00
002039	EMC Property & Casualty Co	IA	100.00
000448	Hamilton Mutual Insurance Co	IA	100.00
002346	Union Ins Co of Providence	IA	100.00
006339	EMC National Life Company	IA	69.34
051371	*EMC National Life Mutual Hldg*	IA	
006339	EMC National Life Company	IA	30.66
051470	**ENTERPRISE FINANCIAL GROUP INC**		
008919	Enterprise Life Ins Co	TX	100.00
078403	Enterprise Finl Performance Co	Saint Kitts And Nevis	100.00
052466	**ENVISION PHARMACEUTICAL HLDGS**		
064969	Envision Insurance Company	OH	100.00
058502	**ERIE INDEMNITY COMPANY**		
007276	Erie Family Life Ins Co	PA	21.63
004272	Erie Insurance Company	PA	100.00
002890	Erie Insurance Company of NY	NY	100.00
011406	Erie Insurance Prop & Cas Co	PA	100.00
000348	Erie Insurance Exchange	PA	
007276	Erie Family Life Ins Co	PA	78.37
011314	Flagship City Insurance Co	PA	100.00
055761	**ESSENCE GROUP HOLDINGS CORP**		
064763	Essence Healthcare Inc	MO	100.00
064986	Essence Healthcare of New York	NY	100.00
055474	**FAIRVIEW HEALTH SERVICES**		
055473	*PreferredOne Admin Svces, Inc.*	MN	50.00
013851	PreferredOne Insurance Co	MN	100.00
064054	PreferredOne Community Hlth Pl	MN	50.00
060160	**FALLON COMMUNITY HEALTH PLAN**		
068728	Fallon Health & Life Assur	MA	100.00
087110	**FAMGUARD CORPORATION LIMITED**		
087111	Family Guardian Insurance Co	Bahamas	100.00
002395	**FARMERS AUTOMOBILE INS ASSN**		
002396	Pekin Insurance Company	IL	100.00
006901	Pekin Life Ins Co	IL	7.60

AMB#	COMPANY	DOMICILE	% OWN
006901	Pekin Life Ins Co	IL	64.20
009525	Pekin Financial Life Ins Co	AZ	100.00
000384	**FEDERATED MUTUAL INS CO**		
006381	Federated Life Ins Co	MN	100.00
004273	Federated Service Ins Co	MN	100.00
052509	**FHC HEALTH SYSTEMS INC**		
052510	*ValueOptions Inc*	VA	100.00
064550	Value Behavioral Health of PA	PA	100.00
068511	Value Health Reinsurance Inc	AZ	100.00
008624	Wellington Life Ins Co	AZ	100.00
064981	ValueOptions of Kansas Inc	KS	100.00
060719	ValueOptions of New Mexico Inc	NM	100.00
064514	ValueOptions of Texas Inc	TX	100.00
051543	**FIDELIS SENIORCARE INC**		
064849	Fidelis SecureCare of Michigan	MI	100.00
064861	Fidelis SecureCare of NC	NC	100.00
064860	Fidelis SecureCare of Texas	TX	100.00
055359	**FIDELITY VENTURES INC**		
007408	Standard Life & Casualty Ins	UT	97.96
050792	**FINANCIAL HOLDING CORPORATION**		
058012	*Americo Life Inc*	MO	100.00
058043	*Financial Industries Corp*	TX	100.00
058056	*Intercontinental Life Corp*	TX	100.00
007169	United Fidelity Life Ins Co	TX	100.00
006233	Americo Financial Lf & Annuity	TX	100.00
050793	*College Insurance Group Inc*		100.00
008094	Financial Assurance Life Ins	TX	100.00
006412	Investors Life of North Amer	TX	100.00
006491	Great Southern Life Ins Co	TX	100.00
006772	National Farmers Union Life	TX	100.00
006853	Ohio State Life Ins Co	TX	100.00
051868	**FIRST COMMAND FINL SVCES, INC.**		
620737	*First Command Bank*	TX	100.00
068133	First Command LIC	TX	100.00
051541	**FIRST INVESTORS CONSOLIDATED**		
620470	*First Investors Fed Svgs Bank*	NJ	100.00
006413	First Investors Life Ins Co	NY	100.00
051506	**FIRSTHEALTH OF THE CAROLINAS**		
064268	FirstCarolinaCare Insurance Co	NC	100.00
030709	**FMR LLC**		
009138	Fidelity Investments Life Ins	UT	100.00
060055	Empire Fidelity Investments Lf	NY	100.00
050293	**FORD MOTOR COMPANY**		
058373	*Ford Holdings LLC*	DE	100.00
050295	*Ford Motor Credit Company*	DE	100.00
000152	American Road Insurance Co	MI	100.00
008549	Vista Life Ins Co	MI	100.00
051542	*Ford Credit International Inc*	DE	100.00
057698	FCE Reinsurance Co Ltd	Ireland	100.00
075288	FDI Insurance Limited	Ireland	100.00
051097	*Ford Motor Service Company*	MI	100.00
073006	Gentle Winds Reins Limited	Cayman Islands	100.00
056556	Transcon Insurance Ltd	Bermuda	100.00
055380	**FORETHOUGHT FINANCIAL GRP, INC**		
055379	*Forethought Finl Services, Inc*	IN	100.00
068262	Forethought National Life Ins	TX	100.00
009053	Forethought Life Ins Co	IN	100.00
000402	**FRANKENMUTH MUTUAL INS CO**		
012300	Ansur America Insurance Co	MI	100.00
012555	ASure Worldwide Insurance Co	MI	100.00
012299	Fortuity Insurance Company	MI	100.00
011495	Patriot Insurance Company	ME	100.00
008973	Patriot Life Ins Co	ME	100.00
052539	**GALAXIE CORPORATION**		
052538	*Capitol Street Corporation*	MS	100.00
051307	*First Tower Corp.*	MS	62.78
000357	American Federated Ins Co	MS	100.00
068071	American Federated Life Ins	MS	100.00
055352	**GARDINER LIMITED PARTNERSHIP**		
050883	*NANRe Holding Corp*	AZ	50.00
060310	North American Natl Re Ins Co	AZ	100.00
055354	*PLIC Investment Partnership*	CO	50.00
009426	Programmed Life Ins Co	AZ	100.00
050004	**GATEWAY HEALTH PLAN L.P.**		
060129	Gateway Health Plan Inc	PA	100.00
064850	Gateway Health Plan of Ohio	OH	100.00
032795	**GEISINGER HEALTH SYSTEM FNDN**		
072606	Geisinger Assurance Company	Cayman Islands	100.00
052749	*Geisinger Clinic*	PA	100.00
076514	Geisinger Insurance Corp, RRG	VT	61.00
068588	Geisinger Health Plan	PA	100.00
012003	Geisinger Indemnity Ins Co	PA	100.00
050408	**GENERAL ELECTRIC COMPANY**		
050409	*General Electric Cap Serv Inc*	DE	100.00
006976	Employers Reassurance Corp	KS	100.00
006297	Union Fidelity Life Ins Co	IL	100.00
003595	Heritage Casualty Ins Co	IL	100.00
055438	**GENEVE HOLDINGS, INC.**		
055411	*Geneve Corporation*	DE	100.00
055403	*GHC Corporation*	DE	100.00
055405	*SIC Securities Corp*	DE	100.00
058054	*Independence Holding Company*	CT	52.89
055407	*Independence Capital Corp.*	DE	100.00
006678	Madison Natl Life Ins Co Inc	WI	100.00
013836	Credico Life Insurance Co.	Saint Kitts And Nevis	100.00
055406	*Madison Investors Corp*	DE	100.00
051320	*American Independence Corp*	DE	49.71
055408	*Independence American Hldgs*	DE	100.00
003552	Independence American Ins Co	DE	100.00
007075	Standard Security Life of NY	NY	100.00
055410	*Honor Capital Corp*	DE	100.00
007055	Southern Life and Health Ins	WI	100.00
059197	**GENWORTH FINANCIAL, INC**		
051191	*Genworth Financial Intl Hldgs*	DE	100.00
075195	Brookfield Life Assurance Co	Bermuda	100.00
052647	*Genworth Finl Australia Hldgs*	DE	100.00
052648	*Genworth Finl Mtge Ins Fin Pty*	Australia	100.00
055386	*Genworth Finl Mtge Ins Hldgs*	Australia	63.34
078927	Genworth Finl Mtge Ins Pty Ltd	Australia	100.00
078928	Genworth Finl Mtge Ind Ltd	Australia	100.00
055388	*Genworth Finl European Grp Hld*	United Kingdom	100.00
055389	*Genworth Finl UK Hldgs Ltd*	United Kingdom	100.00
078207	Financial Assurance Co Limited	United Kingdom	100.00
086422	Consolidated Insurance Grp Ltd	United Kingdom	100.00
085812	Financial Insurance Co Ltd	United Kingdom	100.00
078932	Genworth Finl Ins Compania Seg	Spain	100.00
078931	Genworth Finl Lf Compania Seg	Spain	100.00
084206	Genworth Financial Mtge Ins	United Kingdom	100.00
052774	*Genworth MI Canada, Inc.*	Canada	57.50
052775	*Genworth Canada Hldgs I Ltd*	Canada	100.00
078929	Genworth Finl Mtge Ins Co CA	Canada	100.00
076028	Financial Insurance GG PCC Ltd	Guernsey	99.99
055390	*Genworth Finl Mauritius Hldgs*	Mauritius	100.00
078930	Genworth Finl Mtge Guar India	India	100.00
056532	Genworth Mortgage Ins Ltd	Guernsey	100.00
078933	Genworth Seguros de Credito	Mexico	100.00
051014	*Genworth Mortgage Hldgs, LLC*	NC	100.00
002742	Genworth Mortgage Ins Corp	NC	100.00
012432	Genworth Mortgage Reins Corp	NC	100.00
004820	Genworth Residential Mtg Assur	NC	100.00
004966	Genworth Mtge Ins Corp of NC	NC	100.00
003577	Genworth Residential Mtge NC	NC	100.00
002782	Genworth Home Equity Ins Corp	NC	100.00
010676	Genworth Financial Assur Corp	NC	100.00
057597	Sponsored Captive Re	VT	100.00
050428	*Genworth North America Corp*	WA	100.00
007183	Genworth Life Insurance Co	DE	100.00
009502	Continental Life Brentwood TN	TN	100.00
060568	American Continental Ins Co	TN	100.00
006648	Genworth Life and Annuity Ins	VA	100.00
060026	Genworth Life Insurance Co NY	NY	34.50
009188	Jamestown Life Ins Co	VA	100.00
076111	River Lake Insurance Company	SC	100.00
060561	River Lake Insurance Co II	SC	100.00
060576	River Lake Insurance Co III	SC	100.00
078934	River Lake Ins Co IV Ltd	Bermuda	100.00
060686	River Lake Insurance Co V	VT	100.00
060692	River Lake Insurance Co VI	DE	100.00
071302	River Lake Insurance Co VII	VT	100.00
060718	River Lake Insurance Co VIII	VT	100.00
060594	Rivermont Life Insurance Co I	SC	100.00
060026	Genworth Life Insurance Co NY	NY	65.50
086570	Viking Insurance Company, Ltd	Bermuda	100.00
003687	**GERMANIA FARM MUTUAL INS ASSN**		
002779	Germania Fire & Casualty Co	TX	100.00
012564	Germania Select Ins Co	TX	100.00
003840	Germania Insurance Company	TX	100.00
009530	Germania Life Ins Co	TX	100.00
013135	Texas Heritage Insurance Co	TX	100.00
051806	**GIBRALTAR GROUP, INC.**		
007604	Colonial Security Life Ins Co	TX	100.00
052794	**GLOBAL LIFE ACQUISITION LLC**		
052795	*Global Life Holdings LLC*	DE	100.00
008077	Western United Life Assur Co	WA	100.00
031750	**GOLDMAN SACHS GROUP INC**		
078449	Arrow Capital Reins Co Limited	Bermuda	100.00

AMB#	COMPANY	DOMICILE	% OWN
086904	Arrow Reinsurance Company	Bermuda	100.00
060579	Columbia Capital Life Reins Co	DC	100.00
076825	Charleston Capital Re LLC	DC	100.00
008491	Commonwealth Annuity and Life	MA	100.00
007086	First Allmerica Financial Life	MA	100.00
075138	Pearl Street Insurance Co Inc	VT	100.00
051727	**GRAND VALLEY HLTH CORP**		
068632	Grand Valley Health Plan Inc	MI	100.00
003917	**GRANGE MUTUAL CASUALTY POOL**		
000422	Grange Mutual Casualty Co	OH	
011777	Grange Indemnity Insurance Co	OH	100.00
012470	Grange Insurance Company of MI	OH	100.00
007332	Grange Life Ins Co	OH	79.21
012717	Grange Property & Casualty Ins	OH	100.00
010778	Trustgard Insurance Co	OH	100.00
000516	Integrity Mutual Ins Co	WI	
007332	Grange Life Ins Co	OH	20.79
013841	Integrity Prop & Cas Ins Co.	WI	100.00
052048	**GRAY FAMILY**		
007992	Service Life & Casualty Ins Co	TX	
001956	Service Lloyds Insurance Co	TX	
051037	*Texas General Assurance Corp*	TX	100.00
011636	Heartland Lloyds Insurance Co	TX	100.00
051447	**GREAT CORNERSTONE CORPORATION**		
060385	Great Cornerstone L&H Ins Co	OK	100.00
064044	**GROUP HEALTH COOPERATIVE**		
068643	Group Health Northwest	WA	100.00
064531	Group Health Options	WA	100.00
064627	KPS Health Plans	WA	100.00
055814	**GS ADMINISTRATORS INC**		
075084	Gulf States Casualty Company	British Virgin Islands	100.00
013875	Sentruity Casualty Company	TX	100.00
068023	Servco Life Insurance Company	TX	100.00
006503	**GUARANTEE TRUST LIFE INS CO**		
008401	Guarantee Security Life of AZ	AZ	89.00
051694	*Independence Holding Inc*	IL	21.29
006236	United National Life of Amer	IL	100.00
051653	**GUARANTY CORPORATION**		
051654	*Guaranty Income Life Hldg LLC*		98.96
006504	Guaranty Income Life Ins Co	LA	100.00
087118	**GUARDIAN HOLDINGS LIMITED**		
055659	*Fatum Holding N.V.*	Netherlands Antilles	100.00
088710	Fatum Accident & Health N.V.	Netherlands Antilles	100.00
088711	Fatum General Insurance N.V.	Netherlands Antilles	100.00
088712	Fatum Life N.V.	Netherlands Antilles	100.00
055660	*Guardian General Limited*	Trinidad And Tobago	100.00
086364	Guardian General Insurance Ltd	Trinidad And Tobago	100.00
086254	N.E.M. (West Indies) Ins Ltd	Trinidad And Tobago	100.00
088708	Trans-Nemwil Ins (GD) Ltd	Grenada	54.00
078641	*NEMWIL Holdings (GI) Limited*	Gibraltar	100.00
078640	Link Insurance Company Limited	Gibraltar	100.00
071001	Seguro Insurance PCC Ltd	Guernsey	100.00
078646	Zenith Insurance Plc	Gibraltar	100.00
088911	Royal Caribbean Ins Ltd	Trinidad And Tobago	100.00
084725	West Indies Alliance Ins Co	Jamaica	100.00
088713	Guardian Insurance Limited	Trinidad And Tobago	100.00
088709	BancAssurance Caribbean Ltd	Trinidad And Tobago	100.00
084191	Guardian Life of the Caribbean	Trinidad And Tobago	100.00
078600	Guardian Life Limited	Jamaica	100.00
006508	**GUARDIAN LIFE INS CO OF AMER**		
007409	Berkshire Life Ins Co of Amer	MA	100.00
058147	*First Commonwealth Inc*		100.00
060300	First Commonwealth Ins Co	IL	100.00
065719	First Commonwealth Ltd H Svcs	IL	100.00
064819	First Commonwealth Ltd Hth Svc	WI	100.00
065734	First Commonwealth of Missouri	MO	100.00
064818	First Commonwlth Ltd H Svcs MI	MI	100.00
008197	Guardian Ins & Annuity Co Inc	DE	100.00
064657	Managed Dental Care of CA	CA	100.00
064646	Managed DentalGuard Inc	TX	100.00
064822	Managed DentalGuard Inc	NJ	100.00
006000	Park Avenue Life Ins Co	DE	100.00
007650	Family Service Life Ins Co	TX	100.00
007987	Sentinel American Life Ins Co	TX	100.00
052565	**GUGGENHEIM CAPITAL LLC**		
052566	*Guggenheim Partners LLC*	DE	100.00
052567	*GP Holdco LLC*	DE	99.50
052568	*GPFT Holdco LLC*	DE	100.00
009504	Guggenheim Life and Annuity Co	IA	100.00
008081	**GULF GUARANTY LIFE INS CO**		
011128	Gulf Guaranty Insurance Co	MS	100.00
051378	**GUNDERSEN LUTHERAN, INC.**		
064204	Gundersen Lutheran Health Plan	WI	100.00
040429	*Gundersen Lutheran Med Ctr Inc*	WI	100.00
051368	**H & J CAPITAL LLC**		
009370	Starmount Life Ins Co	LA	100.00
000462	**HARLEYSVILLE MUTUAL INS CO**		
058389	*Harleysville Group Inc*	DE	52.60
011668	Harleysville Insurance Co OH	OH	100.00
000176	Harleysville-Atlantic Ins Co	GA	100.00
001921	Harleysville Ins Co of NJ	NJ	100.00
003779	Harleysville Preferred Ins Co	PA	100.00
000603	Harleysville Lake States Ins	MI	100.00
000643	Harleysville Insurance Company	PA	100.00
003656	Harleysville Insurance Co NY	NY	100.00
002483	Harleysville Worcester Ins Co	PA	100.00
006517	Harleysville Life Ins Co	PA	100.00
012051	Mainland Insurance Company	PA	100.00
011087	Harleysville Pennland Ins Co	PA	100.00
050870	**HARRIS INSURANCE HOLDINGS INC**		
006222	Central United Life Ins Co	AR	100.00
008588	Investors Consolidated Ins Co	NH	100.00
050871	*Manhattan Insurance Group Inc*	TX	100.00
006686	Manhattan Life Ins Co	NY	100.00
006360	Family Life Ins Co	TX	100.00
058707	**HARTFORD FINANCIAL SERV GRP**		
002231	Hartford Fire Insurance Co	CT	100.00
002230	Hartford Accident & Indem Co	CT	100.00
002229	Hartford Casualty Ins Co	IN	100.00
002611	Hartford Insurance Co of IL	IL	100.00
002614	Hartford Lloyd's Insurance Co	TX	100.00
002232	Hartford Underwriters Ins Co	CT	100.00
002235	Twin City Fire Insurance Co	IN	100.00
051098	*Hartford Holdings, Inc*	DE	100.00
058047	*Hartford Life Inc*	DE	100.00
007285	Hartford Life & Accident Ins	CT	100.00
008480	American Maturity Life Ins Co	CT	100.00
006518	Hartford Life Ins Co	CT	100.00
009117	Hartford Internat Life Reassur	CT	100.00
007325	Hartford Life and Annuity Ins	CT	100.00
051256	*Hartford Life International*	CT	100.00
089068	Hartford Life Limited	Ireland	100.00
087992	Icatu Hartford Seguros S.A.	Brazil	50.00
056393	Hartford Life Ltd	Bermuda	100.00
083094	Hartford Life Insurance KK	Japan	100.00
002706	Nutmeg Insurance Company	CT	100.00
050049	*HartRe Group LLC*	CT	100.00
072485	Fencourt Reinsurance Co Ltd	Bermuda	100.00
078730	Hartford Fin Prod Int'l Ltd	United Kingdom	100.00
050380	*Hartford Management Ltd*	Bermuda	100.00
072844	Hartford Insurance Ltd	Bermuda	100.00
002612	Hartford Ins Co of Midwest	IN	100.00
002613	Hartford Ins Co of Southeast	CT	100.00
050339	*Heritage Holdings Inc*	CT	100.00
073249	Heritage Reinsurance Co Ltd	Bermuda	100.00
085602	Excess Insurance Co Ltd	United Kingdom	100.00
002187	First State Insurance Co	CT	100.00
001907	New England Insurance Company	CT	100.00
002188	New England Reinsurance Corp	CT	100.00
073287	New Ocean Insurance Co Ltd	Bermuda	100.00
011654	Pacific Insurance Company, Ltd	CT	100.00
010777	Prop & Cas Ins Co Hartford	IN	100.00
002234	Sentinel Insurance Company Ltd	CT	100.00
002610	Trumbull Insurance Company	CT	100.00
060711	White River Life Reinsurance	VT	100.00
068973	**HARVARD PILGRIM HEALTH CARE**		
064342	Harvard Pilgrim Hlth Care ofNE	MA	100.00
011367	HPHC Insurance Company Inc	MA	100.00
064035	**HAWAII MEDICAL SERVICE ASSN**		
050721	*Benefit Services of Hawaii Inc*	HI	100.00
011875	WorkComp Hawaii Ins Co, Inc	HI	100.00
012099	WorkComp Hawaii Select Ins Co	HI	100.00
052027	**HCC HOLDINGS LLC**		
051424	*Homeshield Capital Co*		52.00
009458	LifeShield National Ins Co	OK	100.00
011818	Homeshield Fire & Cas Ins Co	OK	100.00
058391	**HCC INSURANCE HOLDINGS, INC**		
058331	*Avemco Corporation*	DE	100.00
000191	Avemco Insurance Company	MD	100.00
012531	HCC Specialty Ins Co	OK	100.00
051534	*HCC Ins Holdings (INTL) Ltd*	United Kingdom	100.00
051535	*HCC Specialty Hldgs (No.1) Ltd*	United Kingdom	100.00

AMB#	COMPANY	DOMICILE	% OWN
047525	*Pepys Holdings Ltd*	United Kingdom	100.00
051638	*HCCI Group Limited*	United Kingdom	100.00
087312	HCC International Ins. Co. Plc	United Kingdom	100.00
083642	Houston Cas Co Europe Seg Reas	Spain	100.00
072473	HCC Reinsurance Company Ltd	Bermuda	100.00
051532	*Illium, Inc.*	DE	100.00
003286	Houston Casualty Company	TX	100.00
003833	HCC Insurance Company	IN	100.00
009081	HCC Life Insurance Company	IN	100.00
008618	Perico Life Insurance Company	DE	100.00
000747	U.S. Specialty Insurance Co	TX	100.00
055634	*Ponderosa Management Inc*	CO	100.00
010383	Pioneer General Insurance Co	CO	100.00
051196	*Surety Associates Holdings Co*	NM	100.00
011019	American Contractors Indem Co	CA	100.00
051238	*USSC Holdings Inc*	MD	100.00
012009	United States Surety Company	MD	100.00
085068	**HDI V.A.G.**		
084651	*Talanx AG*	Germany	100.00
078502	PB Pensionskasse AG	Germany	100.00
088855	CiV Hayat Sigorta A.S.	Turkey	90.00
073088	Euro Int'l Reinsurance	Luxembourg	100.00
077335	*GERLING Beteiligungs-GmbH*	Germany	100.00
084092	Hannover Rueckversicherung AG	Germany	50.20
050648	*Hannover Finance Inc*	DE	100.00
050639	*Clarendon Insurance Group Inc*	DE	100.00
001975	Clarendon National Ins Co	NJ	100.00
001845	Clarendon America Ins Co	NJ	100.00
010827	Clarendon Select Insurance Co	FL	100.00
011783	Harbor Specialty Insurance Co	NJ	100.00
051778	*Hannover Finance (UK) Limited*	United Kingdom	100.00
085551	Hannover Life Reasr (UK) Ltd	United Kingdom	100.00
086486	International Insurance Co	United Kingdom	100.00
077905	Hannover Life Re Australasia	Australia	100.00
078848	Hannover Re Gestion Re France	France	100.00
085128	Hannover Reinsurance Group ZA	South Africa	100.00
086007	Hannover Life Reassur ZA Ltd	South Africa	100.00
086008	Hannover Reinsurance Africa	South Africa	100.00
077691	Compass Insurance Company Ltd	South Africa	100.00
051775	*Hannover Ruck-Beiligung Ver*	Germany	100.00
086580	E+S Reinsurance (Ireland)	Ireland	100.00
085064	E+S Rueckversicherungs AG	Germany	63.78
085314	Hannover Re (Bermuda) Ltd	Bermuda	100.00
086922	Hannover Reins (Dublin)	Ireland	100.00
073703	Hannover Re (Guernsey) PCC Ltd	Guernsey	100.00
078849	Hannover Re Takaful B.S.C. (c)	Bahrain	95.00
086581	Hannover Reinsurance (Ireland)	Ireland	100.00
051777	HR Hannover Re, Correduria	Spain	100.00
075471	Kaith Re Ltd	Bermuda	88.00
051776	*Zweite Hannover Ruck Beteil*	Germany	100.00
068031	Hannover Life Reassurance Amer	FL	100.00
088859	Hannover Life Reasr BM Ltd	Bermuda	100.00
084133	Hannover Life Reasr (Ireland)	Ireland	100.00
055247	*HDI-Gerling Leben SvceHldg*	Germany	100.00
078507	ASPECTA Assurance Intl AG	Liechtenstein	100.00
078508	ASPECTA Assr Intl Luxembourg	Luxembourg	100.00
087855	ASPECTA Lebensversicherung AG	Germany	100.00
078506	ASPECTA Zycle Towarzystwo Ubez	Poland	100.00
085842	HDI-Gerling Lebensversicherung	Germany	94.90
077693	HDI-Gerling Friedrich Wilhelm	Germany	100.00
078513	Gerling Polska Towarzystwo Ube	Poland	100.00
089642	HDI-Gerling Pensionsfonds AG	Germany	100.00
077778	HDI-Gerling Pensionskasse AG	Germany	100.00
055435	*HDI-Gerling Sach Servicehldg*	Germany	100.00
083336	HDI Direckt Versicherung AG	Germany	100.00
084449	HDI-Gerling Firmen & Privat	Germany	100.00
084535	HDI-Gerling Rechtsschutz Vers	Germany	100.00
077779	HDI-Gerling Industrie Vers AG	Germany	100.00
078321	HDI-Gerling Welt Service AG	Germany	100.00
002878	HDI-Gerling America Ins Co	IL	100.00
086923	HDI-Gerling de Mexico Seg S.A.	Mexico	99.90
086451	Sul America Companhia de Seg	Brazil	50.00
086943	HDI-Gerling Australia Ins Co	Australia	100.00
084009	HDI-Gerling Ins Co S Africa	South Africa	100.00
086944	HDI-Gerling Polska TU S.A.	Poland	100.00
083844	POIST'OVNA HDI-GERLING	Slovakia	100.00
051780	*HDI-Gerling Intl Hldg AG*	Germany	100.00
078504	HDI Asekuracja TU S.A.	Poland	100.00
078777	HDI Assicurazioni S.p.A.	Italy	100.00
087866	HDI-Gerling Verzeker NV	Netherlands	100.00
089500	HDI Gerling S.A.	Belgium	100.00
083393	HDI Hannover Intl Espana Seg	Spain	100.00
077131	HDI Versicherung AG	Austria	99.97
078512	HDI Seguros S.A.	Spain	100.00
087985	HDI Seguros S/A	Brazil	99.99
083228	HDI Sigorta A.S.	Turkey	99.99
089568	HDI Zahstrahovane AD	Bulgaria	94.00
088860	OOO Strakhovaya Kompania CiV	Russia	90.00
055746	*ProACTIV Vermoegensverwaltungs*	Germany	100.00
084060	PBV Lebensversicherung AG	Germany	100.00
087848	TARGO Lebensversicherung AG	Germany	94.90
087849	TARGO Versicherung AG	Germany	100.00

AMB#	COMPANY	DOMICILE	% OWN
078510	Magyar Posta Biztosito Rt.	Hungary	66.90
078511	Magyar Posta Eletbiztosito Rt.	Hungary	66.90
084586	*neue leben Holding Aktiengesel*	Germany	67.50
084587	Neue leben Lebensversicherung	Germany	100.00
051779	*neue leben Pensionsverwaltung*	Germany	49.00
077785	neue leben Pensionskasse AG	Germany	100.00
084588	neue leben Unfallversicherung	Germany	100.00
084612	PB Lebensversicherung AG	Germany	100.00
084613	PB Versicherung AG	Germany	100.00
089200	PB Pensionsfonds AG	Germany	100.00
009193	**HEALTH CARE SERVICE CORP**		
068658	BCI HMO Inc	IL	51.00
007322	Fort Dearborn Life Ins Co	IL	100.00
068158	Fort Dearborn Life Ins Co NY	NY	100.00
050787	*Preferred Financial Corp*	CO	100.00
008502	Colorado Bankers Life Ins Co	CO	100.00
068932	GHS Health Maintenance Org	OK	100.00
011405	GHS Property & Casualty Ins Co	OK	100.00
007048	HCSC Insurance Services Co	IL	100.00
034014	**HEALTH FIRST, INC.**		
035211	*Cape Canaveral Hospital Inc*	FL	100.00
051364	*Health First Holding Corp Inc*		100.00
064115	Health First Health Plans	FL	100.00
035108	*Holmes Regional Medical Center*	FL	100.00
058046	**HEALTH NET INC**		
068713	Health Net of Arizona Inc	AZ	100.00
068507	Health Net of California Inc	CA	100.00
006722	Health Net Life Insurance Co	CA	100.00
076221	Health Net Life Reinsurance Co	Cayman Islands	100.00
050763	*Health Net of the Northeast*	DE	100.00
052464	*FOHP Inc*	NJ	100.00
050766	*HSI Advantage Health Holdings*	DE	100.00
068586	QualMed Plans for Hlth of W PA	PA	100.00
050938	*Managed Health Network Inc*	DE	100.00
064673	Managed Health Network	CA	100.00
050764	*QualMed Inc*	DE	100.00
068947	Health Net Health Plan of OR	OR	100.00
064188	QualMed Plans for Health of PA	PA	100.00
055167	**HEALTH ONE ALLIANCE, LLC**		
064891	Alliant Health Plans Inc	GA	100.00
064201	**HEALTH PLAN OF UPPER OH VALLEY**		
060350	THP Insurance Company	WV	100.00
068576	Hometown Health Plan	OH	100.00
052494	**HEALTHFIRST INC**		
064346	Managed Health Inc	NY	100.00
068731	**HEALTHPARTNERS INC**		
068667	Group Health Plan Inc	MN	100.00
055345	*HealthPartners Administrators*	MN	100.00
011695	Midwest Assurance Company	MN	100.00
051609	**HEALTHPLEX INC**		
013569	Healthplex Insurance Co	NY	100.00
064959	Healthplex of NJ Inc	NJ	100.00
064782	International HealthCare Svcs	NJ	100.00
068555	**HEALTHPLUS OF MICHIGAN INC**		
060672	HealthPlus Insurance Company	MI	100.00
064762	HealthPlus Partners Inc	MI	100.00
055219	**HEALTHSPRING, INC.**		
055212	*NewQuest, LLC*	TN	100.00
055214	*HealthSpring Management, Inc.*	TN	100.00
064300	HealthSpring of Tennessee	TN	100.00
060673	HealthSpring Life and Health	TX	100.00
068784	HealthSpring of Alabama Inc	AL	100.00
064756	Leon Medical Centers Hlth Plns	FL	100.00
064828	Texas HealthSpring LLC	TX	100.00
034012	**HEARTLAND HEALTH**		
064182	Community Health Plan	MO	100.00
009101	Community Health Plan Ins Co	MO	100.00
052520	**HEARTLAND HOLDING COMPANY INC**		
006730	Heartland National Life Ins Co	IN	100.00
055635	**HENRY FORD HEALTH SYSTEM**		
068810	Health Alliance Plan of MI	MI	100.00
060220	Alliance Health and Life Ins	MI	100.00
056444	Onika Insurance Co Ltd	Cayman Islands	100.00
052490	**HF MANAGEMENT SERVICES LLC**		
064974	Healthfirst Health Plan of NJ	NJ	100.00
064010	**HIGHMARK INC.**		
075494	HCI, Inc	VT	100.00
060570	Highmark Senior Resources Inc	PA	100.00
006128	HM Health Insurance Company	PA	100.00
050693	*HM Insurance Group*	PA	100.00
010086	Highmark Casualty Ins Co	PA	100.00
071254	HM Captive Insurance Co	VT	100.00

AMB#	COMPANY	DOMICILE	% OWN
013871	HM Casualty Insurance Co	PA	100.00
009063	HM Life Insurance Company	PA	100.00
060209	HM Life Insurance Company NY	NY	100.00
068833	Keystone Health Plan West Inc	PA	100.00
050692	United Concordia Companies Inc	PA	100.00
064649	United Concordia Dental Cp AL	AL	100.00
065705	United Concordia Dental Plans	MD	100.00
064008	United Concordia Dental Pls CA	CA	100.00
065704	United Concordia Dental Pls FL	FL	100.00
065702	United Concordia Dental Pls KY	KY	100.00
065700	United Concordia D Pls the MW	MI	100.00
064353	United Concordia Dental Pls PA	PA	100.00
064351	United Concordia Dental Pls TX	TX	100.00
060255	United Concordia Ins Co of NY	NY	100.00
006265	United Concordia Life & Health	PA	100.00
008651	United Concordia Insurance Co	AZ	100.00
058706	**HORACE MANN EDUCATORS CORP**		
006324	Allegiance Life Ins Co	IL	100.00
006535	Horace Mann Life Ins Co	IL	100.00
007867	Educators Life Ins Co	AZ	100.00
003359	Horace Mann Insurance Company	IL	100.00
054011	*Horace Mann Lloyds Mgmt Corp*	TX	100.00
012314	Horace Mann Lloyds	TX	100.00
004148	Horace Mann Prop & Cas Ins Co	CA	100.00
000884	Teachers Insurance Company	IL	100.00
064022	**HORIZON HEALTHCARE SERVICES**		
050982	*Enterprise Holding Company Inc*		100.00
050979	*Rayant Dental Services, Inc.*		100.00
064696	Horizon Healthcare Dental	NJ	100.00
060303	Horizon Healthcare Ins of DE	DE	100.00
012278	Rayant Insurance Co of PA	PA	100.00
050981	*Horizon Healthcare Plan Hldg*		100.00
064397	Horizon Healthcare of Delaware	DE	100.00
068960	Horizon Healthcare of NJ	NJ	100.00
064704	Horizon Healthcare of NY	NY	100.00
060327	Rayant Insurance Company of NY	NY	100.00
064307	**HOSPITAL SERVICE ASSN OF NE PA**		
060298	First Priority Life Ins Co	PA	60.00
068780	HMO of Northeastern PA	PA	60.00
055304	*AllOne Health Group, Inc.*	AK	100.00
006902	Significa Insurance Group Inc	PA	100.00
030884	**HSBC HOLDINGS PLC**		
623171	*Bank of Bermuda Limited*	Bermuda	100.00
071212	HSBC Ins (Bermuda) Limited	Bermuda	100.00
055678	*Grupo Financiero HSBC SA de CV*	Mexico	99.90
078100	HSBC Seguros, S.A. de C.V.	Mexico	99.90
078099	HSBC Pensiones, S.A.	Mexico	99.90
078008	HSBC Vida, S.A. de C.V.	Mexico	99.90
063038	*HSBC Bank plc*	United Kingdom	100.00
055685	*HSBC Europe (Netherlands) B.V.*	Netherlands	100.00
089051	HSBC Insurance (Ireland) Ltd	Ireland	100.00
075369	HSBC Life (Europe) Limited	Ireland	100.00
075290	HSBC Reinsurance Limited	Ireland	100.00
087461	HSBC Life (UK) Limited	United Kingdom	100.00
052075	*Marks & Spencer Retail Fin*	United Kingdom	100.00
087452	Marks & Spencer Lf Assur Ltd	United Kingdom	100.00
055679	*HSBC Finance (Netherlands)*	Netherlands	100.00
055686	*HSBC Holdings B.V.*	Netherlands	100.00
055682	*HSBC Asia Holdings (UK)*	United Kingdom	100.00
055683	*HSBC Asia Holdings B.V.*	Netherlands	100.00
623173	*Hongkong & Shanghai Banking*	Hong Kong	100.00
030819	*Hang Seng Bank Ltd*	Hong Kong	62.10
085377	Hang Seng Insurance Co Ltd	Hong Kong	100.00
078904	Hang Seng General Ins (HK) Co	Hong Kong	100.00
084723	Hang Seng Life Limited	Hong Kong	100.00
084722	*HSBC Ins Asia-Pacific Holdings*	Hong Kong	100.00
088760	HSBC Amanah Takaful (MY)	Malaysia	49.00
086812	HSBC Insurance (Asia) Limited	Hong Kong	100.00
072362	HSBC Life (International) Ltd	Bermuda	100.00
089436	HSBC Insurance (SG) Pte Ltd	Singapore	100.00
055687	*HSBC Insurance Holdings Ltd*	United Kingdom	100.00
049073	*HSBC Ins Brokers Hldgs Ltd*	United Kingdom	100.00
087872	HSBC Insurance (UK) Limited	United Kingdom	100.00
084107	London & Leith Ins Co Ltd	United Kingdom	100.00
076032	HSBC Insurance PCC Limited	Guernsey	
055689	*HSBC Latin America Hldgs (UK)*	United Kingdom	100.00
623174	*HSBC Bank Brasil*	Brazil	100.00
086973	HSBC Seguros (Brasil) S.A.	Brazil	100.00
077884	HSBC Vida e Previdencia	Brazil	100.00
055688	*HSBC Latin America B.V.*	Netherlands	100.00
055681	*HSBC Argentina Holdings S.A.*	Argentina	100.00
086948	HSBC La Buenos Aires Seguros	Argentina	99.20
055684	*HSBC Chacabuco Inversiones AR*	Argentina	60.00
077661	HSBC-New York Life Se Retiro	Argentina	60.00
077662	HSBC-New York Life Seg Vida AR	Argentina	60.00
051273	*HSBC Overseas Hldgs (UK) Ltd*	United Kingdom	100.00
051274	*HSBC North America Hdgs Inc*	DE	100.00
051275	*HSBC Investments (NA) Inc*	DE	100.00
050643	*HSBC Finance Corporation*	DE	100.00
055677	*BFC Ireland (Holdings) Limited*	Ireland	100.00
077705	BFC Insurance Limited	Ireland	100.00
089026	BFC Insurance (Life) Limited	Ireland	100.00
088759	BFC Reinsurance Limited	Ireland	100.00
050633	*HFC Company LLC*	DE	100.00
050292	*Household Insurance Group*	DE	100.00
004698	HSBC Insurance Company of DE	DE	100.00
060344	Household Life Ins Co of DE	DE	100.00
009129	Household Life Ins Co	MI	100.00
008256	First Central Nat Life of NY	NY	100.00
009573	Household Life Ins Co of AZ	AZ	100.00
055676	*Household Global Funding, Inc.*	DE	100.00
055680	*Household Intl Europe Ltd*	United Kingdom	100.00
623172	*HFC Bank Limited*	Ireland	100.00
086142	Hamilton Insurance Company Ltd	United Kingdom	100.00
055429	*HSBC North America Inc*		100.00
030885	*HSBC USA Inc*	MD	100.00
614867	*HSBC Bank USA National Assoc*	VA	100.00
076809	HSBC Reinsurance (USA), Inc.	VT	100.00
075553	HSBC Life Insurance (Cayman)	Cayman Islands	100.00
073501	HSBC Insurance SPC Ltd	Cayman Islands	
058052	**HUMANA INC**		
050929	*CareNetwork Inc*	WI	100.00
007574	Humana Insurance Company	WI	100.00
064068	Humana Employers Hth Pln of GA	GA	100.00
060248	Humana Insurance Company of KY	KY	100.00
051649	*Humana Health Plan Interests*	LA	100.00
068835	Humana Health Benefit Pl of LA	LA	100.00
068626	Humana Wisconsin Health	WI	100.00
064794	Independent Care Health Plan	WI	50.00
055164	*CompBenefits Corporation*	DE	100.00
055165	*Humana/CompBenefits Inc*	FL	100.00
064631	American Dental Plan of NC	NC	100.00
064491	American Dental Providers AR	AR	100.00
064760	CompBenefits Company	FL	100.00
006118	CompBenefits Insurance Co	TX	100.00
055162	*Dental Care Plus Management*	IL	100.00
064759	CompBenefits Dental Inc	IL	100.00
064522	DentiCare Inc	TX	100.00
055163	*HumanaCares Inc*	FL	100.00
064885	CompBenefits of Alabama Inc	AL	100.00
051284	*CPHP Holdings Inc*	FL	100.00
068925	CarePlus Health Plans Inc	FL	100.00
059270	*KMG America Corporation*	SC	100.00
006604	Kanawha Insurance Company	SC	100.00
050778	*Emphesys Inc*	DE	100.00
008845	Emphesys Insurance Company	TX	100.00
060099	Humana Benefit Plan of IL	IL	100.00
050779	*HumanaDental Inc*	DE	100.00
068645	Dental Concern Inc	KY	100.00
060182	Dental Concern Ltd	IL	100.00
007254	HumanaDental Insurance Company	WI	100.00
009494	Humana Health Ins Co FL Inc	FL	100.00
068898	Humana Health Plan Inc	KY	100.00
051648	*CHA Service Company*	KY	100.00
064403	CHA HMO Inc	KY	100.00
068573	Humana Health Plan of Ohio	OH	100.00
060162	Humana Health Plans of PR Inc	PR	100.00
068903	Humana Health Plan of TX	TX	100.00
060595	Humana Insurance Company of NY	NY	100.00
008265	Humana Ins of Puerto Rico Inc	PR	100.00
068907	Humana Medical Plan Inc	FL	100.00
064915	Humana AdvantageCare Plan	FL	100.00
064893	Humana Medical Plan of Utah	UT	100.00
052029	*PHP Companies Incorporated*	TN	100.00
064425	Cariten Health Plan Inc	TN	100.00
007835	Cariten Insurance Company	TN	100.00
064302	Preferred Hlth Partnership	TN	100.00
050854	**IAC GROUP INC**		
008437	Individual Assur Lf Hlth & Acc	MO	100.00
068070	Westport Life Ins Co	AZ	100.00
050668	**ILLINOIS AGRICULTURAL ASSN**		
002249	COUNTRY Mutual Insurance Co	IL	
006292	Cotton States Life Ins Co	GA	25.00
000299	Cotton States Mutual Ins Co	GA	
002133	Shield Insurance Company	GA	100.00
002248	COUNTRY Casualty Ins Co	IL	100.00
002250	COUNTRY Preferred Insurance Co	IL	100.00
000480	Holyoke Mutual Ins Co in Salem	MA	
000608	Middlesex Mutual Assurance Co	CT	
001888	MSI Preferred Insurance Co	IL	100.00
004035	Modern Service Insurance Co	IL	100.00
050669	*Illinois Agricultural Hldng Co*	IL	
006294	COUNTRY Life Ins Co	IL	100.00
006292	Cotton States Life Ins Co	GA	75.00
009084	COUNTRY Investors Life Assur	IL	100.00
620841	*COUNTRY Trust Bank*	IL	100.00
064553	**INDEPENDENCE BLUE CROSS**		
050966	*AmeriHealth Inc*	PA	100.00
012357	AmeriHealth Casualty Ins Co	DE	100.00
007887	AmeriHealth Ins Co of NJ	NJ	100.00

AMB#	COMPANY	DOMICILE	% OWN
050967	*AmeriHealth Integrated Benefit*	DE	100.00
064139	AmeriHealth HMO Inc	PA	100.00
051831	*AmeriHealth Integrated C Mgmt*	PA	100.00
051832	*AmeriHealth Mercy Health Plan*	PA	50.00
064003	Select Health of S Carolina	SC	100.00
068924	Keystone Health Plan East Inc	PA	100.00
064191	Vista Health Plan Inc	PA	100.00
064396	Healthcare Delaware Inc	DE	100.00
050968	*Independence Holdings Inc*	PA	100.00
060163	Puerto Rico Health Plan Inc	PR	100.00
060332	Independence Insurance Inc	DE	100.00
009137	QCC Insurance Company	PA	100.00
064944	Region 6 Rx Corporation	PA	100.00
064466	Inter-County Health Plan Inc	PA	50.00
064467	Inter-County Hospitalization	PA	50.00
060132	**INDEPENDENT ORDER OF FORESTERS**		
055508	*Forester Holdings (Europe) Ltd*	United Kingdom	100.00
087352	Forester Life Limited	United Kingdom	100.00
066847	Unity Life of Canada	Canada	100.00
050666	**INDIANA FARM BUREAU INC**		
007168	United Farm Family Life Ins Co	IN	100.00
007172	United Home Life Ins Co	IN	75.00
000350	United Farm Family Mutual Ins	IN	
003206	Countryway Insurance Co	NY	100.00
000527	UFB Casualty Insurance Company	IN	100.00
007172	United Home Life Ins Co	IN	25.00
006554	**INDUSTRIAL ALLIANCE INS & FINL**		
052462	*Corporation Financiere L'Excel*		100.00
066890	Excellence Life Insurance Co	Canada	98.00
060682	IA American Life Insurance Co	GA	100.00
067738	Industrial Alliance Auto Home	Canada	100.00
006838	Industrial Alliance Pac I&F Sv	Canada	99.90
076394	IAP Insurance Corporation	British Virgin Islands	100.00
087008	Industrial-Alliance Pacif Gen	Canada	100.00
085144	**ING GROEP N.V.**		
085143	*ING Verzekeringen N.V.*	Netherlands	100.00
090082	ING Afore S.A. de C.V.	Mexico	100.00
090083	ING Asigurari de Viata S.A.	Romania	100.00
077290	*ING Australia Holdings Limited*	Australia	100.00
078524	*ING Australia Limited*	Australia	51.00
077668	ANZ Life Assurance Co Ltd	Australia	100.00
090084	ING General Ins Pty Ltd	Australia	100.00
052174	*ING Life Australia Hldgs Pty*	Australia	100.00
086826	ING Life Limited	Australia	100.00
090081	Armstrong Jones Life Asr Pty	Australia	100.00
090086	ING Greek Life Ins Co SA	Greece	100.00
090085	ING Greek General Ins Co SA	Greece	100.00
051113	*ING Insurance Intern BV*	Netherlands	100.00
050817	*ING America Insurance Holdings*	DE	100.00
050821	*Lion Connecticut Holdings Inc*	CT	100.00
052172	*IB Holdings LLC*	VA	100.00
075040	New Providence Insurance Co	Cayman Islands	100.00
051079	*ING International Ins Holdings*	CT	100.00
052173	*ILICA, Inc.*	CT	100.00
090093	ING Life Insurance Company Ltd	China	100.00
006895	ING Life Insurance and Annuity	CT	100.00
008388	ING USA Annuity & Life Ins Co	IA	100.00
006846	ReliaStar Life Insurance Co	MN	100.00
087558	ING Re (UK) Limited	United Kingdom	100.00
006157	ReliaStar Life Ins Co of NY	NY	100.00
007029	Security Life of Denver Ins Co	CO	100.00
006718	Midwestern United Life Ins Co	IN	100.00
060685	Whisperingwind III LLC	SC	100.00
090091	Security Life of Denver Intl	Bermuda	100.00
090080	ING Life Ins Co (Japan) Ltd	Japan	100.00
087173	ING Life Insurance Korea Ltd	South Korea	85.10
090088	ING Nat-Nederlanden Magyar	Hungary	100.00
089153	ING pojist'ovna, a.s.	Czech Republic	100.00
052175	*ING Re Holding (NL) BV*	Netherlands	100.00
077340	ING Re (Netherlands) N.V.	Netherlands	100.00
083419	Nat-Nederlanden Intl Schadever	Netherlands	100.00
077078	ING Seguros de Vida S.A.	Chile	100.00
052177	*ING Verzekeringen NL BV*	Netherlands	100.00
052176	*ING SFE B.V.*	Netherlands	100.00
052178	*Nat-Nederlanden NL BV*	Netherlands	100.00
083308	Movir N.V. te Nieuwegein	Netherlands	100.00
083322	Nat-Nederlanden Levensverzek	Netherlands	100.00
083420	Nat-Nederlanden Schadeverz Mij	Netherlands	100.00
083320	ING Insurance Services N.V.	Netherlands	100.00
089817	Koolhaas Verzekeringen N.V.	Netherlands	100.00
083426	RVS Levensverzekering N.V.	Netherlands	100.00
083415	RVS Schadeverzekering N.V.	Netherlands	100.00
090089	ING Zivotna Poistvna a.s.	Slovakia	100.00
077710	ING Zivotni pojist'ovna N.V.	Czech Republic	100.00
083658	Nationale-Nederlanden General	Spain	100.00
083660	Nationale-Nederlanden Vida	Spain	100.00
090087	*Seguros de Comercial SA de CV*	Mexico	100.00

AMB#	COMPANY	DOMICILE	% OWN
051482	**INSURANCE INVESTMENT COMPANY**		
006342	Equitable Life & Casualty	UT	100.00
055417	**INTERDENT SERVICE CORPORATION**		
064720	Dedicated Dental Systems Inc	CA	100.00
051365	**INTERMOUNTAIN HEALTH CARE INC**		
064078	SelectHealth Inc	UT	100.00
068430	SelectHealth Benefit Assur Co	UT	100.00
076775	Healthcare Captive Ins Co	AZ	100.00
005920	**INVESTORS HERITAGE CAP CORP.**		
006580	Investors Heritage Life Ins Co	KY	100.00
050233	**IOWA FARM BUREAU FEDERATION**		
058512	*FBL Financial Group Inc*	IA	64.60
060315	EquiTrust Life Insurance Co	IA	100.00
006362	Farm Bureau Life Ins Co	IA	100.00
003757	**ISMIE MUTUAL INSURANCE CO**		
012435	ISMIE Indemnity Company	IL	100.00
007004	Physicians Benefits Trust Life	IL	100.00
055418	**IVORY HOLDCO INC**		
055419	*Bright Now! Dental Inc*	CA	100.00
060166	ConsumerHealth Inc	CA	100.00
050664	**J AND P HOLDINGS, INC.**		
003138	First Chicago Insurance Co	IL	100.00
051626	*United National Ins Grp, Inc.*	IL	85.00
008442	United Security Lf & H Ins Co	IL	100.00
050712	**J. MACK ROBINSON & FAMILY**		
058017	*Atlantic American Corporation*	GA	66.67
000158	American Southern Insurance Co	KS	100.00
010644	American Safety Insurance Co	GA	100.00
006145	Bankers Fidelity Life Ins Co	GA	100.00
003050	Delta Fire & Casualty Ins Co	GA	100.00
006307	Delta Life Ins Co	GA	100.00
051564	**JAMEL LTD.**		
009362	Great Western Ins Co	UT	100.00
006458	Great Western Life Ins Co	MT	100.00
051872	**JEFFERSON NATIONAL FINANCIAL**		
006475	Jefferson National Life Ins Co	TX	100.00
058949	**JM FAMILY ENTERPRISES, INC**		
010863	Courtesy Insurance Company	FL	100.00
008994	JMIC Life Insurance Company	FL	100.00
064585	**KAISER FOUNDATION HEALTH PLAN**		
068585	Kaiser Fdn Health Pl of the NW	OR	100.00
068551	Kaiser Fdn H Pl of the Mid-Atl	MD	100.00
068516	Kaiser Fdn Health Plan of CO	CO	100.00
068528	Kaiser Foundation Hlth P of GA	GA	100.00
068577	Kaiser Foundation Hth Pl of OH	OH	100.00
060154	Kaiser Permanente Ins Co	CA	100.00
075666	Lokahi Assurance, Ltd.	HI	100.00
057375	Oak Tree Assurance Ltd	VT	100.00
088613	Ordway International, Ltd.	Bermuda	100.00
075119	Ordway Indemnity Ltd	Bermuda	100.00
006605	**KANSAS CITY LIFE INS CO**		
006854	Old American Ins Co	MO	100.00
007104	Sunset Life Ins Co of America	MO	100.00
055892	**KHL HOLDINGS LLC**		
060296	Kentucky Home Life Ins Co	KY	100.00
055427	**LAWRENZ FAMILY TRUST**		
055428	*Pension Administrators Inc*		97.00
007246	BEST Life and Health Ins Co	TX	100.00
086120	**LEGAL & GENERAL GROUP PLC**		
055754	*Legal & General Hldgs (France)*	France	100.00
083080	Legal & General (France)	France	99.90
083081	Legal Gen Risques Divers (FR)	France	88.70
055755	*Legal & General Ins Hldgs Ltd*	United Kingdom	100.00
084279	Legal & General Assur Society	United Kingdom	100.00
087423	Legal & General Ins Ltd	United Kingdom	100.00
088783	Legal & General Pensions Ltd	United Kingdom	100.00
087482	Nationwide Life Ltd	United Kingdom	100.00
055753	*Legal & Gen Invest Mgmt Hldgs*	United Kingdom	100.00
087422	Legal&Gen Assur Pens Mgmt Ltd	United Kingdom	100.00
051875	*Legal & Gen Overseas Oper Ltd*	United Kingdom	100.00
074305	BLG Insurance Ltd	Guernsey	100.00
051876	*Legal & Gen America Inc*	DE	100.00
006468	Banner Life Ins Co	MD	100.00
076681	First British American Reins	SC	100.00
060588	First British American Re II	SC	100.00
088887	First British Bermuda Reins Co	Bermuda	100.00
006734	William Penn Life Ins Co of NY	NY	100.00
083264	Legal &Gen Nederland Leven	Netherlands	100.00
051581	**LEWER FINANCIAL SERVICES L. P.**		
007393	Lewer Life Ins Co	MO	100.00

AMB#	COMPANY	DOMICILE	% OWN
051114	**LIBERTY MUTUAL HOLDING CO INC**		
051115	*LMHC Mass Holdings Inc*	MA	100.00
051116	*Liberty Mutual Group Inc*	MA	100.00
002159	Employers Ins Co of Wausau	WI	100.00
002282	Liberty Mutual Fire Ins Co	WI	100.00
002283	Liberty Mutual Insurance Co	MA	100.00
050249	*Berkeley Management Corp*	TX	100.00
012410	Liberty Lloyds of Texas Ins Co	TX	100.00
010764	First Liberty Ins Corp	IL	100.00
001812	Liberty Insurance Corporation	IL	100.00
050206	*Liberty Insurance Holdings Inc*	DE	93.06
050209	*LIH US P&C Corporation*	DE	100.00
051117	*Gulf States AIF Inc.*	TX	100.00
012568	America First Lloyds Ins Co	TX	100.00
002254	Indiana Insurance Company	IN	100.00
002253	Consolidated Insurance Co	IN	100.00
002394	Peerless Insurance Company	NH	100.00
002186	America First Insurance Co	NH	100.00
011325	Colorado Casualty Ins Co	NH	100.00
000349	Excelsior Insurance Company	NH	100.00
012076	Golden Eagle Insurance Corp	CA	100.00
000900	Hawkeye-Security Insurance Co	WI	100.00
001814	Liberty Northwest Ins Corp	OR	100.00
012533	North Pacific Insurance Co	OR	100.00
012532	Oregon Automobile Ins Co	OR	100.00
050207	*Liberty-USA Corporation*	DE	100.00
050208	*National Corporation*	DE	100.00
003672	National Insurance Association	IN	100.00
002088	Peerless Indemnity Ins Co	IL	100.00
002323	Midwestern Indemnity Company	OH	100.00
002322	Mid-American Fire & Cas Co	OH	100.00
002393	Netherlands Insurance Co	NH	100.00
058437	*Ohio Casualty Corporation*	OH	8.00
050204	*Summit Holding Southeast Inc*	FL	100.00
012158	Bridgefield Employers Ins Co	FL	100.00
011812	Bridgefield Casualty Ins Co	FL	100.00
058462	*Safeco Corporation*	WA	100.00
002286	American Economy Insurance Co	IN	100.00
002290	American States Ins Co of TX	TX	100.00
002287	American States Insurance Co	IN	100.00
002289	American States Preferred Ins	IN	100.00
002446	First National Ins Co of Amer	WA	100.00
050093	*General America Corp*	WA	100.00
050094	*General America Corp of Texas*	TX	100.00
003610	American States Lloyds Ins Co	TX	100.00
001896	Safeco Lloyds Insurance Co	TX	100.00
002447	General Ins Co of America	WA	100.00
012053	Safeco Insurance Company IN	IN	100.00
002448	Safeco Ins Co of America	WA	100.00
012425	Safeco Insurance Company of OR	OR	100.00
004240	Safeco National Insurance Co	NH	100.00
001867	Safeco Surplus Lines Ins Co	WA	100.00
002709	Safeco Ins Co of Illinois	IL	100.00
004938	Insurance Company of Illinois	IL	100.00
002087	Liberty Insurance Underwriters	NY	100.00
055255	*Liberty Intl Hldgs LLC*	DE	100.00
050211	*Liberty International Holdings*	DE	100.00
078738	Liberty Insurance Limited	Vietnam	100.00
050216	*Liberty Intern Asia Pac Hldgs*	DE	100.00
050106	*Liberty Citystate Holdings PTE*	Singapore	100.00
083999	Liberty Insurance PTE Ltd	Singapore	100.00
055250	*CI Investments Ltd.*	Hong Kong	99.99
089000	Liberty International Ins Ltd	Hong Kong	68.00
089002	Liberty Intl (H.K.) Ltd.	Hong Kong	85.37
051119	*Kritiya Tun Co. Ltd.*	Thailand	49.00
051120	*Tun Kaoklai Co. Ltd.*	Thailand	99.99
089001	LMG Insurance Company Limited	Thailand	74.99
083996	Liberty Intl Iberia S.L.S.	Spain	92.70
050215	*Liberty Intern Brazil Ltda*	Brazil	70.51
086854	Indiana Seguros S/A	Brazil	55.21
087994	Liberty Seguros S.A.	Brazil	100.00
084357	Seguros Caracas de Liberty Mut	Venezuela	99.11
055252	*Liberty International Chile SA*	Chile	99.99
077058	Liberty Cia de Seg Generales	Chile	99.88
050213	*Liberty Intern Latin Amer Hldg*	DE	100.00
051121	*LI (Columbia) Holdings Ltd*	Bermuda	100.00
050214	*LILA (Colombia) Holdings Ltd*	Bermuda	100.00
090722	Liberty Seguros S.A.	Colombia	94.70
090723	Liberty Seguros de Vida S.A.	Colombia	57.59
084356	Liberty ART SA	Argentina	99.90
089971	Liberty Seguros Argentina S.A.	Argentina	99.90
051122	*Liberty Intl (Spain) Hldgs LLC*	DE	100.00
083996	Liberty Intl Iberia S.L.S.	Spain	7.30
087425	Liberty Mutual Ins Europe Ltd	United Kingdom	100.00
055251	*Liberty Spain Insurance Group*	DE	100.00
086393	Liberty Seguros, Cia Seg y Re	Spain	99.98
083442	Genesis Seg Generales Seg Reas	Spain	100.00
089970	Liberty Seguros S.A.	Portugal	100.00
085905	Liberty Sigorta A.S.	Turkey	98.20
078741	Seker Hayat A.S.	Turkey	98.76
006627	Liberty Life Assur of Boston	MA	90.00
055253	*Liberty Mut Captive Hldgs LLC*	DE	100.00
056785	Lexco Limited	Bermuda	100.00
055254	*Liberty Mutual Hldgs (BM) Ltd*	Bermuda	100.00
075757	Arlington Insurance Co Ltd	Bermuda	100.00
050194	*Liberty Mutual Equity LLC*	MA	100.00
003028	Liberty Personal Insurance Co	NH	100.00
012078	Liberty Surplus Ins Corp	NH	100.00
003795	LM General Insurance Company	IL	100.00
010765	LM Insurance Corporation	IL	100.00
003794	LM Personal Insurance Company	IL	100.00
004785	LM Property & Casualty Ins Co	IN	100.00
058437	*Ohio Casualty Corporation*	OH	78.00
002378	Ohio Casualty Insurance Co	OH	100.00
000128	American Fire & Casualty Co	OH	100.00
002379	Ohio Security Insurance Co	OH	100.00
011354	West American Insurance Co	IN	100.00
012077	San Diego Insurance Company	CA	100.00
085093	Wausau Insurance Co (UK) Ltd	United Kingdom	100.00
050205	*Wausau Service Corporation*	WI	100.00
002550	Wausau Business Insurance Co	WI	100.00
004274	Wausau General Insurance Co	WI	100.00
000956	Wausau Underwriters Ins Co	WI	100.00
013107	Liberty Mutual Personal Ins Co	MA	100.00
089972	St. James Insurance Co Ltd	Bermuda	100.00
012569	Liberty County Mutual Ins Co	TX	
000588	Liberty Mutual Mid-Atlantic	PA	
000662	Montgomery Mutual Ins Co	MD	
052358	**LIECHTENSTEINISCHE LANDESBANK**		
052359	*swisspartners Invest Network*	Switzerland	61.74
072461	swisspartners Ins Co SPC Ltd	Cayman Islands	100.00
090233	swisspartners Versicherung AG	Liechtenstein	100.00
050837	**LIFETIME HEALTHCARE INC**		
055374	*Excellus Ventures, Inc.*	NY	.02
060082	Excellus Health Plan Inc	NY	100.00
055374	*Excellus Ventures, Inc.*	NY	99.98
007131	MedAmerica Insurance Co	PA	22.40
073224	MIG Assurance Cayman Ltd	Cayman Islands	100.00
050838	*MedAmerica Inc*	NY	100.00
007131	MedAmerica Insurance Co	PA	77.60
060658	MedAmerica Ins Co of Florida	FL	100.00
060021	MedAmerica Ins Co of New York	NY	100.00
058709	**LINCOLN NATIONAL CORPORATION**		
006904	First Penn-Pacific Life Ins Co	IN	100.00
006664	Lincoln National Life Ins Co	IN	100.00
051557	*Lincoln Financial Holdings LLC*	DE	100.00
060591	LFG South Carolina Reinsurance	SC	100.00
052535	*Lincoln Financial Hldgs LLC II*	DE	100.00
060704	Lincoln Reinsurance Co of VT I	VT	100.00
006239	Lincoln Life & Annuity Co NY	NY	100.00
066532	Lincoln Reinsurance Co of SC	SC	100.00
060705	Lincoln Reinsurance Co SC II	SC	100.00
057025	Lincoln Nat Reins Co Barbados	Barbados	100.00
076657	Lincoln Re Co of Bermuda Ltd	Bermuda	100.00
050177	**LOEWS CORPORATION**		
058705	*CNA Financial Corporation*	DE	90.10
059021	*CNA Financial Capital I*	DE	100.00
059022	*CNA Financial Capital II*	DE	100.00
059023	*CNA Financial Capital III*	DE	100.00
050185	*Continental Corporation*	NY	100.00
002128	Continental Casualty Company	IL	100.00
050184	*CNA Europe Holdings Ltd*	United Kingdom	72.72
086301	CNA Insurance Company Limited	United Kingdom	100.00
078547	Maritime Insurance Company Ltd	United Kingdom	100.00
002127	American Cas Co Reading, PA	PA	100.00
002132	Valley Forge Insurance Co	PA	100.00
077526	CNA Aseg Riesgo Trabajo SA	Argentina	98.00
058155	*CNA Surety Corp*	DE	60.14
000974	Western Surety Company	SD	100.00
011333	Surety Bonding Co of America	SD	100.00
002785	Universal Surety of America	SD	100.00
003538	Columbia Casualty Company	IL	100.00
006280	Continental Assurance Co	IL	100.00
002118	Continental Insurance Co	PA	100.00
084388	CNA Ins (Intern Ag) AU Pty Ltd	Australia	100.00
001882	Continental Ins Co of NJ	NJ	100.00
002212	First Insurance Co of Hawaii	HI	50.00
001747	First Fire & Cas Ins of Hawaii	HI	100.00
001748	First Indemnity Ins of Hawaii	HI	100.00
012228	First Security Insurance of HI	HI	100.00
002129	National Fire Ins Hartford	IL	100.00
086627	North Rock Insurance Co Ltd	Bermuda	100.00
002131	Transportation Insurance Co	IL	100.00
072376	Continental Reins Corp Int	Bermuda	100.00
050801	**LOUISIANA DEALER SERVICES INS**		
009125	First Assur Life of America	LA	100.00
009325	Performance Life of America	LA	100.00
013840	Loss Deficiency Surety Ins Co	LA	100.00
050802	*Versant Holdings Inc*	MS	57.20

AMB#	COMPANY	DOMICILE	% OWN
012477	Versant Casualty Insurance Co	MS	100.00
060339	Versant Life Insurance Company	MS	100.00
068440	**LOUISIANA HLTH SVC & INDEMNITY**		
068990	HMO Louisiana Inc	LA	100.00
060085	Southern National Life Ins	LA	100.00
051261	**LSV PARTNERS LLC**		
060033	Florida Combined Life Ins Co	FL	100.00
052454	*Life & Specialty Ventures LLC*		9.90
052454	*Life & Specialty Ventures LLC*		44.10
009350	USAble Life	AR	100.00
052502	**LUXOTTICA US HOLDINGS CORP**		
052787	*United States Shoe Corporation*	DE	100.00
064516	Pearle Vision Mgd Cr - HMO TX	TX	100.00
050907	**MAGELLAN HEALTH SERVICES INC**		
055482	*Green Spring Health Services*		100.00
055483	*Advocare of Tennessee, Inc.*		100.00
055484	*Premier Holdings, Inc.*		100.00
064433	Premier Behavioral Systs of TN	TN	100.00
064650	Magellan Health Services of CA	CA	100.00
052514	*Magellan Behavioral Health Inc*		100.00
064880	Tennessee Behavioral Health	TN	100.00
066866	**MANULIFE FINANCIAL CORPORATION**		
006688	Manufacturers Life Ins Co	Canada	100.00
087846	First North American Ins Co	Canada	100.00
078479	Manufacturers Life Ins Co (PH)	Philippines	100.00
624313	*Manulife Bank of Canada*	Canada	100.00
066879	Manulife Canada Ltd	Canada	100.00
084570	Manulife Europe Rueckvers-AG	Germany	100.00
051579	*Manulife Holdings (Alberta)*	Canada	100.00
051762	*John Hancock Holdings (DE) LLC*	DE	100.00
050895	*Manufacturers Investment Corp*	MI	100.00
006681	John Hancock Life Ins Co USA	MI	100.00
009074	John Hancock Life & Health Ins	MA	100.00
060056	John Hancock Life Ins Co NY	NY	100.00
057397	*Manulife Reinsurance Ltd*	Bermuda	100.00
078405	Manulife Reinsurance (BM) Ltd		100.00
073955	John Hancock Ins Co of VT	VT	100.00
051763	*John Hancock Intl Hldgs Inc*	MA	100.00
086348	Manulife Hldgs Berhad	Malaysia	45.90
051764	*John Hancock International Inc*	MA	100.00
078478	John Hancock Tianan Life Ins	China	50.00
078473	CIMB Sun Life, PT	Indonesia	96.00
051765	*Manulife Holdings (Bermuda)*	Bermuda	100.00
073838	Manufacturers Life Reins Ltd	Barbados	100.00
072646	Manufacturers P&C Ltd	Barbados	100.00
051766	*Manulife International Hldgs*	Bermuda	100.00
078477	Manulife (International) Ltd	Hong Kong	100.00
078474	Manulife-Sinochem Life Ins Co	China	51.00
078475	Manulife Ins (TH) Public Co	Thailand	100.00
083988	Manulife (Singapore) Pte Ltd	Singapore	100.00
078476	Manulife (Vietnam) Limited	Vietnam	100.00
051767	*MLI Resources Inc.*	Canada	100.00
084418	Manulife Life Insurance Co	Japan	100.00
078472	Manulife Indonesia, PT	Indonesia	80.00
052554	*Manulife Holdings (USA) LLC*	DE	100.00
073255	John Hancock Reassr Co Ltd	Bermuda	100.00
085419	**MAPFRE S.A.**		
090072	Caja Castilla la Mancha	Spain	50.00
086989	*MAPFRE America S. A.*	Spain	88.90
086149	Aseguradora Mundial, S.A.	Panama	65.00
084817	Centro Americana, S.A.	El Salvador	72.90
055186	*Inversiones Peruanas*	Spain	100.00
084337	Mapfre Peru Vida Cia Seg Reas	Peru	67.30
055188	*Mapfre Argentina Holding S.A.*	Argentina	100.00
084211	Mapfre Argentina A.R.T. S.A.	Argentina	99.40
084212	Mapfre Argentina Seguros SA	Argentina	100.00
077463	Aconcagua Seg de Retiro SA	Argentina	76.40
090074	Mapfre Salud S.A.	Argentina	95.00
084213	Mapfre Argentina Seg de Vida	Argentina	80.00
077221	Mapfre Atlas Cia de Seg SA	Ecuador	58.20
050864	*MAPFRE Chile Seguros S.A.*	Chile	100.00
077000	Mapfre Cia Seg Gen Chile SA	Chile	75.50
055189	*Mapfre Chile Vida S.A.*	Chile	100.00
084815	Mapfre Cia de Seg Vida Chile	Chile	100.00
084814	MAPFRE Colombia Vida Seg S.A.	Colombia	94.30
084813	MAPFRE Paraguay Cia de Seguros	Paraguay	89.30
084338	Mapfre Peru, Cia Seg y Reaseg	Peru	99.00
050640	*MAPFRE PRAICO Corp.*	PR	100.00
055190	*Mapfre Dominicana S.A.*	Dominican Republic	100.00
084257	Mapfre BHD Cia de Se SA	Dominican Republic	50.00
007981	MAPFRE Life Insurance Company	PR	65.40
004290	MAPFRE Pan American Ins Co	PR	100.00
011116	MAPFRE PRAICO Insurance Co	PR	100.00
003649	MAPFRE Preferred Risk Ins Co	PR	100.00
077616	Mapfre La Seguridad CA de Seg	Venezuela	99.50
084812	MAPFRE Seg Generales Colombia	Colombia	94.20
086287	Mapfre Tepeyac S.A.	Mexico	55.70
084811	Mapfre Uruguay Cia de Seg SA	Uruguay	100.00

AMB#	COMPANY	DOMICILE	% OWN
085883	Mapfre Vera Cruz Seguradora	Brazil	90.20
052702	*MAPFRE Participacoes Ltda.*	Brazil	99.90
088770	MAPFRE NOSSA CAIXA Vida e Prev	Brazil	51.00
089989	MAPFRE Riscos Especiais	Brazil	100.00
085565	Mapfre Vera Cruz Vida e Prev.	Brazil	86.30
077174	Real Uruguaya de Seguros S.A.	Uruguay	100.00
087130	Mapfre Asistencia Compania	Spain	100.00
086801	Mapfre Empresas Cia de Seg	Spain	100.00
072417	Industrial Re Musini	Luxembourg	100.00
086153	Mapfre Caucion y Credito	Spain	100.00
055187	*Mapfre America Caucion*	Spain	100.00
078688	Mapfre Seg Credito SA Mapfre	Colombia	94.90
077063	Mapfre Garantias y Credito SA	Chile	100.00
077001	Mapfre Seguradora de Garantias	Brazil	100.00
090073	Mapfre Seguradora de Credito	Brazil	100.00
078009	Mapfre Seguros de Credito S.A.	Mexico	100.00
090154	Mapfre Familiar Cia Seg y Reas	Spain	100.00
052169	*Mapfre Internacional S.A.*	Spain	87.50
058350	*Mapfre U.S.A. Corp.*	MA	100.00
050299	*ACIC Holding Company Inc*	RI	100.00
002065	American Commerce Insurance Co	OH	100.00
003131	Commerce West Insurance Co	CA	100.00
000869	State-Wide Insurance Company	NY	100.00
002851	Citation Insurance Company(MA)	MA	100.00
004663	Commerce Insurance Company	MA	100.00
002365	Mapfre Insurance Company	NJ	100.00
010805	MAPFRE Ins Co of Florida	FL	100.00
084974	Mapfre Genel Sigorta A.S.	Turkey	80.00
090597	Mapfre Genel Yasam A.S.	Turkey	100.00
078690	Mapfre Insular Insurance Corp	Philippines	74.90
084226	Mapfre Seguros Gerais SA	Portugal	100.00
086278	MAPFRE RE Cia de Reaseguros SA	Spain	91.50
085880	CIAR (Cie Int Assur de Reassr)	Belgium	100.00
050865	MAPFRE Chile Reaseguros S.A.	Chile	100.00
084818	Caja Reaseguradora de Chile SA	Chile	99.80
090596	Mapfre Re do Brasil Cia Reas	Brazil	100.00
085557	Mapfre Vida SA de Seg y Res	Spain	99.90
083114	Bankinter Seguros de Vida	Spain	50.00
083407	Musini Vida Seguros y Reas	Spain	100.00
056962	Maplux Reinsurance Company Ltd	Luxembourg	100.00
083645	Union Duero Cia Seg Vida	Spain	50.00
055470	**MARSHFIELD CLINIC**		
064207	Security Health Plan of WI	WI	100.00
006695	**MASSACHUSETTS MUTUAL LIFE INS**		
009062	C M Life Insurance Company	CT	100.00
007233	MML Bay State Life Ins Co	CT	100.00
055590	*MassMutual Holding, LLC*	DE	100.00
055589	*MML Capital Partners, LLC*	DE	100.00
055697	*Oppenheimer Acquisition Corp.*	DE	100.00
055695	*MassMutual International, LLC*	DE	100.00
073993	Mass Mutual (Asia) Ltd	Hong Kong	100.00
074226	Mass Mutual (Bermuda) Ltd	Bermuda	100.00
055633	*MassMutual Intl Hldg MSC Inc*	Hong Kong	100.00
089388	Mass Mutual Mercuries Life	Taiwan	100.00
084070	MassMutual Life Insurance Co	Japan	100.00
050892	**MAXIMUM CORPORATION**		
050893	*Insmark Company*	TX	100.00
007559	Champions Life Ins Co	TX	100.00
006204	Central Security Life Ins Co	TX	100.00
007404	Western American Life Ins Co	TX	100.00
052465	**MCS INC**		
064591	MCS Health Management Options	PR	100.00
060379	MCS Life Insurance Company	PR	100.00
051029	**MEDCO HEALTH SOLUTIONS INC**		
010747	Medco Containment Ins Co of NY	NY	100.00
006449	Medco Containment Life Ins Co	PA	100.00
051129	**MEDICA HOLDING COMPANY**		
051130	*Medica Affiliated Services*		100.00
011072	Medica Insurance Company	MN	100.00
068559	Medica Health Plans	MN	100.00
064445	Medica Health Plans of WI	WI	100.00
052511	**MEDICAL ASSOCIATES CLINIC P C**		
068612	Medical Associates Clinic WI	WI	100.00
068542	Medical Associates Health Plan	IA	100.00
004693	**MEDICAL MUTUAL OF OHIO**		
068944	Carolina Care Plan Inc	SC	100.00
006275	Consumers Life Ins Co	OH	100.00
064217	Medical Health Insuring Ohio	OH	100.00
055626	**MEDICAL SAVINGS INVESTMENT INC**		
007677	Medical Savings Insurance Co	IN	100.00
051324	**MEDICO MUTUAL INS HOLDING CO**		
051323	*Medico Holdings Inc*	NE	100.00
003150	Medico Insurance Company	NE	100.00

AMB#	COMPANY	DOMICILE	% OWN
085358	**MEIJI YASUDA LIFE INS CO**		
084179	Meiji Yasuda General Ins Co	Japan	100.00
006883	Pacific Guardian Life Co Ltd	HI	100.00
055883	**MEMBERS MUTUAL HOLDING COMPANY**		
055884	*Fidelity Lifecorp Inc*	DE	100.00
006386	Fidelity Life Association	IL	100.00
051100	**MERITER HEALTH SERVICES INC**		
068683	Physicians Plus Ins Corp	WI	67.00
058175	**METLIFE INC**		
072278	Exeter Reassurance Co Ltd	Bermuda	100.00
006119	First MetLife Investors Ins Co	NY	100.00
612913	*Metlife Bank NA*	NJ	100.00
059064	*MetLife Capital Trust II*	NY	100.00
059130	*MetLife Capital Trust III*	NY	100.00
059297	*MetLife Capital Trust IV*	DE	100.00
059299	*MetLife Capital Trust X*	DE	100.00
078437	*MetLife Chile Invers Limitada*	Chile	100.00
077081	Metlife Chile Seguros de Vida	Chile	100.00
007330	MetLife Insurance Co of CT	CT	86.70
051768	*MetLife European Hldgs Inc*	United Kingdom	100.00
088811	MetLife Assurance Limited	United Kingdom	100.00
078486	MetLife Europe Limited	Ireland	100.00
006125	MetLife Investors USA Ins Co	DE	100.00
051331	*MetLife International Holdings*	DE	100.00
087308	Metlife Insurance Limited	United Kingdom	100.00
077670	MetLife Insurance Limited	Australia	100.00
084308	Metropolitan Life Ins Co of HK	Hong Kong	100.00
078432	MetLife General Insurance Ltd	Australia	100.00
078452	MetLife Ins Co of Korea Ltd	South Korea	85.36
078433	MetLife Insurance S.A./NV	Belgium	99.90
087309	MetLife Limited	United Kingdom	100.00
078103	Metlife Pensiones Mexico, S.A.	Mexico	2.60
051640	*MetLife Worldwide Holdings Inc*	DE	100.00
078434	MetLife Towarystwo Ubezpieczen	Poland	100.00
087986	Metro Life Seg Previdencia	Brazil	74.60
077752	MetLife Seguros de Retiro SA	Argentina	96.90
050055	*MetLife Investors Group Inc*	NY	100.00
007330	MetLife Insurance Co of CT	CT	13.30
009075	MetLife Investors Insurance Co	MO	100.00
084188	Metlife Mexico, S.A.	Mexico	98.70
078436	MetLife Afore, S.A. de C.V.	Mexico	99.90
078452	MetLife Ins Co of Korea Ltd	South Korea	14.64
078103	Metlife Pensiones Mexico, S.A.	Mexico	97.50
076820	MetLife Reinsurance Co of SC	SC	100.00
078438	MetLife Taiwan Ins Co Ltd	Taiwan	100.00
006704	Metropolitan Life Ins Co	NY	100.00
050057	*GenAmerica Financial LLC*	MO	100.00
006439	General American Life Ins Co	MO	100.00
066883	MetLife Canada	Canada	100.00
073673	Missouri Reins (Barbados) Inc	Barbados	100.00
009043	New England Life Ins Co	MA	100.00
077171	Metropolitan Life Seg de Vida	Uruguay	100.00
004675	Metropolitan Prop & Cas Ins Co	RI	100.00
002276	Economy Fire & Casualty Co	IL	100.00
003831	Economy Preferred Insurance Co	IL	100.00
002761	Economy Premier Assurance Co	IL	100.00
003288	Metropolitan Casualty Ins Co	RI	100.00
002496	Metropolitan Direct P & C Ins	RI	100.00
002866	Metropolitan General Ins Co	RI	100.00
003733	Metropolitan Group P&C Ins Co	RI	100.00
087459	Metropolitan Reins Co (UK) Ltd	United Kingdom	100.00
052547	*Metropolitan Lloyds Inc*		100.00
011417	Metropolitan Lloyds Ins Co TX	TX	
009165	Metropolitan Tower Life Ins Co	DE	100.00
060656	MetLife Reinsurance Charleston	SC	100.00
060678	MetLife Reinsurance Co of VT	VT	100.00
056746	Newbury Insurance Co Ltd	Bermuda	100.00
058150	*Safeguard Hlth Enterprises Inc*	DE	100.00
068512	SafeGuard Health Plans (CA)	CA	100.00
064900	Safeguard Health Plans NV Corp	NV	100.00
064671	SafeGuard Health Plans (FL)	FL	100.00
064460	SafeGuard Health Plans (TX)	TX	100.00
008221	SafeHealth Life Ins Co	CA	100.00
055797	**MF SALTA COMPANY INC**		
008115	Westward Life Ins Co	AZ	61.28
050695	**MICHIGAN FARM BUREAU**		
002342	Farm Bureau Mutual Ins of MI	MI	
050696	*Michigan Farm Bureau Fin Corp*	MI	100.00
002341	Farm Bureau General Ins of MI	MI	100.00
006363	Farm Bureau Life Ins Co of MI	MI	100.00
050746	**MINNESOTA MUTUAL COMPANIES INC**		
050752	*Securian Holding Company*		100.00
050751	*Securian Financial Group Inc*		100.00
058027	*CNL Financial Corporation*		100.00
006214	Cherokee National Life Ins Co	GA	100.00
000183	CNL/Insurance America Inc	GA	100.00
006724	Minnesota Life Ins Company	MN	100.00

AMB#	COMPANY	DOMICILE	% OWN
009064	Securian Life Insurance Co	MN	100.00
011605	Securian Casualty Company	MN	100.00
011935	**MISSOURI FARM BUR FEDERATION**		
050902	*Missouri Farm Bureau Serv Inc*	MO	100.00
006364	Farm Bureau Life Ins Co of MO	MO	100.00
013072	Farm Bureau New Horizons Ins	MO	33.30
000360	Farm Bureau Town & Country MO	MO	100.00
013072	Farm Bureau New Horizons Ins	MO	33.30
006737	**MODERN WOODMEN OF AMERICA**		
620893	*MWA Bank*	IL	100.00
051101	**MOLINA HEALTHCARE INC**		
051782	*HCLB, Inc.*	MI	100.00
064179	Alliance for Community Health	MO	100.00
007144	Molina Healthcare Insurance Co	OH	100.00
064260	Molina Healthcare New Mexico	NM	100.00
064685	Molina Healthcare of MI Inc	MI	100.00
064865	Molina Healthcare of Ohio Inc	OH	100.00
064864	Molina Healthcare of Texas Inc	TX	100.00
064341	Molina Healthcare of UT Inc	UT	100.00
068949	Molina Healthcare of WA Inc	WA	100.00
064150	Molina Healthcare of CA Inc	CA	100.00
052543	**MORETON & COMPANY**		
051505	*Town & Country Holding Company*		85.94
008049	Town & Country Life Ins Co	UT	100.00
031216	**MORGAN STANLEY**		
052463	*Morgan Stanley Life Holding*		100.00
060701	Longevity Insurance Company	TX	100.00
018236	**MOTORISTS INSURANCE POOL**		
000132	American Hardware Mut Ins Co	OH	
006744	Motorists Life Ins Co	OH	30.00
000528	Iowa Mutual Insurance Co	IA	
003603	Iowa American Insurance Co	IA	100.00
000652	Motorists Mutual Ins Co	OH	
001760	MICO Insurance Company	OH	100.00
006744	Motorists Life Ins Co	OH	70.00
001964	Wilson Mutual Insurance Co	WI	
002339	Phenix Mutual Fire Ins Co	NH	
051566	**MOUNTAIN SERVICES CORPORATION**		
008354	Mountain Life Ins Co	TN	100.00
051921	**MULHEARN CORPORATION**		
007823	Mulhearn Protective Insurance	LA	95.00
086577	**MUNICH REINS COMPANY**		
052348	*Bell & Clements (Bermuda) Ltd.*	Bermuda	100.00
075591	B&C International Ins Co Ltd	Bermuda	100.00
086893	*ERGO Versicherungsgruppe AG*	Germany	94.70
086530	DKV Deutsche Krankenversicher	Germany	100.00
083124	DKV Belgium S.A.	Belgium	100.00
078750	DKV Luxembourg S.A.	Luxembourg	75.00
083245	DKV Seguros y Reas SA Espanola	Spain	100.00
083630	ERGO Generales Seguros y Re SA	Spain	100.00
083577	ERGO Vida Seguros y Reaseg SA	Spain	100.00
083627	Union Medica la Fuencisla	Spain	100.00
086901	VICTORIA Krankenversicherung	Germany	51.00
055259	*ERGO Achte Beteiligungsgesells*	Germany	100.00
086900	VICTORIA Lebensversicherungs	Germany	90.00
089016	VICTORIA Pensionskasse AG	Germany	100.00
086718	VICTORIA Versicherung AG	Germany	90.00
086902	DAS Deutscher Automobil Schutz	Germany	72.70
083431	DAS Defensa del Automovilista	Spain	100.00
086903	DAS Deutscher Automobil Schutz	Germany	100.00
078743	DAS HELLAS Allgemeine Rechtss	Greece	100.00
055257	*DAS Holding N.V.*	Netherlands	50.00
089681	DAS Nederlandse Rechtsbijstand	Netherlands	100.00
078744	DAS Jogvedelmi Biztosito Reszv	Hungary	99.90
078745	DAS Luxemburg Allgemeine Recht	Luxembourg	100.00
078746	DAS Oigusabikulude Kindlustuse	Estonia	100.00
083713	DAS Osterreichische Allgemeine	Austria	100.00
078747	DAS poist'ovna pravnej ochrany	Slovakia	100.00
083782	DAS pojistovna pravni ochrany	Czech Republic	100.00
078023	DAS Rechtsschutz-Versicherungs	Switzerland	99.80
078748	DAS SA belge d'assur de PJ	Belgium	100.00
078749	DAS Tow U Ochrony Prawnej SA	Poland	99.90
055258	*DAS UK Holdings Limited*	United Kingdom	100.00
087310	DAS Legal Expenses Ins Co Ltd	United Kingdom	100.00
086538	Hamburg-Mannheimer Rechts AG	Germany	51.00
055260	*ERGO International AG*	Germany	100.00
052350	*ERGO Austria Intl AG*	Austria	100.00
090229	ERGO zivotna poistovna	Slovakia	100.00
089175	ERGO Elukindlustuse AS	Estonia	100.00
055261	*ERGO Italia S.p.A.*	Italy	100.00
084893	ERGO Assicurazioni S.p.A.	Italy	80.00
084732	ERGO Previdenza S.p.A.	Italy	70.40
089176	ERGO Kindlustuse AS	Estonia	100.00
089192	Ergo Latvija dziviba AAS	Latvia	100.00
077928	AAS ERGO Latvija	Latvia	99.00
083811	Ergo Lietuva, UAB	Lithuania	100.00

AMB#	COMPANY	DOMICILE	% OWN
083954	Ergo Lietuva Gyvybes Draudimas	Lithuania	100.00
078751	ERGO RUSS Versicherung AG	Russia	73.20
090241	Basko Garant Russisch-Feutsche	Russia	100.00
078752	ERGO Varahalduse AS	Estonia	46.10
083229	ERGOISVICRE Emeklilik Hayat	Turkey	75.00
084970	ERGOISVICRE Sigorta A.S.	Turkey	100.00
086539	Ergo Life N.V.	Belgium	100.00
078754	Sopockie TU Ergo Hestia S.A.	Poland	100.00
052351	*Hestia Financial services S.A.*	Poland	89.30
078753	MTU Moje Towarzystwo Ubez S.A.	Poland	100.00
078755	STU na Zycie Ergo Hestia S.A.	Poland	93.00
078758	VICTORIA General Ins Co S.A.	Greece	100.00
077312	VICTORIA Internacional de PT	Portugal	100.00
078760	VICTORIA-Seguros de Vida, SA	Portugal	100.00
078761	VICTORIA-Seguros S.A.	Portugal	100.00
078759	VICTORIA Life Insurance Co SA	Greece	96.90
090232	Victoria osiguranje d.d.	Croatia	50.10
078762	VICTORIA-VOLKSBANKEN Biztosito	Hungary	50.10
078763	VICTORIA-VOLKSBANKEN Eletbizto	Hungary	50.10
078765	VICTORIA-VOLKSBANKEN Poist'ovn	Slovakia	50.10
078766	VICTORIA-VOLKSBANKEN pojist'ov	Czech Republic	50.50
084937	Victoria-Volksbanken Versich	Austria	74.60
078764	VICTORIA-VOLKSBANKEN Pensions	Austria	23.80
090231	Victoria Zivotno Osiguranje	Croatia	50.10
077817	ERGO Pensionsfonds AG	Germany	100.00
086537	Hamburg-Mannheimer Sachvers	Germany	100.00
086536	Hamburg-Mannheimer Versich AG	Germany	100.00
083893	Hamburg-Mannheimer Pensions	Germany	100.00
084072	KarstadtQuelle Lebensvers AG	Germany	55.00
084979	Quelle Lebensversicherung AG	Austria	100.00
084582	Neckermann Lebensversicherung	Germany	75.00
084583	Neckermann Versicherung AG	Germany	75.00
055267	*QVH Beteiligungs GmbH*	Germany	55.00
084071	KarstadtQuelle Krankenvers AG	Germany	100.00
084073	KarstadtQuelle Versicherung AG	Germany	100.00
087929	Vorsorge Lebensversicherung AG	Germany	100.00
078767	Vorsorge Luxemburg Lebens SA	Luxembourg	100.00
086529	Europaeische Reiseversicherung	Germany	100.00
089924	Compagnie Europeenne d'Asr	France	100.00
052360	*ERV Beteiligungsgesellschaft*	Germany	100.00
083569	Compania Europea de Seguros SA	Spain	100.00
055262	*European Internationl Hldg A/S*	Denmark	100.00
083256	Europaeiske Rejseforsikring AS	Denmark	100.00
083783	Evropska Cestovni Pojist'ovna	Czech Republic	75.00
077033	Europeiska Forsakrings AB	Sweden	100.00
086160	Great Lakes Reinsurance (UK)	United Kingdom	100.00
055263	*Mercur Assistance AG Holding*	Germany	86.00
084576	Almeda Versicherungs-AG	Germany	100.00
050406	*Munich American Holding Corp*	DE	100.00
058390	*HSB Group Inc*	DE	100.00
000465	Hartford Steam Boiler I & I	CT	100.00
055612	*Global Standards LLC*		100.00
011074	Hartford Steam Boiler I & I CT	CT	100.00
086999	HSB Engineering Ins Ltd	United Kingdom	100.00
085707	Boiler Inspection & Ins of Can	Canada	100.00
058415	*Midland Company*	OH	100.00
050263	*Midland Guardian Company*	OH	100.00
050264	*American Modern Ins Group Inc*	OH	100.00
004084	American Family Home Ins Co	FL	100.00
013062	Amer Modern Surpl Lines Ins Co	OH	100.00
003031	American Modern Home Ins Co	OH	100.00
001709	American Modern Lloyds Ins	TX	
002666	American Modern Select Ins Co	OH	100.00
001708	American Southern Home Ins	FL	100.00
013020	American Modern Ins Co FL	FL	100.00
003763	American Western Home Ins Co	OK	100.00
008859	Modern Life Ins Co of Arizona	AZ	100.00
051010	*First Marine Financial Svcs*	MO	100.00
003285	First Marine Insurance Co	MO	100.00
006680	American Modern Life Ins Co	OH	100.00
007521	Southern Pioneer Life Ins Co	AR	100.00
068179	Capitol Life & Accident Ins Co	AR	100.00
051340	*Hyneman Life Corp*		100.00
068314	Arkansas Life Ins Co	AZ	100.00
068362	Ouachita Life Insurance Co	AR	100.00
009489	Union Life Ins Co	AR	100.00
006746	Munich American Reassurance Co	GA	100.00
013971	Munich American Reins Cas Co	SC	100.00
052788	*Munich Health North America*	DE	100.00
052349	*Cairnstone Inc.*	DE	100.00
090230	Excess Reinsurance, Inc.	Turks And Caicos Islands	100.00
008021	Sterling Life Ins Co	IL	100.00
058320	*Munich Re America Corporation*	NJ	100.00
011574	American Alternative Ins Corp	DE	100.00
000149	Munich Reinsurance America Inc	DE	100.00
055265	*Princeton Eagle Holding BM Ltd*	Bermuda	100.00
072124	Princeton Eagle Ins Co Ltd	Bermuda	100.00
055266	*Princeton Eagle West Hldg Inc*	DE	100.00
072317	Princeton Eagle W Ins Co Ltd	Bermuda	100.00
012170	Princeton Excess & Surp Lines	DE	100.00
055268	*Munich Hldgs Australasia Pty*	Australia	100.00
086473	Munich Reins of Australasia	Australia	100.00
050405	*Munich Holdings Ltd*	Canada	100.00
085770	Munich Reinsurance Co Canada	Canada	100.00
085755	Temple Insurance Company	Canada	100.00
078756	Munich Re General (UK) PLC	United Kingdom	100.00
086475	Muenchener Rueck Italia S.p.A.	Italy	100.00
078757	Munich Re Life & Health UK PLC	United Kingdom	100.00
078109	Munich Re Co of Africa Ltd	South Africa	100.00
078768	Munich Mauritius Reins Co Ltd	Mauritius	100.00
078769	Munich Re Co Life Re E.E.C.A.	Russia	100.00
085060	New Reinsurance Company	Switzerland	100.00
078770	Reaseguradora de las Americas	Cuba	100.00
086717	*Tela Aktiengesellschaft*	Germany	100.00
055812	**MUTUAL BENEFIT TRUST**		
055813	*Royal State Corporation*		80.00
007012	Royal State National Ins Co	HI	100.00
007369	**MUTUAL OF OMAHA INS CO**		
050927	*Mutual of Omaha Holdings Inc*		100.00
060694	Omaha Insurance Company	NE	100.00
052552	*Omaha Financial Holdings Inc*	NE	100.00
620616	*Mutual of Omaha Bank*	NE	100.00
004027	Omaha Indemnity Company	WI	100.00
007164	United of Omaha Life Ins Co	NE	100.00
006258	Companion Life Ins Company	NY	100.00
060695	Omaha Life Insurance Company	NE	100.00
007528	United World Life Ins Co	NE	100.00
051622	**MUTUAL TRUST HOLDING COMPANY**		
051623	*MTL Holdings Inc*		100.00
006756	MTL Insurance Company	IL	100.00
059272	**MVP HEALTH CARE INC**		
051299	*MVPHIC Holding Corp*	NY	100.00
051300	*MVPRT Holdings Inc*	NY	100.00
060369	MVP Health Insurance Company	NY	100.00
064829	MVP Health Plan of NH Inc	NH	100.00
060606	MVP Health Ins Co of NH Inc	NH	100.00
064648	MVP Health Services Corp	NY	100.00
064595	Preferred Assurance Company	NY	100.00
051298	*MVPHP Holding Company Inc*	NY	100.00
068567	MVP Health Plan	NY	100.00
006771	**NATIONAL FARM LIFE INS CO**		
060346	American Farm Life Ins Co	TX	100.00
006777	**NATIONAL GUARDIAN LIFE INS CO**		
060371	Preneed Reinsurance Co of Amer	AZ	75.00
009322	Settlers Life Insurance Co	WI	100.00
050781	**NATIONAL LIFE HOLDING COMPANY**		
051127	*NLV Financial Corporation*	VT	100.00
006790	National Life Ins Co	VT	100.00
006647	Life Insurance Co of Southwest	TX	100.00
050586	**NATIONAL PROMOTERS & SERV INC**		
003106	National Insurance Company	PR	65.87
012992	National Group Insurance Co	FL	100.00
007447	National Life Ins Co	PR	48.81
007447	National Life Ins Co	PR	46.56
058428	**NATIONAL SECURITY GRP INC**		
000687	National Security Fire & Cas	AL	100.00
011413	Omega One Insurance Company	AL	100.00
006802	National Security Ins Co	AL	100.00
051454	**NATIONAL SERVICES INC**		
010794	National Insurance Co of WI	WI	100.00
055416	**NATIONAL VISION INC**		
055415	*NVAL Healthcare Systems Inc*	CA	100.00
064717	FirstSight Vision Services Inc	CA	100.00
002358	**NATIONWIDE MUTUAL INS CO**		
058310	*ALLIED Group, Inc*	IA	100.00
001772	ALLIED Property & Cas Ins Co	IA	100.00
002014	AMCO Insurance Company	IA	100.00
052365	*Nationwide Advantage Mortgage*		87.30
090236	AGMC Reinsurance, Ltd.	Turks And Caicos Islands	100.00
001872	Depositors Insurance Company	IA	100.00
002513	Nationwide Insurance Co of Am	IA	100.00
011541	Atlantic Floridian Ins Co	OH	100.00
001987	Crestbrook Insurance Company	OH	100.00
054013	*Lone Star General Agency Inc*	TX	100.00
010346	Colonial County Mutual Ins Co	TX	
003007	National Casualty Company	WI	100.00
078197	Natl Cas Co of America Ltd	United Kingdom	100.00
011802	Nationwide Affinity Ins Co Am	OH	100.00
003539	Nationwide Agribusiness Ins Co	IA	100.00
000277	Nationwide Assurance Company	WI	100.00
050675	*Nationwide Corporation*	OH	95.20
058160	*Nationwide Financial Services*	DE	100.00
006812	Nationwide Life Ins Co	OH	100.00

AMB#	COMPANY	DOMICILE	% OWN
009070	Nationwide Life & Annuity Ins	OH	100.00
620781	*Nationawide Bank*	OH	100.00
076920	NF Reinsurance Ltd	Bermuda	100.00
002356	Nationwide General Ins Co	OH	100.00
011664	Nationwide Indemnity Company	OH	100.00
012238	Nationwide Insurance Co of FL	OH	100.00
002855	Nationwide Lloyds	TX	
002594	Nationwide Prop & Cas Ins Co	OH	100.00
001931	Scottsdale Indemnity Company	OH	100.00
003292	Scottsdale Insurance Company	OH	100.00
013981	Freedom Specialty Insurance Co	OH	100.00
012121	Scottsdale Surplus Lines Ins	AZ	100.00
001722	Veterinary Pet Insurance Co	CA	100.00
000601	Western Heritage Insurance Co	AZ	100.00
050366	*THI Holdings (Delaware) Inc*	DE	100.00
000548	Titan Indemnity Company	TX	100.00
010709	Titan Insurance Company	MI	100.00
000671	Victoria Fire & Casualty Co	OH	100.00
011688	Victoria Automobile Ins Co	IN	100.00
012059	Victoria National Ins Co	OH	100.00
011689	Victoria Select Insurance Co	OH	100.00
012058	Victoria Specialty Ins Co	OH	100.00
000366	Farmland Mutual Insurance Co	IA	
002357	Nationwide Mutual Fire Ins Co	OH	
055442	**NELNET, INC.**		
055443	*Nelnet Academic Serivces, LLC*		100.00
007679	First National Life of USA	NE	100.00
032694	**NESTLE S A**		
052058	*Nestle Holdings Inc*	DE	100.00
052059	*Nestle Insurance Holdings Inc*	DE	100.00
007299	Gerber Life Ins Co	NY	100.00
055820	**NEW CALIFORNIA LIFE HOLDINGS**		
006139	Aurora National Life Assur	CA	100.00
050852	**NEW ERA ENTERPRISES INC**		
007087	New Era Life Ins Co	TX	100.00
007148	New Era Life Ins Co Midwest	TX	100.00
009166	Philadelphia American Life Ins	TX	100.00
006820	**NEW YORK LIFE INS CO**		
051724	Haier New York Life Ins Co Ltd	China	50.00
078463	HSBC NY Life Seg de Retiro	Argentina	100.00
078464	HSBC NY Life Seg de Vida (AR)	Argentina	100.00
009054	New York Life Ins & Annuity	DE	100.00
068015	NYLIFE Ins Co of Arizona	AZ	100.00
055369	*New York Life Intl, LLC*	DE	100.00
090122	Fianzas Monterrey, S.A.	Mexico	100.00
078465	Max NY Life Ins Co Ltd	India	26.00
078468	New York Life Insurance Ltd	South Korea	100.00
078467	New York Life Ins Taiwan Corp	Taiwan	100.00
078923	New York Lf Ins Worldwide Ltd	Hong Kong	100.00
085870	Seg Monterrey New York Life SA	Mexico	100.00
077846	Siam Comm NY Life Ins Pub Co	Thailand	47.33
085457	**NIPPON LIFE INSURANCE COMPANY**		
008419	Nippon Life Ins Co of Amer	IA	96.96
078771	Nissay-Greatwall Life Ins Co	China	50.00
068581	**NORIDIAN MUTUAL INSURANCE CO**		
064370	Dental Service Corp of ND	ND	100.00
006662	Lincoln Mutual Life & Casualty	ND	100.00
064371	North Dakota Vision Services	ND	100.00
055347	**NORMA J HAWKINS**		
055172	*General Partners Hawkins Invst*	KS	90.00
051901	*Hawkins Family Partnership LP*		100.00
008795	American Underwriters Life Ins	AZ	100.00
009124	Century Life Assur Co	OK	100.00
006481	Great Fidelity Life Ins Co	IN	100.00
052798	*Kell & Norma Hawkins Jt Rev Tr*		100.00
073850	First Financial Ins Co Ltd	Saint Kitts And Nevis	100.00
006845	**NORTHWESTERN MUTUAL LIFE INS**		
007067	Northwestern Long Term Care	WI	100.00
059029	*Frank Russell Company*	WA	92.86
050742	**OHIO NATIONAL MUT HOLDINGS INC**		
050741	*Ohio National Financial Serv*	OH	100.00
006852	Ohio National Life Ins Co	OH	100.00
060721	Montgomery Re Inc	VT	100.00
008633	National Security Lf & Annuity	NY	80.50
008930	Ohio National Life Assur Corp	OH	100.00
055881	*ON Global Holdings Inc*		100.00
055882	*Ohio National Sudamerica SA*	Chile	100.00
077084	Ohio National Seguros de Vida	Chile	100.00
090962	Sycamore Re, Ltd.	Bermuda	100.00
084321	**OLD MUTUAL PLC**		
050713	*OM Group (UK) Ltd*	United Kingdom	100.00
090196	Old Mutual (Bermuda) Limited	Bermuda	100.00
052310	*Old Mutual Holdings (GG) Ltd*	Guernsey	100.00
076496	Constantia Ins Co (GG) Ltd	Guernsey	100.00
052311	*Old Mutual Hldgs NA Pty Ltd*	Namibia	100.00
090197	Old Mutual Life Asr Co NA Ltd	Namibia	100.00
089058	Old Mutual Intl (Ireland) Ltd	Ireland	100.00
052313	*Old Mutual Irish Holdings*	Ireland	100.00
075641	Old Mutual Reassur (Ireland)	Ireland	100.00
050715	*Old Mutual (South Africa) Ltd*	South Africa	100.00
050716	*Old Mutual Life Holdings (ZA)*	South Africa	100.00
085861	Old Mutual Life Asr Co ZA	South Africa	100.00
052308	*Mutual & Federal Inv (Pty) Ltd*	South Africa	100.00
085226	Mutual & Federal Ins Co Ltd	South Africa	100.00
052377	*Cougar Investment Holding Ltd*	South Africa	100.00
086788	CGU Insurance Limited	South Africa	100.00
090437	Sentrasure Limited	South Africa	100.00
086789	Credit Guarantee Ins Corp	South Africa	51.00
090194	Mut & Fed Ins Co of BW Ltd	Botswana	100.00
090195	Mut & Fed Ins Co of NA Ltd	Namibia	100.00
090435	Fedsure General Ins Namibia	Namibia	100.00
052388	*Mutual & Federal Co of ZM Ltd*	Zimbabwe	100.00
090436	RM Insurance Company (Pvt) Ltd	Zimbabwe	46.00
052312	*Old Mutual UK Holdings Limited*	United Kingdom	100.00
052307	*Skandia UK Holdings Limited*	United Kingdom	100.00
086306	*Skandia Life Assur (Hldgs) Ltd*	United Kingdom	100.00
077115	Skandia Multifunds Assur Ltd	United Kingdom	100.00
052317	*Skandia Life Holding Co Ltd*	United Kingdom	100.00
086307	Professional Life Assur Ltd	United Kingdom	100.00
090198	Royal Skandia Life Assur Ltd	Isle Of Man	100.00
085619	Skandia Life Assurance Co Ltd	United Kingdom	100.00
089063	Skandia Life Ireland Limited	Ireland	100.00
051652	*Old Mutual (US) Holdings Inc*	DE	100.00
050904	*Old Mutual US Life Holdings*		100.00
006384	OM Financial Life Ins Co	MD	100.00
007122	OM Financial Life Ins Co of NY	NY	100.00
085180	Skandia Insurance Co Ltd (pub)	Sweden	100.00
077024	DIAL Forsakringsaktiebolag	Sweden	100.00
090200	Skandia BSAM Life Ins Co Ltd	China	50.00
052314	*Skandia Holding AB*	Sweden	100.00
052315	*Skandia Holding de Colombia SA*	Colombia	94.90
085465	Skandia Compania Seg Vida SA	Colombia	99.90
083358	Skandia Link Livsforsikring AS	Denmark	100.00
085181	Skandia Liv	Sweden	100.00
089886	Skandia Livsforsikring A/S	Denmark	100.00
078085	Skandia Vida S.A. de C.V.	Mexico	99.90
052309	*Skandia Europe & L America*	United Kingdom	100.00
052316	*Skandia Leben Holding GmbH*	Germany	100.00
084644	Skandia Lebensversicherung AG	Germany	100.00
078044	Skandia Leben AG	Switzerland	100.00
090199	Skandia Leben (FL) AG	Liechtenstein	100.00
083880	Skandia Leben AG, Lebensvers	Austria	100.00
089871	Skandia Link SA Seg y Reas	Spain	100.00
084921	Skandia Vita S.p.A.	Italy	100.00
075874	Skandia Reassurance S.A.	Luxembourg	100.00
058439	**OLD REPUBLIC INTERN CORP**		
050598	*Old Republic Gen Ins Group Inc*	DE	100.00
050599	*Bitco Corporation*	DE	100.00
002075	Bituminous Casualty Corp	IL	100.00
002076	Bituminous Fire & Marine Ins	IL	100.00
055211	*Intl Bus & Merc Ins Hldgs Ltd*	Bermuda	100.00
057139	InterWest Assurance Ltd.	Bermuda	100.00
055210	*Old Republic Construction Prog*	DE	95.96
072486	Old Republic Indemnity Ltd	Bermuda	100.00
002383	Old Republic General Ins Corp	IL	100.00
000733	Old Republic Insurance Co	PA	100.00
004479	Old Republic Lloyds of Texas	TX	100.00
002032	Old Republic Mercantile Ins Co	IL	100.00
000641	Old Republic Security Assur Co	AZ	100.00
050605	*Old Republic Surety Group Inc*	DE	100.00
002814	Old Republic Surety Company	WI	100.00
003769	Old Republic Union Ins Co	IL	100.00
050601	*ORI Great West Holdings Inc*	DE	100.00
000439	Great West Casualty Company	NE	100.00
050606	*Reliable Canadian Holdings Ltd*	Canada	100.00
050607	*Old Republic Canadian Holdings*	Canada	100.00
009049	Reliable Life Ins Co	Canada	100.00
086563	Old Republic Ins Co of Canada	Canada	100.00
050610	*Old Republic Life Ins Grp Inc*	DE	100.00
006863	Old Republic Life Ins Co	IL	100.00
050609	*Old Republic Mtge Guar Grp Inc*	DE	100.00
002750	Republic Mortgage Ins Co	NC	100.00
073243	Group Mortgage Reinsurance Co	VT	100.00
002881	Republic Mortgage Ins Co of FL	FL	100.00
002029	Republic Mortgage Ins Co of NC	NC	100.00
050613	*Old Republic Title Ins Grp Inc*	DE	100.00
050614	*Old Republic Nat Title Hldg Co*	DE	100.00
050615	*American Guaranty Holding Corp*	OK	100.00
011833	American Guaranty Title Ins Co	OK	100.00
011924	Old Republic Nat Title Ins Co	MN	100.00
011423	Mississippi Valley Title Ins	MS	100.00
001751	American Bus & Pers Ins Mut	DE	
055726	**ONEX CORPORATION**		
055381	*Warranty Group, Inc.*	DE	100.00
055382	*TWG Holdings, Inc.*	DE	100.00

AMB#	COMPANY	DOMICILE	% OWN
006176	Resource Life Insurance Co	IL	100.00
055384	*Rockford Holding, Inc.*	DE	70.00
060667	Rockford Life Insurance Co	AZ	100.00
052624	*TWG Europe Limited*	United Kingdom	100.00
087438	London General Insurance Co	United Kingdom	100.00
084203	London General Life Company	United Kingdom	100.00
055383	*TWG Warranty Group, Inc.*	IL	100.00
078924	TWG Argentina Compania	Argentina	69.80
078925	Virginia Surety Compania Seg	Brazil	100.00
002314	Virginia Surety Company, Inc.	IL	100.00
077541	Virginia Surety Cia de Seg SA	Argentina	95.00
031319	**OPTIMUM GROUP INC**		
086608	*Optimum General Inc.*	Canada	86.10
087091	Optimum Insurance Company Inc	Canada	100.00
087724	Optimum Farm Insurance Inc	Canada	100.00
001989	Optimum Prop & Cas Ins Co	TX	100.00
087019	Optimum West Insurance Company	Canada	100.00
051769	*Optimum Re Inc.*		100.00
051770	*Optimum Financiere Europe SAS*	France	100.00
083048	Optimum Vie	France	38.00
050804	*Optimum Re Corp (Canada)*	DE	33.30
083048	Optimum Vie	France	62.00
051771	*ORL Holdings Inc*	DE	100.00
051772	*Optimum Re Life Corporation*	DE	100.00
050803	*Optimum Re Corporation*	DE	100.00
008863	Optimum Re Insurance Company	TX	100.00
050804	*Optimum Re Corp (Canada)*	DE	66.67
066827	Optimum Reassurance Inc	Canada	100.00
050805	*Optimum International (US) Inc*	DE	100.00
068306	Windsor Life Insurance Company	Canada	100.00
057933	Selecta Insurance Inc	Barbados	100.00
050575	**OREGON DENTAL ASSOCIATION**		
064364	Oregon Dental Service	OR	100.00
050576	*Health Services Group*	OR	100.00
010802	Northwest Dentists Ins Co	WA	75.00
011437	ODS Health Plan Inc	OR	100.00
010690	Dentists Benefits Insurance Co	OR	100.00
050799	**PACIFIC MUTUAL HOLDING COMPANY**		
050800	*Pacific LifeCorp*	CA	100.00
071224	Pacific Alliance Reins Ltd.	Bermuda	100.00
006885	Pacific Life Insurance Company	NE	100.00
060670	Pacific Alliance Reins Co VT	VT	100.00
009156	Pacific Life & Annuity Co	AZ	100.00
052402	*Pacific Life Re Holdings LLC*	DE	100.00
052403	*Pacific Life Re Holdings Ltd*	United Kingdom	100.00
052744	*Pacific Life Re Services Ltd*	United Kingdom	100.00
087677	Pacific Life Re Limited	United Kingdom	100.00
052016	**PAN-AMERICAN LIFE MUTUAL HLDG**		
052015	*Pan-American Life Insurance Gr*	LA	100.00
078166	Compania de Seg Panamericana	Guatemala	99.67
075491	INRECO International Reins Co	Cayman Islands	100.00
088749	Pan-American Colombia Cia Seg	Colombia	22.98
057485	Pan American Internat Ins Co	Cayman Islands	100.00
088749	Pan-American Colombia Cia Seg	Colombia	77.01
087146	Pan-American Life Ins Panama	Panama	100.00
006893	Pan-American Life Ins Co	LA	100.00
009058	Pan-American Assurance Company	LA	100.00
088748	Pan-American Life Ins Co of PR	PR	100.00
002415	**PEMCO MUTUAL INSURANCE COMPANY**		
003505	PEMCO Insurance Company	WA	100.00
007420	PEMCO Life Ins Co	WA	100.00
006903	**PENN MUTUAL LIFE INS CO**		
009073	Penn Ins and Annuity Company	DE	100.00
058080	**PENN TREATY AMERICAN CORP**		
006385	Penn Treaty Network America	PA	100.00
007362	American Network Ins Company	PA	100.00
060292	American Indep Network of NY	NY	100.00
052799	**PFHC MEDICAL MANAGEMENT LLC**		
068602	Preservation Life Insurance Co	MO	100.00
000320	**PHARMACISTS MUTUAL INS CO**		
008946	Pharmacists Life Ins Co	IA	100.00
006919	**PHILADELPHIA-UNITED LIFE INS**		
003174	Philadelphia-United Fire Ins	PA	100.00
050888	**PHOENIX COMPANIES INC**		
006922	Phoenix Life Insurance Company	NY	100.00
050820	*PM Holdings Inc*		100.00
068152	American Phoenix Life&Reassur	CT	100.00
050889	*PFG Holdings Inc*	PA	71.00
007142	AGL Life Assurance Company	PA	100.00
009332	PHL Variable Ins Co	CT	100.00
009072	Phoenix Life and Annuity Co	CT	100.00
068237	Phoenix Life and Reassur of NY	NY	100.00
056469	PML International Ins Ltd	Bermuda	100.00

AMB#	COMPANY	DOMICILE	% OWN
068743	**PHYSICIANS HLTH PL-NORTHERN IN**		
055630	*PHP Holding Company*		100.00
064832	PHP Insurance Company of IN	IN	100.00
007372	**PHYSICIANS MUTUAL INSURANCE CO**		
007451	Physicians Life Ins Co	NE	100.00
051053	**PLATEAU GROUP INC**		
012122	Plateau Casualty Insurance Co	TN	100.00
009348	Plateau Ins Co	TN	100.00
068373	Tennessee Life Insurance Co	AZ	100.00
071120	Plateau Reinsurance Co	NV	100.00
078599	Preferred Reinsurance, Ltd.	Turks And Caicos Islands	100.00
078598	Tennessee Dealers Reins Co Ltd	Turks And Caicos Islands	100.00
063036	**POPULAR INC**		
619311	*Banco Popular de Puerto Rico*	PR	100.00
611487	*Popular Auto*	PR	100.00
611941	*Popular Mortgage*	PR	100.00
609182	*Popular Capital Trust I*	PR	100.00
609899	*Popular Capital Trust II*	PR	100.00
624376	*Popular Capital Trust III*	PR	100.00
613348	*Popular Insurance*	PR	100.00
604237	*Popular International Bank Inc*	PR	100.00
604452	*Popular North America, Inc.*	PR	100.00
612776	*Banco Popular North America*	NY	100.00
621332	*E-Loan Inc*	CA	100.00
605581	*Banponce Trust I*	NJ	100.00
609740	*Popular Financial Holdings Inc*	DE	100.00
604102	*Equity One Inc*	NJ	100.00
609865	*Popular North America Cap Tr I*	PR	100.00
060399	Popular Life Re	PR	100.00
050912	**POWER CORPORATION OF CANADA**		
055597	*171263 Canada Inc.*	Canada	100.00
050919	*Power Financial Corporation*		66.30
050910	*Great-West Lifeco Inc.*	Canada	68.60
055609	*Great-West Financial (CA) Inc*	Canada	100.00
055596	*Great-West Financial (NS) Inc*	Canada	100.00
052542	*Great-West Lifeco U S Inc*		100.00
051111	*GWL&A Financial Inc*		100.00
006981	Great-West Life & Ann	CO	100.00
008257	First Great-West Lf & Annuity	NY	100.00
060577	Great-West Life & Annuity SC	SC	100.00
006493	Great-West Life Assurance Co	Canada	100.00
087756	Gold Circle Insurance Company	Canada	100.00
051110	*London Insurance Group Inc*	United Kingdom	100.00
006667	London Life Insurance Company	Canada	100.00
050911	*London Life Financial Corp*	United Kingdom	100.00
086470	London Reinsurance Group	Canada	89.40
086455	London Life & Genl Reins Ltd	Ireland	100.00
086037	London Life & Cas Reins Corp	Barbados	100.00
072095	TRABAJA Reinsurance Co	Cayman Islands	100.00
077342	London Life & Cas (BB) Corp	Barbados	100.00
031107	*LRG (US), Inc.*		100.00
086458	London Life Internat Reins Cp	Barbados	100.00
060237	London Life Reinsurance Co	PA	100.00
050755	*Canada Life Financial Corp*	Canada	100.00
006183	Canada Life Assurance Co	Canada	100.00
050960	*Canada Life Capital Corp*		100.00
050961	*Canada Life International Hldg*		100.00
088687	Canada Life International Ltd	Isle Of Man	100.00
055607	*Canada Life Irish Hldg Co Ltd*	Ireland	100.00
055604	*Canada Life Europe Investment*	Ireland	100.00
089030	Canada Life Asr (Europe) Ltd	Ireland	78.67
089031	Canada Life Asr (Ireland) Ltd	Ireland	100.00
084304	Canada Life Intl Re Ltd	Ireland	100.00
075759	Canada Life Reins Int'l Ltd	Bermuda	100.00
076122	Canada Life Reinsurance Ltd.	Barbados	100.00
055605	*Canada Life Group (UK) Limited*	United Kingdom	100.00
087449	Canada Life Limited	United Kingdom	100.00
055602	*Canada Life (U.K.) Limited*	United Kingdom	100.00
087209	Albany Life Assurance Co Ltd	United Kingdom	100.00
066839	Canada Life Ins Co of Canada	Canada	100.00
006300	Crown Life Insurance Company	Canada	100.00
051131	**PREMERA**		
060076	Premera Blue Cross	WA	100.00
068458	LifeWise Health Plan of AZ	WA	100.00
050808	*Ucentris Insured Solutions Inc*	WA	100.00
009086	LifeWise Assurance Company	WA	100.00
068259	LifeWise Health Plan of Oregon	OR	100.00
064608	LifeWise Health Plan of WA	WA	100.00
052014	**PREMIER DENTAL SERVICES INC**		
052013	*Premier Dental Holdings Inc*	DE	100.00
064821	Premier Choice Dental Inc	AZ	100.00
064651	Western Dental Services Inc	CA	100.00
058084	**PRESIDENTIAL LIFE CORPORATION**		
006948	Presidential Life Ins Co	NY	100.00

AMB#	COMPANY	DOMICILE	% OWN
058179	**PRINCIPAL FINANCIAL GRP INC**		
059080	*Principal Financial Serv Inc*	IA	100.00
055450	*PFG Do Brasil LTDA*	Brazil	100.00
089952	Brasilprev Seguros Previdencia	Brazil	100.00
090206	*Principal Financial Group (MU)*	Mauritius	100.00
090205	Principal PNB Life Ins Co	India	100.00
055451	*Principal Intl de Chile S.A.*	Chile	100.00
077086	Principal Cia Seg Vida Chile	Chile	100.00
055452	*Principal International Inc.*	IA	100.00
055453	*Principal Intl (Asia) Ltd*	Hong Kong	100.00
088566	Principal Ins Co (HK) Ltd	Hong Kong	100.00
078014	Principal Mexico Cia Seg SA CV	Mexico	100.00
090207	Principal Pensiones SA de CV	Mexico	100.00
006150	Principal Life Insurance Co	IA	100.00
060675	Principal Life Insurance Co IA	IA	100.00
059308	Principal Reinsurance Co of DE	IA	100.00
060666	Principal Reinsurance Co of VT	VT	100.00
007326	Principal National Life Ins Co	IA	100.00
031408	**PROMEDICA HEALTH SYSTEM, INC.**		
075338	Promedica Indemnity Corp	VT	100.00
051669	*ProMedica Insurance Corp*	OH	100.00
064833	Paramount Advantage	OH	100.00
068579	Paramount Care Inc	OH	100.00
064294	Paramount Care of Michigan	MI	100.00
064742	Paramount Insurance Company	OH	100.00
058085	**PROTECTIVE LIFE CORPORATION**		
078399	Chesterfield Intl Reins Ltd	Saint Kitts And Nevis	100.00
078400	Dealer Services Reins Ltd	Bermuda	100.00
059075	*PLC Capital Trust III*	DE	100.00
059076	*PLC Capital Trust IV*	DE	100.00
059151	*PLC Capital Trust V*	DE	100.00
059152	*PLC Capital Trust VI*	DE	100.00
059231	*PLC Capital Trust VII*	DE	100.00
059232	*PLC Capital Trust VIII*	DE	100.00
006962	Protective Life Ins Co	TN	100.00
008642	Citizens Accident and Health	AZ	100.00
060295	Golden Gate Captive Insurance	SC	100.00
060214	Golden Gate II Captive Ins Co	SC	100.00
050072	*Lyndon Insurance Group Inc*	MO	100.00
060584	First Protection Company	MN	100.00
060586	First Protection Corp of FL	FL	100.00
003812	Lyndon Property Insurance Co	MO	100.00
008860	Protective Life & Annuity Ins	AL	100.00
060574	Tower Captive Insurance Co	SC	100.00
007222	West Coast Life Ins Co	NE	100.00
060340	Protective Life Insurance NY	NY	100.00
050944	*Western Diversified Services*	IL	100.00
060587	Advantage Warranty Corporation	FL	100.00
034011	**PROVIDENCE HEALTH & SERVICES**		
052522	*Providence Health System OR*		100.00
052521	*Providence Plan Partners*		100.00
068651	Providence Health Plan	OR	100.00
058182	**PRUDENTIAL FINANCIAL INC**		
076310	Pruco Reinsurance Ltd	Bermuda	100.00
051133	*Prudential Annuities Holding*		100.00
051134	*Prudential Annuities Inc*		100.00
008715	Prudential Annuities Life Assr	CT	100.00
060702	Prudential Arizona Reins III	AZ	100.00
051055	*Prudential Holdings LLC*		100.00
006974	Prudential Ins Co of America	NJ	100.00
076547	Prudential Arizona Re Captive	AZ	100.00
008240	Pruco Life Ins Co	AZ	100.00
009371	Pruco Life Insurance Co of NJ	NJ	100.00
009144	Prudential Retirement Ins&Ann	CT	100.00
060647	Universal Prudential AZ Reins	AZ	100.00
624360	*Prudential IBH Holdco Inc*	NJ	100.00
620690	*Prudential Bank & Trust FSB*	CT	100.00
050368	*Prudential Int Ins Hldngs Ltd*		100.00
084917	Pramerica Life S.p.A.	Italy	100.00
078456	Prudential Life Ins Co Taiwan	Taiwan	100.00
088599	Pramerica Zycie TUiR S.A.	Poland	100.00
086614	Prudential Life Ins Co Ltd	Japan	100.00
084305	Prudential Life Ins Co Korea	South Korea	100.00
077749	Prudential Seguros S.A.	Argentina	100.00
050379	*Pruservicos Participacoes SA*	Brazil	100.00
085164	Prudential do Brasil Seg Vida	Brazil	100.00
052644	*Prudential Intl Investments*		100.00
052643	*Prudential Grupo Financiero SA*	Mexico	100.00
090922	Prudential Seguros Mexico SA	Mexico	100.00
051693	*Prudential Japan Holdings Inc.*	Japan	100.00
085460	Gibraltar Life Insurance Co	Japan	100.00
077887	Kyoei do Brasil Cia de Seg	Brazil	100.00
012684	Vantage Casualty Insurance Co	IN	100.00
085925	**PRUDENTIAL PLC**		
090022	CITIC Prudential Life Ins Co	China	50.00
055947	*M & G Group Limited*	United Kingdom	100.00
055935	*M & G Limited*	United Kingdom	100.00
087444	M&G Life Assurance Co Ltd	United Kingdom	100.00
087445	M&G Pensions & Annuity Co Ltd	United Kingdom	100.00
055936	*MM&S (2375) Limited*	United Kingdom	
055944	*Prudential Europe Assur Hldgs*	United Kingdom	92.70
089060	Prudential Internatl Asr plc	Ireland	100.00
087803	Prudential Assurance Co Ltd	United Kingdom	100.00
087544	Prudential (AN) Limited	United Kingdom	100.00
087543	Prudential Annuities Limited	United Kingdom	100.00
089442	Prudential Asr Co SG (Pte) Ltd	Singapore	100.00
078236	Prudential Health Limited	United Kingdom	100.00
087545	Prudential Holborn Life Ltd	United Kingdom	100.00
087546	Prudential Pensions Limited	United Kingdom	100.00
087578	Prudential Retirement Income	United Kingdom	100.00
084362	Scottish Amicable Life plc	United Kingdom	100.00
055946	*Prudential Holdings Limited*	United Kingdom	100.00
055943	*Prudential Corp Hldgs Ltd*	United Kingdom	100.00
090023	PCA Life Assurance Co Ltd	Taiwan	99.00
084746	PCA Life Insurance Company Ltd	Japan	100.00
090027	PCA Life Insurance Co Ltd	South Korea	100.00
090026	Prudential Life Asr TH Public	Thailand	
050743	*Prudential One Limited*	United Kingdom	100.00
055945	*Prudential Four Limited*	United Kingdom	80.00
055934	*Holburn Delaware LLC*	DE	100.00
055941	*Prudential (US Holdco 2) Ltd*	Gibraltar	100.00
055933	*Brooke LLC*	DE	77.00
055939	*Prudential (US Holdco 1) Ltd*	United Kingdom	100.00
055930	*Prudential (US Holdco 1) B.V*	Netherlands	100.00
055940	*Prudential (US Holdco 2) B.V.*	Netherlands	100.00
055942	*Prudential (US Holdco 3) B.V.*	Netherlands	100.00
055931	*Brooke (Holdco 1) Inc.*	DE	100.00
055948	*Brooke (Holdco 2) Inc.*	DE	100.00
055932	*Brooke GP*	DE	99.00
055937	*Nicole Finance Inc.*	DE	100.00
050745	*Brooke Holdings Inc*		100.00
068117	Brooke Life Insurance Co	MI	100.00
006596	Jackson National Life Ins Co	MI	100.00
076006	Jackson National Life (BM) Ltd	Bermuda	100.00
060216	Jackson National Lf Ins of NY	NY	100.00
060698	Squire Reassurance Company LLC	MI	100.00
090024	Prudential Vietnam Asr Pr Ltd	Vietnam	
090025	Prudential Life Assurance, PT	Indonesia	100.00
055938	*Sri Han Suria Sdn Bhd*	Malaysia	100.00
089140	Prudential Asr Malaysia Bhd	Malaysia	100.00
052021	**QUALCHOICE OF ARKANSAS INC**		
064050	QCA Health Plan Inc	AR	81.34
007304	QualChoice Life & Health Ins	AR	100.00
051374	**R & CO. CAPITAL MGMT, L.L.C.**		
051375	*Rosenkranz & Company*		100.00
058036	*Delphi Financial Group Inc*	DE	100.00
009480	Reliance Standard Life of TX	TX	100.00
006990	Reliance Standard Life Ins Co	IL	100.00
009418	First Reliance Standard Life	NY	100.00
050383	*SIG Holdings Inc*	DE	100.00
000818	Safety National Casualty Corp	MO	100.00
012476	Safety First Insurance Company	IL	100.00
072867	Safety National Re SPC	Cayman Islands	100.00
052497	**R D TIPS INC**		
052496	*Fairmount Investments LLC*		100.00
068234	North American Life Ins of TX	TX	55.00
006135	Atlantic Southern Ins Co	PR	100.00
068066	Trans-Western Life Ins Co	TX	100.00
051873	**R J MARTIN MORTGAGE COMPANY**		
006837	North Coast Life Ins Co	WA	53.70
051032	**REALTY ADVISORS INC**		
051030	*Heritage Guaranty Holdings Inc*		100.00
007011	Liberty Bankers Life Ins Co	OK	100.00
060382	American Benefit Life	OK	100.00
006186	Capitol Life Ins Co	TX	100.00
008119	Winnfield Life Ins Co	LA	100.00
051045	**REGENCE GROUP**		
060074	Regence BC/BS of Oregon	OR	100.00
068583	Regence HMO Oregon	OR	100.00
051974	*Capitol Hlth Care Mgmt, Inc.*	OR	100.00
068584	Regence Health Maint of OR	OR	100.00
009345	Regence Life and Health Ins Co	OR	11.00
064412	Regence BlueCross BlueSh of UT	UT	100.00
068604	HealthWise	UT	100.00
009345	Regence Life and Health Ins Co	OR	12.00
060199	Regence BlueShield	WA	100.00
064414	Asuris Northwest Health	WA	100.00
068406	Commencement Bay Life Ins Co	WA	100.00
009345	Regence Life and Health Ins Co	OR	75.00
060266	Regence BlueShield of Idaho	ID	100.00
009345	Regence Life and Health Ins Co	OR	2.00
055760	**REHAB SERVICES CORPORATION**		
009877	First Rehabilitation Lf of Am	NY	100.00
058089	**REINSURANCE GROUP OF AMERICA**		
077487	General American AR Seg Vida	Argentina	95.00

AMB#	COMPANY	DOMICILE	% OWN
050061	Reinsurance Co of Missouri	MO	100.00
065870	Parkway Reinsurance Company	MO	100.00
009080	RGA Reinsurance Company	MO	100.00
051645	*Timberlake Financial L L C*	DE	100.00
060582	Timberlake Reinsurance Co II	SC	100.00
073316	RGA Americas Reins Co Ltd	Barbados	100.00
090222	RGA Atlantic Reins Co, Ltd.	Barbados	100.00
051338	*RGA Australian Holdings Ltd*	Australia	100.00
077907	RGA Reinsurance Co of AU Ltd	Australia	100.00
059087	*RGA Capital Trust I*	MO	100.00
071244	RGA Global Reinsurance Co, Ltd	Bermuda	100.00
050498	*RGA Holdings Ltd*	United Kingdom	100.00
084160	RGA Reinsurance UK Limited	United Kingdom	100.00
076186	RGA International Reinsurance	Ireland	100.00
066817	RGA Life Reinsurance of Canada	Canada	100.00
073031	RGA Reins Co (Barbados) Ltd	Barbados	100.00
051339	*RGA South African Hldg Pty Ltd*	South Africa	100.00
089234	RGA Re Co of South Africa Ltd	South Africa	100.00
078439	RGA Worldwide Reins Co, Ltd.	Barbados	100.00
051973	**RENAISSANCE HEALTH SVCE CORP**		
064485	Delta Dental of Kentucky Inc	KY	
068575	Delta Dental Plan of Michigan	MI	
064694	Delta Dental Plan of Indiana	IN	
064502	Delta Dental Plan of Ohio Inc	OH	
051314	*Renaissance Holding Company*	MI	42.20
006201	Renaissance Lf & Hlth of Amer	IN	100.00
002682	Renaissance Health Ins Co NY	NY	100.00
064537	Delta Dental Plan of NM	NM	
064670	Delta Dental of Tennessee	TN	
051314	*Renaissance Holding Company*	MI	
055306	**RICHARD F JONES**		
007426	Fidelity Security Life Ins Co	MO	100.00
075950	Fidelity Security Assr Company	Cayman Islands	100.00
007899	American Service Life Ins Co	AR	100.00
052495	**RJM COMPANY LLC**		
064518	Midwest Health Plan Inc	MI	100.00
064312	**ROCKY MOUNTAIN HLTH MAINT ORG**		
064561	Rocky Mountain HthCare Options	CO	100.00
031505	**ROYAL BANK OF CANADA**		
055781	*RBC Finance B.V.*	Netherlands	100.00
073743	RBC Reinsurance (Ireland) Ltd	Ireland	100.00
051518	*Royal Bank Holding, Inc.*	Canada	100.00
032886	*R.B.C. Hldgs (Bahamas) Ltd*	Bahamas	100.00
055780	*RBC Caribbean Investment Ltd*	Cayman Islands	100.00
086956	Royal Bank of Canada Ins Co Lt	Barbados	100.00
051517	*RBC Holdings (USA) Inc*	DE	100.00
051516	*RBC USA Holdco Corporation*	DE	100.00
051515	*RBC Ins Holdings (USA) Inc*	DE	100.00
006175	Liberty Life Insurance Company	SC	100.00
057844	LC Insurance Limited	Bermuda	100.00
050903	*RBC Insurance Holdings Inc*	Canada	100.00
087083	RBC General Insurance Company	Canada	100.00
066806	RBC Life Insurance Company	Canada	100.00
086243	RBC Insurance Company Canada	Canada	100.00
055391	**SAFE PARTNERS, LLC**		
051392	*Security American Finl Ent*		100.00
064979	Security Health Ins of Amer NY	NY	100.00
007030	Security Life Ins Co of Amer	MN	100.00
088130	**SAGICOR FINANCIAL CORPORATION**		
055729	*Sagicor Europe Limited*	Cayman Islands	86.00
055727	*Sagicor Corporate Capital Ltd*	United Kingdom	100.00
048299	*Lloyd's Syndicate 1206*	United Kingdom	100.00
052286	*Sagicor Corporate Cap Two Ltd*	United Kingdom	100.00
047737	*Lloyd's Syndicate 44*	United Kingdom	100.00
086569	Sagicor Life Inc.	Barbados	100.00
051330	*LOJ Holdings Ltd*	Jamaica	100.00
086086	Sagicor Life Jamaica Limited	Jamaica	60.00
078642	Sagicor Life Cayman Islands	Cayman Islands	100.00
086807	Sagicor Gen Ins (Cayman) Ltd	Cayman Islands	76.00
076249	Sagicor Re Insurance Co Ltd	Cayman Islands	100.00
078974	Nationwide Insurance Co Ltd	Trinidad And Tobago	100.00
011127	Sagicor Allnation Insurance Co	DE	100.00
086658	Sagicor Capital Life Ins Co	Bahamas	100.00
078975	Capital Life Ins Co Bahamas Lt	Bahamas	100.00
078976	Sagicor Panama S.A.	Panama	100.00
055728	Sagicor Life Aruba N.V.	Aruba	100.00
086979	Sagicor General Insurance Inc.	Barbados	52.80
051268	*Sagicor USA Inc*	DE	100.00
068076	Laurel Life Ins Co	TX	100.00
006057	Sagicor Life Insurance Company	TX	100.00
052460	**ST JOSEPH HEALTH SYSTEM**		
034017	*Covenant Health System*	TX	100.00
052461	*Lubbock Methodist Hospital Svs*		100.00
060114	SHA L L C	TX	66.67
006719	Southwest Life & Health Ins Co	TX	100.00

AMB#	COMPANY	DOMICILE	% OWN
052459	**ST LUKES EPISCOPAL HEALTH SYST**		
052458	*SLEHS Holdings Inc*		100.00
052457	*KS Management Services LLP*	TX	100.00
064972	KS Plan Administrators L L C	TX	100.00
051524	**SAMMONS ENTERPRISES, INC.**		
051525	*Consol Investment Svcs Inc*	NV	100.00
050730	*Sammons Financial Group Inc*	TX	100.00
006711	Midland National Life Ins Co	IA	100.00
060578	SFG Reinsurance Company	SC	100.00
006827	North American Co for L&H	IA	100.00
051979	**SANFORD HEALTH**		
064393	Sanford Health Plan	SD	100.00
064604	Sanford Health Plan of MN	MN	100.00
034026	**SANTAFE HEALTHCARE, INC.**		
064074	AvMed Inc	FL	100.00
006696	**SAVINGS BANK LIFE INS CO OF MA**		
060671	SBLI RE Inc	AZ	100.00
006821	**SBLI USA MUTUAL LIFE INS CO**		
050898	*SBLI USA Holdings Inc*		100.00
060110	S.USA Life Insurance Company	AZ	100.00
052507	**SCAN GROUP**		
060187	SCAN Health Plan	CA	100.00
064846	SCAN Health Plan Arizona	AZ	100.00
086155	**SCOR S.E.**		
002665	General Security National Ins	NY	100.00
077365	SCOR Global Life SE	France	99.99
075241	SCOR Global Life Re (BB) Ltd	Barbados	100.00
055363	*Revios Canada Hldg Corp Ltd.*	Canada	100.00
006460	Revios Reinsurance Canada Ltd	Canada	100.00
078854	SCOR Global Life Reins Ireland	Ireland	100.00
086613	Sweden Reinsurance Co. Ltd.	Sweden	100.00
055362	*Revios US Holdings Inc.*	DE	100.00
073395	SCOR Global Life Re Intl (BB)	Barbados	100.00
006555	SCOR Global Life US Re Ins Co	TX	100.00
006583	Investors Insurance Corp	DE	100.00
060212	SCOR Global Life Re Ins Co TX	TX	100.00
060575	SCOR Global Life Reins Co Amer	DE	100.00
050670	SCOR Financial Services Ltd	Ireland	100.00
078071	SCOR Global Life Re Co Switze	Switzerland	100.00
078344	SCOR Global P&C SE	France	99.99
085445	SCOR Canada Reinsurance Co	Canada	100.00
056935	SCOR Channel Limited	Guernsey	99.98
057336	Arisis Limited	Guernsey	100.00
055528	*SCOR P&C Ireland Holding Ltd*	Ireland	100.00
077713	SCOR Global P&C Ireland Ltd	Ireland	100.00
050672	*SCOR UK Group Ltd*	United Kingdom	100.00
085448	SCOR UK Company Ltd	United Kingdom	100.00
051812	*SCOR Holding (Switzerland) Ltd*	Switzerland	100.00
084820	SCOR Switzerland AG	France	100.00
051813	*SCOR Holding (UK) Limited*	United Kingdom	100.00
089074	SCOR Insurance (UK) Limited	United Kingdom	100.00
075300	SCOR PCC Limited	Guernsey	100.00
085629	SCOR Rueckversicherung (DE) AG	Germany	100.00
088684	SCOR Reins Asia-Pacific Pte	Singapore	100.00
084375	SCOR Reinsurance Co (Asia) Ltd	Hong Kong	100.00
058463	*SCOR U.S. Corporation*	DE	100.00
003599	SCOR Reinsurance Company	NY	100.00
002837	General Security Indem Co AZ	AZ	100.00
060161	**SCOTT & WHITE HEALTH PLAN**		
060393	Insurance Co of Scott & White	TX	100.00
058164	**SCOTTISH RE GROUP LIMITED**		
086896	Scottish Ann&Lf Ins Co(Cayman)	Cayman Islands	100.00
050901	*Scottish Holdings Inc*		100.00
008785	Scottish Re (US) Inc.	DE	100.00
008928	Scottish Re Life Corporation	DE	100.00
051228	*Orkney Holdings, LLC*	DE	100.00
060559	Orkney Re Inc	DE	100.00
078711	Scottish Re Life (Bermuda) Ltd	Bermuda	100.00
072100	Scottish A&L Intl Ins Co (BM)	Bermuda	100.00
075644	Scottish Re (Dublin) Limited	Ireland	100.00
055216	*Scottish Annuity & Life Hldgs*	Bermuda	100.00
073497	Scottish A&L Ins Co BM Ltd	Bermuda	100.00
050748	**SECURITY BENEFIT MUTUAL HLDG**		
051262	*Security Benefit Corporation*		100.00
007025	Security Benefit Life Ins Co	KS	100.00
060104	First Security Benefit L&A NY	NY	100.00
058464	**SECURITY NATIONAL FINANCIAL**		
007127	Security National Life Ins Co	UT	100.00
006184	Capital Reserve Life Ins Co	MO	100.00
068356	Memorial Insurance Co of Amer	AR	100.00
068370	Southern Security Life Ins Co	MS	100.00

AMB#	COMPANY	DOMICILE	% OWN
055810	**SENIOR HEALTH HOLDINGS LLC**		
055811	*Senior Health Holdings Inc*	DE	100.00
064947	Senior Whole Health of NY Inc	NY	100.00
052498	**SENTARA HEALTHCARE**		
068821	OPTIMA Health Plan	VA	100.00
052499	*Sentara Holdings Inc*		100.00
052500	*Sentara Health Plans Inc*		100.00
068490	Optima Health Insurance Co	VA	100.00
002466	**SENTRY INSURANCE A MUTUAL CO**		
000309	Dairyland Insurance Company	WI	100.00
003277	Dairyland Cty Mut Ins Co TX	TX	
002321	Middlesex Insurance Company	WI	100.00
004039	Patriot General Insurance Co	WI	100.00
060403	Parker Centennial Assurance Co	WI	100.00
003588	Sentry Casualty Company	WI	100.00
007041	Sentry Life Ins Co	WI	100.00
007042	Sentry Life Ins Co of New York	NY	100.00
001843	Sentry Lloyds of Texas	TX	
002224	Sentry Select Insurance Co	WI	100.00
004410	Viking Insurance Company of WI	WI	100.00
011414	Peak Prop & Cas Ins Corp	WI	100.00
003626	Viking County Mutual Ins Co	TX	
002319	**SHELTER MUTUAL INSURANCE CO**		
010743	Haulers Insurance Company, Inc	TN	100.00
002318	Shelter General Insurance Co	MO	100.00
006675	Shelter Life Ins Co	MO	100.00
000503	Shelter Reinsurance Company	MO	100.00
031593	**SISTERS OF MERCY HEALTH SYSTEM**		
051077	*MHP Inc*	DE	100.00
060384	Mercy Health Plans	MO	100.00
064419	Mercy Health Plans of MO Inc	MO	100.00
007053	**SOUTHERN FARM BUREAU LIFE INS**		
009118	Southern Capital Life Ins Co	MS	100.00
055471	**SOUTHWEST HEALTH FOUNDATION**		
055472	*Presbyterian Network, Inc.*		100.00
064748	Presbyterian Insurance Company	NM	100.00
068930	Presbyterian Health Plan Inc	NM	100.00
055675	**SOUTHWEST INSURANCE PARTNERS**		
000737	Great Midwest Insurance Co	MI	100.00
008392	National Health Insurance Co	TX	100.00
051903	**SOUTHWEST WASHINGTON HTH SYST**		
064106	Columbia United Providers Inc	WA	89.50
040233	*Southwest Washington Med Ctr*	WA	100.00
051863	**SOUTHWESTERN/GREAT AMER, INC.**		
051864	*Southwestern Ameri Finl Corp*		81.11
068197	Family Heritage Life of Amer	OH	100.00
055209	**SPARROW HEALTH SYSTEM**		
068943	Physicians Hlth Plan of Mid-MI	MI	100.00
060652	PHPMM Insurance Company	MI	100.00
064740	Physicians H P Mid-MI FamCare	MI	100.00
034009	**SPECTRUM HEALTH SYSTEM**		
068977	Priority Health	MI	94.00
060564	Priority Health Insurance Co	MI	100.00
064739	Priority Health Govt Programs	MI	100.00
036921	*Spectrum Health Hospitals*	MI	100.00
036946	*Spectrum Health Reed City Hosp*	MI	100.00
036918	*Spectrum Health United Mem*	MI	100.00
036982	*Spectrum Health Un Meml-Kelsey*	MI	100.00
058174	**STANCORP FINANCIAL GROUP INC**		
007069	Standard Insurance Company	OR	100.00
060342	Standard Life Insurance of NY	NY	100.00
002479	**STATE FARM MUTUAL AUTO INS CO**		
088997	Oglesby Reinsurance Ltd.	Bermuda	100.00
620764	*State Farm Bank FSB*	IL	100.00
002476	State Farm Cty Mutual of TX	TX	
002477	State Farm Fire & Casualty Co	IL	100.00
012235	State Farm Florida Ins Co	FL	100.00
002478	State Farm General Ins Co	IL	100.00
011224	State Farm Indemnity Company	IL	100.00
013016	State Farm Guaranty Ins Co	IL	100.00
007079	State Farm Life & Acc Assur Co	IL	100.00
007080	State Farm Life Ins Co	IL	100.00
009158	State Farm Ann & Life Ins Co	IL	100.00
078618	State Farm Intl Lf Ins Co Ltd	Bermuda	100.00
050159	*State Farm Lloyds Inc*	TX	100.00
001767	State Farm Lloyds	TX	
087157	Top Layer Reinsurance Ltd	Bermuda	50.00
007085	**STATE MUTUAL INS CO**		
007358	Admiral Life Ins Co of America	AZ	100.00
055434	**STERLING HOLDINGS, INC.**		
008841	Sterling Investors Life Ins Co	GA	100.00
051574	**STUDENT ASSURANCE SERVICES INC**		
008650	Investors Growth Life Ins Co	AZ	100.00
034022	**SUMMA HEALTH SYSTEM**		
034073	*Summa Akron City & St Thomas*	OH	100.00
012024	Summa Insurance Company	OH	98.00
060143	SummaCare Inc	OH	100.00
055791	**SUMMIT PARTNERS LP**		
058064	*Fortegra Financial Corp*	GA	78.00
055640	*LOTS Intermediate Co*	DE	100.00
071246	CRC Reassurance Company, Ltd.	Turks And Caicos Islands	100.00
012494	Insurance Company of the South	GA	70.00
008921	Life of the South Insurance Co	GA	100.00
006151	Bankers Life of Louisiana	LA	100.00
012494	Insurance Company of the South	GA	30.00
075015	Lots Reassurance Company	Turks And Caicos Islands	100.00
012167	Lyndon Southern Ins Co	DE	100.00
060271	Southern Financial Life Ins Co	KY	85.00
050913	**SUN LIFE FINANCIAL INC**		
007101	Sun Life Assur Co of Canada	Canada	100.00
055623	*6560016 Canada Inc*	Canada	99.95
088842	Sun Life Reins (BB) No. 2 Corp	Barbados	100.00
052888	*SLF of Canada UK Limited*		100.00
086304	*SLFC Holdings (UK) Plc*	United Kingdom	100.00
087429	SLFC Assurance (UK) Limited	United Kingdom	100.00
078706	Sun Life Financial ID, PT	Indonesia	96.00
072332	Sun Lf Assur Co CN (Barbados)	Barbados	100.00
072333	Sun Life of CA Intl Assur Ltd	Barbados	100.00
055625	*Sun Life Finl of CA (UK)*	United Kingdom	100.00
055624	*Sun Life of Canada (NL) B V*	Netherlands	50.00
088843	Sun Life of Canada (PH), Inc.	Philippines	100.00
090204	Sun Life Everbright Life Ins	China	50.00
055201	*Sun Life Financial (BM) Hldgs*	DE	100.00
078698	Sun Life Finl Ins & Annuity Co	Bermuda	100.00
055205	*Sun Life Finl of Canada UK Ltd*	United Kingdom	100.00
055200	*Sun Life of Canada UK Hldgs*	United Kingdom	100.00
087292	Confederation Life Ins Co (UK)	United Kingdom	100.00
087614	Sun Life Asr Co of Canada (UK)	United Kingdom	100.00
008474	Sun Life and Health Ins Co US	CT	100.00
078701	Sun Life Hong Kong Limited	Hong Kong	100.00
066886	Sun Life Ins (Canada) Ltd	Canada	100.00
074042	Sun Life Reinsurance (IE) Ltd	Ireland	100.00
078700	Sun Life Finl Reins (BB) Ltd	Barbados	100.00
055204	*Sun Life Global Investments*	Canada	100.00
055207	*Sun Life Assr of CA - US Ops H*	Canada	100.00
055202	*Sun Life Financial (US) Hldgs*	Canada	100.00
055203	*Sun Life Financial (US) Invest*	Canada	100.00
055206	*Sun Life of Canada (US) Hldgs*	Canada	100.00
055340	*Dental Holdings Inc*	CT	100.00
064722	California Benefits Dental Pln	CA	100.00
006950	Professional Ins Company	TX	100.00
008226	Sun Life Assur Co of CA (US)	DE	100.00
006547	Independence Life & Annuity Co	RI	100.00
009513	Sun Life Ins & Annuity of NY	NY	100.00
060677	Sun Life Financial US Reins Co	VT	100.00
090967	Sun Life Reins (BB) No 3 Corp	Barbados	100.00
090968	Sun Life Reins (BB) No. 4 Corp	Barbados	100.00
085010	**SWISS REINS CO LTD**		
085830	European Reinsurance Co Zurich	Switzerland	100.00
073415	European Credit & Guarantee	Guernsey	100.00
072587	European Finance Reins Co Ltd	Barbados	100.00
050443	*European Intern Holding Co Ltd*	Barbados	100.00
085982	European Internat Reins Co	Barbados	100.00
050444	*Facility Insurance Holding Cp*	TX	100.00
011239	Facility Insurance Corp	TX	100.00
086792	Swiss Re Africa Limited	South Africa	100.00
050445	*Swiss Re America Holding Corp*	DE	100.00
073394	Stockwood Reinsurance Co Ltd	Barbados	100.00
050068	*Swiss Re L&H Amer Holding Co*	DE	100.00
072639	Life Re International Ltd	Bermuda	100.00
056439	Old Fort Insurance Co Ltd	Bermuda	100.00
007283	Swiss Re Life & Health America	CT	21.00
058081	*Southwestern Life Holdings Inc*	DE	100.00
050972	*SWFC Nevada Inc*	DE	100.00
007283	Swiss Re Life & Health America	CT	79.00
057050	Atlantic Intern Reins Co Ltd	Barbados	100.00
007207	Reassure America Life Ins Co	IN	100.00
076948	Aldgate Reinsurance Co Ltd	Bermuda	100.00
071243	Swiss Re L&H Re Co of BM Ltd	Bermuda	100.00
071299	VFL Intl Life Co SPC Ltd	Cayman Islands	100.00
058158	*Swiss Re Solutions Hldg Corp*	KS	100.00
084295	CORE Reinsurance Company Ltd	Bermuda	100.00
003263	Swiss Reinsurance America Corp	NY	100.00
004101	*Industrial Risk Insurers*	CT	99.50
011135	North American Capacity Ins Co	NH	100.00
010617	North American Elite Ins Co	NH	100.00
001866	North American Specialty Ins	NH	100.00
002695	Washington International Ins	NH	100.00

AMB#	COMPANY	DOMICILE	% OWN
000347	Westport Insurance Corp	MO	100.00
010783	First Specialty Ins Corp	MO	100.00
087159	*Swiss Re Australia Limited*	Australia	100.00
085201	Swiss Re Lf & Hlth Australia L	Australia	100.00
055239	*Swiss Re Management (LU) SA*	Luxembourg	100.00
086847	Swiss Re Europe S.A.	Luxembourg	100.00
085125	Algemene Levensherverzekering	Netherlands	100.00
086463	ERC Frankona Reins (III) Ltd	United Kingdom	100.00
087510	Palatine Insurance Company Ltd	United Kingdom	100.00
086063	Swiss Re Specialty Ins (UK)	United Kingdom	100.00
050424	*Swiss Re Holding ApS*	Denmark	100.00
085501	Swiss Re Denmark Reins A/S	Denmark	100.00
087600	Swiss Re International SE	Luxembourg	100.00
075639	Swiss Re Life&Health (IE) Ltd	Ireland	100.00
086848	Swiss Reinsurance Ireland Ltd	Ireland	100.00
050425	*Swiss Re Frankona Holding GmbH*	Germany	100.00
083891	*Swiss Re Frankona Beteiligungs*	Germany	100.00
055240	*Swiss Re GB Plc*	United Kingdom	100.00
086522	*Admin Re UK Limited*	United Kingdom	77.30
055236	*C Financial Management Limited*	United Kingdom	100.00
087306	C Life Assurance Company Ltd	United Kingdom	100.00
087307	C Life Pensions Limited	United Kingdom	100.00
055237	*G Life H Limited*	United Kingdom	100.00
087358	GL & P Limited	United Kingdom	100.00
055238	*RFSG (UK) Limited*	United Kingdom	100.00
087206	ALAC (UK) Limited	United Kingdom	100.00
085400	Windsor Life Assurance Co Ltd	United Kingdom	100.00
087372	Gresham Life Assur Society Ltd	United Kingdom	100.00
086291	Merc & Gen Re Co plc	United Kingdom	100.00
087480	National Mutual Lf Assur Soc	United Kingdom	100.00
050433	*NM Life Group Limited*	United Kingdom	100.00
087603	NM Life Limited	United Kingdom	100.00
089009	NM Pensions Limited	United Kingdom	100.00
086272	Reassure UK Life Assur Co Ltd	United Kingdom	100.00
087663	XSMA Limited	United Kingdom	100.00
088526	Swiss Re Frankona Reinsurance	United Kingdom	100.00
087622	Swiss Re Life & Health Ltd	United Kingdom	100.00
087621	Swiss Reins Co UK Ltd	United Kingdom	96.20
077618	*Swiss Re Germany Holding AG*	Germany	100.00
085993	Swiss Re Germany AG	Germany	100.00
050447	*Swiss Re Holdings (Canada) Inc*	Canada	100.00
066803	Swiss Re Life & Health Canada	Canada	100.00
086388	Swiss Re Life & Health Africa	South Africa	100.00
073840	Underwriters Reins Co (Barb)	Barbados	
051207	**SYMETRA FINANCIAL CORPORATION**		
007017	Symetra Life Insurance Company	WA	100.00
068147	First Symetra Nat Life Ins NY	NY	100.00
008934	Symetra National Life Ins Co	WA	100.00
055803	**TAKECARE HEALTH SYSTEMS LLP**		
060359	TakeCare Insurance Company Inc	GU	100.00
007112	**TEACHERS INS & ANNUITY ASSOC**		
060222	TIAA-CREF Life Ins Co	NY	100.00
039979	**TEXAS CHILDREN'S HOSPITAL**		
072338	TCH Insurance Co Ltd	Cayman Islands	100.00
064244	Texas Childrens Hlth Plan	TX	100.00
055426	**THOMA CRESSEY BRAVO INC**		
055425	*TC Partners VI L P*		100.00
055421	*Thoma Cressey Fund VI L P*		100.00
050880	*American-Amicable Holding Inc*	DE	100.00
006935	Pioneer Security Life Ins Co	TX	100.00
009122	American-Amicable Life Ins TX	TX	100.00
006849	Occidental Life Ins Co of NC	TX	100.00
006929	Pioneer American Ins Co	TX	100.00
006008	**THRIVENT FINANCIAL LUTHERANS**		
050988	*Thrivent Financial Hldgs Inc*		100.00
620787	*Thrivent Financial Bank*	WI	100.00
009342	Thrivent Life Insurance Co	MN	100.00
052023	**TN RURAL HEALTH IMPROVEMENT AS**		
052024	*RH Group Services Inc*		100.00
009155	Members Health Insurance Co	IN	100.00
060354	TRH Health Insurance Company	TN	100.00
058103	**TORCHMARK CORPORATION**		
006462	Globe Life and Accident Ins Co	NE	100.00
006069	American Income Life Ins Co	IN	100.00
060343	National Income Life Insurance	NY	100.00
006629	Liberty National Life Ins Co	NE	100.00
007175	United Investors Life Ins Co	NE	100.00
074033	TMK Re Ltd	Bermuda	100.00
059282	*Torchmark Capital Trust III*	AL	100.00
007161	United American Ins Co	NE	100.00
009412	First United American Life Ins	NY	100.00
031780	**TORONTO-DOMINION BANK**		
066840	CT Financial Assurance Company	Canada	99.90
055299	*Meloche Monnex Inc*	Canada	100.00
087089	Security National Insurance Co	Canada	100.00
087021	Primmum Insurance Company	Canada	100.00
089791	TD Direct Insurance Inc	Canada	100.00
087028	TD General Insurance Company	Canada	100.00
087725	TD Home and Auto Insurance Co	Canada	100.00
066831	TD Life Insurance Company	Canada	100.00
052658	*TD Vermillion Holdings ULC*	Canada	100.00
055865	*TD Financial International Ltd*	Bermuda	100.00
056952	TD Reinsurance (Barbados) Inc.	Barbados	100.00
055863	*Toronto Dominion Hldgs USA Inc*	IL	100.00
071131	TD USA Insurance, Inc	NY	100.00
064297	**TOTAL HEALTH CARE INC**		
064866	Total Health Care USA Inc	MI	100.00
068742	Total Health Choice Inc	FL	100.00
008051	**TRANS-CITY LIFE INS CO**		
011062	Trans City Casualty Ins Co	AZ	8.50
084090	Trans City Reinsurance Ltd	Turks And Caicos Islands	45.45
084090	Trans City Reinsurance Ltd	Turks And Caicos Islands	45.45
055818	**TREK HOLDINGS INC**		
008304	American Medical and Life Ins	NY	100.00
050905	**TRIPLE-S MANAGEMENT CORP**		
007631	Triple-S Vida, Inc.	PR	100.00
068130	Triple-S Salud Inc	PR	100.00
000370	Triple-S Propiedad, Inc.	PR	100.00
052797	**TRUSTEES SHANNON W TX MEM HSP**		
055166	*Shannon Health System*		
060352	Legacy Health Plan Inc	TX	100.00
064892	Legacy Health Solutions	TX	100.00
039687	*Shannon Medical Center*	TX	100.00
050844	**TRUSTMARK MUTUAL HOLDING CO**		
051167	*Trustmark Group Inc*	IL	100.00
059252	*Trustmark Finance Trust I*	IL	100.00
051166	*Trustmark Insurance Group Inc*	DE	100.00
006165	Trustmark Insurance Company	IL	100.00
006335	Trustmark Life Ins Co	IL	100.00
060706	Trustmark Life Ins Co of NY	NY	100.00
068684	**TUFTS ASSOCIATED HMO INC**		
055798	*Tufts Associated Health Plans*		100.00
060313	Tufts Insurance Co	MA	100.00
050739	**TWA CORPORATION**		
007136	Trans World Assurance Co	CA	100.00
007437	TransAm Assurance Company	AZ	100.00
051370	**21ST CENTURY LIFE & HEALTH CO**		
009200	LifeCare Assurance Co	AZ	100.00
068935	**UCARE MINNESOTA**		
064942	UCare Wisconsin Inc	WI	100.00
051057	**ULLICO INC**		
002623	ULLICO Casualty Company	DE	100.00
011573	Ulico Standard of Amer Cas Co	CA	100.00
007152	Union Labor Life Ins Co	MD	100.00
006316	ULLICO Life Insurance Company	TX	100.00
051337	**UNIFI MUTUAL HOLDING COMPANY**		
050777	*Ameritas Holding Company*	NE	100.00
006152	Ameritas Life Insurance Corp.	NE	100.00
006002	Acacia Life Insurance Company	DC	100.00
052540	*Acacia Financial Corporation*	MD	100.00
620597	*Acacia Federal Savings Bank*	VA	85.21
620597	*Acacia Federal Savings Bank*	VA	14.79
068545	First Ameritas Life of NY	NY	100.00
007150	Union Central Life Ins Co	NE	100.00
055392	**UNITE HERE NATL RETIREMENT FND**		
051479	*Alico Services Corporation*		100.00
006031	Amalgamated Life Ins Co	NY	100.00
055486	**UNITED AMERICAN HEALTHCARE**		
055485	*United American of TN, Inc.*		100.00
064435	UAHC Health Plan of TN Inc	TN	100.00
000928	**UNITED FIRE & CASUALTY COMPANY**		
003223	Addison Insurance Company	IL	100.00
058318	*American Indemnity Finl Corp*	DE	100.00
002038	Texas General Indemnity Co	CO	100.00
000552	Lafayette Insurance Company	LA	100.00
002036	United Fire & Indemn Company	TX	100.00
001775	United Fire Lloyds	TX	
007178	United Life Ins Co	IA	100.00
058796	**UNITED HERITAGE MUTUAL HLDG CO**		
051333	*United Heritage Financial Grp*	ID	100.00
006472	United Heritage Life Ins Co	ID	100.00
010062	United Heritage Prop & Cas Co	ID	100.00
003614	Sublimity Insurance Company	OR	100.00

AMB#	COMPANY	DOMICILE	% OWN
051625	**UNITED INTERNATIONAL CORP**		
060387	United International Life Ins	OK	100.00
000934	**UNITED SERVICES AUTO ASSN**		
013592	Catastrophe Reinsurance Co	TX	100.00
076463	Enterprise Indemnity Captive	AZ	100.00
058488	*USAA Capital Corporation*	TX	100.00
620582	*USAA Federal Savings Bank*	TX	100.00
612200	*USAA Savings Bank*	NV	100.00
004049	USAA Casualty Insurance Co	TX	100.00
012120	Garrison Prop & Cas Ins Co	TX	100.00
011699	USAA County Mutual Ins Co	TX	
054012	*USAA Lloyd's Attorney-In-Fact*	TX	100.00
012460	USAA Texas Lloyd's Company	TX	
004865	USAA General Indemnity Co	TX	100.00
007146	USAA Life Ins Co	TX	100.00
060314	USAA Direct Life Insurance Co	NE	100.00
060247	USAA Life Ins Co of NY	NY	100.00
087660	USAA Limited	United Kingdom	100.00
058106	**UNITEDHEALTH GROUP INC**		
051721	*AmeriChoice Corporation*	DE	100.00
060689	AmeriChoice of Connecticut Inc	CT	100.00
064965	AmeriChoice of Georgia Inc	GA	100.00
064214	AmeriChoice of New Jersey	NJ	100.00
064159	AmeriChoice of Pennsylvania	PA	100.00
064439	Great Lakes Health Plan Inc	MI	100.00
051977	*Three Rivers Holdings Inc*		100.00
064963	Unison Health Plan of Cap Area	DC	100.00
064962	Unison Health Plan of Delaware	DE	100.00
064886	Unison Health Plan of SC Inc	SC	100.00
064879	Unison Health Plan of TN Inc	TN	100.00
051976	*Unison Health Holdings of Ohio*		100.00
064874	Unison Health Plan of Ohio Inc	OH	100.00
064104	Unison Health Plan of PA Inc	PA	100.00
064925	Unison Family Health Plan PA	PA	100.00
068856	UnitedHealthcare of New York	NY	100.00
050853	*Golden Rule Financial Corp*		100.00
009556	All Savers Insurance Co	IN	100.00
060029	All Savers Life Ins Co of CA	CA	100.00
007771	American Medical Security Life	WI	100.00
006263	Golden Rule Ins Co	IN	100.00
073730	H & W Indemnity Ltd	Cayman Islands	100.00
051203	*Mid Atlantic Medical Services*	DE	100.00
006046	MAMSI Life and Health Ins	MD	100.00
068606	MD-Individual Practice Assoc	MD	100.00
068764	Optimum Choice Inc	MD	100.00
051698	*Oxford Health Plans, LLC*	DE	100.00
068520	Health Net of Connecticut Inc	CT	100.00
011859	Health Net Ins of New York Inc	NY	100.00
064005	Health Net of New Jersey Inc	NJ	100.00
068568	Health Net of New York Inc	NY	100.00
068933	Oxford Health Plans (CT) Inc	CT	100.00
068934	Oxford Health Plans (NJ) Inc	NJ	100.00
068716	Oxford Health Plans (NY) Inc	NY	100.00
060022	Oxford Health Ins Inc	NY	100.00
058078	*PacifiCare Health Systems, LLC*	DE	100.00
051254	*PacifiCare Behavioral Health*	DE	100.00
064644	PacifiCare Bhvrl Health of CA	CA	100.00
050932	*PacifiCare Health Plan Admin*	IN	100.00
057272	FHP Reinsurance Ltd	Bermuda	100.00
064840	PacifiCare Dental of Colorado	CO	100.00
007278	PacifiCare Life and Health Ins	IN	99.00
008428	PacifiCare Life Assurance Co	CO	100.00
064218	PacifiCare of Arizona Inc	AZ	100.00
068705	PacifiCare of California	CA	100.00
068639	PacifiCare of Colorado Inc	CO	100.00
064219	PacifiCare of Nevada Inc	NV	100.00
068582	PacifiCare of Oklahoma Inc	OK	100.00
068707	PacifiCare of Oregon Inc	OR	100.00
068706	PacifiCare of Texas Inc	TX	100.00
068591	PacifiCare of Washington	WA	100.00
051697	*Salveo Holding LLC*	DE	100.00
075544	Salveo Insurance Company Ltd	Cayman Islands	100.00
050768	*UnitedHealthcare Services Inc*	MN	100.00
051696	*ACN Group, Inc.*	MN	100.00
064816	ACN Group of California Inc	CA	100.00
050773	*Dental Benefits Providers Inc*	DE	100.00
064716	Dental Benefit Providers of CA	CA	100.00
064690	Dental Benefit Providers of IL	IL	100.00
051205	*Ovations Inc*	DE	100.00
064745	Evercare of Texas LLC	TX	100.00
050769	*OptumHealth Inc*	DE	100.00
033020	*PacificDental Benefits, Inc.*	DE	100.00
068837	National Pacific Dental Inc	TX	100.00
064826	Nevada Pacific Dental Inc	NV	100.00
009065	Unimerica Insurance Company	WI	100.00
050770	*UHIC Holdings Inc*	DE	100.00
008290	UnitedHealthcare Ins Co	CT	100.00
060688	Evercare of New Mexico Inc	NM	100.00
060392	Unimerica Life Ins Co of NY	NY	100.00
060071	UnitedHealthcare Ins Co of IL	IL	100.00
060108	UnitedHealthcare Ins Co of NY	NY	100.00
060046	UnitedHealthcare Ins Co of OH	OH	100.00
051206	*United Behavioral Health*	CA	100.00
064733	U S Behavioral Health Plan CA	CA	100.00
050767	*UnitedHealthcare Inc*	DE	100.00
068102	IBA Health and Life Assur Co	MI	100.00
008297	Midwest Security Life Ins Co	WI	100.00
064001	Neighborhood Hlth Partnership	FL	100.00
058096	*Sierra Health Services Inc*	NV	100.00
068619	Health Plan of Nevada Inc	NV	100.00
007370	Sierra Hlth & Lf Ins Co Inc	CA	100.00
068500	UnitedHealthcare of Alabama	AL	100.00
068847	UnitedHealthcare of Arizona	AZ	100.00
068914	UnitedHealthcare of Arkansas	AR	100.00
068848	UnitedHealthcare of Colorado	CO	100.00
068782	UnitedHealthcare of Florida	FL	100.00
068893	UnitedHealthcare of Georgia	GA	100.00
068532	UnitedHealthcare of Illinois	IL	100.00
068661	UnitedHealthcare of Louisiana	LA	100.00
068987	UnitedHealthcare of Mid-Atl	MD	100.00
068892	UnitedHealthcare of Midlands	NE	100.00
068560	UnitedHealthcare of Midwest	MO	100.00
060118	UnitedHealthcare of MS	MS	100.00
068572	UnitedHealthcare of NC	NC	100.00
068730	UnitedHealthcare of TN Inc	TN	100.00
068841	UnitedHealthcare of TX Inc	TX	100.00
068770	UnitedHealthcare of Utah	UT	100.00
068824	UnitedHealthcare of Wisconsin	WI	100.00
051703	*UnitedHlthcare S River Valley*	DE	100.00
064827	UnitedHealthcare Ins Rvr Vall	IL	100.00
068702	UnitedHealthcare Plan Rvr Vall	IL	100.00
068690	UnitedHealthcare of KY Ltd	KY	94.18
068891	UnitedHealthcare of New Eng	RI	100.00
068580	UnitedHealthcare of Ohio Inc	OH	100.00
058711	**UNITRIN, INC**		
006986	Reliable Life Insurance Co	MO	100.00
003829	Capitol County Mutual Fire	TX	
003807	Old Reliable Casualty Company	MO	100.00
002523	Trinity Universal Ins Co	TX	100.00
002634	Alpha Property & Casualty Ins	WI	100.00
050189	*Direct Response Corporation*	CT	100.00
012149	Response Indemnity Co of CA	CA	100.00
011946	Response Insurance Company	IL	100.00
002701	National Merit Insurance Co	WA	100.00
012032	Response Indemnity Company	NY	100.00
000609	Response Worldwide Ins Co	CT	100.00
002028	Warner Insurance Company	IL	100.00
003045	Response Worldwide Dir Auto	IL	100.00
000391	Financial Indemnity Company	CA	100.00
012213	Kemper Independence Ins Co	IL	100.00
055373	*Merastar Industries, Ltd.*	DE	100.00
003596	Merastar Insurance Company	IN	100.00
003199	Union National Fire Ins Co	LA	100.00
002533	United Casualty Ins Co of Amer	IL	100.00
012163	Unitrin Advantage Ins Co	NY	100.00
012560	Unitrin Auto and Home Ins Co	NY	100.00
011762	Unitrin Direct Insurance Co	IL	100.00
012212	Unitrin Direct Prop & Cas Co	IL	100.00
012561	Unitrin Preferred Ins Co	NY	100.00
003289	Unitrin Safeguard Insurance Co	WI	100.00
050391	*Valley Group Inc*	OR	100.00
050392	*Charter Group Inc*	TX	100.00
010419	Charter Indemnity Company	TX	100.00
001873	Valley Insurance Company	CA	100.00
011979	Valley Property & Casualty Ins	OR	100.00
007155	Union National Life Ins Co	LA	100.00
007174	United Insurance Co of America	IL	100.00
006753	Mutual Savings Life Ins Co	AL	100.00
003655	Mutual Savings Fire Ins Co	AL	100.00
006998	Reserve National Ins Co	OK	100.00
051476	**UNITY FINANCIAL INS GROUP LLC**		
006454	Unity Financial Life Ins Co	PA	100.00
007196	**UNITY MUTUAL LIFE INS CO**		
052519	*Securitas Financial Group LLC*	DE	100.00
009068	Securitas Financial Life Ins	NC	100.00
058109	**UNIVERSAL AMERICAN CORP.**		
051513	*Heritage Health Systems Inc*	DE	100.00
051388	*Harmony Health, Inc.*	OK	100.00
064790	GlobalHealth Inc	OK	100.00
052030	*Heritage Physician Network*	GA	100.00
064744	SelectCare of Texas LLC	TX	25.50
051544	*PSO Management of Texas LLC*	GA	100.00
064744	SelectCare of Texas LLC	TX	74.50
064845	SelectCare Health Plans Inc	TX	100.00
064844	SelectCare of Oklahoma Inc	OK	100.00
064975	SelectCare of Maine	TX	100.00
064977	HHS Health of Oklahoma Inc	OK	100.00
052796	*UAC Holding Inc*	DE	100.00
006090	American Pioneer Life Ins Co	FL	100.00
008411	American Progressive L&H NY	NY	100.00
006273	Constitution Life Ins Co	TX	100.00

AMB#	COMPANY	DOMICILE	% OWN
007311	Marquette National Life Ins Co	TX	100.00
006905	Pennsylvania Life Insurance Co	PA	100.00
006977	Pyramid Life Insurance Company	KS	100.00
007149	Union Bankers Ins Co	TX	100.00
055815	**UNIVERSAL FIDELITY HOLDING CO**		
007198	Universal Fidelity Life Ins Co	OK	100.00
050701	**UNIVERSAL GROUP, INC.**		
003665	Universal Insurance Co (PR)	PR	100.00
012337	Caribbean Alliance Ins Co	PR	100.00
001895	Eastern America Insurance Co	PR	100.00
011864	Richport Insurance Company	PR	100.00
084396	Richport Reinsurance Co Ltd	Bermuda	100.00
060097	Universal Life Insurance Co	PR	100.00
052592	*Universal Overseas, Inc.*		100.00
051259	*Universal Ins Hldgs NA Ins.*	DE	100.00
013118	Universal Specialty Ins Co	FL	100.00
012713	Universal Ins Co North America	FL	100.00
011600	Universal North America Ins Co	TX	100.00
034070	**UNIVERSITY HOSPITALS HLTH SYST**		
011644	QualChoice Health Plan	OH	100.00
051666	**UNIVERSITY OF AL BRD TRUSTEES**		
051667	*Triton Health Systems LLC*		99.00
064257	VIVA Health Inc	AL	100.00
031873	**UNIVERSITY PITTSBURGH MED CTR**		
064549	Community Care Behavioral Hlth	PA	100.00
050976	*UPMC Holding Company Inc*		100.00
050975	*UPMC Coverage Products Inc*		100.00
056295	Forbes Re-Insurance Co Ltd	Cayman Islands	100.00
056202	Cathedral Insurance Co Ltd	Cayman Islands	100.00
056300	Freedom Insurance Co	VT	100.00
072313	Panther Reinsurance Co Ltd	Cayman Islands	100.00
011445	Tri Century Insurance Company	PA	100.00
012486	UPMC Health Benefits Inc	PA	100.00
064808	UPMC Health Network Inc	PA	100.00
064162	UPMC Health Plan Inc	PA	88.66
064807	UPMC For You Inc	PA	100.00
058110	**UNUM GROUP**		
006238	Colonial Life & Accident Ins	SC	100.00
006514	First Unum Life Ins Co	NY	100.00
059632	*Northwind Holdings, LLC*	DE	100.00
013864	Northwind Reinsurance Company	VT	100.00
006899	Paul Revere Life Ins Co	MA	100.00
006900	Paul Revere Variable Annuity	MA	100.00
006968	Provident Life and Accident	TN	85.90
006969	Provident Life and Casualty	TN	100.00
051540	*Tailwind Holdings LLC*	NY	100.00
060589	Tailwind Reinsurance Company	SC	100.00
055748	*Unum European Holding Co Ltd*	United Kingdom	80.00
087658	UNUM Limited	United Kingdom	72.00
006256	Unum Life Ins Co of Amer	ME	100.00
072763	Unumprovident International	Bermuda	100.00
009586	**USABLE MUTUAL INSURANCE CO**		
068964	HMO Partners Inc	AR	50.00
050925	USAble Corporation	AR	100.00
051221	**USIC GROUP, INC.**		
011138	United Surety & Indemnity Co	PR	100.00
010008	USIC of Florida Inc	FL	100.00
060567	USIC Life Insurance Company	PR	100.00
055808	**UTMB HEALTH CARE SYSTEMS INC**		
064511	UTMB Health Plans Inc	TX	100.00
034016	**VALLEY BAPTIST HEALTH SYSTEM**		
052614	*Valley Baptist Hospital Hldgs*		100.00
034077	*Valley Baptist Med Ctr-Brwnvil*	TX	100.00
034076	*Valley Baptist Med C-Harlingen*	TX	100.00
055639	*Valley Baptist Investmnt Hldgs*		100.00
055638	*Valley Baptist Insurance Hldgs*		100.00
064852	Valley Baptist Insurance Co	TX	100.00
051054	**VAN ENTERPRISES**		
010362	Old United Casualty Company	KS	100.00
007879	Old United Life Ins Co	AZ	100.00
007021	**VANTIS LIFE INSURANCE COMPANY**		
060691	Vantis Life Insurance Co of NY	NY	100.00
055420	**VICTORY INSURANCE CORPORATION**		
007132	Trans-Oceanic Life Ins Co	PR	100.00
051834	**VIRGINIA COMMONWEALTH U H SYST**		
051836	*University Health Services Inc*	VA	100.00
051835	*University Health Svcs Mgd Cr*	VA	100.00
064251	Virginia Premier Health Plan	VA	100.00
064607	**VISION SERVICE PLAN**		
050924	*Altair Holding Company (CA)*		100.00
011496	Vision Service Plan Ins Co(MO)	MO	100.00

AMB#	COMPANY	DOMICILE	% OWN
064484	Alaska Vision Services Inc	AK	100.00
064483	Eastern Vision Service Plan	NY	100.00
065725	Indiana Vision Services Inc	IN	100.00
064479	Massachusetts Vision Svc Plan	MA	100.00
064478	Mid-Atlantic Vision Service Pl	VA	100.00
064474	Vision Service Plan Inc	NV	100.00
011105	Vision Service Plan Ins Co(CT)	CT	100.00
064482	Vision Service Plan of Idaho	ID	100.00
064473	Vision Service Plan (OH)	OH	100.00
064476	Vision Services Plan Inc OK	OK	100.00
064834	Vision Service Plan of IL NFP	IL	100.00
064475	Vision Service Plan (WA)	WA	100.00
064477	Wisconsin Vision Service Plan	WI	100.00
051833	**VISTA SERVICE CORPORATION**		
064245	VISTA Health Plan Inc	TX	100.00
058496	**W. R. BERKLEY CORPORATION**		
055588	*Berkley International, LLC*	NY	2.00
006579	Berkley Life and Health Ins Co	IA	100.00
076268	Greenwich Knight Ins Co Ltd	Bermuda	100.00
050255	*J/I Holding Corporation*	DE	100.00
003026	Admiral Insurance Company	DE	100.00
011348	Admiral Indemnity Company	DE	100.00
055588	*Berkley International, LLC*	NY	35.00
055587	*Berkley Intl Latinoamerica S A*	Argentina	97.99
077525	Berkley Intl ART	Argentina	9.93
088726	Berkley Intl do Brasil Seg SA	Brazil	99.60
077383	Berkley International Seg SA	Argentina	99.60
077525	Berkley Intl ART	Argentina	90.07
077491	Indepenedencia Cia Seg Vida SA	Argentina	49.20
090789	Berkley Intl Seg, S.A. Uruguay	Uruguay	100.00
077491	Indepenedencia Cia Seg Vida SA	Argentina	50.80
088726	Berkley Intl do Brasil Seg SA	Brazil	.40
055533	*Berkley London Holdings, Inc.*	DE	67.00
055532	*W.R. Berkley London Hldgs, Ltd*	United Kingdom	100.00
083829	W R Berkley Ins (Europe) Ltd	United Kingdom	100.00
000236	Carolina Casualty Ins Co	IA	100.00
002586	Clermont Insurance Company	IA	100.00
001990	Nautilus Insurance Company	AZ	100.00
055588	*Berkley International, LLC*	NY	14.00
011231	Great Divide Insurance Co	ND	100.00
088725	East Isles Reinsurance, Ltd.	Bermuda	100.00
056478	Queen's Island Ins Co Ltd	Bermuda	100.00
050254	*Signet Star Holdings Inc*	DE	100.00
003630	Berkley Insurance Company	DE	100.00
055533	*Berkley London Holdings, Inc.*	DE	33.00
055588	*Berkley International, LLC*	NY	35.00
011945	Berkley Regional Insurance Co	DE	100.00
011295	Acadia Insurance Company	NH	100.00
055588	*Berkley International, LLC*	NY	14.00
011296	Berkley Regional Specialty Ins	DE	100.00
058944	*CGH Insurance Group, Inc*	AL	100.00
010436	American Mining Insurance Co	AL	100.00
000971	Continental Western Ins Co	IA	100.00
002183	Firemens Ins Co of Wash, DC	DE	100.00
000918	Tri-State Insurance Co of MN	MN	100.00
002532	Union Insurance Company	IA	100.00
002662	Berkley National Insurance Co	IA	100.00
050253	*Union Standard Management Co*	TX	100.00
001876	Union Standard Lloyds	TX	
012118	Gemini Insurance Company	DE	100.00
012190	Key Risk Insurance Company	NC	100.00
000739	Midwest Employers Casualty Co	DE	100.00
012191	Preferred Employers Ins Co	CA	100.00
011017	Riverport Insurance Company	MN	100.00
012245	StarNet Insurance Company	DE	100.00
085802	**WAWANESA MUTUAL INSURANCE CO**		
011976	Wawanesa General Insurance Co	CA	100.00
060079	Wawanesa Life Ins Co	Canada	100.00
052545	**WEA INSURANCE TRUST**		
009506	WEA Insurance Corporation	WI	100.00
051244	**WELLCARE HEALTH PLANS, INC.**		
051407	*WCG Health Management, Inc.*	DE	100.00
051453	*WellCare Management Group Inc*	NY	100.00
076858	Comprehensive Reinsurance Ltd	Cayman Islands	100.00
064956	Harmony Behavioral Health FL	FL	100.00
055221	*Harmony Health Systems Inc*	NJ	100.00
064093	Harmony Health Plan of IL Inc	IL	100.00
064647	HealthEase of Florida Inc	FL	100.00
012173	WellCare Health Ins of NY Inc	NY	100.00
009567	WellCare Health Insurance AZ	AZ	100.00
006530	WellCare Health Insurance IL	IL	100.00
064957	WellCare Health Plans of NJ	NJ	100.00
064118	WellCare of Florida Inc	FL	100.00
051405	WellCare of Georgia Inc	GA	100.00
064820	WellCare of Louisiana Inc	LA	100.00
068750	WellCare of New York Inc	NY	100.00
060116	WellCare of Connecticut Inc	CT	100.00
051406	WellCare of Ohio Inc	OH	100.00
064955	WellCare of South Carolina Inc	SC	100.00

AMB#	COMPANY	DOMICILE	% OWN
064954	WellCare of Texas Inc	TX	100.00
051404	WellCare Prescription Ins Inc	FL	100.00
068347	**WELLMARK INC**		
064385	Wellmark Health Plan of Iowa	IA	85.00
060207	Wellmark of South Dakota Inc	SD	100.00
058180	**WELLPOINT INC.**		
055956	*ATH Holding Company, LLC*	IN	100.00
068044	Anthem Health Plans Inc	CT	100.00
060150	Anthem Health Plans of KY Inc	KY	100.00
064173	Anthem Health Plans of NH Inc	NH	100.00
068999	Matthew Thornton Health Plan	NH	100.00
064391	Anthem Health Plans of ME Inc	ME	100.00
011803	Community Insurance Company	OH	100.00
008665	OneNation Insurance Company	IN	100.00
068817	Rocky Mountain Hosp & Med Svc	CO	100.00
006126	Anthem Life Insurance Company	IN	100.00
068927	HMO Colorado Inc	CO	100.00
058493	*Anthem Holding Corp.*	IN	100.00
050847	*Cerulean Companies Inc*	GA	100.00
068527	BC BS Healthcare Plan of GA	GA	100.00
060075	Blue Cross & Blue Shield of GA	GA	100.00
009177	Greater Georgia Life Ins Co	GA	100.00
051153	*Crossroads Acquisition Corp*	CA	100.00
064315	Blue Cross Blue Shield of WI	WI	100.00
068610	Compcare Health Services Ins	WI	100.00
055385	*DeCare Dental, LLC*		100.00
078926	DeCare Dental Ins Ireland Ltd	Ireland	100.00
051050	*RightCHOICE Managed Care Inc*	DE	100.00
050866	*Healthlink Inc*		100.00
060152	HealthLink HMO Inc	MO	100.00
008217	Healthy Alliance Life Ins Co	MO	100.00
068790	HMO Missouri Inc	MO	100.00
060024	RightCHOICE Insurance Co	IL	100.00
050846	*UNICARE National Services Inc*	DE	100.00
051020	*UNICARE Health Benefit Srvcs*		100.00
060368	UNICARE Health Ins Co of TX	TX	100.00
064240	UNICARE Health Plans of TX	TX	100.00
064878	UNICARE Health Plan of Kansas	KS	100.00
064776	UNICARE Health Plan of WV	WV	100.00
050928	*UNICARE Illinois Services Inc*	IL	100.00
009437	UNICARE Health Ins of Midwest	IL	100.00
068895	UNICARE Health Plans Midwest	IL	100.00
009233	UNICARE Life & Health Ins Co	IN	100.00
064246	UNICARE of TX Hlth Plans Inc	TX	100.00
050845	*WellPoint California Services*		100.00
060057	Anthem BC Life & Health Ins Co	CA	100.00
068970	Blue Cross of California	CA	100.00
064721	Golden West Health Plan Inc	CA	100.00
000607	Anthem Insurance Companies Inc	IN	100.00
051066	*Anthem Southeast Inc*	IN	100.00
068315	Anthem Health Plans of VA	VA	100.00
068669	HealthKeepers Inc	VA	88.89
068745	Peninsula Health Care Inc	VA	51.00
050807	*Priority Inc*		100.00
068916	Priority Health Care Inc	VA	100.00
052020	*WellPoint Acquisition LLC*	IN	100.00
060687	Anthem Lf & Disability Ins Co	NY	100.00
051301	*WellPoint Holding Corp*	DE	100.00
068564	Empire HealthChoice Assurance	NY	100.00
064368	Empire HealthChoice HMO Inc	NY	100.00
601610	**WELLS FARGO & COMPANY**		
607433	*ACO Brokerage Holdings Corp*	IL	100.00
607559	*Wells Fargo Insurance Services*	IL	100.00
050685	*Wells Fargo Insurance Inc*	MN	100.00
054017	*Rural Community Ins Agency Inc*	MN	100.00
002647	Rural Community Insurance Co	MN	100.00
600161	*FNL Insurance Company*	VT	100.00
057252	Superior Guaranty Insurance Co	VT	100.00
031916	*Wachovia Corp (First Union)*	NC	100.00
068201	Financial Life Ins Co of GA	GA	100.00
007498	Wachovia Life Insurance Co	AZ	100.00
055632	*WDS Holdings Inc*	DE	100.00
055631	*WDSI LLC*	DE	100.00
002771	Heritage Indemnity Company	CA	100.00
050412	*Westlake Group Ltd*	Turks And Caicos Islands	100.00
056582	Westlake Insurance Co (BM) Ltd	Bermuda	100.00
050682	*Wells Fargo Financial Serv Inc*	DE	100.00
050683	*Wells Fargo Financial Inc*	IA	100.00
001951	Centurion Casualty Company	IA	100.00
006276	Centurion Life Ins Co	IA	100.00
603899	*Wells Fargo Finl Minnesota*	IA	100.00
604521	*Wells Fargo Finl Acceptance*	IA	100.00
057412	CGT Insurance Co Ltd	Barbados	100.00
606306	*WFC Holdings Corporation*	CA	100.00
615190	*Wells Fargo Bank NA*	SD	100.00
605943	*Mulberry Asset Management Inc*	NV	100.00
052784	*Pelican Asset Management Inc*	DE	100.00
052783	*Violet Asset Management Inc*	DE	100.00
032654	Intrawest Asset Management Inc		100.00
052570	*Carnation Asset Management Inc*	DE	100.00
073390	Golden Pacific Insurance Co	VT	100.00
052782	*Falcon Asset Management Inc*	DE	100.00
007924	Blue Spirit Ins Co	VT	100.00
076290	IWIC Insurance Company	VT	100.00
052781	*Pheasant Asset Management Inc*	DE	100.00
072106	Great Plains Insurance Co	VT	100.00
050735	**WESTERN & SOUTHERN MUT HLDG CO**		
050736	*Western & Southern Finan Grp*	OH	100.00
006617	Lafayette Life Ins Co	IN	100.00
007243	Western and Southern Life Ins	OH	100.00
006244	Columbus Life Insurance Co	OH	100.00
007739	Integrity Life Ins Co	OH	100.00
007798	National Integrity Life Ins Co	NY	100.00
009071	Western-Southern Life Assur	OH	100.00
051824	**WESTERN FINANCIAL GROUP INC**		
066506	SecuriCan General Insurance Co	Canada	100.00
066802	Western Life Assurance Company	Canada	100.00
007248	**WICHITA NATIONAL LIFE INS CO**		
009453	Sheridan Life Ins Co	OK	100.00
064402	**WILLAMETTE DENTAL OF IDAHO INC**		
064529	Willamette Dental of WA Inc	WA	100.00
064497	Willamette Dental Insurance	OR	100.00
052493	**WILLIS-KNIGHTON MEDICAL CENTER**		
064279	Health Plus of Louisiana Inc	LA	100.00
051608	**WILTON RE HOLDINGS LIMITED**		
051607	*Wilton Re U S Holdings Inc*	DE	100.00
060560	Wilton Reassurance Company	MN	100.00
051606	*Redding Re Holdings LLC*	DE	100.00
060593	Redding Reassurance Company	SC	100.00
007118	Texas Life Ins Co	TX	100.00
006084	Wilton Reassurance Life Co NY	NY	100.00
077621	Wilton Reinsurance Bermuda Ltd	Bermuda	100.00
051823	**WINDSOR HEALTH GROUP INC**		
060115	Windsor Health Plan Inc	TN	100.00
060073	**WISCONSIN PHYSICIANS SRVC INS**		
009476	EPIC Life Ins Co	WI	100.00
064830	WPS Health Plan Inc	WI	100.00
003482	**WORKERS COMPENSATION FUND**		
060210	Univantage Insurance Co	UT	100.00
051647	**WORKMEN'S HOLDING COMPANY**		
000980	Workmen's Auto Insurance Co	CA	100.00
008125	Workmen's Life Ins Co	AZ	100.00
054016	**WRIGHT TITUS AGENCY**		
002560	Consolidated Lloyds	TX	
054015	*Consolidated Texas Corporation*	DE	100.00
002559	Consolidated Insurance Assn	TX	
004682	Consumers County Mutual Ins Co	TX	
006653	Life Protection Ins Co	TX	37.71
058361	**XL CAPITAL LTD**		
051043	*EXEL Holdings Ltd*	Cayman Islands	100.00
085633	XL Insurance (Bermuda) Ltd	Bermuda	100.00
058414	*Mid Ocean Limited*	Cayman Islands	100.00
051060	*Mid Ocean Holdings Ltd*	Bermuda	100.00
086106	XL Re Ltd	Bermuda	100.00
078611	ECS Reinsurance Company Inc.	Barbados	100.00
078617	XL Mid Ocean Re Limited	United Kingdom	100.00
078455	XL Re Europe Limited	Ireland	100.00
086824	XL Re Latin America Ltd	Switzerland	100.00
052411	*XL Brazil Holdings AG*	Switzerland	100.00
052413	*XL Re Participacoes Brasil SA*	Brazil	100.00
090491	XL Resseguros Brasil S.A.	Brazil	100.00
051707	*XL Financial Holdings (Ire)*	Ireland	100.00
051041	*XL America Inc*	DE	100.00
055121	*NAC Re Corporation*	DE	100.00
002104	XL Reinsurance America Inc.	NY	100.00
011095	Greenwich Insurance Co	DE	100.00
002423	XL Insurance America Inc	DE	100.00
012182	XL Insurance Co of New York	NY	100.00
002424	XL Select Insurance Company	DE	100.00
000779	XL Specialty Insurance Company	DE	100.00
011340	Indian Harbor Insurance Co	ND	100.00
050958	*XL Life and Annuity Holding Co*	DE	100.00
060395	XL Life Ins and Annuity Co	IL	100.00
052412	*XL Gracechurch Limited*	United Kingdom	100.00
055120	*XL Insurance (UK) Holdings Ltd*	United Kingdom	100.00
084135	XL Ins Argentina SA Cia Seg	Argentina	90.00
087674	XL Insurance Company Limited	United Kingdom	100.00
055119	*XL Holdings (Proprietary) Ltd*	South Africa	100.00
078615	XL Insurance Company Limited	South Africa	100.00
073313	XL Life Ltd	Bermuda	100.00
055114	*XL (Luxembourg) S.a.r.l.*	Luxembourg	100.00
055112	*XL (Finance) S.a.r.l.*	Luxembourg	100.00
055113	*XL (International) S.a.r.l.*	Luxembourg	100.00

Corporate Structures – *Continued*

AMB#	COMPANY	DOMICILE	% OWN
055115	*XL (Services) S.a.r.l.*	Luxembourg	100.00
055116	*XL (Specialty) S.a.r.l.*	Luxembourg	100.00
051062	*XL (Western Europe) S.a.r.l.*	Luxembourg	100.00
051065	*XL Swiss Holdings Ltd*	Switzerland	100.00
078061	Vitodurum Rueckversicherungs	Switzerland	100.00
078108	XL Insurance Mexico SA de CV	Mexico	100.00
078050	XL Versicherungen Schweiz AG	Switzerland	100.00
058498	**ZALE CORPORATION**		
051521	*Zale Delaware, Inc.*	DE	100.00
086138	Jewel Re-Insurance Ltd	Barbados	100.00
003564	Zale Indemnity Company	TX	100.00
007349	Zale Life Ins Co	AZ	100.00
086976	**ZURICH FINANCIAL SERVICES LTD**		
050458	*Allied Zurich PLC*	United Kingdom	100.00
055929	*Dalegate Limited*	Cyprus	100.00
078882	Zurich Retail Insurance Co Ltd	Russia	66.00
078066	Orion Rechtsschutz-Versich	Switzerland	78.00
083271	Zurich Sigorta A.S.	Turkey	100.00
055875	*Zurich Asia Holdings Limited*	Malaysia	
089136	MCIS Zurich Insurance Berhad	Malaysia	40.00
011493	Island Home Insurance Company	GU	100.00
087190	Zuerich Beteiligungs-AG (DE)	Germany	100.00
086269	DA Deutsche Allgemeine Vers AG	Germany	100.00
055872	*Deutscher Herold AG*	Germany	77.80
077719	Deutscher Pensionsfonds AG	Germany	74.90
087183	Zuerich Deutscher Herold Leben	Germany	67.50
087188	Zuerich Versicherung AG (DE)	Germany	100.00
086972	Zurich Brasil Seguros S A	Brazil	
083743	*Zurich Finan Serv Australia*	Australia	100.00
086167	Zurich Australian Ins Ltd	Australia	100.00
083775	Zurich Australia Limited	Australia	100.00
083412	*Zurich Financial Serv UKISA*	United Kingdom	100.00
085950	*Allied Dunbar Assurance plc*	United Kingdom	99.90
085815	*Eagle Star Holdings Limited*	United Kingdom	100.00
085813	Zurich Assurance Ltd	United Kingdom	100.00
084155	Zurich Assurance (2004) plc	United Kingdom	100.00
050442	*Zurich Group Holding*	Switzerland	100.00
058511	*Farmers Group Inc*	CA	86.60
002171	Farmers Insurance Exchange	CA	
003100	Farmers Insurance Company Inc	KS	90.00
004158	Farmers Insurance Co of AZ	AZ	70.00
004159	Farmers Insurance Co of ID	ID	80.00
004305	Farmers Insurance Co of OR	OR	80.00
002784	Farmers Insurance Hawaii, Inc.	HI	80.00
002577	Farmers Ins of Columbus Inc	OH	100.00
058375	*Foremost Corp of America*	MT	80.00
002189	Foremost Insurance Company	MI	100.00
001879	American Federation Ins Co	FL	100.00
003634	Foremost County Mutual Ins Co	TX	
001753	Foremost Lloyds of Texas	TX	
001897	Foremost Prop & Cas Ins Co	MI	100.00
001754	Foremost Signature Ins Co	MI	100.00
004083	Illinois Farmers Ins Co	IL	100.00
012089	Farmers New Century Ins Co	IL	100.00
002173	Mid-Century Insurance Co	CA	80.00
050320	*Bristol West Holdings, Inc.*	FL	47.50
013761	Bristol West Preferred Ins Co	MI	100.00
050321	*Coast National Holding Company*		100.00
000177	Coast National Insurance Co	CA	100.00
012404	Bristol West Casualty Ins Co	OH	100.00
012461	Bristol West Insurance Company	OH	100.00
010796	Security National Ins Co	FL	100.00
000270	Mid-Century Ins Co of Texas	TX	100.00
011780	Neighborhood Spirit P&C Co	CA	80.00
003312	Texas Farmers Insurance Co	TX	86.30
058300	*21st Century Insurance Group*	CA	80.00
000577	21st Century Security Ins Co	PA	100.00
011587	21st Century Advantage Ins Co	MN	100.00
011684	21st Century Auto Ins Co NJ	NJ	100.00
011768	21st Century Indemnity Ins Co	PA	100.00
003786	21st Century National Ins Co	NY	100.00
002796	21st Century Preferred Ins Co	PA	100.00
000876	21st Century Centennial Ins Co	PA	100.00
002123	21st Century Premier Ins Co	PA	100.00
003641	21st Cent North America Ins Co	NY	100.00
011402	21st Century Superior Ins Co	CA	100.00
011109	21st Century Assurance Company	DE	100.00
012021	21st Century Pinnacle Ins Co	NJ	100.00
002359	21st Century Pacific Ins Co	CO	100.00
012039	American Pacific Ins Co, Inc	HI	100.00
010614	21st Century Casualty Co	CA	100.00
003247	21st Century Insurance Co	CA	100.00
011877	21st Century Ins Co Southwest	TX	100.00
006373	Farmers New World Life Ins Co	WA	100.00
060679	Leschi Life Assurance Company	SC	100.00
012131	Farmers Reinsurance Company	CA	100.00
004097	Farmers Texas County Mut Ins	TX	
050440	*Fire Underwriters Association*	CA	100.00
002172	Fire Insurance Exchange	CA	
011778	Civic Property & Casualty Co	CA	80.00

AMB#	COMPANY	DOMICILE	% OWN
011779	Exact Property & Casualty Co	CA	80.00
004306	Farmers Insurance Co of WA	WA	80.00
050441	*Truck Underwriters Association*	CA	100.00
002174	Truck Insurance Exchange	CA	
085397	Eagle Star Insurance Co Ltd	United Kingdom	100.00
084254	City of London Ins Co Ltd	United Kingdom	100.00
084319	Home & Overseas Ins Co Ltd	United Kingdom	100.00
078300	Trent Insurance Co Ltd	United Kingdom	100.00
055873	*Inversiones Suizo Chilena S.A.*	Chile	100.00
086274	Chilena Consolid Seg Generales	Chile	78.90
086275	Chilena Consolidada Seg Vida	Chile	98.90
078306	Midland Assurance Limited	United Kingdom	100.00
084196	Navigators & General Ins Co	United Kingdom	
087533	Preferred Assurance Co Limited	United Kingdom	
090018	Zurich Insurance Indonesia, PT	Indonesia	
087211	Whiteley Partnership Ins Co	United Kingdom	
085261	Zurich Ins Co SA Ltd	South Africa	73.60
078181	African General Ins Co Ltd	South Africa	99.00
078784	Botswana Eagle Insurance Co	Botswana	100.00
090000	Eagle Insurance Company Ltd	Zimbabwe	49.00
086266	Zuerich Versicherungs-AG	Austria	99.90
078340	BONUS Pensionskassen AG	Austria	87.50
077402	Zurich Argentina Cia de Seg SA	Argentina	99.90
077462	Zurich Argentina Cia Seg	Argentina	
090001	Zurich Cie Marocaine d'Asr	Morocco	100.00
086260	Zurich - Companhia de Seguros	Portugal	100.00
090011	Zurich Cia de Seg De Vida SA	Portugal	100.00
086261	Zurich Espana Comp de Seg	Spain	99.80
055876	*Zurich Finanz-Gesellschaft AG*	Switzerland	100.00
077272	Zurich Compania de Seguros SA	Mexico	99.90
078089	Zurich Vida Compania de Seg SA	Mexico	99.90
087680	Zurich GSG Limited	United Kingdom	
050459	*Zurich Holding Co of America*	DE	99.87
058400	*Kemper Corporation*	DE	100.00
006225	Kemper Investors Life Ins Co	IL	100.00
002563	Zurich American Insurance Co	NY	100.00
002562	American Guarantee & Liab Ins	NY	100.00
002147	Empire Fire & Marine Ins Co	NE	100.00
002148	Empire Indemnity Ins Co	OK	100.00
000387	Fidelity and Deposit Co of MD	MD	100.00
003739	Colonial American Cas & Surety	MD	100.00
002306	Maryland Casualty Company	MD	100.00
002303	Assurance Company of America	NY	100.00
002305	Maryland Insurance Company	TX	100.00
002308	Northern Insurance Co of NY	NY	100.00
003557	Steadfast Insurance Company	DE	100.00
002743	American Zurich Insurance Co	IL	100.00
003565	Zurich American Ins Co of IL	IL	100.00
002297	Universal Underwriters Ins Co	KS	100.00
007204	Universal Underwriters Life	KS	100.00
002818	Universal Underwriters of TX	TX	100.00
055878	*Zurich Holdings (UK) Limited*	United Kingdom	100.00
086263	Zurich Specialties London Ltd	United Kingdom	100.00
086273	Zurich International (UK) Ltd	United Kingdom	100.00
090003	Pilot Assurance Company Ltd	United Kingdom	100.00
055928	*Zurich Ins Hldgs (HK) Ltd*	Hong Kong	
090019	Paofoong Ins Co (HK) Ltd	Hong Kong	
086271	Zurich Insurance (Taiwan) Ltd	Taiwan	98.90
089459	Zurich International Belgique	Belgium	99.90
085680	Zurich International Life Ltd	Isle Of Man	100.00
089873	Zurich International (NL) N.V.	Netherlands	100.00
084927	Zurich Investments Life S.p.A.	Italy	100.00
089576	Zurich Life & Pensions S.p.A.	Italy	100.00
084901	Zurich Life Insurance Italia	Italy	100.00
083432	Zurich Life Espana Cia Seg	Spain	100.00
085097	Zurich Life Ins Co Limited	Switzerland	100.00
090020	Zurich Life Ins Philippines	Philippines	
084136	Zurich Vida Cia de Seg y Reas	Spain	100.00
084920	Zuritel S.P.A.	Italy	100.00
055877	*Zurich Holding Ireland Limited*	Ireland	
085676	Zurich Life Assurance plc	Ireland	100.00
089033	Eagle Star European Life Asr	Ireland	100.00
085661	Zurich Insurance plc	Ireland	100.00
086736	Irish National Ins Co plc	Ireland	100.00
085096	Zurich Insurance Co Ltd	Switzerland	100.00
055870	*Aktiengesellschaft Assuricum*	Switzerland	99.60
086134	Zurich Intern (Bermuda) Ltd	Bermuda	40.40
055220	*CMSH Limited*	Bermuda	100.00
055926	*Anglo American Ins Grp UK Ltd*	United Kingdom	100.00
055927	*Anglo American Ins Hldgs Ltd*	United Kingdom	100.00
085546	Anglo American Ins Co Ltd	United Kingdom	100.00
050092	*Centre Group Holdings Limited*	Bermuda	100.00
085566	Centre Solutions (Bermuda) Ltd	Bermuda	100.00
050462	*Centre Group Holdings (US) Ltd*	DE	100.00
086961	Centre Solutions (U.S.) Ltd	Bermuda	100.00
012237	Centre Insurance Company	DE	100.00
007367	Centre Life Insurance Company	MA	100.00
011880	ZC Specialty Insurance Company	TX	100.00
086352	Centre Ins International Co	Ireland	100.00
055869	*Orange Stone Holdings*	Ireland	100.00
055871	*Crown Management Services Ltd*	DE	100.00
090002	Orange Stone Reinsurance	Ireland	100.00

AMB#	COMPANY	DOMICILE	% OWN
050466	*Centre Reins Holdings (DE) Ltd*	DE	100.00
084317	Centre Reinsurance (US) Ltd	Bermuda	100.00
003720	Constellation Reinsurance Co	NY	100.00
090012	Zurich Ins Co (Russia) Ltd	Russia	
078158	Zurich Seguros S.A.	Venezuela	
055874	*Zurich South America Invest AB*	Bolivia	
078955	Boliviana Ciacruz Seg y Reas	Bolivia	51.00
078950	Zurich Boliviana Seg	Bolivia	51.00

U.S. Companies Listed by State

When administrative offices are located elsewhere, the state of incorporation is shown in parentheses after the company's name.

ALABAMA

Alabama Life Reinsurance Co
Alfa Life Ins Corp
Blue Cross & Blue Shield of AL
Citizens Accident and Health (AZ)
DaVita VillageHealth Ins of AL
FirstCommunity Health Plan Inc
HealthSpring of Alabama Inc
Jordan Funeral & Insurance Co
Liberty National Life Ins Co (NE)
Life Insurance Co of Alabama
National Security Ins Co
Peoples Savings Life Ins Co
Protective Life & Annuity Ins
Protective Life Ins Co (TN)
Southern Life and Health Ins (WI)
Southland National Ins Corp
United Concordia Dental Cp AL
United Investors Life Ins Co (NE)
United Trust Ins Co
UnitedHealthcare of Alabama
Universal Life Ins Co
VIVA Health Inc
West Coast Life Ins Co (NE)

ARIZONA

American Savings Life Ins Co
Arizona Dental Insurance Svc
Bird Insurance Company
Canyon State Life Ins Co
Christian Fidelity Life Ins Co (TX)
Congress Life Ins Co
Connecticut Life Ins & Annuity
Dallas General Life Ins Co (TX)
Evercare of Texas LLC (TX)
Futural Life Ins Co
Guarantee Security Life of AZ
IA American Life Insurance Co (GA)
Laurel Life Ins Co (TX)
LifeWise Health Plan of AZ (WA)
Lincoln Heritage Life Ins Co (IL)
North American Ins Co (WI)
Oxford Life Ins Co
Pacific Century Life Ins Corp
PacifiCare of Arizona Inc
Sagicor Life Insurance Company (TX)
SEB Trygg Life (USA) Assur Ltd
Trans-City Life Ins Co
UnitedHealthcare of Arizona

ARKANSAS

American Home Life Ins Co - AR
American Life & Annuity Co
Arkansas Bankers Life Ins Co
Citizens Fidelity Ins Co
Cooperative Life Ins Co
Cosmopolitan Life Ins Co
Delta Dental Plan of Arkansas
First Financial Assurance Co
First Guaranty Insurance Co
Foundation Life Ins Co of AR
Griffin Leggett Burial Ins Co
Higginbotham Burial Ins Co
HMO Partners Inc
Jackson Griffin Insurance Co
New Foundation Life Insurance
Port-O-Call Life Ins Co
QCA Health Plan Inc
QualChoice Life & Health Ins
Selected Funeral & Life Ins Co
Smith Burial & Life Ins Co
Southern Fidelity Life Ins Co
Union Life Ins Co
UnitedHealthcare of Arkansas
USAble Corporation
USAble Life
USAble Mutual Insurance Co
Wonder State Life Ins Co

CALIFORNIA

Access Dental Plan
ACN Group of California Inc
Aetna Dental of CA
Aetna Health of CA
AIDS Healthcare Foundation
Alameda Alliance for Health
Alaska Vision Services Inc (AK)
Alpha Dental Programs Inc (TX)
American Creditors Life Ins Co (DE)
American HealthGuard Corp
American Specialty H Plans CA
Anthem BC Life & Health Ins Co
Arcadian Health Plan Inc (WA)
Arcadian Health Plan of GA Inc (GA)
Arcadian Health Plan of LA Inc (LA)
Arcadian Health Plan of NC Inc (NC)
Arkansas Community Care Inc (AR)
Avante Behavioral Health Plan
Balboa Life Insurance Company
Balboa Life Insurance Co of NY (NY)
BEST Life and Health Ins Co (TX)
Blue Cross of California
Blue Shield of CA Life & Hlth
California Benefits Dental Pln
California Dental Network Inc
California Physicians' Service
Care 1st Health Plan Inc
CareAmerica Life Ins Co
CareMore Health Plan
Central Health Plan of CA
Chinese Community Health Plan
CIGNA Behavioral Health of CA
CIGNA Dental Health of CA Inc
Community Health Group
CONCERN: Employee Assist Prog
ConsumerHealth Inc
Contra Costa Health Plan
County of Los Angeles
County of Ventura
Dedicated Dental Systems Inc
Delta Dental Insurance Co (DE)
Delta Dental of CA
Dental Health Services (CA)
Dental Health Services (WA) (WA)
Dentegra Insurance Company (DE)
Dentegra Ins Co of New England (MA)
Doctors Life Insurance Co
Eastern Vision Service Plan (NY)
Easy Choice Health Plan
EYEXAM of California Inc
First Dental Health
First MetLife Investors Ins Co (NY)
FirstSight Vision Services Inc
For Eyes Vision Plan Inc
Fox Insurance Company
GEMCare Health Plan Inc
General Fidelity Life Ins Co (NC)
Golden State Mutual Life Ins
Golden West Health Plan Inc
Group Ins Trust of CA Soc CPAs
Hallmark Life Insurance Co (AZ)
Health and Human Resource Ctr
Health Net Health Plan of OR (OR)
Health Net Life Insurance Co
Health Net of Arizona Inc (AZ)
Health Net of California Inc
Health Net of Connecticut Inc (CT)
Health Net of New York Inc (NY)
Heritage Provider Network Inc
Holman Professional Counseling
Honored Citizens Choice Hth Pl
Human Affairs Internatl of CA
Indiana Vision Services Inc (IN)
Inland Empire Health Plan
Inter Valley Health Plan Inc
Jaimini Health Inc
Kaiser Foundation Health Plan
Kaiser Foundation Hlth P of GA (GA)
Kaiser Fdn H Pl of the Mid-Atl (MD)
Kern Health Systems
Kern Health Systs Gr Hlth Plan
Landmark Healthplan of CA
Liberty Dental Plan of CA
LifeCare Assurance Co (AZ)
Local Initiative Hlth Auth LA
Magellan Health Services of CA
Managed Dental Care of CA
Managed DentalGuard Inc (NJ)
Managed DentalGuard Inc (TX)
Managed Health Network
March Vision Care Inc
Massachusetts Vision Svc Plan (MA)
Max Vision Care Inc
Medcore HP
Medical Eye Services Inc
MetLife Investors Insurance Co (MO)
MetLife Investors USA Ins Co (DE)
Mid-Atlantic Vision Service Pl (VA)
Molina Healthcare Insurance Co (OH)
Molina Healthcare of CA Inc
Monarch Health Plan
On Lok Senior Health Services
Orange Prev & Trtmt Int Med As
Pacific Life & Annuity Co (AZ)
Pacific Life Insurance Company (NE)
PacifiCare Bhvrl Health of CA
PacifiCare Dental of Colorado (CO)
PacifiCare Life and Health Ins (IN)
PacifiCare Life Assurance Co (CO)
PacifiCare of California
Premier Access Insurance Co
Premier Choice Dental Inc (AZ)
PrimeCare Medical Network Inc
Safeguard Health Plans NV Corp (NV)
SafeGuard Health Plans (CA)
SafeGuard Health Plans (FL) (FL)
SafeHealth Life Ins Co
San Francisco Health Plan
San Joaquin Health Commission
San Mateo Health Commission
San Miguel Health Plan
Santa Barbara Regional H Auth
Santa Clara County
Santa Clara County Health Auth
Santa Cruz-Monterey Mgd Med Cr
SCAN Health Plan
SCAN Health Plan Arizona (AZ)
Scripps Clinic Health Plan Svs
Sharp Health Plan
Sistemas Medicos Nacionales
Solano-Napa-Yolo Comm Med Care
SunAmerica Annuity & Life Assr (AZ)
SunAmerica Life Ins Co (AZ)
Trans World Assurance Co
UNICARE Health Plan of Kansas (KS)
UNICARE Health Plan of WV (WV)
Universal Care
ValueOptions of California Inc
Vision First Eye Care Inc
Vision Plan of America
Vision Service Plan
Vision Service Plan Inc (NV)
Vision Service Plan Ins Co(CT) (CT)
Vision Service Plan Ins Co(MO) (MO)
Vision Service Plan of Idaho (ID)
Vision Service Plan of IL NFP (IL)
Vision Service Plan (OH) (OH)
Vision Service Plan (WA) (WA)
Vision Services Plan Inc OK (OK)
VisionCare of California
Western Dental Services Inc
Western Health Advantage
Westward Life Ins Co (AZ)
Wisconsin Vision Service Plan (WI)
Workmen's Life Ins Co (AZ)

COLORADO

CIGNA Health & Life Insurance (CT)
CIGNA Hthcare-Centennial State
CIGNA HealthCare of CO Inc
CIGNA Healthcare - Pacific Inc (CA)
Colorado Access
Colorado Bankers Life Ins Co
Colorado Choice Health Plans
Colorado Dental Service Inc
Denver Health Medical Plan
Fidelity Standard Life Ins Co (AR)
First Great-West Lf & Annuity (NY)
Great-West Healthcare of IL (IL)
Great-West Life & Ann
HMO Colorado Inc
Imerica Life and Health Ins Co (AR)
Kaiser Fdn Health Plan of CO
North American Natl Re Ins Co (AZ)
Old Reliance Ins Co (AZ)
PacifiCare of Colorado Inc
Programmed Life Ins Co (AZ)
Rocky Mountain Hlth Maint Org
Rocky Mountain HthCare Options
Rocky Mountain Hosp & Med Svc
UnitedHealthcare of Colorado

CONNECTICUT

ACE Life Insurance Company
Aetna Health and Life Ins Co
Aetna Insurance Company of CT
Aetna Life Ins Co
AGL Life Assurance Company (PA)
American Maturity Life Ins Co
American Phoenix Life&Reassur
AmeriChoice of Connecticut Inc
Anthem Health Plans Inc
Aurora National Life Assur (CA)

Berkley Life and Health Ins Co (IA)
Blue Care Health Plan
CIGNA Arbor Life Ins Co
CIGNA HealthCare of AZ Inc (AZ)
CIGNA HealthCare of CA Inc (CA)
CIGNA HealthCare of CT Inc
CIGNA HealthCare of FL Inc (FL)
CIGNA HealthCare of GA Inc (GA)
CIGNA HealthCare of IL Inc (IL)
CIGNA HealthCare of IN Inc (IN)
CIGNA HealthCare of ME Inc (ME)
CIGNA HealthCare of NJ Inc (NJ)
CIGNA HealthCare of NY Inc (NJ)
CIGNA HealthCare of OH Inc (OH)
CIGNA HealthCare of St Lou Inc (MO)
CIGNA HealthCare of TN Inc (TN)
CIGNA HealthCare of TX Inc (TX)
CIGNA HealthCare of UT Inc (UT)
CIGNA Insurance Group Inc (NH)
ConnectiCare Inc
ConnectiCare Insurance Co Inc
ConnectiCare of Massachusetts (MA)
ConnectiCare of New York Inc (NY)
Connecticut General Life Ins
General Re Life Corporation
Hartford Internat Life Reassur
Hartford Life & Accident Ins
Hartford Life and Annuity Ins
Hartford Life Ins Co
Health Net Ins of New York Inc (NY)
Health Net of New Jersey Inc (NJ)
IdeaLife Ins Co
Knights of Columbus
MetLife Insurance Co of CT
Oxford Health Ins Inc (NY)
Oxford Health Plans (CT) Inc
Oxford Health Plans (NJ) Inc (NJ)
Oxford Health Plans (NY) Inc (NY)
PHL Variable Ins Co
Phoenix Life and Annuity Co
Phoenix Life and Reassur of NY (NY)
Phoenix Life Insurance Company (NY)
Prudential Annuities Life Assr
Prudential Retirement Ins&Ann
SCOR Global Life Reins Co Amer (DE)
UnitedHealthcare Ins Co
UnitedHealthcare of New Eng (RI)
UnitedHealthcare of New York (NY)
Vantis Life Insurance Company
Vantis Life Insurance Co of NY (NY)
Wilton Reassurance Company (MN)
Wilton Reassurance Life Co NY (NY)

DELAWARE

American Life Ins Co DE
BCBSD Inc
CIGNA Worldwide Insurance Co

DISTRICT OF COLUMBIA

Advantage Healthplan Inc
CareFirst BlueChoice Inc
DC Chartered Health Plan Inc
Health Right Inc
Heartland Fidelity Ins Co
Hungarian Reformed Fed of Amer
ULLICO Life Insurance Company (TX)
Union Labor Life Ins Co (MD)

FLORIDA

American Bankers Life Assur Co
American Exchange Life Ins Co (TX)
American Fidelity Life Ins Co
American Heritage Life Ins Co
American Pioneer Life Ins Co
America's Hlth Choice Med Plns
AvMed Inc
Bankers Life Insurance Co
Bankers Life of Louisiana (LA)
Best Meridian Ins Co
Blue Cross & Blue Shield of FL
Bupa Insurance Company
Capital Health Plan Inc
Cardif Life Insurance Company (KS)
CarePlus Health Plans Inc
CIGNA Dental Health of CO Inc (CO)
CIGNA Dental Health of DE Inc (DE)
CIGNA Dental Health of FL Inc
CIGNA Dental Health of KS Inc (KS)
CIGNA Dental Health of KY Inc (KY)
CIGNA Dental Health of MD Inc (MD)
CIGNA Dental Health of MO Inc (MO)
CIGNA Dental Health of NJ Inc (NJ)
CIGNA Dental Health of NC Inc (NC)
CIGNA Dental Health of OH Inc (OH)
CIGNA Dental Health of PA Inc (PA)
CIGNA Dental Health of TX Inc (TX)
CIGNA Dental Health of VA Inc (VA)
CIGNA Dental Health Pln AZ Inc (AZ)
Claria Life & Health Ins Co
Constitution Life Ins Co (TX)
Florida Combined Life Ins Co
Florida Health Care Plan Inc
Hannover Life Reassurance Amer
Health First Health Plans
Health Options Inc
Humana AdvantageCare Plan
Humana Health Ins Co FL Inc
Humana Medical Plan Inc
JMIC Life Insurance Company
Life of the South Insurance Co (GA)
Marquette National Life Ins Co (TX)
Neighborhood Hlth Partnership
Pennsylvania Life Insurance Co (PA)
Physicians United Plan Inc
Pyramid Life Insurance Company (KS)
Southern Financial Life Ins Co (LA)
Southern Financial Life Ins Co (KY)
Summit Health Plan Inc
TransAm Assurance Company (AZ)
Union Bankers Ins Co (TX)
UnitedHealthcare of Florida
Vista Healthplan Inc
Vista Healthplan of South FL
WellCare of Ohio Inc (OH)
WellCare of Texas Inc (TX)

GEORGIA

Admiral Life Ins Co of America (AZ)
Alliant Health Plans Inc
American Dental Plan of NC (NC)
American Dental Providers AR (AR)
American Fam Assur Columbus (NE)
American Family Life Assur NY (NY)
AmeriChoice of Georgia Inc
Athens Area Health Plan Select
Atlanta Life Ins Co
Bankers Fidelity Life Ins Co
Blue Cross & Blue Shield of GA
BC BS Healthcare Plan of GA
Cherokee National Life Ins Co
CompBenefits Company (FL)
CompBenefits Dental Inc (IL)
CompBenefits Insurance Co (TX)
Cotton States Life Ins Co
DaVita VillageHealth of GA Inc
Delta Life Ins Co
DentiCare Inc (TX)
Frandisco Life Insurance Co
Greater Georgia Life Ins Co
HCC Life Insurance Company (IN)
Humana Employers Hth Pln of GA
ING Life Insurance and Annuity (CT)
ING USA Annuity & Life Ins Co (IA)
Midwestern United Life Ins Co (IN)
Munich American Reassurance Co
Primerica Life Ins Co (MA)
ReliaStar Life Insurance Co (MN)
ReliaStar Life Ins Co of NY (NY)
Security Life of Denver Ins Co (CO)
Senior Life Insurance Company
State Mutual Ins Co
Sterling Investors Life Ins Co
Suntrust Insurance Co (AZ)
UnitedHealthcare of Georgia

GUAM

Gmhp Health Insurance Limited
MetLife Insurance Limited (GU)
Netcare Life & Health Ins Co

HAWAII

Aloha Care
Hawaii Dental Service
Hawaii Management Alliance Asn
Hawaii Medical Service Assn
Mililani Life Insurance Co
Pacific Beacon Life Reassur
Pacific Guardian Life Co Ltd
Royal State National Ins Co
University Health Alliance

IDAHO

Blue Cross of ID Hlth Service
Delta Dental Plan of Idaho Inc
Regence BlueShield of Idaho
United Heritage Life Ins Co

ILLINOIS

Allegiance Life Ins Co
Allstate Assurance Company
Allstate Life Ins Co
Amalgamated Life and Health
American Capitol Ins Co (TX)
American Life Ins Co IL
BCI HMO Inc
BCS Insurance Company (OH)
BCS Life Insurance Co
Cambridge Life Ins Co (MO)
Catholic Order of Foresters
Celtic Insurance Company
Charter National Life Ins Co
Combined Ins Co of America
Combined Life Ins Co of NY (NY)
Concert Health Plan Ins Co
Continental Assurance Co
COUNTRY Investors Life Assur
COUNTRY Life Ins Co
Dental Concern Ltd
Destiny Health Insurance Co
Educators Life Ins Co (AZ)
Employees Life Co (Mutual)
Federal Life Ins Co (Mutual)
Fidelis SecureCare of Michigan (MI)
Fidelis SecureCare of NC (NC)
Fidelity Life Association
First Commonwealth Ins Co
First Commonwealth Ltd Hth Svc (WI)
First Commonwealth Ltd H Svcs
First Commonwlth Ltd H Svcs MI (MI)
First Commonwealth of Missouri (MO)
First Health Life & Health Ins (TX)
Fort Dearborn Life Ins Co
Fort Dearborn Life Ins Co NY (NY)
Guarantee Trust Life Ins Co
HCSC Insurance Services Co
Health Alliance Medical Plans
Health Alliance-Midwest Inc
Health Care Service Corp
Health Care Service-IL LOB
Horace Mann Life Ins Co
Humana Benefit Plan of IL
Illinois Mutual Life Ins Co
Interstate Bankers Life Ins Co
Life Assurance Co of America
Manhattan National Life Ins Co
Modern Woodmen of America
MTL Insurance Company
Old Republic Life Ins Co
Pekin Financial Life Ins Co (AZ)
Pekin Life Ins Co
PersonalCare Insurance of IL
Physicians Benefits Trust Life
Polish Roman Catholic Union
Professional Life & Casualty
Resource Life Insurance Co
Royal Neighbors of America
State Farm Ann & Life Ins Co
State Farm Life & Acc Assur Co
State Farm Life Ins Co
TruAssure Insurance Company
Trustmark Insurance Company
Trustmark Life Ins Co
Trustmark Life Ins Co of NY (NY)
UNICARE Health Ins Co of TX (TX)
UNICARE Health Ins of Midwest
UNICARE Health Plans of TX (TX)
UNICARE Health Plans Midwest
United National Life of Amer
United Security Lf & H Ins Co
UnitedHealthcare Ins Co of IL
UnitedHealthcare Ins Rvr Vall
UnitedHealthcare of Illinois
UnitedHealthcare Plan Rvr Vall
Universal Guaranty Life Ins Co (OH)
XL Life Ins and Annuity Co

INDIANA

ADVANTAGE Health Solutions Inc
All Savers Insurance Co
All Savers Life Ins Co of CA (CA)
American Health Network IN LLC
American United Life Ins Co
Anthem Insurance Companies Inc
Bankers Conseco Life Insurance (NY)
Bankers Life and Casualty Co (IL)
Clarian Health Plans Inc
Colonial Penn Life Insurance (PA)
Conseco Health Ins Co (AZ)

Conseco Insurance Company (IL)
Conseco Life Insurance Company
Conseco Life Ins Co of Texas (TX)
First Penn-Pacific Life Ins Co
Forethought Life Ins Co
Forethought National Life Ins (TX)
Golden Rule Ins Co
Guggenheim Life and Annuity Co (IA)
Health Resources Inc
HMO Maine (ME)
Integrity Capital Insurance Co
Lincoln National Life Ins Co
M-Plan Inc
MDwise Inc
Medical Savings Insurance Co
Merit Life Insurance Co
MMA Insurance Company
NHP of Indiana LLC
OneNation Insurance Company
PHP Insurance Company of IN
Physicians Hlth Pl-Northern IN
Senior Health Ins Co of PA (PA)
Standard Life Ins Co of IN
State Life Ins Co
UNICARE Life & Health Ins Co
United Farm Family Life Ins Co
United Home Life Ins Co
USA Life One Ins Co of IN
Washington National Ins Co (IL)

IOWA

American Equity Invest Life
American Equity Invest Life NY (NY)
American Republic Ins Co
Aviva Life and Annuity Company
Centurion Life Ins Co
Delta Dental of Iowa
Eagle Life Insurance Company
EMC National Life Company
EquiTrust Life Insurance Co
Farm Bureau Life Ins Co
Hawkeye Life Ins Group Ins
Homesteaders Life Co
Keokuk Area Hosp Org Deliv Sys
Magellan Behavioral Hlth of IA
Medical Associates Clinic WI (WI)
Medical Associates Health Plan
Merrill Lynch Life Ins Co (AR)
ML Life Ins Co of NY (NY)
Monumental Life Ins Co
Pharmacists Life Ins Co
Principal Life Insurance Co
Principal National Life Ins Co
Stonebridge Life Insurance Co (VT)
Transamerica Financial Life (NY)
Transamerica Life Insurance Co
United Life Ins Co
Wellmark Health Plan of Iowa
Wellmark Inc
Western Reserve Lf Assur of OH (OH)

KANSAS

Advance Insurance Co of Kansas
American Home Life Ins Co
American Underwriters Life Ins (AZ)
Blue Cross and Blue Shield KS
Century Life Assur Co (OK)
Coventry Health Care of Kansas
Delta Dental Plan of KS
Employers Reassurance Corp
First Security Benefit L&A NY (NY)
Generali USA Life Reassurance
Great Fidelity Life Ins Co (IN)
Individual Assur Lf Hlth & Acc (MO)
Old United Life Ins Co (AZ)
Preferred Health Systems Ins
Preferred Plus of Kansas Inc
Security Benefit Life Ins Co
Surency Life & Health Ins Co
Unified Life Insurance Company (TX)
Universal Underwriters Life
Westport Life Ins Co (AZ)

KENTUCKY

American Life and Acc of KY
Anthem Health Plans of KY Inc
Bluegrass Family Health Inc
CHA HMO Inc
Citizens Security Life Ins Co
Delta Dental of Kentucky Inc
Dental Choice Inc
Dental Concern Inc
Emphesys Insurance Company (TX)
Humana Health Plan Inc
Humana Insurance Company of KY
Investors Heritage Life Ins Co
Jefferson National Life Ins Co (TX)
Kanawha Insurance Company (SC)
Kentucky Funeral Directors Lf
Kentucky Home Life Ins Co
UnitedHealthcare of KY Ltd

LOUISIANA

Coventry Health Care of LA
Dixie Life Ins Co Inc
Escude Life Ins Co
Evangeline Life Ins Co Inc
First Assur Life of America
Great Central Life Ins Co
Guaranty Income Life Ins Co
Gulf States Life Ins Co Inc
Health Plus of Louisiana Inc
HMO Louisiana Inc
Humana Health Benefit Pl of LA
Jeff Davis Mortuary Ben Assoc
Kilpatrick Life Ins Co of LA
Lafourche Life Ins Co
Life Insurance Co of Louisiana
Louisiana Hlth Svc & Indemnity
Majestic Life Ins Co
Melancon Life Ins Co
Memorial Life Ins Co
Mothe Life Ins Co
Mulhearn Protective Insurance
Pan-American Assurance Company
Pan-American Life Ins Co
Pellerin Life Ins Co
Performance Life of America
Rabenhorst Life Ins Co
Rhodes Life Ins Co of LA
Sabine Life Ins Co
Security Plan Life Ins Co
Southern National Life Ins
Starmount Life Ins Co
UnitedHealthcare of Louisiana
Vantage Health Plan Inc
Versant Life Insurance Company (MS)
Williams Progressive L & A Ins

MAINE

Anthem Health Plans of ME Inc
Patriot Life Ins Co

MARYLAND

Acacia Life Insurance Company (DC)
Baltimore Life Ins Co
Banner Life Ins Co
Bravo Health Insurance Company (DE)
Bravo Health Mid-Atlantic Inc
Bravo Health Pennsylvania Inc (PA)
Bravo Health Texas Inc (TX)
CapitalCare Inc (VA)
Care Improvement Plus of MD
CareFirst of Maryland Inc
CIGNA HealthCare Mid-Atl Inc
Coventry Hlth and Life Ins Co (DE)
Coventry Health Care of DE (DE)
Coventry Health Care of GA Inc (GA)
Coventry Health Care of Iowa (IA)
Coventry Health Care of NE (NE)
Denta-Chek of Maryland Inc
Dental Benefit Providers of IL (IL)
DentaQuest Mid-Atlantic Inc
DentaQuest Virginia Inc (VA)
FirstCare Inc
Graphics Arts Benefit Corp
Group Dental Service of MD Inc
Group Hospital & Medical Svcs (DC)
MAMSI Life and Health Ins
Maryland Care Inc
MD-Individual Practice Assoc
Nevada Pacific Dental Inc (NV)
OM Financial Life Ins Co
OM Financial Life Ins Co of NY (NY)
Optimum Choice Inc
UnitedHealthcare of Mid-Atl
William Penn Life Ins Co of NY (NY)

MASSACHUSETTS

Berkshire Life Ins Co of Amer
Blue Cr & Blue Sh of MA HMO Bl
Blue Cross & Blue Shield of MA
Boston Medical Center Hth Plan
Boston Mutual Life Ins Co
C M Life Insurance Company (CT)
Charleston Capital Re LLC (DC)
CIGNA HealthCare of MA Inc
Columbia Capital Life Reins Co (DC)
Commonwealth Annuity and Life
Dental Service of MA
Empire Fidelity Investments Lf (NY)
Fallon Community Health Plan
Fidelity Investments Life Ins (UT)
First Allmerica Financial Life
Harvard Pilgrim Health Care
Harvard Pilgrim Hlth Care ofNE
Health New England Inc
HPHC Insurance Company Inc
Independence Life & Annuity Co (RI)
John Hancock Life & Health Ins
John Hancock Life Ins Co USA (MI)
Life Ins Co of Boston & NY (NY)
Massachusetts Mutual Life Ins
MML Bay State Life Ins Co (CT)
Monarch Life Ins Co
Neighborhood Health Plan Inc
New England Life Ins Co
Professional Ins Company (TX)
Regal Reinsurance Co
Savings Bank Life Ins Co of MA
Senior Whole Health of CT Inc (CT)
Senior Whole Health of NY Inc (NY)
Sun Life and Health Ins Co US (CT)
Sun Life Assur Co of CA (US) (DE)
Sun Life Ins & Annuity of NY (NY)
Supreme Council Royal Arcanum
Tufts Associated HMO Inc
Tufts Insurance Co

MICHIGAN

AAA Life Insurance Company
Aetna Health Inc (a MI corp)
Alliance Health and Life Ins
American Community Mutual Ins
Associated Mutual
Auto Club Life Insurance Co
Auto-Owners Life Ins Co
Automobile Club of Sthrn CA Lf (CA)
Blue Care Network of Michigan
Blue Care of Michigan Inc
Blue Cross Blue Shield of MI
BlueCaid of Michigan
Brooke Life Insurance Co
CareSource Michigan
Delta Dental Plan of Indiana (IN)
Delta Dental Plan of Michigan
Delta Dental Plan of Ohio Inc (OH)
Farm Bureau Life Ins Co of MI
Gleaner Life Ins Society
Grand Valley Health Plan Inc
Great Lakes Health Plan Inc
Health Alliance Plan of MI
Health Plan of Michigan
HealthPlus Insurance Company
HealthPlus of Michigan Inc
HealthPlus Partners Inc
IBA Health and Life Assur Co
Jackson National Life Ins Co
Jackson National Lf Ins of NY (NY)
Liberty Union Life Assurance
LifeSecure Insurance Company
Locomotive Engineers&Conductor
McLaren Health Plan Inc
Midwest Health Plan Inc
Molina Healthcare of MI Inc
OmniCare Health Plan Inc
Paramount Care of Michigan
PHPMM Insurance Company
Physicians Hlth Plan of Mid-MI
Physicians H P Mid-MI FamCare
Priority Health
Priority Health Govt Programs
Priority Health Insurance Co
ProCare Health Plan
Renaissance Health Ins Co NY (NY)
Renaissance Lf & Hlth of Amer (IN)
Total Health Care Inc
Total Health Care USA Inc
Upper Peninsula Health Plan
US Health and Life Ins Co
Vista Life Ins Co
WellPath of South Carolina (SC)
Woman's Life Ins Society

MINNESOTA

Allianz Life and Annuity Co
Allianz Life Ins Co of NY (NY)
Allianz Life Ins Co N America
Blue Cross & Blue Shield of MN

Delta Dental of MN
Delta Dental of Nebraska (NE)
Dental Benefit Providers of CA (CA)
Federated Life Ins Co
Group Health Plan Inc
Health Tradition Health Plan (WI)
Health Ventures Network
HealthPartners Inc
HMO Minnesota
Investors Growth Life Ins Co (AZ)
Medica Health Plans
Medica Health Plans of WI (WI)
Medica Insurance Company
Metropolitan Health Plan
MII Life Inc
Minnesota Life Ins Company
PreferredOne Community Hlth Pl
PreferredOne Insurance Co
RiverSource Life Ins Co of NY (NY)
RiverSource Life Ins Co
Securian Life Insurance Co
Security Life Ins Co of Amer
Thrivent Financial Lutherans (WI)
Thrivent Life Insurance Co
UCare Minnesota
Unimerica Insurance Company (WI)
UnitedHealthcare of Wisconsin (WI)
U S Behavioral Health Plan CA (CA)

MISSISSIPPI

American Federated Life Ins
American Public Life Ins Co (OK)
AmFirst Insurance Co (OK)
Blue Cross & Blue Shield of MS
Bluebonnet Life Ins Co
Century Credit Life Ins Co
Family Security Life Ins Inc
First M & F Ins Co
Gulf Guaranty Life Ins Co
HMO of Mississippi Inc
Magna Insurance Company
PhysiciansPlus Baptist&St Dom
Pine Belt Life Insurance Co
Security National Life Ins LA (LA)
Southern Capital Life Ins Co
Southern Farm Bureau Life Ins
UnitedHealthcare of MS

MISSOURI

Absolute Total Care Inc (SC)
Alliance for Community Health
American Financial Security
American Service Life Ins Co (AR)
Americo Financial Lf & Annuity (TX)
Bankers Reserve Life Ins of WI (WI)
Blue Advantage Plus of KC Inc
Blue Cross&Blue Shield of K C
Buckeye Community Health Plan (OH)
Capital Reserve Life Ins Co
CeltiCare Health Plan of MA (MA)
Children's Mercy's Fam H Prtnr
Community Health Plan
Community Health Plan Ins Co
Coordinated Care Corp Indiana (IN)
Cox Health Systems HMO
Delta Dental of Missouri
Dental Source of Missouri & KS
Essence Healthcare Inc
Essex Dental Benefits Inc
Family Benefit Life Ins - MO
Farm Bureau Life Ins Co of MO
Fidelity Security Life Ins Co
Financial Assurance Life Ins (TX)
General American Life Ins Co
Good Health HMO Inc
Great Southern Life Ins Co (TX)
Group Health Plan Inc
HealthCare USA of Missouri LLC
HealthLink HMO Inc
Healthy Alliance Life Ins Co
Heartland National Life Ins Co (IN)
HMO Missouri Inc
Investors Life of North Amer (TX)
Kansas City Life Ins Co
Lewer Life Ins Co
Managed Health Services Ins Cp (WI)
Marquette Indemnity & Life Ins (AZ)
Mercy Health Plans
Mercy Health Plans of MO Inc
Missouri Care Incorporated
Missouri Valley Life & Health
Mutual Savings Life Ins Co (AL)
National Farmers Union Life (TX)
National States Ins Co
Ohio State Life Ins Co (TX)
Old American Ins Co
Ozark National Life Ins Co MO
Peach State Health Plan Inc (GA)
Perico Life Insurance Company (DE)
Pioneer Military Insurance Co (NV)
Preservation Life Insurance Co
Reinsurance Co of Missouri
Reliable Life Insurance Co
RGA Reinsurance Company
RightCHOICE Insurance Co (IL)
Shelter Life Ins Co
Sunset Life Ins Co of America
Sunshine State Health Plan Inc (FL)
Superior HealthPlan Inc (TX)
Travelers Protec Assoc of Amer
UDC Dental California Inc (CA)
UDC Ohio Inc (OH)
Union National Life Ins Co (LA)
Union Security DentalCare NJ (NJ)
Union Security Insurance Co (KS)
United Dental Care of AZ Inc (AZ)
United Dental Care of CO Inc (CO)
United Dental Care of MI Inc (MI)
United Dental Care of MO Inc
United Dental Care of NM Inc (NM)
United Dental Care of UT Inc (UT)
United Fidelity Life Ins Co (TX)
United Insurance Co of America (IL)
UnitedHealthcare of Midwest
University Health Plans Inc (NJ)

MONTANA

Big Sky Life Inc
Blue Cross & Blue Shield of MT
Blue Cross Blue Shield MT(HMO)
New West Health Services

NEBRASKA

Ability Insurance Company
American Life & Security Corp
American Republic Corp Ins Co
Ameritas Life Insurance Corp.
Assurity Life Ins Co
Berkshire Hathaway Life of NE
Blue Cross & Blue Shield of NE
Censtat Life Assurance Company (AZ)
Central States H&L Co of Omaha
Companion Life Ins Company (NY)
Cornhusker Life Insurance Co
CSI Life Insurance Company
First Berkshire Hathaway Life (NY)
First Landmark Life Ins Co
First National Life of USA
Lincoln Benefit Life Co
Medico Insurance Company
Mutual of Omaha Ins Co
Omaha Insurance Company
Omaha Life Insurance Company
Physicians Life Ins Co
Physicians Mutual Insurance Co
Southeast Family Life Ins Co (AZ)
Surety Life Ins Co
United of Omaha Life Ins Co
United World Life Ins Co
UnitedHealthcare of Midlands
Woodmen of the World Life Soc
World Corp Insurance Company
World Insurance Company

NEVADA

Health Plan of Nevada Inc
PacifiCare of Nevada Inc
Sierra Hlth & Lf Ins Co Inc (CA)

NEW HAMPSHIRE

Anthem Health Plans of NH Inc
CIGNA HealthCare of NH Inc
Delta Dental Plan of NH
Liberty Life Assur of Boston (MA)
Maine Dental Service Corp (ME)
Matthew Thornton Health Plan

NEW JERSEY

American General Assurance Co (IL)
AmeriChoice of New Jersey
AmeriHealth Ins Co of NJ
Community Dental Associates
Delta Dental of New Jersey Inc
Dental Group of New Jersey Inc
Dental Services Organization
First Central Nat Life of NY (NY)
First Investors Life Ins Co (NY)
Flagship Health Systems Inc
Group Dental H Administrators
Horizon Healthcare Dental
Horizon Healthcare of Delaware (DE)
Horizon Healthcare of NJ
Household Life Ins Co (MI)
Household Life Ins Co of AZ (AZ)
Household Life Ins Co of DE (DE)
John D Kernan DMD PA
Medco Containment Ins Co of NY (NY)
Medco Containment Life Ins Co (PA)
Pruco Life Ins Co (AZ)
Pruco Life Insurance Co of NJ
Prudential Ins Co of America
Rayant Insurance Company of NY (NY)
S.USA Life Insurance Company (AZ)
Ukrainian National Assoc
Unity DPO Inc

NEW MEXICO

Delta Dental Plan of NM
Evercare of New Mexico Inc
Molina Healthcare New Mexico
Presbyterian Health Plan Inc
Presbyterian Insurance Company
Southwest Credit Life Inc

NEW YORK

Allstate Life Ins Co of NY
Amalgamated Life Ins Co
American Intern Life Assur NY
American Medical and Life Ins
American Progressive L&H NY
Anthem Lf & Disability Ins Co
Aviva Life & Annuity Co of NY
AXA Corporate Solutions Lf Re (DE)
AXA Equitable Life Ins Co
Better Life and Health Company (AZ)
Capital District Phys' Hlth Pl
CDPHP Universal Benefits Inc
Centre Life Insurance Company (MA)
Church Life Ins Corporation
Columbian Life Insurance Co (IL)
Columbian Mutual Life Ins Co
Commercial Travelers Mutual
Dentcare Delivery Systems Inc
Elderplan Inc
Empire HealthChoice Assurance
Empire HealthChoice HMO Inc
Excellus Health Plan Inc
Family Service Life Ins Co (TX)
Farm Family Life Ins Co
First Ameritas Life of NY
First Rehabilitation Lf of Am
First SunAmerica Life Ins Co
First Symetra Nat Life Ins NY
First United American Life Ins
Freelancers Insurance Company
Genworth Life Insurance Co NY
Gerber Life Ins Co
GHI HMO Select Inc
Great American Life Ins of NY
Group Health Incorporated
Guardian Ins & Annuity Co Inc (DE)
Guardian Life Ins Co of Amer
Health Ins Plan of Greater NY
Healthfirst Health Plan of NJ (NJ)
HealthNow New York Inc
Healthplex Insurance Co
Healthplex of NJ Inc (NJ)
HIP Insurance Co of New York
HM Life Insurance Company NY
Humana Insurance Company of NY
Independence American Ins Co (DE)
Independent Health Association
Independent Health Benefits
International HealthCare Svcs (NJ)
Intramerica Life Ins Co
John Hancock Life Ins Co NY
Longevity Insurance Company (TX)
Managed Health Inc
MDNY Healthcare Inc
MedAmerica Insurance Co (PA)
MedAmerica Ins Co of Florida (FL)
MedAmerica Ins Co of New York
Metropolitan Life Ins Co
Metropolitan Tower Life Ins Co (DE)
Monitor Life Insurance Co
MONY Life Ins Co
MONY Life Insurance Co of Amer (AZ)
Mutual of America Life Ins Co
MVP Health Insurance Company

MVP Health Ins Co of NH Inc (NH)
MVP Health Plan
MVP Health Plan of NH Inc (NH)
MVP Health Services Corp
National Benefit Life Ins Co
National Income Life Insurance
National Integrity Life Ins Co
National Safety Life Ins Co (PA)
New York Life Ins & Annuity (DE)
New York Life Ins Co
Nippon Life Ins Co of Amer (IA)
NYLIFE Ins Co of Arizona (AZ)
Park Avenue Life Ins Co (DE)
Preferred Assurance Company
Presidential Life Ins Co
Protective Life Insurance NY
Pupil Benefits Plan Inc
Reassure America Life Ins Co (IN)
SBLI USA Mutual Life Ins Co
Security Health Ins of Amer NY
Security Mutual Life of NY
Sentinel American Life Ins Co (TX)
Sentry Life Ins Co of New York
Standard Security Life of NY
Swiss Re Life & Health America (CT)
Teachers Ins & Annuity Assoc
TIAA-CREF Life Ins Co
Unimerica Life Ins Co of NY
Union Security Life Ins NY
United States Life Ins of NY
UnitedHealthcare Ins Co of NY
Unity Mutual Life Ins Co
US Financial Life Ins Co (OH)
Variable Annuity Life Ins Co (TX)

NORTH CAROLINA

AXA Equitable Life & Annuity (CO)
Blue Cross & Blue Shield of NC
CIGNA HealthCare of NC Inc
Delta Dental Plan of NC Inc
Financial Life Ins Co of GA (GA)
First Virginia Life Ins Co (VA)
FirstCarolinaCare Insurance Co
Lincoln Life & Annuity Co NY (NY)
North Carolina Mutual Life Ins
Orkney Re Inc (DE)
PARTNERS Natl Hlth Plns of NC
Scottish Re Life Corporation (DE)
Scottish Re (US) Inc. (DE)
Securitas Financial Life Ins
UnitedHealthcare of NC
WellPath Select Inc

NORTH DAKOTA

Dental Service Corp of ND
Heart of America Health Plan
Lincoln Mutual Life & Casualty
Noridian Mutual Insurance Co
Pioneer Mutual Life Ins Co
Surety Life & Casualty Ins Co

OHIO

American Modern Life Ins Co
Annuity Investors Life Ins Co
Anthem Life Insurance Company (IN)
Arkansas Life Ins Co (AZ)
Capitol Life & Accident Ins Co (AR)
CareSource
Cincinnati Equitable Life
Cincinnati Life Insurance Co
Columbus Life Insurance Co
Community Insurance Company
Consumers Life Ins Co
Dental Care Plus Inc
Envision Insurance Company
Family Heritage Life of Amer
First Catholic Slovak Ladies
First Catholic Slovak Union
Grange Life Ins Co
Great American Life Ins Co
Health Plan of Upper OH Valley (WV)
Hometown Health Plan
Humana Health Plan of Ohio
Integrity Life Ins Co
Kaiser Foundation Hth Pl of OH
Loyal American Life Ins Co
McKinley Life Ins Co
Medical Benefits Mutual Life
Medical Health Insuring Ohio
Medical Mutual of Ohio
Modern Life Ins Co of Arizona (AZ)
Molina Healthcare of Ohio Inc
Motorists Life Ins Co
Mount Carmel Health Plan Inc
National Masonic Provident
National Security Lf & Annuity (NY)
Nationwide Life & Annuity Ins
Nationwide Life Ins Co
Ohio Motorists Life Ins Co
Ohio National Life Assur Corp
Ohio National Life Ins Co
Ouachita Life Insurance Co (AR)
Paramount Advantage
Paramount Care Inc
Paramount Insurance Company
SeeChange Health Insurance Co
Southern Pioneer Life Ins Co (AR)
Summa Insurance Company
SummaCare Inc
Superior Dental Care Inc
Union Central Life Ins Co (NE)
United Transportation Union
UnitedHealthcare Ins Co of OH
UnitedHealthcare of Ohio Inc
Unity Financial Life Ins Co (PA)
Western and Southern Life Ins
Western-Southern Life Assur

OKLAHOMA

American Century Life Ins Co
American Farmers & Ranchers Lf
American Fidelity Assurance Co
CommunityCare HMO Inc
Delta Dental Plan of Oklahoma
Directors Life Assur Co
First Dimension Life Co Inc
GHS Health Maintenance Org
Globe Life and Accident Ins Co (NE)
Great Cornerstone L&H Ins Co
Leaders Life Ins Co
Life Assurance Company
LifeShield National Ins Co
Old Surety Life Ins Co
PacifiCare of Oklahoma Inc
Reserve National Ins Co
Sheridan Life Ins Co
Trinity Life Insurance Company
United International Life Ins
Universal Fidelity Life Ins Co
Wichita National Life Ins Co

OREGON

Advantage Dental Plan Inc
ATRIO Health Plans Inc
ClearOne Health Plans Inc
FamilyCare Health Plans Inc
Health Plan of CareOregon Inc
Kaiser Fdn Health Pl of the NW
M Life Insurance Company (CO)
Marion Polk Community H Pl Adv
Mid Rogue Health Plan
ODS Health Plan Inc
Oregon Dental Service
PacifiCare of Oregon Inc
PacificSource Health Plans
Preferred Health Plan Inc
Providence Health Plan
Regence BC/BS of Oregon
Regence Health Maint of OR
Regence HMO Oregon
Regence Life and Health Ins Co
Samaritan Health Plans Inc
Standard Insurance Company
Standard Life Insurance of NY (NY)
Trillium Community Health Plan
Willamette Dental Insurance
Willamette Dental of Idaho Inc (ID)
Willamette Dental of WA Inc (WA)

PENNSYLVANIA

Advanta Life Ins Co (AZ)
Aetna Better Health Inc (CT) (CT)
Aetna Dental Inc (a NJ corp) (NJ)
Aetna Health Inc (a CO corp) (CO)
Aetna Health Inc (a CT corp) (CT)
Aetna Health Inc (a DE corp) (DE)
Aetna Health Inc (a FL corp) (FL)
Aetna Health Inc (a GA corp) (GA)
Aetna Health Inc (a ME corp) (ME)
Aetna Health Inc (a NJ corp) (NJ)
Aetna Health Inc (a NY corp) (NY)
Aetna Health Inc (a PA corp)
Aetna Health Inc (a WA corp) (WA)
Aetna Health Insurance Company
Aetna Health Ins Co of NY (NY)
Aetna Health of the Carolinas (NC)
AF&L Insurance Company
American Indep Network of NY (NY)
American Labor Life Ins Co (AZ)
American Network Ins Company
AmeriChoice of Pennsylvania
AmeriHealth HMO Inc
Atlantic Southern Dental Fndn (NJ)
Avalon Insurance Company
Capital Advantage Insurance Co
Capital Blue Cross
CIGNA HealthCare of DE Inc (DE)
CIGNA HealthCare of PA Inc
CIGNA Life Ins Co of New York (NY)
Colonial American Life Ins Co
Community Care Behavioral Hlth
Continental Life Ins Co PA
Coventry Health Care of PA Inc
Delta Dental of Delaware (DE)
Delta Dental of New York (NY)
Delta Dental of Pennsylvania
Delta Dental of West Virginia (WV)
Dental Delivery Systems Inc (NJ)
Dental Practice Association NJ (NJ)
Eastern Life and Health Ins Co
Erie Family Life Ins Co
First Dominion Mutual Life (VA)
First Priority Life Ins Co
First Reliance Standard Life (NY)
Gateway Health Plan Inc
Geisinger Health Plan
Greater Beneficial Union
Greek Catholic Union of USA
Harleysville Life Ins Co
Health Partners of Phila
HealthAmerica Pennsylvania
HealthAssurance Pennsylvania
Highmark Inc.
Highmark Senior Resources Inc
HM Health Insurance Company
HM Life Insurance Company
HMO of Northeastern PA
Hospital Service Assn of NE PA
Independence Blue Cross
Independence Insurance Inc (DE)
Inter-County Health Plan Inc
Inter-County Hospitalization
Keystone Health Plan Central
Keystone Health Plan East Inc
Keystone Health Plan West Inc
Life Insurance of North Amer
London Life Reinsurance Co
Magellan Behavioral Hlth of PA
Mellon Life Ins Co (DE)
Mutual Beneficial Assoc Inc (DE)
Penn Ins and Annuity Company (DE)
Penn Mutual Life Ins Co
Penn Treaty Network America
Philadelphia-United Life Ins
Region 6 Rx Corporation
Reliance Standard Life Ins Co (IL)
Reliance Standard Life of TX (TX)
Senior American Life Ins Co
Significa Insurance Group Inc
Slovene National Benefit Soc
Teachers Protective Mutual
UBS Life Insurance Company USA (CA)
Union Fidelity Life Ins Co (IL)
Unison Family Health Plan PA
Unison Health Plan of Ohio Inc (OH)
Unison Health Plan of PA Inc
Unison Health Plan of SC Inc (SC)
Unison Health Plan of TN Inc (TN)
Unison Health Plan of Cap Area (DC)
United Concordia Companies Inc
United Concordia Dental Plans (MD)
United Concordia Dental Pls CA (CA)
United Concordia Dental Pls FL (FL)
United Concordia Dental Pls KY (KY)
United Concordia Dental Pls PA
United Concordia D Pls the MW (MI)
United Concordia Insurance Co (AZ)
United Concordia Ins Co of NY (NY)
United Concordia Life & Health
United Security Assur Co of PA
UPMC For You Inc
UPMC Health Benefits Inc
UPMC Health Network Inc
UPMC Health Plan Inc
Vision Benefits of America
Vista Health Plan Inc
William Penn Association

PUERTO RICO

Atlantic Southern Ins Co
Caribbean American Life Assur

Cooperativa de Seguros de Vida
Humana Health Plans of PR Inc
Humana Ins of Puerto Rico Inc
Island Insurance Corp
MAPFRE Life Insurance Company
MCS Life Insurance Company
National Life Ins Co
Pan-American Life Ins Co of PR
Popular Life Re
Puerto Rico Health Plan Inc
Trans-Oceanic Life Ins Co
Triple-S Salud Inc
Triple-S Vida, Inc.
Universal Life Insurance Co
USIC Life Insurance Company

RHODE ISLAND

Altus Dental Insurance Company
Amica Life Ins Co
Blue Cross & Blue Shield of RI
Delta Dental of Rhode Island
Neighborhood Hlth Plan of RI
Northern National Life of RI

SOUTH CAROLINA

Atlantic Coast Life Ins Co
Blue Cross & Blue Shield of SC
BlueChoice HealthPlan of SC
CIGNA HealthCare of SC Inc
Colonial Life & Accident Ins
Companion Life Insurance Co
Continental American Ins Co
Continental Life Ins Co SC
InStil Health Insurance Co
Liberty Life Insurance Company
Niagara Life and Health Ins Co (NY)
Old Spartan Life Ins Co Inc
Wateree Life Insurance Company

SOUTH DAKOTA

American Memorial Life Ins Co
Avera Health Plans Inc
Delta Dental Plan of SD
Midland National Life Ins Co (IA)
North American Co for L&H (IA)
Sanford Health Plan
Sanford Health Plan of MN (MN)
South Dakota State Med Hldg Co
Wellmark of South Dakota Inc

TENNESSEE

American Continental Ins Co
American General Lf & Accident
BlueCross BlueShield of TN
Cariten Health Plan Inc
Cariten Insurance Company
Caterpillar Life Insurance Co (MO)
Continental Life Brentwood TN
Delta Dental of Tennessee
Direct General Life Insurance (SC)
Direct Life Insurance Company (GA)
First Unum Life Ins Co (NY)
Golden Security Ins Co
HealthSpring Life and Health (TX)
HealthSpring of Tennessee
Mountain Life Ins Co
Paul Revere Life Ins Co (MA)
Paul Revere Variable Annuity (MA)
Plateau Ins Co
Preferred Hlth Partnership
Premier Behavioral Systs of TN
Provident Life and Accident
Provident Life and Casualty
SilverScript Insurance Company
Tennessee Behavioral Health
Tennessee Farmers Life Ins Co
Tennessee Life Insurance Co (AZ)
TRH Health Insurance Company
UAHC Health Plan of TN Inc
UnitedHealthcare of TN Inc
Unum Life Ins Co of Amer (ME)
Volunteer State Health Plan

TEXAS

AECC Total Vision Hth Pl of TX
Aetna Dental Inc (a TX corp)
Aetna Health Inc (a TX corp)
AGC Life Insurance Company (MO)
Allied Financial Ins Co
Ambassador Life Ins Co
American-Amicable Life Ins TX
American Benefit Life (OK)
American Century Life of Texas
American Farm Life Ins Co
American General Life Ins Co
American General Life Ins DE (DE)
American Health and Life Ins
American Income Life Ins Co (IN)
American Industries Life
American National Ins Co
American National Life Ins NY
American Nat'l Life Ins Texas
American Retirement Life Ins (OH)
Bankers Life Ins Co of America
Block Vision of Texas Inc
Brokers National Life Assur (AR)
Capitol Life Ins Co
Capitol Security Life Ins Co
Cass County Life Ins Co
Catholic Life Insurance
Cenpatico Behavioral Hlth TX
Central Reserve Life (OH)
Central Security Life Ins Co
Central United Life Ins Co (AR)
Champions Life Ins Co
Chesapeake Life Ins Co (OK)
CICA Life Ins Co of America (CO)
Citizens National Life Ins Co
Colonial Life Ins Co of Texas
Colonial Security Life Ins Co
Community First Grp Hosp Svc
Community First Health Plans
Community Health Choice Inc
Continental General Ins Co (OH)
Cook Children's Health Plan
Delaware American Life Ins Co (DE)
DentaQuest USA Insurance Co
Dorsey Life Insurance Company
Driscoll Children's Health Pln
El Paso First Health Plans
Employees Life Insurance Co
Enterprise Life Ins Co
Family Liberty Life Ins Co
Family Life Ins Co
Fidelis SecureCare of Texas
First Command LIC
First Continental L & A Ins Co
First National Indemnity
Freedom Life Ins Co of Amer
Fringe Benefit Life Ins Co
Funeral Directors Life Ins Co
Garden State Life Ins Co
Germania Life Ins Co
GlobalHealth Inc (OK)
Government Personnel Mutual
Great American Life Assur Co (OH)
Hawthorn Life Insurance Co
Health Care Service-Texas LOB
HealthMarkets Insurance Co (OK)
HHS Health of Oklahoma Inc (OK)
Humana Health Plan of TX
IBC Life Insurance Company
Insurance Co of Scott & White
International American Life
Investors Consolidated Ins Co (NH)
Investors Insurance Corp (DE)
Jefferson Life Insurance Co
KS Plan Administrators L L C
Landmark Life Insurance Co
Legacy Health Solutions
Lewis Life Insurance Company
Liberty Bankers Life Ins Co (OK)
Life Insurance Co of Southwest
Life of America Insurance Co
Life Protection Ins Co
Lincoln Memorial Life Ins Co
Manhattan Life Ins Co (NY)
McDonald Life Insurance Co
MEGA Life and Health Ins Co (OK)
Memorial Service Life Ins Co
MHNet Life and Health Ins Co
Mid-West National Life of TN
MNM-1997 Inc
Molina Healthcare of Texas Inc
NAP Life Ins Co
National Family Care Life Ins
National Farm Life Ins Co
National Foundation Life Ins
National Health Insurance Co
National Pacific Dental Inc
National Teachers Associates
National Western Life Ins Co (CO)
New Era Life Ins Co
New Era Life Ins Co Midwest
North American Life Ins of TX
Occidental Life Ins Co of NC
Optimum Re Insurance Company
PacifiCare of Texas Inc
Parkland Community Health Plan
Pearle Vision Mgd Cr - HMO TX
Philadelphia American Life Ins
Physicians Health Choice of TX
Pioneer American Ins Co
Pioneer Security Life Ins Co
Preferred Security Life Ins
Presidential Life Ins Co
Provident American Ins Co
Provident American Life & Hlth (OH)
Puritan Life Insurance Company
Regal Life of America Ins Co
SafeGuard Health Plans (TX)
SCOR Global Life Re Ins Co TX
SCOR Global Life US Re Ins Co
Scott & White Health Plan
Sears Life Insurance Company
SelectCare Health Plans Inc
SelectCare of Maine
SelectCare of Oklahoma Inc (OK)
SelectCare of Texas LLC
Servco Life Insurance Company
Service Life & Casualty Ins Co
Seton Health Plan Inc
SHA L L C
Sons of Hermann in Texas
Southwest Life & Health Ins Co
Southwest Service Life Ins Co
SPJST
Standard Life and Accident Ins
Tandy Life Insurance Company
Texas Childrens Hlth Plan
Texas Directors Life Ins Co
Texas HealthSpring LLC
Texas Imperial Life Ins Co
Texas International Life Ins
Texas Life Ins Co
Texas Memorial Life Ins Co
Texas Security Mutual Life Ins
Texas Service Life Ins Co
TJM Life Insurance Company
Tower Life Ins Co
Trans-Western Life Ins Co
United American Ins Co (NE)
United Assurance Life Ins Co
United Benefit Life Ins Co (OH)
United Concordia Dental Pls TX
United Dental Care of TX Inc
United Funeral Benefit Life
United Funeral Dir Benefit
United Teacher Associates Ins
UnitedHealthcare of TX Inc
USAA Direct Life Insurance Co (NE)
USAA Life Ins Co
USAA Life Ins Co of NY (NY)
UTMB Health Plans Inc
Valley Baptist Insurance Co
VISTA Health Plan Inc
Western American Life Ins Co
Western National Life Ins Co
Windsor Life Insurance Company
Winnfield Life Ins Co (LA)
Zale Life Ins Co (AZ)

UTAH

Altius Health Plans
Beneficial Life Ins Co
Deseret Mutual Insurance Co
Educators Hth Plans Lf Acc Hth
Educators Mutual Ins Assoc
Equitable Life & Casualty
Great Western Ins Co
Great Western Life Ins Co (MT)
HealthWise
Humana Medical Plan of Utah
Landcar Life Ins Co
Memorial Insurance Co of Amer (AR)
Regence BlueCross BlueSh of UT
Security National Life Ins Co
Sentinel Security Life Ins Co
Southern Security Life Ins Co (MS)
Standard Life & Casualty Ins
Town & Country Life Ins Co
UnitedHealthcare of Utah
Univantage Insurance Co
Western Mutual Ins Co

VERMONT

Blue Cross & Blue Shield of VT
National Life Ins Co
Vermont Health Plan LLC

VIRGINIA

AMERIGROUP New Jersey Inc (NJ)
AMERIGROUP Ohio Inc (OH)
AMERIGROUP South Carolina Inc (SC)
AMERIGROUP Tennessee Inc (TN)
AMERIGROUP Texas Inc (TX)
AMERIGROUP Virginia Inc
AMGP Georgia Managed Care Co (GA)
Anthem Health Plans of VA
Commonwealth Dealers Life Ins
DaVita VillageHealth of VA Inc
Delta Dental of Virginia
5 Star Life Insurance Co (LA)
Genworth Life and Annuity Ins
Genworth Life Insurance Co (DE)
HealthKeepers Inc
Heritage Union Life Ins Co (AZ)
Jamestown Life Ins Co
Optima Health Insurance Co
OPTIMA Health Plan
Peninsula Health Care Inc
Piedmont Community Healthcare
Priority Health Care Inc
Shenandoah Life Ins Co
Southern Health Services
Value Behavioral Health of PA (PA)
ValueOptions of Texas Inc (TX)
Virginia Premier Health Plan

WASHINGTON

Asuris Northwest Health
Columbia United Providers Inc
Commencement Bay Life Ins Co
Community Health Plan of WA
DaVita VillageHealth of OH Inc (OH)
Farmers New World Life Ins Co
Great Republic Life Ins Co
Group Health Cooperative
Group Health Options
Kemper Investors Life Ins Co (IL)
KPS Health Plans
LifeWise Assurance Company
LifeWise Health Plan of Oregon (OR)
LifeWise Health Plan of WA
Molina Healthcare of WA Inc
North Coast Life Ins Co
Pacific Visioncare WA Inc
PacifiCare of Washington
PEMCO Life Ins Co
Premera Blue Cross
Regence BlueShield
Sterling Life Ins Co (IL)
Symetra Life Insurance Company
Symetra National Life Ins Co
Washington Dental Service
Western United Life Assur Co

WEST VIRGINIA

Carelink Health Plans Inc
Highmark West Virginia Inc

WISCONSIN

Abri Health Plan Inc
American Dental Plan of WI Inc
American Family Life Ins Co
American Medical Security Life
Blue Cross Blue Shield of WI
Care Plus Dental Plans Inc
Catholic Knights
Community Care Health Plan Inc
Compcare Health Services Ins
CUNA Mutual Ins Society (IA)
Dean Health Insurance Inc
Dean Health Plan Inc
Delta Dental of Wisconsin Inc
Dental Protection Plan Inc
DentaQuest Dental Plan of WI
Direct Dental Service Plan Inc
EPIC Life Ins Co
Group Hlth Coop of Eau Claire
Group Health Coop of S Cent WI
Gundersen Lutheran Health Plan
Health Pl for Community Living
Humana Insurance Company
Humana Wisconsin Health
HumanaDental Insurance Company
Independent Care Health Plan
John Alden Life Ins Co
Madison Natl Life Ins Co Inc
MEMBERS Life Ins Co (IA)
MercyCare Insurance Company
Midwest Security Life Ins Co
National Guardian Life Ins Co
National Insurance Co of WI
Network Health Insurance Corp
Network Health Plan
Northwestern Long Term Care
Northwestern Mutual Life Ins
Parker Centennial Assurance Co
Physicians Plus Ins Corp
Preneed Reinsurance Co of Amer (AZ)
Requia Life Insurance Corp
Security Health Plan of WI
Sentry Life Ins Co
Settlers Life Insurance Co
State Life Insurance Fund WI
Time Insurance Company
Vision Care Network Ins Corp
Vision Insurance Plan America
WEA Insurance Corporation
Wisconsin Physicians Srvc Ins
WPS Health Plan Inc
Wyssta Insurance Company Inc

WYOMING

Blue Cross Blue Shield of WY

Caribbean Companies Listed by Country

BAHAMAS

Atlantic Medical Insurance Limited
CLICO (Bahamas) Limited
Colina Insurance Limited
The Family Guardian Insurance Company Limited
Sagicor Capital Life Insurance Company Limited

BARBADOS

Bank of Montreal Insurance (Barbados) Limited
CIBC Reinsurance Company Limited
London Life and Casualty (Barbados) Corporation
London Life and Casualty Reinsurance Corporation
London Life International Reinsurance Corporation
Royal Bank of Canada Insurance Company Ltd
Sagicor Life Inc.
Scotia Insurance (Barbados) Limited
TD Reinsurance (Barbados) Inc.

BERMUDA

AAA Life Re, Ltd.
Ability Reinsurance (Bermuda) Ltd
ACE Tempest Life Reinsurance Ltd.
Aetna Life & Casualty (Bermuda) Ltd.
Amedex Insurance Company (Bermuda) Ltd.
Aurigen Reinsurance Limited
Bermuda International Insurance Services Limited
Bermuda Life Insurance Company Limited
Bermuda Life Worldwide Limited
BF&M Life Insurance Company Limited
Colonial Life Assurance Company Limited
Colonial Medical Insurance Company Limited
Fortis Insurance Company (Asia) Limited
Hannover Life Reassurance Bermuda Limited
Lehman Re Limited
Somers Isles Insurance Company Limited
State Farm International Life Insurance Company Ltd.
Wilton Reinsurance Bermuda Limited
XL Life Ltd

CAYMAN ISLANDS

Best Meridian International Insurance Company SPC
INRECO International Reinsurance Company
Investors Trust Assurance SPC
Sagicor Life of the Cayman Islands Ltd.
Scottish Annuity & Life Insurance Company (Cayman) Ltd.
swisspartners Insurance Company SPC Limited

JAMAICA

Sagicor Life Jamaica Limited

TRINIDAD AND TOBAGO

Colonial Life Insurance Company (Trinidad) Limited
Guardian Life of the Caribbean Limited

Corporate Changes and Retirements
(Since 2005)

For earlier entries access www.ambest.com

Academy Life Insurance Company (AMB Number 006003), St. Louis, Missouri: This company was merged into Life Investors Insurance Company of America on July 1, 2006.

Acadian Life Insurance Company (AMB Number 068118), Metairie, Louisiana: This company was placed in liquidation on May 18, 2006.

Accendo Insurance Company (AMB Number 060681), Bettendorf, Iowa: This company redomesticated from Iowa to Utah on October 3, 2007.

ACE Life Insurance Company (AMB Number 006047), Stamford, Connecticut: This company was acquired by ACE Group on May 9, 2006.

Admiral Life Insurance Company of America (AMB Number 007358), Phoenix, Arizona: This company was acquired by State Mutual Insurance Company on August 18, 2006.

Advance Insurance Company (AMB Number 009567), Phoenix, Arizona: This company was acquired by The Wellcare Management Group, Inc. on June 30, 2006. This company changed its name to WellCare Health Insurance of Arizona, Inc. on July 18, 2006.

AECC Total Vision Health Plan of Texas, Inc. (AMB Number 064512), Dallas, Texas: This company was acquired by Centene Corporation on July 1, 2006.

AET Health Care Plan, Inc. (AMB Number 068787), Dallas, Texas: This company discontinued operation on June 30, 2005.

Aetna Health Inc. (an Arizona corporation) (AMB Number 068971), Phoenix, Arizona: This company was merged into Aetna Health Inc. (a PA Corp.) on June 30, 2009.

Aetna Health Inc. (a Maryland corporation) (AMB Number 068550), Linthicum, Maryland: This company merged into Aetna Health Inc. (a Pennsylvania corporation) on December 31, 2009.

Aetna Health Inc. (a Massachusetts corporation) (AMB Number 068699), Waltham, Massachusetts: This company merged into Aetna Health Inc. (a Pennsylvania corporation) on December 31, 2007.

Aetna Health Inc. (a Missouri corporation) (AMB Number 064369), Chesterfield, Missouri: This company merged into Aetna Health Inc. (a Pennsylvania corporation) on December 31, 2009.

Aetna Health Inc. (a New Hampshire corporation) (AMB Number 068773), Concord, New Hampshire: This company merged into Aetna Health Inc. (a Pennsylvania corporation) on October 10, 2007.

Aetna Health Inc. (an Ohio corporation) (AMB Number 060127), Richfield, Ohio: This company merged into Aetna Health Inc. (a Pennsylvania corporation) on December 31, 2007.

Aetna Health Inc. (an Oklahoma corporation) (AMB Number 064367), Tulsa, Oklahoma: This company was merged into Aetna Health Inc. (a PA Corp.) on June 30, 2009.

Aetna Health Inc. (a Tennessee corporation) (AMB Number 060128), Nashville, Tennessee: This company was merged into Aetna Health Inc. (a PA Corp 68700) effective June 30, 2009.

Aetna Health Inc. (a Louisiana corporation) (AMB Number 060123), Metairie, Louisiana: This company was merged into Corporate Health Insurance Company on August 1, 2006.

Aetna Health of Illinois Inc. (AMB Number 060122), Chicago, Illinois: This company was merged into Aetna Health Inc. (a PA Corp. 68700), effective June 30, 2009.

Aetna Health of the Carolinas Inc. (AMB Number 060134), Charlotte, North Carolina: This company merged into Aetna Health Inc. (a Pennsylvania corporation) on March 31, 2010.

Affinity Dental Health Plan (AMB Number 064928), Culver City, California: This company ceased operation on May 5, 2008.

AIG Annuity Insurance Company (AMB Number 007235), Amarillo, Texas: This company changed its name to Western National Life Insurance Company on March 20, 2009.

AIG Assurance Canada (AMB Number 066828), Toronto, Ontario, Canada: This company merged into AIG Life Insurance Company of Canada on October 1, 2008.

AIG Central Europe & CIS Insurance Holdings Corporation (AMB Number 055277), Delaware: The name of this company was changed to Chartis Central Europe & CIS Insurance Holdings Corporation on July 27, 2009.

AIG Commercial Insurance Group, Inc. (AMB Number 055711), Delaware: The name of this company was changed to Chartis U.S., Inc. on July 27, 2009.

AIG Life Insurance Company (AMB Number 006809), Wilmington, Delaware: This company changed its name to American General Life Insurance Company of Delaware on December 8, 2009.

AIG Life Insurance Company of Canada (AMB Number 066835), Toronto, Ontario, Canada: This company changed its name to BMO Life Assurance Company during April 2009. This company was acquired by BMO Financial Group on April 3, 2009.

AIG Life Insurance Company of Puerto Rico (AMB Number 006073), Hato Rey, Puerto Rico: This company merged into American General Life Insurance Company on March 27, 2008.

AIG SunAmerica Life Assurance Company (AMB Number 006115), Phoenix, Arizona: This company changed its name to SunAmerica Annuity and Life Assurance Company on April 8, 2009.

AIU Africa Holdings, Inc. (AMB Number 055275), Delaware: The name of this company was changed to Chartis Africa Holdings, Inc. on July 27, 2009.

AIU Holdings LLC (AMB Number 055280), Delaware: The name of this company was changed to Chartis International, LLC on July 27, 2009.

Alliance for Community Health (AMB Number 064179), St. Louis, Missouri: This company was acquired by Molina Healthcare, Inc. during October 2007.

Alliance of Poles of America (AMB Number 060052), Cleveland, Ohio: This company was merged into Polish Roman Catholic Union of America during 2005.

Allmerica Financial Life Insurance and Annuity Company (AMB Number 008491), Worcester, Massachusetts: This company changed its name to Commonwealth Annuity and Life Insurance Company on September 1, 2006.

Alpha Maxx Healthcare, Inc. (AMB Number 064770), Jackson, Mississippi: This company surrendered its license on March 23, 2005.

Amedex Insurance Company (AMB Number 008449), Miami, Florida: This company changed its name to BUPA Insurance Company on December 20, 2007.

Americaid Illinois, Inc. (AMB Number 064100), Chicago, Illinois: This company surrendered its license on June 1, 2007.

American Centurion Life Assurance Company (AMB Number 008062), Albany, New York: This company was merged into RiverSource Life Insurance Co. of New York on December 31, 2006.

American Continental Insurance Company (AMB Number 060568), Brentwood, Tennessee: This company was acquired by Genworth Financial, Inc. on May 2, 2006.

American Dental Plan of North Carolina, Inc. (AMB Number 064631), Cary, North Carolina: This company was acquired by Humana Inc. on October 1, 2007.

American Dental Providers of Arkansas, Inc. (AMB Number 064491), Little Rock, Arkansas: This company was acquired by Humana Inc. on October 1, 2007.

American Enterprise Life Insurance Company (AMB Number 009057), Indianapolis, Indiana: This company was merged into RiverSource Life Insurance Company on December 31, 2006.

American Exchange Life Insurance Company (AMB Number 006050), Houston, Texas: This company dissolved on February 26, 2010.

American Financial Life Insurance Company (AMB Number 009107), Fort Worth, Texas: This company was dissolved on February 22, 2007.

American Founders Life Insurance Company (AMB Number 006057), Dallas, Texas: This company was acquired by Sagicor Financial Corporation on September 22, 2005. This company changed its name to Sagicor Life Insurance Company on March 9, 2006.

American Healthcare, Inc. (AMB Number 064898), Springfield, Missouri: This company ceased operation during 2008.

American Industries Family Life Insurance Company (AMB Number 068262), Houston, Texas: This company changed its name to Forethought National Life Insurance Company during January 2005.

American Insurance Company of Texas (AMB Number 008270), Fort Worth, Texas: This company was acquired by Unified Life Insurance Company on December 1, 2006. This company was merged into Unified Life Insurance Company on October 1, 2007.

American Investors Life Insurance Company, Inc. (AMB Number 006075), Topeka, Kansas: This company was acquired by Aviva plc on November 15, 2006. This company merged into Aviva Life and Annuity Company effective August 28, 2009.

American Life and Accident Insurance Company (AMB Number 006079), McKinney, Texas: This company was merged into Globe Life and Accident Insurance Company on August 31, 2007.

American Life & Health Insurance Company (AMB Number 006078), Jefferson City, Missouri: This company merged into First Health Life & Health Insurance Company on December 31, 2008.

American Life Insurance Company of New York (AMB Number 006084), New York, New York: This company changed its name to Wilton Reassurance Life Company of New York on September 27, 2006.

American Mayflower Life Insurance Company of New York (AMB Number 006085), New York, New York: This company was merged into Genworth Life Insurance Company of New York on January 1, 2007.

American Partners Life Insurance Company (AMB Number 009105), Phoenix, Arizona: This company was merged into RiverSource Life Insurance Company on December 31, 2006.

American Pioneer Health Plans Inc. (AMB Number 064867), Orlando, Florida: This company surrendered its license during November, 2008.

American Reserve Life Insurance Company (AMB Number 007486), Edmond, Oklahoma: This company merged into Liberty Bankers Life Insurance Company on December 31, 2008.

American Skandia Life Assurance Corporation (AMB Number 008715), Shelton, Connecticut: This company changed its name to Prudential Annuities Life Assurance Corporation on January 1, 2008.

American States Life Insurance Company (AMB Number 006105), Indianapolis, Indiana: This company was merged into Symetra Life Insurance Company on October 1, 2005.

American Vanguard Life Insurance Company (AMB Number 009113), Des Moines, Iowa: This company was merged into AmerUs Life Insurance Company on September 20, 2005.

AmeriChoice of New York (AMB Number 064290), New York, New York: This company was merged into UnitedHealthcare of New York on December 31, 2007.

Americom Life & Annuity Insurance Company (AMB Number 009505), Houston, Texas: This company was merged into OM Financial Life Insurance Company on September 30, 2007.

Ameritas Variable Life Insurance Company (AMB Number 009364), Lincoln, Nebraska: This company was merged into Ameritas Life Insurance Corp. on April 30, 2007.

AmerUs Life Insurance Company (AMB Number 006199), Des Moines, Iowa: This company was acquired by Aviva plc on November 15, 2006. This company changed its name to Aviva Life and Annuity Company on November 1, 2007.

AMEX Assurance Company (Canada Branch) (AMB Number 066865), Toronto, Ontario, Canada: This company was placed in run off during 2009.

Annuity & Life Reassurance America, Inc. (AMB Number 006281), Windsor, Connecticut: This company changed its name to Heritage Union Life Insurance Company on January 9, 2009.

Anthem Blue Cross Blue Shield Partnership Plan, Inc. (AMB Number 064855), Mason, Ohio: This company merged into Community Insurance Company on December 15, 2009.

Arkansas Blue Cross and Blue Shield, A Mutual Insurance Company (AMB Number 009586), Little Rock, Arkansas: This company changed its name to USAble Mutual Insurance Company on March 23, 2010.

Arkansas Life Insurance Company (AMB Number 068314), Phoenix, Arizona: This company was acquired by American Modern Life Insurance Company on July 7, 2006.

Arkansas National Life Insurance Company (AMB Number 007507), Little Rock, Arkansas: This company was merged into Forethought Life Insurance Company on December 31, 2007.

Arnett HMO, Inc. (AMB Number 064262), Lafayette, Indiana: This company ceased operation on December 31, 2009.

Associated Mutual Hospital Service of Michigan (AMB Number 068042), Grand Rapids, Michigan: This company changed its name to Associated Mutual on January 1, 2009.

Association of Lithuanian Workers (AMB Number 009800), Middletown, New York: This company was merged into Supreme Council of the Royal Arcanum on December 28, 2005.

AtlantiCare Health Plans-HMO (AMB Number 064211), Hammonton, New Jersey: This company surrendered its license on February 28, 2008.

Atrium Health Plan, Inc. (AMB Number 068611), Hudson, Wisconsin: This company was dissolved on March 1, 2006.

Aurigen Canada Limited (AMB Number 066889), Toronto, Ontario, Canada: This Company's name was changed to Aurigen Reinsurance Company on July 23, 2008.

Avalon Health, Ltd. (AMB Number 064426), Harrisburg, Pennsylvania: This company dissolved on November 12, 2008.

Avera Health Plans of Minnesota (AMB Number 064761), Minneapolis, Minnesota: This company was dissolved during 2006.

Aviva Life Insurance Company (AMB Number 006337), Wilmington, Delaware: This company was merged into Aviva Life and Annuity Company effective September 30, 2008.

Aviva Life Insurance Company of New York (AMB Number 009098), Buffalo, New York: This company was merged into Bankers Life Insurance Company of New York on December 27, 2007.

AXA Life and Annuity Company (AMB Number 009516), Denver, Colorado: This company changed its name to AXA Equitable Life and Annuity Company during 2009.

Balboa Life Insurance Company (AMB Number 006965), Irvine, California: This company was acquired by Bank of America Corporation on July 1, 2008.

Balboa Life Insurance Company of New York (AMB Number 060347), New York, New York: This company was acquired by Bank of America Corporation on July 1, 2008.

Banc One Kentucky Insurance Company (AMB Number 009429), Louisville, Kentucky: This company was dissolved on December 30, 2009.

Bankers Life Insurance Company of Illinois (AMB Number 060038), Chicago, Illinois: This company was merged into Bankers Life and Casualty Company on November 20, 2007.

Bankers Life Insurance Company of New York (AMB Number 006467), Woodbury, New York: This company was acquired by Aviva plc on November 15, 2006. This company changed its name to Aviva Life and Annuity Company of New York on December 27, 2007.

BC Life & Health Insurance Company (AMB Number 060057), Woodland Hills, California: This company changed its name to Anthem Blue Cross Life & Health Insurance Company during the third quarter of 2007.

Benefit Life Insurance Company (AMB Number 068113), Richardson, Texas: This company surrendered its license on December 5, 2006.

Benicorp Insurance Company (AMB Number 068104), Indianapolis, Indiana: This company was placed in liquidation on October 5, 2007.

Berkley Life and Health Insurance Company (AMB Number 006579), Urbandale, Iowa: This company redomesticated from California to Iowa during the first quarter of 2008.

BHG Life Insurance Company (AMB Number 060200), Omaha, Nebraska: This company was merged into Berkshire Hathaway Life Insurance Company of Nebraska on December 31, 2006.

Business Men's Assurance Company of America (AMB Number 006175), Greenville, South Carolina: This company changed its name to Liberty Life Insurance Company on June 30, 2006.

California Health Plan (AMB Number 064751), Cerritos, California: This company changed its name to CareMore Health Plan on October 1, 2006.

Cameron Life Insurance Company (AMB Number 068018), Cameron, Missouri: This company was dissolved on January 1, 2005.

Canada Life Insurance Company of New York (AMB Number 008257), White Plains, New York: This company changed its name to First Great-West Life & Annuity Insurance Company on December 31, 2005.

Canada Life Insurance Company of America (AMB Number 060031), Lansing, Michigan: This company was merged into Great-West Life & Annuity Insurance Company on September 30, 2009.

Canassurance Compagnie D'Assurance-Vie Inc. (AMB Number 066878), Montreal, Quebec, Canada: This company changed its name to Canassurance Compagnie D'Assurance on January 1, 2006.

Canassurance Life Insurance Company, Inc. (AMB Number 066878), Montreal, Quebec, Canada: This company changed its name to Canassurance Insurance Company on January 1, 2005.

Cape Health Plan, Inc. (AMB Number 064490), Southfield, Michigan: This company was acquired by Molina Healthcare of Michigan on May 15, 2006. This company was merged into Molina Healthcare of Michigan, Inc. on December 31, 2006.

Capital Health Plans, Inc. (AMB Number 064468), Pittsburgh, Pennsylvania: This company surrendered its license on September 25, 2009.

Capitol Life and Accident Insurance Company (AMB Number 068179), Trumann, Arkansas: This company was acquired by American Modern Life Insurance Company on July 7, 2006.

The Capitol Life Insurance Company (AMB Number 006186), Grand Prairie, Texas: This company was acquired by Liberty Bankers Life Insurance Company on December 4, 2007.

Care Choices HMO (AMB Number 068556), Farmington Hills, Michigan: This company merged into Priority Health on April 1, 2007.

Cariten Health Plan Inc. (AMB Number 064425), Knoxville, Tennessee: This company was acquired by Humana, Inc. on November 1, 2008.

Cariten Insurance Company (AMB Number 007835), Knoxville, Tennessee: This company was acquired by Humana, Inc. on November 1, 2008.

Carolina Care Plan, Inc. (AMB Number 068944), Columbia, South Carolina: This company was merged with MMO/Carolina Acquisition Corp., a wholly owned subsidiary of Medical Mutual of Ohio, an Ohio domiciled mutual casualty insurer. Carolina Care Plan was the surviving corporation of the merger.

Catholic Family Life Insurance (AMB Number 006189), Shorewood, Wisconsin: This company merged into Catholic Knights on April 1, 2010.

Catholic Knights of America (AMB Number 006190), St. Louis, Missouri: This company was merged into Catholic Knights during 2005.

Celtic Insurance Company (AMB Number 006999), Chicago, Illinois: The company was acquired by Centene Corporation effective July 1, 2008.

Central Benefits Mutual Insurance Company (AMB Number 000242), Washington, District of Columbia: This company ceased operation on July 1, 2008.

Central Benefits National Life Insurance Company (AMB Number 006419), Westerville, Ohio: This company ceased operation on July 1, 2008.

Central National Life Insurance Company of Omaha (AMB Number 006201), Wilmington, Delaware: This company changed its name to Renaissance Life & Health Insurance Company of America on November 2, 2005.

Central Oregon Independent Health Services, Inc. (AMB Number 064496), Bend, Oregon: This company was merged into Clear Choice Health Plan, Inc. on March 15, 2007.

Central Reserve Life Insurance Company (AMB Number 006203), Cincinnati, Ohio: This company was acquired by Great American Financial Resources, Inc. on August 7, 2006.

Central United Life Insurance Company (AMB Number 006222), Houston, Texas: This company was redomesticated from Texas to Arkansas on May 15, 2006.

Centurion Life Insurance Company (AMB Number 006276), Lee's Summit, Missouri: This company redomesticated from Missouri to Iowa on December 31, 2006.

Century Life Assurance Company (AMB Number 009124), Oklahoma City, Oklahoma: This company was acquired by American Underwriters Life Insurance Company on October 1, 2006.

CGC Life Insurance Company (AMB Number 060700), Iowa: This company was merged into Transamerica Pacific Insurance Company, Ltd. on July 1, 2009.

CHA HMO, Inc. (AMB Number 064403), Lexington, Kentucky: This company was acquired by Humana Health Plan Inc. on May 1, 2006.

Charleston Capital Reinsurance LLC (AMB Number 076825), Washington, District of Columbia: This company redomesticated from South Carolina to the District of Columbia effective January 21, 2009.

Chase Insurance Life and Annuity Company (AMB Number 006376), Elgin, Illinois: This company was acquired by Protective Life Insurance Company on July 3, 2006. This company was merged into Protective Life Insurance Company on April 1, 2007.

Chase Insurance Life Company (AMB Number 007266), Elgin, Illinois: This company was acquired by Protective Life Insurance Company on July 3, 2006. This company was merged into Protective Life Insurance Company on April 1, 2007.

Chase Insurance Life Company of New York (AMB Number 060360), New York, New York: This company was acquired by Protective Life Insurance Company on July 3, 2006. This company was merged into Protective Life Insurance Company of New York on January 1, 2007.

Chase Life & Annuity Company (AMB Number 006851), Newark, Delaware: This company was acquired by Protective Life Insurance Company on July 3, 2006. This company was merged into Protective Life Insurance Company on January 1, 2007.

Chase Life & Annuity Company of New York (AMB Number 060340), New York, New York: This company was acquired by Protective Life Insurance Company on July 3, 2006. This company changed its name to Protective Life Insurance Company of New York on January 1, 2007.

Cherokee National Life Insurance Company (AMB Number 006214), Macon, Georgia: This company was acquired by Securian Financial Group, Inc. on May 1, 2006.

Christiana Care Health Plans, Inc. (AMB Number 064156), New Castle, Delaware: This company discontinued operation on July 1, 2005.

CIGNA HealthCare of Virginia, Inc. (AMB Number 068880), Richmond, Virginia: This company surrendered its license on December 13, 2006.

CIGNA Insurance Services Company (AMB Number 068344), Charleston, South Carolina: This company was voluntarily dissolved on October 5, 2009.

Citicorp International Insurance Co Ltd (AMB Number 060373), Daytona Beach, Florida: This company changed its name to Metlife International Insurance, Ltd. during 2006.

Citicorp Life Insurance Company (AMB Number 008382), Phoenix, Arizona: This company was acquired by MetLife, Inc. on July 1, 2005. This company was merged into Metropolitan Life Insurance Company on October 5, 2006.

Citizens Insurance Company of America (AMB Number 006228), Denver, Colorado: This company changed its name to CICA Life Insurance Company of America during 2005.

Citizens USA Life Insurance Company (AMB Number 006197), Peoria, Illinois: This company was merged into CICA Life Insurance Company of America on March 31, 2006.

City Holdings Reinsurance Life Company (AMB Number 068180), Phoenix, Arizona: This company was merged into American Health and Life Insurance Company on June 28, 2005.

CM Assurance Company (AMB Number 068010), Enfield, Connecticut: This company was dissolved on December 28, 2006.

CM Benefit Insurance Company (AMB Number 068182), Enfield, Connecticut: This company was dissolved on December 28, 2006.

Columbia Universal Life Insurance Company (AMB Number 060645), Austin, Texas: This company changed its name to LifeSecure Insurance Company on April 1, 2007. This company redomesticated from Texas to Michigan on April 1, 2007.

Columbia Universal Life Insurance Company (AMB Number 009400), Austin, Texas: This company was sold as a shell to Blue Cross and Blue Shield of Michigan during December 2006.

Columbian Family Life Insurance Company (AMB Number 006758), Binghamton, New York: This company was merged into Columbian Mutual Life Insurance Company on November 30, 2005.

Comanche County Hospital Authority (AMB Number 064168), Lawton, Oklahoma: This company surrendered its certificate of authority on September 26, 2006.

Combined Insurance Company of America (AMB Number 006246), Glenview, Illinois: This company was acquired by ACE Limited on April 1, 2008.

Combined Life Insurance Company of New York (AMB Number 008187), Latham, New York: This company was acquired by ACE Limited on April 1, 2008.

Community Bank Life & Health Insurance Comapny, Inc. (AMB Number 007304), Hot Springs, Arkansas: This company was acquired by QualChoice of Arkansas on September 10, 2009.

Community Bank Life & Health Insurance Company (AMB Number 007304), Hot Springs, Arkansas: This company changed its name to QualChoice Life and Health Insurance Company, Inc. on October 20, 2009.

Community Health Plan of Ohio (AMB Number 060145), Fremont, Ohio: This company changed its name to Ion Health of Ohio during January 2005.

Companion HealthCare Corporation (AMB Number 068593), Columbia, South Carolina: This company changed its name to BlueChoice HealthPlan of South Carolina, Inc. on July 1, 2005.

CompBenefits Company (AMB Number 064760), Miami, Florida: This company was acquired by Humana Inc. on October 1, 2007.

CompBenefits Dental, Inc. (AMB Number 064759), Chicago, Illinois: This company was acquired by Humana Inc. on October 1, 2007.

CompBenefits Insurance Company (AMB Number 006118), Houston, Texas: This company was acquired by Humana Inc. on October 1, 2007.

Concord Heritage Life Insurance Company, Inc. (AMB Number 006259), Concord, New Hampshire: This company was acquired by Unified Life Insurance Company on January 1, 2009. This company merged into Unified Life Insurance Company on January 15, 2009.

Congress Life Insurance Company (AMB Number 007600), Phoenix, Arizona: This company was acquired by Lehman Re Limited Bermuda on May 11, 2007.

ConnectiCare, Inc. (AMB Number 068517), Farmington, Connecticut: This company was acquired by Health Insurance Plan of Greater New York (HIP) during 2005.

ConnectiCare of Massachusetts (AMB Number 064464), Boston, Massachusetts: This company was acquired by Health Insurance Plan of Greater New York (HIP) during 2005.

Conseco Life Insurance Company of New York (AMB Number 060002), Jericho, New York: This company changed its name to Bankers Conseco Life Insurance Company on June 26, 2006.

Conseco Senior Health Insurance Company (AMB Number 007910), Bensalem, Pennsylvania: This company changed its name to Senior Health Insurance Company of Pennsylvania on November 12, 2008.

Conseco, Inc. (AMB Number 058030), Delaware: This company changed its name to Conseco, Inc. on May 13, 2010.

Consolidated General Life Insurance Company (AMB Number 006271), Dallas, Texas: This company was merged into Life Protection Insurance Company on December 31, 2007.

Consolidated Healthcare Management, Inc. (AMB Number 064772), Parsippany, New Jersey: This company surrendered its license on February 26, 2009.

Continental American Insurance Company (AMB Number 007411), Columbia, South Carolina: This company was sold to Aflac Incorporated on October 1, 2009.

Continental General Insurance Company (AMB Number 007360), Cincinnati, Ohio: This company was acquired by Great American Financial Resources, Inc. on August 7, 2006. This company redomesticated from Nebraska to Ohio during the fourth quarter of 2008.

Continental Life Insurance Company of Brentwood, Tennessee (AMB Number 009502), Brentwood, Tennessee: This company was acquired by Genworth Financial, Inc. on May 2, 2006.

Coordinated Care Solutions of Texas, Inc. (AMB Number 064746), Houston, Texas: This company surrendered its license on September 11, 2009.

Coordinated Health Partners, Inc. (AMB Number 068592), Providence, Rhode Island: This company was merged into Blue Cross and Blue Shield of Rhode Island on January 1, 2005.

Corporate Health Insurance Company (AMB Number 007443), Blue Bell, Pennsylvania: This company changed its name to Aetna Health Insurance Company on January 1, 2008.

Cotton States Life Insurance Company (AMB Number 006292), Atlanta, Georgia: This company was acquired by COUNTRY Life Insurance Company on January 1, 2005.

COUNTRY Medical Plans, Inc. (AMB Number 060226), Bloomington, Illinois: This company was merged into Cotton States Life Insurance Company on January 1, 2005.

Crocker Life Insurance Company (AMB Number 009334), Concord, California: This company was merged into Centurion Life Insurance Company during 2005.

Crown Life Insurance Company (AMB Number 006300), Regina, Saskatchewan, Canada: This company was acquired by Canada Life Insurance Company on July 5, 2007.

CUMIS Life Insurance Company (AMB Number 008815), Burlington, Ontario, Canada: This company was sold to Co-Operators Life Insurance Company on December 31, 2009.

CUNA Mutual Insurance Society (AMB Number 006302), Madison, Wisconsin: This company redomesticated from Wisconsin to Iowa on May 3, 2007.

CUNA Mutual Life Insurance Company (AMB Number 006674), Waverly, Iowa: This company was merged into CUNA Mutual Insurance Society on December 31, 2007.

Dallas General Life Insurance Company (AMB Number 009442), Dallas, Texas: This company was acquired by Christian Fidelity Life Insurance Company on February 3, 2006.

Davis Vision of Michigan, Inc. (AMB Number 064683), Southfield, Michigan: This company surrendered its license on November 30, 2006.

DaVita VillageHealth of Michigan, Inc. (AMB Number 064937), Brighton, Michigan: This company surrendered their license on November 24, 2008.

Dayton Area Health Plan (AMB Number 068574), Dayton, Ohio: This company changed its name to CareSource on September 9, 2005.

Delaware Health Plan Consortium (AMB Number 064140), New Castle, Delaware: This company discontinued operation on July 1, 2005.

Delaware Physicians Care-Medicare, Incorporated (AMB Number 064901), Newark, Delaware: This company was acquired by Aetna Inc. on August 1, 2007. This company was merged into a non-insurance affiliate on December 31, 2009.

Delmarva Health Plan, Inc. (AMB Number 068756), Easton, Maryland: This company was merged into CareFirst BlueChoice, Inc. during 2005.

Delta Dental of District of Columbia (AMB Number 064672), Washington, District of Columbia: This company surrendered its license during 2009.

Delta Dental Plan of Iowa (AMB Number 060205), Ankeny, Iowa: This company changed its name to Delta Dental of Iowa during 2005.

Delta Dental Plan of Kentucky, Inc. (AMB Number 064485), Louisville, Kentucky: This company changed its name to Delta Dental of Kentucky, Inc. on September 15, 2005.

Delta Dental Plan of Missouri (AMB Number 065732), St. Louis, Missouri: This company changed its name to Delta Dental of Missouri during December 2005.

Delta Dental Plan of Nebraska (AMB Number 064448), Omaha, Nebraska: This company changed its name to Delta Dental of Nebraska on May 10, 2007.

Delta Dental Plan of Minnesota (AMB Number 064440), Eagan, Minnesota: This company changed its name to Delta Dental of Minnesota on February 26, 2008.

Delta Dental Plan of Tennessee (AMB Number 064670), Nashville, Tennessee: This company changed its name to Delta Dental of Tennessee on June 29, 2005.

Delta Dental Plan of Virginia (AMB Number 064565), Roanoke, Virginia: This company changed its name to Delta Dental of Virginia on August 15, 2005.

Delta Dental Plan of Wisconsin, Inc. (AMB Number 064409), Stevens Point, Wisconsin: This company changed its name to Delta Dental of Wisconsin, Inc. on May 19, 2005.

Dental Benefit Providers of New Jersey, Inc. (AMB Number 064753), Newark, New Jersey: This company was dissolved during 2005.

Dental Benefit Providers of Maryland, Inc. (AMB Number 064506), Rockville, Maryland: This company dissolved on May 5, 2008.

Dental Insurance Company of America (AMB Number 060261), New York, New York: This company was merged into United HealthCare Insurance Company of New York on July 17, 2007.

The Dental Network (AMB Number 064786), Towson, Maryland: This company was merged into CareFirst BlueChoice, Inc. during June 2007.

Dental Providers of New Jersey, Inc. (AMB Number 064908), East Orange, New Jersey: This company surrendered its license on February 24, 2010.

DentiCare, Inc. (AMB Number 064522), Houston, Texas: This company was acquired by Humana Inc. on October 1, 2007.

Denticare, Inc. (Florida) (AMB Number 064384), Jacksonville, Florida: This company was merged into Union Security Insurance Company on November 1, 2005.

Denticare, Inc. (Kentucky) (AMB Number 065715), Frankfort, Kentucky: This company was merged into Union Security Insurance Company on November 1, 2005.

Denticare of Oklahoma, Inc. (AMB Number 064376), Tulsa, Oklahoma: This company was merged into Union Security Insurance Company on November 1, 2005.

Dixie National Life Insurance Company (AMB Number 006730), Indianapolis, Indiana: This company changed its name to Heartland National Life Insurance Company during the fourth quarter of 2008.

DOBCO Life Insurance Company (AMB Number 008484), Phoenix, Arizona: This company was dissolved on December 14, 2006.

Doctors Health Plan (AMB Number 064267), Durham, North Carolina: This company was placed in run off during 2005.

Dominion Dental Services, Inc. (AMB Number 064638), Alexandria, Virginia: This company was acquired by Capital Blue Cross on December 31, 2008.

Doral Dental Plan of Wisconsin (AMB Number 064799), Mequon, Wisconsin: This company changed its name to DentaQuest Dental Plan of Wisconsin, Inc. on December 1, 2009.

Doral Dental USA Insurance Company, Inc. (AMB Number 060597), Austin, Texas: This company changed its name to DentaQuest USA Insurance Company, Inc. during December 2009.

Eastern Life and Health Insurance Company (AMB Number 006325), Lancaster, Pennsylvania: This company was acquired by Eastern Insurance Holdings, Inc. on June 19, 2006.

EBL Life Insurance Company (AMB Number 007639), Berwyn, Pennsylvania: This company was liquidated on August 15, 2005.

Educators Mutual Life Insurance Company (AMB Number 006325), Lancaster, Pennsylvania: This company changed its name to Eastern Life and Health Insurance Company on June 16, 2006.

Elder Health Insurance Company Inc (AMB Number 060649), Wilmington, Delaware: This company changed its name to Bravo Health Insurance Company, Inc. during 2007.

Elder Health Maryland HMO, Inc. (AMB Number 064697), Baltimore, Maryland: This company changed its name to Elder Health Mid-Atlantic, Inc. on September 1, 2005.

Elder Health Mid-Atlantic, Inc. (AMB Number 064697), Baltimore, Maryland: This company changed its name to Bravo Health Mid-Atlantic, Inc. during 2007.

Elder Health Pennsylvania HMO, Inc. (AMB Number 064743), Philadelphia, Pennsylvania: This company changed its name to Elder Health Pennsylvania, Inc. during 2005.

Elder Health Pennsylvania, Inc. (AMB Number 064743), Philadelphia, Pennsylvania: This company changed its name to Bravo Health Pennsylvania, Inc. during 2007.

Elder Health Texas, Inc. (AMB Number 064838), San Antonio, Texas: This company changed its name to Bravo Health Texas, Inc. during the first quarter of 2008.

Empire General Life Assurance Corporation (AMB Number 006795), Brentwood, Tennessee: This company was merged into Protective Life Insurance Company on January 1, 2007.

Empire HealthChoice Assurance, Inc. (AMB Number 068564), New York, New York: This company was acquired by WellPoint, Inc. on December 28, 2005.

Empire HealthChoice Inc. (HMO) (AMB Number 064368), New York, New York: This company was acquired by WellPoint, Inc. on December 28, 2005.

Employers Life Insurance Corporation (AMB Number 068027), Spartanburg, South Carolina: This company was dissolved on August 31, 2005.

Essence, Inc. (AMB Number 064763), St. Louis, Missouri: This company changed its name to Essence LLP on March 5, 2007. This company merged into Essence Healthcare LLP on March 5, 2007.

Exclusive Healthcare, Inc. (AMB Number 068629), Omaha, Nebraska: This company was merged into Coventry Health Care of Nebraska, Inc. on July 5, 2007.

Fairlane Life Insurance Company (AMB Number 009508), Phoenix, Arizona: This company was dissolved on December 14, 2006.

Family Health Plan, Inc. (AMB Number 068665), Toledo, Ohio: This company surrendered its license on 12/21/2007.

Family Life Insurance Company (AMB Number 006360), Houston, Texas: This company was acquired by Manhattan Life Insurance Company on December 29, 2006.

Family Unity Holdings, LLC (AMB Number 051476), Wilmington, Delaware: This company changed its name to Unity Financial Insurance Group, LLC during June 2009.

Farmers and Ranchers Life Insurance Company (AMB Number 060341), Oklahoma City, Oklahoma: This company changed its name to American Farmers & Ranchers Life Insurance Company during 2005.

Farmers and Traders Life Insurance Company (AMB Number 006375), Syracuse, New York: This company was merged into Columbian Mutual Life Insurance Company on October 1, 2007.

Federal Home Life Insurance Company (AMB Number 006908), Lynchburg, Virginia: This company was merged into Genworth Life and Annuity Insurance Company on January 1, 2007.

Federated Life Insurance Company of Canada (AMB Number 066802), High River, Alberta, Canada: This company changed its name to Western Life Assurance Company during 2005. This company was acquired by Western Financial on February 28, 2005.

Federation Life Insurance of America (AMB Number 009783), Milwaukee, Wisconsin: This company was merged into Polish Roman Catholic Union of America during 2005.

FFRL Re Corp. (AMB Number 068012), Richmond, Virginia: This company surrendered its license to transact insurance business on December 27, 2006.

Fidelity and Guaranty Life Insurance Company (AMB Number 006384), Baltimore, Maryland: This company changed its name to OM Financial Life Insurance Company on January 2, 2007.

Fidelity and Guaranty Life Insurance Company of New York (AMB Number 007122), Purchase, New York: This company changed its name to OM Financial Life Insurance Company of New York on January 2, 2007.

Fidelity Insurance Company (AMB Number 011531), Rockville, Maryland: This company was merged into MAMSI Life and Health Insurance Company on December 31, 2006.

Fidelity Life Association, A Mutual Legal Reserve Company (AMB Number 006386), Oak Brook, Illinois: This company changed its name to Fidelity Life Association, a Legal Reserve Life Insurance Company on April 30, 2007.

Fidelity Life Insurance Company (AMB Number 009066), Oklahoma City, Oklahoma: This company was acquired by HealthMarkets LLC, a direct subsidiary of HealthMarkets, Inc. on November 29, 2007. This company changed its name to HealthMarkets Insurance Company on July 11, 2008.

Financial American Life Insurance Company (AMB Number 007376), Overland Park, Kansas: This company changed its name to Cardif Life Insurance Company on February 1, 2007.

Financial Benefit Life Insurance Company (AMB Number 009377), Topeka, Kansas: This company was merged into American Investors Life Insurance Company, Inc. on September 30, 2006.

First Alliance Insurance Company (AMB Number 007904), Lexington, Kentucky: This company was merged into Citizens Insurance Company of America on January 1, 2005.

First Allmerica Financial Life Insurance Company (AMB Number 007086), Worcester, Massachusetts: This company was acquired by Commonwealth Annuity and Life Insurance Company on December 31, 2008.

First Choice Health Plan, Inc. (AMB Number 064486), Seattle, Washington: This company surrendered its license on November 9, 2005.

First Citicorp Life Insurance Company (AMB Number 009078), New York, New York: This company was acquired by MetLife, Inc. on July 1, 2005. This company was merged into Metropolitan Life Insurance Company on October 5, 2006.

First Colony Life Insurance Company (AMB Number 006403), Lynchburg, Virginia: This company was merged into Genworth Life and Annuity Insurance Company on January 1, 2007.

First Commonwealth Health Services Corporation (AMB Number 064817), Chicago, Illinois: This company was dissolved during July 2007.

First Commonwealth Reinsurance Company (AMB Number 060358), Phoenix, Arizona: This company was dissolved on May 3, 2007.

First Fortis Life Insurance Company (AMB Number 008533), Syracuse, New York: This company changed its name to Union Security Life Insurance Company of New York on September 6, 2005.

First Great-West Life & Annuity Insurance Company (AMB Number 060244), White Plains, New York: This company was merged into Canada Life Insurance Company of New York on December 31, 2005.

First Life America Corp (AMB Number 060252), Topeka, Kansas: This company redomesticated from Topeka, Kansas to Tulsa, Oklahoma on February 18, 2010. This company changed its name to Trinity Life Insurance Company on February 19, 2010.

First Plan of Minnesota (AMB Number 068757), Duluth, Minnesota: This company changed its name to FirstSolutions during 2007.

FirstCarolinaCare, Inc. (AMB Number 064268), Pinehurst, North Carolina: This company changed its name to FirstCarolinaCare Insurance Company, Inc. on April 30, 2007.

FirstCarolinaCare Insurance Company, Inc. (AMB Number 060657), Pinehurst, North Carolina: This company was merged into FirstCarolinaCare Insurance Company, Inc. on April 30, 2007.

FirstChoice HealthPlans of Connecticut (AMB Number 060116), North Haven, Connecticut: This company changed its name to WellCare of Connecticut, Inc. on April 27, 2005.

FirstGuard Health Plan, Inc. (AMB Number 060191), St. Louis, Missouri: This company surrendered its certificate of authority on June 29, 2007.

FirstGuard Health Plan Kansas, Inc. (AMB Number 064809), Topeka, Kansas: This company surrendered its certificate of authority on March 30, 2007.

FirstSolutions (AMB Number 068757), Duluth, Minnesota: This company surrendered its license during 2009. This company has disaffiliated itself from Aware Integrated Inc. on December 31, 2009. All relationships, common management and common members of the board of directors have been dissolved. The company will operate independently of the BCBS Minnesota organization.

Fleet Life Insurance Company (AMB Number 060328), Phoenix, Arizona: This company was dissolved on December 18, 2009.

Florida Health Care Plan, Inc. (AMB Number 068926), Holly Hill, Florida: This company surrendered its licens on December 31, 2008.

Forethought Life Assurance Company (AMB Number 008321), Indianapolis, Indiana: This company merged into Forethought Life Insurance Company on October 6, 2008.

Forethought Life Insurance Company of New York (AMB Number 060566), New York, New York: This company changed its name to Niagara Life and Health Insurance Company on September 30, 2009. This company was sold to Companion Life Insurance Company on September 30,2009.

Fort Dearborn Life Insurance Company of New York (AMB Number 068158), Pittsford, New York: This company was acquired by Fort Dearborn Life Insurance Company on July 1, 2007.

Fort Wayne Health & Casualty Insurance Company (AMB Number 002736), Fort Wayne, Indiana: This company was merged into North American Specialty Insurance Company on October 1, 2006.

Fortis Benefits DentalCare of New Jersey, Inc. (AMB Number 064677), Marlton, New Jersey: This company changed its name to Union Security DentalCare of New Jersey, Inc. on September 6, 2005.

Fortis Benefits DentalCare of Wisconsin, Inc. (AMB Number 065716), Brookfield, Wisconsin: This company was merged into Union Security Insurance Company on November 1, 2005.

Fortis Benefits Insurance Company (AMB Number 007232), Des Moines, Iowa: This company changed its name to Union Security Insurance Company on September 6, 2005.

Fortis Insurance Company (AMB Number 007126), Milwaukee, Wisconsin: This company changed its name to Time Insurance Company on September 6, 2005.

Gateway Health Plan of Ohio, Inc. (AMB Number 064850), Columbus, Ohio: This company is no longer filing with A.M. Best as of 2009.

GE Capital Life Assurance Company of New York (AMB Number 060026), New York, New York: This company changed its name to Genworth Life Insurance Company of New York on January 1, 2006.

GE Dental & Vision (AMB Number 064726), Agoura Hills, California: This company was acquired by SafeGuard Health Enterprises, Inc. on May 6, 2005. This company surrendered its license during 2006.

GE Group Life Assurance Company (AMB Number 008474), Enfield, Connecticut: This company changed its name to Genworth Life and Health Insurance Company on March 24, 2006.

GE Life and Annuity Assurance Company (AMB Number 006648), Richmond, Virginia: This company changed its name to Genworth Life and Annuity Insurance Company on January 1, 2006.

Gem Insurance Company (AMB Number 009192), Salt Lake City, Utah: This company was merged with SafeHealth Life Insurance Company on February 28, 2005.

General Electric Capital Assurance Company (AMB Number 007183), Wilmington, Delaware: This company changed its name to Genworth Life Insurance Company on January 1, 2006.

General Fidelity Life Insurance Company (AMB Number 006441), San Francisco, California: This company redomesticated from California to South Carolina on December 21, 2005.

Genworth Life and Health Insurance Company (AMB Number 008474), Windsor, Connecticut: This company changed its name to Sun Life and Health Insurance Company (U.S.) on December 1, 2007.

George Washington Life Insurance Company (AMB Number 006450), Charleston, West Virginia: This company was liquidated on January 21, 2005.

George Washington University Health Plan, Inc. (AMB Number 068522), Washington, District of Columbia: This company was dissolved during 2006.

Gerber Life Insurance Company (AMB Number 007299), White Plains, New York: This company was acquired by Nestle SA in August 2007.

GHS Health Maintenance Organization (AMB Number 068932), Tulsa, Oklahoma: This company's parent Group Health Service of Oklahoma, Inc. was merged with Health Care Service Corporation on November 1, 2005.

Glenbrook Life and Annuity Company (AMB Number 007191), Phoenix, Arizona: This company was merged into Allstate Life Insurance Company on January 1, 2005.

Globe Life and Accident Insurance Company (AMB Number 006462), Wilmington, Delaware: This company redomesticated from Delaware to Nebraska during 2007.

GMAC Inc. (AMB Number 051893), Delaware: This company changed its name to Ally Financial Inc. on May 10, 2010.

GMAC LLC (AMB Number 051893), Delaware: This company changed its name to GMAC Inc. on June 30, 2009.

Golden Rule Insurance Company (AMB Number 006263), Lawrenceville, Illinois: This company redomesticated from Illinois to Indiana on October 2, 2006.

Great American Life Assurance Company of Puerto Rico (AMB Number 007631), Rio Piedras, Puerto Rico: This company was acquired by Triple-S Management on January 31, 2006. This company changed its name to Triple-S Vida, Inc. during November 2007.

Great Lakes Delta Insurance Company (AMB Number 008943), Indianapolis, Indiana: This company was merged into Renaissance Life & Health Insurance Company of America on April 1, 2007.

Great Lakes Insurance Company (AMB Number 003218), Newark, Delaware: This company merged into Banc One Insurance Company on December 31, 2007.

Great Plains Reinsurance Company (AMB Number 060090), Phoenix, Arizona: This company changed its name to Express Scripts Insurance Company on March 15, 2005.

Great-West Healthcare of Florida, Inc. (AMB Number 064380), Tampa, Florida: This company surrendered its license during the 4th quarter of 2007.

Great-West Healthcare of Indiana, Inc. (AMB Number 064378), Indianapolis, Indiana: This company surrendered its license during the 4th quarter of 2007.

Great-West Healthcare of Kansas/Missouri, Inc. (AMB Number 064668), Overland Park, Kansas: This company surrendered its license during the 4th quarter of 2007.

Great-West Healthcare of New Jersey, Inc. (AMB Number 064381), Piscataway, New Jersey: This company surrendered its license during the 4th quarter of 2007.

Great-West Healthcare of North Carolina, Inc. (AMB Number 064469), Charlotte, North Carolina: This company surrendered its license during the 4th quarter of 2007.

Great-West Healthcare of Arizona, Inc. (AMB Number 064379), Scottsdale, Arizona: This company surrendered its license in the first quarter of 2008.

Great-West Healthcare of Georgia, Inc. (AMB Number 064025), Atlanta, Georgia: This company was voluntarily dissolved on December 24, 2009.

Great-West Healthcare of Massachusetts, Inc. (AMB Number 064335), Waltham, Massachusetts: This company surrendered its license in the fourth quarter of 2007.

Great-West Healthcare of Texas, Inc. (AMB Number 064027), Dallas, Texas: This company was acquired by CIGNA Corporation on April 1, 2008. This company merged into CIGNA HealthCare of Texas, Inc. on September 30, 2009.

Great-West Healthcare of Ohio, Inc. (AMB Number 064336), North Olmstead, Ohio: This company surrendered its license during the 4th quarter of 2007.

Great-West Healthcare of Oregon, Inc. (AMB Number 064333), Portland, Oregon: This company surrendered its license during the 4th quarter of 2007.

Great-West Healthcare of California, Inc. (AMB Number 064023), Glendale, California: This company was acquired by CIGNA Corporation on April 1, 2008.

Great-West Healthcare of Colorado, Inc. (AMB Number 064024), Greenwood Village, Colorado: This company was acquired by CIGNA Corporation on April 1, 2008.

Great-West Healthcare of Illinois, Inc. (AMB Number 064026), Rosemont, Illinois: This company was acquired by CIGNA Corporation on April 1, 2008.

Great-West Healthcare of Washington, Inc. (AMB Number 064334), Bellevue, Washington: This company discontinued operation on November 30, 2006.

Group Health Service of Oklahoma (AMB Number 060112), Tulsa, Oklahoma: This company was merged into HealthCare Service Corporation, a Mutual Legal Reserve Company on November 1, 2005.

Guarantee Security Life Insurance Company (AMB Number 007654), Jacksonville, Florida: This company was liquidated on July 29, 2005.

Guaranty Insurance and Annuity Company (AMB Number 068128), Houston, Texas: This company surrendered its license on October 5, 2006.

Gulfco Life Insurance Company (AMB Number 007721), Marksville, Louisiana: This company was acquired by Bankers Life of Louisiana on March 20, 2008. This company merged into Bankers Life of Louisiana on December 31, 2008.

Hallmark Life Insurance Company (AMB Number 060297), Phoenix, Arizona: This Company was sold by Westward Life Insurance Company to Centene Corporation on May, 15 2008.

Harrison Life Insurance Company (AMB Number 068221), Gulfport, Mississippi: This company was dissolved on December 31, 2006.

Hart Life Insurance Company (AMB Number 006047), Simsbury, Connecticut: This company was sold as a shell to ACE Life Insurance Company on April 28, 2006.

Hartford Life Group Insurance Company (AMB Number 007681), Chicago, Illinois: This company was merged into Hartford Life and Accident Insurance Company on December 31, 2006.

HCC Insurance Company (AMB Number 003833), Indianapolis, Indiana: This company was sold as a shell to Deere & Company on January 14, 2010.

Health Alliance Medical Plans, Inc. (HMO) (AMB Number 068984), Urbana, Illinois: This company was dissolved on January 1, 2005.

Health Net Insurance of Connecticut, Inc. (AMB Number 011825), Shelton, Connecticut: This company was merged into Health Net Life Insurance Company during 2005.

Health Net Insurance of New York, Inc. (AMB Number 011859), New York, New York: This company was acquired by UnitedHealth Group on December 11, 2009.

Health Net of Connecticut, Inc. (AMB Number 068520), Shelton, Connecticut: This company was acquired by UnitedHealth Group on December 11, 2009.

Health Net of New Jersey, Inc. (AMB Number 064005), Old Bridge, New Jersey: This company was acquired by UnitedHealth Group on December 11, 2009.

Health Net of New York, Inc. (AMB Number 068568), New York, New York: This company was acquired by UnitedHealth Group on December 11, 2009.

Health Net of Pennsylvania, Inc. (AMB Number 068818), Philadelphia, Pennsylvania: This company surrendered its certificate of authority on March 31, 2006.

Health Plan of Nevada, Inc. (AMB Number 068619), Las Vegas, Nevada: This company was acquired by UnitedHealth Group on February 25, 2008.

Health Plan of Nevada LHSO - Lab Services (AMB Number 064734), Las Vegas, Nevada: This company was acquired by UnitedHealth Group on February 25, 2008. This company surrendered its license on December 31, 2009.

Health Plan of Nevada LHSO - Mental Health Services (AMB Number 064735), Las Vegas, Nevada: This company was acquired by UnitedHealthGroup on February 25, 2008. This company surrendered its license on December 31, 2009.

Healthcare, Inc. (AMB Number 064406), Atlanta, Georgia: This company surrendered its license on October 5, 2006.

HealthGuard of Lancaster, Inc. (AMB Number 068714), Camp Hill, Pennsylvania: This company surrendered its certificate of authority on August 1, 2007.

Healthplan of Texas, Inc. (AMB Number 064455), Tyler, Texas: This company surrendered its license on December 20, 2005.

Healthsource Management, Inc. (AMB Number 050761), Bermuda: This company was dissolved on November 1, 2005.

HealthSpring, Inc. (AMB Number 064300), Nashville, Tennessee: This company changed its name to HealthSpring of Tennessee, Inc. during September 2005.

Healthy Palm Beaches, Inc. (AMB Number 064446), West Palm Beach, Florida: This company is no longer filing with A.M. Best as of January 1, 2008.

Heritage Life Insurance Company (AMB Number 006523), Phoenix, Arizona: This company was sold as a shell to HLIC Holdings, Inc. on March 31, 2010.

Heritage Optical Center Inc. (AMB Number 064695), Detroit, Michigan: This company changed its name to Heritage Vision Plans, Inc. on October 1, 2006.

Heritage Union Life Insurance Company (AMB Number 060676), Phoenix, Arizona: This company merged into Annuity & Life Reassurance America, Inc. on January 9, 2009.

Highmark Life Insurance Company of New York (AMB Number 060209), New York, New York: This company changed its name to HM Life Insurance Company of New York on April 4, 2006.

Highmark Life Insurance Company (AMB Number 009063), Pittsburgh, Pennsylvania: This company changed its name to HM Life Insurance Company on April 1, 2006.

HM Health Insurance Company (AMB Number 006128), Richmond, Virginia: This company redomesticated from Virginia to Pennsylvania on August 17, 2006.

HMO Health Plans, Inc. (AMB Number 068945), Alamosa, Colorado: This company changed its name to Colorado Choice Health Plans on April 24, 2006.

HMO New Mexico (AMB Number 068796), Albuquerque, New Mexico: This company was merged into Health Care Service Corporation, a Mutual Legal Reserve Company on December 18, 2007.

Home Owners Life Insurance Company (AMB Number 006530), Chicago, Illinois: This company was acquired by WellCare Healthl Plans, Inc. on July 14, 2006. This company changed its name to WellCare Health Insurance of Illinois, Inc. on September 27, 2006.

Homeshield Insurance Co. (AMB Number 009458), Oklahoma City, Oklahoma: This company changed its name to LifeShield National Insurance Co. on March 20, 2009.

Horizon Healthcare of Pennsylvania, Inc. (AMB Number 064164), Harrisburg, Pennsylvania: This company voluntarily surrendered its certificate of authority on June 7, 2007.

Humana Benefit Plan of Illinois, Inc. (HMO) (AMB Number 064095), Peoria, Illinois: This company is no longer filing with A.M.Best as of January, 1, 2009.

IDS Life Insurance Company (AMB Number 006592), Minneapolis, Minnesota: This company changed its name to RiverSource Life Insurance Company on January 1, 2007.

IDS Life Insurance Company of New York (AMB Number 008345), Albany, New York: This company changed its name to RiverSource Life Insurance Company of New York on January 1, 2007.

IHC Benefit Assurance Company, Inc. (AMB Number 068430), Salt Lake City, Utah: This company changed its name to SelectHealth Benefit Assurance Company, Inc. during 2006.

IHC Health Plans, Inc. (AMB Number 064078), Salt Lake City, Utah: This company changed its name to SelectHealth, Inc. during 2006.

Independent State Life Insurance Company (AMB Number 068115), Austin, Texas: This company changed its name to Puritan Life Insurance Company on November 11, 2008.

Indianapolis Life Insurance Company (AMB Number 006552), Indianapolis, Indiana: This company was acquired by Aviva plc on November 15, 2006. This company merged into Aviva Life and Annuity Company effective September 30, 2008.

Industrial-Alliance Pacific Life Insurance Company (AMB Number 006838), Vancouver, British Columbia, Canada: This company changed its name to Industrial Alliance Pacific Insurance and Financial Services Inc. during 2007.

ING Insurance Company of America (AMB Number 068073), Tampa, Florida: This company was merged into ING Life Insurance and Annuity Company on December 31, 2005.

Insurance Investors Life Insurance Company (AMB Number 008406), Dallas, Texas: This company was dissolved on December 30, 2005.

Integrity Capital Insurance Company (AMB Number 060398), Greenwood, Indiana: This company's parent, Integrity Capital Corporation, was acquired by Citizens Inc. on February 27, 2009.

International Dental Plans, Inc. (AMB Number 065706), Jacksonville, Florida: This company was dissolved during 2006.

Interstate Bankers Life Insurance Company (AMB Number 009095), Chicago, Illinois: This company was dissolved on June 1, 2010.

Investors Guaranty Life Insurance Company (AMB Number 006579), Los Angeles, California: This company was acquired by W. R. Berkley Corporation on September 20, 2007. This company changed its name to Berkley Life and Health Insurance Company on March 7, 2008.

Investors Life Insurance Company of North America (AMB Number 006412), Austin, Texas: This company was purchased by Americo Financial Life and Annuity on July 17, 2008.

Ion Health, Inc. (AMB Number 064781), Erie, Pennsylvania: This company surrendered its certificate of authority on December 20, 2006.

Ion Health of Ohio (AMB Number 060145), Fremont, Ohio: This company surrendered its license on August 4, 2005.

Iowa Fidelity Life Insurance Company (AMB Number 060361), Arizona: This company merged into Transamerica Life Insurance Company during 2009.

IU Health Plan, Inc. (AMB Number 064386), Indianapolis, Indiana: This company changed its name to MDwise, Inc. on January 1, 2007.

Jacksonville Life Insurance Company (AMB Number 009445), Jacksonville, Texas: This company was dissolved on December 21, 2005.

Jefferson Life Insurance Company (AMB Number 068106), Dallas, Texas: This company was merged into Southwest Home Life Insurance Company on December 31, 2005.

Jefferson Pilot Financial Insurance Company (AMB Number 007211), Omaha, Nebraska: This company was acquired by Lincoln National Corporation on April 3, 2006. This company was merged into The Lincoln National Life Insurance Company on July 2, 2007.

Jefferson Pilot LifeAmerica Insurance Company (AMB Number 006239), Florham Park, New Jersey: This company was acquired by Lincoln National Corporation on April 3, 2006. This company redomesticated from New Jersey to New York on April 2, 2007. This company changed its name to Lincoln Life & Annuity Company of New York on April 2, 2007.

Jefferson Standard Life Insurance Company (AMB Number 009068), Winston-Salem, North Carolina: This company was acquired by Lincoln National Corporation on April 3, 2006. This company was sold to Securitas Financial Group, LLC on May 31, 2009. This company changed its name to Securitas Financial Life Insurance Company on May 31, 2009.

Jefferson-Pilot Life Insurance Company (AMB Number 006928), Greensboro, North Carolina: This company was acquired by Lincoln National Corporation on April 3, 2006. This company was merged into Lincoln National Life Insurance Company on April 2, 2007.

John Alden Life Insurance Company (Canada Branch) (AMB Number 069328), Newmarket, Ontario, Canada: This branch was merged into Assurant Life of Canada on June 15, 2006.

John Deere Health Insurance, Inc. (AMB Number 064827), Moline, Illinois: This company was acquired by UnitedHealth Group, Inc. on February 24, 2006. This company changed its name to UnitedHealthcare Insurance Company of the River Valley on March 31, 2006.

John Deere Health Plan, Inc. (AMB Number 068702), Moline, Illinois: This company was acquired by UnitedHealth Group, Inc. on February 24, 2006. This company changed its name to UnitedHealthcare Plan of the River Valley, Inc. on March 31, 2006.

John Hancock Life & Health Insurance Company (AMB Number 009074), Boston, Massachusetts: This company redomesticated from Delaware to Massachusetts on January 1, 2009.

John Hancock Life Insurance Company (AMB Number 006601), Boston, Massachusetts: This company merged into John Hancock Life Insurance Company (USA) on December 31, 2009.

John Hancock Variable Life Insurance Company (AMB Number 008958), Boston, Massachusetts: This company merged into John Hancock Life Insurance Company (USA) on December 31, 2009.

Kaiser Permanente Health Alternatives (AMB Number 064038), Portland, Oregon: This company was merged into Kaiser Foundation Health Plan of the Northwest on December 1, 2007.

Kanawha Insurance Company (AMB Number 006604), Lancaster, South Carolina: This company was acquired by Humana Inc. on November 30, 2007.

Kentucky Investors Inc. (AMB Number 005920), Frankfort, Kentucky: This company changed its name to Investors Heritage Capital Corporation on June 1, 2009.

Key Life Insurance Company (AMB Number 008675), Indianapolis, Indiana: This company merged into Settlers Life Insurance Company on October 1, 2008.

Keystone State Life Insurance Company (AMB Number 008960), Fort Washington, Pennsylvania: This company was acquired by Wilton Re US Group on July 2, 2007. This company was merged into Wilton Reassurance Life Company of New York on October 4, 2007.

The Lafayette Life Insurance Company (AMB Number 006617), Lafayette, Indiana: This company was acquired by Western & Southern Mutual Holding Company on June 15, 2005.

Laurel Life Insurance Company (AMB Number 068076), Austin, Texas: This company was acquired by Sagicor Financial Corporation on September 22, 2005.

LeafRe Reinsurance Company (AMB Number 060102), Tucson, Arizona: This company changed its name to Better Life & Health Company on April 1, 2009.

Leon Medical Centers Health Plans, Inc. (AMB Number 064756), Miami, Florida: This company was acquired by HealthSpring, Inc. on October 1, 2007.

Liberty Life Insurance Company (AMB Number 006628), Greenville, South Carolina: This company was merged into Business Men's Assurance Company of America on June 30, 2006.

Liberty National Life Insurance Company (AMB Number 006629), Omaha, Nebraska: This company redomesticated from Alabama to Nebraska on March 28, 2008.

Life Insurance Company of Georgia (AMB Number 006643), Atlanta, Georgia: This company was acquired by Brooke Life Insurance Company on May 18, 2005. This company was merged into Jackson National Life Insurance Company on December 31, 2005.

Life Insurance Company of Mississippi (AMB Number 008922), Jackson, Mississippi: This company was merged into American Bankers Life Assurance Company of Florida on December 1, 2005.

Life Investors Insurance Company of America (AMB Number 006495), Cedar Rapids, Iowa: This company merged into Transamerica Life Insurance Company on October 2, 2008.

Corporate Changes and Retirements – *Continued*

Life of America Insurance Company (AMB Number 007961), Dallas, Texas: This company merged into Republic American Life Insurance Company on December 1, 2008.

LifeRe Insurance Company (AMB Number 009435), San Antonio, Texas: This company was acquired by Ameritas Life Insurance Corp on July 3, 2007. This company was merged into Ameritas Life Insurance Corporation on October 1, 2008.

LifeSecure Insurance Company (AMB Number 064869), Brighton, Michigan: This company was merged into Columbia Universal Life Insurance Company on April 1, 2007.

Lincoln Direct Life Insurance Company (AMB Number 006663), Lincoln, Nebraska: This company was merged into Assurity Life Insurance Company on January 1, 2005.

Lincoln Life & Annuity Company of New York (AMB Number 060206), Syracuse, New York: This company was merged into Jefferson Pilot LifeAmerica Insurance Company on April 2, 2007.

Longevity Insurance Company (AMB Number 060701), Plano, Texas: This company changed its name to Longevity Insurance Company on August 26, 2008.

Lovelace Sandia Health Systems, Inc. (AMB Number 068562), Albuquerque, New Mexico: This company changed its name to Lovelace Health System, Inc. on May 1, 2006.

Mack H. Hannah Life Insurance Company (AMB Number 068057), Houston, Texas: This company was dissolved on August 31, 2007.

Magellan Behavioral Health of Texas, Inc. (AMB Number 064507), Dallas, Texas: This company voluntarily withdrew its license on December 30, 2005.

Maine Partners Health Plan, Inc. (AMB Number 064394), South Portland, Maine: This company was merged into Anthem Health Plans of Maine, Inc. on January 1, 2005.

Manufacturers Life Insurance Company of America (AMB Number 060381), Bloomfield Hills, Michigan: This company was merged into John Hancock Life Insurance Company (USA) on December 1, 2005.

The Manufacturers Life Insurance Company of New York (AMB Number 060056), Valhalla, New York: This company changed its name to John Hancock Life Insurance Company of New York on January 1, 2005.

The Manufacturers Life Insurance Company (U.S.A.) (AMB Number 006681), Bloomfield Hills, Michigan: This company changed its name to John Hancock Life Insurance Company (USA) on January 1, 2005.

Manulife Insurance Company (AMB Number 009074), Wilmington, Delaware: This company changed its name to John Hancock Life & Health Insurance Company on April 4, 2008.

Marmid Life Insurance Company (AMB Number 009264), Tempe, Arizona: This company was merged into HSBC Reinsurance (USA) Inc. on September 30, 2005.

Maryland Dental Health, Inc. (AMB Number 064785), Baltimore, Maryland: This company surrendered its license on December 1, 2007.

Mayflower National Life Insurance Company (AMB Number 007305), Indianapolis, Indiana: This company was acquired by Assurant, Inc. on July 2, 2007. This company was merged into American Memorial Life Insurance Company on December 1, 2007.

MCAID (AMB Number 064738), Ann Arbor, Michigan: This company was acquired by Blue Care Network on December 31, 2006. This company changed its name to BlueCaid of Michigan on September 25, 2007.

M-Care, Inc. (AMB Number 068783), Ann Arbor, Michigan: This company was acquired by Blue Care Network on December 31, 2006. This company was merged into Blue Care Network of Michigan on December 31, 2007.

MDNY Healthcare, Inc. (AMB Number 064291), Melville, New York: This company was dissolved on May 31, 2008.

Medco Containment Insurance Company of New Jersey (AMB Number 060105), Franklin Lakes, New Jersey: This company was merged into Medco Containment Life Insurance Company on February 1, 2007.

Medico Life Insurance (AMB Number 007378), Omaha, Nebraska: The company changed its name to Ability Insurance Company effective February 10, 2009.

Medico Life Insurance Company (AMB Number 007378), Omaha, Nebraska: This company was acquired by Ability Resources, Inc. on September 28, 2007.

Mediplan Corporation (AMB Number 064842), Canton, Ohio: This company was merged into Buckeye Community Health Plan on June 30, 2006.

Member Service Life Insurance Company (AMB Number 008784), Tulsa, Oklahoma: This company was merged into Fort Dearborn Life Insurance Company on October 1, 2006.

MEMBERS Life Insurance Company (AMB Number 008719), Madison, Wisconsin: This company redomesticated from Wisconsin to Iowa on May 3, 2007.

Memphis Managed Care Corporation (AMB Number 068735), Memphis, Tennessee: This company was acquired by AMERIGROUP Corporation on November 1, 2007.

Mercy MC+, Inc. (AMB Number 064823), Chesterfield, Missouri: This company dissolved on July 15, 2008.

Merit Behavioral Care of California (AMB Number 064736), South San Francisco, California: This company was merged into Magellan Health Services of California on September 30, 2005.

Merrill Lynch Life Insurance Company (AMB Number 009537), Little Rock, Arkansas: This company was acquired by AEGON USA, Inc. on December 28, 2007.

Metcare Health Plans, Inc. (AMB Number 064915), West Palm Beach, Florida: This company was acquired by Humana Medical Plan, Inc., a wholly-owned subsidiary of Humana Inc., on August 29, 2008. This company changed its name to Humana AdvantageCare Plan on September 10, 2008.

MetLife Insurance Company of Connecticut (AMB Number 007330), Hartford, Connecticut: This company was acquired by MetLife, Inc. on July 1, 2005.

MetLife Insurance Company of Connecticut (Canada Branch) (AMB Number 069351), Newmarket, Ontario, Canada: This branch was acquired by MetLife, Inc. on July 1, 2005. This branch surrendered its license in Canada on February 2, 2008.

Metlife International Insurance, Ltd. (AMB Number 060373), Tampa, Florida: This company surrendered its certificate of authority on May 10, 2006.

MetLife Investors Insurance Company of California (AMB Number 008402), Newport Beach, California: This company was merged into MetLife Investors Insurance Company on November 9, 2006.

MetLife Life and Annuity Company of Connecticut (AMB Number 008429), Hartford, Connecticut: This company was acquired by MetLife, Inc. on July 1, 2005. This company was merged into MetLife Insurance Company of Connecticut on December 7, 2007.

Metrowest Health Plan, Inc. (AMB Number 064459), Fort Worth, Texas: This company surrendered its license on March 8, 2006.

MHN Reinsurance Company of Arizona (AMB Number 008907), Phoenix, Arizona: This company was merged into Health Net Life Insurance Company on December 28, 2005.

MIC Life Insurance Corporation (AMB Number 008618), Dover, Delaware: This company changed its name to Perico Life Insurance Company on December 13, 2005. This company was acquired by HCC Insurance Holdings, Inc. on December 13, 2005.

Michigan Health Insurance Company (AMB Number 060400), Southfield, Michigan: This company was acquired by Blue Cross Blue Shield of Michigan on December 31, 2006. This company merged into LifeSecure Insurance Company on March 31, 2009.

Mid Atlantic Life Insurance Company (AMB Number 060562), Charleston, West Virginia: This company merged into Unified Life Insurance Company on January 2, 2007.

Mid-Continent Preferred Life Insurance Company (AMB Number 060382), Edmond, Oklahoma: This company changed its name to American Benefit Life Insurance Company on May 4, 2009.

MidAmerica Life Insurance Company (AMB Number 006906), Omaha, Nebraska: This company changed its name to American Republic Corp Insurance Company on May 18, 2006.

Mid-American Century Life Insurance Company (AMB Number 068241), Jefferson City, Missouri: This company was merged into CICA Life Insurance Company of America on December 31, 2005.

Mid-South Insurance Company (AMB Number 008350), Omaha, Nebraska: This company changed its name to World Corp Insurance Company on April 13, 2006.

Mid-West National Life Insurance Company of Tennessee (AMB Number 006715), Nashville, Tennessee: This company redomesticated from Tennessee to Texas on August 12, 2005.

Missouri Care Health Plan (AMB Number 064416), Columbia, Missouri: This company changed its name to Missouri Care L.C. during 2005.

Missouri Care Incorporated (AMB Number 064921), Columbia, Missouri: This company was acquired by Aetna Inc. on August 1, 2007.

Missouri Care L.C. (AMB Number 064416), Columbia, Missouri: This company discontinued operation on February 1, 2007.

ML Life Insurance Company of New York (AMB Number 008487), New York, New York: This company was acquired by AEGON USA, Inc. on December 28, 2007.

Molina Healthcare of Indiana, Inc. (AMB Number 064841), Merrillville, Indiana: This company voluntarily withdrew from the insurance industry on December 31, 2009.

Montana Benefits, Inc. (AMB Number 060396), Helena, Montana: This company voluntarily surrendered its certificate of authority on December 21, 2005.

Monumental Life Insurance Company (AMB Number 006742), Baltimore, Maryland: This company was redomesticated from Maryland to Iowa on April 1, 2007.

MS Diversified Life Insurance Company (AMB Number 068245), Jackson, Mississippi: This company was merged into American Bankers Life Assurance Company of Florida on November 1, 2006.

MS Life Insurance Company (AMB Number 008902), Jackson, Mississippi: This company was merged into American Bankers Life Assurance Company of Florida on December 1, 2005.

The Municipal Insurance Company of America (AMB Number 006747), Arlington Heights, Illinois: This company was placed in liquidation on October 5, 2007.

Mutual of Detroit Insurance Company (AMB Number 006309), Plymouth, Michigan: This company merged into Columbian Mutual Life Insurance Company on December 1, 2008.

Mutual Protective Insurance Company (AMB Number 003150), Omaha, Nebraska: This company changed its name to Medico Insurance Company on January 1, 2006.

Mutual Security Life Insurance Company (AMB Number 006754), Fort Wayne, Indiana: This company was liquidated on July 29, 2005.

Mutual Service Life Insurance Company (AMB Number 006755), Arden Hills, Minnesota: This company was merged into COUNTRY Life Insurance Company on November 1, 2007.

National Benefit Life Insurance Company (AMB Number 006163), New York, New York: This company was acquired by Citigroup Insurance Holding Corporation on June 30, 2005.

National Capital Life Insurance Company (AMB Number 068193), Austin, Texas: This company was merged into Mayflower National Life Insurance Company on April 1, 2005.

National Financial Insurance Company (AMB Number 006039), Fort Worth, Texas: This company was acquired by Unified Life Insurance Company on December 5, 2006. This company was merged into Unified Life Insurance Company on October 1, 2007.

National Foot Care Program, Inc. (AMB Number 064682), Southfield, Michigan: This company was placed in liquidation on November 19, 2007.

National Fraternal Society of the Deaf (AMB Number 009873), Springfield, Illinois: This company was merged into Catholic Order of Foresters on January 1, 2005.

National Heritage Insurance Company (AMB Number 008760), Plano, Texas: This company surrendered its license on June 27, 2006.

National Life Assurance Company of Canada (AMB Number 006789), Toronto, Ontario, Canada: This company was merged into Industrial-Alliance Insurance and Financial Services Inc. on July 1, 2005.

National Mutual Life Insurance Company (AMB Number 068247), Indianapolis, Indiana: This company changed its name to Buchanan Life Insurance Company during 2005.

NationsBanc Insurance Company, Inc. (AMB Number 007107), Columbia, South Carolina: This company was merged into General Fidelity Life Insurance Company on September 29, 2006.

Nationwide Life and Annuity Company of America (AMB Number 007275), Newark, Delaware: This company merged into National Life & Annuity Insurance Company on December 31, 2009.

Nationwide Life Insurance Company of America (AMB Number 006971), Philadelphia, Pennsylvania: This company merged into Nationwide Life Insurance Company on December 31, 2009.

Nationwide Life Insurance Company of Delaware (AMB Number 060048), Newark, Delaware: This company was dissolved on December 30, 2008.

Neighborhood Health Partnership, Inc. (AMB Number 064001), Miami, Florida: This company was acquired by UnitedHealthCare, Inc. on September 19, 2005.

NGL American Life Insurance Company (AMB Number 009322), Madison, Wisconsin: This company changed its name to Settlers Life Insurance Company on July 1, 2006.

North American Company for Life and Health Insurance (AMB Number 006827), Chicago, Illinois: This company redomesticated from Illinois to Iowa on September 28, 2007.

North American Company for Life and Health Insurance of New York (AMB Number 009044), Garden City, New York: This company was merged into American Life Insurance Company of New York on September 27, 2006. This company was acquired by Wilton Re U.S. Holdings, Inc. on September 27, 2006.

North American National Life Insurance Company (AMB Number 068250), Phoenix, Arizona: This company dissolved during 2008.

Northstar Life Insurance Company (AMB Number 068158), Ithaca, New York: This company changed its name to Fort Dearborn Life Insurance Company of New York on July 1, 2007.

Nutmeg Life Insurance Company (AMB Number 006406), Bettendorf, Iowa: This company was sold as a shell to Accendo Holding Company on September 6, 2007.

Nutmeg Life Insurance Company (AMB Number 060681), Bettendorf, Iowa: This company changed its name to Accendo Insurance Company on October 3, 2007.

NVAL Visioncare Systems of California, Inc. (AMB Number 064717), Upland, California: This company changed its name to FirstSight Vision Services, Inc. on July 1, 2005.

Old Dominion Life Insurance Company (AMB Number 009154), Roanoke, Virginia: This company was merged into Shenandoah Life Insurance Company on December 29, 2006.

Old Republic Life Insurance Company of Arizona (AMB Number 060391), Phoenix, Arizona: This company surrendered its license on March 31, 2008.

Old United Reinsurance Company (AMB Number 060011), Phoenix, Arizona: This company was merged into Old United Life Insurance Company on May 4, 2005.

Old West Annuity & Life Insurance Company (AMB Number 007957), Phoenix, Arizona: This company was acquired by Great American Life Insurance Company on January 1, 2006. This company merged into Great American Life Insurance Company on October 9, 2007.

Omega Reinsurance Corporation (AMB Number 068465), Phoenix, Arizona: This company was dissolved on September 28, 2007.

Omnia Life Insurance Company (AMB Number 060370), Austin, Texas: This company was dissolved on December 30, 2006.

OmniCare Health Plan, Inc. (AMB Number 064435), Memphis, Tennessee: This company changed its name to UAHC Health Plan of Tennessee, Inc on April 21, 2005.

Optimum Choice of the Carolinas, Inc. (AMB Number 064030), Morrisville, North Carolina: This company was merged into UnitedHealthcare of North Carolina, Inc. on December 31, 2006.

Optimum Choice, Inc. of Pennsylvania (AMB Number 064029), Philadelphia, Pennsylvania: This company was merged into AmeriChoice of Pennsylvania, Inc. on December 31, 2006.

Orkney Re, Inc. (AMB Number 060559), Charleston, South Carolina: This company redomesticated from South Carolina to Delaware in early May 2007.

OSF Health Plans, Inc. (AMB Number 060099), Peoria, Illinois: This company was sold to Humana, Inc. on May 27, 2008. This company changed its name to Humana Benefit Plan of Illinois, Inc. during the third quarter of 2008.

Ouachita Life Insurance Company (AMB Number 068362), North Little Rock, Arkansas: This company was acquired by American Modern Life Insurance Company on July 7, 2006.

Owens-Brumley Funeral Insurance Company (AMB Number 068258), Brownwood, Texas: This company changed its name to Texas Memorial Life Insurance Company during September 2006.

OWL Insurance Company (AMB Number 060563), Amarillo, Texas: This company was dissolved on April 18, 2007.

Ozark National Life Insurance Company (AMB Number 006875), Little Rock, Arkansas: This company was acquired by Citizen's, Inc. on October 27, 2008. This company merged into Security Plan Life Insurance Company on October 1, 2009.

Pacific Captive Insurance Company (AMB Number 060214), Charleston, South Carolina: This company changed its name to Golden Gate II Captive Insurance Company during 2007.

Pacific Hospital Association (AMB Number 064500), Springfield, Oregon: This company changed its name to PacificSource Health Plans on July 10, 2006.

Pacific Life and Accident Insurance Company (AMB Number 068078), Dallas, Texas: This company was dissolved on september 30, 2008.

Pacific Life Insurance Company (AMB Number 006885), Newport Beach, California: This company redomesticated from California to Nebraska on September 1, 2005.

Pacific Union Assurance Company (AMB Number 006921), San Francisco, California: This company merged into American General Life Insurance Company on December 31, 2009.

Pacific Union Dental, Inc. (AMB Number 064658), Concord, California: This company merged into Dental Benefit Providers of California, Inc. on October 31, 2008.

PacifiCare Dental (AMB Number 064635), Cypress, California: This company merged into Dental Benefit Providers of California, Inc. on October 31, 2008.

PacifiCare Health Insurance Company of Micronesia (AMB Number 060359), Tamuning, Guam: This company changed its name to TakeCare Insurance Company, Inc. on November 1, 2005.

PacifiCare Insurance Company (AMB Number 060569), Indianapolis, Indiana: This company was dissolved on December 31, 2008.

Paragon Life Insurance Company (AMB Number 009079), St. Louis, Missouri: This company was merged into Metropolitan Life Insurance Company on May 1, 2006.

Paramount Security Life Insurance Company (AMB Number 007902), Shreveport, Louisiana: This company changed its name to Security National Life Insurance Company of Louisiana during 2005.

PartnerRe SA (Canada Branch) (AMB Number 066844), Toronto, Ontario, Canada: This company changed its name to Partner Reinsurance Company Ltd. Canada Branch on January 1, 2008.

Pearle VisionCare, Inc. (AMB Number 064667), San Diego, California: This company surrendered its license in January, 2009.

Pennsylvania Dental Service Corporation (AMB Number 064557), Mechanicsburg, Pennsylvania: This company changed its name to Delta Dental of Pennsylvania on August 15, 2005.

Peoples Benefit Life Insurance Company (AMB Number 006779), Cedar Rapids, Iowa: This company was merged into Monumental Life Insurance Company on October 1, 2007.

The PerfectHealth Insurance Company (AMB Number 064825), New York, New York: This company merged into Group Health Incorporated on December 31, 2009.

PersonalCare Insurance of Illinois, Inc. (HMO) (AMB Number 068765), Champaign, Illinois: This company discontinued operation on January 1, 2005.

The Philanthropic Mutual Life Insurance Company (AMB Number 006920), Plymouth Meeting, Pennsylvania: This company was merged into Columbian Mutual Life Insurance Company on February 28, 2006.

Phoenix National Insurance Company (AMB Number 007144), Cincinnati, Ohio: This company was acquired by Molina Healthcare Inc. on December 22, 2005. This company changed its name to Molina Healthcare Insurance Company on April 24, 2006.

PHP Insurance Plan, Inc. (AMB Number 064123), Green Bay, Wisconsin: This company was dissolved on December 31, 2005.

Physicians Health Plan of Southwest Michigan, Inc. (AMB Number 064620), Kalamazoo, Michigan: This company surrendered its license on December 1, 2007.

Polish National Alliance of Brooklyn, U.S.A. (AMB Number 009871), Brooklyn, New York: This company was merged into Polish National Alliance of the U.S. of N.A. on July 1, 2007.

Preferred Health Partnership of Tennessee, Inc. (AMB Number 064302), Knoxville, Tennessee: This company was acquired by Humana, Inc. on November 1, 2008.

Premier Health, Inc. (AMB Number 064072), Topeka, Kansas: This company was dissolved on June 18, 2009.

Premier Health Insurance Company, Inc. (AMB Number 060384), Chesterfield, Missouri: This company changed its name to Mercy Health Plans on August 23, 2007.

Premier Medical Insurance Group, Inc. (AMB Number 060218), Madison, Wisconsin: This company changed its name to Dean Health Insurance, Inc. on July 1, 2005.

Primary Health Network Inc. (AMB Number 060336), Boise, Idaho: This company was acquired by PacificSource Health Plans on July 30, 2009. This company merged into PacificSource Health Plans on December 31, 2009.

Primerica (AMB Number 058453), Delaware: This company changed its name to Primerica, Inc. during October 2009.

Principal Health Insurance Company (AMB Number 007326), Des Moines, Iowa: This company changed its name to Principal National Life Insurance Company on October 16, 2007.

Principal Life Insurance Company of Iowa II (AMB Number 059308), Des Moines, Iowa: This company redomesticated from Iowa to Delaware on July 15, 2009. This company changed its name to Principal Reinsurance Company of Delaware on July 15, 2009.

Private Medical-Care, Inc. (AMB Number 068640), Cerritos, California: This company was dissolved on December 31, 2006.

Protective Life Insurance Company of Kentucky (AMB Number 060214), Louisville, Kentucky: This company changed its name to Pacific Captive Insurance Company during 2005. This company redomesticated from Kentucky to South Carolina during 2005.

Provident American Life & Health Insurance Company (AMB Number 006932), Cincinnati, Ohio: This company was acquired by Great American Financial Resources, Inc. on August 7, 2006.

The Prudential Insurance Company of America (Canada Branch) (AMB Number 069346), Toronto, Ontario, Canada: This company ceased operation during 2006.

Prudential Select Life Insurance Company of America (AMB Number 060560), Plymouth, Minnesota: This company changed its name to Wilton Reassurance Company on September 30, 2005.

PSO Health Services, LLC (AMB Number 064777), San Antonio, Texas: This company changed its name to Physicians Health Choice of Texas, Inc.on July 31, 2009.

QMedCare of New Jersey, Inc. (AMB Number 064951), Eatontown, New Jersey: This company surrendered its license on June 16, 2008.

QualChoice Select, Inc. (AMB Number 064835), Cleveland, Ohio: This company was acquired by WellPoint, Inc. on August 1, 2006. This company merged into Anthem Blue Cross Blue Shield Partnership Plan, Inc. on December 31, 2007.

Reassure America Life Insurance Company (AMB Number 006676), Jacksonville, Illinois: This company was merged into Valley Forge Life Insurance Company during 2007.

RegenceCare (AMB Number 068633), Seattle, Washington: This company was dissolved on December 31, 2005.

Reinsurance Company of Missouri Inc (AMB Number 050061), Chesterfield, Missouri: This company's ultimate parent, Reinsurance Group of America, was split off of MetLife, Inc. on September 17, 2008.

Reinsurance Group of America Incorporated (AMB Number 058089), Chesterfield, Missouri: This company was split off of MetLife, Inc. on September 17, 2008.

The Reliable Life Insurance Company of Texas (AMB Number 068547), Houston, Texas: This company merged into Reliable Life Insurance Company on October 31, 2008.

Reliance Life Insurance Company (AMB Number 060314), Wilmington, Delaware: This company redomesticated from Delaware to Nebraska during 2007. This company changed its name to USAA Direct Life Insurance Company on September 14, 2007. This company redomesticated from Delaware to Texas on September 14, 2007.

Renaissance Life & Health Insurance Company (AMB Number 009155), Indianapolis, Indiana: This company was sold by its parent, Delta Dental of Indiana, to a third party on July 9, 2009. This company changed its name to Members Health Insurance Company on February 4, 2010.

Renaissance Life & Health Insurance Company of America (AMB Number 006201), Wilmington, Delaware: This company was acquired by Renaissance Holding Company on October 31, 2005. This company redomesticated from Delaware to Indiana on September 1, 2009.

Republic American Life Insurance Company (AMB Number 006574), Dallas, Texas: This company changed its name to Life of America Insurance Company on December 19, 2008.

Resource Life Insurance Company (AMB Number 006176), Chicago, Illinois: This company was acquired by Onex Corporation on November 30, 2006.

Revios Reinsurance U.S. Inc. (AMB Number 060212), Los Angeles, California: This company changed its name to SCOR Global Life Re Insurance Company of Texas on November 14, 2007. This company redomesticated from California to Texas on November 14, 2007.

RGA Life Reinsurance Company of Canada (AMB Number 066817), Toronto, Ontario, Canada: This company's ultimate parent, Reinsurance Group of America, was split off of MetLife, Inc. on September 17, 2008.

RGA Reinsurance Company (AMB Number 009080), Chesterfield, Missouri: This company's ultimate parent, Reinsurance Group of America, was split off of MetLife, Inc. on September 17, 2008.

Rochester Area Health Maintenance Organization, Inc. (AMB Number 064296), Rochester, New York: This company merged into MVP Health Plan, Inc. on May 1, 2009.

Rockford Health Plans (AMB Number 068830), Rockford, Illinois: This company went out of business during 2005.

Rooney Life Insurance Company (AMB Number 060029), Vacaville, California: This company changed its name to All Savers Life Insurance Company of California on May 8, 2008.

Ruffin & Jarrett Insurance Company (AMB Number 068212), Little Rock, Arkansas: This company changed its name to New Foundation Life Insurance Company during 2007.

SafeGuard Health Plans, Inc. (AMB Number 068512), Aliso Viejo, California: This company was acquired by MetLife, Inc. on January 31, 2008.

Safeguard Health Plans, Inc. A Nevada Corporation (AMB Number 064900), Reno, Nevada: This company was acquired by MetLife, Inc. on January 31, 2008.

SafeGuard Health Plans, Inc., a Florida corporation (AMB Number 064671), Plantation, Florida: This company was acquired by MetLife, Inc. on January 31, 2008.

SafeGuard Health Plans, Inc., a Texas corporation (AMB Number 064460), Dallas, Texas: This company was acquired by MetLife, Inc. on January 31, 2008.

SafeHealth Life Insurance Company (AMB Number 008221), Aliso Viejo, California: This company was acquired by MetLife, Inc. on January 31, 2008.

Sage Life Assurance of America, Inc. (AMB Number 009059), Wilmington, Delaware: This company was merged into Valley Forge Life Insurance Company on September 30, 2006.

SCOR Life Insurance Company (AMB Number 006996), Plano, Texas: This company was sold as a shell to Morgan Stanley Life Holding, Inc. on June 30, 2008.

SCOR Life U.S. Re Insurance Company (AMB Number 006555), Plano, Texas: This company changed its name to SCOR Global Life U.S. Re Insurance Company on June 15, 2007.

SCOR VIE (Canada Branch) (AMB Number 066849), Montreal, Quebec, Canada: This company changed its name to SCOR Global Life (Canada Branch) on November 30, 2006.

Security Alliance Insurance Company (AMB Number 068242), Little Rock, Arkansas: This company was merged into CICA Life Insurance Company of America during October 2006.

Security Financial Life Insurance Company (AMB Number 007033), Lincoln, Nebraska: This company was merged into Assurity Life Insurance Company on January 1, 2007.

Security National Life Insurance Company of Louisiana (AMB Number 007902), Shreveport, Louisiana: This company merged into Security National Life Insurance Company on December 31, 2009.

Seguros de Vida Triple-S, Inc. (AMB Number 068131), Guaynabo, Puerto Rico: This company was merged into Great American Life Assurance Company of Puerto Rico on June 30, 2006.

Senate Insurance Company (AMB Number 007612), Phoenix, Arizona: This company was dissolved during 2006.

Senior Health Insurance Company of Pennsylvania (AMB Number 007910), Bensalem, Pennsylvania: This company was acquired by Senior Health Care Oversight Trust, an independent trust on November 12, 2008..

Senior Insurance Services, Inc. (AMB Number 064780), Woodridge, Illinois: This company surrendered their license on December 14, 2006.

Servus Life Insurance Company (AMB Number 007439), Simsbury, Connecticut: This company was sold as a shell to XL Life Insurance and Annuity Company on March 2, 2006.

Servus Life Insurance Company (AMB Number 060575), Stamford, Connecticut: This company redomesticated from Connecticut to Delaware on September 18, 2006. This company changed its name to XL Re Life America Inc. on September 18, 2006.

Settlers Life Insurance Company (AMB Number 068040), Bristol, Virginia: This company merged into NGL American Life Insurance Company on July 1, 2006.

Sierra Health and Life Insurance Company, Inc. (AMB Number 007370), Los Angeles, California: This company was acquired by UnitedHealth Group on February 25, 2008.

Significa Insurance Group, Inc. (AMB Number 006902), Lake Mary, Florida: This company was redomesticated from Florida to Pennsylvania on April 19, 2007.

Sioux Valley Health Plan (AMB Number 064393), Sioux Falls, South Dakota: This company changed its name to Sanford Health Plan during 2007.

Sioux Valley Health Plan of Minnesota (AMB Number 064604), Minneapolis, Minnesota: This company changed its name to Sanford Health Plan of Minnesota during the 4th quarter of 2007.

Southern Pioneer Life Insurance Company (AMB Number 007521), Trumann, Arkansas: This company was acquired by American Modern Life Insurance Company on July 7, 2006.

Southern Security Life Insurance Company (AMB Number 007586), Lake Mary, Florida: This company was merged into Security National Life Insurance Company on December 31, 2006.

Southern Security Life Insurance Company, Incorporated (AMB Number 068370), Louisville, Mississippi: This company was acquired by Security National Financial Corp. during 2008.

Southwest Home Life Insurance Company (AMB Number 009521), Dallas, Texas: This company changed its name to Jefferson Life Insurance Company on December 31, 2005.

Southwest Texas HMO, Inc. (AMB Number 068718), Richardson, Texas: This company changed its name to Health Care Service Corporation HMO-Texas on March 8, 2005.

Southwestern Life Insurance Company (AMB Number 007063), Dallas, Texas: This company merged into Valley Forge Life Insurance Company on December 28, 2006.

Spectera Vision, Inc. (AMB Number 064641), Richmond, Virginia: This company merged into its parent company Spectera, Inc. on March 31, 2007.

Spectera Vision Services of California, Inc. (AMB Number 064714), Culver City, California: This company merged into Spectera, Inc. on September 30, 2007.

Stanford Life Insurance Company (AMB Number 008018), Phoenix, Arizona: This company was merged into Unified Life Insurance Company on April 2, 2007.

State Farm Life Insurance Company (Canada Branch) (AMB Number 069348), Aurora, Ontario, Canada: This company discontinued operation during the 3rd quarter of 2007.

States General Life Insurance Company (AMB Number 007090), Fort Worth, Texas: This company was placed in liquidation on March 9, 2005.

Stonebridge Life Insurance Company (Canada Branch) (AMB Number 069327), Markham, Ontario, Canada: This branch ceased operation on November 26, 2009. Its liabilities were assumed by Stonebridge Life Insurance Company.

Summa Health System Hospitals (AMB Number 034073), Akron, Ohio: This company changed its name to Summa Akron City and St. Thomas Hospitals during 2010.

Summit Health Plan, Inc. (AMB Number 064917), Sunrise, Florida: This company was acquired by Coventry Health Care, Inc. on September 10, 2007.

Summit Insurance Company (AMB Number 068497), Troy, Ohio: This company surrendered its license on December 14, 2007.

Summit National Life Insurance Company (AMB Number 007313), Lancaster, Pennsylvania: This company was liquidated on March 3, 2006.

SunCoast Physicians Health Plan, Inc. (AMB Number 064912), Weston, Florida: This company was placed in liquidation on August 10, 2007.

Templeton Funds Annuity Company (AMB Number 068026), Minneapolis, Minnesota: This company redomesticated from Florida to Minnesota on December 15, 2006. This company was acquired by Allianz Life Insurance Company of North America on April 1, 2007. This company changed its name to Allianz Life and Annuity Company on May 10, 2007.

Tennessee Farmers Life Reassurance Company (AMB Number 009588), Columbia, Tennessee: This company merged into Tennessee Farmers Life Insurance Company on January 1, 2008.

Texas Burial Life Insurance Company (AMB Number 068162), Austin, Texas: This company changed its name to First American Life Insurance Company on April 20, 2006.

Texas Health Choice, L.C. (AMB Number 060138), Dallas, Texas: This company surrendered its license on April 12, 2007.

Texas HealthSpring I, LLC (AMB Number 064828), Houston, Texas: This company changed its name to Texas HealthSpring, LLC on September 15, 2006.

Texas Imperial Life Insurance Company (AMB Number 068290), Austin, Texas: This company was acquired by United Funeral Directors Benefit Life Insurance Company on December 29, 2009.

Texas Life Insurance Company (AMB Number 007118), Waco, Texas: This company was acquired by Wilton Reassurance Company on March 2, 2009.

Three Rivers Health Plans, Inc. (AMB Number 064104), Pittsburgh, Pennsylvania: This company changed its name to Unison Health Plan of Pennsylvania Inc. on November 1, 2005.

Three Rivers Holdings, Inc. (AMB Number 051977), Delaware: This company was acquired by AmeriChoice, a United Health Group company on May 31, 2008.

Touchpoint Health Plan, Inc. (AMB Number 068802), Appleton, Wisconsin: This company was dissolved on March 2, 2007.

Touchpoint Insurance Company, Inc. (AMB Number 060304), Appleton, Wisconsin: This company was dissolved on March 2, 2007.

Transamerica Life Insurance and Annuity Company (AMB Number 007129), Charlotte, North Carolina: This company was merged into Transamerica Life Insurance Company on October 1, 2005.

Transamerica Occidental Life Insurance Company (AMB Number 006848), Cedar Rapids, Iowa: This company merged into Transamerica Life Insurance Company on October 1, 2008.

The Travelers Insurance Company (AMB Number 007330), Hartford, Connecticut: This company changed its name to MetLife Insurance Company of Connecticut on May 1, 2006.

The Travelers Insurance Company (Canada Branch) (AMB Number 069351), Newmarket, Ontario, Canada: This branch changed its name to MetLife Insurance Company of Connecticut (Canada Branch) on May 1, 2006.

The Travelers Life and Annuity Company (AMB Number 008429), Hartford, Connecticut: This company changed its name to MetLife Life and Annuity Company of Connecticut on May 1, 2006.

Triangle Life Insurance Company (AMB Number 009060), Salisbury, North Carolina: This company merged into Life of the South Insurance Company on November 3, 2009.

Trigon Health and Life Insurance Company (AMB Number 006128), Richmond, Virginia: This company was acquired by Highmark Inc. on August 1, 2005. This company changed its name to HM Health Insurance Company on August 1, 2005.

Trinity Life Insurance Company (AMB Number 060653), Tulsa, Oklahoma: This company merged into First Life America Corporation on August 31, 2009.

UBS PaineWebber Life Insurance Company (AMB Number 006882), San Francisco, California: This company changed its name to UBS Life Insurance Company USA on February 2, 2005.

UDC Life and Health Insurance Company (AMB Number 068375), Oklahoma City, Oklahoma: This company was merged into Union Security Insurance Company on November 1, 2005.

UNICARE Health Plan of Oklahoma, Inc. (AMB Number 064633), Oklahoma City, Oklahoma: This company dissolved on December 12, 2007.

UNICARE Health Plan of South Carolina, Inc. (AMB Number 064856), Columbia, South Carolina: This company dissolved on September 15, 2008.

UNICARE Health Plan of Virginia, Inc. (AMB Number 064725), Glen Allen, Virginia: This company was merged into HealthKeepers, Inc. on January 1, 2006.

UNICARE Life & Health Insurance Company (AMB Number 009233), Wilmington, Delaware: This company redomesticated from Delaware to Indiana during 2005.

The Union Central Life Insurance Company (AMB Number 007150), Cincinnati, Ohio: This company redomesticated from Ohio to Nebraska on April 22, 2009.

Union Life Insurance Company (AMB Number 009489), Trumann, Arkansas: This company was acquired by American Modern Life Insurance Company on July 7, 2006.

Union Security Insurance Company (AMB Number 007232), Topeka, Kansas: This company redomesticated from Iowa to Kansas on September 30, 2009.

Union Security Life Insurance Company (AMB Number 007158), Wilmington, Delaware: This company was merged into American Bankers Life Assurance Company of Florida on December 1, 2006.

Union Standard of America Life Insurance Company (AMB Number 068295), Silver Spring, Maryland: This company was merged into Union Labor Life Insurance Company on January 1, 2005.

Unison Family Health Plan of Pennsylvania, Inc. (AMB Number 064925), Churchhill, Pennsylvania: This company's ultimate parent, Three Rivers Holding, Inc., was acquired by AmeriChoice, a United Health Group company on May 31, 2008.

Unison Health Plan of New Jersey, Inc. (AMB Number 064952), West Trenton, New Jersey: This company's ultimate parent, Three Rivers Holding, Inc., was acquired by AmeriChoice, a United Health Group company on May 31, 2008. This company was dissolved on January 7, 2009.

Unison Health Plan of Ohio, Inc. (AMB Number 064874), Cleveland, Ohio: This company's ultimate parent, Three Rivers Holding, Inc., was acquired by AmeriChoice, a United Health Group company on May 31, 2008.

Unison Health Plan of Pennsylvania, Inc. (AMB Number 064104), Pittsburgh, Pennsylvania: This company's ultimate parent, Three Rivers Holding, Inc., was acquired by AmeriChoice, a United Health Group company on May 31, 2008.

Unison Health Plan of South Carolina, Inc. (AMB Number 064886), Greenville, South Carolina: This company's ultimate parent, Three Rivers Holding, Inc., was acquired by AmeriChoice, a United Health Group company on May 31, 2008.

Unison Health Plan of Tennessee, Inc. (AMB Number 064879), Memphis, Tennessee: This company's ultimate parent, Three Rivers Holding, Inc., was acquired by AmeriChoice, a United Health Group company on May 31, 2008.

United American Insurance Company (AMB Number 007161), Wilmington, Delaware: This company redomesticated from Delaware to Nebraska during 2007.

United Benefit Life Insurance Company (AMB Number 006619), Cincinnati, Ohio: This company was acquired by Great American Financial Resources, Inc. on August 7, 2006.

United Concordia Dental Plans of Arizona, Inc. (AMB Number 064605), Phoenix, Arizona: This company was dissolved on June 7, 2007.

United Concordia Dental Plans of Illinois, Inc. (AMB Number 065701), Springfield, Illinois: This company was dissolved on June 25, 2007.

United Concordia Dental Plans of Delaware, Inc. (AMB Number 064401), Hunt Valley, Maryland: This company dissolved on December 17, 2007.

United Dental Care, Inc (AMB Number 064909), Newark, New Jersey: This company surrendered its license on June 2, 2007.

United Dental Care Insurance Company (AMB Number 060035), Phoenix, Arizona: This company was merged into Union Security Insurance Company on November 1, 2005.

United Dental Care of Nebraska, Inc. (AMB Number 065712), Omaha, Nebraska: This company was merged into Union Security Insurance Company on November 1, 2005.

United Dental Care of Pennsylvania, Inc. (AMB Number 064359), Pittsburgh, Pennsylvania: This company was merged into Union Security Insurance Company on November 1, 2005.

United Family Life Insurance Company (AMB Number 007167), Atlanta, Georgia: This company was sold as a shell to Industrial Alliance Insurance and Financial Services on May 1, 2008.

United Heartland Life Insurance Company (AMB Number 060054), Milwaukee, Wisconsin: This company merged into Blue Cross Blue Shield of Wisconsin on December 31, 2006.

United Investors Life Insurance Company (AMB Number 007175), Omaha, Nebraska: This company redomesticated from Missouri to Nebraska on December 21, 2009.

United Liberty Life Insurance Company (AMB Number 007176), Louisville, Kentucky: This company merged into Citizens Security Life Insurance Company on March 31, 2009.

United Lutheran Society (AMB Number 009823), Ligonier, Pennsylvania: This company was merged into Greater Beneficial Union on July 1, 2007.

United Mercantile Life Insurance Company (AMB Number 009089), El Paso, Texas: This company was dissolved on May 31, 2006.

United Security Life Insurance Company of Illinois (AMB Number 008442), Rosemont, Illinois: This company changed its name to United Security Life and Health Insurance Company on March 1, 2005.

UnitedHealthcare of New Jersey, Inc. (AMB Number 068855), Fairfield, New Jersey: This company was merged into Oxford Health Plans (NJ), Inc. on December 31, 2006.

Unity Dental Service Plan Inc. (AMB Number 064559), Parsippany, New Jersey: This company surrendered its license on January 28, 2010.

Unity Health Plans Insurance Corporation (AMB Number 068781), Sauk City, Wisconsin: This company was acquired by University Health Care, Inc. on January 1, 2005.

USAble Life (AMB Number 009350), Little Rock, Arkansas: This company was acquired by Life and Specialty Ventures, LLC during 2005.

USLIFE Credit Life Insurance Company of Arizona (AMB Number 068108), Phoenix, Arizona: This company was dissolved on August 18, 2005.

Utica National Life Insurance Company (AMB Number 006446), New Hartford, New York: This company was merged into American Life Insurance Company of New York on September 27, 2006.

Valley Baptist Health Plan, Inc. (AMB Number 064520), Harlingen, Texas: This company was merged into Valley Baptist Insurance Company on March 1, 2006.

Valley Forge Life Insurance Company (AMB Number 007207), Fort Wayne, Indiana: This company changed its name to Reassure America Life Insurance Company during 2007.

Valley Group Hospital Service Corporation (AMB Number 060376), Harlingen, Texas: This company was merged into Valley Baptist Insurance Company on March 1, 2006.

Valley Health Plan, Inc. (AMB Number 068825), Milwaukee, Wisconsin: This company was merged into Blue Cross Blue Shield of Wisconsin on December 31, 2005.

Venture Life Insurance Company (AMB Number 009472), Phoenix, Arizona: This company was dissolved on December 31, 2006.

Veterans Life Insurance Company (AMB Number 007003), Springfield, Illinois: This company was merged into Stonebridge Life Insurance Company on July 1, 2007.

Victory Health Plan, Inc. (AMB Number 060115), Brentwood, Tennessee: This company changed its name to Windsor Health Plan of Tennessee, Inc. during 2005.

Vista Behavioral Health Plans (AMB Number 064650), El Segundo, California: This company changed its name to Magellan Health Services of California on July 22, 2005.

Vista Healthplan, Inc. (AMB Number 064066), Sunrise, Florida: This company was acquired by Coventry Health Care, Inc. on September 10, 2007.

Vista Healthplan of South Florida, Inc. (AMB Number 064102), Sunrise, Florida: This company was acquired by Coventry Health Care, Inc. on September 10, 2007.

Vista Insurance Plan, Inc. (AMB Number 008878), Sunrise, Florida: This company was acquired by Coventry Health Care, Inc. on September 10, 2007. This company merged into Coventry Health & Life Insurance Company on August 1, 2008.

VMC Behavioral Healthcare Services, Inc. (AMB Number 064814), Pacifica, California: This company surrendered its license during 2008. This company surrendered its license during September 2008.

Vytra Health Plans Long Island, Inc. (AMB Number 068957), Melville, New York: This company was merged into Health Insurance Plan of Greater New York on March 29, 2006.

Vytra Health Services, Inc. (AMB Number 064599), New York, New York: This company was merged into Health Insurance Plan of Greater New York on March 29, 2006.

Washington National Insurance Company (Canada Branch) (AMB Number 066885), Toronto, Ontario, Canada: This company is no longer filing with A.M. Best as of June 2009.

Washington Security Insurance Company (AMB Number 012651), Washington, District of Columbia: This company was dissolved on December 22, 2006.

Watts Health Foundation, Inc. (AMB Number 064151), Inglewood, California: This company surrendered its license on August 31, 2006.

Welborn Clinic (AMB Number 064272), Evansville, Indiana: This company discontinued operation on June 1, 2006.

Welch State Life Insurance Company (AMB Number 068304), Richardson, Texas: This company was dissolved on March 15, 2005.

Wellchoice Insurance of New Jersey, Inc. (AMB Number 068081), Iselin, New Jersey: This company was acquired by WellPoint, Inc. on December 28, 2005. This company was approved for dissolution on October 28, 2008. This company surrendered its license on October 28, 2008.

Wellmark Community Insurance, Inc. (AMB Number 009504), Des Moines, Iowa: This company was sold to GPFT Holdco LLC, a subsidiary of Guggenheim Capital LLC, on August 31, 2009. This company changed its name to Guggenheim Life and Annuity Company on September 1, 2009.

Western United Life Assurance Company (AMB Number 008077), Spokane, Washington: The company was acquired by Global Life Holdings, LLC effective June 5, 2008.

Wilton Reassurance Life Company of New York (AMB Number 006084), New York, New York: This company was acquired by Wilton Re U.S. Holdings, Inc. on September 27, 2006.

Windsor Health Plan of Tennessee, Inc. (AMB Number 060115), Brentwood, Tennessee: This company changed its name to Windsor Health Plan, Inc. on August 8, 2006.

World Life & Health Insurance Company of Pennsylvania (AMB Number 007263), King of Prussia, Pennsylvania: This company was liquidated on April 10, 2006.

XL Re Life America Inc. (AMB Number 060575), Wilmington, Delaware: This company was acquired by SCOR Global Life US on December 4, 2009. This company changed its name to SCOR Global Life Reinsurance Company of America on January 5, 2010.

U.S. States/Territories in Which Companies Are Licensed or Do Business

Company Name	AMB#	AL	AK	AZ	AR	CA	CO	CT	DE	DC	FL	GA	HI	ID	IL	IN	IA	KS	KY	LA	ME	MD	MA	MI	MN	MS	MO	MT	NE	NV	NH	NJ	NM	NY	NC	ND	OH	OK	OR	PA	RI	SC	SD	TN	TX	UT	VT	VA	WA	WV	WI	WY	AS	GU	MP	PR	VI
AAA Life Insurance Company	007424	L	L	L	L	L	L	L	L	L	L	L	L	L	L	L	L	L	L	L	L	L	L	D	L	L	L	L	L	L	L	L	.	L	L	L	L	L	L	L	L	L	L	L	L	L	L	L	L	L	L	L	.	.	.	.	.
Ability Insurance Company	007378	L	L	L	L	L	L	.	L	L	L	L	L	L	L	L	L	L	L	L	.	L	L	L	L	L	L	L	D	L	.	.	L	.	L	L	L	L	L	L	.	L	L	L	L	L	.	L	L	L	L	L	.	.	.	.	.
Abri Health Plan Inc	064811	.	.	.	.	.	.	.	.	.	.	.	.	.	.	.	.	.	.	.	.	.	.	.	.	.	.	.	.	.	.	.	.	.	.	.	.	.	.	.	.	.	.	.	.	.	.	.	.	.	D	.	.	.	.	.	.
Absolute Total Care Inc	064922	.	.	.	.	.	.	.	.	.	.	.	.	.	.	.	.	.	.	.	.	.	.	.	.	.	.	.	.	.	.	.	.	.	.	.	.	.	.	.	.	D	.	.	.	.	.	.	.	.	.	.	.	.	.	.	.
Acacia Life Insurance Company	006002	L	.	L	L	L	L	L	L	D	L	L	L	L	L	L	L	L	L	L	.	L	L	L	L	L	L	L	L	L	L	L	L	.	L	L	L	L	L	L	L	L	L	L	L	L	L	L	L	L	L	L	.	.	.	.	.
Access Dental Plan	064655	.	.	.	.	D	.	.	.	.	.	.	.	.	.	.	.	.	.	.	.	.	.	.	.	.	.	.	.	.	.	.	.	.	.	.	.	.	.	.	.	.	.	.	.	.	.	.	.	.	.	.	.	.	.	.	.
ACE Life Insurance Company	060599	L	L	L	L	L	L	D	L	L	L	L	L	L	L	L	L	L	L	L	L	L	L	L	L	L	L	L	L	L	L	L	L	.	L	L	L	L	L	L	L	L	L	L	L	L	L	L	L	L	L	L	.	.	.	.	.
ACN Group of California Inc	064816	.	.	.	.	D	.	.	.	.	.	.	.	.	.	.	.	.	.	.	.	.	.	.	.	.	.	.	.	.	.	.	.	.	.	.	.	.	.	.	.	.	.	.	.	.	.	.	.	.	.	.	.	.	.	.	.
Admiral Life Ins Co of America	007358	.	.	D	L	L	L	L	.	.	L	L	L	L	L	L	.	L	L	L	.	L	.	.	L	L	L	L	.	.	.	.	L	.	.	L	L	L	.	.	.	.	L	L	L	L	.	.	.	.	L	L	.	L	.	.	.
Advance Insurance Co of Kansas	060404	.	.	.	.	.	.	.	.	.	.	.	.	.	.	.	.	D	.	.	.	.	.	.	.	.	.	.	.	.	.	.	.	.	.	.	.	.	.	.	.	.	.	.	.	.	.	.	.	.	.	.	.	.	.	.	.
Advanta Life Ins Co	008357	.	L	D	L	.	L	.	L	L	L	L	L	L	.	L	.	L	.	L	.	L	.	.	L	.	.	L	L	L	.	.	L	.	.	.	L	L	L	.	.	L	L	L	L	L	.	.	.	L	L	L	.	.	.	.	.
Advantage Dental Plan Inc	064493	.	.	.	.	.	.	.	.	.	.	.	.	L	.	.	.	.	.	.	.	.	.	.	.	.	.	.	.	.	.	.	.	.	.	.	.	.	D	.	.	.	.	.	.	.	.	.	L	.	.	.	.	.	.	.	.
ADVANTAGE Health Solutions Inc	064624	.	.	.	.	.	.	.	.	.	.	.	.	.	.	D	.	.	.	.	.	.	.	.	.	.	.	.	.	.	.	.	.	.	.	.	.	.	.	.	.	.	.	.	.	.	.	.	.	.	.	.	.	.	.	.	.
Advantage Healthplan Inc	064689	.	.	.	.	.	.	.	.	D	.	.	.	.	.	.	.	.	.	.	.	.	.	.	.	.	.	.	.	.	.	.	.	.	.	.	.	.	.	.	.	.	.	.	.	.	.	.	.	.	.	.	.	.	.	.	.
AECC Total Vision Hth Pl of TX	064512	.	.	.	.	.	.	.	.	.	.	.	.	.	.	.	.	.	.	.	.	.	.	.	.	.	.	.	.	.	.	.	.	.	.	.	.	.	.	.	.	.	.	.	D	.	.	.	.	.	.	.	.	.	.	.	.
Aetna Better Health Inc (CT)	064964	.	.	.	.	.	.	D	.	.	.	.	.	.	.	.	.	.	.	.	.	.	.	.	.	.	.	.	.	.	.	.	.	.	.	.	.	.	.	.	.	.	.	.	.	.	.	.	.	.	.	.	.	.	.	.	.
Aetna Dental Inc (a NJ corp)	064709	.	.	.	.	.	.	.	.	.	.	.	.	.	.	.	.	.	.	.	.	.	.	.	.	.	.	.	.	.	.	D	.	.	.	.	.	.	.	.	.	.	.	.	.	.	.	.	.	.	.	.	.	.	.	.	.
Aetna Dental Inc (a TX corp)	064718	.	.	.	.	.	.	.	.	.	.	.	.	.	.	.	.	.	.	.	.	L	.	.	.	.	L	.	.	.	.	.	.	.	.	.	.	.	.	.	.	.	.	.	D	.	.	.	.	.	.	.	.	.	.	.	.
Aetna Dental of CA	064634	.	.	.	.	D	.	.	.	.	.	.	.	.	.	.	.	.	.	.	.	.	.	.	.	.	.	.	.	.	.	.	.	.	.	.	.	.	.	.	.	.	.	.	.	.	.	.	.	.	.	.	.	.	.	.	.
Aetna Health and Life Ins Co	008189	L	L	L	L	L	L	D	L	L	.	L	L	L	L	L	L	L	L	L	L	L	L	L	L	L	.	L	L	L	.	L	L	Q	L	L	L	L	L	L	L	L	L	L	L	L	L	L	L	L	L	L	.	.	.	.	.
Aetna Health Inc (a CO corp)	064071	.	.	.	.	.	D	.	.	.	.	.	.	.	.	.	.	.	.	.	.	.	.	.	.	.	.	.	.	.	.	.	.	.	.	.	.	.	.	.	.	.	.	.	.	.	.	.	.	.	.	.	.	.	.	.	.
Aetna Health Inc (a CT corp)	068698	.	.	.	.	.	.	D	.	.	.	.	.	.	.	.	.	.	.	.	.	.	.	.	.	.	.	.	.	.	.	.	.	.	.	.	.	.	.	.	.	.	.	.	.	.	.	.	.	.	.	.	.	.	.	.	.
Aetna Health Inc (a DE corp)	068697	.	.	.	.	.	.	.	D	.	.	.	.	.	.	.	.	.	.	.	.	.	.	.	.	.	.	.	.	.	.	.	.	.	.	.	.	.	.	.	.	.	.	.	.	.	.	.	.	.	.	.	.	.	.	.	.
Aetna Health Inc (a FL corp)	060120	.	.	.	.	.	.	.	.	.	D	.	.	.	.	.	.	.	.	.	.	.	.	.	.	.	.	.	.	.	.	.	.	.	.	.	.	.	.	.	.	.	.	.	.	.	.	.	.	.	.	.	.	.	.	.	.
Aetna Health Inc (a GA corp)	068701	.	.	.	.	.	.	.	.	.	.	D	.	.	.	.	.	.	.	.	.	.	.	.	.	.	.	.	.	.	.	.	.	.	.	.	.	.	.	.	.	.	.	.	.	.	.	.	.	.	.	.	.	.	.	.	.
Aetna Health Inc (a ME corp)	064155	.	.	.	.	.	.	.	.	.	.	.	.	.	.	.	.	.	.	.	D	.	.	.	.	.	.	.	.	.	.	.	.	.	.	.	.	.	.	.	.	.	.	.	.	.	.	.	.	.	.	.	.	.	.	.	.
Aetna Health Inc (a MI corp)	064366	.	.	.	.	.	.	.	.	.	.	.	.	.	.	.	.	.	.	.	.	.	.	D	.	.	.	.	.	.	.	.	.	.	.	.	.	.	.	.	.	.	.	.	.	.	.	.	.	.	.	.	.	.	.	.	.
Aetna Health Inc (a NJ corp)	068695	.	.	.	.	.	.	.	.	.	.	.	.	.	.	.	.	.	.	.	.	.	.	.	.	.	.	.	.	.	.	D	.	.	.	.	.	.	.	.	.	.	.	.	.	.	.	.	.	.	.	.	.	.	.	.	.
Aetna Health Inc (a NY corp)	068696	.	.	.	.	.	.	.	.	.	.	.	.	.	.	.	.	.	.	.	.	.	.	.	.	.	.	.	.	.	.	.	.	D	.	.	.	.	.	.	.	.	.	.	.	.	.	.	.	.	.	.	.	.	.	.	.
Aetna Health Inc (a PA corp)	068700	.	.	L	.	.	.	.	.	L	.	.	.	.	L	L	.	L	L	.	.	L	L	.	.	.	L	.	.	L	.	.	.	.	.	.	L	L	.	D	.	L	.	L	.	.	.	L	.	.	.	.	.	.	.	.	.
Aetna Health Inc (a TX corp)	068913	.	.	.	.	.	.	.	.	.	.	.	.	.	.	.	.	.	.	.	.	.	.	.	.	.	.	.	.	.	.	.	.	.	.	.	.	.	.	.	.	.	.	.	D	.	.	.	.	.	.	.	.	.	.	.	.
Aetna Health Inc (a WA corp)	068609	.	.	.	.	.	.	.	.	.	.	.	.	.	.	.	.	.	.	.	.	.	.	.	.	.	.	.	.	.	.	.	.	.	.	.	.	.	.	.	.	.	.	.	.	.	.	.	D	.	.	.	.	.	.	.	.
Aetna Health Insurance Company	007443	L	L	L	L	.	L	.	L	L	L	L	L	L	L	L	L	L	L	L	L	L	L	L	L	.	L	L	L	L	L	L	L	.	.	.	L	L	L	D	L	L	L	L	L	L	L	L	L	L	L	L	.	.	.	.	.
Aetna Health Ins Co of NY	009541	.	.	.	.	.	.	.	.	.	.	.	.	.	.	.	.	.	.	.	.	.	.	.	.	.	.	.	.	.	.	.	.	D	.	.	.	.	.	.	.	.	.	.	.	.	.	.	.	.	.	.	.	.	.	.	.
Aetna Health of CA	060119	.	.	.	.	D	.	.	.	.	.	.	.	.	.	.	.	.	.	.	.	.	.	.	.	.	.	.	.	.	.	.	.	.	.	.	.	.	.	.	.	.	.	.	.	.	.	.	.	.	.	.	.	.	.	.	.
Aetna Health of the Carolinas	060134	.	.	.	.	.	.	.	.	.	.	.	.	.	.	.	.	.	.	.	.	.	.	.	.	.	.	.	.	.	.	.	.	.	D	.	.	.	.	.	.	L	.	.	.	.	.	.	.	.	.	.	.	.	.	.	.
Aetna Insurance Company of CT	011023	L	L	L	L	L	L	D	L	L	L	L	L	L	L	L	L	L	L	L	L	L	L	L	L	L	L	L	L	L	L	L	L	L	L	L	L	L	L	L	L	L	L	L	L	L	L	L	L	L	L	L	.	.	.	.	.
Aetna Life Ins Co	006006	L	L	L	L	L	L	D	L	L	L	L	L	L	L	L	L	L	L	L	L	L	L	L	L	L	L	L	L	L	L	L	L	L	L	L	L	L	L	L	L	L	L	L	L	L	L	L	L	L	L	L	.	L	.	L	L
AF&L Insurance Company	011131	.	.	.	L	.	.	.	L	.	.	L	.	L	L	L	.	L	L	.	.	L	.	.	.	.	L	L	L	L	.	.	.	.	.	L	.	L	L	D	.	L	L	.	L	L	.	L	.	L	.	.	.	.	.	.	.
AGC Life Insurance Company	009199	.	.	.	.	.	.	.	.	.	.	.	.	.	.	.	.	.	.	L	.	.	.	.	.	L	D	.	.	.	.	.	.	.	.	.	.	L	.	L	.	L	.	L	.	.	.	.	.	.	.	.	.	.	.	.	.
AGL Life Assurance Company	007142	L	L	L	L	L	L	L	L	L	L	L	L	L	L	L	L	L	L	L	L	L	L	L	L	L	L	L	L	L	.	L	L	.	L	L	L	L	L	D	L	L	L	L	L	L	.	L	L	L	L	L	.	.	.	.	.
AIDS Healthcare Foundation	064843	.	.	.	.	D	.	.	.	.	.	.	.	.	.	.	.	.	.	.	.	.	.	.	.	.	.	.	.	.	.	.	.	.	.	.	.	.	.	.	.	.	.	.	.	.	.	.	.	.	.	.	.	.	.	.	.
Alabama Life Reinsurance Co	060674	D	.	.	.	.	.	.	.	.	.	.	.	.	.	.	.	.	.	.	.	.	.	.	.	.	.	.	.	.	.	.	.	.	.	.	.	.	.	.	.	.	.	.	.	.	.	.	.	.	.	.	.	.	.	.	.
Alameda Alliance for Health	064142	.	.	.	.	D	.	.	.	.	.	.	.	.	.	.	.	.	.	.	.	.	.	.	.	.	.	.	.	.	.	.	.	.	.	.	.	.	.	.	.	.	.	.	.	.	.	.	.	.	.	.	.	.	.	.	.
Alaska Vision Services Inc	064484	.	D	.	.	.	.	.	.	.	.	.	.	.	.	.	.	.	.	.	.	.	.	.	.	.	.	.	.	.	.	.	.	.	.	.	.	.	.	.	.	.	.	.	.	.	.	.	.	.	.	.	.	.	.	.	.
Alfa Life Ins Corp	006293	D	.	.	L	.	.	.	.	.	L	L	.	.	.	.	.	.	.	L	.	.	.	.	.	L	L	.	.	.	.	.	.	.	L	.	.	.	.	.	.	L	.	L	.	.	.	L	.	.	.	.	.	.	.	.	.
All Savers Insurance Co	009556	.	L	L	L	.	L	.	L	L	L	L	.	L	L	D	L	L	L	L	.	L	.	L	.	L	.	L	L	.	.	.	.	.	.	L	L	L	L	L	.	L	L	L	L	.	.	.	.	L	L	L	.	.	.	.	.
All Savers Life Ins Co of CA	060029	.	.	.	.	D	.	.	.	.	.	.	.	.	L	.	.	.	.	.	.	.	.	.	.	.	.	.	.	.	.	.	.	.	.	.	.	.	.	.	.	.	.	.	.	.	.	.	.	.	.	.	.	.	.	.	.
Allegiance Life Ins Co	006324	.	.	L	.	.	L	.	.	.	L	.	L	.	D	.	.	.	.	.	.	.	.	.	.	.	.	.	L	L	.	.	.	.	.	.	L	L	L	.	.	.	.	.	L	.	.	.	L	.	.	.	.	.	.	.	.
Alliance for Community Health	064179	.	.	.	.	.	.	.	.	.	.	.	.	.	.	.	.	.	.	.	.	.	.	.	.	.	D	.	.	.	.	.	.	.	.	.	.	.	.	.	.	.	.	.	.	.	.	.	.	.	.	.	.	.	.	.	.
Alliance Health and Life Ins	060220	.	.	.	.	.	.	.	.	.	.	.	.	.	.	.	.	.	.	.	.	.	.	D	.	.	.	.	.	.	.	.	.	.	.	.	.	.	.	.	.	.	.	.	.	.	.	.	.	.	.	.	.	.	.	.	.
Alliant Health Plans Inc	064891	.	.	.	.	.	.	.	.	.	.	D	.	.	.	.	.	.	.	.	.	.	.	.	.	.	.	.	.	.	.	.	.	.	.	.	.	.	.	.	.	.	.	.	.	.	.	.	.	.	.	.	.	.	.	.	.
Allianz Life and Annuity Co	068026	L	L	L	L	L	L	.	L	L	L	L	L	L	L	L	.	L	L	L	L	L	L	L	D	L	L	L	L	L	.	L	L	.	L	L	L	L	L	L	L	L	L	L	L	L	L	L	L	L	L	L	.	.	.	.	.
Allianz Life Ins Co of NY	009417	.	.	.	.	.	.	L	.	L	.	.	.	.	L	.	.	.	.	.	.	.	.	.	L	.	L	.	.	.	.	.	.	D	.	L	.	.	.	.	.	.	.	.	.	.	.	.	.	.	.	.	.	.	.	.	.
Allianz Life Ins Co N America	006830	L	L	L	L	L	L	L	L	L	L	L	L	L	L	L	L	L	L	L	L	L	L	L	D	L	L	L	L	L	L	L	L	.	L	L	L	L	L	L	L	L	L	L	L	L	L	L	L	L	L	L	L	L	.	L	.
Allied Financial Ins Co	068226	.	.	.	.	.	.	.	.	.	.	.	.	.	.	.	.	.	.	.	.	.	.	.	.	.	.	.	.	.	.	.	.	.	.	.	.	.	.	.	.	.	.	.	D	.	.	.	.	.	.	.	.	.	.	.	.
Allstate Assurance Company	007289	L	L	L	L	L	L	L	L	L	L	L	L	L	D	L	L	L	L	L	L	L	L	L	L	L	L	L	L	L	L	L	L	L	L	L	L	L	L	L	L	L	L	L	L	L	L	L	L	L	L	L	.	.	.	.	.
Allstate Life Ins Co	006027	L	L	L	L	L	L	L	L	L	L	L	L	L	D	L	L	L	L	L	L	L	L	L	L	L	L	L	L	L	L	L	L	Q	L	L	L	L	L	L	L	L	L	L	L	L	L	L	L	L	L	L	.	.	.	L	.
Allstate Life Ins Co of NY	007291	.	.	.	.	L	.	.	L	L	.	.	.	.	L	.	.	.	.	.	.	.	.	.	.	.	L	.	L	.	.	L	.	D	L	.	.	.	.	L	.	.	.	.	L	.	.	.	.	.	.	.	.	.	.	.	.
Aloha Care	064224	.	.	.	.	.	.	.	.	.	.	.	D	.	.	.	.	.	.	.	.	.	.	.	.	.	.	.	.	.	.	.	.	.	.	.	.	.	.	.	.	.	.	.	.	.	.	.	.	.	.	.	.	.	.	.	.
Alpha Dental Programs Inc	064509	.	.	.	.	.	.	.	.	.	.	.	L	L	L	L	.	.	L	.	.	L	.	.	.	.	L	.	.	.	.	L	.	.	.	.	L	.	.	.	.	.	.	.	D	.	.	.	.	.	.	.	.	.	.	.	.
Altius Health Plans	068616	.	.	.	.	.	.	.	.	.	.	.	.	L	.	.	.	.	.	.	.	.	.	.	.	.	.	.	.	L	.	.	.	.	.	.	.	.	.	.	.	.	.	.	.	D	.	.	.	.	.	L	.	.	.	.	.
Altus Dental Insurance Company	060349	.	.	.	.	.	.	.	.	.	.	.	.	.	.	.	.	.	.	.	.	.	L	.	.	.	.	.	.	.	.	.	.	.	.	.	.	.	.	.	D	.	.	.	.	.	.	.	.	.	.	.	.	.	.	.	.
Amalgamated Life and Health	006030	L	.	.	L	L	.	.	.	.	.	.	.	.	D	L	.	.	L	.	.	.	.	L	L	L	L	.	.	.	.	.	.	.	.	.	.	.	.	.	.	.	.	.	.	.	.	.	.	.	L	.	.	.	.	.	.
Amalgamated Life Ins Co	006031	L	L	L	L	L	L	L	L	L	.	L	L	L	L	L	L	L	L	L	L	L	L	L	L	L	L	L	L	L	L	L	.	D	L	L	L	L	L	L	L	L	L	L	L	L	L	L	L	L	L	.	.	.	.	.	.
Ambassador Life Ins Co	009172	.	.	.	.	.	.	.	.	.	.	.	.	.	.	.	.	.	.	.	.	.	.	.	.	.	.	.	.	.	.	.	.	.	.	.	.	.	.	.	.	.	.	.	D	.	.	.	.	.	.	.	.	.	.	.	.
American-Amicable Life Ins TX	009122	L	L	L	L	L	L	L	L	L	L	L	L	L	L	L	.	L	L	L	L	L	.	.	L	L	L	L	L	L	.	.	L	.	L	L	L	L	L	L	.	L	L	L	D	L	.	L	L	L	L	L	.	L	.	.	.
American Bankers Life Assur Co	006040	L	L	L	L	L	L	L	L	L	D	L	L	L	L	L	L	L	L	L	L	L	L	L	L	L	L	L	L	L	L	L	L	.	L	L	L	L	L	L	L	L	L	L	L	L	L	L	L	L	L	L	.	L	.	L	L
American Benefit Life	060382	.	.	L	L	.	L	.	.	L	.	L	.	.	L	L	.	L	.	L	.	.	.	.	L	.	L	L	L	.	.	.	L	.	L	L	.	D	L	.	.	L	L	.	L	.	.	L	.	.	L	.	.	.	.	.	.
American Capitol Ins Co	006043	L	L	L	L	L	L	.	L	L	L	L	.	L	L	L	.	L	.	L	L	L	.	L	.	L	L	L	L	.	L	.	L	.	.	L	.	L	L	L	.	L	L	L	D	L	.	L	L	L	.	L	.	.	.	.	.
American Century Life Ins Co	008932	.	.	.	.	.	.	.	.	.	.	.	.	.	.	.	.	.	.	.	.	.	.	.	.	.	.	.	.	.	.	.	.	.	.	.	.	D	.	.	.	.	.	.	.	.	.	.	.	.	.	.	.	.	.	.	.
American Century Life of Texas	068090	.	.	.	.	.	.	.	.	.	.	.	.	.	.	.	.	.	.	.	.	.	.	.	.	.	.	.	.	.	.	.	.	.	.	.	.	.	.	.	.	.	.	.	D	.	.	.	.	.	.	.	.	.	.	.	.
American Community Mutual Ins	006044	.	L	L	L	.	L	.	L	L	.	L	L	L	L	L	L	L	L	L	L	L	L	D	.	L	L	L	L	L	.	.	L	.	L	L	L	L	L	L	L	L	L	L	L	L	.	L	L	L	L	L	.	.	.	.	.
American Continental Ins Co	060568	L	.	L	L	.	L	.	.	.	L	.	.	.	L	L	L	L	L	.	.	.	.	L	L	L	.	L	L	.	.	.	L	.	L	L	L	L	.	L	.	L	L	D	L	.	.	L	.	L	.	L	.	.	.	.	.
American Creditors Life Ins Co	009097	L	.	.	.	.	.	L	D	.	L	.	.	.	L	.	.	.	.	L	.	.	L	L	.	.	L	L	.	.	.	.	.	.	.	L	.	.	.	L	.	.	.	.	.	.	.	.	.	L	.	.	.	.	.	.	.
American Dental Plan of NC	064631	.	.	.	.	.	.	.	.	.	.	.	.	.	.	.	.	.	.	.	.	.	.	.	.	.	.	.	.	.	.	.	.	.	D	.	.	.	.	.	.	.	.	.	.	.	.	.	.	.	.	.	.	.	.	.	.

D-State of Domicile **L**-Licensed **S**-Surplus Lines Writer **F**-Authorized under the Risk Retention Act **Q**-Qualified or Accredited Reinsurer

U.S. States/Territories in Which Companies Are Licensed or Do Business – *Continued*

Company Name	AMB#	AL	AK	AZ	AR	CA	CO	CT	DE	DC	FL	GA	HI	ID	IL	IN	IA	KS	KY	LA	ME	MD	MA	MI	MN	MS	MO	MT	NE	NV	NH	NJ	NM	NY	NC	ND	OH	OK	OR	PA	RI	SC	SD	TN	TX	UT	VT	VA	WA	WV	WI	WY	AS	GU	MP	PR	VI
American Dental Plan of WI Inc	064796	.	.	.	.	.	.	.	.	.	.	.	.	.	.	.	.	.	.	.	.	.	.	.	.	.	.	.	.	.	.	.	.	.	.	.	.	.	.	.	.	.	.	.	.	.	.	.	.	.	D	.	.	.	.	.	.
American Dental Providers AR	064491	.	.	.	D	.	.	.	.	.	.	.	.	.	.	.	.	.	.	.	.	.	.	.	.	.	.	.	.	.	.	.	.	.	.	.	.	.	.	.	.	.	.	.	.	.	.	.	.	.	.	.	.	.	.	.	.
American Equity Invest Life	009024	L	L	L	L	L	L	L	L	L	L	L	L	L	L	L	D	L	L	L	L	L	L	L	L	L	L	L	L	L	L	L	L	.	L	L	L	L	L	L	L	L	L	L	L	L	L	L	L	L	L	L	.	.	.	.	.
American Equity Invest Life NY	060367	.	.	.	.	.	.	.	.	.	.	.	.	.	.	.	.	.	.	.	.	.	.	.	.	.	.	.	.	.	.	.	.	D	.	.	.	.	.	.	.	.	.	.	.	.	.	.	.	.	.	.	.	.	.	.	.
American Exchange Life Ins Co	006050	.	.	.	.	.	.	.	.	.	.	.	.	.	.	.	.	.	.	L	.	.	.	.	.	.	.	.	.	.	.	.	.	.	.	.	.	.	.	.	.	.	.	.	D	.	.	.	.	.	.	.	.	.	.	.	.
American Fam Assur Columbus	006051	L	L	L	L	L	L	L	L	L	L	L	L	L	L	L	L	L	L	L	L	L	L	L	L	L	L	L	D	L	L	L	L	.	L	L	L	L	L	L	L	L	L	L	L	L	L	L	L	L	L	L	.	L	.	L	L
American Family Life Assur NY	006063	.	.	.	.	.	.	L	.	.	.	.	.	.	.	.	.	.	.	.	.	.	L	.	.	.	.	.	.	.	.	L	.	D	.	L	.	.	.	.	.	.	.	.	.	.	L	.	.	.	.	.	.	.	.	.	.
American Family Life Ins Co	006052	.	.	L	.	L	L	.	.	.	.	L	.	L	L	L	L	L	.	.	.	.	.	L	L	.	L	L	L	L	.	.	L	.	L	L	L	.	L	.	.	L	L	.	L	L	.	.	L	.	D	L	.	.	.	.	.
American Farm Life Ins Co	060346	.	.	.	.	.	.	.	.	.	.	.	.	.	.	.	.	.	.	.	.	.	.	.	.	.	.	.	.	.	.	.	L	.	.	.	.	L	.	.	.	.	.	.	D	.	.	.	.	.	.	.	.	.	.	.	.
American Farmers & Ranchers Lf	060341	.	.	.	.	.	.	.	.	.	.	.	.	L	.	.	.	.	.	.	.	.	.	.	.	.	.	.	.	.	.	.	.	.	.	.	.	D	.	.	.	.	.	.	L	.	.	.	.	.	.	.	.	.	.	.	.
American Federated Life Ins	068071	.	.	.	.	.	.	.	.	.	.	.	.	.	.	.	.	.	.	L	.	.	.	.	.	D	L	.	.	.	.	.	.	.	.	.	.	.	.	.	.	.	.	.	.	.	.	.	.	.	.	.	.	.	.	.	.
American Fidelity Assurance Co	006054	L	L	L	L	L	L	L	L	L	L	L	L	L	L	L	L	L	L	L	L	L	L	L	L	L	L	L	L	L	L	L	L	.	L	L	L	D	L	L	L	L	L	L	L	L	L	L	L	L	L	L	L	L	.	.	.
American Fidelity Life Ins Co	006055	L	L	L	L	L	L	L	L	L	D	L	L	L	L	L	L	L	L	L	L	L	L	L	L	L	L	L	L	L	L	.	L	.	L	L	L	L	L	L	L	L	L	L	L	L	.	L	L	L	L	L	.	L	.	.	.
American Financial Security	007111	.	.	L	L	L	L	L	L	.	.	L	.	.	.	L	L	L	.	.	L	L	.	.	L	L	D	L	L	.	.	.	L	.	.	L	.	.	L	L	L	.	L	.	L	L	.	L	.	L	L	.	.	.	.	.	.
American General Assurance Co	006989	L	L	L	L	L	L	L	L	L	L	L	L	L	D	L	L	L	L	L	L	L	L	L	L	L	L	L	L	L	L	L	L	.	L	L	L	L	L	L	L	L	L	L	L	L	L	L	L	L	L	L	.	.	.	.	.
American General Lf & Accident	006788	L	L	L	L	L	L	L	L	L	L	L	L	L	L	L	L	L	L	L	L	L	L	L	L	L	L	L	L	L	L	L	L	.	L	L	L	L	L	L	L	L	L	D	L	L	L	L	L	L	L	.	.	.	.	.	.
American General Life Ins Co	006058	L	L	L	L	L	L	L	L	L	L	L	L	L	L	L	L	L	L	L	L	L	L	L	L	L	L	L	L	L	L	L	L	.	L	L	L	L	L	L	L	L	L	L	D	L	L	L	L	L	L	L	.	L	.	L	L
American General Life Ins DE	006809	L	L	L	L	L	L	L	D	L	L	L	L	L	L	L	L	L	L	L	L	L	L	L	L	L	L	L	L	L	L	L	L	.	L	L	L	L	L	L	L	L	L	L	L	L	L	L	L	L	L	L	.	.	.	L	.
American Health and Life Ins	006062	L	L	L	L	L	L	L	L	L	L	L	L	L	L	L	L	L	L	L	L	L	L	L	L	L	L	L	L	L	L	L	L	.	L	L	L	L	L	L	L	L	L	L	D	L	L	L	L	L	L	L	.	.	.	.	.
American Health Network IN LLC	064632	.	.	.	.	.	.	.	.	.	.	.	.	.	.	D	.	.	.	.	.	.	.	.	.	.	.	.	.	.	.	.	.	.	.	.	.	.	.	.	.	.	.	.	.	.	.	.	.	.	.	.	.	.	.	.	.
American HealthGuard Corp	064731	.	.	.	.	D	.	.	.	.	.	.	.	.	.	.	.	.	.	.	.	.	.	.	.	.	.	.	.	.	.	.	.	.	.	.	.	.	.	.	.	.	.	.	.	.	.	.	.	.	.	.	.	.	.	.	.
American Heritage Life Ins Co	006064	L	L	L	L	L	L	L	L	L	D	L	L	L	L	L	L	L	L	L	L	L	L	L	L	L	L	L	L	L	L	L	L	.	L	L	L	L	L	L	L	L	L	L	L	L	L	L	L	L	L	L	.	L	.	L	L
American Home Life Ins Co	006065	.	.	L	L	.	L	.	.	.	L	.	.	L	L	L	L	D	.	.	.	.	.	L	L	.	L	L	L	L	.	.	L	.	.	L	L	L	.	.	.	.	L	L	L	.	.	.	.	.	L	L	.	.	.	.	.
American Home Life Ins Co - AR	068161	.	.	.	D	.	.	.	.	.	.	.	.	.	.	.	.	.	.	.	.	.	.	.	.	.	.	.	.	.	.	.	.	.	.	.	.	.	.	.	.	.	.	.	.	.	.	.	.	.	.	.	.	.	.	.	.
American Income Life Ins Co	006069	L	L	L	L	L	L	L	L	L	L	L	L	L	L	D	L	L	L	L	L	L	L	L	L	L	L	L	L	L	L	L	L	.	L	L	L	L	L	L	L	L	L	L	L	L	L	L	L	L	L	L	.	.	.	.	.
American Indep Network of NY	060292	.	.	.	.	.	.	.	.	.	.	.	.	.	.	.	.	.	.	.	.	.	.	.	.	.	.	.	.	.	.	.	.	D	.	.	.	.	.	.	.	.	.	.	.	.	.	.	.	.	.	.	.	.	.	.	.
American Industries Life	008529	.	.	.	.	.	.	.	.	.	.	.	.	.	.	.	.	.	.	.	.	.	.	.	.	.	.	.	.	.	.	.	.	.	.	.	.	.	.	.	.	.	.	.	D	.	.	.	.	.	.	.	.	.	.	.	.
American Intern Life Assur NY	006072	L	L	.	L	L	L	.	L	L	L	L	L	L	L	L	L	L	L	L	L	.	L	L	L	L	L	L	L	L	L	L	L	D	L	L	L	L	L	L	L	L	L	L	L	L	L	L	L	L	L	L	L	L	.	.	L
American Labor Life Ins Co	060390	.	.	D	.	.	.	.	.	.	.	.	.	.	L	L	.	.	.	.	.	.	.	.	.	.	.	.	.	.	.	.	.	.	.	.	.	.	.	L	.	.	.	.	.	.	.	.	.	L	.	.	.	.	.	.	.
American Life and Acc of KY	006077	.	.	.	L	.	.	.	.	.	.	L	.	.	.	L	.	.	D	.	.	L	.	.	.	.	.	.	.	.	.	.	.	.	.	.	L	.	.	L	.	.	.	L	.	.	.	.	.	.	.	.	.	.	.	.	.
American Life & Annuity Co	008622	.	.	.	D	.	.	.	.	.	.	.	.	.	.	.	.	.	.	.	.	.	.	.	.	.	.	.	.	.	.	.	.	.	.	.	.	.	.	.	.	.	.	.	.	.	.	.	.	.	.	.	.	.	.	.	.
American Life Ins Co DE	006081	.	.	.	.	.	.	.	D	.	.	.	.	.	.	.	.	.	.	.	.	.	.	.	.	.	.	.	.	.	.	.	.	.	.	.	.	.	.	.	.	.	.	.	.	.	.	.	.	.	.	.	.	.	.	.	.
American Life Ins Co IL	009091	.	.	.	.	.	.	.	.	.	.	.	.	.	D	.	.	.	.	.	.	.	.	.	.	.	.	.	.	.	.	.	.	.	.	.	.	.	.	.	.	.	.	.	.	.	.	.	.	.	.	.	.	.	.	.	.
American Maturity Life Ins Co	008480	L	L	L	L	L	L	D	L	L	L	L	L	L	L	L	L	L	L	L	L	L	L	L	L	L	L	L	L	L	L	L	L	L	L	L	L	L	L	L	L	L	L	L	L	L	L	L	L	L	L	L	.	.	.	.	.
American Medical and Life Ins	008304	L	L	L	L	.	.	L	L	L	L	L	L	.	L	L	.	L	L	L	.	L	.	L	.	L	L	L	L	L	.	L	.	D	L	L	L	L	L	L	L	L	L	L	L	L	.	.	L	L	L	L	.	.	.	.	.
American Medical Security Life	007771	L	.	L	L	L	L	.	L	L	L	L	.	L	L	L	L	L	L	L	.	L	.	L	L	L	L	L	L	L	.	.	L	.	L	L	L	L	L	L	.	L	L	L	L	L	.	L	L	L	D	L	.	.	.	.	.
American Memorial Life Ins Co	006942	L	L	L	L	L	L	L	L	L	L	L	L	L	L	L	L	L	L	L	L	L	L	L	L	L	L	L	L	L	L	L	L	.	L	L	L	L	L	L	L	L	D	L	L	L	L	L	L	L	L	L	.	.	.	.	L
American Modern Life Ins Co	006680	L	L	L	L	L	L	L	L	L	L	L	L	L	L	L	L	L	L	L	L	L	L	L	L	L	L	L	L	L	.	.	L	L	L	L	D	L	L	L	L	L	L	L	L	L	L	L	L	L	L	L	.	.	.	.	.
American National Ins Co	006087	L	L	L	L	L	L	L	L	L	L	L	L	L	L	L	L	L	L	L	L	L	L	L	L	L	L	L	L	L	L	L	L	.	L	L	L	L	L	L	L	L	L	L	D	L	L	L	L	L	L	L	L	L	.	L	.
American Nat'l Life Ins Texas	007417	L	L	L	L	L	L	L	L	L	L	L	L	L	L	L	L	L	L	L	.	L	L	L	L	L	L	L	L	L	L	.	L	.	L	L	L	L	L	L	L	L	L	L	D	L	.	L	L	L	L	L	.	L	.	.	.
American Network Ins Company	007362	L	.	L	L	L	L	L	L	L	.	L	L	L	L	L	.	L	L	L	L	L	L	.	L	L	L	L	L	L	L	L	.	.	L	L	L	L	L	D	L	L	L	L	L	L	L	L	L	L	.	L	.	.	.	.	.
American Phoenix Life&Reassur	068152	.	L	L	L	L	.	D	L	L	L	L	L	L	L	L	L	L	L	.	.	L	L	L	.	.	Q	Q	L	.	.	L	.	.	L	L	.	.	L	L	.	L	L	L	L	L	Q	.	L	L	.	Q	.	.	.	.	.
American Pioneer Life Ins Co	006090	L	.	L	L	.	L	.	.	L	D	L	.	L	.	L	L	L	L	L	.	L	.	.	.	L	L	L	L	L	.	.	L	.	L	L	L	L	L	.	.	L	L	L	L	L	.	L	L	L	.	L	.	.	.	.	.
American Progressive L&H NY	008411	L	.	.	.	.	L	L	L	L	.	.	L	.	L	L	.	.	.	L	L	L	L	.	L	.	L	.	.	.	L	L	.	D	.	.	L	.	L	L	L	.	.	.	.	.	L	L	.	L	.	.	.	.	.	.	.
American Public Life Ins Co	006094	L	L	L	L	L	L	L	L	L	L	L	L	L	L	L	L	L	L	L	L	L	L	L	L	L	L	L	L	L	L	L	L	.	L	L	L	D	L	L	L	L	L	L	L	L	L	L	L	L	L	L	.	L	.	.	.
American Republic Corp Ins Co	006906	L	.	L	L	.	L	.	L	L	.	L	.	.	L	L	L	L	L	L	.	L	.	.	L	L	L	L	D	L	.	.	L	.	L	L	L	L	L	L	.	L	L	L	L	L	.	L	.	L	L	L	.	.	.	.	.
American Republic Ins Co	006096	L	L	L	L	L	L	L	L	L	L	L	L	L	L	L	D	L	L	L	L	L	L	L	L	L	L	L	L	L	L	L	L	.	L	L	L	L	L	L	L	L	L	L	L	L	L	L	L	L	L	L	.	.	.	.	.
American Retirement Life Ins	008831	L	.	L	L	.	L	.	L	.	L	L	.	.	L	L	L	L	L	L	.	L	.	.	L	L	L	L	L	L	L	.	L	.	L	L	D	L	L	L	.	L	L	L	L	L	.	L	.	L	.	L	.	.	.	.	.
American Savings Life Ins Co	006100	.	.	D	.	.	.	.	.	.	.	.	.	.	.	.	.	.	.	.	.	.	.	.	.	.	.	.	.	.	.	.	.	.	.	.	.	.	.	.	.	.	.	.	.	L	.	.	.	.	.	.	.	.	.	.	.
American Service Life Ins Co	007899	.	.	.	D	.	.	.	.	.	.	.	.	.	.	.	.	.	.	.	.	.	.	.	.	.	.	.	.	.	.	.	.	.	.	.	.	.	.	.	.	.	.	.	.	.	.	.	.	.	.	.	.	.	.	.	.
American Specialty H Plans CA	064802	.	.	.	.	D	.	.	.	.	.	.	.	.	.	.	.	.	.	.	.	.	.	.	.	.	.	.	.	.	.	.	.	.	.	.	.	.	.	.	.	.	.	.	.	.	.	.	.	.	.	.	.	.	.	.	.
American Underwriters Life Ins	008795	.	.	D	.	.	L	.	.	.	.	.	.	L	L	L	.	L	.	L	.	.	.	.	.	.	L	L	L	L	.	.	.	.	.	.	.	L	L	.	.	.	L	.	.	L	.	.	.	L	.	L	.	.	.	.	.
American United Life Ins Co	006109	L	L	L	L	L	L	L	L	L	L	L	L	L	L	D	L	L	L	L	L	L	L	L	L	L	L	L	L	L	L	L	L	Q	L	L	L	L	L	L	L	L	L	L	L	L	L	L	L	L	L	L	.	.	.	.	.
America's Hlth Choice Med Plns	064703	.	.	.	.	.	.	.	.	.	D	.	.	.	.	.	.	.	.	.	.	.	.	.	.	.	.	.	.	.	.	.	.	.	.	.	.	.	.	.	.	.	.	.	.	.	.	.	.	.	.	.	.	.	.	.	.
AmeriChoice of Connecticut Inc	060689	.	.	.	.	.	.	D	.	.	.	.	.	.	.	.	.	.	.	.	.	.	.	.	.	.	.	.	.	.	.	.	.	.	.	.	.	.	.	.	.	.	.	.	.	.	.	.	.	.	.	.	.	.	.	.	.
AmeriChoice of Georgia Inc	064965	.	.	.	.	.	.	.	.	.	.	D	.	.	.	.	.	.	.	.	.	.	.	.	.	.	.	.	.	.	.	.	.	.	.	.	.	.	.	.	.	.	.	.	.	.	.	.	.	.	.	.	.	.	.	.	.
AmeriChoice of New Jersey	064214	.	.	.	.	.	.	.	.	.	.	.	.	.	.	.	.	.	.	.	.	.	.	.	.	.	.	.	.	.	.	D	.	.	.	.	.	.	.	.	.	.	.	.	.	.	.	.	.	.	.	.	.	.	.	.	.
AmeriChoice of Pennsylvania	064159	.	.	.	.	.	.	.	.	.	.	.	.	.	.	.	.	.	.	.	.	.	.	.	.	.	.	.	.	.	.	.	.	.	.	.	.	.	.	D	.	.	.	.	.	.	.	.	.	.	.	.	.	.	.	.	.
Americo Financial Lf & Annuity	006233	L	L	L	L	L	L	L	L	L	L	L	L	L	L	L	L	L	L	L	L	L	L	L	L	L	L	L	L	L	L	L	L	.	L	L	L	L	L	L	L	L	L	L	D	L	L	L	L	L	L	L	.	.	.	L	L
AMERIGROUP New Jersey Inc	064209	.	.	.	.	.	.	.	.	.	.	.	.	.	.	.	.	.	.	.	.	.	.	.	.	.	.	.	.	.	.	D	.	.	.	.	.	.	.	.	.	.	.	.	.	.	.	.	.	.	.	.	.	.	.	.	.
AMERIGROUP Ohio Inc	064873	.	.	.	.	.	.	.	.	.	.	.	.	.	.	.	.	.	.	.	.	.	.	.	.	.	.	.	.	.	.	.	.	.	.	.	D	.	.	.	.	.	.	.	.	.	.	.	.	.	.	.	.	.	.	.	.
AMERIGROUP South Carolina Inc	064887	.	.	.	.	.	.	.	.	.	.	.	.	.	.	.	.	.	.	.	.	.	.	.	.	.	.	.	.	.	.	.	.	.	.	.	.	.	.	.	.	D	.	.	.	.	.	.	.	.	.	.	.	.	.	.	.
AMERIGROUP Tennessee Inc	064927	.	.	.	.	.	.	.	.	.	.	.	.	.	.	.	.	.	.	.	.	.	.	.	.	.	.	.	.	.	.	.	.	.	.	.	.	.	.	.	.	.	.	D	.	.	.	.	.	.	.	.	.	.	.	.	.
AMERIGROUP Texas Inc	064238	.	.	.	.	.	.	.	.	.	.	.	.	.	.	.	.	.	.	.	.	.	.	.	.	.	.	.	.	.	.	.	.	.	.	.	.	.	.	.	.	.	.	.	D	.	.	.	.	.	.	.	.	.	.	.	.
AMERIGROUP Virginia Inc	064899	.	.	.	.	.	.	.	.	.	.	.	.	.	.	.	.	.	.	.	.	.	.	.	.	.	.	.	.	.	.	.	.	.	.	.	.	.	.	.	.	.	.	.	.	.	.	D	.	.	.	.	.	.	.	.	.
AmeriHealth HMO Inc	064139	.	.	.	.	.	.	.	L	.	.	.	.	.	.	.	.	.	.	.	.	.	.	.	.	.	.	.	.	.	.	L	.	.	.	.	.	.	.	D	.	.	.	.	.	.	.	.	.	.	.	.	.	.	.	.	.
AmeriHealth Ins Co of NJ	007887	.	.	.	.	.	.	.	.	.	.	.	.	.	.	.	.	.	.	.	.	.	.	.	.	.	.	.	.	.	.	D	.	.	.	.	.	.	.	.	.	.	.	.	.	.	.	.	.	.	.	.	.	.	.	.	.
Ameritas Life Insurance Corp.	006152	L	L	L	L	L	L	L	L	L	L	L	L	L	L	L	L	L	L	L	L	L	L	L	L	L	L	L	D	L	L	L	L	.	L	L	L	L	L	L	L	L	L	L	L	L	L	L	L	L	L	L	.	.	.	.	.
AmFirst Insurance Co	012998	L	.	L	L	.	.	.	.	.	L	.	.	.	.	.	.	.	.	L	.	L	.	.	.	L	.	.	.	.	.	.	.	.	L	.	L	D	.	L	.	L	.	L	L	.	.	L	.	.	.	.	.	.	.	.	.
AMGP Georgia Managed Care Co	064890	.	.	.	.	.	.	.	.	.	.	D	.	.	.	.	.	.	.	.	.	.	.	.	.	.	.	.	.	.	.	.	.	.	.	.	.	.	.	.	.	.	.	.	.	.	.	.	.	.	.	.	.	.	.	.	.
Amica Life Ins Co	007464	L	L	L	L	L	L	L	L	L	L	L	.	L	L	L	L	L	L	L	L	L	L	L	L	L	L	L	L	L	L	L	L	L	L	L	L	L	L	L	D	L	L	L	L	L	L	L	L	L	L	L	.	.	.	.	.
Annuity Investors Life Ins Co	009088	L	L	L	L	L	L	L	L	L	L	L	L	L	L	L	L	L	L	L	L	L	L	L	L	L	L	L	L	L	L	L	L	.	L	L	D	L	L	L	L	L	L	L	L	L	.	L	L	L	L	L	.	.	.	.	.
Anthem BC Life & Health Ins Co	060057	.	.	.	.	D	.	.	.	.	.	.	.	.	.	.	.	.	.	.	.	.	.	.	.	.	.	.	.	.	.	.	.	.	.	.	.	.	.	.	.	.	.	.	.	.	.	.	.	.	.	.	.	.	.	.	.
Anthem Health Plans Inc	068044	.	.	.	.	.	.	D	.	.	.	.	.	.	.	.	.	.	.	.	.	.	.	.	.	.	.	.	.	.	.	.	.	.	.	.	.	.	.	.	.	.	.	.	.	.	.	.	.	.	.	.	.	.	.	.	.
Anthem Health Plans of KY Inc	060150	.	.	.	.	.	.	.	.	.	.	.	.	.	.	.	.	.	D	.	.	.	.	.	.	.	.	.	.	.	.	.	.	.	.	.	.	.	.	.	.	.	.	.	.	.	.	.	.	.	.	.	.	.	.	.	.
Anthem Health Plans of ME Inc	064391	.	.	.	.	.	.	.	.	.	.	.	.	.	.	.	.	.	.	.	D	.	.	.	.	.	.	.	.	.	.	.	.	.	.	.	.	.	.	.	.	.	.	.	.	.	.	.	.	.	.	.	.	.	.	.	.

D-State of Domicile **L-Licensed** **S-Surplus Lines Writer** **F-Authorized under the Risk Retention Act** **Q-Qualified or Accredited Reinsurer**

U.S. States/Territories in Which Companies Are Licensed or Do Business – *Continued*

Company Name	AMB#	AL	AK	AZ	AR	CA	CO	CT	DE	DC	FL	GA	HI	ID	IL	IN	IA	KS	KY	LA	ME	MD	MA	MI	MN	MS	MO	MT	NE	NV	NH	NJ	NM	NY	NC	ND	OH	OK	OR	PA	RI	SC	SD	TN	TX	UT	VT	VA	WA	WV	WI	WY	AS	GU	MP	PR	VI
Anthem Health Plans of NH Inc	064173	.	.	.	.	.	.	.	.	.	.	.	.	.	.	.	.	.	.	.	.	.	.	.	.	.	.	.	.	.	D	.	.	.	.	.	.	.	.	.	.	.	.	.	.	.	.	.	.	.	.	.	.	.	.	.	.
Anthem Health Plans of VA	068315	.	.	.	.	.	.	.	.	.	.	.	.	.	.	.	.	.	.	.	.	.	.	.	.	.	.	.	.	.	.	.	.	.	.	.	.	.	.	.	.	.	.	.	.	.	.	D	.	.	.	.	.	.	.	.	.
Anthem Insurance Companies Inc	000607	L	.	L	L	.	L	L	.	.	.	L	.	L	L	D	L	L	L	L	L	.	.	.	.	L	L	L	L	L	L	.	L	.	.	.	L	L	L	.	.	L	L	L	L	L	.	L	L	.	L	L	.	.	.	.	.
Anthem Lf & Disability Ins Co	060687	.	.	.	.	.	.	.	.	.	.	.	.	.	.	.	.	.	.	.	.	.	.	.	.	.	.	.	.	.	.	.	.	D	.	.	.	.	.	.	.	.	.	.	.	.	.	.	.	.	.	.	.	.	.	.	.
Anthem Life Insurance Company	006126	L	L	L	L	L	L	L	L	L	L	L	L	L	L	D	L	L	L	L	L	L	L	L	L	L	L	L	L	L	L	L	L	.	L	L	L	L	L	L	.	L	L	L	L	L	.	L	L	L	L	L	.	.	.	.	.
Arcadian Health Plan Inc	064812	.	.	L	.	L	.	.	.	.	.	.	.	.	.	.	.	.	.	.	L	.	.	.	.	.	L	.	.	.	L	.	.	.	.	.	.	.	.	.	.	L	.	.	L	.	.	L	D	.	.	.	.	.	.	.	.
Arcadian Health Plan of GA Inc	064888	.	.	.	.	.	.	.	.	.	.	D	.	.	.	.	.	.	.	.	.	.	.	.	.	.	.	.	.	.	.	.	.	.	.	.	.	.	.	.	.	.	.	.	.	.	.	.	.	.	.	.	.	.	.	.	.
Arcadian Health Plan of LA Inc	064945	.	.	.	.	.	.	.	.	.	.	.	.	.	.	.	.	.	.	D	.	.	.	.	.	.	.	.	.	.	.	.	.	.	.	.	.	.	.	.	.	.	.	.	.	.	.	.	.	.	.	.	.	.	.	.	.
Arcadian Health Plan of NC Inc	064946	.	.	.	.	.	.	.	.	.	.	.	.	.	.	.	.	.	.	.	.	.	.	.	.	.	.	.	.	.	.	.	.	.	D	.	.	.	.	.	.	.	.	.	.	.	.	.	.	.	.	.	.	.	.	.	.
Arizona Dental Insurance Svc	064971	.	.	D	.	.	.	.	.	.	.	.	.	.	.	.	.	.	.	.	.	.	.	.	.	.	.	.	.	.	.	.	.	.	.	.	.	.	.	.	.	.	.	.	.	.	.	.	.	.	.	.	.	.	.	.	.
Arkansas Bankers Life Ins Co	068164	.	.	.	D	.	.	.	.	.	.	.	.	.	.	.	.	.	.	.	.	.	.	.	.	.	.	.	.	.	.	.	.	.	.	.	.	.	.	.	.	.	.	.	.	.	.	.	.	.	.	.	.	.	.	.	.
Arkansas Community Care Inc	064868	.	.	.	D	.	.	.	.	.	.	.	.	.	.	.	.	.	.	.	.	.	.	.	.	.	.	.	.	.	.	.	.	.	.	.	.	L	.	.	.	.	.	.	L	.	.	.	.	.	.	.	.	.	.	.	.
Arkansas Life Ins Co	068314	.	.	D	.	.	.	.	.	.	.	.	.	.	.	.	.	.	.	.	.	.	.	.	.	.	.	.	.	.	.	.	.	.	.	.	.	.	.	.	.	.	.	.	.	.	.	.	.	.	.	.	.	.	.	.	.
Associated Mutual	068042	.	.	.	.	.	.	.	.	.	.	.	.	.	.	.	.	.	.	.	.	.	.	D	.	.	.	.	.	.	.	.	.	.	.	.	L	.	.	.	.	.	.	.	.	.	.	.	.	.	.	.	.	.	.	.	.
Assurity Life Ins Co	007374	L	L	L	L	L	L	L	L	L	L	L	L	L	L	L	L	L	L	L	L	L	L	L	L	L	L	L	D	L	L	L	L	.	L	L	L	L	L	L	L	L	L	L	L	L	L	L	L	L	L	L	.	.	.	.	.
Asuris Northwest Health	064414	.	.	.	.	.	.	.	.	.	.	.	.	.	.	.	.	.	.	.	.	.	.	.	.	.	.	.	.	.	.	.	.	.	.	.	.	.	L	.	.	.	.	.	.	.	.	.	D	.	.	.	.	.	.	.	.
Athens Area Health Plan Select	064556	.	.	.	.	.	.	.	.	.	.	D	.	.	.	.	.	.	.	.	.	.	.	.	.	.	.	.	.	.	.	.	.	.	.	.	.	.	.	.	.	.	.	.	.	.	.	.	.	.	.	.	.	.	.	.	.
Atlanta Life Ins Co	006130	L	.	.	.	.	.	.	.	.	L	D	.	.	L	L	.	L	L	L	.	.	.	L	.	.	L	.	.	.	.	.	.	.	.	.	L	.	.	L	.	L	.	L	L	.	.	L	.	.	L	.	.	.	.	.	.
Atlantic Coast Life Ins Co	006132	L	.	.	.	.	.	.	.	.	L	L	.	.	.	.	.	.	L	.	.	.	.	.	.	L	.	.	.	.	.	.	.	.	L	.	.	.	.	.	.	D	.	L	.	.	.	L	.	.	.	.	.	.	.	.	.
Atlantic Southern Dental Fndn	064783	.	.	.	.	.	.	.	.	.	.	.	.	.	.	.	.	.	.	.	.	L	.	.	.	.	.	.	.	.	.	D	.	.	.	.	.	.	.	.	.	.	.	.	.	.	.	.	.	.	.	.	.	.	.	.	.
Atlantic Southern Ins Co	006135	.	.	.	.	.	.	.	.	.	.	.	.	.	.	.	.	.	.	.	.	.	.	.	.	.	.	.	.	.	.	.	.	.	.	.	.	.	.	.	.	.	.	.	.	.	.	.	.	.	.	.	.	L	.	D	L
ATRIO Health Plans Inc	064904	.	.	.	.	.	.	.	.	.	.	.	.	.	.	.	.	.	.	.	.	.	.	.	.	.	.	.	.	.	.	.	.	.	.	.	.	.	D	.	.	.	.	.	.	.	.	.	.	.	.	.	.	.	.	.	.
Aurora National Life Assur	006139	L	L	L	L	D	L	.	L	L	L	L	L	L	L	L	L	L	L	L	.	L	L	L	L	L	L	L	L	L	.	L	L	.	L	L	L	L	L	L	L	L	L	L	L	L	L	L	L	L	L	L	.	.	.	.	.
Auto Club Life Insurance Co	008525	.	.	L	L	L	L	.	.	.	.	.	.	.	L	L	L	L	L	.	.	L	.	D	L	.	L	.	L	.	.	.	L	.	L	L	L	L	.	L	.	L	L	.	L	.	.	L	L	.	L	.	.	.	.	.	.
Auto-Owners Life Ins Co	006140	L	.	L	L	.	L	.	.	.	L	L	.	L	L	L	L	L	L	.	.	.	.	D	L	L	L	.	L	L	.	.	L	.	L	L	L	.	L	L	.	L	L	L	.	L	.	L	L	.	L	.	.	.	.	.	.
Automobile Club of Sthrn CA Lf	060325	.	.	.	.	D	.	.	.	.	.	.	.	.	.	.	.	.	.	.	.	.	.	Q	.	.	.	.	.	.	.	.	.	.	.	.	.	.	.	.	.	.	.	.	.	.	.	.	.	.	.	.	.	.	.	.	.
Avalon Insurance Company	064854	.	.	.	.	.	.	.	.	.	.	.	.	.	.	.	.	.	.	.	.	.	.	.	.	.	.	.	.	.	.	.	.	.	.	.	.	.	.	D	.	.	.	.	.	.	.	.	.	L	.	.	.	.	.	.	.
Avante Behavioral Health Plan	064803	.	.	.	.	D	.	.	.	.	.	.	.	.	.	.	.	.	.	.	.	.	.	.	.	.	.	.	.	.	.	.	.	.	.	.	.	.	.	.	.	.	.	.	.	.	.	.	.	.	.	.	.	.	.	.	.
Avera Health Plans Inc	064515	.	.	.	.	.	.	.	.	.	.	.	.	.	.	.	L	.	.	.	.	.	.	.	.	.	.	.	L	.	.	.	.	.	.	.	.	.	.	.	.	.	D	.	.	.	.	.	.	.	.	.	.	.	.	.	.
Aviva Life and Annuity Company	006199	L	L	L	L	L	L	L	L	L	L	L	L	L	L	L	D	L	L	L	L	L	L	L	L	L	L	L	L	L	L	L	L	.	L	L	L	L	L	L	L	L	L	L	L	L	L	L	L	L	L	L	.	.	.	.	.
Aviva Life & Annuity Co of NY	006467	.	.	.	.	.	.	L	.	.	L	.	.	.	L	L	L	L	L	.	.	.	L	L	.	L	.	.	.	L	.	L	.	D	L	.	.	.	.	L	L	.	.	.	.	.	L	.	.	.	.	.	.	.	.	.	.
AvMed Inc	064074	.	.	.	.	.	.	.	.	.	D	.	.	.	.	.	.	.	.	.	.	.	.	.	.	.	.	.	.	.	.	.	.	.	.	.	.	.	.	.	.	.	.	.	.	.	.	.	.	.	.	.	.	.	.	.	.
AXA Corporate Solutions Lf Re	009083	L	L	L	L	L	L	L	D	L	.	L	L	L	L	L	L	L	L	L	Q	L	L	L	L	L	L	L	L	L	L	L	L	L	Q	L	L	L	L	L	L	L	L	L	L	L	L	Q	L	L	L	L	.	.	.	.	.
AXA Equitable Life & Annuity	009516	L	L	L	L	L	D	L	L	L	L	L	L	L	L	L	L	L	L	L	L	L	L	L	L	L	L	L	L	L	L	L	L	.	L	L	L	L	L	L	L	L	L	L	L	L	L	L	L	L	L	L	.	.	.	.	.
AXA Equitable Life Ins Co	006341	L	L	L	L	L	L	L	L	L	L	L	L	L	L	L	L	L	L	L	L	L	L	L	L	L	L	L	L	L	L	L	L	D	L	L	L	L	L	L	L	L	L	L	L	L	L	L	L	L	L	L	.	.	.	L	L
Balboa Life Insurance Company	006965	L	L	L	L	D	L	L	L	L	L	L	L	L	L	L	L	L	L	L	L	L	L	L	L	L	L	L	L	L	L	L	L	.	L	L	L	L	L	L	L	L	L	L	L	L	L	L	L	L	L	L	.	L	L	.	L
Balboa Life Insurance Co of NY	060347	.	.	.	.	.	.	.	.	.	.	.	.	.	.	.	.	.	.	.	.	.	.	.	.	.	.	.	.	.	.	.	.	D	.	.	.	.	.	.	.	.	.	.	.	.	.	.	.	.	.	.	.	.	.	.	.
Baltimore Life Ins Co	006143	L	L	L	L	L	L	L	L	L	L	L	L	L	L	L	L	L	L	L	L	D	L	L	L	L	L	L	L	L	L	L	L	.	L	L	L	L	L	L	L	L	L	L	L	L	L	L	L	L	L	L	.	.	.	.	.
Bankers Conseco Life Insurance	060002	.	.	.	.	.	.	.	.	.	.	.	.	.	.	.	.	.	.	.	.	.	.	.	.	.	.	.	.	.	.	.	.	D	.	.	.	.	.	.	.	.	.	.	.	.	.	.	.	.	.	.	.	.	.	.	.
Bankers Fidelity Life Ins Co	006145	L	L	L	L	.	L	.	L	L	L	D	L	L	L	L	L	L	L	L	L	L	L	L	L	L	L	L	L	L	L	L	L	.	L	L	L	L	L	L	L	L	L	L	L	L	.	L	L	L	L	L	.	.	.	.	.
Bankers Life and Casualty Co	006149	L	L	L	L	L	L	L	L	L	L	L	L	L	D	L	L	L	L	L	L	L	L	L	L	L	L	L	L	L	L	L	L	.	L	L	L	L	L	L	L	L	L	L	L	L	L	L	L	L	L	L	.	.	.	.	.
Bankers Life Insurance Co	008448	L	L	L	L	.	.	.	L	L	D	L	L	L	.	L	.	L	L	L	.	L	.	.	.	L	L	L	L	L	.	.	L	.	.	L	L	L	.	L	.	L	L	L	L	L	.	.	L	L	.	L	.	.	.	.	.
Bankers Life Ins Co of America	006153	.	.	.	.	.	L	.	.	.	.	.	.	.	.	.	.	.	L	L	.	.	.	.	.	.	.	.	.	.	.	.	.	.	.	.	.	L	.	.	.	.	.	.	D	L	.	.	.	.	.	.	.	.	.	.	.
Bankers Life of Louisiana	006151	.	.	.	.	.	.	.	.	.	.	.	.	.	.	.	.	.	.	D	.	.	.	.	.	.	.	.	.	.	.	.	.	.	.	.	.	.	.	.	.	.	.	.	.	.	.	.	.	.	.	.	.	.	.	.	.
Bankers Reserve Life Ins of WI	060401	.	.	L	L	.	L	.	L	L	L	L	.	L	L	L	.	L	L	L	L	L	L	L	.	L	L	L	L	L	.	L	L	.	.	.	L	L	L	L	L	L	L	L	L	L	.	L	.	L	D	L	.	.	.	.	.
Banner Life Ins Co	006468	L	L	L	L	L	L	L	L	L	L	L	L	L	L	L	L	L	L	L	L	D	L	L	L	L	L	L	L	L	L	L	L	.	L	L	L	L	L	L	L	L	L	L	L	L	L	L	L	L	L	L	.	.	.	.	.
BCBSD Inc	068578	.	.	.	.	.	.	.	D	.	.	.	.	.	.	.	.	.	.	.	.	.	.	.	.	.	.	.	.	.	.	.	.	.	.	.	.	.	.	.	.	.	.	.	.	.	.	.	.	.	.	.	.	.	.	.	.
BCI HMO Inc	068658	.	.	.	.	.	.	.	.	.	.	.	.	.	D	.	.	.	.	.	.	.	.	.	.	.	.	.	.	.	.	.	.	.	.	.	.	.	.	.	.	.	.	.	.	.	.	.	.	.	.	.	.	.	.	.	.
BCS Insurance Company	003251	L	L	L	L	L	L	L	L	L	L	L	L	L	L	L	L	L	L	L	L	L	L	L	L	L	L	L	L	L	L	L	L	L	L	L	D	L	L	L	L	L	L	L	L	L	L	L	L	L	L	L	.	.	.	L	.
BCS Life Insurance Co	007363	L	L	L	L	L	L	L	L	L	L	L	L	L	D	L	L	L	L	L	L	L	L	L	L	L	L	L	L	L	L	L	L	L	L	L	L	L	L	L	L	L	L	L	L	L	L	L	L	L	L	L	.	.	.	Q	.
Beneficial Life Ins Co	006162	L	L	L	L	L	L	L	L	L	L	L	L	L	L	L	L	L	L	L	L	L	L	L	L	L	L	L	L	L	L	L	L	.	L	L	L	L	L	L	L	L	L	L	L	D	L	L	L	L	L	L	.	.	.	.	.
Berkley Life and Health Ins Co	006579	L	L	L	L	L	L	.	L	L	L	L	L	L	L	L	D	L	L	L	L	L	L	L	L	L	L	L	L	L	L	L	L	.	L	L	L	L	L	L	L	L	L	L	L	L	L	L	L	L	L	L	.	.	.	.	.
Berkshire Hathaway Life of NE	060060	L	L	L	L	L	L	L	L	L	L	L	L	L	L	L	L	L	L	L	L	L	L	L	.	L	L	L	D	L	L	L	L	Q	L	L	L	L	L	L	L	L	L	L	L	L	L	L	L	L	L	L	.	.	.	.	.
Berkshire Life Ins Co of Amer	007409	L	L	L	L	L	L	L	L	L	L	L	L	L	L	L	L	L	L	L	L	L	D	L	L	L	L	L	L	L	L	L	L	L	L	L	L	L	L	L	L	L	L	L	L	L	L	L	L	L	L	L	.	.	.	.	.
BEST Life and Health Ins Co	007246	L	L	L	L	L	L	.	.	L	L	L	L	L	L	L	L	L	L	L	.	L	.	L	.	L	L	L	L	L	.	.	L	.	L	L	L	L	L	.	.	L	L	L	D	L	.	L	L	.	.	L	.	.	.	.	.
Best Meridian Ins Co	060007	.	.	.	.	.	.	.	.	.	D	.	.	.	.	.	.	.	.	.	.	.	.	.	.	.	.	.	.	.	.	.	.	.	.	.	.	.	.	.	.	.	.	.	.	.	.	.	.	.	.	.	.	.	.	.	.
Better Life and Health Company	060102	.	.	D	.	.	.	.	.	.	.	.	.	.	.	.	.	.	.	.	.	.	.	.	.	.	.	.	.	.	.	.	.	.	.	.	.	.	.	.	.	.	.	.	.	.	.	.	.	.	.	.	.	.	.	.	.
Big Sky Life Inc	068171	.	.	.	.	.	.	.	.	.	.	.	.	.	.	.	.	.	.	.	.	.	.	.	.	.	.	D	.	.	.	.	.	.	.	.	.	.	.	.	.	.	.	.	.	.	.	.	.	.	.	.	.	.	.	.	.
Bird Insurance Company	060693	.	.	D	.	.	.	.	.	.	.	.	.	.	.	.	.	.	.	.	.	.	.	.	.	.	.	.	.	.	.	.	.	.	.	.	.	.	.	.	.	.	.	.	.	.	.	.	.	.	.	.	.	.	.	.	.
Block Vision of Texas Inc	064510	.	.	.	.	.	.	.	.	.	.	.	.	.	.	.	.	.	.	.	.	.	.	.	.	.	.	.	.	.	.	.	.	.	.	.	.	.	.	.	.	.	.	.	D	.	.	.	.	.	.	.	.	.	.	.	.
Blue Advantage Plus of KC Inc	064824	.	.	.	.	.	.	.	.	.	.	.	.	.	.	.	.	.	.	.	.	.	.	.	.	.	D	.	.	.	.	.	.	.	.	.	.	.	.	.	.	.	.	.	.	.	.	.	.	.	.	.	.	.	.	.	.
Blue Care Health Plan	064073	.	.	.	.	.	.	D	.	.	.	.	.	.	.	.	.	.	.	.	.	.	.	.	.	.	.	.	.	.	.	.	.	.	.	.	.	.	.	.	.	.	.	.	.	.	.	.	.	.	.	.	.	.	.	.	.
Blue Care Network of Michigan	068741	.	.	.	.	.	.	.	.	.	.	.	.	.	.	.	.	.	.	.	.	.	.	D	.	.	.	.	.	.	.	.	.	.	.	.	.	.	.	.	.	.	.	.	.	.	.	.	.	.	.	.	.	.	.	.	.
Blue Care of Michigan Inc	064870	.	.	.	.	.	.	.	.	.	.	.	.	.	.	.	.	.	.	.	.	.	.	D	.	.	.	.	.	.	.	.	.	.	.	.	.	.	.	.	.	.	.	.	.	.	.	.	.	.	.	.	.	.	.	.	.
Blue Cross & Blue Shield of AL	060080	D	.	.	.	.	.	.	.	.	.	.	.	.	.	.	.	.	.	.	.	.	.	.	.	.	.	.	.	.	.	.	.	.	.	.	.	.	.	.	.	.	.	.	.	.	.	.	.	.	.	.	.	.	.	.	.
Blue Cross & Blue Shield of FL	068174	.	.	.	.	.	.	.	.	.	D	.	.	.	.	.	.	.	.	.	.	.	.	.	.	.	.	.	.	.	.	.	.	.	.	.	.	.	.	Q	.	.	.	.	.	.	.	.	.	.	.	.	.	.	.	.	.
Blue Cross & Blue Shield of GA	060075	.	.	.	.	.	.	.	.	.	.	D	.	.	.	.	.	.	.	.	.	.	.	.	.	.	.	.	.	.	.	.	.	.	.	.	.	.	.	.	.	.	.	.	.	.	.	.	.	.	.	.	.	.	.	.	.
Blue Cross&Blue Shield of K C	064015	.	.	.	.	.	.	.	.	.	.	.	.	.	.	.	.	L	.	.	.	.	.	.	.	.	D	.	.	.	.	.	.	.	.	.	.	.	.	.	.	.	.	.	.	.	.	.	.	.	.	.	.	.	.	.	.
Blue Cross and Blue Shield KS	060070	.	.	.	.	.	.	.	.	.	.	.	.	.	.	.	.	D	.	.	.	.	.	.	.	.	.	.	.	.	.	.	.	.	.	.	.	.	.	.	.	.	.	.	.	.	.	.	.	.	.	.	.	.	.	.	.
Blue Cr & Blue Sh of MA HMO Bl	064847	.	.	.	.	.	.	.	.	.	.	.	.	.	.	.	.	.	.	.	.	.	D	.	.	.	.	.	.	.	.	.	.	.	.	.	.	.	.	.	.	.	.	.	.	.	.	.	.	.	.	.	.	.	.	.	.
Blue Cross & Blue Shield of MA	064562	.	.	.	.	.	.	.	.	.	.	.	.	.	.	.	.	.	.	.	.	.	D	.	.	.	.	.	.	.	.	.	.	.	.	.	.	.	.	.	.	.	.	.	.	.	.	.	.	.	.	.	.	.	.	.	.
Blue Cross & Blue Shield of MN	060077	.	.	.	.	.	.	.	.	.	.	.	.	.	.	.	.	.	.	.	.	.	.	.	D	.	.	.	.	.	.	.	.	.	.	.	.	.	.	.	.	.	.	.	.	.	.	.	.	.	.	.	.	.	.	.	.
Blue Cross & Blue Shield of MS	060217	.	.	.	.	.	.	.	.	.	.	.	.	.	.	.	.	.	.	.	.	.	.	.	.	D	.	.	.	.	.	.	.	.	.	.	.	.	.	.	.	.	.	.	.	.	.	.	.	.	.	.	.	.	.	.	.
Blue Cross & Blue Shield of MT	064338	.	.	.	.	.	.	.	.	.	.	.	.	.	.	.	.	.	.	.	.	.	.	.	.	.	.	D	.	.	.	.	.	.	.	.	.	.	.	.	.	.	.	.	.	.	.	.	.	.	.	.	.	.	.	.	.
Blue Cross & Blue Shield of NE	068172	.	.	.	.	.	.	.	.	.	.	.	.	.	.	.	.	.	.	.	.	.	.	.	.	.	.	.	D	.	.	.	.	.	.	.	.	.	.	.	.	.	.	.	.	.	.	.	.	.	.	.	.	.	.	.	.
Blue Cross & Blue Shield of NC	064070	.	.	.	.	.	.	.	.	.	.	.	.	.	.	.	.	.	.	.	.	.	.	.	.	.	.	.	.	.	.	.	.	.	D	.	.	.	.	.	.	.	.	.	.	.	.	.	.	.	.	.	.	.	.	.	.

D-State of Domicile **L**-Licensed **S**-Surplus Lines Writer **F**-Authorized under the Risk Retention Act **Q**-Qualified or Accredited Reinsurer

U.S. States/Territories in Which Companies Are Licensed or Do Business – *Continued*

Company Name	AMB#	AL	AK	AZ	AR	CA	CO	CT	DE	DC	FL	GA	HI	ID	IL	IN	IA	KS	KY	LA	ME	MD	MA	MI	MN	MS	MO	MT	NE	NV	NH	NJ	NM	NY	NC	ND	OH	OK	OR	PA	RI	SC	SD	TN	TX	UT	VT	VA	WA	WV	WI	WY	AS	GU	MP	PR	VI
Blue Cross & Blue Shield of RI	064570	.	.	.	.	.	.	.	.	.	.	.	.	.	.	.	.	.	.	.	.	.	.	.	.	.	.	.	.	.	.	.	.	.	.	.	.	.	.	.	D	.	.	.	.	.	.	.	.	.	.	.	.	.	.	.	.
Blue Cross & Blue Shield of SC	001727	.	.	.	.	.	.	.	.	.	.	.	.	.	.	.	.	.	.	.	.	.	.	.	.	.	.	.	.	.	.	.	.	.	.	.	.	.	.	.	.	D	.	.	.	.	.	.	.	.	.	.	.	.	.	.	.
Blue Cross & Blue Shield of VT	064541	.	.	.	.	.	.	.	.	.	.	.	.	.	.	.	.	.	.	.	.	.	.	.	.	.	.	.	.	.	.	.	.	.	.	.	.	.	.	.	.	.	.	.	.	.	D	.	.	.	.	.	.	.	.	.	.
BC BS Healthcare Plan of GA	068527	.	.	.	.	.	.	.	.	.	.	D	.	.	.	.	.	.	.	.	.	.	.	.	.	.	.	.	.	.	.	.	.	.	.	.	.	.	.	.	.	.	.	.	.	.	.	.	.	.	.	.	.	.	.	.	.
Blue Cross Blue Shield MT(HMO)	064138	.	.	.	.	.	.	.	.	.	.	.	.	.	.	.	.	.	.	.	.	.	.	.	.	.	.	D	.	.	.	.	.	.	.	.	.	.	.	.	.	.	.	.	.	.	.	.	.	.	.	.	.	.	.	.	.
Blue Cross Blue Shield of MI	060081	.	.	.	.	.	.	.	.	.	.	.	.	.	.	.	.	.	.	.	.	.	.	D	.	.	.	.	.	.	.	.	.	.	.	.	.	.	.	.	.	.	.	.	.	.	.	.	.	.	.	.	.	.	.	.	.
Blue Cross Blue Shield of WI	064315	.	.	.	.	.	.	.	.	.	.	.	.	.	.	.	.	.	.	.	.	.	.	.	.	.	.	.	.	.	.	.	.	.	.	.	.	.	.	.	.	.	.	.	.	.	.	.	.	.	D	.	.	.	.	.	.
Blue Cross Blue Shield of WY	064567	.	.	.	.	.	.	.	.	.	.	.	.	.	.	.	.	.	.	.	.	.	.	.	.	.	.	.	.	.	.	.	.	.	.	.	.	.	.	.	.	.	.	.	.	.	.	.	.	.	.	D	.	.	.	.	.
Blue Cross of California	068970	.	.	.	.	D	.	.	.	.	.	.	.	.	.	.	.	.	.	.	.	.	.	.	.	.	.	.	.	.	.	.	.	.	.	.	.	.	.	.	.	.	.	.	.	.	.	.	.	.	.	.	.	.	.	.	.
Blue Cross of ID Hlth Service	008805	.	.	.	.	.	.	.	.	.	.	.	.	D	.	.	.	.	.	.	.	.	.	.	.	.	.	.	.	.	.	.	.	.	.	.	.	.	.	.	.	.	.	.	.	.	.	.	.	.	.	.	.	.	.	.	.
Blue Shield of CA Life & Hlth	006181	.	.	.	.	D	.	.	.	.	.	.	.	.	.	.	.	.	.	.	.	.	.	.	.	.	.	.	.	.	.	.	.	.	.	.	.	.	.	.	.	.	.	.	.	.	.	.	.	.	.	.	.	.	.	.	.
Bluebonnet Life Ins Co	068175	L	.	.	L	.	.	.	.	.	.	.	.	.	.	.	.	.	.	L	.	.	.	.	.	D	.	.	.	.	.	.	.	.	.	.	.	.	.	.	.	.	.	L	.	.	.	.	.	.	.	.	.	.	.	.	.
BlueCaid of Michigan	064738	.	.	.	.	.	.	.	.	.	.	.	.	.	.	.	.	.	.	.	.	.	.	D	.	.	.	.	.	.	.	.	.	.	.	.	.	.	.	.	.	.	.	.	.	.	.	.	.	.	.	.	.	.	.	.	.
BlueChoice HealthPlan of SC	068593	.	.	.	.	.	.	.	.	.	.	.	.	.	.	.	.	.	.	.	.	.	.	.	.	.	.	.	.	.	.	.	.	.	.	.	.	.	.	.	.	D	.	.	.	.	.	.	.	.	.	.	.	.	.	.	.
BlueCross BlueShield of TN	064002	.	.	.	.	.	.	.	.	.	.	.	.	.	.	.	.	.	.	.	.	.	.	.	.	.	.	.	.	.	.	.	.	.	.	.	.	.	.	.	.	.	.	D	.	.	.	.	.	.	.	.	.	.	.	.	.
Bluegrass Family Health Inc	068747	.	.	.	.	.	.	.	.	.	.	.	.	.	.	L	.	.	D	.	.	.	.	.	.	.	.	.	.	.	.	.	.	.	.	.	.	.	.	.	.	.	.	L	.	.	.	.	.	.	.	.	.	.	.	.	.
Boston Medical Center Hth Plan	064973	.	.	.	.	.	.	.	.	.	.	.	.	.	.	.	.	.	.	.	.	.	D	.	.	.	.	.	.	.	.	.	.	.	.	.	.	.	.	.	.	.	.	.	.	.	.	.	.	.	.	.	.	.	.	.	.
Boston Mutual Life Ins Co	006170	L	L	L	L	L	L	L	L	L	L	L	L	L	L	L	L	L	L	L	L	L	D	L	L	L	L	L	L	L	L	L	L	Q	L	L	L	L	L	L	L	L	L	L	L	L	L	L	L	L	L	L	.	.	.	L	.
Bravo Health Insurance Company	060649	S	S	S	S	L	S	S	D	L	S	S	S	S	L	S	S	S	S	S	.	L	S	L	S	S	S	S	S	S	.	L	S	L	.	.	L	S	.	L	S	S	.	S	L	S	S	S	.	L	S	S	.	.	.	.	.
Bravo Health Mid-Atlantic Inc	064697	.	.	.	.	.	.	.	L	L	.	.	.	.	L	.	.	.	.	.	.	D	.	.	.	.	.	.	.	.	.	.	.	.	.	.	.	.	.	.	.	.	.	.	.	.	.	.	.	.	.	.	.	.	.	.	.
Bravo Health Pennsylvania Inc	064743	.	.	.	.	.	.	.	.	.	.	.	.	.	.	.	.	.	.	.	.	.	.	.	.	.	.	.	.	.	.	.	.	.	.	.	.	.	.	D	.	.	.	.	.	.	.	.	.	.	.	.	.	.	.	.	.
Bravo Health Texas Inc	064838	.	.	.	.	.	.	.	.	.	.	.	.	.	.	.	.	.	.	.	.	.	.	.	.	.	.	.	.	.	.	.	.	.	.	.	.	.	.	.	.	.	.	.	D	.	.	.	.	.	.	.	.	.	.	.	.
Brokers National Life Assur	006023	L	L	L	D	L	L	L	L	L	L	L	L	L	L	L	L	L	L	L	L	L	L	L	L	L	L	L	L	L	.	L	L	.	L	L	L	L	L	L	L	L	L	L	L	L	L	L	L	L	L	L	.	.	.	.	.
Brooke Life Insurance Co	068117	.	.	.	.	.	.	.	.	.	.	.	.	.	.	.	.	.	.	.	.	.	.	D	.	.	.	.	.	.	.	.	.	.	.	.	.	.	.	.	.	.	.	.	.	.	.	.	.	.	.	.	.	.	.	.	.
Buckeye Community Health Plan	064768	.	.	.	.	.	.	.	.	.	.	.	.	.	.	.	.	.	.	.	.	.	.	.	.	.	.	.	.	.	.	.	.	.	.	.	D	.	.	.	.	.	.	.	.	.	.	.	.	.	.	.	.	.	.	.	.
Bupa Insurance Company	008449	.	.	.	.	.	.	.	.	.	D	.	.	.	.	.	.	.	.	.	.	.	.	.	.	.	.	.	.	.	.	.	.	.	.	.	.	.	.	.	.	.	.	.	.	.	.	.	.	.	.	.	.	.	.	.	.
C M Life Insurance Company	009062	L	L	L	L	L	L	D	L	L	L	L	L	L	L	L	L	L	L	L	L	L	L	L	L	L	L	L	L	L	L	L	L	.	L	L	L	L	L	L	L	L	L	L	L	L	L	L	L	L	L	L	.	.	.	L	.
California Benefits Dental Pln	064722	.	.	.	.	D	.	.	.	.	.	.	.	.	.	.	.	.	.	.	.	.	.	.	.	.	.	.	.	.	.	.	.	.	.	.	.	.	.	.	.	.	.	.	.	.	.	.	.	.	.	.	.	.	.	.	.
California Dental Network Inc	064350	.	.	.	.	D	.	.	.	.	.	.	.	.	.	.	.	.	.	.	.	.	.	.	.	.	.	.	.	.	.	.	.	.	.	.	.	.	.	.	.	.	.	.	.	.	.	.	.	.	.	.	.	.	.	.	.
California Physicians' Service	064012	.	.	.	.	D	.	.	.	.	.	.	.	.	.	.	.	.	.	.	.	.	.	.	.	.	.	.	.	.	.	.	.	.	.	.	.	.	.	.	.	.	.	.	.	.	.	.	.	.	.	.	.	.	.	.	.
Cambridge Life Ins Co	008545	.	.	L	L	.	L	.	.	.	.	.	.	.	.	L	.	L	.	L	.	L	.	.	.	L	D	L	L	L	.	.	L	L	L	.	.	L	.	.	.	L	L	L	L	L	.	.	.	L	.	.	.	.	.	.	.
Canyon State Life Ins Co	007537	.	.	D	.	.	.	.	.	.	.	.	.	.	.	.	.	.	.	.	.	.	.	.	.	.	.	.	.	.	.	.	.	.	.	.	.	.	.	.	.	.	.	.	.	.	.	.	.	.	.	.	.	.	.	.	.
Capital Advantage Insurance Co	001783	.	.	.	.	.	.	.	.	.	.	.	.	.	.	.	.	.	.	.	.	.	.	.	.	.	.	.	.	.	.	.	.	.	.	.	.	.	.	D	.	.	.	.	.	.	.	.	.	.	.	.	.	.	.	.	.
Capital Blue Cross	064554	.	.	.	.	.	.	.	.	.	.	.	.	.	.	.	.	.	.	.	.	.	.	.	.	.	.	.	.	.	.	.	.	.	.	.	.	.	.	D	.	.	.	.	.	.	.	.	.	.	.	.	.	.	.	.	.
Capital District Phys' Hlth Pl	068563	.	.	.	.	.	.	.	.	.	.	.	.	.	.	.	.	.	.	.	.	.	.	.	.	.	.	.	.	.	.	.	.	D	.	.	.	.	.	.	.	.	.	.	.	.	.	.	.	.	.	.	.	.	.	.	.
Capital Health Plan Inc	064116	.	.	.	.	.	.	.	.	.	D	.	.	.	.	.	.	.	.	.	.	.	.	.	.	.	.	.	.	.	.	.	.	.	.	.	.	.	.	.	.	.	.	.	.	.	.	.	.	.	.	.	.	.	.	.	.
Capital Reserve Life Ins Co	006184	.	.	.	.	.	.	.	.	.	.	.	.	.	.	.	L	L	.	.	.	.	.	.	.	.	D	.	.	.	.	.	.	.	.	.	.	.	.	.	.	.	.	.	.	.	.	.	.	.	.	.	.	.	.	.	.
CapitalCare Inc	064862	.	.	.	.	.	.	.	.	.	.	.	.	.	.	.	.	.	.	.	.	.	.	.	.	.	.	.	.	.	.	.	.	.	.	.	.	.	.	.	.	.	.	.	.	.	.	D	.	.	.	.	.	.	.	.	.
Capitol Life & Accident Ins Co	068179	.	.	.	D	.	.	.	.	.	.	.	.	.	.	.	.	.	.	.	.	.	.	.	.	.	.	.	.	.	.	.	.	.	.	.	.	.	.	.	.	.	.	.	.	.	.	.	.	.	.	.	.	.	.	.	.
Capitol Life Ins Co	006186	L	L	L	L	L	L	L	L	L	.	L	L	L	L	L	L	L	L	L	L	L	L	L	L	L	L	L	L	L	L	L	L	.	L	L	L	L	L	L	L	L	L	L	D	L	L	L	L	L	L	L	.	.	.	.	.
Capitol Security Life Ins Co	068087	.	.	.	.	.	.	.	.	.	.	.	.	.	.	.	.	.	.	.	.	.	.	.	.	.	.	.	.	.	.	.	.	.	.	.	.	.	.	.	.	.	.	.	D	.	.	.	.	.	.	.	.	.	.	.	.
Cardif Life Insurance Company	007376	L	L	L	L	L	L	L	L	L	L	L	L	L	L	L	L	D	L	L	.	L	L	L	L	L	L	L	L	L	.	.	L	.	L	L	L	L	L	L	L	L	L	L	L	L	.	L	L	.	L	L	.	.	.	.	.
Care 1st Health Plan Inc	064143	.	.	.	.	D	.	.	.	.	.	.	.	.	.	.	.	.	.	.	.	.	.	.	.	.	.	.	.	.	.	.	.	.	.	.	.	.	.	.	.	.	.	.	.	.	.	.	.	.	.	.	.	.	.	.	.
Care Improvement Plus of MD	064894	.	.	.	.	.	.	.	.	.	.	.	.	.	.	.	.	.	.	.	.	D	.	.	.	.	.	.	.	.	.	.	.	.	.	.	.	.	.	.	.	.	.	.	.	.	.	.	.	.	.	.	.	.	.	.	.
Care Plus Dental Plans Inc	065736	.	.	.	.	.	.	.	.	.	.	.	.	.	.	.	.	.	.	.	.	.	.	.	.	.	.	.	.	.	.	.	.	.	.	.	.	.	.	.	.	.	.	.	.	.	.	.	.	.	D	.	.	.	.	.	.
CareAmerica Life Ins Co	007351	.	.	L	.	D	.	.	.	.	.	.	.	.	.	.	.	.	.	L	.	.	.	.	.	.	.	.	.	L	.	.	L	.	.	L	.	.	L	.	.	.	.	.	.	.	.	.	.	.	.	.	.	.	.	.	.
CareFirst BlueChoice Inc	068605	.	.	.	.	.	.	.	.	D	.	.	.	.	.	.	.	.	.	.	.	L	.	.	.	.	.	.	.	.	.	.	.	.	.	.	.	.	.	.	.	.	.	.	.	.	.	L	.	.	.	.	.	.	.	.	.
CareFirst of Maryland Inc	064470	.	.	.	.	.	.	.	.	L	.	.	.	.	.	.	.	.	.	.	.	D	.	.	.	.	.	.	.	.	.	.	.	.	.	.	.	.	.	.	.	.	.	.	.	.	.	.	.	.	.	.	.	.	.	.	.
Carelink Health Plans Inc	064186	.	.	.	.	.	.	.	.	.	.	.	.	.	.	.	.	.	.	.	.	.	.	.	.	.	.	.	.	.	.	.	.	.	.	.	L	.	.	.	.	.	.	.	.	.	.	.	.	D	.	.	.	.	.	.	.
CareMore Health Plan	064751	.	.	.	.	D	.	.	.	.	.	.	.	.	.	.	.	.	.	.	.	.	.	.	.	.	.	.	.	.	.	.	.	.	.	.	.	.	.	.	.	.	.	.	.	.	.	.	.	.	.	.	.	.	.	.	.
CarePlus Health Plans Inc	068925	.	.	.	.	.	.	.	.	.	D	.	.	.	.	.	.	.	.	.	.	.	.	.	.	.	.	.	.	.	.	.	.	.	.	.	.	.	.	.	.	.	.	.	.	.	.	.	.	.	.	.	.	.	.	.	.
CareSource	068574	.	.	.	.	.	.	.	.	.	.	.	.	.	.	.	.	.	.	.	.	.	.	.	.	.	.	.	.	.	.	.	.	.	.	.	D	.	.	.	.	.	.	.	.	.	.	.	.	.	.	.	.	.	.	.	.
CareSource Michigan	064042	.	.	.	.	.	.	.	.	.	.	.	.	.	.	.	.	.	.	.	.	.	.	D	.	.	.	.	.	.	.	.	.	.	.	.	.	.	.	.	.	.	.	.	.	.	.	.	.	.	.	.	.	.	.	.	.
Caribbean American Life Assur	068045	.	.	.	.	.	.	.	.	.	.	.	.	.	.	.	.	.	.	.	.	.	.	.	.	.	.	.	.	.	.	.	.	.	.	.	.	.	.	.	.	.	.	.	.	.	.	.	.	.	.	.	.	.	.	D	L
Cariten Health Plan Inc	064425	.	.	.	.	.	.	.	.	.	.	.	.	.	.	.	.	.	.	.	.	.	.	.	.	.	.	.	.	.	.	.	.	.	.	.	.	.	.	.	.	.	.	D	.	.	.	.	.	.	.	.	.	.	.	.	.
Cariten Insurance Company	007835	.	.	.	.	.	.	.	.	.	.	.	.	.	.	.	.	.	.	.	.	.	.	.	.	.	.	.	.	.	.	.	.	.	.	.	.	.	.	.	.	.	.	D	.	.	.	.	.	.	.	.	.	.	.	.	.
Cass County Life Ins Co	060089	.	.	.	.	.	.	.	.	.	.	.	.	.	.	.	.	.	.	.	.	.	.	.	.	.	.	.	.	.	.	.	.	.	.	.	.	.	.	.	.	.	.	.	D	.	.	.	.	.	.	.	.	.	.	.	.
Caterpillar Life Insurance Co	060402	.	L	L	.	L	.	.	L	L	.	L	.	.	L	L	.	L	L	L	.	L	.	L	.	.	D	L	L	L	.	.	L	.	.	L	.	L	L	.	.	L	L	L	L	L	.	.	.	.	.	L	.	.	.	.	.
Catholic Knights	008188	.	.	.	L	L	.	.	.	.	L	.	.	.	L	L	L	.	.	L	.	.	.	L	L	.	L	.	.	.	.	.	L	.	.	L	L	.	.	L	.	.	L	.	L	.	.	.	.	L	D	.	.	.	.	.	.
Catholic Life Insurance	008827	.	.	L	.	.	.	.	.	.	L	.	.	.	.	.	.	.	.	L	.	.	.	.	.	L	.	.	.	.	.	.	L	.	.	.	.	L	.	.	.	.	.	.	D	.	.	.	.	.	.	.	.	.	.	.	.
Catholic Order of Foresters	006191	.	.	L	.	L	L	L	.	L	.	.	.	.	D	L	L	L	L	L	L	L	L	L	L	.	L	L	L	.	L	.	L	.	.	L	L	L	L	L	L	.	L	.	L	.	L	.	L	.	L	.	.	.	.	.	.
CDPHP Universal Benefits Inc	064596	.	.	.	.	.	.	.	.	.	.	.	.	.	.	.	.	.	.	.	.	.	.	.	.	.	.	.	.	.	.	.	.	D	.	.	.	.	.	.	.	.	.	.	.	.	.	.	.	.	.	.	.	.	.	.	.
Celtic Insurance Company	006999	L	L	L	L	L	L	L	L	L	L	L	L	L	D	L	L	L	L	L	L	L	L	L	L	L	L	L	L	L	L	L	L	.	L	L	L	L	L	L	L	L	L	L	L	L	L	L	L	L	L	L	.	.	.	.	.
CeltiCare Health Plan of MA	064978	.	.	.	.	.	.	.	.	.	.	.	.	.	.	.	.	.	.	.	.	.	D	.	.	.	.	.	.	.	.	.	.	.	.	.	.	.	.	.	.	.	.	.	.	.	.	.	.	.	.	.	.	.	.	.	.
Cenpatico Behavioral Hlth TX	064889	.	.	.	.	.	.	.	.	.	.	.	.	.	.	.	.	.	.	.	.	.	.	.	.	.	.	.	.	.	.	.	.	.	.	.	.	.	.	.	.	.	.	.	D	.	.	.	.	.	.	.	.	.	.	.	.
Censtat Life Assurance Company	060246	.	.	D	.	.	.	.	.	.	.	.	.	.	.	.	.	.	.	.	.	.	.	.	.	.	.	.	.	.	.	.	.	.	.	.	.	.	.	.	.	.	.	.	.	.	.	.	.	.	.	.	.	.	.	.	.
Central Health Plan of CA	064929	.	.	.	.	D	.	.	.	.	.	.	.	.	.	.	.	.	.	.	.	.	.	.	.	.	.	.	.	.	.	.	.	.	.	.	.	.	.	.	.	.	.	.	.	.	.	.	.	.	.	.	.	.	.	.	.
Central Reserve Life	006203	L	.	L	L	.	L	.	L	.	.	L	.	.	L	L	L	L	L	L	.	.	L	.	.	L	L	L	L	L	.	.	L	.	L	L	D	L	L	L	.	L	L	L	L	L	.	L	.	L	L	L	.	.	.	.	.
Central Security Life Ins Co	006204	L	L	L	L	.	L	.	L	L	L	L	.	L	L	L	.	L	L	L	.	L	L	L	.	L	L	L	L	L	.	.	L	.	L	L	L	L	L	.	.	L	L	L	D	L	.	L	L	L	.	L	.	.	.	.	.
Central States H&L Co of Omaha	006206	L	L	L	L	L	L	L	L	L	L	L	L	L	L	L	L	L	L	L	L	L	L	L	L	L	L	L	D	L	L	L	L	.	L	L	L	L	L	L	L	L	L	L	L	L	L	L	L	L	L	L	.	L	.	L	.
Central United Life Ins Co	006222	L	.	L	D	L	L	.	.	.	L	L	.	L	L	L	L	L	L	L	L	L	L	.	L	L	L	L	L	L	L	.	L	.	L	L	L	L	L	L	.	L	L	L	L	L	.	L	L	L	L	L	.	.	.	.	.
Centre Life Insurance Company	007367	L	L	L	L	L	L	L	L	L	L	L	L	L	L	L	L	L	L	L	L	L	D	L	L	L	L	L	L	L	L	L	L	L	L	L	L	L	L	L	L	L	L	L	L	L	L	L	L	L	L	L	.	.	.	.	.
Centurion Life Ins Co	006276	L	L	L	L	L	L	L	L	L	L	L	L	L	L	L	D	L	L	L	.	L	L	L	L	L	L	L	L	L	L	L	L	.	L	L	L	L	L	L	L	L	L	L	L	L	.	L	L	L	L	L	.	L	L	.	.
Century Credit Life Ins Co	008865	.	.	.	.	.	.	.	.	.	.	.	.	.	.	.	.	.	.	.	.	.	.	.	.	D	.	.	.	.	.	.	.	.	.	.	.	.	.	.	.	.	.	.	.	.	.	.	.	.	.	.	.	.	.	.	.
Century Life Assur Co	009124	.	.	.	L	.	.	.	.	.	.	.	.	.	.	.	.	L	.	.	.	.	.	.	.	.	L	.	.	.	.	.	L	.	.	.	.	D	.	.	.	.	.	.	L	.	.	.	.	.	.	.	.	.	.	.	.
CHA HMO Inc	064403	.	.	.	.	.	.	.	.	.	.	.	.	.	.	L	.	.	D	.	.	.	.	.	.	.	.	.	.	.	.	.	.	.	.	.	.	.	.	.	.	.	.	.	.	.	.	.	.	.	.	.	.	.	.	.	.

D-State of Domicile **L**-Licensed **S**-Surplus Lines Writer **F**-Authorized under the Risk Retention Act **Q**-Qualified or Accredited Reinsurer

U.S. States/Territories in Which Companies Are Licensed or Do Business – *Continued*

Company Name	AMB#	AL AK AZ AR CA CO CT DE DC FL GA HI ID IL IN IA KS KY LA ME MD MA MI MN MS MO MT NE NV NH NJ NM NY NC ND OH OK OR PA RI SC SD TN TX UT VT VA WA WV WI WY	AS GU MP PR VI
Champions Life Ins Co	007559	. . . . D	. . . . .
Charleston Capital Re LLC	076825	. . . . D . . . . L	. . . . .
Charter National Life Ins Co	006211	L L L L L L L L L L L L L D L L L L L L L L L L L L L L L L L L . L L L L L L L L L L L L L L L L L L	. . . L .
Cherokee National Life Ins Co	006214	L . . L . L . L . L D . . . . . . L L . L . . . L L . . . . L . . L . L . L . L L . . L . L . .	. . . . .
Chesapeake Life Ins Co	006215	L L L L L L L L L L L L L L L L L L L L L L L L L L L L L L . L . L L L D L L L L L L L L . L L L L L	. . . . .
Children's Mercy's Fam H Prtnr	064183	. . . . L . . . . D	. . . . .
Chinese Community Health Plan	064144	. . . . D	. . . . .
Christian Fidelity Life Ins Co	006217	L . L L . L . . . L L . L L L . L L L . . . . . L L L L L . . L . . L L L L . . L L L D L . L L L . L	. . . . .
Church Life Ins Corporation	006221	L L L L L L L L L L L L L L L L S L L L L S S L L L L L L L L L D L L L L S L L L S L L L L L L L L L	. . . . .
CICA Life Ins Co of America	006228	L . L L . D . . L . L L L . L . L L L . . . . L L L L L L . . L . . L . L L L . L L L L L . . L L . L	. . . . .
CIGNA Arbor Life Ins Co	060710	. . . . . . D	. . . . .
CIGNA Behavioral Health of CA	064789	. . . . D	. . . . .
CIGNA Dental Health of CA Inc	060171	. . . . D	. . . . .
CIGNA Dental Health of CO Inc	060196	. . . . . D	. . . . .
CIGNA Dental Health of DE Inc	060172	. . . . D	. . . . .
CIGNA Dental Health of FL Inc	060173	. . . . D	. . . . .
CIGNA Dental Health of KS Inc	060174	. . . . D . . . . L	. . . . .
CIGNA Dental Health of KY Inc	060175	. . . . D	. . . . .
CIGNA Dental Health of MD Inc	060176	. . . . D	. . . . .
CIGNA Dental Health of MO Inc	064702	. . . . D	. . . . .
CIGNA Dental Health of NJ Inc	060184	. . . . D	. . . . .
CIGNA Dental Health of NC Inc	060178	. . . . D	. . . . .
CIGNA Dental Health of OH Inc	060179	. . . . D	. . . . .
CIGNA Dental Health of PA Inc	060180	. . . . D	. . . . .
CIGNA Dental Health of TX Inc	060181	. . . . D	. . . . .
CIGNA Dental Health of VA Inc	064706	. . . . D	. . . . .
CIGNA Dental Health Pln AZ Inc	060170	. . D	. . . . .
CIGNA Health & Life Insurance	006871	L L L L L L D L L L L L L L L L L L L L L L L L L L L L L L L L . L L L L L L L L L L L L L L L L L L	. . . . .
CIGNA Hlthcare-Centennial State	064024	. . . . . D	. . . . .
CIGNA HealthCare Mid-Atl Inc	068871	. . . . L . . . . D . . . . L	. . . . .
CIGNA HealthCare of AZ Inc	068726	. . D	. . . . .
CIGNA HealthCare of CA Inc	068912	. . . . D	. . . . .
CIGNA HealthCare of CO Inc	068864	. . . . . D	. . . . .
CIGNA HealthCare of CT Inc	068865	. . . . . . D	. . . . .
CIGNA HealthCare of DE Inc	068866	. . . . D	. . . . .
CIGNA HealthCare of FL Inc	068860	. . . . D	. . . . .
CIGNA HealthCare of GA Inc	068753	. . . . D	. . . . .
CIGNA HealthCare of IL Inc	068867	. . . . D L	. . . . .
CIGNA HealthCare of IN Inc	068536	. . . . D	. . . . .
CIGNA HealthCare of ME Inc	068549	. . . . D	. . . . .
CIGNA HealthCare of MA Inc	060201	. . . . D	. . . . .
CIGNA HealthCare of NH Inc	068675	. . . . D	. . . . .
CIGNA HealthCare of NJ Inc	068862	. . . . D	. . . . .
CIGNA HealthCare of NY Inc	068872	. . . . D . L	. . . . .
CIGNA HealthCare of NC Inc	068570	. . . . D	. . . . .
CIGNA HealthCare of OH Inc	068788	. . . . L . . . . L . . . . D	. . . . .
CIGNA HealthCare of PA Inc	068876	. . . . D	. . . . .
CIGNA HealthCare of St Lou Inc	068877	. . . . L . . . . D	. . . . .
CIGNA HealthCare of SC Inc	068594	. . . . D	. . . . .
CIGNA HealthCare of TN Inc	068878	. . . . L . . . . D	. . . . .
CIGNA HealthCare of TX Inc	068828	. . . . D	. . . . .
CIGNA HealthCare of UT Inc	068881	. . . . D	. . . . .
CIGNA Healthcare - Pacific Inc	064023	. . . . D	. . . . .
CIGNA Insurance Group Inc	068124	. . . . D	. . . . .
CIGNA Life Ins Co of New York	006538	L . . . . L . . . . L . . . . . . D . . . . . L . . . L	. . . . .
CIGNA Worldwide Insurance Co	008944	. . . . D	. . . . .
Cincinnati Equitable Life	006757	. . . . L . . . L . . L . . . . D	. . . . .
Cincinnati Life Insurance Co	006568	L L L L L L L L L L L L L L L L L L L L L L L L L L L L L L L L . L L D L L L L L L L L L L L L L L L	. . . . .
Citizens Accident and Health	008642	. . D	. . . . .
Citizens Fidelity Ins Co	068321	. . . D	. . . . .
Citizens National Life Ins Co	008947	L . L L . . . . . L . . . . L . . . . . L L . . . . . L . . . . L . . . . . . D . . L	. . . . .
Citizens Security Life Ins Co	006227	L . . L . . . L L L L . . . L . . D L . L . . . L L . . . . L . . L . L . . L . L . L L . . L . L . .	. . . . .
Clarian Health Plans Inc	064984	. . . . D	. . . . .
Colonial American Life Ins Co	007578	. . . . L . . . . L . . . . . L . . . . D . L . . L	. . . . .
Colonial Life & Accident Ins	006238	L L L L L L L L L L L L L L L L L L L L L L L L L L L L L L L L . L L L L L L L D L L L L L L L L L L	. . . L .
Colonial Life Ins Co of Texas	008864	. . L . . . . L . . . . D . . L	. . . . .
Colonial Penn Life Insurance	006240	L L L L L L L L L L L L L L L L L L L L L L L L L L L L L L L L Q L L L L L D L L L L L L L L L L L L	. . . L L
Colonial Security Life Ins Co	007604	. . . . D	. . . . .
Colorado Access	064310	. . . . . D	. . . . .
Colorado Bankers Life Ins Co	008502	L L L L L D L L L L L L L L L L L L L L L L L L L L L L L L L L . L L L L L L L L L L L L . L L L L L	. L . . .
Colorado Choice Health Plans	068945	. . . . . D	. . . . .
Colorado Dental Service Inc	064558	. . . . . D	. . . . .
Columbia Capital Life Reins Co	060579	. . . . D . . . . Q Q Q . . . . L	. . . . .
Columbia United Providers Inc	064106	. . . . D . . .	. . . . .
Columbian Life Insurance Co	068009	. . L L L L L L L L L L L D L L L L L . L L L L L L L L L L L L . L . L L L L L L L L L L . L L L L L	L . . . .
Columbian Mutual Life Ins Co	006243	L L L L L L L L L L L L L L L L L L L L L L L L L L L L L L L L D L L L L L L L L L L L L L L L L L L	. . . L L

D-State of Domicile **L**-Licensed **S**-Surplus Lines Writer **F**-Authorized under the Risk Retention Act **Q**-Qualified or Accredited Reinsurer

Company Name	AMB#	AL	AK	AZ	AR	CA	CO	CT	DE	DC	FL	GA	HI	ID	IL	IN	IA	KS	KY	LA	ME	MD	MA	MI	MN	MS	MO	MT	NE	NV	NH	NJ	NM	NY	NC	ND	OH	OK	OR	PA	RI	SC	SD	TN	TX	UT	VT	VA	WA	WV	WI	WY	AS	GU	MP	PR	VI
Columbus Life Insurance Co	006244	L	L	L	L	L	L	L	L	L	L	L	L	L	L	L	L	L	L	L	L	L	L	L	L	L	L	L	L	L	L	L	L	.	L	L	D	L	L	L	L	L	L	L	L	L	L	L	L	L	L	L	.	.	.	.	.
Combined Ins Co of America	006246	L	L	L	L	L	L	L	L	L	L	L	L	L	D	L	L	L	L	L	L	L	L	L	L	L	L	L	L	L	L	L	L	.	L	L	L	L	L	L	L	L	L	L	L	L	L	L	L	L	L	L	.	.	L	L	L
Combined Life Ins Co of NY	008187	.	.	.	.	.	.	.	.	.	L	.	.	.	L	.	.	.	.	.	.	.	.	.	.	.	.	.	.	.	.	.	.	D	.	.	.	.	.	.	.	.	.	.	.	.	.	.	.	.	.	.	.	.	.	.	.
Commencement Bay Life Ins Co	068406	.	.	.	.	.	.	.	.	.	.	.	.	.	.	.	.	.	.	.	.	.	.	.	.	.	.	.	.	.	.	.	.	.	.	.	.	.	.	.	.	.	.	.	.	.	.	.	D	.	.	.	.	.	.	.	.
Commercial Travelers Mutual	007361	L	L	L	L	L	L	L	L	L	L	L	.	L	L	L	L	L	L	L	L	L	L	L	L	L	L	L	L	L	L	L	L	D	L	L	L	L	L	L	L	L	L	L	L	L	L	L	L	L	L	L	.	.	.	.	.
Commonwealth Annuity and Life	008491	L	L	L	L	L	L	L	L	L	L	L	L	L	L	L	L	L	L	L	L	L	D	L	L	L	L	L	L	L	L	L	L	.	L	L	L	L	L	L	L	L	L	L	L	L	L	L	L	L	L	L	.	.	.	.	L
Commonwealth Dealers Life Ins	068105	.	.	.	.	.	.	.	L	.	L	L	.	.	.	L	.	.	L	.	.	L	.	.	.	.	.	.	.	.	.	.	.	.	L	.	L	.	.	L	.	L	.	L	.	.	.	D	.	.	.	.	.	.	.	.	.
Community Care Behavioral Hlth	064549	.	.	.	.	.	.	.	.	.	.	.	.	.	.	.	.	.	.	.	.	.	.	.	.	.	.	.	.	.	.	.	.	.	.	.	.	.	.	D	.	.	.	.	.	.	.	.	.	.	.	.	.	.	.	.	.
Community Care Health Plan Inc	064919	.	.	.	.	.	.	.	.	.	.	.	.	.	.	.	.	.	.	.	.	.	.	.	.	.	.	.	.	.	.	.	.	.	.	.	.	.	.	.	.	.	.	.	.	.	.	.	.	.	D	.	.	.	.	.	.
Community Dental Associates	064771	.	.	.	.	.	.	.	.	.	.	.	.	.	.	.	.	.	.	.	.	.	.	.	.	.	.	.	.	.	.	D	.	.	.	.	.	.	.	.	.	.	.	.	.	.	.	.	.	.	.	.	.	.	.	.	.
Community First Grp Hosp Svc	064787	.	.	.	.	.	.	.	.	.	.	.	.	.	.	.	.	.	.	.	.	.	.	.	.	.	.	.	.	.	.	.	.	.	.	.	.	.	.	.	.	.	.	.	D	.	.	.	.	.	.	.	.	.	.	.	.
Community First Health Plans	064049	.	.	.	.	.	.	.	.	.	.	.	.	.	.	.	.	.	.	.	.	.	.	.	.	.	.	.	.	.	.	.	.	.	.	.	.	.	.	.	.	.	.	.	D	.	.	.	.	.	.	.	.	.	.	.	.
Community Health Choice Inc	064454	.	.	.	.	.	.	.	.	.	.	.	.	.	.	.	.	.	.	.	.	.	.	.	.	.	.	.	.	.	.	.	.	.	.	.	.	.	.	.	.	.	.	.	D	.	.	.	.	.	.	.	.	.	.	.	.
Community Health Group	064145	.	.	.	.	D	.	.	.	.	.	.	.	.	.	.	.	.	.	.	.	.	.	.	.	.	.	.	.	.	.	.	.	.	.	.	.	.	.	.	.	.	.	.	.	.	.	.	.	.	.	.	.	.	.	.	.
Community Health Plan	064182	.	.	.	.	.	.	.	.	.	.	.	.	.	.	.	.	L	.	.	.	.	.	.	.	.	D	.	.	.	.	.	.	.	.	.	.	.	.	.	.	.	.	.	.	.	.	.	.	.	.	.	.	.	.	.	.
Community Health Plan Ins Co	009101	.	.	.	.	.	.	.	.	.	.	.	.	.	.	.	.	.	.	.	.	.	.	.	.	.	D	.	.	.	.	.	.	.	.	.	.	.	.	.	.	.	.	.	.	.	.	.	.	.	.	.	.	.	.	.	.
Community Health Plan of WA	064472	.	.	.	.	.	.	.	.	.	.	.	.	.	.	.	.	.	.	.	.	.	.	.	.	.	.	.	.	.	.	.	.	.	.	.	.	.	.	.	.	.	.	.	.	.	.	.	D	.	.	.	.	.	.	.	.
Community Insurance Company	011803	.	.	.	.	.	.	.	.	.	.	.	.	.	.	L	.	.	.	.	.	.	.	.	.	.	.	.	.	.	.	.	.	.	.	.	D	.	.	.	.	.	.	.	.	.	.	.	.	.	.	.	.	.	.	.	.
CommunityCare HMO Inc	064165	.	.	.	.	.	.	.	.	.	.	.	.	.	.	.	.	.	.	.	.	.	.	.	.	.	.	.	.	.	.	.	.	.	.	.	.	D	.	.	.	.	.	.	.	.	.	.	.	.	.	.	.	.	.	.	.
Companion Life Ins Company	006258	.	.	.	.	.	.	L	.	.	.	.	.	.	.	.	.	.	.	.	.	.	.	.	.	.	.	.	.	.	.	L	.	D	.	.	.	.	.	.	.	.	.	.	.	.	.	.	.	.	.	.	.	.	.	.	.
Companion Life Insurance Co	008064	L	L	L	L	.	L	L	L	L	L	L	.	L	L	L	L	L	L	L	L	L	L	L	L	L	L	L	L	L	L	.	L	.	L	L	L	L	L	L	L	D	L	L	L	L	L	L	L	L	L	L	.	.	.	.	.
CompBenefits Company	064760	.	.	.	.	.	.	.	.	.	D	.	.	.	.	.	.	.	.	.	.	.	.	.	.	.	.	.	.	.	.	.	.	.	.	.	.	.	.	.	.	.	.	.	.	.	.	.	.	.	.	.	.	.	.	.	.
CompBenefits Dental Inc	064759	.	.	.	.	.	.	.	.	.	.	.	.	.	D	.	.	.	L	.	.	L	.	.	.	.	L	.	.	.	.	.	.	.	.	.	.	.	.	.	.	.	.	.	.	.	.	.	.	L	.	.	.	.	.	.	.
CompBenefits Insurance Co	006118	L	.	L	L	.	L	.	.	L	L	L	.	L	L	L	L	L	L	L	.	L	.	.	.	L	L	.	L	L	.	.	L	.	L	L	L	L	L	.	.	L	.	L	D	L	.	L	L	L	.	.	.	.	.	.	.
Compcare Health Services Ins	068610	.	.	.	.	.	.	.	.	.	.	.	.	.	.	.	.	.	.	.	.	.	.	.	.	.	.	.	.	.	.	.	.	.	.	.	.	.	.	.	.	.	.	.	.	.	.	.	.	.	D	.	.	.	.	.	.
CONCERN: Employee Assist Prog	064737	.	.	.	.	D	.	.	.	.	.	.	.	.	.	.	.	.	.	.	.	.	.	.	.	.	.	.	.	.	.	.	.	.	.	.	.	.	.	.	.	.	.	.	.	.	.	.	.	.	.	.	.	.	.	.	.
Concert Health Plan Ins Co	060374	.	.	.	.	.	.	.	.	.	.	.	.	.	D	L	.	.	.	.	.	.	.	.	.	.	.	.	.	.	.	.	.	.	.	.	.	.	.	.	.	.	.	.	.	.	.	.	.	.	.	.	.	.	.	.	.
Congress Life Ins Co	007600	L	L	D	L	L	L	.	L	L	L	.	L	L	L	L	L	L	L	L	.	L	.	L	L	L	L	L	L	L	.	.	L	.	.	L	L	L	L	L	L	L	L	L	L	L	L	L	L	L	L	L	.	.	.	.	.
ConnectiCare Inc	068517	.	.	.	.	.	.	D	.	.	.	.	.	.	.	.	.	.	.	.	.	.	.	.	.	.	.	.	.	.	.	.	.	.	.	.	.	.	.	.	.	.	.	.	.	.	.	.	.	.	.	.	.	.	.	.	.
ConnectiCare Insurance Co Inc	064784	.	.	.	.	.	.	D	.	.	.	.	.	.	.	.	.	.	.	.	.	.	.	.	.	.	.	.	.	.	.	.	.	.	.	.	.	.	.	.	.	.	.	.	.	.	.	.	.	.	.	.	.	.	.	.	.
ConnectiCare of Massachusetts	064464	.	.	.	.	.	.	.	.	.	.	.	.	.	.	.	.	.	.	.	.	.	D	.	.	.	.	.	.	.	.	.	.	.	.	.	.	.	.	.	.	.	.	.	.	.	.	.	.	.	.	.	.	.	.	.	.
ConnectiCare of New York Inc	064450	.	.	.	.	.	.	.	.	.	.	.	.	.	.	.	.	.	.	.	.	.	.	.	.	.	.	.	.	.	.	.	.	D	.	.	.	.	.	.	.	.	.	.	.	.	.	.	.	.	.	.	.	.	.	.	.
Connecticut General Life Ins	006266	L	L	L	L	L	L	D	L	L	L	L	L	L	L	L	L	L	L	L	L	L	L	L	L	L	L	L	L	L	L	L	L	L	L	L	L	L	L	L	L	L	L	L	L	L	L	L	L	L	L	L	Q	Q	Q	L	L
Connecticut Life Ins & Annuity	068095	.	.	D	.	.	.	.	.	.	.	.	.	.	.	.	.	.	.	.	.	.	.	.	.	.	.	.	.	.	.	.	.	.	.	.	.	.	.	.	.	.	.	.	.	.	.	.	.	.	.	.	.	.	.	.	.
Conseco Health Ins Co	008101	L	L	D	L	L	L	.	L	L	L	L	L	L	L	L	L	L	L	L	L	L	.	L	L	L	L	L	L	L	L	L	L	.	L	L	L	L	L	L	L	L	L	L	L	L	L	L	L	L	L	L	.	.	.	L	L
Conseco Insurance Company	006080	L	L	L	L	L	L	L	L	L	L	L	L	L	D	L	L	L	L	L	L	L	L	L	L	L	L	L	L	L	L	L	L	.	L	L	L	L	L	L	L	L	L	L	L	L	L	L	L	L	L	L	.	L	.	L	L
Conseco Life Insurance Company	006692	L	L	L	L	L	L	L	L	L	L	L	L	L	L	D	L	L	L	L	L	L	L	L	L	L	L	L	L	L	L	L	L	.	L	L	L	L	L	L	L	L	L	L	L	L	L	L	L	L	L	L	.	L	.	L	L
Conseco Life Ins Co of Texas	068083	.	.	.	.	.	.	.	.	.	.	.	.	.	.	.	.	.	.	.	.	.	.	.	.	.	.	.	.	.	.	.	.	.	.	.	.	.	.	.	.	.	.	.	D	.	.	.	.	.	.	.	.	.	.	.	.
Constitution Life Ins Co	006273	L	L	L	L	L	L	L	L	L	L	L	L	L	L	L	L	L	L	L	L	L	L	L	L	L	L	L	L	L	L	.	L	.	L	L	L	L	L	L	L	L	L	L	D	L	L	L	L	L	L	L	.	.	.	.	.
ConsumerHealth Inc	060166	.	.	.	.	D	.	.	.	.	.	.	.	.	.	.	.	.	.	.	.	.	.	.	.	.	.	.	.	.	.	.	.	.	.	.	.	.	.	.	.	.	.	.	.	.	.	.	.	.	.	.	.	.	.	.	.
Consumers Life Ins Co	006275	.	.	L	L	.	L	.	L	L	L	L	.	.	L	L	L	L	L	L	.	L	.	L	L	L	L	L	L	L	.	L	L	.	.	L	D	L	L	L	.	L	L	.	L	L	.	L	.	L	L	L	.	.	.	.	.
Continental American Ins Co	007411	L	L	L	L	L	L	L	L	L	L	L	L	L	L	L	L	L	L	L	L	L	L	L	L	L	L	L	L	L	L	L	L	.	L	L	L	L	L	L	L	D	L	L	L	L	L	L	L	L	L	L	.	.	.	.	.
Continental Assurance Co	006280	L	L	L	L	L	L	L	L	L	L	L	L	L	D	L	L	L	L	L	L	L	L	L	L	L	L	L	L	L	L	L	L	L	L	L	L	L	L	L	L	L	L	L	L	L	L	L	L	L	L	L	.	.	.	L	L
Continental General Ins Co	007360	L	L	L	L	L	L	L	L	L	L	L	L	L	L	L	L	L	L	L	L	L	L	L	L	L	L	L	L	L	L	L	L	.	L	L	D	L	L	L	L	L	L	L	L	L	L	L	L	L	L	L	.	.	.	.	L
Continental Life Ins Co PA	007603	.	.	.	.	.	.	.	L	.	.	.	.	.	.	.	.	.	.	.	.	.	.	.	.	.	.	.	.	.	.	.	.	.	.	.	.	.	.	D	.	.	.	.	.	.	.	.	.	.	.	.	.	.	.	.	.
Continental Life Brentwood TN	009502	L	.	L	L	.	L	.	L	.	L	L	.	L	L	L	L	L	L	L	.	L	.	L	L	L	L	L	L	L	.	.	L	.	L	L	L	L	.	L	L	L	L	D	L	L	.	L	.	L	L	L	.	.	.	.	.
Continental Life Ins Co SC	006286	.	.	.	.	.	.	.	.	.	.	.	.	.	.	.	.	.	.	.	.	.	.	.	.	.	.	.	.	.	.	.	.	.	.	.	.	.	.	.	.	D	.	.	.	.	.	.	.	.	.	.	.	.	.	.	.
Contra Costa Health Plan	064085	.	.	.	.	D	.	.	.	.	.	.	.	.	.	.	.	.	.	.	.	.	.	.	.	.	.	.	.	.	.	.	.	.	.	.	.	.	.	.	.	.	.	.	.	.	.	.	.	.	.	.	.	.	.	.	.
Cook Children's Health Plan	064508	.	.	.	.	.	.	.	.	.	.	.	.	.	.	.	.	.	.	.	.	.	.	.	.	.	.	.	.	.	.	.	.	.	.	.	.	.	.	.	.	.	.	.	D	.	.	.	.	.	.	.	.	.	.	.	.
Cooperativa de Seguros de Vida	007607	.	.	.	.	.	.	.	.	.	.	.	.	.	.	.	.	.	.	.	.	.	.	.	.	.	.	.	.	.	.	.	.	.	.	.	.	.	.	.	.	.	.	.	.	.	.	.	.	.	.	.	.	.	.	D	.
Cooperative Life Ins Co	068326	.	.	.	D	.	.	.	.	.	.	.	.	.	.	.	.	.	.	.	.	.	.	.	.	.	.	.	.	.	.	.	.	.	.	.	.	.	.	.	.	.	.	.	.	.	.	.	.	.	.	.	.	.	.	.	.
Coordinated Care Corp Indiana	064266	.	.	.	.	.	.	.	.	.	.	.	.	.	.	D	.	.	.	.	.	.	.	.	.	.	.	.	.	.	.	.	.	.	.	.	.	.	.	.	.	.	.	.	.	.	.	.	.	.	.	.	.	.	.	.	.
Cornhusker Life Insurance Co	068186	.	.	.	.	.	.	.	.	.	.	.	.	.	.	.	.	.	.	.	.	.	.	.	.	.	.	.	D	.	.	.	.	.	.	.	.	.	.	.	.	.	.	.	.	.	.	.	.	.	.	.	.	.	.	.	.
Cosmopolitan Life Ins Co	008755	.	.	.	D	.	.	.	.	.	.	.	.	.	.	.	.	.	.	.	.	.	.	.	.	.	.	.	.	.	.	.	.	.	.	.	.	.	.	.	.	.	.	.	.	.	.	.	.	.	.	.	.	.	.	.	.
Cotton States Life Ins Co	006292	L	.	.	.	.	.	.	.	.	L	D	.	.	.	.	.	.	L	L	.	.	.	.	.	L	.	.	.	.	.	.	.	.	L	.	.	.	.	.	.	L	.	L	.	.	.	L	.	.	.	.	.	.	.	.	.
COUNTRY Investors Life Assur	009084	L	L	L	L	.	L	L	L	.	L	L	.	L	D	L	L	L	L	L	L	L	L	L	L	L	L	L	L	L	.	.	L	.	L	L	L	L	L	L	L	L	L	L	L	.	.	L	L	L	L	L	.	.	.	.	.
COUNTRY Life Ins Co	006294	L	L	L	L	.	L	L	L	.	L	L	.	L	D	L	L	L	L	L	L	L	L	L	L	L	L	L	L	L	.	.	L	.	L	L	L	L	L	L	L	L	L	L	L	L	.	L	L	L	L	L	.	.	.	.	.
County of Los Angeles	068680	.	.	.	.	D	.	.	.	.	.	.	.	.	.	.	.	.	.	.	.	.	.	.	.	.	.	.	.	.	.	.	.	.	.	.	.	.	.	.	.	.	.	.	.	.	.	.	.	.	.	.	.	.	.	.	.
County of Ventura	064574	.	.	.	.	D	.	.	.	.	.	.	.	.	.	.	.	.	.	.	.	.	.	.	.	.	.	.	.	.	.	.	.	.	.	.	.	.	.	.	.	.	.	.	.	.	.	.	.	.	.	.	.	.	.	.	.
Coventry Hlth and Life Ins Co	008812	L	L	L	L	.	L	.	D	L	L	L	.	.	L	L	L	L	L	L	L	L	L	L	.	L	L	.	L	L	.	.	.	.	.	.	L	L	.	L	.	L	L	L	L	L	.	L	L	L	L	L	.	.	.	.	.
Coventry Health Care of DE	068687	.	.	.	.	.	.	.	D	.	.	.	.	.	.	.	.	.	.	.	.	L	.	.	.	.	.	.	.	.	.	.	.	.	.	.	.	.	.	.	.	.	.	.	.	.	.	.	.	.	.	.	.	.	.	.	.
Coventry Health Care of GA Inc	068980	.	.	.	.	.	.	.	.	.	.	D	.	.	.	.	.	.	.	.	.	.	.	.	.	.	.	.	.	.	.	.	.	.	.	.	.	.	.	.	.	.	.	.	.	.	.	.	.	.	.	.	.	.	.	.	.
Coventry Health Care of Iowa	068541	.	.	.	.	.	.	.	.	.	.	.	.	.	.	.	D	.	.	.	.	.	.	.	.	.	.	.	.	.	.	.	.	.	.	.	.	.	.	.	.	.	.	.	.	.	.	.	.	.	.	.	.	.	.	.	.
Coventry Health Care of Kansas	064126	.	.	.	.	.	.	.	.	.	.	.	.	.	.	.	.	D	.	.	.	.	.	.	.	.	L	.	.	.	.	.	.	.	.	.	.	.	.	.	.	.	.	.	.	.	.	.	.	.	.	.	.	.	.	.	.
Coventry Health Care of LA	068689	.	.	.	.	.	.	.	.	.	.	.	.	.	.	.	.	.	.	D	.	.	.	.	.	.	.	.	.	.	.	.	.	.	.	.	.	.	.	.	.	.	.	.	.	.	.	.	.	.	.	.	.	.	.	.	.
Coventry Health Care of NE	068544	.	.	.	.	.	.	.	.	.	.	.	.	.	.	.	L	.	.	.	.	.	.	.	.	.	.	.	D	.	.	.	.	.	.	.	.	.	.	.	.	.	.	.	.	.	.	.	.	.	.	.	.	.	.	.	.
Coventry Health Care of PA Inc	064429	.	.	.	.	.	.	.	.	.	.	.	.	.	.	.	.	.	.	.	.	.	.	.	.	.	.	.	.	.	.	.	.	.	.	.	.	.	.	D	.	.	.	.	.	.	.	.	.	.	.	.	.	.	.	.	.
Cox Health Systems HMO	064421	.	.	.	.	.	.	.	.	.	.	.	.	.	.	.	.	.	.	.	.	.	.	.	.	.	D	.	.	.	.	.	.	.	.	.	.	.	.	.	.	.	.	.	.	.	.	.	.	.	.	.	.	.	.	.	.
CSI Life Insurance Company	008488	L	L	L	L	L	L	L	L	L	L	L	L	L	L	L	L	L	L	L	L	L	L	L	L	L	L	L	D	L	.	L	L	.	L	L	L	L	L	L	L	L	L	L	L	L	L	L	L	L	L	L	.	.	.	.	.
CUNA Mutual Ins Society	006302	L	L	L	L	L	L	L	L	L	L	L	L	L	L	L	D	L	L	L	L	L	L	L	L	L	L	L	L	L	L	L	L	L	L	L	L	L	L	L	L	L	L	L	L	L	L	L	L	L	L	L	.	.	.	L	L
Dallas General Life Ins Co	009442	.	.	.	.	.	.	.	.	.	.	.	.	.	.	.	.	.	.	.	.	.	.	.	.	.	.	.	.	.	.	.	.	.	.	.	.	.	.	.	.	.	.	.	D	.	.	.	.	.	.	.	.	.	.	.	.
DaVita VillageHealth Ins of AL	064941	D	.	.	.	.	.	.	.	.	.	.	.	.	.	.	.	.	.	.	.	.	.	.	.	.	.	.	.	.	.	.	.	.	.	.	.	.	.	.	.	.	.	.	.	.	.	.	.	.	.	.	.	.	.	.	.
DaVita VillageHealth of GA Inc	064938	.	.	.	.	.	.	.	.	.	.	D	.	.	.	.	.	.	.	.	.	.	.	.	.	.	.	.	.	.	.	.	.	.	.	.	.	.	.	.	.	.	.	.	.	.	.	.	.	.	.	.	.	.	.	.	.
DaVita VillageHealth of OH Inc	064939	.	.	.	.	.	.	.	.	.	.	.	.	.	.	.	.	.	.	.	.	.	.	.	.	.	.	.	.	.	.	.	.	.	.	.	D	.	.	.	.	.	.	.	.	.	.	.	.	.	.	.	.	.	.	.	.
DaVita VillageHealth of VA Inc	064940	.	.	.	.	.	.	.	.	L	.	.	.	.	.	.	.	.	.	.	.	.	.	.	.	.	.	.	.	.	.	.	.	.	.	.	.	.	.	.	.	.	.	.	.	.	.	D	.	.	.	.	.	.	.	.	.
DC Chartered Health Plan Inc	064625	.	.	.	.	.	.	.	.	D	.	.	.	.	.	.	.	.	.	.	.	.	.	.	.	.	.	.	.	.	.	.	.	.	.	.	.	.	.	.	.	.	.	.	.	.	.	.	.	.	.	.	.	.	.	.	.

D-State of Domicile **L**-Licensed **S**-Surplus Lines Writer **F**-Authorized under the Risk Retention Act **Q**-Qualified or Accredited Reinsurer

U.S. States/Territories in Which Companies Are Licensed or Do Business – *Continued*

Company Name	AMB#	AL	AK	AZ	AR	CA	CO	CT	DE	DC	FL	GA	HI	ID	IL	IN	IA	KS	KY	LA	ME	MD	MA	MI	MN	MS	MO	MT	NE	NV	NH	NJ	NM	NY	NC	ND	OH	OK	OR	PA	RI	SC	SD	TN	TX	UT	VT	VA	WA	WV	WI	WY	AS	GU	MP	PR	VI
Dean Health Insurance Inc	060218	.	.	.	.	.	.	.	.	.	.	.	.	.	.	.	.	.	.	.	.	.	.	.	.	.	.	.	.	.	.	.	.	.	.	.	.	.	.	.	.	.	.	.	.	.	.	.	.	.	D	.	.	.	.	.	.
Dean Health Plan Inc	064203	.	.	.	.	.	.	.	.	.	.	.	.	.	.	.	.	.	.	.	.	.	.	.	.	.	.	.	.	.	.	.	.	.	.	.	.	.	.	.	.	.	.	.	.	.	.	.	.	.	D	.	.	.	.	.	.
Dedicated Dental Systems Inc	064720	.	.	.	.	D	.	.	.	.	.	.	.	.	.	.	.	.	.	.	.	.	.	.	.	.	.	.	.	.	.	.	.	.	.	.	.	.	.	.	.	.	.	.	.	.	.	.	.	.	.	.	.	.	.	.	.
Delaware American Life Ins Co	006305	L	L	L	L	L	L	L	D	L	L	L	L	L	L	L	L	L	L	L	L	L	L	L	.	L	.	L	L	L	.	L	L	.	.	L	L	L	L	L	L	L	L	L	L	L	L	L	L	L	L	L	.	L	.	L	.
Delta Dental Insurance Co	009147	L	L	L	.	L	.	L	D	L	L	L	L	.	L	L	.	L	L	L	L	L	.	.	.	L	L	L	L	L	.	.	L	L	.	.	.	.	L	L	.	L	.	L	L	L	.	.	.	L	.	.	.	.	.	L	L
Delta Dental of CA	068800	.	.	.	.	D	.	.	.	.	.	.	.	.	.	.	.	.	.	.	.	.	.	.	.	.	.	.	.	.	.	.	.	.	.	.	.	.	.	.	.	.	.	.	.	.	.	.	.	.	.	.	.	.	.	.	.
Delta Dental of Delaware	064642	.	.	.	.	.	.	.	D	.	.	.	.	.	.	.	.	.	.	.	.	.	.	.	.	.	.	.	.	.	.	.	.	.	.	.	.	.	.	.	.	.	.	.	.	.	.	.	.	.	.	.	.	.	.	.	.
Delta Dental of Iowa	060205	.	.	.	.	.	.	.	.	.	.	.	.	.	.	.	D	.	.	.	.	.	.	.	.	.	.	.	.	.	.	.	.	.	.	.	.	.	.	.	.	.	.	.	.	.	.	.	.	.	.	.	.	.	.	.	.
Delta Dental of Kentucky Inc	064485	.	.	.	.	.	.	.	.	.	.	.	.	.	.	.	.	.	D	.	.	.	.	.	.	.	.	.	.	.	.	.	.	.	.	.	.	.	.	.	.	.	.	.	.	.	.	.	.	.	.	.	.	.	.	.	.
Delta Dental of MN	064440	.	.	.	.	.	.	.	.	.	.	.	.	.	.	.	.	.	.	.	.	.	.	.	D	.	.	.	.	.	.	.	.	.	.	.	.	.	.	.	.	.	.	.	.	.	.	.	.	.	.	.	.	.	.	.	.
Delta Dental of Missouri	065732	.	.	.	.	.	.	.	.	.	.	.	.	.	.	.	.	.	.	.	.	.	.	.	.	.	D	.	.	.	.	.	.	.	.	.	.	.	.	.	.	L	.	.	.	.	.	.	.	.	.	.	.	.	.	.	.
Delta Dental of Nebraska	064448	.	.	.	.	.	.	.	.	.	.	.	.	.	.	.	F	.	.	.	.	.	.	.	.	.	.	.	D	.	.	.	.	.	.	.	.	.	.	.	.	.	.	.	.	.	.	.	.	.	.	.	.	.	.	.	.
Delta Dental of New Jersey Inc	060194	.	.	.	.	.	.	.	.	.	.	.	.	.	.	.	.	.	.	.	.	.	.	.	.	.	.	.	.	.	.	D	.	.	.	.	.	.	.	.	.	.	.	.	.	.	.	.	.	.	.	.	.	.	.	.	.
Delta Dental of New York	064594	.	.	.	.	.	.	.	.	.	.	.	.	.	.	.	.	.	.	.	.	.	.	.	.	.	.	.	.	.	.	.	.	D	.	.	.	.	.	.	.	.	.	.	.	.	.	.	.	.	.	.	.	.	.	.	.
Delta Dental of Pennsylvania	064557	.	.	.	.	.	.	.	.	.	.	.	.	.	.	.	.	.	.	.	.	L	.	.	.	.	.	.	.	.	.	.	.	.	.	.	.	.	.	D	.	.	.	.	.	.	.	.	.	.	.	.	.	.	.	.	.
Delta Dental of Rhode Island	064571	.	.	.	.	.	.	.	.	.	.	.	.	.	.	.	.	.	.	.	.	.	.	.	.	.	.	.	.	.	.	.	.	.	.	.	.	.	.	.	D	.	.	.	.	.	.	.	.	.	.	.	.	.	.	.	.
Delta Dental of Tennessee	064670	.	.	.	.	.	.	.	.	.	.	.	.	.	.	.	.	.	.	.	.	.	.	.	.	.	.	.	.	.	.	.	.	.	.	.	.	.	.	.	.	.	.	D	.	.	.	.	.	.	.	.	.	.	.	.	.
Delta Dental of Virginia	064565	.	.	.	.	.	.	.	.	.	.	.	.	.	.	.	.	.	.	.	.	.	.	.	.	.	.	.	.	.	.	.	.	.	.	.	.	.	.	.	.	.	.	.	.	.	.	D	.	.	.	.	.	.	.	.	.
Delta Dental of West Virginia	064643	.	.	.	.	.	.	.	.	.	.	.	.	.	.	.	.	.	.	.	.	.	.	.	.	.	.	.	.	.	.	.	.	.	.	.	.	.	.	.	.	.	.	.	.	.	.	.	.	D	.	.	.	.	.	.	.
Delta Dental of Wisconsin Inc	064409	.	.	.	.	.	.	.	.	.	.	.	.	.	.	.	.	.	.	.	.	.	.	.	.	.	.	.	.	.	.	.	.	.	.	.	.	.	.	.	.	.	.	.	.	.	.	.	.	.	D	.	.	.	.	.	.
Delta Dental Plan of Arkansas	064699	.	.	.	D	.	.	.	.	.	.	.	.	.	.	.	.	.	.	.	.	.	.	.	.	.	.	.	.	.	.	.	.	.	.	.	.	.	.	.	.	.	.	.	.	.	.	.	.	.	.	.	.	.	.	.	.
Delta Dental Plan of Idaho Inc	064525	.	.	.	.	.	.	.	.	.	.	.	.	D	.	.	.	.	.	.	.	.	.	.	.	.	.	.	.	.	.	.	.	.	.	.	.	.	.	.	.	.	.	.	.	.	.	.	.	.	.	.	.	.	.	.	.
Delta Dental Plan of Indiana	064694	.	.	.	.	.	.	.	.	.	.	.	.	.	.	D	.	.	.	.	.	.	.	.	.	.	.	.	.	.	.	.	.	.	.	.	.	.	.	.	.	.	.	.	.	.	.	.	.	.	.	.	.	.	.	.	.
Delta Dental Plan of KS	064538	.	.	.	.	.	.	.	.	.	.	.	.	.	.	.	.	D	.	.	.	.	.	.	.	.	F	.	.	.	.	.	.	.	.	.	.	.	.	.	.	.	.	.	.	.	.	.	.	.	.	.	.	.	.	.	.
Delta Dental Plan of Michigan	068575	.	.	.	.	.	.	.	.	.	.	.	.	.	.	.	.	.	.	.	.	.	.	D	.	.	.	.	.	.	.	.	.	.	.	.	.	.	.	.	.	.	.	.	.	.	.	.	.	.	.	.	.	.	.	.	.
Delta Dental Plan of NH	064524	.	.	.	.	.	.	.	.	.	.	.	.	.	.	.	.	.	.	.	.	.	.	.	.	.	.	.	.	.	D	.	.	.	.	.	.	.	.	.	.	.	.	.	.	.	.	.	.	.	.	.	.	.	.	.	.
Delta Dental Plan of NM	064537	.	.	.	.	.	.	.	.	.	.	.	.	.	.	.	.	.	.	.	.	.	.	.	.	.	.	.	.	.	.	.	D	.	.	.	.	.	.	.	.	.	.	.	.	.	.	.	.	.	.	.	.	.	.	.	.
Delta Dental Plan of NC Inc	064526	.	.	.	.	.	.	.	.	.	.	.	.	.	.	.	.	.	.	.	.	.	.	.	.	.	.	.	.	.	.	.	.	.	D	.	.	.	.	.	.	.	.	.	.	.	.	.	.	.	.	.	.	.	.	.	.
Delta Dental Plan of Ohio Inc	064502	.	.	.	.	.	.	.	.	.	.	.	.	.	.	.	.	.	.	.	.	.	.	.	.	.	.	.	.	.	.	.	.	.	.	.	D	.	.	.	.	.	.	.	.	.	.	.	.	.	.	.	.	.	.	.	.
Delta Dental Plan of Oklahoma	064563	.	.	.	.	.	.	.	.	.	.	.	.	.	.	.	.	.	.	.	.	.	.	.	.	.	.	.	.	.	.	.	.	.	.	.	.	D	.	.	.	.	.	.	.	.	.	.	.	.	.	.	.	.	.	.	.
Delta Dental Plan of SD	064488	.	.	.	.	.	.	.	.	.	.	.	.	.	.	.	.	.	.	.	.	.	.	.	.	.	.	.	.	.	.	.	.	.	.	.	.	.	.	.	.	.	D	.	.	.	.	.	.	.	.	.	.	.	.	.	.
Delta Life Ins Co	006307	L	.	.	.	.	.	.	.	.	.	D	.	.	.	.	.	.	.	.	.	.	.	.	.	L	.	.	.	.	.	.	.	.	.	.	.	L	.	.	.	L	.	.	.	.	.	.	.	.	.	.	.	.	.	.	.
Denta-Chek of Maryland Inc	064536	.	.	.	.	.	.	.	.	.	.	.	.	.	.	.	.	.	.	.	.	D	.	.	.	.	.	.	.	.	.	.	.	.	.	.	.	.	.	.	.	.	.	.	.	.	.	.	.	.	.	.	.	.	.	.	.
Dental Benefit Providers of CA	064716	.	.	.	.	D	.	.	.	.	.	.	.	.	.	.	.	.	.	.	.	.	.	.	.	.	.	.	.	.	.	.	.	.	.	.	.	.	.	.	.	.	.	.	.	.	.	.	.	.	.	.	.	.	.	.	.
Dental Benefit Providers of IL	064690	.	.	.	.	.	.	.	.	.	L	.	.	.	D	L	.	.	.	.	.	L	.	.	.	.	L	.	.	.	.	.	.	.	.	.	.	.	.	.	.	.	.	.	.	.	.	.	.	.	.	.	.	.	.	.	.
Dental Care Plus Inc	064698	.	.	.	.	.	.	.	.	.	.	.	.	.	.	L	.	.	L	.	.	.	.	.	.	.	.	.	.	.	.	.	.	.	.	.	D	.	.	.	.	.	.	.	.	.	.	.	.	.	.	.	.	.	.	.	.
Dental Choice Inc	065726	.	.	.	.	.	.	.	.	.	.	.	.	.	.	.	.	.	D	.	.	.	.	.	.	.	.	.	.	.	.	.	.	.	.	.	.	.	.	.	.	.	.	.	.	.	.	.	.	F	.	.	.	.	.	.	.
Dental Concern Inc	068645	.	.	.	.	.	L	.	.	.	L	.	.	.	.	.	.	L	D	.	.	L	.	.	.	.	.	.	.	.	.	.	.	.	.	.	.	.	.	.	.	.	.	.	.	.	.	.	.	.	.	.	.	.	.	.	.
Dental Concern Ltd	060182	.	.	.	.	.	.	.	.	.	.	.	.	.	D	.	.	.	.	.	.	.	.	.	.	.	.	.	.	.	.	.	.	.	.	.	.	.	.	.	.	.	.	.	.	.	.	.	.	.	.	.	.	.	.	.	.
Dental Delivery Systems Inc	064907	.	.	.	.	.	.	.	.	.	.	.	.	.	.	.	.	.	.	.	.	.	.	.	.	.	.	.	.	.	.	D	.	.	.	.	.	.	.	.	.	.	.	.	.	.	.	.	.	.	.	.	.	.	.	.	.
Dental Group of New Jersey Inc	064775	.	.	.	.	.	.	.	.	.	.	.	.	.	.	.	.	.	.	.	.	.	.	.	.	.	.	.	.	.	.	D	.	.	.	.	.	.	.	.	.	.	.	.	.	.	.	.	.	.	.	.	.	.	.	.	.
Dental Health Services (CA)	064730	.	.	.	.	D	.	.	.	.	.	.	.	.	.	.	.	.	.	.	.	.	.	.	.	.	.	.	.	.	.	.	.	.	.	.	.	.	.	.	.	.	.	.	.	.	.	.	.	.	.	.	.	.	.	.	.
Dental Health Services (WA)	064527	.	.	.	.	.	.	.	.	.	.	.	.	.	.	.	.	.	.	.	.	.	.	.	.	.	.	.	.	.	.	.	.	.	.	.	.	.	L	.	.	.	.	.	.	.	.	.	D	.	.	.	.	.	.	.	.
Dental Practice Association NJ	064950	.	.	.	.	.	.	.	.	.	.	.	.	.	.	.	.	.	.	.	.	.	.	.	.	.	.	.	.	.	.	D	.	.	.	.	.	.	.	.	.	.	.	.	.	.	.	.	.	.	.	.	.	.	.	.	.
Dental Protection Plan Inc	064797	.	.	.	.	.	.	.	.	.	.	.	.	.	.	.	.	.	.	.	.	.	.	.	.	.	.	.	.	.	.	.	.	.	.	.	.	.	.	.	.	.	.	.	.	.	.	.	.	.	D	.	.	.	.	.	.
Dental Service Corp of ND	064370	.	.	.	.	.	.	.	.	.	.	.	.	.	.	.	.	.	.	.	.	.	.	.	.	.	.	.	.	.	.	.	.	.	.	D	.	.	.	.	.	.	.	.	.	.	.	.	.	.	.	.	.	.	.	.	.
Dental Service of MA	060193	.	.	.	.	.	.	.	.	.	.	.	.	.	.	.	.	.	.	.	.	.	D	.	.	.	.	.	.	.	.	.	.	.	.	.	.	.	.	.	.	.	.	.	.	.	.	.	.	.	.	.	.	.	.	.	.
Dental Services Organization	064773	.	.	.	.	.	.	.	.	.	.	.	.	.	.	.	.	.	.	.	.	.	.	.	.	.	.	.	.	.	.	D	.	.	.	.	.	.	.	.	.	.	.	.	.	.	.	.	.	.	.	.	.	.	.	.	.
Dental Source of Missouri & KS	065731	.	.	.	.	.	.	.	.	.	.	.	.	.	.	.	.	L	.	.	.	.	.	.	.	.	D	.	.	.	.	.	.	.	.	.	.	.	.	.	.	.	.	.	.	.	.	.	.	.	.	.	.	.	.	.	.
DentaQuest Dental Plan of WI	064799	.	.	.	.	.	.	.	.	.	.	.	.	.	.	.	.	.	.	.	.	.	.	.	.	.	.	.	.	.	.	.	.	.	.	.	.	.	.	.	.	.	.	.	.	.	.	.	.	.	D	.	.	.	.	.	.
DentaQuest Mid-Atlantic Inc	064544	.	.	.	.	.	.	.	.	L	.	.	.	.	.	.	.	.	.	.	.	D	.	.	.	.	.	.	.	.	.	.	.	.	.	.	.	.	.	.	.	.	.	.	.	.	.	.	.	.	.	.	.	.	.	.	.
DentaQuest USA Insurance Co	060597	.	.	.	.	.	.	.	.	.	.	L	.	.	.	.	.	.	.	.	.	.	.	.	.	.	.	.	.	.	.	.	.	.	.	.	.	.	.	.	.	.	.	.	D	.	.	.	.	.	.	.	.	.	.	.	.
DentaQuest Virginia Inc	064637	.	.	.	.	.	.	.	.	.	.	.	.	.	.	.	.	.	.	.	.	.	.	.	.	.	.	.	.	.	.	.	.	.	.	.	.	.	.	.	.	.	.	.	.	.	.	D	.	.	.	.	.	.	.	.	.
Dentcare Delivery Systems Inc	064600	.	.	.	.	.	.	.	.	.	.	.	.	.	.	.	.	.	.	.	.	.	.	.	.	.	.	.	.	.	.	.	.	D	.	.	.	.	.	.	.	.	.	.	.	.	.	.	.	.	.	.	.	.	.	.	.
Dentegra Insurance Company	060383	L	L	L	L	L	L	L	D	L	L	L	L	L	L	L	L	L	L	L	L	L	L	L	L	L	L	L	L	L	L	L	L	L	.	.	L	L	L	L	L	L	L	L	L	L	L	L	L	L	L	L	.	.	.	.	.
Dentegra Ins Co of New England	010110	.	.	.	.	.	.	.	.	L	.	.	.	.	.	.	.	.	.	.	.	.	D	.	.	.	.	.	.	.	L	.	.	L	.	.	.	.	.	.	.	.	.	.	.	.	L	.	.	.	.	.	.	.	.	.	.
DentiCare Inc	064522	.	.	.	.	.	.	.	.	.	.	.	.	.	.	.	.	.	.	.	.	.	.	.	.	.	.	.	.	.	.	.	.	.	.	.	.	.	.	.	.	.	.	.	D	.	.	.	.	.	.	.	.	.	.	.	.
Denver Health Medical Plan	064420	.	.	.	.	.	D	.	.	.	.	.	.	.	.	.	.	.	.	.	.	.	.	.	.	.	.	.	.	.	.	.	.	.	.	.	.	.	.	.	.	.	.	.	.	.	.	.	.	.	.	.	.	.	.	.	.
Deseret Mutual Insurance Co	009490	.	.	.	.	.	.	.	.	.	.	.	L	L	.	.	.	.	.	.	.	.	.	.	.	.	.	.	.	.	.	.	.	.	.	.	.	.	.	.	.	.	.	.	.	D	.	.	.	.	.	.	.	.	.	.	.
Destiny Health Insurance Co	060357	.	.	.	.	.	.	.	.	.	.	.	.	.	D	.	.	.	.	.	.	.	.	.	.	.	.	.	.	.	.	.	.	.	.	.	.	.	.	.	.	.	.	.	.	.	.	.	.	.	.	.	.	.	.	.	.
Direct Dental Service Plan Inc	064798	.	.	.	.	.	.	.	.	.	.	.	.	.	.	.	.	.	.	.	.	.	.	.	.	.	.	.	.	.	.	.	.	.	.	.	.	.	.	.	.	.	.	.	.	.	.	.	.	.	D	.	.	.	.	.	.
Direct General Life Insurance	009373	L	L	L	L	L	L	L	L	L	L	L	.	L	L	L	.	L	L	L	L	L	L	.	L	L	L	L	L	L	.	L	L	.	L	L	L	L	L	L	L	D	L	L	L	L	.	L	L	L	L	.	.	.	.	.	.
Direct Life Insurance Company	007430	L	.	L	L	.	L	.	.	.	L	D	.	.	.	.	.	.	L	L	.	.	.	.	.	L	L	.	.	.	.	.	L	.	.	.	.	.	.	.	.	L	.	L	L	.	.	.	.	.	.	.	.	.	.	.	.
Directors Life Assur Co	007616	.	.	.	L	.	.	.	.	.	.	.	.	.	.	.	.	L	.	.	.	.	.	.	.	.	.	.	.	.	.	.	.	.	.	.	.	D	.	.	.	.	.	.	L	.	.	.	.	.	.	.	.	.	.	.	.
Dixie Life Ins Co Inc	007623	.	.	.	.	.	.	.	.	.	.	.	.	.	.	.	.	.	.	D	.	.	.	.	.	.	.	.	.	.	.	.	.	.	.	.	.	.	.	.	.	.	.	.	.	.	.	.	.	.	.	.	.	.	.	.	.
Doctors Life Insurance Co	009026	.	.	L	.	D	.	.	.	.	.	.	L	.	.	.	.	.	.	.	.	.	.	.	.	.	.	L	.	L	.	.	.	.	.	.	.	.	.	.	.	.	.	.	L	.	.	.	.	.	.	L	.	.	.	.	.
Dorsey Life Insurance Company	068191	.	.	.	.	.	.	.	.	.	.	.	.	.	.	.	.	.	.	.	.	.	.	.	.	.	.	.	.	.	.	.	.	.	.	.	.	.	.	.	.	.	.	.	D	.	.	.	.	.	.	.	.	.	.	.	.
Driscoll Children's Health Pln	064519	.	.	.	.	.	.	.	.	.	.	.	.	.	.	.	.	.	.	.	.	.	.	.	.	.	.	.	.	.	.	.	.	.	.	.	.	.	.	.	.	.	.	.	D	.	.	.	.	.	.	.	.	.	.	.	.
Eagle Life Insurance Company	060690	.	L	L	L	L	.	.	L	L	L	.	.	.	L	L	D	L	L	.	.	.	.	.	.	L	.	L	L	.	.	.	L	.	.	L	L	L	L	L	L	L	L	L	L	L	.	.	L	L	L	L	.	.	.	.	.
Eastern Life and Health Ins Co	006325	L	.	L	L	.	L	L	L	L	L	L	.	L	L	L	.	L	L	L	.	L	.	L	L	L	L	L	L	L	.	L	L	.	L	L	L	L	L	D	L	L	L	L	L	.	L	L	L	L	.	L	.	.	.	.	.
Eastern Vision Service Plan	064483	.	.	.	.	.	.	.	.	.	.	.	.	.	.	.	.	.	.	.	.	.	.	.	.	.	.	.	.	.	.	.	.	D	.	.	.	.	.	.	.	.	.	.	.	.	.	.	.	.	.	.	.	.	.	.	.
Easy Choice Health Plan	064930	.	.	.	.	D	.	.	.	.	.	.	.	.	.	.	.	.	.	.	.	.	.	.	.	.	.	.	.	.	.	.	.	.	.	.	.	.	.	.	.	.	.	.	.	.	.	.	.	.	.	.	.	.	.	.	.
Educators Hth Plans Lf Acc Hth	060648	.	.	L	.	.	.	.	.	.	.	.	.	.	.	.	.	.	.	.	.	.	.	.	.	.	.	.	.	.	.	.	.	.	.	.	.	.	.	.	.	.	.	.	.	D	.	.	.	.	.	.	.	.	.	.	.
Educators Life Ins Co	007867	.	.	D	.	.	.	.	.	.	.	.	.	.	.	.	.	.	.	.	.	.	.	.	.	.	.	.	.	.	.	.	.	.	.	.	.	.	.	.	.	.	.	.	.	.	.	.	.	.	.	.	.	.	.	.	.
Educators Mutual Ins Assoc	009123	.	.	.	.	.	.	.	.	.	.	.	.	L	.	.	.	.	.	.	.	.	.	.	.	.	.	.	.	.	.	.	.	.	.	.	.	.	.	.	.	.	.	.	.	D	.	.	.	.	.	.	.	.	.	.	.
El Paso First Health Plans	064692	.	.	.	.	.	.	.	.	.	.	.	.	.	.	.	.	.	.	.	.	.	.	.	.	.	.	.	.	.	.	.	.	.	.	.	.	.	.	.	.	.	.	.	D	.	.	.	.	.	.	.	.	.	.	.	.

D-State of Domicile **L**-Licensed **S**-Surplus Lines Writer **F**-Authorized under the Risk Retention Act **Q**-Qualified or Accredited Reinsurer

U.S. States/Territories in Which Companies Are Licensed or Do Business – *Continued*

Company Name	AMB#	AL	AK	AZ	AR	CA	CO	CT	DE	DC	FL	GA	HI	ID	IL	IN	IA	KS	KY	LA	ME	MD	MA	MI	MN	MS	MO	MT	NE	NV	NH	NJ	NM	NY	NC	ND	OH	OK	OR	PA	RI	SC	SD	TN	TX	UT	VT	VA	WA	WV	WI	WY	AS	GU	MP	PR	VI
Elderplan Inc	064286	.	.	.	.	.	.	.	.	.	.	.	.	.	.	.	.	.	.	.	.	.	.	.	.	.	.	.	.	.	.	.	.	D	.	.	.	.	.	.	.	.	.	.	.	.	.	.	.	.	.	.	.	.	.	.	.
EMC National Life Company	006339	L	L	L	L	L	L	L	L	L	L	L	L	L	L	L	D	L	L	L	L	L	L	L	L	L	L	L	L	L	L	.	L	.	L	L	L	L	L	L	L	L	L	L	L	L	L	L	L	L	L	L	.	.	.	.	.
Emphesys Insurance Company	008845	.	.	L	.	.	.	.	.	.	.	.	.	.	.	L	.	.	.	.	.	.	.	.	.	.	.	.	.	.	.	.	.	.	.	.	.	.	.	.	.	.	.	.	D	.	.	.	.	.	.	.	.	.	.	.	.
Empire Fidelity Investments Lf	060055	.	.	.	.	.	.	.	.	.	.	.	.	.	.	.	.	.	.	.	.	.	.	.	.	.	.	.	.	.	.	.	.	D	.	.	.	.	.	.	.	.	.	.	.	.	.	.	.	.	.	.	.	.	.	.	.
Empire HealthChoice Assurance	068564	.	.	.	.	.	.	.	.	.	.	.	.	.	.	.	.	.	.	.	.	.	.	.	.	.	.	.	.	.	.	.	.	D	.	.	.	.	.	.	.	.	.	.	.	.	.	.	.	.	.	.	.	.	.	.	.
Empire HealthChoice HMO Inc	064368	.	.	.	.	.	.	.	.	.	.	.	.	.	.	.	.	.	.	.	.	.	.	.	.	.	.	.	.	.	.	.	.	D	.	.	.	.	.	.	.	.	.	.	.	.	.	.	.	.	.	.	.	.	.	.	.
Employees Life Co (Mutual)	008005	.	.	L	L	L	L	.	L	.	L	L	.	L	D	L	L	L	L	L	L	L	.	L	L	L	L	L	L	L	.	.	L	.	L	L	L	L	L	L	.	L	L	L	L	L	.	L	L	L	L	L	.	.	.	.	.
Employees Life Insurance Co	009027	.	.	.	.	.	.	.	.	.	.	.	.	.	.	.	.	.	.	.	.	.	.	.	.	.	.	.	.	.	.	.	.	.	.	.	.	.	.	.	.	.	.	.	D	.	.	.	.	.	.	.	.	.	.	.	.
Employers Reassurance Corp	006976	L	L	L	L	L	L	L	L	L	L	L	L	L	L	L	L	D	L	L	L	L	L	L	L	L	L	L	L	L	L	L	L	.	L	L	L	L	L	L	L	L	L	L	L	L	L	L	L	L	L	L	.	.	.	Q	.
Enterprise Life Ins Co	008919	.	.	L	L	.	.	.	.	.	.	.	.	.	L	.	.	L	.	L	.	.	.	.	.	L	.	.	L	.	.	.	L	.	.	.	.	L	L	.	.	.	.	.	D	.	.	.	.	.	L	.	.	.	.	.	.
Envision Insurance Company	064969	L	L	L	L	L	L	L	L	L	L	L	L	L	L	L	L	L	L	L	.	L	L	.	L	L	L	L	L	L	L	L	L	L	.	.	D	L	L	L	L	L	L	.	L	L	.	L	.	L	L	L	.	.	.	.	.
EPIC Life Ins Co	009476	.	.	L	L	.	L	.	.	.	L	.	.	.	L	L	L	L	L	.	.	L	.	L	L	.	L	.	L	L	.	.	.	.	.	L	L	L	L	L	.	L	L	L	L	.	.	L	.	L	D	.	.	.	.	.	.
Equitable Life & Casualty	006342	L	L	L	L	.	L	L	L	L	.	L	L	L	L	L	L	L	L	L	L	L	L	L	.	L	L	L	L	L	L	.	L	.	L	L	L	L	L	L	L	L	L	L	L	D	L	L	L	L	L	L	.	.	.	.	.
EquiTrust Life Insurance Co	060315	L	L	L	L	L	L	L	L	L	L	L	L	L	L	L	D	L	L	L	L	L	L	L	L	L	L	L	L	L	L	L	L	.	L	L	L	L	L	L	L	L	L	L	L	L	L	L	L	L	L	L	.	.	.	.	.
Erie Family Life Ins Co	007276	.	.	.	.	.	.	.	.	L	.	.	.	.	L	L	.	.	L	.	.	L	.	.	L	.	.	.	.	.	.	.	.	.	L	.	L	.	.	D	.	.	.	L	.	.	.	L	.	L	L	.	.	.	.	.	.
Escude Life Ins Co	009341	.	.	.	.	.	.	.	.	.	.	.	.	.	.	.	.	.	.	D	.	.	.	.	.	.	.	.	.	.	.	.	.	.	.	.	.	.	.	.	.	.	.	.	.	.	.	.	.	.	.	.	.	.	.	.	.
Essence Healthcare Inc	064763	.	.	.	.	.	.	.	.	.	.	.	.	.	L	L	.	.	L	.	.	.	.	.	.	.	D	.	.	.	.	.	.	.	.	.	.	.	.	.	.	.	.	.	.	.	.	.	L	.	.	.	.	.	.	.	.
Essex Dental Benefits Inc	065733	.	.	.	.	.	.	.	.	.	.	.	.	.	.	.	.	.	.	.	.	.	.	.	.	.	D	.	.	.	.	.	.	.	.	.	.	.	.	.	.	.	.	.	.	.	.	.	.	.	.	.	.	.	.	.	.
Evangeline Life Ins Co Inc	007644	.	.	.	.	.	.	.	.	.	.	.	.	.	.	.	.	.	.	D	.	.	.	.	.	.	.	.	.	.	.	.	.	.	.	.	.	.	.	.	.	.	.	.	.	.	.	.	.	.	.	.	.	.	.	.	.
Evercare of New Mexico Inc	060688	.	.	.	.	.	.	.	.	.	.	.	.	.	.	.	.	.	.	.	.	.	.	.	.	.	.	.	.	.	.	.	D	.	.	.	.	.	.	.	.	.	.	.	.	.	.	.	.	.	.	.	.	.	.	.	.
Evercare of Texas LLC	064745	.	.	.	.	.	.	.	.	.	.	.	.	.	.	.	.	.	.	.	.	.	.	.	.	.	.	.	.	.	.	.	.	.	.	.	.	.	.	.	.	.	.	.	D	.	.	.	.	.	.	.	.	.	.	.	.
Excellus Health Plan Inc	060082	.	.	.	.	.	.	.	.	.	.	.	.	.	.	.	.	.	.	.	.	.	.	.	.	.	.	.	.	.	.	.	.	D	.	.	.	.	.	.	.	.	.	.	.	.	.	.	.	.	.	.	.	.	.	.	.
EYEXAM of California Inc	064723	.	.	.	.	D	.	.	.	.	.	.	.	.	.	.	.	.	.	.	.	.	.	.	.	.	.	.	.	.	.	.	.	.	.	.	.	.	.	.	.	.	.	.	.	.	.	.	.	.	.	.	.	.	.	.	.
Fallon Community Health Plan	060160	.	.	.	.	.	.	.	.	.	.	.	.	.	.	.	.	.	.	.	.	.	D	.	.	.	.	.	.	.	.	.	.	.	.	.	.	.	.	.	.	.	.	.	.	.	.	.	.	.	.	.	.	.	.	.	.
Family Benefit Life Ins - MO	007273	.	.	L	.	.	L	.	.	.	.	.	.	L	.	.	.	L	.	.	.	.	.	.	.	.	D	.	L	.	.	.	L	.	.	.	.	L	.	.	.	.	.	.	.	.	.	.	.	.	.	.	.	.	.	.	.
Family Heritage Life of Amer	068197	L	L	L	L	L	L	L	L	L	L	L	L	L	L	L	L	L	L	L	L	L	L	L	L	L	L	L	L	L	L	L	L	.	L	L	D	L	L	L	L	L	L	L	L	L	L	L	L	L	L	L	.	.	.	L	.
Family Liberty Life Ins Co	068198	.	.	.	L	.	.	.	.	.	.	.	.	.	.	.	.	.	.	.	.	.	.	.	.	.	.	.	.	.	.	.	.	.	.	.	.	.	.	.	.	.	.	.	D	.	.	.	.	.	.	.	.	.	.	.	.
Family Life Ins Co	006360	L	L	L	L	L	L	L	L	L	L	L	L	L	L	L	L	L	L	L	L	L	L	L	L	L	L	L	L	L	L	L	L	.	L	L	L	L	L	L	L	L	L	L	D	L	L	L	L	L	L	L	.	.	.	.	L
Family Security Life Ins Inc	068331	.	.	.	.	.	.	.	.	.	.	.	.	.	.	.	.	.	.	L	.	.	.	.	.	D	.	.	.	.	.	.	.	.	.	.	.	.	.	.	.	.	.	.	.	.	.	.	.	.	.	.	.	.	.	.	.
Family Service Life Ins Co	007650	L	L	L	L	L	L	.	L	L	L	L	L	L	L	L	L	L	L	L	.	L	L	L	L	L	L	L	L	L	.	.	L	.	L	L	L	L	L	L	L	L	L	L	D	L	L	.	L	L	L	.	.	.	.	.	L
FamilyCare Health Plans Inc	064499	.	.	.	.	.	.	.	.	.	.	.	.	.	.	.	.	.	.	.	.	.	.	.	.	.	.	.	.	.	.	.	.	.	.	.	.	.	D	.	.	.	.	.	.	.	.	.	.	.	.	.	.	.	.	.	.
Farm Bureau Life Ins Co	006362	.	.	L	.	.	L	.	.	.	.	.	.	L	.	.	D	L	.	.	.	.	.	.	L	.	.	L	L	L	.	.	L	.	.	L	.	L	L	.	.	.	L	.	.	L	.	.	L	.	L	L	.	.	.	.	.
Farm Bureau Life Ins Co of MI	006363	.	.	.	.	.	.	.	.	.	.	.	.	.	.	.	.	.	.	.	.	.	.	D	.	.	.	.	.	.	.	.	.	.	.	.	.	.	.	.	.	.	.	.	.	.	.	.	.	.	.	.	.	.	.	.	.
Farm Bureau Life Ins Co of MO	006364	.	.	.	.	.	.	.	.	.	.	.	.	.	.	.	.	.	.	.	.	.	.	.	.	.	D	.	.	.	.	.	.	.	.	.	.	.	.	.	.	.	.	.	.	.	.	.	.	.	.	.	.	.	.	.	.
Farm Family Life Ins Co	006365	.	.	.	.	.	.	L	L	.	.	.	.	.	.	.	.	.	.	.	L	L	L	.	.	.	.	.	.	.	L	L	.	D	.	.	.	.	.	L	L	.	.	.	.	.	L	L	.	L	.	.	.	.	.	.	.
Farmers New World Life Ins Co	006373	L	L	L	L	L	L	L	L	L	L	L	L	L	L	L	L	L	L	L	L	L	L	L	L	L	L	L	L	L	L	L	L	.	L	L	L	L	L	L	L	L	L	L	L	L	L	L	D	L	L	L	.	.	.	.	.
Federal Life Ins Co (Mutual)	006378	L	L	L	L	L	L	L	L	L	L	L	L	L	D	L	L	L	L	L	.	L	.	L	L	L	L	L	L	L	L	L	L	.	L	L	L	L	L	L	L	L	L	L	L	L	.	L	L	L	L	L	.	.	.	.	.
Federated Life Ins Co	006381	L	.	L	L	L	L	L	L	.	L	L	.	L	L	L	L	L	L	L	L	L	L	L	D	L	L	L	L	L	L	L	L	L	L	L	L	L	L	L	L	L	L	L	L	L	L	L	L	L	L	L	.	.	.	.	.
Fidelis SecureCare of Michigan	064849	.	.	.	.	.	.	.	.	.	.	.	.	.	.	.	.	.	.	.	.	.	.	D	.	.	.	.	.	.	.	.	.	.	.	.	.	.	.	.	.	.	.	.	.	.	.	.	.	.	.	.	.	.	.	.	.
Fidelis SecureCare of NC	064861	.	.	.	.	.	.	.	.	.	.	.	.	.	.	.	.	.	.	.	.	.	.	.	.	.	.	.	.	.	.	.	.	.	D	.	.	.	.	.	.	.	.	.	.	.	.	.	.	.	.	.	.	.	.	.	.
Fidelis SecureCare of Texas	064860	.	.	.	.	.	.	.	.	.	.	.	.	.	L	.	.	.	.	.	.	.	.	.	.	.	.	.	.	.	.	.	.	.	.	.	.	.	.	.	.	.	.	.	D	.	.	.	.	.	.	.	.	.	.	.	.
Fidelity Investments Life Ins	009138	L	L	L	L	L	L	L	L	L	L	L	L	L	L	L	L	L	L	L	L	L	L	L	L	L	L	L	L	L	L	L	L	.	L	L	L	L	L	L	L	L	L	L	L	D	L	L	L	L	L	L	.	.	.	.	.
Fidelity Life Association	006386	L	L	L	L	L	L	L	L	L	L	L	L	L	D	L	L	L	L	L	L	L	L	L	L	L	L	L	L	L	L	L	L	.	L	L	L	L	L	L	L	L	L	L	L	L	L	L	L	L	L	.	.	.	.	.	.
Fidelity Security Life Ins Co	007426	L	L	L	L	L	L	L	L	L	L	L	L	L	L	L	L	L	L	L	L	L	L	L	L	L	D	L	L	L	L	L	L	Q	L	L	L	L	L	L	L	L	L	L	L	L	L	L	L	L	L	L	.	.	.	.	.
Fidelity Standard Life Ins Co	068332	.	.	.	D	.	.	.	.	.	.	.	.	.	.	.	.	.	.	.	.	.	.	.	.	.	.	.	.	.	.	.	.	.	.	.	.	.	.	.	.	.	.	.	.	.	.	.	.	.	.	.	.	.	.	.	.
Financial Assurance Life Ins	008094	.	.	L	L	.	L	.	L	L	.	.	.	L	L	L	.	.	.	L	.	L	.	.	L	L	L	L	L	L	.	.	L	.	.	L	.	.	.	.	.	.	L	L	D	L	.	.	.	L	.	L	.	.	.	.	.
Financial Life Ins Co of GA	068201	.	.	.	.	.	.	.	.	.	.	D	.	.	.	.	.	.	.	.	.	.	.	.	.	.	.	.	.	.	.	.	.	.	.	.	.	.	.	.	.	.	.	.	.	.	.	.	.	.	.	.	.	.	.	.	.
First Allmerica Financial Life	007086	L	L	L	L	L	L	L	L	L	L	L	L	L	L	L	L	L	L	L	L	L	D	L	L	L	L	L	L	L	L	L	L	L	L	L	L	L	L	L	L	L	L	L	L	L	L	L	L	L	L	L	L	L	.	L	L
First Ameritas Life of NY	068545	.	.	.	.	.	.	.	.	.	.	.	.	.	.	.	.	.	.	.	.	.	.	.	.	.	.	.	.	.	.	.	.	D	.	.	.	.	.	.	.	.	.	.	.	.	.	.	.	.	.	.	.	.	.	.	.
First Assur Life of America	009125	L	.	.	.	.	.	.	.	.	.	.	.	.	.	.	.	.	.	D	.	.	.	.	.	L	.	.	.	.	.	.	.	.	.	.	.	.	.	.	.	.	.	L	.	.	.	.	.	.	.	.	.	.	.	.	.
First Berkshire Hathaway Life	060389	.	.	.	.	.	.	.	.	.	.	.	.	.	.	.	.	.	.	.	.	.	.	.	.	.	L	.	L	.	.	.	.	D	.	.	.	.	.	.	.	.	.	.	.	.	.	.	.	.	.	.	.	.	.	.	.
First Catholic Slovak Ladies	009869	L	L	L	L	.	L	L	L	L	L	.	L	L	L	L	L	L	L	L	L	L	L	L	L	.	L	L	L	L	.	L	L	L	L	L	D	L	L	L	L	L	L	L	L	L	L	L	L	L	L	L	.	.	.	.	.
First Catholic Slovak Union	009804	.	.	.	.	.	L	L	.	.	L	.	.	.	L	L	.	.	.	.	.	.	L	L	L	.	L	.	.	.	.	L	.	L	.	.	D	.	.	L	.	.	.	.	.	.	.	.	.	L	L	.	.	.	.	.	.
First Central Nat Life of NY	008256	.	.	.	.	.	.	.	L	.	.	.	.	.	.	.	.	.	.	.	.	.	.	.	.	.	.	.	.	.	.	.	.	D	.	.	.	.	.	.	.	.	.	.	.	.	.	.	.	.	.	.	.	.	.	.	.
First Command LIC	068133	.	.	.	.	.	.	.	.	.	.	.	.	.	.	.	.	.	.	.	.	.	.	.	.	.	.	.	.	.	.	.	.	.	.	.	.	.	.	.	.	.	.	.	D	.	.	.	.	.	.	.	.	.	.	.	.
First Commonwealth Ins Co	060300	.	.	.	.	.	.	.	.	.	.	.	.	.	D	.	.	.	.	.	.	.	.	.	.	.	.	.	.	.	.	.	.	.	.	.	.	.	.	.	.	.	.	.	.	.	.	.	.	.	.	.	.	.	.	.	.
First Commonwealth Ltd Hth Svc	064819	.	.	.	.	.	.	.	.	.	.	.	.	.	.	.	.	.	.	.	.	.	.	.	.	.	.	.	.	.	.	.	.	.	.	.	.	.	.	.	.	.	.	.	.	.	.	.	.	.	D	.	.	.	.	.	.
First Commonwealth Ltd H Svcs	065719	.	.	.	.	.	.	.	.	.	.	.	.	.	D	L	.	.	.	.	.	.	.	.	.	.	.	.	.	.	.	.	.	.	.	.	.	.	.	.	.	.	.	.	.	.	.	.	.	.	.	.	.	.	.	.	.
First Commonwlth Ltd H Svcs MI	064818	.	.	.	.	.	.	.	.	.	.	.	.	.	.	.	.	.	.	.	.	.	.	D	.	.	.	.	.	.	.	.	.	.	.	.	.	.	.	.	.	.	.	.	.	.	.	.	.	.	.	.	.	.	.	.	.
First Commonwealth of Missouri	065734	.	.	.	.	.	.	.	.	.	.	.	.	.	.	.	.	.	.	.	.	.	.	.	.	.	D	.	.	.	.	.	.	.	.	.	.	.	.	.	.	.	.	.	.	.	.	.	.	.	.	.	.	.	.	.	.
First Continental L & A Ins Co	006557	.	L	L	L	L	L	.	L	L	L	L	L	L	L	L	L	L	.	.	L	L	.	.	.	L	L	L	.	.	.	.	L	.	.	L	L	L	L	.	.	L	L	L	D	L	L	L	L	L	L	L	.	.	.	.	.
First Dental Health	064931	.	.	.	.	D	.	.	.	.	.	.	.	.	.	.	.	.	.	.	.	.	.	.	.	.	.	.	.	.	.	.	.	.	.	.	.	.	.	.	.	.	.	.	.	.	.	.	.	.	.	.	.	.	.	.	.
First Dimension Life Co Inc	009499	.	.	.	.	.	.	.	.	.	.	.	.	.	.	.	.	.	.	.	.	.	.	.	.	.	.	.	.	.	.	.	.	.	.	.	.	D	.	.	.	.	.	.	.	.	.	.	.	.	.	.	.	.	.	.	.
First Dominion Mutual Life	006383	.	.	L	.	.	.	L	.	.	.	.	.	.	.	.	.	L	.	.	.	.	.	.	.	.	.	.	.	.	.	L	.	.	.	.	.	.	.	L	.	.	.	.	L	.	.	D	.	.	.	.	.	.	.	.	.
First Financial Assurance Co	060236	.	.	.	D	.	.	.	.	.	.	.	.	.	.	.	.	.	.	.	.	.	.	.	.	.	.	.	.	.	.	.	.	.	.	.	.	.	.	.	.	.	.	.	.	.	.	.	.	.	.	.	.	.	.	.	.
First Great-West Lf & Annuity	008257	.	.	.	.	.	.	.	.	.	.	.	.	.	.	.	.	.	.	.	.	.	.	.	.	.	.	.	.	.	.	.	.	D	.	.	.	.	.	.	.	.	.	.	.	.	.	.	.	.	.	.	.	.	.	.	.
First Guaranty Insurance Co	068218	.	.	.	D	.	.	.	.	.	.	.	.	.	.	.	.	.	.	L	.	.	.	.	.	L	L	.	.	.	.	.	.	.	.	.	.	L	.	.	.	.	.	L	L	.	.	.	.	.	.	.	.	.	.	.	.
First Health Life & Health Ins	008951	L	L	L	L	L	L	L	L	L	L	L	L	L	L	L	L	L	L	L	L	L	L	L	L	L	L	L	L	L	L	L	L	.	L	L	L	L	L	L	L	L	L	L	D	L	L	L	L	L	L	L	.	.	.	.	.
First Investors Life Ins Co	006413	L	L	L	L	L	L	L	L	L	L	L	L	L	L	L	L	L	L	L	L	L	L	L	L	L	L	L	L	L	L	L	L	D	L	L	L	L	L	L	L	L	.	L	L	L	L	L	L	L	L	L	.	.	.	.	.
First Landmark Life Ins Co	068028	.	.	.	.	.	.	.	.	.	.	.	.	.	.	L	.	.	.	.	.	.	.	.	.	.	.	.	D	.	.	.	.	.	.	.	.	.	.	.	.	L	.	.	.	.	.	.	.	.	.	.	.	.	.	.	.
First M & F Ins Co	068336	.	.	.	.	.	.	.	.	.	.	.	.	.	.	.	.	.	.	.	.	.	.	.	.	D	.	.	.	.	.	.	.	.	.	.	.	.	.	.	.	.	.	.	.	.	.	.	.	.	.	.	.	.	.	.	.
First MetLife Investors Ins Co	006119	.	.	.	.	.	.	.	.	.	.	.	.	.	.	.	.	.	.	.	.	.	.	.	.	.	.	.	.	.	.	.	.	D	.	.	.	.	.	.	.	.	.	.	.	.	.	.	.	.	.	.	.	.	.	.	.
First National Indemnity	009159	.	.	.	.	.	.	.	.	.	.	.	.	.	.	.	.	.	.	.	.	.	.	.	.	.	.	.	.	.	.	.	.	.	.	.	.	.	.	.	.	.	.	.	D	.	.	.	.	.	.	.	.	.	.	.	.
First National Life of USA	007679	.	.	.	.	.	.	.	.	.	.	.	.	.	.	.	.	.	.	.	.	.	.	.	.	.	.	.	D	.	.	.	.	.	.	.	.	.	.	.	.	.	.	.	.	.	.	.	.	.	.	.	.	.	.	.	.
First Penn-Pacific Life Ins Co	006904	L	L	L	L	L	L	L	L	L	L	L	L	L	L	D	L	L	L	L	L	L	L	L	L	L	L	L	L	L	L	L	L	.	L	L	L	L	L	L	L	L	L	L	L	L	L	L	L	L	L	L	.	.	.	.	.
First Priority Life Ins Co	060298	.	.	.	.	.	.	.	.	.	.	.	.	.	.	.	.	.	.	.	.	.	.	.	.	.	.	.	.	.	.	.	.	.	.	.	.	.	.	D	.	.	.	.	.	.	.	.	.	.	.	.	.	.	.	.	.

D-State of Domicile **L**-Licensed **S**-Surplus Lines Writer **F**-Authorized under the Risk Retention Act **Q**-Qualified or Accredited Reinsurer

U.S. States/Territories in Which Companies Are Licensed or Do Business – *Continued*

Company Name	AMB#	AL	AK	AZ	AR	CA	CO	CT	DE	DC	FL	GA	HI	ID	IL	IN	IA	KS	KY	LA	ME	MD	MA	MI	MN	MS	MO	MT	NE	NV	NH	NJ	NM	NY	NC	ND	OH	OK	OR	PA	RI	SC	SD	TN	TX	UT	VT	VA	WA	WV	WI	WY	AS	GU	MP	PR	VI
First Rehabilitation Lf of Am	009877	.	.	.	.	.	L	L	L	L	.	.	.	.	L	.	.	.	.	.	.	.	L	L	L	.	.	.	.	.	.	L	.	D	L	.	.	.	.	L	L	L	.	L	.	.	.	.	.	.	.	.	.	.	.	.	.
First Reliance Standard Life	009418	.	.	.	.	.	.	.	L	L	.	.	.	.	.	.	.	.	.	.	.	.	.	.	.	.	.	.	.	.	.	.	.	D	.	.	.	.	.	.	.	.	.	.	.	.	.	.	.	.	.	.	.	.	.	.	.
First Security Benefit L&A NY	060104	.	.	.	.	.	.	.	.	.	.	.	.	.	.	.	.	L	.	.	.	.	.	.	.	.	.	.	.	.	.	.	.	D	.	.	.	.	.	.	.	.	.	.	.	.	.	.	.	.	.	.	.	.	.	.	.
First SunAmerica Life Ins Co	009023	.	.	.	.	.	.	.	.	.	.	.	.	.	.	.	.	.	.	.	.	.	.	.	.	.	.	.	L	.	.	.	L	D	.	.	.	.	.	.	.	.	.	.	.	.	.	.	.	.	.	.	.	.	.	.	.
First Symetra Nat Life Ins NY	068147	.	.	.	.	.	.	.	.	.	.	.	.	.	.	.	.	.	.	.	.	.	.	.	.	.	.	.	.	.	.	.	.	D	.	.	.	.	.	.	.	.	.	.	.	.	.	.	.	.	.	.	.	.	.	.	.
First United American Life Ins	009412	.	.	.	.	.	.	.	.	.	.	.	.	.	.	.	.	.	.	.	.	.	.	.	.	.	.	.	.	.	.	.	.	D	.	.	.	.	.	.	.	.	.	.	.	.	.	.	.	.	.	.	.	.	.	.	.
First Unum Life Ins Co	006514	.	.	.	.	.	.	.	.	.	.	.	.	.	.	.	.	.	.	.	.	.	.	.	.	.	.	.	.	.	.	.	.	D	.	.	.	.	.	.	.	.	.	.	.	.	.	.	.	.	.	.	.	.	.	.	.
First Virginia Life Ins Co	006420	.	.	.	.	.	.	.	.	.	.	.	.	.	.	.	.	.	.	.	.	L	.	.	.	.	.	.	.	.	.	.	.	.	.	.	.	.	.	.	.	.	.	L	.	.	.	D	.	.	.	.	.	.	.	.	.
FirstCare Inc	060307	.	.	.	.	.	.	.	L	L	.	.	.	.	.	.	.	.	.	.	.	D	.	.	.	.	.	.	.	.	.	.	.	.	.	.	.	.	.	.	.	.	.	.	.	.	.	.	.	.	.	.	.	.	.	.	.
FirstCarolinaCare Insurance Co	064268	.	.	.	.	.	.	.	.	.	.	.	.	.	.	.	.	.	.	.	.	.	.	.	.	.	.	.	.	.	.	.	.	.	D	.	.	.	.	.	.	L	.	.	.	.	.	.	.	.	.	.	.	.	.	.	.
FirstCommunity Health Plan Inc	064769	D	.	.	.	.	.	.	.	.	.	.	.	.	.	.	.	.	.	.	.	.	.	.	.	.	.	.	.	.	.	.	.	.	.	.	.	.	.	.	.	.	.	.	.	.	.	.	.	.	.	.	.	.	.	.	.
FirstSight Vision Services Inc	064717	.	.	.	.	D	.	.	.	.	.	.	.	.	.	.	.	.	.	.	.	.	.	.	.	.	.	.	.	.	.	.	.	.	.	.	.	.	.	.	.	.	.	.	.	.	.	.	.	.	.	.	.	.	.	.	.
5 Star Life Insurance Co	008069	L	L	L	L	L	L	L	L	L	L	L	L	L	L	L	L	L	L	D	L	L	L	L	L	L	L	L	L	L	L	L	L	.	L	L	L	L	L	L	L	L	L	L	L	L	L	L	L	L	L	L	L	L	L	L	L
Flagship Health Systems Inc	068631	.	.	.	.	.	.	.	.	.	.	.	.	.	.	.	.	.	.	.	.	.	.	.	.	.	.	.	.	.	.	D	.	.	.	.	.	.	.	L	.	.	.	.	.	.	.	.	.	.	.	.	.	.	.	.	.
Florida Combined Life Ins Co	060033	L	.	.	L	.	.	.	.	.	D	L	.	.	.	.	.	.	.	.	.	.	.	.	.	.	.	.	.	.	.	.	.	.	L	.	.	.	.	.	.	L	.	.	.	.	.	.	.	.	.	.	.	.	.	.	.
Florida Health Care Plan Inc	064968	.	.	.	.	.	.	.	.	.	D	.	.	.	.	.	.	.	.	.	.	.	.	.	.	.	.	.	.	.	.	.	.	.	.	.	.	.	.	.	.	.	.	.	.	.	.	.	.	.	.	.	.	.	.	.	.
For Eyes Vision Plan Inc	064727	.	.	.	.	D	.	.	.	.	.	.	.	.	.	.	.	.	.	.	.	.	.	.	.	.	.	.	.	.	.	.	.	.	.	.	.	.	.	.	.	.	.	.	.	.	.	.	.	.	.	.	.	.	.	.	.
Forethought Life Ins Co	009053	L	L	L	L	L	L	L	L	L	L	L	L	L	L	D	L	L	L	L	L	L	L	L	L	L	L	L	L	L	L	L	L	.	L	L	L	L	L	L	L	L	L	L	L	L	L	L	L	L	L	L	.	.	.	L	.
Forethought National Life Ins	068262	.	.	.	.	.	.	.	.	.	.	.	.	.	.	.	.	.	.	.	.	.	.	.	.	.	.	.	.	.	.	.	.	.	.	.	.	.	.	.	.	.	.	.	D	.	.	.	.	.	.	.	.	.	.	.	.
Fort Dearborn Life Ins Co	007322	L	L	L	L	L	L	L	L	L	L	L	L	L	D	L	L	L	L	L	L	L	L	L	L	L	L	L	L	L	L	L	L	.	L	L	L	L	L	L	L	L	L	L	L	L	L	L	L	L	L	L	.	L	.	L	L
Fort Dearborn Life Ins Co NY	068158	.	.	.	.	.	.	.	.	.	.	.	.	.	.	.	.	.	.	.	.	.	.	.	.	.	.	.	.	.	.	.	.	D	.	.	.	.	.	.	.	.	.	.	.	.	.	.	.	.	.	.	.	.	.	.	.
Foundation Life Ins Co of AR	068338	.	.	.	D	.	.	.	.	.	.	.	.	.	.	.	.	.	.	.	.	.	.	.	.	.	.	.	.	.	.	.	.	.	.	.	.	.	.	.	.	.	.	.	.	.	.	.	.	.	.	.	.	.	.	.	.
Frandisco Life Insurance Co	008800	.	.	.	.	.	.	.	.	.	.	D	.	.	.	.	.	.	.	.	.	.	.	.	.	.	.	.	.	.	.	.	.	.	.	.	.	.	.	.	.	.	.	.	.	.	.	.	.	.	.	.	.	.	.	.	.
Freedom Life Ins Co of Amer	006269	L	.	L	L	.	L	.	L	.	L	L	.	.	L	L	L	L	L	L	.	L	.	L	L	L	L	.	L	L	.	.	L	.	L	.	L	L	L	L	.	L	L	L	D	L	.	L	L	L	.	L	.	.	.	.	.
Freelancers Insurance Company	064970	.	.	.	.	.	.	.	.	.	.	.	.	.	.	.	.	.	.	.	.	.	.	.	.	.	.	.	.	.	.	.	.	D	.	.	.	.	.	.	.	.	.	.	.	.	.	.	.	.	.	.	.	.	.	.	.
Fringe Benefit Life Ins Co	068213	.	.	.	.	.	.	.	.	.	.	.	.	.	.	.	.	.	.	.	.	.	.	.	L	.	.	.	.	.	.	.	.	.	.	.	.	L	.	.	.	.	.	.	D	.	.	.	.	.	.	.	.	.	.	.	.
Funeral Directors Life Ins Co	009492	L	L	L	L	L	L	L	L	.	L	L	L	L	L	L	L	L	L	L	.	L	.	L	L	L	L	L	L	L	.	L	L	.	L	L	L	L	L	L	L	L	L	L	D	L	L	L	L	L	L	.	.	.	.	.	.
Futural Life Ins Co	008138	.	.	D	.	.	.	.	.	.	.	.	.	.	.	.	.	.	.	.	.	.	.	.	.	.	.	.	.	.	.	.	.	.	.	.	.	.	.	.	.	.	.	.	.	.	.	.	.	.	.	.	.	.	.	.	.
Garden State Life Ins Co	006436	L	L	L	L	L	L	L	L	L	L	L	L	L	L	L	L	L	L	L	L	L	L	L	L	L	L	L	L	L	L	L	L	L	L	L	L	L	L	L	L	L	L	L	D	L	L	L	L	L	L	L	.	.	.	.	.
Gateway Health Plan Inc	060129	.	.	.	.	.	.	.	.	.	.	.	.	.	.	.	.	.	.	.	.	.	.	.	.	.	.	.	.	.	.	.	.	.	.	.	.	.	.	D	.	.	.	.	.	.	.	.	.	.	.	.	.	.	.	.	.
Geisinger Health Plan	068588	.	.	.	.	.	.	.	.	.	.	.	.	.	.	.	.	.	.	.	.	.	.	.	.	.	.	.	.	.	.	.	.	.	.	.	.	.	.	D	.	.	.	.	.	.	.	.	.	.	.	.	.	.	.	.	.
GEMCare Health Plan Inc	064876	.	.	.	.	D	.	.	.	.	.	.	.	.	.	.	.	.	.	.	.	.	.	.	.	.	.	.	.	.	.	.	.	.	.	.	.	.	.	.	.	.	.	.	.	.	.	.	.	.	.	.	.	.	.	.	.
General American Life Ins Co	006439	L	L	L	L	L	L	L	L	L	L	L	L	L	L	L	L	L	L	L	L	L	L	L	L	L	D	L	L	L	L	L	L	.	L	L	L	L	L	L	L	L	L	L	L	L	L	L	L	L	L	L	.	.	.	L	.
General Fidelity Life Ins Co	006441	L	L	L	L	L	L	Q	L	L	L	L	L	L	L	L	L	L	L	L	.	L	L	L	L	L	L	L	L	L	L	L	L	.	D	L	L	L	L	L	L	L	L	L	L	L	L	L	L	L	L	L	.	.	.	.	.
General Re Life Corporation	006234	L	L	L	L	L	L	D	L	L	Q	L	Q	L	L	L	L	L	L	L	Q	L	L	L	L	L	Q	L	L	L	Q	L	L	Q	L	L	L	L	L	L	L	L	L	L	L	L	Q	L	L	L	L	L	.	.	.	.	.
Generali USA Life Reassurance	009189	Q	Q	Q	L	L	Q	Q	L	Q	L	L	L	L	L	L	L	D	Q	L	Q	Q	L	L	Q	L	L	Q	Q	L	Q	L	Q	Q	Q	Q	L	L	L	Q	Q	Q	Q	L	L	L	Q	Q	L	Q	L	Q	.	.	.	.	.
Genworth Life and Annuity Ins	006648	L	L	L	L	L	L	L	L	L	L	L	L	L	L	L	L	L	L	L	L	L	L	L	L	L	L	L	L	L	L	L	L	.	L	L	L	L	L	L	L	L	L	L	L	L	L	D	L	L	L	L	.	.	.	.	.
Genworth Life Insurance Co	007183	L	L	L	L	L	L	L	D	L	L	L	L	L	L	L	L	L	L	L	L	L	L	L	L	L	L	L	L	L	L	L	L	.	L	L	L	L	L	L	L	L	L	L	L	L	L	L	L	L	L	L	.	.	.	L	L
Genworth Life Insurance Co NY	060026	.	.	.	.	.	.	L	L	L	L	.	.	.	Q	.	.	.	.	.	.	.	.	.	.	.	.	.	.	.	.	L	.	D	.	.	.	.	.	.	L	.	.	.	.	.	.	L	.	.	.	.	.	.	.	.	.
Gerber Life Ins Co	007299	L	L	L	L	L	L	L	L	L	L	L	L	L	L	L	L	L	L	L	L	L	L	L	L	L	L	L	L	L	L	L	L	D	L	L	L	L	L	L	L	L	L	L	L	L	L	L	L	L	L	L	.	.	.	.	.
Germania Life Ins Co	009530	.	.	.	.	.	.	.	.	.	.	.	.	.	.	.	.	.	.	.	.	.	.	.	.	.	.	.	.	.	.	.	.	.	.	.	.	.	.	.	.	.	.	.	D	.	.	.	.	.	.	.	.	.	.	.	.
GHI HMO Select Inc	064564	.	.	.	.	.	.	.	.	.	.	.	.	.	.	.	.	.	.	.	.	.	.	.	.	.	.	.	.	.	.	.	.	D	.	.	.	.	.	.	.	.	.	.	.	.	.	.	.	.	.	.	.	.	.	.	.
GHS Health Maintenance Org	068932	.	.	.	.	.	.	.	.	.	.	.	.	.	.	.	.	.	.	.	.	.	.	.	.	.	.	.	.	.	.	.	.	.	.	.	.	D	.	.	.	.	.	.	.	.	.	.	.	.	.	.	.	.	.	.	.
Gleaner Life Ins Society	006459	.	.	L	.	.	.	.	.	.	L	.	.	.	L	L	L	L	L	.	.	.	.	D	.	.	L	.	L	.	.	.	.	.	.	.	L	.	.	.	.	.	.	L	.	.	.	L	.	.	.	.	.	.	.	.	.
GlobalHealth Inc	064790	.	.	.	.	.	.	.	.	.	.	.	.	.	.	.	.	.	.	.	.	.	.	.	.	.	.	.	.	.	.	.	.	.	.	.	.	D	.	.	.	.	.	.	.	.	.	.	.	.	.	.	.	.	.	.	.
Globe Life and Accident Ins Co	006462	L	L	L	L	L	L	L	L	L	L	L	L	L	L	L	L	L	L	L	L	L	L	L	L	L	L	L	D	L	L	L	L	.	L	L	L	L	L	L	L	L	L	L	L	L	L	L	L	L	L	L	.	L	.	.	.
Gmhp Health Insurance Limited	068424	.	.	.	.	.	.	.	.	.	.	.	.	.	.	.	.	.	.	.	.	.	.	.	.	.	.	.	.	.	.	.	.	.	.	.	.	.	.	.	.	.	.	.	.	.	.	.	.	.	.	.	.	D	.	.	.
Golden Rule Ins Co	006263	L	L	L	L	L	L	L	L	L	L	L	L	L	L	D	L	L	L	L	L	L	L	L	L	L	L	L	L	L	L	L	L	.	L	L	L	L	L	L	L	L	L	L	L	L	L	L	L	L	L	L	.	L	.	.	.
Golden Security Ins Co	009420	L	.	.	L	.	.	.	.	.	.	.	.	.	.	.	.	.	.	L	.	.	.	.	.	L	.	.	.	.	.	.	.	.	.	.	.	.	.	.	.	.	.	D	L	.	.	.	.	.	.	.	.	.	.	.	.
Golden State Mutual Life Ins	006466	.	.	.	.	D	.	.	.	L	.	L	.	.	L	.	.	.	.	L	.	L	.	L	.	L	L	.	.	L	.	.	.	.	L	.	.	.	.	.	.	.	.	L	L	.	.	.	.	.	.	.	.	.	.	.	.
Golden West Health Plan Inc	064721	.	.	.	.	D	.	.	.	.	.	.	.	.	.	.	.	.	.	.	.	.	.	.	.	.	.	.	.	.	.	.	.	.	.	.	.	.	.	.	.	.	.	.	.	.	.	.	.	.	.	.	.	.	.	.	.
Good Health HMO Inc	068956	.	.	.	.	.	.	.	.	.	.	.	.	.	.	.	.	L	.	.	.	.	.	.	.	.	D	.	.	.	.	.	.	.	.	.	.	.	.	.	.	.	.	.	.	.	.	.	.	.	.	.	.	.	.	.	.
Government Personnel Mutual	006470	L	L	L	L	L	L	L	L	L	L	L	L	L	L	L	L	L	L	L	L	L	L	L	L	L	L	L	L	L	L	.	L	.	L	L	L	L	L	L	L	L	L	L	D	L	L	L	L	L	L	L	.	.	.	.	.
Grand Valley Health Plan Inc	068632	.	.	.	.	.	.	.	.	.	.	.	.	.	.	.	.	.	.	.	.	.	.	D	.	.	.	.	.	.	.	.	.	.	.	.	.	.	.	.	.	.	.	.	.	.	.	.	.	.	.	.	.	.	.	.	.
Grange Life Ins Co	007332	.	.	.	.	.	.	.	.	.	.	L	.	.	L	L	L	L	L	.	.	.	.	L	L	.	L	.	.	.	.	.	.	.	.	.	D	.	.	L	.	L	.	L	.	.	.	L	.	.	L	.	.	.	.	.	.
Graphics Arts Benefit Corp	064539	.	.	.	.	.	.	.	.	L	.	.	.	.	.	.	.	.	.	.	.	D	.	.	.	.	.	.	.	.	.	.	.	.	.	.	.	.	.	.	.	.	.	.	.	.	.	L	.	.	.	.	.	.	.	.	.
Great American Life Assur Co	006253	.	L	L	.	L	.	.	.	L	L	L	.	L	.	L	.	.	L	L	.	.	.	.	.	.	.	L	L	L	.	.	L	.	.	.	D	.	L	.	.	.	L	L	L	.	.	.	.	L	.	.	.	.	.	.	.
Great American Life Ins Co	006474	L	L	L	L	L	L	L	L	L	L	L	L	L	L	L	L	L	L	L	L	L	L	L	L	L	L	L	L	L	L	L	L	.	L	L	D	L	L	L	L	L	L	L	L	L	L	L	L	L	L	L	.	L	.	.	L
Great American Life Ins of NY	006864	.	.	.	.	.	.	.	.	.	.	.	.	.	.	.	.	.	.	.	.	.	.	.	.	L	.	.	.	.	.	.	.	D	.	.	.	.	.	.	.	.	.	.	.	.	.	.	.	.	.	.	.	.	.	.	.
Great Central Life Ins Co	007705	.	.	.	.	.	.	.	.	.	.	.	.	.	.	.	.	.	.	D	.	.	.	.	.	.	.	.	.	.	.	.	.	.	.	.	.	.	.	.	.	.	.	.	.	.	.	.	.	.	.	.	.	.	.	.	.
Great Cornerstone L&H Ins Co	060385	.	.	.	.	.	.	.	.	.	.	.	.	.	.	.	.	.	.	.	.	.	.	.	.	.	.	.	.	.	.	.	.	.	.	.	.	D	.	.	.	.	.	.	L	.	.	.	.	.	.	.	.	.	.	.	.
Great Fidelity Life Ins Co	006481	.	.	L	.	.	.	.	L	.	.	L	.	L	.	D	.	.	L	.	.	.	.	.	.	.	.	.	.	.	.	.	L	.	.	.	L	.	L	.	.	L	.	.	L	.	.	.	.	.	.	.	.	.	.	.	.
Great Lakes Health Plan Inc	064439	.	.	.	.	.	.	.	.	.	.	.	.	.	.	.	.	.	.	.	.	.	.	D	.	.	.	.	.	.	.	.	.	.	.	.	.	.	.	.	.	.	.	.	.	.	.	.	.	.	.	.	.	.	.	.	.
Great Republic Life Ins Co	006888	.	L	L	.	.	.	.	.	.	.	.	.	L	.	.	.	.	.	.	.	.	.	.	.	.	.	.	.	L	.	.	.	.	.	.	.	.	L	.	.	.	.	.	.	L	.	.	D	.	.	.	.	.	.	.	.
Great Southern Life Ins Co	006491	L	L	L	L	L	L	L	L	L	L	L	L	L	L	L	L	L	L	L	L	L	L	L	L	L	L	L	L	L	.	L	L	.	L	L	L	L	L	L	.	L	L	L	D	L	.	L	L	L	L	L	.	.	.	.	L
Great-West Healthcare of IL	064026	.	.	.	.	.	.	.	.	.	.	.	.	.	D	.	.	.	.	.	.	.	.	.	.	.	.	.	.	.	.	.	.	.	.	.	.	.	.	.	.	.	.	.	.	.	.	.	.	.	.	.	.	.	.	.	.
Great-West Life & Ann	006981	L	L	L	L	L	D	L	L	L	L	L	L	L	L	L	L	L	L	L	L	L	L	L	L	L	L	L	L	L	L	L	L	.	L	L	L	L	L	L	L	L	L	L	L	L	L	L	L	L	L	L	.	L	.	L	L
Great Western Ins Co	009362	L	.	L	L	L	L	.	L	L	L	L	.	L	L	L	L	L	L	L	L	L	L	L	L	L	L	L	L	L	L	.	L	.	L	L	L	L	L	L	L	L	L	L	L	D	L	L	L	L	L	L	.	.	.	.	.
Great Western Life Ins Co	006458	.	.	.	.	.	.	.	.	.	.	.	.	.	.	.	.	.	.	.	.	.	.	.	.	.	.	D	.	.	.	.	.	.	.	.	.	.	.	.	.	.	.	.	.	.	.	.	.	.	.	.	.	.	.	.	.
Greater Beneficial Union	008161	.	.	.	.	L	L	.	.	.	L	.	.	.	L	L	.	.	.	.	.	.	.	L	L	.	L	.	.	.	.	L	.	L	.	.	L	.	.	D	.	.	.	.	.	.	.	.	.	.	L	.	.	.	.	.	.
Greater Georgia Life Ins Co	009177	L	.	.	.	.	.	.	.	.	.	D	.	.	.	.	.	.	.	.	.	.	.	.	.	L	.	.	.	.	.	.	.	.	L	.	.	.	.	.	.	L	.	L	.	.	.	L	.	.	.	.	.	.	.	.	.
Greek Catholic Union of USA	009807	.	.	L	.	L	L	L	.	.	L	.	.	.	L	L	.	.	.	.	.	L	.	L	L	.	.	.	.	.	.	L	L	L	.	.	L	.	.	D	.	.	.	.	.	.	.	.	.	L	L	.	.	.	.	.	.
Griffin Leggett Burial Ins Co	068426	.	.	.	D	.	.	.	.	.	.	.	.	.	.	.	.	.	.	.	.	.	.	.	.	.	.	.	.	.	.	.	.	.	.	.	.	.	.	.	.	.	.	.	.	.	.	.	.	.	.	.	.	.	.	.	.
Group Dental H Administrators	064774	.	.	.	.	.	.	.	.	.	.	.	.	.	.	.	.	.	.	.	.	.	.	.	.	.	.	.	.	.	.	D	.	.	.	.	.	.	.	.	.	.	.	.	.	.	.	.	.	.	.	.	.	.	.	.	.
Group Dental Service of MD Inc	064791	.	.	.	.	.	.	.	L	L	.	.	.	.	.	.	.	.	.	.	.	D	.	.	.	.	.	.	.	.	.	.	.	.	.	.	.	.	.	L	.	.	.	.	.	.	.	L	.	.	.	.	.	.	.	.	.
Group Health Cooperative	064044	.	.	.	.	.	.	.	.	.	.	.	.	.	.	.	.	.	.	.	.	.	.	.	.	.	.	.	.	.	.	.	.	.	.	.	.	.	.	.	.	.	.	.	.	.	.	.	D	.	.	.	.	.	.	.	.

D-State of Domicile **L**-Licensed **S**-Surplus Lines Writer **F**-Authorized under the Risk Retention Act **Q**-Qualified or Accredited Reinsurer

U.S. States/Territories in Which Companies Are Licensed or Do Business – *Continued*

Company Name	AMB#	AL	AK	AZ	AR	CA	CO	CT	DE	DC	FL	GA	HI	ID	IL	IN	IA	KS	KY	LA	ME	MD	MA	MI	MN	MS	MO	MT	NE	NV	NH	NJ	NM	NY	NC	ND	OH	OK	OR	PA	RI	SC	SD	TN	TX	UT	VT	VA	WA	WV	WI	WY	AS	GU	MP	PR	VI
Group Hlth Coop of Eau Claire	068654	.	.	.	.	.	.	.	.	.	.	.	.	.	.	.	.	.	.	.	.	.	.	.	.	.	.	.	.	.	.	.	.	.	.	.	.	.	.	.	.	.	.	.	.	.	.	.	.	.	D	.	.	.	.	.	.
Group Health Coop of S Cent WI	068807	.	.	.	.	.	.	.	.	.	.	.	.	.	.	.	.	.	.	.	.	.	.	.	.	.	.	.	.	.	.	.	.	.	.	.	.	.	.	.	.	.	.	.	.	.	.	.	.	.	D	.	.	.	.	.	.
Group Health Incorporated	064601	.	.	.	.	.	.	.	.	.	.	.	.	.	.	.	.	.	.	.	.	.	.	.	.	.	.	.	.	.	.	.	.	D	.	.	.	.	.	.	.	.	.	.	.	.	.	.	.	.	.	.	.	.	.	.	.
Group Health Options	064531	.	.	.	.	.	.	.	.	.	.	.	.	L	.	.	.	.	.	.	.	.	.	.	.	.	.	.	.	.	.	.	.	.	.	.	.	.	.	.	.	.	.	.	.	.	.	.	D	.	.	.	.	.	.	.	.
Group Health Plan Inc	068534	.	.	.	.	.	.	.	.	.	.	.	.	.	L	.	.	.	.	.	.	.	.	.	.	.	D	.	.	.	.	.	.	.	.	.	.	.	.	.	.	.	.	.	.	.	.	.	.	.	.	.	.	.	.	.	.
Group Health Plan Inc	068667	.	.	.	.	.	.	.	.	.	.	.	.	.	.	.	.	.	.	.	.	.	.	.	D	.	.	.	.	.	.	.	.	.	.	.	.	.	.	.	.	.	.	.	.	.	.	.	.	.	.	.	.	.	.	.	.
Group Hospital & Medical Svcs	064471	.	.	.	.	.	.	.	.	D	.	.	.	.	.	.	.	.	.	.	.	L	.	.	.	.	.	.	.	.	.	.	.	.	.	.	.	.	.	.	.	.	.	.	.	.	.	L	.	.	.	.	.	.	.	.	.
Guarantee Security Life of AZ	008401	.	.	D	.	.	.	.	.	.	.	.	.	.	.	.	.	.	.	.	.	.	.	.	.	.	.	.	.	.	.	.	.	.	.	.	.	.	.	.	.	.	.	.	.	.	.	.	.	.	.	.	.	.	.	.	.
Guarantee Trust Life Ins Co	006503	L	L	L	L	L	L	L	L	L	L	L	L	L	D	L	L	L	L	L	L	L	L	L	L	L	L	L	L	L	L	L	L	.	L	L	L	L	L	L	L	L	L	L	L	L	L	L	L	L	L	L	.	.	.	L	.
Guaranty Income Life Ins Co	006504	L	.	L	L	L	L	.	.	.	L	L	.	.	L	L	L	L	L	D	.	.	.	L	.	L	L	L	L	L	.	.	L	.	L	L	L	L	L	.	.	L	.	L	L	L	.	.	L	.	.	L	.	.	.	.	.
Guardian Ins & Annuity Co Inc	008197	L	L	L	L	L	L	L	D	L	L	L	L	L	L	L	L	L	L	L	L	L	L	L	L	L	L	L	L	L	L	L	L	L	L	L	L	L	L	L	L	L	L	L	L	L	L	L	L	L	L	L	.	.	.	.	.
Guardian Life Ins Co of Amer	006508	L	L	L	L	L	L	L	L	L	L	L	L	L	L	L	L	L	L	L	L	L	L	L	L	L	L	L	L	L	L	L	L	D	L	L	L	L	L	L	L	L	L	L	L	L	L	L	L	L	L	L	.	.	.	.	.
Guggenheim Life and Annuity Co	009504	.	L	L	.	.	L	.	L	L	.	.	L	L	L	L	D	L	L	.	.	L	.	.	L	L	L	L	L	L	.	.	L	.	.	.	.	L	L	L	.	L	L	L	.	L	.	.	.	L	L	L	.	.	.	.	.
Gulf Guaranty Life Ins Co	008081	L	.	.	L	.	.	.	.	.	L	.	.	.	.	.	.	.	.	L	.	.	.	.	.	D	.	.	.	.	.	.	.	.	.	.	.	.	.	.	.	.	.	L	.	.	.	.	.	.	.	.	.	.	.	.	.
Gulf States Life Ins Co Inc	007838	.	.	.	.	.	.	.	.	.	.	.	.	.	.	.	.	.	.	D	.	.	.	.	.	L	.	.	.	.	.	.	.	.	.	.	.	.	.	.	.	.	.	.	.	.	.	.	.	.	.	.	.	.	.	.	.
Gundersen Lutheran Health Plan	064204	.	.	.	.	.	.	.	.	.	.	.	.	.	.	.	L	.	.	.	.	.	.	.	.	.	.	.	.	.	.	.	.	.	.	.	.	.	.	.	.	.	.	.	.	.	.	.	.	.	D	.	.	.	.	.	.
Hallmark Life Insurance Co	060297	.	.	D	.	.	.	.	.	.	.	.	.	.	.	.	.	.	.	.	.	.	.	.	.	.	.	.	.	.	.	.	.	.	.	.	.	.	.	.	.	.	.	.	.	.	.	.	.	.	.	.	.	.	.	.	.
Hannover Life Reassurance Amer	068031	Q	L	Q	Q	L	Q	Q	Q	Q	D	Q	Q	Q	Q	L	Q	L	Q	Q	Q	Q	L	L	Q	Q	Q	Q	L	Q	Q	Q	Q	Q	Q	Q	L	Q	Q	Q	Q	Q	Q	Q	Q	L	Q	Q	L	Q	Q	Q	.	.	.	Q	.
Harleysville Life Ins Co	006517	L	.	L	L	.	.	L	L	L	L	L	.	.	L	L	L	.	.	.	.	L	L	L	L	.	.	.	L	.	L	L	L	.	L	.	L	.	.	D	L	L	.	L	L	L	.	L	.	L	L	.	.	.	.	.	.
Hartford Internat Life Reassur	009117	.	L	.	L	L	.	D	L	L	.	.	.	Q	L	L	L	L	Q	.	.	Q	L	L	.	L	.	Q	.	L	Q	L	.	Q	Q	Q	L	.	.	Q	.	L	Q	.	L	L	.	.	L	Q	Q	.	.	.	.	.	.
Hartford Life & Accident Ins	007285	L	L	L	L	L	L	D	L	L	L	L	L	L	L	L	L	L	L	L	L	L	L	L	L	L	L	L	L	L	L	L	L	.	L	L	L	L	L	L	L	L	L	L	L	L	L	L	L	L	L	L	L	L	.	L	.
Hartford Life and Annuity Ins	007325	L	L	L	L	L	L	D	L	L	L	L	L	L	L	L	L	L	L	L	L	L	L	L	L	L	L	L	L	L	L	L	L	.	L	L	L	L	L	L	L	L	L	L	L	L	L	L	L	L	L	L	.	.	.	L	L
Hartford Life Ins Co	006518	L	L	L	L	L	L	D	L	L	L	L	L	L	L	L	L	L	L	L	L	L	L	L	L	L	L	L	L	L	L	L	L	L	L	L	L	L	L	L	L	L	L	L	L	L	L	L	L	L	L	L	.	.	.	.	.
Harvard Pilgrim Health Care	068973	.	.	.	.	.	.	.	.	.	.	.	.	.	.	.	.	.	.	.	L	.	D	.	.	.	.	.	.	.	.	.	.	.	.	.	.	.	.	.	.	.	.	.	.	.	.	.	.	.	.	.	.	.	.	.	.
Harvard Pilgrim Hlth Care ofNE	064342	.	.	.	.	.	.	.	.	.	.	.	.	.	.	.	.	.	.	.	.	.	D	.	.	.	.	.	.	.	L	.	.	.	.	.	.	.	.	.	.	.	.	.	.	.	.	.	.	.	.	.	.	.	.	.	.
Hawaii Dental Service	058183	.	.	.	.	.	.	.	.	.	.	.	D	.	.	.	.	.	.	.	.	.	.	.	.	.	.	.	.	.	.	.	.	.	.	.	.	.	.	.	.	.	.	.	.	.	.	.	.	.	.	.	.	.	.	.	.
Hawaii Management Alliance Asn	064547	.	.	.	.	.	.	.	.	.	.	.	D	.	.	.	.	.	.	.	.	.	.	.	.	.	.	.	.	.	.	.	.	.	.	.	.	.	.	.	.	.	.	.	.	.	.	.	.	.	.	.	.	.	.	.	.
Hawaii Medical Service Assn	064035	.	.	.	.	.	.	.	.	.	.	.	D	.	.	.	.	.	.	.	.	.	.	.	.	.	.	.	.	.	.	.	.	.	.	.	.	.	.	.	.	.	.	.	.	.	.	.	.	.	.	.	.	.	.	.	.
Hawkeye Life Ins Group Ins	009046	.	.	.	.	.	.	.	.	.	.	.	.	.	.	.	D	.	.	.	.	.	.	.	.	.	.	.	.	.	.	.	.	.	.	.	.	.	.	.	.	.	.	.	.	.	.	.	.	.	.	.	.	.	.	.	.
Hawthorn Life Insurance Co	068222	.	.	.	.	.	.	.	.	.	.	.	.	.	.	.	.	.	.	.	.	.	.	.	.	.	.	.	.	.	.	.	.	.	.	.	.	.	.	.	.	.	.	.	D	.	.	.	.	.	.	.	.	.	.	.	.
HCC Life Insurance Company	009081	L	L	L	L	L	L	L	L	L	L	L	L	L	L	D	L	L	L	L	L	L	L	L	L	L	L	L	L	L	L	L	L	L	L	L	L	L	L	L	L	L	L	L	L	L	L	L	L	L	L	L	.	.	.	.	.
HCSC Insurance Services Co	007048	L	L	L	L	L	L	L	L	L	L	L	.	L	D	L	L	L	L	L	.	L	L	L	L	L	L	L	L	L	.	.	L	.	.	.	L	L	L	L	L	L	L	L	L	L	.	L	L	L	L	L	.	.	.	.	.
Health Alliance Medical Plans	068039	.	.	.	.	.	.	.	.	.	.	.	.	.	D	.	.	.	.	.	.	.	.	.	.	.	.	.	.	.	.	.	.	.	.	.	.	.	.	.	.	.	.	.	.	.	.	.	.	.	.	.	.	.	.	.	.
Health Alliance-Midwest Inc	064392	.	.	.	.	.	.	.	.	.	.	.	.	.	D	.	L	.	.	.	.	.	.	.	.	.	.	.	.	.	.	.	.	.	.	.	.	.	.	.	.	.	.	.	.	.	.	.	.	.	.	.	.	.	.	.	.
Health Alliance Plan of MI	068810	.	.	.	.	.	.	.	.	.	.	.	.	.	.	.	.	.	.	.	.	.	.	D	.	.	.	.	.	.	.	.	.	.	.	.	.	.	.	.	.	.	.	.	.	.	.	.	.	.	.	.	.	.	.	.	.
Health and Human Resource Ctr	064749	.	.	.	.	D	.	.	.	.	.	.	.	.	.	.	.	.	.	.	.	.	.	.	.	.	.	.	.	.	.	.	.	.	.	.	.	.	.	.	.	.	.	.	.	.	.	.	.	.	.	.	.	.	.	.	.
Health Care Service Corp	009193	.	L	L	L	.	L	L	L	L	L	.	.	L	D	L	.	.	L	.	L	L	L	L	L	.	L	L	L	.	.	L	L	.	.	.	L	L	L	L	.	L	.	.	L	L	.	L	.	L	L	.	.	.	.	.	.
Health Care Service-IL LOB	068771	.	.	.	.	.	.	.	.	.	.	.	.	.	D	.	.	.	.	.	.	.	.	.	.	.	.	.	.	.	.	.	.	.	.	.	.	.	.	.	.	.	.	.	.	.	.	.	.	.	.	.	.	.	.	.	.
Health Care Service-Texas LOB	068718	.	.	.	.	.	.	.	.	.	.	.	.	.	.	.	.	.	.	.	.	.	.	.	.	.	.	.	.	.	.	.	.	.	.	.	.	.	.	.	.	.	.	.	D	.	.	.	.	.	.	.	.	.	.	.	.
Health First Health Plans	064115	.	.	.	.	.	.	.	.	.	D	.	.	.	.	.	.	.	.	.	.	.	.	.	.	.	.	.	.	.	.	.	.	.	.	.	.	.	.	.	.	.	.	.	.	.	.	.	.	.	.	.	.	.	.	.	.
Health Ins Plan of Greater NY	068985	.	.	.	.	.	.	.	.	.	.	.	.	.	.	.	.	.	.	.	.	.	.	.	.	.	.	.	.	.	.	.	.	D	.	.	.	.	.	.	.	.	.	.	.	.	.	.	.	.	.	.	.	.	.	.	.
Health Net Health Plan of OR	068947	.	.	.	.	.	.	.	.	.	.	.	.	.	.	.	.	.	.	.	.	.	.	.	.	.	.	.	.	.	.	.	.	.	.	.	.	.	D	.	.	.	.	.	.	.	.	.	L	.	.	.	.	.	.	.	.
Health Net Ins of New York Inc	011859	.	.	.	.	.	.	.	.	.	.	.	.	.	.	.	.	.	.	.	.	.	.	.	.	.	.	.	.	.	.	.	.	D	.	.	.	.	.	.	.	.	.	.	.	.	.	.	.	.	.	.	.	.	.	.	.
Health Net Life Insurance Co	006722	L	L	L	L	D	L	L	L	L	L	L	L	L	L	L	L	L	L	L	L	L	L	L	L	L	L	L	L	L	L	L	L	.	L	L	L	L	L	L	L	L	L	L	L	L	L	L	L	L	L	L	.	.	.	.	.
Health Net of Arizona Inc	068713	.	.	D	.	.	.	.	.	.	.	.	.	.	.	.	.	.	.	.	.	.	.	.	.	.	.	.	.	.	.	.	.	.	.	.	.	.	.	.	.	.	.	.	.	.	.	.	.	.	.	.	.	.	.	.	.
Health Net of California Inc	068507	.	.	.	.	D	.	.	.	.	.	.	.	.	.	.	.	.	.	.	.	.	.	.	.	.	.	.	.	.	.	.	.	.	.	.	.	.	.	.	.	.	.	.	.	.	.	.	.	.	.	.	.	.	.	.	.
Health Net of Connecticut Inc	068520	.	.	.	.	.	.	D	.	.	.	.	.	.	.	.	.	.	.	.	.	.	.	.	.	.	.	.	.	.	.	.	.	.	.	.	.	.	.	.	.	.	.	.	.	.	.	.	.	.	.	.	.	.	.	.	.
Health Net of New Jersey Inc	064005	.	.	.	.	.	.	.	.	.	.	.	.	.	.	.	.	.	.	.	.	.	.	.	.	.	.	.	.	.	.	D	.	.	.	.	.	.	.	.	.	.	.	.	.	.	.	.	.	.	.	.	.	.	.	.	.
Health Net of New York Inc	068568	.	.	.	.	.	.	.	.	.	.	.	.	.	.	.	.	.	.	.	.	.	.	.	.	.	.	.	.	.	.	.	.	D	.	.	.	.	.	.	.	.	.	.	.	.	.	.	.	.	.	.	.	.	.	.	.
Health New England Inc	068553	.	.	.	.	.	.	.	.	.	.	.	.	.	.	.	.	.	.	.	.	.	D	.	.	.	.	.	.	.	.	.	.	.	.	.	.	.	.	.	.	.	.	.	.	.	.	.	.	.	.	.	.	.	.	.	.
Health Options Inc	068672	.	.	.	.	.	.	.	.	.	D	.	.	.	.	.	.	.	.	.	.	.	.	.	.	.	.	.	.	.	.	.	.	.	.	.	.	.	.	.	.	.	.	.	.	.	.	.	.	.	.	.	.	.	.	.	.
Health Partners of Phila	064160	.	.	.	.	.	.	.	.	.	.	.	.	.	.	.	.	.	.	.	.	.	.	.	.	.	.	.	.	.	.	.	.	.	.	.	.	.	.	D	.	.	.	.	.	.	.	.	.	.	.	.	.	.	.	.	.
Health Pl for Community Living	064920	.	.	.	.	.	.	.	.	.	.	.	.	.	.	.	.	.	.	.	.	.	.	.	.	.	.	.	.	.	.	.	.	.	.	.	.	.	.	.	.	.	.	.	.	.	.	.	.	.	D	.	.	.	.	.	.
Health Plan of CareOregon Inc	064902	.	.	.	.	.	.	.	.	.	.	.	.	.	.	.	.	.	.	.	.	.	.	.	.	.	.	.	.	.	.	.	.	.	.	.	.	.	D	.	.	.	.	.	.	.	.	.	.	.	.	.	.	.	.	.	.
Health Plan of Michigan	064615	.	.	.	.	.	.	.	.	.	.	.	.	.	.	.	.	.	.	.	.	.	.	D	.	.	.	.	.	.	.	.	.	.	.	.	.	.	.	.	.	.	.	.	.	.	.	.	.	.	.	.	.	.	.	.	.
Health Plan of Nevada Inc	068619	.	.	.	.	.	.	.	.	.	.	.	.	.	.	.	.	.	.	.	.	.	.	.	.	.	.	.	.	D	.	.	.	.	.	.	.	.	.	.	.	.	.	.	.	.	.	.	.	.	.	.	.	.	.	.	.
Health Plan of Upper OH Valley	064201	.	.	.	.	.	.	.	.	.	.	.	.	.	.	.	.	.	.	.	.	.	.	.	.	.	.	.	.	.	.	.	.	.	.	.	L	.	.	.	.	.	.	.	.	.	.	.	.	D	.	.	.	.	.	.	.
Health Plus of Louisiana Inc	064279	.	.	.	.	.	.	.	.	.	.	.	.	.	.	.	.	.	.	D	.	.	.	.	.	.	.	.	.	.	.	.	.	.	.	.	.	.	.	.	.	.	.	.	.	.	.	.	.	.	.	.	.	.	.	.	.
Health Resources Inc	068538	.	.	.	.	.	.	.	.	.	.	.	.	.	.	D	.	.	L	.	.	.	.	.	.	.	.	.	.	.	.	.	.	.	.	.	.	.	.	.	.	.	.	.	.	.	.	.	.	.	.	.	.	.	.	.	.
Health Right Inc	064611	.	.	.	.	.	.	.	.	D	.	.	.	.	.	.	.	.	.	.	.	.	.	.	.	.	.	.	.	.	.	.	.	.	.	.	.	.	.	.	.	.	.	.	.	.	.	.	.	.	.	.	.	.	.	.	.
Health Tradition Health Plan	068620	.	.	.	.	.	.	.	.	.	.	.	.	.	.	.	.	.	.	.	.	.	.	.	.	.	.	.	.	.	.	.	.	.	.	.	.	.	.	.	.	.	.	.	.	.	.	.	.	.	D	.	.	.	.	.	.
Health Ventures Network	064540	.	.	.	.	.	.	.	.	.	.	.	.	.	.	.	.	.	.	.	.	.	.	.	D	.	.	.	.	.	.	.	.	.	.	.	.	.	.	.	.	.	.	.	.	.	.	.	.	.	.	.	.	.	.	.	.
HealthAmerica Pennsylvania	068590	.	.	.	.	.	.	.	.	.	.	.	.	.	.	.	.	.	.	.	.	.	.	.	.	.	.	.	.	.	.	.	.	.	.	.	L	.	.	D	.	.	.	.	.	.	.	.	.	.	.	.	.	.	.	.	.
HealthAssurance Pennsylvania	064719	.	.	.	.	.	.	.	.	.	.	.	.	.	.	.	.	.	.	.	.	.	.	.	.	.	.	.	.	.	.	.	.	.	.	.	.	.	.	D	.	.	.	.	.	.	.	.	.	.	.	.	.	.	.	.	.
HealthCare USA of Missouri LLC	064077	.	.	.	.	.	.	.	.	.	.	.	.	.	.	.	.	.	.	.	.	.	.	.	.	.	D	.	.	.	.	.	.	.	.	.	.	.	.	.	.	.	.	.	.	.	.	.	.	.	.	.	.	.	.	.	.
Healthfirst Health Plan of NJ	064974	.	.	.	.	.	.	.	.	.	.	.	.	.	.	.	.	.	.	.	.	.	.	.	.	.	.	.	.	.	.	D	.	.	.	.	.	.	.	.	.	.	.	.	.	.	.	.	.	.	.	.	.	.	.	.	.
HealthKeepers Inc	068669	.	.	.	.	.	.	.	.	.	.	.	.	.	.	.	.	.	.	.	.	.	.	.	.	.	.	.	.	.	.	.	.	.	.	.	.	.	.	.	.	.	.	.	.	.	.	D	.	.	.	.	.	.	.	.	.
HealthLink HMO Inc	060152	.	.	.	L	.	.	.	.	.	.	.	.	.	L	.	.	.	.	.	.	.	.	.	.	.	D	.	.	.	.	.	.	.	.	.	.	.	.	.	.	.	.	.	.	.	.	.	.	.	.	.	.	.	.	.	.
HealthMarkets Insurance Co	009066	L	L	L	L	L	L	L	L	L	L	L	L	L	L	L	L	L	L	L	L	L	L	L	L	L	L	L	L	L	.	L	L	.	L	L	L	D	L	L	L	L	L	L	L	L	L	L	L	L	L	L	.	.	.	.	.
HealthNow New York Inc	064602	.	.	.	.	.	.	.	.	.	.	.	.	.	.	.	.	.	.	.	.	.	.	.	.	.	.	.	.	.	.	.	.	D	.	.	.	.	.	.	.	.	.	.	.	.	.	.	.	.	.	.	.	.	.	.	.
HealthPartners Inc	068731	.	.	.	.	.	.	.	.	.	.	.	.	.	.	.	.	.	.	.	.	.	.	.	D	.	.	.	.	.	.	.	.	.	.	.	.	.	.	.	.	.	.	.	.	.	.	.	.	.	.	.	.	.	.	.	.
Healthplex Insurance Co	013569	.	.	.	.	.	.	.	.	.	.	.	.	.	.	.	.	.	.	.	.	.	.	.	.	.	.	.	.	.	.	.	.	D	.	.	.	.	.	.	.	.	.	.	.	.	.	.	.	.	.	.	.	.	.	.	.
Healthplex of NJ Inc	064959	.	.	.	.	.	.	.	.	.	.	.	.	.	.	.	.	.	.	.	.	.	.	.	.	.	.	.	.	.	.	D	.	.	.	.	.	.	.	.	.	.	.	.	.	.	.	.	.	.	.	.	.	.	.	.	.
HealthPlus Insurance Company	060672	.	.	.	.	.	.	.	.	.	.	.	.	.	.	.	.	.	.	.	.	.	.	D	.	.	.	.	.	.	.	.	.	.	.	.	.	.	.	.	.	.	.	.	.	.	.	.	.	.	.	.	.	.	.	.	.
HealthPlus of Michigan Inc	068555	.	.	.	.	.	.	.	.	.	.	.	.	.	.	.	.	.	.	.	.	.	.	D	.	.	.	.	.	.	.	.	.	.	.	.	.	.	.	.	.	.	.	.	.	.	.	.	.	.	.	.	.	.	.	.	.
HealthPlus Partners Inc	064762	.	.	.	.	.	.	.	.	.	.	.	.	.	.	.	.	.	.	.	.	.	.	D	.	.	.	.	.	.	.	.	.	.	.	.	.	.	.	.	.	.	.	.	.	.	.	.	.	.	.	.	.	.	.	.	.

D-State of Domicile **L**-Licensed **S**-Surplus Lines Writer **F**-Authorized under the Risk Retention Act **Q**-Qualified or Accredited Reinsurer

Company Name	AMB#	AL	AK	AZ	AR	CA	CO	CT	DE	DC	FL	GA	HI	ID	IL	IN	IA	KS	KY	LA	ME	MD	MA	MI	MN	MS	MO	MT	NE	NV	NH	NJ	NM	NY	NC	ND	OH	OK	OR	PA	RI	SC	SD	TN	TX	UT	VT	VA	WA	WV	WI	WY	AS	GU	MP	PR	VI
HealthSpring Life and Health	060673	L	L	L	L	.	.	L	L	L	.	L	L	.	L	L	L	L	L	L	L	L	L	L	L	L	L	L	L	L	L	.	.	L	.	L	L	L	.	L	L	L	L	L	D	L	L	.	.	L	L	.	.	.	.	.	.
HealthSpring of Alabama Inc	068784	D	.	.	.	.	.	.	.	.	.	.	.	.	.	.	.	.	.	.	.	.	.	.	.	.	.	.	.	.	.	.	.	.	.	.	.	.	.	.	.	.	.	.	.	.	.	.	.	.	.	.	.	.	.	.	.
HealthSpring of Tennessee	064300	.	.	.	.	.	.	.	.	.	.	.	.	.	L	.	.	.	.	.	.	.	.	.	.	L	.	.	.	.	.	.	.	.	.	.	.	.	.	.	.	.	.	D	.	.	.	.	.	.	.	.	.	.	.	.	.
HealthWise	068604	.	.	.	.	.	.	.	.	.	.	.	.	.	.	.	.	.	.	.	.	.	.	.	.	.	.	.	.	.	.	.	.	.	.	.	.	.	.	.	.	.	.	.	.	D	.	.	.	.	.	.	.	.	.	.	.
Healthy Alliance Life Ins Co	008217	L	.	L	L	L	L	.	L	L	.	.	L	L	L	L	L	L	.	L	.	L	.	.	.	L	D	L	L	L	.	.	L	.	L	L	L	L	L	L	.	L	L	L	L	L	.	L	L	L	L	.	.	.	.	.	.
Heart of America Health Plan	064184	.	.	.	.	.	.	.	.	.	.	.	.	.	.	.	.	.	.	.	.	.	.	.	.	.	.	.	.	.	.	.	.	.	.	D	.	.	.	.	.	.	.	.	.	.	.	.	.	.	.	.	.	.	.	.	.
Heartland Fidelity Ins Co	076359	.	.	.	.	.	.	.	.	D	.	.	.	.	.	.	.	.	.	.	.	.	.	.	.	.	.	.	.	.	.	.	.	.	.	.	.	.	.	.	.	.	.	.	.	.	.	.	.	.	.	.	.	.	.	.	.
Heartland National Life Ins Co	006730	L	.	L	L	.	L	.	.	L	L	L	.	.	L	D	.	L	.	L	.	.	.	.	.	L	L	.	L	L	.	.	L	.	.	.	.	L	.	.	.	L	.	L	L	L	.	.	.	.	.	L	.	.	.	.	.
Heritage Provider Network Inc	064580	.	.	.	.	D	.	.	.	.	.	.	.	.	.	.	.	.	.	.	.	.	.	.	.	.	.	.	.	.	.	.	.	.	.	.	.	.	.	.	.	.	.	.	.	.	.	.	.	.	.	.	.	.	.	.	.
Heritage Union Life Ins Co	006281	L	L	D	L	L	L	L	L	L	L	L	.	L	L	L	L	L	L	L	.	L	L	L	L	L	L	L	L	L	.	.	L	.	L	L	L	L	L	L	.	L	L	L	L	L	.	L	L	L	L	L	.	.	.	.	.
HHS Health of Oklahoma Inc	064977	.	.	.	.	.	.	.	.	.	.	.	.	.	.	.	.	.	.	.	.	.	.	.	.	.	.	.	.	.	.	.	.	.	.	.	.	D	L	.	.	.	.	.	.	.	.	.	.	.	.	.	.	.	.	.	.
Higginbotham Burial Ins Co	068345	.	.	.	D	.	.	.	.	.	.	.	.	.	.	.	.	.	.	.	.	.	.	.	.	.	.	.	.	.	.	.	.	.	.	.	.	.	.	.	.	.	.	.	.	.	.	.	.	.	.	.	.	.	.	.	.
Highmark Inc.	064010	.	.	.	.	.	.	.	.	.	.	.	.	.	.	.	.	.	.	.	.	.	.	.	.	.	.	.	.	.	.	.	.	.	.	.	.	.	.	D	.	.	.	.	.	.	.	.	.	.	.	.	.	.	.	.	.
Highmark Senior Resources Inc	060570	.	.	.	.	.	.	.	.	.	.	.	.	.	.	.	.	.	.	.	.	.	.	.	.	.	.	.	.	.	.	.	.	.	.	.	.	.	.	D	.	.	.	.	.	.	.	.	.	L	.	.	.	.	.	.	.
Highmark West Virginia Inc	064415	.	.	.	.	.	.	.	.	.	.	.	.	.	.	.	.	.	.	.	.	.	.	.	.	.	.	.	.	.	.	.	.	.	.	.	.	.	.	.	.	.	.	.	.	.	.	.	.	D	.	.	.	.	.	.	.
HIP Insurance Co of New York	008034	.	.	.	.	.	.	.	.	.	.	.	.	.	.	.	.	.	.	.	.	.	.	.	.	.	.	.	.	.	.	.	.	D	.	.	.	.	.	.	.	.	.	.	.	.	.	.	.	.	.	.	.	.	.	.	.
HM Health Insurance Company	006120	L	L	L	L	L	L	L	L	L	.	L	L	L	L	L	L	L	L	L	.	L	L	L	L	L	L	L	L	L	.	L	L				L	L	L	D	L	L	L	L	L	L	L	L	L	L	L	L	.	.	.	.	.
HM Life Insurance Company	009063	L	L	L	L	L	L	L	L	L	L	L	L	L	L	L	L	L	L	L	L	L	L	L	L	L	L	L	L	L	L	L	L	.	L	L	L	L	L	D	L	L	L	L	L	L	L	L	L	L	L	L	.	.	.	.	.
HM Life Insurance Company NY	060209	.	.	.	.	.	.	.	.	L	.	.	.	.	.	.	.	.	.	.	.	.	.	.	.	.	.	.	.	.	.	.	.	D	.	.	.	.	.	.	L	.	.	.	.	.	.	.	.	.	.	.	.	.	.	.	.
HMO Colorado Inc	068927	.	.	.	.	.	D	.	.	.	.	.	.	.	.	.	.	.	.	.	.	.	.	.	.	.	.	.	.	L	.	.	.	.	.	.	.	.	.	.	.	.	.	.	.	.	.	.	.	.	.	.	.	.	.	.	.
HMO Louisiana Inc	068990	.	.	.	.	.	.	.	.	.	.	.	.	.	.	.	.	.	.	D	.	.	.	.	.	.	.	.	.	.	.	.	.	.	.	.	.	.	.	.	.	.	.	.	.	.	.	.	.	.	.	.	.	.	.	.	.
HMO Maine	064175	.	.	.	.	.	.	.	.	.	.	.	.	.	.	.	.	.	.	.	D	.	.	.	.	.	.	.	.	.	.	.	.	.	.	.	.	.	.	.	.	.	.	.	.	.	.	.	.	.	.	.	.	.	.	.	.
HMO Minnesota	068646	.	.	.	.	.	.	.	.	.	.	.	.	.	.	.	.	.	.	.	.	.	.	.	D	.	.	.	.	.	.	.	.	.	.	.	.	.	.	.	.	.	.	.	.	.	.	.	.	.	.	.	.	.	.	.	.
HMO Missouri Inc	068790	.	.	.	.	.	.	.	.	.	.	.	.	.	L	.	.	.	.	.	.	.	.	.	.	.	D	.	.	.	.	.	.	.	.	.	.	.	.	.	.	.	.	.	.	.	.	.	.	.	.	.	.	.	.	.	.
HMO of Mississippi Inc	064129	.	.	.	.	.	.	.	.	.	.	.	.	.	.	.	.	.	.	.	.	.	.	.	.	D	.	.	.	.	.	.	.	.	.	.	.	.	.	.	.	.	.	.	.	.	.	.	.	.	.	.	.	.	.	.	.
HMO of Northeastern PA	068780	.	.	.	.	.	.	.	.	.	.	.	.	.	.	.	.	.	.	.	.	.	.	.	.	.	.	.	.	.	.	.	.	.	.	.	.	.	.	D	.	.	.	.	.	.	.	.	.	.	.	.	.	.	.	.	.
HMO Partners Inc	068964	.	.	.	D	.	.	.	.	.	.	.	.	.	.	.	.	.	.	.	.	.	.	.	.	.	.	.	.	.	.	.	.	.	.	.	.	.	.	.	.	.	.	.	.	.	.	.	.	.	.	.	.	.	.	.	.
Holman Professional Counseling	064804	.	.	.	.	D	.	.	.	.	.	.	.	.	.	.	.	.	.	.	.	.	.	.	.	.	.	.	.	.	.	.	.	.	.	.	.	.	.	.	.	.	.	.	.	.	.	.	.	.	.	.	.	.	.	.	.
Homesteaders Life Co	006534	L	L	L	L	L	L	L	L	L	L	L	L	L	L	L	D	L	L	L	L	L	L	L	L	L	L	L	L	L	L	L	L	.	L	L	L	L	L	L	L	L	L	L	L	L	L	L	L	L	L	L	.	.	.	.	.
Hometown Health Plan	068576	.	.	.	.	.	.	.	.	.	.	.	.	.	.	.	.	.	.	.	.	.	.	.	.	.	.	.	.	.	.	.	.	.	.	.	D	.	.	.	.	.	.	.	.	.	.	.	.	.	.	.	.	.	.	.	.
Honored Citizens Choice Hth Pl	064815	.	.	.	.	D	.	.	.	.	.	.	.	.	.	.	.	.	.	.	.	.	.	.	.	.	.	.	.	.	.	.	.	.	.	.	.	.	.	.	.	.	.	.	.	.	.	.	.	.	.	.	.	.	.	.	.
Horace Mann Life Ins Co	006535	L	L	L	L	L	L	L	L	L	L	L	L	L	D	L	L	L	L	L	L	L	L	L	L	L	L	L	L	L	L	.	L	.	L	L	L	L	L	L	L	L	L	L	L	L	L	L	L	L	L	L	.	.	.	.	.
Horizon Healthcare Dental	064696	.	.	.	.	.	.	.	.	.	.	.	.	.	.	.	.	.	.	.	.	.	.	.	.	.	.	.	.	.	.	D	.	.	.	.	.	.	.	.	.	.	.	.	.	.	.	.	.	.	.	.	.	.	.	.	.
Horizon Healthcare of Delaware	064397	.	.	.	.	.	.	.	D	.	.	.	.	.	.	.	.	.	.	.	.	.	.	.	.	.	.	.	.	.	.	.	.	.	.	.	.	.	.	.	.	.	.	.	.	.	.	.	.	.	.	.	.	.	.	.	.
Horizon Healthcare of NJ	068960	.	.	.	.	.	.	.	.	.	.	.	.	.	.	.	.	.	.	.	.	.	.	.	.	.	.	.	.	.	.	D	.	.	.	.	.	.	.	.	.	.	.	.	.	.	.	.	.	.	.	.	.	.	.	.	.
Hospital Service Assn of NE PA	064307	.	.	.	.	.	.	.	.	.	.	.	.	.	.	.	.	.	.	.	.	.	.	.	.	.	.	.	.	.	.	.	.	.	.	.	.	.	.	D	.	.	.	.	.	.	.	.	.	.	.	.	.	.	.	.	.
Household Life Ins Co	009129	L	L	L	L	L	L	L	L	L	L	L	L	L	L	L	L	L	L	L	L	L	L	D	L	L	L	L	L	L	L	L	L	.	L	L	L	L	L	L	L	L	L	L	L	L	L	L	L	L	L	L	.	.	.	.	.
Household Life Ins Co of AZ	009573	.	.	D	.	.	.	.	.	.	.	.	.	.	.	.	.	.	.	.	.	.	.	.	.	.	.	.	.	.	.	.	.	.	.	.	.	.	.	.	.	.	.	.	.	.	.	.	.	.	.	.	.	.	.	.	.
Household Life Ins Co of DE	060344	.	.	.	.	.	.	.	D	.	.	.	.	.	.	.	.	.	.	.	.	.	.	.	.	.	.	.	.	.	.	.	.	.	.	.	.	.	.	.	.	.	.	.	.	.	.	.	.	.	.	.	.	.	.	.	.
HPHC Insurance Company Inc	011367	.	.	.	.	.	.	L	.	.	.	.	.	.	.	.	.	.	.	.	L	.	D	.	.	.	.	.	.	.	L	.	.	.	.	.	.	.	.	.	.	.	.	.	.	.	.	.	.	.	.	.	.	.	.	.	.
Human Affairs Internatl of CA	064805	.	.	.	.	D	.	.	.	.	.	.	.	.	.	.	.	.	.	.	.	.	.	.	.	.	.	.	.	.	.	.	.	.	.	.	.	.	.	.	.	.	.	.	.	.	.	.	.	.	.	.	.	.	.	.	.
Humana AdvantageCare Plan	064915	.	.	.	.	.	.	.	.	.	D	.	.	.	.	.	.	.	.	.	.	.	.	.	.	.	.	.	.	.	.	.	.	.	.	.	.	.	.	.	.	.	.	.	.	.	.	.	.	.	.	.	.	.	.	.	.
Humana Benefit Plan of IL	060099	.	.	.	.	.	.	.	.	.	.	.	.	.	D	.	.	.	.	.	.	.	.	.	.	.	.	.	.	.	.	.	.	.	.	.	.	.	.	.	.	.	.	.	.	.	.	.	.	.	.	.	.	.	.	.	.
Humana Employers Hth Pln of GA	064068	.	.	.	.	.	.	.	.	.	.	D	.	.	.	.	.	.	.	.	.	.	.	.	.	.	.	.	.	.	.	.	.	.	.	.	.	.	.	.	.	.	.	.	.	.	.	.	.	.	.	.	.	.	.	.	.
Humana Health Benefit Pl of LA	068835	.	.	.	.	.	.	.	.	.	.	.	.	.	.	.	.	.	.	D	.	.	.	.	.	.	.	.	.	.	.	.	.	.	.	.	.	.	.	.	.	.	.	.	.	.	.	.	.	.	.	.	.	.	.	.	.
Humana Health Ins Co FL Inc	009494	.	.	.	.	.	.	.	.	.	D	.	.	.	.	.	.	.	.	.	.	.	.	.	.	.	.	.	.	.	.	.	.	.	.	.	.	.	.	.	.	.	.	.	.	.	.	.	.	.	.	.	.	.	.	.	.
Humana Health Plan Inc	068898	L	.	L	L	.	L	.	.	.	.	.	.	L	L	L	.	L	D	.	.	.	.	.	.	.	L	.	L	L	.	.	L	.	.	.	.	.	.	.	.	.	.	L	.	.	.	L	L	.	.	.	.	.	.	.	.
Humana Health Plan of Ohio	068573	.	.	.	.	.	.	.	.	.	.	.	.	.	.	.	.	.	.	.	.	.	.	.	.	.	.	.	.	.	.	.	.	.	.	.	D	.	.	.	.	.	.	.	.	.	.	.	.	.	.	.	.	.	.	.	.
Humana Health Plan of TX	068903	.	.	.	.	.	.	.	.	.	.	.	.	.	.	.	.	.	.	.	.	.	.	.	.	.	.	.	.	.	.	.	.	.	.	.	.	.	.	.	.	.	.	.	D	.	.	.	.	.	.	.	.	.	.	.	.
Humana Health Plans of PR Inc	060162	.	.	.	.	.	.	.	.	.	.	.	.	.	.	.	.	.	.	.	.	.	.	.	.	.	.	.	.	.	.	.	.	.	.	.	.	.	.	.	.	.	.	.	.	.	.	.	.	.	.	.	.	.	.	D	.
Humana Insurance Company	007574	L	L	L	L	L	L	L	L	L	L	L	L	L	L	L	L	L	L	L	L	L	L	L	L	L	L	L	L	L	L	L	L	.	L	L	L	L	L	L	L	L	L	L	L	L	L	L	L	L	D	L	.	.	.	.	.
Humana Insurance Company of KY	060248	.	.	.	.	.	.	.	.	.	.	.	.	.	.	.	.	.	D	.	.	.	.	.	.	.	.	.	.	.	.	.	.	.	.	.	.	.	.	.	.	.	.	.	.	.	.	.	.	.	.	.	.	.	.	.	.
Humana Insurance Company of NY	060595	.	.	.	.	.	.	.	.	.	.	.	.	.	.	.	.	.	.	.	.	.	.	.	.	.	.	.	.	.	.	.	.	D	.	.	.	.	.	.	.	.	.	.	.	.	.	.	.	.	.	.	.	.	.	.	.
Humana Ins of Puerto Rico Inc	008265	.	.	.	.	.	.	.	.	.	.	.	.	.	.	.	.	.	.	.	.	.	.	.	.	.	.	.	.	.	.	.	.	.	.	.	.	.	.	.	.	.	.	.	.	.	.	.	.	.	.	.	.	.	.	D	.
Humana Medical Plan Inc	068907	.	.	.	.	.	.	.	.	.	D	.	.	.	.	.	.	.	.	.	.	.	.	.	.	.	.	.	.	.	.	.	.	.	.	.	.	.	.	.	.	.	.	.	.	.	.	.	.	.	.	.	.	.	.	.	.
Humana Medical Plan of Utah	064893	.	.	.	.	.	.	.	.	.	.	.	.	.	.	.	.	.	.	.	.	.	.	.	.	.	.	.	.	.	.	.	.	.	.	.	.	.	.	.	.	.	.	.	.	D	.	.	.	.	.	.	.	.	.	.	.
Humana Wisconsin Health	068626	.	.	.	.	.	.	.	.	.	.	.	.	.	.	.	.	.	.	.	.	.	.	.	.	.	.	.	.	.	.	.	.	.	.	.	.	.	.	.	.	.	.	.	.	.	.	.	.	.	D	.	.	.	.	.	.
HumanaDental Insurance Company	007254	L	L	L	L	L	L	L	L	L	L	L	L	L	L	L	L	L	L	L	.	L	L	L	L	L	L	L	L	L	L	L	L	.	L	L	L	L	L	L	L	L	L	L	L	L	L	L	L	L	D	L	.	.	.	.	.
Hungarian Reformed Fed of Amer	009872	.	.	.	.	L	.	L	.	D	L	.	.	.	L	L	.	.	.	.	.	.	.	L	.	.	.	.	.	.	.	L	.	L	.	.	L	.	.	L	.	.	.	.	.	.	.	.	.	.	.	.	.	.	.	.	.
IA American Life Insurance Co	060682	L	L	L	L	L	L	L	L	L	L	D	L	L	L	L	L	L	L	L	L	L	L	L	L	L	L	L	L	L	L	L	L	.	L	L	L	L	L	L	L	L	L	L	L	L	L	L	L	L	L	L	.	.	.	.	.
IBA Health and Life Assur Co	068102	.	.	.	.	.	.	.	.	.	.	.	.	.	.	.	.	.	.	.	.	.	.	D	.	.	.	.	.	.	.	.	.	.	.	.	.	.	.	.	.	.	.	.	.	.	.	.	.	.	.	.	.	.	.	.	.
IBC Life Insurance Company	068225	.	.	.	.	.	.	.	.	.	.	.	.	.	.	.	.	.	.	.	.	.	.	.	.	.	.	.	.	.	.	.	.	.	.	.	.	.	.	.	.	.	.	.	D	.	.	.	.	.	.	.	.	.	.	.	.
IdeaLife Ins Co	009326	.	L	L	L	L	L	D	L	L	L	L	L	L	L	L	L	L	L	L	L	L	L	L	L	L	L	L	L	L	L	L	L	.	L	L	L	L	L	L	L	L	L	L	L	L	L	L	L	L	L	L	.	.	.	.	.
Illinois Mutual Life Ins Co	006542	L	.	L	L	L	L	L	L	.	L	L	.	L	D	L	L	L	L	L	L	L	L	L	L	L	L	L	L	L	L	L	L	.	L	L	L	L	L	L	L	L	L	L	L	L	L	L	L	L	L	L	.	.	.	.	.
Imerica Life and Health Ins Co	006418	L	L	L	D	L	L	.	L	L	L	L	L	L	L	L	.	L	L	L	.	L	.	.	.	L	L	L	L	L	.	.	L	.	.	.	.	L	L	.	.	L	.	.	L	L	.	.	.	L	.	L	.	.	.	.	.
Independence American Ins Co	003552	L	L	L	L	L	L	L	D	L	L	L	L	L	L	L	L	L	L	L	L	L	L	L	L	L	L	L	L	L	.	L	L	L	L	L	L	L	L	L	L	L	L	L	L	L	L	L	L	L	L	L	.	.	.	.	.
Independence Blue Cross	064553	.	.	.	.	.	.	.	.	.	.	.	.	.	.	.	.	.	.	.	.	.	.	.	.	.	.	.	.	.	.	.	.	.	.	.	.	.	.	D	.	.	.	.	.	.	.	.	.	.	.	.	.	.	.	.	.
Independence Insurance Inc	060332	.	.	.	.	.	.	.	D	.	.	.	.	.	.	.	.	.	.	.	.	.	.	.	.	.	.	.	.	.	.	.	.	.	.	.	.	.	.	.	.	.	.	.	.	.	.	.	.	.	.	.	.	.	.	.	.
Independence Life & Annuity Co	006547	L	L	L	L	L	L	L	L	L	L	L	L	L	L	L	L	L	L	L	L	L	L	L	L	L	L	L	L	L	L	L	L	.	L	L	L	L	L	L	D	L	L	L	L	L	L	L	L	L	L	L	.	.	.	.	.
Independent Care Health Plan	064794	.	.	.	.	.	.	.	.	.	.	.	.	.	.	.	.	.	.	.	.	.	.	.	.	.	.	.	.	.	.	.	.	.	.	.	.	.	.	.	.	.	.	.	.	.	.	.	.	.	D	.	.	.	.	.	.
Independent Health Association	064343	.	.	.	.	.	.	.	.	.	.	.	.	.	.	.	.	.	.	.	.	.	.	.	.	.	.	.	.	.	.	.	.	D	.	.	.	.	.	.	.	.	.	.	.	.	.	.	.	.	.	.	.	.	.	.	.
Independent Health Benefits	064597	.	.	.	.	.	.	.	.	.	.	.	.	.	.	.	.	.	.	.	.	.	.	.	.	.	.	.	.	.	.	.	.	D	.	.	.	.	.	.	.	.	.	.	.	.	.	.	.	.	.	.	.	.	.	.	.
Indiana Vision Services Inc	065725	.	.	.	.	.	.	.	.	.	.	.	.	.	.	D	.	.	.	.	.	.	.	.	.	.	.	.	.	.	.	.	.	.	.	.	.	.	.	.	.	.	.	.	.	.	.	.	.	.	.	.	.	.	.	.	.
Individual Assur Lf Hlth & Acc	008437	L	L	L	L	L	L	.	L	L	L	L	L	L	L	L	L	L	L	L	.	L	.	L	L	L	D	L	L	L	.	L	L	.	L	L	L	L	L	L	.	L	L	L	L	L	.	L	L	L	L	L	L	L	L	.	.
ING Life Insurance and Annuity	006895	L	L	L	L	L	L	D	L	L	L	L	L	L	L	L	L	L	L	L	L	L	L	L	L	L	L	L	L	L	L	L	L	L	L	L	L	L	L	L	L	L	L	L	L	L	L	L	L	L	L	L	.	L	.	L	L
ING USA Annuity & Life Ins Co	008388	L	L	L	L	L	L	L	L	L	L	L	L	L	L	L	D	L	L	L	L	L	L	L	L	L	L	L	L	L	L	L	L	.	L	L	L	L	L	L	L	L	L	L	L	L	L	L	L	L	L	L	.	.	.	.	.

D-State of Domicile **L**-Licensed **S**-Surplus Lines Writer **F**-Authorized under the Risk Retention Act **Q**-Qualified or Accredited Reinsurer

U.S. States/Territories in Which Companies Are Licensed or Do Business – *Continued*

Company Name	AMB#	AL	AK	AZ	AR	CA	CO	CT	DE	DC	FL	GA	HI	ID	IL	IN	IA	KS	KY	LA	ME	MD	MA	MI	MN	MS	MO	MT	NE	NV	NH	NJ	NM	NY	NC	ND	OH	OK	OR	PA	RI	SC	SD	TN	TX	UT	VT	VA	WA	WV	WI	WY	AS	GU	MP	PR	VI
Inland Empire Health Plan	064578	.	.	.	.	D	.	.	.	.	.	.	.	.	.	.	.	.	.	.	.	.	.	.	.	.	.	.	.	.	.	.	.	.	.	.	.	.	.	.	.	.	.	.	.	.	.	.	.	.	.	.	.	.	.	.	.
InStil Health Insurance Co	013586	L	.	L	L	.	.	.	.	.	.	L	.	.	L	.	.	.	L	L	.	.	.	.	.	.	.	.	.	L	.	.	L	.	.	.	.	.	L	.	.	D	.	.	L	L	.	.	.	.	.	.	.	.	.	.	.
Insurance Co of Scott & White	060393	.	.	.	.	.	.	.	.	.	.	.	.	.	.	.	.	.	.	.	.	.	.	.	.	.	.	.	.	.	.	.	.	.	.	.	.	.	.	.	.	.	.	.	D	.	.	.	.	.	.	.	.	.	.	.	.
Integrity Capital Insurance Co	060398	.	.	.	.	.	.	.	.	.	.	.	.	.	.	D	.	.	.	.	.	.	.	.	.	.	.	.	.	.	.	.	.	.	.	.	.	.	.	.	.	.	.	.	.	.	.	.	.	.	.	.	.	.	.	.	.
Integrity Life Ins Co	007739	L	L	L	L	L	L	L	L	L	L	L	L	L	L	L	L	L	L	L	.	L	L	L	L	L	L	L	L	L	.	L	L	.	L	L	D	L	L	L	L	L	L	L	.	L	.	L	L	L	L	L	.	.	.	.	.
Inter-County Health Plan Inc	064466	.	.	.	.	.	.	.	.	.	.	.	.	.	.	.	.	.	.	.	.	.	.	.	.	.	.	.	.	.	.	.	.	.	.	.	.	.	.	D	.	.	.	.	.	.	.	.	.	.	.	.	.	.	.	.	.
Inter-County Hospitalization	064467	.	.	.	.	.	.	.	.	.	.	.	.	.	.	.	.	.	.	.	.	.	.	.	.	.	.	.	.	.	.	.	.	.	.	.	.	.	.	D	.	.	.	.	.	.	.	.	.	.	.	.	.	.	.	.	.
Inter Valley Health Plan Inc	064148	.	.	.	.	D	.	.	.	.	.	.	.	.	.	.	.	.	.	.	.	.	.	.	.	.	.	.	.	.	.	.	.	.	.	.	.	.	.	.	.	.	.	.	.	.	.	.	.	.	.	.	.	.	.	.	.
International American Life	068089	.	.	.	.	.	.	.	.	.	.	.	.	.	.	.	.	.	.	.	.	.	.	.	.	.	.	.	.	.	.	.	.	.	.	.	.	.	.	.	.	.	.	.	D	.	.	.	.	.	.	.	.	.	.	.	.
International HealthCare Svcs	064782	.	.	.	.	.	.	.	.	.	.	.	.	.	.	.	.	.	.	.	.	.	.	.	.	.	.	.	.	.	.	D	.	.	.	.	.	.	.	.	.	.	.	.	.	.	.	.	.	.	.	.	.	.	.	.	.
Interstate Bankers Life Ins Co	009095	.	.	.	.	.	.	.	.	.	.	.	.	.	D	.	.	.	.	.	.	.	.	.	.	.	.	.	.	.	.	.	.	.	.	.	.	.	.	.	.	.	.	.	.	.	.	.	.	.	.	.	.	.	.	.	.
Intramerica Life Ins Co	006572	.	.	L	L	.	.	L	.	.	L	.	L	.	L	L	.	.	L	L	.	L	L	L	.	.	L	.	L	L	.	L	L	D	L	.	.	.	L	L	.	.	.	.	L	L	L	.	.	.	.	L	.	.	.	L	.
Investors Consolidated Ins Co	008588	L	L	L	L	.	.	.	.	L	L	L	L	L	L	L	.	L	L	L	L	L	.	.	.	L	L	L	L	L	D	.	.	.	L	.	.	L	L	L	.	L	L	L	L	L	L	L	L	L	.	.	.	.	.	.	.
Investors Growth Life Ins Co	008650	.	.	D	.	.	.	.	.	.	.	.	.	.	.	.	.	.	.	.	.	.	.	.	.	.	.	.	.	.	.	.	.	.	.	.	.	.	.	.	.	.	.	.	.	.	.	.	.	.	.	.	.	.	.	.	.
Investors Heritage Life Ins Co	006580	L	.	L	L	.	L	.	.	.	L	L	.	.	L	L	.	L	D	L	.	L	.	L	.	L	L	L	L	.	.	.	L	.	L	L	L	L	.	L	.	L	L	L	L	L	.	L	.	L	.	.	.	.	.	.	.
Investors Insurance Corp	006583	.	L	L	L	L	L	L	D	L	L	L	L	L	L	L	L	L	.	L	.	L	L	L	.	L	L	L	L	L	.	.	L	.	L	L	L	L	L	L	.	L	L	L	L	L	.	.	L	L	.	L	.	.	.	.	.
Investors Life of North Amer	006412	L	L	L	L	L	L	L	L	L	L	L	L	L	L	L	L	L	L	L	L	L	L	L	L	L	L	L	L	L	L	L	L	.	L	L	L	L	L	L	L	L	L	L	D	L	L	L	L	L	L	L	.	.	.	.	L
Island Insurance Corp	060581	.	.	.	.	.	.	.	.	.	.	.	.	.	.	.	.	.	.	.	.	.	.	.	.	.	.	.	.	.	.	.	.	.	.	.	.	.	.	.	.	.	.	.	.	.	.	.	.	.	.	.	.	.	.	D	.
JMIC Life Insurance Company	008994	L	L	L	L	.	L	L	L	L	D	L	L	L	L	L	L	L	L	L	L	L	L	.	L	L	L	L	L	L	L	L	L	.	L	L	L	L	L	L	L	L	L	L	L	L	L	L	L	L	L	L	.	.	.	.	.
Jackson Griffin Insurance Co	068351	.	.	.	D	.	.	.	.	.	.	.	.	.	.	.	.	.	.	.	.	.	.	.	.	.	.	.	.	.	.	.	.	.	.	.	.	.	.	.	.	.	.	.	.	.	.	.	.	.	.	.	.	.	.	.	.
Jackson National Life Ins Co	006596	L	L	L	L	L	L	L	L	L	L	L	L	L	L	L	L	L	L	L	L	L	L	D	L	L	L	L	L	L	L	L	L	.	L	L	L	L	L	L	L	L	L	L	L	L	L	L	L	L	L	L	.	.	.	.	.
Jackson National Lf Ins of NY	060216	.	.	.	.	.	.	.	L	.	.	.	.	.	.	.	.	.	.	.	.	.	.	L	.	.	.	.	.	.	.	.	.	D	.	.	.	.	.	.	.	.	.	.	.	.	.	.	.	.	.	.	.	.	.	.	.
Jaimini Health Inc	064732	.	.	.	.	D	.	.	.	.	.	.	.	.	.	.	.	.	.	.	.	.	.	.	.	.	.	.	.	.	.	.	.	.	.	.	.	.	.	.	.	.	.	.	.	.	.	.	.	.	.	.	.	.	.	.	.
Jamestown Life Ins Co	009188	.	.	.	.	.	.	.	.	.	.	.	.	.	.	.	.	.	.	.	.	.	.	.	.	.	.	.	.	.	.	.	.	.	.	.	.	.	.	.	.	.	.	.	.	.	.	D	.	.	.	.	.	.	.	.	.
Jeff Davis Mortuary Ben Assoc	007750	.	.	.	.	.	.	.	.	.	.	.	.	.	.	.	.	.	.	D	.	.	.	.	.	.	.	.	.	.	.	.	.	.	.	.	.	.	.	.	.	.	.	.	.	.	.	.	.	.	.	.	.	.	.	.	.
Jefferson Life Insurance Co	009521	.	.	.	.	.	.	.	.	.	.	.	.	.	.	.	.	.	.	L	.	.	.	.	.	.	.	.	.	.	.	.	.	.	.	.	.	.	.	.	.	.	.	.	D	.	.	.	.	.	.	.	.	.	.	.	.
Jefferson National Life Ins Co	006475	L	L	L	L	L	L	L	L	L	L	L	L	L	L	L	L	L	L	L	L	L	L	L	L	L	L	L	L	L	L	L	L	.	L	L	L	L	L	L	L	L	L	L	D	L	L	L	L	L	L	L	L	L	L	L	L
John Alden Life Ins Co	006600	L	L	L	L	L	L	L	L	L	L	L	L	L	L	L	L	L	L	L	L	L	L	L	L	L	L	L	L	L	L	L	L	.	L	L	L	L	L	L	L	L	L	L	L	L	L	L	L	L	D	L	.	L	.	.	L
John D Kernan DMD PA	064916	.	.	.	.	.	.	.	.	.	.	.	.	.	.	.	.	.	.	.	.	.	.	.	.	.	.	.	.	.	.	D	.	.	.	.	.	.	.	.	.	.	.	.	.	.	.	.	.	.	.	.	.	.	.	.	.
John Hancock Life & Health Ins	009074	L	L	L	L	L	L	L	L	L	L	L	L	L	L	L	L	L	L	L	L	L	D	L	L	L	L	L	L	L	L	L	L	L	L	L	L	L	L	L	L	L	L	L	L	L	L	L	L	L	L	L	.	.	.	L	.
John Hancock Life Ins Co NY	060056	.	.	.	.	.	.	.	.	.	.	.	.	.	.	.	.	.	.	.	.	.	.	.	.	.	.	.	.	.	.	.	.	D	.	.	.	.	.	.	.	.	.	.	.	.	.	.	.	.	.	.	.	.	.	.	.
John Hancock Life Ins Co USA	006681	L	L	L	L	L	L	L	L	L	L	L	L	L	L	L	L	L	L	L	L	L	L	D	L	L	L	L	L	L	L	L	L	.	L	L	L	L	L	L	L	L	L	L	L	L	L	L	L	L	L	L	.	L	.	L	L
Jordan Funeral & Insurance Co	060353	D	.	.	.	.	.	.	.	.	.	.	.	.	.	.	.	.	.	.	.	.	.	.	.	.	.	.	.	.	.	.	.	.	.	.	.	.	.	.	.	.	.	.	.	.	.	.	.	.	.	.	.	.	.	.	.
Kaiser Foundation Health Plan	064585	.	.	.	.	D	.	.	.	.	.	.	.	.	.	.	.	.	.	.	.	.	.	.	.	.	.	.	.	.	.	.	.	.	.	.	.	.	.	.	.	.	.	.	.	.	.	.	.	.	.	.	.	.	.	.	.
Kaiser Fdn Health Plan of CO	068516	.	.	.	.	.	D	.	.	.	.	.	.	.	.	.	.	.	.	.	.	.	.	.	.	.	.	.	.	.	.	.	.	.	.	.	.	.	.	.	.	.	.	.	.	.	.	.	.	.	.	.	.	.	.	.	.
Kaiser Foundation Hlth P of GA	068528	.	.	.	.	.	.	.	.	.	.	D	.	.	.	.	.	.	.	.	.	.	.	.	.	.	.	.	.	.	.	.	.	.	.	.	.	.	.	.	.	.	.	.	.	.	.	.	.	.	.	.	.	.	.	.	.
Kaiser Foundation Hth Pl of OH	068577	.	.	.	.	.	.	.	.	.	.	.	.	.	.	.	.	.	.	.	.	.	.	.	.	.	.	.	.	.	.	.	.	.	.	.	D	.	.	.	.	.	.	.	.	.	.	.	.	.	.	.	.	.	.	.	.
Kaiser Fdn H Pl of the Mid-Atl	068551	.	.	.	.	.	.	.	.	L	.	.	.	.	.	.	.	.	.	.	.	D	.	.	.	.	.	.	.	.	.	.	.	.	.	.	.	.	.	.	.	.	.	.	.	.	.	L	.	.	.	.	.	.	.	.	.
Kaiser Fdn Health Pl of the NW	068585	.	.	.	.	.	.	.	.	.	.	.	.	.	.	.	.	.	.	.	.	.	.	.	.	.	.	.	.	.	.	.	.	.	.	.	.	.	D	.	.	.	.	.	.	.	.	.	L	.	.	.	.	.	.	.	.
Kanawha Insurance Company	006604	L	.	L	L	L	L	L	L	L	L	L	L	L	L	L	L	L	L	L	.	L	L	L	L	L	L	L	L	L	L	L	L	.	L	L	L	L	L	L	L	D	L	L	L	L	L	L	L	L	L	L	.	.	.	.	.
Kansas City Life Ins Co	006605	L	L	L	L	L	L	L	L	L	L	L	L	L	L	L	L	L	L	L	L	L	L	L	L	L	D	L	L	L	L	L	L	.	L	L	L	L	L	L	L	L	L	L	L	L	.	L	L	L	L	L	.	.	.	.	.
Kemper Investors Life Ins Co	006225	L	L	L	L	L	L	L	L	L	L	L	L	L	D	L	L	L	L	L	L	L	L	L	L	L	L	L	L	L	L	L	L	.	L	L	L	L	L	L	L	L	L	L	L	L	L	L	L	L	L	L	.	.	.	.	.
Kentucky Funeral Directors Lf	060365	.	.	.	.	.	.	.	.	.	.	.	.	.	.	.	.	.	D	.	.	.	.	.	.	.	.	.	.	.	.	.	.	.	.	.	.	.	.	.	.	.	.	.	.	.	.	.	.	.	.	.	.	.	.	.	.
Kentucky Home Life Ins Co	060296	.	.	.	.	.	.	.	.	.	.	.	.	.	.	.	.	.	D	.	.	.	.	.	.	.	.	.	.	.	.	.	.	.	.	.	.	.	.	.	.	.	.	.	.	.	.	.	.	.	.	.	.	.	.	.	.
Keokuk Area Hosp Org Deliv Sys	064676	.	.	.	.	.	.	.	.	.	.	.	.	.	.	.	D	.	.	.	.	.	.	.	.	.	.	.	.	.	.	.	.	.	.	.	.	.	.	.	.	.	.	.	.	.	.	.	.	.	.	.	.	.	.	.	.
Kern Health Systems	064084	.	.	.	.	D	.	.	.	.	.	.	.	.	.	.	.	.	.	.	.	.	.	.	.	.	.	.	.	.	.	.	.	.	.	.	.	.	.	.	.	.	.	.	.	.	.	.	.	.	.	.	.	.	.	.	.
Kern Health Systs Gr Hlth Plan	064851	.	.	.	.	D	.	.	.	.	.	.	.	.	.	.	.	.	.	.	.	.	.	.	.	.	.	.	.	.	.	.	.	.	.	.	.	.	.	.	.	.	.	.	.	.	.	.	.	.	.	.	.	.	.	.	.
Keystone Health Plan Central	064051	.	.	.	.	.	.	.	.	.	.	.	.	.	.	.	.	.	.	.	.	.	.	.	.	.	.	.	.	.	.	.	.	.	.	.	.	.	.	D	.	.	.	.	.	.	.	.	.	.	.	.	.	.	.	.	.
Keystone Health Plan East Inc	068924	.	.	.	.	.	.	.	.	.	.	.	.	.	.	.	.	.	.	.	.	.	.	.	.	.	.	.	.	.	.	.	.	.	.	.	.	.	.	D	.	.	.	.	.	.	.	.	.	.	.	.	.	.	.	.	.
Keystone Health Plan West Inc	068833	.	.	.	.	.	.	.	.	.	.	.	.	.	.	.	.	.	.	.	.	.	.	.	.	.	.	.	.	.	.	.	.	.	.	.	.	.	.	D	.	.	.	.	.	.	.	.	.	.	.	.	.	.	.	.	.
Kilpatrick Life Ins Co of LA	007756	.	.	.	L	.	.	.	.	.	.	.	.	.	.	.	.	.	.	D	.	.	.	.	.	L	.	.	.	.	.	.	.	.	.	.	.	L	.	.	.	.	.	.	L	.	.	.	.	.	.	.	.	.	.	.	.
Knights of Columbus	006616	L	L	L	L	L	L	D	L	L	L	L	L	L	L	L	L	L	L	L	L	L	L	L	L	L	L	L	L	L	L	L	L	L	L	L	L	L	L	L	L	L	L	L	L	L	L	L	L	L	L	L	.	L	.	L	L
KPS Health Plans	064627	.	.	.	.	.	.	.	.	.	.	.	.	.	.	.	.	.	.	.	.	.	.	.	.	.	.	.	.	.	.	.	.	.	.	.	.	.	.	.	.	.	.	.	.	.	.	.	D	.	.	.	.	.	.	.	.
KS Plan Administrators L L C	064972	.	.	.	.	.	.	.	.	.	.	.	.	.	.	.	.	.	.	.	.	.	.	.	.	.	.	.	.	.	.	.	.	.	.	.	.	.	.	.	.	.	.	.	D	.	.	.	.	.	.	.	.	.	.	.	.
Lafourche Life Ins Co	007759	.	.	.	.	.	.	.	.	.	.	.	.	.	.	.	.	.	.	D	.	.	.	.	.	.	.	.	.	.	.	.	.	.	.	.	.	.	.	.	.	.	.	.	.	.	.	.	.	.	.	.	.	.	.	.	.
Landcar Life Ins Co	009255	.	.	L	.	.	L	.	.	.	.	.	.	L	.	.	.	.	.	.	.	.	.	.	.	.	.	.	.	.	.	.	L	.	.	.	.	.	L	.	.	.	.	.	L	D	.	.	.	.	.	.	.	.	.	.	.
Landmark Healthplan of CA	064766	.	.	.	.	D	.	.	.	.	.	.	.	.	.	.	.	.	.	.	.	.	.	.	.	.	.	.	.	.	.	.	.	.	.	.	.	.	.	.	.	.	.	.	.	.	.	.	.	.	.	.	.	.	.	.	.
Landmark Life Insurance Co	068055	.	.	.	L	.	.	.	.	.	.	.	.	.	.	.	.	.	.	L	.	.	.	.	.	.	.	.	.	.	.	.	L	.	.	.	.	L	.	.	.	.	.	.	D	.	.	.	.	.	.	.	.	.	.	.	.
Laurel Life Ins Co	068076	.	.	.	.	.	.	.	.	.	.	.	.	.	.	.	.	.	.	.	.	.	.	.	.	.	.	.	.	.	.	.	.	.	.	.	.	.	.	.	.	.	.	.	D	.	.	.	.	.	.	.	.	.	.	.	.
Leaders Life Ins Co	068017	.	.	.	L	.	.	.	.	.	.	.	.	.	.	.	.	L	.	.	.	.	.	.	.	.	.	.	.	.	.	.	.	.	.	.	.	D	.	.	.	.	.	.	L	.	.	.	.	.	.	.	.	.	.	.	.
Legacy Health Solutions	064892	.	.	.	.	.	.	.	.	.	.	.	.	.	.	.	.	.	.	.	.	.	.	.	.	.	.	.	.	.	.	.	.	.	.	.	.	.	.	.	.	.	.	.	D	.	.	.	.	.	.	.	.	.	.	.	.
Lewer Life Ins Co	007393	.	.	L	.	.	.	.	.	.	.	.	.	.	L	.	.	L	.	L	.	.	.	.	.	L	D	.	.	.	.	.	.	.	.	.	.	L	L	.	.	.	L	.	L	.	.	.	.	.	.	.	.	.	.	.	.
Lewis Life Insurance Company	068233	.	.	.	.	.	.	.	.	.	.	.	.	.	.	.	.	.	.	.	.	.	.	.	.	.	.	.	.	.	.	.	.	.	.	.	.	.	.	.	.	.	.	.	D	.	.	.	.	.	.	.	.	.	.	.	.
Liberty Bankers Life Ins Co	007011	.	.	L	L	L	L	.	L	.	L	L	L	L	L	L	L	L	L	L	.	L	.	L	.	L	L	L	L	L	.	.	L	.	L	L	L	D	L	L	.	L	L	L	L	L	.	L	L	L	L	L	.	.	.	.	.
Liberty Dental Plan of CA	064663	.	.	.	.	D	.	.	.	.	.	.	.	.	.	.	.	.	.	.	.	.	.	.	.	.	.	.	.	.	.	.	.	.	.	.	.	.	.	.	.	.	.	.	.	.	.	.	.	.	.	.	.	.	.	.	.
Liberty Life Assur of Boston	006627	L	L	L	L	L	L	L	L	L	L	L	L	L	L	L	L	L	L	L	L	L	D	L	L	L	L	L	L	L	L	L	L	L	L	L	L	L	L	L	L	L	L	L	L	L	L	L	L	L	L	L	.	.	.	.	.
Liberty Life Insurance Company	006175	L	L	L	L	L	L	L	L	L	L	L	L	L	L	L	L	L	L	L	L	L	L	L	L	L	L	L	L	L	L	L	L	.	L	L	L	L	L	L	L	D	L	L	L	L	L	L	L	L	L	L	.	.	.	.	.
Liberty National Life Ins Co	006629	L	L	L	L	L	L	L	L	L	L	L	L	L	L	L	L	L	L	L	L	L	L	L	L	L	L	L	D	L	L	L	L	.	L	L	L	L	L	L	L	L	L	L	L	L	L	L	L	L	L	L	.	L	.	.	.
Liberty Union Life Assurance	006799	.	.	.	.	.	.	.	.	.	.	.	.	.	.	.	.	.	.	.	.	.	.	D	.	.	.	.	.	.	.	.	.	.	.	.	.	.	.	.	.	.	.	.	.	.	.	.	.	L	.	.	.	.	.	.	.
Life Assurance Company	008635	.	.	.	.	.	.	.	.	.	.	.	.	.	.	.	.	.	.	.	.	.	.	.	.	.	.	.	.	.	.	.	.	.	.	.	.	D	.	.	.	.	.	.	.	.	.	.	.	.	.	.	.	.	.	.	.
Life Assurance Co of America	007768	.	.	.	.	.	.	.	.	.	.	.	.	.	D	.	.	.	.	.	.	.	.	.	.	.	.	.	.	.	.	.	.	.	.	.	.	.	.	.	.	.	.	.	.	.	.	.	.	.	.	.	.	.	.	.	.
Life Insurance Co of Alabama	006637	D	.	.	L	.	.	.	.	.	L	L	.	.	.	.	.	.	L	L	.	.	.	.	.	L	.	.	.	.	.	.	.	.	L	.	.	L	.	.	.	L	.	L	.	.	.	.	.	.	.	.	.	.	.	.	.
Life Ins Co of Boston & NY	068126	.	.	.	.	.	.	.	.	.	.	.	.	.	.	.	.	.	.	.	.	.	.	.	.	.	.	.	.	.	.	.	.	D	.	.	.	.	.	.	.	.	.	.	.	.	.	.	.	.	.	.	.	.	.	.	.
Life Insurance Co of Louisiana	007775	.	.	.	.	.	.	.	.	.	.	.	.	.	.	.	.	.	.	D	.	.	.	.	.	.	.	.	.	.	.	.	.	.	.	.	.	.	.	.	.	.	.	.	.	.	.	.	.	.	.	.	.	.	.	.	.
Life Insurance Co of North Amer	006645	L	L	L	L	L	L	L	L	L	L	L	L	L	L	L	L	L	L	L	L	L	L	L	L	L	L	L	L	L	L	L	L	Q	L	L	L	L	L	D	L	L	L	L	L	L	L	L	L	L	L	L	.	.	.	L	L
Life Insurance Co of Southwest	006647	L	L	L	L	L	L	L	L	L	L	L	L	L	L	L	L	L	L	L	L	L	L	L	L	L	L	L	L	L	L	L	L	.	L	L	L	L	L	L	L	L	L	L	D	L	L	L	L	L	L	L	.	.	.	.	.

D-State of Domicile **L**-Licensed **S**-Surplus Lines Writer **F**-Authorized under the Risk Retention Act **Q**-Qualified or Accredited Reinsurer

U.S. States/Territories in Which Companies Are Licensed or Do Business – *Continued*

Company Name	AMB#	AL	AK	AZ	AR	CA	CO	CT	DE	DC	FL	GA	HI	ID	IL	IN	IA	KS	KY	LA	ME	MD	MA	MI	MN	MS	MO	MT	NE	NV	NH	NJ	NM	NY	NC	ND	OH	OK	OR	PA	RI	SC	SD	TN	TX	UT	VT	VA	WA	WV	WI	WY	AS	GU	MP	PR	VI
Life of America Insurance Co	006574	.	.	L	.	.	L	.	.	.	L	L	.	L	.	L	L	.	.	L	.	.	.	.	.	L	.	L	.	L	.	.	.	.	.	.	.	L	.	.	.	.	.	L	D	L	.	.	.	.	.	.	.	.	.	.	.
Life of the South Insurance Co	008921	L	L	L	L	.	.	L	L	L	L	D	L	L	L	L	.	L	L	L	L	L	L	L	L	L	L	L	L	L	L	.	L	.	L	L	L	L	L	L	L	L	L	L	L	L	L	L	L	L	.	L	.	.	.	.	.
Life Protection Ins Co	006653	.	.	.	.	.	.	.	.	.	.	.	.	.	.	.	.	.	.	.	.	.	.	.	.	.	.	.	.	.	.	.	.	.	.	.	.	.	.	.	.	.	.	.	D	.	.	.	.	.	.	.	.	.	.	.	.
LifeCare Assurance Co	009200	.	.	D	.	L	.	.	.	.	.	.	.	.	.	L	.	.	.	.	.	.	.	.	.	L	L	.	.	.	.	.	.	.	L	.	.	.	.	.	.	.	.	.	.	.	.	.	.	.	.	.	.	.	.	.	.
LifeSecure Insurance Company	060645	L	L	L	L	L	L	.	L	L	L	L	L	L	L	L	L	L	L	L	.	L	.	D	L	L	L	L	L	L	.	.	L	.	L	L	L	L	L	L	.	L	L	L	L	L	.	L	L	L	L	L	.	.	.	.	.
LifeShield National Ins Co	009458	.	.	L	L	.	L	.	.	.	.	.	.	L	L	.	.	L	.	.	.	.	.	.	.	.	.	L	L	L	.	.	L	.	.	.	.	D	L	.	.	.	L	.	L	L	.	.	.	.	.	.	.	.	.	.	.
LifeWise Assurance Company	009086	.	L	L	.	L	.	.	.	.	.	.	.	L	.	.	.	.	.	.	.	.	.	.	.	.	.	L	.	.	.	.	L	.	.	L	.	.	L	.	.	.	.	.	.	L	.	.	D	.	.	L	.	.	.	.	.
LifeWise Health Plan of AZ	068458	.	.	L	.	.	.	.	.	.	.	.	.	.	.	.	.	.	.	.	.	.	.	.	.	.	.	.	.	.	.	.	.	.	.	.	.	.	.	.	.	.	.	.	.	.	.	.	D	.	.	.	.	.	.	.	.
LifeWise Health Plan of Oregon	068259	.	.	.	.	.	.	.	.	.	.	.	.	L	.	.	.	.	.	.	.	.	.	.	.	.	.	.	.	.	.	.	.	.	.	.	.	.	D	.	.	.	.	.	.	.	.	.	.	.	.	.	.	.	.	.	.
LifeWise Health Plan of WA	064608	.	.	.	.	.	.	.	.	.	.	.	.	.	.	.	.	.	.	.	.	.	.	.	.	.	.	.	.	.	.	.	.	.	.	.	.	.	.	.	.	.	.	.	.	.	.	.	D	.	.	.	.	.	.	.	.
Lincoln Benefit Life Co	006657	L	L	L	L	L	L	L	L	L	L	L	L	L	L	L	L	L	L	L	L	L	L	L	L	L	L	L	D	L	L	L	L	.	L	L	L	L	L	L	L	L	L	L	L	L	L	L	L	L	L	L	.	L	.	.	L
Lincoln Heritage Life Ins Co	006694	L	L	L	L	L	L	L	L	L	L	L	L	L	D	L	L	L	L	L	L	L	L	L	L	L	L	L	L	L	L	L	L	.	L	L	L	L	L	L	L	L	L	L	L	L	L	L	L	L	L	L	.	.	.	L	.
Lincoln Life & Annuity Co NY	006239	L	L	L	L	L	L	L	L	L	L	L	L	L	L	L	L	L	L	L	L	L	L	L	L	L	L	L	L	L	L	L	L	D	L	L	L	L	L	L	L	L	L	L	L	L	L	L	L	L	L	L	.	.	.	.	L
Lincoln Memorial Life Ins Co	007162	L	L	L	L	L	L	L	L	L	.	L	L	L	L	L	L	L	L	L	L	L	.	.	L	L	L	L	L	L	.	.	.	.	L	L	L	L	L	L	L	L	L	L	D	L	L	L	L	L	L	L	.	.	.	.	.
Lincoln Mutual Life & Casualty	006662	.	.	L	.	.	L	.	.	.	.	.	.	L	.	.	L	L	.	.	.	.	.	.	L	.	.	L	L	.	.	.	.	.	.	D	.	L	L	.	.	.	L	.	.	L	.	.	.	.	L	L	.	.	.	.	.
Lincoln National Life Ins Co	006664	L	L	L	L	L	L	L	L	L	L	L	L	L	L	D	L	L	L	L	L	L	L	L	L	L	L	L	L	L	L	L	L	.	L	L	L	L	L	L	L	L	L	L	L	L	L	L	L	L	L	L	.	L	L	L	L
Local Initiative Hlth Auth LA	064652	.	.	.	.	D	.	.	.	.	.	.	.	.	.	.	.	.	.	.	.	.	.	.	.	.	.	.	.	.	.	.	.	.	.	.	.	.	.	.	.	.	.	.	.	.	.	.	.	.	.	.	.	.	.	.	.
Locomotive Engineers&Conductor	068235	.	.	.	.	.	.	.	.	.	.	.	.	.	.	.	.	.	.	.	.	.	.	D	.	.	.	.	L	.	.	.	L	.	.	.	.	.	.	.	.	.	.	.	L	.	.	.	.	.	.	.	.	.	.	.	.
London Life Reinsurance Co	060237	L	L	L	L	L	L	L	L	L	L	L	L	L	L	L	L	L	L	L	Q	L	L	L	L	L	L	L	L	L	L	L	L	Q	L	L	L	L	L	D	L	L	L	L	L	L	Q	Q	L	L	L	L	.	.	.	Q	.
Longevity Insurance Company	060701	L	L	L	L	L	L	L	L	L	L	L	.	L	L	L	L	L	L	L	.	L	.	L	L	L	L	L	L	L	.	L	L	.	L	.	L	L	L	L	.	L	L	L	D	L	.	L	L	L	L	.	.	.	.	.	.
Louisiana Hlth Svc & Indemnity	068440	.	.	.	.	.	.	.	.	.	.	.	.	.	.	.	.	.	.	D	.	.	.	.	.	.	.	.	.	.	.	.	.	.	.	.	.	.	.	.	.	.	.	.	.	.	.	.	.	.	.	.	.	.	.	.	.
Loyal American Life Ins Co	006671	L	L	L	L	L	L	L	L	L	L	L	L	L	L	L	L	L	L	L	L	L	L	L	L	L	L	L	L	L	L	L	L	.	L	L	D	L	L	L	L	L	L	L	L	L	L	L	L	L	L	L	.	.	.	.	L
M Life Insurance Company	009096	.	.	Q	.	.	D	.	Q	.	.	.	.	.	.	.	.	.	.	.	.	.	.	Q	.	.	.	.	Q	.	.	Q	.	.	.	.	.	.	.	.	.	.	.	.	.	.	.	.	.	.	.	.	.	.	.	.	.
M-Plan Inc	060142	.	.	.	.	.	.	.	.	.	.	.	.	.	.	D	.	.	.	.	.	.	.	.	.	.	.	.	.	.	.	.	.	.	.	.	.	.	.	.	.	.	.	.	.	.	.	.	.	.	.	.	.	.	.	.	.
Madison Natl Life Ins Co Inc	006678	L	L	L	L	L	L	L	L	L	L	L	L	L	L	L	L	L	L	L	L	L	L	L	L	L	L	L	L	L	L	L	L	Q	L	L	L	L	L	L	L	L	L	L	L	L	L	L	L	L	D	L	L	L	.	.	L
Magellan Behavioral Hlth of IA	064675	.	.	.	.	.	.	.	.	.	.	.	.	.	.	.	D	.	.	.	.	.	.	.	.	.	.	.	.	.	.	.	.	.	.	.	.	.	.	.	.	.	.	.	.	.	.	.	.	.	.	.	.	.	.	.	.
Magellan Behavioral Hlth of PA	064552	.	.	.	.	.	.	.	.	.	.	.	.	.	.	.	.	.	.	.	.	.	.	.	.	.	.	.	.	.	.	.	.	.	.	.	.	.	.	D	.	.	.	.	.	.	.	.	.	.	.	.	.	.	.	.	.
Magellan Health Services of CA	064650	.	.	.	.	D	.	.	.	.	.	.	.	.	.	.	.	.	.	.	.	.	.	.	.	.	.	.	.	.	.	.	.	.	.	.	.	.	.	.	.	.	.	.	.	.	.	.	.	.	.	.	.	.	.	.	.
Magna Insurance Company	068127	L	.	.	L	.	.	.	.	.	L	L	.	.	L	L	L	.	L	L	.	.	.	.	.	D	L	.	.	.	.	.	.	.	L	.	.	.	.	.	.	L	.	L	L	.	.	.	.	.	.	.	.	.	.	.	.
Maine Dental Service Corp	064639	.	.	.	.	.	.	.	.	.	.	.	.	.	.	.	.	.	.	.	D	.	.	.	.	.	.	.	.	.	.	.	.	.	.	.	.	.	.	.	.	.	.	.	.	.	.	.	.	.	.	.	.	.	.	.	.
Majestic Life Ins Co	007786	.	.	.	.	.	.	.	.	.	.	.	.	.	.	.	.	.	.	D	.	.	.	.	.	.	.	.	.	.	.	.	.	.	.	.	.	.	.	.	.	.	.	.	.	.	.	.	.	.	.	.	.	.	.	.	.
MAMSI Life and Health Ins	006046	L	.	L	L	L	L	.	L	L	.	L	L	L	L	L	.	L	L	L	.	D	.	.	.	L	L	.	L	L	.	.	L	.	.	.	.	L	.	L	.	L	L	L	L	L	.	L	.	L	.	.	.	.	.	.	.
Managed Dental Care of CA	064657	.	.	.	.	D	.	.	.	.	.	.	.	.	.	.	.	.	.	.	.	.	.	.	.	.	.	.	.	.	.	.	.	.	.	.	.	.	.	.	.	.	.	.	.	.	.	.	.	.	.	.	.	.	.	.	.
Managed DentalGuard Inc	064822	.	.	.	.	.	.	.	.	.	.	.	.	.	.	.	.	.	.	.	.	.	.	.	.	.	.	.	.	.	.	D	.	.	.	.	.	.	.	.	.	.	.	.	.	.	.	.	.	.	.	.	.	.	.	.	.
Managed DentalGuard Inc	064646	.	.	.	.	.	.	.	.	.	.	.	.	.	.	.	.	.	.	.	.	.	.	.	.	.	.	.	.	.	.	.	.	.	.	.	.	.	.	.	.	.	.	.	D	.	.	.	.	.	.	.	.	.	.	.	.
Managed Health Inc	064346	.	.	.	.	.	.	.	.	.	.	.	.	.	.	.	.	.	.	.	.	.	.	.	.	.	.	.	.	.	.	.	.	D	.	.	.	.	.	.	.	.	.	.	.	.	.	.	.	.	.	.	.	.	.	.	.
Managed Health Network	064673	.	.	.	.	D	.	.	.	.	.	.	.	.	.	.	.	.	.	.	.	.	.	.	.	.	.	.	.	.	.	.	.	.	.	.	.	.	.	.	.	.	.	.	.	.	.	.	.	.	.	.	.	.	.	.	.
Managed Health Services Ins Cp	064205	.	.	.	.	.	.	.	.	.	.	.	.	.	.	.	.	.	.	.	.	.	.	.	.	.	.	.	.	.	.	.	.	.	.	.	.	.	.	.	.	.	.	.	.	.	.	.	.	.	D	.	.	.	.	.	.
Manhattan Life Ins Co	006686	L	L	L	L	L	L	L	L	L	L	L	L	L	L	L	L	L	L	L	L	L	L	L	L	L	L	L	L	L	L	L	L	D	L	L	L	L	L	L	L	L	L	L	L	L	L	L	L	L	L	L	.	.	.	.	.
Manhattan National Life Ins Co	006842	L	L	L	L	L	L	L	L	L	L	L	L	L	D	L	L	L	L	L	L	L	L	L	L	L	L	L	L	L	L	L	L	.	L	L	L	L	L	L	L	L	L	L	L	L	L	L	L	L	L	L	.	.	.	.	.
MAPFRE Life Insurance Company	007981	.	.	.	.	.	.	.	.	.	.	.	.	.	.	.	.	.	.	.	.	.	.	.	.	.	.	.	.	.	.	.	.	.	.	.	.	.	.	.	.	.	.	.	.	.	.	.	.	.	.	.	.	.	.	D	L
March Vision Care Inc	064933	.	.	.	.	D	.	.	.	.	.	.	.	.	.	.	.	.	.	.	.	.	.	.	.	.	.	.	.	.	.	.	.	.	.	.	.	.	.	.	.	.	.	.	.	.	.	.	.	.	.	.	.	.	.	.	.
Marion Polk Community H Pl Adv	064905	.	.	.	.	.	.	.	.	.	.	.	.	.	.	.	.	.	.	.	.	.	.	.	.	.	.	.	.	.	.	.	.	.	.	.	.	.	D	.	.	.	.	.	.	.	.	.	.	.	.	.	.	.	.	.	.
Marquette Indemnity & Life Ins	008804	.	.	D	.	.	.	.	.	.	.	.	.	.	L	L	.	.	.	.	.	.	.	.	.	.	L	.	.	.	.	.	.	.	.	.	.	.	.	.	.	.	.	.	.	.	.	.	.	.	.	.	.	.	.	L	.
Marquette National Life Ins Co	007311	L	L	L	L	L	L	.	L	L	L	.	L	L	.	L	L	L	L	L	.	L	L	.	.	L	L	L	L	L	.	.	L	.	.	L	L	L	L	L	L	L	L	L	D	L	L	.	L	L	L	L	.	.	.	.	.
Maryland Care Inc	064897	.	.	.	.	.	.	.	.	.	.	.	.	.	.	.	.	.	.	.	.	D	.	.	.	.	.	.	.	.	.	.	.	.	.	.	.	.	.	.	.	.	.	.	.	.	.	.	.	.	.	.	.	.	.	.	.
Massachusetts Mutual Life Ins	006695	L	L	L	L	L	L	L	L	L	L	L	L	L	L	L	L	L	L	L	L	L	D	L	L	L	L	L	L	L	L	L	L	L	L	L	L	L	L	L	L	L	L	L	L	L	L	L	L	L	L	L	.	.	.	L	.
Massachusetts Vision Svc Plan	064479	.	.	.	.	.	.	.	.	.	.	.	.	.	.	.	.	.	.	.	.	.	D	.	.	.	.	.	.	.	.	.	.	.	.	.	.	.	.	.	.	.	.	.	.	.	.	.	.	.	.	.	.	.	.	.	.
Matthew Thornton Health Plan	068999	.	.	.	.	.	.	.	.	.	.	.	.	.	.	.	.	.	.	.	.	.	.	.	.	.	.	.	.	.	D	.	.	.	.	.	.	.	.	.	.	.	.	.	.	.	.	.	.	.	.	.	.	.	.	.	.
Max Vision Care Inc	064934	.	.	.	.	D	.	.	.	.	.	.	.	.	.	.	.	.	.	.	.	.	.	.	.	.	.	.	.	.	.	.	.	.	.	.	.	.	.	.	.	.	.	.	.	.	.	.	.	.	.	.	.	.	.	.	.
McDonald Life Insurance Co	009570	.	.	.	.	.	.	.	.	.	.	.	.	.	.	.	.	.	.	.	.	.	.	.	.	.	.	.	.	.	.	.	.	.	.	.	.	.	.	.	.	.	.	.	D	.	.	.	.	.	.	.	.	.	.	.	.
McKinley Life Ins Co	068111	.	.	.	.	.	.	.	.	.	.	.	.	.	.	.	.	.	.	.	.	.	.	.	.	.	.	.	.	.	.	.	.	.	.	.	D	.	.	.	.	.	.	.	.	.	.	.	.	.	.	.	.	.	.	.	.
McLaren Health Plan Inc	064616	.	.	.	.	.	.	.	.	.	.	.	.	.	.	.	.	.	.	.	.	.	.	D	.	.	.	.	.	.	.	.	.	.	.	.	.	.	.	.	.	.	.	.	.	.	.	.	.	.	.	.	.	.	.	.	.
MCS Life Insurance Company	060379	.	.	.	.	.	.	.	.	.	.	.	.	.	.	.	.	.	.	.	.	.	.	.	.	.	.	.	.	.	.	.	.	.	.	.	.	.	.	.	.	.	.	.	.	.	.	.	.	.	.	.	.	.	.	D	.
MD-Individual Practice Assoc	068606	.	.	.	.	.	.	.	.	L	.	.	.	.	.	.	.	.	.	.	.	D	.	.	.	.	.	.	.	.	.	.	.	.	.	.	.	.	.	.	.	.	.	.	.	.	.	L	.	.	.	.	.	.	.	.	.
MDNY Healthcare Inc	064291	.	.	.	.	.	.	.	.	.	.	.	.	.	.	.	.	.	.	.	.	.	.	.	.	.	.	.	.	.	.	.	.	D	.	.	.	.	.	.	.	.	.	.	.	.	.	.	.	.	.	.	.	.	.	.	.
MDwise Inc	064386	.	.	.	.	.	.	.	.	.	.	.	.	.	.	D	.	.	.	.	.	.	.	.	.	.	.	.	.	.	.	.	.	.	.	.	.	.	.	.	.	.	.	.	.	.	.	.	.	.	.	.	.	.	.	.	.
MedAmerica Insurance Co	007131	L	L	L	L	L	L	L	L	L	.	L	L	L	L	L	L	L	L	L	L	L	L	L	L	L	L	L	L	L	L	L	L	.	L	L	L	L	L	D	L	L	L	L	L	L	L	L	L	L	L	L	.	.	.	.	.
MedAmerica Ins Co of Florida	060658	.	.	.	.	.	.	.	.	.	D	.	.	.	.	.	.	.	.	.	.	.	.	.	.	.	.	.	.	.	.	.	.	.	.	.	.	.	.	.	.	.	.	.	.	.	.	.	.	.	.	.	.	.	.	.	.
MedAmerica Ins Co of New York	060021	.	.	.	.	.	.	.	.	.	.	.	.	.	.	.	.	.	.	.	.	.	.	.	.	.	.	.	.	.	.	.	.	D	.	.	.	.	.	.	.	.	.	.	.	.	.	.	.	.	.	.	.	.	.	.	.
Medco Containment Ins Co of NY	010747	.	.	.	.	.	.	.	.	.	.	.	.	.	.	.	.	.	.	.	.	.	.	.	.	.	.	.	.	.	.	.	.	D	.	.	.	.	.	.	.	.	.	.	.	.	.	.	.	.	.	.	.	.	.	.	.
Medco Containment Life Ins Co	006449	L	L	L	L	L	L	L	L	L	L	L	L	L	L	L	L	L	L	L	L	L	L	L	L	L	L	L	L	L	L	L	L	.	.	.	L	L	L	D	L	L	L	L	L	L	L	L	L	L	L	L	.	.	.	L	.
Medcore HP	064788	.	.	.	.	D	.	.	.	.	.	.	.	.	.	.	.	.	.	.	.	.	.	.	.	.	.	.	.	.	.	.	.	.	.	.	.	.	.	.	.	.	.	.	.	.	.	.	.	.	.	.	.	.	.	.	.
Medica Health Plans	068559	.	.	.	.	.	.	.	.	.	.	.	.	.	.	.	.	.	.	.	.	.	.	.	D	.	.	.	.	.	.	.	.	.	.	.	.	.	.	.	.	.	L	.	.	.	.	.	.	.	.	.	.	.	.	.	.
Medica Health Plans of WI	064445	.	.	.	.	.	.	.	.	.	.	.	.	.	.	.	.	.	.	.	.	.	.	.	.	.	.	.	.	.	.	.	.	.	.	.	.	.	.	.	.	.	.	.	.	.	.	.	.	.	D	.	.	.	.	.	.
Medica Insurance Company	011072	.	.	.	.	.	.	.	.	.	.	.	.	.	.	.	.	.	.	.	.	.	.	.	D	.	.	.	.	.	.	.	.	.	.	.	.	.	.	.	.	.	L	.	.	.	.	.	.	.	L	.	.	.	.	.	.
Medical Associates Clinic WI	068612	.	.	.	.	.	.	.	.	.	.	.	.	.	.	.	.	.	.	.	.	.	.	.	.	.	.	.	.	.	.	.	.	.	.	.	.	.	.	.	.	.	.	.	.	.	.	.	.	.	D	.	.	.	.	.	.
Medical Associates Health Plan	068542	.	.	.	.	.	.	.	.	.	.	.	.	.	L	.	D	.	.	.	.	.	.	.	.	.	.	.	.	.	.	.	.	.	.	.	.	.	.	.	.	.	.	.	.	.	.	.	.	.	.	.	.	.	.	.	.
Medical Benefits Mutual Life	068036	.	.	.	L	.	.	.	.	.	.	.	.	.	L	L	.	L	.	.	.	.	.	L	.	.	L	.	.	.	.	.	.	.	L	.	D	.	.	.	.	L	.	L	.	.	.	.	.	L	.	.	.	.	.	.	.
Medical Eye Services Inc	064712	.	.	.	.	D	.	.	.	.	.	.	.	.	.	.	.	.	.	.	.	.	.	.	.	.	.	.	.	.	.	.	.	.	.	.	.	.	.	.	.	.	.	.	.	.	.	.	.	.	.	.	.	.	.	.	.
Medical Health Insuring Ohio	064217	.	.	.	.	.	.	.	.	.	.	.	.	.	.	.	.	.	.	.	.	.	.	.	.	.	.	.	.	.	.	.	.	.	.	.	D	.	.	.	.	.	.	.	.	.	.	.	.	.	.	.	.	.	.	.	.
Medical Mutual of Ohio	004693	.	.	.	.	.	.	.	.	.	.	.	.	.	.	L	.	.	.	.	.	.	.	L	.	.	.	.	.	.	.	.	.	.	.	.	D	.	.	L	.	.	.	.	.	.	.	.	.	.	.	.	.	.	.	.	.
Medical Savings Insurance Co	007677	L	L	L	L	L	L	.	.	L	L	L	.	L	L	D	L	L	L	L	.	.	.	.	.	L	L	L	L	L	.	.	L	.	L	L	L	L	L	.	.	L	L	L	L	L	.	L	L	L	.	.	.	.	.	.	.
Medico Insurance Company	003150	L	L	L	L	L	L	.	L	L	L	L	L	L	L	L	L	L	L	L	L	L	L	L	L	L	L	L	D	L	L	.	L	.	.	L	L	L	L	L	L	L	L	L	L	L	L	L	L	L	L	L	.	.	.	.	.
MEGA Life and Health Ins Co	009190	L	L	L	L	L	L	L	L	L	L	L	L	L	L	L	L	L	L	L	L	L	L	L	L	L	L	L	L	L	L	L	L	.	L	L	L	D	L	L	L	L	L	L	L	L	L	L	L	L	L	L	.	.	.	.	.
Melancon Life Ins Co	007794	.	.	.	.	.	.	.	.	.	.	.	.	.	.	.	.	.	.	D	.	.	.	.	.	.	.	.	.	.	.	.	.	.	.	.	.	.	.	.	.	.	.	.	.	.	.	.	.	.	.	.	.	.	.	.	.

D-State of Domicile **L**-Licensed **S**-Surplus Lines Writer **F**-Authorized under the Risk Retention Act **Q**-Qualified or Accredited Reinsurer

U.S. States/Territories in Which Companies Are Licensed or Do Business – *Continued*

Company Name	AMB#	AL	AK	AZ	AR	CA	CO	CT	DE	DC	FL	GA	HI	ID	IL	IN	IA	KS	KY	LA	ME	MD	MA	MI	MN	MS	MO	MT	NE	NV	NH	NJ	NM	NY	NC	ND	OH	OK	OR	PA	RI	SC	SD	TN	TX	UT	VT	VA	WA	WV	WI	WY	AS	GU	MP	PR	VI
Mellon Life Ins Co	009048	.	.	.	.	.	.	.	D	.	.	.	.	.	.	.	.	.	.	.	.	.	.	.	.	.	.	.	.	.	.	.	.	.	.	.	.	.	.	.	.	.	.	.	.	.	.	.	.	.	.	.	.	.	.	.	.
MEMBERS Life Ins Co	008719	L	L	L	L	L	L	L	L	L	L	L	L	L	L	L	D	L	L	L	L	L	L	L	L	L	L	L	L	L	L	L	L	.	L	L	L	L	L	L	L	L	L	L	L	L	L	L	L	L	L	L	.	.	.	.	.
Memorial Insurance Co of Amer	068356	.	.	.	D	.	.	.	.	.	.	.	.	.	.	.	.	.	.	.	.	.	.	.	.	.	.	.	.	.	.	.	.	.	.	.	.	.	.	.	.	.	.	.	.	.	.	.	.	.	.	.	.	.	.	.	.
Memorial Life Ins Co	060053	.	.	.	.	.	.	.	.	.	.	.	.	.	.	.	.	.	.	D	.	.	.	.	.	.	.	.	.	.	.	.	.	.	.	.	.	.	.	.	.	.	.	.	.	.	.	.	.	.	.	.	.	.	.	.	.
Memorial Service Life Ins Co	068059	.	.	.	.	.	.	.	.	.	.	.	.	.	.	.	.	.	.	.	.	.	.	.	.	.	.	.	.	.	.	.	.	.	.	.	.	.	.	.	.	.	.	.	D	.	.	.	.	.	.	.	.	.	.	.	.
Mercy Health Plans	060384	.	.	.	L	.	.	.	.	.	.	.	.	.	.	.	.	.	.	.	.	.	.	.	.	.	D	.	.	.	.	.	.	.	.	.	.	.	.	.	.	.	.	.	.	.	.	.	.	.	.	.	.	.	.	.	.
Mercy Health Plans of MO Inc	064419	.	.	.	.	.	.	.	.	.	.	.	.	.	.	.	.	.	.	.	.	.	.	.	.	.	D	.	.	.	.	.	.	.	.	.	.	.	.	.	.	.	.	.	L	.	.	.	.	.	.	.	.	.	.	.	.
MercyCare Insurance Company	060254	.	.	.	.	.	.	.	.	.	.	.	.	.	L	.	.	.	.	.	.	.	.	.	.	.	.	.	.	.	.	.	.	.	.	.	.	.	.	.	.	.	.	.	.	.	.	.	.	.	D	.	.	.	.	.	.
Merit Life Insurance Co	006703	L	.	L	L	L	L	L	L	L	L	L	L	L	L	D	L	L	L	L	L	L	.	L	L	L	L	L	L	L	L	L	L	Q	L	L	L	L	L	L	L	L	L	L	L	L	.	L	L	L	L	L	.	.	.	Q	L
Merrill Lynch Life Ins Co	009537	L	L	L	D	L	L	L	L	L	L	L	L	L	L	L	L	L	L	L	L	L	L	L	L	L	L	L	L	L	L	L	L	.	L	L	L	L	L	L	L	L	L	L	L	L	L	L	L	L	L	L	.	L	.	.	L
MetLife Insurance Co of CT	007330	L	L	L	L	L	L	D	L	L	L	L	L	L	L	L	L	L	L	L	L	L	L	L	L	L	L	L	L	L	L	L	L	L	L	L	L	L	L	L	L	L	L	L	L	L	L	L	L	L	L	L	.	L	.	L	L
MetLife Investors Insurance Co	009075	L	L	L	L	L	L	L	L	L	L	L	L	L	L	L	L	L	L	L	L	L	L	L	L	L	D	L	L	L	L	L	L	.	L	L	L	L	L	L	L	L	L	L	L	L	L	L	L	L	L	L	.	.	.	.	.
MetLife Investors USA Ins Co	006125	L	L	L	L	L	L	L	D	L	L	L	L	L	L	L	L	L	L	L	L	L	L	L	L	L	L	L	L	L	L	L	L	.	L	L	L	L	L	L	L	L	L	L	L	L	L	L	L	L	L	L	.	.	.	L	.
Metropolitan Health Plan	068558	.	.	.	.	.	.	.	.	.	.	.	.	.	.	.	.	.	.	.	.	.	.	.	D	.	.	.	.	.	.	.	.	.	.	.	.	.	.	.	.	.	.	.	.	.	.	.	.	.	.	.	.	.	.	.	.
Metropolitan Life Ins Co	006704	L	L	L	L	L	L	L	L	L	L	L	L	L	L	L	L	L	L	L	L	L	L	L	L	L	L	L	L	L	L	L	L	D	L	L	L	L	L	L	L	L	L	L	L	L	L	L	L	L	L	L	.	L	L	L	L
Metropolitan Tower Life Ins Co	009165	L	L	L	L	L	L	L	D	L	L	L	L	L	L	L	L	L	L	L	L	L	L	L	L	L	L	L	L	L	L	L	L	L	L	L	L	L	L	L	L	L	L	L	L	L	L	L	L	L	L	L	.	.	.	.	.
MHNet Life and Health Ins Co	060707	.	.	.	.	.	.	.	.	.	.	.	.	.	.	.	.	.	.	.	.	.	.	.	.	.	.	.	.	.	.	.	.	.	.	.	.	.	.	.	.	.	.	.	D	.	.	.	.	.	.	.	.	.	.	.	.
Mid-Atlantic Vision Service Pl	064478	.	.	.	.	.	.	.	.	.	.	.	.	.	.	.	.	.	.	.	.	L	.	.	.	.	.	.	.	.	.	.	.	.	.	.	.	.	.	.	.	.	.	.	.	.	.	.	.	.	.	.	.	.	.	.	.
Mid Rogue Health Plan	064903	.	.	.	.	.	.	.	.	.	.	.	.	.	.	.	.	.	.	.	.	.	.	.	.	.	.	.	.	.	.	.	.	.	.	.	.	.	D	.	.	.	.	.	.	.	.	.	.	.	.	.	.	.	.	.	.
Mid-West National Life of TN	006715	L	L	L	L	L	L	L	L	L	L	L	L	L	L	L	L	L	L	L	.	L	L	L	L	L	L	L	L	L	.	L	L	.	L	L	L	L	L	L	L	L	L	L	D	L	.	L	L	L	L	L	.	.	.	L	.
Midland National Life Ins Co	006711	L	L	L	L	L	L	L	L	L	L	L	L	L	L	L	D	L	L	L	L	L	L	L	L	L	L	L	L	L	L	L	L	.	L	L	L	L	L	L	L	L	L	L	L	L	L	L	L	L	L	L	.	L	L	L	L
Midwest Health Plan Inc	064518	.	.	.	.	.	.	.	.	.	.	.	.	.	.	.	.	.	.	.	.	.	.	D	.	.	.	.	.	.	.	.	.	.	.	.	.	.	.	.	.	.	.	.	.	.	.	.	.	.	.	.	.	.	.	.	.
Midwest Security Life Ins Co	008297	.	L	.	.	.	.	.	.	.	.	.	.	.	L	L	L	L	L	L	.	.	.	L	L	L	.	.	L	L	.	.	.	.	.	.	L	L	.	.	.	.	.	.	L	L	.	.	.	.	D	.	.	.	.	.	.
Midwestern United Life Ins Co	006718	L	L	L	L	L	L	L	L	L	L	L	L	L	L	D	L	L	L	L	L	L	L	L	L	L	L	L	L	L	L	L	L	.	L	L	L	L	L	L	L	L	L	L	L	L	L	L	L	L	L	L	.	.	.	.	L
MII Life Inc	009495	.	.	L	.	.	.	.	.	.	.	.	.	.	.	.	.	.	.	.	.	.	.	L	D	.	.	.	.	.	.	.	.	.	.	L	.	.	.	.	.	.	L	.	.	.	.	.	.	.	L	.	.	.	.	.	.
Mililani Life Insurance Co	068358	.	.	.	.	.	.	.	.	.	.	.	D	.	.	.	.	.	.	.	.	.	.	.	.	.	.	.	.	.	.	.	.	.	.	.	.	.	.	.	.	.	.	.	.	.	.	.	.	.	.	.	.	.	.	.	.
Minnesota Life Ins Company	006724	L	L	L	L	L	L	L	L	L	L	L	L	L	L	L	L	L	L	L	L	L	L	L	D	L	L	L	L	L	L	L	L	Q	L	L	L	L	L	L	L	L	L	L	L	L	L	L	L	L	L	L	.	L	.	L	.
Missouri Care Incorporated	064921	.	.	.	.	.	.	.	.	.	.	.	.	.	.	.	.	.	.	.	.	.	.	.	.	.	D	.	.	.	.	.	.	.	.	.	.	.	.	.	.	.	.	.	.	.	.	.	.	.	.	.	.	.	.	.	.
Missouri Valley Life & Health	068244	.	.	.	.	.	.	.	.	.	.	.	.	.	.	.	.	L	.	.	.	.	.	.	.	.	D	.	.	.	.	.	.	.	.	.	.	.	.	.	.	.	.	.	.	.	.	.	.	.	.	.	.	.	.	.	.
ML Life Ins Co of NY	008487	.	.	.	.	.	.	L	L	.	.	.	.	.	.	.	.	.	.	.	L	.	L	.	.	.	.	.	.	.	L	L	.	D	.	.	.	.	.	.	L	.	.	.	.	.	L	.	.	.	.	.	.	.	.	.	.
MMA Insurance Company	009580	.	.	L	.	L	L	.	.	.	.	.	.	L	L	D	L	L	.	.	.	L	.	L	.	.	.	.	L	.	.	.	.	.	.	.	L	.	L	L	.	.	L	.	.	.	.	L	.	.	.	.	.	.	.	.	.
MML Bay State Life Ins Co	007233	L	L	L	L	L	L	D	L	L	L	L	L	L	L	L	L	L	L	L	L	L	L	L	L	L	L	L	L	L	L	L	L	.	L	L	L	L	L	L	L	L	L	L	L	L	L	L	L	L	L	L	.	.	.	.	.
MNM-1997 Inc	064513	.	.	.	.	.	.	.	.	.	.	.	.	.	.	.	.	.	.	.	.	.	.	.	.	.	.	.	.	.	.	.	.	.	.	.	.	.	.	.	.	.	.	.	D	.	.	.	.	.	.	.	.	.	.	.	.
Modern Life Ins Co of Arizona	008859	.	.	D	.	.	.	.	.	.	.	.	.	.	.	.	.	.	.	.	.	.	.	.	.	.	.	.	.	.	.	.	.	.	.	.	.	.	.	.	.	.	.	.	.	.	.	.	.	.	.	.	.	.	.	.	.
Modern Woodmen of America	006737	L	.	L	L	L	L	L	L	L	L	L	.	L	D	L	L	L	L	L	L	L	L	L	L	L	L	L	.	L	L	L	L	L	L	L	L	L	L	L	L	L	L	L	L	L	L	L	L	L	L	L	.	.	.	.	.
Molina Healthcare Insurance Co	007144	L	L	L	L	L	L	L	L	L	L	L	L	L	L	L	L	L	L	L	.	L	L	L	L	L	L	L	L	L	L	L	L	.	L	L	D	L	L	L	L	L	L	L	L	L	L	L	L	L	L	L	.	.	.	.	.
Molina Healthcare of CA Inc	064150	.	.	.	.	D	.	.	.	.	.	.	.	.	.	.	.	.	.	.	.	.	.	.	.	.	.	.	.	.	.	.	.	.	.	.	.	.	.	.	.	.	.	.	.	.	.	.	.	.	.	.	.	.	.	.	.
Molina Healthcare of MI Inc	064685	.	.	.	.	.	.	.	.	.	.	.	.	.	.	.	.	.	.	.	.	.	.	D	.	.	.	.	.	.	.	.	.	.	.	.	.	.	.	.	.	.	.	.	.	.	.	.	.	.	.	.	.	.	.	.	.
Molina Healthcare New Mexico	064260	.	.	.	.	.	.	.	.	.	.	.	.	.	.	.	.	.	.	.	.	.	.	.	.	.	.	.	.	.	.	.	D	.	.	.	.	.	.	.	.	.	.	.	.	.	.	.	.	.	.	.	.	.	.	.	.
Molina Healthcare of Ohio Inc	064865	.	.	.	.	.	.	.	.	.	.	.	.	.	.	.	.	.	.	.	.	.	.	.	.	.	.	.	.	.	.	.	.	.	.	.	D	.	.	.	.	.	.	.	.	.	.	.	.	.	.	.	.	.	.	.	.
Molina Healthcare of Texas Inc	064864	.	.	.	.	.	.	.	.	.	.	.	.	.	.	.	.	.	.	.	.	.	.	.	.	.	.	.	.	.	.	.	.	.	.	.	.	.	.	.	.	.	.	.	D	.	.	.	.	.	.	.	.	.	.	.	.
Molina Healthcare of WA Inc	068949	.	.	.	.	.	.	.	.	.	.	.	.	.	.	.	.	.	.	.	.	.	.	.	.	.	.	.	.	.	.	.	.	.	.	.	.	.	.	.	.	.	.	.	.	.	.	.	D	.	.	.	.	.	.	.	.
Monarch Health Plan	064936	.	.	.	.	D	.	.	.	.	.	.	.	.	.	.	.	.	.	.	.	.	.	.	.	.	.	.	.	.	.	.	.	.	.	.	.	.	.	.	.	.	.	.	.	.	.	.	.	.	.	.	.	.	.	.	.
Monarch Life Ins Co	006739	L	L	L	L	L	L	L	L	L	.	L	.	.	L	L	L	L	.	.	L	L	D	.	L	L	.	L	L	.	L	L	L	L	L	L	L	L	L	L	L	L	L	L	L	.	L	L	.	L	.	.	.	.	.	.	.
Monitor Life Insurance Co	008664	.	.	L	L	.	L	L	.	L	L	.	.	.	L	L	L	L	.	L	.	L	L	.	.	L	L	L	.	L	.	.	.	D	.	.	L	L	.	L	.	.	.	L	L	L	.	L	.	L	.	.	.	.	.	.	.
Monumental Life Ins Co	006742	L	L	L	L	L	L	L	L	L	L	L	L	L	L	L	D	L	L	L	L	L	L	L	L	L	L	L	L	L	L	L	L	.	L	L	L	L	L	L	L	L	L	L	L	L	L	L	L	L	L	L	.	L	.	L	.
MONY Life Ins Co	006751	L	L	L	L	L	L	L	L	L	L	L	L	L	L	L	L	L	L	L	L	L	L	L	L	L	L	L	L	L	L	L	L	D	L	L	L	L	L	L	L	L	L	L	L	L	L	L	L	L	L	L	.	L	.	L	L
MONY Life Insurance Co of Amer	008091	L	L	D	L	L	L	L	L	L	L	L	L	L	L	L	L	L	L	L	L	L	L	L	L	L	L	L	L	L	L	L	L	.	L	L	L	L	L	L	L	L	L	L	L	L	L	L	L	L	L	L	.	.	.	L	L
Mothe Life Ins Co	006743	.	.	.	.	.	.	.	.	.	.	.	.	.	.	.	.	.	.	D	.	.	.	.	.	.	.	.	.	.	.	.	.	.	.	.	.	.	.	.	.	.	.	.	.	.	.	.	.	.	.	.	.	.	.	.	.
Motorists Life Ins Co	006744	.	.	.	.	.	.	.	.	.	L	L	.	.	L	L	L	.	L	.	.	.	.	L	L	.	.	.	L	.	.	.	.	.	.	.	D	.	.	L	.	L	.	L	.	.	.	L	Q	L	L	.	.	.	.	.	.
Mount Carmel Health Plan Inc	064112	.	.	.	.	.	.	.	.	.	.	.	.	.	.	.	.	.	.	.	.	.	.	.	.	.	.	.	.	.	.	.	.	.	.	.	D	.	.	.	.	.	.	.	.	.	.	.	.	.	.	.	.	.	.	.	.
Mountain Life Ins Co	008354	L	.	L	L	.	.	.	.	.	.	L	.	.	.	L	.	.	L	L	.	.	.	.	.	L	L	.	.	.	.	.	.	.	.	.	.	.	.	.	.	.	.	D	L	.	.	.	.	.	.	.	.	.	.	.	.
MTL Insurance Company	006756	L	.	L	L	L	L	L	L	L	L	L	L	L	D	L	L	L	L	L	L	L	L	L	L	L	L	L	L	L	L	L	L	.	L	L	L	L	L	L	L	L	L	L	L	L	L	L	L	L	L	L	.	.	.	.	.
Mulhearn Protective Insurance	007823	.	.	.	.	.	.	.	.	.	.	.	.	.	.	.	.	.	.	D	.	.	.	.	.	.	.	.	.	.	.	.	.	.	.	.	.	.	.	.	.	.	.	.	.	.	.	.	.	.	.	.	.	.	.	.	.
Munich American Reassurance Co	006746	L	L	L	L	L	Q	L	L	L	L	D	L	L	L	L	L	L	L	L	Q	Q	L	L	L	L	Q	L	L	L	L	L	L	Q	L	Q	L	L	L	L	L	Q	L	L	L	L	Q	L	L	L	L	Q	.	Q	.	L	.
Mutual Beneficial Assoc Inc	009812	.	.	.	.	.	.	.	D	L	.	.	.	.	L	L	.	.	.	.	.	.	.	.	.	.	.	.	.	.	.	L	.	L	.	.	.	.	.	L	.	.	.	.	.	.	.	.	.	.	.	.	.	.	.	.	.
Mutual of America Life Ins Co	008851	L	L	L	L	L	L	L	L	L	L	L	L	L	L	L	L	L	L	L	L	L	L	L	L	L	L	L	L	L	L	L	L	D	L	L	L	L	L	L	L	L	L	L	L	L	L	L	L	L	L	L	.	.	.	.	.
Mutual of Omaha Ins Co	007369	L	L	L	L	L	L	L	L	L	L	L	L	L	L	L	L	L	L	L	L	L	L	L	L	L	L	L	D	L	L	L	L	L	L	L	L	L	L	L	L	L	L	L	L	L	L	L	L	L	L	L	.	.	.	L	L
Mutual Savings Life Ins Co	006753	D	.	.	.	.	.	.	.	.	L	L	.	.	.	L	.	.	.	L	.	.	.	.	.	L	.	.	.	.	.	.	.	.	.	.	.	.	.	.	.	.	.	L	.	.	.	.	.	.	.	.	.	.	.	.	.
MVP Health Insurance Company	060369	.	.	.	.	.	.	.	.	.	.	.	.	.	.	.	.	.	.	.	.	.	.	.	.	.	.	.	.	.	.	.	.	D	.	.	.	.	.	.	.	.	.	.	.	.	L	.	.	.	.	.	.	.	.	.	.
MVP Health Ins Co of NH Inc	060606	.	.	.	.	.	.	.	.	.	.	.	.	.	.	.	.	.	.	.	.	.	.	.	.	.	.	.	.	.	D	.	.	.	.	.	.	.	.	.	.	.	.	.	.	.	.	.	.	.	.	.	.	.	.	.	.
MVP Health Plan	068567	.	.	.	.	.	.	.	.	.	.	.	.	.	.	.	.	.	.	.	.	.	.	.	.	.	.	.	.	.	.	.	.	D	.	.	.	.	.	.	.	.	.	.	.	.	L	.	.	.	.	.	.	.	.	.	.
MVP Health Plan of NH Inc	064829	.	.	.	.	.	.	.	.	.	.	.	.	.	.	.	.	.	.	.	.	.	.	.	.	.	.	.	.	.	D	.	.	.	.	.	.	.	.	.	.	.	.	.	.	.	.	.	.	.	.	.	.	.	.	.	.
MVP Health Services Corp	064648	.	.	.	.	.	.	.	.	.	.	.	.	.	.	.	.	.	.	.	.	.	.	.	.	.	.	.	.	.	.	.	.	D	.	.	.	.	.	.	.	.	.	.	.	.	.	.	.	.	.	.	.	.	.	.	.
NAP Life Ins Co	009485	.	.	.	.	.	.	.	.	.	.	.	.	.	.	.	.	.	.	.	.	.	.	.	.	.	.	.	.	.	.	.	.	.	.	.	.	.	.	.	.	.	.	.	D	.	.	.	.	.	.	.	.	.	.	.	.
National Benefit Life Ins Co	006163	L	L	L	L	L	L	L	L	L	L	L	L	L	L	L	L	L	L	L	L	L	L	L	L	L	L	L	L	L	L	L	L	D	L	L	L	L	L	L	L	L	L	L	L	L	L	L	L	L	L	L	.	.	.	.	L
National Family Care Life Ins	008775	.	.	.	L	.	.	.	.	.	.	.	.	.	.	.	.	.	.	L	.	.	.	.	.	.	.	.	.	.	.	.	.	.	.	.	.	L	.	.	.	.	.	.	D	.	.	.	.	.	.	.	.	.	.	.	.
National Farm Life Ins Co	006771	.	.	.	.	.	.	.	.	.	.	.	.	.	.	.	.	.	.	.	.	.	.	.	.	.	.	.	.	.	.	.	.	.	.	.	.	.	.	.	.	.	.	.	D	.	.	.	.	.	.	.	.	.	.	.	.
National Farmers Union Life	006772	.	L	L	L	L	L	.	.	L	.	.	.	L	L	L	L	L	L	.	.	.	.	L	L	L	L	L	L	L	.	.	L	.	.	L	L	L	L	L	.	.	L	.	D	L	.	L	L	.	L	L	.	.	.	.	.
National Foundation Life Ins	006774	L	L	L	L	L	L	.	L	L	.	L	.	L	.	L	L	L	L	L	L	.	.	.	.	L	L	L	L	L	.	.	L	.	L	L	L	L	L	L	.	L	L	L	D	L	.	Q	L	.	.	L	.	.	.	.	.
National Guardian Life Ins Co	006777	L	L	L	L	L	L	L	L	L	L	L	L	L	L	L	L	L	L	L	L	L	L	L	L	L	L	L	L	L	L	L	L	.	L	L	L	L	L	L	L	L	L	L	L	L	L	L	L	L	D	L	.	.	.	.	.
National Health Insurance Co	008392	L	L	L	L	L	L	L	L	L	.	L	L	L	L	L	L	L	L	L	L	L	L	L	L	L	L	L	L	L	L	L	L	.	L	L	L	L	L	L	L	L	L	L	D	L	L	L	L	L	L	L	.	.	.	.	.
National Income Life Insurance	060343	.	.	.	.	.	.	.	.	.	.	.	.	.	.	.	.	.	.	.	.	.	.	.	.	.	.	.	.	.	.	.	.	D	.	.	.	.	.	.	.	.	.	.	.	.	.	.	.	.	.	.	.	.	.	.	.
National Insurance Co of WI	010794	L	.	.	.	.	L	.	L	.	.	L	.	L	L	L	.	.	L	.	.	L	.	L	L	L	L	L	L	.	.	.	.	.	.	L	.	.	.	.	.	.	L	.	.	.	.	.	L	.	D	L	.	.	.	.	.
National Integrity Life Ins Co	007798	.	.	.	.	.	.	L	.	L	L	.	.	.	.	.	.	.	.	.	L	.	.	.	.	.	.	.	.	.	L	.	.	D	.	.	L	.	.	.	L	.	.	.	.	.	L	.	.	.	.	.	.	.	.	.	.
National Life Ins Co	006790	L	L	L	L	L	L	L	L	L	L	L	L	L	L	L	L	L	L	L	L	L	L	L	L	L	L	L	L	L	L	L	L	L	L	L	L	L	L	L	L	L	L	L	L	L	D	L	L	L	L	L	.	.	.	.	.

D-State of Domicile **L**-Licensed **S**-Surplus Lines Writer **F**-Authorized under the Risk Retention Act **Q**-Qualified or Accredited Reinsurer

Company Name	AMB#	AL	AK	AZ	AR	CA	CO	CT	DE	DC	FL	GA	HI	ID	IL	IN	IA	KS	KY	LA	ME	MD	MA	MI	MN	MS	MO	MT	NE	NV	NH	NJ	NM	NY	NC	ND	OH	OK	OR	PA	RI	SC	SD	TN	TX	UT	VT	VA	WA	WV	WI	WY	AS	GU	MP	PR	VI
National Life Ins Co	007447	.	.	.	.	.	.	.	.	.	.	.	.	.	.	.	.	.	.	.	.	.	.	.	.	.	.	.	.	.	.	.	.	.	.	.	.	.	.	.	.	.	.	.	.	.	.	.	.	.	.	.	.	.	.	D	.
National Masonic Provident	006793	.	.	.	.	.	.	.	L	.	.	.	.	.	.	.	.	.	.	.	.	.	.	L	.	.	.	.	.	.	.	.	.	.	.	.	D	.	.	.	.	.	.	.	.	.	.	.	.	.	.	.	.	.	.	.	.
National Pacific Dental Inc	068837	.	.	.	.	.	.	.	.	.	.	.	.	.	.	.	.	.	.	.	.	.	.	.	.	.	.	.	.	.	.	.	.	.	.	.	.	.	.	.	.	.	.	.	D	.	.	.	.	.	.	.	.	.	.	.	.
National Safety Life Ins Co	007850	.	.	.	.	.	.	.	L	L	.	.	.	.	.	.	.	.	.	.	.	.	.	.	.	.	.	.	.	.	.	.	.	.	.	.	.	.	.	D	.	.	.	.	.	.	.	.	.	L	.	.	.	.	.	.	.
National Security Ins Co	006802	D	.	.	.	.	.	.	.	.	L	L	.	.	.	.	.	.	.	.	.	.	.	.	.	L	.	.	.	.	.	.	.	.	.	.	.	.	.	.	.	L	.	.	L	.	.	.	.	.	.	.	.	.	.	.	.
National Security Lf & Annuity	008633	.	.	L	L	.	.	.	.	L	.	.	.	.	L	L	L	Q	.	L	.	Q	.	.	.	.	.	.	L	.	L	L	.	D	.	.	L	L	L	L	.	Q	L	.	L	L	.	.	.	.	.	.	.	.	.	.	.
National States Ins Co	006071	L	.	L	L	.	L	.	.	.	L	L	.	L	L	L	L	L	L	L	.	L	.	L	L	L	D	L	L	L	.	.	L	.	L	L	L	L	L	L	.	L	L	L	L	L	.	L	L	L	L	.	.	.	.	.	.
National Teachers Associates	006588	L	L	L	L	L	L	L	L	L	L	L	L	L	L	L	L	L	L	L	L	L	.	L	L	L	L	L	L	L	.	L	L	.	L	L	L	L	L	L	.	L	L	L	D	L	.	L	L	L	L	L	.	.	.	.	.
National Western Life Ins Co	006811	L	L	L	L	L	D	L	L	L	L	L	L	L	L	L	L	L	L	L	L	L	L	L	L	L	L	L	L	L	L	L	L	.	L	L	L	L	L	L	L	L	L	L	L	L	L	L	L	L	L	L	L	L	L	L	L
Nationwide Life & Annuity Ins	009070	L	L	L	L	L	L	L	L	L	L	L	L	L	L	L	L	L	L	L	L	L	L	L	L	L	L	L	L	L	L	L	L	.	L	L	D	L	L	L	L	L	L	L	L	L	L	L	L	L	L	L	.	.	.	.	.
Nationwide Life Ins Co	006812	L	L	L	L	L	L	L	L	L	L	L	L	L	L	L	L	L	L	L	L	L	L	L	L	L	L	L	L	L	L	L	L	L	L	L	D	L	L	L	L	L	L	L	L	L	L	L	L	L	L	L	.	L	.	L	L
Neighborhood Hlth Partnership	064001	.	.	.	.	.	.	.	.	.	D	.	.	.	.	.	.	.	.	.	.	.	.	.	.	.	.	.	.	.	.	.	.	.	.	.	.	.	.	.	.	.	.	.	.	.	.	.	.	.	.	.	.	.	.	.	.
Neighborhood Health Plan Inc	068744	.	.	.	.	.	.	.	.	.	.	.	.	.	.	.	.	.	.	.	.	.	D	.	.	.	.	.	.	.	.	.	.	.	.	.	.	.	.	.	.	.	.	.	.	.	.	.	.	.	.	.	.	.	.	.	.
Neighborhood Hlth Plan of RI	064293	.	.	.	.	.	.	.	.	.	.	.	.	.	.	.	.	.	.	.	.	.	.	.	.	.	.	.	.	.	.	.	.	.	.	.	.	.	.	.	D	.	.	.	.	.	.	.	.	.	.	.	.	.	.	.	.
Netcare Life & Health Ins Co	060302	.	.	.	.	.	.	.	.	.	.	.	.	.	.	.	.	.	.	.	.	.	.	.	.	.	.	.	.	.	.	.	.	.	.	.	.	.	.	.	.	.	.	.	.	.	.	.	.	.	.	.	.	D	.	.	.
Network Health Insurance Corp	064708	.	.	.	.	.	.	.	.	.	.	.	.	.	.	.	.	.	.	.	.	.	.	.	.	.	.	.	.	.	.	.	.	.	.	.	.	.	.	.	.	.	.	.	.	.	.	.	.	.	D	.	.	.	.	.	.
Network Health Plan	068627	.	.	.	.	.	.	.	.	.	.	.	.	.	.	.	.	.	.	.	.	.	.	.	.	.	.	.	.	.	.	.	.	.	.	.	.	.	.	.	.	.	.	.	.	.	.	.	.	.	D	.	.	.	.	.	.
Nevada Pacific Dental Inc	064826	.	.	.	.	.	.	.	.	.	.	.	.	.	.	.	.	.	.	.	.	.	.	.	.	.	.	.	.	D	.	.	.	.	.	.	.	.	.	.	.	.	.	.	.	.	.	.	.	.	.	.	.	.	.	.	.
New England Life Ins Co	009043	L	L	L	L	L	L	L	L	L	L	L	L	L	L	L	L	L	L	L	L	L	D	L	L	L	L	L	L	L	L	L	L	L	L	L	L	L	L	L	L	L	L	L	L	L	L	L	L	L	L	L	.	.	.	.	.
New Era Life Ins Co	007087	L	.	L	.	L	L	.	L	.	L	L	.	.	.	L	.	.	.	L	.	.	.	.	.	L	.	.	.	.	.	.	L	.	L	.	L	L	.	L	.	L	L	L	D	L	.	.	.	L	.	.	.	.	.	.	.
New Era Life Ins Co Midwest	007148	.	.	.	.	L	.	.	.	.	L	L	.	.	L	L	.	.	L	L	.	.	.	.	.	L	L	.	.	.	.	.	.	.	L	.	L	L	.	L	.	L	.	L	D	.	.	.	.	.	L	.	.	.	.	.	.
New Foundation Life Insurance	068212	.	.	.	D	.	.	.	.	.	.	.	.	.	.	.	.	.	.	.	.	.	.	.	.	.	.	.	.	.	.	.	.	.	.	.	.	.	.	.	.	.	.	.	.	.	.	.	.	.	.	.	.	.	.	.	.
New West Health Services	064398	.	.	.	.	.	.	.	.	.	.	.	.	.	.	.	.	.	.	.	.	.	.	.	.	.	.	D	.	.	.	.	.	.	.	.	.	.	.	.	.	.	.	.	.	.	.	.	.	.	.	.	.	.	.	.	.
New York Life Ins & Annuity	009054	L	L	L	L	L	L	L	D	L	L	L	L	L	L	L	L	L	L	L	L	L	L	L	L	L	L	L	L	L	L	L	L	L	L	L	L	L	L	L	L	L	L	L	L	L	L	L	L	L	L	L	.	L	.	.	L
New York Life Ins Co	006820	L	L	L	L	L	L	L	L	L	L	L	L	L	L	L	L	L	L	L	L	L	L	L	L	L	L	L	L	L	L	L	L	D	L	L	L	L	L	L	L	L	L	L	L	L	L	L	L	L	L	L	.	L	.	L	L
NHP of Indiana LLC	064857	.	.	.	.	.	.	.	.	.	.	.	.	.	.	D	.	.	L	.	.	.	.	.	.	.	.	.	.	.	.	.	.	.	.	.	.	.	.	.	.	.	.	.	.	.	.	.	.	.	.	.	.	.	.	.	.
Niagara Life and Health Ins Co	060566	.	.	.	.	.	.	.	.	.	.	.	.	.	.	.	.	.	.	.	.	.	.	.	.	.	.	.	.	.	.	.	.	D	.	.	.	.	.	.	.	.	.	.	.	.	.	.	.	.	.	.	.	.	.	.	.
Nippon Life Ins Co of Amer	008419	L	L	L	L	L	L	L	L	L	L	L	L	L	L	L	D	L	L	L	.	L	L	L	L	L	L	L	L	L	.	L	L	L	.	L	L	L	L	L	L	L	L	L	L	L	L	L	L	L	L	.	.	.	.	.	.
Noridian Mutual Insurance Co	068581	.	.	.	.	.	.	.	.	.	.	.	.	.	.	.	.	.	.	.	.	.	.	.	L	.	.	.	.	.	.	.	.	.	.	D	.	.	.	.	.	.	.	.	.	.	.	.	.	.	.	.	.	.	.	.	.
North American Co for L&H	006827	L	L	L	L	L	L	L	L	L	L	L	L	L	L	L	D	L	L	L	L	L	L	L	L	L	L	L	L	L	L	L	L	.	L	L	L	L	L	L	L	L	L	L	L	L	L	L	L	L	L	L	.	.	.	L	.
North American Ins Co	060015	L	.	.	.	.	L	.	.	L	.	.	.	.	L	L	.	L	.	L	.	L	.	L	L	.	L	.	.	.	.	.	L	.	.	L	L	L	L	L	.	L	.	.	L	.	.	.	.	.	D	.	.	.	.	.	.
North American Life Ins of TX	068234	.	.	.	.	.	.	.	.	.	.	.	.	.	.	.	.	.	.	.	.	.	.	.	.	.	.	.	.	.	.	.	.	.	.	.	.	.	.	.	.	.	.	.	D	.	.	.	.	.	.	.	.	.	.	.	.
North American Natl Re Ins Co	060310	.	.	D	.	.	.	.	.	.	.	.	.	.	.	.	.	.	.	.	.	.	.	.	.	.	.	.	.	.	.	.	.	.	.	.	.	.	.	.	.	.	.	.	.	.	.	.	.	.	.	.	.	.	.	.	.
North Carolina Mutual Life Ins	006835	L	.	L	.	L	.	.	.	L	L	L	.	L	L	L	.	.	L	L	.	L	.	L	.	L	L	.	.	L	.	L	.	.	D	.	L	L	.	L	.	L	.	L	L	.	.	L	.	.	.	.	.	.	.	.	.
North Coast Life Ins Co	006837	.	.	L	.	L	L	.	.	.	.	.	L	L	.	.	.	.	.	.	.	.	.	.	.	.	.	L	.	L	.	.	L	.	.	.	.	.	L	.	.	.	.	.	.	L	.	.	D	.	.	L	.	L	L	.	.
Northern National Life of RI	008788	.	.	.	.	.	.	.	.	.	.	.	.	.	.	.	.	.	.	.	.	.	.	.	.	.	.	.	.	.	.	.	.	.	.	.	.	.	.	.	D	.	.	.	.	.	.	.	.	.	.	.	.	.	.	.	.
Northwestern Long Term Care	007067	L	L	L	L	L	L	L	L	L	L	L	L	L	L	L	L	L	L	L	L	L	L	L	L	L	L	L	L	L	L	L	L	L	L	L	L	L	L	L	L	L	L	L	L	L	L	L	L	L	D	L	.	.	.	.	.
Northwestern Mutual Life Ins	006845	L	L	L	L	L	L	L	L	L	L	L	L	L	L	L	L	L	L	L	L	L	L	L	L	L	L	L	L	L	L	L	L	L	L	L	L	L	L	L	L	L	L	L	L	L	L	L	L	L	D	L	.	.	.	.	.
NYLIFE Ins Co of Arizona	068015	L	L	D	L	L	L	L	L	L	L	L	L	L	L	L	L	L	L	L	.	L	L	L	L	L	L	L	L	L	L	L	L	.	L	L	L	L	L	L	L	L	L	L	L	L	L	L	L	L	L	L	.	.	.	.	.
Occidental Life Ins Co of NC	006849	L	L	L	L	L	L	L	L	L	L	L	L	L	L	L	L	L	L	L	L	L	L	L	L	L	L	L	L	L	L	L	L	.	L	L	L	L	L	L	L	L	L	L	D	L	L	L	L	L	L	L	.	L	.	L	L
ODS Health Plan Inc	011437	.	L	.	.	.	.	.	.	.	.	.	.	L	.	.	.	.	.	.	.	.	.	.	.	.	.	.	.	.	.	.	.	.	.	.	.	.	D	.	.	.	.	.	.	.	.	.	L	.	.	.	.	.	.	.	.
Ohio Motorists Life Ins Co	068360	.	.	.	.	.	.	.	.	.	.	.	.	.	.	.	.	.	.	.	.	.	.	.	.	.	.	.	.	.	.	.	.	.	.	.	D	.	.	.	.	.	.	.	.	.	.	.	.	.	.	.	.	.	.	.	.
Ohio National Life Assur Corp	008930	L	.	L	L	L	L	L	L	L	L	L	.	L	L	L	L	L	L	L	L	L	L	L	L	L	L	L	L	L	L	L	L	.	L	L	D	L	L	L	L	L	L	L	L	L	L	L	L	L	L	L	.	.	.	L	.
Ohio National Life Ins Co	006852	L	.	L	L	L	L	L	L	L	L	L	.	L	L	L	L	L	L	L	L	L	L	L	L	L	L	L	L	L	L	L	L	.	L	L	D	L	L	L	L	L	L	L	L	L	L	L	L	L	L	L	.	.	.	L	.
Ohio State Life Ins Co	006853	L	L	L	L	L	L	.	L	L	L	L	L	L	L	L	L	L	L	L	.	L	L	L	L	L	L	L	L	L	L	L	L	.	L	L	L	L	L	L	L	L	L	L	D	L	.	L	L	L	L	L	.	.	.	.	.
Old American Ins Co	006854	L	.	L	L	L	L	L	L	L	L	L	.	L	L	L	L	L	L	L	L	L	L	L	L	L	D	L	L	L	.	L	L	.	L	L	L	L	L	L	L	L	L	L	L	L	L	L	L	L	L	L	.	.	.	.	.
Old Reliance Ins Co	006861	.	.	D	.	.	L	.	.	.	.	.	L	L	L	L	.	.	.	.	.	.	.	L	.	.	L	.	L	.	.	.	L	.	.	.	.	L	.	.	.	.	.	.	L	L	.	.	.	.	.	.	.	.	.	.	L
Old Republic Life Ins Co	006863	L	L	L	L	L	L	L	L	L	L	L	L	L	D	L	L	L	L	L	L	L	L	L	L	L	L	L	L	L	L	L	L	.	L	L	L	L	L	L	L	L	L	L	L	L	L	L	L	L	L	L	.	.	.	L	L
Old Spartan Life Ins Co Inc	007878	.	.	.	.	.	.	.	.	.	.	L	.	.	.	.	.	.	.	.	.	.	.	.	.	.	.	.	.	.	.	.	.	.	.	.	.	.	.	.	.	D	.	.	.	.	.	.	.	.	.	.	.	.	.	.	.
Old Surety Life Ins Co	006867	.	.	.	L	.	L	.	.	.	.	.	.	.	.	.	.	L	.	.	.	.	.	.	.	.	L	L	.	.	.	.	L	.	.	.	.	D	.	.	.	.	.	.	L	.	.	.	.	.	.	.	.	.	.	.	.
Old United Life Ins Co	007879	L	L	D	L	L	L	L	L	L	L	L	L	L	L	L	L	L	L	L	.	L	L	L	L	L	L	L	L	L	.	L	L	.	L	L	L	L	L	L	L	L	L	L	L	L	L	L	L	L	L	L	.	.	.	.	L
OM Financial Life Ins Co	006384	L	L	L	L	L	L	L	L	L	L	L	L	L	L	L	L	L	L	L	L	D	L	L	L	L	L	L	L	L	L	L	L	.	L	L	L	L	L	L	L	L	L	L	L	L	L	L	L	L	L	L	.	.	.	.	.
OM Financial Life Ins Co of NY	007122	.	.	.	.	.	.	.	.	.	.	.	.	.	.	.	.	.	.	.	.	.	.	.	.	.	.	.	.	.	.	.	.	D	.	.	.	.	.	.	.	.	.	.	.	.	.	.	.	.	.	.	.	.	.	.	.
Omaha Insurance Company	060694	.	.	.	.	.	.	.	.	.	.	.	.	.	.	.	.	.	.	.	.	.	.	.	.	.	.	.	D	.	.	.	.	.	.	.	.	.	.	.	.	.	.	.	.	.	.	.	.	.	.	.	.	.	.	.	.
Omaha Life Insurance Company	060695	.	.	.	.	.	.	.	.	.	.	.	.	.	.	.	.	.	.	.	.	.	.	.	.	.	.	.	D	.	.	.	.	.	.	.	.	.	.	.	.	.	.	.	.	.	.	.	.	.	.	.	.	.	.	.	.
OmniCare Health Plan Inc	064810	.	.	.	.	.	.	.	.	.	.	.	.	.	.	.	.	.	.	.	.	.	.	D	.	.	.	.	.	.	.	.	.	.	.	.	.	.	.	.	.	.	.	.	.	.	.	.	.	.	.	.	.	.	.	.	.
On Lok Senior Health Services	064666	.	.	.	.	D	.	.	.	.	.	.	.	.	.	.	.	.	.	.	.	.	.	.	.	.	.	.	.	.	.	.	.	.	.	.	.	.	.	.	.	.	.	.	.	.	.	.	.	.	.	.	.	.	.	.	.
OneNation Insurance Company	008665	L	L	L	L	L	L	L	L	L	L	L	L	L	L	D	L	L	L	L	L	L	L	L	L	L	L	L	L	L	L	L	L	.	.	.	L	L	L	L	L	L	L	L	L	L	L	L	L	L	L	L	.	.	.	.	.
Optima Health Insurance Co	068490	.	.	.	.	.	.	.	.	.	.	.	.	.	.	.	.	.	.	.	.	.	.	.	.	.	.	.	.	.	.	.	.	.	.	.	.	.	.	.	.	.	.	.	.	.	.	D	.	.	.	.	.	.	.	.	.
OPTIMA Health Plan	068821	.	.	.	.	.	.	.	.	.	.	.	.	.	.	.	.	.	.	.	.	.	.	.	.	.	.	.	.	.	.	.	.	.	.	.	.	.	.	.	.	.	.	.	.	.	.	D	.	.	.	.	.	.	.	.	.
Optimum Choice Inc	068764	.	.	.	.	.	.	.	L	L	.	.	.	.	.	.	.	.	.	.	.	D	.	.	.	.	.	.	.	.	.	.	.	.	.	.	.	.	.	.	.	.	.	.	.	.	.	L	.	L	.	.	.	.	.	.	.
Optimum Re Insurance Company	008863	L	.	L	L	L	L	.	.	.	.	L	.	.	L	L	L	L	L	L	.	.	L	L	L	L	.	.	L	L	.	.	.	.	.	.	L	L	.	.	.	.	.	L	D	.	.	.	L	.	L	.	.	.	.	L	.
Orange Prev & Trtmt Int Med As	064713	.	.	.	.	D	.	.	.	.	.	.	.	.	.	.	.	.	.	.	.	.	.	.	.	.	.	.	.	.	.	.	.	.	.	.	.	.	.	.	.	.	.	.	.	.	.	.	.	.	.	.	.	.	.	.	.
Oregon Dental Service	064364	.	L	.	.	.	.	.	.	.	.	.	.	.	.	.	.	.	.	.	.	.	.	.	.	.	.	.	.	.	.	.	.	.	.	.	.	.	D	.	.	.	.	.	.	.	.	.	.	.	.	.	.	.	.	.	.
Orkney Re Inc	060559	.	.	.	.	.	.	.	D	.	.	.	.	.	.	.	.	.	.	.	.	.	.	.	.	.	.	.	.	.	.	.	.	.	.	.	.	.	.	.	.	.	.	.	.	.	.	.	.	.	.	.	.	.	.	.	.
Ouachita Life Insurance Co	068362	.	.	.	D	.	.	.	.	.	.	.	.	.	.	.	.	.	.	.	.	.	.	.	.	.	.	.	.	.	.	.	.	.	.	.	.	.	.	.	.	.	.	.	.	.	.	.	.	.	.	.	.	.	.	.	.
Oxford Health Ins Inc	060022	.	.	.	.	.	.	L	.	.	.	.	.	.	.	.	.	.	.	.	.	.	.	.	.	.	.	.	.	.	.	L	.	D	.	.	.	.	.	L	.	.	.	.	.	.	.	.	.	.	.	.	.	.	.	.	.
Oxford Health Plans (CT) Inc	068933	.	.	.	.	.	.	D	.	.	.	.	.	.	.	.	.	.	.	.	.	.	.	.	.	.	.	.	.	.	.	.	.	.	.	.	.	.	.	.	.	.	.	.	.	.	.	.	.	.	.	.	.	.	.	.	.
Oxford Health Plans (NJ) Inc	068934	.	.	.	.	.	.	.	.	.	.	.	.	.	.	.	.	.	.	.	.	.	.	.	.	.	.	.	.	.	.	D	.	.	.	.	.	.	.	.	.	.	.	.	.	.	.	.	.	.	.	.	.	.	.	.	.
Oxford Health Plans (NY) Inc	068716	.	.	.	.	.	.	.	.	.	.	.	.	.	.	.	.	.	.	.	.	.	.	.	.	.	.	.	.	.	.	.	.	D	.	.	.	.	.	.	.	.	.	.	.	.	.	.	.	.	.	.	.	.	.	.	.
Oxford Life Ins Co	007890	L	L	D	L	L	L	L	L	L	L	L	L	L	L	L	L	L	L	L	L	L	L	L	L	L	L	L	L	L	L	L	L	.	L	L	L	L	L	L	L	L	L	L	L	L	.	L	L	L	L	L	.	.	.	.	.
Ozark National Life Ins Co MO	006877	L	.	L	L	L	L	.	.	.	L	L	.	.	L	L	L	L	L	L	.	.	.	L	L	L	D	L	L	L	.	.	L	.	.	L	L	L	.	.	.	.	L	L	L	L	.	.	.	.	L	L	.	.	.	.	.
Pacific Beacon Life Reassur	060326	.	.	.	.	.	.	.	.	.	.	.	D	.	.	.	.	.	.	.	.	.	.	Q	.	.	.	.	.	.	.	.	.	.	.	.	.	.	.	.	.	.	.	.	.	.	.	.	.	.	.	.	.	.	.	.	.
Pacific Century Life Ins Corp	060335	.	.	D	.	.	.	.	.	.	.	.	L	.	.	.	.	.	.	.	.	.	.	.	.	.	.	.	.	.	.	.	.	.	.	.	.	.	.	.	.	.	.	.	.	.	.	.	.	.	.	.	.	.	.	.	.
Pacific Guardian Life Co Ltd	006883	.	L	L	.	L	L	.	.	.	.	.	D	L	.	.	L	.	.	L	.	.	.	.	.	.	L	L	L	L	.	.	L	.	.	.	.	L	L	.	.	.	L	.	L	L	.	.	L	.	.	L	L	L	L	.	.
Pacific Life & Annuity Co	009156	L	L	D	L	L	L	L	L	L	L	L	L	L	L	L	L	L	L	L	L	L	L	L	L	L	L	L	L	L	L	L	L	L	L	L	L	L	L	L	L	L	L	L	L	L	L	L	L	L	L	L	.	.	.	.	.

D-State of Domicile **L**-Licensed **S**-Surplus Lines Writer **F**-Authorized under the Risk Retention Act **Q**-Qualified or Accredited Reinsurer

U.S. States/Territories in Which Companies Are Licensed or Do Business – *Continued*

Company Name	AMB#	AL	AK	AZ	AR	CA	CO	CT	DE	DC	FL	GA	HI	ID	IL	IN	IA	KS	KY	LA	ME	MD	MA	MI	MN	MS	MO	MT	NE	NV	NH	NJ	NM	NY	NC	ND	OH	OK	OR	PA	RI	SC	SD	TN	TX	UT	VT	VA	WA	WV	WI	WY	AS	GU	MP	PR	VI
Pacific Life Insurance Company	006885	L	L	L	L	L	L	L	L	L	L	L	L	L	L	L	L	L	L	L	L	L	L	L	L	L	L	L	D	L	L	L	L	.	L	L	L	L	L	L	L	L	L	L	L	L	L	L	L	L	L	L	.	.	.	.	.
Pacific Visioncare WA Inc	064628	.	.	.	.	.	.	.	.	.	.	.	.	.	.	.	.	.	.	.	.	.	.	.	.	.	.	.	.	.	.	.	.	.	.	.	.	.	.	.	.	.	.	.	.	.	.	.	D	.	.	.	.	.	.	.	.
PacifiCare Bhvrl Health of CA	064644	.	.	.	.	D	.	.	.	.	.	.	.	.	.	.	.	.	.	.	.	.	.	.	.	.	.	.	.	.	.	.	.	.	.	.	.	.	.	.	.	.	.	.	.	.	.	.	.	.	.	.	.	.	.	.	.
PacifiCare Dental of Colorado	064840	.	.	.	.	.	D	.	.	.	.	.	.	.	.	.	.	.	.	.	.	.	.	.	.	.	.	.	.	.	.	.	.	.	.	.	.	.	.	.	.	.	.	.	.	.	.	.	.	.	.	.	.	.	.	.	.
PacifiCare Life and Health Ins	007278	L	L	L	L	L	L	L	L	L	L	L	L	L	L	D	L	L	L	L	L	L	L	L	L	L	L	L	L	L	L	L	L	.	L	L	L	L	L	L	L	L	L	L	L	L	L	L	L	L	L	L	.	.	.	.	L
PacifiCare Life Assurance Co	008428	.	.	L	.	L	D	.	.	.	.	.	.	.	.	L	.	.	.	.	.	.	.	.	.	.	.	.	.	L	.	.	L	.	.	.	.	L	L	.	.	.	.	.	L	.	.	.	L	.	.	.	.	L	.	.	.
PacifiCare of Arizona Inc	064218	.	.	D	.	.	.	.	.	.	.	.	.	.	.	.	.	.	.	.	.	.	.	.	.	.	.	.	.	.	.	.	.	.	.	.	.	.	.	.	.	.	.	.	.	.	.	.	.	.	.	.	.	.	.	.	.
PacifiCare of California	068705	.	.	.	.	D	.	.	.	.	.	.	.	.	.	.	.	.	.	.	.	.	.	.	.	.	.	.	.	.	.	.	.	.	.	.	.	.	.	.	.	.	.	.	.	.	.	.	.	.	.	.	.	.	.	.	.
PacifiCare of Colorado Inc	068639	.	.	.	.	.	D	.	.	.	.	.	.	.	.	.	.	.	.	.	.	.	.	.	.	.	.	.	.	.	.	.	.	.	.	.	.	.	.	.	.	.	.	.	.	.	.	.	.	.	.	.	.	.	.	.	.
PacifiCare of Nevada Inc	064219	.	.	.	.	.	.	.	.	.	.	.	.	.	.	.	.	.	.	.	.	.	.	.	.	.	.	.	.	D	.	.	.	.	.	.	.	.	.	.	.	.	.	.	.	.	.	.	.	.	.	.	.	.	.	.	.
PacifiCare of Oklahoma Inc	068582	.	.	.	.	.	.	.	.	.	.	.	.	.	.	.	.	.	.	.	.	.	.	.	.	.	.	.	.	.	.	.	.	.	.	.	.	D	.	.	.	.	.	.	.	.	.	.	.	.	.	.	.	.	.	.	.
PacifiCare of Oregon Inc	068707	.	.	.	.	.	.	.	.	.	.	.	.	.	.	.	.	.	.	.	.	.	.	.	.	.	.	.	.	.	.	.	.	.	.	.	.	.	D	.	.	.	.	.	.	.	.	.	L	.	.	.	.	.	.	.	.
PacifiCare of Texas Inc	068706	.	.	.	.	.	.	.	.	.	.	.	.	.	.	.	.	.	.	.	.	.	.	.	.	.	.	.	.	.	.	.	.	.	.	.	.	.	.	.	.	.	.	.	D	.	.	.	.	.	.	.	.	.	.	.	.
PacifiCare of Washington	068591	.	.	.	.	.	.	.	.	.	.	.	.	.	.	.	.	.	.	.	.	.	.	.	.	.	.	.	.	.	.	.	.	.	.	.	.	.	.	.	.	.	.	.	.	.	.	.	D	.	.	.	.	.	.	.	.
PacificSource Health Plans	064500	.	.	.	.	.	.	.	.	.	.	.	.	L	.	.	.	.	.	.	.	.	.	.	.	.	.	.	.	.	.	.	.	.	.	.	.	.	D	.	.	.	.	.	.	.	.	.	L	.	.	.	.	.	.	.	.
Pan-American Assurance Company	009058	L	.	L	L	L	L	L	L	L	L	L	L	L	L	L	.	L	L	D	.	L	.	L	L	L	L	L	L	L	.	L	L	.	L	L	L	L	L	L	.	L	.	L	L	L	.	L	L	L	L	.	.	.	.	L	.
Pan-American Life Ins Co	006893	L	L	L	L	L	L	L	L	L	L	L	L	L	L	L	L	L	L	D	.	L	L	L	L	L	L	L	L	L	L	L	L	.	L	L	L	L	L	L	L	L	L	L	L	L	.	L	L	L	L	L	.	.	.	L	.
Pan-American Life Ins Co of PR	088748	.	.	.	.	.	.	.	.	.	.	.	.	.	.	.	.	.	.	.	.	.	.	.	.	.	.	.	.	.	.	.	.	.	.	.	.	.	.	.	.	.	.	.	.	.	.	.	.	.	.	.	.	.	.	D	.
Paramount Advantage	064833	.	.	.	.	.	.	.	.	.	.	.	.	.	.	.	.	.	.	.	.	.	.	.	.	.	.	.	.	.	.	.	.	.	.	.	D	.	.	.	.	.	.	.	.	.	.	.	.	.	.	.	.	.	.	.	.
Paramount Care Inc	068579	.	.	.	.	.	.	.	.	.	.	.	.	.	.	.	.	.	.	.	.	.	.	.	.	.	.	.	.	.	.	.	.	.	.	.	D	.	.	.	.	.	.	.	.	.	.	.	.	.	.	.	.	.	.	.	.
Paramount Care of Michigan	064294	.	.	.	.	.	.	.	.	.	.	.	.	.	.	.	.	.	.	.	.	.	.	D	.	.	.	.	.	.	.	.	.	.	.	.	.	.	.	.	.	.	.	.	.	.	.	.	.	.	.	.	.	.	.	.	.
Paramount Insurance Company	064742	.	.	.	.	.	.	.	.	.	.	.	.	.	.	.	.	.	.	.	.	.	.	.	.	.	.	.	.	.	.	.	.	.	.	.	D	.	.	.	.	.	.	.	.	.	.	.	.	.	.	.	.	.	.	.	.
Park Avenue Life Ins Co	006000	L	L	L	L	L	L	L	D	L	L	L	.	L	L	L	L	L	L	L	L	L	L	L	L	L	L	L	L	L	L	L	L	.	L	L	L	L	L	L	L	L	L	L	L	L	L	L	L	L	L	L	.	.	.	.	.
Parker Centennial Assurance Co	060403	L	L	L	L	L	L	L	L	L	L	L	L	L	L	L	L	L	L	L	L	L	L	L	L	L	L	L	L	L	L	L	L	.	L	L	L	L	L	L	L	L	L	L	L	L	L	L	L	L	D	L	.	.	.	.	.
Parkland Community Health Plan	064461	.	.	.	.	.	.	.	.	.	.	.	.	.	.	.	.	.	.	.	.	.	.	.	.	.	.	.	.	.	.	.	.	.	.	.	.	.	.	.	.	.	.	.	D	.	.	.	.	.	.	.	.	.	.	.	.
PARTNERS Natl Hlth Plns of NC	068822	.	.	.	.	.	.	.	.	.	.	.	.	.	.	.	.	.	.	.	.	.	.	.	.	.	.	.	.	.	.	.	.	.	D	.	.	.	.	.	.	L	.	.	.	.	.	L	.	.	.	.	.	.	.	.	.
Patriot Life Ins Co	008973	.	.	.	.	.	.	.	.	.	.	.	.	.	.	.	.	.	.	.	D	.	.	.	.	.	.	.	.	.	.	.	.	.	.	.	.	.	.	.	.	.	.	.	.	.	.	.	.	.	.	.	.	.	.	.	.
Paul Revere Life Ins Co	006899	L	L	L	L	L	L	L	L	L	L	L	L	L	L	L	L	L	L	L	L	L	D	L	L	L	L	L	L	L	L	L	L	L	L	L	L	L	L	L	L	L	L	L	L	L	L	L	L	L	L	L	.	.	.	.	.
Paul Revere Variable Annuity	006900	L	.	L	L	L	L	L	L	L	L	L	L	L	L	L	L	L	L	L	L	L	D	L	L	L	L	L	L	L	L	L	L	.	L	L	L	L	L	L	L	L	L	L	L	L	L	L	L	L	L	L	.	.	.	.	.
Peach State Health Plan Inc	064831	.	.	.	.	.	.	.	.	.	.	D	.	.	.	.	.	.	.	.	.	.	.	.	.	.	.	.	.	.	.	.	.	.	.	.	.	.	.	.	.	.	.	.	.	.	.	.	.	.	.	.	.	.	.	.	.
Pearle Vision Mgd Cr - HMO TX	064516	.	.	.	.	.	.	.	.	.	.	.	.	.	.	.	.	.	.	.	.	.	.	.	.	.	.	.	.	.	.	.	.	.	.	.	.	.	.	.	.	.	.	.	D	.	.	.	.	.	.	.	.	.	.	.	.
Pekin Financial Life Ins Co	009525	.	.	D	.	.	.	.	.	.	.	.	.	.	.	.	.	.	.	.	.	.	.	.	.	.	.	.	.	.	.	.	.	.	.	.	.	.	.	.	.	.	.	.	.	.	.	.	.	.	.	.	.	.	.	.	.
Pekin Life Ins Co	006901	.	.	.	.	.	.	.	.	.	.	.	.	.	D	L	L	.	L	.	.	.	.	L	L	.	L	.	.	.	.	.	.	.	.	.	L	.	.	.	.	.	.	.	.	.	.	.	.	.	L	.	.	.	.	.	.
Pellerin Life Ins Co	007909	.	.	.	.	.	.	.	.	.	.	.	.	.	.	.	.	.	.	D	.	.	.	.	.	.	.	.	.	.	.	.	.	.	.	.	.	.	.	.	.	.	.	.	.	.	.	.	.	.	.	.	.	.	.	.	.
PEMCO Life Ins Co	007420	.	.	.	.	.	.	.	.	.	.	.	.	.	.	.	.	.	.	.	.	.	.	.	.	.	.	.	.	.	.	.	.	.	.	.	.	.	L	.	.	.	.	.	.	.	.	.	D	.	.	.	.	.	.	.	.
Peninsula Health Care Inc	068745	.	.	.	.	.	.	.	.	.	.	.	.	.	.	.	.	.	.	.	.	.	.	.	.	.	.	.	.	.	.	.	.	.	.	.	.	.	.	.	.	.	.	.	.	.	.	D	.	.	.	.	.	.	.	.	.
Penn Ins and Annuity Company	009073	L	L	L	L	L	L	L	D	L	L	L	L	L	L	L	L	L	L	L	L	L	L	L	L	L	L	L	L	L	.	L	L	.	L	L	L	L	L	L	L	L	L	L	L	L	L	L	L	L	L	L	.	.	.	.	.
Penn Mutual Life Ins Co	006903	L	L	L	L	L	L	L	L	L	L	L	L	L	L	L	L	L	L	L	L	L	L	L	L	L	L	L	L	L	L	L	L	L	L	L	L	L	L	D	L	L	L	L	L	L	L	L	L	L	L	L	.	.	.	.	.
Penn Treaty Network America	006385	L	L	L	L	L	L	L	L	L	L	L	L	L	L	L	L	.	L	L	.	L	.	L	L	L	L	L	L	L	L	.	L	.	L	L	L	L	L	D	L	L	L	L	L	L	L	L	L	.	L	L	.	.	.	.	.
Pennsylvania Life Insurance Co	006905	L	L	L	L	L	L	L	L	L	L	L	L	L	L	L	L	L	L	L	L	L	L	L	L	L	L	L	L	L	L	L	L	.	L	L	L	L	L	D	L	L	L	L	L	L	L	L	L	L	L	L	.	.	.	L	L
Peoples Savings Life Ins Co	068468	D	.	.	.	.	.	.	.	.	.	.	.	.	.	.	.	.	.	.	.	.	.	.	.	.	.	.	.	.	.	.	.	.	.	.	.	.	.	.	.	.	.	.	.	.	.	.	.	.	.	.	.	.	.	.	.
Performance Life of America	009325	.	.	.	.	.	.	.	.	.	.	.	.	.	.	.	.	.	.	D	.	.	.	.	.	.	.	.	.	.	.	.	.	.	.	.	.	.	.	.	.	.	.	.	.	.	.	.	.	.	.	.	.	.	.	.	.
Perico Life Insurance Company	008618	L	L	L	L	L	L	L	D	L	L	L	L	L	L	L	L	L	L	L	L	L	L	L	L	L	L	L	L	L	L	L	L	.	L	L	L	L	L	L	L	L	L	L	L	L	L	L	L	L	L	L	.	.	.	.	.
PersonalCare Insurance of IL	060028	.	.	.	.	.	.	.	.	.	.	.	.	.	D	.	.	.	.	.	.	.	.	.	.	.	.	.	.	.	.	.	.	.	.	.	.	.	.	.	.	.	.	.	.	.	.	.	.	.	.	.	.	.	.	.	.
Pharmacists Life Ins Co	008946	L	.	L	L	L	L	L	L	L	.	L	.	L	L	L	D	L	L	L	.	L	.	L	L	L	L	L	L	L	.	.	L	.	L	L	L	L	L	L	L	L	L	L	L	L	.	L	L	L	L	L	.	.	.	.	.
Philadelphia American Life Ins	009166	L	L	L	L	L	L	L	L	L	L	L	L	L	L	L	L	L	L	L	L	L	L	L	L	L	L	L	L	L	L	L	L	.	L	L	L	L	L	L	.	L	L	L	D	L	L	L	L	L	L	L	.	.	.	.	L
Philadelphia-United Life Ins	006919	.	.	.	.	.	.	.	L	L	L	.	.	.	L	L	.	.	.	.	.	L	.	L	.	.	L	.	.	.	.	L	.	.	L	.	L	.	.	D	.	.	.	.	.	.	.	L	.	L	.	.	.	.	.	.	.
PHL Variable Ins Co	009332	L	L	L	L	L	L	D	L	L	L	L	L	L	L	L	L	L	L	L	.	L	L	L	L	L	L	L	L	L	L	L	L	.	L	L	L	L	L	L	L	L	L	L	L	L	L	L	L	L	L	L	.	.	.	L	.
Phoenix Life and Annuity Co	009072	L	L	L	L	.	L	D	L	L	L	.	L	L	L	L	L	L	L	L	.	L	.	L	.	L	L	L	L	L	L	L	L	.	L	L	L	L	L	L	L	L	L	L	L	L	L	L	L	L	L	L	.	.	.	.	.
Phoenix Life and Reassur of NY	068237	.	.	.	.	.	.	.	.	.	.	.	.	.	.	.	.	.	.	.	.	.	.	.	.	.	.	.	.	.	.	.	.	D	.	.	.	.	.	.	.	.	.	.	.	.	.	.	.	.	.	.	.	.	.	.	.
Phoenix Life Insurance Company	006922	L	L	L	L	L	L	L	L	L	L	L	L	L	L	L	L	L	L	L	L	L	L	L	L	L	L	L	L	L	L	L	L	D	L	L	L	L	L	L	L	L	L	L	L	L	L	L	L	L	L	L	.	.	.	L	L
PHP Insurance Company of IN	064832	.	.	.	.	.	.	.	.	.	.	.	.	.	.	D	.	.	.	.	.	.	.	.	.	.	.	.	.	.	.	.	.	.	.	.	.	.	.	.	.	.	.	.	.	.	.	.	.	.	.	.	.	.	.	.	.
PHPMM Insurance Company	060652	.	.	.	.	.	.	.	.	.	.	.	.	.	.	.	.	.	.	.	.	.	.	D	.	.	.	.	.	.	.	.	.	.	.	.	.	.	.	.	.	.	.	.	.	.	.	.	.	.	.	.	.	.	.	.	.
Physicians Benefits Trust Life	007004	.	.	.	.	.	.	.	.	.	.	.	.	.	D	L	L	.	.	.	.	.	.	.	.	.	L	.	L	.	.	.	.	.	.	.	.	.	.	.	.	.	.	.	.	.	.	.	.	.	L	.	.	.	.	.	.
Physicians Health Choice of TX	064777	.	.	.	.	.	.	.	.	.	.	.	.	.	.	.	.	.	.	.	.	.	.	.	.	.	.	.	.	.	.	.	.	.	.	.	.	.	.	.	.	.	.	.	D	.	.	.	.	.	.	.	.	.	.	.	.
Physicians Hlth Plan of Mid-MI	068943	.	.	.	.	.	.	.	.	.	.	.	.	.	.	.	.	.	.	.	.	.	.	D	.	.	.	.	.	.	.	.	.	.	.	.	.	.	.	.	.	.	.	.	.	.	.	.	.	.	.	.	.	.	.	.	.
Physicians H P Mid-MI FamCare	064740	.	.	.	.	.	.	.	.	.	.	.	.	.	.	.	.	.	.	.	.	.	.	D	.	.	.	.	.	.	.	.	.	.	.	.	.	.	.	.	.	.	.	.	.	.	.	.	.	.	.	.	.	.	.	.	.
Physicians Hlth Pl-Northern IN	068743	.	.	.	.	.	.	.	.	.	.	.	.	.	.	D	.	.	.	.	.	.	.	.	.	.	.	.	.	.	.	.	.	.	.	.	.	.	.	.	.	.	.	.	.	.	.	.	.	.	.	.	.	.	.	.	.
Physicians Life Ins Co	007451	L	L	L	L	L	L	L	L	L	L	L	L	L	L	L	L	L	L	L	L	L	L	L	L	L	L	L	D	L	L	L	L	.	L	L	L	L	L	L	L	L	L	L	L	L	L	L	L	L	L	L	.	.	.	.	.
Physicians Mutual Insurance Co	007372	L	L	L	L	L	L	L	L	L	L	L	L	L	L	L	L	L	L	L	L	L	L	L	L	L	L	L	D	L	L	L	L	L	L	L	L	L	L	L	L	L	L	L	L	L	L	L	L	L	L	L	.	.	.	.	.
Physicians Plus Ins Corp	068683	.	.	.	.	.	.	.	.	.	.	.	.	.	.	.	.	.	.	.	.	.	.	.	.	.	.	.	.	.	.	.	.	.	.	.	.	.	.	.	.	.	.	.	.	.	.	.	.	.	D	.	.	.	.	.	.
Physicians United Plan Inc	064839	.	.	.	.	.	.	.	.	.	D	.	.	.	.	.	.	.	.	.	.	.	.	.	.	.	.	.	.	.	.	.	.	.	.	.	.	.	.	.	.	.	.	.	.	.	.	.	.	.	.	.	.	.	.	.	.
PhysiciansPlus Baptist&St Dom	064503	.	.	.	.	.	.	.	.	.	.	.	.	.	.	.	.	.	.	.	.	.	.	.	.	D	.	.	.	.	.	.	.	.	.	.	.	.	.	.	.	.	.	.	.	.	.	.	.	.	.	.	.	.	.	.	.
Piedmont Community Healthcare	064390	.	.	.	.	.	.	.	.	.	.	.	.	.	.	.	.	.	.	.	.	.	.	.	.	.	.	.	.	.	.	.	.	.	.	.	.	.	.	.	.	.	.	.	.	.	.	D	.	.	.	.	.	.	.	.	.
Pine Belt Life Insurance Co	060697	.	.	.	.	.	.	.	.	.	.	.	.	.	.	.	.	.	.	.	.	.	.	.	.	D	.	.	.	.	.	.	.	.	.	.	.	.	.	.	.	.	.	.	.	.	.	.	.	.	.	.	.	.	.	.	.
Pioneer American Ins Co	006929	L	L	L	L	L	L	.	.	L	L	L	L	L	L	L	.	L	L	L	.	L	L	.	.	L	L	L	.	L	.	L	L	.	L	.	L	L	L	.	L	L	.	L	D	L	.	L	L	L	.	L	.	.	.	L	.
Pioneer Military Insurance Co	060651	.	.	.	.	.	.	.	.	.	.	.	.	.	.	.	.	.	.	.	.	.	.	.	.	.	.	.	.	D	.	.	.	.	.	.	.	.	.	.	.	.	.	.	.	.	.	.	.	.	.	.	.	.	.	.	.
Pioneer Mutual Life Ins Co	006933	L	.	L	L	L	L	L	L	L	L	L	L	L	L	L	L	L	L	L	L	L	L	L	L	L	L	L	L	L	L	L	L	.	L	D	L	L	L	L	L	L	L	L	L	L	L	L	L	L	L	L	.	.	.	.	.
Pioneer Security Life Ins Co	006935	L	.	.	L	L	L	.	L	L	L	L	L	L	L	L	.	L	L	L	.	L	.	.	L	L	L	L	L	.	.	.	L	.	L	L	.	L	L	L	.	L	L	L	D	L	.	L	L	L	L	.	.	.	.	.	.
Plateau Ins Co	009348	L	.	L	.	.	.	.	.	.	.	L	.	.	.	.	.	.	L	L	.	.	.	.	.	L	.	.	.	.	.	.	.	.	L	.	.	.	.	.	.	L	.	D	.	.	.	.	.	.	.	.	.	.	.	.	.
Polish Roman Catholic Union	006940	.	.	.	L	L	.	L	L	.	L	.	.	.	D	L	.	L	.	.	.	L	L	L	L	.	L	.	L	.	L	L	.	L	.	.	L	.	.	L	L	.	.	.	L	.	L	.	.	L	L	.	.	.	.	.	.
Popular Life Re	060399	.	.	.	.	.	.	.	.	.	.	.	.	.	.	.	.	.	.	.	.	.	.	.	.	.	.	.	.	.	.	.	.	.	.	.	.	.	.	.	.	.	.	.	.	.	.	.	.	.	.	.	.	.	.	D	.
Port-O-Call Life Ins Co	007929	.	.	.	D	.	.	.	.	.	.	.	.	.	.	.	.	.	.	.	.	.	.	.	.	.	.	.	.	.	.	.	.	.	.	.	.	.	.	.	.	.	.	.	.	.	.	.	.	.	.	.	.	.	.	.	.
Preferred Assurance Company	064595	.	.	.	.	.	.	.	.	.	.	.	.	.	.	.	.	.	.	.	.	.	.	.	.	.	.	.	.	.	.	.	.	D	.	.	.	.	.	.	.	.	.	.	.	.	.	.	.	.	.	.	.	.	.	.	.
Preferred Hlth Partnership	064302	.	.	.	.	.	.	.	.	.	.	.	.	.	.	.	.	.	.	.	.	.	.	.	.	.	.	.	.	.	.	.	.	.	.	.	.	.	.	.	.	.	.	D	.	.	.	.	.	.	.	.	.	.	.	.	.
Preferred Health Plan Inc	064793	.	.	.	.	.	.	.	.	.	.	.	.	.	.	.	.	.	.	.	.	.	.	.	.	.	.	.	.	.	.	.	.	.	.	.	.	.	D	.	.	.	.	.	.	.	.	.	.	.	.	.	.	.	.	.	.

D-State of Domicile **L**-Licensed **S**-Surplus Lines Writer **F**-Authorized under the Risk Retention Act **Q**-Qualified or Accredited Reinsurer

Company Name	AMB#	AL	AK	AZ	AR	CA	CO	CT	DE	DC	FL	GA	HI	ID	IL	IN	IA	KS	KY	LA	ME	MD	MA	MI	MN	MS	MO	MT	NE	NV	NH	NJ	NM	NY	NC	ND	OH	OK	OR	PA	RI	SC	SD	TN	TX	UT	VT	VA	WA	WV	WI	WY	AS	GU	MP	PR	VI
Preferred Health Systems Ins	060224	.	.	.	.	.	.	.	.	.	.	.	.	.	.	.	.	D	.	.	.	.	.	.	.	.	.	.	.	.	.	.	.	.	.	.	.	.	.	.	.	.	.	.	.	.	.	.	.	.	.	.	.	.	.	.	.
Preferred Plus of Kansas Inc	068937	.	.	.	.	.	.	.	.	.	.	.	.	.	.	.	.	D	.	.	.	.	.	.	.	.	.	.	.	.	.	.	.	.	.	.	.	.	.	.	.	.	.	.	.	.	.	.	.	.	.	.	.	.	.	.	.
Preferred Security Life Ins	068266	.	.	.	.	.	.	.	.	.	.	.	.	.	.	.	.	.	.	.	.	.	.	.	.	.	.	.	.	.	.	.	.	.	.	.	.	.	.	.	.	.	.	.	D	.	.	.	.	.	.	.	.	.	.	.	.
PreferredOne Community Hlth Pl	064054	.	.	.	.	.	.	.	.	.	.	.	.	.	.	.	.	.	.	.	.	.	.	.	D	.	.	.	.	.	.	.	.	.	.	.	.	.	.	.	.	.	.	.	.	.	.	.	.	.	.	.	.	.	.	.	.
PreferredOne Insurance Co	013851	.	.	.	.	.	.	.	.	.	.	.	.	.	.	.	.	.	.	.	.	.	.	.	D	.	.	.	.	.	.	.	.	.	.	.	.	.	.	.	.	.	.	.	.	.	.	.	.	.	.	.	.	.	.	.	.
Premera Blue Cross	060076	.	L	.	.	.	.	.	.	.	.	.	.	.	.	.	.	.	.	.	.	.	.	.	.	.	.	.	.	.	.	.	.	.	.	.	.	.	.	.	.	.	.	.	.	.	.	.	D	.	.	.	.	.	.	.	.
Premier Access Insurance Co	060375	.	.	L	.	D	L	L	.	.	L	.	.	.	.	.	.	.	L	.	.	.	.	.	.	.	.	.	.	L	.	L	.	L	.	.	.	.	.	L	.	.	.	.	L	.	.	L	.	.	.	.	.	.	.	.	.
Premier Behavioral Systs of TN	064433	.	.	.	.	.	.	.	.	.	.	.	.	.	.	.	.	.	.	.	.	.	.	.	.	.	.	.	.	.	.	.	.	.	.	.	.	.	.	.	.	.	.	D	.	.	.	.	.	.	.	.	.	.	.	.	.
Premier Choice Dental Inc	064821	.	.	D	.	.	.	.	.	.	.	.	.	.	.	.	.	.	.	.	.	.	.	.	.	.	.	.	.	.	.	.	.	.	.	.	.	.	.	.	.	.	.	.	.	.	.	.	.	.	.	.	.	.	.	.	.
Preneed Reinsurance Co of Amer	060371	.	.	D	.	.	.	.	.	.	.	.	.	.	.	.	.	.	.	.	.	.	.	.	.	.	.	.	.	.	.	.	.	.	.	.	.	.	.	.	.	.	.	.	.	.	.	.	.	.	.	.	.	.	.	.	.
Presbyterian Health Plan Inc	068930	.	.	.	.	.	.	.	.	.	.	.	.	.	.	.	.	.	.	.	.	.	.	.	.	.	.	.	.	.	.	.	D	.	.	.	.	.	.	.	.	.	.	.	.	.	.	.	.	.	.	.	.	.	.	.	.
Presbyterian Insurance Company	064748	.	.	.	.	.	.	.	.	.	.	.	.	.	.	.	.	.	.	.	.	.	.	.	.	.	.	.	.	.	.	.	D	.	.	.	.	.	.	.	.	.	.	.	.	.	.	.	.	.	.	.	.	.	.	.	.
Preservation Life Insurance Co	068602	.	.	.	.	.	.	.	.	.	.	.	.	.	.	.	.	.	.	.	.	.	.	.	.	.	D	.	.	.	.	.	.	.	.	.	.	.	.	.	.	.	.	.	.	.	.	.	.	.	.	.	.	.	.	.	.
Presidential Life Ins Co	006948	L	L	L	L	L	L	L	L	L	L	L	L	L	L	L	L	L	L	L	L	L	L	L	L	L	L	L	L	L	.	L	L	D	L	L	L	L	L	L	L	L	L	L	L	L	L	L	L	L	L	L	.	.	.	.	.
Presidential Life Ins Co	007931	.	.	.	.	.	.	.	.	.	.	.	.	.	.	.	.	.	.	.	.	.	.	.	.	.	.	.	.	.	.	.	.	.	.	.	.	.	.	.	.	.	.	.	D	.	.	.	.	.	.	.	.	.	.	.	.
PrimeCare Medical Network Inc	064659	.	.	.	.	D	.	.	.	.	.	.	.	.	.	.	.	.	.	.	.	.	.	.	.	.	.	.	.	.	.	.	.	.	.	.	.	.	.	.	.	.	.	.	.	.	.	.	.	.	.	.	.	.	.	.	.
Primerica Life Inc Co	006693	L	L	L	L	L	L	L	L	L	L	L	L	L	L	L	L	L	L	L	L	L	D	L	L	L	L	L	L	L	L	L	L	.	L	L	L	L	L	L	L	L	L	L	L	L	L	L	L	L	L	L	.	L	L	L	L
Principal Life Insurance Co	006150	L	L	L	L	L	L	L	L	L	L	L	L	L	L	L	D	L	L	L	L	L	L	L	L	L	L	L	L	L	L	L	L	L	L	L	L	L	L	L	L	L	L	L	L	L	L	L	L	L	L	L	.	.	.	L	.
Principal National Life Ins Co	007326	L	L	L	L	L	L	L	L	L	L	L	L	L	L	L	D	L	L	L	L	L	L	L	L	L	L	L	L	L	L	L	L	.	L	L	L	L	L	L	L	L	L	L	L	L	L	L	L	L	L	L	.	.	.	L	.
Priority Health	068977	.	.	.	.	.	.	.	.	.	.	.	.	.	.	.	.	.	.	.	.	.	.	D	.	.	.	.	.	.	.	.	.	.	.	.	.	.	.	.	.	.	.	.	.	.	.	.	.	.	.	.	.	.	.	.	.
Priority Health Care Inc	068916	.	.	.	.	.	.	.	.	.	.	.	.	.	.	.	.	.	.	.	.	.	.	.	.	.	.	.	.	.	.	.	.	.	.	.	.	.	.	.	.	.	.	.	.	.	.	D	.	.	.	.	.	.	.	.	.
Priority Health Govt Programs	064739	.	.	.	.	.	.	.	.	.	.	.	.	.	.	.	.	.	.	.	.	.	.	D	.	.	.	.	.	.	.	.	.	.	.	.	.	.	.	.	.	.	.	.	.	.	.	.	.	.	.	.	.	.	.	.	.
Priority Health Insurance Co	060564	.	.	.	.	.	.	.	.	.	.	.	.	.	.	.	.	.	.	.	.	.	.	D	.	.	.	.	.	.	.	.	.	.	.	.	.	.	.	.	.	.	.	.	.	.	.	.	.	.	.	.	.	.	.	.	.
ProCare Health Plan	064686	.	.	.	.	.	.	.	.	.	.	.	.	.	.	.	.	.	.	.	.	.	.	D	.	.	.	.	.	.	.	.	.	.	.	.	.	.	.	.	.	.	.	.	.	.	.	.	.	.	.	.	.	.	.	.	.
Professional Ins Company	006950	L	.	L	L	L	L	L	.	L	L	L	L	L	L	L	L	L	L	L	.	L	L	L	L	L	L	L	L	L	.	.	L	.	L	L	L	L	L	L	.	L	L	L	D	L	.	L	L	L	L	L	.	.	.	.	.
Professional Life & Casualty	006952	.	.	.	.	.	.	.	.	.	.	.	.	.	D	L	.	.	.	.	.	.	.	.	.	.	.	L	.	.	.	.	.	.	.	L	.	L	.	.	.	.	.	.	.	.	.	.	.	.	.	.	.	.	.	.	.
Programmed Life Ins Co	009426	.	.	D	.	.	.	.	.	.	.	.	.	.	.	.	.	.	.	.	.	.	.	.	.	.	.	.	.	.	.	.	.	.	.	.	.	.	.	.	.	.	.	.	.	.	.	.	.	.	.	.	.	.	.	.	.
Protective Life & Annuity Ins	008860	D	.	L	L	L	L	.	.	.	L	L	.	.	L	L	L	L	L	L	.	.	L	L	.	L	L	.	L	L	.	.	L	L	L	.	L	L	L	.	.	L	.	L	L	L	.	L	L	.	.	.	.	.	.	.	.
Protective Life Ins Co	006962	L	L	L	L	L	L	L	L	L	L	L	L	L	L	L	L	L	L	L	L	L	L	L	L	L	L	L	L	L	L	L	L	.	L	L	L	L	L	L	L	L	L	D	L	L	L	L	L	L	L	L	L	L	L	L	L
Protective Life Insurance NY	060340	.	.	.	.	.	.	.	.	.	.	.	.	.	.	.	.	.	.	.	.	.	.	.	.	.	.	.	.	.	.	.	.	D	.	.	.	.	.	.	.	.	.	.	.	.	.	.	.	.	.	.	.	.	.	.	.
Providence Health Plan	068651	.	.	.	.	.	.	.	.	.	.	.	.	.	.	.	.	.	.	.	.	.	.	.	.	.	.	.	.	.	.	.	.	.	.	.	.	.	D	.	.	.	.	.	.	.	.	.	F	.	.	.	.	.	.	.	.
Provident American Ins Co	006966	.	.	L	.	.	L	.	.	.	.	.	.	.	.	.	.	.	.	L	.	.	.	.	.	F	F	L	.	L	.	.	L	.	.	L	.	L	.	.	.	.	.	F	D	L	.	.	.	.	.	F	.	.	.	.	.
Provident American Life & Hlth	006932	.	L	L	L	L	L	.	L	L	L	L	L	L	L	L	L	L	L	L	.	L	L	.	.	L	L	L	L	L	.	.	.	.	L	L	D	L	L	L	.	L	L	L	L	L	L	.	.	L	L	L	.	.	.	.	.
Provident Life and Accident	006968	L	L	L	L	L	L	L	L	L	L	L	L	L	L	L	L	L	L	L	L	L	L	L	L	L	L	L	L	L	L	L	L	.	L	L	L	L	L	L	L	L	L	D	L	L	L	L	L	L	L	L	.	.	.	L	.
Provident Life and Casualty	006969	.	L	.	L	.	L	L	L	L	.	L	L	L	L	.	L	.	L	L	.	.	L	.	.	L	L	.	L	.	L	L	L	L	L	L	L	L	.	L	L	L	L	D	.	.	.	L	L	.	.	.	.	.	.	.	.
Pruco Life Ins Co	008240	L	L	D	L	L	L	L	L	L	L	L	L	L	L	L	L	L	L	L	L	L	L	L	L	L	L	L	L	L	L	L	L	.	L	L	L	L	L	L	L	L	L	L	L	L	L	L	L	L	L	L	.	L	.	.	.
Pruco Life Insurance Co of NJ	009371	.	.	.	.	.	.	.	.	.	.	.	.	.	.	.	.	.	.	.	.	.	.	.	.	.	.	.	.	.	.	D	.	L	.	.	.	.	.	.	.	.	.	.	.	.	.	.	.	.	.	.	.	.	.	.	.
Prudential Annuities Life Assr	008715	L	L	L	L	L	L	D	L	L	L	L	L	L	L	L	L	L	L	L	L	L	L	L	L	L	L	L	L	L	L	L	L	L	L	L	L	L	L	L	L	L	L	L	L	L	L	L	L	L	L	L	.	.	.	L	.
Prudential Ins Co of America	006974	L	L	L	L	L	L	L	L	L	L	L	L	L	L	L	L	L	L	L	L	L	L	L	L	L	L	L	L	L	L	D	L	L	L	L	L	L	L	L	L	L	L	L	L	L	L	L	L	L	L	L	.	L	.	L	L
Prudential Retirement Ins&Ann	009144	L	L	L	L	L	L	D	L	L	L	L	L	L	L	L	L	L	L	L	L	L	L	L	L	L	L	L	L	L	L	L	L	L	L	L	L	L	L	L	L	L	L	L	L	L	L	L	L	L	L	L	.	.	.	.	.
Puerto Rico Health Plan Inc	060163	.	.	.	.	.	.	.	.	.	.	.	.	.	.	.	.	.	.	.	.	.	.	.	.	.	.	.	.	.	.	.	.	.	.	.	.	.	.	.	.	.	.	.	.	.	.	.	.	.	.	.	.	.	.	D	.
Pupil Benefits Plan Inc	064598	.	.	.	.	.	.	.	.	.	.	.	.	.	.	.	.	.	.	.	.	.	.	.	.	.	.	.	.	.	.	.	.	D	.	.	.	.	.	.	.	.	.	.	.	.	.	.	.	.	.	.	.	.	.	.	.
Puritan Life Insurance Company	068115	.	.	.	.	.	.	.	.	.	.	.	.	.	.	.	.	.	.	.	.	.	.	.	.	.	.	.	.	.	.	.	.	.	.	.	.	.	.	.	.	.	.	.	D	.	.	.	.	.	.	.	.	.	.	.	.
Pyramid Life Insurance Company	006977	L	.	L	L	L	L	.	L	.	L	L	.	L	L	L	L	D	L	L	.	L	L	L	L	L	L	L	L	L	.	.	L	.	L	L	L	L	L	L	.	L	L	L	L	L	.	L	L	.	L	L	.	.	.	.	.
QCA Health Plan Inc	064050	.	.	.	D	.	.	.	.	.	.	.	.	.	.	.	.	.	.	.	.	.	.	.	.	.	.	.	.	.	.	.	.	.	.	.	.	.	.	.	.	.	.	.	.	.	.	.	.	.	.	.	.	.	.	.	.
QualChoice Life & Health Ins	007304	.	.	.	D	.	.	.	.	.	.	.	.	.	.	.	.	.	.	.	.	.	.	.	.	.	.	.	.	.	.	.	.	.	.	.	.	.	.	.	.	.	.	.	.	.	.	.	.	.	.	.	.	.	.	.	.
Rabenhorst Life Ins Co	007954	.	.	.	.	.	.	.	.	.	.	.	.	.	.	.	.	.	.	D	.	.	.	.	.	.	.	.	.	.	.	.	.	.	.	.	.	.	.	.	.	.	.	.	.	.	.	.	.	.	.	.	.	.	.	.	.
Rayant Insurance Company of NY	060327	.	.	.	.	.	.	.	.	.	.	.	.	.	.	.	.	.	.	.	.	.	.	.	.	.	.	.	.	.	.	.	.	D	.	.	.	.	.	.	.	.	.	.	.	.	.	.	.	.	.	.	.	.	.	.	.
Reassure America Life Ins Co	007207	L	L	L	L	L	L	L	L	L	L	L	L	L	L	D	L	L	L	L	L	L	L	L	L	L	L	L	L	L	L	L	L	.	L	L	L	L	L	L	L	L	L	L	L	L	L	L	L	L	L	L	.	L	.	L	.
Regal Life of America Ins Co	068098	.	.	.	.	.	.	.	.	.	.	.	.	.	.	.	.	.	.	.	.	.	.	.	.	.	.	.	.	.	.	.	.	.	.	.	.	.	.	.	.	.	.	.	D	.	.	.	.	.	.	.	.	.	.	.	.
Regal Reinsurance Co	060045	.	.	.	.	.	.	.	.	.	.	.	.	.	.	.	.	.	.	.	.	.	D	.	.	.	.	.	.	.	.	.	.	.	.	.	.	.	.	.	.	.	.	.	.	.	.	.	.	.	.	.	.	.	.	.	.
Regence BC/BS of Oregon	060074	.	.	.	.	.	.	.	.	.	.	.	.	.	.	.	.	.	.	.	.	.	.	.	.	.	.	.	.	.	.	.	.	.	.	.	.	.	D	.	.	.	.	.	.	.	.	.	F	.	.	.	.	.	.	.	.
Regence BlueCross BlueSh of UT	064412	.	.	.	.	.	.	.	.	.	.	.	.	.	.	.	.	.	.	.	.	.	.	.	.	.	.	.	.	.	.	.	.	.	.	.	.	.	.	.	.	.	.	.	.	D	.	.	.	.	.	.	.	.	.	.	.
Regence BlueShield	060199	.	.	.	.	.	.	.	.	.	.	.	.	.	.	.	.	.	.	.	.	.	.	.	.	.	.	.	.	.	.	.	.	.	.	.	.	.	.	.	.	.	.	.	.	.	.	.	D	.	.	.	.	.	.	.	.
Regence BlueShield of Idaho	060266	.	.	.	.	.	.	.	.	.	.	.	.	D	.	.	.	.	.	.	.	.	.	.	.	.	.	.	.	.	.	.	.	.	.	.	.	.	.	.	.	.	.	.	.	.	.	.	F	.	.	.	.	.	.	.	.
Regence Health Maint of OR	068584	.	.	.	.	.	.	.	.	.	.	.	.	.	.	.	.	.	.	.	.	.	.	.	.	.	.	.	.	.	.	.	.	.	.	.	.	.	D	.	.	.	.	.	.	.	.	.	.	.	.	.	.	.	.	.	.
Regence HMO Oregon	068583	.	.	.	.	.	.	.	.	.	.	.	.	.	.	.	.	.	.	.	.	.	.	.	.	.	.	.	.	.	.	.	.	.	.	.	.	.	D	.	.	.	.	.	.	.	.	.	.	.	.	.	.	.	.	.	.
Regence Life and Health Ins Co	009345	.	F	.	.	.	.	.	.	.	.	.	.	F	.	.	.	.	.	.	.	.	.	.	.	.	.	.	.	.	.	.	.	.	.	.	.	.	D	.	.	.	.	.	.	F	.	.	F	.	.	.	.	.	.	.	.
Region 6 Rx Corporation	064944	.	.	.	.	.	.	.	.	.	.	.	.	.	.	.	.	.	.	.	.	.	.	.	.	.	.	.	.	.	.	.	.	.	.	.	.	.	.	D	.	.	.	.	.	.	.	.	.	.	.	.	.	.	.	.	.
Reinsurance Co of Missouri	050061	.	.	.	.	.	.	.	.	.	.	.	.	.	.	.	.	.	.	.	.	.	.	.	.	.	D	.	.	.	.	.	.	.	.	.	.	.	.	.	.	.	.	.	.	.	.	.	.	.	.	.	.	.	.	.	.
Reliable Life Insurance Co	006986	L	L	L	L	L	L	L	L	L	L	L	L	L	L	L	L	L	L	.	L	L	L	L	L	L	D	L	L	L	L	L	L	.	L	L	L	L	L	L	L	L	L	L	L	L	L	L	L	L	L	L	.	.	.	.	.
Reliance Standard Life Ins Co	006990	L	L	L	L	L	L	L	L	L	L	L	L	L	D	L	L	L	L	L	L	L	L	L	L	L	L	L	L	L	L	L	L	Q	L	L	L	L	L	L	L	L	L	L	L	L	L	L	L	L	L	L	.	L	.	L	L
Reliance Standard Life of TX	009480	.	.	.	.	.	.	.	.	.	.	.	.	.	.	.	.	.	.	.	.	.	.	.	.	.	.	.	.	.	.	.	.	.	.	.	.	.	.	.	.	.	.	.	D	.	.	.	.	.	.	.	.	.	.	.	.
ReliaStar Life Insurance Co	006846	L	L	L	L	L	L	L	L	L	L	L	L	L	L	L	L	L	L	L	L	L	L	L	D	L	L	L	L	L	L	L	L	Q	L	L	L	L	L	L	L	L	L	L	L	L	L	L	L	L	L	L	.	L	.	L	.
ReliaStar Life Ins Co of NY	006157	L	L	L	L	L	L	L	L	L	L	L	L	L	L	L	L	L	L	L	L	L	L	L	L	L	L	L	L	L	L	L	L	D	L	L	L	L	L	L	L	L	L	L	L	L	L	L	L	L	L	L	.	.	.	.	.
Renaissance Health Ins Co NY	002682	.	.	.	.	.	.	.	.	.	.	.	.	.	.	.	.	.	.	.	.	.	.	.	.	.	.	.	.	.	.	.	.	D	.	.	.	.	.	.	.	.	.	.	.	.	.	.	.	.	.	.	.	.	.	.	.
Renaissance Lf & Hlth of Amer	006201	L	L	L	L	L	L	L	L	L	L	L	L	L	L	D	L	L	L	L	L	L	L	L	L	L	L	L	L	L	L	L	L	.	.	.	L	L	L	L	L	L	L	L	L	L	L	L	L	L	L	L	.	.	.	.	L
Reserve National Ins Co	006998	L	.	L	L	.	L	.	.	.	L	L	.	L	L	L	L	L	L	L	.	.	L	.	.	L	L	L	L	L	.	.	L	.	L	.	L	D	L	L	.	L	L	L	L	L	.	L	L	L	.	L	.	.	.	.	.
Resource Life Insurance Co	006176	L	L	L	L	L	L	L	L	L	L	L	L	L	D	L	L	L	L	L	L	L	L	L	L	L	L	L	L	L	L	.	L	L	L	L	L	L	L	L	L	L	L	L	L	L	L	L	L	L	L	L	.	.	.	L	.
RGA Reinsurance Company	009080	L	L	L	L	L	L	Q	L	L	L	L	L	L	L	L	L	L	L	L	Q	L	L	L	L	L	D	L	L	L	Q	L	L	Q	L	L	L	L	L	L	L	L	L	L	L	L	L	L	L	L	L	L	.	.	.	.	.
Rhodes Life Ins Co of LA	008092	.	.	.	.	.	.	.	.	.	.	.	.	.	.	.	.	.	.	D	.	.	.	.	.	.	.	.	.	.	.	.	.	.	.	.	.	.	.	.	.	.	.	.	.	.	.	.	.	.	.	.	.	.	.	.	.
RightCHOICE Insurance Co	060024	.	.	.	.	.	.	.	.	.	.	.	.	.	D	.	.	.	.	.	.	.	.	.	.	.	.	.	.	.	.	.	.	.	.	.	.	.	.	.	.	.	.	.	.	.	.	.	.	.	.	.	.	.	.	.	.
RiverSource Life Ins Co of NY	008345	.	.	.	.	.	.	.	L	.	.	.	.	.	.	.	.	.	.	.	.	.	.	.	.	.	.	.	.	.	.	.	.	D	.	L	.	.	.	.	.	.	.	.	.	.	.	.	.	.	.	.	.	.	.	.	.
RiverSource Life Ins Co	006592	L	L	L	L	L	L	L	L	L	L	L	L	L	L	L	L	L	L	L	L	L	L	L	D	L	L	L	L	L	L	L	L	.	L	L	L	L	L	L	L	L	L	L	L	L	L	L	L	L	L	L	.	.	.	.	.
Rocky Mountain Hlth Maint Org	064312	.	.	.	.	.	D	.	.	.	.	.	.	.	.	.	.	.	.	.	.	.	.	.	.	.	.	.	.	.	.	.	.	.	.	.	.	.	.	.	.	.	.	.	.	.	.	.	.	.	.	L	.	.	.	.	.
Rocky Mountain HthCare Options	064561	.	.	.	.	.	D	.	.	.	.	.	.	.	.	.	.	.	.	.	.	.	.	.	.	.	.	.	.	.	.	.	.	.	.	.	.	.	.	.	.	.	.	.	.	.	.	.	.	.	.	.	.	.	.	.	.

D-State of Domicile **L**-Licensed **S**-Surplus Lines Writer **F**-Authorized under the Risk Retention Act **Q**-Qualified or Accredited Reinsurer

U.S. States/Territories in Which Companies Are Licensed or Do Business – *Continued*

Company Name	AMB#	AL	AK	AZ	AR	CA	CO	CT	DE	DC	FL	GA	HI	ID	IL	IN	IA	KS	KY	LA	ME	MD	MA	MI	MN	MS	MO	MT	NE	NV	NH	NJ	NM	NY	NC	ND	OH	OK	OR	PA	RI	SC	SD	TN	TX	UT	VT	VA	WA	WV	WI	WY	AS	GU	MP	PR	VI
Rocky Mountain Hosp & Med Svc	068817	.	.	.	.	.	D	.	.	.	.	.	.	.	.	.	.	.	.	.	.	.	.	.	.	.	.	.	.	L	.	.	.	.	.	.	.	.	.	.	.	.	.	.	.	.	.	.	.	.	.	.	.	.	.	.	.
Royal Neighbors of America	007010	.	.	L	L	L	L	L	L	L	L	L	.	L	D	L	L	L	L	.	L	L	.	L	L	L	L	L	L	L	.	L	L	.	L	L	L	L	L	L	L	.	L	L	L	L	L	L	L	L	L	L	.	.	.	.	.
Royal State National Ins Co	007012	.	.	.	.	.	.	.	.	.	.	.	D	.	.	.	.	.	.	.	.	.	.	.	.	.	.	.	.	.	.	.	.	.	.	.	.	.	.	.	.	.	.	.	.	.	.	.	.	.	.	.	.	L	.	.	.
S.USA Life Insurance Company	060110	L	L	D	L	L	L	.	L	L	L	L	L	L	L	L	.	L	L	L	L	L	L	L	L	.	L	L	L	L	.	L	L	.	.	L	L	L	L	L	L	L	L	L	L	L	L	L	L	L	L	L	.	.	.	.	L
Sabine Life Ins Co	007970	.	.	.	.	.	.	.	.	.	.	.	.	.	.	.	.	.	.	D	.	.	.	.	.	.	.	.	.	.	.	.	.	.	.	.	.	.	.	.	.	.	.	.	.	.	.	.	.	.	.	.	.	.	.	.	.
Safeguard Health Plans NV Corp	064900	.	.	.	.	.	.	.	.	.	.	.	.	.	.	.	.	.	.	.	.	.	.	.	.	.	.	.	.	D	.	.	.	.	.	.	.	.	.	.	.	.	.	.	.	.	.	.	.	.	.	.	.	.	.	.	.
SafeGuard Health Plans (CA)	068512	.	.	.	.	D	.	.	.	.	.	.	.	.	.	.	.	.	.	.	.	.	.	.	.	.	.	.	.	.	.	.	.	.	.	.	.	.	.	.	.	.	.	.	.	.	.	.	.	.	.	.	.	.	.	.	.
SafeGuard Health Plans (FL)	064671	.	.	.	.	.	.	.	.	.	D	.	.	.	.	.	.	.	.	.	.	.	.	.	.	.	.	.	.	.	.	.	.	.	.	.	.	.	.	.	.	.	.	.	.	.	.	.	.	.	.	.	.	.	.	.	.
SafeGuard Health Plans (TX)	064460	.	.	.	.	.	.	.	.	.	.	.	.	.	.	.	.	.	.	.	.	.	.	.	.	.	.	.	.	.	.	.	.	.	.	.	.	.	.	.	.	.	.	.	D	.	.	.	.	.	.	.	.	.	.	.	.
SafeHealth Life Ins Co	008221	.	.	L	.	D	L	.	L	.	L	L	.	.	L	.	.	L	L	.	.	L	.	.	.	.	L	.	.	L	.	.	L	.	.	.	L	.	L	L	.	L	.	.	L	L	.	.	.	.	L	.	.	.	.	.	.
Sagicor Life Insurance Company	006057	L	.	L	L	L	L	.	L	L	L	L	L	L	L	L	L	L	L	L	Q	L	L	L	L	L	L	L	L	L	.	L	L	.	L	L	L	L	L	L	L	L	L	L	D	L	Q	L	L	L	L	L	.	.	.	.	.
Samaritan Health Plans Inc	064906	.	.	.	.	.	.	.	.	.	.	.	.	.	.	.	.	.	.	.	.	.	.	.	.	.	.	.	.	.	.	.	.	.	.	.	.	.	D	.	.	.	.	.	.	.	.	.	.	.	.	.	.	.	.	.	.
San Francisco Health Plan	064582	.	.	.	.	D	.	.	.	.	.	.	.	.	.	.	.	.	.	.	.	.	.	.	.	.	.	.	.	.	.	.	.	.	.	.	.	.	.	.	.	.	.	.	.	.	.	.	.	.	.	.	.	.	.	.	.
San Joaquin Health Commission	064006	.	.	.	.	D	.	.	.	.	.	.	.	.	.	.	.	.	.	.	.	.	.	.	.	.	.	.	.	.	.	.	.	.	.	.	.	.	.	.	.	.	.	.	.	.	.	.	.	.	.	.	.	.	.	.	.
San Mateo Health Commission	064575	.	.	.	.	D	.	.	.	.	.	.	.	.	.	.	.	.	.	.	.	.	.	.	.	.	.	.	.	.	.	.	.	.	.	.	.	.	.	.	.	.	.	.	.	.	.	.	.	.	.	.	.	.	.	.	.
San Miguel Health Plan	064949	.	.	.	.	D	.	.	.	.	.	.	.	.	.	.	.	.	.	.	.	.	.	.	.	.	.	.	.	.	.	.	.	.	.	.	.	.	.	.	.	.	.	.	.	.	.	.	.	.	.	.	.	.	.	.	.
Sanford Health Plan	064393	.	.	.	.	.	.	.	.	.	.	.	.	.	.	.	L	.	.	.	.	.	.	.	.	.	.	.	.	.	.	.	.	.	.	.	.	.	.	.	.	.	D	.	.	.	.	.	.	.	.	.	.	.	.	.	.
Sanford Health Plan of MN	064604	.	.	.	.	.	.	.	.	.	.	.	.	.	.	.	.	.	.	.	.	.	.	.	D	.	.	.	.	.	.	.	.	.	.	.	.	.	.	.	.	.	.	.	.	.	.	.	.	.	.	.	.	.	.	.	.
Santa Barbara Regional H Auth	064710	.	.	.	.	D	.	.	.	.	.	.	.	.	.	.	.	.	.	.	.	.	.	.	.	.	.	.	.	.	.	.	.	.	.	.	.	.	.	.	.	.	.	.	.	.	.	.	.	.	.	.	.	.	.	.	.
Santa Clara County	064152	.	.	.	.	D	.	.	.	.	.	.	.	.	.	.	.	.	.	.	.	.	.	.	.	.	.	.	.	.	.	.	.	.	.	.	.	.	.	.	.	.	.	.	.	.	.	.	.	.	.	.	.	.	.	.	.
Santa Clara County Health Auth	064576	.	.	.	.	D	.	.	.	.	.	.	.	.	.	.	.	.	.	.	.	.	.	.	.	.	.	.	.	.	.	.	.	.	.	.	.	.	.	.	.	.	.	.	.	.	.	.	.	.	.	.	.	.	.	.	.
Santa Cruz-Monterey Mgd Med Cr	064656	.	.	.	.	D	.	.	.	.	.	.	.	.	.	.	.	.	.	.	.	.	.	.	.	.	.	.	.	.	.	.	.	.	.	.	.	.	.	.	.	.	.	.	.	.	.	.	.	.	.	.	.	.	.	.	.
Savings Bank Life Ins Co of MA	006696	.	.	L	L	L	L	L	L	L	L	L	L	.	L	L	L	L	L	L	L	L	D	L	.	L	L	.	.	L	L	L	L	.	L	.	L	L	L	L	L	L	.	L	L	L	L	L	L	L	L	.	.	.	.	.	.
SBLI USA Mutual Life Ins Co	006821	.	.	.	.	.	.	.	.	.	.	.	.	.	L	.	L	.	.	.	.	.	.	L	.	L	.	.	.	.	L	L	.	D	L	.	L	.	.	L	.	.	L	.	.	.	L	.	.	.	.	.	.	.	.	L	.
SCAN Health Plan	060187	.	.	.	.	D	.	.	.	.	.	.	.	.	.	.	.	.	.	.	.	.	.	.	.	.	.	.	.	.	.	.	.	.	.	.	.	.	.	.	.	.	.	.	.	.	.	.	.	.	.	.	.	.	.	.	.
SCAN Health Plan Arizona	064846	.	.	D	.	.	.	.	.	.	.	.	.	.	.	.	.	.	.	.	.	.	.	.	.	.	.	.	.	.	.	.	.	.	.	.	.	.	.	.	.	.	.	.	.	.	.	.	.	.	.	.	.	.	.	.	.
SCOR Global Life Re Ins Co TX	060212	.	L	L	L	L	L	Q	L	L	L	L	L	L	L	L	L	L	Q	L	Q	L	Q	L	L	L	L	L	L	L	Q	Q	L	Q	L	L	L	L	L	Q	Q	L	L	L	D	L	Q	Q	L	L	L	L	.	.	.	Q	.
SCOR Global Life Reins Co Amer	060575	L	L	L	L	L	L	L	D	L	L	L	L	L	L	L	L	L	L	L	L	L	L	L	L	L	L	L	L	L	L	Q	L	.	L	L	L	L	L	L	L	L	L	L	L	L	L	L	L	L	L	L	.	.	.	.	.
SCOR Global Life US Re Ins Co	006555	L	L	L	L	L	L	Q	L	L	L	L	L	L	L	L	L	L	L	L	Q	L	L	L	L	L	L	L	L	L	Q	L	L	.	Q	L	L	L	L	L	L	L	L	L	D	L	L	L	L	L	L	L	.	.	.	.	.
Scott & White Health Plan	060161	.	.	.	.	.	.	.	.	.	.	.	.	.	.	.	.	.	.	.	.	.	.	.	.	.	.	.	.	.	.	.	.	.	.	.	.	.	.	.	.	.	.	.	D	.	.	.	.	.	.	.	.	.	.	.	.
Scottish Re Life Corporation	008928	Q	Q	L	L	L	Q	Q	D	L	Q	L	Q	L	L	L	L	L	Q	L	Q	Q	L	L	Q	L	L	Q	L	L	Q	L	Q	Q	Q	Q	L	L	Q	Q	Q	Q	Q	Q	L	L	Q	Q	L	Q	Q	L	.	L	.	.	.
Scottish Re (US) Inc.	008785	Q	Q	L	Q	L	Q	Q	D	L	Q	L	Q	Q	L	L	L	L	Q	L	Q	Q	Q	Q	L	L	Q	Q	Q	L	Q	Q	Q	Q	Q	Q	L	L	Q	.	Q	Q	Q	Q	L	Q	Q	Q	L	Q	Q	Q	.	.	.	.	.
Scripps Clinic Health Plan Svs	064661	.	.	.	.	D	.	.	.	.	.	.	.	.	.	.	.	.	.	.	.	.	.	.	.	.	.	.	.	.	.	.	.	.	.	.	.	.	.	.	.	.	.	.	.	.	.	.	.	.	.	.	.	.	.	.	.
Sears Life Insurance Company	007170	L	L	L	L	L	L	L	L	L	L	L	L	L	L	L	L	L	L	L	L	L	L	L	L	L	L	L	L	L	L	L	L	.	L	L	L	L	L	L	L	L	L	L	D	L	L	L	L	L	L	L	.	.	.	.	.
SEB Trygg Life (USA) Assur Ltd	060372	.	.	D	.	.	.	.	.	.	.	.	.	.	.	.	.	.	.	.	.	.	.	.	.	.	.	.	.	.	.	.	.	.	.	.	.	.	.	.	.	.	.	.	.	.	.	.	.	.	.	.	.	.	.	.	.
Securian Life Insurance Co	009064	L	L	L	L	L	L	L	L	L	L	L	L	L	L	L	L	L	L	L	L	L	L	L	D	L	L	L	L	L	L	L	L	L	L	L	L	L	L	L	L	L	L	L	L	L	L	L	L	L	L	L	.	.	.	.	.
Securitas Financial Life Ins	009068	.	.	L	L	.	L	.	L	L	.	L	.	L	.	L	.	.	.	L	.	.	.	.	.	L	L	.	.	L	.	.	L	.	D	.	.	L	L	.	.	L	.	L	L	.	.	L	L	L	.	.	.	.	.	.	.
Security Benefit Life Ins Co	007025	L	L	L	L	L	L	L	L	L	L	L	L	L	L	L	L	D	L	L	L	L	L	L	L	L	L	L	L	L	L	L	L	Q	L	L	L	L	L	L	L	L	L	L	L	L	L	L	L	L	L	L	.	L	.	.	.
Security Health Ins of Amer NY	064979	.	.	.	.	.	.	.	.	.	.	.	.	.	.	.	.	.	.	.	.	.	.	.	.	.	.	.	.	.	.	.	.	D	.	.	.	.	.	.	.	.	.	.	.	.	.	.	.	.	.	.	.	.	.	.	.
Security Health Plan of WI	064207	.	.	.	.	.	.	.	.	.	.	.	.	.	.	.	.	.	.	.	.	.	.	.	.	.	.	.	.	.	.	.	.	.	.	.	.	.	.	.	.	.	.	.	.	.	.	.	.	.	D	.	.	.	.	.	.
Security Life Ins Co of Amer	007030	L	L	L	L	L	L	L	L	L	L	L	L	L	L	L	L	L	L	L	L	L	L	L	D	L	L	L	L	L	L	L	L	.	L	L	L	L	L	L	L	L	L	L	L	L	L	L	L	L	L	L	.	.	.	.	.
Security Life of Denver Ins Co	007029	L	L	L	L	L	D	L	L	L	L	L	L	L	L	L	L	L	L	L	L	L	L	L	L	L	L	L	L	L	L	L	L	Q	L	L	L	L	L	L	L	L	L	L	L	L	L	L	L	L	L	L	.	L	.	L	L
Security Mutual Life of NY	007034	L	L	L	L	L	L	L	L	L	L	L	L	L	L	L	L	L	L	L	L	L	L	L	L	L	L	L	L	L	L	L	L	D	L	L	L	L	L	L	L	L	L	L	L	L	L	L	L	L	L	L	.	.	.	L	L
Security National Life Ins Co	007127	L	L	L	L	L	L	.	L	L	L	L	L	L	L	L	L	L	L	L	.	L	.	L	L	L	L	L	L	L	.	.	L	.	.	L	.	L	L	.	.	L	L	L	L	D	.	L	.	.	L	L	.	.	.	.	.
Security National Life Ins LA	007902	.	.	.	.	.	.	.	.	.	.	.	.	.	.	.	.	.	.	D	.	.	.	.	.	.	.	.	.	.	.	.	.	.	.	.	.	.	.	.	.	.	.	.	.	.	.	.	.	.	.	.	.	.	.	.	.
Security Plan Life Ins Co	007450	.	.	.	L	.	.	.	.	.	.	.	.	.	.	.	.	.	.	D	.	.	.	.	.	L	.	.	.	.	.	.	.	.	.	.	.	.	.	.	.	.	.	.	.	.	.	.	.	.	.	.	.	.	.	.	.
SeeChange Health Insurance Co	060717	.	.	.	.	.	.	.	.	.	.	.	.	.	.	.	.	.	.	.	.	.	.	.	.	.	.	.	.	.	.	.	.	.	.	.	D	.	.	.	.	.	.	.	.	.	.	.	.	.	.	.	.	.	.	.	.
SelectCare Health Plans Inc	064845	.	.	.	.	.	.	.	.	.	.	.	.	.	.	.	.	.	.	.	.	.	.	.	.	.	.	.	.	.	.	.	.	.	.	.	.	.	.	.	.	.	.	.	D	.	.	.	.	.	.	.	.	.	.	.	.
SelectCare of Maine	064975	.	.	.	.	.	.	.	.	.	.	.	.	.	.	.	.	.	.	.	L	.	.	.	.	.	.	.	.	.	.	.	.	.	.	.	.	.	.	.	.	.	.	.	D	.	.	.	.	.	.	.	.	.	.	.	.
SelectCare of Oklahoma Inc	064844	.	.	.	.	.	.	.	.	.	.	.	.	.	.	.	.	.	.	.	.	.	.	.	.	.	.	.	.	.	.	.	.	.	.	.	.	D	.	.	.	.	.	.	.	.	.	.	.	.	.	.	.	.	.	.	.
SelectCare of Texas LLC	064744	.	.	.	.	.	.	.	.	.	.	.	.	.	.	.	.	.	.	.	.	.	.	.	.	.	.	.	.	.	.	.	.	.	.	.	.	.	.	.	.	.	.	.	D	.	.	.	.	.	.	.	.	.	.	.	.
Selected Funeral & Life Ins Co	068277	.	.	.	D	.	.	.	.	.	.	.	.	.	.	.	.	.	.	L	.	.	.	.	.	L	.	.	.	.	.	.	.	.	.	.	.	L	.	.	.	.	.	.	.	.	.	.	.	.	.	.	.	.	.	.	.
Senior American Life Ins Co	060294	L	.	L	.	.	L	.	.	.	.	.	.	.	.	.	.	.	.	L	.	.	.	.	.	L	.	.	.	.	.	.	L	.	.	.	L	.	.	D	.	.	.	.	.	.	.	L	.	.	.	.	.	.	.	.	.
Senior Health Ins Co of PA	007910	L	L	L	L	L	L	.	L	L	L	L	L	L	L	L	L	L	L	L	L	L	L	L	L	L	L	L	L	L	L	L	L	.	L	L	L	L	L	D	.	L	L	L	L	L	.	L	L	L	L	L	.	.	.	.	L
Senior Life Insurance Company	008148	L	.	.	L	.	.	.	L	L	L	D	.	L	L	L	.	.	L	L	.	L	.	.	.	L	L	.	.	.	.	.	.	.	L	.	.	L	L	L	.	L	.	L	L	L	.	.	.	.	.	.	.	.	.	.	.
Senior Whole Health of CT Inc	064958	.	.	.	.	.	.	D	.	.	.	.	.	.	.	.	.	.	.	.	.	.	.	.	.	.	.	.	.	.	.	.	.	.	.	.	.	.	.	.	.	.	.	.	.	.	.	.	.	.	.	.	.	.	.	.	.
Senior Whole Health of NY Inc	064947	.	.	.	.	.	.	.	.	.	.	.	.	.	.	.	.	.	.	.	.	.	.	.	.	.	.	.	.	.	.	.	.	D	.	.	.	.	.	.	.	.	.	.	.	.	.	.	.	.	.	.	.	.	.	.	.
Sentinel American Life Ins Co	007987	.	.	L	L	.	L	.	.	.	L	.	.	.	.	.	.	.	.	L	.	.	.	.	.	L	L	L	.	.	.	.	.	.	.	.	.	L	.	.	.	.	.	L	D	L	.	.	.	.	.	.	.	.	.	.	.
Sentinel Security Life Ins Co	007040	.	.	L	.	L	L	.	.	.	.	.	L	L	.	.	L	L	.	.	.	.	.	.	L	.	.	L	L	L	.	.	L	.	.	L	.	L	L	.	.	.	L	.	L	D	.	.	L	.	.	L	.	.	.	.	.
Sentry Life Ins Co	007041	L	L	L	L	L	L	L	L	L	L	L	L	L	L	L	L	L	L	L	L	L	L	L	L	L	L	L	L	L	L	L	L	.	L	L	L	L	L	L	L	L	L	L	L	L	L	L	L	L	D	L	.	.	.	.	.
Sentry Life Ins Co of New York	007042	.	.	.	.	.	.	.	.	.	.	.	.	.	.	.	.	.	.	.	.	.	.	.	L	.	.	.	.	.	.	.	.	D	.	L	.	.	.	.	.	.	.	.	.	.	.	.	.	.	.	.	.	.	.	.	.
Servco Life Insurance Company	068023	.	.	.	L	.	.	.	.	.	.	.	.	.	.	.	.	.	.	L	.	.	.	.	.	L	.	.	.	.	.	.	.	.	.	.	.	L	.	.	.	.	.	.	D	.	.	.	.	.	.	.	.	.	.	.	.
Service Life & Casualty Ins Co	007992	.	.	L	.	.	L	.	.	.	.	.	.	.	.	.	.	.	.	L	.	.	.	.	.	L	.	.	.	.	.	.	L	.	.	.	.	L	.	.	.	L	.	.	D	.	.	.	.	.	.	.	.	.	.	.	.
Seton Health Plan Inc	064252	.	.	.	.	.	.	.	.	.	.	.	.	.	.	.	.	.	.	.	.	.	.	.	.	.	.	.	.	.	.	.	.	.	.	.	.	.	.	.	.	.	.	.	D	.	.	.	.	.	.	.	.	.	.	.	.
Settlers Life Insurance Co	009322	L	L	L	L	L	L	L	L	L	L	L	L	L	L	L	L	L	L	L	L	L	L	L	L	L	L	L	L	L	L	L	L	.	L	L	L	L	L	L	L	L	L	L	L	L	L	L	L	L	D	L	.	.	.	.	.
SHA L L C	060114	.	.	.	.	.	.	.	.	.	.	.	.	.	.	.	.	.	.	.	.	.	.	.	.	.	.	.	.	.	.	.	.	.	.	.	.	.	.	.	.	.	.	.	D	.	.	.	.	.	.	.	.	.	.	.	.
Sharp Health Plan	064064	.	.	.	.	D	.	.	.	.	.	.	.	.	.	.	.	.	.	.	.	.	.	.	.	.	.	.	.	.	.	.	.	.	.	.	.	.	.	.	.	.	.	.	.	.	.	.	.	.	.	.	.	.	.	.	.
Shelter Life Ins Co	006675	.	.	.	L	.	L	.	.	.	.	.	.	.	L	L	L	L	L	L	.	.	.	.	.	L	D	.	L	L	.	.	.	.	.	.	.	L	.	.	.	.	.	L	.	.	.	.	.	.	.	.	.	.	.	.	.
Shenandoah Life Ins Co	007044	L	.	L	L	.	L	.	L	L	L	L	.	.	L	L	L	L	L	L	.	L	.	L	L	L	L	.	L	.	.	L	L	.	L	.	L	L	.	L	.	L	.	L	L	.	.	D	.	L	L	.	.	.	.	.	.
Sheridan Life Ins Co	009453	.	.	.	.	.	.	.	.	.	.	.	.	.	.	.	.	.	.	.	.	.	.	.	.	.	.	.	.	.	.	.	.	.	.	.	.	D	.	.	.	.	.	.	.	.	.	.	.	.	.	.	.	.	.	.	.
Sierra Hlth & Lf Ins Co Inc	007370	L	L	L	L	D	L	L	L	L	.	L	L	L	L	L	L	L	L	L	L	L	L	.	.	L	L	L	L	L	.	L	L	.	L	L	L	L	L	L	L	L	L	L	L	L	.	L	L	L	.	L	.	.	.	.	.
Significa Insurance Group Inc	006902	L	L	L	L	L	L	.	L	L	.	L	.	L	L	L	.	L	L	L	L	L	L	.	L	L	L	L	L	.	.	.	L	.	.	.	L	L	L	D	.	L	L	L	L	L	.	L	L	L	L	L	.	.	.	.	.
SilverScript Insurance Company	064967	L	L	L	L	L	L	L	L	L	L	L	L	L	L	L	L	L	L	L	L	L	L	L	L	L	L	L	L	L	L	L	L	L	.	.	L	L	L	L	L	L	L	D	L	L	L	L	L	L	L	L	.	.	.	L	.
Sistemas Medicos Nacionales	064711	.	.	.	.	D	.	.	.	.	.	.	.	.	.	.	.	.	.	.	.	.	.	.	.	.	.	.	.	.	.	.	.	.	.	.	.	.	.	.	.	.	.	.	.	.	.	.	.	.	.	.	.	.	.	.	.
Slovene National Benefit Soc	007046	.	.	L	.	L	L	.	.	.	L	.	.	.	L	L	.	L	.	.	.	.	.	L	L	.	L	L	.	.	.	.	L	L	.	.	L	.	L	D	.	.	.	.	.	L	.	.	L	L	L	L	.	.	.	.	.
Smith Burial & Life Ins Co	068368	.	.	.	D	.	.	.	.	.	.	.	.	.	.	.	.	.	.	.	.	.	.	.	.	.	.	.	.	.	.	.	.	.	.	.	.	.	.	.	.	.	.	.	.	.	.	.	.	.	.	.	.	.	.	.	.

D-State of Domicile **L**-Licensed **S**-Surplus Lines Writer **F**-Authorized under the Risk Retention Act **Q**-Qualified or Accredited Reinsurer

U.S. States/Territories in Which Companies Are Licensed or Do Business – *Continued*

Company Name	AMB#	AL	AK	AZ	AR	CA	CO	CT	DE	DC	FL	GA	HI	ID	IL	IN	IA	KS	KY	LA	ME	MD	MA	MI	MN	MS	MO	MT	NE	NV	NH	NJ	NM	NY	NC	ND	OH	OK	OR	PA	RI	SC	SD	TN	TX	UT	VT	VA	WA	WV	WI	WY	AS	GU	MP	PR	VI
Solano-Napa-Yolo Comm Med Care	064877	.	.	.	.	D	.	.	.	.	.	.	.	.	.	.	.	.	.	.	.	.	.	.	.	.	.	.	.	.	.	.	.	.	.	.	.	.	.	.	.	.	.	.	.	.	.	.	.	.	.	.	.	.	.	.	.
Sons of Hermann in Texas	068030	.	.	.	.	.	.	.	.	.	.	.	.	.	.	.	.	.	.	.	.	.	.	.	.	.	.	.	.	.	.	.	.	.	.	.	.	.	.	.	.	.	.	.	D	.	.	.	.	.	.	.	.	.	.	.	.
South Dakota State Med Hldg Co	068969	.	.	.	.	.	.	.	.	.	.	.	.	.	.	.	.	.	.	.	.	.	.	.	.	.	.	.	.	.	.	.	.	.	.	.	.	.	.	.	.	.	D	.	.	.	.	.	.	.	.	.	.	.	.	.	.
Southeast Family Life Ins Co	009520	.	.	D	.	.	.	.	.	.	.	.	.	.	.	.	.	.	.	.	.	.	.	.	.	.	.	.	.	.	.	.	.	.	.	.	.	.	.	.	.	.	.	.	.	.	.	.	.	.	.	.	.	.	.	.	.
Southern Capital Life Ins Co	009118	.	.	.	L	.	.	.	.	.	.	L	.	.	.	.	.	.	L	L	.	.	.	.	.	D	.	.	.	.	.	.	.	.	L	.	.	.	.	.	.	L	.	.	L	.	.	L	.	.	.	.	.	.	.	.	.
Southern Farm Bureau Life Ins	007053	L	.	.	L	.	.	.	.	.	L	L	.	.	.	.	.	.	L	L	.	.	.	.	.	D	.	.	.	.	.	.	.	.	L	.	.	.	.	.	.	L	.	L	L	.	.	L	.	.	.	.	.	.	.	L	.
Southern Fidelity Life Ins Co	068491	.	.	.	D	.	.	.	.	.	.	.	.	.	.	.	.	.	.	.	.	.	.	.	.	.	.	.	.	.	.	.	.	.	.	.	.	.	.	.	.	.	.	.	.	.	.	.	.	.	.	.	.	.	.	.	.
Southern Financial Life Ins Co	060006	.	.	.	.	.	.	.	.	.	.	.	.	.	.	.	.	.	.	D	.	.	.	.	.	.	.	.	.	.	.	.	.	.	.	.	.	.	.	.	.	.	.	.	L	.	.	.	.	.	.	.	.	.	.	.	.
Southern Financial Life Ins Co	060271	.	.	.	.	.	.	.	.	.	.	.	.	.	.	.	.	.	D	.	.	.	.	.	.	.	.	.	.	.	.	.	.	.	.	.	.	.	.	.	.	.	.	.	.	.	.	.	.	.	.	.	.	.	.	.	.
Southern Health Services	068607	.	.	.	.	.	.	.	.	.	.	.	.	.	.	.	.	.	.	.	.	.	.	.	.	.	.	.	.	.	.	.	.	.	.	.	.	.	.	.	.	.	.	.	.	.	.	D	.	.	.	.	.	.	.	.	.
Southern Life and Health Ins	007055	L	.	.	.	.	.	.	L	.	L	.	.	.	.	.	.	.	.	L	.	.	.	.	.	L	.	.	.	.	.	.	.	.	.	.	.	.	.	.	.	.	.	.	L	.	.	.	.	.	D	.	.	.	.	.	.
Southern National Life Ins	060085	.	.	.	.	.	.	.	.	.	.	.	.	.	.	.	.	.	.	D	.	.	.	.	.	.	.	.	.	.	.	.	.	.	.	.	.	.	.	.	.	.	.	.	.	.	.	.	.	.	.	.	.	.	.	.	.
Southern Pioneer Life Ins Co	007521	L	.	.	D	.	.	.	.	.	.	L	.	.	.	L	.	L	L	L	.	.	.	.	.	L	L	.	.	.	.	.	L	.	.	.	.	L	.	.	.	L	.	L	L	.	.	.	.	.	.	.	.	.	.	.	.
Southern Security Life Ins Co	068370	.	.	.	.	.	.	.	.	.	.	.	.	.	.	.	.	.	.	.	.	.	.	.	.	D	.	.	.	.	.	.	.	.	.	.	.	.	.	.	.	.	.	.	.	.	.	.	.	.	.	.	.	.	.	.	.
Southland National Ins Corp	008225	D	.	L	L	.	L	.	.	.	L	L	.	.	.	L	.	.	L	L	.	.	.	.	.	L	.	.	.	.	.	.	L	.	L	.	L	L	.	.	.	L	.	L	L	.	.	L	.	.	.	.	.	.	.	.	.
Southwest Credit Life Inc	068282	.	.	.	.	.	.	.	.	.	.	.	.	.	.	.	.	.	.	.	.	.	.	.	.	.	.	.	.	.	.	.	D	.	.	.	.	.	.	.	.	.	.	.	.	.	.	.	.	.	.	.	.	.	.	.	.
Southwest Life & Health Ins Co	006719	.	.	.	.	.	.	.	.	.	.	.	.	.	.	.	.	.	.	L	.	.	.	.	.	.	.	.	.	.	.	.	L	.	.	.	.	.	.	.	.	.	.	.	D	.	.	.	.	.	.	.	.	.	.	.	.
Southwest Service Life Ins Co	068099	.	.	.	.	.	.	.	.	.	.	.	.	.	.	.	.	.	.	.	.	.	.	.	.	.	.	.	.	.	.	.	.	.	.	.	.	.	.	.	.	.	.	.	D	.	.	.	.	.	.	.	.	.	.	.	.
SPJST	009606	.	.	.	.	.	.	.	.	.	.	.	.	.	.	.	.	.	.	.	.	.	.	.	.	.	.	.	.	.	.	.	.	.	.	.	.	.	.	.	.	.	.	.	D	.	.	.	.	.	.	.	.	.	.	.	.
Standard Insurance Company	007069	L	L	L	L	L	L	L	L	L	L	L	L	L	L	L	L	L	L	L	L	L	L	L	L	L	L	L	L	L	L	L	L	.	L	L	L	L	D	L	L	L	L	L	L	L	L	L	L	L	L	L	.	L	.	.	L
Standard Life and Accident Ins	007070	L	L	L	L	L	L	L	L	L	L	L	L	L	L	L	L	L	L	L	.	L	L	L	L	L	L	L	L	L	.	.	L	.	L	L	L	L	L	L	L	L	L	L	D	L	L	L	L	L	L	L	.	.	.	.	.
Standard Life & Casualty Ins	007408	L	.	.	.	.	L	.	.	.	L	L	.	.	.	.	.	.	L	L	.	.	.	.	.	L	.	.	.	L	.	.	.	.	L	.	.	.	.	.	.	L	.	L	L	D	.	.	.	.	.	.	.	.	.	.	.
Standard Life Ins Co of IN	007073	.	.	.	.	.	.	.	.	.	.	.	.	.	.	D	.	.	.	.	.	.	.	.	.	.	.	.	.	.	.	.	.	.	.	.	.	.	.	.	.	.	.	.	.	.	.	.	.	.	.	.	.	.	.	.	.
Standard Life Insurance of NY	060342	.	.	.	.	.	.	.	.	.	.	.	.	.	.	.	.	.	.	.	.	.	.	.	.	.	.	.	.	.	.	.	.	D	.	.	.	.	.	.	.	.	.	.	.	.	.	.	.	.	.	.	.	.	.	.	.
Standard Security Life of NY	007075	L	L	L	L	L	L	L	L	L	L	L	L	L	L	L	L	L	L	L	L	L	L	L	L	L	L	L	L	L	L	L	L	D	L	L	L	L	L	L	L	L	L	L	L	L	L	L	L	L	L	L	.	.	.	L	L
Starmount Life Ins Co	009370	L	L	L	L	L	L	L	L	L	L	L	L	L	L	L	L	L	L	D	L	L	L	L	L	L	L	L	L	L	.	L	L	.	L	L	L	L	L	L	L	L	L	L	L	L	L	L	L	L	L	.	.	.	.	.	.
State Farm Ann & Life Ins Co	009158	L	L	L	L	L	L	.	L	L	.	L	L	L	D	L	.	L	L	L	.	L	.	L	.	L	L	L	L	L	.	L	L	.	.	L	L	L	L	.	.	L	L	L	.	L	L	L	L	L	.	L	.	.	.	.	.
State Farm Life & Acc Assur Co	007079	.	.	.	.	.	.	L	.	.	.	.	.	.	D	.	.	.	.	.	.	.	.	.	.	.	.	.	.	.	.	.	.	L	.	.	.	.	.	.	.	.	.	.	.	.	.	.	.	.	L	.	.	.	.	.	.
State Farm Life Ins Co	007080	L	L	L	L	L	L	L	L	L	L	L	L	L	D	L	L	L	L	L	L	L	.	L	L	L	L	L	L	L	L	L	L	.	L	L	L	L	L	L	L	L	L	L	L	L	L	L	L	L	.	L	.	.	.	.	.
State Life Ins Co	007082	L	L	L	L	L	L	L	L	L	L	L	L	L	L	D	L	L	L	L	L	L	L	L	L	L	L	L	L	L	L	L	L	.	L	L	L	L	L	L	L	L	L	L	L	L	L	L	L	L	L	L	.	.	.	.	.
State Life Insurance Fund WI	007255	.	.	.	.	.	.	.	.	.	.	.	.	.	.	.	.	.	.	.	.	.	.	.	.	.	.	.	.	.	.	.	.	.	.	.	.	.	.	.	.	.	.	.	.	.	.	.	.	.	D	.	.	.	.	.	.
State Mutual Ins Co	007085	L	.	L	L	.	L	.	L	L	L	D	L	L	L	L	L	L	L	L	.	L	.	.	L	L	L	L	L	L	.	.	L	.	L	L	L	L	L	L	L	L	L	L	L	L	L	L	L	L	L	L	.	.	.	.	.
Sterling Investors Life Ins Co	008841	L	L	L	L	L	L	.	L	L	L	D	L	L	L	L	L	L	L	L	.	L	L	.	.	L	L	L	.	L	.	.	L	.	.	L	L	L	L	L	.	L	L	L	L	L	.	L	L	L	.	.	L	L	L	.	.
Sterling Life Ins Co	008021	L	L	L	L	L	L	L	L	L	L	L	L	L	D	L	L	L	L	L	L	L	L	L	L	L	L	L	L	L	L	L	L	L	.	.	L	L	L	L	L	L	L	L	L	L	L	L	L	L	L	L	.	.	.	.	.
Stonebridge Life Insurance Co	006594	L	L	L	L	L	L	L	L	L	L	L	L	L	L	L	L	L	L	L	L	L	L	L	L	L	L	L	L	L	L	L	L	.	L	L	L	L	L	L	L	L	L	L	L	L	D	L	L	L	L	L	.	.	.	.	.
Summa Insurance Company	012024	.	.	.	.	.	.	.	.	.	.	.	.	.	.	.	.	.	.	.	.	.	.	.	.	.	.	.	.	.	.	.	.	.	.	.	D	.	.	.	.	.	.	.	.	.	.	.	.	.	.	.	.	.	.	.	.
SummaCare Inc	060143	.	.	.	.	.	.	.	.	.	.	.	.	.	.	.	.	.	.	.	.	.	.	.	.	.	.	.	.	.	.	.	.	.	.	.	D	.	.	.	.	.	.	.	.	.	.	.	.	.	.	.	.	.	.	.	.
Summit Health Plan Inc	064917	.	.	.	.	.	.	.	.	.	D	.	.	.	.	.	.	.	.	.	.	.	.	.	.	.	.	.	.	.	.	.	.	.	.	.	.	.	.	.	.	.	.	.	.	.	.	.	.	.	.	.	.	.	.	.	.
Sun Life and Health Ins Co US	008474	L	L	L	L	L	L	D	L	L	L	L	L	L	L	L	L	L	L	L	L	L	L	L	L	L	L	L	L	L	L	L	L	L	L	L	L	L	L	L	L	L	L	L	L	L	L	L	L	L	L	L	.	.	.	L	.
Sun Life Assur Co of CA (US)	008226	L	L	L	L	L	L	L	D	L	L	L	L	L	L	L	L	L	L	L	L	L	L	L	L	L	L	L	L	L	L	L	L	.	L	L	L	L	L	L	L	L	L	L	L	L	L	L	L	L	L	L	.	.	.	L	L
Sun Life Ins & Annuity of NY	009513	.	.	.	.	.	.	Q	.	.	.	.	.	.	.	.	.	.	.	.	.	.	.	.	.	.	.	.	.	.	.	.	.	D	.	.	.	.	.	.	L	.	.	.	.	.	.	.	.	.	.	.	.	.	.	.	.
SunAmerica Annuity & Life Assr	006115	L	L	D	L	L	L	L	L	L	L	L	L	L	L	L	L	L	L	L	L	L	L	L	L	L	L	L	L	L	L	L	L	.	L	L	L	L	L	L	L	L	L	L	L	L	L	L	L	L	L	L	.	.	.	.	.
SunAmerica Life Ins Co	007102	L	L	D	L	L	L	L	L	L	L	L	L	L	L	L	L	L	L	L	L	L	L	L	L	L	L	L	L	L	L	L	L	.	L	L	L	L	L	L	L	L	L	L	L	L	L	L	L	L	L	L	.	.	.	.	.
Sunset Life Ins Co of America	007104	.	L	L	L	L	L	L	L	L	L	L	L	L	L	L	L	L	L	L	L	L	L	L	L	L	D	L	L	L	.	.	L	.	L	L	L	L	L	L	L	L	L	.	L	L	.	L	L	L	.	L	.	.	.	.	.
Sunshine State Health Plan Inc	064960	.	.	.	.	.	.	.	.	.	D	.	.	.	.	.	.	.	.	.	.	.	.	.	.	.	.	.	.	.	.	.	.	.	.	.	.	.	.	.	.	.	.	.	.	.	.	.	.	.	.	.	.	.	.	.	.
Suntrust Insurance Co	068107	.	.	D	.	.	.	.	.	.	.	L	.	.	.	.	.	.	.	.	.	.	.	.	.	.	.	.	.	.	.	.	.	.	.	.	.	.	.	.	.	.	.	.	.	.	.	.	.	.	.	.	.	.	.	.	.
Superior Dental Care Inc	065724	.	.	.	.	.	.	.	.	.	.	.	.	.	.	L	.	.	L	.	.	.	.	.	.	.	.	.	.	.	.	.	.	.	.	.	D	.	.	.	.	.	.	.	.	.	.	.	.	.	.	.	.	.	.	.	.
Superior HealthPlan Inc	064457	.	.	.	.	.	.	.	.	.	.	.	.	.	.	.	.	.	.	.	.	.	.	.	.	.	.	.	.	.	.	.	.	.	.	.	.	.	.	.	.	.	.	.	D	.	.	.	.	.	.	.	.	.	.	.	.
Supreme Council Royal Arcanum	007008	.	.	L	.	L	L	L	.	L	L	L	.	.	L	.	.	.	.	.	L	L	D	L	.	.	L	.	L	.	L	L	.	L	L	.	L	.	L	L	L	L	.	.	.	.	.	L	L	.	.	L	.	.	.	.	.
Surency Life & Health Ins Co	060699	.	.	.	.	.	.	.	.	.	.	.	.	.	.	.	.	D	.	.	.	.	.	.	.	.	L	.	.	.	.	.	.	.	.	.	.	.	.	.	.	.	.	.	.	.	.	.	.	.	.	.	.	.	.	.	.
Surety Life & Casualty Ins Co	007110	.	.	.	.	.	.	.	.	.	.	.	.	.	.	.	.	.	.	.	.	.	.	.	.	.	.	.	.	.	.	.	.	.	.	D	.	.	.	.	.	.	L	.	.	.	.	.	.	.	.	.	.	.	.	.	.
Surety Life Ins Co	007109	L	L	L	L	L	L	L	L	L	L	L	L	L	L	L	L	L	L	L	L	L	L	L	L	L	L	L	D	L	L	L	L	.	L	L	L	L	L	L	L	L	L	L	L	L	L	L	L	L	L	L	.	L	.	.	L
Swiss Re Life & Health America	007283	L	L	L	L	L	L	D	L	L	L	Q	L	L	L	L	L	L	L	L	Q	L	Q	L	L	L	L	L	L	L	Q	L	L	L	L	L	L	L	L	L	L	L	L	L	L	L	L	L	L	L	L	Q	.	.	.	Q	.
Symetra Life Insurance Company	007017	L	L	L	L	L	L	L	L	L	L	L	L	L	L	L	L	L	L	L	L	L	L	L	L	L	L	L	L	L	L	L	L	.	L	L	L	L	L	L	L	L	L	L	L	L	L	L	D	L	L	L	.	.	.	.	.
Symetra National Life Ins Co	008934	L	.	L	L	L	L	L	L	L	L	L	.	L	L	L	.	L	L	L	.	L	.	L	L	L	L	L	L	L	.	.	L	.	L	L	L	L	L	L	.	L	L	L	L	L	.	L	D	L	L	.	.	.	.	.	.
Tandy Life Insurance Company	009052	.	.	.	.	.	.	.	.	.	.	.	.	.	.	.	.	.	.	.	.	.	.	.	.	.	.	.	.	.	.	.	.	.	.	.	.	.	.	.	.	.	.	.	D	.	.	.	.	.	.	.	.	.	.	.	.
Teachers Ins & Annuity Assoc	007112	L	L	L	L	L	L	L	L	L	L	L	L	L	L	L	L	L	L	L	L	L	L	L	L	L	L	L	L	L	L	L	L	D	L	L	L	L	L	L	L	L	L	L	L	L	L	L	L	L	L	L	.	.	.	L	L
Teachers Protective Mutual	007114	.	.	.	.	.	.	.	L	L	.	.	.	.	.	L	.	.	L	.	.	L	.	.	.	.	.	.	.	.	.	L	.	.	.	.	L	.	.	D	.	.	.	L	.	.	.	L	.	L	.	.	.	.	.	.	.
Tennessee Behavioral Health	064880	.	.	.	.	.	.	.	.	.	.	.	.	.	.	.	.	.	.	.	.	.	.	.	.	.	.	.	.	.	.	.	.	.	.	.	.	.	.	.	.	.	.	D	.	.	.	.	.	.	.	.	.	.	.	.	.
Tennessee Farmers Life Ins Co	008443	.	.	.	.	.	.	.	.	.	.	.	.	.	.	.	.	.	.	.	.	.	.	.	.	.	.	.	.	.	.	.	.	.	.	.	.	.	.	.	.	.	.	D	.	.	.	.	.	.	.	.	.	.	.	.	.
Tennessee Life Insurance Co	068373	.	.	D	.	.	.	.	.	.	.	.	.	.	.	.	.	.	.	.	.	.	.	.	.	.	.	.	.	.	.	.	.	.	.	.	.	.	.	.	.	.	.	.	.	.	.	.	.	.	.	.	.	.	.	.	.
Texas Childrens Hlth Plan	064244	.	.	.	.	.	.	.	.	.	.	.	.	.	.	.	.	.	.	.	.	.	.	.	.	.	.	.	.	.	.	.	.	.	.	.	.	.	.	.	.	.	.	.	D	.	.	.	.	.	.	.	.	.	.	.	.
Texas Directors Life Ins Co	068292	.	.	.	.	.	.	.	.	.	.	.	.	.	.	.	.	.	.	.	.	.	.	.	.	.	.	.	.	.	.	.	.	.	.	.	.	.	.	.	.	.	.	.	D	.	.	.	.	.	.	.	.	.	.	.	.
Texas HealthSpring LLC	064828	.	.	.	.	.	.	.	.	.	.	.	.	.	.	.	.	.	.	.	.	.	.	.	.	.	.	.	.	.	.	.	.	.	.	.	.	.	.	.	.	.	.	.	D	.	.	.	.	.	.	.	.	.	.	.	.
Texas Imperial Life Ins Co	068290	.	.	.	.	.	.	.	.	.	.	.	.	.	.	.	.	.	.	.	.	.	.	.	.	.	.	.	.	.	.	.	.	.	.	.	.	.	.	.	.	.	.	.	D	.	.	.	.	.	.	.	.	.	.	.	.
Texas International Life Ins	008686	.	.	.	.	.	.	.	.	.	.	.	.	.	.	.	.	.	.	L	.	.	.	.	.	.	.	.	.	.	.	.	.	.	.	.	.	.	.	.	.	.	.	.	D	.	.	.	.	.	.	.	.	.	.	.	.
Texas Life Ins Co	007118	L	L	L	L	L	L	L	L	L	L	L	L	L	L	L	L	L	L	L	L	L	L	L	L	L	L	L	L	L	L	L	L	.	L	L	L	L	L	L	L	L	L	L	D	L	L	L	L	L	L	L	.	.	.	.	.
Texas Memorial Life Ins Co	068258	.	.	.	.	.	.	.	.	.	.	.	.	.	.	.	.	.	.	.	.	.	.	.	.	.	.	.	.	.	.	.	.	.	.	.	.	.	.	.	.	.	.	.	D	.	.	.	.	.	.	.	.	.	.	.	.
Texas Security Mutual Life Ins	068499	.	.	.	.	.	.	.	.	.	.	.	.	.	.	.	.	.	.	.	.	.	.	.	.	.	.	.	.	.	.	.	.	.	.	.	.	.	.	.	.	.	.	.	D	.	.	.	.	.	.	.	.	.	.	.	.
Texas Service Life Ins Co	068291	.	.	.	.	.	.	.	.	.	.	.	.	.	.	.	.	.	.	.	.	.	.	.	.	.	.	.	.	.	.	.	.	.	.	.	.	.	.	.	.	.	.	.	D	.	.	.	.	.	.	.	.	.	.	.	.
Thrivent Financial Lutherans	006008	L	L	L	L	L	L	L	L	L	L	L	L	L	L	L	L	L	L	L	L	L	L	L	L	L	L	L	L	L	L	L	L	L	L	L	L	L	L	L	L	L	L	L	L	L	L	L	L	L	D	L	.	.	.	.	.
Thrivent Life Insurance Co	009342	L	L	L	L	L	L	L	L	L	L	.	L	L	L	L	L	L	L	L	.	L	.	L	D	L	L	L	L	L	.	L	L	.	.	L	L	L	L	L	.	L	L	L	L	L	.	L	L	L	L	.	.	.	.	.	.
TIAA-CREF Life Ins Co	060222	L	L	L	L	L	L	L	L	L	L	L	L	L	L	L	L	L	L	L	L	L	L	L	L	L	L	L	L	L	L	L	L	D	L	L	L	L	L	L	L	L	L	L	L	L	L	L	L	L	L	L	.	.	.	.	.
Time Insurance Company	007126	L	L	L	L	L	L	L	L	L	L	L	.	L	L	L	L	L	L	L	L	L	L	L	L	L	L	L	L	L	L	L	L	.	L	L	L	L	L	L	L	L	L	L	L	L	L	L	L	L	D	L	.	.	.	.	.
TJM Life Insurance Company	068286	.	.	.	.	.	.	.	.	.	.	.	.	.	.	.	.	.	.	.	.	.	.	.	.	.	.	.	.	.	.	.	.	.	.	.	.	.	.	.	.	.	.	.	D	.	.	.	.	.	.	.	.	.	.	.	.
Total Health Care Inc	064297	.	.	.	.	.	.	.	.	.	.	.	.	.	.	.	.	.	.	.	.	.	.	D	.	.	.	.	.	.	.	.	.	.	.	.	.	.	.	.	.	.	.	.	.	.	.	.	.	.	.	.	.	.	.	.	.

D-State of Domicile **L**-Licensed **S**-Surplus Lines Writer **F**-Authorized under the Risk Retention Act **Q**-Qualified or Accredited Reinsurer

U.S. States/Territories in Which Companies Are Licensed or Do Business – *Continued*

Company Name	AMB#	AL	AK	AZ	AR	CA	CO	CT	DE	DC	FL	GA	HI	ID	IL	IN	IA	KS	KY	LA	ME	MD	MA	MI	MN	MS	MO	MT	NE	NV	NH	NJ	NM	NY	NC	ND	OH	OK	OR	PA	RI	SC	SD	TN	TX	UT	VT	VA	WA	WV	WI	WY	AS	GU	MP	PR	VI
Total Health Care USA Inc	064866	.	.	.	.	.	.	.	.	.	.	.	.	.	.	.	.	.	.	.	.	.	.	D	.	.	.	.	.	.	.	.	.	.	.	.	.	.	.	.	.	.	.	.	.	.	.	.	.	.	.	.	.	.	.	.	.
Tower Life Ins Co	007128	.	.	.	.	.	.	.	.	.	.	.	.	.	.	.	.	.	.	.	.	.	.	.	.	.	.	.	.	.	.	.	L	.	.	.	.	L	.	.	.	.	.	.	D	.	.	.	.	.	.	.	.	.	.	.	.
Town & Country Life Ins Co	008049	.	.	L	.	.	.	.	.	.	.	.	.	L	L	.	.	.	.	.	.	.	.	.	.	.	.	.	.	.	.	.	.	.	.	.	.	L	.	.	.	.	.	.	.	D	.	.	.	.	.	.	.	.	.	.	.
Trans-City Life Ins Co	008051	.	.	D	.	.	.	.	.	.	.	.	.	.	.	.	.	.	.	.	.	.	.	.	.	.	.	.	.	.	.	.	.	.	.	.	.	.	.	.	.	.	.	.	.	.	.	.	.	.	.	.	.	.	.	.	.
Trans-Oceanic Life Ins Co	007132	.	.	.	.	.	.	.	.	.	L	.	.	.	.	.	.	.	.	.	.	.	.	.	.	.	.	.	.	.	.	.	.	.	.	.	.	.	.	.	.	.	.	.	.	.	.	.	.	.	.	.	.	.	.	D	L
Trans-Western Life Ins Co	068066	.	.	.	.	.	.	.	.	.	.	.	.	.	.	.	.	.	.	.	.	.	.	.	.	.	.	.	.	.	.	.	.	.	.	.	.	.	.	.	.	.	.	.	D	.	.	.	.	.	.	.	.	.	.	.	.
Trans World Assurance Co	007136	L	L	L	L	D	L	L	L	L	L	L	L	L	L	L	L	L	L	L	L	L	L	L	L	L	L	L	L	L	.	L	L	.	L	L	L	L	L	L	L	L	L	L	L	L	.	L	L	L	L	L	.	L	L	.	.
TransAm Assurance Company	007437	.	.	D	.	.	.	.	.	.	.	.	.	.	.	.	.	.	.	.	.	.	.	.	.	.	.	.	.	.	.	.	L	.	.	.	.	.	.	.	.	.	.	.	.	.	.	.	.	.	.	.	.	.	.	.	.
Transamerica Financial Life	007267	L	L	L	L	L	L	L	L	L	L	L	L	L	L	L	L	L	L	L	L	L	L	L	L	L	L	L	L	L	L	L	L	D	L	L	L	L	L	L	L	L	L	L	L	L	L	L	L	L	L	L	.	.	.	.	.
Transamerica Life Insurance Co	006095	L	L	L	L	L	L	L	L	L	L	L	L	L	L	L	D	L	L	L	L	L	L	L	L	L	L	L	L	L	L	L	L	.	L	L	L	L	L	L	L	L	L	L	L	L	L	L	L	L	L	L	.	L	.	L	L
Travelers Protec Assoc of Amer	009769	L	.	L	.	L	L	.	.	.	L	L	.	.	L	L	L	L	L	L	.	L	.	L	L	L	D	.	L	.	.	.	.	.	L	.	L	L	.	L	L	L	.	L	L	L	.	L	L	L	L	.	.	.	.	.	.
TRH Health Insurance Company	060354	.	.	.	.	.	.	.	.	.	.	.	.	.	.	.	.	.	.	.	.	.	.	.	.	.	.	.	.	.	.	.	.	.	.	.	.	.	.	.	.	.	.	D	.	.	.	.	.	.	.	.	.	.	.	.	.
Trillium Community Health Plan	064863	.	.	.	.	.	.	.	.	.	.	.	.	.	.	.	.	.	.	.	.	.	.	.	.	.	.	.	.	.	.	.	.	.	.	.	.	.	D	.	.	.	.	.	.	.	.	.	.	.	.	.	.	.	.	.	.
Trinity Life Insurance Company	060252	.	.	.	.	.	.	.	.	.	.	.	.	.	L	.	.	L	L	.	.	.	.	.	.	.	.	.	L	.	.	.	.	.	.	L	L	D	.	.	.	.	.	.	L	.	.	.	.	.	.	.	.	.	.	.	.
Triple-S Salud Inc	068130	.	.	.	.	.	.	.	.	.	.	.	.	.	.	.	.	.	.	.	.	.	.	.	.	.	.	.	.	.	.	.	.	.	.	.	.	.	.	.	.	.	.	.	.	.	.	.	.	.	.	.	.	.	.	D	.
Triple-S Vida, Inc.	007631	.	.	.	.	.	.	.	.	.	.	.	.	.	.	.	.	.	.	.	.	.	.	.	.	.	.	.	.	.	.	.	.	.	.	.	.	.	.	.	.	.	.	.	.	.	.	.	.	.	.	.	.	.	.	D	L
TruAssure Insurance Company	008957	.	.	L	.	.	.	.	L	L	L	.	.	.	D	.	.	L	.	L	.	L	L	L	.	.	L	L	L	L	.	.	L	.	L	.	.	L	L	L	.	.	.	L	L	L	.	.	.	.	.	L	.	.	.	.	.
Trustmark Insurance Company	006165	L	L	L	L	L	L	L	L	L	L	L	L	L	D	L	L	L	L	L	L	L	L	L	L	L	L	L	L	L	L	L	L	L	L	L	L	L	L	L	L	L	L	L	L	L	L	L	L	L	L	L	.	.	.	L	.
Trustmark Life Ins Co	006335	L	L	L	L	L	L	L	L	L	L	L	L	L	D	L	L	L	L	L	L	L	L	L	L	L	L	L	L	L	L	L	L	Q	L	L	L	L	L	L	L	L	L	L	L	L	L	L	L	L	L	L	.	.	.	.	.
Trustmark Life Ins Co of NY	060706	.	.	.	.	.	.	.	.	.	.	.	.	.	.	.	.	.	.	.	.	.	.	.	.	.	.	.	.	.	.	.	.	D	.	.	.	.	.	.	.	.	.	.	.	.	.	.	.	.	.	.	.	.	.	.	.
Tufts Associated HMO Inc	068684	.	.	.	.	.	.	.	.	.	.	.	.	.	.	.	.	.	.	.	.	.	D	.	.	.	.	.	.	.	.	.	.	.	.	.	.	.	.	.	L	.	.	.	.	.	.	.	.	.	.	.	.	.	.	.	.
Tufts Insurance Co	060313	.	.	.	.	.	.	.	.	.	.	.	.	.	.	.	.	.	.	.	.	.	D	.	.	.	.	.	.	.	.	.	.	.	.	.	.	.	.	.	L	.	.	.	.	.	.	.	.	.	.	.	.	.	.	.	.
UAHC Health Plan of TN Inc	064435	.	.	.	.	.	.	.	.	.	.	.	.	.	.	.	.	.	.	.	.	.	.	.	.	.	.	.	.	.	.	.	.	.	.	.	.	.	.	.	.	.	.	D	.	.	.	.	.	.	.	.	.	.	.	.	.
UBS Life Insurance Company USA	006882	L	L	L	L	D	L	.	L	L	L	L	L	L	L	L	L	L	L	L	L	L	L	L	L	L	L	L	L	L	L	L	L	.	L	L	L	L	L	L	L	L	L	L	L	L	L	L	L	L	L	L	.	.	.	.	L
UCare Minnesota	068935	.	.	.	.	.	.	.	.	.	.	.	.	.	.	.	.	.	.	.	.	.	.	.	D	.	.	.	.	.	.	.	.	.	.	.	.	.	.	.	.	.	.	.	.	.	.	.	.	.	.	.	.	.	.	.	.
UDC Dental California Inc	064361	.	.	.	.	D	.	.	.	.	.	.	.	.	.	.	.	.	.	.	.	.	.	.	.	.	.	.	.	.	.	.	.	.	.	.	.	.	.	.	.	.	.	.	.	.	.	.	.	.	.	.	.	.	.	.	.
UDC Ohio Inc	065707	.	.	.	.	.	.	.	.	.	.	.	.	.	.	.	.	.	L	.	.	.	.	.	.	.	.	.	.	.	.	.	.	.	.	.	D	.	.	.	.	.	.	.	.	.	.	.	.	.	.	.	.	.	.	.	.
Ukrainian National Assoc	009821	.	.	.	.	.	.	L	L	.	L	.	.	.	L	L	.	L	.	.	.	L	L	L	L	.	.	.	.	.	.	D	.	L	.	.	L	.	.	L	L	.	.	.	.	.	.	.	.	.	.	.	.	.	.	.	.
ULLICO Life Insurance Company	006316	L	L	L	L	L	L	L	L	L	L	L	L	L	L	L	L	L	L	L	L	L	L	.	L	L	L	L	L	L	.	L	L	.	.	L	L	L	L	L	L	L	L	L	D	L	.	L	L	L	L	L	.	.	.	.	.
UNICARE Health Ins Co of TX	060368	.	.	.	.	.	.	.	.	.	.	.	.	.	.	.	.	.	.	.	.	.	.	.	.	.	.	.	.	.	.	.	.	.	.	.	.	.	.	.	.	.	.	.	D	.	.	.	.	.	.	.	.	.	.	.	.
UNICARE Health Ins of Midwest	009437	.	.	.	.	.	.	.	.	.	.	.	.	.	D	L	.	.	.	.	.	.	.	.	.	.	.	.	.	.	.	.	.	.	.	.	.	.	.	.	.	.	.	.	.	.	.	.	.	.	.	.	.	.	.	.	.
UNICARE Health Plan of Kansas	064878	.	.	.	.	.	.	.	.	.	.	.	.	.	.	.	.	D	.	.	.	.	.	.	.	.	.	.	.	.	.	.	.	.	.	.	.	.	.	.	.	.	.	.	.	.	.	.	.	.	.	.	.	.	.	.	.
UNICARE Health Plan of WV	064776	.	.	.	.	.	.	.	.	.	.	.	.	.	.	.	.	.	.	.	.	.	.	.	.	.	.	.	.	.	.	.	.	.	.	.	.	.	.	.	.	.	.	.	.	.	.	.	.	D	.	.	.	.	.	.	.
UNICARE Health Plans of TX	064240	.	.	.	.	.	.	.	.	.	.	.	.	.	.	.	.	.	.	.	.	.	.	.	.	.	.	.	.	.	.	.	.	.	.	.	.	.	.	.	.	.	.	.	D	.	.	.	.	.	.	.	.	.	.	.	.
UNICARE Health Plans Midwest	068895	.	.	.	.	.	.	.	.	.	.	.	.	.	D	L	.	.	.	.	.	.	.	.	.	.	.	.	.	.	.	.	.	.	.	.	.	.	.	.	.	.	.	.	.	.	.	.	.	.	.	.	.	.	.	.	.
UNICARE Life & Health Ins Co	009233	L	L	L	L	L	L	L	L	L	L	L	L	L	L	D	L	L	L	L	L	L	L	L	L	L	L	L	L	L	L	L	L	L	L	L	L	L	L	L	L	L	L	L	L	L	L	L	L	L	L	L	.	.	.	L	.
Unified Life Insurance Company	060366	L	L	L	L	L	L	L	L	L	L	L	L	L	L	L	L	L	L	L	L	L	L	L	L	L	L	L	L	L	L	L	L	.	L	L	L	L	L	L	L	L	L	L	D	L	L	L	L	L	L	L	.	.	.	.	.
Unimerica Insurance Company	009065	L	L	L	L	L	L	L	L	L	L	L	L	L	L	L	L	L	L	L	L	L	L	L	L	L	L	L	L	L	L	L	L	.	L	L	L	L	L	L	L	L	L	L	L	L	L	L	L	L	D	L	.	.	.	.	.
Unimerica Life Ins Co of NY	060392	.	.	.	.	.	.	.	.	L	.	.	.	.	.	.	.	.	.	.	.	.	.	.	.	.	.	.	.	.	.	.	.	D	.	.	.	.	.	.	.	.	.	.	.	.	.	.	.	.	.	.	.	.	.	.	.
Union Bankers Ins Co	007149	L	L	L	L	L	L	.	L	L	L	L	L	L	L	L	L	L	L	L	L	L	.	L	L	L	L	L	L	L	L	.	L	.	L	L	L	L	L	L	.	L	L	L	D	L	L	L	L	L	L	L	.	.	.	.	.
Union Central Life Ins Co	007150	L	L	L	L	L	L	L	L	L	L	L	L	L	L	L	L	L	L	L	L	L	L	L	L	L	L	L	D	L	L	L	L	L	L	L	L	L	L	L	L	L	L	L	L	L	L	L	L	L	L	L	.	.	.	.	.
Union Fidelity Life Ins Co	006297	L	L	L	L	L	L	L	L	L	L	L	L	L	D	L	L	L	L	L	L	L	L	L	L	L	L	L	L	L	L	L	L	.	L	L	L	L	L	L	L	L	L	L	L	L	L	L	L	L	L	L	.	.	.	.	.
Union Labor Life Ins Co	007152	L	L	L	L	L	L	L	L	L	L	L	L	L	L	L	L	L	L	L	L	D	L	L	L	L	L	L	L	L	L	L	L	L	L	L	L	L	L	L	L	L	L	L	L	L	L	L	L	L	L	L	.	.	.	.	.
Union Life Ins Co	009489	.	.	.	D	.	.	.	.	.	.	.	.	.	.	.	.	.	.	.	.	.	.	.	.	.	.	.	.	.	.	.	.	.	.	.	.	.	.	.	.	.	.	.	.	.	.	.	.	.	.	.	.	.	.	.	.
Union National Life Ins Co	007155	L	.	.	L	.	.	.	.	.	L	L	.	.	.	.	.	.	.	D	.	.	.	.	.	L	.	.	.	.	.	.	.	.	.	.	.	L	.	.	.	.	.	L	L	.	.	.	.	.	.	.	.	.	.	.	.
Union Security DentalCare NJ	064677	.	.	.	.	.	.	.	.	.	.	.	.	.	.	.	.	.	.	.	.	.	.	.	.	.	.	.	.	.	.	D	.	.	.	.	.	.	.	.	.	.	.	.	.	.	.	.	.	.	.	.	.	.	.	.	.
Union Security Insurance Co	007232	L	L	L	L	L	L	L	L	L	L	L	L	L	L	L	L	D	L	L	L	L	L	L	L	L	L	L	L	L	L	L	L	.	L	L	L	L	L	L	L	L	L	L	L	L	L	L	L	L	L	L	.	L	.	.	.
Union Security Life Ins NY	008533	.	.	.	.	.	.	.	.	.	.	.	.	.	.	.	.	.	.	.	.	.	.	.	.	.	.	.	.	.	.	.	.	D	.	.	.	.	.	.	.	.	.	.	.	.	.	.	.	.	.	.	.	.	.	.	.
Unison Family Health Plan PA	064925	.	.	.	.	.	.	.	.	.	.	.	.	.	.	.	.	.	.	.	.	.	.	.	.	.	.	.	.	.	.	.	.	.	.	.	.	.	.	D	.	.	.	.	.	.	.	.	.	.	.	.	.	.	.	.	.
Unison Health Plan of Ohio Inc	064874	.	.	.	.	.	.	.	.	.	.	.	.	.	.	.	.	.	.	.	.	.	.	.	.	.	.	.	.	.	.	.	.	.	.	.	D	.	.	.	.	.	.	.	.	.	.	.	.	.	.	.	.	.	.	.	.
Unison Health Plan of PA Inc	064104	.	.	.	.	.	.	.	.	.	.	.	.	.	.	.	.	.	.	.	.	.	.	.	.	.	.	.	.	.	.	.	.	.	.	.	.	.	.	D	.	.	.	.	.	.	.	.	.	.	.	.	.	.	.	.	.
Unison Health Plan of SC Inc	064886	.	.	.	.	.	.	.	.	.	.	.	.	.	.	.	.	.	.	.	.	.	.	.	.	.	.	.	.	.	.	.	.	.	.	.	.	.	.	.	.	D	.	.	.	.	.	.	.	.	.	.	.	.	.	.	.
Unison Health Plan of TN Inc	064879	.	.	.	L	.	.	.	.	.	.	.	.	.	.	.	.	.	.	.	.	.	.	.	.	L	.	.	.	.	.	.	.	.	.	.	.	.	.	.	.	.	.	D	.	.	.	.	.	.	.	.	.	.	.	.	.
Unison Health Plan of Cap Area	064963	.	.	.	.	.	.	.	.	D	.	.	.	.	.	.	.	.	.	.	.	.	.	.	.	.	.	.	.	.	.	.	.	.	.	.	.	.	.	.	.	.	.	.	.	.	.	.	.	.	.	.	.	.	.	.	.
United American Ins Co	007161	L	L	L	L	L	L	L	L	L	L	L	L	L	L	L	L	L	L	L	L	L	L	L	L	L	L	L	D	L	L	L	L	.	L	L	L	L	L	L	L	L	L	L	L	L	L	L	L	L	L	L	.	.	.	.	.
United Assurance Life Ins Co	068091	.	.	.	.	.	.	.	.	.	.	.	.	.	.	.	.	.	.	.	.	.	.	.	.	.	.	.	.	.	.	.	.	.	.	.	.	.	.	.	.	.	.	.	D	.	.	.	.	.	.	.	.	.	.	.	.
United Benefit Life Ins Co	006619	L	.	L	.	L	L	.	L	L	.	L	.	L	L	L	.	L	L	L	.	.	.	.	.	.	L	L	L	L	.	.	L	.	.	L	D	L	L	L	.	.	L	L	L	L	.	.	.	L	.	.	.	.	.	.	.
United Concordia Companies Inc	050692	.	.	.	.	.	.	.	.	.	.	.	.	.	.	.	.	.	.	.	.	.	.	.	.	.	.	.	.	.	.	.	.	.	.	.	.	.	.	D	.	.	.	.	.	.	.	.	.	.	.	.	.	.	.	.	.
United Concordia Dental Cp AL	064649	D	.	.	.	.	.	.	.	.	.	.	.	.	.	.	.	.	.	.	.	.	.	.	.	.	.	.	.	.	.	.	.	.	.	.	.	.	.	.	.	.	.	.	.	.	.	.	.	.	.	.	.	.	.	.	.
United Concordia Dental Plans	065705	.	.	.	.	.	.	.	.	.	.	.	.	.	.	.	.	.	.	.	.	D	.	.	.	.	.	.	.	.	.	L	.	.	.	.	.	.	.	.	.	.	.	.	.	.	.	.	.	.	.	.	.	.	.	.	.
United Concordia Dental Pls CA	064008	.	.	.	.	D	.	.	.	.	.	.	.	.	.	.	.	.	.	.	.	.	.	.	.	.	.	.	.	.	.	.	.	.	.	.	.	.	.	.	.	.	.	.	.	.	.	.	.	.	.	.	.	.	.	.	.
United Concordia Dental Pls FL	065704	.	.	.	.	.	.	.	.	.	D	.	.	.	.	.	.	.	.	.	.	.	.	.	.	.	.	.	.	.	.	.	.	.	.	.	.	.	.	.	.	.	.	.	.	.	.	.	.	.	.	.	.	.	.	.	.
United Concordia Dental Pls KY	065702	.	.	.	.	.	.	.	.	.	.	.	.	.	.	.	.	.	D	.	.	.	.	.	.	.	.	.	.	.	.	.	.	.	.	.	.	.	.	.	.	.	.	.	.	.	.	.	.	.	.	.	.	.	.	.	.
United Concordia Dental Pls PA	064353	.	.	.	.	.	.	.	.	.	.	.	.	.	.	.	.	.	.	.	.	.	.	.	.	.	.	.	.	.	.	.	.	.	.	.	.	.	.	D	.	.	.	.	.	.	.	.	.	.	.	.	.	.	.	.	.
United Concordia Dental Pls TX	064351	.	.	.	.	.	.	.	.	.	.	.	.	.	.	.	.	.	.	.	.	.	.	.	.	.	.	.	.	.	.	.	.	.	.	.	.	.	.	.	.	.	.	.	D	.	.	.	.	.	.	.	.	.	.	.	.
United Concordia D Pls the MW	065700	.	.	.	.	.	.	.	.	.	.	L	.	.	.	.	.	.	.	.	.	.	.	D	.	.	L	.	.	.	.	.	.	.	.	.	L	.	.	.	.	.	.	.	.	.	.	.	.	.	.	.	.	.	.	.	.
United Concordia Insurance Co	008651	.	L	D	L	L	L	L	.	.	L	L	L	L	.	L	L	L	.	L	L	.	L	L	L	L	.	.	L	L	L	.	L	.	.	.	L	L	L	.	.	L	L	L	L	L	L	L	L	L	L	L	.	.	.	.	.
United Concordia Ins Co of NY	060255	.	.	.	.	.	.	.	.	.	.	.	.	.	.	.	.	.	.	.	.	.	.	.	.	.	.	.	.	.	.	.	.	D	.	.	.	.	.	.	.	.	.	.	.	.	.	.	.	.	.	.	.	.	.	.	.
United Concordia Life & Health	006265	.	.	.	.	.	.	.	L	L	.	.	.	.	L	.	.	.	L	.	.	L	.	.	.	.	L	.	.	.	.	L	.	.	.	.	.	.	.	D	.	.	.	.	.	.	.	.	.	.	.	.	.	.	.	L	.
United Dental Care of AZ Inc	065711	.	.	D	.	.	.	.	.	.	.	.	.	.	.	.	.	.	.	.	.	.	.	.	.	.	.	.	.	.	.	.	.	.	.	.	.	.	.	.	.	.	.	.	.	.	.	.	.	.	.	.	.	.	.	.	.
United Dental Care of CO Inc	064674	.	.	.	.	.	D	.	.	.	.	.	.	.	.	.	.	.	.	.	.	.	.	.	.	.	.	.	.	.	.	.	.	.	.	.	.	.	.	.	.	.	.	.	.	.	.	.	.	.	.	.	.	.	.	.	.
United Dental Care of MI Inc	065709	.	.	.	.	.	.	.	.	.	.	.	.	.	.	.	.	.	.	.	.	.	.	D	.	.	.	.	.	.	.	.	.	.	.	.	.	.	.	.	.	.	.	.	.	.	.	.	.	.	.	.	.	.	.	.	.
United Dental Care of MO Inc	065710	.	.	.	.	.	.	.	.	.	.	.	.	.	.	.	.	L	.	.	.	.	.	.	.	.	D	.	.	.	.	.	.	.	.	.	.	.	.	.	.	.	.	.	.	.	.	.	.	.	.	.	.	.	.	.	.
United Dental Care of NM Inc	064360	.	.	.	.	.	.	.	.	.	.	.	.	.	.	.	.	.	.	.	.	.	.	.	.	.	.	.	.	.	.	.	D	.	.	.	.	.	.	.	.	.	.	.	.	.	.	.	.	.	.	.	.	.	.	.	.
United Dental Care of TX Inc	064363	.	.	.	.	.	.	.	.	.	.	.	.	.	.	.	.	.	.	.	.	.	.	.	.	.	.	.	.	.	.	.	.	.	.	.	.	.	.	.	.	.	.	.	D	.	.	.	.	.	.	.	.	.	.	.	.
United Dental Care of UT Inc	064362	.	.	.	.	.	.	.	.	.	.	.	.	.	.	.	.	.	.	.	.	.	.	.	.	.	.	.	.	.	.	.	.	.	.	.	.	.	.	.	.	.	.	.	.	D	.	.	.	.	.	.	.	.	.	.	.

D-State of Domicile **L**-Licensed **S**-Surplus Lines Writer **F**-Authorized under the Risk Retention Act **Q**-Qualified or Accredited Reinsurer

U.S. States/Territories in Which Companies Are Licensed or Do Business – *Continued*

Company Name	AMB#	AL	AK	AZ	AR	CA	CO	CT	DE	DC	FL	GA	HI	ID	IL	IN	IA	KS	KY	LA	ME	MD	MA	MI	MN	MS	MO	MT	NE	NV	NH	NJ	NM	NY	NC	ND	OH	OK	OR	PA	RI	SC	SD	TN	TX	UT	VT	VA	WA	WV	WI	WY	AS	GU	MP	PR	VI
United Farm Family Life Ins Co	007168	.	.	L	.	L	.	.	.	.	.	.	.	.	L	D	.	.	.	.	.	L	L	.	.	.	.	.	.	.	.	L	.	.	.	L	L	.	.	L	.	.	.	.	.	.	.	.	.	.	.	.	.	.	.	.	.
United Fidelity Life Ins Co	007169	L	L	L	L	L	L	.	L	L	.	L	.	L	L	L	L	L	L	L	.	L	L	.	.	L	L	L	L	L	.	.	L	.	L	L	L	L	L	L	L	L	L	L	D	L	.	L	L	L	L	L	.	.	.	.	.
United Funeral Benefit Life	008301	.	.	.	.	.	.	.	.	.	.	.	.	.	.	.	.	.	.	.	.	.	.	.	.	.	.	.	.	.	.	.	.	.	.	.	.	L	.	.	.	.	.	.	D	.	.	.	.	.	.	.	.	.	.	.	.
United Funeral Dir Benefit	068068	.	.	.	.	.	.	.	.	.	.	.	.	.	.	.	.	.	.	.	.	.	.	.	.	.	.	.	.	.	.	.	.	.	.	.	.	.	.	.	.	.	.	.	D	.	.	.	.	.	.	.	.	.	.	.	.
United Heritage Life Ins Co	006472	.	L	L	L	L	L	.	.	.	.	L	L	D	L	L	L	L	L	L	.	.	.	L	L	.	L	L	L	L	.	.	L	.	L	L	L	L	L	L	.	L	L	L	L	L	.	L	L	.	L	L	.	.	.	.	.
United Home Life Ins Co	007172	L	.	L	L	L	L	L	L	L	L	L	L	L	L	D	L	L	L	L	L	L	.	L	L	L	L	L	L	L	.	L	L	.	.	L	L	L	L	L	L	L	.	L	L	L	L	L	L	L	L	.	.	.	.	.	.
United Insurance Co of America	007174	L	.	L	L	L	L	L	L	L	L	L	L	L	D	L	L	L	L	L	L	L	L	L	L	L	L	L	L	L	L	L	L	.	L	L	L	L	L	L	L	L	L	L	L	L	L	L	L	L	L	L	.	.	.	.	.
United International Life Ins	060387	.	.	.	.	.	.	.	.	.	.	.	.	.	.	.	.	.	.	.	.	.	.	.	.	.	.	.	.	.	.	.	.	.	.	.	.	D	.	.	.	.	.	.	.	.	.	.	.	.	.	.	.	.	.	.	.
United Investors Life Ins Co	007175	L	L	L	L	L	L	L	L	L	L	L	L	L	L	L	L	L	L	L	L	L	L	L	L	L	L	L	D	L	L	L	L	.	L	L	L	L	L	L	L	L	L	L	L	L	L	L	L	L	L	L	.	.	.	.	.
United Life Ins Co	007178	L	.	L	L	.	L	.	.	.	L	.	.	L	L	L	D	L	L	L	.	.	.	L	L	L	L	L	L	.	.	.	L	.	.	L	L	L	.	.	.	.	L	L	L	L	.	.	.	.	L	L	.	.	.	.	.
United National Life of Amer	006236	.	.	.	L	.	L	.	.	.	.	.	.	L	D	L	.	L	.	.	.	.	.	.	L	.	L	.	L	L	.	.	L	.	.	L	.	L	.	.	.	.	L	L	L	L	.	.	.	L	.	L	.	.	.	.	.
United of Omaha Life Ins Co	007164	L	L	L	L	L	L	L	L	L	L	L	L	L	L	L	L	L	L	L	L	L	L	L	L	L	L	L	D	L	L	L	L	.	L	L	L	L	L	L	L	L	L	L	L	L	L	L	L	L	L	L	.	L	.	L	L
United Security Assur Co of PA	001850	.	L	L	.	L	.	.	L	L	L	.	.	L	L	.	.	L	.	L	.	L	L	.	L	L	L	L	L	L	.	.	.	.	.	L	L	L	L	D	.	L	L	.	L	L	.	L	L	L	.	.	.	.	.	.	.
United Security Lf & H Ins Co	008442	.	.	L	L	.	.	.	.	.	.	.	.	.	D	L	.	.	.	.	.	.	.	.	.	.	L	.	L	.	.	.	.	.	.	.	.	.	.	.	.	.	.	.	.	.	.	.	.	.	.	.	.	.	.	.	.
United States Life Ins of NY	007192	L	L	L	L	L	L	L	L	L	L	L	L	L	L	L	L	L	L	L	L	L	L	L	L	L	L	L	L	L	L	L	L	D	L	L	L	L	L	L	L	L	L	L	L	L	L	L	L	L	L	L	.	L	.	.	L
United Teacher Associates Ins	006410	L	L	L	L	L	L	L	L	L	L	L	L	L	L	L	L	L	L	L	L	L	L	L	L	L	L	L	L	L	.	L	L	.	L	L	L	L	L	L	.	L	L	L	D	L	.	L	L	L	L	L	.	.	.	L	L
United Transportation Union	008272	.	.	.	.	L	L	.	.	L	.	.	.	.	.	.	.	.	.	.	.	.	.	.	.	.	.	.	.	.	.	.	L	.	.	.	D	.	.	L	.	.	.	.	.	.	.	.	.	L	.	.	.	.	.	.	.
United Trust Ins Co	007379	D	.	.	.	.	.	.	.	.	.	.	.	.	.	.	.	.	.	.	.	.	.	.	.	.	.	.	.	.	.	.	.	.	.	.	.	.	.	.	.	.	.	.	.	.	.	.	.	.	.	.	.	.	.	.	.
United World Life Ins Co	007528	L	L	L	L	L	L	.	L	L	L	L	L	L	L	L	L	L	L	L	L	L	L	L	L	L	L	L	D	L	L	L	L	.	L	L	L	L	L	L	L	L	L	L	L	L	L	L	L	L	L	L	.	.	.	.	.
UnitedHealthcare Ins Co	008290	L	L	L	L	L	L	D	L	L	L	L	L	L	L	L	L	L	L	L	L	L	L	L	L	L	L	L	L	L	L	L	L	.	L	L	L	L	L	L	L	L	L	L	L	L	L	L	L	L	L	L	L	L	L	L	L
UnitedHealthcare Ins Co of IL	060071	.	.	.	.	.	.	.	.	.	.	.	.	.	D	.	.	.	.	.	.	.	.	.	.	.	.	.	.	.	.	.	.	.	.	.	.	.	.	.	.	.	.	.	.	.	.	.	.	.	.	.	.	.	.	.	.
UnitedHealthcare Ins Co of NY	060108	.	.	.	.	.	.	.	.	L	.	.	.	.	.	.	.	.	.	.	.	.	.	.	.	.	.	.	.	.	.	.	.	D	.	.	.	.	.	.	.	.	.	.	.	.	.	.	.	.	.	.	.	.	.	.	.
UnitedHealthcare Ins Co of OH	060046	.	.	.	.	.	.	.	.	.	.	.	.	.	.	.	.	.	.	.	.	.	.	.	.	.	.	.	.	.	.	.	.	.	.	.	D	.	.	.	.	.	.	.	.	.	.	.	.	.	.	.	.	.	.	.	.
UnitedHealthcare Ins Rvr Vall	064827	.	.	.	L	.	.	.	.	.	.	.	.	.	D	.	L	.	.	.	.	.	.	.	.	.	.	.	.	.	.	.	.	.	.	.	L	.	.	.	.	.	.	L	.	.	.	.	.	.	.	.	.	.	.	.	.
UnitedHealthcare of Alabama	068500	D	.	.	.	.	.	.	.	.	.	.	.	.	.	.	.	.	.	.	.	.	.	.	.	.	.	.	.	.	.	.	.	.	.	.	.	.	.	.	.	.	.	.	.	.	.	.	.	.	.	.	.	.	.	.	.
UnitedHealthcare of Arizona	068847	.	.	D	.	.	.	.	.	.	.	.	.	.	.	.	.	.	.	.	.	.	.	.	.	.	.	.	.	.	.	.	.	.	.	.	.	.	.	.	.	.	.	.	.	.	.	.	.	.	.	.	.	.	.	.	.
UnitedHealthcare of Arkansas	068914	.	.	.	D	.	.	.	.	.	.	.	.	.	.	.	.	.	.	.	.	.	.	.	.	.	.	.	.	.	.	.	.	.	.	.	.	.	.	.	.	.	.	.	.	.	.	.	.	.	.	.	.	.	.	.	.
UnitedHealthcare of Colorado	068848	.	.	.	.	.	D	.	.	.	.	.	.	.	.	.	.	.	.	.	.	.	.	.	.	.	.	.	.	.	.	.	.	.	.	.	.	.	.	.	.	.	.	.	.	.	.	.	.	.	.	.	.	.	.	.	.
UnitedHealthcare of Florida	068782	.	.	.	.	.	.	.	.	.	D	.	.	.	.	.	.	.	.	.	.	.	.	.	.	.	.	.	.	.	.	.	.	.	.	.	.	.	.	.	.	.	.	.	.	.	.	.	.	.	.	.	.	.	.	.	.
UnitedHealthcare of Georgia	068893	.	.	.	.	.	.	.	.	.	.	D	.	.	.	.	.	.	.	.	.	.	.	.	.	.	.	.	.	.	.	.	.	.	.	.	.	.	.	.	.	.	.	.	.	.	.	.	.	.	.	.	.	.	.	.	.
UnitedHealthcare of Illinois	068532	.	.	.	.	.	.	.	.	.	.	.	.	.	D	L	.	.	.	.	.	.	.	.	.	.	.	.	.	.	.	.	.	.	.	.	.	.	.	.	.	.	.	.	.	.	.	.	.	.	.	.	.	.	.	.	.
UnitedHealthcare of KY Ltd	068690	.	.	.	.	.	.	.	.	.	.	.	.	.	.	L	.	.	D	.	.	.	.	.	.	.	.	.	.	.	.	.	.	.	.	.	.	.	.	.	.	.	.	.	.	.	.	.	.	.	.	.	.	.	.	.	.
UnitedHealthcare of Louisiana	068661	.	.	.	.	.	.	.	.	.	.	.	.	.	.	.	.	.	.	D	.	.	.	.	.	.	.	.	.	.	.	.	.	.	.	.	.	.	.	.	.	.	.	.	.	.	.	.	.	.	.	.	.	.	.	.	.
UnitedHealthcare of MS	060118	.	.	.	.	.	.	.	.	.	.	.	.	.	.	.	.	.	.	.	.	.	.	.	.	D	.	.	.	.	.	.	.	.	.	.	.	.	.	.	.	.	.	.	.	.	.	.	.	.	.	.	.	.	.	.	.
UnitedHealthcare of New Eng	068891	.	.	.	.	.	.	.	.	.	.	.	.	.	.	.	.	.	.	.	.	.	L	.	.	.	.	.	.	.	.	.	.	.	.	.	.	.	.	.	D	.	.	.	.	.	.	.	.	.	.	.	.	.	.	.	.
UnitedHealthcare of New York	068856	.	.	.	.	.	.	.	.	.	.	.	.	.	.	.	.	.	.	.	.	.	.	.	.	.	.	.	.	.	.	.	.	D	.	.	.	.	.	.	.	.	.	.	.	.	.	.	.	.	.	.	.	.	.	.	.
UnitedHealthcare of NC	068572	.	.	.	.	.	.	.	.	.	.	.	.	.	.	.	.	.	.	.	.	.	.	.	.	.	.	.	.	.	.	.	.	.	D	.	.	.	.	.	.	.	.	.	.	.	.	.	.	.	.	.	.	.	.	.	.
UnitedHealthcare of Ohio Inc	068580	.	.	.	.	.	.	.	.	.	.	.	.	.	.	.	.	.	L	.	.	.	.	.	.	.	.	.	.	.	.	.	.	.	.	.	D	.	.	.	.	.	.	.	.	.	.	.	.	.	.	.	.	.	.	.	.
UnitedHealthcare of TN Inc	068730	.	.	.	.	.	.	.	.	.	.	.	.	.	.	.	.	.	.	.	.	.	.	.	.	.	.	.	.	.	.	.	.	.	.	.	.	.	.	.	.	.	.	D	.	.	.	.	.	.	.	.	.	.	.	.	.
UnitedHealthcare of TX Inc	068841	.	.	.	.	.	.	.	.	.	.	.	.	.	.	.	.	.	.	.	.	.	.	.	.	.	.	.	.	.	.	.	.	.	.	.	.	.	.	.	.	.	.	.	D	.	.	.	.	.	.	.	.	.	.	.	.
UnitedHealthcare of Mid-Atl	068987	.	.	.	.	.	.	.	.	L	.	.	.	.	.	.	.	.	.	.	.	D	.	.	.	.	.	.	.	.	.	.	.	.	.	.	.	.	.	.	.	.	.	.	.	.	.	L	.	.	.	.	.	.	.	.	.
UnitedHealthcare of Midlands	068892	.	.	.	.	.	.	.	.	.	.	.	.	.	.	.	L	.	.	.	.	.	.	.	.	.	.	.	D	.	.	.	.	.	.	.	.	.	.	.	.	.	.	.	.	.	.	.	.	.	.	.	.	.	.	.	.
UnitedHealthcare of Midwest	068560	.	.	.	.	.	.	.	.	.	.	.	.	.	L	.	.	L	.	.	.	.	.	.	.	.	D	.	.	.	.	.	.	.	.	.	.	.	.	.	.	.	.	.	.	.	.	.	.	.	.	.	.	.	.	.	.
UnitedHealthcare of Utah	068770	.	.	.	.	.	.	.	.	.	.	.	.	.	.	.	.	.	.	.	.	.	.	.	.	.	.	.	.	.	.	.	.	.	.	.	.	.	.	.	.	.	.	.	.	D	.	.	.	.	.	.	.	.	.	.	.
UnitedHealthcare of Wisconsin	068824	.	.	.	.	.	.	.	.	.	.	.	.	.	.	.	.	.	.	.	.	.	.	.	.	.	.	.	.	.	.	.	.	.	.	.	.	.	.	.	.	.	.	.	.	.	.	.	.	.	D	.	.	.	.	.	.
UnitedHealthcare Plan Rvr Vall	068702	.	.	.	.	.	.	.	.	.	.	.	.	.	D	.	L	.	.	.	.	.	.	.	.	.	.	.	.	.	.	.	.	.	.	.	.	.	.	.	.	.	.	L	.	.	.	L	.	.	.	.	.	.	.	.	.
Unity DPO Inc	064747	.	.	.	.	.	.	.	.	.	.	.	.	.	.	.	.	.	.	.	.	.	.	.	.	.	.	.	.	.	.	D	.	.	.	.	.	.	.	.	.	.	.	.	.	.	.	.	.	.	.	.	.	.	.	.	.
Unity Financial Life Ins Co	006454	L	.	L	L	L	L	L	L	L	L	L	.	L	L	L	.	L	L	L	L	L	L	.	L	L	L	L	L	L	.	L	L	.	L	L	L	L	L	D	.	L	L	L	L	L	.	L	L	L	L	L	.	.	.	.	.
Unity Mutual Life Ins Co	007196	L	L	L	L	L	L	L	L	L	.	L	L	L	L	L	L	L	L	L	L	L	L	L	L	L	L	L	L	L	L	L	L	D	L	L	L	L	L	L	L	L	L	L	L	L	L	L	L	L	L	L	.	.	.	L	L
Univantage Insurance Co	060210	.	.	.	.	.	.	.	.	.	.	.	.	.	.	.	.	.	.	.	.	.	.	.	.	.	.	.	.	.	.	.	.	.	.	.	.	.	.	.	.	.	.	.	.	D	.	.	.	.	.	.	.	.	.	.	.
Universal Care	068894	.	.	.	.	D	.	.	.	.	.	.	.	.	.	.	.	.	.	.	.	.	.	.	.	.	.	.	.	.	.	.	.	.	.	.	.	.	.	.	.	.	.	.	.	.	.	.	.	.	.	.	.	.	.	.	.
Universal Fidelity Life Ins Co	007198	.	.	L	L	.	.	.	.	.	.	.	.	.	.	.	.	.	.	.	.	.	.	.	.	L	.	.	L	.	.	.	L	.	.	.	.	D	.	.	.	.	.	.	L	.	.	.	.	.	.	.	.	.	.	.	.
Universal Guaranty Life Ins Co	007199	L	.	L	L	.	L	.	L	.	L	L	.	L	L	L	L	L	L	L	.	.	L	.	L	L	L	L	L	L	.	.	L	.	L	L	D	L	L	L	L	L	L	L	L	L	.	L	L	L	L	.	.	.	.	.	.
Universal Life Ins Co	007201	D	.	.	L	L	.	.	.	L	.	.	.	.	.	.	.	L	.	L	.	.	.	.	.	L	L	.	.	.	.	.	.	.	.	.	.	L	.	.	.	.	.	L	L	.	.	L	.	.	.	.	.	.	.	.	.
Universal Life Insurance Co	060097	.	.	.	.	.	.	.	.	.	.	.	.	.	.	.	.	.	.	.	.	.	.	.	.	.	.	.	.	.	.	.	.	.	.	.	.	.	.	.	.	.	.	.	.	.	.	.	.	.	.	.	.	.	.	D	.
Universal Underwriters Life	007204	L	L	L	L	L	L	L	L	L	L	L	L	L	L	L	L	D	L	L	L	L	L	L	L	L	L	L	L	L	L	L	L	.	L	L	L	L	L	L	L	L	L	L	L	L	L	L	L	L	L	L	.	.	.	.	.
University Health Alliance	064548	.	.	.	.	.	.	.	.	.	.	.	D	.	.	.	.	.	.	.	.	.	.	.	.	.	.	.	.	.	.	.	.	.	.	.	.	.	.	.	.	.	.	.	.	.	.	.	.	.	.	.	.	.	.	.	.
University Health Plans Inc	060157	.	.	.	.	.	.	.	.	.	.	.	.	.	.	.	.	.	.	.	.	.	.	.	.	.	.	.	.	.	.	D	.	.	.	.	.	.	.	.	.	.	.	.	.	.	.	.	.	.	.	.	.	.	.	.	.
Unum Life Ins Co of Amer	006256	L	L	L	L	L	L	L	L	L	L	L	L	L	L	L	L	L	L	L	D	L	L	L	L	L	L	L	L	L	L	L	L	Q	L	L	L	L	L	L	L	L	L	L	L	L	L	L	L	L	L	L	.	L	.	L	.
UPMC For You Inc	064807	.	.	.	.	.	.	.	.	.	.	.	.	.	.	.	.	.	.	.	.	.	.	.	.	.	.	.	.	.	.	.	.	.	.	.	.	.	.	D	.	.	.	.	.	.	.	.	.	.	.	.	.	.	.	.	.
UPMC Health Benefits Inc	012486	.	.	.	.	.	.	.	.	.	.	.	.	.	.	.	.	.	.	.	.	.	.	.	.	.	.	.	.	.	.	.	.	.	.	.	L	.	.	D	.	.	.	.	.	.	.	.	.	L	.	.	.	.	.	.	.
UPMC Health Network Inc	064808	.	.	.	.	.	.	.	.	.	.	.	.	.	.	.	.	.	.	.	.	.	.	.	.	.	.	.	.	.	.	.	.	.	.	.	.	.	.	D	.	.	.	.	.	.	.	.	.	.	.	.	.	.	.	.	.
UPMC Health Plan Inc	064162	.	.	.	.	.	.	.	.	.	.	.	.	.	.	.	.	.	.	.	.	.	.	.	.	.	.	.	.	.	.	.	.	.	.	.	L	.	.	D	.	.	.	.	.	.	.	.	.	L	.	.	.	.	.	.	.
Upper Peninsula Health Plan	064619	.	.	.	.	.	.	.	.	.	.	.	.	.	.	.	.	.	.	.	.	.	.	D	.	.	.	.	.	.	.	.	.	.	.	.	.	.	.	.	.	.	.	.	.	.	.	.	.	.	.	.	.	.	.	.	.
U S Behavioral Health Plan CA	064733	.	.	.	.	D	.	.	.	.	.	.	.	.	.	.	.	.	.	.	.	.	.	.	.	.	.	.	.	.	.	.	.	.	.	.	.	.	.	.	.	.	.	.	.	.	.	.	.	.	.	.	.	.	.	.	.
US Financial Life Ins Co	008492	L	L	L	L	L	L	L	L	L	L	L	L	L	L	L	L	L	L	L	L	L	L	L	L	L	L	L	L	L	L	L	L	.	L	L	D	L	L	L	L	L	L	L	L	L	L	L	L	L	L	L	.	.	.	.	.
US Health and Life Ins Co	009184	.	L	L	.	.	.	.	L	L	.	.	.	L	L	L	.	.	.	L	.	.	.	D	.	.	.	.	L	.	.	.	L	.	.	L	L	.	L	.	.	L	L	L	L	L	.	L	.	.	.	.	.	.	.	.	.
USA Life One Ins Co of IN	006161	.	.	.	L	L	.	.	.	.	.	.	.	.	L	D	L	.	L	.	.	.	.	L	.	.	L	.	.	.	.	.	.	.	L	.	L	.	.	L	.	.	.	L	.	.	.	.	.	.	.	.	.	.	.	.	.
USAA Direct Life Insurance Co	060314	L	L	L	L	L	L	.	L	L	L	L	L	L	L	L	L	L	L	L	L	L	L	.	L	L	L	L	D	L	.	L	L	.	L	L	L	L	L	L	.	L	L	L	L	L	L	L	L	L	L	L	.	.	.	.	.
USAA Life Ins Co	007146	L	L	L	L	L	L	L	L	L	L	L	L	L	L	L	L	L	L	L	L	L	L	L	L	L	L	L	L	L	L	L	L	.	L	L	L	L	L	L	L	L	L	L	D	L	L	L	L	L	L	L	.	.	.	.	.
USAA Life Ins Co of NY	060247	.	.	.	.	.	.	.	.	.	.	.	.	.	.	.	.	.	.	.	.	.	.	.	.	.	.	.	.	.	.	.	.	D	.	.	.	.	.	.	.	.	.	.	.	.	.	.	.	.	.	.	.	.	.	.	.
USAble Life	009350	L	.	L	D	L	L	L	L	L	L	L	L	L	L	L	L	L	L	L	L	L	L	L	L	L	L	L	L	L	L	L	L	.	L	L	L	L	L	L	L	L	L	L	L	L	L	L	L	L	L	L	.	.	.	.	.
USAble Mutual Insurance Co	009586	.	.	.	D	.	.	.	.	.	.	.	.	.	.	.	.	.	.	.	.	.	.	.	.	.	.	.	.	.	.	.	.	.	.	.	.	.	.	.	.	.	.	.	.	.	.	.	.	.	.	.	.	.	.	.	.
USIC Life Insurance Company	060567	.	.	.	.	.	.	.	.	.	.	.	.	.	.	.	.	.	.	.	.	.	.	.	.	.	.	.	.	.	.	.	.	.	.	.	.	.	.	.	.	.	.	.	.	.	.	.	.	.	.	.	.	.	.	D	.
UTMB Health Plans Inc	064511	.	.	.	.	.	.	.	.	.	.	.	.	.	.	.	.	.	.	.	.	.	.	.	.	.	.	.	.	.	.	.	.	.	.	.	.	.	.	.	.	.	.	.	D	.	.	.	.	.	.	.	.	.	.	.	.
Valley Baptist Insurance Co	064852	.	.	.	.	.	.	.	.	.	.	.	.	.	.	.	.	.	.	.	.	.	.	.	.	.	.	.	.	.	.	.	.	.	.	.	.	.	.	.	.	.	.	.	D	.	.	.	.	.	.	.	.	.	.	.	.

D-State of Domicile **L**-Licensed **S**-Surplus Lines Writer **F**-Authorized under the Risk Retention Act **Q**-Qualified or Accredited Reinsurer

Company Name	AMB#	AL	AK	AZ	AR	CA	CO	CT	DE	DC	FL	GA	HI	ID	IL	IN	IA	KS	KY	LA	ME	MD	MA	MI	MN	MS	MO	MT	NE	NV	NH	NJ	NM	NY	NC	ND	OH	OK	OR	PA	RI	SC	SD	TN	TX	UT	VT	VA	WA	WV	WI	WY	AS	GU	MP	PR	VI
Value Behavioral Health of PA	064550																																							D																	
ValueOptions of California Inc	064653					D																																																			
ValueOptions of Texas Inc	064514																																												D												
Vantage Health Plan Inc	064282																			D																																					
Vantis Life Insurance Company	007021	L	L	L	L	L	L	D	L	L	L	L	L	L	L	L	L	L	L	L	L	L	L	L	L	L	L	L	L	L	L	L	L		L	L	L	L	L	L	L	L	L	L	L	L	L	L	L	L	L	L					
Vantis Life Insurance Co of NY	060691																																	D																							
Variable Annuity Life Ins Co	007208	L	L	L	L	L	L	L	L	L	L	L	L	L	L	L	L	L	L	L	L	L	L	L	L	L	L	L	L	L	L	L	L	L	L	L	L	L	L	L	L	L	L	L	D	L	L	L	L	L	L	L					
Vermont Health Plan LLC	064124																																														D										
Versant Life Insurance Company	060339																									D																															
Virginia Premier Health Plan	064251																																															D									
Vision Benefits of America	064636																										L													D										L							
Vision Care Network Ins Corp	064801																																																		D						
Vision First Eye Care Inc	064654					D																																																			
Vision Insurance Plan America	064800																																																		D						
Vision Plan of America	068816					D																																																			
Vision Service Plan	064607					D																																																			
Vision Service Plan Inc	064474																													D																											
Vision Service Plan Ins Co(CT)	011105	L	L	L	L		L	D	L	L			L		L	L	L	L	L	L	L		L	L	L	L		L	L	L	L	L					L	L	L	L	L	L	L	L	L	L	L	L	L	L	L	L					
Vision Service Plan Ins Co(MO)	011496										L	L		L								L					D						L																								
Vision Service Plan of Idaho	064482													D																																											
Vision Service Plan of IL NFP	064834														D																																										
Vision Service Plan (OH)	064473																																				D																				
Vision Service Plan (WA)	064475																																																D								
Vision Services Plan Inc OK	064476																																					D																			
VisionCare of California	064660					D																																																			
Vista Health Plan Inc	064191																																							D																	
VISTA Health Plan Inc	064245																																												D												
Vista Healthplan Inc	064066										D																																														
Vista Healthplan of South FL	064102										D																																														
Vista Life Ins Co	008549	L	L	L	L	L	L	L	L	L	L	L	L	L	L	L	L	L	L	L	L	L	L	D	L	L	L	L	L	L	L	L	L		L	L	L	L	L	L	L	L	L	L	L	L		L	L		L	L					
VIVA Health Inc	064257	D																																																							
Volunteer State Health Plan	064304																																											D													
Washington Dental Service	064410																																																D								
Washington National Ins Co	007218	L	L	L	L	L	L	L	L	L	L	L	L	L	D	L	L	L	L	L	L	L	L	L	L	L	L	L	L	L	L	L	L		L	L	L	L	L	L	L	L	L	L	L	L	L	L	L	L	L	L		L			
Wateree Life Insurance Company	068303											L																							L							D															
WEA Insurance Corporation	009506																																																		D						
WellCare of Ohio Inc	051406																																				D																				
WellCare of Texas Inc	064954																																												D												
Wellmark Health Plan of Iowa	064385																D																																								
Wellmark Inc	068347																D																										L														
Wellmark of South Dakota Inc	060207																																										D														
WellPath of South Carolina	064871																																									D															
WellPath Select Inc	064274																																		D							L															
West Coast Life Ins Co	007222	L	L	L	L	L	L	L	L	L	L	L	L	L	L	L	L	L	L	L	L	L	L	L	L	L	L	L	D	L	L	L	L		L	L	L	L	L	L	L	L	L	L	L	L	L	L	L	L	L	L					
Western American Life Ins Co	007404																																												D												
Western and Southern Life Ins	007243	L		L	L	L	L		L	L	L	L	L	L	L	L	L	L	L	L		L		L	L	L	L	L	L	L		L	L		L	L	D	L	L	L	L	L	L	L	L	L		L	L	L	L	L					
Western Dental Services Inc	064651					D																																																			
Western Health Advantage	064577					D																																																			
Western Mutual Ins Co	068150			L										L														L		L			L													D			L								
Western National Life Ins Co	007235	L	L	L	L	L	L	L	L	L	L	L	L	L	L	L	L	L	L	L	L	L	L	L	L	L	L	L	L	L	L	L	L		L	L	L	L	L	L	L	L	L	L	D	L	L	L	L	L	L	L				L	
Western Reserve Lf Assur of OH	007239	L	L	L	L	L	L	L	L	L	L	L	L	L	L	L	L	L	L	L	L	L	L	L	L	L	L	L	L	L	L	L	L		L	L	D	L	L	L	L	L	L	L	L	L	L	L	L	L	L	L		L		L	
Western-Southern Life Assur	009071	L		L	L	L	L	L	L	L	L	L	L	L	L	L	L	L	L	L		L	L	L	L	L	L	L	L	L		L	L		L	L	D	L	L	L		L	L	L	L	L	L	L	L	L	L	L					
Western United Life Assur Co	008077		L	L									L	L		L												L	L	L						L		L	L				L		L	L			D			L					
Westport Life Ins Co	068070			D																																																					
Westward Life Ins Co	008115		L	D	L	L				L	L		L	L	L	L	L		L			L		L		L	L	L	L	L		L	L		L	L	L		L	L	L	L	L	L	L	L		L	L		L						
Wichita National Life Ins Co	007248				L																																	D																			
Willamette Dental Insurance	064497																																						D																		
Willamette Dental of Idaho Inc	064402													D																																											
Willamette Dental of WA Inc	064529																																																D								
William Penn Association	007249					L		L		L	L				L	L			L			L	L	L			L		L			L		L			L			D								L		L	L						
William Penn Life Ins Co of NY	006734							L		L	L			L								L										L		D				L	L	L	L	L	L														
Williams Progressive L & A Ins	008118																			D																																					
Wilton Reassurance Company	060560	L	L	L	L	L	L	L	L	L	Q	L	L	L	L	L	L	L	L	L	Q	L	L	L	D	L	L	L	L	L	Q	L	L		L	L	L	L	L	L	L	L	L	L	L	L	L	L	L	L	L	L					
Wilton Reassurance Life Co NY	006084	L	L	L	L	L	L	L	L	L	L	L	L	L	L	L	L	L	L	L	L	L	L	L	L	L	L	L	L	L	L	L	L	D	L	L	L	L	L	L	L	L	L	L	L	L	L	L	L	L	L	L					L
Windsor Life Insurance Company	068306			L	L																					L	L						L					L							D												
Winnfield Life Ins Co	008119																			D						L																															
Wisconsin Physicians Srvc Ins	060073														L									L													L														D						
Wisconsin Vision Service Plan	064477																																																		D						
Woman's Life Ins Society	006826	L		L	L	L	L	L	L	L	L	L	L	L	L	L	L	L	L	L	L	L		D	L	L	L	L	L	L	L	L	L	L	L	L	L	L	L	L	L	L	L	L	L	L	L	L	L	L	L	L					
Wonder State Life Ins Co	068529				D																																																				
Woodmen of the World Life Soc	007259	L	L	L	L	L	L	L	L	L	L	L	L	L	L	L	L	L	L	L	L	L	L	L	L	L	L	L	D	L	L	L	L	L	L	L	L	L	L	L	L	L	L	L	L	L	L	L	L	L	L	L					
Workmen's Life Ins Co	008125			D		L																																																			
World Corp Insurance Company	008350	L		L	L		L		L	L	L	L		L	L	L	L	L	L	L		L		L		L	L	L	D	L			L		L	L	L	L	L	L		L	L	L	L	L		L		L	L	L					L
World Insurance Company	007262	L		L	L	L	L	L	L	L	L	L	L	L	L	L	L	L	L	L	L	L		L	L	L	L	L	D	L	L	L	L		L	L	L	L	L	L	L	L	L	L	L	L	L	L	L	L	L	L					
WPS Health Plan Inc	064830																																																		D						
Wyssta Insurance Company Inc	064836																																																		D						

D-State of Domicile **L**-Licensed **S**-Surplus Lines Writer **F**-Authorized under the Risk Retention Act **Q**-Qualified or Accredited Reinsurer

Company Name	AMB#	AL	AK	AZ	AR	CA	CO	CT	DE	DC	FL	GA	HI	ID	IL	IN	IA	KS	KY	LA	ME	MD	MA	MI	MN	MS	MO	MT	NE	NV	NH	NJ	NM	NY	NC	ND	OH	OK	OR	PA	RI	SC	SD	TN	TX	UT	VT	VA	WA	WV	WI	WY	AS	GU	MP	PR	VI
XL Life Ins and Annuity Co	060395	L	L	L	L	L	L	L	L	L	L	L	L	L	D	L	L	L	L	L	L	L	L	L	L	L	L	L	L	L	L	L	L	.	L	L	L	L	L	L	L	L	L	L	L	L	L	L	L	L	L	L	.	.	.	.	L
Zale Life Ins Co	007349	L	L	D	L	L	L	L	L	L	L	L	L	L	L	L	.	L	L	L	L	L	L	L	.	L	L	L	L	L	L	L	L	.	L	L	L	L	L	L	L	L	L	L	L	L	L	L	L	L	L	L	.	.	.	.	.

D-State of Domicile **L**-Licensed **S**-Surplus Lines Writer **F**-Authorized under the Risk Retention Act **Q**-Qualified or Accredited Reinsurer

Top 100 U.S. Life/Health Companies

Ranked By 2009 Total Admitted Assets

All figures in thousands of U.S. dollars.

Rank	Company Name	AMB#	Assets
1	Metropolitan Life Insurance Company	006704	289,575,344
2	Prudential Insurance Co of America	006974	225,787,699
3	John Hancock Life Insurance Company USA	006681	203,396,347
4	Teachers Insurance & Ann Assn of America	007112	201,727,945
5	Northwestern Mutual Life Ins Co	006845	166,746,624
6	Lincoln National Life Insurance Co	006664	143,345,609
7	Hartford Life Insurance Company	006518	140,231,960
8	AXA Equitable Life Insurance Company	006341	126,783,596
9	Massachusetts Mutual Life Insurance Co	006695	121,329,281
10	Principal Life Insurance Company	006150	118,786,258
11	New York Life Insurance Company	006820	117,835,521
12	Transamerica Life Insurance Company	006095	101,455,188
13	Pacific Life Insurance Company	006885	94,738,487
14	American Life Insurance Company	006081	91,042,803
15	Nationwide Life Insurance Company	006812	88,955,178
16	New York Life Insurance and Annuity Corp	009054	88,832,647
17	RiverSource Life Insurance Company	006592	81,313,114
18	Jackson National Life Insurance Company	006596	77,789,118
19	American Family Lf Assur Co of Columbus	006051	75,798,442
20	Allianz Life Insurance Co of NA	006830	75,453,862
21	Hartford Life and Annuity Insurance Co	007325	73,406,512
22	ING USA Annuity and Life Insurance Co	008388	71,917,082
23	MetLife Insurance Company of Connecticut	007330	67,232,743
24	Allstate Life Insurance Company	006027	63,008,532
25	ING Life Insurance and Annuity Company	006895	62,474,626
26	Prudential Retirement Ins & Annuity Co	009144	59,982,602
27	Variable Annuity Life Insurance Co	007208	59,451,514
28	Thrivent Financial for Lutherans	006008	54,372,055
29	Prudential Annuities Life Assurance Corp	008715	49,615,991
30	State Farm Life Insurance Company	007080	47,959,821
31	Western National Life Insurance Company	007235	43,440,973
32	Sun Life Assurance Company of CA (US)	008226	42,453,649
33	Aviva Life and Annuity Company	006199	41,990,392
34	MetLife Investors USA Insurance Company	006125	40,666,152
35	Great-West Life & Annuity Insurance Co	006981	40,039,587
36	American General Life Insurance Company	006058	39,653,080
37	Kaiser Foundation Health Plan Inc	064585	37,797,981
38	Monumental Life Insurance Company	006742	34,727,978
39	Genworth Life Insurance Company	007183	32,974,558
40	Guardian Life Ins Co of America	006508	30,895,175
41	Pruco Life Insurance Company	008240	29,252,495
42	Protective Life Insurance Company	006962	26,654,688
43	Midland National Life Insurance Company	006711	26,496,854
44	SunAmerica Annuity and Life Assurance Co	006115	25,887,982
45	Genworth Life and Annuity Insurance Co	006648	25,113,007
46	Minnesota Life Insurance Company	006724	22,800,080
47	Aetna Life Insurance Company	006006	22,490,327
48	Transamerica Financial Life Insurance Co	007267	20,937,072
49	Symetra Life Insurance Company	007017	20,799,084
50	Security Life of Denver Insurance Co	007029	20,770,378
51	ReliaStar Life Insurance Company	006846	20,673,305
52	Connecticut General Life Insurance Co	006266	19,036,994
53	Union Fidelity Life Insurance Company	006297	18,377,842
54	SunAmerica Life Insurance Company	007102	17,549,131
55	Unum Life Insurance Company of America	006256	17,214,784
56	OM Financial Life Insurance Company	006384	16,742,277
57	American Equity Investment Life Ins Co	009024	16,697,568
58	Reassure America Life Insurance Company	007207	16,106,982
59	Ohio National Life Insurance Company	006852	15,785,004
60	Knights of Columbus	006616	15,548,928
61	American National Insurance Company	006087	15,359,313
62	Sun Life Assurance Co of Canada USB	009867	15,278,469
63	RGA Reinsurance Company	009080	14,893,433
64	American United Life Insurance Company	006109	14,839,168
65	USAA Life Insurance Company	007146	14,780,134
66	Phoenix Life Insurance Company	006922	14,654,500
67	Standard Insurance Company	007069	14,524,929
68	Fidelity Investments Life Insurance Co	009138	14,513,448
69	Hartford Life and Accident Insurance Co	007285	14,254,524
70	United of Omaha Life Insurance Company	007164	14,037,295
71	Kemper Investors Life Insurance Company	006225	13,324,913
72	Liberty Life Assurance Company of Boston	006627	12,983,175
73	CUNA Mutual Insurance Society	006302	12,441,231
74	Mutual of America Life Insurance Company	008851	12,427,574
75	Bankers Life and Casualty Company	006149	12,318,840
76	Swiss Re Life & Health America Inc	007283	12,176,227
77	UnitedHealthcare Insurance Company	008290	11,899,664
78	AGC Life Insurance Company	009199	11,801,538
79	MetLife Investors Insurance Company	009075	11,670,931
80	Health Care Svc Corp Mut Legal Reserve	009193	11,377,915
81	Merrill Lynch Life Insurance Company	009537	11,102,780
82	General American Life Insurance Company	006439	11,049,153
83	Penn Mutual Life Insurance Company	006903	10,939,523
84	Western-Southern Life Assurance Company	009071	10,884,697
85	New England Life Insurance Company	009043	10,718,859
86	Southern Farm Bureau Life Insurance Co	007053	10,545,745
87	Great American Life Insurance Company	006474	9,962,026
88	Security Benefit Life Insurance Company	007025	9,862,138
89	Employers Reassurance Corporation	006976	9,604,673
90	Lincoln Life & Annuity Company of NY	006239	9,375,138
91	American General Life and Acc Ins Co	006788	9,359,041
92	American General Life Insurance Co of DE	006809	9,357,652
93	Modern Woodmen of America	006737	9,266,005
94	MONY Life Insurance Company	006751	9,181,461
95	North American Company for L & H Ins	006827	9,117,526
96	Guardian Insurance & Annuity Co Inc	008197	9,022,922
97	First SunAmerica Life Insurance Company	009023	8,949,760
98	Western Reserve Life Assurance Co of OH	007239	8,821,381
99	John Hancock Life Insurance Company NY	060056	8,770,571
100	National Life Insurance Company	006790	8,501,197

The data used to rank entities on these pages were sourced from A.M. Best's ***Global Insurance & Banking Database***. For additional or related data, please visit ***www.ambest.com/research*** and search our online Statistical Study database or ***www.ambest.com/sales***.

Top 100 U.S. Life/Health Companies

Ranked By 2009 Capital & Surplus

All figures in thousands of U.S. dollars.

Rank	Company Name	AMB#	Capital & Surplus
1	Teachers Insurance & Ann Assn of America	007112	22,843,951
2	New York Life Insurance Company	006820	13,686,268
3	Metropolitan Life Insurance Company	006704	12,633,855
4	Northwestern Mutual Life Ins Co	006845	12,402,560
5	Kaiser Foundation Health Plan Inc	064585	11,837,629
6	Prudential Insurance Co of America	006974	10,041,654
7	Massachusetts Mutual Life Insurance Co	006695	9,258,844
8	AGC Life Insurance Company	009199	8,154,648
9	Health Care Svc Corp Mut Legal Reserve	009193	6,692,380
10	Lincoln National Life Insurance Co	006664	6,245,064
11	Hartford Life and Accident Insurance Co	007285	6,005,261
12	American General Life Insurance Company	006058	5,954,032
13	American Family Lf Assur Co of Columbus	006051	5,767,939
14	State Farm Life Insurance Company	007080	5,662,640
15	Hartford Life Insurance Company	006518	5,365,015
16	Transamerica Life Insurance Company	006095	5,026,824
17	John Hancock Life Insurance Company USA	006681	5,018,613
18	Pacific Life Insurance Company	006885	5,005,942
19	New York Life Insurance and Annuity Corp	009054	4,997,629
20	MetLife Insurance Company of Connecticut	007330	4,928,675
21	Aetna Life Insurance Company	006006	4,858,175
22	Principal Life Insurance Company	006150	4,588,745
23	Guardian Life Ins Co of America	006508	4,187,965
24	American Life Insurance Company	006081	4,146,527
25	Thrivent Financial for Lutherans	006008	4,126,774
26	Hartford Life and Annuity Insurance Co	007325	4,085,601
27	SunAmerica Life Insurance Company	007102	4,023,612
28	Jackson National Life Insurance Company	006596	3,972,694
29	Allianz Life Insurance Co of NA	006830	3,923,209
30	Variable Annuity Life Insurance Co	007208	3,625,701
31	Allstate Life Insurance Company	006027	3,467,413
32	Western and Southern Life Ins Co	007243	3,464,875
33	UnitedHealthcare Insurance Company	008290	3,425,789
34	Highmark Inc.	064010	3,394,765
35	RiverSource Life Insurance Company	006592	3,370,671
36	California Physicians' Service	064012	3,189,653
37	Western National Life Insurance Company	007235	3,185,303
38	Genworth Life Insurance Company	007183	3,164,850
39	Nationwide Life Insurance Company	006812	3,129,557
40	AXA Equitable Life Insurance Company	006341	3,115,942
41	Swiss Re Life & Health America Inc	007283	3,039,453
42	Connecticut General Life Insurance Co	006266	2,919,212
43	Brooke Life Insurance Company	068117	2,674,214
44	Protective Life Insurance Company	006962	2,616,531
45	Blue Cross Blue Shield of Michigan	060081	2,562,230
46	Aviva Life and Annuity Company	006199	2,282,876
47	Mutual of Omaha Insurance Company	007369	2,237,934
48	ReliaStar Life Insurance Company	006846	2,190,310
49	Humana Insurance Company	007574	2,182,713
50	Blue Cross and Blue Shield of FL Inc	068174	2,091,886
51	Genworth Life and Annuity Insurance Co	006648	1,935,719
52	American National Insurance Company	006087	1,892,467
53	ING Life Insurance and Annuity Company	006895	1,762,126
54	Sun Life Assurance Company of CA (US)	008226	1,749,838
55	Minnesota Life Insurance Company	006724	1,741,622
56	Primerica Life Insurance Company	006693	1,705,595
57	Security Life of Denver Insurance Co	007029	1,697,472
58	Southern Farm Bureau Life Insurance Co	007053	1,669,157
59	Knights of Columbus	006616	1,647,504
60	Unum Life Insurance Company of America	006256	1,541,119
61	Blue Cross&Blue Shield of South Carolina	001727	1,500,109
62	ING USA Annuity and Life Insurance Co	008388	1,485,056
63	Monumental Life Insurance Company	006742	1,436,586
64	Blue Cross & BS of NC	064070	1,423,751
65	RGA Reinsurance Company	009080	1,416,550
66	Symetra Life Insurance Company	007017	1,415,435
67	Reinsurance Company of Missouri Inc	050061	1,412,945
68	MetLife Investors USA Insurance Company	006125	1,406,057
69	Midland National Life Insurance Company	006711	1,391,869
70	Blue Cross of California	068970	1,377,338
71	Great-West Life & Annuity Insurance Co	006981	1,375,267
72	Penn Mutual Life Insurance Company	006903	1,364,335
73	Empire HealthChoice Assurance Inc	068564	1,363,198
74	USAA Life Insurance Company	007146	1,295,124
75	Independence Blue Cross	064553	1,285,628
76	Health Net of California Inc	068507	1,283,591
77	Ameritas Life Insurance Corp	006152	1,248,997
78	United of Omaha Life Insurance Company	007164	1,245,139
79	CUNA Mutual Insurance Society	006302	1,201,075
80	Standard Insurance Company	007069	1,193,708
81	American Equity Investment Life Ins Co	009024	1,193,130
82	Prudential Retirement Ins & Annuity Co	009144	1,166,402
83	BlueCross BlueShield of Tennessee Inc	064002	1,137,123
84	Modern Woodmen of America	006737	1,136,447
85	National Life Insurance Company	006790	1,134,203
86	Centurion Life Insurance Company	006276	1,023,395
87	John Hancock Life Insurance Company NY	060056	1,016,982
88	Western-Southern Life Assurance Company	009071	1,005,041
89	General American Life Insurance Company	006439	995,160
90	Medical Mutual of Ohio	004693	975,032
91	Excellus Health Plan Inc	060082	965,053
92	Health Insurance Pln of Greater NY	068985	923,059
93	COUNTRY Life Insurance Company	006294	918,023
94	Transamerica Financial Life Insurance Co	007267	911,627
95	Regence BlueShield	060199	892,796
96	PacifiCare of California	068705	891,112
97	Prudential Annuities Life Assurance Corp	008715	880,978
98	Wellmark Inc	068347	880,454
99	Pruco Life Insurance Company	008240	874,836
100	Great American Life Insurance Company	006474	874,636

The data used to rank entities on these pages were sourced from A.M. Best's ***Global Insurance & Banking Database***. For additional or related data, please visit ***www.ambest.com/research*** and search our online Statistical Study database or ***www.ambest.com/sales***.

Top 100 U.S. Life/Health Companies

Ranked By 2009 Gross Premiums Written

All figures in thousands of U.S. dollars.

Rank	Company Name	AMB#	GPW
1	Metropolitan Life Insurance Company	006704	72,985,106
2	Kaiser Foundation Health Plan Inc	064585	39,407,845
3	UnitedHealthcare Insurance Company	008290	36,040,138
4	John Hancock Life Insurance Company USA	006681	28,973,548
5	Prudential Insurance Co of America	006974	27,039,521
6	Lincoln National Life Insurance Co	006664	23,030,507
7	MetLife Insurance Company of Connecticut	007330	18,019,327
8	Health Care Svc Corp Mut Legal Reserve	009193	17,662,253
9	Aetna Life Insurance Company	006006	16,917,080
10	American Family Lf Assur Co of Columbus	006051	16,894,660
11	New York Life Insurance Company	006820	16,428,812
12	Northwestern Mutual Life Ins Co	006845	16,404,387
13	Principal Life Insurance Company	006150	16,152,720
14	Transamerica Life Insurance Company	006095	15,933,413
15	Humana Insurance Company	007574	14,246,583
16	Massachusetts Mutual Life Insurance Co	006695	13,892,387
17	Jackson National Life Insurance Company	006596	13,702,847
18	New York Life Insurance and Annuity Corp	009054	13,124,570
19	American Life Insurance Company	006081	12,249,167
20	Prudential Annuities Life Assurance Corp	008715	11,738,464
21	AXA Equitable Life Insurance Company	006341	11,334,054
22	Blue Cross of California	068970	11,079,124
23	MetLife Investors USA Insurance Company	006125	10,956,278
24	Teachers Insurance & Ann Assn of America	007112	10,076,825
25	Pacific Life Insurance Company	006885	10,045,907
26	RiverSource Life Insurance Company	006592	10,033,451
27	Nationwide Life Insurance Company	006812	9,552,022
28	Allianz Life Insurance Co of NA	006830	8,875,456
29	Health Net of California Inc	068507	8,721,298
30	Connecticut General Life Insurance Co	006266	8,667,783
31	Hartford Life Insurance Company	006518	8,625,237
32	ING Life Insurance and Annuity Company	006895	8,555,433
33	ING USA Annuity and Life Insurance Co	008388	8,392,843
34	California Physicians' Service	064012	8,369,551
35	Aviva Life and Annuity Company	006199	7,051,095
36	PacifiCare of California	068705	6,967,812
37	Blue Cross Blue Shield of Michigan	060081	6,857,124
38	Great-West Life & Annuity Insurance Co	006981	6,762,980
39	Guardian Life Ins Co of America	006508	6,522,093
40	Hannover Life Reassurance Co of America	068031	6,495,875
41	Blue Cross and Blue Shield of FL Inc	068174	6,265,825
42	Highmark Inc.	064010	6,112,813
43	Pruco Life Insurance Company	008240	6,047,313
44	Security Life of Denver Insurance Co	007029	6,006,562
45	Empire HealthChoice Assurance Inc	068564	5,868,804
46	RGA Reinsurance Company	009080	5,780,882
47	UnitedHealthcare Insurance Co of NY	060108	5,539,574
48	State Farm Life Insurance Company	007080	5,277,971
49	Variable Annuity Life Insurance Co	007208	5,247,196
50	Anthem Insurance Companies Inc	000607	4,951,158
51	Excellus Health Plan Inc	060082	4,888,135
52	Hartford Life and Accident Insurance Co	007285	4,875,448
53	Thrivent Financial for Lutherans	006008	4,789,999
54	Health Insurance Pln of Greater NY	068985	4,766,046
55	Blue Cross & BS of NC	064070	4,731,289
56	Transamerica Financial Life Insurance Co	007267	4,730,991
57	Minnesota Life Insurance Company	006724	4,730,444
58	Humana Medical Plan Inc	068907	4,569,476
59	Sun Life Assurance Company of CA (US)	008226	4,435,921
60	Blue Cross & Blue Shield of MA HMO Blue	064847	4,400,791
61	Oxford Health Insurance Incorporated	060022	4,359,344
62	Blue Cross and Blue Shield of Alabama	060080	4,325,884
63	Protective Life Insurance Company	006962	4,325,079
64	Anthem BC Life and Health Insurance Co	060057	4,314,370
65	Unum Life Insurance Company of America	006256	4,306,018
66	ReliaStar Life Insurance Company	006846	4,212,130
67	Canada Life Assurance Co USB	009863	4,197,481
68	Hartford Life and Annuity Insurance Co	007325	4,124,748
69	Keystone Health Plan East Inc	068924	4,106,077
70	Community Insurance Company	011803	4,073,452
71	American General Life Insurance Company	006058	3,988,645
72	Aetna Health Inc (a PA corp)	068700	3,957,328
73	Swiss Re Life & Health America Inc	007283	3,927,646
74	Anthem Health Plans of Virginia	068315	3,774,234
75	Standard Insurance Company	007069	3,774,212
76	Allstate Life Insurance Company	006027	3,761,694
77	American Equity Investment Life Ins Co	009024	3,726,141
78	Western National Life Insurance Company	007235	3,579,589
79	United of Omaha Life Insurance Company	007164	3,524,097
80	Sun Life Assurance Co of Canada USB	009867	3,475,479
81	Coventry Health and Life Insurance Co	008812	3,340,123
82	Group Hospitalization and Medical Svcs	064471	3,337,618
83	Prudential Retirement Ins & Annuity Co	009144	3,335,428
84	Ohio National Life Insurance Company	006852	3,222,782
85	Genworth Life Insurance Company	007183	3,212,121
86	Group Health Incorporated	064601	3,160,757
87	BlueCross BlueShield of Tennessee Inc	064002	3,159,668
88	Bankers Life and Casualty Company	006149	3,156,009
89	First Health Life & Health Insurance Co	008951	3,006,318
90	Symetra Life Insurance Company	007017	3,003,939
91	American National Insurance Company	006087	2,959,497
92	Delta Dental of California	068800	2,846,970
93	Midland National Life Insurance Company	006711	2,820,181
94	Blue Cross and Blue Shield of Minnesota	060077	2,819,138
95	American United Life Insurance Company	006109	2,814,880
96	Horizon Healthcare of New Jersey Inc	068960	2,766,785
97	USAA Life Insurance Company	007146	2,707,738
98	CUNA Mutual Insurance Society	006302	2,663,000
99	Genworth Life and Annuity Insurance Co	006648	2,652,984
100	Anthem Health Plans Inc	068044	2,639,574

The data used to rank entities on these pages were sourced from A.M. Best's ***Global Insurance & Banking Database***. For additional or related data, please visit ***www.ambest.com/research*** and search our online Statistical Study database or ***www.ambest.com/sales***.

Gross Premium Written includes deposits received during the year for deposit type contracts.

Top 100 U.S. Life/Health Companies

Ranked By 2009 Net Premiums Written

All figures in thousands of U.S. dollars.

Rank	Company Name	AMB#	NPW
1	Kaiser Foundation Health Plan Inc	064585	39,407,845
2	UnitedHealthcare Insurance Company	008290	35,846,046
3	Metropolitan Life Insurance Company	006704	25,241,130
4	Health Care Svc Corp Mut Legal Reserve	009193	17,619,725
5	Prudential Insurance Co of America	006974	17,192,703
6	American Family Lf Assur Co of Columbus	006051	16,829,938
7	Lincoln National Life Insurance Co	006664	16,101,551
8	Aetna Life Insurance Company	006006	15,428,580
9	Humana Insurance Company	007574	14,243,936
10	Jackson National Life Insurance Company	006596	13,419,931
11	Northwestern Mutual Life Ins Co	006845	12,938,577
12	John Hancock Life Insurance Company USA	006681	12,925,206
13	American Life Insurance Company	006081	12,861,021
14	Massachusetts Mutual Life Insurance Co	006695	12,389,488
15	New York Life Insurance and Annuity Corp	009054	12,027,172
16	Prudential Annuities Life Assurance Corp	008715	11,596,194
17	New York Life Insurance Company	006820	11,161,524
18	Blue Cross of California	068970	11,079,124
19	AXA Equitable Life Insurance Company	006341	10,215,622
20	Teachers Insurance & Ann Assn of America	007112	9,778,487
21	RiverSource Life Insurance Company	006592	9,759,168
22	MetLife Investors USA Insurance Company	006125	8,893,349
23	Nationwide Life Insurance Company	006812	8,885,854
24	Health Net of California Inc	068507	8,721,298
25	Pacific Life Insurance Company	006885	8,579,269
26	Allianz Life Insurance Co of NA	006830	8,403,348
27	California Physicians' Service	064012	8,369,551
28	ING Life Insurance and Annuity Company	006895	8,320,208
29	Transamerica Life Insurance Company	006095	8,085,118
30	PacifiCare of California	068705	6,967,812
31	Blue Cross Blue Shield of Michigan	060081	6,855,338
32	ING USA Annuity and Life Insurance Co	008388	6,835,447
33	Connecticut General Life Insurance Co	006266	6,821,024
34	Blue Cross and Blue Shield of FL Inc	068174	6,247,975
35	Highmark Inc.	064010	6,107,969
36	Great-West Life & Annuity Insurance Co	006981	6,056,018
37	Principal Life Insurance Company	006150	6,021,396
38	Guardian Life Ins Co of America	006508	5,925,405
39	Empire HealthChoice Assurance Inc	068564	5,868,804
40	Hartford Life Insurance Company	006518	5,824,521
41	Variable Annuity Life Insurance Co	007208	5,247,196
42	Anthem Insurance Companies Inc	000607	4,949,943
43	Excellus Health Plan Inc	060082	4,888,135
44	Health Insurance Pln of Greater NY	068985	4,761,800
45	Pruco Life Insurance Company	008240	4,727,576
46	Blue Cross & BS of NC	064070	4,716,353
47	Minnesota Life Insurance Company	006724	4,434,859
48	Blue Cross & Blue Shield of MA HMO Blue	064847	4,400,791
49	Humana Medical Plan Inc	068907	4,352,585
50	Transamerica Financial Life Insurance Co	007267	4,327,163
51	Blue Cross and Blue Shield of Alabama	060080	4,320,066
52	Anthem BC Life and Health Insurance Co	060057	4,277,799
53	State Farm Life Insurance Company	007080	4,275,149
54	Sun Life Assurance Company of CA (US)	008226	4,207,662
55	Keystone Health Plan East Inc	068924	4,106,077
56	Community Insurance Company	011803	4,073,144
57	Thrivent Financial for Lutherans	006008	4,019,477
58	Aetna Health Inc (a PA corp)	068700	3,957,047
59	Anthem Health Plans of Virginia	068315	3,774,149
60	Western National Life Insurance Company	007235	3,601,122
61	Standard Insurance Company	007069	3,359,365
62	Hartford Life and Accident Insurance Co	007285	3,350,845
63	Allstate Life Insurance Company	006027	3,261,847
64	Coventry Health and Life Insurance Co	008812	3,198,751
65	Group Health Incorporated	064601	3,160,112
66	BlueCross BlueShield of Tennessee Inc	064002	3,159,668
67	Group Hospitalization and Medical Svcs	064471	2,927,358
68	Ohio National Life Insurance Company	006852	2,882,320
69	Delta Dental of California	068800	2,846,970
70	Symetra Life Insurance Company	007017	2,827,928
71	American Equity Investment Life Ins Co	009024	2,826,956
72	Blue Cross and Blue Shield of Minnesota	060077	2,812,069
73	MetLife Insurance Company of Connecticut	007330	2,767,416
74	Horizon Healthcare of New Jersey Inc	068960	2,766,785
75	First Health Life & Health Insurance Co	008951	2,729,212
76	Unum Life Insurance Company of America	006256	2,635,197
77	American National Insurance Company	006087	2,630,028
78	Anthem Health Plans Inc	068044	2,628,849
79	Bankers Life and Casualty Company	006149	2,601,534
80	Sun Life Assurance Co of Canada USB	009867	2,600,058
81	CUNA Mutual Insurance Society	006302	2,540,543
82	Blue Cross and Blue Shield of GA Inc.	060075	2,524,203
83	Protective Life Insurance Company	006962	2,504,636
84	Regence BlueCross BlueShield of Oregon	060074	2,455,280
85	Premera Blue Cross	060076	2,446,292
86	Keystone Health Plan West Inc	068833	2,445,962
87	HealthNow New York Inc	064602	2,444,886
88	CareSource	068574	2,440,659
89	UNICARE Life & Health Insurance Company	009233	2,429,212
90	United of Omaha Life Insurance Company	007164	2,416,311
91	Regence BlueShield	060199	2,400,318
92	Kaiser Foundation Health Plan of NW	068585	2,379,593
93	UnitedHealthcare Plan of River Valley	068702	2,376,529
94	MVP Health Plan Inc	068567	2,352,133
95	Health Care Service Corp-IL Line of Bus	068771	2,343,518
96	Berkshire Hathaway Life Ins Co of NE	060060	2,338,888
97	Blue Cross and Blue Shield of MA	064562	2,315,615
98	Life Insurance Company of North America	006645	2,304,469
99	Empire HealthChoice HMO Inc	064368	2,294,564
100	Tufts Associated Health Maint Org Inc	068684	2,273,001

The data used to rank entities on these pages were sourced from A.M. Best's ***Global Insurance & Banking Database***. For additional or related data, please visit ***www.ambest.com/research*** and search our online Statistical Study database or ***www.ambest.com/sales***.

U.S. State Capital Requirements for HMOs

State	
Alabama	Capital Requirements: $100,000 capital; and $100,000 Statutory deposit and expenses - $100,000. HMOs are covered by guaranty funds. HMORBC requirements have not been implemented.
Alaska	Capital Requirements: $250,000 or the greater of 10% of estimated expenditures for health care or twice estimated average monthly uncovered expenditures for the first year services (AS 21.86.140b) HMOs are not covered by guaranty funds. HMORBC requirements have been implemented.
Arizona	Capital Requirements: Greater than $1 million or 200% of calculated NAIC formula authorized control level risk-based capital. HMOs are not covered by guaranty funds. Each HMO provides a plan for the risk of insolvency to continue benefits for 60 days or until the end of the contract period, whichever is longer, and continue inpatient benefits for those confined on date of insolvency until discharge. HMORBC requirements have been implemented.
Arkansas	Capital Requirements: The applicant has paid-in capital in an amount not less than $100,000 and additional working capital and surplus funds in an amount deemed by the Commissioner to be adequate in relation to the proposed plan of operation. HMOs are not covered by guaranty funds. HMORBC requirements have been implemented.
California	Capital Requirements: Rules and regulations may require a minimum capital or net worth, limitations on indebtedness, procedures for the handling of funds or assets, including segregation of funds, assets and net worth, the maintenance of appropriate insurance and a fidelity bond and the maintenance of a surety bond in an amount not exceeding $50,000. The Commissioner may, by regulation, designate requirements of this section or regulations adopted pursuant to this section, from which public entities and political subdivisions of the state shall be exempt. HMOs are not covered by guaranty funds. HMORBC requirements have not been implemented.
Colorado	Capital Requirements: The regulatory minimum capital requirement for an HMO is $1 million. HMOs are not covered by guaranty funds, due to a harmless clause in provider contracts. HMORBC requirements have been implemented.
Connecticut	Capital Requirements: Initial net worth of $1.5 million is needed, and after licensing, the net worth must be $1 million or 2% of the annual premium revenue, subject to RBC requirements. HMOs are not covered by guaranty funds. HMORBC requirements have been adopted.
Delaware	Capital Requirements: $450,000 minus $300 capital and $150 free surplus is the minimum capital requirement. HMOs are not covered by guaranty funds. HMORBC requirements have not been implemented.
District of Columbia, Washington	Capital Requirements: Must have a minimum regulatory net worth of $1 million. HMOs are not covered by guaranty funds. HMORBC requirements have been implemented.
Florida	Capital Requirements: $1.5 million or 10% of total liabilities, or 2% of annualized premium, whichever is greater. HMOs are not covered by guaranty funds. HMORBC requirements have not been implemented.
Georgia	Capital Requirements: $3 million in total net worth is the regulatory minimum requirement for an HMO. HMOs are not covered by guaranty funds. HMORBC requirements are statutorily required.
Hawaii	Capital Requirements: HMOs are required to maintain a minimum net worth equal to the greater of 1) $2 million, 2) 2% of annual premium revenues on the first $150 million and 1% of annual premium on the premium in excess of $150 million, 3) An amount equal to the sum of three months uncovered health care expenditures, and 4) An amount equal to the sum of a) 8% of annual health care expenditures (except those paid on a capitated basis or managed hospital payment basis), and b) 4% of annual hospital expenditures paid on a managed hospital payment basis. HMOs are not covered by guaranty funds. HMORBC requirements have not been implemented.
Idaho	Capital Requirements: $1 million and an additional surplus of $1 million. MCO's (Managed Care Organizations) are covered by guaranty funds. Managed Care Organizations are subject to Idaho Code Title 41, Chapter 54, "Risked-Based Capital for Insurers Act".
Illinois	Capital Requirements: $ 2 million is required as an initial net worth. Upon receiving a license, an HMO must maintain a minimum net worth of $1.5 million. HMOs are covered by a guaranty fund; the aggregate liability of the Association shall not exceed $300,000 with respect to any one natural person. HMORBC requirements are in effect.
Indiana	Capital Requirements: The greater of 1) $1 million of net worth maintained, 2) 2% of annual premium revenues on the first $150 million and 1% of annual premium in excess of $150 million. 3) Three months uncovered health care expenditures or, 4) An amount equal to the same (a) 8% of annual health care expenditures except those paid on a capitated basis, and (b) 4% of annual hospital expenditures paid on a managed hospital payment basis. HMOs are not covered by guaranty funds. HMORBC requirements have been implemented.
Iowa	Capital Requirements: 1) An HMO shall not be authorized to transact business with a net worth less than $1 million. 2) No HMO incorporated by or organized under the laws of any other state or government shall transact business in this state unless it possesses the net worth required of an HMO organized by the laws of this state and is authorized to do business in this state. 3) As deemed necessary by the Division, each health maintenance organization that is a subsidiary of another person shall file with the division, in a form satisfactory to it, a guarantee of the HMO's obligations issued by the ultimate controlling parent or such other person satisfactory to the division. 4) Each health maintenance organization shall, at the time of application, pay to the division a one-time, non-refundable fee of $10,000 to be used by the Division to create a special fund solely for the payment of administrative expenses in connection with the solvency of an HMO. See Iowa Administrative Code 191-40.12 HMOs are not covered by guaranty funds. HMORBC requirements have been implemented. See Iowa Code, Chapter 521F (2003)
Kansas	Capital Requirements: Effective 7/1/2000, HMOs licensed in Kansas are required to comply with K.S.A. 40-3227 - Minimum net worth; trust deposits; reserves; insolvency plan. HMOs are not covered by guaranty funds. HMORBC requirements: Effective 7/1/2000, health organizations (including HMO) are required to comply with K.S.A. 40-2d01 et seq. — Health Organization Risk-Based Capital Requirements.
Kentucky	Capital Requirements: Ongoing requirements consist of $1 million in capital and $250,000 in surplus. HMOs are not covered by guaranty funds. HMORBC requirements have been implemented.

State	
Louisiana	Capital Requirements: $3 million initial minimum surplus in accordance with La R.S. 22:254. HMOs are not covered by guaranty funds. HMORBC requirements have been implemented.
Maine	Capital Requirements: $1.5 million initial minimum surplus in accordance with Title 24-A MRSA 4204-A. HMOs are not covered by guaranty funds. HMORBC requirements have not been implemented for domestics.
Maryland	Capital Requirements: Initial surplus of at least $1.5 million, maintain surplus funds at least equal to the greater of $750,000 or 5% of subscription charges earned during the prior calendar year, up to a maximum of $3 million. HMOs are not covered by guaranty funds. HMORBC requirements have been implemented.
Massachusetts	Capital Requirements: Initial license: Initial net worth of $1.5 million. Subsequent requirement, greater of (1) $1 million; (2) 2% of annual premium revenues as reported on the most recent annual financial statement filed with the commissioner on the first $150 million of premium and 1% of annual premium on the premium in excess of $150 million; (3) An amount equal to the sum of three months uncovered health care expenditures as reported on the most recent financial statement filed with the commissioner; or (4) An amount equal to the sum of: (i) 8% of annual health care expenditures except those paid on a capitated basis or managed hospital payment basis as reported on the most recent financial statement filed with the commissioner; and (ii) 4% of annual hospital expenditures paid on a managed hospital basis as reported on the most recent financial statement filed with the commissioner. (iii) A health maintenance organization licensed before January 1, 2004 must maintain a minimum adjusted net worth of: (1) 10% of the amount required by subsection (b) by December 31, 2004; (2) 25% of the amount required by subsection (b) by December 31, 2005; (3) 40% of the amount required by subsection (b) by December 31, 2006; (4) 55% of the amount required by subsection (b) by December 31, 2007; (5) 70% of the amount required by subsection (b) by December 31, 2008; (6) 85% of the amount required by subsection (b) by December 31, 2009; and (7) 100% of the amount required by subsection (b) by December 31, 2010. HMOs are not covered by guaranty funds. HMORBC was implemented 211 CMR 25, Risk based capital for health companies, in 2007 to regulate Health filers RBC.
Michigan	Capital Requirements: In June 2000, Michigan enacted new legislation regarding HMOs. There are new capital and surplus requirements for HMOs. Some of these requirements are being phased in over several years. The following is Section 500.3551: Health maintenance organization; net worth. Sec. 3551: (1) A health maintenance organization's minimum net worth shall be determined using accounting procedures approved by the commissioner that ensure that a health maintenance organization is financially and actuarially sound. (2) A health maintenance organization licensed under former part 210 of the public health code, 1978 PA 368, on the effective date of this chapter that automatically received a certificate of authority under section 3505 (1) shall possess and maintain unimpaired net worth as required under former section 21034 of the public health code, 1978 PA 368, until the earlier of the following: (a) The health maintenance organization attains a level of net worth as provided in subsection (3) at which time the health maintenance organization shall continue to maintain that level of net worth. (b) December 31, 2003. (3) A health maintenance organization applying for a certificate of authority on or after the effective date of this chapter and a health maintenance organization wishing to maintain a certificate of authority in this state after December 31, 2003 shall possess and maintain unimpaired net worth in an amount determined adequate by the commissioner to continue to comply with section 403 but not less than the following: (a) For a health maintenance organization that contracts or employs providers in numbers sufficient to provide 90% of the health maintenance organization's benefit payout, minimum net worth is the greatest of the following: (i) $1.5 million. (ii) 4% of the health maintenance organization's subscription revenue. (iii) Three months uncovered expenditures. (b) For a health maintenance organization that does not contract or employ providers in numbers sufficient to provide 90% of the health maintenance organization's benefit payout, minimum net worth is the greatest of the following: (i) $3 million. (ii) 10% of the health maintenance organization's subscription revenue. (iii) Three months' uncovered expenditures. (4) The commissioner shall take into account the risk-based capital requirements as developed by the National Association of Insurance Commissioners in order to determine adequate compliance with section 403 under this section. HMOs are not covered by guaranty funds. HMORBC requirements have been implemented for domestics.
Minnesota	Capital Requirements: Must have an initial net worth of at least 8 1/3% of the sum of all expenses expected to be incurred in the 12 months following the date the certificate of authority is granted, or $1,500,000 whichever is greater. HMOs are not covered by guaranty funds. HMORBC requirements have been implemented. See Minnesota Statutes, sections 60A.50 – 60A.696.
Mississippi	Capital Requirements: Must have an initial net worth of $1.5 million, and shall thereafter maintain the minimum net worth of $1 million or 2% of annual premium revenues. HMOs are not covered by guaranty funds. HMORBC requirements have not been implemented.
Missouri	Capital Requirements: An HMO that obtains a certificate of authority after September 28, 1983 shall have and maintain a capital account of at least $150,000 for a medical group/staff model, or $300,000 for an individual practice association in addition to any deposit requirements. After the first full year of operation, minimum capital and surplus requirements are the greater of 2% of net premiums or $150,000 for medical group/staff model or $300,000 for an individual practice association. HMOs are not covered by guaranty funds. HMORBC requirements have recently been implemented. At this time there are no particular statutes in place.
Montana	Capital Requirements: $750,000 is the current capital in accordance with Section 33-31-216(9)(b), MCA. HMOs are not covered by guaranty funds. HMORBC requirements have been implemented.
Nebraska	Capital Requirements: $1.5 million initial minimum net worth. An HMO must maintain a minimum net worth equal to the greater of (a) $1 million dollars; or (b) Two percent of annual premium revenue as reported on the most recent annual financial statement filed with the director on the first $150 million dollars of premium revenue and one percent of annual premium revenue on the premium revenue in excess of $150 million. (See 44-32,138) HMO's are not covered by guaranty funds unless it is controlled by an insurance company licensed by the Insurance Department under Chapter 44. HMORBC requirements have been implemented.
Nevada	Capital Requirements: $1.5 million is the regulatory minimum requirement for an HMO. HMOs are not covered by guaranty funds. HMORBC requirements have been implemented.

State	
New Hampshire	Capital Requirements: $6.0 million initial minimum surplus in accordance with Title XXXVII Chapter 420-B, Section 420-B:25 Capital Requirements. HMOs are not covered by guaranty funds. HMORBC requirements have been implemented.
New Jersey	The minimum capital requirement as of July 1, 2010 for an initial HMO will be $2,544,239 and for an existing HMO will be $1,696,158. All other items remain the same. HMOs are not covered by guaranty funds. HMORBC requirements became a Statute effective April 1, 2005. It mirrors the NAIC Model Act.
New Mexico	Capital Requirements: HMOs must maintain a minimum net worth equal to the greater of: (1) $1 million; (2) 2% of the annual premium revenues as reported on the most recent annual financial statement filed with the superintendent on the first $150 million of premium revenues and 1% of annual premium on the premium in excess of $150 million; (3) an amount equal to the sum of three months uncovered health care expenditures as reported on the most recent financial statement filed with the superintendent; or (4) an amount equal to the sum of: (a) 8% of annual health care expenditures for enrollees under prepaid contracts except those paid on a capitated basis or managed hospital payment basis as reported on the most recent financial statement filed with the superintendent; and (b) 4% of annual hospital expenditures for enrollees under prepaid contracts paid on a capitated basis and a managed hospital payment basis as reported on the most recent financial statement filed with the superintendent. HMOs are not covered by guaranty funds. HMORBC requirements have not been implemented.
New York	Capital Requirements: Escrow deposit at the greater of 5% of projected annual medical costs, or $100,000: for 2010 the contingent reserve is 9.5% of net premium income. The contingent reserve requirement increases by 1% per year until it reaches 12.5% of net premium income where it remains thereafter. The net worth requirement is the greater of the escrow or contingent reserve. HMOs are not covered by guaranty funds. HMORBC This information is under the purview of the State Insurance Department.
North Carolina	Capital Requirements: $1.5 million initial working capital in accordance with NCGS 58-67-20(a)(4) for full service HMOs. Thereafter, the minimum capital and surplus for a full service HMO is the greater of $1 million (per 58-67-110(b)) or the amount required pursuant to RBC provisions of Article 12 of Chapter 58. HMOs are not covered by guaranty funds. HMORBC requirements have been implemented. HMOs must comply with these requirements pursuant to NC General Statute 58-12.
North Dakota	Capital Requirements: Minimum Net Worth: $1,000,000 HMOs are not covered by guaranty funds. HMORBC requirements have been implemented.
Ohio	Capital Requirements: $1.2 million in net worth is required by Basic Health Care Services. HMOs are not covered by guaranty funds. HMORBC requirements have not been implemented.
Oklahoma	Capital Requirements: $1.5 million net worth and $500,000 deposit. HMOs are not covered by guaranty funds. HMORBC requirements have been implemented pursuant to Title 36, Chapter 6937.
Oregon	Capital Requirements: $2.5 million minimum surplus plus an additional $500,000 when applying for an initial certificate of authority in accordance with ORS 750.045 (1) and (4). HMOs are not covered by guaranty funds; contracts with doctors or hospitals must contain hold harmless provisions. HMORBC requirements have been adopted. OAR 836.011-0500 to 0550.
Pennsylvania	Capital Requirements: Must have an initial net worth of $1.5 million. Operational HMOs must have minimum net worth equal to the greater of $1 million or three months of uncovered heath care expenditures for Pennsylvania enrollees. HMOs are not covered by guaranty funds. HMORBC requirements have been implemented.
Puerto Rico	Deposit Requirements: HMOs shall deposit with the Commissioner the sum of $600,000 in eligible assets, as provided in Section 19.140 of the Insurance Code of Puerto Rico. HMOs are not covered by guaranty funds. HMORBC requirements have not been implemented.
Rhode Island	Capital Requirements: $1.5 million initial minimum surplus in accordance with R.I.G.L. 27-41-13 (h) HMOs are not covered by guaranty funds. HMORBC requirements have been implemented.
South Carolina	Capital Requirements: S.C. Code Ann. Section 38-33-100(A) No health maintenance organization may be issued a certificate of authority unless it is possessed of net worth of at least one million two hundred thousand dollars, six hundred thousand dollars of which must be capital if it is a stock health maintenance organization. HMOs are not covered by guaranty funds. HMORBC requirements have not been codified for domestics.
South Dakota	Capital Requirements: Mutually agreed between SD HMO's & Division of Insurance, $1 million; SDCL 58-41. HMOs are not covered by guaranty funds. HMORBC requirements have not been implemented.
Tennessee	Capital Requirements: $1.5 million initial minimum surplus in accordance with Title 24-A MRSA 4204-A. HMOs are not covered by guaranty funds. HMORBC requirements have not been implemented in accordance with the law since Tennessee's RBC requirements do not include HMO's, however, the Department does consider the RBC Ratio to be a valid regulatory tool and should an HMO RBC level indicate a negative trend or fall below particular levels, the Department would follow the same guide lines indicated in the RBC statute.
Texas	Capital Requirements: i) Capital requirements for an HMO offering basic health services: $1.5 million is the minimum net worth; $100,000 is the minimum initial statutory deposit with deposit increases required each year sufficient to equal "uncovered health care expenses" incurred for the previous calendar year. ii) Capital requirements for an HMO offering limited health services: $1 million is the minimum net worth; $75,000 is the minimum initial statutory deposit with deposit increases required each year sufficient to equal "uncovered health care expenses" incurred for the previous calendar year. iii) Capital requirements for an HMO offering single health services: $500,000 is the minimum net worth; $50,000 is the minimum initial statutory deposit with deposit increases required each year sufficient to equal "uncovered health care expenses" incurred for the previous calendar year. HMOs are not covered by guaranty funds. HMORBC requirements: An insurer reporting total adjusted capital of 150 percent to 200 percent of authorized control level risk-based capital institutes a company action level

State	
	under which the insurer must prepare a comprehensive financial plan that identifies the conditions that contribute to the company's financial condition.
Utah	Capital Requirements: Minimum Asset Requirements = Total Liabilities + $100,000 +)the Greater of $1.3 million or 2 times the RBC authorized control level). 1.) Minimum Capital must equal $100,000. 2.) RBC must be greater than 200%. HMOs are not covered by guaranty funds. HMORBC requirements have been implemented.
Vermont	Capital Requirements: $1.5 million initial minimum surplus in accordance with Title 24-A MRSA 4204-A. HMOs are not covered by guaranty funds. HMORBC requirements have not been implemented in status or regulation.
Virginia	Capital Requirements: $600,000 to $4 million uncovered expenses for regulatory minimum requirements. HMOs are not covered by guaranty funds. HMORBC requirements are implemented in filing requirements by NAIC and are in Chapter 55 of Title 38.2 of the Insurance Code.
Washington	Capital Requirements: Pursuant to RCW 48.46.235 the initial and ongoing minimum requirement for health maintenance organizations is $3 million, two percent of annual premiums on the first $150 million of premiums and one percent of annual premiums in excess of $150 million, or the amount equal to three months of uncovered expenditures, which ever is greater. HMOs are not covered by guaranty funds. HMORBC requirements have been implemented.
West Virginia	Capital Requirements: $2 million minimum capital and surplus. HMOs are not covered by guaranty funds, but participate in the West Virginia HMO Guaranty Association. HMO's are required to prepare and submit to the Commissioner a report of its RBC levels as of the end of the calendar year just ended.
Wisconsin	Capital Requirements: $750,000 or 3% of annual premium. HMOs are covered by $300,000 after a $200 deductible guaranty fund. HMORBC requirements have been implemented.
Wyoming	Capital Requirements: $1.5 million minimum requirements. W.S. 26-34-114. HMOs are covered under the Life and Health Guaranty Association. HMORBC requirements are in statute.

Appendix B
Canada

Canadian Province/Territory Officials Having Charge of Insurance Affairs

Address	Name	Official Title	Telephone
Alberta, CN Edmonton T5K 2C3	Dennis Gartner	Superintendent of Financial Institutions	780-415-9226
British Columbia, CN Surrey V3T 5X3	Alan Clark	CEO-Superintendent of Fin'l Institutions	604-953-5300
Manitoba, CN Winnipeg R3C 3L6	Jim Scalena	Superintendent of Financial Institutions	204-945-2542
New Brunswick, CN Fredericton E3B 5H1	Deborah J. McQuade	Superintendent of Insurance	506-453-2512
Newfoundland, CN St. Johns A1B 4J6	Doug Connolly	Superintendent of Insurance	709-729-4909
Northwest Territories, CN Yellowknife X1A 2L9	Douglas Doak	Director & Superintendent of Insurance	867-920-3423
Nova Scotia, CN Halifax B3J 3C8	Douglas Murphy	Superintendent of Insurance	902-424-7552
Ontario, CN North York M2N 6L9	Philip Howell	CEO-Superintendent of Fin'l Services	416-250-7250
Pr. Edward Island, CN Charlottetown C1A 7N8	Robert Bradley	Superintendent of Insurance	902-368-4550
Quebec, CN Quebec G1V 5C1	Danielle Boulet	Superintendent of Insurance	418-525-0558
Saskatchewan, CN Regina S4P 3V7	James Hall	Superintendent of Insurance	306-787-6700
Yukon Territory, CN Whitehorse Y1A 2C6	Fiona Charbonneau	Superintendent of Insurance	867-667-5111

Canadian Companies Listed by Province/Territory

ALBERTA

Western Life Assurance Company

BRITISH COLUMBIA

Industrial Alliance Pac I&F Sv

MANITOBA

Great-West Life Assurance Co
Wawanesa Life Ins Co

NEW BRUNSWICK

Assumption Mutual Life Ins Co
Blue Cross Life Ins Co of CA

ONTARIO

ACE INA Life Insurance
Aetna Life Ins Co CAB
Allianz Life Ins of NA CAB
Allstate Life Ins Co of Canada
American Bankers Lf Assr CAB
American Health & Life Ins CAB
American Income Life Ins CAB
AMEX Assurance Company CAB
Assurant Life of Canada
Aurigen Reinsurance Company
AXA Equitable Life Ins Co CAB
BMO Life Assurance Company
BMO Life Insurance Company
Canada Life Assurance Co
Canada Life Ins Co of Canada
Canadian Premier Life Ins Co
CIBC Life Insurance Co Ltd
CIGNA Life Ins Co of Canada
Combined Ins Co of Amer CAB
CompCorp Life Insurance Co
Connecticut General Life CAB
CUMIS Life Insurance Company
CUNA Mutual Ins Society CAB
Empire Life Ins Co
Employers Reassurance CAB
Equitable Life Ins Co of CA
First Allmerica Finl Lf CAB
General Re Life Corp CAB
Gerber Life Insurance Co CAB
Hartford Life Ins Co CAB
Household Life Ins Co CAB
Independent Order of Foresters
Knights of Columbus CAB
Liberty Life Assr Boston CAB
Life Ins Co of North Amer CAB
London Life Insurance Company
Manufacturers Life Ins Co
Manulife Canada Ltd
Massachusetts Mutual Lf CAB
MD Life Insurance Company
MetLife Canada
Metropolitan Life Ins Co CAB
Minnesota Life Ins Co CAB
Munich Reinsurance Co CAB
New York Life Ins Co CAB
Partner Reinsurance Co Ltd CAB
PennCorp Life Insurance Co
Phoenix Life Insurance Co CAB
Primerica Life Ins Co of CA
Principal Life Ins Co CAB
RBC Life Insurance Company
Reassure America Life Ins CAB
Reliable Life Ins Co
ReliaStar Life Ins Co CAB
RGA Life Reinsurance of Canada
Scotia Life Insurance Company
State Farm Intl Lf Ins Co CAB
Sun Life Assur Co of Canada
Sun Life Ins (Canada) Ltd
Swiss Re Life & Health Canada
Swiss Reinsurance Co CAB
TD Life Insurance Company
Transamerica Life Canada
Ukrainian National Assoc CAB
United American Ins Co CAB
Unity Life of Canada
Woman's Life Ins Society CAB

QUEBEC

Canassurance Hosp Svc Assn
Canassurance Insurance Company
Colisee Re CAB
Excellence Life Insurance Co
GAN Vie Co Francaise Assr CAB
General American Life CAB
Industrial Alliance Ins & Finl
Optimum Reassurance Inc
SCOR Global Life CAB
Standard Life Assurance Co
Standard Life Assur Ltd CAB

SASKATCHEWAN

Co-operators Life Ins Co
Crown Life Insurance Company

Canadian Provinces/Territories in Which Companies Are Licensed or Do Business

Company Name	AMB#	Alberta	British Columbia	Manitoba	New Brunswick	Newfoundland	Northwest Territories	Nova Scotia	Nunavut	Ontario	Prince Edward Island	Quebec	Saskatchewan	Yukon
ACE INA Life Insurance	066873	L	L	L	L	L	L	L	L	D	L	L	L	L
Aetna Life Ins Co CAB	069358	L	L	L	L	L	.	L	.	D	L	L	L	L
Allianz Life Ins of NA CAB	069312	L	L	L	L	L	L	L	L	D	L	L	L	L
Allstate Life Ins Co of Canada	006028	L	L	L	L	L	L	L	L	D	L	L	L	L
American Bankers Lf Assr CAB	069313	L	L	L	L	L	L	L	L	D	L	L	L	L
American Health & Life Ins CAB	066870	L	L	L	L	L	L	L	L	D	L	L	L	L
American Income Life Ins CAB	069314	L	L	L	L	L	L	L	.	D	L	L	L	L
AMEX Assurance Company CAB	066865	L	L	L	L	L	L	L	L	D	L	L	L	L
Assurant Life of Canada	066882	L	L	L	L	L	L	L	L	D	L	L	L	L
AXA Equitable Life Ins Co CAB	066819	L	L	L	L	L	.	L	.	D	.	L	L	.
Blue Cross Life Ins Co of CA	068557	L	L	L	D	L	L	L	L	L	L	L	L	.
BMO Life Assurance Company	066835	L	L	L	L	L	L	L	L	D	L	L	L	L
BMO Life Insurance Company	066874	.	.	.	.	.	.	.	.	D	.	.	.	.
Canada Life Assurance Co	006183	L	L	L	L	L	L	L	L	D	L	L	L	L
Canada Life Ins Co of Canada	066839	L	L	L	L	L	L	L	L	D	L	L	L	L
Canadian Premier Life Ins Co	066801	L	L	L	L	L	L	L	L	D	L	L	L	L
Canassurance Hosp Svc Assn	066881	.	.	.	.	.	.	.	.	L	.	D	.	.
Canassurance Insurance Company	066878	L	L	L	L	L	L	L	L	L	L	D	L	L
CIBC Life Insurance Co Ltd	066838	L	L	L	L	L	L	L	L	D	L	L	L	L
CIGNA Life Ins Co of Canada	068625	L	L	L	L	L	L	L	.	D	L	L	L	L
Co-operators Life Ins Co	006290	L	L	L	L	L	L	L	L	L	L	L	D	L
Colisee Re CAB	066868	.	.	.	.	.	.	.	.	L	.	D	.	.
Combined Ins Co of Amer CAB	069320	L	L	L	L	L	.	L	.	D	L	L	L	L
CompCorp Life Insurance Co	066880	.	.	.	.	.	.	.	.	D	.	.	.	.
Connecticut General Life CAB	069322	L	.	L	.	.	.	L	.	D	.	L	L	.
Crown Life Insurance Company	006300	L	.	.	.	.	.	.	.	L	.	L	D	.
CUMIS Life Insurance Company	008815	L	L	L	L	L	L	L	L	D	L	L	L	L
CUNA Mutual Ins Society CAB	069318	L	L	L	L	L	.	L	.	D	.	L	L	.
Empire Life Ins Co	006329	L	L	L	L	L	L	L	L	D	L	L	L	L
Employers Reassurance CAB	066867	.	.	.	.	.	.	.	.	D	.	.	.	.
Equitable Life Ins Co of CA	006343	L	L	L	L	L	L	L	L	D	L	L	L	L
First Allmerica Finl Lf CAB	069349	.	.	.	.	.	.	.	.	D	.	L	.	.
GAN Vie Co Francaise Assr CAB	066861	.	.	.	.	.	.	.	.	.	.	D	.	.
General American Life CAB	066822	L	L	L	L	.	.	L	.	L	L	D	L	.
General Re Life Corp CAB	069319	.	L	.	.	.	.	.	.	D	.	L	.	.
Gerber Life Insurance Co CAB	066871	L	L	L	L	L	.	L	.	D	L	L	L	.
Great-West Life Assurance Co	006493	L	L	D	L	L	L	L	L	L	L	L	L	L
Hartford Life Ins Co CAB	069326	L	L	L	L	L	L	L	L	D	L	L	L	L
Household Life Ins Co CAB	066830	L	L	L	L	L	L	L	L	D	L	L	L	L
Independent Order of Foresters	060132	L	L	L	L	L	.	L	.	D	L	L	L	.
Industrial Alliance Ins & Finl	006554	L	L	L	L	L	L	L	L	L	L	D	L	L
Industrial Alliance Pac I&F Sv	006838	L	D	L	L	L	L	L	L	L	L	L	L	L
Knights of Columbus CAB	066815	L	L	L	L	L	L	L	.	D	L	L	L	L
Liberty Life Assr Boston CAB	069357	L	L	L	L	L	L	L	L	D	L	L	L	L
Life Ins Co of North Amer CAB	069330	L	L	L	L	L	.	L	.	D	L	L	L	.
London Life Insurance Company	006667	L	L	L	L	L	L	L	L	D	L	L	L	L
Manufacturers Life Ins Co	006688	L	L	L	L	L	L	L	L	D	L	L	L	L
Manulife Canada Ltd	066879	L	L	L	L	L	L	L	L	D	L	L	L	L
Massachusetts Mutual Lf CAB	069335	L	L	L	L	.	.	.	.	D	.	L	L	.
MD Life Insurance Company	066875	.	.	.	.	.	.	.	.	D	.	.	.	.
MetLife Canada	066883	.	.	.	.	.	.	.	.	D	.	.	.	.
Metropolitan Life Ins Co CAB	069336	L	L	L	L	L	L	L	L	D	L	L	L	L
Minnesota Life Ins Co CAB	069337	L	L	L	.	.	.	L	.	D	.	L	L	.
Munich Reinsurance Co CAB	066862	.	.	.	.	.	.	.	.	D	.	L	.	.
New York Life Ins Co CAB	069340	L	L	L	L	L	L	L	L	D	L	L	L	L
Optimum Reassurance Inc	066827	L	L	L	L	L	L	L	L	L	L	D	L	L
Partner Reinsurance Co Ltd CAB	066891	.	.	.	.	.	.	.	.	D	.	.	.	.
PennCorp Life Insurance Co	060155	L	L	L	L	L	L	L	L	D	L	L	L	L
Phoenix Life Insurance Co CAB	069343	.	.	.	.	.	.	.	.	D	.	L	.	.
Primerica Life Ins Co of CA	060156	L	L	L	L	L	L	L	L	D	L	L	L	L
Principal Life Ins Co CAB	069355	L	L	L	.	.	.	L	.	D	.	L	L	.
RBC Life Insurance Company	066806	L	L	L	L	L	L	L	L	D	L	L	L	L
Reassure America Life Ins CAB	069347	L	L	.	.	.	.	.	.	D	.	L	.	.
Reliable Life Ins Co	009049	L	L	L	L	L	L	L	L	D	L	L	L	L
ReliaStar Life Ins Co CAB	066843	.	.	.	.	.	.	.	.	D	.	L	.	.
RGA Life Reinsurance of Canada	066817	.	L	L	.	.	.	.	.	D	.	L	L	.
SCOR Global Life CAB	066849	.	.	.	.	.	.	.	.	L	.	D	.	.
Scotia Life Insurance Company	066845	L	L	L	L	L	L	L	L	D	L	L	L	L
Standard Life Assurance Co	066846	.	.	.	.	.	.	.	.	.	.	D	.	.
State Farm Intl Lf Ins Co CAB	066884	L	.	.	L	.	.	.	.	D	.	.	.	.
Sun Life Assur Co of Canada	007101	L	L	L	L	L	L	L	L	D	L	L	L	L
Sun Life Ins (Canada) Ltd	066886	L	L	L	L	L	.	L	.	D	L	.	L	.

D-Domiciled L-Licensed

Canadian Provinces/Territories in Which Companies Are Licensed or Do Business – *Continued*

Company Name	AMB#	Alberta	British Columbia	Manitoba	New Brunswick	Newfoundland	Northwest Territories	Nova Scotia	Nunavut	Ontario	Prince Edward Island	Quebec	Saskatchewan	Yukon
Swiss Re Life & Health Canada	066803	.	L	L	.	.	.	.	.	D	.	L	L	.
Swiss Reinsurance Co CAB	066833	.	L	L	.	.	.	.	.	D	.	L	L	.
TD Life Insurance Company	066831	L	L	L	L	L	L	L	L	D	L	L	L	L
Transamerica Life Canada	066805	L	L	L	L	L	L	L	L	D	L	L	L	L
Ukrainian National Assoc CAB	066825	L	.	L	.	.	.	.	.	D	.	L	L	.
United American Ins Co CAB	069354	L	L	L	L	.	.	L	.	D	.	L	L	.
Unity Life of Canada	066847	L	L	L	L	L	L	L	L	D	L	L	L	L
Wawanesa Life Ins Co	060079	L	L	D	L	L	L	L	.	L	L	.	L	.
Western Life Assurance Company	066802	D	L	L	L	L	L	L	L	L	L	L	L	L
Woman's Life Ins Society CAB	066813	L	L	L	L	.	.	.	.	D	.	L	.	.

D-Domiciled L-Licensed

Top 50 Canadian Life/Health Companies

Ranked By 2009 Assets

All figures in thousands of Canadian dollars.

Rank	Company Name	AMB#	Assets
1	Manufacturers Life Insurance Company	006688	80,452,512
2	Sun Life Assurance Company of Canada	007101	73,419,938
3	Great-West Life Assurance Company	006493	26,958,975
4	London Life Insurance Company	006667	24,835,435
5	Canada Life Assurance Company	006183	22,397,733
6	Standard Life Assurance Co of Canada	066846	17,209,995
7	Industrial Alliance Ins & Financial Svcs	006554	15,007,920
8	Sun Life Insurance (Canada) Limited	066886	11,137,092
9	Canada Life Insurance Company of Canada	066839	8,835,176
10	Transamerica Life Canada	066805	6,440,120
11	RBC Life Insurance Company	066806	6,149,892
12	Munich Reinsurance Company CAB	066862	5,602,360
13	Empire Life Insurance Company	006329	4,411,783
14	Independent Order of Foresters	060132	4,408,911
15	BMO Life Assurance Company	066835	3,897,106
16	RGA Life Reinsurance Company of Canada	066817	3,622,393
17	Swiss Re Life & Health Canada	066803	3,484,003
18	Industrial Alliance Pacific Ins & Fn Svc	006838	2,689,876
19	Co-operators Life Insurance Company	006290	2,630,383
20	Swiss Reinsurance Company CAB	066833	2,135,142
21	Knights of Columbus CAB	066815	2,002,759
22	Manulife Canada Ltd	066879	1,401,356
23	Equitable Life Insurance Co of CA	006343	1,317,606
24	General American Life Ins Co CAB	066822	1,256,211
25	State Farm International Life Ins Co CAB	066884	1,155,588
26	Employers Reassurance Corporation CAB	066867	1,086,490
27	Unity Life of Canada	066847	992,373
28	Assurant Life of Canada	066882	812,834
29	Primerica Life Insurance Company of CA	060156	627,217
30	CUMIS Life Insurance Company	008815	596,235
31	Assumption Mutual Life Insurance Company	008074	567,259
32	Wawanesa Life Insurance Company	060079	546,934
33	Combined Insurance Co of America CAB	069320	543,011
34	Crown Life Insurance Company	006300	448,064
35	BMO Life Insurance Company	066874	436,991
36	Blue Cross Life Insurance Company of CA	068557	367,165
37	PennCorp Life Insurance Company	060155	353,270
38	Optimum Reassurance Inc	066827	347,807
39	SCOR Global Life CAB	066849	344,920
40	New York Life Insurance Company CAB	069340	339,898
41	Canassurance Hospital Service Assn	066881	295,040
42	Partner Reinsurance Company Ltd CAB	066891	262,414
43	American Bankers Life Assur of FL CAB	069313	236,296
44	Metropolitan Life Insurance Co CAB	069336	220,016
45	Household Life Insurance Company CAB	066830	181,830
46	Canadian Premier Life Insurance Company	066801	176,176
47	American Income Life Insurance Co CAB	069314	167,686
48	Allianz Life Ins Co of North Amer CAB	069312	139,841
49	ReliaStar Life Insurance Company CAB	066843	116,729
50	American Health & Life Insurance Co CAB	066870	115,065

The data used to rank entities on these pages were sourced from A.M. Best's ***Global Insurance & Banking Database***. For additional or related data, please visit ***www.ambest.com/research*** and search our online Statistical Study database or ***www.ambest.com/sales***.

Top 50 Canadian Life/Health Companies

Ranked By 2009 Capital & Surplus

All figures in thousands of Canadian dollars.

Rank	Company Name	AMB#	Capital & Surplus
1	Manufacturers Life Insurance Company	006688	31,431,193
2	Great-West Life Assurance Company	006493	11,704,649
3	Sun Life Assurance Company of Canada	007101	10,512,067
4	Canada Life Assurance Company	006183	8,172,555
5	London Life Insurance Company	006667	2,812,617
6	Industrial Alliance Ins & Financial Svcs	006554	2,167,253
7	Munich Reinsurance Company CAB	066862	1,762,516
8	RBC Life Insurance Company	066806	1,527,221
9	Standard Life Assurance Co of Canada	066846	1,383,897
10	Independent Order of Foresters	060132	1,357,316
11	Sun Life Insurance (Canada) Limited	066886	1,322,048
12	Swiss Reinsurance Company CAB	066833	1,081,381
13	Transamerica Life Canada	066805	892,576
14	Empire Life Insurance Company	006329	811,866
15	Canada Life Insurance Company of Canada	066839	790,396
16	General American Life Ins Co CAB	066822	760,391
17	Co-operators Life Insurance Company	006290	676,197
18	Primerica Life Insurance Company of CA	060156	608,374
19	Employers Reassurance Corporation CAB	066867	507,824
20	RGA Life Reinsurance Company of Canada	066817	451,586
21	BMO Life Insurance Company	066874	405,507
22	Industrial Alliance Pacific Ins & Fn Svc	006838	394,479
23	Swiss Re Life & Health Canada	066803	373,402
24	BMO Life Assurance Company	066835	368,745
25	Knights of Columbus CAB	066815	354,448
26	Combined Insurance Co of America CAB	069320	325,739
27	Manulife Canada Ltd	066879	272,486
28	Equitable Life Insurance Co of CA	006343	269,643
29	Canassurance Hospital Service Assn	066881	246,275
30	State Farm International Life Ins Co CAB	066884	214,240
31	New York Life Insurance Company CAB	069340	211,446
32	Metropolitan Life Insurance Co CAB	069336	150,077
33	American Bankers Life Assur of FL CAB	069313	132,644
34	Household Life Insurance Company CAB	066830	129,381
35	Wawanesa Life Insurance Company	060079	111,987
36	American Income Life Insurance Co CAB	069314	110,558
37	SCOR Global Life CAB	066849	107,172
38	Canadian Premier Life Insurance Company	066801	103,676
39	CIBC Life Insurance Company Limited	066838	98,881
40	Partner Reinsurance Company Ltd CAB	066891	98,081
41	PennCorp Life Insurance Company	060155	93,744
42	Assumption Mutual Life Insurance Company	008074	88,001
43	American Health & Life Insurance Co CAB	066870	84,748
44	Blue Cross Life Insurance Company of CA	068557	84,340
45	Unity Life of Canada	066847	82,870
46	Crown Life Insurance Company	006300	80,778
47	Scotia Life Insurance Company	066845	79,702
48	Aurigen Reinsurance Company	066889	73,523
49	Assurant Life of Canada	066882	70,497
50	CUMIS Life Insurance Company	008815	66,784

The data used to rank entities on these pages were sourced from A.M. Best's ***Global Insurance & Banking Database***. For additional or related data, please visit ***www.ambest.com/research*** and search our online Statistical Study database or ***www.ambest.com/sales***.

Top 50 Canadian Life/Health Companies

Ranked By 2009 Gross Premiums Written

All figures in thousands of Canadian dollars.

Rank	Company Name	AMB#	GPW
1	Sun Life Assurance Company of Canada	007101	12,440,232
2	Manufacturers Life Insurance Company	006688	9,705,948
3	Great-West Life Assurance Company	006493	5,069,456
4	Munich Reinsurance Company CAB	066862	4,233,713
5	Canada Life Assurance Company	006183	4,222,584
6	London Life Insurance Company	006667	3,366,540
7	Industrial Alliance Ins & Financial Svcs	006554	2,459,897
8	Standard Life Assurance Co of Canada	066846	1,665,102
9	Sun Life Insurance (Canada) Limited	066886	1,249,175
10	RBC Life Insurance Company	066806	1,204,264
11	Canada Life Insurance Company of Canada	066839	1,061,965
12	Empire Life Insurance Company	006329	908,091
13	RGA Life Reinsurance Company of Canada	066817	856,304
14	Swiss Reinsurance Company CAB	066833	779,204
15	Swiss Re Life & Health Canada	066803	742,163
16	Transamerica Life Canada	066805	708,126
17	Co-operators Life Insurance Company	006290	694,440
18	BMO Life Assurance Company	066835	638,632
19	Industrial Alliance Pacific Ins & Fn Svc	006838	612,101
20	Equitable Life Insurance Co of CA	006343	520,887
21	American Bankers Life Assur of FL CAB	069313	400,748
22	CUMIS Life Insurance Company	008815	303,909
23	Canadian Premier Life Insurance Company	066801	294,827
24	Independent Order of Foresters	060132	252,060
25	Knights of Columbus CAB	066815	242,365
26	Combined Insurance Co of America CAB	069320	232,407
27	Primerica Life Insurance Company of CA	060156	223,386
28	General American Life Ins Co CAB	066822	222,912
29	Blue Cross Life Insurance Company of CA	068557	182,409
30	Employers Reassurance Corporation CAB	066867	175,648
31	Optimum Reassurance Inc	066827	154,376
32	Assurant Life of Canada	066882	148,708
33	Canassurance Hospital Service Assn	066881	131,655
34	State Farm International Life Ins Co CAB	066884	126,050
35	Unity Life of Canada	066847	118,778
36	SCOR Global Life CAB	066849	102,100
37	ACE INA Life Insurance	066873	101,105
38	Wawanesa Life Insurance Company	060079	98,465
39	Crown Life Insurance Company	006300	94,665
40	Excellence Life Insurance Company	066890	93,290
41	Assumption Mutual Life Insurance Company	008074	89,122
42	American Income Life Insurance Co CAB	069314	77,644
43	PennCorp Life Insurance Company	060155	76,342
44	Reliable Life Insurance Company	009049	72,629
45	BMO Life Insurance Company	066874	71,261
46	TD Life Insurance Company	066831	65,043
47	Partner Reinsurance Company Ltd CAB	066891	52,296
48	Western Life Assurance Company	066802	51,610
49	Aurigen Reinsurance Company	066889	47,531
50	CIBC Life Insurance Company Limited	066838	41,857

The data used to rank entities on these pages were sourced from A.M. Best's ***Global Insurance & Banking Database***. For additional or related data, please visit ***www.ambest.com/research*** and search our online Statistical Study database or ***www.ambest.com/sales***.

Top 50 Canadian Life/Health Companies

Ranked By 2009 Net Premiums Written

All figures in thousands of Canadian dollars.

Rank	Company Name	AMB#	NPW
1	Sun Life Assurance Company of Canada	007101	9,494,829
2	Manufacturers Life Insurance Company	006688	7,116,787
3	Munich Reinsurance Company CAB	066862	3,897,551
4	Great-West Life Assurance Company	006493	3,859,259
5	London Life Insurance Company	006667	2,950,429
6	Industrial Alliance Ins & Financial Svcs	006554	2,288,589
7	Standard Life Assurance Co of Canada	066846	1,605,640
8	Canada Life Assurance Company	006183	1,306,859
9	Sun Life Insurance (Canada) Limited	066886	1,249,175
10	RBC Life Insurance Company	066806	1,084,119
11	Canada Life Insurance Company of Canada	066839	1,013,506
12	Empire Life Insurance Company	006329	839,876
13	Co-operators Life Insurance Company	006290	631,608
14	Industrial Alliance Pacific Ins & Fn Svc	006838	537,560
15	Equitable Life Insurance Co of CA	006343	414,119
16	Transamerica Life Canada	066805	390,327
17	BMO Life Assurance Company	066835	379,644
18	Independent Order of Foresters	060132	250,593
19	Knights of Columbus CAB	066815	242,392
20	General American Life Ins Co CAB	066822	205,832
21	Primerica Life Insurance Company of CA	060156	202,836
22	Combined Insurance Co of America CAB	069320	185,608
23	Employers Reassurance Corporation CAB	066867	174,185
24	CUMIS Life Insurance Company	008815	170,311
25	Canadian Premier Life Insurance Company	066801	168,874
26	Assurant Life of Canada	066882	148,708
27	Blue Cross Life Insurance Company of CA	068557	139,281
28	Canassurance Hospital Service Assn	066881	131,199
29	State Farm International Life Ins Co CAB	066884	125,992
30	RGA Life Reinsurance Company of Canada	066817	115,645
31	Swiss Reinsurance Company CAB	066833	104,788
32	SCOR Global Life CAB	066849	92,980
33	Unity Life of Canada	066847	90,573
34	Wawanesa Life Insurance Company	060079	86,359
35	American Income Life Insurance Co CAB	069314	77,618
36	Swiss Re Life & Health Canada	066803	75,336
37	PennCorp Life Insurance Company	060155	74,812
38	Assumption Mutual Life Insurance Company	008074	67,100
39	BMO Life Insurance Company	066874	66,377
40	ACE INA Life Insurance	066873	59,767
41	Reliable Life Insurance Company	009049	53,671
42	Partner Reinsurance Company Ltd CAB	066891	52,309
43	Excellence Life Insurance Company	066890	50,285
44	TD Life Insurance Company	066831	46,270
45	Optimum Reassurance Inc	066827	41,589
46	Western Life Assurance Company	066802	38,670
47	American Bankers Life Assur of FL CAB	069313	36,248
48	Household Life Insurance Company CAB	066830	35,774
49	Canassurance Insurance Company	066878	35,750
50	New York Life Insurance Company CAB	069340	35,346

The data used to rank entities on these pages were sourced from A.M. Best's ***Global Insurance & Banking Database***. For additional or related data, please visit ***www.ambest.com/research*** and search our online Statistical Study database or ***www.ambest.com/sales***.

U.S. GUIDE TO QUANTITATIVE TESTS - HEALTH

For a Complete Description of Annual Statement Data Items and Tests—Refer to the Preface.

Profitability Tests

- **Benefits Paid to Net Premiums Written & Fee For Service:** Total medical and hospital and non-health expenses, plus increase in reserves as a percent of net premiums written and fee for service. Other expenses can include non-health related expenses. Also included with net premiums written and fee for service are risk revenues and change in unearned premium reserves.
- **Commission and Expenses to Net Premiums Written & Fee For Service:** Total claims adjustment expense and general administrative expenses as a percentage of net premiums written and fee for service. Also included with net premiums written and fee for service are risk revenues and change in unearned premium reserves.
- **NOG to Total Assets:** Net income excluding net realized capital gains (losses) as a percent of the average between prior year and current year assets. This test measures post-tax insurance earnings in relation to the mean of the company's current and prior year total admitted assets.
- **NOG to Revenue:** Net income excluding net realized capital gains (losses) as a percent of total revenue. This ratio measures post-tax earnings in relationship to total funds provided from operations.
- **Operating Return on Equity:** Net income excluding net realized capital gains (losses) as a percent of the average between prior year and current year capital and surplus. This test measures earnings in relation to the company's total capital and contingency reserve base.
- **Net Yield:** Net investment income as a percentage of the average between prior year and current year invested assets and accrued investment income less borrowed money. It does not reflect the impact of realized and unrealized capital gains or income taxes.
- **Total Return:** The net yield plus realized and unrealized capital gains and losses.

Leverage Tests

- **Liabilities to Assets:** The ratio of total liabilities to total assets. This test measures the proportion of liabilities covered by a company's asset base.
- **Net Premium Written to Capital:** The ratio of premiums to total capital and surplus. This test measures the leverage associated with the level of premiums compared to the capital and surplus of the company. The higher the number the more leveraged the company.
- **Debt to Capital and Surplus:** The ratio of a company's total debt to its total capital and surplus. In this ratio, debt is defined as loans and notes payable on both a current and long term basis, as well as surplus notes.
- **Best's Capital Adequacy Ratio (BCAR):** The BCAR ratio incorporates into a single measure the financial impacts of several distinct risk components. BCAR utilizes the C1 (Credit Risk), C2 (Underwriting Risk), C3 (Interest Rate Risk) and C4 (Business Risk) classifications, from which a required level of capital to support these broad risks is derived. BCAR contains a covariance adjustment, in recognition of the fact that certain risk categories are mutually exclusive.
- **Equity PMPM:** The ratio of capital and surplus to member months. This test measures the amount of capital and surplus spread over a company's membership base.
- **Capital and Surplus to Total Assets:** The ratio of total capital and surplus to net admitted assets. This test measures the relationship of a company's asset base to its capital and surplus.
- **Months Reserves:** The ratio of a company's total capital and surplus to monthly average total expenses. This test provides a measure of the duration of a particular company's capital and surplus versus its expense commitments.

Liquidity Tests

- **Current Liquidity:** This test measures the proportion of liabilities (excluding conditional reserves) covered by cash and unaffiliated holdings, excluding mortgages and real estate.
- **Overall Liquidity:** This ratio measures the proportion of total liabilities covered by a company's total assets, to reflect a company's ability to meet its maturing obligations.
- **Premium Receivable Turnover (Months):** The ratio of premium receivables to commercial revenue. This ratio is expressed in months and measures the liquidity level of a company's total premium and fee-for-service revenue in light of its premium receivables for a specific period.
- **Cash and Invested Assets to Claims and Trade Payables:** The total of cash, short and long-term investments as a percentage of the total claims payable and accounts payable.
- **Claims to Net Premiums Earned:** The ratio of total claims payable to net premiums earned.
- **Average Claims Payment Period:** The ratio of claims payable to total medical expenses per year in days (365).
- **Total IBNR Pay Period:** The ratio of total incurred but not reported claims divided by total medical expenses per year in days (365).

Note: Ratios of 999.9 and -99.9 are maximum and minimum values, respectively.

Version 061610

CANADIAN GUIDE TO QUANTITATIVE TESTS - L/H

For a Complete Description of Annual Statement Data Items and Tests—Refer to the Preface.

Profitability Tests

- **Benefits Paid to NPW:** Benefits paid include death benefits, matured endowments, annuity benefits, accident and health benefits, disability and surrender benefits, group conversions, coupons and payments on supplementary contracts, interest on policy or contract funds and other miscellaneous benefits.
- **Commissions and Expenses to NPW:** Commissions and expenses include payments on both direct and assumed business, general insurance expenses, insurance taxes, licenses and fees, increase in loading and other miscellaneous expenses, and exclude commissions and expense allowances received on reinsurance ceded.
- **NOG to Total Assets:** This test measures after-tax insurance earnings in relation to the mean of the company's current and prior year total general account assets.
- **NOG to Total Revenue:** This test measures after-tax insurance earnings in relation to total funds provided.
- **Operating Return on Equity:** This test measures after-tax insurance earnings in relation to the mean of the company's current and prior year policyholders' and shareholders' surplus base.
- **Net Yield:** This test measures net investment income expressed as a percent of mean invested assets and accrued investment income less borrowed money. It also reflects the impact of amortized realized and unrealized capital gains and income taxes.
- **Total Return:** The net yield plus the change in accumulated other comprehensive income (loss).

Leverage Tests

- **Capital & Surplus to Liabilities:** This test measures the relationship of capital and surplus to the company's unpaid obligations after reinsurance assumed and ceded. It reflects the extent to which the company has leveraged its capital and surplus base.
- **Surplus Relief**: The use of surplus relief can be the result of "surplus strain", a term used to describe any insurance transaction wherein the funds collected are not sufficient to cover the liabilities established.
- **Reinsurance Leverage:** The relationship of total reserves ceded to total capital and surplus.
- **Best's Capital Adequacy Ratio (BCAR):** The BCAR ratio incorporates into a single measure the financial impacts of several distinct risk components. BCAR utilizes the C1 (Credit Risk), C2 (Underwriting Risk), C3 (Interest Rate Risk) and C4 (Business Risk) classifications, from which a required level of capital to support these broad risks is derived. BCAR contains a covariance adjustment, in recognition of the fact that certain risk categories are mutually exclusive.
- **NPW to Total Capital:** This test measures the company's net retained premium writings, after reinsurance assumed and ceded in relation to its capital and surplus.
- **Change in NPW:** This test is a measure of growth in underwriting commitments.
- **Change in Capital:** The annual percentage change in the sum of current year capital & surplus over the prior year's sum.

Liquidity Tests

- **Quick Liquidity:** This test measures the proportion of liabilities (excluding subordinated debt and segregated fund liabilities) covered by cash and investments which can be quickly converted to cash. It indicates a company's ability to meet its maturing obligations without requiring the sale of long-term investments or borrowing money.
- **Current Liquidity:** This test measures the proportion of liabilities (excluding subordinated debt and segregated fund liabilities) covered by cash and unaffiliated holdings, excluding mortgages and real estate.
- **Non-Investment Grade Bonds to Capital:** This test measures exposure to non-investment grade bonds as a percentage of capital and surplus. Generally, non-investment grade bonds carry higher default and liquidity risks. The designation as non-investment grade utilizes the bond quality classifications that coincide with different bond ratings assigned by major credit rating agencies.
- **Delinquent & Foreclosed Mortgages to Capital:** The sum of long-term mortgages upon which interest is overdue more than three months, in process of foreclosure and foreclosed to real estate as a percentage of capital and surplus funds.
- **Mortgages and Credit Tenant Loans and Real Estate to Capital:** Mortgage loans and real estate (home office property, property held for income and property held for sale) as a percentage of capital and surplus funds.
- **Affiliated Investments to Capital:** Affiliated investments (including home office property) as a percentage of capital and surplus funds.

Note: Ratios of 999.9 and -99.9 are maximum and minimum values, respectively.

Version 062408